THE Wadsworth Anthology OF DRAMA

W. B. WORTHEN

University of California, Berkeley

THOMSON

WADSWORTH

Australia • Canada • Mexico • Singapore • Spain • United Kingdom • United States

THOMSON
™
WADSWORTH

The Wadsworth Anthology of Drama
Fourth Edition
W.B. Worthen

Publisher: *Michael Rosenberg*
Senior Editor: *Aron Keesbury*
English Editorial Assistant: *Marita Sermolins*
Editorial Assistant: *Catherine Black*
Production Editor: *Eunice Yeates-Fogle*
Director of Marketing: *Lisa Kimball*
Marketing Manager: *Katrina Byrd*
Senior Print Buyer: *Mary Beth Hennebury*

Compositor, Text Designer: *Graphic World*
Project Manager: *Mike McConnell*
Photo Researcher: *Lili Weiner*
Photo Manager: *Sheri Blaney*
Cover Illustrator: *Lamberto Alvarez*
Cover Designer: *Gina Petti*
Printer: *Von Hoffmann Graphics*

For permission to use materials from this text or
product contact us:
Tel   1-800-730-2214
Fax   1-800-730-2215
Web   www.thomsonrights.com

ISBN: 0-8384-0750-1
Library of Congress Control Number: 2003106615

Preface

Studying drama is more than reading plays. It requires us to study the theaters where the plays were produced, the cultures that framed those theaters, and the critical and performance history that has framed the meanings of drama over time. *The Wadsworth Anthology of Drama* (formerly *The Harcourt Anthology of Drama*) presents drama in these two important contexts: in the play's original theater and the society that sustained it, and in *our* culture, where the play continues to live both as literature and as theatrical performance.

The Wadsworth Anthology of Drama offers a comprehensive collection of classic and contemporary plays from Europe, the Americas, Africa, and Asia. Designed to be used in a variety of drama and theater courses, in general surveys of drama and theater, in courses on tragedy and/or comedy, or in classes on modern theater, *The Wadsworth Anthology of Drama* offers an unusually comprehensive collection of classic theater and an unrivaled selection of contemporary drama drawn from around the world.

A UNIQUE ORGANIZATION

The fourth edition of *The Wadsworth Anthology of Drama* builds on the strengths and success of previous editions of *The Harcourt Anthology of Drama*. It is divided into seven units, each focused on a significant period and place in the history of drama and theater: Athens in the fifth century BCE (four plays); feudal Japan (two plays); England in the late Middle Ages and Renaissance (five plays); England, France, Spain, and colonial Mexico in the seventeenth and eighteenth centuries (five plays); Europe from 1850 through the twentieth century (thirteen plays); the United States (sixteen plays); and contemporary stages around the world (twelve plays).

As in previous editions, each unit of the fourth edition begins with an extensive introduction, placing drama in the context of a specific historical era and using illustrations of theater design to develop a precise sense of stage practice. The unit introductions include a new dimension in this edition: a section, "Reading the Material Theater," which presents original documents from the history of the theater for students' consideration. Each play is accompanied by a brief biography of the playwright and a short introduction to the play. Each unit concludes with a selection of critical readings: essays drawn from the period; essays reconstructing the history of performance in the period; essays by the creators of theater (actors, directors, playwrights, designers); and a contemporary theater review of one play in the unit. *The Wadsworth Anthology of Drama* emphasizes the diversity of drama and theater throughout history, both in its selection of plays and essays and in the issues and ideas raised for discussion as well.

The fourth edition of *The Wadsworth Anthology of Drama* has been extensively revised and is now a more comprehensive and useful volume for contemporary students of dramatic literature and of theater history. At the same time, it significantly expands on previous editions, offering several distinctive features.

NEW PLAYS IN THE FOURTH EDITION

The fourth edition retains plays by Aeschylus, Sophocles, Euripides, Aristophanes, Marlowe, Shakespeare, Calderón, Molière, Racine, Ibsen, Chekhov, Shaw, Pirandello, Brecht, Beckett, Pinter, Churchill, Glaspell, Baraka/Jones, Valdez, Shepard, Wilson, Hwang, Kushner, Soyinka, Friel, and Highway. In addition, this revision of *The Wadsworth Anthology of Drama* has also retained the modern play by Argentine playwright Griselda Gambaro to accompany plays from the Chicano theater and from the Spanish Golden Age theater, and two plays by Native playwrights: Tomson Highway's *Dry Lips Oughta Move to Kapuskasing* and Jack Davis's *No Sugar,* about the resettlement of aboriginal peoples in Australia in the 1930s. The following revisions strengthen the fourth edition:

- **15 new plays** provide a deeper texture for the study of drama, including Marguerite Duras's *India Song,* Arthur Miller's perennial classic, *Death of a Salesman,* and David Edgar's allegory of the new Europe, *Pentecost,* among the others listed below. More plays by women and by a diverse selection of American and international playwrights address the changing conception of drama and performance in the contemporary world.

- **A significant expansion of the unit on American drama,** which now includes a nineteenth-century melodrama—Boucicault's *Octoroon*—as well as plays by Angelina Weld Grimké, Maria Irene Fornes, and Naomi Iizuka; the unit also includes Arthur Miller's *Death of a Salesman.* In addition, the unit on American drama now includes significant focus on race, including plays by Angelina Weld Grimké (*Rachel*), Amiri Baraka/LeRoi Jones (*Dutchman*), Luis Valdez (*Los Vendidos*), August Wilson (*Fences*), David Henry Hwang (*M. Butterfly*), Anna Deavere Smith (*Fires in the Mirror*), and two recent plays, Naomi Iizuka's *36 Views* and Suzan-Lori Parks's Pulitzer Prize–winning *Topdog/Underdog.*

- **A significant expansion of the unit on modern European theater,** including a greater emphasis on women's playwriting throughout the period (Elizabeth Robins, *Votes for Women!;* Marguerite Duras, *India Song;* Caryl Churchill, *Cloud Nine*)

- **An expanded unit on world theater,** focusing on postcolonial drama and theater, including plays from China— Nobel Prize–winner Gao Xingjiang's *The Other Shore*— and India, among plays from modern Japan, Martinique,

Argentina, Nigeria, Northern Ireland, South Africa, Canada, and Australia. Two modern Asian plays—one from Japan and one from China—in addition to the unit on classical Japanese theater make it possible to study one Asian theater tradition in greater depth. This edition also includes, as part of its treatment of early modern drama, a short play by colonial Mexico's most brilliant writer and intellectual, Sor Juana Inés de la Cruz.

- **A larger selection of plays by women** (fourteen), including not only plays by contemporary women such as Naomi Iizuka, Maria Irene Fornes, and Suzan-Lori Parks, for example, but also the classic suffrage play *Votes for Women!* by Elizabeth Robins, and Aphra Behn's *The Rover.*

DEEPER CONTEXTUAL COVERAGE FOR STUDYING DRAMA

The fourth edition retains many of the critical essays of the second edition, such as selections by Aristotle, Nietzsche, Sue-Ellen Case, Niall Slater, Zeami, Sir Philip Sidney, Michael Pennington, John Dryden, Katharine Maus, Émile Zola, Martin Esslin, Fredric Jameson, Bertolt Brecht, Antonin Artaud, Arthur Miller, Amiri Baraka/LeRoi Jones, Arnold Aronson, Frantz Fanon, Homi Bhabha, and Helen Gilbert and Joanne Tompkins. However, the fourth edition adds several important essays, particularly essays devoted to performance practice and theory: an interview with the actress Fiona Shaw on her performance as Medea; Graham Ley on the relationship between Aristotle, Bharatamuni, and Zeami; Rhyllis Rackin on "misogyny" in early modern culture and contemporary scholarship; Hippolyte Clairon on the requirements of acting on the neoclassical stage; Una Chaudhuri on the geography of modern drama; the debate between August Wilson and Robert Brustein on race in American theater; and a selection from the *Notebooks* of Athol Fugard. *The Wadsworth Anthology of Drama* continues its effort to enable students and teachers to explore the issues of representation in the theater and the ways that culture shapes identity, gender and sexuality, power, and race.

In addition to these essays, the fourth edition retains the popular "Aside" sections in each unit-opening essay, devoted to topics of special importance: Roman drama and theater, Sanskrit drama and theater, the masque, the new Shakespeare's Globe Theatre in London, commedia dell' arte, melodrama, the Federal Theater Project, performance art, and intercultural performance. Other additions also help contextualize the plays in *The Wadsworth Anthology of Drama:*

- **New "Behind the Scenes" perspectives in each unit** feature the perspective of an actor, director, designer, or playwright on one of the plays in the unit, giving students a chance to engage more directly with the process of dramatic writing and stage performance.
- **New "Reading the Material Theater" section** of the unit introduction presents a significant document from the history of theater, enabling students and instructors to *practice* methods of historical investigation.

- **New "Performance in History" essays** bring critical issues in the history of drama and theater into a contemporary focus.
- **54 new photos** add to the existing photos and illustrations from the previous editions to alert students and instructors to elements of the plays in performance. Each chapter now begins with a representative photograph, and nearly every play is accompanied by a photograph that illustrates a seminal performance or pivotal aspect of the play. In addition, over 30 illustrations appear throughout the book, clarifying aspects of stage history, theater architecture, and design.

OTHER FEATURES FOR STUDYING DRAMA

The Wadsworth Anthology of Drama is designed for both beginning and advanced students. An introduction to writing about drama and theater furnishes beginning students with an outline of the formal and rhetorical practices used in writing about plays and includes two student essays focusing on different approaches to Caryl Churchill's *Cloud Nine;* this section extends the anthology's commitment to the teaching of drama and theater, expressed in the documentary material gathered in the "Reading the Material Theater" in each unit. The book also includes a useful glossary of dramatic, theatrical, and literary terms as well as an extensive bibliography of drama and theater history and theory and of works about plays and playwrights included in the volume. The book concludes with a selected list of video, film, and sound recordings. *The Wadsworth Anthology of Drama* provides a wide-ranging survey of drama and theater, one that presents both traditional issues and the materials to interrogate those traditions.

ACKNOWLEDGMENTS

With the acquisition of Harcourt College Publishing by Thomson/Wadsworth, this edition of *The Wadsworth Anthology of Drama* has faced many unique challenges, and I am grateful to the editorial staff of Wadsworth for bringing this fourth edition to fruition. I'm especially grateful to Michael Rosenberg and Aron Keesbury for their involvement in the project, to Kathleen Gough for her superb work on the *Instructor's Manual,* and to several members of the Wadsworth staff: Marita Sermolins, Editorial Assistant, for her superb assistance with the photographs; Catherine Black, Editorial Assistant, for her work on the manuscript; Karyn Morrison for the complex task of clearing permissions; Eunice Yeates-Fogle for shepherding the production process; Suzanne Wakefield, the copyeditor; and Mike McConnell, the project manager.

I would also like to thank the many instructors and scholars who commented on the third edition, suggesting ways we might improve this edition:

Sherri Dienstfrey, *Idaho State University*
Stephani Etheridge Woodson, *Arizona State University*
Oliver Gerland, *University of Colorado at Boulder*
Sue Hagedorn, *Virginia Tech*
Michael Harrawood, *Florida Atlantic University*

...n Carolina at Chapel Hill
...e University
...Iowa
...w York University
...ourn University
..., Lake Sumter Community College
...ers, University of Akron
...a Strukus, Boston College

I would also like to thank those who responded to our survey on the second edition, suggesting ways we might improve the third edition:

David Adamson, *University of North Carolina, Chapel Hill*
Gilbert L. Bloom, *Ball State University*
Brian Boney, *University of Texas*
Cynthia Bowers, *Loyola University*
Karen Buckley, *University of Wisconsin, Whitewater*
Susan Carlson, *Iowa State University*
Allen Chesler, *Northern Illinois University*
Barbara Clayton, *University of Wisconsin, Madison*
Kathleen Colligan Cleary, *Clark State Community College*
Jill Dolan, *City University of New York*
David S. Escoffery, *University of Pittsburgh*
Anthony Graham-White, *University of Illinois at Chicago*
John E. Hallwas, *Western Illinois University*
L.W. Harrison, *Santa Rosa Junior College*
Anne-Charlotte Harvey, *San Diego State University*
Gregory Kable, *University of North Carolina, Chapel Hill*
Lawrence Kinsman, *New Hampshire College*
Ann Klautsch, *Boise State University*
Margaret Knapp, *Arizona State University*
Josephine Lee, *University of Minnesota*
Michael J. Longrie, *University of Wisconsin, Whitewater*
Kim Marra, *University of Iowa*
Carla McDonough, *Eastern Illinois University*
John F. O'Malley, *DePaul University*
Michael Peterson, *Millikin University*
Carol Rocamora, *NYU Tisch School of the Arts*
Hans Rudnick, *Southern Illinois University*
Terry Donovan Smith, *University of Washington*
Tramble Turner, *Penn State University*
Jon W. Tuttle, *Francis Marion University*
Timothy Wiles, *Indiana University*
Barry Yzereef, *University of Calgary*

I would also like to thank those who responded to the survey for the third edition:

George Adams, *University of Wisconsin, Whitewater*
Ruth Anderson, *San Diego State University*
Cynthia Bowers, *Loyola University*
Ruth Contrell, *New Mexico State University*
Kenneth Cox, *Oklahoma State University*
Mary Emery, *University of Wisconsin, Whitewater*
Tom Empy, *Casper College*

Lawrence Fink, *Ohio State University*
James Fisher, *Wabash College*
Kay Forston, *Phillips University*
Melissa Gibson, *University of Pittsburgh*
Marsha Morrison, *Genesee Community College*
Chris Mullen, *University of North Carolina, Chapel Hill*
Lurana O'Malley, *University of Hawai'i*
Gwendolyn Orel, *University of Pittsburgh*
Eva Patton, *Fordham University*
Richard Schauer, *University of Wisconsin, Whitewater*
John Terhes, *Chemeketa Community College*
Charles Trainer, *Siena College*
Tramble Turner, *Penn State University*

I am also indebted to Stanton Garner, Jr., University of Tennessee; Josephine Lee, University of Minnesota; Sarah Bryant-Bertail, University of Washington; Jorge Huerta, University of California, San Diego; Kristin Pauka, Univerrsity of Hawai'i; and Barbara Sellars-Young, University of California, Davis, for their help and advice on the third edition. My special thanks to Lurana Donnels O'Malley, of the University of Hawai'i, for her assistance with Units 2 and 7; to James Brandon, again of the University of Hawai'i, for graciously providing photographs and other materials related to the University's productions of *Matsukaze* and *Chūshingura;* and to Octavio Rivera, of la Universidad de las Américas, for his help in providing photographs of his excellent production of Sor Juana's *Loa to The Divine Narcissus.*

I would also like to thank reviewers for the second edition:

George R. Adams, *University of Wisconsin, Whitewater*
Bonnie M. Anderson, *San Diego State University*
Karen Buckley, *University of Wisconsin, Whitewater*
Kathleen Colligan Cleary, *Clark State Community College*
Mary Ann Emery, *University of Wisconsin, Whitewater*
Lawrence E. Fink, *Ohio State University*
Melissa Gibson, *University of Pittsburgh*
Kiki Gounaridou, *University of Pittsburgh*
Anne-Charlotte Harvey, *San Diego State University*
Dennis Kennedy, *Trinity College, Dublin*
Chris Mullen, *University of North Carolina, Chapel Hill*
Lurana O'Malley, *University of Hawai'i*
Gwen Orel, *University of Pittsburgh*
Angela Peckenpaugh, *University of Wisconsin, Whitewater*
Ruth Schauer, *University of Wisconsin, Whitewater*

In addition, I am grateful to the following reviewers of the manuscript of the second edition for their valuable revision suggestions:

Anne Brannen, *Duquesne University*
Bradley Boney, *University of Texas, Austin*
Susan Carlson, *Iowa State University*
S. Alan Chesler, *Northern Illinois University*
Jill Dolan, *City University of New York*

Anthony J. Fichera, *University of North Carolina, Chapel Hill*
L. W. Harrison, *Santa Rosa Junior College*
Margaret Knapp, *Arizona State University*
Josephine Lee, *University of Minnesota*
Michael Longrie, *University of Wisconsin, Whitewater*
Michael Peterson, *University of Wisconsin, Madison*
Eula Thompson, *Jefferson State Community College*
Jon Tuttle, *Francis Marion University*

My thanks to the people who read and commented on the manuscript of the first edition, making it more accurate and useful for instructors:

Stanton B. Garner Jr., *University of Tennessee*
Josephine Lee, *University of Minnesota*
Don Moore, *Louisiana State University*
Cyndia Susan Clegg, *Pepperdine University*

I remain grateful to Sharon Mazer, of the Univer[sity of] Canterbury (New Zealand), for her superb work on the *Instructor's Manual* to previous editions. I would also like to thank Kathleen M. Gough for her superb work on the new edition of the *Instructor's Manual*. And my sincere thanks to Stephen T. Jordan for originally proposing this project, to Oscar G. Brockett of the University of Texas at Austin for allowing me to think out loud about what a book like this one might accomplish, and to Shannon Steen for sharing her ideas on the project.

Finally, I would like to encourage anyone using this book to feel free to drop me a line with ideas and suggestions for later editions. To the many students and colleagues who have called, sent me a note to correct my oversights and omissions, or have graciously spoken to me about the book at professional meetings and conferences, my sincere thanks for your attention and kindness. The flaws and faults that remain are, of course, entirely my own doing.

—W. B. W.

Contents

UNIT I

UNIT V

Modern Europe 529

UNIT VI

The United States 949

UNIT VII

World Stages 1339

Introduction: Drama, Theater, and Culture

Of the many kinds of literature, drama is perhaps the most immediately involved in the life of its community. Drama shares with such other literary modes as lyric poetry, the novel, the epic, and romance the ability to represent and challenge social, political, philosophical, and esthetic attitudes. But unlike most literature, drama has generally been composed for performance, confronting the audience in the public, sociable confines of a theater.

To understand **DRAMA**, we need to understand **THEATER**, because the theater forges the active interplay between drama and its community.[1] On a practical level, for instance, the community must determine where drama will take place, and it is in the theater that a space is carved out for dramatic performance. Not surprisingly, the place of the theater in a city's social and physical geography often symbolizes drama's place in the culture at large. In classical Athens, the theater adjoined a sacred precinct, and plays were part of an extensive religious and civic festival. Greek drama accordingly engages questions of moral, political, and religious authority. In seventeenth-century Paris, the close affiliation between the theater and the court of Louis XIV is embodied in drama's concern with power, authority, and the regulation of rebellious passions. In the United States today, most live theater takes place either in the privileged setting of colleges and universities or in the "theater districts" of major cities, competing for an audience alongside movie theaters, nightclubs, and other entertainments. Drama also seems to be struggling to define itself as part of an established cultural tradition reaching back to Aeschylus and as part of the lively diversity of contemporary popular culture. Social attitudes are reflected in the theater in other ways, too; during performance, the theater constructs its own "society" of performers and spectators. Staging a play puts it immediately into a dynamic social exchange: the interaction between dramatic characters, between characters and the actors who play them, between the performers and the audience, between the drama onstage and the drama of life outside the theater.

READING DRAMA AND SEEING THEATRE

The Greek word for theater, *THEATRON,* means "seeing place," and plays performed in the theater engage their audiences largely through visual means. Less than a century ago, live plays could be seen only on the stage; today, most of us see drama in a variety of media: on film and television as well as in the theater. Yet for the past 500 years or so we have also had access to plays in another, nontheatrical venue: by reading them in books. To see a play performed and to read it in a book are two very different activities, but these distinct experiences of drama can be made to enrich one another in a number of ways.

In the theater, a dramatic text is fashioned into an event, something existing in space and time. The space of the stage, with whatever setting is devised, becomes the place of the drama. The characters are embodied by specific individuals. How a given actor interprets a role tends to shape the audience's sense of that dramatic character; for the duration of the play, it is difficult to imagine another kind of performance—a different Oedipus, Lear, or Nora Helmer than the one standing before us in the flesh. The drama onstage is also bound by the temporal exigencies of performance. The process of performance is irreversible; for the duration of the performance, each moment becomes significant and yet unrecoverable—we can't flip back a few pages to an earlier scene, or rewind the videotape. When a company puts a play into stage production, it inevitably confronts these material facts of the theater: a specific cast of actors, a given theatrical space, a certain amount of money to spend, and the necessity of transforming the rich possibilities offered by the play into a clear and meaningful performance. To make the drama active and concrete, theatrical production puts a specific interpretation of the play on the stage. Whether or

---

[1]Terms in boldface small capital letters are defined in the Glossary; italicized terms are non-English terms.

not to play Caliban in Shakespeare's *The Tempest* as a native of the West Indies; whether to play Torvald Helmer in Ibsen's *A Doll House* as a patriarchal autocrat or as someone bewildered by a changing world; whether to set *Phaedra* in a classical, neoclassical, or a modern setting; whether to use cross-gender or intercultural casting in *The Homecoming*—these are some of the kinds of questions that a production must face, and how the production decides such issues inevitably leads the audience toward a particular sense of the play. Everything that happens onstage becomes meaningful for an audience, something to interpret. Even apparently irrelevant facts—a short actor cast to play Hamlet in Shakespeare's play, or a beautiful actress playing Brecht's Mother Courage—become part of the audience's experience of the play, particularizing the play, lending it a definite flavor and meaning.

Reading a play presents us with a different experience of the drama. Reading plays is, first of all, a relatively recent phenomenon. In early theaters, such as those of classical Athens and Rome, medieval Europe, and even Renaissance Europe of the sixteenth century, drama was almost entirely a theatrical mode, rather than a mode of literature. Although the texts of plays were written down, by and large, audiences came into contact with drama primarily through theatrical performance. By the late sixteenth century, though, the status of drama began to change. The recovery and prestige of Greek and Latin literature led to pervasive familiarity with classical texts, including plays. Throughout Europe, schooling was conducted mainly in Latin, and the plays of Roman playwrights such as Plautus, Terence, and Seneca were frequently used to teach Latin grammar and rhetoric. These plays were widely imitated by playwrights writing drama in vernacular languages for emerging secular, commercial theaters. Printing made it possible to disseminate texts more widely, and plays slowly came to be regarded as worthy of publication and preservation in book form. By the late nineteenth century, widespread literacy created a large reading public and a great demand for books; continued improvements in printing technology provided the means to meet the demand. Playwrights often published their plays as books before they could be produced onstage, with some profound effects. The detailed narrative stage directions in plays by Bernard Shaw, Eugene O'Neill, or Henrik Ibsen, for instance, are useful to a stage director and set designer, but they principally fill in a kind of novelistic background for the reading audience who will experience the play only on the page.

Theater audiences are bound to the temporality and specificity of the stage, but readers have the freedom to compose the play in much more varied ways. A reader can pause over a line, teasing out possible meanings, in effect stopping the progress of the play. Readers are not bound by the linear progress of the play's action, in that they can flip back and forth in the play, looking for clues, confirmations, or connections. Nor are readers bound by the stringent physical economy of the stage, the need to embody the characters with individual actors, to specify the dramatic locale as a three-dimensional space. While actors and directors must decide on a specific interpretation of each moment and every character in the play, readers can keep several competing interpretations alive in the imagination at the same time.

Both ways of thinking about drama are demanding, and students of drama should try to develop a sensitivity to both approaches. Treating the play like a novel or poem, decomposing and recomposing it critically, leads to a much fuller sense of the play's potential meanings, its gaps and inconsistencies; it allows us to question the text without the need to come to definite conclusions. Treating the play as a design for the stage forces us to make commitments, to articulate and defend a particular version of the play, and to find ways of making those meanings active onstage, visible in performance. As readers, one way to develop a sense of the reciprocity between stage and page is to think of the play as constructed mainly of actions, not of words. Think of seeing a play in an unknown language: the *action* of the play would still emerge in its larger outlines, carried by the deeds of the characters. Not knowing the words would not prevent the audience from understanding what a character is doing onstage—threatening, lying, persuading, boasting.

When reading a play, it is easy to be seduced by the text, to think of the play's language as mainly narrative, describing the attitudes of the character. For performers onstage, however, speech—language in action—is always a way of doing something. One way for readers to attune themselves to this active quality of dramatic writing is to ask questions of the text from the point of view of performers or characters. What do I—Lysistrata, Everyman, Miranda—want in this speech? How can I use this speech to help me get it? What am I trying to do by speaking in this way? Although questions like these are still removed from the actual practice of performance, they can help readers unfamiliar with drama begin to read plays in theatrical terms.

Another way to enrich the reading experience of drama is to imagine staging the play: how could the design of the set, the movements of the actors, the pacing of the scenes affect the play's meaning, make the play mean something in particular? Questions of this kind can help to make the play seem more concrete, but they have one important limitation. When asking questions like these, it is tempting to imagine the play being performed in today's theaters, according to our conventions of acting and stagecraft, and within the social and cultural context that frames the theater now. To imagine the play on our stage is, of course, to produce it in our contemporary idiom, informed by our notions both of theater and of the world our theater represents. However, while envisioning performance, we should also imagine the play in the circumstances of its original theater, a theater located in a different culture and possibly sharing few practices of stage-craft with the modern theater. How would Hamlet's advice to the players have appeared on the Globe theater's empty platform stage in 1601? Are there ways in which the text capitalizes on this likeness between Shakespeare's company of actors and those Hamlet addresses fictively in the play? In a theater where a complete, "realistic" illusion was not possible (and, possibly, not even desirable), how does Shakespeare's play turn the conditions of theatrical performance to dramatic advantage? Both reading drama and staging drama involve a complex double-consciousness, inviting us to see the plays with contemporary questions in mind, while at the same time imagining them on their original stages. In this doubleness lies an important dramatic principle: plays can speak to us in our theater but perhaps always retain something of their original accents.

DRAMA AND THEATER IN HISTORY

Throughout its development, dramatic art has changed as the theater's place in the surrounding society has changed. The categories that we apply to drama and theater today—art versus entertainment, popular versus classic, literary versus theatrical—are of relatively recent vintage. They imply ways of thinking about drama and theater that are foreign to the function of theater in many other cultures. Much as drama and theater today emerge in relation to other media of dramatic performance like film and television, so in earlier eras the theater defined itself in relation to other artistic, social, and religious institutions. Placed in a different sphere of culture, drama and theater gained a different kind of significance than they have in the United States today.

Drama and theater often arise in relation to religious observance. In ancient Egypt, for instance, religious rituals involved the imitation of events in a god's or goddess's life. In Greece, drama may have had similar origins; by the sixth century BCE, the performance of plays had become part of a massive religious festival celebrating the god Dionysus. The plays performed in this theater—including those of Aeschylus, Sophocles, Euripides, and Aristophanes gathered here—were highly wrought and intellectually, morally, and esthetically complex and demanding works. Aristotle classes drama among other forms of poetry, but in classical Athens these plays occupied a very different position in the spectrum of culture than do drama or "art" today, precisely because of their central role in the City Dionysia. The Roman theater set drama in the context of a much greater variety of performance—chariot racing, juggling, gladiatorial shows—and while plays were performed on religious holidays, drama was more clearly related to secular entertainments than it had been in Athens. Theater waned in Europe with the decline of the Roman Empire and the systematic efforts of the Catholic church to prevent theatrical performance. Yet when theater was revived in the late Middle Ages, it emerged with the support of the church itself. By the year 1000, brief dramatizations illustrated the liturgy of the Catholic Mass; by the fourteenth century, a full range of dramatic forms—plays dramatizing the lives of saints, morality plays, narrative plays on Christian history—was used to illustrate Christian doctrine and to celebrate important days in the Christian year. Like plays in classical Athens, these plays were produced through community effort rather than by specialized "theaters" in the modern sense. Although we now regard medieval drama as extraordinarily rich and complex "literature," in its own era it was part of a different strand of culture, sharing space with other forms of pageantry and religious celebration, rather than being read with the poetry of Chaucer or Dante.

Similarly, in feudal Japan, the Buddhists developed a form of theater to illustrate the central concepts of their faith. Throughout the twelfth and thirteenth centuries, an increasing number of professional players came to imitate these dramatic performances on secular occasions, and for secular audiences. By the fourteenth century, it became conventional for the great samurai lords, or *SHOGUNS,* to patronize a theatrical company, giving rise to the classical era of the Noh theater. The social history of theater in Japan was complicated by other factors as well. The aristocratic **NOH** theater was rivaled by the popular, often quite contemporary, **KABUKI** theater. Government restrictions on the professions (which tended to make acting a family business, passed on through generations), and Japan's militant isolationism (coming to an end only in the mid-nineteenth century), have contributed to making Japan's classical theater survive in many ways unchanged. Moreover, in many parts of Asia, including China and India, theater was understood as a mixed medium, more centrally emphasizing song and dance as a way of developing the narrative, and many forms of performance—the wide variety of Indian folk theater forms, and of Chinese traditional forms, including **BEIJING OPERA**—developed extremely disciplined and highly stylized performance conventions. These traditional theaters, sometimes tied to aristocratic privilege, sometimes to religious ritual, sometimes to civic celebration, were sharply challenged by the influence of Western dramatic and theatrical practices—spoken drama, dramatic realism, and the notion of a secular, profit-making entertainment-theater—beginning in the eighteenth and nineteenth centuries. The rise of *SHINGEKI* or modern theater in the early twentieth century in Japan, of "spoken drama" at the same time in China, and of Western theatrical methods in India are closely tied to the characteristic forms of globalization of that period, economic imperialism and political colonialism; anticolonial, nationalist, and independence movements throughout Asia have tended both to revive classical forms of traditional theater, and to force a rapprochement with the imported forms of Western theater.

Secular performance did, of course, also take place in classical and medieval Europe, including improvised farces on contemporary life, fairground shows, puppetry, mimes, and other quasi-dramatic events. Many plays were performed only on religious occasions, though, and their performers were usually itinerant, lacking the social and institutional support that would provide them with lasting and continuous existence. Only in the Renaissance of the fifteenth and sixteenth centuries did the Western theater begin to assume the function it has today: a fully secular, profit-making, commercial enterprise. Although Renaissance theaters continually vied with religious and state officials for the freedom to practice their trade, by the sixteenth century, the European theater was part of a secular entertainment market, competing with bear-baiting, animal shows, athletic contests, public executions, royal and civic pageants, public preaching, and many other attractions to draw a paying public. The theater emerged in this period as a distinct institution, supported by its own income; the theater became a trade, a profession, a business, rather than a necessary function of the state or of religious worship. Indeed, if drama in classical Athens was conceived more as religious ritual than as "art" in a modern sense, drama in Renaissance London was classed mainly as popular "entertainment." The theater only gradually became recognized as an arena for "literary" accomplishment, for literary status in this period was reserved mainly for skill demonstrated in forms like the sonnet, the prose romance, or the epic—forms that could win the authors a measure of aristocratic prestige and patronage. As part of the motley, vulgar world of the public theater, plays were not considered serious, permanent literature.

However, the desire to transform drama from ephemeral theatrical "entertainment" into permanent literary "art" begins to be registered in the Renaissance. The poet and playwright Ben Jonson included plays in the 1616 edition of his *Works,* insisting on the literary importance of the volume by publishing it in the large, **FOLIO** format generally reserved for classical authors. In 1623, seven years after his death, William Shakespeare's friends and colleagues published a similar, folio-sized collection of his plays, a book that was reprinted several times throughout the seventeenth century. By the 1660s and 1670s, writers at the court of Louis XIV in Paris could achieve both literary and social distinction as dramatists; Jean Racine's reputation as a playwright, in part at least, helped to win his appointment as Louis's royal historiographer. Yet, despite many notable exceptions, the theatrical origins of drama prevented contemporary plays from being regarded as "literature"—although plays from earlier eras were increasingly republished and gradually seen to have "literary" merit. Indeed, by the nineteenth century, contemporary plays often achieved "literary" recognition by avoiding the theater altogether. English poets like Lord Byron and Percy Bysshe Shelley, for instance, wrote plays that were in many ways unstageable, and so preserved them from degrading contact with the tawdry stage. The English critic Charles Lamb remarked in a famous essay that he preferred reading Shakespeare's plays to seeing them in the theater; for Lamb, the practical mechanics of acting and the stage intruded on the experience of the drama's poetic dimension. In fact, the great playwrights of the late nineteenth century—Henrik Ibsen, Anton Chekhov, August Strindberg, and even the young Bernard Shaw—carved a space for themselves as dramatists by writing plays *in opposition* to the values of their contemporary audiences and to the practice of their contemporary theater—a strategy that would have seemed unimaginable to Aeschylus, Shakespeare, or even Molière. To bring their plays successfully to the stage, new theaters and new theater practices had to be devised, and a new audience had to be found, or made.

This split between the "literary drama" and the "popular theater" has become the condition of twentieth-century drama and theater: plays of the artistic **AVANT-GARDE** are more readily absorbed into the **CANON** of literature, while more conventional entertainments—television screenplays, for instance—remain outside it. The major modern playwrights from Ibsen to Luigi Pirandello to Samuel Beckett first wrote for small theaters and were produced by experimental companies playing to coterie audiences on the fringes of the theatrical "mainstream." This sense of modernist "art" as opposed to the values of bourgeois culture was not confined to drama and theater. Modernist fiction and poetry, cubist and abstract painting and sculpture, modern dance, and modern music all developed a new formal complexity, thematic abstraction, and critical self-consciousness in opposition to the sentimental superficiality they found in conventional art forms. This modernist tendency has itself produced a kind of reaction, a desire to bring the devices of popular culture and mass culture into drama, as a way of altering the place of the theater in society and changing the relationship between the spectators and the stage. Bertolt Brecht's **ALIENATION EFFECT,** Samuel Beckett's importation of circus and film clowns to absurdist theater, Heiner Müller's **PASTICHE** of *Hamlet* in his **POSTMODERN** *Hamletmachine,* or Wole Soyinka's interweaving of African ritual and fourth-wall realism in *Death and the King's Horseman* are all examples of this reaction. For the theater has been challenged by film and television to define its space in contemporary culture, and, given the pervasive availability of other media, theater has increasingly seemed to occupy a place akin to that of opera, among the privileged, elite forms of "high culture." As a result, innovation in today's theater often takes place on the margins or fringes of mainstream theater and mainstream culture: in smaller companies experimenting with new performance forms, in subversive theaters confronting political oppression in many parts of the world, and in theaters working to form a new audience and a new sense of theater by conceiving new forms of drama.

DRAMATIC GENRES

Perhaps because its meaning must emerge rapidly and clearly in performance, drama tends to be compressed and condensed; its characters tend toward types, and its action tends toward certain general patterns as well. It is conventional to speak of these kinds of drama as **GENRES,** each with its own identifying formal structure and typical themes. In the Western theater, following Aristotle's *The Poetics,* **TRAGEDY** is usually considered to concern the fate of an individual hero, singled out from the community through circumstances and through his or her own actions. In the course of the drama, the hero's course of action entwines with events and circumstances beyond his or her control. As a result, the hero's final downfall—usually, but not always, involving death—seems at once both chosen and inevitable. **COMEDY** on the other hand, focuses on the fortunes of the community itself. While the hero of tragedy is usually unique, the heroes of comedy often come in pairs—the lovers who triumph over their parents in romantic comedies, the dupe and the trickster at the center of more ironic or satirical comic modes. While tragedy points toward the hero's downfall or death, comedy generally points toward some kind of broader reform or remaking of society, usually signaled by a wedding or other celebration at the end of the play.

To speak of genre in this way, though, is to suggest that these ideal critical abstractions actually exist in some form, exemplified more or less adequately by particular plays. Yet, as the very different genres of Japanese or Indian theater suggest, terms like *tragedy* and *comedy,* or **MELODRAMA, TRAGOCOMEDY, FARCE,** and others, arise from our efforts to find continuities between extraordinarily different kinds of drama: between plays written in different theaters, for different purposes, to please different audiences, under different historical pressures. When we impose these terms in a prescriptive way, we usually find that the drama eludes them or even calls them into question. Aristotle's brilliant sense of Greek tragedy in *The Poetics,* for instance, hardly "applies" with equal force to Greek plays as different as *Agamemnon, Oedipus the King,* and *Medea,* or Kan'ami's elegant Noh drama, *Matsukaze,* let alone later plays like *Hamlet* or *Endgame.* In his essay, "Tragedy and the Common Man," Arthur Miller tries to preserve "tragedy" for modern drama by redefining Aristotle's description of the hero of tragedy. Instead of Aristotle's hero, a man (not a woman) of an elevated social station, Miller argues that the modern hero should be an average, "common" man (not a woman), precisely because the "best families" do not seem normative to us or representative of our basic values, a goal he pursued in his classic American tragedy, *Death of a Salesman.* Our exemplary characters are taken from the middle classes. Yet to redefine the hero in this way calls Aristotle's other qualifications—the idea of the hero's character and actions, the meaning of the tragic "fall"—into question as well, forcing us to redefine Aristotelian tragedy in ways that make it something entirely new, something evocative in modern terms.

In approaching the question of genre, then, it is often useful to avoid asking how a play exemplifies the universal and unchanging features of tragedy or comedy. Instead, one could ask how a play or a theater *invents* tragedy or comedy for its contemporary audience. What terms does the drama present, what formal features does it use, to represent human experience? How do historically "local" genres—Renaissance **REVENGE TRAGEDY,** French **NEOCLASSICAL DRAMA,** modern **THEATER OF THE ABSURD, KABUKI,** or even the **KATHAKALI** of southern India—challenge, preserve, or redefine broader notions of genre?

DRAMATIC FORM

In about 335 BCE, Aristotle's *The Poetics* set down the formal elements of drama, and the influence of Aristotle's description has been massive: today we still speak of dramatic form in terms of its **PLOT, CHARACTERS, LANGUAGE, THEME,** and its performative elements, what Aristotle called **MUSIC** and **SPECTACLE.** Any student of drama can profit by thinking about how these formal elements function in a given play. How are the incidents of the play—its plot—arranged? What effects are achieved by *this* ordering, rather than by another? How does the plot relate to the play's narrative story, which includes events dating from before the play begins? How does the plot, the structure of the events—for instance, Nora Helmer's first act in *A Doll House* is to enter the house, and her last act is to leave it—develop the play's themes? We might then ask how the play defines its characters. What elements of human experience—family history, psychological motivation, public action—seem to be most prominent in a play's conception of "character"? How do the formal conventions of characterization, such as blank verse in Shakespeare's plays and the densely poetic language of Noh theater, affect our reading of the characters and our understanding of them as representations of human beings?

Although Aristotle presents these elements of drama as distinct, in practice they are mutually defining, making it very difficult to speak of them separately. A play's language, for example, can be analyzed purely for its verbal and rhetorical features, but it is more interesting to ask how the language affects our understanding of the characters or invests the play with certain thematic possibilities. Similarly, while we may regard a play's themes as inside the play, they actually arise only in our interpretation of the play. The themes are something we create by asking certain questions about the play's plotting, its characterization, its use of language. The artificiality of separating these features becomes especially clear when we turn to a play's theatrical dimension. Although Aristotle suggests that a play's literary and theatrical dimensions are independent, to get a real sense of drama we must see the play both as literature and as theater. We must assess how an audience's sense of the play's plot, characters, and themes are shaped by the kinds of spectacle demanded by the play and provided by the theater. The "meaning" of Greek drama cannot be separated from its conditions of performance: the religious festival, the huge amphitheater, the masked actors, the singing, dancing chorus. The barren "sterile promontory" of *Hamlet,* Phaedra's claustral chamber, cross-dressed performance in Churchill's *Cloud Nine:* these elements of the theatrical spectacle are not outside the meaning of the drama; they are its means, the vehicle for achieving that meaning on the stage.

In a book like this one—indeed, in any book—it is difficult to convey a real sense of the power of theater. It is possible, though, to imagine this experience and to discuss it through the materials collected here: dramatic texts, descriptions of stage practice, illustrations of theaters, photographs, essays. However, an obstacle to understanding arises from a split between the disciplines we use to understand drama and theater. At many colleges and universities, this split is represented in the geography of the campus itself, where the English or Literature departments, which teach dramatic literature, are housed in one building, and the Theater or Drama department, which teaches acting, directing, design, and which actually stages the plays, is housed in another. "Literary" approaches to drama focus our attention initially, sometimes exclusively, on the text of a play and train the complex strategies of poetics and poetic interpretation on it. Such interpretation regards the dramatic text as incomplete and specifies the text's range of possible meanings by placing it in various textual and cultural contexts; in a sense, the negotiation between the text and these contexts determines what we can say the play *means*.

"Theatrical" approaches to drama tend to see a play in terms of stage practice, both in the terms of the play's original production and in the light of performance practice today. This approach interrogates the play's staging: how it can be set, what obstacles it presents to acting and casting, what the dramatic effects of costume and design will be. "Theatrical" interpretation regards the dramatic text as an incomplete design for performance and trains the complex machinery of stage representation—directing, acting, design, costuming on the task of fleshing the script out as performed action. The meaning of the play in this regard emerges from what we can make the play *do*.

The literary and theatrical approaches to drama and theater share the assumption that plays are not fully meaningful in themselves; they share the sense that the meaning of drama emerges from the kinds of questions we ask of it, the contexts—literary, historical, theoretical, theatrical—in which we can make it perform, and make it mean something in particular. Although each approach can seem needlessly mysterious, involving its own specialized language and critical practice, its own set of "right" questions and "right" answers, this book has been assembled with the belief that the literary and the theatrical approaches are necessary complements to each other.

In the units that follow, each introductory essay attempts to provide an overview of the dense implication of drama and theater in its culture, and, often, how dramatic literature and theatrical practices have been revived, engaged, or transformed by succeeding generations. Each essay, in other words, introduces the social, political, and cultural milieu of the theater; the theater's physical and symbolic position in the landscape of its culture; the theater's representation of gendered, sexual, and racial identities; the physical design of theaters, and the practices of acting and staging; and the dynamic impact of dramatic—literary—innovation on the work of performance. Although these issues are treated differently, given different prominence in each essay, this constellation of questions stems from a single conviction: that thinking about drama requires that we think about how plays perform as literature, in culture and history, and on the stage.

THE STAGE IN CRITICAL PRACTICE

One of the greatest challenges, for professional scholars and students alike, to understanding the history of drama and theater has to do with the nature of evidence. As any detective drama illustrates—think of Sherlock Holmes—"facts" only become "evidence" when they are subjected to a coherent interpretation, an explanatory narrative. So, too, understanding the "facts" of the theatrical past means transforming them into "evidence," evidence that materializes a certain understanding, interpretation, or explanation of the meaning of drama and theater in history. The difficulties of historiography—the writing of history—with regard to early drama and theater are self-evident. Most of the plays of classical Athens, for example, have been lost; those that survive represent only a small percentage of the "evidence" for the practice of Greek playwrights. Much of the evidence for theatrical practice—how actors worked, the movements of the chorus, the function of music, the behavior of audiences, even the composition of audiences—has had to be adduced from written documents and visual images often far-removed from the theater itself, for these practices (much like the teaching of acting

READING THE MATERIAL THEATER

today) were part of an ongoing tradition that was handed directly from performer to performer, or citizen to citizen. Many theatrical traditions around the world originated in nonliterate oral cultures, which successfully preserved the developing forms and practices of performance over centuries, as long as the communities who sustained them continued to flourish. Often regarded as "primitive," "uncivilized," or simply subversive by invading colonial powers, even traditional practices that survived well into the historical period have sometimes been eradicated (Wole Soyinka's *Death and the King's Horseman* provides a striking image of the ways the English governors of Nigeria regarded several centuries-old traditional performance practices). Nonetheless, some of these traditions survive: though they date from about the sixteenth century, *kathakali* performances in southern India seem to preserve some of the dramatic and performance traditions of ancient Sanskrit performance, as it was described in Bharatamuni's *Natyasastra*. Of course, the rise of print not only forged a fissure between literary drama and theatrical performance: it also provided the means to document a wide variety of theatrical practice and—since the purpose of print is to multiply texts in great numbers—to provide a greater chance that such documents would survive. For this reason, beginning in the sixteenth century, the print-record provides a massive archive of information about the practices of performance: in the publication of plays; in the efflorescence of diaries and memoirs containing information about the stage; in the rise of theatrical journalism in the eighteenth century; in playbills, posters, programs; and in a wide variety of theatrical illustrations—pictures of actors, plays, theaters. In combination with the increasing likelihood that theatrical buildings, sets, costumes, and the records of theater companies have survived, the history of the modern theater is, comparatively speaking, an embarrassment of riches. Needless to say, it has recently become possible even to record performance, on still photographs and film, videotape, and digital media. While it is important to recognize that such recordings are themselves only partial "evidence" for the work of a given production—What is the camera leaving out of the picture? How is close-up distorting what an audience might see? How did the production change in order to be filmed? How did the live production change after it was filmed?—they do provide an invaluable resource for future generations of students.

In each unit, this edition of *The Wadsworth Anthology of Drama* provides a piece of that material past, a document or an image that provides some insight into theatrical practice. Some of these records are visual, and indeed may have had no direct relation to performance in their day: scholars now use them to attempt to reconstruct elements of lost theaters. Several of these records are written documents, often chestnuts in the history of drama and theater. The purpose of including these records here is experimental: how can you use such records to interrogate some aspect of a past performance? What kind of story does the document tell, and what stories does it conceal? What kind of interpretation of theater history does the document enable? What kinds of evidentiary problems does it pose? Reading the documents of the theater's material past is one way to engage in the challenging work of imagining the power of dramatic performance.

I

Classical Athens

Greek amphitheater at the site of the ancient city of Morgtantina, Sicily.

G reat drama arises where the theater occupies an important place in the life of the community. In many respects, Western understanding of drama originated in fifth-century (500–400) BCE classical Athens, where the theater played a central role in politics, religion, and society. The Athenians invented forms of **TRAGEDY** and **COMEDY** that persist to the present day. In tragedy, the Greeks dramatized climactic events in the lives of legendary heroes from prehistory and myth, bringing ethical problems of motive and action to the stage. In comedy, the theater staged satiric portraits of the life of the *POLIS* (the city-state), vividly depicting the energetic conflicts of contemporary Athens in matters of politics, war, education—even the arts of drama. Playwrights through the long history of the theater have continued to find in Greek drama both a model and a point of resistance against which to practice their own craft (see, for example, Jean Racine's *Phaedra* or Bernard Shaw's *Major Barbara* in this book). And we need only recall Sigmund Freud's understanding of the "Oedipus complex" to sense the influence of models of action derived from the Greek theater on later Western culture.

Athens and Sparta were dominant rival powers in fifth-century Greece, which comprised many small independent city-states, each with its own political and cultural institutions, form of government, and alliances. Dramatic performances took place under a variety of circumstances in all Greek cities, but drama as we know it developed in Athens. Dramatic performance in Athens was part of citywide religious festivals honoring the god Dionysus, the most important being the **CITY DIONYSIA.** Plays were produced for contests in which playwrights, actors, and choruses competed for prizes and for distinction among their fellow citizens. These contests, held in an outdoor amphitheater adjoining the sacred temple of the god, followed several days of religious parades and sacrifices. This connection between early drama and religion suggests that the essential nature of Greek drama lies in its supposed "origins" in religious ritual. But the City Dionysia was also a massive civic spectacle that went far beyond religious worship, emphasizing the theater's implication in other areas of public life. Dramatic performance contributed to this celebration of Athens' economic power, cultural accomplishment, and military might. The City Dionysia united religion and politics, enabling Athenians to celebrate both Dionysus and the achievements of their *polis.*

THE CITY DIONYSIA

The City Dionysia was the most prominent of four religious festivals held in Athens and the surrounding province of Attica between December and April; it took place in the month of Elaphebolion (March–April), one month after the previous festival. Although its purpose was primarily a religious one, the City Dionysia was structured around a series of contests between individual citizens and between major Athenian social groups—the ten (later twelve to fifteen) "tribes" that formed the city's basic political and military units. Dramatic performance was introduced to the City Dionysia during the sixth century BCE and became the centerpiece of the elaborate festival. Each year a city magistrate, or *ARCHON,* honored selected wealthy citizens by choosing them to finance one of the three principal tragic dramatists competing for a prize at the festival. Each sponsor, called a *CHOREGOS,* was responsible for hiring the **CHORUS** of young men who sang and danced in the plays. The *choregos* hired musicians and provided costumes and other support for the playwright to whom he was assigned. Later in the period, the state assigned the leading actor to the *choregos* as well, and this actor also competed for a prize. The playwright was responsible for training the chorus and the actors, and for some of the acting himself, and he shared his prize with the *choregos*. Serving as a *choregos* was both a civic duty and an important honor, equivalent to other tasks imposed on the wealthy—maintaining a battleship for a year or training athletes for the Olympic games.

Taking place over several days, the City Dionysia opened with a display of actors and choruses to the city; on the next day there was a lavish parade of religious officials through the city, followed by religious observances and sacrifices held in the theater. Athens also received its annual tribute of goods, money, and slaves from subject and allied states at this time, and war orphans raised at state expense were displayed to the audience. After this display of religious worship and civic pride, two days were devoted to contests of **DITHYRAMBS,** hymns sung and danced by a large chorus. Each of Athens' tribes sponsored two choruses: one consisting of fifty men, another consisting of fifty boys. The city's politics revolved around the tribes, and their contribution to the festival was prominent in this contest. The dithyrambic contest involved a thousand Athenian citizens directly in the performance, a significant portion of the adult male citizens. (It is estimated that Athens in the fifth century had a total population of about 300,000: 100,000 slaves, 30,000 noncitizen foreigners, and 30,000 to 40,000 adult male citizens; women and children were not citizens.) Following the dithyrambs, the main dramatic contest began. The competing playwrights each produced a **TRILOGY** of tragedies, staged over three days. A trilogy could take a single theme or series of events as its subject (like the three plays of Aeschylus' *Oresteia,* 458 BCE), or present three distinct, unrelated dramas. A rugged farce called a **SATYR PLAY** followed the performance of each complete trilogy and was considered part of it; these plays parodied a god's activities, with actors dressed as satyrs—half-man, half-goat. After 486 BCE, comedies were also awarded prizes, but it is unclear whether the comedies were performed on a single day or spread over several days. Prominent citizens representing each of the tribes served as judges and awarded prizes to the playwrights, their *choregoi,* and the actors.

THE THEATER OF DIONYSUS

The Greek theater was a public spectacle, a kind of combination of Inauguration Day, the Super Bowl, the Academy Awards, Memorial Day, and a major religious holiday. Plays were first produced in the **AGORA** (marketplace), which often served as a performance place for festivals in Athens and in the surrounding **DEMES** of Attica, which also staged dramatic performances. However, the size and importance of the City Dionysia required a separate site, and a theater was built on the slope of the Acropolis, near the precinct of Dionysus. The original theater, a ring of wooden seats facing a circular floor, was later refined, enlarged, and constructed of stone. By the time of Aeschylus, Euripides, Sophocles, and Aristophanes, the Athenian theater had achieved its basic design: a circular floor for dancing and acting, ringed by a hillside **AMPHITHEATER** and backed by a low, rectangular building.

The focus of the classical amphitheater, which seated about 14,000 people, was the round **ORCHESTRA** ("dancing place") containing the central altar of Dionysus, at which the festival sacrifices were performed. The dithyrambic choruses performed their ecstatic dances in the orchestra, and most of the action of the plays took place there as well. Facing the orchestra, the hillside was divided into wedge-shaped seating areas. The citizens sat on wooden benches with their tribes: leaders and priests in the front of the sections, women perhaps toward the rear or possibly in a separate section. *Metics* (resident aliens) and visitors were probably seated in a separate area. Special front and center seats, called *prohedria,* were reserved for the judges and the priests of Dionysus.

Behind the *orchestra,* a low building called the **SKENE** faced the audience. Although the *skene* became a permanent stone structure in the fourth century BCE, in the fifth century it was a temporary wooden building, used for changing masks and possibly also for changing costumes. Playwrights quickly found the theatrical potential latent in the *skene's* facade and

EARLY AMPHITHEATER

This is an artist's reconstruction of an early theater in Eretria, Greece. Notice that the seating is constructed of wooden benches and the *skene* is a temporary structure.

set of doors; through these doors the audience heard Agamemnon being murdered in his bath, or saw eyeless Oedipus return to confront the Chorus and his future in exile. In Aeschylus' *Agamemnon,* the Watchman awaits the signal fires on the palace roof, and in performance he may have waited on the roof of the *skene.* The theater also used some machinery for scenic effects: a rolling platform (the **EKKYKLEMA**) used to bring objects or bodies from the *skene* into the orchestra; a crane (**MACHINA**) to raise or lower characters—the gods, for instance—from the orchestra over the roof of the *skene;* later, in the fourth century, painted panels were used to indicate the play's setting or location.

The experience of theater in classical Athens was in some ways akin to participation in other institutions of civic life. Athens was a participatory democracy for its citizens, although citizenship was restricted to adult male Athenians: women, foreigners, slaves, freed slaves, and children were not citizens. Citizens sat in the assembly to discuss and vote on matters of state policy, and they were eligible to serve in all public and military offices as well. Attendance at the City Dionysia was, then, like other aspects of Athenian public life, a privilege and an

THEATER AND SOCIAL LIFE

THEATER OF DIONYSUS

ORCHESTRA

PARODOS   PARODOS

PROSKENION

SKENE

OLD TEMPLE

NEW TEMPLE

N

S

ALTAR

0   5   10M

This ground plan is of the sacred precinct of Dionysus in Athens, fourth century BCE. Notice that the theater is much larger than the earlier theater at provincial Eretria. The large and permanent *skene* was constructed after the fifth century BCE.

obligation mainly reserved for citizens. Citizens received tickets to the festival from officials in their neighborhood, or *DEME;* tickets may have been awarded on the basis of participation in other civic obligations—serving in the courts, the assembly, the army. At the theater, citizens sat together with members of their tribe. In a sense, the theater offered a visual map of the organization of Athenian society, for the tribes formed the basis of political participation outside the theater: The Athenian Assembly and the army were similarly arranged by tribe. Organized by tribes, with precedence given to religious officials and with inferior status or nonparticipation accorded to noncitizens such as women, slaves, and foreigners, the theater of Dionysus mirrored the structure of Athenian society.

The fifth century BCE was the era of Athens' greatest political power and cultural vitality and an era of intense reciprocity between Athenian theater and society. Yet the tension manifest in Greek drama perhaps points to the precarious stability of the Athenian *polis.* The Athenian maritime empire, forged after the defeat of massive Persian forces in 479, was resisted by the smaller Greek states and opposed by Athens' chief rival, the military state of Sparta. Following a long period of hostility and skirmishing, Athens and Sparta declared war against each other in 431 BCE, resulting in Athens' utter defeat in 404. Athenian democracy was replaced by an oppressive oligarchy, the Thirty Tyrants. Although the tyrants were rapidly overthrown and democracy restored, Athens never regained the dynamic cultural life and political power it enjoyed during the fifth century. And although dramatic performance continued after the restoration of democracy, the theater's central role in the *polis* seems to have declined after the Spartan victory. Yet, the theater became one of Greece's most widely disseminated cultural products. When Alexander the Great conquered Greece, the Near East, and northern Africa, he took Greek culture—including theater and drama—with him throughout his empire. And when the Roman Empire later absorbed Alexander's former dominions, it also appropriated Greek dramatic traditions, the design of Greek theaters, and the arts and religion of Greece, as well.

DRAMA AND PERFORMANCE

In his *Poetics,* Aristotle suggests that drama originated in the singing of the dithyrambic choruses; a masked actor was first used to respond to the chorus as an individualized "character" in the mid–sixth century BCE, an innovation attributed to the playwright Thespis, about whom little else is known. Aeschylus was the first to use two actors, probably taking one of the parts himself; in the 460s, Sophocles introduced a third actor and was successfully imitated by Aeschylus in his *Oresteia* in 458 BCE. In general, classical tragedy can be performed with three actors and comedy with four, although each actor may play several parts. All of the performers in the Greek theater—the dramatists, actors, musicians, and chorus members—were male citizens of Athens, as was most of the audience. The dramatic choruses were perhaps composed of young men between the ages of seventeen, when military training began, and twenty-one, when Athenian men entered into adulthood.

The chorus of tragedy both sang and danced, and it was expected to perform with grace and precision. Actors and choruses wore full-head masks made of painted linen or lightweight wood. The main characters' masks were individualized, but the members of the chorus all wore identical masks, giving a special force to the conflict between the unique claims of the protagonist and the more diffuse claims of his society. Costuming in comedy was somewhat more complex. Aristophanes' plays suggest that the chorus at times wore animal masks. The comic protagonists' masks, though, were again individualized; since Aristophanes often put his contemporaries in his plays—Socrates in *Clouds,* for instance, or Euripides in *Frogs*—the masks probably resembled these citizens quite closely. Comic actors often sported a leather **PHALLUS,** clearly visible in statues depicting comic actors and of much dramatic use in plays like *Lysistrata.*

In reading Greek drama, we should remember that its leading parts—both the leading character and the chorus—were designed for competition, as instruments for the actor and chorus to win prizes. The literary brilliance of the plays is, in this sense, a means to enable a particular virtuosity in performance.

WOMEN IN THE ATHENIAN THEATER

In Athenian tragedy and comedy, female characters were played by men. Not only did men sponsor and write the plays, but the "women" onstage were literally men in disguise. Yet, many plays throw the theatrical convention of men playing women into relief. In Euripides' play *The Bacchae,* Pentheus is possessed by Dionysus when he dresses up as a woman and Dionysus admires his good looks; in *Lysistrata,* the Spartan woman Lampito is closely and physically examined by Lysistrata and the other women in ways that focus the audience's attention precisely on the fact that the woman is being played by a man. Drama, then, participated fully in Athens' denial of equality to women. Athena says as much in Aeschylus' *The Eumenides* when she judges Orestes' murder of his mother as a lesser crime than Clytaemnestra's murder of her husband. Looking closely at both the drama and its performance can help us to see how justice, power, and gender came to be arranged in Athenian society.

Although the theater—like Athenian society—was a male-dominated institution, Greek drama repeatedly inquires into the nature of gendered behavior and uses female characters to focus some of its most challenging questions. Given the absence of women from the stage and their marginal status in the theater and in the state, it is fascinating to note how many plays turn on the action of female characters. Women were not themselves citizens of Athens, and their prerogatives, which were considerable, in the *polis* were defined only through marriage to a citizen. Yet many of the plays raise critical moral, ethical, and political problems through the actions of women: Clytaemnestra and Cassandra in Aeschylus' *Agamemnon,* Medea in Euripides' *Medea,* and the women of Aristophanes' *Lysistrata* and *Assembly of Women.* Although Aristotle probably voices his contemporaries' views when he remarks in his *Poetics* that "a woman can be good, or a slave, although one of these classes [women] is inferior and the other, as a class, worthless," the theater stages women in ways that implicitly challenge the authority of this "natural" connection between the good, the legitimate, and the masculine. As a category that troubles the "natural" linkage between masculinity and humanity itself, women in Greek drama often appear to stage a crisis in how the state imagines and justifies itself.

FORMS OF GREEK DRAMA

Formally, the organization of Greek tragedy is somewhat different from that of modern plays, because Greek drama is based on the singing and dancing of the chorus, for whom many of the plays were named. Most plays begin with a **PROLOGUE,** such as the Watchman's speech at the opening of *Agamemnon,* followed by the *PARODOS* (entrance) of the singing and dancing chorus. Several **EPISODES** follow, in which the central characters engage one another and the chorus; the chorus itself often sings (and dances) several **ODES,** which are used to enunciate and enlarge on the play's pivotal issues, and the chorus often becomes a decisive character in the play, as it does in Aeschylus' *Agamemnon* or Euripides' *The Bacchae.* The choral odes are written in lyric meters different from the meters used for the characters' speeches. The play's *CATASTROPHE,* literally its "down turn," marks some change in the hero's status and is followed by the departure of the characters from the stage and the *EXODOS,* or final song, dance, and departure of the chorus. Comedy—at least for Aristophanes, whose plays are the only surviving comedies from the period—is structured similarly, although Aristophanes' plays usually include a long *PARABASIS* a choral ode delivered to the audience discussing political issues, and a final *KOMOS* a scene of choral dancing and revelry.

This formal description, however, hardly accounts for the real and continued power of Greek drama, which arises from an intense and economical relationship between (1) a situation, usually at the point of climax as the play opens, (2) a complex of characters, each with distinctive goals and motives, (3) a chorus used both as a character and as a commentator on the action, and (4) a series of incidents that precipitates a crisis and brings the meaning of the **PROTAGONIST**'s actions into focus. Aristotle called this crisis the ***PERIPETEIA*** or "reversal," in the external situation or fortunes of the main character, and he argued that it should be accompanied by an act of ***ANAGNORISIS,*** or "recognition," in which the character responds to this change. Indeed, Aristotle argued that when the pressure of the tragic action produces a close relationship between reversal and recognition, it instills in the audience intense feelings of fear and pity and then effects ***CATHARSIS*** a purgation of these emotions.

Because the plays were written for a contest, it is not surprising that their language and construction provide opportunity for powerful acting, particularly since the plays were judged only in performance. Yet the stage action of Greek drama is hardly spectacular in the modern sense. Although the visual dimension of Agamemnon's descent from the chariot onto the blood-red tapestry, or Medea's appearance in the dragon-drawn chariot, or even the aching gait of the men in *Lysistrata* is critical to any understanding of these plays, scenes of murder, suicide, or battle usually take place offstage, to be vividly reported by messengers—as in the reports of Jocasta's death and Oedipus' blinding, or of the death of Jason's young bride in *Medea*. Cassandra's graphic prophecy of Agamemnon's murder likewise provides a brutal counterpoint to the slaughter taking place offstage.

The scenic simplicity of the Greek theater enabled playwrights to achieve a special kind of concentration, one that capitalized on the special circumstances of the open-air, festival theater. Greek comedy has come down to us in the work of only two playwrights, Aristophanes and Menander (c. 342–c. 291 BCE). While Aristophanes' plays—usually called **OLD COMEDY**—are energetic and sometimes ribald comedies lampooning the Athenian *polis* and its leading citizens, Menander's comedies—called **NEW COMEDY**—are more generally concerned with mores and manners. Menander wrote more than 100 plays, but only one of his comedies—*The Grouch*—survives in its entirety. Menander's plays were often focused on a comic conflict between parents and children, devising situations and characters that forged an important link between the Greek and Roman theaters, and helped to establish the enduring traditions of stage comedy.

While the comedies center on the life of the community, the stage action of Greek tragedy focuses on the relation between the hero's intention, action, and consequence in ways that typically pit the hero's greatest talents against his unavoidable destiny, his society, his family, and himself. This recipe has provided—in plays from the era of Aeschylus, Sophocles, and Euripides to our own—the substance of tragic drama. The characteristic concerns of Greek drama speak undeniably of classical Athens, but the plays also represent trials of decision, suffering, and desperation with a power and purpose that continue to speak to us in accents very much our own.

GREEK DRAMA IN PERFORMANCE HISTORY

The forms of Greek drama and theater remained in use after the fall of Athens to Sparta; indeed, they were both exported to Rome, Egypt, and the Middle East by Alexander. Yet while tragedy and comedy continued to be written and performed throughout the Greek Mediterranean throughout the Hellenistic period (fourth and third centuries BCE) and beyond, and theater design continued to develop and refine the classical amphitheater, in an important sense the tradition of dramatic writing and performance inaugurated in fifth-century Athens was confined to the Greek provinces. The modes of Greek drama and (to a lesser extent) performance survived somewhat longer in the eastern reaches of the Roman Empire, but in the west they gradually disappeared under the influence of Roman culture. Moreover, although the manuscripts of Greek drama—and of important collateral texts, such as Aristotle's *Poetics*—continued

(ASIDE)
ROMAN DRAMA AND THEATER

Although many of their traditions were absorbed from Greece, the Romans developed a distinctive theater, quite different from the Athenian stage. From its beginnings, Roman theater was more varied than the Greek stage, including acrobatics, juggling, athletic events, gladiatorial combats, and skits. In the sixth and seventh centuries BCE, Rome was a relatively unimportant town, ruled by the Etruscan kingdoms of northern Italy. In 509 the Romans drove out the Etruscans and founded a republic; the republic expanded its influence throughout the fourth century BCE and eventually came to control many territories once governed by the Greeks and by Alexander. Much as the Romans absorbed other Greek cultural institutions, they also absorbed Greek theater and drama, which were first performed in Rome in the mid–third century, in 240 BCE. As Rome's political influence expanded, particularly under the Roman Empire (27 BCE–476 CE), the Romans disseminated their characteristic cultural institutions—including theater and drama—throughout Europe, North Africa, and the Middle East.

Like the Greeks, the Romans associated the drama with festivals, but the Romans not only produced plays on festival occasions throughout the year, they also developed a much wider va-

riety of theatrical entertainments, of which drama was only a small part. Some of the Roman entertainments descended from the sixth-century BCE *ludi Romani,* which included chariot racing, boxing, and other athletic contests, and Greek drama was first performed in Rome at these games. Moreover, Greek drama not only competed with other nondramatic entertainment, it also was rivaled by an indigenous dramatic form known as **ATELLAN FARCE.** Associated with the town of Atella (near present-day Naples), these farces were probably improvised comic skits, involving stock characters and played by masked actors.

After the introduction of tragedy and comedy to the *ludi Romani* in 240 BCE, dramatic performances were introduced to several other festivals, and by 179 BCE, drama was being performed at major religious festivals throughout the year: at the *ludi Romani* honoring Jupiter in September, at a second festival consecrated to Jupiter in November, at festivals honoring Flora and the Great Mother in April, and at a festival honoring Apollo in July. Dramatic performances, though still associated with festivals, were much more common in Rome than in fifth-century Athens, not only because special celebrations sometimes included theatrical performance, but also because any disruption in the rituals connected with the festivals required that the entire festival be repeated, including the dramatic performances.

Given the variety of entertainments offered in Rome—including the chariot races and gladiatorial combats that became increasingly popular in the later Empire, especially after 300 CE—it is not surprising that the Romans built several different kinds of entertainment buildings, stadiums and racecourses as well as theaters. Yet until 55 BCE, theaters in Rome were temporary, built and taken down for each festival. In the first century BCE, the Romans began to build permanent theaters with some regularity. Like their Greek predecessors, the Roman theaters were outdoor amphitheaters, but the Romans built their theaters on level ground, and their superior engineering—particularly the Romans' use of arches in construction—enabled them to build much more massive buildings. Roman theaters were generally three stories in height. A rectangular stage house, or **SCAENA,** stood like the Greek *skene* behind the semicircular orchestra and faced a steeply tiered semicircular auditorium. The facade of the *scaena* was elaborately ornamented with columns and porticos. The Romans built theaters of stone throughout the Empire; many of the Greek theaters that remain today were refurbished and redesigned by the Romans.

Although the Romans continued to perform plays from the Greek theater, they also developed a native strain of drama—represented in the plays of Plautus, Terence, and Seneca. Titus Maccius Plautus (c. 254–c. 184 BCE) is

to be copied for students and readers, they fell out of public circulation. The few texts that have survived of the plays of Aeschylus, Sophocles, Euripides, and Aristophanes are based on copies made for teachers and scholars in Byzantium, dating from the third and fourth centuries CE. Not only have most of their plays been lost (Sophocles is said to have written 123 plays, of which we have seven; Aeschylus is thought to have written more than seventy, of which seven remain; Euripides' nineteen plays are all that remain of more than ninety), but the entire dramatic output of 700 years of theater was lost as well—the names of Agathon, Thespis, Chairemon, Theodektes, Philokles, Ariastas, and others are all that remain of their work. Moreover, since these manuscripts were collected in scholarly or monastic libraries, they have been subject to the destructive forces of history. Many Greek plays were lost in the burning of the library at Alexandria during Caesar's invasion of Egypt; the crusaders sacked Constantinople (previously known as Byzantium) in 1204, and in the process destroyed a city that had joined eastern and western cultures for centuries.

probably the most influential Roman comic playwright. His earliest surviving plays date from 205 BCE, or about thirty-five years after Greek drama was first introduced to Rome; Plautus is thought to have based many of his comedies on Greek New Comedy, but none of these prototypes survives. Plautus is thought to have written more than 100 comedies, many of which— *Amphitryon, The Braggart Warrior, The Rope,* and *The Menaechmus Twins,* for example—established the formal conventions of later comedy. Publius Terentius Afer (c. 195–159 BCE), usually called Terence, was probably born in Carthage and brought to Rome as a slave. Unlike the prolific Plautus, Terence wrote only six comedies, all of which survive, and strove throughout his career to adapt Greek originals to the Roman stage: *The Woman of Andros, Mother-in-Law, Self-Tormentor, Eunuch, Phormio,* and *The Brothers.* The plays of Plautus and Terence have been particularly influential on the form and structure of later European comedy; not only did they establish many of the forms and character types developed by later playwrights, but in the late Middle Ages and Renaissance, their plays were often used to teach Latin in the schools, giving rise to generations of playwrights—including William Shakespeare, Christopher Marlowe, and Molière—who found in Roman drama a form for their own contemporary plays.

The only surviving Roman tragedies were written by Lucius An-

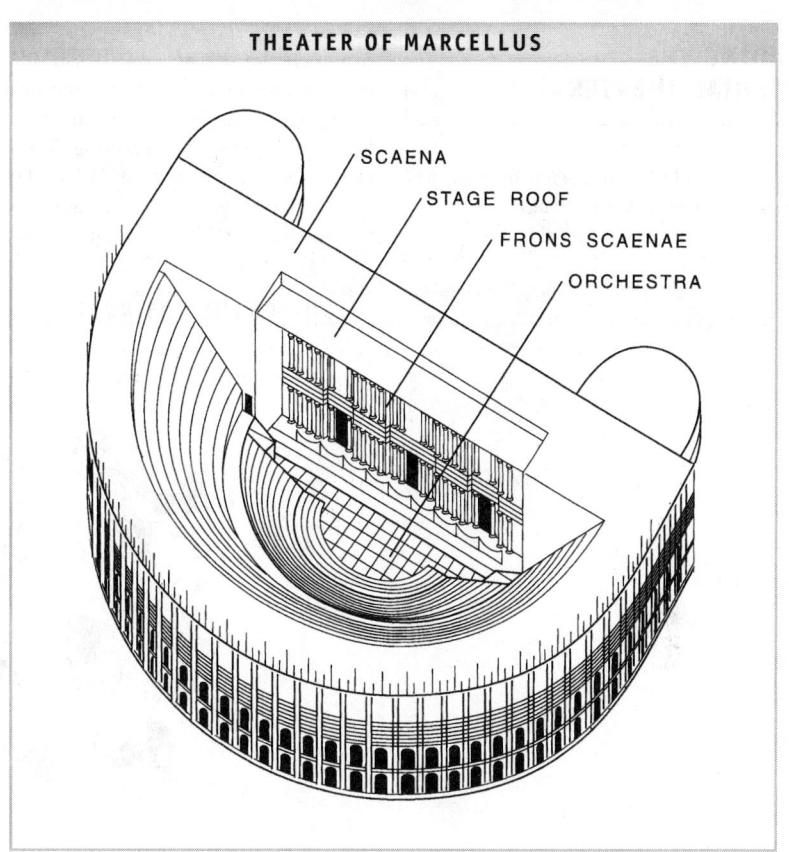

THEATER OF MARCELLUS

SCAENA

STAGE ROOF

FRONS SCAENAE

ORCHESTRA

The Theater of Marcellus was built in Rome, 13–11 BCE.

naeus Seneca (5 BCE–65 CE). Seneca's tragedies were adapted from Greek plays but tend to be more sensational and violent; indeed, it is doubtful that they were performed in the theater. Although only nine of Seneca's plays survive—*The Trojan Women, Medea, Oedipus, Phaedra, Thyestes, Hercules on Oeta, Hercules Mad, The Phoenecian Women, Agamemnon*—Senecan tragedy also exerted an important influence on later drama, especially in the English Renaissance, where Senecan tragedy provided a prototype for the nascent English drama of the sixteenth century.

However, for all their violence, the Crusades also reopened cultural contact with the Islamic Middle East; many of the texts of Greek and Roman culture had been translated into Arabic or had been preserved by Islamic scholars and libraries. With the reopening of European trading and military contacts in the fourteenth, fifteenth, and sixteenth centuries, Europe was able to rediscover the literature of classical Greece, sometimes in Latin translations, sometimes only through commentaries on still-lost texts (such as Aristotle's *Poetics*). In many respects, though, this recovery was principally of Roman theater and drama. The prestige and availability of texts by Latin authors like Plautus, Terence, and Seneca meant that these playwrights were widely taught in schools, convents (such as Gandersheim, where the canoness Hrosvitha [953–973 CE] wrote six comedies modeled on Terence's plays), and universities, where their plays were often performed; the influence of these playwrights can be felt everywhere in European drama of the sixteenth century, most familiarly in Shakespeare's early comedies (like *A Comedy of Errors,* based on Plautus' *The Menaechmus Twins*) and in the

READING THE MATERIAL THEATER

This illustration, taken from an Attic red-figure volute *krater* painted by the "Pronomos painter" c. 450 BCE, is an important document in the history of Greek theater. While it doesn't directly represent the performance of a satyr play onstage, there is much to learn from this vase painting. Look closely at the illustration: What distinctions can you make among the various figures? First, of course, many of the figures seem to be holding their theatrical masks, and several seem to be gazing at them. But among the male figures, several are bearded adult men, while a larger number are beardless, suggesting that they are younger, adolescents. What role do you think they play in the performance? One

THE PRONOMOS *KRATER*

These actors, apparently in a satyr play, appear on a vase painting by the Pronomos painter. Notice that the central seated figure of Dionysus (holding the polelike *thyrsus*) is surrounded by actors holding their masks. The older, bearded actor to the right of Dionysus, wearing the lionskin over his shoulder, is apparently playing Hercules, the

vogue for violent tragedies reminiscent of Seneca's unstaged dramas, plays like Shakespeare's *Titus Andronicus* (see Unit III). The rediscovery of Vitruvius' first-century book on Roman architecture, *De Architectura,* in 1414 (it was printed—a new technology—in 1486) also led a generation of fifteenth- and sixteenth-century architects to design and build theaters on what they took to be a Roman model.

In many respects, though, Greek drama only became widely known in Europe in the later seventeenth and eighteenth centuries, where Greek plays often provided the models for contemporary playwrights, such as Jean Racine (see Unit IV), as well as for the first operas. And it was only in the nineteenth and twentieth centuries that the restoration of classical amphitheaters and the historical and archaeological recovery of the theatrical practices of classical Athens began to make possible experiments in staging classical Greek drama in ways that attempted to approximate the circumstances of classical theater or that attempted to translate those circumstances into a more effective modern idiom. Since the late nineteenth century, for example, the amphitheater at Epidaurus has often been used to stage classical Greek plays in ways that attempt to approximate the traditions of fifth-century Athenian performance.

Clearly, of course, much has changed in the last 2,500 years, and performing classical hint here may be the figure dancing in the bottom row of figures: He has put on his mask, is wearing the *phallos,* and seems to have a satyr's tail. The central figure seated on the throne, with the *thyrsus* in his hand and vines growing just to the left, is labeled "Dionysus," as though the god were seated among the players (he shares the seat with his wife, Ariadne), but there are several other characters who seem to be in costume; the most identifiable is looking at his mask, wearing a full-body costume and carrying the lion-skin of Heracles. Although the illustration seems to provide some fascinating clues to the nature of theatrical performance, it is also misleading in some obvious ways: Just to the right of Ariadne is a seated female figure holding a mask.

protagonist of the play. The other, younger and beardless figures may compose the chorus. While Hercules holds an individualized mask, the chorus members all hold masks similar to each other, and they wear costumes suggestive of satyrs.

drama poses a series of challenges to modern performers. First, the chorus—both its singing and dancing performance style and its function in the drama—has posed a critical problem for modern companies and audiences: German director Max Reinhardt staged a production of *The Oresteia* in 1919 that was among the first of his productions to experiment with large crowds onstage; later productions have tended to make the chorus smaller and more energetic in an attempt to recapture the exciting movement of the classical chorus. Beyond that, the use of masks in classical theater is no longer conventional on the modern stage, although many modern playwrights—Eugene O'Neill, for example, in *Strange Interlude* (1928)—have experimented with masks in an attempt to render psychological complexity with what they take to be "classical" decorum. The 1981 National Theatre (London) production of *The Oresteia,* directed by Sir Peter Hall, used an entirely male cast and performed the play in masks; this production was the first English-language production of a Greek tragedy to be performed in the classical theater at Epidaurus. Although this effort to "recover" the initial circumstances and flavor of Greek performance has driven many performances, Greek drama has also provided the framework for a number of important **AVANT-GARDE** theatrical experiments in the modern era. Of course, Racine's adaptation of Euripides in *Phaedra* might be considered an "updating" of this kind, but in the modern era, stage practices have often been used not so much to recover the classical past as to restage the plays in a modern idiom. Josef Svoboda's brilliant 1963 production of *Oedipus the King* in Prague, for example, took place on a thirty-foot-wide staircase that rose from the bottom of the orchestra pit to beyond the top of the proscenium. The French director Ariane Mnouchkine staged a production of Euripides' *Iphigeneia at Aulis* as an introduction to her staging of *The Oresteia* in 1990 (under the overall title *Les Atrides*); this brilliant production used makeup, costume, movement, and dance idioms from classical Indian and Indonesian theater, implying that a contemporary staging of the Greek classics might well turn to another tradition of "classical" performance to find a still-living stage language. Both for directors—Peter Sellars' 1993 staging of Aeschylus' *The Persians* framed the play with allusions to the Gulf War—and for writers, such as Heiner Müller (*Medeamaterial*), Charles Mee, Jr. (*Orestes*), Caryl Churchill (*A Mouthful of Birds,* based on Euripides' *The Bacchae,* and written with David Lan), Timberlake Wertenbaker (who has translated several Greek plays), Wole Soyinka (*The Bacchae of Euripides*), and others, the theater and drama of classical Athens continue to provide a way to see and understand ourselves.

Framed by a masked member of the Chorus and Jocasta, Oedipus—played here by Laurence Olivier in the landmark 1945 production of *Oedipus the King*—seems finally to recognize the "truth" that he has been seeking.

Framed in a doorway and lit in profile, Diana Rigg embodies the isolation and abandonment of Euripides' Medea.

Aeschylus

Aeschylus (c. 523–456 BCE), whose life spanned the first half of the Athenian fifth century, witnessed Athens' chief political and military conflicts and became its preeminent dramatist. His epitaph suggests that he fought at the battle of Marathon against the Persians, and the detailed description of the naval battle at Salamis in his play *The Persians* implies that he may have fought there as well. Aeschylus added the second actor to dramatic performance, only one of his many achievements in the theater. He won his first victory as a playwright at the City Dionysia in 484 BCE, and in 472 BCE produced *The Persians,* for which Pericles served as his sponsoring *choregos.* In 468 BCE he was defeated by Sophocles, but was again victorious with his trilogy *The Oresteia* and the accompanying satyr play *Proteus* (now lost) in 458. Aeschylus died in Sicily in 456 BCE. Of about seventy plays that he is said to have written, seven survive: *The Suppliants, The Persians, Seven Against Thebes, Prometheus Bound,* and *The Oresteia* trilogy—*Agamemnon, The Libation Bearers,* and *The Eumenides.*

Agamemnon is the first of three plays—including *The Libation Bearers* and *The Eumenides*—collectively called *The Oresteia.* Working from the model of Homer's *Odyssey,* Aeschylus fashioned a complex and original narrative of injustice and retribution, relying on events and characters well-known to his Athenian audience. Indeed, *The Oresteia* depends on the audience's understanding of events that took place a generation before the opening of the first play, *Agamemnon.* In the previous generation, the two sons of Pelops—Atreus and Thyestes—began a bitter feud for control of Argos. Thyestes disputed his brother's claim to the throne and seduced his wife; for this he was exiled, but later returned to Argos with his children to ask Atreus' forgiveness. Atreus received his brother but had the children secretly murdered and baked into a dish that he served to Thyestes. When the truth was revealed to him, Thyestes fled with his one remaining child, Aegisthus, leaving a terrible curse on Atreus, his family, and his descendants.

This curse gives rise to the action of *The Oresteia,* because Aeschylus shows how murder and revenge are played out across the next two generations of the house of Atreus, involving Thyestes' son, Aegisthus; Atreus' two sons, Menelaus and Agamemnon; and Agamemnon's wife, Clytaemnestra, and their children, Iphigeneia, Electra, and Orestes.

The force of much of Aeschylus' drama lies in a powerful economy of action and character, everywhere visible in *Agamemnon. Agamemnon* opens with a watchman awaiting the signal fire that will announce the end of the war on Troy and the return of Agamemnon. This nighttime scene immediately invests the play with a dark sense of foreboding. The opening lyrics of the Chorus provide the context for Agamemnon's arrival by recounting the events of ten years before, when Agamemnon, to secure favorable winds for sailing against

In this production of *Agamemnon* by the American Repertory Theater, the imagery of the "net" used throughout Aeschylus' play is realized in the scenic design of the play.

Troy, sacrificed his own daughter Iphigeneia. Clytaemnestra, eager to punish Agamemnon for his brutal murder of their daughter, is recognized at once as a deceptive and powerful queen, feared by the Argive elders of the Chorus. Cassandra's curse—that her prophecies will never be believed—is appallingly enacted before us at the moment of Agamemnon's murder, and Aegisthus appears as a kind of thug, dehumanized by his cruel and vengeful mission. For a modern audience, the most problematic character is Agamemnon himself, seen onstage in only one scene. Yet this brief scene testifies to the intricate knotting of history and temperament in the design of Aeschylus' tragedy and in the design of *The Oresteia* as a whole. We see Agamemnon's lordly ambition for success and glory, his malleability, his insensitivity to his own wrongdoing. Treading on the crimson tapestries, Agamemnon follows a trail of blood leading him into the house of Atreus, to his accounting for the murder of Iphigeneia, to Aegisthus' fulfillment of Thyestes' curse, and to his own death.

The cycle of retribution continues in the remaining plays of the trilogy. In *The Libation Bearers,* Agamemnon's son, Orestes, returns to Argos from exile, where he had been sent by Aegisthus and Clytaemnestra, to avenge the murder of his father. He arrives in secret and surprises his sister, Electra (and the chorus of slave women bearing libations), at Agamemnon's grave. Brother and sister vow to avenge Agamemnon's death. Returning to the palace, they murder Aegisthus, and then Orestes executes justice on his mother, Clytaemnestra, as well. But this act summons the Furies (or Eumenides), horrible demons who haunt and torment Orestes for his crime. The final play, *The Eumenides,* follows Orestes' search for purification. He first appeals to Apollo to release him and then to Athena. Athena calls the Furies and Orestes to a trial before a jury of mortal Athenian judges. Casting her tie-breaking vote for Orestes, Athena releases him from the Furies; to placate them, she invites them to serve as the honorary deities of Athens itself. The terrible curse of the house of Atreus is finally healed by redefining the process of justice. Revenge is replaced by the code of law.

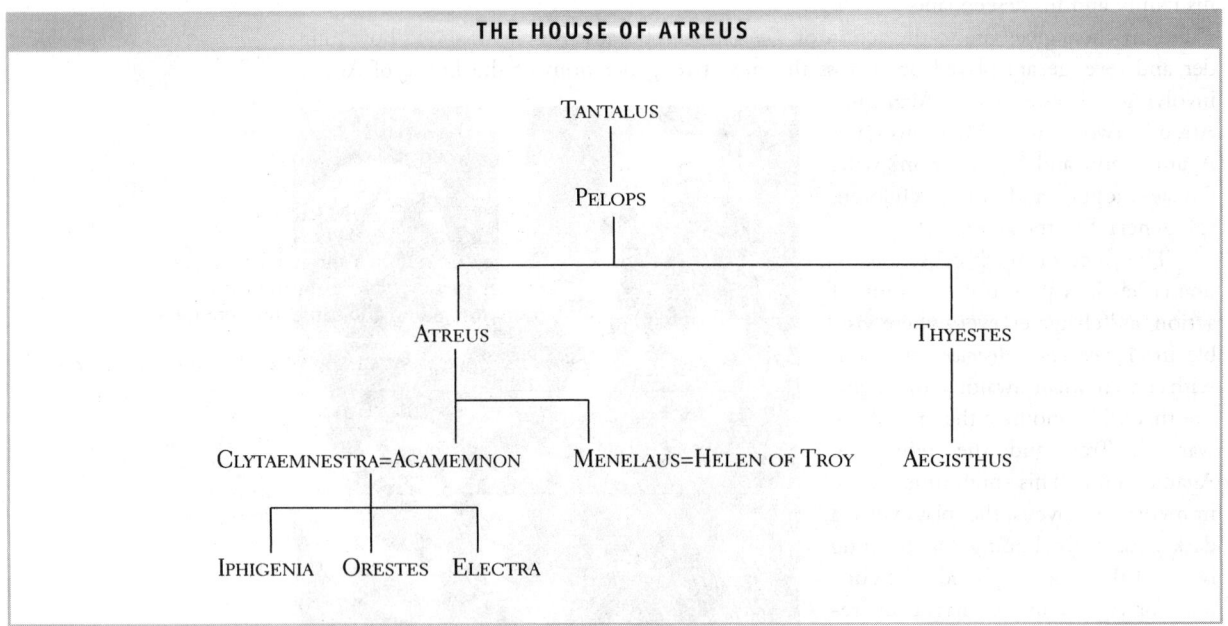

THE HOUSE OF ATREUS

TANTALUS

PELOPS

ATREUS   THYESTES

CLYTAEMNESTRA=AGAMEMNON   MENELAUS=HELEN OF TROY   AEGISTHUS

IPHIGENIA   ORESTES   ELECTRA

The family of Atreus, King of Mycenae and father of Agamemnon and Menelaus, is the focus of powerfully tragic myths and dramas.

AGAMEMNON

Aeschylus

TRANSLATED BY ROBERT FAGLES

CHARACTERS

WATCHMAN   CHORUS, THE OLD MEN OF
CLYTAEMNESTRA   ARGOS *and their* LEADER
HERALD   ATTENDANTS *of Clytaemnestra*
AGAMEMNON   *and of Agamemnon*
CASSANDRA   BODYGUARD *of Aegisthus*
AEGISTHUS

TIME AND SCENE: *A night in the tenth and final autumn of the Trojan War. The house of Atreus in Argos. Before it, an altar stands unlit; a watchman on the high roof fights to stay awake.*

WATCHMAN: Dear gods, set me free from all the pain,
    the long watch I keep, one whole year awake . . .
    propped on my arms, crouched on the roofs of Atreus
    like a dog.
          I know the stars by heart,
5   the armies of the night, and there in the lead
    the ones that bring us snow or the crops of summer,
    bring us all we have—
    our great blazing kings of the sky,
    I know them, when they rise and when they fall . . .
10   and now I watch for the light, the signal-fire
    breaking out of Troy, shouting Troy is taken.
    So she commands, full of her high hopes.
    That woman—she manoeuvres like a man.

    And when I keep to my bed, soaked in dew,
15   and the thoughts go groping through the night
    and the good dreams that used to guard my sleep . . .
    not here, it's the old comrade, terror, at my neck.
    I mustn't sleep, no—

(Shaking himself awake.)

          Look alive, sentry.
    And I try to pick out tunes, I hum a little,
20   a good cure for sleep, and the tears start,
    I cry for the hard times come to the house,
    no longer run like the great place of old.

    Oh for a blessed end to all our pain,
    some godsend burning through the dark—

(Light appears slowly in the east; he struggles to his feet and scans it.)

          I salute you!
25   You dawn of the darkness, you turn night to day—
    I see the light at last.
    They'll be dancing in the streets of Argos
    thanks to you, thanks to this new stroke of—
          Aieeeeee!
    There's your signal clear and true, my queen!
30   Rise up from bed—hurry, lift a cry of triumph

through the house, praise the gods for the beacon,
if they've taken Troy . . .
          But there it burns,
fire all the way. I'm for the morning dances.
Master's luck is mine. A throw of the torch
has brought us triple-sixes—we have won!   35
My move now—

(Beginning to dance, then breaking off, lost in thought.)

          Just bring him home. My king.
I'll take your loving hand in mine and then . . .
the rest is silence. The ox is on my tongue.
Aye, but the house and these old stones,
give them a voice and what a tale they'd tell.   40
And so would I, gladly . . .
I speak to those who know; to those who don't
my mind's a blank. I never say a word.

(He climbs down from the roof and disappears into the palace through a side entrance. A CHORUS, the old men of Argos who have not learned the news of victory, enters and marches round the altar.)

CHORUS: Ten years gone, ten to the day
    our great avenger went for Priam—   45
      Menelaus and lord Agamemnon,
    two kings with the power of Zeus,
    the twin throne, twin sceptre,
    Atreus' sturdy yoke of sons
    launched Greece in a thousand ships,   50
    armadas cutting loose from the land,
    armies massed for the cause, the rescue—

(From within the palace CLYTAEMNESTRA *raises a cry of triumph.)*

    the heart within them screamed for all-out war!
    Like vultures robbed of their young,
      the agony sends them frenzied,   55
    soaring high from the nest, round and
    round they wheel, they row their wings,
    stroke upon churning thrashing stroke,
    but all the labour, the bed of pain,
      the young are lost forever.   60
    Yet someone hears on high—Apollo,

---

8 **our great blazing kings** major constellations that demarcate the seasons

36 **triple-sixes** a winning throw of dice

Pan or Zeus—the piercing wail
these guests of heaven raise,
and drives at the outlaws, late
65   but true to revenge, a stabbing Fury!

(CLYTAEMNESTRA *appears at the doors and pauses with her entourage.*)

So towering Zeus the god of guests
drives Atreus' sons at Paris,
all for a woman manned by many
the generations wrestle, knees
70   grinding the dust, the manhood drains,
the spear snaps in the first blood rites
       that marry Greece and Troy.
And now it goes as it goes
and where it ends is Fate.
75   And neither by singeing flesh
nor tipping cups of wine
nor shedding burning tears can you
enchant away the rigid Fury.

(CLYTAEMNESTRA *lights the altar-fires.*)

We are the old, dishonoured ones,
80   the broken husks of men.
Even then they cast us off,
the rescue mission left us here
to prop a child's strength upon a stick.
What if the new sap rises in his chest?
85   He has no soldiery in him,
       no more than we,
and we are aged past ageing,
gloss of the leaf shrivelled,
three legs at a time we falter on.
90   Old men are children once again,
       a dream that sways and wavers
into the hard light of day.
                              But you,
daughter of Leda, queen Clytaemnestra,
what now, what news, what message
95   drives you through the citadel
       burning victims? Look,
the city gods, the gods of Olympus,
gods of the earth and public markets—
all the altars blazing with your gifts!
100   Argos blazes! Torches
race the sunrise up her skies—
drugged by the lulling holy oils,
       unadulterated,
run from the dark vaults of kings.
105   Tell us the news!
What you can, what is right—
Heal us, soothe our fears!
Now the darkness comes to the fore,
now the hope glows through your victims,
110   beating back this raw, relentless anguish
       gnawing at the heart.

(CLYTAEMNESTRA *ignores them and pursues her rituals; they assemble for the opening chorus.*)

O but I still have power to sound the god's command at
       the roads
that launched the kings. The gods breathe power through
       my song,
       my fighting strength. Persuasion grows with the years—
I sing how the flight of fury hurled the twin command,   115
       one will that hurled young Greece
and winged the spear of vengeance straight for Troy!
The kings of birds to kings of the beaking prows, one black,
       one with a blaze of silver
              skimmed the palace spearhand right   120
              and swooping lower, all could see,
                     plunged their claws in a hare, a mother
              bursting with unborn young—the babies spilling,
quick spurts of blood—cut off the race just dashing
       into life!
Cry, cry for death, but good win out in glory in the end.   125
But the loyal seer of the armies studied Atreus' sons,
two sons with warring hearts—he saw two eagle-kings
       devour the hare and spoke the things to come,
"Years pass, and the long hunt nets the city of Priam,
       the flocks beyond the walls,   130
a kingdom's life and soul—Fate stamps them out.
Just let no curse of the gods lour on us first,
       shatter our giant armour
              forged to strangle Troy. I see
                     pure Artemis bristle in pity—   135
                     yes, the flying hounds of the Father
       slaughter for armies . . . their own victim . . . a
              woman
trembling young, all born to die—She loathes the eagles'
       feast!"
Cry, cry for death, but good win out in glory in the end.
       "Artemis, lovely Artemis, so kind   140
to the ravening lion's tender, helpless cubs,
the suckling young of beasts that stalk the wilds—
       bring this sign for all its fortune,
              all its brutal torment home to birth!
I beg you, Healing Apollo, soothe her before   145
her crosswinds hold us down and moor the ships too long,
pressing us on to another victim . . .
              nothing sacred, no,
                     no feast to be eaten
                            the architect of vengeance   150

(*Turning to the palace.*)

                     growing strong in the house
                     with no fear of the husband
here she waits
the terror raging back and back in the future
       the stealth, the law of the hearth, the mother—   155
              Memory womb of Fury child-avenging
                     Fury!"
So as the eagles wheeled at the crossroads,

---

89 **three legs** a reference to the use of a walking stick as a third
leg in old age

126 **the loyal seer** Calchas, who foretold much hardship at the
outset of the Trojan War

Calchas clashed out the great good blessings mixed with
doom
        for the halls of kings, and singing with our fate
160 we cry, cry for death, but good win out in glory in the end.

                Zeus, great nameless all in all,
                if that name will gain his favour,
                I will call him Zeus.
                I have no words to do him justice,
165   weighing all in the balance,
                all I have is Zeus, Zeus—
        lift this weight, this torment from my spirit,
                cast it once for all.

                He who was so mighty once,
170   storming for the wars of heaven,
                he has had his day.
        And then his son who came to power
                met his match in the third fall
                and he is gone. Zeus, Zeus—
175 raise your cries and sing him Zeus the Victor!
                You will reach the truth:

                Zeus has led us on to know,
                the Helmsman lays it down as law
                that we must suffer, suffer into truth.
180 We cannot sleep, and drop by drop at the heart
        the pain of pain remembered comes again,
        and we resist, but ripeness comes as well.
From the gods enthroned on the awesome rowing-bench
                there comes a violent love.

185   So it was that day the king,
                the steersman at the helm of Greece,
        would never blame a word the prophet said—
        swept away by the wrenching winds of fortune
        he conspired! Weatherbound we could not sail,
190 our stores exhausted, fighting strength hard-pressed,
        and the squadrons rode in the shallows off Chalkis
                where the riptide crashes, drags,

and winds from the north pinned down our hulls at Aulis,
port of anguish . . . head winds starving,
195   sheets and the cables snapped
        and the men's minds strayed,
                the pride, the bloom of Greece
                was raked as time ground on,
        ground down, and then the cure for the storm
200   and it was harsher—Calchas cried,
        "My captains, Artemis must have blood!"—
                so harsh the sons of Atreus
                dashed their sceptres on the rocks,
                could not hold back the tears,

205 and I still can hear the older warlord saying,
        "Obey, obey, or a heavy doom will crush me!—
        Oh but doom will crush me
                once I rend my child,
                the glory of my house—
210   a father's hands are stained,
        blood of a young girl streaks the altar.
        Pain both ways and what is worse?
        Desert the fleets, fail the alliance?
                No, but stop the winds with a virgin's blood,
215   feed their lust, their fury?—feed their fury!—

Law is law!—
                Let all go well."
And once he slipped his neck in the strap of Fate,
his spirit veering black, impure, unholy,
once he turned he stopped at nothing,   220
                seized with the frenzy
                        blinding driving to outrage—
wretched frenzy, cause of all our grief!
Yes, he had the heart
                to sacrifice his daughter,
                to bless the war that avenged a woman's loss,   225
                a bridal rite that sped the men-of-war.
"My father, father!"—she might pray to the winds;
no innocence moves her judges mad for war.
Her father called his henchmen on,
                on with a prayer,   230
                "Hoist her over the altar
like a yearling, give it all your strength!
She's fainting—lift her,
                sweep her robes around her,
                but slip this strap in her gentle curving lips . . .   235
                        here, gag her hard, a sound will curse the house"—

and the bridle chokes her voice . . . her saffron robes
pouring over the sand
                        her glance like arrows showering
wounding every murderer through with pity
                clear as a picture, live,   240
she strains to call their names . . .
I remember often the days with father's guests
when over the feast her voice unbroken,
                pure as the hymn her loving father
bearing third libations, sang to Saving Zeus—   245
transfixed with joy, Atreus' offspring
                throbbing out their love.

What comes next? I cannot see it, cannot say.
The strong techniques of Calchas do their work.
But Justice turns the balance scales,   250
                sees that we suffer
and we suffer and we learn.
And we will know the future when it comes.
Greet it too early, weep too soon.
                It all comes clear in the light of day.   255
Let all go well today, well as she could want,

(*Turning to* CLYTAEMNESTRA.)

our midnight watch, our lone defender,
                single-minded queen.
LEADER: We've come,
Clytaemnestra. We respect your power.
Right it is to honour the warlord's woman   260
once he leaves the throne.
                                But why these fires?
Good news, or more good hopes? We're loyal,
we want to hear, but never blame your silence.

---

245 **third libations** offered to Zeus, following libations to the
gods of Olympus and the spirits of the dead

CLYTAEMNESTRA: Let the new day shine—as the proverb says—
265   glorious from the womb of Mother Night.

(*Lost in prayer, then turning to the* CHORUS.)

You will hear a joy beyond your hopes.
Priam's citadel—the Greeks have taken Troy!
LEADER: No, what do you mean? I can't believe it.
CLYTAEMNESTRA: Troy is ours. Is that clear enough?
LEADER: The joy of it,
270   stealing over me, calling up my tears—
CLYTAEMNESTRA: Yes, your eyes expose your loyal hearts.
LEADER: And you have proof?
CLYTAEMNESTRA: I do,
I must. Unless the god is lying.
LEADER: That,
or a phantom spirit sends you into raptures.
275 CLYTAEMNESTRA: No one takes me in with visions—senseless
dreams.
LEADER: Or giddy rumour, you haven't indulged yourself—
CLYTAEMNESTRA: You treat me like a child, you mock me?
LEADER: Then when did they storm the city?
CLYTAEMNESTRA: Last night, I say, the mother of this
morning.
280 LEADER: And who on earth could run the news so fast?
CLYTAEMNESTRA: The god of fire—rushing fire from Ida!
And beacon to beacon rushed it on to me,
my couriers riding home the torch.
                              From Troy
to the bare rock of Lemnos, Hermes' Spur,
285   and the Escort winged the great light west
to the Saving Father's face, Mount Athos hurled it
third in the chain and leaping Ocean's back
the blaze went dancing on to ecstasy—pitch-pine
streaming gold like a new-born sun—and brought
290   the word in flame to Mount Makistos' brow.
No time to waste, straining, fighting sleep,
that lookout heaved a torch glowing over
the murderous straits of Euripos to reach
Messapion's watchmen craning for the signal.
295   Fire for word of fire! tense with the heather
withered gray, they stack it, set it ablaze—
the hot force of the beacon never flags,
it springs the Plain of Asôpos, rears
like a harvest moon to hit Kithairon's crest
300   and drives new men to drive the fire on.
That relay pants for the far-flung torch,
they swell its strength outstripping my commands
and the light inflames the marsh, the Gorgon's Eye,
it strikes the peak where the wild goats range—
305   my laws, my fire whips that camp!
They spare nothing, eager to build its heat,
and a huge beard of flame overcomes the headland
beetling down the Saronic Gulf, and flaring south
it brings the dawn to the Black Widow's face—
310   the watch that looms above your heads—and now
the true son of the burning flanks of Ida

---

281 **Ida** mountain near Troy   286 **Saving Father's face** Mount
Athos, a seat of Zeus the Savior in northern Greece   309 **Black
Widow's face** "Spider Mountain," perhaps the citadel of Mycenae

crashes on the roofs of Atreus' sons!
And I ordained it all.
Torch to torch, running for their lives,
one long succession racing home my fire.   315
                                        One,
first in the laps and last, wins out in triumph.
There you have my proof, my burning sign, I tell you—
the power my lord passed on from Troy to me!
LEADER: We'll thank the gods, my lady—first this story,
let me lose myself in the wonder of it all!   320
Tell it start to finish, tell us all.
CLYTAEMNESTRA: The city's ours—in our hands this very day!
I can hear the cries in crossfire rock the walls.
Pour oil and wine in the same bowl,
what have you, friendship? A struggle to the end.   325
So with the victors and the victims—the outcries,
you can hear them clashing like their fates.

They are kneeling by the bodies of the dead,
embracing men and brothers, infants over
the aged loins that gave them life, and sobbing,   330
as the yoke constricts their last free breath,
for every dear one lost.
                    And the others,
there, plunging breakneck through the night—
the labour of battle sets them down, ravenous,
to breakfast on the last remains of Troy.   335
Not by rank but chance, by the lots they draw,
they lodge in the houses captured by the spear,
settling in so soon, released from the open sky,
the frost and dew. Lucky men, off guard at last,
they sleep away their first good night in years.   340
If only they are revering the city's gods,
the shrines of the gods who love the conquered land,
no plunderer will be plundered in return.
Just let no lust, no mad desire seize the armies
to ravish what they must not touch—   345
overwhelmed by all they've won!
                          The run for home
and safety waits, the swerve at the post,
the final lap of the gruelling two-lap race.
And even if the men come back with no offence
to the gods, the avenging dead may never rest—   350
Oh let no new disaster strike! And here
you have it, what a woman has to say.
Let the best win out, clear to see.
A small desire but all that I could want.
LEADER: Spoken like a man, my lady, loyal,   355
full of self-command. I've heard your sign
and now your vision.

(*Reaching towards her as she turns and re-enters the palace.*)

                    Now to praise the gods.
The joy is worth the labour.
CHORUS: O Zeus my king and Night, dear Night,
queen of the house who covers us with glories,   360
you slung your net on the towers of Troy,
neither young nor strong could leap
the giant dredge net of slavery,
    all-embracing ruin.
I adore you, iron Zeus of the guests   365

and your revenge—you drew your longbow
year by year to a taut full draw
till one bolt, not falling short
or arching over the stars,
370   could split the mark of Paris!
The sky stroke of god!—it is all Troy's to tell,
but even I can trace it to its cause:
god does as god decrees.
        And still some say
375   that heaven would never stoop to punish men
who trample the lovely grace of things
untouchable. How wrong they are!
        A curse burns bright on crime—
            full-blown, the father's crimes will blossom,
380   burst into the son's.
Let there be less suffering . . .
give us the sense to live on what we need.

            Bastions of wealth
            are no defence for the man
385   who treads the grand altar of Justice
                down and out of sight.

Persuasion, maddening child of Ruin
overpowers him—Ruin plans it all.
And the wound will smoulder on,
390   there is no cure,
a terrible brilliance kindles on the night.
He is bad bronze scraped on a touchstone:
put to the test, the man goes black.
        Like the boy who chases
395   a bird on the wing, brands his city,
            brings it down and prays,
but the gods are deaf
to the one who turns to crime, they tear him down.

            So Paris learned:
400   he came to Atreus' house
            and shamed the tables spread for guests,
                he stole away the queen.

And she left her land chaos, clanging shields,
companions tramping, bronze prows, men in bronze,
405   and she came to Troy with a dowry, death,
strode through the gates
        defiant in every stride,
as prophets of the house looked on and wept,
"Oh the halls and the lords of war,
410   the bed and the fresh prints of love.
I *see* him, unavenging, unavenged,
the stun of his desolation is so clear—
        he longs for the one who lies across the sea
until her phantom seems to sway the house.
415   Her curving images,
                her beauty hurts her lord,
                the eyes starve and the touch
                of love is gone,

"and radiant dreams are passing in the night,
420   the memories throb with sorrow, joy with pain . . .
        it is pain to dream and see desires
slip through the arms,
        a vision lost for ever

winging down the moving drifts of sleep."
So he grieves at the royal hearth   425
        yet others' grief is worse, far worse.
All through Greece for those who flocked to war
they are holding back the anguish now,
        you can feel it rising now in every house;
I tell you there is much to tear the heart.   430

            They knew the men they sent,
            but now in place of men
            ashes and urns come back
                to every hearth.

War, War, the great gold-broker of corpses   435
holds the balance of the battle on his spear!
Home from the pyres he sends them,
        home from Troy to the loved ones,
heavy with tears, the urns brimmed full,
        the heroes return in gold-dust,   440
dear, light ash for men; and they weep,
they praise them, "He had skill in the swordplay,"
        "He went down so tall in the onslaught,"
"All for another's woman." So they mutter
in secret and the rancour steals   445
towards our staunch defenders, Atreus' sons.

            And there they ring the walls, the young,
            the lithe, the handsome hold the graves
            they won in Troy; the enemy earth
                rides over those who conquered.   450

The people's voice is heavy with hatred,
now the curses of the people must be paid,
and now I wait, I listen . . .
        there—there is something breathing
under the night's shroud. God takes aim   455
        at the ones who murder many;
the swarthy Furies stalk the man
gone rich beyond all rights—with a twist
        of fortune grind him down, dissolve him
into the blurring dead—there is no help.   460
The reach for power can recoil,
the bolt of god can strike you at a glance.

            Make me rich with no man's envy,
            neither a raider of cities, no,
            nor slave come face to face with life   465
                overpowered by another.

(Speaking singly.)

—Fire comes and the news is good,
        it races through the streets
but is it true? Who knows?
Or just another lie from heaven?   470

—Show us the man so childish, wonderstruck,
        he's fired up with the first torch,
then when the message shifts
he's sick at heart.
                —Just like a woman
to fill with thanks before the truth is clear.   475

—So gullible. Their stories spread like wildfire,
        they fly fast and die faster;
rumours voiced by women coming to nothing.

LEADER: Soon we'll know her fires for what they are,
480   her relay race of torches hand-to-hand—
know if they're real or just a dream,
the hope of a morning here to take our senses.
I see a herald running from the beach
and a victor's spray of olive shades his eyes
485   and the dust he kicks, twin to the mud of Troy,
shows he has a voice—no kindling timber
on the cliffs, no signal-fires for him.
He can shout the news and give us joy,
or else . . . please, not that.
                                 Bring it on,
490   good fuel to build the first good fires.
And if anyone calls down the worst on Argos
let him reap the rotten harvest of his mind.

(*The* HERALD *rushes in and kneels on the ground.*)

HERALD: Good Greek earth, the soil of my fathers!
Ten years out, and a morning brings me back.
495   All hopes snapped but one—I'm home at last.
Never dreamed I'd die in Greece, assigned
the narrow plot I love the best.
                                 And now
I salute the land, the light of the sun,
our high lord Zeus and the king of Pytho—
500   no more arrows, master, raining on our heads!
At Scamander's banks we took our share,
your longbow brought us down like plague.
Now come, deliver us, heal us—lord Apollo!
Gods of the market, here, take my salute.
505   And you, my Hermes, Escort,
loving Herald, the herald's shield and prayer!—
And the shining dead of the land who launched the armies,
warm us home . . . we're all the spear has left.
You halls of the kings, you roofs I cherish,
510   sacred seats—you gods that catch the sun,
if your glances ever shone on him in the old days,
greet him well—so many years are lost.
He comes, he brings us light in the darkness,
free for every comrade, Agamemnon lord of men.
515   Give him the royal welcome he deserves!
He hoisted the pickaxe of Zeus who brings revenge,
he dug Troy down, he worked her soil down,
the shrines of her gods and the high altars, gone!—
and the seed of her wide earth he ground to bits.
520   That's the yoke he claps on Troy. The king,
the son of Atreus comes. The man is blest,
the one man alive to merit such rewards.

Neither Paris nor Troy, partners to the end,
can say their work outweighs their wages now.
525   Convicted of rapine, stripped of all his spoils,
and his father's house and the land that gave it life—
he's scythed them to the roots. The sons of Priam
pay the price twice over.

499–502 **the king of Pytho . . . plague** at Troy, when Agamemnon refused to release a daughter of Apollo's priest, Apollo ("king
of Pytho") visited a plague upon the Greeks by shooting his arrows among them   528 **pay the price twice over** in ancient
Greek law, double damages were the penalty for theft

LEADER: Welcome home
from the wars, herald, long live your joy.
HERALD: *Our* joy—
now I could die gladly. Say the word, dear gods.   530
LEADER: Longing for your country left you raw?
HERALD: The tears fill my eyes, for joy.
LEADER: You too,
down the sweet disease that kills a man
with kindness . . .
HERALD: Go on, I don't see what you—
LEADER: Love
for the ones who love you—that's what took you.   535
HERALD: You mean
the land and the armies hungered for each other?
LEADER: There were times I thought I'd faint with longing.
HERALD: So anxious for the armies, why?
LEADER: For years now,
only my silence kept me free from harm.
HERALD: What,
with the kings gone did someone threaten you?   540
LEADER: So much . . .
now as you say, it would be good to die.
HERALD: True, we *have* done well.
Think back in the years and what have you?
A few runs of luck, a lot that's bad.
Who but a god can go through life unmarked?   545
A long, hard pull we had, if I would tell it all.
The iron rations, penned in the gangways
hock by jowl like sheep. Whatever miseries
break a man, our quota, every sun-starved day.

Then on the beaches it was worse. Dug in   550
under the enemy ramparts—deadly going.
Out of the sky, out of the marshy flats
the dews soaked us, turned the ruts we fought from
into gullies, made our gear, our scalps
crawl with lice.   555
                   And talk of the cold,
the sleet to freeze the gulls, and the big snows
come avalanching down from Ida. Oh but the heat,
the sea and the windless noons, the swells asleep,
dropped to a dead calm . . .

But why weep now?   560
It's over for us, over for them.
The dead can rest and never rise again;
no need to call their muster. We're alive,
do we have to go on raking up old wounds?
Good-bye to all that. Glad I am to say it.   565

For us, the remains of the Greek contingents,
the good wins out, no pain can tip the scales,
not now. So shout this boast to the bright sun—
fitting it is—wing it over the seas and rolling earth:

"Once when an Argive expedition captured Troy   570
they hauled these spoils back to the gods of Greece,
they bolted them high across the temple doors,
the glory of the past!"
                       And hearing that,
men will applaud our city and our chiefs,
and Zeus will have the hero's share of fame—   575
he did the work.

That's all I have to say.
LEADER: I'm convinced, glad that I was wrong.
Never too old to learn; it keeps me young.

(CLYTAEMNESTRA *enters with her women.*)

First the house and the queen, it's their affair,
580 but I can taste the riches.
CLYTAEMNESTRA: I cried out long ago!—
for joy, when the first herald came burning
through the night and told the city's fall.
And there were some who smiled and said,
"A few fires persuade you Troy's in ashes.
585 Women, women, elated over nothing."

You made me seem deranged.
For all that I sacrificed—a woman's way,
you'll say—station to station on the walls
we lifted cries of triumph that resounded
590 in the temples of the gods. We lulled and blessed
the fires with myrrh and they consumed our victims.

(*Turning to the* HERALD.)

But enough. Why prolong the story?
From the king himself I'll gather all I need.
Now for the best way to welcome home
595 my lord, my good lord . . .
No time to lose!
What dawn can feast a woman's eyes like this?
I can see the light, the husband plucked from war
by the Saving God and open wide the gates.

Tell him that, and have him come with speed,
600 the people's darling—how they long for him.
And for his wife,
may he return and find her true at hall,
just as the day he left her, faithful to the last.
A watchdog gentle to him alone,

(*Glancing towards the palace.*)

savage
605 to those who cross his path. I have not changed.
The strains of time can never break our seal.
In love with a new lord, in ill repute I am
as practised as I am in dyeing bronze.

That is my boast, teeming with the truth.
610 I am proud, a woman of my nobility—
I'd hurl it from the roofs!

(*She turns sharply, enters the palace.*)

LEADER: She speaks well, but it takes no seer to know
she only says what's right.

(*The* HERALD *attempts to leave; the* LEADER *takes him by the arm.*)

Wait, one thing.
Menelaus, is he home too, safe with the men?
615 The power of the land—dear king.
HERALD: I doubt that lies will help my friends,
in the lean months to come.

---

580 **I can taste the riches** according to custom, the bearer of good news was rewarded

LEADER: Help us somehow, tell the truth as well.
But when the two conflict it's hard to hide—
out with it. 620
HERALD: He's lost, gone from the fleets!
He and his ship, it's true.
LEADER: After you watched him
pull away from Troy? Or did some storm
attack you all and tear him off the line?
HERALD: There,
like a marksman, the whole disaster cut to a word.
LEADER: How do the escorts give him out—dead or alive? 625
HERALD: No clear report. No one knows . . .
only the wheeling sun that heats the earth to life.
LEADER: But then the storm—how did it reach the ships?
How did it end? Were the angry gods on hand?
HERALD: This blessed day, ruin it with *them*? 630
Better to keep their trophies far apart.

When a runner comes, his face in tears,
saddled with what his city dreaded most,
the armies routed, two wounds in one,
one to the city, one to hearth and home . . . 635
our best men, droves of them, victims
herded from every house by the two-barb whip
that Ares likes to crack,
that charioteer
who packs destruction shaft by shaft,
careering on with his brace of bloody mares— 640
When he comes in, I tell you, dragging that much pain,
wail your battle-hymn to the Furies, and high time!
But when he brings salvation home to a city
singing out her heart—
how can I mix the good with so much bad 645
and blurt out this?—
"Storms swept the Greeks,
and not without the anger of the gods!"
Those enemies for ages, fire and water,
sealed a pact and showed it to the world—
they crushed our wretched squadrons. 650
Night looming,
breakers lunging in for the kill
and the black gales come brawling out of the north—
ships ramming, prow into hooking prow, gored
by the rush-and-buck of hurricane pounding rain
by the cloudburst— 655
ships stampeding into the darkness,
lashed and spun by the savage shepherd's hand!

But when the sun comes up to light the skies
I see the Aegean heaving into a great bloom
of corpses . . . Greeks, the pick of a generation
scattered through the wrecks and broken spars. 660

But not us, not our ship, our hull untouched.
Someone stole us away or begged us off.
No mortal—a god, death grip on the tiller,
or lady luck herself, perched on the helm,
she pulled us through, she saved us. Aye, 665
we'll never battle the heavy surf at anchor,
never shipwreck up some rocky coast.

---

648 **fire and water** lightning and the sea

But once we cleared that sea-hell, not even
trusting luck in the cold light of day,
670 we battened on our troubles, they were fresh—
the armada punished, bludgeoned into nothing.
And now if one of them still has the breath
he's saying *we* are lost. Why not?
We say the same of him. Well,
675 here's to the best.
                    And Menelaus?
Look to it, he's come back, and yet . . .
if a shaft of the sun can track him down,
alive, and his eyes full of the old fire—
thanks to the strategies of Zeus, Zeus
680 would never tear the house out by the roots—
then there's hope our man will make it home.

You've heard it all. Now you have the truth.

(*Rushing out.*)

CHORUS: Who—what power named the name that drove your
                    fate?—
what hidden brain could divine your future,
685 steer that word to the mark,
to the bride of spears,
        the whirlpool churning armies,
                    Oh for all the world a Helen!
Hell at the prows, hell at the gates
690 hell on the men-of-war,
from her lair's sheer veils she drifted
        launched by the giant western wind,
                and the long tall waves of men in armour,
huntsmen trailing the oar-blades' dying spoor
695 slipped into her moorings,
        Simois' mouth that chokes with foliage,
                    bayed for bloody strife,
for Troy's Blood Wedding Day—she drives her word,
her burning will to the birth, the Fury
700 late but true to the cause,
to the tables shamed
        and Zeus who guards the hearth—
            the Fury makes the Trojans pay!
Shouting their hymns, hymns for the bride
705 hymns for the kinsmen doomed
to the wedding march of Fate.
        Troy changed her tune in her late age,
            and I think I hear the dirges mourning
"Paris, born and groomed for the bed of Fate!"
710 They mourn with their life breath,
        they sing their last, the sons of Priam
                    born for bloody slaughter.
        So a man once reared
a lion cub at hall, snatched
715 from the breast, still craving milk
        in the first flush of life.
A captivating pet for the young,
and the old men adored it, pampered it
        in their arms, day in, day out,
720 like an infant just born.
Its eyes on fire, little beggar,
fawning for its belly, slave to food.

        But it came of age
and the parent strain broke out
and it paid its breeders back.   725
    Grateful it was, it went
through the flock to prepare a feast,
an illicit orgy—the house swam with blood,
        none could resist that agony—
                    massacre vast and raw!   730
From god there came a priest of ruin,
adopted by the house to lend it warmth.
And the first sensation Helen brought to Troy . . .
call it a spirit
        shimmer of winds dying   735
                glory light as gold
            shaft of the eyes dissolving, open bloom
        that wounds the heart with love.
But veering wild in mid-flight
she whirled her wedding on to a stabbing end,   740
slashed at the sons of Priam—hearthmate, friend to the
        death,
            sped by Zeus who speeds the guest,
a bride of tears, a Fury.

There's an ancient saying, old as man himself:
men's prosperity   745
        never will die childless,
                once full-grown it breeds.
        Sprung from the great good fortune in the race
    comes bloom on bloom of pain—
insatiable wealth! But not I,   750
I alone say this. Only the reckless act
can breed impiety, multiplying crime on crime,
        while the house kept straight and just
is blessed with radiant children.

        But ancient Violence longs to breed,   755
                new Violence comes
        when its fatal hour comes, the demon comes
        to take her toll—no war, no force, no prayer
            can hinder the midnight Fury stamped
with parent Fury moving through the house.   760

        But Justice shines in sooty hovels,
                loves the decent life.
        From proud halls crusted with gilt by filthy hands
            she turns her eyes to find the pure in spirit—
spurning the wealth stamped counterfeit with praise,   765
        she steers all things towards their destined end.

(AGAMEMNON *enters in his chariot, his plunder borne before him by
his entourage; behind him, half hidden, stands* CASSANDRA. *The*
OLD MEN *press towards him.*)

Come, my king, the scourge of Troy,
        the true son of Atreus—
How to salute you, how to praise you
neither too high nor low, but hit   770
the note of praise that suits the hour?
So many prize some brave display,

---

725 **it paid its breeders back** on reaching maturity, children
customarily made thank offerings to their parents

they prefer some flaunt of honour
   once they break the bounds.
775 When a man fails they share his grief,
but the pain can never cut them to the quick.
When a man succeeds they share his glory,
torturing their faces into smiles.
But the good shepherd knows his flock.
780 When the eyes seem to brim with love
   and it is only unction, fawning,
he will know, better than we can know.
That day you marshalled the armies
all for Helen—no hiding it now—
785 I drew you in my mind in black;
you seemed a menace at the helm,
   sending men to the grave
to bring her home, that hell on earth.
But now from the depths of trust and love
790 I say Well fought, well won—
   the end is worth the labour!
Search, my king, and learn at last
who stayed at home and kept their faith
   and who betrayed the city.

AGAMEMNON: First,
795 with justice I salute my Argos and my gods,
my accomplices who brought me home and won
my rights from Priam's Troy—the just gods.
No need to hear our pleas. Once for all
they consigned their lots to the urn of blood,
800 they pitched on death for men, annihilation
for the city. Hope's hand, hovering
over the urn of mercy, left it empty.
Look for the smoke—it is the city's seamark,
building even now.
          The storms of ruin live!
805 Her last dying breath, rising up from the ashes
sends us gales of incense rich in gold.

For that we must thank the gods with a sacrifice
our sons will long remember. For their mad outrage
of a queen we raped their city—we were right.
810 The beast of Argos, foals of the wild mare,
thousands massed in armour rose on the night
the Pleiades went down, and crashing through
their walls our bloody lion lapped its fill,
gorging on the blood of kings.
          Our thanks to the gods,
815 long drawn out, but it is just the prelude.

(CLYTAEMNESTRA *approaches with her* ATTENDANTS; *they are carrying dark red tapestries.* AGAMEMNON *turns to the leader.*)

And your concern, old man, is on my mind.
I hear you and agree, I will support you.
How rare, men with the character to praise
820 a friend's success without a trace of envy,
poison to the heart—it deals a double blow.
Your own losses weigh you down but then,

look at your neighbour's fortune and you weep.
Well I know. I understand society,
the flattering mirror of the proud.
          My comrades . . .
they're shadows, I tell you, ghosts of men   825
who swore they'd die for me. Only Odysseus:
I dragged that man to the wars but once in harness
he was a trace-horse, he gave his all for me.
Dead or alive, no matter, I can praise him.

And now this cause involving men and gods.   830
We must summon the city for a trial,
found a national tribunal. Whatever's healthy,
shore it up with law and help it flourish.
Wherever something calls for drastic cures
we make our noblest effort: amputate or wield   835
the healing iron, burn the cancer at the roots.

Now I go to my father's house—
I give the gods my right hand, my first salute.
The ones who sent me forth have brought me home.

(*He starts down from the chariot, looks at* CLYTAEMNESTRA, *stops, and offers up a prayer.*)

Victory, you have sped my way before,   840
now speed me to the last.

(CLYTAEMNESTRA *turns from the king to the* CHORUS.)

CLYTAEMNESTRA: Old nobility of Argos
gathered here, I am not ashamed to tell you
how I love the man. I am older,
and the fear dies away . . . I am human.
Nothing I say was learned from others.   845
This is my life, my ordeal, long as the siege
he laid at Troy and more demanding.
          First,
when a woman sits at home and the man is gone,
the loneliness is terrible,
unconscionable . . .   850
and the rumours spread and fester,
a runner comes with something dreadful,
close on his heels the next and his news worse,
and they shout it out and the whole house can hear:
and wounds—if he took one wound for each report   855
to penetrate these walls, he's gashed like a dragnet,
more, if he had only died . . .
for each death that swelled his record, he could boast
like a triple-bodied Geryon risen from the grave,
"Three shrouds I dug from the earth, one for every body   860
that went down!"
          The rumours broke like fever,
broke and then rose higher. There were times
they cut me down and eased my throat from the noose.
I wavered between the living and the dead.

(*Turning to* AGAMEMNON.)

          And so
our child is gone, not standing by our side,   865

799–802 **they consigned . . . empty** Athenian citizens voted in law cases by placing one hand over each of two urns and dropping a voting-pebble into either the urn for acquittal or the urn for condemnation   810 **the wild mare** the Trojan Horse

826–828 **Only Odysseus . . . trace-horse** to try to evade conscription for the Trojan War, Odysseus feigned madness, but performed loyally once at war   859 **Geryon** a three-bodied giant killed by Heracles

the bond of our dearest pledges, mine and yours;
by all rights our child should be here . . .
Orestes. You seem startled.
You needn't be. Our loyal brother-in-arms
870 will take good care of him, Strophios the Phocian.
He warned from the start we court two griefs in one.
You risk all on the wars—and what if the people
rise up howling for the king, and anarchy
should dash our plans?
                            Men, it is their nature,
875 trampling on the fighter once he's down.
Our child is gone. That is my self-defence
and it is true.
        For me, the tears that welled
like springs are dry. I have no tears to spare.
I'd watch till late at night, my eyes still burn,
880 I sobbed by the torch I lit for you alone.

(*Glancing towards the palace.*)

I never let it die . . . but in my dreams
the high thin wail of a gnat would rouse me,
piercing like a trumpet—I could see you
suffer more than all
885 the hours that slept with me could ever bear.

I endured it all. And now, free of grief,
I would salute that man the watchdog of the fold,
the mainroyal, saving stay of the vessel,
rooted oak that thrusts the roof sky-high,
890 the father's one true heir.
Land at dawn to the shipwrecked past all hope,
light of the morning burning off the night of storm,
the cold clear spring to the parched horseman—
O the ecstasy, to flee the yoke of Fate!
895 It is right to use the titles he deserves.
Let envy keep her distance. We have suffered
long enough.

(*Reaching towards* AGAMEMNON.)

                    Come to me now, my dearest,
down from the car of war, but never set the foot
that stamped out Troy on earth again, my great one.

900 Women, why delay? You have your orders.
Pave his way with tapestries.

(*They begin to spread the crimson tapestries between the king and the palace doors.*)

                    Quickly.
Let the red stream flow and bear him home
to the home he never hoped to see—Justice,
lead him in!
        Leave all the rest to me.
905 The spirit within me never yields to sleep.
We will set things right, with the god's help.
We will do whatever Fate requires.
AGAMEMNON: There
is Leda's daughter, the keeper of my house.

908 **Leda** visited by Zeus in the form of a swan, Leda conceived both Clytaemnestra and Helen

And the speech to suit my absence, much too long.
But the praise that does us justice,   910
let it come from others, then we prize it.
                            This—
you treat me like a woman. Grovelling, gaping up at me—
what am I, some barbarian peacocking out of Asia?
Never cross my path with robes and draw the lightning.
Never—only the gods deserve the pomps of honour   915
and the stiff brocades of fame. To walk on them . . .
I am human, and it makes my pulses stir
with dread.
        Give me the tributes of a man
and not a god, a little earth to walk on,
not this gorgeous work.   920
There is no need to sound my reputation.
I have a sense of right and wrong, what's more—
heaven's proudest gift. Call no man blest
until he ends his life in peace, fulfilled.
If I can live by what I say, I have no fear.   925
CLYTAEMNESTRA: One thing more. Be true to your ideals and
    tell me—
AGAMEMNON: True to my ideals? Once I violate them I am
    lost.
CLYTAEMNESTRA: Would you have sworn this act to god in a
    time of terror?
AGAMEMNON: Yes, if a prophet called for a last, drastic rite.
CLYTAEMNESTRA: But Priam—can you see him if he had your   930
    success?
AGAMEMNON: Striding on the tapestries of god, I see him
    now.
CLYTAEMNESTRA: And *you* fear the reproach of common
    men?
AGAMEMNON: The voice of the people—aye, they have
    enormous power.
CLYTAEMNESTRA: Perhaps, but where's the glory without a
    little gall?
AGAMEMNON: And where's the woman in all this lust for   935
    glory?
CLYTAEMNESTRA: But the great victor—it becomes him to
    give way.
AGAMEMNON: Victory in this . . . war of ours, it means so
    much to you?
CLYTAEMNESTRA: O give way! The power is yours if you
    surrender,
all of your own free will, to me!
AGAMEMNON: Enough.
If you are so determined—   940

(*Turning to the* ATTENDANTS, *pointing to his boots.*)

Let someone help me off with these at least.
Old slaves, they've stood me well.
                            Hurry,
and while I tread his splendours dyed red in the sea,
may no god watch and strike me down with envy
from on high. I feel such shame—   945
to tread the life of the house, a kingdom's worth
of silver in the weaving.

(*He steps down from the chariot to the tapestries and reveals* CASSANDRA, *dressed in the sacred regalia, the fillets, robes, and sceptre of Apollo.*)

Done is done.
Escort this stranger in, be gentle.
Conquer with compassion. Then the gods
950   shine down upon you, gently. No one chooses
the yoke of slavery, not of one's free will—
and she least of all. The gift of the armies,
flower and pride of all the wealth we won,
she follows me from Troy.
                              And now,
955   since you have brought me down with your insistence,
just this once I enter my father's house,
trampling royal crimson as I go.

(*He takes his first steps and pauses.*)

CLYTAEMNESTRA: There is the sea
and who will drain it dry? Precious as silver,
inexhaustible, ever-new, it breeds the more we reap it—
960   tides on tides of crimson dye our robes blood-red.
Our lives are based on wealth, my king,
the gods have seen to that.
Destitution, our house has never heard the word.
I would have sworn to tread on legacies of robes,
965   at one command from an oracle, deplete the house—
suffer the worst to bring that dear life back!

(*Encouraged,* AGAMEMNON *strides to the entrance.*)

When the root lives on, the new leaves come back,
spreading a dense shroud of shade across the house
to thwart the Dog Star's fury. So you return
970   to the father's hearth, you bring us warmth in winter
like the sun—
                    And you are Zeus when Zeus
tramples the bitter virgin grape for new wine
and the welcome chill steals through the halls, at last
the master moves among the shadows of his house,
fulfilled.

(AGAMEMNON *goes over the threshold; the* ATTENDANTS *gather up the tapestries while* CLYTAEMNESTRA *prays.*)

975   Zeus, Zeus, master of all fulfilment, now fulfil our
        prayers—
speed our rites to their fulfilment once for all!

(*She enters the palace, the doors close, the* OLD MEN *huddle in terror.*)

CHORUS: Why, why does it rock me, never stops,
this terror beating down my heart,
            this seer that sees it all—
980   it beats its wings, uncalled unpaid
thrust on the lungs
the mercenary song beats on and on
singing a prophet's strain—
            and I can't throw it off
985   like dreams that make no sense,
and the strength drains
that filled the mind with trust,
and the years drift by and the driven sand
            has buried the mooring lines

---

969 **Dog Star** Sirius, whose rising commonly marks the hot "dog days" of summer

---

that churned when the armoured squadrons cut for Troy …   990
and now I believe it, I can prove he's home,
            my own clear eyes for witness—
                                            Agamemnon!
Still it's chanting, beating deep so deep in the heart
this dirge of the Furies, oh dear god,
not fit for the lyre, its own master   995
    it kills our spirit
kills our hopes
and it's real, true, no fantasy—
            stark terror whirls the brain
                and the end is coming   1000
                    Justice comes to birth—
I pray my fears prove false and fall
and die and never come to birth!
Even exultant health, well we know,
    exceeds its limits, comes so near disease   1005
it can breach the wall between them.

Even a man's fate, held true on course,
    in a blinding flash rams some hidden reef;
but if caution only casts the pick of the cargo—
one well-balanced cast—   1010
the house will not go down, not outright;
labouring under its wealth of grief
the ship of state rides on.

Yes, and the great green bounty of god,
sown in the furrows year by year and reaped each fall   1015
can end the plague of famine.

But a man's life-blood
    is dark and mortal.
Once it wets the earth
what song can sing it back?   1020
Not even the master-healer
    who brought the dead to life—
Zeus stopped the man before he did more harm.

Oh, if only the gods had never forged
the chain that curbs our excess,   1025
    one man's fate curbing the next man's fate,
my heart would outrace my song, I'd pour out all I feel—
            but no, I choke with anguish,
                mutter through the nights.
Never to ravel out a hope in time   1030
and the brain is swarming, burning—

(CLYTAEMNESTRA *emerges from the palace and goes to* CASSANDRA, *impassive in the chariot.*)

CLYTAEMNESTRA: Won't you come inside? I mean you,
    Cassandra.
Zeus in all his mercy wants you to share
some victory libations with the house.
The slaves are flocking. Come, lead them   1035
up to the altar of the god who guards
our dearest treasures.

---

995 **not fit for the lyre** the lyre-god, Apollo, required songs of joy, not mourning   1021 **the master-healer** the physician Asclepius, who restored a dead man to life and was struck dead in consequence by Zeus

                                   Down from the chariot,
          this is no time for pride. Why even Heracles,
          they say, was sold into bondage long ago,
1040   he had to endure the bitter bread of slaves.
          But if the yoke descends on you, be grateful
          for a master born and reared in ancient wealth.
          Those who reap a harvest past their hopes
          are merciless to their slaves.
                                   From us
1045   you will receive what custom says is right.

          (CASSANDRA *remains impassive.*)

LEADER: It's *you* she is speaking to, it's all too clear.
          You're caught in the nets of doom—obey
          if you can obey, unless you cannot bear to.
CLYTAEMNESTRA: Unless she's like a swallow, possessed
1050   of her own barbaric song, strange, dark.
          I speak directly as I can—she must obey.
LEADER: Go with her. Make the best of it, she's right.
          Step down from the seat, obey her.
CLYTAEMNESTRA: Do it now—
          I have no time to spend outside. Already
1055   the victims crowd the hearth, the Navelstone,
          to bless this day of joy I never hoped to see!—
          our victims waiting for the fire and the knife,
          and you,
          if you want to taste our mystic rites, come now.
1060   If my words can't reach you—

          (*Turning to the* LEADER.)

                                   Give her a sign,
          one of her exotic handsigns.
LEADER: I think
          the stranger needs an interpreter, someone clear.
          She's like a wild creature, fresh caught.
CLYTAEMNESTRA: She's mad,
          her evil genius murmuring in her ears.
1065   She comes from a *city* fresh caught.
          She must learn to take the cutting bridle
          before she foams her spirit off in blood—
          and that's the last I waste on her contempt!

          (*Wheeling, re-entering the palace. The* LEADER *turns to* CASSAN-
          DRA, *who remains transfixed.*)

LEADER: Not I, I pity her. I will be gentle.
1070   Come, poor thing. Leave the empty chariot—
          Of your own free will try on the yoke of Fate.
CASSANDRA: Aieeeeee! Earth—Mother—
                                   Curse of the Earth—Apollo Apollo!
LEADER: Why cry to Apollo?
          He's not the god to call with sounds of mourning.
1075 CASSANDRA: Aieeeeee! Earth—Mother—
                                   Rape of the Earth—Apollo Apollo!
LEADER: Again, it's a bad omen.
          She cries for the god who wants no part of grief.

          (CASSANDRA *steps from the chariot, looks slowly towards the
          rooftops of the palace.*)

1038–1040 **Why even Heracles . . . slaves** as punishment,
Heracles was sold in bondage by Hermes to Omphale, queen of
Lydia   1055 **the Navelstone** an allusion to Apollo's "World
Navel," a stone erected at Delphi

CASSANDRA: God of the long road,
                    Apollo *Apollo* my destroyer—
          you destroy me once, destroy me twice—   1080
LEADER: She's about to sense her own ordeal, I think.
          Slave that she is, the god lives on inside her.
CASSANDRA: God of the iron marches,
                    Apollo *Apollo* my destroyer—
          where, where have you led me now? what house—   1085
LEADER: The house of Atreus and his sons. Really—
          don't you know? It's true, see for yourself.
CASSANDRA: No . . . the house that hates god,
          an echoing womb of guilt, kinsmen
                    torturing kinsmen, severed heads,   1090
          slaughterhouse of heroes, soil streaming blood—
LEADER: A keen hound, this stranger.
          Trailing murder, and murder she will find.
CASSANDRA: See, my witnesses—
          I trust to them, to the babies   1095
                    wailing, skewered on the sword,
          their flesh charred, the father gorging on their parts—
LEADER: We'd heard your fame as a seer,
          but no one looks for seers in Argos.
CASSANDRA: Oh no, what horror, what new plot,   1100
          new agony this?—
          it's growing, massing, deep in the house,
                    a plot, a monstrous—*thing*
                    to crush the loved ones, no,
          there is no cure, and rescue's far away and—   1105
LEADER: I can't read these signs; I knew the first,
          the city rings with them.
CASSANDRA: You, you godforsaken—you'd do *this*?
          The lord of your bed,
          you bathe him . . . his body glistens, then—   1110
                    how to tell the climax?—
                    comes so quickly, see,
          hand over hand shoots out, hauling ropes—
                                             then lunge!
LEADER: Still lost. Her riddles, her dark words of god—
          I'm groping, helpless.   1115
CASSANDRA: No no, look *there*!—
          what's that? some net flung out of hell—
                    No, she is the snare,
          the bedmate, deathmate, murder's strong right arm!
                    Let the insatiate discord in the race
          rear up and shriek "Avenge the victim—stone them dead!" 1120
LEADER: What Fury is this? Why rouse it, lift its wailing
          through the house? I hear you and lose hope.
CHORUS: Drop by drop at the heart, the gold of life ebbs out.
          We are the old soldiers . . . wounds will come
          with the crushing sunset of our lives.   1125
          Death is close, and quick.
CASSANDRA: Look out! *look out!*—
          Ai, drag the great bull from the mate!—
          a thrash of robes, she traps him—
          writhing—
                    black horn glints, twists—
                                   she gores him through!
          And now he buckles, look, the bath swirls red—   1130
          There's stealth and murder in the cauldron, do you hear?
LEADER: I'm no judge, I've little skill with the oracles,
          but even I know danger when I hear it.

CHORUS: What good are the oracles to men? Words, more
    words,
1135   and the hurt comes on us, endless words
and a seer's techniques have brought us
terror and the truth.
CASSANDRA: The agony—O I am breaking!—Fate's so hard,
and the pain that floods my voice is mine alone.
1140   Why have you brought me here, tormented as I am?
Why, unless to die with him, why else?
LEADER AND CHORUS: Mad with the rapture—god speeds
    you on
        to the song, the deathsong,
like the nightingale that broods on sorrow,
1145   mourns her son, her son,
her life inspired with grief for him,
she lilts and shrills, dark bird that lives for night.
CASSANDRA: The nightingale—O for a song, a fate like hers!
    The gods gave her a life of ease, swathed her in wings,
1150   no tears, no wailing. The knife waits for me.
They'll splay me on the iron's double edge.
LEADER AND CHORUS: Why?—what god hurls you on, stroke
    on stroke
        to the long dying fall?
Why the horror clashing through your music,
1155   terror struck to song?—
why the anguish, the wild dance?
Where do your words of god and grief begin?
CASSANDRA: Ai, the wedding, wedding of Paris,
death to the loved ones. Oh Scamander,
1160   you nursed my father . . . once at your banks
    I nursed and grew, and now at the banks
of Acheron, the stream that carries sorrow,
it seems I'll chant my prophecies too soon.
LEADER AND CHORUS: What are you saying? Wait, it's clear,
1165   a child could see the truth, it wounds within,
               like a bloody fang it tears—
I hear your destiny—breaking sobs,
        cries that stab the ears.
CASSANDRA: Oh the grief, the grief of the city
1170   ripped to oblivion. Oh the victims,
the flocks my father burned at the wall,
    rich herds in flames . . . no cure for the doom
that took the city after all, and I,
her last ember, I go down with her.
1175 LEADER AND CHORUS: You cannot stop, your song goes on—
some spirit drops from the heights and treads you down
             and the brutal strain grows—
your death-throes come and come and
        I cannot see the end!
1180 CASSANDRA: Then off with the veils that hid the fresh
    young bride—
we will see the truth.
Flare up once more, my oracle! Clear and sharp
as the wind that blows towards the rising sun,
I can feel a deeper swell now, gathering head
1185   to break at last and bring the dawn of grief.

1145 **her son** Itys, son of Philomela, the mother was transformed into a nightingale after she inadvertently tricked her
husband, Tereus, into eating their son's flesh

No more riddles. I will teach you.
Come, bear witness, run and hunt with me.
We trail the old barbaric works of slaughter.

These roofs—look up—there is a dancing troupe
that never leaves. And they have their harmony   1190
but it is harsh, their words are harsh, they drink
beyond the limit. Flushed on the blood of men
their spirit grows and none can turn away
their revel breeding in the veins—the Furies!
They cling to the house for life. They sing,   1195
sing of the frenzy that began it all,
strain rising on strain, showering curses
on the man who tramples on his brother's bed.

There. Have I hit the mark or not? Am I a fraud,
a fortune-teller babbling lies from door to door?   1200
Swear how well I know the ancient crimes
that live within this house.
LEADER: And if I did?
Would an oath bind the wounds and heal us?
But you amaze me. Bred across the sea,
your language strange, and still you sense the truth   1205
as if you had been here.
CASSANDRA: Apollo the Prophet
introduced me to his gift.
LEADER: A *god*—and moved with love?
CASSANDRA: I was ashamed to tell this once,
but now . . .   1210
LEADER: We spoil ourselves with scruples,
long as things go well.
CASSANDRA: He came like a wrestler,
magnificent, took me down and breathed his fire
through me and—
LEADER: You bore him a child?
CASSANDRA: I yielded,
then at the climax I recoiled—I deceived Apollo!
LEADER:
But the god's skills—they seized you even then?   1215
CASSANDRA: Even then I told my people all the grief to come.
LEADER: And Apollo's anger never touched you?—is it
    possible?
CASSANDRA: Once I betrayed him I could never be believed.
LEADER: We believe you. Your visions seem so true.
CASSANDRA: Aieeeee!—
the pain, the terror! the birth-pang of the seer   1220
who tells the truth—
               it whirls me, oh,
the storm comes again, the crashing chords!
Look, you see them nestling at the threshold?
Young, young in the darkness like a dream,
like children really, yes, and their loved ones   1225
brought them down . . .
              their hands, they fill their hands
with their own flesh, they are serving it like food,
holding out their entrails . . . now it's clear,
I can see the armfuls of compassion, see the father
reach to taste and—   1230
           For so much suffering,
I tell you, someone plots revenge.
A lion who lacks a lion's heart,
he sprawled at home in the royal lair

and set a trap for the lord on his return.
1235 My lord . . . I must wear his yoke, I am his slave.
The lord of the men-of-war, he obliterated Troy—
he is so blind, so lost to that detestable hellhound
who pricks her ears and fawns and her tongue draws out
her glittering words of welcome—
                              No, he cannot see
1240 the stroke that Fury's hiding, stealth, and murder.
What outrage—the woman kills the man!
                              What to call
that . . . monster of Greece, and bring my quarry down?
Viper coiling back and forth?
                              Some sea-witch?—
Scylla crouched in her rocky nest—nightmare of sailors?
1245 Raging mother of death, storming deathless war against
the ones she loves!
                              And how she howled in triumph,
boundless outrage. Just as the tide of battle
broke her way, she seems to rejoice that he
is safe at home from war, saved for her.
1250 Believe me if you will. What will it matter
if you won't? It comes when it comes,
and soon you'll see it face to face
and say the seer was all too true.
You will be moved with pity.

LEADER: Thyestes' feast,
1255 the children's flesh—that I know,
and the fear shudders through me. It's true,
real, no dark signs about it. I hear the rest
but it throws me off the scent.

CASSANDRA: Agamemnon.
You will see him dead.

LEADER: Peace, poor girl!
1260 Put those words to sleep.

CASSANDRA: No use,
the Healer has no hand in this affair.

LEADER: Not if it's true—but god forbid it is!

CASSANDRA: You pray, and they close in to kill!

LEADER: What man prepares this, this dreadful—

CASSANDRA: Man?
1265 You *are* lost, to every word I've said.

LEADER: Yes—
I don't see who can bring the evil off.

CASSANDRA: And yet I know my Greek, too well.

LEADER: So does the Delphic oracle,
but he's hard to understand.

CASSANDRA: His *fire!*—
1270 sears me, sweeps me again—the torture!
Apollo Lord of the Light, you burn,
you blind me—
              Agony!
                    She is the lioness,
she rears on her hind legs, she beds with the wolf
when her lion king goes ranging—
                              she will kill me—
1275 Ai, the torture!
              She is mixing her drugs,
adding a measure more of hate for me.

1244 **Scylla** a many-headed monster who terrorized sailors

She gloats as she whets the sword for him.
He brought me home and we will pay in carnage.

Why mock yourself with these—trappings, the rod,
the god's wreath, his yoke around my throat?   1280
Before I die I'll tread you—

(Ripping off her regalia, stamping it into the ground.)

                              Down, out,
die die die!
Now you're down. I've paid you back.
Look for another victim—I am free at last—
make her rich in all your curse and doom.   1285

(Staggering backwards as if wrestling with a spirit tearing at her robes.)

                              See,
Apollo himself, his fiery hands—I feel him again,
he's stripping off my robes, the Seer's robes!
And after he looked down and saw me mocked,
even in these, his glories, mortified by friends
I loved, and they hated me, they were so blind   1290
to their own demise—
                    I went from door to door,
I was wild with the god, I heard them call me
"Beggar! Wretch! Starve for bread in hell!"

And I endured it all, and now he will
extort me as his due. A seer for the Seer.   1295
He brings me here to die like this,
not to serve at my father's altar. No,
the block is waiting. The cleaver steams
with my life blood, the first blood drawn
for the king's last rites.   1300

(Regaining her composure and moving to the altar.)

                    We will die,
but not without some honour from the gods.
There will come another to avenge us,
born to kill his mother, born
his father's champion. A wanderer, a fugitive
driven off his native land, he will come home   1305
to cope the stones of hate that menace all he loves.
The gods have sworn a monumental oath: as his father lies
upon the ground he draws him home with power like a
     prayer.

Then why so pitiful, why so many tears?
I have seen my city faring as she fared,   1310
and those who took her, judged by the gods,
faring as they fare. I must be brave.
It is my turn to die.

(Approaching the doors.)

I address you as the Gates of Death.
I pray it comes with one clear stroke,   1315
no convulsions, the pulses ebbing out
in gentle death. I'll close my eyes and sleep.

LEADER: So much pain, poor girl, and so much truth,
you've told so much. But if you *see* it coming,
clearly—how can you go to your own death,   1320
like a beast to the altar driven on by god,
and hold your head so high?

CASSANDRA: No escape, my friends,
   not now.
LEADER: But the last hour should be savoured.
CASSANDRA: My time has come. Little to gain from flight.
1325 LEADER: You're brave, believe me, full of gallant heart.
CASSANDRA: Only the wretched go with praise like that.
LEADER: But to go nobly lends a man some grace.
CASSANDRA: My noble father—you and your noble children.

(*She nears the threshold and recoils, groaning in revulsion.*)

LEADER: What now? what terror flings you back?
1330   Why? Unless some horror in the brain—
CASSANDRA: Murder.
   The house breathes with murder—bloody shambles!
LEADER: No, no, only the victims at the hearth.
CASSANDRA: I know that odour. I smell the open grave.
LEADER: But the Syrian myrrh, it fills the halls with
   splendour,
1335   can't you sense it?
CASSANDRA: Well, I must go in now,
   mourning Agamemnon's death and mine.
   Enough of life!

(*Approaching the doors again and crying out.*)

              Friends—I cried out,
   not from fear like a bird fresh caught,
   but that you will testify to how I died.
1340   When the queen, woman for woman, dies for me,
   and a man falls for the man who married grief.
   That's all I ask, my friends. A stranger's gift
   for one about to die.
LEADER: Poor creature, you
   and the end you see so clearly. I pity you.
1345 CASSANDRA: I'd like a few words more, a kind of dirge,
   it is my own. I pray to the sun,
   the last light I'll see,
   that when the avengers cut the assassins down
   they will avenge me too, a slave who died,
1350   an easy conquest.
              Oh men, your destiny.
   When all is well a shadow can overturn it.
   When trouble comes a stroke of the wet sponge,
   and the picture's blotted out. And that,
   I think that breaks the heart.

(*She goes through the doors.*)

1355 CHORUS: But the lust for power never dies—
   men cannot have enough.
   No one will lift a hand to send it
   from his door, to give it warning,
   "Power, never come again!"
1360   Take this man: the gods in glory
   gave him Priam's city to plunder,
   brought him home in splendour like a god.
   But now if he must pay for the blood
   his fathers shed, and die for the deaths
1365   he brought to pass, and bring more death
   to avenge his dying, show us one
      who boasts himself born free
   of the raging angel, once he hears—

(*Cries break out within the palace.*)

AGAMEMNON: Aagh!
   Struck deep—the death-blow, deep—
LEADER: Quiet. Cries,
   but who? Someone's stabbed—   1370
AGAMEMNON: Aaagh, again . . .
   second blow—struck home.
LEADER: The work is done,
   you can feel it. The king, and the great cries—
   Close ranks now, find the right way out.

(*But the* OLD MEN *scatter, each speaks singly.*)

CHORUS: —I say send out heralds, muster the guard,
   they'll save the house.   1375
           —And I say rush in now,
   catch them red-handed—butchery running on their
     blades.
   —Right with you, do something—now or never!
   —Look at them, beating the drum for insurrection.
                   —Yes,
   we're wasting time. They rape the name of caution,
   their hands will never sleep.   1380
          —Not a plan in sight.
   Let men of action do the planning, too.
   —I'm helpless. Who can raise the dead with words?
   —What, drag out our lives? bow down to the tyrants,
   the ruin of the house?
          —Never, better to die
   on your feet than live on your knees.   1385
               —Wait,
   do we take the cries for signs, prophesy like seers
   and give him up for dead?
         —No more suspicions,
   not another word till we have proof.
           —Confusion
   on all sides—one thing to do. See how it stands
   with Agamemnon, once and for all we'll see—   1390

(*He rushes at the doors. They open and reveal a silver cauldron that holds the body of* AGAMEMNON *shrouded in bloody robes, with the body of* CASSANDRA *to his left and* CLYTAEMNESTRA *standing to his right, sword in hand. She strides towards the* CHORUS.)

CLYTAEMNESTRA: Words, endless words I've said to serve the
   moment—
   now it makes me proud to tell the truth.
   How else to prepare a death for deadly men
   who seem to love you? How to rig the nets
   of pain so high no man can overleap them?   1395
   I brooded on this trial, this ancient blood feud
   year by year. At last my hour came.
   Here I stand and here I struck
   and here my work is done.
   I did it all. I don't deny it, no.   1400
   He had no way to flee or fight his destiny—

(*Unwinding the robes from* AGAMEMNON's *body, spreading them before the altar where the* OLD MEN *cluster around them, unified as a chorus once again.*)

our never-ending, all embracing net, I cast it
wide for the royal haul, I coil him round and round
in the wealth, the robes of doom, and then I strike him
1405 once, twice, and at each stroke he cries in agony—
he buckles at the knees and crashes here!
And when he's down I add the third, last blow,
to the Zeus who saves the dead beneath the ground
I send that third blow home in homage like a prayer.

1410 So he goes down, and the life is bursting out of him—
great sprays of blood, and the murderous shower
wounds me, dyes me black and I, I revel
like the Earth when the spring rains come down,
the blessed gifts of god, and the new green spear
1415 splits the sheath and rips to birth in glory!

So it stands, elders of Argos gathered here.
Rejoice if you can rejoice—I glory.
And if I'd pour upon his body the libation
it deserves, what wine could match my words?
1420 It is right and more than right. He flooded
the vessel of our proud house with misery,
with the vintage of the curse and now
he drains the dregs. My lord is home at last.
LEADER: You appal me, you, your brazen words—
1425 exulting over your fallen king.
CLYTAEMNESTRA: And you,
you try me like some desperate woman.
My heart is steel, well you know. Praise me,
blame me as you choose. It's all one.
Here is Agamemnon, my husband made a corpse
1430 by this right hand—a masterpiece of Justice.
Done is done.
CHORUS: Woman!—what poison cropped from the soil
or strained from the heaving sea, what nursed you,
drove you insane? You brave the curse of Greece.
You have cut away and flung away and now
1435 the people cast you off to exile,
broken with our hate.
CLYTAEMNESTRA: And now you sentence me?—
you banish *me* from the city, curses breathing
down my neck? But *he*—
name one charge you brought against him then.
1440 He thought no more of it than killing a beast,
and his flocks were rich, teeming in their fleece,
but he sacrificed his own child, our daughter,
the agony I laboured into love
to charm away the savage winds of Thrace.
1445 Didn't the law demand you banish him?—
hunt him from the land for all his guilt?
But now you witness what I've done
and you are ruthless judges.
                Threaten away!
I'll meet you blow for blow. And if I fall
1450 the throne is yours. If god decrees the reverse,
late as it is, old men, you'll learn your place.
CHORUS: Mad with ambition,
                shrilling pride!—some Fury
crazed with the carnage rages through your brain—
1455 I can see the flecks of blood inflame your eyes!
But vengeance comes—you'll lose your loved ones,
stroke for painful stroke.

CLYTAEMNESTRA: Then learn this, too, the power of my
oaths.
By the child's Rights I brought to birth,
by Ruin, by Fury—the three gods to whom   1460
I sacrificed this man—I swear my hopes
will never walk the halls of fear so long
as Aegisthus lights the fire on my hearth.
Loyal to me as always, no small shield
to buttress my defiance.   1465
                Here he lies.
He brutalized me. The darling of all
the golden girls who spread the gates of Troy.
And here his spear-prize . . . what wonders she beheld!—
the seer of Apollo shared my husband's bed,
his faithful mate who knelt at the rowing-benches,   1470
worked by every hand.
                They have their rewards.
He as you know. And she, the swan of the gods
who lived to sing her latest, dying song—
his lover lies beside him.
She brings a fresh, voluptuous relish to my bed!   1475
CHORUS: Oh quickly, let me die—
no bed of labour, no, no wasting illness . . .
bear me off in the sleep that never ends,
                now that he has fallen,
now that our dearest shield lies battered—   1480
                Woman made him suffer,
                        woman struck him down.

Helen the wild, maddening Helen,
one for the many, the thousand lives
you murdered under Troy. Now you are crowned   1485
with this consummate wreath, the blood
that lives in memory, glistens age to age.
Once in the halls she walked and she was war,
angel of war, angel of agony, lighting men to death.
CLYTAEMNESTRA: Pray no more for death, broken   1490
as you are. And never turn
        your wrath on her, call her
the scourge of men, the one alone
who destroyed a myriad Greek lives—
Helen the grief that never heals.   1495
CHORUS: The *spirit!*—you who tread
the house and the twinborn sons of Tantalus—
you empower the sisters, Fury's twins
                whose power tears the heart!
Perched on the corpse your carrion raven   1500
        glories in her hymn,
                her screaming hymn of pride.
CLYTAEMNESTRA: Now you set your judgement straight,
you summon *him!* Three generations
        feed the spirit in the race.   1505
Deep in the veins he feeds our bloodlust—
aye, before the old wound dies
it ripens in another flow of blood.
CHORUS: The great curse of the house, the spirit,
dead weight wrath—and you can praise it!   1510

1472 **the swan** the bird of Apollo, reputed to sing only when
about to die   1497 **the twinborn sons of Tantalus** here,
Agamemnon and Menelaus

Praise the insatiate doom that feeds
relentless on our future and our sons.
Oh all through the will of Zeus,
the cause of all, the one who works it all.
1515   What comes to birth that is not Zeus?
Our lives are pain, what part not come from god?

    Oh my king, my captain,
how to salute you, how to mourn you?
What can I say with all my warmth and love?
1520   Here in the black widow's web you lie,
gasping out your life
in a sacrilegious death, dear god,
reduced to a slave's bed,
my king of men, yoked by stealth and Fate,
1525   by the wife's hand that thrust the two-edged sword.
CLYTAEMNESTRA: You claim the work is mine, call me
Agamemnon's wife—you are so wrong.
Fleshed in the wife of this dead man,
    the spirit lives within me,
1530   our savage ancient spirit of revenge.
In return for Atreus' brutal feast
he kills his perfect son—for every
murdered child, a crowning sacrifice.
CHORUS: And *you*, innocent of his murder?
1535   And who could swear to that? and how? . . .
and still an avenger could arise,
bred by the fathers' crimes, and lend a hand.
He wades in the blood of brothers,
stream on mounting stream—black war erupts
1540   and where he strides revenge will stride,
clots will mass for the young who were devoured.

    Oh my king, my captain,
how to salute you, how to mourn you?
What can I say with all my warmth and love?
1545   Here in the black widow's web you lie,
gasping out your life
in a sacrilegious death, dear god,
reduced to a slave's bed,
my king of men, yoked by stealth and Fate,
1550   by the wife's hand that thrust the two-edged sword.
CLYTAEMNESTRA: No slave's death, I think—
no stealthier than the death he dealt
our house and the offspring of our loins,
    Iphigeneia, girl of tears.
1555   Act for act, wound for wound!
Never exult in Hades, swordsman,
here you are repaid. By the sword
you did your work and by the sword you die.
CHORUS: The mind reels—where to turn?
1560   All plans dashed, all hope! I cannot think . . .
the roofs are toppling, I dread the drumbeat thunder
the heavy rains of blood will crush the house
    the first light rains are over—
Justice brings new acts of agony, yes,
1565   on new grindstones Fate is grinding sharp the sword of
    Justice.
Earth, dear Earth,
if only you'd drawn me under
long before I saw him huddled
in the beaten silver bath.

Who will bury him, lift his dirge?   1570

(*Turning to* CLYTAEMNESTRA.)

    You, can you dare *this*?
To kill your lord with your own hand
then mourn his soul with tributes, terrible tributes—
do his enormous works a great dishonour.
This god-like man, this hero. Who at the grave   1575
will sing his praises, pour the wine of tears?
Who will labour there with truth of heart?
CLYTAEMNESTRA: This is no concern of yours.
The hand that bore and cut him down
will hand him down to Mother Earth.   1580
This house will never mourn for him.
    Only our daughter Iphigeneia,
by all rights, will rush to meet him
first at the churning straits,
the ferry over tears—   1585
she'll fling her arms around her father,
pierce him with her love.
CHORUS: Each charge meets counter-charge.
    None can judge between them. Justice.
The plunderer plundered, the killer pays the price. 1590
The truth still holds while Zeus still holds the throne:
    the one who acts must suffer—
that is law. Who can tear from the veins
the bad seed, the curse? The race is welded to its ruin.
CLYTAEMNESTRA: At last you see the future and the truth! 1595
But I will swear a pact with the spirit
born within us. I embrace his works,
cruel as they are but done at last,
    if he will leave our house
in the future, bleed another line   1600
with kinsmen murdering kinsmen.
Whatever he may ask. A few things
are all I need, once I have purged
our fury to destroy each other—
    purged it from our halls.   1605

(AEGISTHUS *has emerged from the palace with his* BODYGUARD
and stands triumphant over the body of AGAMEMNON.)

AEGISTHUS: O what a brilliant day
it is for vengeance! Now I can say once more
there are gods in heaven avenging men,
blazing down on all the crimes of earth.
Now at last I see this man brought down
in the Furies' tangling robes. It feasts my eyes—   1610
he pays for the plot his father's hand contrived.

Atreus, this man's father, was king of Argos.
My father, Thyestes—let me make this clear—
Atreus' brother challenged him for the crown,
and Atreus drove him out of house and home   1615
then lured him back, and home Thyestes came,
poor man, a suppliant to his own hearth,
to pray that Fate might save him.
          So it did.

———————————

1585 **the ferry** Charon's ferry across the River Styx into the underworld

1620   There was no dying, no staining our native ground
        with his blood. Thyestes was the guest,
        and this man's godless father––

(*Pointing to* AGAMEMNON.)

        The zeal of the host outstripping a brother's love,
        made my father a feast that seemed a feast for gods,
        a love feast of his children's flesh.
                                        He cuts
1625   the extremities, feet and delicate hands
        into small pieces, scatters them over the dish
        and serves it to Thyestes throned on high.
        He picks at the flesh he cannot recognize,
        the soul of innocence eating the food of ruin––
1630   look,

(*Pointing to the bodies at his feet.*)

                that feeds upon the house! And then,
        when he sees the monstrous thing he's done, he shrieks,
        he reels back head first and vomits up that butchery,
        tramples the feast––brings down the curse of Justice:
        "Crash to ruin, all the race of Pleisthenes, crash down!"
1635   So you see him, down. And I, the weaver of Justice,
        plotted out the kill. Atreus drove us into exile,
        my struggling father and I, a babe-in-arms,
        his last son, but I became a man
        and Justice brought me home. I was abroad
1640   but I reached out and seized my man,
        link by link I clamped the fatal scheme
        together. Now I could die gladly, even I––
        now I see this monster in the nets of Justice.
LEADER: Aegisthus, you revel in pain––you sicken me.
1645   You say you killed the king in cold blood,
        single-handed planned his pitiful death?
        I say there's no escape. In the hour of judgement,
        trust to this, your head will meet the people's
        rocks and curses.
AEGISTHUS: You say! you slaves at the oars––
1650   while the master on the benches cracks the whip?
        You'll learn, in your late age, how much it hurts
        to teach old bones their place. We have techniques––
        chains and the pangs of hunger,
        two effective teachers, excellent healers.
1655   They can even cure old men of pride and gall.
        Look––can't you see? The more you kick
        against the pricks, the more you suffer.
LEADER: You, pathetic––
        the king had just returned from battle.
1660   You waited out the war and fouled his lair,
        you planned my great commander's fall.
AEGISTHUS: Talk on––
        you'll scream for every word, my little Orpheus.
        We'll see if the world comes dancing to your song,
        your absurd barking––snarl your breath away!
1665   I'll make you dance, I'll bring you all to heel.
LEADER: *You* rule Argos? You who schemed his death
        but cringed to cut him down with your own hand?

––––––––––––––––––––

1634 **Pleisthenes** an unidentified ancestral figure, perhaps
Atreus or Pelops   1662 **Orpheus** a musician who enchanted
even rocks and trees with his lyre

AEGISTHUS: The treachery was the woman's work, clearly.
        I was a marked man, his enemy for ages.
        But I will use his riches, stop at nothing   1670
        to civilize his people. All but the rebel:
        him I'll yoke and break––
        no cornfed colt, running free in the traces.
        Hunger, ruthless mate of the dark torture-chamber,
        trains her eyes upon him till he drops!   1675
LEADER: Coward, why not kill the man yourself?
        Why did the woman, the corruption of Greece
        and the gods of Greece, have to bring him down?
        Orestes––
                If he still sees the light of day,
        bring him home, good Fates, home to kill   1680
        this pair at last. Our champion in slaughter!
AEGISTHUS: Bent on insolence? Well, you'll learn, quickly.
        At them, men––you have your work at hand!

(*His men draw swords: the* OLD MEN *take up their sticks.*)

LEADER: At them, first at the hilt, to the last man––
AEGISTHUS: First at the hilt, I'm not afraid to die.   1685
LEADER: It's death you want and death you'll have––
        we'll make that word your last.

(CLYTAEMNESTRA *moves between them, restraining* AEGISTHUS.)

CLYTAEMNESTRA: No more, my dearest,
        no more grief. We have too much to reap
        right here, our mighty harvest of despair.   1690
        Our lives are based on pain. No bloodshed now.

        Fathers of Argos, turn for home before you act
        and suffer for it. What we did was destiny.
        If we could end the suffering, how we would rejoice.
        The spirit's brutal hoof has struck our heart.   1695
        And that is what a woman has to say.
        Can you accept the truth?

(CLYTAEMNESTRA *turns to leave.*)

AEGISTHUS: But these . . . mouths
        that bloom in filth––spitting insults in my teeth.
        You tempt your fates, you insubordinate dogs––
        to hurl abuse at me, your master!   1700
LEADER: No Greek
        worth his salt would grovel at your feet.
AEGISTHUS: I––I'll stalk you all your days!
LEADER: Not if the spirit brings Orestes home.
AEGISTHUS: Exiles feed on hope––well I know.
LEADER: More,   1705
        gorge yourself to bursting––soil justice, while you can.
AEGISTHUS: I promise you, you'll pay, old fools––in good
        time, too!
LEADER: Strut on your own dunghill, you cock beside your
        mate.
CLYTAEMNESTRA: Let them howl––they're impotent. You and
        I have power now.
        We will set the house in order once for all.

(*They enter the palace; the great doors close behind them; the* OLD
MEN *disband and wander off.*)

Sophocles

Like Aeschylus, Sophocles (c. 496–406 BCE) had an important career in the civic life of Athens as well as in the theater. He was treasurer for the Athenian imperial league, and served as one of ten generals who led a campaign against Samos, an island threatening to secede from the Athenian alliance. In 411 BCE, he was appointed to a committee called to examine Athens' disastrous military campaign in Sicily. Sophocles' greatest achievements, though, were in the theater. Sophocles was responsible for introducing a third actor into dramatic performance, an innovation rapidly imitated by other playwrights, including Aeschylus and Euripides. He also enlarged the size of the chorus from twelve to fifteen men. Sophocles won his first victory, against Aeschylus, in 468 BCE; he was victorious twenty-four times in his career and never finished lower than second in the dramatic competition. Of the 120 plays attributed to Sophocles, only seven survive: *Ajax, Trachiniae, Antigone, Oedipus the King, Electra, Philoctetes,* and *Oedipus at Colonus.* Fragments of a satyr play, *The Trackers,* also remain. The three "Theban" plays—*Antigone, Oedipus the King,* and *Oedipus at Colonus*—are thematically related, but, unlike *The Oresteia* of Aeschylus, were not composed as a trilogy. *Antigone,* a play about Oedipus' daughters after his banishment from Thebes, was composed about 441 BCE; *Oedipus the King* was first produced sometime shortly after the declaration of war with Sparta in 431 BCE; and *Oedipus at Colonus* was first produced after Sophocles' death and Athens' defeat.

Oedipus the King is framed by two acts of identification, recognition, and acknowledgment. The action of the play is about the deepening and horrible understanding of what it means for the hero to recognize who he is—what it means to *be* Oedipus.

OEDIPUS THE KING

This production of Sophocles' *Oedipus the King* adapts the ritualized elements of Greek theater to a modern African setting.

In *The Poetics,* written nearly a century later (about 335 BCE), Aristotle frequently refers to *Oedipus the King* as a definitive example of the form and purpose of tragedy. Modern audiences, though, sometimes find the play baffling, in part because the prophecy delivered to Oedipus' parents, Laius and Jocasta—that their son will murder his father and marry his mother—seems to rob Oedipus of the ability to act, to decide his fate through his own deeds. The tension between destiny and discovery is central to the play; to understand it, we should pay attention to the function of the oracle at Delphi both in the Greek world and in Oedipus the King. The Greeks consulted the oracle at Delphi on a variety of matters, ranging from personal decisions to problems of state. For example, in the play, Laius and Jocasta have consulted the oracle to learn the future of their child, and Oedipus turns to Delphi to find out whether Polybus is actually his father. At the same time, the oracle also speaks on important public issues—about the cause of the plague afflicting Thebes and about what should be done with Oedipus after his blinding. Sophocles lived in an era of increasing skepticism, when political conflict and the rise of rhetorical training raised questions about the nature and significance of truth—even the truth of oracular revelation. It is not surprising that characters in *Oedipus the King* frequently question such prophecy or have difficulty learning how to accept and interpret it, as when Oedipus flees Corinth to avoid murdering his father.

Critical as the prophecy is to Oedipus' life, Oedipus' deeds are really at issue in *Oedipus the King.* Sophocles chose to begin and end his drama on the day of Oedipus' discovery of his own identity. The play focuses less on the prophecy than on the course and meaning of Oedipus' actions, on *how* he comes to recognize himself as the criminal he seeks. Oedipus arrives at this recognition only through an extraordinary effort of action and decision: Oedipus calls for the exile of Laius' murderer; he insults Tiresias when the prophet tries to evade his questions; he accuses Creon; he threatens the old shepherd with torture in order to learn the truth of his birth. The oracle says that Oedipus will commit his terrible crimes of murder and incest, but Oedipus *chooses* the relentless, brutal pursuit of the truth himself, even to the point of his own incrimination and destruction. The tragedy of *Oedipus the King* lies in the fearsome turn of events caused by Oedipus' inflexible compulsion to discover the truth.

Aristotle considers the hero of tragedy at some length, in terms that are at once compelling and confusing, particularly in the case of Oedipus. Aristotle suggests in *ThePoetics* that the hero of tragedy should be "a man who is neither a paragon of virtue and justice nor undergoes the change to misfortune through any real badness or wickedness but because of some mistake," a description that leads some to look for the cause of this error within Oedipus' character, in a so-called tragic flaw. But, in fact, when he says that the character's "mistake"—or HAMARTIA—is not the result of "any real badness or wickedness," Aristotle seems to deny that the hero's downfall is the effect of any moral "flaw" at all. It might help us to remember that to his audience, Oedipus may have seemed to share some typically "Athenian" characteristics. Oedipus' passion for inquiry, his abrupt decisiveness, and his impulsive desire to act were seen as the stereotypical traits of Athenian citizens and of Athens as a city. Far from being "flaws," these are just the qualities that made Oedipus (and Athens) successful. What is "tragic" about Oedipus' fate in *Oedipus the King* is the way that his own surest strengths—the aggressive, pragmatic qualities that enabled him to outwit the Sphinx—lead, on this one occasion, to his destruction. Oedipus' "mistake" is neither a moral failing nor a deed that he might have avoided; it is simply that he is Oedipus and acts like Oedipus—intelligent, masterful, assertive, impatient, impulsive. The tragedy lies in the way that acting like Oedipus leads him, as it has always led him in the past, to the discovery of the truth he seeks, this time with ruinous consequences.

OEDIPUS THE KING

Sophocles

TRANSLATED BY ROBERT FAGLES

CHARACTERS

OEDIPUS, *king of Thebes*
A PRIEST *of Zeus*
CREON, *brother of Jocasta*
A CHORUS *of Theban citizens*
   and their LEADER
TIRESIAS, *a blind prophet*
JOCASTA, *the queen, wife of*
   Oedipus

A MESSENGER *from Corinth*
A SHEPHERD
A MESSENGER *from inside the*
   palace
ANTIGONE, ISMENE, *daughters*
   of Oedipus and Jocasta
GUARDS *and* ATTENDANTS
PRIESTS *of Thebes*

TIME AND SCENE: *The royal house of Thebes. Double doors dominate the façade; a stone altar stands at the center of the stage.*

Many years have passed since OEDIPUS *solved the riddle of the Sphinx and ascended the throne of Thebes, and now a plague has struck the city. A procession of* PRIESTS *enters; suppliants, broken and despondent, they carry branches wound in wool and lay them on the altar.*

The doors open. GUARDS *assemble.* OEDIPUS *comes forward, majestic but for a telltale limp, and slowly views the condition of his people.*

OEDIPUS: Oh my children, the new blood of ancient Thebes,
   why are you here? Huddling at my altar,
   praying before me, your branches wound in wool.
   Our city reeks with the smoke of burning incense,
5   rings with cries for the Healer and wailing for the dead.
   I thought it wrong, my children, to hear the truth
   from others, messengers. Here I am myself—
   you all know me, the world knows my fame:
   I am Oedipus.

(Helping a PRIEST *to his feet.)*

              Speak up, old man. Your years,
10   your dignity—you should speak for the others.
   Why here and kneeling, what preys upon you so?
   Some sudden fear? some strong desire?
   You can trust me. I am ready to help,
   I'll do anything. I would be blind to misery
15   not to pity my people kneeling at my feet.
PRIEST: O Oedipus, king of the land, our greatest power!
   You see us before you now, men of all ages
   clinging to your altars. Here are boys,
   still too weak to fly from the nest,
20   and here the old, bowed down with the years,
   the holy ones—a priest of Zeus myself—and here
   the picked, unmarried men, the young hope of Thebes.
   And all the rest, your great family gathers now,
   branches wreathed, massing in the squares,
25   kneeling before the two temples of queen Athena
   or the river-shrine where the embers glow and die
   and Apollo sees the future in the ashes.
                   Our city—
   look around you, see with your own eyes
   our ship pitches wildly, cannot lift her head
30   from the depths, the red waves of death . . .
   Thebes is dying. A blight on the fresh crops
   and the rich pastures, cattle sicken and die,

and the women die in labor, children stillborn,
and the plague, the fiery god of fever hurls down
on the city, his lightning slashing through us—   35
raging plague in all its vengeance, devastating
the house of Cadmus! And black Death luxuriates
in the raw, wailing miseries of Thebes.

Now we pray to you. You cannot equal the gods,
your children know that, bending at your altar.   40
But we do rate you first of men,
both in the common crises of our lives
and face-to-face encounters with the gods.
You freed us from the Sphinx, you came to Thebes
and cut us loose from the bloody tribute we had paid   45
that harsh, brutal singer. We taught you nothing,
no skill, no extra knowledge, still you triumphed.
A god was with you, so they say, and we believe it—
you lifted up our lives.
                 So now again,
Oedipus, king, we bend to you, your power—   50
we implore you, all of us on our knees:
find us strength, rescue! Perhaps you've heard
the voice of a god or something from other men,
Oedipus . . . what do you know?
The man of experience—you see it every day—   55
his plans will work in a crisis, his first of all.

Act now—we beg you, best of men, raise up our city!
Act, defend yourself, your former glory!
Your country calls you savior now
for your zeal, your action years ago.   60
Never let us remember of your reign:
you helped us stand, only to fall once more.
Oh raise up our city, set us on our feet.
The omens were good that day you brought us joy—
be the same man today!   65
Rule our land, you know you have the power,
but rule a land of the living, not a wasteland.
Ship and towered city are nothing, stripped of men
alive within it, living all as one.
OEDIPUS: My children,
I pity you. I see—how could I fail to see   70
what longings bring you here? Well I know
you are sick to death, all of you,
but sick as you are, not one is sick as I.

75 Your pain strikes each of you alone, each
in the confines of himself, no other. But my spirit
grieves for the city, for myself and all of you.
I wasn't asleep, dreaming. You haven't wakened me—
I have wept through the nights, you must know that,
groping, laboring over many paths of thought.
80 After a painful search I found one cure:
I acted at once. I sent Creon,
my wife's own brother, to Delphi—
Apollo the Prophet's oracle—to learn
what I might do or say to save our city.
85 Today's the day. When I count the days gone by
it torments me . . . what is he doing?
Strange, he's late, he's gone too long.
But once he returns, then, then I'll be a traitor
if I do not do all the god makes clear.
90 PRIEST: Timely words. The men over there
are signaling—Creon's just arriving.
OEDIPUS: (*Sighting* CREON, *then turning to the altar.*) Lord Apollo,
let him come with a lucky word of rescue,
shining like his eyes!
PRIEST: Welcome news, I think—he's crowned, look,
95 and the laurel wreath is bright with berries.
OEDIPUS: We'll soon see. He's close enough to hear

(*Enter* CREON *from the side; his face is shaded with a wreath.*)

Creon, prince, my kinsman, what do you bring us?
What message from the god?
CREON: Good news.
I tell you even the hardest things to bear,
100 if they should turn out well, all would be well.
OEDIPUS: Of course, but what were the god's *words?* There's
     no hope
and nothing to fear in what you've said so far.
CREON: If you want my report in the presence of these
people . . .

(*Pointing to the* PRIESTS *while drawing* OEDIPUS *toward the palace.*)

I'm ready now, or we might go inside.
OEDIPUS: Speak out,
105 speak to us all. I grieve for these, my people,
far more than I fear for my own life.
CREON: Very well,
I will tell you what I heard from the god.
Apollo commands us—he was quite clear—
"Drive the corruption from the land,
110 don't harbor it any longer, past all cure,
don't nurse it in your soil—root it out!"
OEDIPUS: How can we cleanse ourselves—what rites?
What's the source of the trouble?
CREON: Banish the man, or pay back blood with blood.
115 Murder sets the plague-storm on the city.
OEDIPUS: Whose murder?
Whose fate does Apollo bring to light?
CREON: Our leader,
my lord, was once a man named Laius,
before you came and put us straight on course.
OEDIPUS: I know—
or so I've heard. I never saw the man myself.

CREON: Well, he was killed, and Apollo commands us now— 120
he could not be more clear,
"Pay the killers back—whoever is responsible."
OEDIPUS: Where on earth are they? Where to find it now,
the trail of the ancient guilt so hard to trace?
CREON: "Here in Thebes," he said.   125
Whatever is sought for can be caught, you know,
whatever is neglected slips away.
OEDIPUS: But where,
in the palace, the fields or foreign soil,
where did Laius meet his bloody death?
CREON: He went to consult an oracle, Apollo said,   130
and he set out and never came home again.
OEDIPUS: No messenger, no fellow-traveler saw what
     happened?
Someone to cross-examine?
CREON: No,
they were all killed but one. He escaped,
terrified, he could tell us nothing clearly,   135
nothing of what he saw—just one thing.
OEDIPUS: What's that?
One thing could hold the key to it all,
a small beginning give us grounds for hope.
CREON: He said thieves attacked them—a whole band,
not single-handed, cut King Laius down.   140
OEDIPUS: A thief,
so daring, so wild, he'd kill a king? Impossible,
unless conspirators paid him off in Thebes.
CREON: We suspected as much. But with Laius dead
no leader appeared to help us in our troubles.
OEDIPUS: Trouble? Your *king* was murdered—royal blood! 145
What stopped you from tracking down the killer
then and there?
CREON: The singing, riddling Sphinx.
She . . . persuaded us to let the mystery go
and concentrate on what lay at our feet.
OEDIPUS: No,
I'll start again—I'll bring it all to light myself!   150
Apollo is right, and so are you, Creon,
to turn our attention back to the murdered man.
Now you have *me* to fight for you, you'll see:
I am the land's avenger by all rights,
and Apollo's champion too.   155
But not to assist some distant kinsman, no,
for my own sake I'll rid us of this corruption.
Whoever killed the king may decide to kill me too,
with the same violent hand—by avenging Laius
I defend myself.   160

(*To the* PRIESTS.)

                               Quickly, my children.
Up from the steps, take up your branches now.

(*To the* GUARDS.)

One of you summon the city here before us,
tell them I'll do everything. God help us,
we will see our triumph—or our fall.

(OEDIPUS *and* CREON *enter the palace, followed by the* GUARDS.)

165 PRIEST: Rise, my sons. The kindness we came for
　　　Oedipus volunteers himself.
　　　Apollo has sent his word, his oracle—
　　　Come down, Apollo, save us, stop the plague.

(*The* PRIESTS *rise, remove their branches, and exit to the side. Enter a*
CHORUS, *the citizens of Thebes, who have not heard the news that*
CREON *brings. They march around the altar, chanting.*)

CHORUS:　　　　　　　　　　　　　Zeus!
　　　Great welcome voice of Zeus, what do you bring?
170　What word from the gold vaults of Delphi
　　　comes to brilliant Thebes? Racked with terror—
　　　　　　　　　　　　terror shakes my heart
　　　and I cry your wild cries, Apollo, Healer of Delos
　　　I worship you in dread . . . what now, what is your price?
175　some new sacrifice? some ancient rite from the past
　　　come round again each spring?—
　　　　　　　what will you bring to birth?
　　　Tell me, child of golden Hope
　　　　　warm voice that never dies!

180　You are the first I call, daughter of Zeus
　　　deathless Athena—I call your sister Artemis,
　　　heart of the market place enthroned in glory,
　　　　　　　　　　　guardian of our earth—
　　　I call Apollo, Archer astride the thunderheads of heaven—
185　O triple shield against death, shine before me now!
　　　If ever, once in the past, you stopped some ruin
　　　launched against our walls
　　　　　　you hurled the flame of pain
　　　far, far from Thebes—you gods
190　　　come now, come down once more!
　　　　　　　　　　　　　　No, no
　　　the miseries numberless, grief on grief, no end—
　　　too much to bear, we are all dying
　　　O my people . . .
　　　　　Thebes like a great army dying
195　and there is no sword of thought to save us, no
　　　and the fruits of our famous earth, they will not ripen
　　　no and the women cannot scream their pangs to birth—
　　　screams for the Healer, children dead in the womb
　　　　　and life on life goes down
200　　　　　　　　　　　　you can watch them go
　　　　like seabirds winging west, outracing the day's fire
　　　down the horizon, irresistibly
　　　　　　　streaking on to the shores of Evening
　　　　　　　　　　　　　　　　Death
　　　so many deaths, numberless deaths on deaths, no end—
205　Thebes is dying, look, her children
　　　stripped of pity . . .
　　　　　generations strewn on the ground
　　　unburied, unwept, the dead spreading death
　　　and the young wives and gray-haired mothers with them
210　cling to the altars, trailing in from all over the city—
　　　Thebes, city of death, one long cortege
　　　　　and the suffering rises
　　　　　　　　wails for mercy rise
　　　and the wild hymn for the Healer blazes out
215　clashing with our sobs our cries of mourning—
　　　　O golden daughter of god, send rescue
　　　radiant as the kindness in your eyes!

Drive him back!—the fever, the god of death
　　　　　　that raging god of war
not armored in bronze, not shielded now, he burns me, 220
battle cries in the onslaught burning on—
O rout him from our borders!
Sail him, blast him out to the Sea-queen's chamber
　　　　　　the black Atlantic gulfs
or the northern harbor, death to all 225
where the Thracian surf comes crashing.
Now what the night spares he comes by day and kills—
the god of death.
　　　　　O lord of the stormcloud,
you who twirl the lightning, Zeus, Father,
thunder Death to nothing! 230

Apollo, lord of the light, I beg you—
　　　whip your longbow's golden cord
showering arrows on our enemies—shafts of power
champions strong before us rushing on!

Artemis, Huntress, 235
torches flaring over the eastern ridges—
　　　　ride Death down in pain!

God of the headdress gleaming gold, I cry to you—
your name and ours are one, Dionysus—
　　　come with your face aflame with wine 240
　　　　　　your raving women's cries
　　your army on the march! Come with the lightning
come with torches blazing, eyes ablaze with glory!
Burn that god of death that all gods hate!

(OEDIPUS *enters from the palace to address the* CHORUS, *as if address-ing the entire city of Thebes.*)

OEDIPUS: You pray to the gods? Let me grant your prayers. 245
　　　Come, listen to me—do what the plague demands:
　　　you'll find relief and lift your head from the depths.

　　　I will speak out now as a stranger to the story,
　　　a stranger to the crime. If I'd been present then,
　　　there would have been no mystery, no long hunt 250
　　　without a clue in hand. So now, counted
　　　a native Theban years after the murder,
　　　to all of Thebes I make this proclamation:
　　　if any one of you knows who murdered Laius,
　　　the son of Labdacus, I order him to reveal 255
　　　the whole truth to me. Nothing to fear,
　　　even if he must denounce himself,
　　　let him speak up
　　　and so escape the brunt of the charge—
　　　he will suffer no unbearable punishment, 260
　　　nothing worse than exile, totally unharmed.

(OEDIPUS *pauses, waiting for a reply.*)

　　　　　　　　　　　　　　Next,
　　　if anyone knows the murderer is a stranger,
　　　a man from alien soil, come, speak up.
　　　I will give him a handsome reward, and lay up
　　　gratitude in my heart for him besides. 265

(*Silence again, no reply.*)

But if you keep silent, if anyone panicking,
trying to shield himself or friend or kin,
rejects my offer, then hear what I will do.
I order you, every citizen of the state
270 where I hold throne and power: banish this man—
whoever he may be—never shelter him, never
speak a word to him, never make him partner
to your prayers, your victims burned to the gods.
Never let the holy water touch his hands.
275 Drive him out, each of you, from every home.
He is the plague, the heart of our corruption,
as Apollo's oracle has just revealed to me.
So I honor my obligations:
I fight for the god and for the murdered man.

280 Now my curse on the murderer. Whoever he is,
a lone man unknown in his crime
or one among many, let that man drag out
his life in agony, step by painful step—
I curse myself as well . . . if by any chance
285 he proves to be an intimate of our house,
here at my hearth, with my full knowledge,
may the curse I just called down on him strike me!

These are your orders: perform them to the last.
I command you, for my sake, for Apollo's, for this
      country
290 blasted root and branch by the angry heavens.
Even if god had never urged you on to act,
how could you leave the crime uncleansed so long?
A man so noble—your king, brought down in blood—
you should have searched. But I am the king now,
295 I hold the throne that he held then, possess his bed
and a wife who shares our seed . . . why, our seed
might be the same, children born of the same mother
might have created blood-bonds between us
if his hope of offspring had not met disaster—
300 but fate swooped at his head and cut him short.
So I will fight for him as if he were my father,
stop at nothing, search the world
to lay my hands on the man who shed his blood,
the son of Labdacus descended of Polydorus,
305 Cadmus of old and Agenor, founder of the line:
their power and mine are one.
                              Oh dear gods,
my curse on those who disobey these orders!
Let no crops grow out of the earth for them—
shrivel their women, kill their sons,
310 burn them to nothing in this plague
that hits us now, or something even worse.
But you, loyal men of Thebes who approve my actions,
may our champion, Justice, may all the gods
be with us, fight beside us to the end!

315 LEADER: In the grip of your curse, my king, I swear
I'm not the murderer, I cannot point him out.
As for the search, Apollo pressed it on us—
he should name the killer.
    OEDIPUS: Quite right,
but to force the gods to act against their will
320 no man has the power.
    LEADER: Then if I might mention
the next best thing . . .

OEDIPUS: The third best too—
don't hold back, say it.
LEADER: I still believe . . .
Lord Tiresias sees with the eyes of Lord Apollo.
Anyone searching for the truth, my king,
might learn it from the prophet, clear as day.   325
OEDIPUS: I've not been slow with that. On Creon's cue
I sent the escorts, twice, within the hour.
I'm surprised he isn't here.
LEADER: We need him—
without him we have nothing but old, useless rumors.
OEDIPUS: Which rumors? I'll search out every word.   330
LEADER: Laius was killed, they say, by certain travelers.
OEDIPUS: I know—but no one can find the murderer.
LEADER: If the man has a trace of fear in him
he won't stay silent long,
not with your curses ringing in his ears.   335
OEDIPUS: He didn't flinch at murder,
he'll never flinch at words.

(*Enter* TIRESIAS, *the blind prophet, led by a boy with escorts in attendance. He remains at a distance.*)

LEADER: Here is the one who will convict him, look,
they bring him on at last, the seer, the man of god.
The truth lives inside him, him alone.   340
OEDIPUS: O Tiresias,
master of all the mysteries of our life,
all you teach and all you dare not tell,
signs in the heavens, signs that walk the earth!
Blind as you are, you can feel all the more
what sickness haunts our city. You, my lord,   345
are the one shield, the one savior we can find.

We asked Apollo—perhaps the messengers
haven't told you—he sent his answer back:
"Relief from the plague can only come one way.
Uncover the murderers of Laius,   350
put them to death or drive them into exile."
So I beg you, grudge us nothing now, no voice,
no message plucked from the birds, the embers
or the other mantic ways within your grasp.
Rescue yourself, your city, rescue me—   355
rescue everything infected by the dead.
We are in your hands. For a man to help others
with all his gifts and native strength:
that is the noblest work.
TIRESIAS: How terrible—to see the truth
when the truth is only pain to him who sees!   360
I knew it well, but I put it from my mind,
else I never would have come.
OEDIPUS: What's this? Why so grim, so dire?
TIRESIAS: Just send me home. You bear your burdens,
I'll bear mine. It's better that way,   365
please believe me.
OEDIPUS: Strange response . . . unlawful,
unfriendly too to the state that bred and reared you—
you withhold the word of god.
TIRESIAS: I fail to see
that your own words are so well-timed.
I'd rather not have the same thing said of me . . .   370

OEDIPUS: For the love of god, don't turn away,
  not if you know something. We beg you,
  all of us on our knees.

TIRESIAS: None of you knows—
  and I will never reveal my dreadful secrets,
375 not to say your own.

OEDIPUS: What? You know and you won't tell?
  You're bent on betraying us, destroying Thebes?

TIRESIAS: I'd rather not cause pain for you or me.
  So why this . . . useless interrogation?
380 You'll get nothing from me.

OEDIPUS: Nothing! You,
  you scum of the earth, you'd enrage a heart of stone!
  You won't talk? Nothing moves you?
  Out with it, once and for all!

TIRESIAS: You criticize my temper . . . unaware
385 of the one *you* live with, you revile me.

OEDIPUS: Who could restrain his anger hearing you?
  What outrage—you spurn the city!

TIRESIAS: What will come will come.
  Even if I shroud it all in silence.

390 OEDIPUS: What will come? You're bound to *tell* me that.

TIRESIAS: I will say no more. Do as you like, build your anger
  to whatever pitch you please, rage your worst—

OEDIPUS: Oh I'll let loose, I have such fury in me—
  now I see it all. You helped hatch the plot,
395 you did the work, yes, short of killing him
  with your own hands—and given eyes I'd say
  you did the killing single-handed!

TIRESIAS: Is that so!
  I charge you, then, submit to that decree
  you just laid down: from this day onward
400 speak to no one, not these citizens, not myself.
  You are the curse, the corruption of the land!

OEDIPUS: You, shameless—
  aren't you appalled to start up such a story?
  You think you can get away with this?

TIRESIAS: I have already.
405 The truth with all its power lives inside me.

OEDIPUS: Who primed you for this? Not your prophet's trade.

TIRESIAS: You did, you forced me, twisted it out of me.

OEDIPUS: What? Say it again—I'll understand it better.

TIRESIAS: Didn't you understand, just now?
410 Or are you tempting me to talk?

OEDIPUS: No, I can't say I grasped your meaning.
  Out with it, again!

TIRESIAS: I say you are the murderer you hunt.

OEDIPUS: That obscenity, twice—by god, you'll pay.

415 TIRESIAS: Shall I say more, so you can really rage?

OEDIPUS: Much as you want. Your words are nothing—
  futile.

TIRESIAS: You cannot imagine . . . I tell you,
  you and your loved ones live together in infamy,
  you cannot see how far you've gone in guilt.

420 OEDIPUS: You think you can keep this up and never suffer?

TIRESIAS: Indeed, if the truth has any power.

OEDIPUS: It does
  but not for you, old man. You've lost your power,
  stone-blind, stone-deaf—senses, eyes blind as stone!

TIRESIAS: I pity you, flinging at me the very insults
425 each man here will fling at you so soon.

OEDIPUS: Blind,
  lost in the night, endless night that nursed you!
  You can't hurt me or anyone else who sees the light—
  you can never touch me.

TIRESIAS: True, it is not your fate
  to fall at my hands. Apollo is quite enough,
  and he will take some pains to work this out.   430

OEDIPUS: Creon! Is this conspiracy his or yours?

TIRESIAS: Creon is not your downfall, no, you are your own.

OEDIPUS: O power—
  wealth and empire, skill outstripping skill
  in the heady rivalries of life,
  what envy lurks inside you! Just for this,   435
  the crown the city gave me—I never sought it,
  they laid it in my hands—for this alone, Creon,
  the soul of trust, my loyal friend from the start
  steals against me . . . so hungry to overthrow me
  he sets this wizard on me, this scheming quack,   440
  this fortune-teller peddling lies, eyes peeled
  for his own profit—seer blind in his craft!

  Come here, you pious fraud. Tell me,
  when did you ever prove yourself a prophet?
  When the Sphinx, that chanting Fury kept her   445
    deathwatch here,
  why silent then, not a word to set our people free?
  There was a riddle, not for some passer-by to solve—
  it cried out for a prophet. Where were you?
  Did you rise to the crisis? Not a word,
  you and your birds, your gods—nothing.   450
  No, but I came by, Oedipus the ignorant,
  I stopped the Sphinx! With no help from the birds,
  the flight of my own intelligence hit the mark.

  And this is the man you'd try to overthrow?
  You think you'll stand by Creon when he's king?   455
  You and the great mastermind—
  you'll pay in tears, I promise you, for this,
  this witch-hunt. If you didn't look so senile
  the lash would teach you what your scheming means!

LEADER: I would suggest his words were spoken in anger,   460
  Oedipus . . . yours too, and it isn't what we need.
  The best solution to the oracle, the riddle
  posed by god—we should look for that.

TIRESIAS: You are the king no doubt, but in one respect,
  at least, I am your equal: the right to reply.   465
  I claim that privilege too.
  I am not your slave. I serve Apollo.
  I don't need Creon to speak for me in public.
                So,
  you mock my blindness? Let me tell you this.
  You with your precious eyes,   470
  you're blind to the corruption of your life,
  to the house you live in, those you live with—
  who *are* your parents? Do you know? All unknowing
  you are the scourge of your own flesh and blood,
  the dead below the earth and the living here above,   475
  and the double lash of your mother and your father's
    curse
  will whip you from this land one day, their footfall
  treading you down in terror, darkness shrouding
  your eyes that now can see the light!

Soon, soon
480   you'll scream aloud—what haven won't reverberate?
What rock of Cithaeron won't scream back in echo?
That day you learn the truth about your marriage,
the wedding-march that sang you into your halls,
the lusty voyage home to the fatal harbor!
485   And a crowd of other horrors you'd never dream
will level you with yourself and all your children.

There. Now smear us with insults—Creon, myself
and every word I've said. No man will ever
be rooted from the earth as brutally as you.
490 OEDIPUS: Enough! Such filth from him? Insufferable—
what, still alive? Get out—
faster, back where you came from—vanish!
TIRESIAS: I would never have come if you hadn't called me here.
OEDIPUS: If I thought you would blurt out such absurdities,
495   you'd have died waiting before I'd had you summoned.
TIRESIAS: Absurd, am I! To you, not to your parents:
the ones who bore you found me sane enough.
OEDIPUS: Parents—who? Wait . . . who is my father?
TIRESIAS: This day will bring your birth and your destruction.
500 OEDIPUS: Riddles—all you can say are riddles, murk and
      darkness.
TIRESIAS: Ah, but aren't you the best man alive at solving
      riddles?
OEDIPUS: Mock me for that, go on, and you'll reveal my
      greatness.
TIRESIAS: Your great good fortune, true, it was your ruin.
OEDIPUS: Not if I saved the city—what do I care?
505 TIRESIAS: Well then, I'll be going.

(*To his* ATTENDANT.)

Take me home, boy.
OEDIPUS: Yes, take him away. You're a nuisance here.
    Out of the way, the irritation's gone.

(*Turning his back on* TIRESIAS, *moving toward the palace.*)

TIRESIAS: I will go,
once I have said what I came here to say.
I will never shrink from the anger in your eyes—
510   you can't destroy me. Listen to me closely:
the man you've sought so long, proclaiming,
cursing up and down, the murderer of Laius—
he is here. A stranger,
you may think, who lives among you,
515   he soon will be revealed a native Theban
but he will take no joy in the revelation.
Blind who now has eyes, beggar who now is rich,
he will grope his way toward a foreign soil,
a stick tapping before him step by step.

(OEDIPUS *enters the palace.*)

520   Revealed at last, brother and father both
to the children he embraces, to his mother
son and husband both—he sowed the loins
his father sowed, he spilled his father's blood!

Go in and reflect on that, solve that.
525   And if you find I've lied
from this day onward call the prophet blind.

(TIRESIAS *and the boy exit to the side.*)

CHORUS: Who—
who is the man the voice of god denounces
resounding out of the rocky gorge of Delphi?
    The horror too dark to tell,
whose ruthless bloody hands have done the work?   530
His time has come to fly
    to outrace the stallions of the storm
               his feet a streak of speed—
Cased in armor, Apollo son of the Father
lunges on him, lightning-bolts afire!   535
And the grim unerring Furies
           closing for the kill.
                     Look,
the word of god has just come blazing
flashing off Parnassus' snowy heights!
    That man who left no trace—   540
after him, hunt him down with all our strength!
Now under bristling timber
    up through rocks and caves he stalks
             like the wild mountain bull—
cut off from men, each step an agony, frenzied, racing blind   545
but he cannot outrace the dread voices of Delphi
ringing out of the heart of Earth,
    the dark wings beating around him shrieking doom
            the doom that never dies, the terror—
The skilled prophet scans the birds and shatters me with   550
    terror!
I can't accept him, can't deny him, don't know what to say,
I'm lost, and the wings of dark foreboding beating—
I cannot see what's come, what's still to come . . .
and what could breed a blood feud between
    Laius' house and the son of Polybus?   555
I know of nothing, not in the past and not now,
no charge to bring against our king, no cause
to attack his fame that rings throughout Thebes—
    not without proof—not for the ghost of Laius,
    not to avenge a murder gone without a trace.   560

Zeus and Apollo know, they know, the great masters
    of all the dark and depth of human life.
But whether a mere man can know the truth,
whether a seer can fathom more than I—
there is no test, no certain proof   565
    though matching skill for skill
a man can outstrip a rival. No, not till I see
these charges proved will I side with his accusers.
We saw him then, when the she-hawk swept against him,
saw with our own eyes his skill, his brilliant triumph—   570
    there was the test—he was the joy of Thebes!
    Never will I convict my king, never in my heart.

(*Enter* CREON *from the side.*)

CREON: My fellow-citizens, I hear King Oedipus
levels terrible charges at me. I had to come.
I resent it deeply. If, in the present crisis,   575
he thinks he suffers any abuse from me,
anything I've done or said that offers him
the slightest injury, why, I've no desire
to linger out this life, my reputation in ruins.

580 The damage I'd face from such an accusation
is nothing simple. No, there's nothing worse:
branded a traitor in the city, a traitor
to all of you and my good friends.
LEADER: True,
but a slur might have been forced out of him,
585 by anger perhaps, not any firm conviction.
CREON: The charge was made in public, wasn't it?
I put the prophet up to spreading lies?
LEADER: Such things were said . . .
I don't know with what intent, if any.
590 CREON: Was his glance steady, his mind right
when the charge was brought against me?
LEADER: I really couldn't say, I never look
to judge the ones in power.

(*The doors open.* OEDIPUS *enters.*)

                                    Wait,
here's Oedipus now.
OEDIPUS: You—here? You have the gall
595 to show your face before the palace gates?
You, plotting to kill me, kill the king—
I see it all, the marauding thief himself
scheming to steal my crown and power!
                                    Tell me,
in god's name, what did you take me for,
600 coward or fool, when you spun out your plot?
Your treachery—you think I'd never detect it
creeping against me in the dark? Or sensing it,
not defend myself? Aren't you the fool,
you and your high adventure. Lacking numbers,
605 powerful friends, out for the big game of empire—
you need riches, armies to bring that quarry down!
CREON: Are you quite finished? It's your turn to listen
for just as long as you've . . . instructed me.
Hear me out, then judge me on the facts.
610 OEDIPUS: You've a wicked way with words, Creon,
but I'll be slow to learn—from you.
I find you a menace, a great burden to me.
CREON: Just one thing, hear me out in this.
OEDIPUS: Just one thing,
don't tell *me* you're not the enemy, the traitor.
615 CREON: Look, if you think crude, mindless stubbornness
such a gift, you've lost your sense of balance.
OEDIPUS: If you think you can abuse a kinsman,
then escape the penalty, you're insane.
CREON: Fair enough, I grant you. But this injury
620 you say I've done you, what is it?
OEDIPUS: Did you induce me, yes or no,
to send for that sanctimonious prophet?
CREON: I did. And I'd do the same again.
OEDIPUS: All right then, tell me, how long is it now
625 since Laius . . .
CREON: Laius—what did *he* do?
OEDIPUS: Vanished,
swept from sight, murdered in his tracks.
CREON: The count of the years would run you far back . . .
OEDIPUS: And that far back, was the prophet at his trade?
CREON: Skilled as he is today, and just as honored.

OEDIPUS: Did he ever refer to me then, at that time? 630
CREON: No,
never, at least, when I was in his presence.
OEDIPUS: But you did investigate the murder, didn't you?
CREON: We did our best, of course, discovered nothing.
OEDIPUS: But the great seer never accused me then—why not?
CREON: I don't know. And when I don't, *I* keep quiet. 635
OEDIPUS: You do know this, you'd tell it too—
if you had a shred of decency.
CREON: What?
If I know, I won't hold back.
OEDIPUS: Simply this:
if the two of you had never put heads together,
we would never have heard about *my* killing Laius. 640
CREON: If that's what he says . . . well, you know best.
But now I have a right to learn from you
as you just learned from me.
OEDIPUS: Learn your fill,
you never will convict me of the murder.
CREON: Tell me, you're married to my sister, aren't you? 645
OEDIPUS: A genuine discovery—there's no denying that.
CREON: And you rule the land with her, with equal power?
OEDIPUS: She receives from me whatever she desires.
CREON: And I am the third, all of us are equals?
OEDIPUS: Yes, and it's there you show your stripes— 650
you betray a kinsman.
CREON: Not at all.
Not if you see things calmly, rationally,
as I do. Look at it this way first:
who in his right mind would rather rule
and live in anxiety than sleep in peace? 655
Particularly if he enjoys the same authority.
Not I, I'm not the man to yearn for kingship,
not with a king's power in my hands. Who would?
No one with any sense of self-control.
Now, as it is, you offer me all I need, 660
not a fear in the world. But if I wore the crown . . .
there'd be many painful duties to perform,
hardly to my taste.
                    How could kingship
please me more than influence, power
without a qualm? I'm not that deluded yet, 665
to reach for anything but privilege outright,
profit free and clear.
Now all men sing my praises, all salute me,
now all who request your favors curry mine.
I am their best hope: success rests in me. 670
Why give up that, I ask you, and borrow trouble?
A man of sense, someone who sees things clearly
would never resort to treason.
No, I have no lust for conspiracy in me,
nor could I ever suffer one who does. 675

Do you want proof? Go to Delphi yourself,
examine the oracle and see if I've reported
the message word-for-word. This too:
if you detect that I and the clairvoyant
have plotted anything in common, arrest me, 680
execute me. Not on the strength of one vote,
two in this case, mine as well as yours.

But don't convict me on sheer unverified surmise.
How wrong it is to take the good for bad,
685   purely at random, or take the bad for good.
But reject a friend, a kinsman? I would as soon
tear out the life within us, priceless life itself.
You'll learn this well, without fail, in time.
Time alone can bring the just man to light—
690   the criminal you can spot in one short day.
LEADER: Good advice,
    my lord, for anyone who wants to avoid disaster.
    Those who jump to conclusions may go wrong.
OEDIPUS: When my enemy moves against me quickly,
    plots in secret, I move quickly too, I must,
695   I plot and pay him back. Relax my guard a moment,
    waiting his next move—he wins his objective,
    I lose mine.
CREON: What do you want?
    You want me banished?
OEDIPUS: No, I want you dead.
CREON: Just to show how ugly a grudge can . . .
OEDIPUS: So,
700   still stubborn? you don't think I'm serious?
CREON: I think you're insane.
OEDIPUS: Quite sane—in my behalf.
CREON: Not just as much in mine?
OEDIPUS: You—my mortal enemy?
CREON: What if you're wholly wrong?
OEDIPUS: No matter—I must rule.
CREON: Not if you rule unjustly.
OEDIPUS: Hear him, Thebes, my city!
705 CREON: My city too, not yours alone!
LEADER: Please, my lords.

(*Enter* JOCASTA *from the palace.*)

                        Look, Jocasta's coming,
    and just in time too. With her help
    you must put this fighting of yours to rest.
JOCASTA: Have you no sense? Poor misguided men,
710   such shouting—why this public outburst?
    Aren't you ashamed, with the land so sick,
    to stir up private quarrels?

(*To* OEDIPUS.)

    Into the palace now. And Creon, you go home.
    Why make such a furor over nothing?
715 CREON: My sister, it's dreadful . . . Oedipus, your husband,
    he's bent on a choice of punishments for me,
    banishment from the fatherland or death.
OEDIPUS: Precisely. I caught him in the act, Jocasta,
    plotting, about to stab me in the back.
720 CREON: Never—curse me, let me die and be damned
    if I've done you any wrong you charge me with.
JOCASTA: Oh god, believe it, Oedipus,
    honor the solemn oath he swears to heaven.
    Do it for me, for the sake of all your people.

(*The* CHORUS *begins to chant.*)

725 CHORUS: Believe it, be sensible
            give way, my king, I beg you!

OEDIPUS: What do you want from me, concessions?
CHORUS: Respect him—he's been no fool in the past
    and now he's strong with the oath he swears to god.
OEDIPUS: You know what you're asking?   730
CHORUS: I do.
OEDIPUS: Then out with it!
CHORUS: The man's your friend, your kin, he's under oath—
    don't cast him out, disgraced,
    branded with guilt on the strength of hearsay only.
OEDIPUS: Know full well, if that is what you want
    you want me dead or banished from the land.   735
CHORUS: Never—
    no, by the blazing Sun, first god of the heavens!
        Stripped of the gods, stripped of loved ones,
    let me die by inches if that ever crossed my mind.
    But the heart inside me sickens, dies as the land dies
    and now on top of the old griefs you pile this,   740
    your fury—both of you!
OEDIPUS: Then let him go,
    even if it does lead to my ruin, my death
    or my disgrace, driven from Thebes for life.
    It's you, not him I pity—your words move me.
    He, wherever he goes, my hate goes with him.   745
CREON: Look at you, sullen in yielding, brutal in your rage—
    you will go too far. It's perfect justice:
    natures like yours are hardest on themselves.
OEDIPUS: Then leave me alone—get out!
CREON: I'm going.
    You're wrong, so wrong. These men know I'm right.   750

(*Exit to the side. The* CHORUS *turns to* JOCASTA.)

CHORUS: Why do you hesitate, my lady
        why not help him in?
JOCASTA: Tell me what's happened first.
CHORUS: Loose, ignorant talk started dark suspicions
    and a sense of injustice cut deeply too.   755
JOCASTA: On both sides?
CHORUS: Oh yes.
JOCASTA: What did they say?
CHORUS: Enough, please, enough! The land's so racked already
    or so it seems to me . . .
    End the trouble here, just where they left it.
OEDIPUS: You see what comes of your good intentions now?   760
    And all because you tried to blunt my anger.
CHORUS: My king,
    I've said it once, I'll say it time and again—
        I'd be insane, you know it,
    senseless, ever to turn my back on you.
    You who set our beloved land—storm-tossed, shattered— 765
    straight on course. Now again, good helmsman,
    steer us through the storm!

(*The* CHORUS *draws away, leaving* OEDIPUS *and* JOCASTA *side by side.*)

JOCASTA: For the love of god,
    Oedipus, tell me too, what is it?
    Why this rage? You're so unbending.
OEDIPUS: I will tell you. I respect you, Jocasta,   770
    much more than these men here . . .

(*Glancing at the* CHORUS.)

Creon's to blame, Creon schemes against me.
JOCASTA: Tell me clearly, how did the quarrel start?
OEDIPUS: He says I murdered Laius—I am guilty.
775 JOCASTA: How does he know? Some secret knowledge
 or simple hearsay?
OEDIPUS: Oh, he sent his prophet in
 to do his dirty work. You know Creon,
 Creon keeps his own lips clean.
JOCASTA: A prophet?
 Well then, free yourself of every charge!
780 Listen to me and learn some peace of mind:
 no skill in the world,
 nothing human can penetrate the future.
 Here is proof, quick and to the point.

 An oracle came to Laius one fine day
785 (I won't say from Apollo himself
 but his underlings, his priests) and it declared
 that doom would strike him down at the hands of a son,
 our son, to be born of our own flesh and blood. But Laius,
 so the report goes at least, was killed by strangers,
790 thieves, at a place where three roads meet . . . my son—
 he wasn't three days old and the boy's father
 fastened his ankles, had a henchman fling him away
 on a barren, trackless mountain.
     There, you see?
 Apollo brought neither thing to pass. My baby
795 no more murdered his father than Laius suffered—
 his wildest fear—death at his own son's hands.
 That's how the seers and all their revelations
 mapped out the future. Brush them from your mind.
 Whatever the god needs and seeks
800 he'll bring to light himself, with ease.
OEDIPUS: Strange,
 hearing you just now . . . my mind wandered,
 my thoughts racing back and forth.
JOCASTA: What do you mean? Why so anxious, startled?
OEDIPUS: I thought I heard you say that Laius
805 was cut down at a place where three roads meet.
JOCASTA: That was the story. It hasn't died out yet.
OEDIPUS: Where did this thing happen? Be precise.
JOCASTA: A place called Phocis, where two branching roads,
 one from Daulia, one from Delphi,
810 come together—a crossroads.
OEDIPUS: When? How long ago?
JOCASTA: The heralds no sooner reported Laius dead
 than you appeared and they hailed you king of Thebes.
OEDIPUS: My god, my god—what have you planned to do to me?
815 JOCASTA: What, Oedipus? What haunts you so?
OEDIPUS: Not yet.
 Laius—how did he look? Describe him.
 Had he reached his prime?
JOCASTA: He was swarthy,
 and the gray had just begun to streak his temples,
 and his build . . . wasn't far from yours.
OEDIPUS: Oh no no,
820 I think I've just called down a dreadful curse
 upon myself—I simply didn't know!

JOCASTA: What are you saying? I shudder to look at you.
OEDIPUS: I have a terrible fear the blind seer can see.
 I'll know in a moment. One thing more—
JOCASTA: Anything,
 afraid as I am—ask, I'll answer, all I can.   825
OEDIPUS: Did he go with a light or heavy escort,
 several men-at-arms, like a lord, a king?
JOCASTA: There were five in the party, a herald among them,
 and a single wagon carrying Laius.
OEDIPUS: Ai—
 now I can see it all, clear as day.   830
 Who told you all this at the time, Jocasta?
JOCASTA: A servant who reached home, the lone survivor.
OEDIPUS: So, could he still be in the palace—even now?
JOCASTA: No indeed. Soon as he returned from the scene
 and saw you on the throne with Laius dead and gone,   835
 he knelt and clutched my hand, pleading with me
 to send him into the hinterlands, to pasture,
 far as possible, out of sight of Thebes.
 I sent him away. Slave though he was,
 he'd earned that favor—and much more.   840
OEDIPUS: Can we bring him back, quickly?
JOCASTA: Easily. Why do you want him so?
OEDIPUS: I am afraid,
 Jocasta, I have said too much already.
 That man—I've got to see him.
JOCASTA: Then he'll come.
 But even I have a right, I'd like to think,   845
 to know what's torturing you, my lord.
OEDIPUS: And so you shall—I can hold nothing back from you,
 now I've reached this pitch of dark foreboding.
 Who means more to me than you? Tell me,
 whom would I turn toward but you   850
 as I go through all this?

 My father was Polybus, king of Corinth.
 My mother, a Dorian, Merope. And I was held
 the prince of the realm among the people there,
 till something struck me out of nowhere,   855
 something strange . . . worth remarking perhaps,
 hardly worth the anxiety I gave it.
 Some man at a banquet who had drunk too much
 shouted out—he was far gone, mind you—
 that I am not my father's son. Fighting words!   860
 I barely restrained myself that day
 but early the next I went to mother and father,
 questioned them closely, and they were enraged
 at the accusation and the fool who let it fly.
 So as for my parents I was satisfied,   865
 but still this thing kept gnawing at me,
 the slander spread—I had to make my move.
     And so,
 unknown to mother and father I set out for Delphi,
 and the god Apollo spurned me, sent me away
 denied the facts I came for,   870
 but first he flashed before my eyes a future
 great with pain, terror, disaster—I can hear him cry,
 "You are fated to couple with your mother, you will bring
 a breed of children into the light no man can bear to see—
 you will kill your father, the one who gave you life!"   875

I heard all that and ran. I abandoned Corinth,
from that day on I gauged its landfall only
by the stars, running, always running
toward some place where I would never see
880 the shame of all those oracles come true.
And as I fled I reached that very spot
where the great king, you say, met his death.

Now, Jocasta, I will tell you all.
Making my way toward this triple crossroad
885 I began to see a herald, then a brace of colts
drawing a wagon, and mounted on the bench . . . a man,
just as you've described him, coming face-to-face,
and the one in the lead and the old man himself
were about to thrust me off the road—brute force—
890 and the one shouldering me aside, the driver,
I strike him in anger!—and the old man, watching me
coming up along his wheels—he brings down
his prod, two prongs straight at my head!
I paid him back with interest!
895 Short work, by god—with one blow of the staff
in this right hand I knock him out of his high seat,
roll him out of the wagon, sprawling headlong—
I killed them all—every mother's son!

Oh, but if there is any blood-tie
900 between Laius and this stranger . . .
what man alive more miserable than I?
More hated by the gods? *I* am the man
no alien, no citizen welcomes to his house,
law forbids it—not a word to me in public,
905 driven out of every hearth and home.
And all these curses I—no one but I
brought down these piling curses on myself!
And you, his wife, I've touched your body with these,
the hands that killed your husband cover you with blood.

910 Wasn't I born for torment? Look me in the eyes!
I am abomination—heart and soul!
I must be exiled, and even in exile
never see my parents, never set foot
on native ground again. Else I am doomed
915 to couple with my mother and cut my father down . . .
Polybus who reared me, gave me life.
But why, why?
Wouldn't a man of judgment say—and wouldn't he be
right—
some savage power has brought this down upon my head?

Oh no, not that, you pure and awesome gods,
920 never let me see that day! Let me slip
from the world of men, vanish without a trace
before I see myself stained with such corruption,
stained to the heart.
LEADER: My lord, you fill our hearts with fear.
925 But at least until you question the witness,
do take hope.
OEDIPUS: Exactly. He is my last hope—
I am waiting for the shepherd. He is crucial.
JOCASTA: And once he appears, what then? Why so urgent?
OEDIPUS: I will tell you. If it turns out that his story
930 matches yours, I've escaped the worst.

JOCASTA: What did I say? What struck you so?
OEDIPUS: You said
thieves—
he told you a whole band of them murdered Laius.
So, if he still holds to the same number,
I cannot be the killer. One can't equal many.
But if he refers to one man, one alone, 935
clearly the scales come down on me:
I am guilty.
JOCASTA: Impossible. Trust me,
I told you precisely what he said,
and he can't retract it now;
the whole city heard it, not just I. 940
And even if he should vary his first report
by one man more or less, still, my lord,
he could never make the murder of Laius
truly fit the prophecy. Apollo was explicit:
my son was doomed to kill my husband . . . my son, 945
poor defenseless thing, he never had a chance
to kill his father. They destroyed him first.

So much for prophecy. It's neither here nor there.
From this day on. I wouldn't look right or left.
OEDIPUS: True, true. Still, that shepherd, 950
someone fetch him—now!
JOCASTA: I'll send at once. But do let's go inside.
I'd never displease you, least of all in this.

(OEDIPUS *and* JOCASTA *enter the palace.*)

CHORUS: Destiny guide me always
Destiny find me filled with reverence 955
pure in word and deed.
Great laws tower above us, reared on high
born for the brilliant vault of heaven—
Olympian Sky their only father,
nothing mortal, no man gave them birth, 960
their memory deathless, never lost in sleep:
within them lives a mighty god, the god does not
grow old.

Pride breeds the tyrant
violent pride, gorging, crammed to bursting
with all that is overripe and rich with ruin— 965
clawing up to the heights, headlong pride
crashes down the abyss—sheer doom!
No footing helps, all foothold lost and gone.
But the healthy strife that makes the city strong—
I pray that god will never end that wrestling: 970
god, my champion, I will never let you go.

But if any man comes striding, high and mighty
in all he says and does,
no fear of justice, no reverence
for the temples of the gods— 975
let a rough doom tear him down,
repay his pride, breakneck, ruinous pride!
If he cannot reap his profits fairly
cannot restrain himself from outrage—
mad, laying hands on the holy things untouchable! 980

Can such a man, so desperate, still boast
he can save his life from the flashing bolts of god?

If all such violence goes with honor now
why join the sacred dance?

985 Never again will I go reverent to Delphi,
the inviolate heart of Earth
or Apollo's ancient oracle at Abae
or Olympia of the fires—
unless these prophecies all come true
990 for all mankind to point toward in wonder.
King of kings, if you deserve your titles
Zeus, remember, never forget!
You and your deathless, everlasting reign.

They are dying, the old oracles sent to Laius,
995 now our masters strike them off the rolls.
Nowhere Apollo's golden glory now—
the gods, the gods go down.

(*Enter* JOCASTA *from the palace, carrying a suppliant's branch wound in wool.*)

JOCASTA: Lords of the realm, it occurred to me,
just now, to visit the temples of the gods,
1000 so I have my branch in hand and incense too.

Oedipus is beside himself. Racked with anguish,
no longer a man of sense, he won't admit
the latest prophecies are hollow as the old—
he's at the mercy of every passing voice
1005 if the voice tells of terror.
I urge him gently, nothing seems to help,
so I turn to you, Apollo, you are nearest.

(*Placing her branch on the altar, while an old herdsman enters from the side, not the one just summoned by the King but an unexpected* MESSENGER *from Corinth.*)

I come with prayers and offerings . . . I beg you,
cleanse us, set us free of defilement!
1010 Look at us, passengers in the grip of fear,
watching the pilot of the vessel go to pieces.
MESSENGER: (*Approaching* JOCASTA *and the* CHORUS.) Strangers,
please, I wonder if you could lead us
to the palace of the king . . . I think it's Oedipus.
Better, the man himself—you know where he is?
1015 LEADER: This is his palace, stranger. He's inside.
But here is his queen, his wife and mother
of his children.
MESSENGER: Blessings on you, noble queen,
queen of Oedipus crowned with all your family—
blessings on you always!
1020 JOCASTA: And the same to you, stranger, you deserve it . . .
such a greeting. But what have you come for?
Have you brought us news?
MESSENGER: Wonderful news—
for the house, my lady, for your husband too.
JOCASTA: Really, what? Who sent you?
MESSENGER: Corinth.
1025 I'll give you the message in a moment.
You'll be glad of it—how could you help it?—
though it costs a little sorrow in the bargain.
JOCASTA: What can it be, with such a double edge?

MESSENGER: The people there, they want to make your Oedipus
king of Corinth, so they're saying now.   1030
JOCASTA: Why? Isn't old Polybus still in power?
MESSENGER: No more. Death has got him in the tomb.
JOCASTA: What are you saying? Polybus, dead?—dead?
MESSENGER: If not,
if I'm not telling the truth, strike me dead too.
JOCASTA: (*To a* SERVANT.) Quickly, go to your master, tell him
this!   1035

You prophecies of the gods, where are you now?
This is the man that Oedipus feared for years,
he fled him, not to kill him—and now he's dead,
quite by chance, a normal, natural death,
not murdered by his son.   1040
OEDIPUS: (*Emerging from the palace.*)
                Dearest,
what now? Why call me from the palace?
JOCASTA: (*Bringing the* MESSENGER *closer.*) Listen to *him*, see for
yourself what all
those awful prophecies of god have come to.
OEDIPUS: And who is he? What can he have for me?
JOCASTA: He's from Corinth, he's come to tell you   1045
your father is no more—Polybus—he's dead!
OEDIPUS: (*Wheeling on the* MESSENGER.) What? Let me have it
from your lips.
MESSENGER: Well,
if that's what you want first, then here it is:
make no mistake, Polybus is dead and gone.
OEDIPUS: How—murder? sickness?—what? what killed him?   1050
MESSENGER: A light tip of the scales can put old bones to rest.
OEDIPUS: Sickness then—poor man, it wore him down.
MESSENGER: That,
and the long count of years he'd measured out.
OEDIPUS: So!
Jocasta, why, why look to the Prophet's hearth,
the fires of the future? Why scan the birds   1055
that scream above our heads? They winged me on
to the murder of my father, did they? That was my doom?
Well look, he's dead and buried, hidden under the earth,
and here I am in Thebes, I never put hand to sword—
unless some longing for me wasted him away,   1060
then in a sense you'd say I caused his death.
But now, all those prophecies I feared—Polybus
packs them off to sleep with him in hell!
They're nothing, worthless.
JOCASTA: There.
Didn't I tell you from the start?   1065
OEDIPUS: So you did. I was lost in fear.
JOCASTA: No more, sweep it from your mind forever.
OEDIPUS: But my mother's bed, surely I must fear—
JOCASTA: Fear?
What should a man fear? It's all chance,
chance rules our lives. Not a man on earth   1070
can see a day ahead, groping through the dark.
Better to live at random, best we can.
And as for this marriage with your mother—
have no fear. Many a man before you,
in his dreams, has shared his mother's bed.   1075
Take such things for shadows, nothing at all—

Live, Oedipus,
   as if there's no tomorrow!
OEDIPUS: Brave words,
   and you'd persuade me if mother weren't alive.
1080   But mother lives, so for all your reassurances
   I live in fear, I must.
JOCASTA: But your father's death,
   that, at least, is a great blessing, joy to the eyes!
OEDIPUS: Great, I know . . . but I fear *her*—she's still alive.
MESSENGER: Wait, who is this woman, makes you so afraid?
1085   OEDIPUS: Merope, old man. The wife of Polybus.
MESSENGER: The queen? What's there to fear in her?
OEDIPUS: A dreadful prophecy, stranger, sent by the gods.
MESSENGER: Tell me, could you? Unless it's forbidden
   other ears to hear.
OEDIPUS: Not at all.
1090   Apollo told me once—it is my fate—
   I must make love with my own mother,
   shed my father's blood with my own hands.
   So for years I've given Corinth a wide berth,
   and it's been my good fortune too. But still,
1095   to see one's parents and look into their eyes
   is the greatest joy I know.
MESSENGER: You're afraid of that?
   That kept you out of Corinth?
OEDIPUS: My *father*, old man—
   so I wouldn't kill my father.
MESSENGER: So that's it.
   Well then, seeing I came with such good will, my king,
1100   why don't I rid you of that old worry now?
OEDIPUS: What a rich reward you'd have for that!
MESSENGER: What do you think I came for, majesty?
   So you'd come home and I'd be better off.
OEDIPUS: Never, I will never go near my parents.
1105   MESSENGER: My boy, it's clear, you don't know what you're
   doing.
OEDIPUS: What do you mean, old man? For god's sake, explain.
MESSENGER: If you ran from *them,* always dodging home . . .
OEDIPUS: Always, terrified Apollo's oracle might come true—
MESSENGER: And you'd be covered with guilt, from both your
   parents.
1110   OEDIPUS: That's right, old man, that fear is always
   with me.
MESSENGER: Don't you know? You've really nothing to fear.
OEDIPUS: But why? If I'm their son—Merope, Polybus?
MESSENGER: Polybus was nothing to you, that's why, not in
   blood.
OEDIPUS: What are you saying—Polybus was not my father?
1115   MESSENGER: No more than I am. He and I are equals.
OEDIPUS: My father—
   how can my father equal nothing? You're nothing to me!
MESSENGER: Neither was he, no more your father than I am.
OEDIPUS: Then why did he call me his son?
MESSENGER: You were a gift,
   years ago—know for a fact he took you
1120   from my hands.
OEDIPUS: No, from another's hands?
   Then how could he love me so? He loved me, deeply . . .
MESSENGER: True, and his early years without a child
   made him love you all the more.

OEDIPUS: And you, did you . . .
   buy me? find me by accident?
MESSENGER: I stumbled on you,
   down the woody flanks of Mount Cithaeron.   1125
OEDIPUS: So close,
   what were you doing here, just passing through?
MESSENGER: Watching over my flocks, grazing them on the
   slopes.
OEDIPUS: A herdsman, were you? A vagabond, scraping for
   wages?
MESSENGER: Your savior too, my son, in your worst hour.
OEDIPUS: Oh—
   when you picked me up, was I in pain? What exactly?   1130
MESSENGER: Your ankles . . . they tell the story. Look at
   them.
OEDIPUS: Why remind me of that, that old affliction?
MESSENGER: Your ankles were pinned together. I set you free.
OEDIPUS: That dreadful mark—I've had it from the cradle.
MESSENGER: And you got your name from that misfortune   1135
   too,
   the name's still with you.
OEDIPUS: Dear god, who did it?—
   mother? father? Tell me.
MESSENGER: I don't know.
   The one who gave you to me, he'd know more.
OEDIPUS: What? You took me from someone else?
   You didn't find me yourself?   1140
MESSENGER: No sir,
   another shepherd passed you on to me.
OEDIPUS: Who? Do you know? Describe him.
MESSENGER: He called himself a servant of . . .
   if I remember rightly—Laius.

(JOCASTA *turns sharply.*)

OEDIPUS: The king of the land who ruled here long ago?   1145
MESSENGER: That's the one. That herdsman was *his* man.
OEDIPUS: Is he still alive? Can I see him?
MESSENGER: They'd know best, the people of these parts.

(OEDIPUS *and the* MESSENGER *turn to the* CHORUS.)

OEDIPUS: Does anyone know that herdsman,
   the one he mentioned? Anyone seen him   1150
   in the fields, here in the city? Out with it!
   The time has come to reveal this once for all.
LEADER: I think he's the very shepherd you wanted to see,
   a moment ago. But the queen, Jocasta,
   she's the one to say.   1155
OEDIPUS: Jocasta,
   you remember the man we just sent for?
   Is *that* the one he means?
JOCASTA: That man . . .
   why ask? Old shepherd, talk, empty nonsense,
   don't give it another thought, don't even think—
OEDIPUS: What—give up now, with a clue like this?   1160
   Fail to solve the mystery of my birth?
   Not for all the world!
JOCASTA: Stop—in the name of god,
   if you love your own life, call off this search!
   My suffering is enough.

OEDIPUS: Courage!
1165   Even if my mother turns out to be a slave,
        and I a slave, three generations back,
        you would not seem common.
JOCASTA: Oh no,
        listen to me, I beg you, don't do this.
OEDIPUS: Listen to you? No more. I must know it all,
1170   must see the truth at last.
JOCASTA: No, please—
        for your sake—I want the best for you!
OEDIPUS: Your best is more than I can bear.
JOCASTA: You're doomed—
        may you never fathom who you are!
OEDIPUS: (*To a servant.*) Hurry, fetch me the herdsman, now!
1175   Leave her to glory in her royal birth.
JOCASTA: Aieeeeee—
                man of agony—
        that is the only name I have for you,
        that, no other—ever, ever, ever!

(*Flinging through the palace doors. A long, tense silence follows.*)

LEADER: Where's she gone, Oedipus?
1180   Rushing off, such wild grief . . .
        I'm afraid that from this silence
        something monstrous may come bursting forth.
OEDIPUS: Let it burst! Whatever will, whatever must!
        I must know my birth, no matter how common
1185   it may be—I must see my origins face-to-face.
        She perhaps, she with her woman's pride
        may well be mortified by my birth,
        but I, I count myself the son of Chance,
        the great goddess, giver of all good things—
1190   I'll never see myself disgraced. She is my mother!
        And the moons have marked me out, my blood-brothers,
        one moon on the wane, the next moon great with power.
        That is my blood, my nature—I will never betray it,
        never fail to search and learn my birth!
1195 CHORUS: Yes—if I am a true prophet
                if I can grasp the truth,
            by the boundless skies of Olympus,
            at the full moon of tomorrow, Mount Cithaeron
            you will know how Oedipus glories in you—
1200   you, his birthplace, nurse, his mountain-mother!
        And we will sing you, dancing out your praise—
        you lift our monarch's heart!
            Apollo, Apollo, god of the wild cry
                may our dancing please you!
                                Oedipus—
1205   son, dear child, who bore you?
        Who of the nymphs who seem to live forever
        mated with Pan, the mountain-striding Father?
        Who was your mother? who, some bride of Apollo
        the god who loves the pastures spreading toward the sun?
1210   Or was it Hermes, king of the lightning ridges?
        Or Dionysus, lord of frenzy, lord of the barren peaks—
        did he seize you in his hands, dearest of all his lucky
                finds?—
            found by the nymphs, their warm eyes dancing, gift
        to the lord who loves them dancing out his joy!

(OEDIPUS *strains to see a figure coming from the distance. Attended by* palace GUARDS, *an old* SHEPHERD *enters slowly, reluctant to approach the king.*)

OEDIPUS: I never met the man, my friends . . . still,   1215
        if I had to guess, I'd say that's the shepherd,
        the very one we've looked for all along.
        Brothers in old age, two of a kind,
        he and our guest here. At any rate
        the ones who bring him in are my own men,   1220
        I recognize them.

(*Turning to the* LEADER.)

                But you know more than I,
        you should, you've seen the man before.
LEADER: I know him, definitely. One of Laius' men,
        a trusty shepherd, if there ever was one.
OEDIPUS: You, I ask you first, stranger,   1225
        you from Corinth—is this the one you mean?
MESSENGER: You're looking at him. He's your man.
OEDIPUS: (*To the* SHEPHERD.) You, old man, come over here—
        look at me. Answer all my questions.
        Did you ever serve King Laius?   1230
SHEPHERD: So I did . . .
        a slave, not bought on the block though,
        born and reared in the palace.
OEDIPUS: Your duties, your kind of work?
SHEPHERD: Herding the flocks, the better part of my life.
OEDIPUS: Where, mostly? Where did you do your grazing?   1235
SHEPHERD: Well,
        Cithaeron sometimes, or the foothills round about.
OEDIPUS: This man—you know him? ever see him there?
SHEPHERD: (*Confused, glancing from the* MESSENGER *to the king.*)
        Doing what? What man do you mean?
OEDIPUS: (*Pointing to the* MESSENGER.) This one here—ever
        have dealings with him?
SHEPHERD: Not so I could say, but give me a chance,   1240
        my memory's bad . . .
MESSENGER: No wonder he doesn't know me, master.
        But let me refresh his memory for him.
        I'm sure he recalls old times we had
        on the slopes of Mount Cithaeron;   1245
        he and I, grazing our flocks, he with two
        and I with one—we both struck up together,
        three whole seasons, six months at a stretch
        from spring to the rising of Arcturus in the fall,
        then with winter coming on I'd drive my herds   1250
        to my own pens, and back he'd go with his
        to Laius' folds.

(*To the* SHEPHERD.)

                Now that's how it was,
        wasn't it—yes or no?
SHEPHERD: Yes, I suppose . . .
        it's all so long ago.
MESSENGER: Come, tell me,
        you gave me a child back then, a boy, remember?   1255
        A little fellow to rear, my very own.
SHEPHERD: What? Why rake up that again?

MESSENGER: Look, here he is, my fine old friend—
  the same man who was just a baby then.
1260 SHEPHERD: Damn you, shut your mouth—quiet!
OEDIPUS: Don't lash out at him, old man—
  you need lashing more than he does.
SHEPHERD: Why,
  master, majesty—what have I done wrong?
OEDIPUS: You won't answer his question about the boy.
1265 SHEPHERD: He's talking nonsense, wasting his breath.
OEDIPUS: So, you won't talk willingly—
  then you'll talk with pain.

(*The* GUARDS *seize the* SHEPHERD.)

SHEPHERD: No, dear god, don't torture an old man!
OEDIPUS: Twist his arms back, quickly!
SHEPHERD: God help us, why?—
1270   what more do you need to know?
OEDIPUS: Did you give him that child? He's asking.
SHEPHERD: I did . . . I wish to god I'd died that day.
OEDIPUS: You've got your wish if you don't tell the truth.
SHEPHERD: The more I tell, the worse the death I'll die.
1275 OEDIPUS: Our friend here wants to stretch things out,
  does he?

(*Motioning to his men for torture.*)

SHEPHERD: No, no, I gave it to him—I just said so.
OEDIPUS: Where did you get it? Your house? Someone else's?
SHEPHERD: It wasn't mine, no, I got it from . . . someone.
OEDIPUS: Which one of them?

(*Looking at the citizens.*)

               Whose house?
SHEPHERD: No—
1280   god's sake, master, no more questions!
OEDIPUS: You're a dead man if I have to ask again.
SHEPHERD: Then—the child came from the house . . .
  of Laius.
OEDIPUS: A slave? or born of his own blood?
SHEPHERD: Oh no,
1285   I'm right at the edge, the horrible truth—I've got to say it!
OEDIPUS: And I'm at the edge of hearing horrors, yes, but I
  must hear!
SHEPHERD: All right! His son, they said it was—his son!
  But the one inside, your wife,
  she'd tell it best.
OEDIPUS: My wife—
1290   *she* gave it to you?
SHEPHERD: Yes, yes, my king.
OEDIPUS: Why, what for?
SHEPHERD: To kill it.
OEDIPUS: Her own child,
1295   how could she?
SHEPHERD: She was afraid—
  frightening prophecies.
OEDIPUS: What?
SHEPHERD: They said—
  he'd kill his parents.
1300 OEDIPUS: But you gave him to this old man—why?

SHEPHERD: I pitied the little baby, master,
  hoped he'd take him off to his own country,
  far away, but he saved him for this, this fate.
  If you are the man he says you are, believe me,
  you were born for pain.   1305
OEDIPUS: O god—
  all come true, all burst to light!
  O light—now let me look my last on you!
  I stand revealed at last—
  cursed in my birth, cursed in marriage,
  cursed in the lives I cut down with these hands!   1310

(*Rushing through the doors with a great cry. The Corinthian* MESSENGER, *the* SHEPHERD, *and* ATTENDANTS *exit slowly to the side.*)

CHORUS: O the generations of men
  the dying generations—adding the total
  of all your lives I find they come to nothing . . .
      does there exist, is there a man on earth
  who seizes more joy than just a dream, a vision?   1315
  And the vision no sooner dawns than dies
  blazing into oblivion.

You are my great example, you, your life
  your destiny, Oedipus, man of misery—
  I count no man blest.   1320

         You outranged all men!
    Bending your bow to the breaking-point
you captured priceless glory, O dear god,
and the Sphinx came crashing down,
        the virgin, claws hooked
like a bird of omen singing, shrieking death—   1325
like a fortress reared in the face of death
you rose and saved our land.

From that day on we called you king
we crowned you with honors, Oedipus, towering over all—
mighty king of the seven gates of Thebes.   1330
But now to hear your story—is there a man more agonized?
More wed to pain and frenzy? Not a man on earth,
the joy of your life ground down to nothing
O Oedipus, name for the ages—
  one and the same wide harbor served you   1335
          son and father both
son and father came to rest in the same bridal chamber.
How, how could the furrows your father plowed
bear you, your agony, harrowing on
in silence O so long?   1340

        But now for all your power
Time, all-seeing Time has dragged you to the light,
judged your marriage monstrous from the start—
the son and the father tangling, both one—
O child of Laius, would to god
  I'd never seen you, never never!   1345
    Now I weep like a man who wails the dead
and the dirge comes pouring forth with all my heart!
I tell you the truth, you gave me life
my breath leapt up in you
and now you bring down night upon my eyes.   1350

(*Enter a* MESSENGER *from the palace.*)

MESSENGER: Men of Thebes, always first in honor,
what horrors you will hear, what you will see,
what a heavy weight of sorrow you will shoulder . . .
if you are true to your birth, if you still have
1355 some feeling for the royal house of Thebes.
I tell you neither the waters of the Danube
nor the Nile can wash this palace clean.
Such things it hides, it soon will bring to light—
terrible things, and none done blindly now,
1360 all done with a will. The pains
we inflict upon ourselves hurt most of all.
LEADER: God knows we have pains enough already.
What can you add to them?
MESSENGER: The queen is dead.
LEADER: Poor lady—how?
1365 MESSENGER: By her own hand. But you are spared the worst,
you never had to watch . . . I saw it all,
and with all the memory that's in me
you will learn what that poor woman suffered.

Once she'd broken in through the gates,
1370 dashing past us, frantic, whipped to fury,
ripping her hair out with both hands—
straight to her rooms she rushed, flinging herself
across the bridal-bed, doors slamming behind her—
once inside, she wailed for Laius, dead so long,
1375 remembering the marriage-bed, cradled high in a woven noose, spinning,

He rips off her brooches, the long gold pins
holding her robes—and lifting them high,
looking straight up into the points,

he digs them down the sockets of his eyes, crying, "You, 1405
you'll see no more the pain I suffered, all the pain I caused!
Too long you looked on the ones you never should have seen,
blind to the ones you longed to see, to know! Blind
from this hour on! Blind in the darkness—blind!"
His voice like a dirge, rising, over and over 1410
raising the pins, raking them down his eyes.
And at each stroke blood spurts from the roots,
splashing his beard, a swirl of it, nerves and clots—
black hail of blood pulsing, gushing down.

These are the griefs that burst upon them both, 1415
coupling man and woman. The joy they had so lately,
the fortune of their old ancestral house
was deep joy indeed. Now, in this one day,
wailing, madness and doom, death, disgrace,
all the griefs in the world that you can name, 1420
all are theirs forever.
LEADER: Oh poor man, the misery—
has he any rest from pain now?

(*A voice within, in torment.*)

MESSENGER: He's shouting,
"Loose the bolts, someone, show me to all of Thebes!
My father's murderer, my mother's—"
No, I can't repeat it, it's unholy. 1425
Now he'll tear himself from his native earth,
not linger, curse the house with his own curse.
But he needs strength, and a guide to lead him on.
This is sickness more than he can bear.

(*The palace doors open.*)

                              Look,
he'll show you himself. The great doors are opening— 1430
you are about to see a sight, a horror
even his mortal enemy would pity.

(*Enter* OEDIPUS, *blinded, led by a boy. He stands at the palace steps,
as if surveying his people once again.*)

CHORUS: Oh, the terror—
the suffering, for all the world to see,
the worst terror that ever met my eyes.
What madness swept over you? What god, 1435
what dark power leapt beyond all bounds,
beyond belief, to crush your wretched life?—
godforsaken, cursed by the gods!
I pity you but I can't bear to look.
I've much to ask, so much to learn, 1440
so much fascinates my eyes,
but you . . . I shudder at the sight.
OEDIPUS: Oh, Ohh—
the agony! I am agony—
where am I going? where on earth?
    where does all this agony hurl me? 1445
where's my voice?—
        winging, swept away on a dark tide—
    My destiny, my dark power, what a leap you made!
CHORUS: To the depths of terror, too dark to hear, to see.
OEDIPUS: Dark, horror of darkness 1450

the life that rose up to destroy him, leaving
its mother to mother living creatures
with the very son she'd borne.
Oh how she wept, mourning the marriage-bed
1380 where she let loose that double brood—monsters—
husband by her husband, children by her child.
                              And then—
but how she died is more than I can say. Suddenly
Oedipus burst in, screaming, he stunned us so
we couldn't watch her agony to the end,
1385 our eyes were fixed on him. Circling
like a maddened beast, stalking, here, there,
crying out to us—
              Give him a sword! His wife,
no wife, his mother, where can he find the mother earth
that cropped two crops at once, himself and all his
    children?
1390 He was raging—one of the dark powers pointing the way,
none of us mortals crowding around him, no,
with a great shattering cry—someone, something leading
    him on—
he hurled at the twin doors and bending the bolts back
out of their sockets, crashed through the chamber.
1395 And there we saw the woman hanging by the neck,
cradled high in a woven noose, spinning,
swinging back and forth. And when he saw her,
giving a low, wrenching sob that broke our hearts,
slipping the halter from her throat, he eased her down,
1400 in a slow embrace he laid her down, poor thing . . .
then, what came next, what horror we beheld!

my darkness, drowning, swirling around me
crashing wave on wave—unspeakable, irresistible
    headwind, fatal harbor! Oh again,
the misery, all at once, over and over
1455   the stabbing daggers, stab of memory
raking me insane.
CHORUS: No wonder you suffer
twice over, the pain of your wounds,
the lasting grief of pain.
OEDIPUS: Dear friend, still here?
Standing by me, still with a care for me,
1460   the blind man? Such compassion,
    loyal to the last. Oh it's you,
I know you're here, dark as it is
I'd know you anywhere, your voice—
it's yours, clearly yours.
CHORUS: Dreadful, what you've done . . .
1465   how could you bear it, gouging out your eyes?
What superhuman power drove you on?
OEDIPUS: Apollo, friends, Apollo—
he ordained my agonies—these, my pains on pains!
But the hand that struck my eyes was mine,
1470   mine alone—no one else—
    I did it all myself!
What good were eyes to me?
Nothing I could see could bring me joy.
CHORUS: No, no, exactly as you say.
OEDIPUS: What can I ever see?
1475   What love, what call of the heart
can touch my ears with joy? Nothing, friends.
    Take me away, far, far from Thebes,
    quickly, cast me away, my friends—
this great murderous ruin, this man cursed to heaven,
1480   the man the deathless gods hate most of all!
CHORUS: Pitiful, you suffer so, you understand so much . . .
I wish you had never known.
OEDIPUS: Die, die—
whoever he was that day in the wilds
who cut my ankles free of the ruthless pins,
1485   he pulled me clear of death, he saved my life
for this, this kindness—
    Curse him, kill him!
If I'd died then, I'd never have dragged myself,
my loved ones through such hell.
CHORUS: Oh if only . . . would to god.
1490 OEDIPUS: I'd never have come to
this,
    my father's murderer—never been branded
mother's husband, all men see me now! Now,
    loathed by the gods, son of the mother I defiled
    coupling in my father's bed, spawning lives in the loins
1495   that spawned my wretched life. What grief can crown this
grief?
    It's mine alone, my destiny—I am Oedipus!
CHORUS: How can I say you've chosen for the best?
Better to die than be alive and blind.
OEDIPUS: What I did was best—don't lecture me,
1500   no more advice. I, with *my* eyes,
how could I look my father in the eyes
when I go down to death? Or mother, so abused . . .

I have done such things to the two of them,
crimes too huge for hanging.
          Worse yet,
the sight of my children, born as they were born,   1505
how could I long to look into their eyes?
No, not with these eyes of mine, never.
Not this city either, her high towers,
the sacred glittering images of her gods—
I am misery! I, her best son, reared   1510
as no other son of Thebes was ever reared,
I've stripped myself, I gave the command myself.
All men must cast away the great blasphemer,
the curse now brought to light by the gods,
the son of Laius—I, my father's son!   1515

Now I've exposed my guilt, horrendous guilt,
could I train a level glance on you, my countrymen?
Impossible! No, if I could just block off my ears,
the springs of hearing, I would stop at nothing—
I'd wall up my loathsome body like a prison,   1520
blind to the sound of life, not just the sight.
Oblivion—what a blessing . . .
for the mind to dwell a world away from pain.

O Cithaeron, why did you give me shelter?
Why didn't you take me, crush my life out on the spot?   1525
I'd never have revealed my birth to all mankind.

O Polybus, Corinth, the old house of my fathers,
so I believed—what a handsome prince you raised—
under the skin, what sickness to the core.
Look at me! Born of outrage, outrage to the core.   1530
O triple roads—it all comes back, the secret,
dark ravine, and the oaks closing in
where the three roads join . . .
You drank my father's blood, my own blood
spilled by my own hands—you still remember me?   1535
What things you saw me do? Then I came here
and did them all once more!
          Marriages! O marriage,
you gave me birth, and once you brought me into the
    world
you brought my sperm rising back, springing to light,
fathers, brothers, sons—one murderous breed—   1540
brides, wives, mothers. The blackest things
a man can do, I have done them all!
          No more—
it's wrong to name what's wrong to do. Quickly,
for the love of god, hide me somewhere,
kill me, hurl me into the sea   1545
where you can never look on me again.

(*Beckoning to the* CHORUS *as they shrink away.*)

          Closer,
it's all right. Touch the man of grief.
Do. Don't be afraid. My troubles are mine
and I am the only man alive who can sustain them.

(*Enter* CREON *from the palace, attended by palace* GUARDS.)

LEADER: Put your requests to Creon. Here he is,   1550
just when we need him. He'll have a plan, he'll act.

Now that he's the sole defense of the country
in your place.
OEDIPUS:　　　　　Oh no, what can I say to him?
How can I ever hope to win his trust?
1555　I wronged him so, just now, in every way.
You must see that—I was so wrong, so wrong.
CREON: I haven't come to mock you, Oedipus,
or to criticize your former failings.

(*Turning to the* GUARDS.)

　　　　　　　　　　　　　　　　You there,
have you lost all respect for human feelings?
1560　At least revere the Sun, the holy fire
that keeps us all alive. Never expose a thing
of guilt and holy dread so great it appalls
the earth, the rain from heaven, the light of day!
Get him into the halls—quickly as you can.
1565　Piety demands no less. Kindred alone
should see a kinsman's shame. This is obscene.
OEDIPUS: Please, in god's name . . . you wipe my fears away,
coming so generously to me, the worst of men.
Do one thing more, for your sake, not mine.
1570　CREON: What do you want? Why so insistent?
OEDIPUS: Drive me out of the land at once, far from sight,
where I can never hear a human voice.
CREON: I'd have done that already, I promise you.
First I wanted the god to clarify my duties.
1575　OEDIPUS: The god? His command was clear, every word:
death for the father-killer, the curse—
he said destroy me!
CREON: So he did. Still. In such a crisis
it's better to ask precisely what to do.
OEDIPUS:　　　　　　　　　So miserable—
1580　you would consult the god about a man like me?
CREON: By all means. And this time, I assume,
even you will obey the god's decrees.
OEDIPUS:　　　　　　　　　I will,
I will. And you, I command you—I beg you . . .
the woman inside, bury her as you see fit.
1585　It's the only decent thing,
to give your own the last rites. As for me,
never condemn the city of my fathers
to house my body, not while I'm alive, no,
let me live on the mountains, on Cithaeron,
1590　my favorite haunt, I have made it famous.
Mother and father marked out that rock
to be my everlasting tomb—buried alive.
Let me die there, where they tried to kill me.

Oh but this I know: no sickness can destroy me,
1595　nothing can. I would never have been saved
from death—I have been saved
for something great and terrible, something strange.
Well let my destiny come and take me on its way!
About my children, Creon, the boys at least,
1600　don't burden yourself. They're men,
wherever they go, they'll find the means to live.
But my two daughters, my poor helpless girls,
clustering at our table, never without me
hovering near them . . . whatever I touched,

they always had their share. Take care of them,　1605
I beg you. Wait, better—permit me, would you?
Just to touch them with my hands and take
our fill of tears. Please . . . my king.
Grant it, with all your noble heart.
If I could hold them, just once, I'd think　1610
I had them with me, like the early days
when I could see their eyes.

(ANTIGONE *and* ISMENE, *two small children, are led in from the palace by a nurse.*)

　　　　　　　　　　　　What's that?
O god! Do I really hear you sobbing?—
my two children. Creon, you've pitied me?
Sent me my darling girls, my own flesh and blood!　1615
Am I right?
CREON:　　　　Yes, it's my doing.
I know the joy they gave you all these years,
the joy you must feel now.
OEDIPUS:　　　　　　　　Bless you, Creon!
May god watch over you for this kindness,
better than he ever guarded me.　1620
　　　　　　　　　　Children, where are you?
Here, come quickly—

(*Groping for* ANTIGONE *and* ISMENE, *who approach their father cautiously, then embrace him.*)

　　　　　　　　　　Come to these hands of mine,
your brother's hands, your own father's hands
that served his once bright eyes so well—
that made them blind. Seeing nothing, children,
knowing nothing, I became your father,　1625
I fathered you in the soil that gave me life.

How I weep for you—I cannot see you now . . .
just thinking of all your days to come, the bitterness,
the life that rough mankind will thrust upon you.
Where are the public gatherings you can join,　1630
the banquets of the clans? Home you'll come,
in tears, cut off from the sight of it all,
the brilliant rites unfinished.
And when you reach perfection, ripe for marriage,
who will he be, my dear ones? Risking all　1635
to shoulder the curse that weighs down my parents,
yes and you too—that wounds us all together.
What more misery could you want?
Your father killed his father, sowed his mother,
one, one and the selfsame womb sprang you—　1640
he cropped the very roots of his existence.

Such disgrace, and you must bear it all!
Who will marry you then? Not a man on earth.
Your doom is clear: you'll wither away to nothing,
single, without a child.　1645

(*Turning to* CREON.)

　　　　　　　　　　Oh Creon,
you are the only father they have now . . .
we who brought them into the world
are gone, both gone at a stroke—

Don't let them go begging, abandoned,
1650 women without men. Your own flesh and blood!
Never bring them down to the level of my pains.
Pity them. Look at them, so young, so vulnerable,
shorn of everything—you're their only hope.
Promise me, noble Creon, touch my hand!

(*Reaching toward* CREON, *who draws back.*)

1655 You, little ones, if you were old enough
to understand, there is much I'd tell you.
Now, as it is, I'd have you say a prayer.
Pray for life, my children,
live where you are free to grow and season.
1660 Pray god you find a better life than mine,
the father who begot you.
CREON: Enough.
You've wept enough. Into the palace now.
OEDIPUS: I must, but I find it very hard.
CREON: Time is the great healer, you will see.
1665 OEDIPUS: I am going—you know on what condition?
CREON: Tell me. I'm listening.
OEDIPUS: Drive me out of Thebes, in exile.
CREON: Not I. Only the gods can give you that.
OEDIPUS: Surely the gods hate me so much—
1670 CREON: You'll get your wish at once.

OEDIPUS: You consent?
CREON: I try to say what I mean; it's my habit.
OEDIPUS: Then take me away. It's time.
CREON: Come along, let go of the children.
OEDIPUS: No—
don't take them away from me, not now! No no no!

(*Clutching his daughters as the* GUARDS *wrench them loose and take them through the palace doors.*)

CREON: Still the king, the master of all things?   1675
No more: here your power ends.
None of your power follows you through life.

(*Exit* OEDIPUS *and* CREON *to the palace. The* CHORUS *comes forward to address the audience directly.*)

CHORUS: People of Thebes, my countrymen, look on Oedipus.
He solved the famous riddle with his brilliance,
he rose to power, a man beyond all power.   1680
Who could behold his greatness without envy?
Now what a black sea of terror has overwhelmed him.
Now as we keep our watch and wait the final day,
count no man happy till he dies, free of pain at last.

(*Exit in procession.*)

Euripides

Euripides (c. 484–406 BCE) was the youngest of the three tragic playwrights whose plays remain today. Although he first competed in the City Dionysia in 455 BCE and won his first victory in 441 BCE, Euripides won only four victories in his lifetime and left Athens about 408 BCE for the court of King Archileus of Macedon, where he died. We do not know why Euripides won so infrequently, but his tragedies are much more bitter and ironic than those of Aeschylus or Sophocles, brilliantly unfolding the selfish capriciousness of gods and heroes alike. Of the roughly ninety plays Euripides is thought to have written, eighteen survive, and most of these were written and produced during the war with Sparta: *Alcestis, Medea, Heracleidae, Hippolytus, Cyclops* (a satyr play), *Heracles, Iphigeneia in Tauris, Helen, Hecuba, Andromache, The Trojan Women, Ion, The Suppliant Women, Orestes, Electra, The Phoenician Women.* Three additional plays—*Iphigeneia at Aulis, The Bacchae,* and *Alcmaeon at Corinth* (now lost)—were written in Macedon and brought to Athens by the playwright's son, Euripides the Younger. This trilogy, produced after Euripides' death, won him his final prize at the City Dionysia.

MEDEA

Although many Greek tragedies center on female characters—think of Clytaemnestra in Aeschylus' *Agamemnon,* for example, or Sophocles' *Antigone*—Euripides was famous in Athens for centering his tragedies so frequently on women. Euripides was hardly a feminist in any modern sense, yet more than his contemporaries, he used his tragic heroines to explore the relationship between gender and the other conceptual, political, social, and esthetic categories organizing Athenian life.

As in all roles in the Athenian theater, the role of Medea was played by a male actor; nonetheless, in many ways *Medea* illustrates Euripides' skeptical and ironic regard for conventional attitudes and his tendency toward a more sensational form of tragic action. Like Shakespeare's *Hamlet, Medea* is a tragedy of revenge, in which Medea poisons her husband Jason's newly married wife and her father, Creon, and in the play's climactic moment executes

In this modernized production of Euripides' *Medea* by the Abbey Theatre of Dublin, Fiona Shaw's Medea enacts the slaughter of the children behind an illuminated plexiglass screen.

her own children from her marriage with Jason. What sometimes seems most monstrous to modern readers and audiences is that Medea herself—in one of Euripides' most striking uses of the *machina*—flees Corinth alive at the end of the play, rising above the *skene* in a dragon-drawn chariot, draped in the bodies of her dead children, taunting and reviling the impotent Jason. That is, modern audiences sometimes feel that Medea herself should die at the play's close if *Medea* is to be a truly tragic drama, as though by dying Medea would be "punished" for her revenge in some appalling vision of tragic "justice." But Euripides seems uninterested in such a moralized version of tragedy. Indeed, as Aristotle implies in *The Poetics,* tragedy is a deeply dialectical, contradictory way of representing human experience: tragedy arises from the unresolvable tension between pity and fear, from the relationship between the hero's actions (remembering that the tragic hero is neither a paragon of virtue nor inherently wicked) and their terrible, somehow fitting consequences. Although Aristotle praises Sophocles' *Oedipus the King* as the best-constructed tragedy, he also remarks that Euripides "is felt by the audience to be the most tragic, at least, of the poets." To grasp Euripides' sense of tragedy means placing Medea's execution of the children within the context of the action as a whole—an act that brings her history to bear in one exacting deed; an act like Agamemnon's treading on the carpet or Oedipus' blistering interrogation of the ancient shepherd.

At the play's opening, Medea is an outcast, a foreign exile in Corinth, and the play repeatedly stresses Medea's otherness—she is an Eastern exotic, she has little respect for Greek culture and its institutions, and she is a sorceress as well. Medea is consistently shown to be a figure of willful passion, brought into exile through her love for Jason. Falling in love with Jason when he went to Colchis in search of the Golden Fleece, Medea used her sorcery to help Jason gain the Fleece, betraying her father and killing her brother in the bargain. When the play opens, Jason has returned to Greece with Medea and their children; in Corinth, however, Jason decides to marry the daughter of King Creon. Creon, no doubt recognizing that Medea and her children will pose a constant threat to his own line of succession, has ruled that Medea and her children must again be sent into exile.

Yet as Medea suggests to the Chorus, the indignity that Jason has thrust upon her—being doubly exiled, from her country and from her marriage—is in an important sense merely an extension of the state of all women in Greek culture. For once women "Buy a husband and take for our bodies / A master," they are exiled from their own homes, and from the mastery of their own lives. Inasmuch as women are represented as creatures of passion, they are "exiled" as well from the organizing principles of the Greek state: Reason, the law, and legitimate society are identified in the play as the preserve of men. Euripides makes Jason the spokesman for these values. When Jason first confronts Medea, he takes pride in his talents as a speaker, listing his arguments in support of taking a new wife almost as though he were arguing in the courtroom or conducting a philosophical demonstration. But while Oedipus, for instance, uses the strategies of philosophic inquiry to discover the truth, Jason's arguments seem to conceal the truth—he is betraying Medea and their children, after all—behind a smokescreen of sophistic rhetoric. Having brought Medea into exile, Jason argues that she is fortunate merely to "inhabit a Greek land and understand our ways / How to live by law instead of the sweet will of force." Yet the law that Jason praises seems designed to enable him to act out his own "sweet will"—taking a second wife—while it prevents Medea from acting on hers. The more Jason insists that he is acting reasonably, the more unreasonable his arguments become; he grows increasingly irritable, and finally insulting: "You women have got into such a state of mind / That, if your life at night is good, you think you have / Everything." Euripides' treatment of Jason is typical of his tendency to present an ironic view of the heroes of Greek mythology. Here, in making Jason the representative of Greek values—reason, law, justice—Euripides suggests the limits of those values. For the Chorus clearly sees Jason's "reason" as a self-indulgent pretense: "Though you have made this speech of yours look well, / . . . / You have betrayed your wife and are acting badly."

As Medea comes to recognize, both Jason and the masculine laws of Corinth are willing to betray her, to call her fidelity and love merely irrational, to force her again into exile. Having poisoned Creon and his daughter, Medea first claims to kill the children in order that they not be slain "by another hand less kindly to them." But it is also clear that in killing the children, Medea revenges herself on Jason in the only way open to her; he has little regard for her love for him, but the children are his property, an extension of himself, of his identity. What is more important, the children are his successors, representing his continued presence in the world. For as Jason laments, Medea has contrived a punishment for him that no Greek woman would have dared: In leaving him childless, Medea transforms Jason into an exile like herself, prophesying that he will die "without distinction."

Medea's acts epitomize the ethical ambiguity that drives Greek tragedy. Agamemnon strides on the blood-red carpet, magisterially desecrating the honor of his family as he had once done in sacrificing Iphigeneia; Oedipus sentences the hidden criminal to exile, only to discover that he is the criminal he seeks. To force Jason into a childless exile, Medea commits the kind of crime that Jason has repeatedly drawn her to enact: She murders what she loves in order to insist on the priority and power of her love for him. As in other classical tragedies, the hero chooses to act in a way that is not only consistent with her past, but a self-conscious reenactment of it. The *peripeteia,* the reversal that defines the tragic action, seems in many ways to be a kind of restoration as well, revealing destructive consequences that have been latent in the action from the beginning.

It should be clear that while Euripides interrogates the relationship between reason and passion, culture and nature, the rational and the irrational, science and magic, *Medea* does not finally disrupt or overturn this relationship. Nor does the play finally question the way that Greek culture gendered these categories as masculine and feminine, expressing the conceptual and political hierarchies of its own making as the "natural" outgrowth of some essential gender difference. Euripides exposes the destructive tension lurking in Greek conceptions of gender, power, and identity, but the language of tragedy is not the language of revolution, because although tragedy frequently exposes the values of its world as contradictory and destructive, it also accepts those values as somehow inevitable, unavoidable. Medea flees Corinth and the abusive Jason, but only by destroying herself in the same way she destroys Jason; Medea triumphs over Jason, but only by destroying her family and becoming an exile yet again. The only alternative that *Medea* offers to the way that Medea—and, she argues, all women—is positioned as an outsider, an "exile" to the governing categories of Greek life, is a deeper, more permanent isolation.

MEDEA

Euripides

TRANSLATED BY REX WARNER

CHARACTERS

MEDEA, *princess of Colchis and wife of*
JASON, *son of Aeson, king of Iolcus*
TWO CHILDREN *of Medea and Jason*
CREON, *king of Corinth*

AEGEUS, *king of Athens*
NURSE *to Medea*
TUTOR *to Medea's children*
MESSENGER
CHORUS *of Corinthian women*
ATTENDANTS

SCENE: *In front of* MEDEA's *house in Corinth.*

Enter from the house Medea's NURSE.

NURSE: How I wish the Argo never had reached the land
    Of Colchis, skimming through the blue Symplegades,
    Nor ever had fallen in the glades of Pelion
    The smitten fir-tree to furnish oars for the hands
5   Of heroes who in Pelias' name attempted
    The Golden Fleece! For then my mistress Medea
    Would not have sailed for the towers of the land of Iolcus,
    Her heart on fire with passionate love for Jason;
    Nor would she have persuaded the daughters of Pelias
10   To kill their father, and now be living here
    In Corinth with her husband and children. She gave
    Pleasure to the people of her land of exile,
    And she herself helped Jason in every way.
    This is indeed the greatest salvation of all—
15   For the wife not to stand apart from the husband.
    But now there's hatred everywhere, Love is diseased.
    For, deserting his own children and my mistress,
    Jason has taken a royal wife to his bed,
    The daughter of the ruler of this land, Creon.
20   And poor Medea is slighted, and cries aloud on the
    Vows they made to each other, the right hands clasped
    In eternal promise. She calls upon the gods to witness
    What sort of return Jason has made to her love.
    She lies without food and gives herself up to suffering,
25   Wasting away every moment of the day in tears.
    So it has gone since she knew herself slighted by him.
    Not stirring an eye, not moving her face from the ground,
    No more than either a rock or surging sea water
    She listens when she is given friendly advice.
30   Except that sometimes she twists back her white neck and
    Moans to herself, calling out on her father's name,
    And her land, and her home betrayed when she came away with
    A man who now is determined to dishonor her.
    Poor creature, she has discovered by her sufferings
35   What it means to one not to have lost one's own country.

---

1 **Argo** Jason's ship on the expedition of the Argonauts, sent by Pelias, king of Iolcus in Thessaly (Jason's uncle, who had usurped the throne), to Colchis on the Black Sea. The Symplegades were clashing rocks, one of the obstacles along the way. Pelion is a mountain in Thessaly. Medea was a princess of Colchis who fell in love with Jason and followed him back to Greece

    She has turned from the children and does not like to see them.
    I am afraid she may think of some dreadful thing,
    For her heart is violent. She will never put up with
    The treatment she is getting. I know and fear her
40   Lest she may sharpen a sword and thrust to the heart,
    Stealing into the palace where the bed is made,
    Or even kill the king and the new-wedded groom,
    And thus bring a greater misfortune on herself.
    She's a strange woman. I know it won't be easy
45   To make an enemy of her and come off best.
    But here the children come. They have finished playing.
    They have no thought at all of their mother's trouble.
    Indeed it is not usual for the young to grieve.

(Enter from the right the slave who is the TUTOR *to Medea's two small children. The* CHILDREN *follow him.)*

TUTOR: You old retainer of my mistress' household,
50   Why are you standing here all alone in front of the
    Gates and moaning to yourself over your misfortune?
    Medea could not wish you to leave her alone.
NURSE: Old man, and guardian of the children of Jason,
    If one is a good servant, it's a terrible thing
55   When one's master's luck is out; it goes to one's heart.
    So I myself have got into such a state of grief
    That a longing stole over me to come outside here
    And tell the earth and air of my mistress' sorrows.
TUTOR: Has the poor lady not yet given up her crying?
60 NURSE: Given up? She's at the start, not halfway through her tears.
TUTOR: Poor fool—if I may call my mistress such a name—
    How ignorant she is of trouble more to come.
NURSE: What do you mean, old man? You needn't fear to speak.
TUTOR: Nothing. I take back the words which I used just now.
65 NURSE: Don't, by your beard, hide this from me, your fellow-servant.
    If need be, I'll keep quiet about what you tell me.
TUTOR: I heard a person saying, while I myself seemed
    Not to be paying attention, when I was at the place
    Where the old draught-players sit, by the holy fountain,
70   That Creon, ruler of the land, intends to drive
    These children and their mother in exile from Corinth.
    But whether what he said is really true or not
    I do not know. I pray that it may not be true.

NURSE: And will Jason put up with it that his children
75   Should suffer so, though he's no friend to their mother?
TUTOR: Old ties give place to new ones. As for Jason, he
    No longer has a feeling for this house of ours.
NURSE: It's black indeed for us, when we add new to old
    Sorrows before even the present sky has cleared.
80 TUTOR: But you be silent, and keep all this to yourself.
    It is not the right time to tell our mistress of it.
NURSE: Do you hear, children, what a father he is to you?
    I wish he were dead—but no, he is still my master.
    Yet certainly he has proved unkind to his dear ones.
85 TUTOR: What's strange in that? Have you only just discovered
    That everyone loves himself more than his neighbor?
    Some have good reason, others get something out of it.
    So Jason neglects his children for the new bride.
NURSE: Go indoors, children. That will be the best thing.
90   And you, keep them to themselves as much as possible.
    Don't bring them near their mother in her angry mood.
    For I've seen her already blazing her eyes at them
    As though she meant some mischief and I am sure that
    She'll not stop raging until she has struck at someone.
95   May it be an enemy and not a friend she hurts!

(MEDEA *is heard inside the house.*)

MEDIA: Ah, wretch! Ah, lost in my sufferings,
    I wish, I wish I might die.
NURSE: What did I say, dear children? Your mother
    Frets her heart and frets it to anger.
100   Run away quickly into the house.
    And keep well out of her sight.
    Don't go anywhere near, but be careful
    Of the wildness and bitter nature
    Of that proud mind.
105   Go now! Run quickly indoors.
    It is clear that she soon will put lightning
    In that cloud of her cries that is rising
    With a passion increasing. O, what will she do,
    Proud-hearted and not to be checked on her course,
110   A soul bitten into with wrong?

(*The* TUTOR *takes the* CHILDREN *into the house.*)

MEDEA: Ah, I have suffered
    What should be wept for bitterly. I hate you,
    Children of a hateful mother. I curse you
    And your father. Let the whole house crash.
115 NURSE: Ah, I pity you, you poor creature.
    How can your children share in their father's
    Wickedness? Why do you hate them? Oh children,
    How much I fear that something may happen!
    Great people's tempers are terrible, always
120   Having their own way, seldom checked.
    Dangerous they shift from mood to mood.
    How much better to have been accustomed
    To live on equal terms with one's neighbors.
    I would like to be safe and grow old in a
125   Humble way. What is moderate sounds best,
    Also in practice is best for everyone.
    Greatness brings no profit to people.
    God indeed, when in anger, brings
    Greater ruin to great men's houses.

(*Enter, on the right, a* CHORUS *of Corinthian women. They have come to inquire about* MEDEA *and to attempt to console her.*)

CHORUS: I heard the voice, I heard the cry   130
    Of Colchis' wretched daughter.
    Tell me, mother, is she not yet
    At rest? Within the double gates
    Of the court I heard her cry. I am sorry
    For the sorrow of this home. O, say, what has happened?   135
NURSE: There is no home. It's over and done with.
    Her husband holds fast to his royal wedding,
    While she, my mistress, cries out her eyes
    There in her room, and takes no warmth from
    Any word of any friend.   140
MEDEA: O, I wish
    That lightning from heaven would split my head open.
    Oh, what use have I now for life?
    I would find my release in death
    And leave hateful existence behind me.   145
CHORUS: O God and Earth and Heaven!
    Did you hear what a cry was that
    Which the sad wife sings?
    Poor foolish one, why should you long.
    For that appalling rest?   150
    The final end of death comes fast.
    No need to pray for that.
    Suppose your man gives honor
    To another woman's bed.
    It often happens. Don't be hurt.   155
    God will be your friend in this.
    You must not waste away
    Grieving too much for him who shared your bed.
MEDEA: Great Themis, lady Artemis, behold
    The things I suffer, though I made him promise,   160
    My hateful husband. I pray that I may see him,
    Him and his bride and all their palace shattered
    For the wrong they dare to do me without cause.
    Oh, my father! Oh, my country! In what dishonor
    I left you, killing my own brother for it.   165
NURSE: Do you hear what she says, and how she cries
    On Themis, the goddess of Promises, and on Zeus,
    Whom we believe to be the Keeper of Oaths?
    Of this I am sure, that no small thing
    Will appease my mistress' anger.   170
CHORUS: Will she come into our presence?
    Will she listen when we are speaking
    To the words we say?
    I wish she might relax her rage
    And temper of her heart.   175
    My willingness to help will never
    Be wanting to my friends.
    But go inside and bring her
    Out of the house to us,
    And speak kindly to her: hurry,   180
    Before she wrongs her own.
    This passion of hers moves to something great.

---

159 **Themis . . . Artemis** goddesses: Themis was the goddess of justice; the virgin Artemis would be sensitive to the plight of women 165 **brother** during the escape from Colchis, to delay her father's pursuit

NURSE: I will, but I doubt if I'll manage
　　　To win my mistress over.
185　　But still I'll attempt it to please you.
　　　Such a look she will flash on her servants
　　　If any comes near with a message.
　　　Like a lioness guarding her cubs,
　　　It is right, I think, to consider
190　　Both stupid and lacking in foresight
　　　Those poets of old who wrote songs
　　　For revels and dinners and banquets.
　　　Pleasant sounds for men living at ease;
　　　But none of them all has discovered
195　　How to put to an end with their singing
　　　Or musical instruments grief,
　　　Bitter grief, from which death and disaster
　　　Cheat the hopes of a house. Yet how good
　　　If music could cure men of this! But why raise
200　　To no purpose the voice at a banquet? For *there* is
　　　Already abundance of pleasure for men
　　　With a joy of its own.

(*The* NURSE *goes into the house.*)

CHORUS: I heard a shriek that is laden with sorrow,
　　　Shrilling out her hard grief she cries out
205　　Upon him who betrayed both her bed and her marriage.
　　　Wronged, she calls on the gods,
　　　On the justice of Zeus, the oath sworn,
　　　Which brought her away
　　　To the opposite shore of the Greeks
210　　Through the gloomy salt straits to the gateway
　　　Of the salty unlimited sea.

(MEDEA, *attended by servants, comes out of the house.*)

MEDEA: Women of Corinth, I have come outside to you
　　　Lest you should be indignant with me; for I know
　　　That many people are overproud, some when alone,
215　　And others when in company. And those who live
　　　Quietly, as I do, get a bad reputation.
　　　For a just judgment is not evident in the eyes
　　　When a man at first sight hates another, before
　　　Learning his character, being in no way injured;
220　　And a foreigner especially must adapt himself.
　　　I'd not approve of even a fellow-countryman
　　　Who by pride and want of manners offends his neighbors.
　　　But on me this thing has fallen so unexpectedly.
　　　It has broken my heart. I am finished. I let go
225　　All my life's joy. My friends, I only want to die.
　　　It was everything to me to think well of one man,
　　　And he, my own husband, has turned out wholly vile.
　　　Of all things which are living and can form a judgment
　　　We women are the most unfortunate creatures.
230　　Firstly, with an excess of wealth it is required
　　　For us to buy a husband and take for our bodies
　　　A master; for not to take one is even worse.
　　　And now the question is serious whether we take
　　　A good or bad one; for there is no easy escape
235　　For a woman, nor can she say no to her marriage.
　　　She arrives among new modes of behavior and manners.
　　　And needs prophetic power, unless she has learned at home,
　　　How best to manage him who shares the bed with her.

And if we work out all this well and carefully.
And the husband lives with us and lightly bears his yoke. 240
Then life is enviable. If not, I'd rather die.
A man, when he's tired of the company in his home,
Goes out of the house and puts an end to his boredom
And turns to a friend or companion of his own age.
But we are forced to keep our eyes on one alone. 245
What they say of us is that we have a peaceful time
Living at home, while they do the fighting in war.
How wrong they are! I would very much rather stand
Three times in the front of battle than bear one child.
Yet what applies to me does not apply to you. 250
You have a country. Your family home is here.
You enjoy life and the company of your friends.
But I am deserted, a refugee, thought nothing of
By my husband—something he won in a foreign land.
I have no mother or brother, nor any relation 255
With whom I can take refuge in this sea of woe.
This much then is the service I would beg from you:
If I can find the means or devise any scheme
To pay my husband back for what he has done to me—
Him and his father-in-law and the girl who married him— 260
Just to keep silent. For in other ways a woman
Is full of fear, defenseless, dreads the sight of cold
Steel; but, when once she is wronged in the matter of love,
No other soul can hold so many thoughts of blood.

CHORUS: This I will promise. You are in the right, Medea, 265
　　　In paying your husband back. I am not surprised at you
　　　For being sad.
　　　　　　　　But look! I see our King Creon
　　　Approaching. He will tell us of some new plan.

(*Enter, from the right,* CREON, *with attendants.*)

CREON: You, with that angry look, so set against your husband.
　　　Medea, I order you to leave my territories 270
　　　An exile, and take along with you your two children,
　　　And not to waste time doing it. It is my decree,
　　　And I will see it done. I will not return home
　　　Until you are cast from the boundaries of my land.

MEDEA: Oh, this is the end for me. I am utterly lost. 275
　　　Now I am in the full force of the storm of hate
　　　And have no harbor from ruin to reach easily.
　　　Yet still, in spite of it all, I'll ask the question:
　　　What is your reason, Creon, for banishing me?

CREON: I am afraid of you—why should I dissemble it?— 280
　　　Afraid that you may injure my daughter mortally.
　　　Many things accumulate to support my feeling.
　　　You are a clever woman, versed in evil arts.
　　　And are angry at having lost your husband's love.
　　　I hear that you are threatening, so they tell me, 285
　　　To do something against my daughter and Jason
　　　And me, too. I shall take my precautions first.
　　　I tell you, I prefer to earn your hatred now
　　　Than to be soft-hearted and afterward regret it.

MEDEA: This is not the first time, Creon. Often previously 290
　　　Through being considered clever I have suffered much.
　　　A person of sense ought never to have his children
　　　Brought up to be more clever than the average.
　　　For, apart from cleverness bringing them no profit,
　　　It will make them objects of envy and ill-will. 295
　　　If you put new ideas before the eyes of fools

They'll think you foolish and worthless into the bargain;
And if you are thought superior to those who have
Some reputation for learning, you will become hated.
300 I have some knowledge myself of how this happens;
For being clever, I find that some will envy me,
Others object to me. Yet all my cleverness
Is not so much.
                    Well, then, are you frightened, Creon,
That I should harm you? There is no need. It is not
305 My way to transgress the authority of a king.
How have you injured me? You gave your daughter away
To the man you wanted. Oh, certainly I hate
My husband, but you, I think, have acted wisely;
Nor do I grudge it you that your affairs go well.
310 May the marriage be a lucky one! Only let me
Live in this land. For even though I have been wronged,
I will not raise my voice, but submit to my betters.
CREON: What you say sounds gentle enough. Still in my heart
I greatly dread that you are plotting some evil,
315 And therefore I trust you even less than before.
A sharp-tempered woman, or, for that matter, a man,
Is easier to deal with than the clever type
Who holds her tongue. No. You must go. No need for more
Speeches. The thing is fixed. By no manner of means
320 Shall you, an enemy of mine, stay in my country.
MEDEA: I beg you. By your knees, by your new-wedded girl.
CREON: Your words are wasted. You will never persuade me.
MEDEA: Will you drive me out, and give no heed to my prayers?
CREON: I will, for I love my family more than you.
325 MEDEA: O my country! How bitterly now I remember you!
CREON: I love my country too—next after my children.
MEDEA: O what an evil to men is passionate love!
CREON: That would depend on the luck that goes along with it.
MEDEA: O God, do not forget who is the cause of this!
330 CREON: Go. It is no use. Spare me the pain of forcing you.
MEDEA: I'm spared no pain. I lack no pain to be spared me.
CREON: Then you'll be removed by force by one of my men.
MEDEA: No. Creon, not that! But do listen, I beg you.
CREON: Woman, you seem to want to create a disturbance.
335 MEDEA: I *will* go into exile. *This* is not what I beg for.
CREON: Why then this violence and clinging to my hand?
MEDEA: Allow me to remain here just for this one day,
So I may consider where to live in my exile.
And look for support for my children, since their father
340 Chooses to make no kind of provision for them.
Have pity on them! You have children of your own.
It is natural for you to look kindly on them.
For myself I do not mind if I go into exile.
It is the children being in trouble that I mind.
345 CREON: There is nothing tyrannical about my nature,
And by showing mercy I have often been the loser.
Even now I know that I am making a mistake.
All the same you shall have your will. But this I tell you,
That if the light of heaven tomorrow shall see you,
350 You and your children in the confines of my land,
You die. This word I have spoken is firmly fixed.
But now, if you must stay, stay for this day alone.
For in it you can do none of the things I fear.

(*Exit* CREON, *with his attendants.*)

CHORUS: Oh, unfortunate one! Oh, cruel!
Where will you turn? Who will help you?   355
What house or what land to preserve you
From ill can you find?
Medea, a god has thrown suffering
Upon you in waves of despair.
MEDEA: Things have gone badly every way. No doubt of that   360
But not these things this far, and don't imagine so.
There are still trials to come for the new-wedded pair,
And for their relations pain that will mean something.
Do you think that I would ever have fawned on that man
Unless I had some end to gain or profit in it?   365
I would not even have spoken or touched him with my hands.
But he has got to such a pitch of foolishness
That, though he could have made nothing of all my plans
By exiling me, he has given me this one day
To stay here, and in this I will make dead bodies   370
Of three of my enemies—father, the girl, and my husband.
I have many ways of death which I might suit to them,
And do not know, friends, which one to take in hand;
Whether to set fire underneath their bridal mansion,
Or sharpen a sword and thrust it to the heart.   375
Stealing into the palace where the bed is made.
There is just one obstacle to this. If I am caught
Breaking into the house and scheming against it,
I shall die, and give my enemies cause for laughter.
It is best to go by the straight road, the one in which   380
I am most skilled, and make away with them by poison.
So be it then.
And now suppose them dead. What town will receive me?
What friend will offer me a refuge in his land,
Or the guaranty of his house and save my own life?   385
There is none. So I must wait a little time yet,
And if some sure defense should then appear for me,
In craft and silence I will set about this murder.
But if my fate should drive me on without help,
Even though death is certain, I will take the sword   390
Myself and kill, and steadfastly advance to crime.
It shall not be—I swear it by her, my mistress,
Whom most I honor and have chosen as partner,
Hecate, who dwells in the recesses of my hearth—
That any man shall be glad to have injured me.   395
Bitter I will make their marriage for them and mournful,
Bitter the alliance and the driving me out of the land.
Ah, come, Medea, in your plotting and scheming
Leave nothing untried of all those things which you know.
Go forward to the dreadful act. The test has come   400
For resolution. You see how you are treated. Never
Shall you be mocked by Jason's Corinthian wedding,
Whose father was noble, whose grandfather Helius.
You have the skill. What is more, you were born a woman,
And women, though most helpless in doing good deeds,   405
Are of every evil the cleverest of contrivers.
CHORUS: Flow backward to your sources, sacred rivers,
And let the world's great order be reversed.
It is the thoughts of *men* that are deceitful,
Their pledges that are loose.   410

394 **Hecate** a goddess of the night   403 **Helius** sun god

Story shall now turn my condition to a fair one,
Women are paid their due.
No more shall evil-sounding fame be theirs.

Cease now, you muses of the ancient singers,
415   To tell the tale of my unfaithfulness;
For not on us did Phoebus, lord of music,
Bestow the lyre's divine
Power, for otherwise I should have sung an answer
To the other sex. Long time
420   Has much to tell of us, and much of them.

You sailed away from your father's home,
With a heart on fire you passed
The double rocks of the sea.
And now in a foreign country
425   You have lost your rest in a widowed bed,
And are driven forth, a refugee
In dishonor from the land.

Good faith has gone, and no more remains
In great Greece a sense of shame.
430   It has flown away to the sky.
No father's house for a haven
Is at hand for you now, and another queen
Of your bed has dispossessed you and
Is mistress of your home.

(*Enter* JASON, *with attendants.*)

435 JASON: This is not the first occasion that I have noticed
How hopeless it is to deal with a stubborn temper.
For, with reasonable submission to our ruler's will,
You might have lived in this land and kept your home.
As it is you are going to be exiled for your loose speaking.
440   Not that I mind myself. You are free to continue
Telling everyone that Jason is a worthless man.
But as to your talk about the king, consider
Yourself most lucky that exile is your punishment.
I, for my part, have always tried to calm down
445   The anger of the king, and wished you to remain.
But you will not give up your folly, continually
Speaking ill of him, and so you are going to be banished.
All the same, and in spite of your conduct, I'll not desert
My friends, but have come to make some provision for you,
450   So that you and the children may not be penniless
Or in need of anything in exile. Certainly
Exile brings many troubles with it. And even
If you hate me, I cannot think badly of you.
    MEDEA: O coward in every way—that is what I call you,
455   With bitterest reproach for your lack of manliness,
You have come, you, my worst enemy, have come to me!
It is not an example of overconfidence
Or of boldness thus to look your friends in the face,
Friends you have injured—no, it is the worst of all
460   Human diseases, shamelessness. But you did well
To come, for I can speak ill of you and lighten
My heart, and you will suffer while you are listening.
And first I will begin from what happened first.
I saved your life, and every Greek knows I saved it.
465   Who was a shipmate of yours aboard the Argo.

When you were sent to control the bulls that breathed fire
And yoke them, and when you would sow that deadly field.
Also that snake, who encircled with his many folds
The Golden Fleece and guarded it and never slept,
I killed, and so gave you the safety of the light.   470
And I myself betrayed my father and my home,
And came with you to Pelias' land of Iolcus.
And then, showing more willingness to help than wisdom,
I killed him, Pelias, with a most dreadful death
At his own daughters' hands, and took away your fear.   475
This is how I behaved to you, you wretched man,
And you forsook me, took another bride to bed,
Though you had children; for, if that had not been,
You would have had an excuse for another wedding.
Faith in your word has gone. Indeed, I cannot tell   480
Whether you think the gods whose names you swore by then
Have ceased to rule and that new standards are set up,
Since you must know you have broken your word to me.
O my right hand, and the knees which you often clasped
In supplication, how senselessly I am treated   485
By this bad man, and how my hopes have missed their mark!
Come, I will share my thoughts as though you were a
    friend—
You! Can I think that you would ever treat me well?
But I will do it, and these questions will make you
Appear the baser. Where am I to go? To my father's?   490
Him I betrayed and his land when I came with you.
To Pelias' wretched daughters? What a fine welcome
They would prepare for me who murdered their father!
For this is my position—hated by my friends
At home, I have, in kindness to you, made enemies   495
Of others whom there was no need to have injured.
And how happy among Greek women you have made me
On your side for all this! A distinguished husband
I have—for breaking promises. When in misery
I am cast out of the land and go into exile,   500
Quite without friends and all alone with my children,
That will be a fine shame for the new-wedded groom,
For his children to wander as beggars and she who saved
    him.
O God, you have given to mortals a sure method
Of telling the gold that is pure from the counterfeit;   505
Why is there no mark engraved upon men's bodies,
By which we could know the true ones from the false ones?
CHORUS: It is a strange form of anger, difficult to cure,
When two friends turn upon each other in hatred.
JASON: As for me, it seems I must be no bad speaker.   510
But, like a man who has a good grip of the tiller,
Reef up his sail, and so run away from under
This mouthing tempest, woman, of your bitter tongue.
Since you insist on building up your kindness to me.
My view is that Cypris was alone responsible   515
Of men and gods for the preserving of my life.
You are clever enough—but really I need not enter
Into the story of how it was love's inescapable
Power that compelled you to keep my person safe.
On this I will not go into too much detail.   520

---

416 **Phoebus** Apollo

515 **Cypris** Aphrodite, goddess of love

In so far as you helped me, you did well enough.
But on this question of saving me, I can prove
You have certainly got from me more than you gave.
Firstly, instead of living among barbarians,
525 You inhabit a Greek land and understand our ways,
How to live by law instead of the sweet will of force.
And all the Greeks considered you a clever woman.
You were honored for it; while, if you were living at
The ends of the earth, nobody would have heard of you.
530 For my part, rather than stores of gold in my house
Or power to sing even sweeter songs than Orpheus,
I'd choose the fate that made me a distinguished man.
There is my reply to your story of my labors.
Remember it was you who started the argument.
535 Next for your attack on my wedding with the princess:
Here I will prove that, first, it was a clever move,
Secondly, a wise one, and, finally, that I made it
In your best interests and the children's. Please keep calm.
When I arrived here from the land of Iolcus,
540 Involved, as I was, in every kind of difficulty,
What luckier chance could I have come across than this,
An exile to marry the daughter of the king?
It was not—the point that seems to upset you—that I
Grew tired of your bed and felt the need of a new bride;
545 Nor with any wish to outdo your number of children.
We have enough already. I am quite content.
But—this was the main reason—that we might live well,
And not be short of anything. I know that all
A man's friends leave him stone-cold if he becomes poor.
550 Also that I might bring my children up worthily
Of my position, and, by producing more of them
To be brothers of yours, we would draw the families
Together and all be happy. You need no children.
And it pays me to do good to those I have now
555 By having others. Do you think this a bad plan?
You wouldn't if the love question hadn't upset you.
But you women have got into such a state of mind
That, if your life at night is good, you think you have
Everything; but, if in that quarter things go wrong,
560 You will consider your best and truest interests
Most hateful. It would have been better far for men
To have got their children in some other way, and women
Not to have existed. Then life would have been good.
CHORUS: Jason, though you have made this speech of yours
look well,
565 Still I think, even though others do not agree,
You have betrayed your wife and are acting badly.
MEDEA: Surely in many ways I hold different views
From others, for I think that the plausible speaker
Who is a villain deserves the greatest punishment.
570 Confident in his tongue's power to adorn evil,
He stops at nothing. Yet he is not really wise.
As in your case. There is no need to put on the airs
Of a clever speaker, for one word will lay you flat.
If you were not a coward, you would not have married
575 Behind my back, but discussed it with me first.
JASON: And you, no doubt, would have furthered the proposal,
If I had told you of it, you who even now
Are incapable of controlling your bitter temper.
MEDEA: It was not that. No, you thought it was not respectable
580 As you got on in years to have a foreign wife.

JASON: Make sure of this: it was not because of a woman
I made the royal alliance in which I now live.
But, as I said before, I wished to preserve you
And breed a royal progeny to be brothers
To the children I have now, a sure defense to us.   585
MEDEA: Let me have no happy fortune that brings pain with it,
Or prosperity which is upsetting to the mind!
JASON: Change your ideas of what you want, and show more
sense.
Do not consider painful what is good for you.
Nor, when you are lucky, think yourself unfortunate.   590
MEDEA: You can insult me. You have somewhere to turn to.
But I shall go from this land into exile, friendless.
JASON: It was what you chose yourself. Don't blame others for it.
MEDEA: And how did I choose it? Did I betray my husband?
JASON: You called down wicked curses on the king's family.   595
MEDEA: A curse, that is what I am become to your house too.
JASON: I do not propose to go into all the rest of it;
But, if you wish for the children or for yourself
In exile to have some of my money to help you,
Say so, for I am prepared to give with open hand,   600
Or to provide you with introductions to my friends
Who will treat you well. You are a fool if you do not
Accept this. Cease your anger and you will profit.
MEDEA: I shall never accept the favors of friends of yours,
Nor take a thing from you, so you need not offer it.   605
There is no benefit in the gifts of a bad man.
JASON: Then, in any case, I call the gods to witness that
I wish to help you and the children in every way,
But you refuse what is good for you. Obstinately
You push away your friends. You are sure to suffer for it.   610
MEDEA: Go! No doubt you hanker for your virginal bride,
And are guilty of lingering too long out of her house.
Enjoy your wedding. But perhaps—with the help of God—
You will make the kind of marriage that you will regret.

(JASON *goes out with his attendants.*)

CHORUS: When love is in excess
It brings a man no honor   615
Nor any worthiness.
But if in moderation Cypris comes,
There is no other power at all so gracious.
O goddess, never on me let loose the unerring
Shaft of your bow in the poison of desire.   620

Let my heart be wise.
It is the gods' best gift.
On me let mighty Cypris
Inflict no wordy wars or restless anger
To urge my passion to a different love.   625
But with discernment may she guide women's weddings,
Honoring most what is peaceful in the bed.

O country and home,
Never, never may I be without you,   630
Living the hopeless life,
Hard to pass through and painful,
Most pitiable of all.
Let death first lay me low and death
Free me from this daylight,   635
There is no sorrow above
The loss of a native land.

I have seen it myself,
Do not tell of a secondhand story.
640   Neither city nor friend
Pitied you when you suffered
The worst of sufferings.
O let him die ungraced whose heart
Will not reward his friends,
645   Who cannot open an honest mind
No friend will he be of mine.

(*Enter* AEGEUS, *king of Athens, an old friend of* MEDEA.)

AEGEUS: Medea, greeting! This is the best introduction
Of which men know for conversation between friends.
MEDEA: Greeting to you too, Aegeus, son of King Pandion.
650   Where have you come from to visit this country's soil?
AEGEUS: I have just left the ancient oracle of Phoebus.
MEDEA: And why did you go to earth's prophetic center?
AEGEUS: I went to inquire how children might be born to me.
MEDEA: Is it so? Your life still up to this point is childless?
655   AEGEUS: Yes. By the fate of some power we have no children.
MEDEA: Have you a wife, or is there none to share your bed?
AEGEUS: There is. Yes, I am joined to my wife in marriage.
MEDEA: And what did Phoebus say to you about children?
AEGEUS: Words too wise for a mere man to guess their
meaning.
660   MEDEA: It is proper for me to be told the god's reply?
AEGEUS: It is. For sure what is needed is cleverness.
MEDEA: Then what was his message? Tell me, if I may hear.
AEGEUS: I am not to loosen the hanging foot of the wineskin …
MEDEA: Until you have done something, or reached some
country?
665   AEGEUS: Until I return again to my hearth and house.
MEDEA: And for what purpose have you journeyed to this
land?
AEGEUS: There is a man called Pittheus, king of Troezen.
MEDEA: A son of Pelops, they say, a most righteous man.
AEGEUS: With him I wish to discuss the reply of the god.
670   MEDEA: Yes. He is wise and experienced in such matters.
AEGEUS: And to me also the dearest of all my spear-friends.
MEDEA: Well, I hope you have good luck, and achieve your
will.
AEGEUS: But why this downcast eye of yours, and this pale
cheek?
MEDEA: O Aegeus, my husband has been the worst of all to me.
675   AEGEUS: What do you mean? Say clearly what has caused this
grief.
MEDEA: Jason wrongs me, though I have never injured him.
AEGEUS: What has he done? Tell me about it in clearer words.
MEDEA: He has taken a wife to his house, supplanting me.
AEGEUS: Surely he would not dare to do a thing like that.
680   MEDEA: Be sure he has. Once dear, I now am slighted by him.
AEGEUS: Did he fall in love? Or is he tired of your love?
MEDEA: He was greatly in love, this traitor to his friends.
AEGEUS: Then let him go, if, as you say, he is so bad.
MEDEA: A passionate love—for an alliance with the king.
685   AEGEUS: And who gave him his wife? Tell me the rest of it.
MEDEA: It was Creon, he who rules this land of Corinth.
AEGEUS: Indeed, Medea, your grief was understandable.
MEDEA: I am ruined. And there is more to come: I am
banished.

AEGEUS: Banished? By whom? Here you tell me of a new
wrong.
MEDEA: Creon drives me an exile from the land of Corinth.   690
AEGEUS: Does Jason consent? I cannot approve of this.
MEDEA: He pretends not to, but he will put up with it.
Ah, Aegeus, I beg and beseech you, by your beard
And by your knees I am making myself your suppliant,
Have pity on me, have pity on your poor friend,   695
And do not let me go into exile desolate,
But receive me in your land and at your very hearth.
So may your love, with God's help, lead to the bearing
Of children, and so may you yourself die happy.
You do not know what a chance you have come on here.   700
I will end your childlessness, and I will make you able
To beget children. The drugs I know can do this.
AEGEUS: For many reasons, woman, I am anxious to do
This favor for you. First, for the sake of the gods,
And then for the birth of children which you promise,   705
For in that respect I am entirely at my wits' end.
But this is my position: if you reach my land,
I, being in my rights, will try to befriend you.
But this much I must warn you of beforehand:
I shall not agree to take you out of this country;   710
But if you by yourself can reach my house, then you
Shall stay there safely. To none will I give you up
But from this land you must make your escape yourself,
For I do not wish to incur blame from my friends.
MEDEA: It shall be so. But, if I might have a pledge from you   715
For this, then I would have from you all I desire.
AEGEUS: Do you not trust me? What is it rankles with you?
MEDEA: I trust you, yes. But the house of Pelias hates me,
And so does Creon. If you are bound by this oath,
When they try to drag me from your land, you will not   720
Abandon me; but if our pact is only words,
With no oath to the gods, you will be lightly armed,
Unable to resist their summons. I am weak,
While they have wealth to help them and a royal house.
AEGEUS: You show much foresight for such negotiations.   725
Well, if you will have it so, I will not refuse.
For, both on my side this will be the safest way
To have some excuse to put forward to your enemies,
And for you it is more certain. You may name the gods.
MEDEA: Swear by the plain of Earth, and Helius, father   730
Of my father, and name together all the gods …
AEGEUS: That I will act or not act in what way? Speak.
MEDEA: That you yourself will never cast me from your land,
Nor, if any of my enemies should demand me,
Will you, in your life, willingly hand me over.   735
AEGEUS: I swear by the Earth, by the holy light of Helius,
By all the gods, I will abide by this you say.
MEDEA: Enough. And, if you fail, what shall happen to you?
AEGEUS: What comes to those who have no regard for heaven.
MEDEA: Go on your way. Farewell. For I am satisfied.   740
And I will reach your city as soon as I can,
Having done the deed I have to do and gained my end.

(AEGEUS *goes out.*)

CHORUS: May Hermes, god of travelers,
Escort you, Aegeus, to your home!
And may you have the things you wish   745
So eagerly; for you

Appear to me to be a generous man.

MEDEA: God, and God's daughter, justice, and light of Helius!
Now, friends, has come the time of my triumph over
750 My enemies, and now my foot is on the road.
Now I am confident they will pay the penalty.
For this man, Aegeus, has been like a harbor to me
In all my plans just where I was most distressed.
To him I can fasten the cable of my safety
755 When I have reached the town and fortress of Pallas.
And now I shall tell to you the whole of my plan.
Listen to these words that are not spoken idly.
I shall send one of my servants to find Jason
And request him to come once more into my sight.
760 And when he comes, the words I'll say will be soft ones.
I'll say that I agree with him, that I approve
The royal wedding he has made, betraying me.
I'll say it was profitable, an excellent idea.
But I shall beg that my children may remain here:
765 Not that I would live in a country that hates me
Children of mine to feel their enemies' insults,
But that by a trick I may kill the king's daughter.
For I will send the children with gifts in their hands
To carry to the bride, so as not to be banished—
770 A finely woven dress and a golden diadem.
And if she takes them and wears them upon her skin
She and all who touch the girl will die in agony;
Such poison will I lay upon the gifts I send.
But there, however, I must leave that account paid.
775 I weep to think of what a deed I have to do
Next after that; for I shall kill my own children.
My children, there is none who can give them safety.
And when I have ruined the whole of Jason's house,
I shall leave the land and flee from the murder of my
780 Dear children, and I shall have done a dreadful deed.
For it is not bearable to be mocked by enemies.
So it must happen. What profit have I in life?
I have no land, no home, no refuge from my pain.
My mistake was made the time I left behind me
785 My father's house, and trusted the words of a Greek,
Who, with heaven's help, will pay me the price for that.
For those children he had from me he will never
See alive again, nor will he on his new bride
Beget another child, for she is to be forced
790 To die a most terrible death by these my poisons.
Let no one think me a weak one, feeble-spirited,
A stay-at-home, but rather just the opposite,
One who can hurt my enemies and help my friends;
For the lives of such persons are most remembered.
795 CHORUS: Since you have shared the knowledge of your plan
    with us,
I both wish to help you and support the normal
Ways of mankind, and tell you not to do this thing.
MEDEA: I can do no other thing. It is understandable
For you to speak thus. You have not suffered as I have.
800 CHORUS: But can you have the heart to kill your flesh and
    blood?
MEDEA: Yes, for this is the best way to wound my husband.

CHORUS: And you, too. Of women you will be most unhappy.
MEDEA: So it must be. No compromise is possible.

(*She turns to the* NURSE.)

Go, you, at once, and tell Jason to come to me.
You I employ on all affairs of greatest trust.   805
Say nothing of these decisions which I have made.
If you love your mistress, if you were born a woman.

CHORUS: From of old the children of Erechtheus are
Splendid, the sons of blessed gods. They dwell
In Athens' holy and unconquered land,   810
Where famous Wisdom feeds them and they pass gaily
Always through that most brilliant air where once, they say,
That golden Harmony gave birth to the nine
Pure Muses of Pieria.

And beside the sweet flow of Cephisus' stream,   815
Where Cypris sailed, they say, to draw the water,
And mild soft breezes breathed along her path,
And on her hair were flung the sweet-smelling garlands
Of flowers of roses by the Lovers, the companions
Of Wisdom, her escort, the helpers of men   820
In every kind of excellence.

How then can these holy rivers
Or this holy land love you,
Or the city find you a home,
You, who will kill your children,   825
You, not pure with the rest?
O think of the blow at your children
And think of the blood that you shed.
O, over and over I beg you,
By your knees I beg you do not   830
Be the murderess of your babes!

O where will you find the courage
Or the skill of hand and heart,
When you set yourself to attempt
A deed so dreadful to do?   835
How, when you look upon them,
Can you tearlessly hold the decision
For murder? You will not be able,
When your children fall down and implore you,
You will not be able to dip   840
Steadfast your hand in their blood.

(*Enter* JASON, *with attendants.*)

JASON: I have come at your request. Indeed, although you are
Bitter against me, this you shall have: I will listen
To what new thing you want, woman, to get from me.
MEDEA: Jason, I beg you to be forgiving toward me   845
For what I said. It is natural for you to bear with
My temper, since we have had much love together.
I have talked with myself about this and I have
Reproached myself. "Fool" I said, "why am I so mad?
Why am I set against those who have planned wisely?   850
Why make myself an enemy of the authorities
And of my husband, who does the best thing for me
By marrying royalty and having children who
Will be as brothers to my own? What is wrong with me?

---

755 **fortress of Pallas** Athens, the town of Athena

808 **children of Erechtheus** the Athenians   815 **beside . . .
stream** at Athens

855 Let me give up anger, for the gods are kind to me.
Have I not children, and do I not know that we
In exile from our country must be short of friends?"
When I considered this I saw that I had shown
Great lack of sense, and that my anger was foolish.
860 Now I agree with you. I think that you are wise
In having this other wife as well as me, and I
Was mad. I should have helped you in these plans of yours,
Have joined in the wedding, stood by the marriage bed,
Have taken pleasure in attendance on your bride.
865 But we women are what we are—perhaps a little
Worthless; and you men must not be like us in this,
Nor be foolish in return when we are foolish.
Now, I give in, and admit that then I was wrong.
I have come to a better understanding now.

(She turns toward the house.)

870 Children, come here, my children, come outdoors to us!
Welcome your father with me, and say goodbye to him,
And with your mother, who just now was his enemy,
Join again in making friends with him who loves us.

(Enter the CHILDREN, *attended by the* TUTOR.)

We have made peace, and all our anger is over.
875 Take hold of his right hand—O God, I am thinking
Of something which may happen in the secret future.
O children, will you just so, after a long life,
Hold out your loving arms at the grave? O children,
How ready to cry I am, how full of foreboding!
880 I am ending at last this quarrel with your father,
And, look my soft eyes have suddenly filled with tears.
CHORUS: And the pale tears have started also in my eyes.
O may the trouble not grow worse than now it is!
JASON: I approve of what you say. And I cannot blame you
Even for what you said before. It is natural
885 For a woman to be wild with her husband when he
Goes in for secret love. But now your mind has turned
To better reasoning. In the end you have come to
The right decision, like the clever woman you are.
And of you, children, your father is taking care.
890 He has made, with God's help, ample provision for you.
For I think that a time will come when you will be
The leading people in Corinth with your brothers.
You must grow up. As to the future, your father
And those of the gods who love him will deal with that.
895 I want to see you, when you have become young men,
Healthy and strong, better men than my enemies.
Medea, why are your eyes all wet with pale tears?
Why is your cheek so white and turned away from me?
Are not these words of mine pleasing for you to hear?
900 MEDEA: It is nothing. I was thinking about these children.
JASON: You must be cheerful. I shall look after them well.
MEDEA: I will be. It is not that I distrust your words,
But a woman is a frail thing, prone to crying.
JASON: But why then should you grieve so much for these
children?
905 MEDEA: I am their mother. When you prayed that they
might live
I felt unhappy to think that these things will be.
But come, I have said something of the things I meant
To say to you, and now I will tell you the rest.

Since it is the king's will to banish me from here— 910
And for me, too, I know that this is the best thing,
Not to be in your way by living here or in
The king's way, since they think me ill-disposed to them—
I then am going into exile from this land;
But do you, so that you may have the care of them, 915
Beg Creon that the children may not be banished.
JASON: I doubt if I'll succeed, but still I'll attempt it.
MEDEA: Then you must tell your wife to beg from her father
That the children may be reprieved from banishment.
JASON: I will, and with her I shall certainly succeed. 920
MEDEA: If she is like the rest of us women, you will.
And I, too, will take a hand with you in this business,
For I will send her some gifts which are far fairer,
I am sure of it, than those which now are in fashion,
A finely woven dress and a golden diadem, 925
And the children shall present them. Quick, let one of you
Servants bring here to me that beautiful dress.

(One of her attendants goes into the house.)

She will be happy not in one way, but in a hundred,
Having so fine a man as you to share her bed,
And with this beautiful dress which Helius of old, 930
My father's father, bestowed on his descendants.

(Enter attendant carrying the poisoned dress and diadem.)

There, children, take these wedding presents in your hands.
Take them to the royal princess, the happy bride,
And give them to her. She will not think little of them.
JASON: No, don't be foolish, and empty your hands of these. 935
Do you think the palace is short of dresses to wear?
Do you think there is no gold there? Keep them, don't
give them
Away. If my wife considers me of any value,
She will think more of me than money, I am sure of it.
MEDEA: No, let me have my way. They say the gods themselves 940
Are moved by gifts, and gold does more with men than words.
Hers is the luck, her fortune that which god blesses;
She is young and a princess; but for my children's reprieve
I would give my very life, and not gold only.
Go children, go together to that rich palace, 945
Be suppliants to the new wife of your father,
My lady, beg her not to let you be banished.
And give her the dress—for this is of great importance,
That she should take the gift into her hand from yours.
Go, quick as you can. And bring your mother good news 950
By your success of those things which she longs to gain.

*(*JASON *goes out with his attendants, followed by the* TUTOR *and the* CHILDREN *carrying the poisoned gifts.)*

CHORUS: Now there is no hope left for the children's lives.
Now there is none. They are walking already to murder.
The bride, poor bride, will accept the curse of the gold,
Will accept the bright diadem. 955
Around her yellow hair she will set that dress
Of death with her own hands.

The grace and the perfume and glow of the golden robe
Will charm her to put them upon her and wear the wreath,
And now her wedding will be with the dead below, 960
Into such a trap she will fall,

Poor thing, into such a fate of death and never
Escape from under that curse.

You, too, O wretched bridegroom, making your match
with kings,
965   You do not see that you bring
Destruction on your children and on her,
Your wife, a fearful death.
Poor soul, what a fall is yours!

In your grief, too, I weep, mother of little children,
970   You who will murder your own,
In vengeance for the loss of married love
Which Jason has betrayed
As he lives with another wife.

(*Enter the* TUTOR *with the* CHILDREN.)

TUTOR: Mistress, I tell you that these children are reprieved,
975   And the royal bride has been pleased to take in her hands
Your gifts. In that quarter the children are secure.
But come,
Why do you stand confused when you are fortunate?
Why have you turned round with your cheek away from me?
980   Are not these words of mine pleasing for you to hear?
MEDEA: Oh! I am lost!
TUTOR: That word is not in harmony with my tidings.
MEDEA: I am lost, I am lost!
TUTOR: Am I in ignorance telling you
Of some disaster, and not the good news I thought?
985   MEDEA: You have told what you have told. I do not blame you.
TUTOR: Why then this downcast eye, and this weeping of tears?
MEDEA: Oh, I am forced to weep, old man. The gods and I,
I in a kind of madness, have contrived all this.
TUTOR: Courage! You, too, will be brought home by your
children.
990   MEDEA: Ah, before that happens I shall bring others home.
TUTOR: Others before you have been parted from their
children.
Mortals must bear in resignation their ill luck.
MEDEA: That is what I shall do. But go inside the house,
And do for the children your usual daily work.

(*The* TUTOR *goes into the house.* MEDEA *turns to her* CHILDREN.)

995   O children, O my children, you have a city,
You have a home, and you can leave me behind you,
And without your mother you may live there forever.
But I am going in exile to another land
Before I have seen you happy and taken pleasure in you,
1000   Before I have dressed your brides and made your marriage
beds
And held up the torch at the ceremony of wedding.
Oh, what a wretch I am in this my self-willed thought!
What was the purpose, children, for which I reared you?
For all my travail and wearing myself away?
1005   They were sterile, those pains I had in the bearing of you.
Oh surely once the hopes in you I had, poor me,
Were high ones: you would look after me in old age,
And when I died would deck me well with your own
hands;
A thing which all would have done. Oh but now it is gone,
1010   That lovely thought. For, once I am left without you,

Sad will be the life I'll lead and sorrowful for me.
And you will never see your mother again with
Your dear eyes, gone to another mode of living.
Why, children, do you look upon me with your eyes?
Why do you smile so sweetly that last smile of all?   1015
Oh, Oh, what can I do? My spirit has gone from me,
Friends, when I saw that bright look in the children's eyes.
I cannot bear to do it. I renounce my plans
I had before. I'll take my children away from
This land. Why should I hurt their father with the pain   1020
They feel, and suffer twice as much of pain myself?
No, no, I will not do it. I renounce my plans.
Ah, what is wrong with me? Do I want to let go
My enemies unhurt and be laughed at for it?
I must face this thing. Oh, but what a weak woman   1025
Even to admit to my mind these soft arguments.
Children, go into the house. And he whom law forbids
To stand in attendance at my sacrifices,
Let him see to it. I shall not mar my handiwork.
Oh! Oh!   1030
Do not, O my heart, you must not do these things!
Poor heart, let them go, have pity upon the children.
If they live with you in Athens they will cheer you.
No! By Hell's avenging furies it shall not be—
This shall never be, that I should suffer my children   1035
To be the prey of my enemies' insolence.
Every way is it fixed. The bride will not escape.
No, the diadem is now upon her head, and she,
The royal princess, is dying in the dress, I know it.
But—for it is the most dreadful of roads for me   1040
To tread, and them I shall send on a more dreadful still—
I wish to speak to the children.

(*She calls the* CHILDREN *to her.*)

                    Come, children, give
Me your hands, give your mother your hands to kiss them.
Oh the dear hands, and O how dear are these lips to me,
And the generous eyes and the bearing of my children!   1045
I wish you happiness, but not here in this world.
What is here your father took. Oh how good to hold you!
How delicate the skin, how sweet the breath of children!
Go, go! I am no longer able, no longer
To look upon you. I am overcome by sorrow.   1050

(*The* CHILDREN *go into the house.*)

I know indeed what evil I intend to do,
But stronger than all my afterthoughts is my fury,
Fury that brings upon mortals the greatest evils.

(*She goes out to the right, toward the royal palace.*)

CHORUS: Often before
I have gone through more subtle reasons,   1055
And have come upon questionings greater
Than a woman should strive to search out.
But we too have a goddess to help us
And accompany us into wisdom.
Not all of us. Still you will find   1060
Among many women a few,
And our sex is not without learning.
This I say, that those who have never
Had children, who know nothing of it,

1065 In happiness have the advantage
Over those who are parents.
The childless, who never discover
Whether children turn out as a good thing
Or as something to cause pain, are spared
1070 Many troubles in lacking this knowledge.
And those who have in their homes
The sweet presence of children, I see that their lives
Are all wasted away by their worries.
First they must think how to bring them up well and
1075 How to leave them something to live on.
And then after this whether all their toil
Is for those who will turn out good or bad,
Is still an unanswered question.
And of one more trouble, the last of all,
1080 That is common to mortals I tell.
For suppose you have found them enough for their living,
Suppose that the children have grown into youth
And have turned out good, still, if God so wills it,
Death will away with your children's bodies,
1085 And carry them off into Hades.
What is our profit, then, that for the sake of
Children the gods should pile upon mortals
After all else
This most terrible grief of all?

(*Enter* MEDEA, *from the spectators' right.*)

1090 MEDEA: Friends, I can tell you that for long I have waited
For the event. I stare toward the place from where
The news will come. And now, see one of Jason's servants
Is on his way here, and that labored breath of his
Shows he has tidings for us, and evil tidings.

(*Enter, also from the right, the* MESSENGER.)

1095 MESSENGER: Medea, you who have done such a dreadful thing,
So outrageous, run for your life, take what you can,
A ship to bear you hence or chariot on land.
MEDEA: And what is the reason deserves such flight as this?
MESSENGER: She is dead, only just now, the royal princess,
1100 And Creon dead, too, her father, by your poisons.
MEDEA: The finest words you have spoken. Now and hereafter
I shall count you among my benefactors and friends.
MESSENGER: What! Are you right in the mind? Are you not mad,
Woman? The house of the king is outraged by you.
1105 Do you enjoy it? Not afraid of such doings?
MEDEA: To what you say I on my side have something too
To say in answer. Do not be in a hurry, friend,
But speak. How did they die? You will delight me twice
As much again if you say they died in agony.
1110 MESSENGER: When those two children, born of you, had
entered in,
Their father with them, and passed into the bride's house,
We were pleased, we slaves who were distressed by your
wrongs.
All through the house we were talking of but one thing,
How you and your husband had made up your quarrel.
1115 Some kissed the children's hands and some their yellow
hair,
And I myself was so full of my joy that I
Followed the children into the women's quarters.

Our mistress, whom we honor now instead of you,
Before she noticed that your two children were there,
Was keeping her eye fixed eagerly on Jason. 1120
Afterwards, however, she covered up her eyes,
Her cheek paled, and she turned herself away from him,
So disgusted was she at the children's coming there.
But your husband tried to end the girl's bad temper,
And said "You must not look unkindly on your friends. 1125
Cease to be angry. Turn your head to me again.
Have as your friends the same ones as your husband has.
And take these gifts, and beg your father to reprieve
These children from their exile. Do it for my sake."
She, when she saw the dress, could not restrain herself. 1130
She agreed with all her husband said, and before
He and the children had gone far from the palace,
She took the gorgeous robe and dressed herself in it,
And put the golden crown around her curly locks,
And arranged the set of the hair in a shining mirror, 1135
And smiled at the lifeless image of herself in it.
Then she rose from her chair and walked about the room,
With her gleaming feet stepping most soft and delicate,
All overjoyed with the present. Often and often
She would stretch her foot out straight and look along it. 1140
But after that it was a fearful thing to see.
The color of her face changed, and she staggered back,
She ran, and her legs trembled, and she only just
Managed to reach a chair without falling flat down.
An aged woman servant who, I take it, thought 1145
This was some seizure of Pan or another god,
Cried out "God bless us," but that was before she saw
The white foam breaking through her lips and her rolling
The pupils of her eyes and her face all bloodless.
Then she raised a different cry from that "God bless us," 1150
A huge shriek, and the women ran, one to the king,
One to the newly wedded husband to tell him
What had happened to his bride; and with frequent sound
The whole of the palace rang as they went running.
One walking quickly round the course of a race-track 1155
Would now have turned the bend and be close to the goal,
When she, poor girl, opened her shut and speechless eye,
And with a terrible groan she came to herself.
For a twofold pain was moving up against her.
The wreath of gold that was resting around her head 1160
Let forth a fearful stream of all-devouring fire,
And the finely woven dress your children gave to her,
Was fastening on the unhappy girl's fine flesh.
She leapt up from the chair, and all on fire she ran,
Shaking her hair now this way and now that, trying 1165
To hurl the diadem away; but fixedly
The gold preserved its grip, and, when she shook her hair,
Then more and twice as fiercely the fire blazed out.
Till, beaten by her fate, she fell down to the ground,
Hard to be recognized except by a parent. 1170
Neither the setting of her eyes was plain to see,
Nor the shapeliness of her face. From the top of
Her head there oozed out blood and fire mixed together.
Like the drops on pine-bark, so the flesh from her bones
Dropped away, torn by the hidden fang of the poison. 1175
It was a fearful sight; and terror held us all
From touching the corpse. We had learned from what had
happened.
But her wretched father, knowing nothing of the event,

Came suddenly to the house, and fell upon the corpse,
1180 And at once cried out and folded his arms about her,
And kissed her and spoke to her, saying, "O my poor child,
What heavenly power has so shamefully destroyed you?
And who has set me here like an ancient sepulcher,
Deprived of you? O let me die with you, my child!"
1185 And when he had made an end of his wailing and crying,
Then the old man wished to raise himself to his feet;
But, as the ivy clings to the twigs of the laurel,
So he stuck to the fine dress, and he struggled fearfully.
For he was trying to lift himself to his knee,
1190 And she was pulling him down, and when he tugged hard
He would be ripping his aged flesh from his bones.
At last his life was quenched, and the unhappy man
Gave up the ghost, no longer could hold up his head.
There they lie close, the daughter and the old father,
1195 Dead bodies, an event he prayed for in his tears.
As for your interests, I will say nothing of them,
For you will find your own escape from punishment.
Our human life I think and have thought a shadow,
And I do not fear to say that those who are held
1200 Wise among men and who search the reasons of things
Are those who bring the most sorrow on themselves.
For of mortals there is no one who is happy.
If wealth flows in upon one, one may be perhaps
Luckier than one's neighbor, but still not happy.

(*Exit.*)

1205 CHORUS: Heaven, it seems, on this day has fastened many
Evils on Jason, and Jason has deserved them.
Poor girl, the daughter of Creon, how I pity you
And your misfortunes, you who have gone quite away
To the house of Hades because of marrying Jason.
1210 MEDEA: Women, my task is fixed: as quickly as I may
To kill my children, and start away from this land,
And not, by wasting time, to suffer my children
To be slain by another hand less kindly to them.
Force every way will have it they must die, and since
1215 This must be so, then I, their mother, shall kill them.
Oh, arm yourself in steel, my heart! Do not hang back
From doing this fearful and necessary wrong.
Oh, come, my hand, poor wretched hand, and take the
sword.
Take it, step forward to this bitter starting point,
1220 And do not be a coward, do not think of them,
How sweet they are, and how you are their mother. Just for
This one short day be forgetful of your children,
Afterward weep; for even though you will kill them,
They were very dear—Oh, I am an unhappy woman!

(*With a cry she rushes into the house.*)

1225 CHORUS: O Earth, and the far shining
Ray of the Sun, look down, look down upon
This poor lost woman, look, before she raises
The hand of murder against her flesh and blood.
Yours was the golden birth from which
1230 She sprang, and now I fear divine
Blood may be shed by men.
O heavenly light, hold back her hand,
Check her, and drive from out the house
The bloody Fury raised by fiends of Hell.

Vain waste, your care of children;   1235
Was it in vain you bore the babes you loved,
After you passed the inhospitable strait
Between the dark blue rocks, Symplegades?
O wretched one, how has it come,
This heavy anger on your heart,   1240
This cruel bloody mind?
For God from mortals asks a stern
Price for the stain of kindred blood
In like disaster falling on their homes.

(*A cry from* ONE OF THE CHILDREN *is heard.*)

CHORUS: Do you hear the cry, do you hear the children's cry? 1245
O you hard heart, O woman fated for evil!
ONE OF THE CHILDREN: (*From within.*) What can I do and how
escape my mother's hands?
ANOTHER CHILD: (*From within.*) O my dear brother, I cannot tell.
We are lost.
CHORUS: Shall I enter the house? Oh, surely I should
Defend the children from murder.   1250
A CHILD: (*From within.*) O help us, in God's name, for now we
need your help.
Now, now we are close to it. We are trapped by the sword.
CHORUS: O your heart must have been made of rock or steel,
You who can kill
With your own hand the fruit of your own womb.   1255
Of one alone I have heard, one woman alone
Of those of old who laid her hands on her children,
Ino, sent mad by heaven when the wife of Zeus
Drove her out from her home and made her wander;
And because of the wicked shedding of blood   1260
Of her own children she threw
Herself, poor wretch, into the sea and stepped away
Over the sea-cliff to die with her two children.
What horror more can be? O women's love,
So full of trouble,   1265
How many evils have you caused already!

(*Enter* JASON, *with attendants.*)

JASON: You women, standing close in front of this dwelling,
Is she, Medea, she who did this dreadful deed,
Still in the house, or has she run away in flight?
For she will have to hide herself beneath the earth,   1270
Or raise herself on wings into the height of air,
If she wishes to escape the royal vengeance.
Does she imagine that, having killed our rulers,
She will herself escape uninjured from this house?
But I am thinking not so much of her as for   1275
The children—her the king's friends will make to suffer
For what she did. So I have come to save the lives
Of my boys, in case the royal house should harm them
While taking vengeance for their mother's wicked deed.
CHORUS: O Jason, if you but knew how deeply you are   1280
Involved in sorrow, you would not have spoken so.
JASON: What is it? That she is planning to kill me also?
CHORUS: Your children are dead, and by their own mother's
hand.
JASON: What! That is it? O woman, you have destroyed me!
CHORUS: You must make up your mind your children are no 1285
more.
JASON: Where did she kill them? Was it here or in the house?

CHORUS: Open the gates and there you will see them murdered.
JASON: Quick as you can unlock the doors, men, and undo
    The fastenings and let me see this double evil,
1290   My children dead and her—Oh her I will repay.

(*His attendants rush to the door.* MEDEA *appears above the house in a chariot drawn by dragons. She has the dead bodies of the* CHILDREN *with her.*)

MEDEA: Why do you batter these gates and try to unbar them,
    Seeking the corpses and for me who did the deed?
    You may cease your trouble, and, if you have need of me,
    Speak, if you wish. You will never touch me with your hand,
1295   Such a chariot has Helius, my father's father,
    Given me to defend me from my enemies.
JASON: You hateful thing, you woman most utterly loathed
    By the gods and me and by all the race of mankind,
    You who have had the heart to raise a sword against
1300   Your children, you, their mother, and left me childless—
    You have done this, and do you still look at the sun
    And at the earth, after these most fearful doings?
    I wish you dead. Now I see it plain, though at that time
    I did not, when I took you from your foreign home
1305   And brought you to a Greek house, you, an evil thing,
    A traitress to your father and your native land.
    The gods hurled the avenging curse of yours on me.
    For your own brother you slew at your own hearthside,
    And then came aboard that beautiful ship, the Argo.
1310   And that was your beginning. When you were married
    To me, your husband, and had borne children to me,
    For the sake of pleasure in the bed you killed them.
    There is no Greek woman who would have dared such deeds,
    Out of all those whom I passed over and chose you
1315   To marry instead, a bitter destructive match,
    A monster, not a woman, having a nature
    Wilder than that of Scylla in the Tuscan sea.
    Ah! no, not if I had ten thousand words of shame
    Could I sting you. You are naturally so brazen.
1320   Go, worker in evil, stained with your children's blood.
    For me remains to cry aloud upon my fate,
    Who will get no pleasure from my newly wedded love,
    And the boys whom I begot and brought up, never
    Shall I speak to them alive. Oh, my life is over!
1325 MEDEA: Long would be the answer which I might have made to
    These words of yours, if Zeus the father did not know
    How I have treated you and what you did to me.
    No, it was not to be that you should scorn my love,
    And pleasantly live your life through, laughing at me;
1330   Nor would the princess, nor he who offered the match,
    Creon, drive me away without paying for it.
    So now you may call me a monster, if you wish,
    A Scylla housed in the caves of the Tuscan sea.
    I too, as I had to, have taken hold of your heart.
1335 JASON: You feel the pain yourself. You share in my sorrow.
    MEDEA: Yes, and my grief is gain when you cannot mock it.
    JASON: O children, what a wicked mother she was to you!
    MEDEA: They died from a disease they caught from their father.

1317 **Scylla** a monster in the *Odyssey*

JASON: I tell you it was not my hand that destroyed them.
MEDEA: But it was your insolence, and your virgin wedding. 1340
JASON: And just for the sake of that you chose to kill them.
MEDEA: Is love so small a pain, do you think, for a woman?
JASON: For a wise one, certainly. But you are wholly evil.
MEDEA: The children are dead. I say this to make you suffer.
JASON: The children, I think, will bring down curses on you. 1345
MEDEA: The gods know who was the author of this sorrow.
JASON: Yes, the gods know indeed, they know your loathsome
    heart.
MEDEA: Hate me. But I tire of your barking bitterness.
JASON: And I of yours. It is easier to leave you.
MEDEA: How then? What shall I do? I long to leave you too. 1350
JASON: Give me the bodies to bury and to mourn them.
MEDEA: No, that I will not. I will bury them myself,
    Bearing them to Hera's temple on the promontory;
    So that no enemy may evilly treat them
    By tearing up their grave. In this land of Corinth 1355
    I shall establish a holy feast and sacrifice
    Each year for ever to atone for the blood guilt.
    And I myself go to the land of Erechtheus
    To dwell in Aegeus' house, the son of Pandion.
    While you, as is right, will die without distinction, 1360
    Struck on the head by a piece of the Argo's timber,
    And you will have seen the bitter end of my love.
JASON: May a Fury for the children's sake destroy you,
    And justice, Requitor of blood.
MEDEA: What heavenly power lends an ear 1365
    To a breaker of oaths, a deceiver?
JASON: Oh, I hate you, murderess of children.
MEDEA: Go to your palace. Bury your bride.
JASON: I go, with two children to mourn for.
MEDEA: Not yet do you feel it. Wait for the future. 1370
JASON: Oh, children I loved!
MEDEA: I loved them, you did not.
JASON: You loved them, and killed them.
MEDEA: To make you feel
    pain.
JASON: Oh, wretch that I am, how I long
    To kiss the dear lips of my children!
MEDEA: Now you would speak to them, now you would kiss 1375
    them.
    Then you rejected them.
JASON: Let me, I beg you,
    Touch my boys delicate flesh.
MEDEA: I will not. Your words are all wasted.
JASON: O God, do you hear it, this persecution,
    These my sufferings from this hateful 1380
    Woman, this monster, murderess of children?
    Still what I can do that I will do:
    I will lament and cry upon heaven,
    Calling the gods to bear me witness
    How you have killed my boys and prevent me from 1385
    Touching their bodies or giving them burial.
    I wish I had never begot them to see them
    Afterward slaughtered by you.
CHORUS: Zeus in Olympus is the overseer
    Of many doings. Many things the gods 1390
    Achieve beyond our judgment. What we thought
    Is not confirmed and what we thought not god
    Contrives. And so it happens in this story.

Aristophanes

Aristophanes (c. 450–c. 388 BCE) pursued his career as a playwright throughout the Peloponnesian War. As he observed the decline and defeat of Athens, his comedies relentlessly attacked the war and the individuals and attitudes that supported it. Aristophanes first entered the City Dionysia in 427 BCE and first won in 426 BCE with a now-lost play that satirized the policies and character of the military leader Cleon. Many of Aristophanes' plays—*Birds, Lysistrata, Assembly of Women*—use a utopian premise to criticize the war, but in other plays, Aristophanes lampoons other aspects of city life. In *Frogs,* for instance, a pompous Aeschylus and an embittered Euripides come from Hades to vie with one another once again; in *Clouds,* Aristophanes ridicules the sophists—professional teachers of rhetoric—for their ability to argue any side of an issue, and he particularly singles out Socrates for blame. The impact of Aristophanes' comedy on Athens should not be underestimated. In Plato's *Apology,* Socrates cites Aristophanes' portrayal of him in *Clouds* as one of the factors that turned Athenian sentiment against him, resulting in his trial and sentence of execution. Aristophanes' plays include *Acharnians, Knights, Clouds, Wasps, Peace, Birds, Lysistrata, Women Celebrating the Thesmophoria, Frogs, Assembly of Women,* and *Plutus.*

Lysistrata is one of several plays critical of Athens' war with Sparta. Produced in 411 BCE, the play follows shortly on a disastrous phase of the war for Athens. Two years earlier, the Athenian raid on Sicily had failed, and the navy was decimated, leaving Athens vulnerable to attack by Sparta. Although the navy was rebuilt before Sparta mounted its final assault, Athens fell to Sparta in 404 BCE.

 Lysistrata explores the premise that the women of Greece—drawn from all the major city-states and regions—could unite to oppose the war. Led by the Athenian Lysistrata (her name means "disband the army"), the women barricade themselves on the Acropolis, withholding sex from the men until peace can be declared. Aristophanes provides each of his

LYSISTRATA

Displaying an "eclectic" design combining classical and modern costume elements, this production of Aristophanes' *Lysistrata* also displays an updated version of the Greek costume *phallus* as well.

women with the physical attributes and accent typical of her region. The large and power-ful Spartan woman Lampito, for example, is both an expert in the Spartan rump-kicking dance and speaks in what was—to an Athenian audience—an outlandish accent (to make this clear for English-speaking readers, this translation gives Lampito an exaggerated South-ern drawl).

Lysistrata addresses the politics of its era in a variety of ways. It is, of course, a passion-ate plea for peace, concluding with a scene of comic feasting and dancing enjoyed by all the characters in the play, Athenians and Spartans, men and women. For modern audiences, though, the play's connection between gender and politics may seem more immediate. On one hand, the play implies an equality between men and women. The women claim that the morality of their domestic sphere is superior to the military morality pursued by the men, and to get the women back, the men are forced to compromise with them. On the other hand, although *Lysistrata* seems to provide women with political power, their power resides wholly in their sexuality; they can interrupt, but not change, the fact that they are the prop-erty of men. The Theater of Dionysus could not, of course, put women on the stage, and Lysistrata, Lampito, Kalonike, and the rest—even the naked girl Harmony—were all played by men in padded costumes. In the play and in the *polis,* women were defined principally through their relation to men. The limited influence women could exert was subordinate to the civil power that Aristophanes and his audience took to be the "natural" preserve of the male audience. Despite the play's earthy humor and apparent feminism, *Lysistrata* documents the actual status of women in classical Athens; their power is restricted to the sphere of the *oikos,* or home, and can be practiced only through their subservience to men, who, as citi-zens, finally can command women's bodies, the home, and the state as well.

LYSISTRATA

Aristophanes

TRANSLATED BY DONALD SUTHERLAND

CHARACTERS

LYSISTRATA ⎱
KALONIKE ⎬ *Athenian women*
MYRRHINA ⎰
LAMPITO, *a Spartan woman*
CHORUS OF OLD MEN
CHORUS OF OLD WOMEN
ATHENIAN COMMISSIONER

OLD MARKET WOMAN
CINESIAS, *an Athenian,*
      husband of Myrrhina
SPARTAN HERALD
SCYTHIAN POLICEMEN
PORTER
ATHENIAN OFFICIAL

ATHENIANS
SPARTAN AMBASSADORS
ATHENIAN AMBASSADORS
HARMONY
LADY COP

A street in Athens before daylight.

LYSISTRATA: If anyone had asked them to a festival
  of Aphrodite or of Bacchus or of Pan,
  you couldn't get through Athens for the tambourines,
  but now there's not one solitary woman here.
5 Except my next-door neighbor. Here she's coming out.
  Hello, Kalonike.
KALONIKE: Hello, Lysistrata.
  What are you so upset about? Don't scowl so, dear.
  You're less attractive when you knit your brows and glare.
LYSISTRATA: I know, Kalonike, but I am smoldering
10 with indignation at the way we women act.
  Men think we are so gifted for all sorts of crime
  that we will stop at nothing—
KALONIKE: Well, we are, by Zeus!
LYSISTRATA: —but when it comes to an appointment here
    with me
  to plot and plan for something really serious
15 they lie in bed and do not come.
KALONIKE: They'll come, my dear.
  You know what trouble women have in going out:
  one of us will be wrapped up in her husband still,
  another waking up the maid, or with a child
  to put to sleep, or give its bath, or feed its pap.
20 LYSISTRATA: But they had other more important things to do
  than those.
KALONIKE: What ever is it, dear Lysistrata?
  What have you called us women all together for?
  How much of a thing is it?
LYSISTRATA: Very big.
KALONIKE: And thick?
LYSISTRATA: Oh very thick indeed.
KALONIKE: Then *how* can we be late?
25 LYSISTRATA: That's not the way it is. Or we would all be here.
  But it is something I have figured out myself
  and turned and tossed upon for many a sleepless night.
KALONIKE: It must be something slick you've turned and
    tossed upon!
30 LYSISTRATA: So slick that the survival of all Greece depends
  upon the women.
KALONIKE: On the women? In that case
  poor Greece has next to nothing to depend upon.
LYSISTRATA: Since now it's we who must decide affairs of state:
  either there is to be no Spartan left alive—
KALONIKE: A very good thing too, if none were left,
  by Zeus!

LYSISTRATA:—and every living soul in Thebes to be destroyed— 35
KALONIKE: Except the eels! Spare the delicious eels of Thebes!
LYSISTRATA: —and as for Athens—I can't bring myself to say
  the like of that for us. But just think what I mean!
  Yet if the women meet here as I told them to
  from Sparta, Thebes, and all of their allies, 40
  and we of Athens, all together we'll save Greece.
KALONIKE: What reasonable thing could women ever do,
  or glorious, we who sit around all prettied up
  in flowers and scandalous saffron-yellow gowns,
  groomed and draped to the ground in oriental stuffs 45
  and fancy pumps?
LYSISTRATA: And those are just the very things
  I count upon to save us—wicked saffron gowns,
  perfumes and pumps and rouge and sheer transparent
    frocks.
KALONIKE: But what use can they be?
LYSISTRATA: So no man in our time
  will raise a spear against another man again— 50
KALONIKE: I'll get a dress dyed saffron-yellow, come what may!
LYSISTRATA:—nor touch a shield—
KALONIKE: I'll slip into the sheerest gown!
LYSISTRATA:—nor so much as a dagger—
KALONIKE: I'll buy a pair of pumps!
LYSISTRATA: So don't you think the women should be here
  by now?
KALONIKE: I don't. They should have *flown* and got here 55
  long ago.
LYSISTRATA: You'll see, my dear. They will, like good Athenians,
  do everything too late. But from the coastal towns
  no woman is here either, nor from Salamis.
KALONIKE: I'm certain those from Salamis have crossed the
    strait:
  they're always straddling *something* at this time of night. 60
LYSISTRATA: Not even those I was expecting would be first
  to get here, from Acharnae, from so close to town,
  not even they are here.
KALONIKE: But one of them, I know,
  is under way, and three sheets to the wind, by now.
  But look—some women are approaching over there. 65
LYSISTRATA: And over here are some, coming this way—
KALONIKE: Phew! Phew!
  Where are they from?
LYSISTRATA: Down by the marshes.
KALONIKE: Yes, by Zeus!
  It smells as if the bottoms had been all churned up!

(*Enter* MYRRHINA, *and others.*)

MYRRHINA: Hello Lysistrata. Are we a little late?
70   What's that? Why don't you speak?
LYSISTRATA: I don't think much of you,
   Myrrhina, coming to this business only now.
MYRRHINA: Well, I could hardly find my girdle in the dark.
   If it's so urgent, tell us what it is. We're here.
KALONIKE: Oh no. Let's wait for just a little while until
75   the delegates from Sparta and from Thebes arrive.
LYSISTRATA: You show much better judgment.

(*Enter* LAMPITO, *and others.*)

                                   Here comes Lampito!
LYSISTRATA: Well, darling Lampito! My dearest Spartan friend!
   How very sweet, how beautiful you look! That fresh
   complexion! How magnificent your figure is!
80   Enough to crush a bull!
LAMPITO: Ah shorely think Ah could.
   Ah take mah exacise. Ah jump and thump mah butt.
KALONIKE: And really, what a handsome set of tits you have!
LAMPITO: You feel me ovah lahk a cow fo sacrafahce!
LYSISTRATA: And this other young thing—where ever is *she* from?
85   LAMPITO: She's prominent, Ah sweah, in Thebes—a delegate
   ample enough.
LYSISTRATA: By Zeus, she represents Thebes well,
   having so trim a ploughland.
KALONIKE: Yes, by Zeus, she does!
   There's not a weed of all her field she hasn't plucked.
LYSISTRATA: And who's the other girl?
LAMPITO: Theah's nothing small, Ah sweah,
90   or tahght about her folks in Corinth.
KALONIKE: No, by Zeus!—
   to judge by this side of her, nothing small or tight.
LAMPITO: But who has called togethah such a regiment
   of all us women?
LYSISTRATA: Here I am. I did.
LAMPITO: Speak up,
   just tell us what you want.
KALONIKE: Oh yes, by Zeus, my dear,
95   do let us know what the important business is!
LYSISTRATA: Let me explain it, then. And yet . . . before I do . . .
   I have one little question.
KALONIKE: Anything you like.
LYSISTRATA: Don't you all miss the fathers of your little ones,
   your husbands who have gone away to war? I'm sure
100   you all have husbands in the armies far from home.
KALONIKE: Mine's been away five months in Thrace—
   a general's guard,
   posted to see his general does not desert.
MYRRHINA: And mine has been away in Pylos seven whole
   months.
LAMPITO: And mahn, though he does get back home on leave
   sometahms,
105   no soonah has he come than he is gone again.
LYSISTRATA: No lovers either. Not a sign of one is left.
   For since our eastern allies have deserted us
   they haven't sent a single six-inch substitute
   to serve as leatherware replacement for our men.
110   Would you be willing, then, if I thought out a scheme,
   to join with me to end the war?

KALONIKE: Indeed I would,
   even if I had to pawn this very wrap-around
   and drink up all the money in one day, I would!
MYRRHINA: And so would I, even if I had to see myself
   split like a flounder, and give half of me away!   115
LAMPITO: And so would Ah! Ah'd climb up Mount
   Taÿgetos
   if Ah just had a chance of seeing peace from theah!
LYSISTRATA: Then I will tell you. I may now divulge my
   plan.
   Women of Greece!—if we intend to force the men
   to make a peace, we must abstain . . .   120
KALONIKE: From what? Speak out!
LYSISTRATA: But will you do it?
KALONIKE: We will, though death should be the price!
LYSISTRATA: Well then, we must abstain utterly from the prick.
   Why do you turn your backs? Where are you off to now?
   And you—why pout and make such faces, shake your heads?
   Why has your color changed? Why do you shed those tears?   125
   Will you do it or will you not? Why hesitate?
KALONIKE: I will not do it. Never. Let the war go on!
MYRRHINA: Neither will I. By Zeus, no! Let the war go on!
LYSISTRATA: How can you say so, Madam Flounder, when just
   now
   you were declaiming you would split yourself in half?   130
KALONIKE: Anything else you like, anything! If I must
   I'll gladly walk through fire. That, rather than the prick!
   Because there's nothing like it, dear Lysistrata.
LYSISTRATA: How about you?
MYRRHINA: I too would gladly walk through fire.
LYSISTRATA: Oh the complete depravity of our whole sex!   135
   It is no wonder tragedies are made of us,
   we have such unrelenting unity of mind!
   But you, my friend from Sparta, dear, if you alone
   stand by me, only you, we still might save the cause.
   Vote on my side!   140
LAMPITO: They'ah hahd conditions, mahty hahd,
   to sleep without so much as the fo'skin of one . . .
   but all the same . . . well . . . yes. We need peace just as
   bad.
LYSISTRATA: Oh dearest friend!—the one real woman of them all!
KALONIKE: And if we really should abstain from what you say—
   which Heaven forbid!—do you suppose on that account   145
   that peace might come to be?
LYSISTRATA: I'm absolutely sure.
   If we should sit around, rouged and with skins well
   creamed,
   with nothing on but a transparent negligé,
   and come up to them with our deltas plucked quite smooth,
   and, once our men get stiff and want to come to grips,   150
   we do not yield to them at all but just hold off,
   they'll make a truce in no time. There's no doubt of that.
LAMPITO: We say in Spahta that when Menelaos saw
   Helen's ba'e apples he just tossed away his swo'd.
KALONIKE: And what, please, if our husbands just toss *us* away?   155
LYSISTRATA: Well, you have heard the good old saying: Know
   Thyself.
KALONIKE: It isn't worth the candle. I hate cheap substitutes.
   But what if they should seize and drag us by brute force
   into the bedroom?
LYSISTRATA: Hang onto the doors!
KALONIKE: And if—
   they beat us?   160

LYSISTRATA: Then you must give in, but nastily,
    and do it badly. There's no fun in it by force.
    And then, just keep them straining. They will give it up
    in no time—don't you worry. For never will a man
    enjoy himself unless the woman coincides.

165 KALONIKE: If both of you are for this plan, then so are we.

LAMPITO: And we of Spahta shall persuade ouah men to keep
    the peace sinceahly and with honah in all ways,
    but how could anyone pe'suade the vulgah mob
    of Athens not to deviate from discipline?

170 LYSISTRATA: Don't worry, we'll persuade our men. They'll keep
    the peace.

LAMPITO: They won't, so long as they have battleships afloat
    and endless money sto'ed up in the Pahthenon.

LYSISTRATA: But that too has been carefully provided for:
    we shall take over the Acropolis today.

175   The oldest women have their orders to do that:
    while *we* meet here, *they* go as if to sacrifice
    up there, but really seizing the Acropolis.

LAMPITO: All should go well. What you say theah is very
    smaht.

LYSISTRATA: In that case, Lampito, what are we waiting for?

180   Let's take an oath, to bind us indissolubly.

LAMPITO: Well, just you show us what the oath is. Then we'll
    sweah.

LYSISTRATA: You're right. Where is that lady cop?

(*To the armed* LADY COP *looking around for a* LADY COP.)

                            What do you think
    you're looking for? Put down your shield in front of us,
    there, on its back, and someone get some scraps of gut.

185 KALONIKE: Lysistrata, what in the world do you intend
    to make us take an oath on?

LYSISTRATA: What? Why, on a shield,
    just as they tell me some insurgents in a play
    by Aeschylus once did, with a sheep's blood and guts.

KALONIKE: Oh *don't*, Lysistrata, don't swear upon a *shield,*

190   not if the oath has anything to do with peace!

LYSISTRATA: Well then, what *will* we swear on? Maybe we
    should get
    a white horse somewhere, like the Amazons, and cut
    some bits of gut from it.

KALONIKE: *Where* would we get a horse?

LYSISTRATA: But what kind of an oath *is* suitable for us?

195 KALONIKE: By Zeus, I'll tell you if you like. First we put down
    a big black drinking-cup, face up, and then we let
    the neck of a good jug of wine bleed into it,
    and take a solemn oath to—add no water in.

LAMPITO: Bah Zeus, Ah jest can't tell you how Ah lahk that
    oath!

200 LYSISTRATA: Someone go get a cup and winejug from inside.

(KALONIKE *goes and is back in a flash.*)

KALONIKE: My dears, my dearest dears—how's *this* for pottery?
    You feel good right away, just laying hold of it.

LYSISTRATA: Well, set it down, and lay your right hand on
    this pig.
    O goddess of Persuasion, and O Loving-cup,

205   accept this victim's blood! Be gracious unto us.

KALONIKE: It's not anaemic, and flows clear. Those are good signs.

LAMPITO: What an aroma, too! Bah Castah it *is* sweet!

KALONIKE: My dears, if you don't mind—I'll be the first to
    swear.

LYSISTRATA: By Aphrodite, no! If you had drawn first place
    by lot—but now let all lay hands upon the cup.   210
    Yes, Lampito—and now, let one of you repeat
    for all of you what I shall say. You will be sworn
    by every word she says, and bound to keep this oath:
    No lover and no husband and no man on earth—

KALONIKE: No lover and no husband and no man on earth—   215

LYSISTRATA: *shall e'er approach me with his penis up.* Repeat.

KALONIKE: shall e'er approach me with his penis up. Oh dear,
    my knees are buckling under me, Lysistrata!

LYSISTRATA: *and I shall lead an unlaid life alone at home,*

KALONIKE: and I shall lead an unlaid life alone at home,   220

LYSISTRATA: *wearing a saffron gown and groomed and beautified*

KALONIKE: wearing a saffron gown and groomed and beautified

LYSISTRATA: *so that my husband will be all on fire for me*

KALONIKE: so that my husband will be all on fire for me

LYSISTRATA: *but I will never willingly give in to him*   225

KALONIKE: but I will never willingly give in to him

LYSISTRATA: *and if he tries to force me to against my will*

KALONIKE: and if he tries to force me to against my will

LYSISTRATA: *I'll do it badly and not wiggle in response*

KALONIKE: I'll do it badly and not wiggle in response   230

LYSISTRATA: *nor toward the ceiling will I lift my Persian pumps*

KALONIKE: nor toward the ceiling will I lift my Persian pumps

LYSISTRATA: *nor crouch down as the lions on cheese-graters do*

KALONIKE: nor crouch down as the lions on cheese-graters do

LYSISTRATA: *and if I keep my promise, may I drink of this—*   235

KALONIKE: and if I keep my promise, may I drink of this—

LYSISTRATA: *but if I break it, then may water fill the cup!*

KALONIKE: but if I break it, then may water fill the cup!

LYSISTRATA: Do you all swear to this with her?

ALL: We do, by Zeus!

LYSISTRATA: I'll consecrate our oath now.   240

KALONIKE: Share alike, my dear,
    so we'll be friendly to each other from the start.

LAMPITO: What was that screaming?

LYSISTRATA: That's what I was telling you:
    the women have already seized the Parthenon
    and the Acropolis. But now, dear Lampito,
    return to Sparta and set things in order there—   245
    but leave these friends of yours as hostages with us—
    And let *us* join the others in the citadel
    and help them bar the gates.

KALONIKE: But don't you think the men
    will rally to the rescue of the citadel,
    attacking us at once?   250

LYSISTRATA: They don't worry me much:
    they'll never bring against us threats or fire enough
    to force open the gates, except upon our terms.

KALONIKE: Never by Aphrodite! Or we'd lose our name
    for being battle-axes and unbearable!

(*Exeunt. The scene changes to the Propylaea of the Acropolis. A*
CHORUS OF VERY OLD MEN *struggles slowly in, carrying logs and
firepots.*)

ONE OLD MAN: Lead on! O Drakës, step by step, although your   255
               shoulder's aching
    and under this green olive log's great weight
               your back be breaking!

ANOTHER: Eh, life is long but always has
260   more surprises for us!
                Now who'd have thought we'd live to hear
                        this, O Strymodorus?—

                The wives we fed and looked upon
                    as helpless liabilities
265   now dare to occupy the Parthenon,
                our whole Acropolis, for once they seize
                    the Propylaea, straightway
                they lock and bar the gateway.
CHORUS: Let's rush to the Acropolis with due precipitation
270   and lay these logs down circlewise, till presently we turn them
        into one mighty pyre to make a general cremation
        of all the women up there—eh! with our own hands we'll
            burn them,
        the leaders and the followers, without discrimination!
AN OLD MAN: They'll never have the laugh on me!
275   Though I may not look it,
                I rescued the Acropolis
                    when the Spartans took it
                about a hundred years ago.
                We laid a siege that kept their king
280   six years unwashed, so when I made him throw
                his armor off, for all his blustering,
                    in nothing but his shirt he
                looked very very dirty.
CHORUS: How strictly I besieged the man! These gates were
            all invested
285   with seventeen ranks of armored men all equally ferocious!
        Shall women—by Euripides and all the gods detested—
        not be restrained—with me on hand—from something so
            atrocious?
        They shall!—or may our trophies won at Marathon be bested!
                But we must go a long way yet
290   up that steep and winding road
                before we reach the fortress where we want to get.
                    How shall we ever drag this load,
                    lacking pack-mules, way up there?
                I can tell you that my shoulder has caved in
            beyond repair!
295   Yet we must trudge ever higher,
                    ever blowing on the fire,
                so its coals will still be glowing when we get
            where we are going
                        Fooh! Fooh!
                        Whoo! I choke!
300   What a smoke!

                Lord Heracles! How fierce it flies
                out against me from the pot!
            and like a rabid bitch it bites me in the eyes!
                It's female fire, or it would not
305   scratch my poor old eyes like this.
                Yet undaunted we must onward, up the high
            Acropolis
                    where Athena's temple stands
                    fallen into hostile hands.
                O my comrades! shall we ever have a greater
            need to save her?
310   Fooh! Fooh!
                        Whoo! I choke!
                        What a smoke!

FIRST OLD MAN: Well, thank the gods, I see the fire is yet
            alive and waking!
SECOND OLD MAN: Why don't we set our lumber down right
            here in handy batches,
        then stick a branch of grape-vine in the pot until it catches   315
THIRD OLD MAN: and hurl ourselves against the gate with
            battering and shaking?
FIRST OLD MAN: and if the women won't unbar at such an
            ultimatum
        we'll set the gate on fire and then the smoke will suffocate
            'em.
SECOND OLD MAN: Well, let's put down our load. Fooh fooh,
            what smoke! But blow as needed!
THIRD OLD MAN: Your ablest generals *these* days would not carry   320
        wood like *we* did.
SECOND OLD MAN: At last the lumber ceases grinding my poor
            back to pieces!
THIRD OLD MAN: These are your orders, Colonel Pot: wake up
            the coals and bid them
        report here and present to me a torch lit up and flaring.
FIRST OLD MAN: O Victory, be with us! If you quell the
            women's daring
        we'll raise a splendid trophy of how you and we undid   325
            them!

(*A* CHORUS OF MIDDLE-AGED WOMEN *appears in the offing.*)

A WOMAN: I think that I perceive a smoke in which appears a
            flurry
        of sparks as of a lighted fire. Women, we'll have to hurry!
CHORUS OF WOMEN: Oh fleetly fly, oh swiftly flit,
            my dears, e'er Kalykë be lit
        and with Kritylla swallowed up alive   330
                in flames which the gales dreadfully drive
                and deadly old men fiercely inflate!
        Yet one thing I'm afraid of: will I not arrive too late?
        for filling up my water-jug has been no easy matter
        what with the crowd at the spring in the dusk and the   335
                clamor and pottery clatter.
            Pushed as I was, jostled by slave-
            women and sluts marked with a brand
            yet with my jug firmly in hand
            here I have come, hoping to save   340
                my burning friends and brave,

            for certain windy, witless, old,
            and wheezy fools, so I was told,
        with wood some tons in weight crept up this path,
            not having in mind heating a bath   345
            but uttering threats, vowing they will
        consume those nasty women into cinders on grill!
        But O Athena! never may I see my friends igniting!
        Nay!—let them save all the cities of Greece and their
                people from folly and fighting!   350
            Goddess whose crest flashes with gold,
            they were so bold taking your shrine
            only for this—Goddess who holds
            Athens—for *this* noble design,
            braving the flames, calling on you   355
                to carry water too!

(ONE OF THE OLD MEN *urinates noisily.*)

CHORUS OF WOMEN: Be still! What was that noise? Aha! Oh, wicked and degraded!

Would any good religious men have ever done what *they* did?

CHORUS OF MEN: Just look! It's a surprise-attack! Oh, dear, we're being raided

360 by swarms of them below us when we've got a swarm above us!

CHORUS OF WOMEN: Why panic at the sight of us? This is not many of us.

We number tens of thousands but you've hardly seen a fraction.

CHORUS OF MEN: O Phaidrias, shall they talk so big and we not take some action?

Oh, should we not be bashing them and splintering our lumber?

(*The* OLD MEN *begin to strip for combat.*)

365 CHORUS OF WOMEN: Let us, too, set our pitchers down, so they will not encumber

our movements if these gentlemen should care to offer battle.

CHORUS OF MEN: Oh someone should have clipped their jaws— twice, thrice, until they rattle—

(as once the poet put it)—then we wouldn't hear their prating.

CHORUS OF WOMEN: Well, here's your chance. Won't someone hit me? Here I stand, just waiting!

370 No other bitch will ever grab your balls, the way I'll treat you!

CHORUS OF MEN: Shut up—or I will drub you so old age will never reach you!

CHORUS OF WOMEN: Won't anyone step and lay one finger on Stratyllis?

CHORUS OF MEN: And if we pulverize her with our knuckles, will you kill us?

CHORUS OF WOMEN: No, only chew your lungs out and your innards and your eyes, sir.

375 CHORUS OF MEN: How clever is Euripides! There is no poet wiser:

he says indeed that women are the worst of living creatures.

CHORUS OF WOMEN: Now is the time, Rhodippe: let us raise our brimming pitchers.

CHORUS OF MEN: Why come up here with water, you, the gods' abomination?

CHORUS OF WOMEN: And why come here with fire, you tomb? To give yourself cremation?

380 CHORUS OF MEN: To set your friends alight upon a pyre erected for them.

CHORUS OF WOMEN: And so we brought our water-jugs. Upon your pyre we'll pour them.

CHORUS OF MEN: *You'll* put my fire out?

CHORUS OF WOMEN: Any time! You'll see there's nothing to it.

CHORUS OF MEN: I think I'll grill you right away, with just this torch to do it!

CHORUS OF WOMEN: Have you some dusting-powder? Here's your wedding-bath all ready.

385 CHORUS OF MEN: *You'll* bathe me, garbage that you are?

CHORUS OF WOMEN: Yes, bridegroom, just hold steady!

CHORUS OF MEN: Friends, you have heard her insolence—

CHORUS OF WOMEN: I'm free-born, not your slave, sir.

CHORUS OF MEN: I'll have this noise of yours restrained—

CHORUS OF WOMEN: Court's out—so be less grave, sir.

CHORUS OF MEN: Why don't you set her hair on fire?

CHORUS OF WOMEN: Oh, Water, be of service!

CHORUS OF MEN: Oh woe is me!

CHORUS OF WOMEN: Was it too hot?

CHORUS OF MEN: Oh, stop! What *is* this? Hot? Oh no! 390

CHORUS OF WOMEN: I'm watering you to make you grow.

CHORUS OF MEN: I'm withered from this chill I got!

CHORUS OF WOMEN: You've got a fire, so warm yourself. You're trembling: are you nervous?

(*Enter* ATHENIAN COMMISSIONER, *escorted by four* SCYTHIAN POLICEMEN *with bows and quivers slung on their backs.*)

COMMISSIONER: Has the extravagance of women broken out into full fury, with their banging tambourines 395 and constant wailings for their oriental gods, and on the roof-tops their Adonis festival, which I could hear myself from the Assembly once? For while Demostratos—that numbskull—had the floor, urging an expedition against Sicily, 400 his wife was dancing and we heard her crying out "Weep for Adonis!"—so the expedition failed with such an omen. When the same Demostratos was urging that we levy troops from our allies his wife was on the roof again, a little drunk: 405 "Weep for Adonis! Beat your breast!" says she. At that, he gets more bellicose, that god-Damn-ox-tratos. To this has the incontinence of women come!

CHORUS OF MEN: You haven't *yet* heard how outrageous they can be!

With other acts of violence, these women here 410 have showered us from their jugs, so now we are reduced to shaking out our shirts as if we'd pissed in them.

COMMISSIONER: Well, by the God of Waters, what do you expect? When we ourselves conspire with them in waywardness and give them good examples of perversity 415 such wicked notions naturally sprout in them. We go into a shop and say something like this: "Goldsmith, about that necklace you repaired: last night my wife was dancing, when the peg that bolts the catch fell from its hole. I have to sail for Salamis, 420 but if you have the time, by all means try to come towards evening, and put in the peg she needs." Another man says to a cobbler who is young and has no child's-play of a prick, "Cobbler," he says, "her sandal-strap is pinching my wife's little toe, 425 which is quite delicate. So please come by at noon and stretch it for her so it has a wider play." Such things as that result of course in things like this: when I, as a Commissioner, have made a deal to fit the fleet with oars and need the money now, 430 I'm locked out by these women from the very gates. But it's no use just standing here. Bring on the bars, so I can keep these women in their proper place. What are *you* gaping at, you poor unfortunate? Where are *you* looking? Only seeing if a bar 435 is open yet downtown? Come, drive these crowbars in under the gates on that side, pry away, and I will pry away on this.

(LYSISTRATA *comes out.*)

LYSISTRATA: No need to pry at all.
I'm coming out, of my own will. What use are bars?
440 It isn't bolts and bars we need so much as brains.
COMMISSIONER: Really, you dirty slut? Where is that officer?
Arrest her, and tie both her hands behind her back.
LYSISTRATA: By Artemis, just let him lift a hand at me
and, public officer or not, you'll hear him howl.
445 COMMISSIONER: You let her scare you? Grab her round the
middle, you.
Then *you* go help him and between you get her tied.

(KALONIKE *comes out.*)

KALONIKE: By Artemis, if you just lay one hand on her
I have a mind to trample the shit out of you.
COMMISSIONER: It's out already! Look! Now where's the other
one?
450 Tie up *that* woman first. She babbles, with it all.

(MYRRHINA *comes out.*)

MYRRHINA: By Hecatë, if you just lay a hand on her
you'll soon ask for a cup—to get your swellings down!

(*The* POLICEMAN *dashes behind the* COMMISSIONER *and clings to
him for protection.*)

COMMISSIONER: What happened? Where's that bowman, now?
Hold onto *her!*

(*He moves quickly away downhill.*)

I'll see that none of you can get away through here!
455 LYSISTRATA: By Artemis, you come near her and I'll bereave
your head of every hair! You'll weep for each one, too.
COMMISSIONER: What a calamity! This one has failed me too.
But never must we let ourselves be overcome
by women. All together now, O Scythians—
460 let's march against them in formation!
LYSISTRATA: You'll find out
that inside there we have four companies
of fighting women perfectly equipped for war.
COMMISSIONER: Charge! Turn their flanks, O Scythians! and tie
their hands!
LYSISTRATA: O allies—comrades—women! Sally forth and fight!
465 O vegetable vendors, O green-grocery-
grain-garlic-bread-bean-dealers and inn-keepers all!

(*A group of fierce* OLD MARKET-WOMEN, *carrying baskets of vegetables, spindles, etc., emerges. There is a volley of vegetables. The*
SCYTHIANS *are soon routed.*)

Come pull them, push them, smite them, smash them
into bits!
Rail and abuse them in the strongest words you know!
Halt, Halt! Retire in order! We'll forego the spoils!
470 COMMISSIONER: (*Tragically, like say Xerxes.*) Oh what reverses
have my bowmen undergone!
LYSISTRATA: But what did you imagine? Did you think you came
against a pack of slaves? Perhaps you didn't know
that women can be resolute?
COMMISSIONER: I know they can—
above all when they spot a bar across the way.

CHORUS OF MEN: Commissioner of Athens, you are spending 475
words unduly,
to argue with these animals, who only roar the louder,
or don't you know they showered us so coldly and so
cruelly,
and in our undershirts at that, and furnished us no powder?
CHORUS OF WOMEN: But beating up your neighbor is
inevitably bringing
a beating on yourself, sir, with your own eyes black and 480
bloody.
I'd rather sit securely like a little girl demurely
not stirring up a single straw nor harming anybody,
So long as no one robs my hive and rouses me to stinging.
CHORUS OF MEN: How shall we ever tame these brutes? We
cannot tolerate
the situation further, so we must investigate 485
this occurrence and find
with what purpose in mind
they profane the Acropolis, seize it, and lock
the approach to this huge and prohibited rock,
to our holiest ground! 490
Cross-examine them! Never believe one word
they tell you—refute them, confound them!
We must get to the bottom of things like this
and the circumstances around them.
COMMISSIONER: Yes indeed! and I want to know first one 495
thing:
just *why* you committed this treason,
barricading the fortress with locks and bars—
I insist on knowing the reason.
LYSISTRATA: To protect all the money up there from you—
you'll have nothing to fight for without it. 500
COMMISSIONER: You think it is *money* we're fighting for?
LYSISTRATA: All the troubles we have are about it.
It was so Peisander and those in power
of his kind could embezzle the treasure
that they cooked up emergencies all the time. 505
Well, let them, if such is their pleasure,
but they'll never get into this money again,
though you men should elect them to spend it.
COMMISSIONER: And just what will *you* do with it?
LYSISTRATA: Can you ask?
Of course we shall superintend it. 510
COMMISSIONER: You will superintend the treasury, *you!?*
LYSISTRATA: And why should it strike you so funny?
when we manage our houses in everything
and it's we who look after your money.
COMMISSIONER: But it's not the same thing! 515
LYSISTRATA: Why not?
COMMISSIONER: It's war,
and *this* money must pay the expenses.
LYSISTRATA: To begin with, you needn't be waging war.
COMMISSIONER: To survive, we don't need our defenses?
LYSISTRATA: You'll survive: we shall save you.
COMMISSIONER: Who? You?
LYSISTRATA: Yes, we.
COMMISSIONER: You absolutely disgust me. 520
LYSISTRATA: You may like it or not, but you *shall* be saved.
COMMISSIONER: I protest!
LYSISTRATA: If you care to, but, trust me,
this has got to be done all the same.

COMMISSIONER: It has?
   It's illegal, unjust, and outrageous!
525 LYSISTRATA: We must save you, sir.
COMMISSIONER: Yes? And if I refuse?
LYSISTRATA: You will much the more grimly engage us.
COMMISSIONER: And whence does it happen that war and peace
   are fit matters for women to mention?
LYSISTRATA: I will gladly explain—
COMMISSIONER: And be quick, or else
530   you'll be howling!
LYSISTRATA: Now, just pay attention
   and keep your hands to yourself, if you can!
COMMISSIONER: But I can't. You can't think how I suffer
   from holding them back in my anger!
AN OLD WOMAN: Sir—
   if you don't you will have it much rougher.
535 COMMISSIONER: You may croak that remark to yourself, you hag!
   Will *you* do the explaining?
LYSISTRATA: I'll do it.
   Heretofore we women in time of war
      have endured very patiently through it,
   putting up with whatever you men might do,
540   for never a peep would you let us
   deliver on your unstatesmanly acts
      no matter how much they upset us,
   but we knew very well, while they sat at home,
      when you'd handled a big issue poorly,
545   and we'd ask you then, with a pretty smile
      though our heart would be grieving us sorely,
   "And what were the terms for a truce, my dear,
      you drew up in assembly this morning?"
   "And what's it to you?" says our husband, "Shut up!"
550   —so, as ever, at this gentle warning
   I of course would discreetly shut up.
KALONIKE: Not me!
   You can bet I would never be quiet!
COMMISSIONER: I'll bet, if you weren't, you were beaten up.
LYSISTRATA: *I'd* shut up, and I do not deny it,
555   but when plan after plan was decided on,
      so bad we could scarcely believe it,
   I would say "This last is so mindless, dear,
      I cannot think how you achieve it!"
   And then he would say, with a dirty look,
560   "Just you think what your spindle is for, dear,
   or your head will be spinning for days on end—
      let the *men* attend to the war, dear."
COMMISSIONER: By Zeus, *he* had the right idea!
LYSISTRATA: You fool!
      Right ideas were quite out of the question,
565   when your reckless policies failed, and yet
      we never could make a suggestion.
   And lately we heard you say so yourselves:
      in the streets there'd be someone lamenting:
   "There's not one man in the country now!"
570   —and we heard many others assenting.
   After that, we conferred through our deputies
      and agreed, having briefly debated,
   to act in common to save all Greece
      at once—for why should we have waited?
575   So now, when we women are talking sense,
      if you'll only agree to be quiet

   and to listen to us as we did to you,
      you'll be very much edified by it.
COMMISSIONER: *You* will edify *us!* I protest!
LYSISTRATA: Shut up!
COMMISSIONER: *I'm* to shut up and listen, you scum, you?!   580
   Sooner death! And a veil on your head at that!
LYSISTRATA: We'll fix that. It may really become you:
   do accept this veil as a present from me.
   Drape it modestly—so—round your head, do you see?
   And now—*not* a word more, sir.   585
KALONIKE: Do accept this dear little wool-basket, too!
   Hitch your girdle and card! Here are beans you may
      chew
   the way all of the nicest Athenians do—
   and the *women* will see to the war, sir!
CHORUS OF WOMEN: Oh women, set your jugs aside and keep   590
   a closer distance:
   our friends may need from us as well some resolute
   assistance.

      Since never shall I weary of the stepping of the dance
   nor will my knees of treading, for these ladies I'll advance
      anywhere they may lead,
      and they're daring indeed,   595
      they have wit, a fine figure, and boldness of heart,
      they are prudent and charming, efficient and smart,
      patriotic and brave!

   But, O manliest grandmothers, onward now!   600
      And you matronly nettles, don't waver!
   but continue to bristle and rage, my dears,
      for you've still got the wind in your favor!

(*The* CHORUS OF WOMEN *and the* OLD MARKET-WOMEN *join.*)

LYSISTRATA: But if only the spirit of tender Love
   and the power of sweet Aphrodite
   were to breathe down over our breasts and thighs   605
      an attraction both melting and mighty,
   and infuse a pleasanter rigor in men,
      raising only their cudgels of passion,
   then I think we'd be known throughout all of Greece
      as makers of peace and good fashion.   610
COMMISSIONER: Having done just what?
LYSISTRATA: Well, first of all
   we shall certainly make it unlawful
   to go madly to market in armor.
AN OLD MARKET-WOMAN: Yes!
   By dear Aphrodite, it's awful!
LYSISTRATA: For now, in the midst of the pottery-stalls   615
   and the greens and the beans and the garlic,
   men go charging all over the market-place
   in full armor and beetling and warlike.
COMMISSIONER: They must do as their valor impels them to!
LYSISTRATA: But it makes a man only look funny   620
   to be wearing a shield with a Gorgon's head
   and be wanting sardines for less money.
OLD MARKET-WOMAN: Well, I saw a huge cavalry-captain once
   on a stallion that scarcely could hold him,
   pouring into his helmet of bronze a pint   625
   of pea-soup an old women had sold him,
   and a Thracian who, brandishing shield and spear
   like some savage Euripides staged once,

when he'd frightened a vendor of figs to death,
630   gobbled up all her ripest and aged ones.
COMMISSIONER: And how, on the international scale,
    can you straighten out the enormous
    confusion among all the states of Greece?
LYSISTRATA: Very easily.
COMMISSIONER: How? Do inform us.
635 LYSISTRATA: When our skein's in a tangle we take it thus
    on our spindles, or haven't you seen us?—
    one on this side and one on the other side,
    and we work out the tangles between us.
    And that is the way we'll undo this war,
640   by exchanging ambassadors, whether
    you like it or not, one from either side,
    and we'll work out the tangles together.
COMMISSIONER: Do you really think that with wools and skeins
    and just being able to spin you
645 can end these momentous affairs, you fools?
LYSISTRATA: With any intelligence in you
    you statesmen would govern as we work wool,
    and in everything Athens would profit.
COMMISSIONER: How so? Do tell.
LYSISTRATA: First, you take raw fleece
650   and you wash the beshittedness off it:
    just so, you should first lay the city out
    on a washboard and beat out the rotters
    and pluck out the sharpers like burrs, and when
    you find tight knots of schemers and plotters
655 who are out for key offices, card them loose,
    but best tear off their heads in addition.
    Then into one basket together card
    all those of a good disposition
    be they citizens, resident aliens, friends,
660   an ally or an absolute stranger,
    even people in debt to the commonwealth,
    you can mix them all in with no danger.
    And the cities which Athens has colonized—
    by Zeus, you should try to conceive them
665 as so many shreddings and tufts of wool
    that are scattered about and not leave them
    to lie around loose, but from all of them
    draw the threads in here, and collect them
    into one big ball and then weave a coat
670   for the people, to warm and protect them.
COMMISSIONER: Now, isn't this awful? They treat the state
    like wool to be beaten and carded,
    who have nothing at all to do with war!
LYSISTRATA: Yes we do, you damnable hard-head!
675 We have none of your honors but we have more
    than double your sufferings by it.
    First of all, we bear sons whom you send to war.
COMMISSIONER: Don't bring up our old sorrows! Be quiet!
LYSISTRATA: And now, when we ought to enjoy ourselves,
680   making much of our prime and our beauty,
    we are sleeping alone because all the men
    are away on their soldierly duty.
    But never mind *us*—when young girls grow old
    in their bedrooms with no men to share them.
685 COMMISSIONER: You seem to forget that men, too, grow old.
LYSISTRATA: By Zeus, but you cannot compare them!

When a man gets back, though he be quite gray,
    he can wed a young girl in a minute,
but the season of woman is very short:
    she must take what she can while she's in it.   690
And you know she must, for when it's past,
    although you're not awfully astute, you're
aware that no man will marry her then
    and she sits staring into the future.
COMMISSIONER: But he who can raise an erection still—   695
LYSISTRATA: Is there some good reason you don't drop dead?
    We'll sell you a coffin if you but will.
    Here's a string of onions to crown your head
    and I'll make a honey-cake large and round
    you can feed to Cerberus underground!   700
FIRST OLD MARKET-WOMAN: Accept these few fillets of leek
    from me!
SECOND OLD MARKET-WOMAN: Let me offer you these for your
    garland, sir!
LYSISTRATA: What now? Do you want something else you see?
    Listen! Charon's calling his passenger—
    will you catch the ferry or still delay   705
    when his other dead want to sail away?
COMMISSIONER: Is it not downright monstrous to treat *me* like
    this?
    By Zeus, I'll go right now to the Commissioners
    and show myself in evidence, just as I am!

(*He begins to withdraw with dignity and his four Scythian policemen.*)

LYSISTRATA: Will you accuse us of not giving you a wake?   710
    But your departed spirit will receive from us
    burnt offerings in due form, two days from now at dawn!

(LYSISTRATA *with the other women goes into the Acropolis. The*
COMMISSIONER, *etc., have left. The* MALE CHORUS *and the mixed*
FEMALE CHORUS *are alone.*)

CHORUS OF MEN: No man now dare fall to drowsing, if he
    wishes to stay free!
    Men, let's strip and gird ourselves for this eventuality!

To me this all begins to have a smell   715
    of bigger things and larger things as well:
    most of all I sniff a tyranny afoot. I'm much afraid
    certain secret agents of the Spartans may have come,
    meeting under cover here, in Cleisthenes' home,
    instigating those damned women by deceit to make a raid   720
    upon our treasury and that great sum
    the city paid my pension from.

Sinister events already!—think of lecturing the state,
    women as they are, and prattling on of things like shields
    of bronze,
    even trying hard to get us reconciled to those we hate—   725
    those of Sparta, to be trusted like a lean wolf when it
    yawns!
    All of this is just a pretext, men, for a dictatorship—
    but to me they shall not dictate! Watch and ward! A
    sword I'll hide
    underneath a branch of myrtle; through the agora I'll slip,
    following Aristogeiton, backing the tyrannicide!   730

(The OLD MEN *pair off to imitate the gestures of the famous group statue of the tyrannicides Harmodius and Aristogeiton.)*

> *Thus* I'll take my stand beside him! Now my rage is
>   goaded raw
> I'm as like as not to clip this damned old woman on the jaw!

CHORUS OF WOMEN: Your own mother will not know you when
>   you come home, if you do!

> Let us first, though, lay our things down, O my dear old
>   friends
> and true.

735
> For now, O fellow-citizens, we would
>   consider what will do our city good.
> Well I may, because it bred me up in wealth and elegance:
>   letting me at seven help with the embroidering
>   of Athena's mantle, and at ten with offering
740
> cakes and flowers. When I was grown and beautiful I had
>   my chance
>   to bear her baskets, at my neck a string
>   of figs, and proud as anything.

> Must I not, then, give my city any good advice I can?
> Need you hold the fact against me that I was not born a man,
745
> when I offer better methods than the present ones, and when
> I've a share in this economy, for I contribute men?
> But, you sad old codgers, *yours* is forfeited on many scores:
> you have drawn upon our treasure dating from the Persian
>   wars,
> what they call grampatrimony, and you've paid no taxes back.
750
> Worse, you've run it nearly bankrupt, and the prospect's
>   pretty black.
> Have you anything to answer? Say you were within the law
> and I'll take this rawhide boot and clip you one across the
>   jaw!

CHORUS OF MEN: Greater insolence than ever!—
>   that's the method that she calls
755
>   "better"—if you would believe her.
> But this threat must be prevented! Every man with both
>   his balls
> must make ready—take our shirts off, for a man must reek
>   of male
> outright—not wrapped up in leafage like an omelet for sale!

760
>   Forward and barefoot: we'll do it again
>   to the death, just as when we resisted
>   tyranny out at Leipsydrion, when
>   we really existed!

765
>   Now or never we must grow
>   young again and, sprouting wings
>   over all our bodies, throw
>   off this heaviness age brings!

> For if any of us give them even just a little hold
> nothing will be safe from their tenacious grasp. They are
>   so bold
> they will soon build ships of war and, with exorbitant intent,
770
> send such navies out against us as Queen Artemisia sent.
> But if they attack with horse, our knights we might as
>   well delete:
> nothing rides so well as woman, with so marvelous a seat,
> never slipping at the gallop. Just look at those Amazons

> in that picture in the Stoa, from their horses bringing bronze
> axes down on men. We'd better grab *these* members of the   775
>   sex
> one and all, arrest them, get some wooden collars on their
>   necks!

CHORUS OF WOMEN: By the gods, if you chagrin me
>   or annoy me, if you dare,
>   I'll turn loose the sow that's in me
> till you rouse the town to help you with the way I've done   780
>   your hair!

> Let us too make ready, women, and our garments quickly
>   doff
> so we'll smell like women angered fit to bite our fingers off!

>   Now I am ready: let one of the men
>   come against me, and *he'll* never hanker
>   after a black bean or garlic again: 785
>   no woman smells ranker!

>   Say a single unkind word,
>   I'll pursue you till you drop,
>   as the beetle did the bird.
>   My revenge will never stop!   790

> Yet you will not worry me so long as Lampito's alive
> and my noble friends in Thebes and other cities still
>   survive.
> You'll not overpower us, even passing seven decrees or eight,
> you, poor brutes, whom everyone and everybody's
>   neighbors hate.
> Only yesterday I gave a party, honoring Hecatë,   795
> but when I invited in the neighbor's child to come and play,
> such a pretty thing from Thebes, as nice and quiet as you
>   please,
> just an eel, they said she couldn't, on account of your
>   decrees.
> You'll go on forever passing such decrees without a check
> till somebody takes you firmly by the leg and breaks your   800
>   neck!

*(*LYSISTRATA *comes out. The* CHORUS OF WOMEN *addresses her in the manner of tragedy.)*

> Oh Queen of this our enterprise and all our hopes,
> wherefore in baleful brooding hast thou issued forth?

LYSISTRATA: The deeds of wicked women and the female mind
>   discourage me and set me pacing up and down.

CHORUS OF WOMEN: What's that? What's that you say?   805

LYSISTRATA: The truth, alas, the truth!

CHORUS OF WOMEN: What is it that's so dreadful? Tell it to
>   your friends.

LYSISTRATA: A shameful thing to tell and heavy not to tell.

CHORUS OF WOMEN: Oh, never hide from me misfortune that is
>   ours!

LYSISTRATA: To put it briefly as I can, we are in heat.   810

CHORUS OF WOMEN: Oh Zeus!

LYSISTRATA: Why call on Zeus? This is the
>   way things are.
> At least it seems I am no longer capable
> of keeping them from men. They are deserting me.
> This morning I caught one of them digging away
> to make a tunnel to Pan's grotto down the slope,   815

another letting herself down the parapet
with rope and pulley, and another climbing down
its sheerest face, and yesterday was one I found
sitting upon a sparrow with a mind to fly
820 down to some well-equipped whoremaster's place in town.
Just as she swooped I pulled her backward by the hair.
They think of every far-fetched excuse they can
for going home. And here comes one deserter now.
You there, where are you running?

FIRST WOMAN: I want to go home,
825   because I left some fine Milesian wools at home
that must be riddled now with moths.

LYSISTRATA: Oh, damn your moths!
Go back inside.

FIRST WOMAN: But I shall come back right away,
just time enough to stretch them out upon my bed.

LYSISTRATA: Stretch nothing out, and don't you go away at all.

830 FIRST WOMAN: But shall I let my wools be ruined?

LYSISTRATA: If you must.

SECOND WOMAN: Oh miserable me! I sorrow for the flax
I left at home unbeaten and unstripped!

LYSISTRATA: One more—
wanting to leave for stalks of flax she hasn't stripped.
Come back here!

SECOND WOMAN: But, by Artemis, I only want
835   to strip my flax. Then I'll come right back here again.

LYSISTRATA: Strip me no strippings! If you start this kind of
thing
some other woman soon will want to do the same.

THIRD WOMAN: O lady Artemis, hold back this birth until
I can get safe to some unconsecrated place!

840 LYSISTRATA: What is this raving?

THIRD WOMAN: I'm about to have a child.

LYSISTRATA: But you weren't pregnant yesterday.

THIRD WOMAN: I am today.
Oh, send me home this instant, dear Lysistrata,
so I can find a midwife.

LYSISTRATA: What strange tale is this?
What is this hard thing you have here?

THIRD WOMAN: The child is male.

845 LYSISTRATA: By Aphrodite, no! You obviously have
some hollow thing of bronze. I'll find out what it is.
You silly thing!—you have Athena's helmet here—
and claiming to be pregnant!

THIRD WOMAN: So I am, by Zeus!

LYSISTRATA: In that case, what's the helmet for?

THIRD WOMAN: So if the pains
850   came on me while I'm still up here, I might give birth
inside the helmet, as I've seen the pigeons do.

LYSISTRATA: What an excuse! The case is obvious. Wait here.
I want to show this bouncing baby helmet off.

(*She passes the huge helmet around the* CHORUS OF WOMEN.)

SECOND WOMAN: But I can't even sleep in the Acropolis,
855   not for an instant since I saw the sacred snake!

FOURTH WOMAN: The owls are what are killing *me.* How can I
sleep
with their eternal whit-to-whoo-to-whit-to-whoo?

LYSISTRATA: You're crazy! Will you stop this hocus-pocus now?

No doubt you miss your husbands: don't you think that they
are missing us as much? I'm sure the nights they pass   860
are just as hard. But, gallant comrades, do bear up,
and face these gruelling hardships yet a little while.
There is an oracle that says we'll win, if we
only will stick together. Here's the oracle.

CHORUS OF WOMAN: Oh, read us what it says!   865

LYSISTRATA: Keep silence, then and hear:
"*Now when to one high place are gathered the fluttering
swallows,
Fleeing the Hawk and the Cock however hotly it follows.
Then will their miseries end, and that which is over be under:
Thundering Zeus will decide.*

A WOMAN: Will *we* lie on top now, I wonder?

LYSISTRATA: *But if the Swallows go fighting each other and*   870
springing and winging
Out of the holy and high sanctuary, then people will never
Say there was any more dissolute bitch of a bird whatsoever."

A WOMAN: The oracle is clear, by Zeus!

LYSISTRATA: By *all* the gods!
So let us not renounce the hardships we endure.
But let us go back in. Indeed, my dearest friends,   875
it would be shameful to betray the oracle.

(*Exeunt into the Acropolis.*)

CHORUS OF MEN: Let me tell you a story I heard one day
when I was a child:
There was once a young fellow Melanion by name
who refused to get married and ran away   880
to the wild.
To the mountains he came
and inhabited there
in a grove
and hunted the hare   885
both early and late
with nets that he wove
and also a hound
and he never came home again, such was his hate,
all women he found   890
so nasty, and we
quite wisely agree.

Let us kiss you, dear old dears!

CHORUS OF WOMEN: With no onions, you'll shed tears!

CHORUS OF MEN: I mean, lift my leg and *kick.*   895

CHORUS OF WOMEN: My, you wear your thicket thick!

CHORUS OF MEN: Great Myronides was rough
at the front and black enough
in the ass to scare his foes.
Just ask anyone who knows: 900
it's with hair that wars are won—
take for instance Phormion.

CHORUS OF WOMEN: Let me tell you a story in answer to
Melanion's case.
There is now a man, Timon, who wanders around   905
in the wilderness, hiding his face from view
in a place
where the brambles abound
so he looks like a chip
off a Fury,   910

curling his lip.
Now Timon retired
in hatred and pure
contempt of all men
915   and he cursed them in words that were truly inspired
     again and again
     but women he found
     delightful and sound.

Would you like your jaw repaired?
920 CHORUS OF MEN: Thank you, no. You've got me scared.
CHORUS OF WOMEN: Let me jump and kick it though.
CHORUS OF MEN: You will let your man-sack show.
CHORUS OF WOMEN: All the same you wouldn't see,
     old and gray as I may be,
925   any superfluity
       of unbarbered hair on me;
       it is plucked and more, you scamp,
       since I singe it with a lamp!

(*Enter* LYSISTRATA *on the wall.*)

LYSISTRATA: Women, O women, come here quickly, here to me!
930 WOMAN: Whatever is it? Tell me! What's the shouting for?
LYSISTRATA: I see a man approaching, shaken and possessed,
     seized and inspired by Aphrodite's power.
     O thou, of Cyprus, Paphos, and Cythera, queen!
     continue straight along this way you have begun!
935 A WOMAN: Whoever he is, where is he?
LYSISTRATA: Near Demeter's shrine.
A WOMAN: Why yes, by Zeus, he is. Whoever can he be?
LYSISTRATA: Well, look at him. Do any of you know him?
MYRRHINA: Yes.
     I do. He's my own husband, too, Cinesias.
LYSISTRATA: Then it's your duty now to turn him on a spit,
940   cajole him and make love to him and not make love,
     to offer everything, short of those things of which
     the wine-cup knows.
MYRRHINA: I'll do it, don't you fear.
LYSISTRATA: And I
     will help you tantalize him. I will stay up here
     and help you roast him slowly. But now, disappear!

(*Enter* CINESIAS.)

945 CINESIAS: Oh how unfortunate I am, gripped by what spasms,
     stretched tight like being tortured on a wheel!
LYSISTRATA: Who's there? Who has got this far past the
     sentries?
CINESIAS: I.
LYSISTRATA: A man?
CINESIAS: A man, for sure.
LYSISTRATA: Then clear away from here.
CINESIAS: Who're you, to throw me out?
LYSISTRATA: The look-out for the day.
950 CINESIAS: Then, for the gods' sake, call Myrrhina out for me.
LYSISTRATA: You don't say! Call Myrrhina out! And who are you?
CINESIAS: Her husband. I'm Cinesias Paionides.
LYSISTRATA: Well, my dear man, hello! Your name is not
     unknown
     among us here and not without a certain fame,
955   because your wife has it forever on her lips.

She can't pick up an egg or quince but she must say:
     Cinesias would enjoy it so!
CINESIAS: How wonderful!
LYSISTRATA: By Aphrodite, yes. And if we chance to talk
     of husbands, your wife interrupts and says the rest
     are nothing much compared to her Cinesias.   960
CINESIAS: Go call her.
LYSISTRATA: Will you give me something if I do?
CINESIAS: Indeed I will, by Zeus, if it is what you want.
     I can but offer what I have, and I have this.
LYSISTRATA: Wait there. I will go down and call her.
CINESIAS: Hurry up!
     because I find no charm whatever left in life   965
     since she departed from the house. I get depressed
     whenever I go into it, and everything
     seems lonely to me now, and when I eat my food
     I find no taste in it at allbecause I'm stiff.
MYRRHINA: (*offstage*) I love him, how I love him! But he   970
     doesn't want
     my love! (*on wall*) So what's the use of calling me to him?
CINESIAS: My sweet little Myrrhina, why do you act like that?
     Come down here.
MYRRHINA: There? By Zeus, I certainly will not.
CINESIAS: Won't you come down, Myrrhina, when I'm calling
     you?
MYRRHINA: Not when you call me without needing   975
     anything.
CINESIAS: Not needing anything? I'm desperate with need.
MYRRHINA: I'm going now.
CINESIAS: Oh no! No, don't go yet! At least
     you'll listen to the baby. Call your mammy, you.
BABY: Mammy mammy mammy!
CINESIAS: What's wrong with you? Have you no pity on your   980
     child
     when it is six days now since he was washed or nursed?
MYRRHINA: Oh, *I* have pity. But his father takes no care of him.
CINESIAS: Come down, you flighty creature, for the child.
MYRRHINA: Oh, what it is to be a mother! I'll come down,
     for what else can I do?   985

(MYRRHINA *exits to reenter below.*)

CINESIAS: It seems to me she's grown
     much younger, and her eyes have a more tender look.
     Even her being angry with me and her scorn
     are just the things that pain me with the more desire.
MYRRHINA: Come let me kiss you, dear sweet little baby mine,
     with such a horrid father. Mammy loves you, though.   990
CINESIAS: But why are you so mean? Why do you listen to
     those other women, giving me such pain?—And you,
     you're suffering yourself.
MYRRHINA: Take your hands off of me!
CINESIAS: But everything we have at home, my things and yours,
     you're letting go to pieces.   995
MYRRHINA: Little do I care!
CINESIAS: Little you care even if your weaving's pecked apart
     and carried off by chickens?
MYRRHINA: (*Bravely.*)   Little I care, by Zeus!
CINESIAS: You have neglected Aphrodite's rituals
     for such a long time now. Won't you come back again?

1000 MYRRHINA: Not I, unless you men negotiate a truce
    and make an end of war.
CINESIAS: Well, if it's so decreed,
    we will do even that.
MYRRHINA: Well, if it's so decreed,
    I will come home again. Not now. I've sworn I won't.
CINESIAS: All right, all right. But now lie down with me once
    more.
1005 MYRRHINA: No! No!—yet I don't say I'm not in love with you.
CINESIAS: You love me? Then why not lie down, Myrrhina dear?
MYRRHINA: Don't be ridiculous! Not right before the child!
CINESIAS: By Zeus, of course not. Manes, carry him back home.
    There now. You see the baby isn't in your way.
1010   Won't you lie down?
MYRRHINA: But *where,* you rogue, just where
    is one to do it?
CINESIAS: Where? Pan's grotto's a fine place.
MYRRHINA: But how could I come back to the Acropolis
    in proper purity?
CINESIAS: Well, there's a spring below
    the grotto—you can very nicely bathe in that.

(*Ekkyklema or inset-scene with grotto.*)

1015 MYRRHINA: And then I'm under oath. What if I break my vows?
CINESIAS: Let me bear all the blame. Don't worry about your
    oath.
MYRRHINA: Wait here, and I'll go get a cot for us.
CINESIAS: No no,
    the ground will do.
MYRRHINA: No, by Apollo! Though you *are*
    so horrid, I can't have you lying on the ground.

(*Leaves.*)

1020 CINESIAS: You know, the woman loves me—*that's* as plain as day.
MYRRHINA: There. Get yourself in bed and I'll take off my
    clothes.
    Oh, what a nuisance! I must go and get a mat.
CINESIAS: What for? I don't need one.
MYRRHINA: Oh yes, by Artemis!
    On the bare cords? How ghastly!
CINESIAS: Let me kiss you now.
1025 MYRRHINA: Oh, very well.
CINESIAS: Wow! Hurry, hurry and come back.

(MYRRHINA *leaves. A long wait.*)

MYRRHINA: Here is the mat. Lie down now, while I get
    undressed.
    Oh, what a nuisance! You don't have a pillow, dear.
CINESIAS: But I don't need one, not one bit!
MYRRHINA: By Zeus, *I* do!

(*Leaves.*)

CINESIAS: Poor prick, the service around here is terrible!
1030 MYRRHINA: Sit up, my dear, jump up! Now I've got
    everything.
CINESIAS: Indeed you have. And now, my golden girl, come
    here.

MYRRHINA: I'm just untying my brassiere. Now don't forget:
    about that treaty—you won't disappoint me, dear?
CINESIAS: By Zeus, no! On my life!
MYRRHINA: You have no blanket, dear.
CINESIAS: By Zeus, I do not need one. I just want to screw. 1035
MYRRHINA: Don't worry, dear, you will. I'll be back right away.

(*Leaves.*)

CINESIAS: This number, with her bedding, means to murder me.
MYRRHINA: Now raise yourself upright.
CINESIAS: But *this* is upright now!
MYRRHINA: Wouldn't you like some perfume?
CINESIAS: By Apollo, no!
MYRRHINA: By Aphrodite, yes! You must—like it or not. 1040

(*Leaves.*)

CINESIAS: Lord Zeus! Just let the perfume spill! That's all I ask!
MYRRHINA: Hold out your hand. Take some of this and rub it on.
CINESIAS: This perfume, by Apollo, isn't sweet at all.
    It smells a bit of stalling—not of wedding nights!
MYRRHINA: I brought the *Rhodian* perfume! How absurd of me! 1045
CINESIAS: It's fine! Let's keep it.
MYRRHINA: You *will* have your little joke.

(*Leaves.*)

CINESIAS: Just let me at the man who first distilled perfumes!
MYRRHINA: Try this, in the long vial.
CINESIAS: I've got one like it, dear.
    But don't be tedious. Lie down. And please don't bring
    anything more. 1050
MYRRHINA: (*Going.*) That's what I'll do, by Artemis!
    I'm taking off my shoes. But dearest, don't forget
    you're going to vote for peace.
CINESIAS: I will consider it.
    She has destroyed me, murdered me, that woman has!
    On top of which she's got me skinned and gone away!

        What shall I do? Oh, whom shall I screw, 1055
        cheated of dear Myrrhina, the first
        beauty of all, a creature divine?
        How shall I tend this infant of mine?
        Find me a pimp: it has to be nursed!
CHORUS OF MEN: (*In tragic style, as if to Prometheus or
    Andromeda bound.*)
        In what dire woe, how heavy-hearted 1060
        I see thee languishing, outsmarted!
          I pity thee, alas I do.
        What kidney could endure such pain,
        what spirit could, what balls, what back,
        what loins, what sacroiliac, 1065
        if they came under such a strain
        and never had a morning screw?
CINESIAS: O Zeus! the twinges! Oh, the twitches!
CHORUS OF MEN: And this is what she did to you,
    that vilest, hatefullest of bitches! 1070
CINESIAS: Oh nay, by Zeus, she's dear and sweet!
CHORUS OF MEN: How can she be? She's vile, O Zeus, she's vile!
    Oh treat her, Zeus, like so much wheat—
    O God of Weather, hear my prayer—

1075   and raise a whirlwind's mighty blast
to roll her up into a pile
and carry her into the sky
far up and up and then at last
drop her and land her suddenly
1080   astride that pointed penis there!

(*The ekkyklema turns, closing the inset-scene. Enter, from opposite sides, a* SPARTAN HERALD *and an* ATHENIAN OFFICIAL.)

SPARTAN: Wheah is the Senate-house of the Athenians?
Ah wish to see the chaihman. Ah have news fo him.
ATHENIAN: And who are you? Are you a Satyr or a man?
SPARTAN: Ah am a herald, mah young friend, yes, by the gods,
1085   and Ah have come from Sparta to negotiate.
ATHENIAN: And yet you come here with a spear under your arm?
SPARTAN: Not Ah, bah Zeus, not Ah!
ATHENIAN: Why do you turn around?
Why throw your cloak out so in front? Has the long trip given you a swelling?
SPARTAN: Ah do think the man is queah!
1090 ATHENIAN: But you have an erection, oh you reprobate!
SPARTAN: Bah Zeus, Ah've no sech thing! And don't you fool around!
ATHENIAN: And what have you got there?
SPARTAN: A Spahtan scroll-stick, suh.
ATHENIAN: Well, if it is, *this* is a Spartan scroll-stick, too.
But look, I know what's up: you can tell *me* the truth.
1095   Just how are things with you in Sparta: tell me that.
SPARTAN: Theah is uprising in all Spahta. Ouah allies
are all erect as well. We need ouah milkin'-pails.
ATHENIAN: From where has this great scourge of frenzy fallen on you?
From Pan?
SPARTAN: No, Ah think Lampito began it all,
1100   and then, the othah women throughout Spahta joined
togethah, just lahk at a signal fo a race,
and fought theah husbands off and drove them from theah cunts.
ATHENIAN: So, how're you getting on?
SPARTAN: We suffah. Through the town
we walk bent ovah as if we were carrying
1105   lamps in the wind. The women will not let us touch
even theah berries, till we all with one acco'd
have made a peace among the cities of all Greece.
ATHENIAN: This is an international conspiracy
launched by the women! Now I comprehend it all!
1110   Return at once to Sparta. Tell them they must send
ambassadors fully empowered to make peace.
And our Assembly will elect ambassadors
from our side, when I say so, showing them this prick.
SPARTAN: Ah'll run! Ah'll flah! Fo all you say is excellent!
1115 CHORUS OF MEN: No wild beast is more impossible than
woman is to fight,
nor is fire, nor has the panther such unbridled appetite!
CHORUS OF WOMEN: Well you know it, yet you go on warring
with me without end,
when you might, you cross-grained creature, have me as a
trusty friend.

CHORUS OF MEN: Listen: I will never cease from hating women
till I die!
CHORUS OF WOMEN: Any time you like. But meanwhile is 1120
there any reason why
I should let you stand there naked, looking so ridiculous?
I am only coming near you, now, to slip your coat on, thus.
CHORUS OF MEN: That was very civil of you, very kind to treat me so,
when in such uncivil rage I took it off a while ago.
CHORUS OF WOMEN: Now you're looking like a man again, 1125
and not ridiculous.
If you hadn't hurt my feelings, I would not have made a fuss,
I would even have removed that little beast that's in your eye.
CHORUS OF MEN: *That* is what was hurting me! Well, won't
you take my ring to pry
back my eyelid? Rake the beast out. When you have it, let me see,
for some time now it's been at my eye and irritating me. 1130
CHORUS OF WOMEN: Very well, I will—though you were *born*
an irritable man.
What a monster of a gnat, by Zeus! Look at it if you can.
Don't you see it? It's a native of great marshes, can't you tell?
CHORUS OF MEN: Much obliged, by Zeus! The brute's been
digging at me like a well!
So that now you have removed it, streams of tears come 1135
welling out.
CHORUS OF WOMEN: I will dry them. You're the meanest man
alive, beyond a doubt,
yet I will, and kiss you, too.
CHORUS OF MEN: Don't kiss me!
CHORUS OF WOMEN: If you will or not!
CHORUS OF MEN: Damn you! Oh, what wheedling flatterers
you all are, born and bred!
That old proverb is quite right and not inelegantly said:
"There's no living *with* the bitches and, without them, 1140
even *less*"—
so I might as well make peace with you, and from now on,
I guess,
I'll do nothing mean to you and, from you, suffer nothing
wrong.
So let's draw our ranks together now and start a little song:

For a change, we're not preparing
any mean remark or daring 1145
aimed at any man in town,
but the very opposite: we plan to do and say
only good to everyone,
when the ills we have already are sufficient anyway.
Any man or woman who 1150
wants a little money, oh
say three minas, maybe two,
kindly let us know.
What we have is right in here.
(Notice we have purses, too!) 1155
And if ever peace appear,
he who takes our loan today
never need repay.

We are having guests for supper,
allies asked in by our upper 1160
classes to improve the town.

There's pea-soup, and I had killed a sucking-pig of mine:
I shall see it is well done,
so you will be tasting something very succulent and fine.

1165 Come to see us, then, tonight
early, just as soon as you
have a bath and dress up right:
bring your children, too.
Enter boldly, never mind
1170 asking anyone in sight.
Go straight in and you will find
you are quite at home there, but
all the doors are shut.

And here come the Spartan ambassadors,
1175 dragging beards that are really the biggest I
have ever beheld, and around their thighs
they are wearing some sort of a pig-sty.

Oh men of Sparta, let me bid you welcome first,
and then you tell us how you are and why you come.
1180 SP. AMB.: What need is theah to speak to you in many words?
Fo you may see youahself in what a fix we come.
CHORUS OF MEN: Too bad! Your situation has become
terribly hard and seems to be at fever-pitch.
SP. AMB.: Unutterably so! And what is theah to say?
1185 Let someone bring us peace on any tuhms he will!
CHORUS OF MEN: And here I see some natives of Athenian soil,
holding their cloaks far off their bellies, like the best
wrestlers, who sicken at the touch of cloth. It seems
that overtraining may bring on this strange disease.
1190 ATH. AMB.: Will someone tell us where to find Lysistrata?
We're men, and here we are, in this capacity.
CHORUS OF MEN: This symptom and that other one sound
much alike.
Toward morning I expect convulsions do occur?
ATH. AMB.: By Zeus, we are exhausted with just doing that,
1195 so, if somebody doesn't reconcile us quick,
there's nothing for it: we'll be screwing Cleisthenes.
CHORUS OF MEN: Be carefulput your cloaks on, or you might
be seen
by some young blade who knocks the phalluses off herms.
ATH. AMB.: By Zeus, an excellent idea!
SP. AMB.: (*Having overheard.*)   Yes, bah the gods!
1200 It altogethah is. Quick, let's put on our cloaks.

(*Both groups cover quick and then recognize each other with full
diplomatic pomp.*)

ATH. AMB.: Greetings, O men of Sparta! (*To his group.*) We have
been disgraced!
SP. AMB.: (*To one of his group.*) Mah dearest fellah, what a
dreadful thing fo *us,*
if these Athenians had seen ouah wo'st defeat!
ATH. AMB.: Come now, O Spartans: one must specify each point.
1205 Why have you come here?
SP. AMB.:   To negotiate a peace.
We ah ambassadahs.
ATH. AMB.:   Well put. And so are we.
Therefore, why do we not call in Lysistrata,
she who alone might get us to agree on terms?
SP. AMB.: Call her or any man, even a Lysistratus!

CHORUS OF MEN: But you will have no need, it seems, to call 1210
her now,
for here she is. She heard you and is coming out.
CHORUS OF MEN *and* CHORUS OF WOMEN: All hail, O manliest
woman of all!
It is time for you now to be turning
into something still better, more dreadful, mean,
unapproachable, charming, discerning, 1215
for here are the foremost nations of Greece,
bewitched by your spells like a lover,
who have come to you, bringing you all their claims,
and to *you* turning everything over.
LYSISTRATA: The work's not difficult, if one can catch them now 1220
while they're excited and not making passes at
each other. I will soon find out. Where's *HARMONY?*

(*A naked maid, perhaps wearing a large ribbon reading* HARMONY,
appears from inside.)

Go take the Spartans first, and lead them over here,
not with a rough hand nor an overbearing one,
nor, as our husbands used to do this, clumsily, 1225
but like a woman, in our most familiar style:
If he won't give his hand, then lead him by the prick.
And now, go bring me those Athenians as well,
leading them by whatever they will offer you.
O men of Sparta, stand right here, close by my side, 1230
and you stand over there, and listen to my words.
I am a woman, yes, but there is mind in me.
In native judgment I am not so badly off,
and, having heard my father and my elders talk
often enough, I have some cultivation, too. 1235
And so, I want to take and scold you, on both sides,
as you deserve, for though you use a lustral urn
in common at the altars, like blood-relatives,
when at Olympia, Delphi, or Thermopylae—
how many others I might name if I took time!— 1240
yet, with barbarian hordes of enemies at hand,
it is Greek men, it is Greek cities, you destroy.
That is one argument so far, and it is done.
ATH. AMB.: My prick is skinned alive—that's what's destroying *me.*
LYSISTRATA: Now, men of Sparta—for I shall address you first— 1245
do you not know that once one of your kings came here
and as a suppliant of the Athenians
sat by our altars, death-pale in his purple robe,
and begged us for an army? For Messenë then
oppressed you, and an earthquake from the gods as well. 1250
Then Cimon went, taking four thousand infantry,
and saved the whole of Lacedaemon for your state.
That is the way Athenians once treated you;
you ravage their land now, which once received you well.
ATH. AMB.: By Zeus, these men are in the wrong, Lysistrata! 1255
SP. AMB.: (*With his eyes on* HARMONY.) We'ah wrong . . .
What an unutterably lovely ass!
LYSISTRATA: Do you suppose I'm letting you Athenians off?
Do you not know that once the Spartans in their turn,
when you were wearing the hide-skirts of slavery,
came with their spears and slew many Thessalians, 1260
many companions and allies of Hippias?

They were the only ones who fought for you that day,
freed you from tyranny and, for the skirt of hide,
gave back your people the wool mantle of free men.
1265 SP. AMB.: Ah nevah saw a woman broadahin her views.
ATH. AMB.: And I have never seen a lovelier little nook.
LYSISTRATA: So why, when you have done each other so much
    good,
    go on fighting with no end of malevolence?
    Why don't you make a peace? Tell me, what's in your way?
1270 SP. AMB.: Whah, *we* ah willin', if *they* will give up to us
    that very temptin' cuhve. (*Of* HARMONY, *as hereafter.*)
LYSISTRATA: What curve, my friend?
SP. AMB.:   The bay
    of Pylos, which we've wanted and felt out so long.
ATH. AMB.: No, by Poseidon, you will not get into that!
LYSISTRATA: Good friend, do let them have it.
ATH. AMB.:   No! What other town
1275   can we manipulate so well?
LYSISTRATA: Ask them for one.
ATH. AMB.: Damn, let me think! Now first suppose you cede
    to us
    that bristling tip of land, Echinos, behind which
    the gulf of Malia recedes, and those long walls,
    the legs on which Megara reaches to the sea.
1280 SP. AMB.: No, mah deah man, not *everything,* bah Castah, no!
LYSISTRATA: Oh, give them up. Why quarrel for a pair of legs?
ATH. AMB.: I'd like to strip and get to plowing right away.
SP. AMB.: And *Ah* would lahk to push manuah, still earliah.
LYSISTRATA: When you have made a peace, then you will do
    all that.
1285   But if you want to do it, first deliberate,
    go and inform your allies and consult with them.
ATH. AMB.: Oh, damn our allies, my good woman! We are stiff.
    Will all of our allies not stand resolved with us—
    namely, to screw?
SP. AMB.:   And so will ouahs, Ah'll guarantee.
1290 ATH. AMB.: Our mercenaries, even, will agree with us.
LYSISTRATA: Excellent. Now to get you washed and purified
    so you may enter the Acropolis, where we
    women will entertain you out of our supplies.
    You will exchange your pledges there and vows for peace.
1295   And after that each one of you will take his wife,
    departing then for home.
ATH. AMB.:   Let's go in right away.
SP. AMB.: Lead on, ma'am, anywheah you lahk.
ATH. AMB.:   Yes, and be quick.

(*Exeunt into Acropolis.*)

CHORUS OF MEN *and* CHORUS OF WOMEN:
    All the rich embroideries, the
    scarves, the gold accessories, the
1300   trailing gowns, the robes I own
    I begrudge to no man: let him take what things he will
    for his children or a grown
    daughter who must dress for the procession up Athena's
    hill.
        Freely of my present stocks
1305   I invite you all to take.
    There are here no seals nor locks

very hard to break.
Search through every bag and box,
Look—you will find nothing there   1310
if your eyesight isn't fine—
sharper far than mine!

Are there any of you needing
food for all the slaves you're feeding,
all your little children, too?

I have wheat in tiny grains for you, the finest sort,   1315
and I also offer you
plenty of the handsome strapping grains that slaves get by the
    quart.

        So let any of the poor
        visit me with bag or sack
        which my slave will fill with more   1320
        wheat than they can pack,
        giving each his ample share.
        Might I add that at my door
        I have watch-dogs? So beware.
        Come too close by day or night,   1325
        you will find they bite.

(*Voice of drunken* ATHENIANS *from inside.*)

FIRST ATHENIAN: Open the door! (*Shoves the* PORTER *aside.*)
                    And will you get out of my way?

(*A second drunken* ATHENIAN *follows. The first sees the* CHORUS.)

    What are you sitting there for? Shall I, with this torch,
    burn you alive? (*Drops character.*)
                    How vulgar! Oh, how commonplace!
    I can not do it!   1330

(*Starts back in. The second* ATHENIAN *stops him and remonstrates
with him in a whisper. The first turns and addresses the audience.*)

                Well, if it really must be done
    to please you, we shall face it and go through with it.
CHORUS OF MEN *and* CHORUS OF WOMEN:
    And we shall face it and go through with it with you.
FIRST ATHENIAN: (*In character again, extravagantly.*)
    Clear out of here! Or you'll be wailing for your hair!

(CHORUS OF WOMEN *scours away in mock terror.*)

    Clear out of here! so that the Spartans can come out
    and have no trouble leaving, after they have dined.   1335

(CHORUS OF MEN *scours away in mock terror.*)

SECOND ATHENIAN: I never saw a drinking-party like this
    one:
    even the Spartans were quite charming, and of course
    we make the cleverest company, when in our cups.
FIRST ATHENIAN: You're right, because when sober we are not
    quite sane.
    If I can only talk the Athenians into it,   1340
    we'll always go on any embassy quite drunk,
    for now, going to Sparta sober, we're so quick
    to look around and see what trouble we can make
    that we don't listen to a single word they say—

1345   instead we think we hear them say what they do not—
   and none of our reports on anything agree.
   But just now everything was pleasant. If a man
   got singing words belonging to another song,
1350   we all applauded and swore falsely it was fine!
   But here are those same people coming back again
   to the same spot! Go and be damned, the pack of you!

(*The* CHORUS OF MEN AND WOMEN, *having thrown off their masks, put on other cloaks, and rushed back on stage, stays put.*)

SECOND ATHENIAN: Yes, damn them, Zeus! Just when the
   party's coming out!

(*The party comes rolling out.*)

A SPARTAN: (*To another.*) Mah very chahmin friend, will you
   take up youah flutes?
1355 Ah'll dance the dipody and sing a lovely song
   of us and the Athenians, of both at once!
FIRST ATHENIAN: (*As pleasantly as he can.*)
   Oh yes, take up your little reeds, by all the gods:
   I very much enjoy seeing you people dance.

SPARTAN: Memory, come,
1360   come inspiah thah young
        votaries to song,
      come inspiah theah dance!

(*Other* SPARTANS *join.*)

      Bring thah daughtah, bring the sweet
        Muse, fo well she knows
1365   us and the Athenians,
      how at Ahtemisium
   they in godlike onslaught rose
   hahd against the Puhsian fleet,
      drove it to defeat!
1370   Well she knows the Spartan waws,
      how Leonidas
      in the deadly pass
      led us on lahk baws
   whettin' shahp theah tusks, how sweat
1375   on ouah cheeks in thick foam flowahed,
   off ouah legs how thick it showahed,
      fo the Puhsian men were mo'
       than the sands along the sho'.
   Goddess, huntress, Ahtemis,
1380   slayeh of the beasts, descend:
   vuhgin goddess, come to this
   feast of truce to bind us fast
   so ouah peace may nevah end.
   Now let friendship, love, and wealth
1385   come with ouah acco'd at last.
   May we stop ouah villainous
   wahly foxy stealth!
      Come, O huntress, heah to us,
      heah, O vuhgin, neah to us!

LYSISTRATA: Come, now that all the rest has been so well
   arranged,
   you Spartans take these women home; these others, you. 1390
   Let husband stand beside his wife, and let each wife
   stand by her husband: then, when we have danced a dance
   to thank the gods for our good fortune, let's take care
   hereafter not tǫ make the same mistakes again.
ATHENIAN: Bring on the chorus! Invite the three Graces to 1395
   follow,
   and then call on Artemis, call her twin brother,
   the leader of choruses, healer Apollo!
CHORUS OF MEN AND WOMEN: (*Joins.*) Pray for their friendliest
   favor, the one and the other.
   Call Dionysus, his tender eyes casting
   flame in the midst of his Maenads ecstatic with dancing. 1400
   Call upon Zeus, the resplendent in fire,
   call on his wife, rich in honor and ire,
   call on the powers who possess everlasting
   memory, call them to aid,
   call them to witness the kindly, entrancing 1405
   peace Aphrodite has made!
      Alalai!
        Bound, and leap high! Alalai!
      Cry, as for victory, cry
      Alalai! 1410
LYSISTRATA: Sing us a new song, Spartans, capping our new song.
SPARTANS: Leave thah favohed mountain's height,
   Spahtan Muse, come celebrate
   Amyclae's lord with us and great
   Athena housed in bronze; 1415
   praise Tyndareus' paih of sons,
   gods who pass the days in spoht
   wheah the cold Eurotas runs.

(*General dancing.*)

   Now to tread the dance,
   now to tread it light, 1420
   praising Spahta, wheah you find
      love of singing quickened bah the pounding beat
        of dancing feet,
   when ouah guhls lahk foals cavoht
   wheah the cold Eurotas runs, 1425
   when they fleetly bound and prance
      till theah haih unfilleted shakes in the wind,
   as of Maenads brandishin'
   ahvied wands and revelin',
      Leda's daughtah, puah and faiah, 1430
      leads the holy dances theah.
FULL CHORUS: (*As everyone leaves dancing.*)
   So come bind up youah haih with youah hand,
      with youah feet make a bound
   lahk a deeah; fo the chorus clap out
      an encouragin' sound, 1435
   singin' praise of the temple of bronze
      housin' her we adaw:
   sing the praise of Athena: the goddess unvanquished in
   waw!

CRITICAL CONTEXTS

ARISTOTLE (384–322 BCE)

from *The Poetics* (c. 335 BCE)

TRANSLATED BY GERALD F. ELSE

Born near Macedonia, Aristotle entered the Academy in Athens at the age of seventeen to study with Plato. After Plato's death, Aristotle conducted research in natural history, mainly botany and zoology, throughout the Aegean region and served as the tutor of the young Alexander the Great in Macedon before returning to Athens to found the Lyceum in 355 BCE.

Aristotle wrote extensively on topics ranging from ethics, rhetoric, and metaphysics to physics and natural history. In The Poetics, *he analyzes the field of poetry into different "species" or genres (epic, tragedy, comedy, dithyramb) and attempts to discover the basic features of each. The Poetics demonstrates Aristotle's extensive knowledge of drama, which he uses to refine a keen sense of the form and purpose of tragedy. We should remember that* The Poetics *was written sometime after 335 BCE, roughly a century after the height of the Athenian theater. And although* The Poetics *is the cornerstone of Western dramatic criticism, the meaning of several of Aristotle's key terms—**MIMESIS** (imitation),* **CATHARSIS** *(purgation), and* **HAMARTIA** *(error)—remain controversial.*

Students approaching The Poetics *for the first time often have difficulty with the compressed logic of Aristotle's text, which may have formed something akin to notes for a lecture—a basis for expansion and discussion. Given Aristotle's representation of poetry according to natural "species," one way into his thinking may be to attempt to relate the functions of the various parts of tragedy: What is the relationship between Aristotle's conception of plot and of character? What is the logic that sustains his claim that plot is the principal element of tragedy, more important than character, language, or spectacle? What is the nature of "imitation," as Aristotle expresses it here? Given Aristotle's sense of just and unjust imitation, should we take imitation as a straightforward synonym for realism?*

BASIC CONSIDERATIONS

The art of poetic composition in general and its various species, the function and effect of each of them; how the plots should be constructed if the composition is to be an artistic success; how many other component elements are involved in the process, and of what kind; and similarly all the other questions that fall under this same branch of inquiry—these are the problems we shall discuss; let us begin in the right and natural way, with basic principles.

Epic composition, then; the writing of tragedy, and of comedy also; the composing of dithyrambs; and the greater part of the making of music with flute and lyre: these are all in point of fact, taken collectively, imitative processes. They differ from each other, however, in three ways, namely by virtue of having (1) different means, (2) different objects, and (3) different methods of imitation.

THE DIFFERENTIATION ACCORDING TO MEDIUM

First, in the same way that certain people imitate a variety of things by means of shapes and colors, making visible replicas of them (some doing this on the basis of art, others out of habit), while another group produces its mimicry with the voice, so in the case of the arts we just mentioned: they all carry on their imitation through the media of rhythm, speech, and melody, but with the latter two used separately or together. Thus the arts of flute and lyre music, and any others of similar nature and effect, such as the art of the panpipe, produce their imitation using melody and rhythm alone, while there is another which does so using speeches or verses alone, bare of music, and either mixing the verses with one another or employing just one certain kind—an art which is, as it happens, nameless up to the present time. In fact, we could not even assign a common name to the mimes of Sophron and Xenarchus and the Socratic discourses: nor again if somebody should compose his imitation in trimeters or elegiac couplets or certain other verses of that kind. (Except people do link up poetic composition with verse and speak of "elegiac poets," "epic poets," not treating them as poets by virtue of their imitation, but employing the term as a common appellation going along with the use of verse. And in fact the name is also applied to anyone who treats a medical or scientific topic in verses, yet Homer and Empedocles actually have nothing in common except their verse; hence the proper term for the one is "poet," for the other, "science-writer" rather than "poet.") and likewise if someone should mix all the kinds of verse together in composing his imitation, as Chaeremon composed a *Centaur* using all the verses.

Such is the disjunction we feel is called for in these cases. There are on the other hand certain arts which use all the aforesaid media, I mean such as rhythm, song, and verse. The composition of dithyrambs and of nomes does so, and both tragedy and comedy. But there is a difference in that some of these arts use all the media at once while others use them in different parts of the work.

These then are the differentiations of the poetic arts with respect to the media in which the poets carry on their imitation.

THE OBJECTS OF IMITATION

Since those who imitate men in action, and these must necessarily be either worthwhile or worthless people (for definite characters tend pretty much to develop in men of action), it follows that they imitate men either better or worse than the average, as the painters do—for Polygnotus used to portray superior and Pauson inferior men; and it is evident that each of the forms of imitation aforementioned will include these differentiations, that is, will differ by virtue of imitating objects which are different in this sense. Indeed, it is possible for these dissimilarities to turn up in flute and lyre playing, and also in prose dialogues and bare verses: Thus Homer imitated superior men and Hegemon of Thasos, the inventor of parody, and Nicochares, the author of the *Deiliad,* inferior ones, likewise in connection with dithyrambs and nomes, for one can make the imitation the way Timotheus and Philoxenus did their *Cyclopes.* Finally, the difference between tragedy and comedy coincides exactly with the master-difference: Namely the one tends to imitate people better, the other one people worse, than the average.

THE MODES OF IMITATION

The third way of differentiating these arts is by the mode of imitation. For it is possible to imitate the same objects, and in the same media, (1) by narrating part of the time and dramatizing the rest of the time, which is the way Homer composes (mixed mode), or (2) with the same person continuing without change (straight narrative), or (3) with all the persons who are performing the imitation acting, that is, carrying on for themselves (straight dramatic mode).

JOTTINGS, CHIEFLY ON COMEDY

Poetic imitation, then, shows these three *differentiae,* as we said at the beginning: in the media, objects, and modes of imitation. So in one way Sophocles would be the same (kind of) imitator as Homer, since they both imitate worthwhile people, and in another way the same as Aristophanes, for they both imitate people engaged in action, doing things. In fact some authorities maintain that that is why plays are called dramas, because the imitation is of men acting (*drôntas,* from *drân,* "do, act"). It is also the reason why both tragedy and comedy are claimed by the Dorians: comedy by

the Megarians, both those from hereabouts, who say that it came into being during the period of their democracy, and those in Sicily, and tragedy by some of those in the Peloponnese. They use the names "comedy" and "drama" as evidence; for *they* say that they call their outlying villages *kômai* while the Athenians call theirs "demes" (*dêmoi*)—the assumption being that the participants in comedy were called *kômôidoi* not from their being revelers but because they wandered from one village to another, being degraded and excluded from the city—and that they call "doing" or "acting" *drân* while the Athenians designate it by *prattein.*

THE ORIGIN AND DEVELOPMENT OF POETRY

So much, then, for the *differentiae* of imitation, their number and identity. As to the origin of the poetic art as a whole, it stands to reason that two operative causes brought it into being, both of them rooted in human nature. Namely (1) the habit of imitating is congenital to human beings from childhood (actually man differs from the other animals in that he is the most imitative and learns his first lessons through imitation), and so is (2) the pleasure that all men take in works of imitation. A proof of this is what happens in our experience. There are things which we see with pain so far as they themselves are concerned but whose images, even when executed in very great detail, we view with pleasure. Such is the case for example with renderings of the least favored animals, or of cadavers. The cause of this also is that learning is eminently pleasurable not only to philosophers but to the rest of mankind in the same way, although their share in the pleasure is restricted. For the reason they take pleasure in seeing the images is that in the process of viewing they find themselves learning, that is, reckoning what kind a given thing belongs to: "This individual is a So-and-so." Because if the viewer happens not to have seen such a thing before, the reproduction will not produce the pleasure *qua* reproduction but through its workmanship or color or something else of that sort.

Since, then, imitation comes naturally to us, and melody and rhythm too (it is obvious that verses are segments of the respective rhythms), in the beginning it was those who were most gifted in these respects who, developing them little by little, brought the making of poetry into being out of improvisations. And the poetic enterprise split into two branches, in accordance with the two kinds of character. Namely, the soberer spirits were imitating noble actions and the actions of noble persons, while the cheaper ones were imitating those of the worthless, producing lampoons and invectives at first just as the other sort were producing hymns and encomia. . . .In them (that is, the invectives), in accordance with what is suitable and fitting, iambic verse also put in its appearance; indeed that is why it is called "iambic" now, because it is the verse in which they used to "iambize," that is, lampoon each other. And so some of the early poets became composers of epic, the others of iambic, verses.

Now it happens that we cannot name anyone before Homer as the author of that kind of poem (that is, an iambic poem), though it stands to reason that there were many who were; but from Homer on we can do so: thus his *Margites* and other poems of that sort. However, just as on the serious side Homer was most truly a poet, since he was the only one who not only composed well but constructed dramatic imitations, so too he was the first to adumbrate the forms of comedy by producing a (1) dramatic presentation, and not of invective but of (2) the ludicrous. For as the *Iliad* stands in relation to our tragedies, so the *Margites* stands in relation to our comedies.

Once tragedy and comedy had been partially brought to light, those who were out in pursuit of the two kinds of poetic activity, in accordance with their own respective natures, became in the one case comic poets instead of iambic poets, in the other case producers of tragedies instead of epics, because these genres were higher and more esteemed than the others. Now to review the question whether even tragedy is adequate to the basic forms or not—a question which is (can be) judged both by itself, in the abstract, and in relationship to our theater audiences—that is another story. However that may be, it did spring from an improvisational beginning (both it and comedy: the one from those who led off the dithyramb, the other from those who did so for the phallic performances [?] which still remain on the program in many of our cities); it did expand gradually, each feature being further developed as it appeared; and after it had gone through a number of phases it stopped upon attaining its full natural growth. Thus Aeschylus was the first to expand the troupe of assisting actors from one to two, shorten the choral parts, and see to it that the dialogue takes first place; (. . .) at the same time the verse became iambic trimeter instead of trochaic tetrameter. For in the beginning they used the tetrameter because the form of composition was "satyr-like," that is, more given over to dancing, but when speech came along the very nature of the case turned up the appropriate verse. For iambic is the most speech-like of verses. An indication of this is that we speak more iambics than any other kind of verse in our conversation with each other, whereas we utter hexameters rarely, and when we do we abandon the characteristic tone-pattern of ordinary speech.

Further, as to plurality of episodes and the other additions which are recorded as having been made to tragedy, let our account stop here; for no doubt it would be burdensome to record them in detail.

COMEDY

Comedy is as we said it was, an imitation of persons who are inferior; not, however, going all the way to full villainy, but imitating the ugly, of which the ludicrous is one part. The ludicrous, that is, is a failing or a piece of ugliness which causes no pain or destruction; thus, to go no farther, the comic mask is something ugly and distorted but painless.

Now the stages of development of tragedy, and the men who were responsible for them, have not escaped notice, but comedy did escape notice in the beginning because it was not taken seriously. (In fact it was late in its history that the presiding magistrate officially "granted a chorus" to the comic poets; until then they were volunteers.) Thus comedy already possessed certain defining characteristics when the first "comic poets," so-called, appear in the record. Who gave it masks, or prologues, or troupes of actors and all that sort of thing, is not known. The composing of plots came originally from Sicily; of the Athenian poets, Crates was the first to abandon the lampooning mode and compose arguments, that is, plots, of a general nature.

EPIC AND TRAGEDY

Well then, epic poetry followed in the wake of tragedy up to the point of being a (1) good-sized (2) imitation (3) in verse (4) of people who are to be taken seriously; but in its having its verse unmixed with any other and being narrative in character, there they differ. Further, so far as its length is concerned tragedy tries as hard as it can to exist during a single daylight period, or to vary but little, while the epic is not limited in its time and so differs in that respect. Yet originally they used to do this in tragedies just as much as they did in epic poems.

The constituent elements are partly identical and partly limited to tragedy. Hence anybody who knows about good and bad tragedy knows about epic also; for the elements that the epic possesses appertain to tragedy as well, but those of tragedy are not all found in the epic.

TRAGEDY AND ITS SIX CONSTITUENT ELEMENTS

Our discussions of imitative poetry in hexameters, and of comedy, will come later; at present let us deal with tragedy, recovering from what has been said so far the definition of its essential nature, as it was in development. Tragedy, then, is a process of imitating an action which has serious implications, is complete, and possesses magnitude; by means of language which has been made sensuously attractive, with each of its varieties found separately in the parts; enacted by the persons themselves and not presented through narrative; through a course of pity and fear completing the purification of tragic acts which have those emotional characteristics. By "language made sensuously attractive" I mean language that has rhythm and melody, and by "its varieties found separately" I mean the fact that certain parts of the play are carried on through spoken verses alone and others the other way round, through song.

Now first of all, since they perform the imitation through action (by acting it), the adornment of their visual appearance will perforce constitute some part of the making of tragedy; and song-composition and verbal expression also, for those are the media in which they perform the imitation. By "verbal expression" I mean the actual composition of the verses, and by "song-composition" something whose meaning is entirely clear.

Next, since it is an imitation of an action and is enacted by certain people who are performing the action, and since those people must necessarily have certain traits both of character and thought (for it is thanks to these two factors that we speak of people's actions also as having a defined character, and it is in accordance with their actions that all either succeed or fail); and since the imitation of the action is the plot, for by "plot" I mean here the structuring of the events, and by the "characters" that in accordance with which we say that the persons who are acting have a defined moral character, and by "thought" all the passages in which they attempt to prove some thesis or set forth an opinion—it follows of necessity, then, that tragedy as a whole has just six constituent elements, in relation to the essence that makes it a distinct species; and they are plot, characters, verbal expression, thought, visual adornment, and song-composition. For the elements by which they imitate are two (i.e., verbal expression and song-composition), the manner in which they imitate is one (visual adornment), the things they imitate are three (plot, characters, thought), and there is nothing more beyond these. These then are the constituent forms they use.

THE RELATIVE IMPORTANCE OF THE SIX ELEMENTS

The greatest of these elements is the structuring of the incidents. For tragedy is an imitation not of men but of a life, an action, and they have moral quality in accordance with their characters but are happy or unhappy in accordance with their actions; hence they are not active in order to imitate their characters, but they include the characters along with the actions for the sake of the latter. Thus the structure of events, the plot, is the goal of tragedy, and the goal is the greatest thing of all.

Again: a tragedy cannot exist without a plot, but it can without characters: thus the tragedies of most of our modern poets are devoid of character, and in general many poets are like that; so also with the relationship between Zeuxis and Polygnotus, among the painters: Polygnotus is a good portrayer of character, while Zeuxis' painting has no dimension of character at all.

Again: if one strings end to end speeches that are expressive of character and carefully worked in thought and expression, he still will not achieve the result which we said was the aim of tragedy; the job will be done much better by a tragedy that is more deficient in these other respects but has a plot, a structure of events. It is much the same case as with painting: the most beautiful pigments smeared on at random will not give as much pleasure as a black-and-white outline picture. Besides, the most powerful means tragedy has for swaying our feelings, namely the peripeties and recognitions, are elements of the plot.

Again: an indicative sign is that those who are beginning a poetic career manage to hit the mark in verbal expression and character portrayal sooner than they do in plot construction; and the same is true of practically all the earliest poets.

So plot is the basic principle, the heart and soul, as it were, of tragedy, and the characters come second: . . . it is the imitation of an action and imitates the persons primarily for the sake of their action.

Third in rank is thought. This is the ability to state the issues and appropriate points pertaining to a given topic, an ability which springs from the arts of politics and rhetoric; in fact the earlier poets made their characters talk "politically," the present-day poets rhetorically. But "character" is that kind of utterance which clearly reveals the bent of a man's moral choice (hence there is no character in that class of utterances in which there is nothing at all that the speaker is choosing or rejecting), while "thought" is the passages in which they try to prove that something is so or not so, or state some general principle.

Fourth is the verbal expression of the speeches. I mean by this the same thing that was said earlier, that the "verbal expression" is the conveyance of thought through language: a statement which has the same meaning whether one says "verses" or "speeches."

The song-composition of the remaining parts is the greatest of the sensuous attractions, and the visual adornment of the dramatic persons can have a strong emotional effect but is the least artistic element, the least connected with the poetic art; in fact the force of tragedy can be felt even without benefit of public performance and actors, while for the production of the visual effect the property man's art is even more decisive than that of the poets.

GENERAL PRINCIPLES OF THE TRAGIC PLOT

With these distinctions out of the way, let us next discuss what the structuring of the events should be like, since this is both the basic and the most important element in the tragic art. We have established, then, that tragedy is an imitation of an action which is complete and whole and has some magnitude (for there is also such a thing as a whole that has no magnitude). "Whole" is that which has beginning, middle, and end. "Beginning" is that which does not necessarily follow on something else, but after it something else naturally is or happens; "end," the other way round, is that which naturally follows on something else, either necessarily or for the most part, but nothing else after it; and "middle" that which naturally follows on something else and something else on it. So, then, well-constructed plots should neither begin nor end at any chance point but follow the guidelines just laid down.

Furthermore, since the beautiful, whether a living creature or anything that is composed of parts, should not only have these in a fixed order to one another but also possess a definite size which does not depend on chance—for beauty depends on size and order; hence neither can a very tiny creature turn out to be beautiful (since our perception of it grows blurred as it approaches the period of imperceptibility) nor an excessively huge one (for then it cannot all be perceived at once and so its unity and wholeness are lost), if for example there were a creature a thousand miles long—so, just as in the case of living creatures they must have some size, but one that can be taken in in a single view, so with plots: they should have length, but such that they are easy to remember. As to a limit of the length, the one is determined by the tragic competitions and the ordinary span of attention. (If they had to compete with a hundred tragedies they would compete by the water clock, as they say used to be done [?].) But the limit fixed by the very nature of the case is: the longer the plot, up to the point of still being perspicuous as a whole, the finer it is so far as size is concerned; or to put it in general terms, the length in which, with things happening in unbroken sequence, a shift takes place either probably or necessarily from bad to good fortune or from good to bad—that is an acceptable norm of length.

But a plot is not unified, as some people think, simply because it has to do with a single person. A large, indeed an indefinite number of things can happen to a given individual, some of which go to constitute no unified event; and in the same way there can be many acts of a given individual from which no single action emerges. Hence it seems clear that those poets are wrong who have composed *Heracleïds, Theseïds,* and the like. They think that since Heracles was a single person it follows that the plot will be single too. But Homer, superior as he is in all other respects, appears to have grasped this point well also, thanks either to art or nature, for in composing an *Odyssey* he did not incorporate into it everything that happened to the hero, for example how he was wounded on Mt. Parnassus or how he feigned madness at the muster, neither of which events, by happening, made it at all necessary or probable that the other should happen. Instead, he composed the *Odyssey*—and the *Iliad* similarly—around a unified action of the kind we have been talking about.

A poetic imitation, then, ought to be unified in the same way as a single imitation in any other mimetic field, by having a single object: since the plot is an imitation of an action, the latter ought to be both unified and complete, and the component events ought to be so firmly compacted that if any one of them is shifted to another place, or removed, the whole is loosened up and dislocated; for an element whose addition or subtraction makes no perceptible extra difference is not really a part of the whole.

From what has been said it is also clear that the poet's job is not to report what has happened but what is likely to happen: that is, what is capable of happening according to the rule of probability or necessity. Thus the difference between the historian and the poet is not in their utterances being in verse or prose (it would be quite possible for Herodotus' work to be translated into verse, and it would not be any the less a history with verse than it is without it); the difference lies in the fact that the historian speaks of what has happened, the poet of the kind of thing that *can* happen. Hence also poetry is a more philosophical and serious business than history; for poetry speaks more of universals, history of particulars. "Universal" in this case is what kind of person is likely to do or say certain kinds of things, according to probability or necessity; that is what poetry aims at, although it gives its persons particular names afterward; while the "particular" is what Alcibiades did or what happened to him.

In the field of comedy this point has been grasped: our comic poets construct their plots on the basis of general probabilities and then assign names to the persons quite arbitrarily, instead of dealing with individuals as the old iambic poets did. But in tragedy they still cling to the historically given names. The reason is that what is possible is persuasive; so what has not happened we are not yet ready to believe is possible, while what has happened is, we feel, obviously possible: for it would not have happened if it were impossible. Nevertheless, it is a fact that even in our tragedies, in some cases only one or two of the names are traditional, the rest being invented, and in some others none at all. It is so, for example, in Agathon's *Antheus*—the names in it are as fictional as the events—and it gives no less pleasure because of that. Hence the poets ought not to cling at all costs to the traditional plots, around which our tragedies are constructed. And in fact it is absurd to go searching for this kind of authentication, since even the familiar names are familiar to only a few in the audience and yet give the same kind of pleasure to all.

So from these considerations it is evident that the poet should be a maker of his plots more than of his verses, insofar as he is a poet by virtue of his imitations and what he imitates is actions. Hence even if it happens that he puts something that has actually taken place into poetry, he is none the less a poet; for there is nothing to prevent some of the things that have happened from being the kind of things that can happen, and that is the sense in which he is their maker.

SIMPLE AND COMPLEX PLOTS

Among simple plots and actions the episodic are the worst. By "episodic" plot I mean one in which there is no probability or necessity for the order in which the episodes follow one another. Such structures are composed by the bad poets because they are bad poets, but by the good poets because of the actors: in composing contest pieces for them, and stretching out the plot beyond its capacity, they are forced frequently to dislocate the sequence.

Furthermore, since the tragic imitation is not only of a complete action but also of events that are fearful and pathetic, and these come about best when they come about contrary to one's expectation yet logically, one following from the other; that way they will be more productive of wonder than if they happen merely at random, by chance— because even among chance occurrences the ones people consider most marvelous are those that seem to have come about as if on purpose: for example the way the statue of Mitys at Argos killed the man who had been the cause of Mitys' death, by falling on him while he was attending the festival; it stands to reason, people think, that such things don't happen by chance—so plots of that sort cannot fail to be artistically superior.

Some plots are simple, others are complex; indeed the actions of which the plots are imitations already fall into these two categories. By "simple" action I mean one the development of which being continuous and unified in the manner stated above, the reversal comes without peripety or recognition, and by "complex" action one in which the reversal is continuous but with recognition or peripety or both. And these developments must grow out of the very structure of the plot itself, in such a way that on the basis of what has happened previously this particular outcome follows either by necessity or in accordance with probability; for there is a great difference in whether these events happen because of those or merely after them.

"Peripety" is a shift of what is being undertaken to the opposite in the way previously stated, and that in accordance with probability or necessity as we have just been saying; as

for example in the *Oedipus* the man who has come, thinking that he will reassure Oedipus, that is, relieve him of his fear with respect to his mother, by revealing who he once was, brings about the opposite; and in the *Lynceus*, as he (Lynceus) is being led away with every prospect of being executed, and Danaus pursuing him with every prospect of doing the executing, it comes about as a result of the other things that have happened in the play that he is executed and Lynceus is saved. And "recognition" is, as indeed the name indicates, a shift from ignorance to awareness, pointing in the direction either of close blood ties or of hostility, of people who have previously been in a clearly marked state of happiness or unhappiness.

The finest recognition is one that happens at the same time as a peripety, as is the case with the one in the *Oedipus*. Naturally, there are also other kinds of recognition: it is possible for one to take place in the prescribed manner in relation to inanimate objects and chance occurrences, and it is possible to recognize whether a person has acted or not acted. But the form that is most integrally a part of the plot, the action, is the one aforesaid; for that kind of recognition combined with peripety will excite either pity or fear (and these are the kinds of action of which tragedy is an imitation according to our definition), because both good and bad fortune will also be most likely to follow that kind of event. Since, further, the recognition is a recognition of persons, some are of one person by the other one only (when it is already known who the "other one" is), but sometimes it is necessary for both persons to go through a recognition, as for example Iphigenia is recognized by her brother through the sending of the letter, but of him by Iphigenia another recognition is required.

These then are two elements of plot: peripety and recognition; third is the *pathos*. Of these, peripety and recognition have been discussed; a *pathos* is a destructive or painful act, such as deaths on stage, paroxysms of pain, woundings, and all that sort of thing.

THE TRAGIC SIDE OF TRAGEDY: PITY AND FEAR AND THE PATTERNS OF THE COMPLEX PLOT

The "parts" of tragedy which should be used as constituent elements were mentioned earlier; . . . but what one should aim at and what one should avoid in composing one's plots, and whence the effect of tragedy is to come, remains to be discussed now, following immediately upon what has just been said.

Since, then, the construction of the finest tragedy should be not simple but complex, and at the same time imitative of fearful and pitiable happenings (that being the special character of this kind of poetry), it is clear first of all that

(1) neither should virtuous men appear undergoing a change from good to bad fortune, for that is not fearful, nor pitiable either, but morally repugnant; nor (2) the wicked from bad fortune to good—that is the most untragic form of all, it has none of the qualities that one wants: it is productive neither of ordinary sympathy nor of pity nor of fear—nor again (3) the really wicked man changing from good fortune to bad, for that kind of structure will excite sympathy but neither pity nor fear, since the one (pity) is directed towards the man who does not deserve his misfortune and the other (fear) towards the one who is like the rest of mankind—what is left is the man who falls between these extremes. Such is a man who is neither a paragon of virtue and justice nor undergoes the change to misfortune through any real badness or wickedness but because of some mistake; one of those who stand in great repute and prosperity, like Oedipus and Thyestes: conspicuous men from families of that kind.

So, then, the artistically made plot must necessarily be single rather than double, as some maintain, and involve a change not from bad fortune to good fortune but the other way round, from good fortune to bad, and not thanks to wickedness but because of some mistake of great weight and consequence, by a man such as we have described or else on the good rather than the bad side. An indication comes from what has been happening in tragedy: at the beginning the poets used to "tick off" whatever plots came their way, but nowadays the finest tragedies are composed about a few houses: they deal with Alcmeon, Oedipus, Orestes, Meleager, Thyestes, Telephus, and whichever others have had the misfortune to do or undergo fearful things.

Thus the technically finest tragedy is based on this structure. Hence those who bring charges against Euripides for doing this in his tragedies are making the same mistake. His practice is correct in the way that has been shown. There is a very significant indication: on our stages and in the competitions, plays of this structure are accepted as the most tragic, *if* they are handled successfully, and Euripides, though he may not make his other arrangements effectively, still is felt by the audience to be the most tragic, at least, of the poets.

Second comes the kind which is rated first by certain people, having its structure double like the *Odyssey* and with opposite endings for the good and bad. Its being put first is due to the weakness of the audiences; for the poets follow along, catering to their wishes. But this particular pleasure is not the one that springs from tragedy but is more characteristic of comedy.

PITY AND FEAR AND THE TRAGIC ACT

Now it is possible for the fearful or pathetic effect to come from the actors' appearance, but it is also possible for it to arise from the very structure of the events, and this is closer to the mark and characteristic of a better poet. Namely, the plot must be so structured, even without benefit of any visual effect, that the one who is hearing the events unroll shudders with fear and feels pity at what happens: which is what one would experience on hearing the plot of the *Oedipus*. To set out to achieve this by means of the masks and costumes is less artistic, and requires technical support in the staging. As for those who do not set out to achieve the fearful through the masks and costumes, but only the monstrous, they have nothing to do with tragedy at all; for one should not seek any and every pleasure from tragedy, but the one that is appropriate to it.

Since it is the pleasure derived from pity and fear by means of imitation that the poet should seek to produce, it is clear that these qualities must be built into the constituent events. Let us determine, then, which kinds of happening are felt by the spectator to be fearful, and which pitiable. Now such acts are necessarily the work of persons who are near and dear (close blood kin) to one another, or enemies, or neither. But when an enemy attacks an enemy there is nothing pathetic about either the intention or the deed, except in the actual pain suffered by the victim; nor when the act is done by "neutrals"; but when the tragic acts come within the limits of close blood relationship, as when brother kills or intends to kill brother or do something else of that kind to him, or son to father or mother to son or son to mother—those are the situations one should look for.

Now although it is not admissible to break up the transmitted stories—I mean for instance that Clytemestra was killed by Orestes, or Eriphyle by Alcmeon—one should be artistic both in inventing stories and in managing the ones that have been handed down. But what we mean by "artistic" requires some explanation.

It is possible, then, (1) for the act to be performed as the older poets presented it, knowingly and wittingly; Euripides did it that way also, in Medea's murder of her children. It is possible (2) to refrain from performing the deed, with knowledge. Or it is possible (3) to perform the fearful act, but unwittingly, then recognize the blood relationship later, as Sophocles' Oedipus does; in that case the act is outside the play, but it can be in the tragedy itself, as with Astydamas' Alcmeon, or Telegonus in the *Wounding of Odysseus*. A further mode, in addition to these, is (4) while intending because of ignorance to perform some black crime, to discover the relationship before one does it. And there is no other mode besides these; for one must necessarily either do the deed or not, and with or without knowledge of what it is.

Of these modes, to know what one is doing but hold off and not perform the act (No. 2) is worst: it has the morally repulsive character and at the same time is not tragic; for there is no tragic act. Hence nobody composes that way, or only rarely, as, for example, Haemon threatens Creon in the *Antigone.* Performing the act (with knowledge) (No. 1) is second (poorest). Better is to perform it in ignorance and recognize what one has done afterward (No. 3); for the repulsive quality does not attach to the act, and the recognition has a shattering emotional effect. But the best is the last (No. 4): I mean a case like the one in the *Cresphontes* where Merope is about to kill her son but does not do so because she recognizes him first; or in *Iphigenia in Tauris* the same happens with sister and brother; or in the *Helle* the son recognizes his mother just as he is about to hand her over to the enemy.

The reason for what was mentioned a while ago, namely that our tragedies have to do with only a few families, is this: It was because the poets, when they discovered how to produce this kind of effect in their plots, were conducting their search on the basis of chance, not art; hence they have been forced to focus upon those families which happen to have suffered tragic happenings of this kind.

THE TRAGIC CHARACTERS

Enough, then, concerning the structure of events and what traits the tragic plots should have. As for the characters, there are four things to be aimed at. First and foremost, that they be good. The persons will have character if in the way previously stated their speech or their action reveals the moral quality of some choice, and good character if a good choice. Good character exists, moreover, in each category of persons; a woman can be good, or a slave, although one of these classes (to wit, women) is inferior and the other, as a class, worthless. Second, that they be appropriate; for it is possible for a character to be brave, but inappropriately to a woman. Third is likeness to human nature in general; for this is different from making the character good and appropriate according to the criteria previously mentioned. And fourth is consistency. For even if the person being imitated is inconsistent, and that kind of character has been taken as the theme, he should be inconsistent in a consistent fashion.

An example of moral depravity that accomplishes no necessary purpose is the Menelaus in Euripides' *Orestes;* of an unsuitable and inappropriate character, the lamentation of Odysseus in the *Scylla* and the speech of Melanippe; and of the inconsistent, *Iphigenia at Aulis,* for the girl who pleads for her life is in no way like the later one.

In character portrayal also, as in plot construction, one should always strive for either the necessary or the probable, so that it is either necessary or probable for that kind of person to do or say that kind of thing, just as it is for one event to follow the other. It is evident, then, that the dénouements of plots also should come out of the character itself, and not from the "machine" as in the *Medea* or with the sailing of the fleet in the *Aulis.* Rather the machine should be used for things that lie outside the drama proper, either previous events that a human being cannot know, or subsequent events which require advance prophecy and exposition; for we grant the gods the ability to foresee everything. But let there be no illogicality in the web of events, or if there is, let it be outside the play like the one in Sophocles' *Oedipus.*

Since tragedy is an imitation of persons who are better than average, one should imitate the good portrait painters, for in fact, while rendering likenesses of their sitters by reproducing their individual appearance, they also make them better-looking; so the poet, in imitating men who are irascible or easygoing or have other traits of that kind, should make them, while still plausibly drawn, morally good, as Homer portrayed Achilles as good yet like other men.

TECHNIQUES OF RECOGNITION

What recognition is generically, was stated earlier; now as to its varieties: First comes the one that is least artistic and is most used, merely out of lack of imagination, that by means of tokens. Of these some are inherited, like "the lance that all the Earth-born wear," or "stars" such as Carcinus employs in his *Thyestes;* some are acquired, and of those some are on the body, such as scars, others are external, like the well-known amulets or the recognition in the *Tyro* by means of the little ark. There are better and poorer ways of using these; for example, Odysseus was recognized in different ways by means of his scar, once by the nurse and again by the swineherds. Those that are deliberately cited for the sake of establishing an identity, and all that kind, are less artistic, while those that develop naturally but unexpectedly, like the one in the foot-washing scene, are better.

Second poorest are those that are contrived by the poet and hence are inartistic; for example the way, in the *Iphigenia,* she recognizes that it is Orestes: *she* was recognized by means of the letter, but *he* goes out of his way to say what the poet, rather than the plot, wants him to say. Thus this mode is close kin to the error mentioned above: he might as well have actually worn some tokens. Similarly, in Sophocles' *Tereus,* the "voice of the shuttle."

Third poorest is that through recollection, by means of a certain awareness that follows on seeing or hearing something, like the one in the *Cypriotes* of Dicaeogenes where the hero bursts into tears on seeing the picture, and the one in Book 8 of the *Odyssey:* Odysseus weeps when he hears the lyre-player and is reminded of the War; in both cases the recognition follows.

Fourth in ascending order is the recognition based on reasoning; for example in the *Libation-Bearers:* "Somebody like me has come; nobody is like me but Orestes; therefore he has come." And the one suggested by the sophist Polyidus in speaking of the *Iphigenia:* it would have been natural, he said, for Orestes to draw the conclusion (aloud): "My sister was executed as a sacrifice, and now it is my turn." Also in the *Tydeus* of Theodectes: "I came expecting to find my son, and instead I am being destroyed myself." Or the one in the *Daughters of Phineus:* when they see the spot they reflect that it was indeed their fate to die here; for they had been exposed here as babies also. There is also one based on mistaken inference on the part of the audience, as in *Odysseus the False Messenger.* In that play, that he and no one else can

string the bow is an assumption, a premise invented by the poet, and also his saying that he would recognize the bow when in fact he had not seen it; whereas the notion that he (the poet) has made his invention for the sake of the other person who would make the recognition, that is a mistaken inference.

The best recognition of all is the one that arises from the events themselves; the emotional shock of surprise is then based on probabilities, as in Sophocles' *Oedipus* and in the *Iphigenia;* for it was only natural that she should wish to send a letter. Such recognitions are the only ones that dispense with artificial inventions and visible tokens. And second-best are those based on reasoning. . . .

PERFORMANCE IN HISTORY

SUE-ELLEN CASE
from "Classic Drag: The Greek Creation of Female Parts" (1985)

A prominent scholar and theoretician of feminism and theater, Sue-Ellen Case examines the complicity of traditional theatrical practices—cross-dressing in the Greek theater, for example—in the patriarchal structure of Western culture. Professor Case has written many influential studies of gender, sexuality, and theater and is the author of Feminism and Theatre *(1988) and of* The Domain-Matrix *(1997).*

In this essay, Case sets the action of classical Greek theater—notably The Oresteia *and* Medea—*in the context of contemporary feminist theory. Given this orientation to the drama, what elements of the plays emerge as most significant in Case's argument? In what ways does this "reading against the grain" open perspectives on the value and belief-system of classical Athens? How are terms like "justice" or "nature" interrogated by this interpretive strategy?*

From a feminist perspective, the initial observations about the history of theatre noted the absences of women within the tradition. Since traditional scholarship has focused on evidence related to written texts, the absence of women playwrights became central to early feminist investigations. The fact that there was no significant number of extant texts written by women for the stage until the seventeenth century produced a rather astounding sense of absence in the classical traditions of the theatre. The silence of women's voices in these traditions led feminist historians who were interested in women playwrights to concentrate on periods in which they did emerge: primarily the seventeenth century in England, the nineteenth century in America, and the twentieth century in Europe and America. These studies produced a number of new anthologies of plays by women and biographies of women playwrights that began to appear in the early seventies.

Work on the classical periods became possible by studying the image of women within plays written by men. Many scholars attribute the beginning of this type of textual discovery to the popular book by Kate Millett entitled *Sexual Politics* (1970). Millett's book illustrated a way to recognize and interpret the images of women in male literature as misogynistic. *Sexual Politics* offered a way to read against texts by becoming aware of their gendered bias and, as the title suggests, to foreground the notion that art is not distinct from politics. While Millett's book concentrated on describing the images of women, other early works such as Judith Fetterly's *The Resisting Reader* articulated a posture for resisting reading texts by men as they were conventionally read. Fetterly outlined ways to read against texts to discover the feminist subtext latent in such subversions. Works on images of women still predominate in the feminist criticism of historical texts. Numerous re-visions of Aeschylus and Shakespeare

are currently being produced. The images are commonly identified as being one of two basic types: positive roles, which depict women as independent, intelligent, and even heroic and a surplus of misogynistic roles commonly identified as the Bitch, the Witch, the Vamp, or the Virgin/Goddess. These roles reflect the perspective of the playwright or of the theatrical tradition on women. Originally, feminist historians used these theatrical images of women as evidence of the kind of lives actual women might have lived in the period. For example, what the characters and situations of Medea or Phaedra might tell us about the lives of powerful women in Greece. This approach was useful because traditional socio-economic histories tend to exhibit the same absence of women as does the literature. In the seventies, groundbreaking work on women in history was done in both realms: the socio-historical evidence identified in theatrical texts, and the publication of newly-collated documents on laws, social practices, and economic restrictions on women in history. This work enabled feminist critics and historians to produce a new kind of cultural analysis, which is based on the interplay of cultural phenomena, such as plays, theatre practice, and socio-economic evidence, to discover the nature of women's lives in the classical periods.

Yet, the discovery of the complicity of art with political projects, as well as the complicity of traditional history with the patriarchy led to new discoveries which reverse the original interpretations of these documents. The feminist critic may no longer believe that the portrayal of women in classical plays by men relates to the lives of actual women. Instead, the feminist critic may assume that the images of women in these plays represent a fiction of women constructed by the patriarchy. This assumption originates in a central practice within classical cultures: the division between private and public life. The public life becomes privileged in the classical plays and histories, while the private life remains relatively invisible. The new feminist analyses prove that this division is gender-specific, i.e., the public life is the property of men and women are relegated to the invisible private sphere. The result of the suppression of actual women in the classical world created the invention of a representation of the gender "Woman" within the culture. This "Woman" appeared on the stage, in the myths, and in the plastic arts, representing the patriarchal values attached to the gender of "Woman" while suppressing the experiences, stories, feelings, and fantasies of actual women.[1] The new feminist approach to these cultural fictions divides this "Woman" as a male-produced fiction from historical women, insisting that there is little connection between the two categories. Within theatre practice, the clearest illustration of this division is in the tradition of the all-male stage. "Woman" was played by male actors in drag, while actual women were banned from the stage. The classical acting practice reveals the construction of the fictional gender created by the patriarchy. The classical plays and theatrical conventions can now be regarded as allies in the project of suppressing actual women and replacing them with the masks of patriarchal production.

The beginning of the activity and literature known as theatre is traditionally assigned to the plays and practices of the Athenian festivals of Dionysos in sixth and fifth century BCE. Our notions of plays, acting, physical theatre space, costume, mask, and relation of play to audience begin with these Athenian festivals. In the sixth century, both women and men participated in these ceremonies, but by the fifth century, when the ceremonies were becoming what is known as theatre, women disappeared from the practice. Scholars do not record any evidence for specific laws or codes forbidding women to appear in the songs and dances, nor is there any evidence for the specific date or occasion of the beginning of their omission. Margarete Bieber, a recognized authority on this history, merely notes that it was part of "Attic morality" which "banished women from public life."[2] This implies, then, that the reason for this practice must be sought in the emerging cultural codes of Athens, rather than in specific political or theatrical practices. Three elements of Athenian culture help to understand the emerging theatrical practice: the new economic practices, the new cultural project and the new genealogy of the gods. The intersection of all of these

elements will be theatrically legitimatized in the text of *The Oresteia*.

Among the new economic practices, the rise of the family unit radically altered the role of women in Greek public life. Ironically, the important role women began to assume within the family unit was the cause of their removal from public life. The family unit became the new site for the creation and transmission of personal wealth. With the rise of the *polis*, the large network inherent in aristocracies gave way to single families. The rise of metals as commodities and the small-scale cultivation of land made it possible for individuals to control their own wealth. Yet while ownership became more individual and located within the family unit, it was limited to the male gender. Women were restricted to limited conditions of ownership and exchange. For example, women could only enter into inheritance transactions in the absence of a male and women were not allowed to barter for property over one *medimnos* (bushel). Within this new economy, women became a medium of exchange and marriage became an institution of ownership.[3] In fact, the word for marriage, *ekdosis*, meant loan—women were loaned to their husbands by their fathers, and in the case of a divorce, they were returned to their fathers.

With this change in the organization of wealth came a concomitant change in the organization of political units. The *oikos*, or household, became the basic unit for citizenship.[4] Citizenship was dependent upon family lines—a son was granted citizenship only if his parents were citizens, but without a son the parents could not retain their citizenship. This new condition for citizenship led to the strict definition and regulation of the sex life of the woman. The mother/wife assumed a new moral/legal dimension for the legitimacy and security of heirs and, by extension, political membership in the *polis*. Clear lines of reproduction were vital to the *polis*, making adultery a crime against society, rather than a sign of personal transgression. At the same time that the household became controlled by needs of the state, its activities became totally separate from those which were considered the business of the state, the mark of the citizen, or the activities of public life. Nancy Hartsock, in her book *Money, Sex, and Power*, describes it this way: The Greeks defined the

[1]See Teresa de Lauretis, *Alice Doesn't: Feminism, Semiotics, Cinema* (Bloomington: Indiana University Press, 1984), for a thorough development of the concept of "Woman."

[2]Margarete Bieber, *The History of the Greek and Roman Theatre* (Princeton: Princeton University Press, 1939), p. 9.

[3]See Gayle Rubin, "The Traffic in Women: Notes on the 'Political Economy' of Sex," in *Toward an Anthropology of Women*, ed. Rayna R. Reiter (New York: Monthly Review Press, 1975), for a discussion of women as a medium of exchange through the institution of marriage and kinship laws.

[4]Marilyn Arthur, "'Liberated' Women: The Classical Era," in *Becoming Visible: Women in European History*, eds. Renate Bridenthal and Claudia Koonz (Boston: Houghton Mifflin, 1977), pp. 67–68.

household as a private, apolitical space from the public, political space of the *polis*. "The result was a theorization of politics and political power as activities that occurred in a masculine arena characterized by freedom from necessary labor, dominance of intellect or soul," while the domestic space was defined by necessary labor and as a place where bodily needs were dominant.[5] Since Athenian women were confined to the house (explicitly in the laws of Solon), they were removed from the public life of the intellect and the soul and confined to the world of domestic labor, childbearing, and concomitant sexual activities. Actual women disappeared from the public life of the *polis,* lost their economic and legal powers and became objects of exchange. Within the socio-economic life of the *polis,* it is not surprising that their participation in the Dionysian festivals was restricted to private practices, resulting in their eventual exclusion from the stage.

Alongside these new legal and economic practices came new cultural institutions. Athens created new architecture, new religions, new myths, and the practice of theatre. These cultural institutions became allied with the suppression of women by creating the new gender role of "Woman" that would privilege the masculine gender and oppress the feminine one. At base, the new cultural categories of gender were constructed as categories of difference and polarity.[6] "Woman" appeared as the opposite of man. This move can best be seen in the new myths and architectural depictions of the amazons. The image of amazons is central to the female gender conflated with the outsider and with polar differences from the Greek male citizen. The amazons, dangerous but defeated, reverse the "natural" gender roles. They are warriors who force men to do "women's" work, such as child rearing, while the women go off to war.[7] The amazons also embody other myths of gender reversal—they keep female babies and dispose of the male ones, while the custom was to dispose of female babies.[8] Moreover, the word "amazon" (no breast) ties such practices to a biological, secondary sex characteristic specific to the female. The new architecture of the Acropolis, the civic center of Athens, displays the downfall of the amazons and the rise of Athena. Central to the new political order, then, is the demise of these women who would defy correct gender associations and the rise of a woman who

would enforce the new image of "Woman" in the *polis.* This demise of the old images of women and the rise of Athena are central themes in *The Oresteia.*

The genealogy of the gods provides the mytho-historical context for this creation of the new "Woman." The history of the gods explains why genders are opposite, locked in conflict, and why the male gender must defeat the former female one. The myth of the first earth-mother-goddess, Gaia, is a story of the dangers of her womb—the story of her children is one of murders and castrations. It concludes with the final conquest by Zeus, who swallows his wife Metis in order to gain her power of reproduction and then gives birth to Athena. Athena represents the end of the dangers of the womb, for she has no mother (breaking with matriarchal and female-identification), has no sexuality (she remains a virgin), defeats the amazons, allies herself with the reign of Zeus and Apollo, and thereby brings order to Athens. About this same time, Dionysos, a new god, appears in Athens and usurps the role of fertility and sexuality which the earlier female goddesses had retained. This male usurpation of female fertility will later be idealized by Plato in his famous midwife metaphor, while the assimilation of female sexuality will be usurped by boys in the social practice of male homosexuality (also later idealized by Plato). The genealogy of the gods thus divides female sexuality from power, assimilating female sexuality in the figure of Dionysos and isolating power in the image of the motherless virgin, Athena.

The rise of drama, within the Athenian state festivals dedicated to the celebration of Dionysos, places theatre securely within this new patriarchal institution of gender wars. Theatre must be gender-specific to the male and enact the suppression of actual women as well as the representation of the new "Woman." The maenads (the female celebrants of the Dionysian festivals) must dance into oblivion, while the satyrs (the male celebrants) must become the first choruses of the drama. "The singer Arion is said to have given to the singers of the dithyramb . . . the costume of the satyrs. The practice of representing someone other than oneself grew out of this ecstasy and led to the mimic art of the actors."[9] In other words, the power of representation was given only to the male celebrants. The invention of acting was gender-specific—the actor was the satyr. The gender-specific quality of the actor in the satyr play was even underscored by his wearing of the leather phallus. Yet in order to dramatize the battle of the genders, the female must somehow be represented: the male actor would need to perform the female role. Though scholars and theatre historians never mention

[5]Nancy Hartsock, *Money, Sex and Power: Toward a Feminist Historical Materialism* (New York: Longman, 1983), p. 187.

[6]Page duBois, *Centaurs and Amazons* (Ann Arbor: University of Michigan Press, 1982), p. 2.

[7]William Blake Tyrell, *Amazons: A Study in Athenian Myth-making* (Baltimore: Johns Hopkins University Press, 1984), p. 47.

[8]Tyrell, p. 55.

[9]Bieber, p. 1.

this strange phenomenon in more than passing remarks, Bieber does note one specific problem for male actors in their representations of women: on the vases, the maenads seem to be in a state of ecstasy—to play maenads, the male actors needed the comprehension of the religious emotion felt by these women.[10] Yet a more central problem emerges: how does one depict a woman? How does the male actor signal to the audience that he is a woman? Along with the female costume of the shorter tunic and the female mask with longer hair, he might have indicated through gesture, movement, and vocal intonation that the character was female. In considering this portrayal, it is important to remember that the notion of the female derived from the male point of view, which remained alien to female experience and reflected the perspective of her gendered opposite. This vocabulary of gestures initiated the image of "Woman" as she is seen on the stage—institutionalized through patriarchal culture and represented by male-originated signs of her appropriate gender behavior. Moreover, the practice of male actors playing women probably encouraged the creation of female roles which lent themselves to generalization and stereotype. The depiction and development of female characters in the written texts must have accommodated the practice of their representation onstage. Though all characters were formalized and masked, the cross-gender casting for female characters distinguished them in kind from the male characters. A subtextual message was delivered about the nature of the female gender, its behavior, appearance, and formal distance from the representation of the male.

The Athenian theatre practice created a political and aesthetic arena for ritualized and codified gender behavior, linking it to civic privileges and restrictions. The elevation of this gender principle to the term "classic" canonizes it as a paradigmatic element of the history of theatre, connoting the expulsion of women from the canon and the ideal. The etymology of "classic," connoting class, indicates that this expulsion is also related to the economic and legal privileges of the "first class"—a class to which women were denied admittance. The consonance of aesthetic criteria with economic ones becomes clear in the term itself. In each of the cultures which has produced "classics" for the stage (not only the Athenian, but the Roman and the Elizabethan) women were denied access to the stage and to legal and economic enfranchisement. These same production values are embedded in the texts of these periods. Female characters are derived from the absence of actual women on the stage and from the reasons for their absence. Each culture which

valorizes the reproduction of those "classic" texts actively participates in the same patriarchal subtext which created those female characters as "Woman." Though we cannot examine a production of the Greek classics, we can examine one of the "classic" texts produced for the Dionysian festivals and reproduced in the history of theatrical productions, history, and criticism within our own contemporary culture. The trilogy of *The Oresteia* exhibits all of the themes and practices discussed above. Moreover, its elevated position in the canon illustrates its lasting value. A feminist reading of *The Oresteia* illustrates the defeat of the old matriarchal genealogy, the nature of "Woman" as portrayed on the stage, the rise of Athena, and the legacy of the suppression of actual women.

THE ORESTEIA

Many feminist critics and historians have analyzed *The Oresteia* as a text central to the formalization of misogyny. Simone de Beauvoir and Kate Millett describe it as the mythical rendering of a patriarchal takeover. Nancy Hartsock argues that it associates the female gender with sexuality and nature, those forces that must be tamed in outside activities and within the inner person for the survival of the *polis*.[11] Hartsock describes *The Oresteia* within the dramatic festivals that are themselves associated with male gender activities. The drama, like the four-horse chariot race, is a contest. It formalizes *agons* (contests) and the notion of winners and losers. The festivals associate the heroic ideal of valor in battle with the peacetime ideal of rhetorical and dramatic competition.[12] The subject of the drama is the subject of war—the male warrior hero. When this *agon* is inscribed with the conflicts of gender, the dramatic dice are loaded for the same gender-specific hero to win. *The Oresteia* enacts the "battle of the sexes," using Athenian cultural and political codes to prescribe that women must lose the battle.

Early in the first play of the trilogy, *Agamemnon,* the chorus of old men explicates the dramatic situation within the perspective of male-female problems. The old men describe a promiscuous woman (Helen) as the cause of the Trojan war in which Agamemnon is presently engaged and they tell of the war fleet launched by Agamemnon's sacrifice of his virgin-daughter Iphigenia. The Trojan war and the relationship of Agamemnon and Clytemnestra are already fraught with conflicts embedded in gender roles. Then the chorus prepares the audience for the entrance of Clytemnestra by linking gender with certain attributes of character. They suggest that steady resolve and intensity of purpose are gender-specific when they refer to the male (inner) strength of Clytemnestra

---

[10]Bieber, p. 9.

[11]Hartsock, p. 192.
[12]Hartsock, p. 198.

(line 13).[13] Within this context Clytemnestra enters, played by a man. After s/he speaks, the chorus congratulates her for thinking like a man and dismisses her announcement of the end of the war as just "like a woman to take rapture before fact" (line 475). These lines presume certain gender roles regarding the judgment of evidence and decision-making. Within the theatre practice, they also play with a certain level of irony since a man in drag plays a woman who "thinks like a man." Clearly, the primary referent is the male. The notion of female, like the notion of the amazon, disrupts the male order. Clytemnestra is introduced as a figure of that disruption. The absence of the male king has provided her with "unnatural" political power. In his absence, she has taken a male lover. By this act, she disrupts the gender code of female sexuality, for the tradition was that women were to remain monogamous even during ten year wars. The chorus treats Clytemnestra's liaison as dangerous. Yet when Agamemnon enters with his sexual war booty, Cassandra, the implication of social disruption is not in the text. In fact, the dramatic pathos of the drama favors Agamemnon, despite his treatment of women as evidenced by his rape of Cassandra or his murder of Iphigenia.

Cassandra provides the Athenian image of the woman in the public arena (even though she is played by a man). She has certain privileges of belonging (she is the priestess of Apollo which assures her of sexual liaisons with citizens of rank such as Agamemnon), but she does not have the privilege of effective public speech because of her prior refusal to be violated by Apollo. Cassandra's entrance, as an outsider, as Agamemnon's booty, mute to Clytemnestra and expelled from effective dialogue, even portrayed by a male actor, projects the strength of the misogyny embedded in the Athenian patriarchal order. What remains in the play is only Clytemnestra's murder of Agamemnon and her complete vilification. At the end, the chorus mourns Agamemnon as one who had to fight a war for a woman and then be killed by one (lines 1481–1482).

The third play, *The Eumenides,* decides the winner of the battle of the sexes within the play, within Athens, and within the genealogy of the gods. From a feminist perspective, it is ironic that this play dramatizes the so-called beginnings of democracy. Moreover, within theatre history, *The Eumenides* is often marked as the play of the new order of civilization which created our western tradition of reason and fair play. This may be an accurate description, for it does make the deciding gender judgments of Athenian culture and condemns

women to their subservient role in Western civilization. The play rests upon a new genealogy of the gods. It opens with the old order, the vile goddesses, the Eumenides. They create an ugly, frightening characterization of the earlier chthonic female religions. The masks created for them were famous for their disgusting appearance. An extant remark about them states that "Aeschylus' Eumenides horrified women into miscarriages,"[14] an interesting anecdote for its gender and sexual connotations. The Eumenides have arrived in Athens, while pursuing Orestes to revenge his murder of his mother. They describe their role as the punishment of matricide (line 210). Orestes appeals to Apollo for help and Athena appears to solve the problem. She institutes a trial, exhibiting Athenian methods of justice, to try Orestes for his murder. The decision is to set Orestes free. This conclusion is damning evidence for the public rationalization of misogyny, for it rests upon establishing the parental line as male. The mother is not the parent, but the nurse of the child. The parent is defined as he who mounts (lines 658–661). Athena is the supreme proof of this fact because she had no mother and was begat by the male god Zeus (lines 734–738). The Eumenides are confined to a cave and their function is no longer to revenge matricide, but to preside over marriages. Thus, the trilogy which began with the end of the Trojan war and proceeded through the house of Agamemnon ends with the institution of democracy deciding the role of gender and the definition of procreation. This ending can be seen as paradigmatic of future plot structures in the Western playwriting tradition. A majority of plays will conclude various kinds of civic, historical, and psychological problems with the institution of marriage. The proper gender role for women is inscribed in this conclusion.

The feminist reader of *The Oresteia* discovers that she must read against the text, resisting not only its internal sense of pathos and conclusion, but also the historical and cultural codes which surround it, including its treatment within theatre history. The pathos the feminist reader feels may be for Iphigenia and Clytemnestra rather than for Agamemnon. She may perceive Athena as a male-identified woman in alliance with the male network of power rather than as a hero of Athens. She definitely feels excluded from the conventions of the stage, bewildered by the conviction of cross-gender casting which is only practiced in terms of female characters. Mimesis is not possible for her. Perhaps the feminist reader will decide that the female roles have nothing to do with women, that these roles should be played by men, as fantasies of "Woman" as "Other" than men, disruptions of a patriarchal society which illustrates its fear and loathing of

[13]All citations of *The Oresteia* are from *Complete Greek Tragedies,* Vol. 1, *Aeschylus,* eds. David Grene, Richmond Lattimore (Chicago: Chicago University Press, 1960).

[14]Sir Arthur Pickard-Cambridge, *The Dramatic Festivals of Athens* (Oxford: Clarendon Press, 1968), p. 265.

the female parts. In fact, the feminist reader might become persuaded that the Athenian roles of Medea, Clytemnestra, Cassandra, or Phaedra are properly played as drag roles. The feminist reader might conclude that women need not relate to these roles or even attempt to identify with them. Moreover, the feminist historian might conclude that these roles contain no information about the experience of real women in the classical world. Nevertheless, the feminist scholars must recognize that theatre originated in this kind of cultural climate and that the Athenian experience will continue to provide a certain paradigm of theatrical practice for the rest of Western theatrical/cultural history. By linking practice, text, and cultural practice in this new way, she may enhance her understanding of how the hegemonic structure of patriarchal practice was instituted in Athens. . . .

NIALL W. SLATER
from "The Idea of the Actor" (1990)

Niall Slater has written widely about the performance of classical Greek and Roman theater and is the author of Plautus in Performance *(1985) and* Reading Petronius *(1990). In this essay, he describes the ways in which the public performance of classical Athenian actors dramatizes a sense of acting as a craft and as an art. Given the paucity of evidence about the actual practice of actors in the classical theater, how does Slater construct his interpretation of classical Greek acting? What kind of information does he find in the range of his source materials? Are there ways in which his reading of plays for the clues they offer to the practice of acting might help you to read Greek drama?*

Before actors there was drama. The actor as a conceptual category is posterior to the playing of drama before an audience. Like so much in the fifth-century theater, the emergence of the actor as a category can be discerned only dimly. Any attempt to deal with it will of necessity involve a great deal of speculation. It is nonetheless worth the effort, for I will argue that the creation of concepts of actor and acting is essential to the process whereby the unique public enactment at a festival which we have so far been describing becomes a portable and repeatable play in very much our modern sense in the next century.

I take my title from a splendid book of the same name by William Worthen.[1] His is a study of the ethics of performance, the changes in the conception and self-conception of the actor in the Renaissance, eighteenth century, and modern theater. My concern here is with the origin of the concept of "actor" and thus is even more precisely ethical—that which is essential to the ethos of acting as opposed to any other mode of public or private performance.

This difference in essence is easily stated: it is dialogic performance. Here I may seem merely to repeat the traditional accounts that say that drama arises from an actor responding to the chorus. Note, though, that mimesis alone is not enough to create the actor. Other types of poetry, other performances had been mimetic before. When Homer has Akhilleus [Achilles] speak in the *Iliad,* that speech mimes real speech, but there is still an enormous gulf between Homer singing of characters speaking (even in dialogue with each other) and placing two physically exemplified voices onstage. In the latter situation the controlling voice of the Homeric narrative has disappeared. The two voices onstage claim an equal status—neither has by nature a better claim to speak for the poet or for any particular order. To borrow and perhaps misuse a term from Bakhtin, acting comes into being through heteroglossia.

It is at this moment that the performance of this type of poetry becomes unreproducible by the individual. Much has been written about the fusion of poetic forms, of iambic and choral meters, of dialogue and song, which creates tragedy and comedy. What has been too little acknowledged is that this is a fusion between that which can, and that which cannot, be reperformed outside its original context.

Here I ought to confront more directly the recent work of C.J. Herington.[2] In his book *Poetry into Drama,* Herington posits a song culture in ancient Greece in which all poetry is created in hopes of endless reperformance. He believes that the music to all the lyric poets and tragedy was passed down to the fourth century by a series of reperformances. He even argues for the survival of some original choreography through reperformance.

---

[1] William B. Worthen, *The Idea of the Actor: Drama and the Ethics of Performance* (Princeton, 1984).

[2] C.J. Herington, *Poetry into Drama: Early Tragedy and the Greek Poetic Tradition* (Berkeley, Los Angeles, and London, 1985).

The problem with this theory is to find both an occasion and a medium for such reperformance. It is immediately apparent that much choral lyric will never have been reperformed by a chorus—as in the case of epinician poetry. It seems unlikely that there was ever an occasion to recruit and train a new chorus for further performances of a Pindaric victory ode after the first celebration. In this case it is indeed possible, as Herington invites us to do, to imagine reperformance of the work by an individual performer.

The example of a scene between Strepsiades and Pheidippides in Aristophanes' *Clouds* is relevant here, though far from unambiguous. Strepsiades asks Pheidippides to sing Simonides; then, when Pheidippides spurns that request, Strepsiades asks him to "recite" (*lexai*) some Aiskhylos [Aeschylus] (1353–1367). This too Pheidippides refuses to do and then, according to the manuscripts, he "sings" a speech or *rhesis* from Euripides.[3]

Whatever Pheidippides then performs apparently came from Euripides' *Aiolos*, but it is not possible to determine whether this is a chorus or a lyric solo. Devotees might well have learned lyric solo passages and sung them at symposiums. Likewise the Aiskhylos requested might have been solo or chorus. It cannot, however, have been an excerpt from the genuinely dramatic part of drama—an exchange between two or more characters. Who would ever have learned a passage of stichomythia by heart? On what occasion would such a passage be reperformed?

If I may be pardoned a modern analogy, early tragedy and comedy, with their "bad plots and laughable diction,"[4] must have been a great deal like early twentieth-century musical comedies—a series of songs stitched together with a few pennyworth of plot. The creators of these early musicals certainly hoped that the shows would promote their songs and lodge them in the public memory; they hoped for sales of sheet music and later recordings, the modern version of imperishable *kleos*. Many songs that still live in our musical memory were introduced in such shows—but the plots and dialogue have long since vanished. So too I am persuaded that the poets of early tragedy and comedy will have written their lyrics in the hope that their songs would catch the audience's imagination and live on through reperformance—but the dialogue was occasional poetry, written for a single performance. Aiskhylos could not have dreamed at the beginning of his career that anyone would want to memorize his dialogue—because on what occasion would two or three people meet to give it an oral performance?

Other evidence for private reperformance of dramatic texts in the fifth century suggests only choruses. The famous story in Plutarch's *Life of Nikias* which tells how prisoners from the Sicilian expedition won their freedom from the mines by their knowledge of Euripides again must mean ability to sing tragic choruses.[5] Nor is it surprising that so many would have such a knowledge of Euripides. John J. Winkler has persuasively argued that the choruses of tragedy were drawn yearly from the ephebes. A large number of young men fresh from military training who were shipped off to join the Sicilian debacle will have recently performed in a Euripidean chorus.[6]

Acting of course did not remain a marginal contribution to the drama. It is a commonplace that over time, the balance between acting and choral performance was reversed. The chorus in its turn became marginal. Less common is any attempt to model or explain this change other than in terms of "degeneracy" of the form. I will suggest a model with three rather loosely delimited stages: first, one in which acting is judged in relation to the myth it enacts; second, one in which actors are compared and judged in similar but not identical performances; and finally a stage in which reperformance has become possible and comparisons can be made of actors playing precisely the same roles.

Tradition tells us the poets were their own first actors, and we have no compelling reason to doubt this. Indeed it has been suggested that a poet as late as Aristophanes played in his own comedies.[7] Obviously the poet was not granted a chorus on the basis of his acting ability but for his skill in composition, and equally obviously poets will have differed in their personal histrionic skills. The *Life of Sophokles* [Sophocles] says that he was the first poet to abandon acting in his own plays because of his weak voice. If true, this would be an important milestone: not merely the quality of the

[3]K.J. Dover in *Aristophanes: Clouds*, 2d ed. (Oxford, 1968), on verse 1371 (see also 251–253) emends the various forms of *aido* found in the manuscripts to *eg'*, from *ago*, quoting a parallel from Theophrastos. Dover himself says that recitation from tragedy after dinner was not usual, and the practice from Theophrastos' day may not be that of the fifth century.

[4]Aristotle, *Poetics* 6, 18, notes that the earlier tragic poets were much better with language and character study than with their plots.

[5]*Life of Nikias* 29. Plutarch speaks first of Euripides' *poemata* in general, but then specifies that some, wandering on the battlefield, were given food and drink for singing a *melos* of Euripides. He connects with this the story of a ship admitted to the harbor because those on board knew *asmata* of the poet.

[6]See the estimate of W. B. Sedgwick, "The Frogs and the Audience," *Classica et Mediaevalia* 9 (1947): 1–9, for the numbers who would have had experience singing in the chorus.

[7]C. Bailey, "Who Played Dicaeopolis?" in *Greek Poetry and Life*, ed. Bailey et al. (Oxford, 1936).

poetry but the quality of the acting now makes a difference to the success of a drama. Though M.R. Lefkowitz dismisses this statement from the *Life* by a chain of reasoning I cannot follow,[8] it seems likely on the whole that early poets did act, while later poets did not. Dating the change to Sophokles' early career may be wrong, but it is not likely to be far out of the actual historical sequence.

From the moment the poet creates a dialogue between characters, he needs another actor for his performance. What little evidence we have suggests that poets regularly employed certain people, presumably friends, as actors. What special qualifications these would have had is unknown—they certainly do not seem to have been themselves poets by and large.[9] Again the *Life of Sophocles* (trans. Lefkowitz) reports on the authority of Ister:

> Ister also says that he discovered the white half-boots that actors and chorus members wear, and that he wrote his dramas to suit their characters.

The statement about writing the *dramata* according to *phuseis auton* is our interest here. Does this mean that Sophokles had in mind the peculiar capacities of his performers in the composition process? Like so much of the lives of the poets, this is a laundry list, and the relation of one item to another is far from clear. Though the grammatical antecedents of *auton* are *hypokritai* and *khoreutai*, these two statements may not have been connected in Ister—what have white boots to do with typecasting? Interpreting this way also presents us with an extreme improbability. What on earth can it mean to write a chorus according to the *phuseis* of its performers? Once again, let us remember that the pool of choristers change every year—did Sophokles walk into rehearsal, look over the pimply throng, and say, "You lads look much more like Lemnian maidens than Argive elders"? But the notion that he wrote *actors'* parts according to their performance capacities is far from improbable.

The principal objection to accepting this as a historical datum is the possibility that actors were allotted to the poets, not chosen by them, in the later fifth century, but there is no proof that allotment of actors was introduced this early, and I shall argue against it on grounds of probability below. A poet who writes according to the capacities of his actors is another important milestone, whoever that poet was. Fifty years ago, A. S. Owen argued that Sophokles was just such a poet, to the extent that he changed distribution of singing parts based on the capacities of his actors.[10]

Thus in the early fifth century, actors existed primarily in relation to the piece they enacted. Their performance was not separable from the overall performance of the drama. Gradually, this began to change. We can describe a parallel evolution in which their part of the drama increased in both size and complexity without yet determining causality between the two. It is only logical to assume that, insofar as the victorious poets tended to employ the same actors, at first in subordinate roles, then later as protagonists, the actors' skills improved apace. At some point the poets ceased to act, in recognition of the fact that mimetic skill was now a significant factor in the success or failure of the piece as a whole.

The narrowing in the choice of tragic subjects which seems to begin in the course of the fifth century may be related to the developing skills of the actors. Aristotle says

[8] In *The Lives of the Greek Poets* (Baltimore, 1981), 77–78, she asserts that this detail is inserted to explain the statement that Sophokles invented the third actor. The sequence where Aiskhylos invents the second actor and Sophokles the third is suspicious. But the *Life* makes no causal link between Sophokles' ceasing to act and the invention of the third actor; indeed the author's statement about Sophokles' changes in the size of the choruses intervenes between the two. I can see no reason to believe that the author of the *Life* or anyone else thought Sophokles' abandonment of acting *explained* his invention of the third actor.

[9] P. Ghiron-Bistagne, *Recherches sur les acteurs dans la Grèce antique* (Paris, 1976), 136–154, summarizes what we know. The *Life of Aiskhylos* gives us the names of his customary actors, Kleandros and Mynniskos, otherwise unknown.

[10] A.S. Owen, "The Date of the Electra of Sophocles," in *Greek Poetry and Life,* ed. Bailey, 145–157. Lefkowitz's citation (*Lives*, 79) of this article by Owen in the course of her argument for allotment is somewhat misleading. Owen doubts the allotment of actors this early. The source of the notion that allotment was introduced at the same time as contest for actors seems to be A.E. Haigh, the source for *DFA* as well. In the first edition of *The Attic Theatre* (Oxford, 1889), 76, Haigh simply states that "long before the end of the fifth century" allotment of actors was introduced, and he offers as evidence an inference from silence: "Towards the end of the fifth century we no longer hear of particular poets and actors being permanently connected together." By the time of the second edition of *The Attic Theatre* (Oxford, 1898), 80, he has decided that "the change in the method of selection was probably introduced about the middle of the fifth century, when the contests in acting were established, and the position of the actors received its first official recognition." He adduces, however, no new evidence in support of this view. Finally, allotment itself need not be a bar to adapting the text to the capacities of the performers. Only if the text were fixed before the allotment and unalterable thereafter would the poet be unable to adapt his text to the performer's capacity. Texts in a working theater are never written in stone. I believe that the text of a Greek drama was quite fluid up until the moment of performance, the arkhōn did not grant a chorus on the basis of one of the Oxford Classical Texts in hand.

that some myths are better suited to tragedy than others.[11] One can only speculate that acting plays a part here. One representation of Orestes can build on another, both histrionically as well as poetically. The urn supposedly containing Orestes' ashes is as much a creation of performance as of poetry, if not more. How an actor realizes a scene onstage creates just as much an anxiety of influence for future performers as do the words of the text. Mrs. Siddons' "tender" Lady Macbeth still exerts an influence over performers today. Thus as the storehouse of myths for tragedy begins to contract ever so slightly, the actors begin to portray characters whom other actors have portrayed before. As this process accelerates, it creates the standards by which quality of acting can be judged and actors typed in their abilities to represent certain kinds of characters.

We have no direct glimpse of this process, unless the vague reference to Sophokles' writing according to his actors' *phuseis* is one. Our real evidence for the process is its result: the institution of contests for actors of tragedy at the City Dionysia almost certainly in 449, at the Lenaia perhaps in 442.

The importance of the institution of the contests cannot be overemphasized. Their existence means that acting is now conceptually separate from the drama. Actors have an ontology in and for themselves. Standards exist by which one actor's performance can be judged superior to another's. If actors do not yet have the same status as the poets, they nonetheless are seen to be doing something very different— for it is now possible for a victorious actor to play in a losing play. No doubt at the beginning the prize for acting tended to go to the protagonist of the victorious play, just as today there is some association of the Oscar for best actor or actress and best picture. Nonetheless the possibility exists that a great play can be inadequately acted or that extraordinary acting can be done in inadequate plays. We first know that this happened in 418, when we have inscriptional evidence for a victorious protagonist in a losing play.[12]

Certainly actors are part of the public consciousness by now, as some of Aristophanes' anecdotes about actors indicate. At *Peace* 781–86 he complains about the dancing of the sons of Karkinos who spoiled his production of *Wasps*.[13] In the *Frogs* (303) he has a good bit of fun at the expense of the unfortunate Hegelokhos and his famous mispronunciation in his performance of *Orestes*. If Aristophanes can have such fun at their expense, actors must now have something of the same public recognition and presence as the other public figures he attacks.

It would be a great help to know when the system of allotment for protagonists began. What we know of it comes from the *Suda,* where we also learn that the victor of one year's contest was entitled to be one of the protagonists the following year. We know nothing else of how the group of actors to be allotted was drawn up. Nor do we know how deuteragonist and tritagonist were selected, although it seems likely that the protagonist would have had some influence on their choice. There is an appeal of economy in Haigh's suggestion that allotment is contemporary with the initiation of the contests, but that seems to me specious. It presupposes an extraordinarily swift change in the status of actors in the middle of the fifth century, from nonentities to a controlled and rationed commodity. The provision that a victor has an automatic right to compete the next year also seems very suspicious this early, and the *Suda* clearly links this with allotment. One would assume that at first a victor in one year's contest would quite naturally be asked to compete the next year. A formal provision securing this right suggests a situation in which there are many more actors than slots for them at the festival. It therefore seems more probable that allotment and the right of a victor to a slot the next year came some time after the introduction of contests, when the number of available actors was large and even the chance to appear had to be fought for, a situation much more likely in the fourth century.

Large numbers of actors do not simply appear; they must be trained. As with any other *tekhnē* in ancient Greece, theater seems to have run in certain families. D.F. Sutton has just published a collection of the evidence for such families.[14] Interestingly, Sutton says that he began collecting evidence for *actors'* families only, but broadened his definition after discovering only father-son combinations among actors. Given average Greek life expectancies, it is perhaps not surprising that there are no families with three successive generations of actors. For a father to train his own son demands that he exceed the average life expectancy.

Necessarily, then, actors must have trained others beside family members. Gregory Sifakis[15] has suggested on the

---

[11]In *The Poetics* 13.7 he discusses the narrowing of the tragic canon, noting that earlier drew their plots from a wide range of sources, but later tragedians focused on the experiences of a few families.

[12]Recorded in the *didascalia,* IG H², 2319. See *DFA,* 95.

[13]See D.M. MacDowell, *Aristophanes: Wasps* (Oxford, 1971), 326–332, on 1501 ff.; M. Platnauer, *Aristophanes: Peace* (Oxford, 1964), 94–95, on 289–291; and 135 ff., on 781 ff.

[14]D.F. Sutton, "The Theatrical Families of Athens," *AJP* 108 (1987): 9–26.

[15]"Boy Actors in New Comedy," in *Arktouros,* ed. G. W. Bowersock. W. Burkert, and M.C.J. Putnam (New York and Berlin, 1979), 199–208.

evidence of the Mytilene mosaics that boy apprentices were used to represent certain nonspeaking parts in the performances of New Comedy. Apprenticeship was surely the natural way to learn the craft of acting in Greece, and a system such as Sifakis suggests whereby apprentices became synagonists and finally protagonists themselves seems quite likely. Child performers certainly would have been used to represent Alkestis' children in Euripides, for example, and these might well have been boys in training.

There are certainly more actors as the century goes on, but it is only in the latter half of the century that they become visible as such in art. In vase painting earlier on, we can distinguish with certainty only choristers. The bird dancers of black-figure . . . are usually considered a theriomorphic chorus and have often been discussed, despite the wide gap in time, in connection with the *Birds* of Aristophanes. There is now at the Getty Museum in Malibu a late fifth-century krater that, according to J.R. Green,[16] may well be a contemporary illustration of the *Birds,* showing two bird choristers dancing around the flute-player . . .

As with animal choruses, so with satyrs. One can usually tell satyr performers from real satyrs; the former wear hairy shorts or trunks which support the phallus and the tail, but the heads are drawn as if they were quite realistic and not masks. Performers representing normal human characters are usually only distinguishable if they have removed or not yet assumed their masks[. . . .] Even in these cases, the performers are choristers. We must wait until near the end of the century to find performers who are definitely actors represented as such. Here we find a few fragmentary representations and the famous Pronomos Vase[. . . .]

Our admittedly impressionistic survey of vase painting and the theater in the fifth century is nonetheless food for thought. It is customary to attribute these results to the conventions of vase painting. Trendall and Webster are probably right, for example, to see behind certain earlier fifth-century vases the inspiration of actors performing Aiskhylean plays, though there is nothing definite to mark the figures as actors.[17] Here the vase painter seems to accept the mimesis as reality and represents it as such in his work. But this merely begs the question—where do conventions come from? When, only gradually and toward the end of the century, the painters do choose to represent actors themselves, seen in moments at which they are separate from the drama which it

is their function to enact, what is causing painting convention to change? Whence comes a consciousness of, and interest in, the process of mimesis?

Some sculptural evidence can be drawn into our study of when the actor as a category emerges. Most germane to our purpose is the famous Peiraeus actors' relief[. . . .] The piece dates from the very end of the fifth century and shows three actors and two figures on a banqueting couch; one figure is labelled (in an inscription which is clearly much later than the carving of the relief) Dionysos. This is a fascinating piece of evidence for the history of actors in the fifth century, but it is unfortunately easier to say what it cannot be, than what it was. This is *not* a victory dedication for any play, and certainly not the *Bakkhai* [Bacchae], as has been suggested.[18] We have victory dedications for plays, but they celebrate the *khorēgos*. Nor is it a victory dedication from the acting contest. That contest was only among protagonists; here the full complement of three actors is represented. Iconographically the relief is very similar to a series of banqueting hero reliefs which we know from this period. These heroes are largely anonymous but do imply some form of cult activity. The question then becomes: who are the worshippers on the Peiraeus relief, and what is their relationship to the figure on the couch?

I have elsewhere attempted to argue back from the subsequent reinscription of the piece to its original context. I will not reiterate all the details of that argument here, but only state that I would connect the reinscription with the formation of the Athenian branch of the Artists of Dionysos in the early third century BCE. I believe the figure on the couch did not originally represent Dionysos, but was one of the customary banqueting heroes.[19]

Are the three human figures then the actual dedicators of the piece or simply representative (as protagonist, deuteragonist, and tritagonist) of a larger group of actors? Both are certainly possibilities. By the end of the fifth century a protagonist may well have regularly worked with the same two synagonists in a master/journeyman relationship. Thus this could be a dedication in gratitude for the success of this partnership. I find the rededication of the piece several generations later suggestive, however. The rededication implies that it remained on display in a place of worship frequented by actors who felt some proprietary interest in the piece, such that they reinscribed it to their patron Dionysos when the new guild was formed. I suggest then that the piece was

[16]J.R. Green, "A Representation of the *Birds* of Aristophanes," *Greek Vases in the J. Paul Getty Museum* (Malibu, 1985), 2:95–118.

[17]IGD, e.g., III 1, 2 (*Khoephoroi*), III 1, 8 (*Eumenides*), III 1, 13 (*Edonoi*), III 1, 24 and 25 (*Phineus*).

[18]The view of T.B.L. Webster—see my article, "Vanished Players: Two Classical Reliefs and Theatre History," *GRBS* 26 (1985): 333–344.

[19]See my "Vanished Players."

in its original use a dedication of a group, perhaps a proto-guild, of Athenian actors to their hero/patron. Worship by actors of a hero, whether as a partnership or a larger group, implies a sense of group identity, a sense if you will of professionalism. Actors now have both public recognition and self-recognition.

Thus at the end of the fifth century, actors had a public presence, though perhaps still not one equal with that of the poet. Once again we must remind ourselves that fifth-century plays were written for single performances. While a poet might then take his play to Syracuse or the court of Macedon, Athens would not see it performed at the Dionysia again. I leave out of account here plays so revised as to be new, such as Euripides' two versions of *Hippolytos* or Aristophanes' two versions of *Clouds* (whose second performance is a matter of grave doubt anyway). The sole exception to the rule of one Athenian performance per play in the fifth century is Aiskhylos, whose plays were accorded the unique right of reperformance after his death. Details of this are very sketchy. Were it not for the evidence of Aristophanes in *Akharnians*[10] where Dikaiopolis refers to his anticipation of a revival of Aiskhylos, we might suspect that the tradition of reperformances of Aiskhylos in the fifth century was a projection backward of later practice. We do not know if a revived Aiskhylos play competed with the works of the living or not. In any case this is the great exception. Thus in the fifth century an actor could not make a reputation in a particular performance. There were no legendary interpretations such as Mrs. Siddons' Lady Macbeth or Irving's Hamlet.

The decisive move to repeated performances and the development of a genuine touring circuit of performances was a phenomenon of the fourth century. While we know of dramatic performances at the theater in the Peiraeus at the end of the fifth century, there do not seem to have been theatri-cal performances at most celebrations of the Rural Dionysia until after the Peloponnesian War.[20] My own belief is that country inhabitants, cooped up in the hated city during the war, nonetheless took back with them to the country in the fourth century a taste for theater.

To review briefly: at the beginning of the fifth century, actors as a category of public attention simply did not exist. As performers they were not differentiated from the singers of dithyramb—volunteer amateurs participating in the city's festival. The principal actors were usually the poets, and thus were simply identified with the pieces they wrote. As the first half of the century progressed, however, acting skill began to be recognized as something apart from the poetry. Histrionic skill could make or mar. The poets gradually abandoned acting to men of more specifically performative skills. The recognition of this change comes with the establishment of acting contests in the middle of the century. Now performances are judged in relation to each other as well as to the work. At the same time the storehouse of myths suitable for dramatic representation seems to be shrinking; it is tempting to speculate that acting helps in this winnowing process as one performance builds on, and of course competes with, another. The art of the second half of the fifth century shows us actors as such for the first time, not only as the painter's eye dwells on the margins, on the transitions into and out of illusion in the theater, but also as the actors see themselves and pay to have themselves represented. Only in the fourth century do we reach the final stage where an actor like Polos can become famous for his representation of a particular role.[21] Only then are plays the repeatable texts we think of today, because a social context for a reperformance has at last been created. The actors through their skills and their assertion of their individuality are a key force in that transformation.

---

[20]Some recent discoveries of small deme theaters, as yet unpublished, may require a revision of the chronology I here argue for; these may be late fifth century. Theaters were not used solely for dramatic performances, however, and even if there were deme theaters in Attica before 403 BCE that still may not prove the existence of an already functioning touring circuit and the expectation that plays from the City Dionysia would be reperformed in such theaters.

[21]*Epiktetos* (*Dissertationes* frag. 11, p. 464, Schenkl, editio minor) tells us of his portrayals of Oidipous [Oedipus], both as king and as beggar. Polus also might be claimed as the inventor of method acting. Aulus Gellius, *Natura animalium* 6.5, tells us how Polus increased the power of his performance as Elektra lamenting over the supposed urn containing Orestes' ashes by using an urn containing the ashes of his own recently deceased son.

AN ACTOR'S PERSPECTIVE

INTERVIEW WITH FIONA SHAW

INTERVIEWED BY AOIFE MONKS. (2001)

Born in Cork, Ireland, Fiona Shaw has become one of the leading actresses of the English-speaking world. After taking a philosophy degree in University College Cork, she emigrated to England to train at the Royal Academy of Dramatic Art. Immediately after her training, she was snapped up to play lead roles in productions in the Royal Shakespeare Company and the Royal National Theatre. Shaw was then cast in Deborah Warner's production of Electra *for the RSC in 1988 and began a collaborative relationship with the director which has had a major impact on both their careers. Shaw and Warner went on to stage Brecht's* The Good Person of Sezchwan *(1989), Ibsen's* Hedda Gabler, *Beckett's* Footfalls *(1994), Shakespeare's* Richard II *(1995), a stage version of T. S. Eliot's* The Waste Land *(1995-7), and most recently, an adaptation of Jeanette Winterson's* The Powerbook. *Shaw also starred in Warner's feature film,* The Last September, *which was released in 2000. Fiona Shaw has also developed an extensive career separately in film, television and theater roles.*

Warner and Shaw collaborated on a celebrated production of Medea *at the Irish National (Abbey) Theatre in Dublin in June 2000. Deborah Warner stated her intention to make the production: "entirely Irish."[1] She directed the chorus to speak in a combination of English and Irish, and a singer sang traditional Irish laments from the auditorium. The entire cast was made up of Irish actors apart from Aegeus, played by the Jamaican actor Leo Wringer, and the Nurse played by Scottish actor, Fiona Bell. The production transferred to the Queen's Theatre in the West End of London in November 2000, where Warner recast the show almost entirely, apart from Shaw as Medea, and replaced the Irish cast with English actors. This move transformed the use of the Irish language, and Shaw's Irishness, in the production.*

Shaw's Medea is a sympathetic, witty, and intelligent woman, and Shaw's performance was praised for its complexity and sense of irony, with one critic dubbing her "the first funny Medea." The production eliminated Euripides' deus-ex-machina escape, showing instead the anti-climactic aftermath of the killings, with Medea still desperately trying to get Jason's attention. The staging of the murder scene was described by one critic as: "one of the most harrowing moments I've seen on stage," and audience members frequently fainted at the sight of the two young boys being killed. The production evoked the anxiety about the abuse and murder of children in contemporary Ireland and Britain, and captivated and horrified audiences by turns in Dublin and in London.

Aoife Monks is a stage director, who has recently completed her Ph.D. in Drama at Trinity College, Dublin. This interview was conducted in February 2001, as part of Monks's dissertation on the use of crossdressing in the work of Deborah Warner and Elizabeth LeCompte.

AM: How did Medea's foreignness work in the Dublin and London productions?

Because I think her nationality changed from Dublin to London: but I wasn't quite sure what her nationality was in Dublin.

FS: Well I don't think that being literal about these things is helpful. In Dublin, I was an outsider to a group much more prescribed by design so that it's very obviously a rather restrictive community, it was almost Islamic wasn't it?

Here [London], because I *am* Irish, there is not as much of a prescription around the chorus, they just are, the local people of here, but in Dublin that wasn't the case, in Dublin they were heightened versions of local people.

AM: And the use of the Irish language changed between the two as well?

FS: The use of Irish is really an extraction which I think is quite good, it's not that it is Irish, it's that it is a local old language which people use to communicate. It just happens to be a useful tool, and in Dublin what it did is that if the chorus did speak Irish, the audience understood the local view. Here [London] I am just using a tiny fragment that she might revert to, a language that the chorus wouldn't understand, that the audience wouldn't understand, which is fundamentally not so sympathetic, because people don't like not understanding things.

AM: So it reversed the use of Irish?

FS: Yeah yeah. I think of it very much as a sort of grace note.

---

[1] Helen Meaney, *The Irish Times*, 27/5/2000

AM: I am interested by the fact that, in interview, you said that the Dublin version of *Medea* was engaging with modern Ireland, with a different Ireland to the one you had left. . .

FS: I felt very out of contemporary Ireland, but actors use whatever the grab bag is in front of them, I mean if you feel out of something, then that helps you feel slightly alienated, it's not saying anything intrinsic about the thing but seeing it as an imaginative inspiration. There are funny things that he (Jason) says: "You come from the sky's backyard" and that is terribly funny if I think of that as Cork . . .

AM: There were people laughing at that in the audience in London, and I wasn't sure about what they were laughing at.

FS: I'm sure they were laughing at the fact that they were from Bolton or something, I don't think that would be again particularly about Ireland, people relate those things to themselves, but it's amazing for me. The "sky's backyard" could be Cork or it could be Ireland, but I don't think people would have any notion of that here particularly.

AM: And then Greece became London in some sense as well, some complex sophisticated place?

FS: I think the Greece Euripides was talking about didn't really exist, he was writing about the world as he knew it. Think of Shakespeare, also taking nominal names of places which form a platform from which a debate can be imaginatively explored, that's all it is. Medea and Jason are microbes of the human consciousness that are made flesh, and in order to make them flesh it helps if you give them a context. It is better if that context is local, so for the Greeks it was Greece, and for us it is better if it is something to do with who we are. And yet we are often helped by the word *Greece,* because if we are too literal about the place, we are sucked into all the provincialism of that place, and the play is not trying to deal with its own provincialism, it's trying to be a platform in which we can be imaginative.

AM: So the detail gives you freedom . . . the specificity gives you freedom to expand from it?

FS: Yes, that is how the imagination works. If this was set in London now people might be worried about who we really were talking about, who was that person really . . . and the great thing about the play and the word universal is that it is profoundly individual to each person watching it, and presumably each person playing it.

AM: I wanted to ask you what the comparison was between working on *Medea* and *Electra.*

FS: It's too long . . . a lifetime! I think I threw myself off the edge of a cliff for *Electra* and Deborah sort of helped me land perfectly well. I needed to move my acting forward. I think we made a leap at that time.

AM: How did they compare as characters? Electra and Medea? What were their differences as people?

FS: I don't think I can answer that at all! Because they're . . . character is merely situation enacted by the choices of the actor, they're not. . . .

AM: Essentially different?

They are, but the differences are the unselfconscious differences of my character to yours. If I start naming my character and your character, I wouldn't be able to play it. The character of Electra was me ten years ago, and that text and that situation. But with Medea, I suppose there's a remarkable difference in the playing of it, because Electra was obsessed with one thing. There's no humour in Electra at all, she had no irony. She's a very very interesting and very very moving aspect of the human soul, Electra, somebody so worn out that if she had a personality once, she was probably very gentle and probably rather lovely. But, by the time you meet her, everything has gone except this aspect of herself, this dreadful woman waiting for her brother's return. That's very very sad, it makes me sad about humans: they can get to that state, and it makes them very unattractive at that moment. That's a very interesting corner of the human experience to explore.

But Medea's grief is much more recent, so she's much nearer sanity.

AM: She has more of a context too, doesn't she?

FS: She has children in her life. And a husband who she could recover quite quickly from if he returned, although if Jason did return she might not take him back either . . . she would be unable to, you know, she really is trapped, she's caught. . .

Of course Medea does get comfort, while in Electra there's no comfort. There are comforts for Medea, one being that the chorus agree with her, that she should do something. She needs this, because she doesn't seem to function on her own at all, whereas Electra is completely on her own. And Aegeus turns up for Medea, that is quite extraordinary, then she knows the entire system, entire fate is on her side, for good or ill. You've no idea if any good will come of it, and in fact pure ill comes.

AM: I never expected there to be dragons in the ending of the show, but I was surprised by the sense right at the end that this really was for nothing, that nothing has changed.

FS: That is hell, that is hell. . . . Reality mustn't serve the play, the play must serve our reality and we now live in a very post-theistic society and so our hell is much more on the earth than in the life beyond. There are people who say there's a great relief in killing somebody, that once you've killed them you feel better, you've done something for that moment, and then you pay for the rest of your life, Maybe we are being more moral by discovering that there is nothing brave in murder, that there is bravery in action but there is no glory in it at all, of any kind, none.

AM: The audience were very sympathetic to Medea, and I think your ending gave a sense of "perhaps we could end up doing that too, maybe if we really do feel sympathetic, then we almost could go along with the murders."

FS: I think that is not an interpretation, I think those things are very simply set up. We see Medea, we hear she's got worse things coming, we know her husband's left her, we think "that's very bad but...." And then we hear she's going to be banished, and we hear the chorus saying "goodness you're worse off than we thought," so that information is being given to the audience, so . . . the structure's very basic. Aegeus turns up and she says "right, I've had enough of being down, up I go," and up we go with her, and then we think "oh my God how far is she going?" and up she goes, and it all happens.

And I think that is very much our experience of the pre-Christian world, pre-sin really, that actions do need encouragement, and once we've encouraged them, we've no idea what we've encouraged, we all live like that. I mean whenever you've done a bad thing, it's very rare you've planned it. You have an affair and then regret it. You don't think "it's a bad thing to have an affair but I will have one," you find yourself agreeing. I mean we all do that, we say "it's a good thing to have a Labour government," and so we vote for a Labour government, and then we regret it, but that's just our action, we can't be responsible at the moment of choice all the time.

But we do become more and more responsible as we go nearer and nearer to the . . . that's what's so interesting about the chorus, they think "you're right you should kill him," and then as she goes nearer to that they think "uh oh!" When she says "what can I do?" and they say "nothing," they've agreed. The chorus are sort of ushers at the side of the audience going "Are we all for this? Yeah yeah . . . I think so . . . intellectually we are yeah . . . we can see that, yeah." *Medea* is a brilliant play for showing how the intellect or law or logic or morality are worryingly different to the messy things in our life.

AM: I wondered about the gender differences in playing Medea and Richard II, in connection with your idea of Richard being a "non-man" and being beyond gender. I wondered how you played that, what happened to you when you played that role?

And by comparison, how you played Medea who is very much a woman, not necessarily because of any essence, but because of her power, what kind of power she had and the things she could and couldn't do.

FS: I just decided Richard was a good idea and did it. Why I thought it was a good idea, or why I subsequently did not think it was a good idea, or why was I in it, why I agreed to it, to are questions that I'm still probably not able to answer, only because I still don't know the answer . . . I don't know what it is to be a man. I know what it is to think like Richard II, on those lines. Of course, you are allowing bits of yourself to disappear, you're battening down your breasts . . . so I think the non-man was my way in. And also, there are many men who play a man better . . . you know the worst man would play a better man than I could so that really wasn't the target, the way in wasn't to try to be a man.

But of course the menu that was open to Richard, which was the menu of power and kingship and a rather moving attachment to a crown, is exactly opposite to what Medea has in relation to her husband, they're absolutely opposite ownerships, one is very male, the ownership of power, and Richard's essence lies in the notion of being not just king but therefore beyond human beings. It's great fun to play that. You're absolutely right that Medea's much nearer home, much nearer the domestic reality enflamed to a kind of poetical dimension.

AM: Why do you think the critics were so resistant to your performance as Richard?

FS: I think it was that the English do need Shakespeare history plays to reflect history and actually *Richard II* had the same set of criticisms as *Medea*. They need the Greek world to reflect some notion of Greekness and the moment you don't fulfill that obligation, when you say "this *Richard II* is a piece of theatre, it's a piece of verse written by a writer 400 years ago, we can do anything we like with it," they get nervous because it has a sort of temple like status in the common community.

AM: Why there was a protectiveness over *Medea*? Why did the English critics become concerned by your changes to the ending of the play?

FS: I think a little knowledge is a dangerous thing. The chariot pulled by dragons is really an assumption, but the theatre has to break its own assumptions, particularly if it's done rigorously, that's my argument. What's the point of somebody bringing an irrelevant thing into it? Or else they don't do the play because they say "the play's irrelevant to me because I don't know what the chariot is," the chariot is just the language of the scene.

I'm very defensive about this . . . I think Deborah and I don't take liberties with things, we work with immense rigour, we don't swash in there and say "well Euripides brought in a chariot there and so will we." It has no meaning, I mean it has no meaning for us. The theatre can do anything it likes. The theatre has no rules, you could do it with dwarves, that's theatre, you could do it with babies if you like, that's theatre. It's extraordinary that people think, "well that should be done in blue," which is really the same issue that was in the Beckett Estate, it should be done like Beckett did it. That is death to the theatre.

Theatre has to respond to us now, and I do think this production is responding to us now if only because we live now. I'm of the same age as Medea, I'm the same type of person who might be in that situation now. So my life and my world that I'm in is the thing that I'm bringing to the text of *Medea*. That is completely valid. It is not in anyway misconstruing our contemporary heightened experience of children's deaths. . .

AM: What do you think you and Deborah have been trying to do with your work, both of you, through the plays you've chosen to do together?

FS: I'm trying to be alive, I'm trying to surprise myself. I know what I should think about things, and through plays I find out what I really think about them. I think reality is a mystery and I get excited when we hit the mystery rather than the expected reality.

I want to wrongfoot the audience in the most pleasant way, I have no wish to upset them, I want to turn their heads around.

I want the production to be worthy of spending so much time doing it, so I want it to be very rigorous. I like when it's hard, I don't enjoy it necessarily. I would love it to have some meaning for others, but I can only say it has meaning for me, when it is hard and when I end up somewhere unexpected. That seems to be to me like traveling, journeying and I love sharing that journey and I'm delighted if it delights an audience or appeals to their sense of wanting to journey, they want to go somewhere they didn't know they were going. I don't want to confirm the audience's biases and their prejudices, I want to humbly go with them and say "I didn't know it was going to be like this either." We place ourselves in a very vulnerable position because I can't defend where we get to, I can only say "this is where we got to, after all these months of working on it. We got here, we didn't decide to get here, we didn't necessarily choose to get here, and we'll take it away if it's the wrong place to have gone, if it is the untrue place we won't go there." There are these wonderful endings but they're not the true endings so we don't do them, the true ones for us anyway.

I think the theatre, it's quite a selfish thing, I need it to be an incredibly rigorous, an extremely difficult place to be. It's probably the same thing that motivates Ranulph Fiennes to go to the South Pole, it may be a complete folly, but it's only interesting if it's hard.

PERFORMANCE REVIEW

The Oresteia

MICHAEL BILLINGTON
Review of The Oresteia

DIRECTED BY SIR PETER HALL, AT THE OLIVIER THEATRE, ROYAL NATIONAL THEATRE, LONDON, 30 NOVEMBER 1981.

Michael Billington is one of the best known and most widely read theater critics writing in London. In November 1981, he reviewed the National Theatre production of The Oresteia. *This production was notable in several ways: it used an entirely male cast; both the leading actors and the chorus were masked; and it was the first English-language production to perform a Greek tragedy in the classical amphitheater at Epidaurus (Greece). Although the production was widely praised, and subsequently filmed, Billington's review honestly records the difficulties of transporting an unfamiliar performance convention—here, the use of masks—into the contemporary theater.*

Peter Hall's production of *The Oresteia* at the Olivier is certainly very daring. But does it work? For the first two plays of Aeschylus's great trilogy, I have to admit that the conventions chosen by Hall and his translator, Tony Harrison—masks, an all-male cast, rough alliterative Anglo-Saxon kind of verse—were like insurmountable barriers between me and the work. Only in the final, fantastically difficult play, *Eumenides,* do the conventions become a bonus with triumph being snatched belatedly from the jaws of Morpheus.

The first problem is that of the masks. You can rationalise till you're blue in the face (and some very strange arguments are used in the programme to justify the masks) but the blunt Emperor-has-no-clothes truth is that masks make language very difficult to hear and deny the actor one of his most basic weapons. Of course they were used in the Greek theatre. But that was partly because the occasion was a religious ritual, partly because one actor (as here) played more than one role and partly because in theatres seating up to 15,000, the facial features had to be exaggerated.

To employ them today (whatever the intellectual motive) seems to me as perverse as making a movie without sound or doing Shakespeare in a mock-Elizabethan playhouse. What was an accepted convention for the Greeks for us becomes an arty device.

Only in the third play, *Eumenides,* do the masks become something more than an obstacle. Agamemnon has been murdered by Clytaemnestra. She, in turn, has been killed by her son Orestes. In the final play Apollo and the ancient Furies are locked in a terrific conflict over the morality of the murder. A hung jury cannot decide the issue and, as Athena finally resolves things, Aeschylus deliberately moves the action onto another plane and the masks at last come into their own.

The most chilling moment in the whole evening is the assembly, one by one, of the Furies, white-masked, gory-locked and to a sound like the murmur of innumerable bees. Their transformation into kindly beings (by a series of political bribes) and their final exit through a silent, standing, astonished Olivier audience is also a moving piece of theatre.

But in the earlier plays the masks so distance the spectator (this spectator anyway) as to leave him detached and unfeeling. Harrison argues that the mask and its language "compel us to keep our eyes open in situations of extremity when we might otherwise flinch away in horror and stop looking." This is absolute poppycock. I've seen *The Oresteia* at the Burgtheater in Vienna and in Peter Stein's magnificent Berlin Schaubühne version and can report that the audience, confronted by recognisable human beings, had rather less difficulty than here in keeping their eyes open.

Time and again the style adopted here alienates (in the Brechtian sense) the spectator and drastically limits the text's emotional variety. Take the return home of Agamemnon. He enters on a mobile trolley, spear-wreathed and adorned with skeletal horses' heads. In his mask he represents one attribute: bluff militaristic might. But given a human face (as he was by Peter Stein) it was possible for him to pause on the threshold and suggest an apprehensive foreknowledge of his death. Likewise Clytemnestra, in an unvaried rouge-streaked gold mask, cannot begin to convey the human subtlety (the guilt under the gilt, so to speak) of the murderous intent underlying her extravagant supplications.

What is extraordinary about this *Oresteia* is that it leaps effortlessly over the hurdle where other productions fall. Stein botched the *Eumenides* because, I suspect, he couldn't accept the divine intervention and the blatant endorsement of male supremacy. But Hall's version here really begins to work. The alienation-effect that has kept us lightly chilled in the first two plays pays off precisely because it enables us to see the contrived absurdity of the arguments. When Apollo, seeking to justify matricide, says, "The mother of what's called her offspring's no parent but only the nurse to the seed that's implanted," one is permitted to scoff.

The imagery of this third play is also infinitely more expressive: there is a fine moment when the body of Orestes sways and ripples under pressure from the Furies before making a slow motion escape like a marathon-runner trudging through mire. And the judgment on Orestes, with the jurors dropping their pebbles into one of two downstage urns, is as engrossing as it must have been in 458 BC.

The production also boasts one other unequivocal success: Harrison Birtwistle's music. Scored for six musicians on either side of the stage, it punctuates the action ceaselessly: jagged percussion for the Chorus's fragmented verse, screeching woodwind wails for Cassandra's cries, amplified harp when the trial reaches its most intense. Instead of being a detachable adornment, the music becomes an inseparable part of the event.

In the end the test of any production of *The Oresteia* is whether it sends you out feeling you've encountered drama's first masterpiece or endured an act of piety; and my feelings, as you may have gathered, were somewhat split.

For the first two plays I felt starved of blood, passion, excitement, emotion as I stared wanly at these hollow-eyed masks from which emerged this indigestible alliterative verse, beating like rain on a corrugated-iron roof. But with the trial of Orestes the language thins out, there is a deliberately ironic contrast between the beaten-gold masks and the tarnished arguments, and we feel a precarious order has been spun out of chaos. What starts as a dehumanised experiment at last achieves a perfervid ritual excitement.

II

Classical Japan

Acting in the Noh theatre.

The drama and theater of the Asian world has a history as complex and multifaceted as the histories of the many civilizations, peoples, and nations that have been said—by the West—to compose the "Asian world." India, for example, has a literature—in **SANSKRIT**—more than 3,000 years old. Although the golden age of Sanskrit theater took place in the fourth and fifth centuries, theater of various kinds—folk, classical, and modern—thrives in India today. The conventions of Indian theater have pervasively influenced the theater of southeast Asia; the Sanskrit epic poems *Mahabharata* and *Ramayana* provide the characters and settings, for example, for the beautiful shadow-puppet theater of Java in Indonesia—the *WAYANG KULIT*—and related forms of performance using dolls or live actors.

The masked dance drama of Korea—called *KAMYONGUK*—is related both to Chinese and Japanese theater, and Korea, like other Asian countries, has developed an important modern theater as well.

European knowledge of China's theater probably dates from Marco Polo's visits (1254–1324); we know of more than 550 playwrights who wrote after the Mongol invasion during China's Yüan dynasty (1279–1368), part of a theatrical tradition that is recorded as early as 1000 BCE and that developed throughout the Han (206 BCE–221 CE), Hui (589–614), T'ang (618–904), and Sung (960–1279) periods. Several plays from the Yüan theater have been adapted by European playwrights; Voltaire's *The Orphan of China* (1755), an adaptation of Chi Chunhsiang's *The House of Chao,* was the first Chinese play to become widely known in Europe, and Li Hsing's *The Story of the Chalk Circle* has been adapted several times, notably by Bertolt Brecht in *The Caucasian Chalk Circle* (1944). After the Mongols were expelled during the Ming dynasty (1368–1644), the center of theatrical activity shifted from northern China toward southern cities such as Hangchow. It was only during the eighteenth and nineteenth centuries, under the Ch'ing dynasty (1644–1912), that the most characteristic form of modern Chinese theater, the *BEIJING OPERA,* began to take the shape that it has today, sharing the stage with both Western and Western-style plays, and with a vigorous experimental theater working in a more distinctly Chinese dramatic idiom.

Although no one theater can be said to represent these rich and diverse theatrical traditions, the classical theater of Japan shares many features common to other Asian theaters: it blends aristocratic and popular affiliations; it descends from social and religious ritual traditions; it coordinates acting, dance, music, and spectacle; many of its plots and characters are derived from familiar literary and historical narratives and legends; its performance conventions are elaborately stylized and refined; and its performers are often trained with a level of formality not found in Western theater. This is hardly surprising, in that the introduction of Buddhism into Japan during the sixth century coincided with an important period of Japanese cultural and political expansion; for the next two centuries, Japan was actively in contact with the vital cultures of India, China, and Korea. Although the period of "classical" Japanese theater—roughly the twelfth through the eighteenth centuries—coincides with an extended period of cultural isolation, the expansion of Japan's military, political, and economic power in the nineteenth and twentieth centuries has again brought Japanese culture into dialogue with Asia and the West. Indeed, while Japan's imperial ambitions—the invasion of China and much of the Pacific Rim before and during World War II—were extinguished with the atomic bombing of Hiroshima and Nagasaki, Japanese theater and drama

125

have continued to develop both in response to Western culture and through the experimental innovation of its own traditions.

The classical Japanese theater is a product of a distinctive period in the history of Japan, extending from 1192, when the emperor gave all civil and secular power to a *SHOGUN,* a hereditary military leader, to 1868, when the emperor regained state as well as religious authority. For better than 750 years the Japanese emperors lived in Kyoto, engaged in largely ceremonial duties, while the *shoguns,* based in Edo, exercised all political and judicial authority. The Genroku period (1680–1730) saw an extraordinary flowering of Japanese art and culture supported by the shogunate; this was the period of Basho, the famous *haiku* poet; of Ihara Saikaku, the novelist; and of Chikamatsu Monzaemon, Japan's greatest playwright. Although the Noh theater was in decline by the Genroku period, the three principal modes of Japanese classical theater—**NOH, DOLL THEATER,** and **KABUKI**—are in different ways the product of the elaborately hierarchical culture of feudal Japan, and of the increasing tension between the class of warriors who ruled Japan and a class of artisans and merchants—sometimes called simply *CHONIN,* or townsmen—whose economic power was centered in Japan's cities. With the rise of the shogunate, Japanese society assumed a feudal character that represented the interests and values of its ruling class of *SAMURAI* warriors. Owing their allegiance to the *shogun,* the ranks of the *samurai* comprised various warrior lords, or *DAIMYO,* and their attendant warriors. As in other feudal societies, in Japan it was both a right and an obligation to display the signs and behavior of one's caste. The *samurai,* for example, were expected to obey a stringent honor code, one that required their absolute loyalty to the *shogun,* to the *samurai* caste, and to its military ethos. If a *samurai* betrayed his lord, he and his followers risked becoming outcasts, called *RŌNIN* or "men adrift." The most famous Kabuki drama, *Chūshingura* (1748), takes the fortunes of such a *samurai* lord and his forty-seven followers as its subject, and *rōnin* are common figures in the Japanese theater. This organization extended throughout Japanese society; not only was Japanese society divided into major castes, but its professions—including theater and prostitution, often closely associated in the popular imagination—were strictly controlled through an elaborate guild system. In the major cities, theaters were built in specifically licensed quarters, and actors were generally required to live in or near those districts. Much as tradespeople had to make their trade known through conventions of dress (a practice common in Europe at this time as well), so actors were required in 1709 to shave their forelocks as a public sign of their profession.

Under the Ashikaga shogunate, which began in 1338 and ended in a civil war in the late sixteenth century, not only were the values of the *samurai* dominant, but the privileges of the *samurai* relative to other castes—such as the many ranks of merchants, artisans, farmers, and peasants—were rigidly observed. The principal forms of theatrical entertainment, especially Noh (or Nō) theater, were both sponsored by and largely reserved for the elite *samurai* castes and represented the literary and cultural values of their patrons. In 1603, Tokugawa Ieyasu (1542–1616) became the Emperor's *shogun,* and in the Tokugawa period (1603–1867; sometimes called the Edo period, after the city that was his seat, present-day Tokyo), Japan entered a period of extended peace and increasing cultural isolation. In the seventeenth century, the *shoguns* began to expel all foreigners from Japan, reserving specific enclaves in port cities like Nagasaki as protected zones where foreign trade might be undertaken. As cities such as Osaka, Tokyo, and Kyoto became significant urban centers, the merchant classes became wealthier and more powerful. Although their status was lower than that of the *samurai,* many of the merchants amassed huge fortunes that far exceeded the wealth of many *samurai.* The *samurai* still exerted political authority—in 1705 the *samurai* confiscated the fortune of a merchant to whom many of them were indebted—but the merchant classes came to dominate the cultural sphere as they became the principal audience for poetry, fiction, and theater. Although all three forms of classical Japanese theater are preserved and performed today, they first became popular in different eras of Japan's history: The Noh, as it is now known, was developed largely between the fourteenth and early seventeenth centuries; the doll theater's greatest popularity was in the late seventeenth century; Kabuki, which is said to have originated when Okuni, a dancer from the Izumo Shrine in Kyoto, began to perform satirical skits in Kyoto in 1603, developed largely between the late seventeenth and mid-eighteenth centuries.

THE DEVELOPMENT OF NOH THEATER

Although Noh theater achieved its highly literary and ceremonial form in the fourteenth century, it is usually said to have developed from performance modes popular throughout the tenth and eleventh centuries, the *SARUGAKU-NO,* and a related form, *DENGAKU-NO.* "Noh" means "accomplishment" or "performance," and both forms of entertainment contributed elements to the development of Noh theater and drama. *Dengaku-no* may have had more explicit ritual elements, and was initially associated with the native Japanese religion of Shinto, but both forms involved acrobatics, comic role-playing, and dance. *Sarugaku* means "monkey music," which may give some idea of the exuberance of these performances. In the twelfth century, however, *sarugaku-no* was adapted by Buddhist priests to illustrate tenets of Buddhist thought and belief, and performances were given to large audiences at major temples, acted by lower-ranking priests. In time, professional players both imitated these performances outside the temples and were hired to replace the priests in temple performances; by the mid-twelfth century, guilds of performers were attached to major temples. In return for free performances during religious ceremonies and festivals, the professional guilds were given a monopoly on performing in the region of the temple.

Although the *sarugaku-no* and *dengaku-no* seem to have been energetic and spirited forms of entertainment, it was the association with the contemplative and literary elements of Buddhism that were to have the greatest effect on the formation of Noh theater. In 1374, Kan'ami Kiyotsugu (1333–1384)—a leader of one of the four main *sarugaku-no* troupes— performed before the *shogun* Yoshimitsu Ashikaga (1358–1408). Kan'ami was one of the great innovators of his era and is thought to have contributed to giving the Noh its current form. He emphasized the rhythmic nature of the musical accompaniment, developed a greater use of mime in acting, and correlated dance and musical elements more closely with a dramatic plot. These innovations might well have been lost, however, had the *shogun* not been so impressed that he took Kan'ami and his son, Zeami Motokiyo (1363–1444), under his patronage. Kan'ami's troupe became the most influential in Japan, and after his father's death Zeami assumed control of the company, until he was exiled from the court in 1434 by one of Yoshimitsu's sons. Together, Kan'ami and Zeami gave the Noh drama its now-traditional ethos and shape. Kan'ami's innovations were explored and formalized by Zeami, who wrote or revised more than 100 of the 241 plays that make up the Noh repertoire and described the philosophical, esthetic, and practical goals of Noh performance in several theoretical essays. In time, the *daimyo,* emulating the *shogun,* came to sponsor their own Noh performers. Because the performers and performances were so closely bound to the status of the *samurai* caste, however, Noh never became a popular or even very public form of theater. Although *samurai* occasionally sponsored "subscription" performances of Noh for the "townsmen," these highly refined, intensely literary dramas were definitively the entertainment of the elite.

The esthetics of Noh derive from the Buddhist emphasis on **ZEN,** or contemplation, an attitude of repose and withdrawal from worldly desire and distraction. Noh performance aims to induce a similar kind of attentive repose in its audience, to evoke what is called *YUGEN* (often translated as "grace," although for Western readers this may have irrelevant Christian connotations), a mood or state of mind responsive to the mysterious, graceful, and impermanent beauty of the performance. For this reason, perhaps, Noh drama is not really driven by the cause-and-effect narrative logic of Western drama. Noh plays are typically centered on scenes of revelation that climax in the main actor's principal dance. Rather than imitating life, a Noh play should evoke the "flower," as Zeami termed the fusion of esthetic, spiritual, and moral beauty arising from the performance.

Noh Dramatic Form

A "typical" Noh play might begin with the *WAKI,* or secondary actor, meeting the *SHITE,* or principal actor, at a site of historical, legendary, or mythological importance. The *waki* enters first, and in his opening song—sometimes called the **TRAVELING SONG,** because he sings it while making his entrance—announces who he is (often a priest), and where he is going. The *shite* then enters, taking the role of an ordinary person. They discuss the significance of the place, perhaps where a legendary warrior was killed in battle. The characters speak a densely literary language, for part of the Noh dramatist's skill is shown in his cunning ability to borrow allusions and quotations from Japanese literature; the actors repeat and emphasize a network of phrases and images that convey the play's central theme. The chorus—kneeling stage left—also contributes to this "literary" texture, narrating some of the action and singing or reciting some of the dialogue. The *shite* then leaves the stage, and in some Noh productions a **KYŌGEN** (a brief farce also descended from *sarugaku*) is performed. When the *shite* returns, however, he reveals who he really is, usually a god, hero, or demon connected with the place whose destiny is troubled; he might, for example, be the ghost of the legendary warrior. In a manner of speaking, the character continues to haunt this place because he or she is unable to let go of the world, of the "character" and its investment in the world that are the essence of his or her being. The ghost is haunted by the tortuous attitude or emotion that keeps him or her connected to the world. Unlike a Greek or Shakespearean tragedy, a Noh play does not conclude with a speech of recognition or response; instead, Noh drama concludes with an intricate dance, a beautiful interplay of dialogue, dance, narration, and music for the audience's contemplation.

Since the active repertoire of Noh drama has remained more or less the same for over 400 years, it is perhaps not surprising that other elements of Noh theater and performance have become highly systematic and conventionalized. There are five types of Noh drama—plays praising the gods, plays about warriors, plays about women, plays about madness or

NOH PERFORMANCE SPACE, FIFTEENTH CENTURY

seats for high-ranking officials

stands

stage

hashigakari

mirror room

This is the ground plan of the performance space in the time of Zeami.

spirits, and plays about demons—and in classical Japan, a program of Noh performance included one play from each of these categories, performed in this order, with a *kyōgen* between each Noh play. In modern Japan it has become more common to perform only two or three plays followed by a *kyōgen,* in part because the pace of performance is much slower today. Although women at one time performed in Noh theater, in 1629 women were banned from the Japanese stage; while women do perform in the modern Japanese theater, Noh companies are now traditionally all male. Plays are performed by the *shite* who is masked, an unmasked *waki,* and actors who play the *shite*'s companions (*TSURE*). A chorus of six to ten men both sings and narrates from a position to the side of the stage, and musicians—a flute and two or three drums—are positioned at the rear of the stage. The drums beat rhythmically, punctuating and accentuating the actors' delivery, while the flute plays in a kind of counterpoint to their speech. The *shite*'s mask is drawn from one of five categories—old person, male, female, gods, monsters—and the clothing of the performers is similarly stylized: The actors sometimes wear elaborate headdresses, and sumptuous silk clothing, arranged and layered in particular ways for certain roles. The members of the chorus wear the traditional dress of the *samurai.* Attendants clothed in black are present onstage throughout the performance, helping the actors with costumes and masks and placing and removing properties when needed; they are always senior actors of the company, because they may also need to step in to finish a performance if an actor is unable to continue. The stage is bare of sets, and hand properties are few and conventional; a bundle of firewood might be represented by a few sticks bound with flowers. Similarly, many of the properties are purely symbolic: A twig carried by a grieving woman is the sign of her madness. Throughout the performance, the actors move slowly and ceremonially; indeed, many of their actions must take place at a prescribed area of the stage.

Although the Noh stage was shaped somewhat differently in Kan'ami's and Zeami's era, by 1615 it had assumed the shape it retains to this day. A stage (*BUTAI*), roughly eighteen feet square, extends into the audience area; the stage is roofed like the early shrines from which

The Noh Stage

This ground plan shows the stage with the mirror room, the *hashigakari,* the *shitebashira,* the *wakibashira,* the *metsukebashira,* and the *fuebashira,* as well as the locations for the musicians and the chorus.

it derives, and the audience is seated in front and on the stage-right side. A painted backdrop behind the stage always pictures the Yogo Pine at the Kasuga Shrine in Nara. The stage is always of highly polished wood, with sounding jars concealed beneath it to resonate with the emphatic stamping that is part of the actors' performance. The musicians are seated directly behind the main stage area on a second, narrow stage (ATOZA); they are in full view of the audience and are able to see the actors and adjust their playing to the actors' performance throughout the play. A small entrance, called the **HURRY DOOR,** leads off the stage-left side of the *atoza,* which is used by the stage assistants, the chorus, and for the exit of dead characters. A second narrow stage runs along the stage-left side of the stage, the *WAKI-ZA,* where the chorus is seated, again in view of the audience and able to adjust their narration and singing to the pace of the actors. Finally, a long bridge, the *HASHIGAKARI,* leads from the upstage right corner of the stage out to the **MIRROR ROOM,** where the costumed actors have been studying themselves to get into the character. The *hashigakari* is six feet wide by thirty-three to fifty-two feet long; it is bordered by a narrow strip of white pebbles, on which stand three pine trees, representing heaven, earth, and man.

The four pillars that support the roof over the stage also have specific functions in the performance and provide a sense of the ceremonial formality of Noh theater. The upstage right pillar closest to the *hashigakari* is called the **SHITEBASHIRA,** or *shite*'s pillar. When the *shite* enters the *hashigakari,* he slides his feet (which are bound in cotton cloth) slowly along the floor; reaching the *shitebashira,* he pauses to announce who he is, where he is coming from, and where he is going (sometimes the *waki* will make this announcement when the *shite* reaches the *shitebashira*). The pillar downstage right is called the **METSUKEBASHIRA,** the gazing or eye-fixing pillar. It is the place where the *shite* looks while delivering his speech and which he watches through the slits in his mask to help orient his performance; given the tiny eye-openings in Noh masks, the *metsukebashira* is nearly all the *shite* can see. Downstage left, diagonally across from the *shitebashira,* is the **WAKIBASHIRA,** where the *waki* is often stationed when the *shite* enters. Upstage left is the **FUEBASHIRA,** the flute-player's pillar, where the flute-player is positioned.

As Zeami suggests in "Teachings on Style and the Flower" (see Critical Contexts), the training of a Noh actor in the fourteenth century was presumed to be lifelong, more a vocation than an occupation. Under the shogunate, Noh performers were given the privileges of the *samurai* caste, and five schools for training Noh actors were founded. These schools were run by hereditary masters, and certain families of Noh performers have influenced the theater over several generations; indeed, we owe the preservation of many documents (including Zeami's treatises), properties, and masks to the unusually closed and traditional ways in which Noh training has been passed from generation to generation. Four of the five current Noh companies were founded in Zeami's lifetime. Although Japan is no longer a caste society, acting in a Noh company today still requires years of dedication and intense training, something between the priesthood and the military. Moreover, because the relatively small number of classical Noh plays was stabilized in the early seventeenth century, Noh actors have generally mastered all the roles of the repertoire and perform without rehearsal. Their intensive training in movement, song, and dance prepares the actors, chorus, musicians, and stage assistants to be closely responsive to the many subtleties of their collective performance. And given the stability of the repertoire, of training, and of performance conventions, Noh theater has been performed in an unbroken tradition from Zeami's era to the present day.

THE DEVELOPMENT OF DOLL THEATER

Like the Noh theater, the doll theater owes something to the desire of Buddhist priests to educate a wider Japanese audience in their teachings. Unlike the Noh, however, the doll theater was not supported or protected directly by the shogunate, and it came to enjoy a more popular audience. The doll theater arose from the confluence of two kinds of performance: puppet shows and storytelling to music. Much like the itinerant performers of *sarugaku-no,* wandering puppeteers became associated with shrines and temples in the twelfth century. At the same time, a form of live storytelling also became popular, the singing and recitation of legends and stories to the accompaniment of the BIWA, a four-stringed, plucked instrument. One of the most popular of these narratives was *The Tale of Jōruri,* a love story about a wealthy girl named Jōruri; although the story dates from the fifteenth century, it became popular when it was performed to a musical instrument imported from the Ryukyu Islands between 1558 and 1569, the SAMISEN. The *samisen,* a three-stringed instrument that is both plucked and struck, has a much wider tonal and dynamic range than the *biwa.* Samisen-accompanied dialogue and narrative became so popular that this kind of performance was termed simply JŌRURI. In effect, the doll theater is a form of *jōruri* in which the song and spoken narrative are accompanied by puppet performance.

Although puppets had been used in Japan for several centuries, puppets were first used in conjunction with *jōruri* performances in the sixteenth century; puppet-*jōruri* performances have been recorded in Kyoto as early as 1596, and by the late seventeenth century there were important doll theaters in both Tokyo and Osaka. As in the Noh, the plays performed in the doll theaters used narrative, dialogue, music, and acting to convey the dramatic action, and in the seventeenth century playwrights writing for the doll theaters adapted plots and characters directly from Noh models. In part, however, because of their derivation from the romantic *jōruri* narratives, in part because their audiences were well-to-do merchants and citizens rather than the aristocratic *samurai,* and in part because they were competing with the more salacious Kabuki theaters for that audience, the doll theaters came to dramatize events more closely approaching contemporary life. Although the earliest doll theater plays were on historical and legendary subjects (like the Noh plays), by the late seventeenth and early eighteenth centuries, doll drama concerned stagings of current events, and romanticized portrayals of contemporary life, called "domestic plays" or SEWAMONO. Although the shogunate forbade the staging of current events in 1703, the shoguns were more concerned about the satirical portrayals of *samurai* common in Kabuki; playwrights continued to write about contemporary events.

The doll theater played a major role in the development of Japanese theater generally. When Gidayu Takemoto (1651–1714), a famous performer of *jōruri,* opened the Takemoto Theater in Osaka in 1684, he began a collaboration with Chikamatsu Monzaemon (1653–1725), now generally recognized as Japan's greatest dramatist. Chikamatsu wrote an important body of plays for the doll theater, on historical subjects as well as on contemporary life. His play *Love Suicides at Sonezaki* (1703) concerns the double suicide of a young merchant and a prostitute in 1703 and was renowned for the beauty of its language and the power of its performance. The genre became so popular that in 1722 the shogunate banned plays about double suicide, which were common in both the doll theater and the Kabuki theater, perhaps fearing that Chikamatsu's play would be imitated by romantic young Japanese. Not only did Chikamatsu and other playwrights—notably Chikamatsu Hanji (1725–1783) and Uemura Bunrakuken (1737–1810), for whom the current puppet theater of Japan, BUNRAKU, is named—produce an extraordinarily rich body of plays, but also these plays were immediately mined by the Kabuki theaters, providing a source of material for living actors as well as the doll theater's elaborate puppets.

The stage of the doll theater is thirty-six feet wide by twenty-six feet deep and is divided into three sections, each separated by a low screen. The three puppeteers who operate each puppet are visible throughout the performance. They are costumed in elegant traditional clothes and are seated behind the screens. The puppeteers and their dolls share the stage with several other performers: the stage assistants, dressed in black as in the Noh theater; the an-

The Doll Theater Stage

nouncer; the narrator; and the *samisen* player. The announcer begins the performance by announcing the title of the play and introducing the narrator and the *samisen* player. The narrator is responsible for the verbal art of the play in a direct development of his role in the *jōruri*: he narrates the story of the play, speaks the dialogue of the characters and expresses their emotions as well, smiling, laughing, weeping, and so on. Later in the eighteenth century several narrators were used, one for each of the major characters in the drama. The *samisen* is played to augment, clarify, and deepen the narrator's performance, lending it a special plangency.

As in the Noh theater, performance in the doll theater is extremely ceremonial and precise, and performers undergo years of training to achieve their craft. Although marionettes were used in the seventeenth century, hand-operated puppets became increasingly popular and by 1736 had supplanted earlier forms. The typical doll is three or four feet tall and is operated by three puppeteers. The most senior operator, dressed in a formal nineteenth-century costume, stands behind the doll and holds it up; he works a system of strings and pulleys within the head that control the doll's head, eyebrows, and eyelids, and he also operates the doll's right arm and right hand by means of hidden strings. His two assistants are clothed in black like the stage assistants, and their faces are covered; one assistant operates the left arm and hand, and the other assistant operates the legs and feet. Much as training in the Noh theater resembles that of a traditional art, so learning to operate the puppets of the doll theater entails a lifetime of commitment. Puppeteers take an apprenticeship of ten years to learn to operate the legs and feet of the dolls with sufficient grace; they then take another ten years to learn the correct operation of the left arm and hand before spending the final ten years on mastering the subtleties of the right arm, right hand, and head.

Doll theater contributed extensively to the dramatic repertoire of the Kabuki theater, and the fixed poses of the puppets are sometimes thought to contribute to the exaggerated expressive stance of the Kabuki actors, the **MIE.** But the doll theater contributed other innovations to Japanese theater and to world theater generally. Much as the dolls increased in complexity throughout the late seventeenth century and early eighteenth century—gaining eye movement in 1730, finger joints and movements in 1733, and so on—so the stage itself became increasingly mechanized. By 1715 the doll theaters were using movable settings, and by 1727 elevator traps were used to raise and lower scenery visibly through the floor of the stage. This machinery not only was put to use in the more spectacular Kabuki theater, but also was adapted and imitated by theaters around the world. Although the doll theater was surpassed in popularity by the Kabuki in the nineteenth century, it continues to be sponsored by the Japanese government and performed regularly in Osaka and Tokyo.

THE DEVELOPMENT OF KABUKI THEATER

Kabuki is in many ways the most energetic and spectacular mode of classical Japanese theater, using live actors to stage intense and passionate dramas whose effect is heightened by a range of powerful performance conventions and by an elaborately mechanized stage. As in the doll theater, Kabuki arose as a popular form of entertainment, supported by audiences outside the aristocratic sphere of Noh performance. Although Kabuki drama, as in the drama of the doll theaters, was initially derived from the plays of the Noh theater, Kabuki theater rapidly developed its own dramatic style and performance esthetics.

Unlike Noh and doll theater, Kabuki did not originate in medieval performance forms like the *sarugaku-no* and the *biwa*-accompanied narratives that became *jōruri*. Instead, Kabuki began in 1603, when Okuni, who claimed to be a priestess from the Izumo Grand Shrine, set up an impromptu stage in the Kyoto riverbed, where she performed dances and satirical skits. Okuni's company was largely composed of women, and within a short time a number of companies—some involving prostitutes, who offered performances as entertainment— were established in Kyoto and elsewhere. Although comic roles—called *SARUWAKA*—were always performed by men, the earliest troupes were composed mainly of women, called either *ONNA KABUKI* (women's Kabuki) or *YŪGO KABUKI* (prostitutes' Kabuki). At the same time, however, other Kabuki companies, composed mainly of adolescent boys, became popular.

Throughout the early period of Kabuki, its performers—both women and boys—were frequently associated with prostitution, which extended in various ways to a variety of leisure activities: to bathhouses, dances, and to the practice of *GEISHA,* which has its origins at this time. All of these activities, however, were distinct from the work of the *YŪGO,* or professional prostitute. As in other respects, the shogunate treated Kabuki like prostitution, beginning in 1624 to license companies and theater districts.

The boundary between theater and prostitution—by men, women, and boys—was difficult to police, though, and in 1652 authorities finally banned the boys' Kabuki—*WAKASHU KABUKI*—outright. Thereafter, the only Kabuki companies that were licensed to perform were the *YARO KABUKI,* or adult male Kabuki companies, which are now traditional.

The repertoire of Kabuki theater contains two kinds of plays, one based on historical or legendary incidents, and *sewamono* or "domestic plays," based on contemporary events. Okuni had once acted the role of a young *samurai* soliciting a prostitute, and plays based on the visit of a wealthy and powerful young man to the "licensed quarter" became a popular Kabuki genre, particularly in Kyoto and Osaka. Many of these plays, including *Love Letter from the Licensed Quarter* (1780), concern the fortunes of Yūgiri, a well-known courtesan of the Osaka Shinmachi quarter who died in 1678. Chikamatsu—whose *Love Suicides at Sonezaki* (1703) adapted the conventions of Kabuki to the doll stage—played a central role in this regard as well: he worked as the house playwright to a famous Kabuki company for more than twenty years. Although plays that dramatize love suicides and plays staging the scandals of the *samurai* caste were banned after 1722, playwrights continued to write about contemporary life under the guise of one of the other major genres of Kabuki theater, the history play. It quickly became apparent that by changing names and setting the drama in the past, playwrights were able to write domestic plays thinly veiled as history. For example, in 1703 the forty-seven retainers of Lord Asano took revenge on their master's disgrace at the hands of a shogunate official by killing the official and then committing *seppuku,* or ritual disembowelment. Within two weeks, a Kabuki play alluding to the incident was staged, and then was rapidly closed by the government. When Chikamatsu turned to these events in 1710, he set the play in the fourteenth century to sidestep the ban, and one of the most famous Kabuki plays—*Chūshingura* (1748)—concerns these events as well.

The Kabuki Stage

Kabuki is very much a performance genre, and its plays were organized around the abilities of its actors rather than around a literary script. For this reason, even the plays written by the most influential Kabuki playwrights—Chikamatsu Monzaemon, Takedo Izumo (1691–1756), and Kawatake Mokuami (1816–1893)—began as outlines of scenes to be elaborated by a cadre of assistant playwrights. A Kabuki company contained forty to sixty actors, each of whom specialized in a certain kind of role and expected the playwright to devise scenes that would allow him to display his talents. Companies generally included a leading-man actor, or *TACHIYAKU,* and specialists in villainous men (*KATAKIYAKU*), in young men and boys (*WAKASHUGATA*), in comic roles (*DOKEKATA*), and in women's roles (*ONNAGATA*), which were also divided according to age and type.

Finally, the unusual duration of a Kabuki performance also demanded the talents of the playwright's staff of assistants. Kabuki performances originally began about three o'clock in the morning and did not conclude until dusk; the fourteen- to fifteen-hour production was composed of a series of scenes arranged around a common theme or mood. The production usually began with a dance play, followed by a familiar play from the company's repertoire. Because the play was familiar to the company, it required little preparation. Then the

KABUKI STAGE, NINETEENTH CENTURY

Notice the screens to the side of the stage, the *hanamichi* (which attaches to the front of the stage in the lower left-center of the picture), and a revolving platform in the center of the stage. (From Brockett, Oscar G. *History of the Theatre,* 7th Edition. Published by Allyn and Bacon, Boston, MA. Copyright © 1995 by Pearson Education. Reprinted by permission of the publisher.)

company would perform one or two short practice plays, written by apprentice playwrights and performed by actors-in-training as part of their education. The main play—the **HON KYŌGEN**—would be performed at about seven o'clock in the morning and lasted until dusk. This play was outlined by the house playwright in collaboration with the company's leading actor and manager, and he would write the most important sections himself; the company's second and third rank playwrights would elaborate dialogue for the rest of the play. The play was customarily divided into four sections: a history section in four to six acts (*JIDAIMONO*) concerning the exploits of the *samurai;* a dance; a *sewamono* (contemporary) section in one to three acts, set in the milieu of artisans, traders, and merchants; and a concluding dance drama. Kabuki performances today are generally given in two programs, lasting from eleven to four o'clock and from four-thirty until nine-thirty in the evening. Although it is rare to see a full-length Kabuki play performed today, the four-part sequence is still followed.

Kabuki is very much an actor's theater. The actors undergo a long period of training, and as in Noh theater, certain families of actors have dominated the history of Kabuki. Indeed, Kabuki actors often wear their family crest in performance, and audiences frequently compare an actor's performance in a given role with his father's or his uncle's. Originating as a form of dance, Kabuki places a premium on choreography, which accompanies gesture and speech as a means of realizing the character's essential tone or feeling in a precise and elegant image. Yet the actors play directly to the audience, and the most striking moments in the performance—the *mie,* a highly conventionalized posed performance of passion—are underscored as performance when the stage assistants clap two pieces of wood loudly and rhythmically together. The actors play conventional roles, and each role in the Kabuki repertoire has a conventional costume associated with it. The costumes are extremely cumbersome, so the actors are often helped by stage assistants clothed in black who position properties and move pieces of the set. The actors are not masked, but wear an elaborate and conventionalized makeup, usually of red and black lines and patterns ranged over a white base; *onnagata* actors generally add only eyebrow lines and rouged cheeks and lips to an otherwise white face. Given its close relationship to *jōruri* and doll theater, it is not surprising that Kabuki usually requires a narrator onstage as well who not only sets the scene, but comments on the action throughout; he also occasionally speaks dialogue. Kabuki actors never sing, so their songs are sung by the narrator and by an onstage chorus. Moreover, each play is accompanied by traditional music, played by musicians wearing the traditional *samurai* costume. The orchestra for Kabuki is considerably larger than that for Noh and makes use of flutes, bells, drums, cymbals, and gongs, as well as the *samisen*.

Although the first Kabuki companies played on impromptu stages, they soon were allowed to use Noh theaters; given their raffish character, however, Kabuki companies were not allowed to have roofed theaters until 1724. Like the doll theater, Kabuki theater quickly made use of scenic technology; the elevator stage was in use by 1736, and by the late eighteenth century it was common for Kabuki theaters to have a revolving stage, sometimes two independent turntables with one turning inside the other. Kabuki makes extensive use of scenery, though much of it is of a symbolic or ornamental nature. Like properties in this theater, which tend to be suggestive of the objects they represent, the scenery of a Kabuki performance is openly theatrical in character: the scenery is changed in view of the audience by visible assistants (who help the actors as well) and aims to suggest the locale of the scene rather than put it on the stage in a realistic way. It is a measure, though, of the relationship between the extroverted Kabuki performance and its audience that its most distinguishing feature involves the audience more directly in the production. In the early eighteenth century, Kabuki theaters added a **HANAMICHI**, or elevated bridge, extending from the rear of the auditorium to the stage. Actors made their exits and entrances here, and scenes could be played on the *hanamichi* as well. By the 1770s, a second *hanamichi* was added, and the area between the two *hanamichi* was divided into floor boxes, while other rows of seating ran along the sides of the auditorium. Although the second *hanamichi* is still required for some plays, it is generally no longer in use.

The restoration of the emperor in 1868 not only brought about the collapse of the shogunate, but also ended Japan's isolation. It also dramatized the economic weakness of the *samurai* relative to the merchant class. In many respects, Japan's theater was vulnerable to extinction, especially the Noh and doll theaters, which had no truly popular audience; Kabuki was the only theater which continued to attract new plays, playwrights, and audiences in the nineteenth and twentieth centuries. But the Japanese worked to preserve their classical theater, and it is still possible today to see plays from the Noh, doll theater, and Kabuki repertoire in excellent, traditional productions.

CLASSICAL JAPANESE DRAMA IN PERFORMANCE HISTORY

After 1868, Japan became open to cultural influence from the West, and a variety of dramatic and theatrical forms came to rival the traditional genres of Noh, *jōruri,* and Kabuki. **SHIMPA,** a theatrical movement originating in Osaka in the 1880s, responded to the Western theater's use of more colloquial language and contemporary dramatic settings. However, because many of the *shimpa* actors were drawn from Kabuki, *shimpa* gradually came to resemble Kabuki in performance, even though its dramas were more evidently based on recent news events, crimes, and political controversies. Although *shimpa* and its successor, **SHINGEKI**—a "realistic" dramatic movement that both imported and imitated the plays of Ibsen, Chekhov, Shaw, and others—marked an important move away from the classical genres, they continued to be performed in the twentieth century.

SANSKRIT DRAMA AND THEATER

The cultures, languages, and theater of the Indian subcontinent have been transformed by three massive invasions: by the Aryans sometime between 3000 and 2000 BCE; by the Moslems, who brought both the Persian language and the Koran, in the tenth and eleventh centuries; and by the British, beginning in the seventeenth century. The Aryan language—Sanskrit (literally, "the perfected tongue")—became the foundation of ancient Indian culture. Sanskrit was a spoken language until early in the first millennium, when Prakit became the vernacular. Something like Latin in medieval Europe, Sanskrit was reserved for ritual, religious, and academic uses, and for India's rich literature and theater. Sanskrit is the language of the *Rgveda*, a collection of prayers and hymns composed between 1500 and 1000 BCE that is the oldest work in any Indo-European language. The two major epics of Indian culture—the *Mahabharata* and the *Ramayana*—date from around 1000 BCE, but took their current form during India's golden age, which lasted from the second century CE into the ninth century. Although it had long been thought in the West that Sanskrit theater gradually disappeared after the Moslem invasions of the tenth and eleventh centuries, Sanskrit plays were still performed in Kerala—a state in the southwest of India—by performers who were part of a hereditary caste connected to religious temples.

Hindu belief and the caste structure of ancient Indian society inform the esthetics of Sanskrit theater and drama. Ancient India was a rigidly stratified society composed of four hereditary castes, each of which was subdivided: the *Brahmins* (priests and intellectuals), *Kshatriyas* (aristocrats, warriors), *Vaisyas* (craftsmen, farmers), and *Sudras* (unskilled workers, peasants). Although these castes were devised and perpetuated along racial and economic lines, they also translated Hindu religious beliefs into the organizing structure of society. Hindu is based on a belief in Brahman, or "world-soul." Although different aspects of Brahman are often represented as distinct gods—Brahma the creator, Siva the destroyer, Vishnu the preserver, for example—these gods are really aspects of Brahman, the only whole, perfect, and unchanging being. The created universe is arrayed hierarchically, according to the degree that each being is able to contemplate or participate in this sense of wholeness or perfection.

In performance, Sanskrit drama emblematizes this dichotomy between the distracting diversity of lived experience and the contemplation of wholeness and perfection; Sanskrit theater offers its audience a richly varied performance while inducing the audience to adopt a unifying and impersonal, even contemplative mood. Most of our understanding of Sanskrit drama derives from the second-century *Natyasastra,* or *Art of the Theater,* usually attributed to the playwright Bharata, from several other treatises, and from the twenty-five plays that remain. Much as ancient Greek plays were based on myth and legend mainly drawn from the *Iliad* and the *Odyssey,* Sanskrit plays were generally based on heroic stories taken from the *Mahabharata* and the *Ramayana* and were divided into two groups: *RUPAKA* (major drama) and *UPA-RUPAKA* (minor drama). *Rupaka* are of various lengths and include the plays of Bharata; Bhasa's second-century plays *The Vision of Vasavadatta* and *Carudatta;* King Sudraka's *The Clay Cart* (written sometime between the fourth and eighth centuries); Kalidasa's fifth-century *Sakuntala;* and the seventh-century plays of King Harsa and Bhavabhuti. As in the Japanese Noh, the narrative of the play is less critical than the attitude it produces: the impersonal and contemplative mood of wholeness called *RASA.* According to the *Natyasastra,* there are eight basic *rasas* or moods that a play should strive to produce—erotic, comic, pathetic, furious, heroic, terrible, odious, and marvelous—and while a given play may include several *rasas,* it should be designed so that one mood dominates. Moreover, these *rasas* are related to the *BHAVA,* the emotions or feelings displayed in the play by the characters. The eight *bhavas*—desire, comic or sympathetic laughter, sadness, anger, vigor or power, fear, loathing, and wonder—are the organizing, "stable" emotions staged in the play, and are complicated by thirty-three "unsta-

Indeed, the Japanese classical theater was perhaps most keenly threatened by Japan's defeat in World War II and the subsequent occupation. As part of the postwar occupation of Japan, the United States established a Civil Information and Education Section, which had as part of its duties both the protection of traditional Japanese culture and the importation of "progressive," democratic culture, including American literature and drama. This office often came into conflict with the occupation's censorship office, concerned as it was to prevent the spread of imperial Japanese political ideas. Although neither Noh nor *jōruri* seemed to pose much of a political threat, the popular Kabuki theater had long been associated with the feudal ideology of Japanese nationalism, and the censors were much more careful in their approval of Kabuki theater. The first Kabuki play to be produced after the end of occupable" emotions. The subtle balance and interplay of the *bhavas* should evoke a sense of harmony and perfection, the dominant *rasa* of the play.

As in Hindu philosophy, Sanskrit drama aims to produce a sense of one-ness from the diversity of experience; *rasa* arises from each play's cunning in-terplay of the range of *bhavas,* of dia-logue written in both verse and prose, of Sanskrit and Prakit, and of character types ranging from gods, kings, and he-roes to servants, peasants, and children. Yet despite this diversity, Sanskrit plays have several common characteristics. Each play not only produces its main mood or *rasa,* it also illustrates the workings of *karma* or cosmic justice. For this reason, Sanskrit drama falls outside the Western understanding of tragedy, and Sanskrit playwrights are urged by the *Natyasastra* not to repre-sent death onstage. Sanskrit is spoken by all the male Brahmin and Kshatriya characters in the play, whereas women, peasants, and children speak Prakit, as does the jester character who appears in most plays, often as the hero's side-kick. Although plays vary in length from one act to ten acts, each act gen-erally takes place within a single day; the action usually takes place in several earthly and heavenly locations.

Plays were performed on a variety of occasions in ancient India—at festi-vals, weddings, coronations, and at other public events—and the play's *rasa* was appropriate to the occasion. The *Natyasastra* describes three kinds of theater structure—square, rectangu-lar, and triangular—each in three dif-ferent sizes. The rectangular theaters

CLASSICAL SANSKRIT PERFORMANCE

These six hand positions are used in a classical Sanskrit performance.

were divided into two equal areas. The audience area was supported by four pillars, representing both the four compass points and the four principal castes. The stage area was divided into two parts—a relatively shallow per-forming space divided from a back-stage area by a wall.

Performances were accompanied by a variety of musical instruments and were elaborately ceremonial in character; actors used an elaborate sys-tem of movement, gesture, and speech. Because the performers were to repre-sent codified *bhavas,* the *Natyasastra* described the gestures appropriate to them: for instance, thirty-two different eye movements, thirty-two positions for the feet, twenty-four gestures for one hand. Both the Sanskrit drama and texts like the *Natyasastra* docu-ment the extraordinary theatrical vi-tality of the golden age of classical Indian culture.

tion censorship in 1948 was, in fact, the great *samurai* revenge play, *Chūshingura,* often known in English as *The Loyal Forty-Seven Samurai.*

Since the war, the traditional modes of Japanese theater have become popular not only in Japan, but throughout the world. Several modern playwrights—notably Mishima Yukio—have either written new Noh or Kabuki plays or have adapted earlier dramas to modern set-tings. Moreover, the revival of Japanese classical theater has been part of an important resur-gence of interest in traditional modes of artistic expression in Japan, which has taken place alongside Japan's emergence as a leading political, economic, and cultural power in the late twentieth century.

In this 1989 English-language production at the University of Hawai'i, *Matsukaze* is played on a traditional Noh stage.

Exemplifying the elegant movement of Kabuki theater, this scene from the University of Hawai'i production of *Chūshingura* shows Kampei protecting Okaru from attackers, who threaten them with cherry-blossom weapons.

This view of the *Matsukaze* shows the musicians and chorus, as well as the *hashigakari*.

In the University of Hawai'i production of *Chūshingura* (1979), Lord Enya Hangan commits *seppuku*, watched by the shogun's messengers.

READING THE MATERIAL THEATER

One of the great traditions of Japan is the art of portraiture, and many of Japan's greatest artists made portraits of celebrated actors. As historical records, however, these portraits are somewhat difficult to use: like Japanese theater, Japanese painting was itself a highly conventionalized activity. Nonetheless, these illustrations provide a striking insight into the power of performance on Japan's classical stage. Here is a portrait of the actor Seki Sanjuro II (1805–1870) in the role of Kyogoku Takumi, by the great artist Kunisada (1786–1865). Kunisada lived toward the end of the Edo period; shortly after his death, in 1867, the last of the Tokugawa shoguns resigned, leading to the increasing openness to the West characteristic of the Meiji period. In this sense, Kunisada's printmaking—which covers natural subjects, as well as the circumscribed life of the court, the brothels, and the theaters—documents the final phases of traditional Japanese culture before the massive impact of European and American modernity.

In his long career, Kunisada made a large number of theatrical portraits which were engraved and printed; he also occasionally illustrated scenes of backstage life. (See the excellent overview of Kunisada's work provided by Sebastian Izzard, J. Thomas Rimer, and John T. Carpenter in *Kunisada's World,* a catalogue of the exhibition "Kunisada's World" shown at the Japan Society Gallery in New York in 1993 [New York: Japan Society, 1993] from which this portrait and descriptive information are taken.) This portrait is part of a series of 150 portraits of Kabuki actors that Kunisada planned to print late in his life; he completed seventy-two. The cartouches—the small bars with engraved Japanese characters—list the actor's name and the role he is playing in the illustration, as well as Kunisada's signature. In many respects these portraits seem heavily conventionalized, even idealized, and we know that Kunisada based many of them on earlier portraits; some portraits—of actors whose careers were over before Kunisada began his work—are based on portraits executed by other artists. Nonetheless, the portraits capture a number of significant features of Kabuki theater. In most of the portraits, Kunisada shows the actor in the *mie*—a moment of intense passion, in which the actor freezes and moves his eyes rapidly, as a way of demonstrating the intensity of his feelings; this action is usually sustained by the musicians' drumming and often prompts shouts of encouragement and applause from the audience.

Beyond that, what features of the portrait seem prominent? What kind of roles do you think were his speciality? Given the conventionality of the portrait, how do you interpret the strong and energetic sense of line in the image, evident especially around his nose and chin?

Seki Sanjūrō II as Kyōgoku Takumi, in a portrait by Kunisada.

Kan'ami Kiyotsugu

Kan'ami Kiyotsugu (1333–1384) was one of the principal performers of *sarugaku-no* and the leader of a prominent company. When he appeared before the *shogun* Yoshimitsu Ashikiga in 1374, the *shogun* was so impressed with the company that he retained them as his players. Kan'ami is generally credited with refining and systematizing the Noh for his aristocratic audience and with writing many of the plays that became part of the standard Noh repertoire. Kan'ami's son, Zeami Motokiyo (1363–1444), succeeded his father as the leader of the company and had a massive influence on the development of the Noh. Zeami both reworked older plays and wrote many new plays of his own; of the 241 plays in the Noh repertoire, more than 100 are connected to Zeami. Zeami influenced the development of Noh in other respects as well, mainly in writing sixteen essays on Noh esthetics. These essays cover a range of topics, including the training of actors, the proper style of dramatic writing, and the goals of performance. Although Zeami enjoyed the favor of Yoshimitsu until the *shogun's* death in 1408, he fared less well under the rule of Yoshimitsu's son, Yoshimochi (1386–1428) and was banished to the remote island of Sado in 1434 when Yoshimochi's younger brother Yoshinori (1394–1441) became *shogun*. The reasons for Yoshinori's hostility to Zeami are not clear but may involve Yoshinori's preference for another playwright, On'ami. Zeami did succeed in passing his essays on to his son-in-law, Komparu Zenchiku (1405–1468), who became an important Noh playwright and theoretician. Not much is known about the end of Zeami's life; legend has it that he was able to return to the mainland after Yoshinori was assassinated in 1441.

MATSUKAZE

Matsukaze was originally written by Kan'ami and extensively reworked by Zeami; it has remained in the Noh repertoire since the fifteenth century and is performed by all Noh companies.

This elegant drama, like most Noh plays, takes place in a setting familiar from the classic literature of Japan, the Bay of Suma. Suma is principally associated with the famous poet, courtier, and scholar Ariwaka no Yukihira (818–893), whose exile at Suma was recounted in his own poetry and formed the basis for many stories and legends. It also inspired the narrative of Genji's exile at Suma in the Japanese epic *Tale of Genji*. The narrative of the play, though, seems to have been invented by Kan'ami. The play opens when the *waki*—playing a priest—enters the stage, singing a traveling song about his arrival at Suma. He asks the *kyōgen* (playing a villager) about the significance of the pine tree, and he is informed that it memorializes two fisher girls, Murasame and Matsukaze, who have long since died. Shortly thereafter, Murasame—played by the *tsure*—enters, followed by the *shite*, Matsukaze. The two girls elaborately mime dipping brine into their cart with their fans, and in speeches that quote from Yukihira and from other poets, they describe their desolation. Their language here is rich with imagery, particularly of the changing sea, the hard lives of the fishermen, and of the moon, a Buddhist symbol of enlightenment. As is typical of the Noh, many of their lines are spoken by the Chorus.

Although the *shite* and his *tsure* do not leave the stage, they retire to the *shitebashira*, where they mime sitting in their small hut. The *waki*—who has observed them throughout the first scene—approaches the hut and asks for shelter, quoting one of Yukihira's poems in passing. The girls then reveal that they are the ghosts of Matsukaze and Murasame, still "steeped in longing" for the exiled poet, even in death. They had fallen in love with Yukihira during his exile at Suma, and he had given them their names, "Wind in the Pines" (*matsukaze*) and "Autumn Rain" (*murasame*), names redolent of the imagery of classical Japanese poetry. The girls were not able to follow Yukihira when he returned to court after his exile;

This production of Kan'ami's *Matsukaze* emphasizes the traditional spatial, costume, and performance elements of Noh theater.

all they have in his memory is his hunting cloak and court hat. Driven nearly to madness with her eternal grief, Matsukaze puts on Yukihira's cloak and hat for her final dance.

Matsukaze is an evocative example of the way Noh theater attempts to capture a particular mood through the collaborative interplay between each of its highly wrought arts. The beauty of the language, the delicacy of characterization, the succinct action, the music of the flute and drums, the chanting of the Chorus, and the refinement of the acting combine to capture the subtle intensity of feeling for which Noh theater is famous.

MATSUKAZE

Kan'ami Kiyotsugu
TRANSLATED BY ROYALL TYLER

CHARACTERS

AN ITINERANT PRIEST *(waki)*   MATSUKAZE *(shite)*
A VILLAGER *(kyōgen)*   MURASAME *(tsure)*

PLACE: *Suma Bay in Settsu Province*
TIME: *Autumn, the Ninth Month*

(The stage assistant places a stand with a pine sapling set into it at the front of the stage. The PRIEST enters and stands at the naming-place. He carries a rosary.)

PRIEST: I am a priest who travels from province to province. Lately I have been in the Capital. I visited the famous sites and ancient ruins, not missing a one. Now I intend to make a pilgrimage to the western provinces. *(He faces for-*
5 *ward.)* I have hurried, and here I am already at the Bay of Suma in Settsu Province. *(His attention is caught by the pine tree.)* How strange! That pine on the beach has a curious look. There must be a story connected with it. I'll ask someone in the neighborhood. *(He faces the bridgeway.)* Do
10 you live in Suma?

(The VILLAGER comes down the bridgeway to the first pine. He wears a short sword.)

VILLAGER: Perhaps I am from Suma; but first tell me what you want.
PRIEST: I am a priest and I travel through the provinces. Here on the beach I see a solitary pine tree with a wooden
15 tablet fixed to it, and a poem slip hanging from the tablet. Is there a story connected with the tree? Please tell me what you know.
VILLAGER: The pine is linked with the memory of two fisher girls, Matsukaze and Murasame. Please say a prayer for
20 them as you pass.
PRIEST: Thank you. I know nothing about them, but I will stop at the tree and say a prayer for them before I move on.
VILLAGER: If I can be of further service, don't hesitate to ask.
PRIEST: Thank you for your kindness.
25 VILLAGER: At your command, sir.

(The VILLAGER exits. The PRIEST goes to stage center and turns toward the pine tree.)

PRIEST: So, this pine tree is linked with the memory of two fisher girls, Matsukaze and Murasame. It is sad! Though their bodies are buried in the ground, their names linger on. This lonely pine tree lingers on also, ever green and
30 untouched by autumn, their only memorial. Ah! While I have been chanting sutras and invoking Amida Buddha for their repose, the sun, as always on autumn days, has quickly set. That village at the foot of the mountain is a long way. Perhaps I can spend the night in this fisherman's
35 salt shed.

(He kneels at the waki-position. The stage assistant brings out the prop, a cart for carrying pails of brine, and sets it by the gazing-pillar. He places a pail on the cart.)

(MURASAME enters and comes down the bridgeway as far as the first pine. She wears the tsure mask. MATSUKAZE follows her and stops at the third pine. She wears the wakaonna mask. Each carries a water pail. They face each other .)

MATSUKAZE AND MURASAME: A brine cart wheeled along the beach
Provides a meager livelihood:
The sad world rolls
Life by quickly and in misery!
MURASAME: Here at Suma Bay   40
The waves shatter at our feet,
And even the moonlight wets our sleeves
With its tears of loneliness.

(MURASAME goes to stage center while MATSUKAZE moves to the shite position.)

MATSUKAZE: The autumn winds are sad.
When the Middle Counselor Yukihira   45
Lived here back a little from the sea,
They inspired his poem,
"Salt winds blowing from the mountain pass. . . ."
On the beach, night after night,
Waves thunder at our door;   50
And on our long walks to the village
We've no companion but the moon.
Our toil, like all of life, is dreary,
But none could be more bleak than ours.
A skiff cannot cross the sea,   55
Nor we this dream world.
Do we exist, even?
Like foam on the salt sea,
We draw a cart, friendless and alone,
Poor fisher girls whose sleeves are wet   60
With endless spray, and tears
From our hearts' unanswered longing.
CHORUS: Our life is so hard to bear
That we envy the pure moon

---

48 **"Salt . . . pass"** from the poem by Yukihira, No. 876 in the *Shinkokinshū*: "The sleeves of the traveler have turned cold; the wind from Suma Bay blows through the pass."   52 **We've . . . moon** a modified quotation from the poem by Hōkyō Chūmei, No. 187 in the *Kin'yōshū*: "Pillow of grass—as I sleep on my journey I realize I have no companion but the moon."   58–59 **salt sea** the words "salt sea," which can also be translated "brine," lead to mention of the brine cart even though the cart does not logically belong in the context   64 **That . . . moon** from the poem by Fujiwara Takamitsu, No. 435 in the *Shūishū*: "In this world which seems difficult to pass through, how I envy the pure moon!"

65   Now rising with the tide.
       But come, let us dip brine,
       Dip brine from the rising tide!
       Our reflections seem to shame us!

       (*They look down as if catching a glimpse of their reflections in the water. The movement of their heads "clouds" the expression on their masks, making it seem sad.*)

       Yes, they shame us!
70   Here, where we shrink from men's eyes,
       Drawing our timorous cart;
       The withdrawing tide
       Leaves stranded pools behind.
       How long do they remain?
75   If we were the dew on grassy fields,
       We would vanish with the sun.
       But we are sea tangle,
       Washed up on the shore,
       Raked into heaps by the fishermen,
80   Fated to be discarded, useless,
       Withered and rotting,
       Like our trailing sleeves,
       Like our trailing sleeves.

       (*They look down again.*)

       Endlessly familiar, still how lovely
85   The twilight at Suma!
       The fishermen call out in muffled voices;
       At sea, the small boats loom dimly.
       Across the faintly glowing face of the moon
       Flights of wild geese streak,
90   And plovers flock below along the shore.
       Fall gales and stiff sea winds:
       These are things, in such a place,
       That truly belong to autumn.
       But oh, the terrible, lonely nights!

       (*They hide their faces.*)

95   MATSUKAZE: Come, dip the brine.
       MURASAME: Where the seas flood and fall,
          Let us tie our sleeves back to our shoulders.
       MATSUKAZE: Think only, "Dip the brine."
       MURUSAME: We ready ourselves for the task,
100   MATSUKAZE: But for women, this cart is too hard.
       CHORUS: While the rough breakers surge and fall,

       (MURASAME *moves upstage to stand beside* MATSUKAZE.)

       While the rough breakers surge and fall,
       And cranes among the reeds
       Fly up with sharp cries.
105   The four winds add their wailing.
       How shall we pass the cold night?

       (*They look up.*)

       The late moon is so brilliant—
       What we dip is its reflection!
       Smoke from the salt fires
110   May cloud the moon—take care!

_____

85 **The twilight** the following description is generally inspired by the "Exile at Suma" chapter of *The Tale of Genji*

Are we always to spend only
The sad autumns of fishermen?
At Ojima in Matsushima

(MATSUKAZE *half-kneels by the brine cart and mimes dipping with her fan.*)

       The fisherfolk, like us,
       Delight less in the moon   115
       Than in the dipping of its reflection;
       There they take delight in dipping
       Reflections of the moon.

(MATSUKAZE *returns to the* shite *position.*)

       We haul our brine from afar,
       As in far-famed Michinoku   120
       And at the salt kilns of Chika—
       Chika, whose name means "close by."
       MATSUKAZE: Humble folk hauled wood for salt fires
          At the ebb tide on Akogi Shore.
       CHORUS: On Ise Bay there's Twice-See Beach—   125
          Oh, could I live my life again!

(MATSUKAZE *looks off into the distance.*)

       MATSUKAZE: On days when pine groves stand hazy,
          And the sea lanes draw back
          From the coast at Narumi—
       CHORUS: You speak of Narumi; this is Naruo,   130
          Where pines cut off the moonlight
          From the reed-thatched roofs of Ashinoya.
       MATSUKAZE: Who is to tell of our unhappiness
          Dipping brine at Nada?
          With boxwood combs set in our hair,   135
          From rushing seas we draw the brine,
          Oh look! I have the moon in my pail!

_____

113 **Ojima** is one of the islands at Matsushima, a place renowned for its scenic beauty. Both names are conventionally associated in poetry with *ama*, fisherwomen   120 **As in far-famed** the following passage is a *tsukushi*, or "exhaustive enumeration," of place-names associated with the sea, including allusions and plays on words. This passage was apparently borrowed from an older work, a play called *Tōei* that was set by Ashinoya Bay. Michinoku is a general name for the northern end of the island of Honshu. Chika was another name for Shiogama ("Salt Kiln"), and sounds like the word meaning "near"   124 **Akogi** the name of a stretch of shore on Ise Bay. The pulling in of the nets and the hauling of the wood for the salt kilns at Akogi were frequently mentioned in poetry   125 **Twice-See Beach** (*Futami-ga-ura*) is a word evocative of Ise and often used in poetry for the meaning of its name 129 **Narumi** often mentioned in poetry because of its dry flats that appeared at low tide   132 **Ashinoya** (modern Ashiya) and Naruo are two places near Suma. Ashinoya means literally "reed house"   134 **Dipping . . . Nada** derived from the poem in the eighty-seventh episode of the *Ise Monogatari*: "At Nada by Ashinoya, I have no respite from boiling brine for salt; I have come without even putting a boxwood comb in my hair."   135 **With boxwood** the line recalls the poem quoted in the previous note, but it is used because of the pivot-word *tsuge no*, "of boxwood," and *tsuge*, "to inform." Similarly, *kushi sashi*, "Setting a comb (in the hair)," leads into *sashi-kuru nami*, "in-rushing waves"

(MURASAME *kneels before the brine cart and places her pail on it.* MATSUKAZE, *still standing, looks into her pail.*)

MATSUKAZE: In my pail too I hold the moon!
CHORUS: How lovely! A moon here too!

(MURASAME *picks up the rope tied to the cart and gives it to* MATSUKAZE, *then moves to the* shite *position.* MATSUKAZE *looks up.*)

140 MATSUKAZE: The moon above is one;
　　Below it has two, no, three reflections

(*She looks into both pails.*)

　　Which shine in the flood tide tonight,

(*She pulls the cart to a spot before the musicians.*)

　　And on our cart we load the moon!
　　No, life is not all misery
145　Here by the sea lanes.

(*She drops the rope. The stage assistant removes the cart.* MATSUKAZE *sits on a low stool and* MURASAME *kneels beside her, a sign that the two women are resting inside their hut. The* PRIEST *rises.*)

PRIEST: The owner of the salt shed has returned. I shall ask for a night's lodging. (*To* MATSUKAZE *and* MURASAME.) I beg your pardon. Might I come inside?
MURASAME: (*Standing and coming forward a little.*) Who might
150　you be?
PRIEST: A traveler, overtaken by night on my journey. I should like to ask lodging for the night.
MURASAME: Wait here. I must ask the owner. (*She kneels before* MATSUKAZE.) A traveler outside asks to come in and spend
155　the night.
MATSUKAZE: That is little enough, but our hut is so wretched we cannot ask him in. Please tell him so.
MURASAME: (*Standing, to the* PRIEST.) I have spoken to the owner. She says the house is too wretched to put anyone up.
160 PRIEST: I understand those feelings
　　Perfectly, but poverty makes
　　No difference at all to me.
　　I am only a priest. Please
　　Say I beg her to let
165　Me spend the night.
MURASAME: No, we really cannot put you up.
MATSUKAZE: (*To* MURASAME.) Wait!
　　I see in the moonlight
　　One who has renounced the world.
170　He will not mind a fisherman's hut,
　　With its rough pine pillars and bamboo fence;
　　I believe it is very cold tonight,
　　So let him come in and warm himself
　　At our sad fire of rushes.
175　You may tell him that.
MURASAME: Please come in.
PRIEST: Thank you very much. Forgive me for intruding.

(*He takes a few steps forward and kneels.* MURASAME *goes back beside* MATSUKAZE.)

MATSUKAZE: I wished from the beginning to invite you in, but this place is so poor I felt I must refuse.

PRIEST: You are very kind. I am a priest and a traveler, and 180 never stay anywhere very long. Why prefer one lodging to another? In any case, what sensitive person would not prefer to live here at Suma, in the quiet solitude. Yukihira wrote,
　　"If ever anyone　　　　　　　　　　　　　　　　185
　　Chances to ask for me,
　　Say I live alone,
　　Soaked by the dripping seaweed
　　On the shore of Suma Bay."
(*He looks at the pine tree.*) A while ago I asked someone the 190 meaning of that solitary pine on the beach. I was told it grows there in memory of two fisher girls, Matsukaze and Murasame. There is no connection between them and me, but I went to the pine anyway and said a prayer for them. (MATSUKAZE *and* MURASAME *weep. The* PRIEST *stares at* 195 *them.*) This is strange! They seem distressed at the mention of Matsukaze and Murasame. Why?
MATSUKAZE AND MURASAME: Truly, when a grief is hidden,
　　Still, signs of it will show.
　　His poem, "If ever anyone　　　　　　　　　　200
　　Chances to ask for me,"
　　Filled us with memories which are far too fond.
　　Tears of attachment to the world
　　Wet our sleeves once again.
PRIEST: Tears of attachment to the world? You speak as 205 though you are no longer of the world. Yukihira's poem overcame you with memories. More and more bewildering! Please, both of you, tell me who you are.
MATSUKAZE AND MURASAME: We would tell you our names,
　　But we are too ashamed!　　　　　　　　　　210
　　No one, ever,
　　Has chanced to ask for us,
　　Long dead as we are,
　　And so steeped in longing
　　For the world by Suma Bay　　　　　　　　215
　　That pain has taught us nothing.
　　Ah, the sting of regret!
　　But having said this,
　　Why should we hide our names any longer?
　　At twilight you said a prayer　　　　　　　220
　　By a mossy grave under the pine
　　For two fisher girls,
　　Matsukaze and Murasame.
　　We are their ghosts, come to you.
　　When Yukihira was here he whiled away　　225
　　Three years of weary exile
　　Aboard his pleasure boat,
　　His heart refreshed
　　By the moon of Suma Bay.
　　There were, among the fisher girls　　　　230
　　Who hauled brine each evening,
　　Two sisters whom he chose for his favors.
　　"Names to fit the season!"
　　He said, calling us
　　Pine Wind and Autumn Rain.　　　　　　235
　　We had been Suma fisher girls,
　　Accustomed to the moon,

185–189 **If ever . . . Bay** poem No. 962 in the *Kokinshū*

But he changed our salt makers' clothing
To damask robes,
240   Burnt with the scent of faint perfumes.
MATSUKAZE: Then, three years later, Yukihira
Returned to the Capital.
MURASAME: Soon, we heard he had died, oh so young!
MATSUKAZE: How we both loved him!
245   Now the message we pined for
Would never, never come.
CHORUS: Pine Wind and Autumn Rain
Both drenched their sleeves with the tears
Of hopeless love beyond their station,
250   Fisher girls of Suma.
Our sin is deep, O priest.
Pray for us, we beg of you!

(*They press their palms together in supplication.*)

Our love grew rank as wild grasses;
Tears and love ran wild.
255   It was madness that touched us.
Despite spring purification,
Performed in our old robes,
Despite prayers inscribed on paper streamers,
The gods refused us their help.
260   We were left to melt away
Like foam on the waves,
And, in misery, we died.

(MATSUKAZE *looks down, shading her mask.*)

Alas! How the past evokes our longing!
Yukihira, the Middle Counselor,

(*The stage assistant puts a man's cloak and court hat in* MAT-
SUKAZE'S *left hand.*)

265   Lived three years here by Suma Bay.
Before he returned to the Capital,
He left us these keepsakes of his stay:
A court hat and a hunting cloak.
Each time we see them,

(*She looks at the cloak.*)

270   Our love grows again,
And gathers like dew
On the tip of a leaf
So that there's no forgetting,
Not for an instant.
275   Oh endless misery!

(*She places the cloak in her lap.*)

"This keepsake
Is my enemy now;
For without it

(*She lifts the cloak.*)

I might forget."

(*She stares at the cloak.*)

The poem says that   280
And it's true:
My anguish only deepens.

(*She weeps.*)

MATSUKAZE: "Each night before I go to sleep,
I take off the hunting cloak
CHORUS: And hang it up . . ."   285

(*The keepsakes in her hand, she stands and, as in a trance, takes a
few steps toward the gazing-pillar.*)

I hung all my hopes
On living in the same world with him,
But being here makes no sense at all
And these keepsakes are nothing.

(*She starts to drop the cloak, only to cradle it in her arms and press
it to her.*)

I drop it, but I cannot let it lie;   290
So I take it up again
To see his face before me yet once more.

(*She turns to her right and goes toward the naming-place, then stares
down the bridgeway as though something were coming after her.*)

"Awake or asleep,
From my pillow, from the foot of my bed,
Love rushes in upon me."   295
Helplessly I sink down,
Weeping in agony.

(*She sits at the* shite *position, weeping. The stage assistant helps her
take off her outer robe and replace it with the cloak. He also helps tie
on the court hat.*)

MATSUKAZE: The River of Three Fords
Has gloomy shallows
Of never-ending tears;   300
I found, even there,
An abyss of wildest love.

---

240 **Burnt** . . . derived from a poem by Fujiwara Tameuji, No.
361 in the *Shingo-senshū:* "The fishermen of Suma are accustomed to the moon, spending the autumn in clothes wet with
waves blown by the salt wind." 258 **Despite prayers** . . . literally, "purification on the day of the serpent." The ceremony
was performed on the first day of the serpent in the third month.
Genji had the ceremony performed while he was at Suma. The
streamers were conventional Shinto offerings

276–279 **This keepsake . . . forget** a slightly modified quotation of the anonymous poem, No. 746 in the *Kokinshū.* It is also
quoted in *Lady Han* 283–285 **Each night . . . up** the first part
of a poem by Ki no Tomomori, No. 593 in the *Kokinshū.* The last
two lines run: "When I wear it there is no instant when I do not
long for him." 293–295 **"Awake . . . me"** the first part of an
anonymous poem, No. 1023 in the *Kokinshū.* The last part runs:
"Helpless, I stay in the middle of the bed." 298 **River . . . Three
Fords** the river of the afterworld

Oh joy! Look! Over there!
Yukihira has returned!

(*She rises, staring at the pine tree.*)

305 He calls me by my name, Pine Wind!
I am coming!

(*She goes to the tree.* MURASAME *hurriedly rises and follows. She catches* MATSUKAZE'S *sleeve.*)

MURASAME: For shame! For such thoughts as these
You are lost in the sin of passion.
All the delusions that held you in life—
310 None forgotten!

(*Both step back from the tree.*)

That is a pine tree.
And Yukihira is not here.
MATSUKAZE: You are talking nonsense!

(*She looks at the pine tree.*)

This pine is Yukihira!
315 "Though we may part for a time,
If I hear you are pining for me,
I'll hurry back."
Have you forgotten those words he wrote?
MURASAME: Yes, I had forgotten!
320 He said, "Though we may part for a time,
If you pine, I will return to you."
MATSUKAZE: I have not forgotten.
And I wait for the pine wind
To whisper word of his coming.
325 MURASAME: If that word should ever come,
My sleeves for a while
Would be wet with autumn rain.
MATSUKAZE: So we await him. He will come,
Constant ever, green as a pine.
330 MURASAME: Yes, we can trust
MATSUKAZE: his poem:
CHORUS: "I have gone away

315–317 **"Though . . . back"** paraphrase of the poem by Yukihira, No. 365 in the *Kokinshū*. Another paraphrase is given in the following speech by Murasame, and the poem is given in its correct form below. In Japanese *matsu* means both "pine tree" and "to wait."

(MURASAME, *weeping, kneels before the flute player.* MATSUKAZE *goes to the first pine on the bridgeway, then returns to the stage and dances.*)

MATSUKAZE: Into the mountains of Inaba,
Covered with pines,
But if I hear you pine,   335
I shall come back at once."
Those are the mountain pines
Of distant Inaba,

(*She looks up the bridgeway.*)

And these are the pines
On the curving Suma shore.   340
Here our dear prince once lived.
If Yukihira comes again,
I shall go stand under the tree

(*She approaches the tree.*)

Bent by the sea-wind,
And, tenderly, tell him   345

(*She stands next to the tree.*)

I love him still!

(*She steps back a little and weeps. Then she circles the tree, her dancing suggesting madness.*)

CHORUS: Madly the gale howls through the pines,
And breakers crash in Suma Bay;
Through the frenzied night
We have come to you   350
In a dream of deluded passion.
Pray for us! Pray for our rest!

(*At stage center,* MATSUKAZE *presses her palms together in supplication.*)

Now we take our leave. The retreating waves
Hiss far away, and a wind sweeps down
From the mountain to Suma Bay.   355
The cocks are crowing on the barrier road.
Your dream is over. Day has come.
Last night you heard the autumn rain;
This morning all that is left
Is the wind in the pines,   360
The wind in the pines.

---

336 **"I . . . once"** the poem by Yukihira mentioned in the previous note

Chūshingura: The Forty-Seven Samurai

In 1701, at the court of the *shogun* in Edo, the *daimyo* of *Akō,* Lord Asano, drew his sword and slightly wounded Lord Kira, one of the *shogun's* officials; as a consequence of drawing his sword at the court—a capital crime—Lord Asano was sentenced to *seppuku,* or ritual suicide. In the following months, Asano's *rōnin,* or retainers, felt themselves to have been dishonored and humiliated by the ruling against their lord, and plotted to take revenge. In January of 1703 they made a bold nighttime raid on Lord Kira's mansion. When they found Kira, they beheaded him, and ceremoniously marched with his head to Lord Asano's tomb. The raid on Lord Kira was, not surprisingly, a major scandal, and posed the shogunate with a difficult legal and political problem: on the one hand, Lord Asano's *rōnin* had acted with superb loyalty, risking their lives to avenge the honor of their feudal lord, upholding the values of the *samurai*; on the other hand, they had formed an illegal secret conspiracy and had carried out murder. Two months after taking revenge on Lord Kira, the *rōnin* were ordered by the *shogun* to commit *seppuku* themselves.

These are the historical events standing behind one of the *jōruri* and Kabuki theaters' most famous and enduring narratives, the tale of *The Forty-Seven Samurai.* Within weeks of the verdict, a host of plays were written and performed, mainly in the *jōruri* theaters; in most cases, however, the Tokagawa edict against staging contemporary events forced playwrights to alter the characters' names, and to set the story in an earlier historical period. In 1710, the great playwright Chikamatsu Monzaemon (1623–1725) wrote a play for the puppet theater entitled *Goban Taiheiki,* which relocated the events of contemporary Edo to the four-

This scene from the University of Hawai'i production of *Chūshingura* emphasizes the formal energy of Kabuki theater.

teenth century. Probably the first professional playwright in Japanese history, Chikamatsu (born Sugimori Nobumori) was the second son of the Sugimori *samurai* family. He moved with his family to Kyoto in his teens, and took the stage name Chikamatsu in his thirties, becoming a celebrated playwright for the *jōruri* theater, and collaborating with the most famous Kabuki actor of his era, Tojuro Sakata (1647–1709). A member of the *rōnin* himself, Chikamatsu was sympathetic with the dishonor done to Asano's retainers, and in his staging of their dramatic revenge established many of the dramatic conventions that would become standard in later versions of the story. In the next thirty years, Chikamatsu's play was one of hundreds of plays on the subject performed before the opening of the classic version of the story—*Kanadehon Chūshingura*—at the Takemoto puppet theater in 1748. Within the year, four Kabuki theaters (three in Edo and one in Kyoto) staged versions of *Chūshingura* which rapidly became part of the standard Kabuki repertory. The story of the forty-seven samurai has been one of the most enduring and popular of all Kabuki plays.

Although the Kabuki versions of *Chūshingura* are based on *jōruri* narratives, the genesis of plays in the Kabuki theater was quite different from that in the puppet theater. While the *jōruri* theaters closely followed the elaborately crafted dramatic text supplied by the playwright, in the Kabuki theater, the performers tended to take existing stories and refashion them in order to showcase their talents. While *Chūshingura* is one of the few plays still occasionally performed in the all-day form of *jōruri*, Kabuki performance tends to concentrate on several scenes from the narrative that have now become standard, which enables the play to be performed within the shorter duration of contemporary Kabuki theater. In this sense, the version of *Chūshingura: The Forty-Seven Samurai* printed here follows traditional Kabuki practice: it is a version of *Kanadehon Chūshingura* prepared by the professional Kabuki actor Nakamura Matagorō II, for a three-hour, English-language production at the University of Hawai'i in 1979. Readers who wish to consult the entire *jōruri* text should consult Donald Keene's *Chūshingura: The Treasury of Loyal Retainers*.

CHŪSHINGURA: THE FORTY-SEVEN SAMURAI

Adaptation by Nakamura Matagorō II and James R. Brandon

TRANSLATED BY JAMES R. BRANDON, JUNKO BERBERICH, AND MICHAEL FELDMAN

CHARACTERS

TADAYOSHI, *younger brother of the shogun*
KŌNO MORONAO, *chief councilor of the shogun and governor of Kamakura*
MOMONOI WAKASANOSUKE, *a young samurai*
ENYA HANGAN, *a young provincial lord*
KAOYO, *wife of Enya Hangan*
KAKOGAWA HONZŌ, *chief retainer of Wakasanosuke*
SAGISAKA BANNAI, *retainer of Moronao*
OKARU, *in love with Kampei, and later his wife*
KAMPEI, *retainer of Enya Hangan*
ISHIDŌ, *the shogun's representative at Hangan's death*
YAKUSHIJI, *envoy from the shogun*
GOEMON, *elderly retainer of Enya Hangan*

RIKIYA, *son of Yuranosuke*
ŌBOSHI YURANOSUKE, *chief retainer of Enya Hangan*
KUDAYŪ, *former retainer of Enya Hangan, now Moronao's spy*
HEIEMON, *older brother of Okaru*
SHIMIZU ICHIGAKU, *Moronao's bodyguard*
TAKEMORI KITAHACHI, *retainer to Enya Hangan*
PROVINCIAL LORDS
FOOTMEN
RETAINERS
LADIES-IN-WAITING
MAIDS
MALE GEISHA
FIGHTING CHORUS
SOLDIERS
STAGE ASSISTANTS
SAMISEN PLAYER
NARRATOR

STAGE MANAGER
SECOND STAGE MANAGER
KIYOMOTO SINGER
JESTER

TIME AND PLACE OF ACTION

Act I   SCENE 1: Hachiman Shrine in Kamakura, 1338.

SCENE 2: Outside the gate of the shogunal mansion in Kamakura, the next evening.

SCENE 3: The Pine Room of the shogunal mansion in Kamakura, a few minutes later.

Act II   SCENE 1: Along the road, near Mt. Fuji, the following morning.

SCENE 2: A reception room in Enya Hangan's mansion, the same day.

SCENE 3: The rear gate of Enya Hangan's mansion, immediately following.

Act III SCENE 1: The Ichiriki Brothel in Kyoto, eighteen months later.

SCENE 2: The garden of Moronao's mansion in Kamakura, several days later.

ACT ONE

SCENE I

Hachiman Shrine

Two sharp clacks of the hardwood ki signal offstage musicians to begin slow and regular drum and flute music, "Kata Shagiri" ("Half-Shagiri"). The deliberate pace of the music gradually accelerates. The lights in the auditorium dim slightly; the audience watches the kabuki curtain of broad rust, black, and green stripes. Very slowly, the curtain is pushed open by a STAGE ASSISTANT walking from stage right to left. Ki clacks intersperse every eighth, every fourth, then every second drum beat. Drumming and ki intermingle as the tempo rapidly increases during the last few feet of the curtain opening. The scene is a ceremonial audience before Hachiman Shrine in Kamakura. The shogun's brother, TADAYOSHI, is seated on the center of a broad stone platform running across the back of the stage. He wears a subdued Chinese-style court robe with bloused trousers and a gold lacquered hat. On his left sits the highest local official of the government, KŌNO MORONAO. A voluminous black robe with large sleeves and trailing trousers encase his body and a high black hat increases his height. Six PROVINCIAL LORDS kneel behind them on the platform. Kneeling on the ground before them are two samurai officials, MOMONOI WAKASANOSUKE and ENYA HANGAN dressed, respectively, in powder blue and yellow robes of the same exaggerated cut as MORONAO's, and HANGAN's wife, KAOYO. She wears a silk embroidered kimono and outer robe of deep blue. Two FOOTMEN sit on the ground cross-legged to the right. The heads of all the charac-

ters are dropped forward limply on their chests, in imitation of puppets before they have been brought to life. Two ki clacks signal the music to stop and the action of the scene to begin.

STAGE MANAGER: (*Rhythmic, prolonged calls from offstage right.*) Hear ye, hear ye, hear ye, hear ye, hear ye, hear ye . . . hear ye!

(*Deep, thick chords of a jōruri, or puppet-style, samisen are heard from the small room above the set stage left. The team of jōruri SAMISEN PLAYER and NARRATOR are not seen, but they can see the action on stage through the thin bamboo blind that hangs in front of them. The NARRATOR constantly shifts his vocal style between a kind of half-spoken chanting and singing. His tones are rich and full and unabashedly project the extremes of human emotion. Each syllable is precisely uttered. Sharp samisen chords punctuate the end of a chanted phrase; they become melodic under sung passages. A syllable can be clipped or staccato, or it can be prolonged into a lengthy obligato, spread over many samisen chords, so that the narrative line compresses or expands in time in order to best project the theatrical needs of the moment.*)

NARRATOR: (*Chants.*) "A banquet laid out before your eyes! Without eating of its food, never will you be able to know its taste!" Likewise, a country in peace . . . its able retainers will hide their gallantry and chivalry. (*Sings.*) Take our story as an example . . . witness here and now . . .

SECOND STAGE MANAGER: (*Calling from offstage left.*) Hear ye, hear ye, hear ye, hear ye . . . hear ye!

5

10 STAGE MANAGER: (*Calling from offstage center.*) Hear ye, hear
ye . . . hear ye!
NARRATOR: (*Chants.*) Ashikaga government chief Takauji has
Kyoto as the headquarters of his reign, his power expanding far. The time is the closing of February, thirteen thirty-
15 eight. The place is Kamakura in the east, at Hachiman
Shrine, now completed in its awesome grandeur. (*Sings.*)
Gathered here to celebrate a battle fought and won are
lords of distinction, in their solemn moments. (*Chants.*)
Acting as government proxy, Ashikaga Tadayoshi has just
20 arrived from the capital . . . of Kyoto!

(*At the mention of his name,* TADAYOSHI *raises his head, opens his
eyes, and elegantly flicks open his sleeves: puppetlike, he has been
"brought to life."*)

Here in Kamakura, he is received by the shogun's official,
Kōno Moronao! The officers of the reception are:
Momonoi Wakasanosuke Yasuchika, Moronao's target of
displeasure for his rough manners, and Hakushu's castle
25 lord, Enya Hangan Takasada. (*Sings.*) Among these men, a
single flower, Lady Kaoyo, wife of Hangan.

(*Each character, as named, comes to life, showing his or her personality through the simple actions of lifting the head, opening the eyes,
and adjusting the trailing kimono sleeves:* MORONAO's *evil
nature—seven abrupt head jerks ending in a fierce* mie *pose with
eyes crossed, arms extending aggressively forward as two loud beats
of the wooden* tsuke *call attention to the pose;* WAKASANOSUKE's
*impetuosity—five strong movements of the head, sudden opening
of the eyes, each arm flicked out independently;* HANGAN's
*composure—three smooth head movements, gentle eye opening, and
both sleeves elegantly adjusted;* KAOYO's *modesty—no movement at
all except for the slow raising of the head. Narrative shifts to song.*)

Moronao casts amorous eyes at this rare beauty. Loyal
men, bowing low. . .

(MORONAO *leers openly at* KAOYO. *Then everyone places their
hands on the floor and they make a ceremonious, deep bow to*
TADAYOSHI. *Narrative returns to chanting.*)

As Tadayoshi speaks, all listen in reverence!

(*All lift their heads and listen respectfully.*)

30 TADAYOSHI: (*Clear, unaffected voice, looking straight ahead.*) Attend, Lady Kaoyo!
KAOYO: (*Bowing.*) My lord.
TADAYOSHI: It is the shogun, not I, who has summoned you
here. You served the emperor Godaigo when he bestowed
35 upon the warrior Yoshisada the imperial battle crown.
Now, with prayers commemorating our victory in battle,
my brother the shogun wills that this battle crown be dedicated to the shrine of Hachiman, god of war. If you can,
confirm that this, and no other, is the one! Come, come!
40 Answer me, answer me!
KAOYO: (*Bowing.*) My lord.
NARRATOR: (*Chants.*) Attendants carry forth the precious battle crown, bending down to open up the heavy wooden
chest. Lifting up the battle crown . . . is it the one of fame?
45 (*Sings.*) Though gazing closely at the battle crown held
high, she will only speak when she is certain . . . and then,
floating famous fragrance of the crown well known . . .

(*The two* FOOTMEN *place a large wooden chest center and remove
its lid. They bring out a samurai helmet. Its golden fittings gleam in
the light.* KAOYO *moves forward the better to observe it, kneels, and
noticing its special perfume, nods decisively.*)

KAOYO: This is the very crown Yoshisada wore in battle, I can
say with certainty.
NARRATOR: (*Chants.*) Saying these words, Kaoyo bows deep 50
in reverence.

(*She bows. A* FOOTMAN *places the helmet at* TADAYOSHI's *feet.
With the second* FOOTMAN, *he carries off the chest.*)

TADAYOSHI: Enya Hangan! Momonoi Wakasanosuke! In conjunction with the dedication, all ceremonies are placed in
your care. Consult Lord Moronao. Kaoyo, you may go!
KAOYO: (*Bowing.*) My lord. 55
NARRATOR: (*Chants.*) Kaoyo has now been freed of her demanding task, waiting as his lordship . . . into the palace goes!

(TADAYOSHI *rises; a* STAGE ASSISTANT *takes off the stool he has
been sitting on. Without looking to the right or left, he walks with a
dignified gait down the steps. He stops and poses. Drum and flute
play stately exit music.* TADAYOSHI *flicks open his sleeves, turns, and
moves slowly off left.* PROVINCIAL LORDS *rise and follow, their formal court trousers trailing behind them.* FOOTMEN *bring up the rear.
They exit. The music continues in the background as* HANGAN,
WAKASANOSUKE, *and* KAOYO *play out in silence their petitions to*
MORONAO *for permission to depart. To* HANGAN's *polite bow of request* MORONAO *nods condescendingly.* HANGAN *rises, and with
unruffled composure, goes off left, carrying the helmet with him, to be
deposited in the shrine.* WAKASANOSUKE *bows brusquely, scarcely
bothering to conceal his contempt for* MORONAO. *In response,*
MORONAO *deliberately and disdainfully averts his gaze. Moving to
where he is in* MORONAO's *line of sight again,* WAKASANOSUKE
bows a second time, more brusquely still. Again MORONAO *ignores
him and looks away. Trembling with fury,* WAKASANOSUKE *moves
directly in front of* MORONAO *and bows a third time.* MORONAO
looks over his head as if the young samurai were not there.
WAKASANOSUKE *leaps up in rage, strikes back his sleeve, and rushes
off left. Music stops.* MORONAO *laughs soundlessly, then looks expectantly to* KAOYO, *who bows politely, rises, and starts to move
away.* MORONAO *rises, a* STAGE ASSISTANT *removing the stool on
which he has been sitting. He stops* KAOYO *with an unctuous, but
clearly threatening, command.*)

MORONAO: One moment, Lady Kaoyo! I wish to have a
word with you. I believe that you and I share in common
an unspoken passion, for the art of writing poetry. Will 60
you accept from me this poem, composed with loving
care, your reply to which I will not be displeased to receive from your own lips, Kaoyo, my lady.
NARRATOR: (*Chants.*) From his sleeve to her sleeve, a love letter from Moronao! (*Sings.*) Saying not a single word, she 65
throws it aside.

(*Crossing to her,* MORONAO *looks around to see that no one is
watching. He passes a love letter into* KAOYO's *sleeve. She takes it
out, and looking at the salutation, knows immediately what it is.
Coldly she drops it to the ground.* MORONAO *scoops it up and tucks
it away in the breast of his kimono.*)

MORONAO: (*Insinuatingly.*) Casually you cast my letter to the ground, but you will not cast down my intentions that easily. Until you accept my love, I will track you, chase you, wear you down. In the palace your husband is my puppet, to rise or to fall in his duties, solely on Moronao's will. Kaoyo, my lady . . . well? Do you not agree?

(*He glances about again, then moves behind her and enfolds her in a rough embrace. She discreetly tries to free herself: their bodies sway back and forth.*)

NARRATOR: (*Sings.*) In her heart are angry words but Kaoyo refrains. Dear Lady Kaoyo, tears in her eyes.

(*Without warning* WAKASANOSUKE *strides on. Taking in the situation at a glance, he turns his back.*)

WAKASANOSUKE: Ahem! Ahem! (*Furious,* MORONAO *breaks away.* WAKASANOSUKE *moves beside* KAOYO.) Lady Kaoyo, Lord Tadayoshi dismissed you long ago. If you linger, you are risking his displeasure. Go! Do not stay a moment longer!

KAOYO: Yes, good Lord Wakasanosuke, with your permission, I shall take my leave.

NARRATOR: (*Sings.*) Burdened with care, to her mansion . . . Kaoyo returns.

(KAOYO *bows and moves quickly onto the* hanamichi, *the rampway which extends from the stage, through the audience, to the rear of the auditorium. She stops at the "seven-three" position, that is, the position seven-tenths of the distance from the back of the auditorium and three-tenths from the stage. She poses, puts her hands inside her kimono sleeves, then regally moves down the* hanamichi. *She passes out of sight as the narration ends.*)

MORONAO: (*Snarling.*) No one summoned you! You are insolent, Wakasanosuke! Kaoyo was entreating me, in private audience, to guide Hangan in his palace duties. That is how even the mighty must grovel before the shogun's chief councilor. And who are you? A country rustic, a nobody. So low a single word from Moronao would send you tumbling into the streets to beg for your food! And you call yourself a samurai? A samurai? (MORONAO *strikes* WAKASANOSUKE's *chest with his heavy fan.*) You . . . a sa-mu-rai? (*On the last three syllables,* MORONAO *strikes* WAKASANOSUKE's *chest, sword hilt, and chest again.* WAKASANOSUKE *falls back.*) B-b-blockhead country bumpkin!

NARRATOR: (*Chants.*) You dare to meddle, little man? Moronao's revenge! Bursting in hot anger, Wakasanosuke . . . here in the sacred shrine before his Majesty, a moment of patience is all I need! One more word decides my life, death may be my fate! Wakasanosuke now holds himself in!

(*To the narration:* WAKASANOSUKE *poses with hand on the hilt of his sword; he notices he is in a sacred shrine and falls back; his hand trembles; he nods with determination, throws his fan into the air, and lunges forward as if to draw his sword.* MORONAO *slaps his fan against* WAKASANOSUKE's *sword arm and glares at his young opponent in alarm and rage. At that moment a cry is heard from offstage announcing the return of* TADAYOSHI.)

VOICES OFF: (*In unison.*) Bow down!
MORONAO: (*Snarling.*) Bow down, I say!

(MORONAO *strikes* WAKASANOSUKE's *sword arm viciously with his closed fan.* WAKASANOSUKE *drops to one knee, glares at* MORONAO, *and poses with his hand on his sword.* MORONAO *rushes up the platform steps, suddenly pivots back to face* WAKASANOSUKE, *flips open his sleeves, and poses in a fierce* mie. MORONAO *crosses his eyes and glares to two loud beats of the* tsuke. WAKASANOSUKE *restrains himself; his chest heaves. The curtain is run closed to accelerating ki* clacks. *A single* ki *clack marks the end of the scene and signals the offstage drum and flute to play "Sagariha" ["Departure"] as the scene is changed.*)

SCENE II
Bribery and Rendezvous

Two ki clacks: *the curtain is run open. Ki* clacks *accelerate, then fade away. The scene is the rear gate of the shogunal mansion in Kamakura where the state ceremonies are to be held. It is night. Pale blue light floods the stage. One ki* clack *signals action to begin.*

NARRATOR: (*Chants.*) Chief retainer of Wakasanosuke, (*Sings.*) Kakogawa Honzō comes in with a tray full of gifts, a self-assigned task.

(HONZŌ, *carrying a tray of silks as a bribe for* MORONAO, *comes onto the* hanamichi. *He stops at the seven-three position, looks toward the gate, and poses.*)

HONZŌ: Bannai. Master Bannai.

(BANNAI, *a comic villain, enters from inside the gate.* HONZŌ *moves quickly onto the stage, places the gifts on the ground, and kneels respectfully before* BANNAI.)

BANNAI: (*Officiously.*) Someone calls me. Who is it, who is it? (*Notices* HONZŌ. *Starts.*) State your business, I am a busy man!
HONZŌ: (*Bowing obsequiously.*) I am Kakogawa Honzō, chief retainer of Momonoi Wakasanosuke.
BANNAI: (*Chuckles delightedly.*) The bluebird Wakasanosuke and his friend, the yellow canary Enya Hangan, are country chickens. What a cackling they will make in the palace. Oh, my master, Lord Moronao, will pluck them clean!
HONZŌ: (*Carefully watching* BANNAI's *expression.*) That is the matter on which I have come, good Bannai. My master is young and untutored in the intricacies of palace etiquette. Only with Lord Moronao's generous guidance will he be able to carry out his important duties. Taking this opportunity, I express my gratitude for your master's favor.

(HONZŌ *bows low.* BANNAI *turns front with a self-satisfied smirk on his face.*)

BANNAI: Everyone needs a chief councilor's favors. But your Wakasanosuke was rude to my master. Go back where you came from, go back, go away! (BANNAI *strikes a pose: feet together, head up, right fist extended toward* HONZŌ.)
HONZŌ: What you say is true, still please accept these gifts on behalf of Wakasanosuke and his grateful followers.

(HONZŌ *bows toward the gifts of silk. He looks about, to be sure they are unseen, then takes out a wrapped package of gold coins. Moving forward on his knees to* BANNAI's *side, he drops the package into the open kimono sleeve.*)

Carry my message to Lord Moronao. Do what is necessary, good Bannai. Will you do so, Bannai? Bannai?

(HONZŌ *tugs lightly on* BANNAI'*s sleeve.*)

NARRATOR: (*Chants.*) Wondering, Bannai takes it in his hand!

(BANNAI *flicks* HONZŌ'*s hand away and in doing so strikes the heavy coins. He clutches his fingers in pain, then wonders what his hand hit. He sneaks a look at the coins. He reacts with delighted surprise.*)

NARRATOR: (*Sings.*) Money talks words of power!

30 BANNAI: (*Effusive, his attitude completely changed.*) Well, well, Kakogawa Honzō, how nice of you to come. (*He squats and bows to* HONZŌ.) You have come at the right moment: the ceremonial rooms are being prepared. Come, come!

(BANNAI *picks up the tray of gifts, rises, and gestures for* HONZŌ *to follow him.*)

HONZŌ: (*Bowing carefully.*) I am a person of no importance, I
35 do not dare enter the palace.
BANNAI: (*Proudly.*) If Lord Moronao is with you, who would dare object? Come, I will show you the rooms.
HONZŌ: I will enter then, most gratefully.
BANNAI: Then come along. Come along!

(BANNAI *poses.* HONZŌ *bows. They cross toward the gate: three times* BANNAI *turns back, chuckling and bowing, to beckon* HONZŌ *forward. At the gate* BANNAI *stops short.*)

40 Master Honzō, the threshold is high.
NARRATOR: (*Sings.*) Moronao is happy. Honzō bought the life of Wakasanosuke. His scheme now is accomplished. Together they go.

(BANNAI *steps carefully over the foot-high threshold of the gate and goes inside, followed by* HONZŌ.)

NARRATOR: (*A nō song, as if part of the entertainment inside the mansion.*)
"At the end of the journey we have reached Takasago Bay;
45 At the end of the journey we have reached Takasago Bay."

(OKARU, *a beautiful young girl in her late teens, enters on the hanamichi. She wears a maiden's trailing kimono with long sleeves, in a purple arrow pattern. She holds a lacquered letter box in her right hand. She stops at the seven-three position, looks toward the gate, and poses.*)

OKARU: My Lady Kaoyo urgently sends this letter to her husband, Lord Enya Hangan. How fortunate that I, her favorite, was allowed to bring it. Dearest Kampei, I cannot bear to be apart from you a single moment.

(*Offstage musicians play nō-style drum and flute music in the background.* KAMPEI, *a young samurai, enters from the gate followed by a* RETAINER. *They wear black kimono under stiff vests; their divided skirts are folded up to their knees, showing that they are on guard duty.* KAMPEI *is in the service of* HANGAN *and is* OKARU'*s lover.* OKARU *sees him and runs to meet him.*)

50 KAMPEI: Okaru, is it you?
OKARU: (*Coquettishly.*) Dearest Kampei, I missed you so.

KAMPEI: (*Flustered and worried about meeting her while he is on duty.*) But why are you here at the palace gate, at night, and all alone?
OKARU: I've come for Lady Kaoyo. "Meet Kampei and tell 55 him he is to ask my husband to deliver this letter to Lord Moronao"—those were her very words.

(OKARU *passes him the letter box.*)

KAMPEI: (*Unsure.*) I am to deliver this directly to Lord Hangan?
HOKARU: Yes, dearest Kampei.

(*She smiles invitingly at him.*)

KAMPEI: Wait for me, Okaru.   60

(*He turns to go.*)

OKARU: (*She holds his sleeve.*) Kampei!
KAMPEI: I should take it to our master myself. I should be with him. It is my duty not to leave his side in the palace. I . . .

(*He is irresolute. He tries to leave; she tugs gently, persuasively at his sleeve. He looks into her pleading eyes. He decides. He turns to the* RETAINER.)

Take this immediately to Lord Hangan.   65
RETAINER: I will.

(*The* RETAINER *takes the letter box, bows, and crosses into the gate.*)

OKARU: I want to be with you so. Now that we are here, together . . .
KAMPEI: You are flushed with excitement, Okaru!
OKARU: (*Taking his hand in hers.*) Please come. I don't care! 70
NARRATOR: (*Sings.*) Seizing fast her lover's hand . . . she leads him away!

(*She presses against him boldly, folding her arm over his. They pose: a sharp ki clack emphasizes the moment. Offstage drum and samisen resume in the background. They look excitedly into each other's eyes and then hurriedly cross into the darkness of the trees beyond the gate. The curtain is run quickly closed to accelerating ki clacks. Music ends. Soft, intermittent ki clacks mark time while the scene is changed.*)

SCENE III
Pine Room

Two ki clacks: the curtain opens. The scene is a large reception room of the shogunal mansion called the Pine Room because of the designs painted on the gold sliding doors extending across the full stage. A single ki clack: action begins.

NARRATOR: (*Chants.*) Utter indignation, for Moronao is late! Impatiently waiting in the palace . . . Wakasanosuke!

(WAKASANOSUKE *rushes onto the* hanamichi. *He drops to one knee at the seven-three position, resolutely slaps his thigh, and poses, waiting for the arrival of* MORONAO. *A sliding door left opens. Rapid drum and flute music.* BANNAI *ushers* MORONAO *on stage, bowing obsequiously. He carries a small paper lantern to light the room. Without a word,* WAKASANOSUKE *leaps to his feet, slips his sword arm free of the restricting formal vest, and rushes to attack* MORONAO. BANNAI *momentarily is able to block* WAKASANOSUKE's *path, but then is hurled to the floor as* WAKASANOSUKE *pushes past.* MORONAO *falls to his knees. He clasps his hands together pleadingly.* BANNAI *throws his arms around* WAKASANOSUKE's *lower leg, holding him fast. Music stops.*)

MORONAO: There you are, there you are, Lord Wakasanosuke, good Wakasanosuke. Your early arrival makes me ashamed,
5 ashamed, so very ashamed. I was rude to you at Hachiman Shrine. I was. (WAKASANOSUKE *edges forward as if to draw.*) Now, now, now, you have every right to be angry. But have pity on a foolish old samurai. I throw my sword at your feet. I clasp my hands and apologize. Bannai, Bannai,
10 you too, bow, apologize to Lord Wakasanosuke.
NARRATOR: (*Sings.*) Flattering, and what is more, detestable words so sweet. Taken aback completely, Wakasanosuke wonders what has happened. There is nothing he can do . . .

(MORONAO *bows his head low to the floor.* WAKASANOSUKE *cannot believe his eyes, seeing the proud councilor abasing himself. He kicks* BANNAI *away, slips his sword arm inside his vest, and strides past* MORONAO. MORONAO *circles to avoid him, crawling on his hands and knees indecorously.* WAKASANOSUKE *turns back, spitting out his words.*)

WAKASANOSUKE: Contemptible samurai!

(*He strides off stage left.*)

15 MORONAO: I was wrong, I was wrong, I apologize, I apologize, I . . .

(*Eyes fearfully on the ground,* MORONAO *continues.* BANNAI *registers comic shock, seeing his master bowing and speaking to no one. He scurries forward on his hands and knees. He pulls* MORONAO's *sleeve. Music stops. Their eyes meet.* BANNAI *nods in the direction of* WAKASANOSUKE's *exit.* MORONAO *sees that he is alone and sighs with relief. Recovering his dignity, he sits up.*)

MORONAO: Bannai, that stupid young puppy meant, I think, to kill me. "A sword in a fool's hand makes the wise man cautious."
20 BANNAI: (*Bowing.*) Oh yes, my lord, how true.
NARRATOR: (*Chants "Jo no Mai" ["Slow Dance"] drum and flute music.*) Who has planned this mischievous fate? (*Sings.*) Enya Hangan . . . innocent of this all, proceeds to Moronao. (*Chants.*) Moronao . . . seeing his victim!

(*Simultaneously,* BANNAI *arranges his master's sword and the lantern and exits stage left while* HANGAN *appears on the hanamichi, carrying in his left hand the letter box given by* KAMPEI's *retainer. Noh-style "Jo no Mai" drum and flute music continues in the background.*)

MORONAO: (*Ominously.*) Late, late, late! You're late, Hangan!

(HANGAN *bows slightly and hurries on stage. He kneels, bowing again.*)

25 HANGAN: I humbly beg your pardon for being a few moments late. I come ready for your instructions. First, however, I have been asked by my wife to place this letter in your hands.

(*He moves forward on his knees, places the letter box on the floor beside* MORONAO, *moves back, and bows respectfully.*)

MORONAO: (*Feigning ignorance.*) Hmm, hmm. A letter from Lady Kaoyo? To me? (*Opens the box and removes the letter card.*) Ah, I understand. My poetic skill is renowned. No 30 doubt she wishes me to place the touch of my pen upon her heartfelt words, to correct any blemishes. There is time before the ceremonies. Sit and be at ease. (*He reads.*) "A woman's love does, not lie in the hopeful eye, of her beholder; not beholden to lie I, aver never to lie with you." 35 (*Music stops.* MORONAO *again.*) "Not beholden to lie I, aver never to lie . . . with you."
NARRATOR: (*Chanting rapidly.*) After weighing the words . . . Kaoyo has rejected my love and this is the proof! This must mean that Hangan has found out my intention! (*Sings.*) 40 Anger and humiliation . . . but pretending ignorance.

(MORONAO *looks straight forward, his face frozen in humiliated rage, his right hand slowly closing into a rigid fist that crushes his brocade silk robe. Masking his emotions he turns toward* HANGAN. *Drum and flute music resume.*)

MORONAO: Hangan, was this poem shown to you?
HANGAN: (*Bows politely.*) I have not seen it until this moment, your Excellency.

(*Reassured that* HANGAN *is not party to* KAOYO's *insult,* MORONAO *proceeds to deliberately humiliate him.*)

MORONAO: Is that so? Well, the lord of little Hakushu castle 45 has a clever wife. She can dash off a subtle poem like this. A woman so talented and famous for her beauty must be a source of great husbandly pride. Such a superlative creature in fact, that her infatuated husband, not bearing to be separated from her, finds his sacred duties at the palace . . . 50 wearisome!

(MORONAO *casually turns his back to* HANGAN, *idly playing with his fan.*)

NARRATOR: (*Chants.*) Moronao is filled with spiteful words of insinuation. Riding on his frustration . . . any may be his prey. Hangan is perplexed at the burst of displeasure. (*Sings.*) Gushing anger, he holds it down, holds it in! 55

(HANGAN *starts. He almost turns to confront* MORONAO, *but then suppresses his anger. He pretends to smile, as if sharing* MORONAO's *joke. Ominous drum beats continue in the background.*)

HANGAN: Ha, ha, ha, ha. I see my lordship is in a playful mood. He has, perhaps, been drinking and is feeling in good humor. Yes, surely my lord has been drinking. Ha, ha, ha, ha.
MORONAO: (*Dangerously, facing* HANGAN.) What is that? When 60 have you seen me drinking? You, who have never offered me as much as a cup of wine? Whether I, Moronao, choose to drink or not, nothing keeps me from *my* duty! The one who's been drinking is you, Hangan. You've come from a drinking party with your charming wife, she 65 pouring for you, and you pouring for her! Isn't that why you come to the palace late?

(HANGAN's *face tightens.* MORONAO *notices and turns away with a malicious look in his eye.*)

Isn't there a story about a stay-at-home like you, helpless beyond his front door? I seem to recall . . . ah, yes, the "Tadpole in the Puddle." There once was a young tadpole that lived in a tiny puddle. He knew no other place between heaven and earth, and so he thought his puddle the most wonderful home in the world. One day a compassionate person passed by, just like Moronao, who, taking pity, lifted him from his stagnant pool and released him in the waters of a broad river. (*Arms out,* MORONAO *deliberately strikes* HANGAN's *chest with his heavy fan.*) Well, the tadpole was out of his depth, dropped suddenly into the great world from his shallow one. Completely at a loss, willy-nilly he went this way, and willy-nilly he went that way. (*Pointing with fan.*) And in the end he ran headfirst smack into a bridgepost. (*Strikes* HANGAN *full in the chest with his fan.*) And shivering and quivering, and shivering and quivering, the little tadpole expired. (*Twirling his fan in limp fingers.*) The tadpole is . . . you! (*Looks full into* HANGAN's *straining face.*) Oh? I do believe the young tadpole has lost his tail and is turning into a toad. (HANGAN *turns and glares furiously at* MORONAO.) Yes, with your eyes bulging out, Hangan, you look exactly like a toad. Ha, ha, ha, ha! This Moronao has lived many years, but this is the first time I've seen in the palace a toad wearing clothes. Oh, come here, come here, Bannai, Hangan's turning into a toad. Hangan *is* a toad, a sa-mu-rai toad! (*Drum beats stop. Silence.* MORONAO *deliberately strikes* HANGAN's *chest, sword hilt, and chest with his fan.*) Ha, ha, ha, ha, ha!
NARRATOR: (*Chants.*) Toad! Devil talk! Demon words!

(MORONAO *rears back, points contemptuously at* HANGAN *with his fan, rotates his head, and poses in a* mie *to two loud* tsuke *beats. Music stops.*)

Hangan can no more take the vile old man!
HANGAN: (*Slowly, with dangerous, suppressed fury.*) Do you dare compare Enya Hangan Takasada, castle lord of Hakushu . . . to a toad? You cannot possibly mean the words you have said! Have you gone out of your mind . . . Councilor Moronao!

(HANGAN *pivots to face* MORONAO, *slapping his thigh for emphasis.*)

MORONAO: (*Darkly.*) Watch yourself, Hangan! Remember I am councilor of the shogun. No one calls me insane. You are ludicrous!
HANGAN: You have been deliberately insulting me? Do you dare tell me that!
MORONAO: (*Insinuating.*) Indeed, I dare. And if I dare, who are you to complain?
HANGAN: (*Drawn out.*) If you dare . . .
MORONAO: (*Leaning in insolently.*) If I dare . . . ?
HANGAN: Hmm!

(HANGAN's *patience snaps. He rises on one knee, his hand on his sword.* MORONAO *instantly parries* HANGAN's *sword arm with his closed fan.*)

MORONAO: (*Commandingly.*) The palace! (MORONAO *slaps* HANGAN's *sword arm away and the two men pull back:* MORONAO *fearfully,* HANGAN *furious.*) The palace! The palace! It is the palace! Don't you know the law? Draw your sword in the palace and your house will be destroyed! Don't you know that! (*Drum beats resume.* MORONAO *slaps his fan commandingly on the floor.* HANGAN, *anguished that he must restrain his rage, folds his arms tightly over the hilts of his swords and slowly sinks back onto his haunches.* MORONAO *notes this and is emboldened to continue his provocation.*) Hm, since you know . . . then go ahead, kill me. Well . . . draw . . . draw . . . draw your sword. Come, kill me! Kill me . . . Hangan!

(MORONAO *forces himself bodily against* HANGAN *and leans against* HANGAN's *swords. They pose. Burning with humiliation,* HANGAN *abases himself in order to fulfill his ceremonial duties. He backs away and bows low.*)

HANGAN: A moment, a moment, Lord Moronao, I beg your indulgence. Without thinking I spoke out of turn. I implore you, instruct me in my duties for the ceremony. I will do as you say. Humbly, I beseech you, your Excellency.

(*Music stops.* HANGAN *looks up from his bow.* MORONAO *smugly turns away, avoiding his gaze.* HANGAN's *patience snaps a second time: his hand leaps for his sword. Instantly* MORONAO *reacts.*)

MORONAO: Your hand!
HANGAN: My hand?
MORONAO: (*With all his authority.*) Yes, your hand!
HANGAN: This hand . . .

(*He hesitates, looks at his trembling hand, then drops his hands to the floor and bows in defeat.*)

. . . humbly begs your forgiveness.
MORONAO: (*Savoring his victory.*) So, you apologize, do you? Very well, very well. Soon instructions in great detail for today's ceremony . . .
HANGAN: (*Looks up hopefully.*) . . . will be given to me?
MORONAO: (*Viciously.*) No, not to you! To Wakasanosuke! (HANGAN *is stunned, motionless. In silence* MORONAO *casually rises, tears* KAOYO's *letter card in two, and throws the pieces in* HANGAN's *face.*) There is no educating a provincial barbarian.

(MORONAO *deliberately turns his back and kicks his left and right trailing trouser legs in* HANGAN's *face.* HANGAN *rears back. Chuckling,* MORONAO *starts to leave.*)

HANGAN: Moronao! Wait!

(HANGAN *steps on* MORONAO's *trailing trouser leg.* MORONAO *is brought up short. He tugs at the trouser; it is held fast.*)

MORONAO: (*Deadly calm.*) Be careful. You'll soil my trousers. Hop. Hop, hop, hop. (MORONAO *turns to leave, but cannot move.*) So, you won't hop away, little toad? Can there be something else you want?
HANGAN: What I want is . . .
MORONAO: What you want is . . . ?

(HANGAN *quietly slips his sword arm free of the stiff vest.* MO-
RONAO *turns and thrusts his sneering face toward* HANGAN.)

150 HANGAN: (*A scream.*) You!

(HANGAN's *short sword flashes out of its sheath and gashes* MORONAO's
forehead. Drum and flute play furious "Haya Mai" ("Fast Dance").
MORONAO *staggers and falls.* BANNAI *rushes on to help his master flee.*
HANGAN *leaps to his feet and is about to finish* MORONAO *with a second blow when* HONZŌ, *who has been hiding behind a decorative screen
stage right, rushes out and seizes* HANGAN *from behind.*)

NARRATOR: "Hold me not! My foe is there!"

(*Six* PROVINCIAL LORDS *run on from right.* HANGAN *struggles to
get free, but he is encircled and held fast. In desperation he hurls his
sword after the disappearing enemy. A single sharp clack of the* ki. *The
sword falls short. He reaches out with both hands after* MORONAO
*and poses: his fingers curl into fists and his chest heaves with sobs of
mortification. But* HONZŌ *and the* PROVINCIAL LORDS *hold him
fast. To gradually accelerating* ki *clacks the curtain is run closed. Offstage musicians play "Shagiri." A single* ki *clack concludes the act.*)

ACT TWO

SCENE I
Fugitive Travel

*The large drum beats melancholy "Yama Oto" ("Mountain Pat-
tern"). To accelerating* ki *clacks the curtain is slowly pushed open. A
sky-blue curtain fills the stage. A single* ki *clack: the blue curtain
drops and is whisked away by black-robed* STAGE ASSISTANTS *to reveal a colorful springtime scene in the country. Snow-covered Mt.
Fuji is seen in the background, pink cherry blossoms bloom everywhere.* OKARU *and* KAMPEI *stand center, their faces hidden behind a
straw hat. A temple bell tolls in the distance. Kiyomoto music begins
from offstage.* KAMPEI *lowers the hat and we see the lovers dressed
for traveling: kimono skirts raised and a bundle over* KAMPEI's *shoulder. They mime in slow dance movements to the kiyomoto lyrics the
story of their disgrace and flight.*)

KIYOMOTO SINGER: Oh, you who flee, do you not see yon
green field, a veil of new green?

(*They look at the flowers at their feet, to the left and the right. They
look into each other's eyes, then pose gazing into the distance.
Singing ends; samisen continues in the background. Facing upstage,
they pass their sandals and* KAMPEI's *hat and bundle to two* STAGE
ASSISTANTS. *They turn front and kneel center stage.* KAMPEI *places
his long sword on the ground beside him.*)

KAMPEI: (*Melancholy.*) Giving myself over in love to you, I failed
    our master when he needed me, and now we are fugitives
5   fleeing in the dead of night I know not where. When I
    think of it, I no longer have the heart to live. Say prayers
    over the grave of this dishonored samurai. Okaru . . .
    farewell.

(KAMPEI *takes his short sword from his sash and is about to draw
the blade. Gently she seizes it and prevents him.*)

OKARU: No, I won't have you saying that again. I am to blame
10   that you were not beside Lord Hangan. I cannot live with-

out you. If you die then so must I. But rather than praising your spirit, people will say we died as lovers frequently
do. Please, live, dearest Kampei. Live . . . in love . . . for me.

(KAMPEI *tries to draw the sword again. She pulls one way, he the
other.* KAMPEI, *irresolute, allows her to take the short sword. She
places it beside her, away from his reach.*)

KIYOMOTO SINGER: " 'Twas then my heart went astray. It was
    when you, yes, you made me love, oh, so imprudently.   15
    Blame my imprudent heart that spoke to me thus: 'So easy
    it is to die, but you must live, live on.' "

(KAMPEI *takes up the long sword to kill himself. Again, she gently
holds the scabbard so that he cannot draw. They rise and move left,
then right, in a delicate struggle for the sword. Allowing himself to be
persuaded, they pose with the sword held firmly in her hands. He
looks away, wiping his falling tears. She takes the sword and places
it out of his reach. They kneel side-by-side.*)

KAMPEI: Your tenderness overwhelms me. (*Nods with resolution.*)
    We will flee across the mountains to your father's home.
OKARU: (*Smiling, relieved.*) You make me so happy.   20
KAMPEI: In time I know I can find a way to atone for desert-
    ing my master. Come, let us go.
OKARU: (*Meekly.*) Yes, Kampei.
KIYOMOTO SINGER: Now for travel they prepare, but who
    should confront them!   25

(KAMPEI *rises and poses facing front.*)

BANNAI: (*Off, at the rear of the* hanamichi.) Hey, hey! Here we go!
FIGHTING CHORUS: (*Also off.*) Haaa!

(*Loud beats of the big drum. Strong accelerating* tsuke *pattern as
BANNAI *runs onto the* hanamichi *followed by eight of his men, the
FIGHTING CHORUS. BANNAI *has his kimono tucked up to his
knees, and a cord holds back his sleeves. His makeup has become ludicrous: bat-shaped eyebrows, drooping eyes, and a tiny blue-gray
mustache. The* FIGHTING CHORUS *is dressed identically in red leggings and arm coverings and red and white patterned kimono that
stop at their knees. Each carries a branch of cherry blossoms as a
weapon.* BANNAI *stops at the seven-three position.* KAMPEI *escorts
OKARU *to the left, out of harm's way, and stands calmly.*)

BANNAI: (*A comic challenge.*) Hey, hey! Kampei!

(*He stamps forward with two steps, each accented by two* tsuke *beats.
He and his men march on stage. The men, alert for their master's call,
kneel upstage in two rows.* BANNAI *faces front, with a supercilious
look. He speaks in a special rhythmical pattern,* nori, *in which each
dialogue phrase fits into an eight-beat* samisen *musical phrase. He
accompanies the tale with comic gestures.*)

Your stupid master, Enya Hangan, Takasada and my hon-
    ored master, Councilor Moronao, met in the palace while,   30
    chittering chattering, chittering chattering, your master
    Hangan, flew into a snit. Taking a teensy sword, he
    whipped it out, he made a slash. He is a traitor, locked up
    in his residence, boxed up like a criminal. Ha ha ha . . . ha
    ha ha . . . haha haha hahaha! Hangan has been hauled   35
    away! I'll catch you like a chick! I'll pluck you like a duck!
    I am claiming Okaru! Well? Well? Well, well? (*Accelerating.*)

Well, well, well, well, well! Kampei! Your goose is cooked! Give her . . . to me!

(BANNAI *stands on tiptoe, holds his sword hilts threateningly, and cocks his head in comic* mie *to two beats of the* tsuke.)

40 KIYOMOTO SINGER: "Give her to me," yells Sagisaka Bannai. Kampei bursts out with mocking laughter.

KAMPEI: (*Laughs, then speaks in rhythmic nori phrases.*) You are a funny bird, Sagisaka Bannai, a little chirping sparrow, I could swallow in a bite. (*Rapidly.*) Kampei's fiery gaze

45 could fry you to a crisp! But instead of eating you, I will make you eat crow!

(KAMPEI *slips his fists out of the breast of his kimono, allowing the black outer kimono to drop. An inner kimono of brilliant crimson color is revealed. He stamps aggressively forward, then poses with arms outstretched, head cocked in a* mie *to two* tsuke *beats.* BAN-NAI *tumbles to the ground terrified.*)

KIYOMOTO SINGER: Glaring and with arms outstretched, Kampei stands before him!

BANNAI: (*Weakly.*) Help!

(KIYOMOTO *samisen and drums play instrumental music as the eight members of the* FIGHTING CHORUS *attack* KAMPEI. KAMPEI *waves half of them past him until he stands center in a* mie *position. Four men face him from either side, holding their cherry branches as if they were swords. They strike at him right, left, right. He forces them back. They fall away. They pose in a* mie *to two* tsuke *beats.* KAMPEI *now fights his opponents in a series of group combats that are executed in delicate, controlled dance patterns. Rhythmic drums and samisen support the action.*)

50 KIYOMOTO SINGER: Cherry, cherry blossoms! A name, oh, so beloved.

(*One man on each side strikes at* KAMPEI *with the cherry branch. Three times* KAMPEI *avoids, then seizing the tips of the branches, he whirls them in a circle and presses them to their knees. He poses in a* mie. *Flicking the branches away, the men are hit on the forehead; they retreat.* KAMPEI *nonchalantly dusts off his hands.*)

"No, no, you can't have her," and why should that be?

(*One man on each side seizes* KAMPEI's *arms. They struggle right, left, right.* KAMPEI *flicks them forward onto their knees. They try to seize his feet, he backs up. They rush in to encircle him. He avoids, then casually taps them on the back. They do a cartwheel and fall prostrate on the ground.* KAMPEI *poses in a* mie.)

So tender, so fine, so frail, never to be won by you!

(*Four men form a square around* KAMPEI. *Two-by-two they attack, but he pivots to avoid them. Six men strike with their cherry branches.* KAMPEI *drops to his knees, deftly knocks the wind out of them with an open-hand blow, and, with a sweeping gesture, knocks them off their feet. They fall on their bottoms in unison.*)

Delightful, though she's only to be seen. How can you

55 ever feel true love, if she won't play with you!

(*The* FIGHTING CHORUS *retires upstage.* BANNAI *pulls* OKARU *by the sleeve. Foolishly flirting, he touches his cheek to her hand.* KAMPEI

pushes him away, and when BANNAI *tries to get past to* OKARU, *blocks his way.* BANNAI *slips under* KAMPEI's *sleeve, but is caught and held by the nape of the neck.* BANNAI *struggles free, strikes at* KAMPEI, *is kicked to his knees, and finally is grasped by the ear, lifted, and spun around.* BANNAI *is near tears in frustration and humiliation. Trying once again, he raises his fist, but* KAMPEI *turns and casually pushes* BANNAI *to the ground.* KAMPEI *stamps forward and poses in a strong* mie *to two* tsuke *beats.*)

BANNAI: (*Plaintively.*) Take him!

(*Large drum and tsuke beats. The* FIGHTING CHORUS *attacks in unison:* KAMPEI *passes them off right and left as he strides from stage left to right; he turns and passes unharmed between them as they strike at him with their cherry branches. One man, coming from hiding, strikes at* KAMPEI *from behind.* KAMPEI *kicks him to the ground, places his foot on his back, and poses in a strong* mie *to two beats of the* tsuke. KAMPEI *kicks the man away and attacks. Booming drum accelerates. The* FIGHTING CHORUS *retreats. They run pell-mell down the hanamichi and out of sight.* KAMPEI *poses in a powerful "stone-throwing"* mie *to two beats of the* tsuke. BANNAI *sneaks up.*)

BANNAI: Kampei, here I come!

(BANNAI *raises his sword to strike.* KAMPEI *catches his wrist, spins him around, forces him to his knees, and raises the sword.*)

KAMPEI: (*Bantering.*) Shall I cut your ears off? (*Terrified,* BANNAI *covers his ears with wildly trembling hands.*) Shall I cut off your nose? (BANNAI *covers his nose.*) Or shall I simply kill you? 60

OKARU: Killing him would bring more trouble. So, please, just let him go.

BANNAI: (*Foolishly, imitating* OKARU's *inflections.*) So, please, just let him go!

(BANNAI *clasps his trembling hands together in prayer.*)

KIYOMOTO SINGER: Oh, how he prattles on, that bird, Sag- 65
isaka! Smoothing his ruffled feathers, slowly, then faster, flirts with death, and yet to live, away he flies!

(KAMPEI *nods agreement. He casually rolls* BANNAI *across the stage away from* OKARU. *He poses facing front.* BANNAI *rubs his throat, then noticing* KAMPEI *is holding his sword, meekly gestures a request that it be returned. Contemptuously,* KAMPEI *tosses the sword on the ground.* BANNAI *leaps back in terror. Gathering his courage, he snares the sword with his foot, then suddenly turns and raises the sword as if to strike. A fierce glance from* KAMPEI *deflates him completely. He turns and escapes off right, lifting his legs high in the air in a "stork walk."*)

KAMPEI: He deserved to die. But his death would be a crime to add to my disloyalty.

(*A cock crows in the distance. They both look up into the sky. They speak in melancholy, poetic tones.*)

Already it is dawning . . .   70
OKARU: . . . on the peaks of the mountains . . .
KAMPEI: . . . the eastern light glows . . .
OKARU and KAMPEI: (*In unison.*) . . . lighting trailing clouds.

(*They pose together center stage, absorbed in their own melancholy.*)

KIYOMOTO SINGER: They fly away at daybreak, like the crows
75   that cry, "caw, caw." So dear to each other, in love, in love.

(*A* STAGE ASSISTANT *passes to* OKARU *the hat, bundle, and swords.
Dutifully,* OKARU *helps* KAMPEI *adjust the bundle and slide the
swords into his sash. They put on their sandals. A temple bell tolls.
They move apart, pose, then move back-to-back.*)

Though they must hasten to depart, their minds are filled
with woe. Who would doubt their loyalty if they proved
the guilt they feel? Away they go.

(*They look into each other's eyes. Restraining tears,* KAMPEI *puts on
a manly bearing, takes* OKARU *by the hand, and turns to begin their
long journey.* BANNAI *sneaks up behind them. He holds* OKARU *by
the waist.*)

BANNAI: Okaru is mine, all mine!

(KAMPEI *moves to block* BANNAI, *passing* OKARU *to safety on the
hanamichi. He pushes* BANNAI *away and turns to join* OKARU.)

80   BANNAI: Kampei, wait!
KAMPEI: (*Turning back at the seven-three position.*) Bannai, you
     want. . . . ?
BANNAI: (*Posing.*) Kampei, I want . . .
KAMPEI: Hmm?
85   BANNAI: (*Deflated.*) Nothing.
KAMPEI: Simpleton!

(*A loud* ki *clack:* BANNAI *collapses to the ground. Drum booms
loudly.* KAMPEI *takes* OKARU's *hand and slowly they exit down the
hanamichi. Kiyomoto samisen plays plaintive chords and* ki *clacks
accelerate as the curtain begins to close.* BANNAI *is in the path of
the curtain. He retreats before it, then, realizing it is hopeless, seizes
the curtain with both hands and, grinning happily, prances across the
stage, closing the curtain and disappearing from sight. A single* ki
clack: drum and flute play lively "Shagiri" to close the scene.)

SCENE II
Hangan's Suicide

Two ki *clacks: the curtain is slowly opened to the rachetlike sound of
an old-fashioned clock. The scene is a large, formal room in* HANGAN's
*mansion. Sliding doors that make up the rear wall are painted powder
blue and covered with silver crests of* HANGAN's *clan. Tatami matting
covers the floor.* HANGAN, *dressed in a simple kimono and vest so pale
a blue-gray that it verges on white, kneels center. He faces two envoys
from the shogun,* ISHIDŌ *and* YAKUSHIJI, *who are sitting stage left on
high stools. They wear dark kimono, vests, and trousers.* ISHIDŌ's *sympathetic manner contrasts sharply with* YAKUSHIJI's *derisive attitude.*
GOEMON, *a senior retainer of* HANGAN, *kneels upstage. Silence.*
ISHIDŌ *rises and faces* HANGAN. *He takes from the breast of his kimono a large folded letter. He holds it reverently to his forehead.*

ISHIDŌ: Hear the shogun's command. (*Removing the letter from
     its envelope, he reads.*) "Whereas, Enya Hangan Takasada,
     you have willfully committed an act of bloodshed against
     our chief councilor, Moronao, and thereby have defiled
5   the palace, know that your estates, large and small, are
     hereby confiscated and you are ordered to end your life by
     seppuku."

(ISHIDŌ *gravely holds the open letter in front of him, so* HANGAN
can read the order with his own eyes. After glancing at it, HANGAN
bows respectfully.)

HANGAN: (*With perfect control.*) In all respects I accept the
     shogun's command.
NARRATOR: (*Chants.*) From the adjoining room, knocking   10
     on the door . . .

(*A* RETAINER *knocks on the sliding door. He speaks in a faint, muffled voice, suggesting tears.*)

RETAINER: (*Off.*) Goemon, Goemon. We, Lord Hangan's re-
     tainers, beg permission to see our master . . .
RETAINERS: (*Off, quietly in unison.*) . . . one last time.
GOEMON: (*Bowing to* HANGAN.) My lord, your retainers wish   15
     to see you.
HANGAN: Tell them not until Chief Retainer Yuranosuke has
     arrived from our province.
GOEMON: (*Facing the door.*) You heard our lord. You may enter
     when Yuranosuke arrives, not before.   20
RETAINERS: (*Scarcely audible.*) Ahhh.
NARRATOR: (*Sings.*) Their plea, not granted . . . no one dares
     utter a single word. In the room, silence prevails.

(HANGAN *rises and retires upstage, where he kneels with his back to
the audience.*)

GOEMON: (*Quietly, facing offstage right.*) Proceed.
RETAINER: (*Faintly, off.*) Yes.   25

(*In complete silence arrangements are made for* HANGAN's *death by
ritual disembowelment.* RETAINERS, *dressed in somber blue and gray
kimono, vests, and split trousers, swiftly and unobtrusively enter. They
place two tatami mats center to make a six-foot square platform. They
cover it with a pure white cloth. Sprigs of green, in small bamboo hold-
ers, are placed at the four corners. With downcast eyes, the* RETAINERS
slip quietly away. GOEMON *bows to* HANGAN *indicating that the place
of suicide is ready.* HANGAN *rises, slowly pivots front, and crosses down
to the cloth seat. Unconsciously his gaze drifts to the hanamichi: he
is waiting for the arrival of his chief retainer,* YURANOSUKE, *and does
not want to die before passing to him his last instructions. His right foot
touches the cloth. He remembers it is obligatory to step into the place
of suicide with the left foot. He glances at the envoys to see if they have
noticed: they are gazing straight ahead. He deliberately steps onto the
cloth and slowly kneels.*)

NARRATOR: (*Chants.*) Rikiya proceeds with the saddest or-
     der. (*Sings.*) The master's suicide blade weighing heavy on
     his heart . . .

(YURANOSUKE's *son,* RIKIYA, *enters from up left. He carries a plain
wooden tray bearing the short dagger with which* HANGAN *will kill
himself. The long sleeves of his black kimono and a delicate forelock
of hair indicate he is a youth, not yet grown to manhood. He places
the tray on the floor before the envoys for their verification. He bows.*
ISHIDŌ *and* YAKUSHIJI *look at the blade, then nod to each other that
it is satisfactory.* ISHIDŌ *nods gravely to* RIKIYA.)

NARRATOR: Before Lord Hangan he lays the blade.

(RIKIYA *places the tray on the cloth before* HANGAN, *bows low, and
then looks up for instructions.* HANGAN *looks gently into* RIKIYA's

eyes and with a single head movement indicates that RIKIYA *is to leave: a boy so young should not have to witness* seppuku. RIKIYA *politely shakes his head: until his father arrives, he must fulfill his father's duties.* HANGAN *repeats the order to leave; again* RIKIYA *shakes his head. Impressed by the boy's loyalty,* HANGAN *nods that he may stay.* RIKIYA *bows gratefully, rises, backs away, and takes a place beside* GOEMON.)

30 NARRATOR: (*Sings.*) Taking off, in hushed silence, his outer clothes to expose his death robe . . . securing the seat of death.

(HANGAN *prepares himself for death with calm deliberation. He slips off the vest, letting it drop to his waist. He tucks the ends under his legs so as to hold his body in place after he has died. He drops the outer kimono to his waist and tucks it in as well. Beneath he is wearing a pure white kimono appropriate for death, an indication to the envoys that he was prepared to die even before they brought the shogun's command. He places his hands firmly on his thighs and looks intently down the* hanamichi.)

HANGAN: (*Softly but urgently.*) Rikiya.
RIKIYA: (*Bowing.*) Yes.
35 HANGAN: Yuranosuke . . . ?
RIKIYA: Yuranosuke . . . (*He looks down the* hanamichi *for a sign that his father has arrived.*) . . . has not as yet arrived.
NARRATOR: (*Sings.*) Proper steps for suicide, he lifts the tray and bows. (*Chants.*) Waiting no longer, the blade in his
40 hand.

(HANGAN *prepares the dagger. He lifts the tray to his forehead respectfully. He ceremoniously takes the dagger in his right hand and a sheet of white paper in his left. He wraps the paper around the blade until only its tip is bare. He is now able to grasp the blade low for extra leverage. He holds the blade at ready on his thigh. The tip points to his stomach. Outwardly calm, his voice betrays his anxiety.*)

HANGAN: Rikiya, Rikiya!
RIKIYA: (*Bowing.*) Yes.
HANGAN: Yuranosuke . . . ?
RIKIYA: Yes! (RIKIYA *bows and rushes to the end of the* hanamichi.
45 *He falls to his knees, looks to the right, the left, then straight ahead, searching for sight of his father. His lip trembles, he is close to tears.*) Yuranosuke . . . (*He rushes back and throws himself on the floor before* HANGAN.) . . . has not as yet arrived!
HANGAN: (*Calmly.*) Tell him that I regret . . . not seeing him
50 one last time. (HANGAN *nods that* RIKIYA *may retire and pivots slightly toward* ISHIDŌ.) Lord Ishidō, I ask that you witness and report my death.
NARRATOR: (*Sings.*) Here at last the time has come, the blade is aimed. Hangan . . . thrusts it in . . . thrusts it deep!

(HANGAN *places the tray behind him. He rises slightly on his knees, looking one last time down the* hanamichi *for* YURANOSUKE. *He holds the dagger under the ribs on his left side. With a sudden jerk he thrusts the blade into his stomach. Involuntarily his body drops forward and his head falls. Rapid narrative shifts to chanting.*)

55 Running at a desperate speed, the awaited person comes! Here at last is Ōboshi Yuranosuke! A frantic gaze at his master: "Is he still alive?" Overcome by the sight, he falls on his knees!

(YURANOSUKE *bursts onto the* hanamichi, *running frantically, all decorum cast aside. He wears a formal gray kimono, vest, and trousers pulled up for travel. Reaching the seven-three position, he sees his master in the midst of suicide. He reels, falls back, then slowly sinks to his knees.*)

ISHIDŌ: (*Rising.*) Is it Ōboshi Yuranosuke?   60
YURANOSUKE: It is.
ISHIDŌ: (*Urgently.*) Approach, approach quickly!

(YURANOSUKE *attempts to rise, but his legs will not function. He weeps unashamedly. To gain control of himself, he reaches inside the breast of his kimono to pull tight the inner cloth binding his waist. With great effort he pushes himself up from the floor and moves unsteadily to* HANGAN's *side. He falls to his knees and bows deeply.*)

NARRATOR: (*Chants.*) The men of Hangan, all, till now forbidden . . . but no longer! They come rushing in!

(*Ten* RETAINERS *enter swiftly from up right. They are barefooted and carry no swords. They fall to their knees in a row upstage and, following* YURANOSUKE's *lead, bow deeply to their master* HANGAN. YURANOSUKE's *eyes remain downcast and* HANGAN, *in pain, does not yet look up.*)

YURANOSUKE: Ōboshi Yuranosuke kneels before my lord.
HANGAN: (*Weakly.*) Yuranosuke?   65
YURANOSUKE: I am here.
HANGAN: At last you've come.
YURANOSUKE: All that I could ever ask is to be at your side in these last moments . . .
HANGAN: Ah, it makes me content as well. (*Slowly their gazes* 70
meet.) You have heard, have you not . . . everything . . . everything . . . ?

(*His voice trails off in pain.* YURANOSUKE *edges closer, looking meaningfully at* HANGAN.)

YURANOSUKE: Yes!
HANGAN: (*Rousing himself.*) I am humiliated . . . !
YURANOSUKE: (*Interrupting.*) No words can express such feel- 75
ings as I hold. Nothing remains now but for me to assure you a just end.
HANGAN: (*Meaningfully.*) One thing remains.
NARRATOR: (*Chants.*) Gripping tight the blade, cutting straight across in disembowelment. (*Sings.*) Such moments 80
of agony . . . exhaling his breath . . .

(HANGAN *cuts his stomach across from left to right. Although the pain is excruciating and his lips tremble and his breathing grows labored,* HANGAN *maintains the stoic decorum expected of a samurai until the blade reaches its final point just under the right ribs. Then breath seems to leave him. His body sags. He braces his left hand on his thigh.*)

HANGAN: (*Faintly.*) Yuranosuke . . . Yuranosuke . . . come close . . .
YURANOSUKE: Yes.

(HANGAN *is near death.* YURANOSUKE *slides forward urgently. Knowing* HANGAN *cannot speak openly because the shogun's envoys are present, he searches his master's face for some command.*)

85 HANGAN: Take this blade . . . to remind you . . . do not forget. Re-ve-n . . . (YURANOSUKE *starts.* HANGAN *must not say "revenge" out loud.* HANGAN *catches himself.*) . . . remember me.

(*Weakly* HANGAN *looks into* YURANOSUKE'S *face, then down the* hanamichi. YURANOSUKE *follows* HANGAN'S *gaze. Master and retainer look deeply into each other's eyes.* YURANOSUKE *understands that in spite of his master's seeming calm acceptance of the death sentence,* HANGAN *passionately desires vengeance against the enemy outside the mansion, that is,* MORONAO.)

YURANOSUKE: (*Passionately.*) I swear!

(YURANOSUKE *slaps his chest for emphasis and bows deeply.* HANGAN *knows that* YURANOSUKE *understands. He is now free to die. He smiles.*)

HANGAN: Ha ha. Ha ha. Ha, ha, ha, ha . . .

(*The laugh fades. With ebbing strength,* HANGAN *pulls the blade from his stomach. He gasps.*)

90 NARRATOR: (*Chants.*) Aiming the blade at his throat . . . one slash across. Breathing his last breath, lifeless he crumples.

(*Weakened hands, trembling violently, lift the blade upward. He tilts his head. His neck is exposed. A quick slash and the jugular vein is cut. His body rises upward in three spasms of breath. His eyes flutter closed. He falls limply forward, dead. Silently* ISHIDŌ *rises. A* STAGE ASSISTANT *whisks his stool offstage.* ISHIDŌ *places the shogun's letter on his open fan and places them on* HANGAN'S *body. He moves stage right and kneels beside* YURANOSUKE.)

ISHIDŌ: (*Quietly.*) Yuranosuke, Yakushiji now assumes authority over Hangan's estates. Hangan's retainers are hereby denied the rank of samurai and are disbanded. I will report
95   to the shogun that the death of Hangan is accomplished. You have my deepest sympathy, Yuranosuke.
NARRATOR: (*Sings.*) Ishidō, the envoy, expresses sympathy. His sad assignment is over.

(ISHIDŌ *rises facing the line of* RETAINERS. *He raises his arms in a gesture of condolence. The* RETAINERS *look up, then bow respectfully. Slowly* ISHIDŌ *walks to the seven-three position on the* hanamichi. *At a signal from* YURANOSUKE, RIKIYA *moves forward to see him out.* ISHIDŌ *turns back.*)

ISHIDŌ: There is no need. There is no need.
100 NARRATOR: He prays silently.

(ISHIDŌ *folds his hands and, with downcast eyes, walks slowly down the* hanamichi *and out of sight.*)

NARRATOR: (*Chants.*) Yakushiji holds them in contempt!

(YAKUSHIJI *rises brusquely. The* STAGE ASSISTANT *takes away his stool.*)

YAKUSHIJI: Now that he's dead, I'm master here! Cart the corpse away, while I settle in. Show me the way! (*He starts to go, then turns back.*) It's a sad time, isn't it! Ha, ha, ha, ha!

(YAKUSHIJI *strides off left, shown out by a* RETAINER. *Complete silence.* YURANOSUKE *moves in to attend to his master's body. He*

straightens the legs and brings kimono and vest up over the torso. He moves closer and tries to take the dagger from HANGAN'S hand. In death HANGAN'S fingers hold it tightly. YURANOSUKE falls back weeping. He gently massages his master's hand until the fingers are warmed, softened, and the dagger slips from their grasp. YURANOSUKE places the dagger carefully into the breast of his kimono. He backs away. He and the RETAINERS bow expectantly.*)

NARRATOR: (*Singing plaintively.*) Lady Kaoyo enters from an- 105
other room. Her hair so long and black, oh, so beautiful, now pitiful, it is no more. She will pray as a nun, till her end.

(KAOYO *and four* LADIES-IN-WAITING *enter from the left, walking with downcast eyes. They are dressed in pure white kimono and hold Buddhist rosaries. The last* LADY-IN-WAITING *carries a small tray on which rests the cloth-wrapped remains of* KAOYO'S *long hair. They kneel left. The* MAIDS *bow deeply.*)

KAOYO: (*Quietly.*) Yuranosuke. When I think of why my husband had to die, and that I was the cause . . .
YURANOSUKE: (*Firmly.*) My lady, please understand our 110
heartfelt feelings. All of us, each retainer offers his deepest condolence.

(YURANOSUKE *bows to* KAOYO, *then nods to* GOEMON. GOEMON *and the* RETAINERS *rise and move in a circle around their master. Silently, they take up the white cloth, the tatami mats, tray, and sprigs of green. They exit upstage right.* HANGAN *moves off behind the cloth. In an instant all sign of the suicide is removed.*)

KAOYO: Yuranosuke.
YURANOSUKE: Yes, my lady.
KAOYO: I offer my lock of hair.

(*The* LADY-IN-WAITING *places the tray with the hair center stage.* YURANOSUKE *sees it and weeps.* KAOYO *turns to show her close-cropped head.*)

NARRATOR: (*Prolonged, melancholy singing.*) Kaoyo is left be- 115
hind, her grief is so . . . o . . . o . . . She yearns to go to the temple . . .

(*She rises, as if to follow her husband, but* YURANOSUKE *stops her with a commanding gesture.*)

YURANOSUKE: My lady!

(*She falls back weakly. A single* ki *clack. They move into a pose:* YURANOSUKE *picks up the tray with one hand and forces her back with the other;* KAOYO *faces front, lifts the rosary to her eyes, and sobs silently.* Ki *clacks accelerate as the curtain is slowly walked closed.*)

SCENE III
Outer Gate

Two ki *clacks signal drum and flute to play "Toki no Taiko" ("Time Drum"). The curtain is pushed quickly open. The scene is outside the massive outer gate of* HANGAN'S *mansion. No one is on stage.*

NARRATOR: (*Chanting rapidly.*) Farewell to Hangan. Now his body lies alone. The young retainers run back from the temple! They no longer can hold the shame inside!

(*To loud, accelerating* tsuke *beats,* RIKIYA *leads a band of* RETAINERS *onto the* hanamichi. *They urge each other on with shouts of "Kill*

them!" "They won't have our lord's mansion!" "We'll fight them!"
"Lord Hangan was unjustly killed!" At the same time YURANOSUKE
and GOEMON *come out of a small door in the gate.* GOEMON *rushes
up to the* RETAINERS *with outstretched arms, shouting, "Stop, stop!"*
YURANOSUKE *roughly pushes* RIKIYA *to the ground.)*

YURANOSUKE: (*Furious.*) What, you too, Rikiya? What are
5   you thinking of, trying to attack the mansion? We are no
     longer samurai. We cannot fight Yakushiji's men. (*Drops to
     one knee, hand on the hilt of his short sword.*) If you do not
     stop, I shall commit seppuku on this very spot! Do you
     want to be my seconds, all of you?
10   RETAINERS: No, but master . . .
     YURANOSUKE: (*Implacably.*) Then will you stop when I tell you?
     RETAINERS: Yes, but . . .
     YURANOSUKE: It will achieve nothing to die now!

(*The* RETAINERS *cannot disobey. Grumbling and rebellious, they begin to fall back.*)

NARRATOR: (*Chants.*) Behind the gate is heard . . . Yakushiji's
15   voice!
     YAKUSHIJI: (*Off.*) Hey, men, there's a sight. Newly hatched
     ex-samurai, milling around like chickens with their heads
     cut off! It's enough to make you laugh!
     YAKUSHIJI'S MEN: (*Off.*) Ha, ha, ha, ha, ha!
20   FIRST RETAINER: Do you . . .
     RETAINERS: . . . hear that?

(*Furious, they turn to storm the gate, hands on the hilts of their
swords.* YURANOSUKE *springs into their path and blocks the way.*)

YURANOSUKE: Have you forgotten our late lord?
RETAINERS: No, but . . .
YURANOSUKE: Not now! Go back, go back! Go back I tell you!

(*YURANOSUKE *draws himself up commandingly. He runs his hand
up the edge of his vest and poses in a furious* mie. *Two* tsuke *beats.*)

25   NARRATOR: (*Sings.*) "Go back," he commands!
     YURANOSUKE: (*Almost in a scolding tone now.*) Back, back, back.

(*YURANOSUKE *waves them away. They fall back grudgingly, then
turn and stride off down the* hanamichi. YURANOSUKE *watches
them leave. He is alone. Silence. He sighs with relief. The hand at his
breast slides down until it accidentally touches the dagger. He slowly
drops to his knees and takes it out. He unwraps the covering purple
cloth. The blade tip is red with* HANGAN's *blood.*)

NARRATOR: (*Sings.*) The suicide blade, red with blood, cries
     out for revenge . . . cries out for revenge! Burning tears rake
     his heart, tears . . . falling . . . falling . . . falling . . . falling . . .

(*Gazing at the blade,* YURANOSUKE's *chest heaves. He covers his
eyes to hide the tears.*)

30   Hangan's last words of vengeance imbedded deep in
     Yuranosuke. (*Chanting.*) We know indeed the motive of
     Yuranosuke, his revenge to be noted for many ages . . .
     forty-seven loyal men immortalized!

(*He wipes blood from the blade onto his palm and then deliberately
brings his hand up to his mouth. He licks the blood as an oath of*

vengeance. Music stops. Silence. YURANOSUKE *begins his long pantomime of departure. He carefully wraps the dagger in the purple
cloth. He holds it to his forehead respectfully. He places it in the
breast of his kimono. He rises and stands. He slaps the dust from his
knees. He adjusts his trousers. He folds both hands inside his kimono
sleeves. He rests his hands on the hilts of his swords. He half-closes
his eyes, regretting deeply that he must abandon his master's mansion. A temple bell tolls in the distance. Pensively, he begins to walk
away from the gate. The gate recedes, indicating* YURANOSUKE *has
covered a long distance. He turns back. A crow caws in the distance.
He resumes the painful separation. A crow caws a second time. A second bell tolls. He stops, stricken with the finality of parting. Then, he
moves onto the* hanamichi. *Once more he turns back and, as if he
has no heart to continue, slides to his knees. A temple bell tolls.
Plaintive, tentative chords of the* samisen *begin. He rises, begins to
walk away, looks sadly over his shoulder for one last glimpse, then
resolutely turns and strides down the* hanamichi *and out of sight.
Music crescendoes and* ki *clacks accelerate: the curtain is run closed.
Drum and flute play rapid "Shagiri" to end the scene.*)

ACT THREE

SCENE I

Ichiriki Brothel

Two ki *clacks: the curtain is pushed open to offstage singing of
"Hana ni Asobaba" ("If You Play in the Flowers"). The scene is the
Ichiriki Brothel in the Gion licensed quarter in Kyoto. Two pavilions
are set in a garden. Lying on his side in the larger room, stage center, is* YURANOSUKE. *He is feigning sleep, his face covered with a
half-open fan. He wears an elegant purple kimono and matching
cloak. Curtains are at the back and a stone water basin is left. Three
steps lead down into the garden. Paper-covered sliding doors conceal
the interior of the smaller pavilion, stage left. It is several feet higher
off the ground than the center pavilion.*

NARRATOR: (*Singing briskly.*) The mountains and the moon.
     From the eastern mountains, just a few miles, breathless
     from running fast, the young man . . . Rikiya.

(RIKIYA *enters on the* hanamichi. *A purple scarf covers his head and
serves as a partial disguise. His black kimono is hiked up at the
sides, to free his legs for running. He stops at a garden gate set on the*
hanamichi *at the seven-three position. He looks back to see if he is
being observed, then swiftly passes through the gate, closing it.*)

     Entering the brothel garden . . . there lies Yuranosuke, pre-
     tending to be drunk. Taking caution to wake his father in   5
     secrecy, he walks softly in, stepping close to him. The
     sword guard speaks!

(RIKIYA *sees his father. He mounts the steps, kneels, and makes a
ringing sound by striking sword guard against sheath.* YURANOSUKE
gestures RIKIYA *away with a sleepy movement of the fan.* RIKIYA
*crosses swiftly back through the gate, closes it, looks around to be cer-
tain they are not being observed, and kneels to wait for his father.
Offstage* samisen *play tentative chords.* YURANOSUKE *rises. He
staggers as if drunk, ad-libbing, "That was heady wine. I need some
air. Don't go away, girls. I'll be in the garden." He looks through the
curtains to see if anyone is watching. He crosses to the gate, stumbling
several times in order to have the chance to look carefully in all directions. He stands swaying, fan before his face. He speaks guardedly.*)

YURANOSUKE: Rikiya, do I hear the sound of urgency in the echo of your sword?

10   RIKIYA: Yes, Father. I bring a secret message from Lady Kaoyo. (RIKIYA *brings out a letter from his right sleeve and passes it to* YURANOSUKE, *who puts it immediately into the breast of his kimono without examining it.*)

YURANOSUKE: (*Carefully.*) Did she say anything to you?

15   RIKIYA: (*Rising on his knees urgently.*) Soon, soon our enemy . . .

YURANOSUKE: Rikiya! "Soon at night our enemy, flees like plovers o'er the sea. . . ."

(*Music swells. To cover the slip of his son's tongue,* YURANOSUKE *sings a well-known passage from a* now *play. He staggers in a circle looking to see if anyone has heard* RIKIYA'S *remark. Simultaneously,* RIKIYA *pivots in the opposite direction, looking for eavesdroppers.* YURANOSUKE *gestures for* RIKIYA *to come closer;* RIKIYA *whispers* KAOYO'S *message in his father's ear. The curtains in the room center part.* KUDAYŪ *peeks out. He is a gray-haired former retainer of* HANGAN, *now secretly working for* MORONAO. *He wears a plain brown kimono and cloak. He watches for a moment, then slips away.*)

YURANOSUKE: Send a palanquin for me tonight. Tell the others to be ready. Go, go!

20   NARRATOR: (*Sings.*) No time left for hesitation . . . to the eastern hills, homeward now . . .

(YURANOSUKE *sharply gestures with the fan.* RIKIYA *bows, rises, and holding firmly onto the hilts of his swords, begins to leave.*)

YURANOSUKE: Rikiya!

RIKIYA: (*Returning and bowing.*) Yes.

YURANOSUKE: Be careful while passing through the quarter.
25   Then hurry! Go now!

RIKIYA: Yes!

NARRATOR: Rikiya returns home.

(RIKIYA *realizes his mistake; he is holding his swords ready to draw, thus calling attention to himself. He hides the hilts with his sleeves. Swiftly, carefully, he hurries down the* hanamichi *out of sight. Offstage* samisen *play "Odoriji Aikata" ("Dance Melody"). Four* MAIDS *and a male* JESTER *enter through the curtain, ad-libbing, "Yura, where are you?" "Come drink with us." "Don't leave us, Yura."* YURANOSUKE *pretends drunkenness again.*)

FIRST MAID: Yura, Yura, are you here?

YURANOSUKE: Hmm. You've come to get me? I'm a lucky
30   man. Come close all of you, let's amuse ourselves. Come, sing and dance for me.

(YURANOSUKE *sits on the steps. The* MAIDS *and the* JESTER *kneel in the garden in a semicircle around him.*)

SECOND MAID: Very well . . .

ALL: . . . let's begin, let's begin!

(*Lilting music of offstage* samisen, *drum, and bell accompanies various dances and songs. These are extemporized by the performers from production to production.* MAIDS *and* JESTER *ad-lib comic banter throughout.*)

MAIDS: (*Clapping as they sing.*) "What will it be like, what will
35   it be like? If you don't be careful, we will make you drink. Ah, what will it be like, what will it be like?"

(JESTER *and* THIRD MAID *rise and move center. They do a game of* jan-ken-po, *"scissors-paper-stone." He loses. She laughingly pushes him. He falls in a heap on the ground. The* MAIDS *rise and form pairs.*)

FOURTH MAID: Come, let's dance!

ALL: "First your left foot, then your right, tap, tap, tap;
   Around we go, back again;
   Are you ready, one, two, three!"   40

(*They circle left, then right, touching palms of their outstretched hands. They turn their backs to each other and bump bottoms on the count of three. With peals of laughter they recover their balance. The* JESTER *and* YURANOSUKE *laugh and applaud.*)

YURANOSUKE: Very good, very good!

FIRST MAID: How about a game, Yura dear?

JESTER: Blind man's bluff!

SECOND MAID: You be It!

ALL: Yes, yes!   45

(YURANOSUKE *tries to wave them away, but they playfully surround him and put a cloth over his eyes. They twirl him around in the center of the garden, and move left, laughing and clapping in time to their song.*)

ALL: "Yura, Yura, over here;
   Listen to our clapping hands."

YURANOSUKE: (*Sings.*) "I'll catch you all, soon enough you'll see."

(*He stumbles in their direction. They easily avoid his outstretched arms and flee to the other side of the garden.*)

ALL: "Yura, Yura over here;
   Come and catch us if you can."   50

YURANOSUKE: "I'll catch you all, and make you drink with me."

(*They duck under his arms. When he turns back to continue pursuit, they take him by the hands and, still singing and clapping, lead him off to the inner room with his blindfold still in place. They are no sooner off than* KUDAYŪ'S *head pops through the curtain on the other side of the stage. Samisen music stops.* KUDAYŪ *peers about intently. He slips into the room.*)

KUDAYŪ: That letter Rikiya gave to Yuranosuke . . . the rumor of a vendetta must be true! He has not forgotten; they are plotting, just as I thought. When I tell Moronao, what will be my great reward? If, of course, it's true. I'll spy him out!   55
   Here's a perfect place to hide.

(*He sees a hiding place. He removes a board under the veranda, opening a space for him to crawl in. He hides behind the steps.* YURANOSUKE *enters alone from upstage, pretending to be drunk.*)

YURANOSUKE: I'll be back . . . don't wait, girls . . . in a minute, I'll be back.

(*Samisen music resumes. He looks around. Seeing he is alone, he drops his pretense. He rinses his mouth with water from the stone basin. He spits it out. It falls on the unsuspecting* KUDAYŪ. *He takes out the letter from* KAOYO *and holds it respectfully to his forehead. He begins to read, slowly unrolling the letter until it reaches the ground. At the same time the paper doors slide open to reveal* OKARU *in the small room left. She wears the elaborate hairstyle and clinging kimono of a courtesan.*)

NARRATOR: (*Sings.*) Evening breeze, brings a courtesan, Kampei's wife Okaru, away from her love. Someone has sent a
60 love letter, "I wish it were for me." Okaru from a room above, tries to see the words. Too far in the evening dusk, the letters are not clear to read. Thinking of a way out, a mirror in her hand, she leans back . . . mirror held up high, reflec-
65 tion of the letter. Under the floor a spy, Kudayū waits . . . the trailing letter glows in the moonlight. (*Chants.*) Who could know someone is reading words of confidence?

(*The three form a tableau:* YURANOSUKE *is engrossed in reading the secret letter;* OKARU *views the letter backwards in a mirror; and* KUDAYŪ, *spectacles on his nose, reads the bottom portion, line-by-line, as it comes down to him. Narrative shifts to singing.*)

Okaru, unaware that her hairpin has loosened! (*Chants.*) It drops to the floor! Surprised by the sound above, he
70 quickly hides the letter . . . Yuranosuke! Underneath Kudayū smirking at his game. (*Sings.*) Okaru pretends nothing has happened here.

(YURANOSUKE *quickly resumes his drunken role. He begins to roll up the letter, but not before* KUDAYŪ *rips off the part he has been reading.* OKARU *puts down the mirror, picks up a fan, and turns to* YURANOSUKE.)

OKARU: (*Languidly.*) Yura dear, is it you?
YURANOSUKE: Hmm, Okaru? So close at hand, what are you
75 doing?
OKARU: (*In poetic form of seven and five syllables.*) Yura dear, it's all your fault, I drank too much wine; my head is whirling round and I can scarcely see; I have come to sober up, wafted by the evening breeze.

(YURANOSUKE *reaches the end of the letter. He feels the ragged edge. Startled, he looks quickly at the letter, then puts it away in the breast of his kimono. He takes out a piece of tissue paper and wads it up, covering his action by improvising conversation with* OKARU.)

80 YURANOSUKE: Hmm. Wafted by the evening breeze, you say? Wafted by the evening breeze? Ah!

(*He drops the wad of paper to the ground.* KUDAYŪ, *thinking it is part of the letter, snatches it and stuffs it into his kimono breast.* YURANOSUKE *falls back, supposedly in a drunken stupor, but actually wanting to ponder what to do next. He decides. Soft samisen plays "Odoriji Aikata" in the background.*)

Hm. Okaru, there is something I want to talk to you about. Come over here.
OKARU: (*Rises as if to leave her room.*) Very well, I'll come
85 around and visit you.
YURANOSUKE: (*Coming down into the garden.*) No, Okaru, if you go that way the maids will catch you. They will force on you more wine. Ah, a ladder. Fortune smiles. Climb down this way and you won't be seen. (*Places a ladder against*
90 OKARU's *pavilion. Bantering.*) Descend for me, Okaru!
OKARU: (*Coquettishly on the ladder.*) I've never climbed a ladder before.
YURANOSUKE: You've climbed other things.

OKARU: I'm not used to this strange position. It frightens me.
YURANOSUKE: You're past the age to be afraid of a new po- 95 sition. Straddle it, open your legs, it'll all go smoothly.
OKARU: Don't be naughty, Yura. I tell you it frightens me. It's swaying like a boat.
YURANOSUKE: Never mind, I'll throw in my anchor. That will hold you down. Where shall I put it? (*He tries to lift* 100 *her skirt with his fan. She brushes his hand away.*)
OKARU: You mustn't peek, Yura.
YURANOSUKE: (*Singing.*) "I adore your crescent moon, glistening in its secret grotto." Ha, ha, ha.
OKARU: (*Pouting.*) If you talk that way, I won't come down. 105
YURANOSUKE: Don't prattle like a virgin. You're a courtesan in the Gion brothel. I'll take you from behind. (YURANOSUKE *embraces her from behind.*)
OKARU: Oh, stop it.
YURANOSUKE: Then come, come. 110
OKARU: I am, I am!

(*Laughing, she slips off the final rung of the ladder and moves away from* YURANOSUKE. *She kneels right, fanning herself.* YURANOSUKE *glances at her sharply, then resumes the drunken pose. He stoops to retrieve the dropped hairpin and crosses to give it to her.*)

YURANOSUKE: (*Casually.*) Just now, Okaru, did something catch your eye?
OKARU: I . . . nothing.
YURANOSUKE: (*Coaxing.*) Come now, didn't you see, didn't 115 you see . . .
OKARU: . . . your interesting letter . . .
YURANOSUKE: . . . from up above?
OKARU: (*Lightly.*) Hmm, yes.
YURANOSUKE: And you read it all? 120
OKARU: Oh, you do go on.

(*Covering his concern, he pretends to stumble. He recovers his balance, singing a now song which both hides and expresses his feelings.*)

YURANOSUKE: "Fate conspires to bring, my life to this crisis. . . ." (*Mimes striking a nō drum.*) Ya, tum, tum, tum! Ha, ha, ha!
OKARU: (*Turns to him, laughing.*) What in the world do you mean? 125
YURANOSUKE: It means that of all the women in the world, I have become enamored of you. Come live with me, Okaru.
OKARU: Stop it. You're such a tease!
YURANOSUKE: (*Grandiloquently.*) I will redeem your contract with the master of the brothel and take you away. 130
OKARU: I don't believe it. You're making fun of me.
YURANOSUKE: I'll prove it's not a lie. Be my mistress for just three days, and after that, Okaru, your spirit will be free to go where it will.
OKARU: (*Taking him seriously for the first time.*) For three days? 135
YURANOSUKE: On my sacred oath as a samurai. Live with me for three days. I'll find the master and buy your contract now. Well, is it agreed?

(OKARU *looks carefully at him to see if it possibly can be true. They pose. She bows low.*)

OKARU: I am grateful, Yuranosuke.
YURANOSUKE: Can it make you happy to be redeemed . . . 140 by this Yuranosuke?

OKARU: Oh, yes!

YURANOSUKE: Such radiance shines in that happy face.

(*They pose: she looks at him with gratitude; flicking open his fan, he covers his face to hide his stricken expression.*)

YURANOSUKE: Don't go away now. I'll be right back.

145 OKARU: Three days? Yes, Yuranosuke. I'll be here.

(*Offstage, sad "Yo ni mo Inga" ["Nighttime Fate"] is sung quietly. They lightly ad-lib to cover his exit. Still pretending to be drunk, he staggers up the steps. He turns back several times. He passes through the curtains in search of the master of the house. When he is gone she kneels center stage, trembling with excitement.*)

OKARU: How happy I am! I must write to dearest Kampei that I am coming home! And to Mother and Father, to tell the wonderful news!

(*She hurries up the steps into the center room, brings out a writing box and roll of letter paper, kneels, and begins to write a letter home. Song ends.*)

NARRATOR: (*Chants.*) Now appears . . . Heiemon!

(*Offstage samisen briskly play "Odoriji Aikata." A young samurai strides on from the right into the garden. His hair is severely drawn back and his plain kimono suggests poverty. It is* HEIEMON, OKARU's *older brother, in search of both* YURANOSUKE *and* OKARU. *He looks around, then seeing a woman in the room, enters and sits behind her. He speaks brusquely, almost rudely.*)

150 HEIEMON: Sorry to trouble you, Miss, but I am looking for a young woman, from my hometown of Yamazaki, by the name of Okaru, brought here a year ago . . .

(*Hearing her name* OKARU *turns. They recognize each other.*)

Sister!

OKARU: Heiemon! Oh! I feel ashamed for you to see me here!

(OKARU's *demeanor completely changes: in the presence of a male family member who is her elder, she becomes submissive, gentle, a little girl seeking approbation. She hides her face. She rushes down the steps, and falls to her knees.* HEIEMON, *though stern, acts protectively toward her. He rises and poses on the steps.*)

155 HEIEMON: What is there to feel ashamed of? When I returned home Mother told me you had sold yourself to this brothel, hoping that with your contract price Kampei could contribute to the vendetta against Lord Hangan's enemy. You have willingly sacrificed yourself for your husband and for Lord Hangan. I am proud of you, Okaru!
160   (*He poses at the top of the steps: right foot forward, right arm extended protectively in her direction.*)

OKARU: (*Hesitantly, looks up at him.*) Then you're not going to scold me?

165 HEIEMON: Scold you? I am filled with admiration, filled with admiration!

(*He crosses down the steps and kneels. He sits proudly, sword placed on the ground beside him.*)

OKARU: I'm happy that you think kindly of me. (*Becoming excited.*) Oh, there are so many things I want to ask my dear big brother. I don't know where to begin . . . how is Kam . . .

HEIEMON: (*Uneasy.*) Kam . . . ?   170

(OKARU *is embarrassed to have asked about her husband first. She changes the subject.*)

OKARU: Come . . . tell me, how is Mother?

HEIEMON: Set your mind at ease. Mother is well.

OKARU: And Father? Nothing troubles him, I hope?

HEIEMON: (*Uncomfortably.*) Hm . . . Father . . . he is at rest . . . he is at rest.   175

OKARU: (*Modestly.*) And what of Kampei?

HEIEMON: Kampei? Ah . . . well . . . he is as well as can be.

OKARU: You set my heart at ease. (*Bubbling.*) Oh, I forgot. . . be happy for me, Brother. Tonight, without warning, Yuranosuke offered to buy out my contract.   180

HEIEMON: Yuranosuke did that? (*Trying to understand how such a thing could be.*) Ah, then he's become your patron?

OKARU: Nonsense. We have only drunk together two or three times. And Heiemon, it's almost too good to be true. After three days he will let me come home.   185

HEIEMON: Hm? Then you told him you are Kampei's wife?

OKARU: How could I, a prostitute, tell him that and bring disgrace to Kampei and to my parents?

HEIEMON: (*Facing front.*) Hm! Then he is no more than a whoremaster! (*He slaps his thigh in anger.*) He has no intention of avenging Hangan, our lord and master!   190

OKARU: Oh, no, Brother, he has. He has. Listen . . .

NARRATOR: (*Sings.*) In whispers, the content of the letter is revealed.

(OKARU *and* HEIEMON *rise. He leans forward. She whispers in his ear. They pose for a moment, then break apart and kneel.*)

OKARU: . . . so you see?   195

HEIEMON: (*Shocked.*) Then you read it all?

OKARU: Yes, and after reading it, his eye met mine, and flirting, he looked me up and down, up and down, and then began to talk of taking me away.

(OKARU *mimes his flirting by pressing the backs of her index fingers together, right on top of left, then left on top of right.* HEIEMON *is puzzled. He tries to understand her words, miming as she did.*)

HEIEMON: What? After reading it, flirting, he looked you up   200 and down, up and down . . . (*He slaps his thigh for emphasis.*) Ah! Now I understand!

OKARU: (*Laughing.*) You startled me.

HEIEMON: (*Facing the inner room, he bows low.*) Forgive me, Master Yuranosuke, I misjudged you! I was wrong, forgive me!   205

OKARU: Dearest Brother, what in the world are you doing?

HEIEMON: (*Turns and looks into* OKARU's *eyes.*) Dear Sister. There is something I must ask of you. Okaru, do now exactly as I say.

OKARU: You sound so very stiff and formal. What must you   210 ask of me?

HEIEMON: What I must ask of you is . . .

OKARU: What you must ask of me is . . . ?

HEIEMON: Okaru, let your brother take your life!

(*He springs to his feet and whips out his long sword. She falls back. Rapid "Odoriji Aikata." To double beats of the* tsuke, *he slashes at her right, left, right. She avoids. She rises and pushes him away. He turns to strike; she distracts him with a shower of tissue paper drawn from her breast and thrown in the air. She runs to the* hanamichi; *he follows. She closes the gate between them. They pose in a* mie *to two loud* tsuke *beats: on the ground, she holds up her hands imploringly; he stands with legs together, the sword directly overhead as if to strike. Music stops.*)

215 OKARU: (*Appealing to him.*) What am I supposed to have done wrong? You have no right to just do as you please. I have my husband and both my parents to care for. Forgive me if I have spoken out of turn. I clasp my hands and beg you to spare me!
220 NARRATOR: (*Sings.*) Seeing his sister's clasped hands . . . a brother's love overwhelms the dutiful heart. He can only cry.

(*He tries to but cannot strike his sister. He falls back distraught, turns upstage to face away from her, holds the sword behind his back, and weeps unashamedly. When the narration is finished, he turns to face* OKARU. *He is contrite. Slow offstage "Odoriji Aikata" resumes in the background.*)

HEIEMON: I was wrong, Okaru, not to explain. Come, come over here.

(*He waves her to him. She flounces.*)

OKARU: No, I will not come near you.
225 HEIEMON: (*Sternly.*) When your elder brother calls, why don't you come?
OKARU: (*Sweetly.*) If you want to know, I'll tell you why: I think you still intend to kill me, and I don't like that at all!

(HEIEMON *notices the long sword in his hand. He puts it on the ground and pushes it toward her.*)

HEIEMON: Ah, this. There is nothing to stop you now. So
230 come, come!
OKARU: Yes, there is. Something else.

(*She points at the short sword in his sash. Annoyed, he pushes it toward her.*)

HEIEMON: There, now. Come over here!

(*She rises and is about to cross through the gate. She looks at him and stops.*)

OKARU: Your face is so frightening.
HEIEMON: I can't help that. This is the face I was born with.
235 OKARU: Well then, please turn around.
HEIEMON: What a nuisance. Like this? Like this?

(*Grumbling, he turns his back. He poses with arms stretched out to either side.*)

OKARU: Now, don't look. Keep your face turned away. (*She cautiously goes through the gate, picks up the swords, and puts them out of his reach. She kneels behind him, placing her hands on his sash. Music stops. She poses.*) All right, here I am.
240

Brother dear, what is it you want? (*He turns to face her. He places his hands protectively on her shoulders. They pose.*)
HEIEMON: (*Voice filled with emotion, he speaks in poetic form of seven and five syllables.*) Once you were a samurai, now a courtesan; combing out your silken hair, while the world 245
has changed; precious Sister how pitiful, totally unaware of the life you left behind!

(HEIEMON *breaks away and kneels left.* OKARU *moves close.*)

OKARU: Totally unaware . . . of what, Heiemon?
HEIEMON: Soon after you left home last year, one rainy night, Father was . . . 250
OKARU: (*Frightened.*) Father was . . . ?
HEIEMON: (*Choked scream.*) . . . struck down by a robber and slain by his sword!
OKARU: (*Falls back slackly.*) That cannot be true.
HEIEMON: You must be strong, Okaru. You look forward to 255
leaving here and being with your husband . . .
OKARU: Yes . . . Kampei . . . what about Kampei?
HEIEMON: Kampei . . .
OKARU: Kampei . . . ?
HEIEMON: (*A terrible scream.*) Cut open his stomach and is dead! 260

(*He mimes the suicide and collapses, weeping.* OKARU *falls back, shocked, hardly able to breathe.*)

OKARU: Kampei . . . oh . . . no. What shall I do? What shall I do?
HEIEMON: I know, I know, I know . . .

(*They speak alternately, then faster and faster, until they are speaking at the same time. Then their grief-stricken voices fade away.* OKARU *crawls to her older brother and puts her head on his lap. She weeps pitiably. At last* HEIEMON *gains control of himself. He gently disengages himself.*)

HEIEMON: Don't you see? Yuranosuke is not a man to be infatuated, and he did not know you were Kampei's wife. 265
Okaru, you were wrong to have read that secret letter. Yuranosuke's loyalty is clear. He cannot risk letting you live and he intends to buy your contract . . . just to kill you! Rather than dying at someone else's hand, let me be the one to take your life. Let me prove to Yuranosuke and his 270
followers that though I am a mere foot soldier, my spirit is as loyal as theirs. Let me serve our late master. Give me your life, dear Sister!
NARRATOR: (*Sings.*) The tragedy is disclosed! Okaru is prepared!

(HEIEMON *is agonized by the conflict between his duty to* HANGAN *and his love for* OKARU. *He beseeches her with clasped hands.* OKARU *willingly prepares to sacrifice herself. Gently she opens his hands.*)

OKARU: It is my karma not to meet my beloved husband and 275
father again. There is no reason for me to live.

(*She crosses to get the swords, returns, and places them before him.*)

Brother dear, please end my life now.

(*She turns her back, clasps her hands in prayer, and drops her head forward, exposing her neck to his sword.*)

HEIEMON: Admirable resolve. Namu Amida Butsu. Praise Buddha the Merciful.

(*He stands. He unsheaths the sword. He raises it to strike.* YURA-NOSUKE's *voice is heard from behind the curtain.*)

280 YURANOSUKE: (*Off.*) Wait, wait! Stop at once! (*He enters.*) Your behavior is admirable, both of you. I acknowledge your loyalty. Heiemon, I hereby permit you to accompany us on our journey to the east.

(HEIEMON *and* OKARU *move right and kneel respectfully.* HEIEMON *is excited by* YURANOSUKE's *acceptance of him into the vendetta group.*)

HEIEMON: Then you are ready? And I may go with you?
285 Okaru, Sister, do you hear? I am forever grateful.

(HEIEMON *bows to* YURANOSUKE. YURANOSUKE *comes down the steps.*)

YURANOSUKE: Okaru, for your loyalty, your husband, Kampei, will be admitted to our league. And since he was unable during his life to kill even a single enemy, let your action, Okaru, serve as his apology to Lord Hangan in the
290 afterlife . . . here and now . . .

(YURANOSUKE *takes* HEIEMON's *long sword and places it in* OKARU's *hands. He guides her to the veranda. They pose.*)

NARRATOR: (*Chants.*) Thrusting deep through the dark of the hiding place. The hateful spy, Kudayū, a fatal blow in his shoulder, rolls and turns in deadly pain!

(*They thrust the sword under the veranda. Double* tsuke *beats.* KU-DAYŪ *cries out.* HEIEMON *drags the mortally wounded* KUDAYŪ *into the garden and throws him to the ground.* YURANOSUKE *kneels, and holding* KUDAYŪ *by the scruff of the neck, strikes furiously with closed fan.*)

YURANOSUKE: Kudayū, you wretch! Traitor! More than forty
295 of us day and night have shed tears of agony. We have parted from our children, deserted our parents, and sold our wives into prostitution all in order to avenge our Lord Hangan's death. And you, who enjoyed wealth and honor in his service, have betrayed your master and become Mo-
300 ronao's spy! Fiend! Demon! You are a monster!
NARRATOR: (*Sings.*) As if to grind him into the ground, Yuranosuke . . . his burst of anger cannot be gratified!

(*He strikes him five times to sharp* tsuke *beats. Then contemptuously he pushes him away. Bringing his hand to his eyes,* YURANOSUKE *openly weeps. Just then the* MAIDS *cry out offstage. Rapid "Odoriji Aikata." Instantly* YURANOSUKE *reverts to his pose as a drunken brothel patron. He rises, staggering. The* MAIDS *enter and kneel in a semicircle in the center room.*)

FIRST MAID: Master Yuranosuke, Master Yuranosuke . . .
SECOND MAID: . . . your palanquin has arrived.
305 YURANOSUKE: You've come for me?
ALL: We will see you out.

(YURANOSUKE *crosses up the steps and stands at the top. He gestures for* OKARU *to join him there and for* HEIEMON *to pick up the nearly dead* KUDAYŪ. *Music stops.*)

YURANOSUKE: Heiemon. Take our drunken friend to the Kamo River. Let him drown his sorrows . . . in the waters there!

(YURANOSUKE *flicks open his fan and raises it overhead.* OKARU *kneels beside* YURANOSUKE, *placing her hands on his sash.* HEIEMON *drapes* KUDAYŪ's *limp body over his shoulder. A single sharp clack of the* ki. *They freeze in a group* mie *pose. Ki clacks accelerate, drum beats speed up, and offstage "Odoriji Aikata" crescendoes as the curtain is slowly pushed closed.*)

SCENE II
Vendetta

Two sharp ki clacks: large drum softly beats "Yuki Oto" ("Snow Sound"). The ki clacks accelerate to accompany the opening of the curtain. The scene is the garden of MORONAO's *mansion in Edo. It is night. Snow is falling. Rocks, trees, ground, and small bridge across a pond are covered with a mantle of white. Soft, rapid tsuke beats. Several* WOMEN *from* MORONAO's *household rush on from the left. They are wearing nightclothes. Frightened and confused they urge each other to flee. They disappear. Drum and tsuke beats crescendo. Two* RETAINERS *with drawn swords rush on from the right. They pose.*

MORONAO'S RETAINER: I am Riku Handayū, retainer of Moronao. Name yourself!
HANGAN'S RETAINER: Akagaki Genzō, loyal to Enya Hangan. Let me pass!

(*They pose. Another two* RETAINERS *run on from the left.*)

MORONAO'S RETAINER: You will burn in hell before you 5 touch Lord Moronao!
HANGAN'S RETAINER: I, Katayama Genta, will take his head for Lord Hangan! Stand aside!

(*Large drum pattern of triple beats, "Mitsudaiko," and loud continuous tsuke beats. The paired opponents fight: they slash and parry with their long swords. In the end* HANGAN's *men gain the upper hand;* MORONAO's *men turn and are pursued off stage. Drumming changes to quiet "Snow Sound."* SHIMIZU *enters on the hanamichi. He is a famous swordsman hired by* MORONAO *as a bodyguard. A woman's kimono is draped over his head as a disguise, to allow him to reach the side of his master without being detained by* HANGAN's *men. He stops at the seven-three position.*)

SHIMIZU: The war drum. Yuranosuke has come at last. But he will not succeed. The moon shall see the severed heads of 10 forty-seven rōnin before it witnesses the death of Lord Moronao!

(SHIMIZU *rushes on stage. He meets* TAKEMORI, *one of* HANGAN's *men. They circle each other warily.* SHIMIZU's *swords are seen.*)

TAKEMORI: Stop! Who are you?
SHIMIZU: (*Dropping the kimono to his waist.*) I am Shimizu Ichigaku, protector of Lord Moronao. 15
TAKEMORI: And I am Takemori Kitahachi! I've come for Moronao's head!
SHIMIZU: Then you must take mine first.
TAKEMORI: Come, fight! Fight!

(*"Mitsudaiko" drumming, loud tsuke beats, and "Chuwya Aikata" samisen music accompany the battle.* TAKEMORI *attacks, rushing past*

SHIMIZU. SHIMIZU *throws tiny daggers at* TAKEMORI, *who falls to the ground to evade. One of* HANGAN's *spearmen rushes on from the right, forcing* SHIMIZU *away from* TAKEMORI. SHIMIZU *is attacked from both sides. He slips free and runs onto the bridge over the pond. He is attacked by spear and sword simultaneously.* TAKEMORI *reaches under his guard and stabs* SHIMIZU *in the chest. A second slash, down his back, sends* SHIMIZU *toppling into the water of the pond and out of sight. Drum crescendoes. A loud whistle is heard off left. It signals* MORONAO's *capture.* MORONAO *is dragged on by several of* HANGAN's *men. He is thrown to the ground. He wears nothing except a white sleeping kimono. He is unarmed.* YURANOSUKE, RIKIYA, GOEMON, HEIEMON, *and other* RETAINERS *enter. They surround* MORONAO, *watching him carefully.* YURANOSUKE *kneels beside* MORONAO *politely.*)

20   YURANOSUKE: We allow you to die, Moronao, by your own
     hand . . . with this blade.

(*He unwraps* HANGAN's *suicide dagger and respectfully places it before* MORONAO, *offering him the opportunity to die with honor, instead of being killed.* MORONAO *is shaking with fright. He picks up the dagger as if to kill himself, then lunges at* YURANOSUKE. *Seizing* MORONAO's *wrist,* YURANOSUKE *turns the dagger against* MORONAO *and plunges it into his breast.* MORONAO *cries out once, then falls back dead. The* RETAINERS *form a ring around* MORONAO, *hiding him from view.* TAKEMORI *raises his sword and with a single stroke cuts off* MORONAO's *head. Two loud* tsuke *beats. It is wrapped in a white cloth and held high at the end of a spear.* MORONAO *moves offstage unseen behind a black cloth held by a* STAGE ASSISTANT. *The* RETAINERS *rise triumphantly.*)

YURANOSUKE: You have fought bravely, all of you. Your years of hardship, endured without thought of self, have brought success to our cherished plan. What joy Lord Hangan's spirit must feel for your deeds. On his behalf I thank you.   25
GOEMON: And now, let us bring Moronao's head to our master!

(*Spoken lightly, the lines are in poetic phrases of seven and five syllables.*)

YURANOSUKE: Deep concerns like drifted snow, melt in the clear of day . . .
RIKIYA: . . . at last our long awaited, vengeance is achieved . . .   30
GOEMON: . . . together with the clearing, of the morning clouds . . .
AGAKI: . . . at the cock's crow announcing, dawn of a new day . . .
TAKEMORI: . . . our hearts filled to overflowing, rise with the   35
rising sun . . .
GOEMON: . . . as we go together to . . .
ALL: . . . our Lord Hangan's grave.
YURANOSUKE: Shout victory together! Victory!

(*Single* ki *clack: offstage drum and* samisen *play "Taka no Hara" ("Hawk Plain") slowly, gradually accelerating until the scene is over. Each person turns to those next to him, nods, wipes tears of gratitude, grips an elbow, or places a hand on a shoulder. Then their thoughts return to their master,* HANGAN, *and all of them stand silent, posed in mingled happiness and grief. The curtain closes to rapidly accelerating* ki *clacks. The offstage musicians play "Shagiri" indicating the play is over.*)

CRITICAL CONTEXTS

ZEAMI MOTOKIYO (1363–1444)

from "A Mirror Held to the Flower" (1424)

TRANSLATED BY J. THOMAS RIMER AND YAMAZAKI MASAKAZU

Although Zeami's treatises describe the practical and esthetic foundations of the Noh (Nō) theater, they were not well known until the twentieth century. Since the Noh was organized around prominent families of actors, Zeami's texts were passed on in private and shown only to those who had been properly initiated. The first definitive edition of the treatises was published in 1940.

In "A Mirror Held to the Flower," Zeami discusses the training of Noh performers, emphasizing the interplay between physical training, spiritual development, and acting style in the production of the "flower"—beauty—in Noh performance. In this translation, the central term yugen *has been translated as "Grace." Although Zeami's language can seem remote to modern students, it is important to pay attention to the ways his understanding of acting relates to the process of Noh drama. How would you relate the kind of skills and attention that Zeami describes here to the demands of Noh drama?*

An actor must not only rehearse thoroughly with his teachers but he must learn through practice to imitate their peerless performances. Indeed, it is precisely because the art of these great performers has been brought to the highest levels of training that they can present in their acting an appearance of total mastery and ease, thus fascinating their audiences. If a beginner wishes merely to imitate this level of accomplishment, he may seem to achieve its semblance, yet there will be nothing moving in his performance. A truly great artist has for many years succeeded in training both his body and his spirit; he can hold back much of his potential in reserve and perform in an easy fashion, so that only seven-tenths of his art is visible. If a beginner tries to perform in this fashion, without the proper practice, he will only imitate what he can observe, and so his spirit and his performance can not reach beyond that seven-tenths he can grasp. What is more, his own progress will be blocked.

Therefore, when a student is learning his craft, the teacher should show not his own high level of ability [in which there is a reserve of artistry], but, as he did when he too was a beginner, indicate to his pupils how to use fully both their minds and bodies. After such lessons have been absorbed the students will gradually reach a level of mastery and attain a level of ease in their own performances, understand how to hold in reserve a certain amount of their own physical energy, and grasp of themselves the principle that "what is felt by the heart is ten, what appears in movement seven."

UNDERSTANDING THE PROPER MEANING OF LEARNING OUR ART

In general, a performance of Perfect Fluency cannot be imitated. And if an actor makes an attempt to imitate it, the very effort involved in the attempt will produce a tension that cannot be a part of Perfect Fluency. Only something that is meant to appear difficult can actually be imitated. "The truth and what looks like it are two different things,"[1] it is said. Thus, could there be any way to imitate the truth of the master actor's easy performance? Indeed, ease and difficulty are two aspects of the same thing. There is a separate teaching on this matter. The means by which a student learns from a teacher are well known, and so no special comment is needed here. However, the teacher's official certification of the student must be based on a thorough examination of his capacities and devotion; otherwise, certification should not be given. If the student's basic abilities are insufficient, no certification is possible. Should certification be given when talent is lacking, a level of accomplishment is suggested that cannot actually be matched. The certification will be fraudulent and the results meaningless; therefore, it should not be given. In the *Book of Changes* it is written that "if suitable teachings are given to those who are not suitable, the hatred of Heaven will be aroused."[2] In order that such a suitable person can be created, three conditions must be present. First, he must possess himself the requisite talent. Secondly, he must adore his art and show a total dedication to the path of *Nō*. Thirdly, he must have a teacher capable of showing him the proper way. If these three conditions cannot be met, the candidate will not be suitable. A suitable person is one who has the capacity to achieve the highest reaches of his art, to be recognized himself as a teacher.

---

[1] A popular saying found in many texts circulated in this period.

[2] The quotation as recorded here does not appear in the *Book of Changes* (*I ching*).

When I observe the artistic abilities of young performers now, it appears that "skipping"[3] has become commonplace. This situation comes about because they imitate without study. An actor must begin by studying the Two Basic Arts and the Three Role Types, continue to practice all that is appropriate for his age, and carry on his studies in the proper sequence, so that he will reach a stage of mastery in all the arts of the Nō that can permit him to perform in any artistic style. To learn only by imitation and so only manage a temporary resolution seems indeed to represent a kind of "skipping." For example, when studying the Two Basic Arts, one must not study the Three Role Types. When the time comes to study the Three Role Types, one must put off for a certain time the study of military roles [as they demand intense physical effort]. When an actor does come to study the military roles, then the demon roles in both the Delicacy within Strength and Rough styles of movement should be put off for a certain time, since there is an appropriate moment to learn them as well. To attempt to learn all these roles at once—what a terribly difficult thing it would be. And the degree of difficulty would be unexpectedly high. Therefore, even if by "skipping" a young performer manages to fool the public into thinking that he is a master, he will achieve a momentary Flower. And as such an artist grows older, his art will decline. And even should his art not decline, it would be impossible for him to achieve true renown. This point must be firmly kept in mind.

Concerning "skipping," there is another matter to consider. If an actor is inordinately fond of new plays, and should he come step by step to abandon the older repertory he performed in the past, he can never master the art of Nō and will only be "skipping." Rather, the actor must fix a repertory of standard plays at which he excels and then mix new plays in with them. If he plays only fresh pieces and neglects the plays to which he is accustomed, the results, in terms of the art of the Nō, will be a disgraceful "skipping" indeed. Besides, if only unusual pieces are performed, then that procedure of itself loses its novelty. If a mixture of old and new is achieved, then both the old and the new alike will seem novel. Such becomes the undying flower. As Confucius said, "He who by reanimating the Old can gain knowledge of the New is fit to be a teacher."[4]

HAVING A REAL UNDERSTANDING OF SKILL

If an actor has become fully proficient at music and dance, he may be called skillful. If he has not become fully accomplished, there will be no denying his shortcomings. On the other hand, there is a kind of real skill based on still different considerations. For example, there are actors whose abilities in dance and chant show no shortcomings, yet who have not achieved a high reputation. Then again, there are actors whose voices are not attractive and whose mastery of dancing and singing show defects, yet who are widely thought of as accomplished performers. The reason for this is that both dancing and gesture are external skills. The essentials of our art lie in the spirit. They represent a true enlightenment established through art. Thus, if an actor knows how to create interest and can perform from an understanding of this spirit, he will gain a reputation as a fine actor even if he has not mastered every aspect of his craft. Such being the case, if an actor really wants to become a master, he cannot simply depend on his skill in dance and gesture. Rather, mastery seems to depend on the actor's own state of self-understanding and the sense of style with which he has been blessed. Real discernment of the nature of the differences between external skill and interior understanding forms the basis of true mastery. Thus it is that an actor who has merely perfected his technique will have little of interest to show. Other actors, from the beginning of their careers, can fascinate their audiences. So it is that an actor, from the time he is young until he masters seven-tenths, eight-tenths, even all of his technique and reaches the level of a master, will continue to interest others for quite separate considerations.

Still higher than the level of interest, there is a level of skill that will simply make the audience gasp, without reflection, in surprise and pleasure. This level will be termed one of a pure Feeling that Transcends Cognition. The response to such a performance is such that there is no occasion for reflection, no time for a spectator to realize how well the performance is contrived. Such a state might be referred to as "purity unmixed."[5] In the Book of Changes, when the Chinese character for "feeling" (kan) is written, the element that stands for "mind" (kokoro) is eliminated [and the character is written as] in order to illustrate the fact that when true feeling is involved, there is no room in the concept for reflection as a function of the mind.[6]

[3]"Skipping" (tendoku) was a term originally used to mean "turning the sutras," chanting the first few lines and then skipping the rest to save time, as a kind of devotional exercise. Zeami of course uses the term ironically.

[4]See Arthur Waley, The Analects of Confucius, Book II, No. 11, page 90.

[5]A term sometimes used to indicate the high level of excellence in waka poetry. The term is probably of Zen origin.

[6]For a translation into English of this section of the I ching, see Richard Wilhelm, tr., The I Ching or Book of Changes, pages 122–125. The interpretation of the passage is evidently Zeami's.

Thus it is that the actor comes to possess various levels of artistic skill. If a beginning actor continues on through all the various stages of his training, he will be called a good actor, but not necessarily anything more. Yet there is still a higher level where real mastery is possible. If the spectators are truly fascinated with an actor's performance, he can be said to have reached the level of a master. If, in addition, he possesses the ability to create for his audience an intensity of pure feeling that goes beyond the workings of the mind, he will have achieved the level of greatest reputation. Thus an actor should pursue his study of *Nō* through these various levels, develop his skills, and through his own spiritual understanding, bring his art to the highest possible level of fulfillment.

SHALLOW AND DEEP

Concerning *Nō* performance, there is one matter that must be given particularly serious consideration. If a performance is given without sufficient attention to detail, it will be without interest. On the other hand, if too much attention is given by the performer to details, the whole performance risks to shrink in scale. Then again, if the actor thinks to play his part as liberally as possible, the opportunities for the audience to witness his skill will be fewer, and there will be a tendency for his performance to become slow and monotonous. An understanding of this distinction is of the greatest importance. An actor might, on first reflection, think that the parts of the play requiring intricate skills should be played in as complex a fashion as possible, while those moments requiring a more general approach should be played as broadly as possible. Yet in fact this kind of distinction cannot be made unless an actor knows the art of *Nō* very well indeed. A student must question his teacher closely on such matters, so that these distinctions become clear. There is, however, one general principle that can be kept in mind. For the chant, the dance, and the various sorts of gestures that will be employed, the actor's spirit should be as delicately attuned as possible, but, at the same time, his physical stance should be as relaxed and broad as possible. An actor must comprehend these principles and stick to them.

In general, it can be said that, in the case of the *Nō*, an art that is based on general and flexible principles can be made subtle and detailed. But a *Nō* that is merely meticulous in conception cannot easily develop on a large and relaxed scale. After all, the small can be contained in the large, but not the large in the small. A great deal of skill needs to be given over to this matter. A *Nō* that possesses both these qualities will truly be full and rich. Indeed, when ice formed during the deep cold melts, the ice formed during a brief chilly spell will melt as well.

ENTERING THE REALM OF GRACE

The aesthetic quality of Grace is considered the highest ideal of perfection in many arts. Particularly in the *Nō*, Grace can be regarded as the highest principle. However, although the quality of Grace is manifested in performance and audiences give it high appreciation, there are very few actors who in fact possess that quality. This is because they have never had a taste of the real Grace themselves. So it is that few actors have entered this world.

What kind of realm is represented by what is termed Grace? For example, if we take the general appearance of the world and observe the various sorts of people who live there, it might be said that Grace is best represented in the character of the nobility, whose deportment is of such a high quality and who receive the affection and respect not given to others in society. If such is the case, then their dignified and mild appearance represents the essence of Grace. Therefore, the stage appearance of Grace is best indicated by their refined and elegant carriage. If an actor examines closely the nobility's beautiful way of speaking and studies the words and habitual means of expression that such elevated persons use, even to observing their tasteful choice of language when saying the smallest things, such can be taken to represent the Grace of speech. In the case of the chant, when the melody flows smoothly and naturally on the ear and sounds suitably mild and calm, this quality can be said to represent the Grace of music. In the case of the dance, if the actor studies until he is truly fluent, so that his appearance on stage will be sympathetic and his carriage both unostentatious and moving to those who observe him, he will surely manifest the Grace of the dance. When he is acting a part, if he makes his appearance beautiful in the Three Role Types, he will have achieved Grace in his performance. Again, when presenting a role of fearsome appearance, a demon's role for example, even should the actor use a rough manner to a certain extent, he must not forget to preserve a graceful appearance, and he must remember the principles of "what is felt in the heart is ten," and "violent body movements, gentle foot movements," so that his stage appearance will remain elegant. Thus he may manifest the Grace of a demon's role.

An actor must come to grasp those various types of Grace and absorb them within himself; for no matter what kind of role he may assume, he must never separate himself from the virtue of Grace. No matter what the role—whether the character be of high or low rank, a man, a woman, a priest or lay person, a farmer or country person, even a beggar or an outcast—it should seem as though each were holding a branch of flowers in his hand. In this one respect they exhibit the same appeal, despite whatever differences they may show in their social positions. This Flower represents the beauty of their stance in the *nō,* and the ability to reveal this kind of stance in performance represents, of course, its spirit. In order to study the Grace of words, the actor must study the art of composing poetry; and to study the Grace of physical appearance, he must study the aesthetic qualities of elegant costume, so that, in every aspect of his art, no matter how the role may change that the actor is playing, he will always maintain one aspect in his performance that shows Grace. Such it is to know the seed of Grace.

However, it may well happen that an actor will put such an importance on his impersonation of the particulars of his role, regarding this aspect of his performance as the highest of his art, that he will neglect to maintain the beauty of the stance he has properly assumed. Thus he will fail to enter the world of Grace. And if he does not enter into the world of Grace, he cannot approach the level of Highest Fruition. And unless he reaches this highest level of accomplishment, he will never be recognized as a great actor. There are indeed few masters who have attained those heights. Thus an actor must rehearse with the utmost diligence on this critical point of the representation of Grace.

This Highest Fruition of an actor represents precisely the appearance of this deeply beautiful posture. I cannot repeat too often that an actor must rehearse with the need for the proper preparation of his body always in mind. Thus it is of crucial importance that, beginning with the Two Basic Arts down to the specifics of any role that may be played, the stance of the actor be attractive so as to represent this Highest Fruition in every circumstance. If the actor's posture is unattractive, his art will invariably appear vulgar. In any case, whatever gestures may be seen or music may be heard, however great the variety, the fact that the actor's stance is beautifully assumed represents the true attainment of Grace. An actor may be said to have entered the world of Grace when he has of his own accord studied these principles and made himself master of them. If an actor does not work to fulfill them and thinks that, without mastering every aspect of his art, he can still try to attain this Grace, he will, in fact, never know it during his entire lifetime.

PAYING HEED TO THE ACCUMULATION OF SKILLS

Studying the art of the *Nō,* having the reputation of a superior actor, and rising in merit as the years pass by depends on a proper accumulation of skills. Yet the nature of such an accumulation will differ depending on where the actor lives and performs. Even if he earns a reputation as a fine actor, if the praise he earns is not from those who live in the capital, it can have little significance for him. Even an actor who has earned genuine praise in the capital, should he return to his native place and continue to perform in the countryside, will

merely expend his energies in attempting not to forget those means of expression that he learned in the capital, and because of his false sense that he still remembers how to perform properly, he will little by little slacken in his persistence in maintaining his beauty of performance. The result will be an accumulation of bad experiences. Such a stagnation of experience must be shunned.

In the capital, on the other hand, the actor will be performing before discerning spectators so that, should he become careless concerning any element in his art and so fail to progress, he will soon notice a response from his audience; then too, as criticism and comment come to him, he will eventually disregard the unsatisfactory elements in his art, accumulate only positive artistic experiences, and discover that his art has become polished. Of its own accord his skill will become as burnished as a jewel. There is a saying that "sagebrush, which has the ability to bend, even should it grow up among flax plants, will come out straight, without correction, while white sand, when mixed with earth, will become black like the rest."[7] Thus by living in the capital, an actor is in the proper environment, and the insufficiencies in his art will naturally disappear. This gradual lessening of error is in itself the accumulation of good experience. There is no way that an artist can simply set out to pile up these experiences of his own accord. Rather, let me repeat again and again a warning that, if an actor does not take cognizance of his good experiences, they will stagnate and turn into an accumulation of bad experiences.

So it is that even a skilled performer as he grows older will come to depend on his increasingly old-fashioned art, which has become so through an accumulation caused by his own stagnation. Although audiences may dislike his performances, he thinks only that he has been recognized as an artist of great merit for a long time. Thus he does not recognize the real feelings of his audiences. He therefore loses the chance to make his final appearances on the stage successful—such an important opportunity in an actor's career.

All of this is the result of piling up of such bad experiences. The greatest caution must be taken against this.

CONNECTING ALL THE ARTS THROUGH ONE INTENSITY OF MIND

It is often commented on by audiences that "many times a performance is effective when the actor does nothing." Such an accomplishment results from the actor's greatest, most

---

[7] An expression widely circulated during the medieval period in various forms, probably originating in the writings of Tseng Ts'an, one of the most important disciples of Confucius.

secret skill. From the techniques involved in the Two Basic Arts down to all the gestures and the various kinds of Role Playing, all such skills are based on the abilities found in the actor's body. Thus to speak of an actor "doing nothing" actually signifies that interval which exists between two physical actions. When one examines why this interval "when nothing happens" may seem so fascinating, it is surely because of the fact that, at the bottom, the artist never relaxes his inner tension. At the moment when the dance has stopped, or the chant has ceased, or indeed at any of those intervals that can occur during the performance of a role, or, indeed, during any pause or interval, the actor must never abandon his concentration but must keep his consciousness of that inner tension. It is this sense of inner concentration that manifests itself to the audience and makes the moment enjoyable.

However, it is wrong to allow an audience to observe the actor's inner state of control directly. If the spectators manage to witness this, such concentration will merely become another ordinary skill or action, and the feeling in the audience that "nothing is happening" will disappear.

The actor must rise to a selfless level of art, imbued with a concentration that transcends his own consciousness, so that he can bind together the moments before and after that instant when "nothing happens." Such a process constitutes that inner force that can be termed "connecting all the arts through one intensity of mind."

"Indeed, when we come to face death, our life might be likened to a puppet on a cart (decorated for a great festival). As soon as one string is cut, the creature crumbles and fades."[8] Such is the image given of the existence of man, caught in the perpetual flow of life and death. This constructed puppet, on a cart, shows various aspects of himself but cannot come to life of itself. It represents a deed performed by moving strings. At the moment when the strings are cut, the figure falls and crumbles. *Sarugaku* too is an art that makes use of just such artifice. What supports these illusions and gives them life is the intensity of mind of the actor. Yet the existence of this intensity must not be shown directly to the audience. Should they see it, it would be as though they could see the strings of a puppet. Let me repeat again: the actor must make his spirit the strings, and without letting his audience become aware of them, he will draw together the forces of his art. In that way, true life will reside in his *Nō*.

In general, such attitudes need not be limited to the moments involved in actual performance. Morning and night alike, and in all the activities of daily life, an actor must never abandon his concentration, and he must retain his resolve.

---

[8]A saying attributed to a priest of the Rinzai sect of Zen Buddhism in Japan, Gettan Sowkow (1316?–1389).

Thus, if without ever slackening, he manages to increase his skills, his art of the *Nō* will grow ever greater. This particular point represents one of the most secret of all the teachings concerning our art. However, in actual rehearsal, there must be within this concentration some variations of tension and relaxation.

THE MOMENT OF PEERLESS CHARM

The character *myō* in the term *myōsho* [Peerless Charm] means "exquisite" or "delicate." But it also has the meaning of an appearance that transcends any specific form. Such a transcendence of form represents an expression of this Peerless Charm.

When one speaks of such moments in terms of the *Nō*, this Charm should exist in every aspect of our art, from the Two Basic Arts to gesture. Yet precisely where can it be located? It seems to be found nowhere. If an actor can possess this arresting power, he must be a performer of surpassing skill. However, if an actor is truly blessed with great talent, he will show from his beginnings some shadow of this Charm. The actor will not himself be conscious of it, but spectators of discernment will always find this quality within him. Ordinary spectators, on the other hand, will merely find that his performances are enjoyable in some mysterious fashion. And indeed even in the case of an actor of the highest skill, he will at best have come only to the realization that he somehow does possess this skill. Still, he will have no consciousness that he is practicing it at any given moment. An actor will possess this quality precisely because he does not recognize it; if such a moment could in any way be put into words, this Charm could no longer exist.

When one ponders carefully the substance of this Peerless Charm, can it not be said that an artist may approach it when he has truly learned his craft and attained Perfect Fluency, when he has transcended all stages of his art to the point where he performs everything with ease and exhibits every skill without care, thus achieving a selfless art that rises above any artifice? When an actor manages to ascend to the aesthetic level of Grace, will he indeed not be somewhat closer to this power of beauty? These matters must be pondered deeply.

JUDGING THE NŌ

When it comes to making crucial judgments concerning the *Nō*, people invariably have different ideas. It is difficult indeed for any particular *Nō* to match the tastes of everyone. Thus the basis of judgment should be made on the strength of the performances of accomplished actors who enjoy a wide reputation.

First of all, one should look and listen with great care during actual performances so as to understand why some plays succeed and why others do not. Plays that succeed possess three qualities: Sight, Sound, and Heart.

As for the *Nō* that succeeds through Sight, the stage atmosphere will be colorful from the beginning, the dancing and music will have an attractive air, the spectators, noblemen and commoners alike, will be spontaneous in their praise, the atmosphere brilliant. Such is the *Nō* that is effective to the eye. It goes without saying that such a performance will please the discriminating; even those who know nothing of the *Nō* will find such a performance enjoyable. However, concerning such performances, there is one point that an actor must keep in mind. If the performance passes by altogether too well and with too much appeal, and if every aspect seems enjoyable, then the feelings of the audience will tend to become over-stimulated, and their sensibilities in appreciating the details of the acting will be coarsened. For this part, an actor may be impetuous and, since he wants to exhaust every aspect of his art, will make no allowance for a slackening of pace, either for himself or for the audience. In an attempt to make every aspect of the performance successful, a surface brilliance is achieved, but the end results may be unsatisfactory. This kind of abuse arises when the play goes too well. On such an occasion, the play should be performed in a more restrained manner, all the artistic appearances made more moderate, and the eyes and ears of the spectators given some surcease, so that they can have an occasion to rest and breathe easily and the audience can be given the quiet necessary to observe the really skillful elements in the performance. Then, if the results are successful, the plays that follow will seem stronger, so that, whatever the number of plays that may be staged, their fascination for the audience will never be exhausted. So it is that an effective *Nō* performance can be said to succeed through the art of Sight.

Nō that can be said to succeed through Sound shows from the very beginning a serious atmosphere. The music and text are chosen in accord with the season [and the time of day], thus creating a gentle, relaxed, and enjoyable effect. Above all, it is the chant that should create the main impression. Only a peerless artist of highest experience can achieve this effect during a performance. However, the kind of sober flavor engendered by such a performance cannot be understood by country audiences and the like.

This kind of *Nō,* when performed by a peerless actor, can give rise through his spiritual resources to various aesthetic qualities that make the play become more and more enjoyable as it goes along. In the case of an artist of the second rank, however, whose art has not fully matured, he will cause the day's performance to lag if he decides to follow such a presentation by a famous actor with one of his own in a *Nō* that is also of this particular variety. When such a player fol-

lows the kind of performance that has successfully created a cool and quiet atmosphere, as he continues on he will only create a gloomy mood in the succeeding plays. An actor must be aware of this difficulty and put his energies into his performance in order to begin to increase the number of stimulating moments in the play, so as to bring an element of surprise to his audience. Of course, as a truly peerless player has naturally a wide repertory and is highly trained in body and mind, his art will be effectively manifested in his dance and chant, so that his performance will naturally progress in an enjoyable manner. A player of the second rank, however, must take great care so that, as the performance continues, the atmosphere does not go dead. Concerning this point, when thinking to keep up the atmosphere of his performance, the actor must not reveal his methods to the audience. The spectators must merely feel that the performance is enjoyable. Such is the actor's secret, based on long-mastered precedents as to how to perform successfully. All I have written above can explain how a *Nō* can succeed through Sound.

When it comes to the *Nō* that succeeds through the Heart, a truly gifted actor of *sarugaku,* after he has mastered the whole repertory, will have the ability even when performing a play of no particular distinction in terms of chant, dance, gesture, or plot, to create even in the midst of a certain dullness a particular poetic quality that can move the hearts of his audience. This level of attainment is not usually grasped even by connoisseurs; how much more beyond any imaginings of a country audience must be such an art. Indeed, such a quality must seem to represent the propitious manifestation of an actor of the highest abilities. Such a performance can be termed a *Nō* that succeeds through the Heart, a *Nō* that surpasses technique, a *Nō* that transcends outward manifestation.

An actor must learn to discriminate between the kinds of artistic qualities that display those various differences. There are spectators of discernment who do not really understand the art of the *Nō*. On the other hand, there are those spectators who possess a true grasp of the essential nature of the *Nō* but who cannot observe subtle differences. Those who have both a practical and a theoretical understanding of *Nō* represent the highest level of spectator. For example, there are occasions when a fine performance does not meet with success, and times when an unskilled performance pleases, but no one must use these exceptions as a basis for one's general judgments. For example, truly gifted players customarily have success with outdoor and other large-scale performances, while lesser actors perform profitably at smaller playing areas at country fairs or on other such occasions.

An actor who understands how to make his performance attractive to his audience brings good fortune to the *Nō*.

Then too, a spectator who understands the heart of the actor as he watches a performance is a gifted spectator. The following might be said concerning making judgments: forget the specifics of a performance and examine the whole. Then forget the performance and examine the actor. Then forget the actor and examine his inner spirit. Then, forget that spirit, and you will grasp the nature of the Nō.

THE MATTER OF MASTERING THE CHANT

There are two aspects to the study of the chant. The person who composes the text should know the principles of music and how to make the words flow together in a euphonious fashion. For his part, the performer who sings must know how to fit the melody to the words and to chant the syllables and words in a clear and correct manner. Since the beauty of the chant derives from the syllables and the words performed, the melodies must be composed in such a way that the pronunciation is always correctly represented, and the linking between the phrases smooth and flexible. When the chant is performed, if the singer has mastered these principles and really knows them well, both the composition and the performance will reinforce each other and produce an enjoyable effect. As this is true, a standard should be established by which the melody is attached to the chant. The flow of the phrases must be attractive, and the sound characteristics of the text must be in harmony with the melody, so that the results will of themselves be musical. That is, the melody provides the basic frame for the musical composition, and the artistic effect derives from the spirit of the performer, who shades the melody in terms of the flow of the phrases. Thus an actor has various elements of music that he must master—the physical problems of using the breath, the development of his own emotional concentration in order to direct it properly, and the understanding of the melody, as well as the music that lies behind the melody. In terms of practicing the musical aspects of Nō, the following should be taken to heart: forget the voice and understand the shading of the melody. Forget the melody and understand the pitch. Forget the pitch and understand the rhythm.

In learning the art of musical performance, there is a proper order to be followed: first, the words of the text must be learned thoroughly; then the melody must be mastered; then the actor must learn how to color the melody; finally, he must learn how to apply the proper pitch accent. After all these steps are taken, the actor must concentrate on how to bring his performances to flower. At every stage, an emphasis must be placed on the rhythm. When practicing the voice, miss no occasion to obtain this kind of training, so beneficial to personal development.

Then there is the matter of accent in musical performance. In the case of auxiliary words or particles, the prob-

lem is not a serious one. However, mistaken accents on such substantive words as nouns, verbs, and adjectives[9] are harmful. Understanding the importance of this distinction is crucial. Serious study must be given to this point. When speaking of mistaken accents on these substantive words, I refer to pronunciations with improper pitch accent, which affect the meaning of the words. In the case of particles and auxiliary words, the problem has to do with the voicing of such sounds as te, ni, ha, and the like. Concerning correct pronunciation for these sounds, when the flow of words in the course of the singing moves effectively, even if the pronunciation becomes altered to some extent, so long as the rhythm is correct, the problem is not a serious one. It is said that words that make a heavy or a light effect, that are clear or complex in sound, depend on the forward flow of the text. In addition, there are various customs and rules concerning sound changes when words are juxtaposed together. Study the transmitted teachings carefully on this matter. As concerns particles that come at the end of phrases, such as ha, ni, no, o, ka, te, mo, shi, and so forth, even if there should be some deviation in their pronunciation, there will be nothing disagreeable in the sound as long as the melody is tasteful. In other words, the movement of the melody should be supported by these various particles. In the chanting, every syllable must not simply be pronounced in a flat manner, with an equal length and emphasis given to all of them. Those sounds which represent substantive words should be pronounced briskly, so that their meaning remains clear, while the sound of the auxiliary syllables can be rather freely regulated—slow or fast—in order to make the melody more colorful.

[Remember that] the principle of using four basic tones is used [in Chinese].[10]

In The History of the Former Han by Pan Ku,[11] it is written [concerning the legendary origin of the melody] that "as for the origins of the twelve-pitch gamut, a man [named Ling

---

[9]That is, independent, uninflected words usually written with Chinese characters.

[10]Zeami doubtless wished to stress the importance of proper pitch accent for substantive words in Japanese, usually written in Chinese characters, by this reference to the Chinese language. For a concise description of the function of tones in classical Chinese, see James J.Y. Liu, The Art of Chinese Poetry, pages 21–22.

[11]Pan Ku's history was the first of the so-called dynastic histories of China. For a general description of the text and its subject matter, see Burton Watson, Early Chinese Literature, pages 103–109. Zeami's quotation contains minor errors. For an explanation of the significance of the passage in the history of Chinese music, see Kenneth J. DeWoskin, A Song for One or Two, pages 59–61.

Lun] climbed Mount Kun-lun and, hearing the voice of the male and female phoenix, created the six *ryo* pitches and six *ritsu* pitches of the twelve-pitch gamut." *Ritsu,* since it is derived from the voice of the male phoenix, represents the principle of *yang. Ryo,* which imitates the voice of the female phoenix, represents *yin. Ritsu* represents the kind of sound that goes from high to low, and the breath is inhaled. *Ryo* represents a sound that goes from low to high, and the breath is exhaled. Breathing appropriate to *ritsu* is produced through a state of tension; *ryo* is produced in a state of ease. Then too, *ritsu* can be considered as appropriate to Non-Being, *ryo* appropriate to Being. Thus, a thin, high voice [a "vertical" voice] is appropriate for *ritsu,* while a thick, low voice [a "horizontal" voice] is appropriate for *ryo.*

In the *Analects,*[12] it is written that "the hides of the bear, the tiger, and the panther are used as targets [for the hunter's] arrow. The tiger is the prince's target, the panther the nobleman's target, and the bear the target of the officers of state." If this sequence is followed, it would doubtless be correct to write "tiger, panther, bear." But for the sake of euphony, the order is changed to "bear, tiger, and panther."

THE ULTIMATE KEYS OF OUR ART

The contents of this work have now all been set forth. There is nothing to learn in addition to what has been set down here. Indeed, there is nothing else involved but to "understand the *Nō*" with one's very being. If this fundamental principle is not observed, the various matters discussed here will serve no purpose. If an actor really wishes to master the *Nō,* he must set aside all other pursuits and truly give his whole soul to our art; then, as his learning increases and his experience grows, he will gradually of himself reach a level of awareness and so come to understand the *Nō.*

First of all, an actor must deeply believe what his teacher tells him and take those instructions to heart. The numerous teachings involved are contained in the various points discussed in this book, but the actor must truly master them and engrave them on his heart, so that, when he is actually in a performance, he can try out in practice the various things that he has learned. Then, as a result, he will value those principles, and, as he comes to revere the art of *Nō,* he will as time passes come to understand the real secret of success in our art. In whatever artistic pursuit, one studies and then understands, so that he will know how to carry out his art in ac-

---

[12]No such passage appears in the *Analects,* but a somewhat similar one does appear in the *Chou li* or *Rites of Chou.* Both this passage and the preceding section on *The History of the Former Han* were added to Zeami's text in the form of notes, and may not be by his hand.

tual practice. In *sarugaku* as well, one must study and learn, so that these various principles can be put into practice.

All these secret teachings can be summed up by saying that an actor must continually earn mastery through constant practice, from his apprenticeship through his old age. When I speak of studying through old age, I refer to the fact that from the time of an actor's apprenticeship until the peak of his maturity there are various arts that must be mastered. It is only from the time that an actor passes forty that he can slowly begin to make use of restraint in his physical performance. In other words, he must learn the means of artistic expression appropriate for an actor of his age. When the actor passes fifty, then he can begin to use the technique of "doing nothing." This represents a crucial stage in an actor's career. The first thing to learn at this point is the necessity to limit the kinds of plays in the actor's repertory. His musical performance now becomes the center of his style of performance, his acting style becomes simpler, and his dancing and gestures grow more restrained. He should only give a hint of his former colorful appearance. In fact, the art of music remains the one area in which an actor at this age can excel. This is true because an older voice will have exhausted its natural and untrained qualities, and the voice that remains will be highly polished, in whatever style of vocal production the actor may wish to use; thus whatever music is chanted, the results will always be enjoyable. This is a sure means to achieve a successful performance. Thus an older actor should learn carefully to make his age serve his own artistic purposes and work all the harder to train himself appropriately.

Concerning roles that can be played by older actors, old men and women are doubtless the most appropriate. However, depending on the strong points of a particular actor, he may not necessarily be limited to these two. Still, an actor who wishes to create an atmosphere of serenity in his performance will find the roles of older characters best suited to him. If his special strength lies in roles demanding energetic movement, however, those will not be suitable for the aesthetic qualities appropriate to the art of older actors. In any case, within these limits, he should perform his dances and gestures while limiting himself to six-tenths or seven-tenths of "what is felt by the heart is ten," so as to perform in a manner appropriate to his age. Such is the means to master the art suitable for the older actor.

In our Kanze school, there is one phrase that is of infinite value concerning the fundamentals of any artistic accomplishment: an actor must never forget the experiences he has undergone as a beginning artist. In the transmitted teaching, there are three explanations provided for this. Accordingly:

—He must never forget the fresh experiences he first went through as a young performer.

—At each level of accomplishment, there are new levels of fresh experience that the actor must encounter for the first time, as though he were a beginner, and then never forget.

—After the actor becomes older, there are still new stages of fresh experience that must never be forgotten.

Here are the teachings contained in these maxims in more detail.

Concerning the maxim that "he must never forget the fresh experiences he first went through as a young performer," it can be said that, if the actor retains the feelings he had at that time, he will profit from them in many ways as he grows older. As the expression has it, "an understanding of errors in the past will turn them into advantages in the future." Or, "seeing the cart in front turn over serves as a warning to the cart that follows." Forgetting the arts one has learned as a beginner amounts in fact to forgetting the skills an actor may possess at a later point in his career. The fact that his art has been perfected and his reputation has been made can only be the result of the development of his own skill. But if he does not take cognizance of how his skills have improved, he will unknowingly revert to the level he possessed as a beginner. Such a reversal means that his art is actually degenerating. His ability to maintain a sense of his present level of accomplishment shows that he has not forgotten the skills learned as a young performer. I cannot stress this principle too strongly: if an actor loses his memory of his unmatured skills, he will be forced to revert to them. On the other hand, if he does not forget them, his later accomplishments will be genuine. And, if they are genuine, his abilities, as they increase, will insure that his art can never retrogress. Thus, this truth can serve as a distinction between truth and error.

Young actors must therefore take cognizance of the current level of their accomplishment, realize that they are still only beginners, and understand that they must not lose sight of their own skills that still remain to be developed. In this way, they can truly work to lift the level of their art. To lose consciousness of the level of one's ability is to forget how to advance in the art; under such circumstances, an artist's skill will not increase. Therefore, young artists must never lose their perceptions of their actual level of ability.

Secondly, there is the principle that "at each level of accomplishment, there are new levels of fresh experience that the actor must encounter for the first time, as though he were a beginner, and then never forget." This means that, for the actor, from his beginnings through the height of his career and into his old age, there are always various suitable means of expression he must practice and learn. On all these occasions he can be seen as a beginner. Therefore, if at each stage he abandons and forgets what has come before, he will

only possess the artistic ability that matches what he is doing at that particular moment in his career. If, on the other hand, he has managed to maintain in himself all the skills that he has previously mastered, so that he can still make use of them, then he can perform in an ever-increasing variety of styles. These "new skills" refer to those he has learned for the first time at every successive stage in his career. Maintaining them all and combining them together at one time means that he has forgotten none of them. It is just through such efforts that a *shite* becomes an artist of wide-ranging abilities. Thus one must never forget what he has learned at each stage of his career.

Finally, "after the actor becomes older, there are still new stages of fresh experience that must never be forgotten." Truly, although there are limits on a human life, the *Nō* never comes to an end. If an actor has mastered every technique appropriate to each stage in his career, then when it comes time to learn what is correct for an older actor, he will still be able to enjoy a new experience even at this late stage in his career. If an actor still possesses this attitude when he reaches this high level, his art will still contain everything about the *Nō* that he has managed to learn before. When he passes the age of fifty, as I have said, an actor need have no other plan than to "do nothing special." To face the challenge of having no other technique than to "do nothing special"—is the art of an older actor really so different than that of a beginner?

So it is that if an actor manages to live his whole life without forgetting how and what he has learned at any one time in his career, the level of his art will steadily increase during his last years, and his abilities will never degenerate. To live one's life without ever exhausting the depths of the *Nō* represents the most profound principle of our school, a principle that must be passed on from child to grandchild, generation to generation as a secret teaching of our house. Passing on the importance of these attitudes I have described above will serve as a means to develop the artistry of all generations to come. On the other hand, if an actor forgets this "experience of a beginner," he will surely not be able to pass the conception along to others in later generations. An artist must not forget this "experience of a beginner," but must convey it to those who follow, for countless generations.

In addition to what I have written here, another who studies the *Nō* may, depending on his own abilities and discernment, be able to discover still other truths.

All of the *Teachings on Style and the Flower*, beginning with the chapter called "The Practice of the *Nō* in Relation to the Age of the Actor" down to the "Separate Secret Teaching," is a secret document that makes clear the *Nō* by using the metaphor of the flower. That text represents an account of various elements in the art of my father Kan'ami, set down twenty years after his death, and serves as a record of what I learned from him. The present treatise, on the other hand, represents discoveries that have occurred to me from time to time concerning the *Nō* over a period of forty years, down to the time of my own advanced age. Summing them up, I have written out my observations in six sections and twenty parts,[13] which I leave behind as a memento of my art.

Ōe 31 [1424], 1st day of the 6th month

Zeami

This teaching was passed on by Zeami himself for the succeeding generations of his house and should not be shown to actors from other troupes. Luckily, thanks to the Will of Heaven, which knows that my heart reveres the art of the *Nō*, this manuscript has come into my hands. This secret teaching forms the very core of the art of our school, and it has been written down to guide the art of our family. It is a text of fearsome power. Thus it must not be shown carelessly to others.

Eikyō 9 [1437], 8th month, 8th day

Komparu Zenchiku[14]

---

[13]The indication of twenty parts suggests that the manuscript was originally arranged in some different fashion.

[14]Komparu's signature is an attribution; the identity of the writer is not altogether certain.

PERFORMANCE IN HISTORY

GRAHAM LEY

"Aristotle's *Poetics*, Bharatamuni's *Natyasastra*, and Zeami's Treatises: Theory as Discourse" (2000)

Graham Ley has written widely about Greek and Renaissance culture and performance, and is the author of From Mimesis to Interculturalism: Readings of Theatrical Theory Before and After Modernism. *In this essay, he compares the understandings of theater and performance expressed by three of the world's major classical theater traditions, as they are expressed by Aristotle, Bharatamuni, and Zeami. Students often find these essays challenging, and Ley offers a number of ways not only to address each author, but to compare between them.*

Comparisons between the Greek and *nō* theatres, and between the Greek and Sanskrit theatres and the theoretical writings associated with them, have their own traditions in modern scholarship and take a variety of forms.[1] Inevitably insights about the qualities of the original theatrical experience are a major objective of such comparisons. The theoretical writings can be seen credibly as repositories of information capable, to a degree, of being recomposed into understanding and appreciation. In addition, certain leading concepts, such as those that gather round the English word "imitation" (Greek *mimesis*, Sanskrit *anukarana*, Japanese *monomane*) predictably attract major critical attention.

Treating all three bodies of writing as forms of composition or discourses in their own right is an alternative approach that can yield different results and illuminate different aspects of theory and its relationship to practice. The material is complex, of course, and any initial treatment is bound to have its limitations. Here I want to consider various characteristics of the *Poetics,* the *Natyasastra,* and Zeami's treatises under two provisional headings. The first, context and status, is documentary in tone. The second, the discourse of theory, includes critical analysis of writings.

CONTEXT AND STATUS

The *Poetics* of Aristotle has a wide and discernible context that embraces texts now known only by name or inference. It begins in the work itself, which almost certainly included a second part on comedy and may well have contained an excursus on katharsis that amplified the minimal mention of the concept in what survives of the text.[2] In addition, Aristotle is known to have written a work, *On Poets,* in dialogue form and in three books, as well as books on *Victories in the Festivals of Dionysos* and on *Records of Production (Didaskaliai).* The last of these were certainly documentary rather than critical or theoretical. These works should be placed alongside six books of *Homeric Problems*—which may have been related to the kind of treatment epic receives in

the later part of the surviving text of the *Poetics*—and a work *On Music.*

The surviving *Poetics* is an esoteric work, which means that it was closely associated with Aristotle's oral teaching in his school, the Lykaion (Lyceum). This status contrasts with the lost *On Poets,* which belonged to the exoteric works designed to be reproduced in manuscript and read outside the school. One should note that the written dialogue form had been thoroughly established by Plato as a mode of promulgating the advantages of the pursuit of spoken, philosophical dialectic. There is, of course, a remarkable irony here: Aristotle's *On Poets* has disappeared into minimal fragments, while his *Poetics* has had a massive influence as writing in the public domain. But further questions remain: what exactly was retained for oral teaching, and why was it retained? Aristotle's intentions cannot be known, nor is it clear how the esoteric writings (all of the works we have by Aristotle) came to replace the exoteric writings in circulation. One possible answer is that this kind of retention within the teaching system might relate to a sense of an exclusive audience (plausibly his pupils) and transmission within the school (of ideas to successive teachers).[3]

Certain aspects of context and status are perhaps less problematic. Aristotle in his documentary works on the dramatic festivals is clearly concerned with the record—and hence with the formation of what we might call a classic sense of achievement in drama. This is plainly a characteristic of the *Poetics,* which is not by any means a manifesto for initiative or change. This consolidation of a classic sense is also apparent in the contemporary activities associated with Lykourgos in Athens, where Aristotle was repeatedly resident. The theatre of Dionysos received a lavish reinstatement in stone, which must have fixed the form in which dramas might be played; Lykourgos also assured a definitive collection of past playscripts and secured finance for statues of playwrights. We can also be reasonably clear about the existence of a kind of writing called a *techne,* or an "art." What these treatises exactly contained is unknown, but they were written on a specific skill often by a practitioner. Sophocles wrote a treatise *On the Chorus;* the sculptor and bronze-caster Polykleitos wrote a *Canon* (his famous statue *Spear-Carrier* or *Doryphoros* was also called "The Canon"); and other specialist works are also testified. The absence of a *techne* on dramaturgy permits Aristotle to write one.

Quite why he should is another matter, and in this respect the evidence of his *Rhetoric* is interesting. The *Rhetoric* is itself a *techne,* of what could be considered an unrespectable art, and Aristotle is clearly aiming to provide rhetoric with a respectable and indeed a philosophically sound status as a public activity. Public speaking, in the political or legal spheres, was a major constituent of Athenian public life, but Aristotle was of the opinion that many of its more serious aspects had not been considered in any previous written treatment (*techne*) of the art. In book 3 of the *Rhetoric,* in writing of the importance of "delivery" or "performance" by the orator or the actor, Aristotle incidentally notes that "in the case of tragedy actors now have more effect than the poets," and it is clear that he is thinking of success in the dramatic competitions (Aristotle 1991, 216).[4] A theory of the emotions related to that in the *Poetics;* a consideration of "style" or *lexis,* also prominent in the *Poetics;* the importance of argument, rhythm, and the arrangement of the parts of a speech—all suggest that the rehabilitation of rhetoric as a serious and social art in the *Rhetoric* offers us a helpful context for understanding the discursive context of the *Poetics.*

The final and overwhelming part of the context is the formulation of the status of philosophy, and I shall return to this issue in the following section. Inherited concepts are of great importance, and much of our understanding of the *Poetics* and its influence depends on appreciating the significance of the Platonic term "mimesis." Platonic philosophy, like that of Aristotle, is deeply political, concerned with the values and practices of the polis and its inhabitants, and the principal claim of Platonic philosophy was to a close relationship with truth. These two characteristics combine to make philosophical discourse supposedly the most powerful and secure discourse, capable of subjecting social practice to a controlling analysis. The *Poetics* is supported by a web of such philosophical analyses and arguments having to do with cognition, ethics, and psychology. Drama is something to be known, not merely practiced, and to be knowable it needs to be identified or fixed in best practice.[5]

The *Natyasastra* is undoubtedly a compendium, and as such it is open to interesting or frustrating questions about authorship and to what one might call the analytic or unitarian tendencies—namely, the inclination to believe that

the compilation is (respectively) the work of many or substantially of one.[6] As a consequence, its date is open to debate, as well, and arguments exist for placing it between about the fourth century B.C. and a millennium later. The situation is not helped by uncertainty about the dates or eras of other significant Sanskrit writings. The mythical figure of Bharata as a sage with disciples, one who is capable of cursing an aberrant performer, is prominent in one of the plays of Kalidasa, *Vikramorvasiya,* and the ironic mythology of the playwright accords perfectly well—in a minimal way—with what is found in the *Natyasastra.* But even a fixed or nearly certain date for the activity of Kalidasa would not in principle inform us greatly about the relationship between theory and practice.[7]

But there are more substantial indicators of a context that is bound up closely with status. The claim of the treatise as it stands is that of a fifth Veda, a position that might otherwise be accorded to *itihasa,* or mythical learning, as represented by epic poetry, notably the *Mahabharata;*[8] I shall return to this issue later. But the status of the theatre itself is far more dubious. The performers of drama are cursed with a position in the lowest caste of Sudras, while the theory and the mythical status of its compiler Bharata are clearly raised above that demeaning level. This dilemma advertises a problematic role for the compendium in its first principles—and in particular for the status of the *natyacarya* and the *sutradhara* who control and direct the activities of a company of players.

There are further aspects of context that present themselves immediately. The compilation of a *sastra* on the theatre plainly invites comparison with the status of other *sastra* writings, such as the *Manu Smrti* on *dharma* (duty, religious and social obligation), the *Arthasastra* (ascribed to Kautilya) on *artha,* worldly good, and hence politics, and the *Kamasutra* (of Vatsyayana) on *kama,* or pleasure, specifically sexual satisfaction. The generally discursive *sastra* literature of treatises follows the esoteric sutra literature of condensed aphorisms, originally associated with cult and the rituals observed in the Veda literature.[9] The *Natyasastra* itself insists (in chapter 35) that knowledge of the other *sastra* writings is essential for the *sutradhara* (usually translated as the "director" of the company); the three varieties of the stage building are originally conceived, it is claimed, in accordance with the *sastra* literature. As a text, the *Natyasastra* is plainly writing itself into a complex intertextuality.

Religious sanction is thoroughly apparent, not only in the founding or charter myth of the opening section (and in chapters 22 and 36), but in the subsequent and precise instructions for preparing a playhouse and for the preliminaries of performance. Bharata is a sage who is invited by the gods to assume the implementation of the fifth Veda invented by Brahma, compiled from elements of the other four, but unlike them open to those of the Sudra caste. Despite this last provision, theatrical performance initially pertains to the gods as audience, and even to the demons, and the gods are installed all over the stage. A further performance concerned with dharma, *kama,* and *artha* is then shown to Siva, who provides the religious sanction for dance in drama. But the extent to which the activity is placed in the ritual world by this fifth Veda is apparent in the roles prescribed for the *natyacarya* in the worship of the stage, where he takes over from the opening prayers of the Brahmins (chapter 3), and for the *sutradhara* in the preliminaries to performance, in which he is succeeded by the *sthapaka* (introducer), who should resemble the *sutradhara* and is himself a Brahmin. The distinction between *natyacarya* and *sutradhara* in the *Natyasastra* is by no means clear, but the treatise affords them the role of priests in ritual observation consonant with the Vedas, and comprehensive in its scope.[10] From conception to the moment of performance the *Natyasastra* ensures an unbroken thread of religious engagement for the theatre.

The ritual is not, however, the only form of status assured to the theatre by the *sastra.* Appropriate conduct, as described and prescribed in the *sastra* literature, will not only be religious in its orientation. The categorization with which the *Natyasastra* abounds is part of a scheme of order, of appropriateness, which may be applied as much to character as to gesture. The discipline of the allocation of Sanskrit and Prakrit speech to characters (in chapter 18) acknowledges the distinctions of caste and the demeaning circumstances that may qualify caste status, while the modes of address to be followed in drama (chapter 19) secure conformity with the established order. In this respect the compilation of rules in the *sastra* is an assurance to authority of respectability for the practice of theatre. Hence what may appear as no more than an established formulaic opening to chapter 19, addressed to the best of the Brahmins who have questioned Bharata from the beginning of the treatise, actually presents order to those at its apex. The creation of a *sastra,* not the creation of drama, is the continuing subject of the *Natyasastra,* and that creation offers both context and status to a theatre practice, which is all the more likely to wish to conform to its precepts for just those reasons.

In the *Natyasastra,* it is the "sons of Bharata" who are to carry on and perform the tradition established by their father and received from Brahma and Siva. In the coda to *Shūgyoku tokka,* Takeda Komparu Hachemon records in 1656 that as a result of the unlucky death of his elder brother, Ujikatsu Shichirō, his father had felt it necessary to pass on the "secret book" to him (Rimer and Yamazaki 1984, 147).[11] He himself is now passing it on to his successor, since "the

line of transmission must not be allowed to be interrupted." This short statement reflects, somewhat pathetically, what had happened at the death of Zeami's older son, Motomasa, in 1432, an event that confirmed the transmission of Zeami's written teachings out of the male succession to his son-in-law Komparu Zenchiku.[12] For Takeda Komparu Hachemon the possession of texts is a signal of the right to succeed: "Since the beginning, these secrets were given to the head of the house alone and it has never been permitted for other children or other descendants to make inquiries concerning these profound secrets" (Rimer and Yamazaki 1984, 147). For Zeami, writing the original treatise on the *nō* (*Fūshikaden;* 1402 with later additions) had been an initiative undertaken explicitly to record the teachings of his father Kan'ami, who had died in 1384. The testament was to serve the "house" of his family, and perhaps the most explicit occasion for its composition was Zeami's sense of a decline in the *nō.* This is first expressed as a fear in *Fūshikaden* (from 1400) but quickly turns into a statement in the same work (from 1402) and reappears later in *Shikadō* of 1420 as a constant if theoretical conviction (pp. 30, 37, and 72 respectively). The motif of decline is not hard to trace in Aristotle's attitude to the art of tragedy, and the threat of decadence is a minor mythical theme in the *Natyasastra* as well. Like success, it is a prominent motive for the creation of theoretical texts, and it is inevitably used to affirm a normative code.

The motif of decline, in alliance with the transmission of a secretive authority, not only issues the strongest imperative to the succession but also presupposes a history of achievement. In his coda to *Shūgyoku tokka,* Takeda Komparu Hachemon takes the line of transmission back to "our ancestor Hata no Kōkatsu." In doing so he reiterates and affirms the genealogy of *nō* constructed for his successors, and in honor of his father, by Zeami at the start of his first treatise, *Fūshikaden.* In this genealogy, Hata no Kōkatsu was commissioned by Prince Shōtokuto provide entertainments called *sarugaku* for the sake of peace, and this art was inherited by his descendants, to be performed at the shrines of Kasuga and Hie. A religious sanction for the ancestral *nō,* performed for the public good, is allied to imperial patronage, in a prefiguring of the patronage extended by the shogun to Kan'ami and his son Zeami. The mythology is elaborated later in *Fūshikaden,* when the actions of Shōtuku are doubled by those of the Emperor Murakami, who revives the patronage by extending it to a successor of Kōkatsu named Hata no Ujiyasu. His descendant is identified as the head of the Komparu company by Zeami (pp. 34–36).

Sarugaku is dignified in its history by these associations. There exists a description of a *sarugaku* entertainment from the eleventh century by Fujiwara no Akihira, which includes mimetic pieces alongside juggling and acrobatics, featuring such figures as an aged local magistrate, a frightened monk, "a respected nun who . . . seeks the gift of swaddling clothes for the baby shortly to be born," and "the official . . . believed to be a serious man [who] one day whistles unintentionally the tune of a flute" (Inoura 1971, 43–44). Chinese *san-yueh,* "which included comic mime, singing and dancing, as well as acrobatics and conjuring tricks," was "transmitted to Japan in the eighth century, both from China itself and from Korea" (Konishi 1991, 520). The performers of *sarugaku* were originally "exempted from taxes and labor levies," and when this exemption was withdrawn in 782 many chose to remain outside the census and hence were considered and effectively classed as outcasts: *semmin* (ibid.). The continuing fragility of social status for the performer even in the later period is reflected in the disapproval of the aristocrat Go-oshikōji Kintada for the favor shown by the shogun to the boy Zeami: "*Sarugaku* like this is the occupation of beggars, and such favor for a *sarugaku* player indicates disorder in the nation" (Hare1986, 16). Indeed, as modern biographical studies have disclosed, patronage was to desert Zeami later.

But *Sarugaku nō* is given more than a recurrent myth of high patronage to enhance its functional discipline of self-respect. Although he seemingly dismisses an origin in India and a time scale that stretches back to the gods at the opening of *Fūshikaden,* Zeami returns to both themes with greater conviction and to greater effect later in the treatise. The story of the dance of Uzume drawing the sun goddess Amaterasu from the cave, which may be found in the cosmogony of the eighth-century *Nihongi,* becomes a foundation myth for *sarugaku* (Rimer and Yamazaki 1984, 31–32).[13] This initiative by Zeami parallels the divine myths for the origin of poetry proposed in the famous preface by Tsurayuki to the first imperial anthology, *Kokin Waka Shū,* of the ninth century. India assumes significance because it permits Zeami to ascribe a Buddhist origin to *sarugaku* and claims precedence over China, the true historical source of *san-yueh,* which is nonetheless permitted to enter the multiple frame as the spiritual nationality of Hatano Kōkatsu (pp. 32–33).

The relationship of the creation and composition of the treatises to the poetics of *waka* and linked verse is most apparent in the adoption of the value term *"yugen"* (often translated as "grace"), but the centrality of the flower imagery cannot be ignored.[14] It is found in Tsurayuki and Yoshimoto, a contemporary of Zeami's father, whose influence on Zeami has been alleged, and Zeami's appropriation of *yugen* and the flower to the actor's performance represents his most profound theoretical elevation of the disciplined art of the *nō.*[15] In *Fūshikaden,* Zeami admitted that *yugen* was traditionally identified with a rival style of *sarugaku,* the *Omi,* in

contrast to the traditional identification of Zeami's own Yamato style with role playing or "imitation," *monomane* (Rimer and Yamazaki 1984, 38). A mediation of these two concepts, under the presiding aspirational imagery of the flower, occupies much of the labor of the treatises, one that is rendered fraught by the elusiveness of taste in the dominant patrons.[16]

In *Fūshikaden,* an outstanding performer is "one whose speech lacks no refinement and whose appearance creates a feeling of grace." In *Kakyō* (1424), "grace is best represented in the character of the nobility," their appearance, and their way of speaking (pp. 3 and 93 respectively). Those from the lower orders who are represented in *nō* must "exhibit the same appeal, despite whatever differences they may show in their social positions." By "living in the capital, an actor is in the proper environment." And "if the praise he earns is not from those who live in the capital, it can have little significance for him" (pp. 94, 96, and 95 respectively). *Yugen* is a certain sign of acceptance and status for Zeami: it is considered "the highest ideal of perfection in many arts" and thus can be regarded as "the highest principle" of the *nō* (p. 92, again from Kakyō). Creating a composed performance that accords with the taste of the nobility—and maintains it with the continuity afforded to poetry—is the intricate and paradoxical aspiration of these written treatises for an ephemeral art.

THE DISCOURSE OF THEORY

European poetics is significantly lacking in a myth of origin, although modernity has often made use of the Greek experience to create one. Epic poetry, of course, alluded to the muse or the Muses, though the Homeric poems are modest on the subject. (The muse is no more than *thea,* "goddess," in the first line of Homer's *Iliad.*) Only Hesiod is expansive in his *Theogony.* In the opening of that poem, Hesiod is approached by these daughters of Zeus on Mount Helicon and more or less compelled to sing of the gods and the Muses. But this seems little more than an elaborate conceit founded on the formulaic, invocatory appeal to a muse found in the opening lines of the Homeric epics. Their specializations were established far later, and for Aristotle they are of no importance whatsoever. Nor, indeed, is the imposing figure of Dionysos, whose ecstatic divinity presided over the theatrical festivals of Athens. The historical or social beginnings of tragedy and comedy do find a place in his introductory discussions in the *Poetics,* but they enter (in chapter 3) as rival claims based on etymology and dialect, or as the barest of developmental schemes, which takes two existing forms of celebration (dithyramb and phallic songs) and posits them cursorily as antecedents.

The lack of a divine charter for both epic and tragedy—or even for comedy and satyric drama, which were nothing if not explicitly Dionysiac—is striking, and its absence must direct us to a substitute. There is, certainly, some possibility of finding one in the briefly stated theory of katharsis, which is perhaps the most fascinating and enigmatic of all the theoretical topics in the *Poetics*. [17] Katharsis has a remarkable resonance in Greek culture, because it combines connotations of medical purging with those of religious purification, allowing Aristotle to claim for tragedy a function that had the widest possible implications for personal and public good. [18] The ceremonies introducing the dramatic festivals included a purification of the theatre, and much of modern criticism and theory has inclined to understand tragedy and comedy as religious drama, often with an emphasis on the ritual scapegoat and the sacrifice. [19] It would not be an exaggeration to state that the lack of a divine charter in the leading theoretical source of antiquity has prompted modern criticism to concentrate at least some of its energies on supplying one— whether in Nietzsche's heady combination of Apollo and Dionysos (Nietzsche 1967) or in Girard's immensely influential sacrificial theory, an anthropological substitute for ancient religious belief (Girard 1977).

Aristotle first defines tragedy at the opening of chapter 6 of the *Poetics* in the famous formulation beginning: "Tragedy, then, is a representation of an action that is worth serious attention, complete in itself, and of some amplitude" (Aristotle 1965, 38–39). The representation is of human beings performing actions, and the definition, like the central concerns of the analysis that follows it, is quite plainly indebted to Plato, who provided his own working definition in his ruthless critique of tragedy in book 10 of the *Republic:* "Drama represents human beings in action, either voluntarily or under compulsion; in that action they fare, as they think, well or ill, and experience joy or sorrow" (Plato 1974, 371). It is interesting that in these typical modern translations the general term "representation" is projected onto antiquity. "Mimesis" and its cognates are used by both Plato and Aristotle. Here Plato actually proposes that "the mimetic [art or skill, *techne*] imitates" (for "drama represents" in the preceding translation). For Plato, the implied reference to a *techne* recalls its fixed place in a descending valuation of "skills": from the user who alone really understands use, to the maker who attempts to provide it, to the artistic imitator. This order parallels an order of truth: from the ideal but intangible "forms" of things, to the skillful manifestation of them in creation, and, at the lowest level, to the realm of their imitation in art. [20] For Plato, the skills of the user and those of the maker (or artisan) are superior to those of the mimic artist.

In stating that Aristotle's definition of tragedy is delayed until chapter 6 of the *Poetics* I am drawing attention to the fact that the presiding definition is present from the beginning and is inherited from Plato. The *Poetics* assumes the challenge posed by Plato in book 10 for "men who are not poets themselves but who love poetry" to mount a defense of poetry in prose, "proving that she doesn't only give pleasure but brings lasting benefit to human life and human society" (Plato 1974, 376). Aristotle's approach to this task is to leave the descriptive definition of mimesis firmly in place for poetry but to alter it significantly—which he does most effectively by identifying it with "nature," or *phusis,* in chapter 4 of the *Poetics*. Mimesis is a natural activity and fundamental to learning. This is a complete contradiction of Plato's censure, which had lack of truth or an extremely remote access to the truth as its negative criterion for poetry and art. Aristotle also deftly plays with one of those Platonic triads mentioned earlier by emphasizing the terms *"poiesis"* and *"poietike"* in relation to the art (*techne*) of poetry. This picks up the second of Plato's levels in skills, that of the maker or artisan (the *techne* of *poiesis*)—and identifies it with the third or lower level of *mimetike*. By implication, both making and imitating are natural, and Plato's presiding skill of the user or consumer is picked up in the second "natural" aspect of mimesis for Aristotle, which is the pleasure derived from looking at or listening to imitations (again in chapter 4 of the *Poetics*). Thus all three Platonic skills are, in this synthesis, rendered natural and functional in learning by Aristotle. It is an immensely subtle resolution of apparent distinctions and difficulties, achieved without rejecting the primary definition established by the master.

Both mimesis and the concept of action entailed by it result in the domination of plot (*muthos*), action, and incident in the theoretical analysis of tragedy as a *poiesis,* and these matters are in the control of the *poietes,* the playwright, who directs his own composition. The beneficial effects to be felt by the community from the proper creation and execution of tragedy depend on the understanding of the playwright, and Aristotle's *Poetics* is almost exclusively a dramaturgical theory. It is conceived from first principles as a contribution to the discourse of philosophy and is addressed—as an esoteric discourse—to that elite which might attend to discussions in the Lykaion. But it is the philosophical discourse and the philosophical *logos* that preside over the foundation of European poetics, and this has had a slightly bizarre result: namely, the ultimate subordination of almost all attempted theories or disciplines of the art to concepts of nature and truth. In this respect, it is interesting to note that there is no evidence whatsoever to suggest that tragedy ever regarded itself as a mimesis or that the concept had any serious artistic viability before its dubious place in the Platonic order of illusion. [21]

The question of authorship in the *Natyasastra* is bound up with the narrative strategies of the compendium. Explicitly there are three gods who provide an impetus: Brahma, who responds to a request from the gods to create a fifth Veda for all the castes; Siva, who responds to an early performance with the categorization of dance (chapter 4); and Visnu, who provides the inspiration for the *vrtti* (styles or modes) of performance by his struggle with the two demons Madhu and Kaitabha (chapter 22). In fact, struggle lies at the heart of the creation of drama, since the demons are insulted by the first play, which takes the form of a fight between the gods and demons, who are defeated. Their anger leads them to paralyze the performers and prompts Indra to thrash the demons with his flagpole, which becomes a symbol of the gods 'protection for the stage. Brahma's resolution of the conflict is to reassure the demons that they are included in a total representation of existence, which pays close attention to *dharma, artha,* and *kama* (chapter 1). In this respect the *Natyasastra* in itself lays claim to the status of *itihasa,* as an instructive account of the affairs of gods, demons, and human beings, at the same time as it claims a comparable status for the products of its guidance as a *sastra*—namely, theatrical plays. This comprehensive scope entails an ambitious concept of *anukarana,* or mimicry, which must include the actions of all creation and by so doing can include the competence of the other *sastras,* as Brahma is made to claim in chapter 1.

The narrative frame of the *Natyasastra* is apparent in the opening and closing chapters, and the form it takes is a result of the foundation myth's emphasis on a divine origin. Drama is conceived as a performance for the gods, with the demons initially a disruptive component of the audience, and the subsequent involvement of Siva as lord of the dance leaves the foundation of a theatre and the establishment of the preliminary rites of performance firmly in that context. The priestly role assigned to the *natyacarya* and the *sutradhara,* and even the *sidhaka,* conforms to this vital charter for the fifth Veda. This divine context is ideal for the presentation of the ordering of an art which is the *sastra,* but it leaves unanswered the inevitable translation of a divinely conceived art to a human level. In chapter 36, the myth of Urvasi, one of the *apsara*s or heavenly dancers created by Brahma to dance gracefully in the original performance, offers a traditional vehicle for a descent from heaven to earth, since she is drawn to the king Pururavas.[22] But since Urvasi herself is withdrawn again to heaven, this myth is itself framed in chapter 36 by a further account, which has the king's grandson, Nahusa, requesting substitutes for Urvasi, who are provided by the sons of Bharata. They are then able to unite with the women of the harem of the king, who had been taught by

Urvasi, and provide a lineage of performers. On the condition of their fulfillment of the prescriptions of the *sastra,* the sons of Bharata are permitted to return to heaven.

The complexity of this translation from heaven to earth, and its narrative postponement in the *sastra,* are the result of the conflict between the aspirational claims of the "art" in its treatise and the low status accorded to performers. In chapter 36 the sons of Bharata became drunk with knowledge of the *Natyaveda* and produced a lampoon of the sages—who cursed them by expelling them from the caste of Brahmins and placing them among the Sudras, the lowest caste. It is Bharata who acts as a mediator and directs them to accept the opportunity presented by the request of the king Nahusa. The effect of this narrative subtlety is to reconcile the existence of a *sastra* and a fifth Veda with the performance of drama for all the classes, including the Sudras, prescribed in the opening chapter of the compendium.[23] But the *sastra* itself must not be compromised, and the concluding sections of chapter 36 reiterate its divine origins as a discourse, promising those who follow it comprehension of all the other *sastra*s and the achievement of a merit that accords with those who practice sacrifice and study the Vedas with divine approval.

The complex charter and justification of the concluding chapter of the *Natyasastra* is, like the treatise as a whole, a narrative recounted to the sages who question Bharata himself. The framework of question and extended answer is made explicit repeatedly in the opening of the treatise (chapters 1, 2, 5, and 6), prompting responses on the origins, on the playhouse, on the preliminaries, and on the *rasa*s, and is understood to cover the categorizing narrative until its renewal at the opening of the final chapter. But this concluding chapter, with its reference to the amplifications made to the *sastra* by Kohala and the sons of Bharata, returns to the subject of the composition of the treatise, which extends beyond the personage of Bharata. In this respect, it exhibits the same embracing knowledge of itself that we find in the very first chapter, where Bharata is initially introduced in the third person in his dialogue with the sages. The narrative and authoritative persona of Bharata is distanced in the frame from absolute ownership of the text as a document.

The text itself contains one further aspect that complicates our understanding of it as a discourse. In the opening to chapter six the sages request of Bharata an explanation of the "digest" or "thesis" (*samgraha*) alongside those of the "memorial verses" (*karika*) and "etymology" (*nirukta*). It is clear from Bharata's response (6.8–11) that the core element of these three terms is the aphoristic sutra, typically expressed in the (memorial) verse or verses that offer a rule or meaning, possibly reliant on etymology; when accompanied by a commentary, these form the digest, or *samgraha*. Chapters 6 and 7, which contain the discussion of the emotional theory of *bhava*s and *rasa*s, with the audience prominent in consideration, are indeed composed as a commentary surrounding and amplifying a set of these memorial verses, which are quoted directly. This format is particularly prominent in chapter 7, where the first memorial verses announce a relatively plain aesthetic order dependent on etymology: a *bhava* is an instrument of causation, which makes something "pervade," and so words and gestures illustrating the *bhava*s permit the meaning of the playwright to "pervade" the audience. In the traditional verse of 7.6, the determinants and consequents that control the *bhava*s are themselves "things which are created by human nature and are in accordance with the ways of human nature and with the ways of the world" (Ghosh 1967, 120). Most noticeably, the traditional verse of 7.7 in referring to *rasa* uses the metaphor of fire, the *rasa* spreading over the body as fire consumes a dry stick. This image seems to be completely detached from the more familiar metaphor of "taste" (itself expressed in other verses in 6.31–33), and apparently is designed to describe an effect rather than analyze a process.

The subsequent account of the *bhava*s, which forms the substance of chapter 7, is heavily based on memorial verses related to each state, with the treatise adding a commentary that is in many respects no more than a recapitulation of what is contained in the verses. Thus love, laughter, sorrow, and so forth are to be shown by an engagingly simple form of physical mimicry, or *anukarana*, appropriate to each state. In its most appealing form, this kind of precept offers observations such as "death . . . should be represented by the absence of any further movement of the body" (7.89; Ghosh 1967, 144). It is noticeable that the concluding *sattvika* states of the chapter, which are themselves perhaps the extreme of physical representation by the actor (sweating and goose pimples are two of them), are accompanied by no memorial verses (7.93–106). Since physicality is the express concern of the imitation already prescribed in the verses for the preceding *bhava*s, this is perhaps not surprising. There is only one reference in the memorial verses quoted in the chapter to the other *sastra*s, and that is descriptive, when the state of "assurance" is to be portrayed in the theatre by an actor instructing pupils and explaining the *sastra*s (7.82). The aesthetics of these verses of chapter 7, as observations on the art of performance, encode a relatively simple if detailed form of imitation, mimicry, or *anukarana*, which is far from carrying the conceptual connotations of the cosmic and universal "representation" determined by Brahma. But that is because the *Natyasastra* is very far from being just a handbook for performance, even for the playwright or the *natyacarya* or *sutradhara* to whom it is often implicitly addressed.

Both etymology and memorial verses play their part in Zeami's discourse, who has one complete treatise (*Kyūi*) composed as a commentary upon mystical aphorisms. But the intertextuality of the treatises is by no means confined to the influence of Zen Buddhism, as might be concluded from Zeami's later life and the tenor of *Kyūi*, including as it does quotations from Mencius, Confucius' *Analects*, and *waka* poetry. Also important in Zeami is a principle of *monomane*, or imitation, a term that modulates in the treatises from the relative simplicity of mimicry—such as that found in chapter 7 of the *Natyasastra*—to an imposing problematic of an art. As role playing is seen to be essential to the characteristics of Zeami's inheritance of Yamato *sarugaku*, so mimicry is essential to role playing, and it features early in *Fūshikaden*. Movement, gesture, and manner of speaking are clearly components of *monomane*, but costume may carry a great deal (emphasized in relation to women, mad persons, and warriors), as may the handling of defining properties (a fan, a sword); facial expression must not be an object of *monomane*. But the presiding prescription is emphatic: "Role playing involves an imitation, in every particular, with nothing left out" (Rimer and Yamazaki 1984, 10).

The governing principle seems simple enough, and in its ideal form would be dependent on observation, but the simplicity is from the beginning subject to qualifications. So "playing the part of a ruler or a high official" will confront the actor with his inevitable ignorance of the manners of the court nobility (ibid.). Similar problems affect the portrayal of women of high rank, but the deficiencies may be made up by feedback from appropriate members of the audience (noble males) and tactful inquiry and investigation (noble women). These comments apply explicitly to compensation for the difficulties of direct observation in given cases, and with regard to "an ordinary woman" or to "persons of high profession" *monomane* can apparently operate directly (pp. 11 and 10 respectively). Yet this apparent simplicity of mimicry may be misleading. The commonplace actions of laborers and rustics must not be "copied too realistically," and a general principle is asserted that "men of lowly occupation should not be imitated in any meticulous fashion, nor shown to men of refined taste." Yet those who "have traditionally been found congenial as poetic subjects" (woodcutters, grass cutters, charcoal burners, salt workers) may be imitated in detail. This leads to the formulation of a second general principle: "The degree of imitation must vary, depending on the kind of role being performed" (p. 10). It is a principle that appears later in *Kakyō* in close association with *yugen* and the governing metaphor of the flower, which is introduced to provide a resolution of the inherent problem:

> No matter what the role—whether the character be of high or low rank, a man, a woman, a priest or lay person, a farmer or country person, even a beggar or an outcast—it should seem as though each were holding a branch of flowers in his hand. In this one respect they exhibit the same appeal, despite whatever differences they may show in their social positions. [p. 94]

As a discursive term of the treatises, *monomane* charts the intense and subtle transition from the overt, satirical mimicry of early *sangaku* to the delicate compromises that reflect the presiding taste of the nobility. But *monomane* also has different operations to perform within the texts. It may, for example, express the relationship between teacher and pupil. Here again the apparent simplicity of *monomane* (representing a sound tradition of in-body learning) contains the problematic of the relationship. A pupil must imitate, but superficial imitation is not the art (*Shikadō*); and the teacher must not expose his highest levels of attainment to imitation by the pupil but should offer only what the pupil can follow (*Kakyō*, pp. 66 and 87 respectively). In this respect, *monomane* in the treatises operates as a control on the effectiveness and possible errors of *monomane* in the tradition of oral teaching: as *Shikadō* states plainly at its conclusion, the treatises are written because not just any training will do (pp. 72–73).[24] A similar operation for the term is found in discussions of the relationships between actors, where *monomane* must not be restricted to the exclusive imitation of what is superior, as might be assumed (*Fūshikaden*, pp. 24–25). It may also introduce the distinction between "function" and "substance," or "externalization" and "internalization," in the imitation of acting, which may follow the surface of excellence rather than the spirit (*Shikadō*, pp. 71 and 66 respectively). In this respect, *monomane* introduces the hidden—much as it does in the discussion of the portrayal of the mad or possessed, where the mimicry of their external state is nothing without the imitation of the dominant feeling or the possessing spirit (*Fūshikaden*, pp. 13–14).

In its ultimate expression, *monomane* will cancel itself completely—as it does in the portrayal of the old man by the "truly gifted player" who becomes the role and has "assumed the personality of an old man." Although the illusion persists for the audience, the actor will actually play the part like the youth the old man would like to be. This inversion is a paradox of imitation, and once again the problematics of *monomane* resolve themselves in the metaphor of the flower: such an outstanding portrayal is like "a flower blooming on an ancient tree" (*Fūshikaden*, pp. 55–56). The instability ascribed to *monomane* by Zeami leads inevitably to the flower as the

governing metaphor of aspiration in the treatises—much as the mastery of the problems of role playing is the absolute preliminary to an understanding of "the flower that does not fade" in *Fūshikaden* (p. 30). The goal of success lies in the image of the flower, but success itself may be illusory if it is only temporary (pp. 37 and 39). While *monomane* may be adjusted to the demands of *yugen*, in the compromise between the Yamato and Omi styles of performance that inspires the composition of the treatises, the metaphorical range of the flower offers a far more impressive set of resolutions. Thus the flower is a mediating principle between styles, even including *dengaku*, which "represents quite a different form of art from our own." *Fūshikaden* contends: "Styles of acting and the basic forms of art may differ variously, but what is effective about each is common to all. This moving quality is the Flower. It is recognised as crucial to Yamato and Omi *sarugaku* and to *dengaku* as well" (p. 39).

"This moving quality" readily expresses the range and capability of metaphor, which may conjoin what is apparently different in the conviction of a resolution. As a consequence, it can mediate between a country audience and the nobility, in the person of the player who possesses it (p. 50), and can cover the appeal of different levels of attainment to such audiences: "Now, as concerns the Nine Levels, it goes without saying that the flower is manifested in the upper three levels, yet in the middle three and lower three levels of our art as well, insofar as they possess elements of interest, there are appropriate flowers for them as well" (*Shūgyoku tokka*, p. 130). The upper three are for the "highly cultivated"; the middle and lower, it seems, are for "farmers and rural people."

The ambition represented by the image of the flower summarizes Zeami's aspirations for the transcendence of cultural obstacles facing the ideal *nō* performer. The ambition is present in the image, which is one of attainment and manifestation (and so of consummate approval from an audience) whenever it is applied. But the aspirations apply to what may appear to be irreconcilable. Thus in chapter 5 of *Fūshikaden*, the actor who has mastered "the real secrets of his art" and has "achieved his Flower" will be respected everywhere and will "perform ably in the style of Yamato and Omi *sarugaku*, and even in the style of *dengaku*, depending on the wishes of his audience" (p. 40). The image contains and transcends a serious paradox, since the claim to universal respect is deeply problematic if an audience without discrimination cannot appreciate a good player. But the flower does not wither in such circumstances: "Thus, while it is true that an untutored audience may not be able to grasp the elements that make a performer good, and thereby appreciate him, nevertheless a truly gifted player, if he really makes use of all his artistic skill, should be able to move even an undiscriminating audience" (pp. 39–40).

The tasks set for the image by aspiration are daunting. Not only must the actor know all the styles, but he must also master his own. And unless he does so he will "not only fail to grasp the fundamentals of his own proper art but will certainly fail to understand any of the others," or the flower will elude him (ibid.). The problem of different flowers and different audiences and their levels of appreciation leads to a variety of evasions. Hence Zeami suggests that in order to please a provincial audience the actor may need to draw on "the easy style of performance he used when a beginner"; yet when a good actor faces a withdrawal of favor "because of some situation over which he has no control," he may retain his flower by performing in the provinces (pp. 41 and 42 respectively).

It is, of course, the image that must be retained by theoretical aspiration, even at the cost of a temporary loss of conviction. And if metaphor is to be retained, it must be allowed to collapse under the strain into something more potent. It cannot hold in all circumstances. A good play may be performed in front of a discerning audience by a good player, but it still may not succeed: although the balance of yin and yang may be to blame, Zeami is obliged to admit that, contradictory as it may seem to the terms in which he has framed the example, one of the only answers is to assume that the actor has actually failed to "achieve the proper flower" (p. 45). It is in the secret teaching of chapter 7 of *Fūshikaden* that Zeami finally acknowledges that the range of metaphor is in fact banal and something further is required for the image. If "the flower can be used . . . as a metaphor for all things in the *nō*," and mostly describes what "seems novel to the imagination of the spectator," then its attempted application to all discursive circumstances will result in its degradation, prompted by an eventual failure to resolve or to reconcile successfully (pp. 52–53). The antidote to this debasement of a vital currency is the discovery, or the invention, of the gold standard—namely, the meta-metaphor, the collapse of the metaphor into itself to emerge as a symbol: "The player who has studied his art to its furthest reaches will come to know the Flower that lies within the Flower" (p. 55).

This extremity of remote aspiration can be located in the "Flower drawn from past and future," a symbol that is introduced toward the close of *Fūshikaden* only to be apparently withdrawn, since "no one has ever heard of such a supremely gifted artist from the beginnings of our art down to the present day" (p. 57). But the composition of the treatises as a compelling charter for the Kanze house ensures that there must be one exemplar, as writing enshrines the founding father of achievement, Kan'ami. Ultimately the treatises are the secret, and the secret lies in the treatises, from which it can never be fully extracted, because once recognized actual achievement vanishes: "Where there are secrets, the Flower exists; without secrets, the Flower does not exist" (p. 60).

CONCLUDING COMMENTS

After opening out a discussion of all three bodies of writing, I do not wish to offer a misrepresentative closure in the form of summarizing conclusions. I have considered related questions of status and discourse, but there are many other issues of equal importance that one might add to a discussion of this kind. Plainly a consideration of the theoretical discourses from the point of the addressees is bound to be intriguing—to different degrees in relation to each—but we should probably resist the temptation to ascribe the composition of theory to a kind of humanist pragmatism. So, with Aristotle, we can assume a manifest address in the *Poetics* to the potential playwright (in contrast to the actor) or poet, but the address to Plato and the continuing discourse of philosophy in the Greek schools is even more pronounced. The *Natyasastra* codifies procedure and possibility most explicitly for the director or supervisor of a company, at times shifting its address to the playwright, but its immediate addressees, the sages who question Bharata, are part of a far more imposing fiction that is essential to the work. With Zeami, the picture is complex in a different way. The head of the school, and the succession, are an overt concern, and the accent lies heavily on excellence by the actor in performance. But there is an accompanying expectation in the dialogic portion of *Fūshikaden* (chapter 3) that figures of this sort should expect to compose their own scripts (pp. 21–22) in a more satisfactory alternative to the task of selection and interpretation; and instruction and ultimately models are given in the later *Sandō* (pp. 148–162). The composition of scripts, as in Aristotle and the *Natyasastra,* is brought firmly under theoretical control and, like performance, is subject to the potentially transcendent model established by the theorist Zeami.[25] If there is an invitation to apparent addressees in all three bodies of material, it is by no means an invitation to the kinds of artistic initiative that created the form.

That theory has its own dynamic of continuity is quite clear, not just from the example of the *Poetics* in Western thought, but from works in the Sanskrit and Japanese traditions that have not entered into this discussion. The *Natyasastra* inspired both commentary and digest, and its modern interpretation would not take the form it has without the vision of Abhinavagupta and his reading in the *Abhinavabharati*.[26] The composition and compilation of *Sarugaku Dangi* by his son Motoyoshi redefined Zeami in the role he had assigned to his own father, and recent publication has explored the quality and significance of Zeami's immediate theoretical successor, Komparu Zenchiku.[27] In Zenchiku's vision of Six Circles and One Dewdrop, the sense of attainment he received from his teacher Zeami is rendered into a symbolism relatively devoid of pragmatic instruction or reference to dramaturgy. In its turn, it is itself then susceptible to commentary from Buddhist and Confucian sources, as Thornhill has closely examined; in fact, the text contains these commentaries and renders them into a further synthesis (Thornhill 1993; Nearman 1995). For Zenchiku, therefore, the first sphere of his symbolic order represents "the spirit that circulates, flowing without ceasing even for a moment," to which Nearman adds the following commentary:

> That is, even though the first sphere is presented by a static, two-dimensional circle, this diagram is intended to convey the idea of ceaseless movement, a circulation of undifferentiated energy that is omnidirectional, and like a bird's egg, it contains all that is necessary for the ultimate production of a vital phenomenal manifestation. [Nearman 1995, 249]

This is theory in its most transcendent mode—and as striking a confirmation of its existence as discourse as one might expect to find.

NOTES

I am grateful to the University of Exeter for a research grant in support of this study and, as well, to the staffs of the Library of the Indian Institute and the Japanese Library in the Nissan Institute in Oxford for their help. My thanks are also due to Samuel L. Leiter and Marvin Carlson.

1. For examples see Megumi (1989), Sukla (1977), Gupt (1994), and Smethurst (1989), who cites Japanese comparative scholarship. Gopalakrishnan (1991) and Rajakaruna (1993) offer short, comparative studies of Indian and *nō* theatre. The reader should note that my bibliography, for reasons of space and proportion, is indicative only.

2. Janko (1984) discusses the evidence for the contents of a second book of the *Poetics* and presents a tentative reconstruction.

3. The ancient Greek tradition holds that Aristotle's esoteric works were transmitted by successive heads of the Peripatetic school of philosophy; see the introduction to Lucas (1968, x).

4. These early chapters of book 3 also refer to the existence of a *techne* literature on the "art" of style and delivery (performative speaking) in rhetoric.

5. Translations and studies of Aristotle's *Poetics* abound. Here I mention one commentary (Halliwell 1986), one collection of essays (Rorty 1992), and one monograph (Belfiore 1992).

6. The debate goes back as far as the earliest major commentator, Abhinavagupta. For discussions see, among others, Gupt (1994, 29ff.) and Dasgupta and De (1962).

7. See the essay by Gerow, "Sanskrit Dramatic Theory and Kalidasa's Plays," in Miller (1984, 42–64). This volume includes a translation of Kalidasa's Vikramorvasiya (Urvasi Won by Valor) by D. Gitomer.

8. See Keith (1924, 12–13) and MacDonell (1900, 284, 288–289, and 294) on Vyasa, the mythical compiler of the epic, who had supposedly arranged the four Vedas.

9. On the sutras see MacDonell (1900, chaps. 2 and 9); part 3 of Keith (1920) is devoted to what he terms the "Scientific Literature," namely the *sastra* writings. The reader should note that the date of Keith's edition is as given on the title page; but his preface indicates (pp. viii and xxviii) that the book was actually published in 1928 and certainly after the publication of Keith (1924).

10. One division of the sutra literature had dealt with the rites that might be performed by the householder and his wife in accordance with the Vedas; see MacDonell (1900, 37). But this should not, in principle, affect our understanding of the status afforded to the *natyacarya* and *sutradhara* by the *Natyasastra* in the context of the ritual dedication of the theatre.

11. All quotations from the treatises of Zeami are taken from this volume of translations, which has become a standard textbook. For comparison, Nearman (1984) gives details in his bibliography of his annotated translations of selected treatises (including *Kakyō*) for *Monumenta Nipponica*, while dePoorter (1986) provides an annotated translation of the *Sarugaku Dangi*, a compilation to which I do not refer in this discussion. De Poorter's "Appendix 1" (1986, 242–249) usefully lists all the writings of Zeami with indications of date and subject, and cites translations in English, French, and German.

12. For the biography of Zeami see Hare (1986, chap. 1).

13. For the myth of Amaterasu in the *Nihongi* see Aston (1896, 41–45).

14. On *yugen* as a criterion in poetic theory see Putzar (1973, 63–64) and de Poorter: "From the twelfth century this word was used in Japan for the judgement of poems" (1986, 55). Compare Ueda Makoto (1991, 40), who declares of the fourteenth-century usage by the poet Yoshimoto that "the term seems to designate a certain idea roughly equivalent to elegance, gracefulness, or polished beauty." On the problems of translation for the term in Zeami see Hare (1986, 300), who seems to prefer "elegance"; compare Rimer and Yamazaki (1984, 260), who opt for the use of "grace" throughout.

15. On the imagery of blossoms and flower in Tsurayuki and Yoshimoto see the examples given by Ueda (1991, 8 and 41).

16. Most biographical and critical accounts attach great importance to the issue of taste in the successive *shoguns* and the audience. See, for example, Raz (1983, 70–122), Hare (1986, 11–38), and Konishi (1991, 520–560).

17. The famous formulation of katharsis occurs at the beginning of chapter 6 of the *Poetics*.

18. For a wide variety of interpretations of katharsis in the *Poetics* see the essays collected by Rorty (1992).

19. On the celebration of the dramatic festivals see the essay by Goldhill, "The City Dionysia and Civic Ideology," in Winkler and Zeitlin (1990); see also the essay by Cole, "Procession and Celebration at the Dionysia," in Scodel (1993).

20. See Plato (1974) on the three skills (pp. 367–369) and on the descending order of knowledge (pp. 359–364).

21. On *mimesis* and related terms before Plato see Else (1958).

22. The myth of Urvasi is found in the most ancient of the four Vedas, the Rig Veda, book 10, number 95; for a translation with notes and a short commentary see O'Flaherty (1981, 252–256).

23. The claim that drama allows for the instruction of all castes, including the Sudras who were excluded from listening to the Vedas, was also made on behalf of the *Mahabharata;* see Mac-Donell (1900, 289).

24. The control exercised by the treatises on the oral or in-body teaching is also made apparent in the *Kakyō's* concern that proper principles should be followed in the certification of pupils (p. 88).

25. Quinn (1993) observes that Zeami's assumption in *Sandō* that performers were "capable of composing both the lines and the music of their own plays" was "unprecedented" but came to be the norm: "Collaboration was the more common practice, *sarugaku* professionals composing the music and poets composing the lines" (p. 55). It is interesting, here, to compare the situation in relation to the substantially untheorized (and later) *kabuki;* see Dunn and Torigoe (1969, 20–21 and 118).

26. On the value of Abhinavagupta see the short summary by Ghosh (1961, xlvii–xlix). Gupt (1994) makes extensive use of the commentary and provides a summary of *rasa* criticism up to and including the *Abhinavabharati* in the eleventh century (pp. 260–271); the analysis on pp. 236–247, which reproduces his own argument in Gupt (1990), is a good example of its weight in the interpretation of significant concepts. There is a translation of the immensely influential part of the *Abhinavabharati* that refers to chapter 6 of the *Natyasastra* in Gnoli (1956); see also Chari (1990).

27. For the *Sarugaku Dangi,* in addition to the translation in Rimer and Yamazaki (1984, 172–256), see de Poorter (1986). On the transmission from Zeami to Komparu Zenchiku see Pinnington (1997). Zenchiku's treatises, and the commentaries upon them from Buddhist and Confucian sources, are the subject of Thornhill (1993); Nearman has provided a series of annotated translations, comparable to those he executed for Zeami, of the *Rokurin Ichiro* treatises of Zenchiku in four successive issues of *Monumenta Nipponica* (beginning with Nearman 1995).

REFERENCES

Aristotle. 1965. *On the Art of Poetry.* Translated by T. S. Dorsch. In *Aristotle, Horace, Longinus: Classical Literary Criticism.* Harmondsworth: Penguin.

——. 1991. *The Art of Rhetoric.* Translated by H. C. Lawson-Tancred. Harmondsworth: Penguin.

Aston, William G., trans. 1896. *Nihongi: Chronicles of Japan from the Earliest Times to A.D. 697.* London: Kegan Paul.

Belfiore, Elizabeth. 1992. *Tragic Pleasures: Aristotle on Plot and Emotion.* Princeton: Princeton University Press.

Chari, V. K. 1990. *Sanskrit Criticism.* Honolulu: University of Hawai'i Press.

Dasgupta, S. N., and S. K. De. 1962. *A History of Sanskrit Literature, Classical Period.* 2nd ed. Calcutta: University of Calcutta Press.

de Poorter, E. 1986. *Zeami's Talks on Sarugaku: An Annotated Translation of the* Sarugaku Dangi. Amsterdam: Gieben.

Dunn, Charles J., and Torigoe Bunzo, eds. and trans. 1969. *The Actors' Analects.* New York: Columbia University Press.

Else, Gerald F. 1958. "Imitation in the Fifth Century." *Classical Philology* 53:73–90.

Ghosh, Manomohan, trans. 1961. *Natyasastra.* Vol. 2. Calcutta: Asiatic Society.

——. 1967. *Natyasastra.* Vol. 1. 2nd ed. Calcutta: Manisha Granthalaya.

Girard, René. 1977. *Violence and the Sacred.* Translated by P. Gregory. Baltimore: Johns Hopkins University Press.

Gnoli, R. 1956. *The Aesthetic Experience According to Abhinavagupta.* Rome: Istituto Italiano per il Medio e Estremo Oriente.

Gopalakrishnan, S. 1991. "Kutiyattam and Noh: Commonalities and Divergences." *Sangeet Natak* 99:35–42.

Gupt, Bharat. 1990. "Clarification on *Lokodharmi* and *Natyadharmi.*" *Sangeet Natak* 95:35–44.

——. 1994. *Dramatic Concepts, Greek and Indian: A Study of the* Poetics *and the* Natyasastra. New Delhi: D. K. Printworld.

Halliwell, Stephen. 1986. *Aristotle's* Poetics. Chapel Hill: University of North Carolina Press.

Hare, Thomas B. 1986. *Zeami's Style: The Noh Plays of Zeami Motokiyo.* Stanford: Stanford University Press.

Inoura Yoshinobo. 1971. *A History of Japanese Theatre.* Vol. 1: *Noh and Kyogen.* Tokyo: Kokusai Bunka Shinkokai.

Janko, Richard. 1984. *Aristotle on Comedy: Towards a Reconstruction of Poetics II.* Berkeley: University of California Press.

Keith, Arthur B. 1920. *A History of Sanskrit Literature.* London: Oxford University Press.

——. 1924. *The Sanskrit Drama.* London: Oxford University Press.

Konishi Jin'ichi. 1991. *A History of Japanese Literature.* Vol. 3: *The High Middle Ages.* Translated by A. Gatten and M. Harrison. Edited by E. Miner. Princeton: Princeton University Press.

Lucas, Donald W., ed. 1968. *Aristotle* Poetics. Oxford: Clarendon Press.

MacDonell, Arthur A. 1900. *A History of Sanskrit Literature.* London: Heinemann.

Megumi Sata. 1989. "Aristotle's *Poetics* and Zeami's Teachings on Style and the Flower." *Asian Theatre Journal* 6(1):47–56.

Miller, Barbara S., ed. 1984. *Theater of Memory: The Plays of Kalidasa*. New York: Columbia University Press.

Nearman, Mark J. 1984. "Feeling in Relation to Acting: An Outline of Zeami's Views." *Asian Theatre Journal* 1(1): 40–51.

———. 1995. "The Visions of a Creative Artist: Zenchiku's *Rokurin Ichiro* Treatises." *Monumenta Nipponica* 50(2): 235–261.

Nietzsche, Friedrich. 1967. *The Birth of Tragedy and The Case of Wagner*. Translated by W. Kaufmann. New York: Vintage.

O'Flaherty, Wendy D. 1981. *The Rig Veda: An Anthology*. Harmondsworth: Penguin.

Pinnington, N. J. 1997. "Crossed Paths: Zeami's Transmission to Zenchiku." *Monumenta Nipponica* 52(2):201–234.

Plato. 1974. *The Republic*. Translated by D. Lee. Harmondsworth: Penguin.

Putzar, E. 1973. *Japanese Literature: A Historical Outline*. Tucson: University of Arizona Press.

Quinn, S. F. 1993. "How to Write a Noh Play: Zeami's *Sandō*." *Monumenta Nipponica* 48(1):53–88.

Rajakaruna, D. A. 1993. "The Classical Noh Theatre of Japan: An Indian Approach." *Sangeet Natak* 108–109:17–22.

Raz, Jacob. 1983. *Audience and Actors: A Study of Their Interaction in the Japanese Traditional Theatre*. Leiden: Brill.

Rimer, J. Thomas, and Yamazaki Masakazu. 1984. *On the Art of the Noh Drama: The Major Treatises of Zeami*. Princeton: Princeton University Press.

Rorty, Amélie O., ed. 1992. *Essays on Aristotle's Poetics*. Princeton: Princeton University Press.

Scodel, Ruth, ed. 1993. *Theater and Society in the Classical World*. Ann Arbor: University of Michigan Press.

Smethurst, Mae. 1989. *The Art of Aeschylus and Zeami*. Princeton: Princeton University Press.

Sukla, A. C. 1977. *The Concept of Imitation in Greek and Indian Aesthetics*. Calcutta: Rupa.

Thornhill, A. H. 1993. *Six Circles, One Dewdrop: The Religio-Aesthetic World of Komparu Zenchiku*. Princeton: Princeton University Press.

Ueda Makoto. 1991. *Literary and Art Theories in Japan*. Ann Arbor: University of Michigan Press.

Winkler, John J., and Froma I. Zeitlin, eds. 1990. *Nothing to Do with Dionysos?: Athenian Drama in Its Social Context*. Princeton: Princeton University Press.

A PLAYWRIGHT'S PERSPECTIVE

ZEAMI MOTOKIYO (1363–1444)

from *Teachings on Style and the Flower* (1402)

TRANSLATED BY J. THOMAS RIMER AND YAMAZAKI MASAKAZU

Although in many respects Zeami's critical writings describe the esthetics of Noh drama, Zeami was necessarily concerned with the practical training of his performers. In this essay, he treats the lifelong discipline of the classical Noh actor. (Introductory material on Zeami can be found on page 168 in the Critical Contexts section.)

In searching for the origins of *sarugaku* and *ennen,* some say they came from India, and some say they have been handed down since the age of the gods. Yet as time moves on and those ages grow remote, any proper skill is lacking to learn the ancient ways precisely. The origin of the *nō,* which all enjoy today, goes back to the reign of the Empress Suiko, when Prince Shōtoku commanded Hata no Kōkatsu (some say for the sake of peace in the country, some say to entertain the people) to create sixty-six public entertainments, which were named *sarugaku.* From that time onward, men in every age must have used images of the beauties of nature as a means to render this entertainment more elegant. Later, the descendants of Kōkatsu inherited this art and served at the Kasuga and Hie shrines.[1] This is why, even now, those performers from Yamato and Ōmi perform rites at both temples, which are still flourishing. Therefore, while studying the old and admiring the new, the great traditions of elegance must never be slighted. A truly skillful player is one whose speech lacks no refinement and whose appearance creates a feeling of Grace. One who wishes to follow the path of the *Nō* must engage himself in no other art. There is one exception: the art of poetry deserves study, for it is a means to open the actor to the profound beauties of nature and enrich his life. I will note here in general various things I have seen and heard since my youth concerning the practice of the *Nō.*

Sensual pleasures, gambling, heavy drinking represent the Three Prohibitions. Such was the precept of my late father.

Rehearse with the greatest effort; do not be overbearing with others.

ITEMS CONCERNING THE PRACTICE OF THE NŌ IN RELATION TO THE AGE OF THE ACTOR
Age Seven

It may be said of our art that one may begin at seven.[2] When a boy practices at this age, he will naturally of his own accord show some elements of beauty in what he does. If, by chance, he should show some special skill in dancing, movement, chanting, or in the kind of powerful gestures required for demon roles, he should be left free to perform them in his own manner, according to his own desires. He should certainly not be instructed as to what he did well and what he did poorly. If rehearsals are too strict, and if the child is admonished too much, he will lose his enthusiasm. If the *Nō* becomes unpleasant for him, then his progress will cease. He should only be taught dancing, movement, and the chant. In particular, he should not be instructed in the fine points of Role Playing, even though he may show aptitude for it. He must not be permitted to perform in a *waki sarugaku,* especially on an open stage. Let him perform at a time that seems appropriate, in the third or fourth play in the day's program, when he can be given a part he can perform with skill.

Age of Eleven or Twelve

From this age onward, the voice begins to achieve its proper pitch, and the actor can begin to comprehend the *Nō.* Therefore, various aspects of the art can now be explained. In the first place, a boy's appearance, no matter in what aspect, will produce the sensation of Grace. And his voice at this age will always sound charming as well. Because of those two strong

---

[1] The Yamato *sarugaku* troupe had an official affiliation with the Kasuga Shrine in Nara. A series of *Nō* performances was included in the important Wakamiya festival held there. The Ōmi troupe had official ties with the Hie Shrine on Mount Hiei, to the north of Kyoto, the site of the great Buddhist temple complex of Enryakuji.

[2] Traditionally, ages were calculated so that a person was considered one year old at birth and two at the beginning of the next calendar year. Thus the ages given here are higher than would have been assigned to a Western actor at the same stage of development. Thus Zeami's actor at the age of seventeen or eighteen would probably be, by Western reckoning, between fourteen and sixteen.

points, any defects can be hidden and the good points will be made all the more evident. On the whole, it is better not to teach any fine points concerning Role Playing for a child's performance, for such knowledge would make his performances at this stage seem inappropriate and, in fact, hinder further progress in his art. Later, as he becomes more skillful, he should be allowed to practice every element of the art. With the appearance and voice of a child, a boy actor, if he shows skill in his performance, can hardly give a bad impression. Still, this Flower is not the true Flower. It is only a temporary bloom. For that reason, practice at this time is easily managed. This does not mean that, because of this one flowering, he will always appear to be so skillful. As rehearsal at this age will always allow the young actor to create the impression of the Flower through his good points, the development of his basic skills is crucial. His movements must be authentic, the words of his chanting distinct, and his positions for dancing must be well fixed. These skills must be carefully and thoroughly rehearsed.

From the Age of Seventeen or Eighteen

This is a particularly crucial period, and not too many kinds of training can be arranged. First of all, since the actor's voice is changing, he loses his first Flower. His physical figure changes as well, and his movements become awkward. Before, his voice was full and beautiful, and it was easy for him to perform; now, realizing that the rules have changed, the actor's will falters. What is more, since the audience may look scornfully at his performance, he now feels embarrassed and discouraged. As concerns training, then, at this age, the actor, even though there are those who may point to him and laugh, must take no note, but retire to his own house, and, in a pitch comfortable to him, practice his chanting, using appropriate techniques for morning and evening.[3] Most important of all, he must vow to himself that, although he is now in a crucial period, he will truly stake his life on the Nō and never abandon it. Should any actor give up his training at this point, his skill can never increase. In general, although the pitch of the individual voice at this age may vary, it usually lies between the ōshiki and the banshiki.[4] If the actor tries to regulate the pitch too strictly [by forcing], he risks

---

[3]Zeami's remark suggests that a certain caution must be used when exercising the voice in the morning, whereas in the evening the voice is freer and can thus be exercised more vigorously.

[4]Ōshiki and banshiki are two of the twelve pitches in the traditional Japanese musical scales. Ōshiki is considered to correspond roughly to the pitch A in the Western musical scale, banshiki to B.

getting into bad habits with his posture. Then too, this may be the cause of damage to the actor's voice in later life.

From Twenty-four or Twenty-five

It is in this period that the level of artistry of the performer begins to become established. The limits of the actor will be fixed by his training and his self-discipline. His voice will by now have settled, and his body will have matured. These are the strong points required in our art: voice and physical appearance. Both of these become fixed at this period. This is the time in an actor's life when the art is born that will lead to the skills of his later years. In the eyes of others, it may well appear that a new and highly skilled performer has appeared. Therefore, even though he is being judged against a performer who is already highly regarded, it may seem on the occasion of his performance that his Flower is a new and fresh one, and, should he win a competition, others may praise him beyond his due, so that the actor himself comes to believe that he is already highly skilled. I cannot stress often enough that such an attitude serves as an enemy to the actor. For such is not the true Flower. A truly novel Flower comes about because of the actor's age and experience, when his spectators can truly be surprised. Spectators of real discernment are able to make this distinction. It would indeed be a shame if this early Flower, which actually represents only the actor's first level of accomplishment, should somehow be fixed in the actor's thoughts, so that he sees this phase as the culmination of his art, and therefore indulges himself in what is a deviation from the true path. Actually, even if an actor is praised by his audience and manages to win a competition over a famous performer, he must take cognizance of the fact that his Flower is merely a temporary one; therefore, he will begin at once to study Role Playing with the utmost seriousness and will ask every detail of those who have already achieved a real reputation for their performances, so that he may rehearse all the more diligently. One who believes that this temporary Flower is the real Flower is one who has separated himself from the true way. And indeed, any performer can be taken in by this temporary Flower and so fail to realize that he is losing the real one. Such is the situation of a young actor.

Here is one point that must be considered carefully. If one has a true ability to understand his own level of perfection in his art, then he can never lose that level of the Flower. If an actor thinks he has attained a higher level of skill than he has reached, however, he will lose even the level that he has achieved. This matter must be thought over carefully.

Thirty-four or Thirty-five Years

This age represents the peak of perfection in our art. If an actor grasps the various items set down here, and masters them, he will truly be acknowledged by the public and will achieve a reputation as a great actor. If such public recognition does not come, however, and he does not obtain such a reputation, then no matter how skillful the actor may be, he must recognize the fact that he is not one who has yet found the true Flower. And if he has not obtained such a Flower by this time, his art will begin to decline when he is forty. The proof of this fact will become clear as the actor grows older. An actor is on the rise until he is thirty-four or thirty-five, and he begins to decline after forty. This fact cannot be repeated too often—those who do not achieve a reputation at this stage of their career have not actually mastered the art of the *nō*. Therefore it is in this period that the actor must perfect his self-discipline. At this time in his career, he can recall all that he has learned: it is also the moment when he is able to plan for the means to accomplish what he wishes to in the future. If such things are not mastered at this age, then, let me repeat again, it will be difficult for an actor to find success with audiences later in his career.

Forty-four, Forty-five Years

From this point on, the actor must find new means of showing his skills. Even if he has achieved a fine reputation and has mastered the art of the *Nō,* he must be able in turn to have in his troupe young actors who will follow him. Although his real art may not decline, yet, as his years advance, his physical presence and the beauty others find in him will be diminished. Leaving aside the exceptionally handsome performer, even a fairly good-looking actor, as he grows older, should no longer be seen playing roles that do not require a mask. Thus this former aspect of his art will now be lacking. From this point onward, it is best not to perform elaborate parts. On the whole, an actor should choose roles that are congenial to him and that can be played in a relaxed manner without physical strain. He should allow the younger actors to show off their own abilities, and he should play with them in a modest fashion, as an associate. Even if he has no young successor of a suitable caliber, an actor should not himself perform any highly complicated and strenuous roles. In any case, the audience will find no Flower in this sort of performance. If, on the other hand, an actor has not lost his Flower by this age, then it will remain truly his possession. If an actor still possesses his Flower as he approaches fifty, then he must have achieved a real reputation before the age of forty. Even an actor who has gained such a reputation however, if he is truly a master, must most of all know himself, and, therefore, work to give the young actors proper training; he will exert himself to the utmost, without performing roles that may betray his own weaknesses. One who truly knows how to see and reflect upon himself it is he who has really grasped the nature of our art.

Fifty Years Old and Later

From this point onward, for the most part, there is little more that can be done. There is a saying that "even *Ch'i lin,* when old, is worse than a worn out packhorse."[5] Nevertheless, an actor who has truly mastered his art, even though he has lost his ability to perform many of his roles, and although he may manifest less and less of his art in performance, will still have something of his Flower left about him.

My late father died at the age of fifty-two on the nineteenth day of the fifth month [of 1384], and on the fourth day of that same month, he performed the *Nō* in connection with religious services at the Sengen shrine in the province of Suruga.[6] The performances that day were particularly colorful, and all the spectators, high-ranking and commoner alike, praised his performances. At that time the various plays were given over to the younger actors, and he performed a few easy roles in a modest way. Yet the beauty of his Flower was all the more striking. For when an artist has achieved a real Flower, then the art of the *nō,* even if the foliage is slight and the tree grows old, still retains its blooms. This is the very proof that, even in an ancient frame, the Flower remains.

What has been written above constitutes the appropriate stages of *Nō* training at various ages.

VARIOUS ITEMS CONCERNING ROLE PLAYING

It would be impossible to describe in writing all the various aspects of Role Playing. Yet as this skill forms the fundamental basis of our art, various roles must be studied with the greatest care. In general, Role Playing involves an imitation, in every particular, with nothing left out. Still, depending on the circumstances, one must know how to vary the degree of imitation involved. For example, when it comes to playing the part of a ruler or a high official, it is extremely difficult to perform with the necessary detail, since the actor cannot know the real way of life of the court nobility, or the bearing appropriate to a great lord. Still, he can study carefully their way of speaking, observe their circumstances, and ask the opinion of those noblemen who watch the performances. Next, he must imitate down to the smallest detail the various things done by persons of high profession, especially those elements related to high artistic pursuits. On the other hand, when it comes to imitating laborers and rustics, their commonplace actions should not be copied too realistically. In

---

[5]*Ch'i-lin* (*kirin* in Japanese) famous in ancient Chinese historical chronicles was, rather like the Greek Pegasus, a horse with the miraculous ability to travel enormous distances very quickly.

[6]Generally identified as the Sengen Shrine in the present city of Shizuoka, a little over 100 miles south of Tokyo.

the case of woodcutters, grass cutters, charcoal burners, and salt workers, however, they should be imitated in detail insofar as they have traditionally been found congenial as poetic subjects. In general, men of lowly occupation should not be imitated in any meticulous fashion, nor shown to men of refined taste. Should they see such things, they will merely find them vulgar, and the performance will hold no attraction for them. The need for prudence in this matter can be fully understood. Thus the degree of imitation must vary, depending on the kind of role being performed.

Women's Roles

In general, a young *shite* is the most suitable actor to play the part of a woman. Nevertheless, playing such a part represents a considerable undertaking. If the actor's style of dress is unseemly, there will be nothing worth watching in the performance. When it comes to impersonating high-ranking women of the court, such as ladies-in-waiting, for example, since the actor cannot easily view their actual deportment, he must make serious, detailed inquiries concerning such matters. As for items of clothing such as the *kinu* and the *hakama,* these too cannot merely be chosen on the basis of the actor's personal preference. The actor must make a proper investigation concerning what is correct. When it comes to impersonating an ordinary woman, however, the actor will be familiar with the appropriate details, and so the task will not be difficult. If the actor dresses in an appropriate *kinu* or *kosode,* that will doubtless suffice. When performing *kusemai, shirabyōshi,* or mad women's roles, the actor should hold a fan or a sprig of flowers, for example, loosely in his hand in order to represent female gentleness. The *kinu* and the *hakama,* as well, should be long enough to conceal his steps, his hips and knees should be straight, and his bodily posture pliable. As for his head posture, if he bends backward, his face will appear coarse. If the actor looks down, on the other hand, his appearance from the back will be unseemly. Then too, if he holds his neck too stiffly, he will not look feminine. He should certainly wear a robe with long sleeves, and he should avoid showing the tips of his hands. His *obi* should be loosely tied. The fact that an actor takes great care with his costume means that he is truly anxious to perform his role as well as possible. No matter what the role, bad costuming will never be effective, and, in the case of a woman's role, proper dressing is essential.

Old Men

Playing the role of an old man represents the very pinnacle of our art. These roles are crucial, since the spectators who watch can gauge immediately the real skills of the actor. There are many *shite* who have mastered the art of *Nō* quite well, but who cannot achieve the appearance of an old man.

When an actor plays a woodcutter, salt scooper, or a similar part that contains conspicuous gestures, it is easy enough for the spectators to be deceived and to make a false judgment too quickly concerning the performer's talents. But to play the part of an old man of high rank whose gestures involve no characteristic movement is truly difficult and requires the skills of a master actor. Unless an actor rehearses over the years until his art is at its peak, he cannot properly present this kind of role. Without a proper Flower, such a restrained performance can have nothing of interest about it.

In terms of stage deportment, most actors, thinking to appear old, bend their loins and hips, shrink their bodies, lose their Flower, and give withered, uninteresting performances. Thus there is little that is attractive in what such actors do. It is particularly important that the actor refrain from performing in a limp or weak manner, but bear himself with grace and dignity. Most crucial of all is the dancing posture chosen for the role of an old man. One must study assiduously the precept: portray an old man while still possessing the Flower. The results should resemble an old tree that puts forth flowers.

Performing Without a Mask

This too represents an important aspect of our art. As such roles are those representing ordinary persons, they may seem to be easy to perform, but, surprisingly, unless the highest level of skill in the *Nō* is used, such a performance will not be worth watching. The actor must of necessity study the object of each role individually [since the face is visible]. Although it is not possible to imitate any particular individual countenance in performance, actors sometimes alter their own ordinary facial expressions in an attempt to create some particular effect. The results are always without interest. The performance should rather be constructed from the movements and general feeling of the person being portrayed. The actor must always use his own natural facial expressions and never try to alter them.

Roles of Mad Persons

This skill represents the most fascinating aspect of our art. In this category there are many types of roles, and an actor who has truly taken up this specialty can play successfully all types of roles. I must repeat again and again that an actor must fully commit himself to rehearse and practice continuously, as I have admonished. In general, there are various types of possessed beings; for example, those inhabited by the curse of a god, a Buddha, the spirit of a living person, or of a dead person. Therefore, if the actor studies the nature of the spirit who possesses the character, he should be able to manage the part well. On the other hand, the really difficult parts involve those characters whose thoughts have become confused because their minds have become crazed—a parent searching for a lost child, for example, a wife thrown over by her husband, or a husband who lives on after his wife. Even a relatively skillful *shite* may fail to make the distinction between them, and he will create his mad gestures in the same manner, so that no emotional response is engendered in those who watch him. In the case of characters of this sort, the actor must have as his intention the manifestation of the precise feelings that can indicate the character's emotional disturbance, and make them the core of his Flower; then, if he feigns madness with all the skill he has at his command, there will certainly be many arresting elements in his performance. If an actor possesses this kind of skill, and if he can make his spectators weep, his art will represent the highest attainment possible. Reflect as fully as possible on what I have written above.

It goes without saying that a costume appropriate for the role of a mad person is essential. Still, as the character is a mad person, the costume might, depending on the occasion, be more gaudy than usual. The actor can carry in his hand a sprig of flowers appropriate to the season.

Then again, while I have spoken in terms of acting that imitates surface realities, there is another point that must be seriously considered. Although I said that the madness of the character must be performed in terms of the being who possesses that character, when it comes to playing a madwoman possessed by a warrior or a demon, for example, the circumstances are made quite difficult for the actor. Thinking to act out the true nature of the being who possesses such a character, the actor will show masculine wrath while playing a woman, and his performance will seem quite inappropriate. On the other hand, if the actor concentrates on the womanly traits of his character, there will be no logic to the possession. Similarly, when a male character is possessed by a woman, the same difficulty arises. In sum, to avoid plays with such characters represents an important secret of our art. Those who compose such texts simply do not understand the nature of our art. A writer who truly understands the art of *Nō* would never compose a text that showed such a lack of harmony. To possess this truth is another secret of our art.

When it comes to playing the role of a mad person without a mask, the performance will not be complete unless the actor has truly mastered his art. For, if the expressions on the actor's face are not properly descriptive, there will be no sense of madness conveyed. If the actor changes his face without a profound understanding of his art, on the other hand, the results will be merely ugly. The deepest arts of Role Playing are required for these paradoxical circumstances.

Thus, in important performances, inexperienced actors must participate with the greatest caution. Playing without a mask is very difficult. Acting a mad role is also very difficult. To combine these two elements into one: how difficult indeed to elevate such a role to the level of the Flower. Rehearsal and study are the only methods possible.

Roles of Buddhist Priests

Although such roles exist, they are few in number and do not require so much practice. In general, when playing a gorgeously robed cleric or a priest of high rank, the actor must use the majesty and dignity of the character as the basis for his performance. When it comes to lesser-ranking priests, such as those who have abandoned the world and practice austerities, their religious pilgrimage is of paramount importance to them, and so it is crucial for the actor to create the impression that such characters are absorbed in their religious devotions. In the end, when it comes to the materials on which to build a performance, more pains may be required than might be expected.

Shura

Here is still another type of role. Such dead warrior roles, even when well performed, are seldom arresting. Thus they should not be performed too often. Nevertheless, when it comes to events dealing with the famous Genji or Heike warriors,[7] if the various elements are knit together with suitable elegance, so that the text is a good one, such a performance can be more moving than one of any other variety. In such plays, some spectacular moment is particularly important. The wildness of the *shura* style may well lead to the kind of behavior appropriate to a demon role. Then again, such a role risks turning entirely into a dance performance. If there is a section in the play that resembles *kusemai,* it is allowable to include some appropriate dancelike gestures. As it is customary for the actor to carry with him a bow and quiver and to wear some variety of sword, the performer should undertake a careful study of how to carry and use such objects, making efforts to exhibit the essence of this type of role. The actor must take special care to avoid both those movements appropriate to a demon role on the one hand, and the use of purely dancelike motions on the other.

Roles of Gods

In general, this kind of Role Playing is related to that appropriate for the demon roles. As the appearance of such a fig-

---

[7]The Genji and Heike clans were the chief rivals in the disastrous civil wars of 1185 that brought an end to the political domination by the Kyoto court. Many important *Nō* texts by Zeami dealt with characters and incidents from those battles.

ure is always fierce, no particular difficulties are created by playing the part in the manner of a demon, depending, of course, on the role of the god involved. However, there is one essential difference between the two types of characters. Dancelike gestures are the most appropriate for the role of a god, but they are not suitable for a demon role. Particularly in the case of a god role, the only means available to the actor to represent such a being lies in his being properly dressed, and therefore he must give particular attention to the creation of a properly noble appearance. The actor must decorate his costume correctly and adjust his clothing in an appropriate manner.

Demon Roles

These roles are a particular specialty of the Yamato school. They are extremely difficult to perform successfully. True, it is simple to play effectively the demon roles of vengeful ghosts or possessed beings, as they offer visible elements of interest that can make them arresting. The performer, directing himself toward his acting partner, should use small foot and hand motions and make his movements in accordance with the effect created by his headgear. In the case of a real demon from hell, however, even if the actor studies well, his performance is likely to be merely frightening. There are no real means to make such roles truly enjoyable for the spectators. In fact, these are such difficult roles to play that there are few actors who can perform them in an effective way, it seems.

The essence of such roles lies in forcefulness and frightfulness. Yet such qualities do not stimulate feelings of enjoyment. For this reason, the role of a demon is particularly difficult to play. Logically, the harder the actor tries to perform them, the less interesting they become. The essence of such a role is frightfulness, yet the qualities of frightfulness and enjoyment are as different as black and white. Thus, it might be said that an actor who can perform such a role in an

enjoyable way would indeed be a performer of the highest talent. Indeed, an actor who strives for nothing but to play demon roles well can never really attain the Flower. Therefore, a performance by a young actor, even if it seems well done, will not really be effective. Is it not then true that an actor who only strives to play demon roles well can never actually perform them well? This paradox must be carefully studied. For the interest the spectator finds in the performance of a demon role is like a flower blooming among the rocks.

Chinese Roles

As these are special kinds of characters, there is no fixed form of practice for the actor. The element of appearance is essential. In choosing a mask—even though the character is of course a human being just like anyone else—it is best for the actor to wear something with an unusual appearance so as to maintain the effect of something somehow out of the ordinary.

Such parts are effectively played by older artists with talent and experience. Still, other than costuming, there are no special techniques required. In any case, since any attempt to imitate the Chinese style directly, either in chant or in movement, will not in itself be effective, it is better to add just one representative element to an ordinary performance. The selection of just such an element, slight in itself, can serve as a means to animate the whole. Although usually such changes are not considered appropriate, there is no way truly to copy the style, and so such a slight change in gesture will add something of the Chinese flavor and can give the spectators an appropriate sensation. Such methods have been practiced for a long time.

In general, such are the various elements of Role Playing. It is difficult to express any finer details in writing. Nevertheless, an actor who has fully grasped the points enumerated above will be able by himself to grasp them.

PERFORMANCE REVIEW

Chūshingura Finest of This Season

SANDRA SCHLANGER
Review of *Chūshingura: The Forty-Seven Samurai*

DIRECTED BY NAKAMURA MATAGORŌ, UNIVERSITY OF HAWAI'I, KENNEDY THEATER, 16 MARCH 1979.

The University of Hawai'i's Department of Theatre is an internationally known center for the study of Asian theater; in 1978–1979, the department engaged in a yearlong effort to study and produce Kabuki theater. The adaptation and translation of Chūshingura: The Forty-Seven Samurai *printed in this collection was produced at the University, and then on an extensive tour of the continental United States. In her review of the production, Sandra Schlanger provides some sense of the spectacular nature of Kabuki theater, not only the disciplined nature of its acting style, but also of the importance of music as well.*

Last Wednesday evening the University Theatre in cooperation with the music department opened its eagerly anticipated production of the Kabuki play, "The Forty-Seven Samurai," a theatrical tour de force and probably the finest happening yet to be seen on Island stages this season.

The play deals with one of the most popular themes in Kabuki repertoire, the secret vendetta of 47 loyal retainers to avenge the forced suicide of their master, and is based on actual events that occurred in 18th-century Edo (present-day Tokyo).

The drama celebrates historical and cultural themes central to Japanese tradition and sentiment and is regularly performed in Japan in December, the month in which the actual episode occurred.

Through the centuries the story has been reworked by Kabuki artists in several versions since its first staging as a puppet drama (*bunraku*) in 1748. The three-hour version that Island audiences are being treated to is an adaptation of the 11-hour original by visiting Kabuki master Nakamura Matagorō of the National Theatre of Japan, and UH drama professor James Brandon

The translation by Brandon, Junko Berberich and Michael Feldman gives this production the distinction of being the first Kabuki play, complete with the puppet-style chanting (*gidayu*), ever to be performed entirely in English.

Wooden clappers announce the opening of the drama, and as offstage flutes and drums begin to sound and Itsuko Tagawa begins to chant the narration, the black sleeve and glove of an "invisible" stage assistant (*koken*) draws aside the curtain to reveal the first scene, the Hachiman shrine in Kamakura.

The narration, intoned in the singsong and exaggerated style of the original Japanese, introduces the characters as they begin to move in the slow, stylized, exact gestures traditional to Kabuki.

Lines are quickly drawn between good and evil, arrogance and modesty, loyalty and malfeasance of duty, with the story being carried forward alternately by the actors and the offstage narration.

Musical accompaniment provided by a *samisen* (a three-stringed instrument), wooden clappers, and sparingly-used drums accompany the action throughout.

Norris Shimabuku as Moronao, the evil governor, is powerful in his low, gravelly voice of authority and station, and loathsome in his grimaces (*mie*). Carol Honda as Bannai, the diminutive, roly-poly retainer of Moronao, becomes very much the imp during the lighter moments of the drama.

Douglas Day as the noble Lord Hangan shows his finest skills in the climactic scene in Act 2 wherein he carries out the shogun's order of death by seppuku (ritual suicide by disembowelment). Dressed in the white mourning garments, Day approaches the prepared mat with its sprigs of evergreen, hesitating suggestively, kneeling, facing the audience, with a subtle play of expression that does indeed suggest all of the struggle for calm preparatory to inflicting the mortal strokes. The tension created is enormous.

Elizabeth Wichmann, who plays a lovely and plaintive Okaru, performs with considerable delicacy of movement and intonation. Her enchanting scene of Act 3 played in the gorgeous silks and ornamented hair-style of the courtesan is possibly the most charming of the evening.

Medieval and Renaissance England

A performance of *The Tempest* at the new Shakespeare's Globe Theatre, on the Bankside in London. The theater is a meticulous reconstruction of the Globe Theatre of 1613.

The fifteenth, sixteenth, and seventeenth centuries saw Europe transformed by the extraordinary cultural revolution we now call the European Renaissance. Fueled by new technology such as printing and by new scientific, political, and religious ideas, explosive change transformed European culture. The known world expanded beyond the sea to embrace the New World; the recovery of Greek and Latin literature spurred a sweeping intellectual revolution; strong centralized monarchies in Spain, Portugal, France, and England created new empires abroad and fought to control an increasingly restive populace at home; the Protestant Reformation undermined the religious and political authority of the Catholic church, beginning a period of violent religious conflict; and the "new philosophy"—modern science—of Copernicus, Bacon, and Galileo seemed to put even the physical world of heaven and earth in doubt. "'Tis all in pieces, all coherence gone," the poet John Donne wrote in 1611, voicing the profound anxiety and exhilaration of many of his contemporaries: "Prince, subject, father, son are things forgot. / For every man alone thinks that he hath got / To be a Phoenix." The changing tides of thought swept away the crumbling edifice of the medieval world—the feudal state, the universal church, scholastic philosophy, an ordered heaven, and revealed truth—and opened the way for the modern world.

This revolution also infused the theater; the Renaissance, especially in Italy, France, Spain, and England, is one of the great ages of theatrical and dramatic achievement. In England, the professional theater as we know it originated at this time: the history of the secular, profit-making, commercial theater is conventionally dated from the opening of the first theater building, The Theatre, in London in 1576. Licensed and protected as an aristocratic entertainment, the theater was also a popular institution in which commoners such as William Shakespeare, Richard Burbage, Edward Alleyn, Inigo Jones, and others, could indeed rise like the phoenix. However, to understand the revolutionary impact of theater and drama in Shakespeare's era, we need to understand their conservative inheritance, their deep indebtedness to the medieval stage that preceded them.

Dramatic performance in medieval Europe was thoroughly conditioned by the Catholic church's central role in the life of the community. Having closed the Roman theaters in the sixth century, the church maintained a vigilant opposition to the secular theater and the vices associated with it. Yet the revival of theater in Europe, beginning in the tenth century, was inspired and sponsored by the church itself. The four major dramatic forms in the late Middle Ages were connected with the church, its rituals, and its calendar of religious observances: LITURGICAL DRAMA enacted as part of the liturgy of the Catholic Mass; CYCLE PLAYS, illustrating scriptural history and performed by craft guilds on the feast of Corpus Christi; MORALITY DRAMA, enacting the symbolic structure of Christian life; and plays written and performed in schools and universities, sometimes imitating classical plays. In England, cycle and morality plays particularly influenced the later, secular drama of the sixteenth century.

The earliest dramatic records, dating from the ninth century, are musical TROPES, brief elaborations of the authorized liturgy, written to amplify the scriptural text and enhance its impact and appeal. These compositions were set to music and sung in ANTIPHONAL

DRAMA AND THEATER IN MEDIEVAL ENGLAND

Liturgical Drama

PERFORMANCE (back and forth, in dialogue) between monks or boy choristers to accompany the liturgy of the Mass. In England, Ethelwold, Bishop of Winchester, wrote a series of lessons concerning the conduct of the Mass, the *Regularis Concordia* (965–975), including instructions for such performances. What follows are his instructions to the priests for representing the visit of the three Marys to the tomb of Christ after the Crucifixion (translated from Latin). This trope is often called the *Quem Quaeritis,* after the Latin text spoken by the "angel": "Whom seek you?":

> While the third lesson is being chanted, let four brethren vest themselves; of whom, let one, vested in an alb, enter as if to take part in the service, and let him without being observed approach the place of the sepulchre [i.e., near the altar], and there, holding a palm in his hand, let him sit down quietly. While the third responsory is being sung, let the remaining three follow, all of them vested in copes, and carrying in their hands censers filled with incense; and slowly, in the manner of seeking something, let them come before the place of the sepulchre. These things are done in imitation of the angel seated in the monument, and of the women coming with spices to anoint the body of Jesus. When therefore that one seated shall see the three, as if straying about and seeking something, approach him, let him begin in a dulcet voice of medium pitch to sing:

> > *Whom seek ye in the sepulchre, O followers of Christ?*

> When he has sung this to the end, let the three respond in unison:

> > *Jesus of Nazareth, which was crucified, O celestial one.*

> To whom that one:

> > *He is not here; he is risen; just as he foretold.*
> > *Go, announce that he is risen from the dead.*

> At the word of this command let those three turn themselves to the choir, saying:

> > *Alleluia! The Lord is risen to-day.*
> > *The strong lion, the Christ, the Son of God. Give thanks to God.*

> This said, let the former, again seating himself, as if recalling them, sing the anthem:

> > *Come, and see the place where the Lord was laid. Alleluia! Alleluia!*

> And saying this, let him rise and let him lift the veil and show them the place bare of the cross, but only the cloths laid there with which the cross was wrapped. Seeing which, let them set down the censers which they carried into the same sepulchre, and let them take up the cloth and spread it out before the eyes of the clergy; and as if making known that the Lord had risen and was not now therein wrapped, let them sing this anthem:

> > *The Lord is risen from the sepulchre.*
> > *Who for us hung upon the cross.*

> And let them place the cloth upon the altar. The anthem being ended, let the Prior, rejoicing with them at the triumph of our King, in that, having conquered death, he arose, begin the hymn:

> > *We praise thee, O God.*

> This begun, all the bells chime out together.[1]

Despite its brevity and the limitations imposed by the liturgy itself, this trope has the elements of drama: a progressive plot, the involvement of specific characters, conflict and resolution. Ethelwold's "stage directions" convey a subtle sense of how character can be created by performance and a fine sense of visual spectacle as well, all within the narrow scope allowed by the Mass.

---

[1]*Regularis Concordia,* in *Chief Pre-Shakespearean Dramas,* ed. Joseph Quincy Adams (Boston: Houghton Mifflin, 1924), 9–10.

Throughout the Middle Ages and beyond, liturgical plays of this kind became increasingly common and complex. Enacted in different locations within the church, called **MAN-SIONS,** liturgical drama provided a model for the forms of religious drama that came to be performed outside the church and outside the framework of the liturgy. In the tenth and eleventh centuries, the church sponsored dramatized scenes from the life of Christ or the lives of the saints, staged on important Christian holidays. For example, a town might commemorate the entrance of Christ into Jerusalem on Palm Sunday with a procession to the cathedral in which townspeople enacted various roles. In addition, the church oversaw the production of cycles of plays, which became a principal mode of theatrical and dramatic innovation. These cycles were performed sixty days after Easter as part of the feast of Corpus Christi, a holiday inaugurated in the fourteenth century to celebrate the doctrine of the Eucharist. The Corpus Christi festival frequently featured the perfor-mance of a series of plays dramatizing scriptural history: the Creation, Old Testament events (Noah and the Flood, Abraham and Isaac), scenes from the New Testament (the Annunciation, Herod and the Slaughter of the Innocents), and prophetic plays concern-ing the Harrowing of Hell and the Last Judgment. The production of these plays could last several days or weeks and called on the services of the entire town. Each craft guild (or *mystery,* as the guilds were called; the cycles are sometimes called **MYSTERY CYCLES**) financed and produced a different play, often on a subject appropriate to the guild. The shipwrights' guild might undertake the Noah play, the Three Kings play might be assigned to the goldsmiths, and so on. The plays were the property of the guilds and passed through generations of guild members. In major towns with many craft guilds, the cycles often included a large number of plays. Of the English cycles, the York cycle is the longest, containing forty-eight plays; the Wakefield cycle has thirty-two; and the Chester cycle has twenty-four.

Cycle Drama

Although they were produced for a popular, largely illiterate audience, the cycle dra-mas are extremely sophisticated and required the talents of trained performers. One of the cycles' most powerful and typical features is their use of **ANACHRONISM**—the blending of the historical past with contemporary events and characters. Many of the characters who appear in the plays are medieval English peasants, who often display an ironic, even theatri-cal sense of their involvement in the scriptural events of the past. One of the most telling uses of this technique occurs in the York *Crucifixion;* the York playwright conveys the Ro-man soldiers' hardness to the message of Christ by making them jest with him about the crucifixion they are performing:

> 1 **SOLDIER:** (*To* CHRIST.) Say, Sir, how likes you now
>   This work that we have wrought?
> 2 **SOLDIER:** We pray you say us how
>   Ye feel, or faint ye aught.
> **JESUS:** . . . My Father, that all bales [evils] may beet [abate].
>   Forgive these men that do me pine [pain].
>   What they work wot [know] they nought;
>   Therefore, my Father, I crave,
>   Let never their sins be sought,
>   But see their souls to save.
> 1 **SOLDIER:** We! Hark! he jangles like a jay.

By characterizing the jesting Roman soldiers as, in effect, contemporaries of the me-dieval audience, the play implies that biblical events are part of the audience's contemporary history. Seeing their neighbors enacting the biblical scenes and seeing contemporary char-acters share the stage with biblical figures must have emphasized the immediacy of the on-going Christian story.

Morality Drama

Like the cycle plays, morality plays dramatized elements of Christian life. Instead of staging events from scriptural history, morality drama stages a symbolic **ALLEGORY** of the Christian's spiritual journey through life. Increasingly popular throughout the fourteenth and fifteenth centuries, plays like *The Castle of Perseverance* (c. 1425), *Mankind* (c. 1470), and *Everyman* (c. 1500) emphasized the individual's struggle with sin, while the cycle plays emphasized the larger patterns of Christian history. Later playwrights, including Shakespeare, found both models useful. The cycles provided a pattern for staging the epic sweep of secular English history, and morality drama provided a supple device for representing psychological and moral conflict. Morality plays often provided the structure for the secular plays written at schools and universities as well, and for the **INTERLUDES** performed at court as a break from holiday feasting. They also provided a staple technique for characterization in the later secular drama. Christopher Marlowe's *Doctor Faustus* (1590) uses the Good and Evil Angels to externalize Faustus's moral conflict, and other playwrights frequently used the devices of morality drama to dramatize the difficulties of political choice. In John Skelton's interlude, *Magnificence* (1516), written for Henry VIII or Thomas Sackville, and Thomas Norton's *Gorboduc* (1561), the monarch is shown to make his decisions framed by a host of allegorized counselors, good and bad advisers who approximate the role played in morality drama by angels and demons.

STAGING MEDIEVAL DRAMA

Medieval plays were often acted on or near **PAGEANT WAGONS.** In some towns the audience seems to have remained stationary at various locations while the wagons and their plays proceeded past them; in other towns, the wagons were drawn in a procession of **TABLEAUX VIVANTS** (posed scenes) through the town and then arranged in an open area for the performance, allowing the audience to move from play to play. In Chester, for example, a list survives of the stations where the plays were performed, and for York it is possible to trace the route of the pageant wagons through the city. Given the size and complexity of these performances, it's not surprising to find that they were not easily performed on one day: the procession took three days at Chester, and began at 4:30 A.M. in York, lasting until past midnight. The plays combined historical and contemporary elements; in performance, the staging produced a close and powerful relationship between the dramatic characters and the audience. In the Coventry play of the Magi, for example, Herod raves when he discovers that the three kings have escaped him:

> I Stamp! I Stare! I look all about!
> Might I them take, I should them burn at a glede [fire]!
> I rant! I run! and now run I wode [mad]
> A! That these villain traitors hath marred this my mood!
> They shall be hanged, if I may come them to!
>
> (*Here Herod rages in the pagond* [pageant wagon] *and in the street also.*)[2]

Herod's rage was certainly one of the highlights of the medieval cycles. Shakespeare, at least, seems to refer to it in *Hamlet* (1600), when he has Hamlet remind his actors that they should be restrained and natural in their performance, because overacting "out-Herods Herod." The stage direction also suggests that Herod's frenzy carried him from the wagon and into the street, into a closer and more effective relationship to his audience. This interaction between actor and audience is characteristic of popular theater and is a feature of medieval performance carried into Renaissance acting. It also suggests that the "place" of

---

[2]The Coventry *Magi, Herod, and the Slaughter of the Innocents,* in *Chief Pre-Shakespearean Dramas,* ed. Joseph Quincy Adams (Boston: Houghton Mifflin, 1924), 163.

medieval drama, the fictitious locale of the play, was not firmly localized onstage; the actors/characters could move easily back and forth between Herod's Jerusalem and the medieval audience, and even onstage places could be rapidly and easily transformed. This flexibility also allowed medieval playwrights to treat stage space symbolically. The ground plot for *The Castle of Perseverance,* for instance—with its scaffolds for various evils, its moat, and its central castle—clearly offers us a symbolic locale rather than an actual geography. The

MEDIEVAL PAGEANT WAGON

One actor is playing in the street in front of the wagon.

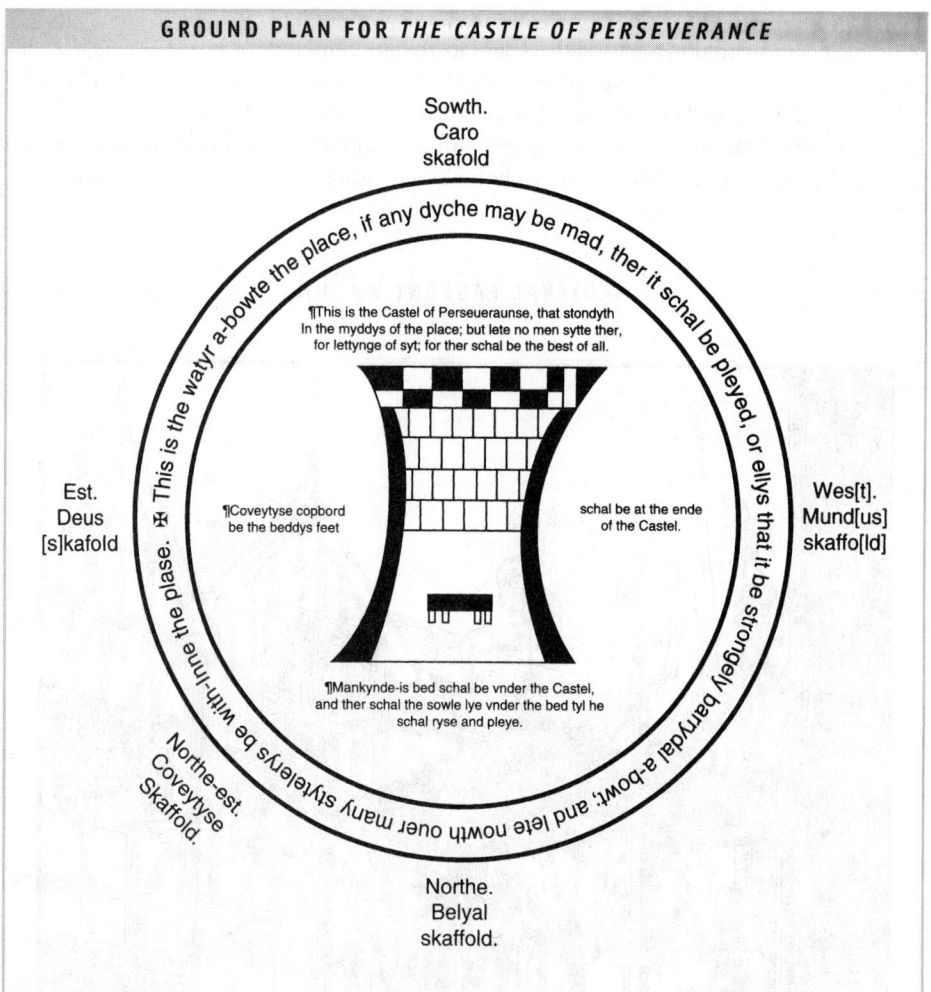

GROUND PLAN FOR *THE CASTLE OF PERSEVERANCE*

Sowth.
Caro
skafold

This is the watyr a-bowte the place, if any dyche may be mad, ther it schal be pleyed, or ellys that it be strongely barryd al a-bowt; and lete nowth ouer many stytelerys be with-inne the plase.

¶This is the Castel of Perseuerraunse, that stondyth
In the myddys of the place; but lete no men sytte ther,
for lettynge of syt; for ther schal be the best of all.

Est.
Deus
[s]kafold

¶Coveytyse copbord
be the beddys feet

schal be at the ende
of the Castel.

Wes[t].
Mund[us]
skaffo[ld]

¶Mankynde-is bed schal be vnder the Castel,
and ther schal the sowle lye vnder the bed tyl he
schal ryse and pleye.

Northe-est.
Coveytyse
Skaffold.

Northe.
Belyal
skaffold.

The ground-plot for the medieval morality play shows five scaffolds (North, Northeast, South, East, and West) arranged around a playing area, with a castle in the center. A ditch enclosed the castle to keep spectators at a distance. In the manuscript, a note beneath the drawing describes the costumes and special effects: "He that shall play Belial (a devil), look that he have gunpowder burning in pipes in his hands and in his ears, and in his arse, when he goes to battle. The four daughters should be clad in mantles; Mercy in white, Ruthwiseness in red, all together, Truth in sad green, and Peace all in black; and they shall play in the place all together until they bring up the soul."

various demons on their scaffolds stand at a symbolic distance, not an actual distance, from the central castle.

This complex of dramatic conventions, staging practices, and audience attitudes is a legacy of the medieval theater passed on to later theater. Although the medieval stage was only one of many influences on it, the drama of the sixteenth and seventeenth centuries is reminiscent of medieval drama in many ways. Renaissance drama frequently treats secular history according to a providential design similar to that of the cycles; it often treats its characters in the symbolic terms of the medieval morality dramas; and it uses both acting and stage space to create an immediacy between the fictive play and its audience. These habits take on very different meanings in Renaissance London, in a city and in a state in which the Anglican Protestant church is the state religion and where signs of Catholicism—or, in fact, of any religious subject matter—in the theater could be read as an act of sedition. The medieval theater provided the forms of drama and the practices of theater that were refashioned by the political, social, and theatrical pressures of the new era.

The explosion of theatrical and dramatic activity in London can be marked by two dates: 1567, when John Brayne built the Red Lion, London's first purpose-built theater (his brother-in-law, James Burbage, built The Theatre in 1576); and 1642, when plays were suspended and theaters were closed at the outbreak of the Civil War. The theater underwent profound changes from the reign of Elizabeth I (ruled 1558–1603) to the reigns of her successors James I (1603–1625) and Charles I (1625–1642, executed 1649), yet at the same time it endured the intense social and cultural upheavals of the period with remarkable consistency. As an institution, the new professional theater witnessed the emergence of England as a modern state; the rise of England as an important mercantile and naval power, aided by the defeat of the Spanish Armada in 1588; the expansion of English interests in the New World; the growth of the city of London to roughly 250,000 inhabitants; and the ascendance of the Puritan faction that closed the theaters and deposed and executed the king.

> ## DRAMA AND THEATER IN RENAISSANCE LONDON

    The professional theater—a new institution in England, though already established on the continent—necessarily reflected the political and social strains of the time. These strains are most readily visible in the many laws regulating theatrical performance. The location of theater buildings, the structure and organization of theater companies, and the entire scene of theatrical activity in Renaissance London epitomized the fundamental tensions of English society as it moved from the medieval to the modern world.

The sixteenth century witnessed intense religious and civil controversy, dating in part from Henry VIII's divorce from Catherine of Aragon in 1532 and his consequent excommunication from the Catholic church in 1533. Once Henry established the Protestant church of England as the religion of the realm in 1535, English politics were often dictated by England's vulnerability to the massive, hostile powers of the Catholic church in Rome and Catholic states such as France and Spain. Within England, a variety of Protestant sects competed with each other, with the government, and with the Church of England for power. This was also a period of profound changes in the ordering of society, a period of growing mercantile power, of aristocratic discontent with the power of the monarchy, and of the rise of new merchants and other social groups into prominence and power. As a result, the Crown was eternally on guard to suppress civil unrest or religious nonconformity.

> ## THE PROFESSIONAL THEATER AND ITS SOCIETY

    Given this volatile political climate, it is not surprising that the Crown sought to limit and control public assembly, including theatrical performances. Laws were frequently directed against the theater, particularly against productions identified with England's Catholic past. In 1548, for example, the English church cancelled the Feast of Corpus Christi, and the production of the cycle plays was systematically suppressed. In 1569, the York cycle was performed for the last time, and in 1575, the mayor of Chester was arrested for allowing cycle plays to be performed. The last cycle performance took place in Coventry in 1576, and the last record of any Corpus Christi play being performed in England (before the modern era) dates from 1605, in Kendal. Morality plays may have seemed less sectarian in the kind of instruction they offered; features of morality drama were more readily absorbed by the secular theater.

    Yet while the Crown limited and censored the stage, it also maintained its traditional patronage of the theater. The population of London nearly tripled in Shakespeare's lifetime, from roughly 80,000 in 1564 to more than 200,000 at his death in 1616. The Elizabethan era was characterized by several large crop failures, a deflation in the value of currency, repeated bouts of the plague, and persistent threats of invasion from without and sedition from within. Not surprisingly, both the queen and her Privy Council, and the local city magistrates throughout England, were fearful both of itinerant travelers and of large—potentially riotous—assemblies. The famous "Act for the punishment of Vagabonds" of 1572 is a case in point. The law prohibited itinerant players and entertainers from wandering throughout the realm, but its ultimate effect was to establish permanent theatrical companies under the protection of noble patrons. The law ordered that "all Fencers, Bearwards, Common Players in Interludes, and Minstrels, not belonging to any Baron of this Realm, or towards any other honorable Personage of greater Degree . . . [who] wander abroad and have not License of two Justices of the Peace at the least . . . shall be taken adjudged and deemed Rogues Vagabonds and Sturdy Beggars." Unless they belonged to the retinue of a nobleman, players were classed with common vagrants and could be arrested and fined. Protected as servants, a company of players could receive a license to perform in public.

The statute points to the strong bond between the theater and the aristocracy, and patents granted by Elizabeth entitled noblemen to retain companies of actors as servants. These patents—granted for the Lord Chamberlain's Men (Shakespeare's company), the Lord Admiral's Men (who produced Marlowe's plays), and others—shaped the professional theater of Renaissance London. Elizabeth authorized such companies to perform "Comedies, Tragedies, Interludes, and stage plays" in public, in London and elsewhere. Yet, in granting these privileges, the Crown made significant qualifications. Elizabeth expanded the powers of her Master of Revels, Edmund Tilney, requiring "all and every plaier or plaiers with their playmakers, either belonging to any noble man or otherwise" to "appear before him with all such plaies, Tragedies, Comedies or showes as they shall in readiness or meane to sett forth," and to receive his approval before their performance. Censorship in the period was extensive, and Elizabeth also stipulated that plays "be not published or shown in the time of common prayer, or in the time of great and common plague in our said City of London." Religious and civic officials exerted considerable authority over when and where plays could actually be performed and where theaters could legally be built, and they often closed theaters for months at a time because of plague or civil strife. In 1594, the Privy Council restricted London to two companies (the Lord Chamberlain's Men and the Lord Admiral's Men) and restricted them to public performance at the Globe and Rose theaters when in London.

Professional Companies

The City of London, as in many towns, had its own ordinances prohibiting plays within the city limits, and for this reason James Burbage—a member of the Earl of Leicester's company—built The Theatre to the north of the city. Within a decade theaters had been built to the north of the city and to the south, across the Thames River.

Although they were technically "servants," the major acting companies—the most famous being the Lord Chamberlain's Men, patented in 1593 and then given royal sponsorship as the King's Men when King James I succeeded Elizabeth in 1603—were organized as stockholding, profit-making corporations; that is, as business enterprises in the modern sense. Their economic survival depended on their public performances, because their patron might command and finance only a few productions per year. Several investors, or **SHARERS,** put up the capital to finance the company and took a percentage of its profits. The sharers were not just investors; they were involved in all aspects of the theater. In 1603, for instance, the sharers of the King's Men included Shakespeare (playwright and actor), Richard Burbage (James Burbage's son and the company's principal actor, who was the first to play Shakespeare's King Lear, Hamlet, and Macbeth), the actors John Heminges and Henry Condell (who later published Shakespeare's plays), and the comic actors William Sly (see *The Taming of the Shrew*) and Robert Armin (who played the Fool in *King Lear*), among others. The sharers were responsible for building or leasing a theater, for purchasing plays, for taking on boy actors as apprentices, and for hiring other actors for each production. They also were liable when legal proceedings were brought against the company.

THEATERS IN RENAISSANCE LONDON, ABOUT 1630

A number of theaters were constructed in London after 1574. The dark line extending from The Tower (lower right) to Blackfriars in the west is the old city wall. Note that, with the exception of the first and second Blackfriars theaters, the theaters are either north of the city (the Fortune, The Theatre, the Curtain, the Red Bull) or south of the Thames River (the Swan, the Hope, the Rose, the Globe).

SKETCH OF THE SWAN THEATER, 1596

Johannes de Witt, a Dutch visitor to London, drew a sketch of a play in progress at the Swan in 1596. He sent the sketch to a friend, who made this copy. The drawing shows the tiring house with its two stage doors, a three-tiered gallery, the platform stage, and the standing pit.

MODERN RECONSTRUCTION OF THE SWAN THEATER

C. Walter Hodges based this reconstruction on the de Witt sketch.

Although several companies flourished during the theater's heyday, life for actors and playwrights was hard. Until 1594, all professional playing companies were forced to perform in a variety of places, in London's various theaters and on tour. Although the scene with the players in *Hamlet* implies that touring was an occasional hardship of the London companies, recent research demonstrates that touring had been commonplace before the building of London's theaters and remained an important aspect of a theater company's vitality throughout the period. Playwrights, who were paid a flat fee by the company for the script of a play, hustled to scrape together a living: Thomas Dekker spent time in debtors' prison, and Ben Jonson died in penury. On the other hand, the theater also provided an opportunity for advancement as well. Several actors, including Richard Burbage and Edward Alleyn, were able to amass considerable fortunes. Shakespeare used the money he received as sharer to invest in property both in London and in his home, Stratford-upon-Avon, where he purchased a large house and land. Such careers were the exception rather than the rule, however, in an era when the theater was widely regarded as illicit and was frequently declared illegal.

The Theaters

English companies performed on three kinds of stage—large, open, outdoor buildings called **PUBLIC THEATERS** that held as many as 3,000 people; smaller, indoor, more elite **PRIVATE THEATERS** holding perhaps 700; and private performances at court or at the home of the patron. Public theaters, inspired both by the innyard booths where companies performed on

(ASIDE)
SHAKESPEARE'S GLOBE

One of the most fascinating constellations of scholarly, architectural, and theatrical ambition in recent years has been the building of a replica of the 1613 Globe theater on the banks of the Thames River, a few hundred yards from the site of Shakespeare's original theater. Although a variety of efforts have been made throughout the world—one is currently under way in Japan—to build models of the Globe or other English Renaissance theaters, the Bankside project has been notable for the scrupulousness of its research into the location, size, and materials of the Globe and for the care with which it has been constructed. Within the limits of modern legal requirements (fire laws) and social conventions (accessible bathrooms), "Shakespeare's Globe" has been built both as an experiment in Tudor and Stuart building practices and to foster an experiential experiment in the performance of Renaissance plays.

The American actor Sam Wanamaker instigated the project and remained its guiding force until his death in 1993. Part of Wanamaker's vision was that the theater should be both a theatrical and a scholarly endeavor, and much of the success of the final project is due to the team he assembled, including the scholar Andrew Gurr, architect Theo Crosby (who died in 1994), and artistic director Mark Rylance. The accuracy of the building was immeasurably helped by the discovery in 1989 of a section of the Globe's foundation beneath a nineteenth-century building adjacent to the Southwark bridge; although Anchor Terrace is protected as a landmark (preventing much excavation of the Globe's foundation), the section of foundation that has been unearthed has enabled scholars, using the familiar seventeenth-century engraving of the London skyline by Wenceslaus Hollar, to deduce that the Globe was a polygon constructed of twenty bays, with an exterior diameter of 100 feet. However, building the theater as part of the Bankside Globe Centre—which will also include a replica of a theater designed by Inigo Jones and has exhibition and other facilities—was not an easy task, and much of what has been learned about the Globe has been the result of scholarly investigation into Tudor building practices and the efforts to reconstruct them.

Shakespeare's Globe is an impressively handmade building, using traditional building practices: the bays are made of oak timbers and are held together by more than 6,000 wooden pegs. Once the bays were erected, the walls were filled in with oak staves, lath, and then plastered: rather than using modern plaster, research showed that Tudor builders used a plaster made of lime and cow's hair. Because the hair of modern English cows is too short, the Globe builders used a lime plaster mixed with goat hair. A fire sheet was put between each wall, and tests on the resulting lath-and-plaster showed that it could resist 1,000 degrees Fahrenheit for three hours—long enough to empty the theater in an emergency (when the Globe burned in 1613, no injuries were reported, either). The building is also the first wood-framed building to be built in London since the great fire of 1666: its thatched roof is applied in the traditional manner and has been treated with a fire-retardant chemical, and a sprinkler system is installed just under the roofline.

By far the most controversial aspect of the building has been the location of the two pillars that hold up the "heavens," and the design of the back wall of the stage, the tiring house wall. Between the Prologue Season (1996) and the Globe's opening in 1997, a variety of changes in both were made, resulting in a sumptuously painted backdrop with additional tapestries, and faux-marble columns. Audiences going to the Globe today find themselves in a theater somewhat less crowded than a full house in Shakespeare's day might have been. Although the original Globe held 3,000, the current Globe seats just over 1,000 and can hold about 500 standing "groundlings" in the pit (today, the average audience member is about 10% larger than his or her Elizabethan predecessor; beyond that, modern audiences are not willing—nor are they allowed by fire regulations—to be jammed together as tightly as Elizabethan patrons probably were). But what they will also find—as the production of *Henry V* in 1997 showed— is a theater operating as a kind of experimental venue, using the container of Shakespeare's drama to explore how the plays might have worked in their original conditions. At the present time, the company intends to do some productions in period dress (the costumes often themselves made with Tudor cloth-making and dye techniques), but to do others in modern dress. The result of a massive and energetic combination of talents, Shakespeare's Globe is finally meant to work as a living theater.[1]

---

[1] The building of the Globe was recorded in a variety of newspaper and scholarly accounts throughout the early 1990s; students interested in learning more about Shakespeare's Globe should consult Shakespeare's Globe Education Centre, Bankside, London SE1 9DT, United Kingdom.

THE GLOBE THEATER FOUNDATION

In 1989, part of the foundation of the Globe theater was discovered. This portion of the Globe foundation extends from beneath a landmark nineteenth-century building; the remainder of the Globe foundation is beneath the building and therefore cannot be excavated. Nonetheless, this section of the inner and outer wall of the theater, and of the exterior stairwell which led to the galleries, has enabled scholars to gauge with much greater accuracy both the size and configuration of Shakespeare's theater.

DESIGNING SHAKESPEARE'S GLOBE

This illustration shows how the archaeological evidence of the Globe theater foundations has been used, along with other evidence, to develop a new understanding of the theater's size and shape. The foundations, which comprise two "bays" or sections of the Globe's exterior structure, enabled Theo Crosby, the architect of the reconstructed Shakespeare's Globe in London, to estimate the overall dimensions of the building (about ninety-nine feet in diameter) and also to determine that the Globe was a twenty-sided polygon.

tour and by the circular arenas used for animal baiting, were outdoor buildings accommodating a large and diverse audience for afternoon performances. Although one theater, the Fortune, was rectangular, most public theaters were polygonal structures. The roughly circular, three-story gallery surrounded an open pit for standing audiences, into which a stage extended at a height of about five feet. The stage was partly roofed, and two doors used for entrances were set into the rear wall, or **TIRING HOUSE.** On the gallery level above the stage, small rooms were used for aristocratic seating, for music, and for scenes requiring action above the stage—as in the balcony scene in *Romeo and Juliet,* or when Prospero appears "aloft" in *The Tempest.* The stage had a central trapdoor (or **GRAVE TRAP**), and its roofed area held a pulley for raising or lowering actors (as in the masque scene in *The Tempest*) or properties. The public theaters catered to a paying audience, charging one penny to enter the pit and an additional penny to enter each of the galleries, where seating was provided on benches. Estimates on the size of the theaters vary, but the largest, such as the Globe or the Fortune, were about 100 feet in external diameter, with a standing yard about 70 feet across, and a stage 45 feet wide and 27 feet deep; they could hold tightly-packed audiences of 2,000 to 3,000 people. Some theaters were considerably smaller. The Rose theater (whose foundation was discovered in 1989) was a twelve-sided building about 70 feet across, with a pit 50 feet in diameter and a stage roughly 25 by 15 feet. Most of the plays we associate with the Renaissance theater—those of Marlowe, Shakespeare, Jonson, John Webster, John Fletcher, and others—were produced in public theaters such as the Globe, the Rose, the Hope, the Swan, and the Fortune.

Although a number of theaters were built in this period, the prestige of the public theaters seems to have declined in the 1620s and 1630s as companies shifted much of their attention to the more lucrative private theaters. These theaters stood within the City of London, on lands called "liberties"; a liberty was a property that had once belonged to monasteries and had remained outside the city's legal jurisdiction, even though it was within the city limit. Best known of these theaters is the Blackfriars playhouse (the property originally belonged to the Dominican friars, who wore black gowns). Blackfriars was used intermittently throughout the 1590s by boys' companies, troupes of boy chapel choristers who were formed into companies for acting plays. Blackfriars was acquired by the King's Men and used by them for performances after 1608. These theaters were modeled along the lines of a great-house banqueting room: long indoor rooms illuminated by candles, with a low stage at one end, faced by benches for seating and flanked by additional seats along side galleries. The private theaters generally charged sixpence or more for basic admission, with additional charges for special seating. Companies performed at private theaters in winter and at public theaters in summer and generally brought the same repertoire to both venues. The private theaters did develop the reputation, however, for originating a more satirical and erudite body of drama.

DRAMA AND PERFORMANCE

Performing plays in **REPERTORY** over perhaps as many as 200 days a year, the London companies competed with each other for their audiences and generated an enormous demand for new plays. The plays that they bought and performed are among the greatest works of English literature. English drama in this period comprises plays on English history (such as Shakespeare's *Henry V* and *Richard III,* or Marlowe's *Edward II*); on classical history (Shakespeare's *Julius Caesar* and *Coriolanus,* Ben Jonson's *Sejanus*); romantic comedies (such as Shakespeare's *A Midsummer Night's Dream*); city comedies (Shakespeare's *Measure for Measure*); heroic tragedies (Shakespeare's *Hamlet* and *King Lear,* John Webster's *The Duchess of Malfi*); and plays of intrigue or satire (John Marston's *The Malcontent,* Thomas Middleton's *The Changeling*). Later in the period, audiences seemed to develop a taste for plays they called **TRAGICOMEDIES,** usually romantic plays that begin in the tragic vein but proceed to a happy resolution. Several of John Fletcher's plays are tragicomedies of this kind, and Shakespeare's *Cymbeline* and *The Tempest* resemble tragicomedy as well.

This list of genres suggests both the fertile range of innovation in the Renaissance theater and the drama's dependence on models drawn from the classical and medieval theaters. Roman drama—the comedies of Plautus and Terence and the tragedies of Seneca—was widely used in schools and universities as part of the teaching of Latin, and university students often staged these plays in Latin. It is not surprising, then, that some features of classical drama made their way into the Renaissance theater. The model of Shakespearean romantic comedy—mistaken identities, separated lovers, an irascible old man or father, a wily servant—derives directly from Plautus's plays; indeed, Shakespeare's *Comedy of Errors* directly adapts Plautus's *The Menaechmus Twins.* In a similar fashion, the violence of Seneca's tragedies makes its way directly into the action of Elizabethan drama. Formally and thematically, however, Renaissance drama also differs sharply from its classical ancestors. Renaissance plays tend to be more diffuse, involving a greater variety of characters and multiple plots; in tragedy, the action is often not quite as closely focused on the fortunes of a single hero as it is in classical tragedy. In these and other ways—in the Christian providence that seems to stand behind the action of many plays, in its variety of contemporary characters, in its use of symbolic anachronism, and in the complex relationship between the dramatic world and the world of the audience—Renaissance drama bears the signs of its medieval inheritance.

Playwrights generally wrote in **BLANK VERSE,** an unrhymed **IAMBIC PENTAMETER** line (ten syllables with alternating stress), and occasionally used other verse forms as well. They often used prose, sometimes for emphasis, sometimes to develop the qualities of a particular character. Although modern editors divided the plays into five acts, in most cases Renaissance playwrights probably did not compose their plays in this form. Performance on the public theater stage was rapid and continuous. The theaters used an open stage, few large properties, and had little or no scenery onstage, so that scenes could follow one another without interruption.

Despite the absence of elaborate stage sets, performance in the Renaissance theater was nonetheless spectacular. Actors used costumes, properties, and language to transform the midafternoon stage into a dramatic locale—Prospero's desert island, Lear's heath, Faustus's study. Some larger properties could be wheeled out from the rear doors, or perhaps raised from the trap: a throne, for instance, or a bed for Desdemona in *Othello,* or the hell-mouth used at the end of *Doctor Faustus.* A cannon fired during a production of Shakespeare's *Henry VIII* in 1613 unfortunately set fire to the Globe and burned it to the ground.

The unlocalized stage of medieval drama can be seen as the forerunner of the Renaissance theater's fluid use of stage space. The open stage made for an almost cinematic flexibility in performance, as the play could range rapidly from scene to scene, place to place. Costuming was eclectic and anachronistic: the actors wore mainly Elizabethan clothing, adding armor, royal finery, motley, or some "classical" style of gowns when needed. The actors—Burbage, Alleyn, Will Kemp, among many others—were widely praised for their power and effectiveness. Their acting style was oratorical in tragedy and extemporaneous in comedy, but there is no doubt that many were consummate performers, in command of dozens of roles that could be put into play at short notice.

WOMEN IN DRAMA AND PERFORMANCE

Boy actors played a significant part in the experience of English theater, for boy actors played the parts of women and girls onstage, including major roles like Lady Macbeth, Ophelia, and Cleopatra. Much as they did in classical Athens, "women" emerged onstage in Renaissance London only as a side-effect of masculine attitudes and performances. In the English theater, this **CROSS-DRESSING** came into special prominence, though, because the romantic, sexual, and political intrigue so popular in Renaissance plays was often focused on

THE JACOBEAN COURT MASQUE

One of the principal obligations of the professional companies was to perform at court or for their patron. Performances at court often took place during holidays and were commanded with increasing frequency by James I and Charles I. The companies performed many of their staple plays at court, but they also performed special entertainments called **MASQUES,** plays written in verse, usually on mythological subjects, that involved dancing, fanciful costumes, music, and special scenic machinery and effects. While the actors spoke the lines in these plays, they shared the stage with members of the court, who performed in the elaborate dances that began, punctuated, and ended the masques. The little play that Prospero puts on for Ferdinand and Miranda in Shakespeare's *The Tempest* resembles court masques in many ways, with its cast of goddesses, its formal singing and dancing, and the ceremonial quality of the occasion it celebrates.

Masques were an elaborate and expensive entertainment; some were performed on special state occasions. Jonson's *Hymenaei* (1605) celebrated the marriage of Lady Essex and *The Masque of Oberon* (1610) was written to celebrate Prince Henry's investiture as Prince of Wales, and all had important implications for the mythology of the Stuart dynasty. Because members of the royal and aristocratic families performed in the masques, the poet was challenged to devise a setting and dramatic narrative that were elevated enough for the courtly audience and to dignify the aristocratic performers. Each masque included several "grand masquing dances," which were performed by members of the court, often costumed as "characters" in the masque.

Jonson was by far the most renowned writer of masques, though the playwrights James Shirley, William Davenant (who became a critically important theater manager after the restoration of the monarchy in 1660), and others also wrote masques. Jonson wrote more than a dozen masques, and in the course of his long career innovated the genre in several ways. While the earlier Stuart masques tend to have a relatively simple narrative, later masques, beginning with *The Masque of Queens* (1609), adopted a more complicated structure. *The Masque of Queens* begins with an **ANTIMASQUE,** a scene involving witches, goblins, or demons who are magically transformed into goddesses or allegorical virtues in the course of the action.

His majesty, then, being set, and the whole company in full expectation, the part of the scene which first presented itself was an ugly hell, which flaming beneath, smoked unto the top of the roof. And in respect all evils are, morally said to come from hell, . . . these witches, with a kind of hollow and infernal music, came forth from thence. First one, then two, and three, and more, till their number increased to eleven, all differently attired: some with rats on their head, some on their shoulders; others with ointment pots at their girdles; all with spindles, timbrels, rattles or other venefical [having to do with witchcraft] instruments, making a confused noise, with strange gestures.

The witches dance and pronounce a series of charms until, suddenly, "with a strange and sudden music,"

they fell into a magical dance full of preposterous change and gesticulation. . . . In the heat of their dance on the sudden was heard a sound of loud music, as if many instruments had made one blast; with which not only the hags themselves but the hell into which they ran quite vanished, and the whole face of the scene altered, scarce suffering the memory of such a thing. But in the place of it appeared a glorious and magnificent building figuring the House of Fame, in the top of which were discovered the twelve masquers sitting upon a throne triumphal erected in form of a pyramid and circled with all store of light. From whom a person, by this time descended, in the furniture of Perseus, and expressing heroic and masculine virtue began to speak.[1]

The antimasque establishes a world of demonic disorder, which suddenly vanishes when the members of the court appear in the House of Fame, among classical heroes and virtues. We can get a sense of the delicacy of Jonson's situation when we recognize that the performers of the masque included the queen herself, as well as the countesses of Arundel, Derby, Huntington, Bedford, Essex, and Montgomery, Viscountess Cranborne, and several ladies in waiting. Members of the court were both performers and the audience of this self-enclosed spectacle, which almost of necessity reflected back on its audience an idealized vision of courtly perfection. Indeed, in the last Stuart masque, *Salmacida Spolia,* written by Davenant, both the king and the queen were among the dancers.

As an ambitious writer, Jonson thought the masques were essentially a vehicle for his splendid poetry. But as even this brief description suggests, the masques were highly dependent on the development of new scenic technology and on the skills of the architect and designer Inigo Jones (1573–1652). The masques were unusually expensive: one of King James's masques cost more than £4,000, and one of King Charles's cost £21,000. Much of

---

[1]From *Ben Jonson: Selected Masques,* ed. Stephen Orgel (New Haven, CT: Yale University Press, 1970).

this money was spent on the elaborate, changeable scenery that accompanied the masques, the first changeable scenery in the English theater. Inigo Jones designed the theater space where masques were performed, the banqueting hall of Whitehall Palace. Jones had visited Italy in 1600; he may have visited again during 1607–1608, and he is known to have been in Italy from 1613 to 1615. In Italy he came into contact with the theater designs of Andrea Palladio (1518–1580), who adapted the design of classical Roman theaters for indoor stages: Palladio's Teatro Olimpico had a curved amphitheater-like auditorium and a proscenium stage. As court architect and designer, Jones had the opportunity both to import Palladio's understanding of theatrical design, and to develop his own interest in elaborate spectacle. The stage at Whitehall was about forty feet wide by twenty-eight feet deep, and gently raked. Although Jones's theater at Whitehall changed during his long tenure at court, it eventually consisted of staggered wings and a backdrop to convey a sense of perspective. Unlike both the public and private theaters of Renaissance London, Jones's theater was the first to use changeable scenery, and when the theaters reopened in 1660, the English companies brought this aristocratic inheritance with them: Jones's **WINGS-AND-BACKDROP** designs became the basic model for changeable scenery throughout the eighteenth century.

Jones's interest in spectacle was far reaching, and he devised the instruments to execute many of Jonson's most elaborate poetic images: flying machines, a globe that opened to reveal several aristocratic dancers, and brilliant costumes to dress the masques' allegorical characters. But it was Jones's development of a perspective in the theater that was most deeply implicated in the rhetoric of court life. At Whitehall performances, the King sat on a raised, central dais directly in front of the stage; since none of the other courtiers could be seated with their backs to the King,

FIERY SPIRIT

Inigo Jones created this costume for a fiery spirit in 1635.

those closer to the stage were seated along the side walls of the room, while others were seated behind the royal spectator. It has been argued that the king was positioned in a complex relation to the stage and to the rest of the audience: not only was he the only spectator for whom the illusion of perspective was complete (the other spectators could probably see between the wings, for example), but the rest of the audience could *see* that only the king had a perfect vision of the world onstage. The closer one sat to the royal seat, the more one's view of the illusion onstage approximated the king's ideal vantage. Spectators and performers, in other words, engaged in a richly hierarchical sense of illusion in which the King's centrality—and, in a sense, his omniscience—was constantly displayed, and each spectator's distance from that sense of illusion was constantly experienced. Like Jonson, whose texts frequently betray his intense

awareness of his royal audience and aristocratic performers, Jones's perspective theater reflects the increasingly absolutist ideology of the Stuart monarchy.

The banqueting hall at Whitehall played one more ironic role in the history of performance. Charles I became increasingly hostile to Parliament—he refused to call Parliament from 1629 to 1640—and when civil war broke out in 1642, Charles fled London. The Royalist forces were concentrated in Oxford, and in 1647 Charles was defeated and captured by the Parliamentary army. In 1649, he was sentenced to death by Parliament, and he visited the Whitehall banquet hall on his way to his execution. The executioner's block was set on a large public stage outside a window of the banquet hall; Charles was led through the room where the masques' brilliant fantasies had been staged for him to his own last performance—the public stage where he was beheaded.

COSTUMES FOR SHAKESPEARE'S *TITUS ANDRONICUS*

Dating from about 1595, this drawing appears to show a scene from *Titus Andronicus,* by William Shakespeare.
Two of the actors wear pseudoclassical Roman costumes; the others are dressed in Elizabethan clothing.

female characters and therefore on the performance of the boy actors. Indeed, the drama frequently uses cross-dressing as a way of interrogating the power and perquisites of gender, in ways that sometimes confirm and sometimes question the role of gender in English society. English society was an overtly hierarchical one, and despite the power of the "Virgin Queen," women had little access to education, most could not hold property, and they were generally subject to discrimination of many kinds. In this social economy and in a theater in which Puritan opposition to the stage frequently criticized the theater's "effeminacy," the absence of women from the stage became a powerful sign of their absence from other scenes of power. Much as sumptuary laws prevented individuals from wearing jewels and clothing above their social station, so too was cross-dressing a legal offense in sixteenth-century England, punishable by whipping and a prison sentence. The license of the theater, the freedom to create magical new worlds on the stage, was, like other forms of power in the period, the prerogative of men, and the images that men created for the stage are in important ways imprinted with the signs of a specifically masculine imagination. As with all stage conventions, cross-dressing was deeply implicated in the values of the culture outside the theater, so much so that when women did perform onstage in England—a French company used actresses at Blackfriars in 1629—they met with hostility, ridicule, and rejection.

Nonetheless, women not only attended the theater, but a few—aristocratic women, who often patronized poets and other artists—also wrote plays, and sometimes performed in them at court. Queen Elizabeth is thought to have translated a passage from Seneca's *Hercules on Mount Oeta,* and other women similarly adapted or wrote plays. Mary Sidney, Countess of Pembroke and sister of Sir Philip Sidney, translated Robert Garnier's play *The Tragedy of Antonie* in the 1590s. Her niece, Lady Mary Wroth (daughter of Mary Sidney's brother, Robert, and a frequent participant in Jacobean court masques), wrote a mythological play,

Love's Victory, probably in the early 1620s. Perhaps the best-known plays today are Elizabeth Cary, Viscountess of Falkland's *Tragedy of Miriam* (published in 1613) and the plays published by Margaret Cavendish, Marchioness of Newcastle, in 1662 and 1668. Although these plays were not staged—aristocratic women did not traffic in theater business—they have since become a critical part of our understanding of English Renaissance drama.

The theater had an extraordinary hold on the English imagination. In their many progresses, pageants, and allegorical entertainments, the English monarchs revealed a keen sense of the power of fictive images to represent reality, or a version of it, and so to shape their subjects' understanding of royal power. Playwrights and audiences also found in the theater a magical image of human possibility. Think of Prospero summoning the storm, Ariel, and other spirits with his stagey magic; or of the playwright John Webster's description of "an excellent actor": "All men have been of his occupation, and indeed what he doth feignedly, that do others essentially: this day one plays a Monarch, the next a private person. Here one acts a Tyrant, on the morrow an Exile; a Parasite [sponger] this man tonight, tomorrow a Precisian [Puritan], and so of divers others." Acting and the theater provided a liberating image of human—or, at least, masculine—power: the power to transform oneself and the world. However, the rich, strange, transforming freedom of the theater could also seem empty and terrifying, even demonic. Rather than an image of human potential, the theater could seem to offer an image of the poverty of human action, the sterile and deceptive emptiness of the world we make and inhabit. As King Lear preaches to blinded Gloucester, "When we are born, we cry that we are come / To this great stage of fools." Puritan critics of the theater insistently reminded audiences that the stage's methods—to seduce with the vain and showy image of a false reality—were also Satan's, and that the theater subversively invited audiences to "unman, unChristian, uncreate themselves." Yet it is precisely this transforming power that lies at the heart of the Renaissance theater's fascination for its audience. Although the theater sometimes seemed to depict a world threatened with constant change and loss, it also presented the power of illusion to recreate the real.

MEDIEVAL AND RENAISSANCE DRAMA IN PERFORMANCE AND HISTORY

Although the banning of the cycle dramas in England in the sixteenth century marked an ending of the traditions of medieval drama and theater there, the same was not true on the continent, where both cycle dramas and morality dramas continued to be performed. In Spain, for example, the **AUTOS SACRAMENTALES**—morality plays on Christian themes—were produced in major cities such as Madrid, and had an important influence on dramatic writing as well (see Unit IV). Similarly, staging short pageants—like the shepherd plays or *pastorelas* performed today throughout Latin America, and in many Latino communities in the United States, before Christmas—has remained a part of religious festivities in many places; perhaps the most striking of these is the processional staging of the Passion held in Oberammergau, Germany.

In many respects, though, the vivid and popular style of the cycle plays had to wait until the late nineteenth and early twentieth centuries to find an audience; when the manuscripts of the four English cycles first began to be studied seriously in the nineteenth century, their plays were seen merely as primitive precursors to the more finished, literary achievement of English Renaissance dramatists. However, this model of the "evolution" of dramatic forms, from "simple" to "complex," is not really borne out by a close examination of the plays themselves, which use a popular literary and theatrical medium to undertake a drama of enormous subtlety, scope, and power. Beginning in the twentieth century, a number of efforts were made to stage medieval drama—both the cycle plays and morality plays, such as *Everyman*—and the force and theatrical vitality of the plays became immediately apparent. In recent years, the cycle plays have been staged frequently, both in their traditional locations (at York, for instance), and elsewhere: the University of Toronto and the Court Theater at the University of Chicago have mounted very well received versions.

Although the English theaters were closed in 1642, interrupting the practices both of playwriting and of theatrical performance, the secular drama of Renaissance England has had in many respects a more sustained tradition. When the theaters reopened in 1660, they reopened in a very different form—indoor theaters, using lights and stage machinery, replaced the outdoor public theaters of the Jacobean and Caroline periods—and to a much more narrowly circumscribed audience (see Unit IV). And while there was considerable demand for new plays, for many years some plays of the Renaissance period held the stage, and indeed provided the dramatic conventions on which new plays were mapped. While today we tend to think of Shakespeare as the preeminent writer of his era, in the Restoration period, Shakespeare's plays were revived less frequently than those of other playwrights, notably Ben Jonson, James Shirley, and Francis Beaumont and John Fletcher; it was only in the eighteenth century that Shakespeare's plays began to have something approaching their current popularity.

The history of Shakespeare in the theater, however, is a history of adaptation: the concept that Shakespeare's plays have an inner logic and should be performed "as they were written" is a purely modern idea. Shakespeare's plays were, of course, altered in the practice of his own company, and playwrights in the later seventeenth and eighteenth centuries adapted the plays to the taste of their era. John Dryden, for example, transformed Shakespeare's erotically supercharged Antony and Cleopatra into an honorable Roman and his staid matron in his version of *Antony and Cleopatra,* called *All for Love* (1677). Nahum Tate's version of Shakespeare's *King Lear* (1681) concludes with Edgar marrying Cordelia (yes, she lives) and retiring happily offstage with Lear (he lives, too) and Kent; this version of *Lear* held the stage well into the nineteenth century. Rather than regarding these revisions as quaintly misguided, we should recognize that theatrical production always rewrites the drama in the idiom of the day; to their audiences, these productions were fully "Shakespearean," just as recent films—Kenneth Branagh's setting of *Hamlet* in the nineteenth century, Baz Luhrmann's framing *Romeo and Juliet* as a gang war in a Latin American Verona, or Michael Almereyda's use of Ethan Hawke as an alienated, technologically adept modern New Yorker in his *Hamlet*—are efforts to make Shakespeare speak in ways that will be powerful to audiences today.

Indeed, today we tend to think of Shakespeare across a variety of media: in film and television and advertising as well as in a range of theatrical venues. But for the seventeenth, eighteenth, and nineteenth centuries, Shakespeare was the property of the theater, and many actors and actresses became famous for their portrayals of Shakespearean roles: Thomas Betterton (1635–1710), Charles Macklin (1700–1797), Sarah Siddons (1755–1831), Edmund Kean (1789–1833), Sir Henry Irving (1838–1905), the first English actor to be knighted, and Ellen Terry (1847–1928) are just a few. In many respects, though, David Garrick (1717–1779) had the greatest impact as a Shakespearean actor. In part through his celebrated performances—he was renowned as Hamlet, Macbeth, and Richard III—Garrick helped to create a new interest in Shakespeare in the theater: he had his portrait painted frequently in Shakespearean roles (Hogarth's painting of Garrick as Richard III is a famous example), and he used his popularity to advance Shakespeare's reputation, not least by staging a Shakespeare Jubilee in Stratford. Garrick was a friend of the great literary critic Samuel Johnson, and Garrick's efforts in the theater coincided with a series of attempts to produce better, more accurate editions of Shakespeare's plays. But although Garrick had the reputation of restoring "Shakespeare's" original texts to the stage, he could hardly hope to succeed in the face of a century of popular stage adaptations. Although Garrick did introduce some Shakespearean material that had previously been cut from performances, his King Lear survived the play just as Nahum Tate's did, and his Richard III bawled out—as he had ever since Colley Cibber revised the play in 1700—"Off with his head!" (Indeed, Cibber's version of *Richard III* cuts several characters and persisted on-stage well into the twentieth century; it also partly informs Laurence Olivier's film of the play.)

The stage production of Shakespearean drama has always responded to the beliefs and values of its contemporary audiences. Tate's adaptation of *King Lear* was praised by Johnson, for example, for its happy ending seemed to restore justice in the theater; Johnson thought Shakespeare's original ending fine for readers, but too bleak and destructive for the stage. Shakespeare's plays were adapted to the more melodramatic and sentimental tastes of the eighteenth century; in the nineteenth century, a vogue for historical accuracy and stage realism led to a series of splendid efforts to reconstruct the historical setting of the plays: medieval Scotland in Charles Kean's 1853 *Macbeth* or Christian-era England in Henry Irving's *Cymbeline* (1896). These changes in taste are reflected in acting style as well: Betterton's portrayal of Hamlet was renowned in the late seventeenth century for its gravity and grace; Betterton is said never to have raised his arms above his waist, an illustration of neoclassical decorum in performance. By the early decades of the nineteenth century, Samuel Taylor Coleridge remarked that watching Edmund Kean in performance was akin to reading Shakespeare "by flashes of lightning"; Kean's performance impressed his audiences precisely through his well-crafted *lack* of decorum, in accord with Romantic beliefs about emotional expressivity. Irving is in many ways the first modern actor in what we would recognize as a psychological tradition of acting; although his career preceded the Russian director Constantin Stanislavski's pioneering work on the style of realistic performance (see Unit V), Irving's penchant for subtle physical details of characterization—his enemies called them mannerisms—gave his work a psychological concreteness and complexity that was powerful to an audience whose understanding of dramatic character was trained on the novels of Charles Dickens and George Eliot.

The theater also registers its culture's changing social attitudes in its portrayal of Shakespearean roles. Charles Macklin, for example, was probably the first actor to take a more sympathetic portrayal of the Jewish moneylender Shylock in *The Merchant of Venice;* the role had traditionally been performed as a satiric stereotype. Yet even Macklin retained the comic red wig and beard with which Shylock had always been performed; Edmund Kean was the first actor to get rid of them. Henry Irving's production of the play ended after the Act IV trial scene: in his version, *The Merchant of Venice* becomes something more like "The Tragedy of Shylock." In 1994, Peter Sellars set the play in a version of Los Angeles and drew explicit parallels to the police beating of Rodney King and the uprising that followed the acquittal of the officers involved. In Sellars's production the play's Jews were all played as African Americans; the Venetians were all played as Latinos and Latinas; and Portia and her retinue were all played as Asian Americans. Although Sellars's production was deservedly controversial, it illustrates a sense that Shakespeare's drama is capable of entering into new situations unimagined by Shakespeare, and of saying new things as well.

In the twentieth century, the pictorial style favored by Victorian theaters has largely been replaced in an effort to stage the plays in the simpler style of Shakespeare's theater. The first experiments of this kind were undertaken by William Poel (1852–1934), who used his Elizabethan Stage Society to produce versions of *Twelfth Night* and other plays on an open stage, and using a text more closely approximating Shakespeare's. Poel made it possible to see Shakespeare's plays as lively and fast-moving (all those scene changes in Victorian productions had made a Shakespeare play a very long evening, requiring many cuts to compensate for all the time it took to raise and lower sets), and regardless of whether directors (a new role in the theater also dating to this period) have chosen to stage the plays in Elizabethan or other settings, the sense of a rapidly changing series of scenes, localized not by extensive sets onstage but by the language and action, informs most twentieth-century Shakespeare. Indeed, it is often said that filmic techniques—quick cutting between scenes made possible by camera work and editing—provided a means to understand how Shakespearean drama might be played differently onstage.

It is now possible to see a range of Shakespeares on the contemporary stage—not only Shakespeare performed in languages other than English, but through the eclectic range of theatrical styles characteristic of the modern stage. Some productions—the "restored" versions, such as the 1997 *Henry V,* at Shakespeare's Globe in London—work hard to use Elizabethan costumes to produce the flavor of Shakespeare's theater. Other productions set the plays in a different historical era (there have been several recent *Henry V* productions set in the American Civil War, for example) to make the workings of the play's society visible to us in more familiar circumstances. Still others use eclectic staging, combining set and costume elements from a variety of periods to take Shakespeare out of history—in the Royal Shakespeare Company's 1991 *Troilus and Cressida,* for example, Agamemnon appeared in a breastplate and a ratty old cardigan sweater: a kind of timeless image of the doddering old general.

Of course, the ability of the modern stage to bring a great technological flexibility to Shakespeare is matched by the possibilities of film. Shakespeare plays were among the first subjects of silent filmmakers, and many of the most distinguished films of the twentieth century are versions of Shakespearean drama. Indeed, contemporary students of Shakespeare are often much more likely to see a Shakespeare film than a live Shakespeare performance, especially with the number of exciting Shakespeare films produced in the 1990s: Kenneth Branagh in *Henry V, Much Ado About Nothing,* and *Hamlet;* Ian McKellan in *Richard III;* Mel Gibson in *Hamlet;* Leonardo Di Caprio and Claire Danes in *Romeo + Juliet.* As a part of the common cultural inheritance of the West—and indeed, frequently challenged as such by resistant, postcolonial productions in India, Canada, Africa, and elsewhere—Shakespeare is produced today across the spectrum of performance.

Michael Pennington appears as Hamlet in the Royal Shakespeare Company production, 1980.

In this scene from an American Shakespeare Theater production of *The Tempest,* Ariel describes how he has performed Prospero's commands.

As the "cavalier" costumes suggest, John Gielgud's acclaimed 1934 production of *Hamlet* was set in the later seventeenth century, rather than in the Elizabethan era; here, Hamlet and Laertes duel in the play's final scene.

READING THE MATERIAL THEATER

One of the most chastening facts concerning the early modern theater is that most of the drama performed on its stages has been lost: plays were given to the theater companies in handwritten manuscript; they were copied out by hand into parts—scrolls containing each actor's part, with cues for each of his speeches—and the copy of the play maintained by the company was, likewise, a handwritten copy. Needless to say, nearly all such manuscripts have been lost.

Although by the later sixteenth century typesetting was a familiar technology in Renaissance England, the proliferation of printed documents —volumes of classical Latin texts, broadsides, ballads, religious pamphlets, guides to domestic work, conduct books for courtiers—presented Shakespeare's audiences with an information explosion much akin to the one we face in the digital age. At the same time, print was not understood to be an appropriate vehicle for all forms of writing. Poets, for example, saw print—associated with declassé mercantile world—as an inferior mode for circulating their poems: to gain the kind of aristocratic prestige (and patronage) they most desired, poets typically circulated their poems in manuscript among the aristocrats at court.

Beyond that, printing was a relatively expensive endeavor, and theater companies—who owned the text of the play, having purchased it from the playwright—had little incentive to publish a successful play. Yet plays were published, frequently in a small, inexpensive format; because the sheet of paper on which the text is printed is folded twice (into four) before the book is bound, these small books are known bibliographically as **QUARTOS.** Because of their size, the sometimes slipshod character of their presswork, and their association with the theater, quarto volumes of plays were also stigmatized; Sir Thomas Bodley—whose library, the Bodleian, remains the Oxford University library—famously refused to purchase such "idle riffe-raffes" for his collection. Since quarto-sized volumes of individual plays were usually published in very small quantities, they are today quite rare.

Many of Shakespeare's plays were published in quarto form during his lifetime (*Hamlet,* for example, was published in two very different quarto versions), but nearly half of his plays—including *Macbeth, Antony and Cleopatra, The Tempest* and others—would be unknown to us without the efforts of two of his fellow-sharers, John Heminges and Henry Condell, who published a nearly complete collection of Shakespeare's plays (in the large-size **FOLIO** format) in 1623, seven years after the playwright's death. This was a signal event in the history of dramatic publishing—in 1623, only one other English dramatist, Ben Jonson, had published a collected *Works* on this scale.

We can learn a lot about the condition of the theater and about the relationship between theater practice and the emerging norms of print culture by closely examining the printed texts of Shakespeare's plays in both quarto and folio versions. Here, for example, is the title page of *Titus Andronicus,* one of Shakespeare's earliest successes, a play that has recently been adapted for film by the director and designer Julie Taymor, and a play that testifies to the fascination that Senecan drama held for playwrights and audiences in the 1580s and 1590s. It is a violent, rhetorically rich play. What can we learn about the theater, and about Renaissance attitudes toward theater, drama, and literature, from this title page? Some aspects to consider: How is the page designed? What are its most prominent visual features? How are different typefaces used to highlight different kinds of information? How is the book designed to appeal to a potential purchaser? What elements are visually prominent and which are less prominent? Is there information missing that might seem necessary to a modern purchaser? How can we read the information presented here as an index of the relation between two newly emerging industries—professional theater and literary publishing—in the period?

THE MOST LAmentable Romaine Tragedie of Titus Andronicus:

As it was Plaide by the Right Honourable the Earle of *Darbie,* Earle of *Pembrooke,* and Earle of *Suffex* their Seruants.

LONDON,

Printed by Iohn Danter, and are to be fold by *Edward White* & *Thomas Millington,* at the little North doore of Paules at the figne of the Gunne.

1594.

THE WAKEFIELD SECOND SHEPHERDS' PAGEANT

The cycle of Corpus Christi plays performed in the Yorkshire town of Wakefield is one of the best known of the cycles, not least due to the influence of an unknown writer known now as "the Wakefield Master." But while there is considerable information about the performance of the cycles in Chester and in York, much less is known about performance at Wakefield. In York, for example, each play in the Corpus Christi cycle was probably performed on a separate pageant wagon; the wagons were arranged in the order of the plays—from the first play, *The Fall of the Angels,* to the last, *The Last Judgment*—and proceeded through the city, stopping at each of twelve stations. Although we know that this procession began at 4:30 in the morning and proceeded until past midnight, scholars are still not entirely clear on the logistics of the entire cycle's performance.

The data recording productions at Wakefield are much sketchier than for York; Martial Rose suggests in his book, *The Wakefield Mystery Plays,* that the plays might have been staged at Wakefield in a different way. After a procession through the city, the wagons might have been brought to a single location—a square, or perhaps before the cathedral—where all the plays could be performed in sequence for a single audience. As in other towns, however, each pageant could have been performed by a different guild, and the guild would have had the responsibility both for developing the text of the play, and for maintaining appropriate costumes and properties, as well as the pageant wagon. However, the single surviving manuscript of the plays from Wakefield (usually called the Towneley manuscript) is somewhat less complete than the records of other towns: only three of the pageants are specifically assigned to individual guilds.

But the Wakefield cycle is interesting for many other reasons, though, not least for the work of the "Wakefield Master," who probably wrote in the early part of the fifteenth century. Although many of the pageants in the Wakefield cycle are similar to those in York—Wakefield had once been a part of York—six of the pageants in the manuscript use an unusual nine-line stanza. Although it's not clear whether these pageants were originally composed by the same individual or merely revised by the same hand, they share similar stylistic elements and are usually attributed to a single author. As is the case in *The Second Shepherds' Pageant,* these plays are distinctive in their hard-nosed portrayal of the tough conditions of rural life in medieval England and are written in a pungent south Yorkshire dialect. The Wakefield Master is usually said to have written, revised, or contributed to the Wakefield *Killing of Abel* play (possibly produced by the Glovers' guild), its *Noah* play, two plays on the subject of the shepherds, and a brilliant version of *The Buffeting of Christ.*

The Second Shepherds' Pageant is typical of the medieval cycle plays in its insis-

In this scene from *The Second Shepherds' Play* Mak confronts one of the Shepherds.

tent counterpoint between the human world and the promise of eternal salvation, and this counterpoint is handled with the Wakefield Master's typical energy and subtlety. The first half of the play is a comedy, involving Mak's unsuccessful—and hilarious—attempt to pass off the lamb he has stolen from a group of local shepherds as his child; the second portion of the play begins with the Angel's appearance and summoning of the shepherds to Bethlehem. On one level, of course, the play's explicit parallel between Mak's lamb/child and the annunciation of the birth of Jesus, the Lamb of God, suggests a discontinuity between the tricky, trivial, and ultimately deceptive human world and the salvation that is to come. Indeed, it's a measure of the Wakefield Master's sure grasp of the sensibilities of his audience that this potentially blasphemous parody of the Nativity (Mak's wife swaddling the lamb to disguise it as their newborn baby) works not to undermine the miracle of the Christian narrative, but to distinguish the distractions of the fallen, human world from the powerful promise of salvation incarnated in the Nativity itself. The Angel appears to the shepherds at the moment they toss Mak in a blanket, and it should be noted that he does not accompany them to Bethlehem.

While *The Second Shepherds' Pageant* makes a searching formal comparison between human and divine events, it also uses anachronism in particularly effective ways: the Wakefield Master portrays the shepherds at the outset of the play not as long-ago characters in the faraway Holy Land; they are vividly characterized as the contemporaries of their medieval audience. We can hear the accents of a hard-working, overtaxed rural population irritated by their landed, supercilious masters throughout the opening moments of the play: when the First Shepherd complains of being "Fortaxed and rammed / We are made hand-tamed / With these gentlery-men" or when the Third Shepherd says that we "that sweats and swinks, / Eat our bread full dry, and that me forthinks. / We are oft wet and weary when mastermen winks." The plot of the play, in other words, enforces a formal contrast between the world of Mak and the promised deliverance of the Savior; in its insistent staging of the Christian narrative as something happening now, among us in its audience, the play forges a likeness between the past and the present, linking them together in a common Christian time. Like many cycle plays, the Wakefield *Second Shepherds' Pageant* asks its audience to contemplate the relationship between the eternal and the temporal by staging the Christian narrative in the everyday terms of medieval life.

THE WAKEFIELD SECOND SHEPHERDS' PAGEANT

Anonymous

CHARACTERS

FIRST SHEPHERD, *Coll*   WIFE OF MAK, *Gill*
SECOND SHEPHERD, *Gib*   ANGEL
THIRD SHEPHERD, *Daw*   MARY, *with the Christ-child*
MAK, *the Sheep-stealer*

SCENE ONE

The open fields.

1 SHEPHERD: Lord, what these weathers are cold! And I am
     ill happed.
    I am near-hand dold, so long have I napped;
    My legs they fold, my fingers are chapped,
    It is not as I would, for I am all lapped
5   In sorrow.
     In storms and tempest,
     Now in the east, now in the west,
     Woe is him has never rest
     Mid-day nor morrow!

10   But we sely husbands that walk on the moor,
    In faith, we are near-hands out of the door.
    No wonder, as it stands, if we be poor,
    For the tilth of our lands lies fallow as the floor,
    As ye ken.
15   We are so hammed,
     Fortaxed and rammed,
     We are made hand-tamed
     With these gentlery-men.

    Thus they reave us our rest, our Lady them wary!
20   These men that are lord-fast, they cause the plough tarry.
    That, men say, is for the best; we find it contrary.
    Thus are husbands oppressed, in point to miscarry
    On live.
     Thus hold they us under,
25   Thus they bring us in blunder;
     It were great wonder
     And ever should we thrive.

    For may he get a paint sleeve or a brooch, nowadays,
    Woe is him that him grieve, or once again-says!

Dare no man him repreve, what mastery he mays;   30
And yet may no man lieve one word that he says—
No letter.
He can make purveyance
With boast and braggance,
And all is through maintenance   35
Of men that are greater.

There shall come a swain as proud as a po;
He must borrow my wain, my plough also;
Then I am full fain to grant ere he go.
Thus live we in pain, anger, and woe   40
By night and day.
He must have, if he langed,
If I should forgang it;
I were better be hanged
Than once say him nay.   45

It does me good, as I walk thus by mine own,
Of this world for to talk in manner of moan.
To my sheep will I stalk and harken anon,
There abide on a balk, or sit on a stone
Full soon;   50
For I trow, pardie,
True men if they be,
We get more company
Ere it be noon.

(*Enter* SECOND SHEPHERD.)

2 SHEPHERD: Benste and Dominus, what may this bemean?   55
Why fares this world thus? Oft have we not seen.
Lord, these weathers are spitous, and the winds full keen,
And the frosts so hideous they water mine een—
No lie.
Now in dry, now in wet,   60
Now in snow, now in sleet,
When my shoon freeze to my feet
It is not all easy.

---

1 **what . . . happed** how cold this weather is! And I am poorly clad   2 **near-hand dold** nearly numb   3 **they fold** give way   4 **lapped** wrapped   10 **But . . . husbands** but we poor husbandmen   11 **we . . . door** we are nearly homeless   13 **tilth** arable part   15 **hammed** crippled   16 **fortaxed and rammed** overtaxed and crushed   17–18 **We . . . gentlery-men** we are reduced to submission by these gentry   19 **They . . . wary** they rob us of our rest, our Lady curse them!   20 **lord-fast** bound to a lord   22–23 **in . . . live** in danger of coming to mortal harm   25 **blunder** trouble   27 **ever** if   28 **For . . . brooch** if he is able to get an embroidered sleeve, i.e., a lord's livery   29 **again-says** gainsays

30 **Dare . . . mays** no man dare repreve him, no matter what force he uses   31 **lieve** believe   33 **He . . . purveyance** he can requisition [our belongings]   34 **braggance** bragging   35 **maintenance** support   37 **po** peacock   42–43 **He . . . it** he must have what he wants, even if I have to go without it   46 **mine own** myself   47 **moan** grumble   49 **balk** a strip of rough grassland dividing two ploughed portions of a common field   51 **pardie** by God   55 **Benste** benedicite (bless us); **bemean** mean   56 **oft . . . seen** we have not often seen the like   57 **spitous** cruel   58 **een** eyes

But as far as I ken, or yet as I go,
65 We sely wedmen dree mickle woe:
We have sorrow then and then; it falls oft so.
Silly Copple, our hen, both to and fro
She cackles;
But begin she to croak,
70 To groan or to cluck,
Woe is him our cock,
For he is in the shackles.

These men that are wed have not all their will;
When they are full hard sted, they sigh full still.
75 God wot they are led full hard and full ill;
In bower nor in bed they say nought theretill.
This tide
My part have I fun,
I know my lesson:
80 Woe is him that is bun,
For he must abide.

But now late in our lives—a marvel to me,
That I think my heart rives such wonders to see;
What that destiny drives it should so be—
85 Some men will have two wives, and some men three
In store;
Some are woe that have any.
But so far can I:
Woe is him that has many,
90 For he feels sore.

But, young men, of wooing, for God that you bought,
Be well ware of wedding, and think in your thought:
'Had I wist' is a thing that serveth of nought.
Mickle still mourning has wedding home brought,
95 And griefs,
With many a sharp shower;
For thou mayst catch in an hour
That shall sow thee full sour
As long as thou lives.

100 For, as ever read I epistle, I have one to my fere
As sharp as thistle, as rough as a briar.
She is browed like a bristle, with a sour-loten cheer;
Had she once wet her whistle, she could sing full clear
Her paternoster.

She is as great as a whale,   105
She has a gallon of gall;
By him that died for us all,
I would I had run to I had lost her!
1 SHEPHERD: God look over the raw! Full deafly ye stand,
2 SHEPHERD: Yea, the devil in thy maw, so tariand!   110
Saw'st thou awre of Daw?
1 SHEPHERD: Yea, on a lea-land
Heard I him blow. He comes here at hand,
Not far.
Stand still.
2 SHEPHERD: Why?
1 SHEPHERD: For he comes, hope I.   115
2 SHEPHERD: He will make us both a lie,
But if we beware.

(*Enter* THIRD SHEPHERD.)

3 SHEPHERD: Christ's cross me speed, and Saint Nicholas!
Thereof had I need; it is worse than it was.
Whoso could take heed and let the world pass,   120
It is ever in dread and brickle as glass,
And slithes.
This world fared never so,
With marvels mo and mo—
Now in weal, now in woe,   125
And all thing writhes.

Was never since Noah's flood such floods seen,
Winds and rains so rude, and storms so keen:
Some stammered, some stood in doubt, as I ween.
Now God turn all to good! I say as I mean,   130
For ponder:
These floods so they drown,
Both in fields and in town,
And bear all down;
And that is a wonder.   135

We that walk on the nights our cattle to keep,
We see sudden sights when other men sleep.
Yet methink my heart lights; I see shrews peep.
Ye are two all-wights—I will give my sheep
A turn.   140
But full ill have I meant;
As I walk on this bent,
I may lightly repent,
My toes if I spurn.

64–66 **But . . . then** but as far as I know or as my experience goes, we poor married men suffer much woe: we have sorrow time and again   71 **Woe . . . cock** unhappy is our cock   74 **When . . . still** when they are hard put to it they sigh unceasingly   76–79 **they . . . lesson** they never answer back. Now I've found out what I have to do   80 **bun** bound (in marriage)   81 **abide** remain so   83 **rives** breaks   84 **What . . . be** whatever destiny compels must come to pass   87 **woe** miserable   88 **can** know   90 **sore** pain   91 **But . . . bought** but young men, as for wooing, by God who redeemed you   92 **well ware** very wary   93 **Had . . . nought** 'If only I had known' is something that doesn't help you   94 **mickle** constant   96 **shower** pang   98 **That . . . sour** what shall grieve you most bitterly   100 **I . . . fere** I have one for my mate   102 **She . . . cheer** she has bristly brows and a sour-looking face

---

108 **to** till   109 **God . . . stand** God save the audience! You stand there as deaf as a post (the First Shepherd has evidently been trying to attract the other's attention)   110–112 **Yea . . . blow** the devil in your belly for tarrying so long! Have you seen Daw anywhere? . . . Yea, in a fallow field I heard him blow [his horn]   115 **hope** think   116 **make** tell   117 **if** unless   119 **it** i.e., the world   120–23 **Whose . . . so** anyone who could look on and let the world go by [would see that] it is always fearful and as brittle as glass, and slides away (that is, is transitory). But the world never behaved in this way before   124 **mo** more   126 **writhes** changes   129 **ween** fear   131 **ponder** consider   138 **lights** grows light; **shrews** rogues   139 **all-wights** monsters   139–144 **I . . . spurn** I will turn my sheep away. But I have been ill disposed [to the shepherds], as I walk on this field, I may stub my toes in easy penance

145   Ah, sir, God you save, and master mine!
      A drink fain would I have, and somewhat to dine.
      1 SHEPHERD: Christ's curse, my knave, thou art a lither hine!
      2 SHEPHERD: What, the boy list rave! Abide unto syne;
      We have made it.
150   Ill thrift on thy pate!
      Though the shrew came late,
      Yet is he, in state
      To dine—if he had it.

      3 SHEPHERD: Such servants as I, that sweat and swinks,
155   Eat our bread full dry, and that me forthinks.
      We are oft wet and weary when master-men winks;
      Yet come full lately both dinners and drinks.
      But nately
      Both our dame and our sire,
160   When we have run in the mire,
      They can nip at our hire,
      And pay us full lately.

      But hear my truth, master: for the fare that ye make,
      I shall do thereafter—work as I take.
165   I shall do a little, sir, and among ever lake,
      For yet lay my supper never on my stomach
      In fields.
      Whereto should I threap?
      With my staff can I leap;
170   And men say 'Light cheap
      Litherly foryields.'

      1 SHEPHERD: Thou wert an ill lad to ride on wooing
      With a man that had but little of spending.
      2 SHEPHERD: Peace, boy, I bade. No more jangling,
175   Or I shall make thee full rad, by the heaven's king!
      With thy gauds—
      Where are our sheep, boy?—we scorn.
      3 SHEPHERD: Sir, this same day at morn
      I them left in the corn,
180   When they rang Lauds.

      They have pasture good, they cannot go wrong.
      1 SHEPHERD: That is right. By the rood, these nights are long!
      Yet I would, ere we yode, one gave us a song.
      2 SHEPHERD: So I thought as I stood, to mirth us among.
185   3 SHEPHERD: I grant.

---

147 **lither hine** lazy hind   148–149 **What . . . it** what, the boy is pleased to rave! Wait till later; we have finished it (i.e., our meal)   150 **thrift** luck   152 **in state** ready   154 **swinks** toil   155 **for-thinks** displeases   156 **winks** sleep   157 **full lately** tardily   158 **nately** thoroughly   161 **They . . . hire** they can stint our wages   163–167 **But . . . fields** but hear my promise, master: in return for the food you provide, I shall do accordingly work as I'm paid. I shall do but little, sir, and betweenwhiles play all the time   168 **threap** haggle   170–173 **Light . . . spending** 'A cheap bargain repays badly.' . . . You'd be the wrong lad for anyone that's hard up to take a-wooing with him (cf. *Othello* 3.3.71)   174–177 **Peace . . . boy** stop your wrangling, or I'll quickly make you, by the king of heaven. We scorn your pranks—where are our sheep, boy?   180 **Lauds** the first of the seven canonical offices, usually sung at daybreak   182 **rood** cross   183 **yode** went   184 **to . . . among** to gladden us meanwhile

---

      1 SHEPHERD: Let me sing the tenory.
      2 SHEPHERD: And I the treble so high.
      3 SHEPHERD: Then the mean falls to me.
      Let see how ye chant.

      (*They sing. Then* MAK *enters with a cloak covering his tunic.*)

      MAK: Now, Lord, for thy names seven, that made both moon   190
      and starns
      Well more than I can neven, thy will, Lord, of me tharns.
      I am all uneven; that moves oft my harns.
      Now would God I were in heaven, for there weep no bairns
      So still.
      1 SHEPHERD: Who is that pipes so poor?   195
      MAK: Would God ye wist how I foor!
      Lo, a man that walks on the moor,
      And has not all his will.
      2 SHEPHERD: Mak, where hast thou gone? Tell us tiding.
      3 SHEPHERD: Is he come? Then ilkone take heed to his thing.   200

      (*He takes* MAK's *cloak from him.*)

      MAK: What! I be a yeoman, I tell you, of the king,
      The self and the same, sond from a great lording,
      And sich.
      Fie on you! Go hence
      Out of my presence!   205
      I must have reverence.
      Why, who be ich?
      1 SHEPHERD: Why make ye it so quaint? Mak, ye do wrong.
      2 SHEPHERD: But, Mak, list ye saint? I trow that ye long.
      3 SHEPHERD: I trow the shrew can paint, the devil might him   210
      hang!
      MAK: I shall make complaint, and make you all to thwang
      At a word,
      And tell even how ye doth.
      1 SHEPHERD: But, Mak, is that sooth?
      Now take out that Southern tooth,   215
      And set in a turd!
      2 SHEPHERD: Mak, the devil in your eye! A stroke would I
      lene you.
      3 SHEPHERD: Mak, know ye not me? By God, I could teen you.
      MAK: God look you all three! Methought I had seen you.
      Ye are a fair company.   220
      1 SHEPHERD: Can ye now mean you?
      2 SHEPHERD: Shrew, peep!

---

186 **tenory** tenor   190–192 **Now . . . harns** now, Lord, by thy seven names, who made both moon and stars far more than I can name, thy will concerning me, Lord, is lacking. I am all at sixes and sevens; that often unsettles my brain   194 **still** incessantly   195 **Who . . . poor** who is it that cries so piteously?   196 **wist** knew; **foor** fared   199 **tiding** news   200 **ilkone** everyone   202 **sond** messenger   203 **sich** such like   208 **Why . . . quaint** why are you so uppish?   209 **But . . . long** but, Mak, do you want to play saint? I believe you do   210 **paint** deceive   211 **and . . . thwang** and have you all flogged   213 **doth** do   215 **Now . . . tooth** southern speech. (Mak has been trying to talk southern English)   216 **set** put   217 **lene** give   218 **teen** hurt   219 **look** save   220 **Can . . . you** can you remember now?   221 **peep** pry about

Thus late as thou goes,
What will men suppose?
And thou hast an ill noise
225   Of stealing of sheep.
    MAK: And I am true as steel, all men wot;
        But a sickness I feel that holds me full hot:
        My belly fares not well, it is out of estate.
    3 SHEPHERD: Seldom lies the devil dead by the gate.
230   MAK: Therefore
        Full sore am I and ill;
        If I stand stone-still,
        I eat not a needle
        This month and more.
235   1 SHEPHERD: How fares thy wife? By my hood, how fares she?
    MAK: Lies waltering—by the rood—by the fire, lo!
        And a house full of brood. She drinks well, too;
        Ill speed other good that she will do!
        But she
240   Eats as fast as she can,
        And ilk year that comes to man
        She brings forth a lakan—
        And, some years, two.

        But were I now more gracious, and richer by far,
245   I were eaten out of house and of harbour.
        Yet is she a foul dowse, if ye come near;
        There is none that trows nor knows a war
        Than ken I.
        Now will ye see what I proffer?
250   To give all in my coffer
        To-morn at next to offer
        Her head-masspenny.

    2 SHEPHERD: I wot so forwaked is none in this shire;
        I would sleep if I taked less to my hire.
255   3 SHEPHERD: I am cold and naked, and would have a fire.
    1 SHEPHERD: I am weary, forraked, and run in the mire—
        Wake thou!
    2 SHEPHERD: Nay, I will lie down by.
        For I must sleep, truly.
260   3 SHEPHERD: As good a man's son was I
        As any of you.

        But, Mak, come hither! Between shalt thou lie down.
    MAK: Then might I let you bedene of that ye would rown,
        No dread.

From my top to my toe, (*He recites a night-spell.*)   265
Manus tuas commendo,
Pontio Pilato.
Christ's cross me speed!

Now were time for a man that lacks what he would
To stalk privily then unto a fold,   270
And nimbly to work then, and be not too bold,
For he might abuy the bargain, if it were told
At the ending.
Now were time for to reel;
But he needs good counsel   275
That fain would fare well,
And has but little spending.

But about you a circle, as round as a moon,
To I have done what I will, till that it be noon,
That ye lie stone-still to that I have done;   280
And I shall say theretill of good words a fone:
'On height,
Over your heads, my hand I lift.
Out go your eyes! Fordo your sight!'
But yet I must make better shift,   285
And it be right.

Lord, what they sleep hard!—that may ye all hear.
Was I never a shepherd, but now will I lere.
If the flock be scared, yet shall I nip near.
How! draw hitherward! Now mends our cheer   290
From sorrow
A fat sheep, I dare say,
A good fleece, dare I lay.
Eft-quit when I may,
But this will I borrow.   295

(*He goes home with the sheep.*)

SCENE TWO

Mak's cottage.

MAK: How, Gill, art thou in? Get us some light.
WIFE: Who makes such din this time of the night?
    I am set for to spin; I hope not I might
    Rise a penny to win, I shrew them on height!
    So fares   5
    A housewife that has been,
    To be raised thus between.
    Here may no note be seen
    For such small chares.

---

223 **suppose** suspect   224 **noise** reputation   225 **Of** for
227 **full hot** severely   228 **estate** condition   229 **Seldom . . .
gate** seldom lies the devil dead by the roadside, i.e., appearances
may be deceptive   232–233 **If . . . needle** may I be turned to stone
if I have eaten a morsel   236 **waltering** sprawling   237 **brood**
children   238 **Ill speed** i.e., there is no hope of her doing much
else   241 **ilk** every   242 **lakan** baby   244 **gracious** prosperous
245 **harbour** home   246 **dowse** wench   247 **There . . . war**
there is none who believes [he knows] or [really] knows a worse
one   250–252 **To give . . . head-masspenny** tomorrow at the
latest to give all in my coffer as an offering for her soul   253 **for-
waked** wearied with waking   254 **if . . . hire** even if I should get
less wages   256 **forraked** worn out with walking   258 **by** near
by   262 **between** between us   263–264 **Then . . . dread** then
I might keep you from whispering what you want, no doubt

272–273 **For . . . ending** for he might pay dearly for it, if it
came to a final reckoning   274 **reel** move quickly   277
spending money   278 **circle** (magic) circle   279 **To till**   281
And . . . fone and I shall also say a few good words   282 **On
height** high   284–287 **Out . . . hard** 'Lose your power of
sight.' But yet I must make better efforts, if things are to come
right. Lord, how soundly they sleep!   288 **lere** learn   289 **yet
. . . near** yet I shall grab [a sheep] tightly   290–292 **Now . . .
sheep** now a fat sheep shall comfort us   294 **Eft-quit** repay
ii. 3–9 **I . . . chares** I don't think I can earn a penny by getting
up [from my spinning], curse them! Any woman who has been
a housewife knows what it means to be got up from her work
continually. I have no work to show because of such small chores

10 MAK: Good wife, open the heck! See'st thou not what I
        bring?
WIFE: I may thole thee draw the sneck. Ah, come in, my
        sweeting!
MAK: Yea, thou thar not reck of my long standing.
WIFE: By the naked neck art thou like for to hang.
MAK: Do way!
15   I am worthy my meat,
    For in a strait can I get
    More than they that swink and sweat
    All the long day.

    Thus it fell to my lot, Gill; I had such grace.
20 WIFE: It were a foul blot to be hanged for the case.
MAK: I have scaped, Jelott, oft as hard a glase.
WIFE: 'But so long goes the pot to the water,' men says,
    'At last
    Comes it home broken.'
25 MAK: Well know I the token,
    But let it never be spoken!
    But come and help fast.
    I would he were flain; I list well eat.
    This twelvemonth was I not so fain of one sheep-meat.
30 WIFE: Come they ere he be slain, and hear the sheep bleat—
MAK: Then might I be ta'en: that were a cold sweat!
    Go spar
    The gate-door.
WIFE: Yes, Mak,
    For and they come at thy back—
35 MAK: Then might I buy, for all the pack,
    The devil of the war.

    WIFE: A good bourd have I spied, since thou canst none:
    Here shall we him hide, till they be gone,
    In my cradle. Abide! Let me alone,
40   And I shall lie beside in childbed and groan.
MAK: Thou red,
    And I shall say thou wast light
    Of a knave-child this night.
WIFE: Now well is me day bright
45   That ever was I bred!

    This is a good guise and a far cast;
    Yet a woman's advice helps at the last.
    I wot never who spies; again go thou fast.
MAK: But I come ere they rise, else blows a cold blast!

---

10 **heck** inner door 11 **I . . . sneck** I will let you draw the
latch 12 **Yea . . . standing** you needn't mind about my standing [outside] so long 14 **Do way!** enough! 15 **meat** food
16 **strait** fix 17 **swink** toil 20 **blot** deed 21 **glase** blow
25 **token** portent 28–29 **I . . . meat** I wish he were skinned;
I am eager to eat. At no time this year have I been so glad of a
meal of mutton 32 **spar** fasten 33 **gate-door** enter door
34 **and** if 35–36 **Then . . . war** then I may get the devil of a
bad time from the whole pack of them 37 **bourd** jest; **canst**
knowest 41 **red** ready 42 **light** delivered 43 **knave-child**
boy 44–46 **Now . . . cast** I'm happy when I think of the
bright day I was born! This is a good method and a cunning trick
48 **again . . . fast** return again quickly [to the others] 49 **else**
unless

I will go sleep.   50
Yet sleep all this meny;
And I shall go stalk privily,
As it had never been I
That carried their sheep.

SCENE THREE

The open fields.

1 SHEPHERD: *Resurrex a mortuus!* have hold my hand!
    Judas carnas dominus! I may not well stand:
    My foot sleeps, by Jesus, and I walter fastand.
    I thought that we laid us full near England.
2 SHEPHERD: Ah, yea?   5
    Lord, what I have slept well!
    As fresh as an eel,
    As light I me feel
    As leaf on a tree.

3 SHEPHERD: Benste be herein! So me quakes,   10
    My heart is out of skin, what-so it makes.
    Who makes all this din? So my brow blakes,
    To the door will I win. Hark, fellows, wakes!
    We were four:
    See ye awre of Mak now?   15
1 SHEPHERD: We were up ere thou.
2 SHEPHERD: Man, I give God avow
    Yet yede he nawre.

3 SHEPHERD: Methought he was lapped in a wolf-skin.
1 SHEPHERD: So are many happed now—namely within.   20
3 SHEPHERD: When we had long napped, methought with a
        gin
    A fat sheep he trapped; but he made no din.
2 SHEPHERD: Be still!
    Thy dream makes thee wood;
    It is but phantom, by the rood.   25
1 SHEPHERD: Now God turn all to good,
    If it be his will.

2 SHEPHERD: Rise, Mak, for shame! Thou liest right long.
MAK: Now Christ's holy name be us among!
    What is this? For Saint Jame, I may not well gang!   30
    I trow I be the same. Ah, my neck has lain wrong
    Enough. (*They help him to get up.*)
    Mickle thank! Since yester-even,
    Now by Saint Stephen,
    I was flayed with a sweven—   35
    My heart out of slough.

---

51 **meny** company

iii. 3 **I . . . fastand** I'm tottering with hunger 5 **Ah, yea?** Oh,
really? 6 **Lord . . . well** how well I have slept! 10 **Benste** blessing 10–11 **So . . . makes** I tremble so much, my heart is in my
mouth, whatever the reason for it 12 **blakes** darkens 13 **win**
go; **wakes** wake up 15 **See . . . now?** have you seen Mak anywhere? 17–18 **Man . . . nawre** I vow to God he's gone nowhere
yet 20 **So . . . within** many are covered like that nowadays, especially underneath 21 **gin** snare 24 **wood** mad 30 **For
. . . Jame** by Saint James; **gang** walk 31–32 **Ah . . . Enough**
my neck has been lying very crookedly 35–36 **I . . . slough** I
was terrified by a dream—I nearly jumped out of my skin

I thought Gill began to croak and travail full sad,
Well-night at the first cock, of a young lad
For to mend our flock. Then be I never glad;
40   I have tow on my rock more than ever I had.
Ah, my head!
A house full of young tharms,
The devil knock out their harns!
Woe is him has many bairns,
45   And thereto little bread.

I must go home, by your leave, to Gill, as I thought.
I pray you look my sleeve, that I steal nought;
I am loath you to grieve or from you take aught.
3 SHEPHERD: Go forth, ill might thou chieve! Now would I
    we sought,
50   This morn,
That we had all our store.
1 SHEPHERD: But I will go before.
Let us meet.
2 SHEPHERD: Where?
3 SHEPHERD: At the crooked thorn.

SCENE FOUR

Mak's cottage.

MAK: Undo this door! Who is here? How long shall I stand?
WIFE: Who makes such a bere? Now walk in the wenyand!
MAK: Ah, Gill, what cheer? It is I, Mak, your husband.
WIFE: Then may we see here the devil in a band,
5   Sir Guile!
Lo, he comes with a lote,
As he were holden in the throat.
I may not sit at my note
A hand-long while.
10 MAK: Will ye hear what fare she makes to get her a glose?
And does naught but lakes, and claws her toes.
WIFE: Why, who wanders, who wakes? Who comes, who
    goes?
Who brews, who bakes? What makes me thus hoarse?
And then
15   It is ruth to behold—
Now in hot, now in cold,
Full woeful is the household
That wants a woman.

But what end hast thou made with the herds, Mak?
20 MAK: The last word that they said when I turned my back,
They would look that they had their sheep, all the pack.

I hope they will not be well paid when they their sheep
    lack,
Pardie!
But how-so the game goes,
To me they will suppose,   25
And make a foul noise,
And cry out upon me.

But thou must do as thou hight.
WIFE: I accord me theretill;
I shall swaddle him right in my cradle.
If it were a greater sleight, yet could I help till.   30
I will lie down straight. Come hap me.
MAK: I will.
WIFE: Behind!
Come Coll and his marrow,
They will nip us full narrow.
MAK: But I may cry 'Out, harrow!'   35
The sheep if they find.

WIFE: Harken ay when they call; they will come anon.
Come and make ready all, and sing by thine own;
Sing lullay thou shall, for I must groan,
And cry out by the wall on Mary and John,   40
For sore.
Sing lullay on fast,
When thou hearest at the last;
And but I play a false cast,
Trust me no more.   45

SCENE FIVE

The crooked thorn.

3 SHEPHERD: Ah, Coll, good morn! Why sleepest thou not?
1 SHEPHERD: Alas, that ever was I born! We have a foul blot—
A fat wether have we lorn.
3 SHEPHERD: Marry, God's forbot!
2 SHEPHERD: Who should do us that scorn? That were a foul
    spot.
1 SHEPHERD: Some shrew.   5
I have sought with my dogs
All Horbury shrogs,
And, of fifteen hogs,
Found I but one ewe.

3 SHEPHERD: Now trow me, if ye will—by Saint Thomas of 10
    Kent,
Either Mak or Gill was at that assent.

---

37 **full sad** hard   39 **mend** increase   40 **I . . . had** I have more
tow on my distaff (i.e., more trouble in store) than ever I had
42 **tharms** bellies   43 **harns** brains   46 **thought** intended
47 **look** examine   49 **chieve** prosper   49–51 **Now . . . store**
now I want us this morning to see that we have all our stock
iv. 2 **bere** din; **Now . . . wenyand** walk in the waning moon,
i.e., at an unlucky time   4 **band** noose   6 **lote** noise   7 **holden**
held my   8 **note** work   9 **hand-long** brief   10 **Will . . . glose**
will you listen to the fuss she makes in the hope of excusing herself?   11 **lakes** play   15 **ruth** a pity   16 **Now . . . cold** i.e., at
all times   18 **wants** lacks   19 **herds** shepherds

22 **hope** think; **well paid** pleased   24 **how-so** however   25
To . . . suppose they will suspect me   28 **hight** promised; **I .
. . theretill** I agree to that   30 **sleight** trick; **Yet . . . till** I could
still help with it   31 **straight** straightway; **hap** cover   33 **marrow** make   34 **narrow** hard   35 **Out, harrow!** a cry for help
39 **lullay** lullaby   41 **sore** pain   42 **on fast** quickly   44 **And
. . . cast** and if I don't play a false trick
v. 3 **lorn** lost; **God's forbot!** God forbid!   4 **scorn** insult; **spot**
disgrace   7 **Horbury** Horbury, near Wakefield; **shrogs** thickets
8–9 **And . . . ewe** among fifteen hogs (or young sheep) I found
only a ewe, i.e., the wether was missing   10 **Saint Thomas of
Kent** St. Thomas of Canterbury   11 **Either . . . assent** either
Mak or Gill was a party to it

1 SHEPHERD: Peace, man, be still! I saw when he went.
    Thou slander'st him ill; thou ought to repent
    Good speed.
15   2 SHEPHERD: Now as ever might I thee,
    If I should even here die,
    I would say it were he
    That did that same deed.

    3 SHEPHERD: Go we thither, I rede, and run on our feet.
20   Shall I never eat bread, the sooth to I wit.
    1 SHEPHERD: Nor drink in my head, with him till I meet.
    2 SHEPHERD: I will rest in no stead till that I him greet,
    My brother.
    One I will hight:
25   Till I see him in sight,
    Shall I never sleep one night
    There I do another.

SCENE SIX

Mak's cottage.

3 SHEPHERD: Will ye hear how they hack? Our sire list croon.
1 SHEPHERD: Heard I never none crack so clear out of tone.
    Call on him.
2 SHEPHERD: Mak, undo your door soon!
MAK: Who is it that spake, as it were noon,
5   On loft?
    Who is that, I say?
3 SHEPHERD: Good fellows, were it day.
MAK: As far as ye may,
    Good, speak soft,
10   Over a sick woman's head, that is at malease;
    I had liefer be dead ere she had any disease.
WIFE: Go to another stead! I may not well quease;
    Each foot that ye tread goes thorough my nose
    So high.
15   1 SHEPHERD: Tell us, Mak, if ye may,
    How fare ye, I say?
MAK: But are ye in this town to-day?
    Now how fare ye?

    Ye have run in the mire, and are wet yet;
20   I shall make you a fire, if ye will sit.
    A nurse would I hire. Think ye on yet?

Well quit is my hire—my dream, this is it—
A season.
I have bairns, if ye knew,
Well more than enew;
But we must drink as we brew,   25
And that is but reason.

I would ye dined ere ye yode. Methink that ye sweat.
2 SHEPHERD: Nay, neither mends our mood drink nor
    meat.
MAK: Why, sir, ails you aught but good?   30
3 SHEPHERD: Yea, our sheep that we gete
    Are stolen as they yode. Our loss is great.
MAK: Sirs, drink!
    Had I been there,
    Some should have bought it full sore.
1 SHEPHERD: Marry, some men trow that ye were,   35
    And that us forthinks.
2 SHEPHERD: Mak, some men trows that it should be ye.
3 SHEPHERD: Either ye or your spouse, so say we.
MAK: Now if ye have suspouse to Gill or to me,
    Come and rip our house, and then may ye see   40
    Who had her.
    If I any sheep fot,
    Either cow or stot—
    And Gill, my wife, rose not
    Here since she laid her—   45

    As I am true and leal, to God here I pray
    That this be the first meal that I shall eat this day.
1 SHEPHERD: Mak, as have I sele, advise thee, I say:
    He learned timely to steal that could not say nay.
WIFE: I swelt!   50
    Out, thieves, from my wones!
    Ye come to rob us for the nonce.
MAK: Hear ye not how she groans?
    Your hearts should melt.

WIFE: Out, thieves, from my bairn! Nigh him not there.   55
MAK: Wist ye how she had farn, your hearts would be sore.
    Ye do wrong, I you warn, that thus come before
    To a woman that has farn; but I say no more.
WIFE: Ah, my middle!
    I pray to God so mild,   60
    If ever I you beguiled,
    That I eat this child
    That lies in this cradle.

MAK: Peace, woman, for God's pain, and cry not so!
    Thou spillest thy brain, and makest me full woe.   65

---

14 **Good speed** quickly   15 **Now . . . thee** as I hope to prosper
19 **rede** advise   20 **the . . . wit** Till I know the truth   22 **stead**
place   23 **My brother** a friendly form of address   24 **One . . .**
hight one thing I will promise   27 **There** where
vi. 1 **Will . . . croon** do you hear them trilling? Our gentleman is
pleased to croon   2 **crack** bawl; **tone** tune   3 **soon** immediately
4–5 **Who . . . loft?** who is it that spoke aloud, as though it were
noon?   7 **were it** if only it were   9 **Good** good sirs   10–11 **Over**
. . . disease because of a sick woman who is in distress; I had rather
die than she should suffer any discomfort   12 **quease** breathe
13–14 **Each . . . high** every step you tread goes through my nose
so strongly, i.e., goes right through my head   21–23 **A nurse . . .**
season I would like to hire a nurse. Do you still remember [my
dream about a new addition to the family]? I've been paid my wages
in full for a while—this is my dream come true

---

25 **enew** enough   28 **yode** went   30 **Why . . . good** why, sir,
is anything wrong with you?; **gete** tend   34 **bought** paid for
36 **forthinks** displeases   37 **trows** believe   39 **suspouse** suspicion   40 **rip** ransack   42 **fot** fetched   43 **stot** heifer   46 **leal**
honest   48–49 **Mak . . . nay** Mak, as I hope for happiness, take
thought I say: he learned early to steal who could not say no [to
another's property]   50 **swelt** feel faint   51 **wones** house
52 **Ye . . . nonce** you come on purpose to rob us   55 **Nigh . . .**
there do not go near him there   56 **Wist . . . farn** if you knew
what she had been through   58 **To . . . farn** to a woman who
has been in labour   62 **eat** may eat   65 **spillest** injurest

2 SHEPHERD: I trow our sheep be slain. What find ye two?
3 SHEPHERD: All work we in vain; as well may we go.
> But hatters!
> I can find no flesh,
70 Hard nor nesh,
> Salt nor fresh,
> But two tome platters.

> Quick cattle but this, tame nor wild,
> None, as have I bliss, as loud as he smelled.
75 WIFE: No, so God me bless, and give me joy of my child!
1 SHEPHERD: We have marked amiss; I hold us beguiled.
2 SHEPHERD: Sir, don.
> Sir—our Lady him save!—
> Is your child a knave?
80 MAK: Any lord might him have,
> This child, to his son.

> When he wakens he kips, that joy is to see.
3 SHEPHERD: In good time to his hips, and in sely.
> But who were his gossips so soon ready?
85 MAK: So fair fall their lips!
1 SHEPHERD: (*Aside.*)   Hark now, a lie!
MAK: So God them thank,
> Parkin, and Gibbon Waller, I say,
> And gentle John Horne, in good fay—
> He made all the garray—
90 With the great shank.
2 SHEPHERD: Mak, friends will we be, for we are all one.
MAK: We? Now I hold for me, for mends get I none.
> Farewell all three!—all glad were ye gone.
3 SHEPHERD: Fair words may there be, but love is there none
95 This year. (*They leave the cottage.*)
1 SHEPHERD: Gave ye the child anything?
2 SHEPHERD: I trow not one farthing.
3 SHEPHERD: Fast again will I fling;
> Abide ye me there. (*He returns to the cottage.*)

100 Mak, take it to no grief, if I come to thy bairn.
MAK: Nay, thou dost me great reprief, and foul hast thou farn.
3 SHEPHERD: The child will it not grieve, that little day-starn
> Mak, with your leave, let me give your bairn
> But sixpence.

---

68 **hatters** confound it   70 **nesh** soft   72 **But** only; **tome** empty   73–74 **Quick . . . smelled** live stock but this (i.e., the 'baby' in the cradle), tame or wild, none [have I found], as I hope to be happy, that smelled as loud as he (i.e., the missing sheep)   76 **We . . . amiss** aimed wrongly, i.e., made a mistake   77 **don** completely   79 **knave** boy   82 **kips** snatches   83 **In . . . sely** a good and happy future to him   84 **gossips** godparents   85 **So . . . lips** good luck to them   88 **John Horne** the shepherd in the *First Shepherds' Pageant* who quarrels with Gib about the pasturing of an imaginary flock of sheep; **fay** good faith   89 **garray** commotion   90 **shank** long legs   91 **all one** agreed   92 **Now . . . none** for my own part, I'm holding back, for I get no amends   93 **all . . . gone** [I should be] very glad if you were gone (probably an aside)   98 **Fast . . . fling** I will dash back   100 **take . . . grief** don't take offence   101 **Nay . . . farn** nay, you do me great shame, and you have behaved badly   102 **day-starn** star

MAK: Nay, do way! He sleeps.   105
3 SHEPHERD: Methink he peeps.
MAK: When he wakens he weeps.
> I pray you go hence.

3 SHEPHERD: Give me leave him to kiss, and lift up the clout.

(*He glimpses the sheep.*)

> What the devil is this? He has a long snout!   110
1 SHEPHERD: He is marked amiss. We wait ill about.
2 SHEPHERD: Ill-spun weft, iwis, ay comes foul out.
> Aye, so! (*He recognizes the sheep.*)
> He is like to our sheep!
3 SHEPHERD: How, Gib, may I peep?   115
1 SHEPHERD: I trow kind will creep
> Where it may not go.

2 SHEPHERD: This was a quaint gaud and a far cast;
> It was a high fraud.
3 SHEPHERD: Yea, sirs, was't.
> Let burn this bawd and bind her fast.   120
> A false scold hangs at the last;
> So shalt thou.
> Will ye see how they swaddle
> His four feet in the middle?
> Saw I never in a cradle.   125
> A horned lad ere now.

MAK: Peace, bid I. What, let be your fare!
> I am he that him begat, and yond woman him bare.
1 SHEPHERD: What devil shall he hat, Mak? Lo, God, Mak's heir!
2 SHEPHERD: Let be all that. Now God give him care,   130
> I sagh.
WIFE: A pretty child is he
> As sits on a woman's knee;
> A dillydown, pardie,
> To gar a man laugh.   135

3 SHEPHERD: I know him by the ear-mark; that is a good token.
MAK: I tell you, sirs, hark! his nose was broken.
> Since told me a clerk that he was forspoken.
1 SHEPHERD: This is a false work; I would fain be wroken.
> Get weapon!   140
WIFE: He was taken with an elf,
> I saw it myself;
> When the clock struck twelve,
> Was he forshapen.
2 SHEPHERD: Ye two are well feft sam in a stead.   145

---

109 **clout** cloth   111–112 **He . . . out** he is misshapen. We do wrong to pry about . . . Ill-spun weft, indeed, always comes out badly, i.e., what is bred in the bone will come out in the flesh   116–118 **I . . . cast** nature will creep where it cannot walk, i.e., assert itself in one way or another . . . This was a clever dodge and a cunning trick   127 **fare** uproar   129 **he hat** be called   130 **care** sorrow   131 **I sagh** I saw [the sheep myself]   134 **dilly-down** darling   135 **gar** make   138 **forspoken** bewitched   139 **wroken** avenged   141 **with** by   144 **forshapen** transformed   145 **Ye . . . stead** you two are well endowed together in one place, i.e., are as clever a pair of rascals as ever lived under one roof

1 SHEPHERD: Since they maintain their theft, let do them to
    dead.
MAK: If I trespass eft, gird off my head.
    With you will I be left.
3 SHEPHERD: Sirs, do my rede:
    For this trespass
150   We will neither ban ne flite,
    Fight nor chide,
    But have done as tite,
    And cast him in canvas.

(*They toss* MAK *in a blanket.*)

SCENE SEVEN

The open fields.

1 SHEPHERD: Lord, what I am sore, in point for to burst!
    In faith, I may no more; therefore will I rest.
2 SHEPHERD: As a sheep of seven score he weighed in my fist.
    For to sleep aywhere methink that I list.
5 3 SHEPHERD: Now I pray you
    Lie down on this green.
1 SHEPHERD: On these thieves yet I mean.
3 SHEPHERD: Whereto should ye teen?
    Do as I say you.

(*An* ANGEL *sings 'Gloria in excelsis,' and then says:*)

10 ANGEL: Rise, herdmen hend, for now is he born
    That shall take from the fiend that Adam had lorn;
    That warlock to shend, this night is he born.
    God is made your friend now at this morn,
    He behests.
15   At Bedlem go see
    There lies that free
    In a crib full poorly,
    Betwixt two beasts.
1 SHEPHERD: This was a quaint steven that ever yet I heard.
20   It is a marvel to neven, thus to be scared.
2 SHEPHERD: Of God's son of heaven he spoke upward.
    All the wood on a leven methought that he gard
    Appear.
3 SHEPHERD: He spake of a bairn
25   In Bedlem, I you warn.
1 SHEPHERD: That betokens yond starn;
    Let us seek him there.

2 SHEPHERD: Say, what was his song? Heard ye not how he
    cracked it,

Three breves to a long?
3 SHEPHERD: Yea, marry, he hacked it:
    Was no crochet wrong, nor no thing that lacked it.   30
1 SHEPHERD: For to sing us among, right as he knacked it,
    I can.
2 SHEPHERD: Let see how ye croon.
    Can ye bark at the moon?
3 SHEPHERD: Hold your tongues! Have done!   35
1 SHEPHERD: Hark after, then.

(*Sings.*)

2 SHEPHERD: To Bedlem he bade that we should gang;
    I am full adrad that we tarry too long.
3 SHEPHERD: Be merry and not sad—of mirth is our song!
    Everlasting glad to meed may we fang   40
    Without noise.
1 SHEPHERD: Hie we thither forthy,
    If we be wet and weary,
    To that child and that lady;
    We have it not to lose.   45
2 SHEPHERD: We find by the prophecy—let be your din!—
    Of David and Isay, and more than I min—
    They prophesied by clergy—that in a virgin
    Should he light and lie, to sloken our sin,
    And slake it,   50
    Our kind, from woe;
    For Isay said so:
    Ecce virgo
    Concipiet a child that is naked.

3 SHEPHERD: Full glad may we be, and abide that day   55
    That lovely to see, that all mights may.
    Lord, well were me for once and for ay,
    Might I kneel on my knee, some word for to say
    To that child.
    But the angel said   60
    In a crib was he laid;
    He was poorly arrayed,
    Both meek and mild.

1 SHEPHERD: Patriarchs that have been, and prophets beforn,
    They desired to have seen this child that is born.   65
    They are gone full clean; that have they lorn.
    We shall see him, I ween, ere it be morn,
    To token.
    When I see him and feel,
    Then wot I full well   70
    It is true as steel

---

146 **dead** death 147 **eft** again; **gird** strike 148 **With . . .
rede** I throw myself on your mercy. . . . Take my advice
150 **ban** curse; **flite** quarrel 152 **as tite** at once
vii. 4 For . . . list I think I would be glad to sleep anywhere
7 **mean** think 8 **teen** vex yourself 10 **hend** gentle 12 **warlock** the devil; **shend** destroy 14 **behests** promises
15 **Bedlem** Bethlehem 16 **There** where; **free** noble one
19 **quaint steven** elegant voice 20 **neven** tell of 21 **upward**
on high 22–23 **All . . . Appear** I thought he made the whole
wood appear as if lit up by lightning 28 **cracked** sang

29 **hacked** trilled 30 **Was . . . it** No crochet was wrong, and
there was nothing it lacked 31 **knacked** sang 37 **gang** go
38 **adrad** afraid 40–41 **Everlasting . . . noise** we can get
everlasting joy as our reward without any fuss 42 **Hie** therefore
43 **If** even if 45 **We . . . lose** we must not forget it 47 **Isay**
Isaiah; **min** remember 48 **clergy** learning 49 **light** alight;
sloken quench 50 **slake** relieve 51 **kind** race 53–54 *Ecce
. . . Concipiet* behold, a virgin shall conceive 56–57 **That . . .
ay** to see that lovely one who is almighty. Lord, I would be happy
for once and all 64 **beforn** in the past 66 **They . . . lorn** that
chance have they lost 68 **token** as a sign

That prophets have spoken:
To so poor as we are that he would appear,
First find and declare by his messenger.
75 2 SHEPHERD: Go we now, let us fare; the place is us near.
3 SHEPHERD: I am ready and yare; go we in fere
To that bright.
Lord, if thy will be—
We are lewd all three—
80 Thou grant us some kins glee
To comfort thy wight.

SCENE EIGHT

The stable in Bethlehem.

1 SHEPHERD: Hail, comely and clean; hail, young child!
Hail, maker, as I mean, of a maiden so mild!
Thou hast waried, I ween, the warlock so wild:
The false guiler of teen, now goes he beguiled.
5 Lo, he merries,
Lo, he laughs, my sweeting!
A well fare meeting!
I have holden my heting:
Have a bob of cherries.
10 2 SHEPHERD: Hail, sovereign saviour, for thou hast us
sought!
Hail, freely food and flower, that all thing hast
wrought!
Hail, full of favour, that made all of nought!
Hail! I kneel and I cower. A bird have I brought
To my bairn.
15 Hail, little tiny mop!

Of our creed thou art crop;
I would drink on thy cop,
Little daystarn.
3 SHEPHERD: Hail, darling dear, full of Godhead!
I pray thee be near when that I have need.   20
Hail, sweet is thy cheer! My heart would bleed
To see thee sit here in so poor weed,
With no pennies.
Hail! Put forth thy dall!
I bring thee but a ball: 25
Have and play thee withal,
And go to the tennis.
MARY: The Father of heaven, God omnipotent,
That set all on seven, his Son has he sent.
My name could he neven, and light ere he went.   30
I conceived him full even through might, as he meant;
And now is he born.
He keep you from woe!—
I shall pray him so.
Tell forth as ye go,   35
And min on this morn.
1 SHEPHERD: Farewell, lady, so fair to behold,
With thy child on thy knee.
2 SHEPHERD: But he lies full cold.
Lord, well is me! Now we go, thou behold.
3 SHEPHERD: Forsooth, already it seems to be told   40
Full oft.
1 SHEPHERD: What grace we have fun!
2 SHEPHERD: Come forth; now are we won!
3 SHEPHERD: To sing are we bun:
Let take on loft.   45

---

74 **First . . . messenger** find [us] first of all, and make known [his birth] through his messenger   76 **yare** eager; **in fere** together   77 **bright** bright one   79 **lewd** simple   80–81 **Thou . . . wight** grant us some joyful way of comforting thy child **viii.** 1 **clean** pure   2 **of** born of   3 **waried** cursed; **warlock** the false and malicious deceiver i.e., the devil   5 **merries** is merry   7 **well fare** very fine   8 **I . . . heting** I have kept my promise   9 **bob** bunch   11 **flower** noble child   15 **mop** moppet

---

16–17 **Of . . . cop** you are the head of our faith; I would drink in your cup (i.e., the cup of the eucharist)   22 **weed** clothing 24 **dall** hand   29 **That . . . seven** that made all the world in seven days   30–31 **My . . . meant** he named my name and alighted in me before He went. I conceived him indeed through God's might, as His purpose was   36 **min** remember   43 **won** redeemed   44 **bun** bound   45 **Let . . . loft** let us begin loudly

EVERYMAN

Everyman was written late in the fifteenth century and strongly resembles a Flemish play, *Elckerlijc* ("Everyman"), which was printed in 1495. It seems likely that one of the two plays is a translation of the other, but scholars are uncertain about which is the original. Given the play's subtle treatment of the Catholic doctrine of salvation, it has sometimes been argued that *Everyman* was written by a monk or cleric. Yet *Everyman* is hardly a theological treatise; it brims with a vitality that brings the reality of impending death vividly to the stage.

In the play, God orders Death to seek out Everyman and prepare him to die. Like most people, though, Everyman is not ready to meet his end. He first tries to bribe Death and then pleads unsuccessfully for mercy. When Death does not relent, Everyman begins a kind of spiritual journey, confronting several allegorical figures and asking them to accompany him to the grave. Medieval allegory often involved the personification of moral or psychological abstractions, much like the characters that Everyman meets: Fellowship, Kindred, Goods, Good Deeds, Knowledge, and so on. In performance, however, these abstractions become vividly fleshed-out, for the playwright gives these characters traits and behaviors that make them powerfully "real" and recognizable as individuals on the stage rather than as abstract moral emblems. As Everyman proceeds toward death, he is deserted by most of his worldly attributes, but Good Deeds remains faithful to him, especially once he has repented. Although the playwright concludes *Everyman* with a moralizing sermon by the Doctor, we may well feel that the theatrical lesson of the play has at least as much to do with the humanizing of Everyman and his poignant confrontation with our common mortality.

This production of *Everyman* transforms what may at first seem a statically "allegorical" drama into a visceral, choreographed spectacle.

EVERYMAN

Anonymous

TRANSLATED BY A. C. CAWLEY

CHARACTERS

GOD	COUSIN	STRENGTH
MESSENGER	GOODS	DISCRETION
DEATH	GOOD DEEDS	FIVE WITS
EVERYMAN	KNOWLEDGE	ANGEL
FELLOWSHIP	CONFESSION	DOCTOR
KINDRED	BEAUTY	

Here beginneth a treatise how the High Father of Heaven sendeth death to summon every creature to come and give account of their lives in this world, and is in manner of a moral play.

MESSENGER: I pray you all give your audience,
   And hear this matter with reverence,
   By figure a moral play:
   The *Summoning of Everyman* called it is,
5   That of our lives and ending shows
   How transitory we be all day.
   This matter is wondrous precious,
   But the intent of it is more gracious,
   And sweet to bear away.
10   The story saith: Man, in the beginning
   Look well, and take good heed to the ending,
   Be you never so gay!
   Ye think sin in the beginning full sweet,
   Which in the end causeth the soul to weep,
15   When the body lieth in clay.
   Here shall you see how Fellowship and Jollity,
   Both Strength, Pleasure, and Beauty,
   Will fade from thee as flower in May;
   For ye shall hear how our Heaven King
20   Calleth Everyman to a general reckoning:
   Give audience, and hear what he doth say.   *(Exit.)*

(GOD *speaketh:*)

GOD: I perceive, here in my majesty,
   How that all creatures be to me unkind,
   Living without dread in worldly prosperity:
25   Of ghostly sight the people be so blind,
   Drowned in sin, they know me not for their God;
   In worldly riches is all their mind,
   They fear not my righteousness, the sharp rod.
   My law that I showed, when I for them died,
30   They forget clean, and shedding of my blood red;
   I hanged between two, it cannot be denied;
   To get them life I suffered to be dead;
   I healed their feet, with thorns hurt was my head.
   I could do no more than I did, truly;
35   And now I see the people do clean forsake me:
   They use the seven deadly sins damnable,
   As pride, covetise, wrath, and lechery
   Now in the world be made commendable;

And thus they leave of angels the heavenly company.
Every man liveth so after his own pleasure,   40
And yet of their life they be nothing sure:
I see the more that I them forbear
The worse they be from year to year.
All that liveth appaireth fast;
Therefore I will, in all the haste,   45
Have a reckoning of every man's person;
For, and I leave the people thus alone
In their life and wicked tempests,
Verily they will become much worse than beasts;
For now one would by envy another up eat;   50
Charity they do all clean forget.
I hoped well that every man
In my glory should make his mansion,
And thereto I had them all elect;
But now I see, like traitors deject,   55
They thank me not for the pleasure that I to them meant,
Nor yet for their being that I them have lent,
I proffered the people great multitude of mercy,
And few there be that asketh it heartily.
They be so cumbered with worldly riches   60
That needs on them I must do justice,
On every man living without fear.
Where art thou, Death, thou mighty messenger?

(*Enter* DEATH.)

DEATH: Almighty God, I am here at your will,
   Your commandment to fulfill.   65
GOD: Go thou to Everyman,
   And show him, in my name,
   A pilgrimage he must on him take,
   Which he in no wise may escape;
   And that he bring with him a sure reckoning   70
   Without delay or any tarrying.

(GOD *withdraws.*)

DEATH: Lord, I will in the world go run overall,
   And cruelly outsearch both great and small;
   Every man will I beset that liveth beastly
   Out of God's laws, and dreadeth not folly.   75

---

3 **By figure** in form 6 **all day** always 8 **But . . . gracious** but the purpose of it is more devout 23 **unkind** ungrateful 25 **Of ghostly sight** in spiritual vision 32 **I . . . dead** I consented to die 37 **covetise** covetousness

41 **And . . . sure** and yet their lives are by no means obscure 44 **appaireth** degenerates 47 **and** if 48 **tempests** tumults 55 **deject** abject 59 **heartily** earnestly 72 **overall** everywhere

He that loveth riches I will strike with my dart,
His sight to blind, and from heaven to depart—
Except that alms be his good friend—
In hell for to dwell, world without end.
80   Lo, yonder I see Everyman walking.
Full little he thinketh on my coming;
His mind is on fleshly lusts and his treasure,
And great pain it shall cause him to endure
Before the Lord, Heaven King.

(*Enter* EVERYMAN.)

85   Everyman, stand still! Whither art thou going
Thus gaily? Hast thou thy Maker forget?
EVERYMAN: Why askest thou?
      Wouldest thou wit?
DEATH: Yea, sir; I will show you:
90   In great haste I am sent to thee
From God out of his majesty.
EVERYMAN: What, sent to me?
DEATH: Yea, certainly.
      Though thou have forget him here,
95   He thinketh on thee in the heavenly sphere,
As, ere we depart, thou shalt know.
EVERYMAN: What desireth God of me?
DEATH: That shall I show thee:
      A reckoning he will needs have
100   Without any longer respite.
EVERYMAN: To give a reckoning longer leisure I crave;
This blind matter troubleth my wit.
DEATH: On thee thou must take a long journey;
Therefore thy book of count with thee thou bring,
105   For turn again thou cannot by no way.
And look thou be sure of thy reckoning,
For before God thou shalt answer, and show
Thy many bad deeds, and good but a few;
How thou hast spent thy life, and in what wise,
110   Before the chief Lord of paradise.
Have ado that we were in that way,
For, wit thou well, thou shalt make none attorney.
EVERYMAN: Full unready I am such reckoning to give.
I know thee not. What messenger art thou?
115   DEATH: I am Death, that no man dreadeth,
For every man I rest, and no man spareth;
For it is God's commandment
That all to me should be obedient.
EVERYMAN: O Death, thou comest when I had thee least in
      mind!
120   In thy power it lieth me to save;
Yet of my good will I give thee, if thou will be kind:
Yea, a thousand pound shalt thou have,
And defer this matter till another day.
DEATH: Everyman, it may not be, by no way.
125   I set not by gold, silver, nor riches,

Ne by pope, emperor, king, duke, ne princes;
For, and I would receive gifts great,
All the world I might get;
But my custom is clean contrary.
I give thee no respite. Come hence, and not tarry.   130
EVERYMAN: Alas, shall I have no longer respite?
I may say Death giveth no warning!
To think on thee, it maketh my heart sick,
For all unready is my book of reckoning.
But twelve year and I might have abiding,   135
My counting-book I would make so clear
That my reckoning I should not need to fear.
Wherefore, Death, I pray thee, for God's mercy,
Spare me till I be provided of remedy.
DEATH: Thee availeth not to cry, weep, and pray;   140
But haste thee lightly that thou were gone that journey,
And prove thy friends if thou can;
For, wit thou well, the tide abideth no man,
And in the world each living creature
For Adam's sin must die of nature.   145
EVERYMAN: Death, if I should this pilgrimage take,
And my reckoning surely make,
Show me, for saint charity,
Should I not come again shortly?
DEATH: No, Everyman; and thou be once there,   150
Thou mayst never more come here,
Trust me verily.
EVERYMAN: O gracious God in the high seat celestial,
Have mercy on me in this most need!
Shall I have no company from this vale terrestrial   155
Of mine acquaintance, that way me to lead?
DEATH: Yea, if any be so hardy
That would go with thee and bear thee company.
Hie thee that thou were gone to God's magnificence,
Thy reckoning to give before his presence.   160
What, weenest thou thy life is given thee,
And thy worldly goods also?
EVERYMAN: I had wend so, verily.
DEATH: Nay, nay; it was but lent thee;
For as soon as thou art go,   165
Another a while shall have it, and then go therefro,
Even as thou hast done.
Everyman, thou art mad! Thou hast thy wits five,
And here on earth will not amend thy life;
For suddenly I do come.   170
EVERYMAN: O wretched caitiff, whither shall I flee,
That I might scape this endless sorrow?
Now, gentle Death, spare me till to-morrow,
That I may amend me
With good advisement.   175
DEATH: Nay, thereto I will not consent,
Nor no man will I respite;
But to the heart suddenly I shall smite
Without any advisement.
And now out of thy sight I will me hie;   180
See thou make thee ready shortly,

---

77 **depart** separate   88 **wit** know   102 **blind** obscure   104 **count** account   105 **turn again** return   111 **Have . . . way** i.e., let's see about making that journey   112 **none attorney** no one [your] advocate   115 **that . . . dreadeth** who fears no man   116 **rest** arrest   121 **good** goods   123 **And defer** if you defer   125 **set not by** care not for

143 **tide** time   161 **weenest** suppose   163 **wend** supposed   165 **go** gone   166 **therefro** from it   175 **advisement** reflection

For thou mayst say this is the day
That no man living may scape away.

(*Exit* DEATH.)

EVERYMAN: Alas, I may well weep with sighs deep!
185 Now have I no manner of company
To help me in my journey, and me to keep;
And also my writing is full unready.
How shall I do now for to excuse me?
I would to God I had never be get!
190 To my soul a full great profit it had be;
For now I fear pains huge and great.
The time passeth, Lord, help, that all wrought!
For though I mourn it availeth nought.
The day passeth. and is almost ago;
195 I wot not well what for to do.
To whom were I best my complaint to make?
What and I to Fellowship thereof spake,
And showed him of this sudden chance?
For in him is all mine affiance;
200 We have in the world so many a day
Be good friends in sport and play.
I see him yonder, certainly.
I trust that he will bear me company;
Therefore to him will I speak to ease my sorrow.
205 Well met, good Fellowship, and good morrow!

(FELLOWSHIP *speaketh:*)

FELLOWSHIP: Everyman, good morrow, by this day!
Sir, why lookest thou so piteously?
If any thing be amiss, I pray thee me say,
That I may help to remedy.
210 EVERYMAN: Yea, good Fellowship, yea;
I am in great jeopardy.
FELLOWSHIP: My true friend, show to me your mind;
I will not forsake thee to my life's end,
In the way of good company.
215 EVERYMAN: That was well spoken, and lovingly.
FELLOWSHIP: Sir, I must needs know your heaviness;
I have pity to see you in any distress.
If any have you wronged, ye shall revenged be,
Though I on the ground be slain for thee—
220 Though that I know before that I should die.
EVERYMAN: Verily, Fellowship, gramercy.
FELLOWSHIP: Tush! by thy thanks I set not a straw.
Show me your grief, and say no more.
EVERYMAN: If I my heart should to you break,
225 And then you to turn your mind from me,
And would not me comfort when ye hear me speak,
Then should I ten times sorrier be.
FELLOWSHIP: Sir, I say as I will do indeed.
EVERYMAN: Then be you a good friend at need:
230 I have found you true herebefore.
FELLOWSHIP: And so ye shall evermore;
For, in faith; and thou go to hell,

I will not forsake thee by the way.
EVERYMAN: Ye speak like a good friend; I believe you well.
I shall deserve it, and I may.   235
FELLOWSHIP: I speak of no deserving, by this day!
For he that will say, and nothing do,
Is not worthy with good company to go;
Therefore show me the grief of your mind,
As to your friend most loving and kind.   240
EVERYMAN: I shall show you how it is:
Commanded I am to go a journey,
A long way, hard and dangerous,
And give a strait count, without delay,
Before the high Judge, Adonai.   245
Wherefore, I pray you, bear me company,
As ye have promised, in this journey.
FELLOWSHIP: That is matter indeed. Promise is duty;
But, and I should take such a voyage on me,
I know it well, it should be to my pain;   250
Also it maketh me afeard, certain.
But let us take counsel here as well as we can,
For your words would fear a strong man.
EVERYMAN: Why, ye said if I had need
Ye would me never forsake, quick ne dead,   255
Though it were to hell, truly.
FELLOWSHIP: So I said, certainly,
But such pleasures be set aside, the sooth to say;
And also, if we took such a journey,
When should we come again?   260
EVERYMAN: Nay, never again, till the day of doom.
FELLOWSHIP: In faith, then will not I come there!
Who hath you these tidings brought?
EVERYMAN: Indeed, Death was with me here.
FELLOWSHIP: Now, by God that all hath bought,   265
If Death were the messenger,
For no man that is living to-day
I will not go that loath journey—
Not for the father that begat me!
EVERYMAN: Ye promised, otherwise, pardie.   270
FELLOWSHIP: I wot well I said so, truly;
And yet if thou wilt eat, and drink, and make good cheer,
Or haunt to women the lusty company,
I would not forsake you while the day is clear,
Trust me verily.   275
EVERYMAN: Yea, thereto ye would be ready!
To go to mirth, solace, and play,
Your mind will sooner apply,
Than to bear me company in my long journey.
FELLOWSHIP: Now, in good faith, I will not that way.   280
But and thou will murder, or any man kill,
In that I will help thee with a good will.
EVERYMAN: O, that is a simple advice indeed.
Gentle fellow, help me in my necessity!
We have loved long, and now I need;   285
And now, gentle Fellowship, remember me.

---

186 **keep** guard 187 **writing** the writing of Everyman's accounts 189 **be get** been born 194 **ago** gone 197 **and if** 199 **affiance** trust 206 **by this day** an asseveration 216 **heaviness** sorrow 224 **break** open

235 **deserve** repay 244 **strait count** strict account 245 **Adonai** a Hebrew name for God 248 **That . . . indeed** that is a good reason indeed [for asking me] 253 **fear** frighten 265 **bought** redeemed 268 **loath** loathsome 270 **pardie** by God 273 **Or . . . company** or frequent the pleasant company of women 274 **while . . . clear** until daybreak 278 **apply** attend

FELLOWSHIP: Whether ye have loved me or no,
By Saint John, I will not with thee go.

EVERYMAN: Yet, I pray thee, take the labour, and do so much
for me
290   To bring me forward, for saint charity,
And comfort me till I come without the town.

FELLOWSHIP: Nay, and thou would give me a new gown,
I will not a foot with thee go;
But, and thou had tarried, I would not have left thee so.
295   And as now God speed thee in thy journey,
For from thee I will depart as fast as I may.

EVERYMAN: Whither away, Fellowship? Will thou forsake me?

FELLOWSHIP: Yea, by my fay! To God I betake thee.

EVERYMAN: Farewell, good Fellowship; for thee my heart is
sore.
300   Adieu for ever! I shall see thee no more.

FELLOWSHIP: In faith, Everyman, farewell now at the ending;
For you I will remember that parting is mourning.

(*Exit* FELLOWSHIP.)

EVERYMAN: Alack! shall we thus depart indeed—
Ah, Lady, help!—without any more comfort?
305   Lo, Fellowship forsaketh me in my most need.
For help in this world whither shall I resort?
Fellowship herebefore with me would merry make,
And now little sorrow for me doth he take.
It is said, 'In prosperity men friends may find,
310   Which in adversity be full unkind.'
Now whither for succour shall I flee,
Sith that Fellowship hath forsaken me?
To my kinsmen I will, truly,
Praying them to help me in my necessity;
315   I believe that they will do so,
For kind will creep where it may not go.
I will go say, for yonder I see them.
Where be ye now, my friends and kinsmen?

(*Enter* KINDRED *and* COUSIN.)

KINDRED: Here be we now at your commandment.
320   Cousin, I pray you show us your intent
In any wise, and do not spare.

COUSIN: Yea, Everyman, and to us declare
If ye be disposed to go anywhither;
For, wit you well, we will live and die together.
325   KINDRED: In wealth and woe we will with you hold,
For over his kin a man may be bold.

EVERYMAN: Gramercy, my friends and kinsmen kind.
Now shall I show you the grief of my mind:
I was commanded by a messenger,
330   That is a high king's chief officer;
He bade me go a pilgrimage, to my pain,

And I know well I shall never come again;
Also I must give a reckoning strait,
For I have a great enemy that hath me in wait,
Which intendeth me for to hinder.   335

KINDRED: What account is that which ye must render?
That would I know.

EVERYMAN: Of all my works I must show
How I have lived and my days spent;
Also of ill deeds that I have used   340
In my time, sith life was me lent;
And of all virtues that I have refused.
Therefore, I pray you, go thither with me
To help to make mine account, for saint charity.

COUSIN: What, to go thither? Is that the matter?   345
Nay, Everyman, I had liefer fast bread and water
All this five year and more.

EVERYMAN: Alas, that ever I was bore!
For now shall I never be merry,
If that you forsake me.   350

KINDRED: Ah, sir, what ye be a merry man!
Take good heart to you, and make no moan.
But one thing I warn you, by Saint Anne—
As for me, ye shall go alone.

EVERYMAN: My Cousin, will you not with me go?   355

COUSIN: No, by our Lady! I have the cramp in my toe.
Trust not to me, for, so God me speed,
I will deceive you in your most need.

KINDRED: It availeth not us to tice.
Ye shall have my maid with all my heart;   360
She loveth to go to feasts, there to be nice,
And to dance, and abroad to start:
I will give her leave to help you in that journey,
If that you and she may agree.

EVERYMAN: Now show me the very effect of your mind: 365
Will you go with me, or abide behind?

KINDRED: Abide behind? Yea, that will I, and I may!
Therefore farewell till another day.

(*Exit* KINDRED.)

EVERYMAN: How should I be merry or glad?
For fair promises men to me make,   370
But when I have most need they me forsake.
I am deceived; that maketh me sad.

COUSIN: Cousin Everyman, farewell now,
For verily I will not go with you.
Also of mine own an unready reckoning   375
I have to account; therefore I make tarrying.
Now God keep thee, for now I go.

(*Exit* COUSIN.)

---

290 **bring me forward** escort me   298 **fay** faith; **betake** commend   303 **depart** part   312 **Sith** since   316 **For . . . go** For kinship will creep where it cannot walk, that is, blood is thicker than water   317 **go say** essay, try   321 **In . . . spare** without fail, and do not hold back   323 **anywhither** anywhere   325 **hold** side   326 **For . . . bold** for a man may be sure of his kinsfolk

334 **For . . . wait** a great enemy (the devil) who has me under observation   340 **used** practised   346 **I . . . water** I had rather fast on bread and water   348 **bore** born   351 **what . . . man** what a merry man you are   359 **It . . . tice** it is no use trying to entice us   361 **nice** wanton   362 **abroad to start** go out and about   365 **effect** tenor

EVERYMAN: Ah, Jesus, is all come hereto?
    Lo, fair words maketh fools fain;
380   They promise, and nothing will do, certain.
    My kinsmen promised me faithfully
    For to abide with me steadfastly,
    And now fast away do they flee:
    Even so Fellowship promised me.
385   What friend were best me of to provide?
    I lose my time here longer to abide.
    Yet in my mind a thing there is:
    All my life I have loved riches;
    If that my Good now help me might,
390   He would make my heart full light.
    I will speak to him in this distress—
    Where art thou, my Goods and riches?

(GOODS *speaks from a corner.*)

GOODS: Who calleth me? Everyman? What! hast thou haste?
    I lie here in corners, trussed and piled so high,
395   And in chests I am locked so fast,
    Also sacked in bags. Thou mayst see with thine eye
    I cannot stir; in packs low I lie.
    What would ye have? Lightly me say.
EVERYMAN: Come hither, Goods, in all the haste thou may,
400   For of counsel I must desire thee.
GOODS: Sir, and ye in the world have sorrow or adversity,
    That can I help you to remedy shortly.
EVERYMAN: It is another disease that grieveth me;
    In this world it is not, I tell thee so.
405   I am sent for, another way to go,
    To give a strait count general
    Before the highest Jupiter of all;
    And all my life I have had joy and pleasure in thee,
    Therefore, I pray thee, go with me;
410   For, peradventure, thou mayst before God Almighty
    My reckoning help to clean and purify;
    For it is said ever among
    That money maketh all right that is wrong.
GOODS: Nay, Everyman, I sing another song.
415   I follow no man in such voyages;
    For, and I went with thee,
    Thou shouldst fare much the worse for me;
    For because on me thou did set thy mind,
    Thy reckoning I have made blotted and blind,
420   That thine account thou cannot make truly;
    And that hast thou for the love of me.
EVERYMAN: That would grieve me full sore,
    When I should come to that fearful answer.
    Up, let us go thither together.
425 GOODS: Nay, not so! I am too brittle, I may not endure;
    I will follow no man one foot, be ye sure.
EVERYMAN: Alas, I have thee loved, and had great pleasure
    All my life-days on good and treasure.

GOODS: That is to thy damnation, without leasing,
    For my love is contrary to the love everlasting;   430
    But if thou had me loved moderately during,
    As to the poor to give part of me,
    Then shouldst thou not in this dolour be,
    Nor in this great sorrow and care.
EVERYMAN: Lo, now was I deceived ere I was ware,   435
    And all I may wite misspending of time.
GOODS: What, weenest thou that I am thine?
EVERYMAN: I had wend so.
GOODS: Nay, Everyman, I say no.
    As for a while I was lent thee;   440
    A season thou hast had me in prosperity.
    My condition is man's soul to kill;
    If I save one, a thousand I do spill.
    Weenest thou that I will follow thee?
    Nay, not from this world, verily.   445
EVERYMAN: I had wend otherwise.
GOODS: Therefore to thy soul Goods is a thief;
    For when thou art dead, this is my guise—
    Another to deceive in this same wise
    As I have done thee, and all to his soul's reprief.   450
EVERYMAN: O false Goods, cursed may thou be.
    Thou traitor to God, that hast deceived me
    And caught me in thy snare!
GOODS: Marry, thou brought thyself in care,
    Whereof I am glad;   455
    I must needs laugh, I cannot be sad.
EVERYMAN: Ah, Goods, thou hast had long my heartly love;
    I gave thee that which should be the Lord's above.
    But wilt thou not go with me indeed?
    I pray thee truth to say.   460
GOODS: No, so God me speed!
    Therefore farewell, and have good day.

(*Exit* GOODS.)

EVERYMAN: O, to whom shall I make my moan
    For to go with me in that heavy journey?
    First Fellowship said he would with me gone;   465
    His words were very pleasant and gay,
    But afterward he left me alone.
    Then spake I to my kinsmen, all in despair,
    And also they gave me words fair;
    They lacked no fair speaking,   470
    But all forsook me in the ending.
    Then went I to my Goods, that I loved best,
    In hope to have comfort, but there had I least;
    For my Goods sharply did me tell
    That he bringeth many into hell.   475
    Then of myself I was ashamed,

---

385 **me . . . provide** to provide myself with   389 **Good** Goods
398 **Lightly** quickly   400 **For . . . thee** for I must entreat your
advice   403 **disease** trouble   412 **For . . . among** for it is
sometimes said   419 **blind** obscure

429 **without leasing** without a lie, that is, truly   431–432 **But
. . . me** but if you had loved me moderately during your lifetime,
so as to give part of me to the poor   433 **dolour** distress
435 **ware** aware   436 **And . . . time** and I may blame it all on
the bad use I have made of time   438 **wend** supposed   442 **condition** nature   443 **spill** ruin   448 **guise** practice   450 **reprief** shame   457 **heartly** heartfelt

And so I am worthy to be blamed;
Thus may I well myself hate.
Of whom shall I now counsel take?
480 I think that I shall never speed
Till that I go to my Good Deed.
But, alas, she is so weak
That she can neither go nor speak;
Yet will I venture on her now.
485 My Good Deeds, where be you?

(GOOD DEEDS *speaks from the ground.*)

GOOD DEEDS: Here I lie, cold in the ground;
Thy sins hath me sore bound,
That I cannot stir.
EVERYMAN: O Good Deeds, I stand in fear!
490 I must you pray of counsel,
For help now should come right well.
GOOD DEEDS: Everyman, I have understanding
That ye be summoned account to make
Before Messias, of Jerusalem King;
495 And you do by me, that journey with you will I take.
EVERYMAN: Therefore I come to you, my moan to make;
I pray you that ye will go with me,
GOOD DEEDS: I would full fain, but I cannot stand, verily.
EVERYMAN: Why, is there anything on you fall?
500 GOOD DEEDS: Yea, sir, I may thank you of all;
If ye had perfectly cheered me,
Your book of count full ready had be.
Look, the books of your works and deeds eke!
Behold how they lie under the feet,
505 To your soul's heaviness.
EVERYMAN: Our Lord Jesus help me!
For one letter here I cannot see.
GOOD DEEDS: There is a blind reckoning in time of distress.
EVERYMAN: Good Deeds, I pray you help me in this need,
510 Or else I am for ever damned indeed;
Therefore help me to make reckoning
Before the Redeemer of all thing,
That King is, and was, and ever shall.
GOOD DEEDS: Everyman, I am sorry of your fall,
515 And fain would I help you, and I were able.
EVERYMAN: Good Deeds, your counsel I pray you give me.
GOOD DEEDS: That shall I do verily;
Though that on my feet I may not go,
I have a sister that shall with you also,
520 Called Knowledge, which shall with you abide,
To help you to make that dreadful reckoning.

(*Enter* KNOWLEDGE.)

KNOWLEDGE: Everyman, I will go with thee, and be thy guide,
In thy most need to go by thy side.
EVERYMAN: In good condition I am now in every thing,
And am wholly content with this good thing, 525
Thanked be God my creator.
GOOD DEEDS: And when she hath brought you there
Where thou shalt heal thee of thy smart,
Then go you with your reckoning and your Good Deeds together,
For to make you joyful at heart 530
Before the blessed Trinity.
EVERYMAN: My Good Deeds, gramercy!
I am well content, certainly,
With your words sweet.
KNOWLEDGE: Now go we together lovingly 535
To Confession, that cleansing river.
EVERYMAN: For joy I weep; I would we were there!
But, I pray you, give me cognition
Where dwelleth that holy man, Confession.
KNOWLEDGE: In the house of salvation: 540
We shall find him in that place,
That shall us comfort, by God's grace.

(KNOWLEDGE *takes* EVERYMAN *to* CONFESSION.)

Lo, this is Confession. Kneel down and ask mercy,
For he is in good conceit with God Almighty.
EVERYMAN: O glorious fountain, that all uncleanness doth clarify, 545
Wash from me the spots of vice unclean,
That on me no sin may be seen.
I come with Knowledge for my redemption,
Redempt with heart and full contrition;
For I am commanded a pilgrimage to take, 550
And great accounts before God to make.
Now I pray you, Shrift, mother of salvation,
Help my Good Deeds for my piteous exclamation.
CONFESSION: I know your sorrow well, Everyman.
Because with Knowledge ye come to me, 555
I will you comfort as well as I can,
And a precious jewel I will give thee,
Called penance, voider of adversity;
Therewith shall your body chastised be,
With abstinence and perseverance in God's service. 560
Here shall you receive that scourge of me,
Which is penance strong that ye must endure,
To remember thy Saviour was scourged for thee
With sharp scourges, and suffered it patiently;
So must thou, ere thou scape that painful pilgrimage. 565
Knowledge, keep him in this voyage,
And by that time Good Deeds will be with thee.
But in any wise be siker of mercy,
For your time draweth fast; and ye will saved be,
Ask God mercy, and he will grant truly. 570

---

483 **go** walk   484 **venture** gamble   491 **For . . . well** for help would now be very welcome   495 **And . . . me** if you do as I advise   499 **fall** befallen   500 **of** for   501 **If . . . me** if you had encouraged me fully   503 **eke** also   508 **There . . . distress** a sinful person in this hour of need finds that the account of his good deeds is dimly written and difficult to read   520 **Knowledge** the meaning of Knowledge here is acknowledgment or recognition of sins

---

528 **smart** pain   538 **cognition** knowledge   540 **In . . . salvation** in the church   544 **conceit** esteem   549 **Redempt . . . contrition** redeemed by heartfelt and full contrition   552 **Shrift** confession   553 **for . . . exclamation** in answer to my piteous cry   558 **voider** expeller   568 **siker** sure   569 **draweth fast** draws quickly to an end; **and** if

When with the scourge of penance man doth him bind,
The oil of forgiveness then shall he find.
EVERYMAN: Thanked be God for his gracious work!
For now I will my penance begin;
575   This hath rejoiced and lighted my heart,
Though the knots be painful and hard within.
KNOWLEDGE: Everyman, look your penance that ye fulfil,
What pain that ever it to you be;
And Knowledge shall give you counsel at will
580   How your account ye shall make clearly.
EVERYMAN: O eternal God, O heavenly figure,
O way of righteousness, O goodly vision,
Which descended down in a virgin pure
Because he would every man redeem,
585   Which Adam forfeited by his disobedience:
O blessed Godhead, elect and high divine,
Forgive my grievous offence;
Here I cry thee mercy in this presence.
O ghostly treasure, O ransomer and redeemer,
590   Of all the world hope and conductor,
Mirror of joy, and founder of mercy,
Which enlumineth heaven and earth thereby,
Hear my clamorous complaint, though it late be;
Receive my prayers, of thy benignity;
595   Though I be a sinner most abominable,
Yet let my name be written in Moses' table.
O Mary, pray to the Maker of all thing,
Me for to help at my ending;
And save me from the power of my enemy,
600   For Death assaileth me strongly.
And, Lady, that I may by mean of thy prayer
Of your Son's glory to be partner,
By the means of his passion, I it crave;
I beseech you help my soul to save.
605   Knowledge, give me the scourge of penance;
My flesh therewith shall give acquittance:
I will now begin, if God give me grace.
KNOWLEDGE: Everyman, God give you time and space!
Thus I bequeath you in the hands of our Saviour;
610   Now may you make your reckoning sure.
EVERYMAN: In the name of the Holy Trinity,
My body sore punished shall be:
Take this, body, for the sin of the flesh!

(*Scourges himself.*)

Also thou delightest to go gay and fresh,
And in the way of damnation thou did me bring,   615
Therefore suffer now strokes and punishing.
Now of penance I will wade the water clear,
To save me from purgatory, that sharp fire.

(GOOD DEEDS *rises from the ground.*)

GOOD DEEDS: I thank God, now I can walk and go,
And am delivered of my sickness and woe.   620
Therefore with Everyman I will go, and not spare;
His good works I will help him to declare.
KNOWLEDGE: Now, Everyman, be merry and glad!
Your Good Deeds cometh now; ye may not be sad.
Now is your Good Deeds whole and sound,   625
Going upright upon the ground.
EVERYMAN: My heart is light, and shall be evermore;
Now will I smite faster than I did before.
GOOD DEEDS: Everyman, pilgrim, my special friend,
Blessed be thou without end;   630
For thee is preparate the eternal glory.
Ye have me made whole and sound,
Therefore I will bide by thee in every stound.
EVERYMAN: Welcome, my Good Deeds; now I hear thy voice,
I weep for very sweetness of love.   635
KNOWLEDGE: Be no more sad, but ever rejoice;
God seeth thy living in his throne above.
Put on this garment to thy behoof,
Which is wet with your tears,
Or else before God you may it miss,   640
When ye to your journey's end come shall.
EVERYMAN: Gentle Knowledge, what do ye it call?
KNOWLEDGE: It is a garment of sorrow:
From pain it will you borrow;
Contrition it is,   645
That geteth forgiveness;
It pleaseth God passing well.
GOOD DEEDS: Everyman, will you wear it for your heal?
EVERYMAN: Now blessed be Jesu, Mary's Son,
For now have I on true contrition.   650
And let us go now without tarrying;
Good Deeds, have we clear our reckoning?
GOOD DEEDS: Yea, indeed, I have it here.
EVERYMAN: Then I trust we need not fear;
Now, friends, let us not part in twain.   655
KNOWLEDGE: Nay, Everyman, that will we not, certain.
GOOD DEEDS: Yet must thou lead with thee
Three persons of great might.
EVERYMAN: Who should they be?
GOOD DEEDS: Discretion and Strength they hight,   660
And thy Beauty may not abide behind.
KNOWLEDGE: Also ye must call to mind
Your Five Wits as for your counsellors.
GOOD DEEDS: You must have them ready at all hours.
EVERYMAN: How shall I get them hither?   665

---

571 **him** himself   575 **lighted** lightened   576 **Though . . . within** though the knots [of the scourge] be painful and hard to my body   586 **divine** divinity   588 **in this presence** in the presence of this company   592 **thereby** besides   596 **Yet . . . table** medieval theologians regarded the two tables given on Sinai as symbols of baptism and penance, respectively. Thus Everyman is asking to be numbered among those who have escaped damnation by doing penance for their sins   599 **my enemy** the devil   601–603 **And . . . crave** and, Lady, I beg that through the mediation of thy prayer I may share in your Son's glory, in consequence of His passion   606 **acquittance** satisfaction (as a part of the sacrament of penance)   608 **space** opportunity

---

631 **preparate** prepared   633 **stound** trial   638 **behoof** advantage   644 **borrow** release   647 **passing** exceedingly   648 **heal** salvation   660 **hight** are called   663 **Wits** senses

KNOWLEDGE: You must call them all together,
    And they will hear you incontinent.
EVERYMAN: My friends, come hither and be present,
    Discretion, Strength, my Five Wits, and Beauty.

(*Enter* BEAUTY, STRENGTH, DISCRETION, *and* FIVE WITS.)

670 BEAUTY: Here at your will we be all ready.
    What will ye that we should do?
    GOOD DEEDS: That ye would with Everyman go,
    And help him in his pilgrimage.
    Advise you, will ye with him or not in that voyage?
675 STRENGTH: We will bring him all thither,
    To his help and comfort, ye may believe me.
    DISCRETION: So will we go with him all together.
    EVERYMAN: Almighty God, lofed may thou be!
    I give thee laud that I have hither brought
680 Strength, Discretion, Beauty, and Five Wits. Lack
        I nought.
    And my Good Deeds, with Knowledge clear,
    All be in my company at my will here;
    I desire no more to my business.
    STRENGTH: And I, Strength, will by you stand in distress,
685 Though thou would be in battle fight on the ground.
    FIVE WITS: And though it were through the world round,
    We will not depart for sweet ne sour.
    BEAUTY: No more will I unto death's hour
    Whatsoever thereof befall.
690 DISCRETION: Everyman, advise you first of all;
    Go with a good advisement and deliberation.
    We all give you virtuous monition
    That all shall be well.
    EVERYMAN: My friends, harken what I will tell:
695 I pray God reward you in his heavenly sphere.
    Now harken, all that be here,
    For I will make my testament
    Here before you all present:
    In alms half my good I will give with my hands twain
700 In the way of charity, with good intent,
    And the other half still shall remain
    In queth, to be returned there it ought to be.
    This I do in despite of the fiend of hell,
    To go quit out of his peril
705 Ever after and this day.
    KNOWLEDGE: Everyman, harken what I say:
    Go to priesthood, I you advise,
    And receive of him in any wise
    The holy sacrament and ointment together.
710 Then shortly see ye turn again hither;
    We will all abide you here.
    FIVE WITS: Yea, Everyman, hie you that ye ready were.

There is no emperor, king, duke, ne baron,
    That of God hath commission
    As hath the least priest in the world being;   715
    For of the blessed sacraments pure and benign
    He beareth the keys, and thereof hath the cure
    For man's redemption—it is ever sure—
    Which God for our soul's medicine
    Gave us out of his heart with great pine.   720
    Here in this transitory life, for thee and me,
    The blessed sacraments seven there be:
    Baptism, confirmation, with priesthood good,
    And the sacrament of God's precious flesh and blood,
    Marriage, the holy extreme unction, and penance;   725
    These seven be good to have in remembrance,
    Gracious sacraments of high divinity.
EVERYMAN: Fain would I receive that holy body,
    And meekly to my ghostly father I will go.
FIVE WITS: Everyman, that is the best that ye can do.   730
    God will you to salvation bring,
    For priesthood exceedeth all other thing:
    To us Holy Scripture they do teach,
    And converteth man from sin heaven to reach;
    God hath to them more power given   735
    Than to any angel that is in heaven.
    With five words he may consecrate,
    God's body in flesh and blood to make,
    And handleth his Maker between his hands.
    The priest bindeth and unbindeth all bands,   740
    Both in earth and in heaven.
    Thou ministers all the sacraments seven;
    Though we kissed thy feet, thou were worthy;
    Thou art surgeon that cureth sin deadly:
    No remedy we find under God   745
    But all only priesthood.
    Everyman, God gave priests that dignity,
    And setteth them in his stead among us to be;
    Thus be they above angels in degree.

(EVERYMAN *goes to the priest to receive the last sacraments.*)

KNOWLEDGE: If priests be good, it is so, surely.   750
    But when Jesus hanged on the cross with great smart,
    There he gave out of his blessed heart
    The same sacrament in great torment:
    He sold them not to us, that Lord omnipotent.
    Therefore Saint Peter the apostle doth say   755
    That Jesu's curse hath all they
    Which God their Saviour do buy or sell,
    Or they for any money do take or tell.
    Sinful priests giveth the sinners example bad;
    Their children sitteth by other men's fires, I have heard;   760

---

667 **incontinent** immediately   674 **Advise** consider
678 **lofed** praised   683 **to** for   687 **for . . . sour** that is, in happiness or adversity   688 **unto** until   691 **advisement** reflection   692 **monition** forewarning   701–702 **And . . . be** the
meaning seems to be that Everyman's immovable property (his
body) will lie at rest in the earth   704–705 **To . . . day** to go
free out of his power today and ever after   708 **in any wise**
without fail   712 **hie . . . were** hurry and prepare yourself

714 **commission** authority   715 **being** living   720 **pine** suffering   728 **that holy body** the sacrament   729 **ghostly** spiritual   737 **five words** *Hoc est enim corpus meum* ("This is my
body")   742 **ministers** administer   746 **But . . . priesthood**
except only from the priesthood   750 **it is so** that they are
above the angels   755–757 **Therefore . . . sell** the reference
here is to the sin of simony (Acts 8:18 ff.)   760 **Their . . . fires**
their children are illegitimate

And some haunteth women's company
With unclean life, as lusts of lechery:
These be with sin made blind.
FIVE WITS: I trust to God no such may we find;
765   Therefore let us priesthood honour,
And follow their doctrine for our souls' succour.
We be their sheep, and they shepherds be
By whom we all be kept in surety.
Peace, for yonder I see Everyman come,
770   Which hath made true satisfaction.
GOOD DEEDS: Methink it is he indeed.

(*Re-enter* EVERYMAN.)

EVERYMAN: Now Jesu be your alder speed!
I have received the sacrament for my redemption,
And then mine extreme unction:
775   Blessed be all they that counselled me to take it!
And now, friends, let us go without longer respite;
I thank God that ye have tarried so long.
Now set each of you on this rood your hand,
And shortly follow me:
780   I go before there I would be; God be our guide!
STRENGTH: Everyman, we will not from you go
Till ye have done this voyage long.
DISCRETION: I, Discretion, will bide by you also.
KNOWLEDGE: And though this pilgrimage be never so strong,
785   I will never part you fro.
STRENGTH: Everyman, I will be as sure by thee
As ever I did by Judas Maccabee.

(EVERYMAN *comes to his grave.*)

EVERYMAN: Alas, I am so faint I may not stand;
My limbs under me doth fold.
790   Friends, let us not turn again to this land,
Not for all the world's gold;
For into this cave must I creep
And turn to earth, and there to sleep.
BEAUTY: What, into this grave? Alas!
795   EVERYMAN: Yea, there shall ye consume, more and less.
BEAUTY: And what, should I smother here?
EVERYMAN: Yea, by my faith, and never more appear.
In this world live no more we shall,
But in heaven before the highest Lord of all.
800   BEAUTY: I cross out all this; adieu, by Saint John!
I take my cap in my lap, and am gone.
EVERYMAN: What, Beauty, whither will ye?
BEAUTY: Peace, I am deaf; I look not behind me,
Not and thou wouldest give me all the gold in thy chest.

(*Exit* BEAUTY.)

---

772 **be . . . speed** be the helper of you all   778 **rood** cross
784 **strong** grievous   785 **you fro** from you   786–787 **Everyman . . . Maccabee** I will stand by you as steadfastly as ever I
did by Judas Maccabaeus (I Macc. 3)   795 **consume . . . less** decay, all of you   800 **I . . . this** I cancel all this, that is, my promise
to stay with you   801 **I . . . lap** I doff my cap (so low that it
comes) into my lap

EVERYMAN: Alas, whereto may I trust?   805
Beauty goeth fast away from me;
She promised with me to live and die.
STRENGTH: Everyman, I will thee also forsake and deny;
Thy game liketh me not at all.
EVERYMAN: Why, then, ye will forsake me all?   810
Sweet Strength, tarry a little space.
STRENGTH: Nay, sir, by the rood of grace!
I will hie me from thee fast,
Though thou weep till thy heart to-brast.
EVERYMAN: Ye would ever bide by me, ye said.   815
STRENGTH: Yea, I have you far enough conveyed.
Ye be old enough, I understand,
Your pilgrimage to take on hand;
I repent me that I hither came.
EVERYMAN: Strength, you to displease I am to blame;   820
Yet promise is debt, this ye well wot.
STRENGTH: In faith, I care not.
Thou art but a fool to complain;
You spend your speech and waste your brain.
Go thrust thee into the ground!   825

(*Exit* STRENGTH.)

EVERYMAN: I had wend surer I should you have found.
He that trusteth in his Strength
She him deceiveth at the length.
Both Strength and Beauty forsaketh me;
Yet they promised me fair and lovingly.   830
DISCRETION: Everyman, I will after Strength be gone;
As for me, I will leave you alone.
EVERYMAN: Why, Discretion, will you forsake me?
DISCRETION: Yea, in faith, I will go from thee,
For when Strength goeth before   835
I follow after evermore.
EVERYMAN: Yet, I pray thee, for the love of the Trinity,
Look in my grave once piteously.
DISCRETION: Nay, so nigh will I not come;
Farewell, every one!   840

(*Exit* DISCRETION.)

EVERYMAN: O, all thing faileth, save God alone—
Beauty, Strength, and Discretion;
For when Death bloweth his blast,
They all run from me full fast.
FIVE WITS: Everyman, my leave now of thee I take;   845
I will follow the other, for here I thee forsake.
EVERYMAN: Alas, then may I wail and weep,
For I took you for my best friend.
FIVE WITS: I will no longer thee keep;
Now farewell, and there an end.   850

(*Exit* FIVE WITS.)

EVERYMAN: O Jesu, help! All hath forsaken me.
GOOD DEEDS: Nay, Everyman; I will bide with thee.
I will not forsake thee indeed;

---

809 **liketh** pleases   811 **space** while   814 **to-brast** break
820 **you . . . blame** I am to blame for displeasing you

Thou shalt find me a good friend at need.

855 EVERYMAN: Gramercy, Good Deeds! Now may I true friends
see.

They have forsaken me, every one;

I loved them better than my Good Deeds alone.

Knowledge, will ye forsake me also?

KNOWLEDGE: Yea, Everyman, when ye to Death shall go;

860 But not yet, for no manner of danger.

EVERYMAN: Gramercy, Knowledge, with all my heart.

KNOWLEDGE: Nay, yet I will not from hence depart

Till I see where ye shall become.

EVERYMAN: Methink, alas, that I must be gone

865 To make my reckoning and my debts pay,

For I see my time is nigh spent away.

Take example, all ye that this do hear or see,

How they that I loved best do forsake me,

Except my Good Deeds that bideth truly.

870 GOOD DEEDS: All earthly things is but vanity:

Beauty, Strength, and Discretion do man forsake,

Foolish friends, and kinsmen, that fair spake—

All fleeth save Good Deeds, and that am I.

EVERYMAN: Have mercy on me, God most mighty;

875 And stand by me, thou mother and maid, holy Mary.

GOOD DEEDS: Fear not; I will speak for thee.

EVERYMAN: Here I cry God mercy.

GOOD DEEDS: Short our end, and minish our pain;

Let us go and never come again.

880 EVERYMAN: Into thy hands, Lord, my soul I commend;

Receive it, Lord, that it be not lost,

As thou me boughtest, so me defend,

And save me from the fiend's boast,

That I may appear with that blessed host

885 That shall be saved at the day of doom.

In manus tuas, of mights most

For ever, *commendo spiritum meum.*

(*He sinks into his grave.*)

KNOWLEDGE: Now hath he suffered that we all shall endure;

The Good Deeds shall make all sure.

Now hath he made ending; 890

Methinketh that I hear angels sing,

And make great joy and melody

Where Everyman's soul received shall be.

ANGEL: Come, excellent elect spouse, to Jesu!

Hereabove thou shalt go 895

Because of thy singular virtue.

Now the soul is taken the body fro,

Thy reckoning is crystal-clear.

Now shalt thou into the heavenly sphere,

Unto the which all ye shall come 900

That liveth well before the day of doom.

(*Enter* DOCTOR.)

DOCTOR: This moral men may have in mind.

Ye hearers, take it of worth, old and young,

And forsake Pride, for he deceiveth you in the end;

And remember Beauty, Five Wits, Strength, and 905
Discretion,

They all at the last do every man forsake,

Save his Good Deeds there doth he take.

But beware, for and they be small

Before God, he hath no help at all;

None excuse may be there for every man. 910

Alas, how shall he do then?

For after death amends may no man make,

For then mercy and pity doth him forsake.

If his reckoning be not clear when he doth come,

God will say: '*Ite, maledicti, in ignem eternum.*' 915

And he that hath his account whole and sound,

High in heaven he shall be crowned;

Unto which place God bring us all thither,

That we may live body and soul together.

Thereto help the Trinity! 920

Amen, say ye, for saint charity.

THUS ENDETH THIS MORAL PLAY OF EVERYMAN

863 **where . . . become** what shall become of you   878 **Short
. . . pain** shorten our end, and diminish our pain   886–887 *In
. . . meum* Into thy hands, most mighty One for ever, I commend
my spirit

894 **spouse** bride of Jesus [a common medieval metaphor to express the idea of the soul's union with God]   903 **take . . .
worth** value it   907 **Save** unless   915 *Ite . . . eternum* depart,
ye cursed, into everlasting fire (Matthew xxv.41)

Christopher Marlowe

Born in the same year as Shakespeare, Christopher Marlowe (1564–1593) pursued a very different kind of life than his famous contemporary. Unlike Shakespeare, Marlowe had a university education; schooled at the King's School in Canterbury, Marlowe then attended Corpus Christi College, Cambridge. Marlowe left Cambridge in 1587, and his first play—*Tamburlaine,* in two full-length parts—was produced later that year. He wrote several important plays in the course of the next six years: *Doctor Faustus* (c. 1589), *The Jew of Malta* (c. 1590), and *Edward II* (c. 1591). Marlowe also wrote *Dido, Queen of Carthage,* possibly while still at Cambridge, and a play about the St. Bartholomew massacre of Huguenots in Paris, *The Massacre at Paris* (1593). Marlowe was an accomplished poet and wrote the narrative poem *Hero and Leander* (published in 1598), among many others. He was known at court and to influential advisers to Queen Elizabeth, such as Sir Walter Raleigh and Sir Francis Walsingham. It is not surprising that Marlowe's life has been much romanticized, especially given his reputation for iconoclasm, his association with occultists, and his service as one of Elizabeth's spies in Europe. Marlowe was arrested on several occasions for fighting and died from injuries he received in a tavern fight in 1593; there is some speculation that he may have been assassinated. He was twenty-nine years old.

Despite the brevity of his career, Marlowe is deservedly ranked among the greatest of English playwrights. The rhetorical flourish of what Ben Jonson called his "mighty line" and the brilliance of his language are unsurpassed in their majesty and power. His plays were popular in part no doubt because they starred Edward Alleyn, the major actor of the 1580s and early 1590s. Alleyn was the son-in-law of Philip Henslowe, a theatrical entrepreneur who built several theaters in London; their efforts, and Marlowe's plays, made them rich men. Indeed, Marlowe's plays remain alive today through the depth and force of their principal roles. In Faustus and Tamburlaine, Marlowe created roles of a rich and involved subjectivity, characters of the psychological complexity that would become one of the hallmarks of English drama.

DOCTOR FAUSTUS

Marlowe based his play on a popular German narrative, the *History of Doctor Johann Faust,* published in 1587. Audiences might also have seen in Faustus some resemblance to John Dee, Queen Elizabeth's royal astrologer. *Doctor Faustus* was celebrated in its day and would certainly have made a spectacular impression on audiences in the public theater. We know from Henslowe's accounts that his theater had a "hell mouth for Doctor Faustus," some kind of grotesque opening from which the devils could leap to snare Faustus and haul him off to damnation. The devils themselves were covered with flames, fireworks, and firecrackers. Tradition has it that Alleyn—clearly a real showman—wore a cross prominently displayed around his neck as a way of "defending" himself should real devils be summoned by his performance of Faustus.

The magic of the play, however, arises from the attraction exerted by Faustus himself. Like many of Marlowe's heroes, Faustus is an "overreacher," a man who magnificently and self-destructively tries to go beyond his own limitations, perhaps even beyond the limits of human nature itself. We can see this magnificent energy at the play's opening, when Faustus turns away from Aristotle and philosophy, from medicine, from the law, and from theology to the seductive arts of magic, striking the bargain with the devil that gives him the power to gratify his insatiable curiosity in exchange for his mortal soul.

Modern readers are sometimes confused by *Doctor Faustus*'s morality play elements, the pageant of the Seven Deadly Sins, and the Good and Bad angels who frame Faustus's temptation. Marlowe brings a medieval vision of the tragic "fall of those who stood in high degree" into collision with the more psychologically oriented vision of tragedy that is characteristic of the modern secular world. Certainly the Good and Bad angels point to what is right and wrong about Faustus's temptation. What is fascinating about the play is the way that Faustus's desire to be ravished by new experiences not only overcomes his scruples, but ours as well. Marlowe's play relies on the fact that despite the angels' warnings, we will want to see where Faustus's overreaching will take him.

Faustus—like Prospero in Shakespeare's *The Tempest*—could be taken as a figure for the Renaissance sense of human potential, here realized in its negative or self-destructive dimension. Faustus also seems to provide a figure for the morality of the theater itself, because the power that Faus-

Mephostophilis confronts Faustus in Marlowe's *Doctor Faustus*.

tus exercises in the play increasingly seems to be illusory, merely theatrical. The spectacles that Faustus conjures are finally only shows—Mephostophilis and Helen are just devils in disguise—and the power he wields has increasingly trivial results: tricking the Pope degenerates into hoodwinking the horse-courser and setting antlers on Benvolio's head. Faustus is damned for bargaining away his soul, but what finally seems to turn the play toward tragedy is what he sells his soul for: not for the world, but for the illusion of a world, a kind of endless and impoverished theater. We might well recall that the illusions that damn Faustus are, in many ways, the same illusions we have come to the theater to see. The theater makes Faustus's temptation real to its audience by tempting it with many of the same arts.

DOCTOR FAUSTUS

Christopher Marlowe
EDITED BY SYLVAN BARNET

CHARACTERS

CHORUS
DOCTOR FAUSTUS
WAGNER, *his student and servant*
GOOD ANGEL
BAD ANGEL
VALDES ⎫
CORNELIUS ⎭ *magicians*
THREE SCHOLARS
LUCIFER, *prince of devils*
MEPHOSTOPHILIS, *a devil*
ROBIN, *a clown*
BELZEBUB, *a devil*
PRIDE ⎫
COVETOUSNESS
ENVY
WRATH ⎬ *the Seven Deadly Sins*
GLUTTONY
SLOTH
LECHERY ⎭
DICK, *a clown*
POPE ADRIAN
RAYMOND, *King of Hungary*

BRUNO, *rival Pope appointed by the Emperor*
TWO CARDINALS
ARCHBISHOP OF RHEIMS
FRIARS
VINTNER
MARTINO ⎫
FREDERICK ⎬ *gentlemen at the Emperor's court*
BENVOLIO ⎭
THE GERMAN EMPEROR, CHARLES THE FIFTH
DUKE OF SAXONY
TWO SOLDIERS
HORSE-COURSER, *a clown*
CARTER, *a clown*
HOSTESS OF A TAVERN
DUKE OF VANHOLT
DUCHESS OF VANHOLT
SERVANT
OLD MAN
DARIUS OF PERSIA, ALEXANDER THE GREAT, ALEXANDER'S
  PARAMOUR, HELEN OF TROY, DEVILS, PIPER, CARDINALS,
  MONKS, FRIARS, ATTENDANTS, SOLDIERS, SERVANTS, TWO
  CUPIDS

PROLOGUE

Enter CHORUS.

Not marching in the fields of Trasimene
Where Mars did mate the warlike Carthagens,
Nor sporting in the dalliance of love
In courts of kings where state is overturned,
5   Nor in the pomp of proud audacious deeds
Intends our muse to vaunt his heavenly verse.
Only this, gentles—We must now perform
The form of Faustus' fortunes, good or bad:
And now to patient judgments we appeal
10   And speak for Faustus in his infancy.
Now is he born of parents base of stock
In Germany within a town called Rhode;
At riper years to Wittenberg he went
Whereas his kinsmen chiefly brought him up.

So much he profits in divinity   15
That shortly he was graced with doctor's name,
Excelling all, and sweetly can dispute
In th' heavenly matters of theology;
Till swoll'n with cunning, of a self-conceit,
His waxen wings did mount above his reach   20
And melting, heavens conspired his overthrow!
For falling to a devilish exercise
And glutted now with learning's golden gifts
He surfeits upon cursèd necromancy:
Nothing so sweet as magic is to him   25
Which he prefers before his chiefest bliss—
And this the man that in his study sits.

(*Exit.*)

Prologue s.d. **Chorus** a single actor (here, perhaps, Wagner, Faustus' servant-student)   1 **Trasimene** Lake Trasimene, site of one of Hannibal's victories over the Romans, 217 BCE (Marlowe is not known to have written on this subject, though lines 3–4 may refer to his Edward II, and line 5 to his Tamburlaine) 2 **Mars did mate** i.e., the Roman army encountered   4 **state** government   6 **muse** poet; **vaunt** proudly display   12 **Rhode** Roda   14 **Whereas** where

16 **graced** alluding to the official "grace" permitting the student to take his degree   19 **cunning, of a self-conceit** ingenuity, born of arrogance   20 **waxen wings** alluding to Icarus, who flew by means of wings made of feathers waxed to a framework; despite the warning of his father, Icarus soared too near the sun, the wax melted, and he plunged to his death   24 **necromancy** literally, divination by means of the spirits of the dead, but here probably equivalent to black magic   26 **prefers before his chiefest bliss** sets above his hope of salvation

ACT ONE

SCENE I

FAUSTUS *in his study.*

FAUSTUS: Settle thy studies Faustus, and begin
To sound the depth of that thou wilt profess.
Having commenced, be a divine in show—
Yet level at the end of every art
5 And live and die in Aristotle's works.
Sweet *Analytics,* 'tis thou hast ravished me.
Bene disserere est finis logices.
Is to dispute well logic's chiefest end?
Affords this art no greater miracle?
10 Then read no more, thou has attained that end.
A greater subject fitteth Faustus' wit:
Bid *on kai me on* farewell, and Galen come:
Be a physician Faustus, heap up gold,
And be eternized for some wondrous cure.
15 *Summum bonum medicinae sanitas,*
The end of physic is our body's health.
Why Faustus hast thou not attained that end?
Are not thy bills hung up as monuments
Whereby whole cities have escaped the plague
20 And thousand desperate maladies been cured?
Yet art thou still but Faustus and a man.
Could'st thou make men to live eternally
Or being dead raise them to life again,
Then this profession were to be esteemed.
25 Physic farewell! Where is Justinian?
Si una eademque res legatur duobus, alter rem, alter
valorem rei, et cetera.
A petty case of paltry legacies.
Exhereditare filium non potest pater, nisi—
30 Such is the subject of the *Institute*
And universal body of the law!
This study fits a mercenary drudge
Who aims at nothing but external trash,
Too servile and illiberal for me.
35 When all is done, divinity is best.
Jerome's Bible, Faustus, view it well.

Stipendium peccati mors est. Ha! *Stipendium et cetera.* The reward of sin is death? That's hard: *Si peccasse negamus, fallimur, et nulla est in nobis veritas.* If we say that we have no sin, we deceive ourselves, and there is no truth in us. Why, 40 then belike, we must sin, and so consequently die.
Ay, we must die an everlasting death.
What doctrine call you this? *Che serà, serà:*
What will be, shall be! Divinity, adieu!
These metaphysics of magicians 45
And negromantic books are heavenly;
Lines, circles, letters, characters—
Ay, these are those that Faustus most desires.
O, what a world of profit and delight,
Of power, of honor, and omnipotence 50
Is promised to the studious artisan!
All things that move between the quiet poles
Shall be at my command: emperors and kings
Are but obeyed in their several provinces
But his dominion that exceeds in this 55
Stretcheth as far as doth the mind of man:
A sound magician is a demi-god!
Here tire my brains to get a deity!

(*Enter* WAGNER.)

Wagner, commend me to my dearest friends.
The German Valdes and Cornelius. 60
Request them earnestly to visit me.
WAGNER: I will, sir.

(*Exit.*)

FAUSTUS: Their conference will be a greater help to me
Than all my labors, plod I ne'er so fast.

(*Enter the* [GOOD] ANGEL *and the* [EVIL] SPIRIT.)

GOOD ANGEL: O Faustus, lay that damnèd book aside 65
And gaze not on it lest it tempt thy soul
And heap God's heavy wrath upon thy head!
Read, read the Scriptures—that is blasphemy!
BAD ANGEL: Go forward Faustus, in that famous art
Wherein all nature's treasure is contained. 70
Be thou on earth as Jove is in the sky,
Lord and commander of these elements!

I.i. s.d. **Faustus in his study** probably at his last line the Chorus drew back a curtain at the rear of the stage, disclosing Faustus 2 **profess** study and teach 3 **commenced** taken a degree 4 **level** aim 6 **Analytics** title of two treatises by Aristotle on logic 7 *Bene . . . logices* the end (i.e., purpose) of logic is to argue well (Latin) 11 **wit** intelligence 12 **on kai me on** being and not being (Greek); **Galen** Greek authority on medicine, second century CE 15 *Summum . . . sanitas* health is the greatest good of medicine (Latin, translated from Aristotle's *Nichomachean Ethics*) 16 **physic** medicine 18 **bills** prescriptions 25 **Justinian** Roman emperor and authority on law (483–565) who ordered the compilation of the *Institutes* 26–27 *Si . . . et cetera* if one thing is willed to two persons, one of them shall have the thing itself, the other the value of the thing, and so forth (Latin) 29 *Exhereditare . . . nisi* a father cannot disinherit his son unless (Latin) 36 **Jerome's Bible** the Latin translation made by St. Jerome (c. 340–420)

---

37 *Stipendium . . . est* the wages of sin is death (Romans vi.23; if Faustus had gone on to read the rest of the verse, he would have found that "the gift of God is eternal life through Jesus Christ our Lord") 38–39 *Si . . . veritas* from 1 John 1:8, translated in the next two lines: Faustus neglects the following verse: "If we confess our sins, He is faithful and just to forgive us our sins, and to cleanse us from all unrightheousness" 43 *Che serà, serà* (Italian, translated in the first half of the next line) 45 **metaphysics** subjects lying beyond (or studied after) physics 46 **negromantic** black magical (though probably here also associated with "necromantic," i.e., concerned with raising the spirits of the dead) 51 **artisan** i.e., expert 52 **quiet** motionless 55 **this** i.e., magic 58 **get** beget 63 **conference** conversation. 64 s.d. **Spirit** Bad Angel, devil (the two angels probably enter the stage from separate doors) 68 **that** i.e., the book of magic

(*Exeunt* ANGELS.)

FAUSTUS: How am I glutted with conceit of this!
    Shall I make spirits fetch me what I please?
75   Resolve me of all ambiguities?
    Perform what desperate enterprise I will?
    I'll have them fly to India for gold,
    Ransack the ocean for orient pearl,
    And search all corners of the new-found world
80   For pleasant fruits and princely delicates;
    I'll have them read me strange philosophy
    And tell the secrets of all foreign kings;
    I'll have them wall all Germany with brass
    And make swift Rhine circle fair Wittenberg;
85   I'll have them fill the public schools with silk
    Wherewith the students shall be bravely clad.
    I'll levy soldiers with the coin they bring
    And chase the Prince of Parma from our land
    And reign sole king of all the provinces!
90   Yea, stranger engines for the brunt of war
    Than was the fiery keel at Antwerp bridge
    I'll make my servile spirits to invent.

(*Enter* VALDES *and* CORNELIUS.)

    Come German Valdes and Cornelius
    And make me blest with your sage conference.
95   Valdes, sweet Valdes, and Cornelius,
    Know that your words have won me at the last
    To practice magic and concealèd arts.
    Philosophy is odious and obscure,
    Both law and physic are for petty wits,
100   Divinity is basest of the three—
    Unpleasant, harsh, contemptible, and vile.
    'Tis magic, magic, that hath ravished me!
    Then, gentle friends, aid me in this attempt
    And I, that have with subtle syllogisms
105   Graveled the pastors of the German church
    And made the flow'ring pride of Wittenberg
    Swarm to my problems as th' infernal spirits
    On sweet Musaeus when he came to hell,
    Will be as cunning as Agrippa was,
110   Whose shadows made all Europe honor him.
VALDES: Faustus, these books, thy wit, and our experience
    Shall make all nations to canonize us.

As Indian Moors obey their Spanish lords,
So shall the spirits of every element
Be always serviceable to us three: 115
Like lions shall they guard us when we please,
Like Almain rutters with their horsemen's staves
Or Lapland giants trotting by our sides;
Sometimes like women or unwedded maids
Shadowing more beauty in their airy brows   120
Than has the white breasts of the queen of love;
From Venice shall they drag huge argosies
And from America the golden fleece
That yearly stuffs old Philip's treasury,
If learnèd Faustus will be resolute.   125
FAUSTUS: Valdes, as resolute am I in this
    As thou to live; therefore object it not.
CORNELIUS: The miracles that magic will perform
    Will make thee vow to study nothing else.
    He that is grounded in astrology,   130
    Enriched with tongues, well seen in minerals,
    Hath all the principles magic doth require.
    Then doubt not Faustus but to be renowned
    And more frequented for this mystery
    Than heretofore the Delphian oracle.   135
    The spirits tell me they can dry the sea
    And fetch the treasure of all foreign wracks,
    Yea, all the wealth that our forefathers hid
    Within the massy entrails of the earth.
    Then tell me Faustus, what shall we three want?   140
FAUSTUS: Nothing, Cornelius. O, this cheers my soul!
    Come, show me some demonstrations magical
    That I may conjure in some bushy grove
    And have these joys in full possession.
VALDES: Then haste thee to some solitary grove,   145
    And bear wise Bacon's and Albanus' works,
    The Hebrew Psalter, and New Testament;
    And whatsoever else is requisite
    We will inform thee ere our conference cease.
CORNELIUS: Valdes, first let him know the words of art,   150
    And then, all other ceremonies learned,
    Faustus may try his cunning by himself.
VALDES: First I'll instruct thee in the rudiments,
    And then wilt thou be perfecter than I.
FAUSTUS: Then come and dine with me, and after meat   155
    We'll canvass every quiddity thereof,
    For ere I sleep I'll try what I can do:
    This night I'll conjure though I die therefor!

(*Exeunt omnes.*)

---

73 **conceit of this** i.e., the conception of being a magician
75 **Resolve me of** explain to me   77 **India** either the West Indies (America) or the East Indies   78 **orient** lustrous and precious 85 **public schools** universities 86 **bravely** splendidly
88 **Prince of Parma** Spanish governor-general of the Low Countries during 1579–1592 90 **brunt** assault 91 **fiery keel** burning ship sent by the Netherlanders in 1585 against a bridge erected by Parma to blockade Antwerp (Antwerp here is adjectival, not genitive) 105 **Graveled** confounded 107 **problems** questions proposed for disputation 108 **Musaeus** legendary Greek poet 109 **Agrippa** Cornelius Agrippa of Nettesheim (1486–1535), German author of *De occulta philosophia,* a survey of Renaissance magic; Agrippa was believed to have raised spirits ("shadows") from the dead

---

113 **Indian Moors** American Indians 117 **Almain rutters** German cavalrymen 120 **Shadowing** sheltering 124 **Philip** King Philip II of Spain (1527–1598) 131 **well seen** skilled 134 **frequented for this mystery** resorted to for this art 135 **Delphian oracle** oracle of Apollo at Delphi 139 **massy** massive 140 **want** lack 143 **conjure** raise spirits 146 **Bacon** Roger Bacon, medieval friar and scientist; **Albanus** perhaps Pietro d'Abano, medieval writer on medicine and philosophy 156 **canvass every quiddity** discuss every essential detail 158 s.d. ***omnes*** all (Latin)

SCENE II

Enter two SCHOLARS.

1 SCHOLAR: I wonder what's become of Faustus that was wont to make our schools ring with *sic probo.*

(*Enter* WAGNER.)

2 SCHOLAR: That shall we presently know. Here comes his boy.

1 SCHOLAR: How now sirrah, where's thy master?

5 WAGNER: God in heaven knows.

1 SCHOLAR: Why, dost not thou know then?

WAGNER: Yes, I know, but that follows not.

1 SCHOLAR: Go to sirrah, leave your jesting and tell us where he is.

10 WAGNER: That follows not by force of argument, which you, being licentiates, should stand upon; therefore, acknowledge your error and be attentive.

2 SCHOLAR: Then you will not tell us?

WAGNER: You are deceived, for I will tell you. Yet if you were

15 not dunces, you would never ask me such a question. For is he not corpus naturale? And is not that mobile? Then wherefore should you ask me such a question? But that I am by nature phlegmatic, slow to wrath, and prone to lechery—to love. I would say—it were not for you to come within forty

20 foot of the place of execution—although I do not doubt but to see you both hanged the next sessions. Thus, having triumphed over you, I will set my countenance like a precisian and begin to speak thus: Truly, my dear brethren, my master is within at dinner, with Valdes and Cornelius, as this wine, if

25 it could speak, would inform your worships; and so, the Lord bless you, preserve you, and keep you, my dear brethren.

(*Exit.*)

1 SCHOLAR: O Faustus, then I fear that which I have long suspected,
    That thou art fall'n into that damnèd art
    For which they two are infamous through the world.

30 2 SCHOLAR: Were he a stranger, not allied to me,
    The danger of his soul would make me mourn.
    But come, let us go and inform the rector.
    It may be his grave counsel may reclaim him.

1 SCHOLAR: I fear me nothing will reclaim him now.

35 2 SCHOLAR: Yet let us see what we can do.

(*Exeunt.*)

I.ii. 2 *sic probo* thus I prove it (Latin)   3 **presently** at once; **boy** servant (an impoverished student)   4 **sirrah** term of address used to an inferior   8 **Go to** exclamation of impatience   11 **licentiates** possessors of a degree preceding the master's degree; **stand upon** make much of   15 **dunces** (1) fools (2) hair-splitters   16 **corpus naturale . . . mobile** natural matter . . . movable (Latin, scholastic definition of the subject-matter of physics)   18 **phlegmatic** sluggish   20 **the place of execution** the place of action, i.e., the dining room (with quibble on gallows)   21 **sessions** sittings of a court   22 **precisian** Puritan (Wagner goes on to parody the style of the Puritans)   32 **rector** head of the university

SCENE III

Thunder. Enter LUCIFER *and four* DEVILS. FAUSTUS *to them with this speech.*

FAUSTUS: Now that the gloomy shadow of the night,
    Longing to view Orion's drizzling look,
    Leaps from th' antarctic world unto the sky
    And dims the welkin with her pitchy breath,
    Faustus, begin thine incantations   5
    And try if devils will obey thy hest,
    Seeing thou hast prayed and sacrificed to them.
    Within this circle is Jehovah's name
    Forward and backward anagrammatized,
    Th' abbreviated names of holy saints,   10
    Figures of every adjunct to the heavens,
    And characters of signs and erring stars,
    By which the spirits are enforced to rise:
    Then fear not, Faustus, to be resolute
    And try the utmost magic can perform.   15

(*Thunder.*)

Sint mihi dei Acherontis propitii! Valeat numen triplex Iehovae! Ignei, aerii, aquatici, spiritus, salvete! Orientis princeps, Belzebub inferni ardentis monarcha, et Demogorgon, propitiamus vos ut appareat et surgat Mephostophilis! Quid tu moraris? Per Iehovam, Gehennam, et consecratam aquam quam nunc spargo, 20 *signumque crucis quod nunc facio, et per vota nostra, ipse nunc surgat nobis dicatus Mephostophilis!*

(*Enter a* DEVIL.)

I charge thee to return and change thy shape,
    Thou art too ugly to attend on me.
    Go, and return an old Franciscan friar: 25
    That holy shape becomes a devil best.

(*Exit* DEVIL.)

I.iii. s.d. **Enter . . . Devils** (they are invisible to Faustus; perhaps they enter through a trapdoor and climb to the upper playing area, as implied in 5.2 s.d.)   2 **Orion** constellation appearing at the beginning of winter, associated with rain   4 **welkin** sky   8 **circle** circle the conjuror draws around him on the ground, to call the spirits and to protect himself from them   11 **adjunct to** heavenly body fixed to   12 **signs and erring stars** signs of the Zodiac and planets   16–22 *Sint . . . Mephostophilis* may the gods of the lower region be favorable to me. Away with the trinity of Jehovah. Hail, spirits of fire, air, water. Prince of the east, Belzebub monarch of burning hell, and Demogorgon, we pray to you that Mephostophilis may appear and rise. Why do you delay? By Jehovah, Gehenna, and the holy water which now I sprinkle, and the sign of the cross which now I make, and by our vows, may Mephostophilis himself now rise to serve us (Latin)   22 s.d. **Devil** the word "dragon" oddly appears, after "surgat Mephostophilis," in the preceding conjuration. It makes no sense in the sentence, and it has therefore been omitted from the present text, but perhaps it indicates that a dragon briefly appears at that point, or perhaps the devil referred to in the present stage direction is disguised as a dragon

I see there's virtue in my heavenly words.
Who would not be proficient in this art?
How pliant is this Mephostophilis,
30   Full of obedience and humility,
Such is the force of magic and my spells.

(*Enter* MEPHOSTOPHILIS.)

MEPHOSTOPHILIS: Now Faustus, what wouldst thou have me do?
FAUSTUS: I charge thee wait upon me whilst I live
To do whatever Faustus shall command,
35   Be it to make the moon drop from her sphere
Or the ocean to overwhelm the world.
MEPHOSTOPHILIS: I am a servant to great Lucifer
And may not follow thee without his leave.
No more than he commands must we perform.
40   FAUSTUS: Did not he charge thee to appear to me?
MEPHOSTOPHILIS: No, I came now hither of mine own accord.
FAUSTUS: Did not my conjuring raise thee? Speak.
MEPHOSTOPHILIS: That was the cause, but yet *per accidens:*
For when we hear one rack the name of God,
45   Abjure the Scriptures and his savior Christ.
We fly in hope to get his glorious soul.
Nor will we come unless he use such means
Whereby he is in danger to be damned.
Therefore the shortest cut for conjuring
50   Is stoutly to abjure the Trinity
And pray devoutly to the prince of hell.
FAUSTUS: So Faustus hath already done, and holds this principle,
There is no chief but only Belzebub:
To whom Faustus doth dedicate himself.
55   This word "damnation" terrifies not me
For I confound hell in Elysium:
My ghost be with the old philosophers!
But leaving these vain trifles of men's souls,
Tell me, what is that Lucifer thy Lord?
60   MEPHOSTOPHILIS: Arch-regent and commander of all spirits.
FAUSTUS: Was not that Lucifer an angel once?
MEPHOSTOPHILIS: Yes Faustus, and most dearly loved of God.
FAUSTUS: How comes it then that he is prince of devils?
MEPHOSTOPHILIS: O, by aspiring pride and insolence.
65   For which God threw him from the face of heaven.
FAUSTUS: And what are you that live with Lucifer?
MEPHOSTOPHILIS: Unhappy spirits that fell with Lucifer,
Conspired against our God with Lucifer,
And are forever damned with Lucifer.
70   FAUSTUS: Where are you damned?
MEPHOSTOPHILIS: In hell.
FAUSTUS: How comes it then that thou art out of hell?
MEPHOSTOPHILIS: Why this is hell, nor am I out of it.
Think'st thou that I who saw the face of God
75   And tasted the eternal joys of heaven
Am not tormented with ten thousand hells
In being deprived of everlasting bliss?

O Faustus, leave these frivolous demands
Which strikes a terror to my fainting soul!
FAUSTUS: What, is great Mephostophilis so passionate   80
For being deprivèd of the joys of heaven?
Learn thou of Faustus manly fortitude
And scorn those joys thou never shalt possess.
Go bear these tidings to great Lucifer:
Seeing Faustus hath incurred eternal death   85
By desperate thoughts against Jove's deity,
Say he surrenders up to him his soul
So he will spare him four and twenty years,
Letting him live in all voluptuousness,
Having thee ever to attend on me,   90
To give me whatsoever I shall ask,
To tell me whatsoever I demand,
To slay mine enemies and to aid my friends
And always be obedient to my will.
Go and return to mighty Lucifer   95
And meet me in my study at midnight,
And then resolve me of thy master's mind.
MEPHOSTOPHILIS: I will, Faustus.
FAUSTUS: Had I as many souls as there be stars
I'd give them all for Mephostophilis.   100
By him I'll be great emperor of the world,
And make a bridge through the moving air
To pass the ocean with a band of men;
I'll join the hills that bind the Afric shore
And make that country continent to Spain,   105
And both contributary to my crown;
The Emperor shall not live but by my leave,
Nor any potentate of Germany.
Now that I have obtained what I desired
I'll live in speculation of this art   110
Till Mephostophilis return again.

(*Exit.*)

(*Exeunt* LUCIFER *and* DEVILS.)

SCENE IV

Enter WAGNER *and* [ROBIN] *the clown.*

WAGNER: Come hither, sirrah boy.
ROBIN: Boy! O, disgrace to my person! Zounds, boy in your
   face! You have seen many boys with such pickadevants, I
   am sure.
WAGNER: Sirrah, hast thou no comings in?   5
ROBIN: Yes, and goings out too, you may see sir.

---

43 *per accidens* the immediate (but not ultimate) cause (Latin)
44 **rack** torture   46 **glorious** (1) splendid (2) presumptuous
56 **confound hell in Elysium** do not distinguish between hell
and Elysium   57 **ghost** spirit; **old** i.e., pre-Christian   60 **spirits** devils

---

79 **strikes** it is not unusual to have a plural subject—especially
when it has a collective force—take a verb ending in *-s*   80 **passionate** emotional   97 **resolve** inform   102 **through** pronounced "thorough"   105 **continent to** continuous with
110 **speculation** contemplation

I.iv. s.d. **Clown** buffoon   2 **Zounds** by God's wounds   3
pickadevants pointed beards   5 **comings in** income (the
Clown then quibbles on "goings out," i.e., expenses and also
holes in his clothes through which his body pokes

WAGNER: Alas, poor slave! See how poverty jests in his nakedness. I know the villain's out of service, and so hungry that
I know he would give his soul to the devil for a shoulder
10   of mutton, though it were blood-raw.

ROBIN: Not so, neither! I had need to have it well roasted, and
good sauce to it, if I pay so dear, I can tell you.

WAGNER: Sirrah, wilt thou be my man and wait on me? And
I will make thee go like *Qui mihi discipulus.*

15   ROBIN: What, in verse?

WAGNER: No, slave, in beaten silk and stavesacre.

ROBIN: Stavesacre? That's good to kill vermin! Then, belike,
if I serve you I shall be lousy.

WAGNER: Why, so thou shalt be, whether thou dost it or no;
20   for sirrah, if thou dost not presently bind thyself to me for
seven years, I'll turn all the lice about thee into familiars
and make them tear thee in pieces.

ROBIN: Nay sir, you may save yourself a labor, for they are as
familiar with me as if they paid for their meat and drink,
25   I can tell you.

WAGNER: Well sirrah, leave your jesting and take these guilders.

ROBIN: Yes marry sir, and I thank you too.

WAGNER: So, now thou art to be at an hour's warning when-
soever and wheresoever the devil shall fetch thee.

30   ROBIN: Here, take your guilders, I'll none of 'em!

WAGNER: Not I, thou art pressed. Prepare thyself, for I will
presently raise up two devils to carry thee away. Banio!
Belcher!

ROBIN: Belcher! And Belcher come here I'll belch him. I am
35   not afraid of a devil!

(*Enter two* DEVILS.)

WAGNER: How now sir, will you serve me now?

ROBIN: Ay, good Wagner, take away the devil then.

WAGNER: Spirits, away! (*Exeunt* DEVILS.) Now sirrah, follow me.

ROBIN: I will sir! But hark you master, will you teach me this
40   conjuring occupation?

WAGNER: Ay sirrah, I'll teach thee to turn thyself to a dog or
a cat or a mouse or a rat or anything.

ROBIN: A dog or a cat or a mouse or a rat? O brave Wagner!

WAGNER: Villain, call me Master Wagner. And see that you
45   walk attentively, and let your right eye be always diametrally fixed upon my left heel, that thou mayst *quasi vestigiis nostris insistere.*

ROBIN: Well sir, I warrant you.

(*Exeunt.*)

---

14 *Qui mihi discipulus* one who is my disciple, i.e., like the
servant of a learned man (the Latin is the beginning of a
poem, familiar to Renaissance schoolboys, on proper behavior)
16 **beaten** embroidered (leading to the quibble on the sense
"hit"); **stavesacre** preparation from seeds of delphinium, used to
kill vermin   21 **familiars attendant** demons   26 **guilders**
Dutch coins   27 **marry** indeed (a mild oath, from "by the Virgin
Mary")   31 **pressed** enlisted into service   34 **And** if   43 **brave**
splendid   45 **diametrally** directly   46–47 *quasi vestigiis nostris
insistere* as if to step in our footsteps

ACT TWO

SCENE I

Enter FAUSTUS *in his study.*

FAUSTUS: Now, Faustus, must thou needs be damned;
Canst thou not be saved!
What boots it then to think on God or heaven?
Away with such vain fancies, and despair—
Despair in God and trust in Belzebub!   5
Now go not backward, Faustus, be resolute!
Why waverst thou? O something soundeth in mine ear,
"Abjure this magic, turn to God again."
Ay, and Faustus will turn to God again.
To God? He loves thee not;   10
The god thou serv'st is thine own appetite
Wherein is fixed the love of Belzebub!
To him I'll build an altar and a church
And offer lukewarm blood of newborn babies!

(*Enter the two* ANGELS.)

BAD ANGEL: Go forward, Faustus, in that famous art.   15

GOOD ANGEL: Sweet Faustus, leave that execrable art.

FAUSTUS: Contrition, prayer, repentance, what of these?

GOOD ANGEL: O, they are means to bring thee unto heaven.

BAD ANGEL: Rather illusions, fruits of lunacy,
That make men foolish that do use them most.   20

GOOD ANGEL: Sweet Faustus, think of heaven and heavenly
things.

BAD ANGEL: No Faustus, think of honor and of wealth.

(*Exeunt* ANGELS.)

FAUSTUS: Wealth!
Why, the signory of Emden shall be mine!
When Mephostophilis shall stand by me   25
What power can hurt me? Faustus, thou art safe.
Cast no more doubts! Mephostophilis, come,
And bring glad tidings from great Lucifer.
Is't not midnight? Come Mephostophilis,
Veni, veni, Mephostophile!   30

(*Enter* MEPHOSTOPHILIS.)

Now tell me, what saith Lucifer thy Lord?

MEPHOSTOPHILIS: That I shall wait on Faustus whilst he lives,
So he will buy my service with his soul.

FAUSTUS: Already Faustus hath hazarded that for thee.

MEPHOSTOPHILIS: But now thou must bequeath it solemnly   35
And write a deed of gift with thine own blood,
For that security craves Lucifer.
If thou deny it I must back to hell.

FAUSTUS: Stay Mephostophilis and tell me
What good will my soul do thy lord?   40

MEPHOSTOPHILIS: Enlarge his kingdom.

II.i. 3 **boots** avails   24 **signory of Emden** lordship of the
rich German port at the mouth of the Ems   30 *Veni, veni,
Mephostophile* come, come, Mephostophilis (Latin)

FAUSTUS: Is that the reason why he tempts us thus?
MEPHOSTOPHILIS: *Solamen miseris socios habuisse doloris.*
FAUSTUS: Why, have you any pain that torture other?
45   MEPHOSTOPHILIS: As great as have the human souls of men.
      But tell me, Faustus, shall I have thy soul—
      And I will be thy slave and wait on thee
      And give thee more than thou hast wit to ask?
FAUSTUS: Ay Mephostophilis. I'll give it him.
50   MEPHOSTOPHILIS: Then, Faustus, stab thy arm courageously
      And bind thy soul that at some certain day
      Great Lucifer may claim it as his own.
      And then be thou as great as Lucifer!
FAUSTUS: Lo, Mephostophilis, for love of thee
55   Faustus hath cut his arm and with his proper blood
      Assures his soul to be great Lucifer's,
      Chief lord and regent of perpetual night.
      View here this blood that trickles from mine arm
      And let it be propitious for my wish.
60   MEPHOSTOPHILIS: But Faustus,
      Write it in manner of a deed of gift.
FAUSTUS: Ay so I do—But Mephostophilis,
      My blood congeals and I can write no more.
MEPHOSTOPHILIS: I'll fetch thee fire to dissolve it straight.

(*Exit.*)

65   FAUSTUS: What might the staying of my blood portend?
      Is it unwilling I should write this bill?
      Why streams it not that I may write afresh:
      "Faustus gives to thee his soul"? O there it stayed.
      Why shouldst thou not? Is not thy soul thine own?
70   Then write again: "Faustus gives to thee his soul."

(*Enter* MEPHOSTOPHILIS *with the chafer of fire.*)

MEPHOSTOPHILIS: See Faustus, here is fire. Set it on.
FAUSTUS: So, now the blood begins to clear again.
      Now will I make an end immediately.
MEPHOSTOPHILIS: (*Aside.*) What will not I do to obtain his soul!
75   FAUSTUS: *Consummatum est!* This bill is ended:
      And Faustus hath bequeathed his soul to Lucifer.
      —But what is this inscription on mine arm?
      Homo fuge! Whither should I fly?
      If unto God, He'll throw me down to hell.
80   My senses are deceived, here's nothing writ.
      O yes, I see it plain! Even here is writ.
      Homo fuge! Yet shall not Faustus fly!
MEPHOSTOPHILIS: (*Aside.*) I'll fetch him somewhat to delight
      his mind.

(*Exit.*)

(*Enter* DEVILS *giving crowns and rich apparel to* FAUSTUS. *They dance and then depart.*)

(*Enter* MEPHOSTOPHILIS.)

FAUSTUS: What means this show? Speak. Mephostophilis.
MEPHOSTOPHILIS: Nothing Faustus, but to delight thy mind   85
      And let thee see what magic can perform.
FAUSTUS: But may I raise such spirits when I please?
MEPHOSTOPHILIS: Ay Faustus, and do greater things than
      these.
FAUSTUS: Then, Mephostophilis, receive this scroll,
      A deed of gift of body and of soul: 90
      But yet conditionally that thou perform
      All covenants and articles between us both.
MEPHOSTOPHILIS: Faustus, I swear by hell and Lucifer
      To effect all promises between us both.
FAUSTUS: Then hear me read it, Mephostophilis: 95

      "On these conditions following:
          First, that Faustus may be a spirit in form and substance.
          Secondly, that Mephostophilis shall be his servant and
      be by him commanded.
          Thirdly, that Mephostophilis shall do for him and bring   100
      him whatsoever.
          Fourthly, that he shall be in his chamber or house in-
      visible.
          Lastly, that he shall appear to the said John Faustus at all
      times in what form or shape soever he please:
          I, John Faustus of Wittenberg, Doctor, by these pre-   105
      sents, do give both body and soul to Lucifer, prince of the
      east, and his minister Mephostophilis, and furthermore
      grant unto them that, four and twenty years being expired,
      and these articles above written being inviolate, full power
      to fetch or carry the said John Faustus, body and soul, flesh,   110
      blood, or goods, into their habitation wheresoever.
                                  By me John Faustus."

MEPHOSTOPHILIS: Speak Faustus, do you deliver this as your
      deed?
FAUSTUS: Ay, take it, and the devil give thee good of it!
MEPHOSTOPHILIS: So now Faustus, ask me what thou wilt.   115
FAUSTUS: First will I question with thee about hell.
      Tell me, where is the place that men call hell?
MEPHOSTOPHILIS: Under the heavens.
FAUSTUS: Ay, so are all things else, but whereabouts?
MEPHOSTOPHILIS: Within the bowels of these elements   120
      Where we are tortured and remain forever.
      Hell hath no limits nor is circumscribed
      In one self place, but where we are is hell,
      And where hell is there must we ever be.
      And to be short, when all the world dissolves   125
      And every creature shall be purified
      All places shall be hell that is not heaven!
FAUSTUS: I think hell's a fable.
MEPHOSTOPHILIS: Ay, think so still—till experience change
      thy mind!

---

43 *Solamen . . . doloris* misery loves company (Latin)   44 **other** others   49 **him** i.e., to Lucifer   55 **proper** own   56 **Assures** conveys by contract   66 **bill** contract   s.d. **chafer** portable grate 71 **it** i.e., the receptacle containing the congealed blood   75 *Consummatum est* it is finished (Latin: a blasphemous repetition of Christ's words on the cross; see John xix.30)   78 *Homo fuge* fly, man (Latin)

97 **spirit** evil spirit, devil (but to see Faustus as transformed now into a devil deprived of freedom to repent is to deprive the remainder of the play of much of its meaning)   109 **inviolate** unviolated

130 FAUSTUS: Why, dost thou think that Faustus shall be damned?
MEPHOSTOPHILIS: Ay, of necessity, for here's the scroll
    In which thou hast given thy soul to Lucifer.
FAUSTUS: Ay, and body too; but what of that?
    Think'st thou that Faustus is so fond to imagine
135 That after this life there is any pain?
    No, these are trifles and mere old wives' tales.
MEPHOSTOPHILIS: But I am an instance to prove the contrary,
    For I tell thee I am damned and now in hell!
FAUSTUS: Nay, and this be hell, I'll willingly be damned—
140 What, sleeping, eating, walking, and disputing?
    But leaving this, let me have a wife, the fairest maid in
        Germany, for I am wanton and lascivious and cannot
        live without a wife.
MEPHOSTOPHILIS: Well Faustus, thou shalt have a wife.

(*He fetches in a woman* DEVIL [*with fireworks*].)

145 FAUSTUS: What sight is this?
MEPHOSTOPHILIS: Now Faustus, will thou have a wife?
FAUSTUS: Here's a hot whore indeed! No, I'll no wife.
MEPHOSTOPHILIS: Marriage is but a ceremonial toy, (*Exit*
    SHE-DEVIL.)
    And if thou lovest me, think no more of it.
150 I'll cull thee out the fairest courtesans
    And bring them every morning to thy bed.
    She whom thine eye shall like thy heart shall have,
    Were she as chaste as was Penelope,
    As wise as Saba, or as beautiful
155 As was bright Lucifer before his fall.
    Here, take this book and peruse it well.
    The iterating of these lines brings gold;
    The framing of this circle on the ground
    Brings thunder, whirlwinds, storm, and lightning;
160 Pronounce this thrice devoutly to thyself,
    And men in harness shall appear to thee,
    Ready to execute what thou command'st.
FAUSTUS: Thanks Mephostophilis for this sweet book.
    This will I keep as chary as my life.

(*Exeunt.*)

SCENE II

Enter FAUSTUS *in his study and* MEPHOSTOPHILIS.

FAUSTUS: When I behold the heavens, then I repent
    And curse thee, wicked Mephostophilis,
    Because thou has deprived me of those joys.
MEPHOSTOPHILIS: 'Twas thine own seeking Faustus, thank
    thyself.

But think'st thou heaven is such a glorious thing? 5
    I tell thee, Faustus, it is not half so fair
    As thou or any man that breathe on earth.
FAUSTUS: How prov'st thou that?
MEPHOSTOPHILIS: 'Twas made for man; then he's more excellent.
FAUSTUS: If heaven was made for man, 'twas made for me! 10
    I will renounce this magic and repent.

(*Enter the two* ANGELS.)

GOOD ANGEL: Faustus, repent: yet God will pity thee!
BAD ANGEL: Thou art a spirit: God cannot pity thee!
FAUSTUS: Who buzzeth in mine ears I am a spirit?
    Be I a devil, yet God may pity me— 15
    Yea, God will pity me if I repent.
BAD ANGEL: Ay, but Faustus never shall repent.

(*Exit* ANGELS.)

FAUSTUS: My heart is hardened, I cannot repent.
    Scarce can I name salvation, faith, or heaven,
    Swords, poison, halters, and envenomed steel 20
    Are laid before me to dispatch myself.
    And long ere this I should have done the deed
    Had not sweet pleasure conquered deep despair.
    Have not I made blind Homer sing to me
    Of Alexander's love and Oenon's death? 25
    And hath not he that built the walls of Thebes
    With ravishing sound of his melodious harp
    Made music with my Mephostophilis?
    Why should I die then or basely despair?
    I am resolved, Faustus shall not repent! 30
    Come Mephostophilis, let us dispute again
    And reason of divine astrology.
    Speak, are there many spheres above the moon?
    Are all celestial bodies but one globe
    As is the substance of this centric earth? 35
MEPHOSTOPHILIS: As are the elements, such are the heavens,
    Even from the moon unto the empyreal orb
    Mutually folded in each others' spheres,
    And jointly move upon one axle-tree,
    Whose terminé is termed the world's wide pole. 40
    Nor are the names of Saturn, Mars, or Jupiter
    Feigned but are erring stars.
FAUSTUS: But have they all one motion,
    Both *situ et tempore?*
MEPHOSTOPHILIS: All move from east to west in four and 45
    twenty hours upon the poles of the world but differ in
    their motions upon the poles of the zodiac.

---

134 **fond** foolish   148 **toy** trifle   150 **cull thee out** select for
you   153 **Penelope** wife of Ulysses, famed for her fidelity
154 **Saba** the Queen of Sheba   157 **iterating** repetition
158 **framing** drawing   161 **harness** armor   164 s.d. **Exeunt** a
scene following this stage direction has probably been lost. Earlier
Wagner hired the Clown; later the Clown is an ostler possessed of
one of Faustus' conjuring books. Possibly, then, the lost scene was
a comic one, showing the Clown stealing a book and departing

II.ii.   12 **yet** still, even now   25 **Alexander . . . Oenon's** Paris,
also called Alexander, was Oenone's lover, but he later deserted
her for Helen of Troy, causing the Trojan War, the subject of
Homer's Iliad   26 **he** Amphion, whose music charmed stones to
form the walls of Thebes   35 **centric** central   36 **such** i.e.,
separate but combined; the idea is that the heavenly bodies are
separate but their spheres are concentric ("folded"), and all—
from the nearest (the moon) to the farthest ("the empyreal orb"
or empyrean)—move on one axletree   40 **terminé** end, extremity   42 **erring stars** planets   44 *situ et tempore* in place
and in time

FAUSTUS: These slender questions Wagner can decide.
Hath Mephostophilis no greater skill?
50 Who knows not the double motion of the planets?
That the first is finished in a natural day.
The second thus: Saturn in thirty years;
Jupiter in twelve; Mars in four; the sun, Venus, and Mer-
cury in a year; the moon in twenty-eight days. These are
55 fresh-men's suppositions. But tell me, hath every sphere a
dominion or *intelligentia*?
MEPHOSTOPHILIS: Ay.
FAUSTUS: How many heavens or spheres are there?
MEPHOSTOPHILIS: Nine: the seven planets, the firmament, and
60 the empyreal heaven.
FAUSTUS: But is there not *coelum igneum et crystallinum?*
MEPHOSTOPHILIS: No Faustus, they be but fables.
FAUSTUS: Resolve me then in this one question. Why are not
conjunctions, oppositions, aspects, eclipses all at one time,
65 but in some years we have more, in some less?
MEPHOSTOPHILIS: *Per inaqualem motum respectu totius.*
FAUSTUS: Well, I am answered. Now tell me, who made the
world?
MEPHOSTOPHILIS: I will not.
70 FAUSTUS: Sweet Mephostophilis, tell me.
MEPHOSTOPHILIS: Move me not, Faustus!
FAUSTUS: Villain, have not I bound thee to tell me any-
thing?
MEPHOSTOPHILIS: Ay, that is not against our kingdom. This is.
Thou art damned. Think thou of hell!
75 FAUSTUS: Think, Faustus, upon God, that made the world.
MEPHOSTOPHILIS: Remember this!

(*Exit.*)

FAUSTUS: Ay, go accursèd spirit to ugly hell!
'Tis thou hast damned distressèd Faustus' soul—
Is't not too late?

(*Enter the two* ANGELS.)

80 BAD ANGEL: Too late.
GOOD ANGEL: Never too late, if Faustus will repent.
BAD ANGEL: If thou repent, devils will tear thee in pieces.
GOOD ANGEL: Repent, and they shall never raze thy skin.

(*Exeunt* ANGELS.)

FAUSTUS: O Christ, my savior, my savior!
85 Help to save distressèd Faustus' soul.

(*Enter* LUCIFER, BELZEBUB, *and* MEPHOSTOPHILIS.)

LUCIFER: Christ cannot save thy soul, for He is just.
There's none but I have interest in the same.
FAUSTUS: O, what art thou that look'st so terribly?

LUCIFER: I am Lucifer
And this is my companion prince in hell.   90
FAUSTUS: O Faustus, they are come to fetch thy soul!
BELZEBUB: We are come to tell thee thou dost injure us.
LUCIFER: Thou call'st on Christ contrary to thy promise.
BELZEBUB: Thou should'st not think on God.
LUCIFER: Think on the Devil.
BELZEBUB: And his dam too.   95
FAUSTUS: Nor will Faustus henceforth. Pardon him for this,
And Faustus vows never to look to heaven!
Never to name God or to pray to Him,
To burn His Scriptures, slay His ministers,
And make my spirits pull His churches down.   100
LUCIFER: So shalt thou show thyself an obedient servant,
And we will highly gratify thee for it.
BELZEBUB: Faustus, we are come from hell in person to show
thee some pastime. Sit down and thou shalt behold the
Seven Deadly Sins appear to thee in their own proper   105
shapes and likeness.
FAUSTUS: That sight will be as pleasant to me as Paradise was
to Adam the first day of his creation.
LUCIFER: Talk not of Paradise or creation but mark the show.
Go Mephostophilis, fetch them in.   110

(*Enter the* SEVEN DEADLY SINS [*led by a* PIPER].)

BELZEBUB: Now Faustus, question them of their names and
dispositions.
FAUSTUS: That shall I soon. What art thou, the first?
PRIDE: I am Pride. I disdain to have any parents. I am like to
Ovid's flea, I can creep into every corner of a wench: 115
sometimes, like a periwig I sit upon her brow; next, like
a necklace I hang about her neck; then, like a fan of feathers I kiss her; and then, turning myself to a wrought
smock, do what I list—But fie, what a smell is here! I'll
not speak a word more for a king's ransom unless the   120
ground be perfumed and covered with cloth of arras.
FAUSTUS: Thou art a proud knave indeed. What art thou, the
second?
COVETOUSNESS: I am Covetousness, begotten of an old churl
in a leather bag; and might I now obtain my wish, this   125
house, you and all, should turn to gold that I might lock
you safe into my chest. O my sweet gold!
FAUSTUS: And what art thou, the third?
ENVY: I am Envy, begotten of a chimney-sweeper and an oysterwife. I cannot read and therefore wish all books burned. 130
I am lean with seeing others eat. O, that there would come
a famine over all the world that all might die and I live
alone! Then thou shouldst see how fat I'd be. But must
thou sit and I stand? Come down, with a vengeance!
FAUSTUS: Out, envious wretch! But what art thou, the fourth? 135

---

51 **natural day** twenty-four hours   55 **suppositions** premises
55–56 **dominion or *intelligentia*** governing angel or intelligence
(believed to impart motion to the sphere)   61 *coelum igneum et
crystallinum* a heaven of fire and a crystaline sphere (Latin)
64 **at one time** i.e., at regular intervals   66 *Per . . . totius* because of unequal speed within the system (Latin)   71 **Move**
anger   83 **raze** scratch   87 **interest in** legal claim on

95 **dam** mother   105 **Seven Deadly Sins** so called because
they cause spiritual death; they are Pride, Covetousness, Envy,
Wrath, Gluttony, Sloth, Lechery   115 **Ovid's flea** flea in
Carmen de pulce, a lewd poem mistakenly attributed to Ovid
118 **wrought smock** decorated petticoat   121 **cloth of arras**
Flemish cloth used for tapestries   125 **leather bag** moneybag (?)
129–130 **chimney-sweeper . . . oysterwife** i.e., dirty and smelly

WRATH: I am Wrath. I had neither father nor mother. I leapt out of a lion's mouth when I was scarce an hour old and ever since have run up and down the world with these case of rapiers, wounding myself when I could get none
140 to fight withal. I was born in hell! And look to it, for some of you shall be my father.

FAUSTUS: And what art thou, the fifth?

GLUTTONY: I am Gluttony. My parents are all dead, and the devil a penny they have left me, but a small pension: and
145 that buys me thirty meals a day and ten bevers, a small trifle to suffice nature. I come of a royal pedigree. My father was a gammon of bacon, and my mother was a hogshead of claret wine. My godfathers were these: Peter Pickledherring and Martin Martlemas-beef. But my godmother.
150 O, she was an ancient gentlewoman: her name was Margery March-beer. Now Faustus, thou hast heard all my progeny, wilt thou bid me to supper?

FAUSTUS: Not I.

GLUTTONY: Then the devil choke thee!

155 FAUSTUS: Choke thyself, glutton! What art thou, the sixth?

SLOTH: Heigh-ho! I am Sloth. I was begotten on a sunny bank. Heigh-ho, I'll not speak a word more for a king's ransom.

FAUSTUS: And what are you, Mistress Minx, the seventh and last?

LECHERY: Who, I, I sir? I am one that loves an inch of raw
160 mutton better than an ell of fried stockfish, and the first letter of my name begins with Lechery.

LUCIFER: Away to hell, away! On, piper!

(*Exeunt the* SEVEN SINS.)

FAUSTUS: O, how this sight doth delight my soul!

LUCIFER: But Faustus, in hell is all manner of delight.

165 FAUSTUS: O, might I see hell and return again safe, how happy were I then!

LUCIFER: Faustus, thou shalt. At midnight I will send for thee. Meanwhile peruse this book and view it thoroughly, And thou shalt turn thyself into what shape thou wilt.

170 FAUSTUS: Thanks mighty Lucifer.
This will I keep as chary as my life.

LUCIFER: Now Faustus, farewell.

FAUSTUS: Farewell great Lucifer. Come Mephostophilis.

(*Exeunt omnes several ways.*)

SCENE III

Enter [ROBIN] *the clown.*

ROBIN: What, Dick, look to the horses there till I come again! I have gotten one of Doctor Faustus' conjuring books, and now we'll have such knavery as't passes.

(*Enter* DICK.)

DICK: What, Robin, you must come away and walk the horses.

ROBIN: I walk the horses? I scorn't, faith. I have other matters 5
in hand. Let the horses walk themselves an they will. (*Reading.*) A *per se*—a; t, h, e—the; o *per se*—o; deny orgon—gorgon. Keep further from me, O thou illiterate and unlearned hostler!

DICK: 'Snails, what hast thou got there, a book? Why, thou 10
canst not tell ne'er a word on't.

ROBIN: That thou shalt see presently. Keep out of the circle, I say, lest I send you into the hostry with a vengeance.

DICK: That's like, 'faith! You had best leave your foolery, for an my master come, he'll conjure you, 'faith. 15

ROBIN: My master conjure me? I'll tell thee what. An my master come here, I'll clap as fair a pair of horns on's head as e'er thou sawest in thy life.

DICK: Thou need'st not do that, for my mistress hath done it.

ROBIN: Ay, there be of us here that have waded as deep into 20
matters as other men—if they were disposed to talk.

DICK: A plague take you! I thought you did not sneak up and down after her for nothing. But I prithee tell me in good sadness Robin, is that a conjuring book?

ROBIN: Do but speak what thou't have me to do, and I'll do't. 25
If thou't dance naked, put off thy clothes, and I'll conjure thee about presently. Or if thou't go but to the tavern with me, I'll give thee white wine, red wine, claret wine, sack, muscadine, malmsey, and whippin—crusthold-belly-hold. And we'll not pay one penny for it. 30

DICK: O brave! Prithee let's to it presently, for I am as dry as a dog.

ROBIN: Come then, let's away.

(*Exeunt.*)

ACT THREE

Enter the CHORUS.

Learnèd Faustus,
To find the secrets of astronomy
Graven in the book of Jove's high firmament,
Did mount him up to scale Olympus' top:
Where, sitting in a chariot burning bright 5
Drawn by the strength of yokèd dragons' necks,
He views the clouds, the planets, and the stars,
The tropics, zones, and quarters of the sky,
From the bright circle of the hornèd moon
Even to the height of *primum mobile:* 10

---

138 **these case** this pair   145 **bevers** snacks (literally drinks)
147 **gammon** haunch   149 **Martlemas-beef** cattle slaughtered at Martinmas (11 November) and salted for winter consumption   151 **March-beer** strong beer brewed in March; **progeny** ancestry   156 **Heigh-ho** a yawn or tired greeting 159 **inch of raw mutton** i.e., penis ("mutton" in a bawdy sense commonly alludes to a prostitute, but since here the speaker is a woman, the allusion must be to a male)   160 **an ell of . . . stockfish** forty-five inches of dried cod   171 **chary** carefully 178 s.d. **several** various

II.iii. 6 **an** if   7 *per se* by itself (Latin; the idea is, "A by itself spells A")   7–8 **deny orgon—gorgon** Robin is trying to read the name "Demogorgon"   10 **'Snails** by God's nails   13 **hostry** hostelry inn   17 **horns** as the next speech indicates, horns were said to adorn the head of a man whose wife was unfaithful   23 **in good sadness** seriously   28 **sack** sherry   29 **whippincrust** illiterate pronunciation of "hippocras," a spiced wine

III Chorus 8 **zones** segments of the sky   9 **circle** orbit 10 **primum mobile** the outermost sphere, the empyrean

And whirling round with this circumference
Within the concave compass of the pole,
From east to west his dragons swiftly glide
And in eight days did bring him home again.
15   Not long he stayed within his quiet house
To rest his bones after his weary toil
But new exploits do hale him out again.
And mounted then upon a dragon's back,
That with his wings did part the subtle air,
20   He now is gone to prove cosmography,
That measures coasts and kingdoms of the earth,
And as I guess will first arrive at Rome
To see the Pope and manner of his court
And take some part of holy Peter's feast,
25   The which this day is highly solemnized.

(*Exit.*)

SCENE I

Enter FAUSTUS *and* MEPHOSTOPHILIS.

FAUSTUS: Having now, my good Mephostophilis,
   Passed with delight the stately town of Trier,
   Environed round with airy mountain tops,
   With walls of flint, and deep-entrenchèd lakes,
5   Not to be won by any conquering prince:
   From Paris next, coasting the realm of France,
   We saw the river Main fall into Rhine,
   Whose banks are set with groves of fruitful vines:
   Then up to Naples, rich Campania,
10   Whose buildings fair and gorgeous to the eye,
   The streets straight forth and paved with finest brick,
   Quarters the town in four equivalents.
   There saw we learnèd Maro's golden tomb,
   The way he cut an English mile in length
15   Through a rock of stone in one night's space.
   From thence to Venice, Padua, and the rest,
   In one of which a sumptuous temple stands
   That threats the stars with her aspiring top,
   Whose frame is paved with sundry colored stones
20   And roofed aloft with curious work in gold.
   Thus hitherto hath Faustus spent his time.
   But tell me now, what resting-palace is this?
   Hast thou, as erst I did command,
   Conducted me within the walls of Rome?
25 MEPHOSTOPHILIS: I have, my Faustus, and for proof thereof
   This is the goodly palace of the Pope,
   And cause we are no common guests
   I choose his privy chamber for our use.
FAUSTUS: I hope his Holiness will bid us welcome.
30 MEPHOSTOPHILIS: All's one, for we'll be bold with his venison.
   But now my Faustus, that thou may'st perceive
   What Rome contains for to delight thine eyes,

Know that this city stands upon seven hills
That underprop the groundwork of the same:
Just through the midst runs flowing Tiber's stream   35
With winding banks that cut it in two parts,
Over the which four stately bridges lean
That make safe passage to each part of Rome.
Upon the bridge called Ponte Angelo
Erected is a castle passing strong   40
Where thou shalt see such store of ordinance
As that the double cannons forged of brass
Do match the number of the days contained
Within the compass of one complete year,
Beside the gates and high pyramides   45
That Julius Caesar brought from Africa.
FAUSTUS: Now, by the kingdoms of infernal rule,
   Of Styx, of Acheron, and the fiery lake
   Of ever-burning Phlegethon, I swear
   That I do long to see the monuments   50
   And situation of bright-splendent Rome.
   Come therefore, let's away.
MEPHOSTOPHILIS: Nay stay my Faustus. I know you'd see the
     Pope
   And take some part of holy Peter's feast,
   The which this day with high solemnity,   55
   This day, is held through Rome and Italy
   In honor of the Pope's triumphant victory.
FAUSTUS: Sweet Mephostophilis, thou pleasest me.
   Whilst I am here on earth let me be cloyed
   With all things that delight the heart of man.   60
   My four and twenty years of liberty
   I'll spend in pleasure and in dalliance,
   That Faustus' name, whilst this bright frame doth stand,
   May be admirèd through the furthest land.
MEPHOSTOPHILIS: 'Tis well said, Faustus, come then, stand   65
     by me
   And thou shalt see them come immediately.
FAUSTUS: Nay stay, my gentle Mephostophilis,
   And grant me my request, and then I go.
   Thou know'st, within the compass of eight days
   We viewed the face of heaven, of earth, and hell.   70
   So high our dragons soared into the air
   That looking down the earth appeared to me
   No bigger than my hand in quantity—
   There did we view the kingdoms of the world,
   And what might please mine eye I there beheld.   75
   Then in this show let me an actor be
   That this proud Pope may Faustus' cunning see!
MEPHOSTOPHILIS: Let it be so, my Faustus, but first stay
   And view their triumphs as they pass this way.
   And then devise what best contents thy mind   80
   By cunning in thine art to cross the Pope
   Or dash the pride of this solemnity—
   To make his monks and abbots stand like apes
   And point like antics at his triple crown,

---

20 **prove cosmography** test maps, i.e., explore the universe

III.i. 2 Trier German city on the Moselle, also known as Trèves
4 **deep-entrenchèd lakes** moats   13 **Maro** Vergil (Publius
Vergilius Maro, 70–19 BCE)   15 **Through** pronounced "thorough"

---

37 **lean** bend   45 **pyramides** obelisk (pronounced py-ràm-i-des)
48–49 **Styx, Acheron, Phlegethon** rivers of the underworld
79 **triumphs** spectacular displays   84 **antics** grotesque figures,
buffoons

85　To beat the beads about the friars' pates,
　　Or clap huge horns upon the cardinals' heads,
　　Or any villainy thou canst devise—
　　And I'll perform it, Faustus. Hark, they come!
　　This day shall make thee be admired in Rome!

(*Enter the* CARDINALS *and* BISHOPS, *some bearing crosiers, some the*
pillars; MONKS *and* FRIARS *singing their procession; then the* POPE
and RAYMOND *King of Hungary, with* BRUNO *led in chains.*)

90　POPE: Cast down our footstool.
　　RAYMOND:　　　　　　　　Saxon Bruno, stoop,
　　Whilst on thy back his Holiness ascends
　　Saint Peter's chair and state pontifical.
　　BRUNO: Proud Lucifer, that state belongs to me—
　　But thus I fall to Peter, not to thee.
95　POPE: To me and Peter shalt thou grov'ling lie
　　And crouch before the papal dignity!
　　Sound trumpets then, for thus Saint Peter's heir
　　From Bruno's back ascends Saint Peter's chair!

(*A flourish while he ascends.*)

　　Thus as the gods creep on with feet of wool
100　Long ere with iron hands they punish men,
　　So shall our sleeping vengeance now arise
　　And smite with death thy hated enterprise.
　　Lord Cardinals of France and Padua,
　　Go forthwith to our holy consistory
105　And read amongst the statutes decretal
　　What by the holy council held at Trent
　　The sacred synod hath decreed for him
　　That doth assume the papal government
　　Without election and a true consent.
110　Away, and bring us word with speed!
　　1 CARDINAL: We go my lord.

(*Exeunt [two]* CARDINALS.)

POPE: Lord Raymond—

(*Talks to him apart.*)

FAUSTUS: Go haste thee, gentle Mephostophilis,
　　Follow the cardinals to the consistory
115　And as they turn their superstitious books
　　Strike them with sloth and drowsy idleness
　　And make them sleep so sound that in their shapes
　　Thyself and I may parley with this Pope,
　　This proud confronter of the Emperor!
120　—And in despite of all his holiness
　　Restore this Bruno to his liberty
　　And bear him to the states of Germany!

_____

89 **admired** wondered at; s.d. **Raymond King of Hungary**
. . . Bruno unhistorical figures; Bruno is the emperor's nominee
for the papal throne　92 **state** throne　98 s.d. **flourish** trumpet fanfare　104 **consistory** i.e., meeting-place of the papal
consistory or senate　105 **statutes decretal** i.e., ecclesiastical
laws　106 **council held at Trent** intermittently from 1545 to
1563　107 **synod** council

MEPHOSTOPHILIS: Faustus, I go.
FAUSTUS: Dispatch it soon.
　　The Pope shall curse that Faustus came to Rome.　125

(*Exit* FAUSTUS *and* MEPHOSTOPHILIS.)

BRUNO: Pope Adrian, let me have some right of law:
　　I was elected by the Emperor.
POPE: We will depose the Emperor for that deed
　　And curse the people that submit to him.
　　Both he and thou shalt stand excommunicate　130
　　And interdict from church's privilege
　　And all society of holy men.
　　He grows too proud in his authority,
　　Lifting his lofty head above the clouds,
　　And like a steeple overpeers the church.　135
　　But we'll pull down his haughty insolence.
　　And as Pope Alexander, our progenitor,
　　Trod on the neck of German Frederick,
　　Adding this golden sentence to our praise:
　　"That Peter's heirs should tread on emperors　140
　　And walk upon the dreadful adder's back,
　　Treading the lion and the dragon down,
　　And fearless spurn the killing basilisk"—
　　So will we quell that haughty schismatic
　　And by authority apostolical　145
　　Depose him from his regal government.
BRUNO: Pope Julius swore to princely Sigismond,
　　For him and the succeeding Popes of Rome,
　　To hold the emperors their lawful lords.
POPE: Pope Julius did abuse the church's rites　150
　　And therefore none of his decrees can stand.
　　Is not all power on earth bestowed on us?
　　And therefore though we would, we cannot err.
　　Behold this silver belt whereto is fixed
　　Seven golden keys fast sealed with seven seals　155
　　In token of our sevenfold power from heaven
　　To bind or loose, lock fast, condemn, or judge,
　　Resign or seal, or whatso pleaseth us.
　　Then he and thou and all the world shall stoop—
　　Or be assurèd of our dreadful curse　160
　　To light as heavy as the pains of hell.

(*Enter* FAUSTUS *and* MEPHOSTOPHILIS *like the* CARDINALS.)

MEPHOSTOPHILIS: (*Aside.*) Now tell me Faustus, are we not
　　fitted well?
FAUSTUS: (*Aside.*) Yes Mephostophilis, and two such cardinals
　　Ne'er served a holy Pope as we shall do.
　　But whilst they sleep within the consistory　165
　　Let us salute his reverend Fatherhood.
RAYMOND: Behold my lord, the cardinals are returned.
POPE: Welcome grave fathers, answer presently,
　　What have our holy council there decreed
　　Concerning Bruno and the Emperor　170

_____

137 **Pope Alexander** Pope Alexander III (d. 1181) compelled
the Emperor Frederick Barbarossa to kneel before him; **progenitor** predecessor　143 **basilisk** fabulous monster said to kill with
a glance　158 **Resign** unseal　168 **presently** immediately

In quittance of their late conspiracy
Against our state and papal dignity?
FAUSTUS: Most sacred patron of the church of Rome,
By full consent of all the synod
175 Of priests and prelates it is thus decreed:
That Bruno and the German Emperor
Be held as lollards and bold schismatics
And proud disturbers of the church's peace.
And if that Bruno by his own assent,
180 Without enforcement of the German peers,
Did seek to wear the triple diadem
And by your death to climb Saint Peter's chair,
The statutes decretal have thus decreed:
He shall be straight condemned of heresy
185 And on a pile of fagots burnt to death.
POPE: It is enough. Here, take him to your charge
And bear him straight to Ponte Angelo
And in the strongest tower enclose him fast.
Tomorrow, sitting in our consistory
190 With all our college of grave cardinals
We will determine of his life or death.
Here, take his triple crown along with you
And leave it in the church's treasury.
Make haste again, my good lord cardinals,
195 And take our blessing apostolical.
MEPHOSTOPHILIS: (*Aside.*) So, so! Was never devil thus
blessed before.
FAUSTUS: (*Aside.*) Away sweet Mephostophilis, be gone!
The cardinals will be plagued for this anon.

(*Exeunt* FAUSTUS *and* MEPHOSTOPHILIS [*with* BRUNO].)

POPE: Go presently and bring a banquet forth,
200 That we may solemnize Saint Peter's feast
And with Lord Raymond, King of Hungary,
Drink to our late and happy victory.

(*Exeunt.*)

SCENE II

A sennet while the banquet is brought in, and then enter FAUSTUS
and MEPHOSTOPHILIS *in their own shapes.*

MEPHOSTOPHILIS: Now Faustus, come prepare thyself for
mirth.
The sleepy cardinals are hard at hand
To censure Bruno, that is posted hence,
And on a proud-paced steed as swift as thought
5 Flies o'er the Alps to fruitful Germany,
There to salute the woeful Emperor.
FAUSTUS: The Pope will curse them for their sloth today
That slept both Bruno and his crown away.
But now, that Faustus may delight his mind
10 And by their folly make some merriment,

Sweet Mephostophilis, so charm me here
That I may walk invisible to all
And do whate'er I please unseen of any.
MEPHOSTOPHILIS: Faustus, thou shalt. Then kneel down
presently,
Whilst on thy head I lay my hand   15
And charm thee with this magic wand.
First wear this girdle, then appear
Invisible to all are here:
The planets seven, the gloomy air,
Hell, and the Furies' forkèd hair,   20
Pluto's blue fire, and Hecat's tree
With magic spells so compass thee
That no eye may thy body see.
So Faustus, now for all their holiness,
Do what thou wilt, thou shalt not be discerned.   25
FAUSTUS: Thanks Mephostophilis. Now friars, take heed
Lest Faustus make your shaven crowns to bleed.
MEPHOSTOPHILIS: Faustus, no more. See where the cardinals
come.

(*Enter* POPE [*and* FRIARS] *and all the* LORDS [*with* KING RAY-
MOND *and the* ARCHBISHOP OF RHEIMS]. *Enter the* [*two*] CAR-
DINALS *with a book.*)

POPE: Welcome lord cardinals. Come, sit down.
Lord Raymond, take your seat. Friars, attend,   30
And see that all things be in readiness
As best beseems this solemn festival.
1 CARDINAL: First may it please your sacred Holiness
To view the sentence of the reverend synod
Concerning Bruno and the Emperor.   35
POPE: What needs this question? Did I not tell you
Tomorrow we would sit i' th' consistory
And there determine of his punishment?
You brought us word, even now, it was decreed
That Bruno and the cursèd Emperor   40
Were by the holy council both condemned
For loathèd lollards and base schismatics.
Then wherefore would you have me view that book?
1 CARDINAL: Your Grace mistakes. You gave us no such charge.
RAYMOND: Deny it not; we all are witnesses   45
That Bruno here was late delivered you
With his rich triple crown to be reserved
And put into the church's treasury.
BOTH CARDINALS: By holy Paul we saw them not.
POPE: By Peter you shall die   50
Unless you bring them forth immediately.
Hale them to prison, lade their limbs with gyves.
False prelates, for this hateful treachery
Cursed be your souls to hellish misery.

(*Exeunt* ATTENDANTS *with two* CARDINALS.)

---

171 **quittance of** requital for   177 **lollards** heretics   194 **again**
i.e., to return

III.ii. s.d. **sennet** set of notes played on a trumpet signaling an
approach or a departure

---

20 **Furies' forkèd hair** the hair of the Furies consisted of
snakes, whose forked tongues may be implied here   21 **Hecat**
Hecate, goddess of magic (possibly her "tree" is the gallows-tree,
but possibly "tree" is a slip for "three," Hecate being the triple
goddess of heaven, earth, and hell)   52 **gyves** fetters

55 FAUSTUS: So, they are safe. Now Faustus, to the feast.
   The Pope had never such a frolic guest.
POPE: Lord Archbishop of Rheims, sit down with us.
ARCHBISHOP: I thank your Holiness.
FAUSTUS: Fall to, the devil choke you an you spare!
60 POPE: Who's that spoke? Friars, look about.
   Lord Raymond, pray fall to. I am beholding
   To the Bishop of Milan for this so rare a present.
FAUSTUS: (*Aside.*) I thank you, sir!

(*Snatches the dish.*)

POPE: How now! Who snatched the meat from me?
65   Villains, why speak you not?
   My good Lord Archbishop, here's a most dainty dish
   Was sent me from a cardinal in France.
FAUSTUS: (*Aside.*) I'll have that too!

(*Snatches the dish.*)

POPE: What lollards do attend our Holiness
70   That we receive such great indignity!
   Fetch me some wine.
FAUSTUS: (*Aside.*) Ay, pray do, for Faustus is adry.
POPE: Lord Raymond, I drink unto your Grace.
FAUSTUS: (*Aside.*) I pledge your Grace.

(*Snatches the goblet.*)

75 POPE: My wine gone too? Ye lubbers, look about
   And find the man that doth this villainy,
   Or by our sanctitude you all shall die.
   I pray, my lords, have patience at this troublesome banquet.
ARCHBISHOP: Please it your Holiness, I think it be some
80   ghost crept out of purgatory, and now is come unto your
   Holiness for his pardon.
POPE: It may be so:
   Go then, command our priests to sing a dirge
   To lay the fury of this same troublesome ghost.

(*Exit* ATTENDANT.)

(*The* POPE *crosses himself before eating.*)

85 FAUSTUS: How now! Must every bit be spicèd with a cross?
   Nay then, take that!

(*Strikes the* POPE.)

POPE: O, I am slain! Help me my lords!
   O come and help to bear my body hence.
   Damned be this soul forever for this deed.

(*Exeunt the* POPE *and his train.*)

90 MEPHOSTOPHILIS: Now Faustus, what will you do now?
   For I can tell you, you'll be cursed with bell, book, and
   candle.

---

59 **Fall to** set to work (here, as commonly, "start eating")
91–92 **bell, book, and candle** implements used in excommunicating (the bell was tolled, the book closed, the candle extinguished)

FAUSTUS: Bell, book, and candle. Candle, book, and bell.
   Forward and backward, to curse Faustus to hell!

(*Enter the* FRIARS, *with bell, book, and candle for the dirge.*)

1 FRIAR: Come brethren, let's about our business with good   95
   devotion.
   Cursèd be he that stole his Holiness' meat from the table.
   Maledicat Dominus!
   Cursèd be he that struck his Holiness a blow on the face.
   Maledicat Dominus!

(FAUSTUS *strikes a* FRIAR.)

   Cursèd be he that took Friar Sandelo a blow on the pate.   100
   Maledicat Dominus!
   Cursèd be he that disturbeth our holy dirge.
   Maledicat Dominus!
   Cursèd be he that took away his Holiness' wine.
   Maledicat Dominus!   105

([FAUSTUS *and* MEPHOSTOPHILIS] *beat the* FRIARS, *fling fireworks among them and exeunt.*)

SCENE III

Enter [ROBIN] *the clown and* DICK *with a cup.*

DICK: Sirrah Robin, we were best look that your devil can
   answer the stealing of this same cup, for the vintner's boy
   follows us at the hard heels.
ROBIN: 'Tis no matter, let him come! An he follow us I'll so
   conjure him as he was never conjured in his life, I warrant   5
   him. Let me see the cup.

(*Enter* VINTNER.)

DICK: Here 'tis. Yonder he comes. Now Robin, now or never
   show thy cunning.
VINTNER: O, are you here? I am glad I have found you. You
   are a couple of fine companions! Pray, where's the cup you   10
   stole from the tavern?
ROBIN: How, how! We steal a cup? Take heed what you say.
   We look not like cup-stealers, I can tell you.
VINTNER: Never deny't, for I know you have it, and I'll search
   you.   15
ROBIN: Search me? Ay, and spare not! (*Aside.*) Hold the cup,
   Dick. Come, come. Search me, search me.

(VINTNER *searches him.*)

VINTNER: Come on sirrah, let me search you now.
DICK: Ay ay, do do. (*Aside.*) Hold the cup, Robin. I fear not
   your searching. We scorn to steal your cups, I can tell you.   20

(VINTNER *searches him.*)

---

97 *Maledicat Dominus* may the Lord curse him (Latin)

III.iii. 3 **at the hard heels** hard at heel, closely   10 **companions** fellows (contemptuous)

VINTNER: Never outface me for the matter, for sure the cup
is between you two.

ROBIN: Nay, there you lie! 'Tis beyond us both.

VINTNER: A plague take you. I thought 'twas your knavery to
25 take it away. Come, give it me again.

ROBIN: Ay, much! When, can you tell? (*Aside.*) Dick, make
me a circle and stand close at my back and stir not for thy
life. Vintner, you shall have your cup anon. (*Aside.*) Say
nothing, Dick! O *per se,* o; Demogorgon, Belcher, and
30 Mephostophilis!

(*Enter* MEPHOSTOPHILIS. *Exit* VINTNER.)

MEPHOSTOPHILIS: You princely legions of infernal rule,
How am I vexèd by these villains' charms!
From Constantinople have they brought me now
Only for pleasure of these damnèd slaves.

35 ROBIN: By lady sir, you have had a shrewd journey of it. Will
it please you to take a shoulder of mutton to supper and
a tester in your purse and go back again?

DICK: Ay, I pray you heartily, sir. For we called you but in jest,
I promise you.

40 MEPHOSTOPHILIS: To purge the rashness of this cursèd deed,
First be thou turnèd to this ugly shape,
For apish deeds transformèd to an ape.

ROBIN: O brave! An ape! I pray sir, let me have the carrying
of him about to show some tricks.

45 MEPHOSTOPHILIS: And so thou shalt. Be thou transformed to
a dog and carry him upon thy back. Away, be gone!

ROBIN: A dog! That's excellent. Let the maids look well to
their porridge-pots, for I'll into the kitchen presently.
Come Dick, come.

(*Exeunt the two* CLOWNS.)

50 MEPHOSTOPHILIS: Now with the flames of ever-burning fire
I'll wing myself and forthwith fly amain
Unto my Faustus, to the Great Turk's count.

(*Exit.*)

ACT FOUR

Enter CHORUS.

When Faustus had with pleasure ta'en the view
Of rarest things and royal courts of kings,
He stayed his course and so returnèd home,
Where such as bare his absence but with grief,
5 I mean his friends and nearest companions,
Did gratulate his safety with kind words.
And in their conference of what befell
Touching his journey through the world and air
They put forth questions of astrology
10 Which Faustus answered with such learnèd skill

As they admired and wondered at his wit
Now is his fame spread forth in every land.
Amongst the rest the Emperor is one,
Carolus the Fifth, at whose palace now
Faustus is feasted 'mongst his noblemen.   15
What there he did in trial of his art
I leave untold, your eyes shall see performed.

(*Exit.*)

SCENE I

Enter MARTINO *and* FREDERICK *at several doors.*

MARTINO: What ho, officers, gentlemen!
Hie to the presence to attend the Emperor.
Good Frederick, see the rooms be voided straight,
His Majesty is coming to the hall.
Go back and see the state in readiness.   5

FREDERICK: But where is Bruno, our elected Pope,
That on a fury's back came post from Rome?
Will not his Grace consort the Emperor?

MARTINO: O yes, and with him comes the German conjurer,
The learnèd Faustus, fame of Wittenberg,   10
The wonder of the world for magic art:
And he intends to show great Carolus
The race of all his stout progenitors
And bring in presence of his Majesty
The royal shapes and warlike semblances   15
Of Alexander and his beauteous paramour.

FREDERICK: Where is Benvolio?

MARTINO: Fast asleep, I warrant you.
He took his rouse with stoups of Rhenish wine
So kindly yesternight to Bruno's health
That all this day the sluggard keeps his bed.   20

FREDERICK: See, see, his window's ope. We'll call to him.

MARTINO: What ho, Benvolio!

(*Enter* BENVOLIO *above at a window, in his nightcap, buttoning.*)

BENVOLIO: What a devil ail you two?

MARTINO: Speak softly sir, lest the devil hear you,
For Faustus at the court is late arrived   25
At his heels a thousand furies wait
To accomplish whatsoever the doctor please.

BENVOLIO: What of this?

MARTINO: Come, leave thy chamber first, and thou shalt see
This conjurer perform such rare exploits   30
Before the Pope and royal Emperor
As never yet was seen in Germany.

BENVOLIO: Has not the Pope enough of conjuring yet?
He was upon the devil's back late enough!

---

23 **beyond us both** apparently Robin has managed to place the
cup at some distance from where he now stands   26 **When,
can you tell** a scornful reply   35 **shrewd** bad   37 **tester** sixpence   42 **apish** (1) foolish (2) imitative

IV Chorus 6 **gratulate** express joy in   7 **conference** discussion

14 **Carolus the Fifth** Charles V (1500–1558), Holy Roman
Emperor

IV.i. s.d. **several** separate   2 **presence** presence-chamber
3 **voided straight** emptied immediately   5 **state** chair of state,
throne   8 **consort** attend   16 **Alexander and his beauteous
paramour** Alexander the Great and his mistress, Thaïs   18 **took
his rouse with stoups** had drinking bouts with full goblets
31 **the Pope** i.e., Bruno

35   And if he be so far in love with him
      I would he would post with him to Rome again.
      FREDERICK: Speak, wilt thou come and see this sport?
      BENVOLIO: Not I.
      MARTINO: Wilt thou stand in thy window and see it then?
      BENVOLIO: Ay, and I fall not asleep i'th' meantime.
40   MARTINO: The Emperor is at hand, who comes to see
      What wonders by black spells may compassed be.
      BENVOLIO: Well, go you attend the Emperor. I am content for
      this once to thrust my head out at a window, for they say
      if a man be drunk overnight the devil cannot hurt him in
45   the morning. If that be true, I have a charm in my head
      shall control him as well as the conjurer, I warrant you.

(*Exit* [MARTINO *with* FREDERICK. BENVOLIO *remains at window*].)

SCENE II

A sennet. CHARLES *the German Emperor,* BRUNO, [DUKE OF] SAXONY, FAUSTUS, MEPHOSTOPHILIS, FREDERICK, MARTINO, *and* ATTENDANTS.

      EMPEROR: Wonder of men, renownèd magician,
      Thrice-learnèd Faustus, welcome to our court,
      This deed of thine in setting Bruno free
      From his and our professèd enemy,
5   Shall add more excellence unto thine art
      Than if by powerful necromantic spells
      Thou could'st command the world's obedience.
      For ever be beloved of Carolus!
      And if this Bruno thou hast late redeemed
10   In peace possess the triple diadem
      And sit in Peter's chair despite of chance,
      Thou shalt be famous through all Italy
      And honored of the German Emperor.
      FAUSTUS: These gracious words, most royal Carolus
15   Shall make poor Faustus to his utmost power
      Both love and serve the German Emperor
      And lay his life at holy Bruno's feet.
      For proof whereof, if so your Grace be pleased,
      The doctor stands prepared by power of art
20   To cast his magic charms that shall pierce through
      The ebon gates of ever-burning hell,
      And hale the stubborn furies from their caves
      To compass whatsoe'er your Grace commands.
      BENVOLIO: Blood! He speaks terribly. But for all that I do not
25   greatly believe him. He looks as like a conjurer as the
      Pope to a costermonger.
      EMPEROR: Then Faustus, as thou late didst promise us,
      We would behold that famous conqueror

---

46 s.d. **Benvolio remains at window** because Benvolio does not leave the stage, this scene cannot properly be said to be ended. But the present edition, following its predecessors for convenience of reference, begins a new scene

IV.ii. s.d. **sennet** trumpet fanfare (the absence of a verb in the rest of the stage direction perhaps indicates that the Emperor and his party do not enter but rather are "discovered," as Faustus may have been discovered at the beginning of 1.1, if the Chorus drew back a curtain)   9 **redeemed** freed   26 **costermonger** fruit-seller

      Great Alexander and his paramour
      In their true shapes and state majestical,   30
      That we may wonder at their excellence.
      FAUSTUS: Your Majesty shall see them presently.—
      Mephostophilis away,
      And with a solemn noise of trumpets' sound
      Present before this royal Emperor   35
      Great Alexander and his beauteous paramour.
      MEPHOSTOPHILIS: Faustus, I will.

(*Exit.*)

      BENVOLIO: Well master doctor, an your devils come not away
      quickly, you shall have me asleep presently. Zounds, I
      could eat myself for anger to think I have been such an ass   40
      all this while to stand gaping after the devils' governor and
      can see nothing.
      FAUSTUS: I'll make you feel something anon if my art fail me
      not!
      My lord, I must forewarn your Majesty
      That when my spirits present the royal shapes   45
      Of Alexander and his paramour,
      Your Grace demand no questions of the King
      But in dumb silence let them come and go.
      EMPEROR: Be it as Faustus please; we are content.
      BENVOLIO: Ay ay, and I am content too. And thou bring   50
      Alexander and his paramour before the Emperor, I'll be
      Actaeon and turn myself to a stag.
      FAUSTUS: (*Aside.*) And I'll play Diana and send you the horns
      presently.

(*Sennet. Enter at one* [door] *the* EMPEROR ALEXANDER, *at the other* DARIUS. *They meet.* DARIUS *is thrown down.* ALEXANDER *kills him, takes off his crown, and offering to go out, his* PARAMOUR *meets him. He embraceth her and sets* DARIUS' *crown upon her head, and coming back both salute the* EMPEROR; *who leaving his state offers to embrace them, which* FAUSTUS *seeing suddenly stays him. Then trumpets cease and music sounds.*)

      My gracious lord, you do forget yourself.   55
      These are but shadows, not substantial.
      EMPEROR: O pardon me, my thoughts are so ravished
      With sight of this renownèd Emperor,
      That in mine arms I would have compassed him.
      But Faustus, since I may not speak to them,   60
      To satisfy my longing thoughts at full,
      Let me this tell thee: I have heard it said
      That this fair lady whilst she lived on earth,
      Had on her neck a little wart or mole.
      How may I prove that saying to be true?   65
      FAUSTUS: Your Majesty may boldly go and see.
      EMPEROR: Faustus, I see it plain!
      And in this sight thou better pleasest me
      Than if I gained another monarchy.

---

39 **Zounds** by God's wounds   52 **Actaeon** legendary hunter who saw the naked goddess Diana bathing. She transformed him into a stag, and he was torn to pieces by his own hounds   54 s.d. **Darius** King of Persia, defeated by Alexander in 334 BCE   59 **compassed** encompassed, embraced

70 FAUSTUS: Away, be gone! (*Exit show.*)
　　See, see my gracious lord, what strange beast is yon that
　　thrusts his head out at the window!
　　EMPEROR: O wondrous sight! See, Duke of Saxony,
　　Two spreading horns most strangely fastened
75　　Upon the head of young Benvolio.
　　SAXONY: What, is he asleep or dead?
　　FAUSTUS: He sleeps my lord, but dreams not of his horns.
　　EMPEROR: This sport is excellent. We'll call and wake him.
　　What ho, Benvolio!
80 BENVOLIO: A plague upon you! Let me sleep awhile.
　　EMPEROR: I blame thee not to sleep much, having such a head
　　of thine own.
　　SAXONY: Look up Benvolio! 'Tis the Emperor calls.
　　BENVOLIO: The Emperor! Where? O zounds, my head!
85 EMPEROR: Nay, and thy horns hold, 'tis no matter for thy head,
　　for that's armed sufficiently.
　　FAUSTUS: Why, how now Sir Knight? What, hanged by the
　　horns? This is most horrible! Fie fie, pull in your head for
　　shame! Let not all the world wonder at you.
90 BENVOLIO: Zounds doctor, is this your villainy?
　　FAUSTUS: Oh, say not so sir: The doctor has no skill,
　　No art, no cunning to present these lords
　　Or bring before this royal Emperor
　　The mighty monarch, warlike Alexander.
95　　If Faustus do it, you are straight resolved
　　In bold Actaeon's shape to turn a stag.
　　And therefore my lord, so please your Majesty,
　　I'll raise a kennel of hounds shall hunt him so
　　As all his footmanship shall scarce prevail
100　　To keep his carcass from their bloody fangs.
　　Ho, Belimote, Argiron, Asterote!
　　BENVOLIO: Hold, hold! Zounds, he'll raise up a kennel of dev-
　　ils I think, anon. Good my lord, entreat for me. 'Sblood, I
　　am never able to endure these torments.
105 EMPEROR: Then good master doctor,
　　Let me entreat you to remove his horns.
　　He has done penance now sufficiently.
　　FAUSTUS: My gracious lord, not so much for injury done to
　　me, as to delight your Majesty with some mirth, hath
110　　Faustus justly requited this injurious knight; which being all
　　I desire, I am content to remove his horns. Mephostophilis,
　　transform him. And hereafter sir, look you speak well of
　　scholars.
　　BENVOLIO: (*Aside.*) Speak well of ye! 'Sblood, and scholars be
115　　such cuckold-makers to clap horns on honest men's heads
　　o' this order, I'll ne'er trust smooth faces and small ruffs
　　more. But an I be not revenged for this, would I might be
　　turned to a gaping oyster and drink nothing but salt water.

　　(*Exit.*)

　　EMPEROR: Come Faustus, while the Emperor lives,
120　　In recompense of this thy high desert,

────────────

87–88 **hanged by the horns** the spreading horns prevent Benvolio from pulling his head inside of the window   103 **'Sblood**
by God's blood   110 **injurious** insulting   116 **small ruffs**
(worn by scholars, in contrast to the large ruffs worn by
courtiers)

Thou shalt command the state of Germany
And live beloved of mighty Carolus.

(*Exeunt omnes.*)

SCENE III

Enter BENVOLIO, MARTINO, FREDERICK, *and* SOLDIERS.

MARTINO: Nay, sweet Benvolio, let us sway thy thoughts
　　From this attempt against the conjurer.
BENVOLIO: Away! You love me not to urge me thus.
　　Shall I let slip so great an injury
　　When every servile groom jests at my wrongs　　　　5
　　And in their rustic gambols proudly say,
　　"Benvolio's head was graced with horns today"?
　　O, may these eyelids never close again
　　Till with my sword I have that conjurer slain!
　　If you will aid me in this enterprise,　　　　　　　10
　　Then draw your weapons and be resolute;
　　If not, depart. Here will Benvolio die
　　But Faustus' death shall quit my infamy.
FREDERICK: Nay, we will stay with thee, betide what may,
　　And kill that doctor if he come this way.　　　　　15
BENVOLIO: Then, gentle Frederick, hie thee to the grove
　　And place our servants and our followers
　　Close in an ambush there behind the trees.
　　By this, I know, the conjurer is near.
　　I saw him kneel and kiss the Emperor's hand　　　20
　　And take his leave laden with rich rewards.
　　Then soldiers, boldly fight. If Faustus die,
　　Take you the wealth, leave us the victory.
FREDERICK: Come soldiers, follow me unto the grove.
　　Who kills him shall have gold and endless love.　　25

(*Exit* FREDERICK *with the* SOLDIERS.)

BENVOLIO: My head is lighter than it was by th' horns—
　　But yet my heart more ponderous than my head,
　　And pants until I see that conjurer dead.
MARTINO: Where shall we place ourselves, Benvolio?
BENVOLIO: Here will we stay to bide the first assault.　　30
　　O, were that damnèd hell-hound but in place
　　Thou soon should'st see me quit my foul disgrace.

(*Enter* FREDERICK.)

FREDERICK: Close, close! The conjurer is at hand
　　And all alone comes walking in his gown.
　　Be ready then and strike the peasant down!　　　　35
BENVOLIO: Mine be that honor then! Now sword, strike home!
　　For horns he gave I'll have his head anon.

(*Enter* FAUSTUS *with the false head.*)

MARTINO: See see, he comes.
BENVOLIO:　　　　　　　No words. This blow ends all!

(*Strikes* FAUSTUS.)

────────────

IV.iii. **let slip** ignore   13 **But** unless; **quit** avenge   35 **peasant**
low fellow

FAUSTUS: O!

40 FREDERICK: Groan you, master doctor?

BENVOLIO: Break may his heart with groans! Dear Frederick, see,

Thus will I end his griefs immediately.

(*Cuts off* FAUSTUS' *false head.*)

MARTINO: Strike with a willing hand! His head is off.

BENVOLIO: The devil's dead, the furies now may laugh.

45 FREDERICK: Was this that stern aspect, that awful frown,

Made the grim monarch of infernal spirits

Tremble and quake at his commanding charms?

MARTINO: Was this that damnèd head whose heart conspired

Benvolio's shame before the Emperor?

50 BENVOLIO: Ay, that's the head, and here the body lies

Justly rewarded for his villainies.

FREDERICK: Come let's devise how we may add more shame

To the black scandal of his hated name.

BENVOLIO: First, on his head in quittance of my wrongs

55 I'll nail huge forkèd horns and let them hang

Within the window where he yoked me first

That all the world may see my just revenge.

MARTINO: What use shall we put his beard to?

BENVOLIO: We'll sell it to a chimney-sweeper. It will wear out

60 ten birchen brooms, I warrant you.

FREDERICK: What shall eyes do?

BENVOLIO: We'll put out his eyes, and they shall serve for buttons to his lips to keep his tongue from catching cold.

65 MARTINO: An excellent policy! And now sirs, having divided him, what shall the body do?

(FAUSTUS *rises.*)

BENVOLIO: Zounds, the devil's alive again!

FREDERICK: Give him his head for God's sake!

FAUSTUS: Nay keep it. Faustus will have heads and hands,

70 Ay, all your hearts, to recompense this deed.

Knew you not, traitors, I was limited

For four and twenty years to breathe on earth?

And had you cut my body with your swords

Or hewed this flesh and bones as small as sand,

75 Yet in a minute had my spirit returned

And I had breathed a man made free from harm.

But wherefore do I dally my revenge?

Asteroth, Belimoth, Mephostophilis!

(*Enter* MEPHOSTOPHILIS *and other* DEVILS.)

Go horse these traitors on your fiery backs

80 And mount aloft with them as high as heaven,

Thence pitch them headlong to the lowest hell.

Yet stay, the world shall see their misery,

And hell shall after plague their treachery.

Go Belimoth, and take this caitiff hence

85 And hurl him in some lake of mud and dirt:

---

84 **caitiff** wretch

Take thou this other, drag him through the woods

Amongst the pricking thorns and sharpest briars:

Whilst with my gentle Mephostophilis

This traitor flies unto some steepy rock

That rolling down may break the villain's bones   90

As he intended to dismember me.

Fly hence, dispatch my charge immediately!

FREDERICK: Pity us, gentle Faustus, save our lives!

FAUSTUS: Away!

FREDERICK: He must needs go that the devil drives.

(*Exeunt* SPIRITS *with the* KNIGHTS.)

(*Enter the ambushed* SOLDIERS.)

1 SOLDIER: Come sirs, prepare yourselves in readiness.   95

Make haste to help these noble gentlemen.

I heard them parley with the conjurer.

2 SOLDIER: See where he comes, dispatch, and kill the slave!

FAUSTUS: What's here, an ambush to betray my life?

Then Faustus, try thy skill. Base peasants, stand!   100

For lo, these trees remove at my command

And stand as bulwarks 'twixt yourselves and me

To shield me from your hated treachery!

Yet to encounter this your weak attempt

Behold an army comes incontinent.   105

(FAUSTUS *strikes the door, and enter a* DEVIL *playing on a drum, after him another bearing an ensign, and divers with weapons:* MEPHOSTOPHILIS *with fireworks: they set upon the* SOLDIERS *and drive them out.* [*Exeunt all.*])

SCENE IV

Enter at several doors BENVOLIO, FREDERICK, *and* MARTINO, *their heads and faces bloody and besmeared with mud and dirt, all having horns on their heads.*

MARTINO: What ho, Benvolio!

BENVOLIO: Here! What, Frederick, ho!

FREDERICK: O, help me gentle friend. Where is Martino?

MARTINO: Dear Frederick, here,

Half smothered in a lake of mud and dirt,

Through which the furies dragged me by the heels.   5

FREDERICK: Martino, see, Benvolio's horns again.

MARTINO: O misery! How now Benvolio?

BENVOLIO: Defend me, heaven! Shall I be haunted still?

MARTINO: Nay fear not man, we have no power to kill.

BENVOLIO: My friends transformed thus! O hellish spite,   10

Your heads are all set with horns.

FREDERICK: You hit it right:

It is your own you mean. Feel on your head.

BENVOLIO: Zounds, horns again!

MARTINO: Nay chafe not man, we all are sped.

BENVOLIO: What devil attends this damned magician,

That spite of spite our wrongs are doubled?   15

---

101 **remove** move   105 **incontinent** immediately

IV.iv. 8 **haunted** the following line suggests that there is a quibble on "hunted," Benvolio now resembling a stag   13 **chafe** fret; **sped** done for, ruined (because of the horns)

FREDERICK: What may we do that we may hide our shames?
BENVOLIO: If we should follow him to work revenge
He'd join long asses' ears to these huge horns
And make us laughing-stocks to all the world.
20 MARTINO: What shall we then do, dear Benvolio?
BENVOLIO: I have a castle joining near these woods,
And thither we'll repair and live obscure
Till time shall alter this our brutish shapes.
Sith black disgrace hath thus eclipsed our fame,
25 We'll rather die with grief than live with shame.

(*Exeunt omnes.*)

SCENE V

Enter FAUSTUS *and the* HORSE-COURSER.

HORSE-COURSER: I beseech your worship, accept of these
forty dollars.
FAUSTUS: Friend, thou canst not buy so good a horse for so
small a price. I have no great need to sell him, but if thou
5 likest him for ten dollars more, take him, because I see
thou hast a good mind to him.
HORSE-COURSER: I beseech you sir, accept of this. I am a
very poor man and have lost very much of late by horse-
flesh, and this bargain will set me up again.
10 FAUSTUS: Well, I will not stand with thee. Give me the
money. Now sirrah, I must tell you that you may ride him
o'er hedge and ditch and spare him not. But, do you hear,
in any case ride him not into the water.
HORSE-COURSER: How sir, not into the water! Why, will he
15 not drink of all waters?
FAUSTUS: Yes, he will drink of all waters, but ride him not
into the water: o'er hedge and ditch or where thou wilt,
but not into the water. Go bid the hostler deliver him
unto you, and remember what I say.
20 HORSE-COURSER: I warrant you sir. O joyful day! Now am I
a made man forever.

(*Exit.*)

FAUSTUS: What art thou, Faustus, but a man condemned to die?
Thy fatal time draws to a final end;
Despair doth drive distrust into my thoughts.
25 Confound these passions with a quiet sleep.
Tush, Christ did call the thief upon the cross!
Then rest thee Faustus, quiet in conceit.

(*He sits to sleep.*)

(*Enter the* HORSE-COURSER *wet.*)

---

24 **Sith** since
IV.v. s.d. **Horse-courser** horse trader   2 **dollars** German
coins   8 **horse-flesh** the possibility of a quibble on "whores
flesh" is increased by "set me up" and "stand" in the ensuing dialogue   10 **stand** haggle   16 **drink of all waters** i.e., go anywhere   23 **fatal time** life span   26 **Christ . . . cross** in Luke
xxiii.39–43 Christ promised one of the thieves that he would be
with Christ in paradise   27 **quiet in conceit** with a quiet mind

HORSE-COURSER: O what a cozening doctor was this! I riding my horse into the water, thinking some hidden mystery had been in the horse, I had nothing under me but a 30
little straw and had much ado to escape drowning. Well,
I'll go rouse him and make him give me my forty dollars
again. Ho, sirrah doctor, you cozening scab! Master doctor, awake and rise, and give me my money again, for your
horse is turned to a bottle of hay. Master doctor!   35

(*He pulls off his leg.*)

Alas, I am undone! What shall I do? I have pulled off his leg.
FAUSTUS: O help, help! The villain hath murdered me!
HORSE-COURSER: Murder or not murder, now he has but
one leg I'll outrun him, and cast this leg into some ditch
or other.
FAUSTUS: Stop him, stop him, stop him!—Ha, ha, ha! Faustus 40
hath his leg again, and the horse-courser a bundle of hay
for his forty dollars.

(*Enter* WAGNER.)

How now, Wagner? What news with thee?
WAGNER: If it please you, the Duke of Vanholt doth earnestly
entreat your company, and hath sent some of his men to 45
attend you with provision fit for your journey.
FAUSTUS: The Duke of Vanholt's an honorable gentleman,
and one to whom I must be no niggard of my cunning.
Come, away!

(*Exeunt.*)

SCENE VI

Enter [ROBIN] *the clown,* DICK, HORSE-COURSER, *and a* CARTER.

CARTER: Come my masters, I'll bring you to the best beer in
Europe. What ho, hostess! Where be these whores?

(*Enter* HOSTESS.)

HOSTESS: How now? What lack you? What, my old guests,
welcome.
ROBIN: (*Aside.*) Sirrah Dick, dost thou know why I stand so 5
mute?
DICK: (*Aside.*) No Robin, why is't?
ROBIN: (*Aside.*) I am eighteen pence on the score. But say
nothing. See if she have forgotten me.
HOSTESS: Who's this that stands so solemnly by himself? 10
What, my old guest!
ROBIN: O, hostess, how do you? I hope my score stands still.
HOSTESS: Ay, there's no doubt of that, for methinks you make
no haste to wipe it out.
DICK: Why hostess, I say, fetch us some beer!   15
HOSTESS: You shall, presently.—Look up into th' hall there, ho!

(*Exit.*)

---

28 **cozening** deceiving   35 **bottle** bundle
IV.vi. 8 **on the score** in debt

DICK: Comes sirs, what shall we do now till mine hostess comes?

CARTER: Marry sir, I'll tell you the bravest tale how a con-
20 jurer served me. You know Doctor Faustus?

HORSE-COURSER: Ay, a plague take him! Here's some on's have cause to know him. Did he conjure thee too?

CARTER: I'll tell you how he served me. As I was going to Wittenberg t'other day with a load of hay, he met me and
25 asked me what he should give me for as much hay as he could eat. Now sir, I, thinking that a little would serve his turn, bad him take as much as he would for three far-things. So he presently gave me my money and fell to eat-ing; and as I am a cursen man, he never left eating till he
30 had eat up all my load of hay.

ALL: O monstrous, eat a whole load of hay!

ROBIN: Yes yes, that may be, for I have heard of one that has eat a load of logs.

HORSE-COURSER: Now sirs, you shall hear how villainously
35 he served me. I went to him yesterday to buy a horse of him, and he would by no means sell him under forty dol-lars. So sir, because I knew him to be such a horse as would run over hedge and ditch and never tire, I gave him his money. So, when I had my horse, Doctor Faustus bade
40 me ride him night and day and spare him no time. "But," quoth he, "in any case ride him not into the water." Now sir, I thinking the horse had had some quality that he would not have me know of, what did I but rid him into a great river—and when I came just in the midst, my horse
45 vanished away and I sate straddling upon a bottle of hay.

ALL: O brave doctor!

HORSE-COURSER: But you shall hear how bravely I served him for it. I went me home to his house, and there I found him asleep. I kept ahallowing and whooping in his ears,
50 but all could not wake him. I seeing that, took him by the leg and never rested pulling till I had pulled me his leg quite off, and now 'tis at home in mine hostry.

DICK: And has the doctor but one leg then? That's excellent, for one of his devils turned me into the likeness of an ape's face.

55 CARTER: Some more drink, hostess!

ROBIN: Hark you, we'll into another room and drink awhile, and then we'll go seek out the doctor.

(*Exeunt omnes.*)

SCENE VII

Enter the DUKE OF VANHOLT, *his* [SERVANTS,] DUCHESS, FAUS-TUS, *and* MEPHOSTOPHILIS.

DUKE: Thanks master doctor, for these pleasant sights. Nor know I how sufficiently to recompense your great deserts in erecting that enchanted castle in the air, the sight whereof so delighted me,
5 As nothing in the world could please me more.

FAUSTUS: I do think myself, my good lord, highly recompensed in that it pleaseth your Grace to think but well of that which Faustus hath performed.—But gracious lady, it may be that you have taken no pleasure in those sights. There-

fore I pray you tell me what is the thing you most desire to 10 have: be it in the world it shall be yours. I have heard that great-bellied women do long for things are rare and dainty.

DUCHESS: True master doctor, and since I find you so kind, I will make known unto you what my heart desires to have: and were it now summer, as it is January, a dead time of 15 the winter, I would request no better meat than a dish of ripe grapes.

FAUSTUS: This is but a small matter. Go Mephostophilis, away!

(*Exit* MEPHOSTOPHILIS.)

Madam, I will do more than this for your content.

(*Enter* MEPHOSTOPHILIS *again with the grapes.*)

Here, now taste ye these. They should be good, 20
For they come from a far country, I can tell you.

DUKE: This makes me wonder more than all the rest, that at this time of the year when every tree is barren of his fruit, from whence you had these ripe grapes.

FAUSTUS: Please it your Grace, the year is divided into two 25 circles over the whole world, so that when it is winter with us, in the contrary circle it is likewise summer with them, as in India, Saba, and such countries that lie far east, where they have fruit twice a year. From whence, by means of a swift spirit that I have, I had these grapes 30 brought as you see.

DUCHESS: And trust me, they are the sweetest grapes that e'er I tasted.

(*The* CLOWNS [ROBIN, DICK, CARTER, *and* HORSE-COURSER] *bounce at the gate within.*)

DUKE: What rude disturbers have we at the gate?
Go pacify their fury, set it ope, 35
And then demand of them what they would have.

(*They knock again and call out to talk with* FAUSTUS.)

A SERVANT: Why, how now masters, what a coil is there!
What is the reason you disturb the Duke?

DICK: We have no reason for it, therefore a fig for him!

SERVANT: Why saucy varlets, dare you be so bold! 40

HORSE-COURSER: I hope sir, we have wit enough to be more bold than welcome.

SERVANT: It appears so. Pray be bold elsewhere
And trouble not the Duke.

DUKE: What would they have? 45

SERVANT: They all cry out to speak with Doctor Faustus.

CARTER: Ay, and we will speak with him.

DUKE: Will you sir? Commit the rascals.

DICK: Commit with us! He were as good commit with his father as commit with us! 50

---

29 **cursen** i.e., Christian (dialect form)   32–33 **eat a load of logs** been drunk   52 **hostry** inn

IV.vii. 12 **great-bellied** i.e., pregnant   16 **meat** food   25 **two circles** i.e., the northern and the southern hemispheres (though later in the speech he talks of east and west rather than of north and south)   s.d. **bounce** knock   37 **coil** turmoil   38 **reason** pro-nounced like "raisin," leading to the quibble on "fig"; a "fig" here is an obscene contemptuous gesture in which the hand is clenched and the thumb is thrust between the first and second fingers, making the thumb resemble the stem of a fig, or a penis   48 **Commit** imprison (Dick proceeds to quibble on the idea of committing adultery)

FAUSTUS: I do beseech your Grace, let them come in.
 They are good subject for a merriment.
DUKE: Do as thou wilt, Faustus, I give thee leave.
FAUSTUS: I thank your Grace.

(*Enter* [ROBIN] *the clown,* DICK, CARTER, *and* HORSE-COURSER.)

 Why, how now my good friends?
55 'Faith, you are too outrageous; but come near,
 I have procured your pardons. Welcome all.
ROBIN: Nay sir, we will be welcome for our money, and we
 will pay for what we take. What ho, give's half a dozen of
 beer here, and be hanged!
60 FAUSTUS: Nay, hark you, can you tell me where you are?
CARTER: Ay, marry can I, we are under heaven.
SERVANT: Ay, but Sir Sauce-box, know you in what place?
HORSE-COURSER: Ay ay, the house is good enough to drink
 in. Zounds, fill us some beer, or we'll break all the barrels
65 in the house and dash out all your brains with your bottles.
FAUSTUS: Be not so furious. Come, you shall have beer.
 My lord, beseech you give me leave awhile;
 I'll gage my credit 'twill content your Grace.
DUKE: With all my heart, kind doctor, please thyself.
70 Our servants and our court's at thy command.
FAUSTUS: I humbly thank your Grace.—Then fetch some beer.
HORSE-COURSER: Ay marry, there spake a doctor indeed! And
 'faith, I'll drink a health to thy wooden leg for that word.
FAUSTUS: My wooden leg? What dost thou mean by that?
75 CARTER: Ha, ha, ha, dost hear him Dick? He has forgot his leg.
HORSE-COURSER: Ay ay, he does not stand much upon that.
FAUSTUS: No, 'faith, not much upon a wooden leg.
CARTER: Good lord, that flesh and blood should be so frail
 with your worship! Do not you remember a horse-
80 courser you sold a horse to?
FAUSTUS: Yes, I remember I sold one a horse.
CARTER: And do you remember you bid he should not ride
 into the water?
FAUSTUS: Yes, I do very well remember that.
85 CARTER: And do you remember nothing of your leg?
FAUSTUS: No, in good sooth.
CARTER: Then I pray remember your curtsy.
FAUSTUS: I thank you sir.
CARTER: 'Tis not so much worth. I pray you tell me one thing.
90 FAUSTUS: What's that?
CARTER: Be both your legs bedfellows every night together?
FAUSTUS: Would'st thou make a colossus of me that thou ask-
 est me such questions?
CARTER: No, truly sir, I would make nothing of you, but I
95 would fain know that.

(*Enter* HOSTESS *with drink.*)

FAUSTUS: Then I assure thee certainly they are.
CARTER: I thank you, I am fully satisfied.
FAUSTUS: But wherefore dost thou ask?

CARTER: For nothing, sir, but methinks you should have a
 wooden bedfellow of one of 'em.   100
HORSE-COURSER: Why, do you hear sir, did not I pull off one
 of your legs when you were asleep?
FAUSTUS: But I have it again now I am awake. Look you here sir.
ALL: O horrible! Had the doctor three legs?
CARTER: Do you remember sir, how you cozened me and eat   105
 up my load of—

(FAUSTUS *charms him dumb.*)

DICK: Do you remember how you made me wear an ape's—

(FAUSTUS *charms him.*)

HORSE-COURSER: You whoreson conjuring scab! Do you remember how you cozened me with a ho—

(FAUSTUS *charms him.*)

ROBIN: Ha' you forgotten me? You think to carry it away   110
 with your "hey-pass" and "re-pass"? Do you remember
 the dog's fa—

([FAUSTUS *charms him.*] *Exeunt* CLOWNS.)

HOSTESS: Who pays for the ale? Hear you master doctor, now
 you have sent away my guests, I pray who shall pay me for
 my a—   115

([FAUSTUS *charms her.*] *Exit* HOSTESS.)

DUCHESS: My Lord,
 We are much beholding to this learnèd man.
DUKE: So are we madam, which we will recompense
 With all the love and kindness that we may:
 His artful sport drives all sad thoughts away.   120

(*Exeunt.*)

ACT FIVE

SCENE I

Thunder and lightning. Enter DEVILS *with covered dishes:*
MEPHOSTOPHILIS *leads them into* FAUSTUS' *study. Then enter*
WAGNER.

WAGNER: I think my master means to die shortly. He has
 made his will and given me his wealth: his house, his
 goods, and store of golden plate—besides two thousand
 ducats ready coined. I wonder what he means. If death
 were nigh, he would not frolic thus. He's now at supper   5
 with the scholars, where there's such belly-cheer as Wagner in his life ne'er saw the like! And see where they
 come. Belike the feast is done.

(*Exit.*)

---

68 **gage** pledge   76 **stand much upon** quibble on "attach
much importance to"   87 **curtsy** also called "a leg," hence
there is a quibble on the Carter's previous speech   92 **colossus**
huge statue in the harbor at Rhodes, between whose legs ships
were said to have sailed

---

111 **hey-pass, re-pass** conjuring expressions

V.i. 7 **Belike** most likely   1–7 **I think . . . done** though
printed as prose in the quarto, as here, perhaps this speech should
be verse, the lines ending *shortly, wealth, plate, coined, nigh, supper,
belly-cheer, like, done*

(*Enter* FAUSTUS, MEPHOSTOPHILIS, *and two or three* SCHOLARS.)

1 SCHOLAR: Master Doctor Faustus, since our conference
about fair ladies, which was the beautifulest in all the
10 world, we have determined with ourselves that Helen of
Greece was the admirablest lady that ever lived. Therefore
master doctor, if you will do us so much favor as to let us
see that peerless dame of Greece, whom all the world ad-
mires for majesty, we should think ourselves much be-
15 holding unto you.
FAUSTUS: Gentlemen,
For that I know your friendship is unfeigned,
It is not Faustus' custom to deny
The just request of those that wish him well:
20 You shall behold that peerless dame of Greece
No otherwise for pomp or majesty
Than when Sir Paris crossed the seas with her
And brought the spoils to rich Dardania.
Be silent then, for danger is in words.

(*Music sounds.* MEPHOSTOPHILIS *brings in* HELEN: *she passeth over
the stage.*)

25 2 SCHOLAR: Was this fair Helen, whose admired worth
Made Greece with ten years' wars afflict poor Troy?
3 SCHOLAR: Too simple is my wit to tell her worth,
Whom all the world admires for majesty.
1 SCHOLAR: Now we have seen the pride of nature's work,
30 We'll take our leaves, and for this blessèd sight
Happy and blest be Faustus evermore.
FAUSTUS: Gentlemen, farewell, the same wish I to you.

(*Exeunt* SCHOLARS.)

(*Enter an* OLD MAN.)

OLD MAN: O gentle Faustus, leave this damnèd art,
This magic that will charm thy soul to hell
35 And quite bereave thee of salvation.
Though thou hast now offended like man,
Do not persever in it like a devil.
Yet, yet, thou hast an amiable soul
If sin by custom grow not into nature.
40 Then, Faustus, will repentance come too late!
Then, thou are banished from the sight of heaven!
No mortal can express the pains of hell!
It may be this my exhortation
Seems harsh and all unpleasant. Let it not.
45 For gentle son, I speak it not in wrath
Or envy of thee but in tender love
And pity of thy future misery:
And so have hope that this my kind rebuke,
Checking thy body, may amend thy soul.
50 FAUSTUS: Where art thou, Faustus? Wretch, what hast thou
done!

(MEPHOSTOPHILIS *gives him a dagger.*)

Hell claims his right and with a roaring voice
Says "Faustus, come, thine hour is almost come!"
And Faustus now will come to do thee right!
OLD MAN: O stay, good Faustus, stay thy desperate steps!
I see an angel hover o'er thy head,   55
And with a vial full of precious grace
Offers to pour the same into thy soul:
Then call for mercy and avoid despair.
FAUSTUS: O friend,
I feel thy words to comfort my distressèd soul: 60
Leave me awhile to ponder on my sins.
OLD MAN: Faustus, I leave thee, but with grief of heart,
Fearing the enemy of thy hapless soul.

(*Exit.*)

FAUSTUS: Accursèd Faustus! Wretch, what hast thou done!
I do repent, and yet I do despair: 65
Hell strives with grace for conquest in my breast!
What shall I do to shun the snares of death?
MEPHOSTOPHILIS: Thou traitor Faustus, I arrest thy soul
For disobedience to my sovereign lord.
Revolt, or I'll in piecemeal tear thy flesh.   70
FAUSTUS: I do repent I e'er offended him.
Sweet Mephostophilis, entreat thy lord
To pardon my unjust presumption,
And with my blood again I will confirm
The former vow I made to Lucifer.   75
MEPHOSTOPHILIS: Do it then, Faustus, with unfeignèd heart
Lest greater dangers do attend thy drift.
FAUSTUS: Torment, sweet friend, that base and agèd man
That durst dissuade me from thy Lucifer,
With greatest torment that our hell affords.   80
MEPHOSTOPHILIS: His faith is great. I cannot touch his soul.
But what I may afflict his body with
I will attempt, which is but little worth.
FAUSTUS: One thing, good servant, let me crave of thee
To glut the longing of my heart's desire: 85
That I may have unto my paramour
That heavenly Helen which I saw of late,
Whose sweet embraces may extinguish clear
Those thoughts that do dissuade me from my vow,
And keep mine oath I made to Lucifer.   90
MEPHOSTOPHILIS: This or what else my Faustus shall desire
Shall be performed in twinkling of an eye.

(*Enter* HELEN *again, passing over between two* CUPIDS.)

FAUSTUS: Was this the face that launched a thousand ships
And burnt the topless towers of Ilium?
Sweet Helen, make me immortal with a kiss.   95
Her lips suck forth my soul. See where it flies!
Come Helen, come, give me my soul again.
Here will I dwell, for heaven is in these lips
And all is dross that is not Helena.

---

23 **spoils** booty (including Helen); **Dardania** Troy 35 **bereave** deprive 37 **persever** accent on second syllable 38 **an
amiable soul** a soul worthy of love 49 **Checking** rebuking

---

70 **Revolt** return (to your allegiance) 94 **topless** i.e., so tall
their tops are beyond sight; **Ilium** Troy

100   I will be Paris, and for love of thee
      Instead of Troy shall Wittenberg be sacked:
      And I will combat with weak Menelaus
      And wear thy colors on my plumèd crest.
      Yea, I will wound Achilles in the heel
105   And then return to Helen for a kiss.
      O, thou art fairer than the evening's air
      Clad in the beauty of a thousand stars,
      Brighter art thou than flaming Jupiter
      When he appeared to hapless Semele,
110   More lovely than the monarch of the sky
      In wanton Arethusa's azure arms,
      And none but thou shalt be my paramour.

(*Exeunt.*)

SCENE II

Thunder. Enter LUCIFER, BELZEBUB, *and* MEPHOSTOPHILIS.

LUCIFER: Thus from infernal Dis do we ascend
      To view the subjects of our monarchy,
      Those souls which sin seals the black sons of hell.
      'Mong which as chief, Faustus, we come to thee,
5   Bringing with us lasting damnation
      To wait upon thy soul. The time is come
      Which makes it forfeit.
MEPHOSTOPHILIS: And this gloomy night
      Here in this room will wretched Faustus be.
BELZEBUB: And here we'll stay
10   To mark him how he doth demean himself.
MEPHOSTOPHILIS: How should he but in desperate lunacy?
      Fond worldling, now his heart blood dries with grief.
      His conscience kills it, and his laboring brain
      Begets a world of idle fantasies
15   To overreach the devil; but all in vain:
      His store of pleasures must be sauced with pain!
      He and his servant Wagner are at hand.
      Both come from drawing Faustus' lastest will.
      See where they come.

(*Enter* FAUSTUS *and* WAGNER.)

20   FAUSTUS: Say Wagner, thou hast perused my will;
      How dost thou like it?
WAGNER: Sir, so wondrous well
      As in all humble duty I do yield
      My life and lasting service for your love.

(*Enter the* SCHOLARS.)

FAUSTUS: Gramercies, Wagner—Welcome gentlemen.

(*Exit* WAGNER.)

1 SCHOLAR: Now worthy Faustus, methinks your looks are   25
      changed.
FAUSTUS: O gentlemen!
2 SCHOLAR: What ails Faustus?
FAUSTUS: Ah my sweet chamber-fellow, had I lived with thee,
      then had I lived still!—But now must die eternally. Look
      sirs, comes he not, comes he not?   30
1 SCHOLAR: O my dear Faustus, what imports this fear?
2 SCHOLAR: Is all our pleasure turned to melancholy?
3 SCHOLAR: He is not well with being over-solitary.
2 SCHOLAR: If it be so, we'll have physicians and Faustus shall
      be cured.   35
3 SCHOLAR: 'Tis but a surfeit sir, fear nothing.
FAUSTUS: A surfeit of deadly sin that hath damned both body
      and soul!
2 SCHOLAR: Yet Faustus, look up to heaven and remember
      mercy is infinite.   40
FAUSTUS: But Faustus' offense can ne'er be pardoned. The
      serpent that tempted Eve may be saved, but not Faustus!
      O gentlemen, hear with patience and tremble not at my
      speeches. Though my heart pant and quiver to remember
      that I have been a student here these thirty years. O, would   45
      I had never seen Wittenberg, never read book.—And
      what wonders I have done all Germany can witness, yea
      all the world, for which Faustus hath lost both Germany
      and the world, yea heaven itself—heaven, the seat of God,
      the throne of the blessed, the kingdom of joy—and must   50
      remain in hell for ever! hell, O hell forever! Sweet friends,
      what shall become of Faustus being in hell forever?
2 SCHOLAR: Yet Faustus, call on God.
FAUSTUS: On God, whom Faustus hath abjured? On God,
      whom Faustus hath blasphemed? O my God, I would weep,   55
      but the devil draws in my tears! Gush forth blood instead of
      tears, yea life and soul! O, he stays my tongue! I would lift
      up my hands, but see, they hold 'em, they hold 'em!
ALL: Who, Faustus?
FAUSTUS: Why, Lucifer and Mephostophilis. O gentlemen, I   60
      gave them my soul for my cunning.
ALL: O, God forbid!
FAUSTUS: God forbade it indeed, but Faustus hath done it.
      For the vain pleasure of four and twenty years hath Faus-
      tus lost eternal joy and felicity, I writ them a bill with   65
      mine own blood. The date is expired. This is the time.
      And he will fetch me.
1 SCHOLAR: Why did not Faustus tell us of this before, that
      divines might have prayed for thee?
FAUSTUS: Oft have I thought to have done so, but the devil   70
      threatened to tear me in pieces if I named God—to fetch
      me body and soul if I once gave ear to divinity; and now
      'tis too late! Gentlemen, away, lest you perish with me.
2 SCHOLAR: O, what may we do to save Faustus?
FAUSTUS: Talk not of me but save yourselves and depart.   75
3 SCHOLAR: God will strengthen me. I will stay with Faustus.

---

102 **Menelaus** Greek king, deserted by Helen for Paris
104 **Achilles** greatest of the Greek warriors   109 **Semele**
beloved by Jupiter, who promised to do whatever she wished; she
asked to see him in his full splendor, and the sight incinerated her
111 **Arethusa** a nymph, here apparently loved by Jupiter, "the
monarch of the sky"

V.ii. s.d. **Enter Lucifer, Belzebub, and Mephostophilis** probably they rise out of a trapdoor and ascend to the upper stage,
Mephostophilis descending to the main stage at line 86   1 **infernal Dis** the underworld (named for its ruler)   12 **Fond** foolish

---

24 **Gramercies** thank you   36 **a surfeit** indigestion

1 SCHOLAR: Tempt not God, sweet friend, but let us into the
next room and pray for him.

FAUSTUS: Ay, pray for me, pray for me. And what noise soever
80   you hear come not unto me, for nothing can rescue me.

2 SCHOLAR: Pray thou, and we will pray that God may have
mercy upon thee.

FAUSTUS: Gentlemen, farewell! If I live till morning, I'll visit
you. If not, Faustus is gone to hell.

85 ALL: Faustus, farewell.

(*Exeunt* SCHOLARS.)

MEPHOSTOPHILIS: Ay, Faustus, now thou hast no hope of
heaven.
    Therefore, despair! Think only upon hell,
    For that must be thy mansion, there to dwell.

FAUSTUS: O thou bewitching fiend, 'twas thy temptation
90   Hath robbed me of eternal happiness.

MEPHOSTOPHILIS: I do confess it Faustus, and rejoice.
    'Twas I, that when thou wert i'the way to heaven
    Damned up thy passage. When thou took'st the book
    To view the Scriptures, then I turned the leaves
95   And led thine eye.
    What, weep'st thou! 'Tis too late, despair, farewell!
    Fools that will laugh on earth, most weep in hell.

(*Exit.*)

(*Enter the* GOOD ANGEL *and the* BAD ANGEL *at several doors.*)

GOOD ANGEL: O Faustus, if thou hadst given ear to me
    Innumerable joys had followèd thee.
100   But thou did'st love the world.

BAD ANGEL: Gave ear to me,
    And now must taste hell's pains perpetually.

GOOD ANGEL: O, what will all thy riches, pleasures, pomps
    Avail thee now?

BAD ANGEL: Nothing but vex thee more,
    To want in hell, that had on earth such store.

(*Music while the throne descends.*)

105 GOOD ANGEL: O, thou hast lost celestial happiness,
    Pleasures unspeakable, bliss without end.
    Had'st thou affected sweet divinity,
    Hell or the devil had had no power on thee.
    Had'st thou kept on that way, Faustus behold
110   In what resplendent glory thou had'st sat
    In yonder throne, like those bright shining saints,
    And triumphed over hell! That hast thou lost.

(*Throne ascends.*)

    And now, poor soul, must thy good angel leave thee,
    The jaws of hell are open to receive thee.

(*Exit.*)

(*Hell is discovered.*)

---

104 s.d. **throne** symbolic of heaven   107 **affected** preferred

BAD ANGEL: Now Faustus, let thine eyes with horror stare   115
    Into that vast perpetual torture-house.
    There are the furies, tossing damnèd souls
    On burning forks. Their bodies boil in lead.
    There are live quarters broiling on the coals,
    That ne'er can die: this ever-burning chair   120
    Is for o'er-tortured souls to rest them in.
    These that are fed with sops of flaming fire
    Were gluttons and loved only delicates
    And laughed to see the poor starve at their gates.
    But yet all these are nothing. Thou shalt see   125
    Ten thousand tortures that more horrid be.

FAUSTUS: O, I have seen enough to torture me.

BAD ANGEL: Nay, thou must feel them, taste the smart of all:
    He that loves pleasure must for pleasure fall.
    And so I leave thee Faustus, till anon: 130
    Then wilt thou tumble in confusion.

(*Exit.*)

(*The clock strikes eleven.*)

FAUSTUS: O Faustus!
    Now hast thou but one bare hour to live
    And then thou must be damned perpetually.
    Stand still, you ever-moving spheres of Heaven   135
    That time may cease and midnight never come:
    Fair nature's eye, rise, rise again and make
    Perpetual day, or let this hour be but a year,
    A month, a week, a natural day—
    That Faustus may repent and save his soul.   140
    O lente lente currite noctis equi!
    The stars move still, time runs, the clock will strike:
    The devil will come, and Faustus must be damned!
    O, I'll leap up to my God! Who pulls me down?
    See, see where Christ's blood streams in the firmament!   145
    One drop of blood will save me. O my Christ!—
    Rend not my heart for naming of my Christ!
    Yet will I call on Him! O spare me, Lucifer!—
    Where is it now? 'Tis gone: and see where God
    Stretcheth out His arm and bends His ireful brows!   150
    Mountains and hills, come, come and fall on me
    And hide me from the heavy wrath of God!
    No?
    Then will I headlong run into the earth.
    Gape earth! O no, it will not harbor me.   155
    You stars that reigned at my nativity,
    Whose influence hath allotted death and hell,
    Now draw up Faustus like a foggy mist
    Into the entrails of yon laboring cloud
    That when you vomit forth into the air,   160
    My limbs may issue from your smoky mouths—
    But let my soul mount and ascend to heaven!

(*The watch strikes.*)

---

119 **quarters** bodies   131 **confusion** destruction   141 **O . . .
equi** slowly, slowly run, O horses of the night (Latin, adapted
from Ovid's *Amores*, I.xiii.40, where a lover regretfully thinks of
the coming of the dawn)

O half the hour is passed! 'Twill all be passed anon!
O God,
165 If thou wilt not have mercy on my soul
Yet for Christ's sake, whose blood hath ransomed me,
Impose some end to my incessant pain!
Let Faustus live in hell a thousand years,
A hundred thousand, and at last be saved!
170 No end is limited to damnèd souls!
Why wert thou not a creature wanting soul?
Or why is this immortal that thou hast?
O, Pythagoras' metempsychosis, were that true
This soul should fly from me and I be changed
175 Into some brutish beast.
All beasts are happy, for when they die
Their souls are soon dissolved in elements.
But mine must live still to be plagued in hell!
Cursed be the parents that engendered me!
180 No Faustus, curse thyself, curse Lucifer
That hath deprived thee of the joys of heaven.

(*The clock strikes twelve.*)

It strikes, it strikes! Now body, turn to air,
Or Lucifer will bear thee quick to hell!
O soul, be changed into small water-drops
185 And fall into the ocean, ne'er be found.

(*Thunder, and enter the* DEVILS.)

My God, my God! Look not so fierce on me!
Adders and serpents, let me breathe awhile!
Ugly Hell, gape not! Come not Lucifer!
I'll burn my books!—O Mephostophilis!

(*Exeunt* [DEVILS *with* FAUSTUS].)

SCENE III

Enter the SCHOLARS.

1 SCHOLAR: Come gentlemen, let us go visit Faustus,
For such a dreadful night was never seen
Since first the world's creation did begin!
Such fearful shrieks and cries were never heard!
Pray heaven, the doctor have escaped the danger.   5
2 SCHOLAR: O, help us heaven, see, here are Faustus' limbs
All torn asunder by the hand of death!
3 SCHOLAR: The devils whom Faustus served have torn him
thus:
For 'twixt the hours of twelve and one, methought
I heard him shriek and call aloud for help,   10
At which self time the house seemed all on fire
With dreadful horror of these damnèd fiends.
2 SCHOLAR: Well gentlemen, though Faustus' end be such
As every Christian heart laments to think on,
Yet for he was a scholar once admired   15
For wondrous knowledge in our German schools,
We'll give his mangled limbs due burial;
And all the students, clothed in mourning black,
Shall wait upon his heavy funeral.

(*Exeunt.*)

(*Enter* CHORUS.)

Cut is the branch that might have grown full straight   20
And burnèd is Apollo's laurel bough
That sometime grew within this learnèd man.
Faustus is gone: regard his hellish fall,
Whose fiendful fortune may exhort the wise
Only to wonder at unlawful things,   25
Whose deepness doth entice such forward wits
To practice more than heavenly power permits.

(*Exit.*)

(*Terminat hora diem; terminat Author opus.*)

---

170 **limited to** set for   173 **metempsychosis** transmigration of souls (a doctrine held by Pythagoras, philosopher of the sixth century BCE)   178 **still** always   183 **quick** alive   189 s.d. **Exeunt [Devils with Faustus]** possibly the devils drag Faustus into the "hell" that was "discovered" at 5.2.114, and then toss his limbs onto the stage, or possibly the limbs are revealed in 5.3.6 by withdrawing a curtain at the rear of the stage

V.iii. 11 **self** same

---

19 **wait upon** attend; **heavy** sad   21 **laurel bough** symbol of wisdom, here associated with Apollo, god of divination   25 **Only to wonder** at i.e., merely to observe at a distance, with awe   27 s.d. **Terminat . . . opus** the hour ends the day; the author ends his work (this Latin tag probably is not Marlowe's but the printer's, though it is engaging to believe Marlowe wrote it, ending his play at midnight, the hour of Faustus' death)

William Shakespeare

Given the fact that William Shakespeare (1564–1616) was a commoner and that he worked in the ephemeral trades of the theater, what we know about his life is extraordinarily rich and revealing, especially in comparison to the lives of other playwrights of the period, such as Christopher Marlowe or John Webster. William Shakespeare was born in Stratford-upon-Avon, a town to the northwest of London in Warwickshire. He was baptized on April 26, 1564, and was probably born a few days earlier—his birth date is conventionally given as April 23, the feast day of St. George, the patron saint of England, and the day on which Shakespeare died fifty-two years later in 1616, again at his home in Stratford. One of eight children, Shakespeare was the son of a glover—a tradesman who worked with a variety of leather goods. It is not known whether Shakespeare attended the local school, the King's New School, but like other schools of the period, it would have provided him with an extensive grounding in Latin grammar, rhetoric, and literature. Later in his career, Shakespeare often drew on works he could have read at such a school: plays by Terence and Plautus, the poetry of Virgil and Ovid, the writings of Caesar.

He married Anne Hathaway in November 1582; she was twenty-six and he was eighteen. In May 1583 they had their first daughter, Susannah, followed by twins, Hamnet and Judith, born in 1585. Although his wife and children remained in Stratford throughout his career, Shakespeare went to London sometime in the late 1580s, possibly joining one of the theater companies that passed through Stratford.

By the 1590s, Shakespeare was established in London as an up-and-coming playwright; he was associated with the Lord Chamberlain's Men; he had written several plays on English history; and he was at work on several comedies and tragedies. When plague closed the theaters in London from the summer of 1592 through the spring of 1594, Shakespeare wrote two narrative poems, *Venus and Adonis* and *The Rape of Lucrece,* which he dedicated to Henry Wriothesley, the third Earl of Southampton, in a bid for patronage. He later wrote *The Phoenix and the Turtle* and circulated a brilliant and ambitious sequence of sonnets in manuscript before publishing it in 1609. As a shareholder of the Lord Chamberlain's Men, Shakespeare would have had many duties; no doubt he acted many parts, and we know he

In the celebrated 1954 production of Shakespeare's *Hamlet,* Richard Burton takes leave of Claire Bloom as Ophelia.

appeared in two plays by his contemporary, Ben Jonson—*Every Man in His Humour* and *Sejanus*. In 1598, the Lord Chamberlain's men tore down The Theatre, brought the timbers south of the city, and used them to build a new theater, the Globe. The Globe would remain the principal public-theater venue for the rest of Shakespeare's career, complemented by court and private-theater performances.

Shakespeare became the most popular playwright in London. He profited handsomely from his efforts at the Globe and from the patronage of the court, particularly after James I came to the throne in 1603 and took on the Lord Chamberlain's company as his own King's Men. Shakespeare used his income to buy a large house, called New Place, in Stratford, and throughout his career added to his property there; he retired and returned to Stratford in 1613. He drew up a will shortly before he died in 1616, leaving property to his family and mentioning gifts for several of his friends, including members of the King's Men: Richard Burbage, John Heminges, and Henry Condell. Heminges and Condell proved true to Shakespeare, for in 1623 they took Shakespeare's plays and published them in a single large volume. In an era when plays were not regarded as "literature," this was an important event. Although many of Shakespeare's plays had been published individually during his lifetime, roughly half of Shakespeare's plays (*Macbeth, Antony and Cleopatra,* and *The Tempest,* for instance) existed only in manuscript form at Shakespeare's death and certainly would not have survived without the efforts of Heminges and Condell. This complete volume is now usually called the "First Folio," because it is printed in a large, **FOLIO**-sized format (about twice the dimensions of this book). The First Folio contains thirty-six of Shakespeare's plays; two more plays all or partly by Shakespeare and published in his lifetime (*Pericles* and *The Two Noble Kinsmen*) were left out of the Folio, and it is generally thought that Shakespeare contributed to a thirty-ninth play, *Sir Thomas More,* of which only a short manuscript section survives. More recently, several scholars have argued that Shakespeare collaborated on a history play, *Edward III.* Finally, although many people have advanced the thesis that someone else actually wrote the "Shakespeare" plays—Sir Francis Bacon, Francis Walsingham, the Earl of Oxford, among others—these claims belong to the realm of myth, not to the realm of history.

The range of Shakespeare's accomplishment as a playwright is astonishing. Early in his career, Shakespeare wrote two cycles of plays on English history—*Henry VI* (Parts 1, 2, and 3) and *Richard III;* and *Richard II, Henry IV* (Parts 1 and 2), and *Henry V*—that not only established a vogue for history plays but gave the English audience an epic version of the struggles that founded the Tudor and Stuart dynasties. Shakespeare's early comedies—*The Comedy of Errors, Two Gentlemen of Verona*—are very much in the vein of Plautus. Later comedies—*A Midsummer Night's Dream, As You Like It, Twelfth Night, The Merchant of Venice*—explore a variety of complex relations between love, sexuality, adulthood, ethnic discrimination, power, politics, and money. To many audiences today, Shakespeare is most remembered for *Hamlet* and the magisterial series of tragedies that followed, including *Othello, King Lear,* and *Macbeth.* Shakespeare's achievements often began with experimentation. The major tragedies benefitted from his earlier efforts in the mode of the Roman playwright Seneca in *Titus Andronicus,* in morality drama in *Richard III,* in romantic tragedy in *Romeo and Juliet,* and political intrigue–drama in *Julius Caesar.* In his final years as a playwright, Shakespeare seems to have collaborated with John Fletcher on a few occasions and to have turned his hand to plays in the vein of "tragicomedy," now generally called **ROMANCE:** *Pericles, Cymbeline, The Winter's Tale,* and *The Tempest.*

In his landmark study, *The Idea of a Theater,* actor/scholar Francis Fergusson characterized *Hamlet* as one of the "sphinxes of literature," a play that has repeatedly drawn actors, audiences, and scholars into its labyrinthine mystery. Yet while *Hamlet,* like the brooding young

HAMLET

prince of Denmark, may now seem like a difficult and philosophical problem, to its original audiences the play was a version of a popular genre on the Elizabethan stage, the revenge
tragedy. As in many of his other plays, Shakespeare adapted his tragedy from a variety of
known materials. The story of Amlethus, a disinherited Danish prince who uses feigned
madness and cunning to avenge his father's murder and regain the throne from his villainous uncle, dates from the twelfth-century *Historia Danica* of the Danish historian Saxo
Grammaticus; it was later adapted as a tragic narrative by François de Belleforest and included in his *Histoires tragiques* in 1576. Although Shakespeare may have known these versions, it is more certain that he knew a now-lost play on the subject of Hamlet's revenge
that was staged in the 1580s. This play—usually called the *Ur-Hamlet* by scholars—was possibly written by Thomas Kyd, the author of another popular revenge tragedy, *The Spanish
Tragedy*. While little is known about this play, we do know that it had at least one element
of Shakespeare's play; in 1596, the playwright and novelist Thomas Lodge remarked on a
play in which a pale ghost "cried so miserably at the Theater, like an oyster-wife, 'Hamlet,
revenge!'"

A ghost, a sinister and deceptive family, a court full of busybodies and spies, a broken
romance, an elaborate play-within-the-play, a command, sometimes from beyond the grave,
to take revenge, an elaborate finale in which the stage is littered with corpses—these devices
were common in revenge tragedies preceding Shakespeare's play, such as *The Spanish Tragedy*,
and common also in those which capitalized on *Hamlet*'s success in 1601, plays like John
Marston's *The Malcontent* and Cyril Tourneur's *The Revenger's Tragedy* (which opens with a
man speaking to a skull) and John Webster's *The White Devil*. *Hamlet* avails itself of all these
devices, but it also reflects and refracts them; the play seems to question what it means to
take action, simply to act, let alone take revenge, in a world of such complete duplicity that
any behavior might seem the treacherous "actions that a man might play." In his famous essay, "The World of *Hamlet*," Maynard Mack suggests that the play is in the "interrogative
mood": not only does Hamlet repeatedly ask questions of himself and others ("To be or not
to be . . . ," "Is it not monstrous . . . ," and so on), but much of the action of the play involves, as Polonius suggests, using theatrical "indirections" to "find directions out": Polonius
sends Reynaldo to spread dishonorable rumors about Laertes, to see whether Laertes is being virtuous in Paris; Claudius and Polonius "stage" Ophelia for Hamlet, hoping to discover
whether he's mad for revenge or madly in love; Hamlet hopes that the players' *The Murder
of Gonzago* will reveal Claudius's guilt; Polonius hides fatally behind the arras while Hamlet
interrogates Gertrude; Claudius stages a "duel" between Hamlet and Laertes that is really a
design for murder.

The world of *Hamlet* is a world in which appearances sometimes deceive and sometimes speak the truth: not being able to read the signs—as Ophelia, Rosencrantz and
Guildenstern, and Polonius all discover—can be fatal. Indeed, the play's obsession with
seeming ("Seems, madam? Nay, it is. I know not 'seems,'" Hamlet declares in his first scene
in the play) perhaps explains its obsession with the arts of seeming, with acting, performance, theater. In *Hamlet*, Shakespeare undertakes an extended meditation on the purpose
and limits of theater. Hamlet, of course, is quite familiar with the theater, and Shakespeare
clearly characterizes the troupe of players as his audience's contemporaries; not only is the
company all male, but they seem to have left the city—as many professional companies did
in the late 1590s—as a result of the "war of the theaters," the contemporary vogue for companies of boy-actors performing satirical plays. Moreover, Hamlet's famous advice to the
players (3.2) suggests that he has a keen eye for performance. He chastens the actors not to
"mouth it, as many of our players do," not to "saw the air too much with your hand," but
to "Suit the action to the word, the word to the action." Yet in *Hamlet*, words and actions
are more often than not suited to deception, to the extent that to Hamlet "this goodly
frame, the earth, seems . . . a sterile promontory." Hamlet's blatant reference to the Globe

itself—an actor, surrounded by the circular frame of the Globe, standing on the bare platform of the stage—suggests a skeptical regard for the theater's creation. While plays like *A
Midsummer Night's Dream* or perhaps *The Tempest* suggest the theater's ability to present healing fictions, the theater in *Hamlet* is presented from a more ironic, even disaffected perspective: to be trapped in a theatrical world, a world where performance outruns truth, is to be
trapped in a world of empty and sterile pretending.

Shakespeare was clearly captivated by the character of Hamlet, which is often described
as the richest acting role in the theatrical repertoire. But the theatricality that besets
Hamlet in the shady world of Elsinore also poses problems for Hamlet's many interpreters,
not only for Polonius and Claudius—who spend much of the play trying to "read"
Hamlet, figure him out—but for the generations of actors, audiences, and scholars who have
attempted to "pluck out the heart of [his] mystery." The difficulties of sounding Hamlet, however, are also part of the play's elaborate design. From his opening scene in the play, in which
Hamlet both wears the conventional black of mourning and chides his mother for presuming
that he is seeming to be in mourning, Hamlet's performance challenges his audiences (both
onstage and off) to "read" him, to interpret his character through the signs and signals of his
behavior. That is, Hamlet presents the audience with the same challenges that any actor does,
inviting us to interpret "that within" from the various behaviors that pass "show." And, contrary to Laurence Olivier—whose brilliant film of the play opens with a voice intoning that
Hamlet is the story "of a man who could not make up his mind"—Hamlet seems to act decisively throughout the play; what's difficult about reading Hamlet is that it's hard to tell when
he's *acting* and when he's "acting in earnest." Hamlet feigns madness in some scenes, but seems
madly out of control in others, such as the "nunnery" scene with Ophelia or the scene in
Gertrude's closet. He asks the player to act the part of vengeful Pyrrhus, then seems to adopt
the murderous swagger of the stage revenger, and then to question his performance ("Why,
what an ass am I"). He directs the players to insert a scene into *The Murder of Gonzago* to trick
Claudius into revealing his guilt, and then can't seem to keep himself off the stage, interrupting and interpreting the play as they play it. He's so offended when Laertes stagily leaps into
Ophelia's grave that he outperforms Laertes's overacting: "Nay, an thou'lt mouth, / I'll rant as
well as thou." Even Hamlet's soliloquies are problematic in this regard. For although we might
think that we hear the "true" Hamlet when he speaks alone onstage, how can we know that
Hamlet isn't trying on another role, either for his own benefit or ours—as he seems to do
when he plays the revenger in the "O what a rogue and peasant slave am I" speech? And as
the play proceeds, Hamlet's soliloquies become less frequent, and less revealing: when he returns from England in Act 5—having sent his friends Rosencrantz and Guildenstern to their
death—the play provides him with no more solo speeches; like the court, we have only
Hamlet's abrupt and irritable actions to go on.

Hamlet was evidently a success when it was first performed in 1600 or 1601; a pirated
version of the play (the so-called bad quarto, Q1) was published in 1603, presumably because the play's popularity suggested that a published text could make some money. A version of the play authorized by the King's Men was published in 1604 (the second quarto,
Q2), and the play was later included in the 1623 Folio (F); although Q1 is the most corrupt
version of the play, Q2 and F are by no means identical, and most modern texts collate elements of both versions.

From its inception, *Hamlet* has been a popular play with actors and audiences, and
from Richard Burbage's creation of the role, Hamlet has been a mark of distinction in
the history of English acting: the Restoration actor Thomas Betterton and the great
eighteenth-century actor David Garrick were both admired in the part (Henry Fielding's
novel *Tom Jones* contains a memorable parody of Garrick's performance). In the late nineteenth century Sir Henry Irving, the first actor to be knighted in England, gave a celebrated performance in which Hamlet never left the stage, but several other characters

(Rosencrantz and Guildenstern, for instance) were cut entirely. In the twentieth century, the play has, if anything, confirmed its reputation as an obligatory test for great actors, who have given a host of brilliant performances: Sir John Gielgud and Sir Laurence Olivier both produced fine stage versions of the play, and Olivier later won a Best Film Academy Award for his film version. Since World War II, Richard Burton, Jonathan Pryce, Derek Jacobi, and Michael Pennington are among the many actors to have given distinguished performances of this demanding play. The complexity of the play is something that faces actors even more immediately than readers of the play, because they will have to find a way to suit their acting to Hamlet's wild and whirling character. As Michael Pennington remarks in an essay on playing Hamlet, "To pull it off will take the actor further down into his psyche, memory and imagination, and further outwards to the limits of his technical knowledge and equipment, than he has probably been before."[1]

---

[1] Philip Brockbank, ed., *Players of Shakespeare: Essays in Shakespearean Performance by Twelve Players with the Royal Shakespeare Company* (Cambridge: Cambridge University Press, 1985), 117.

HAMLET

William Shakespeare

EDITED BY CYRUS HOY

CHARACTERS

CLAUDIUS, *King of Denmark*
HAMLET, *son to the late, and nephew to the present king*
POLONIUS, *Lord Chamberlain*
HORATIO, *friend to Hamlet*
LAERTES, *son to Polonius*
VOLTEMAND
CORNELIUS
ROSENCRANTZ
GUILDENSTERN } *courtiers*
OSRIC
A GENTLEMAN
A PRIEST
MARCELLUS } *officers*
BERNARDO

FRANCISCO, *a soldier*
REYNALDO, *servant to Polonius*
PLAYERS
TWO CLOWNS, *grave-diggers*
FORTINBRAS, *Prince of Norway*
A NORWEGIAN CAPTAIN
ENGLISH AMBASSADORS
GERTRUDE, *Queen of Denmark, and mother of Hamlet*
OPHELIA, *daughter to Polonius*
GHOST OF HAMLET'S FATHER
LORDS, LADIES, OFFICERS, SOLDIERS, SAILORS, MESSENGERS, *and* ATTENDANTS

SCENE: *Denmark.*

ACT ONE

SCENE I

Enter BERNARDO *and* FRANCISCO, *two sentinels.*

BERNARDO: Who's there?
FRANCISCO: Nay, answer me. Stand, and unfold yourself.
BERNARDO: Long live the king!
FRANCISCO: Bernardo?
5 BERNARDO: He.
FRANCISCO: You come most carefully upon your hour.
BERNARDO: 'Tis now struck twelve. Get thee to bed, Francisco.
FRANCISCO: For this relief much thanks. 'Tis bitter cold,
　And I am sick at heart.
10 BERNARDO: Have you had quiet guard?
FRANCISCO:　　　　　　　　　　Not a mouse stirring.
BERNARDO: Well, good night.
　If you do meet Horatio and Marcellus,
　The rivals of my watch, bid them make haste.

(Enter HORATIO *and* MARCELLUS.)

FRANCISCO: I think I hear them. Stand, ho! Who is there?
15 HORATIO: Friends to this ground.
MARCELLUS:　　　　　　　　　And liegemen to the Dane.
FRANCISCO: Give you good night.
MARCELLUS:　　　　　　　　O, farewell, honest soldier!
　Who hath relieved you?
FRANCISCO:　　　　　　Bernardo hath my place.
　Give you good night.

(Exit FRANCISCO.)

MARCELLUS:　　　　　Holla, Bernardo!
BERNARDO:　　　　　　　　　　Say—
　What, is Horatio there?

HORATIO:　　　　　　　　　A piece of him.
BERNARDO: Welcome, Horatio. Welcome, good Marcellus.　20
HORATIO: What, has this thing appeared again to-night?
BERNARDO: I have seen nothing.
MARCELLUS: Horatio says 'tis but our fantasy,
　And will not let belief take hold of him
　Touching this dreaded sight twice seen of us.　25
　Therefore I have entreated him along
　With us to watch the minutes of this night,
　That if again this apparition come,
　He may approve our eyes and speak to it.
HORATIO: Tush, tush, 'twill not appear.　30
BERNARDO:　　　　　　　　　　Sit down awhile,
　And let us once again assail your ears,
　That are so fortified against our story,
　What we have two nights seen.
HORATIO:　　　　　　　　Well, sit we down,
　And let us hear Bernardo speak of this.
BERNARDO: Last night of all,　35
　When yond same star that's westward from the pole
　Had made his course t' illume that part of heaven
　Where now it burns, Marcellus and myself,
　The bell then beating one—

(Enter GHOST.)

MARCELLUS: Peace, break thee off. Look where it comes again.　40
BERNARDO: In the same figure like the king that's dead.
MARCELLUS: Thou art a scholar; speak to it, Horatio.
BERNARDO: Looks 'a not like the king? Mark it, Horatio.
HORATIO: Most like. It harrows me with fear and wonder.
BERNARDO: It would be spoke to.　45
MARCELLUS:　　　　　　　　Question it, Horatio.
HORATIO: What art thou that usurp'st this time of night
　Together with that fair and warlike form

I.i. **13 rivals** partners　**15 Dane** King of Denmark

29 approve confirm　**36 pole** polestar　**44 harrows** afflicts, distresses

In which the majesty of buried Denmark
Did sometimes march? By heaven I charge thee, speak.
50 MARCELLUS: It is offended.
BERNARDO: See, it stalks away.
HORATIO: Stay. Speak, speak. I charge thee, speak.

(*Exit* GHOST.)

MARCELLUS: 'Tis gone and will not answer.
BERNARDO: How now, Horatio! You tremble and look pale.
Is not this something more than fantasy?
55   What think you on't?
HORATIO: Before my God, I might not this believe
Without the sensible and true avouch
Of mine own eyes.
MARCELLUS: Is it not like the king?
HORATIO: As thou art to thyself.
60   Such was the very armour he had on
When he the ambitious Norway combated.
So frowned he once when, in an angry parle,
He smote the sledded Polacks on the ice.
'Tis strange.
65 MARCELLUS: Thus twice before, and jump at this dead hour,
With martial stalk hath he gone by our watch.
HORATIO: In what particular thought to work I know not,
But in the gross and scope of mine opinion,
This bodes some strange eruption to our state.
70 MARCELLUS: Good now, sit down, and tell me he that knows,
Why this same strict and most observant watch
So nightly toils the subject of the land,
And why such daily cast of brazen cannon
And foreign mart for implements of war;
75   Why such impress of shipwrights, whose sore task
Does not divide the Sunday from the week.
What might be toward that this sweaty haste
Doth make the night joint-laborer with the day?
Who is't that can inform me?
HORATIO: That can I.
80   At least, the whisper goes so. Our last king,
Whose image even but now appeared to us,
Was as you know by Fortinbras of Norway,
Thereto pricked on by a most emulate pride,
Dared to the combat; in which our valiant Hamlet
85   (For so this side of our known world esteemed him)
Did slay this Fortinbras; who by a sealed compact
Well ratified by law and heraldry,
Did forfeit, with his life, all those his lands
Which he stood seized of, to the conqueror;
90   Against the which a moiety competent

Was gagèd by our king; which had returned
To the inheritance of Fortinbras,
Had he been vanquisher; as, by the same comart
And carriage of the article designed,
His fell to Hamlet. Now, sir, young Fortinbras,   95
Of unimprovèd mettle hot and full,
Hath in the skirts of Norway here and there
Sharked up a list of lawless resolutes
For food and diet to some enterprise
That hath a stomach in't; which is no other,   100
As it doth well appear unto our state,
But to recover of us by strong hand
And terms compulsatory, those foresaid lands
So by his father lost; and this, I take it,
Is the main motive of our preparations,   105
The source of this our watch, and the chief head
Of this post-haste and romage in the land.
BERNARDO: I think it be no other but e'en so.
Well may it sort that this portentous figure
Comes armèd through our watch; so like the king   110
That was and is the question of these wars.
HORATIO: A mote it is to trouble the mind's eye.
In the most high and palmy state of Rome,
A little ere the mightiest Julius fell,
The graves stood tenantless and the sheeted dead   115
Did squeak and gibber in the Roman streets;
As stars with trains of fire, and dews of blood,
Disasters in the sun; and the moist star,
Upon whose influence Neptune's empire stands,
Was sick almost to doomsday with eclipse.   120
And even the like precurse of feared events,
As harbingers preceding still the fates
And prologue to the omen coming on,
Have heaven and earth together demonstrated
Unto our climatures and countrymen.   125

(*Enter* GHOST.)

But soft, behold, lo where it comes again!
I'll cross it though it blast me.—Stay, illusion.

([GHOST] *spreads his arms.*)

If thou hast any sound or use of voice,
Speak to me.
If there be any good thing to be done,   130
That may to thee do ease, and grace to me,
Speak to me.
If thou art privy to thy country's fate,
Which happily foreknowing may avoid,

---

135   O, speak!
    Or if thou hast uphoarded in thy life
    Extorted treasure in the womb of earth,
    For which, they say, you spirits oft walk in death,

(The cock crows.)

    Speak of it. Stay, and speak. Stop it, Marcellus.
140 MARCELLUS: Shall I strike at it with my partisan?
HORATIO: Do, if it will not stand.
BERNARDO: 'Tis here.
HORATIO: 'Tis here!

(Exit GHOST.*)*

MARCELLUS: 'Tis gone!
    We do it wrong, being so majestical,
    To offer it the show of violence;
145   For it is as the air, invulnerable,
    And our vain blows malicious mockery.
BERNARDO: It was about to speak when the cock crew.
HORATIO: And then it started like a guilty thing
    Upon a fearful summons. I have heard
150   The cock, that is the trumpet to the morn,
    Doth with his lofty and shrill-sounding throat
    Awake the god of day and at his warning,
    Whether in sea or fire, in earth or air,
    Th' extravagant and erring spirit hies
155   To his confine; and of the truth herein
    This present object made probation.
MARCELLUS: It faded on the crowing of the cock.
    Some say that ever 'gainst that season comes
    Wherein our Saviour's birth is celebrated,
160   The bird of dawning singeth all night long,
    And then, they say, no spirit dare stir abroad.
    The nights are wholesome, then no planets strike,
    No fairy takes, nor witch hath power to charm,
    So hallowed and so gracious is that time.
165 HORATIO: So have I heard and do in part believe it.
    But look, the morn in russet mantle clad
    Walks o'er the dew of yon high eastward hill.
    Break we our watch up, and by my advice
    Let us impart what we have seen to-night
170   Unto young Hamlet, for, upon my life
    This spirit, dumb to us, will speak to him.
    Do you consent we shall acquaint him with it,
    As needful in our loves, fitting our duty?
MARCELLUS: Let's do't, I pray, and I this morning know
175   Where we shall find him most convenient.

(Exeunt.)

SCENE II

Flourish. Enter CLAUDIUS, KING OF DENMARK, GERTRUDE THE
QUEEN, COUNCILLORS, *[including]* POLONIUS *and his son* LAERTES,
HAMLET, *cum aliis [including* VOLTEMAND *and* CORNELIUS.*]*

KING: Though yet of Hamlet our dear brother's death
    The memory be green, and that it us befitted
    To bear our hearts in grief, and our whole kingdom
    To be contracted in one brow of woe,
    Yet so far hath discretion fought with nature   5
    That we with wisest sorrow think on him,
    Together with remembrance of ourselves.
    Therefore our sometime sister, now our queen,
    Th' imperial jointress to this warlike state,
    Have we, as 'twere with a defeated joy,   10
    With an auspicious and a dropping eye,
    With mirth in funeral and with dirge in marriage,
    In equal scale weighing delight and dole,
    Taken to wife; nor have we herein barred
    Your better wisdoms, which have freely gone   15
    With this affair along. For all, our thanks.
    Now follows that you know young Fortinbras,
    Holding a weak supposal of our worth,
    Or thinking by our late dear brother's death
    Our state to be disjoint and out of frame,   20
    Colleaguèd with this dream of his advantage,
    He hath not failed to pester us with message
    Importing the surrender of those lands
    Lost by his father, with all bands of law,
    To our most valiant brother. So much for him.   25
    Now for ourself, and for this time of meeting,
    Thus much the business is: we have here writ
    To Norway, uncle of young Fortinbras—
    Who, impotent and bedrid, scarcely hears
    Of this his nephew's purpose—to suppress   30
    His further gait herein, in that the levies,
    The lists, and full proportions are all made
    Out of his subject; and we here dispatch
    You, good Cornelius, and you, Voltemand,
    For bearers of this greeting to old Norway,   35
    Giving to you no further personal power
    To business with the king, more than the scope
    Of these delated articles allow.
    Farewell, and let your haste commend your duty.
CORNELIUS: ⎫
VOLTEMAND: ⎬ In that and all things will we show our duty   40
KING: We doubt it nothing, heartily farewell.

(Exeunt VOLTEMAND *and* CORNELIUS.*)*

    And now, Laertes, what's the news with you?
    You told us of some suit. What is't, Laertes?
    You cannot speak of reason to the Dane
    And lose your voice. What wouldst thou beg, Laertes,   45
    That shall not be my offer, not thy asking?
    The head is not more native to the heart,
    The hand more instrumental to the mouth,
    Than is the throne of Denmark to thy father.
    What wouldst thou have, Laertes?   50

---

140 **partisan** pike   154 **extravagant** straying, vagrant; **erring**
wandering   156 **probation** proof   158 **'gainst** just before
162 **strike** blast, destroy by malign influence   163 **takes** be-
witches

I.ii. s.d. **cum aliis** with others

---

9 **jointress** a widow who holds a jointure or life interest in an
estate   14 **barred** excluded   21 **Colleaguèd** united   31 **gait**
proceeding   32 **proportions** forces or supplies for war   38
delated expressly stated   44 **Dane** King of Denmark   45 **lose
your voice** speak in vain   47 **native** joined by nature   48 **instrumental** serviceable

LAERTES: My dread lord,
Your leave and favour to return to France,
From whence, though willingly, I came to Denmark
To show my duty in your coronation,
Yet now I must confess, that duty done,
55 My thoughts and wishes bend again toward France,
And bow them to your gracious leave and pardon.
KING: Have you your father's leave? What says Polonius?
POLONIUS: He hath, my lord, wrung from me my slow leave
By laborsome petition, and at last
60 Upon his will I sealed my hard consent.
I do beseech you give him leave to go.
KING: Take thy fair hour, Laertes. Time be thine,
And thy best graces spend it at thy will.
But now, my cousin Hamlet, and my son—
65 HAMLET: (Aside.) A little more than kin, and less than kind.
KING: How is it that the clouds still hang on you?
HAMLET: Not so, my lord. I am too much in the sun.
QUEEN: Good Hamlet, cast thy nighted color off,
And let thine eye look like a friend on Denmark.
70 Do not for ever with thy vailèd lids
Seek for thy noble father in the dust.
Thou know'st 'tis common—all that lives must die,
Passing through nature to eternity.
HAMLET: Ay, madam, it is common.
QUEEN: If it be,
75 Why seems it so particular with thee?
HAMLET: Seems, madam? Nay, it is. I know not 'seems.'
'Tis not alone my inky cloak, good mother,
Nor customary suits of solemn black,
Nor windy suspiration of forced breath,
80 No, nor the fruitful river in the eye,
Nor the dejected haviour of the visage,
Together with all forms, moods, shapes of grief,
That can denote me truly. These indeed seem,
For they are actions that a man might play,
85 But I have that within which passeth show—
These but the trappings and the suits of woe.
KING: 'Tis sweet and commendable in your nature, Hamlet,
To give these mourning duties to your father,
But you must know your father lost a father,
90 That father lost, lost his, and the survivor bound
In filial obligation for some term
To do obsequious sorrow. But to persever
In obstinate condolement is a course
Of impious stubbornness. 'Tis unmanly grief.
95 It shows a will most incorrect to heaven,
A heart unfortified, a mind impatient,
An understanding simple and unschooled.
For what we know must be, and is as common
As any the most vulgar thing to sense,
100 Why should we in our peevish opposition
Take it to heart? Fie, 'tis a fault to heaven,
A fault against the dead, a fault to nature,

To reason most absurd, whose common theme
Is death of fathers, and who still hath cried,
From the first corse till he that died to-day,   105
'This must be so.' We pray you throw to earth
This unprevailing woe, and think of us
As of a father, for let the world take note
You are the most immediate to our throne,
And with no less nobility of love   110
Than that which dearest father bears his son
Do I impart toward you. For your intent
In going back to school in Wittenberg,
It is most retrograde to our desire,
And we beseech you, bend you to remain   115
Here in the cheer and comfort of our eye,
Our chiefest courtier, cousin, and our son.
QUEEN: Let not thy mother lose her prayers, Hamlet.
I pray thee stay with us, go not to Wittenberg.
HAMLET: I shall in all my best obey you, madam.   120
KING: Why, 'tis a loving and a fair reply.
Be as ourself in Denmark. Madam, come.
This gentle and unforced accord of Hamlet
Sits smiling to my heart, in grace whereof,
No jocund health that Denmark drinks to-day   125
But the great cannon to the clouds shall tell,
And the king's rouse the heaven shall bruit again,
Respeaking earthly thunder. Come away.

(Flourish. Exeunt all but HAMLET.)

HAMLET: O, that this too too sallied flesh would melt,
Thaw and resolve itself into a dew,   130
Or that the Everlasting had not fixed
His canon 'gainst self-slaughter. O God, God,
How weary, stale, flat, and unprofitable
Seem to me all the uses of this world!
Fie on't, ah, fie, 'tis an unweeded garden   135
That grows to seed. Things rank and gross in nature
Possess it merely. That it should come to this,
But two months dead, nay, not so much, not two.
So excellent a king, that was to this
Hyperion to a satyr, so loving to my mother,   140
That he might not beteem the winds of heaven
Visit her face too roughly. Heaven and earth,
Must I remember? Why, she would hang on him
As if increase of appetite had grown
By what it fed on, and yet, within a month—   145
Let me not think on't. Frailty, thy name is woman—
A little month, or ere those shoes were old
With which she followed my poor father's body

---

56 **pardon** indulgence 60 **hard** reluctant 64 **cousin** kinsman of any kind except parent, child, brother, or sister 65 **kin** related as nephew; **kind** (1) affectionate (2) natural, lawful 70 **vailèd** lowered 75 **particular** personal, individual 92 **obsequious** dutiful in performing funeral obsequies or manifesting regard for the dead; **persever** persevere

105 **corse** corpse 114 **retrograde** contrary 127 **rouse** full draught of liquor; **bruit** echo 129 **sallied** sullied. "Sallied" is the reading of *Quarto 2* (Q2, also Q1). *Folio* (F) reads "solid." Since Hamlet's primary concern is with the fact of the flesh's impurity, not with its corporeality, the choice as between Q and F clearly lies with Q. "Sally" is a legitimate sixteenth-century form of "sully"; it occurs in Dekker's *Patient Grissil* (1.1.12), printed in 1603, as F.T. Bowers has pointed out (in "Hamlet's 'Sullied' or 'Solid' Flesh. A Bibliographical Case-History," *Shakespeare Survey* 9 [1956]: p. 44); and it occurs as a noun at 2.1.39 of *Hamlet* 132 **canon** law 137 **merely** entirely 140 **Hyperion** the sun god 141 **beteem** allowed

Like Niobe, all tears, why she—
150 O God, a beast that wants discourse of reason
Would have mourned longer—married with my uncle,
My father's brother, but no more like my father
Than I to Hercules. Within a month,
Ere yet the salt of most unrighteous tears
155 Had left the flushing in her gallèd eyes,
She married. O, most wicked speed, to post
With such dexterity to incestuous sheets!
It is not, nor it cannot come to good.
But break my heart, for I must hold my tongue.

(*Enter* HORATIO, MARCELLUS, *and* BERNARDO.)

160 HORATIO: Hail to your lordship!
HAMLET: I am glad to see you well.
Horatio—or I do forget myself.
HORATIO: The same, my lord, and your poor servant ever.
HAMLET: Sir, my good friend, I'll change that name with you.
And what make you from Wittenberg, Horatio?
165 Marcellus?
MARCELLUS: My good lord!
HAMLET: I am very glad to see you. (*To* BERNARDO.) Good
      even, sir.—
But what, in faith, make you from Wittenberg?
HORATIO: A truant disposition, good my lord.
170 HAMLET: I would not hear your enemy say so,
Nor shall you do my ear that violence
To make it truster of your own report
Against yourself. I know you are no truant.
But what is your affair in Elsinore?
175 We'll teach you to drink deep ere you depart.
HORATIO: My lord, I came to see your father's funeral.
HAMLET: I prithee, do not mock me, fellow-student,
I think it was to see my mother's wedding.
HORATIO: Indeed, my lord, it followed hard upon.
180 HAMLET: Thrift, thrift, Horatio. The funeral baked meats
Did coldly furnish forth the marriage tables.
Would I had met my dearest foe in heaven
Or ever I had seen that day, Horatio!
My father—methinks I see my father.
185 HORATIO: Where, my lord?
HAMLET: In my mind's eye, Horatio.
HORATIO: I saw him once, 'a was a goodly king.
HAMLET: 'A was a man, take him for all in all,
I shall not look upon his like again.
HORATIO: My lord, I think I saw him yesternight.
190 HAMLET: Saw who?
HORATIO: My lord, the king your father.
HAMLET: The king my father?
HORATIO: Season your admiration for a while
With an attent ear, till I may deliver

Upon the witness of these gentlemen
This marvel to you.   195
HAMLET: For God's love, let me hear!
HORATIO: Two nights together had these gentlemen,
Marcellus and Bernardo, on their watch
In the dead waste and middle of the night
Been thus encountered. A figure like your father,
Armed at point exactly, cap-a-pe,   200
Appears before them, and with solemn march
Goes slow and stately by them. Thrice he walked
By their oppressed and fear-surprisèd eyes
Within his truncheon's length, whilst they, distilled
Almost to jelly with the act of fear,   205
Stand dumb and speak not to him. This to me
In dreadful secrecy impart they did,
And I with them the third night kept the watch,
Where, as they had delivered, both in time,
Form of the thing, each word made true and good,   210
The apparition comes. I knew your father.
These hands are not more like.
HAMLET: But where was this?
MARCELLUS: My lord, upon the platform where we watch.
HAMLET: Did you not speak to it?
HORATIO: My lord, I did,
But answer made it none. Yet once methought   215
It lifted up it head and did address
Itself to motion, like as it would speak;
But even then the morning cock crew loud,
And at the sound it shrunk in haste away
And vanished from our sight.   220
HAMLET: 'Tis very strange.
HORATIO: As I do live, my honoured lord, 'tis true,
And we did think it writ down in our duty
To let you know of it.
HAMLET: Indeed, sirs, but
This troubles me. Hold you the watch to-night?
ALL: We do, my lord.   225
HAMLET: Armed, say you?
ALL: Armed, my lord.
HAMLET: From top to toe?
ALL: My lord, from head to foot.
HAMLET: Then saw you not his face.
HORATIO: O yes, my lord, he wore his beaver up.
HAMLET: What, looked he frowningly?
HORATIO: A countenance more in sorrow than in anger.   230
HAMLET: Pale or red?
HORATIO: Nay, very pale.
HAMLET: And fixed his eyes upon you?
HORATIO: Most constantly.
HAMLET: I would I had been there.
HORATIO: It would have much amazed you.
HAMLET: Very like.
Stayed it long?   235
HORATIO: While one with moderate haste might tell
a hundred.
BOTH: Longer, longer.

---

149 **Niobe** wife of Amphion, King of Thebes, she boasted of having more children than Leto and was punished when her seven sons and seven daughters were slain by Apollo and Artemis, children of Leto; in her grief she was changed by Zeus into a stone, which continually dropped tears   150 **wants** lacks; **discourse of reason** the reasoning faculty   155 **gallèd** sore from rubbing or chafing   163 **change** exchange   164 **make** do   182 **dearest** direst   192 **Season** temper, moderate; **admiration** wonder, astonishment

---

200 **at point** exactly in every particular; **cap-a-pe** from head to foot   204 **truncheon** military leader's baton   216 **it** its   228 **beaver** the part of the helmet that was drawn down to cover the face   235 **tell** count

HORATIO: Not when I saw't.

HAMLET: His beard was grizzled, no?

HORATIO: It was as I have seen it in his life,
    A sable silvered.

HAMLET: I will watch to-night.
240   Perchance 'twill walk again.

HORATIO: I warr'nt it will.

HAMLET: If it assume my noble father's person,
    I'll speak to it though hell itself should gape
    And bid me hold my peace. I pray you all,
    If you have hitherto concealed this sight,
245   Let it be tenable in your silence still,
    And whatsomever else shall hap to-night,
    Give it an understanding but no tongue.
    I will requite your loves. So fare you well.
    Upon the platform 'twixt eleven and twelve
250   I'll visit you.

ALL: Our duty to your honor.

HAMLET: Your loves, as mine to you. Farewell.

(*Exeunt* [*all but* HAMLET].)

    My father's spirit in arms? All is not well.
    I doubt some foul play. Would the night were come!
    Till then sit still, my soul. Foul deeds will rise,
255   Though all the earth o'erwhelm them, to men's eyes.

(*Exit.*)

SCENE III

Enter LAERTES *and* OPHELIA *his sister.*

LAERTES: My necessaries are embarked. Farewell.
    And, sister, as the winds give benefit
    And convoy is assistant, do not sleep,
    But let me hear from you.

OPHELIA: Do you doubt that?

5 LAERTES: For Hamlet, and the trifling of his favor,
    Hold it a fashion and a toy in blood,
    A violet in the youth of primy nature,
    Forward, not permanent, sweet, not lasting,
    The perfume and suppliance of a minute,
10   No more.

OPHELIA: No more but so?

LAERTES: Think it no more.
    For nature crescent does not grow alone
    In thews and bulk, but as this temple waxes
    The inward service of the mind and soul
    Grows wide withal. Perhaps he loves you now,
15   And now no soil nor cautel doth besmirch
    The virtue of his will, but you must fear,
    His greatness weighed, his will is not his own,
    For he himself is subject to his birth.

He may not, as unvalued persons do,
Carve for himself, for on his choice depends   20
The safety and health of this whole state,
And therefore must his choice be circumscribed
Unto the voice and yielding of that body
Whereof he is the head. Then if he says he loves you,
It fits your wisdom so far to believe it   25
As he in his particular act and place
May give his saying deed, which is no further
Than the main voice of Denmark goes withal.
Then weigh what loss your honor may sustain
If with too credent ear you list his songs,   30
Or lose your heart, or your chaste treasure open
To his unmastered importunity.
Fear it, Ophelia, fear it, my dear sister,
And keep you in the rear of your affection,
Out of the shot and danger of desire.   35
The chariest maid is prodigal enough
If she unmask her beauty to the moon.
Virtue itself scapes not calumnious strokes.
The canker galls the infants of the spring
Too oft before their buttons be disclosed,   40
And in the morn and liquid dew of youth
Contagious blastments are most imminent.
Be wary then; best safety lies in fear.
Youth to itself rebels, though none else near.

OPHELIA: I shall the effect of this good lesson keep   45
    As watchman to my heart. But, good my brother,
    Do not as some ungracious pastors do,
    Show me the steep and thorny way to heaven,
    Whiles like a puffed and reckless libertine
    Himself the primrose path of dalliance treads   50
    And recks not his own rede.

LAERTES: O, fear me not.

(*Enter* POLONIUS.)

    I stay too long. But here my father comes.
    A double blessing is a double grace;
    Occasion smiles upon a second leave.

POLONIUS: Yet here, Laertes? Aboard, aboard, for shame!   55
    The wind sits in the shoulder of your sail,
    And you are stayed for. There, my blessing with thee,
    And these few precepts in thy memory
    Look thou character. Give thy thoughts no tongue,
    Nor any unproportioned thought his act.   60
    Be thou familiar, but by no means vulgar.
    Those friends thou hast, and their adoption tried,
    Grapple them to thy soul with hoops of steel,
    But do not dull thy palm with entertainment
    Of each new-hatched, unfledged courage. Beware   65
    Of entrance to a quarrel, but being in,

---

237 **grizzled** grayish   239 **sable silvered** black mixed with
white   245 **tenable** retained   246 **whatsomever** whatsover
253 **doubt** suspect

I.iii.   6 **fashion** the creation of a season only; **toy in blood** passing
fancy   7 **primy** of the springtime   11 **crescent** growing   12
thews sinews, strength; **this temple** the body   15 **cautel** deceit
16 **will** desire   17 **greatness weighed** high position considered

---

19 **unvalued persons** persons of no social importance   20
Carve for himself act according to his own inclination   23
yielding assent   30 **credent** trusting   34 **affection** feeling
39 **canker** canker-worm (which feeds on roses); **galls** injures
40 **buttons** buds   42 **blastments** blights   51 **recks** regards;
rede counsel   59 **character** engrave   60 **unproportioned**
inordinate   61 **vulgar** common   65 **courage** young blood,
man of spirit

Bear't that th' opposèd may beware of thee.
Give every man thy ear, but few thy voice;
Take each man's censure, but reserve thy judgement.
70 Costly thy habit as thy purse can buy,
But not expressed in fancy; rich not gaudy,
For the apparel oft proclaims the man,
And they in France of the best rank and station
Are of a most select and generous chief in that.
75 Neither a borrower nor a lender be,
For loan oft loses both itself and friend,
And borrowing dulls th' edge of husbandry.
This above all, to thine own self be true,
And it must follow as the night the day
80 Thou canst not then be false to any man.
Farewell. My blessing season this in thee!
LAERTES: Most humbly do I take my leave, my lord.
POLONIUS: The time invites you. Go, your servants tend.
LAERTES: Farewell, Ophelia, and remember well
85 What I have said to you.
OPHELIA: 'Tis in my memory locked,
And you yourself shall keep the key of it.
LAERTES: Farewell.

(*Exit* LAERTES.)

POLONIUS: What is 't, Ophelia, he hath said to you?
OPHELIA: So please you, something touching the Lord
    Hamlet.
90 POLONIUS: Marry, well bethought.
'Tis told me he hath very oft of late
Given private time to you, and you yourself
Have of your audience been most free and bounteous.
If it be so—as so 'tis put on me,
95 And that in way of caution—I must tell you,
You do not understand yourself so clearly
As it behooves my daughter and your honor.
What is between you? Give me up the truth.
OPHELIA: He hath, my lord, of late made many tenders
100 Of his affection to me.
POLONIUS: Affection? Pooh! You speak like a green girl,
Unsifted in such perilous circumstance.
Do you believe his tenders, as you call them?
OPHELIA: I do not know, my lord, what I should think.
105 POLONIUS: Marry, I will teach you. Think yourself a baby
That you have ta'en these tenders for true pay
Which are not sterling. Tender yourself more dearly,
Or (not to crack the wind of the poor phrase,
Running it thus) you'll tender me a fool.
110 OPHELIA: My lord, he hath importuned me with love
In honorable fashion.
POLONIUS: Ay, fashion you may call it. Go to, go to.
OPHELIA: And hath given countenance to his speech, my lord,
With almost all the holy vows of heaven.
115 POLONIUS: Ay, springes to catch woodcocks. I do know,
When the blood burns, how prodigal the soul
Lends the tongue vows. These blazes, daughter,
Giving more light than heat, extinct in both

Even in their promise, as it is a-making,
You must not take for fire. From this time   120
Be something scanter of your maiden presence.
Set your entreatments at a higher rate
Than a command to parle. For Lord Hamlet,
Believe so much in him that he is young,
And with a larger tether may he walk   125
Than may be given you. In few, Ophelia,
Do not believe his vows, for they are brokers,
Not of that dye which their investments show,
But mere implorators of unholy suits,
Breathing like sanctified and pious bawds,   130
The better to beguile. This is for all:
I would not, in plain terms, from this time forth
Have you so slander any moment leisure
As to give words or talk with the Lord Hamlet.
Look to't, I charge you. Come your ways.   135
OPHELIA: I shall obey, my lord.

(*Exeunt.*)

SCENE IV

Enter HAMLET, HORATIO, *and* MARCELLUS.

HAMLET: The air bites shrewdly; it is very cold.
HORATIO: It is a nipping and an eager air.
HAMLET: What hour now?
HORATIO: I think it lacks of twelve.
MARCELLUS: No, it is struck.
HORATIO: Indeed? I heard it not. It then draws near the season 5
    Wherein the spirit held his wont to walk.

(*A flourish of trumpets, and two pieces go off.*)

What does this mean, my lord?
HAMLET: The king doth wake to-night and takes his rouse,
Keeps wassail, and the swagg'ring up-spring reels,
And as he drains his draughts of Rhenish down,   10
The kettledrum and trumpet thus bray out
The triumph of his pledge.
HORATIO: Is it a custom?
HAMLET: Ay, marry, is't,
But to my mind, though I am native here
And to the manner born, it is a custom   15
More honored in the breach than the observance.
This heavy-headed revel east and west
Makes us traduced and taxed of other nations.
They clepe us drunkards, and with swinish phrase
Soil our addition, and indeed it takes   20
From our achievements, though performed at height,
The pith and marrow of our attribute.
So oft it chances in particular men,
That for some vicious mole of nature in them,

---

74 **chief** eminence   77 **husbandry** thriftiness   81 **season**
ripen   83 **tend** attend, wait   90 **Marry** by Mary   99 **tenders**
offers   102 **Unsifted** untried   115 **springes** snares

122 **entreatments** military negotiations for surrender   127
brokers go-betweens   128 **investments** clothes   129 **implorators** solicitors

I.iv. 2 **eager** sharp   9 **wassail** carousal; **up-spring** a German
dance   18 **taxed of** censured by   19 **clepe** call   20 **addition**
title added to a man's name to denote his rank   22 **attribute**
reputation

25 As, in their birth, wherein they are not guilty
(Since nature cannot choose his origin),
By the o'ergrowth of some complexion,
Oft breaking down the pales and forts of reason,
Or by some habit that too much o'er-leavens
30 The form of plausive manners—that these men,
Carrying, I say, the stamp of one defect,
Being nature's livery or fortune's star,
His virtues else, be they as pure as grace,
As infinite as man may undergo,
35 Shall in the general censure take corruption
From that particular fault. The dram of evil
Doth all the noble substance often doubt
To his own scandal.

(*Enter* GHOST.)

HORATIO: Look, my lord, it comes.
HAMLET: Angels and ministers of grace defend us!
40 Be thou a spirit of health or goblin damned,
Bring with thee airs from heaven or blasts from hell,
Be thy intents wicked or charitable,
Thou com'st in such a questionable shape
That I will speak to thee. I'll call thee Hamlet,
45 King, father, royal Dane. O, answer me!
Let me not burst in ignorance, but tell
Why thy canonized bones, hearsèd in death,
Have burst their cerements; why the sepulchre
Wherein we saw thee quietly interred,
50 Hath oped his ponderous and marble jaws
To cast thee up again. What may this mean
That thou, dead corse, again in complete steel
Revisits thus the glimpses of the moon,
Making night hideous, and we fools of nature
55 So horridly to shake our disposition
With thoughts beyond the reaches of our souls?
Say, why is this? wherefore? What should we do?

([GHOST] *beckons*.)

HORATIO: It beckons you to go away with it,
As if it some impartment did desire
60 To you alone.
MARCELLUS: Look, with what courteous action
It waves you to a more removèd ground.
But do not go with it.
HORATIO: No, by no means.
HAMLET: It will not speak; then I will follow it.
HORATIO: Do not, my lord.
HAMLET: Why, what should be the fear?
65 I do not set my life at a pin's fee,
And for my soul, what can it do to that,
Being a thing immortal as itself?
It waves me forth again. I'll follow it.

----

26 **his** its   27 **complexion** one of the four temperaments (sanguine, melancholy, choleric, and phlegmatic)   29 **o'er-leavens** works change throughout   30 **plausive** pleasing   32 **livery** badge; **star** a person's fortune, rank, or destiny, viewed as determined by the stars   37 **doubt** put out, obliterate   38 **his** its   47 **canonized** buried according to the church's rule; **hearsèd** coffined, buried   59 **impartment** communication

HORATIO: What if it tempt you toward the flood, my lord,
Or to the dreadful summit of the cliff   70
That beetles o'er his base into the sea,
And there assume some other horrible form,
Which might deprive your sovereignty of reason
And draw you into madness? Think of it.
The very place puts toys of desperation,   75
Without more motive, into every brain
That looks so many fathoms to the sea
And hears it roar beneath.
HAMLET: It waves me still.
Go on. I'll follow thee.
MARCELLUS: You shall not go, my lord.   80
HAMLET: Hold off your hands.
HORATIO: Be ruled; You shall not go.
HAMLET: My fate cries out,
And makes each petty artere in this body
As hardy as the Nemean lion's nerve.
Still am I called. Unhand me, gentlemen.
By heaven, I'll make a ghost of him that lets me.   85
I say, away—Go on. I'll follow thee.

([*Exeunt*] GHOST *and* HAMLET.)

HORATIO: He waxes desperate with imagination.
MARCELLUS: Let's follow. 'Tis not fit thus to obey him.
HORATIO: Have after. To what issue will this come?
MARCELLUS: Something is rotten in the state of Denmark.   90
HORATIO: Heaven will direct it.
MARCELLUS: Nay, let's follow him.

(*Exeunt*.)

SCENE V

Enter GHOST *and* HAMLET.

HAMLET: Whither wilt thou lead me? Speak. I'll go no further.
GHOST: Mark me.
HAMLET: I will.
GHOST: My hour is almost come
When I to sulph'rous and tormenting flames
Must render up myself.
HAMLET: Alas, poor ghost!
GHOST: Pity me not, but lend thy serious hearing   5
To what I shall unfold.
HAMLET: Speak. I am bound to hear.
GHOST: So art thou to revenge, when thou shalt hear.
HAMLET: What?
GHOST: I am thy father's spirit,
Doomed for a certain term to walk the night,   10
And for the day confined to fast in fires,
Till the foul crimes done in my days of nature
Are burnt and purged away. But that I am forbid
To tell the secrets of my prison house,
I could a tale unfold whose lightest word   15
Would harrow up thy soul, freeze thy young blood,

----

71 **beetles** juts out   73 **sovereignty of reason** state of being ruled by reason   75 **toys** fancies, impules   82 **artere** artery   83 **Nemean lion** slain by Hercules in the performance of one of his twelve labors   85 **lets** hinders

Make thy two eyes like stars start from their spheres,
Thy knotted and combinèd locks to part,
And each particular hair to stand an end,
20   Like quills upon the fretful porpentine.
But this eternal blazon must not be
To ears of flesh and blood. List, list, O, list!
If thou didst ever thy dear father love—
HAMLET: O God!
25 GHOST: Revenge his foul and most unnatural murder.
HAMLET: Murder!
GHOST: Murder most foul, as in the best it is,
But this most foul, strange, and unnatural.
HAMLET: Haste me to know't, that I, with wings as swift
30   As meditation or the thoughts of love,
May sweep to my revenge.
GHOST: I find thee apt,
And duller shouldst thou be than the fat weed
That roots itself in ease on Lethe wharf,
Wouldst thou not stir in this. Now, Hamlet, hear.
35   'Tis given out that, sleeping in my orchard,
A serpent stung me. So the whole ear of Denmark
Is by a forgèd process of my death
Rankly abused. But know, thou noble youth,
The serpent that did sting thy father's life
40   Now wears his crown.
HAMLET: O my prophetic soul!
My uncle!
GHOST: Ay, that incestuous, that adulterate beast,
With witchcraft of his wits, with traitorous gifts—
O wicked wit and gifts that have the power
45   So to seduce!—won to his shameful lust
The will of my most seeming virtuous queen.
O Hamlet, what a falling off was there,
From me, whose love was of that dignity
That it went hand in hand even with the vow
50   I made to her in marriage, and to decline
Upon a wretch whose natural gifts were poor
To those of mine!
But virtue, as it never will be moved,
Though lewdness court it in a shape of heaven,
55   So lust, though to a radiant angel linked,
Will sate itself in a celestial bed
And prey on garbage.
But soft, methinks I scent the morning air.
Brief let me be. Sleeping within my orchard,
60   My custom always of the afternoon,
Upon my secure hour thy uncle stole,
With juice of cursed hebona in a vial,
And in the porches of my ears did pour
The leperous distilment, whose effect
65   Holds such an enmity with blood of man
That swift as quicksilver it courses through
The natural gates and alleys of the body,
And with a sudden vigor it doth posset
And curd, like eager droppings into milk,

The thin and wholesome blood. So did it mine,   70
And a most instant tetter barked about
Most lazar-like with vile and loathsome crust
All my smooth body.
Thus was I sleeping by a brother's hand
Of life, of crown, of queen, at once dispatched,   75
Cut off even in the blossoms of my sin,
Unhouseled, disappointed, unaneled,
No reck'ning made, but sent to my account
With all my imperfections on my head.
O, horrible! O, horrible! most horrible!   80
If thou hast nature in thee, bear it not,
Let not the royal bed of Denmark be
A couch for luxury and damnèd incest.
But howsomever thou pursues this act,
Taint not thy mind, nor let thy soul contrive   85
Against thy mother aught. Leave her to heaven,
And to those thorns that in her bosom lodge
To prick and sting her. Fare thee well at once.
The glowworm shows the matin to be near,
And gins to pale his uneffectual fire.   90
Adieu, adieu, adieu. Remember me.

(*Exit.*)

HAMLET: O all you host of heaven! O earth! What else?
And shall I couple hell? O, fie! Hold, hold, my heart,
And you, my sinews, grow not instant old,
But bear me stiffly up. Remember thee?   95
Ay, thou poor ghost, whiles memory holds a seat
In this distracted globe. Remember thee?
Yea, from the table of my memory
I'll wipe away all trivial fond records,
All saws of books, all forms, all pressures past   100
That youth and observation copied there,
And thy commandment all alone shall live
Within the book and volume of my brain,
Unmixed with baser matter. Yes, by heaven!
O most pernicious woman!   105
O villain, villain, smiling, damnèd villain!
My tables—meet it is I set it down
That one may smile, and smile, and be a villain
At least I am sure it may be so in Denmark.   (*Writing.*)
So, uncle, there you are. Now to my word: 110
It is 'Adieu, adieu! Remember me,'
I have sworn't.

(*Enter* HORATIO *and* MARCELLUS.)

HORATIO: My lord, my lord!
MARCELLUS: Lord Hamlet!
HORATIO: Heavens secure him!
HAMLET: So be it!

I.v. 19 **an** on   20 **porpentine** porcupine   21 **eternal blazon** proclamation of the secrets of eternity   33 **Lethe** the river in Hades that brings forgetfulness   37 **process** account   61 **secure** free from suspicion   62 **hebona** an imaginary poison, associated with henbane   68 **posset** curdle   69 **eager** acid

71 **tetter** a skin eruption; **barked** covered as with bark   77 **Unhouseled** without having received the sacrament; **disappointed** unprepared; **unaneled** without extreme unction   83 **luxury** lust   89 **matin** morning   97 **globe** head   98 **table** writing tablet, memorandum book (as at line 107, below; here metaphorically of the mind)   99 **fond** foolish   100 **saws** sayings; **forms** concepts; **pressures** impressions

115 MARCELLUS: Illo, ho, ho, my lord!
    HAMLET: Hillo, ho, ho, boy! Come, bird, come.
    MARCELLUS: How is't, my noble lord?
    HORATIO: What news, my lord?
    HAMLET: O, wonderful!
    HORATIO: Good my lord, tell it.
    HAMLET: No, you will reveal it.
120 HORATIO: Not I, my lord, by heaven.
    MARCELLUS: Nor I, my lord.
    HAMLET: How say you then, would heart of man once think it?
       But you'll be secret?
    BOTH: Ay, by heaven, my lord.
    HAMLET: There's never a villain dwelling in all Denmark
       But he's an arrant knave.
125 HORATIO: There needs no ghost, my lord, come from the grave
       To tell us this.
    HAMLET: Why, right, you are in the right,
       And so without more circumstance at all
       I hold it fit that we shake hands and part,
       You, as your business and desire shall point you,
130   For every man has business and desire
       Such as it is, and for my own poor part,
       I will go pray.
    HORATIO: These are but wild and whirling words, my lord.
    HAMLET: I am sorry they offend you, heartily;
135   Yes, faith, heartily.
    HORATIO: There's no offence, my lord.
    HAMLET: Yes, by Saint Patrick, but there is, Horatio,
       And much offence too. Touching this vision here,
       It is an honest ghost, that let me tell you
       For your desire to know what is between us,
140   O'ermaster't as you may. And now, good friends,
       As you are friends, scholars, and soldiers,
       Give me one poor request.
    HORATIO: What is't, my lord? We will.
    HAMLET: Never make known what you have seen to-night.
145   BOTH: My lord, we will not.
    HAMLET: Nay, but swear't.
    HORATIO: In faith,
       My lord, not I.
    MARCELLUS: Nor I, my lord, in faith.
    HAMLET: Upon my sword.
    MARCELLUS: We have sworn, my lord, already.
    HAMLET: Indeed, upon my sword, indeed.

(GHOST *cries under the stage.*)

    GHOST: Swear.
    HAMLET: Ha, ha, boy, say'st thou so? Art thou there, truepenny?
150   Come on. You hear this fellow in the cellarage.
       Consent to swear.
    HORATIO: Propose the oath, my lord.
    HAMLET: Never to speak of this that you have seen,
       Swear by my sword.
    GHOST: (*Beneath.*) Swear.
155 HAMLET: Hic et ubique? Then we'll shift our ground.

---

115 **Illo, ho, ho** cry of the falconer to summon his hawk   136
Saint Patrick associated, in the late middle ages, with purgatory,
whence the ghost has presumably come   149 **truepenny** honest fellow   155 **Hic et ubique** here and everywhere

Come hither, gentlemen,
   And lay your hands again upon my sword.
   Swear by my sword
   Never to speak of this that you have heard.
GHOST: (*Beneath.*) Swear by his sword.   160
HAMLET: Well said, old mole! Canst work i' th' earth so fast?
   A worthy pioneer! Once more remove, good friends.
HORATIO: O day and night, but this is wondrous strange!
HAMLET: And therefore as a stranger give it welcome.
   There are more things in heaven and earth, Horatio,   165
   Than are dreamt of in your philosophy.
   But come.
   Here as before, never, so help you mercy,
   How strange or odd some'er I bear myself
   (As I perchance hereafter shall think meet   170
   To put an antic disposition on),
   That you, at such times, seeing me, never shall,
   With arms encumbered thus, or this head-shake,
   Or by pronouncing of some doubtful phrase,
   As 'Well, well, we know,' or 'We could, and if we would'   175
   Or 'If we list to speak,' or 'There be, and if they might'
   Or such ambiguous giving out, to note
   That you know aught of me—this do swear,
   So grace and mercy at your most need help you.
GHOST: (*Beneath.*) Swear.   180
HAMLET: Rest, rest, perturbèd spirit! So, gentlemen,
   With all my love I do commend me to you,
   And what so poor a man as Hamlet is
   May do t' express his love and friending to you,
   God willing, shall not lack. Let us go in together,   185
   And still your fingers on your lips, I pray.
   The time is out of joint. O cursèd spite
   That ever I was born to set it right!
   Nay, come, let's go together.

(*Exeunt.*)

ACT TWO

SCENE I

Enter old POLONIUS *with his man* [REYNALDO].

POLONIUS: Give him this money and these notes. Reynaldo.
REYNALDO: I will, my lord.
POLONIUS: You shall do marvellous wisely, good Reynaldo,
   Before you visit him, to make inquire
   Of his behavior.   5
REYNALDO: My lord, I did intend it.
POLONIUS: Marry, well said, very well said. Look you, sir,
   Enquire me first what Danskers are in Paris,
   And how, and who, what means, and where they keep,
   What company, at what expense; and finding
   By this encompassment and drift of question   10
   That they do know my son, come you more nearer
   Than your particular demands will touch it.
   Take you as 'twere some distant knowledge of him,

---

162 **pioneer** miner   171 **antic** mad   173 **encumbered** folded
II.i. 7 **Danskers** Danes   8 **means** wealth   10 **encompassment** talking round the matter

As thus, 'I know his father and his friends,
15   And in part him,' do you mark this, Reynaldo?
REYNALDO: Ay, very well, my lord.
POLONIUS: 'And in part him, but,' you may say, 'not well,
    But if 't be he I mean, he's very wild,
    Addicted so and so.' And there put on him
20   What forgeries you please; marry, none so rank
    As may dishonour him. Take heed of that.
    But, sir, such wanton, wild, and usual slips
    As are companions noted and most known
    To youth and liberty.
REYNALDO: As gaming, my lord?
25 POLONIUS: Ay, or drinking, fencing, swearing, quarrelling,
    Drabbing—you may go so far.
REYNALDO: My lord, that would dishonour him.
POLONIUS: Faith, no, as you may season it in the charge.
    You must not put another scandal on him,
30   That he is open to incontinency.
    That's not my meaning. But breathe his faults so quaintly
    That they may seem the taints of liberty,
    The flash and outbreak of a fiery mind,
    A savageness in unreclaimèd blood,
35   Of general assault.
REYNALDO: But, my good lord—
POLONIUS: Wherefore should you do this?
REYNALDO: Ay, my lord,
    I would know that.
POLONIUS: Marry, sir, here's my drift,
    And I believe it is a fetch of warrant.
    You laying these slight sullies on my son,
40   As 'twere a thing a little soiled i' th' working,
    Mark you,
    Your party in converse, him you would sound,
    Having ever seen in the prenominate crimes
    The youth you breathe of guilty, be assured
45   He closes with you in this consequence,
    'Good sir', or so, or 'friend', or 'gentleman',
    According to the phrase or the addition
    Of man and country.
REYNALDO: Very good, my lord.
POLONIUS: And then, sir, does 'a this—'a does—What was I
      about to say?
50   By the mass, I was about to say something.
    Where did I leave?
REYNALDO: At 'closes in the consequence.'
POLONIUS: At 'closes in the consequence'—ay, marry,
    He closes thus: 'I know the gentleman.
55   I saw him yesterday, or th' other day,
    Or then, or then, with such, or such, and as you say,
    There was 'a gaming, there o'ertook in 's rouse;
    There falling out at tennis', or perchance
    'I saw him enter such a house of sale',
60   Videlicet, a brothel, or so forth.

See you, now—
    Your bait of falsehood takes this carp of truth,
    And thus do we of wisdom and of reach,
    With windlasses and with assays of bias,
    By indirections find directions out;   65
    So by my former lecture and advice
    Shall you my son. You have me, have you not?
REYNALDO: My lord, I have.
POLONIUS: God bye ye; fare ye well.
REYNALDO: Good my lord.
POLONIUS: Observe his inclination in yourself.   70
REYNALDO: I shall, my lord.
POLONIUS: And let him ply his music.
REYNALDO: Well, my lord.
POLONIUS: Farewell.

(*Exit* REYNALDO.)

(*Enter* OPHELIA.)

                          How now, Ophelia! what's the matter?
OPHELIA: O my lord, my lord, I have been so affrighted!
POLONIUS: With what, i' th' name of God?   75
OPHELIA: My lord, as I was sewing in my closet,
    Lord Hamlet, with his doublet all unbraced,
    No hat upon his head, his stockings fouled,
    Ungartered, and down-gyvèd to his ankle,
    Pale as his shirt, his knees knocking each other,   80
    And with a look so piteous in purport
    As if he had been loosèd out of hell
    To speak of horrors—he comes before me.
POLONIUS: Mad for thy love?
OPHELIA: My lord, I do not know,
    But truly I do fear it.   85
POLONIUS: What said he?
OPHELIA: He took me by the wrist, and held me hard,
    Then goes he to the length of all his arm,
    And with his other hand thus o'er his brow,
    He falls to such perusal of my face
    As 'a would draw it. Long stayed he so.   90
    At last, a little shaking of mine arm
    And thrice his head thus waving up and down,
    He raised a sigh so piteous and profound
    As it did seem to shatter all his bulk
    And end his being. That done, he lets me go,   95
    And with his head over his shoulder turned,
    He seemed to find his way without his eyes,
    For out adoors he went without their helps,
    And to the last bended their light on me.
POLONIUS: Come, go with me. I will go seek the king.   100
    This is the very ecstasy of love,
    Whose violent property fordoes itself,
    And leads the will to desperate undertakings
    As oft as any passion under heaven
    That does afflict our natures. I am sorry.   105
    What, have you given him any hard words of late?

---

20 **forgeries** invented wrongdoings 24 **liberty** license 26 **Drabbing** whoring 28 **season** moderate 31 **quaintly** delicately 34 **unreclaimèd** untamed 35 **Of general assault** assailing all 38 **fetch of warrant** allowable device 43 **prenominate** before-named 45 **closes** agrees; **in this consequence** as follows 47 **addition** title 60 **Videlicet** namely

---

63 **reach** ability 64 **windlasses** roundabout approaches; **assays of bias** indirect attempts 68 **God buy ye** God be with you 76 **closet** private room 77 **unbraced** unlaced 79 **down-gyvèd** hanging down, like gyves or fetters on a prisoner's ankles 101 **ecstasy** madness 102 **fordoes** destroys

OPHELIA: No, my good lord, but as you did command
　　　I did repel his letters, and denied
　　　His access to me.
POLONIUS:　　　　That hath made him mad.
110　I am sorry that with better heed and judgement
　　　I had not quoted him. I feared he did but trifle,
　　　And meant to wrack thee; but beshrew my jealousy.
　　　By heaven, it is as proper to our age
　　　To cast beyond ourselves in our opinions
115　As it is common for the younger sort
　　　To lack discretion. Come, go we to the king.
　　　This must be known, which being kept close, might move
　　　More grief to hide than hate to utter love.
　　　Come.

(*Exeunt.*)

SCENE II

Flourish. Enter KING *and* QUEEN, ROSENCRANTZ, *and*
GUILDENSTERN [*and* ATTENDANTS].

KING: Welcome, dear Rosencrantz and Guildenstern.
　　　Moreover that we much did long to see you,
　　　The need we have to use you did provoke
　　　Our hasty sending. Something have you heard
5　　Of Hamlet's transformation—so call it,
　　　Sith nor th' exterior nor the inward man
　　　Resembles that it was. What it should be,
　　　More than his father's death, that thus hath put him
　　　So much from th' understanding of himself,
10　I cannot dream of. I entreat you both
　　　That, being of so young days brought up with him,
　　　And sith so neighboured to his youth and havior,
　　　That you vouchsafe your rest here in our court
　　　Some little time, so by your companies
15　To draw him on to pleasures, and to gather
　　　So much as from occasion you may glean,
　　　Whether aught to us unknown afflicts him thus,
　　　That opened, lies within our remedy.
QUEEN: Good gentlemen, he hath much talked of you,
20　And sure I am two men there is not living
　　　To whom he more adheres. If it will please you
　　　To show us so much gentry and good will
　　　As to expend your time with us awhile
　　　For the supply and profit of our hope,
25　Your visitation shall receive such thanks
　　　As fits a king's remembrance.
ROSENCRANTZ:　　　　Both your majesties
　　　Might, by the sovereign power you have of us,
　　　Put your dread pleasures more into command
　　　Than to entreaty.
GUILDENSTERN:　　　But we both obey,
30　And here give up ourselves in the full bent
　　　To lay our service freely at your feet,
　　　To be commanded.
KING: Thanks, Rosencrantz and gentle Guildenstern.

QUEEN: Thanks, Guildenstern and gentle Rosencrantz.
　　　And I beseech you instantly to visit　　　35
　　　My too much changed son. Go, some of you,
　　　And bring these gentlemen where Hamlet is.
GUILDENSTERN: Heavens make our presence and our practices
　　　Pleasant and helpful to him!
QUEEN:　　　　Ay, amen!

(*Exeunt* ROSENCRANTZ *and* GUILDENSTERN [*with some* AT-
TENDANTS].)

(*Enter* POLONIUS.)

POLONIUS: Th' ambassadors from Norway, my good lord,　40
　　　Are joyfully returned.
KING: Thou still hast been the father of good news.
POLONIUS: Have I, my lord? I assure my good liege,
　　　I hold my duty as I hold my soul,
　　　Both to my God and to my gracious king;　　45
　　　And I do think—or else this brain of mine
　　　Hunts not the trail of policy so sure
　　　As it hath used to do—that I have found
　　　The very cause of Hamlet's lunacy.
KING: O, speak of that, that do I long to hear.　　50
POLONIUS: Give first admittance to th' ambassadors.
　　　My news shall be the fruit to that great feast.
KING: Thyself do grace to them, and bring them in.

(*Exit* POLONIUS.)

　　　He tells me, my dear Gertrude, he hath found
　　　The head and source of all your son's distemper.　55
QUEEN: I doubt it is no other but the main,
　　　His father's death and our o'erhasty marriage.
KING: Well, we shall sift him.

(*Enter* AMBASSADORS [VOLTEMAND *and* CORNELIUS], *with*
POLONIUS.)

　　　　　　　Welcome, my good friends,
　　　Say, Voltemand, what from our brother Norway?
VOLTEMAND: Most fair return of greetings and desires.　60
　　　Upon our first, he sent out to suppress
　　　His nephew's levies, which to him appeared
　　　To be a preparation 'gainst the Polack,
　　　But better looked into, he truly found
　　　It was against your highness, whereat grieved,　65
　　　That so his sickness, age, and impotence
　　　Was falsely borne in hand, sends out arrests
　　　On Fortinbras, which he in brief obeys,
　　　Receives rebuke from Norway, and in fine,
　　　Makes vow before his uncle never more　　70
　　　To give th' assay of arms against your majesty.
　　　Whereon old Norway, overcome with joy,
　　　Gives him three score thousand crowns in annual fee,
　　　And his commission to employ those soldiers,
　　　So levied as before, against the Polack,　　75
　　　With an entreaty, herein further shown,　(*Gives a paper.*)
　　　That it might please you to give quiet pass
　　　Through your dominions for this enterprise,

---

111 **quoted** observed　112 **wrack** ruin　113 **proper to** characteristic of　117 **close** secret; **move** cause

II.ii. 6 Sith **since**　18 **opened** disclosed　22 **gentry** courtesy

---

42 **still** ever　56 **doubt** suspect　63 **the Polack** the Polish
nation　67 **borne in hand** deceived　69 **in fine** in the end
71 **assay** trial

On such regards of safety and allowance
80   As therein are set down.
    KING: It likes us well,
    And at our more considered time we'll read,
    Answer, and think upon this business.
    Meantime we thank you for your well-took labor.
    Go to your rest; at night we'll feast together.
85   Most welcome home!

    (*Exeunt* AMBASSADORS.)

    POLONIUS: This business is well ended.
    My liege and madam, to expostulate
    What majesty should be, what duty is,
    Why day is day, night night, and time is time,
    Were nothing but to waste night, day and time.
90   Therefore, since brevity is the soul of wit,
    And tediousness the limbs and outward flourishes,
    I will be brief. Your noble son is mad.
    Mad call I it, for to define true madness,
    What is't but to be nothing else but mad?
95   But let that go.
    QUEEN: More matter with less art.
    POLONIUS: Madam, I swear I use no art at all.
    That he is mad, 'tis true: 'tis true 'tis pity.
    And pity 'tis 'tis true. A foolish figure,
    But farewell it, for I will use no art.
100   Mad let us grant him, then, and now remains
    That we find out the cause of this effect,
    Or rather say the cause of this defect,
    For this effect defective comes by cause.
    Thus it remains, and the remainder thus.
105   Perpend.
    I have a daughter—have while she is mine—
    Who in her duty and obedience, mark,
    Hath given me this. Now gather, and surmise.   (*Reads.*)
            'To the celestial, and my soul's idol, the most beautified
110   Ophelia'—That's an ill phrase, a vile phrase, 'beautified' is
            a vile phrase. But you shall hear. Thus: (*Reads.*)
            'In her excellent white bosom, these, etc.'
    QUEEN: Came this from Hamlet to her?
    POLONIUS: Good madam, stay awhile. I will be faithful.
    (*Reads letter.*)

115   'Doubt thou the stars are fire,
                    Doubt that the sun doth move;
                Doubt truth to be a liar;
                    But never doubt I love.

            'O dear Ophelia, I am ill at these numbers. I have not
120   art to reckon my groans, but that I love thee best, O most
    best, believe it. Adieu.
                    'Thine evermore, most dear lady, whilst
                            this machine is to him, Hamlet.'
    This in obedience hath my daughter shown me,
125   And more above, hath his solicitings,
    As they fell out by time, by means and place,
    All given to mine ear.

    KING: But how hath she
    Received his love?
    POLONIUS: What do you think of me?
    KING: As of a man faithful and honourable.
    POLONIUS: I would fain prove so. But what might you think,   130
    When I had seen this hot love on the wing,
    (As I perceived it, I must tell you that,
    Before my daughter told me), what might you,
    Or my dear majesty your queen here, think,
    If I had played the desk or table-book,   135
    Or given my heart a winking, mute and dumb,
    Or looked upon this love with idle sight,
    What might you think? No, I went round to work,
    And my young mistress thus I did bespeak:
    'Lord Hamlet is a prince out of thy star.   140
    This must not be'. and then I prescripts gave her,
    That she should lock herself from his resort,
    Admit no messengers, receive no tokens.
    Which done, she took the fruits of my advice;
    And he repelled, a short tale to make,   145
    Fell into a sadness, then into a fast,
    Thence to a watch, thence into a weakness,
    Thence to a lightness, and, by this declension,
    Into the madness wherein now he raves,
    And all we mourn for.   150
    KING: Do you think 'tis this?
    QUEEN: It may be, very like.
    POLONIUS: Hath there been such a time—I would fain
            know that—
        That I have positively said ''Tis so,'
        When it proved otherwise?
    KING: Not that I know.
    POLONIUS: (*Pointing to his head and shoulder.*) Take this from   155
            this, if this be otherwise:
        If circumstances lead me, I will find
        Where truth is hid, though it were hid indeed
        Within the centre.
    KING: How may we try it further?
    POLONIUS: You know, sometimes he walks four hours together
        Here in the lobby.   160
    QUEEN: So he does, indeed.
    POLONIUS: At such a time I'll loose my daughter to him.
        Be you and I behind an arras then.
        Mark the encounter. If he love her not,
        And be not from his reason fall'n thereon,
        Let me be no assistant for a state,   165
        But keep a farm and carters.
    KING: We will try it.

    (*Enter* HAMLET [*reading on a book*].)

    QUEEN: But look where sadly the poor wretch comes reading.
    POLONIUS: Away, I do beseech you both away,
        I'll board him presently.

    ([*Exeunt*] king and queen [*with attendants*].)

                    O, give me leave.

---

79 **regards** considerations   90 **wit** understanding   95 **matter**
meaning, sense   105 **Perpend** consider   119 **numbers** verses
123 **machine** body

135 **played . . . table-book** acted as silent go-between   138
round directly   147 **watch** sleeplessness   148 **lightness** light-
headedness   158 **centre** centre of the earth and of the Ptole-
maic universe   169 **board** accost; **presently** immediately

170 How does my good Lord Hamlet?

HAMLET: Well, God-a-mercy.

POLONIUS: Do you know me, my lord?

HAMLET: Excellent well, you are a fishmonger.

POLONIUS: Not I, my lord.

175 HAMLET: Then I would you were so honest a man.

POLONIUS: Honest, my lord?

HAMLET: Ay, sir, to be honest as this world goes, is to be one man picked out of ten thousand.

POLONIUS: That's very true, my lord.

180 HAMLET: For if the sun breed maggots in a dead dog, being a good kissing carrion—Have you a daughter?

POLONIUS: I have, my lord.

HAMLET: Let her not walk i' th' sun. Conception is a blessing, but as your daughter may conceive—friend, look to 't.

185 POLONIUS: (Aside.) How say you by that? Still harping on my daughter. Yet he knew me not at first. 'A said I was a fishmonger. 'A is far gone. And truly in my youth I suffered much extremity for love, very near this. I'll speak to him again.—What do you read, my lord?

190 HAMLET: Words, words, words.

POLONIUS: What is the matter, my lord?

HAMLET: Between who?

POLONIUS: I mean the matter that you read, my lord.

HAMLET: Slanders, sir; for the satirical rogue says here that old
195 men have grey beards, that their faces are wrinkled, their eyes purging thick amber and plum-tree gum, and that they have a plentiful lack of wit, together with most weak hams—all which, sir, though I most powerfully and potently believe, yet I hold it not honesty to have it thus set
200 down, for yourself, sir, shall grow old as I am, if like a crab you could go backward.

POLONIUS: (Aside.) Though this be madness, yet there is method in 't.—Will you walk out of the air, my lord?

HAMLET: Into my grave?

205 POLONIUS: (Aside.) Indeed, that's out of the air. How pregnant sometimes his replies are! a happiness that often madness hits on, which reason and sanity could not so prosperously be delivered of. I will leave him, and suddenly contrive the means of meeting between him and
210 my daughter.—My lord, I will take my leave of you.

HAMLET: You cannot take from me anything that I will not more willingly part withal—except my life, except my life, except my life.

(Enter GUILDENSTERN and ROSENCRANTZ.)

POLONIUS: Fare you well, my lord.

215 HAMLET: These tedious old fools!

POLONIUS: You go to seek the Lord Hamlet. There he is.

ROSENCRANTZ: (To POLONIUS.) God save you, sir!

(Exit POLONIUS.)

GUILDENSTERN: My honored lord!

ROSENCRANTZ: My most dear lord!

220 HAMLET: My excellent good friends! How dost thou, Guildenstern?

Ah, Rosencrantz! Good lads, how do ye both?

ROSENCRANTZ: As the indifferent children of the earth.

GUILDENSTERN: Happy in that we are not over-happy;
On Fortune's cap we are not the very button.   225

HAMLET: Nor the soles of her shoe?

ROSENCRANTZ: Neither, my lord.

HAMLET: Then you live about her waist, or in the middle of her favors?

GUILDENSTERN: Faith, her privates we.   230

HAMLET: In the secret parts of Fortune? O, most true, she is a strumpet. What news?

ROSENCRANTZ: None, my lord, but that the world's grown honest.

HAMLET: Then is doomsday near. But your news is not true.   235
Let me question more in particular. What have you, my good friends, deserved at the hands of Fortune, that she sends you to prison hither?

GUILDENSTERN: Prison, my lord!

HAMLET: Denmark's a prison.   240

ROSENCRANTZ: Then is the world one.

HAMLET: A goodly one, in which there are many confines, wards, and dungeons, Denmark being one o' th' worst.

ROSENCRANTZ: We think not so, my lord.

HAMLET: Why then 'tis none to you; for there is nothing either   245
good or bad, but thinking makes it so. To me it is a prison.

ROSENCRANTZ: Why then your ambition makes it one. 'Tis too narrow for your mind.

HAMLET: O God, I could be bounded in a nutshell and count myself a king of infinite space, were it not that I have bad   250
dreams.

GUILDENSTERN: Which dreams indeed are ambition; for the very substance of the ambitious is merely the shadow of a dream.

HAMLET: A dream itself is but a shadow.   255

ROSENCRANTZ: Truly, and I hold ambition of so airy and light a quality that it is but a shadow's shadow.

HAMLET: Then are our beggars bodies, and, our monarchs and outstretched heroes the beggars' shadows. Shall we to th' court? for, by my fay, I cannot reason.   260

BOTH: We'll wait upon you.

HAMLET: No such matter. I will not sort you with the rest of my servants; for, to speak to you like an honest man, I am most dreadfully attended. But in the beaten way of friendship, what make you at Elsinore?   265

ROSENCRANTZ: To visit you, my lord; no other occasion.

HAMLET: Beggar that I am, I am ever poor in thanks, but I thank you; and sure, dear friends, my thanks are too dear a halfpenny. Were you not sent for? Is it your own inclining? Is it a free visitation? Come, come, deal justly with   270
me. Come, come, nay speak.

GUILDENSTERN: What should we say, my lord?

HAMLET: Anything but to the purpose. You were sent for, and there is a kind of confession in your looks, which your modesties have not craft enough to color. I know the   275
good king and queen have sent for you.

ROSENCRANTZ: To what end, my lord?

HAMLET: That you must teach me. But let me conjure you by the rights of our fellowship, by the consonancy of our

---

205 **pregnant** full of meaning   206 **happiness** aptness

---

223 **indifferent** average   225 **button** knob on the top of the cap   260 **fay** faith   262 **sort you with** put you in the same class with

280   youth, by the obligation of our ever-preserved love, and by
        what more dear a better proposer can charge you withal be
        even and direct with me whether you were sent for or no.

ROSENCRANTZ: (*Aside to* GUILDENSTERN.) What say you?

HAMLET: (*Aside.*) Nay, then, I have an eye of you.—If you
285   love me, hold not off.

GUILDENSTERN: My lord, we were sent for.

HAMLET: I will tell you why; so shall my anticipation prevent
       your discovery, and your secrecy to the king and queen
       moult no feather. I have of late—but wherefore I know
290   not—lost all my mirth, forgone all custom of exercises; and
       indeed it goes so heavily with my disposition, that this
       goodly frame the earth seems to me a sterile promontory,
       this most excellent canopy the air, look you, this brave
       o'er-hanging firmament, this majestical roof fretted with
295   golden fire, why it appeareth nothing to me but a foul and
       pestilent congregation of vapors. What a piece of work is a
       man, how noble in reason, how infinite in faculties, in form
       and moving, how express and admirable in action, how like
       an angel in apprehension, how like a god: the beauty of the
300   world, the paragon of animals. And yet to me, what is this
       quintessence of dust? Man delights not me, nor woman
       neither, though by your smiling you seem to say so.

ROSENCRANTZ: My lord, there was no such stuff in my
       thoughts.

305 HAMLET: Why did ye laugh, then, when I said 'Man delights
       not me'?

ROSENCRANTZ: To think, my lord, if you delight not in man,
       what lenten entertainment the players shall receive from
       you. We coted them on the way, and hither are they com-
310   ing to offer you service.

HAMLET: He that plays the king shall be welcome—his
       majesty shall have tribute on me; the adventurous knight
       shall use his foil and target; the lover shall not sigh gratis;
       the humorous man shall end his part in peace; the clown
315   shall make those laugh whose lungs are tickle o' th' sere;
       and the lady shall say her mind freely, or the blank verse
       shall halt for 't. What players are they?

ROSENCRANTZ: Even those you were wont to take such de-
       light in, the tragedians of the city.

320 HAMLET: How chances it they travel? Their residence, both in
       reputation and profit, was better both ways.

ROSENCRANTZ: I think their inhibition comes by the means
       of the late innovation.

HAMLET: Do they hold the same estimation they did when I
       was in the city? Are they so followed?   325

ROSENCRANTZ: No, indeed, are they not.

HAMLET: How comes it? Do they grow rusty?

ROSENCRANTZ: Nay, their endeavour keeps in the wonted pace;
       but there is, sir, an eyrie of children, little eyases, that cry out
       on the top of question, and are most tyrannically clapped 330
       for't. These are now the fashion, and so berattle the common
       stages (so they call them) that many wearing rapiers are afraid
       of goose quills and dare scarce come thither.

HAMLET: What, are they children? Who maintains 'em? How
       are they escoted? Will they pursue the quality no longer 335
       than they can sing? Will they not say afterwards, if they
       should grow themselves to common players (as it is most
       like, if their means are no better), their writers do them
       wrong to make them exclaim against their own succession?

ROSENCRANTZ: 'Faith, there has been much to do on both 340
       sides; and the nation holds it no sin to tarre them to con-
       troversy. There was for a while no money bid for argument,
       unless the poet and the player went to cuffs in the question.

HAMLET: Is't possible?

GUILDENSTERN: O, there has been much throwing about of 345
       brains.

HAMLET: Do the boys carry it away?

ROSENCRANTZ: Ay, that they do, my lord, Hercules and his
       load too.

HAMLET: It is not very strange, for my uncle is King of Den- 350
       mark, and those that would make mouths at him while
       my father lived give twenty, forty, fifty, a hundred ducats
       apiece for his picture in little. 'Sblood, there is something
       in this more than natural, if philosophy could find it out.

(*A flourish.*)

GUILDENSTERN: There are the players.   355

HAMLET: Gentlemen, you are welcome to Elsinore. Your
       hands. Come then th' appurtenance of welcome is fashion
       and ceremony. Let me comply with you in this garb, lest
       my ex-tent to the players, which I tell you must show
       fairly outwards, should more appear like entertainment 360
       than yours. You are welcome. But my uncle-father and
       aunt-mother are deceived.

GUILDENSTERN: In what, my dear lord?

HAMLET: I am but mad north-north-west; when the wind is
       southerly I know a hawk from a handsaw.   365

---

287 **prevent** forestall   288 **discovery** disclosure   294 **fretted**
decorated with fretwork   308 **lenten** scanty   309 **coted** passed
313 **foil and target** spear and shield   313–314 **humorous
man** the actor who plays the eccentric character dominated by
one of the four humors   315 **tickle o' th' sere** easily set off
(**sere** is that part of a gunlock which keeps the hammer at full or
half cock)   316 **halt** limp   322 **inhibition** prohibition of plays
by authority (possibly with reference to decree of the Privy
Council of 22 June 1600, limiting the number of London theater
companies to two, and stipulating that the two were to perform
only twice a week)   323 **innovation** meaning uncertain (sometimes taken to refer to the reintroduction, ca. 1600, on the London theatrical scene of companies of boy actors performing in
private theaters; sometimes interpreted as "political upheaval,"
with special reference to Essex's rebellion, February, 1601)

329 **eyrie** nest; **eyases** nestling hawks (here, the boys in the children's companies training as actors)   330 **on the top of question** louder than all others on matter of dispute   331–332
common stages public theaters of the **common players** (below, line 337), organized in companies composed mainly of adult
actors   333 **goose quills** pens (of the satiric dramatists writing
for the private theaters)   335 **escoted** maintained; **pursue the
quality** continue in the profession of acting   336 **sing** i.e., until their voices change   341 **tarre** incite   342 **argument** plot
of a play   349 **load** i.e., the world (the sign of the Globe theater represented Hercules bearing the world on his shoulders)
351 **mouths** grimaces   353 **in little** in miniature   357 **ap-
purtenance** adjuncts   358–359 **extent** welcome   365 **hawk**
mattock or pickaxe (also called "hack," here used with a play on
hawk as a bird); **handsaw** a saw managed with one hand (here
used with a play on some corrupt form of *hernshaw,* "heron")

(*Enter* POLONIUS.)

POLONIUS: Well be with you, gentlemen.

HAMLET: Hark you, Guildenstern—and you too—at each ear a hearer. That great baby you see there is not yet out of his swaddling clouts.

370 ROSENCRANTZ: Happily he is the second time come to them, for they say an old man is twice a child.

HAMLET: I will prophesy he comes to tell me of the players. Mark it.—You say right, sir, a Monday morning, 'twas then indeed.

375 POLONIUS: My lord, I have news to tell you.

HAMLET: My lord, I have news to tell you. When Roscius was an actor in Rome—

POLONIUS: The actors are come hither, my lord.

HAMLET: Buzz, buzz.

380 POLONIUS: Upon my honor—

HAMLET: Then came each actor on his ass—

POLONIUS: The best actors in the world, either for tragedy, comedy, history, pastoral, pastoral-comical, historical-pastoral, tragical-historical, tragical-comical-historical-

385 pastoral, scene individable, or poem unlimited. Seneca cannot be too heavy nor Plautus too light. For the law of writ and the liberty, these are the only men.

HAMLET: O Jephthah, judge of Israel, what a treasure hadst thou!

390 POLONIUS: What a treasure had he, my lord?

HAMLET: Why—

> 'One fair daughter, and no more,
> The which he loved passing well.'

POLONIUS: (*Aside.*) Still on my daughter.

395 HAMLET: Am I not i' th' right, old Jephthah?

POLONIUS: If you call me Jephthah, my lord, I have a daughter that I love passing well.

HAMLET: Nay, that follows not.

POLONIUS: What follows then, my lord?

400 HAMLET: Why—

> 'As by lot, God wot,'

and then, you know,

> 'It came to pass, as most like it was.'

The first row of the pious chanson will show you more,

405 for look where my abridgement comes.

(*Enter the* PLAYERS.)

You are welcome, masters; welcome, all.—I am glad to see thee well.—Welcome, good friends. O, old friend! Why thy face is valanced since I saw thee last. Come'st thou to beard me in Denmark?—What, my young lady and mistress? By'r lady, your ladyship is nearer to heaven than 410 when I saw you last by the altitude of a chopine. Pray God, your voice, like a piece of uncurrent gold, be not cracked within the ring.—Masters, you are all welcome. We'll e'en to't like French falconers, fly at any thing we see. We'll have a speech straight. Come give us a taste of 415 your quality, come a passionate speech.

1 PLAYER: What speech, my good lord?

HAMLET: I heard thee speak me a speech once, but it was never acted, or if it was, not above once, for the play, I remember, pleased not the million; 'twas caviary to the general. But it 420 was—as I received it, and others whose judgements in such matters cried in the top of mine—an excellent play, well digested in the scenes, set down with as much modesty as cunning. I remember one said there were no sallets in the lines to make the matter savory, nor no matter in the phrase 425 that might indict the author of affectation, but called it an honest method, as wholesome as sweet, and by very much more handsome than fine. One speech in't I chiefly loved. 'Twas Æneas' tale to Dido and thereabout of it especially when he speaks of Priam's slaughter. If it live in your mem- 430 ory, begin at this line—let me see, let me see:

> 'The rugged Pyrrhus, like th' Hyrcanian beast'—

'tis not so;—it begins with Pyrrhus—

> 'The rugged Pyrrhus, he whose sable arms,
> Black as his purpose, did the night resemble 435
> When he lay couchèd in the ominous horse,
> Hath now this dread and black complexion smeared
> With heraldry more dismal; head to foot
> Now is he total gules, horridly tricked
> With blood of fathers, mothers, daughters, sons, 440
> Baked and impasted with the parching streets,
> That lend a tyrannous and a damnèd light
> To their lord's murder. Roasted in wrath and fire,
> And thus o'er-sizèd with coagulate gore,
> With eyes like carbuncles, the hellish Pyrrhus 445
> Old grandsire Priam seeks.'

So, proceed you.

POLONIUS: Fore God, my lord, well spoken, with good accent and good discretion.

1 PLAYER: 'Anon he finds him 450
> Striking too short at Greeks. His antique sword,
> Rebellious to his arm, lies where it falls,

---

370 **Happily** perhaps   376 **Roscius** the greatest of Roman comic actors, though regarded by the Elizabethans as a tragic one   384–385 **scene individable** i.e., a play that observes the unities of time and place   385 **poem unlimited** a play that does not observe the unities; **Seneca** Roman writer of tragedies   386 **Plautus** Roman comic dramatist; **law of writ and the liberty** i.e., plays according to strict classical rules, and those that ignored the unities of time and place   388 **Jephthah** was compelled to sacrifice a beloved daughter (Judges 2). Hamlet quotes from a contemporary ballad titled *Jephthah, Judge of Israel* at lines 392–393, 401, and 403   404 **row** stanza

408 **valanced** bearded   409 **young lady** i.e., the boy who plays female roles   411 **chopine** a shoe with high cork heel and sole   412–413 **cracked within the ring** a coin cracked within the circle surrounding the head of the sovereign was no longer legal tender and so *uncurrent*   415 **straight** immediately   420 **caviary** caviare; **general** multitude   422–423 **digested** arranged   424 **sallets** salads, highly seasoned passages   428 **more handsome than fine** admirable rather than appealing by mere cleverness   432 **Hyrcanian beast** tiger   436 **horse** i.e., the Trojan horse   439 **gules** heraldic term for red; tricked delineated   444 **o'er-sizèd** covered as with size; **coagulate** clotted

Repugnant to command. Unequal matched,
Pyrrhus at Priam drives, in rage strikes wide.
455   But with the whiff and wind of his fell sword
Th' unnervèd father falls. Then senseless Ilium,
Seeming to feel this blow, with flaming top
Stoops to his base, and with a hideous crash
Takes prisoner Pyrrhus' ear. For, lo! his sword,
460   Which was declining on the milky head
Of reverend Priam, seemed i' th' air to stick.
So as a painted tyrant Pyrrhus stood,
And like a neutral to his will and matter,
Did nothing.
465   But as we often see, against some storm,
A silence in the heavens, the rack stand still,
The bold winds speechless, and the orb below
As hush as death, anon the dreadful thunder
Doth rend the region; so, after Pyrrhus' pause,
470   A rousèd vengeance sets him new awork,
And never did the Cyclops' hammers fall
On Mars's armor, forged for proof eterne
With less remorse than Pyrrhus' bleeding sword
Now falls on Priam.
475   Out, out, thou strumpet, Fortune! All you gods,
In general synod take away her power,
Break all the spokes and fellies from her wheel,
And bowl the round nave down the hill of heaven
As low as to the fiends.'
480   POLONIUS: This is too long.
HAMLET: It shall to the barber's with your beard.—Prithee,
say on. He's for a jig, or a tale of bawdry, or he sleeps. Say
on, come to Hecuba.
1 PLAYER: 'But who, ah woe! had seen the mobled queen—'
485   HAMLET: 'The mobled queen'?
POLONIUS: That's good.
1 PLAYER: 'Run barefoot up and down, threat'ning the flames
With bisson rheum; a clout upon that head
Where late the diadem stood, and for a robe,
490   About her lank and all o'er-teemèd loins,
A blanket, in the alarm of fear caught up—
Who this had seen, with tongue in venom steeped,
'Gainst Fortune's state would treason have pronounced.
But if the gods themselves did see her then,
495   When she saw Pyrrhus make malicious sport
In mincing with his sword her husband's limbs,
The instant burst of clamor that she made,
Unless things mortal move them not at all,
Would have made milch the burning eyes of heaven,
500   And passion in the gods.'
POLONIUS: Look whe'r he has not turned his color, and has
tears in's eyes. Prithee no more.

---

453 **Repugnant** refractory   455 **fell** fierce, cruel   465 **against**
just before   466 **rack** mass of cloud   469 **region** air   471
Cyclops giant workmen who made armor in the smithy of Vulcan   472 **proof eterne** to be forever impenetrable   477 **fellies**
the curved pieces forming the rim of a wheel   478 **nave** hub of
a wheel   484 **mobled** muffled   488 **bisson rheum** blinding
tears   490 **o'er-teemed** exhausted by many births   493 **state**
government   499 **milch** moist, tearful (lit., milk, giving)

HAMLET: 'Tis well. I'll have thee speak out the rest of this
soon.—Good my lord, will you see the players well bestowed? Do you hear, let them be well used, for they are   505
the abstract and brief chronicles of the time; after your
death you were better have a bad epitaph than their ill report while you live.
POLONIUS: My lord, I will use them according to their desert.
HAMLET: God's bodkin, man, much better. Use every man af-   510
ter his desert, and who shall 'scape whipping? Use them
after your own honor and dignity. The less they deserve,
the more merit is in your bounty. Take them in.
POLONIUS: Come, sirs.
HAMLET: Follow him, friends. We'll hear a play tomorrow.   515
(*Aside to* 1 PLAYER.) Dost thou hear me, old friend, can
you play the 'Murder of Gonzago'?
1 PLAYER: Ay, my lord.
HAMLET: We'll ha't tomorrow night. You could for a need
study a speech of some dozen or sixteen lines which I   520
would set down and insert in't, could you not?
1 PLAYER: Ay, my lord.
HAMLET: Very well. Follow that lord, and look you mock him
not.

(*Exeunt* POLONIUS *and* PLAYERS.)

My good friends, I'll leave you till night. You are welcome   525
to Elsinore.
ROSENCRANTZ: Good my lord!

(*Exeunt* [ROSENCRANTZ *and* GUILDENSTERN].)

HAMLET: Ay, so God by to you. Now I am alone.
O, what a rogue and peasant slave am I!
Is it not monstrous that this player here,   530
But in a fiction, in a dream of passion,
Could force his soul so to his own conceit
That from her working all his visage wanned;
Tears in his eyes, distraction in his aspect,
A broken voice, and his whole function suiting   535
With forms to his conceit? And all for nothing,
For Hecuba!
What's Hecuba to him or he to Hecuba,
That he should weep for her? What would he do
Had he the motive and the cue for passion   540
That I have? He would drown the stage with tears,
And cleave the general ear with horrid speech,
Make mad the guilty, and appal the free,
Confound the ignorant, and amaze indeed
The very faculties of eyes and ears.   545
Yet I,
A dull and muddy-mettled rascal, peak
Like John-a-dreams, unpregnant of my cause,
And can say nothing; no, not for a king
Upon whose property and most dear life   550
A damned defeat was made. Am I a coward?
Who calls me villain, breaks my pate across,

---

506 **abstract** summary account   510 **God's bodkin** by God's
dear body   532 **conceit** imagination   542 **general** public
547 **muddy-mettled** dull-spirited; **peak** mope   548 **unpregnant** not quickened to action

Plucks off my beard and blows it in my face,
Tweaks me by the nose, gives me the lie i' th' throat
555 As deep as to the lungs? Who does me this?
Ha, 'swounds, I should take it; for it cannot be
But I am pigeon-livered and lack gall
To make oppression bitter, or ere this
I should 'a fatted all the region kites
560 With this slave's offal. Bloody, bawdy villain!
Remorseless, treacherous, lecherous, kindless villain!
Why, what an ass am I! This is most brave,
That I, the son of a dear father murdered,
Prompted to my revenge by heaven and hell,
565 Must like a whore unpack my heart with words,
And fall a-cursing like a very drab,
A scullion! Fie upon 't! foh!
About, my brains! Hum—I have heard
That guilty creatures sitting at a play,
570 Have by the very cunning of the scene
Been struck so to the soul that presently
They have proclaimed their malefactions:
For murder, though it have no tongue, will speak
With most miraculous organ. I'll have these players
575 Play something like the murder of my father
Before mine uncle. I'll observe his looks.
I'll tent him to the quick. If 'a do blench,
I know my course. The spirit that I have seen
May be the devil, and the devil hath power
580 T' assume a pleasing shape, yea, and perhaps
Out of my weakness and my melancholy,
As he is very potent with such spirits,
Abuses me to damn me. I'll have grounds
More relative than this. The play's the thing
585 Wherein I'll catch the conscience of the king.

(*Exit.*)

ACT THREE

SCENE I

Enter KING, QUEEN, POLONIUS, OPHELIA, ROSENCRANTZ, GUILDENSTERN, LORDS.

KING: And can you by no drift of conference
Get from him why he puts on this confusion,
Grating so harshly all his days of quiet
With turbulent and dangerous lunacy?
5 ROSENCRANTZ: He does confess he feels himself distracted,
But from what cause 'a will by no means speak.

---

559 **region kites** kites of the air   561 **kindless** unnatural. Following this line, *F* adds the words "Oh Vengeance!" Their inappropriateness to the occasion is noted by Professor Harold Jenkins (in his "Playhouse Interpolations in the Folio Text of Hamlet," *Studies in Bibliography* 13 [1960]: 37). Professor Jenkins remarks that the folio text, by introducing Hamlet's "call for vengeance while he is still absorbed in self-reproaches, both anticipates and misconstrues" the crisis of his passion and of the speech, which comes in fact at line 568 ("**About, my brains**"), when "he abandons his self-reproaches and plans action"   567 **scullion** kitchen wench   571 **presently** immediately   577 **tent** probe; **blench** flinch   583 **Abuses** deludes   584 **relative** relevant

GUILDENSTERN: Nor do we find him forward to be sounded,
But with a crafty madness keeps aloof
When we would bring him on to some confession
Of his true state.   10
QUEEN: Did he receive you well?
ROSENCRANTZ: Most like a gentleman.
GUILDENSTERN: But with much forcing of his disposition.
ROSENCRANTZ: Niggard of question, but of our demands
Most free in his reply.
QUEEN: Did you assay him
To any pastime?   15
ROSENCRANTZ: Madam, it so fell out that certain players
We o'er-raught on the way. Of these we told him,
And there did seem in him a kind of joy
To hear of it. They are here about the court,
And as I think, they have already order   20
This night to play before him.
POLONIUS: 'Tis most true,
And he beseeched me to entreat your majesties
To hear and see the matter.
KING: With all my heart, and it doth much content me
To hear him so inclined.   25
Good gentlemen, give him a further edge,
And drive his purpose into these delights.
ROSENCRANTZ: We shall, my lord.

(*Exeunt* ROSENCRANTZ *and* GUILDENSTERN.)

KING: Sweet Gertrude, leave us too;
For we have closely sent for Hamlet hither,
That he, as 'twere by accident, may here   30
Affront Ophelia.
Her father and myself (lawful espials)
We'll so bestow ourselves that, seeing unseen,
We may of their encounter frankly judge,
And gather by him, as he is behaved,   35
If't be th' affliction of his love or no
That thus he suffers for.
QUEEN: I shall obey you.—
And for your part, Ophelia, I do wish
That your good beauties be the happy cause
Of Hamlet's wildness. So shall I hope your virtues   40
Will bring him to his wonted way again,
To both your honors.
OPHELIA: Madam, I wish it may.

(*Exit* QUEEN *with* LORDS.)

POLONIUS: Ophelia, walk you here.—Gracious, so please you,
We will bestow ourselves.—(*To* OPHELIA.) Read on this book,
That show of such an exercise may color   45
Your loneliness.—We are oft to blame in this,
'Tis too much proved, that with devotion's visage
And pious action we do sugar o'er
The devil himself.

III.i. 7 **forward** willing   14 **assay** try to win   17 **o'er-raught** overtook   26 **give him a further edge** sharpen his inclination   29 **closely** privately   31 **Affront** meet face to face   32 **espials** spies   45 **exercise** act of devotion; **color** give an appearance of naturalness to

KING: (*Aside.*)   O, 'tis too true.
50   How smart a lash that speech doth give my conscience!
       The harlot's cheek, beautied with plast'ring art,
       Is not more ugly to the thing that helps it
       Then is my deed to my most painted word.
       O heavy burden!
55   POLONIUS: I hear him coming. Let's withdraw, my lord.

(*Exeunt* KING *and* POLONIUS.)

(*Enter* HAMLET.)

HAMLET: To be, or not to be, that is the question:
       Whether 'tis nobler in the mind to suffer
       The slings and arrows of outrageous fortune,
       Or to take arms against a sea of troubles,
60   And by opposing end them. To die, to sleep—
       No more; and by a sleep to say we end
       The heartache, and the thousand natural shocks
       That flesh is heir to: 'tis a consummation
       Devoutly to be wished. To die, to sleep—
65   To sleep, perchance to dream, ay there's the rub;
       For in that sleep of death what dreams may come
       When we have shuffled off this mortal coil
       Must give us pause. There's the respect
       That makes calamity of so long life:
70   For who would bear the whips and scorns of time,
       Th' oppressor's wrong, the proud man's contumely,
       The pangs of despised love, the law's delay,
       The insolence of office, and the spurns
       That patient merit of th' unworthy takes,
75   When he himself might his quietus make
       With a bare bodkin? Who would fardels bear,
       To grunt and sweat under a weary life,
       But that the dread of something after death,
       The undiscovered country, from whose bourn
80   No traveller returns, puzzles the will,
       And makes us rather bear those ills we have
       Than fly to others that we know not of?
       Thus conscience does make cowards of us all,
       And thus the native hue of resolution
85   Is sicklied o'er with the pale cast of thought,
       And enterprises of great pitch and moment
       With this regard their currents turn awry
       And lose the name of action. Soft you now,
       The fair Ophelia.—Nymph, in thy orisons
90   Be all my sins remembered.
       OPHELIA: Good my lord,
       How does your honor for this many a day?
       HAMLET: I humbly thank you, well.
       OPHELIA: My lord, I have remembrances of yours
       That I have longed long to re-deliver.
95   I pray you now receive them.
       HAMLET: No, not I,
       I never gave you aught.

OPHELIA: My honored lord, you know right well you did,
       And with them words of so sweet breath composed
       As made the things more rich. Their perfume lost,
       Take these again, for to the noble mind   100
       Rich gifts wax poor when givers prove unkind.
       There, my lord.
HAMLET: Ha, ha! are you honest?
OPHELIA: My lord?
HAMLET: Are you fair?   105
OPHELIA: What means your lordship?
HAMLET: That if you be honest and fair, your honesty should
       admit no discourse to your beauty.
OPHELIA: Could beauty, my lord, have better commerce than
       with honesty?   110
HAMLET: Ay, truly, for the power of beauty will sooner trans-
       form honesty from what it is to a bawd than the force of
       honesty can translate beauty into his likeness. This was
       sometime a paradox, but now the time gives it proof. I did
       love you once.   115
OPHELIA: Indeed, my lord, you made me believe so.
HAMLET: You should not have believed me, for virtue cannot
       so inoculate our old stock but we shall relish of it. I loved
       you not.
OPHELIA: I was the more deceived.   120
HAMLET: Get thee to a nunnery. Why wouldst thou be a
       breeder of sinners? I am myself indifferent honest, but yet I
       could accuse me of such things that it were better my
       mother had not borne me: I am very proud, revengeful, am-
       bitious, with more offences at my beck than I have thoughts 125
       to put them in, imagination to give them shape, or time to
       act them in. What should such fellows as I do crawling be-
       tween earth and heaven? We are arrant knaves all; believe
       none of us. Go thy ways to a nunnery. Where's your father?
OPHELIA: At home, my lord.   130
HAMLET: Let the doors be shut upon him, that he may play
       the fool nowhere but in's own house. Farewell.
OPHELIA: O, help him, you sweet heavens!
HAMLET: If thou dost marry, I'll give thee this plague for thy
       dowry: be thou as chaste as ice, as pure as snow, thou shalt 135
       not escape calumny. Get thee to a nunnery, farewell. Or if
       thou wilt needs marry, marry a fool, for wise men know
       well enough what monsters you make of them. To a nun-
       nery, go, and quickly too. Farewell.
OPHELIA: Heavenly powers, restore him!   140
HAMLET: I have heard of your paintings well enough. God
       hath given you one face, and you make yourselves another.
       You jig and amble, and you lisp; you nickname God's crea-
       tures, and make your wantonness your ignorance. Go to, I'll
       no more on't, it hath made me mad. I say we will have no   145
       moe marriage. Those that are married already, all but one,
       shall live. The rest shall keep as they are. To a nunnery, go.

(*Exit.*)

OPHELIA: O, what a noble mind is here o'erthrown!
       The courtier's, soldier's, scholar's, eye, tongue, sword,

---

52 **to** compared to 65 **rub** obstacle (lit., obstruction encountered by bowler's ball) 67 **coil** bustle, turmoil 75 **quietus** settlement 76 **bodkin** dagger; **fardels** burdens 79 **bourn** realm
86 **pitch** height 87 **regard** consideration 89 **orisons** prayers

---

103 **honest** chaste 118 **inoculate** graft 122 **indifferent**
honest moderately respectable 144 **make your wantonness
your ignorance** excuse your wanton behavior with the plea
that you don't know any better 145 **moe** more

150   Th' expectancy and rose of the fair state,
        The glass of fashion and the mould of form,
        Th' observed of all observers, quite quite down!
        And I of ladies most deject and wretched,
        That sucked the honey of his musiced vows,
155   Now see that noble and most sovereign reason
        Like sweet bells jangled, out of time and harsh;
        That unmatched form and feature of blown youth
        Blasted with ecstasy. O, woe is me
        T' have seen what I have seen, see what I see!

(*Enter* KING *and* POLONIUS.)

160 KING: Love? His affections do not that way tend,
        Nor what he spake, though it lacked form a little,
        Was not like madness. There's something in his soul,
        O'er which his melancholy sits on brood,
        And I do doubt the hatch and the disclose
165   Will be some danger; which for to prevent,
        I have in quick determination
        Thus set it down: he shall with speed to England
        For the demand of our neglected tribute.
        Haply the seas and countries different,
170   With variable objects, shall expel
        This something-settled matter in his heart
        Whereon his brains still beating puts him thus
        From fashion of himself. What think you on't?
    POLONIUS: It shall do well. But yet do I believe
175   The origin and commencement of his grief
        Sprung from neglected love.—How now, Ophelia?
        You need not tell us what Lord Hamlet said;
        We heard it all.—My lord, do as you please,
        But if you hold it fit, after the play
180   Let his queen-mother all alone entreat him
        To show his grief. Let her be round with him,
        And I'll be placed, so please you, in the ear
        Of all their conference. If she find him not,
        To England send him; or confine him where
185   Your wisdom best shall think.
    KING: It shall be so.
        Madness in great ones must not unwatched go.

(*Exeunt.*)

SCENE II

Enter HAMLET *and three of the* PLAYERS.

HAMLET: Speak the speech, I pray you, as I pronounced it to
    you, trippingly on the tongue; but if you mouth it as many
    of our players do, I had as lief the town-crier spoke my
    lines. Nor do not saw the air too much with your hand
5   thus, but use all gently; for in the very torrent, tempest, and
    as I may say, whirlwind of your passion, you must acquire
    and beget a temperance that may give it smoothness. O, it
    offends me to the soul to hear a robustious periwig-pated
    fellow tear a passion to tatters, to very rags, to split the ears

of the groundlings, who for the most part are capable of 10
nothing but inexplicable dumb shows and noise. I would
have such a fellow whipped for o'erdoing Termagant. It
out-Herods Herod. Pray you avoid it.
1 PLAYER: I warrant your honour.
HAMLET: Be not too tame neither, but let your own discre- 15
    tion be your tutor. Suit the action to the word, the word
    to the action, with this special observance, that you o'er-
    step not the modesty of nature; for any thing so o'erdone
    is from the purpose of playing, whose end both at the first,
    and now, was and is, to hold as 'twere the mirror up to na- 20
    ture, to show virtue her own feature, scorn her own im-
    age, and the very age and body of the time his form and
    pressure. Now this overdone, or come tardy off, though it
    make the unskilful laugh, cannot but make the judicious
    grieve, the censure of the which one must in your al- 25
    lowance o'erweigh a whole theatre of others. O, there be
    players that I have seen play—and heard others praise, and
    that highly—not to speak it profanely, that neither having
    th' accent of Christians, nor the gait of Christian, pagan,
    nor man, have so strutted and bellowed that I have thought 30
    some of nature's journeymen had made men, and not
    made them well, they imitated humanity so abominably.
1 PLAYER: I hope we have reformed that indifferently with us.
HAMLET: O, reform it altogether. And let those that play your
    clowns speak no more than is set down for them, for there 35
    be of them that will themselves laugh, to set on some
    quantity of barren spectators to laugh too, though in the
    meantime some necessary question of the play be then to
    be considered. That's villanous, and shows a most pitiful
    ambition in the fool that uses it. Go, make you ready. 40

(*Exeunt* PLAYERS.)

(*Enter* POLONIUS, GUILDENSTERN, *and* ROSENCRANTZ.)

    How now, my lord? Will the king hear this piece of work?
POLONIUS: And the queen too, and that presently.
HAMLET: Bid the players make haste. (*Exit* POLONIUS.)
    Will you two help to hasten them?
ROSENCRANTZ: Ay, my lord. 45

(*Exeunt they two.*)

HAMLET: What, ho! Horatio!

(*Enter* HORATIO.)

HORATIO: Here, sweet lord, at your service.
HAMLET: Horatio, thou art e'en as just a man
    As e'er my conversation coped withal.
HORATIO: O my dear lord! 50
HAMLET: Nay, do not think I flatter,
    For what advancement may I hope from thee,
    That no revenue hast but thy good spirits

---

150 **expectancy** hope   151 **glass** mirror   157 **blown** blooming   158 **ecstasy** madness   160 **affections** emotions   164
doubt fear   181 **round** plain-spoken

III.ii. 10 **groundlings** spectators who paid least and stood on
the ground   12 **Termagant** thought to be a Mohammedan deity, and represented in medieval mystery plays as a violent and
ranting personage; **Herod** represented in the mystery plays as a
blustering tyrant   25 **censure** judgment, opinion   33 **indifferently** fairly well   49 **coped** encountered

To feed and clothe thee? Why should the poor be flattered?
No, let the candied tongue lick absurd pomp,
55 And crook the pregnant hinges of the knee
Where thrift may follow fawning. Dost thou hear?
Since my dear soul was mistress of her choice
And could of men distinguish her election,
S'hath sealed thee for herself, for thou hast been
60 As one in suff'ring all that suffers nothing,
A man that Fortune's buffets and rewards
Hast ta'en with equal thanks; and blest are those
Whose blood and judgment are so well comeddled
That they are not a pipe for Fortune's finger
65 To sound what stop she please. Give me that man
That is not passion's slave, and I will wear him
In my heart's core, ay, in my heart of heart,
As I do thee. Something too much of this.
There is a play to-night before the king.
70 One scene of it comes near the circumstance
Which I have told thee of my father's death.
I prithee, when thou seest that act afoot,
Even with the very comment of thy soul
Observe my uncle. If his occulted guilt
75 Do not itself unkennel in one speech,
It is a damnèd ghost that we have seen,
And my imaginations are as foul
As Vulcan's stithy. Give him heedful note,
For I mine eyes will rivet to his face,
80 And after we will both our judgements join
In censure of his seeming.
HORATIO: Well, my lord.
If 'a steal aught the whilst this play is playing,
And 'scape detecting, I will pay the theft.

(*Enter Trumpets and Kettledrums,* KING, QUEEN, POLONIUS, OPHELIA, [ROSENCRANTZ, GUILDENSTERN, *and other* LORDS *attendant*].)

HAMLET: They are coming to the play. I must be idle.
85   Get you a place.
KING: How fares our cousin Hamlet?
HAMLET: Excellent, i' faith, of the chameleon's dish. I eat the
      air, promise-crammed. You cannot feed capons so.
KING: I have nothing with this answer, Hamlet. These words
90   are not mine.
HAMLET: No, nor mine now. (*To* POLONIUS.) My lord, you
      played once i' th' university, you say?
POLONIUS: That did I, my lord; and was accounted a good
      actor.
95 HAMLET: What did you enact?
POLONIUS: I did enact Julius Caesar. I was killed i' th' Capi-
      tol; Brutus killed me.
HAMLET: It was a brute part of him to kill so capital a calf
      there. Be the players ready?
100 ROSENCRANTZ: Ay, my lord, they stay upon your patience.

QUEEN: Come hither, my dear Hamlet, sit by me.
HAMLET: No, good mother, here's metal more attractive.
POLONIUS: (*To the* KING.) O, ho! do you mark that?
HAMLET: Lady, shall I lie in your lap?

(*Lying down at* OPHELIA's *feet*.)

OPHELIA: No, my lord.   105
HAMLET: I mean, my head upon your lap?
OPHELIA: Ay, my lord.
HAMLET: Do you think I meant country matters?
OPHELIA: I think nothing, my lord.
HAMLET: That's a fair thought to lie between maids' legs.   110
OPHELIA: What is, my lord?
HAMLET: Nothing.
OPHELIA: You are merry, my lord.
HAMLET: Who, I?
OPHELIA: Ay, my lord.   115
HAMLET: O God, your only jig-maker! What should a man
      do but be merry? For look you how cheerfully my
      mother looks, and my father died within's two hours.
OPHELIA: Nay, 'tis twice two months, my lord.
HAMLET: So long? Nay then, let the devil wear black, for I'll 120
      have a suit of sables. O heavens! die two months ago, and
      not forgotten yet? Then there's hope a great man's mem-
      ory may outlive his life half a year, but, by'r lady 'a must
      build churches then, or else shall 'a suffer not thinking on,
      with the hobby-horse, whose epitaph is   125

      'For O, for O, the hobby-horse is forgot!'

(*The trumpets sound. Dumb Show follows.*)

(*Enter a* KING *and a* QUEEN [*very lovingly*]; *the* QUEEN *embracing him and he her.* [*She kneels, and makes show of protestation unto him.*] *He takes her up, and declines his head upon her neck. He lies him down upon a bank of flowers; she, seeing him asleep, leaves him. Anon comes in another man, takes off his crown, kisses it, pours poison in the sleeper's ears, and leaves him. The* QUEEN *returns, finds the* KING *dead, makes passionate action. The* POISONER *with some three or four come in again, seem to condole with her. The dead body is carried away. The* POISONER *woos the* QUEEN *with gifts; she seems harsh awhile, but in the end accepts love.*)

(*Exeunt.*)

OPHELIA: What means this, my lord?
HAMLET: Marry, this is miching mallecho; it means mischief.
OPHELIA: Belike this show imports the argument of the play.

(*Enter* PROLOGUE.)

HAMLET: We shall know by this fellow. The players cannot   130
      keep counsel; they'll tell all.
OPHELIA: Will 'a tell us what this show meant?
HAMLET: Ay, or any show that you will show him. Be not you
      ashamed to show, he'll not shame to tell you what it means.

---

55 **pregnant** ready   56 **thrift** profit   58 **election** choice   63
co-meddled mingled   73 **the very comment of thy soul**
with a keenness of observation that penetrates to the very being
74 **occulted** hidden   75 **unkennel** reveal   78 **stithy** forge
81 **censure** opinion   84 **idle** crazy   87 **chameleon's dish** the
air, on which the chameleon was supposed to feed

---

125 **hobby-horse** the figure of a horse fastened round the waist
of a morris dancer. Puritan efforts to suppress the country sports
in which the hobby-horse figured led to a popular ballad
lamenting the fact that "the hobby-horse is forgot"   128 **miching mallecho** skulking or crafty crime

135 OPHELIA: You are naught, you are naught. I'll mark the play.
PROLOGUE:
> For us, and for our tragedy,
> Here stooping to your clemency,
> We beg your hearing patiently.

(*Exit.*)

HAMLET: Is this a prologue, or the posy of a ring?
140 OPHELIA: 'Tis brief, my lord.
HAMLET: As woman's love.

(*Enter [the* PLAYER] KING *and* QUEEN.)

PLAYER KING: Full thirty times hath Phoebus' cart gone round
> Neptune's salt wash and Tellus' orbèd ground,
> And thirty dozen moons with borrowed sheen
145 About the world have times twelve thirties been,
> Since love our hearts and Hymen did our hands
> Unite comutual in most sacred bands.
PLAYER QUEEN: So many journeys may the sun and moon
> Make us again count o'er ere love be done!
150 But woe is me, you are so sick of late,
> So far from cheer and from your former state,
> That I distrust you. Yet though I distrust,
> Discomfort you, my lord, it nothing must.
> For women's fear and love hold quantity,
155 In neither aught, or in extremity.
> Now what my love is proof hath made you know,
> And as my love is sized, my fear is so.
> Where love is great, the littlest doubts are fear;
> Where little fears grow great, great love grows there.
160 PLAYER KING: Faith, I must leave thee, love, and shortly too;
> My operant powers their functions leave to do.
> And thou shalt live in this fair world behind,
> Honored, beloved; and haply one as kind
> For husband shalt thou—
PLAYER QUEEN: O, confound the rest!
165 Such love must needs be treason in my breast.
> In second husband let me be accurst!
> None wed the second but who killed the first.
HAMLET: That's wormwood.
PLAYER QUEEN: The instances that second marriage move
170 Are base respects of thrift, but none of love.
> A second time I kill my husband dead,
> When second husband kisses me in bed.
PLAYER KING: I do believe you think what now you speak,
> But what we do determine oft we break.
175 Purpose is but the slave to memory,
> Of violent birth, but poor validity;
> Which now, like fruit unripe, sticks on the tree,
> But fall unshaken when they mellow be.
> Most necessary 'tis that we forget
180 To pay ourselves what to ourselves is debt.

What to ourselves in passion we propose,
The passion ending, doth the purpose lose.
The violence of either grief or joy
Their own enactures with themselves destroy.
Where joy most revels, grief doth most lament;   185
Grief joys, joy grieves, on slender accident.
This world is not for aye, nor 'tis not strange
That even our loves should with our fortunes change;
For 'tis a question left us yet to prove,
Whether love lead fortune, or else fortune love.   190
The great man down, you mark his favorite flies;
The poor advanced makes friends of enemies;
And hitherto doth love on fortune tend,
For who not needs shall never lack a friend,
And who in want a hollow friend doth try,   195
Directly seasons him his enemy.
But orderly to end where I begun,
Our wills and fates do so contrary run
That our devices still are overthrown;
Our thoughts are ours, their ends none of our own.   200
So think thou wilt no second husband wed,
But die thy thoughts when thy first lord is dead.
PLAYER QUEEN: Nor earth to me give food, nor heaven light,
> Sport and repose lock from me day and night.
> To desperation turn my trust and hope,   205
> An anchor's cheer in prison be my scope,
> Each opposite that blanks the face of joy
> Meet what I would have well, and it destroy,
> Both here and hence pursue me lasting strife,
> If once a widow, ever I be wife!   210
HAMLET: If she should break it now!
PLAYER KING: 'Tis deeply sworn. Sweet, leave me here awhile.
> My spirits grow dull, and fain I would beguile
> The tedious day with sleep.

(*Sleeps.*)

PLAYER QUEEN: Sleep rock thy brain.
> And never come mischance between us twain!   215

(*Exit.*)

HAMLET: Madam, how like you this play?
QUEEN: The lady doth protest too much, methinks.
HAMLET: O, but she'll keep her word.
KING: Have you heard the argument? Is there no offence in't?
HAMLET: No, no, they do but jest, poison in jest; no offence   220
i' th' world.
KING: What do you call the play?
HAMLET: 'The Mouse-trap.' Marry, how? Tropically. This play
is the image of a murder done in Vienna. Gonzago is the
duke's name; his wife, Baptista. You shall see anon. 'Tis a   225
knavish piece of work, but what of that? Your majesty, and
we that have free souls, it touches us not. Let the galled
jade winch, our withers are unwrung.

(*Enter* LUCIANUS.)

---

135 **naught** naughty, lewd   139 **posy** brief motto engraved on
a fingerring   142 **Phoebus' cart** the sun's chariot   143 **Tellus'
orbed ground** the earth (Tellus was the Roman goddess of the
earth)   146 **Hymen** god of marriage   152 **distrust** fear for
154 **hold quantity** are proportional, weigh alike   157 **as my
love is sized** according to the greatness of my love   161 **op-
erant** vital   169 **instances** motives   176 **validity** endurance

---

184 **enactures** enactments   187 **aye** ever   196 **seasons him**
ripens him into   206 **anchor's** anchorite's   227 **galled jade**
sorebacked horse

This is one Lucianus, nephew to the king.

230 OPHELIA: You are as good as a chorus, my lord.

HAMLET: I could interpret between you and your love, if I could see the puppets dallying.

OPHELIA: You are keen, my lord, you are keen.

HAMLET: It would cost you a groaning to take off mine edge.

235 OPHELIA: Still better, and worse.

HAMLET: So you mis-take your husbands.—Begin, murderer. Leave thy damnable faces and begin. Come, the croaking raven doth bellow for revenge.

LUCIANUS: Thoughts black, hands apt, drugs fit, and time

240 agreeing,
Confederate season, else no creature seeing.
Thou mixture rank, of midnight weeds collected,
With Hecate's ban thrice blasted, thrice infected,
Thy natural magic and dire property
On wholesome life usurp immediately.

(Pours the poison in his ears.)

245 HAMLET: 'A poisons him i' th' garden for his estate. His name's Gonzago. The story is extant, and written in very choice Italian. You shall see anon how the murderer gets the love of Gonzago's wife.

OPHELIA: The king rises.

250 HAMLET: What, frighted with false fire?

QUEEN: How fares my lord?

POLONIUS: Give o'er the play.

KING: Give me some light. Away!

POLONIUS: Lights, lights, lights!

(Exeunt all but HAMLET and HORATIO.)

255 HAMLET: Why, let the strucken deer go weep,
The hart ungallèd play.
For some must watch, while some must sleep;
Thus runs the world away.

Would not this, sir, and a forest of feathers—if the rest of
260 my fortunes turn Turk with me—with two Provincial roses on my razed shoes, get me a fellowship in a cry of players?

HORATIO: Half a share.

HAMLET: A whole one, I.

For thou dost know, O Damon dear,
265 This realm dismantled was
Of Jove himself, and now reigns here
A very, very—pajock.

HORATIO: You might have rhymed.

HAMLET: O good Horatio, I'll take the ghost's word for a
270 thousand pound. Didst perceive?

HORATIO: Very well, my lord.

HAMLET: Upon the talk of the poisoning.

HORATIO: I did very well note him.

HAMLET: Ah, ha! Come, some music. Come, the recorders.

For if the king like not the comedy,   275
Why then, belike, he likes it not, perdy.

Come, some music.

(Enter ROSENCRANTZ *and* GUILDENSTERN.*)*

GUILDENSTERN: Good my lord, vouchsafe me a word with you.

HAMLET: Sir, a whole history.

GUILDENSTERN: The king, sir—   280

HAMLET: Ay, sir what of him?

GUILDENSTERN: Is in his retirement marvellous distempered.

HAMLET: With drink, sir?

GUILDENSTERN: No, my lord, with choler.

HAMLET: Your wisdom should show itself more richer to sig- 285
nify this to the doctor, for for me to put him to his purgation would perhaps plunge him into more choler.

GUILDENSTERN: Good my lord, put your discourse into some
frame, and start not so wildly from my affair.

HAMLET: I am tame, sir. Pronounce.   290

GUILDENSTERN: The queen, your mother, in most great affliction of spirit, hath sent me to you.

HAMLET: You are welcome.

GUILDENSTERN: Nay, good my lord, this courtesy is not of the
right breed. If it shall please you to make me a wholesome 295
answer, I will do your mother's commandment. If not, your
pardon and my return shall be the end of my business.

HAMLET: Sir, I cannot.

GUILDENSTERN: What, my lord?

HAMLET: Make you a wholesome answer; my wit's diseased. 300
But, sir, such answer as I can make, you shall command, or
rather, as you say, my mother. Therefore no more, but to
the matter. My mother, you say—

ROSENCRANTZ: Then thus she says: your behaviour hath
struck her into amazement and admiration.   305

HAMLET: O wonderful son, that can so stonish a mother! But
is there no sequel at the heels of this mother's admiration?
Impart.

ROSENCRANTZ: She desires to speak with you in her closet
ere you go to bed.   310

HAMLET: We shall obey, were she ten times our mother. Have
you any further trade with us?

ROSENCRANTZ: My lord, you once did love me.

HAMLET: And do still, by these pickers and stealers.

ROSENCRANTZ: Good my lord, what is your cause of distem- 315
per? You do surely bar the door upon your own liberty, if
you deny your griefs to your friend.

HAMLET: Sir, I lack advancement.

ROSENCRANTZ: How can that be, when you have the voice
of the king himself for your succession in Denmark?   320

HAMLET: Ay, sir, but 'While the grass grows'—the proverb is
something musty.

---

242 **Hecate** goddess of witchcraft; **blasted** fallen under a blight
259 **feathers** plumes for actors' costumes 260 **Provincial
roses** i.e., Provençal roses. Ribbon rosettes resembling these
French roses were used to decorate shoes 261 **razed** with ornamental slashing; **cry** company 267 **pajock** presumably a
variant form of "patch-cock," a despicable person. Cf. 3.4.104

---

275 **For if . . . comedy** a seeming parody of *The Spanish Tragedy*,
4.1.197–98 ("And if the world like not this tragedy, / Hard is the
hap of old Hieronimo"), where another revenger's dramatic entertainment is referred to 287 **choler** one of the four bodily
humors, an excess of which gave rise to anger 295 **wholesome** reasonable 307 **admiration** wonder 314 **pickers and
stealers** hands 321 **'while the grass grows'** a proverb ending 'the horse starves'

(Enter the PLAYERS *with recorders.)*

O, the recorders! Let me see one. To withdraw with you—why do you go about to recover the wind of me, as
325 if you would drive me into a toil?

GUILDENSTERN: O, my lord, if my duty be too bold, my love is too unmannerly.

HAMLET: I do not well understand that. Will you play upon this pipe?

330 GUILDENSTERN: My lord, I cannot.

HAMLET: I pray you.

GUILDENSTERN: Believe me, I cannot.

HAMLET: I beseech you.

GUILDENSTERN: I know no touch of it, my lord.

335 HAMLET: It is easy as lying. Govern these ventages with your fingers and thumb, give it breath with your mouth, and it will discourse most eloquent music. Look you, these are the stops.

GUILDENSTERN: But these cannot I command to any ut-
340 t'rance of harmony. I have not the skill.

HAMLET: Why look you now, how unworthy a thing you make of me! You would play upon me, you would seem to know my stops, you would pluck out the heart of my mystery, you would sound me from my lowest note to the top of my com-
345 pass; and there is music, excellent voice, in this little organ, yet cannot you make it speak. 'Sblood, do you think I am easier to be played on than a pipe? Call me what instrument you will, though you can fret me, you cannot play upon me.

(Enter POLONIUS.)

350 God bless you, sir!

POLONIUS: My lord, the queen would speak with you, and presently.

HAMLET: Do you see yonder cloud that's almost in shape of a camel?

355 POLONIUS: By th' mass and 'tis, like a camel indeed.

HAMLET: Methinks it is like a weasel.

POLONIUS: It is backed like a weasel.

HAMLET: Or like a whale.

POLONIUS: Very like a whale.

360 HAMLET: Then I will come to my mother by and by. *(Aside.)* They fool me to the top of my bent.—I will come by and by.

POLONIUS: I will say so.

(Exit POLONIUS.)

HAMLET: 'By and by' is easily said. Leave me, friends.

(Exeunt all but HAMLET.)

'Tis now the very witching time of night,
365 When churchyards yawn and hell itself breathes out
Contagion to this world. Now could I drink hot blood,
And do such bitter business as the day
Would quake to look on. Soft, now to my mother.
O heart, lose not thy nature; let not ever
370 The soul of Nero enter this firm bosom.

Let me be cruel, not unnatural;
I will speak daggers to her, but use none.
My tongue and soul in this be hypocrites:
How in my words somever she be shent,
To give them seals never my soul consent! 375

(Exit.)

SCENE III

Enter KING, ROSENCRANTZ, *and* GUILDENSTERN.

KING: I like him not, nor stands it safe with us
To let his madness range. Therefore prepare you.
I your commission will forthwith dispatch,
And he to England shall along with you.
The terms of our estate may not endure 5
Hazard so near's as doth hourly grow
Out of his brows.

GUILDENSTERN: We will ourselves provide,
Most holy and religious fear it is
To keep those many many bodies safe
That live and feed upon your majesty. 10

ROSENCRANTZ: The single and peculiar life is bound
With all the strength and armor of the mind
To keep itself from noyance, but much more
That spirit upon whose weal depends and rests
The lives of many. The cess of majesty 15
Dies not alone, but like a gulf doth draw
What's near it with it. It is a massy wheel
Fixed on the summit of the highest mount,
To whose huge spokes ten thousand lesser things
Are mortised and adjoined, which when it falls, 20
Each small annexment, petty consequence,
Attends the boist'rous ruin. Never alone
Did the king sigh, but with a general groan.

KING: Arm you, I pray you, to this speedy voyage,
For we will fetters put about this fear, 25
Which now goes too free-footed.

ROSENCRANTZ: We will haste us.

(Exeunt Gentlemen [ROSENCRANTZ *and* GUILDENSTERN].)

(Enter POLONIUS.)

POLONIUS: My lord, he's going to his mother's closet.
Behind the arras I'll convey myself
To hear the process. I'll warrant she'll tax him home,
And as you said, and wisely was it said, 30
'Tis meet that some more audience than a mother,
Since nature makes them partial, should o'erhear
The speech of vantage. Fare you well, my liege.
I'll call upon you ere you go to bed,
And tell you what I know. 35

374 **somever,** soever; **shent** reproved, abused

III.iii. 5 terms of our estate conditions required for our rule as king   **7 brows** threatening looks that suggest the dangerous plots Hamlet's brain is hatching   **11 peculiar** private   **13 noyance** harm   **15 cess** cessation, extinction   **20 mortised** jointed (as with mortise and tenon)   **33 of vantage** (1) in addition; (2) from a convenient place for listening

323 **withdraw** step aside for private conversation   325 **toil** net, snare   335 **ventages** holes or stops in the recorder   348 **fret** (1) a stop on the fingerboard of a guitar (2) annoy   370 **Nero** Roman emperor who murdered his mother

KING: Thanks, dear my lord. (*Exit* POLONIUS.)
    O, my offence is rank, it smells to heaven;
    It hath the primal eldest curse upon't,
    A brother's murder. Pray can I not,
    Though inclination be as sharp as will.
40   My stronger guilt defeats my strong intent,
    And like a man to double business bound,
    I stand in pause where I shall first begin,
    And both neglect. What if this cursèd hand
    Were thicker than itself with brother's blood,
45   Is there not rain enough in the sweet heavens
    To wash it white as snow? Whereto serves mercy
    But to confront the visage of offence?
    And what's in prayer but this twofold force,
    To be forestallèd ere we come to fall,
50   Or pardoned being down? Then I'll look up.
    My fault is past. But, O, what form of prayer
    Can serve my turn? 'Forgive me my foul murder'?
    That cannot be, since I am still possessed
    Of those effects for which I did the murder—
55   My crown, mine own ambition, and my queen.
    May one be pardoned and retain th' offence?
    In the corrupted currents of this world
    Offence's gilded hand may shove by justice,
    And oft 'tis seen the wicked prize itself
60   Buys out the law. But 'tis not so above
    There is no shuffling: there the action lies
    In his true nature, and we ourselves compelled,
    Even to the teeth and forehead of our faults,
    To give in evidence. What then? What rests?
65   Try what repentance can. What can it not?
    Yet what can it when one can not repent?
    O wretched state! O bosom black as death!
    O limèd soul, that struggling to be free
    Art more engaged! Help, angels! Make assay.
70   Bow, stubborn knees, and heart with strings of steel,
    Be soft as sinews of the new-born babe.
    All may be well.

(*He kneels.*)

(*Enter* HAMLET.)

HAMLET: Now might I do it pat, now 'a is a-praying,
    And now I'll do't—and so 'a goes to heaven,
75   And so am I revenged. That would be scanned.
    A villain kills my father, and for that,
    I, his sole son, do this same villain send
    To heaven.
    Why, this is hire and salary, not revenge.
80   'A took my father grossly, full of bread,
    With all his crimes broad blown, as flush as May;
    And how his audit stands who knows save heaven?
    But in our circumstance and course of thought
    'Tis heavy with him; and am I then revenged

    To take him in the purging of his soul,   85
    When he is fit and seasoned for his passage?
    No.
    Up, sword, and know thou a more horrid hent.
    When he is drunk asleep, or in his rage,
    Or in th' incestuous pleasure of his bed,   90
    At game a-swearing, or about some act
    That has no relish of salvation in't—
    Then trip him, that his heels may kick at heaven,
    And that his soul may be as damned and black
    As hell, whereto it goes. My mother stays.   95
    This physic but prolongs thy sickly days.

(*Exit.*)

KING: (*Rising.*) My words fly up, my thoughts remain below.
    Words without thoughts never to heaven go.

(*Exit.*)

SCENE IV

Enter [QUEEN] GERTRUDE *and* POLONIUS.

POLONIUS: 'A will come straight. Look you lay home to him.
    Tell him his pranks have been too broad to bear with,
    And that your grace hath screened and stood between
    Much heat and him. I'll silence me even here.
    Pray you be round.   5
QUEEN: I'll warrant you. Fear me not.
    Withdraw, I hear him coming.

(POLONIUS *goes behind the arras.*)

(*Enter* HAMLET.)

HAMLET: Now, mother, what's the matter?
QUEEN: Hamlet, thou hast thy father much offended.
HAMLET: Mother, you have my father much offended.
QUEEN: Come, come, you answer with an idle tongue.   10
HAMLET: Go, go, you question with a wicked tongue.
QUEEN: Why, how, now, Hamlet?
HAMLET: What's the matter now?
QUEEN: Have you forgot me?
HAMLET: No, by the rood, not so:
    You are the queen, your husband's brother's wife,
    And would it were not so, you are my mother.   15
QUEEN: Nay, then I'll set those to you that can speak.
HAMLET: Come, come, and sit you down. You shall not budge.
    You go not till I set you up a glass
    Where you may see the inmost part of you.
QUEEN: What will thou do? Thou wilt not murder me?   20
    Help, ho!
POLONIUS: (*Behind.*) What, ho! help!
HAMLET: (*Draws.*) How now! a rat?
    Dead for a ducat, dead!

(*Thrusts his sword through the arras and kills* POLONIUS.)

---

39 **will** carnal desire   61 **shuffling** doubledealing; **action** legal action   68 **limèd** soul caught by sin as the bird by lime   69 **assay** an effort   80 **grossly** unprepared spiritually   81 **as flush as May** in full flower   83 **in our circumstance** considering all evidence; **course** beaten way, habit

88 **hent** occasion, opportunity

III.iv. 5 Following Polonius's "Pray you be round" (which in *F* reads "Pray you round with him"), *F* adds the line: "*Hamlet within.* Mother, mother, mother"   13 **rood** cross

25 POLONIUS: (*Behind.*) O, I am slain!
   QUEEN: O me, what hast thou done?
   HAMLET: Nay, I know not.
     Is it the king?
   QUEEN: O, what a rash and bloody deed is this!
   HAMLET: A bloody deed? Almost as bad, good mother,
30   As kill a king and marry with his brother.
   QUEEN: As kill a king?
   HAMLET: Ay, lady, it was my word.

(*Lifts up the arras and sees the body of* POLONIUS.)

     Thou wretched, rash, intruding fool, farewell!
     I took thee for thy better. Take thy fortune.
     Thou find'st to be too busy is some danger.—
35   Leave wringing of your hands. Peace, sit you down
     And let me wring your heart, for so I shall
     If it be made of penetrable stuff,
     If damnèd custom have not brazed it so
     That it be proof and bulwark against sense.
40 QUEEN: What have I done that thou dar'st wag thy tongue
     In noise so rude against me?
   HAMLET: Such an act
     That blurs the grace and blush of modesty,
     Calls virtue hypocrite, takes off the rose
     From the fair forehead of an innocent love,
45   And sets a blister there, makes marriage-vows
     As false as dicers' oaths. O, such a deed
     As from the body of contraction plucks
     The very soul, and sweet religion makes
     A rhapsody of words. Heaven's face does glow
50   O'er this solidity and compound mass
     With heated visage, as against the doom—
     Is thought-sick at the act.
   QUEEN: Ay me, what act,
     That roars so loud, and thunders in the index?
   HAMLET: Look here, upon this picture and on this.
55   The counterfeit presentment of two brothers.
     See what a grace was seated on this brow:
     Hyperion's curls, the front of Jove himself,
     An eye like Mars, to threaten and command,
     A station like the herald Mercury
60   New lighted on a heaven-kissing hill—
     A combination and a form indeed
     Where every god did seem to set his seal
     To give the world assurance of a man.
     This was your husband. Look you now what follows.
65   Here is your husband, like a mildewed ear
     Blasting his wholesome brother. Have you eyes?
     Could you on this fair mountain leave to feed,
     And batten on this moor? Ha! have you eyes?
     You cannot call it love, for at your age
70   The heyday in the blood is tame, it's humble,

And waits upon the judgement, and what judgement
Would step from this to this? Sense sure you have,
Else could you not have motion, but sure that sense
Is apoplexed, for madness would not err
Nor sense to ecstasy was ne'er so thralled   75
But it reserved some quantity of choice
To serve in such a difference. What devil was't
That thus hath cozened you at hoodman-blind?
Eyes without feeling, feeling without sight,
Ears without hands or eyes, smelling sans all,   80
Or but a sickly part of one true sense
Could not so mope. O shame! where is thy blush?
Rebellious hell,
If thou canst mutine in a matron's bones,
To flaming youth let virtue be as wax   85
And melt in her own fire. Proclaim no shame
When the compulsive ardor gives the charge,
Since frost itself as actively doth burn,
And reason pandars will.
QUEEN: O Hamlet, speak no more!
   Thou turn'st mine eyes into my very soul,   90
   And there I see such black and grainèd spots
   As will not leave their tinct.
HAMLET: Nay, but to live
   In the rank sweat of an enseamèd bed,
   Stewed in corruption, honeying and making love
   Over the nasty sty—   95
QUEEN: O, speak to me no more!
   These words like daggers enter in mine ears.
   No more, sweet Hamlet.
HAMLET: A murderer and a villain,
   A slave that is not twentieth part the tithe
   Of your precedent lord, a vice of kings,
   A cutpurse of the empire and the rule,   100
   That from a shelf the precious diadem stole
   And put it in his pocket—
QUEEN: No more.

(*Enter* GHOST.)

HAMLET: A king of shreds and patches—
   Save me and hover o'er me with your wings,   105
   You heavenly guards! What would your gracious figure?
QUEEN: Alas, he's mad.
HAMLET: Do you not come your tardy son to chide,
   That lapsed in time and passion lets go by
   Th' important acting of your dread command?   110
   O, say!
GHOST: Do not forget. This visitation
   Is but to whet thy almost blunted purpose.
   But look, amazement on thy mother sits.
   O, step between her and her fighting soul!   115

---

38 **brazed** plated it as with brass   39 **proof** impenetrable, as of armor   47 **contraction** the contract of marriage   50 **this solidity and compound mass** the earth, as compounded of the four elements   51 **doom** Judgment Day   53 **index** table of contents; thus, indication of what is to follow   55 **counterfeit presentment** portrait   57 **front** forehead   59 **station** bearing figure   68 **batten** feed like an animal   70 **heyday** ardor

72 **Sense** the senses collectively, which according to Aristotelian tradition are found in all creatures that have the power of locomotion   75 **ecstasy** madness   78 **hoodman-blind** blindman's bluff   80 **sans** without   82 **mope** act without full use of one's wits   89 **will** desire   91 **grainèd spots** indelible stains   92 **tinct** color   93 **enseamèd** greasy   99 **vice** a character in the morality plays, presented often as a buffoon (here, a caricature)

Conceit in weakest bodies strongest works.
Speak to her, Hamlet.
HAMLET: How is it with you, lady?
QUEEN: Alas, how is't with you,
That you do bend your eye on vacancy,
120   And with th' incorporal air do hold discourse?
Forth at your eyes your spirits wildly peep,
And as the sleeping soldiers in th' alarm,
Your bedded hair like life in excrements
Start up and stand an end. O gentle son,
125   Upon the heat and flame of thy distemper
Sprinkle cool patience. Whereon do you look?
HAMLET: On him, on him! Look you how pale he glares.
His form and cause conjoined, preaching to stones,
Would make them capable.—Do not look upon me,
130   Lest with this piteous action you convert
My stern effects. Then what I have to do
Will want true color—tears perchance for blood.
QUEEN: To whom do you speak this?
HAMLET: Do you see nothing there?
135 QUEEN: Nothing at all, yet all that is I see.
HAMLET: Nor did you nothing hear?
QUEEN: No, nothing but ourselves.
HAMLET: Why, look you there. Look, how it steals away.
My father, in his habit as he lived!
140   Look where he goes even now out at the portal.

(*Exit* GHOST.)

QUEEN: This is the very coinage of your brain.
This bodiless creation ecstasy
Is very cunning in.
HAMLET: My pulse as yours doth temperately keep time,
145   And makes us healthful music. It is not madness
That I have uttered. Bring me to the test,
And I the matter will re-word, which madness
Would gambol from. Mother, for love of grace,
Lay not that flattering unction to your soul,
150   That not your trespass but my madness speaks.
It will but skin and film the ulcerous place
Whiles rank corruption, mining all within,
Infects unseen. Confess yourself to heaven,
Repent what's past, avoid what is to come,
155   And do not spread the compost on the weeds,
To make them ranker. Forgive me this my virtue,
For in the fatness of these pursy times
Virtue itself of vice must pardon beg,
Yea, curb and woo for leave to do him good.
160 QUEEN: O Hamlet, thou hast cleft my heart in twain.
HAMLET: O, throw away the worser part of it,
And live the purer with the other half.
Good night—but go not to my uncle's bed.
Assume a virtue, if you have it not.
165   That monster custom, who all sense doth eat,

Of habits devil, is angel yet in this,
That to the use of actions fair and good
He likewise gives a frock or livery
That aptly is put on. Refrain to-night,
And that shall lend a kind of easiness   170
To the next abstinence; the next more easy;
For use almost can change the stamp of nature,
And either curb the devil, or throw him out
With wondrous potency. Once more, good night,
And when you are desirous to be blest,   175
I'll blessing beg of you. For this same lord,
I do repent; but heaven hath pleased it so,
To punish me with this, and this with me,
That I must be their scourge and minister.
I will bestow him and will answer well   180
The death I gave him. So, again, good night.
I must be cruel only to be kind.
This bad begins and worse remains behind.
One word more, good lady.
QUEEN: What shall I do?
HAMLET: Not this, by no means, that I bid you do: 185
Let the bloat king tempt you again to bed,
Pinch wanton on your cheek, call you his mouse,
And let him, for a pair of reechy kisses,
Or paddling in your neck with his damned fingers,
Make you to ravel all this matter out,   190
That I essentially am not in madness,
But mad in craft. 'Twere good you let him know,
For who that's but a queen, fair, sober, wise,
Would from a paddock, from a bat, a gib,
Such dear concernings hide? Who would so do?   195
No, in despite of sense and secrecy,
Unpeg the basket on the house's top,
Let the birds fly, and like the famous ape,
To try conclusions, in the basket creep
And break your own neck down.   200
QUEEN: Be thou assured, if words be made of breath
And breath of life, I have no life to breathe
What thou hast said to me.
HAMLET: I must to England; you know that?
QUEEN: Alack,
I had forgot. 'Tis so concluded on.   205
HAMLET: There's letters sealed, and my two school-fellows,
Whom I will trust as I will adders fanged,
They bear the mandate; they must sweep my way
And marshal me to knavery. Let it work,

---

116 **Conceit** imagination   123 **excrements** nails, hair (whatever grows out of the body)   124 **an** on   129 **capable** able to respond   132 **want** lack   148 **gambol** leap or start, as a shying horse   149 **unction** ointment; hence, soothing notion   152 **mining** undermining   157 **fatness** grossness, slackness; **pursy** corpulent   165 **who all sense doth eat** who consumes all human sense, both bodily and spiritual

166 **Of habits devil** being a devil in, or in respect of, habits (with a play on "habits," as meaning both settled practices and garments, whereby devilish practices contrast with "actions fair and good," line 167, and devilish garments contrast with the "frock or livery" of line 168, which custom in its angelic aspect provides)   183 **This** i.e., the death of Polonius (cf. line 178); **remains behind** is yet to come   188 **reechy** dirty   191 **essentially** in fact   194 **paddock** toad; **gib** tom-cat   197–200 **Unpeg the basket . . . neck down** the story is lost (in it, apparently, the ape carries a cage of birds to the top of a house, releases them by accident, and, surprised at their flight, imagines he can imitate it by first creeping into the basket and then leaping out. The moral of the story, for the queen, is not to expose herself to destruction by making public what good sense decrees should be kept secret.)

210 For 'tis the sport to have the engineer
     Hoist with his own petar; and 't shall go hard
     But I will delve one yard below their mines
     And blow them at the moon. O, 'tis most sweet
     When in one line two crafts directly meet.
215 This man shall set me packing.
     I'll lug the guts into the neighbour room.
     Mother, good night indeed. This counsellor
     Is now most still, most secret and most grave,
     Who was in life a foolish prating knave.
220 Come sir, to draw toward an end with you.
     Good night, mother.

(*Exit* [HAMLET *tugging in* POLONIUS].)

ACT FOUR

SCENE I

Enter KING [*to the*] QUEEN, *with* ROSENCRANTZ *and* GUILDEN-
STERN.

KING: There's matter in these sighs, these profound heaves,
     You must translate, 'tis fit we understand them.
     Where is your son?
QUEEN: Bestow this place on us a little while.

(*Exeunt* ROSENCRANTZ *and* GUILDENSTERN.)

5   Ah, mine own lord, what have I seen to-night!
KING: What, Gertrude, how does Hamlet?
QUEEN: Mad as the sea and wind when both contend
     Which is the mightier. In his lawless fit,
     Behind the arras hearing something stir,
10   Whips out his rapier, cries 'A rat, a rat!'
     And in this brainish apprehension kills
     The unseen good old man.
KING: O heavy deed!
     It had been so with us had we been there.
     His liberty is full of threats to all—
15   To you yourself, to us, to every one.
     Alas, how shall this bloody deed be answered?
     It will be laid to us, whose providence
     Should have kept short, restrained, and out of haunt,
     This mad young man. But so much was our love,
20   We would not understand what was most fit,
     But like the owner of a foul disease,
     To keep it from divulging, let it feed
     Even on the pith of life. Where is he gone?
QUEEN: To draw apart the body he hath killed,
25   O'er whom his very madness, like some ore
     Among a mineral of metals base,
     Shows itself pure: 'a weeps for what is done.
KING: O Gertrude, come away!
     The sun no sooner shall the mountains touch
30   But we will ship him hence, and this vile deed

     We must with all our majesty and skill,
     Both countenance and excuse. Ho, Guildenstern!

(*Enter* ROSENCRANTZ *and* GUILDENSTERN.)

     Friends both, go join you with some further aid.
     Hamlet in madness hath Polonius slain,
     And from his mother's closet hath he dragged him.   35
     Go seek him out; speak fair, and bring the body
     Into the chapel. I pray you haste in this.

(*Exeunt* ROSENCRANTZ *and* GUILDENSTERN.)

     Come, Gertrude, we'll call up our wisest friends
     And let them know both what we mean to do
     And what's untimely done; so haply slander—   40
     Whose whisper o'er the world's diameter,
     As level as the cannon to his blank,
     Transports his poisoned shot—may miss our name,
     And hit the woundless air. O, come away!
     My soul is full of discord and dismay.   45

(*Exeunt.*)

SCENE II

Enter HAMLET.

HAMLET: Safely stowed.—But soft, what noise? who calls on
     Hamlet? O, here they come.

([*Enter*] ROSENCRANTZ, [GUILDENSTERN,] *and* OTHERS.)

ROSENCRANTZ: What have you done, my lord, with the dead
     body?
HAMLET: Compounded it with dust, whereto 'tis kin.   5
ROSENCRANTZ: Tell us where 'tis, that we may take it thence
     And bear it to the chapel.
HAMLET: Do not believe it.
ROSENCRANTZ: Believe what?
HAMLET: That I can keep your counsel and not mine own.   10
     Besides, to be demanded of a sponge—what replication
     should be made by the son of a king?
ROSENCRANTZ: Take you me for a sponge, my lord?
HAMLET: Ay, sir, that soaks up the king's countenance, his re-
     wards, his authorities. But such officers do the king best   15
     service in the end. He keeps them, like an apple in the
     corner of his jaw, first mouthed to be last swallowed.
     When he needs what you have gleaned, it is but squeez-
     ing you and, sponge, you shall be dry again.
ROSENCRANTZ: I understand you not, my lord.   20
HAMLET: I am glad of it. A knavish speech sleeps in a foolish
     ear.
ROSENCRANTZ: My lord, you must tell us where the body is,
     and go with us to the king.
HAMLET: The body is with the king, but the king is not with   25
     the body.
     The king is a thing—

---

211 **petar** a bomb or charge for blowing in gates   217 **indeed**
in earnest (cf. lines 163, 174, 181)

IV.i. The action is continuous with that of the preceding scene.
The Queen does not leave the stage.   2 **translate** explain   11
brainish apprehension frenzied delusion   18 **out of haunt**
away from society   26 **mineral** mine

---

42 **As level as** sure of aim; **blank** target

IV.ii. 1 After the words "Safely stowed," *F* adds the line: "*Gentlemen within. Hamlet, Lord Hamlet.*" Here, as at 3.4.5 "when a
character speaks of hearing someone coming, *F* provides, though
Q does not, for the audience to hear it too" (Jenkins, *SB*, 13.35)
11 **replication** reply

GUILDENSTERN: A thing, my lord!

HAMLET: Of nothing. Bring me to him. Hide fox, and all after.

(*Exeunt.*)

SCENE III

Enter KING, *and two or three.*

KING: I have sent to seek him, and to find the body.
How dangerous is it that this man goes loose!
Yet must not we put the strong law on him.
He's loved of the distracted multitude,
5 Who like not in their judgement but their eyes,
And where 'tis so, th' offender's scourge is weighed,
But never the offence. To bear all smooth and even,
This sudden sending him away must seem
Deliberate pause. Diseases desperate grown
10 By desperate appliance are relieved,
Or not at all.

(*Enter* ROSENCRANTZ, [GUILDENSTERN,] *and all the rest.*)

                    How now! what hath befall'n?

ROSENCRANTZ: Where the dead body is bestowed, my lord,
We cannot get from him.

KING: But where is he?

ROSENCRANTZ: Without, my lord; guarded, to know your
pleasure.

15 KING: Bring him before us.

ROSENCRANTZ: Ho! bring in the lord.

(*They enter* [*with* HAMLET].)

KING: Now, Hamlet, where's Polonius?

HAMLET: At supper.

KING: At supper? Where?

HAMLET: Not where he eats, but where 'a is eaten. A certain
20 convocation of politic worms are e'en at him. Your worm
is your only emperor for diet. We fat all creatures else to
fat us, and we fat ourselves for maggots. Your fat king and
your lean beggar is but variable service—two dishes, but
to one table. That's the end.

25 KING: Alas, alas!

HAMLET: A man may fish with the worm that hath eat of a
king, and eat of the fish that hath fed of that worm.

KING: What dost thou mean by this?

HAMLET: Nothing but to show you how a king may go a
30 progress through the guts of a beggar.

KING: Where is Polonius?

HAMLET: In heaven. Send thither to see. If your messenger
find him not there, seek him i' th' other place yourself. But
if, indeed, you find him not within this month, you shall
35 nose him as you go up the stairs into the lobby.

KING: (*To* ATTENDANTS.) Go seek him there.

HAMLET: 'A will stay till you come.

(*Exeunt* ATTENDANTS.)

KING: Hamlet, this deed, for thine especial safety—
Which we do tender, as we dearly grieve
For that which thou hast done—must send thee hence   40
With fiery quickness. Therefore prepare thyself.
The bark is ready, and the wind at help,
Th' associates tend, and everything is bent
For England.

HAMLET: For England?

KING: Ay, Hamlet.

HAMLET: Good.

KING: So is it, if thou knew'st our purposes.   45

HAMLET: I see a cherub that sees them. But come, for England!
Farewell, dear mother.

KING: Thy loving father, Hamlet.

HAMLET: My mother. Father and mother is man and wife, man
and wife is one flesh. So, my mother. Come, for England. 50

(*Exit.*)

KING: Follow him at foot: tempt him with speed aboard.
Delay it not: I'll have him hence to-night.
Away! for every thing is sealed and done
That else leans on th' affair. Pray you make haste.

(*Exeunt all but the* KING.)

And, England, if my love thou hold'st at aught—   55
As my great power thereof may give thee sense,
Since yet thy cicatrice looks raw and red
After the Danish sword, and thy free awe
Pays homage to us—thou mayst not coldly set
Our sovereign process, which imports at full   60
By letters congruing to that effect
The present death of Hamlet. Do it, England.
For like the hectic in my blood he rages,
And thou must cure me. Till I know 'tis done,
Howe'er my haps, my joys were ne'er begun.   65

(*Exit.*)

SCENE IV

Enter FORTINBRAS *with his* ARMY *over the stage.*

FORTINBRAS: Go, captain, from me greet the Danish king.
Tell him that by his license Fortinbras
Craves the conveyance of a promised march
Over his kingdom. You know the rendezvous.
If that his majesty would aught with us,   5
We shall express our duty in his eye,
And let him know so.

CAPTAIN: I will do't, my lord.

---

29 **Hide fox, and all after** presumably a cry in some game such
as hide-and-seek. The words, which do not occur in *Q2,* may
be an actor's addition

IV.iii. 9 **Deliberate pause** carefully considered   30 **progress**
the state journey of a ruler

39 **tender** value   46 **cherub** one of the cherubim, the watchmen or sentinels of heaven, and thus endowed with the keenest
vision   57 **cicatrice** scar, used here of memory of a defeat   59
coldly set regard with indifference   60 **process** mandate   61
congruing to in accordance with   63 **hectic** consumptive
fever   65 **haps** fortunes

IV.iv. 3 **conveyance** conduct   6 **eye** presence

FORTINBRAS: Go softly on.

(*Exeunt all but the* CAPTAIN.)

(*Enter* HAMLET, ROSENCRANTZ, [GUILDENSTERN,] *and* OTHERS.)

HAMLET: Good sir, whose powers are these?
10 CAPTAIN: They are of Norway, sir.
HAMLET: How purposed, sir, I pray you?
CAPTAIN: Against some part of Poland.
HAMLET: Who commands them, sir?
CAPTAIN: The nephew to old Norway, Fortinbras.
15 HAMLET: Goes it against the main of Poland, sir,
    Or for some frontier?
CAPTAIN: Truly to speak, and with no addition,
    We go to gain a little patch of ground
    That hath in it no profit but the name.
20   To pay five ducats, five, I would not farm it;
    Nor will it yield to Norway or the Pole
    A ranker rate should it be sold in fee.
HAMLET: Why, then the Polack never will defend it.
CAPTAIN: Yes, it is already garrisoned.
25 HAMLET: Two thousand souls and twenty thousand ducats
    Will not debate the question of this straw.
    This is th' imposthume of much wealth and peace,
    That inward breaks, and shows no cause without
    Why the man dies. I humbly thank you, sir.
30 CAPTAIN: God buy you, sir.

(*Exit.*)

ROSENCRANTZ: Will 't please you go, my lord?
HAMLET: I'll be with you straight. Go a little before.

(*Exeunt all but* HAMLET.)

    How all occasions do inform against me,
    And spur my dull revenge! What is a man,
    If his chief good and market of his time
35   Be but to sleep and feed? A beast, no more.
    Sure he that made us with such large discourse,
    Looking before and after, gave us not
    That capability and godlike reason
    To fust in us unused. Now, whether it be
40   Bestial oblivion, or some craven scruple
    Of thinking too precisely on th' event—
    A thought which, quartered, hath but one part wisdom
    And ever three parts coward—I do not know
    Why yet I live to say 'This thing's to do',
45   Sith I have cause, and will, and strength, and means,
    To do 't. Examples gross as earth exhort me:
    Witness this army of such mass and charge,
    Led by a delicate and tender prince,
    Whose spirit, with divine ambition puffed,
50   Makes mouths at the invisible event,
    Exposing what is mortal and unsure
    To all that fortune, death, and danger dare,

Even for an eggshell. Rightly to be great
Is not to stir without great argument,
But greatly to find quarrel in a straw   55
When honor's at the stake. How stand I then,
That have a father killed, a mother stained,
Excitements of my reason and my blood,
And let all sleep, while to my shame I see
The imminent death of twenty thousand men   60
That for a fantasy and trick of fame
Go to their graves like beds, fight for a plot
Whereon the numbers cannot try the cause,
Which is not tomb enough and continent
To hide the slain? O, from this time forth,   65
My thoughts be bloody, or be nothing worth!

(*Exit.*)

SCENE V

Enter HORATIO, [QUEEN] GERTRUDE, *and a* GENTLEMAN.

QUEEN: I will not speak with her.
GENTLEMAN: She is importunate, indeed distract.
    Her mood will needs be pitied.
QUEEN: What would she have?
GENTLEMAN: She speaks much of her father, says she hears
    There's tricks i' th' world, and hems, and beats her heart,   5
    Spurns enviously at straws, speaks things in doubt
    That carry but half sense. Her speech is nothing,
    Yet the unshaped use of it doth move
    The hearers to collection; they aim at it,
    And botch the words up fit to their own thoughts,   10
    Which, as her winks and nods and gestures yield them,
    Indeed would make one think there might be thought,
    Though nothing sure, yet much unhappily.
HORATIO: 'Twere good she were spoken with, for she may strew
    Dangerous conjectures in ill-breeding minds.   15
QUEEN: Let her come in. (*Exit* GENTLEMAN.)
    (*Aside.*) To my sick soul, as sin's true nature is,
    Each toy seems prologue to some great amiss.
    So full of artless jealousy is guilt,
    It spills itself in fearing to be spilt.   20

(*Enter* OPHELIA [*distracted*].)

OPHELIA: Where is the beauteous majesty of Denmark?
QUEEN: How now, Ophelia!
OPHELIA: (*She sings.*)

53–56 **Rightly to be great . . . honor's at the stake** i.e., to be rightly great is *not* to refuse to act ("stir") in a dispute ("argument") because the grounds are insufficient, but to be moved to action even in trivial circumstances where a question of honor is involved   63 **try the cause** settle by combat   64 **continent** receptacle

IV.v. 6 **Spurns enviously at straws** takes exception, spitefully, to trifles   7 **nothing** nonsense   8 **unshaped use** disordered manner   9 **collection** attempts at shaping meaning; **aim** guess   13 **sure** certain   18 **toy** trifle   19 **artless jealousy** ill-concealed suspicion   20 **spills** destroys

---

15 **main** chief part   17 **addition** exaggeration   20 **To pay** i.e., for a yearly rental   22 **a ranker rate** a greater price; **sold in fee** sold with absolute and perpetual possession   27 **imposthume** abscess   32 **inform** take shape   34 **market** profit   36 **discourse** power of reasoning   39 **fust** grow musty   50 **Makes mouths at** makes scornful faces at, derides

How should I your true love know
From another one?
25 By his cockle hat and staff,
And his sandal shoon.

QUEEN: Alas, sweet lady, what imports this song?
OPHELIA: Say you? Nay, pray you mark. (*Song.*)

He is dead and gone, lady,
30 He is dead and gone;
At his head a grass-green turf,
At his heels a stone.

O, ho!

QUEEN: Nay, but Ophelia—
OPHELIA: Pray you mark.

(*Sings.*)

35   White his shroud as the mountain snow—

(*Enter* KING.)

QUEEN: Alas, look here, my lord.
OPHELIA: (*Song.*)

Larded all with sweet flowers;
Which bewept to the grave did not go
With true-love showers.

40 KING: How do you, pretty lady?
OPHELIA: Well, good dild you! They say the owl was a baker's
daughter. Lord, we know what we are, but know not what
we may be. God be at your table!
KING: Conceit upon her father.
45 OPHELIA: Pray let's have no words of this, but when they ask
you what it means, say you this:

(*Song.*)

To-morrow is Saint Valentine's day,
All in the morning betime,
And I a maid at your window,
50   To be your Valentine.
Then up he rose, and donned his clo'es,
And dupped the chamber-door,
Let in the maid, that out a maid
Never departed more.

55 KING: Pretty Ophelia—
OPHELIA: Indeed, without an oath, I'll make an end on't:

(*Sings.*)

By Gis and by Saint Charity,
Alack, and fie for shame!
Young men will do't, if they come to't;

By cock, they are to blame.   60
Quoth she 'Before you tumbled me,
You promised me to wed.'

He answers:

'So would I a' done, by yonder sun,
An thou hadst not come to my bed.'   65

KING: How long hath she been thus?
OPHELIA: I hope all will be well. We must be patient, but I
cannot choose but weep, to think they would lay him i' th'
cold ground. My brother shall know of it, and so I thank
you for your good counsel. Come, my coach! Good night,   70
ladies, good night. Sweet ladies, good night, good night.

(*Exit.*)

KING: Follow her close; give her good watch, I pray you.

(*Exeunt* HORATIO *and* GENTLEMEN.)

O, this is the poison of deep grief; it springs
All from her father's death, and now behold!
O Gertrude, Gertrude,   75
When sorrows come, they come not single spies,
But in battalions: first, her father slain;
Next, your son gone, and he most violent author
Of his own just remove; the people muddied,
Thick and unwholesome in their thoughts and whispers   80
For good Polonius' death; and we have done but greenly
In hugger-mugger to inter him; poor Ophelia
Divided from herself and her fair judgement,
Without the which we are pictures, or mere beasts;
Last, and as much containing as all these,   85
Her brother is in secret come from France,
Feeds on his wonder, keeps himself in clouds,
And wants not buzzers to infect his ear
With pestilent speeches of his father's death.
Wherein necessity, of matter beggared,   90
Will nothing stick our person to arraign
In ear and ear, O my dear Gertrude, this,
Like to a murd'ring piece, in many places
Gives me superfluous death. Attend,   (*A noise within.*)

(*Enter a* MESSENGER.)

Where are my Switzers? Let them guard the door.   95
What is the matter?
MESSENGER: Save yourself, my lord.
The ocean, overpeering of his list,
Eats not the flats with more impiteous haste
Then young Laertes, in a riotous head,
O'erbears your officers. The rabble call him lord,   100
And as the world were now but to begin,

---

25 **cockle hat** hat bearing a cockle shell, worn by a pilgrim who
had been to the shrine of St. James of Compostella, in Spain   26
shoon shoes   37 **Larded** garnished, strewn   41 **good dild you**
God yield (requite) you   41–42 **They say the owl was a baker's
daughter** allusion to a folktale in which a baker's daughter was
transformed into an owl because of her ungenerous behavior (giving short measure) when Christ asked for bread in the baker's shop
44 **Conceit upon her father** i.e., obsessed with her father's death
48 **betime** early   52 **dupped** opened   57 **Gis** Jesus

60 **cock** corruption of God   79 **remove** banishment, departure; **muddied** stirred up and confused   81 **greenly** without
judgment   82 **hugger-mugger** secrecy and disorder   87 **in
clouds** i.e., of suspicion and rumor   88 **wants** lacks   90 **of
matter beggared** lacking facts   91 **nothing stick** in no way
hesitate   93 **murd'ring piece** cannon loaded with shot meant
to scatter   94 F omits the King's 'Attend,' but substitutes, by way
of drawing attention to the "noise within"   95 **Switzers** Swiss
bodyguard   97 **list** boundary   99 **riotous head** turbulent mob

Antiquity forgot, custom not known,
The ratifiers and props of every word,
They cry 'Choose we, Laertes shall be king'.
105 Caps, hands, and tongues, applaud it to the clouds,
'Laertes shall be king, Laertes king!'
QUEEN: How cheerfully on the false trail they cry!

(*A noise within.*)

O, this is counter, you false Danish dogs!
KING: The doors are broke.

(*Enter* LAERTES *with* OTHERS.)

110 LAERTES: Where is this king?—Sirs, stand you all without.
ALL: No, let's come in.
LAERTES: I pray you give me leave.
ALL: We will, we will.

(*Exeunt his followers.*)

LAERTES: I thank you. Keep the door.—O thou vile king,
Give me my father!
QUEEN: Calmly, good Laertes,
115 LAERTES: That drop of blood that's calm proclaims me bastard,
Cries cuckold to my father, brands the harlot
Even here between the chaste unsmirchèd brow
Of my true mother.
KING: What is the cause, Laertes,
That thy rebellion looks so giant-like?
120 Let him go, Gertrude. Do not fear our person.
There's such divinity doth hedge a king
That treason can but peep to what it would,
Acts little of his will. Tell me, Laertes.
Why thou art thus incensed. Let him go, Gertrude.
125 Speak, man.
LAERTES: Where is my father?
KING: Dead.
QUEEN: But not by him.
KING: Let him demand his fill.
LAERTES: How came he dead? I'll not be juggled with.
To hell allegiance, vows to the blackest devil,
130 Conscience and grace to the profoundest pit!
I dare damnation. To this point I stand,
That both the worlds I give to negligence,
Let come what comes, only I'll be revenged
Most throughly for my father.
135 KING: Who shall stay you?
LAERTES: My will, not all the world's.
And for my means, I'll husband them so well
They shall go far with little.
KING: Good Laertes,
If you desire to know the certainty
Of your dear father, is't writ in your revenge
140 That, swoopstake, you will draw both friend and foe,
Winner and loser?
LAERTES: None but his enemies.

---

108 **counter** hunting backward on the trail   120 **fear** fear for
134 **throughly** thoroughly   140 **swoopstake** sweepstake, taking all the stakes on the gambling table

KING: Will you know them, then?
LAERTES: To his good friends thus wide I'll ope my arms,
And like the kind life-rend'ring pelican,
Repast them with my blood.   145
KING: Why, now you speak
Like a good child and a true gentleman.
That I am guiltless of your father's death,
And am most sensibly in grief for it,
It shall as level to your judgement 'pear
As day does to your eye.   150

(*A noise within:* 'Let her come in.')

LAERTES: How now! what noise is that?

(*Enter* OPHELIA.)

O heat, dry up my brains! tears seven times salt
Burn out the sense and virtue of mine eye!
By heaven, thy madness shall be paid with weight
Till our scale turn the beam. O rose of May,   155
Dear maid, kind sister, sweet Ophelia!
O heavens! is 't possible a young maid's wits
Should be as mortal as an old man's life?
Nature is fine in love, and where 'tis fine
It sends some precious instance of itself   160
After the thing it loves.
OPHELIA: (*Song.*)

They bore him barefac'd on the bier;
Hey non nonny, nonny, hey nonny;
And in his grave rain'd many a tear—

Fare you well, my dove!   165
LAERTES: Hadst thou thy wits, and didst persuade revenge,
It could not move thus.
OPHELIA: You must sing 'A-down, a-down,' and you 'Call him
a-down-a.' O, how the wheel becomes it! It is the false
stew ard, that stole his master's daughter.   170
LAERTES: This nothing's more than matter.
OPHELIA: There's rosemary, that's for remembrance. Pray you,
love, remember. And there is pansies, that's for thoughts.
LAERTES: A document in madness, thoughts and remem-
brance fitted.   175

---

144 **pelican** supposed to feed her young with her own blood
149 **level** plain   153 **virtue** power   159 **fine** refined to purity
169 **wheel** burden, refrain   172–180 Harold Jenkins, in his Arden edition of *Hamlet* (London and New York, 1982) 536–542, suggests that Ophelia gives rosemary (emblematic of remembrance) and pansies (of thoughts) to Laertes; that she gives fennel and columbines (both signifying marital infidelity) to the queen; she gives rue (for repentance) to the king (keeping some for herself as a sign of her sorrow, but noting that the king is to wear his rue with a **difference,** an heraldic term designating a mark for distinguishing one branch of a family from another in a coat-of-arms). The daisy, an emblem of love's victims, is given to the king as substitute for the absent Hamlet, whose absence he has caused. The king would also be given the violets (emblems of faithfulness, associated both with Ophelia's love for Hamlet, and Polonius's service to the state, both now lost) were these still available. Each gift of flowers represents a symbolic reproach to the recipient

OPHELIA: There's fennel for you, and columbines. There's rue
for you, and here's some for me. We may call it herb of grace
a Sundays. O, you must wear your rue with a difference.
There's a daisy. I would give you some violets, but they with
180   ered all when my father died. They say 'a made a good end,

    (*Sings.*)   For bonny sweet Robin is all my joy.

LAERTES: Thought and affliction, passion, hell itself,
    She turns to favor and to prettiness.
OPHELIA: (*Song.*)

        And will 'a not come again?
185   And will 'a not come again?
        No, no, he is dead:
        Go to thy death-bed:
        He never will come again.

        His beard was as white as snow,
190   All flaxen was his poll:
        He is gone, he is gone,
        And we cast away moan:
        God ha' mercy on his soul!

    And of all Christian souls, I pray God. God buy you. (*Exit.*)
195 LAERTES: Do you see this, O God?
KING: Laertes, I must commune with your grief,
    Or you deny me right. Go but apart,
    Make choice of whom your wisest friends you will,
    And they shall hear and judge 'twixt you and me.
200   If by direct or by collateral hand
    They find us touched, we will our kingdom give,
    Our crown, our life, and all that we call ours,
    To you in satisfaction; but if not,
    Be you content to lend your patience to us,
205   And we shall jointly labour with your soul
    To give it due content.
LAERTES: Let this be so.
    His means of death, his obscure funeral—
    No trophy, sword, nor hatchment, o'er his bones,
    No noble rite nor formal ostentation—
210   Cry to be heard, as 'twere from heaven to earth,
    That I must call't in question.
KING: So you shall;
    And where th' offence is let the great axe fall.
    I pray you go with me.

(*Exeunt.*)

SCENE VI

Enter HORATIO *and* OTHERS.

HORATIO: What are they that would speak with me?
GENTLEMAN: Sea-faring men, sir. They say they have letters
    for you.
HORATIO: Let them come in. (*Exit* GENTLEMAN.)
    I do not know from what part of the world
5   I should be greeted, if not from Lord Hamlet.

(*Enter* SAILORS.)

---

190 **poll** head   208 **hatchment** coat of arms

SAILOR: God bless you, sir.
HORATIO: Let him bless thee too.
SAILOR: 'A shall sir, an't please him. There's a letter for you,
    sir—it comes from th' ambassador that was bound for En-
    gland—if your name be Horatio, as I am let to know it is. 10
HORATIO: (*Reads.*) 'Horatio, when thou shalt have over-
    looked this, give these fellows some means to the king.
    They have letters for him. Ere we were two days old at
    sea, a pirate of very warlike appointment gave us chase.
    Finding ourselves too slow of sail, we put on a compelled 15
    valor, and in the grapple I boarded them. On the instant
    they got clear of our ship, so I alone became their pris-
    oner. They have dealt with me like thieves of mercy, but
    they knew what they did; I am to do a good turn for
    them. Let the king have the letters I have sent, and repair 20
    thou to me with as much speed as thou wouldest fly
    death. I have words to speak in thine ear will make thee
    dumb; yet are they much too light for the bore of the
    matter. These good fellows will bring thee where I am.
    Rosencrantz and Guildenstern hold their course for En- 25
    gland. Of them I have much to tell thee, Farewell.
                 'He that thou knowest thine, Hamlet.'
    Come, I will give you way for these your letters,
    And do't the speedier that you may direct me
    To him from whom you brought them.

(*Exeunt.*)

SCENE VII

Enter KING *and* LAERTES.

KING: Now must your conscience my acquittance seal,
    And you must put me in your heart for friend,
    Sith you have heard, and with a knowing ear,
    That he which hath your noble father slain
    Pursued my life.   5
LAERTES: It well appears. But tell me
    Why you proceeded not against these feats,
    So criminal and so capital in nature,
    As by your safety, wisdom, all things else,
    You mainly were stirred up.
KING: O, for two special reasons,
    Which may to you, perhaps, seem much unsinewed, 10
    But yet to me th' are strong. The queen his mother
    Lives almost by his looks, and for myself—
    My virtue or my plague, be it either which—
    She's so conjunctive to my life and soul
    That, as the star moves not but in his sphere, 15
    I could not but by her. The other motive,
    Why to a public count I might not go,
    Is the great love the general gender bear him,
    Who, dipping all his faults in their affection,
    Work, like the spring that turneth wood to stone, 20
    Convert his gyves to graces; so that my arrows,
    Too slightly timbered for so loud a wind,

IV.vi. 23 **bore** *literally, caliber of a gun; hence, size, importance*

IV.vii. 7 **capital** *punishable by death* 10 **unsinewed** *weak*
14 **conjunctive** *closely joined* 17 **count** *reckoning* 18 **general gender** *common people* 21 **gyves** *fetters*

Would have reverted to my bow again,
And not where I had aimed them.

25 LAERTES: And so have I a noble father lost,
A sister driven into desp'rate terms,
Whose worth, if praises may go back again,
Stood challenger on mount of all the age
For her perfections. But my revenge will come.

30 KING: Break not your sleeps for that. You must not think
That we are made of stuff so flat and dull
That we can let our beard be shook with danger,
And think it pastime. You shortly shall hear more.
I loved your father, and we love our self,

35 And that, I hope, will teach you to imagine—

(*Enter a* MESSENGER *with letters.*)

MESSENGER: These to your majesty; this to the queen.
KING: From Hamlet! Who brought them?
MESSENGER: Sailors, my lord, they say. I saw them not.
They were given me by Claudio; he received them

40 Of him that brought them.
KING: Laertes, you shall hear them.—
Leave us. (*Exit* MESSENGER.)
(*Reads.*) 'High and mighty, you shall know I am set naked
on your kingdom. To-morrow shall I beg leave to see
your kingly eyes, when I shall, first asking your pardon,

45 thereunto recount the occasion of my sudden and more
strange return.   Hamlet.'
What should this mean? Are all the rest come back?
Or is it some abuse, and no such thing?
LAERTES: Know you the hand?

50 KING: 'Tis Hamlet's character. 'Naked!'
And in a postscript here, he says 'alone.'
Can you devise me?
LAERTES: I am lost in it, my lord. But let him come.
It warms the very sickness in my heart

55 That I shall live and tell him to his teeth
'Thus didst thou.'
KING: If it be so, Laertes—
As how should it be so, how otherwise?—
Will you be ruled by me?
LAERTES: Ay, my lord,
So you will not o'errule me to a peace.

60 KING: To thine own peace. If he be now returned,
As checking at his voyage, and that he means

No more to undertake it, I will work him
To an exploit now ripe in my device,
Under the which he shall not choose but fall;
And for his death no wind of blame shall breathe   65
But even his mother shall uncharge the practice
And call it accident.
LAERTES: My lord, I will be ruled;
The rather if you could devise it so
That I might be the organ.
KING: It falls right.
You have been talked of since your travel much,   70
And that in Hamlet's hearing, for a quality
Wherein they say you shine. Your sum of parts
Did not together pluck such envy from him
As did that one, and that, in my regard,
Of the unworthiest siege.   75
LAERTES: What part is that, my lord?
KING: A very riband in the cap of youth,
Yet needful too, for youth no less becomes
The light and careless livery that it wears
Than settled age his sables and his weeds,
Importing health and graveness. Two months since   80
Here was a gentleman of Normandy.
I have seen myself, and served against, the French,
And they can well on horseback, but this gallant
Had witchcraft in't. He grew unto his seat,
And to such wondrous doing brought his horse,   85
As had he been incorpsed and demi-natured
With the brave beast. So far he topped my thought
That I, in forgery of shapes and tricks,
Come short of what he did.
LAERTES: A Norman was't?
KING: A Norman.   90
LAERTES: Upon my life, Lamord.
KING: The very same.
LAERTES: I know him well. He is the brooch indeed
And gem of all the nation.
KING: He made confession of you,
And gave you such a masterly report   95
For art and exercise in your defence,
And for your rapier most especial,
That he cried out 'twould be a sight indeed
If one could match you. The scrimers of their nation,
He swore had neither motion, guard, nor eye,   100
If you opposed them. Sir, this report of his
Did Hamlet so envenom with his envy
That he could nothing do but wish and beg
Your sudden coming o'er, to play with you.
Now out of this—   105
LAERTES: What out of this, my lord?
KING: Laertes, was your father dear to you?
Or are you like the painting of a sorrow,
A face without a heart?
LAERTES: Why ask you this?

---

35 Following the entrance of the Messenger, the King says in *F* "How now? What Newes?" and the Messenger replies, "Letters my Lord from *Hamlet*." Jenkins comments (*SB* 13.36): "In *Q* the King is not told the letters come from Hamlet; he is left to find this out as he reads, and his cry 'From *Hamlet*' betokens his astonishment on doing so. I think Hamlet would not have approved of the *F* messenger who robs his bomb of the full force of its explosion. Shakespeare's messenger did not even know he carried such a bomb, for the letters had reached him via sailors who were ignorant of their sender. They took him for 'th' Embassador that was bound for *England*' (4.4.9). *F,* with its too knowledgeable messenger, by seeking to enhance the effect, destroys it" 52 **devise** explain to 61 **checking at** turning aside from (like a falcon turning from its quarry for other prey)

---

66 **uncharge the practice** regard the deed as free from villainy 69 **organ** instrument 75 **siege** rank 79 **weeds** garments 86 **incorpsed** made one body; **demi-natured** like a centaur, half man half horse 87 **topped** excelled 88 **forgery** invention 99 **scrimers** fencers (French *escrimeurs*)

KING: Not that I think you did not love your father,
110　But that I know love is begun by time,
　　And that I see, in passages of proof,
　　Time qualifies the spark and fire of it.
　　There lives within the very flame of love
　　A kind of wick or snuff that will abate it,
115　And nothing is at a like goodness still,
　　For goodness, growing to a plurisy,
　　Dies in his own too much. That we would do,
　　We should do when we would; for this 'would' changes,
　　And hath abatements and delays as many
120　As there are tongues, are hands, are accidents,
　　And then this 'should' is like a spendthrift's sigh,
　　That hurts by easing. But to the quick of th' ulcer—
　　Hamlet comes back; what would you undertake
　　To show yourself in deed your father's son
125　More than in words?
LAERTES:　　　　　　　To cut his throat i' th' church.
KING: No place, indeed, should murder sanctuarize;
　　Revenge should have no bounds. But good Laertes,
　　Will you do this, keep close within your chamber;
　　Hamlet returned shall know you are come home;
130　We'll put on those shall praise your excellence,
　　And set a double varnish on the fame
　　The Frenchman gave you, bring you in fine together,
　　And wager on your heads. He, being remiss,
　　Most generous, and free from all contriving,
135　Will not peruse the foils, so that with ease,
　　Or with a little shuffling, you may choose
　　A sword unbated, and in a pass of practice
　　Requite him for your father.
LAERTES:　　　　　　　　I will do't,
　　And for that purpose I'll anoint my sword.
140　I bought an unction of a mountebank
　　So mortal that but dip a knife in it,
　　Where it draws blood no cataplasm so rare,
　　Collected from all simples that have virtue
　　Under the moon, can save the thing from death
145　That is but scratched withal. I'll touch my point
　　With this contagion, that if I gall him slightly,
　　It may be death.
KING:　　　　　Let's further think of this,
　　Weigh what convenience both of time and means
　　May fit us to our shape. If this should fail,
150　And that our drift look through our bad performance,
　　'Twere better not assayed. Therefore this project
　　Should have a back or second that might hold
　　If this should blast in proof. Soft! let me see.
　　We'll make a solemn wager on your cunnings—
155　I ha't.
　　When in your motion you are hot and dry—

As make your bouts more violent to that end—
And that he calls for drink, I'll have preferred him
A chalice for the nonce, whereon but sipping,
If he by chance escape your venomed stuck,　　　160
Our purpose may hold there.—But stay, what noise?

(*Enter* QUEEN.)

QUEEN: One woe doth tread upon another's heel,
　　So fast they follow. Your sister's drowned, Laertes.
LAERTES: Drowned! O, where?
QUEEN: There is a willow grows askant the brook　　165
　　That shows his hoar leaves in the glassy stream.
　　Therewith fantastic garlands did she make
　　Of crowflowers, nettles, daisies, and long purples
　　That liberal shepherds give a grosser name,
　　But our cold maids do dead men's fingers call them.　170
　　There on the pendent boughs her crownet weeds
　　Clamb'ring to hang, an envious sliver broke,
　　When down her weedy trophies and herself
　　Fell in the weeping brook. Her clothes spread wide,
　　And mermaid-like awhile they bore her up,　　175
　　Which time she chanted snatches of old lauds,
　　As one incapable of her own distress,
　　Or like a creature native and indued
　　Unto that element. But long it could not be
　　Till that her garments, heavy with their drink,　　180
　　Pulled the poor wretch from her melodious lay
　　To muddy death.
LAERTES:　　　　Alas, then, she is drowned?
QUEEN: Drowned, drowned.
LAERTES: Too much of water hast thou, poor Ophelia,
　　And therefore I forbid my tears; but yet　　185
　　It is our trick; nature her custom holds,
　　Let shame say what it will. When these are gone,
　　The woman will be out. Adieu, my lord.
　　I have a speech o' fire that fain would blaze
　　But that this folly drowns it.　　190

(*Exit.*)

KING:　　　　　　　　Let's follow, Gertrude.
　　How much I had to do to calm his rage!
　　Now fear I this will give it start again;
　　Therefore let's follow.

(*Exeunt.*)

ACT FIVE

SCENE I

Enter two CLOWNS.

---

111 **passages of proof** incidents of experience　112 **qualifies** weakens　116 **plurisy** excess　122 **quick** sensitive flesh　126 **sanctuarize** give sanctuary to　133 **remiss** careless　135 **peruse** inspect　137 **unbated** not blunted; **pass of practice** treacherous thrust　142 **cataplasm** poultice　143 **simples** medicinal herbs　149 **shape** plan　150 **drift** scheme　152 **back or second** something in support　153 **blast in proof** burst during trial (like a faulty cannon)　156 **motion** exertion

158 **preferred** offered to　159 **nonce** occasion　160 **stuck** thrust　165 **askant** alongside　166 **hoar** gray　169 **liberal** free-spoken, licentious　170 **cold** chaste　171 **crownet** coronet　172 **envious** malicious　176 **lauds** hymns　177 **incapable of** insensible to　178 **indued** endowed　188 **woman** unmanly part of nature

V.i. s.d. **clowns** rustics

CLOWN: Is she to be buried in Christian burial when she wil-
fully seeks her own salvation?

OTHER: I tell thee she is, therefore make her grave straight.
The crowner hath sat on her, and finds it Christian burial.

5 CLOWN: How can that be, unless she drowned herself in her
own defence?

OTHER: Why, 'tis found so.

CLOWN: It must be 'se offendendo', it cannot be else. For here
lies the point: if I drown myself wittingly, it argues an act,
10 and an act hath three branches—it is to act, to do, and to
perform; argal, she drowned herself wittingly.

OTHER: Nay, but hear you, Goodman Delver.

CLOWN: Give me leave. Here lies the water; good. Here
stands the man; good. If the man go to this water and
15 drown himself, it is, will he, nill he, he goes—mark you
that. But if the water come to him and drown him, he
drowns not himself. Argal, he that is not guilty of his own
death shortens not his own life.

OTHER: But is this law?

20 CLOWN: Ay, marry, is't; crowner's quest law.

OTHER: Will you ha' the truth on 't? If this had not been a
gentlewoman, she should have been buried out o' Christian burial.

CLOWN: Why, there thou say'st. And the more pity that great
25 folk should have count'nance in this world to drown or
hang themselves more than their even-Christen. Come, my
spade. There is no ancient gentlemen but gard'ners, ditch-
ers, and grave-makers. They hold up Adam's profession.

OTHER: Was he a gentleman?

30 CLOWN: 'A was the first that ever bore arms.

OTHER: Why, he had none.

CLOWN: What, art a heathen? How dost thou understand the
Scripture? The Scripture says Adam digged. Could he dig
without arms? I'll put another question to thee. If thou
35 answerest me not to the purpose, confess thyself—

OTHER: Go to.

CLOWN: What is he that builds stronger than either the mason, the shipwright, or the carpenter?

OTHER: The gallows-maker for that frame outlives a thousand
40 tenants.

CLOWN: I like thy wit well, in good faith. The gallows does
well. But how does it well? It does well to those that do
ill. Now thou dost ill to say the gallows is built stronger
than the church. Argal, the gallows may do well to thee.
45 To't again, come.

OTHER: 'Who builds stronger than a mason, a shipwright, or
a carpenter?'

CLOWN: Ay tell me that, and unyoke.

OTHER: Marry, now I can tell.

50 CLOWN: To't.

OTHER: Mass, I cannot tell.

(*Enter* HAMLET *and* HORATIO *afar off.*)

CLOWN: Cudgel thy brains no more about it, for your dull ass
will not mend his pace with beating. And when you are
asked this question next, say 'a grave-maker.' The houses
he makes lasts till doomsday. Go, get thee in, and fetch me 55
a stoup of liquor. (*Exit* OTHER CLOWN.)

(HAMLET *and* HORATIO *come forward as* CLOWN *digs and sings.*)

(*Song.*)

In youth, when I did love, did love,
    Methought it was very sweet,
To contract-O-the time, for-a-my behove,
    O, methought, there-a-was nothing-a-meet.   60

HAMLET: Has this fellow no feeling of his business, that 'a
sings at gravemaking?

HORATIO: Custom hath made it in him a property of easiness.

HAMLET: 'Tis e'en so. The hand of little employment hath
the daintier sense.   65

CLOWN: (*Song.*)

But age, with his stealing steps,
    Hath clawed me in his clutch,
And hath shipped me into the land,
    As if I had never been such.

(*Throws up a skull.*)

HAMLET: That skull had a tongue in it, and could sing once. 70
How the knave jowls it to the ground, as if 'twere Cain's
jawbone, that did the first murder! This might be the pate
of a politician, which this ass now o'erreaches; one that
would circumvent God, might it not?

HORATIO: It might, my lord.   75

HAMLET: Or of a courtier, which could say 'Good morrow,
sweet lord! How dost thou, sweet lord?' This might be my
Lord Such-a-one, that praised my Lord Such-a-one's
horse, when 'a went to beg it, might it not?

HORANTIO: Ay, my lord.   80

HAMLET: Why, e'en so, and now my Lady Worm's, chopless,
and knock'd about the mazzard with a sexton's spade.
Here's fine revolution, an we had the trick to see't. Did
these bones cost no more the breeding but to play at loggats with them? Mine ache to think on't.   85

CLOWN: (*Song.*)

A pick-axe and a spade, a spade,
    For and a shrouding sheet:
O, a pit of clay for to be made
    For such a guest is meet.

(*Throws up another skull.*)

HAMLET: There's another. Why may not that be the skull of 90
a lawyer? Where be his quiddities now, his quillets, his

---

4 **crowner** coroner   8 **se offendendo** the Clown's blunder for
se defendendo ("in self-defense")   11 **argal** therefore (corrupt form of *ergo*)   20 **quest** inquest   26 **even-Christen** fellow Christian   48 **tell me that, and unyoke** answer the
question and then you can relax

---

56 **stoup** tankard   59 **behove** benefit   59–60 The repeated *a*
and *o* may represent the Clown's vocal embellishments, but more
probably they represent his grunting as he takes breath in the
course of his digging   63 **a property of easiness** a habit that
comes easily to him   71 **jowls** hurls   74 **circumvent** cheat
81 **chopless** with lower jaw missing   82 **mazzard** head
84–85 **loggats** small logs of wood for throwing at a mark   91
quiddities subtle distinctions; **quillets** quibbles

cases, his tenures, and his tricks? Why does he suffer this mad knave now to knock him about the sconce with a dirty shovel, and will not tell him of his action of battery?
95 Hum! This fellow might be in's time a great buyer of land, with his statutes, his recognizances, his fines, his double vouchers, his recoveries. Is this the fine of his fines, and the recovery of his recoveries, to have his fine pate full of fine dirt? Will his vouchers vouch him no more of his pur-
100 chases, and double ones too, than the length and breadth of a pair of indentures? The very conveyances of his lands will scarcely lie in this box, and must th' inheritor himself have no more, ha?

HORATIO: Not a jot more, my lord.

105 HAMLET: Is not parchment made of sheepskins?

HORANTIO: Ay, my lord, and of calves' skins too.

HAMLET: They are sheep and calves which seek out assurance in that. I will speak to this fellow. Whose grave's this, sirrah?

CLOWN: Mine, sir. (*Sings.*)

110   O, a pit of clay for to be made—

HAMLET: I think it be thine indeed, for thou liest in't.

CLOWN: You lie out on't, sir, and therefore 'tis not yours. For my part, I do not lie in't, yet it is mine.

HAMLET: Thou dost lie in't, to be in't and say it is thine. 'Tis
115 for the dead, not for the quick; therefore thou liest.

CLOWN: 'Tis a quick lie, sir; 'twill away again from me to you.

HAMLET: What man dost thou dig it for?

CLOWN: For no man, sir.

HAMLET: What woman, then?

120 CLOWN: For none neither.

HAMLET: Who is to be buried in't?

CLOWN: One that was a woman, sir; but, rest her soul, she's dead.

HAMLET: How absolute the knave is! We must speak by the
125 card, or equivocation will undo us. By the Lord, Horatio, this three years I have took note of it, the age is grown so picked that the toe of the peasant comes so near the heel of the courtier, he galls his kibe. How long hast thou been a grave-maker?

130 CLOWN: Of all the day i' th' year, I came to't that day that our last King Hamlet overcame Fortinbras.

HAMLET: How long is that since?

CLOWN: Cannot you tell that? Every fool can tell that. It was that very day that young Hamlet was born—he that is
135 mad, and sent into England.

HAMLET: Ay, marry, why was he sent into England?

CLOWN: Why, because 'a was mad. 'A shall recover his wits there; or, if a do not, 'tis no great matter there.

HAMLET: Why?

140 CLOWN: 'Twill not be seen in him there. There the men are as mad as he.

---

96 **recognizances** legal bonds, defining debts; vouchers persons vouched or called on to warrant a title 97 **recoveries** legal processes to break an entail 100–101 **pair of indentures** deed or legal agreement in duplicate 101 **conveyances** deeds by which property is transferred 124 **absolute** positive 125 **card** card on which the points of the mariner's compass are marked (i.e., absolutely to the point) 127 **picked** fastidious 128 **kibe** chilblain

HAMLET: How came he mad?

CLOWN: Very strangely, they say.

HAMLET: How strangely?

CLOWN: Faith, e'en with losing his wits. 145

HAMLET: Upon what ground?

CLOWN: Why, here in Denmark. I have been sexton here, man and boy, thirty years.

HAMLET: How long will a man lie i' th' earth ere he rot?

CLOWN: Faith, if 'a be not rotten before 'a die—as we have 150
many pocky corses now-a-days that will scarce hold the laying in—'a will last you some eight year or nine year. A tanner will last you nine year.

HAMLET: Why he more than another?

CLOWN: Why, sir, his hide is so tanned with his trade that 'a 155
will keep out water a great while and your water is a sore decayer of your whoreson dead body. Here's a skull now hath lain you i' th' earth three and twenty years.

HAMLET: Whose was it?

CLOWN: A whoreson mad fellow's it was. Whose do you 160
think it was?

HAMLET: Nay, I know not.

CLOWN: A pestilence on him for a mad rogue! 'a poured a flagon of Rhenish on my head once. This same skull, sir, was, sir, Yorick's skull, the king's jester. 165

HAMLET: (*Takes the skull.*) This?

CLOWN: E'en That.

HAMLET: Alas, poor Yorick! I knew him, Horatio—a fellow of infinite jest, of most excellent fancy. He hath bore me on his back a thousand times, and now how abhorred in my 170
imagination it is! My gorge rises at it. Here hung those lips that I have kissed I know not how oft. Where be your gibes now, your gambols, your songs, your flashes of merriment that were wont to set the table on a roar? Not one now to mock your own grinning? Quite chop-fall'n? 175
Now get you to my lady's chamber, and tell her, let her paint an inch thick, to this favour she must come. Make her laugh at that. Prithee, Horatio, tell me one thing.

HORATIO: What's that, my lord?

HAMLET: Dost thou think Alexander looked o' this fashion i' 180
th' earth?

HORATIO: E'en so.

HAMLET: And smelt so? Pah!

(*Throws down the skull.*)

HORATIO: E'en so, my lord.

HAMLET: To what base uses we may return, Horatio! Why 185
may not imagination trace the noble dust of Alexander till 'a find it stopping a bung-hole?

HORATIO: 'Twere to consider too curiously to consider so.

HAMLET: No, faith, not a jot, but to follow him thither with modesty enough, and likelihood to lead it. Alexander died, 190
Alexander was buried, Alexander returneth to dust; the dust is earth; of earth we make loam; and why of that loam whereto he was converted might they not stop a beer-barrel?

       Imperious Caesar, dead and turned to clay,
       Might stop a hole to keep the wind away. 195

---

151 **pocky** infected with pox (syphilis) 164 **Rhenish** Rhine wine 188 **too curiously** over ingeniously

O, that that earth which kept the world in awe
Should patch a wall t'expel the winter's flaw!

But soft, but soft awhile! Here comes the king,
The queen, the courtiers.

(*Enter* KING, QUEEN, LAERTES, *and the Corse* [*with a Doctor of Divinity as* PRIEST *and* LORDS *attendant*].)

         Who is this they follow?
200 And with such maimèd rites? This doth betoken
The corse they follow did with desperate hand
Fordo it own life. 'Twas of some estate.
Couch we awhile and mark.

(*Retires with* HORATIO.)

LAERTES: What ceremony else?
205 HAMLET: That is Laertes, a very noble youth. Mark.
LAERTES: What ceremony else?
DOCTOR: Her obsequies have been as far enlarged
As we have warranty. Her death was doubtful,
And but that great command o'ersways the order,
210 She should in ground unsanctified been lodged
Till the last trumpet. For charitable prayers,
Shards, flints and pebbles should be thrown on her.
Yet here she is allowed her virgin crants,
Her maiden strewments and the bringing home
215 Of bell and burial.
LAERTES: Must there no more be done?
DOCTOR: No more be done.
We should profane the service of the dead
To sing a requiem and such rest to her
As to peace-parted souls.
LAERTES: Lay her i' th' earth,
220 And from her fair and unpolluted flesh
May violets spring! I tell thee, churlish priest,
A minist'ring angel shall my sister be
When thou liest howling.
HAMLET: What, the fair Ophelia!
QUEEN: Sweets to the sweet. Farewell!

(*Scatters flowers.*)

225 I hoped thou shouldst have been my Hamlet's wife.
I thought thy bride-bed to have decked, sweet maid,
And not have strewed thy grave.
LAERTES: O treble woe
Fall ten times treble on that cursèd head,
Whose wicked deed thy most ingenious sense
230 Deprived thee of! Hold off the earth awhile,
Till I have caught her once more in mine arms.

(*Leaps into the grave.*)

Now pile your dust upon the quick and dead,
Till of this flat a mountain you have made

T' o'er-top old Pelion or the skyish head
Of blue Olympus.   235
HAMLET: (*Coming forward.*) What is he whose grief
Bears such an emphasis, whose phrase of sorrow
Conjures the wand'ring stars, and makes them stand
Like wonder-wounded hearers? This is I,
Hamlet the Dane.

(LAERTES *climbs out of the grave.*)   240

LAERTES: The devil take thy soul!

(*Grappling with him.*)

HAMLET: Thou pray'st not well.
I prithee take thy fingers from my throat,
For though I am not splenitive and rash,
Yet have I in me something dangerous,
Which let thy wisdom fear. Hold off thy hand.
KING: Pluck them asunder.   245
QUEEN: Hamlet! Hamlet!
ALL: Gentlemen!
HORATIO: Good my lord, be quiet.

(*The* ATTENDANTS *part them.*)

HAMLET: Why, I will fight with him upon this theme
Until my eyelids will no longer wag.   250
QUEEN: O my son, what theme?
HAMLET: I loved Ophelia. Forty thousand brothers
Could not with all their quantity of love
Make up my sum. What wilt thou do for her?
KING: O, he is mad, Laertes.   255
QUEEN: For love of God, forbear him.
HAMLET: 'Swounds, show me what thou't do.
Woo't weep, woo't fight, woo't fast, woo't tear thyself,
Woo't drink up eisel, eat a crocodile?
I'll do't. Dost come here to whine?   260
To outface me with leaping in her grave?
Be buried quick with her, and so will I,
And if thou prate of mountains, let them throw
Millions of acres on us, till our ground,
Singeing his pate against the burning zone, 265
Make Ossa like a wart! Nay, an thou'lt mouth,
I'll rant as well as thou.
QUEEN: This is mere madness;
And thus awhile the fit will work on him.
Anon, as patient as the female dove
When that her golden couplets are disclosed, 270
His silence will sit drooping.
HAMLET: Hear you, sir.
What is the reason that you use me thus?

---

234 **Pelion** a mountain in Thessaly, like Olympus, line 235, and Ossa, line 266 (the allusion is to the war in which the Titans fought the gods and, in their attempt to scale heaven, heaped Ossa and Olympus on Pelion, or Pelion and Ossa on Olympus) 237 **such an emphasis** so vehement an expression or display 242 **splenitive** fiery-tempered (from the spleen, seat of anger) 258 **Woo't** wilt (thou) 259 **eisel** vinegar 270 **couplets** newly hatched pair

---

197 **flaw** gust 202 **Fordo** destroy; **it** its 212 **Shards** bits of broken pottery 213 **crants** garland 229 **most ingenious** of quickest apprehension

I loved you ever. But it is no matter.
Let Hercules himself do what he may,
275   The cat will mew, and dog will have his day.
KING: I pray thee, good Horatio, wait upon him.

(*Exit* HAMLET *and* HORATIO.)

(*To* LAERTES.) Strengthen your patience in our last night's
speech.
We'll put the matter to the present push.—
Good Gertrude, set some watch over your son.—
280   This grave shall have a living monument.
An hour of quiet shortly shall we see;
Till then in patience our proceeding be.

(*Exeunt.*)

SCENE II

Enter HAMLET *and* HORATIO.

HAMLET: So much for this, sir; now shall you see the other.
You do remember all the circumstance?
HORATIO: Remember it, my lord!
HAMLET: Sir, in my heart there was a kind of fighting
5   That would not let me sleep. Methought I lay
Worse than the mutines in the bilboes. Rashly,
And praised be rashness for it—let us know,
Our indiscretion sometime serves us well,
When our deep plots do pall; and that should learn us
10   There's a divinity that shapes our ends,
Rough-hew them how we will—
HORATIO: That is most certain.
HAMLET: Up from my cabin,
My sea-gown scarfed about me, in the dark
Groped I to find out them, had my desire,
15   Fingered their packet, and in fine withdrew
To mine own room again, making so bold,
My fears forgetting manners, to unseal
Their grand commission; where I found, Horatio—
Ah, royal knavery!—an exact command,
20   Larded with many several sorts of reasons
Importing Denmark's health and England's too,
With, ho! such bugs and goblins in my life,
That on the supervise, no leisure bated,
No, not to stay the grinding of the axe,
25   My head should be struck off.
HORATIO: Is't possible?
HAMLET: Here's the commission; read it at more leisure.
But will thou hear me how I did proceed?
HORATIO: I beseech you.
HAMLET: Being thus benetted round with villainies,
30   Or I could make a prologue to my brains,
They had begun the play. I sat me down,
Devised a new commission, wrote it fair.

I once did hold it, as our statists do,
A baseness to write fair, and laboured much
How to forget that learning; but sir, now   35
It did me yeoman's service. Wilt thou know
Th' effect of what I wrote?
HORATIO: Ay, good my lord.
HAMLET: An earnest conjuration from the king,
As England was his faithful tributary,
As love between them like the palm might flourish, 40
As peace should still her wheaten garland wear
And stand a comma 'tween their amities,
And many such like as's of great charge,
That on the view and knowing of these contents,
Without debatement further more or less,   45
He should the bearers put to sudden death,
Not shriving-time allowed.
HORATIO: How was this sealed?
HAMLET: Why, even in that was heaven ordinant,
I had my father's signet in my pursue,
Which was the model of that Danish seal,   50
Folded the writ up the form of th' other,
Subscribed it, gave't th' impression, placed it safely,
The changeling never known. Now the next day
Was our sea-fight, and what to this was sequent
Thou knowest already.   55
HORATIO: So Guildenstern and Rosencrantz go to't.
HAMLET: Why, man, they did make love to this employment.
They are not near my conscience; their defeat
Does by their own insinuation grow.
'Tis dangerous when the baser nature comes   60
Between the pass and fell incensèd points
Of mighty opposites.
HORATIO: Why, what a king is this!
HAMLET: Does it not, think thee, stand me now upon—
He that hath killed my king and whored my mother,
Popped in between th' election and my hopes,   65
Thrown out his angle for my proper life,
And with such coz'nage—is't not perfect conscience,
To quit him with this arm? And is't not to be damned
To let this canker of our nature come
In further evil?   70
HORATIO: It must be shortly known to him from England
What is the issue of the business there.
HAMLET: It will be short; the interim is mine.
And a man's life's no more than to say 'one.'
But I am very sorry, good Horatio,   75
That to Laertes I forgot myself;
For by the image of my cause I see
The portraiture of his. I'll court his favours.

V.ii. 6 **mutines** mutineers; **bilboes** fetters   9 **pall** fail   15
Fingered filched   20 **Larded** garnished   22 **bugs and goblins** imaginary horrors (here, horrendous crimes attributed to
Hamlet, and represented as dangers should he be allowed to live)
23 **supervise** perusal; **bated** deducted, allowed   24 **stay** await
30 **Or** ere

33 **statists** statesmen   42 **comma** a connective that also acknowledges separateness   43 **charge** (1) importance (2) burden
(the double meaning fits the play that makes "as's" into "asses")
48 **ordinant** guiding   52 **Subscribed** signed   59 **insinuation**
intrusion   61 **pass** thrust; **fell** fierce   63 **Does it not . . .
stand me now upon** is it not incumbent upon me   65 **election** i.e., to the kingship. Denmark being an elective monarchy
66 **angle** fishing line; **proper** own   68 **quit** repay

But sure the bravery of his grief did put me
80 Into a tow'ring passion.
HORATIO: Peace; who comes here?

(*Enter* [OSRIC] *a courtier.*)

OSRIC: Your lordship is right welcome back to Denmark.
HAMLET: I humbly thank you, sir. (*Aside to* HORATIO.) Dost
    know this water-fly?
HORATIO: (*Aside to* HAMLET.) No, my good lord.
85 HAMLET: (*Aside to* HORATIO.) Thy state is the more gracious,
    for 'tis a vice to know him. He hath much land, and fer-
    tile. Let a beast be lord of beasts, and his crib shall stand at
    the king's mess. 'Tis a chough, but as I say, spacious in the
    possession of dirt.
90 OSRIC: Sweet lord, if your lordship were at leisure, I should
    impart a thing to you from his majesty.
HAMLET: I will receive it, sir, with all diligence of spirit. Put
    your bonnet to his right use. 'Tis for the head.
OSRIC: I thank you lordship, it is very hot.
95 HAMLET: No, believe me, 'tis very cold; the wind is northerly.
OSRIC: It is indifferent cold, my lord, indeed.
HAMLET: But yet methinks it is very sultry and hot for my
    complexion.
OSRIC: Exceedingly, my lord; it is very sultry, as 'twere—I can
100   not tell how. My lord, his majesty bade me signify to you
    that 'a has laid a great wager on your head. Sir, this is the
    matter—
HAMLET: I beseech you, remember.

(HAMLET *moves him to put on his hat.*)

OSRIC: Nay, good my lord; for my ease, in good faith. Sir, here
105   is newly come to court Laertes; believe me, an absolute
    gentleman, full of most excellent differences, of very soft
    society and great showing. Indeed, to speak feelingly of
    him, he is the card or calendar of gentry, for you shall find
    in him the continent of what part a gentleman would see.
110 HAMLET: Sir, his definement suffers, no perdition in you,
    though I know to divide him inventorially would dozy th'
    arithmetic of memory, and yet but yaw neither in respect
    of his quick sail. But in the verity of extolment, I take him
    to be a soul of great article, and his infusion of such dearth
115   and rareness as, to make true diction of him, his semblable
    is his mirror, and who else would trace him, his umbrage,
    nothing more.
OSRIC: Your lordship speaks most infallibly of him.
HAMLET: The concernancy, sir? Why do we wrap the gentle-
120   man in our more rawer breath?
OSRIC: Sir?

HORATIO: It's not possible to understand in another tongue?
    You will to't, sir, really.
HAMLET: What imports the nomination of this gentleman?
OSRIC: Of Laertes?   125
HORATIO: (*Aside.*) His purse is empty already. All's golden
    words are spent.
HAMLET: Of him, sir.
OSRIC: I know you are not ignorant—
HAMLET: I would you did, sir; yet, in faith, if you did, it would   130
    not much approve me. Well, sir.
OSRIC: You are not ignorant of what excellence Laertes is—
HAMLET: I dare not confess that, lest I should compare with
    him in excellence; but to know a man well were to know
    himself.   135
OSRIC: I mean, sir, for his weapon; but in the imputation laid
    on him by them in his meed, he's unfellowed.
HAMLET: What's his weapon?
OSRIC: Rapier and dagger.
HAMLET: That's two of his weapons—but well.   140
OSRIC: The king, sir, hath wagered with him six Barbary
    horses, against the which he has impawned, as I take it, six
    French rapiers and poniards, with their assigns, as girdle,
    hangers, and so. Three of the carriages, in faith, are very
    dear to fancy, very responsive to the hilts, most delicate   145
    carriages, and of very liberal conceit.
HAMLET: What call you the carriages?
HORATIO: (*Aside to* HAMLET.) I knew you must be edified by
    the margent ere you had done.
OSRIC: The carriages, sir, are the hangers.   150
HAMLET: The phrase would be more germane to the matter
    if we could carry cannon by our sides. I would it might
    be hangers till then. But on! Six Barbary horses against six
    French swords, their assigns, and three liberal conceited
    carriages; that's the French bet against the Danish. Why is   155
    this all impawned, as you call it?
OSRIC: The king, sir, hath laid, sir, that in a dozen passes be-
    tween yourself and him he shall not exceed you three hits;
    he hath laid on twelve for nine, and it would come to im-
    mediate trial if your lordship would vouchsafe the answer.   160
HAMLET: How if I answer no?
OSRIC: I mean, my lord, the opposition of your person in trial.
HAMLET: Sir, I will walk here in the hall. If it please his
    majesty, it is the breathing time of day with me. Let the
    foils be brought, the gentleman willing, and the king hold   165
    his purpose; I will win for him an I can. If not, I will gain
    nothing but my shame and the odd hits.

---

79 **bravery** ostentatious display   88 **mess** table; **chough** jackdaw; thus, a chatterer   96 **indifferent** somewhat   98 **complexion** temperament   106 **differences** distinguishing
qualities   107 **great showing** distinguished appearance   108
card map   109 **continent** all-containing embodiment   110
definement definition   111 **divide him inventorially** classify
him in detail; **dozy** dizzy   112 **yaw** hold to a course unsteadily,
like a ship that steers wild   114 **article** scope, importance; **in-
fusion** essence; **dearth** scarcity   115 **semblable** likeness   116
trace (1) draw, (2) follow; **umbrage** shadow   119 **concernancy** import, relevance

123 **to't** i.e., to get an understanding   124 **nomination** mention
131 **approve** commend   133 **compare** compete   137 **meed**
pay; **unfellowed** unequaled   142 **impawned** staked   143 **assigns** appendages   144 **carriages** an affected word for hangers,
i.e., straps from which the weapon was hung   146 **liberal conceit**
elaborate design   149 **margent** margin (where explanatory notes
were printed)   157–158 **in a dozen passes . . . he shall not exceed you three hits** the odds the King proposes seem to be that in
a match of twelve bouts, Hamlet will win at least five. Laertes would
need to win by at least eight to four   159 **he hath laid on twelve
for nine** "he" apparently is Laertes, who has seemingly raised the
odds against himself by wagering that out of twelve bouts he will win
nine   164 **breathing time** time for taking exercise   166 **an** if

OSRIC: Shall I deliver you so?

HAMLET: To this effect, sir, after what flourish your nature will.

170 OSRIC: I commend my duty to your lordship.

HAMLET: Yours. (*Exit* OSRIC.) He does well to commend it himself; there are no tongues else for's turn.

HORATIO: This lapwing runs away with the shell on his head.

HAMLET: 'A did comply, sir, with his dug, before 'a sucked it.

175 Thus has he, and many more of the same bevy that I know the drossy age dotes on, only got the tune of the time; and out of an habit of encounter, a kind of yesty collection which carries them through and through the most fanned and winnowed opinions; and do but blow them to their

180 trial, the bubbles are out.

(*Enter a* LORD.)

LORD: My lord, his majesty commended him to you by young Osric, who brings back to him that you attend him in the hall. He sends to know if your pleasure hold to play with Laertes, or that you will take longer time.

185 HAMLET: I am constant to my purposes: they follow the king's pleasure. If his fitness speaks, mine is ready; now or when-soever, provided I be so able as now.

LORD: The king and queen and all are coming down.

HAMLET: In happy time.

190 LORD: The queen desires you to use some gentle entertain-ment to Laertes before you fall to play.

HAMLET: She well instructs me.

(*Exit* LORD.)

HORATIO: You will lose, my lord.

HAMLET: I do not think so. Since he went into France, I have

195 been in continual practice. I shall win at the odds. But thou wouldst not think how ill all's here about my heart. But it is no matter.

HORATIO: Nay, good my lord—

HAMLET: It is but foolery, but it is such a kind of gaingiving

200 as would perhaps trouble a woman.

HORATIO: If your mind dislike any thing, obey it. I will fore-stall their repair hither, and say you are not fit.

HAMLET: Not a whit, we defy augury. There is a special prov-idence in the fall of a sparrow. If it be now, 'tis not to

205 come; if it be not to come, it will be now; if it be not now, yet it will come. The readiness is all. Since no man of aught he leaves knows, what is't to leave betimes? Let be.

(*A table prepared.* [*Enter*] *trumpets, drums, and* OFFICERS *with cushions;* KING, QUEEN, [OSRIC,] *and all the* STATE, [*with*] *foils, daggers, and* LAERTES.)

KING: Come, Hamlet, come, and take this hand from me.

(*The* KING *puts* LAERTES' *hand into* HAMLET's.)

HAMLET: Give me your pardon, sir. I have done you wrong,
But pardon 't as you are a gentleman.   210
This presence knows, and you must needs have heard,
How I am punished with a sore distraction.
What I have done
That might your nature, honour, and exception,
Roughly awake, I here proclaim was madness.   215
Was 't Hamlet wronged Laertes? Never Hamlet.
If Hamlet from himself be ta'en away,
And when he's not himself does wrong Laertes,
Then Hamlet does it not. Hamlet denies it.
Who does it then? His madness. If 't be so,   220
Hamlet is of the faction that is wronged;
His madness is poor Hamlet's enemy.
Sir, in this audience,
Let my disclaiming from a purposed evil
Free me so far in your most generous thoughts   225
That I have shot mine arrow o'er the house,
And hurt my brother.

LAERTES: I am satisfied in nature,
Whose motive in this case should stir me most
To my revenge. But in my terms of honor
I stand aloof, and will no reconcilement   230
Till by some elder masters of known honor,
I have a voice and precedent of peace
To keep my name ungored. But till that time
I do receive your offered love like love,
And will not wrong it.   235

HAMLET: I embrace if freely,
And will this brother's wager frankly play.
Give us the foils.

LAERTES: Come, one for me.

HAMLET: I'll be your foil, Laertes. In mine ignorance
Your skill shall, like a star i' th' darkest night,
Stick fiery off indeed.   240

LAERTES: You mock me, sir.

HAMLET: No, by this hand.

KING: Give them the foils, young Osric. Cousin Hamlet,
You know the wager?

HAMLET: Very well, my lord;
Your Grace has laid the odds o'th' weaker side.

KING: I do not fear it, I have seen you both;   245
But since he is bettered, we have therefore odds.

LAERTES: This is too heavy; let me see another.

HAMLET: This likes me well. These foils have all a length?

(*They prepare to play.*)

OSRIC: Ay, my good lord.

KING: Set me the stoups of wine upon that table.   250
If Hamlet give the first or second hit,
Or quit in answer of the third exchange,
Let all the battlements their ordnance fire.

---

173 **lapwing** a bird reputedly so precocious as to run as soon as hatched   174 **comply** observe the formalities of courtesy; **dug** mother's nipple   175 **bevy** a covey of quails or lapwings   176 **drossy** frivolous   177 **encounter** manner of address or accost-ing; **yesty collection** a frothy and superficial patchwork of terms from the conversation of others   179 **winnowed** tested, freed from inferior elements   186 **fitness** convenience, inclina-tion   199 **gaingiving** misgiving

---

232 **voice and precedent** authoritative statement justified by precedent   238 **foil** (1) setting for gem (2) weapon   246 **bet-tered** perfected through training   248 **have all a length** are all of the same length   252 **quit in answer** literally, give as good as he gets (i.e., if the third bout is a draw)

The king shall drink to Hamlet's better breath,
255 And in the cup an union shall he throw,
Richer than that which four successive kings
In Denmark's crown have worn. Give me the cups,
And let the kettle to the trumpet speak,
The trumpet to the cannoneer without,
260 The cannons to the heavens, the heaven to earth,
'Now the king drinks to Hamlet.' Come begin—

(*Trumpets the while.*)

And you, the judges, bear a wary eye.
HAMLET: Come on, sir.
LAERTES: Come, my lord.

(*They play.*)

HAMLET: One.
LAERTES: No.
HAMLET: Judgment.
OSRIC: A hit, a very palpable hit.

(*Drums, trumpets, and shot. Flourish; a piece goes off.*)

265 LAERTES: Well, again.
KING: Stay, give me drink. Hamlet, this pearl is thine.
Here's to thy health. Give him the cup.
HAMLET: I'll play this bout first; set it by awhile.
Come.

(*They play.*)

270 Another hit; what say you?
LAERTES: I do confess't.
KING: Our son shall win.
QUEEN: He's fat, and scant of breath.
Here, Hamlet, take my napkin, rub thy brows.
The queen carouses to thy fortune, Hamlet.
275 HAMLET: Good madam!
KING: Gertrude, do not drink.
QUEEN: I will, my lord; I pray you pardon me.
KING: (*Aside.*) It is the poisoned cup; it is too late.
HAMLET: I dare not drink yet, madam; by and by.
280 QUEEN: Come, let me wipe thy face.
LAERTES: My lord, I'll hit him now.
KING: I do not think't.
LAERTES: (*Aside.*) And yet it is almost against my conscience.
HAMLET: Come, for the third, Laertes. You but dally.
I pray you pass with your best violence;
285 I am afeard you make a wanton of me.
LAERTES: Say you so? come on.

(*They play.*)

OSRIC: Nothing, neither way.
LAERTES: Have at you now!

(LAERTES *wounds* HAMLET; *then, in scuffling, they change rapiers.*)

KING: Part them. They are incensed.
HAMLET: Nay, come again.   290

(HAMLET *wounds* LAERTES. *The* QUEEN *falls.*)

OSRIC: Look to the queen there, ho!
HORATIO: They bleed on both sides. How is it, my lord?
OSRIC: How is't Laertes?
LAERTES: Why, as a woodcock to mine own springe, Osric.
I am justly killed with mine own treachery.   295
HAMLET: How does the queen?
KING: She swoons to see them bleed.
QUEEN: No, no, the drink, the drink! O my dear Hamlet!
The drink, the drink! I am poisoned.

(*Dies.*)

HAMLET: O villany! Ho! let the door be locked.
Treachery! Seek it out.   300

(LAERTES *falls. Exit* OSRIC.)

LAERTES: It is here, Hamlet. Hamlet, thou art slain;
No med'cine in the world can do thee good.
In thee there is not half an hour's life.
The treacherous instrument is in thy hand,
Unbated and envenomed. The foul practice   305
Hath turned itself on me. Lo, here I lie,
Never to rise again. Thy mother's poisoned.
I can no more. The king, the king's to blame.
HAMLET: The point envenomed too!
Then, venom, to thy work.   310

(*Wounds the* KING.)

ALL: Treason! treason!
KING: O, yet defend me, friends. I am but hurt.
HAMLET: Here, thou incestuous, murd'rous, damnèd Dane,
Drink off this potion. Is thy union here?
Follow my mother.   315

(KING *dies.*)

LAERTES: He is justly served.
It is a poison tempered by himself.
Exchange forgiveness with me, noble Hamlet.
Mine and my father's death come not upon thee,
Nor thine on me!

(*Dies.*)

HAMLET: Heaven make thee free of it! I follow thee.   320
I am dead, Horatio. Wretched queen, adieu!
You that look pale and tremble at this chance,
That are but mutes or audience to this act,
Had I but time, as this fell sergeant Death
Is strict in his arrest, O, I could tell you—   325
But let it be. Horatio, I am dead:

---

255 **union** pearl   272 **fat** out of training   285 **make a wanton of me** trifle with me

294 **springe** trap   305 **Unbated** unblunted; **practice** plot   324
fell cruel; **sergeant** an officer whose duty is to summon persons
to appear before a court

Thou livest; report me and my cause aright
To the unsatisfied.

HORATIO: Never believe it:
I am more an antique Roman than a Dane.
330   Here's yet some liquor left.

HAMLET: As th'art a man,
Give me the cup. Let go. By heaven, I'll ha't.
O God, Horatio, what a wounded name,
Things standing thus unknown, shall live behind me!
If thou didst ever hold me in thy heart,
335   Absent thee from felicity awhile,
And in this harsh world draw thy breath in pain,
To tell my story.

(A march afar off.)

            What warlike noise is this?

(Enter OSRIC.)

OSRIC: Young Fortinbras, with conquest come from Poland,
To th' ambassadors of England gives
340   This warlike volley.

HAMLET: O, I die, Horatio!
The potent poison quite o'er-crows my spirit.
I cannot live to hear the news from England,
But I do prophesy th' election lights
On Fortinbras. He has my dying voice.
345   So tell him, with th' occurrents, more and less,
Which have solicited—the rest is silence.

(Dies.)

HORATIO: Now cracks a noble heart. Good night, sweet
prince, And flights of angels sing thee to thy rest!

(March within.)

      Why does the drum come hither?

(Enter FORTINBRAS, with the AMBASSADORS [and with drum, colors, and ATTENDANTS].)

350   FORTINBRAS: Where is this sight?

HORATIO: What is it you would see?
If aught of woe or wonder, cease your search.

FORTINBRAS: This quarry cries on havoc. O proud Death,
What feast is toward in thine eternal cell

That thou so many princes at a shot
So bloodily hast struck?   355

AMBASSADORS: The sight is dismal;
And our affairs from England come too late.
The ears are senseless that should give us hearing
To tell him his commandment is fulfilled,
That Rosencrantz and Guildenstern are dead.
Where should we have our thanks?   360

HORATIO: Not from his mouth,
Had it th' ability of life to thank you.
He never gave commandment for their death.
But since, so jump upon this bloody question,
You from the Polack wars, and you from England,
Are here arrived, give order that these bodies   365
High on a stage be placèd to the view,
And let me speak to th' yet unknowing world
How these things came about. So shall you hear
Of carnal, bloody, and unnatural acts;
Of accidental judgements, casual slaughters;   370
Of deaths put on by cunning and forced cause;
And, in this upshot, purposes mistook
Fall'n on th' inventors' heads. All this can I
Truly deliver.

FORTINBRAS: Let us haste to hear it.
And call the noblest to the audience.   375
For me, with sorrow I embrace my fortune.
I have some rights of memory in this kingdom,
Which now to claim my vantage doth invite me.

HORATIO: Of that I shall have also cause to speak,
And from his mouth whose voice will draw on more. 380
But let this same be presently performed,
Even while men's minds are wild, lest more mischance
On plots and errors happen.

FORTINBRAS: Let four captains
Bear Hamlet like a soldier to the stage,
For he was likely, had he been put on,   385
To have proved most royal; and for his passage
The soldier's music and the rite of war
Speak loudly for him.
Take up the bodies. Such a sight as this
Becomes the field, but here shows much amiss.   390
Go, bid the soldiers shoot.

(Exeunt [marching. A peal of ordnance shot off].)

---

341 **o'er-crows** triumphs over   344 **voice** vote   345 **more and less** great and small   346 **solicited** incited, prompted

352 **quarry** pile of dead   353 **toward** impending   363 **jump** exactly   371 **put on** instigated; **forced cause** by reason of compulsion   385 **put on** set to perform in office   386 **passage** death

THE TEMPEST

The Tempest was staged at court in 1611. It is probably the last play that Shakespeare wrote without a collaborator, and generations of readers and audiences have taken Prospero as an image of Shakespeare himself: when Prospero puts aside his powerful, theatrical magic, Shakespeare may in a sense be making his farewell to the stage.

Renaissance audiences might have taken *The Tempest* as an example of a new kind of play becoming increasingly popular in the early seventeenth century: tragicomedy. Renaissance tragicomedy generally opens in the severe, disturbing mood of tragedy and builds to a moment of crisis; it then resolves into a comic finale of festivity, marriage, and harmony. That is, this version of "tragicomedy" concerns the play's plot structure, rather than its tone or mood. Shakespeare's company, the King's Men, had staged several plays by John Fletcher, one of the premier writers of tragicomedy, and it is inviting to see Shakespeare trying out his hand at the new genre late in his career in plays such as *Pericles, Cymbeline, The Winter's Tale,* and *The Tempest. The Tempest* begins as something like a revenge tragedy: Prospero plots to revenge himself on his usurping brother Antonio, and Sebastian's plot to murder Alonso also smacks of tragic intrigue. However, The Tempest, while raising the problems of tragedy, resolves them in the mode of comedy. Instead of murdering his brother, Prospero marries his daughter, Miranda, to Alonso's son, Ferdinand. The spirit Ariel prompts Prospero to discover that "The rarer action is / In virtue than in vengeance."

In other respects, *The Tempest* shares the forms and moods of Shakespearean comedy. In a plot reminiscent of many of Shakespeare's earlier comedies, Prospero's daughter, Miranda, falls instantly in love with Alonso's son, Ferdinand, for in *The Tempest,* virtue "naturally" recognizes virtue in others. The marriage also promises to heal the political rifts between Milan and Naples, and Prospero devises an elegant entertainment to lend the engagement an aura of sanctity. In its mythological characters, verse, song, and dance, Prospero's play resembles the masques frequently performed at court on such occasions. The romantic comedy of Ferdinand and Miranda is balanced by the play's more ironic treatment of Caliban, Stephano, and Trinculo. If the magical meeting of the lovers urges us to believe that the virtuous are drawn naturally together, the fact that Caliban takes the boozy Stephano and Trinculo for gods, and that the three of them try to over-

Patrick Stewart as Prospero conjures the storm in the Joseph Papp Public Theater production of Shakespeare's *The Tempest.*

throw Prospero from his second kingdom, suggests a parallel recognition—that bad nature also seeks itself out in others.

Although Prospero and Doctor Faustus may practice different kinds of magic, both are figures of the common desire to transcend nature through art. But much as Faustus is finally damned for his bargain with Mephostophilis, so Prospero learns that his own nature, and human nature generally, cannot be overcome. Prospero must learn to forgive to return to the world from his magic island-prison. Indeed, if the power of Prospero's artful magic is symbolized by the capable spirit Ariel, its limitations are suggested by Caliban. In some ways, Caliban represents a European imagination of human nature in its elemental form, an image of human nature that in the sixteenth and seventeenth centuries was often reinforced by European contacts with the indigenous peoples of the Americas and Africa. For although Prospero's island is located in the Mediterranean, many of its features—and the shipwreck motif—seem to be drawn from pamphlets describing the exploration of the New World. In 1609, a fleet of English ships bound for Virginia was wrecked by a storm in the Bermudas; and while many of the ships eventually reached Jamestown, one, the Sea Adventure, remained lost for nearly a year. When the ship finally reached Virginia in May of 1610, the Englishmen's story of survival and their encounters with the natives of the "still-vexed Bermoothes" was widely published in pamphlets that Shakespeare seems to have read while writing the play.

The play's setting and sources have led critics to see *The Tempest* as a play not only about the state of human nature, but also about the conquest and subjection of the native peoples represented by Caliban. Caliban is clearly seen from the point of view of the European settlers: Prospero calls him a devil and a slave and uses him as a beast of burden; his language is simple; and instead of using the arts of romance on Miranda, as Ferdinand does, he tries to rape Miranda in an effort to people the island with Calibans. Caliban was the master of the island's nature, its "fresh springs, brine pits, barren place and fertile," but in attempting to civilize Caliban, Prospero has succeeded only in deforming him. Caliban is now neither "natural" nor civilized, but a parody of European "humanity": "You taught me language, and my profit on't / Is, I know how to curse."

Prospero's stagey magic, his ability to conjure storms and spectacles, is a glorious image of Renaissance "overreaching." As in *A Midsummer Night's Dream* or *Hamlet*, Shakespeare uses *The Tempest* to frame his final, most subtle imaging of the extraordinary powers of art—the arts of magic, of civilization, of the theater. At the same time, *The Tempest* also expresses the limitations of that art: neither Sebastian nor Antonio seems fundamentally changed by Prospero's magic. And much as Caliban has been changed, the play finally can find no voice, no language for Caliban to speak. In recent years, stage productions have sometimes taken the play as an opportunity to investigate the dynamics of colonialism. Lewis Baumander's production (Toronto, 1987) set the play on the Queen Charlotte Islands, off the coast of British Columbia, Canada, during the late eighteenth century, when these islands were being explored and settled by British seamen. Not only have other productions (Jonathan Miller's 1988 *Tempest*) more generally interrogated the questions of cultural and racial domination posed in Shakespeare's play, but many writers—Roberto Fernández Retamar, for example, in *Caliban* (1989)—have seen in Shakespeare's play an allegory of the West's continued representational power over its colonial and postcolonial subjects. Aimé Césaire's play *A Tempest* is perhaps the best-known dramatic response to *The Tempest,* and it is included in Unit VII.

The Tempest is also the subject of one of the most famous and experimental Shakespeare films of the 1990s, Peter Greenaway's *Prospero's Books* (1991).

THE TEMPEST

William Shakespeare

EDITED BY DAVID BEVINGTON

CHARACTERS

ALONSO, *King of Naples*
SEBASTIAN, *his brother*
PROSPERO, *the right Duke of Milan*
ANTONIO, *his brother, the usurping Duke of Milan*
FERDINAND, *son to the King of Naples*
GONZALO, *an honest old Counselor*
ADRIAN *and* } *Lords*
FRANCISCO }
CALIBAN, *a savage and deformed Slave*
TRINCULO, *a Jester*
STEPHANO, *a drunken Butler*

MASTER *of a Ship*
BOATSWAIN
MARINERS
MIRANDA, *daughter to Prospero*
ARIEL, *an airy Spirit*
IRIS
CERES
JUNO } *[presented by]* SPIRITS
NYMPHS
REAPERS
[*Other* SPIRITS *attending on Prospero.*]

ACT ONE

SCENE I

An uninhabited island.

A tempestuous noise of thunder and lightning heard. Enter a SHIP-MASTER *and a* BOATSWAIN.

MASTER: Boatswain!
BOATSWAIN: Here, master. What cheer?
MASTER: Good speak to th' mariners. Fall to 't, yarely, or we run ourselves aground. Bestir, bestir.

(Exit.)

(Enter MARINERS.*)*

5 BOATSWAIN: Heigh, my hearts! Cheerly, cheerly, my hearts! Yare, yare! Take in the topsail. Tend to th' master's whistle.— Blow till thou burst thy wind, if room enough!

(Enter ALONSO, SEBASTIAN, ANTONIO, FERDINAND, GONZALO, *and others.*)

ALONSO: Good boatswain, have care. Where's the master? Play the men.
10 BOATSWAIN: I pray now, keep below.
ANTONIO: Where is the master, bos'n?
BOATSWAIN: Do you not hear him? You mar our labor. Keep your cabins; you do assist the storm.
GONZALO: Nay, good, be patient.
15 BOATSWAIN: When the sea is. Hence! What cares these roarers for the name of king? To cabin! Silence! Trouble us not.
GONZALO: Good, yet remember whom thou hast aboard.
BOATSWAIN: None that I more love than myself. You are a counselor; if you can command these elements to silence, 20 and work the peace of the present, we will not hand a rope more. Use your authority. If you cannot, give thanks you have liv'd so long, and make yourself ready in your cabin for the mischance of the hour, if it so hap.— Cheerly, good hearts!—Out of our way, I say.

(Exit.)

GONZALO: I have great comfort from this fellow. Methinks he 25 hath no drowning mark upon him; his complexion is perfect gallows. Stand fast, good Fate, to his hanging! Make the rope of his destiny our cable, for our own doth little advantage. If he be not born to be hang'd, our case is miserable.

(Exeunt.)

(Enter BOATSWAIN.*)*

BOATSWAIN: Down with the topmast! Yare! Lower, lower! 30 Bring her to try with main-course. (*A cry within.*) A plague upon this howling! They are louder than the weather or our office.

(Enter SEBASTIAN, ANTONIO, *and* GONZALO.*)*

Yet again? What do you here? Shall we give o'er and drown? Have you a mind to sink? 35
SEBASTIAN: A pox o' your throat, you bawling, blasphemous, incharitable dog!
BOATSWAIN: Work you then.
ANTONIO: Hang, cur! Hang, you whoreson, insolent noise-maker! We are less afraid to be drown'd than thou art. 40
GONZALO: I'll warrant him for drowning, though the ship were no stronger than a nutshell and as leaky as an unstanch'd wench.

I.i. Location: On a ship at sea. 3 Good i.e., it's good you've come; or, my good fellow; **yarely** nimbly **6 Tend** attend **7 Blow** (addressed to the wind); **if room enough** as long as we have searoom enough **8–9 Play the men** act like men (?) ply, urge the men to exert themselves (?) **15 roarers** waves or winds, or both; spoken to as though they were "bullies" or "blusterers" **20 hand** handle

26–27 complexion . . . gallows appearance shows he was born to be hanged (and therefore, according to the proverb, in no danger of drowning) **28 our . . . advantage** i.e., our own cable is of little benefit **31 Bring . . . course** sail her close to the wind by means of the mainsail **32 our office** i.e., the noise we make at our work **41 warrant him for drowning** guarantee that he will never be drowned **42 unstanch'd** insatiable, loose, unrestrained

BOATSWAIN: Lay her a-hold, a-hold! Set her two courses off
45   to sea again! Lay her off!

(*Enter* MARINERS *wet.*)

MARINERS: All lost! To prayers, to prayers! All lost!

(*Exeunt.*)

BOATSWAIN: What, must our mouths be cold?
GONZALO: The King and Prince at prayers! Let's assist them,
    For our case is as theirs.
SEBASTIAN: I am out of patience.
50 ANTONIO: We are merely cheated of our lives by drunkards.
    This wide-chopp'd rascal! Would thou mightst lie drowning
    The washing of ten tides!
GONZALO: He'll be hang'd yet,
    Though every drop of water swear against it
    And gape at wid'st to glut him.

(*A confused noise within:*)

                              "Mercy on us!"—
55   "We split, we split!"—"Farewell my wife and children!"–
    "Farewell, brother!"—"We split, we split, we split!"

(*Exit* BOATSWAIN.)

ANTONIO: Let's all sink wi' th' King.
SEBASTIAN: Let's take leave of him.

(*Exit* [*with* ANTONIO].)

GONZALO: Now would I give a thousand furlongs of sea for an
60   acre of barren ground, long heath, brown furze, anything.
    The wills above be done! But I would fain die a dry death.

(*Exit.*)

SCENE II

Enter PROSPERO [*in his magic robes*] *and* MIRANDA.

MIRANDA: If by your art, my dearest father, you have
    Put the wild waters in this roar, allay them.
    The sky, it seems, would pour down stinking pitch,
    But that the sea, mounting to th' welkin's cheek,
5   Dashes the fire out. O, I have suffered
    With those that I saw suffer! A brave vessel,
    Who had, no doubt, some noble creature in her,
    Dash'd all to pieces. O, the cry did knock
    Against my very heart! Poor souls, they perish'd.

---

44 **a-hold** a-hull, close to the wind; **courses** sails, i.e., foresail as
well as mainsail, set in an attempt to get the ship back out into
open water   47 **must . . . cold** i.e., let us heat up our mouths
with liquor   50 **merely** quite   51 **wide-chopp'd** with mouth
wide open   51–52 **lie . . . tides** (Pirates were hanged on the
shore and left until three tides had come in.)   54 **glut** swallow
60 **heath** uncultivated ground; heather; **furze** a weed growing
on waste land

I.ii. Location: The island. Before Prospero's cell.   4 **welkin's
cheek** sky's face   6 **brave** gallant, splendid

Had I been any god of power, I would   10
Have sunk the sea within the earth or ere
It should the good ship so have swallow'd and
The fraughting souls within her.
PROSPERO: Be collected.
    No more amazement. Tell your piteous heart
    There's no harm done.   15
MIRANDA: O, woe the day!
PROSPERO: No harm.
    I have done nothing but in care of thee,
    Of thee, my dear one, thee, my daughter, who
    Art ignorant of what thou art, nought knowing
    Of whence I am, nor that I am more better
    Than Prospero, master of a full poor cell,   20
    And thy no greater father.
MIRANDA: More to know
    Did never meddle with my thoughts.
PROSPERO: 'Tis time
    I should inform thee farther. Lend thy hand,
    And pluck my magic garment from me. So,

(*Lays down his magic robe and staff.*)

    Lie there, my art. Wipe thou thine eyes; have comfort. 25
    The direful spectacle of the wrack, which touch'd
    The very virtue of compassion in thee,
    I have with such provision in mine art
    So safely ordered that there is no soul—
    No, not so much perdition as an hair   30
    Betid to any creature in the vessel
    Which thou heard'st cry, which thou saw'st sink. Sit
        down;
    For thou must now know farther.
MIRANDA: You have often
    Begun to tell me what I am, but stopp'd
    And left me to a bootless inquisition,   35
    Concluding, "Stay, not yet."
PROSPERO: The hour's now come;
    The very minute bids thee ope thine ear.
    Obey and be attentive. Canst thou remember
    A time before we came unto this cell?
    I do not think thou canst, for then thou wast not   40
    Out three years old.
MIRANDA: Certainly, sir, I can.
PROSPERO: By what? By any other house or person?
    Of anything the image, tell me, that
    Hath kept with thy remembrance.
MIRANDA: 'Tis far off,
    And rather like a dream than an assurance   45
    That my remembrance warrants. Had I not
    Four or five women once that tended me?
PROSPERO: Thou hadst, and more, Miranda. But how is it
    That this lives in thy mind? What seest thou else
    In the dark backward and abysm of time?   50

---

11 **or ere** before   13 **fraughting** forming the cargo; **collected**
calm, composed   14 **amazement** consternation   20 **full** very
30 **perdition** loss   31 **Betid** happened   35 **bootless inquisition** profitless inquiry   41 **Out** fully   45–46 **assurance . . .
warrants** certainty that my memory guarantees

If thou rememb'rest aught ere thou cam'st here,
How thou cam'st here thou mayst.
MIRANDA: But that I do not.
PROSPERO: Twelve year since, Miranda, twelve year since,
       Thy father was the Duke of Milan and
55   A prince of power.
MIRANDA: Sir, are not you my father?
PROSPERO: Thy mother was a piece of virtue, and
       She said thou wast my daughter; and thy father
       Was Duke of Milan; and thou his only heir
       And princess no worse issued.
MIRANDA: O the heavens!
60   What foul play had we, that we came from thence?
       Or blessed was 't we did?
PROSPERO: Both, both, my girl.
       By foul play, as thou say'st, were we heav'd thence,
       But blessedly holp hither.
MIRANDA: O, my heart bleeds
       To think o' th' teen that I have turn'd you to,
65   Which is from my remembrance! Please you, farther.
PROSPERO: My brother and thy uncle, call'd Antonio—
       I pray thee mark me—that a brother should
       Be so perfidious!—he whom next thyself
       Of all the world I lov'd, and to him put
70   The manage of my state, as at that time
       Through all the signories it was the first
       And Prospero the prime duke, being so reputed
       In dignity, and for the liberal arts
       Without a parallel; those being all my study,
75   The government I cast upon my brother
       And to my state grew stranger, being transported
       And rapt in secret studies. Thy false uncle—
       Dost thou attend me?
MIRANDA: Sir, most heedfully.
PROSPERO: Being once perfected how to grant suits,
80   How to deny them, who t' advance and who
       To trash for overtopping, new created
       The creatures that were mine, I say, or chang'd 'em,
       Or else new form'd 'em; having both the key
       Of officer and office, set all hearts i' th' state
85   To what tune pleas'd his ear, that now he was
       The ivy which had hid my princely trunk,
       And suck'd my verdure out on 't. Thou attend'st not.
MIRANDA: O, good sir, I do.
PROSPERO: I pray thee mark me.
       I, thus neglecting worldly ends, all dedicated
90   To closeness and the bettering of my mind
       With that which, but by being so retir'd,
       O'er-priz'd all popular rate, in my false brother
       Awak'd an evil nature; and my trust,

Like a good parent, did beget of him
A falsehood in its contrary as great   95
As my trust was, which had indeed no limit,
A confidence sans bound. He being thus lorded,
Not only with what my revenue yielded,
But what my power might else exact—like one
Who having into truth, by telling of it,   100
Made such a sinner of his memory
To credit his own lie—he did believe
He was indeed the Duke, out o' th' substitution,
And executing th' outward face of royalty,
With all prerogative. Hence his ambition growing—   105
Dost thou hear?
MIRANDA: Your tale, sir, would cure deafness.
PROSPERO: To have no screen between this part he play'd
       And him he play'd it for, he needs will be
       Absolute Milan. Me, poor man, my library
       Was dukedom large enough. Of temporal royalties   110
       He thinks me now incapable; confederates—
       So dry he was for sway—wi' th' King of Naples
       To give him annual tribute, do him homage,
       Subject his coronet to his crown, and bend
       The dukedom yet unbow'd—alas, poor Milan!—   115
       To most ignoble stooping.
MIRANDA: O the heavens!
PROSPERO: Mark his condition and th' event, then tell me
       If this might be a brother.
MIRANDA: I should sin
       To think but nobly of my grandmother.
       Good wombs have borne bad sons   120
PROSPERO: Now the condition.
       This King of Naples, being an enemy
       To me inveterate, hearkens my brother's suit,
       Which was that he, in lieu o' th' premises
       Of homage and I know not how much tribute,
       Should presently extirpate me and mine   125
       Out of the dukedom and confer fair Milan
       With all the honors on my brother. Whereon,
       A treacherous army levied, one midnight
       Fated to th' purpose, did Antonio open
       The gates of Milan, and, i' th' dead of darkness,   130
       The ministers for th' purpose hurried thence
       Me and thy crying self.
MIRANDA: Alack, for pity!
       I, not rememb'ring how I cried out then,

---

56 **piece** masterpiece, exemplar   59 **issued** born, descended
63 **holp** helped   64 **teen . . . to** trouble I've caused you to remember, or put you to   65 **from** out of   71 **signories** i.e.,
city-states of northern Italy   79 **perfected** grown skillful   81
trash check a hound by tying a weight to its neck; **overtopping**
running too far ahead of the pack; or, growing too tall   82
creatures dependents; **or** either   83 **key** (1) key for unlocking
(2) tool for tuning stringed instruments   90 **closeness** retirement, seclusion   91–92 **but . . . rate** except that it was done in
retirement, (would have) surpassed in value all popular estimate

94 **good parent** alludes to the proverb that good parents often
bear bad children; see also line 120   97 **sans** without; **lorded**
raised to lordship, with power and wealth   100–102 **Who . . .
lie** i.e., who, by repeatedly telling the lie (that he was indeed
Duke of Milan), made his memory such a confirmed sinner
against truth that he began to believe his own lie   103 **out o'**
as a result of   104 **And . . . royalty** and (as a result) his carrying out all the ceremonial functions of royalty   108 **him** i.e.,
himself   109 **Absolute Milan** unconditional Duke of Milan
110 **temporal royalties** practical prerogatives and responsibilities of a sovereign   111 **confederates** conspires, allies himself
112 **dry** thirsty   113 **him** i.e., the King of Naples   114 **his . . .
his** Antonio's . . . the King of Naples'   117 **condition** pact;
event outcome   123 **in . . . premises** in return for the stipu-
lation   125 **presently extirpate** at once remove

     Will cry it o'er again. It is a hint
135   That wrings mine eyes to 't.
PROSPERO: Hear a little further,
     And then I'll bring thee to the present business
     Which now's upon 's, without the which this story
     Were most impertinent.
MIRANDA: Wherefore did they not
     That hour destroy us?
PROSPERO: Well demanded, wench.
140   My tale provokes that question. Dear, they durst not,
     So dear the love my people bore me, nor set
     A mark so bloody on the business, but
     With colors fairer painted their foul ends.
     In few, they hurried us aboard a bark,
145   Bore us some leagues to sea, where they prepar'd
     A rotten carcass of a butt, not rigg'd,
     Nor tackle, sail, nor mast; the very rats
     Instinctively have quit it. There they hoist us,
     To cry to th' sea that roar'd to us, to sigh
150   To th' winds whose pity, sighing back again,
     Did us but loving wrong.
MIRANDA: Alack, what trouble
     Was I then to you!
PROSPERO: O, a cherubin
     Thou wast that did preserve me. Thou didst smile,
     Infused with a fortitude from heaven,
155   When I have deck'd the sea with drops full salt,
     Under my burden groan'd, which rais'd in me
     An undergoing stomach, to bear up
     Against what should ensue.
MIRANDA: How came we ashore?
PROSPERO: By Providence divine.
160   Some food we had, and some fresh water, that
     A noble Neapolitan, Gonzalo,
     Out of his charity, who being then appointed
     Master of this design, did give us, with
     Rich garments, linens, stuffs, and necessaries,
165   Which since have steaded much. So, of his gentleness,
     Knowing I lov'd my books, he furnish'd me
     From mine own library with volumes that
     I prize above my dukedom.
MIRANDA: Would I might
     But ever see that man!
PROSPERO: Now I arise.

(*Resumes his magic robes.*)

170   Sit still, and hear the last of our sea-sorrow.
     Here in this island we arriv'd; and here
     Have I, thy schoolmaster, made thee more profit
     Than other princess' can that have more time
     For vainer hours and tutors not so careful.

MIRANDA: Heavens thank you for 't! And now, I pray you, sir, 175
     For still 'tis beating in my mind, your reason
     For raising this sea-storm?
PROSPERO: Know thus far forth.
     By accident most strange, bountiful Fortune,
     Now my dear lady, hath mine enemies
     Brought to this shore; and by my prescience 180
     I find my zenith doth depend upon
     A most auspicious star, whose influence
     If now I court not but omit, my fortunes
     Will ever after droop. Here cease more questions.
     Thou art inclin'd to sleep; 'tis a good dullness, 185
     And give it way. I know thou canst not choose.

(MIRANDA *sleeps.*)

     Come away, servant, come! I am ready now.
     Approach, my Ariel, come.

(*Enter* ARIEL.)

ARIEL: All hail, great master! Grave sir, hail! I come
     To answer thy best pleasure; be 't to fly, 190
     To swim, to dive into the fire, to ride
     On the curl'd clouds. To thy strong bidding, task
     Ariel and all his quality.
PROSPERO: Hast thou, spirit,
     Perform'd to point the tempest that I bade thee?
ARIEL: To every article. 195
     I boarded the King's ship; now on the beak,
     Now in the waist, the deck, in every cabin,
     I flam'd amazement. Sometime I'd divide,
     And burn in many places; on the topmast,
     The yards, and boresprit, would I flame distinctly, 200
     Then meet and join. Jove's lightnings, the precursors
     O' th' dreadful thunder-claps, more momentary
     And sight-outrunning were not; the fire and cracks
     Of sulphurous roaring the most mighty Neptune
     Seem to besiege and make his bold waves tremble, 205
     Yea, his dread trident shake.
PROSPERO: My brave spirit!
     Who was so firm, so constant, that this coil
     Would not infect his reason?
ARIEL: Not a soul
     But felt a fever of the mad and play'd
     Some tricks of desperation. All but mariners 210
     Plung'd in the foaming brine and quit the vessel;
     Then all afire with me, the King's son, Ferdinand,
     With hair up-staring—then like reeds, not hair—
     Was the first man that leapt; cried, "Hell is empty,
     And all the devils are here." 215

---

134 **hint** occasion   138 **impertinent** irrelevant   144 **few** few words   146 **butt** cask, tub   151 **loving wrong** i.e., the winds pitied Prospero and Miranda though of necessity they blew them from shore   155 **deck'd** covered (with salt tears); adorned   156 **which** i.e., the smile   157 **undergoing stomach** courage to go on   165 **steaded much** been of much use   172 **more profit** profit more   173 **princess'** princesses

181 **zenith** height of fortune (astrological term)   182 **influence** astrological power   187 **Come away** come   192 **task** make demands upon   193 **quality** (1) fellow-spirits (2) abilities   194 **to point** to the smallest detail   196 **beak** prow   197 **waist** midships; **deck** poopdeck at the stern   198 **flam'd amazement** struck terror in the guise of fire, i.e., St. Elmo's fire   200 **boresprit** bowsprit; distinctly in different places   207 **coil** tumult   209 **of the mad** i.e., such as madmen feel   213 **up-staring** standing on end

PROSPERO: Why, that's my spirit!
But was not this nigh shore?
ARIEL: Close by, my master.
PROSPERO: But are they, Ariel, safe?
ARIEL: Not a hair perish'd.
On their sustaining garments not a blemish,
But fresher than before; and, as thou bad'st me,
220   In troops I have dispers'd them 'bout the isle.
The King's son have I landed by himself,
Whom I left cooling of the air with sighs
In an odd angle of the isle and sitting,
His arms in this sad knot.

(Folds his arms.)

PROSPERO: Of the King's ship,
225   The mariners, say how thou hast dispos'd,
And all the rest o' th' fleet.
ARIEL: Safely in harbor
Is the King's ship; in the deep nook, where once
Thou call'dst me up at midnight to fetch dew
From the still-vex'd Bermoothes, there she's hid;
230   The mariners all under hatches stow'd,
Who, with a charm join'd to their suff'red labor,
I have left asleep; and for the rest o' th' fleet,
Which I dispers'd, they all have met again
And are upon the Mediterranean flote
235   Bound sadly home for Naples,
Supposing that they saw the King's ship wrack'd
And his great person perish.
PROSPERO: Ariel, thy charge
Exactly is perform'd. But there's more work.
What is the time o' th' day?
ARIEL: Past the mid season.
240   PROSPERO: At least two glasses. The time 'twixt six and now
Must by us both be spent most preciously.
ARIEL: Is there more toil? Since thou dost give me pains,
Let me remember thee what thou hast promis'd,
Which is not yet perform'd me.
PROSPERO: How now? Moody?
245   What is 't thou canst demand?
ARIEL: My liberty.
PROSPERO: Before the time be out? No more!
ARIEL: I prithee,
Remember I have done thee worthy service,
Told thee no lies, made thee no mistakings, serv'd
Without or grudge or grumblings. Thou didst promise
250   To bate me a full year.
PROSPERO: Dost thou forget
From what a torment I did free thee?
ARIEL: No.

---

218 **sustaining garments** garments that buoyed them up in the
sea   223 **angle** corner   224 **sad knot** folded arms are indicative of melancholy   227 **nook** bay   229 **still-vex'd
Bermoothes** ever stormy Bermudas. Perhaps refers to the then-
recent Bermuda shipwreck; see Play Introduction   231 **with
. . . labor** by means of a spell added to all the labor they have
undergone   234 **flote** sea   239 **mid season** noon   240
glasses i.e., hourglasses   243 **remember** remind   250 **bate**
remit, deduct

PROSPERO: Thou dost, and think'st it much to tread the ooze
Of the salt deep,
To run upon the sharp wind of the north,
To do me business in the veins o' th' earth   255
When it is bak'd with frost.
ARIEL: I do not, sir.
PROSPERO: Thou liest, malignant thing! Hast thou forgot
The foul witch Sycorax, who with age and envy
Was grown into a hoop? Hast thou forgot her?
ARIEL: No, sir.   260
PROSPERO: Thou hast. Where was she born? Speak. Tell me.
ARIEL: Sir, in Argier.
PROSPERO: O, was she so? I must
Once in a month recount what thou hast been,
Which thou forget'st. This damn'd witch Sycorax,
For mischiefs manifold and sorceries terrible   265
To enter human hearing, from Argier,
Thou know'st, was banish'd; for one thing she did
They would not take her life. Is not this true?
ARIEL: Ay, sir.
PROSPERO: This blue-ey'd hag was hither brought with child 270
And here was left by th' sailors. Thou, my slave,
As thou report'st thyself, was then her servant;
And, for thou wast a spirit too delicate
To act her earthy and abhorr'd commands,
Refusing her grand hests, she did confine thee,   275
By help of her more potent ministers,
And in her most unmitigable rage,
Into a cloven pine, within which rift
Imprison'd thou didst painfully remain
A dozen years; within which space she died   280
And left thee there, where thou did'st vent thy groans
As fast as mill-wheels strike. Then was this island—
Save for the son that she did litter here,
A freckled whelp hag-born—not honor'd with
A human shape.   285
ARIEL: Yes, Caliban her son.
PROSPERO: Dull thing, I say so; he, that Caliban
Whom now I keep in service. Thou best know'st
What torment I did find thee in; thy groans
Did make wolves howl and penetrate the breasts
Of ever angry bears. It was a torment   290
To lay upon the damn'd, which Sycorax
Could not again undo. It was mine art,
When I arriv'd and heard thee, that made gape
The pine and let thee out.
ARIEL: I thank thee, master.
PROSPERO: If thou more murmur'st, I will rend an oak   295
And peg thee in his knotty entrails till
Thou hast howl'd away twelve winters.
ARIEL: Pardon, master;
I will be correspondent to command
And do my spriting gently.

---

258 **envy** malice   262 **Argier** Algiers   267 **one . . . did** perhaps a reference to her pregnancy, for which her life would be
spared   270 **blue-ey'd** with dark circles under the eyes   273
for because   275 **hests** commands   296 **his** its   298 **correspondent** responsive, submissive

300   PROSPERO: Do so, and after two days
       I will discharge thee.
       ARIEL: That's my noble master!
       What shall I do? Say what? What shall I do?
       PROSPERO: Go make thyself like a nymph o' th' sea.
          Be subject
       To no sight but thine and mine, invisible
305   To every eyeball else. Go take this shape
       And hither come in 't. Go, hence with diligence!

       (*Exit* [ARIEL].)

       Awake, dear heart, awake! Thou hast slept well;
       Awake!
       MIRANDA: The strangeness of your story put
310   Heaviness in me.
       PROSPERO: Shake it off. Come on;
       We'll visit Caliban my slave, who never
       Yields us kind answer.
       MIRANDA: 'Tis a villain, sir,
       I do not love to look on.
       PROSPERO: But, as 'tis,
       We cannot miss him. He does make our fire,
315   Fetch in our wood, and serves in offices
       That profit us. What, ho! Slave! Caliban!
       Thou earth, thou! Speak.
       CALIBAN: (*Within.*)   There's wood enough within.
       PROSPERO: Come forth, I say! There's other business for thee.
       Come, thou tortoise! When?

       (*Enter* ARIEL *like a water-nymph.*)

320   Fine apparition! My quaint Ariel,
       Hark in thine ear.

       (*Whispers.*)

       ARIEL: My lord, it shall be done.

       (*Exit.*)

       PROSPERO: Thou poisonous slave, got by the devil himself
       Upon thy wicked dam, come forth!

       (*Enter* CALIBAN.)

       CALIBAN: As wicked dew as e'er my mother brush'd
325   With raven's feather from unwholesome fen
       Drop on you both! A south-west blow on ye
       And blister you all o'er!
       PROSPERO: For this, be sure, tonight thou shalt have cramps,
       Side-stitches that shall pen thy breath up; urchins
330   Shall, for that vast of night that they may work,
       All exercise on thee. Thou shalt be pinch'd

As thick as honeycomb, each pinch more stinging
Than bees that made 'em.
CALIBAN: I must eat my dinner.
    This island's mine, by Sycorax my mother,
    Which thou tak'st from me. When thou cam'st first,   335
    Thou strok'st me and made much of me, wouldst give me
    Water with berries in 't, and teach me how
    To name the bigger light, and how the less,
    That burn by day and night; and then I lov'd thee
    And show'd thee all the qualities o' th' isle,   340
    The fresh springs, brine-pits, barren place and fertile.
    Curs'd be I that did so! All the charms
    Of Sycorax, toads, beetles, bats, light on you!
    For I am all the subjects that you have,
    Which first was mine own king; and here you sty me   345
    In this hard rock, whiles you do keep from me
    The rest o' th' island.
PROSPERO: Thou most lying slave,
    Whom stripes may move, not kindness! I have us'd thee,
    Filth as thou art, with humane care, and lodg'd thee
    In mine own cell, till thou didst seek to violate   350
    The honor of my child.
CALIBAN: O ho, O ho! Would't had been done!
    Thou didst prevent me; I had peopled else
    This isle with Calibans.
MIRANDA: Abhorred slave,
    Which any print of goodness wilt not take,   355
    Being capable of all ill! I pitied thee,
    Took pains to make thee speak, taught thee each hour
    One thing or other. When thou didst not, savage,
    Know thine own meaning, but wouldst gabble like
    A thing most brutish, I endow'd thy purposes   360
    With words that made them known. But thy vile race,
    Though thou didst learn, had that in 't which good natures
    Could not abide to be with; therefore wast thou
    Deservedly confin'd into this rock,
    Who hadst deserv'd more than a prison.   365
CALIBAN: You taught me language, and my profit on 't
    Is, I know how to curse. The red plague rid you
    For learning me your language!
PROSPERO: Hag-seed, hence!
    Fetch us in fuel; and be quick, thou'rt best,
    To answer other business. Shrug'st thou, malice?   370
    If thou neglect'st or dost unwillingly
    What I command, I'll rack thee with old cramps,
    Fill all thy bones with aches, make thee roar
    That beasts shall tremble at thy din.
CALIBAN: No, pray thee.
    (*Aside.*) I must obey. His art is of such pow'r,   375

---

314 **miss** do without   320 **quaint** ingenious   323 **wicked** mischievous, harmful   326 **south-west** i.e., wind thought to bring disease   329 **urchins** hedgehogs; here, suggesting goblins in the guise of hedgehogs   330 **vast** lengthy, desolate time; **that . . . work** malignant spirits were thought to be restricted to the hours of darkness

348 **stripes** lashes   354–365 **Abhorred . . . prison** sometimes assigned by editors to Prospero   360 **purposes** meanings, desires   361 **race** natural disposition; species, nature   367 **red plague** bubonic plague; **rid** destroy   368 **learning** teaching; **Hag-seed** offspring of a female demon   369 **thou'rt best** you'd be well advised   372 **old** such as old people suffer; or, plenty of   373 **aches** pronounced "aitches"

It would control my dam's god, Setebos,
And make a vassal of him.
PROSPERO: So, slave, hence!

(*Exit* CALIBAN.)

(*Enter* FERDINAND; *and* ARIEL, *invisible, playing and singing.*
[FERDINAND *does not see* PROSPERO *and* MIRANDA.])

(ARIEL'*s song.*)

    Come unto these yellow sands,
       And then take hands.
380   Curtsied when you have and kiss'd,
       The wild waves whist,
    Foot it featly here and there;
    And, sweet sprites, the burden bear.
       Hark, hark!

(*Burden, dispersedly* [*within*].)

385   Bow-wow.
    The watch-dogs bark.

(*Burden, dispersedly* [*within*].)

    Bow-wow.
    Hark, hark! I hear
    The strain of strutting chanticleer
390   Cry, Cock-a-diddle-dow.

FERDINAND: Where should this music be? I' th' air or th'
    earth?
    It sounds no more; and, sure, it waits upon
    Some god o' th' island. Sitting on a bank,
    Weeping again the King my father's wrack,
395   This music crept by me upon the waters,
    Allaying both their fury and my passion
    With its sweet air. Thence I have follow'd it,
    Or it hath drawn me rather. But 'tis gone.
    No, it begins again.

(ARIEL'*s song.*)

400   Full fathom five thy father lies;
       Of his bones are coral made;
    Those are pearls that were his eyes.
       Nothing of him that doth fade
    But doth suffer a sea-change
405   Into something rich and strange.
    Sea-nymphs hourly ring his knell:

(*Burden* [*within*].)

    Ding-dong.
    Hark, now I hear them—Ding-dong,
    bell.

410 FERDINAND: The ditty does remember my drown'd father.
    This is no mortal business, nor no sound
    That the earth owes. I hear it now above me.

---

381 **whist** being hushed   382 **featly** nimbly   383 **burden** refrain, undersong   384 s.d. **dispersedly** i.e., from all directions   409 **remember** commemorate   411 **owes** owns

PROSPERO: The fringed curtains of thine eye advance
    And say what thou seest yond.
MIRANDA: What is 't! A spirit!
    Lord, how it looks about! Believe me, sir,
    It carries a brave form. But 'tis a spirit.   415
PROSPERO: No, wench, it eats and sleeps and hath such
    senses
    As we have, such. This gallant which thou seest
    Was in the wrack; and, but he's something stain'd
    With grief, that's beauty's canker, thou mightst call him
    A goodly person. He hath lost his fellows   420
    And strays about to find 'em.
MIRANDA: I might call him
    A thing divine, for nothing natural
    I ever saw so noble.
PROSPERO: (*Aside.*)   It goes on, I see,
    As my soul prompts it. Spirit, fine spirit, I'll free thee
    Within two days for this.   425
FERDINAND: (*Seeing* MIRANDA.) Most sure, the goddess
    On whom these airs attend!—Vouchsafe my pray'r
    May know if you remain upon this island,
    And that you will some good instruction give
    How I may bear me here. My prime request,
    Which I do last pronounce, is, O you wonder!   430
    If you be maid or no?
MIRANDA: No wonder, sir,
    But certainly a maid.
FERDINAND: My language? Heavens!
    I am the best of them that speak this speech,
    Were I but where 'tis spoken.
PROSPERO: (*Coming forward.*)   How? The best?
    What wert thou, if the King of Naples heard thee?   435
FERDINAND: A single thing, as I am now, that wonders
    To hear thee speak of Naples. He does hear me;
    And that he does I weep. Myself am Naples,
    Who with mine eyes, never since at ebb, beheld
    The King my father wrack'd.   440
MIRANDA: Alack, for mercy!
FERDINAND: Yes, faith, and all his lords, the Duke of Milan
    And his brave son being twain.
PROSPERO: (*Aside.*)   The Duke of Milan
    And his more braver daughter could control thee,
    If now 'twere fit to do 't. At the first sight
    They have chang'd eyes. Delicate Ariel,   445
    I'll set thee free for this. (*To* FERDINAND.) A word, good sir.
    I fear you have done yourself some wrong. A word!

---

412 **advance** raise   415 **brave** excellent   418 **but** except that; **something stain'd** somewhat disfigured   419 **canker** cankerworm (feeding on buds and leaves)   423 **It goes on** i.e., my plan works   427 **remain** dwell   429 **bear me** conduct myself; **prime** chief   433 **best** i.e., in birth   436 **single** (1) solitary (2) feeble   437–438 **He . . . weep** i.e., this man to whom I speak (Prospero) hears me as I hear him, proving to me I am indeed alive, not dreaming, and am in the sad plight I imagined (?)   438 **Naples** the King of Naples (also in line 437)   442 **son** the only reference in the play to a son of Antonio   443 **control** confute   445 **chang'd eyes** exchanged amorous glances   447 **done . . . wrong** i.e., spoken falsely

MIRANDA: (*Aside.*) Why speaks my father so ungently? This
Is the third man that e'er I saw, the first
450 That e'er I sigh'd for. Pity move my father
To be inclin'd my way!
FERDINAND: O, if a virgin,
And your affection not gone forth, I'll make you
The Queen of Naples.
PROSPERO: Soft, sir! One word more.
(*Aside.*) They are both in either's pow'rs; but this swift
business
455 I must uneasy make, lest too light winning
Make the prize light. (*To* FERDINAND.) One word more:
I charge thee
That thou attend me. Thou dost here usurp
The name thou ow'st not, and hast put thyself
Upon this island as a spy, to win it
460 From me, the lord on 't.
FERDINAND: No, as I am a man.
MIRANDA: There's nothing ill can dwell in such a temple.
If the ill spirit have so fair a house,
Good things will strive to dwell with 't.
PROSPERO: Follow me.—
Speak not you for him; he's a traitor.—Come,
465 I'll manacle thy neck and feet together.
Sea-water shalt thou drink; thy food shall be
The fresh-brook mussels, wither'd roots, and husks
Wherein the acorn cradled. Follow.
FERDINAND: No.
I will resist such entertainment till
470 Mine enemy has more pow'r.

(*He draws, and is charmed from moving.*)

MIRANDA: O dear father,
Make not too rash a trial of him, for
He's gentle, and not fearful.
PROSPERO: What, I say,
My foot my tutor?—Put thy sword up, traitor,
Who mak'st a show but dar'st not strike, thy conscience
475 Is so possess'd with guilt. Come, from thy ward,
For I can here disarm thee with this stick
And make thy weapon drop.

(*Brandishes his staff.*)

MIRANDA: (*Trying to hinder him.*)   Beseech you, father.
PROSPERO: Hence! Hang not on my garments.
MIRANDA: Sir, have pity!
I'll be his surety.
PROSPERO: Silence! One word more
480 Shall make me chide thee, if not hate thee. What,
An advocate for an imposter! Hush!
Thou think'st there is no more such shapes as he,
Having seen but him and Caliban. Foolish wench,

To th' most of men this is a Caliban
And they to him are angels.   485
MIRANDA: My affections
Are then most humble; I have no ambition
To see a goodlier man.
PROSPERO: (*To* FERDINAND.) Come on, obey.
Thy nerves are in their infancy again
And have no vigor in them.
FERDINAND: So they are.
My spirits, as in a dream, are all bound up.   490
My father's loss, the weakness which I feel,
The wrack of all my friends, nor this man's threats
To whom I am subdu'd, are but light to me,
Might I put through my prison once a day
Behold this maid. All corners else o' th' earth   495
Let liberty make use of; space enough
Have I in such a prison.
PROSPERO: (*Aside.*) It works. (*To* FERDINAND.) Come on.—
Thou hast done well, fine Ariel! (*To* FERDINAND.) Follow
me.
(*To* ARIEL.) Hark what thou else shalt do me.
MIRANDA: (*To* FERDINAND.)   Be of comfort.
My father's of a better nature, sir,   500
Than he appears by speech. This is unwonted
Which now came from him.
PROSPERO: (*To* ARIEL.)   Thou shalt be as free
As mountain winds, but then exactly do
All points of my command.
ARIEL: To th' syllable.
PROSPERO: (*To* FERDINAND.) Come, follow. (*To* MIRANDA.)   505
Speak not for him.

(*Exeunt.*)

ACT TWO

SCENE I

Enter ALONSO, SEBASTIAN, ANTONIO, GONZALO, ADRIAN,
FRANCISCO, *and others.*

GONZALO: Beseech you, sir, be merry. You have cause,
So have we all, of joy, for our escape
Is much beyond our loss. Our hint of woe
Is common; every day some sailor's wife,
The masters of some merchant, and the merchant,   5
Have just our theme of woe; but for the miracle,
I mean our preservation, few in millions
Can speak like us. Then wisely, good sir, weigh
Our sorrow with our comfort.
ALONSO: Prithee, peace.
SEBASTIAN: (*To* ANTONIO.) He receives comfort like cold   10
porridge.

---

455 **uneasy** difficult   455–456 **light . . . light** easy . . . cheap
458 **ow'st** ownest   469 **entertainment** treatment   472 **gen-**
tle wellborn; **fearful** cowardly   473 **foot** subordinate (Miranda,
the foot, presumes to instruct Prospero, the head)   475 **ward**
defensive posture (in fencing)

---

484 **To** compared to   488 **nerves** sinews   499 **me** for me

II.i. Location: Another part of the island.   3 **hint of** occasion for   5 **masters . . . the merchant** officers of some merchant vessel and the merchant himself, the owner   11 **porridge**
with a pun on *peace* and *pease,* a usual ingredient of porridge

ANTONIO: (*To* SEBASTIAN.) The visitor will not give him o'er so.

SEBASTIAN: Look, he's winding up the watch of his wit; by
15 and by it will strike.

GONZALO: Sir—

SEBASTIAN: (*To* ANTONIO.) One. Tell.

GONZALO: When every grief is entertain'd that's offer'd,
Comes to th' entertainer—

20 SEBASTIAN: A dollar.

GONZALO: Dolor comes to him, indeed. You have spoken
truer than you purpos'd.

SEBASTIAN: You have taken it wiselier than I meant you should.

GONZALO: Therefore, my lord—

25 ANTONIO: Fie, what a spendthrift is he of his tongue!

ALONSO: I prithee, spare.

GONZALO: Well, I have done. But yet—

SEBASTIAN: He will be talking.

ANTONIO: Which, of he or Adrian, for a good wager, first
30 begins to crow?

SEBASTIAN: The old cock.

ANTONIO: The cock'rel.

SEBASTIAN: Done. The wager?

ANTONIO: A laughter.

35 SEBASTIAN: A match!

ADRIAN: Though this island seem to be desert—

SEBASTIAN: Ha, ha, ha!

ANTONIO: So, you're paid.

ADRIAN: Uninhabitable and almost inaccessible—

40 SEBASTIAN: Yet—

ADRIAN: Yet—

ANTONIO: He could not miss 't.

ADRIAN: It must needs be of subtle, tender, and delicate
temperance.

45 ANTONIO: Temperance was a delicate wench.

SEBASTIAN: Ay, and a subtle, as he most learnedly deliver'd.

---

12 **visitor** one taking nourishment and comfort to the sick, i.e., Gonzalo; **give him o'er** abandon him   17 **Tell** keep count   18–19 **When . . . entertainer** when every sorrow that presents itself is accepted without resistance, there comes to the recipient   20 **dollar** widely circulated coin, the German *Thaler* and the Spanish *piece of eight.* Sebastian puns on *entertainer* in the sense of *innkeeper;* to Gonzalo, *dollar* suggests *dolor,* grief.   29–30 **Which . . . crow** which of the two, Gonzalo or Adrian, do you bet will speak (crow) first   31 **old cock** i.e., Gonzalo   32 **cock'rel** i.e., Adrian   34 **laughter** (1) burst of laughter (2) sitting of eggs. When Adrian, the *cock'rel,* begins to speak two lines later, Sebastian loses the bet. Some editors alter the speech prefixes in lines 37–38 so that Antonio enjoys his laugh as the prize for winning, but possibly Sebastian pays for losing with a laugh   35 **A match** a bargain; agreed   42 **miss 't** (1) avoid saying "Yet" (2) miss the island   44 **temperance** climate   45 **Temperance** a girl's name; **delicate** here it means *given to pleasure, voluptuous;* in line 43, *pleasant.* Antonio is evidently suggesting that "tender, and delicate temperance" sounds like a Puritan phrase, which Antonio then mocks by applying the words to a woman rather than an island. He began this bawdy comparison with a double entendre on *inaccessible,* line 39   46 **subtle** here it means *tricky;* in line 43, *delicate;* **deliver'd** uttered. Sebastian joins in the Puritan baiting of Antonio with his use of the pious cant phrase "learnedly deliver'd"

ADRIAN: The air breathes upon us here most sweetly.

SEBASTIAN: As if it had lungs, and rotten ones.

ANTONIO: Or as 'twere perfum'd by a fen.

GONZALO: Here is everything advantageous to life.   50

ANTONIO: True, save means to live.

SEBASTIAN: Of that there's none, or little.

GONZALO: How lush and lusty the grass looks! How green!

ANTONIO: The ground indeed is tawny.

SEBASTIAN: With an eye of green in 't.   55

ANTONIO: He misses not much.

SEBASTIAN: No; he doth but mistake the truth totally.

GONZALO: But the rarity of it is—which is indeed almost beyond credit—

SEBASTIAN: As many vouch'd rarities are.   60

GONZALO: That our garments, being, as they were, drench'd in the sea, hold notwithstanding their freshness and glosses, being rather new-dyed than stain'd with salt water.

ANTONIO: If but one of his pockets could speak, would it not say he lies?   65

SEBASTIAN: Ay, or very falsely pocket up his report.

GONZALO: Methinks our garments are now as fresh as when we put them on first in Afric, at the marriage of the King's fair daughter Claribel to the King of Tunis.

SEBASTIAN: 'Twas a sweet marriage, and we prosper well in   70
our return.

ADRIAN: Tunis was never grac'd before with such a paragon to their queen.

GONZALO: Not since widow Dido's time.

ANTONIO: Widow! A pox o' that! How came that widow in?   75
Widow Dido!

SEBASTIAN: What if he had said "widower Aeneas" too? Good Lord, how you take it!

ADRIAN: "Widow Dido" said you? You make me study of that. She was of Carthage, not of Tunis.   80

GONZALO: This Tunis, sir, was Carthage.

ADRIAN: Carthage?

GONZALO: A assure you, Carthage.

ANTONIO: His word is more than the miraculous harp.

SEBASTIAN: He hath rais'd the wall and houses too.   85

ANTONIO: What impossible matter will he make easy next?

SEBASTIAN: I think he will carry this island home in his pocket and give it his son for an apple.

ANTONIO: And, sowing the kernels of it in the sea, bring forth more islands.   90

GONZALO: Ay.

---

53 **lusty** healthy   54 **tawny** dull brown, yellowish   55 **eye** tinge, or spot (perhaps with reference to Gonzalo's eye or judgment)   60 **vouch'd** certified   64 **pockets** i.e., because they are muddy   66 **pocket up** receive unprotestingly, fail to respond to a challenge   72 **to** for   74 **widow Dido** Queen of Carthage, deserted by Aeneas. She was in fact a widow when Aeneas, a widower, met her, but Antonio may be amused at the term "widow" to describe a woman deserted by her lover   84 **miraculous harp** alludes to Amphion's harp with which he raised the walls of Thebes; Gonzalo has exceeded that deed by creating a modern Carthage—walls *and* houses—mistakenly on the site of Tunis   91 **Ay** Gonzalo may be reasserting his point about Carthage, or he may be responding ironically to Antonio who in turn answers sarcastically

ANTONIO: Why, in good time.

GONZALO: (*To* ALONSO.) Sir, we were talking that our garments seem now as fresh as when we were at Tunis at the
95   marriage of your daughter, who is now queen.

ANTONIO: And the rarest that e'er came there.

SEBASTIAN: Bate, I beseech you, widow Dido.

ANTONIO: O, widow Dido? Ay, widow Dido.

GONZALO: Is not, sir, my doublet as fresh as the first day I
100   wore it? I mean, in a sort.

ANTONIO: That "sort" was well fish'd for.

GONZALO: When I wore it at your daughter's marriage?

ALONSO: You cram these words into mine ears against
    The stomach of my sense. Would I had never
105   Married my daughter there! For, coming thence,
    My son is lost and, in my rate, she too,
    Who is so far from Italy removed
    I ne'er again shall see her. O thou mine heir
    Of Naples and of Milan, what strange fish
110   Hath made his meal on thee?

FRANCISCO: Sir, he may live.
    I saw him beat the surges under him,
    And ride upon their backs. He trod the water,
    Whose enmity he flung aside, and breasted
    The surge most swoll'n that met him. His bold head
115   'Bove the contentious waves he kept, and oared
    Himself with his good arms in lusty stroke
    To th' shore, that o'er his wave-worn basis bowed,
    As stooping to relieve him. I not doubt
    He came alive to land.

ALONSO: No, no, he's gone.

120 SEBASTIAN: Sir, you may thank yourself for this great loss,
    That would not bless our Europe with your daughter,
    But rather loose her to an African,
    Where she at least is banish'd from your eye,
    Who hath cause to wet the grief on 't.

ALONSO: Prithee, peace.

125 SEBASTIAN: You were kneel'd to and importun'd otherwise
    By all of us, and the fair soul herself
    Weigh'd between loathness and obedience, at
    Which end o' th' beam should bow. We have lost your son,
    I fear, for ever. Milan and Naples have
130   Moe widows in them of their business' making
    Than we bring men to comfort them.
    The fault's your own.

ALONSO: So is the dear'st o' th' loss.

GONZALO: My lord Sebastian,
    The truth you speak doth lack some gentleness,

And time to speak it in. You rub the sore,   135
    When you should bring the plaster.

SEBASTIAN: Very well.

ANTONIO: And most chirurgeonly.

GONZALO: It is foul weather in us all, good sir,
    When you are cloudy.

SEBASTIAN: (*To* ANTONIO.) Foul weather?

ANTONIO: (*To* SEBASTIAN.)   Very foul.

GONZALO: Had I plantation of this isle, my lord—   140

ANTONIO: He'd sow 't with nettle-seed.

SEBASTIAN: Or docks, or mallows.

GONZALO: And were the king on 't, what would I do?

SEBASTIAN: Scape being drunk for want of wine.

GONZALO: I' th' commonwealth I would by contraries
    Execute all things; for no kind of traffic   145
    Would I admit; no name of magistrate;
    Letters should not be known; riches, poverty,
    And use of service, none; contract, succession,
    Bourn, bound of land, tilth, vineyard, none;
    No use of metal, corn, or wine, or oil;   150
    No occupation; all men idle, all,
    And women too, but innocent and pure;
    No sovereignty—

SEBASTIAN: Yet he would be king on 't.

ANTONIO: The latter end of his commonwealth forgets the
    beginning.

GONZALO: All things in common nature should produce   155
    Without sweat or endeavor. Treason, felony,
    Sword, pike, knife, gun, or need of any engine,
    Would I not have; but nature should bring forth,
    Of it own kind, all foison, all abundance,
    To feed my innocent people.   160

SEBASTIAN: No marrying 'mong his subjects?

ANTONIO: None, man; all idle—whores and knaves.

GONZALO: I would with such perfection govern, sir,
    T' excel the golden age.

SEBASTIAN: Save his Majesty!

ANTONIO: Long live Gonzalo!   165

GONZALO: And—do you mark me, sir?

ALONSO: Prithee, no more. Thou dost talk nothing to me.

GONZALO: I do well believe your Highness, and did it to min-
    ister occasion to these gentlemen, who are of such sensible
    and nimble lungs that they always use to laugh at nothing.

ANTONIO: 'Twas you we laugh'd at.   170

GONZALO: Who in this kind of merry fooling am nothing to
    you; so you may continue and laugh at nothing still.

---

92 **in good time** an expression of ironical acquiescence or amazement; i.e., *sure, right away*   96 **rarest** most remarkable, beautiful   97 **Bate** abate, except, leave out (i.e., don't forget Dido; or, let's have no more talk of Dido)   100 **in a sort** in a way   104 **stomach** appetite   105 **Married** given in marriage   106 **rate** estimation, consideration   116 **lusty** vigorous   117 **that . . . bowed** that hung out over its wave-worn foot   118 **As** as if   124 **Who** which, i.e., the eye   126–128 **the fair . . . bow** i.e., Claribel herself was poised uncertain between unwillingness to marry and obedience to her father as to which end of the scale should sink, which should prevail   130 **Moe** more   133 **dear'st** heaviest, most costly

135 **time** appropriate time   137 **chirurgeonly** like a skilled surgeon. Antonio mocks Gonzalo's medical analogy of a *plaster* applied curatively to a wound   140 **plantation** colonization (with subsequent wordplay on the literal meaning)   141 **docks, mallows** various weeds   144 **by contraries** by what is directly opposite to usual custom   145 **traffic** trade   147 **Letters** learning   148 **use of service** custom of employing servants; **succession** holding of property by right of inheritance   149 **Bourn** boundaries; bound of land landmarks; **tilth** tillage of soil   150 **corn** grain   157 **engine** instrument of warfare   159 **it** its; **foison** plenty   164 **Save** God save   167–168 **minister occasion** furnish opportunity   168 **sensible** sensitive

ANTONIO: What a blow was there given!

SEBASTIAN: An it had not fall'n flat-long.

175 GONZALO: You are gentlemen of brave mettle; you would lift the moon out of her sphere, if she would continue in it five weeks without changing.

(Enter ARIEL [invisible] playing solemn music.)

SEBASTIAN: We would so, and then go a-batfowling.

ANTONIO: Nay, good my lord, be not angry.

180 GONZALO: No, I warrant, you, I will not adventure my discretion so weakly. Will you laugh me asleep? For I am very heavy.

ANTONIO: Go sleep, and hear us.

(All sleep except ALONSO, SEBASTIAN, and ANTONIO.)

ALONSO: What, all so soon asleep? I wish mine eyes
185   Would, with themselves, shut up my thoughts. I find
They are inclin'd to do so.

SEBASTIAN: Please you, sir,
Do not omit the heavy offer of it.
It seldom visits sorrow; when it doth,
It is a comforter.

ANTONIO: We two, my lord,
190   Will guard your person while you take your rest,
And watch your safety.

ALONSO: Thank you. Wondrous heavy.

(ALONSO sleeps. Exit ARIEL.)

SEBASTIAN: What a strange drowsiness possesses them!

ANTONIO: It is the quality o' th' climate.

SEBASTIAN: Why
Doth it not then our eyelids sink? I find not
195   Myself dispos'd to sleep.

ANTONIO: Nor I; my spirits are nimble.
They fell together all, as by consent;
They dropp'd, as by a thunder-stroke. What might,
Worthy Sebastian? O, what might—? No more—
And yet methinks I see it in thy face,
200   What thou shouldst be. Th' occasion speaks thee, and
My strong imagination sees a crown
Dropping upon thy head.

SEBASTIAN: What, art thou waking?

ANTONIO: Do you not hear me speak?

SEBASTIAN: I do; and surely
It is a sleepy language and thou speak'st
205   Out of thy sleep. What is it thou didst say?

---

174 **An** if; **flat-long** with the flat of the sword, i.e., ineffectually. (Cf. *fallen flat.*) 178 **a-batfowling** hunting birds at night with lantern and stick; also, gulling a simpleton. Gonzalo is the simpleton, or fowl, and Sebastian will use the moon as his lantern 180–81 **adventure . . . weakly** risk my reputation for discretion for so trivial a cause (by getting angry at these sarcastic fellows) 182 **heavy** sleep 183 **Go . . . us** let our laughing send you to sleep, or, go to sleep and hear us laugh at you 187 **omit** neglect; **heavy** drowsy 200 **speaks** calls upon; or, pronounces, proclaims. Sebastian as usurper of Alonso's crown

This is a strange repose, to be asleep
With eyes wide open—standing, speaking, moving—
And yet so fast asleep.

ANTONIO: Noble Sebastian,
Thou let'st thy fortune sleep—die, rather; wink'st
Whiles thou art waking.   210

SEBASTIAN: Thou dost snore distinctly;
There's meaning in thy snores.

ANTONIO: I am more serious than my custom. You
Must be so too, if heed me; which to do
Trebles thee o'er.

SEBASTIAN: Well, I am standing water.

ANTONIO: I'll teach you how to flow.   215

SEBASTIAN: Do so. To ebb
Hereditary sloth instructs me.

ANTONIO: O,
If you but knew how you the purpose cherish
Whiles thus you mock it! How, in stripping it,
You more invest it! Ebbing men, indeed,
Most often do so near the bottom run   220
By their own fear or sloth.

SEBASTIAN: Prithee say on.
The setting of thine eye and cheek proclaim
A matter from thee, and a birth indeed
Which throes thee much to yield.

ANTONIO: Thus, sir:
Although this lord of weak remembrance, this,   225
Who shall be of as little memory
When he is earth'd, hath here almost persuaded—
For he's a spirit of persuasion, only
Professes to persuade—the King his son's alive,
'Tis as impossible that he's undrown'd   230
As he that sleeps here swims.

SEBASTIAN: I have no hope
That he's undrown'd.

ANTONIO: O, out of that "no hope"
What great hope have you! No hope that way is
Another way so high a hope that even
Ambition cannot pierce a wink beyond,   235

---

209 **wink'st** shut your eyes   214 **Trebles thee o'er** makes you three times as great and rich; **standing water** water which neither ebbs nor flows, at a standstill, indecisive   216 **Hereditary sloth** natural laziness   217 **purpose** i.e., of being king; **cherish** i.e., make dear, enrich   219 **invest** clothe. Antonio's paradox is that by skeptically stripping away illusions Sebastian can see the essence of a situation and the opportunity it presents, or that by disclaiming and deriding his purpose Sebastian shows how he values it   220 **the bottom** i.e., on which unadventurous men may go aground and miss the tide of fortune   222 **setting** set expression (of earnestness)   223 **matter** matter of importance   224 **throes** causes pain, as in giving birth   225 **this lord** i.e., Gonzalo; **remembrance** (1) power of remembering (2) being remembered after his death   227 **earth'd** buried   228–229 **only . . . persuade** i.e., whose whole function (as a privy councilor) is to persuade   233 **that way** i.e., in regard to Ferdinand's being saved   235–236 **Ambition . . . there** ambition itself cannot see any further than that hope (of the crown), but is unsure of itself in seeing even so far, is dazzled by daring to think so high

But doubt discovery there. Will you grant with me
That Ferdinand is drown'd?
SEBASTIAN: He's gone.
ANTONIO: Then, tell me,
Who's the next heir of Naples?
SEBASTIAN: Claribel.
ANTONIO: She that is Queen of Tunis; she that dwells
240   Ten leagues beyond man's life; she that from Naples
Can have no note, unless the sun were post—
The man i' th' moon's too slow—till new-born chins
Be rough and razorable; she that from whom
We all were sea-swallow'd, though some cast again,
245   And by that destiny to perform an act
Whereof what's past is prologue, what to come
In yours and my discharge.
SEBASTIAN: What stuff is this? How say you?
'Tis true, my brother's daughter's Queen of Tunis;
250   So is she heir of Naples; 'twixt which regions
There is some space.
ANTONIO: A space whose ev'ry cubit
Seems to cry out, "How shall that Claribel
Measure us back to Naples? Keep in Tunis,
And let Sebastian wake." Say this were death
255   That now hath seiz'd them; why, they were no worse
Than now they are. There be that can rule Naples
As well as he that sleeps; lords that can prate
As amply and unnecessarily
As this Gonzalo; I myself could make
260   A chough of as deep chat. O, that you bore
The mind that I do! What a sleep were this
For your advancement! Do you understand me?
SEBASTIAN: Methinks I do.
ANTONIO: And how does your content
Tender your own good fortune?
SEBASTIAN: I remember
265   You did supplant your brother Prospero.
ANTONIO: True.
And look how well my garments sit upon me,
Much feater than before. My brother's servants
Were then my fellows; now they are my men.
SEBASTIAN: But, for your conscience?
270 ANTONIO: Ay, sir, where lies that? If 'twere a kibe,
'Twould put me to my slipper; but I feel not
This deity in my bosom. Twenty consciences,
That stand 'twixt me and Milan, candied be they
And melt ere they molest! Here lies your brother,
275   No better than the earth he lies upon,

If he were that which now he's like—that's dead,
Whom I, with this obedient steel, three inches of it,
Can lay to bed forever; whiles you, doing thus,
To the perpetual wink for aye might put
This ancient morsel, this Sir Prudence, who   280
Should not upbraid our course. For all the rest,
They'll take suggestion as a cat laps milk;
They'll tell the clock to any business that
We say befits the hour.
SEBASTIAN: Thy case, dear friend,
Shall be my precedent. As thou got'st Milan,   285
I'll come by Naples. Draw thy sword. One stroke
Shall free thee from the tribute which thou payest,
And I the king shall love thee.
ANTONIO: Draw together;
And when I rear my hand, do you the like,
To fall it on Gonzalo.   290

(*They draw.*)

SEBASTIAN: O, but one word.

(*They talk apart.*)

(*Enter* ARIEL [*invisible*], *with music and song.*)

ARIEL: My master through his art foresees the danger
That you, his friend, are in, and sends me forth—
For else his project dies—to keep them living.

(*Sings in* GONZALO's *ear.*)

While you here do snoring lie,
Open-ey'd conspiracy   295
His time doth take.
If of life you keep a care,
Shake off slumber, and beware.
Awake, awake!

ANTONIO: Then let us both be sudden.   300
GONZALO: (*Waking.*) Now, good angels preserve the King!

(*The others wake.*)

ALONSO: Why, how now, ho, awake? Why are you drawn?
Wherefore this ghastly looking?
GONZALO: What's the matter?
SEBASTIAN: Whiles we stood here securing your repose,
Even now, we heard a hollow burst of bellowing   305
Like bulls, or rather lions. Did 't not wake you?
It struck mine ear most terribly.
ALONSO: I heard nothing.
ANTONIO: O, 'twas a din to fright a monster's ear,
To make an earthquake! Sure it was the roar
Of a whole herd of lions.   310
ALONSO: Heard you this, Gonzalo?
GONZALO: Upon mine honor, sir, I heard a humming,
And that a strange one too, which did awake me.

---

240 **Ten . . . life** i.e., it would take more than a lifetime to get
there   241 **note** news, intimation; **post** messenger   243 **from**
on our voyage from   244 **cast** were disgorged (with a pun on
casting of parts for a play)   247 **discharge** performance   253
Measure us i.e., traverse the cubits, find her way   254 **wake**
i.e., to his good fortune   259–260 **I . . . chat** I could teach a
jackdaw to talk as wisely, or, be such a garrulous talker myself
263 **content** desire, inclination   264 **Tender** regard, look after
267 **feater** more becomingly, fittingly   270 **kibe** chilblain, sore
on the heel   271 **put me to** oblige me to wear   273 **Milan**
the dukedom of Milan; **candied** frozen, congealed in crystalline
form

---

279 **wink** sleep, closing of eyes   283 **tell the clock** i.e., answer
appropriately, chime   287 **tribute** (See 1.2.113–24)   296 **time**
opportunity   304 **securing** standing guard over

315 I shak'd you, sir, and cried. As mine eyes open'd,
I saw their weapons drawn. There was a noise,
That's verily. 'Tis best we stand upon our guard,
Or that we quit this place. Let's draw our weapons.
ALONSO: Lead off this ground, and let's make further search
For my poor son.
320 GONZALO: Heavens keep him from these beasts!
For he is, sure, i' th' island.
ALONSO: Lead away.
ARIEL: (*Aside.*) Prospero my lord shall know what I have done.
So, King, go safely on to seek thy son.

(*Exeunt [severally].*)

SCENE II

Enter CALIBAN *with a burden of wood. A noise of thunder heard.*

CALIBAN: All the infections that the sun sucks up
From bogs, fens, flats, on Prosper fall and make him
By inch-meal a disease! His spirits hear me,
And yet I needs must curse. But they'll nor pinch,
5 Fright me with urchin-shows, pitch me i' th' mire,
Nor lead me, like a firebrand, in the dark
Out of my way, unless he bid 'em; but
For every trifle are they set upon me;
Sometime like apes that mow and chatter at me
10 And after bite me, then like hedgehogs which
Lie tumbling in my barefoot way and mount
Their pricks at my footfall; sometime am I
All wound with adders who with cloven tongues
Do hiss me into madness.

(*Enter* TRINCULO.)

                    Lo, now, lo!
15 Here comes a spirit of his, and to torment me
For bringing wood in slowly. I'll fall flat;
Perchance he will not mind me.

(*Lies down.*)

TRINCULO: Here's neither bush nor shrub, to bear off any
weather at all, and another storm brewing; I hear it sing i'
20 th' wind. Yond same black cloud, yond huge one, looks like
a foul bombard that would shed his liquor. If it should
thunder as it did before, I know not where to hide my
head. Yond same cloud cannot choose but fall by pailfuls.
(*Sees* CALIBAN.) What have we here? A man or a fish? Dead
25 or alive? A fish, he smells like a fish; a very ancient and fish-
like smell; a kind of not of the newest Poor-John. A strange
fish! Were I in England now, as once I was, and had but this
fish painted, not a holiday fool there but would give a piece

of silver. There would this monster make a man; any strange
beast there makes a man. When they will not give a doit to   30
relieve a lame beggar, they will lay out ten to see a dead Indian. Legg'd like a man! And his fins like arms! Warm, o' my
troth! I do now let loose my opinion, hold it no longer: this
is no fish, but an islander, that hath lately suffer'd by a thunderbolt. (*Thunder.*) Alas, the storm is come again! My best   35
way is to creep under his gaberdine; there is no other shelter hereabout. Misery acquaints a man with strange bedfellows. I will here shroud till the dregs of the storm be past.

(*Creeps under* CALIBAN's *garment.*)

(*Enter* STEPHANO, *singing,* [*a bottle in his hand*].)

STEPHANO: "I shall no more to sea, to sea,   40
          Here shall I die ashore—"

This is a very scurvy tune to sing at a man's funeral.
Well, here's my comfort.

(*Drinks.*)

(*Sings.*)

    "The master, the swabber, the boatswain and I,
        The gunner and his mate
    Lov'd Mall, Meg, and Marian, and Margery,   45
        But none of us car'd for Kate;
        For she had a tongue with a tang,
        Would cry to a sailor, 'Go hang!'
    She lov'd not the savor of tar nor of pitch,
    Yet a tailor might scratch her where'er she did itch.   50
        Then to sea, boys, and let her go hang!"

This is a scurvy tune too; but here's my comfort.

(*Drinks.*)

CALIBAN: Do not torment me! Oh!
STEPHANO: What's the matter? Have we devils here? Do you
put tricks upon 's with savages and men of Ind, ha? I have   55
not scap'd drowning to be afeard now of your four legs;
for it hath been said, "As proper a man as ever went on
four legs cannot make him give ground"; and it shall be
said so again while Stephano breathes at' nostrils.
CALIBAN: This spirit torments me! Oh!   60
STEPHANO: This is some monster of the isle with four legs,
who hath got, as I take it, an ague. Where the devil should
he learn our language? I will give him some relief, if it be
but for that. If I can recover him and keep him tame and
get to Naples with him, he's a present for any emperor   65
that ever trod on neat's-leather.
CALIBAN: Do not torment me, prithee. I'll bring my wood
home faster.

II.ii. Location: Another part of the island. 3 **By inch-
meal** inch by inch   4 **nor** neither   5 **urchin-shows** apparitions shaped like hedgehogs   6 **like a firebrand** in the guise of
a will-o'-the-wisp   9 **mow** make faces   17 **mind** notice   18
bear off keep off   21 **foul bombard** dirty leathern bottle; his
its   26 **Poor-John** salted hake, type of poor fare   28 **painted**
i.e., painted on a sign set up outside a booth or tent at a fair

---

29 **make a man** make one's fortune   30 **doit** small coin   36
gaberdine cloak, loose upper garment   38 **shroud** take shelter;
dregs i.e., last remains   55 **Ind** India   57 **proper** handsome;
four legs the conventional phrase would supply *two legs*   59 **at'**
at the   64 **for that** i.e., for knowing our language; recover restore   66 **neat's-leather** cowhide

STEPHANO: He's in his fit now and does not talk after the wis-
70   est. He shall taste of my bottle; if he have never drunk
wine afore, it will go near to remove his fit. If I can recover
him and keep him tame, I will not take too much for him;
he shall pay for him that hath him, and that soundly.

CALIBAN: Thou dost me yet but little hurt;
75   Thou wilt anon, I know it by thy trembling.
Now Prosper works upon thee.

STEPHANO: Come on your ways; open your mouth; here is
that which will give language to you, cat. Open your
mouth; this will shake your shaking, I can tell you, and
80   that soundly. (*Gives* CALIBAN *drink*.) You cannot tell who's
your friend. Open your chaps again.

TRINCULO: I should know that voice. It should be—but he is
drown'd; and these are devils. O defend me!

STEPHANO: Four legs and two voices; a most delicate mon-
85   ster! His forward voice now is to speak well of his friend;
his backward voice is to utter foul speeches and to detract.
If all the wine in my bottle will recover him, I will help
his ague. Come. (*Gives drink*.) Amen! I will pour some in
thy other mouth.

90 TRINCULO: Stephano!

STEPHANO: Doth thy other mouth call me? Mercy, mercy!
This is a devil, and no monster. I will leave him; I have no
long spoon.

TRINCULO: Stephano! If thou beest Stephano, touch me and
95   speak to me; for I am Trinculo—be not afeard—thy good
friend Trinculo.

STEPHANO: If thou beest Trinculo, come forth. I'll pull thee by
the lesser legs. If any be Trinculo's legs, these are they. (*Pulls
him out*.) Thou art very Trinculo indeed! How cam'st thou
100   to be the siege of this moon-calf? Can he vent Trinculos?

TRINCULO: I took him to be kill'd with a thunder-stroke. But
art thou not drown'd, Stephano? I hope now thou art not
drown'd. Is the storm overblown? I hid me under the dead
moon-calf's gaberdine for fear of the storm. And art thou
105   living, Stephano? O Stephano, two Neapolitans scap'd!

STEPHANO: Prithee, do not turn me about; my stomach is not
constant.

CALIBAN: These be fine things, an if they be not sprites.
That's a brave god and bears celestial liquor.
110   I will kneel to him.

STEPHANO: How didst thou scape? How cam'st thou hither?
Swear by this bottle how thou cam'st hither. I escap'd
upon a butt of sack which the sailors heav'd o'erboard—
by this bottle, which I made of the bark of a tree with
115   mine own hands since I was cast ashore.

CALIBAN: (*Kneeling*.) I'll swear upon that bottle to be thy true
subject, for the liquor is not earthly.

STEPHANO: Here; swear then how thou escap'dst.

TRINCULO: Swum ashore, man, like a duck. I can swim like a
duck, I'll be sworn.   120

STEPHANO: Here, kiss the book. Though thou canst swim like
a duck, thou art made like a goose.

(*Gives drink*.)

TRINCULO: O Stephano, hast any more of this?

STEPHANO: The whole butt, man. My cellar is in a rock by
the sea-side where my wine is hid. How now, moon-calf? 125
How does thine ague?

CALIBAN: Hast thou not dropp'd from heaven?

STEPHANO: Out o' th' moon, I do assure thee. I was the man
i' th' moon when time was.

CALIBAN: I have seen thee in her and I do adore thee.   130
My mistress show'd me thee and thy dog and thy bush.

STEPHANO: Come, swear to that; kiss the book. I will furnish
it anon with new contents. Swear.

(*Gives drink*.)

TRINCULO: By this good light, this is a very shallow monster!
I afeard of him? A very weak monster! The man i' th' 135
moon? A most poor credulous monster! Well drawn, monster, in good sooth!

CALIBAN: I'll show thee every fertile inch o' th' island;
And I will kiss thy foot. I prithee, by my god.

TRINCULO: By this light, a most perfidious and drunken 140
monster! When's god's asleep, he'll rob his bottle.

CALIBAN: I'll kiss thy foot. I'll swear myself thy subject.

STEPHANO: Come on then; down, and swear.

(CALIBAN *swears*.)

TRINCULO: I shall laugh myself to death at this puppy-headed
monster. A most scurvy monster! I could find in my heart 145
to beat him—

STEPHANO: Come, kiss.

TRINCULO: But that the poor monster's in drink. An abominable monster!

CALIBAN: I'll show thee the best springs; I'll pluck thee berries; 150
I'll fish for thee and get thee wood enough.
A plague upon the tyrant that I serve!
I'll bear him no more sticks, but follow thee,
Thou wondrous man.

TRINCULO: A most ridiculous monster, to make a wonder of 155
a poor drunkard!

CALIBAN: I prithee, let me bring thee where crabs grow;
And I with my long nails will dig thee pig-nuts,
Show thee a jay's nest, and instruct thee how
To snare the nimble marmoset. I'll bring thee   160

---

72 **I will . . . much** i.e., no sum can be too much   73 **hath**
possesses, receives   78 **cat . . . mouth** allusion to the proverb,
"Good liquor will make a cat speak"   81 **chaps** jaws   92–93
long spoon allusion to the proverb, "He that sups with the devil
has need of a long spoon"   100 **siege** excrement; **moon-calf**
monster, abortion. Supposed to be caused by the influence of the
moon; **vent** emit   106–107 not constant unsteady   108 **an if**
if   109 **brave** fine, magnificent   113 **butt of sack** barrel of
Canary wine

---

121 **book** i.e., bottle   129 **when time was** once upon a time
131 **dog . . . bush** the man in the moon was popularly imagined to have with him a dog and a bush of thorn   134 **By . . .
light** by God's light, by this good light from heaven   136 **Well
drawn** well pulled (on the bottle)   157 **crabs** crab apples   158
pig-nuts peanuts   160 **marmoset** small monkey

To clust'ring filberts, and sometimes I'll get thee
Young scamels from the rock. Wilt thou go with me?

STEPHANO: I prithee now, lead the way without any more
talking. Trinculo, the King and all our company else being
165 drown'd, we will inherit here. Here! Bear my bottle. Fellow Trinculo, we'll fill him by and by again.

CALIBAN: (*Sings drunkenly.*)

Farewell, master; farewell, farewell!

TRINCULO: A howling monster; a drunken monster!

CALIBAN: No more dams I'll make for fish,
170   Nor fetch in firing
       At requiring,
       Nor scrape trenchering, nor wash dish.
          'Ban, 'Ban, Ca-Caliban
          Has a new master, get a new man.
175   Freedom, high-day! High-day, freedom!
          Freedom, high-day, freedom!

STEPHANO: O brave monster! Lead the way.

(*Exeunt.*)

ACT THREE

SCENE I

Enter FERDINAND, *bearing a log.*

FERDINAND: There be some sports are painful, and their labor
Delight in them sets off; some kinds of baseness
Are nobly undergone; and most poor matters
Point to rich ends. This my mean task
5 Would be as heavy to me as odious, but
The mistress which I serve quickens what's dead
And makes my labors pleasures. O, she is
Ten times more gentle than her father's crabbed,
And he's compos'd of harshness. I must remove
10 Some thousands of these logs and pile them up,
Upon a sore injunction. My sweet mistress
Weeps when she sees me work, and says such baseness
Had never like executor. I forget;
But these sweet thoughts do even refresh my labors,
15 Most busy lest, when I do it.

(*Enter* MIRANDA; *and* PROSPERO [*at a distance, unseen*].)

MIRANDA: Alas, now, pray you,
Work not so hard. I would the lightning had
Burnt up those logs that you are enjoin'd to pile!
Pray, set it down and rest you. When this burns,

'Twill weep for having wearied you. My father
Is hard at study; pray now, rest yourself.   20
He's safe for these three hours.

FERDINAND: O most dear mistress,
The sun will set before I shall discharge
What I must strive to do.

MIRANDA: If you'll sit down,
I'll bear your logs the while. Pray give me that.
I'll carry it to the pile.   25

FERDINAND: No, precious creature,
I had rather crack my sinews, break my back,
Than you should such dishonor undergo
While I sit lazy by.

MIRANDA: It would become me
As well as it does you; and I should do it
With much more ease, for my good will is to it,   30
And yours it is against.

PROSPERO: (*Aside.*)   Poor worm, thou art infected!
This visitation shows it.

MIRANDA: You look wearily.

FERDINAND: No, noble mistress, 'tis fresh morning with me
When you are by at night. I do beseech you—
Chiefly that I might set it in my prayers—   35
What is your name?

MIRANDA: Miranda.—O my father,
I have broke your hest to say so.

FERDINAND: Admir'd Miranda!
Indeed the top of admiration! Worth
What's dearest to the world! Full many a lady
I have ey'd with best regard, and many a time   40
Th' harmony of their tongues hath into bondage
Brought my too diligent ear. For several virtues
Have I lik'd several women, never any
With so full soul but some defect in her
Did quarrel with the noblest grace she ow'd   45
And put it to the foil. But you, O you,
So perfect and so peerless, are created
Of every creature's best!

MIRANDA: I do not know
One of my sex; no woman's face remember,
Save, from my glass, mine own. Nor have I seen   50
More that I may call men than you, good friend,
And my dear father. How features are abroad,
I am skilless of; but, by my modesty,
The jewel in my dower, I would not wish
Any companion in the world but you,   55
Nor can imagination form a shape,
Besides yourself, to like of. But I prattle
Something too wildly, and my father's precepts
I therein do forget.

FERDINAND: I am in my condition
A prince, Miranda; I do think, a king—   60
I would, not so!—and would no more endure
This wooden slavery than to suffer
The flesh-fly blow my mouth. Hear my soul speak:

---

162 **scamels** possibly "seamews," mentioned in Strachey's letter, or shellfish; or perhaps from *squamelle*, furnished with little scales. Contemporary French and Italian travel accounts report that the natives of Patagonia in South America ate small fish described as *fort scameux* and *square* 165 **inherit** take possession 172 **trenchering** trenchers, wooden plates 175 **high-day** holiday (?)

III.i. Location: Before Prospero's cell. 2 **sets off** makes seem greater by contrast 6 **quickens** gives life to 11 **sore injunction** severe command 15 **Most . . . it** i.e., least troubled by my labor when I think of her (?) The line may be in need of emendation

---

32 **visitation** (1) visit (2) visitation of the plague, i.e., infection of love 37 **hest** command 45 **ow'd** owned 46 **put . . . foil** (1) overthrew it (as in wrestling) (2) served as a "foil" or contrast to set it off 53 **skilless** ignorant 63 **blow** befoul with fly-eggs

The very instant that I saw you, did
65 My heart fly to your service; there resides,
    To make me slave to it; and for your sake
    Am I this patient log-man.
MIRANDA: Do you love me?
FERDINAND: O heaven, O earth, bear witness to this sound,
    And crown what I profess with kind event
70 If I speak true! If hollowly, invert
    What best is boded me to mischief! I
    Beyond all limit of what else i' th' world
    Do love, prize, honor you.
MIRANDA: (*Weeping.*)   I am a fool
    To weep at what I am glad of.
PROSPERO: (*Aside.*)   Fair encounter
75 Of two most rare affections! Heavens rain grace
    On that which breeds between 'em!
FERDINAND: Wherefore weep you?
MIRANDA: At mine unworthiness, that dare offer
    What I desire to give, and much less take
    What I shall die to want. But this is trifling,
80 And all the more it seeks to hide itself
    The bigger bulk it shows. Hence, bashful cunning,
    And prompt me, plain and holy innocence!
    I am your wife, if you will marry me;
    If not, I'll die your maid. To be your fellow
85 You may deny me, but I'll be your servant,
    Whether you will or no.
FERDINAND: My mistress, dearest,
    And I thus humble ever.
MIRANDA: My husband, then?
FERDINAND: Ay, with a heart as willing
    As bondage e'er of freedom. Here's my hand.
90 MIRANDA: And mine, with my heart in 't. And now farewell
    Till half an hour hence.
FERDINAND: A thousand thousand!

(*Exeunt* [FERDINAND *and* MIRANDA *severally*].)

PROSPERO: So glad of this as they I cannot be,
    Who are surpris'd with all; but my rejoicing
    At nothing can be more. I'll to my book,
95 For yet ere supper-time must I perform
    Much business appertaining.

SCENE II

Enter CALIBAN, STEPHANO, *and* TRINCULO.

STEPHANO: Tell not me. When the butt is out, we will drink
    water, not a drop before. Therefore bear up, and board
    'em. Servant-monster, drink to me.
TRINCULO: Servant-monster? The folly of this island! They
5   say there's but five upon this isle; we are three of them. If
    th' other two be brain'd like us, the state totters.

STEPHANO: Drink, servant-monster, when I bid thee. Thy
    eyes are almost set in thy head.

(*Gives drink.*)

TRINCULO: Where should they be set else? He were a brave
    monster indeed if they were set in his tail.   10
STEPHANO: My man-monster hath drown'd his tongue in sack.
    For my part, the sea cannot drown me; I swam, ere I could
    recover the shore, five and thirty leagues off and on. By this
    light, thou shalt be my lieutenant, monster, or my standard.
TRINCULO: Your lieutenant, if you list; he's no standard.   15
STEPHANO: We'll not run, Monsieur Monster.
TRINCULO: Nor go neither, but you'll lie like dogs and yet
    say nothing neither.
STEPHANO: Moon-calf, speak once in thy life, if thou beest a
    good moon-calf.   20
CALIBAN: How does thy honor? Let me lick thy shoe.
    I'll not serve him; he is not valiant.
TRINCULO: Thou liest, most ignorant monster, I am in case to
    justle a constable. Why, thou debosh'd fish thou, was there
    ever man a coward that hath drunk so much sack as I to-   25
    day? Wilt thou tell a monstrous lie, being but half a fish
    and half a monster?
CALIBAN: Lo, how he mocks me! Wilt thou let him, my lord?
TRINCULO: "Lord," quoth he? That a monster should be such
    a natural!   30
CALIBAN: Lo, lo, again! Bite him to death, I prithee.
STEPHANO: Trinculo, keep a good tongue in your head. If you
    prove a mutineer—the next tree! The poor monster's my
    subject and he shall not suffer indignity.
CALIBAN: I thank my noble lord. Wilt thou be pleas'd   35
    To hearken once again to the suit I made to thee?
STEPHANO: Marry, will I. Kneel and repeat it; I will stand, and
    so shall Trinculo.

(CALIBAN *kneels.*)

(*Enter* ARIEL, *invisible.*)

CALIBAN: As I told thee before, I am subject to a tyrant,
    A sorcerer, that by his cunning hath   40
    Cheated me of the island.
ARIEL: Thou liest.
CALIBAN: Thou liest, thou jesting monkey, thou!
    I would my valiant master would destroy thee.
    I do not lie.
STEPHANO: Trinculo, if you trouble him any more in 's tale,   45
    by this hand, I will supplant some of your teeth.

---

69 **kind event** favorable outcome   70 **hollowly** insincerely,
falsely   71 **boded** destined for   79 **want** lack   84 **fellow**
mate, equal

III.ii. Location: Another part of the island.   1 **out** empty
2 **bear . . . 'em** Stephano uses the terminology of maneuvering
at sea and boarding a vessel under attack as a way of urging an
assault on the liquor supply

8 **set** fixed in a drunken stare; or sunk, like the sun   9 **brave**
fine, splendid   13 **recover** arrive at   14 **standard** standard-
bearer, ancient, i.e., ensign (as distinguished from *lieutenant,* line
15)   15 **list** prefer; **no standard** i.e., not able to stand up   16
run (1) retreat (2) urinate (taking Trinculo's *standard* line 15, in
the old sense of *conduit*)   17 **go** walk; **lie** (1) tell lies (2) lie prostrate (3) excret   23–24 **case . . . constable** i.e., in fit condition,
made valiant by drink, to taunt or challenge the police; **debosh'd**
i.e., debauched   30 **natural** (1) idiot (2) natural as opposed to
unnatural, monster-like   33 **the next tree** i.e., you'll hang   37
Marry i.e., indeed (originally an oath by the Virgin Mary)

TRINCULO: Why, I said nothing.

STEPHANO: Mum, then, and no more.—Proceed.

CALIBAN: I say, by sorcery he got this isle;

50   From me he got it. If thy greatness will
Revenge it on him—for I know thou dar'st,
But this thing dare not—

STEPHANO: That's most certain.

CALIBAN: Thou shalt be lord of it, and I'll serve thee.

55   STEPHANO: How now shall this be compass'd? Canst thou
bring me to the party?

CALIBAN: Yea, yea, my lord. I'll yield him thee asleep,
Where thou mayst knock a nail into his head.

ARIEL: Thou liest; thou canst not.

60   CALIBAN: What a pied ninny's this! Thou scurvy patch!
I do beseech thy greatness, give him blows
And take his bottle from him. When that's gone
He shall drink nought but brine, for I'll now show him
Where the quick freshes are.

65   STEPHANO: Trinculo, run into no further danger. Interrupt
the monster one word further, and, by this hand, I'll turn
my mercy out o' doors and make a stock-fish of thee.

TRINCULO: Why, what did? I did nothing. I'll go farther off.

STEPHANO: Didst thou not say he lied?

70   ARIEL: Thou liest.

STEPHANO: Do I so? Take thou that. (*Beats* TRINCULO.) As
you like this, give me the lie another time.

TRINCULO: I did not give the lie. Out o' your wits and hearing
too? A pox o' your bottle! This can sack and drinking do. A

75   murrain on your monster, and the devil take your fingers!

CALIBAN: Ha, ha, ha!

STEPHANO: Now, forward with your tale.

(*To* TRINCULO.)

Prithee, stand further off.

CALIBAN: Beat him enough. After a little time

80   I'll beat him too.

STEPHANO: Stand farther.—Come, proceed.

CALIBAN: Why, as I told thee, 'tis a custom with him
I' th' afternoon to sleep. There thou mayst brain him,
Having first seiz'd his books, or with a log

85   Batter his skull, or paunch him with a stake,
Or cut his wezand with thy knife. Remember
First to possess his books; for without them
He's but a sot, as I am, nor hath not
One spirit to command. They all do hate him

90   As rootedly as I. Burn but his books.
He has brave utensils—for so he calls them—
Which, when he has a house, he'll deck withal.
And that most deeply to consider is
The beauty of his daughter. He himself

95   Calls her a nonpareil. I never saw a woman,
But only Sycorax my dam and she;

But she as far surpasseth Sycorax
As great'st does least.

STEPHANO: Is it so brave a lass?

CALIBAN: Ay, lord; she will become thy bed, I warrant,   100
And bring thee forth brave brood.

STEPHANO: Monster, I will kill this man. His daughter and I will
be king and queen—save our Graces!—and Trinculo and
thyself shall be viceroys. Dost thou like the plot, Trinculo?

TRINCULO: Excellent.   105

STEPHANO: Give me thy hand. I am sorry I beat thee; but,
while thou liv'st, keep a good tongue in thy head.

CALIBAN: Within this half hour will he be asleep.
Wilt thou destroy him then?

STEPHANO: Ay, on mine honor.   110

ARIEL: (*Aside.*) This will I tell my master.

CALIBAN: Thou mak'st me merry; I am full of pleasure.
Let us be jocund. Will you troll the catch
You taught me but while-ere?

STEPHANO: At thy request, monster, I will do reason, any rea-   115
son. Come on, Trinculo, let us sing.

(*Sings.*)

"Flout 'em and scout 'em
And scout 'em and flout 'em!
Thought is free."

CALIBAN: That's not the tune.   120

(ARIEL *plays the tune on a tabor and pipe.*)

STEPHANO: What is this same?

TRINCULO: This is the tune of our catch, play'd by the picture of Nobody.

STEPHANO: If thou beest a man, show thyself in thy likeness.
If thou beest a devil, take 't as thou list.   125

TRINCULO: O, forgive me my sins!

STEPHANO: He that dies pays all debts. I defy thee. Mercy
upon us!

CALIBAN: Art thou afeard?

STEPHANO: No, monster, not I.   130

CALIBAN: Be not afeard. This isle is full of noises,
Sounds and sweet airs, that give delight and hurt not.
Sometimes a thousand twangling instruments
Will hum about mine ears, and sometimes voices
That, if I then had wak'd after long sleep,   135
Will make me sleep again; and then, in dreaming,
The clouds methought would open and show riches
Ready to drop upon me, that, when I wak'd,
I cried to dream again.

STEPHANO: This will prove a brave kingdom to me, where I   140
shall have my music for nothing.

CALIBAN: When Prospero is destroy'd.

STEPHANO: That shall be by and by. I remember the story.

---

52 **this thing** i.e., Trinculo   60 **pied ninny** fool in motley;
patch fool   64 **quick freshes** running springs   67 **stock-fish**
dried cod beaten before cooking   72 **give me the lie** call me
a liar to my face   75 **murrain** plague (literally, a cattle disease)
85 **paunch** stab in the belly   86 **wezand** windpipe   88 **sot**
fool   91 **brave utensils** fine furnishings

---

113 **troll the catch** sing the round   114 **while-ere** a short
time ago   118 **scout** deride   s.d. **tabor** small drum   122–123
picture of Nobody refers to a familiar figure with head, arms,
and legs, but no trunk   125 **take 't . . . list** i.e., take my defiance as you please, as best you can

TRINCULO: The sound is going away. Let's follow it, and after
145   do our work.
STEPHANO: Lead, monster; we'll follow. I would I could see
    this taborer; he lays it on.
TRINCULO: Wilt come? I'll follow, Stephano.

(*Exeunt [following* ARIEL's *music].*)

SCENE III

Enter ALONSO, SEBASTIAN, ANTONIO, GONZALO, ADRIAN,
FRANCISCO, *etc.*

GONZALO: By 'r lakin, I can go no further, sir;
    My old bones aches. Here's a maze trod indeed
    Through forth-rights and meanders! By your patience,
    I needs must rest me.
ALONSO: Old lord, I cannot blame thee,
5   Who am myself attach'd with weariness,
    To th' dulling of my spirits. Sit down, and rest.
    Even here I will put off my hope and keep it
    No longer for my flatterer. He is drown'd
    Whom thus we stray to find, and the sea mocks
10   Our frustrate search on land. Well, let him go.

(ALONSO *and* GONZALO *sit.*)

ANTONIO: (*Aside to* SEBASTIAN.) I am right glad that he's so
    out of hope.
    Do not, for one repulse, forego the purpose
    That you resolv'd t' effect.
SEBASTIAN: (*To* ANTONIO.)   The next advantage
    Will we take throughly.
15 ANTONIO: (*To* SEBASTIAN.) Let it be tonight,
    For, now they are oppress'd with travail, they
    Will not, nor cannot, use such vigilance
    As when they are fresh.
SEBASTIAN: (*To* ANTONIO.) I say tonight. No more.

(*Solemn and strange music; and* PROSPERO *on the top, invisible.*)

ALONSO: What harmony is this? My good friends, hark!
GONZALO: Marvelous sweet music!

(*Enter several strange shapes, bringing in a banquet, and dance about
it with gentle actions of salutations; and, inviting* [ALONSO], *etc., to
eat, they depart.*)

20 ALONSO: Give us kind keepers, heavens! What were these?
SEBASTIAN: A living drollery. Now I will believe
    That there are unicorns, that in Arabia
    There is one tree, the phoenix' throne, one phoenix
    At this hour reigning there.

ANTONIO: I'll believe both;
    And what does else want credit, come to me,   25
    And I'll be sworn 'tis true. Travelers ne'er did lie,
    Though fools at home condemn 'em.
GONZALO: If in Naples
    I should report this now, would they believe me
    If I should say I saw such islanders?
    For, certes, these are people of the island,   30
    Who, though they are of monstrous shape, yet, note,
    Their manners are more gentle, kind, than of
    Our human generation you shall find
    Many, nay, almost any.
PROSPERO: (*Aside.*)   Honest lord,
    Thou hast said well; for some of you there present   35
    Are worse than devils.
ALONSO: I cannot too much muse
    Such shapes, such gesture, and such sound, expressing,
    Although they want the use of tongue, a kind
    Of excellent dumb discourse.
PROSPERO: (*Aside.*)   Praise in departing.
FRANCISCO: They vanish'd strangely.   40
SEBASTIAN: No matter, since
    They have left their viands behind; for we have stomachs.
    Will 't please you taste of what is here?
ALONSO: Not I.
GONZALO: Faith, sir, you need not fear. When we were boys,
    Who would believe that there were mountaineers
    Dew-lapp'd like bulls, whose throats had hanging at 'em   45
    Wallets of flesh? Or that there were such men
    Whose heads stood in their breasts? Which now we find
    Each putter-out of five for one will bring us
    Good warrant of.
ALONSO: I will stand to and feed,
    Although my last—no matter, since I feel   50
    The best is past. Brother, my lord the Duke,
    Stand to and do as we.

(*They approach the table.*)

(*Thunder and lightning. Enter* ARIEL, *like a harpy; claps his wings
upon the table; and, with a quaint device, the banquet vanishes.*)

ARIEL: You are three men of sin, whom Destiny,
    That hath to instrument this lower world
    And what is in 't, the never-surfeited sea   55

III.iii. Location: Another part of the island. **1 By 'r lakin**
by our Ladykin, by our Lady **3 forth-rights and meanders**
paths straight and crooked **5 attach'd** seized **12 for** because
of **14 throughly** thoroughly **17 s.d. on the top** at some
high point of the tiring-house or the theatre **20 kind keepers**
guardian angels **21 drollery** puppet show

25 **want credit** lack credence 30 **certes** certainly 36 **muse**
wonder at 39 **Praise in departing** i.e., save your praise until
the end of the performance 45 **Dew-lapp'd** having a dewlap,
or fold of skin hanging from the neck, like cattle 47 **in their
breasts** i.e., like the Anthropophagi described in Othello 48
putter-out . . . one one who invests money, or gambles on the
risks of travel on the condition that, if he returns safely, he is to
receive five times the amount deposited; hence, any traveler 49
stand to fall to; take the risk 52 s.d. **harpy** a fabulous monster
with a woman's face and vulture's body, supposed to be a minister of divine vengeance; **quaint device** ingenious stage contrivance; **banquet vanishes** i.e., the food vanishes; the table
remains until line 82 54 **to** i.e., as its

Hath caus'd to belch up you, and on this island
Where man doth not inhabit—you 'mongst men
Being most unfit to live. I have made you mad;
And even with such-like valor men hang and drown
60 Their proper selves.

(ALONSO, SEBASTIAN, *and* ANTONIO *draw their swords.*)

                       You fools! I and my fellows
Are ministers of Fate. The elements,
Of whom your swords are temper'd, may as well
Wound the loud winds, or with bemock'd-at stabs
Kill the still-closing waters, as diminish
65 One dowle that's in my plume. My fellow-ministers
Are like invulnerable. If you could hurt,
Your swords are now too massy for your strengths
And will not be uplifted. But remember—
For that's my business to you—that you three
70 From Milan did supplant good Prospero;
Expos'd unto the sea, which hath requit it,
Him and his innocent child; for which foul deed
The pow'rs, delaying, not forgetting, have
Incens'd the seas and shores, yea, all the creatures,
75 Against your peace. Thee of thy son, Alonso,
They have bereft; and do pronounce by me
Ling'ring perdition, worse than any death
Can be at once, shall step by step attend
You and your ways; whose wraths to guard you from—
80 Which here, in this most desolate isle, else falls
Upon your heads—is nothing but heart's sorrow
And a clear life ensuing.

(*He vanishes in thunder; then, to soft music, enter the shapes again, and dance, with mocks and mows, and carrying out the table.*)

PROSPERO: Bravely the figure of this harpy hast thou
Perform'd, my Ariel; a grace it had devouring.
85 Of my instruction hast thou nothing bated
In what thou hadst to say. So, with good life
And observation strange, my meaner ministers
Their several kinds have done. My high charms work,
And these mine enemies are all knit up
90 In their distractions. They now are in my pow'r;
And in these fits I leave them, while I visit
Young Ferdinand, whom they suppose is drown'd,
And his and mine lov'd darling.

---

59 **such-like valor** i.e., the reckless valor derived from madness 60 **proper** own 62 **whom** which 64 **still-closing** always closing again when parted 65 **dowle** soft, fine feather 66 **like** likewise, similarly; **If** even if 71 **requit** requited, avenged 79 **whose** refers to the heavenly powers s.d. **mocks and mows** mocking gestures and grimaces 83 **Bravely** finely, dashing 84 **a grace ... devouring** i.e., you gracefully caused the banquet to disappear as if you had consumed it (with puns on *grace* meaning "gracefulness" and "a blessing on the meal," and on *devouring* meaning "a literal eating" and "an all-consuming or ravishing grace") 85 **bated** abated, diminished 86 **good life** faithful reproduction 87 **observation strange** exceptional attention to detail; **meaner** i.e., subordinate to Ariel 88 **several kinds** individual parts

(*Exit above.*)

GONZALO: I' th' name of something holy, sir, why stand you
In this strange stare? 95
ALONSO: O, it is monstrous, monstrous!
Methought the billows spoke and told me of it;
The winds did sing it to me, and the thunder,
That deep and dreadful organ-pipe, pronounc'd
The name of Prosper; it did bass my trespass.
Therefore my son i' th' ooze is bedded, and 100
I'll seek him deeper than e'er plummet sounded
And with him there lie mudded.

(*Exit.*)

SEBASTIAN: But one fiend at a time,
I'll fight their legions o'er.
ANTONIO: I'll be thy second.

(*Exeunt* [SEBASTIAN *and* ANTONIO].)

GONZALO: All three of them are desperate. Their great guilt, 105
Like poison given to work a great time after,
Now 'gins to bite the spirits. I do beseech you,
That are of suppler joints, follow them swiftly
And hinder them from what this ecstasy
May now provoke them to. 110
ADRIAN: Follow, I pray you.

(*Exeunt omnes.*)

ACT FOUR

SCENE I

Enter PROSPERO, FERDINAND, *and* MIRANDA.

PROSPERO: If I have too austerely punish'd you,
Your compensation makes amends, for I
Have given you here a third of mine own life,
Or that for which I live; who once again
I tender to thy hand. All thy vexations 5
Were but my trials of thy love, and thou
Hast strangely stood the test. Here, afore Heaven,
I ratify this my rich gift. O Ferdinand,
Do not smile at me that I boast her off,
For thou shalt find she will outstrip all praise 10
And make it halt behind her.
FERDINAND: I do believe it
Against an oracle.

---

94 **why** Gonzalo was not addressed in Ariel's speech to the "three men of sin," line 53, and is not as they are in a maddened state; see lines 105–107 95 **it** i.e., my sin 99 **bass my trespass** proclaim my trespass like a bass note in music 104 **o'er one** after another

IV.i. Location: Before Prospero's cell. 3 **a third** i.e., Miranda, into whose education Prospero has put a third of his life (?) or who represents a large part of what he cares about, along with his dukedom and his learned study (?) 7 **strangely** extraordinarily 9 **boast her off** i.e., praise her so 11 **halt** limp 12 **Against an oracle** i.e., even if an oracle should declare otherwise

PROSPERO: Then, as my gift and thine own acquisition
Worthily purchas'd, take my daughter. But
15   If thou dost break her virgin-knot before
All sanctimonious ceremonies may
With full and holy rite be minist'red,
No sweet aspersion shall the heavens let fall
To make this contract grow; but barren hate,
20   Sour-ey'd disdain, and discord shall bestrew
The union of your bed with weeds so loathly
That you shall hate it both. Therefore take heed,
As Hymen's lamps shall light you.
FERDINAND: As I hope
For quiet days, fair issue, and long life,
25   With such love as 'tis now, the murkiest den,
The most opportune place, the strong'st suggestion
Our worser genius can, shall never melt
Mine honor into lust, to take away
The edge of that day's celebration
30   When I shall think or Phoebus' steeds are founder'd
Or Night kept chain'd below.
PROSPERO: Fairly spoke.
Sit then and talk with her; she is thine own.

(FERDINAND *and* MIRANDA *sit*.)

What, Ariel! My industrious servant, Ariel!

(*Enter* ARIEL.)

ARIEL: What would my potent master? Here I am.
35 PROSPERO: Thou and thy meaner fellows your last service
Did worthily perform; and I must use you
In such another trick. Go bring the rabble,
O'er whom I give thee pow'r, here to this place.
Incite them to quick motion, for I must
40   Bestow upon the eyes of this young couple
Some vanity of mine art. It is my promise,
And they expect it from me.
ARIEL: Presently?
PROSPERO: Ay, with a twink.
ARIEL: Before you can say "come" and "go,"
45   And breathe twice and cry "so, so,"
Each one, tripping on his toe,
Will be here with mop and mow.
Do you love me, master? No?
50 PROSPERO: Dearly, my delicate Ariel. Do not approach
Till thou dost hear me call.
ARIEL: Well, I conceive.

(*Exit*.)

PROSPERO: Look thou be true; do not give dalliance
Too much the rein. The strongest oaths are straw
To th' fire i' th' blood. Be more abstemious,
Or else good night your vow!
FERDINAND: I warrant you, sir;
The white cold virgin snow upon my heart   55
Abates the ardor of my liver.
PROSPERO: Well.
Now come, my Ariel! Bring a corollary,
Rather than want a spirit. Appear, and pertly!
No tongue! All eyes! Be silent.

(*Soft music*.)

(*Enter* IRIS.)

IRIS: Ceres, most bounteous lady, thy rich leas   60
Of wheat, rye, barley, vetches, oats, and pease;
Thy turfy mountains, where live nibbling sheep,
And flat meads thatch'd with stover, them to keep;
Thy banks with pioned and twilled brims,
Which spongy April at thy hest betrims,   65
To make cold nymphs chaste crowns; and thy broom-
     groves,
Whose shadow the dismissed bachelor loves,
Being lass-lorn; thy pole-clipt vineyard;
And thy sea-marge, sterile and rocky-hard,
Where thou thyself dost air—the queen o' th' sky,   70
Whose wat'ry arch and messenger am I,
Bids thee leave these, and with her sovereign grace.

(JUNO *descends* [*slowly in her car*].)

Here on this grass-plot, in this very place,
To come and sport. Her peacocks fly amain.
Approach, rich Ceres, her to entertain.   75

(*Enter* CERES.)

CERES: Hail, many-color'd messenger, that ne'er
Dost disobey the wife of Jupiter,
Who with thy saffron wings upon my flow'rs
Diffusest honey-drops, refreshing show'rs,
And with each end of thy blue bow dost crown   80
My bosky acres and my unshrubb'd down,

---

16 **sanctimonious** sacred   18 **aspersion** dew, shower   23 **Hymen's** Hymen was the Greek and Roman god of marriage   27 **worser genius** evil genius, or evil attendant spirit   30 **or** either; **founder'd** broken down, made lame (i.e., Ferdinand will wait impatiently for the bridal night)   37 **rabble** band, i.e., the *meaner* fellows of line 35   41 **vanity** illusion   47 **mop and mow** gestures and grimaces   50 **conceive** understand

56 **liver** as the presumed seat of the passions   57 **corollary** surplus, extra supply   58 **want** lack; **pertly** briskly s.d. **Iris** goddess of the rainbow, and Juno's messenger   60 **Ceres** goddess of the generative power of nature; **leas** meadows   61 **vetches** plants for forage, fodder   63 **stover** winter fodder for cattle   64 **pioned and twilled** undercut by the swift current and protected by roots and branches woven into a mat (?)   66 **broom-groves** clumps of broom, gorse, yellow-flowered shrub   67 **dismissed bachelor** rejected male lover   68 **pole-clipt** hedged in with poles; or pruned   70 **queen o' th' sky** i.e., Juno   71 **wat'ry arch** rainbow   72 s.d. **Juno descends** i.e., starts her descent from the "heavens" above the stage (?)   74 **peacocks** birds sacred to Juno, and used to pull her chariot; **amain** with full speed   75 **entertain** receive   81 **bosky** wooded; **down** upland

Rich scarf to my proud earth; why hath thy Queen
Summon'd me hither, to this short-grass'd green?

IRIS: A contract of true love to celebrate,
85   And some donation freely to estate
On the bless'd lovers.

CERES: Tell me, heavenly bow,
If Venus or her son, as thou dost know,
Do now attend the Queen? Since they did plot
The means that dusky Dis my daughter got,
90   Her and her blind boy's scandal'd company
I have forsworn.

IRIS: Of her society
Be not afraid. I met her deity
Cutting the clouds towards Paphos, and her son
Dove-drawn with her. Here thought they to have done
95   Some wanton charm upon this man and maid,
Whose vows are, that no bed-right shall be paid
Till Hymen's torch be lighted; but in vain;
Mars's hot minion is return'd again;
Her waspish-headed son has broke his arrows,
100   Swears he will shoot no more, but play with sparrows
And be a boy right out.

(JUNO *alights.*)

CERES: Highest Queen of state,
Great Juno, comes; I know her by her gait.

JUNO: How does my bounteous sister? Go with me
To bless this twain, that they may prosperous be
105   And honor'd in their issue.

(*They sing.*)

JUNO: Honor, riches, marriage-blessing,
          Long continuance, and increasing,
          Hourly joys be still upon you!
          Juno sings her blessings on you.

110 CERES: Earth's increase, foison plenty,
          Barns and garners never empty,
          Vines with clust'ring bunches growing,
          Plants with goodly burden bowing;
          Spring come to you at the farthest
115   In the very end of harvest!
          Scarcity and want shall shun you;
          Ceres' blessing so is on you.

FERDINAND: This is a most majestic vision, and
Harmonious charmingly. May I be bold
120   To think these spirits?

PROSPERO: Spirits, which by mine art
I have from their confines call'd to enact
My present fancies.

FERDINAND: Let me live here ever;
So rare a wond'red father and a wife
Makes this place Paradise.

(JUNO *and* CERES *whisper, and send* IRIS *on employment.*)

PROSPERO: Sweet now, silence!
Juno and Ceres whisper seriously;   125
There's something else to do. Hush and be mute,
Or else our spell is marr'd.

IRIS: You nymphs, call'd Naiads, of the windring brooks,
With your sedg'd crowns and ever-harmless looks,
Leave your crisp channels, and on this green land   130
Answer your summons; Juno does command.
Come, temperate nymphs, and help to celebrate
A contract of true love; be not too late.

(*Enter certain* NYMPHS.)

You sunburnt sicklemen, of August weary,
Come hither from the furrow and be merry.   135
Make holiday; your rye-straw hats put on
And these fresh nymphs encounter every one
In country footing.

(*Enter certain* REAPERS, *properly habited. They join with the* NYMPHS *in a graceful dance, towards the end whereof* PROSPERO *starts suddenly, and speaks; after which, to a strange, hollow, and confused noise, they heavily vanish.*)

PROSPERO: (*Aside.*) I had forgot that foul conspiracy
Of the beast Caliban and his confederates   140
Against my life. The minute of their plot
Is almost come. (*To the* SPIRITS.) Well done! Avoid; no
    more!

FERDINAND: This is strange. Your father's in some passion
That works him strongly.

MIRANDA: Never till this day
Saw I him touch'd with anger so distemper'd.   145

PROSPERO: You do look, my son, in a mov'd sort,
As if you were dismay'd. Be cheerful, sir.
Our revels now are ended. These our actors,
As I foretold you, were all spirits and
Are melted into air, into thin air;   150
And, like the baseless fabric of this vision,
The cloud-capp'd tow'rs, the gorgeous palaces,
The solemn temples, the great globe itself,
Yea, all which it inherit, shall dissolve
And, like this insubstantial pageant faded,   155
Leave not a rack behind. We are such stuff
As dreams are made on, and our little life
Is rounded with a sleep. Sir, I am vex'd.
Bear with my weakness; my old brain is troubled.

---

85 **estate** bestow   87 **son** i.e., Cupid   89 **Dis . . . got** Pluto, or Dis, god of the infernal regions, carried off Persephone, daughter of Ceres, to be his bride in Hades   90 **Her** i.e., Venus; **scandal'd** scandalous   92 **her deity** i.e., her highness   93 **Paphos** place on the island of Cyprus, sacred to Venus   98 **Mars' hot minion** i.e., Venus, the beloved of Mars   99 **waspish-headed** fiery, hotheaded, peevish   100 **sparrows** supposed lustful, and sacred to Venus   101 **right out** outright   110 **foison plenty** plentiful harvest   111 **garners** granaries

123 **wond'red** wonder-performing, wondrous; **wife** sometimes emended to *wise*   128 **windring** wandering, winding (?)   130 **crisp** curled, rippled   132 **temperate** chaste   138 **country footing** country dancing; s.d. **heavily** slowly, dejectedly   142 **Avoid** depart, withdraw   146 **mov'd sort** troubled state, condition   148 **revels** entertainments, pageants   151 **baseless** without substance   154 **which it inherit** who occupy it   156 **rack** wisp of cloud   157 **on** of

160 Be not disturb'd with my infirmity.
If you be pleas'd, retire into my cell
And there repose. A turn or two I'll walk
To still my beating mind.
FERDINAND, MIRANDA: We wish your peace.

(*Exeunt.*)

PROSPERO: Come with a thought! I thank thee, Ariel. Come.

(*Enter* ARIEL.)

165 ARIEL: Thy thoughts I cleave to. What's thy pleasure?
PROSPERO: Spirit,
We must prepare to meet with Caliban.
ARIEL: Ay, my commander. When I presented Ceres,
I thought to have told thee of it, but I fear'd
Lest I might anger thee.
170 PROSPERO: Say again, where didst thou leave these varlets?
ARIEL: I told you, sir, they were red-hot with drinking,
So full of valor that they smote the air
For breathing in their faces; beat the ground
For kissing of their feet; yet always bending
175 Towards their project. Then I beat my tabor,
At which, like unback'd colts, they prick'd their ears,
Advanc'd their eyelids, lifted up their noses
As they smelt music. So I charm'd their ears
That calf-like they my lowing follow'd through
180 Tooth'd briers, sharp furzes, pricking goss, and thorns,
Which ent'red their frail shins. At last I left them
I' th' filthy-mantled pool beyond your cell,
There dancing up to th' chins, that the foul lake
O'erstunk their feet.
PROSPERO: This was well done, my bird.
185 Thy shape invisible retain thou still.
The trumpery in my house, go bring it hither,
For stale to catch these thieves.
ARIEL: I go, I go.

(*Exit.*)

PROSPERO: A devil, a born devil, on whose nature
Nurture can never stick; on whom my pains,
190 Humanely taken, all, all lost, quite lost!
And as with age his body uglier grows,
So his mind cankers. I will plague them all,
Even to roaring.

(*Enter* ARIEL, *loaden with glistering apparel, etc.*)

Come, hang them on this line.

([ARIEL *hangs up the showy finery;* PROSPERO *and* ARIEL *remain, invisible.*] Enter CALIBAN, STEPHANO, *and* TRINCULO, *all wet.*)

CALIBAN: Pray you, tread softly, that the blind mole may not
Hear a foot fall. We now are near his cell.   195
STEPHANO: Monster, your fairy, which you say is a harmless
fairy, has done little better than play'd the Jack with us.
TRINCULO: Monster, I do smell all horse-piss, at which my
nose is in great indignation.
STEPHANO: So is mine. Do you hear, monster? If I should take   200
a displeasure against you, look you—
TRINCULO: Thou wert but a lost monster.
CALIBAN: Good my lord, give me thy favor still.
Be patient, for the prize I'll bring thee to
Shall hoodwink this mischance. Therefore speak softly.   205
All's hush'd as midnight yet.
TRINCULO: Ay, but to lose our bottles in the pool—
STEPHANO: There is not only disgrace and dishonor in that,
monster, but an infinite loss.
TRINCULO: That's more to me than my wetting. Yet this is   210
your harmless fairy, monster!
STEPHANO: I will fetch off my bottle, though I be o'er ears
for my labor.
CALIBAN: Prithee, my King, be quiet. See'st thou here,
This is the mouth o' th' cell. No noise, and enter.   215
Do that good mischief which may make this island
Thine own for ever, and I, thy Caliban,
For aye thy foot-licker.
STEPHANO: Give me thy hand. I do begin to have bloody
thoughts.   220
TRINCULO: (*Seeing the finery.*) O King Stephano! O peer! O
worthy Stephano! Look what a wardrobe here is for thee!
CALIBAN: Let it alone, thou fool! It is but trash.
TRINCULO: O, ho, monster! We know what belongs to a frip-
pery. O King Stephano! (*Takes a gown.*)   225
STEPHANO: Put off that gown, Trinculo. By this hand, I'll have
that gown.
TRINCULO: Thy Grace shall have it.
CALIBAN: The dropsy drown this fool! What do you mean
To dote thus on such luggage? Let's alone   230
And do the murder first. If he awake,
From toe to crown he'll fill our skins with pinches,
Make us strange stuff.
STEPHANO: Be you quiet, monster. Mistress line, is not this
my jerkin? (*Takes it down.*) Now is the jerkin under the   235
line. Now, jerkin, you are like to lose your hair and prove
a bald jerkin.
TRINCULO: Do, do! We steal by line and level, an 't like your
Grace.

---

164 **with a thought** i.e., on the instant, or summoned by my thought, no sooner thought on than here   167 **presented** acted the part of, or introduced   176 **unback'd** unbroken, unridden   177 **Advanc'd** lifted up   180 **goss** gorse, a prickly shrub   182 **filthy-mantled** covered with a slimy coating   186 **trumpery** cheap goods, the *glistering apparel* mentioned in the following stage direction   187 **stale** (1) decoy (2) out of fashion garments (with possible further suggestions of *fit for a stale* or prostitute, *stale* meaning "horse-piss," line 198, and *steal,* pronounced like *stale*)   192 **cankers** festers, grows malignant   193 **line** lime tree or linden

---

197 **Jack** (1) Knave (2) will-o-the-wisp   205 **hoodwink** cover up, make you not see (a hawking term)   221 **King . . . peer** alludes to the old ballad beginning, "King Stephen was a worthy peer"   224 **frippery** place where cast-off clothes are sold   230 **luggage** cumbersome trash   235 **jerkin** jacket make of leather; **under the line** under the lime tree (with punning sense of being south of the equinoctial line or equator; sailors to the southern regions were popularly supposed to lose their hair from scurvy or other diseases. Stephano also quibbles bawdily on losing hair through syphilis, and in *Mistress* and *jerkin*)   238 **by line and level** i.e., by means of plumb-line and carpenter's level, methodically (with pun on *line,* "lime tree," line 235, and *steal* pronounced *stale,* i.e., prostitute, continuing Stephano's bawdy quibble); **an 't like** if it please

240 STEPHANO: I thank thee for that jest. Here's a garment for 't.
(*Gives a garment.*) Wit shall not go unrewarded while I am
king of this country. "Steal by line and level" is an excellent pass of pate. There's another garment for 't.

TRINCULO: Monster, come, put some lime upon your fingers,
245 and away with the rest.

CALIBAN: I have none on 't. We shall lose our time,
And all be turn'd to barnacles, or to apes
With foreheads villainous low.

STEPHANO: Monster, lay to your fingers. Help to bear this
250 away where my hogshead of wine is, or I'll turn you out
of my kingdom. Go to, carry this.

TRINCULO: And this.

STEPHANO: Ay, and this.

(*They collect more and more garments.*)

(*A noise of hunters heard. Enter divers* SPIRITS, *in shape of dogs and
hounds, hunting them about,* PROSPERO *and* ARIEL *setting them on.*)

PROSPERO: Hey, Mountain, hey!
255 ARIEL: Silver! There it goes, Silver!

PROSPERO: Fury, Fury! There, Tyrant, there! Hark! Hark!

(CALIBAN, STEPHANO, *and* TRINCULO *are driven out.*)

Go charge my goblins that they grind their joints
With dry convulsions, shorten up their sinews
With aged cramps, and more pitch-spotted make them
260 Than pard or cat o' mountain.

ARIEL: Hark, they roar!

PROSPERO: Let them be hunted soundly. At this hour
Lies at my mercy all mine enemies.
Shortly shall all my labors end, and thou
Shalt have the air at freedom. For a little
265 Follow, and do me service.

(*Exeunt.*)

ACT FIVE

SCENE I

Enter PROSPERO *in his magic robes,* [*with his staff,*] *and* ARIEL.

PROSPERO: Now does my project gather to a head.
My charms crack not, my spirits obey, and Time
Goes upright with his carriage. How's the day?

ARIEL: On the sixth hour; at which time, my lord,
5 You said our work should cease.

---

243 **pass of pate** sally of wit   244 **lime** birdlime, sticky substance (to give Caliban sticky fingers)   247 **barnacles** barnacle
geese, formerly supposed to be hatched from seashells attached
to trees and to fall thence into the water; here evidently used, like
apes, as types of simpletons   248 **villainous** miserably   258
dry associated with age, arthritic (?); **convulsions** cramps   259
aged characteristic of old age   260 **pard** panther or leopard;
cat o' mountain wildcat

V.i. Location: Before Prospero's cell.   3 **his carriage** its
burden (i.e., Time is unstopped, runs smoothly)

PROSPERO: I did say so,
When first I rais'd the tempest. Say, my spirit,
How fares the King and 's followers?

ARIEL: Confin'd together
In the same fashion as you gave in charge,
Just as you left them; all prisoners, sir,
In the line-grove which weather-fends your cell.   10
They cannot budge till your release. The King,
His brother, and yours, abide all three distracted,
And the remainder mourning over them,
Brimful of sorrow and dismay; but chiefly
Him that you term'd, sir, "The good old lord, Gonzalo."   15
His tears runs down his beard like winter's drops
From eaves of reeds. Your charm so strongly works 'em
That if you now beheld them, your affections
Would become tender.

PROSPERO: Dost thou think so, spirit?

ARIEL: Mine would, sir, were I human.   20

PROSPERO: And mine shall.
Hast thou, which art but air, a touch, a feeling
Of their afflictions, and shall not myself,
One of their kind, that relish all as sharply,
Passion as they, be kindlier mov'd than thou art?
Though with their high wrongs I am struck to th' quick,   25
Yet with my nobler reason 'gainst my fury
Do I take part. The rarer action is
In virtue than in vengeance. They being penitent,
The sole drift of my purpose doth extend
Not a frown further. Go release them, Ariel.   30
My charms I'll break, their senses I'll restore,
And they shall be themselves.

ARIEL: I'll fetch them, sir.

(*Exit.*)

(PROSPERO *traces a charmed circle with his staff.*)

PROSPERO: Ye elves of hills, brooks, standing lakes, and groves,
And ye that on the sands with printless foot
Do chase the ebbing Neptune, and do fly him   35
When he comes back; you demi-puppets that
By moonshine do the green sour ringlets make,
Whereof the ewe not bites; and you whose pastime
Is to make midnight mushrooms, that rejoice
To hear the solemn curfew; by whose aid,   40
Weak masters though ye be, I have bedimm'd
The noontide sun, call'd forth the mutinous winds,
And 'twixt the green sea and the azur'd vault
Set roaring war; to the dread rattling thunder
Have I given fire, and rifted Jove's stout oak   45

---

10 **line-grove** grove of lime trees; **weather-fends** protects from
the weather   11 **your release** you release them   17 **eaves of
reeds** thatched roofs   23 **relish all** experience quite   24 **Passion** experience deep feeling   27 **rarer** nobler   33–50 **Ye . . .
art** this famous passage is an embellished paraphrase of Golding's
translation of Ovid's *Metamorphoses,* 7.197–219   36 **demi-
puppets** puppets of half-size, i.e., elves and fairies   37 **green
sour ringlets** fairy rings, circles in grass (actually produced by
mushrooms)   44–45 **to . . . fire** I have discharged the dread rattling thunderbolt   45 **rifted** riven, split

With his own bolt; the strong-bas'd promontory
Have I made shake, and by the spurs pluck'd up
The pine and cedar; graves at my command
Have wak'd their sleepers, op'd, and let 'em forth
50   By my so potent art. But this rough magic
I here abjure, and, when I have requir'd
Some heavenly music, which even now I do,
To work mine end upon their senses that
This airy charm is for, I'll break my staff,
55   Bury it certain fathoms in the earth,
And deeper than did ever plummet sound
I'll drown my book.

(*Solemn music.*)

(*Here enters* ARIEL *before; then* ALONSO, *with a frantic gesture, attended by* GONZALO; SEBASTIAN *and* ANTONIO *in like manner, attended by* ADRIAN *and* FRANCISCO. *They all enter the circle which* PROSPERO *had made, and there stand charm'd; which* PROSPERO *observing, speaks:*)

A solemn air, and the best comforter
To an unsettled fancy, cure thy brains,
60   Now useless, boil'd within thy skull! There stand,
For you are spell-stopp'd.
Holy Gonzalo, honorable man,
Mine eyes, ev'n sociable to the show of thine,
Fall fellowly drops. The charm dissolves apace,
65   And as the morning steals upon the night,
Melting the darkness, so their rising senses
Begin to chase the ignorant fumes that mantle
Their clearer reason. O good Gonzalo,
My true preserver, and a loyal sir
70   To him thou follow'st! I will pay thy graces
Home both in word and deed. Most cruelly
Didst thou, Alonso, use me and my daughter.
Thy brother was a furtherer in the act.
Thou art pinch'd for 't now, Sebastian. Flesh and blood,
75   You, brother mine, that entertain'd ambition,
Expell'd remorse and nature, who, with Sebastian,
Whose inward pinches therefore are most strong,
Would here have kill'd your king, I do forgive thee,
Unnatural though thou art.—Their understanding
80   Begins to swell, and the approaching tide
Will shortly fill the reasonable shore
That now lies foul and muddy. Not one of them
That yet looks on me, or would know me. Ariel,
Fetch me the hat and rapier in my cell.

(ARIEL *goes to the cell and returns immediately.*)

85   I will discase me, and myself present
As I was sometime Milan. Quickly, spirit;
Thou shalt ere long be free.

(ARIEL *sings and helps to attire him.*)

ARIEL: Where the bee sucks, there suck I;
In a cowslip's bell I lie;
There I couch when owls do cry.   90
On the bat's back I do fly
After summer merrily.
Merrily, merrily shall I live now
Under the blossom that hangs on the bough.

PROSPERO: Why, that's my dainty Ariel! I shall miss thee;   95
But yet thou shalt have freedom. So, so, so.
To the King's ship, invisible as thou art!
There shalt thou find the mariners asleep
Under the hatches. The master and the boatswain
Being awake, enforce them to this place,   100
And presently, I prithee.
ARIEL: I drink the air before me, and return
Or ere your pulse twice beat. (*Exit.*)
GONZALO: All torment, trouble, wonder, and amazement
Inhabits here. Some heavenly power guide us   105
Out of this fearful country!
PROSPERO: Behold, sir King,
The wronged Duke of Milan, Prospero.
For more assurance that a living prince
Does now speak to thee, I embrace thy body;
And to thee and thy company I bid   110
A hearty welcome.

(*Embraces him.*)

ALONSO: Whe'er thou be'st he or no,
Or some enchanted trifle to abuse me,
As late I have been, I not know. Thy pulse
Beats as of flesh and blood; and, since I saw thee,
Th' affliction of my mind amends, with which,   115
I fear, a madness held me. This must crave,
An if this be at all, a most strange story.
Thy dukedom I resign, and do entreat
Thou pardon me my wrongs. But how should Prospero
Be living and be here?   120
PROSPERO: (*To* GONZALO.)   First, noble friend,
Let me embrace thine age, whose honor cannot
Be measur'd or confin'd.

(*Embraces him.*)

GONZALO: Whether this be
Or be not, I'll not swear.
PROSPERO: Yet do yet taste
Some subtleties o' th' isle, that will not let you
Believe things certain. Welcome, my friends all!   125
(*Aside to* SEBASTIAN *and* ANTONIO.) But you, my brace of
lords, were I so minded,

---

47 **spurs** roots   51 **requir'd** requested   58 **and** i.e., which is
63 **sociable** sympathetic; **show** appearance   64 **Fall** let fall   70
pay thy graces reward your favors   71 **Home** fully   76 **remorse** pity; **nature** natural feeling   85 **discase** disrobe   86 **As
. . . Milan** in my former appearance as Duke of Milan

96 **So, so, so** expresses approval of Ariel's help as valet   112 **trifle** trick of magic; **abuse** deceive   116 **crave** require   117 **An
. . . all** if this is actually happening   118 **Thy . . . resign** Alonso
made arrangement with Antonio at the time of Prospero's banishment for Milan to pay tribute to Naples; see 1.2.113–127
124 **subtleties** illusions, magical powers

I here could pluck his Highness' frown upon you
And justify you traitors. At this time
I will tell no tales.

SEBASTIAN: The devil speaks in him.

PROSPERO: No.

130   For you, most wicked sir, whom to call brother
Would even infect my mouth, I do forgive
Thy rankest fault—all of them; and require
My dukedom of thee, which perforce I know
Thou must restore.

ALONSO: If thou be'st Prospero,

135   Give us particulars of thy preservation,
How thou hast met us here, who three hours since
Were wrack'd upon this shore; where I have lost—
How sharp the point of this remembrance is!—
My dear son Ferdinand.

PROSPERO: I am woe for 't, sir.

140 ALONSO: Irreparable is the loss, and Patience
Says it is past her cure.

PROSPERO: I rather think
You have not sought her help, of whose soft grace
For the like loss I have her sovereign aid
And rest myself content.

ALONSO: You the like loss?

145 PROSPERO: As great to me as late; and, supportable
To make the dear loss, have I means much weaker
Than you may call to comfort you, for I
Have lost my daughter.

ALONSO: A daughter?

150   O heavens, that they were living both in Naples,
The king and queen there! That they were, I wish
Myself were mudded in that oozy bed
Where my son lies. When did you lose your daughter?

PROSPERO: In this last tempest. I perceive these lords

155   At this encounter do so much admire
That they devour their reason and scarce think
Their eyes do offices of truth, their words
Are natural breath. But, howsoev'r you have
Been justled from your senses, know for certain

160   That I am Prospero and that very duke
Which was thrust forth of Milan, who most strangely
Upon this shore, where you were wrack'd, was landed,
To be the lord on 't. No more yet of this,
For 'tis a chronicle of day by day,

165   Not a relation for a breakfast nor
Befitting this first meeting. Welcome, sir;
This cell's my court. Here have I few attendants
And subjects none abroad. Pray you look in.
My dukedom since you have given me again,

170   I will requite you with as good a thing,
At least bring forth a wonder, to content ye
As much as me my dukedom.

(Here PROSPERO *discovers* FERDINAND *and* MIRANDA, *playing at chess.)*

---

128 **justify you** prove you to be   139 **woe** sorry   145 **late** recent   155 **admire** wonder   156–158 **scarce . . . breath** scarcely believe that their eyes inform them accurately what they see or that their words are naturally spoken   172 s.d. **discovers** i.e., by opening a curtain, presumably rear-stage

MIRANDA: Sweet lord, you play me false.

FERDINAND: No, my dearest love,
I would not for the world.   175

MIRANDA: Yes, for a score of kingdoms you should wrangle,
And I would call it fair play.

ALONSO: If this prove
A vision of the island, one dear son
Shall I twice lose.

SEBASTIAN: A most high miracle!

FERDINAND: Though the seas threaten, they are merciful;   180
I have curs'd them without cause. (*Kneels.*)

ALONSO: Now all the blessings
Of a glad father compass thee about!
Arise, and say how thou cam'st here.

MIRANDA: O, wonder!
How many goodly creatures are there here!
How beauteous mankind is! O brave new world,   185
That has such people in 't!

PROSPERO: 'Tis new to thee.

ALONSO: What is this maid with whom thou wast at play?
Your eld'st acquaintance cannot be three hours.
Is she the goddess that hath sever'd us,
And brought us thus together?   190

FERDINAND: Sir, she is mortal;
But by immortal Providence she's mine.
I chose her when I could not ask my father
For his advice, nor thought I had one. She
Is daughter to this famous Duke of Milan,
Of whom so often I have heard renown,   195
But never saw before; of whom I have
Receiv'd a second life; and second father
This lady makes him to me.

ALONSO: I am hers.
But, O, how oddly will it sound that I
Must ask my child forgiveness!   200

PROSPERO: There, sir, stop.
Let us not burden our remembrances with
A heaviness that's gone.

GONZALO: I have inly wept
Or should have spoke ere this. Look down, you gods,
And on this couple drop a blessed crown!
For it is you that have chalk'd forth the way   205
Which brought us hither.

ALONSO: I say Amen, Gonzalo!

GONZALO: Was Milan thrust from Milan, that his issue
Should become kings of Naples? O, rejoice
Beyond a common joy, and set it down
With gold on lasting pillars: In one voyage   210
Did Claribel her husband find at Tunis,
And Ferdinand, her brother, found a wife

176–177 **Yes . . . play** i.e., yes, even if we were playing for twenty kingdoms, something less than the whole world, you would still contend mightily against me and play me false, and I would let you do it as though it were fair play; or, if you were to play not just for stakes but literally for kingdoms, my accusation of false play would be out of order in that your "wrangling" would be proper   185 **brave** splendid, gorgeously appareled, handsome   188 **eld'st** longest   207 **Was Milan** was the Duke of Milan

Where he himself was lost; Prospero his dukedom
In a poor isle; and all of us ourselves
215 When no man was his own.
ALONSO: (*To* FERDINAND *and* MIRANDA.) Give me your hands.
Let grief and sorrow still embrace his heart
That doth not wish you joy!
GONZALO: Be it so! Amen!

(*Enter* ARIEL, *with the* MASTER *and* BOATSWAIN *amazedly following.*)

O, look, sir, look, sir! Here is more of us.
I prophesied, if a gallows were on land,
220 This fellow could not drown. Now, blasphemy,
That swear'st grace o'erboard, not an oath on shore?
Hast thou no mouth by land? What is the news?
BOATSWAIN: The best news is that we have safely found
Our King and company; the next, our ship—
225 Which, but three glasses since, we gave out split—
Is tight and yare and bravely rigg'd as when
We first put out to sea.
ARIEL: (*Aside to* PROSPERO.) Sir, all this service
Have I done since I went.
PROSPERO: (*Aside to* ARIEL.) My tricksy spirit!
ALONSO: These are not natural events; they strengthen
230 From strange to stranger. Say, how came you hither?
BOATSWAIN: If I did think, sir, I were well awake,
I'd strive to tell you. We were dead of sleep,
And—how we know not—all clapp'd under hatches;
Where but even now with strange and several noises
235 Of roaring, shrieking, howling, jingling chains,
And moe diversity of sounds, all horrible,
We were awak'd; straightway, at liberty;
Where we, in all her trim, freshly beheld
Our royal, good, and gallant ship, our master
240 Cap'ring to eye her. On a trice, so please you,
Even in a dream, were we divided from them
And were brought moping hither.
ARIEL: (*Aside to* PROSPERO.)   Was 't well done?
PROSPERO: (*Aside to* ARIEL.) Bravely, my diligence. Thou
shalt be free.
ALONSO: This is as strange a maze as e'er men trod,
245 And there is in this business more than nature
Was ever conduct of. Some oracle
Must rectify our knowledge.
PROSPERO: Sir, my liege,
Do not infest your mind with beating on
The strangeness of this business. At pick'd leisure,
250 Which shall be shortly, single I'll resolve you,
Which to you shall seem probable, of every
These happen'd accidents; till when, be cheerful
And think of each thing well. (*Aside to* ARIEL.) Come
hither, spirit.
Set Caliban and his companions free;

Untie the spell. (*Exit* ARIEL.) How fares my gracious sir?   255
There are yet missing of your company
Some few odd lads that you remember not.

(*Enter* ARIEL, *driving in* CALIBAN, STEPHANO, *and* TRINCULO, *in their stol'n apparel.*)

STEPHANO: Every man shift for all the rest, and let no man
take care of himself; for all is but fortune. Coragio, bully-
monster, coragio!   260
TRINCULO: If these be true spies which I wear in my head,
here's a goodly sight.
CALIBAN: O Setebos, these be brave spirits indeed!
How fine my master is! I am afraid
He will chastise me.   265
SEBASTIAN: Ha, ha!
What things are these, my lord, Antonio?
Will money buy 'em?
ANTONIO: Very like. One of them
Is a plain fish, and no doubt marketable.
PROSPERO: Mark but the badges of these men, my lords,   270
Then say if they be true. This misshapen knave,
His mother was a witch, and one so strong
That could control the moon, make flows and ebbs,
And deal in her command without her power.
These three have robb'd me; and this demi-devil—   275
For he's a bastard one—had plotted with them
To take my life. Two of these fellows you
Must know and own; this thing of darkness I
Acknowledge mine.
CALIBAN: I shall be pinch'd to death.
ALONSO: Is not this Stephano, my drunken butler?   280
SEBASTIAN: He is drunk now. Where had he wine?
ALONSO: And Trinculo is reeling ripe. Where should they
Find this grand liquor that hath gilded 'em?
How cam'st thou in this pickle?
TRINCULO: I have been in such a pickle since I saw you last   285
that, I fear me, will never out of my bones. I shall not fear
flyblowing.
SEBASTIAN: Why, how now, Stephano?
STEPHANO: O, touch me not! I am not Stephano, but a cramp.   290
PROSPERO: You'd be king o' the isle, sirrah?
STEPHANO: I should have been a sore one then.
ALONSO: (*Pointing to* CALIBAN.) This is a strange thing as e'er
I look'd on.

---

216 **still** always; **his** that man's   217 **That** who   225 **glasses**
i.e., hours; **gave** out reported   226 **yare** ready   240 **Cap'ring**
to eye dancing for joy to see   242 **moping** in a daze   246
conduct guide, leader   248 **infest** harass, disturb   249 **pick'd**
chosen, convenient   250 **single** i.e., by my own human powers
252 **accidents** occurrences

259 **Coragio** courage; bully-monster gallant monster (ironical)
264 **fine** splendidly attired   270 **badges** emblems of cloth or
silver worn on the arms of retainers. Prospero refers here to the
stolen clothes as emblems of their villainy   271 **true** honest
274 **deal . . . power** wield the moon's power, either without
her authority or beyond her influence   278 **own** recognize, admit as belonging to you   283 **gilded** (1) flushed, made drunk
(2) covered with gilt (suggesting the horse-urine)   284 **pickle**
(1) fix, predicament (2) pickling brine (in this case, horse urine)
286–287 **fly-blowing** i.e., being fouled by fly-eggs (from which
he is saved by being pickled)   291 **sirrah** Standard form of address to an inferior   292 **sore** (1) tyrannical (2) wracked by
pain

PROSPERO: He is as disproportion'd in his manners
295   As in his shape. Go, sirrah, to my cell;
         Take with you your companions. As you look
         To have my pardon, trim it handsomely.
CALIBAN: Ay, that I will; and I'll be wise hereafter
         And seek for grace. What a thrice-double ass
300   Was I to take this drunkard for a god
         And worship this dull fool!
PROSPERO: Go to; away!
ALONSO: Hence, and bestow your luggage where you found it.
SEBASTIAN: Or stole it, rather.

(*Exeunt* CALIBAN, STEPHANO, *and* TRINCULO.)

PROSPERO: Sir, I invite your Highness and your train
305   To my poor cell, where you shall take your rest
         For this one night; which, part of it, I'll waste
         With such discourse as, I not doubt, shall make it
         Go quick away—the story of my life,
         And the particular accidents gone by
310   Since I came to this isle. And in the morn
         I'll bring you to your ship, and so to Naples,
         Where I have hope to see the nuptial
         Of these our dear-belov'd solemnized;
         And thence retire me to my Milan, where
315   Every third thought shall be my grave.
ALONSO: I long
         To hear the story of your life, which must
         Take the ear strangely.
PROSPERO: I'll deliver all;
         And promise you calm seas, auspicious gales,
         And sail so expeditious that shall catch
320   Your royal fleet far off. (*Aside to* ARIEL.) My Ariel, chick,

That is thy charge. Then to the elements
Be free, and fare thou well!—Please you, draw near.

(*Exeunt omnes.*)

EPILOGUE

Spoken by PROSPERO.

         Now my charms are all o'erthrown,
         And what strength I have 's mine own,
         Which is most faint. Now, 'tis true,
         I must be here confin'd by you,
         Or sent to Naples. Let me not,   5
         Since I have my dukedom got
         And pardon'd the deceiver, dwell
         In this bare island by your spell,
         But release me from my bands
         With the help of your good hands.   10
         Gentle breath of yours my sails
         Must fill, or else my project fails,
         Which was to please. Now I want
         Spirits to enforce, art to enchant,
         And my ending is despair,   15
         Unless I be reliev'd by prayer,
         Which pierces so that it assaults
         Mercy itself and frees all faults.
         As you from crimes would pardon'd be,
         Let your indulgence set me free.   20

(*Exit.*)

---

322 **draw near** i.e., enter my cell

Epilogue 9 **bands** bonds 10 **hands** i.e., applause (the noise of which would break the spell of silence) 13 **want** lack 16 **prayer** i.e., Prospero's petition to the audience 17 **assaults** rightfully gains the attention of 18 **frees** obtains forgiveness of 19 **crimes** sins

---

306 **waste** spend 309 **accidents** occurrences 317 **Take** take effect upon, enchant; **deliver** declare, relate

CRITICAL CONTEXTS

SIR PHILIP SIDNEY (1554–1586)

from *Apology for Poetry* (1598)

EDITED BY FORREST G. ROBINSON

Philip Sidney was one of the preeminent courtiers of his day. He was a familiar figure at the court of Queen Elizabeth I, led an ill-fated military expedition to the Netherlands (where he was fatally wounded), wrote an important sonnet sequence, Astrophil and Stella, *and a prose romance,* Arcadia. *His* Apology for Poetry *develops a defense of poets and poetry based on their ability to offer a fictive "golden world," an idealized image of reality that can edify, entertain, and instruct.*

Reading Sidney's Apology, *it is useful to bear several questions in mind: What is the problem that Sidney is attempting to address here? Is there a moral or ethical problem posed by poetry, particularly by the fact that poetry is a form of fiction, of lying? Why is it important to Sidney to compare the poet with the historian and the philosopher? What are the underlying problems that Sidney is attempting to address in his assessment of contemporary dramatic genres?*

. . . There is no art delivered to mankind that hath not the works of nature for his principal object, without which they could not consist, and on which they so depend, as they become actors and players, as it were, of what nature will have set forth. So doth the astronomer look upon the stars, and by that he seeth, setteth down what order nature hath taken therein. So do the geometrician and arithmetician in their diverse sorts of quantities. So doth the musician in times tell you which by nature agree, which not. The natural philosopher thereon hath his name, and the moral philosopher standeth upon the natural virtues, vices, and passions of man; and follow nature (saith he) therein, and thou shalt not err. The lawyer saith what men have determined; the historian what men have done. The grammarian speaketh only of the rules of speech, and the rhetorician and logician, considering what in nature will soonest prove and persuade, thereon give artificial[1] rules, which still are compassed within the circle of a question, according to the proposed matter. The physician weigheth the nature of a man's body, and the nature of things helpful or hurtful unto it. And the metaphysic, though it be in the second and abstract notions, and therefore be counted supernatural, yet doth he indeed build upon the depth of nature. Only the poet, disdaining to be tied to any such subjection, lifted up with the vigor of his own invention, doth grow in effect another nature, in making things either better than nature bringeth forth, or quite anew, forms such as never were in nature, as the Heroes, Demigods, Cyclops, Chimeras, Furies, and such like; so as he goeth hand in hand with nature, not enclosed within the narrow warrant of her gifts, but freely ranging only within the zodiac of his own wit.

Nature never set forth the earth in so rich tapestry as divers poets have done, neither with pleasant rivers, fruitful trees, sweet smelling flowers, nor whatsoever else may make the too much loved earth more lovely. Her world is brazen, the poets only deliver a golden. . . .

Our tragedies and comedies (not without cause cried out against), observing rules neither of honest civility nor of skillful poetry, excepting *Gorboduc*[2] (again I say, of those that I have seen), which notwithstanding, as it is full of stately speeches and well sounding phrases, climbing to the height of Seneca his[3] style, and as full of notable morality, which it doth most delightfully teach, and so obtain the very end of poesy; yet in troth it is very defectious in the circumstances, which grieveth me, because it might not remain as an exact model of all tragedies. For it is faulty both in place and time, the two necessary companions of all corporal actions. For where the stage should always represent but one place, and the uttermost time presupposed in it should be, both by Aristotle's precept and common reason, but one day, there is both many days and many places inartificially[4] imagined.

But if it be so in *Gorboduc,* how much more in all the rest? where you shall have Asia of the one side, and Afric of the other, and so many other under-kingdoms, that the player, when he cometh in, must ever begin with telling where he is, or else the tale will not be conceived. Now ye shall have three ladies walk to gather flowers, and then we must believe the stage to be a garden. By and by we hear news of shipwreck in

[1] **artificial** humanly contrived, rather than natural

[2] **Gorboduc** an early English play (first performed in 1562), modeled on the tragedies of Seneca

[3] **Seneca his** Seneca's

[4] **inartificially** artlessly

the same place, and then we are to blame if we accept it not for a rock. Upon the back of that comes out a hideous monster with fire and smoke, and then the miserable beholders are bound to take it for a cave. While in the meantime two armies fly in, represented with four swords and bucklers, and then what hard heart will not receive it for a pitched field?

Now of time they are much more liberal, for ordinary it is that two young princes fall in love. After many traverses, she is got with child, delivered of a fair boy, he is lost, groweth a man, falls in love, and is ready to get another child, and all this in two hours' space: which, how absurd it is in sense, even sense may imagine, and art hath taught, and all ancient examples justified, and at this day, the ordinary players in Italy will not err in. Yet will some bring in an example of Eunuchus in Terence, that containeth matter of two days, yet far short of twenty years. True it is, and so was it to be played in two days, and so fitted to the time it set forth. And though Plautus hath in one place done amiss, let us hit with him, and not miss with him. But they will say, how then shall we set forth a story which containeth both many places and many times? And do they not know that a tragedy is tied to the laws of poesy, and not of history, not bound to follow the story, but having liberty, either to feign a quite new matter, or to frame the history to the most tragical conveniency? Again, many things may be told which cannot be showed, if they know the difference betwixt reporting and representing. . . .

PERFORMANCE IN HISTORY

PHYLLIS RACKIN
"Misogyny Is Everywhere" (2000)

Phyllis Rackin is an important American scholar of Shakespeare and Renaissance drama and culture, whose books include Stages of History: Shakespeare's English Chronicles *and (with Jean E. Howard)* Engendering a Nation: A Feminist Account of Shakespeare's English Histories. *In this essay, Rackin undertakes a double-barreled argument: she at once attempts to assess the treatment of women in contemporary Renaissance scholarship, and the actual place of women in Renaissance society. How does she go about these two complementary tasks? What do you take to be the purpose of her effort to throw light on the day-to-day working lives of women in Shakespeare's era? Are there ways in which the silence of women in the literature of Shakespeare's era is prolonged by the critical discourse of today?*

> Misogyny presents an interpretive embarrassment of riches: it is everywhere, unabashed in its articulation and so overdetermined in its cultural roots that individual instances sometimes seem emotionally underdetermined, rote and uninflected expressions of what would go without saying if it weren't said so often.
>
> Mullaney (1994: 141)

This description of late sixteenth-century English culture is likely to ring true for readers of current feminist/historicist Shakespeare criticism. "In historical research," as a wise old teacher once warned me, "you're likely to find what you are looking for"; and what most of us have been looking for in recent years is a history of men's anxiety in the face of female power, of women's disempowerment, and of outright misogyny. I want to interrogate that history, not because it is necessarily incorrect but because it is incomplete. It constitutes only one of many stories that could be told about women's place in Shakespeare's world, and I think we need to consider the implications of its current hegemony. Why does the evidence for misogyny in Shakespeare's world strike the writer as "an interpretive embarrassment of riches"? Who is enriched by the many "rote and uninflected expressions of what would go without saying if it weren't said so often" in recent feminist criticism?

One reason the story of patriarchal oppression has become so influential is that it has been disseminated in recent textbooks. The editor of a reader designed to illustrate *The Cultural Identity of Seventeenth-Century Woman*, for instance, states flatly that

> Woman's place was within doors, her business domestic. . . . Women of evident intelligence themselves accepted this divorce between the private (feminine) and public (masculine) spheres

From *A Feminist Companion to Shakespeare*, ed. Dympna Callaghan (Oxford: Blackwell, 2000), 43–55.

and, despite the recent precedents of Mary Queen of Scots, Mary Tudor and Elizabeth, they shared the age's "distaste . . . for the notion of women's involvement in politics." (Keeble 1994: 186)

However, even the most sophisticated scholarship often includes similar claims. For example, in what is likely to become a standard history of gender in early modern England, Anthony Fletcher writes,

> It was conventional, as we have seen, to assume men and women had clearly defined gender roles indoors and out of doors. . . . Femininity, as we have seen, was presented as no more than a set of negatives. The requirement of chastity was, as we have seen, the overriding measure of female gender. Woman not only had to be chaste but had to be seen to be chaste: silence, humility and modesty were the signifiers that she was so. (1995: 120–2)

Some of the most important recent feminist/historicist literary scholarship includes reminders that "the period was fraught with anxiety about rebellious women and particularly their rebellion through language" (Newman 1991: 40); that "women's reading was policed and their writing prohibited or marked as transgressive even when they were not engaged in other criminal activities" (Dolan 1996: 159); and that "an obsessive energy was invested in exerting control over the unruly woman—the woman who was exercising either her sexuality or her tongue under her own control rather than under the rule of a man" (Boose 1991: 195). In a sense, of course, these quotations are misleading because they are taken out of context, and they belie the subtlety and complexity of the arguments from which they were taken. Nonetheless, I believe the excerpts are significant because they indicate how often even the best feminist scholarship feels the need to situate itself within a patriarchal master narrative.

Feminist scholars found a brilliant explication of that narrative in Peter Stallybrass's essay, "Patriarchal Territories: The Body Enclosed," which argued that women's bodies were assumed to be "*naturally* 'grotesque'" and that women were therefore "subjected to constant surveillance . . . because, as Bakhtin says of the grotesque body, it is 'unfinished, outgrows itself, transgresses its own limits.'" This constant surveillance, Stallybrass continued, focused on "three specific areas: the mouth, chastity, the threshold of the house," which "were frequently collapsed into each other." "Silence, the closed mouth, is made a sign of chastity. And silence and chastity are, in turn, homologous to woman's enclosure within the house" (Stallybrass 1986: 126–7). Published in 1986, "Patriarchal Territories" theorized the relationships between sexual loathing, the silencing of women's voices, and the constriction of women's activities in a beautifully articulated analysis that has proved to have remarkable influence and explanatory power in subsequent feminist criticism. It is significant, I believe, that the conclusion of Stallybrass's article, where he suggests that the figure of the unruly woman was also valorized as a rallying point for protest against social injustice, was often ignored.

The pervasive scholarly investment in Renaissance misogyny has lead to a massive rereading of Shakespeare's plays. As Valerie Traub observes, "It is by now a commonplace that Shakespeare was preoccupied with the uncontrollability of women's sexuality; witness the many plots concerning the need to prove female chastity, the threat of adultery, and, even when female fidelity is not a major theme of the play, the many references to cuckoldry in songs, jokes, and passing remarks" (1995: 121). Reminders that women were expected to be chaste, silent, and obedient probably occur more frequently in recent scholarship than they did in the literature of Shakespeare's time; the connections between female speech and female sexual transgression are retraced and the anxieties evoked by the possibility of female power are discovered in play after play. "Female sexuality in Shakespeare's plays," we are told, "is invariably articulated as linguistic transgression—that is, a verbal replication of female obliquity" (Carroll 1995: 184). If speech is transgressive, reading and writing are even more dangerous. Lavinia's gruesome fate in *Titus Andronicus,* for instance, is "expressive of the anxieties she generates as an educated, and hence potentially unruly, woman" (Eaton, cited by Garner and Sprengnether 1996: 12–13).

Plays with overtly repressive and misogynist themes have proved increasingly popular, and the stories they tell are held up as historically accurate expressions of beliefs generally endorsed in Shakespeare's time. *The Taming of the Shrew,* for instance, is the subject of 105 listings for the years 1985–97 in the online *MLA Bibliography,* far more than any of the other early comedies (for those same years, the *Bibliography* lists

twenty-eight for *Two Gentlemen of Verona,* forty-seven for *Comedy of Errors,* and sixty-one for *Love's Labour's Lost*). Other plays are reinterpreted. *The Merchant of Venice,* for example, "instructs its audience that daughters who submit, who know their place, will ultimately fare better than daughters who rebel" (Leventen 1991: 75). The heroines of Shakespeare's middle comedies were especially attractive to the feminist critics of the 1970s, when it seemed important to mobilize Shakespeare's authority in the service of our own political goals. In the 1980s, however, a more pessimistic picture emerged as scholars marshaled historical evidence to demonstrate the pervasiveness of patriarchal beliefs and practices and discredit the optimistic feminist readings of the 1970s as unhistorical.

One of the characteristics that traditionally made the heroines of Shakespeare's middle comedies attractive is their erotic appeal, but influential critics associated that attraction with the fact that they were portrayed by male actors. Stephen Greenblatt's widely cited article on "Fiction and Friction" used Thomas Laqueur's arguments about the conception of a single-sexed body in Renaissance anatomical theory to argue that "the open secret of identity—that within differentiated individuals is a single structure, identifiably male—is presented literally in the all-male cast." "Men," Greenblatt wrote, "love women precisely as *representations,* a love the original performances of these plays literalized in the person of the boy actor" (1988: 93). For Lisa Jardine, the heroines of these plays were "sexually enticing *qua* transvestied boys, and the plays encourage the audience to view them as such" (1991: 61). Moreover, at the same time that criticism like Greenblatt's and Jardine's taught us to recognize that cross-dressed boys may have been objects of desire for Shakespeare's original audience, we were also taught that sexualized women were not: female sexual desire, we are repeatedly told, was regarded as threatening. In *Antony and Cleopatra,* for instance, "Egypt's queen . . . resembles other Jacobean females who in desiring or being desired become a source of pollution" (Tennenhouse 1986: 144). In *II Henry VI,* depicting "Margaret as a figure of open and unrestrained sexual passion is one way of demonizing her and representing the dangers of a femininity not firmly under the control of a father or husband" (Howard and Rackin 1997: 74).

Sexual passion is not the only characteristic that makes women threatening in recent feminist Shakespeare criticism, where it seems that virtually any manifestation of female strength or ability, even if it is admired by other characters on stage, would have had to evoke anxiety in the original audiences. Helena in *All's Well That Ends Well* is a good example. In the playtext her virtues are celebrated and her aspirations endorsed by the King and the Countess. The Introduction to the play in the Riverside Shakespeare summed up the traditional view of the character: "Helena is prized by the older generation not only because they recognize her intrinsic worth, but because she is a living example of the attitudes of the past" (Evans et al. 1997: 535). She is also the center of dramatic interest, with the longest part in the play. According to the Spevack *Concordance* (1968), she speaks 15.858 percent of the words in the script; Bertram speaks only 9.042 percent, a total that is exceeded not only by Helena, but also by his mother, who has 9.618 percent. Nonetheless, according to a leading male feminist critic,

> Helena's gender makes impossible any one-sided identification with Helena against Bertram. . . . Reacting against Helena's triumph, Shakespeare remains in part sympathetically bound to the besieged male positions of both Bertram and the king; the play thereby gives voice not only to the two male characters' discomfiture but also to Shakespeare's. The authorial division that blocks a convincing resolution is significant because it dramatizes a much larger cultural quandary: the society's inability to accommodate, without deep disturbance, decisive female control. (Erickson 1991: 73–4)

The last two sentences are carefully worded, attributing ambivalence about Helena's achievement and anxiety about the spectacle of "decisive female control" to Shakespeare and to the culture in which he wrote, thus authorizing ambivalence and anxiety as the historically appropriate responses to Helena's triumph. But the first sentence I quoted—"Helena's gender makes impossible any one-sided identification with Helena against Bertram"—seems to claim even more. The present tense of the verb seems to universalize Erickson's reading and deny its historical specificity, implying that ambivalence and anxiety are the only possible responses to the character for any reader or viewer in any time or place.

It may be unfair to make too much of Erickson's use of the present tense, but it points to a larger problem for historicist literary criticism, which has pressing implications for feminist/historicist scholarship. The conventions of scholarly writing have been to write about literary texts in the present tense, thus expressing their imaginative presence, and about historical events in the past tense to mark their temporal distance from the writer who recounts them. This distinction is breaking down, both in popularized history, where the present tense is increasingly used to describe past events, and in postmodern historical theory, which is shaped by the recognition that history, no less than fiction, is constantly updated to fit the shapes of present interests and assumptions. The question of grammatical tense poses an especially pressing problem for new historicist literary criticism. The present tense effaces historical distance, the past

denies literary presence, and the distinction between past tense for history and present tense for fiction implicitly denies the imbrication of the literary text in its historical context that animates the entire new historicist project. If the text and its historical context are components of a seamless discursive web, it is difficult to sustain the grammatical distinction between present and past tenses that marks the separation of literary text from its historical context. But if that distinction is elided, where does the new historicist scholar situate herself in relation to the literary/historical objects of her analysis? Using the present tense, as Erickson does in the passage I quoted, seems to claim universal validity for a historically situated response. At the same time, however, it implicitly acknowledges that the version of past experience being constructed is a projection of current interests and anxieties.

The present tense is also the conventional form for references to the work of other scholars, as if it too existed in a timeless, ahistorical space. As we all know, however, scholarly texts, no less than the texts scholars study, are imbricated in the historical contexts in which they were produced and shaped by the social locations and personal interests and desires of their writers, even though the conventions of academic civility make those factors difficult to discuss. Nonetheless, I believe it is important to note, not only that the feminist/historicist Shakespeare criticism of the 1980s often tended to privilege male experience, emphasizing masculine anxiety in the face of powerful women, but also that some of the most influential work of that period was, in fact, the work of male critics.

One of the most influential modern readings of *As You Like It*, for instance, Louis Adrian Montrose's 1981 article, "'The Place of a Brother,'" proposed to reverse the then prevailing view of the play by arguing that "what happens to Orlando at home is not Shakespeare's contrivance to get him into the forest; what happens to Orlando in the forest is Shakespeare's contrivance to remedy what has happened to him at home" (Montrose 1981: 29). Just as Oliver has displaced Orlando from his rightful place in the patriarchy, Montrose's reading displaces Rosalind from her place as the play's protagonist, focusing instead upon the relationships among brothers, fathers, and sons. Although Oliver appears only briefly on stage and the brothers' reconciliation is narrated, not shown, the main issue in the play is said to be Orlando's troubled relationship with his brother and consequent loss of his rightful place in society; Rosalind is reduced to a vehicle for its restoration: marrying her enables Orlando to become "heir apparent to the reinstated Duke" (Montrose 1981: 38). Montrose does not cite Gayle Rubin's 1975 article on "the traffic in women," but this is the paradigm that seems to lie behind his argument.[1] The power of Rubin's paradigm is so great that it supersedes the textual evidence that the marriage satisfies Rosalind's own long-standing desire (see, e.g., I.iii.9) and that it is she, not her father, who tells Orlando "To you I give myself" (V.iv.106). In fact, none of the marriages in the play is arranged by a father. The only marriage that can be said to be arranged is that of Silvius and Phoebe, which Rosalind herself arranges. Rosalind dominates the action of the play (she has the longest part in the script, speaking, according to the Spevack *Concordance* (1968), 26.744 percent of the words in the playscript). Nonetheless, Montrose's argument that the play "is a structure for her containment" (1981: 52) has been widely influential in subsequent criticism.

With the turn to history in literary studies generally, and especially in the field of the Renaissance, feminist Shakespeare criticism has been almost completely shaped by the scholarly consensus about the pervasiveness of masculine anxiety and women's disempowerment in Shakespeare's world. Much of this criticism is sympathetic to women's plights, exposing women's oppression and describing the sociological, psychological, and ideological mechanisms that produced it, but it poses problems which are simultaneously intellectual and political. Feminist scholarship needs history, and it needs the analytic instruments the new historicism provides. The problem is that the conceptual categories that shape contemporary scholarly discourse, no less than the historical records of the past, are often man-made and shaped by men's anxieties, desires, and interests. As such, they constitute instruments of women's exclusion, and often of women's oppression. What Kathleen McLuskie wrote about *Measure for Measure* in 1985 seems increasingly applicable to the entire Shakespearean canon and to historical accounts of the world in which he wrote: "Feminist criticism," she argued, "is restricted to exposing its own exclusion from the text. It has no point of entry into it, for the dilemmas of the narrative and the sexuality under discussion are constructed in completely male terms" (McLuskie 1994: 97). How then can we enter the discourse of current feminist/historicist Shakespeare criticism without becoming so thoroughly inscribed within its categories that we are forced to imagine both the plays and the culture in which they were produced from a male point of view?

It is important to remember that feminist criticism began with a political agenda, although—especially in the United States—it has increasingly entered the mainstream of academic discourse. The current interest in issues of sex and gender has provided increased academic visibility for feminist concerns and increased professional visibility for academic feminists, but it has not come without costs. Adopted as a conceptual tool by women and men without a serious political commitment to feminist political agendas, criticism designated as "feminist" has provided arguments that can just as easily be used to naturalize women's oppression as to oppose it. Among the consequences of this selective history for feminist students of Shakespeare's plays is the fact that we are being taught to read from the subject position of a man, and a misogynist man at that. The cultural prestige of Shakespeare makes his plays a model for contemporary values and the privileged site where past history is reconstructed. Even academic historians often turn to Shakespeare for evidence of past practices and attitudes (the index to Anthony Fletcher's *Gender, Sex and Subordination in England 1500-1800,* for instance, lists fifty-four references to Shakespeare's plays). For the feminist political project, there are obvious dangers in contemplating our past from the point of view of late twentieth-century academic men who may—consciously or not—be anxious or ambivalent about the progress women have made in the wake of the contemporary women's movement. The stories we tell about the past have consequences for the present and future, and if the story of misogyny and oppression is the only story we tell about the past, we risk a dangerous complacency in the present. Like the Virginia Slims ads that tell us, "You've come a long way, baby" because we can now smoke openly rather than hiding our habits from our menfolk, an oversimplified history that emphasizes past oppression is likely to encourage an equally oversimplified optimism about our present situation. As Lena Cowen Orlin observes, "if we have enjoyed this construction of women, perhaps it is because it offers us the comforting reassurance that history has made progress and that we have come a long way (baby) from our early modern predecessors."[2]

This is not to deny that there is ample evidence for a history of misogyny and of women's oppression in Shakespeare's world and that there are good reasons why it needed to be told. All the statements I have cited are documented with quotations from early modern texts and citations of early modern cultural practice; and, as Linda Boose has eloquently written in her brilliant study of *The Taming of the Shrew,* it is essential to "assert an intertextuality that binds the obscured records of a painful women's history" to the Shakespearean text because "that history has paid for the right to speak itself"; and "the impulse to rewrite the more oppressively patriarchal material in this play serves the very ideologies about gender that it makes less visible by making less offensive" (1991: 181–2). However, as Boose also makes clear, although the history of male misogyny is inextricably entangled with the history of women's oppression, those histories had strikingly different consequences for women and men. In considering the evidence for Renaissance misogyny and the oppressive practices it produced, it is essential to remember an essential axiom of postmodern historical study—the fact that, as Sandra Harding has wittily remarked, there is no such thing as a "view from nowhere." We need to view the textual evidence for misogyny and oppression more critically, considering both the social locations of the original writers and those of the contemporary scholars who have put those texts back into circulation.

As Deborah Payne has argued in another context, certain anecdotes, texts, and passages from texts are repeatedly cited and assumed "to represent dominant social views: for positivists, a historical transparency; for poststructuralists, a sign within a culturally determined system of signification. This 'short-circuit fallacy' . . . can occur only by ignoring [the writer of the text's or the recorder of the anecdote's] vexed position within the social space" from which he writes (1995: 22). Payne adopts the phrase "short-circuit fallacy" from Pierre Bourdieu, who defines it as ignoring "the crucial mediation provided by . . . the field of cultural production . . . a social space with its own logic, within which agents struggle over stakes of a particular kind." "The most essential bias," he goes on to warn, is the "'ethnocentrism of the scientist,' which consists in ignoring everything that the analyst injects into his perception of the object by virtue of the fact that he is placed outside of the object, that he observes it from afar and from above" (Bourdieu and Wacquant 1992: 69–70). Carol Thomas Neely makes a similar point in a recent study of madness and gender in Shakespeare's tragedies and early modern culture:

> The complexities of reading the discourse of madness in Shakespeare and his culture reveal the difficulty and necessity of historicizing: examining one's own position and that of one's subject(s) in contemporary culture in relation to the construction of those subject(s) which emerged in early modern culture, working to tease out disjunctions and connections. This project reveals that the shape of gender difference cannot be assumed but must always be reformulated in specific historical contexts. (1996: 96)

The lesson, in the words of Jean E. Howard's famous essay on the new historicism, is that "there is no transcendent space from which one can perceive the past 'objectively.'" "Our view," she continues, "is always informed by our present position" (Howard 1986: 22). It follows from this that "objectivity is not in any pure form a possibility," that "interpretive and even descriptive acts" are inevitably political, and that "any move into history is [therefore] an intervention" (Howard 1986: 43).

One strategy for intervention adopted by feminist scholars in the 1980s and 1990s has been to look for places for fe-male agency within patriarchal scripts. In 1981, for instance, Coppélia Kahn argued in *Man's Estate* that the power over women given to men by patriarchy made men paradoxically "vulnerable to women" because "a woman's subjugation to her husband's will was the measure of his patriarchal authority and thus of his manliness" (Kahn 1981: 15–17). In 1985, Catherine Belsey pointed out in *The Subject of Tragedy* that women convicted of witchcraft were empowered at the moment of their execution by the "requirement for confessions from the scaffold," which, "paradoxically . . . offered women a place from which to speak in public with a hitherto unimagined authority which was not diminished by the fact that it was demonic" (Belsey 1985: 190–1). In 1994, Frances E. Dolan focused in *Dangerous Familiars* on early modern representations of domestic crimes perpetrated by women in an effort "to uncover the possibilities, however contingent and circumscribed, for human agency in historical process" because "accounts of domestic violence" are "one set of scripts in which women could be cast as agents, albeit in problematic terms" (Dolan 1994: 5).

Increasingly, however, feminist scholars are challenging the patriarchal narrative itself, recovering the materials for alternative narratives and emphasizing that repressive prescriptions should not be regarded as descriptions of actual behavior. In her 1993 study of *Women and Property in Early Modern England,* Amy Louise Erickson points out that

> it is one thing to observe that early modern male writers invariably described women's place in the social hierarchy, the "great chain of being", entirely in terms of marriage. It is quite another to remember that they did so in a society in which most adult women in the population at any given time were not married—they were either widowed or they had never married. (Erickson 1993: 8–9)

Similarly, in a 1997 essay, Diana E. Henderson reminds us that

> Some aristocratic women, in fact, managed to avoid being confined to any of their numerous homes, much less "the" home; those at the other end of the social scale might have no home at all, and they could hardly afford to create gendered space. . . . Texts (especially literary ones) tend to preserve the voices and perspectives of those who dominated within society; we must supplement them with both historical data and our scholarly imaginations if we wish to hear more of the conversation. Female-headed households in *Gammer Gurton's Needle* may be only a schoolmaster's source of comedy or deflected anxiety, but it is also true that there were many female-headed households in town and city alike; historical study of Southwark, the theater district itself, reveals that at least 16 percent of households were headed by a woman. The type of historical evidence we bring to bear when interpreting plays undoubtedly informs what types of domesticity we see represented, what gaps we notice, how we value them. (Henderson 1997: 192)

Thus, while *As You Like It* is a fantasy, the female household that Rosalind and Celia establish in the forest had precedents in the very district where the theater was located. Moreover, Rosalind's role in arranging her own marriage and Phoebe's as well also had ample precedents in the real world. As Margaret Ezell has demonstrated, early modern women played central roles in arranging marriages, not only their own, but those of their daughters, nieces, and granddaughters as well. Far more fathers than mothers had died by the time their children reached marriageable age (Ezell 1987: 18). Moreover, even when both parents were alive, great numbers of women lived away from their parents' homes, often supporting themselves independently and negotiating their own marriages. Vivien Brodsky Elliott's study of single women in the London marriage market during the years 1598 to 1619 shows that women who had migrated from the country to work in London tended to marry later than London-born women and to marry men who were closer to their own age, statistics which, Elliott concludes, suggest "a greater freedom of choice of spouse and a more active role for women in the courtship and marriage process" (Elliott 1982: 89): "without the control or influence of their parents the marriage process for them was one in which they had an active role in initiating their own relationships, in finding suitable partners, and in conducting courtships" (Elliott 1982: 97). Among the upper levels of society where there was more property involved and parents were more likely to take an active role in arranging their children's marriages, Ezell's study of women's correspondence with other women reveals that mothers, grandmothers, and aunts played central roles in negotiating marriages for their children (Ezell 1987: 20–34).

Women's power and authority extended beyond the limits of their families. The example of the Tudor queens Mary and Elizabeth is well known, and the "anomaly" of Elizabeth's position has been endlessly noted; but they were not the only women who exercised political authority. Patricia Crawford's examination of voting registers reveals that in some parts of England, "women had been regularly voting in parliamentary elections during the seventeenth century into the 1650s at least" (Orgel 1996: 74). Women also possessed considerable economic power, not only through inheritance from fathers and husbands (and from mothers and other female relatives as well), but also by virtue of their own gainful employment. Widows were usually named executrix in their husband's wills, and when a husband died intestate, the widow was legally entitled to administer the estate (Erickson 1993: 19, 61–78, 175). Bess of Hardwick began with a marriage portion of forty marks, but ended, after inheriting the property of four successive husbands, as the Countess of Shrewsbury and one of the wealthiest women in England (Hogrefe 1977).

Women lower on the social scale earned their livings, not only as servants, but also in a variety of trades that took them outside the household. Itinerant chapwomen peddled a variety of goods, and Amy Louise Erickson has noted that "prohibitions upon girls and women appearing in public places like markets and fairs are entirely absent from early modern ballads and broadsides" (Erickson 1993: 10). Women's prominence in the marketplace is also attested by the drawings of thirteen London food markets produced by Hugh Alley in 1598, which include numerous images of women, both alone and with other women or men, both buying and selling. These images are particularly significant, because Alley's text is not specifically concerned with the activities of women in the markets; the women are simply there, apparently as a matter of course.

Even the guilds, generally believed to be bastions of male privilege, included women. The Statute of Artificers referred to apprentices as "persons"; and individual acts mentioned girls as well as boys and mistresses as well as masters: women were legally entitled, not only to enter apprenticeship, but also to take on apprentices of their own (Snell 1985: 177). As Stephen Orgel points out,

> until late in the seventeenth century women in one place or another, were admitted into practically every English trade or guild. Women did not, moreover, limit their efforts to ladylike pursuits: in Chester, in 1575, there were five women blacksmiths. Elsewhere, women were armourers, bootmakers, printers, pewterers, goldsmiths, farriers, and so forth . . . and they pursued these trades not as wives, widows, or surrogates, but as fully independent, legally responsible craftspersons. This point needs especially to be stressed, since a common modern way of ignoring the presence of women in the Renaissance workforce is to claim that they were there only as emanations of absent or dead husbands: this is not the case. The *percentage* of female apprentices is especially notable, for a practice that Lawrence Stone and E. P. Thompson believe did not exist. In Southampton, for example, at the beginning of the seventeenth century, 48 percent—almost half—the apprentices were women. (Orgel 1996: 73; see also Clark 1992; Snell 1985)

The historical evidence I have sampled undermines the current scholarly consensus that respectable women were expected to stay at home, that they were economically dependent on fathers and husbands, and that they were subjected to constant surveillance by jealous men, obsessively anxious about their sexual fidelity. I found it because I was looking for it. Historical evidence, as my old teacher reminded me, is subject to selective citation and motivated interpretation. The same, of course, is true of literary texts. In a 1985 study of *King John*, I easily discovered that

> Lady Faulconbridge's infidelity has created the nightmare situation that haunts the patriarchal imagination—a son not of her husband's getting destined to inherit her husband's lands and ti-

tle. Like Shakespeare's ubiquitous cuckold jokes, the Faulconbridge episode bespeaks the anxiety that motivates the stridency of patriarchal claims and repressions. (Rackin 1985: 341)

That reading seemed valid to me because it confirmed the paradigmatic view of women's place in Shakespeare's world. Looking at it now, I realize that it elided a number of features of the text: the facts that the revelation of Lady Faulconbridge's adultery is depicted in humorous terms, that the Bastard it produced is a sympathetic character, that he welcomes the revelation of his bastardy, and that it results in his acceptance as the son of Richard Cordelion and consequent social elevation. Of course, the lady's husband, who might indeed have been jealous, is no longer alive when the revelation occurs.

Nonetheless, if we reexamine the representations of male sexual jealousy in Shakespeare's other plays, it is difficult to sustain the assumption that it expresses a normative view. Othello's jealousy of Desdemona is the source of tragedy, Leontes's jealousy of Hermione is the source of near-tragedy, Ford's jealousy of his wife is the subject of comic debunking. And all are mistaken. To be sure, Shakespeare does depict unfaithful wives. Goneril and Margaret are obvious examples. But it is worth noting that in neither case is the woman's infidelity her only, or even her chief, offense; and neither husband is wracked by jealousy. In other plays of the period, unfaithful wives are forgiven. Sometimes, in fact, their infidelity goes undetected. Consider, for instance, the case of Winnifride in *The Witch of Edmonton,* who is pregnant by another man when she marries Frank Thorney, who believes the baby is his. Never punished for her transgression, she is depicted throughout in sympathetic terms and, at the end of the play, is welcomed into the home of the supremely virtuous Carters. Sir Arthur Clarington, the coldhearted aristocrat who seduced Winnifride when she was his maidservant, is denounced as "the instrument that wrought all" the "misfortunes" of the other characters. According to Old Carter, he is "worthier to be hang'd" than Frank Thorney, who murdered Carter's daughter (V.ii).

In attempting to interpret plays historically, probably the best starting place for a feminist critic is Jean E. Howard's reminder that women were paying customers in early modern theaters (Howard 1988: 439–40; see also Gurr 1996: 61–5 and appendices 1 and 2; Levin 1989). According to the records of early English playgoers compiled by Andrew Gurr, these included respectable women, such as the wife of John Overall, who was Regius Professor of Theology at Cambridge from 1596 to 1607 and Dean of St. Paul's from 1602 to 1618 (Gurr 1996: 207). In fact, Gurr found far more references to citizens' wives and ladies than to whores (1996: 62), even though references to prostitutes seeking customers are

more familiar to modern readers whose assumptions about the women in the playhouses have been shaped by scholarly citations of anti-theatrical literature. Those assumptions were not, apparently, shared by the players, who explicitly defer to female playgoers in prologues and epilogues and express the players' awareness that the women in the audience, as well as the men, had to be pleased. The Epilogue to *As You Like It* is a good case in point. Spoken by the actor who played Rosalind, it addresses female and male playgoers separately, beginning with the women, whom it charges "to like as much of this play as please you," thus suggesting that the "you" in the play's title refers primarily to them. The Epilogue to Shakespeare's *Henry VIII* expects to hear "good" about the play "only in / The merciful construction of good women, / For such a one we showed 'em," acknowledging that positive representations of female characters were likely to appeal to female playgoers. In *The Knight of the Burning Pestle,* a citizen and his wife repeatedly interrupt the players to demand changes in the represented action, and although both are the subjects of satire, there is no suggestion that her interruptions are more inappropriate than his because she is a woman or that her husband's wishes are more to be honored than hers. Ben Jonson, whom it would be difficult to accuse of excessive deference to women, dedicated *The Alchemist* to Lady Mary Wroth, and declared in the Prologue to *Epicoene* his intention to provide a dramatic feast "fit for ladies . . . lords, knights, squires, . . . your waiting-wench and city-wires [i.e., citizens' wives who wore fashionable ruffs supported by wires], . . . your men, and daughters of Whitefriars." Jonson's assumption that women's interests might be different from men's and that both needed to be pleased is supported by no less a personage than Queen Anne, who not only patronized two companies of players (The Children of the Queen's Revels and Queen Anne's Men), but also, according to the French ambassador, attended plays in which "the comedians of the metropolis bring [King James] upon the stage." The Queen, the ambassador reported, "attends these representations in order to enjoy the laugh against her husband" (Chambers 1951: I, 325).

It is generally assumed that private playhouse audiences were more homogeneous than those in the large public amphitheaters like Shakespeare's Globe, but even the private playhouses catered to women as well as men, and, as these examples show, those women came into the playhouses with tastes, interests, and allegiances which were not necessarily the same as men's. Moreover, it is difficult to imagine a totalizing master narrative that would account for the varied experience, tastes, interests, and allegiances of all the women who enjoyed playgoing in Shakespeare's England. They included applewives and fishwives, doxies and respectable citizens, queens and great ladies (Gurr 1996: 60–4). Because playing was a commercial enterprise, it was in the players' interests to please as many of the paying customers as they could, the women no less than the men. The female playgoers in Shakespeare's London brought their own perspectives to the action. Perhaps we should try harder to emulate their example. *Women* were everywhere in Shakespeare's England, but the variety of their roles in life and in the scripts of plays too often "goes without saying." If we wanted to look for it, I think we could find "an interpretive embarrassment of riches" for a revitalized feminist criticism.[3]

NOTES

1. "The Traffic in Women" is a core text for contemporary feminist/historicist criticism, but, as Stephen Orgel observes, this "brilliant, classic essay" illustrates how "even the most powerful feminist analyses are often in collusion with precisely the patriarchal assumptions they undertake to displace." "To define Renaissance culture simply as a patriarchy," he explains, is "to limit one's view to the view the dominant culture took of itself; to assert that within it women were domestic creatures and a medium of exchange is to take Renaissance ideology at its word, and thereby to elide and suppress the large number of women who operated outside the family system, and the explicit social and legal structures that enabled them, in this patriarchy, to do so" (Orgel 1996: 125).

2. I am grateful to Lena Cowen Orlin for sharing with me her brilliant unpublished essay, "The Witness Who Spoke When the Cock Crowed," and allowing me to quote from it. Here is the context of her comment: "Here [in second-wave feminism], the female victim has been an object of our scholarly desires. Literary historians have so often repeated the mantra that women were enjoined to be chaste, silent, and obedient; have so often described the spatial restrictions on women; have so often 'explained' playtexts in terms taken from the most conservative literatures of their time, that the reigning orthodoxy of historiography has become that of patriarchal philosophy. I have myself been oppressed by the sheer weight of the homiletic record, by the sermons and conduct books that are so readily available, so generically familiar, so textually congenial. I and perhaps others have been seduced by the efforts of our own research into thinking these prescriptions were culturally operative in a way that they cannot have been in many women's daily lives. Even though we have reminded ourselves that such admonitions would not have been necessary had their strictures been more generally observed, we have nonetheless persisted in depicting women as victims of unrelenting misogyny, patriarchy, and oppression. If we have enjoyed this construction of women, perhaps it is because it offers us the comforting reassurance that history has made progress and that we have come a long way (baby) from our early modern predecessors" (Orlin 1998).

3. I wish to thank Rebecca Bushnell, Jean E. Howard, Lena Cowen Orlin, and Donald Rackin for helpful critical readings of drafts of this essay.

REFERENCES AND FURTHER READING

Archer, I., Barron, C., and Harding, V. (eds.) 1988: *Hugh Alley's Caveat: The Markets of London in 1598*. London: London Topographical Society Publication No. 137.

Belsey, C. 1985: *The Subject of Tragedy: Identity and Difference in Renaissance Drama*. London: Methuen.

Boose, L. E. 1991: "Scolding Brides and Bridling Scolds: Taming the Woman's Unruly Member." *Shakespeare Quarterly*, 42, 179–213.

Bourdieu, P. and Wacquant, L. J. D. 1992: *An Invitation to Reflexive Sociology*. Chicago: University of Chicago Press.

Carroll, W. C. 1995: "The Virgin Not: Language and Sexuality in Shakespeare." In Deborah E. Barker and Ivo Kamps (eds.), *Shakespeare and Gender: A History*. London and New York: Verso, 283–301.

Chambers, E. K. 1951: *The Elizabethan Stage*. Oxford: Clarendon Press. Reprinted with corrections. (Original work published 1923.)

Clark, A. 1992: *Working Life of Women in the Seventeenth Century*. Third edition. London and New York: Routledge.

Dolan, F. E. 1994: *Dangerous Familiars: Representations of Domestic Crime in England 1550-1700*. Ithaca and London: Cornell University Press.

——1996: "Reading, Writing, and Other Crimes." In Valerie Traub, M. Lindsay Kaplan, and Dympna Callaghan (eds.), *Feminist Readings of Early Modern Culture: Emerging Subjects*. Cambridge: Cambridge University Press, 142–67.

Eaton, S. 1996: "A Woman of Letters: Lavinia in *Titus Andronicus*." In Shirley Nelson Carner and Madelon Sprengnether (eds.), *Shakespearean Tragedy and Gender*. Bloomington: Indiana University Press, 54–74.

Elliott, V. B. 1982: "Single Women in the London Marriage Market: Age, Status and Mobility, 1598–1619." In R. B. Outhwaite (ed.), *Marriage and Society: Studies in the Social History of Marriage*. New York: St. Martin's Press, 81–100.

Erickson, A. L. 1993: *Women and Property in Early Modern England*. London and New York: Routledge.

Erickson, P. 1991: *Rewriting Shakespeare, Rewriting Ourselves*. Berkeley: University of California Press.

Evans, G. B. et al. 1997: *The Riverside Shakespeare*. Second edition. Boston and New York: Houghton Mifflin.

Ezell, M. 1987: *The Patriarch's Wife: Literary Evidence and the History of the Family*. Chapel Hill and London: University of North Carolina Press.

Fletcher, A. 1995: *Gender, Sex and Subordination in England 1500-1800*. New Haven and London: Yale University Press.

Garner, S. N. and Sprengnether, M. (eds.) 1996: *Shakespearean Tragedy and Gender*. Bloomington: Indiana University Press.

Greenblatt, S. 1988: "Fiction and Friction." In *Shakespearean Negotiations: The Circulation of Social Energy in Renaissance England*. Berkeley: University of California Press, 66–93.

Gurr, A. 1996: *Playgoing in Shakespeare's London*. Second edition. Cambridge: Cambridge University Press.

Henderson, D. E. 1997: "The Theater and Domestic Culture." In John D. Cox and David Scott Kastan (eds.), *A New History of Early English Drama*. New York: Columbia University Press, 173–94.

Hogrefe, P. 1977: *Women of Action in Tudor England*. Ames, IA: Iowa State University Press.

Howard, J. E. 1986: "The New Historicism in Renaissance Studies." *English Literary Renaissance*, 16, 13–43.

——1988: "Crossdressing, the Theatre, and Gender Struggle in Early Modern England." *Shakespeare Quarterly*, 39, 418–40.

——and Rackin, P. 1997: *Engendering a Nation: A Feminist Account of Shakespeare's English Histories*. London and New York: Routledge.

Jardine, L. 1991: "Boy Actors, Female Roles, and Elizabethan Eroticism." In David Scott Kastan and Peter Stallybrass (eds.), *Staging the Renaissance: Reinterpretations of Elizabethan and Jacobean Drama*. New York and London: Routledge, 57–67.

Kahn, C. 1981: *Man's Estate: Masculine Identity in Shakespeare*. Berkeley: University of California Press.

Keeble, N. H. (ed.) 1994: *The Cultural Identity of Seventeenth-Century Woman: A Reader*. London: Routledge.

Leventen, C. 1991: "Patrimony and Patriarchy in *The Merchant of Venice*." In Valerie Wayne (ed.), *The Matter of Difference: Materialist Feminist Criticism of Shakespeare*. Ithaca: Cornell University Press, 59–79.

Levin, R. 1989: "Women in the Renaissance Theatre Audience." *Shakespeare Quarterly*, 40, 165–74.

McLuskie, K. 1994: "The Patriarchal Bard: Feminist Criticism and Shakespeare: *King Lear* and *Measure for Measure*." In Jonathan Dollimore and Alan Sinfield (eds.), *Political Shakespeare: Essays in Cultural Materialism*. Second edition. Ithaca: Cornell University Press, 88–108.

Montrose, L. A. 1981: "'The Place of a Brother' in *As You Like It*: Social Process and Comic Form." *Shakespeare Quarterly*, 32, 28–54.

Mullaney, S. 1994: "Mourning and Misogyny: *Hamlet, The Revenger's Tragedy*, and the Final Progress of Elizabeth I, 1600–1607." *Shakespeare Quarterly*, 45, 139–62.

Neely, C. T. 1996: "'Documents in Madness': Reading Madness and Gender in Shakespeare's Tragedies and Early Modern Culture." In Shirley Nelson Garner and Madelon Sprengnether (eds.), *Shakespearean Tragedy and Gender*. Bloomington: Indiana University Press, 75–104.

Newman, K. 1991: *Fashioning Femininity and English Renaissance Drama*. Chicago: University of Chicago Press.

Orgel, S. 1996: *Impersonations: The Performance of Gender in Shakespeare's England*. Cambridge: Cambridge University Press.

Orlin, L. C. 1998: "The Witness Who Spoke When the Cock Crowed." Unpublished essay.

Payne, D. C. 1995: "Reified Object or Emergent Professional? Retheorizing the Restoration Actress." In J. Douglas Canfield and Deborah C. Payne (eds.), *Cultural Readings of Restoration and Eighteenth-Century English Theater*. Athens and London: University of Georgia Press, 13–38.

Rackin, P. 1985: "Anti-Historians: Women's Roles in Shakespeare's Histories." *Theatre Journal*, 37, 329–44.

Rubin, G. 1975: "The Traffic in Women: Notes on the 'Political Economy' of Sex." In Reina Reiter (ed.), *Towards an Anthropology of Women*. New York: Monthly Review Press, 157–210.

Snell, K. D. M. 1985: "The Apprenticeship of Women." In *Annals of the Labouring Poor: Social Change and Agrarian England, 1660-1900*. Cambridge: Cambridge University Press, 270–319.

Spevack, M. 1968: *A Complete and Systematic Concordance to the Works of Shakespeare*. Hildesheim: Georg Olms.

Stallybrass, P. 1986: "Patriarchal Territories: The Body Enclosed." In Margaret W. Ferguson, Maureen Quilligan, and Nancy J. Vickers (eds.), *Rewriting the Renaissance: The Discourses of Sexual Difference in Early Modern Europe*. Chicago: University of Chicago Press, 123–42.

Tennenhouse, L. 1986: *Power on Display: The Politics of Shakespeare's Genres*. New York and London: Methuen.

Traub, V. 1995: "Jewels, Statues, and Corpses: Containment of Female Erotic Power." In Deborah E. Barker and Ivo Kamps (eds.), *Shakespeare and Gender: A History*. London and New York: Verso, 120–41.

AN ACTOR'S PERSPECTIVE

MICHAEL PENNINGTON

"Hamlet" (1985)

Michael Pennington is a notable British actor, and was a member of the Royal Shakespeare Company (RSC) in the 1980s, before becoming a founding member, with Michael Bogdanov, of The English Shakespeare Company. He played the role of Hamlet in the 1980 RSC production of Hamlet *and recorded his understanding of the demands of playing Hamlet in an essay written for the* Players of Shakespeare *series.*

Pennington's description of the process of the production and of his own preparation here is meticulous: what strikes you as important about his strategies for preparing to play Hamlet? What elements of the play do you think would be magnified by his vision of the role? How would Pennington's preparation, on the other hand, tend to make potential elements of the part less visible?

Hamlet is a white-magic play, as white as *Macbeth* is black. *Macbeth* remains an unholy riddle that we still hesitate to name for fear of retribution; but *Hamlet* is potently on the side of life, for all its catastrophes, and clearly occupies a special place in the lives of those who have to do with it. Among actors, the central part is supposedly the object of much professional rivalry; among those who have played it, it is the source, surprisingly often, of regret, and occasionally of real self-definition. Directors seem to identify with the play and the character as much as actors; most productions have their directors' sensibilities written all over them, and everyone is agreed the play should show the age and body of the time his form and pressure as well as, inevitably, refracting the personal preoccupations of those working on it. From an habituated audience it still calls out a nervy sense of expectation; and, perhaps more important, to a young audience it can give a theatrical taste that will last a lifetime.

Occasionally an actor may come to the part innocently, having neither seen it nor played anything in it before; but this must be exceptional, and an accumulated peripheral knowledge of the play is a burden most Hamlets arrive with. I had had a shot at it at twenty, as a student, and I suppose in hindsight this was the beginning of a preparation. However, perhaps mercifully, I can remember little about that occasion except a sense of surprise when I found that the playing of the part was enjoyable, fun, a release; at that stage I in no way associated acting with enjoyment, more with the direst self-analysis, and I was astonished not to feel more of a failure. I couldn't believe it. Now I can, because I can see that the part had in some sense contracted to fit the lineaments of a twenty-year-old, just as it has a way of expanding or tightening to suit the extraordinary variety of bodies that have climbed into it. In that limited sense the character is extremely obliging—the greatest straight role ever written—which does not contradict the fact that finally to pull it off will take the actor further down into his psyche, memory and imagination, and further outwards to the limits of his technical knowledge and equipment, than he has probably been before.

A couple of other involvements with the play in the interim being really neither here nor there, I came to the part again inside a company with which I had been absorbed for five years, with a director with whom I already had a working relationship, and with the part in a sense having been quietly bubbling away since my student days. The readiness was, it was to be hoped, all. So that by the time John Barton and I began a series of roughly weekly meetings in the January before April rehearsals, a certain amount of preparation could be said to have been done, in a way that could not be said of other projects. Many of these meetings were, on the face of it, surprisingly inconclusive. I recalled that, in the case of Barry Kyle's *Measure for Measure* two years previously, a number of firm decisions, clarifying images, had formed between us before rehearsals began, in response to the riddles of the play and the elusive character of the Duke; but this tentative shaping up to Hamlet, although based on a good working knowledge of the play, produced mostly caveats, a few long-range hunches, and naturally a determination to open the book freshly and forget the past. The closer we moved at this time to definitions of character and ambience, the more my imagination contracted and the play seemed to burst out of our confining thoughts. As we veered away from these issues, the cutting of the text became a priority. An early impulse of mine to play the uncut text having been rightly dismissed as a Wagnerian folly, it was soon agreed that there was a need to cut radically, preferably by means of filleting rather than major surgery, and pretty soon John Barton had come up with a text from which hardly more than half a dozen lines at a stretch had gone, but which would have a Stratford audience on the street by eleven o'clock without any cherished area of the play having been brutalized. (Amidst these rigours there were some whimsical moments. A passage from the bad quarto in the advice to the Players about their jester "blabbering with his lips, and thus keeping in his cinquepace of jests" was deemed so baroque and unfamiliar that it was left in until after a month of rehearsal it was decided it was a great nuisance and should be dumped.)

Some specific ideas were floated at this time which have survived: the Ghost was to be as alarmingly human as possible and should be seen by Gertrude as by everyone else; the Players are professionals and should be good at their job, even though they have lost their base and are on the road; and there seemed no reason to suppose that Hamlet himself does not have the predominantly graceful qualities in his make-up credited to him by Ophelia, Horatio and Fortinbras. Generally speaking, though, it seemed the best service we could do ourselves was to lay off and let the play operate on us, through us, in rehearsal. In line with this, the setting would probably need to be simple, very simple; and in the obvious absence of theoretical overlay, the narrative would be likely to be clear and swift, catching its audience by surprise, however well they knew the story.

We finally edged sidelong into rehearsal by means of small meetings of two or three characters at a time—Hamlet and Ophelia, Gertrude and Claudius, Hamlet and Rosencrantz and Guildenstern—rather than with a read-through or head-on company call; and a rather unassuming enquiry into the connections between us and into the groundplan of the play was, I suppose, the feature of the early days. In the face of the play's riches, we needed to be fairly hard-nosed. Every famous passage and every operatic opportunity for the actor was to be tested against its contribution to the story or to the development of a relationship, and the relationships themselves were to be explored in tight harness to the action. I had to trick myself into being as naïve as possible; to grasp simply the A to B of every passage; to try to identify the precise purpose of, say, the closet scene, and so free myself from its famousness in the hope of approaching Hamlet's alienation, his struggle with himself and the others, and his particular bravery, only through what lay in front of me on the page. Grace-notes could wait.

Inevitably, we found that Shakespeare had been there before us; each famous passage does of course contain its particular momentum, its own means of pressing the events forward. The play began forming itself in my mind as a brilliant narrative exploding on the one hand into set pieces like the first court scene, the play scene and the duel; and sustained on the other by a series of essential interviews, duologues that define Hamlet's relations with his neighbours—the Ghost, Ophelia and Gertrude above all, but also Polonius, Rosencrantz and Guildenstern, Horatio and the Gravediggers: a kind of character dialectic that is further refined at four crucial moments into Hamlet's purest and most distinctive encounters, those with his audience. These form the character's most confidential relationship; and in practice it meant preparing to meet the audience on terms as open and mutual as possible. Given what we know of the social circumstances of Shakespeare's theatre, and given the immediacy that a theatrical event should have at any time, it still seems natural to expect at least half an answer to his blazing questions:

> Am I a coward?
> Who calls me villain? Breaks my pate across? . . .
> Tweaks me by the nose? Gives me the lie i' the throat
> As deep as to the lungs? Who does me this?
> Ha?   (2.2.571–6)

Once this had begun to emerge, specific questions of design became clearer. The physical setting needed to be open enough to accommodate the sweep of the set pieces, uncluttered enough to focus sharply on the interviews (a bed would be an unwanted third character in the closet scene) and confrontational enough to allow as close a contact as possible with the house for the soliloquies. The costumes would tend to reflect character and humour rather than a social or political moment. Very soon a raked platform in front of a large open space was modelled.

Meanwhile, moving through rehearsals, John Barton was becoming more and more interested in the theatre image that was to become central to the production—the sense in which the chance arrival of a troupe of players at the court not only provokes action in the dramatic narrative sense, a means to catch the conscience of the King, but also precipitates in Hamlet an enquiry into the validity of his own emotions next to the supposedly counterfeit ones of the actors, into his own role as avenger, and into the appearance of his world as against its corrupt reality. At the time I did not really understand this theme and rather feared it, thinking it might draw us into a sort of Pirandellian "angle" on the play, and not really seeing how it helped; but it became very important to me later. Among other things, it gives a clue to the peculiar balances in some of Hamlet's language; though he is rarely highly poetic in the manner of Lear or Macbeth, there are vertiginous switches in him from the humdrum to the hypermetaphorical and back which I could understand better when I saw that he sees himself simultaneously as a private man and also as a miscast avenging angel in some atavistic tragedy:

> Now could I drink hot blood,
> And do such bitter business as the day
> Would quake to look on. Soft! Now to my mother . . . (3.2.390–2)

Often too his sharp perception of the immediate physical world is linked to a literary taste:

> or e'er those shoes were old
> With which she followed my poor father's body,
> Like Niobe, all tears . . . (1.2.147–9)

Clearly the distinction between self-dramatization and real feeling, theatricality and life, runs right through the play, and was beginning to influence my reception of the text; and soon the theatrical world itself—hampers, cloaks and property swords—began to appear in rehearsals.

This initial hesitation in picking up an idea of the director's may serve to illustrate the working relationship of actor and director a little. Without a base of agreement in most matters a venture such as this would be fraught with all sorts of danger—inadvisable in fact; and the fact in this case of having worked with John Barton before, and having discussed things at length before rehearsal, was, mutually I hope, reassuring. But differences there will always be, if only of bias—a conflict one hopes will be creative and without animus, either resolved by compromise or perhaps remaining through the production as a sort of mutual check and balance. Throughout rehearsals of the earlier part of the play John Barton would be inviting me wherever possible to take gentler options with the part, feeling for instance that I should find restraint and courtesy in the first court scene, albeit under great strain, while I was inclined towards sarcasm and sharpness. There may be no final resolution to this sort of thing—individual performances in a run will veer to and fro, and our debate continues. What was constant in John Barton's guidance of me was his encouragement always to use the language as a necessary funnel for the emotions in a scene. This may sound obvious, but in a part as emotionally turbulent as Hamlet the actor may sometimes allow a tide of feeling to distort highly-wrought areas of language and so make them obscure. In fact of course the feelings require those words, and only those words, to define them and make them communicable—it is all one thing, the feeling, the pressure, the need to speak, the image that defines. It can be like pressing a tornado through the eye of a needle, but a persistent attention to colour, texture, rhythm and characteristic music goes beyond textual piety to become an emotional necessity.

Other things were emerging. Characterization is difficult to talk about in relation to Hamlet, for the player is working in a specially subjective way, and the production is likely to be reflecting his own basic personality. It would be surprising to find him reaching very far from his theatrical self or a director asking him to do so. A man's Hamlet tends to be one of a kind, and the main challenge is to express fully the deep crises of the part through your own spirit. Nevertheless, there is a responsibility too, and periods of objectivity. The essentially young man of the opening seemed to me the least like the prime mover of a tragedy. Grief seems to have sharpened his sense of falsehood in the world around him, but in other ways the immeasurable shock he has received has sent him to sleep. The torpor is deep and disturbing to watch, lifting in utterances—"My father, methinks I see my father"—which are more hallucinatory than sentimental. Anybody familiar with bereavement can recognize the symptoms. In dramatic terms, until the news of the Ghost's appearance animates him, gives him something to believe in, he is a dramatic hero of whom nothing much can be expected. During the early stages of the play the pressure of events makes him into a hero of whom much must be expected, and yet his characteristic response to challenge is to step back, into "wild and whirling words," secretiveness, and indeed to fall in all too easily with a series of chance encounters in Act 2, Scene 2 which allows him almost to forget himself—until right at the end of the "rogue and peasant slave" soliloquy a glimmer of purpose appears. This moment seemed to us to demand the first of two theatre intervals, leaving an image on the eye of a still man in the act of beginning to walk.

So the man of the first third of the play is non-initiating, relatively passive, immobilized by his burdens; and if he is a rebel, whether the production is politically inclined or not, he is a very conservative rebel. He has a yearning for the past that seems to go beyond his personal crisis to be a cultural need. His world is based not only on a contemporary sense of reason but also on an older, deeper morality, and his vision is traduced by a new world of sexually aggressive men, court espionage and seemingly opportunistic women. A deep concern for the past and its values runs through him and he perhaps never speaks of the future. As a physical consequence of this idea, we began to get a picture of a man in the first court scene who was soberly and traditionally dressed amid the tawdry theatricality of the new court; and in general an almost formal courtesy and restraint began to creep into my dealings with acquaintances and visitors to the court, alongside an open enthusiasm for my friends. Hamlet has a kind of sweet optimism, bitterly disappointed; and the struggle to overcome the maelstrom inside him seems truer, and potentially more moving, than a continual public display of his demons.

On the other hand, it became obvious in rehearsing the scenes with Ophelia and Gertrude that alongside the evident generosity and grace in the man there was now a strong current of violence, particularly towards the women in his life, aggravated by a sense of betrayal, and sadly misdirected towards them rather than towards his real enemy. In the nunnery scene we moved towards an openly expressed viciousness—the tenderness of the early part of the scene turned on its head—and it occurred to me that this is paralleled in the still more violent language of the closet, where the arrival of the Ghost perhaps forestalls another physical outbreak. It seemed a rich streak for the production to mine, not least because the opportunity for the audience to question the hero's morality, and even to project an antipathy back to the stage, is an important counterpoint to the mainly sympathetic appeal on which the part rests. Conversely again, his generosity in unbetrayed friendship, as with Horatio, remains to me one of the most touching things about Hamlet; he protects his less imaginative friend from his "curious considerations," the darker recesses of his thinking, so that, even on the edge of catastrophe at the end of the play, he will not let Horatio take the strain of his premonitions—"Let be." It is a spirit both highly demanding and very solicitous, its artistic potential cruelly wasted.

All these things were developing out of a daily exposure to the play in as innocent a frame of mind as possible, and all the time hints were being thrown out that sent us ferreting through the play for corroboration. What was the man's characteristic language? While John Barton was pointing out to me how often theatrical words were recurring in the script—"cue," "act," "action"—I too was out hunting, finding how often Hamlet returns to "dust," to "nothing," to triplets—"well, well, well," "except my life, except my life, except my life,"—and noting that in three of the four confessional soliloquies, but never elsewhere, he emphatically uses the word "coward." Then again, what is one to make of the sudden explosion of three lines of ferocious monosyllables in "How all occasions do inform against me":

> I do not know
> Why yet I live to say "This thing's to do,"
> Sith I have cause and will and strength and means
> To do't . . .   (4.4.43–6)

These are small bricks in a big wall, but necessary; and I suppose at this time we were going in some sort of sequence from early hunches to a radar scanning of the text to a grasp of the converging lines of the part.

It all sounds fairly calculated, this daytime enquiry; my night-time exposure to the play was rather different. Waiting for the emotional flashpoints that would bring all these things together, I found myself writing Hamlet-riddles in an attempt to rein the kaleidoscopic impressions of the day into some sort of documentary coherence:

> The external world is proceeding smoothly. The society is attractive, warmhearted, congenial; they all understand one another. The really difficult thing is to stand apart from such a seductive world. Nevertheless one man, already grief-stricken and prey to morbid reflection, has a nightmare in which he receives a message, supposedly from beyond the grave, which declares that the external world is in fact riddled with corruption, its leader a murderer and adulterer, and his wife guilty by implication. It is inconceivable. Vainly the benighted dreamer scans the external world for corroboration of his fantastic dream but finds none. The external world is the same as it was before. Nobody acknowledges even the possibility of guilt. Even a carefully prepared entertainment devised to expose the guilty is taken simply as a piece of social bad taste. The man must be mistaken, and his dream truly a nightmare. He persuades himself otherwise, his reason totters and he begins to despair. Events overtake him and he finds himself caught up in an adventure story that finally destroys him. Before dying he does in fact destroy his enemy, though still without having any conclusive proof of that man's original guilt or the woman's involvement. By the time he dies the man has killed three people and indirectly caused the death of others. He still has not exposed the original crime to the eyes of the world. He has only trusted his instinct, in the form of a visitation from the other world that is most akin to a dream, and by an extraordinary and deep irony, his instinct was true.

Could we really be meaning to confront critics and audiences with yet another *Hamlet* without an angle beyond our developing hunches? Should we not have a couple of tricks up our sleeves? The play is swamped in a miasma of interpretation—this director's line, this actor's forte, 350 years of all kinds of enquiry. *Hamlet* as a good yarn? How plain can plain theatre get? But then how good it would be if we could ambush our audiences into catching their breath at a turn in the story that their conscious minds have known since school, but which under theatrical pressure they have forgotten. And there is always a new, younger, audience too. Anyway, what was I myself on the verge of, asking all these questions? I was beginning to taste the famous isolation of the part, feeling the emotional tides of a man adrift from the behaviour, the humour, the very language of his neighbours: a disorientation that in some equivalent way was beginning to separate me from colleagues and friends:

> Nothing could have less to do with ghosts, shadows, uncertainty of mind, the jolting of the earth beneath your feet, doubt between dream and waking, than the bright busy practicality of this court, with its clear vocabulary and shared purposes. The family is intact—Claudius with my mother, Polonius with Laertes and Ophelia—good humour and self-confidence everywhere. In this easy and comfortable world, a man dressed stubbornly in black, white with tiredness and a grinding grief, speaks in riddles: worms, skulls, words of leaping, boggling insanity uttered in

tones of even normality. He is like a damaged animal they would leave for dead rather than take a step to save—a madman at a chamber concert.

But then dawn would break and each day we would have another go. By this time, a couple of weeks before previews, frequent run-throughs were planned, largely to allow me to have a look at the course. The formidable athletic geometry of the part requires a training to match, and I needed to know where the stress points lay, where the tricky corners were and where I could take a breath. The first third of the play is deceptive; as the character is passive, the central actor loses his usual responsibility for driving the play forward, and instead should be carried by it. But I soon found that the great middle arc of the play, from the nunnery through to the departure for England, was the most taxing stretch, the action moving precipitately in rhythm with Hamlet's direct organization of events. For the character, this progress is like a tunnel in which success lies next to defeat; where more violent impulses to action are checked by still deeper introspections; where the supernatural once again regulates the real world; where emotional and rational certainties are rocked once more. A rapprochement is unexpectedly reached with Gertrude which will alter the course of both their lives; and above all a murder is committed by accident which finally puts Hamlet outside his own moral framework for good and all. For the actor, this is where the part shakes you like a rat, racing you from one crisis to the next with scarcely time to draw breath; and at the end of the sequence both actor and character are washed up on the chilly plateau of "How all occasions do inform against me," where rationality begins to seep back into the character and the actor once again meets the audience and is offered the prospect of rest. On the return from England, an eerie calm descends; but even here the earth is moving under his feet and violent action waits in ambush. Thinking forward as usual—narrative momentum always!—the actor has to realize that the point of the graveyard scene is not primarily Yorick, who is really a cadenza, but the discovery that the grave of "one that was a woman" will turn out by a wicked irony to be ready for Ophelia, and that the fight in the grave, soon to be followed by the duel, is waiting just when he thought that things were settling down. It's not a part to play on an empty stomach.

In discussing the athletics rather than the aesthetics, I have moved out of rehearsal into describing the experience of performance, and indeed, these things being what they are, I remember little of the immediate run-up to opening except, as ever, the attempt to keep my performing head above water amidst the necessarily long hours and technical adjustments. The preview period is one of fourteen-hour days, re-rehearsal after the experience of meeting an audience,

and changes to be absorbed before each evening; so that it is largely a matter of surviving. However, open we did, and at the time of writing I have played the part some 120 times and have not yet finished. Nevertheless, I will not really know much objectively about Hamlet until it is all over. Seen in retrospect for these purposes, the seemingly haphazard process of planning and rehearsal, with its chance discoveries, its missed opportunities, its dry calculations and intuitive hunches—a process that bemuses and frustrates outside observers, so invisible are its movements—might seem to have had some kind of form and pressure. However, a good deal of what I have described may never really have happened in rehearsal at all; but in performance—or been only realized in performance. Sustaining a role during a run is obviously the actor's province more particularly than the director's or critic's; and amidst all the interpreting and judgement, the actor is qualified by the experience of Hamlet for nothing except to go out the next day and do it again. He hopes that the peculiar gift bestowed on him is the aptitude to take a nightly jump in the dark, knowing only the broadest topography of the jump and little of the outcome. I do not know whether audiences realize, even in a relatively structured piece of work, the extent to which they, entering the building from one end, share with those entering from the other a real curiosity about the outcome of the evening. Certainly in playing the part I am more than usually aware of the narrowness of the margin separating a performance that is okay, even good, from one that is special—and how crucial the margin is, since no one wants to come so far to see a Hamlet that is just okay. People do expect to be changed, or at least moved over slightly. What the margin depends on goes beyond application and hard work into some speculative area too numinous to pursue. On some nights the part ups and plays you effortlessly; on others it is like labouring with an out-of-tune violin. Fortunately there is no knowing: on a night like the first, someone will come round and tell you you did nothing for them, and even in the latter case somebody may have been thrilled. An individual performance in the theatre is a live thing, with its own conditions and unpredictability; and to an extent the actor, given a base of discipline and control, must allow himself to be carried by the prevailing winds. Everyone wants the occasion to be special; everyone, including the actors, waits for lightning to strike.

At any event, a performance is one of a kind, and a slightly different man is presented every night; the emotional landscape the actor inhabits is variable, and this particularly volatile part has a way of changing shape in your hands. There are matters in the part that I have never in any case been happy to discuss, such as Hamlet's "madness," which seems to me undiscussable outside the terms of performance. Whether Hamlet is "mad," whatever that is, depends very much on how mad the spectator or actor happens to be. Sometimes it is the theatre's job to pass on a riddle, not to solve it. Certainly by the end of the cellarage scene Shakespeare has brought his character to a fork in the road—a man in extreme nervous disarray decides to feign a nervous breakdown. The irony is obvious. From there on, the exact contours of the divergence inside his personality are an option that as a performer I claim, just as I claim the right to vary within a discipline and over a period of time. The changes that take place through a run are not usually consciously planned, though in the repertoire system, with its frequent breaks, it is necessary to keep some kind of conscious stock; more frequently they arise, for better or worse, out of impulse—as on the evening when a sense of conscience suddenly replaced self-confidence in my attitude to the death of Rosencrantz and Guildenstern, and has remained ever since. The rationalization comes after. "To be or not to be" varies quite a lot, possibly because it is really a relatively unimportant speech in the line of the part, though of course a beautiful thing in itself, and so it can afford to vary. Still, you do not notice a person ageing if you see them all the time, and a frequent attender of a production may be better placed than I am to assess changes in my performance. All that is really necessary for the actor working in repertoire is to be ready each time, to stay on his toes, in the knowledge that things will vary, and that the whole tissue of private references that underpin his performance will quietly change with the patterns of his own life and even the world news: "What a piece of work is a man." Above all he must retain a sense of occasion. There are many mistakes, many disappointments, a sense of defeat amidst the various elations. A particular kind of empathy between actor and audience seems to me crucial in this particular part, and therefore the actor's third ear, by which he monitors as far as he can the nature of the silence in the house on a particular night, the response to the comedy and so on—the strange process by which 1500 separate minds come to be thought of as one thing, an audience—will be specially at work. It is not a matter of ingratiation, but in the end the whole thing does depend on the invisible lines of contact that either complete the event or not. Sometimes there seems no way, and the actor making his series of rapid choices on the stage feels he has never hit on the ones that will deliver Shakespeare's man to the public. But he may be wrong, and above all the play is always there, the next day or the next year (when somebody else will be struggling with the problem). Meanwhile we go back to the beginning each time, hopeful not to waste.

A man with a sword comes upon his enemy, whom he has sworn to destroy, at prayer. The promised act of revenge can at this point be performed with relatively little difficulty—indeed with no greater fear of discovery than that of the praying man on an earlier occasion when he destroyed his enemy in an orchard. With exultation the armed man approaches his victim and raises his sword.

At this point we stop and see where we are. There is no question in the mind of the spectator but that the sword will certainly come down on the neck of the praying man with all the fury with which it was raised. There is also no question in the mind of the armed man but that he will now do the deed—no question at all. Most oddly of all, in the mind of the actor personifying the man with the sword there is a momentary certainty that tonight will be different, and that his colleague on the floor is about to suffer a severe and unexpected injury.

The alarming question arises: who is actually in charge? If the actor himself is in doubt, then who is masterminding the event and guiding us towards the next action? Everyone waits, the spectators, the two men, the two actors playing the two men, all held for a moment on the same edge, holding the same breath.

Needless to say, things don't always go so sweetly, and I do not mean to mystify. But perhaps it is on hinges such as this that this formidable play finally swings. Certainly all our planning, decisions conscious and unconscious, hunches, strategies and jumps in the dark would add up to very little if they did not in the end lead to just such a small moment of suspense.

PERFORMANCE REVIEW

An Innovative Season at Stratford-upon-Avon

MEL GUSSOW
Review of *Hamlet*

DIRECTED BY JOHN BARTON, ROYAL SHAKESPEARE COMPANY, AT STRATFORD-UPON-AVON, 27 JULY 1980.

Mel Gussow's review, "An Innovative Season at Stratford-upon-Avon," for the New York Times *provides at once an interesting overview of a landmark year in the history of the Royal Shakespeare Company, and a thoughtful account of its production of* Hamlet; *it is especially provocative to read his comments on Michael Pennington's performance alongside Pennington's commentary on preparing the part for performance, printed on pp. 362-367.*

In John Barton's new production of *Hamlet,* the first in 10 years on the main stage at Stratford-upon-Avon, Michael Pennington is a scholar prince, a poet of action and, perhaps most of all, a performer. This choice of a *Hamlet* in 1980 as the Royal Shakespeare Company's first entry in what appears to be a contest to find a definitive Dane of the decade says something about the state of Stratford.

Over the years, the RSC has repeatedly diversified its interests, approaching its resident playwright from divergent directions, performing him faithfully in period and also in drastically transformed versions. Audiences are often surprised at Stratford. There is no assurance of traditionalism, particularly at the Other Place, the company's smaller, experimental theater. Under the artistic direction of Ron Daniels, the Other Place has increasingly generated innovative work (some of it versions of Shakespeare), which often moves from Stratford to the RSC's London workshop stage, the Warehouse, just as major Shakespearean productions move to the Aldwych. The main Stratford stage, with seasons alternately led by one of the company's co-artistic directors, Trevor Nunn and Terry Hands (this summer belongs to Mr. Hands), does not neglect its devotion to Shakespeare as source. At its heart, the RSC remains as authoritative as its august name.

For the new *Hamlet,* there is no fog on the battlements and there is no murkiness at the court within. Bright lights illuminate the stage even when the Ghost walks at night. As played by Raymond Westwell, the Ghost is a most corporeal presence; he could be a tenured tutor from Wittenberg checking up on an errant student. In direct contrast, in Jonathan Pryce's recent radical *Hamlet* at the Royal Court Theater in London, Hamlet spoke for the ghost of his father; it was as if he were possessed and were exorcising a demon. In an English theater lately visited by controversial Hamlets—including an actress in the role and a "skinhead"—the Pennington performance is not so much a variation as a reversion to the age of Gielgud, when a Hamlet could be well-spoken as well as ill-mannered. This Hamlet is in several senses an exceptional actor.

In her introduction to the forthcoming new Penguin edition of the play, Anne Barton, the wife of the director, apparently speaks for her husband when she stresses the "theatrical self-reference" of the text. "For Hamlet," she writes, "the theater becomes a means of deciphering a treacherous world." Art assumes control over life. To accent Hamlet's use of artifice, the designer, Ralph Koltai, takes us backstage at Elsi-

nore. The court is a raised platform surrounded by the accoutrements of the evening's performance. There is even a thundersheet ready to be rattled. Hamlet stage manages the play within the play and appears to be understudying all the roles; he could step in as Player King or Queen at a second's notice. Similarly, he manipulates Polonius, Ophelia and others. He is feigning madness, and he entreats us to share his sham.

His dialogue with Polonius (Tony Church) is the most playful within memory; we are made aware of a genuine bond between the prince and the good old man. They enjoy their banter. This Polonius is much more Hamlet's philosophic equal than, for example, stolid Horatio. Escorting the players onto their stage, Polonius dons a foolscap and, briefly, he and Hamlet caper as if they were partners in a vaudeville team. During the players' performance, Hamlet himself is costumed in crazy-quilt. When Polonius is slain (there are entirely too many stabs and slashes behind and through the arras in this occasionally overstated production), Hamlet's dismay is evident.

Mr. Pennington rarely raises his voice, but he can be suddenly explosive. He rations his temper. With Ophelia—a tenderly passionate portrayal by Carol Royle in her first major role at Stratford—his initial "Get thee to a nunnery" is an expression of concern, almost a verbalized caress: please, do it for your own good. Hamlet manipulates his own emotions until he is in a fever. By the end of the speech, he is fueled with ire and resentment—and in a physical frenzy, he actually strikes Ophelia. With Mr. Pennington, we always feel the potential for violence. He has a look of fixed intensity and it is a feeling that carries into his reading of the soliloquies. With flawless diction and without ever becoming arbitrary, he makes the speeches seem both vital and conversational.

There are shortcomings in the production, beginning with the Ghost. The evening lacks a sense of omen and mystery. A few of the actors, such as Derek Godfrey as Claudius, retreat into blandness; they become faceless in Elsinore. One problem in *Hamlet* and in other productions in repertory at Stratford is a thinning of the acting ranks. In each of the plays, with the notable exception of Beaumont and Fletcher's *The Maid's Tragedy* at the Other Place, the performances fall short of a cohesive ensemble.

Many of the R.S.C.'s strongest actors are working in London, where the company is performing the epic two-part *Nicholas Nickleby* at the Aldwych and the Kaufman-Hart *Once in a Lifetime* in repertory with Pam Gems's *Piaf* at the Picadilly. The resources of this estimable company are not inexhaustible, and by that I mean scenery and costumes as well as actors. The spareness of the productions at Stratford and the largely unimaginative design could be attributed to artistic fallowness as well as to economic stringency.

It would take an extremely close line reading to distinguish the differences between the Stratford seasons of its two directors. Each is party to the other's decisions. Perhaps the hallmark of Mr. Hands's current repertory is his own bucolic production of *As You Like It*. By turn fanciful and pragmatic, womanly and hoydenish, Susan Fleetwood is a radiant Rosalind with a voice of the purest quicksilver. As her conspiratorial partner, Celia, Sinead Cusack invites our affection; she makes this supporting role seem consequential. In court—the setting is oddly fleece-lined with wall-to-wall lambs wool—the production is somewhat stiff-jointed, except for a most convincing bout between Orlando and Charles the wrestler. However, the young women's flight to Arden, in consort with Joe Melia's madcap minstrel Touchstone, is an airy and frolicsome journey.

Stratford's primary experiment is Ron Daniels's *Romeo and Juliet,* the sort of venture that is usually presented in small scale at the Other Place, but is now seen in larger dimension on the main stage. The major roles are played by young actors: Judy Buxton is a dewy Juliet, Anton Lesser a youthfully headstrong, although not a particularly romantic Romeo. Mr. Daniels has unmoored the play in a never-never land that is closer to the *West Side Story* turf of the Jets and the Sharks than it is to Shakespeare's Verona. Romeo and his mates, lounging like lizards on street corners, are garbed in leatherboots, pants and jackets. They carry canes concealing swords—a very free interpretation of what Shakespeare meant by "fiddle-sticks."

We keep waiting for bars of Leonard Bernstein; what is heard is an exchange of sneers and hisses, underscored by Italian street music. Ralph Koltai's set consists of large museum-size slabs of abstract paintings, white with a few slashes of color, which are used for walls and doors with equal inefficiency. For the balcony scene, Juliet appears to perch on top of an abstract painting as a short Romeo struggles on tiptoe to touch her fingers. I vastly prefer Stratford's *Romeo and Juliet* of several seasons ago, starring Ian McKellen, and, as an attempt at modernization, the 1978 *Taming of the Shrew* in which Jonathan Pryce played Petruchio on a motorcycle. That Michael Bogdanov production was a reinterpretation with a pronounced comic purpose.

While *Hamlet, As You Like It* and *Romeo and Juliet* compete for a large audience on the main stage, in the Other Place there is a rousing production of *The Maid's Tragedy*. This seldom-performed tale of melodramatic revenge and fearful conscience has a plot of labyrinthine complexity and a visceral resolution that covers the stage with gore. The RSC cast, directed by Barry Kyle, glides through the intricate intrigues with the confidence of a ship's navigator, binding us in the spell of the tragic story.

There is only one false note. Once again a play is not enriched by its setting—in this case wicker furniture to represent the court at Rhodes—and costumes (the characters seem more outfitted for a harem than for a court). However, the cast is first-rate, especially the ladies—Sinead Cusack in the pivotal role as a predatory woman who sets the spinning plot in motion, Domini Blythe and Carol Royle. Led by Susan Fleetwood in *As You Like It,* there is a garland of talented young actresses this season at Stratford—and there is also Michael Pennington offering an intelligent and articulate Hamlet.

IV

Early Modern Europe

The 1993 Willamette College production of Aphra Behn's *The Rover*.

I n London, Paris, and Madrid, theater and drama experienced a second "renais-
        sance" in the later seventeenth century. In these cities, the theater came under
        the influence and protection of the king and his court, and the theaters of both
London and Paris adapted Italian staging practices, as did the theaters of the Spanish court.
As scenic technology became increasingly complex and spectacular, theater buildings
achieved the form they would hold well into the nineteenth century, and the work of new
playwrights and new dramatic designs invigorated the dramatic repertoire.

Yet for all their similarities, the theaters of Restoration England, of Louis XIV's France,
and of the Spanish "Golden Age" were sustained by very different social and political climates. In France, Louis XIV declared *"L'état, c'est moi"*—"I am the state"—in 1660, confidently drawing all state authority into the person of the king and his magnificent court. The
later seventeenth century in France was a period of royal absolutism, as the throne worked
to consolidate its power. In England, conditions were very different, for 1660 brought the
restoration of the monarchy. The Restoration period saw an ongoing negotiation between
newly installed Charles II and Parliament for power, in which Parliament gradually gained
control of many royal prerogatives. In both countries, the theater became associated with the
throne and reflected the tensions animating social and political life.

THE POLITICAL CLIMATE

In France, a character in Molière's play *Tartuffe* drew the official portrait of the absolute
monarch: "A Prince who sees into our inmost hearts, / And can't be fooled by any trickster's arts." Yet the authoritarian policies of the French government, the internecine competition among members of the court, and even the fortunes of the theater suggest that the
king's claim of absolute power was challenged in a variety of ways. Under Louis XIII
(reigned 1610–1643) and Louis XIV (reigned 1643–1715), the Crown strove to centralize
its power by crushing the claims of the landed nobility and by expanding French rule in a
series of costly wars. Since Louis XIII came to the throne at the age of nine, when his father—Henry IV—was assassinated, much of this expansion was carried on by his chief minister, Cardinal Richelieu (1585–1642), and Richelieu's successor, Cardinal Mazarin
(1602–1661). The suppression of the traditional nobility was achieved largely through
Richelieu's formation of a new bureaucracy loyal to the Crown, partly composed of politically active clergy and partly of commoners promoted over the heads of the nobility to critical positions in the government. Allowing these "new men" to buy aristocratic titles, the
Crown raised money and further diluted the power of the nobility. The Crown's ravenous
appetite for cash to pay for the lavish life of the court and for expensive building projects,
such as the palace of Versailles (built by Louis XIV in 1673), further weakened the nobility
and alienated the peasantry. Using tax-farmers, who paid a fixed sum to the government in
exchange for the authority to collect taxes and pocket the excess as profit, the Crown
squeezed the nobles' wealth directly into the royal coffers, impoverishing their lands and
making the peasantry increasingly rebellious.

A poor and disaffected peasantry, a jealous aristocracy, an upstart bourgeoisie, and an increasingly authoritarian and isolated monarchy: this became the recipe for revolution. Although the French Revolution did not erupt until 1789, France suffered civil convulsions
throughout the seventeenth century that dramatize the tension between Louis' absolutist
rhetoric and the political realities of his reign. The nobles led a series of rebellions called

the Fronde throughout the 1640s and 1650s, in an effort to unseat Louis and his powerful ministers. Louis defeated these uprisings and finally sealed the fate of his enemies when he required the nobility to attend him at Versailles, so he could keep his eye on their activities. However, the Fronde was part of a more pervasive unrest. Relentless taxation, economic stagnation, and repeated famines throughout the seventeenth century made the peasants angry as well, and peasant riots and rebellions took place in nearly every province of France in nearly every decade of the century. Finally, Louis XIV also had difficulty with the most volatile issue of seventeenth-century Europe—religious dissent. The close ties between the Crown and the church often resulted in the suppression of Protestant sects, particularly the Calvinist French Huguenots. Protestant rebellion had forced the enactment of the Edict of Nantes in 1598, granting the Huguenots considerable religious freedom. Louis XIV revoked the Edict in 1685, giving the government wider latitude to suppress increasingly energetic religious protest. Louis XIV carefully crafted the image of the "Le Roi Soleil"—the Sun King—whose absolute authority seemed almost a force of nature, not a fact of politics. Throughout his reign, though, Louis had to contend with recalcitrant factions who refused to accept completely his characterization of the king's power.

In England, resistance to royal authority had been much more successful. Between 1603 and 1642, the Stuart kings James I (reigned 1603–1625) and his son, Charles I (reigned 1625–1649), worked to limit the power of Parliament and to enforce increasingly strict religious laws that suppressed the Protestant Puritan sects and demanded conformity with the Church of England. In 1642, Parliament passed legislation limiting the powers of the throne, and Civil War between Parliamentary and Royalist forces erupted. Charles I was executed in 1649; his wife and children (including the future king, Charles II) escaped to France. From 1653 to 1658, Oliver Cromwell served as Lord Protector of the realm, but Royalist sentiments eventually prevailed and established Charles II (reigned 1660–1685) on the throne.

Although the monarchy was restored—the term *Restoration* refers generally to the period of Charles II's reign and the remainder of the seventeenth century—Charles II was in no position to command the nation, and English politics in the later seventeenth century mainly concerned the negotiation of power between the Crown and Parliament. Charles' death in 1685 spurred a crisis in that his son James II (reigned 1685–1688) was Catholic and threatened to compromise English religious and civil autonomy from the Catholic church and the Catholic states of Europe. In 1689, Parliament effectively deposed James, inviting his Protestant daughter Mary (reigned as Mary II, 1689–1694) and her husband, William of Orange (reigned as William III, 1689–1702), to return to England and assume the throne. While Louis XIV increasingly insisted on the autonomous power of the throne in France, the Parliament in England finally achieved a lasting compromise with the Crown in the form of a constitutional monarchy. In bringing William and Mary into power, Parliament gained the authority of consent over royal succession, a power it confirmed in 1702 in naming James II's daughter Anne as successor (reigned as Queen Anne, 1702–1714).

While in an important sense the gulf separating French and English culture has always been narrow and deep, like the English Channel, Spanish culture in the Renaissance arises from a very different history. Spain was occupied by the Moors in 711 and is still marked by its five centuries of Islamic culture. In 1479, Ferdinand of Aragon and Isabella of Castile were married, forming the alliance that gave rise to modern Spain. In 1480 they joined forces with the Catholic Inquisition, expelling Jews from the country. At the Conquest of Granada in 1492, the Moors were finally driven out of Spain.

Having formed a single state, the Spanish monarchy successfully expanded its reach into a global empire during the sixteenth century. Under Charles V, Spain's territory included its many New World colonies as well as the Netherlands and the Holy Roman Empire of central Europe, and the culture of the Spanish court was unrivaled in Europe; this was the era of Velásquez and El Greco. During the reign of Philip II (1556–1598), however, Spain's domination of Europe began to wane. Spain became involved in a brutal and expensive effort to retain control of the Netherlands, a hotbed of Protestant resistance. English soldiers—Sir Philip Sidney and Ben Jonson, among others—fought the Spanish in the Netherlands, and Philip tried in several ways to outmaneuver the English. He proposed marriage to Queen Elizabeth, but as with other suitors, she strung him along for political purposes and finally refused him. He also mounted a massive naval invasion of England, the Spanish Armada of 1588, which was surprisingly defeated. Spain continued to wane in the seventeenth century, eventually losing the Netherlands and losing Portugal in 1657. By 1665, Spain was ruled by the last of the Hapsburg kings, the deformed imbecile Charles II (1665–1700). The death of Charles II drew all of Europe into the Wars of the Spanish Succession.

THEATER IN FRANCE, 1660–1700

Louis XIV's familiar sobriquet, "Le Roi Soleil," derives from a role he played in a court ballet devised for him in 1653. A fine dancer, Louis sponsored and took part in a wide variety of entertainments. Moreover, the centralization of power in the king and the court paralleled the increasing institutionalization of the arts under Louis XIV, as a means of advancing his own prestige and of keeping control over potentially seditious activities. The most famous of these institutions—the ACADÉMIE FRANÇAISE—was chartered in 1637 and used by Cardinal Richelieu to evaluate a critical controversy surrounding Pierre Corneille's play *The Cid*. Corneille's detractors had sharply attacked the play, and Richelieu urged the Académie to resolve whether *The Cid* could legitimately be described as effective tragedy in neoclassical terms (on *neoclassicism,* see p. 384). In return, Richelieu promoted the Académie and its aims, the purification of French language and literature, and the advancement of official French culture. Louis XIV assumed the role of official protector of the Académie Française in 1672 and sponsored other institutions as ornaments to his reign: the Académie Royale de Musique (1672), the Académie Royale de Peinture et de Sculpture (1648), the Académie des Inscriptions (1663), the Académie des Sciences (1666), and the Académie de l'Architecture (1671). The institution of the stage was no exception. Theatrical companies had always needed the king's license to play in Paris, and Louis licensed several companies and named Molière's company as the *Troupe du roi*. After Molière's death in 1673, the leading tragic actress in Paris, Mademoiselle Champmeslé, joined with Molière's troupe and gained the king's patronage. The new company—the COMÉDIE FRANÇAISE— opened in August of 1680. It held a MONOPOLY on the production of all spoken drama in French, and although this monopoly has long since vanished, the Comédie Française remains the principal company performing the French classical repertoire.

In Louis XIV's Paris, the institutions of art—including the theater—were identified with the prerogatives of the king and his court, though the structure of the theater had its roots in practices dating back to the Middle Ages. Throughout the later Middle Ages and into the sixteenth century, stage production in Paris was controlled by the Confrérie de la Passion, a guildlike corporation initially formed to stage religious drama. In 1545 the Confrérie purchased land in Paris from the Duke of Burgundy and erected the Hôtel de Bourgogne, at the time probably the only permanent theater building in Europe (*hôtel* in this case means "hall" or "large building"). Extensively remodeled in 1647, the Hôtel de Bourgogne served as the model for other theaters built in the seventeenth century: the Théâtre du Marais (built in a tennis court in 1629, rebuilt in 1644); the Palais-Cardinal (built by Richelieu in 1640; later renamed the Palais-Royal); the Salle des Machines (1642), and the Comédie Française (1689).

The shape of these theaters owes something to the Hôtel de Bourgogne, and something to tennis courts as well, for tennis courts were often used as theaters. (In the sixteenth and seventeenth centuries, tennis courts were long indoor rooms with side galleries.) These

GROUND PLAN OF THE COMÉDIE FRANÇAISE THEATER

The Comédie Française had this basic design from 1689 to 1770. Note the open *parterre,* the wings (marked Y), and the backdrops (Z). The benches on the stage were added during the eighteenth century.

theaters generally had deep, **RAKED STAGES** (40 feet deep, 45 feet wide at the Hôtel de Bourgogne) that faced an open **PIT** called the **PARTERRE** (literally, "on the ground") which was used for standing spectators. The auditorium had **BOXES** on three sides; **GALLERY** seating rose above the boxes opposite the stage; some patrons were also seated on the stage itself. The theaters were large—the Hôtel de Bourgogne initially held 1,600 spectators, the Comédie Française held 2,000—and many theaters made extensive use of stage scenery, sometimes concocting extraordinary spectacles. In a fantasy celebrating Louis XIV's wedding in 1662, the entire royal family and its entourage were "flown" by machines in the Salle des Machines; in a production in 1671, 300 deities were lifted aloft. The dramatic theaters— the Hôtel de Bourgogne, the Palais-Royal, the Comédie Française—tended to avoid such effects, using instead a single setting for each play, depending on the genre of the play. The theaters generally used a series of staggered **WINGS AND BACKDROP** to create the effect of perspective, adapting both scenic practices and scene-changing technology from Italian theaters.

Acting companies in Paris were organized as investment corporations requiring the patronage of the Crown and had long included women in their ranks. Louis XIV's reign saw a series of great actresses take the stage, Mademoiselle DuParc and Mademoiselle Champmeslé among them. Companies were comprised of twelve members (eight men, four women), who shared the company's profits. The company hired additional actors when necessary. The Comédie Française standardized this practice: its twelve main actors— called

SOCIÉTAIRES—ran the company for twenty years, and new *sociétaires* could be recruited only after the retirement of current members. Actors in the Comédie Française received an annual subsidy from the Crown and a retirement pension if they completed their twenty years with the company. The company purchased plays, which were cast by the author. Throughout the 1650s and 1660s the major companies kept about 70 plays in repertoire and generally played three or four times per week. After the 1680s, the Comédie Française began daily performances, beginning at 5 P.M.

We should recall that life at court was itself a kind of performance, and that attending the theater provided ample opportunity for aristocrats, courtiers, and aspiring courtiers to display and preen themselves. In a milieu so dependent on the king's preference, we can easily imagine how stage seating and side boxes emphasized that the evening's entertainment included the audience's performances as well as the actors'. This sense of the reciprocity between court and stage is signaled more concretely by the fortunes of the Parisian theaters after Louis XIV moved the court to Versailles. Although five companies flourished in Paris while Louis kept court in the city, by 1700 only two remained.

THEATER IN ENGLAND, 1660–1737

At the outbreak of the English Civil War in 1642, Parliament closed the London theaters, putting a stop to dramatic performance. Some companies managed to mount secret productions between 1642 and 1660, but Parliament and city officials moved quickly to suppress them, sometimes by destroying the theater buildings. In the 1650s, however, William Davenant (1606–1668), a Royalist supporter of Charles I and successor to Ben Jonson as writer of court masques, attempted to mount operas. In 1656 he succeeded in staging a production of *The Siege of Rhodes* at Rutland House, performing it again in 1658 and 1659 at the Cockpit theater and elsewhere in London.

The restoration of Charles II to the throne in 1660 inaugurated a period of renewed theatrical vitality. As in France—where Charles developed a taste for theater during his exile—the theater was closely associated with royal prerogatives. Upon his return, Charles rewarded **PATENTS** to William Davenant and Thomas Killegrew (1612–1683) to open theaters under royal authority. These **PATENT THEATERS** (also called "theaters royal")—Davenant's Duke's company, and Killigrew's King's company—thus held a royal monopoly on the production of spoken English drama. Although they underwent huge modifications, the patent theaters dominated the legitimate theater until the mid-nineteenth century, when legislation was passed that finally broke their monopoly. Yet monopoly could not guarantee support. The two companies, unable to turn a profit, were united into a single company from 1682 to 1695.

When the theaters reopened in 1660, theatrical taste had changed significantly. Although a few of the older, pre-1642 theater buildings were still standing, they could not handle the new theater technology. For, as in the French theater, the English theater rapidly encouraged the development of scenic practices already well-known in Italy—a **PROSCENIUM** stage and moveable painted wings and backdrop used to create a visual setting for the play. Onstage, theaters used stock sets—one for classical tragedy, one for romantic comedy, and so on—that conformed to the dramatic genre of the play. In 1661, Davenant converted Lisle's Tennis Court to the Lincoln's Inn Fields Theater, which measured 30 by 70 feet; he replaced this theater with the Dorset Garden Theater in 1671. Killegrew erected his Theatre Royal in Bridges Street in 1663. When it burned in 1672, he built a new Theatre Royal in Drury Lane, which opened in 1674; a theater has occupied this site down to the present time.

The new English theaters were much smaller than the French theaters. The Drury Lane theater, for example, held 650 to 700 people, though it was expanded throughout the late seventeenth and eighteenth centuries and eventually held more than 2,000. Nonetheless,

CHRISTOPHER WREN'S THEATRE ROYAL, DRURY LANE

In 1674, Christopher Wren designed a new Theatre Royal, Drury Lane. Note that the acting area extends to the apron, in front of the wing and backdrop stage scenery. Pit seating, side boxes, and two galleries also are visible.

like the French theaters, the English houses also introduced new design and staging practices: a proscenium stage flanked by a large **APRON,** footlights to illuminate the stage, a raked pit with benches (the French *parterre* was flat and had no seats), side and rear box seats, and a rear gallery. This division of the house accorded with social and class distinctions in the audience, which was in any event a narrow selection of the English public, in part because the theater was recognized as the ornament of the privileged, and—not incidentally—because plays were produced in the afternoon, when working people could not easily attend. The entire auditorium was lighted by chandeliers, making the audience itself very much a part of the show: in an important sense the performance did not stop at the edge of the stage. Although the theaters were not at the court itself, they were frequently patronized by courtiers and the nobility, who preened and displayed themselves to the audience—sometimes from seats onstage. Charles II—who numbered the well-known actress Nell Gwynn (1650–1687) among his many mistresses—was also frequently in the audience.

Companies were generally managed by one of the actors, and they avoided the need for lengthy casting and rehearsal by developing **LINES OF BUSINESS,** in which each actor would specialize in a particular type of character: heroic lead, comic lead, male heavy, female heavy, utility player, and so on. Acting style was relatively formal, and actors often played downstage on the apron directly to the audience; a famous speech—one of Hamlet's soliloquies, for example—would be delivered directly to the audience, something like an operatic aria today, a practice called **POINTING.** As the theater developed in the later seventeenth century, sharing companies were replaced by companies financed by outside investors, who paid the actors salaries and took a percentage of the profits. Companies were large and salaries low; actors were compensated by **BENEFIT** performances, in which the actor (on his or her benefit night) received the entire profit from a given evening's performance, minus the operating expenses of the house. The practice of supplementing salaries with benefit performances continued well into the nineteenth century, and although most benefit nights—after the house expenses were deducted—left the actors with little additional pay, benefits provided an excuse to keep actors' salaries low.

By far the greatest innovation in the English theater, though, was the introduction of actresses onstage. English comedies in this period were often frankly concerned with sexual intrigue, and the actresses who played in them—and in the new heroic tragedies, and in the plays by Shakespeare, Jonson, Fletcher, and other Renaissance playwrights who continued to hold the stage—also had a reputation for sexual licentiousness. Yet, while several actresses, like Nell Gwynne, were mistresses of the famous and powerful, the phenomenon of regarding actresses as sexual objects, of classing them with prostitutes, has more to do with the status and vulnerability of working women in a highly stratified and patriarchal society than it does with the immorality of the stage or its performers. Indeed, actresses' ongoing struggle to assert themselves as legitimate performers was born at this time as well, epitomized in the careers of Elizabeth Barry (1658–1713), Anne Bracegirdle (1663–1748), and many others.

THEATER IN SPAIN'S GOLDEN AGE, 1580–1680

As in medieval England and France, medieval Spanish theater was strongly influenced by the church, which saw in the drama a source of instruction and inspiration. Although there is some evidence for liturgical drama as early as the twelfth century, the principal form of medieval theater was the *AUTO SACRAMENTALE,* a form of allegorical religious drama initially devised to celebrate the feast of Corpus Christi. But while the mystery cycles were suppressed in Protestant England, the Spanish *autos* continued to be performed alongside the secular theater until they were banned in 1765. Like the English cycles, the *autos* were in civic hands, and by the late sixteenth century major cities would perform *autos* as many as three times per year, usually in the central city plaza before a gathering of citizens and civic officials. Professional actors were hired for the *autos* and were drawn through the city on wagons (*CARROS*); the *carros* were heavily decorated, and a prize was given for the most spectacular *carro.* Despite their abstract themes, the *autos* remained extremely popular and drew on the talents of the best playwrights of the era—between 1647 and 1681, for instance, all the *autos* performed in Madrid were written by Pedro Calderón de la Barca.

Philip II, Philip III, and Philip IV were all interested in theater and commissioned playwrights to devise entertainments; during the reign of Philip III, Spain developed an impressive court theater. Early in the seventeenth century, this court theater merely occupied a hall at the Alcázar palace, as Ben Jonson and Inigo Jones had done at Whitehall palace in England, and it produced a similar kind of entertainment: mythological dramas that required spectacular scenery, effects, and costumes. But by the 1630s, the center of court theater shifted to the new palace of Buen Retiro. Here, in 1640 Cosme Lotti (d. 1643) was retained to build a permanent theater that could perform the scenic effects of the Italian theater. This theater was roofed, but in its basic design resembled the most influential of Spanish theaters in the Golden Age, the public theater or *CORRAL.*

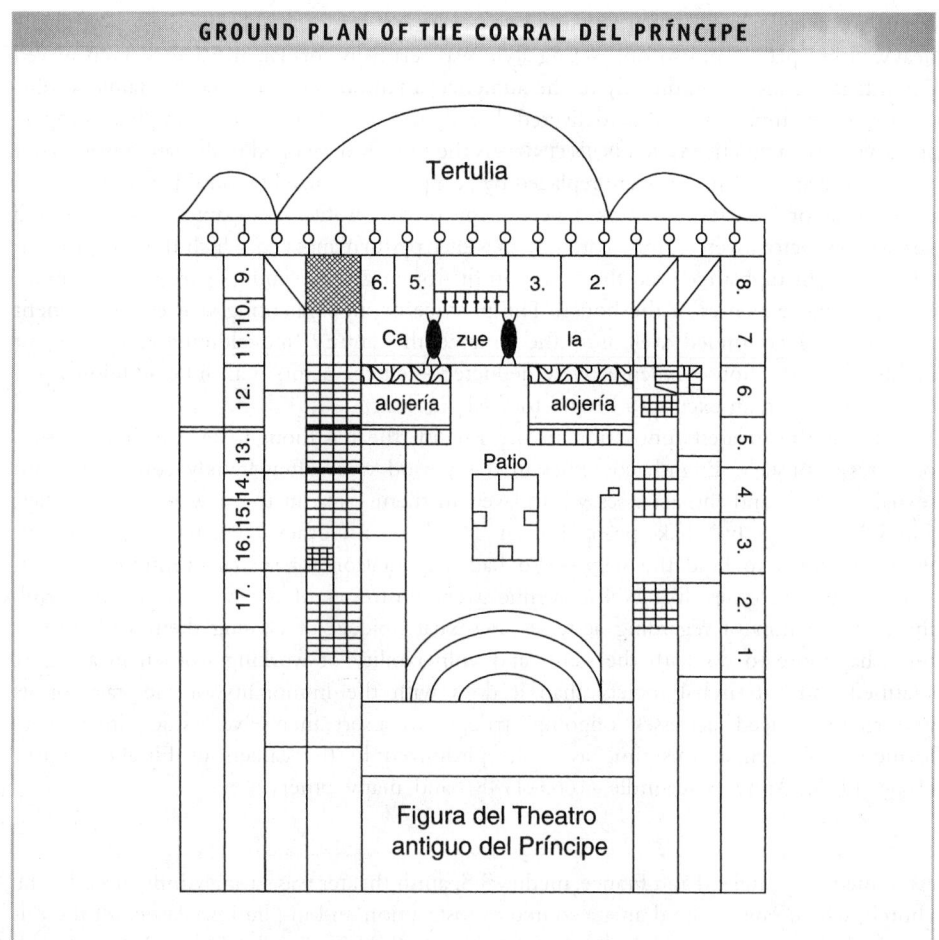

GROUND PLAN OF THE CORRAL DEL PRÍNCIPE

Made in 1730, this drawing of the Corral del Príncipe shows the important features of the theater: the *patio,* the *alojería,* the *gradas,* and the *cazuela.*

Although the Spanish public theater resembled the public theaters of Elizabethan London, it stood in a much different relationship to city life. While the English theaters were banned from the city proper and were erected across the Thames in Southwark, the Spanish theaters were public institutions. Since the medieval church held the rights to theatrical production, the public theaters were licensed by religious confraternities in the sixteenth century, which used the funds for various charitable purposes, including maintaining the general hospital of Madrid. By the early seventeenth century, these funds were paid directly to the city, and theaters continued to subsidize charities well into the nineteenth century. Companies of actors were licensed to play in the city, and took a lease on a *corral* for a stated period of time. In general, Spanish companies toured major cities and towns, and only Seville and Madrid allowed two companies to perform at the same time. While playwrights were initially associated with individual companies, by the seventeenth century playwrights would sell their plays to the company: they were paid very well for an *auto,* and adequately for a regular play—about 500 reales, or about 10 times the daily wage of a laborer. Although companies were composed of men and boys until 1587, when women were allowed to appear onstage, the church issued a decree banning women from performing onstage in 1596. By 1599, however, a royal council ruled that actresses could be permitted, providing they were married to a member of the company; it also ruled against cross-dressing, so that when

VIEW OF THE CORRAL DEL PRÍNCIPE

This illustration provides a view of the Corral del Príncipe from the rear of the *patio,* perhaps from the *cazuela.*

Rosaura appeared dressed as a man in Calderón's *Life Is a Dream,* the actress wore a man's costume only down to the waist with a skirt below.

The reciprocity between the city and the theater is also revealed in the design of public theaters of the golden age, particularly the two principal theaters of Madrid, the Corral de la Cruz, opened in 1579 as Spain's first theater, and the Corral del Príncipe, opened in 1583. The theaters were originally merely stages placed in a courtyard enclosed on three or four sides by four-story buildings; over time the theaters gradually acquired possession of these structures, but in the meantime the buildings' galleries and windows could be sold to spectators separately. The central courtyard or *PATIO* was unroofed, and like the pit of English theaters was occupied by standing spectators. In the seventeenth century, a few rows of benches (called *TABURETES*) were erected near the stage, on a raised and fenced dais. Along the sides of the *patio* rose the *GRADAS,* steeply raked rows of seats that rose to the second floor. The *ALOJERÍA,* a tavern, served refreshments, and was located at the rear of the *patio;* above the *alojería,* were several stories of galleries: the *CAZUELA,* or women's gallery, on the second floor; above it galleries for the City of Madrid and Council of Castile officials; and a gallery for intellectual and church officials, the *TERTULIA*. Above the *gradas*, the grated windows of the houses served as box seats. The third and fourth floors of the buildings were converted to *DESVANES* or "attics," small open galleries.

DRAMATIC INNOVATION IN FRANCE, ENGLAND, AND SPAIN

Although theatrical production extended into a number of other forms—ballet, opera, royal pageants, and the special-effects extravaganzas called **MACHINE PLAYS**—prevailing attitudes, particularly in France, prohibited the mixing of dramatic genres: Tragedy and comedy were firmly discriminated from one another and from others kinds of entertainment. In France, comedy—and, indeed, the organization of theatrical companies—was particularly influenced by the techniques of the Italian *COMMEDIA DELL'ARTE*. French tragic drama inherited a taste for classical subject matter from the schools and universities, which had led Europe in translating Greek and Roman playwrights into French. Throughout the sixteenth century, the court sponsored a variety of efforts to classicize the theater, supporting several important playwrights, including Robert Garnier and Étienne Jodelle, who created highly wrought and refined tragedies based on the model of classical drama. The heroic tragedies of Pierre Corneille (1606–1684) and Jean Racine (1639–1699) epitomize this tradition while also turning it in a new direction, refracting contemporary moral, political, and philosophical issues through the lens of a classical style.

English drama in the Restoration also was affected by the **HEROIC TRAGEDIES** of France and Spain, by the comedies of Ben Jonson and James Shirley, and by the tragedies of Shakespeare and of Francis Beaumont and John Fletcher, which continued to be performed, though often in revised or adapted form. John Dryden (1631–1700), for example, not only adapted versions of *The Tempest* and *Antony and Cleopatra* (the latter as *All for Love*, 1677), but also wrote plays in the mode of heroic tragedy, such as *Aureng-Zebe* (1675) and *The Conquest of Granada* (1669). Heroic tragedy generally represents the idealized passions of characters forced to choose between love and personal honor. Comic drama took its inspiration both from European models—Molière's plays, for example—and from the earlier plays of Ben Jonson, but in the plays of William Wycherly (1640–1716), Sir George Etherege (1635–1692), and William Congreve (1670–1729), English comedy rapidly developed its own original style. Restoration comedies are most often in the vein of **COMEDY OF MANNERS**, contemporary dramas in which witty aristocrats, city dupes and dandies, and dull country gentlemen are engaged in an elaborate adventure of sexual intrigue. Restoration comedy is often elegant and verbally polished, and obsessed with issues of class, privilege, manners, and sex. In addition, much as the Restoration theater witnessed the rise of actresses onstage, it also saw the first women to achieve success as playwrights: Aphra Behn (1640–1689), Catharine Trotter (1679–1749), and Susanna Centlivre (1670–1723).

After the turn of the century, the risqué character of many plays spurred one of the perennial movements to restrain the theater as an immoral institution. Partly as a result of Jeremy Collier's diatribe *A Short View of the Immorality and Profaneness of the English Stage* (1698), and partly as a result of changing attitudes and social mores, English comedy after 1700—the plays of Sir Richard Steele (1672–1729), Colley Cibber (1671–1757), George Farquhar (1678–1707), Oliver Goldsmith (1728–1774), and Richard Brinsley Sheridan (1751–1816), for instance—became more romantic and sentimental. Moreover, political satire in English theater was also sharply limited with the passing of the Stage Licensing Act of 1737. After 1737, all plays produced for public entertainment had to be submitted for censorship prior to production. The censor could require changes, delete words, passages, or scenes, or refuse to grant permission entirely. Confronting the Act by producing a nonlicensed play was to risk the fining and imprisonment of everyone involved in the production. While theaters found a variety of ways to subvert or sidestep the law, the censorship remained in effect—with some modifications—until 1968, inhibiting the possibility of dramatic innovation.

(ASIDE)
COMMEDIA DELL' ARTE

The term *commedia dell' arte* means the "comedy of the professional players," and *commedia* became popular throughout Europe in the sixteenth century. *Commedia* companies were itinerant (though one was established in Paris for part of Louis XIV's reign), organized around ten or twelve actors, men and women, each of whom played a stock character who could be easily recognized by typical and routine behavior. Although the characters were fixed, the plots that *commedia* companies played were generally improvised; the actor relied on the traits of his or her character and a core of stage business from which to invent action and dialogue. The cast usually included one or two pairs of young lovers (the **INNAMORATO** and **INNAMORATA**), good-looking, aristocratic, or fashionable characters played without masks. The rest of the cast was masked and played more stereotypical roles: the **CAPITANO,** a military braggart and coward, played with sword and cape; the **PANTALONE,** an elderly dupe, often in love, played in stockings, breeches, and slippers; the **DOTTORE,** sometimes actually a doctor, but otherwise a pedantic friend of the Pantalone; and a variety of comic parts called **ZANNI,** usually sly servants. The most familiar of these parts is *Arlecchino,* or **HARLEQUIN,** a cunning character who is usually an acrobat, wearing a patched costume (later refined to a diamond-shaped pattern), a black cap, and carrying his slapstick—the origin of our term "slapstick," which gives some idea of what *commedia* humor was like. *Commedia* was also popular in England, but it had fewer long-term effects on the comic drama than on the rise of English **PANTOMIME.** In England, plays were often followed by a short **AFTERPIECE,** which frequently led Harlequin into adventures with mythological characters. John Rich (1692–1761), taking the name Lun, was the most famous Harlequin of the early eighteenth-century English stage.

PANTALONE AND HARLEQUIN

Note the mask and breeches of the Pantalone (left), and the mask, slapstick, and diamond-shaped patches of the Harlequin (right).

In the early sixteenth century, a Spanish theatrical manager may well have written his own plays and acted in them himself. Lope de Rueda (1510–1565), for example, was a touring performer and the author of both *autos* and secular plays. But by the late sixteenth century, companies would pay a playwright for the play, and the theaters had made several genres popular: the *CAPA Y ESPADA* or heroic/romantic "cape and sword" play was very popular, as was the *RUIDO* or "noise" play. But the forms of Golden Age drama were in many ways determined by the extraordinary and prolific career of Lope Félix de Vega Carpio (1562–1635). Lope de Vega is frequently said to have written more than 1,500 plays—which points to the immense popularity of the theater and its constant need for new material—and more than 450 of his plays have survived. He is particularly associated with *COMEDIA NUEVA,* a genre mixing the tragic and the comic, high and low characters (including the *GRACIOSO,* a comic fool), and usually having a romantic plot. In the intervals between the acts of his plays, short interludes (*ENTREMESES*) were performed, which were coherent plays in themselves. Like other playwrights in this period, Lope de Vega also wrote *autos,* but his best-known work is *Fuente Ovejuna* (1614), a play about a vicious tyrant that critics have seen as an allegory on Portuguese independence.

Lope shared the stage with several equally brilliant playwrights, principally with Pedro Calderón de la Barca (1600–1681), who succeeded Lope de Vega as Spain's most influential dramatist. Miguel de Cervantes (1547–1616), the author of *Don Quixote,* wrote about thirty plays, of which sixteen remain. Tirso de Molina (1584–1648) was a friar who had written more than 400 plays—eighty survive—before he was reprimanded by the Council of Castile; his best-known play, *El Burlador de Seville* (*The Trickster of Seville*) is the earliest play on the subject of Don Juan. The playwright Guillén de Castro (1569–1631) was a friend of Lope de Vega; his influence on the French theater is perhaps as marked as it was in Spain. Guillén de Castro wrote *Las Mocedades del Cid* (*The Youthful Adventures of the Cid*), which was adapted by Corneille as *Le Cid* and ignited a furious controversy about neoclassical esthetics.

NEOCLASSICISM, DRAMA, AND THEATER

In both France and England, the arts in general and drama in particular were closely regulated by the state, a state of affairs sustained by the rise of **NEOCLASSICISM.** Neoclassicism is, in the simplest sense, the revival of what was taken to be a "classical" ordering of the arts. The literature of classical Greece and Rome began to be recovered in the fourteenth and fifteenth centuries, first through the dissemination of texts preserved in monasteries and later through expanded contact with the Islamic world in the sixteenth and seventeenth centuries. Translating, imitating, and adapting classical texts, European writers in the later seventeenth century appeared to "revive" the principles of classical art. In practice, however, neoclassicism offered an *interpretation* of the classics, emphasizing order, control, decorum, reason, and harmony.

In many respects, neoclassicism relied on the authority of Aristotle's *Poetics,* published first in Latin translation in 1498 and then in Italian in 1549, and on the series of critical commentaries written on Aristotle throughout the sixteenth century. Aristotle's *Poetics* is something of a naturalist's description of the several species of poetry and their characteristics, but readers in the sixteenth and seventeenth centuries fell under the influence of Aristotle's enormous authority (see *Doctor Faustus,* Act 1) and quickly transformed the *Poetics* into a prescription, a series of rules, for producing the most perfect and effective tragedies. Two central precepts of the *Poetics* regard the tragic hero's actions: Those acts must seem both necessary and probable, and they should not entirely violate moral expectations. Neoclassical critics and playwrights schematized Aristotle's descriptions as necessary features of dramatic composition, arguing that a tragedy should be rigorously and causally plotted and should reveal the workings of providential justice through the actions of universalized or typical characters. These goals were transformed into the famous "unities" of neoclassicism: A play should take place within a single day (unity of time), in one location (unity of place), and consist of a single line of action, a single plot (unity of action). The action of neoclassical tragedy, therefore, is concentrated, maintaining a uniformity of tone and style called **DECORUM.** Plays in this mode maintain a single, narrow range of language and behavior; the action is either idealized (rather than realistic) in tragedy, or commonplace in comedy: tragic characters are classic and heroic, while comic characters are contemporary, even bourgeois; tragedy undertakes the conflict between the ideal passions of love and honor, while comedy takes its cue from more earthly desires—lust, greed, hypocrisy, and so on. Following the recovery of Vitruvius' *De Architectura* (15 BCE) in 1414, this neoclassical sensibility urged the modern stage to imitate Vitruvius' distinction between the proper stage settings of tragedy and comedy: classical architecture for tragedy, urban architecture for comedy. Especially in seventeenth-century Paris, theaters adjusted their stagecraft to these ideals of regularity and decorum, assigning a generalized palace setting to the elevated world of tragedy, and the *chambre à quatre portes*—the room with four doors—to the lower, contemporary world of comedy.

Writing later in the eighteenth century, the Englishman Thomas Davies characterized the differences between French and English audiences and suggests that neoclassical ideals did not take root as deeply in the English theater as they did in France:

> The Frenchman, when he goes to a play, seems to make his entertainment a matter of importance. The long speeches in the plays of Corneille, Racine, Crébillon, and Voltaire, which would disgust an English ear, are extremely pleasing to our light neighbours: they sit in silence, and enjoy the beauty of sentiment, and energy of language; and are taught habitually to cry at scenes of distress. The Englishman looks upon the theatre as a place of amusement; he does not expect to be alarmed with terror, or wrought upon by scenes of commiseration; but he is surprised into the feeling of those passions, and sheds tears because he cannot avoid it. The theatre, to most Englishmen, becomes a place of instruction by chance.

Davies, of course, betrays a common chauvinism of the English toward the French: while the French are pedantic and calculating, the English are spontaneous. But this distinction between English and French theaters—one for "art," one for "entertainment"; one tragic, one comic—conceals the fundamental likenesses between the two institutions and the plays they put on the stage. As the plays of Corneille, Racine, and Dryden suggest, neoclassical tragedy imposes severe and artificial forms on the irrepressible forces of the passions, which inevitably break through the formal speech and decorous behavior of the characters to destroy them and sometimes the state as well. Comedy of the period in England and in France reveals a cognate tension, as the formal acting styles and stereotyped characters common in Restoration comedy seem barely able to contain the bottomless appetites of the plays' heroes. To this extent, neoclassical decorum embodies a barely contained anxiety about the power of forms—forms of conduct, forms of art, forms of state—to prevent a revolution of unreason and disorder.

EARLY MODERN DRAMA IN PERFORMANCE AND HISTORY

In many respects, the theater of seventeenth-century Europe is continuous with our own. Given the fact that the European monarchies were rapidly expanding their political and mercantile influence around the globe, it's not surprising to find that their culture became exported as well, often to the cultivated elites of their new colonies. In Mexico, for example, the seventeenth-century nun Sor Juana Inés de la Cruz (1651–1695) composed both *autos* and full-length dramas that echo—and, indeed, rival—the plays of the Spanish playwrights Calderón and Lope de Vega. The English drama of this period was exported as well; Farquhar's *The Recruiting Officer* was the first play to be performed in the penal colony of Australia. Moreover, the seventeenth century saw the institutionalization of theater as a commercial activity: in its architecture (indoor theaters, proscenium stages), in its greater appeal to a bourgeois audience, even in institutions like the Comédie Française (which, of course, continues to produce the plays of Molière and Racine), this theater is the direct forebear of the modern European theater, and in many ways the progenitor of its colonial theaters as well.

While the plays in this unit are all still in the classical repertory of modern theaters, these plays tend to pose particular problems to modern directors and actors. Although many

READING THE MATERIAL THEATER

One of the most challenging elements of theater history is the interpretation of the documentary record. Indeed, with the rise of print, the theater spawned its own information explosion, as newspaper descriptions, reviews, memoirs, and even published letters provide accounts of the practices of the stage. Yet these documents themselves often require a skeptical eye. Anthony Aston's *A Brief Supplement to Colley Cibber, Exq: His Lives of the Late Famous Actors and Actresses* (published in London in 1748) provides what seems to be an eyewitness account of the acting style of Thomas Betterton (1635–1710). What features of Betterton's physique and style emerge most strongly to Aston? Are there class or cultural implications in the various terms Aston uses to praise Betterton? How does Aston distinguish between Betterton's success in comic and tragic roles? How does he distinguish between Betterton's style in comedy and that of Estcourt and Harper?

Mr. Betterton (although a superlative good Actor) labour'd under ill Figure, being clumsily made, having a great Head, a short thick Neck, stoop'd in the Shoulders, and had fat short Arms, which he rarely lifted higher than his Stomach. –His Left Hand frequently lodg'd in his Breast, between his Coat and Waistcoat, while, with his Right, he prepar'd his Speech. –His Actions were few, but just. –He had little Eyes, and a broad Face, a little Pock-fretten, a corpulent Body, and thick Legs, with large Feet. –He was better to meet, than to follow; for his Aspect was serious, venerable, and majestic; in his latter Time a little Paralytic. –His Voice was low and grumbling; yet he could Time it by an artificial *Climax,* which enforc'd universal Attention, even from the *Fops* and *Orange-girls.* –He was incapable of dancing, even in a Country-Dance; as was MRS. BARRY: But their good Qualities were more than equal to their Deficiencies. –While MRS. BRACEGIRDLE sung very agreeably in the LOVES of *Mars and Venus,* and danced in a Country-Dance, as well as MR. WILKS, though not with so much Art and Foppery, but like a well-bred Gentleman. –Mr. BETTERTON was the most extensive Actor, from *Alexander* to *Sir John Falstaff;* but in that last Character, he wanted the Waggery of ESTCOURT, the Drollery of HARPER, and Sallaciousness of JACK EVANS. –But, then *Estcourt* was too trifling; *Harper* had too much of the *Bartholomew-Fair;* and *Evans* misplac'd his Humour. –Thus, you see what *Flaws* are in *bright Diamonds;* –And I have often wish'd that Mr. *Betterton* would have resign'd the Part of HAMLET to some young Actor, (who might have Personated, though not have Acted, it better) for, when he threw himself at *Ophelia's* Feet, he appear'd a little too grave for a young Student, lately come from the University of *Wirtemberg;* and his *Repartees* seem'd rather as *Apophthegms* from a *sage Philosopher,* than the *sporting Flashes* of a young HAMLET; and no one else could have pleas'd the Town, he was so rooted in their Opinion. His younger Contemporary (*Betterton* 63, *Powell* 40 Years old), POWELL attempted several of *Betterton's* Parts, as *Alexander, Jaffeir, &c,* but lost his Credit; as, in *Alexander,* he maintain'd not the Dignity of a King, but Out-Heroded HEROD; and in his poison'd mad Scene, *outrav'd all Probability;* while *Betterton* kept his Passion under, and shew'd it most (as Fame smoaks most, when stifled). *Betterton,* from the Time he was dress'd to the End of the Play, kept his Mind in the same Temperament and Adaptness, as the present Character required.

plays of this period—*Tartuffe* or *The Rover*—are given a contemporary setting, and concern themselves with relatively familiar characters, their language and characterization tends to be quite formal. Molière, for example, writes in a rich and fluid verse, even for the part of Tartuffe; Behn's cavaliers speak in prose, but their language is nonetheless dynamic and rhetorically complex. For modern actors, the elegance of this language often provides a point of entry to these characters, a way of seizing on the carefully discriminated social hierarchies at work in the cultures of these plays. Indeed, this verbal formality often becomes a kind of keynote to other aspects of performance as well, leading to a certain stateliness of physical movement and gesture, and an elegant balance of design elements as well. And yet in part because they are part of a classical repertoire, these plays have also inspired experiment and adaptation, a challenge to directors, designers, and actors to make it new.

PEDRO CALDERÓN DE LA BARCA

Like many of his contemporaries, Pedro Calderón de la Barca (1600–1681) was a prolific playwright; he is thought to have written more than 200 plays, of which about 100 survive. Calderón was born in Madrid on January 17, 1600, the son of a minor court official. He was educated at a Jesuit "college," or preparatory school, before attending the University of Alcalá de Henares and the University of Salamanca. In 1620 he entered and won a poetry competition in honor of St. Isidore, which brought his writing to the attention of Lope de Vega, one of the judges of the contest. His first play, *Love, Honor, and Power,* was performed at court in 1623, but Calderón—who served intermittently in the military in the early 1620s—did not become established as a playwright until some time after 1626, when his plays were popular both at court and in the public theaters. With the death of Lope in 1635, Calderón became the most important playwright in Spain; he was knighted by Philip IV and became the principal court playwright in 1636.

Many of Calderón's plays in this period are either *capa y espada* plays, like *The Phantom Lady* (1629), or "love and honor" plays. *El alcalde de Zalamea* (*The Mayor of Zalamea,* 1642) is typical of the "love and honor" genre. In the play, a peasant's daughter is raped by a soldier; through a series of coincidents, the peasant becomes the mayor just as the soldier is apprehended, and he is torn between his desire for revenge, his obligation to enforce the process of law, and Christian charity. Calderón's most important play, *La vida es sueño* (*Life Is a Dream*) was produced in 1636. Throughout his career, Calderón also wrote *autos sacramentales,* but these became more significant later in his life. Calderón's mistress died in 1648, and Calderón entered the priesthood in 1651, possibly in grief over her loss; he also adopted and raised her child, who may have been his natural son. He was appointed priest of a Toledo parish, but the bishop objected to his playwriting, and Calderón devoted himself to *autos* thereafter; his *autos* were so popular that between 1647 and 1681 the only *autos* performed in Madrid were by Calderón. Calderón was made chaplain to the king in 1663 and died in retirement in 1681.

LIFE IS A DREAM

Life Is a Dream typifies the concerns of Calderón's mature drama: It is a play that tests the relationship between love and honor and conducts a searching meditation on human nature itself. The play is set in a mythological Poland, ruled by King Basil. Several years before the current action, it was predicted that if Basil's son, Segismund, were to succeed to the throne, he "would be the most outrageous / Of all men, the most cruel of all princes, / And impious of all monarchs, by whose acts / The kingdom would be torn up and divided." Basil, not willing to murder his son to save his country, has had Segismund removed from court and imprisoned in a cave, where he is attended only by the old courtier Clotaldo. This is where Rosaura—a well-born woman, also forsaken by her father—finds Segismund at the opening of the play.

Calderón begins his interrogation of human nature in the characterization of Segismund. Raised like a beast, Segismund is impulsive and untamed; though he opens the play complaining about his life of constant punishment, when he sees Rosaura (disguised as a man) watching him, he seizes and threatens to kill her. Yet when Rosaura kneels to him and begs for mercy, Segismund feels a strange sensation:

> Your voice has softened me, your presence halted me,
> And now, confusingly, I feel respect
> For you.

In the opening of Pedro Calderon de la Barca's *Life is a Dream,* Rosaura defends herself against Segismund, who is clothed in animal hides.

Living in captivity and isolation, Segismund is a "human monster": his behavior is ruled neither by reason nor by the conventions of polite society. Yet Segismund responds to Rosaura's plea for mercy as though some element of human sympathy were native to him. At the outset of the play, Calderón presents two contrasting views of human nature. In one perspective, human beings—like other animals—are ruled by their passions, which can only be governed by the civilizing force of law and reason; since Segismund has been raised without benefit of culture, he represents humanity in this unadorned state. Yet at the same time, Segismund's innate response to Rosaura suggests a second view of human nature, one in which sympathy, kindness, and morality are not imposed on human nature by education and society, but are somehow innate to humanity itself.

Just as Segismund relents toward Rosaura, Clotaldo suddenly bursts in and arrests her; Basil has decreed that even the existence of his son must remain a secret. But in arresting Rosaura, Clotaldo takes her sword, which he immediately recognizes as the sword he had left "fair Violante" years before: Rosaura—who has traveled to Poland disguised as a man for protection—must be Clotaldo's "son." Clotaldo is now caught in the classic "love-and-honor" bind. His duty to his king requires him to arrest and eventually execute anyone who spies Basil's secret son; yet to honor his bond to the king, he must betray the natural love he should show to his own child.

As the play proceeds, Clotaldo's effort to reclaim his son is paralleled by Basil's guilty desire to restore his own son to society. Basil hits on an experiment: he will put Segismund to sleep and awaken him at court; when he awakens, Segismund will be told that he is now the king. If his behavior is civilized and restrained, then Basil will know that the prophecy was wrong and will acknowledge Segismund as his heir; if his behavior is threatening, he will be sent back to prison. But Basil's plan has one flaw: having been raised in solitude, Segismund has no understanding of the elaborate conventions of courtly behavior. When he awakens as "king," he is rude to Prince Astolfo, offensively forward to Stella, and murderously impulsive to the servants who try to restrain and control his behavior. His behavior is so outrageous that he is again knocked unconscious and sent back to his prison.

Returned to captivity, Segismund can only understand his sojourn at court as a beautiful dream, a dream that becomes an image for the fleeting and illusory joys of life itself. But this recognition reforms Segismund, enables him to recognize that he can only assume his full humanity by governing his passions. In the play's final moments, Segismund is released from prison by a rebellious mob, who have come to release Segismund in order to overthrow Basil. When Segismund and his army confront Basil, the old king not only as-sumes that he has lost his kingdom, but that Segismund will kill him, in part to repay Basil for stealing the better part of his life. But Segismund now understands that although Basil's treatment has made him "savage" in his passions—an "inhuman monster"—the only way to regain his humanity is to govern his desire for revenge. So Segismund submits himself to Basil, who recognizes that his son has been reformed and gives him the kingdom: in con-quering himself, Segismund wins the throne as well.

Calderón's drama is a deeply philosophical play, and the characters meditate extensively on the nature and meaning of their behavior. But *Life Is a Dream* is in some sense also a po-litical play; its rich examination of "human nature" is conducted from a deeply aristocratic perspective. The only way that Segismund can demonstrate his humanity, after all, is to rec-ognize and accept the conventions of courtly behavior as "natural." It is a sign of Segismund's acceptance of those values that his first act as king is to sentence the soldier who liberated him from prison to a life imprisonment of his own.

LIFE IS A DREAM

Pedro Calderón de la Barca

TRANSLATED BY ROY CAMPBELL

CHARACTERS

BASIL, *King of Poland*
SEGISMUND, *Prince*
ASTOLFO, *Duke of Muscovy*
CLOTALDO, *old man*
CLARION, *a comical servant*
ROSAURA, *a lady*

STELLA, *a princess*
SOLDIERS, GUARDS, MUSICIANS, SERVANTS, RETINUES, WOMEN

The scene is laid in the court of Poland, a nearby fortress, and the open country

---

ACT ONE

On one side a craggy mountain: on the other a rude tower whose base serves as a prison for SEGISMUND. *The door facing the spectators is open. The action begins at nightfall.*

ROSAURA, *dressed as a man, appears on the rocks climbing down to the plain: behind her comes* CLARION.

ROSAURA: You headlong hippogriff who match the gale
    In rushing to and fro, you lightning-flicker
    Who give no light, you scaleless fish, you bird
    Who have no coloured plumes, you animal
5   Who have no natural instinct, tell me whither
    You lead me stumbling through this labyrinth
    Of naked crags! Stay here upon this peak
    And be a Phaëthon to the brute-creation!
    For I, pathless save only for the track
10   The laws of destiny dictate for me,
    Shall, blind and desperate, descend this height
    Whose furrowed brows are frowning at the sun.
    How rudely, Poland, you receive a stranger
    (Hardly arrived, but to be treated hardly)
15   And write her entry down in blood with thorns.
    My plight attests this well, but after all,
    Where did the wretchèd ever pity find?
CLARION: Say *two* so wretchèd. Don't you leave me out
    When you complain! If we two sallied out
20   From our own country, questing high adventure,
    And after so much madness and misfortune
    Are still two here, and were two when we fell
    Down those rough crags—shall I not be offended
    To share the trouble yet forego the credit?
25 ROSAURA: I did not give you shares in my complaint
    So as not to rob you of the right to sorrow
    Upon your own account. There's such relief
    In venting grief that a philosopher
    Once said that sorrows should not be bemoaned
30   But sought for pleasure.
CLARION: Philosopher?
    I call him a long-bearded, drunken sot
    And would they'd cudgelled him a thousand blows
    To give him something worth his while lamenting!
    But, madam, what should we do, by ourselves,
35   On foot and lost at this late hour of day,

Here on this desert mountain far away—
    The sun departing after fresh horizons?
ROSAURA: Clarion, how can I answer, being both
    The partner of your plight and your dilemma?
CLARION: Would anyone believe such strange events?   40
ROSAURA: If there my sight is not deceived by fancy,
    In the last timid light that yet remains
    I seem to see a building.
CLARION: Either my hopes
    Are lying or I see the signs myself.
ROSAURA: Between the towering crags, there stands so small 45
    A royal palace that the lynx-eyed sun
    Could scarce perceive it at midday, so rude
    In architecture that it seems but one
    Rock more down-toppled from the sun-kissed crags
    That form the jaggèd crest.   50
CLARION: Let's go closer,
    For we have stared enough: it would be better
    To let the inmates makes us welcome.
ROSAURA: See:
    The door, or, rather, that funeral gap,
    Is yawning wide—whence night itself seems born,
    Flowing out from its black, rugged centre.   55

(A sound of chains is heard.)

CLARION: Heavens! What's that I hear?
ROSAURA: I have become
    A block immovable of ice and fire.
CLARION: Was that a little chain? Why, I'll be hanged
    If that is not the clanking ghost of some
    Past galley-slave—my terror proves it is!   60
SEGISMUND: Oh, miserable me! Unhappy me!
ROSAURA: How sad a cry that is! I fear new trials
    And torments.
CLARION: It's a fearful sound.
ROSAURA: Oh, come,
    My Clarion, let us fly from suffering!
CLARION: I'm in such sorry trim, I've not the spirit   65
    Even to run away.
ROSAURA: And if you had,
    You'd not have seen that door, not known of it.
    When one's in doubt, the common saying goes
    One walks between two lights.
CLARION: I'm the reverse.

70   It's not that way with me.
        ROSAURA: What then disturbs you?
        CLARION: I walk in doubt between two darknesses.
        ROSAURA: Is not that feeble exhalation there
            A light? That pallid star whose fainting tremors,
            Pulsing a doubtful warmth of glimmering rays,
75   Make even darker with its spectral glow
            That gloomy habitation? Yes! because
            By its reflection (though so far away)
            I recognise a prison, grim and sombre,
            The sepulchre of some poor living carcase.
80   And, more to wonder at, a man lies there
            Clothed in the hides of savage beasts, with limbs
            Loaded with fetters, and a single lamp
            For company. So, since we cannot flee,
            Let us stay here and listen to his plaint
85   And what his sorrows are.
            SEGISMUND: Unhappy me!
            Oh, miserable me! You heavens above,
            I try to think what crime I've done against you
            By being born. Although to have been born,
            I know, is an offence, and with just cause
90   I bear the rigours of your punishment:
            Since to be born is man's worst crime. But yet
            I long to know (to clarify my doubts)
            What greater crime, apart from being born,
            Can thus have earned my greater chastisement.
95   Aren't others born like me? And yet they seem
            To boast a freedom that I've never known.
            The bird is born, and in the hues of beauty
            Clothed with its plumes, yet scarce has it become
            A feathered posy—or a flower with wings—
100   When through ethereal halls it cuts its way,
            Refusing the kind shelter of its nest.
            And I, who have more soul than any bird,
            Must have less liberty?
            The beast is born, and with its hide bright-painted,
105   In lovely tints, has scarce become a spangled
            And starry constellation (thanks to the skilful
            Brush of the Painter) than its earthly needs
            Teach it the cruelty to prowl and kill,
            The monster of its labyrinth of flowers.
110   Yet I, with better instincts than a beast,
            Must have less liberty?
            The fish is born, the birth of spawn and slime,
            That does not even live by breathing air.
            No sooner does it feel itself a skiff
115   Of silver scales upon the wave than swiftly
            It roves about in all directions taking
            The measure of immensity as far
            As its cold blood's capacity allows.
            Yet I, with greater freedom of the will,
120   Must have less liberty?
            The brook is born, and like a snake unwinds
            Among the flowers. No sooner, silver serpent,
            Does it break through the blooms than it regales
            And thanks them with its music for their kindness,
125   Which opens to its course the majesty
            Of the wide plain. Yet I, with far more life,
            Must have less liberty?

            This fills me with such passion, I become
            Like the volcano Etna, and could tear
            Pieces of my own heart out of my breast!   130
            What law, justice, or reason can decree
            That man alone should never know the joys
            And be alone excepted from the rights
            God grants a fish, a bird, a beast, a brook?
        ROSAURA: His words have filled me full of fear and pity.   135
        SEGISMUND: Who is it overheard my speech? Clotaldo?
        CLARION: Say "yes!"
        ROSAURA: It's only a poor wretch, alas,
            Who in these cold ravines has overheard
            Your sorrows.
        SEGISMUND: Then I'll kill you

        (*Seizes her.*)

            So as to leave no witness of my frailty.   140
            I'll tear you into bits with these strong arms!
        CLARION: I'm deaf. I wasn't able to hear that.
        ROSAURA: If you were human born, it is enough
            That I should kneel to you for you to spare me.
        SEGISMUND: Your voice has softened me, your presence   145
            halted me,
            And now, confusingly, I feel respect
            For you. Who are you? Though here I have learned
            So little of the world, since this grim tower
            Has been my cradle and my sepulchre;
            And though since I was born (if you can say   150
            I really have been born) I've only seen
            This rustic desert where in misery
            I dwell alone, a living skeleton,
            An animated corpse; and though till now,
            I never spoke, save to one man who hears   155
            My griefs and through whose converse I have heard
            News of the earth and of the sky; and though,
            To astound you more, and make you call me
            A human monster, I dwell here, and am
            A man of the wild animals, a beast   160
            Among the race of men; and though in such
            Misfortune, I have studied human laws,
            Instructed by the birds, and learned to measure
            The circles of the gentle stars, you only
            Have curbed my furious rage, amazed my vision,   165
            And filled with wonderment my sense of hearing.
            Each time I look at you, I feel new wonder!
            The more I see of you, the more I long
            To go on seeing more of you. I think
            My eyes are dropsical, to go on drinking   170
            What it is death for them to drink, because
            They go on drinking that which I am dying
            To see and that which, seen, will deal me death.
            Yet let me gaze on you and die, since I
            Am so bewitched I can no longer think   175
            What not seeing you would do to me—the sight
            Itself being fatal! that would be more hard
            Than dying, madness, rage, and fiercest grief:
            It would be life—worst fate of all because
            The gift of life to such a wretchèd man   180
            Would be the gift of death to happiness!

ROSAURA: Astonished as I look, amazed to hear,
I know not what to say nor what to ask.
All I can say is that heaven guided me
185 Here to be comforted, if it is comfort
To see another sadder than oneself.
They say a sage philosopher of old,
Being so poor and miserable that he
Lived on the few plain herbs he could collect,
190 One day exclaimed: "Could any man be poorer
Or sadder than myself?"—when, turning round,
He saw the very answer to his words.
For there another sage philosopher
Was picking up the scraps he'd thrown away.
195 I lived cursing my fortune in this world
And asked within me: "Is there any other
Suffers so hard a fate?" Now out of pity
You've given me the answer. For within me
I find upon reflection that my griefs
200 Would be as joys to you and you'd receive them
To give you pleasure. So if they perchance
In any measure may afford relief,
Listen attentively to my misfortune
And take what is left over for yourself.
205 I am . . .
CLOTALDO: (*Within.*) Guards of the tower! You sluggards
Or cowards, you have let two people pass
Into the prison bounds . . .
ROSAURA: Here's more confusion!
SEGISMUND: That is Clotaldo, keeper of my prison.
Are my misfortunes still not at an end?
210 CLOTALDO: Come. Be alert, and either seize or slay them
Before they can resist!
VOICES: (*Within.*)   Treason! Betrayal!
CLARION: Guards of the tower who let us pass unhindered,
Since there's a choice, to seize us would be simpler.

(*Enter* CLOTALDO *with* SOLDIERS. *He holds a pistol and they all wear masks.*)

CLOTALDO: (*Aside to the* SOLDIERS.) Cover your faces, all! It's
a precaution
215 Imperative that nobody should know us
While we are here.
CLARION: What's this? A masquerade?
CLOTALDO: O you, who ignorantly passed the bounds
And limits of this region, banned to all—
Against the king's decree which has forbidden
220 That any should find out the prodigy
Hidden in these ravines—yield up your weapons
Or else this pistol, like a snake of metal,
Will spit the piercing venom of two shots
With scandalous assault upon the air.
225 SEGISMUND: Tyrannic master, ere you harm these people
Let my life be the spoil of these sad bonds
In which (I swear it by Almighty God)
I'll sooner rend myself with hands and teeth
Amid these rocks than see them harmed and mourn
230 Their suffering.
CLOTALDO: Since you know, Segismund,
That your misfortunes are so huge that, even

Before your birth, you died by heaven's decree,
And since you know these walls and binding chains
Are but the brakes and curbs to your proud frenzies,
What use is it to bluster?   235

(*To the* GUARDS.)

                                    Shut the door
Of this close prison! Hide him in its depths!
SEGISMUND: Ah, heavens, how justly you denied me freedom!
For like a Titan I would rise against you,
Pile jasper mountains high on stone foundations
And climb to burst the windows of the sun!   240
CLOTALDO: Perhaps you suffer so much pain today
Just to forestall that feat.
ROSAURA: Now that I see
How angry pride offends you, I'd be foolish
Not to plead humbly at your feet for life.
Be moved by me to pity. It would be   245
Notoriously harsh that neither pride
Nor humbleness found favour in your eyes!
CLARION: And if neither Humility nor Pride
Impress you (characters of note who act
And motivate a thousand mystery plays)   250
Let me, here, who am neither proud nor humble,
But merely something halfway in between,
Plead to you both for shelter and for aid.
CLOTALDO: Ho, there!
SOLDIER: Sir?
CLOTALDO: Take their weapons. Bind their eyes
So that they cannot see the way they're led.   255
ROSAURA: This is my sword. To nobody but you
I yield it, since you're, after all, the chief.
I cannot yield to one of meaner rank.
CLARION: My sword is such that I will freely give it
To the most mean and wretched.   260

(*To one* SOLDIER.)

                                    Take it, you!
ROSAURA: And if I have to die, I'll leave it to you
In witness of your mercy. It's a pledge
Of great worth and may justly be esteemed
For someone's sake who wore it long ago.
CLOTALDO: (*Apart.*) Each moment seems to bring me new   265
misfortune!
ROSAURA: Because of that, I ask you to preserve
This sword with care. Since if inconstant Fate
Consents to the remission of my sentence,
It has to win me honour. Though I know not
The secret that it carries, I do know   270
It has got one—unless I trick myself—
And prize it just as the sole legacy
My father left me.
CLOTALDO: Who then was your father?
ROSAURA: I never knew.
CLOTALDO: And why have you come here?
ROSAURA: I came to Poland to avenge a wrong.   275
CLOTALDO: (*Apart.*) Sacred heavens!

(*On taking the sword he becomes very perturbed.*)

What's this? Still worse and worse.
I am perplexed and troubled with more fears.

(*Aloud.*)

Tell me: who gave that sword to you?
ROSAURA: A woman.
CLOTALDO: Her name?
ROSAURA: A secret I am forced to keep.
280 CLOTALDO: What makes you think this sword contains a
        secret?
ROSAURA: That she who gave it to me said: "Depart
        To Poland. There with subtlety and art
        Display it so that all the leading people
        And noblemen can see you wearing it,
285   And I know well that there's a lord among them
        Who will both shelter you and grant you favour."
        But, lest he should be dead, she did not name him.
CLOTALDO: (*Aside.*) Protect me, heavens! What is this I hear?
        I cannot say if real or imagined
290   But here's the sword I gave fair Violante
        In token that, whoever in the future
        Should come from her to me wearing this sword,
        Would find in me a tender father's love.
        Alas, what can I do in such a pass,
295   When he who brings the sword to win my favour
        Brings it to find his own red death instead
        Arriving at my feet condemned already?
        What strange perplexity! How hard a fate!
        What an inconstant fortune to be plagued with!
300   This is my son not only by all signs
        But also by the promptings of my heart,
        Since, seeing him, my heart seems to cry out
        To him, and beat its wings, and, though unable
        To break the locks, behaves as one shut in,
305   Who, hearing noises in the street outside,
        Cranes from the window-ledge. Just so, not knowing
        What's really happening, but hearing sounds,
        My heart runs to my eyes which are its windows
        And out of them flows into bitter tears.
310   Protect me, heaven! What am I to do?
        To take him to the king is certain death.
        To hide him is to break my sacred oath
        And the strong law of homage. From one side
        Love of one's own, and from the other loyalty—
315   Call me to yield. Loyalty to my king
        (Why do I doubt?) comes before life and honour.
        Then live my loyalty, and let him die!
        When I remember, furthermore, he came
        To avenge an injury—a man insulted
320   And unavenged is in disgrace. My son
        Therefore he is not, nor of noble blood.
        But if some danger has mischanced, from which
        No one escapes, since honour is so fragile
        That any act can smash it, and it takes
325   A stain from any breath of air, what more
        Could any nobleman have done than he,
        Who, at the cost of so much risk and danger,
        Comes to avenge his honour? Since he's so brave
        He is my son, and my blood's in his veins.

And so betwixt the one doubt and the other,   330
The most important mean between extremes
Is to go to the king and tell the truth—
That he's my son, to kill, if so he wishes.
Perhaps my loyalty thus will move his mercy
And if I thus can merit a live son   335
I'll help him to avenge his injury.
But if the king prove constant in his rigour
And deal him death, he'll die in ignorance
That I'm his father.

(*Aloud to* ROSAURA *and* CLARION.)

                            Come then, strangers, come!
And do not fear that you have no companions   340
In your misfortunes, since, in equal doubt,
Tossed between life and death, I cannot guess
Which is the greater evil or the less.

A hall at the royal palace, in court

Enter ASTOLFO *and* SOLDIERS *at one side: from the other side*
PRINCESS STELLA *and* [WOMEN]. *Military music and salvos.*

ASTOLFO: To greet your excellent bright beams
        As brilliant as a comet's rays,   345
        The drums and brasses mix their praise
        With those of fountains, birds, and streams.
        With sounds alike, in like amaze,
        Your heavenly face each voice salutes,
        Which puts them in such lively fettle,   350
        The trumpets sound like birds of metal,
        The songbirds play like feathered flutes.
        And thus they greet you, fair señora—
        The salvos, as their queen, the brasses,
        As to Minerva when she passes,   355
        The songbirds to the bright Aurora,
        And all the flowers and leaves and grasses
        As doing homage unto Flora,
        Because you come to cheat the day
        Which now the night has covered o'er—   360
        Aurora in your spruce array,
        Flora in peace, Pallas in war,
        But in my heart the queen of May.
STELLA: If human voice could match with acts
        You would have been unwise to say   365
        Hyperboles that a few facts
        May well refute some other day
        Confounding all this martial fuss
        With which I struggle daringly,
        Since flatteries you proffer thus   370
        Do not accord with what I see.
        Take heed that it's an evil thing
        And worthy of a brute accursed,
        Loud praises with your mouth to sing
        When in your heart you wish the worst.   375
ASTOLFO: Stella, you have been badly misinformed
        If you doubt my good faith. Here let me beg you
        To listen to my plea and hear me out.
        The third Eugtorgius died, the King of Poland.

380 Basil, his heir, had two fair sisters who
    Bore you, my cousin, and myself. I would not
    Tire you with all that happened here. You know
    Clorilene was your mother who enjoys,
    Under a better reign, her starry throne.

385 She was the elder. Lovely Recisunda
    (Whom may God cherish for a thousand years!)
    The younger one, my mother and your aunt,
    Was wed in Muscovy. Now to return:
    Basil has yielded to the feebleness

390 Of age, loves learnèd study more than women,
    Has lost his wife, is childless, will not marry.
    And so it comes that you and I both claim
    The heirdom of the realm. You claim that you
    Were daughter to the elder daughter. I

395 Say that my being born a man, although
    Son of the younger daughter, gives me title
    To be preferred. We've told the king, our uncle,
    Of both of our intentions. And he answered
    That he would judge between our rival claims,

400 For which the time and place appointed was
    Today and here. For the same reason I
    Have left my native Muscovy. With that
    Intent I come—not seeking to wage war
    But so that you might thus wage war on me!

405 May Love, wise god, make true what people say
    (Your "people" is a wise astrologer)
    By settling this through your being chosen queen—
    Queen and my consort, sovereign of my will;
    My uncle crowning you, for greater honour;

410 Your courage conquering, as it deserves;
    My love applauding you, its emperor!
    STELLA: To such chivalrous gallantry, my breast
    Cannot hold out. The imperial monarchy
    I wish were mine only to make it yours—

415 Although my love is not quite satisfied
    That you are to be trusted since your speech
    Is somewhat contradicted by that portrait
    You carry in the locket round your neck.
    ASTOLFO: I'll give you satisfaction as to that.

    (*Drums.*)

420 But these loud instruments will not permit it
    That sound the arrival of the king and council.

    (Enter KING BASIL *with his following.*)

    STELLA: Wise Thales . . .
    ASTOLFO: Learned Euclid . . .
    STELLA: Among the signs . . .
    ASTOLFO: Among the stars . . .
    STELLA: Where you preside in power . . .
    ASTOLFO: Where you reside . . .
    STELLA: And plot their paths . . .
425 ASTOLFO: And trace their fiery trails . . .
    STELLA: Describing . . .
    ASTOLFO: . . . Measuring and judging them . . .
    STELLA: Please read my stars that I, in humble bonds . . .
    ASTOLFO: Please read them, so that I in soft embraces . . .
    STELLA: May twine as ivy to this tree!

ASTOLFO: May find
    Myself upon my knees before these feet!   430
BASIL: Come and embrace me, niece and nephew. Trust me,
    Since you're both loyal to my loving precepts,
    And come here so affectionately both—
    In nothing shall I leave you cause to cavil,
    And both of you as equals will be treated.   435
    The gravity of what I have to tell
    Oppresses me, and all I ask of you
    Is silence: the event itself will claim
    Your wonderment. So be attentive now,
    Belovèd niece and nephew, illustrious courtiers,   440
    Relatives, friends, and subjects! You all know
    That for my learning I have merited
    The surname of The Learnèd, since the brush
    Of great Timanthes, and Lisippus' marbles—
    Stemming oblivion (consequence of time)—   445
    Proclaimed me to mankind Basil the Great.
    You know the science that I most affect
    And most esteem is subtle mathematics
    (By which I forestall time, cheat fame itself)
    Whose office is to show things gradually.   450
    For when I look my tables up and see,
    Present before me, all the news and actions
    Of centuries to come, I gain on Time—
    Since Time recounts whatever I have said
    After I say it. Those snowflaking haloes,   455
    Those canopies of crystal spread on high,
    Lit by the sun, cut by the circling moon,
    Those diamond orbs, those globes of radiant crystal
    Which the bright stars adorn, on which the signs
    Parade in blazing excellence, have been   460
    My chiefest study all through my long years.
    They are the volumes on whose adamantine
    Pages, bound up in sapphire, heaven writes,
    In lines of burnished gold and vivid letters,
    All that is due to happen, whether adverse   465
    Or else benign. I read them in a flash,
    So quickly that my spirit tracks their movements—
    Whatever road they take, whatever goal
    They aim at. Would to heaven that before
    My genius had been the commentary   470
    Writ in their margins, or the index to
    Their pages, that my life had been the rubble,
    The ruin, and destruction of their wrath,
    And that my tragedy in them had ended,
    Because, to the unlucky, even their merit   475
    Is like a hostile knife, and he whom knowledge
    Injures is but a murderer to himself.
    And this I say myself, though my misfortunes
    Say it far better, which, to marvel at,
    I beg once more for silence from you all.   480
    With my late wife, the queen, I had a son,
    Unhappy son, to greet whose birth the heavens
    Wore themselves out in prodigies and portents.
    Ere the sun's light brought him live burial
    Out of the womb (for birth resembles death)   485
    His mother many times, in the delirium
    And fancies of her sleep, saw a fierce monster
    Bursting her entrails in a human form,

Born spattered with her lifeblood, dealing death,
490 The human viper of this century!
The day came for his birth, and every presage
Was then fulfilled, for tardily or never
Do the more cruel ones prove false. At birth
His horoscope was such that the bright sun,
495 Stained in its blood, entered ferociously
Into a duel with the moon above.
The whole earth seemed a rampart for the strife
Of heaven's two lights, who—though not hand-to-hand—
Fought light-to-light to gain the mastery!
500 The worst eclipse the sun has ever suffered
Since Christ's own death horrified earth and sky.
The whole earth overflowed with conflagrations
So that it seemed the final paroxysm
Of existence. The skies grew dark. Buildings shook.
505 The clouds rained stones. The rivers ran with blood.
In this delirious frenzy of the sun,
Thus, Segismund was born into the world,
Giving a foretaste of his character
By killing his own mother, seeming to speak thus
510 By his ferocity: "I am a man,
Because I have begun now to repay
All kindnesses with evil." To my studies
I went forthwith, and saw in all I studied
That Segismund would be the most outrageous
515 Of all men, the most cruel of all princes,
And impious of all monarchs, by whose acts
The kingdom would be torn up and divided
So as to be a school of treachery
And an academy of vices. He,
520 Risen in fury, amidst crimes and horrors,
Was born to trample me (with shame I say it)
And make of my grey hairs his very carpet.
Who is there but believes an evil Fate?
And more if he discovers it himself,
525 For self-love lends its credit to our studies.
So I, believing in the Fates, and in
The havoc that their prophecies predestined,
Determined to cage up this newborn tiger
To see if on the stars we sages have
530 Some power. I gave out that the prince had died
Stillborn, and, well-forewarned, I built a tower
Amidst the cliffs and boulders of yon mountains
Over whose tops the light scarce finds its way,
So stubbornly their obelisks and crags
535 Defend the entry to them. The strict laws
And edicts that I published then (declaring
That nobody might enter the forbidden
Part of the range) were passed on that account.
There Segismund lives to this day, a captive,
540 Poor and in misery, where, save Clotaldo,
His guardian, none have seen or talked to him.
The latter has instructed him in all
Branches of knowledge and in the Catholic faith,
Alone the witness of his misery.
545 There are three things to be considered now:
Firstly, Poland, that I love you greatly,
So much that I would free you from the oppression
And servitude of such a tyrant king.

He would not be a kindly ruler who
Would put his realm and homeland in such danger.   550
The second fact that I must bear in mind
Is this: that to deny my flesh and blood
The rights which law, both human and divine,
Concedes, would not accord with Christian charity,
For no law says that, to prevent another   555
Being a tyrant, I may be one myself,
And if my son's a tyrant, to prevent him
From doing outrage, I myself should do it.
Now here's the third and last point I would speak of,
Namely, how great an error it has been   560
To give too much belief to things predicted,
Because, even if his inclination should
Dictate some headlong, rash precipitancies,
They may perhaps not conquer him entirely,
For the most accursèd destiny, the most   565
Violent inclination, the most impious
Planet—all can but influence, not force,
The free will which man holds direct from God.
And so, between one motive and another
Vacillating discursively, I hit   570
On a solution that will stun you all.
I shall tomorrow, but without his knowing
He is my son—your king—place Segismund
(For that's the name with which he was baptised)
Here on my throne, beneath my canopy,   575
Yes, in my very place, that he may govern you
And take command. And you must all be here
To swear him fealty as his loyal subjects.
Three things may follow from this test, and these
I'll set against the three which I proposed.   580
The first is that should the prince prove prudent,
Stable, and benign—thus giving the lie
To all that prophecy reports of him—
Then you'll enjoy in him your rightful ruler
Who was so long a courtier of the mountains   585
And neighbour to the beasts. Here is the second:
If he prove proud, rash, cruel, and outrageous,
And with a loosened rein gallop unheeding
Across the plains of vice, I shall have done
My duty, and fulfilled my obligation   590
Of mercy. If I then re-imprison him,
That's incontestably a kingly deed—
Not cruelty but merited chastisement.
The third thing's this: that if the prince should be
As I've described him, then—by the love I feel   595
For you, my vassals—I shall give you worthier
Rulers to wear the sceptre and the crown;
Because your king and queen will be my nephew
And niece, each with an equal right to rule,
Each gaining the inheritance he merits,   600
And joined in faith of holy matrimony.
This I command you as a king, I ask you
As a kind father, as a sage I pray you,
As an experienced old man I tell you,
And (if it's true, as Spanish Seneca   605
Says, that the king is slave unto his nation)
This, as a humble slave, I beg of you.
ASTOLFO: If it behoves me to reply (being

The person most involved in this affair)
610   Then, in the name of all, let Segismund
Appear! It is enough that he's your son!
ALL: Give us our prince: we want him for our king!
BASIL: Subjects, I thank you for your kindly favour.
Accompany these, my two Atlases,
615   Back to their rooms. Tomorrow you shall see him.
ALL: Long live the great King Basil! Long live Basil!

(*Exeunt all, accompanying* STELLA *and* ASTOLFO. *The king remains.*)

(*Enter* CLOTALDO *with* ROSAURA *and* CLARION.)

CLOTALDO: May I have leave to speak, sire?
BASIL: Oh, Clotaldo!
You're very welcome.
CLOTALDO: Thus to kneel before you
Is always welcome, sire—yet not today
620   When sad and evil Fate destroys the joy
Your presence normally concedes.
BASIL: What's wrong?
CLOTALDO: A great misfortune, sire, has come upon me
Just when I should have met it with rejoicing.
BASIL: Continue.
CLOTALDO: Sire, this beautiful young man
625   Who inadvertently and daringly
Came to the tower, wherein he saw the prince,
Is my . . .
BASIL: Do not afflict yourself, Clotaldo.
Had it not been just now, I should have minded,
I must confess. But I've revealed the secret,
630   And now it does not matter if he knows it.
Attend me afterwards. I've many things
To tell you. You in turn have many things
To do for me. You'll be my minister,
I warn you, in the most momentous action
635   The world has ever seen. These prisoners, lest you
Should think I blame your oversight, I'll pardon.

(*Exit.*)

CLOTALDO: Long may you live, great sire! A thousand years!

(*Aside.*)

Heaven improves our fates. I shall not tell him
Now that he is my son, since it's not needed
640   Till he's avenged.

(*Aloud.*)

Strangers, you may go free.
ROSAURA: Humbly I kiss your feet.
CLARION: Whilst I'll just *miss* them—
Old friends will hardly quibble at one letter.
ROSAURA: You've granted me my life, sir. I remain
645   Your servant and eternally your debtor.
CLOTALDO: No! It was not your life I gave you. No!
Since any wellborn man who, unavenged,
Nurses an insult does not live at all.
And seeing you have told me that you came

For that sole reason, it was not life I spared—   650
Life in disgrace is not a life at all.

(*Aside.*)

I see this spurs him.
ROSAURA: Freely I confess it—
Although you spared my life, it was no life.
But I will wipe my honour's stain so spotless
That after I have vanquished all my dangers   655
Life well may seem a shining gift from you.
CLOTALDO: Take here your burnished steel: 'twill be enough,
Bathed in your enemies' red blood, to right you.
For steel that once was mine (I mean of course
Just for the time I've had it in my keeping)   660
Should know how to avenge you.
ROSAURA: Now, in your name I gird it on once more
And on it I will swear to take revenge
Although my foe were even mightier.
CLOTALDO: Is he so powerful?   665
ROSAURA: So much so that . . .
Although I have no doubt in your discretion . . .
I say no more because I'd not estrange
Your clemency.
CLOTALDO: You would have won me had you told me, since
That would prevent me helping him.   670

(*Aside.*)

If only I could discover who he is!
ROSAURA: So that you'll not think that I value lightly
Such confidence, know that my adversary
Is no less than Astolfo, Duke of Muscovy.
CLOTALDO: (*Aside.*) (I hardly can withstand the grief it   675
    gives me
For it is worse than aught I could imagine!
Let us inquire of him some further facts.)

(*Aloud.*)

If you were born a Muscovite, your ruler
Could never have affronted you. Go back
Home to your country. Leave this headstrong valour.   680
It will destroy you.
ROSAURA: Though he's been my prince,
I know that he has done me an affront.
CLOTALDO: Even though he slapped your face, that's no
    affront.

(*Aside.*)

O heavens!
ROSAURA: My insult was far deeper!
CLOTALDO: Tell it:
Since nothing I imagine could be deeper.   685
ROSAURA: Yes. I will tell it, yet, I know not why,
With such respect I look upon your face,
I venerate you with such true affection,
With such high estimation do I weigh you,
That I scarce dare to tell you—these men's clothes   690
Are an enigma, not what they appear.
So now you know. Judge if it's no affront

695   That here Astolfo comes to wed with Stella
    Although betrothed to me. I've said enough.

(*Exeunt* ROSAURA *and* CLARION.)

CLOTALDO: Here! Listen! Wait! What mazed confusion!
    It is a labyrinth wherein the reason
    Can find no clue. My family honour's injured.
    The enemy's all powerful. I'm a vassal
    And she's a woman. Heavens! Show a path
700   Although I don't believe there is a way!
    There's nought but evil bodings in the sky.
    The whole world is a prodigy, say I.

ACT TWO

A hall in the royal palace.

Enter BASIL *and* CLOTALDO.

CLOTALDO: All has been done according to your orders.
BASIL: Tell me, Clotaldo, how it went?
CLOTALDO: Why, thus:
    I took to Segismund a calming drug
    Wherein are mixed herbs of especial virtue,
5   Tyrannous in their overpowering strength
    Which seize and steal and alienate man's gift
    Of reasoning, thus making a live corpse
    Of him. His violence evaporated
    With all his faculties and senses too.
10   There is no need to prove it's possible
    Because experience teaches us that medicine
    Is full of natural secrets, that there is no
    Animal, plant, or stone that has not got
    Appointed properties. If human malice
15   Explores a thousand poisons which deal death,
    Who then can doubt, that being so, that other
    Poisons, less violent, cause only sleep?
    But (leaving that doubt aside, as proven false
    By every evidence) hear then the sequel:
20   I went down into Segismund's close prison
    Bearing the drink wherein, with opium,
    Henbane and poppies had been mixed. With him
    I talked a little while of the humanities,
    In which dumb Nature has instructed him,
25   The mountains and the heavens and the stars,
    In whose divine academies he learned
    Rhetoric from the birds and the wild creatures.
    To lift his spirit to the enterprise
    Which you require of him, I chose for subject
30   The swiftness of a stalwart eagle, who,
    Deriding the base region of the wind,
    Rises into the sphere reserved for fire,
    A feathered lightning, an untethered comet.
    Then I extolled such lofty flight and said:
35   "After all, he's the king of birds, and so
    Takes precedence, by right, over the rest."
    No more was needful for, in taking up
    Majesty for his subject, he discoursed
    With pride and high ambition, as his blood

    Naturally moves, incites, and spurs him on   40
    To grand and lofty things, and so he said
    That in the restless kingdom of the birds
    There should be those who swear obedience, too!
    "In this, my miseries console me greatly,
    Because if I'm a vassal here, it's only   45
    By force, and not by choice. Of my own will
    I would not yield in rank to any man."
    Seeing that he grew furious—since this touched
    The theme of his own griefs—I gave the potion
    And scarcely had it passed from cup to breast   50
    Before he yielded all his strength to slumber.
    A chill sweat ran through all his limbs and veins.
    Had I not known that this was mere feigned death
    I would have thought him dead. Then came the men
    To whom you've trusted this experiment,   55
    Who placed him in a coach and brought him here
    To your own rooms, where all things were prepared
    In royalty and grandeur as befitting
    His person. In your own bed they have laid him
    Where, when the torpor wanes, they'll do him service   60
    As if he were Your Majesty himself.
    All has been done as you have ordered it,
    And if I have obeyed you well, my lord,
    I'd beg a favour (pardon me this freedom)—
    To know what your intention is in thus   65
    Transporting Segismund here to the palace.
BASIL: Your curiosity is just, Clotaldo,
    And yours alone I'll satisfy. The star
    Which governs Segismund, my son, in life,
    Threatens a thousand tragedies and woes.   70
    And now I wish to see whether the stars
    (Which never lie—and having shown to us
    So many cruel signs seem yet more certain)
    May yet be brought to moderate their sentence,
    Whether by prudence charmed or valour won,   75
    For man does have the power to rule his stars.
    I would examine this, bringing him here
    Where he may know he is my son, and make
    Trial of his talent. If magnanimously
    He conquers and controls himself, he'll reign,   80
    But if he proves a tyrant and is cruel,
    Back to his chains he'll go. Now, you will ask,
    Why did we bring him sleeping in this manner
    For the experiment? I'll satisfy you,
    Down to the smallest detail, with my answer.   85
    If he knows that he is my son today,
    And if tomorrow he should find himself
    Once more reduced to prison, to misery,
    He would despair entirely, knowing truly
    Who, and whose son, he is. What consolation   90
    Could he derive, then, from his lot? So I
    Contrive to leave an exit for such grief,
    By making him believe it was a dream.
    By these means we may learn two things at once:
    First, his character—for he will really be   95
    Awake in all he thinks and all his actions;
    Second, his consolation—which would be
    (If he should wake in prison on the morrow,
    Although he saw himself obeyed today)
    That he might understand he had been dreaming,   100

And he will not be wrong, for in this world,
Clotaldo, all who live are only dreaming.
CLOTALDO: I've proofs enough to doubt of your success,
But now it is too late to remedy it.
105 From what I can make out, I think he's awakened
And that he's coming this way, by the sound.
BASIL: I shall withdraw. You, as his tutor, go
And guide him through his new bewilderments
By answering his queries with the truth.
110 CLOTALDO: You give me leave to tell the truth of it?
BASIL: Yes, because knowing all things, he may find
Known perils are the easiest to conquer.

(*Exit* BASIL. *Enter* CLARION.)

CLARION: It cost me four whacks to get here so quickly.
I caught them from a red-haired halberdier
115 Sprouting a ginger beard over his livery,
And I've come to see what's going on.
No windows give a better view than those
A man brings with him in his head, not asking
For tickets of admission or paid seats,
120 Since at all functions, festivals, or feasts
He looks out with the same nice self-composure.
CLOTALDO: (*Aside.*) Here's Clarion who's the servant of that
person—
That trader in woes, importer from Poland
Of my disgrace.

(*Aloud.*)

Come, Clarion, what news?
125 CLARION: Item the first: encouraged by the fact
Your clemency's disposed to venge her insult,
Rosaura has resumed her proper clothing.
CLOTALDO: That's right: it's less indecorous and bold.
CLARION: Item: she's changed her name, and given out
130 That she's your niece. And now they've made so much
Of her that she's been raised to maid of honour
To the unique and only princess, Stella.
CLOTALDO: That's right: her honour stands to my account.
CLARION: Indeed she merely bides the time till you
135 Will settle all accounts about her honour.
CLOTALDO: Biding the time is wise, for in the end
It's Time that's going to settle all accounts!
CLARION: Item: that she's attended like a queen,
Because they take her for your niece. Item:
140 That I, who trudged along with her, am dying
Of hunger. Nobody remembers me,
Nor yet remembers that I'm like my name
And (should I sound my Clarion) could tell
All to the king and Stella and Astolfo.
145 For I am both a Clarion and a servant—
Two things which ill-accord with secrecy.
If silence should, by chance, let slip my hand,
Then there's a chorus which would fit me well:
"Dawn-breaking Clarion plays no better tune!"
150 CLOTALDO: You've reason for complaint. I'll satisfy it
If you'll but serve me . . .
CLARION: Hush, here's Segismund!

(*Enter* MUSICIANS, *singing, and* SERVANTS *arraying* SEGISMUND,
who seems amazed.)

SEGISMUND: Heavens above! What's this that I am seeing?
I wonder at it all, with naught of fear!
But with a mighty doubt, I disbelieve it!
I?—in a sumptuous palace? I—encircled   155
With rich brocades and silks? I—overwhelmed
With servants in such brilliant liveries?
I—to awake in such a gorgeous bed?
I—in the middle of so many footmen
Who clothe me in rich garments? I'm awake: 160
It would be false to take this for a dream.
Am I not Segismund? Heavens! disabuse me
If I'm mistaken. Say, what could have happened
In my imagination while I slept—
That I should find myself in such a place?   165
But why should I worry, whatever it was?
I'll let myself be served and entertained—
Befall what may.
FIRST SERVANT: (*Aside to* SECOND SERVANT *and* CLARION.)
He's very melancholy!
SECOND SERVANT: Who would not be, considering all that's
happened
To him?   170
CLARION: I would not be!
SECOND SERVANT: You, speak to him.
FIRST SERVANT: Shall they begin to sing again?
SEGISMUND: Why, no,
I would not have them sing.
SECOND SERVANT: You're so distraught,
I wish you entertained.
SEGISMUND: My griefs are such
That no mere voices can amuse me now—
Only the martial music pleased my mind.   175
CLOTALDO: Your Highness, mighty prince, give me your hand
To kiss. I'm glad to be the first to offer
Obedience at your feet.
SEGISMUND: (*Aside.*) This is Clotaldo.
How is it he, that tyrannised my thralldom,
Should now be treating me with such respect?   180

(*Aloud.*)

Tell me what's happening all round me here.
CLOTALDO: With the perplexities of your new state,
Your reason will encounter many doubts,
But I shall try to free you from them all
(If that may be) because you now must know   185
You are hereditary Prince of Poland.
If you have been withdrawn from public sight
Under restraint, it was in strict obedience
To Fate's inclemency, which will permit
A thousand woes to fall upon this empire   190
The moment that you wear the sovereign's crown.
But trusting that you'll prudently defeat
Your own malignant stars (since they can be
Controlled by magnanimity) you've been
Brought to this palace from the tower you knew   195
Even while your soul was yielded up to sleep.
My lord the king, your father, will be coming
To see you, and from him you'll learn the rest.
SEGISMUND: Then, vile, infamous traitor, what have I
To know more than this fact of who I am,   200
To show my pride and power from this day onward?

How have you played your country such a treason
    As to deny me, against law and right,
    The rank which is my own?
CLOTALDO: Unhappy me!
205 SEGISMUND: You were a traitor to the law, a flattering liar
    To your own king, and cruel to myself.
    And so the king, the law, and I condemn you,
    After such fierce misfortunes as I've borne,
    To die here by my hands.
SECOND SERVANT: My lord!
SEGISMUND: Let none
210 Get in the way. It is in vain. By God!
    If you intrude, I'll throw you through the window.
SECOND SERVANT: Clotaldo, fly!
CLOTALDO: Alas, poor Segismund!
    That you should show such pride, all unaware
    That you are dreaming this.

(*Exit.*)

SECOND SERVANT: Take care! Take care!
215 SEGISMUND: Get out!
SECOND SERVANT: He was obeying the king's orders.
SEGISMUND: In an injustice, no one should obey
    The king, and I'm his prince.
SECOND SERVANT: He had no right
    To look into the rights and wrongs of it.
SEGISMUND: You must be mad to answer back at me.
220 CLARION: The prince is right. It's you who're in the
        wrong!
SECOND SERVANT: Who gave you right to speak?
CLARION: I simply took it.
SEGISMUND: And who are you?
CLARION: I am the go-between,
    And in this art I think I am a master—
    Since I'm the greatest jackanapes alive.
225 SEGISMUND: (*To* CLARION.) In all this new world, you're the
        only one
    Of the whole crowd who pleases me.
CLARION: Why, my lord,
    I am the best pleaser of Segismunds
    That ever was: ask anybody here!

(*Enter* ASTOLFO.)

ASTOLFO: Blessèd the day, a thousand times, my prince,
230 On which you landed here on Polish soil
    To fill with so much splendour and delight
    Our wide horizons, like the break of day!
    For you arise as does the rising sun
    Out of the rugged mountains, far away.
235 Shine forth then! And although so tardily
    You bind the glittering laurels on your brows,
    The longer may they last you still unwithered.
SEGISMUND: God save you.
ASTOLFO: That you do not know me, sir,
    Is some excuse for greeting me without
240 The honour due to me. I am Astolfo
    The Duke of Muscovy. You are my cousin.
    We are of equal rank.
SEGISMUND: Then if I say,
    "God save you," do I not display good feeling?

But since you take such note of who you are,
    The next time that I see you, I shall say   245
    "God save you *not*," if you would like that better.
SECOND SERVANT: (*To* ASTOLFO.) Your Highness, make
        allowance for his breeding
    Amongst the mountains. So he deals with all.

(*To* SEGISMUND.)

    Astolfo does take precedence, Your Highness—
SEGISMUND: I have no patience with the way he came   250
    To make his solemn speech, then put his hat on!
SECOND SERVANT: He's a grandee!
SEGISMUND: I'm grander than grandees!
SECOND SERVANT: For all that, there should be respect
        between you,
    More than among the rest.
SEGISMUND: And who told you
    To mix in my affairs?   255

(*Enter* STELLA.)

STELLA: Many times welcome to Your Royal Highness,
    Now come to grace the dais that receives him
    With gratitude and love. Long may you live
    August and eminent, despite all snares,
    And count your life by centuries, not years!   260
SEGISMUND: (*Aside to* CLARION.) Now tell me, who's this
        sovereign deity
    At whose divinest feet Heaven lays down
    The fleece of its aurora in the east?
CLARION: Sir, it's your cousin Stella.
SEGISMUND: She were better
    Named "sun" than "star"!   265

(*To* STELLA.)

                          Though your speech was fair,
    Just to have seen you and been conquered by you
    Suffices for a welcome in itself.
    To find myself so blessed beyond my merit
    What can I do but thank you, lovely Stella,
    For you could add more brilliance and delight   270
    To the most blazing star? When you get up
    What work is left the sun to do? O give me
    Your hand to kiss, from out whose cup of snow
    The solar horses drink the fires of day!
STELLA: Be a more gentle courtier.   275
ASTOLFO: I am lost.
SECOND SERVANT: I know Astolfo's hurt. I must divert him.

(*To* SEGISMUND.)

    Sir, you should know that thus to woo so boldly
    Is most improper. And, besides, Astolfo . . .
SEGISMUND: Did I not tell you not to meddle with me?
SECOND SERVANT: I only say what's just.   280
SEGISMUND: All this annoys me.
    Nothing seems just to me but what I want.
SECOND SERVANT: Why, sir, I heard you say that no obedience
    Or service should be lent to what's unjust.
SEGISMUND: You also heard me say that I would throw
    Anyone who annoys me from that balcony.   285

SECOND SERVANT: With men like me you cannot do such
 things.
SEGISMUND: No? Well, by God, I'll have to prove it then!

(*He takes him in his arms and rushes out, followed by many, to return soon after.*)

ASTOLFO: What on earth have I seen? Can it be true?
STELLA: Go, all, and stop him!
SEGISMUND: (*Returning.*) From the balcony
290 He's fallen in the sea. How strange it seems!
ASTOLFO: Measure your acts of violence, my lord:
 From crags to palaces, the distance is
 As great as that between man and the beasts.
SEGISMUND: Well, since you are for speaking out so boldly,
295 Perhaps one day you'll find that on your shoulders
 You have no head to place your hat upon.

(*Exit* ASTOLFO. *Enter* BASIL.)

BASIL: What's happened here?
SEGISMUND: Nothing at all. A man
 Wearied me, so I threw him in the sea.
CLARION: (*To* SEGISMUND.) Be warned. That is the king.
BASIL: On the first day,
300 So soon, your coming here has cost a life?
SEGISMUND: He said I couldn't: so I won the bet.
BASIL: It grieves me, Prince, that, when I hoped to see you
 Forewarned, and overriding Fate, in triumph
 Over your stars, the first thing I should see
305 Should be such rigour—that your first deed here
 Should be a grievous homicide. Alas!
 With what love, now, can I offer my arms,
 Knowing your own have learned to kill already?
 Who sees a dirk, red from a mortal wound,
310 But does not fear it? Who can see the place
 Soaking in blood, where late a man was murdered,
 But even the strongest must respond to nature?
 So in your arms seeing the instrument
 Of death, and looking on a blood-soaked place,
315 I must withdraw myself from your embrace,
 And though I thought in loving bonds to bind
 Your neck, yet fear withholds me from your arms.
SEGISMUND: Without your loving arms I can sustain
 Myself as usual. That such a loving father
320 Could treat me with such cruelty, could thrust me
 From his side ungratefully, could rear me
 As a wild beast, could hold me for a monster,
 And pray that I were dead, that such a father
 Withholds his arms from winding round my neck,
325 Seems unimportant, seeing that he deprives
 Me of my very being as a man.
BASIL: Would to heaven I had never granted it,
 For then I never would have heard your voice,
 Nor seen your outrages.
SEGISMUND: Had you denied
330 Me being, then I would not have complained,
 But that you took it from me when you gave it—
 That is my quarrel with you. Though to give
 Is the most singular and noble action,
 It is the basest action if one gives

Only to take away.   335
BASIL: How well you thank me
 For being raised from pauper to a prince!
SEGISMUND: In this what is there I should thank you for?
 You tyrant of my will! If you are old
 And feeble, and you die, what can you give me
 More than what is my own by right of birth? 340
 You are my father and my king, therefore
 This grandeur comes to me by natural law.
 Therefore, despite my present state, I'm not
 Indebted to you, rather can I claim
 Account of all those years in which you robbed me 345
 Of life and being, liberty, and honour.
 You ought to thank me that I press no claim
 Since you're my debtor, even to bankruptcy.
BASIL: Barbarous and outrageous brute! The heavens
 Have now fulfilled their prophecy: I call 350
 Them to bear witness to your pride. Although
 You know now, disillusioned, who you are,
 And see yourself where you take precedence,
 Take heed of this I say: be kind and humble
 Since it may be that you are only dreaming, 355
 Although it seems to you you're wide-awake.

(*Exit* BASIL.)

SEGISMUND: Can I perhaps be dreaming, though I seem
 So wide-awake? No: I am not asleep,
 Since I can touch, and realise what I
 Have been before, and what I am today. 360
 And if you even now relented, Father,
 There'd be no cure since I know who I am
 And you cannot, for all your sighs and groans,
 Cheat me of my hereditary crown.
 And if I was submissive in my chains 365
 Before, then I was ignorant of what I am,
 Which I now know (and likewise know that I
 Am partly man but partly beast as well).

(*Enter* ROSAURA *in woman's clothing.*)

ROSAURA: (*Aside.*) I came in Stella's train. I am afraid
 Of meeting with Astolfo, since Clotaldo 370
 Says he must not know who I am, not see me,
 Because (he says) it touches on my honour.
 And well I trust Clotaldo since I owe him
 The safety of my life and honour both.
CLARION: What pleases you, and what do you admire 375
 Most, of the things you've seen here in the world?
SEGISMUND: Why, nothing that I could not have foreseen—
 Except the loveliness of women! Once,
 I read among the books I had out there
 That who owes God most grateful contemplation 380
 Is Man: who is himself a tiny world.
 But I think who owes God more grateful study
 Is Woman—since she is a tiny heaven,
 Having as much more beauty than a man
 As heaven than earth. And even more, I say, 385
 If she's the one that I am looking at.
ROSAURA: (*Aside.*) That is the prince. I'll go.
SEGISMUND: Stop! Woman! Wait!

Don't join the sunset with the breaking day
By fading out so fast. If east and west
390   Should clash like that, the day would surely suffer
A syncope. But what is this I see?
ROSAURA: What I am looking at I doubt, and yet
Believe.
SEGISMUND: (*Aside.*) This beauty I have seen before.
ROSAURA: (*Aside.*) This pomp and grandeur I have seen before
395   Cooped in a narrow dungeon.
SEGISMUND: (*Aside.*)   I have found
My life at last.

(*Aloud.*)

Woman (for that sole word
Outsoars all wooing flattery of speech
From one that is a man), woman, who are you?
If even long before I ever saw you
400   You owed me adoration as your prince,
How much the more should you be conquered by me
Now I recall I've seen you once before!
Who are you, beauteous woman?
ROSAURA: (*Aside.*)   I'll pretend.

(*Aloud.*)

In Stella's train, I am a luckless lady.
405 SEGISMUND: Say no such thing. You are the sun from which
The minor star that's Stella draws its life,
Since she receives the splendour of your rays.
I've seen how in the kingdom of sweet odours,
Commander of the squadrons of the flowers,
410   The rose's deity presides, and is
Their empress by divine right of her beauty.
Among the precious stones which can be listed
In the academy of mines, I've seen
The diamond much preferred above the rest,
415   And crowned their emperor, for shining brightest.
In the revolving empire of the stars
The morning star takes pride among the others.
In their perfected spheres, when the sun calls
The planets to his council, he presides
420   And is the very oracle of day.
Then if among stars, gems, planet, and flowers
The fairest are exalted, why do you
Wait on a lesser beauty than yourself
Who are, in greater excellence and beauty,
425   The sun, the morning star, the diamond, and the rose!

(*Enter* CLOTALDO, *who remains by the stage-curtain.*)

CLOTALDO: (*Aside.*) I wish to curb him, since I brought
him up.
But, what is this?
ROSAURA: I reverence your favour,
And yet reply, rhetorical, with silence,
For when one's mind is clumsy and untaught,
430   He answers best who does not speak at all.
SEGISMUND: Stay! Do not go! How can you wish to go
And leave me darkened by my doubts?
ROSAURA: Your Highness,

I beg your leave to go.
SEGISMUND: To go so rudely
Is not to beg my leave but just to take it.
ROSAURA: But if you will not grant it, I must take it.   435
SEGISMUND: That were to change my courtesy to rudeness.
Resistance is like venom to my patience.
ROSAURA: But even if this deadly, raging venom
Should overcome your patience, yet you dare not
And could not treat me with dishonour, sir.   440
SEGISMUND: Why, just to see then if I can, and dare to—
You'll make me lose the fear I bear your beauty,
Since the impossible is always tempting
To me. Why, only now I threw a man
Over this balcony who said I couldn't: 445
And so to find out if I can or not
I'll throw your honour through the window too.
CLOTALDO: (*Aside.*) He seems determined in this course.
Oh, heavens!
What's to be done that for a second time
My honour's threatened by a mad desire?   450
ROSAURA: Then with good reason it was prophesied
Your tyranny would wreak this kingdom
Outrageous scandals, treasons, crimes, and deaths.
But what can such a creature do as you
Who are not even a man, save in the name—   455
Inhuman, barbarous, cruel, and unbending
As the wild beasts amongst whom you were nursed?
SEGISMUND: That you should not insult me in this way
I spoke to you most courteously, and thought
I'd thereby get my way; but if you curse me thus   460
Even when I am speaking gently, why,
By the living God, I'll really give you cause.
Ho there! Clear out, the lot of you, at once!
Leave her to me! Close all the doors upon us.
Let no one enter!   465

(*Exeunt* CLARION *and other* ATTENDANTS.)

ROSAURA: I am lost . . . I warn you . . .
SEGISMUND: I am a tyrant and you plead in vain.
CLOTALDO: (*Aside.*) Oh, what a monstrous thing! I must
restrain him
Even if I die for it.

(*Aloud.*)

Sir! Wait! Look here!
SEGISMUND: A second time you have provoked my anger,
You feeble, mad old man! Do you prize lightly   470
My wrath and rigour that you've gone so far?
CLOTALDO: Brought by the accents of her voice, I came
To tell you you must be more peaceful
If still you hope to reign, and warn you that
You should not be so cruel, though you rule—   475
Since this, perhaps, is nothing but a dream.
SEGISMUND: When you refer to disillusionment
You rouse me near to madness. Now you'll see,
Here as I kill you, if it's truth or dreaming!

(*As he tries to pull out his dagger,* CLOTALDO *restrains him and throws himself on his knees before him.*)

480 CLOTALDO: It's thus I'd save my life: and hope to do so—
SEGISMUND: Take your presumptuous hand from off this steel.
CLOTALDO: Till people come to hold your rage and fury
    I shall not let you go.
ROSAURA: O heavens!
SEGISMUND: Loose it,

(*They struggle.*)

    I say, or else—you interfering fool—
485   I'll crush you to your death in my strong arms!
ROSAURA: Come quickly! Here's Clotaldo being killed!

(*Exit.*)

(ASTOLFO *appears as* CLOTALDO *falls on the floor, and the former stands between* SEGISMUND *and* CLOTALDO.)

ASTOLFO: Why, what is this, most valiant prince? What?
    Staining
    Your doughty steel in such old, frozen blood?
    For shame! For shame! Sheathe your illustrious weapon!
490 SEGISMUND: When it is stained in his infamous blood!
ASTOLFO: At my feet here he has found sanctuary
    And there he's safe, for it will serve him well.
SEGISMUND: Then serve me well by dying, for like this
    I will avenge myself for your behaviour
495   In trying to annoy me first of all.
ASTOLFO: To draw in self-defence offends no king,
    Though in his palace.

(ASTOLFO *draws his sword and they fight.*)

CLOTALDO: (*To* ASTOLFO.) Do not anger him!

(*Enter* BASIL, STELLA, *and* ATTENDANTS.)

BASIL: Hold! Hold! What's this? Fighting with naked swords?
STELLA: (*Aside.*) It is Astolfo! How my heart misgives me!
500 BASIL: Why, what has happened here?
ASTOLFO: Nothing, my Lord,
    Since you've arrived.

(*Both sheathe their swords.*)

SEGISMUND: Much, though you *have* arrived.
    I tried to kill the old man.
BASIL: Had you no
    Respect for those white hairs?
CLOTALDO: Sire, since they're only
    Mine, as you well can see, it does not matter!
505 SEGISMUND: It is in vain you'd have me hold white hairs
    In such respect, since one day you may find
    Your own white locks prostrated at my feet
    For still I have not taken vengeance on you
    For the foul way in which you had me reared.

(*Exit.*)

510 BASIL: Before that happens you will sleep once more
    Where you were reared, and where what's happened may
    Seem just a dream (being mere earthly glory).

(*All save* ASTOLFO *and* STELLA *leave.*)

ASTOLFO: How seldom does prediction fail, when evil!
    How oft, foretelling good! Exact in harm,
    Doubtful in benefit! Oh, what a great   515
    Astrologer would be one who foretold
    Nothing but harms, since there's no doubt at all
    That they are always due! In Segismund
    And me the case is illustrated clearly.
    In him, crimes, cruelties, deaths, and disasters   520
    Were well predicted, since they all came true.
    But in my own case, to predict for me
    (As I foresaw beholding rays which cast
    The sun into the shade and outface heaven)
    Triumphs and trophies, happiness and praise,   525
    Was false—and yet was true: it's only just
    That when predictions start with promised favours
    They should end in disdain.
STELLA: I do not doubt
    Your protestations are most heartfelt; only
    They're not for me, but for another lady   530
    Whose portrait you were wearing round your neck
    Slung in a locket when you first arrived.
    Since it is so, she only can deserve
    These wooing flatteries. Let her repay you
    For in affairs of love, flatteries and vows   535
    Made for another are mere forged credentials.

(ROSAURA *enters but waits by the curtain.*)

ROSAURA: (*Aside.*) Thanks be to God, my troubles are near
    ended!
    To judge from what I see, I've naught to fear.
ASTOLFO: I will expel that portrait from my breast
    To make room for the image of your beauty   540
    And keep it there. For there where Stella is
    Can be no room for shade, and where the sun is
    No place for any star. I'll fetch the portrait.

(*Aside.*)

    Forgive me, beautiful Rosaura, that,
    When absent, men and women seldom keep   545
    More faith than this.

(*Exit.*)

(ROSAURA *comes forward.*)

ROSAURA: (*Aside.*)   I could not hear a word. I was afraid
    That they would see me.
STELLA: Oh, Astrea!
ROSAURA: My lady!
STELLA: I am delighted that you came. Because
    To you alone would I confide a secret.
ROSAURA: Thereby you greatly honour me, your servant.   550
STELLA: Astrea, in the brief time I have known you
    I've given you the latchkey of my will.
    For that, and being who you are, I'll tell you
    A secret which I've very often hidden
    Even from myself.   555

ROSAURA: I am your slave.
STELLA: Then, briefly:
　　Astolfo, who's my cousin (the word cousin
　　Suffices, since some things are plainly said
　　Even by thinking them), is to wed me
　　If Fortune thus can wipe so many cares
560　Away with one great joy. But I am troubled
　　In that, the day he first came here, he carried
　　A portrait of a lady round his neck.
　　I spoke to him about it courteously.
　　He was most amiable, he loves me well,
565　And now he's gone for it. I am embarrassed
　　That he should give it me himself. Wait here,
　　And tell him to deliver it to you.
　　Do not say more. Since you're discreet and fair:
　　You'll surely know just what love is.

(Exit.)

ROSAURA: Great heavens!
570　How I wish that I did not! For who could be
　　So prudent or so skilful as would know
　　What to advise herself in such a case?
　　Lives there a person on this earth today
　　Who's more beset by the inclement stars,
575　Who has more cares besieging him, or fights
　　So many dire calamities at once?
　　What can I do in such bewilderment
　　Wherein it seems impossible to find
　　Relief or comfort? Since my first misfortune
580　No other thing has chanced or happened to me
　　But was a new misfortune. In succession
　　Inheritors and heirs of their own selves
　　(Just like the Phoenix, his own son and father)
　　Misfortunes reproduce themselves, are born,
585　And live by dying. In their sepulchre
　　The ashes they consume are hot forever.
　　A sage once said misfortunes must be cowards
　　Because they never dare to walk alone
　　But come in crowds. I say they are most valiant
590　Because they always charge so bravely on
　　And never turn their backs. Who charges with them
　　May dare all things because there is no fear
　　That they'll ever desert him; and I say it
　　Because in all my life I never once
595　Knew them to leave me, nor will they grow tired
　　Of me till, wounded and shot through and through
　　By Fate, I fall into the arms of death.
　　Alas, what can I do in this dilemma?
　　If I reveal myself, then old Clotaldo,
600　To whom I owe my life, may take offence,
　　Because he told me to await the cure
　　And mending of my honour in concealment.
　　If I don't tell Astolfo who I am
　　And he detects me, how can I dissimulate?
605　Since even if I say I am not I,
　　The voice, the language, and the eyes will falter,
　　Because the soul will tell them that they lie.
　　What shall I do? It is in vain to study
　　What I should do, when I know very well

　　That, whatsoever way I choose to act,   610
　　When the time comes I'll do as sorrow bids,
　　For no one has control over his sorrows.
　　Then since my soul dares not decide its actions
　　Let sorrow fill my cup and let my grief
　　Reach its extremity and, out of doubts   615
　　And vain appearances, once and for all
　　Come out into the light—and Heaven shield me!

(Enter ASTOLFO.*)*

ASTOLFO: Here, lady, is the portrait . . . but . . . great God!
ROSAURA: Why does Your Highness halt, and stare
　　astonished?
ASTOLFO: Rosaura! Why, to see you here!   620
ROSAURA: Rosaura?
　　Sir, you mistake me for some other lady.
　　I am Astrea, and my humble station
　　Deserves no perturbation such as yours.
ASTOLFO: Enough of this pretence, Rosaura, since
　　The soul can never lie. Though as Astrea   625
　　I see you now, I love you as Rosaura.
ROSAURA: Not having understood Your Highness' meaning
　　I can make no reply except to say
　　That Stella (who might be the star of Venus)
　　Told me to wait here and to tell you from her   630
　　To give to me the portrait you were fetching
　　(Which seems a very logical request)
　　And I myself will take it to my lady.
　　Thus Stella bids: even the slightest things
　　Which do me harm are governed by some star.   635
ASTOLFO: Even if you could make a greater effort
　　How poorly you dissimulate, Rosaura!
　　Tell your poor eyes they do not harmonise
　　With your own voice, because they needs must jangle
　　When the whole instrument is out of time.   640
　　You cannot match the falsehood of your words
　　With the sincerity of what you're feeling.
ROSAURA: All I can say is—that I want the portrait.
ASTOLFO: As you require a fiction, with a fiction
　　I shall reply. Go and tell Stella this: 645
　　That I esteem her so, it seems unworthy
　　Only to send the counterfeit to her
　　And that I'm sending her the original.
　　And you, take the original along with you,
　　Taking yourself to her.   650
ROSAURA: When a man starts
　　Forth on a definite task, resolved and valiant,
　　Though he be offered a far greater prize
　　Than what he seeks, yet he returns with failure
　　If he returns without his task performed.
　　I came to get that portrait. Though I bear   655
　　The original with me, of greater value,
　　I would return in failure and contempt
　　Without the copy. Give it me, Your Highness,
　　Since I cannot return without it.
ASTOLFO: But
　　If I don't give it you, how can you do so?   660
ROSAURA: Like this, ungrateful man! I'll take it from you.

(She tries to wrest it from him.)

ASTOLFO: It is in vain.
ROSAURA: By God, it shall not come
   Into another woman's hands!
ASTOLFO: You're terrifying!
ROSAURA: And you're perfidious!
ASTOLFO: Enough, my dear
665   Rosaura!
ROSAURA: I, your dear? You lie, you villain!

(*They are both clutching the portrait.*)

(*Enter* STELLA.)

STELLA: Astrea and Astolfo, what does this mean?
ASTOLFO: (*Aside.*) Here's Stella.
ROSAURA: (*Aside.*)   Love, grant me the strength to win
   My portrait.

(*To* STELLA.)

                   If you want to know, my lady,
   What this is all about, I will explain.
670   ASTOLFO: (*To* ROSAURA, *aside.*) What do you mean?
ROSAURA: You told me to await
   Astolfo here and ask him for a portrait
   On your behalf. I waited here alone
   And as one thought suggests another thought,
   Thinking of portraits, I recalled my own
675   Was here inside my sleeve. When one's alone,
   One is diverted by a foolish trifle
   And so I took it out to look at it.
   It slipped and fell, just as Astolfo here,
   Bringing the portrait of the other lady,
680   Came to deliver it to you as promised.
   He picked my portrait up, and so unwilling
   Is he to give away the one you asked for,
   Instead of doing so, he seized upon
   The other portrait which is mine alone
685   And will not give it back though I entreated
   And begged him to return it. I was angry
   And tried to snatch it back. That's it he's holding,
   And you can see yourself if it's not mine.
STELLA: Let go the portrait.

(*She snatches it from him.*)

ASTOLFO: Madam!
STELLA: The draughtsman
690   Was not unkind to truth.
ROSAURA: Is it not mine?
STELLA: Why, who could doubt it?
ROSAURA: Ask him for the other.
STELLA: Here, take your own, Astrea. You may leave us.
ROSAURA: (*Aside.*) Now I have got my portrait, come what
   will.

(*Exit.*)

STELLA: Now give me up the portrait that I asked for
695   Although I'll see and speak to you no more.
   I do not wish to leave it in your power
   Having been once so foolish as to beg it.

ASTOLFO: (*Aside.*) Now how can I get out of this foul trap?

(*To* STELLA.)

   Beautiful Stella, though I would obey you,
   And serve you in all ways, I cannot give you   700
   The portrait, since . . .
STELLA: You are a crude, coarse villain
   And ruffian of a wooer. For the portrait—
   I do not want it now, since, if I had it,
   It would remind me I had asked you for it.

(*Exit.*)

ASTOLFO: Listen! Look! Wait! Let me explain!   705

(*Aside.*)

                                   Oh, damn
   Rosaura! How the devil did she get
   To Poland for my ruin and her own?

The prison of SEGISMUND *in the tower.*

SEGISMUND *lying on the ground loaded with fetters and clothed in skins as before.* CLOTALDO, *two* ATTENDANTS, *and* CLARION.

CLOTALDO: Here you must leave him—since his reckless pride
   Ends here today where it began.
ATTENDANT: His chain
   I'll rivet as it used to be before.   710
CLARION: O Prince, you'd better not awake too soon
   To find how lost you are, how changed your fate,
   And that your fancied glory of an hour
   Was but a shade of life, a flame of death!
CLOTALDO: For one who knows so well to wield his tongue 715
   It's fit a worthy place should be provided
   With lots of room and lots of time to argue.
   This is the fellow that you have to seize

(*To the* ATTENDANTS.)

   And that's the room in which you are to lock him.

(*Points to the nearest cell.*)

CLARION: Why me?   720
CLOTALDO: Because a Clarion who knows
   Too many secrets must be kept in gaol—
   A place where even clarions are silent.
CLARION: Have I, by chance, wanted to kill my father
   Or thrown an Icarus from a balcony?
   Am I asleep or dreaming? To what end   725
   Do you imprison me?
CLOTALDO: You're Clarion.
CLARION: Well, say I swear to be a cornet now,
   A silent one, a wretched instrument . . . ?

(*They hustle him off.* CLOTALDO *remains.*)

(*Enter* BASIL, *wearing a mask.*)

BASIL: Clotaldo.

CLOTALDO: Sire . . . and is it thus alone
730   Your Majesty has come?
BASIL: Vain curiosity
         To see what happens here to Segismund.
CLOTALDO: See where he lies, reduced to misery!
BASIL: Unhappy prince! Born at a fatal moment!
         Come waken him, now he has lost his strength
735   With all the opium he's drunk.
CLOTALDO: He's stirring
         And talking to himself.
BASIL: What is he dreaming?
         Let's listen now.
SEGISMUND: He who chastises tyrants
         Is a most pious prince . . . Now let Clotaldo
         Die by my hand . . . my father kiss my feet . . .
740 CLOTALDO: He threatens me with death!
BASIL: And me with insult
         And cruelty.
CLOTALDO: He'd take my life away.
BASIL: And he'd humiliate me at his feet.
SEGISMUND: (*Still in a dream.*) Throughout the expanse of
              this world's theatre
         I'll show my peerless valour, let my vengeance
745   Be wreaked, and the Prince Segismund be seen
         To triumph—over his father . . . but, alas!

         (*Awakening.*)

         Where am I?
BASIL: (*To* CLOTALDO.) Since he must not see me here,
         I'll listen further off. You know your cue.

(*Retires to one side.*)

SEGISMUND: Can this be I? Am I the same who, chained
750   And long imprisoned, rose to such a state?
         Are you not still my sepulchre and grave,
         You dismal tower? God! What things I have dreamed!
CLOTALDO: (*Aside.*) Now I must go to him to disenchant him.

(*Aloud.*)

         Awake already?
SEGISMUND: Yes: it was high time.
755 CLOTALDO: What? Do you have to spend all day asleep?
         Since I was following the eagle's flight
         With tardy discourse, have you still lain here
         Without awaking?
SEGISMUND: No. Nor even now
         Am I awake. It seems I've always slept,
760   Since, if I've dreamed what I've just seen and heard
         Palpably and for certain, then I am dreaming
         What I see now—nor is it strange I'm tired,
         Since what I, sleeping, see, tells me that I
         Was dreaming when I thought I was awake.
765 CLOTALDO: Tell me your dream.
SEGISMUND: That's if it *was* a dream!
         No, I'll not tell you what I dreamed; but what
         I lived and saw, Clotaldo, I *will* tell you.
         I woke up in a bed that might have been
         The cradle of the flowers, woven by Spring.
770   A thousand nobles, bowing, called me Prince,

         Attiring me in jewels, pomp, and splendour.
         My equanimity you turned to rapture
         Telling me that I was the Prince of Poland.
CLOTALDO: I must have got a fine reward!
SEGISMUND: Not so:
         For as a traitor, twice, with rage and fury,   775
         I tried to kill you.
CLOTALDO: Such cruelty to me?
SEGISMUND: I was the lord of all, on all I took revenge,
         Except I loved one woman . . . I believe
         That *that* was true, though all the rest has faded.

(*Exit* BASIL.)

CLOTALDO: (*Aside.*) I see the king was moved, to hear him   780
         speak.

(*Aloud.*)

         Talking of eagles made you dream of empires,
         But even in your dreams it's good to honour
         Those who have cared for you and brought you up.
         For Segismund, even in dreams, I warn you
         Nothing is lost by trying to do good.   785

(*Exit.*)

SEGISMUND: That's true, and therefore let us subjugate
         The bestial side, this fury and ambition,
         Against the time when we may dream once more,
         As certainly we shall, for this strange world
         Is such that but to live here is to dream.   790
         And now experience shows me that each man
         Dreams what he is until he is awakened.
         The king dreams he's a king and in this fiction
         Lives, rules, administers with royal pomp.
         Yet all the borrowed praises that he earns   795
         Are written in the wind, and he is changed
         (How sad a fate!) by death to dust and ashes.
         What man is there alive who'd seek to reign
         Since he must wake into the dream that's death.
         The rich man dreams his wealth which is his care   800
         And woe. The poor man dreams his sufferings.
         He dreams who thrives and prospers in this life.
         He dreams who toils and strives. He dreams who injures,
         Offends, and insults. So that in this world
         Everyone dreams the thing he is, though no one   805
         Can understand it. I dream I am here,
         Chained in these fetters. Yet I dreamed just now
         I was in a more flattering, lofty station.
         What is this life? A frenzy, an illusion,
         A shadow, a delirium, a fiction.   810
         The greatest good's but little, and this life
         Is but a dream, and dreams are only dreams.

ACT THREE

The tower.

Enter CLARION.

CLARION: I'm held in an enchanted tower, because
         Of all I know. What would they do to me
         For all I don't know, since—for all I know—
         They're killing me by starving me to death.

5   O that a man so hungry as myself
   Should live to die of hunger while alive!
   I am so sorry for myself that others
   May well say "I can well believe it," since
   This silence ill accords with my name "Clarion,"
10   And I just can't shut up. My fellows here?
   Spiders and rats—fine feathered songsters those!
   My head's still ringing with a dream of fifes
   And trumpets and a lot of noisy humbug
   And long processions as of penitents
15   With crosses, winding up and down, while some
   Faint at the sight of blood besmirching others.
   But now to tell the truth, I am in prison.
   For knowing secrets, I am kept shut in,
   Strictly observed as if I were a Sunday,
20   And feeling sadder than a Tuesday, where
   I neither eat nor drink. They say a secret
   Is sacred and should be as strictly kept
   As any saint's day on the calendar.
   Saint Secret's Day for me's a working day
25   Because I'm never idle then. The penance
   I suffer here is merited, I say:
   Because being a lackey, I was silent,
   Which, in a servant, is a sacrilege.

(*A noise of drums and trumpets.*)

FIRST SOLDIER: (*Within.*) Here is the tower in which he is
   imprisoned.
30   Smash in the door and enter, everybody!
CLARION: Great God! They've come to seek me. That is
   certain
   Because they say I'm here. What can they want?

(*Enter several* SOLDIERS.)

FIRST SOLDIER: Go in.
SECOND SOLDIER: He's here!
CLARION: No, he's not here!
ALL THE SOLDIERS: Our lord!
CLARION: What, are they drunk?
FIRST SOLDIER: You are our rightful prince.
35   We do not want and never shall allow
   A stranger to supplant our trueborn prince.
   Give us your feet to kiss!
ALL THE SOLDIERS: Long live the prince!
CLARION: Bless me, if it's not real! In this strange kingdom
   It seems the custom, everyday, to take
40   Some fellow and to make him prince and then
   Shut him back in this tower. That *must* be it!
   So I must play my role.
ALL THE SOLDIERS: Give us your feet.
CLARION: I can't. They're necessary. After all
   What sort of use would be a footless prince?
45 SECOND SOLDIER: All of us told your father, as one man,
   We want no prince of Muscovy but you!
CLARION: You weren't respectful to my father? Shame!
FIRST SOLDIER: It was our loyalty that made us tell him.
CLARION: If it was loyalty, you have my pardon.
50 SECOND SOLDIER: Restore your empire. Long live Segismund!

CLARION: (*Aside.*) That is the name they seem to give to all
   These counterfeited princes.

(*Enter* SEGISMUND.)

SEGISMUND: Who called Segismund?
CLARION: (*Aside.*) I seem to be a hollow sort of prince.
FIRST SOLDIER: Which of you's Segismund?
SEGISMUND: I am.
SECOND SOLDIER: (*To* CLARION.)   Then why,
   Rash fool, did you impersonate the prince   55
   Segismund?
CLARION: What? I, Segismund? Yourselves
   Be-Segismunded me without request.
   All yours was both the rashness and the folly.
FIRST SOLDIER: Prince Segismund, whom we acclaim our lord,
   Your father, great King Basil, in his fear   60
   That heaven would fulfil a prophecy
   That one day he would kneel before your feet
   Wishes now to deprive you of the throne
   And give it to the Duke of Muscovy.
   For this he called a council, but the people   65
   Discovered his design and knowing, now,
   They have a native king, will have no stranger.
   So scorning the fierce threats of destiny,
   We've come to seek you in your very prison,
   That aided by the arms of the whole people,   70
   We may restore you to the crown and sceptre,
   Taking them from the tyrant's grasp. Come, then:
   Assembling here, in this wide desert region,
   Hosts of plebeians, bandits, and freebooters,
   Acclaim you king. Your liberty awaits you!   75
   Hark to its voice!

(*Shouts within.*)

           Long life to Segismund!
SEGISMUND: Once more, you heavens will that I should dream
   Of grandeur, once again, 'twixt doubts and shades,
   Behold the majesty of pomp and power
   Vanish into the wind, once more you wish   80
   That I should taste the disillusion and
   The risk by which all human power is humbled,
   Of which all human power should live aware.
   It must not be. I'll not be once again
   Put through my paces by my fortune's stars.   85
   And since I know this life is all a dream,
   Depart, vain shades, who feign, to my dead senses,
   That you have voice and body, having neither!
   I want no more feigned majesty, fantastic
   Display, nor void illusions, that one gust   90
   Can scatter like the almond tree in flower,
   Whose rosy buds, without advice or warning,
   Dawn in the air too soon and then, as one,
   Are all extinguished, fade, and fall, and wither
   In the first gust of wind that comes along!   95
   I know you well. I know you well by now.
   I know that all that happens in yourselves
   Happens as in a sleeping man. For me
   There are no more delusions and deceptions
   Since I well know this life is all a dream.   100

SECOND SOLDIER: If you think we are cheating, just sweep
    Your gaze along these towering peaks, and see
    The hosts that wait to welcome and obey you.
SEGISMUND: Already once before I've seen such crowds
105   Distinctly, quite as vividly as these:
    And yet it was a dream.
SECOND SOLDIER: No great event
    Can come without forerunners to announce it
    And this is the real meaning of your dream.
SEGISMUND: Yes, you say well. It was the fore-announcement
110   And just in case it was correct, my soul,
    (Since life's so short) let's dream the dream anew!
    But it must be attentively, aware
    That we'll awake from pleasure in the end.
    Forewarned of that, the shock's not so abrupt,
115   The disillusion's less. Evils anticipated
    Lose half their sting. And armed with this precaution—
    That power, even when we're sure of it, is borrowed
    And must be given back to its true owner—
    We can risk anything and dare the worst.
120   Subjects, I thank you for your loyalty.
    In me you have a leader who will free you,
    Bravely and skilfully, from foreign rule.
    Sound now to arms, you'll soon behold my valour.
    Against my father I must march and bring
125   Truth from the stars. Yes: he must kneel to me.

(*Aside.*)

    But yet, since I may wake before he kneels,
    Perhaps I'd better not proclaim what may not happen.
ALL: Long live Segismund!

(*Enter* CLOTALDO.)

CLOTALDO: Gracious heavens! What is
    This riot here?
SEGISMUND: Clotaldo!
CLOTALDO: Sir!

(*Aside.*)

               He'll prove
130   His cruelty on me.
CLARION: I bet he throws him
    Over the mountain.
CLOTALDO: At your royal feet
    I kneel, knowing my penalty is death.
SEGISMUND: Rise, rise, my foster father, from the ground,
    For you must be the compass and the guide
135   In which I trust. You brought me up, and I
    Know what I owe your loyalty. Embrace me!
CLOTALDO: What's that you say?
SEGISMUND: I know I'm in a dream,
    But I would like to act well, since good actions,
    Even in a dream, are not entirely lost.
140 CLOTALDO: Since doing good is now to be your glory,
    You will not be offended that I too
    Should do what's right. You march against your father!
    I cannot give you help against my king.
    Here at your feet, my lord, I plead for death.

SEGISMUND: (*Aloud.*) Villain!   145

(*Aside.*)

              But let us suffer this annoyance.
    Though my rage would slay him, yet he's loyal.
    A man does not deserve to die for that.
    How many angry passions does this leash
    Restrain in me, this curb of knowing well
    That I must wake and find myself alone!   150
SECOND SOLDIER: All this fine talk, Clotaldo, is a cruel
    Spurn of the public welfare. We are loyal
    Who wish our own prince to reign over us.
CLOTALDO: Such loyalty, after the king were dead,
    Would honour you. But while the king is living   155
    He is our absolute, unquestioned lord.
    There's no excuse for subjects who oppose
    His sovereignty in arms.
FIRST SOLDIER: We'll soon see well
    Enough, Clotaldo, what this loyalty
    Is worth.   160
CLOTALDO: You would be better if you had some.
    It is the greatest prize.
SEGISMUND: Peace, peace, I pray you.
CLOTALDO: My lord!
SEGISMUND: Clotaldo, if your feelings
    Are truly thus, go you, and serve the king;
    That's prudence, loyalty, and common sense.
    But do not argue here with anyone   165
    Whether it's right or wrong, for every man
    Has his own honour.

CLOTALDO: Humbly I take my leave.

(*Exit.*)

SEGISMUND: Now sound the drums and march in rank and
    order
    Straight to the palace.
ALL: Long live Segismund!
SEGISMUND: Fortune, we go to reign! Do not awake me   170
    If I am dreaming! Do not let me fall
    Asleep if it is true! To act with virtue
    Is what matters, since if this proves true,
    That truth's sufficient reason in itself;
    If not, we win us friends against the time   175
    When we at last awake.

A room in the royal palace.

Enter BASIL *and* ASTOLFO.

BASIL: Whose prudence can rein in a bolting horse?
    Who can restrain a river's pride, in spate?
    Whose valour can withstand a crag dislodged
    And hurtling downwards from a mountain peak?   180
    All these are easier by far than to hold back
    A crowd's proud fury, once it has been roused.
    It has two voices, both proclaiming war,
    And you can hear them echoing through the mountains,

185   Some shouting "Segismund," others "Astolfo."
       The scene I set for swearing of allegiance
       Lends but an added horror to this strife:
       It has become the back cloth to a stage
       Where Fortune plays out tragedies in blood.
190   ASTOLFO: My lord, forget the happiness and wealth
       You promised me from your most blessèd hand.
       If Poland, which I hope to rule, refuses
       Obedience to my right, grudging me honour,
       It is because I've got to earn it first.
195   Give me a horse, that I with angry pride
       May match the thunder in my voice and ride
       To strike, like lightning, terror far and wide.

(*Exit* ASTOLFO.)

       BASIL: No remedy for what's infallible!
       What is foreseen is perilous indeed!
200   If something has to be, there's no way out;
       In trying to evade it, you but court it.
       This law is pitiless and horrible.
       Thinking one can evade the risk, one meets it:
       My own precautions have been my undoing,
205   And I myself have quite destroyed my kingdom.

(*Enter* STELLA.)

       STELLA: If you, my lord, in person do not try
       To curb the vast commotion that has started
       In all the streets between the rival factions,
       You'll see your kingdom, swamped in waves of crimson,
210   Swimming in its own blood, with nothing left
       But havoc, dire calamity, and woe.
       So frightful is the damage to your empire
       That, seen, it strikes amazement; heard, despair.
       The sun's obscured, the very winds are hindered.
215   Each stone is a memorial to the dead.
       Each flower springs from a grave while every building
       Appears a mausoleum, and each soldier
       A premature and walking skeleton.

(*Enter* CLOTALDO.)

       CLOTALDO: Praise be to God, I reach your feet alive!
220   BASIL: Clotaldo! What's the news of Segismund?
       CLOTALDO: The crowd, a headstrong monster blind with rage,
       Entered his dungeon tower and set him free.
       He, now exalted for the second time,
       Conducts himself with valour, boasting how
225   He will bring down the truth out of the stars.
       BASIL: Give me a horse, that I myself, in person,
       May vanquish such a base, ungrateful son!
       For I, in the defence of my own crown,
       Shall do by steel what science failed to do.

(*Exit.*)

230   STELLA: I'll be Bellona to your Sun, and try
       To write my name next yours in history.
       I'll ride as though I flew on outstretched wings
       That I may vie with Pallas.

(*Exit.*)

(*Enter* ROSAURA, *holding back* CLOTALDO.)

       ROSAURA: I know that all is war, Clotaldo, yet
       Although your valour calls you to the front,   235
       First hear me out. You know quite well that I
       Arrived in Poland poor and miserable,
       Where, shielded by your valour, I found mercy.
       You told me to conceal myself, and stay
       Here in the palace, hiding from Astolfo.   240
       He saw me in the end, and so insulted
       My honour that (although he saw me clearly)
       He nightly speaks with Stella in the garden.
       I have the key to it and I will show you
       How you can enter there and end my cares.   245
       Thus bold, resolved, and strong, you can recover
       My honour, since you're ready to avenge me
       By killing him.
       CLOTALDO: It's true that I intended,
       Since first I saw you (having heard your tale)
       With my own life to rectify your wrongs.   250
       The first step that I took was bid you dress
       According to your sex, for fear Astolfo
       Might see you as you were, and deem you wanton.
       I was devising how we could recover
       Your honour (so much did it weigh on me)   255
       Even though we had to kill him. (A wild plan—
       Though since he's not my king, I would not flinch
       From killing him.) But then, when suddenly
       Segismund tried to kill me, it was he
       Who saved my life with his surpassing valour.   260
       Consider: how can I requite Astolfo
       With death for giving me my life so bravely,
       And when my soul is full of gratitude?
       So torn between the two of you I stand—
       Rosaura, whose life I saved, and Astolfo,   265
       Who saved my life. What's to be done? Which side
       To take, and whom to help, I cannot judge.
       What I owe you in that I gave you life
       I owe to him in that he gave me life.
       And so there is no course that I can take   270
       To satisfy my love. I am a person
       Who has to act, yet suffer either way.
       ROSAURA: I should not have to tell so brave a man
       That if it is nobility to give,
       It's baseness to receive. That being so   275
       You owe no gratitude to him, admitting
       That it was he who gave you life, and you
       Who gave me life, since he forced you to take
       A meaner role, and through me you assumed
       A generous role. So you should side with me: 280
       My cause is so far worthier than his own
       As giving is than taking.
       CLOTALDO: Though nobility
       Is with the giver, it is gratitude
       That dwells with the receiver. As a giver
       I have the name of being generous: 285
       Then grant me that of being grateful too
       And let me earn the title and be grateful,
       As I am liberal, giving or receiving.
       ROSAURA: You granted me my life, at the same time
       Telling me it was worthless, since dishonoured,   290

And therefore was no life. Therefore from you
I have received no life at all. And since
You should be liberal first and grateful after
(Since so you said yourself) I now entreat you
295 Give me the life, the life you never gave me!
As giving magnifies the most, give first
And then be grateful after, if you will!
CLOTALDO: Won by your argument, I will be liberal.
Rosaura, I shall give you my estate
300 And you shall seek a convent, there to live.
This measure is a happy thought, for, see,
Fleeing a crime, you find a sanctuary.
For when the empire's threatened with disasters
And is divided thus, I, born a noble,
305 Am not the man who would augment its woes.
So with this remedy which I have chosen
I remain loyal to the kingdom, generous
To you, and also grateful to Astolfo.
And thus I choose the course that suits you best.
310 Were I your father, what could I do more?
ROSAURA: Were you my father, then I would accept
The insult. Since you are not, I refuse.
CLOTALDO: What do you hope to do then?
ROSAURA: Kill the duke!
CLOTALDO: A girl who never even knew her father
315 Armed with such courage?
ROSAURA: Yes.
CLOTALDO: What spurs you on?
ROSAURA: My good name.
CLOTALDO: In Astolfo you will find . . .
ROSAURA: My honour rides on him and strikes him
down!
CLOTALDO: Your king, too, Stella's husband!
ROSAURA: Never, never
Shall that be, by almighty God, I swear!
320 CLOTALDO: Why, this is madness!
ROSAURA: Yes it is!
CLOTALDO: Restrain it.
ROSAURA: That I cannot.
CLOTALDO: Then you are lost forever!
ROSAURA: I know it!
CLOTALDO: Life and honour both together!
ROSAURA: I well believe it!
CLOTALDO: What do you intend?
ROSAURA: My death.
CLOTALDO: This is despair and desperation.
325 ROSAURA: It's honour.
CLOTALDO: It is nonsense.
ROSAURA: It is valour.
CLOTALDO: It's frenzy.
ROSAURA: Yes, it's anger! Yes, it's fury!
CLOTALDO: In short you cannot moderate your passion?
ROSAURA: No.
CLOTALDO: Who is there to help you?
ROSAURA: I, myself.
CLOTALDO: There is no cure?
ROSAURA: There is no cure!
CLOTALDO: Think well
330 If there's not some way out . . .
ROSAURA: Some other way
To do away with me . . .

(*Exit.*)

CLOTALDO: If you are lost,
My daughter, let us both be lost together!

In the country.

Enter SEGISMUND *clothed in skins.* SOLDIERS *marching.* CLARION.
Drums beating.

SEGISMUND: If Rome, today, could see me here, renewing
Her olden triumphs, she might laugh to see
A wild beast in command of mighty armies,   335
A wild beast, to whose fiery aspirations
The firmament were all too slight a conquest!
But stoop your flight, my spirit. Do not thus
Be puffed to pride by these uncertain plaudits
Which, when I wake, will turn to bitterness   340
In that I won them only to be lost.
The less I value them, the less I'll miss them.

(*A trumpet sounds.*)

CLARION: Upon a rapid courser (pray excuse me,
Since if it comes to mind I must describe it)
In which it seems an atlas was designed   345
Since if its body is earth, its soul is fire
Within its breast, its foam appears the sea,
The wind its breath, and chaos its condition,
Since in its soul, its foam, its breath and flesh,
It seems a monster of fire, earth, sea, and wind,   350
Upon the horse, all of a patchwork colour,
Dappled, and rushing forward at the will
Of one who plies the spur, so that it flies
Rather than runs—see how a woman rides
Boldly into your presence.   355
SEGISMUND: Her light blinds me.
CLARION: Good God! Why, here's Rosaura!
SEGISMUND: It is heaven
That has restored her to my sight once more.

(*Enter* ROSAURA *with sword and dagger in riding costume.*)

ROSAURA: Generous Segismund, whose majesty
Heroically rises in the lustre
Of his great deeds out of his night of shadows,   360
And as the greatest planet, in the arms
Of his aurora, lustrously returns
To plants and roses, over hills and seas,
When, crowned with gold, he looks abroad, dispersing
Radiance, flashing his rays, bathing the summits,   365
And broidering the fringes of the foam,
So may you dawn upon the world, bright sun
Of Poland, that a poor unhappy woman
May fall before your feet and beg protection
Both as a woman and unfortunate—   370
Two things that must oblige you, sire, as one
Who prizes yourself as valiant, each of them
More than suffices for your chivalry.

343–355 **Upon a . . . presence** Clarion's speech is a parody of
exaggerated style including Calderón's [R.C.]

Three times you have beheld me now, three times
375 Been ignorant of who I am, because
Three times you saw me in a different clothing.
The first time you mistook me for a man,
Within that rigorous prison, where your hardships
Made mine seem pleasure. Next time, as a woman,
380 You saw me, when your pomp and majesty
Were as a dream, a phantasm, a shade.
The third time is today when, as a monster
Of both the sexes, in a woman's costume
I bear a soldier's arms. But to dispose you
385 The better to compassion, hear my story.
My mother was a noble in the court
Of Moscow, who, since most unfortunate,
Must have been beautiful. Then came a traitor
And cast his eyes on her (I do not name him,
390 Not knowing who he is). Yet I deduce
That he was valiant too from my own valour,
Since he gave form to me—and I could wish
I had been born in pagan times, that I might
Persuade myself he was some god of those
395 Who rain in showers of gold, turn into swans
Or bulls, for Danaës, Ledas, or Europas.
That's strange: I thought I was just rambling on
By telling old perfidious myths, yet find
I've told you how my mother was cajoled.
400 Oh, she was beautiful as no one else
Has been, but was unfortunate like all.
He swore to wed her (that's an old excuse)
And this trick reached so nearly to her heart
That thought must weep, recalling it today.
405 The tyrant left her only with his sword
As Aeneas left Troy. I sheathed its blade here
Upon my thigh, and I will bare it too
Before the ending of this history.
Out of this union, this poor link which neither
410 Could bind the marriage nor handcuff the crime,
Myself was born, her image and her portrait,
Not in her beauty, but in her misfortune,
For mine's the same. That's all I need to say.
The most that I can tell you of myself
415 Is that the man who robbed me of the spoils
And trophies of my honour is Astolfo.
Alas! to name him my heart rages so
(As hearts will do when men name enemies).
Astolfo was my faithless and ungrateful
420 Lord, who (quite forgetful of our happiness,
Since of a past love even the memory fades)
Came here to claim the throne and marry Stella
For she's the star who rises as I set.
It's hard to credit that a star should sunder
425 Lovers the stars had made conformable!
So hurt was I, so villainously cheated,
That I became mad, brokenhearted, sick,
Half wild with grief, and like to die, with all
Hell's own confusion ciphered on my mind
430 Like Babel's incoherence. Mutely I told
My griefs (since woes and griefs declare themselves
Better than can the mouth, by their effects),
When, with my mother (we were by ourselves),

She broke the prison of my pent-up sorrows
And from my breast they all rushed forth in troops.   435
I felt no shyness, for in knowing surely
That one to whom one's errors are recounted
Has also been an ally in her own,
One finds relief and rest, since bad example
Can sometimes serve for a good purpose too.   440
She heard my plaint with pity, and she tried
To palliate my sorrows with her own.
How easily do judges pardon error
When they've offended too! An example,
A warning, in herself, she did not trust   445
To idleness, or the slow cure of time,
Nor try to find a remedy for her honour
In my misfortunes, but, with better counsel,
She bade me follow him to Poland here
And with prodigious gallantry persuade him   450
To pay the debt to honour that he owes me.
So that it would be easier to travel,
She bade me don male clothing, and took down
This ancient sword which I am wearing now.
Now it is time that I unsheathe the blade   455
As I was bid, for, trusting in its sign,
She said: "Depart to Poland, show this sword
That all the nobles may behold it well,
And it may be that one of them will take
Pity on you, and counsel you, and shield you."   460
I came to Poland and, you will remember,
Entered your cave. You looked at me in wonder.
Clotaldo passionately took my part
To plead for mercy to the king, who spared me,
Then, when he heard my story, bade me change   465
Into my own clothes and attend on Stella,
There to disturb Astolfo's love and stop
Their marriage. Again you saw me in woman's dress
And were confused by the discrepancy.
But let's pass to what's new: Clotaldo, now   470
Persuaded that Astolfo must, with Stella,
Come to the throne, dissuades me from my purpose,
Against the interests of my name and honour.
But seeing you, O valiant Segismund,
Are claiming your revenge, now that the heavens   475
Have burst the prison of your rustic tower,
(Wherein you were the tiger of your sorrows,
The rock of sufferings and direful pains)
And sent you forth against your sire and country,
I come to aid you, mingling Dian's silks   480
With the hard steel of Pallas. Now, strong Captain,
It well behoves us both to stop this marriage—
Me, lest my promised husband should be wed,
You, lest, when their estates are joined, they weigh
More powerfully against your victory.   485
I come, as a mere woman, to persuade you
To right my shame; but, as a man, I come
To help you battle for your crown. As woman,
To melt your heart, here at your feet I fall;
But, as a man, I come to serve you bravely   490
Both with my person and my steel, and thus,
If you today should woo me as a woman,
Then I should have to kill you as a man would

In honourable service of my honour;
495   Since I must be three things today at once—
Passionate, to persuade you: womanly,
To ply you with my woes: manly, to gain
Honour in battle.
SEGISMUND: Heavens! If it is true I'm dreaming,
Suspend my memory, for in a dream
500   So many things could not occur. Great heavens!
If I could only come free of them all!
Or never think of any! Who ever felt
Such grievous doubts? If I but dreamed that triumph
In which I found myself, how can this woman
505   Refer me to such sure and certain facts?
Then all of it was true and not a dream.
But if it be the truth, why does my past life
Call it a dream? This breeds the same confusion.
Are dreams and glories so alike, that fictions
510   Are held for truths, realities for lies?
Is there so little difference in them both
That one should question whether what one sees
And tastes is true or false? What? Is the copy
So near to the original that doubt
515   Exists between them? Then if that is so,
And grandeur, power, majesty, and pomp,
Must all evaporate like shades at morning,
Let's profit by it, this time, to enjoy
That which we only can enjoy in dreams.
520   Rosaura's in my power: my soul adores her beauty.
Let's take the chance. Let love break every law
On which she has relied in coming here
And kneeling, trustful, prostrate at my feet.
This is a dream. If so, dream pleasures now
525   Since they must turn to sorrows in the end!
But with my own opinions, I begin
Once again to convince myself. Let's think.
If it is but vainglory and a dream,
Who for mere human vainglory would lose
530   True glory? What past blessing is not merely
A dream? Who has known heroic glories,
That deep within himself, as he recalls them
Has never doubted that they might be dreams?
But if this all should end in disenchantment,
535   Seeing that pleasure is a lovely flame
That's soon converted into dust and ashes
By any wind that blows, then let us seek
That which endures in thrifty, lasting fame
In which no pleasures sleep, nor grandeurs dream.
540   Rosaura's without honour. In a prince
It's worthier to restore it than to steal it.
I shall restore it, by the living God,
Before I win my throne! Let's shun the danger
And fly from the temptation which is strong!
545   Then sound to arms!

(*To a* SOLDIER.)

Today I must give battle before darkness
Buries the rays of gold in green-black waves!
ROSAURA: My lord! Alas, you stand apart, and offer
No word of pity for my plight. How is it

You neither hear nor see me nor even yet   550
Have turned your face on me?
SEGISMUND: Rosaura, for your honour's sake
I must be cruel to you, to be kind.
My voice must not reply to you because
My honour must reply to you. I am silent
Because my deeds must speak to you alone.   555
I do not look at you since, in such straits,
Having to see your honour is requited,
I must not see your beauty.

(*Exit with* SOLDIERS.)

ROSAURA: What strange enigma's this? After such trouble
Still to be treated with more doubtful riddles!   560

(*Enter* CLARION.)

CLARION: Madam, may you be visited just now?
ROSAURA: Why, Clarion, where have you been all this time?
CLARION: Shut in the tower, consulting cards
About my death: "to be or not to be."
And it was a near thing.   565
ROSAURA: Why?
CLARION: Because I know
The secret who you are: in fact, Clotaldo . . .

(*Drums.*)

But hush what noise is that?
ROSAURA: What can it be?
CLARION: From the beleaguered palace a whole squadron
Is charging forth to harry and defeat
That of fierce Segismund.   570
ROSAURA: Why, what a coward
Am I, not to be at his side, the terror
And scandal of the world, while such fierce strife
Presses all round in lawless anarchy.

(*Exit.*)

VOICES OF SOME: Long live our king!
VOICES OF OTHERS: Long live our liberty!
CLARION: Long live both king and liberty. Yes, live!   575
And welcome to them both! I do not worry.
In all this pother, I behave like Nero
Who never grieved at what was going on.
If I had anything to grieve about
It would be me, myself. Well hidden here   580
Now, I can watch the sport that's going on.
This place is safe and hidden between crags,
And since death cannot find me here, two figs for death!

(*He hides. Drums and the clash of arms are heard.*)

(*Enter* BASIL, CLOTALDO, *and* ASTOLFO, *fleeing.*)

BASIL: Was ever king so hapless as myself
Or father more ill used?   585
CLOTALDO: Your beaten army
Rush down, in all directions, in disorder.
ASTOLFO: The traitors win!

BASIL: In battles such as these
         Those on the winning side are ever "loyal,"
         And traitors the defeated. Come, Clotaldo,
590   Let's flee from the inhuman cruelty
         Of my fierce son!

(*Shots are fired within.* CLARION *falls wounded.*)

CLARION: Heavens, save me!
ASTOLFO: Who is this
         Unhappy soldier bleeding at our feet?
CLARION: I am a most unlucky man who, wishing
         To guard myself from death, have sought it out
595   By fleeing from it. Shunning it, I found it,
         Because, to death, no hiding-place is secret.
         So you can argue that whoever shuns it
         Most carefully runs into it the quickest.
         Turn, then, once more into the thick of battle:
600   There is more safety there amidst the fire
         And clash of arms than here on this secluded
         Mountain, because no hidden path is safe
         From the inclemency of Fate; and so,
         Although you flee from death, yet you may find it
605   Quicker than you expect, if God so wills.

(*He falls dead.*)

BASIL: "If God so wills" . . . With what strange eloquence
         This corpse persuades our ignorance and error
         To better knowledge, speaking from the mouth
         Of its fell wound, where the red liquid flowing
610   Seems like a bloody tongue which teaches us
         That the activities of man are vain
         When they are pitted against higher powers.
         For I, who wished to liberate my country
         From murder and sedition, gave it up
615   To the same ills from which I would have saved it.
CLOTALDO: Though Fate, my lord, knows every path, and finds
         Him whom it seeks even in the midst of crags
         And thickets, it is not a Christian judgment
         To say there is no refuge from its fury.
620   A prudent man can conquer Fate itself.
         Though you are not exempted from misfortune,
         Take action to escape it while you can!
ASTOLFO: Clotaldo speaks as one mature in prudence,
         And I as one in valour's youthful prime.
625   Among the thickets of this mount is hidden
         A horse, the very birth of the swift wind.
         Flee on him, and I'll guard you in the rear.
BASIL: If it is God's will I should die, or if
         Death waits here for my coming, I will seek
630   Him out today, and meet him face to face.

(*Enter* SEGISMUND, STELLA, ROSAURA, SOLDIERS, *and their* TRAIN.)

A SOLDIER: Amongst the thickets of this mountain
635   The king is hiding.
SEGISMUND: Seek him out at once!
         Leave no foot of the summit unexplored
         But search from stem to stem and branch to branch!
CLOTALDO: Fly, sir!

BASIL: What for?
ASTOLFO: What do you mean to do?
BASIL: Astolfo, stand aside!
CLOTALDO: What is your wish?
BASIL: To take a cure I've needed for sometime.

(*To* SEGISMUND.)

         If you have come to seek me, here I am.

(*Kneeling.*)

         Your father, prince, kneels humbly at your feet.
         The white snow of my hair is now your carpet.   640
         Tread on my neck and trample on my crown!
         Lay low and drag my dignity in dust!
         Take vengeance on my honour! Make a slave
         Of me and, after all I've done to thwart them,
         Let Fate fulfil its edict and claim homage   645
         And Heaven fulfil its oracles at last!
SEGISMUND: Illustrious court of Poland, who have been
         The witnesses of such unwonted wonders,
         Attend to me, and hear your prince speak out.
         What Heaven decrees and God writes with his finger 650
         (Whose prints and ciphers are the azure leaves
         Adorned with golden lettering of the stars)
         Never deceives nor lies. They only lie
         Who seek to penetrate the mystery
         And, having reached it, use it to ill purpose.   655
         My father, who is here to evade the fury
         Of my proud nature, made me a wild beast:
         So, when I, by my birth of gallant stock,
         My generous blood, and inbred grace and valour,
         Might well have proved both gentle and forbearing,   660
         The very mode of life to which he forced me,
         The sort of bringing up I had to bear
         Sufficed to make me savage in my passions.
         What a strange method of restraining them!
         If one were to tell any man: "One day   665
         You will be killed by an inhuman monster,"
         Would it be the best method he could choose
         To wake that monster when it was asleep?
         Or if they told him: "That sword which you're wearing
         Will be your death," what sort of cure were it   670
         To draw it forth and aim it at his breast?
         Or if they told him: "Deep blue gulfs of water
         Will one day be your sepulchre and grave
         Beneath a silver monument of foam,"
         He would be mad to hurl himself in headlong   675
         When the sea highest heaved its showy mountains
         And crystalline sierras plumed with spray.
         The same has happened to the king as to him
         Who wakes a beast which threatens death, to him
         Who draws a naked sword because he fears it,   680
         To him who dives into the stormy breakers.
         Though my ferocious nature (hear me now)
         Was like a sleeping beast, my inborn rage
         A sheathèd sword, my wrath a quiet ripple,
         Fate should not be coerced by man's injustice—   685
         This rouses more resentment. So it is
         That he who seeks to tame his fortune must

Resort to moderation and to measure.
He who foresees an evil cannot conquer it
690 Thus in advance, for though humility
Can overcome it, this it can do only
When the occasion's there, for there's no way
To dodge one's fate and thus evade the issue.
Let this strange spectacle serve as example—
695 This prodigy, this horror, and this wonder,
Because it is no less than one, to see,
After such measures and precautions taken
To thwart it, that a father thus should kneel
At his son's feet, a kingdom thus be shattered.
700 This was the sentence of the heavens above,
Which he could not evade, much though he tried.
Can I, younger in age, less brave, and less
In science than the king, conquer that fate?

(*To the* KING.)

Sire, rise, give me your hand, now that the heavens
705 Have shown you that you erred as to the method
To vanquish them. Humbly I kneel before you
And offer you my neck to tread upon.
BASIL: Son, such a great and noble act restores you
Straight to my heart. Oh, true and worthy prince!
710 You have won both the laurel and the palm.
Crown yourself with your deeds! For you *have* conquered!
ALL: Long live Segismund! Long live Segismund!
SEGISMUND: Since I have other victories to win,
The greatest of them all awaits me now:
715 To conquer my own self. Astolfo, give
Your hand here to Rosaura, for you know
It is a debt of honour and must be paid.
ASTOLFO: Although, it's true, I owe some obligations—
She does not know her name or who she is,
720 It would be base to wed a woman who . . .
CLOTALDO: Hold! Wait! Rosaura's of as noble stock
As yours, Astolfo. In the open field
I'll prove it with my sword. She is my daughter

And that should be enough.
ASTOLFO: What do you say?
CLOTALDO: Until I saw her married, righted, honoured,   725
I did not wish for it to be discovered.
It's a long story but she is my daughter.
ASTOLFO: That being so, I'm glad to keep my word.
SEGISMUND: And now, so that the princess Stella here
Will not remain disconsolate to lose   730
A prince of so much valour, here I offer
My hand to her, no less in birth and rank.
Give me your hand.
STELLA: I gain by meriting
So great a happiness.
SEGISMUND: And now, Clotaldo,
So long so loyal to my father, come   735
To my arms. Ask me anything you wish.
FIRST SOLDIER: If thus you treat a man who never served you,
What about me who led the revolution
And brought you from your dungeon in the tower?
What will you give me?   740
SEGISMUND: That same tower and dungeon
From which you never shall emerge till death.
No traitor is of use after his treason.
BASIL: All wonder at your wisdom!
ASTOLFO: What a change
Of character!
ROSAURA: How wise and prudent!
SEGISMUND: Why
Do you wonder? Why do you marvel, since   745
It was a dream that taught me and I still
Fear to wake up once more in my close dungeon?
Though that may never happen, it's enough
To dream it might, for thus I came to learn
That all our human happiness must pass   750
Away like any dream, and I would here
Enjoy it fully ere it glide away,
Asking (for noble hearts are prone to pardon)
Pardon for faults in the actors or the play.

Molière

Jean-Baptiste Poquelin (1622–1773) was born into a prosperous mercantile family with connections at court; his father, Jean Poquelin, secured the honor of *tapissier ordinaire du roi,* the upholsterer to the court, which carried an annual pension. Jean Poquelin also educated his son in the traditional disciplines of the humanities, philosophy, and the classics and must have intended a life at court for him. In 1643, Jean-Baptiste joined with the Illustre Théâtre, a theatrical company run by the Béjart family, took the stage name Molière, and after a brief period performing in Parisian tennis courts, left with the company to play in the provinces. In 1658, after several hard and impoverished years of touring, when Molière is thought to have mastered the techniques of *commedia dell' arte,* the company was invited to perform in Paris.

Molière's career was closely tied to the court. When his brother died in 1660, he received the position of court upholsterer and the income it provided. More important, Molière became a significant playwright and both wrote and acted in a splendid series of plays that satirized the manners and morals of elegant society: *Les Précieuses Ridicules* (1659), *Sganarelle* (1660), *School for Husbands* (1661), *School for Wives* (1662), *Dom Juan* (1665), *The Misanthrope* (1666), *The Doctor in Spite of Himself* (1666), *The Miser* (1668), *The Learned Ladies* (1672), and *The Imaginary Invalid* (1673). Molière also prepared other entertainments at court, including many royal pageants, ballets, and machine plays devised by and for Louis XIV. In addition to being a great dramatist, Molière was a fine comic actor as well and performed in his own plays; he died shortly after playing the title role in the fourth performance of *The Imaginary Invalid.*

The fortunes of *Tartuffe* suggest Molière's importance at court. When Molière initially produced the first three acts of the play in 1664, the clergy protested and banned the play from production in Paris. Many of Molière's plays had excited controversy, and in this case Molière appealed to the king and proceeded to revise the play. Louis's attitude is perhaps revealed by the fact that he made Molière's company the *Troupe du roi* ("King's Company") in 1665, but even the throne could not prevent the clergy from censoring Molière's second version of the play in 1667, newly titled *The Impostor.* Molière finally produced the play to acclaim in 1669, and the record of his efforts is preserved in the series of letters and prefaces included here.

Molière's theatrical company was the most influential of its day. After his death, his young wife Amanda Béjart and the actress Mademoiselle Champmeslé—newly defected from the rival company at the Hôtel de Bourgogne—established a new company, the Comédie Française. Yet although Molière achieved extraordinary status at court, because he was an actor he remained stigmatized in ways that playwrights like Racine and Corneille were not. Following its standard practice, and perhaps because of *Tartuffe*'s notoriety, the church refused to bury Molière in sacred ground. Louis XIV intervened, but was only able to persuade the Archbishop of Paris to bury Molière in a parish cemetery. The burial was conducted at night, by two priests, with no funeral ceremony.

TARTUFFE

The Catholic church criticized *Tartuffe* for its portrait of hypocritical piety, but the fact that Molière played the part of Orgon may suggest that the play is as much about Tartuffe's effect on that benighted householder as it is about the title character. For if Tartuffe is hypocritical, Orgon is obsessed, less with piety than with his own desire to achieve a kind of total power and authority in his household, a kind of domestic absolutism; he is, in a sense, a comic, bourgeois Louis XIV in miniature. Moreover, Tartuffe dupes Orgon not by tricking him, but by inviting Orgon to fulfill his own fantasy of autonomy and authority. As he brags

Tartuffe seduces Elmire while Orgon hides beneath the table in Molière's *Tartuffe*.

to the sensible Cléante, under Tartuffe's teaching, "my soul's been freed / From earthly loves, and every human tie: / My mother, children, brother, and wife could die, / And I'd not feel a single moment's pain." Helping Orgon to realize this fantasy, Tartuffe transforms him into a kind of monster: Orgon comes near to selling his daughter, disinheriting his son, allowing his wife to be raped, and losing his family's property and fortune.

Tartuffe is very much a play of the world, a satiric comedy. Set in an urban landscape, the play insistently translates the idealized passions of tragedy and romantic comedy—love, honor, loyalty—into their ironic counterparts—lust, hypocrisy, betrayal. Molière peoples the play with individualized versions of the unchanging types of *commedia dell' arte* and the Roman comedy that inspired it: the reasonable and attractive heroes; an old, pedantic, self-absorbed dupe; a wily and conniving villain; a clever and witty servant. Yet Molière reinvents this range of stock characters, brilliantly turning his play toward an exploration of the folly of self-deception. For while we might take the neoclassical conflict between reason and the passions to be the hallmark of tragedy, it surges through this play as well. Orgon's passionate solipsism is, for all its ridiculousness, no less profound, troubling, or destructive than the obsessed affections of Racine's Phaedra and Hippolytus. Also, Orgon's redemption, by fiat of the king, seems no less arbitrary than the vengeful caprice of Venus or Neptune in Racine's tragedy.

Since the characters cannot change in Molière's comedy, change must happen to them. Molière's most brilliant device here arises in the person of the king's officer, who appears to apprehend Tartuffe and to restore Orgon and his family to their property: property is what establishes the position, the place, the social and individual identity of these characters. Although Molière's DEUS EX MACHINA might be regarded as an elegant (though somewhat clumsy) compliment to the king—and, perhaps, as a sly jab at the clerical critics who attacked *Tartuffe*—this device plays a subtle role in dramatizing the nature of royal authority. For in *Tartuffe,* the king has the power to assign every person to his or her proper place, to see into our inmost hearts, to structure the moral and social order of the world as the reflection of his own will and judgment: *"L'état, c'est moi."* In this sense, even though *Tartuffe* unleashes the uncontrollable power of self-delusion and the power and destructive fantasies of absolute authority, the play concludes by asserting the legitimacy of that absolute power. Molière's *deus ex machina* testifies both to the power and to the arbitrariness of the king's authority.

PREFACE[1]
TRANSLATED BY RICHARD WILBUR

Here is a comedy that has excited a good deal of discussion and that has been under attack for a long time; and the persons who are mocked by it have made it plain that they are more powerful in France than all whom my plays have satirized up to this time. Noblemen, ladies of fashion, cuckolds, and doctors all kindly consented to their presentation, which they themselves seemed to enjoy along with everyone else; but hypocrites do not understand banter: they became angry at once, and found it strange that I was bold enough to represent their actions and to care to describe a profession shared by so many good men. This is a crime for which they cannot forgive me, and they have taken up arms against my comedy in a terrible rage. They were careful not to attack it at the point that had wounded them: they are too crafty for that and too clever to reveal their true character. In keeping with their lofty custom, they have used the cause of God to mask their private interests; and *Tartuffe,* they say, is a play that offends piety: It is filled with abominations from beginning to end, and nowhere is there a line that does not deserve to be burned. Every syllable is wicked, the very gestures are criminal, and the slightest glance, turn of the head, or step from right to left conceals mysteries that they are able to explain to my disadvantage. In vain did I submit the play to the criticism of my friends and the scrutiny of the public: all the corrections I could make, the judgment of the king and queen who saw the play,[2] the approval of great princes and ministers of state who honored it with their presence, the opinion of good men who found it worthwhile; all this did not help. They will not let go of their prey, and every day of the week they have pious zealots abusing me in public and damning me out of charity.

I would care very little about all they might say except that their devices make enemies of men whom I respect and gain the support of genuinely good men, whose faith they know and who, because of the warmth of their piety, readily accept the impressions that others present to them. And it is this which forces me to defend myself. Especially to the truly devout do I wish to vindicate my play, and I beg of them with all my heart not to condemn it before seeing it, to rid themselves of preconceptions, and not aid the cause of men dishonored by their actions.

If one takes the trouble to examine my comedy in good faith, he will surely see that my intentions are innocent throughout, and tend in no way to make fun of what men revere; that I have presented the subject with all the precautions that its delicacy imposes; and that I have used all the art and skill that I could to distinguish clearly the character of the hypocrite from that of the truly devout man. For that purpose I used two whole acts to prepare the appearance of my scoundrel. Never is there a moment's doubt about his character; he is known at once from the qualities I have given him; and from one end of the play to the other, he does not say a word, he does not perform an action which does not depict to

---

[1]Molière added his three petitions to Louis XIV; they follow the preface.
[2]Louis XIV was married to Marie Thérèse of Austria.

the audience the character of a wicked man, and which does not bring out in sharp relief the character of the truly good man which I oppose to it.

I know full well that by way of reply, these gentlemen try to insinuate that it is not the role of the theater to speak of these matters; but with their permission, I ask them on what do they base this fine doctrine. It is a proposition they advance as no more than a supposition, for which they offer not a shred of proof; and surely it would not be difficult to show them that comedy, for the ancients, had its origin in religion and constituted a part of its ceremonies; that our neighbors, the Spaniards, have hardly a single holiday celebration in which a comedy is not a part; and that even here in France, it owes its birth to the efforts of a religious brotherhood who still own the Hôtel de Bourgogne, where the most important mystery plays of our faith were presented[3]; that you can still find comedies printed in gothic letters under the name of a learned doctor of the Sorbonne[4]; and without going so far, in our own day the religious dramas of Pierre Corneille[5] have been performed to the admiration of all France.

If the function of comedy is to correct men's vices, I do not see why any should be exempt. Such a condition in our society would be much more dangerous than the thing itself; and we have seen that the theater is admirably suited to provide correction. The most forceful lines of a serious moral statement are usually less powerful than those of satire; and nothing will reform most men better than the depiction of their faults. It is a vigorous blow to vices to expose them to public laughter. Criticism is taken lightly, but men will not tolerate satire. They are quite willing to be mean, but they never like to be ridiculed.

I have been attacked for having placed words of piety in the mouth of my impostor. Could I avoid doing so in order to represent properly the character of a hypocrite? It seemed to me sufficient to reveal the criminal motives which make him speak as he does, and I have eliminated all ceremonial phrases, which nonetheless he would not have been found using incorrectly. Yet some say that in the fourth act he sets forth a vicious morality; but is not this a morality which everyone has heard again and again? Does my comedy say anything new here? And is there any fear that ideas so thoroughly detested by everyone can make an impression on men's minds; that I make them dangerous by presenting them in the theater; that they acquire authority from the lips of a scoundrel? There is not the slightest suggestion of any of this; and one must either approve the comedy of *Tartuffe* or condemn all comedies in general.

This has indeed been done in a furious way for some time now, and never was the theater so much abused.[6] I cannot deny that there were Church Fathers who condemned comedy; but neither will it be denied me that there were some who looked on it somewhat more favorably. Thus authority, on which censure is supposed to depend, is destroyed by this disagreement; and the only conclusion that can be drawn from this difference of opinion among men enlightened by the same wisdom is that they viewed comedy in different ways, and that some considered it in its purity, while others regarded it in its corruption and confused it with all those wretched performances which have been rightly called performances of filth.

---

[3]A reference to the *Confrérie de la Passion et Résurrection de Notre-Seigneur* (the Fraternity of the Passion and Resurrection of Our Saviour), founded in 1402. The Hôtel de Bourgogne was a rival theater of Molière.

[4]Probably Maitre Jehán Michel, a medical doctor who wrote mystery plays.

[5]Pierre Corneille (1606–1684) and Racine were France's two greatest writers of classic tragedy. The two dramas Molière doubtlessly had in mind were *Polyeucte* (1643) and *Théodore, vierge et martyre* (1645).

[6]Molière had in mind Nicole's two attacks on the theater: *Visionnaries* (1666) and *Traité de Comédie*, and the Prince de Condé's *Traité de Comédie* (1666).

And in fact, since we should talk about things rather than words, and since most misunderstanding comes from including contrary notions in the same word, we need only to remove the veil of ambiguity and look at comedy in itself to see if it warrants condemnation. It will surely be recognized that as it is nothing more than a clever poem which corrects men's faults by means of agreeable lessons, it cannot be condemned without injustice. And if we listened to the voice of ancient times on this matter, it would tell us that its most famous philosophers have praised comedy—they who professed so austere a wisdom and who ceaselessly denounced the vices of their times. It would tell us that Aristotle spent his evenings at the theater[7] and took the trouble to reduce the art of making comedies to rules. It would tell us that some of its greatest and most honored men took pride in writing comedies themselves,[8] and that others did not disdain to recite them in public; that Greece expressed its admiration for this art by means of handsome prizes and magnificent theaters to honor it; and finally, that in Rome this same art also received extraordinary honors; I do not speak of Rome run riot under the license of the emperors, but of disciplined Rome, governed by the wisdom of the consuls, and in the age of the full vigor of Roman dignity.

I admit that there have been times when comedy became corrupt. And what do men not corrupt every day? There is nothing so innocent that men cannot turn it to crime; nothing so beneficial that its values cannot be reversed; nothing so good in itself that it cannot be put to bad uses. Medical knowledge benefits mankind and is revered as one of our most wonderful possessions; and yet there was a time when it fell into discredit, and was often used to poison men. Philosophy is a gift of Heaven; it has been given to us to bring us to the knowledge of a God by contemplating the wonders of nature; and yet we know that often it has been turned away from its function and has been used openly in support of impiety. Even the holiest of things are not immune from human corruption, and every day we see scoundrels who use and abuse piety, and wickedly make it serve the greatest of crimes. But this does not prevent one from making the necessary distinctions. We do not confuse in the same false inference the goodness of things that are corrupted with the wickedness of the corrupt. The function of an art is always distinguished from its misuse; and as medicine is not forbidden because it was banned in Rome,[9] nor philosophy because it was publicly condemned in Athens,[10] we should not suppress comedy simply because it has been condemned at certain times. This censure was justified then for reasons which no longer apply today; it was limited to what was then seen; and we should not seize on these limits, apply them more rigidly than is necessary, and include in our condemnation the innocent along with the guilty. The comedy that this censure attacked is in no way the comedy that we want to defend. We must be careful not to confuse the one with the other. There may be two persons whose morals may be completely different. They may have no resemblance to one another except in their names, and it would be a terrible injustice to want to condemn Olympia, who is a good woman, because there is also an Olympia who is lewd. Such procedures would make for great confusion everywhere. Everything under the sun would be condemned; now since this rigor is not applied to the countless instances of abuse we see every day, the same should hold for comedy, and those plays should be approved in which instruction and virtue reign supreme.

---

[7]A reference to Aristotle's *The Poetics* (composed between 335 and 322 BCE, the year of his death).

[8]The Roman consul and general responsible for the final destruction of Carthage in 146 BCE, Scipio Africanus Minor (c. 185–129 BCE), collaborated with the writer of comedies, Terence (Publius Terentius Afer, c. 195 or 185–c. 159 BCE).

[9]Pliny the Elder says that the Romans expelled their doctors at the same time that the Greeks did theirs.

[10]An allusion to Socrates' condemnation to death.

I know there are some so delicate that they cannot tolerate a comedy, who say that the most decent are the most dangerous, that the passions they present are all the more moving because they are virtuous, and that men's feelings are stirred by these presentations. I do not see what great crime it is to be affected by the sight of a generous passion; and this utter insensitivity to which they would lead us is indeed a high degree of virtue! I wonder if so great a perfection resides within the strength of human nature, and I wonder if it is not better to try to correct and moderate men's passions than to try to suppress them altogether. I grant that there are places better to visit than the theater; and if we want to condemn every single thing that does not bear directly on God and our salvation, it is right that comedy be included, and I should willingly grant that it be condemned along with everything else. But if we admit, as is in fact true, that the exercise of piety will permit interruptions, and that men need amusement, I maintain that there is none more innocent than comedy. I have dwelled too long on this matter. Let me finish with the words of a great prince on the comedy, *Tartuffe*.[11]

Eight days after it had been banned, a play called *Scaramouche the Hermit*[12] was performed before the court; and the king, on his way out, said to this great prince: "I should really like to know why the persons who make so much noise about Molière's comedy do not say a word about *Scaramouche*." To which the prince replied, "It is because the comedy of *Scaramouche* makes fun of Heaven and religion, which these gentlemen do not care about at all, but that of Molière makes fun of *them,* and that is what they cannot bear."

Molière

First Petition[13]

(PRESENTED TO THE KING ON THE COMEDY OF TARTUFFE)

Sire,

As the duty of comedy is to correct men by amusing them, I believed that in my occupation I could do nothing better than attack the vices of my age by making them ridiculous; and as hypocrisy is undoubtedly one of the most common, most improper, and most dangerous, I thought, Sire, that I would perform a service for all good men of your kingdom if I wrote a comedy which denounced hypocrites and placed in proper view all of the contrived poses of these incredibly virtuous men, all of the concealed villainies of these counterfeit believers who would trap others with a fraudulent piety and a pretended virtue.

I have written this comedy, Sire, with all the care and caution that the delicacy of the subject demands; and so as to maintain all the more properly the admiration and respect due to truly devout men, I have delineated my character as sharply as I could; I have left no room for doubt; I have removed all that might confuse good with evil, and have used for this painting only the specific colors and essential lines that make one instantly recognize a true and brazen hypocrite.

Nevertheless, all my precautions have been to no avail. Others have taken advantage of the delicacy of your feelings on religious matters, and they have been able to deceive you

---

[11]One of Molière's benefactors who liked the play was the Prince de Condé; the Prince had *Tartuffe* read to him and also privately performed for him.

[12]A troupe of Italian comedians had just performed the licentious farce, where a hermit dressed as a monk makes love to a married woman, announcing that *questo e per mortificar la carne* ("this is to mortify the flesh").

[13]The first of the three *petitions* or *placets* to Louis XIV concerning the play. On May 12, 1664, *Tartuffe*— or at least the first three acts roughly as they now stand—was performed at Versailles. A cabal unfavorable to Molière, including the Archbishop of Paris, Hardouin de Péréfixe, Queen-Mother Anne of Austria, certain influential courtiers, and the Brotherhood or Company of the Holy Sacrament (formed in 1627 to enforce morality), arranged that the play be banned and Molière censured.

on the only side of your character which lies open to deception: your respect for holy things. By underhanded means, the Tartuffes have skillfully gained Your Majesty's favor, and the models have succeeded in eliminating the copy, no matter how innocent it may have been and no matter what resemblance was found between them.

Although the suppression of this work was a serious blow for me, my misfortune was nonetheless softened by the way in which Your Majesty explained his attitude on the matter; and I believed, Sire, that Your Majesty removed any cause I had for complaint, as you were kind enough to declare that you found nothing in this comedy that you would forbid me to present in public.

Yet, despite this glorious declaration of the greatest and most enlightened king in the world, despite the approval of the Papal Legate[14] and of most of our churchmen, all of whom, at private readings of my work, agreed with the views of Your Majesty, despite all this, a book has appeared by a certain priest[15] which boldly contradicts all of these noble judgments. Your Majesty expressed himself in vain, and the Papal Legate and churchmen gave their opinion to no avail: Sight unseen, my comedy is diabolical, and so is my brain; I am a devil garbed in flesh and disguised as a man,[16] a libertine, a disbeliever who deserves a punishment that will set an example. It is not enough that fire expiate my crime in public, for that would be letting me off too easily: The generous piety of this good man will not stop there; he will not allow me to find any mercy in the sight of God; he demands that I be damned, and that will settle the matter.

This book, Sire, was presented to Your Majesty; and I am sure that you see for yourself how unpleasant it is for me to be exposed daily to the insults of these gentlemen, what harm these abuses will do my reputation if they must be tolerated, and finally, how important it is for me to clear myself of these false charges and let the public know that my comedy is nothing more than what they want it to be. I will not ask, Sire, for what I need for the sake of my reputation and the innocence of my work: enlightened kings such as you do not need to be told what is wished of them; like God, they see what we need and know better than we what they should give us. It is enough for me to place my interests in Your Majesty's hands, and I respectfully await whatever you may care to command.

(August, 1664)

Second Petition[17]

(PRESENTED TO THE KING IN HIS CAMP BEFORE THE CITY OF LILLE, IN FLANDERS)

Sire,

It is bold indeed for me to ask a favor of a great monarch in the midst of his glorious victories; but in my present situation, Sire, where will I find protection anywhere but where I seek it, and to whom can I appeal against the authority of the power that crushes me,[18] if not to the source of power and authority, the just dispenser of absolute law, the sovereign judge and master of all?

---

[14]Cardinal Legate Chigi, nephew to Pope Alexander VII, heard a reading of *Tartuffe* at Fontainebleau on August 4, 1664.

[15]Pierre Roullé, the curate of St. Barthélémy, who wrote a scathing attack on the play and sent his book to the king.

[16]Molière took some of these phrases from Roullé.

[17]On August 5, 1667, *Tartuffe* was performed at the Palais-Royal. The opposition—headed by the First President of Parliament—brought in the police, and the play was stopped. Since Louis was campaigning in Flanders, friends of Molière brought the second *placet* to Lille. Louis had always been favorable toward the playwright; in August 1665, Molière's company, the *Troupe de Monsieur* (nominally sponsored by Louis's brother Philippe, Duc d'Orléans) had become the *Troupe du Roi.*

[18]President de Lanvignon, in charge of the Paris police.

My comedy, Sire, has not enjoyed the kindnesses of Your Majesty. All to no avail, I produced it under the title of *The Hypocrite* and disguised the principal character as a man of the world; in vain I gave him a little hat, long hair, a wide collar, a sword, and lace clothing,[19] softened the action and carefully eliminated all that I thought might provide even the shadow of grounds for discontent on the part of the famous models of the portrait I wished to present; nothing did any good. The conspiracy of opposition revived even at mere conjecture of what the play would be like. They found a way of persuading those who in all other matters plainly insist that they are not to be deceived. No sooner did my comedy appear than it was struck down by the very power which should impose respect; and all that I could do to save myself from the fury of this tempest was to say that Your Majesty had given me permission to present the play and I did not think it was necessary to ask this permission of others, since only Your Majesty could have refused it.

I have no doubt, Sire, that the men whom I depict in my comedy will employ every means possible to influence Your Majesty, and will use, as they have used already, those truly good men who are all the more easily deceived because they judge of others by themselves.[20] They know how to display all of their aims in the most favorable light; yet, no matter how pious they may seem, it is surely not the interests of God which stir them; they have proven this often enough in the comedies they have allowed to be performed hundreds of times without making the least objection. Those plays attacked only piety and religion, for which they care very little; but this play attacks and makes fun of them, and that is what they cannot bear. They will never forgive me for unmasking their hypocrisy in the eyes of everyone. And I am sure that they will not neglect to tell Your Majesty that people are shocked by my comedy. But the simple truth, Sire, is that all Paris is shocked only by its ban, that the most scrupulous persons have found its presentation worthwhile, and men are astounded that individuals of such known integrity should show so great a deference to people whom everyone should abominate and who are so clearly opposed to the true piety which they profess.

I respectfully await the judgment that Your Majesty will deign to pronounce: But it's certain, Sire, that I need not think of writing comedies if the Tartuffes are triumphant, if they thereby seize the right to persecute me more than ever, and find fault with even the most innocent lines that flow from my pen.

Let your goodness, Sire, give me protection against their envenomed rage, and allow me, at your return from so glorious a campaign, to relieve Your Majesty from the fatigue of his conquests, give him innocent pleasures after such noble accomplishments, and make the monarch laugh who makes all Europe tremble!

(August, 1667)

Third Petition

(PRESENTED TO THE KING)

Sire,

A very honest doctor[21] whose patient I have the honor to be, promises and will legally contract to make me live another thirty years if I can obtain a favor for him from Your Majesty. I told him of his promise that I do not deserve so much, and that I should be glad to help him if he will merely agree not to kill me. This favor, Sire, is a post of canon at your royal chapel of Vincennes, made vacant by death.

---

[19]There is evidence that in 1664 Tartuffe played his role dressed in a cassock, thus allying him more directly to the clergy.

[20]Molière apparently did not know that de Lanvignon had been affiliated with the Company of the Holy Sacrament for the previous ten years.

[21]A physician friend, M. de Mauvillain, who helped Molière with some of the medical details of *Le Malade imaginaire*.

May I dare to ask for this favor from Your Majesty on the very day of the glorious resurrection of *Tartuffe*, brought back to life by your goodness? By this first favor I have been reconciled with the devout, and the second will reconcile me with the doctors.[22] Undoubtedly this would be too much grace for me at one time, but perhaps it would not be too much for Your Majesty, and I await your answer to my petition with respectful hope.

(February, 1669)

---

[22]Doctors are ridiculed to varying degrees in earlier plays of Molière: *Dom Juan, L'Amour médecin,* and *Le Médecin malgré lui.*

TARTUFFE

Molière

TRANSLATED BY RICHARD WILBUR

CHARACTERS

MADAME PERNELLE, *Orgon's mother*
ORGON, *Elmire's husband*
ELMIRE, *Orgon's wife*
DAMIS, *Orgon's son, Elmire's stepson*
MARIANE, *Orgon's daughter, Elmire's stepdaughter, in love with Valère*
VALÈRE, *in love with Mariane*
CLÉANTE, *Orgon's brother-in-law*

TARTUFFE, *a hypocrite*
DORINE, *Mariane's lady's-maid*
M. LOYAL, *a bailiff*
A POLICE OFFICER
FLIPOTE, *Madame Pernelle's maid*

The scene throughout: Orgon's house in Paris

ACT ONE

SCENE I

MADAME PERNELLE *and* FLIPOTE, *her maid,* ELMIRE, MARIANE, DORINE, DAMIS, CLÉANTE

MADAME PERNELLE: Come, come, Flipote; it's time I left this
    place.
ELMIRE: I can't keep up, you walk at such a pace.
MADAME PERNELLE: Don't trouble, child; no need to show
    me out.
    It's not your manners I'm concerned about.
5 ELMIRE: We merely pay you the respect we owe.
    But, Mother, why this hurry? Must you go?
MADAME PERNELLE: I must. This house appals me. No one in it
    Will pay attention for a single minute.
    Children, I take my leave much vexed in spirit.
10   I offer good advice, but you won't hear it.
    You all break in and chatter on and on.
    It's like a madhouse with the keeper gone.
DORINE: If . . .
MADAME PERNELLE: Girl, you talk too much, and I'm afraid
    You're far too saucy for a lady's-maid.
15   You push in everywhere and have your say.
DAMIS: But . . .
MADAME PERNELLE: You, boy, grow more foolish every day.
    To think my grandson should be such a dunce!
    I've said a hundred times, if I've said it once,
    That if you keep the course on which you've started,
20   You'll leave your worthy father broken-hearted.
MARIANE: I think . . .
MADAME PERNELLE: And you, his sister, seem so pure,
    So shy, so innocent, and so demure.
    But you know what they say about still waters.
    I pity parents with secretive daughters.
25 ELMIRE: Now, Mother . . .
MADAME PERNELLE: And as for you, child, let me add
    That your behavior is extremely bad,
    And a poor example for these children, too.
    Their dear, dead mother did far better than you.
    You're much too free with money, and I'm distressed
30   To see you so elaborately dressed.
    When it's one's husband that one aims to please,
    One has no need of costly fripperies.
CLÉANTE: Oh, Madam, really . . .
MADAME PERNELLE: You are her brother, Sir,
    And I respect and love you; yet if I were
    My son, this lady's good and pious spouse, 35
    I wouldn't make you welcome in my house.
    You're full of worldly counsels which, I fear,
    Aren't suitable for decent folk to hear.
    I've spoken bluntly, Sir; but it behooves us
    Not to mince words when righteous fervor moves us. 40
DAMIS: Your man Tartuffe is full of holy speeches . . .
MADAME PERNELLE: And practises precisely what he preaches.
    He's a fine man, and should be listened to.
    I will not hear him mocked by fools like you.
DAMIS: Good God! Do you expect me to submit 45
    To the tyranny of that carping hypocrite?
    Must we forgo all joys and satisfactions
    Because that bigot censures all our actions?
DORINE: To hear him talk—and he talks all the time—
    There's nothing one can do that's not a crime. 50
    He rails at everything, your dear Tartuffe.
MADAME PERNELLE: Whatever he reproves deserves reproof.
    He's out to save your souls, and all of you
    Must love him, as my son would have you do.
DAMIS: Ah no, Grandmother, I could never take 55
    To such a rascal, even for my father's sake.
    That's how I feel, and I shall not dissemble.
    His every action makes me seethe and tremble
    With helpless anger, and I have no doubt
    That he and I will shortly have it out. 60
DORINE: Surely it is a shame and a disgrace
    To see this man usurp the master's place—
    To see this beggar who, when first he came,
    Had not a shoe or shoestring to his name
    So far forget himself that he behaves 65
    As if the house were his, and we his slaves.
MADAME PERNELLE: Well, mark my words, your souls would
    fare far better
    If you obeyed his precepts to the letter.
DORINE: You see him as a saint. I'm far less awed;
    In fact, I see right through him. He's a fraud. 70
MADAME PERNELLE: Nonsense!
DORINE: His man Laurent's the same, or worse;
    I'd not trust either with a penny purse.
MADAME PERNELLE: I can't say what his servant's morals may be;

His own great goodness I can guarantee.
75 You all regard him with distaste and fear
Because he tells you what you're loath to hear,
Condemns your sins, points out your moral flaws,
And humbly strives to further Heaven's cause.
DORINE: If sin is all that bothers him, why is it
80 He's so upset when folk drop in to visit?
Is Heaven so outraged by a social call
That he must prophesy against us all?
I'll tell you what I think: if you ask me,
He's jealous of my mistress' company.
85 MADAME PERNELLE: Rubbish! (*To* ELMIRE.) He's not alone,
child, in complaining
Of all of your promiscuous entertaining.
Why, the whole neighborhood's upset, I know,
By all these carriages that come and go,
With crowds of guests parading in and out
90 And noisy servants loitering about.
In all of this, I'm sure there's nothing vicious;
But why give people cause to be suspicious?
CLÉANTE: They need no cause; they'll talk in any case.
Madam, this world would be a joyless place
95 If, fearing what malicious tongues might say,
We locked our doors and turned our friends away.
And even if one did so dreary a thing,
D'you think those tongues would cease their chattering?
One can't fight slander; it's a losing battle;
100 Let us instead ignore their tittle-tattle.
Let's strive to live by conscience' clear decrees,
And let the gossips gossip as they please.
DORINE: If there is talk against us, I know the source:
It's Daphne and her little husband, of course.
105 Those who have greatest cause for guilt and shame
Are quickest to besmirch a neighbor's name.
When there's a chance for libel, they never miss it;
When something can be made to seem illicit
They're off at once to spread the joyous news,
110 Adding to fact what fantasies they choose.
By talking up their neighbor's indiscretions
They seek to camouflage their own transgressions,
Hoping that others' innocent affairs
Will lend a hue of innocence to theirs,
115 Or that their own black guilt will come to seem
Part of a general shady color-scheme.
MADAME PERNELLE: All that is quite irrelevant. I doubt
That anyone's more virtuous and devout
Than dear Orante; and I'm informed that she
120 Condemns your mode of life most vehemently.
DORINE: Oh, yes, she's strict, devout, and has no taint
Of worldliness; in short, she seems a saint.
But it was time which taught her that disguise;
She's thus because she can't be otherwise.
125 So long as her attractions could enthrall,
She flounced and flirted and enjoyed it all,
But now that they're no longer what they were
She quits a world which fast is quitting her,
And wears a veil of virtue to conceal
130 Her bankrupt beauty and her lost appeal.
That's what becomes of old coquettes today:
Distressed when all their lovers fall away,
They see no recourse but to play the prude,

And so confer a style on solitude.
Thereafter, they're severe with everyone,   135
Condemning all our actions, pardoning none,
And claiming to be pure, austere, and zealous
When, if the truth were known, they're merely jealous,
And cannot bear to see another know
The pleasures time has forced them to forgo.   140
MADAME PERNELLE: (*Initially to* ELMIRE.) That sort of talk is
what you like to hear;
Therefore you'd have us all keep still, my dear,
While Madam rattles on the livelong day.
Nevertheless, I mean to have my say.
I tell you that you're blest to have Tartuffe   145
Dwelling, as my son's guest, beneath this roof;
That Heaven has sent him to forestall its wrath
By leading you, once more, to the true path;
That all he reprehends is reprehensible,
And that you'd better heed him, and be sensible.   150
These visits, balls, and parties in which you revel
Are nothing but inventions of the Devil.
One never hears a word that's edifying:
Nothing but chaff and foolishness and lying,
As well as vicious gossip in which one's neighbor   155
Is cut to bits with épée, foil, and saber.
People of sense are driven half-insane
At such affairs, where noise and folly reign
And reputations perish thick and fast.
As a wise preacher said on Sunday last,   160
Parties are Towers of Babylon, because
The guests all babble on with never a pause;
And then he told a story which, I think . . .

(*To* CLÉANTE.)

I heard that laugh, Sir, and I saw that wink!
Go find your silly friends and laugh some more!   165
Enough; I'm going; don't show me to the door.
I leave this household much dismayed and vexed;
I cannot say when I shall see you next.

(*Slapping* FLIPOTE.)

Wake up, don't stand there gaping into space!
I'll slap some sense into that stupid face.   170
Move, move, you slut.

SCENE II

CLÉANTE, DORINE

CLÉANTE: I think I'll stay behind;
I want no further pieces of her mind.
How that old lady . . .
DORINE: Oh, what wouldn't she say
If she could hear you speak of her that way!
She'd thank you for the *lady*, but I'm sure   5
She'd find the *old* a little premature.
CLÉANTE: My, what a scene she made, and what a din!
And how this man Tartuffe has taken her in!
DORINE: Yes, but her son is even worse deceived;
His folly must be seen to be believed.   10

In the late troubles, he played an able part
And served his king with wise and loyal heart,
But he's quite lost his senses since he fell
Beneath Tartuffe's infatuating spell.
15 He calls him brother, and loves him as his life,
Preferring him to mother, child, or wife.
In him and him alone will he confide;
He's made him his confessor and his guide;
He pets and pampers him with love more tender
20 Than any pretty mistress could engender,
Gives him the place of honor when they dine,
Delights to see him gorging like a swine,
Stuffs him with dainties till his guts distend,
And when he belches, cries "God bless you, friend!"
25 In short, he's mad; he worships him; he dotes,
His deeds he marvels at, his words he quotes,
Thinking each act a miracle, each word
Oracular as those that Moses heard.
Tartuffe, much pleased to find so easy a victim,
30 Has in a hundred ways beguiled and tricked him,
Milked him of money, and with his permission
Established here a sort of Inquisition.
Even Laurent, his lackey, dares to give
Us arrogant advice on how to live;
35 He sermonizes us in thundering tones
And confiscates our ribbons and colognes.
Last week he tore a kerchief into pieces
Because he found it pressed in a *Life of Jesus*:
He said it was a sin to juxtapose
40 Unholy vanities and holy prose.

SCENE III

ELMIRE, MARIANE, DAMIS, CLÉANTE, DORINE

ELMIRE: (*To* CLÉANTE.) You did well not to follow; she stood
          in the door
          And said *verbatim* all she'd said before.
          I saw my husband coming. I think I'd best
          Go upstairs now, and take a little rest.
5 CLÉANTE: I'll wait and greet him here; then I must go.
          I've really only time to say hello.
   DAMIS: Sound him about my sister's wedding, please.
          I think Tartuffe's against it, and that he's
          Been urging Father to withdraw his blessing.
10   As you well know, I'd find that most distressing.
          Unless my sister and Valère can marry,
          My hopes to wed *his* sister will miscarry,
          And I'm determined . . .
   DORINE: He's coming.

SCENE IV

ORGON, CLÉANTE, DORINE

ORGON: Ah, Brother, good-day.
CLÉANTE: Well, welcome back. I'm sorry I can't stay.
          How was the country? Blooming, I trust, and green?
ORGON: Excuse me, Brother; just one moment.

(*To* DORINE.)

                                            Dorine . . .

(*To* CLÉANTE.)

          To put my mind at rest, I always learn   5
          The household news the moment I return.

(*To* DORINE.)

          Has all been well, these two days I've been gone?
          How are the family? What's been going on?
DORINE: Your wife, two days ago, had a bad fever,
          And a fierce headache which refused to leave her.   10
ORGON: Ah. And Tartuffe?
DORINE: Tartuffe? Why, he's round and red,
          Bursting with health, and excellently fed.
ORGON: Poor fellow!
DORINE: That night, the mistress was unable
          To take a single bite at the dinner-table.
          Her headache-pains, she said, were simply hellish.   15
ORGON: Ah. And Tartuffe?
DORINE: He ate his meal with relish,
          And zealously devoured in her presence
          A leg of mutton and a brace of pheasants.
ORGON: Poor fellow!
DORINE: Well, the pains continued strong,
          And so she tossed and tossed the whole night long,   20
          Now icy-cold, now burning like a flame.
          We sat beside her bed till morning came.
ORGON: Ah. And Tartuffe?
DORINE: Why, having eaten, he rose
          And sought his room, already in a doze,
          Got into his warm bed, and snored away   25
          In perfect peace until the break of day.
ORGON: Poor fellow!
DORINE: After much ado, we talked her
          Into dispatching someone for the doctor.
          He bled her, and the fever quickly fell.
ORGON: Ah. And Tartuffe?   30
DORINE: He bore it very well.
          To keep his cheerfulness at any cost,
          And make up for the blood *Madame* had lost,
          He drank, at lunch, four beakers full of port.
ORGON: Poor fellow!
DORINE: Both are doing well, in short.
          I'll go and tell *Madame* that you've expressed   35
          Keen sympathy and anxious interest.

SCENE V

ORGON, CLÉANTE

CLÉANTE: That girl was laughing in your face, and though
          I've no wish to offend you, even so
          I'm bound to say that she had some excuse.
          How can you possibly be such a goose?
          Are you so dazed by this man's hocus-pocus   5
          That all the world, save him, is out of focus?
          You've given him clothing, shelter, food, and care;
          Why must you also . . .
ORGON: Brother, stop right there.
          You do not know the man of whom you speak.
CLÉANTE: I grant you that. But my judgment's not so weak   10
          That I can't tell, by his effect on others . . .

ORGON: Ah, when you meet him, you two will be like brothers!
   There's been no loftier soul since time began.
   He is a man who . . . a man who . . . an excellent man.
15   To keep his precepts is to be reborn,
   And view this dunghill of a world with scorn.
   Yes, thanks to him I'm a changed man indeed.
   Under his tutelage my soul's been freed
   From earthly loves, and every human tie:
20   My mother, children, brother, and wife could die,
   And I'd not feel a single moment's pain.
CLÉANTE: That's a fine sentiment, Brother; most humane.
ORGON: Oh, had you seen Tartuffe as I first knew him,
   Your heart, like mine, would have surrendered to him.
25   He used to come into our church each day
   And humbly kneel nearby, and start to pray.
   He'd draw the eyes of everybody there
   By the deep fervor of his heartfelt prayer;
   He'd sigh and weep, and sometimes with a sound
30   Of rapture he would bend and kiss the ground;
   And when I rose to go, he'd run before
   To offer me holy-water at the door.
   His serving-man, no less devout than he,
   Informed me of his master's poverty;
35   I gave him gifts, but in his humbleness
   He'd beg me every time to give him less.
   "Oh, that's too much," he'd cry, "too much by twice!
   I don't deserve it. The half, Sir, would suffice."
   And when I wouldn't take it back, he'd share
40   Half of it with the poor, right then and there.
   At length, Heaven prompted me to take him in
   To dwell with us, and free our souls from sin.
   He guides our lives, and to protect my honor
   Stays by my wife, and keeps an eye upon her;
45   He tells me whom she sees, and all she does,
   And seems more jealous than I ever was!
   And how austere he is! Why, he can detect
   A mortal sin where you would least suspect;
   In smallest trifles, he's extremely strict.
50   Last week, his conscience was severely pricked
   Because, while praying, he had caught a flea
   And killed it, so he felt, too wrathfully.
CLÉANTE: Good God, man! Have you lost your common sense—
   Or is this all some joke at my expense?
55   How can you stand there and in all sobriety . . .
ORGON: Brother, your language savors of impiety.
   Too much free-thinking's made your faith unsteady,
   And as I've warned you many times already,
   'Twill get you into trouble before you're through.
60 CLÉANTE: So I've been told before by dupes like you:
   Being blind, you'd have all others blind as well;
   The clear-eyed man you call an infidel,
   And he who sees through humbug and pretense
   Is charged, by you, with want of reverence.
65   Spare me your warnings, Brother; I have no fear
   Of speaking out, for you and Heaven to hear,
   Against affected zeal and pious knavery.
   There's true and false in piety, as in bravery,
   And just as those whose courage shines the most
70   In battle, are the least inclined to boast,
   So those whose hearts are truly pure and lowly
   Don't make a flashy show of being holy.
   There's a vast difference, so it seems to me,

Between true piety and hypocrisy:
How do you fail to see it, may I ask?   75
Is not a face quite different from a mask?
Cannot sincerity and cunning art,
Reality and semblance, be told apart?
Are scarecrows just like men, and do you hold
That a false coin is just as good as gold?   80
Ah, Brother, man's a strangely fashioned creature
Who seldom is content to follow Nature,
But recklessly pursues his inclination
Beyond the narrow bounds of moderation,
And often, by transgressing Reason's laws,   85
Perverts a lofty aim or noble cause.
A passing observation, but it applies.
ORGON: I see, dear Brother, that you're profoundly wise;
   You harbor all the insight of the age.
   You are our one clear mind, our only sage,   90
   The era's oracle, its Cato too,
   And all mankind are fools compared to you.
CLÉANTE: Brother, I don't pretend to be a sage,
   Nor have I all the wisdom of the age.
   There's just one insight I would dare to claim: 95
   I know that true and false are not the same;
   And just as there is nothing I more revere
   Than a soul whose faith is steadfast and sincere,
   Nothing that I more cherish and admire
   Than honest zeal and true religious fire,   100
   So there is nothing that I find more base
   Than specious piety's dishonest face—
   Than these bold mountebanks, these histrios
   Whose impious mummeries and hollow shows
   Exploit our love of Heaven, and make a jest   105
   Of all that men think holiest and best;
   These calculating souls who offer prayers
   Not to their Maker, but as public wares,
   And seek to buy respect and reputation
   With lifted eyes and sighs of exaltation;   110
   These charlatans, I say, whose pilgrim souls
   Proceed, by way of Heaven, toward earthly goals,
   Who weep and pray and swindle and extort,
   Who preach the monkish life, but haunt the court,
   Who make their zeal the partner of their vice—   115
   Such men are vengeful, sly, and cold as ice,
   And when there is an enemy to defame
   They cloak their spite in fair religion's name,
   Their private spleen and malice being made
   To seem a high and virtuous crusade,   120
   Until, to mankind's reverent applause,
   They crucify their foe in Heaven's cause.
   Such knaves are all too common; yet, for the wise,
   True piety isn't hard to recognize,
   And, happily, these present times provide us   125
   With bright examples to instruct and guide us.
   Consider Ariston and Périandre;
   Look at Oronte, Alcidamas, Clitandre;
   Their virtue is acknowledged; who could doubt it?
   But you won't hear them beat the drum about it.   130
   They're never ostentatious, never vain,
   And their religion's moderate and humane;
   It's not their way to criticize and chide:
   They think censoriousness a mark of pride,
   And therefore, letting others preach and rave,   135

They show, by deeds, how Christians should behave.
They think no evil of their fellow man,
But judge of him as kindly as they can.
They don't intrigue and wangle and conspire;
140 To lead a good life is their one desire;
The sinner wakes no rancorous hate in them;
It is the sin alone which they condemn;
Nor do they try to show a fiercer zeal
For Heaven's cause than Heaven itself could feel.
145 These men I honor, these men I advocate
As models for us all to emulate.
Your man is not their sort at all, I fear:
And, while your praise of him is quite sincere,
I think that you've been dreadfully deluded.
150 ORGON: Now then, dear Brother, is your speech concluded?
CLÉANTE: Why, yes.
ORGON: Your servant, Sir.

(*He turns to go.*)

CLÉANTE: No, Brother; wait.
There's one more matter. You agreed of late
That young Valère might have your daughter's hand.
ORGON: I did.
CLÉANTE: And set the date, I understand.
155 ORGON: Quite so.
CLÉANTE: You've now postponed it; is that true?
ORGON: No doubt.
CLÉANTE: The match no longer pleases you?
ORGON: Who knows?
CLÉANTE: D'you mean to go back on your word?
ORGON: I won't say that.
CLÉANTE: Has anything occurred
Which might entitle you to break your pledge?
160 ORGON: Perhaps.
CLÉANTE: Why must you hem, and haw, and hedge?
The boy asked me to sound you in this affair . . .
ORGON: It's been a pleasure..
CLÉANTE: But what shall I tell Valère?
ORGON: Whatever you like.
CLÉANTE: But what have you decided?
What are your plans?
ORGON: I plan, Sir, to be guided
165 By Heaven's will.
CLÉANTE: Come, Brother, don't talk rot.
You've given Valère your word; will you keep it, or not?
ORGON: Good day.
CLÉANTE: This looks like poor Valère's undoing;
I'll go and warn him that there's trouble brewing.

ACT TWO

SCENE I

ORGON, MARIANE

ORGON: Mariane.
MARIANE: Yes, Father?
ORGON: A word with you; come here.
MARIANE: What are you looking for?
ORGON: (*Peering into a small closet.*)
                         Eavesdroppers, dear.

I'm making sure we shan't be overheard.
Someone in there could catch our every word.
Ah, good, we're safe. Now, Mariane, my child,   5
You're a sweet girl who's tractable and mild,
Whom I hold dear, and think most highly of.
MARIANE: I'm deeply grateful, Father, for your love.
ORGON: That's well said, Daughter; and you can repay me
If, in all things, you'll cheerfully obey me.   10
MARIANE: To please you, Sir, is what delights me best.
ORGON: Good, good. Now, what d'you think of Tartuffe, our
    guest?
MARIANE: I, Sir?
ORGON: Yes. Weigh your answer; think it through.
MARIANE: Oh, dear. I'll say whatever you wish me to.
ORGON: That's wisely said, my Daughter. Say of him, then,   15
That he's the very worthiest of men,
And that you're fond of him, and would rejoice
In being his wife, if that should be my choice.
Well?
MARIANE: What?
ORGON: What's that?
MARIANE: I . . .
ORGON: Well?
MARIANE: Forgive me, pray.
ORGON: Did you not hear me?   20
MARIANE: Of *whom*, Sir, must I say
That I am fond of him, and would rejoice
In being his wife, if that should be your choice?
ORGON: Why, of Tartuffe.
MARIANE: But, Father, that's false, you know.
Why would you have me say what isn't so?
ORGON: Because I am resolved it shall be true.   25
That it's my wish should be enough for you.
MARIANE: You can't mean, Father . . .
ORGON: Yes, Tartuffe shall be
Allied by marriage to this family,
And he's to be your husband, is that clear?
It's a father's privilege . . .   30

SCENE II

DORINE, ORGON, MARIANE

ORGON: (*To DORINE.*)   What are you doing in here?
Is curiosity so fierce a passion
With you, that you must eavesdrop in this fashion?
DORINE: There's lately been a rumor going about—
Based on some hunch or chance remark, no doubt—   5
That you mean Mariane to wed Tartuffe.
I've laughed it off, of course, as just a spoof.
ORGON: You find it so incredible?
DORINE: Yes, I do.
I won't accept that story, even from you.
ORGON: Well, you'll believe it when the thing is done.   10
DORINE: Yes, yes, of course. Go on and have your fun.
ORGON: I've never been more serious in my life.
DORINE: Ha!
ORGON: Daughter, I mean it; you're to be his wife.
DORINE: No, don't believe your father; it's all a hoax.
ORGON: See here, young woman . . .   15
DORINE: Come, Sir, no more jokes;

You can't fool us.

ORGON: How dare you talk that way?

DORINE: All right, then: we believe you, sad to say.
But how a man like you, who looks so wise
And wears a moustache of such splendid size,

20   Can be so foolish as to . . .

ORGON: Silence, please!
My girl, you take too many liberties.
I'm master here, as you must not forget.

DORINE: Do let's discuss this calmly; don't be upset.
You can't be serious, Sir, about this plan.

25   What should that bigot want with Mariane?
Praying and fasting ought to keep him busy.
And then, in terms of wealth and rank, what is he?
Why should a man of property like you
Pick out a beggar son-in-law?

ORGON: That will do.

30   Speak of his poverty with reverence.
His is a pure and saintly indigence
Which far transcends all worldly pride and pelf.
He lost his fortune, as he says himself,
Because he cared for Heaven alone, and so

35   Was careless of his interests here below.
I mean to get him out of his present straits
And help him to recover his estates—
Which, in his part of the world, have no small fame.
Poor though he is, he's a gentleman just the same.

40   DORINE: Yes, so he tells us; and, Sir, it seems to me
Such pride goes very ill with piety.
A man whose spirit spurns this dungy earth
Ought not to brag of lands and noble birth;
Such worldly arrogance will hardly square

45   With meek devotion and the life of prayer.
. . . But this approach, I see, has drawn a blank;
Let's speak, then, of his person, not his rank.
Doesn't it seem to you a trifle grim
To give a girl like her to a man like him?

50   When two are so ill-suited, can't you see
What the sad consequences is bound to be?
A young girl's virtue is imperilled, Sir,
When such a marriage is imposed on her;
For if one's bridegroom isn't to one's taste,

55   It's hardly an inducement to be chaste,
And many a man with horns upon his brow
Has made his wife the thing that she is now.
It's hard to be a faithful wife, in short,
To certain husbands of a certain sort,

60   And he who gives his daughter to a man she hates
Must answer for her sins at Heaven's gates.
Think, Sir, before you play so risky a role.

ORGON: This servant-girl presumes to save my soul!

DORINE: You would do well to ponder what I've said.

65   ORGON: Daughter, we'll disregard this dunderhead.
Just trust your father's judgment. Oh, I'm aware
That I once promised you to young Valère;
But now I hear he gambles, which greatly shocks me;
What's more, I've doubts about his orthodoxy.

70   His visits to church, I note, are very few.

DORINE: Would you have him go at the same hours as you,
And kneel nearby, to be sure of being seen?

ORGON: I can dispense with such remarks, Dorine.

(*To* MARIANE.)

Tartuffe, however, is sure of Heaven's blessing,
And that's the only treasure worth possessing.   75
This match will bring you joys beyond all measure;
Your cup will overflow with every pleasure;
You two will interchange your faithful loves
Like two sweet cherubs, or two turtle-doves.
No harsh word shall be heard, no frown be seen,   80
And he shall make you happy as a queen.

DORINE: And she'll make him a cuckold, just wait and see.

ORGON: What language!

DORINE: Oh, he's a man of destiny;
He's *made* for horns, and what the stars demand
Your daughter's virtue surely can't withstand.   85

ORGON: Don't interrupt me further. Why can't you learn
That certain things are none of your concern?

DORINE: It's for your own sake that I interfere.

(*She repeatedly interrupts* ORGON *just as he is turning to speak to his daughter.*)

ORGON: Most kind of you. Now, hold your tongue, d'you
     hear?

DORINE: If I didn't love you . . .   90

ORGON: Spare me your affection.

DORINE: I'll love you, Sir, in spite of your objection.

ORGON: Blast!

DORINE: I can't bear, Sir, for your honor's sake,
To let you make this ludicrous mistake.

ORGON: You mean to go on talking?

DORINE: If I didn't protest
This sinful marriage, my conscience couldn't rest.   95

ORGON: If you don't hold your tongue, you little shrew . . .

DORINE: What, lost your temper? A pious man like you?

ORGON: Yes! Yes! You talk and talk. I'm maddened by it.
Once and for all, I tell you to be quiet.

DORINE: Well, I'll be quiet. But I'll be thinking hard.   100

ORGON: Think all you like, but you had better guard
That saucy tongue of yours, or I'll . . .

(*Turning back to* MARIANE.)

                              Now, child,
I've weighed this matter fully.

DORINE: (*Aside.*)   It drives me wild
That I can't speak.

(ORGON *turns his head, and she is silent.*)

ORGON: Tartuffe is no young dandy,
But, still, his person . . .   105

DORINE: (*Aside.*)   Is as sweet as candy.

ORGON: Is such that, even if you shouldn't care
For his other merits . . .

(*He turns and stands facing* DORINE, *arms crossed.*)

DORINE: (*Aside.*)   They'll make a lovely pair.
If I were she, no man would marry me
Against my inclination, and go scot-free.
He'd learn, before the wedding-day was over,   110
How readily a wife can find a lover.

ORGON: (*To* DORINE.) It seems you treat my orders as a joke.
DORINE: Why, what's the matter? 'Twas not to you I spoke.
ORGON: What *were* you doing?
DORINE: Talking to myself, that's all.
115 ORGON: Ah! (*Aside.*) One more bit of impudence and gall,
    And I shall give her a good slap in the face.

(*He puts himself in position to slap her;* DORINE, *whenever he
glances at her, stands immobile and silent.*)

    Daughter, you shall accept, and with good grace,
    The husband I've selected . . . Your wedding-day . . .

(*To* DORINE.)

    Why don't you talk to yourself?
DORINE: I've nothing to say.
120 ORGON: Come, just one word.
DORINE: No thank you, Sir. I pass.
    ORGON: Come, speak; I'm waiting.
DORINE: I'd not be such an ass.
    ORGON: (*Turning to* MARIANE.) In short, dear Daughter, I
        mean to be obeyed,
    And you must bow to the sound choice I've made.
DORINE: (*Moving away.*) I'd not wed such a monster, even in jest.

(ORGON *attempts to slap her, but misses.*)

125 ORGON: Daughter, that maid of yours is a thorough pest;
    She makes me sinfully annoyed and nettled.
    I can't speak further; my nerves are too unsettled.
    She's so upset me by her insolent talk,
    I'll calm myself by going for a walk.

SCENE III

DORINE, MARIANE

DORINE: (*Returning.*) Well, have you lost your tongue, girl?
    Must I play
    Your part, and say the lines you ought to say?
    Faced with a fate so hideous and absurd,
    Can you not utter one dissenting word?
5 MARIANE: What good would it do? A father's power is great.
DORINE: Resist him now, or it will be too late.
MARIANE: But . . .
DORINE: Tell him one cannot love at a father's whim;
    That you shall marry for yourself, not him;
    That since it's you who are to be the bride,
10   It's you, not he, who must be satisfied;
    And that if his Tartuffe is so sublime,
    He's free to marry him at any time.
MARIANE: I've bowed so long to Father's strict control,
    I couldn't oppose him now, to save my soul.
15 DORINE: Come, come, Mariane. Do listen to reason, won't you?
    Valère has asked your hand. Do you love him, or don't you?
MARIANE: Oh, how unjust of you! What can you mean
    By asking such a question, dear Dorine?
    You know the depth of my affection for him;
20   I've told you a hundred times how I adore him.
DORINE: I don't believe in everything I hear;
    Who knows if your professions were sincere?

MARIANE: They were, Dorine, and you do me wrong to
        doubt it;
    Heaven knows that I've been all too frank about it.
DORINE: You love him, then?   25
MARIANE: Oh, more than I can express.
DORINE: And he, I take it, cares for you no less?
MARIANE: I think so.
DORINE: And you both, with equal fire,
    Burn to be married?
MARIANE: That is our one desire.
DORINE: What of Tartuffe, then? What of your father's plan?
MARIANE: I'll kill myself, if I'm forced to wed that man.   30
DORINE: I hadn't thought of that recourse. How splendid!
    Just die, and all your troubles will be ended!
    A fine solution. Oh, it maddens me
    To hear you talk in that self-pitying key.
MARIANE: Dorine, how harsh you are! It's most unfair.   35
    You have no sympathy for my despair.
DORINE: I've none at all for people who talk drivel
    And, faced with difficulties, whine and snivel.
MARIANE: No doubt I'm timid, but it would be wrong . . .
DORINE: True love requires a heart that's firm and strong.   40
MARIANE: I'm strong in my affection for Valère,
    But coping with my father is his affair.
DORINE: But if your father's brain has grown so cracked
    Over his dear Tartuffe that he can retract
    His blessing, though your wedding-day was named,   45
    It's surely not Valère who's to be blamed.
MARIANE: If I defied my father, as you suggest,
    Would it not seem unmaidenly, at best?
    Shall I defend my love at the expense
    Of brazenness and disobedience?   50
    Shall I parade my heart's desires, and flaunt . . .
DORINE: No, I ask nothing of you. Clearly you want
    To be Madame Tartuffe, and I feel bound
    Not to oppose a wish so very sound.
    What right have I to criticize the match?   55
    Indeed, my dear, the man's a brilliant catch.
    Monsieur Tartuffe! Now, there's a man of weight!
    Yes, yes, Monsieur Tartuffe, I'm bound to state,
    Is quite a person; that's not to be denied;
    'Twill be no little thing to be his bride.   60
    The world already rings with his renown;
    He's a great noble—in his native town;
    His ears are red, he has a pink complexion,
    And all in all, he'll suit you to perfection.
MARIANE: Dear God!   65
DORINE: Oh, how triumphant you will feel
    At having caught a husband so ideal!
MARIANE: Oh, do stop teasing, and use your cleverness
    To get me out of this appalling mess.
    Advise me, and I'll do whatever you say.
DORINE: Ah no, a dutiful daughter must obey   70
    Her father, even if he weds her to an ape.
    You've a bright future; why struggle to escape?
    Tartuffe will take you back where his family lives,
    To a small town aswarm with relatives—
    Uncles and cousins whom you'll be charmed to meet.   75
    You'll be received at once by the elite,
    Calling upon the bailiff's wife, no less—
    Even, perhaps, upon the mayoress,

Who'll sit you down in the *best* kitchen chair.
80   Then, once a year, you'll dance at the village fair
To the drone of bagpipes—two of them, in fact—
And see a puppet-show, or an animal act.
Your husband . . .
MARIANE: Oh, you turn my blood to ice!
Stop torturing me, and give me your advice.
DORINE: (*Threatening to go.*)
85   Your servant, Madam.
MARIANE: Dorine, I beg of you . . .
DORINE: No, you deserve it; this marriage must go through.
MARIANE: Dorine!
DORINE: No.
MARIANE: Not Tartuffe! You know I think him . . .
DORINE: Tartuffe's your cup of tea, and you shall drink him.
MARIANE: I've always told you everything, and relied . . .
90 DORINE: No. You deserve to be tartuffified.
MARIANE: Well, since you mock me and refuse to care,
I'll henceforth seek my solace in despair:
Despair shall be my counsellor and friend,
And help me bring my sorrows to an end.

(*She starts to leave.*)

95 DORINE: There now, come back; my anger has subsided.
You do deserve some pity, I've decided.
MARIANE: Dorine, if Father makes me undergo
This dreadful martyrdom, I'll die, I know.
DORINE: Don't fret; it won't be difficult to discover
100   Some plan of action . . . But here's Valère, your lover.

SCENE IV

VALÈRE, MARIANE, DORINE

VALÈRE: Madam, I've just received some wondrous news
Regarding which I'd like to hear your views.
MARIANE: What news?
VALÈRE: You're marrying Tartuffe.
MARIANE: I find
That Father does have such a match in mind.
5 VALÈRE: Your father, Madam . . .
MARIANE: . . . has just this minute said
That it's Tartuffe he wishes me to wed.
VALÈRE: Can he be serious?
MARIANE: Oh, indeed he can;
He's clearly set his heart upon the plan.
VALÈRE: And what position do you propose to take,
10   Madam?
MARIANE: Why—I don't know.
VALÈRE: For heaven's sake—
You don't know?
MARIANE: No.
VALÈRE: Well, well!
MARIANE: Advise me, do.
VALÈRE: Marry the man. That's my advice to you.
MARIANE: That's your advice?
VALÈRE: Yes.
MARIANE: Truly?
VALÈRE: Oh, absolutely.
You couldn't choose more wisely, more astutely.
15 MARIANE: Thanks for this counsel; I'll follow it, of course.

VALÈRE: Do, do; I'm sure 'twill cost you no remorse.
MARIANE: To give it didn't cause your heart to break.
VALÈRE: I gave it, Madam, only for your sake.
MARIANE: And it's for your sake that I take it, Sir.
DORINE: (*Withdrawing to the rear of the stage.*) Let's see which 20
fool will prove the stubborner.
VALÈRE: So! I am nothing to you, and it was flat
Deception when you . . .
MARIANE: Please, enough of that.
You've told me plainly that I should agree
To wed the man my father's chosen for me,
And since you've deigned to counsel me so wisely, 25
I promise, Sir, to do as you advise me.
VALÈRE: Ah, no, 'twas not by me that you were swayed.
No, your decision was already made;
Though now, to save appearances, you protest
That you're betraying me at my behest. 30
MARIANE: Just as you say.
VALÈRE: Quite so. And I now see
That you were never truly in love with me.
MARIANE: Alas, you're free to think so if you choose.
VALÈRE: I choose to think so, and here's a bit of news:
You've spurned my hand, but I know where to turn 35
For kinder treatment, as you shall quickly learn.
MARIANE: I'm sure you do. Your noble qualities
Inspire affection . . .
VALÈRE: Forget my qualities, please.
They don't inspire you overmuch, I find.
But there's another lady I have in mind 40
Whose sweet and generous nature will not scorn
To compensate me for the loss I've borne.
MARIANE: I'm no great loss, and I'm sure that you'll transfer
Your heart quite painlessly from me to her.
VALÈRE: I'll do my best to take it in my stride. 45
The pain I feel at being cast aside.
Time and forgetfulness may put an end to.
Or if I can't forget, I shall pretend to.
No self-respecting person is expected
To go on loving once he's been rejected. 50
MARIANE: Now, that's a fine, high-minded sentiment.
VALÈRE: One to which any sane man would assent.
Would you prefer it if I pined away
In hopeless passion till my dying day?
Am I to yield you to a rival's arms 55
And not console myself with other charms?
MARIANE: Go then: console yourself; don't hesitate.
I wish you to; indeed, I cannot wait.
VALÈRE: You wish me to?
MARIANE: Yes.
VALÈRE: That's the final straw.
Madam, farewell. Your wish shall be my law. 60

(*He starts to leave, and then returns: this repeatedly.*)

MARIANE: Splendid.
VALÈRE: (*Coming back again.*)
    This breach, remember, is of your making;
It's you who've driven me to the step I'm taking.
MARIANE: Of course.
VALÈRE: (*Coming back again.*)
    Remember, too, that I am merely
Following your example.

MARIANE: I see that clearly.
65 VALÈRE: Enough. I'll go and do your bidding, then.
MARIANE: Good.
VALÈRE: (*Coming back again.*)
                    You shall never see my face again.
MARIANE: Excellent.
VALÈRE: (*Walking to the door, then turning about.*)
                    Yes?
MARIANE: What?
VALÈRE: What's that? What did you say?
MARIANE: Nothing. You're dreaming.
VALÈRE: Ah. Well, I'm on my way.
     Farewell, *Madame.*

(*He moves slowly away.*)

MARIANE: Farewell.
DORINE: (*To* MARIANE.)   If you ask me,
70   Both of you are as mad as mad can be.
     Do stop this nonsense, now. I've only let you
     Squabble so long to see where it would get you.
     Whoa there, Monsieure Valère!

(*She goes and seizes* VALÈRE *by the arm; he makes a great show of resistance.*)

VALÈRE: What's this, Dorine?
DORINE: Come here.
VALÈRE: No, no, my heart's too full of spleen.
75   Don't hold me back; her wish must be obeyed.
DORINE: Stop!
VALÈRE: It's too late now; my decision's made.
DORINE: Oh, pooh!
MARIANE: (*Aside.*)
                    He hates the sight of me, that's plain.
     I'll go, and so deliver him from pain.
DORINE: (*Leaving* VALÈRE, *running after* MARIANE.) And now
     you run away! Come back.
MARIANE: No, no.
80   Nothing you say will keep me here. Let go!
VALÈRE: (*Aside.*) She cannot bear my presence, I perceive.
     To spare her further torment, I shall leave.
DORINE: (*Leaving* MARIANE, *running after* VALÈRE.) Again!
     You'll not escape, Sir; don't you try it.
     Come here, you two. Stop fussing, and be quiet.

(*She takes* VALÈRE *by the hand, then* MARIANE, *and draws them together.*)

VALÈRE: (*To* DORINE.)
85   What do you want of me?
MARIANE: (*To* DORINE.)
                    What is the point of this?
DORINE: We're going to have a little armistice.

(*To* VALÈRE.)

     Now, weren't you silly to get so overheated?
VALÈRE: Didn't you see how badly I was treated?
DORINE: (*To* MARIANE.) Aren't you a simpleton, to have lost
     your head?
90 MARIANE: Didn't you hear the hateful things he said?

DORINE: (*To* VALÈRE.) You're both great fools. Her sole
     desire, Valère,
     Is to be yours in marriage. To that I'll swear.

(*To* MARIANE.)

     He loves you only, and he wants no wife
     But you, Mariane. On that I'll stake my life.
MARIANE: (*To* VALÈRE.) Then why you advised me so, I
     cannot see.   95
VALÈRE: (*To* MARIANE.) On such a question, why ask advice
     of *me?*
DORINE: Oh, you're impossible. Give me your hands, you two.

(*To* VALÈRE.)

     Yours first.
VALÈRE: (*Giving* DORINE *his hand.*)
                    But why?
DORINE: (*To* MARIANE.)
                    And now a hand from you.
MARIANE: (*Also giving* DORINE *her hand.*)
     What are you doing?
DORINE: There: a perfect fit.
     You suit each other better than you'll admit.   100

(VALÈRE *and* MARIANE *hold hands for some time without looking at each other.*)

VALÈRE: (*Turning toward* MARIANE.) Ah, come, don't be so
     haughty. Give a man
     A look of kindness, won't you, Mariane?

(MARIANE *turns toward* VALÈRE *and smiles.*)

DORINE: I tell you, lovers are completely mad!
VALÈRE: (*To* MARIANE.) Now come, confess that you were
     very bad
     To hurt my feelings as you did just now.   105
     I have a just complaint, you must allow.
MARIANE: *You* must allow that you were most unpleasant . . .
DORINE: Let's table that discussion for the present;
     Your father has a plan which must be stopped.
MARIANE: Advise us, then; what means must we adopt?   110
DORINE: We'll use all manner of means, and all at once.

(*To* MARIANE.)

     Your father's addled; he's acting like a dunce.
     Therefore you'd better humor the old fossil.
     Pretend to yield to him, be sweet and docile,
     And then postpone, as often as necessary,   115
     The day on which you have agreed to marry.
     You'll thus gain time, and time will turn the trick.
     Sometimes, for instance, you'll be taken sick,
     And that will seem good reason for delay;
     Or some bad omen will make you change the day—   120
     You'll dream of muddy water, or you'll pass
     A dead man's hearse, or break a looking-glass.
     If all else fails, no man can marry you
     Unless you take his ring and say "I do."
     But now, let's separate. If they should find   125
     Us talking here, our plot might be divined.

(*To* VALÈRE.)

      Go to your friends, and tell them what's occurred,
      And have them urge her father to keep his word.
      Meanwhile, we'll stir her brother into action,
130   And get Elmire, as well, to join our faction.
      Good-bye.
  VALÈRE: (*To* MARIANE.)
               Though each of us will do his best,
      It's your true heart on which my hopes shall rest.
  MARIANE: (*To* VALÈRE.) Regardless of what Father may decide,
      None but Valère shall claim me as his bride.
135 VALÈRE: Oh, how those words content me! Come what will …
  DORINE: Oh, lover, lovers! Their tongues are never still.
      Be off, now.
  VALÈRE: (*Turning to go, then turning back.*)
               One last word …
  DORINE: No time to chat:
      You leave by this door; and *you* leave by that.

(DORINE *pushes them, by the shoulders, toward opposing doors.*)

ACT THREE

SCENE I

DAMIS, DORINE

  DAMIS: May lightning strike me even as I speak,
      May all men call me cowardly and weak,
      If any fear or scruple holds me back
      From settling things, at once, with that great quack!
5 DORINE: Now, don't give way to violent emotion.
      Your father's merely talked about this notion,
      And words and deeds are far from being one.
      Much that is talked about is left undone.
  DAMIS: No, I must stop that scoundrel's machinations;
10   I'll go and tell him off; I'm out of patience.
  DORINE: Do calm down and be practical. I had rather
      My mistress dealt with him—and with your father.
      She has some influence with Tartuffe, I've noted.
      He hangs upon her words, seems most devoted,
15   And may, indeed, be smitten by her charm.
      Pray Heaven it's true! 'Twould do our cause no harm.
      She sent for him, just now, to sound him out
      On this affair you're so incensed about;
      She'll find out where he stands, and tell him, too,
20   What dreadful strife and trouble will ensue
      If he lends countenance to your father's plan.
      I couldn't get in to see him, but his man
      Says that he's almost finished with his prayers.
      Go, now. I'll catch him when he comes downstairs.
25 DAMIS: I want to hear this conference, and I will.
  DORINE: No, they must be alone.
  DAMIS: Oh, I'll keep still.
  DORINE: Not you. I know your temper. You'd start a brawl,
      And shout and stamp your foot and spoil it all.
      Go on.
  DAMIS: I won't; I have a perfect right …
30 DORINE: Lord, you're a nuisance! He's coming; get out of
      sight.

(DAMIS *conceals himself in a closet at the rear of the stage.*)

SCENE II

TARTUFFE, DORINE

  TARTUFFE: (*Observing* DORINE, *and calling to his manservant
      offstage.*)
      Hang up my hair-shirt, put my scourge in place,
      And pray, Laurent, for Heaven's perpetual grace.
      I'm going to the prison now, to share
      My last few coins with the poor wretches there.
  DORINE: (*Aside.*) Dear God, what affectation! What a fake! 5
  TARTUFFE: You wished to see me?
  DORINE: Yes …
  TARTUFFE: (*Taking a handkerchief from his pocket.*)
                    For mercy's sake,
      Please take this handkerchief, before you speak.
  DORINE: What?
  TARTUFFE: Cover that bosom, girl. The flesh is weak,
      And unclean thoughts are difficult to control.
      Such sights as that can undermine the soul. 10
  DORINE: Your soul, it seems, has very poor defenses,
      And flesh makes quite an impact on your senses.
      It's strange that you're so easily excited;
      My own desires are not so soon ignited,
      And if I saw you naked as a beast, 15
      Not all your hide would tempt me in the least.
  TARTUFFE: Girl, speak more modestly; unless you do,
      I shall be forced to take my leave of you.
  DORINE: Oh, no, it's I who must be on my way;
      I've just one little message to convey. 20
      Madame is coming down, and begs you, Sir,
      To wait and have a word or two with her.
  TARTUFFE: Gladly.
  DORINE: (*Aside.*) *That* had a softening effect!
      I think my guess about him was correct.
  TARTUFFE: Will she be long? 25
  DORINE: No: that's her step I hear.
      Ah, here she is, and I shall disappear.

SCENE III

ELMIRE, TARTUFFE

  TARTUFFE: May Heaven, whose infinite goodness we adore,
      Preserve your body and soul forevermore,
      And bless your days, and answer thus the plea
      Of one who is its humblest votary.
  ELMIRE: I thank you for that pious wish. But please, 5
      Do take a chair and let's be more at ease.

(*They sit down.*)

  TARTUFFE: I trust that you are once more well and strong?
  ELMIRE: Oh, yes: the fever didn't last for long.
  TARTUFFE: My prayers are too unworthy, I am sure,
      To have gained from Heaven this most gracious cure; 10
      But lately, Madam, my every supplication
      Has had for object your recuperation.
  ELMIRE: You shouldn't have troubled so. I don't deserve it.

TARTUFFE: Your health is priceless, Madam, and to preserve it
15   I'd gladly give my own, in all sincerity.
ELMIRE: Sir, you outdo us all in Christian charity.
      You've been most kind. I count myself your debtor.
TARTUFFE: 'Twas nothing, Madam. I long to serve you better.
ELMIRE: There's a private matter I'm anxious to discuss.
20   I'm glad there's no one here to hinder us.
TARTUFFE: I too am glad; it floods my heart with bliss
      To find myself alone with you like this.
      For just this chance I've prayed with all my power—
      But prayed in vain, until this happy hour.
25 ELMIRE: This won't take long, Sir, and I hope you'll be
      Entirely frank and unconstrained with me.
TARTUFFE: Indeed, there's nothing I had rather do
      Than bare my inmost heart and soul to you.
      First, let me say that what remarks I've made
30   About the constant visits you are paid
      Were prompted not by any mean emotion,
      But rather by a pure and deep devotion,
      A fervent zeal . . .
ELMIRE: No need for explanation.
      Your sole concern, I'm sure, was my salvation.
TARTUFFE: (*Taking* ELMIRE*'s hand and pressing her fingertips.*)
35   Quite so; and such great fervor do I feel . . .
ELMIRE: Ooh! Please! You're pinching!
TARTUFFE: 'Twas from excess of zeal.
      I never meant to cause you pain, I swear.
      I'd rather . . .

(*He places his hand on* ELMIRE*'s knee.*)

ELMIRE: What can your hand be doing there?
TARTUFFE: Feeling your gown; what soft, fine-woven stuff!
40 ELMIRE: Please, I'm extremely ticklish. That's enough.

(*She draws her chair away;* TARTUFFE *pulls his after her.*)

TARTUFFE: (*Fondling the lace collar of her gown.*) My, my, what
         lovely lacework on your dress!
      The workmanship's miraculous, no less.
      I've not seen anything to equal it.
ELMIRE: Yes, quite. But let's talk business for a bit.
45   They say my husband means to break his word
      And give his daughter to you, Sir. Had you heard?
TARTUFFE: He did once mention it. But I confess
      I dream of quite a different happiness.
      It's elsewhere, Madam, that my eyes discern
50   The promise of that bliss for which I yearn.
ELMIRE: I see: you care for nothing here below.
TARTUFFE: Ah, well—my heart's not made of stone, you know.
ELMIRE: All your desires mount heavenward, I'm sure,
      In scorn of all that's earthly and impure.
55 TARTUFFE: A love of heavenly beauty does not preclude
      A proper love for earthly pulchritude;
      Our senses are quite rightly captivated
      By perfect works our Maker has created.
      Some glory clings to all that Heaven has made;
60   In you, all Heaven's marvels are displayed.
      On that fair face, such beauties have been lavished,
      The eyes are dazzled and the heart is ravished;
      How could I look on you, O flawless creature,

And not adore the Author of all Nature,
Feeling a love both passionate and pure   65
For you, his triumph of self-portraiture?
At first, I trembled lest that love should be
A subtle snare that Hell had laid for me;
I vowed to flee the sight of you, eschewing
A rapture that might prove my soul's undoing;   70
But soon, fair being, I became aware
That my deep passion could be made to square
With rectitude, and with my bounden duty.
I thereupon surrendered to your beauty.
It is, I know, presumptuous on my part   75
To bring you this poor offering of my heart,
And it is not my merit, Heaven knows,
But your compassion on which my hopes repose.
You are my peace, my solace, my salvation;
On you depends my bliss—or desolation;   80
I bide your judgment and, as you think best,
I shall be either miserable or blest.
ELMIRE: Your declaration is most gallant, Sir,
      But don't you think it's out of character?
      You'd have done better to restrain your passion   85
      And think before you spoke in such a fashion.
      It ill becomes a pious man like you . . .
TARTUFFE: I may be pious, but I'm human too:
      With your celestial charms before his eyes,
      A man has not the power to be wise.   90
      I know such words sound strangely, coming from me,
      But I'm no angel, nor was meant to be,
      And if you blame my passion, you must needs
      Reproach as well the charms on which it feeds.
      Your loveliness I had no sooner seen   95
      Than you became my soul's unrivalled queen;
      Before your seraph glance, divinely sweet,
      My heart's defenses crumbled in defeat,
      And nothing fasting, prayer, or tears might do
      Could stay my spirit from adoring you.   100
      My eyes, my sighs have told you in the past
      What now my lips make bold to say at last,
      And if, in your great goodness, you will deign
      To look upon your slave, and ease his pain,—
      If, in compassion for my soul's distress,   105
      You'll stoop to comfort my unworthiness,
      I'll raise to you, in thanks for that sweet manna,
      An endless hymn, an infinite hosanna.
      With me, of course, there need be no anxiety.
      No fear of scandal or of notoriety.   110
      These young court gallants, whom all the ladies fancy,
      Are vain in speech, in action rash and chancy;
      When they succeed in love, the world soon knows it;
      No favor's granted them but they disclose it
      And by the looseness of their tongues profane   115
      The very altar where their hearts have lain.
      Men of my sort, however, love discreetly,
      And one may trust our reticence completely.
      My keen concern for my good name insures
      The absolute security of yours;   120
      In short, I offer you, my dear Elmire,
      Love without scandal, pleasure without fear.
ELMIRE: I've heard your well-turned speeches to the end,

And what you urge I clearly apprehend.
125   Aren't you afraid that I may take a notion
To tell my husband of your warm devotion,
And that, supposing he were duly told,
His feelings toward you might grow rather cold?
TARTUFFE: I know, dear lady, that your exceeding charity
130   Will lead your heart to pardon my temerity;
That you'll excuse my violent affection
As human weakness, human imperfection;
And that—O fairest!—you will bear in mind
That I'm but flesh and blood, and am not blind.
135   ELMIRE: Some women might do otherwise, perhaps,
But I shall be discreet about your lapse;
I'll tell my husband nothing of what's occurred
If, in return, you'll give your solemn word
To advocate as forcefully as you can
140   The marriage of Valère and Mariane,
Renouncing all desire to dispossess
Another of his rightful happiness,
And . . .

SCENE IV

DAMIS, ELMIRE, TARTUFFE

DAMIS: *(Emerging from the closet where he has been hiding.)*
              No! We'll not hush up this vile affair;
I heard it all inside that closet there,
Where Heaven, in order to confound the pride
Of this great rascal, prompted me to hide.
5   Ah, now I have my long-awaited chance
To punish his deceit and arrogance,
And give my father clear and shocking proof
Of the black character of his dear Tartuffe.
ELMIRE: Ah no, Damis; I'll be content if he
10   Will study to deserve my leniency.
I've promised silence—don't make me break my word;
To make a scandal would be too absurd.
Good wives laugh off such trifles, and forget them;
Why should they tell their husbands, and upset them?
15   DAMIS: You have your reasons for taking such a course,
And I have reasons, too, of equal force.
To spare him now would be insanely wrong.
I've swallowed my just wrath for far too long
And watched this insolent bigot bringing strife
20   And bitterness into our family life.
Too long he's meddled in my father's affairs,
Thwarting my marriage-hopes, and poor Valère's.
It's high time that my father was undeceived,
And now I've proof that can't be disbelieved—
25   Proof that was furnished me by Heaven above.
It's too good not to take advantage of.
This is my chance, and I deserve to lose it
If, for one moment, I hesitate to use it.
ELMIRE: Damis . . .
DAMIS: No, I must do what I think right.
30   Madam, my heart is bursting with delight,
And, say whatever you will, I'll not consent
To lose the sweet revenge on which I'm bent.
I'll settle matters without more ado;
And here, most opportunely, is my cue.

SCENE V

ORGON, DAMIS, TARTUFFE, ELMIRE

DAMIS: Father, I'm glad you've joined us. Let us advise you
Of some fresh news which doubtless will surprise you.
You've just now been repaid with interest
For all your loving-kindness to our guest.
He's proved his warm and grateful feelings toward you;   5
It's with a pair of horns he would reward you.
Yes, I surprised him with your wife, and heard
His whole adulterous offer, every word.
She, with her all too gentle disposition,
Would not have told you of his proposition;   10
But I shall not make terms with brazen lechery,
And feel that not to tell you would be treachery.
ELMIRE: And I hold that one's husband's peace of mind
Should not be spoilt by tattle of this kind.
One's honor doesn't require it: to be proficient   15
In keeping men at bay is quite sufficient.
These are my sentiments, and I wish, Damis,
That you had heeded me and held your peace.

SCENE VI

ORGON, DAMIS, TARTUFFE

ORGON: Can it be true, this dreadful thing I hear?
TARTUFFE: Yes, Brother, I'm a wicked man, I fear:
A wretched sinner, all depraved and twisted,
The greatest villain that has ever existed.
My life's one heap of crimes, which grows each minute;   5
There's naught but foulness and corruption in it;
And I perceive that Heaven, outraged by me,
Has chosen this occasion to mortify me.
Charge me with any deed you wish to name;
I'll not defend myself, but take the blame.   10
Believe what you are told, and drive Tartuffe
Like some base criminal from beneath your roof;
Yes, drive me hence, and with a parting curse:
I shan't protest, for I deserve far worse.
ORGON: *(To DAMIS.)* Ah, you deceitful boy, how dare you try   15
To stain his purity with so foul a lie?
DAMIS: What! Are you taken in by such a bluff?
Did you not hear . . . ?
ORGON: Enough, you rogue, enough!
TARTUFFE: Ah, Brother, let him speak: you're being unjust.
Believe his story; the boy deserves your trust.   20
Why, after all, should you have faith in me?
How can you know what I might do, or be?
Is it on my good actions that you base
Your favor? Do you trust my pious face?
Ah, no, don't be deceived by hollow shows;   25
I'm far, alas, from being what men suppose;
Though the world takes me for a man of worth,
I'm truly the most worthless man on earth.

(To DAMIS.)

Yes, my dear son, speak out now: call me the chief
Of sinners, a wretch, a murderer, a thief;   30

Load me with all the names men most abhor;
I'll not complain; I've earned them all, and more;
I'll kneel here while you pour them on my head
As a just punishment for the life I've led.
ORGON: (*To* TARTUFFE.)
35   This is too much, dear Brother.

(*To* DAMIS.)

                                        Have you no heart?
DAMIS: Are you so hoodwinked by this rascal's art. . . ?
ORGON: Be still, you monster.

(*To* TARTUFFE.)

                            Brother, I pray you, rise.

(*To* DAMIS.)

     Villain!
DAMIS: But . . .
ORGON: Silence!
DAMIS: Can't you realize. . . ?
ORGON: Just one word more, and I'll tear you limb from limb.
40   TARTUFFE: In God's name, Brother, don't be harsh with him.
     I'd rather far be tortured at the stake
     Than see him bear one scratch for my poor sake.
ORGON: (*To* DAMIS.)
     Ingrate!
TARTUFFE: If I must beg you, on bended knee,
     To pardon him . . .
ORGON: (*Falling to his knees, addressing* TARTUFFE.)
                         Such goodness cannot be!

(*To* DAMIS.)

45   Now, *there's* true charity!
DAMIS: What, you. . . ?
ORGON: Villain, be still!
     I know your motives; I know you wish him ill:
     Yes, all of you—wife, children, servants, all—
     Conspire against him and desire his fall,
     Employing every shameful trick you can
50   To alienate me from this saintly man.
     Ah, but the more you seek to drive him away,
     The more I'll do to keep him. Without delay,
     I'll spite this household and confound its pride
     By giving him my daughter as his bride.
55   DAMIS: You're going to force her to accept his hand?
ORGON: Yes, and this very night, d'you understand?
     I shall defy you all, and make it clear
     That I'm the one who gives the orders here.
     Come, wretch, kneel down and clasp his blessed feet,
60   And ask his pardon for your black deceit.
DAMIS: I ask that swindler's pardon? Why, I'd rather . . .
ORGON: So! You insult him, and defy your father!
     A stick! A stick! (*To* TARTUFFE.) No, no—release me, do.

(*To* DAMIS.)

     Out of my house this minute! Be off with you,
65   And never dare set foot in it again.
DAMIS: Well, I shall go, but . . .

ORGON: Well, go quickly, then.
     I disinherit you; an empty purse
     Is all you'll get from me—except my curse!

SCENE VII

ORGON, TARTUFFE

ORGON: How he blasphemed your goodness! What a son!
TARTUFFE: Forgive him, Lord, as I've already done.

(*To* ORGON.)

     You can't know how it hurts when someone tries
     To blacken me in my dear Brother's eyes.
ORGON: Ahh!   5
TARTUFFE: The mere thought of such ingratitude
     Plunges my soul into so dark a mood . . .
     Such horror grips my heart . . . I gasp for breath,
     And cannot speak, and feel myself near death.
ORGON:

(*He runs, in tears, to the door through which he has just driven his son.*)

     You blackguard! Why did I spare you? Why did I not
     Break you in little pieces on the spot?   10
     Compose yourself, and don't be hurt, dear friend.
TARTUFFE: These scenes, these dreadful quarrels, have got to
          end.
     I've much upset your household, and I perceive
     That the best thing will be for me to leave.
ORGON: What are you saying!   15
TARTUFFE: They're all against me here;
     They'd have you think me false and insincere.
ORGON: Ah, what of that? Have I ceased believing in you?
TARTUFFE: Their adverse talk will certainly continue,
     And charges which you now repudiate
     You may find credible at a later date.   20
ORGON: No, Brother, never.
TARTUFFE: Brother, a wife can sway
     Her husband's mind in many a subtle way.
ORGON: No, no.
TARTUFFE: To leave at once is the solution;
     Thus only can I end their persecution.
ORGON: No, no, I'll not allow it; you shall remain.   25
TARTUFFE: Ah, well; 'twill mean much martyrdom and pain,
     But if you wish it . . .
ORGON: Ah!
TARTUFFE: Enough; so be it.
     But one thing must be settled, as I see it.
     For your dear honor, and for our friendship's sake,
     There's one precaution I feel bound to take.   30
     I shall avoid your wife, and keep away . . .
ORGON: No, you shall not, whatever they may say.
     It pleases me to vex them, and for spite
     I'd have them see you with her day and night.
     What's more, I'm going to drive them to despair   35
     By making you my only son and heir;
     This very day, I'll give to you alone
     Clear deed and title to everything I own.
     A dear, good friend and son-in-law-to-be

40   Is more than wife, or child, or kin to me.
       Will you accept my offer, dearest son?
   TARTUFFE: In all things, let the will of Heaven be done.
   ORGON: Poor fellow! Come, we'll go draw up the deed.
       Then let them burst with disappointed greed!

ACT FOUR

SCENE I

CLÉANTE, TARTUFFE

   CLÉANTE: Yes, all the town's discussing it, and truly,
       Their comments do not flatter you unduly.
       I'm glad we've met, Sir, and I'll give my view
       Of this sad matter in a word or two.
5   As for who's guilty, that I shan't discuss;
       Let's say it was Damis who caused the fuss;
       Assuming, then, that you have been ill-used
       By young Damis, and groundlessly accused,
       Ought not a Christian to forgive, and ought
10   He not to stifle every vengeful thought?
       Should you stand by and watch a father make
       His only son an exile for your sake?
       Again I tell you frankly, be advised:
       The whole town, high and low, is scandalized;
15   This quarrel must be mended, and my advice is
       Not to push matters to a further crisis.
       No, sacrifice your wrath to God above,
       And help Damis regain his father's love.
   TARTUFFE: Alas, for my part I should take great joy
20   In doing so. I've nothing against the boy.
       I pardon all, I harbor no resentment;
       To serve him would afford me much contentment.
       But Heaven's interest will not have it so:
       If he comes back, then I shall have to go.
25   After his conduct—so extreme, so vicious—
       Our further intercourse would look suspicious.
       God knows what people would think! Why, they'd describe
       My goodness to him as a sort of bribe;
       They'd say that out of guilt I made pretense
30   Of loving-kindness and benevolence—
       That, fearing my accuser's tongue, I strove
       To buy his silence with a show of love.
   CLÉANTE: Your reasoning is badly warped and stretched,
       And these excuses, Sir, are most far-fetched.
35   Why put yourself in charge of Heaven's cause?
       Does Heaven need our help to enforce its laws?
       Leave vengeance to the Lord, Sir; while we live,
       Our duty's not to punish, but forgive;
       And what the Lord commands, we should obey
40   Without regard to what the world may say.
       What! Shall the fear of being misunderstood
       Prevent our doing what is right and good?
       No, no; let's simply do what Heaven ordains,
       And let no other thoughts perplex our brains.
45 TARTUFFE: Again, Sir, let me say that I've forgiven
       Damis, and thus obeyed the laws of Heaven;
       But I am not commanded by the Bible
       To live with one who smears my name with libel.
   CLÉANTE: Were you commanded, Sir, to indulge the whim

Of poor Orgon, and to encourage him   50
In suddenly transferring to your name
A large estate to which you have no claim?
TARTUFFE: 'Twould never occur to those who know me best
    To think I acted from self-interest.
    The treasures of this world I quite despise;   55
    Their specious glitter does not charm my eyes;
    And if I have resigned myself to taking
    The gift which my dear Brother insists on making,
    I do so only, as he well understands,
    Lest so much wealth fall into wicked hands,   60
    Lest those to whom it might descend in time
    Turn it to purposes of sin and crime,
    And not, as I shall do, make use of it.
    For Heaven's glory and mankind's benefit.
CLÉANTE: Forget these trumped-up fears. Your argument   65
    Is one the rightful heir might well resent;
    It is a moral burden to inherit
    Such wealth, but give Damis a chance to bear it.
    And would it not be worse to be accused
    Of swindling, than to see that wealth misused?   70
    I'm shocked that you allowed Orgon to broach
    This matter, and that you feel no self-reproach;
    Does true religion teach that lawful heirs
    May freely be deprived of what is theirs?
    And if the Lord has told you in your heart   75
    That you and young Damis must dwell apart,
    Would it not be the decent thing to beat
    A generous and honorable retreat,
    Rather than let the son of the house be sent,
    For your convenience, into banishment?   80
    Sir, if you wish to prove the honesty
    Of your intentions . . .
TARTUFFE: Sir, it is half-past three.
    I've certain pious duties to attend to,
    And hope my prompt departure won't offend you.
CLÉANTE: (*Alone.*) Damn.   85

SCENE II

ELMIRE, MARIANE, CLÉANTE, DORINE

DORINE: Stay, Sir, and help Mariane, for Heaven's sake!
    She's suffering so, I fear her heart will break.
    Her father's plan to marry her off tonight
    Has put the poor child in a desperate plight.
    I hear him coming. Let's stand together, now,   5
    And see if we can't change his mind, somehow,
    About this match we all deplore and fear.

SCENE III

ORGON, ELMIRE, MARIANE, CLÉANTE, DORINE

ORGON: Hah! Glad to find you all assembled here.

(*To* MARIANE.)

    This contract, child, contains your happiness,
    And what it says I think your heart can guess.
MARIANE: (*Falling to her knees.*) Sir, by that Heaven which
        sees me here distressed,

5   And by whatever else can move your breast,
       Do not employ a father's power, I pray you,
       To crush my heart and force it to obey you,
       Nor by your harsh commands oppress me so
       That I'll begrudge the duty which I owe—
10   And do not so embitter and enslave me
       That I shall hate the very life you gave me.
       If my sweet hopes must perish, if you refuse
       To give me to the one I've dared to choose,
       Spare me at least—I beg you, I implore—
15   The pain of wedding one whom I abhor;
       And do not, by a heartless use of force,
       Drive me to contemplate some desperate course.
   ORGON: (*Feeling himself touched by her.*) Be firm, my soul.
          No human weakness, now.
   MARIANE: I don't resent your love for him. Allow
20   Your heart free rein, Sir; give him your property,
       And if that's not enough, take mine from me;
       He's welcome to my money; take it, do,
       But don't, I pray, include my person too.
       Spare me, I beg you; and let me end the tale
25   Of my sad days behind a convent veil.
   ORGON: A convent! Hah! When crossed in their amours,
       All lovesick girls have the same thought as yours.
       Get up! The more you loathe the man, and dread him,
       The more ennobling it will be to wed him.
30   Marry Tartuffe, and mortify your flesh!
       Enough; don't start that whimpering afresh.
   DORINE: But why. . . ?
   ORGON: Be still, there. Speak when you're
          spoken to.
       Not one more bit of impudence out of you.
   CLÉANTE: If I may offer a word of counsel here . . .
35 ORGON: Brother, in counseling you have no peer;
       All your advice is forceful, sound, and clever;
       I don't propose to follow it, however.
   ELMIRE: (*To* ORGON.) I am amazed, and don't know what
          to say;
       Your blindness simply takes my breath away.
40   You are indeed bewitched, to take no warning
       From our account of what occurred this morning.
   ORGON: Madam, I know a few plain facts, and one
       Is that you're partial to my rascal son;
       Hence, when he sought to make Tartuffe the victim
45   Of a base lie, you dared not contradict him.
       Ah, but you underplayed your part, my pet;
       You should have looked more angry, more upset.
   ELMIRE: When men make overtures, must we reply
       With righteous anger and a battle-cry?
50   Must we turn back their amorous advances
       With sharp reproaches and with fiery glances?
       Myself, I find such offers merely amusing,
       And make no scenes and fusses in refusing;
       My taste is for good-natured rectitude,
55   And I dislike the savage sort of prude
       Who guards her virtue with her teeth and claws,
       And tears men's eyes out for the slightest cause;
       The Lord preserve me from such honor as that,
       Which bites and scratches like an alley-cat!
60   I've found that a polite and cool rebuff
       Discourages a lover quite enough.

ORGON: I know the facts, and I shall not be shaken.
ELMIRE: I marvel at your power to be mistaken.
       Would it, I wonder, carry weight with you
       If I could *show* you that our tale was true?   65
ORGON: Show me?
ELMIRE: Yes.
ORGON: Rot.
ELMIRE: Come, what if I found a way
       To make you see the facts as plain as day?
ORGON: Nonsense.
ELMIRE: Do answer me; don't be absurd.
       I'm not now asking you to trust our word.
       Suppose that from some hiding-place in here   70
       You learned the whole sad truth by eye and ear—
       What would you say of your good friend, after that?
ORGON: Why, I'd say . . . nothing, by Jehoshaphat!
       It can't be true.
ELMIRE: You've been too long deceived,
       And I'm quite tired of being disbelieved.   75
       Come now: let's put my statements to the test,
       And you shall see the truth made manifest.
ORGON: I'll take that challenge. Now do your uttermost.
       We'll see how you make good your empty boast.
ELMIRE: (*To* DORINE.)
       Send him to me.   80
DORINE: He's crafty; it may be hard
       To catch the cunning scoundrel off his guard.
ELMIRE: No, amorous men are gullible. Their conceit
       So blinds them that they're never hard to cheat.
       Have him come down. (*To* CLÉANTE *and* MARIANE.)
          Please leave us, for a bit.

SCENE IV

ELMIRE, ORGON

ELMIRE: Pull up this table, and get under it.
ORGON: What?
ELMIRE: It's essential that you be well-hidden.
ORGON: Why there?
ELMIRE: Oh, Heavens! Just do as you are bidden
       I have my plans; we'll soon see how they fare.
       Under the table, now; and once you're there,   5
       Take care that you are neither seen nor heard.
ORGON: Well, I'll indulge you, since I gave my word
       To see you through this infantile charade.
ELMIRE: Once it is over, you'll be glad we played.

(*To her husband, who is now under the table.*)

       I'm going to act quite strangely, now, and you   10
       Must not be shocked at anything I do.
       Whatever I may say, you must excuse
       As part of that deceit I'm forced to use.
       I shall employ sweet speeches in the task
       Of making that impostor drop his mask;   15
       I'll give encouragement to his bold desires,
       And furnish fuel to his amorous fires.
       Since it's for your sake, and for his destruction,
       That I shall seem to yield to his seduction,
       I'll gladly stop whenever you decide   20

That all your doubts are fully satisfied.
I'll count on you, as soon as you have seen
What sort of man he is, to intervene,
And not expose me to his odious lust
25 One moment longer than you feel you must.
Remember: you're to save me from my plight
Whenever . . . He's coming! Hush! Keep out of sight!

SCENE V

TARTUFFE, ELMIRE, ORGON

TARTUFFE: You wish to have a word with me, I'm told.
ELMIRE: Yes. I've a little secret to unfold.
    Before I speak, however, it would be wise
    To close that door, and look about for spies.

(TARTUFFE *goes to the door, closes it, and returns.*)

5   The very last thing that must happen now
    Is a repetition of this morning's row.
    I've never been so badly caught off guard.
    Oh, how I feared for you! You saw how hard
    I tried to make that troublesome Damis
10   Control his dreadful temper, and hold his peace.
    In my confusion, I didn't have the sense
    Simply to contradict his evidence;
    But as it happened, that was for the best,
    And all has worked out in our interest.
15   This storm has only bettered your position;
    My husband doesn't have the least suspicion,
    And now, in mockery of those who do,
    He bids me be continually with you.
    And that is why, quite fearless of reproof,
20   I now can be alone with my Tartuffe,
    And why my heart—perhaps too quick to yield—
    Feels free to let its passion be revealed.
    TARTUFFE: Madam, your words confuse me. Not long ago,
    You spoke in quite a different style, you know.
25 ELMIRE: Ah, Sir, if that refusal made you smart,
    It's little that you know of woman's heart,
    Or what that heart is trying to convey
    When it resists in such a feeble way!
    Always, at first, our modesty prevents
30   The frank avowal of tender sentiments;
    However high the passion which inflames us,
    Still, to confess its power somehow shames us.
    Thus we reluct, at first, yet in a tone
    Which tells you that our heart is overthrown,
35   That what our lips deny, our pulse confesses,
    And that, in time, all noes will turn to yesses.
    I fear my words are all too frank and free,
    And a poor proof of woman's modesty;
    But since I'm started, tell me, if you will—
40   Would I have tried to make Damis be still,
    Would I have listened, calm and unoffended,
    Until your lengthy offer of love was ended,
    And been so very mild in my reaction,
    Had your sweet words not given me satisfaction?
45   And when I tried to force you to undo

The marriage-plans my husband has in view,
What did my urgent pleading signify
If not that I admired you, and that I
Deplored the thought that someone else might own
Part of a heart I wished for mine alone?   50
TARTUFFE: Madam, no happiness is so complete
    As when, from lips we love, come words so sweet;
    Their nectar floods my every sense, and drains
    In honeyed rivulets through all my veins.
    To please you is my joy, my only goal;   55
    Your love is the restorer of my soul;
    And yet I must beg leave, now, to confess
    Some lingering doubts as to my happiness
    Might this not be a trick? Might not the catch
    Be that you wish me to break off the match   60
    With Mariane, and so have feigned to love me?
    I shan't quite trust your fond opinion of me
    Until the feelings you've expressed so sweetly
    Are demonstrated somewhat more concretely,
    And you have shown, by certain kind concessions,   65
    That I may put my faith in your professions.
ELMIRE:

(*She coughs, to warn her husband.*)

    Why be in such a hurry? Must my heart
    Exhaust its bounty at the very start?
    To make that sweet admission cost me dear,
    But you'll not be content, it would appear,   70
    Unless my store of favors is disbursed
    To the last farthing, and at the very first.
TARTUFFE: The less we merit, the less we dare to hope,
    And with our doubts, mere words can never cope.
    We trust no promised bliss till we receive it;   75
    Not till a joy is ours can we believe it.
    I, who so little merit your esteem,
    Can't credit this fulfillment of my dream,
    And shan't believe it, Madam, until I savor
    Some palpable assurance of your favor.   80
ELMIRE: My, how tyrannical your love can be,
    And how it flusters and perplexes me!
    How furiously you take one's heart in hand,
    And make your every wish a fierce command!
    Come, must you hound and harry me to death?   85
    Will you not give me time to catch my breath?
    Can it be right to press me with such force,
    Give me no quarter, show me no remorse,
    And take advantage, by your stern insistence,
    Of the fond feelings which weaken my resistance?   90
TARTUFFE: Well, if you look with favor upon my love,
    Why, then, begrudge me some clear proof thereof?
ELMIRE: But how can I consent without offense
    To Heaven, toward which you feel such reverence?
TARTUFFE: If Heaven is all that holds you back, don't worry.   95
    I can remove that hindrance in a hurry.
    Nothing of that sort need obstruct our path.
ELMIRE: Must one not be afraid of Heaven's wrath?
TARTUFFE: Madam, forget such fears, and be my pupil,
    And I shall teach you how to conquer scruple.   100
    Some joys, it's true, are wrong in Heaven's eyes;

Yet Heaven is not averse to compromise;
There is a science, lately formulated,
Whereby one's conscience may be liberated,
105   And any wrongful act you care to mention
May be redeemed by purity of intention.
I'll teach you, Madam, the secrets of that science;
Meanwhile, just place on me your full reliance.
Assuage my keen desires, and feel no dread:
110   The sin, if any, shall be on my head.

(ELMIRE *coughs, this time more loudly.*)

You've a bad cough.
ELMIRE: Yes, yes. It's bad indeed.
TARTUFFE: (*Producing a little paper bag.*) A bit of licorice may
     be what you need.
ELMIRE: No, I've a stubborn cold, it seems. I'm sure it
     Will take much more than licorice to cure it.
115   TARTUFFE: How aggravating.
ELMIRE: Oh, more than I can say.
TARTUFFE: If you're still troubled, think of things this way:
     No one shall know our joys, save us alone,
     And there's no evil till the act is known;
     It's scandal, Madam, which makes it an offense,
120   And it's no sin to sin in confidence.
ELMIRE: (*Having coughed once more.*) Well, clearly I must do as
     you require,
     And yield to your importunate desire.
     It is apparent, now, that nothing less
     Will satisfy you, and so I acquiesce.
125   To go so far is much against my will;
     I'm vexed that it should come to this; but still,
     Since you are so determined on it, since you
     Will not allow mere language to convince you,
     And since you ask for concrete evidence, I
130   See nothing for it, now, but to comply.
     If this is sinful, if I'm wrong to do it,
     So much the worse for him who drove me to it.
     The fault can surely not be charged to me.
TARTUFFE: Madam, the fault is mine, if fault there be,
135   And . . .
ELMIRE: Open the door a little, and peek out;
     I wouldn't want my husband poking about.
TARTUFFE: Why worry about the man? Each day he grows
     More gullible; one can lead him by the nose.
     To find us here would fill him with delight,
140   And if he saw the worst, he'd doubt his sight.
ELMIRE: Nevertheless, do step out for a minute
     Into the hall, and see that no one's in it.

SCENE VI

ORGON, ELMIRE

ORGON: (*Coming out from under the table.*) That man's a
     perfect monster, I must admit!
     I'm simply stunned. I can't get over it.
ELMIRE: What, coming out so soon? How premature!
     Get back in hiding, and wait until you're sure.
5   Stay till the end, and be convinced completely;

We mustn't stop till things are proved concretely.
ORGON: Hell never harbored anything so vicious!
ELMIRE: Tut, don't be hasty. Try to be judicious.
     Wait, and be certain that there's no mistake.
     No jumping to conclusions, for Heaven's sake!   10

(*She places* ORGON *behind her, as* TARTUFFE *re-enters.*)

SCENE VII

TARTUFFE, ELMIRE, ORGON

TARTUFFE: (*Not seeing* ORGON.) Madam, all things have
     worked out to perfection;
     I've given the neighboring rooms a full inspection;
     No one's about; and now I may at last . . .
ORGON: (*Intercepting him.*) Hold on, my passionate fellow,
     not so fast!
     I should advise a little more restraint.   5
     Well, so you thought you'd fool me, my dear saint!
     How soon you wearied of the saintly life—
     Wedding my daughter, and coveting my wife!
     I've long suspected you, and had a feeling
     That soon I'd catch you at your double-dealing.   10
     Just now, you've given me evidence galore;
     It's quite enough; I have no wish for more.
ELMIRE: (*To* TARTUFFE.) I'm sorry to have treated you so
     slyly.
     But circumstances forced me to be wily.
TARTUFFE: Brother, you can't think . . .   15
ORGON: No more talk from you;
     Just leave this household, without more ado.
TARTUFFE: What I intended . . .
ORGON: That seems fairly clear.
     Spare me your falsehoods and get out of here.
TARTUFFE: No, I'm the master, and you're the one to go!
     This house belongs to me, I'll have you know,   20
     And I shall show you that you can't hurt *me*
     By this contemptible conspiracy,
     That those who cross me know not what they do,
     And that I've means to expose and punish you,
     Avenge offended Heaven, and make you grieve   25
     That ever you dared order me to leave.

SCENE VIII

ELMIRE, ORGON

ELMIRE: What was the point of all that angry chatter?
ORGON: Dear God, I'm worried. This is no laughing
     matter.
ELMIRE: How so?
ORGON: I fear I understood his drift.
     I'm much disturbed about that deed of gift.
ELMIRE: You gave him . . . ?   5
ORGON: Yes, it's all been drawn and signed.
     But one thing more is weighing on my mind.
ELMIRE: What's that?
ORGON: I'll tell you; but first let's see if there's
     A certain strong-box in his room upstairs.

ACT FIVE

SCENE I

ORGON, CLÉANTE

CLÉANTE: Where are you going so fast?
ORGON: God knows!
CLÉANTE: Then wait;
    Let's have a conference, and deliberate
    On how this situation's to be met.
ORGON: That strong-box has me utterly upset;
5   This is the worst of many, many shocks.
CLÉANTE: Is there some fearful mystery in that box?
ORGON: My poor friend Argas brought that box to me
    With his own hands, in utmost secrecy;
    'Twas on the very morning of his flight.
10   It's full of papers which, if they came to light,
    Would ruin him—or such is my impression.
CLÉANTE: Then why did you let it out of your possession?
ORGON: Those papers vexed my conscience, and it seemed
      best
    To ask the counsel of my pious guest.
15   The cunning scoundrel got me to agree
    To leave the strong-box in his custody,
    So that, in case of an investigation,
    I could employ a slight equivocation
    And swear I didn't have it, and thereby,
20   At no expense to conscience, tell a lie.
CLÉANTE: It looks to me as if you're out on a limb.
    Trusting him with that box, and offering him
    That deed of gift, were actions of a kind
    Which scarcely indicate a prudent mind.
25   With two such weapons, he has the upper hand,
    And since you're vulnerable, as matters stand,
    You erred once more in bringing him to bay.
    You should have acted in some subtler way.
ORGON: Just think of it: behind that fervent face,
30   A heart so wicked, and a soul so base!
    I took him in, a hungry beggar, and then . . .
    Enough, by God! I'm through with pious men:
    Henceforth I'll hate the whole false brotherhood.
    And persecute them worse than Satan could.
35 CLÉANTE: Ah, there you go—extravagant as ever.
    Why can you not be rational? You never
    Manage to take the middle course, it seems,
    But jump, instead, between absurd extremes
    You've recognized your recent grave mistake
40   In falling victim to a pious fake;
    Now, to correct that error, must you embrace
    An even greater error in its place,
    And judge our worthy neighbors as a whole
    By what you've learned of one corrupted soul?
45   Come, just because one rascal made you swallow
    A show of zeal which turned out to be hollow,
    Shall you conclude that all men are deceivers,
    And that, today, there are no true believers?
    Let atheists make that foolish inference;
50   Learn to distinguish virtue from pretense,
    Be cautious in bestowing admiration,
    And cultivate a sober moderation.

    Don't humor fraud, but also don't asperse
    True piety; the latter fault is worse,
    And it is best to err, if err one must,   55
    As you have done, upon the side of trust.

SCENE II

DAMIS, ORGON, CLÉANTE

DAMIS: Father, I hear that scoundrel's uttered threats
    Against you; that he pridefully forgets
    How, in his need, he was befriended by you,
    And means to use your gifts to crucify you.
ORGON: It's true, my boy. I'm too distressed for tears.   5
DAMIS: Leave it to me, Sir; let me trim his ears.
    Faced with such insolence, we must not waver.
    I shall rejoice in doing you the favor
    Of cutting short his life, and your distress.
CLÉANTE: What a display of young hotheadedness!   10
    Do learn to moderate your fits of rage.
    In this just kingdom, this enlightened age,
    One does not settle things by violence.

SCENE III

MADAME PERNELLE, MARIANE, ELMIRE, DORINE, DAMIS, OR-
GON, CLÉANTE

MADAME PERNELLE: I hear strange tales of very strange
    events.
ORGON: Yes, strange events which these two eyes beheld.
    The man's ingratitude is unparalleled.
    I save a wretched pauper from starvation.
    House him, and treat him like a blood relation,   5
    Shower him every day with my largesse,
    Give him my daughter, and all that I possess;
    And meanwhile the unconscionable knave
    Tries to induce my wife to misbehave;
    And not content with such extreme rascality,   10
    Now threatens me with my own liberality,
    And aims, by taking base advantage of
    The gifts I gave him out of Christian love,
    To drive me from my house, a ruined man,
    And make me end a pauper, as he began.   15
DORINE: Poor fellow!
MADAME PERNELLE: No, my son, I'll never bring
    Myself to think him guilty of such a thing.
ORGON: How's that?
MADAME PERNELLE: The righteous always were maligned.
ORGON: Speak clearly, Mother. Say what's on your mind.
MADAME PERNELLE: I mean that I can smell a rat, my dear.   20
    You know how everybody hates him, here.
ORGON: That has no bearing on the case at all.
MADAME PERNELLE: I told you a hundred times, when you
    were small,
    That virtue in this world is hated ever;
    Malicious men may die, but malice never.   25
ORGON: No doubt that's true, but how does it apply?
MADAME PERNELLE: They've turned you against him by a
    clever lie.
ORGON: I've told you, I was there and saw it done.

MADAME PERNELLE: Ah, slanderers will stop at nothing, Son.

30 ORGON: Mother, I'll lose my temper . . . For the last time,
   I tell you I was witness to the crime.

MADAME PERNELLE: The tongues of spite are busy night and
      noon
   And to their venom no man is immune.

ORGON: You're talking nonsense. Can't you realize

35   I saw it; saw it; saw it with my eyes?
   Saw, do you understand me? Must I shout it
   Into your ears before you'll cease to doubt it?

MADAME PERNELLE: Appearances can deceive, my son.
      Dear me,
   We cannot always judge by what we see.

40 ORGON: Drat! Drat!

MADAME PERNELLE: One often interprets things awry;
   Good can seem evil to a suspicious eye.

ORGON: Was I to see his pawing at Elmire
   As an act of charity?

MADAME PERNELLE: Till his guilt is clear,
   A man deserves the benefit of the doubt.

45   You should have waited, to see how things turned out.

ORGON: Great God in Heaven, what more proof did I need?
   Was I to sit there, watching, until he'd . . .
   You drive me to the brink of impropriety.

MADAME PERNELLE: No, no, a man of such surpassing piety

50   Could not do such a thing. You cannot shake me.
   I don't believe it, and you shall not make me.

ORGON: You vex me so that, if you weren't my mother,
   I'd say to you . . . some dreadful thing or other.

DORINE: It's your turn now, Sir, not to be listened to;

55   You'd not trust us, and now she won't trust you.

CLÉANTE: My friends, we're wasting time which should be
      spent
   In facing up to our predicament.
   I fear that scoundrel's threats weren't made in sport.

DAMIS: Do you think he'd have the nerve to go to court?

60 ELMIRE: I'm sure he won't: they'd find it all too crude
   A case of swindling and ingratitude.

CLÉANTE: Don't be too sure. He won't be at a loss
   To give his claims a high and righteous gloss;
   And clever rogues with far less valid cause

65   Have trapped their victims in a web of laws.
   I say again that to antagonize
   A man so strongly armed was most unwise.

ORGON: I know it; but the man's appalling cheek
   Outraged me so, I couldn't control my pique.

70 CLÉANTE: I wish to Heaven that we could devise
   Some truce between you, or some compromise.

ELMIRE: If I had known what cards he held, I'd not
   Have roused his anger by my little plot.

ORGON: (*To* DORINE, *as* M. LOYAL *enters.*) What is that fellow
      looking for? Who is he?

75   Go talk to him—and tell him that I'm busy.

SCENE IV

MONSIEUR LOYAL, MADAME PERNELLE, ORGON, DAMIS, MARI-
ANE, DORINE, ELMIRE, CLÉANTE

MONSIEUR LOYAL: Good day, dear sister. Kindly let me see
   Your master.

DORINE: He's involved with company,
   And cannot be disturbed just now, I fear.

MONSIEUR LOYAL: I hate to intrude; but what has brought
      me here
   Will not disturb your master, in any event.   5
   Indeed, my news will make him most content.

DORINE: Your name?

MONSIEUR LOYAL: Just say that I bring greetings from
   Monsieur Tartuffe, on whose behalf I've come.

DORINE: (*To* ORGON.) Sir, he's a very gracious man, and bears
   A message from Tartuffe, which, he declares,   10
   Will make you most content.

CLÉANTE: Upon my word,
   I think this man had best be seen, and heard.

ORGON: Perhaps he has some settlement to suggest.
   How shall I treat him? What manner would be best?

CLÉANTE: Control your anger, and if he should mention   15
   Some fair adjustment, give him your full attention.

MONSIEUR LOYAL: Good health to you, good Sir. May
      Heaven confound
   Your enemies, and may your joys abound.

ORGON: (*Aside, to* CLÉANTE.) A gentle salutation: it confirms
   My guess that he is here to offer terms.   20

MONSIEUR LOYAL: I've always held your family most dear;
   I served your father, Sir, for many a year.

ORGON: Sir, I must ask your pardon; to my shame,
   I cannot now recall your face or name.

MONSIEUR LOYAL: Loyal's my name; I come from   25
      Normandy,
   And I'm a bailiff, in all modesty.
   For forty years, praise God, it's been my boast
   To serve with honor in that vital post,
   And I am here, Sir, if you will permit
   The liberty, to serve you with this writ . . .   30

ORGON: To—*what?*

MONSIEUR LOYAL: Now, please, Sir, let us have no friction:
   It's nothing but an order of eviction.
   You are to move your goods and family out
   And make way for new occupants, without
   Deferment or delay, and give the keys . . .   35

ORGON: I? Leave this house?

MONSIEUR LOYAL: Why yes, Sir, if you please.
   This house, Sir, from the cellar to the roof,
   Belongs now to the good Monsieur Tartuffe,
   And he is lord and master of your estate
   By virtue of a deed of present date,   40
   Drawn in due form, with clearest legal phrasing . . .

DAMIS: Your insolence is utterly amazing!

MONSIEUR LOYAL: Young man, my business here is not with
      you,
   But with your wise and temperate father, who,
   Like every worthy citizen, stands in awe   45
   Of justice, and would never obstruct the law.

ORGON: But . . .

MONSIEUR LOYAL: Not for a million, Sir, would you rebel
   Against authority; I know that well.
   You'll not make trouble, Sir, or interfere
   With the execution of my duties here.   50

DAMIS: Someone may execute a smart tattoo
   On that black jacket of yours, before you're through.

MONSIEUR LOYAL: Sir, bid your son be silent. I'd much regret

Having to mention such a nasty threat
55 Of violence, in writing my report.
DORINE: (*Aside.*) This man Loyal's a most disloyal sort!
MONSIEUR LOYAL: I love all men of upright character,
And when I agreed to serve these papers, Sir,
It was your feelings that I had in mind.
60 I couldn't bear to see the case assigned
To someone else, who might esteem you less
And so subject you to unpleasantness.
ORGON: What's more unpleasant than telling a man to leave
His house and home?
MONSIEUR LOYAL: You'd like a short reprieve?
65 If you desire, Sir, I shall not press you,
But wait until tomorrow to dispossess you.
Splendid. I'll come and spend the night here, then,
Most quietly, with half a score of men.
For form's sake, you might bring me, just before
70 You go to bed, the keys to the front door.
My men, I promise, will be on their best
Behavior, and will not disturb your rest.
But bright and early, Sir, you must be quick
And move out all your furniture, every stick;
75 The men I've chosen are both young and strong,
And with their help it shouldn't take you long.
In short, I'll make things pleasant and convenient,
And since I'm being so extremely lenient,
Please show me, Sir, a like consideration,
80 And give me your entire cooperation.
ORGON: (*Aside.*) I may be all but bankrupt, but I vow
I'd give a hundred louis, here and now,
Just for the pleasure of landing one good clout
Right on the end of that complacent snout.
85 CLÉANTE: Careful; don't make things worse.
DAMIS: My bootsole itches
To give that beggar a good kick in the breeches.
DORINE: Monsieur Loyal, I'd love to hear the whack
Of a stout stick across your fine broad back.
MONSIEUR LOYAL: Take care: a woman too may go to jail if
90 She uses threatening language to a bailiff.
CLÉANTE: Enough, enough, Sir. This must not go on.
Give me that paper, please, and then begone.
MONSIEUR LOYAL: Well, *au revoir.* God give you all good cheer!
ORGON: May God confound you, and him who sent you
here!

SCENE V

ORGON, CLÉANTE, MARIANE, ELMIRE, MADAME PERNELLE,
DORINE, DAMIS

ORGON: Now, Mother, was I right or not? This writ
Should change your notion of Tartuffe a bit.
Do you perceive his villainy at last?
MADAME PERNELLE: I'm thunderstruck. I'm utterly aghast.
5 DORINE: Oh, come, be fair. You mustn't take offense
At this new proof of his benevolence.
He's acting out of selfless love, I know.
Material things enslave the soul, and so
He kindly has arranged your liberation
10 From all that might endanger your salvation.
ORGON: Will you not ever hold your tongue, you dunce?

CLÉANTE: Come, you must take some action, and at once.
ELMIRE: Go tell the world of the low trick he's tried.
The deed of gift is surely nullified
By such behavior, and public rage will not   15
Permit the wretch to carry out his plot.

SCENE VI

VALÈRE, ORGON, CLÉANTE, ELMIRE, MARIANE, MADAME PER-
NELLE, DAMIS, DORINE

VALÈRE: Sir, though I hate to bring you more bad news,
Such is the danger that I cannot choose.
A friend who is extremely close to me
And knows my interest in your family
Has, for my sake, presumed to violate   5
The secrecy that's due to things of state,
And sends me word that you are in a plight
From which your one salvation lies in flight.
That scoundrel who's imposed upon you so
Denounced you to the King an hour ago   10
And, as supporting evidence, displayed
The strong-box of a certain renegade
Whose secret papers, so he testified,
You had disloyally agreed to hide.
I don't know just what charges may be pressed,   15
But there's a warrant out for your arrest;
Tartuffe has been instructed, furthermore,
To guide the arresting officer to your door.
CLÉANTE: He's clearly done this to facilitate
His seizure of your house and your estate.   20
ORGON: That man, I must say, is a vicious beast!
VALÈRE: Quick, Sir; you mustn't tarry in the least.
My carriage is outside, to take you hence;
This thousand louis should cover all expense.
Let's lose no time, or you shall be undone;   25
The sole defense, in this case, is to run.
I shall go with you all the way, and place you
In a safe refuge to which they'll never trace you.
ORGON: Alas, dear boy, I wish that I could show you
My gratitude for everything I owe you.   30
But now is not the time; I pray the Lord
That I may live to give you your reward.
Farewell, my dears; be careful . . .
CLÉANTE: Brother, hurry.
We shall take care of things; you needn't worry.

SCENE VII

The OFFICER, TARTUFFE, VALÈRE, ORGON, ELMIRE, MARIANE,
MADAME PERNELLE, DORINE, CLÉANTE, DAMIS

TARTUFFE: Gently, Sir, gently; stay right where you are.
No need for haste; your lodging isn't far.
You're off to prison, by order of the Prince.
ORGON: This is the crowning blow, you wretch; and since
It means my total ruin and defeat,   5
Your villainy is now at last complete.
TARTUFFE: You needn't try to provoke me; it's no use.
Those who serve Heaven must expect abuse.
CLÉANTE: You are indeed most patient, sweet, and blameless.

10 DORINE: How he exploits the name of Heaven! It's shameless.
TARTUFFE: Your taunts and mockeries are all for naught;
   To do my duty is my only thought.
MARIANE: Your love of duty is more meritorious,
   And what you've done is little short of glorious.
15 TARTUFFE: All deeds are glorious, Madam, which obey
   The sovereign prince who sent me here today.
ORGON: I rescued you when you were destitute,
   Have you forgotten that, you thankless brute?
TARTUFFE: No, no, I well remember everything;
20   But my first duty is to serve my King.
   That obligation is so paramount
   That other claims, beside it, do not count;
   And for it I would sacrifice my wife,
   My family, my friend, or my own life.
25 ELMIRE: Hypocrite!
DORINE: All that we most revere, he uses
   To cloak his plots and camouflage his ruses.
CLÉANTE: If it is true that you are animated
   By pure and loyal zeal, as you have stated,
   Why was this zeal not roused until you'd sought
30   To make Orgon a cuckold, and been caught?
   Why weren't you moved to give your evidence
   Until your outraged host had driven you hence?
   I shan't say that the gift of all his treasure
   Ought to have damped your zeal in any measure;
35   But if he is a traitor, as you declare,
   How could you condescend to be his heir?
TARTUFFE: (*To the* OFFICER.) Sir, spare me all this clamor; it's
     growing shrill.
   Please carry out your orders, if you will.
OFFICER: Yes, I've delayed too long, Sir. Thank you kindly.
40   You're just the proper person to remind me.
   Come, you are off to join the other boarders
   In the King's prison, according to his orders.
TARTUFFE: Who? I, Sir?
OFFICER: Yes.
TARTUFFE: To prison? This can't be true!
OFFICER: I owe an explanation, but not to you.

(*To* ORGON.)

45   Sir, all is well; rest easy, and be grateful.
   We serve a Prince to whom all sham is hateful,
   A Prince who sees into our inmost hearts,
   And can't be fooled by any trickster's arts.
   His royal soul, though generous and human,
50   Views all things with discernment and acumen;
   His sovereign reason is not lightly swayed,
   And all his judgments are discreetly weighed.
   He honors righteous men of every kind,
   And yet his zeal for virtue is not blind,

Nor does his love of piety numb his wits   55
And make him tolerant of hypocrites.
'Twas hardly likely that this man could cozen
A King who's foiled such liars by the dozen.
With one keen glance, the King perceived the whole
Perverseness and corruption of his soul,   60
And thus high Heaven's justice was displayed:
Betraying you, the rogue stood self-betrayed.
The King soon recognized Tartuffe as one
Notorious by another name, who'd done
So many vicious crimes that one could fill   65
Ten volumes with them, and be writing still.
But to be brief: our sovereign was appalled
By this man's treachery toward you, which he called
The last, worst villainy of a vile career,
And bade me follow the impostor here   70
To see how gross his impudence could be,
And force him to restore your property.
Your private papers, by the King's command,
I hereby seize and give into your hand.
The King, by royal order, invalidates   75
The deed which gave this rascal your estates,
And pardons, furthermore, your grave offense
In harboring an exile's documents.
By these decrees, our Prince rewards you for
Your loyal deeds in the late civil war,   80
And shows how heartfelt is his satisfaction
In recompensing any worthy action,
How much he prizes merit, and how he makes
More of men's virtues than of their mistakes.
DORINE: Heaven be praised!   85
MADAME PERNELLE: I breathe again, at last.
ELMIRE: We're safe.
MARIANE: I can't believe the danger's past.
ORGON: (*To* TARTUFFE.)
   Well, traitor, now you see . . .
CLÉANTE: Ah, Brother, please,
   Let's not descend to such indignities.
   Leave the poor wretch to his unhappy fate,
   And don't say anything to aggravate   90
   His present woes; but rather hope that he
   Will soon embrace an honest piety,
   And mend his ways, and by a true repentance
   Move our just King to moderate his sentence.
   Meanwhile, go kneel before your sovereign's throne   95
   And thank him for the mercies he has shown.
ORGON: Well said: let's go at once and, gladly kneeling,
   Express the gratitude which all are feeling.
   Then, when that first great duty has been done,
   We'll turn with pleasure to a second one,   100
   And give Valère, whose love has proven so true,
   The wedded happiness which is his due.

Jean Racine

Jean Racine (1639–1699) pursued a career closely connected with the dominant institutions of Parisian culture: the court, the church, and the stage. Racine's parents both died in his early childhood, and he was raised by his grandfather and enrolled at the school of the famous and controversial abbey at Port-Royal. Port-Royal was associated with an emphatically unworldly Catholic sect, the Jansenists, that was brutally suppressed in the seventeenth century. Racine's education at Port-Royal played a decisive role in his intellectual life and in the course of his career as a dramatist.

At Port-Royal, Racine perfected his study of Greek and Latin, considered a career in the church, and became ambitious for public success and for a life at court. By the early 1660s he had written several courtly poems—on Louis XIV's marriage, on his illness—that brought him to the attention of the established writers at court: Jean La Fontaine, Nicholas Boileau-Despréaux, and Molière. His first surviving play, *La Thebaïde,* was performed by Molière's company in 1664. In 1665, he gave *Alexandre* to Molière's company as well, but he was dissatisfied with Molière's production. He then gave the play to the rival company at the Hôtel de Bourgogne, where it played opposite Molière's production. Molière withdrew the play, and the hostilities between the two playwrights intensified in 1667 when Mademoiselle DuParc, Molière's leading lady—and possibly Racine's mistress—defected from Molière's company to create the title role in Racine's *Andromaque.* This play initiates the stunning series of Racine's major plays, *Britannicus* (1669), *Bérénice* (1670), *Bajazet* (1672), *Mithridate* (1673), *Iphigénie* (1674), and *Phèdre* (1677).

Phaedra (as it is known in English) is Racine's most celebrated play—and his most controversial. The play, originally entitled *Phèdre et Hippolyte,* opened in January 1677 at the Hôtel de Bourgogne, but Racine's enemies at court persuaded Jacques Pradon (1632–1698), a minor playwright, to open his own play about Phaedra at the Palais-Royal theater. The plays ran against one another, inviting comparison and criticism. After *Phaedra,* Racine married and retired from Paris to Port-Royal. He was also appointed to the coveted position of court historiographer and in 1684 wrote a history of Louis XIV's wars. Racine's two last plays, *Esther* (1688) and *Athalie* (1690), are religious dramas, written at the request of Louis's second wife, Madame de Maintenon, to be performed privately at St. Cyr, a girls' academy. Racine was buried at Port-Royal in 1699, and his remains were moved when the abbey was subsequently destroyed.

Throughout his career, Racine maintained contact with Port-Royal, responding to its criticism of his work in the theater, defending Port-Royal in ecclesiastical matters, and writing a history of the abbey. However, Port-Royal's most pervasive influence on Racine's drama has to do with the Jansenist sense of sin, of the impossibility of redeeming human action. Inspired by the writing of Cornelius Otto Jansen (1558–1638), the Jansenists held that mankind lives in a state of essential sin and corruption and summoned their followers to retire from the world in order to contemplate the moral abyss dividing mankind from God's mercy. What made Jansenism particularly threatening to the church in the seventeenth century was its resistance to the authority of Rome and its call for a solitary and contemplative clergy, which challenged the massive public and political role played by the church in the affairs of the French state. Racine's plays touch only metaphorically on the strictly religious issues surrounding the Jansenist debate, but they are directly concerned with the philosophical themes of Jansenist belief: the sense of unavoidable guilt, the tortuous process of introspection, and the desire to escape the world of action.

PHAEDRA

If René Descartes' famous *cogito ergo sum* ("I think, therefore I am") can be taken to represent a neoclassical concern for rational order, *Phaedra* might be said to illustrate a similar

One of Phaedra's celebrated tirades from Racine's *Phaedra,* produced by the American Repertory Theatre.

principle in terms of tragedy: "I feel, therefore I suffer." The play's main characters, particularly Hippolytus and Phaedra, feel and suffer precisely because reason fails to control the massive passions welling up within them, passions that deepen the rift between the corruption they feel and the uncorrupted ideals they never can achieve.

Racine's Jansenist beliefs have an indirect but profound impact in *Phaedra.* The world of the play is a world of unavoidable sin in which action leads inevitably to wrongdoing and catastrophe and in which flight is impossible. The characters define themselves according to fixed and unattainable ideals that are subverted by their irresistible, even criminal passions. Hippolytus pursues an ideal of heroic innocence and self-containment, violated in his own eyes by his love for Aricia. Theseus is consumed by his passion for power, conquest, and authority and feels betrayed when he believes that he has been usurped by his son. Phaedra's honor, and even her humanity, are shattered by her adulterous, incestuous desire for her stepson. The play's elegant compression concentrates the action exclusively on these characters; their confidants—Theramenes and Oenone—function largely as screens on which Racine projects the tempestuous passions of the main characters. Although the characters blame the gods for the desire they suffer, the destructive force of the characters' passions really rises from within. In the world of *Phaedra,* action is impossible and sin is inevitable. The characters are each destroyed by the monsters they become.

PREFACE
TRANSLATED BY R.C. KNIGHT

Here is another tragedy on a subject taken from Euripides. The action follows a somewhat different course, but I have enriched my play with everything in his that I considered most strikingly beautiful. Had I borrowed no more than the conception of Phaedra's character, I might say I owe him the most reasonable thing, perhaps, that I have given to the theatre. I am not surprised that this character was so successful in Euripides' time, and now again in our own, considering that it has every quality required by Aristotle in the tragic hero, and proper to arouse compassion and terror. For Phaedra is not altogether guilty, and not altogether innocent. She is drawn by her destiny, and the anger of the Gods, into an unlawful passion which she is the first to hold in horror. She makes every endeavour to overcome it. She chooses death rather than disclose it to anyone. And when forced to reveal it, she speaks of it with such shame and confusion as leave no doubt that her crime is rather a punishment from the Gods, than an impulse of her own will.

I have even taken pains to make her a little less odious than she is in the tragedies of antiquity, where she brings herself, unprompted, to accuse Hippolytus. I felt that a false testimony was something too base, too black, to put into the mouth of a Princess possessed otherwise of sentiments so noble and virtuous. Such baseness seemed to me more fitting to a Nurse, who might have more slave-like propensities; though even she only enters upon the lying accusation to save the life and honour of her mistress. If Phaedra acquiesces, it is because she is beside herself in the agitation of her thoughts, and the next moment she comes on with the intention of vindicating the guiltless and publishing the truth.

Hippolytus is accused, in Euripides and in Seneca, of actually raping his step-mother—*vim corpus tulit;* here, of no more than the intention. I desired to spare Theseus a sense of shame which might have made him less acceptable to my audience.

As for the figure of Hippolytus, I had read in ancient authors that Euripides was blamed for depicting him as a philosopher free of all imperfection—so that the death of the youthful Prince gave rise to far more indignation than pity. I felt I should give him a failing that might render him somewhat guilty towards his father, without detracting at all from that magnanimity which makes him spare Phaedra's honour and go to his doom without accusing her. By failing I mean his involuntary passion for Aricia, the daughter and the sister of his father's mortal enemies.

This Aricia is not a child of my invention. Virgil relates that Hippolytus married her, and she bore him a son, after Aesculapius had brought him back to life. And I have read too, in certain authors, that Hippolytus had married and brought into Italy an Athenian maiden of high birth, named Aricia, who had given her name to an Italian township.

I adduce these authorities, because I have most scrupulously endeavoured to keep close to the legend. I have even taken the history of Theseus just as it is in Plutarch.

It is this historian who mentions that the belief in Theseus' descent to the underworld to abduct Proserpine was occasioned by a journey he made into Epirus towards the source of the Acheron, where a King, whose wife Pirithous sought to carry off, held Theseus prisoner after putting Pirithous to death. Thus I have tried to retain the verisimilitude of history, and yet to lose none of the embellishments of fable, so rich in the stuff of poetry. And the rumour of Theseus' death, based on the legendary journey, gives rise to that declaration of Phaedra's love which proves one of the principal causes of her unhappy plight, and which she would never have dared utter while she believed her husband to be alive.

For the rest, I dare not yet assert this play to be in truth the best of my tragedies. I leave my readers, and time, to set its rightful price upon it. What I can assert is that I have composed none where virtue is shown to more advantage than here. The slightest faults are severely punished. The bare thought of crime is regarded with no less horror than crime itself. The failings of love are treated as real failings. The passions are offered to view only to show all the ravage they create. And vice is everywhere painted in such hues, that its hideous face may be recognised and loathed. Here is the proper aim for every man to keep in sight who works for the public. And this, above all, was the purpose of the earliest tragic poets. Their stage was a school where virtue was taught no less well than in the schools of the philosophers. Thus Aristotle consented to draw up the rules of the dramatic poem; Socrates, the sagest of the philosophers, thought it no shame to set his hand to the tragedies of Euripides. It were much to be desired that our works should be found as serious and as full of useful instruction as the pages of those poets. It might bring about a reconciliation between the tragic art and a number of persons, noted for their religion and learning, who have denounced it of late, but might well look upon it with less disfavour if authors cared as much to instruct as to entertain their audience, and carried out thereby the true purpose of tragedy.

Jean Racine
(1677)

PHAEDRA

Jean Racine

TRANSLATED BY R.C. KNIGHT

CHARACTERS

THESEUS, *son of Aegeus, King of Athens*
PHAEDRA, *wife of Theseus, daughter of Minos and Pasiphaë*
HIPPOLYTUS, *son of Theseus by Antiope, Queen of the Amazons*
ARICIA, *daughter of Pallas, descended from the ancient kings of Athens*
OENONE, *nurse and confidant of Phaedra*

THERAMENES, *tutor of Hippolytus*
ISMENE, *confidant to Aricia*
PANOPE, *one of Phaedra's women*
GUARDS

The scene is in Trozen, a town in the Peloponnese

ACT ONE

HIPPOLYTUS, THERAMENES

HIPPOLYTUS: My mind's made up: I sail, Theramenes.
    No more for me the tranquil days of Trozen,
    For in the mortal tempest of my doubts
    I am dishonoured if I linger here.
5   Six months ago my father sailed and left me
    Ignorant what befalls a head so cherished,
    Ignorant even where he may be hidden—
THERAMENES: So where will you go to look for him, my lord?
    Already, to relieve a fear I shared,
10   I have scoured the two seas that Corinth holds asunder.
    Demanded Theseus of the tribes that live
    Where Acheron drives down headlong into Hell,
    Searched Elis, skirted Taenarum, and even
    Traversed the waves where Icarus fell and perished.
15   What hope new-risen or what happier skies
    Will light you to his footsteps? Why, perhaps,
    Who knows, perhaps the King your father wishes
    Not to unveil the mystery of his venture,
    And while his peril fills your thought and ours,
20   Serene, weaving the latest of his loves,
    The hero waits to seize the unguarded moment—
HIPPOLYTUS: Stop, good Theramenes. You slander Theseus;
    There is a nobler cause for these delays;
    After the follies of forgotten youth
25   The wanderings of his inconstant heart
    Are fixed at length, and Phaedra fears no rival.
    So once more—I shall go where duty points
    And fly a land I cannot bear to see.
THERAMENES: But my lord, how long have you despised the presence
30   Of these calm fields, the pleasure of your childhood
    Whose solitude was dearer to you than
    The splendid stir of Athens and the court?
    What fear has banished you, or else what heartache?
HIPPOLYTUS: Those days are past. Pleasure and peace have vanished
35   Since first the Gods directed to our shore
    The child of Minos and Pasiphaë.
THERAMENES: I see: there is the cause, the hated presence—
    Phaedra, who came, your father's dangerous bride,
    Looked on you once, and by your prompt exile
40   Gave the first measure of her new-won power.

    But all that dogged hate and old aversion
    Has passed with time, passed or at least abated;
    And after all what danger lies in her,
    A woman dying, crying out for death?
    Stricken by ills that none can make her utter,   45
    Tired of her life, tired of the day that lights her,
    What can she do to you?
HIPPOLYTUS: I do not fear
    Anything her aversion could devise.
    I sail to fly another enemy,
    I do admit: I fly Aricia,   50
    The youngest and the last of all that house
    In fatal league against ours.
THERAMENES: You, my lord,
    Are turned against her too? But Pallas' daughter
    Surely had no part in her brothers' treason,
    And must you hate that unoffending grace?   55
HIPPOLYTUS: I would not fly her if I hated her.
THERAMENES: My lord, have I permission to interpret
    Your flight? Must I suppose that you are not
    The old implacable Hippolytus,
    The outlaw of Love's empire, he that vowed   60
    Never to wear the yoke his father wore?
    Can it be that a slighted and a smarting Goddess
    Will press you to the service of her shrine,
    Reduce you to the rank of common men
    And vindicate that father by your fate?   65
    Can it be love, my lord?
HIPPOLYTUS: How can you say it,
    My friend, that knew the childhood of my heart
    And all its growth in pride and fierce resolve?
    Shall I dishonour it, disown myself?
    First, as a babe, at an Amazonian breast   70
    I drank the resolution that astounds you,
    But once of age to look upon myself
    I wished to be no other than I was.
    Then, in the faithful service of your kindness
    As you rehearsed for me my father's story,   75
    Do you remember how my soul blazed up
    At each particular in the noble toils
    Of the intrepid hero, as we showed him
    Turning the world from thoughts of lost Alcides
    By monsters strangled and by brigands slain—   80
    Procrustes, Sinnis, Sciro, Cercyon
    And Epidaurus scattered with the limbs
    Of her gigantic tyrant, and the gore

Reeking from all Crete, of the Minotaur?
85 But when you told other ignobler feats—
A faith so cheaply pledged, and ever new,
Helen torn from a mother's arms in Sparta,
In Salamis the sighs of Periboea,
So many more than he can even name,
90 Victims too credulous of a lover's tongue;
What barren rocks heard Ariadne's sorrows;
How Phaedra, last and under happier auspice,
Followed him—then I wished the tale untold;
Often I urged you hasten and be done;
95 And would my wishes had redeemed from fame
That darker half of such a fair renown!
And now, by the spite of Heaven, shall I be
Degraded to the same indignity?
—Baseness beyond excuse, for those were frailties
100 Unseen amid a multitude of honours,
While not one trophy of a monster slain
Entitles me to fail as he has failed.
Even if I lost my freedom and my pride
How could I yield them to Aricia?
105 How could my disobedient sense forget
That which divides us irremovably?
The King denies her, denies her fallen brothers,
By violent laws, continuance of their line;
Their name must die for ever in her death,
110 Their guilty branch must bear no other fruit,
And till the tomb, submissive and sequestered,
The torch of wedlock must not burn for her.
Am I to oppose my father and his wrath?
Embrace her claims? and give a precedent
115 To treason? and embark my youth—
THERAMENES: My lord,
If the marked hour draws on, our arguments
Escape the notice of the incurious Heavens.
No. Theseus wished you blind, and gave you eyes;
His hate inflames the passion he forbids you,
120 And adds enchantment to his prisoner's charms.
But come, why look askance at honest love?
Why not make trial where its sweetness lies?
Why be enchained by vain and foolish scruples?
Who fears to stray that follows Hercules?
125 Many a stubborn heart has Venus bent—
Where would you be yourself and your defiance
Had chaste Antiope been as chaste as you
And never warmed to Theseus' flame? But why
Face out a falsehood with the pride of words?
130 Confess how things have changed: not now as once,
Aloof, intractable, we see you guide
A skimming chariot along the beaches
Or, adept in the mystery Neptune taught,
Break an unmastered courser to the curb;
135 Less often our halloos awake the forests;
Your eyes droop, weighted with a secret fire . . .
The case is clear—you are in love, in flame,
In torment, and you will not show your wound.
Is it Aricia?
HIPPOLYTUS: Theramenes,
140 I sail today, and go to find my father.
THERAMENES: Without an audience of Phaedra?
HIPPOLYTUS: No.

I will see her; I cannot well do less.
You may send word.—But what is the fresh misfortune
Disturbs her favorite Oenone so?

(*Enter* OENONE.)

OENONE: Alas, my lord, what grief can equal mine?   145
The Queen is near her utmost bourne of fate;
She that I watch by night and day unsleeping
Dies in my arms, and will not tell her sickness.
Her thought is all at variance with itself;
Her sick disquiet drives her from her bed   150
To see the light of day. But by her orders
No eye of man may see her suffering.
—Here she is.
HIPPOLYTUS: Very well; then I retire
Not to offend with this unwelcome face.

(*Exeunt* HIPPOLYTUS *and* THERAMENES.)

(*Enter* PHAEDRA.)

PHAEDRA: No more, for I can move no more, Oenone.   155
Let me rest; I am faint, my strength has left me.
My darkened eyes are dazzled by the light,
My wavering knees are weak beneath my weight.
Ah me!

(*Sits.*)

OENONE: High Gods, relent and see our tears!
PHAEDRA: These fripperies, these veils, they hang so heavy!   160
Whose was the unkind hand that piled and bound
These clustering locks that weigh upon my brow?
So feeble and so weary, all these things
Grieve me and weary me.
OENONE: How can we please you?
Yourself, repentant of your wicked thoughts,   165
You called in haste for clothes and ornaments;
Yourself you rallied your forgotten vigour,
You wanted to be out and see the sunlight.
Now you are here, my lady, and it seems
You loathe the very light that you desired.   170
PHAEDRA: Splendid begetter of a seed afflicted,
Father from whom my mother claimed her birth,
O blushing Sun ashamed of my despair,
Now, for the last time, I salute thy face.
OENONE: What, still possessed of such a fearful purpose?   175
Shall I for ever see you, turned from life,
Enact the mournful ritual of your death?
PHAEDRA: Oh give me the shadow of the forest glades!
Or let my eye piercing the glorious dust
Follow the wheeling chariot in the course!   180
OENONE: My lady?
PHAEDRA: Oh, I am mad. What have I said?
Where am I, where are my thoughts, my wandering mind?
Lost, for the Gods have taken it away.
My face is hot, Oenone, with my shame;
I cannot hide my guilty sufferings   185
And tears descend that I cannot restrain.
OENONE: Blush if you must, but blush to keep a silence

That doubles all the misery you suffer.
Rebellious to all tending, deaf to all pleas,
190 Will you unpitying allow your life
To flow away? What madness cuts it short?
What spell, what poison stanches up its course?
Thrice has the sky been muffled up in shade
And still is sleep a stranger to your eyes;
195 Thrice has the day displaced the gloom of night
And still you fast, and still your body wastes.
What dark temptation leads you on? What right
Invests you with the power to take your life—
Wronging the Gods from whom you draw your being,
200 Failing the husband who received your promise,
Failing still more your helpless children, doomed
To bitter lives of bondage; for reflect,
The very day that takes their mother from them
Rebuilds the hope of that Barbarian's child,
205 That arrogant enemy of you and yours,
The boy the Amazonian stranger bore,
Hippolytus—
PHAEDRA: O Gods!
OENONE: That charge strikes home!
PHAEDRA: Woman, how dare you name that name to me?
OENONE: Why, now your anger is most justly roused.
210 It heartens me that you should shrink to hear
That fatal name. Then live. For love, for duty,
Live; if you would not have the Scythian's son,
Bending your children to his hated yoke,
Lord it over the fairest blood of Greece
215 And of the Gods. But do not wait, each moment
You die. Rally, betimes, your prostrate vigour
While yet your almost spent and guttering life
Still glows, and may be kindled once again.
PHAEDRA: I have outlived the right to live already.
220 OENONE: Why, is there some remorse that feeds upon you?
What have you done that drives you so distraught?
Your hands have never dipped in guiltless blood?
PHAEDRA: I thank the Gods my hands are free of evil.
Would that my heart were innocent as they!
225 OENONE: What resolution, then, have you conceived
To terrify your heart before the time?
PHAEDRA: I have said enough. Ask me no more, have pity;
For if I die it is to keep within me
This dreadful secret.
OENONE: Keep it then, and die;
230 But other hands, not mine, will close your eyes.
Yours is a weak and flickering fire, but I
Will lose my spirit first among the dead;
There are many avenues and all unbarred;
An injured heart will soon perceive the best.—
235 Ungrateful mistress, when did I betray you?
Have you forgotten that these hands received you
When you were born? My children and my home,
I have left all for you: and all for this.
PHAEDRA: What do you think to gain by this beseeching?
240 You will shrink with horror if I break my silence.
OENONE: What can you tell me then more horrible
Than thus to see you die before my face?
PHAEDRA: And when you know my destiny and my weakness
Still I shall die, and only die more guilty.

OENONE: My lady, by the tears I shed for you,   245
By these your trembling knees I hold entwined,
Deliver me from deadly fear and doubt.
PHAEDRA: You wish it. Rise.
OENONE: Speak on, and I will listen.
PHAEDRA: How shall I tell, ye Gods, or where begin?
OENONE: Your fears are insults to my loyalty.   250
PHAEDRA: O deathless hate of Venus, fatal vengeance!
O heavy doom of love upon my mother!
OENONE: Forget, my lady. Hide that memory
And keep it from the ears of later times.
PHAEDRA: Love left thee dying, sweet sister Ariadne, 255
Lying forsaken by the alien waters.
OENONE: Let by, my lady. Must your mortal grief
Be vented on the dearest of your blood?
PHAEDRA: Of this doomed blood, I, by the will of Venus,
I perish now the last and most accursed.   260
OENONE: You love!
PHAEDRA: To madness and to ecstasy.
OENONE: Who?
PHAEDRA: There's the horror that surpasses horror:
I love . . . at the fatal name I blench and tremble—
I love . . .
OENONE: But who?
PHAEDRA: You know the Amazon's son,
The young Prince who endured so much, through me . . . 265
OENONE: O Gods! Hippolytus!
PHAEDRA: You spoke the name!
OENONE: Sweet Heavens! You have chilled my very blood.
O race polluted, hopeless, lamentable!
Woe worth the day that brought us to these shores!
Why did we venture?   270
PHAEDRA: It was long ago
And far from here. When first the rite of Hymen
Bound my obedience to the son of Aegeus—
My happiness, my peace then seemed so plain—
Careless in Athens stood my conqueror.
I saw and gazed, I blushed and paled again,   275
A blind amazement rose and blurred my mind;
My eyes were dim, my lips forgot to speak,
This, I knew, was the awful flame of Venus,
The fated torment of her chosen victims.
I tried to ward it off with prayers, with vows   280
And offerings, a temple built and decked,
And in the midst of endless sacrifices
I searched the entrails for my erring wisdom.
Weak drugs for irremediable love!
Even as my hand spilt incense at the shrine,   285
Even as my lips invoked the name of Venus
I prayed Hippolytus, my eyes beheld
Hippolytus, and while the altars steamed
I offered all to him I dared not name.
I fled him everywhere. O bitterness,   290
He looked upon me in his father's features.
At last, I turned upon myself. I forced
Myself to play the torturer against
The dreaded enemy I loved too well,
Put on the bride's abhorrence of the stepson,   295
Pleaded and pressed until I banished him
Out of his father's arms, his father's heart.

Once more I breathed; and after this, Oenone,
My life, serener, flowed in blameless ways,
300   Pleasing my husband, covering my pain,
Tending the fruits of his unhappy bed:
Foolish expedients! and inexorable
Hardness of destiny!—My lord himself
Brought me to Trozen and my banished foe.
305   The ancient wound gaped deep, and bled again.
No longer is it a secret flame that flickers
About my veins: headlong in onset Venus
Hangs on her quarry! I abhorred my guilt,
Life was a curse, my love a misery;
310   I looked for death to save my name, and bury
Far from the day the darkness of these fires.
I could not face your strivings and your tears.
Now you know all; and it is well, if you
Stand but aside from my advancing death.
315   Abstain at last from undeserved reproaches,
And leave your useless effort to revive
The embers of a fast-expiring fire.

(*Enter* PANOPE.)

PANOPE: I wish that I could hide the news, my lady,
That I am forced to bring you. Death has taken
320   Your lord, our most indomitable King;
And you alone are ignorant of your loss.
OENONE: What is this, Panope?
                                My lady's prayers
Will never now bring Theseus back to Athens,
And mariners that landed here today
325   Have told Hippolytus that he is dead.
PHAEDRA: Gods!
PANOPE: Athens wavers in the choice of masters.
One boasts allegiance to the Prince your son;
One, reckless of the statutes of the land,
Presumes to favour the Barbarian's child,
330   My lady; and they say a rank sedition
Proclaims Aricia and the blood of Pallas.
I knew it was my duty to report
Such perils. Hippolytus is ready now
To sail, and many fear if he arrives
335   In this tempestuous season, he will sway
A fickle multitude.
OENONE: Panope, thank you:
Your news was precious, and the Queen has heard.

(*Exit* PANOPE.)

OENONE: My lady, I had thrown away all pleadings,
All hope to move you, and my only thought
340   Was to attend you past the gates of the tomb,
But new disaster points new purposes,
An altered fortune, and an altered duty.
      Theseus is dead, and you are his successor,
My lady, with a son that looks to you—
345   A slave alone, and if you live a king.
No other will uphold his friendless quarrel,
No other wipe away his orphan tears;
Only in Heaven will his hearers be

The Gods, your judges and his ancestors.
Live then, in liberty from all misgiving;   350
Your love is now as unremarkable
As any love, for death disjoins the bond
That made its foulness and its infamy.
Henceforth the image of Hippolytus
Is not so terrible, and you may see him   355
With perfect guiltlessness. But what if now,
Despairing of a better understanding,
He takes command of these rebellious throngs?
Open his eyes, soften that stubborn heart.
Prince of these smiling coasts, his patrimony   360
Is here in Trozen, but he knows the laws;
He knows that they deliver to your son
The queenly ramparts that Minerva reared.
Your rightful enemy is also his:
Unite your forces to defeat Aricia.   365
PHAEDRA: So be it. I commit my way to you.
I will live, if I still have strength to live
And if a mother's love can even now
Revive in my wasted flesh the seeds of life.

ACT TWO

ARICIA, ISMENE

ARICIA: He asked to see me here? Hippolytus
Wanted to see me and to say farewell?
Are you quite certain? Is this true, Ismene?
ISMENE: Much more than this, now that the King is dead.
Prepare yourself, my lady; all the hearts   5
He kept at bay will cluster at your feet.
All Greece will bring its tributes to Aricia,
Enfranchised now and sovereign of her fortunes.
ARICIA: So then, Ismene, it is no idle talk.
And I have no oppressor and no foe?   10
ISMENE: My lady, none. The Heavens have relented
And Theseus walks among your fathers' shades.
ARICIA: What enterprise has brought him to his death?
Do they say?
ISMENE: Rumours wild and past belief;
Some say that in a lover's last adventure   15
The seas have claimed this ever-wandering husband;
Some say, and everywhere the news is sown,
That with Pirithous he went down to Hell,
Saw the Cocytus and the coasts of darkness
And stood alive amid a world of shadows,   20
But could not scale the gloomy track again
Nor pass the bourne men never pass but once.
ARICIA: Shall mortal men, before the last leave-taking,
Fathom those sullen deeps of the Departed?
What sorcery lured him to their awful shore?   25
ISMENE: My lady, he is dead, and you alone
Doubt it. All Athens grieves for him, all Trozen
Knows, and salutes Hippolytus for Prince.
And in these walls, despairing for her son,
Phaedra takes counsel of her trembling friends.   30
ARICIA: And you suppose that, kinder than his father,
Hippolytus will make my bondage sweeter
And pity me?

ISMENE: My lady, yes, I do.

ARICIA: But do you know the hard Hippolytus?

35   What makes you fancy he could feel compassion
        For me alone, who never felt for woman?
        He never joins our customary paths
        And hides himself wherever we are not.

ISMENE: Oh, I know all the legend of his coldness;

40   But when you met the proud Hippolytus
        I own the strangeness of his reputation
        Sharpened the edge of my curiosity.
        I saw a face at variance with the fable;
        At once your eyes disturbed that hard assurance

45   And his, avoiding you but all in vain,
        Melted at once, and could not turn away.
        His pride may yet refuse the name of lover
        But I'll believe his looks, and not his tongue.

ARICIA: Ah, sweet Ismene, how my heart devours

50   The unhoped-for comfort of a mere perhaps!
        You that have known me, did you once imagine
        This heart, the plaything of unpitying Fortune,
        Starved of all sustenance except despair,
        Would learn of love and the wild woes of love?

55   Child of Earth's child, last of a royal lineage,
        Sole remnant spared by battlefield and hatred,
        I lost the last proud blossoms of our tree,
        Six brothers, in the springtime of their year.
        The steel reaped all, and Earth's unwilling furrows

60   Drank her own blood, the blood of her Erechtheus.
        Since then you know what rigorous decree
        Defies all Greeks to lift their eyes to mine—
        For a mutinous ardour in the sister's breast
        Might wake the embers in her brothers' urns—

65   And you remember how I laughed to scorn
        Those calculations of the victor's fear;
        I held that love itself was slavery
        And even thanked the King for a constraint
        So fit and favourable to my distaste—

70   Then, yes; but then I had not seen his son.
        Not that subservient to the eye's seduction
        I love him for that beauty, that demeanour,
        Graces of partial Nature, gifts that he
        Ignores, if ever he has noticed them;

75   I see richer and dearer treasures in him—
        His father's parts, and not his father's failings;
        For I confess I love the manly pride
        That never bent under the yoke of Love.
        Phaedra was flattered by the doubtful glory

80   Of Theseus' courtly sighs: but I am prouder
        And will not stoop to share an easy prize
        Or occupy an undefended heart.
        No, but to shape a will as yet unbending,
        To waken pain in a proof-armoured bosom,

85   To lead a slave that never thought to serve,
        Vainly at war against the pleasing chain—
        There's a reward worthy of my ambition;
        Hercules was an easier adversary
        Who readily disarmed and quick to yield

90   Lent no such lustre to his overthrow.
        But dear Ismene, these are reckless dreams:
        Resistance there will be, and all too stubborn,
        And you shall hear me soon in humbler strain

Lament the coldness that I praise today.
He love, Hippolytus? What heights of fortune   95
Could ever bring him—

ISMENE: Only let him speak;
        He is coming now.

(*Enter* HIPPOLYTUS.)

HIPPOLYTUS: My lady, before I sail
        I owe you some account of my intentions.
        My father's dead: and well enough my fears
        Foretold the causes of his late homecoming—   100
        Death only, and the closure of his toils
        Could hold him from the world so long. The Gods
        At last abandon to the fatal Spinners
        Alcides' friend, his fellow, his successor.
        —I know your enmity will not forbid   105
        His son to assert these titles he has earned.—
        One hope alleviates my deepest sorrow,
        For I can end a harsh and long subjection:
        I here revoke laws that have caused me grief—
        The full bestowal of your life and hand   110
        Is yours alone, and in my patrimony,
        This Trozen, seat of Pittheus my grandfather,
        Which willingly defers his crown to me
        I leave you free and freer than its Prince.

ARICIA: Show me less kindness, I could bear it better. 115
        So much regard for me in my abjection
        Binds me, my lord, more even than you know,
        To that constraint you would have put away.

HIPPOLYTUS: Doubtful who stands the next in title, Athens
        Canvasses you, and me, and Phaedra's son.   120

ARICIA: Me, my lord?

HIPPOLYTUS: I have never shut my eyes
        To arrogant laws that seem to bar my claim:
        The Greeks reject me for my mother's race.
        But if my brother were my only rival
        I could appeal to certain natural laws   125
        And make them good against the law's caprice.
        I have a better reason to refrain:
        To you I yield, say rather I restore
        The seat, the sceptre, that your fathers held
        Of the illustrious mortal, son of Earth.   130
        It only passed to Aegeus by adoption;
        And next my father, Athens' second founder,
        Was hailed and crowned for all his benefits
        While your unhappy brothers lay forgotten.
        Now, Athens calls you home within her ramparts, 135
        Too long the ancient quarrel lives in pain,
        Too long your blood, that flowed along her fields,
        Reeks from the furrows where it found its birth.—
        Trozen I hold. As for the son of Phaedra
        The Cretan acres yield him rich retirement.   140
        Attica falls to you. I sail, to join
        My partisans with yours, in your support.

ARICIA: At every word more troubled and bewildered,
        Can I, or dare I, think I heard you rightly?
        Have I my senses, is this your intent?   145
        What God, my lord, what God inspired your mind?
        Rightly your glory sounds in every climate
        But reputation falls behind the truth.

What, will you cheat yourself on my behalf?
150   It was enough indeed to think that you
      Hated me not, and held a mind untainted
      By this long enmity—
HIPPOLYTUS: How could I hate you?
      Men may deride this proud unconquered heart
      But do they think a monster gave me birth?
155   What brutishness or what inveterate malice
      Could see your face and not forget its fury?
      And how should I withstand this subtle spell—
ARICIA: My lord! . . .
HIPPOLYTUS: My tongue has carried me too far;
      But wisdom fails and yields to the compulsion . . .
160   Now that my silence has been partly broken,
      My lady, I must needs go on, and speak
      The secret that my soul cannot contain.—
      Here stands a Prince of all men most unhappy,
      A monument of overthrown presumption;
165   I, long a truant from the law of love
      And long a mocker of its votaries,
      That stayed ashore watching the luckless sailor
      And never thought myself to fight the tempest,
      Levelled at last beneath the common fate
170   By strange tides I am borne far from myself.
      My wanton liberty has learnt to yield
      And in an instant this bold heart was tamed.
      Six months or nearly, in despair and shame,
      I've borne the arrow burning in my side;
175   Vainly I pit my strength against myself
      And you. I fly you where you are, and find you
      Where you are not; deep in the forest glade
      Your picture chases me; sunlight and shade
      Alike retrace your features and alike
180   Betray the fugitive that would be free,
      And I, for all my fruitless pains, look round
      To find Hippolytus, and know him not.
      My bow, my bounds, my spear, my chariot,
      Weary me. Neptune's lessons are forgotten;
185   Only my lamentations fill the groves,
      My stabled coursers know my voice no more.
         Perhaps this tale I tell of uncouth passion
      Will make you blush to own your handiwork:
      Wild terms, indeed, to offer up a heart!
190   And chains too fair for such a slave to claim!
      And yet my tribute therefore ranks the higher;
      Consider that I speak an unknown language
      And do not spurn these faltered words of love
      That you alone could teach Hippolytus.

(*Enter* THERAMENES.)

195   THERAMENES: Close on my heels, my lord, the Queen
         approaches
      Asking for you.
HIPPOLYTUS: For me?
THERAMENES: In what intention
      I do not know, but messengers have come
      Bidding you wait on her before you sail.
HIPPOLYTUS: The Queen? What should I say to her? Or she . . .
200   ARICIA: You cannot disappoint her wish, my lord.
      Even to such an enemy is due

Some sign of formal pity for her grief.
HIPPOLYTUS: So you go. And I sail. And still I know not
      Whether my worship has incensed my goddess,
      Whether this heart I leave in your two hands . . .   205
ARICIA: Sail, Prince. Pursue your noble purposes;
      Bring me the realm of Athens for dominion;
      Whatever gift you make shall be accepted,
      But that imperial, that unhoped-for state
      Is not the dearest of your offerings.   210

(*Exeunt* ARICIA *and* ISMENE.)

HIPPOLYTUS: Good friend, are all things ready?—But I hear
      The Queen.—Have all things ordered for our sailing.
      Send out the signal. Haste, command, return
      And free me from the burden of this meeting.

(*Exit* THERAMENES.)

(*Enter* PHAEDRA *and* OENONE.)

PHAEDRA: He is here. My blood retreats toward my heart.   215
      I see him, and forget what I should speak.
OENONE: Be mindful of the son that trusts in you!
PHAEDRA: They say that you are taking ship at once,
      My lord. I came to join my grief with yours,
      And with the story of a mother's terrors—   220
      My child is fatherless, and soon the day
      Will dawn that brings him to another deathbed;
      So fiercely even now assailed and threatened,
      Your strength alone can champion his weakness.—
      But deep within me throbs the preying thought   225
      That his complaint will never reach your ear,
      That through my child your angry justice soon
      Will strike a hated memory.
HIPPOLYTUS: My lady,
      So infamous a wish was never mine.
PHAEDRA: But you have seen me unremittingly   230
      Pursue your hate, my lord; and how could you
      Explore the bottom of my soul and read
      My secret there? I threw myself upon
      Your just resentment; I would not suffer you
      Within the self-same frontiers; privily   235
      And openly I waged my war, and set
      The width of seas between your path and mine.
      I even gave explicit orders not
      To breathe your name before my presence. Yet,
      If by the wrong the penalty were measured,   240
      If only hatred could achieve your hatred,
      Never did woman more deserve your tears,
      My lord, and less your enmity.
HIPPOLYTUS: No mother
      That watches for her children's interest
      Forgives the other children of her house;   245
      I know, my lady. Untoward mistrust
      Is always near when men have married twice.
      Another in your place would have conceived
      No less suspicion, and I might have suffered
      Deeper indignities.   250
PHAEDRA: Ah but, my lord,

The Gods—as now they stand my witnesses—
Deigned to release me from this general law.
How different are the thoughts that ravage me!
HIPPOLYTUS: It is too soon, my lady, for such thoughts;
255   The sunshine may still light your husband's eye,
And Heaven still may yield him to our prayers;
Neptune's his friend, and that high patronage
Will not in vain be canvassed by my father.
PHAEDRA: No man has twice explored the coasts of Death,
260   My lord. If Theseus touched the sullen shores
Vainly we look for Gods to send him home:
Harsh Acheron is grasping and holds fast
His prey. But did I say that he is dead?
He breathes again in you; I see the King,
265   See him, speak to him, thrill . . . My mind is wandering,
My lord, my madness speaks the thing it should not.
HIPPOLYTUS: This is a prodigy of loyal love:
Theseus is gone, yet lives within your mind
And fires the ardour of your loving heart.
270 PHAEDRA: Yes, Prince, for him indeed I yearn, I languish;
I love him—not the man that Hell has claimed,
The butterfly that every beauty lured,
The adulterous ravisher that would have stained
The God of Hell's own bed; but faithful, fine,
275   Sometimes aloof, and pure, gallant and gay,
Young, stealing every heart upon his road—
So do they character our Gods, and so
I see you now; those eyes, that voice, were his,
That generous red of virtue in your cheek,
280   When first he drove across the Cretan foam,
Meet meditation for the virgin dreams
Of Minos' daughters. You, where were you then
Among the flower and chivalry of Greece?
Where was Hippolytus—alas, too young—
285   The day his vessel grounded on our shore?
You would have slain the terror of the island,
The monster lapped in labyrinthine wiles;
Into your hand my sister would have thrust,
To unweave those riddling and deceitful ways,
290   The thread of life and death. But no, she would not—
Love would have found a readier wit in me,
And I, Prince, I, devoted and assured,
Could have resolved the devious Labyrinth;
What would I not have done for that sweet head?
295   How should a thread content your fearful lover?
Half-claimant in the peril that you claimed
I would have walked before you in the way,
And Phaedra, steadfast in the Labyrinth,
Would have returned again with you, or else
300   With you remained.
HIPPOLYTUS: Great Gods, what have you said?
My lady, can it be that you forget
That Theseus is my father, and your husband?
PHAEDRA: And why do you suppose I had forgotten,
Prince? Do I appear so careless of my honour?
305 HIPPOLYTUS: Forgive, my lady. I own, I blush to own
How blameless are the words that I reproved.
My shame can face it out no more before you,
So let me go . . .
PHAEDRA: Ah, leave your heartless lying.
You understand and you have heard enough.

Very well then, you shall learn what Phaedra is   310
And all her frenzy. Yes; I am in love.
But never think that even while I love you
I can absolve myself, or hide my face
From my own guiltiness. And never think
The wanton love that blurs my better mind   315
Grew with the treachery of my consent.
I, singled out for a celestial vengeance,
Unpitied victim, I abhor myself
More than you hate me. Let the Gods bear witness,
Those Gods that set the fire within my breast,   320
The fatal fire of my accursed line;
Those Gods whose majesty and might exulted
In the beguiling of a mortal's weakness.
Turn back the past yourself; how I have laboured
To seem malignant, savage, how I fostered   325
Your hatred as my ally in the fight.
Did I escape you? No, I banished you.
What fruit repaid these unavailing cares?
You loathed me more, I could not love you less;
Your suffering doubled the spell that binds me,   330
The withering ravage of my flames, my tears.
Your eyes can testify that this is true—
If for one moment they could bear my sight.
Why, this confession of my bitter secret,
My shameful secret, do you think that I   335
Have made it willingly? I came in fear
For one defenceless that I dare not fail:
I came to pray you not to hate my child.
Precarious resolution of a mind
Too full of what it loves! I came, and spoke   340
Of nothing else but you. So now, do justice.
Punish me for this execrable passion.
Approve yourself a hero's son indeed
And sweep this monster from the universe.
Dare Theseus' widow love Hippolytus?   345
Truly so vile a monster must not live.
My heart is here, and here is where you strike.
Eager to make atonement for its fault
I feel it swell and bound to meet your hand:
Strike. Or am I unworthy of your steel,   350
Or will your hate refuse so sweet a doom,
Or would ignoble blood sully your fingers?
Then hold your hand and let me have your sword.
Give it me.
OENONE: Stop, my lady. Heavenly powers!
What would you do? But somebody is coming: 355
Escape their sight, be quick, come back, or face
Inevitable shame.

(*Exeunt* PHAEDRA *and* OENONE. *Enter* THERAMENES.)

THERAMENES: Was that the Queen
Half dragged, half rushing out? What, my lord, what
Are all these marks of grief? You stand disarmed,
Dumb, pale . . .   360
HIPPOLYTUS: Come, let us go, Theramenes.
I cannot think of what I have heard and witnessed;
I cannot see myself without disgust.
Phaedra . . . No more, great Gods! Oblivion
Must shroud away the secret and the shame.

365 THERAMENES: If you would leave, my lord, the sail hangs
     ready;
    But Athens is beforehand with her answer:
    Her chiefs have counted votes among the tribes;
    Your brother has their suffrage, Phaedra wins.
HIPPOLYTUS: Phaedra!
THERAMENES: A herald of the will of Athens
370   Will bring the reins of state into her hands.
    Her son is King.
HIPPOLYTUS: Ye Gods that know her heart,
    Is it her righteousness you would repay?
THERAMENES: And now dark rumours speak again of
     Theseus:
    Some tell that men have seen him in Epirus
375   Alive; though, I, who went to seek him there,
    I know full well, my lord . . .
HIPPOLYTUS: It may be so.
    But I would hear whatever rumour tells,
    Consult this public cry, divine its sources.
    If it be worthless to delay our journey
380   We sail; and cost the venture what it will
    I'll save the sceptre for a worthy hand.

ACT THREE

PHAEDRA, OENONE

PHAEDRA: Send them away, these heralds and these honours.
    Have they a balm to ease a tortured mind?
    Unkind, is Phaedra fit for public show?
    Rather conceal me, for my secret's out:
5   Intemperate desire has seen the light,
    And what these lips had never thought to utter
    He heard. Immortal Gods! and how he listened,
    How long he parried, how deviously he turned
    To baffle the approaches of my speech!
10   How visibly he yearned to leave my presence!
    How painfully his blush revived my shame!
    Why did you disappoint me of my death?
    Ah, when his weapon pointed at my breast
    Did he blench? Did he stir to snatch it back?
15   Enough for him my fingers at the hilt
    And in his heartless reckoning it was vile,
    Profaned, a blade that would defile his hand.
OENONE: And so complaining, dwelling on your sorrow,
    You feed a fire that wisdom would have quenched.
20   Should not a worthy child of Minos' blood
    Look for serenity in nobler tasks,
    Fly from a struggle that you cannot win,
    Learn to assume the guidance of a kingdom
    And be a Queen?
PHAEDRA: Queen, I? And hold command,
25   While my own senses rage in mutiny,
    While in my soul wisdom has lost dominion,
    While shame and slavery has bowed my head,
    And death is waiting?
OENONE: Fly.
PHAEDRA: I cannot leave him.
OENONE: You drove him away, and cannot go from him?
30 PHAEDRA: I cannot now. He has seen my raging soul,
    Seen me transgress the rigid pale of virtue;

    Before those stony eyes I have poured out
    My shame, and now, unbidden, secret hope
    Has slipped into my breast. Ay, you yourself,
    Rallying the wasted forces of my life,   35
    The parting spirit ready on my lips,
    Wooed me from death with false and soothing words;
    You half persuaded me that I might love.
OENONE: Ah, call me guilty, or call me innocent,
    I would do worse if anything could save you.   40
    But, if resentment ever stung your mind,
    Can you forget the blow of his rebuff,
    The insolence, the icy cruelty
    That eyed you all but prostrate at his feet,
    The arrogant disdain?—how odious   45
    Had Phaedra only seen him as I saw!
PHAEDRA: What if he lost this arrogance, Oenone?
    He has the harshness of his forest ways,
    And in his arduous life Hippolytus
    Has never heard of love until today.   50
    What if surprise had robbed him of his speech?
    What if we blamed him more than he deserved?
OENONE: He was conceived in a Barbarian's womb.
PHAEDRA: Barbarian, Scythian, still she learned to love.
OENONE: He hates our sex with firm and deadly hate.   55
PHAEDRA: So I shall never fear another woman.
    Enough: such counsels had their season once;
    My passion now commands you, and not my reason.
    Though hard and inaccessible to love,
    Another side lies weaker to attack—   60
    The sweets of empire tempted him, I think;
    Athens allured him more than he could hide.
    His ships already turned their prows to sea
    With canvas rigged and offered to the breeze.
    Find him, Oenone, find the ambitious boy,   65
    Show him the glitter of the Athenian crown,
    Bid him assume the diadem and the glory;
    I only ask to lay it on his brow,
    Into his hand descends authority
    I cannot grasp, and he shall teach my son   70
    The science of command—even he might
    Look as a father on him. In his power
    I now resign the orphan and the mother.
    Incline his heart by any means you know,
    Use—do not blush—the voice of supplication,   75
    I sanction all. I have no other hope;
    Go, till you come again I cannot tell
    What else I have to do.

(*Exit* OENONE.)

PHAEDRA: (*Alone.*)   O Thou, that knowest
    How deep in shame my soul is overwhelmed,
    Venus, O Venus unappeasable,   80
    This is the consummation of thy hatred.
    These must be the limits of thy cruelty.
    Thy triumph is entire, each shot has told.
    Art thou not sated yet with victory?
    Find tougher quarry then: Hippolytus   85
    Rejects thy deity, derides thy wrath,
    He never bent the knee before thy altar;
    Thy name seems hideous in his stubborn ears,

Goddess, avenge; our grievances are one!
90   Teach him to love . . . Oenone, here so soon?
        I am rejected then, you were not heard.

(*Enter* OENONE.)

OENONE: Stifle the memory of a hopeless passion,
        My lady; summon up your earlier virtue.
        The King's not dead, and you will see him soon.
95   Theseus has landed. He is coming here.
        The populace are rushing to salute him,
        And as I passed obedient to your mission
        Unending cheers rose up on every hand—
PHAEDRA: He is not dead. Nothing else signifies,
100   Oenone. I revealed a lawless love
        That wounds him in his honour. And he lives.
        What needs there more?
OENONE: But yet—
PHAEDRA: I told you so;
        And you would not. Foreboding and remorse
        Have yielded to your tears. Only this morning
105   My death was not unworthy to be pitied:
        I took your counsel, and I die disgraced.
OENONE: Die?
PHAEDRA: Righteous Gods! The things this day has seen!
        And now, as I meet my husband and his son
        I know this witness of adulterous passion
110   Studies my countenance before his father—
        My heart heavy with sighs he would not hear,
        My eyelids drenched with tears that he despised.
        Do you think his tenderness for Theseus' honour
        Would hide away the memory of my falsehood,
115   My treason to a father and a King?
        Will he repress the loathing I inspire?
        What if he did? I know my treachery,
        Oenone. And if there are intrepid women
        Who taste a flawless quietude in crime
120   And force their countenance to show no shame,
        I am not such. My misdeeds rise before me;
        And even now these over-arching walls
        Seem full of tongues, impatient to accuse me
        Before my husband, and proclaim his wrong.
125   Oh for a death, and surcease from this anguish!
        Is life so precious and so hard to leave?
        Need the tormented hesitate to die?
        Only I fear the name I leave behind—
        The legacy of horror for my children,
130   Whose blood, the very blood of Jupiter,
        Should swell their hearts with pride: now they must lift
        The burden of a mother's infamy.
        My soul foretells that malice, soon or late,
        Will throw my black reproach into their faces,
135   And crushed so cruelly they may never dare
        To look with level eyes upon their kind.
OENONE: It is most true. They both are to be pitied,
        And never sorrow was foretold more surely.
        But why abandon them to the ordeal?
140   Why be the witness that betrays your cause?
        For all is lost; and all the world will judge
        That Phaedra knows her guilt, and dare not wait

The awful presence of an outraged husband.
        Hippolytus should thank you for a deed
        Stronger than all his words on his behalf;   145
        And what can I respond to your accuser?
        Confounded, tongue-tied, I must live to see
        Him taste a hideous triumph undisturbed
        And chronicle your shame to all mankind.
        May fire from Heaven fall upon me sooner!   150
        But tell me this, and tell without dissembling:
        Do you still love him, this presumptuous Prince?
        How does he now appear . . . ?
PHAEDRA: I see him now
        Grim as a monster and as terrible.
OENONE: Then why concede him victory unresisted?   155
        Do you fear him? Attack before he strikes
        And use the imputation he prepares
        For you. What can refute you? Every sign
        Informs against him—first his sword that Fortune
        Leaves in your hands, and then this day's distress,   160
        And those disconsolate months of misery,
        And long ago his father's mind prepared
        When long ago you claimed his banishment.
PHAEDRA: Shall I defame and murder innocence?
OENONE: Lend me but silence and my zeal suffices.   165
        Like you I shudder at my remedy
        And dread it deeper than a thousand deaths.
        But either this, or else I lose my mistress,
        And in your loss all other values fade.
        So I will speak. Theseus will rage, but still   170
        He'll take no more revenge than banishment.
        A father punishing is still a father
        Whose love is louder than the voice of justice;
        But guiltless blood is nothing in the scales
        Against the imperilled honour of your name.   175
        That is a jewel far too dear to hazard;
        It is a law we dare not disobey;
        And when our honour stands at such a cost
        Virtue itself must go for sacrifice.
        —Here they are. I see Theseus.   180
PHAEDRA: And I see
        Hippolytus, and his unflinching eyes
        Spell my dishonour. Do what you will, Oenone.
        I am in your hands. In this tormented hour
        To save myself is more than I can do.

(*Enter* THESEUS, HIPPOLYTUS, *and* THERAMENES.)

THESEUS: Fortune has smiled again, my dearest lady,   185
        And now your sweet embrace—
PHAEDRA: No, Theseus; stop,
        Do not pollute this love and this delight.
        No longer I deserve this tenderness.
        You have been wronged. The jealousy of Fortune
        Has not respected her you left behind you;   190
        And now, unworthy to approach your love,
        My sole desire must be for solitude.

(*Exit* PHAEDRA.)

THESEUS: What is this cheerless welcome that I find here,
        My son?

HIPPOLYTUS: A riddle Phaedra must interpret,
195   No one else can. But now if prayers can move
I ask but this, my lord, never to see
Her face again, but to live out my life
Safe, far away, forgotten by the Queen.
THESEUS: Now you, my son, forsake me!
HIPPOLYTUS: For you know
200   I never sought her, but you brought her here
At your departure; and the coasts of Trozen
Became the dwelling of Aricia
And of the Queen. I was to be their guardian.
But now what duty keeps me from my life?
205   Inglorious victories among the forests
Weary my idle youth, my wasted skill.
I long to waken from obscurity
And tip my hunter's spear in a nobler red.
Before you had spent the years that I have counted
210   What robbers, what oppressors, and what monsters
Had known the weight of that revengeful arm,
Victor and scourge of wanton insolence!
While on the quiet shore of either sea
The traveller learnt to take his road in peace;
215   Hercules heard your prowess and drew breath,
Leaving his triumphs and his toils to you—
And I, the unknown son of such a father,
Have much to do to reach my mother's footsteps.
Now let my unfledged valour learn to dare;
220   Let me, if anywhere some monster yet
Escapes you, drag its trophy to your feet,
Or by the record of a glorious failure
Find life for ever in a fitting death
And show posterity I was your son.
225   THESEUS: What is it, what invading blast of fear
Empties my very home at my approach?
Why, O ye Gods, to face these shrinking looks,
This lack of love, did ye deliver me?
I had one friend. His unregarding passion
230   Conspired to carry back from far Epirus
The tyrant's Queen. I helped, against my will,
But Fate was pitiless, and we were blind.
The villain caught me all unarmed, unwatching,
And these two eyes—that weep him yet—beheld
235   Pirithous under the fangs of beasts
Fatted on human slaughter; and I spent
Deep in the sightless silence of his dungeons
Down near the horrible empire of the Dead,
Six months. Then Heaven thought on me again.
240   I tricked the watchful eyes. I purged creation
Of one perfidious enemy, and his blood
Glutted his own fell monsters. Now at length
Free, and restored to all that's left to love,
Now that my soul aspires to nothing more
245   Than the enjoyment of their blessed sight,
Grief and lament is all my salutation,
None will abide to suffer my embraces;
And, chilled by the contagion of the fears
That breathe about my path, I'd rather be
250   A prisoner again and in Epirus.
     Speak out. Phaedra declares I've been betrayed.
Who wronged me? Why is not the wrong avenged?

Has Greece, so long beholden to this arm,
Offered a refuge to the criminal?
—You will not answer? Is my son, my son,   255
A shield and ally of my enemies?
I will go in, for this suspense unmans me.
I will find out the culprit and the offence.
Phaedra must tell me what her sorrow is.

(*Exit* THESEUS.)

HIPPOLYTUS: What did her words portend? They froze my   260
     blood:
Would Phaedra in her ecstasy of frenzy
Denounce her guilt and give her case away?
Gods, when the King is told! Death-dealing Love,
What blighting mists thou hast wrapped around his
     house!
And I with my secret of disloyal passion,   265
What was I once, what will he think me now!
My mind is dark with unaccomplished shapes
Of evil: but need innocence be afraid?
I must look for better times and better ways
To move my father's heart, and then reveal   270
Love he may doom to parting and to tears
But fixed beyond his force to overthrow.

ACT FOUR

THESEUS, OENONE

THESEUS: Ah! What have you said? The rebel, the betrayer
Conceived this outrage on his father's honour?
How unrelenting is thy hand upon me,
O Destiny! I know not where I go,
I know not what I do. All my long kindness   5
Wasted, paid with this hideous wanton plot!
And with the argument and threat of steel
To enforce his dark design! I know that sword,
I gave it him, I strapped it to his side—
For nobler work than this. Not all the bonds   10
Of blood itself could hold him back; and she
Could hesitate to punish, and her silence
Showed mercy to the wrongdoer!
OENONE: Say rather
Showed mercy to a father's suffering.
Shamed by a lover's frenzy, and ashamed   15
That her chaste eyes could kindle such a fire,
She would have died, my lord, and dimmed for ever
Herself the innocent lustre of those eyes.
The arm was raised. I hastened, I preserved
Her life for the embraces of her lord,   20
And pitying your fears and her confusion
Became the unwilling spokesman of her tears.
THESEUS: The perfidy! Yes, for all his craft, he paled;
He quaked with fear, I saw it as he came;
I marvelled then to feel his joylessness   25
And froze against the chill of his embrace.
—Did you not say, the love that burns in him
Had shown itself in Athens long before?
OENONE: My lord, remember how the Queen abhorred him;

30   It was unhallowed love that caused her hatred.
THESEUS: And now, in Trozen, it has flared again?
OENONE: I have told you all, my lord; but I have left
      My lady too long now with her deadly sorrow,
      And, by your leave, my place is at her side.

(*Exit* OENONE. *Enter* HIPPOLYTUS.)

35   THESEUS: So, here he comes. Great Gods, that noble carriage
      Would it not blind another's eye, as mine?
      Then sacrilegious and adulterous heads
      May flaunt the sacred emblem of the pure?
      Why is there no infallible badge to blazon
40   The minds of our dissembling race of men?
      HIPPOLYTUS: May I not know, my lord, why such a weight
      Of cloud darkens the majesty of your brow?
      Must this be secret from my loyalty?
      THESEUS: Dissembler! Dare you come so near to me?
45   Monster the thunderbolts reprieve too long,
      Corrupted straggler of the brigand race
      I cleansed the earth of once, how dare you still
      Parade that odious face, here where your frenzy
      Clutched at a father's bed? How dare you pace
50   These halls where all things tell of your dishonour?
      Why are you not far hence, where skies unknown
      Illumine coasts that never knew my name?
      Away, you traitor. Do not stand and tempt
      A hate, an anger hardly to be stayed.
55   Enough for me the indelible reproach
      Of fathering you, without the soil of murder
      To smother my bright deeds from memory.
      —Away. And if you would not share the sentence
      Of all the villains that this hand has felled
60   Take care that never again the sun that lights us
      Finds your rebellious feet upon this shore.
      Away, I tell you, out of my dominions
      And cleanse them for ever of your loathsome presence.
            And now hear, Neptune, hear. If once my courage
65   Scoured off a scum of bandits from thy coasts
      Remember thou hast sworn in recompense
      To grant one prayer. In long and stern confinement
      I called not thy undying power; I saved thee
      Thrifty of all the aid I hoped for, till
70   A greater need. Today I pray: avenge
      A mourning father. To thy wrath I leave
      This profligate. Still his lust in his blood.
      Let Theseus read thy kindness in thy rage.
      HIPPOLYTUS: With such a love Hippolytus is charged
75   By Phaedra! Weight of horror crushes me;
      So many assaults unlooked-for, stroke on stroke,
      Leave me no words.
      THESEUS: And so you judged that Phaedra's
      Compliant silence would have muffled up
      Your savage insolence. You might have waited
80   To gather up the sword that now, in her hands,
      Helps to convict you. Or why not, better still,
      Heap up the measure of your infamy
      With one good blow to finish breath and life?
      HIPPOLYTUS: After a calumny so infamous
85   I should let truth be heard—but for a secret
      That touches you, my lord. I beg you sanction

Respect that silences what I might say;
Labour no more to probe into your pain,
Look on my life, consider what I am:
The greatest crimes have lesser crimes before them;   90
The rest is easy when the way is known;
Like virtue, vice is gradual. No one day
Made any good man vile, murderous, incestuous,
And innocence is slow to dare, and slow
To push beyond the boundaries of law.   95
I had a mother, as chaste as she was valiant,
Nor have I derogated from my blood;
Pittheus, wise among men, took up my nurture
After her hands. I would not praise myself,
But, if one virtue was allotted mine,   100
May I not claim, my lord, to loathe that act
My enemies presume to speak of? This
Has made Hippolytus his name in Greece—
Unstudied honour rude in its excess,
Rugged, intractable austerity.   105
The daylight is no cleaner than the deeps
Of this my heart. What, sacrilegious lust
Could stain Hippolytus?
THESEUS: And this condemns you:
That was the foul source fed your vaunted coldness—
No one but Phaedra could bewitch your eyes;   110
No other woman's love was worth your interest
Unless it offered pleasures more than lawful.
HIPPOLYTUS: No, father, you shall hear the truth. This heart
      Has not refused an honourable yoke.
      Here at your feet I will confess—I love,   115
      And love in disobedience to your will.
      Aricia's beauty holds my heart enslaved
      And Pallas' daughter has subdued your son.
      I worship her, forgetful of my duty
      And have no room to feel another passion.   120
THESEUS: You love her! No—a pitiful pretence;
      You feign that crime to clear yourself of this.
HIPPOLYTUS: These six months I have hid from love, and
            loved,
      My lord; I came here to confess to you
      In trembling. But is it so? Will nothing move you?   125
      What fearful oath will win you to believe?
      Witness the Earth, the Heavens, and all Nature . . .
THESEUS: What felon ever feared a perjury?
      Peace, peace. Waste no more time on idle stories
      If that fine virtue rests on aids like these.   130
HIPPOLYTUS: You see it as a mockery, a lie:
      But Phaedra in her heart of hearts knows better.
THESEUS: Shall I endure so much effrontery?
HIPPOLYTUS: What place of exile, and how long a time
      Do you appoint?   135
THESEUS: Past the Pillars of Hercules
      A traitor's presence is too close for me.
HIPPOLYTUS: What friendship shall I find to comfort me
      When you have cast me out, dishonoured thus?
THESEUS: Find yourself friends whose dangerous regard
      Goes to adultery and honours incest,   140
      Deceivers, ingrates, free of law and shame,
      Fit to protect a criminal like you.
HIPPOLYTUS: And still you taunt me with adultery
      And incest. How can I reply? But Phaedra

145   Came of a mother, Phaedra's is a blood,
        My lord, you do not need me to recall it,
        More laden with their awful taint than mine.
        THESEUS: How dare you go so far before my face?
        For the last time, villain, avoid my sight,
150   Leave me; or force a father in his rage
        To have you flung with infamy from the place.

(*Exit* HIPPOLYTUS.)

        And now you go towards your waiting doom
        Irrevocably. For by that River's name
        Terrible even to the immortal Gods,
155   Neptune has sworn his oath, and will perform it.
        Yes, and I loved you, and in spite of all,
        Before the hour is come, my bowels yearn
        For pity of you. But I have too much cause—
        Did ever a deeper injury wound a father?
160   Ye righteous Gods, that see me thus prostrated,
        Did I give being to a son like this?

(*Enter* PHAEDRA.)

        PHAEDRA: My lord, you see me here impelled by terror:
        Just now, when that terrible voice assailed my ears,
        I thought the threat might come to a fulfilment.
165   Let me beg you, if there still is time, have pity
        On your own race, your own blood; do not force me,
        My lord, to hear it crying from the earth.
        Spare me the endless misery of laying
        That fearful stain on a paternal hand.
170 THESEUS: My lady, I have kept my hand unstained
        And still the unnatural boy has not escaped;
        Immortal hands will undertake his doom,
        Neptune's my debtor; you shall be avenged.
        PHAEDRA: Your debtor, Neptune! Then your prayer of hate . . .
175 THESEUS: Are you afraid it might be heard too soon?
        No, join your own entreaty with my curses,
        Paint me his crimes once more in all their blackness
        Inflame my faint and still-too-sluggish rage—
        He has added guilt more than the guilt you knew;
180   His frenzy spends itself in railing on you,
        He swears that all your words are perjuries,
        He says Aricia claims his heart, his love,
        His loyalty.
        PHAEDRA: No, my lord!
        THESEUS: That is what he told me;
        Not that a flimsy lie could impose on me.
185   I hope to hear that Neptune's justice falls
        Swiftly, and till that hour I'll ply his altars
        And keep him mindful of his undying word.

(*Exit* THESEUS.)

        PHAEDRA: He leaves me, with this dreadful news, alone.
        Ah Gods, the fire that I dreamed was safely stifled
190   To wake no more! Dreadful, unlooked-for news!
        All trepidation and remorse, all speed
        Out of Oenone's clinging arms of fear
        I came to save his son. And who can tell
        What might have been had conscience had its way?
195   Whether I might have spoken of my guilt,

        Might have let slip, had he but left me time,
        The entire and awful truth?—He has felt love,
        Hippolytus, who never felt for me;
        Aricia claims his loyalty, his heart . . .
        Gods! while I pleaded, while my prayer beat   200
        On those rigid eyes, that unrelenting brow,
        I thought he bore impenetrable armour
        Always the same and closed to all alike.
        And now another has overthrown his pride,
        Another finds favour in the tyrant's eyes;   205
        Perhaps his heart is easy to entreat
        And condescends to any plea but mine.
        And I am fool enough to be his friend!

(*Enter* OENONE.)

        —Oenone, do you know what I have heard?
        OENONE: No; I have tried to find you in alarm,   210
        Wondering what sudden impulse drove you here
        And how it may imperil you . . .
        PHAEDRA: Oenone,
        Who would have thought there was another woman?
        OENONE: You say—
        PHAEDRA: Hippolytus, I tell you, loves—
        The adversary I could never shake,   215
        Vexed by submission, impatient of complaining,
        The ogre that I never could encounter
        Undaunted; he is tamed and brought to heel,
        Aricia has forced the access to his heart.
        OENONE: Aricia!   220
        PHAEDRA: Oh, I never thought of these,
        These newest tortures that I live to taste:
        All the old despairs, the ecstasies, the broodings,
        Raging of flame, and horror of remorse,
        And that slight of unendurable denial
        Were barely foretastes of my torment here.   225
        They, lovers! Did they bewitch these watchful eyes?
        What time did they find to meet? Since when? What
          place?
        What furtive means? You knew. Why was I left
        To treasure foolish dreams? You might have told me
        Of their stolen pleasure. Were they often seen   230
        Speaking, or lingering? Was it the forest shades
        That sheltered them? Ah, but they had liberty
        To see the face they sought. The Heavens smiled
        On the innocence of their embrace, no fear
        Restrained their eager steps, and each fair day   235
        Rose clear and candid on their love. And I
        Disowned, dishonoured in the whole creation
        I fled the sun, I could not face the daylight,
        Death was the only godhead I could pray;
        Gall on my tongue, and tears my only drink;   240
        Happy, if any privacy of grief
        Had left me this one pitiable solace,
        To taste a last precarious luxury;
        But the forced travesty of a smiling face
        Deprived me even of the right to weep.   245
        OENONE: They reap no harvest of their vain desires:
        They'll meet no more.
        PHAEDRA: They'll love for evermore.
        Now as I speak—the poison of the thought!—

Mocking the fury of a rival wronged,
250   Forgetful of the exile that divides them,
They swear a thousand times never to part.
No, I will not yield to the insult of their joy,
Oenone. Help me, pity my jealousy.
Aricia must be crushed. I must stir up
255   My husband's wrath against that hated house—
No feeble sentence serves, the sister's crime
Is more than all her brothers'. I'll entreat him
In rage and jealousy.
                          What am I doing?
Where is reason in my wandering mind? I, jealous?
260   I, entreat Theseus? He, my husband, lives
And still I burn—for whom? Still yearn—for whom?
At every word each separate hair lifts up
Upon my head. My guilt has filled the measure—
I crave for incest, dream of calumny,
265   My murderous hands, avid of vengeance, burn
To bathe in the blood of innocence. Misery!
And dare I live, and dare I face the sight
Of that sacred Sun, the giver of my life,
I, grandchild of the high Father of the Gods,
270   My forebears crowding Heaven and all creation?
Where may I hide? Flee to the night of Hell?
No, no, not there; for there my father's hands
Inexorable lift the doomsday urn,
They say, and Minos stands in deathly justice
275   Over the pallid multitudes of men.
Will that great shade not start in ghastly anger
When I in shame before his awful gaze,
His daughter, plead my guilt, and deeds perhaps
Unheard in all the calendar of Hell?
280   Father, what will you say to these? I see
The tremendous urn roll thundering at your feet;
I see you ponder unknown penalties
To execute yourself upon your own . . .
Forgive. A cruel God detests your seed,
285   A heavenly vengeance breathed in me the frenzy
You see. Alas, and still of all the guilt
And all the shame that never will release me
My fearful heart has never reaped the sweets.
Pursued while yet I breathe by ceaseless evils
290   I wait to yield a bruised and broken life.
OENONE: My lady, come, dismiss a causeless terror,
Be more indulgent to a venial failing—
You love; but driven by a fatal charm.
It is not ours to challenge Destiny.
295   Was this a wonder never seen till now?
Were you the first that Love has overthrown?
Weakness was ever part of man's condition;
So, mortal, bow to a mortal's destiny.
You struggle against an immemorial yoke:
300   Even the Gods that live in high Olympus
Whose judgements hold a guilty world in dread
Have loved, and sometimes loved against the law.
PHAEDRA: Still you dare speak? And this is your advice,
And till the end you mean to drug my mind?
305   I hate you. All your help has been my downfall.
You dragged me back to the unbearable sunshine;
Your prayers were louder than the voice of right;
The man that I shunned, you made me see.

Was it your business? And now have all the lies
Of those false lips dared blacken such a life?   310
You may have killed him. His father's impious vows
And blind revenge perhaps are gratified
Already. I'll hear no more. Leave me alone,
Loathly inhuman monster; leave my sight,
Leave me alone to shape my bitter future.   315
On you I pray the justice of the Gods;
And may they make you the eternal warning
Of all cringing cunning sycophants that nourish
Their masters' dearest weakness, urge the way
Their cravings tend, and smooth the slope of crime; 320
Accursed flatterers, deadliest gift of all
That angry Heaven inflicts upon a King! (*Exit.*)
OENONE: (*Alone.*) O ye Gods! To have borne so much for
   her, forgone
So much!—This is my pay. And it is just.

ACT FIVE

HIPPOLYTUS, ARICIA, ISMENE

ARICIA: And in this extremity you will not speak
And will not undeceive a loving father?
Cruel, if you can disregard my tears
And lightly say goodbye to me for ever,
Then sail, and leave Aricia with her grief;   5
But do not go in certainty of death.
Fight the foul imputation on your honour,
Constrain your father to unsay his curses.
There is time yet. What reason, or what folly
Makes you leave all the advantage to the accuser?   10
Tell Theseus what you know.
HIPPOLYTUS: Have I not told
What may be told? Would you have me reveal
To light the shameful mystery of his bed
Or by too scrupulous report bring down
Confusion on a father's honoured head?   15
Alone you know this horror. You, and the Gods,
Alone receive the outpouring of my heart.
See if I love you: I have shown to you
What I would fain have veiled from my own thoughts.
But under what a seal, you know. Forget,   20
My lady, if you can, that I have spoken;
Let me believe this hideous affair
Will never be breathed between those blameless lips.
We set our trust upon the righteous Heavens.
My cause is theirs; and Phaedra, whether soon   25
Or in the slow procedure of their justice,
Will not escape disgrace. This deference
I ask of you; and all the rest I sweep
Before the liberty of my wrath. I bid you
No longer be a slave. I bid you dare   30
To come with me, dare to be banned with me.
Break from a poisoned house where Virtue breathes
A deathly and a desecrated air;
Turn into profit for a headlong flight
All the disorder following on my fall.   35
The means I offer: you have still no guard
But my own men. Most powerful patrons wait us—
Argos extends her arms, and Sparta welcomes;

Let common friends receive our just laments,
40   Otherwise Phaedra rakes our wreckage up,
Evicts us both from a throne our fathers left us,
And strips us both for spoils to deck her son.
The moment beckons, grasp it. But what fear
Restrains you? What suspends your doubtful mind?
45   Only for your sake have I dared so far.
When I am all on fire, why are you ice?
Are you unwilling to adventure on
An outlaw's path?

ARICIA: Oh, but how happily,
My lord, I'd taste of exile so; how eagerly
50   Embrace a life forgotten of all beside
And linked with yours! But lacking that sweet bond
Can I in honour join your wanderings?
I know the sternest laws do not forbid me
To fly your father's power: he is not mine,
55   I owe him no obedience; and to fly
From an oppressor is the right of all.
But you, my lord, love me. And anxious honour . . .

HIPPOLYTUS: And can you think I rate that honour cheaply?
No, no. I came with worthier designs—
60   Escape your foes, and follow as my bride.
Free in adversity, since Heaven has freed us,
Our pledges need no words but ours, and Hymen
Robbed of his torchlit rites is Hymen still.
     By Trozen's gates, among those sepulchres,
65   Antique memorials of my father's pride,
A wayside temple holy and renowned
Stands grim protector of the plighted word;
There falsehood dare not raise her voice, or falls
Blasted at once, and certitude of death
70   Lays chains invincible on perjury.
May we not there with solemn mutual oath
Give and receive our hearts' enduring faith
Before the shrine, and pray the Deity
For his protection and paternal love?
75   I will invoke each mighty God to hear me—
Maiden Diana, Juno's majesty,
And every name whose present patronage
Shall seal and sanctify my true intent.

ARICIA: The King is here. Fly, Prince, depart at once.
80   I shall remain awhile to hide my purpose.
Away—but send me back a trusty servant
To guide my footsteps safely to your side.

(*Exit* HIPPOLYTUS.)

(*Enter* THESEUS.)

THESEUS: Lighten the mists, ye Gods, and show my eyes
The truth they seek for here!
                    Now, sweet Ismene,
85   See everything is done. Be ready quickly.

(*Exit* ISMENE.)

THESEUS: You seem disturbed, your colour fails, my lady.
What was Hippolytus doing in this place?
ARICIA: Taking an everlasting leave, my lord.
THESEUS: And so your eyes have tamed that rebel heart
90   And brought him to his earliest thoughts of love.

ARICIA: I must not hide the truth from you, my lord.
He has not learnt your unjust hate from you;
He did not treat me like a criminal.
THESEUS: You mean he vowed you everlasting passion.
I should not build on that unsettled heart.   95
He swore as deep to others.
ARICIA: He, my lord?
THESEUS: I wish you could have taught him constancy.
How could you bear that loathsome competition?
ARICIA: And how can you bear loathsome calumnies
To blacken all the lustre of his fame?   100
Have you so little knowledge of his nature?
Can you not tell the guiltless from the guilty?
Only your eyes are darkened by a cloud
That lets his goodness gleam on all the world.
Oh stop, relent. He must not be the victim   105
Of false accusers. Repent your murderous curses.
Tremble, my lord, tremble, lest frowning Heaven
Hate you enough to take you at your word—
Gods may accept our offerings in anger
And punish with the presents we entreated.   110
THESEUS: No, blind as you are with ill-requited love
You will not blind me to his villainy;
For I have witnesses, beyond reproach,
Beyond suspicion—I have seen tears flow,
Tears that were true.   115
ARICIA: Look to yourself, my lord:
Your matchless weight of arm redeemed mankind
From monsters past all counting—but not all,
The breed is not destroyed, and you have saved
One . . . I must say no more; your son forbids me.
Knowing what deference his heart still holds   120
I should increase his suffering too much
Dared I continue. Let me imitate
His generous scruple, and excuse myself
While nothing forces me to break my silence.

(*Exit* ARICIA.)

THESEUS: (*Alone.*) But what is in her mind? What lurks   125
    below
A tale so often broached, and never told?
Is it a stratagem without a meaning?
Is it conspiracy to bind me on
A rack of doubt? And secret in my heart
Steeled to be cruel, what is the small voice   130
That pleads for mercy, and unmans my wrath,
Perplexes me and tears me?—I must see
Her woman once again; I know too little.
—Guard! Fetch Oenone, and send her in alone.

(*Enter* PANOPE.)

PANOPE: I cannot say what thoughts are in her heart,   135
But the distraction motions of the Queen
Fill me with fear, my lord. Death and despair
Are painted on her face, and the deathly tint
Sits even now upon her cheeks. Already
Pursued with scorn and chiding from her side,   140
Oenone has plunged to death among the waves.
None knows what wild will drove her, and her voice
Is covered in the murmur of the tide.

THESEUS: What have you said?

PANOPE: Her going gave no peace;
145   Confusion gains in the Queen's divided soul:
       One moment, soothing her mysterious grief,
       She takes her children, bathes them in her tears;
       And suddenly, her motherhood dismissed,
       She drives them from her with a look of loathing.
150   Her restless steps come and go purposeless
       And we are strangers in her fevered eyes.
       Thrice she has written, only to repent,
       And thrice destroyed the message uncompleted.
       My lord, be gracious: see her, comfort her.
155   THESEUS: Is it so? Oenone's dead, and Phaedra waits
       For death? Call for my son, let him plead his cause,
       Let him speak to me, and I will listen.

       (*Exit* PANOPE.)

                                    Neptune,
       Delay thy deadly gift, be not too sudden,
       Rather refuse it utterly. What if
160   I was seduced too soon by worthless words?
       What if my cruel hands were raised too rashly?
       What wretchedness would follow from that vow!

       (*Enter* THERAMENES.)

       THESEUS: Is it you, Theramenes? Where is my son?
       What have you done with him? His careful tending
165   Has been your charge from earliest infancy.
       But why the tears I see upon your cheeks?
       What of my son?
       THERAMENES: O late, O vain regret,
       O useless love! Hippolytus is no more.
       THESEUS: Oh Gods!
       THERAMENES: I saw him die, the best and sweetest
170   Of human kind—and, let me say, my lord,
       The purest also.
       THESEUS: Is my son dead? Now,
       Now that these arms reached out for him, the Gods
       Impatient urged his execution on?
       How did I lose him? What immortal stroke . . . ?
175   THERAMENES: Still close behind us lay the gates of Trozen.
       He drove his chariot, his grieving guard
       Matching his silence, marched on either hand.
       Sunk in his thought, the loose reins lying free,
       He brought us on the causeway to Mycenae;
180   And the noble beasts, so eager once to leap
       At the least inflexion of a master's voice,
       Now bent dull eyes to earth and drooping crests
       As if communing with his bitter mood.
       —Suddenly from the sea an awful cry
185   Shattered the silence of the air. And then
       A second voice wailed answer from the landward.
       Our blood was frozen in our inmost hearts.
       Stiffly rose up the listening horses' manes.
       And now from the level deep immense there heaves
190   A boiling mount of brine, and still it swells,
       Rears wavelike foaming down on us and breaks
       To belch a ravening monster at our feet
       Whose threatening brow is broadened with huge horns,
       Whose body, cased in golden glint of scales,

Thrashes a train of sinuous writhing whorls.   195
Indomitable bull, malignant dragon,
Its long-drawn bellows rumble down the shore;
Heaven quails, earth shudders at the portent, air
Reeks with its pestilential breath. The wave
Withdraws again, aghast at what it bore.   200
We fly to the nearby temple; not one lingers
Or wraps himself in unavailing valour.
Hippolytus, honouring his hero blood,
Hippolytus alone checks, wheels his team,
Snatches the spears, charges upon the creature,   205
Aims, and unerring flings. A gaping slash
Fair in the monster's flank drives it in bounds
Of pain and fury to the horses' feet
To roar and wallow and from flaming jaws
To spatter them with blood and cloud and fire.   210
Reckless, they plunge aside. They hear no more,
Answer no more to bridle or to voice.
The charioteer spends all his strength in vain
While they redden the bits with spume that is bright
   with blood.
Even, men say, some more than mortal shape   215
Borne on the horrible confusion plied
Their dusty flanks with goads. Where terror leads them
Stand rocks. The axle screeches, snaps. The car
Crashes in fragments; and my fearless master
Drops tangled in the reins . . . —Forgive my weakness.   220
In that tormenting image lives a source
Of quenchless tears.—I watched, my lord, I watched
Your helpless son dragging behind the steeds
His hands had fed. He tried to call to them:
Instead, his cries startle them. So they gallop   225
And make one wound of all his living flesh.
   Now as the plain is pealing with our grief
The violent fit is spent. They slacken speed,
And stop, where close at hand his father's tombs
And ancient sculptures hold the chill remains   230
And memories of Kings. I run, behind me
Run all his guard, reading the traces painted
By his gallant blood, past the empurpled crags,
Past dripping brambles hung about with spoils
Of bloody hair. I reach him, I speak; he gives me   235
A hand and greets me with a dying gaze
That quickly closes. And I hear these words:
   'My guiltless days are forfeit to the Gods.
Do you after my death be watchful over
The sad Aricia; and, sweet friend, if ever   240
My father undeceived should come to mourn
The misadventure of a slandered son,
To lay in peace my blood and wailing shade
Bid him be gentle to the captive maiden,
Render her . . .' On the word the lifeless youth   245
Fell back into my arms a ravaged corpse,
The dreadful triumph of an angry Heaven,
Where not a father's eye could undertake
To know his child.
THESEUS: O child! O dearest hope
I cast away! Gods, ye unswerving Gods,   250
Too faithfully ye served me! Now must life
Henceforward be a death of long-drawn sorrow.
THERAMENES: And now in fear and haste Aricia,

Stealing, my lord, from your captivity
255 To hear his nuptial vow before the Gods,
Approached. There are the red and steaming grasses,
And there—what welcome for a bride's regard!—
There is Hippolytus, but motionless,
Featureless, bloodless. First she seeks to question
260 Her misery, and, seeing, still demands
Hippolytus. Then, too pitifully assured,
After one glance reproachful to the skies
Cold, with one cry, lifeless upon the dead
She falls. Ismene, weeping, is beside her
265 And draws her back to life and life's despair;
And I, still subject to the hostile daylight,
Return to speak a hero's last desires
And so fulfil the grievous ministry
His dying heart committed to my love.
270 —But here I see the deadliest of his foes.

(*Enter* PHAEDRA, PANOPE, *and* GUARDS.)

THESEUS: Well, victory is yours: my son is gone.
Much, much I could suspect; deep rankling doubt
Acquits him in my heart and troubled mind—
But he is dead: your sacrifice, my lady;
275 Take it, find satisfaction in the forfeit
Unmerited or just. It matters little
That evermore my eyes be blindfolded;
Let him be criminal if you accuse.
His loss alone is theme enough for sorrow,
280 No need to look for new and fearful knowledge
That, impotent to bring the dead again,
Could pile at most new suffering on the old.
Let me escape, leave you and leave these shores,
Flying the bloody image of a son
285 Mangled—before that harrying memory
I could long for exile from the world of men.
All things upbraid me, all increase my anguish—
My very name (for nameless, I could hide),
The very honours that the Gods bestowed,
290 Whose murderous grace I'll mourn, and not again
Importune them with fruitless prayers of mine;
Do what they might, their fatal condescension

Could not console for what they took away.
PHAEDRA: Theseus, I have repented of my silence.
Your son requires his innocence from my lips;   295
Yes, he was guiltless.
THESEUS: This to me, his father!
And on your solemn faith I sentenced him.
Can any pretext for an act so vile—
PHAEDRA: My time is measured. Listen to me, Theseus.
I, on your dutiful and temperate son,   300
Looked with profaning and incestuous eyes—
The flame of Heaven lighted in my bosom
A fatal fire. Oenone did the rest;
She feared Hippolytus, my passion known,
Would publish all the madness that he loathed;   305
Presuming on my feebleness, she came
With that base story of my victim's guilt.
Self-chosen, easy death among the waves
Punished her perfidy and foiled my anger,
And by now the knife would have cleft my destiny,   310
But goodness still cried out for vindication.
I chose the slower path. I chose to pour
Into your ears before I joined the dead
The chronicle of my remorse. I have drained
And mingled with my burning blood a draught   315
Medea left in Athens. Now already
Her poison makes it progress toward my heart
Striking that heart with cold it never knew;
Faintly already I perceive the daylight
And you I wrong by my unworthy presence;   320
And death, blurring the sunbeams from these eyes
Whose glance polluted them, restores the light
To perfect purity.
PANOPE: My lord, she is dying.
THESEUS: And would the dark remembrance too might die
Of what she has done! Come, all is now too plain.   325
I must enfold what still remains to touch
Of my dear son, and expiate in tears
The blind curse I shall evermore bewail
With dear-bought honours rendered at his tomb;
And, better to placate his injured spirit,   330
I will forget the voice of ancient vengeance
And look upon his lover as my child.

Aphra Behn

Little is known about the early life of England's first female professional playwright, Aphra Behn (1640–1689), who may have been born Eaffrey Johnson in Kent. She left England just after the restoration of Charles II for the South American colony of Surinam, where she lived from 1663 to 1664. Again, many of the details about her life there are unknown, though Surinam provided the setting for her great novel, *Oronooko: or, The Royal Slave,* published in 1688. Returning to England, she appears to have married someone named Behn; in *The Passionate Shepherdess: Aphra Behn 1640–89* (London: Jonathan Cape, 1977; p. 48), Maureen Duffy accounts for several possible candidates, but also suggests that Aphra Behn's marriage may have been a legitimating fiction: "Mr. Behn, her putative husband, has less substance than any character she invented." By the mid-1660s, however, Aphra Behn was serving Charles II as a spy in Antwerp and seems to have been caught up in the politics surrounding the Dutch invasion of Surinam. When she returned to England penniless in 1667, she was sent to debtors' prison and appealed to the government for her wages. Between 1670 and her death in 1689, however, Behn emerged as a famous and influential writer; in addition to her novel *Orinooko,* Behn had a successful career as a poet and celebrated playwright. She wrote fifteen plays, beginning with *The Forced Marriage: or, The Jealous Bridegroom* (1668), a tragicomedy produced by Thomas Betterton at Lincoln's Inn Fields. Behn's major plays are mainly in the mode of Restoration comedy and were successful both in their day and well into the eighteenth century: her best-known plays today are *The Rover* (1677), *The Feigned Courtesans* (1679), which was dedicated to her friend and supporter (and the King's mistress), the actress Nell Gwynn, *The Second Part of The Rover* (1681), and *The City Heiress* (1682). Her novel *Oronooko* was dramatized by Thomas Southerne in 1695 and was popular onstage throughout the eighteenth century. Aphra Behn was part of the elite milieu of intellectual culture of her day, the friend of courtiers such as Buckingham and Rochester, and of writers like Otway and Dryden. Although her work was, in a sense, recovered for modern readers by Virginia Woolf's famous essay *A Room of One's Own,* Behn's plays have been increasingly popular and successful in the theater. Aphra Behn is buried in Westminster Abbey.

THE ROVER *The Rover* is a comedy of intrigue, set in Naples during the Carnival. The play concerns the sexual adventures of a band of Englishmen—Belvile, Willmore (the Rover), and Blunt—and their efforts to seduce the heroine Florinda and her sister Hellena. As in many Restoration comedies, *The Rover* takes a frank attitude toward sexual and financial negotiations, which are often paired in the play. The play opens with Hellena's rejection of a life in the convent and her decision to "provide my self this Carnival, if there be e'er a handsome proper fellow." In the course of the play, Hellena flirts with Willmore; Willmore wins the services (and, unfortunately, the love) of the courtesan Angelica, who eventually tries to murder him; Willmore and Blunt nearly rape Florinda on several occasions; and Blunt is tricked by a prostitute and turned out into the street in his shirt and underwear, "before consummation."

Yet despite the licentiousness of its action, the play clearly depends on a deeply ingrained sense of propriety, much of which operates through class distinctions. While it "would anger us vilely to be trussed up for a rape upon a maid of quality," one of the gentlemen declares, it seems otherwise acceptable to "ruffle a harlot." Morality, in *The Rover,* is in many ways determined by class and wealth. These distinctions are both troubled and confirmed by the important function of disguise and masking in the play. Since the action of *The Rover* takes place during Carnival, the main characters meet only in disguise. Masking enables the characters both to flirt without dishonoring themselves and to discover the truth

The Williamstown Theatre Festival production of *The Rover*, featuring Edward Hermann, Harry Groener, Christopher Reeve, and Stephen Collins.

about one another. In fact, masking in the play empowers the women, in that the temporary masking of the Carnival allows the women to escape their enforced lives at home and to meet men in public. Florinda and Hellena, for instance, can marry only with their brother Pedro's permission. He wants to marry his sisters to the wealthiest—and oldest—suitors, who will be able to settle large fortunes on them. However, the young Englishmen who attract the two sisters are Royalist supporters of Charles II, currently exiled from Cromwell's Protectorate because they support the Crown. As a result, although they are well-born, they are currently without funds and so are a poor match for Florinda and Hellena, at least in Pedro's eyes.

Masking also enables the women to escape Pedro's control, to act on their own behalf. Indeed, although the women are more modest than the Rover, they are equally devious in their pursuit of a lover—though the women insist on marriage as the price of their virginity. In Behn's brilliant comedy, the women emerge as the agents—as well as the objects—of the play's erotic intrigue.

In recent years, *The Rover* has received a number of excellent stage productions—at Minneapolis's Guthrie Theater, the Royal Shakespeare Company, and on many university campuses.

THE ROVER

OR THE BANISH'D CAVALIERS

Aphra Behn

EDITED BY MONTAGUE SUMMERS

CHARACTERS

Don ANTONIO, *the Vice-Roy's Son*
Don PEDRO, *a Noble Spaniard, his Friend*
BELVILE, *an English Colonel in love with Florinda*
WILLMORE, *the Rover*
FREDERICK, *an English Gentleman, and Friend to Belvile and Blunt*
BLUNT, *an English Country Gentleman*
STEPHANO, *Servant to Don Pedro*
PHILIPPO, *Lucetta's Gallant*
SANCHO, *Pimp to Lucetta*
BISKEY *and* SEBASTIAN, *two Bravoes to Angelica*
DIEGO, *Page to Don Antonio*
PAGE *to Hellena*
BOY, *Page to Belvile*

Blunt's MAN
OFFICERS *and* SOLDIERS
FLORINDA, *Sister to Don Pedro*
HELLENA, *a gay young Woman design'd for a Nun, and Sister to Florinda*
VALERIA, *a Kinswoman to Florinda*
ANGELICA BIANCA, *a famous Curtezan*
MORETTA, *her Woman*
CALLIS, *Governess to Florinda and Hellena*
LUCETTA, *a jilting Wench*
SERVANTS, *other* MASQUERADERS, MEN *and* WOMEN

SCENE: *Naples, in Carnival-time.*

PROLOGUE

Written by a Person of Quality

WITS, like Physicians, never can agree,
When of a different Society;
And Rabel's Drops were never more cry'd down
By all the Learned Doctors of the Town,
5 Than a new Play, whose Author is unknown:
Nor can those Doctors with more Malice sue
(And powerful Purses) the dissenting Few,
Than those with an insulting Pride do rail
At all who are not of their own Cabal.
10 If a Young Poet hit your Humour right,
You judge him then out of Revenge and Spite;
So amongst Men there are ridiculous Elves,
Who Monkeys hate for being too like themselves:
So that the Reason of the Grand Debate,
15 Why Wit so oft is damn'd, when good Plays take,
Is, that you censure as you love or hate.
Thus, like a learned Conclave, Poets sit
Catholick Judges both of Sense and Wit,
And damn or save, as they themselves think fit.
20 Yet those who to others Faults are so severe,
Are not so perfect, but themselves may err.
Some write correct indeed, but then the whole
(Bating their own dull Stuff i'th' Play) is stole:
As Bees do suck from Flowers their Honey-dew,
25 So they rob others, striving to please you.
     Some write their Characters genteel and fine,
But then they do so toil for every Line,
That what to you does easy seem, and plain,
Is the hard issue of their labouring Brain.
30 And some th' Effects of all their Pains we see,
Is but to mimick good Extempore.
Others by long Converse about the Town,
Have Wit enough to write a leud Lampoon,

But their chief Skill lies in a Baudy Song.
In short, the only Wit that's now in Fashion   35
Is but the Gleanings of good Conversation.
As for the Author of this coming Play,
I ask'd him what he thought fit I should say,
In thanks for your good Company to day:
He call'd me Fool, and said it was well known,   40
You came not here for our sakes, but your own.
New Plays are stuff'd with Wits, and with Debauches,
That croud and sweat like Cits in *May*-day Coaches.

ACT ONE

SCENE I

A Chamber.

Enter FLORINDA *and* HELLENA.

FLORINDA: What an impertinent thing is a young Girl bred in a Nunnery! How full of Questions! Prithee no more, Hellena; I have told thee more than thou understand'st already.

HELLENA: The more's my Grief; I wou'd fain know as much as you, which makes me so inquisitive; nor is't enough to know   5
you're a Lover, unless you tell me too, who 'tis you sigh for.

FLORINDA: When you are a Lover, I'll think you fit for a Secret of that nature.

HELLENA: 'Tis true, I was never a Lover yet—but I begin to have a shreud Guess, what 'tis to be so, and fancy it very   10
pretty to sigh, and sing, and blush and wish, and dream and wish, and long and wish to see the Man; and when I do, look pale and tremble; just as you did when my Brother brought home the fine *English* Colonel to see you—what do you call him? Don *Belvile.*

FLORINDA: Fie, *Hellena.*   15

HELLENA: That Blush betrays you—I am sure 'tis so—or is it Don *Antonio* the Vice-Roy's Son?—or perhaps the rich

old Don *Vincentio,* whom my father designs for your Hus-
20 band?—Why do you blush again?
FLORINDA: With Indignation; and how near soever my Father
thinks I am to marrying that hated Object, I shall let him
see I understand better what's due to my Beauty, Birth and
Fortune, and more to my Soul, than to obey those unjust
25 Commands.
HELLENA: Now hang me, if I don't love thee for that dear
Disobedience. I love Mischief strangely, as most of our Sex
do, who are come to love nothing else—But tell me, dear
Florinda, don't you love that fine *Anglese?*—for I vow next
30 to loving him my self, 'twill please me most that you do
so, for he is so gay and so handsom.
FLORINDA: *Hellena,* a Maid design'd for a Nun ought not to
be so curious in a Discourse of Love.
HELLENA: And dost thou think that ever I'll be a Nun? Or at
35 least till I'm so old, I'm fit for nothing else. Faith no, Sister; and that which makes me long to know whether you
love *Belvile,* is because I hope he has some mad Companion or other, that will spoil my Devotion; nay I'm resolv'd
to provide my self this Carnival, if there be e'er a hand-
40 som Fellow of my Humour above Ground, tho I ask first.
FLORINDA: Prithee be not so wild.
HELLENA: Now you have provided your self with a Man, you
take no Care for poor me—Prithee tell me, what dost thou
see about me that is unfit for Love—have not I a world of
45 Youth? a Humour gay? a Beauty passable? a Vigour desirable? well shap'd? clean limb'd? sweet breath'd? and Sense
enough to know how all these ought to be employ'd to the
best Advantage: yes, I do and will. Therefore lay aside your
Hopes of my Fortune, by my being a Devotee, and tell me
50 how you came acquainted with this *Belvile;* for I perceive
you knew him before he came to *Naples.*
FLORINDA: Yes, I knew him at the Siege of *Pampelona,* he was
then a Colonel of *French* Horse, who when the Town was
ransack'd, nobly treated my Brother and my self, preserv-
55 ing us from all Insolencies; and I must own, (besides great
Obligations) I have I know not what, that pleads kindly
for him about my Heart, and will suffer no other to enter—But see my Brother.

(*Enter Don* PEDRO, STEPHANO, *with a Masquing Habit, and* CALLIS.)

PEDRO: Good morrow, Sister. Pray, when saw you your Lover
60 Don *Vincentio?*
FLORINDA: I know not, Sir—*Callis,* when was he here? for I
consider it so little, I know not when it was.
PEDRO: I have a Command from my Father here to tell you,
you ought not to despise him, a Man of so vast a Fortune,
65 and such a Passion for you—*Stephano,* my things—

(*Puts on his Masquing Habit.*)

FLORINDA: A Passion for me! 'tis more than e'er I saw, or had
a desire should be known—I hate *Vincentio,* and I would
not have a Man so dear to me as my Brother follow the
ill Customs of our Country, and make a Slave of his Sis-
70 ter—And Sir, my Father's Will, I'm sure, you may divert.

---

52 **Siege of *Pampelona*** Pampluna, the strongly fortified capital
of Navarra and very frequently a center of military operations

PEDRO: I know not how dear I am to you, but I wish only to
be rank'd in your Esteem, equal with the *English* Colonel
Belvile—Why do you frown and blush? Is there any Guilt
belongs to the Name of that Cavalier?
FLORINDA: I'll not deny I value *Belvile:* when I was expos'd to such 75
Dangers as the licens'd Lust of common Soldiers threatened,
when Rage and Conquest flew thro the City—then *Belvile,*
this Criminal for my sake, threw himself into all Dangers to
save my Honour, and will you not allow him my Esteem?
PEDRO: Yes, pay him what you will in Honour—but you must 80
consider Don *Vincentio's* Fortune, and the Jointure he'll
make you.
FLORINDA: Let him consider my Youth, Beauty and Fortune;
which ought not to be thrown away on his Age and Jointure.
PEDRO: 'Tis true, he's not so young and fine a Gentleman as 85
that *Belvile*—but what Jewels will that Cavalier present
you with? those of his Eyes and Heart?
HELLENA: And are not those better than any Don *Vincentio*
has brought from the *Indies?*
PEDRO: Why how now! Has your Nunnery-breeding taught 90
you to understand the Value of Hearts and Eyes?
HELLENA: Better than to believe *Vincentio* deserves Value from
any woman—He may perhaps encrease her Bags, but not
her Family.
PEDRO: This is fine—Go up to your Devotion, you are not 95
design'd for the Conversation of Lovers.
HELLENA: (*Aside.*) Nor Saints yet a while I hope.
Is't not enough you make a Nun of me, but you must cast
my Sister away too, exposing her to a worse confinement
than a religious Life? 100
PEDRO: The Girl's mad—Is it a Confinement to be carry'd
into the Country, to an antient Villa belonging to the
Family of the *Vincentio's* these five hundred Years, and have
no other Prospect than that pleasing one of seeing all her
own that meets her Eyes—a fine Air, large Fields and Gar- 105
dens, where she may walk and gather Flowers?
HELLENA: When? By Moon-Light? For I'm sure she dares not
encounter with the heat of the Sun; that were a Task only
for Don *Vincentio* and his *Indian* Breeding, who loves it in
the Dog-days—And if these be her daily Divertisements, 110
what are those of the Night? to lie in a wide Moth-eaten
Bed-Chamber with Furniture in Fashion in the Reign of
King *Sancho* the First; the Bed that which his Forefathers
liv'd and dy'd in.
PEDRO: Very well. 115
HELLENA: This Apartment (new furbisht and fitted out for the
young Wife) he (out of Freedom) makes his Dressing-
room; and being a frugal and a jealous Coxcomb, instead of
a Valet to uncase his feeble Carcase, he desires you to do that
Office—Signs of Favour, I'll assure you, and such as you 120
must not hope for, unless your Woman be out of the way.
PEDRO: Have you done yet?
HELLENA: That Honour being past, the Giant stretches it self,
yawns and sighs a Belch or two as loud as a Musket, throws

---

113 **King *Sancho* the First** Sancho I, 'the Fat,' of Castile and
Leon, reigned 955–967: Sancho I of Aragon 1067–1094. But the
phrase is here only in a vague general sense to denote some
musty and immemorial antiquity without any exact reference

125 himself into Bed, and expects you in his foul Sheets, and e'er you can get your self undrest, calls you with a Snore or two—And are not these fine Blessings to a young Lady?

PEDRO: Have you done yet?

HELLENA: And this man you must kiss, nay, you must kiss
130 none but him too—and nuzle thro his Beard to find his Lips—and this you must submit to for threescore Years, and all for a Jointure.

PEDRO: For all your Character of Don *Vincentio,* she is as like to marry him as she was before.

135 HELLENA: Marry Don *Vincentio!* hang me, such a Wedlock would be worse than Adultery with another Man: I had rather see her in the *Hostel de Dieu,* to waste her Youth there in Vows, and be a Handmaid to Lazers and Cripples, than to lose it in such a Marriage.

140 PEDRO: You have consider'd, Sister, that *Belvile* has no Fortune to bring you to, is banisht his Country, despis'd at home, and pity'd abroad.

HELLENA: What then? the Vice-Roy's Son is better than that Old Sir Fisty. Don *Vincentio!* Don *Indian!* he thinks he's
145 trading to *Gambo* still, and wou'd barter himself (that Bell and Bawble) for your Youth and Fortune.

PEDRO: *Callis,* take her hence, and lock her up all this Carnival, and at Lent she shall begin her everlasting Penance in a Monastery.

150 HELLENA: I care not, I had rather be a Nun, than be oblig'd to marry as you wou'd have me, if I were design'd for't.

PEDRO: Do not fear the Blessing of that Choice—you shall be a Nun.

HELLENA: Shall I so? you may chance to be mistaken in my
155 way of Devotion—(*Aside.*) A Nun! yes I am like to make a fine Nun! I have an excellent Humour for a Grate: No, I'll have a Saint of my own to pray to shortly, if I like any that dares venture on me.

PEDRO: *Callis,* make it your Business to watch this wild Cat.
160 As for you, *Florinda,* I've only try'd you all this while, and urg'd my Father's Will; but mine is, that you would love *Antonio,* he is brave and young, and all that can compleat the Happiness of a gallant Maid—This Absence of my Father will give us opportunity to free you from *Vincentio,*
165 by marrying here, which you must do to morrow.

FLORINDA: To morrow!

PEDRO: To morrow, or 'twill be too late—'tis not my Friendship to *Antonio,* which makes me urge this, but Love to thee, and Hatred to *Vincentio*—therefore resolve upon't to morrow.

170 FLORINDA: Sir, I shall strive to do, as shall become your Sister.

PEDRO: I'll both believe and trust you—Adieu.

(*Exeunt* PEDRO *and* STEPHANO.)

HELLENA: As become his Sister!—That is, to be as resolved your way, as he is his—

(HELLENA *goes to* CALLIS.)

FLORINDA: I ne'er till now perceiv'd my Ruin near,
175 I've no Defence against *Antonio's* Love,

---

137 **Hostel de Dieu** the first Spanish hospital was erected at Granada by St. Juan de Dios before 1550   145 **Gambo** the Gambia in West Africa has been a British Colony since 1664, when a fort, now Fort James, was founded at the mouth of the river

For he has all the Advantages of Nature,
The moving Arguments of Youth and Fortune.

HELLENA: But hark you, *Callis,* you will not be so cruel to lock me up indeed: will you?

CALLIS: I must obey the Commands I hate—besides, do you 180 consider what a Life you are going to lead?

HELLENA: Yes, *Callis,* that of a Nun: and till then I'll be indebted a World of Prayers to you, if you let me now see, what I never did, the Divertisements of a Carnival.

CALLIS: What, go in Masquerade? 'twill be a fine farewell to 185 the World I take it—pray what wou'd you do there?

HELLENA: That which all the World does, as I am told, be as mad as the rest, and take all innocent Freedom—Sister, you'll go too, will you not? come prithee be not sad— We'll out-wit twenty Brothers, if you'll be rul'd by me— 190 Come put off this dull Humour with your Clothes, and assume one as gay, and as fantastick as the Dress my Cousin *Valeria* and I have provided, and let's ramble.

FLORINDA: *Callis,* will you give us leave to go?

CALLIS: (*Aside.*) I have a youthful Itch of going my self. 195 —Madam, if I thought your Brother might not know it, and I might wait on you, for by my troth I'll not trust young Girls alone.

FLORINDA: Thou see'st my Brother's gone already, and thou shalt attend and watch us. 200

(*Enter* STEPHANO.)

STEPHANO: Madam, the Habits are come, and your Cousin *Valeria* is drest, and stays for you.

FLORINDA: 'Tis well—I'll write a Note, and if I chance to see *Belvile,* and want an opportunity to speak to him, that shall let him know what I've resolv'd in favour of him. 205

HELLENA: Come, let's in and dress us.

(*Exeunt.*)

SCENE II

A Long Street.

Enter BELVILE, MELANCHOLY, BLUNT, *and* FREDERICK.

FREDERICK: Why, what the Devil ails the Colonel, in a time when all the World is gay, to look like mere Lent thus? Hadst thou been long enough in *Naples* to have been in love, I should have sworn some such Judgment had befall'n thee.

BELVILE: No, I have made no new Amours since I came to 5 Naples.

FREDERICK: You have left none behind you in Paris.

BELVILE: Neither.

FREDERICK: I can't divine the Cause then; unless the old Cause, the want of Mony. 10

BLUNT: And another old Cause, the want of a Wench— Wou'd not that revive you?

BELVILE: You're mistaken, *Ned.*

BLUNT: Nay, 'Sheartlikins, then thou art past Cure.

FREDERICK: I have found it out; thou hast renew'd thy Ac- 15 quaintance with the Lady that cost thee so many Sighs at the Siege of *Pampelona*—pox on't, what d'ye call her—her Brother's a noble *Spaniard*—Nephew to the dead General—

---

14 **'Sheartlikins** by God's heart

Florinda—ay, *Florinda*—And will nothing serve thy turn but
that damn'd virtuous Woman, whom on my Consience
thou lov'st in spite too, because thou seest little or no possibility of gaining her?

BELVILE: Thou art mistaken, I have Interest enough in that
lovely Virgin's Heart, to make me proud and vain, were it
not abated by the Severity of a Brother, who perceiving
my Happiness—

FREDERICK: Has civilly forbid thee the House?

BELVILE: 'Tis so, to make way for a powerful Rival, the Vice-
Roy's Son, who has the advantage of me, in being a Man of
Fortune, a *Spaniard,* and her Brother's Friend; which gives
him liberty to make his Court, whilst I have recourse only to
Letters, and distant Looks from her Window, which are as soft
and kind as those which Heav'n sends down on Penitents.

BLUNT: Hey day! 'Sheartlikins, Simile! by this Light the Man
is quite spoil'd—*Frederick,* what the Devil are we made of,
that we cannot be thus concern'd for a Wench?—'Sheartlikins, our *Cupids* are like the Cooks of the Camp, they
can roast or boil a Woman, but they have none of the fine
Tricks to set 'em off, no Hogoes to make the Sauce pleasant, and the Stomach sharp.

FREDERICK: I dare swear I have had a hundred as young, kind
and handsom as this *Florinda;* and Dogs eat me, if they
were not as troublesom to me i'th' Morning as they were
welcome o'er night.

BLUNT: And yet, I warrant, he wou'd not touch another
Woman, if he might have her for nothing.

BELVILE: That's thy Joy, a cheap Whore.

BLUNT: Why, 'dsheartlikins, I Love a frank Soul—When did
you ever hear of an honest Woman that took a Man's
Mony? I warrant 'em good ones—But, Gentlemen, you
may be free, you have been kept so poor with Parliaments
and Protectors, that the little Stock you have is not worth
preserving—but I thank my Stars, I have more Grace than
to forfeit my Estate by Cavaliering.

BELVILE: Methinks only following the Court should be sufficient to entitle 'em to that.

BLUNT: 'Sheartlikins, they know I follow it to do it no good,
unless they pick a hole in my Coat for lending you Mony
now and then; which is a greater Crime to my Conscience, Gentlemen, than to the Common-wealth.

(*Enter* WILLMORE.)

WILLMORE: Ha! dear *Belvile!* noble Colonel!

BELVILE: *Willmore!* welcome ashore, my dear Rover!—what
happy Wind blew us this good Fortune?

WILLMORE: Let me salute you my dear *Fred,* and then command me—How is't honest Lad?

FREDERICK: Faith, Sir, the old Complement, infinitely the
better to see my dear mad *Willmore* again—Prithee why
camest thou ashore? and where's the Prince?

WILLMORE: He's well, and reigns still Lord of the watery Element—I must aboard again within a Day or two, and my
Business ashore was only to enjoy my self a little this Carnival.

BELVILE: Pray know our new Friend, Sir, he's but bashful, a
raw Traveller, but honest, stout, and one of us.

---

39 **Hogoes** Haut-goût, a relish

(*Embraces* BLUNT.)

WILLMORE: That you esteem him, gives him an Interest here.

BLUNT: Your Servant, Sir.

WILLMORE: But well—Faith I'm glad to meet you again in a
warm Climate, where the kind Sun has its god-like Power
still over the Wine and Woman.—Love and Mirth are my
Business in *Naples;* and if I mistake not the Place, here's an
excellent Market for Chapmen of my Humour.

BELVILE: See here be those kind Merchants of Love you look
for.

(*Enter several* MEN *in masquing Habits, some playing on Musick,
others dancing after;* WOMEN *drest like Curtezans, with Papers pin-
n'd to their Breasts, and Baskets of Flowers in their Hands.*)

BLUNT: 'Sheartlikins, what have we here!

FREDERICK: Now the Game begins.

WILLMORE: Fine pretty Creatures! may a stranger have leave
to look and love?—What's here—(*Reads the Paper.*): *Roses
for every Month!*

BLUNT: Roses for every Month! what means that?

BELVILE: They are, or wou'd have you think they're Curtezans,
who here in *Naples* are to be hir'd by the Month.

WILLMORE: Kind and obliging to inform us—Pray where do
these Roses grow? I would fain plant some of 'em in a
Bed of mine.

WOMAN: Beware such Roses, Sir.

WILLMORE: A Pox of fear: I'll be bak'd with thee between a
pair of Sheets, and that's thy proper Still, so I might but
strow such Roses over me and under me—Fair one,
wou'd you wou'd give me leave to gather at your Bush
this idle Month, I wou'd go near to make some Body
smell of it all the Year after.

BELVILE: And thou hast need of such a Remedy, for thou
stinkest of Tar and Rope-ends, like a Dock or Pesthouse.

(*The* WOMAN *puts her self into the Hands of a* MAN, *and Exit.*)

WILLMORE: Nay, nay, you shall not leave me so.

BELVILE: By all means use no Violence here.

WILLMORE: Death! just as I was going to be damnably in
love, to have her led off! I could pluck that Rose out of
his Hand, and even kiss the Bed, the Bush it grew in.

FREDERICK: No Friend to Love like a long Voyage at Sea.

BLUNT: Except a Nunnery, *Frederick.*

WILLMORE: Death! but will they not be kind, quickly be
kind? Thou know'st I'm no tame Sigher, but a rampant
Lion of the Forest.

(*Two* MEN *drest all over with Horns of several sorts, making Grimaces at one another, with Papers pinn'd on their Backs, advance
from the farther end of the Scene.*)

BELVILE: Oh the fantastical Rogues, how they are dress'd! 'tis
a Satir against the whole Sex.

WILLMORE: Is this a Fruit that grows in this warm Country?

BELVILE: Yes: 'Tis pretty to see these *Italian* start, swell, and stab
at the Word *Cuckold,* and yet stumble at Horns on every
Threshold.

WILLMORE: See what's on their Back—(*Reads.*) *Flowers for
every Night.*—Ah Rogue! And more sweet than Roses of
ev'ry Month! This is a Gardiner of *Adam's* own breeding.

(*They dance.*)

BELVILE: What think you of those grave People?—is a Wake in *Essex* half so mad or extravagant?

WILLMORE: I like their sober grave way, 'tis a kind of legal au-
125   thoriz'd Fornication, where the Men are not chid for 't, nor the Women despis'd, as amongst our dull *English;* even the Monsieurs want that part of good Manners.

BELVILE: But here in *Italy* a Monsieur is the humblest best-bred Gentleman—Duels are so baffled by Bravos that an
130   age shews not one, but between a *Frenchman* and a Hang-man, who is as much too hard for him on the Piazza, as they are for a *Dutchman* on the new Bridge—But see an-other Crew.

(*Enter* FLORINDA, HELLENA, *and* VALERIA, *drest like Gipsies;* CALLIS *and* STEPHANO, LUCETTA, PHILIPPO, *and* SANCHO *in Masquerade.*)

HELLENA: Sister, there's your *Englishman,* and with him a
135   handsome proper Fellow—I'll to him, and instead of telling him his Fortune, try my own.

WILLMORE: Gipsies, on my Life—Sure these will prattle if a Man cross their Hands. (*Goes to* HELLENA.)—Dear pretty (and I hope) young Devil, will you tell an amorous
140   Stranger what Luck he's like to have?

HELLENA: Have a care how you venture with me, Sir, lest I pick your Pocket, which will more vex your *English* Hu-mour, than an *Italian* Fortune will please you.

WILLMORE: How the Devil cam'st thou to know my Coun-
145   try and Humour?

HELLENA: The first I guess by a certain forward Impudence, which does not displease me at this time; and the Loss of your Money will vex you, because I hope you have but very little to lose.

150   WILLMORE: Egad Child, thou'rt i'th' right; it is so little, I dare not offer it thee for a Kindness—But cannot you divine what other things of more value I have about me, that I would more willingly part with?

HELLENA: Indeed no, that's the Business of a Witch, and I am
155   but a Gipsy yet—Yet, without looking in your Hand, I have a parlous Guess, 'tis some foolish Heart you mean, an inconstant *English* Heart, as little worth stealing as your Purse.

WILLMORE: Nay, then thou dost deal with the Devil, that's
160   certain—Thou hast guess'd as right as if thou hadst been one of that Number it has languisht for—I find you'll be better acquainted with it; nor can you take it in a better time, for I am come from Sea, Child; and *Venus* not being propitious to me in her own Element, I have a world of
165   Love in store—Wou'd you would be good-natur'd, and take some on't off my Hands.

HELLENA: Why—I could be inclin'd that way—but for a fool-ish Vow I am going to make—to die a Maid.

WILLMORE: Then thou art damn'd without Redemption; and
170   as I am a good Christian, I ought to charity to divert so wicked a Design—therefore prithee, dear Creature, let me know quickly when and where I shall begin to set a help-ing hand to so good a Work.

HELLENA: If you should prevail with my tender Heart (as I
175   begin to fear you will, for you have horrible loving Eyes) there will be difficulty in't that you'll hardly undergo for my sake.

WILLMORE: Faith, Child, I have been bred in Dangers, and wear a Sword that has been employ'd in a worse Cause, than for a handsom kind Woman—Name the Danger—let it be any thing but a long Siege, and I'll undertake it.   180

HELLENA: Can you storm?

WILLMORE: Oh, most furiously.

HELLENA: What think you of a Nunnery-wall? for he that wins me, must gain that first.

WILLMORE: A Nun! Oh how I love thee for't! there's no Sin-   185
ner like a young Saint—Nay, now there's no denying me: the old Law had no Curse (to a Woman) like dying a Maid; witness *Jephtha's* Daughter.

HELLENA: A very good Text this, if well handled; and I perceive, Father Captain, you would impose no severe Penance on her   190
who was inclin'd to console her self before she took Orders.

WILLMORE: If she be young and handsom.

HELLENA: Ay, there's it—but if she be not—

WILLMORE: By this Hand, Child, I have an implicit Faith, and dare venture on thee with all Faults—besides, 'tis more   195
meritorious to leave the World when thou hast tasted and prov'd the Pleasure on't; then 'twill be a Virtue in thee, which now will be pure Ignorance.

HELLENA: I perceive, good Father Captain, you design only to make me fit for Heaven—but if on the contrary you   200
should quite divert me from it, and bring me back to the World again, I should have a new Man to seek I find; and what a grief that will be—for when I begin, I fancy I shall love like any thing: I never try'd yet.

WILLMORE: Egad, and that's kind—Prithee, dear Creature,   205
give me Credit for a Heart, for faith, I'm a very honest Fel-low—Oh, I long to come first to the Banquet of Love; and such a swinging Appetite I bring—Oh, I'm impatient. Thy Lodging, Sweetheart, thy Lodging, or I'm a dead man.

HELLENA: Why must we be either guilty of Fornication or Mur-   210
der, if we converse with you Men?—And is there no differ-ence between leave to love me, and leave to lie with me?

WILLMORE: Faith, Child, they were made to go together.

LUCETTA: (*Pointing to* BLUNT.) Are you sure this is the Man?

SANCHO: When did I mistake your Game?   215

LUCETTA: This is a stranger, I know by his gazing; if he be brisk he'll venture to follow me; and then, if I understand my Trade, he's mine: he's *English* too, and they say that's a sort of good natur'd loving People, and have generally so kind an opinion of themselves, that a Woman with any   220
Wit may flatter 'em into any sort of Fool she pleases.

BLUNT: 'Tis so—she is taken—I have Beauties which my false Glass at home did not discover.

(*She often passes by* BLUNT *and gazes on him; he struts, and cocks, and walks, and gazes on her.*)

FLORINDA: This Woman watches me so, I shall get no Op-portunity to discover my self to him, and so miss the in-   225
tent of my coming—But as I was saying, Sir—(*Looking in his Hand.*) by this Line you should be a Lover.

BELVILE: I thought how right you guess'd, all Men are in love, or pretend to be so—Come, let me go, I'm weary of this fooling.   230

(*Walks away.*)

FLORINDA: I will not, till you have confess'd whether the Passion that you have vow'd *Florinda* be true or false.

(*She holds him, he strives to get from her.*)

BELVILE: *Florinda!*

(*Turns quick towards her.*)

235 FLORINDA: Softly.
BELVILE: Thou hast nam'd one will fix me here for ever.
FLORINDA: She'll be disappointed then, who expects you this Night at the Garden-gate, and if you'll fail not—as let me see the other Hand—you will go near to do—she vows to
240 die or make you happy.

(*Looks on* CALLIS, *who observes 'em.*)

BELVILE: What canst thou mean?
FLORINDA: That which I say—Farewell.

(*Offers to go.*)

BELVILE: Oh charming Sybil, stay, complete that Joy, which, as it is, will turn into Distraction!—Where must I be? at the
245 Garden-gate? I know it—at night you say—I'll sooner forfeit Heaven than disobey.

(*Enter* DON PEDRO *and other Masquers, and pass over the Stage.*)

CALLIS: Madam, your Brother's here.
FLORINDA: Take this to instruct you farther.

(*Gives him a Letter, and goes off.*)

FREDERICK: Have a care, Sir, what you promise; this may be
250 a Trap laid by her Brother to ruin you.
BELVILE: Do not disturb my Happiness with Doubts.

(*Opens the Letter.*)

WILLMORE: My dear pretty Creature, a Thousand Blessings on thee; still in this Habit, you say, and after Dinner at this Place.
HELLENA: Yes, if you will swear to keep your Heart, and not
255 bestow it between this time and that.
WILLMORE: By all the little Gods of Love I swear, I'll leave it with you; and if you run away with it, those Deities of Justice will revenge me.

(*Exeunt all the* WOMEN *except* LUCETTA.)

FREDERICK: Do you know the Hand?
260 BELVILE: 'Tis *Florinda's*.
All Blessings fall upon the virtuous Maid.
FREDERICK: Nay, no Idolatry, a sober Sacrifice I'll allow you.
BELVILE: Oh Friends! the welcom'st News, the softest Letter!—nay, you shall see it; and could you now be serious,
265 I might be made the happiest Man the Sun shines on.
WILLMORE: The Reason of this mighty Joy.
BELVILE: See how kindly she invites me to deliver her from the threaten'd Violence of her Brother—will you not assist me?
WILLMORE: I know not what thou mean'st, but I'll make one
270 at any Mischief where a Woman's concern'd—but she'll be grateful to us for the Favour, will she not?
BELVILE: How mean you?
WILLMORE: How should I mean? Thou know'st there's but one way for a Woman to oblige me.
275 BELVILE: Don't prophane—the Maid is nicely virtuous.

WILLMORE: Who pox, then she's fit for nothing but a Husband; let her e'en go, Colonel.
FREDERICK: Peace, she's the Colonel's Mistress, Sir.
WILLMORE: Let her be the Devil; if she be thy Mistress, I'll serve her—name the way.   280
BELVILE: Read here this Postcript.

(*Gives him a Letter.*)

WILLMORE: (*Reads.*) *At Ten at night—at the Garden-Gate—of which, if I cannot get the Key, I will contrive a way over the Wall—come attended with a Friend or two.*—Kind heart, if we three cannot weave a String to let her down a Garden-   285
Wall, 'twere pity but the Hangman wove one for us all.
FREDERICK: Let her alone for that: your Woman's Wit, your fair kind Woman, will not out-trick a Brother or a Jew, and contrive like a Jesuit in Chains—but see, *Ned Blunt* is stoln out after the Lure of a Damsel.   290

(*Exit* BLUNT *and* LUCETTA.)

BELVILE: So he'll scarce find his way home again, unless we get him cry'd by the Bell-man in the Market-place, and 'twou'd sound prettily—a lost *English* Boy of Thirty.
FREDERICK: I hope 'tis some common crafty Sinner, one that will fit him; it may be she'll sell him for *Peru*, the Rogue's   295
sturdy and would work well in a Mine; at least I hope she'll dress him for our Mirth; cheat him of all, then have him well-favour'dly bang'd, and turn'd out naked at Midnight.
WILLMORE: Prithee what Humour is he of, that you wish him so well?   300
BELVILE: Why, of an *English* Elder Brother's Humour, educated in a Nursery, with a Maid to tend him till Fifteen, and lies with his Grand-mother till he's of Age; one that knows no Pleasure beyond riding to the next Fair, or going up to *London* with his right Worshipful Father in Par-   305
liament-time; wearing gay Clothes, or making honourable Love to his Lady Mother's Landry-Maid; gets drunk at a Hunting-Match, and ten to one then gives some Proofs of his Prowess—A pox upon him, he's our Banker, and has all our Cash about him, and if he fail we are all broke.   310
FREDERICK: Oh let him alone for that matter, he's of a damn'd stingy Quality, that will secure our Stock. I know not in what Danger it were indeed, if the Jilt should pretend she's in love with him, for 'tis a kind believing Coxcomb; otherwise if he part with more than a Piece of   315
Eight—geld him: for which offer he may chance to be beaten, if she be a Whore of the first Rank.
BELVILE: Nay the Rogue will not be easily beaten, he's stout enough; perhaps if they talk beyond his Capacity, he may chance to exercise his Courage upon some of them; else   320
I'm sure they'll find it as difficult to beat as to please him.
WILLMORE: 'Tis a lucky Devil to light upon so kind a Wench!
FREDERICK: Thou hadst a great deal of talk with thy little Gipsy, coud'st thou do no good upon her? for mine was hard-hearted.   325
WILLMORE: Hang her, she was some damn'd honest Person of Quality, I'm sure, she was so very free and witty. If her Face

---

314 **a Piece of Eight** a piastre, a coin of varying values in different countries

be but answerable to her Wit and Humour, I would be bound to Constancy this Month to gain her. In the mean 330 time, have you made no kind Acquaintance since you came to Town?—You do not use to be honest so long, Gentlemen.

FREDERICK: Faith Love has kept us honest, we have been all fir'd with a Beauty newly come to Town, the famous *Pad-uana Angelica Bianca.*

335 WILLMORE: What, the Mistress of the dead *Spanish* General?

BELVILE: Yes, she's now the only ador'd Beauty of all the Youth in *Naples,* who put on all their charms to appear lovely in her sight, their Coaches, Liveries, and themselves, all gay, as on a Monarch's Birth-Day, to attract the Eyes of this fair 340 Charmer, while she has the Pleasure to behold all languish for her that see her.

FREDERICK: 'Tis pretty to see with how much Love the Men regard her, and how much Envy the Women.

WILLMORE: What Gallant has she?

345 BELVILE: None, she's exposed to Sale, and four Days in the Week she's yours—for so much a Month.

WILLMORE: The very Thought of it quenches all manner of Fire in me—yet prithee let's see her.

BELVILE: Let's first to Dinner, and after that we'll pass the Day 350 as you please—but at Night ye must all be at my Devotion.

WILLMORE: I will not fail you.

(*Exeunt.*)

ACT TWO

SCENE I

The Long Street.

Enter BELVILE *and* FREDERICK *in Masquing-Habits, and* WILLMORE *in his own Clothes, with a Vizard in his Hand.*

WILLMORE: But why thus disguis'd and muzzl'd?

BELVILE: Because whatever Extravagances we commit in these Faces, our own may not be oblig'd to answer 'em.

WILLMORE: I should have chang'd my Eternal Buff too: but 5 no matter, my little Gipsy wou'd not have found me out then: for if she should change hers, it is impossible I should know her, unless I should hear her prattle—A Pox on't, I cannot get her out of my Head: Pray Heaven, if ever I do see her again, she prove damnable ugly, that I may 10 fortify my self against her Tongue.

BELVILE: Have a care of Love, for o' my conscience she was not of a Quality to give thee any hopes.

WILLMORE: Pox on 'em, why do they draw a Man in then? She has play'd with my Heart so, that 'twill never lie still 15 till I have met with some kind Wench, that will play the Game out with me—Oh for my Arms full of soft, white, kind—Woman! such as I fancy *Angelica.*

BELVILE: This is her House, if you were but in stock to get admittance; they have not din'd yet; I perceive the Picture is 20 not out.

(*Enter* BLUNT.)

WILLMORE: I long to see the Shadow of the fair Substance, a Man may gaze on that for nothing.

BLUNT: Colonel, thy Hand—and thine, *Frederick.* I have been an Ass, a deluded Fool, a very Coxcomb from my Birth till this Hour, and heartily repent my little Faith. 25

BELVILE: What the Devil's the matter with thee *Ned?*

BLUNT: Oh such a Mistress, *Frederick,* such a Girl!

WILLMORE: Ha! where? *Frederick.* Ay where!

BLUNT: So fond, so amorous, so toying and fine! and all for sheer Love, ye Rogue! Oh how she lookt and kiss'd! and 30 sooth'd my Heart from my Bosom. I cannot think I was awake, and yet methinks I see and feel her Charms still—*Frederick.*—Try if she have not left the Taste of her balmy Kisses upon my Lips—

(*Kisses him.*)

BELVILE: Ha, ha, ha! *Willmore.* Death Man, where is she? 35

BLUNT: What a Dog was I to stay in dull *England* so long—How have I laught at the Colonel when he sigh'd for Love! but now the little Archer has reveng'd him, and by his own Dart, I can guess at all his Joys, which then I took for Fancies, mere Dreams and Fables—Well, I'm resolved 40 to sell all in Essex, and plant here for ever.

BELVILE: What a Blessing 'tis, thou hast a Mistress thou dar'st boast of; for I know thy Humour is rather to have a proclaim'd Clap, than a secret Amour.

WILLMORE: Dost know her Name? 45

BLUNT: Her Name? No, 'sheartlikins: what care I for Names?—She's fair, young, brisk and kind, even to ravishment: and what a Pox care I for knowing her by another Title?

WILLMORE: Didst give her anything?

BLUNT: Give her!—Ha, ha, ha! why, she's a Person of Quality 50 —That's a good one, give her! 'sheartlikins dost think such Creatures are to be bought? Or are we provided for such a Purchase? Give her, quoth ye? Why she presented me with this Bracelet, for the Toy of a Diamond I us'd to wear: No, Gentlemen, *Ned Blunt* is not every Body—She 55 expects me again to night.

WILLMORE: Egad that's well; we'll all go.

BLUNT: Not a Soul: No, Gentlemen, you are Wits; I am a dull Country Rogue, I.

FREDERICK: Well, Sir, for all your Person of Quality, I shall be 60 very glad to understand your Purse be secure; 'tis our whole Estate at present, which we are loth to hazard in one Bottom: come, Sir, unload.

BLUNT: Take the necessary Trifle, useless now to me, that am belov'd by such a Gentlewoman—'sheartlikins Money! 65 Here take mine too.

FREDERICK: No, keep that to be cozen'd, that we may laugh.

WILLMORE: Cozen'd!—Death! wou'd I cou'd meet with one, that wou'd cozen me of all the Love I cou'd spare to night.

FREDERICK: Pox 'tis some common Whore upon my Life. 70

BLUNT: A Whore! yes with such Clothes! such Jewels! such a House! such Furniture, and so attended! a Whore!

BELVILE: Why yes, Sir, they are Whores, tho they'll neither entertain you with Drinking, Swearing, or Baudy; are Whores in all those gay Clothes, and right Jewels; are 75 Whores with great Houses richly furnisht with Velvet Beds, Store of Plate, handsome Attendance, and fine Coaches, are Whores and errant ones.

WILLMORE: Pox on't, where do these fine Whores live?

80 BELVILE: Where no Rogue in Office yclep'd Constables dare give 'em laws, nor the Wine-inspired Bullies of the Town break their Windows; yet they are Whores, tho this *Essex Calf* believe them Persons of Quality.

BLUNT: 'Sheartlikins, y'are all Fools, there are things about
85 this *Essex* Calf, that shall take with the Ladies, beyond all your Wits and Parts—This Shape and Size, Gentlemen, are not to be despis'd; my Waste tolerably long, with other inviting Signs, that shall be nameless.

WILLMORE: Egad I believe he may have met with some Per-
90 son of Quality that may be kind to him.

BELVILE: Dost thou perceive any such tempting things about him, should make a fine Woman, and of Quality, pick him out from all Mankind, to throw away her Youth and Beauty upon, nay, and her dear Heart too?—no, no, *An-*
95 *gelica* has rais'd the Price too high.

WILLMORE: May she languish for Mankind till she die, and be damn'd for that one Sin alone.

(*Enter two* BRAVOES, *and hang up a great Picture of* ANGELICA's *against the Balcony, and two little ones at each side of the Door.*)

BELVILE: See there the fair Sign to the Inn, where a Man may lodge that's Fool enough to give her Price.

(WILLMORE *gazes on the Picture.*)

100 BLUNT: 'Sheartlikins, Gentlemen, what's this?

BELVILE: A famous Curtezan that's to be sold.

BLUNT: How! to be sold! nay then I have nothing to say to her—sold! what Impudence is practis'd in this Country?—With Order and Decency Whoring's established
105 here by virtue of the Inquisition—Come let's be gone, I'm sure we're no Chapmen for this Commodity.

FREDERICK: Thou art none, I'm sure, unless thou could'st have her in thy Bed at the Price of a Coach in the Street.

WILLMORE: How wondrous fair she is—a Thousand Crowns
110 a Month—by Heaven as many Kingdoms were too little. A plague of this Poverty—of which I ne'er complain, but when it hinders my Approach to Beauty, which Virtue ne'er could purchase.

(*Turns from the Picture.*)

BLUNT: What's this?—(*Reads.*) *A Thousand Crowns a Month!*—
115 'Sheartlikins, here's a Sum! sure 'tis a mistake.—Hark you, Friend, does she take or give so much by the Month!

FREDERICK: A Thousand Crowns! Why, 'tis a Portion for the *Infanta.*

BLUNT: Hark ye, Friends, won't she trust?
120 BRAVO: This is a Trade, Sir, that cannot live by Credit.

(*Enter* DON PEDRO *in Masquerade, follow'd by* STEPHANO.)

BELVILE: See, here's more Company, let's walk off a while.

(PEDRO *reads.* Exeunt ENGLISH. *Enter* ANGELICA *and* MORETTA *in the Balcony, and draw a Silk Curtain.*)

PEDRO: Fetch me a Thousand Crowns, I never wish to buy this Beauty at an easier Rate.

(*Passes off.*)

ANGELICA: Prithee what said those Fellows to thee?

BRAVO: Madam, the first were Admirers of Beauty only, but
125 no purchasers; they were merry with your Price and Pic-ture, laught at the Sum, and so past off.

ANGELICA: No matter, I'm not displeas'd with their rallying; their Wonder feeds my Vanity, and he that wishes to buy, gives me more Pride, than he that gives my Price can
130 make me Pleasure.

BRAVO: Madam, the last I knew thro all his disguises to be Don *Pedro,* Nephew to the General, and who was with him in *Pampelona.*

ANGELICA: Don *Pedro*! my old Gallant's Nephew! When his
135 Uncle dy'd, he left him a vast Sum of Money; it is he who was so in love with me at *Padua,* and who us'd to make the General so jealous.

MORETTA: Is this he that us'd to prance before our Window and take such care to shew himself an amorous Ass? if I am
140 not mistaken, he is the likeliest Man to give your Price.

ANGELICA: The Man is brave and generous, but of an Hu-mour so uneasy and inconstant, that the victory over his Heart is as soon lost as won; a Slave that can add little to the Triumph of the Conqueror; but inconstancy's the Sin
145 of all Mankind, therefore I'm resolv'd that nothing but Gold shall charm my Heart.

MORETTA: I'm glad on't; 'tis only interest that Women of our Profession ought to consider: tho I wonder what has kept you from that general Disease of our Sex so long, I mean
150 that of being in love.

ANGELICA: A kind, but sullen Star, under which I had the Happiness to be born; yet I have had no time for Love; the bravest and noblest of Mankind have purchas'd my Favours at so dear a Rate, as if no Coin but Gold were
155 current with our Trade—But here's Don *Pedro* again, fetch me my Lute—for 'tis for him or Don *Antonio* the Vice-Roy's Son, that I have spread my Nets.

(*Enter at one Door Don* PEDRO, *and* STEPHANO; *Don* ANTONIO *and* DIEGO [*his page*], *at the other Door, with people following him in Masquerade, antickly attir'd, some with Musick: they both go up to the Picture.*)

ANTONIO: A thousand Crowns! had not the Painter flatter'd
160 her, I should not think it dear.

PEDRO: Flatter'd her! by Heaven he cannot. I have seen the Original, nor is there one Charm here more than adorns her Face and Eyes; all this soft and sweet, with a certain languishing Air, that no Artist can represent.

ANTONIO: What I heard of her Beauty before had fir'd my
165 Soul, but this confirmation of it has blown it into a flame.

PEDRO: Ha!

PAGE: Sir, I have known you throw away a Thousand Crowns on a worse Face, and tho y' are near your Marriage, you may venture a little Love here; *Florinda*—will not miss it.
170 PEDRO: (*Aside.*) Ha! *Florinda*! Sure 'tis *Antonio.*

ANTONIO: *Florinda*! name not those distant Joys, there's not one thought of her will check my Passion here.

PEDRO: Florinda scorn'd! and all my Hopes defeated of the Possession of Angelica! (*A noise of a Lute above. Antonio*
175 *gazes up.*) Her Injuries by Heaven he shall not boast of.

(*Song to a Lute above.*)

Song

When *Damon* first began to love,
He languisht in a soft Desire,
And knew not how the Gods to move,
180   To lessen or increase his Fire,
For *Caelia* in her charming Eyes
    Wore all Love's Sweet, and all his Cruelties.

II

But as beneath a Shade he lay,
Weaving of Flow'rs for *Caelia's* Hair,
185 She chanc'd to lead her Flock that way,
And saw the am'rous Shepherd there.
She gaz'd around upon the Place,
And saw the Grove (resembling Night)
To all the Joys of Love invite,
190   Whilst guilty Smiles and Blushes drest her Face.
At this the bashful Youth all Transport grew,
And with kind Force he taught the Virgin how
To yield what all his Sighs cou'd never do.

ANTONIO: By Heav'n she's charming fair!

(ANGELICA *throws open the Curtains, and bows to* ANTONIO, *who pulls off his Vizard, and bows and blows up Kisses.* PEDRO *unseen looks in his Face.*)

195 PEDRO: 'Tis he, the false *Antonio!*
ANTONIO: Friend, where must I pay my offering of Love?

(*To the bravo.*)

    My Thousand Crowns I mean.
PEDRO: That offering I have design'd to make,
    And yours will come too late.
200 ANTONIO: Prithee be gone, I shall grow angry else,
    And then thou art not safe.
PEDRO: My Anger may be fatal, Sir, as yours;
    And he that enters here may prove this Truth.
ANTONIO: I know not who thou art, but I am sure thou'rt
205   worth my killing, and aiming at *Angelica.*

(*They draw and fight.*)

(*Enter* WILLMORE *and* BLUNT, *who draw and part 'em*)

BLUNT: 'Sheartlikins, here's fine doings.
WILLMORE: Tilting for the Wench I'm sure—nay gad, if that
    wou'd win her, I have as good a Sword as the best of ye—
    Put up—put up, and take another time and place, for this
210   is design'd for Lovers only.

(*They all put up.*)

PEDRO: We are prevented; dare you meet me to morrow on
    the *Molo?*
For I've a Title to a better quarrel,
That of *Florinda,* in whose credulous Heart
Thou'st made an Int'rest, and destroy'd my Hopes.
215 ANTONIO: Dare?
    I'll meet thee there as early as the Day.

PEDRO: We will come thus disguis'd, that whosoever chance
    to get the better, he may escape unknown.
ANTONIO: It shall be so.

(*Exit* PEDRO *and* STEPHANO.)

Who shou'd this Rival be? unless the *English* Colonel, of 220
whom I've often heard Don Pedro speak; it must be he, and
time he were removed, who lays a Claim to all my Happiness.

(WILLMORE *having gaz'd all this while on the Picture, pulls down a little one.*)

WILLMORE: This posture's loose and negligent,
    The sight on't wou'd beget a warm desire
    In Souls, whom Impotence and Age had chill'd.   225
    —This must along with me.
BRAVO: What means this rudeness, Sir?—restore the Picture.
ANTONIO: Ha! Rudeness committed to the fair *Angelica!*—
    Restore the Picture, Sir.
WILLMORE: Indeed I will not, Sir.   230
ANTONIO: By Heav'n but you shall.
WILLMORE: Nay, do not shew your Sword; if you do, by this
    dear Beauty—I will shew mine too.
ANTONIO: What right can you pretend to't?
WILLMORE: That of Possession which I will maintain—you 235
    perhaps have 1000 Crowns to give for the Original.
ANTONIO: No matter, Sir, you shall restore the Picture.
ANGELICA: Oh, *Moretta!* what's the matter?

(ANGELICA *and* MORETTA *above.*)

ANTONIO: Or leave your Life behind.
WILLMORE: Death! you lye—I will do neither.   240
ANGELICA: Hold, I command you, if for me you fight.

(*They fight, the Spaniards join with* ANTONIO, BLUNT *laying on like mad. They leave off and bow.*)

WILLMORE: How heavenly fair she is!—ah Plague of her Price.
ANGELICA: You Sir in Buff, you that appear a Soldier, that first
    began this Insolence.
WILLMORE: 'Tis true, I did so, if you call it Insolence for a 245
    Man to preserve himself; I saw your charming Picture, and
    was wounded: quite thro my Soul each pointed Beauty
    ran; and wanting a Thousand Crowns to procure my
    Remedy, I laid this little Picture to my Bosom—which if
    you cannot allow me, I'll resign.   250
ANGELICA: No, you may keep the Trifle.
ANTONIO: You shall first ask my leave, and this.

(*Fight again as before.*)

(*Enter* BELVILE *and* FREDERICK *who join with the English.*)

ANGELICA: Hold; will you ruin me?—*Biskey, Sebastian,* part them.

(*The* SPANIARDS *are beaten off.*)

MORETTA: Oh Madam, we're undone, a pox upon that rude
    Fellow, he's set on to ruin us: we shall never see good days, 255
    till all these fighting poor Rogues are sent to the Gallies.

(*Enter* BELVILE, BLUNT *and* WILLMORE, *with his shirt bloody.*)

BLUNT: 'Sheartlikins, beat me at this Sport, and I'll ne'er wear Sword more.

BELVILE: The Devil's in thee for a mad Fellow, thou art always
260   one at an unlucky Adventure.—Come, let's be gone whilst we're safe, and remember these are *Spaniards,* a sort of People that know how to revenge an Affront.

FREDERICK: (*To* WILLMORE.) You bleed; I hope you are not wounded.

265 WILLMORE: Not much:—a plague upon your Dons, if they fight no better they'll ne'er recover *Flanders.*—What the Devil was't to them that I took down the Picture?

BLUNT: Took it! 'Sheartlikins, we'll have the great one too; 'tis ours by Conquest.—Prithee, help me up, and I'll pull it
270   down.—

ANGELICA: Stay, Sir, and e'er you affront me further, let me know how you durst commit this Outrage—To you I speak, Sir, for you appear like a Gentleman.

WILLMORE: To me, Madam?—Gentlemen, your Servant.

(BELVILE *stays him.*)

275 BELVILE: Is the Devil in thee? Do'st know the danger of en-tring the house of an incens'd Curtezan?

WILLMORE: I thank you for your care—but there are other matters in hand, there are, tho we have no great Tempta-tion.—Death! let me go.

280 FREDERICK: Yes, to your Lodging, if you will, but not in here.—Damn these gay Harlots—by this Hand I'll have as sound and hansome a Whore for a Patacoone.—Death, Man, she'll murder thee.

WILLMORE: Oh! fear me not, shall I not venture where a
285   Beauty calls? a lovely charming Beauty? for fear of dan-ger! when by Heaven there's none so great as to long for her, whilst I want Money to purchase her.

FREDERICK: Therefore 'tis loss of time, unless you had the thousand Crowns to pay.

290 WILLMORE: It may be she may give a Favour, at least I shall have the pleasure of saluting her when I enter, and when I depart.

BELVILE: Pox, she'll as soon lie with thee, as kiss thee, and sooner stab than do either—you shall not go.

ANGELICA: Fear not, Sir, all I have to wound with, is my Eyes.

295 BLUNT: Let him go, 'Sheartlikins, I believe the Gentlewoman means well.

BELVILE: Well, take thy Fortune, we'll expect you in the next Street.—Farewell Fool,—farewell—

WILLMORE: B'ye Colonel—

(*Goes in.*)

300 FREDERICK: The Rogue's stark mad for a Wench.

(*Exeunt.*)

SCENE II

A Fine Chamber.

Enter WILLMORE, ANGELICA, *and* MORETTA.

ANGELICA: Insolent, Sir, how durst you pull down my Picture?
WILLMORE: Rather, how durst you set it up, to tempt poor amorous Mortals with so much Excellence? which I find you have but too well consulted by the unmerciful price you set upon't.—Is all this Heaven of Beauty shewn to 5 move Despair in those that cannot buy? and can you think the effects of that Despair shou'd be less extravagant than I have shewn?

ANGELICA: I sent for you to ask my Pardon, Sir, not to aggra-vate your Crime.—I thought I shou'd have seen you at 10 my Feet imploring it.

WILLMORE: You are deceived, I came to rail at you, and talk such Truths, too, as shall let you see the Vanity of that Pride, which taught you how to set such a Price on Sin. For such it is, whilst that which is Love's due is meanly barter'd for. 15

ANGELICA: Ha, ha, ha, alas, good Captain, what pity 'tis your edifying Doctrine will do no good upon me—*Moretta,* fetch the Gentleman a Glass, and let him survey himself, to see what Charms he has,—(*Aside in a soft tone.*) and guess my Business. 20

MORETTA: He knows himself of old, I believe those Breeches and he have been acquainted ever since he was beaten at *Worcester.*

ANGELICA: Nay, do not abuse the poor Creature.—

MORETTA: Good Weather-beaten Corporal, will you march 25 off? we have no need of your Doctrine, tho you have of our Charity; but at present we have no Scraps, we can af-ford no kindness for God's sake; in fine, Sirrah, the Price is too high i'th' Mouth for you, therefore troop, I say.

WILLMORE: Here, good Fore-Woman of the Shop, serve me, 30 and I'll be gone.

MORETTA: Keep it to pay your Landress, your Linen stinks of the Gun-Room; for here's no selling by Retail.

WILLMORE: Thou hast sold plenty of thy stale Ware at a cheap Rate. 35

MORETTA: Ay, the more silly kind Heart I, but this is an Age wherein Beauty is at higher Rates.—In fine, you know the price of this.

WILLMORE: I grant you 'tis here set down a thousand Crowns a Month—Baud, take your black Lead and sum it up, that 40 I may have a Pistole-worth of these vain gay things, and I'll trouble you no more.

MORETTA: Pox on him, he'll fret me to Death:—abominable Fellow, I tell thee, we only sell by the whole Piece.

WILLMORE: 'Tis very hard, the whole Cargo or nothing— 45 Faith, Madam, my Stock will not reach it, I cannot be your Chapman.—Yet I have Countrymen in Town, Mer-chants of Love, like me; I'll see if they'll put for a share, we cannot lose much by it, and what we have no use for, we'll sell upon the *Friday's* Mart, at—*Who gives more?* I am 50 studying, Madam, how to purchase you, tho at present I am unprovided of Money.

ANGELICA: Sure, this from any other Man would anger me— nor shall he know the Conquest he has made—Poor an-gry Man, how I despise this railing. 55

WILLMORE: Yes, I am poor—but I'm a Gentleman,
    And one that scorns this Baseness which you practise.
    Poor as I am, I would not sell my self,
    No, not to gain your charming high-priz'd Person.

---

282 **Patacoone** a Spanish coin

41 **Pistole** a gold coin

60   Tho I admire you strangely for your Beauty,
       Yet I contemn your Mind.
       —And yet I wou'd at any rate enjoy you;
       At your own rate—but cannot—See here
       The only Sum I can command on Earth;
65   I know not where to eat when this is gone:
       Yet such a Slave I am to Love and Beauty,
       This last reserve I'll sacrifice to enjoy you.
       —Nay, do not frown, I know you are to be bought,
       And wou'd be bought by me, by me,
70   For a mean trifling Sum, if I could pay it down.
       Which happy knowledge I will still repeat,
       And lay it to my Heart, it has a Virtue in't,
       And soon will cure those Wounds your Eyes have made.
       —And yet—there's something so divinely powerful there—
75   Nay, I will gaze—to let you see my Strength.

(Holds her, looks on her, and pauses and sighs.)

       By Heaven, bright Creature—I would not for the World
       Thy Fame were half so fair as thy Face.

(Turns her away from him.)

ANGELICA: *(Aside.)* His words go thro me to the very Soul.
       —If you have nothing else to say to me.
80 WILLMORE: Yes, you shall hear how infamous you are—
       For which I do not hate thee:
       But that secures my Heart, and all the Flames it feels
       Are but so many Lusts,
       I know it by their sudden bold intrusion.
85   The Fire's impatient and betrays, 'tis false—
       For had it been the purer Flame of Love,
       I should have pin'd and languish'd at your Feet,
       E'er found the Impudence to have discover'd it.
       I now dare stand your Scorn, and your Denial.
90 MORETTA: Sure she's bewitcht, that you can stand thus tamely,
       and hear his saucy railing.—Sirrah, will you be gone?
ANGELICA: How dare you take this liberty?—(*To* MORETTA.)
       Withdraw.—Pray, tell me, Sir, are not you guilty of the
       same mercenary Crime? When a Lady is proposed to you
95   for a Wife, you never ask, how fair, discreet, or virtuous she
       is; but what's her Fortune—which if but small, you cry—
       She will not do my business—and basely leave her, tho she
       languish for you.—Say, is not this as poor?
WILLMORE: It is a barbarous Custom, which I will scorn to
100   defend in our Sex, and do despise in yours.
ANGELICA: Thou art a brave Fellow! put up thy Gold, and know
       That were thy Fortune large, as is thy Soul,
       Thou shouldst not buy my Love,
       Couldst thou forget those mean Effects of Vanity,
105   Which set me out to sale; and as a Lover, prize
       My yielding Joys.
       Canst thou believe they'l be entirely thine,
       Without considering they were mercenary?
WILLMORE: *(Aside.)* I cannot tell, I must bethink me first—
110   ha, Death, I'm going to believe her.
ANGELICA: Prithee, confirm that Faith—or if thou canst
       not—flatter me a little, 'twill please me from thy Mouth.
WILLMORE: Curse on thy charming Tongue! dost thou return
       My feign'd Contempt with so much subtilty?

(Aside.)

Thou'st found the easiest way into my Heart,   115
Tho I yet know that all thou say'st is false.

(Turning from her in a Rage.)

ANGELICA: By all that's good 'tis real,
       I never lov'd before, tho oft a Mistress.
       —Shall my first Vows be slighted?
WILLMORE: *(Aside.)* What can she mean?   120
ANGELICA: *(In an angry tone.)* I find you cannot credit me.
WILLMORE: I know you take me for an errant Ass,
       An Ass that may be sooth'd into Belief,
       And then be us'd at pleasure.
       —But, Madam, I have been so often cheated   125
       By perjur'd, soft, deluding Hypocrites,
       That I've no Faith left for the cozening Sex,
       Especially for Women of your Trade.
ANGELICA: The low esteem you have of me, perhaps
       May bring my Heart again: 130
       For I have Pride that yet surmounts my Love.

(She turns with Pride, he holds her.)

WILLMORE: Throw off this Pride, this Enemy to Bliss,
       And shew the Power of Love: 'tis with those Arms
       I can be only vanquisht, made a Slave.
ANGELICA: Is all my mighty Expectation vanisht?   135
       —No, I will not hear thee talk,—thou hast a Charm
       In every word, that draws my Heart away.
       And all the thousand Trophies I design'd,
       Thou hast undone—Why are thou soft?
       Thy Looks are bravely rough, and meant for War.   140
       Could thou not storm on still?
       I then perhaps had been as free as thou.
WILLMORE: *(Aside.)* Death! how she throws her Fire about
       my Soul!
       —Take heed, fair Creature, how you raise my Hopes,
       Which once assum'd pretend to all Dominion.   145
       There's not a Joy thou hast in store
       I shall not then command:
       For which I'll pay thee back my Soul, my Life.
       Come, let's begin th' account this happy minute.
ANGELICA: And will you pay me then the Price I ask?   150
WILLMORE: Oh, why dost thou draw me from an awful
       Worship,
       By shewing thou art no Divinity?
       Conceal the Fiend, and shew me all the Angel;
       Keep me but ignorant, and I'll be devout,
       And pay my Vows for ever at this Shrine.   155

(Kneels, and kisses her Hand.)

ANGELICA: The Pay I mean is but thy Love for mine.—Can
       you give that?
WILLMORE: Intirely—come, let's withdraw: where I'll renew
       my vows,—and breathe 'em with such Ardour, thou shalt
       not doubt my Zeal.   160
ANGELICA: Thou hast a Power too strong to be resisted.

(Exit WILLMORE *and* ANGELICA.*)*

MORETTA: Now my Curse go with you—Is all our Project
fallen to this? to love the only Enemy to our Trade? Nay,
to love such a Shameroon, a very Beggar; nay, a Pirate-
165   Beggar, whose Business is to rifle and be gone, a No-Pur-
chase, No-Pay Tatterdemalion, an English Piccaroon; a
Rogue that fights for daily Drink, and takes a Pride in being loyally lousy—Oh, I could curse now, if I durst—This
is the Fate of most Whores.

170   *Trophies, which from believing Fops we win,*
       Are Spoils to those who cozen us again.

ACT THREE

SCENE I

A Street.

Enter FLORINDA, VALERIA, HELLENA, *in Antick different Dresses
from what they were in before,* CALLIS *attending.*

FLORINDA: I wonder what should make my Brother in so ill
a Humour: I hope he has not found out our Ramble this
Morning.

HELLENA: No, if he had, we should have heard on't at both
5   Ears, and have been mew'd up this Afternoon; which I
would not for the World should have happen'd—Hey ho!
I'm sad as a Lover's Lute.

VALERIA: Well, methinks we have learnt this Trade of Gipsies
as readily as if we had been bred upon the Road to *Loretto:*
10   and yes I did so fumble, when I told the Stranger his Fortune, that I was afraid I should have told my own and
yours by mistake—But methinks *Hellena* has been very serious ever since.

FLORINDA: I would give my Garters she were in love, to be
15   reveng'd upon her, for abusing me—How is't, *Hellena?*

HELLENA: Ah!—would I had never seen my mad Monsieur—and
yet for all your laughing I am not in love—and yet this small
Acquaintance, o'my Conscience, will never out of my Head.

VALERIA: Ha, ha, ha—I laugh to think how thou art fitted with a
20   Lover, a Fellow that, I warrant, loves every new Face he sees.

HELLENA: Hum—he has not kept his Word with me here—
and may be taken up—that thought is not very pleasant to
me—what the Duce should this be now that I feel?

VALERIA: What is't like?

25 HELLENA: Nay, the Lord knows—but if I should be hanged, I
cannot chuse but be angry and afraid, when I think that mad
Fellow should be in love with any Body but me—What to
think of my self I know not—Would I could meet with
some true damn'd Gipsy, that I might know my Fortune.

30 VALERIA: Know it! why there's nothing so easy; thou wilt love
this wandering Inconstant till thou find'st thy self hanged
about his Neck, and then be as mad to get free again.

FLORINDA: Yes, *Valeria;* we shall see her bestride his Baggage-
horse, and follow him to the Campaign.

35 HELLENA: So, so; now you are provided for, there's no care
taken of poor me—But since you have set my Heart a
wishing, I am resolv'd to know for what. I will not die of
the Pip, so I will not.

---

164 **shameroon** a trickster, a cozening rascal

FLORINDA: Art thou mad to talk so? Who will like thee well
enough to have thee, that hears what a mad Wench thou art?   40

HELLENA: Like me! I don't intend every he that likes me shall
have me, but he that I like: I shou'd have staid in the Nunnery still, if I had lik'd my Lady Abbess as well as she lik'd
me. No, I came thence, not (as my wise Brother imagines)
to take an eternal Farewel of the World, but to love and to   45
be belov'd; and I will be belov'd, or I'll get one of your
Men, so I will.

VALERIA: Am I put into the Number of Lovers?

HELLENA: You! my Couz, I know thou art too good natur'd to
leave us in any Design: Thou wou't venture a Cast, tho thou   50
comest off a Loser, especially with such a Gamester—I ob-
serv'd your Man, and your willing ears incline that way; and
if you are not a Lover, 'tis an Art soon learnt—that I find.

(Sighs.)

FLORINDA: I wonder how you learnt to love so easily, I had a
thousand Charms to meet my Eyes and Ears, e'er I cou'd   55
yield; and 'twas the knowledge of *Belvile's* Merit, not the
surprising Person, took my Soul—Thou art too rash to
give a Heart at first sight.

HELLENA: Hang your considering Lover; I ne'er thought beyond the Fancy, that 'twas a very pretty, idle, silly kind of   60
Pleasure to pass ones time with, to write little, soft, non-
sensical Billets, and with great difficulty and danger receive Answers; in which I shall have my Beauty prais'd, my
Wit admir'd (tho little or none) and have the Vanity and
Power to know I am desirable; then I have the more In-   65
clination that way, because I am to be a Nun, and so shall
not be suspected to have any such earthly Thoughts about
me—But when I walk thus—and sigh thus—they'll think
my Mind's upon my Monastery, and cry, how happy 'tis
she's so resolv'd!—But not a Word of Man.   70

FLORINDA: What a mad Creature's this!

HELLENA: I'll warrant, if my Brother hears either of you sigh,
he cries (gravely)—I fear you have the Indiscretion to be in
love, but take heed of the Honour of our House, and your
own unspotted Fame; and so he conjures on till he has laid   75
the soft-wing'd God in your Hearts, or broke the Bird-
snest— But see here comes your Lover: but where's my inconstant? let's stop aside, and we may learn something.

(Go aside.)

(Enter BELVILE, FREDERICK, *and* BLUNT.)

BELVILE: What means this? the Picture's taken in.

BLUNT: It may be the Wench is good-natur'd, and will be   80
kind *gratis.* Your Friend's a proper handsom Fellow.

BELVILE: I rather think she has cut his Throat and is fled: I am
mad he should throw himself into Dangers—Pox on't, I
shall want him to night—let's knock and ask for him.

HELLENA: My heart goes a-pit a-pat, for fear 'tis my Man they   85
talk of.

(Knock, MORETTA *above.)*

MORETTA: What would you have?

BELVILE: Tell the Stranger that enter'd here about two Hours
ago, that his Friends stay here for him.

90 MORETTA: A Curse upon him for *Moretta,* would he were at the Devil—but he's coming to you.

(*Enter* WILLMORE.)

HELLENA: I, I, 'tis he. Oh how this vexes me.

BELVILE: And how, and how, dear Lad, has Fortune smil'd? Are we to break her Windows, or raise up Altars to her! hah!

95 WILLMORE: Does not my Fortune sit triumphant on my Brow? dost not see the little wanton God there all gay and smiling? have I not an Air about my Face and Eyes, that distinguish me from the Croud of common Lovers? By Heav'n, *Cupid*'s Quiver has not half so many Darts as her 100 Eyes—Oh such a Bona Roba, to sleep in her Arms is lying in Fresco, all perfum'd Air about me.

HELLENA: (*Aside.*) Here's fine encouragement for me to fool on.

WILLMORE: Hark ye, where didst thou purchase that rich Canary we drank to-day? Tell me, that I may adore the 105 Spigot, and sacrifice to the Butt: the Juice was divine, into which I must dip my Rosary, and then bless all things that I would have bold or fortunate.

BELVILE: Well, Sir, let's go take a Bottle, and hear the Story of your Success.

110 FREDERICK: Would not *French* Wine do better?

WILLMORE: Damn the hungry Balderdash; cheerful Sack has a generous Virtue in't, inspiring a successful Confidence, gives Eloquence to the Tongue, and Vigour to the Soul; and has in a few Hours compleated all my Hopes and Wishes. There's 115 nothing left to raise a new Desire in me—Come let's be gay and wanton—and, Gentlemen, study, study what you want, for here are Friends,—that will supply, Gentlemen,—hark! what a charming sound they make—'tis he and she Gold whilst here, shall beget new Pleasures every moment.

120 BLUNT: But hark ye, Sir, you are not married, are you?

WILLMORE: All the Honey of Matrimony, but none of the Sting, Friend.

BLUNT: 'Sheartlikins, thou'rt a fortunate Rogue.

WILLMORE: I am so, Sir, let these inform you.—Ha, how 125 sweetly they chime! Pox of Poverty, it makes a Man a Slave, makes Wit and Honour sneak, my Soul grew lean and rusty for want of Credit.

BLUNT: 'Sheartlikins, this I like well, it looks like my lucky Bargain! Oh how I long for the Approach of my Squire, 130 that is to conduct me to her House again. Why! here's two provided for.

FREDERICK: By this light y're happy Men.

BLUNT: Fortune is pleased to smile on us, Gentlemen,—to smile on us.

(*Enter* SANCHO, *and pulls* BLUNT *by the Sleeve. They go aside.*)

135 SANCHO: Sir, my Lady expects you—she has remov'd all that might oppose your Will and Pleasure—and is impatient till you come.

BLUNT: Sir, I'll attend you—Oh the happiest Rogue! I'll take no leave, lest they either dog me, or stay me.

(*Exit with* SANCHO.)

140 BELVILE: But then the little Gipsy is forgot?

WILLMORE: A Mischief on thee for putting her into my thoughts; I had quite forgot her else, and this Night's Debauch had drunk her quite down.

HELLENA: Had it so, good Captain?

(*Claps him on the Back.*)

WILLMORE: Ha! I hope she did not hear.   145

HELLENA: What, afraid of such a Champion!

WILLMORE: Oh! you're a fine Lady of your word, are you not? to make a Man languish a whole day—

HELLENA: In tedious search of me.

WILLMORE: Egad, Child, thou'rt in the right, hadst thou seen   150 what a melancholy Dog I have been ever since I was a Lover, how I have walkt the Streets like a *Capuchin,* with my Hands in my Sleeves—Faith, Sweetheart, thou wouldst pity me.

HELLENA: Now, if I should be hang'd, I can't be angry with him, he dissembles so heartily—Alas, good Captain, what   155 pains you have taken—Now were I ungrateful not to reward so true a Servant.

WILLMORE: Poor Soul! that's kindly said, I see thou bearest a Conscience—come then for a beginning shew me thy dear Face.   160

HELLENA: I'm afraid, my small Acquaintance, you have been staying that swinging stomach you boasted of this morning; I remember then my little Collation would have gone down with you, without the Sauce of a handsom Face— Is your Stomach so quesy now?   165

WILLMORE: Faith long fasting, Child, spoils a Man's Appetite—yet if you durst treat, I could so lay about me still.

HELLENA: And would you fall to, before a Priest says Grace?

WILLMORE: Oh fie, fie, what an old out-of-fashion'd thing hast thou nam'd? Thou could'st not dash me more out of   170 Countenance, shouldst thou shew me an ugly Face.

(*Whilst he is seemingly courting* HELLENA, *enter* ANGELICA, MORETTA, BISKEY, *and* SEBASTIAN, *all in Masquerade:* ANGELICA *sees* WILLMORE *and starts.*)

ANGELICA: Heavens, is't he? and passionately fond to see another Woman?

MORETTA: What cou'd you expect less from such a Swaggerer?

ANGELICA: Expect! as much as I paid him, a Heart intire,   175 Which I had pride enough to think when e'er I gave It would have rais'd the Man above the Vulgar, Made him all Soul, and that all soft and constant.

HELLENA: You see, Captain, how willing I am to be Friends with you, till Time and Ill-luck make us Lovers; and ask   180 you the Question first, rather than put your Modesty to the blush, by asking me: for alas, I know you Captains are such strict Men, severe Observers of your Vows to Chastity, that 'twill be hard to prevail with your tender Conscience to marry a young willing Maid.   185

WILLMORE: Do not abuse me, for fear I should take thee at thy word, and marry thee indeed, which I'm sure will be Revenge sufficient.

HELLENA: O' my Conscience, that will be our Destiny, because we are both of one humour; I am as inconstant as you, for   190 I have considered, Captain, that a handsom Woman has a great deal to do whilst her Face is good, for then is our Harvest- time to gather Friends; and should I in these days of my Youth, catch a fit of foolish Constancy, I were undone; 'tis loitering by day-light in our great Journey: there-   195 fore declare, I'll allow but one year for Love, one year for Indifference, and one year for Hate—and then—go hang your self—for I profess myself the gay, the kind, and the inconstant—the Devil's in't if this won't please you.

200 WILLMORE: Oh most damnably!—I have a Heart with a hole quite thro it too, no Prison like mine to keep a Mistress in.

ANGELICA: (*Aside.*) Purjur'd Man! how I believe thee now!

HELLENA: Well, I see our Business as well as Humours are alike, yours to cozen as many Maids as will trust you, and
205 I as many Men as have Faith—See if I have not as desperate a lying look, as you can have for the heart of you.

(*Pulls off her Vizard; he starts.*)

—How do you like it, Captain?

WILLMORE: Like it! by Heav'n, I never saw so much Beauty. Oh the Charms of those sprightly black Eyes, that strangely
210 fair Face, full of Smiles and Dimples! those soft round melting cherry Lips! and small even white Teeth! not to be exprest, but silently adored!—Oh one Look more, and strike me dumb, or I shall repeat nothing else till I am mad.

(*He seems to court her to pull off her Vizard: she refuses.*)

ANGELICA: I can endure no more—nor is it fit to interrupt
215 him; for if I do, my Jealousy has so destroy'd my Reason,—I shall undo him—Therefore I'll retire. And you *Sebastian* (*To one of her bravoes.*) follow that Woman, and learn who 'tis; (*To the other bravo.*) while you tell the Fugitive, I would speak to him instantly.

(*Exit.*)

(*This while* FLORINDA *is talking to* BELVILE, *who stands sullenly.* FREDERICK *courting* VALERIA.)

220 VALERIA: Prithee, dear Stranger, be not so sullen; for tho you have lost your Love, you see my Friend frankly offers you hers, to play with in the mean time.

BELVILE: Faith, Madam, I am sorry I can't play at her Game.

FREDERICK: Pray leave your Intercession, and mind your own
225 Affair, they'll better agree apart; he's a model Sigher in Company, but alone no Woman escapes him.

FLORINDA: Sure he does but rally—yet if it should be true— I'll tempt him farther—Believe me, noble Stranger, I'm no common Mistress—and for a little proof on't—wear this
230 Jewel—nay, take it, Sir, 'tis right, and Bills of Exchange may sometimes miscarry.

BELVILE: Madam, why am I chose out of all Mankind to be the Object of your Bounty?

VALERIA: There's another civil Question askt.

235 FREDERICK: Pox of's Modesty, it spoils his own Markets, and hinders mine.

FLORINDA: Sir, from my Window I have often seen you; and Women of Quality have so few opportunities for Love, that we ought to lose none.

240 FREDERICK: Ay, this is something! here's a Woman!—When shall I be blest with so much kindness from your fair Mouth? (*Aside to* BELVILE.) Take the Jewel, Fool.

BELVILE: You tempt me strangely, Madam, every way.

FLORINDA: (*Aside.*) So, if I find him false, my whole Repose
245 is gone.

BELVILE: And but for a Vow I've made to a very fine Lady, this Goodness had subdu'd me.

FREDERICK: Pox on't be kind, in pity to me be kind, for I am to thrive here but as you treat her Friend.

250 HELLENA: Tell me what did you in yonder House, and I'll unmasque.

WILLMORE: Yonder House—oh—I went to—a—to—why, there's a Friend of mine lives there.

HELLENA: What a she, or a he Friend?

255 WILLMORE: A Man upon my Honour! a Man—A she Friend! no, no, Madam, you have done my Business, I thank you.

HELLENA: And was't your Man Friend, that had more Darts in's Eyes than *Cupid* carries in a whole Budget of Arrows?

WILLMORE: So—

260 HELLENA: Ah such a *Bona Roba*: to be in her Arms is lying in *Fresco,* all perfumed Air about me—Was this your Man Friend too?

WILLMORE: So—

HELLENA: That gave you the He, and the She—Gold, that begets young Pleasures.
265

WILLMORE: Well, well, Madam, then you see there are Ladies in the World, that will not be cruel—there are, Madam, there are—

HELLENA: And there be Men too as fine, wild, inconstant Fellows as your self, there be, Captain, there be, if you go to
270 that now—therefore I'm resolv'd—

WILLMORE: Oh!

HELLENA: To see your Face no more—

WILLMORE: Oh!

HELLENA: Till to morrow.
275

WILLMORE: Egad you frighted me.

HELLENA: Nor then neither, unless you'l swear never to see that Lady more.

WILLMORE: See her!—why! never to think of Womankind again?
280

HELLENA: Kneel, and swear.

(*Kneels, she gives him her Hand.*)

WILLMORE: I do, never to think—to see—to love—nor lie with any but thy self.

HELLENA: Kiss the Book.

WILLMORE: Oh, most religiously.
285

(*Kisses her Hand.*)

HELLENA: Now what a wicked Creature am I, to damn a proper Fellow.

CALLIS: (*To* FLORINDA.) Madam, I'll stay no longer, 'tis e'en dark.

FLORINDA: However, Sir, I'll leave this with you—that when I'm gone, you may repent the opportunity you have lost
290 by your modesty.

(*Gives him the Jewel, which is her Picture, and Exits. He gazes after her.*)

WILLMORE: 'Twill be an Age till to morrow,—and till then I will most impatiently expect you—Adieu, my dear pretty Angel.

(*Exeunt all the* WOMEN.)

BELVILE: Ha! *Florinda's* Picture! 'twas she her self—what a dull
295 Dog was I? I would have given the World for one minute's discourse with her.—

FREDERICK: This comes of your Modesty,—ah pox on your Vow, 'twas ten to one but we had lost the Jewel by't.

300 BELVILE: *Willmore!* the blessed'st Opportunity lost!—*Florinda,* Friends, *Florinda!*

WILLMORE: Ah Rogue! such black Eyes, such a Face, such a Mouth, such Teeth,—and so much Wit!

BELVILE: All, all, and a thousand Charms besides.

305 WILLMORE: Why, dost thou know her?

BELVILE: Know her! ay, ay, and a Pox take me with all my Heart for being modest.

WILLMORE: But hark ye, Friend of mine, are you my Rival? and have I been only beating the Bush all this while?

310 BELVILE: I understand thee not—I'm mad—see here—

(*Shews the Picture.*)

WILLMORE: Ha! whose Picture is this?—'tis a fine Wench.

FREDERICK: The Colonel's Mistress, Sir.

WILLMORE: Oh, oh, here—I thought it had been another Prize—come, come, a Bottle will set thee right again.

(*Gives the Picture back.*)

315 BELVILE: I am content to try, and by that time 'twill be late enough for our Design.

WILLMORE: Agreed.

Love does all day the Soul's great Empire keep,
But Wine at night lulls the soft God asleep.

(*Exeunt.*)

SCENE II

LUCETTA's House.

Enter BLUNT and LUCETTA with a Light.

LUCETTA: Now we are safe and free, no fears of the coming home of my old jealous Husband, which made me a little thoughtful when you came in first—but now Love is all the business of my Soul.

5 BLUNT: (*Aside.*) I am transported—Pox on't, that I had but some fine things to say to her, such as Lovers use—I was a Fool not to learn of *Frederick* a little by Heart before I came—something I must say.—'Sheartlikins, sweet Soul, I am not us'd to complement, but I'm an honest Gentle-

10 man, and thy humble Servant.

LUCETTA: I have nothing to pay for so great a Favour, but such a Love as cannot but be great, since at first sight of that sweet Face and Shape it made me your absolute Captive.

BLUNT: (*Aside.*) Kind heart, how prettily she talks! Egad I'll

15 show her Husband a *Spanish* Trick; send him out of the World, and marry her: she's damnably in love with me, and will ne'er mind Settlements, and so there's that sav'd.

LUCETTA: Well, Sir, I'll go and undress me, and be with you instantly.

20 BLUNT: Make haste then, for 'dsheartlikins, dear Soul, thou canst not guess at the pain of a longing Lover, when his Joys are drawn within the compass of a few minutes.

LUCETTA: You speak my Sense, and I'll make haste to provide it.

(*Exit.*)

BLUNT: 'Tis a rare Girl, and this one night's enjoyment with 25 her will be worth all the days I ever past in Essex.—Would she'd go with me into *England,* tho to say truth, there's plenty of Whores there already.—But a pox on 'em they are such mercenary prodigal Whores, that they want such a one as this, that's free and generous, to give 'em good Ex- 30 amples:—Why, what a House she has! how rich and fine!

(*Enter* SANCHO.)

SANCHO: Sir, my Lady has sent me to conduct you to her Chamber.

BLUNT: Sir, I shall be proud to follow—Here's one of her Ser-vants too: 'dsheartlikins, by his Garb and Gravity he might 35 be a Justice of Peace in *Essex,* and is but a Pimp here.

(*Exeunt.*)

(*The Scene changes to a Chamber with an Alcove-Bed in it, a Table, &c.* LUCETTA *in Bed. Enter* SANCHO *and* BLUNT, *who takes the Candle of* SANCHO *at the Door.*)

SANCHO: Sir, my Commission reaches no farther.

BLUNT: Sir, I'll excuse your Complement:—what, in Bed, my sweet Mistress?

LUCETTA: You see, I still out-do you in kindness. 40

BLUNT: And thou shalt see what haste I'll make to quit scores—oh the luckiest Rogue!

(*Undresses himself.*)

LUCETTA: Shou'd you be false or cruel now!

BLUNT: False, 'Sheartlikins, what dost thou take me for a *Jew?* an insensible Heathen,—A Pox of thy old jealous Hus- 45 band: and he were dead, egad, sweet Soul, it shou'd be none of my fault, if I did not marry thee.

LUCETTA: It never shou'd be mine.

BLUNT: Good Soul, I'm the fortunatest Dog!

LUCETTA: Are you not undrest yet? 50

BLUNT: As much as my Impatience will permit.

(*Goes towards the Bed in his Shirt and Drawers.*)

LUCETTA: Hold, Sir, put out the Light, it may betray us else.

BLUNT: Any thing, I need no other Light but that of thine Eyes!—(*Aside.*) 'sheartlikins, there I think I had it.

(*Puts out the Candle, the Bed descends, he gropes about to find it.*)

—Why—why—where am I got? what, not yet?—where 55 are your sweetest?—ah, the Rogue's silent now—a pretty Love-trick this—how she'll laugh at me anon!—you need not, my dear Rogue! you need not! I'm all on a fire al-ready—come, come, now call me in for pity—Sure I'm enchanted! I have been round the Chamber, and can find 60 neither Woman, nor Bed—I lockt the Door, I'm sure she cannot go that way; or if she cou'd, the Bed cou'd not—Enough, enough, my pretty Wanton, do not carry the Jest too far—Ha, betray'd! Dogs! Rogues! Pimps! help! help!

(*Lights on a Trap, and is let down. Enter* LUCETTA, PHILIPPO, *and* SANCHO *with a Light.*)

65　PHILIPPO: Ha, ha, ha, he's dispatcht finely.

LUCETTA: Now, Sir, had I been coy, we had mist of this Booty.

PHILIPPO: Nay when I saw 'twas a substantial Fool, I was mollified; but when you doat upon a Serenading Coxcomb, upon a Face, fine Clothes, and a Lute, it makes me rage.

70　LUCETTA: You know I never was guilty of that Folly, my dear *Philippo,* but with your self—But come let's see what we have got by this.

PHILIPPO: A rich Coat!—Sword and Hat!—these Breeches too—are well lin'd!—see here a Gold Watch!—a Purse—

75　ha! Gold!—at least two hundred Pistoles! a bunch of Diamond Rings; and one with the Family Arms!—a Gold Box!—with a Medal of his King! and his Lady Mother's Picture!—these were sacred Reliques, believe me!—see, the Wasteband of his Breeches have a Mine of Gold!—

80　Old Queen *Bess's.* We have a Quarrel to her ever since Eighty Eight, and may therefore justify the Theft, the Inquisition might have committed it.

LUCETTA: See, a Bracelet of bow'd Gold, these his Sister ty'd about his Arm at parting—but well—for all this, I fear his

85　being a Stranger may make a noise, and hinder our Trade with them hereafter.

PHILIPPO: That's our security; he is not only a Stranger to us, but to the Country too—the Common-Shore into which he is descended, thou know'st, conducts him into another

90　Street, which this Light will hinder him from ever finding again—he knows neither your Name, nor the Street where your House is, nay, nor the way to his own Lodgings.

LUCETTA: And art not thou an unmerciful Rogue, not to afford him one Night for all this?—I should not have been

95　such a *Jew.*

PHILIPPO: Blame me not, *Lucetta,* to keep as much of thee as I can to my self—come, that thought makes me wanton,—let's to Bed,—*Sancho,* lock up these.

This is the Fleece which Fools do bear,
100　*Design'd for witty Men to sheer.*

(*Exeunt.*)

(*The Scene changes, and discovers* BLUNT, *creeping out of a Common Shore, his Face, &c., all dirty.*)

BLUNT: Oh Lord!

(*Climbing up.*)

I am got out at last, and (which is a Miracle) without a Clue—and now to Damning and Cursing—but if that would ease me, where shall I begin? with my Fortune, my

105　self, or the Quean that cozen'd me—What a dog was I to believe in Women! Oh Coxcomb—ignorant conceited Coxcomb! to fancy she cou'd be enamour'd with my Person, at the first sight enamour'd—Oh, I'm a cursed Puppy, 'tis plain, Fool was writ upon my Forehead, she perceiv'd it,—saw the

110　*Essex* Calf there—for what Allurements could there be in this Countenance? which I can indure, because I'm acquainted with it—Oh, dull silly Dog! to be thus sooth'd into a Cozening! Had I been drunk, I might fondly have credited

---
83 **bow'd Gold** *bowed* is still used in the North of England for bent: 'a bowed pin'

---

the young Quean! but as I was in my right Wits, to be thus cheated, confirms I am a dull believing *English* Country 115 Fop.—But my Comrades! Death and the Devil, there's the worst of all—then a Ballad will be sung to Morrow on the *Prado,* to a lousy Tune of the enchanted Squire, and the annihilated Damsel—But *Frederick* that Rogue, and the Colonel, will abuse me beyond all Christian patience—had she left 120 me my Clothes, I have a Bill of Exchange at home wou'd have sav'd my Credit—but now all hope is taken from me— Well, I'll home (if I can find the way) with this Consolation, that I am not the first kind believing Coxcomb; but there are, Gallants, many such good Natures amongst ye. 125

And tho you've better Arts to hide your Follies,
Adsheartlikins y'are all as errant Cullies.

SCENE III

The Garden, in the Night.

Enter FLORINDA, *undress'd, with a Key, and a little Box.*

FLORINDA: Well, thus far I'm in my way to Happiness; I have got my self free from *Callis;* my Brother too, I find by yonder light, is gone into his Cabinet, and thinks not of me: I have by good Fortune got the Key of the Garden Back-door,— I'll open it, to prevent *Belvile's* knocking,—a little noise will 5 now alarm my Brother. Now am I as fearful as a young Thief. (*Unlocks the Door.*)—Hark,—what noise is that?— Oh, 'twas the Wind that plaid amongst the Boughs.—*Belvile* stays long, methinks—it's time—stay—for fear of a surprize, I'll hide these Jewels in yonder Jessamin. 10

(*She goes to lay down the Box.*)

(*Enter* WILLMORE *drunk.*)

WILLMORE: What the Devil is become of these Fellows, *Belvile* and *Frederick?* They promis'd to stay at the next corner for me, but who the Devil knows the corner of a full Moon?— Now—whereabouts am I?—hah—what have we here? a Garden!—a very convenient place to sleep in—hah—what 15 has God sent us here?—a Female—by this light, a Woman; I'm a Dog if it be not a very Wench.—

FLORINDA: He's come!—hah—who's there?

WILLMORE: Sweet Soul, let me salute thy Shoe-string.

FLORINDA: 'Tis not my *Belvile*—good Heavens, I know him 20 not.—Who are you, and from whence come you!

WILLMORE: Prithee—prithee, Child—not so many hard Questions—let it suffice I am here, Child—Come, come kiss me.

FLORINDA: Good Gods! what luck is mine?

WILLMORE: Only good luck, Child, parlous good luck.—Come 25 hither,—'tis a delicate shining Wench,—by this Hand she's perfum'd, and smells like any Nosegay.—Prithee, dear Soul, let's not play the Fool, and lose time,—precious time—for as Gad shall save me, I'm as honest a Fellow as breathes, tho I am a little disguis'd at present.—Come, I say,—why, thou may'st 30 be free with me, I'll be very secret. I'll not boast who 'twas oblig'd me, not I—for hang me if I know thy Name.

---
30 **disguis'd** a common phrase for drunk

FLORINDA: Heavens! what a filthy beast is this!

WILLMORE: I am so, and thou oughtst the sooner to lie with
35 me for that reason,—for look you, Child, there will be no
Sin in't, because 'twas neither design'd nor premeditated;
'tis pure Accident on both sides—that's a certain thing
now—Indeed should I make love to you, and you vow Fidelity—and swear and lye till you believ'd and yielded—
40 Thou art therefore (as thou art a good Christian) oblig'd
in Conscience to deny me nothing. Now—come, be
kind, without any more idle prating.

FLORINDA: Oh, I am ruin'd—wicked Man, unhand me.

WILLMORE: Wicked! Egad, Child, a Judge, were he young and
45 vigorous, and saw those Eyes of thine, would know 'twas
they gave the first blow—the first provocation.—Come,
prithee let's lose no time, I say—this is a fine convenient
place.

FLORINDA: Sir, let me go, I conjure you, or I'll call out.

50 WILLMORE: Ay, ay, you were best to call Witness to see how
finely you treat me—do.—

FLORINDA: I'll cry Murder, Rape, or any thing, if you do not
instantly let me go.

WILLMORE: A Rape! Come, come, you lye, you Baggage, you
55 lye: What, I'll warrant you would fain have the World believe now that you are not so forward as I. No, not you,—
why at this time of Night was your Cobweb-door set
open, dear Spider—but to catch Flies?—Hah come—or I
shall be damnably angry.—Why what a Coil is here.—

60 FLORINDA: Sir, can you think—

WILLMORE: That you'd do it for nothing? oh, oh, I find what
you'd be at—look here, here's a Pistole for you—here's a
work indeed—here—take it, I say.—

FLORINDA: For Heaven's sake, Sir, as you're a Gentleman—

65 WILLMORE: So—now—she would be wheedling me for
more—what, you will not take it then—you're resolv'd
you will not.—Come, come, take it, or I'll put it up again;
for, look ye, I never give more.—Why, how now, Mistress,
are you so high i'th' Mouth, a Pistole won't down with
70 you?—hah—why, what a work's here—in good time—
come, no struggling, be gone—But an y'are good at a
dumb Wrestle, I'm for ye,—look ye,—I'm for ye.—

(*She struggles with him.*)

(*Enter* BELVILE *and* FREDERICK.)

BELVILE: The Door is open, a Pox of this mad Fellow, I'm angry
that we've lost him, I durst have sworn he had follow'd us.

75 FREDERICK: But you were so hasty, Colonel, to be gone.

FLORINDA: Help, help,—Murder!—help—oh, I'm ruin'd.

BELVILE: Ha, sure that's *Florinda*'s Voice.

(*Comes up to them.*)

—A Man! Villain, let go that Lady.

(*A noise.*)

(WILLMORE *turns and draws,* FREDERICK *interposes.*)

FLORINDA: *Belvile!* Heavens! my Brother too is coming, and
80 'twill be impossible to escape.—*Belvile,* I conjure you to
walk under my Chamber-window, from whence I'll give

you some instructions what to do—This rude Man has
undone us.

(*Exit.*)

WILLMORE: *Belvile!*

(*Enter* PEDRO, STEPHANO, *and other Servants with Lights.*)

PEDRO: I'm betray'd; run, *Stephano,* and see if *Florinda* be safe. 85

(*Exit* STEPHANO.)

So who'er they be, all is not well, I'll to *Florinda*'s Chamber.

(*They fight, and* PEDRO's *Party beats 'em out; going out, meets*
STEPHANO.)

STEPHANO: You need not, Sir, the poor Lady's fast asleep, and
thinks no harm: I wou'd not wake her, Sir, for fear of
frightning her with your danger.

PEDRO: I'm glad she's there—Rascals, how came the Garden- 90
Door open?

STEPHANO: That Question comes too late, Sir: some of my
Fellow-Servants Masquerading I'll warrant.

PEDRO: Masquerading! a leud Custom to debauch our
Youth—there's something more in this than I imagine. 95

(*Exeunt.*)

SCENE IV

Changes to the Street.

Enter BELVILE *in Rage,* FREDERICK *holding him, and* WILLMORE
melancholy.

WILLMORE: Why, how the Devil shou'd I know *Florinda?*

BELVILE: Ah plague of your ignorance! if it had not been
Florinda, must you be a Beast?—a Brute, a senseless
Swine?

WILLMORE: Well, Sir, you see I am endu'd with Patience—I 5
can bear—tho egad y're very free with me methinks,—I
was in good hopes the Quarrel wou'd have been on my
side, for so uncivilly interrupting me.

BELVILE: Peace, Brute, whilst thou'rt safe—oh, I'm distracted.

WILLMORE: Nay, nay, I'm an unlucky Dog, that's certain. 10

BELVILE: Ah curse upon the Star that rul'd my Birth! or whatsoever other Influence that makes me still so wretched.

WILLMORE: Thou break'st my Heart with these Complaints;
there is no Star in fault, no Influence but Sack, the cursed
Sack I drank. 15

FREDERICK: Why, how the Devil came you so drunk?

WILLMORE: Why, how the Devil came you so sober?

BELVILE: A curse upon his thin Skull, he was always beforehand that way.

FREDERICK: Prithee, dear Colonel, forgive him, he's sorry for 20
his fault.

BELVILE: He's always so after he has done a mischief—a
plague on all such Brutes.

WILLMORE: By this Light I took her for an errant Harlot.

BELVILE: Damn your debaucht Opinion: tell me, Sot, hadst thou 25
so much sense and light about thee to distinguish her to be

a Woman, and could'st not see something about her Face
and Person, to strike an awful Reverence into thy Soul?

30   WILLMORE: Faith no, I consider'd her as mere a Woman as I
could wish.

BELVILE: 'Sdeath I have no patience—draw, or I'll kill you.

WILLMORE: Let that alone till to morrow, and if I set not all
right again, use your Pleasure.

BELVILE: To morrow, damn it.
35   The spiteful Light will lead me to no happiness.
To morrow is *Antonio's*, and perhaps
Guides him to my undoing;—oh that I could meet
This Rival, this powerful Fortunate.

WILLMORE: What then?

40   BELVILE: Let thy own Reason, or my Rage instruct thee.

WILLMORE: I shall be finely inform'd then, no doubt; hear
me, Colonel—hear me—shew me the Man and I'll do his
Business.

BELVILE: I know him no more than thou, or if I did, I should
45   not need thy aid.

WILLMORE: This you say is *Angelica's* House, I promis'd the
kind Baggage to lie with her to Night.

(*Offers to go in.*)

(*Enter* ANTONIO *and his Page.* ANTONIO *knocks on the Hilt of his
Sword.*)

ANTONIO: You paid the thousand Crowns I directed?

PAGE: To the Lady's old Woman, Sir, I did.

50   WILLMORE: Who the Devil have we here?

BELVILE: I'll now plant my self under *Florinda's* Window, and
if I find no comfort there, I'll die.

(*Exit* BELVILE *and* FREDERICK. *Enter* MORETTA.)

MORETTA: Page!

PAGE: Here's my Lord.

55   WILLMORE: How is this, a Piccaroon going to board my
Frigate! here's one Chase-Gun for you.

(*Drawing his Sword, justles* ANTONIO *who turns and draws. They
fight,* ANTONIO *falls.*)

MORETTA: Oh, bless us, we are all undone!

(*Runs in, and shuts the Door.*)

PAGE: Help, Murder!

(BELVILE *returns at the noise of fighting.*)

BELVILE: Ha, the mad Rogue's engag'd in some unlucky Ad-
60   venture again.

(*Enter two or three* MASQUERADERS.)

MASQUERADER: Ha, a Man kill'd!

WILLMORE: How! a Man kill'd! then I'll go home to sleep.

(*Puts up, and reels out. Exeunt* MASQUERADERS *another way.*)

BELVILE: Who shou'd it be! pray Heaven the Rogue is safe, for
all my Quarrel to him.

(*As* BELVILE *is groping about, enter an* OFFICER *and six* SOL-
DIERS.)

SOLDIER: Who's there?   65

OFFICER: So, here's one dispatcht—secure the Murderer.

BELVILE: Do not mistake my Charity for Murder: I came to
his Assistance.

(SOLDIERS *sieze on* BELVILE.)

OFFICER: That shall be tried, Sir.—St. *Jago*, Swords drawn in
the Carnival time!   70

(*Goes to* ANTONIO.)

ANTONIO: Thy Hand prithee.

OFFICER: Ha, Don *Antonio*! look well to the Villain there.—
How is't, Sir?

ANTONIO: I'm hurt.

BELVILE: Has my Humanity made me a Criminal?   75

OFFICER: Away with him.

BELVILE: What a curst Chance is this!

(*Exeunt* SOLDIERS *with* BELVILE.)

ANTONIO: (*To the* OFFICER.) This is the Man that has set upon
me twice—carry him to my Apartment till you have further Orders from me.   80

(*Exit.* ANTONIO *led.*)

ACT FOUR

SCENE I

A fine Room.

Discovers BELVILE, *as by Dark alone.*

BELVILE: When shall I be weary of railing on Fortune, who is
resolv'd never to turn with Smiles upon me?—Two such
Defeats in one Night—none but the Devil and that mad
Rogue could have contriv'd to have plagued me with—I
am here a Prisoner—but where?—Heaven knows—and if   5
there be Murder done, I can soon decide the Fate of a
Stranger in a Nation without Mercy—Yet this is nothing
to the Torture my Soul bows with, when I think of losing
my fair, my dear *Florinda.*—Hark—my Door opens—a
Light—a Man—and seems of Quality—arm'd too.—   10
Now shall I die like a Dog without defence.

(*Enter* ANTONIO *in a Night-Gown, with a Light; his Arm in a
Scarf, and a Sword under his Arm: He sets the Candle on the Table.*)

ANTONIO: Sir, I come to know what Injuries I have done
you, that could provoke you to so mean an Action, as to
attack me basely, without allowing time for my Defence.

BELVILE: Sir, for a Man in my Circumstances to plead Inno-   15
cence, would look like Fear—but view me well, and you
will find no marks of a Coward on me, nor any thing that
betrays that Brutality you accuse me of.

ANTONIO: In vain, Sir, you impose upon my Sense,
You are not only he who drew on me last Night,   20

But yesterday before the same House, that of *Angelica.*
Yet there is something in your Face and Mein—

BELVILE: I own I fought to day in the defence of a Friend of
mine, with whom you (if you're the same) and your
25   Party were first engag'd.
Perhaps you think this Crime enough to kill me,
But if you do, I cannot fear you'll do it basely.

ANTONIO: No, Sir, I'll make you fit for a Defence with this.

(*Gives him the Sword.*)

BELVILE: This Gallantry surprizes me—nor know I how to
30   use this Present, Sir, against a Man so brave.

ANTONIO: You shall not need;
For know, I come to snatch you from a Danger
That is decreed against you;
Perhaps your Life, or long Imprisonment:
35   And 'twas with so much Courage you offended,
I cannot see you punisht.

BELVILE: How shall I pay this Generosity?

ANTONIO: It had been safer to have kill'd another,
Than have attempted me;
40   To shew your Danger, Sir, I'll let you know my Quality;
And 'tis the Vice-Roy's Son whom you have wounded.

BELVILE: (*Aside.*) The Vice-Roy's Son!
Death and Confusion! was this Plague reserved
To compleat all the rest?—oblig'd by him!
45   The Man of all the World I would destroy.

ANTONIO: You seem disorder'd, Sir.

BELVILE: Yes, trust me, Sir, I am, and 'tis with pain
That Man receives such Bounties,
Who wants the pow'r to pay 'em back again.

50 ANTONIO: To gallant Spirits 'tis indeed uneasy;
—But you may quickly over-pay me, Sir.

BELVILE: Then I am well—(*Aside.*) kind Heaven! but set us
even,
That I may fight with him, and keep my Honour safe.
—Oh, I'm impatient, Sir, to be discounting
55   The mighty Debt I owe you; command me quickly—

ANTONIO: I have a Quarrel with a Rival, Sir,
About the Maid we love.

BELVILE: (*Aside.*) Death, 'tis *Florinda* he means—
That Thought destroys my Reason, and I shall kill him—

60 ANTONIO: My Rival, Sir,
Is one has all the Virtues Man can boast of.

BELVILE: Death! who shou'd this be?

ANTONIO: He challeng'd me to meet him on the *Molo,*
As soon as Day appear'd; but last Night's quarrel
65   Has made my Arm unfit to guide a Sword.

BELVILE: I apprehend you, Sir, you'd have me kill the Man
That lays a claim to the Maid you speak of.
—I'll do't—I'll fly to do it.

ANTONIO: Sir, do you know her?

70 BELVILE: —No, Sir, but 'tis enough she is admired by you.

ANTONIO: Sir, I shall rob you of the Glory on't,
For you must fight under my Name and Dress.

BELVILE: That Opinion must be strangely obliging that makes
You think I can personate the brave *Antonio,*
75   Whom I can but strive to imitate.

ANTONIO: You say too much to my Advantage.

Come, Sir, the Day appears that calls you forth.
Within, Sir, is the Habit.

(*Exit* ANTONIO.)

BELVILE: Fantastick Fortune, thou deceitful Light,
That cheats the wearied Traveller by Night,   80
Tho on a Precipice each step you tread,
I am resolv'd to follow where you lead.

(*Exit.*)

SCENE II

The Molo.

Enter FLORINDA *and* CALLIS *in Masques, with* STEPHANO.

FLORINDA: (*Aside.*) I'm dying with my fears; *Belvile's* not coming,
As I expected, underneath my Window,
Makes me believe that all those Fears are true.
—Canst thou not tell with whom my Brother fights?

STEPHANO: No, Madam, they were both in Masquerade, I was   5
by when they challeng'd one another, and they had decided the Quarrel then, but were prevented by some Cavaliers; which made 'em put it off till now—but I am sure
'tis about you they fight.

FLORINDA: (*Aside.*) Nay then 'tis with *Belvile,* for what other   10
Lover have I that dares fight for me, except *Antonio?* and
he is too much in favour with my Brother—If it be he, for
whom shall I direct my Prayers to Heaven?

STEPHANO: Madam, I must leave you; for if my Master see me,
I shall be hang'd for being your Conductor.—I escap'd nar-   15
rowly for the Excuse I made for you last night i'th' Garden.

FLORINDA: And I'll reward thee for't—prithee no more.

(*Exit* STEPHANO.)

(*Enter Don* PEDRO *in his Masquing Habit.*)

PEDRO: *Antonio's* late to day, the place will fill, and we may be
prevented.

(*Walks about.*)

FLORINDA: (*Aside.*) Antonio! sure I heard amiss.   20

PEDRO: But who would not excuse a happy Lover.
When soft fair Arms comfine the yielding Neck;
And the kind Whisper languishingly breathes,
Must you be gone so soon?
Sure I had dwelt for ever on her Bosom.   25
—But stay, he's here.

(*Enter* BELVILE *drest in* ANTONIO's *Clothes.*)

FLORINDA: 'Tis not *Belvile,* half my Fears are vanisht.

PEDRO: *Antonio!*—

BELVILE: (*Aside.*) This must be he.
You're early, Sir,—I do not use to be out-done this way.   30

PEDRO: The wretched, Sir, are watchful, and 'tis enough
You have the advantage of me in *Angelica.*

BELVILE: (*Aside.*) Angelica!
Or I've mistook my Man! Or else *Antonio,*

35   Can he forget his Interest in *Florinda*,
        And fight for common Prize?
PEDRO: Come, Sir, you know our terms—
BELVILE: (*Aside.*) Be Heaven, not I.
        —No talking, I am ready, Sir.

(*Offers to fight.* FLORINDA *runs in.*)

40 FLORINDA: (*To* BELVILE.) Oh, hold! who'er you be, I do con-
        jure you hold. If you strike here—I die—
PEDRO: *Florinda!*
BELVILE: *Florinda* imploring for my Rival!
PEDRO: Away, this Kindness is unseasonable.

(*Puts her by, they fight; she runs in just as* BELVILE *disarms* PEDRO.)

45 FLORINDA: Who are you, Sir, that dare deny my Prayers?
BELVILE: Thy Prayers destroy him; if thou wouldst preserve him.
        Do that thou'rt unacquainted with, and curse him.

(*She holds him.*)

FLORINDA: By all you hold most dear, by her you love,
        I do conjure you, touch him not.
50 BELVILE: By her I love!
        See—I obey—and at your Feet resign
        The useless Trophy of my Victory.

(*Lays his sword at her Feet.*)

PEDRO: *Antonio,* you've done enough to prove you love *Florinda.*
BELVILE: Love *Florinda!*
55   Does Heaven love Adoration, Pray'r, or Penitence?
        Love her! here Sir,—your Sword again.

(*Snatches up the Sword, and gives it him.*)

        Upon this Truth I'll fight my Life away.
PEDRO: No, you've redeem'd my Sister, and my Friendship.
BELVILE: Don *Pedro!*

(*He gives him* FLORINDA *and pulls off his Vizard to shew his Face, and puts it on again.*)

60 PEDRO: Can you resign your Claims to other Women,
        And give your Heart intirely to *Florinda?*
BELVILE: Intire, as dying Saints Confessions are.
        I can delay my happiness no longer.
        This minute let me make *Florinda* mine:
65 PEDRO: This minute let it be—no time so proper,
        This Night my Father will arrive from *Rome,*
        And possibly may hinder what we propose.
FLORINDA: Oh Heavens! this Minute!

(*Enter* MASQUERADERS, *and pass over.*)

BELVILE: Oh, do not ruin me!
70 PEDRO: The place begins to fill; and that we may not be ob-
        serv'd, do you walk off to St. *Peter's* Church, where I will
        meet you, and conclude your Happiness.
BELVILE: I'll meet you there—(*Aside.*) if there be no more
        Saints Churches in *Naples.*

FLORINDA: Oh stay, Sir, and recall your hasty Doom: 75
        Alas I have not yet prepar'd my Heart
        To entertain so strange a Guest.
PEDRO: Away, this silly Modesty is assum'd too late.
BELVILE: Heaven, Madam! what do you do?
FLORINDA: Do! despise the Man that lays a Tyrant's Claim   80
        To what he ought to conquer by Submission.
BELVILE: You do not know me—move a little this way.

(*Draws her aside.*)

FLORINDA: Yes, you may even force me to the Altar,
        But not the holy Man that offers there
        Shall force me to be thine.   85

(PEDRO *talks to* CALLIS *this while.*)

BELVILE: Oh do not lose so blest an opportunity!
        See—'tis your *Belvile*—not *Antonio,*
        Whom your mistaken Scorn and Anger ruins.

(*Pulls off his Vizard.*)

FLORINDA: *Belvile!*
        Where was my Soul it cou'd not meet thy Voice,   90
        And take this knowledge in?

(*As they are talking, enter* WILLMORE *finely drest, and* FREDERICK.)

WILLMORE: No Intelligence! no News of *Belvile* yet—well I am
        the most unlucky Rascal in Nature—ha!—am I deceiv'd—
        or is it he—look, *Frederick*—'tis he—my dear *Belvile.*

(*Runs and embraces him.* BELVILE'S *Vizard falls out on's Hand.*)

BELVILE: Hell and Confusion seize thee!   95
PEDRO: Ha! *Belvile!* I beg your Pardon, Sir.

(*Takes* FLORINDA *from him.*)

BELVILE: Nay, touch her not, she's mine by Conquest, Sir.
        I won her by my Sword.
WILLMORE: Did'st thou so—and egad, Child, we'll keep her
        by the Sword.   100

(*Draws on* PEDRO, BELVILE *goes between.*)

BELVILE: Stand off.
        Thou'rt so profanely leud, so curst by Heaven,
        All Quarrels thou espousest must be fatal.
WILLMORE: Nay, an you be so hot, my Valour's coy,
        And shall be courted when you want it next.   105

(*Puts up his Sword.*)

BELVILE: You know I ought to claim a Victor's Right,

(*To* PEDRO.)

        But you're the Brother to divine *Florinda,*
        To whom I'm such a Slave—to purchase her,
        I durst not hurt the Man she holds so dear.
PEDRO: 'Twas by *Antonio's,* not by *Belvile's* Sword,   110
        This Question should have been decided, Sir:

I must confess much to your Bravery's due,
Both now, and when I met you last in Arms.
But I am nicely punctual in my word,
115   As Men of Honour ought, and beg your Pardon.

(*Aside to* FLORINDA *as they are going out.*)

—For this Mistake another Time shall clear.
—This was some Plot between you and *Belvile*:
But I'll prevent you.

(BELVILE *looks after her, and begins to walk up and down in a Rage.*)

WILLMORE: Do not be modest now, and lose the Woman: but
120   if we shall fetch her back, so—
BELVILE: Do not speak to me.
WILLMORE: Not speak to you!—Egad, I'll speak to you, and
    will be answered too.
BELVILE: Will you, Sir?
125 WILLMORE: I know I've done some mischief, but I'm so dull
    a Puppy, that I am the Son of a Whore, if I know how, or
    where—prithee inform my Understanding.—
BELVILE: Leave me I say, and leave me instantly.
WILLMORE: I will not leave you in this humour, nor till I
130   know my Crime.
BELVILE: Death, I'll tell you, Sir—

(*Draws and runs at* WILLMORE; *he runs out;* BELVILE *after him,* FREDERICK *interposes.*)

(*Enter* ANGELICA, MORETTA, *and* SEBASTIAN.)

ANGELICA: Ha—*Sebastian*—Is not that *Willmore?* haste, haste,
    and bring him back.
FREDERICK: The Colonel's mad—I never saw him thus be-
135   fore; I'll after 'em, lest he do some mischief, for I am sure
    Willmore will not draw on him.

(*Exit.*)

ANGELICA: I am all Rage! my first desires defeated
    For one, for ought he knows, that has no
    Other Merit than her Quality,—
140   Her being Don *Pedro*'s Sister—He loves her:
    I know 'tis so—dull, dull, insensible—
    He will not see me now tho oft invited;
    And broke his Word last night—false perjur'd Man!
    —He that but yesterday fought for my Favours,
145   And would have made his Life a Sacrifice
    To've gain'd one Night with me,
    Must now be hired and courted to my Arms.
MORETTA: I told you what wou'd come on't, but *Moretta*'s an
    old doating Fool—Why did you give him five hundred
150   Crowns, but to set himself out for other Lovers? You
    shou'd have kept him poor, if you had meant to have had
    any good from him.
ANGELICA: Oh, name not such mean Trifles.—Had I given him all
    My Youth has earn'd from Sin,
155   I had not lost a Thought nor Sigh upon't.
    But I have given him my eternal Rest,
    My whole Repose, my future Joys, my Heart;
    My Virgin Heart. *Moretta*! oh 'tis gone!

MORETTA: Curse on him, here he comes;
    How fine she has made him too!   160

(*Enter* WILLMORE *and* SEBASTIAN. ANGELICA *turns and walks away.*)

WILLMORE: How now, turn'd Shadow?
    Fly when I pursue, and follow when I fly!

(*Sings.*)

    Stay gentle Shadow of my Dove,
        And tell me e'er I go,
    Whether the Substance may not prove   165
        A fleeting Thing like you.

There's a soft kind Look remaining yet.

(*As she turns she looks on him.*)

ANGELICA: Well, Sir, you may be gay; all Happiness, all Joys
    pursue you still, Fortune's your Slave, and gives you every
    hour choice of new Hearts and Beauties, till you are cloy'd 170
    with the repeated Bliss, which others vainly languish
    for—But know, false Man, that I shall be reveng'd.

(*Turns away in a Rage.*)

WILLMORE: So, 'gad, there are of those faint-hearted Lovers,
    whom such a sharp Lesson next their Hearts would make
    as impotent as Fourscore—pox o' this whining—my 175
    Bus'ness is to laugh and love—a pox on't; I hate your
    sullen Lover, a Man shall lose as much time to put you in
    Humour now, as would serve to gain a new Woman.
ANGELICA: I scorn to cool that Fire I cannot raise,
    Or do the Drudgery of your virtuous Mistress. 180
WILLMORE: A virtuous Mistress! Death, what a thing thou
    hast found out for me! why what the Devil should I do
    with a virtuous Woman?—a sort of ill'natur'd Creatures,
    that take a Pride to torment a Lover. Virtue is but an In-
    firmity in Women, a Disease that renders even the hand- 185
    som ungrateful; whilst the ill-favour'd, for want of
    Sollicitations and Address, only fancy themselves so.—I
    have lain with a Woman of Quality, who has all the while
    been railing at Whores.
ANGELICA: I will not answer for your Mistress's Virtue, 190
    Tho she be young enough to know no Guilt:
    And I could wish you would persuade my Heart,
    'Twas the two hundred thousand Crowns you courted.
WILLMORE: Two hundred thousand Crowns! what Story's
    this?—what Trick?—what Woman?—ha. 195
ANGELICA: How strange you make it! have you forgot the
    Creature you entertain'd on the Piazza last night?
WILLMORE: Ha, my Gipsy worth two hundred thousand
    Crowns!—oh how I long to be with her—pox, I knew
    she was of Quality. 200
ANGELICA: False Man, I see my Ruin in thy Face.
    How many vows you breath'd upon my Bosom,
    Never to be unjust—have you forgot so soon?
WILLMORE: Faith no, I was just coming to repeat 'em—but
    here's a Humour indeed—would make a Man a Saint— 205
    (*Aside.*) Wou'd she'd be angry enough to leave me, and
    command me not to wait on her.

(*Enter* HELLENA, *drest in Man's Clothes.*)

HELLENA: This must be *Angelica,* I know it by her mumping
    Matron here—Ay, ay, 'tis she: my mad Captain's with her
210   too, for all his swearing—how this unconstant Humour
    makes me love him:—pray, good grave Gentlewoman, is
    not this *Angelica?*
MORETTA: My too young Sir, it is—I hope 'tis one from Don
    Antonio.

(*Goes to* ANGELICA.)

215 HELLENA: (*Aside.*) Well, something I'll do to vex him for this.
ANGELICA: I will not speak with him; am I in humour to re-
    ceive a Lover?
WILLMORE: Not speak with him! why I'll be gone—and wait
    your idler minutes—Can I shew less Obedience to the
220   thing I love so fondly?

(*Offers to go.*)

ANGELICA: A fine Excuse this—stay—
WILLMORE: And hinder your Advantage: should I repay your
    Bounties so ungratefully?
ANGELICA: Come, hither, Boy,—that I may let you see
225   How much above the Advantages you name
    I prize one Minute's Joy with you.
WILLMORE: Oh, you destroy me with this Endearment.

(*Impatient to be gone.*)

    —Death, how shall I get away!—Madam, 'twill not be fit
    I should be seen with you—besides, it will not be conve-
230   nient—and I've a Friend—that's dangerously sick.
ANGELICA: I see you're impatient—yet you shall stay.
WILLMORE: And miss my Assignation with my Gipsy.

(*Aside, and walks about impatiently.* MORETTA *brings* HELLENA,
who addresses her self to ANGELICA.)

HELLENA: Madam, You'l hardly pardon my Intrusion,
    When you shall know my Business;
235   And I'm too young to tell my Tale with Art:
    But there must be a wondrous store of Goodness
    Where so much Beauty dwells.
ANGELICA: A pretty Advocate, whoever sent thee,
    —Prithee proceed—Nay, Sir, you shall not go.

(*To* WILLMORE *who is stealing off.*)

240 WILLMORE: Then shall I lose my dear Gipsy for ever.
    (*Aside.*)—Pox on't, she stays me out of spite.
HELLENA: I am related to a Lady, Madam,
    Young, rich, and nobly born, but has the fate
    To be in love with a young *English* Gentleman.
245   Strangely she loves him, at first sight she lov'd him,
    But did adore him when she heard him speak;
    For he, she said, had Charms in every word,
    That fail'd not to surprize, to wound, and conquer—
WILLMORE: (*Aside.*) Ha, Egad I hope this concerns me.
250 ANGELICA: 'Tis my false Man, he means—wou'd he were gone.
    This Praise will raise his Pride and ruin me—(*To*
        WILLMORE.) Well,

Since you are so impatient to be gone.
I will release you, Sir.
WILLMORE: (*Aside.*) Nay, then I'm sure 'twas me he spoke of,
    this cannot be the Effects of Kindness in her.   255
    —No, Madam, I've consider'd better on't,
    And will not give you cause of Jealousy.
ANGELICA: But, Sir, I've—business, that—
WILLMORE: This shall not do, I know 'tis but to try me.
ANGELICA: (*Aside.*) Well, to your Story, Boy,—tho 'twill undo me. 260
HELLENA: With this Addition to his other Beauties,
    He won her unresisting tender Heart,
    He vow'd and sigh'd, and swore he lov'd her dearly;
    And she believ'd the cunning Flatterer,
    And thought her self the happiest Maid alive: 265
    To day was the appointed time by both,
    To consummate their Bliss;
    The Virgin, Altar, and the Priest were drest,
    And whilst she languish't for the expected Bridegroom,
    She heard, he paid his broken Vows to you.   270
WILLMORE: (*Aside.*) So, this is some dear Rogue that's in love
    with me, and this way lets me know it; or if it be not me,
    she means some one whose place I may supply.
ANGELICA: Now I perceive
    The cause of thy Impatience to be gone,   275
    And all the business of this glorious Dress.
WILLMORE: Damn the young Prater, I know not what he means.
HELLENA: Madam,
    In your fair Eyes I read too much concern
    To tell my farther Business.   280
ANGELICA: Prithee, sweet Youth, talk on, thou may'st perhaps
    Raise here a Storm that may undo my Passion,
    And then I'll grant thee any thing.
HELLENA: Madam, 'tis to intreat you, (oh unreasonable!)
    You wou'd not see this Stranger;   285
    For if you do, she vows you are undone,
    Tho Nature never made a Man so excellent;
    And sure he'ad been a God, but for Inconstancy.
WILLMORE: (*Aside.*) Ah, Rogue, how finely he's instructed!
    —'Tis plain some Woman that has seen me *en passant.* 290
ANGELICA: Oh, I shall burst with Jealousy! do you know the
    Man you speak of?—
HELLENA: Yes, Madam, he us'd to be in Buff and Scarlet.
ANGELICA: (*To* WILLMORE.) Thou, false as Hell, what canst
    thou say to this?   295
WILLMORE: By Heaven—
ANGELICA: Hold, do not damn thy self—
HELLENA: Nor hope to be believ'd.

(*He walks about, they follow.*)

ANGELICA: Oh, perjur'd Man!
    Is't thus you pay my generous Passion back?   300
HELLENA: Why wou'd you, Sir, abuse my Lady's Faith?
ANGELICA: And use me so unhumanly?
HELLENA: A Maid so young, so innocent—
WILLMORE: Ah, young Devil!
ANGELICA: Dost thou not know thy Life is in my Power?   305
HELLENA: Or think my Lady cannot be reveng'd?
WILLMORE: (*Aside.*) So, so, the Storm comes finely on.
ANGELICA: Now thou art silent, Guilt has struck thee dumb.

Oh, hadst thou still been so, I'd liv'd in safety.

(*She turns away and weeps.*)

310 WILLMORE: (*Aside to* HELLENA, *looks towards* ANGELICA *to watch her turning; and as she comes towards them, he meets her.*) Sweetheart, the Lady's Name and House—quickly: I'm impatient to be with her.—

HELLENA: (*Aside.*) So now is he for another Woman.

315 WILLMORE: The impudent'st young thing in Nature! I cannot persuade him out of his Error, Madam.

ANGELICA: I know he's in the right,—yet thou'st a Tongue That wou'd persuade him to deny his Faith.

(*In Rage walks away.*)

WILLMORE: (*Said softly to* HELLENA.) Her Name, her Name, dear Boy—

320 HELLENA: Have you forgot it, Sir?

WILLMORE: (*Aside.*) Oh, I perceive he's not to know I am a Stranger to his Lady.

—Yes, yes, I do know—but—I have forgot the—

(ANGELICA *turns.*)

—By Heaven, such early confidence I never saw.

ANGELICA: Did I not charge you with this Mistress, Sir?
325 Which you denied, tho I beheld your Perjury. This little Generosity of thine has render'd back my Heart.

(*Walks away.*)

WILLMORE: So, you have made sweet work here, my little mischief; Look your Lady be kind and good-natur'd now, or I shall have but a cursed Bargain on't.

(ANGELICA *turns towards them.*)

330 —The Rogue's bred up to Mischief, Art thou so great a Fool to credit him?

ANGELICA: Yes, I do; and you in vain impose upon me. —Come hither, Boy—Is not this he you speak of?

HELLENA: (HELLENA *looks in his Face, he gazes on her.*) I think—
335 it is; I cannot swear, but I vow he has just such another lying Lover's look.

WILLMORE: (*Aside.*) Hah! do not I know that Face?— By Heaven, my little Gipsy! what a dull Dog was I? Had I but lookt that way, I'd known her.
340 Are all my hopes of a new Woman banisht? —Egad, if I don't fit thee for this, hang me. —Madam, I have found out the Plot.

HELLENA: Oh Lord, what does he say? am I discover'd now?

WILLMORE: Do you see this young Spark here?
345 HELLENA: He'll tell her who I am.

WILLMORE: Who do you think this is?

HELLENA: Ay, ay, he does know me.—Nay, dear Captain, I'm undone if you discover me.

WILLMORE: Nay, nay, no cogging; she shall know what a pre-
350 cious Mistress I have.

_____

349 **cogging** to cog = to trick, wheedle, or cajole

HELLENA: Will you be such a Devil?

WILLMORE: Nay, nay, I'll teach you to spoil sport you will not make.—This small Ambassador comes not from a Person of Quality, as you imagine, and he says; but from a very er- rant Gipsy, the talkingst, pratingst, cantingst little Animal 355 thou ever saw'st.

ANGELICA: What news you tell me! that's the thing I mean.

HELLENA: (*Aside.*) Wou'd I were well off the place.—If ever I go a Captain-hunting again.—

WILLMORE: Mean that thing? that Gipsy thing? thou may'st 360 as well be jealous of thy Monkey, or Parrot as her: a *Ger- man* Motion were worth a dozen of her, and a Dream were a better Enjoyment, a Creature of Constitution fit- ter for Heaven than Man.

HELLENA: (*Aside.*) Tho I'm sure he lyes, yet this vexes me. 365

ANGELICA: You are mistaken, she's a *Spanish* Woman Made up of no such dull Materials.

WILLMORE: Materials! Egad, and she be made of any that will either dispense, or admit of Love, I'll be bound to conti- nence. 370

HELLENA: (*Aside to him.*) Unreasonable Man, do you think so?

WILLMORE: You may Return, my little Brazen Head, and tell your Lady, that till she be handsom enough to be belov'd, or I dull enough to be religious, there will be small hopes of me.

ANGELICA: Did you not promise then to marry her? 375

WILLMORE: Not I, by Heaven.

ANGELICA: You cannot undeceive my fears and torments, till you have vow'd you will not marry her.

HELLENA: If he swears that, he'll be reveng'd on me indeed for all my Rogueries. 380

ANGELICA: I know what Arguments you'll bring against me, Fortune and Honour.

WILLMORE: Honour! I tell you, I hate it in your Sex; and those that fancy themselves possest of that Foppery, are the most impertinently troublesom of all Woman-kind, and 385 will transgress nine Commandments to keep one: and to satisfy your Jealousy I swear—

HELLENA: (*Aside to him.*) Oh, no swearing, dear Captain—

WILLMORE: If it were possible I should ever be inclin'd to marry, it should be some kind young Sinner, one that has 390 Generosity enough to give a favour handsomely to one that can ask it discreetly, one that has Wit enough to man- age an Intrigue of Love—oh, how civil such a Wench is, to a Man than does her the Honour to marry her.

ANGELICA: By Heaven, there's no Faith in any thing he says. 395

(*Enter* SEBASTIAN.)

SEBASTIAN: Madam, *Don Antonio*—

ANGELICA: Come hither.

HELLENA: Ha, *Antonio!* he may be coming hither, and he'll cer- tainly discover me, I'll therefore retire without a Ceremony.

(*Exit* HELLENA.)

ANGELICA: I'll see him, get my Coach ready. 400

SEBASTIAN: It waits you, Madam.

WILLMORE: This is lucky: what, Madam, now I may be gone and leave you to the enjoyment of my Rival?

ANGELICA: Dull Man, that canst not see how ill, how poor That false dissimulation looks—Be gone, 405 And never let me see thy cozening Face again,

Lest I relapse and kill thee.

WILLMORE: Yes, you can spare me now,—farewell till you are
in a better Humour—I'm glad of this release—

410   Now for my Gipsy:
For tho to worse we change, yet still we find
New Joys, New Charms, in a new Miss that's kind.

(*Exit* WILLMORE.)

ANGELICA: He's gone, and in this Ague of My Soul
The shivering Fit returns;

415   Oh with what willing haste he took his leave,
As if the long'd for Minute were arriv'd,
Of some blest Assignation.
In vain I have consulted all my Charms,
In vain this Beauty priz'd, in vain believ'd

420   My eyes cou'd kindle any lasting Fires.
I had forgot my Name, my Infamy,
And the Reproach that Honour lays on those
That dare pretend a sober passion here.
Nice Reputation, tho it leave behind

425   More Virtues than inhabit where that dwells,
Yet that once gone, those virtues shine no more.
—Then since I am not fit to belov'd,
I am resolv'd to think on a Revenge
On him that sooth'd me thus to my undoing.

(*Exeunt.*)

SCENE III

A Street.

Enter FLORINDA *and* VALERIA *in Habits different from what they
have been seen in.*

FLORINDA: We're happily escap'd, yet I tremble still.
VALERIA: A Lover and fear! why, I am but half a one, and yet
I have Courage for any Attempt. Would *Hellena* were here.
I wou'd fain have had her as deep in this Mischief as we,

5   she'll fare but ill else I doubt.
FLORINDA: She pretended a Visit to the *Augustine* Nuns, but
I believe some other design carried her out, pray Heavens
we light on her.
VALERIA: When I saw no reason wou'd go good on her, I fol-

10   low'd her into the Wardrobe, and as she was looking for
something in a great Chest, I tumbled her in by the Heels,
snatcht the Key of the Apartment where you were confin'd, lockt her in, and left her bauling for help.
FLORINDA: 'Tis well you resolve to follow my Fortunes, for

15   thou darest never appear at home again after such an Action.
VALERIA: That's according as the young Stranger and I shall
agree—But to our business—I deliver'd your Letter, your
Note to *Belvile,* when I got out under pretence of going
to Mass, I found him at his Lodging, and believe me it

20   came seasonably; for never was Man in so desperate a
Condition. I told him of your Resolution of making your
escape to day, if your Brother would be absent long
enough to permit you; if not, die rather than be *Antonio's.*
FLORINDA: Thou shou'dst have told him I was confin'd to my

25   Chamber upon my Brother's suspicion, that the Business
on the *Molo* was a Plot laid between him and I.

VALERIA: I said all this, and told him your Brother was now
gone to his Devotion, and he resolves to visit every
Church till he find him; and not only undeceive him in
that, but caress him so as shall delay his return home.   30
FLORINDA: Oh Heavens! he's here, and *Belvile* with him too.

(*They put on their Vizards.*)

(*Enter Don* PEDRO, BELVILE, WILLMORE; BELVILE, *and Don* PE-
DRO *seeming in serious Discourse.*)

VALERIA: Walk boldly by them, I'll come at a distance, lest he
suspect us.

(*She walks by them, and looks back on them.*)

WILLMORE: Ha! A Woman! and of an excellent Mien!
PEDRO: She throws a kind look back on you.   35
WILLMORE: Death, tis a likely Wench, and that kind look shall
not be cast away—I'll follow her.
BELVILE: Prithee do not.
WILLMORE: Do not! By Heavens to the Antipodes, with such
an Invitation.   40

(*She goes out, and* WILLMORE *follows her.*)

BELVILE: 'Tis a mad Fellow for a Wench.

(*Enter* FREDERICK.)

FREDERICK: Oh Colonel, such News.
BELVILE: Prithee what?
FREDERICK: News that will make you laugh in spite of Fortune.
BELVILE: What, *Blunt* has had some damn'd Trick put upon   45
him, cheated, bang'd, or clapt?
FREDERICK: Cheated, Sir, rarely cheated of all but his Shirt
and Drawers; the unconscionable Whore too turn'd him
out before Consummation, so that traversing the Streets at
Midnight, the Watch found him in this *Fresco,* and con-   50
ducted him home: By Heaven 'tis such a slight, and yet I
durst as well have been hang'd as laugh at him, or pity
him; he beats all that do but ask him a Question, and is in
such an Humour—
PEDRO: Who is't has met with this ill usage, Sir?   55
BELVILE: (*Aside.*) A Friend of ours, whom you must see for
Mirth's sake. I'll imploy him to give *Florinda* time for an
escape.
PEDRO: Who is he?
BELVILE: A young Countryman of ours, one that has been ed- 60
ucated at so plentiful a rate, he yet ne'er knew the want of
Money, and 'twill be a great Jest to see how simply he'll
look without it. For my part I'll lend him none, and the
Rogue knows not how to put on a borrowing Face, and
ask first. I'll let him see how good 'tis to play our parts   65
whilst I play his—Prithee, *Frederick* do go home and keep
him in that posture till we come.

(*Exeunt.*)

(*Enter* FLORINDA *from the farther end of the Scene, looking behind her.*)

FLORINDA: I am follow'd still—hah—my Brother too advancing this way, good Heavens defend me from being
seen by him.   70

(*She goes off.*)

(*Enter* WILLMORE, *and after him* VALERIA, *at a little distance.*)

WILLMORE: Ah! There she sails, she looks back as she were willing to be boarded, I'll warrant her Prize.

(*He goes out,* VALERIA *following.*)

(*Enter* HELLENA, *just as he goes out, with a* PAGE.)

75
HELLENA: Hah, is not that my Captain that has a Woman in chase?—'tis not *Angelica*. Boy, follow those People at a distance, and bring me an Account where they go in.—I'll find his Haunts, and plague him every where.—ha—my Brother!

(*Exit* PAGE. BELVILE, WILLMORE, *and* PEDRO *cross the Stage:* HELLENA *runs off.*)

(*Scene changes to another Street. Enter* FLORINDA.)

80
FLORINDA: What shall I do, my Brother now pursues me. Will no kind Power protect me from his Tyranny?—Hah, here's a Door open, I'll venture in, since nothing can be worse than to fall into his Hands, my Life and Honour are at stake, and my Necessity has no choice.

(*She goes in. Enter* VALERIA, *and Hellena's* PAGE *peeping after* FLORINDA.)

PAGE: Here she went in, I shall remember this House.

(*Exit* PAGE.)

85
VALERIA: This is *Belvile's* Lodgings; she's gone in as readily as if she knew it—hah—here's that mad Fellow again, I dare not venture in—I'll watch my Opportunity.

(*Goes aside. Enter* WILLMORE, *gazing about him.*)

WILLMORE: I have lost her hereabouts—Pox on't she must not scape me so.

(*Goes out.*)

(*Scene changes to* BLUNT'*s chamber, discovers him sitting on a couch in his shirt and drawers, reading.*)

90

95
BLUNT: So, now my Mind's a little at Peace, since I have resolv'd Revenge—A Pox on this Taylor tho, for not bringing home the Clothes I bespoke; and a Pox of all poor Cavaliers, a Man can never keep a spare Suit for 'em; and I shall have these Rogues come in and find me naked; and then I'm undone; but I'm resolv'd to arm my self—the Rascals shall not insult over me too much.

(*Puts on an old rusty Sword and Buff-Belt.*)

100
—Now, how like a Morrice-Dancer I am equipt—a fine Lady-like Whore to cheat me thus, without affording me a Kindness for my Money, a Pox light on her, I shall never be reconciled to the Sex more, she has made me as faithless as a Physician, as uncharitable as a Churchman, and as ill-natur'd as a Poet. O how I'll use all Womenkind hereafter! what wou'd I give to have one of 'em within my reach now!

105
any Mortal thing in Petticoats, kind Fortune, send me; and I'll forgive thy last Night's Malice—Here's a cursed Book too, (a Warning to all young Travellers) that can instruct me how to prevent such Mischiefs now 'tis too late. Well 'tis a rare convenient thing to read a little now and then, as well as hawk and hunt.

(*Sits down again and reads.*)

(*Enter to him* FLORINDA.)

110
FLORINDA: This House is haunted sure, 'tis well furnisht and no living thing inhabits it—hah—a Man! Heavens how he's attir'd! sure 'tis some Rope-dancer, or Fencing-Master; I tremble now for fear, and yet I must venture now to speak to him—Sir, if I may not interrupt your Meditations—

(*He starts up and gazes.*)

115
BLUNT: Hah—what's here? Are my wishes granted? and is not that a she Creature? Adsheartlikins 'tis! what wretched thing art thou—hah!

120
FLORINDA: Charitable Sir, you've told your self already what I am; a very wretched Maid, forc'd by a strange unlucky Accident, to seek a safety here, and must be ruin'd, if you do not grant it.

125
BLUNT: Ruin'd! Is there any Ruin so inevitable as that which now threatens thee? Dost thou know, miserable Woman, into what Den of Mischiefs thou art fall'n? what a Bliss of Confusion?—hah—dost not see something in my looks that frights thy guilty Soul, and makes thee wish to change that Shape of Woman for any humble Animal, or Devil? for those were safer for thee, and less mischievous.

130
FLORINDA: Alas, what mean you, Sir? I must confess your Looks have something in 'em makes me fear; but I beseech you, as you seem a Gentleman, pity a harmless Virgin, that takes your House for Sanctuary.

135
BLUNT: Talk on, talk on, and weep too, till my faith return. Do, flatter me out of my Senses again—a harmless Virgin with a Pox, as much one as t'other, adsheartlikins. Why, what the Devil can I not be safe in my House for you? not in my Chamber? nay, even being naked too cannot secure me. This is an Impudence greater than has invaded me yet.—Come, no Resistance.

(*Pulls her rudely.*)

FLORINDA: Dare you be so cruel?

140

145

150
BLUNT: Cruel, adsheartlikins as a Gally-slave, or a *Spanish* Whore: Cruel, yes, I will kiss and beat thee all over; kiss, and see thee all over; thou shalt lie with me too, not that I care for the Injoyment, but to let you see I have ta'en deliberated Malice to thee, and will be revenged on one Whore for the Sins of another; I will smile and deceive thee, flatter thee, and beat thee, kiss and swear, and lye to thee, imbrace thee and rob thee, as she did me, fawn on thee, and strip thee stark naked, then hang thee out at my Window by the Heels, with a Paper of scurvey Verses fasten'd to thy Breast, in praise of damnable Women—Come, come along.

FLORINDA: Alas, Sir, must I be sacrific'd for the Crimes of the most infamous of my Sex? I never understood the Sins you name.

BLUNT: Do, persuade the Fool you love him, or that one of you
155   can be just or honest; tell me I was not an easy Coxcomb, or
      any strange impossible Tale: it will be believ'd sooner than
      thy false Showers or Protestations. A Generation of damn'd
      Hypocrites, to flatter my very Clothes from my back! dis-
      sembling Witches! are these the Returns you make an hon-
160   est Gentleman that trusts, believes, and loves you?—But if I
      be not even with you—Come along, or I shall—

(*Pulls her again.*)

(*Enter* FREDERICK.)

FREDERICK: Hah, what's here to do?
BLUNT: Adsheartlikins, *Frederick* I am glad thou art come, to
      be a Witness of my dire Revenge.
165 FREDERICK: What's this, a Person of Quality too, who is upon
      the Ramble to supply the Defects of some grave impotent
      Husband?
BLUNT: No, this has another Pretence, some very unfortunate
      Accident brought her hither, to save a Life pursued by I
170   know not who, or why, and forc'd to take Sanctuary here
      at Fools Haven. Adsheartlikins to me of all Mankind for
      Protection? Is the Ass to be cajol'd again, think ye? No,
      young one, no Prayers or Tears shall mitigate my Rage;
      therefore prepare for both my Pleasure of Enjoyment and
175   Revenge, for I am resolved to make up my Loss here on
      thy Body, I'll take it out in kindness and in beating.
FREDERICK: Now, Mistress of mine, what do you think of this?
FLORINDA: I think he will not—dares not be so barbarous.
FREDERICK: Have a care, *Blunt,* she fetch'd a deep Sigh, she is
180   inamour'd with thy Shirt and Drawers, she'll strip thee
      even of that. There are of her Calling such unconscionable
      Baggages, and such dexterous Thieves, they'll flea a Man,
      and he shall ne'er miss his Skin, till he feels the Cold.
      There was a Country-man of ours robb'd of a Row of
185   Teeth whilst he was sleeping, which the Jilt made him buy
      again when he wak'd—You see, Lady, how little Reason
      we have to trust you.
BLUNT: 'Dsheartlikins, why, this is most abominable.
FLORINDA: Some such Devils there may be, but by all that's
190   holy I am none such, I entered here to save a Life in danger.
BLUNT: For no goodness I'll warrant her.
FREDERICK: Faith, Damsel, you had e'en confess the plain
      Truth, for we are Fellows not to be caught twice in the
      same Trap: Look on that Wreck, a tight Vessel when he set
195   out of Haven, well trim'd and laden, and see how a Female
      Piccaroon of this Island of Rogues has shatter'd him, and
      canst thou hope for any Mercy?
BLUNT: No, no, Gentlewoman, come along, adsheartlikins we
      must be better acquainted—we'll both lie with her, and
200   then let me alone to bang her.
FREDERICK: I am ready to serve you in matters of Revenge,
      that has a double Pleasure in't.
BLUNT: Well said. You hear, little one, how you are condem-
      n'd by publick Vote to the Bed within, there's no resisting
205   your Destiny, Sweetheart.

(*Pulls her.*)

FLORINDA: Stay, Sir, I have seen you with *Belvile,* an *English*
      Cavalier, for his sake use me kindly; you know how, Sir.

BLUNT: *Belvile!* why, yes, Sweeting, we do know *Belvile,* and
      wish he were with us now, he's a Cormorant at Whore and
      Bacon, he'd have a Limb or two of thee, my Virgin Pullet: 210
      but 'tis no matter, we'll leave him the Bones to pick.
FLORINDA: Sir, if you have any Esteem for that *Belvile,* I con-
      jure you to treat me with more Gentleness; he'll thank
      you for the Justice.
FREDERICK: Hark ye, *Blunt,* I doubt we are mistaken in this 215
      matter.
FLORINDA: Sir, If you find me not worth *Belvile's* Care, use
      me as you please; and that you may think I merit better
      treatment than you threaten—pray take this Present—

(*Gives him a Ring: He looks on it.*)

BLUNT: Hum—A Diamond! why, 'tis a wonderful Virtue now 220
      that lies in this Ring, a mollifying Virtue; adsheartlikins
      there's more persuasive Rhetorick in't, than all her Sex
      can utter.
FREDERICK: I begin to suspect something; and 'twou'd anger
      us vilely to be truss'd up for a Rape upon a Maid of Qual- 225
      ity, when we only believe we ruffle a Harlot.
BLUNT: Thou art a credulous Fellow, but adsheartlikins I have
      no Faith yet; why, my Saint prattled as parlously as this
      does, she gave me a Bracelet too, a Devil on her: but I sent
      my Man to sell it to day for Necessaries, and it prov'd as 230
      counterfeit as her Vows of Love.
FREDERICK: However let it reprieve her till we see *Belvile.*
BLUNT: That's hard, yet I will grant it.

(*Enter a* SERVANT.)

SERVANT: Oh, Sir, the Colonel is just come with his new
      Friend and a *Spaniard* of Quality, and talks of having you 235
      to Dinner with 'em.
BLUNT: 'Dsheartlikins, I'm undone—I would not see 'em for
      the World: Harkye, *Frederick* lock up the Wench in your
      Chamber.
FREDERICK: Fear nothing, Madam, whate'er he threatens, 240
      you're safe whilst in my Hands.

(*Exit* FREDERICK *and* FLORINDA.)

BLUNT: And, Sirrah—upon your Life, say—I am not at
      home—or that I am asleep—or—or any thing—away—
      I'll prevent them coming this way.

(*Locks the Door and Exeunt.*)

ACT FIVE

SCENE I

BLUNT'*s Chamber.*

After a great knocking as at his Chamber-door, enter BLUNT *softly,*
crossing the Stage in his Shirt and Drawers, as before.

(*Call within.*) *Ned, Ned Blunt, Ned Blunt.*

BLUNT: The Rogues are up in Arms, 'dsheartlikins, this vil-
      lainous *Frederick* has betray'd me, they have heard of my
      blessed Fortune.

(*And knocking within.*) *Ned Blunt, Ned, Ned—*   5

BELVILE: Why, he's dead, sir, without dispute dead, he has not
  been seen to day; let's break open the Door—here—Boy—

BLUNT: Ha, break open the Door! 'dsheartlikins that mad Fellow will be as good as his word.

10 BELVILE: Boy, bring something to force the Door.

(*A great noise within at the Door again.*)

BLUNT: So, now must I speak in my own Defence, I'll try
  what Rhetorick will do—hold—hold, what do you
  mean, Gentlemen, what do you mean?

BELVILE: Oh Rogue, art alive? prithee open the Door, and
15   convince us.

BLUNT: Yes, I am alive, Gentlemen—but at present a little busy.

BELVILE: (*Within.*) How! *Blunt* grown a man of Business!
  come, come, open, and let's see this Miracle.

BLUNT: No, no, no, no, Gentlemen, 'tis no great Business—
20   but—I am—at—my Devotion,—'dsheartlikins, will you
  not allow a man time to pray?

BELVILE: (*Within.*) Turn'd religious! a greater Wonder than the
  first, therefore open quickly, or we shall unhinge, we shall.

BLUNT: This won't do—Why, hark ye, Colonel; to tell you
25   the plain Truth, I am about a necessary Affair of Life.—I
  have a Wench with me—you apprehend me? the Devil's
  in't if they be so uncivil as to disturb me now.

WILLMORE: How, a Wench! Nay, then we must enter and partake; no Resistance,—unless it be your Lady of Quality,
30   and then we'll keep our distance.

BLUNT: So, the Business is out.

WILLMORE: Come, come, lend more hands to the Door,—
  now heave altogether—so, well done, my Boys—

(*Breaks open the Door. Enter* BELVILE, WILLMORE, FREDERICK,
PEDRO, *and* BELVILE'*s page:* BLUNT *looks simply, they all laugh at
him, he lays his hand on his Sword, and comes up to* WILLMORE.)

BLUNT: Hark ye, Sir, laugh out your laugh quickly, d'ye hear,
35   and be gone, I shall spoil your sport else; 'dsheartlikins, Sir,
  I shall—the Jest has been carried on too long,—(*Aside.*) a
  Plague upon my Taylor—

WILLMORE: 'Sdeath, how the Whore has drest him! Faith, Sir,
  I'm sorry.

40 BLUNT: Are you so, Sir? keep't to your self then, Sir, I advise you,
  d'ye hear? for I can as little endure your Pity as his Mirth.

(*Lays his Hand on's Sword.*)

BELVILE: Indeed, *Willmore,* thou wert a little too rough with
  Ned Blunt's Mistress; call a Person of Quality Whore, and
  one so young, so handsome, and so eloquent!—ha, ha, ha.

45 BLUNT: Hark ye, Sir, you know me, and know I can be angry; have a care—for 'dsheartlikins I can fight too—I can,
  Sir,—do you mark me—no more.

BELVILE: Why so peevish, good *Ned?* some Disappointments,
  I'll warrant—What! did the jealous Count her Husband
50   return just in the nick?

(*They laugh.*)

BLUNT: Or the Devil, Sir,—d'ye laugh?
  Look ye, settle me a good sober Countenance, and that
  quickly too, or you shall know *Ned Blunt* is not—

BELVILE: Not every Body, we know that.

BLUNT: Not an Ass, to be laught at, Sir.   55

WILLMORE: Unconscionable Sinner, to bring a Lover so near
  his Happiness, a vigorous passionate Lover, and then not
  only cheat him of his Moveables, but his Desires too.

BELVILE: Ah, Sir, a Mistress is a Trifle with *Blunt,* he'll have a
  dozen the next time he looks abroad; his Eyes have   60
  Charms not to be resisted: There needs no more than to
  expose that taking Person to the view of the Fair, and he
  leads 'em all in Triumph.

PEDRO: Sir, tho I'm a stranger to you, I'm ashamed at the
  rudeness of my Nation; and could you learn who did it,   65
  would assist you to make an Example of 'em.

BLUNT: Why, ay, there's one speaks sense now, and handsomly;
  and let me tell you Gentlemen, I should not have shew'd my
  self like a Jack-Pudding, thus to have made you Mirth, but that
  I have revenge within my power; for know, I have got into my   70
  possession a Female, who had better have fallen under any
  Curse, than the Ruin I design her: 'dsheartlikins, she assaulted
  me here in my own Lodgings, and had doubtless committed a
  Rape upon me, had not this Sword defended me.

FREDERICK: I knew not that, but o' my Conscience thou   75
  hadst ravisht her, had she not redeem'd her self with a
  Ring—let's see't, *Blunt.*

(BLUNT *shews the Ring.*)

BELVILE: (*Goes to whisper to him.*) Hah!—the Ring I gave
  Florinda when we exchang'd our Vows!—hark ye, *Blunt*—

WILLMORE: No whispering, good Colonel, there's a Woman   80
  in the case, no whispering.

BELVILE: Hark ye, Fool, be advis'd, and conceal both the Ring
  and the Story, for your Reputation's sake; don't let People
  know what despis'd Cullies we *English* are: to be cheated
  and abus'd by one Whore, and another rather bribe thee   85
  than be kind to thee, is an Infamy to our Nation.

WILLMORE: Come, come, where's the Wench! we'll see her,
  let her be what she will, we'll see her.

PEDRO: Ay, ay, let us see her, I can soon discover whether she
  be of Quality, or for your Diversion.   90

BLUNT: She's in *Frederick's* Custody.

WILLMORE: Come, come, the Key.

(*To* FREDERICK *who gives him the Key, they are going.*)

BELVILE: Death! what shall I do?—stay, Gentlemen—yet if I
  hinder 'em, I shall discover all—hold, let's go one at
  once—give me the Key.   95

WILLMORE: Nay, hold there, Colonel, I'll go first.

FREDERICK: Nay, no Dispute, *Ned* and I have the property of her.

WILLMORE: Damn Property—then we'll draw Cuts.

(BELVILE *goes to whisper* WILLMORE.)

  Nay, no Corruption, good Colonel: come, the longest
  Sword carries her.—   100

(*They all draw, forgetting Don* PEDRO, *being a Spaniard, had the
longest.*)

BLUNT: I yield up my Interest to you Gentlemen, and that
  will be Revenge sufficient.

WILLMORE: The Wench is yours—(*To* PEDRO.) Pox of his
Toledo, I had forgot that.

105 FREDERICK: Come, Sir, I'll conduct you to the Lady.

(*Exit* FREDERICK *and* PEDRO.)

BELVILE: (*Aside.*) To hinder him will certainly discover—
Dost know, dull Beast, what Mischief thou hast done?

(WILLMORE *walking up and down out of Humour.*)

WILLMORE: Ay, ay, to trust our Fortune to Lots, a Devil on't,
'twas madness, that's the Truth on't.

110 BELVILE: Oh intolerable Sot!

(*Enter* FLORINDA, *running masqu'd,* PEDRO *after her,* WILLMORE
gazing round her.)

FLORINDA: (*Aside.*) Good Heaven, defend me from discovery.
PEDRO: 'Tis but in vain to fly me, you are fallen to my Lot.
BELVILE: Sure she is undiscover'd yet, but now I fear there is
no way to bring her off.
115 WILLMORE: Why, what a Pox is not this my Woman, the same
I follow'd but now?

(PEDRO *talking to* FLORINDA, *who walks up and down.*)

PEDRO: As if I did not know ye, and your Business here.
FLORINDA: (*Aside.*) Good Heaven! I fear he does indeed—
PEDRO: Come, pray be kind, I know you meant to be so
120 when you enter'd here, for these are proper Gentlemen.
WILLMORE: But, Sir—perhaps the Lady will not be impos'd
upon, she'll chuse her Man.
PEDRO: I am better bred, than not to leave her Choice free.

(*Enter* VALERIA, *and is surpriz'd at the Sight of Don* PEDRO.)

VALERIA: (*Aside.*) Don *Pedro* here! there's no avoiding him.
125 FLORINDA: (*Aside.*) *Valeria*! then I'm undone—
VALERIA: (*To* PEDRO, *running to him.*) Oh! have I found you,
Sir—
—The strangest Accident—if I had breath—to tell it.
PEDRO: Speak—is *Florinda* safe? *Hellena* well?
130 VALERIA: Ay, ay, Sir—*Florinda*—is safe—from any fears of you.
PEDRO: Why, where's *Florinda*?—speak.
VALERIA: Ay, where indeed, Sir? I wish I could inform you,—
But to hold you no longer in doubt—
FLORINDA: (*Aside.*) Oh, what will she say!
135 VALERIA: She's fled away in the Habit of one of her Pages,
Sir—but *Callis* thinks you may retrieve her yet, if you
make haste away; she'll tell you, Sir, the rest—(*Aside.*) if
you can find her out.
PEDRO: Dishonourable Girl, she has undone my Aim—Sir—
140 you see my necessity of leaving you, and I hope you'll pardon it: my Sister, I know, will make her flight to you; and
if she do, I shall expect she should be render'd back.
BELVILE: I shall consult my Love and Honour, Sir.

(*Exit* PEDRO.)

FLORINDA: (*To* VALERIA.) My dear Preserver, let me imbrace
145 thee.
WILLMORE: What the Devil's all this?

BLUNT: Mystery by this Light.
VALERIA: Come, come, make haste and get your selves married quickly, for your Brother will return again.
BELVILE: I am so surpriz'd with Fears and Joys, so amaz'd to 150
find you here in safety, I can scarce persuade my Heart
into a Faith of what I see—
WILLMORE: Harkye, Colonel, is this that Mistress who has cost
you so many Sighs, and me so many Quarrels with you?
BELVILE: It is—(*To* FLORINDA.) Pray give him the Honour of 155
your Hand.
WILLMORE: Thus it must be receiv'd then.

(*Kneels and kisses her Hand.*)

And with it give your Pardon too.
FLORINDA: The Friend to *Belvile* may command me anything.
WILLMORE: (*Aside.*) Death, wou'd I might, 'tis a surprizing 160
Beauty.
BELVILE: Boy, run and fetch a Father instantly.

(*Exit* PAGE.)

FREDERICK: So, now do I stand like a Dog, and have not a
Syllable to plead my own Cause with: by this Hand,
Madam, I was never thorowly confounded before, nor 165
shall I ever more dare look up with Confidence, till you
are pleased to pardon me.
FLORINDA: Sir, I'll be reconcil'd to you on one Condition,
that you'll follow the Example of your Friend, in marry-
ing a Maid that does not hate you, and whose Fortune (I 170
believe) will not be unwelcome to you.
FREDERICK: Madam, had I no Inclinations that way, I shou'd
obey your kind Commands.
BELVILE: Who, *Frederick* marry; he has so few Inclinations for
Womankind, that had he been possest of Paradise, he 175
might have continu'd there to this Day, if no Crime but
Love cou'd have disinherited him.
FREDERICK: Oh, I do not use to boast of my Intrigues.
BELVILE: Boast! why thou do'st nothing but boast; and I dare
swear, wer't thou as innocent from the Sin of the Grape, as 180
thou art from the Apple, thou might'st yet claim that right
in *Eden* which our first Parents lost by too much loving.
FREDERICK: I wish this Lady would think me so modest a Man.
VALERIA: She shou'd be sorry then, and not like you half so
well, and I shou'd be loth to break my Word with you; 185
which was, That if your Friend and mine are agreed, it
shou'd be a Match between you and I.

(*She gives him her Hand.*)

FREDERICK: Bear witness, Colonel, 'tis a Bargain.

(*Kisses her Hand.*)

BLUNT: (*To* FLORINDA.) I have a Pardon to beg too; but adsheartlikins I am so out of Countenance, that I am a Dog 190
if I can say any thing to purpose.
FLORINDA: Sir, I heartily forgive you all.
BLUNT: That's nobly said, sweet Lady—*Belvile,* prithee present her her Ring again, for I find I have not Courage to
approach her my self. 195

(*Gives him the Ring, he gives it to* FLORINDA. *Enter* BOY.)

BOY: Sir, I have brought the Father that you sent for.

BELVILE: 'Tis well, and now my dear *Florinda,* let's fly to compleat that mighty Joy we have so long wish'd and sigh'd for. Come, *Frederick* you'll follow?

200 FREDERICK: Your Example, Sir, 'twas ever my Ambition in War, and must be so in Love.

WILLMORE: And must not I see this juggling Knot ty'd?

BELVILE: No, thou shalt do us better Service, and be our Guard, lest Don *Pedro's* sudden Return interrupt the Ceremony.

205 WILLMORE: Content; I'll secure this Pass.

(*Exit* BELVILE, FLORINDA, FREDERICK, *and* VALERIA. *Enter page.*)

BOY: (*To* WILLMORE.) Sir, there's a Lady without wou'd speak to you.

WILLMORE: Conduct her in, I dare not quit my Post.

BOY: And, Sir, your Taylor waits you in your Chamber.

210 BLUNT: Some comfort yet, I shall not dance naked at the Wedding.

(*Exit* BLUNT *and* BOY.)

(*Enter again the* BOY, *conducting in* ANGELICA *in a masquing Habit and a Vizard,* WILLMORE *runs to her.*)

WILLMORE: This can be none but my pretty Gipsy—Oh, I see you can follow as well as fly—Come, confess thy self the most malicious Devil in Nature, you think you have done
215 my Bus'ness with *Angelica*—

ANGELICA: Stand off, base Villain—

(*She draws a Pistol and holds to his Breast.*)

WILLMORE: Hah, 'tis not she: who art thou? and what's thy Business?

ANGELICA: One thou hast injur'd, and who comes to kill thee
220 for't.

WILLMORE: What the Devil canst thou mean?

ANGELICA: By all my Hopes to kill thee—

(*Holds still the Pistol to his Breast, he going back, she following still.*)

WILLMORE: Prithee on what Acquaintance? for I know thee not.

ANGELICA: Behold this Face!—so lost to thy Remembrance!
225 And then call all thy Sins about thy Soul,

(*Pulls off her Vizard.*)

And let them die with thee.

WILLMORE: *Angelica!*

ANGELICA: Yes, Traitor.
Does not thy guilty Blood run shivering thro thy Veins?
230 Hast thou no Horrour at this Sight, that tells thee,
Thou hast not long to boast thy shameful Conquest?

WILLMORE: Faith, no Child, my Blood keeps its old Ebbs and Flows still, and that usual Heat too, that cou'd oblige thee with a Kindness, had I but opportunity.

235 ANGELICA: Devil! dost wanton with my Pain—have at thy Heart.

WILLMORE: Hold, dear Virago! hold thy Hand a little,
I am not now at leisure to be kill'd—hold and hear me—
(*Aside.*) Death, I think she's in earnest.

ANGELICA: (*Aside, turning from him.*) Oh if I take not heed,
My coward Heart will leave me to his Mercy. 240
—What have you, Sir, to say?—but should I hear thee,
Thoud'st talk away all that is brave about me:

(*Follows him with the Pistol to his Breast.*)

And I have vow'd thy Death, by all that's sacred.

WILLMORE: Why, then, there's an end of a proper handsom Fellow, that might have liv'd to have done good Service 245
yet:—That's all I can say to't.

ANGELICA: (*Pausingly.*) Yet—I wou'd give thee—time for Penitence.

WILLMORE: Faith, Child, I thank God, I have ever took care to lead a good, sober, hopeful Life, and am of a Religion that teaches me to believe, I shall depart in Peace. 250

ANGELICA: So will the Devil: tell me
How many poor believing Fools thou hast undone;
How many Hearts thou hast betray'd to ruin!
—Yet, these are little Mischiefs to the Ills
Thou'st taught mine to commit: thou'st taught it Love. 255

WILLMORE: Egad, 'twas shrewdly hurt the while.

ANGELICA: —Love, that has robb'd it of its Unconcern,
Of all that Pride that taught me how to value it,
And in its room a mean submissive Passion was convey'd,
That made me humbly bow, which I ne'er did 260
To any thing but Heaven.
—Thou, perjur'd Man, didst this, and with thy Oaths,
Which on thy Knees thou didst devoutly make,
Soften'd my yielding Heart—And then, I was a Slave—
Yet still had been content to've worn my Chains, 265
Worn 'em with Vanity and Joy for ever,
Hadst thou not broke those Vows that put them on.
—'Twas then I was undone.

(*All this while follows him with a Pistol to his Breast.*)

WILLMORE: Broke my Vows! why, where hast thou lived?
Amongst the Gods! For I never heard of mortal Man, 270
That has not broke a thousand Vows.

ANGELICA: Oh, Impudence!

WILLMORE: *Angelica!* that Beauty has been too long tempting,
Not to have made a thousand Lovers languish,
Who in the amorous Favour, no doubt have sworn 275
Like me; did they all die in that Faith? still adoring?
I do not think they did.

ANGELICA: No, faithless Man: had I repaid their Vows, as I did thine, I wou'd have kill'd the ungrateful that had abandon'd me. 280

WILLMORE: This old General has quite spoil'd thee, nothing makes a Woman so vain, as being flatter'd; your old Lover ever supplies the Defects of Age, with intolerable Dotage, vast Charge, and that which you call Constancy; and attributing all this to your own Merits, you domineer, and 285
throw your Favours in's Teeth, upbraiding him still with the Defects of Age, and cuckold him as often as he deceives your Expectations. But the gay, young, brisk Lover, that brings his equal Fires, and can give you Dart for Dart, he'll be as nice as you sometimes. 290

ANGELICA: All this thou'st made me know, for which I hate thee.

Had I remain'd in innocent Security,
I shou'd have thought all Men were born my Slaves;
And worn my Pow'r like Lightning in my Eyes,
295   To have destroy'd at Pleasure when offended.
—But when Love held the Mirror, the undeceiving Glass
Reflected all the Weakness of my Soul, and made me
    know,
My richest Treasure being lost, my Honour,
All the remaining Spoil cou'd not be worth
300   The Conqueror's Care or Value.
—Oh how I fell like a long worship'd Idol,
Discovering all the Cheat!
Wou'd not the Incense and rich Sacrifice,
Which blind Devotion offer'd at my Altars,
305   Have fall'n to thee?
Why woud'st thou then destroy my fancy'd Power?
WILLMORE: By Heaven thou art brave, and I admire thee
    strangely.
I wish I were that dull, that constant thing,
Which thou woud'st have, and Nature never meant me:
310   I must, like chearful Birds, sing in all Groves,
And perch on every Bough,
Billing the next kind She that flies to meet me;
Yet after all cou'd build my Nest with thee,
Thither repairing when I'd lov'd my round,
315   And still reserve a tributary Flame.

(*Offers her a Purse of Gold.*)

—To gain your Credit, I'll pay you back your Charity,
And be oblig'd for nothing but for Love.
ANGELICA: Oh that thou wert in earnest!
So mean a Thought of me,
320   Wou'd turn my Rage to Scorn, and I shou'd pity thee,
And give thee leave to live;
Which for the publick Safety of our Sex,
And my own private Injuries, I dare not do.
Prepare—

(*Follows still, as before.*)

325   —I will no more be tempted with Replies.
WILLMORE: Sure—
ANGELICA: Another Word will damn thee! I've heard thee talk
    too long.

(*She follows him with a Pistol ready to shoot: he retires still amaz'd.*)

(*Enter Don* ANTONIO, *his Arm in a Scarf, and lays hold on the Pistol.*)

ANTONIO: Hah! *Angelica!*
ANGELICA: *Antonio!* What Devil brought thee hither?
330 ANTONIO: Love and Curiosity, seeing your Coach at Door.
Let me disarm you of this unbecoming Instrument of
    Death.—

(*Takes away the Pistol.*)

Amongst the Number of your Slaves, was there not one
    worthy the Honour to have fought your Quarrel?
335   —Who are you, Sir, that are so very wretched

To merit Death from her?
WILLMORE: One, sir, that cou'd have made a better End of an
amorous Quarrel without you, than with you.
ANTONIO: Sure 'tis some Rival—hah—the very Man took
down her Picture yesterday—the very same that set on me 340
last night—Blest opportunity—

(*Offers to shoot him.*)

ANGELICA: Hold, you're mistaken, Sir.
ANTONIO: By Heaven the very same!
—Sir, what pretensions have you to this Lady?
WILLMORE: Sir, I don't use to be examin'd, and am ill at all 345
    Disputes but this—

(*Draws,* ANTONIO *offers to shoot.*)

ANGELICA: (*To* WILLMORE.) Oh, hold! you see he's arm'd
    with certain Death:
—And you, *Antonio,* I command you hold,
By all the Passion you've so lately vow'd me.

(*Enter Don* PEDRO, *sees* ANTONIO, *and stays.*)

PEDRO: (*Aside.*) Hah, *Antonio!* and *Angelica!*   350
ANTONIO: When I refuse Obedience to your Will,
May you destroy me with your mortal Hate.
By all that's Holy I adore you so,
That even my Rival, who has Charms enough
To make him fall a Victim to my Jealousy,   355
Shall live, nay, and have leave to love on still.
PEDRO: (*Aside.*) What's this I hear?
ANGELICA: (*Pointing to* WILLMORE.) Ah thus, 'twas thus he
    talk'd, and I believ'd.
—*Antonio,* yesterday,
I'd not have sold my Interest in his Heart,   360
For all the Sword has won and lost in Battle.
—But now to show my utmost of Contempt,
I give thee Life—which if thou would'st preserve,
Live where my Eyes may never see thee more,
Live to undo some one, whose Soul may prove   365
So bravely constant to revenge my Love.

(*Goes out,* ANTONIO *follows, but* PEDRO *pulls him back.*)

PEDRO: *Antonio*—stay.
ANTONIO: Don *Pedro*—
PEDRO: What Coward Fear was that prevented thee
From meeting me this Morning on the *Molo?*   370
ANTONIO: Meet thee?
PEDRO: Yes me; I was the Man that dar'd thee to't.
ANTONIO: Hast thou so often seen me fight in War,
To find no better Cause to excuse my Absence?
—I sent my Sword and one to do thee Right,   375
Finding my self uncapable to use a Sword.
PEDRO: But 'twas *Florinda's* Quarrel that we fought,
And you to shew how little you esteem'd her,
Sent me your Rival, giving him your Interest.
—But I have found the Cause of this Affront,   380
But when I meet you fit for the Dispute,
—I'll tell you my Resentment.

ANTONIO: I shall be ready, Sir, e'er long to do your Reason.

(*Exit* ANTONIO.)

PEDRO: If I cou'd find *Florinda,* now whilst my Anger's high, I
385   think I shou'd be kind, and give her to *Belvile* in Revenge.

WILLMORE: Faith, Sir, I know not what you wou'd do, but I
be-lieve the Priest within has been so kind.

PEDRO: How! my Sister married?

WILLMORE: I hope by this time she is, and bedded too, or he
390   has not my longings about him.

PEDRO: Dares he do thus? Does he not fear my Pow'r?

WILLMORE: Faith not at all. If you will go in, and thank him
for the Favour he has done your Sister, so; if not, Sir, my
Power's greater in this House than yours; I have a damn'd
395   surly Crew here, that will keep you till the next Tide, and
then clap you an board my Prize; my Ship lies but a
League off the *Molo,* and we shall show your Donship a
damn'd *Tramontana* Rover's Trick.

(*Enter* BELVILE.)

BELVILE: This Rogue's in some new Mischief—hah, *Pedro* re-
400   turn'd!

PEDRO: Colonel *Belvile,* I hear you have married my Sister.

BELVILE: You have heard truth then, Sir.

PEDRO: Have I so? then, Sir, I wish you Joy.

BELVILE: How!

405   PEDRO: By this Embrace I do, and I glad on't.

BELVILE: Are you in earnest?

PEDRO: By our long Friendship and my Obligations to thee,
I am. The sudden Change I'll give you Reasons for anon.
Come lead me into my Sister, that she may know I now
410   approve her Choice.

(*Exit* BELVILE *with* PEDRO. WILLMORE *goes to follow them. Enter*
HELLENA *as before in Boy's Clothes, and pulls him back.*)

WILLMORE: Ha! my Gipsy—Now a thousand Blessings on
thee for this Kindness. Egad, Child, I was e'en in despair
of ever seeing thee again; my Friends are all provided for
within, each Man his kind Woman.

415   HELLENA: Hah! I thought they had serv'd me some such Trick.

WILLMORE: And I was e'en resolv'd to go aboard, condemn
my self to my lone Cabin, and the Thoughts of thee.

HELLENA: And cou'd you have left me behind? wou'd you
have been so ill-natur'd?

420   WILLMORE: Why, 'twou'd have broke my Heart, Child—but
since we are met again, I defy foul Weather to part us.

HELLENA: And wou'd you be a faithful Friend now, if a Maid
shou'd trust you?

WILLMORE: For a Friend I cannot promise, thou art of a
425   Form so excellent, a Face and Humour too good for cold
dull Friendship; I am parlously afraid of being in love,
Child, and you have not forgot how severely you have us'd
me.

HELLENA: That's all one, such Usage you must still look for,
to find out all your Haunts, to rail at you to all that love

you, till I have made you love only me in your own De-   430
fence, because no body else will love.

WILLMORE: But hast thou no better Quality to recommend
thy self by?

HELLENA: Faith none, Captain—Why, 'twill be the greater
Charity to take me for thy Mistress, I am a lone Child, a   435
kind of Orphan Lover; and why I shou'd die a Maid, and
in a Captain's Hands too, I do not understand.

WILLMORE: Egad, I was never claw'd away with Broad-Sides
from any Female before, thou hast one Virtue I adore,
good-Nature; I hate a coy demure Mistress, she's as trou-   440
blesom as a Colt, I'll break none; no, give me a mad Mistress when mew'd, and in flying on[e] I dare trust upon
the Wing, that whilst she's kind will come to the Lure.

HELLENA: Nay, as kind as you will, good Captain, whilst it
lasts, but let's lose no time.   445

WILLMORE: My time's as precious to me, as thine can be;
therefore, dear Creature, since we are so well agreed, let's
retire to my Chamber, and if ever thou were treated with
such savory Love—Come—My Bed's prepar'd for such a
Guest, all clean and sweet as thy fair self; I love to steal a   450
Dish and a Bottle with a Friend, and hate long Graces—
Come, let's re-tire and fall to.

HELLENA: 'Tis but getting my Consent, and the Business is
soon done; let but old Gaffer *Hymen* and his Priest say Amen
to't, and I dare lay my Mother's Daughter by as proper a Fel-   455
low as your Father's Son, without fear or blushing.

WILLMORE: Hold, hold, no Bugg Words, Child, Priest and
Hymen: prithee add Hangman to 'em to make up the
Consort—No, no, we'll have no Vows but Love, Child, nor
Witness but the Lover; the kind Diety injoins naught but   460
love and enjoy. *Hymen* and Priest wait still upon Portion,
and Joynture; Love and Beauty have their own Cere-
monies. Marriage is as certain a Bane to Love, as lending
Money is to Friendship: I'll neither ask nor give a Vow, tho
I could be content to turn Gipsy, and become a Left-hand   465
Bridegroom, to have the Pleasure of working that great
Miracle of making a Maid a Mother, if you durst venture;
'tis upse Gipsy that, and if I miss, I'll lose my Labour.

HELLENA: And if you do not lose, what shall I get? A Cradle
full of Noise and Mischief, with a Pack of Repentance at   470
my Back? Can you teach me to weave Incle to pass my
time with? 'Tis upse Gipsy that too.

WILLMORE: I can teach thee to weave a true Love's Knot better.

HELLENA: So can my Dog.

WILLMORE: Well, I see we are both upon our Guard, and I see   475
there's no way to conquer good Nature, but by yielding—
here—give me thy Hand—one Kiss and I am thine—

HELLENA: One Kiss! How like my Page he speaks; I am resolv'd
you shall have none, for asking such a sneaking Sum—He
that will be satisfied with one Kiss, will never die of that   480
Longing; good Friend single-Kiss, is all your talking come
to this? A Kiss, a Caudle! farewel, Captain single-Kiss.

(*Going out he stays her.*)

---

398 **Tramontana** Italian and Spanish *tramontano* = from beyond
the mountains

468 **upse** *Op zijn* (Dutch) = in the fashion or manner of, *Upse
Gipsy* = like a gipsy   471 **Incle** linen thread or yarn which was
woven into a tape once very much in use

WILLMORE: Nay, if we part so, let me die like a Bird upon a
Bough, at the Sheriff's Charge. By Heaven, both the *Indies*
485 shall not buy thee from me. I adore thy Humour and will
marry thee, and we are so of one Humour, it must be a
Bargain—give me thy Hand—

(*Kisses her hand.*)

And now let the blind ones (Love and Fortune) do their worst.
HELLENA: Why, God-a-mercy, Captain!
490 WILLMORE: But harkye—The Bargain is now made; but is it
not fit we should know each other's Names? That when
we have Reason to curse one another hereafter, and People ask me who 'tis I give to the Devil, I may at least be
able to tell what Family you came of.
495 HELLENA: Good reason, Captain; and where I have cause, (as I
doubt not but I shall have plentiful) that I may know at
whom to throw my—Blessings—I beseech ye your Name.
WILLMORE: I am call'd *Robert the Constant*.
HELLENA: A very fine Name! pray was it your Faulkner or
500 Butler that christen'd you? Do they not use to whistle
when then call you?
WILLMORE: I hope you have a better, that a Man may name
without crossing himself, you are so merry with mine.
HELLENA: I am call'd *Hellena the Inconstant*.

(*Enter* PEDRO, BELVILE, FLORINDA, FREDERICK, *and* VALERIA.)

505 PEDRO: Hah! *Hellena!*
FLORINDA: *Hellena!*
HELLENA: The very same—hah my Brother! now, Captain,
shew your Love and Courage; stand to your Arms, and defend me bravely, or I am lost for ever.
510 PEDRO: What's this I hear? false Girl, how came you hither,
and what's your Business? Speak.

(*Goes roughly to her.*)

WILLMORE: Hold off, Sir, you have leave to parly only.

(*Puts himself between.*)

HELLENA: I had e'en as good tell it, as you guess it. Faith,
Brother, my Business is the same with all living Creatures
515 of my Age, to love, and be loved, and here's the Man.
PEDRO: Perfidious Maid, hast thou deceiv'd me too, deceiv'd
thy self and Heaven?
HELLENA: 'Tis time enough to make my Peace with that: Be
you but kind, let me alone with Heaven.
520 PEDRO: *Belvile,* I did not expect this false Play from you; was't
not enough you'd gain *Florinda* (which I pardon'd) but
your leud Friends too must be inrich'd with the Spoils of
a noble Family?
BELVILE: Faith, Sir, I am as much surpriz'd at this as you can be:
525 Yet, Sir, my Friends are Gentlemen, and ought to be esteem'd for their Misfortunes, since they have the Glory to
suffer with the best of Men and Kings; 'tis true, he's a Rover
of Fortune, yet a Prince aboard his little wooden World.
PEDRO: What's this to the maintenance of a Woman or her
530 Birth and Quality?
WILLMORE: Faith, Sir, I can boast of nothing but a Sword
which does me Right where-e'er I come, and has de-

fended a worse Cause than a Woman's: and since I lov'd
her before I either knew her Birth or Name, I must pursue my Resolution, and marry her.   535
PEDRO: And is all your holy Intent of becoming a Nun debauch'd into a Desire of Man?
HELLENA: Why—I have consider'd the matter, Brother, and
find the Three hundred thousand Crowns my Uncle left
me (and you cannot keep from me) will be better laid out 540
in Love than in Religion, and turn to as good an Account—let most Voices carry it, for Heaven or the Captain?
ALL CRY: Captain, a Captain.
HELLENA: Look ye, Sir, 'tis a clear Case.
PEDRO: (*Aside.*) Oh I am mad—if I refuse, my Life's in Dan- 545
ger—Come—There's one motive induces me—take
her—I shall now be free from the fear of her Honour;
guard it you now, if you can, I have been a Slave to't long
enough.

(*Gives her to him.*)

WILLMORE: Faith, Sir, I am of a Nation, that are of opinion a
Woman's Honour is not worth guarding when she has a 550
mind to part with it.
HELLENA: Well said, Captain.
PEDRO: (*To* VALERIA.) This was your Plot, Mistress, but I hope
you have married one that will revenge my Quarrel to
you—   555
VALERIA: There's no altering Destiny, Sir.
PEDRO: Sooner than a Woman's Will, therefore I forgive you
all—and wish you may get my Father's Pardon as easily;
which I fear.

(*Enter* BLUNT *drest in a Spanish Habit, looking very ridiculously;
his* MAN *adjusting his Band.*)

MAN: 'Tis very well, Sir.   560
BLUNT: Well, Sir, 'dsheartlikins I tell you 'tis damnable ill,
Sir—a Spanish Habit, good Lord! cou'd the Devil and my
Taylor devise no other Punishment for me, but the Mode
of a Nation I abominate?
BELVILE: What's the matter, *Ned?*   565
BLUNT: Pray view me round, and judge—

(*Turns round.*)

BELVILE: I must confess thou art a kind of an odd Figure.
BLUNT: In a Spanish Habit with a Vengeance! I had rather be
in the Inquisition for Judaism, than in this Doublet and
Breeches; a Pillory were an easy Collar to this, three   570
Hand-fuls high; and these Shoes too are worse than the
Stocks, with the Sole an Inch shorter than my Foot: In
fine, Gentlemen, methinks I look altogether like a Bag of
Bays stuff'd full of Fools Flesh.
BELVILE: Methinks 'tis well, and makes the look *en Cavalier:*   575
Come, Sir, settle your Face, and salute our Friends, Lady—
BLUNT: Hah! Say'st thou so, my little Rover?

(*To* HELLENA.)

Lady—(if you be one) give me leave to kiss your Hand,
and tell you, adsheartlikins, for all I look so, I am your
humble Servant—A Pox of my *Spanish* Habit.   580

WILLMORE: Hark—what's this?

(*Musick is heard to Play. Enter* BOY.)

BOY: Sir, as the Custom is, the gay People in Masquerade, who make every Man's House their own, are coming up.

(*Enter several* MEN *and* WOMEN *in masquing Habits, with Musick, they put themselves in order and dance.*)

585 BLUNT: Adsheartlikins, wou'd 'twere lawful to pull off their false Faces, that I might see if my Doxy were not amongst 'em.

BELVILE: Ladies and Gentlemen, since you are come so *a propos,* you must take a small Collation with us.

(*To the* MASQUERADERS.)

WILLMORE: Whilst we'll to the Good Man within, who stays
590   to give us a Cast of his Office.

(*To* HELLENA.)

—Have you no trembling at the near approach?

HELLENA: No more than you have in an Engagement or a Tempest.

595 WILLMORE: Egad, thou'rt a brave Girl, and I admire thy
      Love and Courage.
      Lead on, no other Dangers they can dread,
      Who venture in the Storms o'th' Marriage-Bed.

(*Exeunt.*)

EPILOGUE

THE banisht Cavaliers! a Roving Blade!
A popish Carnival! a Masquerade!
The Devil's in't if this will please the Nation,
In these our blessed Times of Reformation,
5   When Conventicling is so much in Fashion.
And yet—
That mutinous Tribe less Factions do beget,
Than your continual differing in Wit;

Your Judgment's (as your Passions) a Disease:
Nor Muse nor Miss your Appetite can please;   10
You're grown as nice as queasy Consciences,
Whose each Convulsion, when the Spirit moves,
Damns every thing that Maggot disapproves.
   With canting Rule you wou'd the Stage refine,
And to dull Method all our Sense confine.   15
With th' Insolence of Common-wealths you rule,
Where each gay Fop, and politick brave Fool
On Monarch Wit impose without controul.
As for the last who seldom sees a Play,
Unless it be the old Black-Fryers way,   20
Shaking his empty Noodle o'er *Bamboo,*
He crys—Good Faith, these Plays will never do.
—Ah, Sir, in my young days, what lofty Wit,
What high-strain'd Scenes of Fighting there were writ:
These are slight airy Toys. But tell me, pray,   25
What has the *House of Commons* done to day?
Then shews his Politicks, to let you see
Of State Affairs he'll judge as notably,
As he can do of Wit and Poetry.
The younger Sparks, who hither do resort,   30
Cry—
Pox o' your gentle things, give us more Sport;
—Damn me, I'm sure 'twill never please the Court.
   Such Fops are never pleas'd, unless the Play
Be stuff'd with Fools, as brisk and dull as they: 35
Such might the Half-Crown spare, and in a Glass
At home behold a more accomplisht Ass,
Where they may set their Cravats, Wigs and Faces,
And practice all their Buffoonry Grimaces;
See how this—Huff becomes—this Dammy—flare—   40
Which they at home may act, because they dare,
But—must with prudent Caution do elsewhere.
Oh that our *Nokes,* or *Tony Lee* could show
A Fop but half so much to th' Life as you.

---

43 **Nokes, or *Tony Lee*** James Nokes and Antony Leigh, the two famous actors, were the leading low comedians of the day

Sor Juana Inés de la Cruz

Juana Inés de Asbaje y Ramírez de Santillana (1648/1651–1695) was probably born in late November or early December of 1648 to the daughter of a wealthy landowner (Isabel Ramírez de Santillana) and an army officer (Pedro Manuel de Asbaje y Vargas Manchucha) serving in the Spanish New World colony of New Spain—present-day Mexico. Although her parents had two other children (Isabel Ramírez had three additional children with another officer), they were not married, and Juana Inés was born an illegitimate "daughter of the church." Raised in the provincial town of Panoyan, Juana had access to her grandfather's library and, by her own account, was a voracious reader, as she later wrote in her *Answer to Sor Filotea* (written 1691):

> When I was six or seven years old and already knew how to read and write, along with all the other skills like embroidery and sewing that women learn, I heard that in Mexico City there were a University and Schools where they studied sciences. As soon as I heard this I began to slay my poor mother with insistent and annoying pleas, begging her to dress me in men's clothes and send me to the capital, to the home of some relatives she had there, so that I could enter the University and study. She refused, and was right in doing so; but I quenched my desire by reading a great variety of books that belonged to my grandfather, and neither punishments nor scoldings could prevent me. And so when I did go to Mexico City, people marveled not so much at my intelligence as at my memory and the facts I knew at an age when it seemed I had scarcely had time to speak.[1]

Juana was sent to live with her mother's relatives in Mexico City in 1659. She lived with them for five years until she moved into the home of the viceroy, where she served in the court of the vicereine, Doña Leonor Carreto, Marquisa de Mancera.

Although she began to write on both religious and secular subjects while at court, Juana's career was closely tied to the church. In 1666, she joined the Carmelite convent of San José, but the penitential strictness of the order seems to have caused her health to suffer, and she left the convent after three months. Still eager to join a convent, she agreed to sit for an examination by the viceroy and forty scholars assembled to test the range of her knowledge, as a means to confirm her suitability for religious life. According to Diego Callega, a priest who wrote the first biography of Sor Juana, she performed like a "royal galleon attacked by canoes," and was admitted to the convent of Santa Paula in 1669, where she took the name Sor Juana Inés de la Cruz. (Illegitimate children were not admissible to convent life; at this time, Juana claimed that her parents had been married, and that her birth date was November 12, 1651; a baptismal record for 1648—listing Juana's aunt and uncle as godparents of an infant "Inés"—is now usually taken as evidence for her birth in that year.)

Although the convent was cloistered, Sor Juana received money to support her servants and was able to receive guests, to study, and to write; she was also closely connected to the social life of New Spain's capital city. The Aztec city of Tenochtitlán had supported some 250,000 inhabitants before the conquest in 1520, but Mexico City was a much smaller city in the seventeenth century. While war, disease, and enslavement drastically reduced the native population, the general population was augmented not only by the annual arrival of *peninsulares* (new inhabitants from Spain), but by an increasing population of *criollos* (people of European descent born in Mexico, like Sor Juana) and *mestizos,* as well as by a growing number of African slaves and immigrants from other Spanish colonies. In the 1800 census, for example, the population of Mexico City was 137,000, making it the largest city in the Americas. The church wielded extensive political power in Mexico (there were sixteen convents in Mexico City alone), and—as in Europe—the leaders of the church and of the state were often drawn from the same aristocratic families. In this sense, it's not surprising that

[1] See *The Answer/La Respuesta, Including a Selection of Poems,* ed. and trans. Electa Arenal and Amanda Powell (New York: Feminist Press, 1994).

Religion, costumed as a Spanish nobleman, surveys the fallen Aztec men and women after the battle between Zeal and Occident, in the 1997 Universidad de las Americas production of the *Loa* to *The Divine Narcissus* by Sor Juana Inés de la Cruz.

throughout her life, Sor Juana was an intimate acquaintance of aristocratic circles in Mexico City, particularly of the viceroys and vicereines.

One vicereine, Maria Luisa Manrique de Lara y Gonzaga (whose husband was viceroy 1680–1686), was the inspiration of several of Sor Juana's poems and had her first volume, *Inundación Castálida,* published in Madrid in 1689 (the title refers to the nymph Castálida, who drowned herself rather than be seduced by Apollo); the title-page described Sor Juana as "the Tenth Muse." By 1690, Sor Juana was arguably the most accomplished secular and philosophical writer in the Americas: She mastered the baroque forms of secular Spanish poetry, writing not only sixty-five sonnets and many ballads and occasional poems, but two well-known comedies (including *Los empeños de una casa*) that were staged. She also wrote sixteen sets of **VILLANCICOS,** carols performed at the Mass; these often incorporate her understanding both of African dialects and of the indigenous Nahua language and were performed at cathedrals throughout Mexico during her lifetime. She wrote three *auto sacramentales,* two of which were performed; thirty-two **LOAS;** a brilliant philosophical treatise *The First Dream* (1685); and a defense of women's claim to an intellectual and spiritual life, *Answer to Sor Filotea.*

Yet despite her fame, Sor Juana was under continual pressure from the church to conform to the more "feminine" role of quiet devotion and service. Early in her career she struggled with her confessor, Antonio Núñez de Miranda, who regarded writing as improper for women, especially for women of the church. Although Sor Juana succeeded in dismissing him as her confessor, he continued to agitate for her silence with higher church officials, including the misogynist archbishop Francisco Aguian y Seijas. In 1690—shortly after her second volume of poetry had been published in Madrid, and her brilliant *auto The Divine Narcissus,* had been published in Mexico—the church's opposition came to a head. During that year, Sor Juana wrote a theological critique of a sermon written forty years earlier, an essay clearly not intended for publication; her friend, the bishop of Puebla, Manuel

Fernández de Santa Cruz, asked her to send it to him. Without her permission, he published Sor Juana's essay under the title *Carta atenagórica*—"Letter Worthy of Athena." Despite the praise implied in the title, the bishop was in fact eager to expose Sor Juana to censure and appended his own corrective letter to her treatise—from "Sor Filotea," "lover of God." This public rebuke spurred Sor Juana's brilliant *Answer to Sor Filotea de la Cruz,* a passionate defense of both her intellectual life and its contribution to her faith, written in 1691 but published only after her death in 1700. Despite her defense, however, Sor Juana acceded to the will of the church in 1692. Her last set of *villancicos* was performed at the cathedral in Oaxaca; she sold both her musical instruments and her extensive library (among the largest private libraries in the Americas at the time), and in 1694 she signed—in blood—a new declaration of faith, vowing to give up secular studies as well. She died during an epidemic that swept Mexico City in April 1695.

Sor Juana's poetry, plays, and philosophical writings are well known in Spanish, and many have been published in English translations (see the Bibliography); the Mexican poet Octavio Paz has written a celebrated biography of Sor Juana: *Sor Juana, or, The Traps of Faith,* trans. Margaret Sayers Peden (Cambridge: Harvard University Press, 1988).

LOA TO THE DIVINE NARCISSUS

The Divine Narcissus is a full-length *auto sacramental,* an allegorical drama on the subject of the Eucharist that Sor Juana wrote in 1687. She intended to submit it to be performed in Madrid as part of a competition for new *autos* following the death of Calderón, who had been the sole author of *autos* performed in the Spanish capital before his death in 1681. Although the death of the queen in 1689 forced the cancellation of the festival, Sor Juana's *The Divine Narcissus* and its introductory *loa* remain among the most accomplished examples of this important genre of Spanish-language drama.

Although the *loa* can be used for either secular or sacred purposes, Sor Juana uses it here specifically to introduce the themes of the *auto,* which uses the Greek story of Echo and Narcissus to allegorize the theological doctrine of the Eucharist. However, to modern readers and audiences, the *loa* is perhaps more interesting for its staging of colonial conflict; through an allegorical conversation between Zeal (a *conquistador*), Religion (a Spanish lady), and the Aztec rulers (Occident and America), the short play also stages an allegory of the conquest of Mexico and its consequences. Although there is no record of the play being performed in Sor Juana's lifetime, it clearly records aspects of Aztec life—the opening dance and ritual worship of the God of the Seeds—that were legally prohibited in seventeenth-century New Spain, while staging a debate between the Aztec leaders and the Spanish invaders who insist on replacing the native religion with the practice of Christianity. While the bullheaded *conquistador,* Zeal, is on the point of murdering the defeated Aztecs, they are spared by Religion, who hears in their account of their religious rituals a profane version of the miracle of the Eucharist:

> What images,
> what dark designs, what shadowings
> of truths most sacred to our Faith
> do these lies seek to imitate?

Religion works to bring Christian salvation to Occident and America by pointing out the similarities between their religion and the mysteries of the Eucharist:

> a God composed
> of human blood, an offering
> of sacrifice, and in himself
> does He combine with bloody death
> the life-sustaining seeds of earth?

To instruct Occident and America, Religion decides to

> make for you a metaphor
> a concept clothed in rhetoric
> so colorful that what I show
> to you, your eyes will clearly see.

The *auto* that follows, *The Divine Narcissus,* is Religion's illustrative "metaphor," her way of explaining the Eucharist to the inhabitants of the New World.

Written by a *criolla,* as part of a competition to take place in Madrid, Sor Juana's play is in many ways a barometer of the situation of colonial writing; the final dialogue between Zeal and Religion considers whether such a play, written in the colony about colonial subjects, will be received in "the crown city of Madrid, / which is the center of the Faith, / the seat of Catholic majesty" as an act of "impropriety." Although written at the height of Spain's imperial expansion, and indeed in many ways written to celebrate that expansion, Sor Juana's *loa* to *The Divine Narcissus* deftly registers many of the tensions that typically inform colonial writing: between the colony and the capital, between the native population and their invaders, for instance. But particularly in the brittle relationship between Zeal and Religion and the more charitable relationship between Religion and America, Sor Juana seems to open another kind of critique as well; Religion refuses, for example, to sanction the extermination, or even the subjugation, of Occident and America. While the *loa* testifies unambiguously to Sor Juana's confidence in the universality of her faith, it also seems to question some of the ways religion is used to advance Spain's political and economic mission in this new and distinct society.

LOA TO THE DIVINE NARCISSUS

Sor Juana Inés de la Cruz

TRANSLATED BY PATRICIA A. PETERS AND RENÉE DOMEIER, O.S.B.

CHARACTERS

OCCIDENT	RELIGION	AZTECS
AMERICA	MUSIC	DANCERS
ZEAL	SOLDIERS	

SCENE ONE

Enter OCCIDENT, *a gallant-looking Aztec, wearing a crown. By his side is* AMERICA, *an Aztec woman of poised self-possession. They are dressed in the mantas and huipiles worn for singing a tocotín. They seat themselves on two chairs. On each side, Aztec men and women dance with feathers and rattles in their hands, as is customary for those doing this dance. While they dance,* MUSIC *sings.*

MUSIC: O, Noble Mexicans,
   whose ancient ancestry
   comes forth from the clear light
   and brilliance of the Sun,
5 since this, of all the year,
   is your most happy feast
   in which you venerate
   your greatest deity,
   come and adorn yourselves
10 with vestments of your rank;
   let your holy fervor be
   made one with jubilation;
   and celebrate in festive pomp
   the great God of the Seeds!

15 MUSIC: Since the abundance of
   our native fields and farms
   is owed to him alone
   who gives fertility,
   then offer him your thanks,
20 for it is right and just
   to give from what has grown,
   the first of the new fruits.
   From your own veins, draw out
   and give, without reserve,
25 the best blood, mixed with seed,
   so that his cult be served,
   and celebrate in festive pomp,
   the great God of the Seeds!

(OCCIDENT *and* AMERICA *sit, and* MUSIC *ceases.*)

OCCIDENT: Of all the deities to whom
30 our rites demand I bend my knee—
   among two thousand gods or more
   who dwell within this royal city
   and who require the sacrifice
   of human victims still entreating
35 for life until their blood is drawn
   and gushes forth from hearts still beating
   and bowels still pulsing—I declare,
   among all these, (it bears repeating),

   whose ceremonies we observe,
   the greatest is, surpassing all   40
   this pantheon's immensity
   the great God of the Seeds.
AMERICA: And you are right, since he alone
   daily sustains our monarchy
   because our lives depend on his 45
   providing crops abundantly;
   and since he gives us graciously
   the gift from which all gifts proceed,
   our fields rich with golden maize,
   the source of life through daily bread, 50
   we render him our highest praise.
   Then how will it improve our lives
   if rich America abounds
   in gold from mines whose smoke deprives
   the fields of their fertility 55
   and with their clouds of filthy soot
   will not allow the crops to grow
   which blossom now so fruitfully
   from seeded earth? Moreover, his
   protection of our people far 60
   exceeds our daily food and drink,
   the body's sustenance. Indeed,
   he feeds us with his very flesh
   (first purified of every stain).
   We eat his body, drink his blood, 65
   and by this sacred meal are freed
   and cleansed from all that is profane,
   and thus, he purifies our soul.
   And now, attentive to his rites,
   together let us all proclaim: 70
OCCIDENT, AMERICA, DANCERS and MUSIC: We celebrate in
   festive pomp,
   the great God of the Seeds!

SCENE TWO

They exit dancing. Enter Christian RELIGION *as a Spanish lady,* ZEAL *as a Captain General in armor, and Spanish* SOLDIERS.

RELIGION: How, being Zeal, can you suppress
   the flames of righteous Christian wrath
   when here before your very eyes
   idolatry, so blind with pride, 5
   adores, with superstitious rites
   an idol, leaving your own bride,
   the holy faith of Christ disgraced?
ZEAL: Religion, trouble not your mind
   or grieve my failure to attack,

10   complaining that my love is slack,
for now the sword I wear is bared,
its hilt in hand, clasped ready and
my arm raised high to take revenge.
Please stand aside and deign to wait
15   till I requite your grievances.

(*Enter* OCCIDENT *and* AMERICA *dancing, and accompanied by* MUSIC, *who enters from the other side.*)

MUSIC: And celebrate in festive pomp,
the great God of the Seeds!
ZEAL: Here they come! I will confront them.
RELIGION: And I, in peace, will also go
20   (before your fury lays them low)
for justice must with mercy kiss;
I shall invite them to arise
from superstitious depths to faith.
ZEAL: Let us approach while they are still
25   absorbed in their lewd rituals.
MUSIC: And celebrate in festive pomp,
the great God of the Seeds!

(ZEAL *and* RELIGION *cross the stage.*)

RELIGION: Great Occident, most powerful;
America, so beautiful
30   and rich; you live in poverty
amid the treasures of your land.
Abandon this irreverent cult
with which the demon has waylaid you.
Open your eyes! Follow the path
35   that leads straightforwardly to truth,
to which my love yearns to persuade you.
OCCIDENT: Who are these unknown people, so
intrusive in my sight, who dare
to stop us in our ecstasy?
40   Heaven forbid such infamy!
AMERICA: Who are these nations, never seen,
that wish, by force, to pit themselves
against my ancient power supreme?
OCCIDENT: Oh, you alien beauty fair;
45   oh, pilgrim woman from afar,
who comes to interrupt my prayer,
please speak and tell me who you are.
RELIGION: Christian Religion is my name,
and I intend that all this realm
50   will make obeisance unto me.
OCCIDENT: An impossible concession!
AMERICA: Yours is but a mad obsession!
OCCIDENT: You will meet with swift repression.
AMERICA: Pay no attention; she is mad!
55   Let us go on with our procession.
MUSIC and AZTECS: And celebrate in festive pomp,
the great God of the Seeds!
ZEAL: How is this, barbarous Occident?
Can it be, sightless Idolatry,
60   that you insult Religion,
the spouse I cherish tenderly?
Abomination fills your cup
and overruns the brim, but see
that God will not permit you to

continue drinking down delight,   65
and I am sent to deal your doom.
OCCIDENT: And who are you who frightens all
who only look upon your face?
ZEAL: I am Zeal. Does that surprise you?
Take heed! for when your excesses   70
bring disgrace to fair Religion,
then will Zeal arise to vengeance;
for insolence I will chastise you.
I am the minister of God,
Who growing weary with the sight   75
of overreaching tyrannies
so sinful that they reach the height
of error, practiced many years,
has sent me forth to penalize you.
And thus, these military hosts   80
with flashing thunderbolts of steel,
the ministers of His great wrath
are sent, His anger to reveal.
OCCIDENT: What god? What sin? What tyranny?
What punishment do you foresee?   85
Your reasons make no sense to me,
nor can I make the slightest guess
who you might be with your insistence
on tolerating no resistance,
impeding us with rash persistence   90
from lawful worship as we sing.
MUSIC: And celebrate with festive pomp,
the great God of the Seeds!
AMERICA: Madman, blind, and barbarous,
with mystifying messages   95
you try to mar our calm and peace,
destroying the tranquility
that we enjoy. Your plots must cease,
unless, of course, you wish to be
reduced to ashes, whose existence   100
even the winds will never sense.
(*To* OCCIDENT.) And you, my spouse, and your cohort,
close off your hearing and your sight
to all their words; refuse to heed
their fantasies of zealous might;   105
proceed to carry out your rite.
Do not concede to insolence
from foreigners intent to dull
our ritual's magnificence.
MUSIC: And celebrate with festive pomp,   110
the great God of the Seeds!
ZEAL: Since our initial offering
of peaceful terms, you held so cheap,
the dire alternative of war,
I guarantee you'll count more dear.   115
Take up your arms! To war! To war!

(*Drums and trumpets sound.*)

OCCIDENT: What miscarriages of justice
has heaven sent against me?
What are these weapons, blazing fire,
before my unbelieving eyes?   120
Get ready, guards! Aim well, my troops,
Your arrows at this enemy!

AMERICA: What lightening bolts does heaven send
    to lay me low? What molten balls
125 of burning lead so fiercely rain?
    What centaurs crush with monstrous force
    and cause my people such great pain?
(*Within.*) To arms! To arms! War! War!

([*Drums and trumpets*] *sound.*)

(*Within.*) Long life to Spain! Long live her king!

(*The battle begins. Indians enter through one door and flee through
another with the Spanish pursuing at their heels. From back stage,*
OCCIDENT *backs away from* RELIGION *and* AMERICA *retreats before* ZEAL's *onslaught.*)

SCENE THREE

RELIGION: Give up, arrogant Occident!
OCCIDENT: I must bow to your aggression,
    but not before your arguments.
ZEAL: Die, impudent America!
5 RELIGION: Desist! Do not give her to Death;
    her life is of some worth to us.
ZEAL: How can you now defend this maid
    who has so much offended you?
RELIGION: America has been subdued
10 because your valor won the strife,
    but now my mercy intervenes
    in order to preserve her life.
    It was your part to conquer her
    by force with military might;
15 mine is to gently make her yield,
    persuading her by reason's light.
ZEAL: But you have seen the stubbornness
    with which these blind ones still abhor
    your creed; is it not better far
20 that they all die?
RELIGION: Good Zeal, restrain
    your justice, and do not kill them.
    My gentle disposition deigns
    to forbear vengeance and forgive.
    I want them to convert and live.
25 AMERICA: If your petition for my life
    and show of Christian charity
    are motivated by the hope
    that you, at last, will conquer me,
    defeating my integrity
30 with verbal steel where bullets failed,
    then you are sadly self-deceived.
    A weeping captive, I may mourn
    for liberty, yet my will grows
    beyond these bonds; my heart is free,
35 and I will worship my own gods!
OCCIDENT: Forced to surrender to your power,
    I have admitted my defeat,
    but still it must be clearly said
    that violence cannot devour
40 my will, nor force constrain its right.
    Although in grief, I now lament,
    a prisoner, your cruel might

has limits. You cannot prevent
my saying here within my heart
I worship the great God of Seeds! 45

SCENE FOUR

RELIGION: Wait! What you perceive as force
    is not coercion, but affection.
    What god is this that you adore?
OCCIDENT: The great God of the Seeds
    who causes fields to bring forth fruit. 5
    To him the lofty heavens bow;
    to him the rains obedience give;
    and when, at last, he cleanses us
    from stains of sin, then he invites
    us to the meal that he prepares. 10
    Consider whether you could find
    a god more generous and good
    who blesses more abundantly
    than he whom I describe to you.
RELIGION: (*Aside.*) O God, help me! What images, 15
    what dark designs, what shadowings
    of truths most sacred to our Faith
    do these lies seek to imitate?
    O false, sly, and deceitful snake!
    O asp, with sting so venomous! 20
    O hydra, that from seven mouths
    pours noxious poisons, every one
    a passage to oblivion!
    To what extent, with this facade
    do you intend maliciously 25
    to mock the mysteries of God?
    Mock on! for with your own deceit,
    if God empowers my mind and tongue,
    I'll argue and impose defeat.
AMERICA: Why do you find yourself perplexed? 30
    Do you not see there is no god
    other than ours who verifies
    with countless blessings his great works?
RELIGION: In doctrinal disputes, I hold
    with the apostle Paul, for when 35
    he preached to the Athenians
    and found they had a harsh decree
    imposing death on anyone
    who tried to introduce new gods,
    since he had noticed they were free 40
    to worship at a certain shrine,
    an altar to "the Unknown God,"
    he said to them, "This Lord of mine
    is no new god, but one unknown
    that you have worshipped in this place, 45
    and it is He, my voice proclaims."
    And thus I—

(OCCIDENT *and* AMERICA *whisper to each other.*)

      Listen, Occident!
and hear me, blind Idolatry!
for all your happiness depends
on listening attentively. 50
These miracles that you recount,

these prodigies that you suggest,
these apparitions and these rays
of light in superstition dressed
55 are glimpsed but darkly through a veil.
These portents you exaggerate,
attributing to your false gods
effects that you insinuate,
but wrongly so, for all these works
60 proceed from our true God alone,
and of His Wisdom come to birth.
Then if the soil richly yields,
and if the fields bud and bloom,
if fruits increase and multiply,
65 if seeds mature in earth's dark womb,
if rains pour forth from leaden sky,
all is the work of His right hand;
for neither the arm that tills the soil
nor rains that fertilize the land
70 nor warmth that calls life from the tomb
of winter's death can make plants grow;
for they lack reproductive power
if Providence does not concur,
by breathing into each of them
75 a vegetative soul.
AMERICA: That might be so;
then tell me, is this God so kind—
this deity whom you describe—
that I might touch Him with my hands,
these very hands that carefully
80 create the idol, here before you,
an image made from seeds of earth
and innocent, pure human blood
shed only for this sacred rite?
RELIGION: Although the Essence of Divinity
85 is boundless and invisible,
because already It has been
eternally united with
our nature, He resembles us
so much in our humanity
90 that He permits unworthy priests
to take Him in their humble hands.
AMERICA: In this, at least, we are agreed,
for to my god no human hands
are so unstained that they deserve
95 to touch him; nonetheless, he gives
this honor graciously to those
who serve him with their priestly lives.
No others dare to touch the god,
nor in the sanctuary stand.
100 ZEAL: A reverence most worthily
directed to the one true God!
OCCIDENT: Whatever else you claim, now tell
me this: Is yours a God composed
of human blood, an offering
105 of sacrifice, and in Himself
does He combine with bloody death
the life-sustaining seeds of earth?
RELIGION: As I have said, His boundless
Majesty is insubstantial,
110 but in the Holy Sacrifice

of Mass, His blessed humanity
is placed unbloody under the
appearances of bread, which comes
from seeds of wheat and is transformed
into His Body and His Blood;   115
and this most holy Blood of Christ,
contained within a sacred cup,
is verily the offering
most innocent, unstained, and pure
that on the altar of the cross   120
was the redemption of the world.
AMERICA: Such miracles, unknown to us,
make me desire to believe;
but would the God that you reveal
offer Himself so lovingly   125
transformed for me into a meal
as does the god that I adore?
RELIGION: In truth, He does. For this alone
His Wisdom came upon the earth
to dwell among all humankind.   130
AMERICA: And so that I can be convinced,
may I not see this Deity?
OCCIDENT: And so that I can be made free
of old beliefs that shackle me?
RELIGION: Yes, you will see when you are bathed   135
in crystal waters from the font
of baptism.
OCCIDENT: And well I know,
in preparation to attend
a banquet, I must bathe, or else
our ancient custom I offend.   140
ZEAL: Your vain ablutions will not do
the cleansing that your stains require.
OCCIDENT: Then what?
RELIGION: There is a sacrament
of living waters, which can cleanse
and purify you of your sins.   145
AMERICA: Because you deluge my poor mind
with concepts of theology,
I've just begun to understand;
there is much more I want to see,
and my desire to know is now   150
by holy inspiration led.
OCCIDENT: And I desire more keenly still
to know about the life and death
of the God you say is in the bread.
RELIGION: Then come along with me, and I   155
shall make for you a metaphor,
a concept clothed in rhetoric
so colorful that what I show
to you, your eyes will clearly see;
for now I know that you require   160
objects of sight instead of words,
by which faith whispers in your ears
too deaf to hear; I understand,
for you necessity demands
that through the eyes, faith find her way   165
to her reception in your hearts.
OCCIDENT: Exactly so. I do prefer
to see the things you would impart.

SCENE FIVE

RELIGION: Then come.
ZEAL: Religion, answer me:
   what metaphor will you employ
   to represent these mysteries?
RELIGION: An *auto* will make visible
5   through allegory images
   of what America must learn
   and Occident implores to know
   about the questions that now burn
   within him so.
ZEAL: What will you call
10   this play in allegory cast?
RELIGION: *Divine Narcissus*, let it be,
   because if that unhappy maid
   adored an idol which disguised
   in such strange symbols the attempt
15   the demon made to counterfeit
   the great and lofty mystery
   of the most Blessed Eucharist,
   then there were also, I surmise,
   among more ancient pagans hints
20   of such high marvels symbolized.
ZEAL: Where will your drama be performed?
RELIGION: In the crown city of Madrid,
   which is the center of the Faith,
   the seat of Catholic majesty,
25   to whom the Indies owe their best
   beneficence, the blessed gift
   of Holy Writ, the Gospel light
   illuminating all the West.
ZEAL: That you should write in Mexico
30   for royal patrons don't you see
   to be an impropriety?
RELIGION: Is it beyond imagination
   that something made in one location
   can in another be of use?
35   Furthermore, my writing it
   comes, not of whimsical caprice,
   but from my vowed obedience
   to do what seems beyond my reach.
   Well, then, this work, however rough
40   and little polished it might be,
   results from my obedience,
   and not from any arrogance.
ZEAL: Then answer me, Religion, how
   (before you leave the matter now),
45   will you respond when you are chid
   for loading the whole Indies on

a stage to transport to Madrid?
RELIGION: The purpose of my play can be
   none other than to glorify
   the Eucharistic Mystery;   50
   and since the cast of characters
   are no more than abstractions which
   depict the theme with clarity,
   then surely no one should object
   if they are taken to Madrid;   55
   distance can never hinder thought
   with persons of intelligence,
   nor seas impede exchange of sense.
ZEAL: Then, prostrate at his royal feet,
   beneath whose strength two worlds are joined   60
   we beg for pardon of the King;
RELIGION: and from her eminence, the Queen;
AMERICA: whose sovereign and anointed feet
   the humble Indies bow to kiss;
ZEAL: and from the Royal High Council;   65
RELIGION: and from the ladies, who bring light
   into their hemisphere;
AMERICA: and from
   their poets, I most humbly beg
   forgiveness for my crude attempt,
   desiring with these awkward lines   70
   to represent the Mystery.
OCCIDENT: Let's go, for anxiously I long to see
   exactly how this God of yours
   will give Himself as food to me.

(AMERICA, OCCIDENT, *and* ZEAL *sing:*)

   The Indies know   75
   and do concede
   who is the true
   God of the Seeds.
   In loving tears
   which joy prolongs   80
   we gladly sing
   our happy songs.
ALL: Blest be the day
   when I could see
   and worship the   85
   great God of Seeds.

(*They all exit, dancing and singing.*)

CRITICAL CONTEXTS

JOHN DRYDEN (1631–1700)

"Preface to *Troilus and Cressida*, Containing the Grounds of Criticism in Tragedy" (1679)

EDITED BY ARTHUR C. KIRSCH

John Dryden is the most important English critic and poet of the late seventeenth century; he was appointed poet laureate and royal historiographer in 1668 and was also the author of many plays, both comedies and heroic tragedies. In 1679, he wrote an adaptation of Shakespeare's Troilus and Cressida, *and in his "Preface" to the play Dryden argues for neoclassical principles of unity and decorum.*

In the "Preface," Dryden frames a specifically neoclassical sense of the purpose and function of tragedy. One way into this essay is through a comparison with Aristotle, and indeed, with Greek tragedy. How do Dryden's criteria at once invoke and revise the sense of tragic construction in Aristotle's The Poetics? *Beyond that, what are the features of Shakespearean drama that seem to require Dryden's attention as a reviser? What is the sense of decorum that Dryden wishes to urge, and that Shakespeare's original play seems to violate?*

The poet Aeschylus was held in the same veneration by the Athenians of after ages as Shakespeare is by us; and Longinus has judged, in favor of him, that he had a noble boldness of expression, and that his imaginations were lofty and heroic; but, on the other side, Quintilian affirms that he was daring to extravagance. 'Tis certain that he affected pompous words, and that his sense too often was obscured by figures. Notwithstanding these imperfections, the value of his writings after his decease was such that his countrymen ordained an equal reward to those poets who could alter his plays to be acted on the theater, with those whose productions were wholly new, and of their own. The case is not the same in England; though the difficulties of altering are greater, and our reverence for Shakespeare much more just, than that of the Grecians for Aeschylus. In the age of that poet, the Greek tongue was arrived to its full perfection; they had then amongst them an exact standard of writing and of speaking. The English language is not capable of such a certainty; and we are at present so far from it that we are wanting in the very foundation of it, a perfect grammar. Yet it must be allowed to the present age that the tongue in general is so much refined since Shakespeare's time that many of his words, and more of his phrases, are scarce intelligible. And of those which we understand, some are ungrammatical, others coarse; and his whole style is so pestered with figurative expressions, that it is as affected as it is obscure. 'Tis true, that in his later plays he had worn off somewhat of the rust; but the tragedy which I have undertaken to correct was, in all probability, one of his first endeavors on the stage.[1]

The original story was written by one Lollius, a Lombard, in Latin verse, and translated by Chaucer into English; intended, I suppose, a satire on the inconstancy of women: I find nothing of it among the Ancients; not so much as the name Cressida once mentioned. Shakespeare (as I hinted), in the apprenticeship of his writing, modeled it into that play which is now called by the name of *Troilus and Cressida*; but so lamely is it left to us, that it is not divided into acts; which fault I ascribe to the actors who printed it after Shakespeare's death; and that too so carelessly, that a more uncorrect copy I never saw. For the play itself, the author seems to have begun it with some fire; the characters of Pandarus and Thersites are promising enough; but as if he grew weary of his task, after an entrance or two, he lets 'em fall: and the later part of the tragedy is nothing but a confusion of drums and trumpets, excursions and alarms. The chief persons, who give name to the tragedy, are left alive; Cressida is false, and is not punished. Yet after all, because the play was Shakespeare's, and that there appeared in some places of it the admirable genius of the author, I undertook to remove that heap of rubbish under which many excellent thoughts lay wholly buried. Accordingly, I new modeled the plot; threw out many unnecessary persons; improved those characters which were begun and left unfinished: as Hector, Troilus, Pandarus, and Thersites; and added that of Andromache. After this I made, with no small trouble, an order and connection of all the scenes; removing them from the places where they were inartificially set; and though it was impossible to keep 'em all unbroken, because the scene must be sometimes in the city and sometimes in the camp, yet I have so ordered them that there is a coherence of 'em with one another, and a dependence on the main design: no leaping from Troy to

---

[1]Actually, *Troilus and Cressida*, which was probably written around 1602, came at the midpoint of Shakespeare's career.

the Grecian tents, and thence back again in the same act; but a due proportion of time allowed for every motion. I need not say that I have refined his language, which before was obsolete; but I am willing to acknowledge that as I have often drawn his English nearer to our times, so I have sometimes conformed my own to his; and consequently, the language is not altogether so pure as it is significant. The scenes of Pandarus and Cressida, of Troilus and Pandarus, of Andromache with Hector and the Trojans, in the second act, are wholly new; together with that of Nestor and Ulysses with Thersites, and that of Thersites with Ajax and Achilles. I will not weary my reader with the scenes which are added of Pandarus and the lovers, in the third; and those of Thersites, which are wholly altered; but I cannot omit the last scene in it, which is almost half the act, betwixt Troilus and Hector. The occasion of raising it was hinted to me by Mr. Betterton: the contrivance and working of it was my own. They who think to do me an injury by saying that it is an imitation of the scene betwixt Brutus and Cassius, do me an honor by supposing I could imitate the incomparable Shakespeare; but let me add that if Shakespeare's scene, or that faulty copy of it in *Amintor and Melantius*, had never been, yet Euripides had furnished me with an excellent example in his *Iphigenia*, between Agamemnon and Menelaus; and from thence, indeed, the last turn of it is borrowed.[2] The occasion which Shakespeare, Euripides, and Fletcher have all taken is the same; grounded upon friendship: and the quarrel of two virtuous men, raised by natural degrees to the extremity of passion, is conducted in all three to the declination of the same passion, and concludes with a warm renewing of their friendship. But the particular groundwork which Shakespeare has taken is incomparably the best; because he has not only chosen two of the greatest heroes of their age, but has likewise interested the liberty of Rome, and their own honors who were the redeemers of it, in this debate. And if he has made Brutus, who was naturally a patient man, to fly into excess at first, let it be remembered in his defense that, just before, he has received the news of Portia's death; whom the poet, on purpose neglecting a little chronology, supposes to have died before Brutus, only to give him an occasion of being more easily exasperated. Add to this that the injury he had received from Cassius had long been brooding in his mind; and that a melancholy man, upon consideration of an affront, es-

pecially from a friend, would be more eager in his passion than he who had given it, though naturally more choleric.

Euripides, whom I have followed, has raised the quarrel betwixt two brothers who were friends. The foundation of the scene was this: the Grecians were windbound at the port of Aulis, and the oracle had said that they could not sail, unless Agamemnon delivered up his daughter to be sacrificed: he refuses; his brother Menelaus urges the public safety; the father defends himself by arguments of natural affection, and hereupon they quarrel. Agamemnon is at last convinced, and promises to deliver up Iphigenia, but so passionately laments his loss that Menelaus is grieved to have been the occasion of it and, by a return of kindness, offers to intercede for him with the Grecians, that his daughter might not be sacrificed. But my friend Mr. Rymer has so largely, and with so much judgment, described this scene, in comparing it with that of Melantius and Amintor, that it is superfluous to say more of it; I only named the heads of it, that any reasonable man might judge it was from thence I modeled my scene betwixt Troilus and Hector. I will conclude my reflections on it with a passage of Longinus, concerning Plato's imitation of Homer: "We ought not to regard a good imitation as a theft, but as a beautiful idea of him who undertakes to imitate, by forming himself on the invention and the work of another man; for he enters into the lists like a new wrestler, to dispute the prize with the former champion. This sort of emulation, says Hesiod, is honorable, 'this strife is wholesome to man,'[3] when we combat for victory with a hero, and are not without glory even in our overthrow. Those great men whom we propose to ourselves as patterns of our imitation serve us as a torch, which is lifted up before us to enlighten our passage; and often elevate our thoughts as high as the conception we have of our author's genius."[4]

I have been so tedious in three acts that I shall contract myself in the two last. The beginning scenes of the fourth act are either added or changed wholly by me; the middle of it is Shakespeare altered, and mingled with my own; three or four of the last scenes are altogether new. And the whole fifth act, both the plot and the writing, are my own additions.

But having written so much for imitation of what is excellent, in that part of the preface which related only to myself, methinks it would neither be unprofitable nor unpleasant to inquire how far we ought to imitate our own poets, Shakespeare and Fletcher, in their tragedies: and this will occasion another inquiry, how those two writers differ between themselves. But since neither of these questions

---

[2]The comparison of the quarrels between Amintor and Melantius in Beaumont and Fletcher's *Maid's Tragedy* and Agamemnon and Menelaus in Euripides's *Iphigenia in Aulis* had already been made by Rymer in his *Tragedies of the Last Age* (1678), as Dryden acknowledges in the following paragraph.

[3]ἀγαθὴ δ' ἔρις ἐστὶ βροτοῖσιν (*Works and Days*, 1.24).

[4]*On the Sublime*, 13.4.

can be solved unless some measures be first taken by which we may be enabled to judge truly of their writings, I shall endeavor, as briefly as I can, to discover the grounds and reason of all criticism, applying them in this place only to tragedy. Aristotle with his interpreters, and Horace, and Longinus, are the authors to whom I owe my lights; and what part soever of my own plans, or of this, which no mending could make regular, shall fall under the condemnation of such judges, it would be impudence in me to defend. . . .

THE GROUNDS OF CRITICISM IN TRAGEDY

Tragedy is thus defined by Aristotle (omitting what I thought unnecessary in his definition). 'Tis an imitation of one entire, great, and probable action; not told, but represented; which, by moving in us fear and pity, is conducive to the purging of those two passions in our minds. More largely thus, tragedy describes or paints an action, which action must have all the proprieties above named. First, it must be one or single, that is, it must not be a history of one man's life; suppose of Alexander the Great, or Julius Caesar, but one single action of theirs. This condemns all Shakespeare's historical plays, which are rather chronicles represented than tragedies, and all double action of plays. As to avoid a satire upon others, I will make bold with my own *Marriage à-la-Mode,* where there are manifestly two actions, not depending on one another: but in *Oedipus* there cannot properly be said to be two actions, because the love of Adrastus and Eurydice has a necessary dependence on the principal design, into which it is woven. The natural reason of rule is plain; for two different independent actions distract the attention and concernment of the audience, and consequently destroy the intention of the poet: if his business be to move terror and pity, and one of his actions be comical, the other tragical, the former will divert the people, and utterly make void his greater purpose. Therefore, as in perspective, so in tragedy, there must be a point of sight in which all the lines terminate; otherwise the eye wanders, and the work is false. This was the practice of the Grecian stage. But Terence made an innovation in the Roman: all his plays have double actions; for it was his custom to translate two Greek comedies, and to weave them into one of his, yet so that both the actions were comical, and one was principal, the other but secondary or subservient. And this has obtained on the English stage, to give us the pleasure of variety.

As the action ought to be one, it ought, as such, to have order in it, that is, to have a natural beginning, a middle, and an end. A natural beginning, says Aristotle, is that which could not necessarily have been placed after another thing, and so of the rest. This consideration will arraign all plays after the new model of Spanish plots, where accident is heaped upon accident, and that which is first might as reasonably be

last: an inconvenience not to be remedied but by making one accident naturally produce another, otherwise 'tis a farce and not a play. Of this nature is the *Slighted Maid,*[5] where there is no scene in the first act which might not by as good reason be in the fifth. And if the action ought to be one, the tragedy ought likewise to conclude with the action of it. Thus in *Mustapha,*[6] the play should naturally have ended with the death of Zanger, and not have given us the grace cup after dinner of Solyman's divorce from Roxolana.

The following properties of the action are so easy that they need not my explaining. It ought to be great, and to consist of great persons, to distinguish it from comedy, where the action is trivial, and the persons of inferior rank. The last quality of the action is that it ought to be *probable,* as well as admirable and great. 'Tis not necessary that there should be historical truth in it; but always necessary that there should be a likeness of truth, something that is more than barely possible, *probable* being that which succeeds or happens oftener than it misses. To invent therefore a probability, and to make it wonderful, is the most difficult undertaking in the art of poetry; for that which is not wonderful is not great; and that which is not probable will not delight a reasonable audience. This action, thus described, must be represented and not told, to distinguish dramatic poetry from epic: but I hasten to the end or scope of tragedy, which is to rectify or purge our passions, fear and pity.

To instruct delightfully is the general end of all poetry. Philosophy instructs, but it performs its work by precept: which is not delightful, or not so delightful as example. To purge the passions by example is therefore the particular instruction which belongs to tragedy. Rapin, a judicious critic, has observed from Aristotle that pride and want of commiseration are the most predominant vices in mankind: therefore, to cure us of these two, the inventors of tragedy have chosen to work upon two other passions, which are fear and pity. We are wrought to fear by their setting before our eyes some terrible example of misfortune, which happened to persons of the highest quality; for such an action demonstrates to us that no condition is privileged from the turns of fortune; this must of necessity cause terror in us, and consequently abate our pride. But when we see that the most virtuous, as well as the greatest, are not exempt from such misfortunes, that consideration moves pity in us, and insensibly works us to be helpful to, and tender over, the distressed, which is the noblest and most god-like of moral virtues. Here 'tis observable that it is absolutely necessary to make a man virtuous, if we desire he should be pitied: we

---

[5] By Sir Robert Stapylton (1663).

[6] By Roger Boyle, Earl of Orrery (first performed in 1665).

lament not, but detest, a wicked man; we are glad when we behold his crimes are punished, and that poetical justice[7] is done upon him. Euripides was censured by the critics of his time for making his chief characters too wicked: for example, Phaedra, though she loved her son-in-law with reluctancy, and that it was a curse upon her family for offending Venus, yet was thought too ill a pattern for the stage. Shall we therefore banish all characters of villainy? I confess I am not of that opinion; but it is necessary that the hero of the play be not a villain; that is, the characters which should move our pity ought to have virtuous inclinations, and degrees of moral goodness in them. As for a perfect character of virtue, it never was in nature, and therefore there can be no imitation of it; but there are allays of frailty to be allowed for the chief persons, yet so that the good which is in them shall outweigh the bad, and consequently leave room for punishment on the one side, and pity on the other.

After all, if anyone will ask me whether a tragedy cannot be made upon any other grounds than those of exciting pity and terror in us, Bossu,[8] the best of modern critics, answers thus in general: that all excellent arts, and particularly that of poetry, have been invented and brought to perfection by men of a transcendent genius; and that therefore they who practice afterwards the same arts are obliged to tread in their footsteps, and to search in their writings the foundation of them; for it is not just that new rules should destroy the authority of the old. But Rapin writes more particularly thus[9]: that no passions in a story are so proper to move our concernment as fear and pity; and that it is from our concernment we receive our pleasure, is undoubted; when the soul becomes agitated with fear for one character, or hope for another, then it is that we are pleased in tragedy by the interest which we take in their adventures.

Here, therefore, the general answer may be given to the first question, how far we ought to imitate Shakespeare and Fletcher in their plots: namely, that we ought to follow them so far only as they have copied the excellencies of those who invented and brought to perfection dramatic poetry: those things only excepted which religion, customs of countries, idioms of languages, etc., have altered in the superstructures, but not in the foundation of the design.

How defective Shakespeare and Fletcher have been in all their plots, Mr. Rymer has discovered in his criticisms: neither can we who follow them be excused from the same or greater errors; which are the more unpardonable in us, because we want their beauties to countervail our faults. The best of their designs, the most approaching to antiquity, and the most conducing to move pity, is the *King and No King;* which, if the farce of Bessus were thrown away, is of that inferior sort of tragedies which end with a prosperous event. 'Tis probably derived from the story of Oedipus, with the character of Alexander the Great, in his extravagancies, given to Arbaces. The taking of this play, amongst many others, I cannot wholly ascribe to the excellency of the action; for I find it moving when it is read: 'tis true, the faults of the plot are so evidently proved that they can no longer be denied. The beauties of it must therefore lie either in the lively touches of the passion: or we must conclude, as I think we may, that even in imperfect plots there are less degrees of nature, by which some faint emotions of pity and terror are raised in us: as a less engine will raise a less proportion of weight, though not so much as one of Archimedes' making; for nothing can move our nature, but by some natural reason, which works upon passions. And since we acknowledge the effect, there must be something in the cause.

The difference between Shakespeare and Fletcher in their plotting seems to be this: that Shakespeare generally moves more terror, and Fletcher more compassion. For the first had a more masculine, a bolder and more fiery genius; the second, a more soft and womanish. In the mechanic beauties of the plot, which are the observation of the three unities, time, place, and action, they are both deficient; but Shakespeare most. Ben Jonson reformed those errors in his comedies, yet one of Shakespeare's was regular before him; which is, *The Merry Wives of Windsor.* For what remains concerning the design, you are to be referred to our English critic. That method which he has prescribed to raise it from mistake, or ignorance of the crime, is certainly the best, though 'tis not the only: for amongst all the tragedies of Sophocles, there is but one, *Oedipus,* which is wholly built after that model.

After the plot, which is the foundation of the play, the next thing to which we ought to apply our judgment is the manners, for now the poet comes to work above ground: the ground-work indeed is that which is most necessary, as that upon which depends the firmness of the whole fabric; yet it strikes not the eye so much as the beauties or imperfections of the manners, the thoughts, and the expressions.

The first rule which Bossu prescribes to the writer of an heroic poem, and which holds too by the same reason in all dramatic poetry, is to make the moral of the work, that is, to lay down to yourself what that precept of morality shall be, which you would insinuate into the people; as namely, Homer's (which I have copied in my *Conquest of Granada*) was, that union preserves a commonwealth, and discord

---

[7]A phrase first coined by Rymer in *The Tragedies of the Last Age.*

[8]Le Bossu, author of *Traité du poème épique* (1675).

[9]In *Réflexions sur la poétique d'Aristote* (1674).

destroys it; Sophocles, in his *Oedipus,* that no man is to be accounted happy before his death. 'Tis the moral that directs the whole action of the play to one center; and that action or fable is the example built upon the moral, which confirms the truth of it to our experience: when the fable is designed, then and not before, the persons are to be introduced with their manners, characters, and passions.

The manners in a poem are understood to be those inclinations, whether natural or acquired, which move and carry us to actions, good, bad, or indifferent, in a play; or which incline the persons to such or such actions. I have anticipated part of this discourse already, in declaring that a poet ought not to make the manners perfectly good in his best persons; but neither are they to be more wicked in any of his characters than necessity requires. To produce a villain, without other reason than a natural inclination to villainy is, in poetry, to produce an effect without a cause; and to make him more a villain than he has just reason to be, is to make an effect which is stronger than the cause.

The manners arise from many causes; and are either distinguished by complexion, as choleric and phlegmatic, or by the differences of age or sex, of climates, or quality of the persons, or their present condition. They are likewise to be gathered from the several virtues, vices, or passions, and many other commonplaces which a poet must be supposed to have learned from natural philosophy, ethics, and history; of all which whosoever is ignorant, does not deserve the name of poet.

But as the manners are useful in this art, they may be all comprised under these general heads: first, they must be apparent; that is, in every character of the play, some inclinations of the person must appear: and these are shown in the actions and discourse. Secondly, the manners must be suitable, or agreeing to the persons; that is, to the age, sex, dignity, and the other general heads of manners: thus, when a poet has given the dignity of a king to one of his persons, in all his actions and speeches, that person must discover majesty, magnanimity, and jealousy of power, because these are suitable to the general manners of a king. The third property of manners is resemblance; and this is founded upon the particular characters of men, as we have them delivered to us by relation or history; that is, when a poet has the known character of this or that man before him, he is bound to represent him such, at least not contrary to that which fame has reported him to have been. Thus, it is not a poet's choice to make Ulysses choleric, or Achilles patient, because Homer has described 'em quite otherwise. Yet this is a rock on which ignorant writers daily split; and the absurdity is as monstrous as if a painter should draw a coward running from a battle, and tell us it was the picture of Alexander the Great.

The last property of manners is that they be constant and equal, that is, maintained the same through the whole design: thus, when Virgil had once given the name of *pious* to Aeneas, he was bound to show him such, in all his words and actions through the whole poem. All these properties Horace has hinted to a judicious observer: "1. you must mark the manners of each age; 2. or follow tradition; 3. or create your own convention; 4. let each character remain constant and consistent with itself."[10]

From the manners, the characters of persons are derived; for indeed the characters are no other than the inclinations, as they appear in the several persons of the poem; a character being thus defined, that which distinguishes one man from another. Not to repeat the same things over again which have been said of the manners, I will only add what is necessary here. A character, or that which distinguishes one man from all others, cannot be supposed to consist of one particular virtue, or vice, or passion only; but 'tis a composition of qualities which are not contrary to one another in the same person; thus the same man may be liberal and valiant, but not liberal and covetous; so in a comical character, or humour (which is an inclination to this or that particular folly), Falstaff is a liar, and a coward, a glutton, and a buffoon, because all these qualities may agree in the same man; yet it is still to be observed that one virtue, vice, and passion ought to be shown in every man, as predominant over all the rest; as covetousness in Crassus, love of his country in Brutus; and the same in characters which are feigned.

The chief character or hero in a tragedy, as I have already shown, ought in prudence to be such a man who has so much more in him of virtue than of vice, that he may be left amiable to the audience, which otherwise cannot have any concernment for his sufferings; and 'tis on this one character that the pity and terror must be principally, if not wholly, founded—a rule which is extremely necessary, and which none of the critics that I know have fully enough discovered to us. For terror and compassion work but weakly when they are divided into many persons. If Creon had been the chief character in *Oedipus,* there had neither been terror nor compassion moved; but only detestation of the man and joy for his punishment; if Adrastus and Eurydice had been made more appealing characters, then the pity had been divided, and lessened on the part of Oedipus: but making Oedipus the best and bravest person, and even Jocasta but an underpart to him, his virtues and the punishment of his fatal crime drew both the pity and the terror to himself.

---

[10] 1. *notandi sunt tibi mores;* 2. *aut famam sequere;* 3. *aut sibi convenientia finge;* 4. *servetur ad imum, qualis ab incepto processerit, et sibi constet (Ars poetica,* 11.156, 119, 126–127).

By what had been said of the manners, it will be easy for a reasonable man to judge whether the characters be truly or falsely drawn in a tragedy; for if there be no manners appearing in the characters, no concernment for the persons can be raised; no pity or horror can be moved, but by vice or virtue; therefore, without them, no person can have any business in the play. If the inclinations be obscure, 'tis a sign the poet is in the dark, and knows not what manner of man he presents to you; and consequently you can have no idea, or very imperfect, of that man; nor can judge what resolutions he ought to take; or what words or actions are proper for him. Most comedies made up of accidents or adventures are liable to fall into this error; and tragedies with many turns are subject to it; for the manners never can be evident where the surprises of fortune take up all the business of the stage; and where the poet is more in pain to tell you what happened to such a man than what he was. 'Tis one of the excellencies of Shakespeare that the manners of his persons are generally apparent, and you see their bent and inclinations. Fletcher comes far short of him in this, as indeed he does almost in everything: there are but glimmerings of manners in most of his comedies, which run upon adventures: and in his tragedies, *Rollo, Otto, A King and No King*, Melantius,[11] and many others of his best, are but pictures shown you in the twilight; you know not whether they resemble vice or virtue, and they are either good, bad, or indifferent, as the present scene requires it. But of all poets, this commendation is to be given to Ben Jonson, that the manners even of the most inconsiderable persons in his plays are everywhere apparent.

By considering the second quality of manners, which is that they be suitable to the age, quality, country, dignity, etc., of the character, we may likewise judge whether a poet has followed nature. In this kind, Sophocles and Euripides have more excelled among the Greeks than Aeschylus; and Terence more than Plautus among the Romans. Thus Sophocles gives to Oedipus the true qualities of a king, in both those plays which bear his name; but in the latter, which is the *Oedipus Colonœus*, he lets fall on purpose his tragic style; his hero speaks not in the arbitrary tone, but remembers, in the softness of his complaints, that he is an unfortunate blind old man, that he is banished from his country, and persecuted by his next relations. The present French poets are generally accused that wheresoever they lay the scene, or in whatsoever age, the manners of their heroes are wholly French. Racine's Bajazet is bred at Constantinople, but his civilities are conveyed to him, by some secret passage, from Versailles into the Seraglio. But our Shakespeare, having as-

cribed to Henry the Fourth the character of a king and of a father, gives him the perfect manners of each relation, when either he transacts with his son or with his subjects. Fletcher, on the other side, gives neither to Arbaces, nor to his King in the *Maid's Tragedy*, the qualities which are suitable to a monarch; though he may be excused a little in the latter, for the King there is not uppermost in the character; 'tis the lover of Evadne, who is King only in a second consideration; and though he be unjust, and has other faults which shall be nameless, yet he is not the hero of the play. 'Tis true, we find him a lawful prince (though I never heard of any King that was in Rhodes), and therefore Mr. Rymer's criticism stands good; that he should not be shown in so vicious a character. Sophocles has been more judicious in his *Antigone;* for though he represents in Creon a bloody prince, yet he makes him not a lawful king, but an usurper, and Antigona herself is the heroine of the tragedy. But when Philaster wounds Arethusa and the boy; and Perigot his mistress, in the *Faithful Shepherdess,* both these are contrary to the character of manhood. Nor is Valentinian managed much better, for though Fletcher has taken his picture truly, and shown him as he was, an effeminate, voluptuous man, yet he has forgotten that he was an Emperor, and has given him none of those royal marks which ought to appear in a lawful successor of the throne. If it be inquired what Fletcher should have done on this occasion: ought he not to have represented Valentinian as he was? Bossu shall answer this question for me, by an instance of the like nature: Mauritius, the Greek Emperor, was a prince far surpassing Valentinian, for he was endued with many kingly virtues; he was religious, merciful, and valiant, but withal he was noted of extreme covetousness, a vice which is contrary to the character of a hero, or a prince: therefore, says the critic, that emperor was no fit person to be represented in a tragedy, unless his good qualities were only to be shown, and his covetousness (which sullied them all) were slurred over by the artifice of the poet.[12] To return once more to Shakespeare: no man ever drew so many characters, or generally distinguished 'em better from one another, excepting only Jonson. I will instance but in one, to show the copiousness of his invention: 'tis that of Caliban, or the Monster in the *Tempest*. He seems there to have created a person which was not in nature, a boldness which at first sight would appear intolerable; for he makes him a species of himself, begotten by an incubus on a witch; but this, as I have elsewhere proved, is not wholly beyond the bounds of credibility, at least the vulgar still believe it. We have the separated notions of a spirit, and of a witch (and spirits,

---

[11]Otto is Rollo's brother; Melantius is a character in *The Maid's Tragedy.*

[12]*Traité du poème épique,* 4.7.

according to Plato, are vested with a subtle body; according to some of his followers, have different sexes); therefore, as from the distinct apprehensions of a horse, and of a man, imagination has formed a centaur; so from those of an incubus and a sorceress, Shakespeare has produced his monster. Whether or no his generation can be defended, I leave to philosophy; but of this I am certain, that the poet has most judiciously furnished him with a person, a language, and a character, which will suit him, both by father's and mother's side: he has all the discontents and malice of a witch, and of a devil, besides a convenient proportion of the deadly sins; gluttony, sloth, and lust are manifest; the dejectedness of a slave is likewise given him, and the ignorance of one bred up in a desert island. His person is monstrous, as he is the product of unnatural lust; and his language is as hobgoblin as his person; in all things he is distinguished from other mortals. The characters of Fletcher are poor and narrow, in comparison of Shakespeare's; I remember not one which is not borrowed from him; unless you will except that strange mixture of a man in the *King and No King;* so that in this part Shakespeare is generally worth our imitation; and to imitate Fletcher is but to copy after him who was a copier.

Under this general head of manners, the passions are naturally included, as belonging to the characters. I speak not of pity and of terror, which are to be moved in the audience by the plot; but of anger, hatred, love, ambition, jealousy, revenge, etc., as they are shown in this or that person of the play. To describe these naturally, and to move them artfully, is one of the greatest commendations which can be given to a poet: to write pathetically, says Longinus, cannot proceed but from a lofty genius. A poet must be born with this quality; yet, unless he help himself by an acquired knowledge of the passions, what they are in their own nature, and by what springs they are to be moved, he will be subject either to raise them where they ought not to be raised, or not to raise them by the just degrees of nature, or to amplify them beyond the natural bounds, or not to observe the crisis and turns of them, in their cooling and decay: all which errors proceed from want of judgment in the poet, and from being unskilled in the principles of moral philosophy. Nothing is more frequent in a fanciful writer than to foil himself by not managing his strength; therefore, as in a wrestler, there is first required some measure of force, a well-knit body, and active limbs, without which all instruction would be vain; yet, these being granted, if he want the skill which is necessary to a wrestler, he shall make but small advantage of his natural robustuousness: so, in a poet, his inborn vehemence and force of spirit will only run him out of breath the sooner, if it be not supported by the help of art. The roar of passion indeed may please an audience, three parts of which are igno-

rant enough to think all is moving which is noise, and it may stretch the lungs of an ambitious actor, who will die upon the spot for a thundering clap; but it will move no other passion than indignation and contempt from judicious men. Longinus, whom I have hitherto followed, continues thus: *If the passions be artfully employed, the discourse becomes vehement and lofty: if otherwise, there is nothing more ridiculous than a great passion out of season:* and to this purpose he animadverts severely upon Aeschylus, who writ nothing in cold blood, but was always in a rapture, and in fury with his audience:[13] the inspiration was still upon him, he was ever tearing it upon the tripos[14]; or (to run off as madly as he does, from one similitude to another) he was always at high flood of passion, even in the dead ebb and lowest water-mark of the scene. He who would raise the passion of a judicious audience, says a learned critic, must be sure to take his hearers along with him; if they be in a calm, 'tis in vain for him to be in a huff: he must move them by degrees, and kindle with 'em; otherwise he will be in danger of setting his own heap of stubble on a fire, and of burning out by himself without warming the company that stand about him. They who would justify the madness of poetry from the authority of Aristotle have mistaken the text, and consequently the interpretation: I imagine it to be false read, where he says of poetry that it is εὐφυοῦς ἢ μανικοῦ, that it had always somewhat in it either of a genius, or of a madman. 'Tis more probable that the original ran thus, that poetry was εὐφυοῦς οὐ μανικοῦ, that it belongs to a witty man, but not to a madman.[15] Thus then the passions, as they are considered simply and in themselves, suffer violence when they are perpetually maintained at the same height; for what melody can be made on that instrument, all whose strings are screwed up at first to their utmost stretch, and to the same sound? But this is not the worst: for the characters likewise bear a part in the general calamity, if you consider the passions embodied in them; for it follows of necessity that no man can be distinguished from another by his discourse, when every man is ranting, swaggering, and exclaiming with the same excess: as if it were the only business of all the characters to contend with each other for the prize at Billingsgate; or that the scene of the tragedy lay in Bet'lem.[16] Suppose the poet should intend this man to be choleric, and that man to be patient; yet when they are confounded in the writing, you cannot distinguish

---

[13] *On the Sublime,* 3.

[14] A reference to the tripod at Delphi on which the priestess of Apollo delivered her raving oracles.

[15] Aristotle, *The Poetics,* 17.

[16] Bedlam, a London hospital for the insane.

them from one another: for the man who was called patient and tame is only so before he speaks; but let his clack be set a-going, and he shall tongue it as impetuously, and as loudly, as the errantest hero in the play. By this means, the characters are only distinct in name; but, in reality, all the men and women in the play are the same person. No man should pretend to write who cannot temper his fancy with his judgment: nothing is more dangerous to a raw horseman than a hot-mouthed jade without a curb.

'Tis necessary therefore for a poet who would concern an audience by describing of a passion, first to prepare it, and not to rush upon it all at once. Ovid has judiciously shown the difference of these two ways, in the speeches of Ajax and Ulysses: Ajax, from the very beginning, breaks out into his exclamations, and is swearing by his Maker, "'By Jupiter,' he cried."[17] Ulysses, on the contrary, prepares his audience with all the submissiveness he can practice, and all the calmness of a reasonable man; he found his judges in a tranquillity of spirit, and therefore set out leisurely and softly with 'em, till he had warmed 'em by degrees; and then he began to mend his pace, and to draw them along with his own impetuousness: yet so managing his breath, that it might not fail him at his need, and reserving his utmost proofs of ability even to the last. The success, you see, was answerable; for the crowd only applauded the speech of Ajax:

and the applause of the crowd followed his closing words.[18]

But the judges awarded the prize for which they contended to Ulysses:

the assembly was very moved; and the power of eloquence was revealed, and the skillful orator carried off the hero's arms.[19]

The next necessary rule is to put nothing into the discourse which may hinder your moving of the passions. Too many accidents, as I have said, encumber the poet, as much as the arms of Saul did David; for the variety of passions which they produce are ever crossing and jostling each other out of the way. He who treats of joy and grief together is in a fair way of causing neither of those effects. There is yet another obstacle to be removed, which is pointed wit, and sentences affected out of season; these are nothing of kin to the violence of passion: no man is at leisure to make sentences

and similes when his soul is in an agony. I the rather name this fault that it may serve to mind me of my former errors; neither will I spare myself, but give an example of this kind from my *Indian Emperor.* Montezuma, pursued by his enemies, and seeking sanctuary, stands parleying without the fort, and describing his danger to Cydaria, in a simile of six lines:

As on the sands the frighted traveller
Sees the high seas come rolling from afar, etc.[20]

My Indian potentate was well skilled in the sea for an inland prince, and well improved since the first act, when he sent his son to discover it. The image had not been amiss from another man, at another time: "but not now, in this place"[21]; he destroyed the concernment which the audience might otherwise have had for him; for they could not think the danger near when he had the leisure to invent a simile.

If Shakespeare be allowed, as I think he must, to have made his characters distinct, it will easily be inferred that he understood the nature of the passions: because it has been proved already that confused passions make undistinguishable characters. Yet I cannot deny that he has his failings; but they are not so much in the passions themselves as in his manner of expression: he often obscures his meaning by his words, and sometimes makes it unintelligible. I will not say of so great a poet that he distinguished not the blown puffy style from true sublimity; but I may venture to maintain that the fury of his fancy often transported him beyond the bounds of judgment, either in coining of new words and phrases or racking words which were in use into the violence of a catachresis.[22] 'Tis not that I would explode[23] the use of metaphors from passions, for Longinus thinks 'em necessary to raise it: but to use 'em at every word, to say nothing without a metaphor, a simile, an image, or description, is I doubt to smell a little too strongly of the buskin. I must be forced to give an example of expressing passion figuratively; but that I may do it with respect to Shakespeare, it shall not be taken from anything of his: 'tis an exclamation against Fortune, quoted in his *Hamlet,* but written by some other poet:

Out, out, thou strumpet Fortune! all you gods,
In general synod, take away her power;
Break all the spokes and felleys from her wheel,
And bowl the round nave down the hill of Heav'n,
As low as to the fiends.

[17] *agimus, pro Jupiter, inquit* (*Metamorphoses,* 13.5).

[18]   *vulgique secutum*
 ultima mumur erat.
   Ibid., 123.

[19] *mota manus procerum est; et quid facundia posset tum patuit, fortisque viri tulit arma disertus.*
   Ibid., 282–83.

[20] Act 5.

[21] *sed nunc non erat hisce locus* (*Ars poetica,* 1.19).

[22] A misuse of terms.

[23] Banish, reject.

And immediately after, speaking of Hecuba, when Priam was killed before her eyes:

> The mobled queen ran up and down,
> Threatening the flame with bisson rheum; a clout about that head
> Where late the diadem stood; and for a robe,
> About her lank and all o'er-teemed loins,
> A blanket in th' alarm of fear caught up.
> Who this had seen, with tongue in venom steep'd
> 'Gainst Fortune's state would treason have pronounced;
> But if the gods themselves did see her then,
> When she saw Pyrrhus make malicious sport
> In mincing with his sword her husband's limbs,
> The instant burst of clamour that she made
> (Unless things mortal move them not at all)
> Would have made milch the burning eyes of Heaven,
> And passion in the gods.[24]

What a pudder is here kept in raising the expression of trifling thoughts! Would not a man have thought that the poet had been bound prentice to a wheelwright, for his first rant? and had followed a ragman for the clout and blanket, in the second? Fortune is painted on a wheel, and therefore the writer, in a rage, will have poetical justice down upon every member of that engine: after this execution, he bowls the nave down hill, from Heaven to the fiends (an unreasonable long mark, a man would think); 'tis well there are no solid orbs to stop it in the way, or no element of fire to consume it: but when it came to the earth, it must be monstrous heavy, to break ground as low as to the center. His making milch the burning eyes of Heaven was a pretty tolerable flight too: and I think no man ever drew milk out of eyes before him: yet to make the wonder greater, these eyes were burning. Such a sight indeed were enough to have raised passion in the gods; but to excuse the effects of it, he tells you perhaps they did not see it. Wise men would be glad to find a little sense couched under all those pompous words; for bombast is commonly the delight of that audience which loves poetry, but understands it not: and as commonly has been the practice of those writers who, not being able to infuse a natural passion into the mind, have made it their business to ply the ears and to stun their judges by the noise. But Shakespeare does not often thus; for the passions in his scene between Brutus and Cassius are extremely natural, the thoughts are such as arise from the matter, and the expression of 'em not viciously figurative. I cannot leave this subject before I do justice to that divine poet by giving you one of his passionate descriptions:

'tis of Richard the Second when he was deposed, and led in triumph through the streets of London by Henry of Bolingbroke: the painting of it is so lively, and the words so moving, that I have scarce read anything comparable to it in any other language. Suppose you have seen already the fortunate usurper passing through the crowd, and followed by the shouts and acclamations of the people; and now behold King Richard entering upon the scene: consider the wretchedness of his condition, and his carriage in it; and refrain from pity if you can:

> As in a theater, the eyes of men,
> After a well-graced actor leaves the stage,
> Are idly bent on him that enters next,
> Thinking his prattle to be tedious:
> Even so, or with much more contempt, men's eyes
> Did scowl on Richard: no man cried, God save him:
> No joyful tongue gave him his welcome home,
> But dust was thrown upon his sacred head,
> Which with such gentle sorrow he shook off,
> His face still combating with tears and smiles
> (The badges of his grief and patience),
> That had not God (for some strong purpose) steel'd
> The hearts of men, they must perforce have melted,
> And barbarism itself have pitied him.[25]

To speak justly of this whole matter: 'tis neither height of thought that is discommended, nor pathetic vehemence, nor any nobleness of expression in its proper place; but 'tis a false measure of all these, something which is like 'em, and is not them; 'tis the Bristol-stone,[26] which appears like a diamond; 'tis an extravagant thought, instead of a sublime one; 'tis roaring madness, instead of vehemence; and a sound of words, instead of sense. If Shakespeare were stripped of all the bombast in his passions, and dressed in the most vulgar words, we should find the beauties of his thoughts remaining; if his embroideries were burnt down, there would still be silver at the bottom of the melting-pot: but I fear (at least let me fear it for myself) that we who ape his sounding words have nothing of his thought, but are all outside; there is not so much as a dwarf within our giant's clothes. Therefore, let not Shakespeare suffer for our sakes; 'tis our fault, who succeed him in an age which is more refined, if we imitate him so ill that we copy his failings only, and make a virtue of that in our writings which in his was an imperfection.

For what remains, the excellency of that poet was, as I have said, in the more manly passions; Fletcher's in the softer: Shakespeare writ better betwixt man and man; Fletcher, betwixt man and woman: consequently, the one described friendship better; the other love: yet Shakespeare

---

[24] *Hamlet*, 2.2.475–79, 487–500. [Line numbers cited here are those in this anthology; the lines that Dryden quotes differ slightly from this anthology because of his use of another version of Shakespeare's play.—Editor]

[25] *Richard II*, 5.2.23–36.

[26] A rock crystal.

taught Fletcher to write love: and Juliet, and Desdemona, are originals. 'Tis true, the scholar had the softer soul; but the master had the kinder. Friendship is both a virtue and a passion essentially; love is a passion only in its nature, and is not a virtue but by accident: good nature makes friendship, but effeminacy love. Shakespeare had an universal mind, which comprehended all characters and passions; Fletcher a more confined and limited: for though he treated love in perfection, yet honor, ambition, revenge, and generally all the stronger passions, he either touched not, or not masterly. To conclude all, he was a limb of Shakespeare.

I had intended to have proceeded to the last property of manners, which is that they must be constant, and the characters maintained the same from the beginning to the end; and from thence to have proceeded to the thoughts and expressions suitable to a tragedy: but I will first see how this will relish with the age. 'Tis, I confess, but cursorily written;

yet the judgment which is given here is generally founded upon experience: but because many men are shocked at the name of rules, as if they were a kind of magisterial prescription upon poets, I will conclude with the words of Rapin, in his reflections on Aristotle's work of poetry: "If the rules be well considered, we shall find them to be made only to reduce nature into method, to trace her step by step, and not to suffer the least mark of her to escape us: 'tis only by these that probability in fiction is maintained, which is the soul of poetry. They are founded upon good sense, and sound reason, rather than on authority; for though Aristotle and Horace are produced, yet no man must argue that what they write is true because they writ it; but 'tis evident, by the ridiculous mistakes and gross absurdities which have been made by those poets who have taken their fancy only for their guide, that if this fancy be not regulated, 'tis a mere caprice, and utterly incapable to produce a reasonable and judicious poem."[27]

---

[27]*Réflexions*, 12.

518 UNIT IV · EARLY MODERN EUROPE

PERFORMANCE IN HISTORY

KATHARINE EISAMAN MAUS

from "'Playhouse Flesh and Blood': Sexual Ideology and the Restoration Actress" (1979)

Katharine Eisaman Maus has written widely about seventeenth-century literature, including a book on the playwright Ben Jonson. In this essay, Maus explores the relationship between Restoration actresses, their reputation for sexual promiscuity, and the politics of gender in the Restoration theater and society.

Sometime in the fall of 1660—no one is quite sure when or at which theater—the first professional English actress made her debut on the public stage. Her appearance was not entirely without precedents. In the first half of the seventeenth century, Queen Henrietta Maria and her ladies performed extensively in the English court theater. During the interregnum, when the theaters were officially closed, William D'Avenant used at least one woman—a Mrs. Edward Coleman—in his opera *The Siege of Rhodes*. On the Continent, women had been employed on the stage since the sixteenth century, and many royalists became familiar with the French custom when they followed Prince Charles into exile. However, women had never been used on the English stage in any regular or systematic way.

Before the war, adolescent boys had performed the women's parts in the public theater. In November, 1629, when a French company with actresses came to London, Thomas Brand informed Archbishop Laud that "those women . . . giving just offense to all virtuous and well disposed persons in this town . . . were hissed, hooted, and pippin-pelted from the stage."[1] By the Restoration, though, attitudes toward women on the stage seem to have changed radically. The new actresses were accepted almost immediately into the life of the theater, and there was surprisingly little controversy over their suitability for the stage.

What caused this striking reversal of audience attitudes? Was it merely a case of English theater-goers belatedly relinquishing a set of absurd scruples? Discussions of seventeenth-century actresses have assumed that they succeeded on the stage because they could provide a more plausible portrayal of women characters than transvestite actors

could.[2] There are two objections to this kind of explanation. For one thing, there is no evidence which implies that the female impersonators were incompetent. Female parts written by Shakespeare, Webster, Ford, Middleton, and others suggests no mean estimate by the playwrights of the boys' abilities; Elizabethan and Jacobean audiences applauded male Juliets, Rosalinds, and Cleopatras. The usual explanation of the actresses' success further assumes that naturalism is an obvious and desirable goal in theatrical representation—an assumption which is questionable to say the least. E.H. Gombrich has shown that standards of naturalism—what will seem "true to life" in a drawing or painting—vary from generation to generation depending upon the conventions which inform and have informed artistic production. What seems natural or conventional is not universal across time and space, but is historically and culturally conditioned.[3] There is no reason to suppose that naturalism in the theater

[1] John Payne Collier, *History of Dramatic Poetry to the Time of Shakespeare: And Annals of the Stage to the Restoration* (London: John Murray, 1831), II, pp. 23–24.

[2] e.g., Colley Cibber, *An Apology of the Life of Colley Cibber* (London, 1740), p. 55: "The characters of Women, on former Theatres, were perform'd by Boys, or young Men of the most effeminate Aspect. And what Grace, or Master-Stroke of Action, can we conceive such ungain Hoydens to have been capable of?"

Allardyce Nicoll, *The History of Restoration Drama 1660–1700* (Cambridge: Cambridge U P, 1928), p. 71: "the actresses certainly made possible a more charming presentation of Shakespearean tragedy and comedy, shedding a fresh light on the Desdemonas and Ophelias of the past."

Rosamund Gilder, *Enter the Actresses* (London: George C. Harrup, 1931), pp. 134–35: "In England the curtain of legal prohibition drops in 1642 on a stage peopled by squeaking Cleopatras, and rises eighteen years later on a rout of beautiful, witty, and accomplished actresses."

John Harold Wilson, *All the King's Ladies: Actresses of the Restoration* (Chicago: U Chicago Press, 1958), p. 90: "As creators of character there can be little doubt that the new actresses were superior to their juvenile predecessors . . . the stage life of the female impersonator was usually short, and his interpretation of a character could never be more than superficially correct."

[3] E.H. Gombrich, *Art and Illusion* (New York: Pantheon, 1960), esp. pp. 181–287.

is any less problematic than naturalism in the visual arts. Why should male impersonation of women seem more intolerable than other kinds of artificiality—extravagantly exotic sets, or a highly rhetorical acting style? The Restoration audience expected, and enjoyed, stage conventions which grievously ignore the demands of realism as understood by, say, Ibsen or Chekhov.

The orthodox explanation of the actresses' new acceptability is, if not entirely wrong, at least seriously insufficient. What is required is an examination of the issues in terms of the attitudes prevailing in Restoration culture. This examination logically begins with the contemporary accounts of the actresses, and inevitably widens to include analysis of Restoration attitudes toward women and the theater in general.

Unfortunately, there is very little comment upon the actresses in the years when they are first introduced, when the quality of contemporary response might best help illuminate the reasons for their professional success. Since no one seriously questioned women's fitness for the stage, the few attempts to account for the innovation involve no very elaborate process of justification. In 1660, the players and owners of theatrical companies were complaining that the hiatus in the theatrical tradition had created a dearth of well-trained female impersonators. The available actors were all too masculine-looking, they claimed, to excel in women's parts. As Thomas Jordan lamented in his preface to a revival of *Othello*:

> Our women are defective, and so siz'd
> You'ld think they were some of the guard disguis'd
> For to speak truth, men act that are between
> Forty and fifty, wenches of fifteen
> With bone so large and nerve so incompliant
> When you call Desdemona, enter Geant.[4]

According to this line of argument, the peculiar circumstances of the Restoration theater necessitated the employment of women. The closing of the theaters during the interregnum had interrupted the old system of apprenticeship, which had supplied the Elizabethan and Jacobean companies with adequately-trained female impersonators.

This explanation, even if true, would only reveal by what chance women arrived on the stage, and not how and why they were successful once they got there. Furthermore, the plight of the producers was not nearly so severe as Jordan represents it. According to John Downes in *Roscius Angli-*

canus, the King's Company at its inception included four actors "Bred up from Boys, under the Master ACTORS."[5] The Duke's Company included six actors, who "commonly Acted Women's Parts"—notably Edward Kynaston, who "being young made a complete Femal Stage Beauty, performing his part so well . . . that it hath since been disputable among the Judicious, whether any Woman that succeeded him so sensibly touched the audience as he."[6] Pepys and Cibber, as well as Downes, comment upon the excellence of Kynaston's impersonations, as well as upon the more than passable abilities of the lesser actors.[7] Surely if the Restoration audience had greeted the women players with the hisses and orange pips of an earlier generation, the companies would have made do for a while with ungainly performances by untrained adolescent boys. The perceived unsuitability of male actors for female roles is really more a symptom than an explanation of changing attitudes.

As the theaters reopened, actors and producers urged yet another argument for the introduction of actresses, which seems at least in retrospect equally unsatisfactory as a real explanation. Initially some people hoped that the presence of women on the stage would eliminate the obscene and corrupt aspects of English drama, and encourage the adoption of purer standards for theatrical spectacle. The patents issued to William D'Avenant and Thomas Killigrew in 1660, and reissued in 1662, contain the following clause:

> forasmuch as many plays formerly acted, do conteine severall prophane, obscene, and scurrilous passages, and the women's parts therein have been acted by men in the habit of women, at which some have taken offense; for the preventing of these abuses for the future, we doe straitly charge, command, and enjoyn that henceforth no . . . play shall be acted by either of the said companies conteining any passages offensive to piety or good manners . . . And we doe likewise permit and give leave that all the women's parts to be acted in either of the said two companies may be performed by women so long as these recreations, which by reason of the abuses aforesaid were scandalous and offensive, may by such reformation be esteemed not only harmlesse delight but useful instruction.[8]

By this account the actresses were introduced in order to help the dramatic arts exert a beneficial effect upon the community. Whether or not this apparently pious hope was initially a sincere one, it remained unrealized on the Restoration

[4]Thomas Jordan, "A Prologue, to introduce the first Woman that came to act on the Stage, in the tragedy called The Moor of Venice," in *A Royal Arbour of Loyal Poesie* (London, 1664), p. 22.

[5]John Downes, *Roscius Anglicanus, or An Historical View of the Stage* (London, 1708), p. 2.

[6]Ibid., p. 19.

[7]Samuel Pepys, *The Diary of Samuel Pepys,* ed. R. Latham and W. Matthews (London: G. Bell, 1970), I, 224 (August 18, 1660) and II, 7 (January 7, 1660–61). Cibber, p. 71.

[8]Nicoll, pp. 285–86n.

stage. Restoration drama, especially comedy, tends to be sexually more explicit and morally more subversive than the drama of earlier decades—and the sexual explicitness, at least, largely depends upon the physical presence of genuine women on the stage. "We can only conclude," writes a twentieth century critic, "that [the actresses'] chief effect on dramatic literature was to push it steadily in the direction of sex and sensuality."[9] The threat implied in the language of the patents—that the women's continued employment depended upon their moral efficacy—was of course never carried out. If women were now considered appropriate on the public stage, it was not for their purifying influence, any more than it was due to a shortage of teenage boys.

Since the overt attempts at contemporary justification seem inadequate, it is reasonable to suspect that the new acceptability of actresses is associated with ideological changes more fundamental or far-reaching than a mere modification of theatrical custom might indicate. The first such change which needs to be examined is the transformation in audience attitudes toward players in the latter part of the seventeenth century—a change which makes the success of the Restoration actress even more striking. Before the war, even the most appreciative playgoers seem not have been particularly interested in the offstage lives of Burbage, Kempe, or Alleyn. In the more intimate Restoration theater, though, the personalities of both male and female players intrigued the comparatively small and loyal audience. Actresses as well as actors were praised not for their ability to depict any character with equal skill, but for their ability to inform their dramatic portrayals with the force of their personal talent and idiosyncratic vision. In James Wright's *Historia Histrionica* (London, 1699), Truewit assumes that even in reading an old play one is curious about the personalities of the original actors:

> I wish they had printed in the last age (so I call the times before the rebellion) the actors names over against the parts they acted, as they have done since the restoration: and thus one might have guess'd at the action of the men, by the parts which we now read in the old plays. (page 3)

Restoration theater did not really challenge the actor to submit himself to the demands of a fictional role; rather it provided, at least for the leading players, manifold opportunities for self-expression. In the case of women like Nell Gwynn, Elizabeth Barry, or Ann Bracegirdle, this kind of attention constituted a virtually unprecedented celebration of female personality—at least of middle- and lower-class female personality.

As Restoration playwrights worked very closely with the theatrical companies, they inevitably wrote with particular performers in mind. They were thus able to play upon the spectator's sense of the relationship between an actor's personality and the roles he was required to enact. Nell Gwynn and Charles Hart, lovers behind the scenes, played witty, amoral "mad couples" together—Florimel and Celadon in Dryden's *Secret Love,* Miridia and Philidor in Howard's *All Mistaken,* Jacintha and Wildblood in Dryden's *Evening's Love,* Olivia and Wildish in Sedley's *Mulberry Garden.* Ann Bracegirdle, who resisted the advances of enamored aristocrats throughout her career, and who was the object of a melodramatic rape attempt, became famous for her portrayal of chaste women in distress. She was applauded when, as Cordelia in the revised *Lear,* she described herself as "Arm'd in my Virgin Innocence"—although the promiscuous Mrs. Barry, "in the same part, more fam'd for her Stage Performance than the other, at the words, *Virgin Innocence,* has created a Horse-laugh . . . and the scene of generous Pity and Compassion at the close turn'd to Ridicule."[10]

Prologues and epilogues, with their ambiguous position between the fictional and the real, provided ideal opportunities to exploit the relation between the player and the part. The most extreme, and probably the funniest, example occurs at the end of Dryden's *Tyrannic Love.* Nell Gwynn, playing a doomed princess despite her generally recognized ineptitude in tragic roles, finally expires. Servants load her corpse onto a litter and are carrying it out when she suddenly sits bolt upright and exclaims, "Hold, are you mad? You damn'd confounded Dog! I am to rise, and speak the Epilogue!" She leaps off the bier and begins the final speech:

> I come, kind Gentlemen, strange news to tell ye
> I am the ghost of poor departed Nelly . . .
> To tell you truth, I walk because I die
> Out of my calling, in a Tragedy.
> O Poet, dam'd dull Poet, who could prove
> So senseless to make Nelly die for love! . . .
> As for my epitaph when I am gone,
> I'll trust no poet, but will write my own:
> "Here Nelly lies, who, though she liv'd a Slattern
> Yet dy'd a princess, acting in Saint Cathar'n."[11]

In *An Essay of Dramatic Poetry, and The Grounds of Criticism in Tragedy,* Dryden's qualified admiration for the French tradition testifies to his interest in and sensitivity to the require-

[9]Wilson, p. 107.

[10]William Chetwood, *A General History of the Stage* (London, 1749), p. 28.

[11]John Dryden, *The Dramatic Works,* ed. Montague Summers (London: Nonesuch, 1931), II, p. 395.

ments of theatrical decorum. But the demands of the tragic situation, even for Dryden, are overridden by the demands of Nell's personality.

It is tempting to think of the new acceptance of female assertiveness on the stage as part of a general revaluation of women's status—a reassessment that would eventually allow them to participate more fully in all aspects of public life. Certainly all the evidence suggests that although the actresses were never as numerous or as well-paid as their male colleagues, they participated extensively in the life of the companies to which they belonged. They were granted the same special privileges as the actors—most significantly a relative immunity from prosecution for debt. And with the formation of the Lincoln's Inn Fields Company in 1695, two actresses—Ann Bracegirdle and Mary Saunderson Betterton—became shareholders, with a right to a certain percentage of the company's profits.

The employment of actresses does not, however, coincide with a more general broadening of female participation in public life. In fact, during the second half of the seventeenth century women seem to have been losing rather than acquiring opportunities for gainful employment. Men were encroaching upon such traditionally female occupations as brewing, textile manufacture, dressmaking, and midwifery. Women were less and less likely to run businesses or enter trades independently of their husbands, to help their husbands in a family venture, or to continue such a venture when they were widowed. By the beginning of the eighteenth century, there were few alternatives for undowered, unmarried women—or married women whose husbands could not support them—other than domestic service or prostitution.[12] The success of the actress has to be explained in ways which take into account the drastically different experience of women in other professions.

Actresses, in other words, seem to be anomalous rather than typical; the task is to isolate the factors that make their case so special. It is reasonable to look more closely to the audience's actual response to the women on the stage, in order to establish revealing patterns of assumptions. One such pattern is so obvious as to be unavoidable. Everyone from Dryden on has remarked upon the audience's extraordinarily lively, even obsessive, concern with the actresses' sexuality.

John Downes, in *Roscius Angelicanus,* regales the reader with sly anecdotes:

> And all the Women's Parts admirably Acted: chiefly *Celia* [Moll Davis], a Shepherdess being Mad for Love; especially in Singing several Wild and Mad Songs. *My Lodging is on the Cold Ground,* etc. She perform'd that so Charmingly, that not long after, it Rais'd her from her Bed on the Cold Ground, to a Bed Royal.
>
> *Note, Mrs. Johnson in this Comedy, Dancing a Jigg so Charming Well, Love's power in a little time after Coerc'd her to Dance more Charming else where.*[13]

Others were less delicate. The anonymous author of "Satyr on Players" (London, c. 1685), declares that actresses are "so lewd in every kind / You'd swear that Rogue and Whore had both combin'd," and goes on to support his claim in explicit detail:

> Sue Percival so long has known the Stage
> She grows in Lewdness faster, than in Age:
> From Eight or Nine she there has swiving been;
> So calls that Nature, which is truly Sin. (page 2)

Despite the difference in tone, Downes and the author of the "Satyr" both assume that the sexual exploits of the actress are an extension of her histrionic function rather than an irrelevant side-issue. Moll Davis's change of beds is described as the direct result of her fine performance; Mrs. Johnson gets invited to dance elsewhere because she has danced so well on the stage; Sue Percival's theatrical and sexual exploits coincide. Modern critics like John Harold Wilson and Allardyce Nicoll conclude that the presence of the actresses debased the theater, by lending it the atmosphere of a brothel.[14] . . .

No doubt the fuss is partly due to the fact that the actresses' sex lives really were fairly unorthodox. As Allardyce Nicoll primly declares, "very few of these women led chaste lives."[15] Elizabeth Barry was the mistress of John, Earl of Rochester; Elizabeth Hall the mistress of Sir Philip Howard; the Mrs. Johnson of Downes's anecdote the mistress of Henry, Earl of Peterborough. Margaret Hughes was the mistress of Prince Rupert, Susannah Hall the mistress of Sir Robert Howard, Ann Reeves the mistress of Dryden, Elizabeth Barry (again) of Otway, and Ann Bracegirdle (perhaps) of Congreve. Hester Davenport was irregularly married to the Earl of Oxford—when she refused to become his mistress he dressed up one of his servants as a parson, and had an invalid marriage ceremony performed. Nell Gwynn and Moll Davis went all the way to the top, and became mistresses of Charles

---

[12]The standard work on the subject is still Alice Clark's *Working Life of Women in the Seventeenth Century* (London: Routledge and Sons, 1919). Her conclusion—that women were progressively excluded from the job market during the seventeenth century—though not her Marxist analysis, has recently been supported by Roger Thompson, *Women In Stuart England and America* (London: Routledge and Kegan Paul, 1974), pp. 74–75.

[13]Downes, pp. 23–24, page 33.

[14]Wilson, *passim.;* Nicoll, p. 72.

[15]Nicoll, p. 72.

II. Others, like Elizabeth Boutell and Rebecca Marshall, played the field.

Nonetheless, there were alternative models, like Mary Saunderson Betterton, who was the leading tragic actress before Mrs. Barry, and who seems to have led a faithful married life throughout her long career. An actress like Nell Gwynn, however, whose stage career lasted only five years, and whose histrionic talents were probably much smaller, seemed a much more exemplary specimen. When Ann Bracegirdle proved unexpectedly chaste, the audience did not divert its attention from her sexuality, but focused upon it all the more sharply.

> RAMBLE: And Mrs. Bracegirdle . . .
> CRITIC: Is a haughty conceited Woman, that has got more Money by dissembling her Lewdness, than others by professing it.
> SULLEN: But does that Romantick Virgin still keep up her great reputation?
> CRITIC: D'ye mean her Reputation for Acting?
> SULLEN: I mean her Reputation for not acting; you understand me.—[16]

By contrast, audience interest in the male players tended not to involve such an avid concern with their sex lives. Actors like Charles Hart, Edward Kynaston, and Cardell Goodman were "kept" by aristocratic ladies—in Goodman's case his connection with Lady Castlemaine obtained him a pardon after he had been convicted of highway robbery, a capital crime. But contemporary comment on their situation is muted; their sexuality is not considered part and parcel with their histrionic vocation. . . .

If hierarchical assumptions dominate conceptions of gender difference, boys and women occupy a similar position—they are inferior versions of mature men, *hommes manqués*. From one point of view, as *As You Like It*'s Rosalind-Ganymede knows, boys and women are cattle of the same color. The convention of the boy-actress has a certain logic; at any rate it does not pose a profound or necessary challenge to the audience's ideological convictions. If sexual difference is understood in terms of opposition, however, transvestite role-playing involves a much greater rupture of decorum—a rupture which may be ludicrous, implausible, or titillating depending upon the context. Boys no longer seem appropriate in women's tragic roles; a Cleopatra who shaves is the occasion for a jest.[17] The Restoration audience was more eager to see women in male disguise, but arguably this eagerness is rooted in the same attitudes which make the boy impersonators seem obsolete. John Harold Wilson has remarked upon the surprisingly "indelicate" methods by which women players in male disguise were unmasked in Restoration comedy.[18] Surely all the loosened hair, all the naked breasts in the fifth act are meant to heighten an incongruity of which the audience was already aware; the unmasking reinforces a histrionic appeal which depends upon the seductive appeal of female difference.

From this perspective one can see why the actresses appeared on the public stage for the first time at the Restoration; why their success could coincide with a more general withdrawal of women from public life; and also why their achievement took the specific forms that it did. It is not merely new attitudes toward women and the theater, but the persistence of old ones, which make possible the novel phenomenon of the Restoration actress, and which condition the highly selective enthusiasm of her audience.

---

[16]Anon. (sometimes ascribed to Charles Gildon), *A Comparison between The Two Stages* (London, 1702), p. 17.

[17]Cibber, p. 71.
[18]Wilson, p. 85.

AN ACTRESS'S PERSPECTIVE

HYPPOLITE CLAIRON

from *Memoirs of Hyppolite Clairon, the Celebrated French Actress: with Reflections Upon the Dramatic Art* (1798).

Hyppolite Clairon (Claire-Josèphe-Hippolyte Léris de la Tude, 1723-1803), known professionally as Mlle. Clairon, was the principal actress of the Comédie Française in the mid-eighteenth century. Although little is known of her early years, she attracted attention in smaller roles at the Comédie-Italienne in Paris; she first performed at the Comédie Française in the role of Phaedra in 1743. She is know to have studied vocal delivery with the philosophe *Denis Diderot (whose essay,* The Paradox of the Actor, *was written in the 1770s), and played leading roles in several of Voltaire's plays as well. She was imprisoned in 1765, and upon her release gave up professional acting; she was supported by Voltaire, and wrote her* Memoirs. *She died in penury after the French Revolution.*

In this selection from her Memoirs, *Mlle. Clairon provides a vivid sense of the way neoclassical actors understood the practice and purpose of acting. What elements of the actor's training seem particularly important to her? How do those elements seem to you to relate to the kind of acting called for in the neoclassical repertory—in a play like* Phaedra, *for example, in which Clairon gave a celebrated performance? How does Clairon's emphasis on dancing, drawing, and music help us to understand notions of the kind of "decorum" required of neoclassical performance?*

It is the wish of many that I should write sentiments relative to an art which I have long professed. It is supposed that the reflections I have made, in order to render myself supportable in the eyes of the public, may be of some use to those who are destined to pursue the same career. Perhaps the public, or, at least, the admirers of theatrical representations will contemplate with some degree of pleasure the road I have followed, in order to acquire their favor. But reflection and writing are two such different things: it appears so extraordinary to me to comprehend anything without the aid of physiognomy, gesture and speech; I am so diffident of myself, that I tremble as much in taking up the pen as I once did in appearing before the public. . . . Without any regular plan, perhaps without system, but certainly without vanity, I am about to trace what I deem necessary to the attainment of this art—an art much more difficult than it is generally supposed to be.

ENUNCIATION: OR THE MANAGEMENT OF THE VOICE

As it must be the chief object of the actress to be heard distinctly in all parts of the theatre, it is therefore an indispensable requisite that she should be possessed of a strong and sonorous voice.

In order that she may be enabled to give the necessary shade to the picture she means to represent, her voice must be clear, harmonious, flexible, and susceptible of every possible intonation.

From *Actors and Acting*, ed. Toby Cole and Helen Krich Chinoy (New York: Crown, 1949), 171–74.

A voice which is deficient in point of compass or expression can never be adequate to characters where the stronger passions are displayed. . . .

STRENGTH

A good constitution is a material point: there is no profession more fatiguing. Irritable nerves, weak lungs, or delicate constitutions, cannot long sustain the weight of tragic characters.

I have found, in the course of my time, a number of young authors and fine ladies who have thought that nothing was more easy than to perform Mahomet, Mérope, etc.; that the author had done all that was necessary; that to learn the parts, and to leave the rest to nature was all the actor had to do. Nature! How many use this word without knowing its meaning. The difference of sex, of age, of situation, of time, of countries, of manners and of customs demand different modes of expression. What infinite pains and study must it not require to make an actor forget his own character; to identify himself with every personage he represents; to acquire the faculty of representing love, hatred, ambition, and every passion of which human nature is susceptible,—every shade, every gradation by which these sentiments are depicted with their full extent of coloring and expression.

There are no arts or professions but have certain defined principles. Are there then none required to direct the tragedian? Is it only in the history of mankind he must obtain his information? Reading of itself would be nothing; he must mediate upon and render himself familiar with, what he reads . . . he must adapt to every character the genius of the nation to which it belongs; he must reflect without intermission; repeat a hundred and a hundred times the same thing, in order to surmount the difficulties he meets with at every step. It is not enough to study the character; he must study the history of it, in order to develop the intention of the author, feel the beauties of his composition and adapt his character to the general scope of the work: he must scrutinize the hearts of all connected with the scene, attend the relations they bear towards each other; and finally, he must be able to comprehend why what he hears, and what he sees, is so represented or expressed. . . .

In addition to what I have said, the most arduous test is to be enumerated: it is the indispensable necessity of having one's mind continually impressed with events the most dreadful and terrible and with images of the most horrid nature. The actor who does not identify himself with the character he represents is like a scholar who repeats his lessons; but he who does so identify himself with the personage he is portraying—whose tears seem the effect of nature, who absorbs the idea of his own existence in the miseries of an assumed character; such a person must be wretched: and I maintain it requires a degree of strength almost beyond what human nature is endowed with to perform the characters of tragedy well for more than ten years.

• • •

In recalling to mind my plan of study, I hope I shall be pardoned for observing that I have often smiled at the folly of those who have upbraided me for having recourse to art. Alas! What should I have been without it? Could I have personated Roxane, Amenaide, or Viriate? Should I be consistent if I was to apply my own feelings and habits to such characters? Doubtless not. How am I enabled to substitute the ideas, sentiments and feelings, which should distinguish those characters in lieu of my own? It is by art alone that it can be done: for if ever I have seemed to personate them in a manner purely natural, is is because my studies, joined to some happy gifts which I may have derived from nature, have conducted me to the perfection of art.

All men are not endowed with creative genius. I will endeavor to direct those who are inadequate to the pursuit of an original system of their own, and for that purpose will resume my examination.

[Memory and Exteriors, figure or appearance, are the two additional major qualities listed as necessary to an actor.]

DANCING AND DRAWING
In order to be able to tread the stage with ease and grace, to give facility to the motions of the body, dignity to the whole appearance, and to prevent the acquirement of habits repug-

nant to nature, it is indispensably necessary that those who dedicate themselves to a theatrical profession should pay the utmost attention to the art of dancing. They must carefully avoid contracting the airs and manner of a dancing-master; but, in every other respect, a knowledge of the art is requisite.

It were to be wished that every actor should be more or less initiated in the art of drawing: they would thereby become more susceptible of the good effect of preserving proper distances; they would more easily discover the point of perspective, which is so important on the stage, both with respect to their figure and their dress. In pantomimic representations, or pieces calculated for show, the performers who are to set off the principal personages are placed more advantageously, and are better adapted to fill up the picture with its proper shade or effect. Such actors as are unacquainted with this art, I advise to study the works of the most eminent painters and sculptors.

MUSIC
Without pretending to acquire a fundamental knowledge of the science of music, it is, nevertheless, necessary for an actor to study its elements, in order to be enabled to form a proper judgment as to the extend of his voice, to render every intonation easy and familiar, to avoid discordance, to regulate his sounds, to preserve and vary them at pleasure, and to impart to every accent, whether vehement or plaintive, that degree of modulation which is necessary.

Without this study, it is almost impossible to play Corneille to advantage. He is either so sublime, or so familiar, that, unless the actor is perfectly sure of his intonation, he runs the risk of appearing bombastical or trivial.

LANGUAGE, GEOGRAPHY, AND BELLES LETTRES
The study of language is of more importance to an actor than any other. The theatre ought to be the school for foreigners, and of that part of the public who have neither time, nor the means of procuring proper masters, to learn the language of the country in its most perfect purity.

It is almost incredible, that persons who are selected to represent the *chef d'oeuvres* of the most eminent writers of the nation should be unacquainted with the difference between a long and a short syllable, or the distinction between the singular number and the plural; that they should confound the genders of the nouns; that they should scarce know the masculine from the feminine; and that provincial accents should destroy the grandeur and purity of our language. Such, however, is the case with reference to the greater part of our actors. He who is unacquainted with the extent and value of words can never comprehend the meaning of things: if he should stumble upon it, it is only by chance; and I am at a loss to conceive how the public can tolerate those who appear before them with such defects, or who betray such unpardonable ignorance.

It is impossible to read history, with any advantage or improvement, without a knowledge of geography. The right of judging of the merits of such authors as write for the theatre imposes upon an actor the necessity of acquiring every species of knowledge which may enable him to judge with accuracy, and to determine, by a single perusal, the merits of a work which the author has been a year composing. An intimate acquaintance with stage-effect and the rules of the theatre, an accurate ear, a good taste, a sound, discriminating, and attentive judgment, are not all that is required: it is necessary to be acquainted with mythology, history, geography, and language; he must be acquainted with every description of poetry, and the writings of every dramatic author, ancient or modern. He will then be enabled to judge whether an author has made the most of his subject; he will perceive how much has been drawn from the times, places, and characters of which he has written; in short, whether the author has shown a creative fancy, is a servile imitator, or a plagiarist. The approbation of the critic is no ways flattering, nor his censure any disgrace, unless he is known to possess those qualities necessary to enable him to form his judgment with accuracy. It is not enough to approve or reject a work; the man who does either, ought to show himself capable of judging. About two years before my retirement from the theatre, there was a league among certain authors to pay no attention whatever to the judgment of actors. This attempt to invalidate the opinions of a class of men, without whom the authors could be of no use, was as unjust as the pretence for it was false and groundless.

Unless a superior power destroys the right of the actors, it is impossible that any of them should ever consent to such an injustice and degradation. Corneille, Voltaire, and Racine, demanded no other tribunal: their works, however, unlike those of the present day, did not require the illusions of the theatre, or the talents of the actors. It has been said by authors, that the actors robbed them of the reward due to their exertions: the trifling recompense they received was, they said, a proof of it. I can state, in reply to this observation without the least fear of contradiction, that, with respect to the two and tweny years I have been upon the theatre, it is unfounded in truth. . . .

PERFORMANCE REVIEW

Femmes Fatales

FRANK RICH
Review of *The Rover*

DIRECTED BY JOHN RUBINSTEIN, AT THE WILLIAMSTOWN THEATER, WILLIAMSTOWN, MA, 27 JULY 1987.

Frank Rich reviewed this summer festival production of Aphra Behn's The Rover *for the* New York Times. *The Williamstown Theater has a distinguished history of offering summer audiences in Western Massachusetts fine professional theater, and this production is no exception: the cast included Edward Herrmann as Blunt, Ann Reinking as Lucetta, and Christopher Reeve as Willmore. Rich notes the play's sprawling and energetic plot, and also comments—somewhat negatively—on the production's efforts to underline the play's incipient feminism.*

From the moment Christopher Reeve swaggers on stage in 17th-century cavalier finery, shirt open and sword at the ready, it's clear why the Williamstown Theater Festival has chosen to revive "The Rover." This infrequently staged Restoration comedy, written by Aphra Behn in 1677, gives Mr. Reeve and his dashing companions—Stephen Collins, Harry Groener, Edward Herrmann—a chance to duel and flirt and clown and play drunk, all in the name of culture.

"The Rover" is about exiled English adventurers in single-minded pursuit of more than one kind of sack at pre-Lenten carnival time. As with "The Three Musketeers" or "The Pirates of Penzance," or maybe "Mister Roberts," it seems like just the thing to unite rambunctious actors and vacationing audiences in macho bonhomie during a heat wave.

Paradoxically, however, the evening turns out to be somewhat more interesting and substantially less rollicking than it first appears. The festive spirit expires before intermission, and for an unsurprising reason. A high-gloss Restoration performance style cannot be churned out overnight by the summer-theater assembly line, no matter what the caliber of actors involved. But if "The Rover" finally sinks into its endless plot of disguises and mix-ups, its tedious second half is preceded by the unexpected assertion of a subversive playwright's sensibility. Aphra Behn was England's first professional woman writer, and not even Mr. Reeve and his swashbuckling buddies can keep this good woman's sprightly voice down.

Although Behn has been the subject of feminist scholarship in recent years, one needn't apply a contemporary ideological yardstick to take the measure of her independent spirit. Almost six decades ago, Virginia Woolf saluted Behn for giving women "the right to speak their minds." That outspokenness is built into the fabric of "The Rover," which might well be indistinguishable from the work of Behn's friend Wycherley, were it not for the fact that the female characters freely express their sexual desires and decry their economic and social subjugation. While the men—starting with Mr. Reeve's title character, Willmore—may have top billing and the most farcical scenes, it is the women who have the last word.

This is particularly true of the two heroines entangled with the hero. Robin Strasser plays a high-priced courtesan named Angelica Bianca, and it is commonly believed that the character shares the point of view as well as the initials of the playwright. "Who made the laws by which you judge me?" she asks Willmore. "Men! Men who would rove and ramble, but require that women must be nice." Ms. Strasser's double-edged wielding of the word "nice" is far sharper than her adversary's sword. The actress captures that rare prostitute with a mind of steel rather than a heart of gold—a woman who bristles at the oppressive male double standard even as she keeps a tiny, everdimming candle lit for love.

As Hellena, the "proper" girl after Willmore's heart, Faye Grant integrates Behn's sexual politics, wry sense of humor and erotic playfulness into a seamless characterization. Chafing at a world that offers her only the choice of the nunnery or an imprisoning marriage, Hellena takes to outwitting Willmore at his own masculine game, gleefully demanding her own right to carnal inconstancy. The diminutive Ms. Grant is more than up to the task of bringing Mr. Reeve to her feet; indeed, her puckish presence and witty vocal delivery, always true to both the feminist and the feminine, are so beguiling that the audience can't (and doesn't) get enough of her. This actress has come a long way since she made her name in New York for her broad Jean Hagen impersonation in the musical "Singin' in the Rain."

The director, John Rubinstein, is sympathetic to the polemical undertow delicately illuminated by Ms. Grant and Ms. Strasser. There is one early chilling moment, when Hellena and her uninhibitedly chatting sisters turn into subservient ninnies the instant their domineering brother enters their room. But such staging niceties are a luxury the director can infrequently afford. On a tight deadline, he has his hands full just getting a show of this size on its feet.

Following the example of John Barton, who directed an acclaimed Royal Shakespeare Company "Rover" in Stratford-on-Avon last year, Mr. Rubinstein tries to juice up the pace by trimming the play's text and switching its setting from Naples to an unnamed Spanish colony blighted by an excess of strolling guitar players. He might profitably have cut even deeper in the low-comedy scenes featuring the miscast Mr. Herrmann as the archetypal Essex lout, Ned Blunt.

Among the rest of Mr. Rubinstein's large company, Mr. Groener and Ann Reinking (as another self-protective prostitute) are the most engagingly relaxed, while Mr. Collins, Kate Burton, and David Purdham may snap into comic focus if they push a little less hard during the remaining week of the run.

As for Mr. Reeve, his stage acting remains a puzzlement. He speaks and moves well, yet his considerable efforts at charm (including his oft-recycled Cary Grant accent) still seem studied and cold. But while there is no verve to this performance, the alienating, smarmy narcissism of his Willmore does prevent "The Rover" from teetering over into the summertime celebration of locker-room machismo that a more likable hero might have prompted. Though perhaps more by default than design, it is the women who deliver the punch in Williamstown's hunk-heavy rendition of Behn's pioneering play.

Modern Europe

Hamm in one of the definitive spaces of modern drama, the empty room of Samuel Beckett's *Endgame,* in the 2000 Rude Mechanicals Theater Company production.

I n many ways the world we live in today was forged between 1850 and 1950. Since the mid-nineteenth century, enormous political changes have redrawn the map of the planet: two world wars; the rise of the United States and the rise and fall of the Union of Soviet Socialist Republics as world superpowers; revolutions in Russia and China; worldwide liberation from European colonial rule in Mexico, the Philippines, Latin America, Africa, India, and Southeast Asia. Political change was spurred by a series of industrial and technological revolutions. This century saw the introduction of the telephone, radio, film, and television; of the automobile and the highway; of the airplane and the rocket; of penicillin, anesthetics, vaccinations, and artificial organs; of the assembly line and mass production; of multinational corporations extending their markets and influence around the globe. The acceleration of technological change altered the fabric of daily life, creating new forms of living, working, and relating to one another, and new ways of measuring our lives: suburbs and housing developments, trade unions and public corporations, the time clock and the wristwatch, public education and compulsory retirement. It witnessed huge changes in the landscape of life: the growth of the modern cityscape, of modern slums, skyscrapers, subways, and even city streets; of massive public projects like the Panama and Suez canals, the Empire State Building, the Eiffel Tower, and their grim cousins—the gas chambers of Auschwitz and the nuclear bombing of Hiroshima and Nagasaki.

Political and social changes were rivaled by the intellectual and cultural revolutions that gave—or attempted to give—meaning to modern experience. This was the century of Darwin and the theory of evolution; of Marx and Lenin; of Gandhi's nonviolent resistance; of Einstein, Oppenheimer, and Teller, and a revolution in our understanding of the physical cosmos; of Freud's discovery of the unconscious; of Proust, Joyce, Stein, Eliot, and Woolf; of the Impressionist painters, and of Picasso, and Pollock; of Diaghilev and Nijinsky, of Fred Astaire and Ginger Rogers, of Isadora Duncan and Martha Graham; of Wagner, of Stravinsky and Schoenberg, of ragtime and jazz.

This complex of revolutions extends to the modern theater. Technological innovation, political developments, and two major wars encouraged an increasing internationalism across the arts of Europe, evident in the "international" style of architecture popularized by Le Corbusier, the Bauhaus, and their followers; in Cubist painting and sculpture; and in modernist writing and music. This internationalism, however, hardly fostered a single, monolithic sense of "modernism" in the arts. Instead, it gave rise to a series of fragmentary **AVANT-GARDE** movements—imagism, cubism, vorticism, futurism, symbolism, surrealism, Dada, and so on—each with its own ideals, esthetics, and audience, and usually with its own resistant posture toward society as well. The fragment—the poetic image, Joyce's "epiphanies," Schoenberg's twelve-tone row, montage in film—came to be valued as a means of expression in itself. Since the 1950s, a variety of social, political, and esthetic challenges have been made to modernism—usually under the general rubric of **POSTMODERNISM.** These challenges are discussed later in this essay.

Modernist art also developed a distinction between "high art" and the esthetics of mass culture that parallels the modern division of labor and implies a division between highbrow and lowbrow, the elite and the popular. In many respects, the modernist theater became definitive of "high art" as it was edged from the center of cultural life by other performance media—film, radio, and later, television—which claimed greater immediacy and wider distribution. After the turn of the twentieth century, the modern theater and drama were

531

increasingly pressed to define what is germane, special, essential to live dramatic performance.

Units V, VI, and VII survey the theater more widely than previous units, focusing not on a single city or site of performance, but instead on the broader developments of national and international movements. For although the theaters of Chekhov's Moscow, Shaw's London, and Brecht's Berlin reflected very different social dynamics, they were engaged in a common, distinctly modernist project: bringing the stage into a critical relation to the forms of modern life by taking an experimental attitude toward theatrical production. And many of these projects have a visible legacy in the work of their successors: in Beckett's sterile chambers, in Müller's assault on the dynamics of temporality and identity, in Churchill's parallel between sexual and colonial politics, in the critical **HYBRIDIZATION** of Soyinka's drama.

The Modern Theater

Theatrical innovation always takes place on three fronts: as technology, as esthetics, and as ideology. The history of the modern theater is in one sense a history of new strategies and techniques for stage production: electric lighting, revolving stages, increasingly spectacular and illusionistic stage machinery, and new techniques of stage design, acting, and direction. What makes these changes meaningful is how they are used to represent and explain the world around us.

Reviewing the history of nineteenth-century drama, Brander Matthews, the first professor of dramatic literature in the United States, remarked in 1910 that modern drama owed its innovation more to Edison than to Ibsen, that the new drama was "the inevitable consequence of the incandescent bulb." The technological revolutions that brought engines and electricity to the public transformed theater throughout Europe and America: the replacement of candle lighting and gas lighting with more flexible electric lighting; the installation of the **PROSCENIUM** frame, emphasizing the pictorial coherence of the stage; the gradual disappearance of galleries and boxes in favor of seating the audience in darkened, fan-shaped theaters, emphasizing a perspective view of the proscenium; elevators to raise and lower sets; revolving stages on which several settings could be placed at one time. This technology could be put to a variety of uses, and the nineteenth-century theaters of Europe and America had an extraordinarily spectacular dimension, fostering a taste for **EXTRAVAGANZAS, MELODRAMAS, NAUTICAL SHOWS, PANTOMIMES,** and **TABLEAUX.** However, the apparatus of the modern theater came increasingly to be dominated by the notion of **SCENIC UNITY,** the idea that the stage set, the costumes, the behavior of the actors, and the dramatic action all should correspond to a single historical era and social milieu. Shakespeare's actors had mixed contemporary Elizabethan dress with "antique" costumes in the production of plays with classical settings. Throughout the eighteenth century, actors wore contemporary clothing regardless of the historical era of the play. By the late nineteenth century, however— following the example of Charles Kean and Henry Irving in England, the company of George II, the Duke of Saxe-Meiningen in Germany, and others—productions increasingly strove to establish a unified style on the stage, in which the dialogue, acting style, costumes, setting, and dramatic action all conformed to a single point-of-view.

The use of a unified theatrical style to assert a thorough **VERISIMILITUDE,** a photographic "slice of life" onstage, became the cornerstone of modern **REALISM** in drama and theater and of the movement called **NATURALISM** in which it began. In a series of essays calling for a "naturalism in the theater," published in the 1870s, the French novelist and playwright Émile Zola argued that the technology of the late nineteenth-century theater could be used to represent a more clinical or scientific attitude toward the world. He urged the stage to adopt a more lifelike and "naturalistic" style by adopting the "objective" methods and perspective of the natural sciences. By filling the stage with objects—real doors, real walls, pictures, furniture, fireplaces—the theater could place men and women in their "environment" rather than in the idealized "setting" of the classical theater, and the characters could then be

A PROSCENIUM STAGE: SHAKESPEARE MEMORIAL THEATRE

The Shakespeare Memorial Theatre, Stratford-upon-Avon, 1932, displays an extensive backstage area used for scenic machinery.

seen as influenced by that material environment. In contrast to the ideal heroes of earlier drama, the characters of modern plays would become part of that stage milieu, influenced by the forces of history, society, economy, and psychology. Naturalism uses the technology of the stage to claim a "scientific" attitude toward social problems, usually emphasizing the determining role that the social environment plays in the characters' actions. It organized the theater's new technology and the idea of scenic unity it made possible, and provided modern theater with a characteristic kind of meaning: the achievement of verisimilitude.

Naturalism and realism are notoriously difficult to distinguish; here we can describe them as two phases in the history of modern theater and drama. In this sense, naturalism provides the thematic inspiration and many of the dramatic techniques we now associate with modern realistic drama. Realism in the theater is also committed to verisimilitude, but usually develops a wider range of style and a more problematic sense of the relationship of character and environment. While naturalistic plays tend to be preoccupied with the duplication of material reality onstage, realistic plays sometimes distort the verisimilitude of the stage picture in order to dramatize an inner, psychological truth. The domestic space of Sam

Shepard's *True West* (see Unit VI), for example, at first seems to frame a reunion between two brothers but rapidly transforms itself into the landscape of fantasy. Realism extends and refines the techniques first explored by Zola's generation of playwrights, directors, and actors: a simple and direct speaking style that usually masks a **SUBTEXT** of subtle, unspoken motives; middle- or lower-class characters; action that revolves around the discovery of some past crime or indiscretion; a three-dimensional stage set, usually a domestic interior. Rather than using the play as a vehicle for a single "star" actor, realistic performance emphasizes the ensemble playing of the cast, so that each character becomes important in the overall action. Onstage, realism often treats the boundary of the proscenium as an invisible fourth wall dividing the environment onstage from the audience. The **FOURTH WALL** prevents the actors from playing to the audience and so from destroying the unity of illusion onstage.

Realism has become the dominant mode of dramatic performance today, so pervasive that it may be difficult for us to recapture its special excitement and danger when first introduced in the 1880s and 1890s. In the first blush of the modern era, the ability to picture an untheatrical, apparently "real" world on the stage was in itself a kind of spectacle, akin to the magic of the new, competing art of photography. Moreover, the first generation of realistic playwrights often adopted a critical posture toward the pieties of the middle-class audience whose attitudes were embodied in the "realistic" vision of the world. Plays such as Ibsen's *Ghosts* and *A Doll House,* Strindberg's *The Father,* and even Glaspell's *Trifles* raised the scandalous topics of sexual betrayal, marital discord, class conflict, sexual freedom, and gender politics in ways that challenged the conventional morality of the bourgeois audience.

The realistic theater developed many of the practices we are familiar with today: new sets for each production, rather than the same furniture recycled from show to show, in order to create the play's specific environment; the fourth wall; the darkened auditorium. Although realistic drama became pervasive, it first flourished in the small avant-garde theaters of the **INDEPENDENT THEATER MOVEMENT** at the turn of the century. Throughout Europe and the United States, playwrights and directors worked to carve a place for themselves outside the commercial mainstream, which often resisted and sometimes censored the controversial plays of the new realism. André Antoine founded the Théâtre Libre ("Free Theater") in Paris as a subscription theater in 1887; since the shows were open only to subscribers and not to the general public, he was able to avoid censorship and to produce plays like Ibsen's *Ghosts* and Strindberg's *The Father.* Antoine's work was paralleled by the German Freie Bühne ("Free Stage") in 1889. In England, the actress Janet Achurch mounted a production of Ibsen's *A Doll House* in 1889; J.T. Grein's Independent Theater opened in 1891 with a production of *Ghosts* and went on to produce plays by Ibsen, Shaw, and other contemporary playwrights. In Russia, Constantin Stanislavski and Vladimir Nemirovich-Danchenko founded the Moscow Art Theater in 1898, launching one of the most influential of modern theaters with their production of Chekhov's *The Seagull.* Independent theaters were often part of nationalist movements as well, especially in Norway, Sweden, Finland, Italy, and Ireland. In Ireland, W.B. Yeats, Lady Augusta Gregory, John Millington Synge, and a solid cast of amateur actors established a nationalist theater company in 1902 and opened The Abbey Theater in 1904. Here, the artistic resistance of the independent theater was allied to political resistance and national self-definition. The influence of these theaters was felt in the United States throughout the first decades of the twentieth century. David Belasco's minute fidelity to detail had firmly established a realistic idiom in the American theater, but it took the **LITTLE THEATER MOVEMENT,** inaugurated by Eugene O'Neill, Susan Glaspell, and the Provincetown Playhouse in 1915, to establish a repertoire of modern drama in the United States, and they were soon followed by other companies.

Forms of Modern Drama

The rise of the independent theaters also points to the theater's fragmentation and its marginalization in modern society. The theater no longer commands the cultural centrality that it had in classical Athens or in London and Paris in the sixteenth and seventeenth centuries.

SHAKESPEARE MEMORIAL THEATRE, INTERIOR VIEW

Although the Shakespeare Memorial Theatre has a forestage apron extending toward the audience, it is in many respects typical of the proscenium theaters of the early twentieth century. The audience is seated in a fan-shaped auditorium, in fixed seats, facing the illuminated stage.

Instead, it has become the site for a diverse, sometimes confusing array of artistic experiments. Naturalism and realism were the first dramatic modes to consider themselves not as expressing the dominant political and ideological order, but as criticizing the values and institutions of middle-class society. The major plays of the realistic canon often tend to criticize modern life, particularly its dehumanizing, exploitative routine. The major heroes of the realistic mode—Nora Helmer, Major Barbara, Laura Wingfield—are all characters whose desire for freedom, vitality, and life is threatened by the deadening, deceptive world in which they live. Because realistic drama usually sees that world as an all-embracing "environment," though, its social themes don't finally lead to a call for social change. Modern society may be a prison, but the liberation urged by realistic drama is imagined on the individual level; the characters' search for freedom, value, and meaning leaves the world unchanged. Despite its critical stance toward modern society, realistic drama tacitly accepts the world and its values as an unchanging, and unchangeable, environment in which the characters live out their lives.

For this reason, realistic drama has often seemed an inadequate vehicle for a sustained critique of the forces of modern life, and almost from the moment of its inception in the 1880s and 1890s, realism inspired antagonistic forms of drama and theater. The history of modern drama is a series of reactions against bourgeois society and its values, and against the realistic drama that seemed to represent it and its vision of the world.

Although it was finally concerned with many of the same issues, the **EXPRESSIONIST THEATER** popular from the turn of the century through the 1930s marked an exciting stylistic departure from the realistic mode. Expressionist plays like Strindberg's *A Dream Play,* or American plays like Elmer Rice's *The Adding Machine,* Sophie Treadwell's *Machinal,* or Eugene O'Neill's *The Hairy Ape* (see Unit VI), transformed the terms of realistic theater and drama. Rather than showing a character whose inner vitality is crushed by the bourgeois environment, expressionist plays try to show the mind and heart of the character visually, to express it directly in the objects and actions of the stage. The stage set becomes distorted, nearly dreamlike, and it is often peopled by characters who are exaggerated, mechanized, or fantastic, as a way of conveying the emotional coloring of the central character's experience. In O'Neill's *The Emperor Jones,* for instance, Jones is haunted by his "Little Formless Fears" when he flees into the forest; his flight is accompanied by the sound of a drum, which beats faster and louder as the play proceeds. More often, characters in expressionist drama are unnamed, like the Young Woman of *Machinal* or Mr. Zero of *The Adding Machine,* emphasizing that they have become cogs in the modern social and industrial machine. The action of expressionist drama is episodic and much like morality drama. Ernst Toller even named the scenes of his play *Transfiguration* "stations" to stress the play's likeness to a Christian passion play.

Thematically, expressionist theater resembles realism in its attention to character psychology and in its portrayal—however distorted or exaggerated—of the dehumanizing process of modern life. However, the style of expressionism also subverts realism in important ways, challenging both the logical, causal ordering of realistic dramatic action and the visual verisimilitude of the realistic theater. The **SYMBOLIST THEATER** also developed anti-realistic attitudes toward drama and staging and extended the expressionist theater's repudiation of the drama of modern life. Written in prose or in verse, symbolic drama created a dim and mysterious other world, sometimes drawn from mythology or simply from the poet's imagination. The Belgian playwright Maurice Maeterlinck created a vogue for this kind of drama at the turn of the century, a drama which finds analogies in the work of Stéphane Mallarmé, August Strindberg, T. S. Eliot, W. B. Yeats, and Samuel Beckett. Yeats's mythological plays—such as *On Baile's Strand*—are typical of this special and influential mode. Relatively static in action, the plays rely on a densely figurative language to enlarge and energize the "poetic" meaning of events onstage.

Finally, an explicitly Marxist theory of the ideologically coercive dimension of realism—the sense that realism claims that its special perspective of the world is *natural;* that is, unavoidable and *real*—stands at the center of modern **EPIC THEATER.** Though usually associated with Bertolt Brecht, many of the techniques of epic theater were developed by Erwin Piscator in Berlin during the 1920s and early 1930s and by Vsevolod Meyerhold in his brilliant experiments with **CONSTRUCTIVIST THEATER** after the Russian Revolution of 1917. Brecht assimilated these techniques to a political purpose that he called epic theater. Rather than claiming to represent reality directly onstage by concealing the workings of the theater, epic theater alerts the audience to the ideological dimension of theater practice by constantly keeping the stage's "means of production" in view. Brecht developed the **ALIENATION EFFECT** as a way of alerting the audience to the constructed nature of stage events. While the realistic theater claims that the theater and drama, actor and character, stage and dramatic locale are the same, epic theater shows how they are different. In so doing, Brecht argued, the epic theater enables the audience to ask how—with what purpose, to what effect—stage practice is making this dramatic effect come about, and so leads the audience to take a more critical view of the process of the theater. Epic acting, then, comments on itself as "acting." The stage is not unified as a single dramatic locale, but always remains visibly a stage. Brecht also argued that epic drama should be structured differently than realistic plays. Instead of the apparently organic, "causal" action of realistic drama, Brecht's plays are written in a series of episodes. This technique, Brecht argued, allows the actors and the audience to reconsider the character's possibilities for action and change afresh in each scene. By calling the audience's attention to how the play comes into being onstage, epic theater encourages the audience to develop a dialectical sense of how social reality—in the theater and in the world at large—comes into being, how it is made through the interaction of individual and social forces and the interaction of material reality and **IDEOLOGY.** Epic theater has had an enormous influence on drama and theater around the world.

Stage practice has developed its own rich history, too—again often in reaction to realistic verisimilitude. Throughout the twentieth century, for instance, designers and architects have experimented with different ways of orienting the audience to the stage, in **THEATER IN THE ROUND** and in **ENVIRONMENTAL THEATER,** for instance. To see the dramatic action surrounded by spectators or to have the play take place among the audience members alters the audience's relationship to both the drama and its performance and changes how they can read the production. The Constructivist experiments of Vsevolod Meyerhold following the Russian Revolution placed a nonrepresentational "construction" onstage, a structure that the actors used as a "machine for acting" rather than as a realistic set. Similarly, experimental performance altered notions of what dramatic and theatrical representation could be like. Following World War I, writers such as Tristan Tzara called for an art that was formless and irrational, a process rather than a product; such "Dada"—a nonsense term—poems, plays, and monologues were often given **CABARET PERFORMANCE** in Zurich, Berlin, and Paris. **DADA** and **SURREALIST THEATER** developed a kind of hallucinatory intimacy between stage and audience, laying the foundations for Artaud's **THEATER OF CRUELTY.** In all of these experiments, the theater worked to disperse the visual unity characteristic of the realistic stage in ways that led to new configurations of the relationship between the audience and the performers and to new interpretive perspectives on drama and the possibilities of theater.

Realism, expressionism, symbolist theater, and *epic theater*—these useful labels necessarily limit and categorize the rich variety of the stage in ways that are artificial and untrue to the dynamics of change in the modern theater, for new innovations tend to draw their techniques from several of these modes. Modern plays, for instance, often blend representational techniques as a way of challenging the audience's understanding of the drama and its implication in the world. Despite their "realistic" anchoring in a material, lifelike setting, for example, Chekhov's plays sometimes disturb the stability of that illusion with odd, almost "symbolic" effects—the breaking string in *The Cherry Orchard,* for instance. The action of Strindberg's *The Father,* too, for all the play's emphasis on domestic and social environment, seems to lurch and accelerate in ways more characteristic of an "expressionist" linking of the dramatic form to the characters' psychological experience. In Pirandello's *Six Characters in Search of an Author*—a play indebted in many ways to the "symbolist" theater—the Characters want the Actors to produce a play much in the manner of Ibsen's drama, a realistic drama of hidden crime and its discovery. These labels are useful in helping us to describe some of the outlines of a given play, but we should remember that many modern playwrights wrote in a variety of modes, and that each play is itself a kind of experiment.

The modern theater's radical redefinitions of the style and purpose of drama required similar redefinitions of acting and performance. At the turn of the century, a theatrical company would have been organized according to each actor's typical **LINE OF BUSINESS.** Something like the company in Pirandello's *Six Characters,* companies had a leading comic actor, a villain or "heavy," a leading man, a leading lady, a comic old man, a comic woman, and a variety of other parts. Unlike *commedia dell' arte,* actors each played a variety of different characters; nonetheless, each actor would have elaborated some relatively conventional "business" for acting the kind of character he or she usually played. The unity of illusion demanded by the realistic theater, however, required each character to be more finely individualized. Much as the stage designer provided a new set for each production and the

Acting And Performance

(ASIDE)
MELODRAMA

Although most of the plays included in *The Heinle Anthology of Drama* have been popular in the theater, they are all to some extent plays that have been canonized for their qualities as dramatic "literature": rich language and characterization, complex engagement with social and moral issues, deft and original use of dramatic convention, and so on. However, theater and drama pose special problems to the idea of a single literary canon. As popular entertainments, plays have not always been regarded as having "literary" merit. Plays were published only irregularly in Shakespeare's era partly for this reason, and even today few publishers have much commitment to keeping contemporary plays in print—which makes it particularly difficult for contemporary drama to become part of *any* literary canon. More important, plays are produced under very different conditions than novels and poems. Plays are made to be meaningful in a specific theater; their "literary" impact on readers is often secondary to their original purpose, which is to make a theatrical impact on a given body of spectators.

In late-eighteenth and nineteenth-century Europe—in part as a result of the relaxing of restrictions on theatrical performance, and in part as a reflection of a sense of "literature" as part of a circumscribed sphere of "high culture"—a variety of new dramatic genres became popular, of which the most important is **MELODRAMA.** The term was initially used to indicate plays in which music was used to accentuate the emotional coloring of the action; the term became more generally applied to plays with a conventionalized set of characters, a clear narrative structure, and a distinct moral cosmos. In the nineteenth-century theater, melodrama was an extremely popular genre, fusing the theater's increasing capacity for visual spectacle with a strongly colored and direct dramatic action. The world of melodrama is a world of clear-cut moral absolutes: the hero and heroine are thoroughly virtuous and are threatened by villains who are proportionately unscrupulous. The action is organized in a series of episodes, in each of which the hero/heroine's happiness, virtue, fortune, or life is threatened with destruction; each act of a melodrama usually ends with some striking crisis, often calling for an elaborate stage effect—an explosion, train wreck, or storm. The action of melodrama is often highly involved and coincidental, yet usually works eventually toward a happy—or at least sentimental—ending. If the hero must die, he usually dies in the heroine's arms; more often, the couple are restored to one another and live happily ever after.

Melodrama is usually dated from the popularity of plays like Johann Christoph Friedrich von Schiller's (1759–1805) *The Robbers* (1782), August Friedrich Ferdinand von Kotzebue's (1761–1819) *Menschenhass und Reue* (1789), and René Charles Guilbert de Pixérécourt's (1773–1844) *Coelina* (1800); although Kotzebue and Pixérécourt are now rarely read, their plays were widely adapted throughout Europe. Thirty-six of Kotzebue's plays were translated into English, and several remained popular throughout the nineteenth century. Richard Brinsley Sheridan (1751–1816) adapted Kotzebue's *Der Spanier in Peru* as *Pizarro* in 1799, which became a brilliant success for the actor John Philip Kembel; Thomas Holcroft (1744–1809) adapted Pixérécourt's *Coelina* as *A Tale of Mystery* in 1802. While early nineteenth-century melodrama tended toward Gothic settings—mysterious castles, ghostly visitors, and the like—by later in the century melodrama's typical formal and moral patterns were applied to plays with local and contemporary settings. Pierce Egan's novel *Life in London* was adapted as *Tom and Jerry; or, Life in London* in 1821; Edward George Bulwer-Lytton's (1803–1873) *Money* (1840) was one of several plays that held

costume designer provided clothing appropriate to the character and his or her setting, so the actors were forced to particularize their performances in new ways.

A second stimulus for this innovation was the drama itself. Playwrights like Ibsen and Chekhov typically created characters against the grain of theatrical stereotypes. Nora Helmer, for example, seems like a typical **SOUBRETTE** at the opening of *A Doll House,* the pert and clever young woman of light comedy. However, as the play develops, Ibsen challenges this convention and forces the actress to discover new ways of producing the character. Realistic plays frequently ask actors to work against the apparent "type" of the role, to discover the psychological subtext of will and desire beneath the spoken words that motivates the character's actions. Actors and actresses at the turn of the century frequently had difficulty reading the new realistic plays, precisely because they could not see how to represent the more indirect action and individualized characters through the kinds of stage behavior they had been trained to use.

the stage through the end of the century.

Since melodrama drew a wide audience, and often centered on poor-but-virtuous heroes and heroines, it has sometimes been thought to articulate social resistance. For while early versions like Douglas Jerrold's (1803–1857) hugely popular nautical melodrama *Black Ey'd Susan* (1829) emphasized the undying loyalty and patriotism of British navy sailors (or "tars"), the polarized moral ethos of melodrama could be turned into a vehicle for social critique. In the United States, melodrama became one vehicle for dramatizing ethnic and racial conflict. John Augustus Stone's (1800–1834) *Metamora; or, The Last of the Wampanoags* (1829), dramatized a heroic Indian chief's losing battle to save the land of his ancestors from his rapacious white enemies. In *The Octoroon* (1859), Dion Boucicault (1820–1890) staged the fatal love story between the octoroon Zoe, the virtuous plantation owner who loves her, and the wicked Yankee overseer, McCloskey, who threatens to buy her when it emerges that Zoe was never actually freed from slavery. Although these plays end with "tragic" consequences for their heroes and heroines, melodrama tends to locate its evils in the character of its villains, rather than in the structure of society itself: for this reason, melodrama is usually unable to

MELODRAMA: THE BELLS

Sir Henry Irving's (1838–1905) performance in Leopold Lewis's melodrama *The Bells* was one of his greatest roles. The illustration presents both the emotionally exaggerated quality of melodramatic acting and melodrama's use of special effects. In the play, Mathias (Irving's role) has murdered and concealed the body of a Polish Jew. Although many years have passed since the murder, Mathias is haunted by the sound of his victim's sleigh bells. In this scene, he staggers before a vision of the crime itself.

develop a deeper analysis of the social institutions—racism, for example—that afflict its characters' lives. When Bernard Shaw turned to melodrama as a vehicle for his own drama of social critique, he strategically inverted its patterns of characterization as a way of opening its social order to criticism: one way *Major Barbara,* for example, attempts to jolt the audience into examining its attitudes about society at large is by casting Andrew Undershaft—so similar to the scheming and all-powerful industrialist villain of countless popular melodramas—as the moral "hero" of the play.

A new kind of drama requires a new kind of acting, and companies throughout Europe developed ways of acting more behavioristically onstage. The most systematic approach to acting was undertaken by the actor and director Constantin Stanislavski at the Moscow Art Theater around the turn of the twentieth century. Although Stanislavski thought that his techniques could be applied to any play, he discovered the need for such acting largely in his work on Chekhov's plays. Chekhov's plays were frustrating to actors of the old school, because the characters did not conform to traditional types and the action seemed so indirect and inconsequential, lacking familiar dramatic rhythms and climaxes. Stanislavski developed techniques for approaching each character as an individual, techniques that were later systematized as a "method" of actor-training. Stanislavski trained the actor to associate his or her personal history with the invented actions of the dramatic character so that the actor could tap that emotional spontaneity, a "life in art," as part of the performance. By using the **MAGIC IF**—imagining themselves *as* the character, rather than applying a stock line of business—and using their own **EMOTION MEMORY** to vivify the character's inner life, Stanislavski's actors were taught to bring authentic emotional experience into their performances. Of course, Stanislavski also emphasized the many other abilities that an actor must develop—physical training, vocal control, grace, concentration—but his real contribution to the modern stage is the emphasis on the actor's emotional reality in performance. The realistic theater uses real objects to create a persuasive material environment, and its characters come alive through the actor's real feeling. Stanislavski's work has been extremely influential, particularly in the United States, where it was adapted as the school of **METHOD ACTING** in the 1930s, and it remains—in very different and modified forms—at the center of much actor-training today.

Antirealistic drama also called for the development of new styles of performance. Meyerhold developed **BIOMECHANICS** as a way to make the actor's performance more physical, less directly concerned with the behavioral and psychological verisimilitude typical of Stanislavskian realistic acting. His work has analogies in the use of dance and ritualized performance in symbolist theater and in the nonrepresentational physicality of Antonin Artaud's Theater of Cruelty. Symbolist theater also repudiated the lifelike quality of realistic acting. It required a highly artificial and statuesque stillness from performers, allowing the actors to strike powerful but ethereal poses in order to deliver the densely poetic language of the play without interference. Yeats—whose antipathy to realism was profound—thought of training his actors in barrels, to keep them from moving and gesturing as they would do in everyday life: the art of the symbolist theater should be emphatically artificial, thoroughly apart from the conduct of life beyond the stage.

Brecht, again, voiced the most thorough critique of realistic acting. To Brecht, the problem of realistic acting was that it showed the "character" as a finished product, a commodity, rather than revealing *how* the character had come into being, both through the social forces described in the drama and through the decisions taken by the actor as part of the performance. Brecht argued that the actor should acknowledge that he or she both empathizes with the character and demonstrates the character to the audience, that acting is both feeling and showing at the same time. This dialectical approach invites the audience to see how the actor is making the "character" and allows the public to interpret both the process and the product of theater art, the dramatic "character" and the actor's labor.

Women in Modern Drama and Theater

Most readers of modern drama immediately note the prominence of women characters in the plays—Nora Helmer in *A Doll House,* Vida Levering in *Votes for Women!*, Barbara in *Major Barbara,* Courage in *Mother Courage.* Playwrights frequently associated the political and social limitations of middle-class life with male characters and used female characters to pose subversive questions about that social order. However, in the drama, as in society, this subversive freedom sometimes emerges as illusory or problematic. Ibsen, for instance, enables Nora to recognize how she has been defined by the men in her life, but the world outside her home hardly seems inviting; is there really anywhere for her to go? Many of the women—the Stepdaughter of Pirandello's *Six Characters,* Major Barbara—are also assigned an erotic power opposed to the "reason" of their male antagonists. While this power, too, can be disruptive, it sometimes also reinforces traditional gender stereotypes. Feminine erotic power in the drama carries with it other ascribed values, defining women as more emotional, as more subject to the influence of the body, as closer to "nature." Men retain a pragmatic, "rational" authority that places them at the center of society, and that defines the arena of culture and civilization as an implicitly male domain. The apparent freedom of these stage women, that is, often signals their deeper captivity to the gendered economy of modern society, a captivity shared by actresses in the period as well. Although this is also a period in which actresses—Sarah Bernhardt, Eleonora Duse, Elizabeth Robins, or Ellen Terry, for example—could earn an international reputation, they worked in a theater in which men greatly outnumbered women in the audience and in which nearly all of the managers and producers were men. Women were also important playwrights throughout Europe in the first decades of the twentieth century: Elizabeth Robins's *Votes for Women!* brought the "woman question" to the English stage in 1907; Minna Canth was the leading playwright of the Finnish Theater (her portrait graces the proscenium of the National Theater today); Marieluise Fleisser's *Pioneers in Ingolstadt* (1924) in many ways rivaled Brecht's early vision of epic theater. In a male-dominated industry like the modern theater, it is not surprising that women onstage—both dramatic characters and performers—should reflect fundamentally masculine attitudes about the place of women in society.

To think of the history of theater and drama since Ibsen is to think of an increasingly large and problematic array of dramatic styles, modes of theatrical production, and conceptions of the audience and its world. Many of these innovations were local at first, responding to the social and theatrical conditions of a specific time and place: Brecht's Marxist theater arose in the cabaret culture of Berlin in the late 1920s; Pirandello's **METATHEATER** was part of the lively Italian avant-garde following World War I; Shaw's drama was informed by the progressive politics of the British Fabian Society and by dramatic conventions drawn from the popular plays of the late Victorian stage. The drama of modern Europe develops a posture of resistant inquiry toward the pieties of contemporary social life. It works both to represent that world and to change it, to affect our ideas about character and personality, about the political realities of our world, and even about the metaphysical certainties we have come to believe. But it is the impact of global political and cultural change that marks the theater of the second half of the twentieth century.

The impact of film and television has forced the theater to work to define what kinds of performance are specific to the stage, how live dramatic performances can offer something unique, something not already available in other performance media. For this reason, perhaps, theater and drama since 1950 have necessarily been "experimental," working to develop new kinds of plays, new practices of stage production, and new kinds of theatrical experience for their audiences. Much as the proscenium theaters of the early twentieth century have given way to other, more flexible kinds of theater spaces, so dramatic writing has become much more varied and experimental. Even stage realism—the mode of Ibsen and Chekhov, Miller and Williams—has undergone an important reworking in the plays of Sam Shepard, Harold Pinter, Heiner Müller, and others.

THEATER AND CULTURE SINCE 1950

Here, we can identify three patterns of innovation as a way of organizing our thinking about the diversity of the contemporary stage. One strategy—inspired most directly by Antonin Artaud's **THEATER OF CRUELTY**—attacks the notion that the theater is essentially a *representational* medium, emphasizing instead the *experiential* aspect of theater. Rather than staging images of some fictive world to an audience of passive spectators, this kind of theater works to structure the *present experience* of the audience in new ways, as in the participatory and ritualistic theater experiments of the 1960s and 1970s. The influence of Artaud's assault on representation is evident in the contemporary theater in several ways: in absurdist drama, in the focus on the body in Griselda Gambaro's *Information for Foreigners,* in the dreamlike density of Müller's *Hamletmachine,* among others.

The second mode of innovation, **THEATER OF THE ABSURD,** originated as a new form of playwriting rather than as theatrical experimentation. The plays of Samuel Beckett, Slawomir Mrozek, Eugène Ionesco, Boris Vian, Edward Albee, Harold Pinter, and others create a strangely dislocated dramatic world, in which arbitrary or "absurd" events both confront and mystify the characters.

While Artaud inspired an existential or experiential theater, Bertolt Brecht—whose work became widely known and imitated only after World War II—inspired a different kind

THEATER IN THE ROUND

In a theater in the round, the audience surrounds the action, rather than facing the stage as in a proscenium theater. Theater space of this kind lends itself to greater immediacy and contact between the performers and the audience.

of assault on the conventions of realistic theater. Contemporary **POLITICAL THEATER** also criticizes the notion of "representation," but in different terms than Artaud or theater of the absurd, *representation* is a word with two senses: in "representing" a picture of the world, the arts necessarily claim that their images are "representative" in some way. Political theater frequently shows how a social or political order uses its power to "represent" others coercively—for example, by depicting those others through demeaning or limiting stereotypes. For this reason, political theater today is intent on using live performance to change the prejudicial attitudes concealed in conventional ideas of representation.

Of course, no plays fit easily or fully into these three categories, but to think of the drama of the postwar period as raising questions of our existential or our political relation to the theater—and so to the world—provides a useful and powerful way of opening that drama to our understanding. Each of these modes of theater creates a different relationship between the stage and its audience, and we should examine each of them in some detail.

The writings of Antonin Artaud, particularly the essays collected in the volume *The Theater and Its Double* (written in the late 1920s and 1930s, published in France in 1938, translated to English in 1958), have had an extraordinary impact on our sense of theater. Like many innovators of his generation—think of Brecht or Pirandello—Artaud worked to undermine the notion that the theater can only show its audiences realistic vignettes of daily life. Instead, Artaud argued that the theater should alter the balance between presentation—the actual, immediate activities of actors and audiences, their *presence* in the theater—and representation, the fictive "drama" that had seemed to define the purpose and scope of theater. Artaud—who used the term *theater of cruelty* for this project—advocated transforming the theater into an all-consuming spectacle, akin both to rituals like the Catholic Mass and to public festivals, in which the boundaries between acting and observing, actor and spectator, fiction and reality, conscious and unconscious would be broken or transgressed. The idea that the theater would "communicate," but not through rational means, is captured in one of Artaud's most powerful metaphors for this nearly unimaginable theater: the plague. Artaud envisioned a theater that would transmit its experiences corporeally, through the body, like disease, like mystical wisdom, alchemically transforming all of its participants. To avoid staging conventional dramas, Artaud called for a theater of "no more masterpieces," one that would use the dramatic text to transform the relations between stage and spectator by making the production a total experience—visual, auditory, gustatory, olfactory, tactile, physical—for the audience.

Stage director Peter Brook once remarked that "Artaud applied is Artaud betrayed," and it is true that Artaud's sense of theater is deeply metaphorical, a kind of theater experience that is almost unimaginable to us, and certainly not imaginable to us as theater. Artaud rarely offers a practical description of how this theater could come into being. Instead, the value and influence of Artaud's writing has been indirect and inspirational, bearing in a variety of tangential ways on kinds of theater that are not in any literal sense "Artaudian." In that Artaud imagines a theater of *presence*—not of representation—involving the audience in an experience rather than showing them a picture, his theater comes into contact with several very different kinds of innovation. Although the American experimental theater of the 1960s and 1970s is the most direct application—and betrayal—of Artaud, Artaud's conception of theater stands distantly behind a variety of more formally constructed plays: the dislocating imagery of Beckett and Müller; the ritualized, hallucinatory violence of Pinter's plays; the elaborate physical rituals of Gao Xingjian's *The Other Shore*. Of course, as *written* plays, "masterpieces," these plays are specifically opposed to the ideals of Artaud's unrealizable theater, while at the same time they explore part of the terrain opened by Artaud's vision.

Coined by the theater critic Martin Esslin in 1961, the phrase *theater of the absurd* tries to capture the special irrationality and unpredictability of a certain wave of dramatic writing of the late 1950s and 1960s, including the plays of Samuel Beckett and Harold Pinter, for example. Taking as his keynote Beckett's famous play *Waiting for Godot* (1953)—a play in which two Chaplinesque tramps wait for a mysterious man named Godot, who never arrives—Esslin finds the theater of the absurd to have certain stylistic and thematic characteristics. It rejects the sense of causality found in realistic plays, the sense that it is possible to find the causes for events either in the environment or in the psychological motives of the characters themselves. Instead, theater of the absurd tends to be about a world in which inexplicable, arbitrary, or irrational events happen. Although the events usually seem to be part of some kind of order or scheme, it is an order that the characters and their audience cannot quite grasp. As Hamm says in Beckett's play *Endgame,* "Something is taking its course," but neither the characters nor the audience are ever sure what that "something" is. In Eugène Ionesco's play *Rhinoceros* (1960), the inhabitants of a small French village begin to turn inexplicably into rhinoceroses. In each act of Boris Vian's *The Empire Builders* (1959), a family moves to a smaller room in an apartment building, always accompanied by a mysterious, bandaged figure. In Slawomir Mrozek's

Artaud and the Theater of Cruelty

Theater of the Absurd

Striptease (1961), two men are commanded by a huge, silent finger to remove their clothes and don huge conical hats that conceal and blind them. As Esslin suggests, this drama insists that the fictions we use to make sense of our world—ideas of order, causality, rationality—are just that: fictions imposed on an arbitrary and mysterious reality, whose meanings remain fugitive and elusive.

Absurdist drama treats its audience somewhat differently than realistic plays do, rejecting the "dramatic irony" of the traditional theater, in which the audience understands more than the characters onstage. Instead, the theater of the absurd refuses to provide this privilege to its spectators. We are as baffled and frustrated by our attempts to make the events mean something as the characters are; "Mean something!" a character remarks in *Endgame*, "You and I, mean something! (*Brief laugh*)." Our *present* experience as an audience is structured and made significant by absurdist theatrical production. In the theater, we don't just observe the "absurd" drama onstage, we are forced to undergo it, to live it through. For this reason, both the drama onstage and the audience's experience in the theater are sometimes described as *existential*. We have to *decide* the meaning of our being in the theater, without the comfort, solace, or guidance of some transcendent, predetermined world view.

Political Theater

Much as theater of the absurd works to make the spectators' situation in the theater an extension of the characters' situation on the stage, political theater since Brecht has worked to make the audience's performance in the theater a recognizably political one. By fragmenting the stage space, by showing how the illusion is made rather than concealing its means of production, and by involving the audience more overtly in deciding the meaning of the play's events, the theater is shown to be a political instrument. Like television, newspapers, universities, the courts, and so on, the theater is an institution that produces the ideas and images with which we govern our lives. Both the example of Brecht's plays and his challenging theory of performance have been absorbed and redefined by the world theater. In common with theater of the absurd, political theater works to resist and complicate realistic representation, the "slice of life" of Ibsen, Chekhov, and Miller. Instead of staging an arbitrarily unreal and absurd world, political theater examines "representative" images of reality. Who makes those images? Who benefits from them? Who is injured, governed, or oppressed by them? How do they help to maintain the social *status quo*?

For this reason, much political theater connects representation onstage with representation in society, showing how various social groups—women, gay men, lesbians, ethnic and racial groups, the poor—have been staged in society and in the theater. A fundamental assumption of political theater is that these stereotypes are part of the larger system of discrimination that operates in society, and that they reveal the dominant attitudes of those who govern, control, or influence society from positions of power. In plays like Amiri Baraka's *Dutchman,* Caryl Churchill's *Cloud Nine,* and Wole Soyinka's *Death and the King's Horseman,* the racial conflicts informing contemporary society and culture are explored in very different ways: in relation to colonialism, to the mythologies of imperial history, to women's experience. These plays are very different in style, ranging from a kind of realism in *Death and the King's Horseman* to the testifying monologues of Anna Deavere Smith. It is not a single point of view or a single dramatic style that defines political theater, but the use of theatrical representation itself as a way to analyze representation in society at large.

A similar approach to theater informs many of the modern plays gathered in this anthology, for many of them explore the issue of representation: how Asia is represented in the minds of the West in David Henry Hwang's *M. Butterfly,* how the English remapped and so represented the Irish in their own language and political system in Brian Friel's *Translations,* how African tribal traditions are tragically misunderstood by British imperialists in Wole Soyinka's *Death and the King's Horseman,* how the Chicano and Anglo cultures interact in Luis Valdez's *Los Vendidos,* how torture and tourism are connected in Griselda Gambaro's *In-*

formation for Foreigners, or the literal consumption of the Third World by the First in Manjula Padmanabhan's *Harvest.* Political theater sometimes seems highly message oriented, overtly didactic to readers and audiences used to the more subtle instruction offered by realistic plays. Yet the messages of contemporary political theater tend to be fused into the process of theater, so that the politics of the play come into being not in the prepared script of the play but in our experience as an audience. All of these plays disrupt the expectations, attitudes, and preconceptions of the empowered audience and invite the audience to develop different ways of reading their society as part of their involvement in the play.

Drama, Theater, and the "Postmodern"

On the contemporary stage, though, these modes of theater do not work in isolation from one another, but interact with one another, as part of the dynamic means the theater uses to engage its audiences in an understanding of the world. Indeed, to describe the contemporary theater in terms of its historical inheritance from the modernist theater of Brecht, Artaud, and the absurdists is in an important sense to overlook what is most significant about the stage today: its break from the traditions of modernism. If we look at the range of contemporary performance activity, much of it has little to do with traditional drama. Think of the performance-art monologues of Spalding Gray (one of his best-known, *Swimming to Cambodia,* was made into a film by Jonathan Demme) or Karen Finley (whose work was at the center of the 1990 censorship controversy at the National Endowment for the Arts); of the music of Laurie Anderson; of video art and film; of music television and advertising; of the disorienting stage spectacles of Robert Wilson; even of "plays" like Peter Handke's *Offending the Audience* and *The Ride Across Lake Constance,* or Heiner Müller's *Hamletmachine,* or Samuel Beckett's later work for the theater, *Not I, Footfalls,* and *Ohio Impromptu.*

Theorists of culture and the arts have related these developments to innovations in the visual arts, in architecture, and in writing, characterizing their common features as **POSTMODERN.** The term itself is a difficult one, suggesting that these works often share some of the features of earlier, "modernist" art; the literary and cultural theorist Fredric Jameson suggests that the distinguishing feature of postmodern art is its attitude toward history. Jameson points out that postmodern works frequently invoke or appropriate the style of earlier historical periods, as in the use of neoclassical ornamentation in recent architecture, or the recollection of earlier film styles in more recent movies (**FILM NOIR** in *Chinatown* or *L.A. Confidential*). Jameson labels this technique **PASTICHE.** What is striking about these postmodern quotations of style, though, is not any systematic reinterpretation of tradition or any statement of value, but their tonelessness, their neutrality, the absence of the kind of moral and historical sense we might expect from the act of confronting history. In postmodern pastiche, the recollection of an earlier style does not provide a new understanding of the past, nor does it illuminate our contemporary historical situation. Instead, pastiche denatures that style by removing it from history, and history from it. Style becomes exactly that: simply another option. Hamm's many quotations from English literature in *Endgame* or the pastiche of Gilbert and Sullivan operetta in Churchill's *Cloud Nine* are perhaps part of this complex problem, for in each case the "past" is presented to the audience in terms of an artistic style that is largely emptied of its force as history.

Moreover, Jameson's discussion of pastiche also emphasizes the importance of the esthetic *surface* in postmodern art. Music video and advertising are sometimes taken as the paradigmatic postmodern forms, forms whose "message" lies almost exclusively in a rapidly changing, brilliantly seductive, series of images. Although this technique relates to the modernist use of **MONTAGE** in film and theater, it is different in several important ways. Modernist montage uses a series of images narratively, to tell a story. Although the camera cuts quickly from image to image, the audience assembles the images in a single complete narrative. Both the narrative and the interpreting spectator achieve a sense of wholeness. In contrast, postmodern images are juxtaposed in striking, sometimes contradictory combinations that resist our ability to impose a single narrative explanation, a single story line. Postmodern performance—on film or video or in the theater—is insistently fragmentary; it asserts the incompletion of the artistic object and the incomplete quality of the spectator's experience as well. Postmodern arts resist imposing a single explanatory interpretation that would both complete the narrative and confirm the audience's sense of wholeness, of self-integration. In this sense, postmodern arts are sometimes described as concerned with the "death of the subject." They question the possibility both of a comprehensible world and of a comprehending individual. By disorienting language, fragmenting narrative, and dispensing with such organizing principles as "plot" and "character," postmodern art claims that we have entered a new age in which the complex disconnections of modern culture have made obsolete many of our beliefs about the world and our ways of representing the world and ourselves.

MODERN EUROPEAN DRAMA IN PERFORMANCE AND HISTORY

The understanding of theater that was inaugurated in the mid-nineteenth century is in many respects continuous with our own today: although various experiments—environmental theater, theater of cruelty, performance art—have contributed to a rich sense of the diversity of theatrical performance forms today, to many people "going to the theater" means going to a specially designated building, sitting in a darkened auditorium, and watching the events that take place on the stage. Of course, this activity is shaped today by social and economic forces still just emerging in the early-modern period: whereas earlier audiences usually had a small number of theaters to turn to for performance, performances are available today in a wide range of spaces—subsidized state and municipal theaters throughout Europe, commercial theaters like those in London's West End and New York's Broadway, college and university playhouses, festival theaters like the annual festival at Grahamstown in South Africa or the Shaw Festival in Stratford, Ontario, and many more. Theater in the twentieth century is characterized by its "optional" character: we choose theater from among a range of other forms of dramatic performance, like film and television; the theaters we attend are positioned in their ambient cultures in a much wider variety of ways; and the performances we see tend to value their "uniqueness" rather than their conventionality in typically modern ways.

Moreover, while the performance practices of earlier European theaters were highly conventionalized—masks and *cothurni* for tragedy in Athens, the phallus for comedy; a standard comic or tragic stage set in the neoclassical theaters of France and Italy—in the modern period, the style of dramatic production has become much more varied, not only as a sign of the director's and designer's artistic signature in the production, but also as part of what the play has to sell to its audiences. Indeed, the invention of the stage director in the late nineteenth century is symptomatic of a trend in modernist esthetics more generally, a trend from the polished deployment of convention to an emphasis on the artwork's originality—an originality that signals the individual creative presence of an author or *auteur*. In earlier theaters, of course, someone usually had the responsibility of organizing and rehearsing the actors: this was sometimes the playwright in classical Athenian theater, or the company's leading actor, like David Garrick, in the later eighteenth century. But in these theaters, performance practice was extremely conventionalized: actors, like Shakespeare's, who have a solid line of business, don't really need much rehearsal—an actor whose typical line of business is comic old men will more or less have an approach ready for characters like Polonius. In the modern theater, however, the director has the responsibility for shaping the diverse talents of the company—set, costume, and lighting designs; acting; music—into a single whole, one that seems to deploy the performance in a unique way. Much as we think of a film as embodying the director's vision, so too in the theater the performance is often understood as an expression of the director's ability to shape the play, the players, and the physical milieu of the stage into a uniquely expressive whole.

For this reason, the modern theater is often called the "director's theater," and in many respects the history of modern stage practice is the history of the innovations of brilliant directors. Although naturalistic or realistic drama—the plays of Ibsen and Chekhov and O'Neill—are duly appreciated for their striking departures from the standard practices of nineteenth-century playwriting, transforming these innovations from the page to the stage required a generation of brilliant directors: Antoine, Stanislavski, Meyerhold, Max Reinhardt. Indeed, throughout the history of the modern theater, actors and directors have sometimes been baffled by the new demands of these scripts; Stanislavski, for example, can be understood to have devised his famous Method in response to the obliquity of Chekhov's plays. Similarly, when one thinks of the landmark theatrical productions of the twentieth-century European theater, they are always associated with the director: Stanislavski's productions of Chekhov at the turn of the century; Meyerhold's brilliant *Hedda Gabler,* with its white set and Hedda's brilliant, snakelike green dress; Piscator's work with Brecht in the 1920s, and Brecht's direction of the Berliner Ensemble in his own and others' plays after World War II; Peter Brook's use of the circus to realize the "magic" of Shakespeare's *A Midsummer Night's Dream* in 1970; Robert Wilson's visualization of Heiner Müller's *Hamletmachine* in the 1980s. As a consequence, one of the most energetic kinds of experiment in the later part of the century has been in the area of a more collaborative theater practice. Many contemporary theater companies are organized as collectives, in which responsibility for the "artistic" decisions is shared, rather than given over to a single person. But even in more conventional circumstances, companies often work to make the playwright's, actors', and designers' work have a more direct impact on the final stage of theater work. Caryl Churchill's play *Cloud Nine,* for example, arose from a series of workshops undertaken by members of the Joint Stock Company, in which the actors experimented by playing different gender, sexual, or racial roles in a variety of situations: Churchill wrote the text of the play out of the workshops, and director Max Stafford-Clark used the results of the workshops as a foundation for the play's theatrical performance. Given the increasing complexity of theatrical production—the use not only of complex technology backstage, but the inclusion of multimedia production as part of the performance itself—we can expect that this struggle to shape the authority of the stage will continue well into the future.

Notes for the Modern Tragedy

Rome, 19. 10, 78.

There are two kinds of spiritual law, two kinds of conscience, one in man and another, altogether different, in woman. They do not understand each other; but in practical life the woman is judged by man's law, as though she were not a woman but a man.

The wife in the play ends by having no idea of what is right or wrong; natural feeling on the one hand and belief in authority on the other have altogether bewildered her.

A woman cannot be herself in the society of the present day, which is an exclusively masculine society, with laws framed by men and with a judicial system that judges feminine conduct from a masculine point of view.

She has committed forgery, and she is proud of it; for she did it out of love for her husband, to save his life. But this husband with his commonplace principles of honour is on the side of the law and regards the question with masculine eyes.

Spiritual conflicts. Oppressed and bewildered by the belief in authority, she loses faith in her moral right and ability to bring up her children. Bitterness. A mother in modern society, like certain insects who go away and die when she has done her duty in the propagation of the race.[1] Love of life, of home, of husband and children and family. Here and there a wom-

---

[1] The sentence is elliptical in the original.

READING THE MATERIAL THEATER

Compared with the documentary record of earlier theaters, the modern theater offers an embarrassment of riches: not only is the print tradition rich in reviews, memoirs, and other accounts of the production and reception of plays in the theater, but also playwrights themselves have often left working drafts of their plays. Henrik Ibsen is particularly notable in this regard: an extremely disciplined and methodical writer, Ibsen not only began most of his plays with a detailed scenario; he retained many of the successive drafts of his plays. These materials provide a unique insight into the process of Ibsen's imagination, and indeed into his practice as a writer as well.

What follows are Ibsen's "Notes for the Modern Tragedy," dated 19 October 1878, and his original scenario for *A Doll House*. Not surprisingly, perhaps, many of the elements of the finished play remain in this outline. At the same time, this document differs from the final drama in a number of respects (including some of the characters' names). Granted that a scenario necessarily tends to streamline the action and emphasize the plot of the play, do you find this scenario surprising in any way? Does it seem to present the same kinds of moral or ethical emphases you find in the play? Are there elements of the finished play that seem larger or more powerful than you might have expected from this scenario alone? Are there elements of the scenario that are less prominent in the final draft? The final lines of the scenario are particularly chilling: "Five:—seven hours till midnight. Twenty-four hours till the next midnight. Twenty-four and seven—thirty-one. Thirty-one hours to live. . . ." How do these lines figure in Ibsen's final imagining of the action of the finale of *A Doll House?*

anly shaking-off of her thoughts. Sudden return of anxiety and terror. She must bear it all alone. The catastrophe approaches, inexorably, inevitably. Despair, conflict and destruction.

(Krogstad has acted dishonourably and thereby become well-to-do; now his prosperity does not help him, he cannot recover his honour.)

PERSONS

STENBORG, a Government clerk.

NORA, his wife.

MISS (MRS.) LIND (, a widow).

ATTORNEY KROGSTAD.

KAREN, nurse at the Stenborgs'.

A PARLOUR-MAID at the Stenborgs'.

A PORTER.

THE STENBORGS' THREE LITTLE CHILDREN.

DOCTOR HANK.

SCENARIO

FIRST ACT

A room comfortably, but not showily, furnished. In the back, on the right, a door leads to the hall; on the left another door leads to the room or office of the master of the house, which can be seen when the door is opened. A fire in the stove. Winter day.

She enters from the back, humming gaily; she is in outdoor dress and carries several parcels, has been shopping. As she opens the door, a Porter is seen in the hall, carrying a Christmas-tree. She: Put it down there for the present. (Taking out her purse) How much? Porter: Fifty öre. She: Here is a crown. No, keep the change. The Porter thanks her and goes. She continues humming and smiling with quiet glee as she opens several of the parcels she has brought. Calls off, is he at home? Yes! At first, conversation through the closed door; then he opens it and goes on talking to her while continuing to work most of the time, standing at his desk. There is a ring at the hall-door; he does not want to be disturbed; shuts himself in. The maid opens the door to her mistress's friend, just arrived in town. Happy surprise. Mutual explanation of the position of affairs. He has received the post of manager in the new joint-stock bank and is to enter on his duties at the New Year; all financial worries are at an end. The friend has come to town to look for some small employment in an office or whatever may present itself. Mrs. Stenborg gives her good hopes, is certain that all will turn out well. The maid opens the front-door to the debt-collector. Mrs. Stenborg terrified; they exchange a few words; he is shown into the office. Mrs. Stenborg and her friend; the circumstances of the debt-collector are touched upon. Stenborg enters in his overcoat; has sent the collector out the other way. Conversation about the friend's affairs; hesitation on his part. He and the friend go out; his wife follows them into the hall; the Nurse enters with the children. Mother and children play. The collector enters. Mrs. Stenborg sends the children out to the left. Great scene between her and him. He goes. Stenborg enters; has met him on the stairs; displeased; wants to know what he came back for? Her support? No intrigues. His wife cautiously tries to pump him. Strict legal answers. Exit to his room. She (repeating her words when the collector went out) But that's impossible. Why, I did it from love!

SCENARIO

SECOND ACT

The last day of the year. Midday. Nora and the old Nurse. Nora, impelled by uneasiness, is putting on her things to go out. Anxious random questions of one kind and another give a hint that thoughts of death are in her mind. Tries to banish these thoughts, to turn it off, hopes that something or other may intervene. But what? The Nurse goes off to the left.—Stenborg enters from his room. Short dialogue between him and Nora.—The Nurse re-enters, looking for Nora; the youngest child is crying. Annoyance and questioning on Stenborg's part; exit the Nurse; Stenborg is going in to the children.—Doctor Hank enters. Scene between him and Stenborg.—Nora soon re-enters; she has turned back; anxiety has driven her home again. Scene between her, the Doctor and Stenborg. Stenborg goes into his room.—Scene between Nora and the Doctor. The Doctor goes out.—Nora alone.—Mrs. Linde enters. Scene between her and Nora.—Krogstad enters. Short scene between him, Mrs. Linde and Nora. Mrs. Linde goes in to the children.—Scene between Krogstad and Nora.—she entreats and implores him for the sake of her little children; in vain. Krogstad goes out. The letter is seen to fall from outside into the letter-box.—Mrs. Linde re-enters after a short pause. Scene between her and Nora. Half confession. Mrs. Linde goes out.—Nora alone.—Stenborg enters. Scene between him and Nora. He wants to empty the letter-box. Entreaties, jests, half playful persuasion. He promises to let business wait till after New Year's Day; but at 12 o'clock midnight—! Exit. Nora alone. Nora (looking at the clock:) It is five o'clock. Five;—seven hours till midnight. Twenty-four hours till the next midnight. Twenty-four and seven—thirty-one. Thirty-one hours to live.—

THIRD ACT

(A muffled sound of dance music is heard from the floor above. A lighted lamp on the table. Mrs. Linde sits in an armchair and absently turns the pages of a book, tries to read, but seems unable to fix her attention; once or twice she looks at her watch. Nora comes down from the dance; uneasiness has driven her; surprise at finding Mrs. Linde, who pretends that she wanted to see Nora in her costume. Helmer, displeased at her going away, comes to fetch her back. The Doctor also enters, but to say good-bye. Meanwhile Mrs. Linde has gone into the side room on the right. Scene between the Doctor, Helmer and Nora. He is going to bed, he says, never to get up again; they are not to come and see him; there is ugliness about a death-bed. He goes out. Helmer goes upstairs again with Nora, after the latter has exchanged a few words of farewell with Mrs. Linde. Mrs. Linde alone. Then Krogstad. Scene and explanation between them. Both go out. Nora and the children. Then she alone. Then Helmer. He takes the letters out of the letter-box. Short scene; good-night; he goes into his room. Nora in despair prepares for the final step; is ready at the door when Helmer enters with the open letter in his hand. Great scene. A ring. Letter to Nora from Krogstad. Final scene. Divorce. Nora leaves the house.—

In this production of Luigi Pirandello's *Six Characters in Search of an Author*, the statuesque "characters" arrive at the stage door, clothed in black and bathed in an eerie light.

In this scene from Henrik Ibsen's *A Doll House*, Doctor Rank, Helmer, and Nora have just returned from the party; Nora wears her tarantella costume, and Helmer has been given a "mask" of middle-class respectability.

The photograph of the Moscow Art Theater's original production of Anton Chekhov's *The Cherry Orchard* shows the naturalistic detail for which Constantin Stanislavski's company was famous; Stanislavski is at the left in the role of Gaev, gesturing to the bookcase.

Henrik Ibsen

At the turn of the century, Henrik Ibsen's name was synonymous with modernity in the European theater; much of the territory of modern drama was first explored in Ibsen's work. Born into a mercantile family in provincial Norway, Ibsen (1828–1906) had planned to study medicine; however, after failing to matriculate at the university, he turned to a career as a writer. From 1850 through 1864, Ibsen worked for the nationalist Norwegian Theater in Bergen and then for the Mollergate Theater in Christiania (now Oslo). As literary manager, stage manager, and assistant to the director, Ibsen learned the craft of practical theater firsthand. He also wrote a series of romantic history plays, some in prose and some in verse. Although his fame now rests on the realistic plays he wrote later in his career, in his own lifetime these history plays—such as *The Vikings at Helgeland* (1858)—were quite popular, especially in Norway.

In 1864, Ibsen left Norway and settled in Rome, where he wrote two pivotal plays, *Brand* (1866) and *Peer Gynt* (1867). The story of an idealistic minister, *Brand* established Ibsen as an important European writer and announced one of his central themes: the cost of moral idealism in the modern world. *Peer Gynt* is often taken as a companion-piece to *Brand,* for Peer's picaresque journey throughout Europe is undertaken simply for the purpose of his own self-satisfaction: while Brand's motto is "Be wholly what you are," Peer Gynt's is "To thine own self be . . . enough." In 1877, after extensive work on the Hegelian history drama *Emperor and Galilean,* Ibsen wrote *Pillars of Society,* a prose drama of modern life, inaugurating the stunning series of plays that made him famous and established the contours of modern realistic drama. In *A Doll House* (1879), *Ghosts* (1881), and *An Enemy of the People* (1882), Ibsen explored the conflict between the social and moral restrictions of bourgeois society and the psychological, often unconscious, demands of individual freedom. Ibsen adapted the suspenseful, rigorously plotted form of the **WELL-MADE PLAY** (or *pièce bien faite*) popularized throughout Europe by French playwrights Eugène Scribe and Victorien Sardou and used it in plays of modern life critical of bourgeois morality and society. The well-made play is notoriously difficult to define, even though its features are familiar: a rigorously "causal" plot, a secret gradually revealed to the audience, a "necessary scene" (the *scène-à-faire*) in which the secret is revealed to the characters, a character (the *raisonneur*) who explains and moralizes the action to the others, and a predominance of coincidental events. In his earlier plays, Ibsen takes these formal conventions and makes them function as forces in the dramatic world. The world of the play comes to seem mechanistic, determined by a secret that will out, full of busybodies explaining and interpreting the action. The mechanics of the well-made play, that is, are identified with the deadening force of social convention, which painfully threatens to extinguish the vitality of the central characters. This conflict between deadening social convention and a mysterious inner vitality pervades Ibsen's mature plays as well, which increasingly moved away from the "well-made" form: *The Wild Duck* (1885), *Rosmersholm* (1887), *The Lady from the Sea* (1888), and *Hedda Gabler* (1890). Ibsen's last plays seem more poetic or symbolic, though they take place in the familiar milieu of the realistic stage: *The Master Builder* (1892), *Little Eyolf* (1894), *John Gabriel Borkman* (1896), and the unfinished *When We Dead Awaken* (1900). Ibsen suffered a paralyzing series of strokes in 1900 that left him unable to write. He died in 1906.

Ibsen's effect on his contemporaries and his influence on the course of modern drama were immediate and profound. His plays were rapidly translated into the major European languages, and stage productions—which often inaugurated the new "independent" theaters—frequently became the subject of sensation and controversy. Indeed, "Ibsenism" came to be a catchword for a variety of social causes, though Ibsen himself generally avoided politics. Although Ibsen's plays brought new issues to the stage, it was his practice as a playwright that proved truly revolutionary. Many playwrights had adopted the realistic theater's use of a material stage environment, its emphasis on the burden of the past, and its sense of a mechanized and constricting society. Ibsen not only used this material with powerful subtlety and resonance, he gave the stage its first distinctively modern characters: complex, contradictory individuals driven by a desire for something—the "joy of life," a sense of themselves—that they can barely recognize or name.

A DOLL HOUSE

A Doll House was inspired by a series of incidents that came to Ibsen's attention in 1878 when a woman named Laura Kieler contacted him. Kieler had signed a secret—and illegal—loan to raise money for a cure for her tubercular husband. She wrote to Ibsen asking him to recommend the novel she had written to his publisher, in hopes that the profits from its sale would allow her to repay the loan. Ibsen refused. Kieler forged a check and was caught. Her husband committed her to an asylum, had her charged as an unfit mother, and demanded a legal separation. When she was released from the asylum, however, the family remained together.

We can see the shaping power of Ibsen's imagination in his transformation of Laura Kieler's tragedy into the ironic masterpiece, *A Doll House*. The play, which by the turn of the century was a rallying point for international feminist demands for the vote and for other legal rights and protections for women, organizes the conflict between Nora and Helmer around a subtle set of contrasts: the childlike and protected Nora and the world-weary Mrs. Linde; the upright and protective Helmer and the shady—yet finally generous—Krogstad; the privations of the past and the financial freedom Nora sees on the horizon. However, as the play proceeds, the stable, bourgeois world that Helmer represents is revealed as a tissue of deception; the institutions of marriage, respectability, and social justice turn out to be fictions that the privileged use to manipulate their world. Nora comes to seem effective, efficient, worldly wise, and finally independent, while Helmer readily compromises his principles to save his reputation. The world of financial freedom Nora glimpses at the play's outset turns out to be a kind of prison and is replaced by another kind of freedom at the end of the play: the frightening freedom to cut herself loose from the bonds of marriage, family, and society.

Helmer had more authority with audiences in the 1880s and 1890s than he does today, and Nora was conventionally criticized as an "unwomanly woman" for taking the loan, deceiving her husband, and leaving her family. Indeed, the first English actress to be offered

Owen Teale and Janet McTeer in Henrik Ibsen's *A Doll House*, in the 1997 production using a new translation by Frank McGuinness.

the part turned it down, because she didn't want audiences to think of her as the kind of woman who would desert her children. Yet the play tends to validate Nora's personal growth and her final decision to leave her family and cannily uses the material environment of the stage setting to convey the suffocating situation in which Nora finds herself.

The play takes place in one room: the drawing room where the upwardly mobile Helmers (deluxe books on the shelf, piano against the wall, framed art prints) receive their guests and conduct their lives. The room itself represents the Helmers' concern for social status and assumes a symbolic importance as well: it stands between the unseen privacy of the kitchen and bedroom—the domestic world of marriage and children—and the threatening public world beyond the front door, the world of Krogstad, of the dark and icy river, of Nora's final escape. The room becomes a kind of prison, a room in which Rank's declaration of love for Nora seems inappropriate, in which Helmer criticizes her dizzying tarantella—a Sicilian dance thought to imitate the death throes of someone bitten by a tarantula—as too abandoned, and in which Nora's final discussion with Helmer makes her submission to him impossible. That is, the room makes concrete the play's concern for the social constraints on a woman's life, becoming a visual image of how Helmer's masculine, bourgeois moral authority imprisons Nora. It is not entirely clear that Nora can survive in the harsh social and economic climate outside the comfortable parlor, but it is clear that escape from the parlor is her final alternative.

A Doll House was a successful—and a scandalous—play throughout Europe in the last decades of the nineteenth century, and it has remained in the repertoire ever since. Nora has always been associated with feminist politics, and several productions in the 1960s and 1970s saw in *A Doll House* an anticipatory allegory of the women's movement. Indeed, whereas Helmer appeared to 1880s audiences as a romantic leading man, the challenge for contemporary productions is to make him appear sympathetic, someone worth Nora's years of sacrifice, and someone she will have to struggle to leave.

A DOLL HOUSE

Henrik Ibsen

TRANSLATED BY ROLF FJELDE

CHARACTERS

TORVALD HELMER, *a lawyer*
NORA, *his wife*
DR. RANK
MRS. LINDE
NILS KROGSTAD, *a bank clerk*
THE HELMERS' THREE SMALL CHILDREN

ANNE-MARIE, *their nurse*
A MAID, *Helene*
A DELIVERY BOY

The action takes place in Helmer's residence

ACT ONE

A comfortable room, tastefully but not expensively furnished. A door to the right in the back wall leads to the entryway; another to the left leads to HELMER's *study. Between these doors, a piano. Midway in the left-hand wall a door, and further back a window. Near the window a round table with an armchair and a small sofa. In the right-hand wall, toward the rear, a door, and nearer the foreground a porcelain stove with two armchairs and a rocking chair beside it. Between the stove and the side door, a small table. Engravings on the walls. An etagère with china figures and other small art objects; a small bookcase with richly bound books; the floor carpeted; a fire burning in the stove. It is a winter day.*

A bell rings in the entryway; shortly after we hear the door being unlocked. NORA *comes into the room, humming happily to herself; she is wearing street clothes and carries an armload of packages, which she puts down on the table to the right. She has left the hall door open; and through it a* DELIVERY BOY *is seen, holding a Christmas tree and a basket, which he gives to the* MAID *who let them in.*

NORA: Hide the tree well, Helene. The children mustn't get a glimpse of it till this evening, after it's trimmed. (*To the* DELIVERY BOY, *taking out her purse.*) How much?

DELIVERY BOY: Fifty, ma'am.

5   NORA: There's a crown. No, keep the change. (*The* BOY *thanks her and leaves.* NORA *shuts the door. She laughs softly to herself while taking off her street things. Drawing a bag of macaroons from her pocket, she eats a couple, then steals over and listens at her husband's study door.*) Yes, he's home. (*Hums again as she*

10 *moves to the table right.*)

HELMER: (*From the study.*) Is that my little lark twittering out there?

NORA: (*Busy opening some packages.*) Yes, it is.

HELMER: Is that my squirrel rummaging around?

15 NORA: Yes!

HELMER: When did my squirrel get in?

NORA: Just now. (*Putting the macaroon bag in her pocket and wiping her mouth.*) Do come in, Torvald, and see what I've bought.

20 HELMER: Can't be disturbed. (*After a moment he opens the door and peers in, pen in hand.*) Bought, you say? All that there? Has the little spendthrift been out throwing money around again?

NORA: Oh, but Torvald, this year we really should let ourselves

25 go a bit. It's the first Christmas we haven't had to economize.

HELMER: But you know we can't go squandering.

NORA: Oh yes, Torvald, we can squander a little now. Can't we? Just a tiny, wee bit. Now that you've got a big salary and are going to make piles and piles of money.

HELMER: Yes—starting New Year's. But then it's a full three   30
months till the raise comes through.

NORA: Pooh! We can borrow that long.

HELMER: Nora! (*Goes over and playfully takes her by the ear.*) Are your scatterbrains off again? What if today I borrowed a thousand crowns, and you squandered them over Christ-   35
mas week, and then on New Year's Eve a roof tile fell on my head, and I lay there—

NORA: (*Putting her hand on his mouth.*) Oh! Don't say such things!

HELMER: Yes, but what if it happened—then what?   40

NORA: If anything so awful happened, then it just wouldn't matter if I had debts or not.

HELMER: Well, but the people I'd borrowed from?

NORA: Them? Who cares about them! They're strangers.

HELMER: Nora, Nora, how like a woman! No, but seriously,   45
Nora, you know what I think about that. No debts! Never borrow! Something of freedom's lost—and something of beauty, too—from a home that's founded on borrowing and debt. We've made a brave stand up to now, the two of us; and we'll go right on like that the little while we have to.   50

NORA: (*Going toward the stove.*) Yes, whatever you say, Torvald.

HELMER: (*Following her.*) Now, now, the little lark's wings mustn't droop. Come on, don't be a sulky squirrel. (*Taking out his wallet.*) Nora, guess what I have here.

NORA: (*Turning quickly.*) Money!   55

HELMER: There, see. (*Hands her some notes.*) Good grief, I know how costs go up in a house at Christmastime.

NORA: Ten—twenty—thirty—forty. Oh, thank you, Torvald; I can manage no end on this.

HELMER: You really will have to.   60

NORA: Oh yes, I promise I will! But come here so I can show you everything I bought. And so cheap! Look, new clothes for Ivar here—and a sword. Here a horse and a trumpet for Bob. And a doll and a doll's bed here for Emmy; they're nothing much, but she'll tear them to bits in no time any-   65
way. And here I have dress material and handkerchiefs for the maids. Old Anne-Marie really deserves something more.

HELMER: And what's in that package there?

NORA: (*With a cry.*) Torvald, no! You can't see that till tonight!

HELMER: I see. But tell me now, you little prodigal, what have   70
you thought of for yourself?

NORA: For myself? Oh, I don't want anything at all.

HELMER: Of course you do. Tell me just what—within reason—you'd most like to have.

75 NORA: I honestly don't know. Oh, listen, Torvald—

HELMER: Well?

NORA: (*Fumbling at his coat buttons, without looking at him.*) If you want to give me something, then maybe you could— you could—

80 HELMER: Come on, out with it.

NORA: (*Hurriedly.*) You could give me money, Torvald. No more than you think you can spare; then one of these days I'll buy something with it.

HELMER: But Nora—

85 NORA: Oh, please, Torvald darling, do that! I beg you, please. Then I could hang the bills in pretty gilt paper on the Christmas tree. Wouldn't that be fun?

HELMER: What are those little birds called that always fly through their fortunes?

90 NORA: Oh yes, spendthrifts; I know all that. But let's do as I say, Torvald; then I'll have time to decide what I really need most. That's very sensible, isn't it?

HELMER: (*Smiling.*) Yes, very—that is, if you actually hung onto the money I give you, and you actually used it to buy your-

95 self something. But it goes for the house and for all sorts of foolish things, and then I only have to lay out some more.

NORA: Oh, but Torvald—

HELMER: Don't deny it, my dear little Nora. (*Putting his arm around her waist.*) Spendthrifts are sweet, but they use up a

100 frightful amount of money. It's incredible what it costs a man to feed such birds.

NORA: Oh, how can you say that! Really, I save everything I can.

HELMER: (*Laughing.*) Yes, that's the truth. Everything you can.

105 But that's nothing at all.

NORA: (*Humming, with a smile of quiet satisfaction.*) Hm, if you only knew what expenses we larks and squirrels have, Torvald.

HELMER: You're an odd little one. Exactly the way your father

110 was. You're never at a loss for scaring up money; but the moment you have it, it runs right out through your fingers; you never know what you've done with it. Well, one takes you as you are. It's deep in your blood. Yes, these things are hereditary, Nora.

115 NORA: Ah, I could wish I'd inherited many of Papa's qualities.

HELMER: And I couldn't wish you anything but just what you are, my sweet little lark. But wait; it seems to me you have a very—what should I call it?—a very suspicious look today—

120 NORA: I do?

HELMER: You certainly do. Look me straight in the eye.

NORA: (*Looking at him.*) Well?

HELMER: (*Shaking an admonitory finger.*) Surely my sweet tooth hasn't been running riot in town today, has she?

125 NORA: No. Why do you imagine that?

HELMER: My sweet tooth really didn't make a little detour through the confectioner's?

NORA: No, I assure you, Torvald—

HELMER: Hasn't nibbled some pastry?

130 NORA: No, not at all.

HELMER: Not even munched a macaroon or two?

NORA: No, Torvald, I assure you, really—

HELMER: There, there now. Of course I'm only joking.

NORA: (*Going to the table, right.*) You know I could never think of going against you.   135

HELMER: No, I understand that; and you *have* given me your word. (*Going over to her.*) Well, you keep your little Christmas secrets to yourself, Nora darling. I expect they'll come to light this evening, when the tree is lit.

NORA: Did you remember to ask Dr. Rank?   140

HELMER: No. But there's no need for that; it's assumed he'll be dining with us. All the same, I'll ask him when he stops by here this morning. I've ordered some fine wine. Nora, you can't imagine how I'm looking forward to this evening.

NORA: So am I. And what fun for the children, Torvald!   145

HELMER: Ah, it's so gratifying to know that one's gotten a safe, secure job, and with a comfortable salary. It's a great satisfaction, isn't it?

NORA: Oh, it's wonderful!

HELMER: Remember last Christmas? Three whole weeks be-   150 fore, you shut yourself in every evening till long after midnight, making flowers for the Christmas tree, and all the other decorations to surprise us. Ugh, that was the dullest time I've ever lived through.

NORA: It wasn't at all dull for me.   155

HELMER: (*Smiling.*) But the outcome *was* pretty sorry, Nora.

NORA: Oh, don't tease me with that again. How could I help it that the cat came in and tore everything to shreds.

HELMER: No, poor thing, you certainly couldn't. You wanted so much to please us all, and that's what counts. But it's   160 just as well that the hard times are past.

NORA: Yes, it's really wonderful.

HELMER: Now I don't have to sit here alone, boring myself, and you don't have to tire your precious eyes and your fair little delicate hands—   165

NORA: (*Clapping her hands.*) No, is it really true, Torvald, I don't have to? Oh, how wonderfully lovely to hear! (*Taking his arm.*) Now I'll tell you just how I've thought we should plan things. Right after Christmas—(*The doorbell rings.*) Oh, the bell. (*Straightening the room up a bit.*) Some-   170 body would have to come. What a bore!

HELMER: I'm not at home to visitors, don't forget.

MAID: (*From the hall doorway.*) Ma'am, a lady to see you—

NORA: All right, let her come in.

MAID: (*To* HELMER.) And the doctor's just come too.   175

HELMER: Did he go right to my study?

MAID: Yes, he did.

(HELMER *goes into his room. The* MAID *shows in* MRS. LINDE, *dressed in traveling clothes, and shuts the door after her.*)

MRS. LINDE: (*In a dispirited and somewhat hesitant voice.*) Hello, Nora.

NORA: (*Uncertain.*) Hello—   180

MRS. LINDE: You don't recognize me.

NORA: No, I don't know—but wait, I think—(*Exclaiming.*) What! Kristine! Is it really you?

MRS. LINDE: Yes, it's me.

NORA: Kristine! To think I didn't recognize you. But then,   185 how could I? (*More quietly.*) How you've changed, Kristine!

MRS. LINDE: Yes, no doubt I have. In nine—ten long years.

NORA: Is it so long since we met! Yes, it's all of that. Oh, these last eight years have been a happy time, believe me. And

190 so now you've come in to town, too. Made the long trip in the winter. That took courage.

MRS. LINDE: I just got here by ship this morning.

NORA: To enjoy yourself over Christmas, of course. Oh, how lovely! Yes, enjoy ourselves, we'll do that. But take your
195 coat off. You're not still cold? (*Helping her.*) There now, let's get cozy here by the stove. No, the easy chair there! I'll take the rocker here. (*Seizing her hands.*) Yes, now you have your old look again; it was only in that first moment. You're a bit more pale, Kristine—and maybe a bit thinner.

200 MRS. LINDE: And much, much older, Nora.

NORA: Yes, perhaps a bit older; a tiny, tiny bit; not much at all. (*Stopping short; suddenly serious.*) Oh, but thoughtless me, to sit here, chattering away. Sweet, good Kristine, can you forgive me?

205 MRS. LINDE: What do you mean, Nora?

NORA: (*Softly.*) Poor Kristine, you've become a widow.

MRS. LINDE: Yes, three years ago.

NORA: Oh, I knew it, of course; I read it in the papers. Oh, Kristine, you must believe me; I often thought of writing
210 you then, but I kept postponing it, and something always interfered.

MRS. LINDE: Nora dear, I understand completely.

NORA: No, it was awful of me, Kristine. You poor thing, how much you must have gone through. And he left you noth-
215 ing?

MRS. LINDE: No.

NORA: And no children?

MRS. LINDE: No.

NORA: Nothing at all, then?

220 MRS. LINDE: Not even a sense of loss to feed on.

NORA: (*Looking incredulously at her.*) But Kristine, how could that be?

MRS. LINDE: (*Smiling wearily and smoothing her hair.*) Oh, sometimes it happens, Nora.

225 NORA: So completely alone. How terribly hard that must be for you. I have three lovely children. You can't see them now; they're out with the maid. But now you must tell me everything—

MRS. LINDE: No, no, no, tell me about yourself.

230 NORA: No, you begin. Today I don't want to be selfish. I want to think only of you today. But there *is* something I must tell you. Did you hear of the wonderful luck we had recently?

MRS. LINDE: No, what's that?

235 NORA: My husband's been made manager in the bank, just think!

MRS. LINDE: Your husband? How marvelous!

NORA: Isn't it? Being a lawyer is such an uncertain living, you know, especially if one won't touch any cases that aren't
240 clean and decent. And of course Torvald would never do that, and I'm with him completely there. Oh, we're simply delighted, believe me! He'll join the bank right after New Year's and start getting a huge salary and lots of commissions. From now on we can live quite differ-
245 ently—just as we want. Oh, Kristine, I feel so light and happy! Won't it be lovely to have stacks of money and not a care in the world?

MRS. LINDE: Well, anyway, it would be lovely to have enough for necessities.

250 NORA: No, not just for necessities, but stacks and stacks of money!

MRS. LINDE: (*Smiling.*) Nora, Nora, aren't you sensible yet? Back in school you were such a free spender.

NORA: (*With a quiet laugh.*) Yes, that's what Torvald still says.
255 (*Shaking her finger.*) But "Nora, Nora" isn't as silly as you all think. Really, we've been in no position for me to go squandering. We've had to work, both of us.

MRS. LINDE: You too?

NORA: Yes, at odd jobs—needlework, crocheting, embroidery,
260 and such—(*Casually.*) and other things too. You remember that Torvald left the department when we were married? There was no chance of promotion in his office, and of course he needed to earn more money. But that first year he drove himself terribly. He took on all kinds of ex-
265 tra work that kept him going morning and night. It wore him down, and then he fell deathly ill. The doctors said it was essential for him to travel south.

MRS. LINDE: Yes, didn't you spend a whole year in Italy?

NORA: That's right. It wasn't easy to get away, you know. Ivar
270 had just been born. But of course we had to go. Oh, that was a beautiful trip, and it saved Torvald's life. But it cost a frightful sum, Kristine.

MRS. LINDE: I can well imagine.

NORA: Four thousand, eight hundred crowns it cost. That's
275 really a lot of money.

MRS. LINDE: But it's lucky you had it when you needed it.

NORA: Well, as it was, we got it from Papa.

MRS. LINDE: I see. It was just about the time your father died.

NORA: Yes, just about then. And, you know, I couldn't make
280 that trip out to nurse him. I had to stay here, expecting Ivar any moment, and with my poor sick Torvald to care for. Dearest Papa, I never saw him again, Kristine. Oh, that was the worst time I've known in all my marriage.

MRS. LINDE: I know how you loved him. And then you went
285 off to Italy?

NORA: Yes. We had the means now, and the doctors urged us. So we left a month after.

MRS. LINDE: And your husband came back completely cured?

NORA: Sound as a drum!

290 MRS. LINDE: But—the doctor?

NORA: Who?

MRS. LINDE: I thought the maid said he was a doctor, the man who came in with me.

NORA: Yes, that was Dr. Rank—but he's not making a sick call.
295 He's our closest friend, and he stops by at least once a day. No, Torvald hasn't had a sick moment since, and the children are fit and strong, and I am, too. (*Jumping up and clapping her hands.*) Oh, dear God, Kristine, what a lovely thing to live and be happy! But how disgusting of me—I'm talk-
300 ing of nothing but my own affairs. (*Sits on a stool close by* KRISTINE, *arms resting across her knees.*) Oh, don't be angry with me! Tell me, is it really true that you weren't in love with your husband? Why did you marry him, then?

MRS. LINDE: My mother was still alive, but bedridden and
305 helpless—and I had my two younger brothers to look after. In all conscience, I didn't think I could turn him down.

NORA: No, you were right there. But was he rich at the time?

MRS. LINDE: He was very well off, I'd say. But the business was shaky, Nora. When he died, it all fell apart, and nothing
310 was left.

NORA: And then—?

MRS. LINDE: Yes, so I had to scrape up a living with a little shop and a little teaching and whatever else I could find. The last

315 three years have been like one endless workday without a rest for me. Now it's over, Nora. My poor mother doesn't need me, for she's passed on. Nor the boys, either; they're working now and can take care of themselves.

NORA: How free you must feel—

320 MRS. LINDE: No—only unspeakably empty. Nothing to live for now. (*Standing up anxiously.*) That's why I couldn't take it any longer out in that desolate hole. Maybe here it'll be easier to find something to do and keep my mind occupied. If I could only be lucky enough to get a steady job, some office work—

325 NORA: Oh, but Kristine, that's so dreadfully tiring, and you already look so tired. It would be much better for you if you could go off to a bathing resort.

MRS. LINDE: (*Going toward the window.*) I have no father to give me travel money, Nora.

330 NORA: (*Rising.*) Oh, don't be angry with me.

MRS. LINDE: (*Going to her.*) Nora dear, don't you be angry with me. The worst of my kind of situation is all the bitterness that's stored away. No one to work for, and yet you're always having to snap up your opportunities. You

335 have to live; and so you grow selfish. When you told me the happy change in your lot, do you know I was delighted less for your sakes than for mine?

NORA: How so? Oh, I see. You think maybe Torvald could do something for you.

340 MRS. LINDE: Yes, that's what I thought.

NORA: And he will, Kristine! Just leave it to me; I'll bring it up so delicately—find something attractive to humor him with. Oh, I'm so eager to help you.

MRS. LINDE: How very kind of you, Nora, to be so concerned

345 over me—doubly kind, considering you really know so little of life's burdens yourself.

NORA: I—? I know so little—?

MRS. LINDE: (*Smiling.*) Well, my heavens—a little needlework and such—Nora, you're just a child.

350 NORA: (*Tossing her head and pacing the floor.*) You don't have to act so superior.

MRS. LINDE: Oh?

NORA: You're just like the others. You all think I'm incapable of anything serious—

355 MRS. LINDE: Come now—

NORA: That I've never had to face the raw world.

MRS. LINDE: Nora dear, you've just been telling me all your troubles.

NORA: Hm! Trivia! (*Quietly.*) I haven't told you the big thing.

360 MRS. LINDE: Big thing? What do you mean?

NORA: You look down on me so, Kristine, but you shouldn't. You're proud that you worked so long and hard for your mother.

MRS. LINDE: I don't look down on a soul. But it is true: I'm

365 proud—and happy, too—to think it was given to me to make my mother's last days almost free of care.

NORA: And you're also proud thinking of what you've done for your brothers.

MRS. LINDE: I feel I've a right to be.

370 NORA: I agree. But listen to this, Kristine—I've also got something to be proud and happy for.

MRS. LINDE: I don't doubt it. But whatever do you mean?

NORA: Not so loud. What if Torvald heard! He mustn't, not for anything in the world. Nobody must know, Kristine.

375 No one but you.

MRS. LINDE: But what is it, then?

NORA: Come here. (*Drawing her down beside her on the sofa.*) It's true—I've also got something to be proud and happy for. I'm the one who saved Torvald's life.

MRS. LINDE: Saved—? Saved how? 380

NORA: I told you about the trip to Italy. Torvald never would have lived if he hadn't gone south—

MRS. LINDE: Of course; your father gave you the means—

NORA: (*Smiling.*) That's what Torvald and all the rest think, but— 385

MRS. LINDE: But—?

NORA: Papa didn't give us a pin. I was the one who raised the money.

MRS. LINDE: You? That whole amount?

NORA: Four thousand, eight hundred crowns. What do you 390 say to that?

MRS. LINDE: But Nora, how was it possible? Did you win the lottery?

NORA: (*Disdainfully.*) The lottery? Pooh! No art to that.

MRS. LINDE: But where did you get it from then? 395

NORA: (*Humming, with a mysterious smile.*) Hmm, tra-la-la-la.

MRS. LINDE: Because you couldn't have borrowed it.

NORA: No? Why not?

MRS. LINDE: A wife can't borrow without her husband's consent.

NORA: (*Tossing her head.*) Oh, but a wife with a little business 400 sense, a wife who knows how to manage—

MRS. LINDE: Nora, I simply don't understand—

NORA: You don't have to. Whoever said I borrowed the money? I could have gotten it other ways. (*Throwing herself back on the sofa.*) I could have gotten it from some ad- 405 mirer or other. After all, a girl with my ravishing appeal—

MRS. LINDE: You lunatic.

NORA: I'll bet you're eaten up with curiosity, Kristine.

MRS. LINDE: Now listen here, Nora—you haven't done something indiscreet? 410

NORA: (*Sitting up again.*) Is it indiscreet to save your husband's life?

MRS. LINDE: I think it's indiscreet that without his knowledge you—

NORA: But that's the point: he mustn't know! My Lord, can't 415 you understand? He mustn't ever know the close call he had. It was to *me* the doctors came to say his life was in danger—that nothing could save him but a stay in the south. Didn't I try strategy then! I began talking about how lovely it would be for me to travel abroad like other 420 young wives; I begged and I cried; I told him please to remember my condition, to be kind and indulge me; and then I dropped a hint that he could easily take out a loan. But at that, Kristine, he nearly exploded. He said I was frivolous, and it was his duty as man of the house not to 425 indulge me in whims and fancies—as I think he called them. Aha, I thought, now you'll just have to be saved— and that's when I saw my chance.

MRS. LINDE: And your father never told Torvald the money wasn't from him? 430

NORA: No, never. Papa died right about then. I'd considered bringing him into my secret and begging him never to tell. But he was too sick at the time—and then, sadly, it didn't matter.

MRS. LINDE: And you've never confided in your husband since? 435

NORA: For heaven's sake, no! Are you serious? He's so strict on that subject. Besides—Torvald, with all his masculine pride—how painfully humiliating for him if he ever found out he was in debt to me. That would just ruin our relationship. Our beautiful, happy home would never be the same.

MRS. LINDE: Won't you ever tell him?

NORA: (*Thoughtfully, half smiling.*) Yes—maybe sometime, years from now, when I'm no longer so attractive. Don't laugh! I only mean when Torvald loves me less than now, when he stops enjoying my dancing and dressing up and reciting for him. Then it might be wise to have something in reserve—(*Breaking off.*) How ridiculous! That'll never happen—Well, Kristine, what do you think of my big secret? I'm capable of something too, hm? You can imagine, of course, how this thing hangs over me. It really hasn't been easy meeting the payments on time. In the business world there's what they call quarterly interest and what they call amortization, and these are always so terribly hard to manage. I've had to skimp a little here and there, wherever I could, you know. I could hardly spare anything from my house allowance, because Torvald has to live well. I couldn't let the children go poorly dressed; whatever I got for them, I felt I had to use up completely—the darlings!

MRS. LINDE: Poor Nora, so it had to come out of your own budget, then?

NORA: Yes, of course. But I was the one most responsible, too. Every time Torvald gave me money for new clothes and such, I never used more than half; always bought the simplest, cheapest outfits. It was a godsend that everything looks so well on me that Torvald never noticed. But it did weigh me down at times, Kristine. It *is* such a joy to wear fine things. You understand.

MRS. LINDE: Oh, of course.

NORA: And then I found other ways of making money. Last winter I was lucky enough to get a lot of copying to do. I locked myself in and sat writing every evening till late in the night. Ah, I was tired so often, dead tired. But still it was wonderful fun, sitting and working like that, earning money. It was almost like being a man.

MRS. LINDE: But how much have you paid off this way so far?

NORA: That's hard to say, exactly. These accounts, you know, aren't easy to figure. I only know that I've paid out all I could scrape together. Time and again I haven't known where to turn. (*Smiling.*) Then I'd sit here dreaming of a rich old gentleman who had fallen in love with me—

MRS. LINDE: What! Who is he?

NORA: Oh, really! And that he'd died, and when his will was opened, there in big letters it said, "All my fortune shall be paid over in cash, immediately, to that enchanting Mrs. Nora Helmer."

MRS. LINDE: But Nora dear—who was this gentleman?

NORA: Good grief, can't you understand? The old man never existed; that was only something I'd dream up time and again whenever I was at my wits' end for money. But it makes no difference now; the old fossil can go where he pleases for all I care; I don't need him or his will—because now I'm free. (*Jumping up.*) Oh, how lovely to think of that, Kristine! Carefree! To know you're carefree, utterly carefree; to be able to romp and play with the children, and to keep up a beautiful, charming home—everything just the way Torvald likes it! And think, spring is coming, with big blue skies. Maybe we can travel a little then.

Maybe I'll see the ocean again. Oh yes, it is so marvelous to live and be happy!

(*The front doorbell rings.*)

MRS. LINDE: (*Rising.*) There's the bell. It's probably best that I go.

NORA: No, stay. No one's expected. It must be for Torvald.

MAID: (*From the hall doorway.*) Excuse me, ma'am—there's a gentleman here to see Mr. Helmer, but I didn't know— since the doctor's with him—

NORA: Who is the gentleman?

KROGSTAD: (*From the doorway.*) It's me, Mrs. Helmer.

(MRS. LINDE *starts and turns away toward the window.*)

NORA: (*Stepping toward him, tense, her voice a whisper.*) You? What is it? Why do you want to speak to my husband?

KROGSTAD: Bank business—after a fashion. I have a small job in the investment bank, and I hear now your husband is going to be our chief—

NORA: In other words, it's—

KROGSTAD: Just dry business, Mrs. Helmer. Nothing but that.

NORA: Yes, then please be good enough to step into the study. (*She nods indifferently as she sees him out by the hall door, then returns and begins stirring up the stove.*)

MRS. LINDE: Nora—who was that man?

NORA: That was a Mr. Krogstad—a lawyer.

MRS. LINDE: Then it really was him.

NORA: Do you know that person?

MRS. LINDE: I did once—many years ago. For a time he was a law clerk in our town.

NORA: Yes, he's been that.

MRS. LINDE: How he's changed.

NORA: I understand he had a very unhappy marriage.

MRS. LINDE: He's a widower now.

NORA: With a number of children. There now, it's burning. (*She closes the stove door and moves the rocker a bit to one side.*)

MRS. LINDE: They say he has a hand in all kinds of business.

NORA: Oh? That may be true; I wouldn't know. But let's not think about business. It's so dull.

(DR. RANK *enters from* HELMER'S *study.*)

RANK: (*Still in the doorway.*) No, no, really—I don't want to intrude, I'd just as soon talk a little while with your wife. (*Shuts the door, then notices* MRS. LINDE.) Oh, beg pardon. I'm intruding here too.

NORA: No, not at all. (*Introducing him.*) Dr. Rank, Mrs. Linde.

RANK: Well now, that's a name much heard in this house. I believe I passed the lady on the stairs as I came.

MRS. LINDE: Yes, I take the stairs very slowly. They're rather hard on me.

RANK: Uh-hm, some touch of internal weakness?

MRS. LINDE: More overexertion, I'd say.

RANK: Nothing else? Then you're probably here in town to rest up in a round of parties?

MRS. LINDE: I'm here to look for work.

RANK: Is that the best cure for overexertion?

MRS. LINDE: One has to live, Doctor.

RANK: Yes, there's a common prejudice to that effect.

NORA: Oh, come on, Dr. Rank—you really do want to live yourself.

RANK: Yes, I really do. Wretched as I am, I'll gladly prolong my torment indefinitely. All my patients feel like that. And it's quite the same, too, with the morally sick. Right at this moment there's one of those moral invalids in there with Helmer—

MRS. LINDE: (*Softly.*) Ah!

NORA: Who do you mean?

RANK: Oh, it's a lawyer, Krogstad, a type you wouldn't know. His character is rotten to the root—but even he began chattering all-importantly about how he had to *live*.

NORA: Oh? What did he want to talk to Torvald about?

RANK: I really don't know. I only heard something about the bank.

NORA: I didn't know that Krog—that this man Krogstad had anything to do with the bank.

RANK: Yes, he's gotten some kind of berth down there. (*To* MRS. LINDE.) I don't know if you also have, in your neck of the woods, a type of person who scuttles about breathlessly, sniffing out hints of moral corruption, and then maneuvers his victim into some sort of key position where he can keep an eye on him. It's the healthy these days that are out in the cold.

MRS. LINDE: All the same, it's the sick who most need to be taken in.

RANK: (*With a shrug.*) Yes, there we have it. That's the concept that's turning society into a sanatorium.

(NORA, *lost in her thoughts, breaks out into quiet laughter and claps her hands.*)

RANK: Why do you laugh at that? Do you have any real idea of what society is?

NORA: What do I care about dreary old society? I was laughing at something quite different—something terribly funny. Tell me, Doctor—is everyone who works in the bank dependent now on Torvald?

RANK: Is that what you find so terribly funny?

NORA: (*Smiling and humming.*) Never mind, never mind! (*Pacing the floor.*) Yes, that's really immensely amusing: that we—that Torvald has so much power now over all those people. (*Taking the bag out of her pocket.*) Dr. Rank, a little macaroon on that?

RANK: See here, macaroons! I thought they were contraband here.

NORA: Yes, but these are some that Kristine gave me.

MRS. LINDE: What? I—?

NORA: Now, now, don't be afraid. You couldn't possibly know that Torvald had forbidden them. You see, he's worried they'll ruin my teeth. But hmp! Just this once! Isn't that so, Dr. Rank? Help yourself! (*Puts a macaroon in his mouth.*) And you too, Kristine. And I'll also have one, only a little one—or two, at the most. (*Walking about again.*) Now I'm really tremendously happy. Now there's just one last thing in the world that I have an enormous desire to do.

RANK: Well! And what's that?

NORA: It's something I have such a consuming desire to say so Torvald could hear.

RANK: And why can't you say it?

NORA: I don't dare. It's quite shocking.

MRS. LINDE: Shocking?

RANK: Well, then it isn't advisable. But in front of us you certainly can. What do you have such a desire to say so Torvald could hear?

NORA: I have such a huge desire to say—to hell and be damned!

RANK: Are you crazy?

MRS. LINDE: My goodness, Nora!

RANK: Go on, say it. Here he is.

NORA: (*Hiding the macaroon bag.*) Shh, shh, shh!

(HELMER *comes in from his study, hat in hand, overcoat over his arm.*)

NORA: (*Going toward him.*) Well, Torvald dear, are you through with him?

HELMER: Yes, he just left.

NORA: Let me introduce you—this is Kristine, who's arrived here in town.

HELMER: Kristine—? I'm sorry, but I don't know—

NORA: Mrs. Linde, Torvald dear. Mrs. Kristine Linde.

HELMER: Of course. A childhood friend of my wife's, no doubt?

MRS. LINDE: Yes, we knew each other in those days.

NORA: And just think, she made the long trip down here in order to talk with you.

HELMER: What's this?

MRS. LINDE: Well, not exactly—

NORA: You see, Kristine is remarkably clever in office work, and so she's terribly eager to come under a capable man's supervision and add more to what she already knows—

HELMER: Very wise, Mrs. Linde.

NORA: And then when she heard that you'd become a bank manager—the story was wired out to the papers—then she came in as fast as she could and—Really, Torvald, for my sake you can do a little something for Kristine, can't you?

HELMER: Yes, it's not at all impossible. Mrs. Linde, I suppose you're a widow?

MRS. LINDE: Yes.

HELMER: Any experience in office work?

MRS. LINDE: Yes, a good deal.

HELMER: Well, it's quite likely that I can make an opening for you—

NORA: (*Clapping her hands.*) You see, you see!

HELMER: You've come at a lucky moment, Mrs. Linde.

MRS. LINDE: Oh, how can I thank you?

HELMER: Not necessary. (*Putting his overcoat on.*) But today you'll have to excuse me—

RANK: Wait, I'll go with you. (*He fetches his coat from the hall and warms it at the stove.*)

NORA: Don't stay out long, dear.

HELMER: An hour; no more.

NORA: Are you going too, Kristine?

MRS. LINDE: (*Putting on her winter garments.*) Yes, I have to see about a room now.

HELMER: Then perhaps we can all walk together.

NORA: (*Helping her.*) What a shame we're so cramped here, but it's quite impossible for us to—

MRS. LINDE: Oh, don't even think of it! Good-bye, Nora dear, and thanks for everything.

NORA: Good-bye for now. Of course you'll be back this evening. And you too, Dr. Rank. What? If you're well enough? Oh, you've got to be! Wrap up tight now.

(*In a ripple of small talk the company moves out into the hall; children's voices are heard outside on the steps.*)

665 NORA: There they are! There they are! (*She runs to open the door. The* CHILDREN *come in with their nurse,* ANNE-MARIE.) Come in, come in! (*Bends down and kisses them.*) Oh, you darlings—! Look at them, Kristine. Aren't they lovely!

RANK: No loitering in the draft here.

670 HELMER: Come, Mrs. Linde—this place is unbearable now for anyone but mothers.

(DR. RANK, HELMER, *and* MRS. LINDE *go down the stairs.* ANNE-MARIE *goes into the living room with the* CHILDREN. NORA *follows, after closing the hall door.*)

NORA: How fresh and strong you look. Oh, such red cheeks you have! Like apples and roses. (*The* CHILDREN *interrupt her throughout the following.*) And it was so much fun? That's
675 wonderful. Really? You pulled both Emmy and Bob on the sled? Imagine, all together! Yes, you're a clever boy, Ivar. Oh, let me hold her a bit, Anne-Marie. My sweet little doll baby! (*Takes the smallest from* ANNE-MARIE *and dances with her.*) Yes, yes, Mama will dance with Bob as well. What? Did you
680 throw snowballs? Oh, if I'd only been there! No, don't bother, Anne-Marie—I'll undress them myself. Oh yes, let me. It's such fun. Go in and rest; you look half frozen. There's hot coffee waiting for you on the stove. (ANNE-MARIE *goes into the room to the left.* NORA *takes the* CHILDREN'S
685 *winter things off, throwing them around, while the children talk to her all at once.*) Is that so? A big dog chased you? But it didn't bite? No, dogs never bite little, lovely doll babies. Don't peek in the packages, Ivar! What is it? Yes, wouldn't you like to know. No, no, it's an ugly something. Well? Shall we play?
690 What shall we play? Hide-and-seek? Yes, let's play hide-and-seek. Bob must hide first. I must? Yes, let me hide first. (*Laughing and shouting, she and the* CHILDREN *play in and out of the living room and the adjoining room to the right. At last* NORA *hides under the table. The* CHILDREN *come storming in, search,*
695 *but cannot find her, then hear her muffled laughter, dash over to the table, lift the cloth up and find her. Wild shouting. She creeps forward as if to scare them. More shouts. Meanwhile, a knock at the hall door; no one has noticed it. Now the door half opens, and* KROGSTAD *appears. He waits a moment; the game goes on.*)

700 KROGSTAD: Beg pardon, Mrs. Helmer—

NORA: (*With a strangled cry, turning and scrambling to her knees.*) Oh! What do you want?

KROGSTAD: Excuse me. The outer door was ajar; it must be someone forgot to shut it—

705 NORA: (*Rising.*) My husband isn't home, Mr. Krogstad.

KROGSTAD: I know that.

NORA: Yes—then what do you want here?

KROGSTAD: A word with you.

NORA: With—? (*To the* CHILDREN, *quietly.*) Go in to Anne-
710 Marie. What? No, the strange man won't hurt Mama. When he's gone, we'll play some more. (*She leads the* CHILDREN *into the room to the left and shuts the door after them. Then, tense and nervous:*) You want to speak to me?

KROGSTAD: Yes, I want to.

715 NORA: Today? But it's not yet the first of the month—

KROGSTAD: No, it's Christmas Eve. It's going to be up to you how merry a Christmas you have.

NORA: What is it you want? Today I absolutely can't—

KROGSTAD: We won't talk about that till later. This is something else. You do have a moment to spare, I suppose? 720

NORA: Oh yes, of course—I do, except—

KROGSTAD: Good. I was sitting over at Olsen's Restaurant when I saw your husband go down the street—

NORA: Yes?

KROGSTAD: With a lady. 725

NORA: Yes. So?

KROGSTAD: If you'll pardon my asking: wasn't that lady a Mrs. Linde?

NORA: Yes.

KROGSTAD: Just now come into town? 730

NORA: Yes, today.

KROGSTAD: She's a good friend of yours?

NORA: Yes, she is. But I don't see—

KROGSTAD: I also knew her once.

NORA: I'm aware of that. 735

KROGSTAD: Oh? You know all about it. I thought so. Well, then let me ask you short and sweet: is Mrs. Linde getting a job in the bank?

NORA: What makes you think you can cross-examine me, Mr. Krogstad—you, one of my husband's employees? But 740 since you ask, you might as well know—yes, Mrs. Linde's going to be taken on at the bank. And I'm the one who spoke for her, Mr. Krogstad. Now you know.

KROGSTAD: So I guessed right.

NORA: (*Pacing up and down.*) Oh, one does have a tiny bit of 745 influence, I should hope. Just because I am a woman, don't think it means that—When one has a subordinate position, Mr. Krogstad, one really ought to be careful about pushing somebody who—hm—

KROGSTAD: Who has influence? 750

NORA: That's right.

KROGSTAD: (*In a different tone.*) Mrs. Helmer, would you be good enough to use your influence on my behalf?

NORA: What? What do you mean?

KROGSTAD: Would you please make sure that I keep my sub- 755 ordinate position in the bank?

NORA: What does that mean? Who's thinking of taking away your position?

KROGSTAD: Oh, don't play the innocent with me. I'm quite aware that your friend would hardly relish the chance of 760 running into me again; and I'm also aware now whom I can thank for being turned out.

NORA: But I promise you—

KROGSTAD: Yes, yes, yes, to the point: there's still time, and I'm advising you to use your influence to prevent it. 765

NORA: But Mr. Krogstad, I have absolutely no influence.

KROGSTAD: You haven't? I thought you were just saying—

NORA: You shouldn't take me so literally. I! How can you believe that I have any such influence over my husband?

KROGSTAD: Oh, I've known your husband from our student 770 days. I don't think the great bank manager's more steadfast than any other married man.

NORA: You speak insolently about my husband, and I'll show you the door.

KROGSTAD: The lady has spirit. 775

NORA: I'm not afraid of you any longer. After New Year's, I'll soon be done with the whole business.

KROGSTAD: (*Restraining himself.*) Now listen to me, Mrs. Helmer. If necessary, I'll fight for my little job in the bank
780   as if it were life itself.

NORA: Yes, so it seems.

KROGSTAD: It's not just a matter of income; that's the least of it. It's something else—All right, out with it! Look, this is the thing. You know, just like all the others, of course, that
785   once, a good many years ago, I did something rather rash.

NORA: I've heard rumors to that effect.

KROGSTAD: The case never got into court; but all the same, every door was closed in my face from then on. So I took up those various activities you know about. I had to grab
790   hold somewhere; and I dare say I haven't been among the worst. But now I want to drop all that. My boys are growing up. For their sakes, I'll have to win back as much respect as possible here in town. That job in the bank was like the first rung in my ladder. And now your husband
795   wants to kick me right back down in the mud again.

NORA: But for heaven's sake, Mr. Krogstad, it's simply not in my power to help you.

KROGSTAD: That's because you haven't the will to—but I have the means to make you.

800 NORA: You certainly won't tell my husband that I owe you money?

KROGSTAD: Hm—what if I told him that?

NORA: That would be shameful of you. (*Nearly in tears.*) This secret—my joy and my pride—that he should learn it in
805   such a crude and disgusting way—learn it from you. You'd expose me to the most horrible unpleasantness—

KROGSTAD: Only unpleasantness?

NORA: (*Vehemently.*) But go on and try. It'll turn out the worse for you, because then my husband will really see what a
810   crook you are, and then you'll *never* be able to hold your job.

KROGSTAD: I asked if it was just domestic unpleasantness you were afraid of?

NORA: If my husband finds out, then of course he'll pay what I owe at once, and then we'd be through with you for good.

815 KROGSTAD: (*A step closer.*) Listen, Mrs. Helmer—you've either got a very bad memory, or else no head at all for business. I'd better put you a little more in touch with the facts.

NORA: What do you mean?

KROGSTAD: When your husband was sick, you came to me
820   for a loan of four thousand, eight hundred crowns.

NORA: Where else could I go?

KROGSTAD: I promised to get you that sum—

NORA: And you got it.

KROGSTAD: I promised to get you that sum, on certain condi-
825   tions. You were so involved in your husband's illness, and so eager to finance your trip, that I guess you didn't think out all the details. It might just be a good idea to remind you. I promised you the money on the strength of a note I drew up.

NORA: Yes, and that I signed.

830 KROGSTAD: Right. But at the bottom I added some lines for your father to guarantee the loan. He was supposed to sign down there.

NORA: Supposed to? He did sign.

KROGSTAD: I left the date blank. In other words, your father
835   would have dated his signature himself. Do you remember that?

NORA: Yes, I think—

KROGSTAD: Then I gave you the note for you to mail to your father. Isn't that so?

NORA: Yes.   840

KROGSTAD: And naturally you sent it at once—because only some five, six days later you brought me the note, properly signed. And with that, the money was yours.

NORA: Well, then; I've made my payments regularly, haven't I?

KROGSTAD: More or less. But—getting back to the point—   845
those were hard times for you then, Mrs. Helmer.

NORA: Yes, they were.

KROGSTAD: Your father was very ill, I believe.

NORA: He was near the end.

KROGSTAD: He died soon after?   850

NORA: Yes.

KROGSTAD: Tell me, Mrs. Helmer, do you happen to recall the date of your father's death? The day of the month, I mean.

NORA: Papa died the twenty-ninth of September.

KROGSTAD: That's quite correct; I've already looked into that.   855
And now we come to a curious thing—(*Taking out a paper.*) which I simply cannot comprehend.

NORA: Curious thing? I don't know—

KROGSTAD: This is the curious thing: that your father co-signed the note for your loan three days after his death.   860

NORA: How—? I don't understand.

KROGSTAD: Your father died the twenty-ninth of September. But look. Here your father dated his signature October second. Isn't that curious, Mrs. Helmer? (*NORA is silent.*) Can you explain it to me? (*NORA remains silent.*) It's also   865
remarkable that the words "October second" and the year aren't written in your father's hand, but rather in one that I think I know. Well, it's easy to understand. Your father forgot perhaps to date his signature, and then someone or other added it, a bit sloppily, before anyone knew of his   870
death. There's nothing wrong in that. It all comes down to the signature. And there's no question about *that*, Mrs. Helmer. It really *was* your father who signed his own name here, wasn't it?

NORA: (*After a short silence, throwing her head back and looking*   875
squarely at him.) No, it wasn't. *I* signed Papa's name.

KROGSTAD: Wait, now—are you fully aware that this is a dangerous confession?

NORA: Why? You'll soon get your money.

KROGSTAD: Let me ask you a question—why didn't you send   880
the paper to your father?

NORA: That was impossible. Papa was so sick. If I'd asked him for his signature, I also would have had to tell him what the money was for. But I couldn't tell him, sick as he was, that my husband's life was in danger. That was just impossible.   885

KROGSTAD: Then it would have been better if you'd given up the trip abroad.

NORA: I couldn't possibly. The trip was to save my husband's life. I couldn't give that up.

KROGSTAD: But didn't you ever consider that this was a fraud   890
against me?

NORA: I couldn't let myself be bothered by that. You weren't any concern of mine. I couldn't stand you, with all those cold complications you made, even though you knew how badly off my husband was.   895

KROGSTAD: Mrs. Helmer, obviously you haven't the vaguest idea of what you've involved yourself in. But I can tell you this: it was nothing more and nothing worse that I once did—and it wrecked my whole reputation.

900 NORA: You? Do you expect me to believe that you ever acted bravely to save your wife's life?

KROGSTAD: Laws don't inquire into motives.

NORA: Then they must be very poor laws.

KROGSTAD: Poor or not—if I introduce this paper in court, 905 you'll be judged according to law.

NORA: This I refuse to believe. A daughter hasn't a right to protect her dying father from anxiety and care? A wife hasn't a right to save her husband's life? I don't know much about laws, but I'm sure that somewhere in the 910 books these things are allowed. And you don't know anything about it—you who practice the law? You must be an awful lawyer, Mr. Krogstad.

KROGSTAD: Could be. But business—the kind of business we two are mixed up in—don't you think I know about that? 915 All right. Do what you want now. But I'm telling you *this*: if I get shoved down a second time, you're going to keep me company. (*He bows and goes out through the hall.*)

NORA: (*Pensive for a moment, then tossing her head.*) Oh, really! Trying to frighten me! I'm not so silly as all that. (*Begins* 920 *gathering up the* CHILDREN'S *clothes, but soon stops.*) But—? No, but that's impossible! I did it out of love.

THE CHILDREN: (*In the doorway, left.*) Mama, that strange man's gone out the door.

NORA: Yes, yes, I know it. But don't tell anyone about the 925 strange man. Do you hear? Not even Papa!

THE CHILDREN: No, Mama. But now will you play again?

NORA: No, not now.

THE CHILDREN: Oh, but Mama, you promised.

NORA: Yes, but I can't now. Go inside; I have too much to do. 930 Go in, go in, my sweet darlings. (*She herds them gently back in the room and shuts the door after them. Settling on the sofa, she takes up a piece of embroidery and makes some stitches, but soon stops abruptly.*) No! (*Throws the work aside, rises, goes to the hall door and calls out.*) Helene! Let me have the tree in 935 here. (*Goes to the table, left, opens the table drawer, and stops again.*) No, but that's utterly impossible!

MAID: (*With the Christmas tree.*) Where should I put it, ma'am?

NORA: There. The middle of the floor.

MAID: Should I bring anything else?

940 NORA: No, thanks. I have what I need.

(*The* MAID, *who has set the tree down, goes out.*)

NORA: (*Absorbed in trimming the tree.*) Candles here—and flowers here. That terrible creature! Talk, talk, talk! There's nothing to it at all. The tree's going to be lovely. I'll do anything to please you, Torvald. I'll sing for you, dance for you—

945

(HELMER *comes in from the hall, with a sheaf of papers under his arm.*)

NORA: Oh! You're back so soon?

HELMER: Yes. Has anyone been here?

NORA: Here? No.

HELMER: That's odd. I saw Krogstad leaving the front door.

950 NORA: So? Oh yes, that's true. Krogstad was here a moment.

HELMER: Nora, I can see by your face that he's been here, begging you to put in a good word for him.

NORA: Yes.

HELMER: And it was supposed to seem like your own idea? You were to hide it from me that he'd been here. He asked 955 you that, too, didn't he?

NORA: Yes, Torvald, but—

HELMER: Nora, Nora, and you could fall for that? Talk with that sort of person and promise him anything? And then in the bargain, tell me an untruth. 960

NORA: An untruth—?

HELMER: Didn't you say that no one had been here? (*Wagging his finger.*) My little songbird must never do that again. A songbird needs a clean beak to warble with. No false notes. (*Putting his arm about her waist.*) That's the way it 965 should be, isn't it? Yes, I'm sure of it. (*Releasing her.*) And so, enough of that. (*Sitting by the stove.*) Ah, how snug and cozy it is here. (*Leafing among his papers.*)

NORA: (*Busy with the tree, after a short pause.*) Torvald!

HELMER: Yes. 970

NORA: I'm so much looking forward to the Stenborgs' costume party, day after tomorrow.

HELMER: And I can't wait to see what you'll surprise me with.

NORA: Oh, that stupid business!

HELMER: What? 975

NORA: I can't find anything that's right. Everything seems so ridiculous, so inane.

HELMER: So my little Nora's come to *that* recognition?

NORA: (*Going behind his chair, her arms resting on its back.*) Are you very busy, Torvald? 980

HELMER: Oh—

NORA: What papers are those?

HELMER: Bank matters.

NORA: Already?

HELMER: I've gotten full authority from the retiring manage- 985 ment to make all necessary changes in personnel and procedure. I'll need Christmas week for that. I want to have everything in order by New Year's.

NORA: So that was the reason this poor Krogstad—

HELMER: Hm. 990

NORA: (*Still leaning on the chair and slowly stroking the nape of his neck.*) If you weren't so very busy, I would have asked you an enormous favor, Torvald.

HELMER: Let's hear. What is it?

NORA: You know, there isn't anyone who has your good 995 taste—and I want so much to look well at the costume party. Torvald, couldn't you take over and decide what I should be and plan my costume?

HELMER: Ah, is my stubborn little creature calling for a lifeguard? 1000

NORA: Yes, Torvald, I can't get anywhere without your help.

HELMER: All right—I'll think it over. We'll hit on something.

NORA: Oh, how sweet of you. (*Goes to the tree again. Pause.*) Aren't the red flowers pretty—? But tell me, was it really such a crime that this Krogstad committed? 1005

HELMER: Forgery. Do you have any idea what that means?

NORA: Couldn't he have done it out of need?

HELMER: Yes, or thoughtlessness, like so many others. I'm not so heartless that I'd condemn a man categorically for just one mistake. 1010

NORA: No, of course not, Torvald!

HELMER: Plenty of men have redeemed themselves by openly confessing their crimes and taking their punishment.

NORA: Punishment—?

1015 HELMER: But now Krogstad didn't go that way. He got himself out by sharp practices, and that's the real cause of his moral breakdown.

NORA: Do you really think that would—?

HELMER: Just imagine how a man with that sort of guilt in 1020 him has to lie and cheat and deceive on all sides, has to wear a mask even with the nearest and dearest he has, even with his own wife and children. And with the children, Nora—that's where it's most horrible.

NORA: Why?

1025 HELMER: Because that kind of atmosphere of lies infects the whole life of a home. Every breath the children take in is filled with the germs of something degenerate.

NORA: (*Coming closer behind him.*) Are you sure of that?

HELMER: Oh, I've seen it often enough as a lawyer. Almost 1030 everyone who goes bad early in life has a mother who's a chronic liar.

NORA: Why just—the mother?

HELMER: It's usually the mother's influence that's dominant, but the father's works in the same way, of course. Every 1035 lawyer is quite familiar with it. And still this Krogstad's been going home year in, year out, poisoning his own children with lies and pretense; that's why I call him morally lost. (*Reaching his hands out toward her.*) So my sweet little Nora must promise me never to plead his cause. Your hand 1040 on it. Come, come, what's this? Give me your hand. There, now. All settled. I can tell you it'd be impossible for me to work alongside of him. I literally feel physically revolted when I'm anywhere near such a person.

NORA: (*Withdraws her hand and goes to the other side of the Christ-* 1045 *mas tree.*) How hot it is here! And I've got so much to do.

HELMER: (*Getting up and gathering his papers.*) Yes, and I have to think about getting some of these read through before dinner. I'll think about your costume, too. And something to hang on the tree in gilt paper, I may even see about that. 1050 (*Putting his hand on her head.*) Oh you, my darling little songbird. (*He goes into his study and closes the door after him.*)

NORA: (*Softly, after a silence.*) Oh, really! it isn't so. It's impossible. It must be impossible.

ANNE-MARIE: (*In the doorway, left.*) The children are begging 1055 so hard to come in to Mama.

NORA: No, no, no, don't let them in to me! You stay with them, Anne-Marie.

ANNE-MARIE: Of course, ma'am. (*Closes the door.*)

NORA: (*Pale with terror.*) Hurt my children—! Poison my 1060 home? (*A moment's pause; then she tosses her head.*) That's not true. Never. Never in all the world.

ACT TWO

Same room. Beside the piano the Christmas tree now stands stripped of ornament, burned-down candle stubs on its ragged branches. NORA'S *street clothes lie on the sofa.* NORA, *alone in the room, moves restlessly about; at last she stops at the sofa and picks up her coat.*

NORA: (*Dropping the coat again.*) Someone's coming! (*Goes toward the door, listens.*) No—there's no one. Of course—no-body's coming today, Christmas Day—or tomorrow, either. But maybe—(*Opens the door and looks out.*) No, nothing in the mailbox. Quite empty. (*Coming forward.*) What nonsense! 5 He won't do anything serious. Nothing terrible could happen. It's impossible. Why, I have three small children.

(ANNE-MARIE, *with a large carton, comes in from the room to the left.*)

ANNE-MARIE: Well, at last I found the box with the masquerade clothes.

NORA: Thanks. Put it on the table. 10

ANNE-MARIE: (*Does so.*) But they're all pretty much of a mess.

NORA: Ahh! I'd love to rip them in a million pieces!

ANNE-MARIE: Oh, mercy, they can be fixed right up. Just a little patience.

NORA: Yes, I'll go get Mrs. Linde to help me. 15

ANNE-MARIE: Out again now? In this nasty weather? Miss Nora will catch cold—get sick.

NORA: Oh, worse things could happen—How are the children?

ANNE-MARIE: The poor mites are playing with their Christmas presents, but— 20

NORA: Do they ask for me much?

ANNE-MARIE: They're so used to having Mama around, you know.

NORA: Yes, but Anne-Marie, I *can't* be together with them as much as I was. 25

ANNE-MARIE: Well, small children get used to anything.

NORA: You think so? Do you think they'd forget their mother if she was gone for good?

ANNE-MARIE: Oh, mercy—gone for good!

NORA: Wait, tell me, Anne-Marie—I've wondered so often— 30 how could you ever have the heart to give your child over to strangers?

ANNE-MARIE: But I had to, you know, to become little Nora's nurse.

NORA: Yes, but how could you *do* it? 35

ANNE-MARIE: When I could get such a good place? A girl who's poor and who's gotten in trouble is glad enough for that. Because that slippery fish, he didn't do a thing for me, you know.

NORA: But your daughter's surely forgotten you. 40

ANNE-MARIE: Oh, she certainly has not. She's written to me, both when she was confirmed and when she was married.

NORA: (*Clasping her about the neck.*) You old Anne-Marie, you were a good mother for me when I was little.

ANNE-MARIE: Poor little Nora, with no other mother but me. 45

NORA: And if the babies didn't have one, then I know that you'd—What silly talk! (*Opening the carton.*) Go in to them. Now I'll have to—Tomorrow you can see how lovely I'll look.

ANNE-MARIE: Oh, there won't be anyone at the party as 50 lovely as Miss Nora. (*She goes off into the room, left.*)

NORA: (*Begins unpacking the box, but soon throws it aside.*) Oh, if I dared to go out. If only nobody would come. If only nothing would happen here while I'm out. What craziness—nobody's coming. Just don't think. This muff— 55 needs a brushing. Beautiful gloves, beautiful gloves. Let it go. Let it go! One, two, three, four, five, six—(*With a cry.*)

Oh, there they are! (*Poises to move toward the door, but re-mains irresolutely standing.* MRS. LINDE *enters from the hall,*
60 *where she has removed her street clothes.*)
NORA: Oh, it's you, Kristine. There's no one else out there? How good that you've come.
MRS. LINDE: I hear you were up asking for me.
NORA: Yes, I just stopped by. There's something you really
65 can help me with. Let's get settled on the sofa. Look, there's going to be a costume party tomorrow evening at the Stenborgs' right above us, and now Torvald wants me to go as a Neapolitan peasant girl and dance the tarantella that I learned in Capri.
70 MRS. LINDE: Really, are you giving a whole performance?
NORA: Torvald says yes, I should. See, here's the dress. Torvald had it made for me down there; but now it's all so tattered that I just don't know—
MRS. LINDE: Oh, we'll fix that up in no time. It's nothing more
75 than the trimmings—they're a bit loose here and there. Needle and thread? Good, now we have what we need.
NORA: Oh, how sweet of you!
MRS. LINDE: (*Sewing.*) So you'll be in disguise tomorrow, Nora. You know what? I'll stop by then for a moment and
80 have a look at you all dressed up. But listen, I've absolutely forgotten to thank you for that pleasant evening yesterday.
NORA: (*Getting up and walking about.*) I don't think it was as pleasant as usual yesterday. You should have come to town a bit sooner, Kristine—Yes, Torvald really knows how to
85 give a home elegance and charm.
MRS. LINDE: And you do, too, if you ask me. You're not your father's daughter for nothing. But tell me, is Dr. Rank al-ways so down in the mouth as yesterday?
NORA: No, that was quite an exception. But he goes around
90 critically ill all the time—tuberculosis of the spine, poor man. You know, his father was a disgusting thing who kept mistresses and so on—and that's why the son's been sickly from birth.
MRS. LINDE: (*Lets her sewing fall to her lap.*) But my dearest
95 Nora, how do you know about such things?
NORA: (*Walking more jauntily.*) Hmp! When you've had three children, then you've had a few visits from—from women who know something of medicine, and they tell you this and that.
100 MRS. LINDE: (*Resumes sewing; a short pause.*) Does Dr. Rank come here every day?
NORA: Every blessed day. He's Torvald's best friend from childhood, and *my* good friend, too. Dr. Rank almost be-longs to this house.
105 MRS. LINDE: But tell me—is he quite sincere? I mean, doesn't he rather enjoy flattering people?
NORA: Just the opposite. Why do you think that?
MRS. LINDE: When you introduced us yesterday, he was pro-claiming that he'd often heard my name in this house; but
110 later I noticed that your husband hadn't the slightest idea who I really was. So how could Dr. Rank—?
NORA: But it's all true, Kristine. You see, Torvald loves me be-yond words, and, as he puts it, he'd like to keep me all to himself. For a long time he'd almost be jealous if I even
115 mentioned any of my old friends back home. So of course I dropped that. But with Dr. Rank I talk a lot about such things, because he likes hearing about them.
MRS. LINDE: Now listen, Nora; in many ways you're still like a child. I'm a good deal older than you, with a little more

experience. I'll tell you something: you ought to put an 120 end to all this with Dr. Rank.
NORA: What should I put an end to?
MRS. LINDE: Both parts of it, I think. Yesterday you said something about a rich admirer who'd provide you with money— 125
NORA: Yes, one who doesn't exist—worse luck. So?
MRS. LINDE: Is Dr. Rank well off?
NORA: Yes, he is.
MRS. LINDE: With no dependents?
NORA: No, no one. But— 130
MRS. LINDE: And he's over here every day?
NORA: Yes, I told you that.
MRS. LINDE: How can a man of such refinement be so grasping?
NORA: I don't follow you at all.
MRS. LINDE: Now don't try to hide it, Nora. You think I can't 135 guess who loaned you the forty-eight hundred crowns?
NORA: Are you out of your mind? How could you think such a thing! A friend of ours, who comes here every single day. What an intolerable situation that would have been!
MRS. LINDE: Then it really wasn't him. 140
NORA: No, absolutely not. It never even crossed my mind for a moment—And he had nothing to lend in those days; his inheritance came later.
MRS. LINDE: Well, I think that was a stroke of luck for you, Nora dear. 145
NORA: No, it never would have occurred to me to ask Dr. Rank—Still, I'm quite sure that if I had asked him—
MRS. LINDE: Which you won't, of course.
NORA: No, of course not. I can't see that I'd ever need to. But I'm quite positive that if I talked to Dr. Rank— 150
MRS. LINDE: Behind your husband's back?
NORA: I've got to clear up this other thing; *that's* also behind his back. I've *got* to clear it all up.
MRS. LINDE: Yes, I was saying that yesterday, but—
NORA: (*Pacing up and down.*) A man handles these problems 155 so much better than a woman—
MRS. LINDE: One's husband does, yes.
NORA: Nonsense. (*Stopping.*) When you pay everything you owe, then you get your note back, right?
MRS. LINDE: Yes, naturally. 160
NORA: And can rip it into a million pieces and burn it up—that filthy scrap of paper!
MRS. LINDE: (*Looking hard at her, laying her sewing aside, and ris-ing slowly.*) Nora, you're hiding something from me.
NORA: You can see it in my face? 165
MRS. LINDE: Something's happened to you since yesterday morning. Nora, what is it?
NORA: (*Hurrying toward her.*) Kristine! (*Listening.*) Shh! Tor-vald's home. Look, go in with the children a while. Tor-vald can't bear all this snipping and stitching. Let 170 Anne-Marie help you.
MRS. LINDE: (*Gathering up some of the things.*) All right, but I'm not leaving here until we've talked this out. (*She disappears into the room, left, as* TORVALD [HELMER] *enters from the hall.*)
NORA: Oh, how I've been waiting for you, Torvald dear. 175
HELMER: Was that the dressmaker?
NORA: No, that was Kristine. She's helping me fix up my cos-tume. You know, it's going to be quite attractive.
HELMER: Yes, wasn't that a bright idea I had?
NORA: Brilliant! But then wasn't I good as well to give in to 180 you?

HELMER: Good—because you give in to your husband's judgment? All right, you little goose, I know you didn't mean it like that. But I won't disturb you. You'll want to
185   have a fitting, I suppose.

NORA: And you'll be working?

HELMER: Yes. (*Indicating a bundle of papers.*) See, I've been down to the bank. (*Starts toward his study.*)

NORA: Torvald.

190 HELMER: (*Stops.*) Yes.

NORA: If your little squirrel begged you, with all her heart and soul, for something—?

HELMER: What's that?

NORA: Then would you do it?

195 HELMER: First, naturally, I'd have to know what it was.

NORA: Your squirrel would scamper about and do tricks, if you'd only be sweet and give in.

HELMER: Out with it.

NORA: Your lark would be singing high and low in every
200   room—

HELMER: Come on, she does that anyway.

NORA: I'd be a wood nymph and dance for you in the moonlight.

HELMER: Nora—don't tell me it's that same business from this
205   morning?

NORA: (*Coming closer.*) Yes, Torvald, I beg you, please!

HELMER: And you actually have the nerve to drag that up again?

NORA: Yes, yes, you've got to give in to me; you *have* to let
210   Krogstad keep his job in the bank.

HELMER: My dear Nora, I've slated his job for Mrs. Linde.

NORA: That's awfully kind of you. But you could just fire another clerk instead of Krogstad.

HELMER: This is the most incredible stubbornness! Because
215   you go and give an impulsive promise to speak up for him, I'm expected to—

NORA: That's not the reason, Torvald. It's for your own sake. That man does writing for the worst papers; you said it yourself. He could do you any amount of harm. I'm
220   scared to death of him—

HELMER: Ah, I understand. It's the old memories haunting you.

NORA: What do you mean by that?

HELMER: Of course, you're thinking about your father.

NORA: Yes, all right. Just remember how those nasty gossips
225   wrote in the papers about Papa and slandered him so cruelly. I think they'd have had him dismissed if the department hadn't sent you up to investigate, and if you hadn't been so kind and open-minded toward him.

HELMER: My dear little Nora, there's a notable difference between
230   your father and me. Your father's official career was hardly above reproach. But mine is; and I hope it'll stay that way as long as I hold my position.

NORA: Oh, who can ever tell what vicious minds can invent? We could be so snug and happy now in our quiet, care-
235   free home—you and I and the children, Torvald! That's why I'm pleading with you so—

HELMER: And just by pleading for him you make it impossible for me to keep him on. It's already known at the bank that I'm firing Krogstad. What if it's rumored around now
240   that the new bank manager was vetoed by his wife—

NORA: Yes, what then—?

HELMER: Oh yes—as long as our little bundle of stubbornness gets her way—! I should go and make myself ridicu-

lous in front of the whole office—give people the idea I can be swayed by all kinds of outside pressure. Oh, you can 245 bet I'd feel the effects of that soon enough! Besides—there's something that rules Krogstad right out at the bank as long as I'm the manager.

NORA: What's that?

HELMER: His moral failings I could maybe overlook if I had 250 to—

NORA: Yes, Torvald, why not?

HELMER: And I hear he's quite efficient on the job. But he was a crony of mine back in my teens—one of those rash friendships that crop up again and again to embarrass you 255 later in life. Well, I might as well say it straight out: we're on a first-name basis. And that tactless fool makes no effort at all to hide it in front of others. Quite the contrary—he thinks that entitles him to take a familiar air around me, and so every other second he comes booming out with 260 his "Yes, Torvald!" and "Sure thing, Torvald!" I tell you, it's been excruciating for me. He's out to make my place in the bank unbearable.

NORA: Torvald, you can't be serious about all this.

HELMER: Oh no? Why not? 265

NORA: Because these are such petty considerations.

HELMER: What are you saying? Petty? You think I'm petty!

NORA: No, just the opposite, Torvald dear. That's exactly why—

HELMER: Never mind. You call my motives petty; then I 270 might as well be just that. Petty! All right! We'll put a stop to this for good. (*Goes to the hall door and calls.*) Helene!

NORA: What do you want?

HELMER: (*Searching among his papers.*) A decision. (*The* MAID *comes in.*) Look here; take this letter; go out with it at once. 275 Get hold of a messenger and have him deliver it. Quick now. It's already addressed. Wait, here's some money.

MAID: Yes, sir. (*She leaves with the letter.*)

HELMER: (*Straightening his papers.*) There, now, little Miss Willful. 280

NORA: (*Breathlessly.*) Torvald, what was that letter?

HELMER: Krogstad's notice.

NORA: Call it back, Torvald! There's still time. Oh, Torvald, call it back! Do it for my sake—for your sake, for the children's sake! Do you hear, Torvald; do it! You don't know 285 how this can harm us.

HELMER: Too late.

NORA: Yes, too late.

HELMER: Nora dear, I can forgive you this panic, even though basically you're insulting me. Yes, you are! Or isn't it an 290 insult to think that I should be afraid of a courtroom hack's revenge? But I forgive you anyway, because this shows so beautifully how much you love me. (*Takes her in his arms.*) This is the way it should be, my darling Nora. Whatever comes, you'll see: when it really counts, I have 295 strength and courage enough as a man to take on the whole weight myself.

NORA: (*Terrified.*) What do you mean by that?

HELMER: The whole weight, I said.

NORA: (*Resolutely.*) No, never in all the world. 300

HELMER: Good. So we'll share it, Nora, as man and wife. That's as it should be. (*Fondling her.*) Are you happy now? There, there, there—not these frightened dove's eyes. It's nothing at all but empty fantasies—Now you should run through your tarantella and practice your tambourine. I'll 305

go to the inner office and shut both doors, so I won't hear a thing; you can make all the noise you like. (*Turning in the doorway.*) And when Rank comes, just tell him where he can find me. (*He nods to her and goes with his papers into the*
310 *study, closing the door.*)

NORA: (*Standing as though rooted, dazed with fright, in a whisper.*) He really could do it. He will do it. He'll do it in spite of everything. No, not that, never, never! Anything but that! Escape! A way out—(*The doorbell rings.*) Dr. Rank! Any-
315 thing but that! Anything, whatever it is! (*Her hands pass over her face, smoothing it; she pulls herself together, goes over and opens the hall doo. DR. RANK stands outside, hanging his fur coat up. During the following scene, it begins getting dark.*)

NORA: Hello, Dr. Rank. I recognized your ring. But you
320 mustn't go in to Torvald yet; I believe he's working.

RANK: And you?

NORA: For you, I always have an hour to spare—you know that. (*He has entered, and she shuts the door after him.*)

RANK: Many thanks. I'll make use of these hours while I can.

325 NORA: What do you mean by that? While you can?

RANK: Does that disturb you?

NORA: Well, it's such an odd phrase. Is anything going to happen?

RANK: What's going to happen is what I've been expecting so
330 long—but I honestly didn't think it would come so soon.

NORA: (*Gripping his arm.*) What is it you've found out? Dr. Rank, you have to tell me!

RANK: (*Sitting by the stove.*) It's all over with me. There's nothing to be done about it.

335 NORA: (*Breathing easier.*) Is it you—then—?

RANK: Who else? There's no point in lying to one's self. I'm the most miserable of all my patients, Mrs. Helmer. These past few days I've been auditing my internal accounts. Bankrupt! Within a month I'll probably be laid out and
340 rotting in the churchyard.

NORA: Oh, what a horrible thing to say.

RANK: The thing itself is horrible. But the worst of it is all the other horror before it's over. There's only one final exami-nation left; when I'm finished with that, I'll know about
345 when my disintegration will begin. There's something I want to say. Helmer with his sensitivity has such a sharp dis-taste for anything ugly. I don't want him near my sickroom.

NORA: Oh, but Dr. Rank—

RANK: I won't have him in there. Under no condition. I'll
350 lock my door to him—As soon as I'm completely sure of the worst, I'll send you my calling card marked with a black cross, and you'll know then the wreck has started to come apart.

NORA: No, today you're completely unreasonable. And I
355 wanted you so much to be in a really good humor.

RANK: With death up my sleeve? And then to suffer this way for somebody else's sins. Is there any justice in that? And in every single family, in some way or another, this in-evitable retribution of nature goes on—

360 NORA: (*Her hands pressed over her ears.*) Oh, stuff! Cheer up! Please—be gay!

RANK: Yes, I'd just as soon laugh at it all. My poor, innocent spine, serving time for my father's gay army days.

NORA: (*By the table, left.*) He was so infatuated with asparagus
365 tips and *pâté de foie gras,* wasn't that it?

RANK: Yes—and with truffles.

NORA: Truffles, yes. And then with oysters, I suppose?

RANK: Yes, tons of oysters, naturally.

NORA: And then the port and champagne to go with it. It's so
370 sad that all these delectable things have to strike at our bones.

RANK: Especially when they strike at the unhappy bones that never shared in the fun.

NORA: Ah, that's the saddest of all.

RANK: (*Looks searchingly at her.*) Hm.

375 NORA: (*After a moment.*) Why did you smile?

RANK: No, it was you who laughed.

NORA: No, it was you who smiled, Dr. Rank!

RANK: (*Getting up.*) You're even a bigger tease than I'd thought.

NORA: I'm full of wild ideas today.

380 RANK: That's obvious.

NORA: (*Putting both hands on his shoulders.*) Dear, dear Dr. Rank, you'll never die for Torvald and me.

RANK: Oh, that loss you'll easily get over. Those who go away are soon forgotten.

385 NORA: (*Looks fearfully at him.*) You believe that?

RANK: One makes new connections, and then—

NORA: Who makes new connections?

RANK: Both you and Torvald will when I'm gone. I'd say you're well under way already. What was that Mrs. Linde
390 doing here last evening?

NORA: Oh, come—you can't be jealous of poor Kristine?

RANK: Oh yes, I am. She'll be my successor here in the house. When I'm down under, that woman will probably—

NORA: Shh! Not so loud. She's right in there.

395 RANK: Today as well. So you see.

NORA: Only to sew on my dress. Good gracious, how unrea-sonable you are. (*Sitting on the sofa.*) Be nice now, Dr. Rank. Tomorrow you'll see how beautifully I'll dance; and you can imagine then that I'm dancing only for you—yes, and of course for Torvald, too—that's under-
400 stood. (*Takes various items out of the carton.*) Dr. Rank, sit over here and I'll show you something.

RANK: (*Sitting.*) What's that?

NORA: Look here. Look.

RANK: Silk stockings.

405 NORA: Flesh-colored. Aren't they lovely? Now it's so dark here, but tomorrow—No, no, no, just look at the feet. Oh well, you might as well look at the rest.

RANK: Hm—

NORA: Why do you look so critical? Don't you believe they'll
410 fit?

RANK: I've never had any chance to form an opinion on that.

NORA: (*Glancing at him a moment.*) Shame on you. (*Hits him lightly on the ear with the stockings.*) That's for you. (*Puts them away again.*)

415 RANK: And what other splendors am I going to see now?

NORA: Not the least bit more, because you've been naughty. (*She hums a little and rummages among her things.*)

RANK: (*After a short silence.*) When I sit here together with you like this, completely easy and open, then I don't know—
420 I simply can't imagine—whatever would have become of me if I'd never come into this house.

NORA: (*Smiling.*) Yes, I really think you feel completely at ease with us.

RANK: (*More quietly, staring straight ahead.*) And then to have to
425 go away from it all—

NORA: Nonsense, you're not going away.

RANK: (*His voice unchanged.*)—and not even be able to leave
some poor show of gratitude behind, scarcely a fleeting
430 regret—no more than a vacant place that anyone can fill.

NORA: And if I asked you now for—? No—

RANK: For what?

NORA: For a great proof of your friendship—

RANK: Yes, yes?

435 NORA: No, I mean—for an exceptionally big favor—

RANK: Would you really, for once, make me so happy?

NORA: Oh, you haven't the vaguest idea what it is.

RANK: All right, then tell me.

NORA: No, but I can't, Dr. Rank—it's all out of reason. It's
440 advice and help, too—and a favor—

RANK: So much the better. I can't fathom what you're hint-
ing at. Just speak out. Don't you trust me?

NORA: Of course. More than anyone else. You're my best and
truest friend, I'm sure. That's why I want to talk to you.
445 All right, then, Dr. Rank: there's something you can help
me prevent. You know how deeply, how inexpressibly
dearly Torvald loves me; he'd never hesitate a second to
give up his life for me.

RANK: (*Leaning close to her.*) Nora—do you think he's the only
450 one—

NORA: (*With a slight start.*) Who—?

RANK: Who'd gladly give up his life for you.

NORA: (*Heavily.*) I see.

RANK: I swore to myself you should know this before I'm
455 gone. I'll never find a better chance. Yes, Nora, now you
know. And also you know now that you can trust me beyond anyone else.

NORA: (*Rising, natural and calm.*) Let me by.

RANK: (*Making room for her, but still sitting.*) Nora—

460 NORA: (*In the hall doorway.*) Helene, bring the lamp in. (*Goes over
to the stove.*) Ah, dear Dr. Rank, that was really mean of you.

RANK: (*Getting up.*) That I've loved you just as deeply as
somebody else? Was *that* mean?

NORA: No, but that you came out and told me. That was
465 quite unnecessary—

RANK: What do you mean? Have you known—?

(*The* MAID *comes in with the lamp, sets it on the table, and goes out
again.*)

RANK: Nora—Mrs. Helmer—I'm asking you: have you
known about it?

NORA: Oh, how can I tell what I know or don't know?
470 Really, I don't know what to say—Why did you have to
be so clumsy, Dr. Rank! Everything was so good.

RANK: Well, in any case, you now have the knowledge that
my body and soul are at your command. So won't you
speak out?

475 NORA: (*Looking at him.*) After that?

RANK: Please, just let me know what it is.

NORA: You can't know anything now.

RANK: I have to. You mustn't punish me like this. Give me
the chance to do whatever is humanly possible for you.

480 NORA: Now there's nothing you can do for me. Besides, actually, I don't need any help. You'll see—it's only my fantasies. That's what it is. Of course! (*Sits in the rocker, looks
at him, and smiles.*) What a nice one you are, Dr. Rank.
Aren't you a little bit ashamed, now that the lamp is here?

RANK: No, not exactly. But perhaps I'd better go—for good? 485

NORA: No, you certainly can't do that. You must come here just
as you always have. You know Torvald can't do without you.

RANK: Yes, but *you?*

NORA: You know how much I enjoy it when you're here.

RANK: That's precisely what threw me off. You're a mystery 490
to me. So many times I've felt you'd almost rather be with
me than with Helmer.

NORA: Yes—you see, there are some people that one loves most
and other people that one would almost prefer being with.

RANK: Yes, there's something to that. 495

NORA: When I was back home, of course I loved Papa most.
But I always thought it was so much fun when I could
sneak down to the maids' quarters, because they never
tried to improve me, and it was always so amusing, the
way they talked to each other. 500

RANK: Aha, so it's *their* place that I've filled.

NORA: (*Jumping up and going to him.*) Oh, dear, sweet Dr.
Rank, that's not what I meant at all. But you can understand that with Torvald it's just the same as with Papa—

(*The* MAID *enters from the hall.*)

MAID: Ma'am—please! (*She whispers to* NORA *and hands her a* 505
calling card.)

NORA: (*Glancing at the card.*) Ah! (*Slips it into her pocket.*)

RANK: Anything wrong?

NORA: No, no, not at all. It's only some—it's my new dress—

RANK: Really? But—there's your dress. 510

NORA: Oh, that. But this is another one—I ordered it—
Torvald mustn't know—

RANK: Ah, now we have the big secret.

NORA: That's right. Just go in with him—he's back in the inner study. Keep him there as long as— 515

RANK: Don't worry. He won't get away. (*Goes into the study.*)

NORA: (*To the* MAID.) And he's standing waiting in the kitchen?

MAID: Yes, he came up by the back stairs.

NORA: But didn't you tell him somebody was here?

MAID: Yes, but that didn't do any good. 520

NORA: He won't leave?

MAID: No, he won't go till he's talked with you, ma'am.

NORA: Let him come in, then—but quietly. Helene, don't
breathe a word about this. It's a surprise for my husband.

MAID: Yes, yes, I understand—(*Goes out.*) 525

NORA: This horror—it's going to happen. No, no, no, it can't
happen, it mustn't. (*She goes and bolts* HELMER's *door. The*
MAID *opens the hall door for* KROGSTAD *and shuts it behind
him. He is dressed for travel in a fur coat, boots, and a fur cap.*)

NORA: (*Going toward him.*) Talk softly. My husband's home. 530

KROGSTAD: Well, good for him.

NORA: What do you want?

KROGSTAD: Some information.

NORA: Hurry up, then. What is it?

KROGSTAD: You know, of course, that I got my notice. 535

NORA: I couldn't prevent it, Mr. Krogstad. I fought for you to
the bitter end, but nothing worked.

KROGSTAD: Does your husband's love for you run so thin?
He knows everything I can expose you to, and all the
same he dares to— 540

NORA: How can you imagine he knows anything about this?

KROGSTAD: Ah, no—I can't imagine it either, now. It's not at
all like my fine Torvald Helmer to have so much guts—

NORA: Mr. Krogstad, I demand respect for my husband!

545 KROGSTAD: Why, of course—all due respect. But since the lady's keeping it so carefully hidden, may I presume to ask if you're also a bit better informed than yesterday about what you've actually done?

NORA: More than you ever could teach me.

550 KROGSTAD: Yes, I *am* such an awful lawyer.

NORA: What is it you want from me?

KROGSTAD: Just a glimpse of how you are, Mrs. Helmer. I've been thinking about you all day long. A cashier, a night—court scribbler, a—well, a type like me also has a little of

555 what they call a heart, you know.

NORA: Then show it. Think of my children.

KROGSTAD: Did you or your husband ever think of mine? But never mind. I simply wanted to tell you that you don't need to take this thing too seriously. For the present,

560 I'm not proceeding with any action.

NORA: Oh no, really! Well—I knew that.

KROGSTAD: Everything can be settled in a friendly spirit. It doesn't have to get around town at all; it can stay just among us three.

565 NORA: My husband must never know anything of this.

KROGSTAD: How can you manage that? Perhaps you can pay me the balance?

NORA: No, not right now.

KROGSTAD: Or you know some way of raising the money in

570 a day or two?

NORA: No way that I'm willing to use.

KROGSTAD: Well, it wouldn't have done you any good, anyway. If you stood in front of me with a fistful of bills, you still couldn't buy your signature back.

575 NORA: Then tell me what you're going to do with it.

KROGSTAD: I'll just hold onto it—keep it on file. There's no outsider who'll even get wind of it. So if you've been thinking of taking some desperate step—

NORA: I have.

580 KROGSTAD: Been thinking of running away from home—

NORA: I have!

KROGSTAD: Or even of something worse—

NORA: How could you guess that?

KROGSTAD: You can drop those thoughts.

585 NORA: How could you guess I was thinking of *that*?

KROGSTAD: Most of us think about *that* at first. I thought about it too, but I discovered I hadn't the courage—

NORA: (*Lifelessly.*) I don't either.

KROGSTAD: (*Relieved.*) That's true, you haven't the courage?

590 You too?

NORA: I don't have it—I don't have it.

KROGSTAD: It would be terribly stupid, anyway. After that first storm at home blows out, why, then—I have here in my pocket a letter for your husband—

595 NORA: Telling everything?

KROGSTAD: As charitably as possible.

NORA: (*Quickly.*) He mustn't ever get that letter. Tear it up. I'll find some way to get money.

KROGSTAD: Beg pardon, Mrs. Helmer, but I think I just told

600 you—

NORA: Oh, I don't mean the money I owe you. Let me know how much you want from my husband, and I'll manage it.

KROGSTAD: I don't want any money from your husband.

NORA: What do you want, then? 605

KROGSTAD: I'll tell you what. I want to recoup, Mrs. Helmer; I want to get on in the world—and there's where your husband can help me. For a year and a half I've kept myself clean of anything disreputable—all that time struggling with the worst conditions; but I was satisfied, 610 working my way up step by step. Now I've been written right off, and I'm just not in the mood to come crawling back. I tell you, I want to move on. I want to get back in the bank—in a better position. Your husband can set up a job for me— 615

NORA: He'll never do that!

KROGSTAD: He'll do it. I know him. He won't dare breathe a word of protest. And once I'm in there together with him, you just wait and see! Inside of a year, I'll be the manager's righthand man. It'll be Nils Krogstad, not Tor- 620 vald Helmer, who runs the bank.

NORA: You'll never see the day!

KROGSTAD: Maybe you think you can—

NORA: I have the courage now—for *that*.

KROGSTAD: Oh, you don't scare me. A smart, spoiled lady like 625 you—

NORA: You'll see; you'll see!

KROGSTAD: Under the ice, maybe? Down in the freezing, coal-black water? There, till you float up in the spring, ugly, unrecognizable, with your hair falling out— 630

NORA: You don't frighten me.

KROGSTAD: Nor do you frighten me. One doesn't do these things, Mrs. Helmer. Besides, what good would it be? I'd still have him safe in my pocket.

NORA: Afterwards? When I'm no longer—? 635

KROGSTAD: Are you forgetting that *I'll* be in control then over your final reputation? (NORA *stands speechless, staring at him.*) Good; now I've warned you. Don't do anything stupid. When Helmer's read my letter, I'll be waiting for his reply. And bear in mind that it's your husband himself who's 640 forced me back to my old ways. I'll never forgive him for that. Good-bye, Mrs. Helmer. (*He goes out through the hall.*)

NORA: (*Goes to the hall door, opens it a crack, and listens.*) He's gone. Didn't leave the letter. Oh no, no, that's impossible too! (*Opening the door more and more.*) What's that? He's 645 standing outside—not going downstairs. He's thinking it over? Maybe he'll—? (*A letter falls in the mailbox; then* KROGSTAD's *footsteps are heard, dying away down a flight of stairs.* NORA *gives a muffled cry and runs over toward the sofa table. A short pause.*) In the mailbox. (*Slips warily over to the* 650 *hall door.*) It's lying there. Torvald, Torvald—now we're lost!

MRS. LINDE: (*Entering with the costume from the room, left.*) There now, I can't see anything else to mend. Perhaps you'd like to try—

NORA: (*In a hoarse whisper.*) Kristine, come here. 655

MRS. LINDE: (*Tossing the dress on the sofa.*) What's wrong? You look upset.

NORA: Come here. See that letter? *There!* Look—through the glass in the mailbox.

MRS. LINDE: Yes, yes, I see it. 660

NORA: That letter's from Krogstad—

MRS. LINDE: Nora—it's Krogstad who loaned you the money!

NORA: Yes, and now Torvald will find out everything.

MRS. LINDE: Believe me, Nora, it's best for both of you.

665 NORA: There's more you don't know. I forged a name.

MRS. LINDE: But for heaven's sake—?

NORA: I only want to tell you that, Kristine, so that you can be my witness.

MRS. LINDE: Witness? Why should I—?

670 NORA: If I should go out of my mind—it could easily happen—

MRS. LINDE: Nora!

NORA: Or anything else occurred—so I couldn't be present here—

MRS. LINDE: Nora, Nora, you aren't yourself at all!

675 NORA: And someone should try to take on the whole weight, all of the guilt, you follow me—

MRS. LINDE: Yes, of course, but why do you think—?

NORA: Then you're the witness that it isn't true, Kristine. I'm very much myself; my mind right now is perfectly clear; 680 and I'm telling you: nobody else has known about this; I alone did everything. Remember that.

MRS. LINDE: I will. But I don't understand all this.

NORA: Oh, how could you ever understand it? It's the miracle now that's going to take place.

685 MRS. LINDE: The miracle?

NORA: Yes, the miracle. But it's so awful, Kristine. It mustn't take place, not for anything in the world.

MRS. LINDE: I'm going right over and talk with Krogstad.

NORA: Don't go near him; he'll do you some terrible harm!

690 MRS. LINDE: There was a time once when he'd gladly have done anything for me.

NORA: He?

MRS. LINDE: Where does he live?

NORA: Oh, how do I know? Yes. (Searches in her pocket.) Here's 695 his card. But the letter, the letter—!

HELMER: (From the study, knocking on the door.) Nora!

NORA: (With a cry of fear.) Oh! What is it? What do you want?

HELMER: Now, now, don't be so frightened. We're not coming in. You locked the door—are you trying on the dress?

700 NORA: Yes, I'm trying it. I'll look just beautiful, Torvald.

MRS. LINDE: (Who has read the card.) He's living right around the corner.

NORA: Yes, but what's the use? We're lost. The letter's in the box.

705 MRS. LINDE: And your husband has the key?

NORA: Yes, always.

MRS. LINDE: Krogstad can ask for his letter back unread; he can find some excuse—

NORA: But it's just this time that Torvald usually—

710 MRS. LINDE: Stall him. Keep him in there. I'll be back as quick as I can. (She hurries out through the hall entrance.)

NORA: (Goes to HELMER's door, opens it, and peers in.) Torvald!

HELMER: (From the inner study.) Well—does one dare set foot in one's own living room at last? Come on, Rank, now 715 we'll get a look—(In the doorway.) But what's this?

NORA: What, Torvald dear?

HELMER: Rank had me expecting some grand masquerade.

RANK: (In the doorway.) That was my impression, but I must have been wrong.

720 NORA: No one can admire me in my splendor—not till tomorrow.

HELMER: But Nora dear, you look so exhausted. Have you practiced too hard?

NORA: No, I haven't practiced at all yet.

HELMER: You know, it's necessary— 725

NORA: Oh, it's absolutely necessary, Torvald. But I can't get anywhere without your help. I've forgotten the whole thing completely.

HELMER: Ah, we'll soon take care of that.

NORA: Yes, take care of me, Torvald, please! Promise me that? 730 Oh, I'm so nervous. That big party—You must give up everything this evening for me. No business—don't even touch your pen. Yes? Dear Torvald, promise?

HELMER: It's a promise. Tonight I'm totally at your service— you little helpless thing. Hm—but first there's one thing I 735 want to—(Goes toward the hall door.)

NORA: What are you looking for?

HELMER: Just to see if there's any mail.

NORA: No, no, don't do that, Torvald!

HELMER: Now what? 740

NORA: Torvald, please. There isn't any.

HELMER: Let me look, though. (Starts out. NORA, at the piano, strikes the first notes of the tarantella. HELMER, at the door, stops.) Aha!

NORA: I can't dance tomorrow if I don't practice with you. 745

HELMER: (Going over to her.) Nora dear, are you really so frightened?

NORA: Yes, so terribly frightened. Let me practice right now; there's still time before dinner. Oh, sit down and play for me, Torvald. Direct me. Teach me, the way you always 750 have.

HELMER: Gladly, if it's what you want. (Sits at the piano.)

NORA: (Snatches the tambourine up from the box, then a long, varicolored shawl, which she throws around herself, whereupon she springs forward and cries out:) Play for me now! Now I'll 755 dance!

(HELMER plays and NORA dances. RANK stands behind HELMER at the piano and looks on.)

HELMER: (As he plays.) Slower. Slow down.

NORA: Can't change it.

HELMER: Not so violent, Nora!

NORA: Has to be just like this. 760

HELMER: (Stopping.) No, no, that won't do at all.

NORA: (Laughing and swinging her tambourine.) Isn't that what I told you?

RANK: Let me play for her.

HELMER: (Getting up.) Yes, go on. I can teach her more easily 765 then.

(RANK sits at the piano and plays; NORA dances more and more wildly. HELMER has stationed himself by the stove and repeatedly gives her directions; she seems not to hear them; her hair loosens and falls over her shoulders; she does not notice, but goes on dancing. MRS. LINDE enters.)

MRS. LINDE: (Standing dumbfounded at the door.) Ah—!

NORA: (Still dancing.) See what fun, Kristine!

HELMER: But Nora darling, you dance as if your life were at stake. 770

NORA: And it is.

HELMER: Rank, stop! This is pure madness. Stop it, I say!

(RANK *breaks off playing, and* NORA *halts abruptly*).

HELMER: (*Going over to her.*) I never would have believed it. You've forgotten everything I taught you.

775 NORA: (*Throwing away the tambourine.*) You see for yourself.

HELMER: Well, there's certainly room for instruction here.

NORA: Yes, you see how important it is. You've got to teach me to the very last minute. Promise me that, Torvald?

HELMER: You can bet on it.

780 NORA: You mustn't, either today or tomorrow, think about anything else but me; you mustn't open any letters—or the mailbox—

HELMER: Ah, it's still the fear of that man—

NORA: Oh yes, yes, that too.

785 HELMER: Nora, it's written all over you—there's already a letter from him out there.

NORA: I don't know. I guess so. But you mustn't read such things now; there mustn't be anything ugly between us before it's all over.

790 RANK: (*Quietly to* HELMER.) You shouldn't deny her.

HELMER: (*Putting his arm around her.*) The child can have her way. But tomorrow night, after you've danced—

NORA: Then you'll be free.

MAID: (*In the doorway, right.*) Ma'am, dinner is served.

795 NORA: We'll be wanting champagne, Helene.

MAID: Very good, ma'am. (*Goes out.*)

HELMER: So—a regular banquet, hm?

NORA: Yes, a banquet—champagne till daybreak! (*Calling out.*) And some macaroons, Helene. Heaps of them—just

800 this once.

HELMER: (*Taking her hands.*) Now, now, now—no hysterics. Be my own little lark again.

NORA: Oh, I will soon enough. But go on in—and you, Dr. Rank. Kristine, help me put up my hair.

805 RANK: (*Whispering, as they go.*) There's nothing wrong—really wrong, is there?

HELMER: Oh, of course not. It's nothing more than this childish anxiety I was telling you about. (*They go out, right.*)

NORA: Well?

810 MRS. LINDE: Left town.

NORA: I could see by your face.

MRS. LINDE: He'll be home tomorrow evening. I wrote him a note.

NORA: You shouldn't have. Don't try to stop anything now. After all, it's a wonderful joy, this waiting here for the miracle.

815 MRS. LINDE: What is it you're waiting for?

NORA: Oh, you can't understand that. Go in to them; I'll be along in a moment.

(MRS. LINDE *goes into the dining room.* NORA *stands a short while as if composing herself; then she looks at her watch.*)

NORA: Five. Seven hours to midnight. Twenty-four hours to

820 the midnight after, and then the tarantella's done. Seven and twenty-four? Thirty-one hours to live.

HELMER: (*In the doorway, right.*) What's become of the little lark?

NORA: (*Going toward him with open arms.*) Here's your lark!

ACT THREE

Same scene. The table, with chairs around it, has been moved to the center of the room. A lamp on the table is lit. The hall door stands open. Dance music drifts down from the floor above. MRS. LINDE *sits at the table, absently paging through a book, trying to read, but apparently unable to focus her thoughts. Once or twice she pauses, tensely listening for a sound at the outer entrance.*

MRS. LINDE: (*Glancing at her watch.*) Not yet—and there's hardly any time left. If only he's not—(*Listening again.*) Ah, there he is. (*She goes out in the hall and cautiously opens the outer door. Quiet footsteps are heard on the stairs. She whispers:*) Come in. Nobody's here.   5

KROGSTAD: (*In the doorway.*) I found a note from you at home. What's back of all this?

MRS. LINDE: I just *had* to talk to you.

KROGSTAD: Oh? And it just *had* to be here in this house?

MRS. LINDE: At my place it was impossible; my room hasn't a   10 private entrance. Come in; we're all alone. The maid's asleep, and the Helmers are at the dance upstairs.

KROGSTAD: (*Entering the room.*) Well, well, the Helmers are dancing tonight? Really?

MRS. LINDE: Yes, why not?   15

KROGSTAD: How true—why not?

MRS. LINDE: All right, Krogstad, let's talk.

KROGSTAD: Do we two have anything more to talk about?

MRS. LINDE: We have a great deal to talk about.

KROGSTAD: I wouldn't have thought so.   20

MRS. LINDE: No, because you've never understood me, really.

KROGSTAD: Was there anything more to understand—except what's all too common in life? A calculating woman throws over a man the moment a better catch comes by.

MRS. LINDE: You think I'm so thoroughly calculating? You   25 think I broke it off lightly?

KROGSTAD: Didn't you?

MRS. LINDE: Nils—is that what you really thought?

KROGSTAD: If you cared, then why did you write me the way you did?   30

MRS. LINDE: What else could I do? If I had to break off with you, then it was my job as well to root out everything you felt for me.

KROGSTAD: (*Wringing his hands.*) So that was it. And this—all this, simply for money!   35

MRS. LINDE: Don't forget I had a helpless mother and two small brothers. We couldn't wait for you, Nils; you had such a long road ahead of you then.

KROGSTAD: That may be; but you still hadn't the right to abandon me for somebody else's sake.   40

MRS. LINDE: Yes—I don't know. So many, many times I've asked myself if I did have that right.

KROGSTAD: (*More softly.*) When I lost you, it was as if all the solid ground dissolved from under my feet. Look at me; I'm a half-drowned man now, hanging onto a wreck.   45

MRS. LINDE: Help may be near.

KROGSTAD: It was near—but then you came and blocked it off.

MRS. LINDE: Without my knowing it, Nils. Today for the first time I learned that it's you I'm replacing at the bank.

KROGSTAD: All right—I believe you. But now that you know,   50 will you step aside?

MRS. LINDE: No, because that wouldn't benefit you in the slightest.

KROGSTAD: Not "benefit" me, hm! I'd step aside anyway.

MRS. LINDE: I've learned to be realistic. Life and hard, bitter   55 necessity have taught me that.

KROGSTAD: And life's taught me never to trust fine phrases.

MRS. LINDE: Then life's taught you a very sound thing. But you do have to trust in actions, don't you?

60 KROGSTAD: What does that mean?

MRS. LINDE: You said you were hanging on like a half-drowned man to a wreck.

KROGSTAD: I've good reason to say that.

MRS. LINDE: I'm also like a half-drowned woman on a wreck.
65 No one to suffer with; no one to care for.

KROGSTAD: You made your choice.

MRS. LINDE: There wasn't any choice then.

KROGSTAD: So—what of it?

MRS. LINDE: Nils, if only we two shipwrecked people could
70   reach across to each other.

KROGSTAD: What are you saying?

MRS. LINDE: Two on one wreck are at least better off than each on his own.

KROGSTAD: Kristine!

75 MRS. LINDE: Why do you think I came into town?

KROGSTAD: Did you really have some thought of me?

MRS. LINDE: I have to work to go on living. All my born days, as long as I can remember, I've worked, and it's been my best and my only joy. But now I'm completely alone
80   in the world; it frightens me to be so empty and lost. To work for yourself—there's no joy in that. Nils, give me something—someone to work for.

KROGSTAD: I don't believe all this. It's just some hysterical feminine urge to go out and make a noble sacrifice.

85 MRS. LINDE: Have you ever found me to be hysterical?

KROGSTAD: Can you honestly mean this? Tell me—do you know everything about my past?

MRS. LINDE: Yes.

KROGSTAD: And you know what they think I'm worth
90   around here.

MRS. LINDE: From what you were saying before, it would seem that with me you could have been another person.

KROGSTAD: I'm positive of that.

MRS. LINDE: Couldn't it happen still?

95 KROGSTAD: Kristine—you're saying this in all seriousness? Yes, you are! I can see it in you. And do you really have the courage, then—?

MRS. LINDE: I need to have someone to care for; and your children need a mother. We both need each other. Nils, I
100   have faith that you're good at heart—I'll risk everything together with you.

KROGSTAD: (*Gripping her hands.*) Kristine, thank you, thank you—Now I know I can win back a place in their eyes. Yes—but I forgot—

105 MRS. LINDE: (*Listening.*) Shh! The tarantella. Go now! Go on!

KROGSTAD: Why? What is it?

MRS. LINDE: Hear the dance up there? When that's over, they'll be coming down.

KROGSTAD: Oh, then I'll go. But—it's all pointless. Of course,
110   you don't know the move I made against the Helmers.

MRS. LINDE: Yes, Nils, I know.

KROGSTAD: And all the same, you have the courage to—?

MRS. LINDE: I know how far despair can drive a man like you.

KROGSTAD: Oh, if I only could take it all back.

115 MRS. LINDE: You easily could—your letter's still lying in the mailbox.

KROGSTAD: Are you sure of that?

MRS. LINDE: Positive. But—

KROGSTAD: (*Looks at her searchingly.*) Is that the meaning of it, then? You'll save your friend at any price. Tell me straight 120 out. Is that it?

MRS. LINDE: Nils—anyone who's sold herself for somebody else once isn't going to do it again.

KROGSTAD: I'll demand my letter back.

MRS. LINDE: No, no. 125

KROGSTAD: Yes, of course. I'll stay here till Helmer comes down; I'll tell him to give me my letter again—that it only involves my dismissal—that he shouldn't read it—

MRS. LINDE: No, Nils, don't call the letter back.

KROGSTAD: But wasn't that exactly why you wrote me to 130 come here?

MRS. LINDE: Yes, in that first panic. But it's been a whole day and night since then, and in that time I've seen such incredible things in this house. Helmer's got to learn everything; this dreadful secret has to be aired; those two have to come to a 135 full understanding; all these lies and evasions can't go on.

KROGSTAD: Well, then, if you want to chance it. But at least there's one thing I can do, and do right away—

MRS. LINDE: (*Listening.*) Go now, go, quick! The dance is over. We're not safe another second. 140

KROGSTAD: I'll wait for you downstairs.

MRS. LINDE: Yes, please do; take me home.

KROGSTAD: I can't believe it; I've never been so happy. (*He leaves by way of the outer door; the door between the room and the hall stays open.*) 145

MRS. LINDE: (*Straightening up a bit and getting together her street clothes.*) How different now! How different! Someone to work for, to live for—a home to build. Well, it is worth the try! Oh, if they'd only come! (*Listening.*) Ah, there they are. Bundle up. (*She picks up her hat and coat.* NORA's *and* 150 HELMER's *voices can be heard outside; a key turns in the lock, and* HELMER *brings* NORA *into the hall almost by force. She is wearing the Italian costume with a large black shawl about her; he has on evening dress, with a black domino open over it.*)

NORA: (*Struggling in the doorway.*) No, no, no, not inside! I'm 155 going up again. I don't want to leave so soon.

HELMER: But Nora dear—

NORA: Oh, I beg you, please, Torvald. From the bottom of my heart, *please*—only an hour more!

HELMER: Not a single minute, Nora darling. You know our 160 agreement. Come on, in we go; you'll catch cold out here. (*In spite of her resistance, he gently draws her into the room.*)

MRS. LINDE: Good evening.

NORA: Kristine!

HELMER: Why, Mrs. Linde—are you here so late? 165

MRS. LINDE: Yes, I'm sorry, but I did want to see Nora in costume.

NORA: Have you been sitting here, waiting for me?

MRS. LINDE: Yes. I didn't come early enough; you were all upstairs; and then I thought I really couldn't leave without 170 seeing you.

HELMER: (*Removing* NORA's *shawl.*) Yes, take a good look. She's worth looking at, I can tell you that, Mrs. Linde. Isn't she lovely?

MRS. LINDE: Yes, I should say— 175

HELMER: A dream of loveliness, isn't she? That's what everyone thought at the party, too. But she's horribly stubborn—this sweet little thing. What's to be done with her?

Can you imagine, I almost had to use force to pry her away.

180 NORA: Oh, Torvald, you're going to regret you didn't indulge me, even for just a half hour more.

HELMER: There, you see. She danced her tarantella and got a tumultuous hand—which was well earned, although the performance may have been a bit too naturalistic—I mean
185 it rather overstepped the proprieties of art. But never mind—what's important is, she made a success, an overwhelming success. You think I could let her stay on after that and spoil the effect? Oh no; I took my lovely little Capri girl—my capricious little Capri girl, I should say—
190 took her under my arm; one quick tour of the ballroom, a curtsy to every side, and then—as they say in novels—the beautiful vision disappeared. An exit should always be effective, Mrs. Linde, but that's what I can't get Nora to grasp. Phew, it's hot in here. (*Flings the domino on a chair and opens*
195 *the door to his room.*) Why's it dark in here? Oh yes, of course. Excuse me. (*He goes in and lights a couple of candles.*)

NORA: (*In a sharp, breathless whisper.*) So?

MRS. LINDE: (*Quietly.*) I talked with him.

NORA: And—?

200 MRS. LINDE: Nora—you must tell your husband everything.

NORA: (*Dully.*) I knew it.

MRS. LINDE: You've got nothing to fear from Krogstad, but you have to speak out.

NORA: I won't tell.

205 MRS. LINDE: Then the letter will.

NORA: Thanks, Kristine. I know now what's to be done. Shh!

HELMER: (*Reentering.*) Well, then, Mrs. Linde—have you admired her?

MRS. LINDE: Yes, and now I'll say good night.

210 HELMER: Oh, come, so soon? Is this yours, this knitting?

MRS. LINDE: Yes, thanks. I nearly forgot it.

HELMER: Do you knit, then?

MRS. LINDE: Oh yes.

HELMER: You know what? You should embroider instead.

215 MRS. LINDE: Really? Why?

HELMER: Yes, because it's a lot prettier. See here, one holds the embroidery so, in the left hand, and then one guides the needle with the right—so—in an easy, sweeping curve—right?

MRS. LINDE: Yes, I guess that's—

220 HELMER: But, on the other hand, knitting—it can never be anything but ugly. Look, see here, the arms tucked in, the knitting needles going up and down—there's something Chinese about it. Ah, that was really a glorious champagne they served.

225 MRS. LINDE: Yes, good night, Nora, and don't be stubborn anymore.

HELMER: Well put, Mrs. Linde!

MRS. LINDE: Good night, Mr. Helmer.

HELMER: (*Accompanying her to the door.*) Good night, good
230 night. I hope you get home all right. I'd be very happy to—but you don't have far to go. Good night, good night. (*She leaves. He shuts the door after her and returns.*) There, now, at last we got her out the door. She's a deadly bore, that creature.

235 NORA: Aren't you pretty tired, Torvald?

HELMER: No, not a bit.

NORA: You're not sleepy?

HELMER: Not at all. On the contrary, I'm feeling quite exhilarated. But you? Yes, you really look tired and sleepy.

240 NORA: Yes, I'm very tired. Soon now I'll sleep.

HELMER: See! You see! I was right all along that we shouldn't stay longer.

NORA: Whatever you do is always right.

HELMER: (*Kissing her brow.*) Now my little lark talks sense. Say,
245 did you notice what a time Rank was having tonight?

NORA: Oh, was he? I didn't get to speak with him.

HELMER: I scarcely did either, but it's a long time since I've seen him in such high spirits. (*Gazes at her a moment, then comes nearer her.*) Hm—it's marvelous, though, to be back
250 home again—to be completely alone with you. Oh, you bewitchingly lovely young woman!

NORA: Torvald, don't look at me like that!

HELMER: Can't I look at my richest treasure? At all that beauty that's mine, mine alone—completely and utterly.

255 NORA: (*Moving around to the other side of the table.*) You mustn't talk to me that way tonight.

HELMER: (*Following her.*) The tarantella is still in your blood, I can see—and it makes you even more enticing. Listen. The guests are beginning to go. (*Dropping his voice.*)
260 Nora—it'll soon be quiet through this whole house.

NORA: Yes, I hope so.

HELMER: You do, don't you, my love? Do you realize—when I'm out at a party like this with you—do you know why I talk to you so little, and keep such a distance away; just
265 send you a stolen look now and then—you know why I do it? It's because I'm imagining then that you're my secret darling, my secret young bride-to-be, and that no one suspects there's anything between us.

NORA: Yes, yes; oh, yes, I know you're always thinking of me.

270 HELMER: And then when we leave and I place the shawl over those fine young rounded shoulders—over that wonderful curving neck—then I pretend that you're my young bride, that we're just coming from the wedding, that for the first time I'm bringing you into my house—that for the first
275 time I'm alone with you—completely alone with you, your trembling young beauty! All this evening I've longed for nothing but you. When I saw you turn and sway in the tarantella—my blood was pounding till I couldn't stand it—that's why I brought you down here so early—

280 NORA: Go away, Torvald! Leave me alone. I don't want all this.

HELMER: What do you mean? Nora, you're teasing me. You will, won't you? Aren't I your husband—?

(*A knock at the outside door.*)

NORA: (*Startled.*) What's that?

HELMER: (*Going toward the hall.*) Who is it?

285 RANK: (*Outside.*) It's me. May I come in a moment?

HELMER: (*With quiet irritation.*) Oh, what does he want now? (*Aloud.*) Hold on. (*Goes and opens the door.*) Oh, how nice that you didn't just pass us by!

RANK: I thought I heard your voice, and then I wanted so badly to have a look in. (*Lightly glancing about.*) Ah, me, these old
290 familiar haunts. You have it snug and cozy in here, you two.

HELMER: You seemed to be having it pretty cozy upstairs, too.

RANK: Absolutely. Why shouldn't I? Why not take in everything in life? As much as you can, anyway, and as long as you can. The wine was superb—
295 HELMER: The champagne especially.

RANK: You noticed that too? It's amazing how much I could guzzle down.

NORA: Torvald also drank a lot of champagne this evening.

300 RANK: Oh?

NORA: Yes, and that always makes him so entertaining.

RANK: Well, why shouldn't one have a pleasant evening after a well-spent day?

HELMER: Well spent? I'm afraid I can't claim that.

305 RANK: (*Slapping him on the back.*) But I can, you see!

NORA: Dr. Rank, you must have done some scientific research today.

RANK: Quite so.

HELMER: Come now—little Nora talking about scientific re-
310 search!

RANK: Indeed you may.

NORA: Then they were good?

RANK: The best possible for both doctor and patient—certainty.

315 NORA: (*Quickly and searchingly.*) Certainty?

RANK: Complete certainty. So don't I owe myself a gay evening afterwards?

NORA: Yes, you're right, Dr. Rank.

HELMER: I'm with you—just so long as you don't have to suf-
320 fer for it in the morning.

RANK: Well, one never gets something for nothing in life.

NORA: Dr. Rank—are you very fond of masquerade parties?

RANK: Yes, if there's a good array of odd disguises—

NORA: Tell me, what should we two go as at the next mas-
325 querade?

HELMER: You little featherhead—already thinking of the next!

RANK: We two? I'll tell you what: you must go as Charmed Life—

HELMER: Yes, but find a costume for *that*!

330 RANK: Your wife can appear just as she looks every day.

HELMER: That was nicely put. But don't you know what you're going to be?

RANK: Yes, Helmer, I've made up my mind.

HELMER: Well?

335 RANK: At the next masquerade I'm going to be invisible.

HELMER: That's a funny idea.

RANK: They say there's a hat—black, huge—have you never heard of the hat that makes you invisible? You put it on, and then no one on earth can see you.

340 HELMER: (*Suppressing a smile.*) Ah, of course.

RANK: But I'm quite forgetting what I came for. Helmer, give me a cigar, one of the dark Havanas.

HELMER: With the greatest pleasure. (*Holds out his case.*)

RANK: Thanks. (*Takes one and cuts off the tip.*)

345 NORA: (*Striking a match.*) Let me give you a light.

RANK: Thank you. (*She holds the match for him; he lights the cigar.*) And now good-bye.

HELMER: Good-bye, good-bye, old friend.

NORA: Sleep well, Doctor.

350 RANK: Thanks for that wish.

NORA: Wish me the same.

RANK: You? All right, if you like—Sleep well. And thanks for the light. (*He nods to them both and leaves.*)

HELMER: (*His voice subdued.*) He's been drinking heavily.

355 NORA: (*Absently.*) Could be. (HELMER *takes his keys from his pocket and goes out in the hall.*) Torvald—what are you after?

HELMER: Got to empty the mailbox; it's nearly full. There won't be room for the morning papers.

NORA: Are you working tonight?

360 HELMER: You know I'm not. Why—what's this? Someone's been at the lock.

NORA: At the lock—?

HELMER: Yes, I'm positive. What do you suppose—? I can't imagine one of the maids—? Here's a broken hairpin. Nora, it's yours— 365

NORA: (*Quickly.*) Then it must be the children—

HELMER: You'd better break them of that. Hm, hm—well, opened it after all. (*Takes the contents out and calls into the kitchen.*) Helene! Helene, would you put out the lamp in the hall. (*He returns to the room, shutting the hall door, then* 370
displays the handful of mail.) Look how it's piled up. (*Sorting through them.*) Now what's this?

NORA: (*At the window.*) The letter! Oh, Torvald, no!

HELMER: Two calling cards—from Rank.

NORA: From Dr. Rank? 375

HELMER: (*Examining them.*) "Dr. Rank, Consulting Physician." They were on top. He must have dropped them in as he left.

NORA: Is there anything on them?

HELMER: There's a black cross over the name. See? That's a gruesome notion. He could almost be announcing his 380
own death.

NORA: That's just what he's doing.

HELMER: What! You've heard something? Something he's told you?

NORA: Yes. That when those cards came, he'd be taking his 385
leave of us. He'll shut himself in now and die.

HELMER: Ah, my poor friend! Of course I knew he wouldn't be here much longer. But so soon—And then to hide himself away like a wounded animal.

NORA: If it has to happen, then it's best it happens in si- 390
lence—don't you think so, Torvald?

HELMER: (*Pacing up and down.*) He'd grown right into our lives. I simply can't imagine him gone. He with his suffering and loneliness—like a dark cloud setting off our sunlit happiness. Well, maybe it's best this way. For him, at 395
least. (*Standing still.*) And maybe for us too, Nora. Now we're thrown back on each other, completely. (*Embracing her.*) Oh you, my darling wife, how can I hold you close enough? You know what, Nora—time and again I've wished you were in some terrible danger, just so I could 400
stake my life and soul and everything, for your sake.

NORA: (*Tearing herself away, her voice firm and decisive.*) Now you must read your mail, Torvald.

HELMER: No, no, not tonight. I want to stay with you, dearest.

NORA: With a dying friend on your mind? 405

HELMER: You're right. We've both had a shock. There's ugliness between us—these thoughts of death and corruption. We'll have to get free of them first. Until then—we'll stay apart.

NORA: (*Clinging about his neck.*) Torvald—good night! Good night! 410

HELMER: (*Kissing her on the cheek.*) Good night, little songbird. Sleep well, Nora. I'll be reading my mail now. (*He takes the letters into his room and shuts the door after him.*)

NORA: (*With bewildered glances, groping about, seizing* HELMER's *domino, throwing it around her, and speaking in short, hoarse,* 415
broken whispers.) Never see him again. Never, never. (*Putting her shawl over her head.*) Never see the children either—them, too. Never, never. Oh, the freezing black water! The depths—down—Oh, I wish it were over—He has it now; he's reading it—now. Oh no, no, not yet. Tor- 420
vald, good-bye, you and the children—(*She starts for the hall; as she does,* HELMER *throws open his door and stands with an open letter in his hand.*)

HELMER: Nora!

425 NORA: (*Screams.*) Oh—!

HELMER: What is this? You know what's in this letter?

NORA: Yes, I know. Let me go! Let me out!

HELMER: (*Holding her back.*) Where are you going?

NORA: (*Struggling to break loose.*) You can't save me, Torvald!

430 HELMER: (*Slumping back.*) True! Then it's true what he writes! How horrible! No, no, it's impossible—it can't be true.

NORA: It is true. I've loved you more than all this world.

HELMER: Ah, none of your slippery tricks.

NORA: (*Taking one step toward him.*) Torvald—!

435 HELMER: What *is* this you've blundered into!

NORA: Just let me loose. You're not going to suffer for my sake. You're not going to take on my guilt.

HELMER: No more playacting. (*Locks the hall door.*) You stay right here and give me a reckoning. You understand what 440 you've done? Answer! You understand?

NORA: (*Looking squarely at him, her face hardening.*) Yes. I'm beginning to understand everything now.

HELMER: (*Striding about.*) Oh, what an awful awakening! In all these eight years—she who was my pride and joy—a hyp-445 ocrite, a liar—worse, worse—a criminal! How infinitely disgusting it all is! The shame! (*NORA says nothing and goes on looking straight at him. He stops in front of her.*) I should have suspected something of the kind. I should have known. All your father's flimsy values—Be still! All your father's flimsy 450 values have come out in you. No religion, no morals, no sense of duty—Oh, how I'm punished for letting him off! I did it for your sake, and you repay me like this.

NORA: Yes, like this.

HELMER: Now you've wrecked all my happiness—ruined my 455 whole future. Oh, it's awful to think of. I'm in a cheap little grafter's hands; he can do anything he wants with me, ask for anything, play with me like a puppet—and I can't breathe a word. I'll be swept down miserably into the depths on account of a featherbrained woman.

460 NORA: When I'm gone from this world, you'll be free.

HELMER: Oh, quit posing. Your father had a mess of those speeches too. What good would that ever do me if you were gone from this world, as you say? Not the slightest. He can still make the whole thing known; and if he does, I could be 465 falsely suspected as your accomplice. They might even think that I was behind it—that I put you up to it. And all that I can thank you for—you that I've coddled the whole of our marriage. Can you see now what you've done to me?

NORA: (*Icily calm.*) Yes.

470 HELMER: It's so incredible, I just can't grasp it. But we'll have to patch up whatever we can. Take off the shawl. I said, take it off! I've got to appease him somehow or other. The thing has to be hushed up at any cost. And as for you and me, it's got to seem like everything between us is just 475 as it was—to the outside world, that is. You'll go right on living in this house, of course. But you can't be allowed to bring up the children; I don't dare trust you with them— Oh, to have to say this to someone I've loved so much, and that I still—! Well, that's done with. From now on 480 happiness doesn't matter; all that matters is saving the bits and pieces, the appearance—(*The doorbell rings.* HELMER *starts.*) What's that? And so late. Maybe the worst—? You think he'd—? Hide, Nora! Say you're sick. (*NORA remains standing motionless.* HELMER *goes and opens the door.*)

MAID: (*Half dressed, in the hall.*) A letter for Mrs. Helmer. 485

HELMER: I'll take it. (*Snatches the letter and shuts the door.*) Yes, it's from him. You don't get it; I'm reading it myself.

NORA: Then read it.

HELMER: (*By the lamp.*) I hardly dare. We may be ruined, you and I. But—I've got to know. (*Rips open the letter, skims* 490 *through a few lines, glances at an enclosure, then cries out joyfully.*) Nora! (NORA *looks inquiringly at him.*) Nora! Wait— better check it again—Yes, yes, it's true. I'm saved. Nora, I'm saved!

NORA: And I? 495

HELMER: You too, of course. We're both saved, both of us. Look. He's sent back your note. He says he's sorry and ashamed—that a happy development in his life—oh, who cares what he says! Nora, we're saved! No one can hurt you. Oh, Nora, Nora—but first, this ugliness all has to go. 500 Let me see—(*Takes a look at the note.*) No, I don't want to see it; I want the whole thing to fade like a dream. (*Tears the note and both letters to pieces, throws them into the stove and watches them burn.*) There—now there's nothing left—He wrote that since Christmas Eve you—Oh, they must have 505 been three terrible days for you, Nora.

NORA: I fought a hard fight.

HELMER: And suffered pain and saw no escape but—No, we're not going to dwell on anything unpleasant. We'll just be grateful and keep on repeating: it's over now, it's 510 over! You hear me, Nora? You don't seem to realize—it's over. What's it mean—that frozen look? Oh, poor little Nora, I understand. You can't believe I've forgiven you. But I have, Nora; I swear I have. I know that what you did, you did out of love for me. 515

NORA: That's true.

HELMER: You loved me the way a wife ought to love her husband. It's simply the means that you couldn't judge. But you think I love you any the less for not knowing how to handle your affairs? No, no—just lean on me; I'll guide 520 you and teach you. I wouldn't be a man if this feminine helplessness didn't make you twice as attractive to me. You mustn't mind those sharp words I said—that was all in the first confusion of thinking my world had collapsed. I've forgiven you, Nora; I swear I've forgiven you. 525

NORA: My thanks for your forgiveness. (*She goes out through the door, right.*)

HELMER: No, wait—(*Peers in.*) What are you doing in there?

NORA: (*Inside.*) Getting out of my costume.

HELMER: (*By the open door.*) Yes, do that. Try to calm yourself 530 and collect your thoughts again, my frightened little songbird. You can rest easy now; I've got wide wings to shelter you with. (*Walking about close by the door.*) How snug and nice our home is, Nora. You're safe here; I'll keep you like a hunted dove I've rescued out of a hawk's claws. I'll 535 bring peace to your poor, shuddering heart. Gradually it'll happen, Nora; you'll see. Tomorrow all this will look different to you; then everything will be as it was. I won't have to go on repeating I forgive you; you'll feel it for yourself. How can you imagine I'd ever conceivably want 540 to disown you—or even blame you in any way? Ah, you don't know a man's heart, Nora. For a man there's something indescribably sweet and satisfying in knowing he's forgiven his wife—and forgiven her out of a full and open heart. It's as if she belongs to him in two ways now: in a 545

sense he's given her fresh into the world again, and she's become his wife and his child as well. From now on that's what you'll be to me—you little, bewildered, helpless thing. Don't be afraid of anything, Nora; just open your
550 heart to me, and I'll be conscience and will to you both— (NORA *enters in her regular clothes.*) What's this? Not in bed? You've changed your dress?

NORA: Yes, Torvald, I've changed my dress.

HELMER: But why now, so late?

555 NORA: Tonight I'm not sleeping.

HELMER: But Nora dear—

NORA: (*Looking at her watch.*) It's still not so very late. Sit down, Torvald; we have a lot to talk over. (*She sits at one side of the table.*)

560 HELMER: Nora—what is this? That hard expression—

NORA: Sit down. This'll take some time. I have a lot to say.

HELMER: (*Sitting at the table directly opposite her.*) You worry me, Nora. And I don't understand you.

NORA: No, that's exactly it. You don't understand me. And
565 I've never understood you either—until tonight. No, don't interrupt. You can just listen to what I say. We're closing out accounts, Torvald.

HELMER: How do you mean that?

NORA: (*After a short pause.*) Doesn't anything strike you about
570 our sitting here like this?

HELMER: What's that?

NORA: We've been married now eight years. Doesn't it occur to you that this is the first time we two, you and I, man and wife, have ever talked seriously together?

575 HELMER: What do you mean—seriously?

NORA: In eight whole years—longer even—right from our first acquaintance, we've never exchanged a serious word on any serious thing.

HELMER: You mean I should constantly go and involve you in
580 problems you couldn't possibly help me with?

NORA: I'm not talking of problems. I'm saying that we've never sat down seriously together and tried to get to the bottom of anything.

HELMER: But dearest, what good would that ever do you?

585 NORA: That's the point right there: you've never understood me. I've been wronged greatly, Torvald—first by Papa, and then by you.

HELMER: What! By us—the two people who've loved you more than anyone else?

590 NORA: (*Shaking her head.*) You never loved me. You've thought it fun to be in love with me, that's all.

HELMER: Nora, what a thing to say!

NORA: Yes, it's true now, Torvald. When I lived at home with Papa, he told me all his opinions, so I had the same ones
595 too; or if they were different I hid them, since he wouldn't have cared for that. He used to call me his doll-child, and he played with me the way I played with my dolls. Then I came into your house—

HELMER: How can you speak of our marriage like that?

600 NORA: (*Unperturbed.*) I mean, then I went from Papa's hands into yours. You arranged everything to your own taste, and so I got the same taste as you—or I pretended to; I can't remember. I guess a little of both, first one, then the other. Now when I look back, it seems as if I'd lived here
605 like a beggar—just from hand to mouth. I've lived by doing tricks for you, Torvald. But that's the way you wanted

it. It's a great sin what you and Papa did to me. You're to blame that nothing's become of me.

HELMER: Nora, how unfair and ungrateful you are! Haven't you been happy here? 610

NORA: No, never. I thought so—but I never have.

HELMER: Not—not happy!

NORA: No, only lighthearted. And you've always been so kind to me. But our home's been nothing but a playpen. I've been your doll-wife here, just as at home I was Papa's 615 doll-child. And in turn the children have been my dolls. I thought it was fun when you played with me, just as they thought it fun when I played with them. That's been our marriage, Torvald.

HELMER: There's some truth in what you're saying—under all 620 the raving exaggeration. But it'll all be different after this. Playtime's over; now for the schooling.

NORA: Whose schooling—mine or the children's?

HELMER: Both yours and the children's, dearest.

NORA: Oh, Torvald, you're not the man to teach me to be a 625 good wife to you.

HELMER: And you can say that?

NORA: And I—how am I equipped to bring up children?

HELMER: Nora!

NORA: Didn't you say a moment ago that that was no job to 630 trust me with?

HELMER: In a flare of temper! Why fasten on that?

NORA: Yes, but you were so very right. I'm not up to the job. There's another job I have to do first. I have to try to educate myself. You can't help me with that. I've got to do 635 it alone. And that's why I'm leaving you now.

HELMER: (*Jumping up.*) What's that?

NORA: I have to stand completely alone, if I'm ever going to discover myself and the world out there. So I can't go on living with you. 640

HELMER: Nora, Nora!

NORA: I want to leave right away. Kristine should put me up for the night—

HELMER: You're insane! You've no right! I forbid you!

NORA: From here on, there's no use forbidding me anything. 645 I'll take with me whatever is mine. I don't want a thing from you, either now or later.

HELMER: What kind of madness is this!

NORA: Tomorrow I'm going home—I mean, home where I came from. It'll be easier up there to find something to do. 650

HELMER: Oh, you blind, incompetent child!

NORA: I must learn to be competent, Torvald.

HELMER: Abandon your home, your husband, your children! And you're not even thinking what people will say.

NORA: I can't be concerned about that. I only know how es- 655 sential this is.

HELMER: Oh, it's outrageous. So you'll run out like this on your most sacred vows.

NORA: What do you think are my most sacred vows?

HELMER: And I have to tell you that! Aren't they your duties 660 to your husband and children?

NORA: I have other duties equally sacred.

HELMER: That isn't true. What duties are they?

NORA: Duties to myself.

HELMER: Before all else, you're a wife and a mother. 665

NORA: I don't believe in that anymore. I believe that, before all else, I'm a human being, no less than you—or anyway,

I ought to try to become one. I know the majority thinks
you're right, Torvald, and plenty of books agree with you,
670 too. But I can't go on believing what the majority says, or
what's written in books. I have to think over these things
myself and try to understand them.
HELMER: Why can't you understand your place in your own
home? On a point like that, isn't there one everlasting
675 guide you can turn to? Where's your religion?
NORA: Oh, Torvald, I'm really not sure what religion is.
HELMER: What—?
NORA: I only know what the minister said when I was confirmed. He told me religion was this thing and that.
680 When I get clear and away by myself, I'll go into that
problem too. I'll see if what the minister said was right,
or, in any case, if it's right for me.
HELMER: A young woman your age shouldn't talk like that. If
religion can't move you, I can try to rouse your con-
685 science. You do have some moral feeling? Or, tell me—
has that gone too?
NORA: It's not easy to answer that, Torvald. I simply don't
know. I'm all confused about these things. I just know I
see them so differently from you. I find out, for one thing,
690 that the law's not at all what I'd thought—but I can't get
it through my head that the law is fair. A woman hasn't a
right to protect her dying father or save her husband's life!
I can't believe that.
HELMER: You talk like a child. You don't know anything of
695 the world you live in.
NORA: No, I don't. But now I'll begin to learn for myself. I'll
try to discover who's right, the world or I.
HELMER: Nora, you're sick; you've got a fever. I almost think
you're out of your head.
700 NORA: I've never felt more clearheaded and sure in my life.
HELMER: And—clearheaded and sure—you're leaving your
husband and children?
NORA: Yes.
HELMER: Then there's only one possible reason.
705 NORA: What?
HELMER: You no longer love me.
NORA: No. That's exactly it.
HELMER: Nora! You can't be serious!
NORA: Oh, this is so hard, Torvald—you've been so kind to
710 me always. But I can't help it. I don't love you anymore.
HELMER: (Struggling for composure.) Are you also clearheaded
and sure about that?
NORA: Yes, completely. That's why I can't go on staying here.
HELMER: Can you tell me what I did to lose your love?
715 NORA: Yes, I can tell you. It was this evening when the miraculous thing didn't come—then I knew you weren't the
man I'd imagined.
HELMER: Be more explicit; I don't follow you.
NORA: I've waited now so patiently eight long years—for, my
720 Lord, I know miracles don't come every day. Then this
crisis broke over me, and such a certainty filled me: now
the miraculous event would occur. While Krogstad's letter was lying out there, I never for an instant dreamed that
you could give in to his terms. I was so utterly sure you'd
725 say to him: go on, tell your tale to the whole wide world.
And when he'd done that—
HELMER: Yes, what then? When I'd delivered my own wife
into shame and disgrace—!

NORA: When he'd done that, I was so utterly sure that you'd
step forward, take the blame on yourself and say: I am the 730
guilty one.
HELMER: Nora—!
NORA: You're thinking I'd never accept such a sacrifice from
you? No, of course not. But what good would my protests
be against you? That was the miracle I was waiting for, in 735
terror and hope. And to stave that off, I would have taken
my life.
HELMER: I'd gladly work for you day and night, Nora—and
take on pain and deprivation. But there's no one who
gives up honor for love. 740
NORA: Millions of women have done just that.
HELMER: Oh, you think and talk like a silly child.
NORA: Perhaps. But you neither think nor talk like the man
I could join myself to. When your big fright was over—
and it wasn't from any threat against me, only for what 745
might damage you—when all the danger was past, for you
it was just as if nothing had happened. I was exactly the
same, your little lark, your doll, that you'd have to handle
with double care now that I'd turned out so brittle and
frail. (Gets up.) Torvald—in that instant it dawned on me 750
that for eight years I've been living here with a stranger,
and that I'd even conceived three children—oh, I can't
stand the thought of it! I could tear myself to bits.
HELMER: (Heavily.) I see. There's a gulf that's opened between
us—that's clear. Oh, but Nora, can't we bridge it somehow? 755
NORA: The way I am now, I'm no wife for you.
HELMER: I have the strength to make myself over.
NORA: Maybe—if your doll gets taken away.
HELMER: But to part! To part from you! No, Nora, no—I
can't imagine it. 760
NORA: (Going out, right.) All the more reason why it has to be.
(She reenters with her coat and a small overnight bag, which she
puts on a chair by the table.)
HELMER: Nora, Nora, not now! Wait till tomorrow.
NORA: I can't spend the night in a strange man's room. 765
HELMER: But couldn't we live here like brother and sister—
NORA: You know very well how long that would last. (Throws
her shawl about her.) Good-bye, Torvald. I won't look in on
the children. I know they're in better hands than mine.
The way I am now, I'm no use to them. 770
HELMER: But someday, Nora—someday—?
NORA: How can I tell? I haven't the least idea what'll become
of me.
HELMER: But you're my wife, now and wherever you go.
NORA: Listen, Torvald—I've heard that when a wife deserts 775
her husband's house just as I'm doing, then the law frees
him from all responsibility. In any case, I'm freeing you
from being responsible. Don't feel yourself bound, any
more than I will. There has to be absolute freedom for us
both. Here, take your ring back. Give me mine. 780
HELMER: That too?
NORA: That too.
HELMER: There it is.
NORA: Good. Well, now it's all over. I'm putting the keys
here. The maids know all about keeping up the house— 785
better than I do. Tomorrow, after I've left town, Kristine
will stop by to pack up everything that's mine from home.
I'd like those things shipped up to me.
HELMER: Over! All over! Nora, won't you ever think about me?

790   NORA: I'm sure I'll think of you often, and about the children and the house here.

HELMER: May I write you?

NORA: No—never. You're not to do that.

HELMER: Oh, but let me send you—

795   NORA: Nothing. Nothing.

HELMER: Or help you if you need it.

NORA: No. I accept nothing from strangers.

HELMER: Nora—can I never be more than a stranger to you?

NORA: (*Picking up the overnight bag.*) Ah, Torvald—it would

800   take the greatest miracle of all—

HELMER: Tell me the greatest miracle!

NORA: You and I both would have to transform ourselves to the point that—Oh, Torvald, I've stopped believing in miracles.

HELMER: But I'll believe. Tell me! Transform ourselves to the point that—? 805

NORA: That our living together could be a true marriage. (*She goes out down the hall.*)

HELMER: (*Sinks down on a chair by the door, face buried in his hands.*) Nora! Nora! (*Looking about and rising.*) Empty. She's gone. (*A sudden hope leaps in him.*) The greatest miracle—? 810

(*From below, the sound of a door slamming shut.*)

August Strindberg

The Swedish playwright August Strindberg (1849–1912) was a modern Renaissance man: he wrote some fifty plays, several autobiographical novels, and a variety of scientific and occult works as well. A series of tempestuous marriages marked Strindberg's life and are reflected in his corrosively misogynistic attitudes and in his hostility toward Ibsen, who seemed to Strindberg to advocate a new order of feminine domination. Calling *A Doll House* "sick like its father," Strindberg wrote *The Father* (1887) in reply to Ibsen, a play in which a calculating woman drives her husband into madness. Although Strindberg considered the play to be an experiment in the new "naturalism," it is really a kind of psychological thriller: the characters are so consumed by their sexual combat with one another that the worldly environment hardly seems important. Strindberg sent the play to Émile Zola, who found it absorbing and curious, but lacking in the material social reality he demanded of the new drama. Strindberg then wrote *Miss Julie* (1888) and considered the play's use of naturalism in his famous preface to the play. The battle of the sexes is one of Strindberg's preoccupations, examined in a series of plays including *Creditors* (1888) and *The Dance of Death, Parts 1 and 2* (1901).

The battle of the sexes was also the battle that occupied Strindberg's life outside the theater. His three marriages all involved periods of psychological breakdown and creative fertility. His breakdown of the mid-1890s after marrying his second wife is documented in *The Inferno* (1897) and is symptomatic of Strindberg's volatile and unstable frame of mind. Much of Strindberg's manic energy was focused on women—he believed that his wife was attempting to drive him mad by sending rays through the walls. Strindberg also developed a passion for the occult and for alchemy, and in addition to his plays, poems, and novels, he wrote a number of scientific and pseudoscientific treatises. Unlike Ibsen, Strindberg experimented in a variety of dramatic genres throughout his career. Calling himself the "Zola of the occult," Strindberg wrote an influential series of expressionist and symbolic plays; the best known today are *To Damascus* (in three parts, 1898–1901) and *A Dream Play* (1901). He also wrote several important plays on Swedish history, including *Erik XIV* (1899), *Gustav Adolph* (1900), and *Gustav III* (1902). In 1907 he founded a small theater—the Intimate Theater—which brought the independent theater movement to Sweden and produced his intense and often symbolic series of "chamber plays," including *The Ghost Sonata* (1907) and *The Pelican* (1907). When Strindberg died in 1912, he had become not only the most significant literary and theatrical figure in Swedish history, but also a major influence on the course of modern drama.

THE FATHER   *The Father* provides a strongly colored illustration of Strindberg's energetic exploitation of the implicit sexual politics of naturalistic theater. Written in reply to Ibsen's *A Doll House, The Father* reworks much of Ibsen's material: this play, too, concerns a battle for domestic freedom between a sensible "pillar of the community" and his emotionally engaging and powerful wife. But where Ibsen saw in Nora a model for the ways patriarchal social conventions slowly suffocate women, Strindberg's play works in much the opposite direction. At the outset of the play, the Captain is nearly the paradigmatic naturalistic hero: a man of the world, a freethinker, widely read in literature and philosophy, and—most important—a man of science, using his spectroscope to conduct astronomical research. Yet the Captain represents the impact of naturalism in another respect as well; much as Zola wanted to see character determined by its environment, so in *The Father* the environment of suspicion created by Laura ultimately drives the Captain's fate, robbing him both of his daughter and his reason. For the claustral room of *The Father* is urgently feminized: not only is the Captain's

The Father is comforted by Bertha in August Strindberg's *The Father*.

Nurse a part of his family, but Laura deftly manages to control the *appearance* of reality in the box set onstage. In their duel to control the fate of their daughter Bertha, Laura plays on the Captain's sense that only the mother knows for certain who is the father of her child; undermining the Captain's confidence in his paternity, Laura also creates the impression that his behavior has become irregular, suggestively leading the Doctor to see the Captain's behavior as providing grounds for a declaration of mental incompetence, and the transferal of control of their property to Laura. In this respect, *The Father* seems to verge on a kind of expressionistic theater, in that the action of the play increasingly takes place inside the Captain's mind and is externalized in the physical world of the play—the wallpapered room, which seems to close in on the Captain, the straitjacket he's tricked into wearing by the Nurse.

The action of *The Father* is often traced to Strindberg's tempestuous first marriage to Siri von Essen, an independent-minded actress, and it was immediately accepted for production by André Antoine's Théâtre Libre in Paris. By 1890, it had been performed in Denmark, Sweden, and Germany and had entered the repertoire of the "new drama" that was changing European theaters.

THE FATHER

August Strindberg

TRANSLATED BY EVERT SPRINCHORN

CHARACTERS

CAPTAIN, *in the cavalry* (ADOLF)
LAURA, *his wife*
BERTHA, *their daughter, about 14 years old*
DR. EASTLAND
PASTOR, *Protestant, Laura's brother* (JONAS)
MARGARET, *a maid, the Captain's old nurse*

HAPPY, *a corporal in the cavalry*
ORDERLY, *the Captain's*
VOICE OF THE MOTHER-IN-LAW

The action takes place in Sweden in a December in the 1880s.

ACT ONE

The parlor of the CAPTAIN's *house. A door in the rear wall, to the right, leads to the entrance hall. In the middle of the room, a large round table, with newspapers, magazines, and scientific journals on it. To the right, a leather sofa with a table in front of it. To the far right, a wallpapered jib door, of the sort common in nineteenth-century Swedish homes. To the left, a secretary; a pendulum clock above it. Also to the left, the door to the inner rooms. Weapons of various sorts, hunting rifles and game-bags, hanging on the walls. Near the rear door, a clothes tree with military coats hanging on it. A lamp is burning on the center table.*

SCENE I

The CAPTAIN *and the* PASTOR *are sitting on the leather sofa. The* CAPTAIN *is in undress uniform except for his boots and spurs. The* PASTOR *is dressed in black and white neck-cloth but without clerical collar. He is smoking a pipe.*

The CAPTAIN *rings.*

ORDERLY: Sir?

CAPTAIN: Is Happy out there?

ORDERLY: Waiting your orders, sir, in the kitchen.

CAPTAIN: In the kitchen again! Damn! Get him in here right

5   away!

ORDERLY: Yes, sir! (*Exits.*)

CAPTAIN: That son-of-a-gun has been too familiar with the help. Got the kitchen maid pregnant. A hot little devil, isn't he?

PASTOR: You mean Happy? He was in trouble last year! Same

10   thing!

CAPTAIN: Ah, you remember. Why don't you help the cavalry out and talk to him—friendly. Might set him right. I've bawled him out, sworn at him, even thrashed him. Nothing makes an impression.

15   PASTOR: And you want me to read a sermon to him? What impression do you think God's word makes on a cavalry trooper?

CAPTAIN: Well, as my brother-in-law you know it makes no impression on me.

20   PASTOR: I do indeed.

CAPTAIN: However, it might on him. Give it a try, hm?

SCENE II

HAPPY *enters.*

CAPTAIN: All right, Happy, out with it!

HAPPY: With your permission, sir, I can't talk about it—I mean with the pastor here.

PASTOR: Don't be embarrassed on my account, my lad.

CAPTAIN: Come on now, let's have it, the whole story. It's that   5
   or punishment duty.

HAPPY: Well, you see—well—we went to dance at Gabriel's house, and then—well, then Louis said that—

CAPTAIN: What's Louis got to do with it? Don't go making up stories.   10

HAPPY: Well, you see, after a while Emma said let's go to the barn.

CAPTAIN: I see. It was Emma who seduced you!

HAPPY: Not exactly, but that ain't far wrong. Let me tell you, if the girl doesn't want to, nothing happens.   15

CAPTAIN: We're wasting time. Are you or are you not the father of this baby?

HAPPY: How should I know?

CAPTAIN: What! If you don't know, who does?

HAPPY: Well, sir, how can you ever know?   20

CAPTAIN: You mean you weren't the only one?

HAPPY: Oh, sure, that time I was; but you still can't be certain you're the only one. I mean—

CAPTAIN: Are you trying to implicate Louis in this? Is that your game?   25

HAPPY: It's hard to know who's at fault.

CAPTAIN: Now just a minute. You told Emma that you wanted to marry her.

HAPPY: Well, you always gotta say that—

CAPTAIN: (*To the* PASTOR.) My God, what's the world coming to?   30

PASTOR: The same old refrain.—But tell me, Happy, you must be man enough to know if you're the father.

HAPPY: Well, sure I know I got it off with her. But Pastor, you know yourself that don't necessarily mean anything comes of it.   35

PASTOR: Listen, young man, we are talking about you!—Surely you can't leave the girl to take care of the child by herself. You cannot be forced to marry her, perhaps, but you certainly must help care for the child. I'll see to that.

HAPPY: Then Louis has got to go in with it too!   40

CAPTAIN: All right! We'll have to let the courts settle it. I can't untangle this mess. I find it rather tedious. That's all. Dismissed.

NOTE: The stage directions in this translation follow the nineteenth-century Scandinavian custom of indicating left and right from the point of view of the audience, not the actor.

PASTOR: Happy! Just a second. . . . Don't you think it's a bit
45 unfair to toss the poor girl out into the street like that,
with her baby? Don't you? You must realize that conduct
like that can only . . . well . . .

HAPPY: Naturally, if I really knew I was the father, but, well,
how can you ever know that? Go slaving through life for
50 somebody else's child—I ain't cut out for that. Pastor, you
and the captain, sir, you can understand what I mean.

CAPTAIN: Dismissed!

HAPPY: Yes, sir! (*Exits.*)

CAPTAIN: Not that way! Stay out of the kitchen!

SCENE III

CAPTAIN: Why didn't you whale the daylights out of him?

PASTOR: What do you mean? I thought I really let him have it.

CAPTAIN: Ha! You just sat there sputtering.

PASTOR: Frankly, I don't know what to say. I feel sorry for the
5 girl. And I feel sorry for the boy. Suppose he isn't the father?
The girl can put the baby in a maternity hospital, nurse it for
four months, and the child is taken care of thereafter. Not the
boy—he can't wet-nurse it. The girl can get a good place afterward in some decent home, but the boy's whole future
10 might be ruined—dishonorable discharge and all that.

CAPTAIN: I damn well wouldn't want to sit on the bench and
pass judgment in this case. The lad isn't exactly blameless.
How can one tell? One thing is certain; the girl is guilty
to some extent—if there's any guilt at all.

15 PASTOR: Yes, that's true. I don't presume to judge anyone. . . .
What were we talking about before we got involved in
this damned mess?—Bertha and her confirmation.

CAPTAIN: More than her confirmation; it was the question of
her whole upbringing. This house is filled with women,
20 and every one of them wants to bring up my little girl. Your
stepmother wants her to be a spiritualist; Laura hopes to
make an artist out of her; the governess wants her to be a
Methodist; old Margaret steers her to the Baptists; and the
kitchen help want her to join the Salvation Army. You can't
25 pull a person in several different directions at once without
their coming apart. The trouble is that I, who have the primary responsibility for developing her mind and talents, am
constantly thwarted. I've got to get her out of this house.

PASTOR: The trouble is you have too many women running
30 things.

CAPTAIN: You can say that again. I live in a cage filled with
tigers. If I didn't hold an iron red-hot under their noses,
they would tear me to pieces.—All right, laugh, you bastard. It wasn't bad enough that I married your sister; you
35 had to foist your old stepmother on me too.

PASTOR: For heaven's sake, a man can't have his stepmother
living in the same house with him.

CAPTAIN: No, you prefer a mother-in-law as a boarder—in
somebody else's house.

40 PASTOR: Yes, well, everyone has his lot in life.

CAPTAIN: Maybe. But I've got a lot too much to bear. I've still
got my old nurse, from the time I was a child, and she
treats me as if I were still wearing a bib. Oh, she's very
kind, Lord knows, but she just doesn't belong here.

45 PASTOR: You've got to learn to keep the womenfolk in line.
You let them run things too much.

CAPTAIN: All right, you old horse, would you be so good as to
enlighten me on how women are supposed to be kept in line?

PASTOR: To tell the truth, Laura was always—. She's my own
sister, but she certainly could be quarrelsome.   50

CAPTAIN: Laura? Oh, she can be difficult, but she's not the
worst. I can handle her.

PASTOR: Come on, get it off your chest. I know what she's like.

CAPTAIN: She was brought up like a sentimental schoolgirl
and she's having a little difficulty getting adjusted. That's   55
all. After all, she's my wife—

PASTOR: And therefore she can do no wrong? No, you don't
fool me; she's the one who's putting the screws on you.

CAPTAIN: Anyway, the point is that now the whole house is
in an uproar. Laura won't let our child leave, while I can't   60
let her stay in this nuthouse.

PASTOR: Ah, ha, just as I thought: Laura *won't*. In that case, I fear
the worst. When she was a child she would lie stiff and still,
playing dead, until she got what she wanted. And when she
got it, she gave it back, saying it wasn't the thing that she   65
wanted so much, she just wanted to have her own way.

CAPTAIN: Really. Already like that! . . . You know, she gets
herself into such a state sometimes, she scares me. I think
something's the matter with her.

PASTOR: Now what is it that you and Laura want for Bertha   70
that is so impossible to agree on? Can't you reach a compromise?

CAPTAIN: Don't get the idea that I want to make her into a
Wunderkind or a prodigy or remake her in my own image.
And I don't want to be a matchmaker to my own daugh-   75
ter, bringing her up just so she can get married. If you do
that, and things don't work out, she'll turn into a sour old
maid. On the other hand, I don't want her to pursue a
man's profession, which would take years of study. And all
that education would be absolutely wasted if she decided   80
to get married.

PASTOR: So what do you want?

CAPTAIN: I want her to be a teacher. If she doesn't get married, she can still support herself and won't be any worse
off than those poor teachers who have to share their   85
salaries with their families. If she gets married, she can use
what she's learned to educate her own children. Now
what's wrong with that?

PASTOR: Nothing. Nothing's wrong with it. On the other
hand, could it be that she has shown such a talent for   90
painting that it would be a crime not to encourage it?

CAPTAIN: No, not at all! I showed some samples of her work to
a well-known painter who said it was ordinary, uninspired
stuff, the kind of thing one learns in art classes. But then last
summer some young whippersnapper, with all the answers—   95
you know the type—comes along and says Bertha has a
colossal talent. And that closed the case in favor of Laura.

PASTOR: I suppose he had a crush on Bertha?

CAPTAIN: Of course, what else!

PASTOR: Well then, old boy, God help you. You're going to   100
need His help. Really sad—I mean, Laura has her own
faction—in there. (*Pointing to the inner rooms.*)

CAPTAIN: You can bet on that! The whole house is ready to
explode. And just between you and me, it isn't exactly
what I'd call a fair fight that's being fought on that side.   105

PASTOR: (*Rising.*) You think I don't know?

CAPTAIN: You know, eh?

PASTOR: Who'd know better?

CAPTAIN: The worst of it is, it seems to me that Bertha's career
110   is being decided in there on the basis of some pretty vile
reasons. "This will teach the men."—"Women can do this
and women can do that." Man against woman—that's all I
hear, all day long.—You're not leaving, are you? No, no,
stay for supper. I don't know what we've got in the house;
115   we'll find something. The new doctor is going to drop in.
I told you I was waiting for him. Have you seen him?

PASTOR: I caught a glimpse of him as I rode by. Looked like
a proper and sensible sort.

CAPTAIN: Good, that's something. Do you think I can find an
120   ally in him?

PASTOR: Who knows? All depends on how long he has lived
with women.

CAPTAIN: Oh, come on now, won't you stay?

PASTOR: No, thanks very much, old friend. I promised I'd be
125   home for supper—and the old lady gets so worried if I'm
late.

CAPTAIN: Worried? Furious, you mean. Well, as you wish.
Here, let me help you with your overcoat.

PASTOR: Must be awfully cold tonight. Ah, thank you, thank
130   you. You should look after yourself, Adolf. You seem so
tense and nervous.

CAPTAIN: Do I act nervous?

PASTOR: Well, a little. Are you sure you're feeling all right?

CAPTAIN: What's Laura been telling you? For twenty years
135   now she's been treating me as if I had one foot in the grave.

PASTOR: Laura? No, no, no. It's just that you worry me. Take
care of yourself; a bit of free advice. Goodnight, you old
horse.—Wait, I thought you wanted to talk about Bertha's
confirmation?

140   CAPTAIN: Not at all. Let me tell you, I'm not going to interfere with the public conscience. Let it run its appointed
course. I'm neither a proselytizer nor a martyr. We're beyond all that, right? Say hello to those at home.

PASTOR: Goodnight, Adolf. Say hello to Laura.

SCENE IV

CAPTAIN: (*Opens the leaf of the secretary and sits down to do the
accounts.*) Thirty-four, -nine, forty-three, -seven, -eight,
fifty-six.

LAURA: (*Enters through the door at left.*) Would you mind telling
5   me—

CAPTAIN: Just a second.—Sixty-six, seventy-one, eighty-four,
eighty-nine, ninety-two, one hundred. What did you want?

LAURA: Maybe I'm bothering you.

CAPTAIN: Not at all. The household money, I suppose?

10   LAURA: That's right. The household money.

CAPTAIN: Put the bills there, and I'll go through them.

LAURA: Bills?

CAPTAIN: Yes.

LAURA: What's this about bills?

15   CAPTAIN: I've got to have the receipts, obviously. Our financial position isn't too good, and in case of an audit, you've
got to produce the bills and receipts; otherwise our creditors could accuse us of negligence.

LAURA: If our finances are that bad, it isn't my fault.

20   CAPTAIN: That's exactly what we'll find out by going through
the accounts.

LAURA: Listen, if that tenant farmer of ours doesn't pay up,
it's not my fault.

CAPTAIN: And who gave that tenant farmer the highest recommendation? You did! And why did you recommend   25
this—this—shall we say, wastrel?

LAURA: And why did you give this—this—wastrel a lease?

CAPTAIN: Because you wouldn't let me eat in peace, sleep in
peace, or work in peace until you got him here. You
wanted him here because your brother wanted to get rid   30
of him. Your mother wanted him because I *didn't* want
him. The governess wanted him because he was a Bible-
reading pietist. And old Margaret wanted him because she
knew his grandmother when they were children. That's
why he was hired. And if I hadn't taken him on, by now   35
I'd be raving in the madhouse or pushing up daisies.—
Anyway, here's the budget money and your allowance.
You can give me the bills and receipts later.

LAURA: (*Curtseying.*) Thank you so much! . . . What about
you?—Do you keep track of what you spend apart from   40
housekeeping expenses?

CAPTAIN: I don't think that's any of your business.

LAURA: No, apparently not—just as little as my child's education is. I see the House and Senate met this evening. What
did you and my brother decide?   45

CAPTAIN: I had already reached my decision, and therefore I
had merely to convey it to the only friend I and the rest
of my family have in common. Bertha is going to live in
town. She will be leaving in two weeks.

LAURA: And where will she be living—if I may ask?   50

CAPTAIN: She'll be boarding with the Savbergs, the judge advocate.

LAURA: That atheist!

CAPTAIN: A child is to brought up in the faith of its father—
that's the law.   55

LAURA: And the mother has nothing to say about it?

CAPTAIN: Nothing at all. She sold her birthrights in a legal
exchange, relinquishing her rights in return for the husband's support of her and her children.

LAURA: So the mother has no rights over her child?   60

CAPTAIN: None whatsoever. Once you've sold something,
you can't take it back and keep the money.

LAURA: What if the father and the mother should come to an
agreement . . . ?

CAPTAIN: An agreement? I want her to live in town, you want   65
her to live out here. Averaging it out arithmetically, she'd
move into the railway station, halfway between here and
the town. It's a problem without a solution. Do you understand?

LAURA: Then we'll have to invent one, won't we? . . . What   70
did Happy want with you just now?

CAPTAIN: That's a military secret.

LAURA: And the talk of the whole kitchen.

CAPTAIN: Then you must know all about it!

LAURA: I most certainly do!   75

CAPTAIN: And no doubt you have already handed down your
decision.

LAURA: It's in the law books!

CAPTAIN: The law books don't tell who the father of the child is.

LAURA: One usually knows.   80

CAPTAIN: People with any sense say one can never really know.

LAURA: Isn't that remarkable! You mean you can't know who
the father is?

CAPTAIN: So they say.

85 LAURA: Really remarkable! Then tell me, how can the father have rights over the mother's child?

CAPTAIN: He has them only if he takes on certain responsibilities—or has them forced on him. Besides, in marriage there's no question about who the father is.

90 LAURA: No question?

CAPTAIN: I should hope not.

LAURA: Not even when the wife has been unfaithful?

CAPTAIN: That doesn't have any application in the present case. Anything else you want to ask?

95 LAURA: Not a thing.

CAPTAIN: Good. Then I'm going up to my room, and maybe you'll be good enough to inform me when the doctor comes. (*Closes the secretary and stands up*).

LAURA: Yes, sir, my captain!

100 CAPTAIN: (*Opening the wallpapered door at the right.*) As soon as he comes, mind you. I don't want to seem rude to him. Understand? (*Exits.*)

LAURA: I understand. Perfectly.

SCENE V

LAURA *looks at the money she is holding in her hand.*

VOICE OF THE MOTHER-IN-LAW: (*From within.*) Laura!

LAURA: Yes, what is it?

VOICE OF THE MOTHER-IN-LAW: Where's my tea?

LAURA: (*In the doorway to the inner rooms.*) Coming—in a moment.

(LAURA *is going to the entrance door at the rear when the door is opened, and the* ORDERLY *enters, followed by* DR. EASTLAND.)

5 ORDERLY: Doctor Eastland.

DR. EASTLAND: How do you do?

LAURA: (*Going to meet him and offering her hand.*) How good of you to come, Doctor. Welcome to our house. The captain is out just now, I'm afraid, but he'll be back soon.

10 DR. EASTLAND: I beg your pardon for coming so late, but I have already had to make a house call.

LAURA: Please sit down, won't you?

DR. EASTLAND: Thank you.

LAURA: Yes, there seems to be quite a lot of illness in this area
15 right now, but I do hope you'll find everything to your liking here. You know, for us who are rather isolated here in the country it's very important to find a doctor who takes a genuine interest in his patients. I've heard so many good things about you, Doctor. I do hope we shall get
20 along well together.

DR. EASTLAND: Very kind of you, madam. Let me say on my part that I hope my calls here will be social ones and not professional ones. Your family is quite healthy and—

LAURA: Yes, fortunately we haven't had any severe illnesses.
25 Still, things aren't the way they should be.

DR. EASTLAND: Really?

LAURA: Yes, things aren't as good as we might wish.

DR. EASTLAND: I'm sorry to hear that.

LAURA: There are certain situations in family life that, for the
30 sake of propriety and one's conscience, one is compelled to conceal from the world.

DR. EASTLAND: Not from one's doctor, I trust.

LAURA: True. That is why I feel it is my painful duty to let you know right from the start what the true situation is.

DR. EASTLAND: I see. I wonder if we should not put off this 35 discussion until I've met your husband?

LAURA: No! No, you must hear me out *before* you see him.

DR. EASTLAND: So the matter concerns him?

LAURA: Yes, him—my dearly beloved husband.

DR. EASTLAND: How distressing. I assure you, you have my 40 sympathy.

LAURA: (*Taking out a handkerchief.*) My husband is mentally ill. . . . There, I've said it. Now you can judge for yourself.

DR. EASTLAND: I can't believe it! I've read the captain's papers on mineralogy. I've admired them; they reveal a very clear 45 and penetrating intellect.

LAURA: Indeed! You don't know how happy it would make all of us here in the family if we were mistaken.

DR. EASTLAND: Of course it may be that his mind is disturbed in other areas. Perhaps you could tell me—? 50

LAURA: That's exactly what we fear! You see, sometimes he gets the strangest ideas. He's entitled to them, I suppose— as a scientist, I mean, if only they didn't affect the well-being of the whole family. For instance, he has an absolute mania for buying all sorts of things. 55

DR. EASTLAND: Oh? What sort of things?

LAURA: Books! Boxes and boxes of them—which he never reads.

DR. EASTLAND: Well, scientists do buy books; that doesn't seem so strange. 60

LAURA: You don't believe me?

DR. EASTLAND: Madam, I'm convinced that you believe what you say.

LAURA: Then tell me, is it reasonable to think that you can see in a microscope what happens on another planet? 65

DR. EASTLAND: He says he can do that?

LAURA: That's what he says.

DR. EASTLAND: In a microscope?

LAURA: Yes, in a microscope!

DR. EASTLAND: I must admit that doesn't sound good, if it's 70 true.

LAURA: If it's true! I see you have no confidence in me, Doctor. And here I sit confiding the family secrets to you.

DR. EASTLAND: Now, now, now, madam, what you say will go no further. I'm gratified you feel you can trust me. But as 75 a doctor I have to examine—I have to test things before I can make a diagnosis. Has the captain shown any symptoms of instability, of extreme vacillation?

LAURA: Oh, the stories I could tell you! We've been married for twenty years, and he's never once made up his mind 80 without changing it.

DR. EASTLAND: Is he obstinate? Rigid and difficult to reason with?

LAURA: He always wants his own way, in everything. And once he gets it, he shrugs it off and tells *me* to make the decision. 85

DR. EASTLAND: Does give one pause, I must say. Perhaps this does need looking into. You see, madam, it's volition, the will, the ability to make decisions, that constitutes the backbone of the psyche; and if that is weakened, the whole mind may collapse. 90

LAURA: Oh, God knows what I've had to put up with during all these trying years, forcing myself to agree to everything he says. If you only knew how I've struggled with him to keep things going. If you only knew!

95 DR. EASTLAND: Madam, your misfortune touches me deeply. I assure you I shall do whatever can be done. You have my heartfelt sympathies. I beg you to rely completely on me. From what you tell me there's one thing that I would like to suggest. Avoid bringing up any thoughts with strong

100 emotional associations. In a weak mind they spread like wildfire and turn into obsessions and manias. I think you know what I mean.

LAURA: Yes. You mean anything that would arouse his suspicions.

105 DR. EASTLAND: Precisely. A sick man can convince himself of anything; he's so susceptible.

LAURA: Yes, of course. . . . Yes, I understand. . . . Yes.

(A bell rings from within.)

Excuse me, my mother is ringing for me. Could you wait just a moment, please?—Oh, why here's Adolf now—

(LAURA leaves.)

SCENE VI

The CAPTAIN enters through the jib door.

CAPTAIN: What, are you already here, Doctor? Welcome, welcome.

DR. EASTLAND: Captain. It's a great pleasure for me to make the acquaintance of such a well-known scientist.

5 CAPTAIN: Oh, please, please. My military duties don't allow me much time for deep research. Still, I think I may be on the track of an important discovery.

DR. EASTLAND: Really!

CAPTAIN: Yes, yes! I've been subjecting meteor stones to spec-

10 troscopy, and I've found carbon, in other words, vestiges of organic life! What do you say to that?

DR. EASTLAND: You can see that in a microscope?

CAPTAIN: No, damnation, man, in the spectroscope!

DR. EASTLAND: Ah, spectroscope! Excuse me, of course, of

15 course. Pretty soon I suppose you'll be telling us what's happening on Jupiter.

CAPTAIN: Not what's happening, but what has happened. If only that damned bookseller in Paris would send me the books. I think all the bookdealers of the world are in a

20 plot against me. For two months I have not had a single reply from any one of them. Imagine, no answers to my orders, my letters, my abusive telegrams, nothing! It's driving me out of my mind. I don't know what's behind it.

DR. EASTLAND: Oh, it's probably just plain ordinary careless-

25 ness. You shouldn't get yourself so worked up over that.

CAPTAIN: But, devil take it, I won't be able to get my paper ready in time. And I know that right now in Berlin they're working along the same lines.—But we're not supposed to be talking about this. Forgive me. Now let's

30 get at *your* problem. If you want to live here, we can offer the small flat in the wing of the house. Or do you want to live in the old servants' quarters?

DR. EASTLAND: Just as you wish. Makes no difference to me.

CAPTAIN: No, it's up to you. Take your pick.

35 DR. EASTLAND: No, I'll let you decide that.

CAPTAIN: No. I'll decide nothing of the sort. It's up to you to say what you want. I have no preference, none at all.

DR. EASTLAND: Well, I can't decide—

CAPTAIN: For Christ's sake man, just say what you want! I don't care. I have no preference, no wish in this matter. 40 What are you, a milksop? Come, come, make up your mind. Infuriating!

DR. EASTLAND: Well, if it's up to me—all right, I'll move in here.

CAPTAIN: Good! That's more like it. Thank you.—I'm sorry, 45 Doctor, but there's nothing that irks me so much as hearing someone say "makes no difference to me." *(He rings.)*

(The nurse MARGARET enters.)

CAPTAIN: Oh, so it's you, Margaret. Say, do you know if the apartment in the wing is ready for the doctor?

MARGARET: Yes, Captain. It's all ready. 50

CAPTAIN: Good. Then I won't detain you, Doctor. You must be tired. Goodnight. Make yourself at home. I'll see you in the morning, I hope.

DR. EASTLAND: Good evening, Captain.

CAPTAIN: I trust my wife has made things clear to you— 55 given you the lay of the land, as it were.

DR. EASTLAND: Yes, your splendid wife has given me some pointers that it might be good for an outsider to know. Well, goodnight, Captain.

SCENE VII

CAPTAIN: Ah, dear old Margaret! Now what can I do for you?

MARGARET: My big boy Adolf! Could I speak to you for a moment?

CAPTAIN: My dear old nurse, you go right ahead and say whatever's on your mind. You're the only one I can listen 5 to around here without climbing the walls.

MARGARET: Now Adolf, don't you think you could meet Laura halfway and work out something with her about your child? After all, she's the mother and—

CAPTAIN: After all, I'm the father, Margaret. 10

MARGARET: Yes, yes, yes. But a father has other things to think about; the mother has only her child.

CAPTAIN: That's exactly it. She's only got one burden to carry, while I have three. And what she carries I also have to carry. Don't you think I would have been something other 15 than an old soldier by now if I didn't have a wife and child?

MARGARET: Well, that isn't what I mean.

CAPTAIN: No, I'm sure it isn't. You're just trying to put me in the wrong.

MARGARET: Oh, Adolf, my boy, don't you believe that I want 20 only the best for you?

CAPTAIN: Of course, I believe it, you dear old girl. But you don't know what is best for me. You see, it isn't enough for me just to have given life to a child; I also want to give it my mind and soul. 25

MARGARET: Well, I wouldn't know about things like that. I just think that people should make an effort to get along together.

CAPTAIN: You're not my old friend, are you, Margaret?

MARGARET: Me? What are you saying, Adolf? Do you think 30 I can forget you were my baby boy when you were a little tyke?

CAPTAIN: No, old girl. Do you think I can forget? You've been like a mother to me. You've given me aid and comfort—up to now—when everyone else was against me. But now when the chips are down, you betray me and join the enemy.

MARGARET: Enemy?

CAPTAIN: Yes, enemy! You know how things stand in this house. You've seen it all, from beginning to end.

MARGARET: Yes, I've seen—more than enough. For heaven's sake, why should two people torture each other like this— two good people so kind to everybody else? Laura is never like that to me or to the others.

CAPTAIN: No, only to me. I know. But let me tell you, Margaret, if you abandon me now, you'll be doing a bad thing. They're spinning a web around me. And that doctor is no friend of mine.

MARGARET: Oh, Adolf, Adolf, you think the worst of everybody. You know why? Adolf, it's because you don't have the true faith. That's why, Adolf.

CAPTAIN: But you and the Baptists have found the one and only true faith. How fortunate you are.

MARGARET: I am not as unfortunate as you, Adolf, let me tell you. If you would humble your heart you would see that God would make you happy. Thou shalt love thy neighbor.

CAPTAIN: It's remarkable; you just so much as talk of God and love and your voice gets as hard as iron and your eyes glint like steel. No, no, Margaret, you certainly haven't found the true faith.

MARGARET: All right, you be proud and almighty with your books and learning. You'll see how far that gets you when it really counts.

CAPTAIN: How haughtily speak the humble at heart! Of course learning doesn't mean much to cows like you!

MARGARET: You ought to be ashamed! . . . But I still love my boy, my big, silly boy, and he'll come back to his old nurse, like a poor runaway boy, when the winds begin to howl.

CAPTAIN: Margaret! I'm sorry . . . Margaret, you've got to believe me, no one here wants to help me—no one but you. Help me. I know something is going to happen. I don't know what, but whatever it is, it's all wrong.

(*A sharp cry from within.*)

What's that? Who's screaming?

SCENE VIII

BERTHA *enters from the right.*

BERTHA: Papa, Papa! Help, help! Save me!

CAPTAIN: There, there, my dear child! There, there. What's the matter?

BERTHA: Oh, Daddy, help me! She wants to hurt me!

CAPTAIN: Now, now, who wants to hurt you? Hm? Tell me. Come on now, tell me.

BERTHA: Grandma does.—But it was my fault. I tricked her.

CAPTAIN: All right, now you tell me just what happened.

BERTHA: You've got to promise not to tell. Promise? Promise?

CAPTAIN: Yes, yes. Now what is this all about?

(MARGARET *exits.*)

BERTHA: It happens at night. Grandma comes in, and turns the lamp down low, and then she sets me down at the table with a pen in my hand over a piece of paper. And then she says the spirits will write.

CAPTAIN: What kind of nonsense—! And you haven't told me about this before?

BERTHA: I'm sorry. I didn't dare. Grandma said the spirits would get back at me if I told on them. And then the pen begins to write, and I don't know if I'm doing it or not. And sometimes it writes a lot, and sometimes nothing comes. But it has to come, she says, it has to. And tonight I thought I was doing good, and then Grandma says it was from Shakespeare, and that I had tricked her. And then she got awfully mad.

CAPTAIN: Do you think there are spirits?

BERTHA: I don't know.

CAPTAIN: But I know that there aren't any.

BERTHA: Grandma says that you don't understand such things, and that you have much worse things that can see what's going on on other planets.

CAPTAIN: Is that what she says? What else does she say?

BERTHA: She says that you really can't do any conjuring.

CAPTAIN: I never said I could. You know what meteor stones are? Stones that have fallen from other heavenly bodies. Well, I can examine them and find out if they contain the same elements as our earth. That's all that I can see.

BERTHA: Grandma says that there are things that she can see but that you can't see.

CAPTAIN: Well, Bertha, that's not true.

BERTHA: Grandma wouldn't tell a lie.

CAPTAIN: Why not?

BERTHA: Then Mama is lying too.

CAPTAIN: Uh huh.

BERTHA: If you say Mama is lying, I'll never believe you again.

CAPTAIN: I haven't said that. And that's why you must believe me when I say that it's best for you, best for your future, that you get away from this house. Do you want to do that? Do you want to go and live in town and learn something practical?

BERTHA: Oh, Daddy, how I want to live in town! Get away from here, anywhere! As long as I could still see you now and then. Often. Everything here is so gloomy—dark like a long winter night. But when you come home, Daddy, it's like a spring morning.

CAPTAIN: You dear little chatterbox! My dearest little girl!

BERTHA: But, Daddy, if only you could be nice to Mommy, you know. She cries a lot.

CAPTAIN: (*Murmurs noncommittally, and then says.*) So you want to live in town?

BERTHA: Yes, I do, I do!

CAPTAIN: Suppose Mama doesn't want you to?

BERTHA: But she has to want me to!

CAPTAIN: Just suppose she doesn't?

BERTHA: Then I don't know what to do. She has to want me to, she has to!

CAPTAIN: Will you ask her if you can go?

BERTHA: No, you ask her, ask her nice and sweet. She doesn't pay any mind to me.

CAPTAIN: Hmmm. . . . Well now, if you want to go, and I want you to go, and she *doesn't* want you to go, what do we do then?

BERTHA: Oh, no. Then the bickering will start again. Why can't you both—?

SCENE IX

LAURA *enters.*

LAURA: Ah, so this is where you are, Bertha! This seems to be a good time for hearing what she thinks. We've got to settle the question of her future sooner or later.

CAPTAIN: The child can scarcely have any sound opinion
5   about her future. She doesn't know what lies ahead for a young girl. We on the other hand have a pretty good idea. We've seen a lot of girls grow up and go through life.

LAURA: But since we don't see eye to eye, why not let Bertha's opinion tip the scales?

10   CAPTAIN: No! I won't allow anyone to usurp my rights, neither women nor children. Bertha, leave us.

(BERTHA *leaves.*)

LAURA: You were afraid of what she would say. You knew she would come around to me.

CAPTAIN: I know that she herself wants to get away from
15   home. I also know that you have the power to change her mind any way you wish.

LAURA: Really. Am I so strong?

CAPTAIN: You've got the strength of the devil in getting your own way. So has anyone who has no scruples about the
20   means he uses. For example, how did you get rid of Doctor Norling, and how did you get the new doctor out here?

LAURA: Yes, how *did* I manage that?

CAPTAIN: You kept insulting Norling until he left in disgust, and you got your brother to "arrange" the appointment of
25   the new one.

LAURA: What was wrong with that? Very simple and perfectly legal. Is Bertha leaving soon?

CAPTAIN: Yes, in two weeks she'll move into town.

LAURA: That is your decision?

30   CAPTAIN: Yes!

LAURA: Have you spoken to Bertha about it?

CAPTAIN: Yes.

LAURA: Then I guess I shall have to try to put a stop to it.

CAPTAIN: You can't!

35   LAURA: Oh, no? Do you suppose a real mother will allow her daughter to go and live with trash and to have the child learn that everything she has implanted in her mind is stupid, so that for the rest of her life she'll be despised by her own daughter?

40   CAPTAIN: Do you suppose that a real father will allow ignorant superstitious women to teach his daughter that he is a charlatan?

LAURA: It doesn't mean as much in the case of the father.

CAPTAIN: Why not?

45   LAURA: Because the mother is closer to the child. It's a fact that no one can really know who the father of a child is.

CAPTAIN: I don't see the application in the present case.

LAURA: You don't know if you are Bertha's father.

CAPTAIN: I don't know?

50   LAURA: Since no one knows, how can you?

CAPTAIN: This is a poor joke.

LAURA: Who's joking? I'm only making use of your teachings. Besides, how do you know I haven't been unfaithful?

CAPTAIN: I can believe you capable of almost anything, but
55   not that. And you wouldn't talk about it if it were true.

LAURA: Suppose I were willing to endure anything, to be shunned, despised, anything to hold on to my child and bring her up as I see fit, and suppose I am sincere when I declare: "Bertha is my child but not yours." Suppose—

CAPTAIN: That's enough!   60

LAURA: Just suppose. Then your power would be at an end.

CAPTAIN: That is, if you could prove that I was not the father.

LAURA: That shouldn't be difficult. Would you like me to try?

CAPTAIN: I said that's enough!

LAURA: All I would have to do is reveal the name of the real   65
father, specify the time and place. For example—when was Bertha born?—three years after we got married—

CAPTAIN: For the last time I'm telling you—!

LAURA: Telling me what?—You're right, we've had enough. But be very careful what you do and what you decide.   70
And above all, don't make yourself ridiculous.

CAPTAIN: Ridiculous? I think it's tragic.

LAURA: The more you think so, the more comical you become.

CAPTAIN: I get the laughs and you get the tears. Is that it?

LAURA: Yes. Aren't we women clever?   75

CAPTAIN: That's why we can't fight against you.

LAURA: Then why do you get yourself involved in a fight with a superior enemy?

CAPTAIN: Superior?

LAURA: Yes. It's strange, but I could never look at a man with-   80
out feeling superior.

CAPTAIN: Well, you'll soon learn who your master is. And you won't forget it.

LAURA: That should be interesting.

MARGARET: (*Entering.*) The table's set. Would you like to have   85
something to eat now?

LAURA: Yes, Margaret, thank you.

(*The* CAPTAIN *hesitates. Sits in the armchair near the table in front of the divan.*)

LAURA: Aren't you going to have supper?

CAPTAIN: No thanks. I don't care for anything.

LAURA: What's the matter? Depressed?   90

CAPTAIN: No, just not hungry.

LAURA: Come, otherwise they'll start asking questions, unnecessary questions. . . . You can have the decency—. . . . All right, if you won't, then sit there! (*She leaves.*)

MARGARET: Adolf, now what's going on here?   95

CAPTAIN: I don't know what's going on. Can you tell me how you women can handle a grown man as if he were a child?

MARGARET: I don't know. I suppose it's because you are all born of women, all of you, big and small . . .

CAPTAIN: And no woman is born of man. But I've got to be   100
Bertha's father. Tell me, Margaret, you believe that, don't you? You believe it?

MARGARET: Heavens, but you're silly! Of course you're your own child's father. Come on now and get something to eat. Don't sit there putting a face on. There, there. Come on now.   105

CAPTAIN: (*Standing up.*) Get out of here, you old woman! To hell with all you witches! (*At the door to the hallway.*) Corporal! Orderly!

ORDERLY: (*Entering.*) Yes, sir!

CAPTAIN: Harness up the one-horse sleigh. Immediately!   110

MARGARET: Adolf! Don't do anything—!

CAPTAIN: Get out, woman!—At once, do you hear!

MARGARET: Lord help us, what are you up to?

CAPTAIN: (*Putting on his military cap and great coat, etc.*) Don't
115   expect me home. Not before midnight. (*Leaves.*)

MARGARET: God have mercy! Now what's he up to?

ACT TWO

Same set as first act. The kerosene lamp is burning on the table. Night.

SCENE I

DR. EASTLAND *and* LAURA *are in conversation.*

DR. EASTLAND: According to what I gathered from our conversation, I'm still not convinced about his condition. In the
first place, you were mistaken in saying he had arrived at
some astonishing conclusions about the other planets by
5   looking through a microscope. Now that I've found out that
it was a spectroscope, I would say that not only is he sane but
that he merits the highest praise for his work as a scientist.

LAURA: But, Doctor, I never said anything of the kind!

DR. EASTLAND: Madam, I took notes on our conversation,
10   and I distinctly recall that I asked about this crucial point,
fearing that I had not heard you correctly. One has to be
extremely scrupulous in making accusations that could
lead to a man's being certified and committed.

LAURA: Certified?

15 DR. EASTLAND: You surely know that a person who is declared insane loses his civil and domestic rights.

LAURA: No, I wasn't aware of that.

DR. EASTLAND: And there's another point that strikes me as
questionable. He mentioned that his letters to the book-
20   sellers had gone unanswered. Forgive me for asking, but I
must know whether you—with the best intentions in the
world—have interfered with his correspondence?

LAURA: Yes, I have. I felt it was my duty to look after the best
interests of the family. I could not let him ruin us all with-
25   out doing something.

DR. EASTLAND: Forgive me for saying this, but I don't believe
you have seriously considered the possible consequences
of your actions. If he finds out that you have been secretly
meddling in his affairs, there is no telling what will hap-
30   pen. One confirmed suspicion can set off an avalanche of
doubts. Or to put it another way: interfering in his business is like putting a spoke in a wheel, the worst thing for
his nervous condition. I'm sure you yourself know how
the mind is fretted and torn when your deepest wishes are
35   thwarted, your will paralyzed.

LAURA: Yes, I certainly know.

DR. EASTLAND: Then you know what he must have felt.

LAURA: (*Rising.*) It's midnight and he's still not home. We can
fear the worst now.

40 DR. EASTLAND: Madam, I beg of you to tell me what happened tonight after I left. I must know.

LAURA: He let his imagination run away with him. He had
the craziest notions. He was seized with the idea that he
was not the father of his own child.

45 DR. EASTLAND: Strange. Very strange. What brought that up?

LAURA: I can't imagine—unless—well, he was questioning
one of his troopers about the parentage of some child, and
when I defended the girl in the case, he got all excited and
said no one could tell who was the father of a child. God

knows I did everything I could to quiet him, but now I 50
think the whole thing's hopeless. (*Cries.*)

DR. EASTLAND: This can't be allowed to continue. Something
has to be done—without arousing his suspicions, of
course. I wonder if you could tell me if the captain has had
such odd notions before? 55

LAURA: Six years ago there was a similar situation. That time
he admitted—in his own letter to his doctor—that he
feared for his sanity.

DR. EASTLAND: I see, I see. A case with roots deep in the past.
And the sanctity of the family—and now this—I can't pry 60
into everything; I must keep to what meets the eye.
What's done can't be undone, unfortunately, and the treatment should have begun at that time. . . . Where do you
think he is now?

LAURA: I don't have the slightest notion. I only know he gets 65
the wildest ideas.

DR. EASTLAND: Do you want me to wait up for him? To
avoid arousing his suspicions I could say that I was making a call on your mother—some complaint or ailment.

LAURA: Yes, that's excellent. And, Doctor, please don't leave us. If 70
you only knew how upset I am. I wonder, wouldn't it be better if we told him right out what you think of his condition?

DR. EASTLAND: That's something one never tells the mentally
disturbed before they themselves bring it up, and only
then in exceptional cases. It all depends on how things de- 75
velop. But we shouldn't be sitting here. Perhaps I should
slip into the next room; things would look more natural.

LAURA: Yes, that would be better. And Margaret can sit in
here. She always waits up for him. She's the only one who
knows how to handle him. (*Goes to the door at left.*) Mar- 80
garet! Margaret!

MARGARET: Yes, is there something you want? Has the captain come home?

LAURA: No, I want you to sit here and wait for him. And
when he comes, you're to tell him that my mother is ill, 85
and that's why the doctor is here.

MARGARET: Yes, yes. All right, I'll tend to it.

LAURA: (*Opens the door to the inner rooms.*) Doctor, would you
mind stepping this way?

(DR. EASTLAND *leaves with* LAURA.)

SCENE II

MARGARET: (*Sitting at the table. Produces a hymnbook and a pair
of spectacles.*) Ah, yes, yes. Yes, yes. (*Reading half to herself.*)

> A vale of tears, dark and drear,
> Is this our life, and short its span.
> Death's angel is ever near 5
> Warning every living man:
>   All are mortal, all is vain.

All mortal. If that isn't the truth.

> Yea, all that lives on earth must die
> And to the scythe of death succumb. 10
> Only sorrow stays to sigh

II.ii. 3–7 **A vale . . . vain** a hymn by J. O. Wallin, the most prolific of Swedish hymnists

And etch with tears the silent tomb:
All are mortal, all is vain.

Etch with tears, yes. Yes.

(*During this* BERTHA *has entered, carrying a tray with a coffee pot and a piece of embroidery on it.*)

15 BERTHA: (*Softly.*) Margaret, can I sit here with you? It's so gloomy upstairs.

MARGARET: God in Heaven, are you still up?

BERTHA: I have to work on Daddy's Christmas present. And here's coffee for you.

20 MARGARET: Ah, you're a sweet child, but this just won't do. You have to get up in the morning, and it's after midnight.

BERTHA: What difference does that make? I don't dare sit alone upstairs. There are ghosts up there, I'm sure there are.

MARGARET: I knew it, I knew it, just what I said! Mark my

25 words, there's no good fairy watching over this house. What did you hear, Bertha?

BERTHA: I—I heard someone singing in the attic.

MARGARET: In the attic! At this time of night!

BERTHA: Such a moaning, mournful song, the most mourn-

30 ful song I've ever heard. And it sounded like it came from the storage room up in the attic, where the cradle is, you know, the room to the left—

MARGARET: Hooo, hooo! . . . And Lord what weather tonight!

Alas, what is this life we lead on earth?
35 Unending toil and pain, and nothing worth.
Even on the best of days we found
Cares and tribulations did abound.

Yes, dear child, may God grant us a happy Christmas.

BERTHA: Margaret, is it true that Daddy is sick?

40 MARGARET: Yes, I'm afraid he is.

BERTHA: Then we won't be allowed to celebrate Christmas. Why isn't he in bed if he's sick?

MARGARET: Well, Bertha, he has the kind of an illness where he can be up and about.—Shhh! There's someone out in

45 the hall. Now, you be a good girl and go to bed. And take the coffee pot with you; otherwise your daddy will be mad.

BERTHA: (*Goes out with the serving tray.*) Goodnight, Margaret.

MARGARET: Goodnight, child. God bless you.

SCENE III

CAPTAIN: (*Enters, covered with snow. Takes off his overcoat.*) You still up? Go to bed.

MARGARET: I was only waiting for . . .

(*The* CAPTAIN *lights a candle. Opens the leaf of the secretary. Sits down and takes some letters and newspapers from his pocket.*)

MARGARET: Adolf—?

5 CAPTAIN: What do you want?

MARGARET: Laura's mother is sick. And the doctor is here.

CAPTAIN: Anything serious?

MARGARET: No, I don't think so. Only a cold.

CAPTAIN: (*Standing up.*) Who was the father of your child,

10 Margaret?

34–37 **Alas, . . . abound** from a hymn by J. Rosenthal.

MARGARET: I've told you the whole story so many times. It was that good-for-nothing Johnson.

CAPTAIN: Are you certain it was him?

MARGARET: Don't be silly—of course I'm certain, since he
15 was the only one.

CAPTAIN: Yes—but was *he* certain he was the only one? No, he couldn't be certain, but you could. There's the difference.

MARGARET: I don't see any difference.

CAPTAIN: No, you can't see it; but it's there all the same. (*He leafs through a photograph album on the table.*) Do you think 20 Bertha looks like me? (*Contemplates a portrait in the album.*)

MARGARET: Why, you're as like as two peas in a pod.

CAPTAIN: Did Johnson admit he was the father?

MARGARET: He had to—what else could he do?

CAPTAIN: Awful! Incredible. 25

SCENE IV

DR. EASTLAND *enters.*

CAPTAIN: Good evening, Doctor. How is my mother-in-law feeling?

DR. EASTLAND: Oh, it's nothing serious. She sprained her left ankle slightly.

CAPTAIN: I thought I heard Margaret say it was a cold. There 5 seems to be a slight difference of opinion. Go to bed, Margaret.

(MARGARET *exits.*)

(*Pause.*)

CAPTAIN: Sit down, won't you? Sit down, Doctor.

DR. EASTLAND: (*Seating himself.*) Thank you.

CAPTAIN: Is it true that if you cross a zebra with a mare, the 10 foal is striped?

DR. EASTLAND: (*Taken aback.*) Quite true! Absolutely.

CAPTAIN: And is it true that if you continue the breeding with a studhorse, the succeeding foals will also be striped?

DR. EASTLAND: Yes, that's also true. 15

CAPTAIN: So: under certain conditions a studhorse can be the sire of striped foals, and under other conditions, not.

DR. EASTLAND: Yes, so it would seem.

CAPTAIN: In other words, similarity between offspring and father proves nothing. 20

DR. EASTLAND: I, ah—

CAPTAIN: In other words, fatherhood cannot be proved.

DR. EASTLAND: Ah, ha . . .

CAPTAIN: You're a widower, aren't you? And have had children?

DR. EASTLAND: Yes, I— 25

CAPTAIN: Didn't you feel ridiculous at times? Being a father, I mean. I don't know anything so comical as seeing a father parading his children down the street. Or hearing a father talk about *his* children. "My wife's children"—
that's what he should say. Didn't you ever sense how false 30 your position was?—Never any little stabs of doubt?—I won't say suspicions; as a gentleman, I presume your wife was above suspicion.

DR. EASTLAND: No, I never had that. But, Captain, you have to accept the parentage of your children in good faith. As 35 Goethe says. I believe it was Goethe.

CAPTAIN: Good faith where a woman is involved? That's taking a big risk, isn't it?

DR. EASTLAND: Well, Captain, there are all kinds of women.

40 CAPTAIN: No, Doctor! Only three kinds—and only one genus. The latest research has made that clear. When I was young and strong and—let me boast—handsome—I recall now two fleeting impressions that since then have left me appre-hensive. I was traveling one time by steamboat. I sat in the
45 forward salon, some friends and I. The young woman who ran the restaurant came and sat down opposite me, sat down sobbing, and told us her fiancé had gone down with his ship. We offered our sympathies, and I ordered champagne. After the second glass, I touched her foot; after the fourth,
50 her knee; and by morning I had completely consoled her.

DR. EASTLAND: We all have our failings and weaknesses. There are spots even on the sun.

CAPTAIN: Yes, and on the leopard, too. You know what they say about them. . . . My second example: I was at a resort, and
55 there was a young wife there who had her children with her while her husband was in town on business. Very religious woman, with the strictest principles, always preaching to me, and utterly honorable, I'm sure. A very plain woman, phys-ically unattractive. I avoided her. I fled from her. But she, on
60 the pretext of borrowing books from me, dogged my heels. I loaned her a book—two books—and when she was about to move, she—strangely enough—returned the books. Have you heard of such a thing! Three months later I found in these selfsame books a visiting card with a sufficiently clear
65 declaration of her feelings. Quite innocent—as innocent as any avowal of love from a married woman to a strange man who has never made any advances to her can be.

DR. EASTLAND: A vulgar, scheming woman, obviously.

CAPTAIN: No, not at all, no! No! She was sincere in her reli-
70 gious beliefs, sincere in her morality, sincere in her mari-tal fidelity. The proof: she actually confided in her husband that she was infatuated with me. You see, therein lies the great peril. This is what fills me with apprehen-sion. They are utterly unconscious of their instinctive de-
75 ceitfulness. Such is the genus "woman."

DR. EASTLAND: You must not let these morbid thoughts get the better of you, Captain. You'll end up a sick man.

CAPTAIN: Sick? Such an imprecise word for a doctor to use. All steam boilers explode when the manometer goes past
80 one hundred. But one hundred doesn't represent the same pressure on different boilers. Understand? Besides, are you not here to watch over me? If I were not a man, I would have the right to present my case—or to make a case, slyly, out of insinuations. I might in fact provide you with a
85 complete diagnosis, a clinical account of my illness. Alas, and unfortunately, I am only a man, and can do nothing but fold my arms on my chest like an ancient Roman and hold my breath until I die. Goodnight.

DR. EASTLAND: Captain! . . . If you are ill or deeply disturbed, it
90 would do no offense to your honor as a man to tell me all there is to tell. I want to hear the other side of the story, too.

CAPTAIN: Hearing one side of this story is enough, I should think.

DR. EASTLAND: No, Captain. When I saw *Ghosts* and heard Mrs. Alving giving us a postmortem on her husband, I
95 said to myself, "Damned shame the dead can't speak."

CAPTAIN: Do you think he would speak if he were alive? And if *any* dead husband rose up and spoke, do you think he'd be believed? Goodnight, Doctor. You can see I am quite calm. You can go to bed. Go home.

DR. EASTLAND: Very well, Captain, goodnight. I have done all 100
I can do.

CAPTAIN: Do we part as enemies?

DR. EASTLAND: Not at all. I very much regret that we can't be friends. Goodnight. (*Exits.*)

(*The* CAPTAIN *follows* DR. EASTLAND *to the door at rear. Then he goes to the door at left and opens it halfway.*)

CAPTAIN: Come in; let's have a talk. I knew you were eaves- 105
dropping.

SCENE V

LAURA *enters, somewhat abashed. The* CAPTAIN *sits down at the secretary, the leaf of which is still down.*

CAPTAIN: I know it's late, but we've got to have this out. Sit down. (*Pause.*) I went to the post office tonight and picked up some letters. From them I learn that you have held back both my incoming and outgoing mail. The imme-diate consequence of this is that, because of the loss of 5
time, others shall rush ahead of me in my research, and I shall fall into the shade.

LAURA: I did what I did for your own good. You were ne-glecting your military duties for this other work.

CAPTAIN: My good? No! You were quite certain that one day 10
I'd win more honor with my scientific work than with my military duties. And your primary aim was to see to it that I didn't win any honors, because that would emphasize your insignificance. But there's more: I've intercepted some letters addressed to you.   15

LAURA: What a gentleman you are!

CAPTAIN: From which it appears you have special plans for me. For a long time now you have been gathering my for-mer friends against me by spreading rumors about my mental condition. And you have succeeded in your efforts 20
to the extent that from the colonel down to the cook, there is scarcely anyone who believes I'm not mad. Now as far as my illness is concerned, these are the facts. My mind is clear, as you know, so that I can carry out my du-ties and my responsibilities as a father. My emotions are 25
still pretty much within my control and will be as long as my willpower remains in working order. But you have gnawed and chewed on it so that the cogs are worn smooth, and soon the gear wheels will slip and the whole mechanism will spin backward and fly to pieces. I won't 30
appeal to your feelings—since you lack them: therein lies your strength. I do, however, appeal to your best interests.

LAURA: What does that mean?

CAPTAIN: Your behavior has succeeded in arousing my suspi-cions to the point where my acumen is blunted and my 35
thoughts run wild—the onset of madness—what you have been waiting for, and which might come at any mo-ment. Now I put this question to you: is it in your better interest that I am of sound or unsound mind? Think about it. If I collapse, I lose my position in the army, and where 40
would you be? If I die, you get my insurance. However, if I should take my own life, you would receive nothing. So you see, it is in your interest that I live my life out.

LAURA: Is this supposed to be a trap?

45 CAPTAIN: Of course! It's up to you to set your foot in it or go around it.

LAURA: You say you'll kill yourself. You won't!

CAPTAIN: Can you be sure? Do you think a man can live when he has nothing and no one to live for?

50 LAURA: So you capitulate?

CAPTAIN: No, I'm suggesting an armistice.

LAURA: On what conditions?

CAPTAIN: That I retain my reason and sanity. Rid me of my suspicions and I lay down my arms.

55 LAURA: What suspicions?

CAPTAIN: Concerning Bertha's parentage.

LAURA: Are there any suspicions about that?

CAPTAIN: With me there are. Suspicions you have fed and nourished.

60 LAURA: I? How?

CAPTAIN: You have dropped them like hebona in the porches of my ear, and circumstances have made them doubly poisonous. Free me from uncertainty. Tell me plainly I'm right, and I shall forgive you in advance.

65 LAURA: You don't expect me to assume a guilt that's not mine!

CAPTAIN: What difference does that make, since you can be certain that I won't reveal it. A man doesn't go around trumpeting his shame.

LAURA: If I say your suspicions are wrong, you can't be certain; but if I say they are right, then you can be certain. So you want your suspicions to be right.

70

CAPTAIN: Fantastic, but true. The first instance cannot be proved, you see; only the second.

LAURA: Have you any grounds for these suspicions?

75 CAPTAIN: Yes and no.

LAURA: I know what you are up to. You want me to admit my guilt so you can get rid of me and keep the child entirely to yourself. No, you won't catch me in that trap.

CAPTAIN: Do you think I'd want to bring up somebody else's child if I were certain of your guilt?

80

LAURA: I'm confident you wouldn't. And that's why I realize you were lying a moment ago when you said you'd forgive me in advance.

CAPTAIN: (Rising.) Laura, save me and my reason. You don't understand what I'm trying to say. If the child isn't mine, I have no rights over it, and want none. Isn't that exactly what you want? Do you want more? What else? You want power over the child, with me on hand to support both her and you? Is that it?

85

90 LAURA: Yes, power. What is this whole life-and-death struggle but a struggle for power?

CAPTAIN: For me, since I do not believe in a life in the hereafter, my child was my life in the future. It was my form of immortality, the only form of it that has any basis in reality. Take that from me, and you cut the thread of life.

95

LAURA: Why didn't we separate before?

CAPTAIN: Because the child held us together. But the child became a chain. How did it happen? How? How? . . . I never thought about it before, but now I remember something that happened—a memory that implicates and condemns you. We had been married two years and had no children—you best know why. I fell ill and lay near death. One time when the fever left me, I heard voices in the sitting room. You and the lawyer talking about the money I

100

possessed—at that time. He explained that you couldn't 105 inherit any of it since we didn't have any children, and he asked if you were pregnant. What you said I couldn't hear. I recovered—and we had a child. Who is the father?

LAURA: You!

CAPTAIN: No, not me, not me! There's a crime buried in the past, 110 a crime now coming to light. And what a devilish crime! Your tender consciences made you free the black slaves, but you held on to the white. I have worked and slaved for you, for your child, your mother, your maids. I have sacrificed my career and promotion; I've been whipped from pillar to post, 115 gone without sleep, worried myself sick about taking care of you until my hair has turned gray—gone through hell in order that you might enjoy a trouble-free life and spend your old age enjoying life again through your child. I've endured it all without complaining because I thought I was father of 120 this child. This is the lowest form of theft, the most brutal slavery. I've suffered seventeen years at hard labor as an innocent man; how can you repay me for that?

LAURA: Now you are mad!

CAPTAIN: (Sitting down.) That's what you want, isn't it? I've 125 seen how you've worked to conceal your crime. I took pity on you because I didn't understand what was troubling you. I often lulled your troubled conscience, thinking I was chasing away a nightmare. I have heard you cry out in your sleep. I didn't want to listen. I remember 130 now—the other night—the night before Bertha's birthday. Between two and three in the morning, I was still up, reading. You shrieked as if someone were choking you. "Go away, go away—or I'll tell!" I pounded on the wall— I—didn't want to hear more. I've harbored my suspicions 135 a long time, afraid to hear them confirmed. This I have suffered for you; what will you do for me?

LAURA: What can I do? I swear by God and everything that's holy that you are Bertha's father.

CAPTAIN: What good does that do when you've already said 140 that a mother may and should commit any crime for the sake of her child? I beg you, by the memory of all that's past—I beg you like a wounded man asking for the *coup de grace*—tell me all. Don't you see I am as helpless as a child; can't you hear I have come to cry to you as to my 145 mother; can't you forget that I am a man, a soldier commanding man and beast? I ask only for the pity you would show a dying man; I surrender the tokens of my power; I beseech you, have mercy on me. (*He is on his knees.*)

LAURA: (*Puts her hand on his head.*) What! You're crying. A 150 man like you crying!

CAPTAIN: Yes, I am crying. A man and crying. Hath not a man eyes? Hath not a man hands, organs, senses, affections, passions? Is he not fed with the same food, hurt with the same weapons, warmed and cooled by the same summer 155 and winter as a woman is? If you prick us, do we not bleed? If you tickle us, do we not laugh? If you poison us, do we not die? Why should not a man be allowed to wail, a soldier to cry? Because it is unmanly? Why is it unmanly?

160

LAURA: Cry, cry, my boy, and your mother will comfort you, as she did before. Remember? It was as your second mother that I came into your life. Your big, strong body was a bundle of nerves. You were a giant child who had come into the world too early, or perhaps had come unwanted. 165

CAPTAIN: It's true. My mother and father did not want me, and so I was born without strength of will. I hoped that I could make myself whole by becoming one with you. And so I let you take charge. I who in the field, who be-
170 fore the troops gave the orders, became with you the one who obeyed. I couldn't do without you. I looked up to you as a higher, more intelligent being, listening to your every word like a stupid child.

LAURA: It's true, it was like that. And I loved you for the child
175 in you. But—oh, you saw it well enough, every time your nature changed and you came to me as my lover, I blushed with shame, and your lovemaking was a joy followed by the anguish of incest. The mother became her boy's lover—. Disgusting!

180 CAPTAIN: Yes, I felt your disgust but I didn't understand the cause of it. When I saw in you what I thought was your contempt for my unmanliness, I sought to win the woman in you by being a man.

LAURA: That was the mistake. The mother in me was your
185 friend, you see. The woman was your enemy, and love be-tween the sexes is war. And don't think I gave myself. I didn't give, I took—what I wanted. But you had the up-per hand, and I always felt it, and longed for the day it would be mine.

190 CAPTAIN: You always had the upper hand. You could hypno-tize me blind and deaf, so that I neither saw nor heard, only obeyed. You could hand me a raw potato and make me believe it was a peach. You could convince me that your silly whims were flashes of genius. You could have
195 induced me to commit a crime—to do the cheapest, most contemptible things. How? Why? Because you didn't think, you didn't reason, you didn't listen to me; you did whatever came into your head. But when I woke from your spell, reflected on what had happened, I saw that my
200 honor was stained, my reputation tarnished. I wanted to restore it by doing something grand—a daring exploit, a great discovery, at least a face-saving suicide. I wanted to fight in the field; I was denied my request. So I turned to science, made it my life. And now when I am about to
205 reach out and pluck the fruit of my endeavors, you hack off my arm. Now I have no honor, and my life is at an end; for a man cannot live without honor.

LAURA: And a woman?

CAPTAIN: Yes. She has her children; but he doesn't.—What
210 are you getting at? Feminism, women's emancipation, Ib-senism? . . . We—all of us—lived our little lives, uncon-scious as children, full of ideals, illusions, delusions. And then we woke up. Right enough, but we woke up all turned round, with our feet on the pillow, and he who
215 woke us was himself walking in his sleep. When women grow old and cease to be women, they grow beards; I wonder what happens to men when they grow old and cease to be men? Those emanipators who crowed to make the sun rise were no longer cocks but capons, and those
220 who answered the cockcrow were sexless hens, so that when the sun was to rise we found it was nothing but moonshine, and we were still sitting among ruins, just as in the good old days. It had all been nothing but a little morning nap, a crazy dream, and no waking up at all.

225 LAURA: You know, you should have been a writer.

CAPTAIN: Who knows?

LAURA: Well, I'm sleepy. If you have any more fantasies, save them for morning.

CAPTAIN: Just one word more about realities. Do you hate me?

LAURA: Yes, sometimes. When you act the man. 230

CAPTAIN: It's like race hate. If it's true that we are descended from the apes, it must have been from two different species. We're not like each other, are we?

LAURA: What are you getting at?

CAPTAIN: I feel that in this struggle one of us has to go under. 235

LAURA: Which one?

CAPTAIN: The weaker, naturally.

LAURA: And the stronger is in the right?

CAPTAIN: Always, since he has the power.

LAURA: Then I am in the right. 240

CAPTAIN: You mean you are already in power?

LAURA: Yes—and legally! As of tomorrow morning when you'll be declared incapable of managing your affairs.

CAPTAIN: Certified?

LAURA: That's right. And I'll be free to bring up my child 245 without having to put up with your wild ideas.

CAPTAIN: And who'll pay for this upbringing when I'm no longer around?

LAURA: Your army pension.

CAPTAIN: (*Goes toward her threateningly.*) How can you have 250 me put under guardianship?

LAURA: (*Taking out a letter.*) With this letter, a certified copy of which is now in the hands of the court.

CAPTAIN: What letter?

LAURA: (*Moving backward toward the door at the left.*) Yours! Your 255 declaration to your doctor that you are insane!

(*The* CAPTAIN *stares at her dumbly.*)

LAURA: You have fulfilled your function as an unfortunately indispensable father and family provider. Now you're no longer needed. You're dismissed. You can go. Go—now that you see my mind is as strong as my will. I'm sure you 260 won't want to stay and face up to that!

(*The* CAPTAIN *crosses to the table; takes the burning lamp and throws it at* LAURA, *who has exited backward toward the door.*)

ACT THREE

The same set. A different lamp is on the table. The jib door is bar-ricaded with a chair.

SCENE I

LAURA *and* MARGARET *on stage.*

LAURA: Did he give you the keys?

MARGARET: Give! No, Lord help me, I took them from the captain's clothes when Happy was brushing them outside.

LAURA: So Happy is on duty today.

MARGARET: Yes, that he is. 5

LAURA: Give me the keys.

MARGARET: All right, but it's no better than stealing. Listen to him walking up there—back and forth, back and forth.

LAURA: Are you sure he can't get in through that door?

MARGARET: Locked, bolted, barricaded—and Happy on 10 guard outside.

LAURA: (*Opening the secretary and seating herself at it.*) Control yourself, Margaret. We've got to be calm if we want to save ourselves.

(*A knocking at the hall door.*)

15   Who is that?

MARGARET: (*Opening the door to the hall.*) It's Happy.

LAURA: Let him in.

HAPPY: (*Entering.*) A dispatch from the colonel.

LAURA: Give it here. (*Reads it.*) I see. . . . Happy, have you re-
20   moved all the cartridges from all the guns and all the hunting bags?

HAPPY: I did exactly as you ordered.

LAURA: Wait outside until I've answered the colonel's letter.

(HAPPY *exits.* LAURA *sits down to write.*)

MARGARET: Listen! Do you hear that? What do you suppose
25   he's doing up there now?

LAURA: Quiet! Can't you see I'm writing?

(*The sounds of someone sawing can be heard.*)

MARGARET: (*Half aloud, to herself.*) God have mercy. . . . Where's it all going to end?

LAURA: There. Give this to Happy. And don't breathe a word
30   of this to my mother. Do you hear?

(MARGARET *goes to the door.* LAURA *opens the drawers of the secretary and takes out some papers.*)

SCENE II

The PASTOR *enters and takes a chair. Sits down next to* LAURA *at the secretary.*

PASTOR: Good evening, Laura. I've been gone the whole day and just now got back. It's been a bad day for you, hasn't it?

LAURA: The worst night and day I've ever been through.

PASTOR: Well, I see you weren't harmed, in any event.

5   LAURA: No, thank God. But just think what might have happened.

PASTOR: Tell me, what started it all? I've heard so many different stories.

LAURA: It started with his crazy idea that he wasn't Bertha's
10   father and ended with his throwing a lighted lamp right in my face.

PASTOR: That's appalling! He's completely insane. What are you going to do now?

LAURA: We have to prevent further outbreaks of violence.
15   The doctor has sent for a straitjacket from the hospital. In the meantime I've sent word to the colonel, and I'm trying to familiarize myself with the household finances, which he has completely mismanaged.

PASTOR: What a wretched affair. I can't say I'm surprised
20   though. Fire—water—pressure. Explosion! What have you got in that box?

(LAURA *has taken a drawer from the secretary.*)

LAURA: Look at this! Here's where he's kept everything.

PASTOR: (*Going through the contents.*) Dear God. . . . He's kept your little doll . . . and here's your christening cap—and

Bertha's rattle . . . and all your letters . . . and your 25
locket. . . . (*Drying his eyes.*) He must have held you very dear, Laura, sister. I haven't kept mementos like that.

LAURA: He may have held me dear once upon a time. But time—time brings so many changes.

PASTOR: What's that large piece of paper?—The deed to a 30
cemetery plot. Yes, rather the cemetery than the asylum. Laura—tell me: are you quite blameless in all this?

LAURA: Me? Why blame me because somebody goes insane?

PASTOR: Yes. . . . Well, I shan't say anything. Blood is still thicker than water. 35

LAURA: Exactly what are you insinuating?

PASTOR: (*Confronting her.*) Listen to me.

LAURA: Well?

PASTOR: You certainly can't deny that this fits in perfectly with your plans to bring up Bertha on your own terms. 40

LAURA: I don't understand.

PASTOR: I really admire you, Laura.

LAURA: Me? Huh!

PASTOR: I'll be appointed guardian to that atheist! Fact is, I've always regarded him as a weed in our garden. 45

LAURA: (*Gives a short laugh, quickly stifled; abruptly serious.*) You dare to say this to me, his wife!

PASTOR: God, but you're strong, Laura! Unbelievably strong! Like a fox in a trap, you'd rather bite off your own leg than be caught. Like a master thief—no accomplices, not even 50
your own conscience.—Look at yourself in the mirror. You wouldn't dare.

LAURA: I never use a mirror.

PASTOR: No, you don't dare!—Let me look at your hands. Not a spot of incriminating blood, not a trace of the se- 55
cret poison. A little innocent murder, beyond the law's reach. An unconscious crime! Unconscious? Marvelous invention!—Listen to him sawing away up there.—Watch out! If he gets loose, he'll saw you in half.

LAURA: Talk, talk, talk—as if your conscience bothered you. 60
If you think I'm guilty, accuse me—if you can.

PASTOR: I cannot.

LAURA: You see? You cannot. Therefore I am innocent. Now you take charge of your ward, and I'll tend to mine.—Ah, the doctor. 65

SCENE III

DR. EASTLAND *enters.*

LAURA: (*Getting up.*) Hello, my dear Doctor. You will help, won't you? Though I'm afraid there isn't much that can be done. Do you hear how he's carrying on upstairs? Are you convinced now?

DR. EASTLAND: I am convinced that an act of violence was 5
committed. The question is, should this act be regarded as due to an outburst of rage or of insanity?

PASTOR: Putting aside the outburst, you have to admit he was obsessed with certain fixed ideas.

DR. EASTLAND: In my view, Pastor, your ideas are even more 10
fixed. Are they obsessions?

PASTOR: I have definite views regarding higher spiritual matters. They are not—

DR. EASTLAND: Shall we leave our views out of this? . . . Madam, the decision is up to you whether you want to 15 see your husband fined and imprisoned or sent to the asylum. How do you judge his behavior?

LAURA: I can't answer that now.

DR. EASTLAND: In other words, you have no definite views regarding the best interests of the family? Is that right, Pastor?

PASTOR: Either way there will be a scandal. . . . It's difficult to say.

LAURA: If he's only fined for assault and battery, he might become violent again.

DR. EASTLAND: And if he's sent to jail, he'll soon be out again. I take it we're agreed: it's best for all concerned that he be treated as insane.—Where's his old nurse?

LAURA: Why?

DR. EASTLAND: She will have to put the straitjacket on him, after I've spoken to him and given the order. But not before! I have the—the garment out here. (*Goes out into the hall and returns with a large parcel.*) Would you please ask Miss Margaret to step in here?

(LAURA *rings.*)

PASTOR: I don't like this one bit. "It is a fearful thing to fall into the hands of the living God."

(MARGARET *enters.*)

DR. EASTLAND: (*Unwrapping the straitjacket.*) Now listen to me carefully. You must slip this jacket on the captain from behind, if and when I think the need should arise, to prevent any violence on his part. As you can see, it's got these unusually long arms, designed to restrain any movement. These arms are to be tied behind his back. Now these two straps go through these buckles and are then fastened to a chair or the sofa, or whatever is convenient. That's all there's to it. Are you willing to do it?

MARGARET: No, Doctor, I can't. Oh, I couldn't, I couldn't.

LAURA: Why don't you do it yourself, Doctor?

DR. EASTLAND: Because he mistrusts me, Madam. You, of course, would be the obvious choice, but I'm afraid he mistrusts you too.

(LAURA *gives him a sharp look, then turns away.*)

DR. EASTLAND: Perhaps you, Pastor?

PASTOR: No, I'm afraid I must decline.

SCENE IV

HAPPY *enters.*

LAURA: Have you already delivered the message?

HAPPY: As you ordered.

DR. EASTLAND: Ah, my lad. You know the situation here, don't you? The captain is mentally ill, and you've got to help us with him.

HAPPY: Anything I can do to help the captain, sir, I'll be glad to do.

DR. EASTLAND: You've got to get him into this straitjacket—

MARGARET: No. No, he mustn't touch him. I don't want the captain hurt. I'd rather do it myself, gently, very gently. But you can stand outside, Happy, in case I need help. Now that's the way it has to be.

(*A pounding on the wallpapered door.*)

DR. EASTLAND: That's him! Hide the straitjacket under your shawl on the chair, and all of you go out—the pastor and I will receive him—that door won't last much longer. Out, out!

MARGARET: (*Exiting to the left.*) Lord help us!

(LAURA *closes the secretary and exits to the left.* HAPPY *exits at the rear.*)

SCENE V

The door is broken in. The lock is torn from its seat, and the chair blocking the door is hurled out into the room. The CAPTAIN, *wearing a wool shirt, enters with several books under one arm, a saw in one hand, his hair rumpled, a wild expression on his face.*

CAPTAIN: (*Placing the books on the table.*) The same thing in every book! And that proves it—I'm not crazy! The *Odyssey,* first book, line 215. Telemachus talking to Athena: "My mother calls me the son of the man"—meaning Odysseus—"but I myself do not know. No one has ever been certain of his father." And this is the suspicion entertained by Telemachus of Penelope, the most virtuous of all women! Beautiful, eh? Beautiful! . . . And here we have the prophet Ezekiel: "The fool says: Lo here is my father, but who can know whose loins have engendered him?" What could be clearer?— And what have I here? History of Russian literature by Merzlyakov. Alexander Pushkin, Russia's greatest poet, tormented to death by the widespread rumors of his wife's unfaithfulness. That was more the cause of his death than the bullet fired into his chest during a duel. On his deathbed he swore that she was innocent. What an ass! Ass! How could he swear to that? You see I've been doing my homework.— Ah, Jonas, so you are here! And the good doctor, naturally. Have you heard how I replied to an English lady who complained that Irish husbands threw lighted kerosene lamps right in the faces of their wives? "My God, what women!" I said. "W-w-women?" she stammered. "Of course," said I. "When things have gone so far that a man, a man who has loved and adored his woman, takes a lighted lamp and throws it in her face—then you can be sure!"

PASTOR: Sure of what?

CAPTAIN: Nothing. One can't be sure of anything, one can only have faith. Right, Jonas? Believe and you'll be saved. That's the way, isn't it Jonas? No! One is damned for believing! I know that for a fact.

DR. EASTLAND: Captain—!

CAPTAIN: Quiet! I don't wish to talk to you. The human telephone transmitting what they tell you in there. In there! (*Indicates the inner rooms.*) You know. You know.—Tell me, Jonas, do you think you are the father of your children? I seem to remember that you once employed a tutor in your house—pretty face, dimpled cheeks—people talked about him. Oh, yes.

PASTOR: Adolf, that's enough!

CAPTAIN: Feel under your wig and see if there aren't two bumps there. Upon my soul, I do believe he's turning pale. Come, come, it's only tittle-tattle.—But, my God, they tattle so much! Ain't we a lovely bunch of ridiculous rascals, we husbands? Right, Doctor? Right? By the way, how were

45 things in your marriage bed? Wasn't there a lieutenant staying in the house—hmm? Just a minute now, his name—his
name was—(*Whispers in* DR. EASTLAND'*s ear.*) Look at that!
He's turning pale, too. Oh, don't look so upset. She's dead
and buried, and what's done cannot be undone. However, I
50 did know the fellow and can tell you that he is now—look
at me, Doctor—no, no, right in my eyes—a major in the
dragoons! My God, I swear you've got horns, too!

DR. EASTLAND: (*Irritated.*) Captain can't you find something
else to talk about?

55 CAPTAIN: Now look at that! Right away he wants to talk
about something else when I want to talk about horns.

PASTOR: Adolf . . . you know that you are mentally ill.

CAPTAIN: I know that well enough. And could I treat your
antlered brains some space of time, I would soon have you
60 locked up too. Crazy I may be, but what made me crazy?
That doesn't concern you; it doesn't concern anyone.
Now let us talk of other things. (*Takes the photograph album
from the table.*) My God, there she is!—My child. My? That
we cannot know. You know what we should do in order
65 that we might know? First, get married for appearance's
sake, get divorced soon after, become lovers, and then
adopt the child. That way you can at least be certain that
it is your adopted child. Isn't that logical? What good does
it do me now—now that you have taken my kind of im-
70 mortality from me? What good is philosophy and science
when I have nothing to live for? What does life mean to
me when honor is gone? I grafted my right arm, half my
brain, half my spinal cord on another stem. I thought they
would grow together, entwine to form a single, more
75 nearly perfect tree. And then someone comes with a knife
and cuts just under the graft, leaving me as a mere half-
tree. But the other shoots up with my right arm and half
my brain, while I wither and die, for those were the best
parts of me that I gave away. Now I want to die. Do with
80 me what you will. I no longer exist.

(DR. EASTLAND *and the* PASTOR *whisper together. They go into the
inner rooms off left. Shortly thereafter* BERTHA *enters.*)

SCENE VI

The CAPTAIN *is sitting at the table, hunched over.*

BERTHA: (*Approaching him.*) Are you sick, Daddy?

CAPTAIN: (*Looking up dully.*) I?

BERTHA: You know what you have done? Don't you know
that you threw the lamp at Mommy?

5 CAPTAIN: Did I?

BERTHA: Yes, you did. Suppose she had been hurt?

CAPTAIN: What difference would that make?

BERTHA: You can't be my father if you talk like that!

CAPTAIN: What? Not your father? How do you know? Who
10 told you? And who is your father? Who?

BERTHA: Well, certainly not you!

CAPTAIN: Still not me? Then who? You appear to be well informed. Who informed you? That I should live to see the
day when my child comes to me and tells me to my face
15 that I am not her father! Don't you realize that you disgrace your mother when you say this? Don't you understand that if it's true, your mother is shamed?

BERTHA: Don't say anything bad about Mother! I won't have it!

CAPTAIN: No, you all stick together, all against me. And
you've done it from the very start! 20

BERTHA: Daddy!

CAPTAIN: Don't ever use that word again!

BERTHA: Daddy, Daddy!

CAPTAIN: (*Holding her close.*) Bertha, my dearest own child,
you are my child! Yes, yes, it's true. It can't be any other 25
way. The rest was only a sick thought brought by the
wind like fever or the plague. Look at me so that I may
see my soul in your eyes. . . . But I see her soul, too! You
have two souls, and you love me with the one and hate
me with the other. You must love only me! You must have 30
only one soul, otherwise you will never have peace, nor
shall I. You must have only one mind, the child of my
mind; you must have only one will, which is my will.

BERTHA: No, I don't want that! I want to be myself.

CAPTAIN: That you may not be! You see, I am a cannibal and 35
I want to eat you. Your mother wanted to eat me, but she
couldn't. I am Saturn who ate his own children because it
had been prophesied that they would eat him. Eat or be
eaten—that is the question! If I don't eat you, you will eat
me—and you've already bared your teeth. Don't be afraid 40
now, my dearest girl, I'm not going to hurt you. (*Goes over
to the wall where the weapons hang and takes a revolver.*)

BERTHA: (*Trying to get away, going toward the door.*) Help,
Mommy! Mommy, help, help! He'll kill me!

MARGARET: (*Entering.*) Adolf, what is going on here? 45

CAPTAIN: (*Examining the revolver.*) Did you remove the cartridges?

MARGARET: Yes, I've put them away. But if you just sit nice
and still here, I'll bring them out again.

(*Takes the* CAPTAIN *by the arm and seats him in the chair, where he
remains seated, dull and apathetic. She picks up the straitjacket and
stands behind the chair.* BERTHA *slips out to the left.*)

MARGARET: Adolf, do you remember when you were my dear 50
little boy, and I tucked you into bed at night, and we would
say, "Now I lay me down to sleep"? Remember how I would
get up at night and give you a glass of water? Remember
how I would light the candle and tell you lovely fairy tales
when you had bad dreams and couldn't sleep. Remember? 55

CAPTAIN: Go on talking, Margaret; it soothes my head and feels
so good. When I was a child and you were my nanny . . .

MARGARET: All right, but you must listen. . . . Remember the
time you took the big kitchen knife to carve boats and
how I had to trick you into giving it to me. You were be- 60
ing very difficult, and so I had to trick you, because you
didn't believe it was for your own good. . . . "Give me that
snake," I said, "before it bites you!" And then you let me
have the knife. (*Takes the revolver from the* CAPTAIN'*s hand.*)
And then there were the times you were to get dressed 65
and didn't want to. I had to coax and wheedle and say you
were going to have a golden coat and be dressed like a
prince. And then I took the little undershirt, which was
only green wool, and held it in front of you and said, "Pop
in your arms, both arms." And then I would say, "Now 70
you just sit still while I button up the back." (*She has the
straitjacket on him by this time.*) And then I would say, "Now

stand up and let's see how it looks. Walk across the floor so we can see how it fits." (*She leads him to the sofa.*) And then I would say, "Now it's time to go to bed."

CAPTAIN: Bed? Go to bed when you've just dressed me?— Damn! Damn! What have you done to me! (*Struggles to get loose.*) Oh, you damned deceitful woman! Who would have thought you could be so clever! (*Lying down on the sofa.*) Captured, shorn, outwitted, and not even allowed to die!

MARGARET: Forgive me, Adolf, forgive me, but I couldn't let you kill the child.

CAPTAIN: Why did you not let me kill the child? Life on earth is hell and death is the kingdom of heaven, and the children belong to heaven.

MARGARET: What can you know of what comes after death?

CAPTAIN: That's all we do know. Of life we know nothing. Oh, if we had only known that from the beginning.

MARGARET: Adolf, bow your head, humble your proud heart, and call on God for mercy. It is still not too late. It was not too late for the thief on the cross when the Redeemer said, "Today shalt thou be with me in Paradise!"

CAPTAIN: What, croaking over the corpse already, you old crow!

(MARGARET *takes her hymnbook from her apron pocket.*)

CAPTAIN: (*Calling.*) Happy! Are you there, Happy? Orderly!

(HAPPY *enters.*)

CAPTAIN: Throw this woman out of here! She wants to suffocate me in the fumes of her psalms. Throw her out the window or up the chimney, wherever you damn please!

HAPPY: (*Looking at* MARGARET.) Lord, help me, Captain, really, I mean—I just can't. Honestly, I can't. Six guys, sure, but not a woman.

CAPTAIN: Can't manage one woman, is that what you mean?

HAPPY: Sure I can, but they're something special. I mean, you don't want to do violence to them.

CAPTAIN: Something special? Haven't they done violence to me?

HAPPY: I can't, sir, I mean—well, I can't, sir. It's just like you asking me to hit the pastor here, sir. It's something inside, like religion. I can't.

SCENE VII

LAURA *enters and signals* HAPPY *to leave.*

CAPTAIN: Omphale! Omphale! You play with his club while Hercules spins your wool.

LAURA: (*Crosses to the sofa.*) Adolf, look at me. Do you think I am your enemy?

CAPTAIN: Yes, I do believe that. I believe that you are all my enemies. My mother, who didn't want me to come into this world because my birth would cause her pain; she was my enemy. She deprived my first cells of nourishment, stunting and crippling me before I was born. My sister was my enemy when she taught me to be meek and sweet to her. The first woman I made love to was my enemy for she gave me ten years of disease in exchange for the love I gave her. My daughter became my enemy when she had to choose between you and me. And you, my wife, are my mortal enemy, for you would not leave me until I had been cast down lifeless.

LAURA: I don't know that I have ever thought about or intended any of the things you imagine. Perhaps some dim desire to remove you as an obstacle ruled my actions at times. If you see some design in them, it's possible it was there, though I wasn't aware of it. I never laid any plans. Things merely rolled along the rails you yourself laid out. And before God and my conscience I feel that I am innocent, even if I am not. Your presence was like a stone weighing on my breast, pressing and hurting until I had to shake off the burden. That's how it was, and if I have struck you, as a reflex action, I ask you to forgive me.

CAPTAIN: Sounds plausible enough. But what good does it do me? And where does the blame lie? In modern marriage, perhaps, the marriage of minds. One used to marry a wife; now one goes into partnership with a career woman, or sets up housekeeping with a friend. After which one either copulates with the business partner or rapes the friend. What happened to love? Good, sound, carnal love? Died in the process of incorporation. And what about the offspring in this marriage corporation where no one assumes responsibility and love dividends are periodically payable to the stockholder? Who owns the assets when the crash comes? Who is the physical father to the spiritual child?

LAURA: Your suspicions about the child, Adolf—they're completely groundless.

CAPTAIN: That's just what's so terrible. If only there were some grounds for them, there would be something to hang on to—to take hold of. Now there are only goblins hiding in the bushes, sticking their heads out to laugh. It's just shadowboxing, a sham battle fought with blanks. Against something real and deadly one can fight with brain and brawn. But now my thoughts dissolve into nothingness: the grist is gone and my brain grinds on stone until it catches fire. Put a pillow under my head. And throw something over me. I'm freezing. I'm freezing to death.

(LAURA *takes her shawl and spreads it out over him.*)

(MARGARET *goes out for a pillow.*)

LAURA: Give me your hand as a friend.

CAPTAIN: My hand! Which you tied behind me. . . . Omphale, Omphale! I feel your soft shawl against my mouth—as warm and soft as your arm. It smells like vanilla, as your hair did when you were young. Laura, when you were young, and we walked among the birch trees—cowslips and thrushes—beautiful, heavenly! How beautiful life was—and look at it now. You didn't want it to be like this; I didn't want it; and still it got to be like this. Who is it makes our lives?

LAURA: God, only God—

CAPTAIN: The god of war, then! Or goddess nowadays. Take away this cat on my chest! Take it away!

(MARGARET *comes in with the pillow; removes the shawl.*)

CAPTAIN: Give me my army coat. Throw it over me.

(MARGARET *takes his army overcoat from the clothes tree and spreads it over him.*)

CAPTAIN: Ah, my hard lion skin that you wanted to take from me, Omphale, Omphale! What a cunning woman—the peace lover who invented disarmament. Awaken, Hercules, before they take your club from you! You want to
70 cheat us of our armor, too, and have us believe it is only for show. No, lady, it was iron before it became tassels and braids. The blacksmith used to make the tunic, now it's the seamstress. Omphale, Omphale! Brute strength has fallen before wily weakness. I spit on you, you devil of a
75 woman! To hell with your whole damned sex! (*He raises himself up to spit at her but falls back on the sofa.*) What kind of a pillow have you given me, Margaret? So hard and cold, so cold. Come and sit here on the chair, next to me. Like that, yes. Let me lay my head in your lap. There! . . .
80 That's better. So warm. Lean over me so I can feel your breast. . . . How soft and lovely it is to sleep on a woman's bosom, a mother's or a mistress's, but loveliest a mother's.

LAURA: Do you want to see your child, Adolf? . . . Adolf, do you?

85 CAPTAIN: My child? A man has no children; only women have children. That's why the future can be theirs, since we die childless. . . . Now I lay me down to sleep, I—

MARGARET: Listen, he's praying to God.

CAPTAIN: No, to you, to lull me to sleep. I'm tired, so tired. . . .
90 Goodnight, Margaret, and blessed be thou among women. (*He raises himself up but falls with a cry back into* MARGARET'*s lap.*)

SCENE VIII

Crossing to the left, LAURA *calls in* DR. EASTLAND, *who enters with the* PASTOR.

LAURA: Help us, Doctor, if it's not too late! He's not breathing.

DR. EASTLAND: (*Taking the* CAPTAIN'*s pulse.*) He's had a stroke.

PASTOR: Is he dead?

DR. EASTLAND: No, he may still come to life, but to which life one cannot say. 5

PASTOR: "Once to die, but after this the judgment."

DR. EASTLAND: No judgment. And no incriminations. You who believe that a god governs our destinies can take the matter up with Him.

MARGARET: Pastor, he prayed to God in his last moment. 10

PASTOR: (*To* LAURA.) Is that true?

LAURA: Yes, it's true.

DR. EASTLAND: If it is—and I can no more judge of that than of his illness—then my skills can do no more for him. Now try yours, Pastor. 15

LAURA: Is that all you can find to say at a man's deathbed, Doctor?

DR. EASTLAND: Yes, that's all. I know no more. Let him who knows more speak.

BERTHA: (*Entering from the left, running to her mother's arms.*) 20 Mother, Mother!

LAURA: My child! My own child!

PASTOR: Amen.

Anton Chekhov

The work of Anton Chekhov (1860–1904) is noted for its objectivity, its sympathetic yet almost clinical examination of turn-of-the-century Russian life. Born in the provincial town of Taganrog, Chekhov trained for a career in medicine and began practicing as a physician in the mid-1880s. At that time he also began to write his first short stories. In his fiction, as in his later plays, Chekhov adopted a mildly ironic attitude toward his subjects, one that resisted sensation and melodrama in favor of a more neutral stance; as he wrote in a letter, "It is necessary that on stage everything should be as complex and as simple as in life. People are having dinner, and while they're having it, their future happiness may be decided or their lives may be about to be shattered." Chekhov's life was shattered in just this way, simply, suddenly, and casually. In 1884 he coughed up blood, the sure sign that he had contracted tuberculosis. The disease could not be cured and required repeated periods of convalescence; an early death was a certainty.

Chekhov began writing plays in the 1880s as well, mainly short comic sketches he called "vaudevilles," among them *The Bear* (1888), *The Proposal* (1889), and *The Wedding* (1890). In 1896, the Alexandrinsky Theater in St. Petersburg performed his full-length drama, *The Seagull*. The play's indirect plotting and its avoidance of the conventional climaxes of melodrama confused actors and audiences alike, and it failed. Chekhov was persuaded by Constantin Stanislavski and Vladimir Nemirovich-Danchenko to mount the play in their newly founded Moscow Art Theater (MAT) in 1898. Stanislavski's commitment to a restrained style of performance, emphasizing psychological complexity and balanced playing by the entire ensemble is generally credited with making the MAT production a success; a seagull became the company's signature. Chekhov produced three more major plays with the MAT. He revised *The Wood Demon* (1889) as *Uncle Vanya* in 1899 and then produced *Three Sisters* (1901) and *The Cherry Orchard* (1904). Chekhov married the actress Olga Knipper, who played leading roles in his plays, including Madame Ranevskaya in *The Cherry Orchard* in 1901, and spent the final years of his life convalescing in Yalta.

THE CHERRY ORCHARD

The action of Chekhov's plays is usually indirect, not progressive and consequential, in the manner of Ibsen's work. Instead, a Chekhov play generally opens with the arrival of some well-to-do characters in the provincial scene of the play and closes with their departure: Yelena and Serbryakov in *Uncle Vanya,* the regiment and its romantic Lieutenant Colonel Vershinin in *Three Sisters,* Madame Ranevskaya and her entourage in *The Cherry Orchard*. In between, we see how the lives of the characters are changed and yet somehow remain the same, as though their interaction worked to reveal the fundamentally static condition of their lives.

More than Chekhov's earlier plays, perhaps, *The Cherry Orchard* also seems to prefigure the fall of a class: the leisured, ineffectual, yet attractive Madame Ranevskaya and her brother, who own the estate but are incapable of bringing it into the twentieth century. We are left with the final vision of the ancient servant Firs, himself a relic of the emancipation of the serfs half a century before, locked in the house while the orchard falls to the axes. The future seems to promise a brutal and sudden change, which the main characters of the play are unable to face. The play takes, at best, an ironic attitude toward the fortunes of Lyubov and Gaev. Tragedies in Chekhov's plays occur in the momentary actions of daily life; they are casual and haphazard, almost accidental, and yet alter the course of life irrevocably. Varya and Lopakhin, for example, bumble their way through the long-expected scene of their engagement, but the scene doesn't come off. Lopakhin remains uncommitted and Varya remains a poor relation dependent on the charity of her family, soon to be sent away to work as a governess. For Varya, the misplayed scene has a bitter and tragic finality.

A scene from Anton Chekhov's *The Cherry Orchard*.

Chekhov calls the play a "comedy," and despite its mournful tone we might consider what he might have had in mind. Chekhov seems sympathetic to the tragedies of daily life, but often trains a skeptical eye on characters who assume the self-regarding accents of high tragedy, or whose sense of themselves verges on self-delusion, the solipsistic inability to see the world around them. Throughout *The Cherry Orchard,* some characters seem lost in a world of dreams: think of Gaev and his sister arriving in their childhood nursery, of Trofimov's vague and clumsy plans for the future, of kindly old Firs. Chekhov forces us to regard his characters with a certain distance, largely by weaving a texture of comedy into the fabric of the play. Everyone ridicules Gaev's sentimental apostrophe to the bookcase in act 1, and Chekhov adds a list of vaudeville tricks to his characters' performances: Lopakhin's "Ba-a-a" at the opening of the play, Yepikhodov crushing the hatbox with the suitcase in act 4, Trofimov tumbling down the stairs, Charlotta's music-hall turns, Firs's feeble efforts to keep everyone warm. The famous, inexplicable sound effect of act 2—the breaking string—may work in this way as well. It both underscores the mournful tone of the scene and interrupts the illusionistic surface of the action, forcing the audience out of a fully sympathetic engagement with Chekhov's sentimental characters. The play, in this light, seems "tragic" only if we accept the main characters' view of their predicament and accept their idle, self-absorbed fantasies as the stuff of tragedy.

Chekhov went to some lengths to keep the play's tone unsettled, in part because he knew that Stanislavski tended to regard his work as high tragedy. Chekhov suggested to Stanislavski that he play the part of Lopakhin: "When I was writing Lopakhin," he wrote in a letter to the actor, "I thought of it as a part for you. . . . Lopakhin is a merchant, of course, but he is a very decent person in every sense. He must behave with perfect decorum, like an educated man, with no petty ways or tricks of any sort, and it seemed to me that this part, the central one of the play, would come out brilliantly in your hands. . . . you must remember that Varya, a serious and religious girl, is in love with Lopakhin; she wouldn't be in love with a mere money-grubber." Describing Lopakhin in terms of Varya is typical of

Chekhov's tendency to think of the ensemble as a whole, rather than in terms of individual characters; but we might also think that Chekhov has strategic designs on Stanislavski as well. Fearing that Stanislavski would want to play the part of Gaev, and would play the part too sympathetically, Chekhov tried to persuade him to train his talents on the comic part of Lopakhin. Imagining Stanislavski as Lopakhin, we begin to see the kind of drama Chekhov had imagined: had he taken the part (Stanislavski played Gaev after all), Stanislavski would have played against the grain of broad humor that underlies Lopakhin, humanizing the role, creating neither a fully sympathetic character nor a vulgar comedian, but something in between. Similarly, *The Cherry Orchard* as a whole strikes a balance somewhere between comedy and tragedy, in which comic and tragic possibilities strain against one another as ways of interpreting the play and the experience of our lives.

As it turned out, Stanislavski's direction emphasized the play's sombre tone, the sense of a generation falling before modern progress as the orchard falls to the axes. After the Russian Revolution in 1917, *The Cherry Orchard* came to be regarded as nearly a prophetic allegory of the progress of history, the displacing of the feudal past by the modern, industrial present.

A pronunciation guide for Russian names appears on pp. 619-620.

THE CHERRY ORCHARD

Anton Chekhov

TRANSLATED BY CAROL ROCAMORA

CHARACTERS

RANEVSKAYA, LYUBOV ANDREEVNA, *a landowner*
ANYA, *her daughter, age seventeen*
VARYA, *her adopted daughter, age twenty-four*
GAEV, *Leonid Andreevich, Ranevskaya's brother*
LOPAKHIN, *Yermolai Alekseevich, a merchant*
TROFIMOV, *Pyotr Sergeevich, a student*
SIMEONOV-PISHCHIK, *Boris Borisovich, a landowner*
CHARLOTTA IVANOVNA, *a governess*
YEPIKHODOV, *Semyon Panteleevich, a clerk*
DUNYASHA, *a maid*

FIRS, *a servant, an old man of eighty-seven*
YASHA, *a young servant*
A PASSERBY
A STATIONMASTER
A POST OFFICE CLERK
GUESTS, SERVANTS, CARRIAGE DRIVERS

The action takes place on the estate of Lyubov Andreevna Ranevskaya

ACT ONE

A room, which is still called the nursery. One of the doors leads to ANYA's *room. It is dawn, just before sunrise. It is already May, the cherry trees are all in bloom, but outside it is still cold; there is an early morning frost in the orchard. The windows in the room are closed.*

Enter DUNYASHA *with a candle, and* LOPAKHIN *with a book in his hand.*

LOPAKHIN: The train's arrived, thank God. What time is it?
DUNYASHA: Almost two. (*Puts out the candle.*) It's already getting light out.
5 LOPAKHIN: So how late is the train, then? A couple of hours, at least. (*Yawns and stretches.*) Well, I've made a fool of myself, then, haven't I! Hm? Came all the way out here, just to meet the train, and fell fast asleep . . . Sat here waiting and dozed right off. Annoying, isn't it . . . You should have woken me up.
10 DUNYASHA: I thought you'd already gone. (*Listens.*) Listen, I think they're here.
LOPAKHIN: (*Listens.*) No . . . They've got to get their baggage first, you know, that sort of thing . . .

(*Pause.*)

15 Lyubov Andreevna, she's been living abroad for five years, I don't know, I can't even imagine what's become of her now . . . She's a fine person, you know . . . a warm, kind person. I remember, once, when I was a boy, oh, about fifteen years old, say, and my father—he had a shop here in the village then—my father, he hit me in the face with his
20 fist, blood was pouring from my nose . . . We'd come out into the courtyard together, somehow, and he was drunk. And there was Lyubov Andreevna, I remember her so vividly, so young then, so graceful, so slender, she took me by the hand, brought me over to the washstand, right into
25 this very room, into the nursery. "Don't cry, little peasant," she said, "it will heal before your wedding day . . ."

(*Pause.*)

Little peasant . . . Yes, my father was a peasant, it's true enough, and here I am in a three-piece suit and fancy shoes. A silk purse from a sow's ear, or something like that, isn't that how the expression goes . . . Yes . . . The only dif- 30 ference is, now I'm rich, I've got a lot of money, but don't look too closely, once a peasant . . . (*Leafs through the book.*) Look at me, I read through this entire book and didn't understand a word of it. Read it and dozed right off.

(*Pause.*)

DUNYASHA: The dogs didn't sleep at all last night, they can 35 sense their masters are coming home.
LOPAKHIN: What's wrong with you, Dunyasha . . .
DUNYASHA: My hands are trembling. I'm going to faint, I know I am.
LOPAKHIN: You're much too high-strung, Dunyasha. And 40 look at you, all dressed up like a young lady, hair done up, too. You mustn't do that. Remember who you are.

(*Enter* YEPIKHODOV *with a bouquet; he is wearing a jacket and highly polished boots, which squeak loudly; upon entering, he drops the bouquet.*)

YEPIKHODOV: (*Picks up the bouquet.*) Look what the gardener sent. Put them on the dining room table. That's what he said. (*Gives the bouquet to* DUNYASHA.) 45
LOPAKHIN: And bring me some kvass, will you?
DUNYASHA: Yes, sir. (*Leaves.*)
YEPIKHODOV: We have an early morning frost, we have three degrees below zero, and we have the cherry blossoms all in bloom. I don't approve of our climate. (*Sighs.*) Really, I 50 don't. Our climate doesn't work, it just doesn't work. It's not conducive. And would you like to hear more, Yermolai Alekseich, well, then you will, because the day before yesterday, I bought these boots, and, trust me, they squeak so much, that they are beyond hope. Now how can I oil 55 them? Tell me? How?
LOPAKHIN: Enough. You're getting on my nerves.
YEPIKHODOV: Every day some new disaster befalls me. A new day, a new disaster. But do I grumble, do I complain, no, I don't, I accept it, look, I'm smiling, even. 60

(DUNYASHA *enters, gives* LOPAKHIN *some kvass.*)

I'm going now. (*Stumbles against a chair, which falls down.*) There . . . (*As if vindicated.*) You see? I mean, that's the situation, and excuse me for saying so . . . Remarkable, even . . . isn't it! (*Exits.*)

65 DUNYASHA: Yermolai Alekseich, I have something to tell you . . . Yepikhodov has proposed to me.

LOPAKHIN: Ah!

DUNYASHA: But I don't know, really . . . He's a nice enough fellow, you know, quiet and all, it's just that whenever he
70 starts to talk, I can't understand a word he's saying. I mean, it all sounds so sweet and sincere, only it just doesn't make any sense. I like him, I mean, I think I like him. And he? He adores me. But he's such an unfortunate fellow, you know, really, every day it's something else. They even have
75 a name for him, do you know what they call him: "Mister Disaster" . . .

LOPAKHIN: (*Listens.*) I think they're coming . . .

DUNYASHA: They're coming! What's happening to me . . . I'm freezing, look, I'm shivering all over.

80 LOPAKHIN: They're really coming! Let's go meet them. Will she recognize me? We haven't seen each other in five years.

DUNYASHA: (*Agitated.*) I'm going to faint, I know I am . . . Look, I'm fainting!

(*Two carriages are heard pulling up to the house.* LOPAKHIN *and* DUNYASHA *exit quickly. The stage is empty. Then there is noise in the adjacent rooms.* FIRS *hurries across the stage to meet* LYUBOV ANDREEVNA; *he is leaning on a cane, and is dressed in old-fashioned livery and a high hat; he mutters something to himself, but it is impossible to make out a single word. The offstage noise crescendos. A voice calls out: "Let's go this way through here . . ." Enter* LYUBOV ANDREEVNA, ANYA, *and* CHARLOTTA IVANOVNA *with a little dog on a leash; they are all dressed in traveling clothes. Enter* VARYA, *wearing a coat and a shawl,* GAEV, SIMEONOV-PISHCHIK, LOPAKHIN, DUNYASHA *carrying a bundle and an umbrella,* SERVANTS *carrying luggage—they all come through the room.*)

ANYA: This way! Mama, do you remember what room this is?
85 LYUBOV ANDREEVNA: (*Ecstatic, in tears.*) The nursery!

VARYA: How cold it is, my hands are numb. (*To* LYUBOV ANDREEVNA.) Look, Mamochka, your rooms, violet and white, just as you left them.

LYUBOV ANDREEVNA: My nursery, my darling nursery, my
90 beautiful room . . . I slept here, when I was a child . . . (*Weeps.*) And now, I'm a child again . . . (*Kisses her brother,* VARYA, *and her brother again.*) And Varya looks the same as ever, just like a little nun. And Dunyasha I recognize, of course . . . (*Kisses* DUNYASHA.)

95 GAEV: The train was two hours late. How do you like that? How's that for efficiency!

CHARLOTTA: (*To* PISHCHIK.) My dog eats walnuts, too.

PISHCHIK: (*Amazed.*) Imagine that!

(*They all exit, except for* ANYA *and* DUNYASHA.)

DUNYASHA: We've been waiting forever . . . (*Takes* ANYA's *coat*
100 *and hat.*)

ANYA: I didn't sleep one moment the whole journey long, four whole nights . . . and now I'm absolutely frozen!

DUNYASHA: You left during Lent, we had snow then, and frost, and now! My darling! (*Bursts out laughing, kisses her.*) I've waited forever for you, my precious, my joy . . . And I've got 105 something to tell you, I can't wait one minute longer. . . .

ANYA: (*Listlessly.*) Now what . . .

DUNYASHA: Yepikhodov, the clerk, proposed to me just after Easter.

ANYA: Not again . . . (*Adjusts her hair.*) I've lost all my hair- 110 pins . . . (*She is exhausted; she almost sways on her feet.*)

DUNYASHA: No, really, I don't know what to think, any more. He adores me, God, how he adores me!

ANYA: (*Gazes at the door to her room, tenderly.*) My very own room, my windows, it's as if I never left. I'm home! And to- 115 morrow I'll wake up, and I'll run out into the orchard . . . Oh, if only I could rest! I'm so exhausted—I didn't sleep one moment the whole way, I was so worried.

DUNYASHA: Pyotr Sergeich arrived the day before yesterday.

ANYA: (*Overjoyed.*) Petya! 120

DUNYASHA: He's out in the bathhouse, asleep, that's where he's staying. "I'm afraid of being in the way," he said. (*Glances at her pocket watch.*) We ought to wake him up, but Varvara Mikhailovna gave us strict orders not to. "Don't you dare wake him up," she said. 125

(*Enter* VARYA, *a bunch of keys hanging from her belt.*)

VARYA: Dunyasha, go, quickly, bring the coffee . . . Mamochka wants coffee.

DUNYASHA: Right away. (*Exits.*)

VARYA: So, thank God, you're here. You're home at last! (*Embracing her.*) My darling's home! My angel is home! 130

ANYA: I've been through so much.

VARYA: I can imagine.

ANYA: I left during Holy Week, it was so cold then, remember? And Charlotta Ivanovna talked the whole way, talked and played card tricks. How could you have stuck me 135 with Charlotta! . . .

VARYA: You can't travel alone, darling. At seventeen!

ANYA: When we arrived in Paris, it was cold there, too, and snowing. My French is terrible. Mama lived on the fifth floor, and when I finally got there, the flat was filled with 140 all sorts of French people, ladies, an old Catholic priest with a little book, and, oh, it was so uncomfortable there, so stuffy, the room was filled with smoke. And suddenly I felt sorry for Mama, so very sorry, I threw my arms around her neck, I held her so tight, I couldn't let go. And Mama 145 kept clinging to me, and weeping . . .

VARYA: (*In tears.*) Enough, enough . . .

ANYA: She had already sold the dacha near Menton, she had nothing left, nothing at all. And neither did I, not a single kopek, we hardly had enough money to get home. And 150 Mama just doesn't understand it, still! There we are, sitting in the station restaurant, and she orders the most expensive thing on the menu, she gives the waiter a ruble tip for tea. Charlotta, too. And Yasha orders a complete dinner, it's simply terrible. Yasha is Mama's butler, you know. We 155 brought him with us . . .

VARYA: I'm seen him, the devil . . .

ANYA: So, tell me! Have we paid the interest yet?

VARYA: With what?

ANYA: Dear God, dear God . . . 160

VARYA: And in August, the estate will be sold . . .

ANYA: Dear God . . .

LOPAKHIN: (*Peeks through the door and makes a 'bleating' sound.*) Ba-a-a . . . (*Exits.*)

165 VARYA: (*In tears.*) I'd like to give him such a . . . (*Makes a threatening gesture with her fist.*)

ANYA: (*Embraces* VARYA, *softly.*) Varya, has he proposed yet? (VARYA *shakes her head "no."*) But he loves you, he does . . . Why don't you talk about it, what are you two waiting

170 for?

VARYA: I know nothing will ever come of it, nothing. He's so busy, he has no time for me, really . . . he pays no attention to me at all. Well, God bless him, but it's too painful for me even to look at him . . . Everyone talks about our wed-

175 ding, everyone congratulates us, but the fact is, there's absolutely nothing to it, it's all a dream . . . (*Changes tone.*) Your brooch looks just like a little bee.

ANYA: (*Sadly.*) Mama bought it. (*She goes to her room, speaking in a gay, child-like voice.*) And in Paris, I went up in a hot air

180 balloon!

VARYA: My darling's home! My angel is home!

(DUNYASHA *has already returned with the coffee pot and prepares the coffee.*)

(*Stands by the doorway.*) All day long, darling, I go about my business, I run the household, I do my chores, but all the time I'm thinking, dreaming. If only we could marry you

185 off to a rich man, then I'd find peace, I'd go to a cloister, and then on a pilgrimage to Kiev, to Moscow, and on and on, from one holy place to the next . . . on and on. A blessing!

ANYA: The birds are singing in the orchard. What time is it?

VARYA: After two, it must be . . . Time for you to sleep, dar-

190 ling. (*Goes into* ANYA'*s room.*) Yes, a blessing!

(YASHA *enters with a rug, and a traveling bag.*)

YASHA: (*Crosses the stage, discreetly.*) May I?

DUNYASHA: I wouldn't have recognized you, Yasha. How you've changed, since you've been abroad.

YASHA: Hm . . . And who are you?

195 DUNYASHA: When you left, I was about 'so' high . . . (*Indicates.*) Dunyasha, Fyodor Kozoedov's daughter. Don't you remember!

YASHA: Hm . . . Ripe as a cucumber! (*Glances around, and then grabs her and embraces her; she screams and drops a saucer.*

200 YASHA *exits quickly.*)

VARYA: (*In the doorway, displeased.*) What's going on here?

DUNYASHA: (*In tears.*) I broke a saucer . . .

VARYA: That means good luck.

ANYA: (*Coming out of her room.*) We'd better warn Mama:

205 Petya's here . . .

VARYA: I gave strict orders not to wake him up.

ANYA: (*Deep in thought.*) Father died six years ago, and one month later my little brother Grisha drowned in the river, a lovely little seven-year-old boy. Mama couldn't endure it,

210 she ran away, she ran away without once looking back . . . (*Shudders.*) How well I understand her, if only she knew!

(*Pause.*)

And Petya Trofimov was Grisha's tutor, he might remind her of it all . . .

(*Enter* FIRS, *in a jacket and white waistcoat.*)

FIRS: (*Goes to the coffee pot, anxiously.*) The mistress will take her coffee here . . . (*Puts on white gloves.*) Is the coffee 215 ready? (*Sternly, to* DUNYASHA.) You! Where is the cream?

DUNYASHA: Oh, my God . . . (*Rushes out.*)

FIRS: (*Fusses with the coffee pot.*) Pathetic fool . . . (*Mutters to himself under his breath.*) They've just returned from Paris . . . Now in the old days, the master used to go to Paris, too . . . 220 by horse and carriage . . . (*Bursts out laughing.*)

VARYA: What is it, Firs?

FIRS: Yes, and what may I do for you? (*Overjoyed.*) My mistress has come home! I've waited for so long! Now I can die . . . (*Weeps with joy.*) 225

(*Enter* LYUBOV ANDREEVNA, GAEV, LOPAKHIN, *and* SIMEONOV-PISHCHIK; SIMEONOV-PISHCHIK *wears a lightweight coat, fitted at the waist, and wide trousers. As he walks,* GAEV *gestures, as if he were playing a game of billiards.*)

LYUBOV ANDREEVNA: How does it go? Wait—don't tell me, let me think . . . "Yellow into the corner pocket! Double into the middle!"

GAEV: "Cut shot into the corner!" Once upon a time, sister dearest, we slept in this very room, you and I, and now I'm 230 fifty-one years old, strange, isn't? . . .

LOPAKHIN: Yes, time flies.

GAEV: Beg pardon?

LOPAKHIN: As I was saying, time flies.

GAEV: It smells of patchouli in here. 235

ANYA: I'm going to bed. Good night, Mama. (*Kisses her mother.*)

LYUBOV ANDREEVNA: My beloved child. (*Kisses her hands.*) Are you glad you're home? I simply can't get hold of myself.

ANYA: Good night, Uncle.

GAEV: (*Kisses her face, hands.*) God bless you. You are the im- 240 age of your mother! (*To his sister.*) Lyuba, you looked exactly like this at her age.

(ANYA *gives her hand to* LOPAKHIN *and* PISHCHIK; *she exits, and closes the door behind her.*)

LYUBOV ANDREEVNA: She's exhausted, really.

PISHCHIK: A tiring journey, no doubt.

VARYA: (*To* LOPAKHIN *and* PISHCHIK.) So, gentlemen? It's almost 245 three o'clock in the morning, let's not overstay our welcome.

LYUBOV ANDREEVNA: (*Laughs.*) You're the same as ever, Varya. (*Draws her close and kisses her.*) First I'll have my coffee, then we'll all go, yes?

(FIRS *places a cushion under her feet.*)

Thank you, dearest. I've gotten so used to coffee. I drink 250 it day and night. Thank you, my darling old man. (*Kisses* FIRS.)

VARYA: I'll go see if they've brought everything in . . . (*Exits.*)

LYUBOV ANDREEVNA: Am I really sitting here? (*Bursts out laughing.*) I feel like jumping up and down, and waving my 255 arms in the air! (*Covers her face with her hands.*) No, really, I must be dreaming! God knows, I love my country, I love it passionately, I couldn't even see out of the train window, I wept the whole way. (*In tears.*) Never mind, we must have our coffee. Thank you, Firs, thank you, my darling 260 old man. I'm so glad you're still alive.

FIRS: The day before yesterday.

GAEV: He's hard of hearing.

LOPAKHIN: I'd better be going; I leave for Kharkov at five this
265 morning. What a nuisance! I only wanted to see you, that's
      all, to talk to you a little . . . You're as lovely as ever . . .

PISHCHIK: (*Sighs heavily.*) Even lovelier . . . All dressed up,
      Parisian style . . . I'm head-over-heels, as they say!

LOPAKHIN: People like Leonid Andreich here, they say all
270 sorts of things about me, call me a boor, a kulak, but re-
      ally, it doesn't matter, I couldn't care less. Let them say
      whatever they like. I only want you to believe in me, as
      you always did, to look at me with those beautiful, soulful
      eyes, as you used to, once. Merciful God! My father was a
275 serf, he belonged to your grandfather and then to your fa-
      ther, but it was you, yes, you, who did so much for me
      once, so much, and I've forgotten everything now, I love
      you like my own flesh and blood . . . more, even, than my
      own flesh and blood.

280 LYUBOV ANDREEVNA: I can't sit still, I'm in such a state . . .
      (*Jumps up and walks around the room, agitated.*) I simply can't
      bear all this joy . . . Go ahead, laugh at me, I'm being fool-
      ish, I know it . . . My dear little bookcase . . . (*Kisses the
      bookcase.*) My own little table.

285 GAEV: Nanny died while you were gone.

LYUBOV ANDREEVNA: (*Sits and drinks coffee.*) Yes, God rest her
      soul. They wrote me.

GAEV: Anastasy died, too. And cross-eyed Petrushka—you re-
      member him—he ran away, he lives in town now, at the
290 district superintendent's. (*Takes a box of fruit drops out of his
      pocket, pops one into his mouth.*)

PISHCHIK: My daughter, Dashenka . . . she sends her regards . . .

LOPAKHIN: I'd like to tell you some good news, if I may, some
      cheerful news, all right? (*Looks at his watch.*) I've got to go,
295 there's no time to talk . . . so, very briefly, then. As you al-
      ready know, your cherry orchard is being sold to pay off the
      debts, the auction date has been set for the twenty-second
      of August, but don't you worry, my dear, you don't have to
      lose any sleep over this, rest assured, there is a way out . . .
300 Here's my plan. Your attention, please! Your estate is located
      only thirteen miles from town, roughly, a railroad runs
      nearby, so if the cherry orchard and the land along the river
      are divided up into plots and then leased for summer homes,
      why then you'll receive at least 25,000 in yearly income.

305 GAEV: Forgive me, but what nonsense!

LYUBOV ANDREEVNA: I don't quite understand you, Yermolai
      Alekseich.

LOPAKHIN: You'll receive at least twenty-five rubles a year per
      three acre plot from the summer tenants, and if you ad-
310 vertise right away, I'll guarantee you, by autumn, there
      won't be a single plot left, they'll all be bought up. In a
      word, congratulations, you're saved. The site is marvelous,
      the river is deep. Only, of course, you'll have to clear it
      out, get rid of some things . . . for example, let us say, tear
315 down all the old buildings, and this house, too, which isn't
      much good for anything any more, cut down the old
      cherry orchard . . .

LYUBOV ANDREEVNA: Cut it down? Forgive me, my darling,
      but you have no idea what you're talking about. If there is
320 one thing in the entire province that's of interest, that's re-
      markable, even, why it's our own cherry orchard.

LOPAKHIN: The only thing remarkable about this orchard is
      that it's so big. There's a cherry crop once every two

years, and yes, there are a lot of them, but what good are
      they, nobody buys them.   325

GAEV: There is a reference to this cherry orchard in the
      Encyclopaedia.

LOPAKHIN: (*Looks at his watch.*) Unless we come up with a plan,
      unless we reach a decision, then on the twenty-second of
      August the cherry orchard and the entire estate will be auc- 330
      tioned off. Make up your minds, will you, please! There is
      no other way, I swear to you. None. Absolutely none.

FIRS: Once upon a time, forty—fifty years ago, they used to
      dry the cherries, soak them, marinate them, preserve
      them, and often . . .   335

GAEV: Hush, Firs.

FIRS: And often, they would send cart loads of dried cherries
      to Moscow and Kharkov. Brought in heaps of money!
      And those dried cherries, oh, how soft they were, soft,
      sweet, plump, juicy, fragrant . . . They knew the recipe in 340
      those days . . .

LYUBOV ANDREEVNA: Yes, where is that recipe now?

FIRS: Forgotten. No one remembers it any more.

PISHCHIK: (*To LYUBOV ANDREEVNA.*) Tell us! What is it like in
      Paris? Did you eat frogs' legs?   345

LYUBOV ANDREEVNA: I ate crocodile.

PISHCHIK: Imagine that . . .

LOPAKHIN: Up until now, we've only had landowners and
      peasants living in our countryside, but now, the summer
      people are starting to appear among us. All the towns,   350
      even the smallest ones, are surrounded by summer homes
      now. And, it's possible to predict that, in twenty years or
      so, the summer population will multiply beyond our
      wildest dreams. Now they're just sitting out on their bal-
      conies, drinking their tea, but just wait, soon it will come 355
      to pass, you'll see, they'll start cultivating their little plots
      of land, and your cherry orchard will bloom again with
      wealth, prosperity, happiness . . .

GAEV: (*Indignant.*) What nonsense!

(*Enter* VARYA *and* YASHA.)

VARYA: Two telegrams came for you, Mamochka. (*Takes keys*   360
      *and unlocks the antique bookcase; the keys make a clinking
      sound.*) Here they are.

LYUBOV ANDREEVNA: From Paris. (*Rips them up, without read-
      ing them.*) I'm through with Paris.

GAEV: And do you know, Lyuba, how old this bookcase is?   365
      Only one week ago, I pull out the bottom drawer, I look,
      and what do I see—a mark burned into it, a number. This
      bookcase was built exactly one hundred years ago. How
      do you like that? Eh? We may now celebrate the jubilee
      anniversary of this bookcase, ladies and gentlemen. Yes,   370
      it's an inanimate object, of course, but nevertheless, it is
      still a *book* case.

PISHCHIK: (*Amazed.*) One hundred years old. Imagine that! . . .

GAEV: Yes . . . a work of art . . . (*Touching the bookcase.*) O ven-
      erable bookcase! I salute thy existence. For over a century, 375
      thou hast sought the pure ideals of truth and justice; thy
      silent exhortation for fruitful labor has not yet faltered
      these one hundred years, inspiring courage and hope for
      the brightest future (*In tears.*) in generation after genera-
      tion of our kin, and fostering in us the noble ideals of   380
      charity and good.

(*Pause.*)

LOPAKHIN: Yes . . .

LYUBOV ANDREEVNA: You haven't changed a bit, Lyonya.

GAEV: (*A bit embarrassed.*) "Off the ball . . . right-hand corner!
385 Cut shot into the middle."

LOPAKHIN: (*Glances at his watch.*) Time for me to go.

YASHA: (*Gives* LYUBOV ANDREEVNA *medicine.*) Perhaps you'll
take your pills now . . .

PISHCHIK: Why bother taking medicine, lovely lady . . .
390 doesn't do any harm, doesn't do any good either . . . Do
let me have them . . . dearest lady. (*Takes the pills, pours them
into the palm of his hand, blows on them, puts them in his
mouth, and washes them down with kvass.*) There!

LYUBOV ANDREEVNA: (*Frightened.*) You've gone mad!

395 PISHCHIK: Took them all.

LOPAKHIN: There's an appetite.

(*Everyone laughs.*)

FIRS: When he was here during Holy Week, he ate half a
bucket of cucumbers . . . (*Mutters to himself.*)

LYUBOV ANDREEVNA: What is he saying?

400 VARYA: He's been muttering like that for three years now.
We're used to it.

YASHA: Old age.

(*Enter* CHARLOTTA IVANOVNA *wearing a white dress; she is very
thin and tightly laced, with a lorgnette on her belt; she crosses the
stage.*)

LOPAKHIN: Forgive me, Charlotta Ivanovna, I didn't have the
chance to greet you. (*Goes to kiss her hand.*)

405 CHARLOTTA IVANOVNA: (*Takes her hand away.*) If I let you kiss
my hand, next you'll want to kiss my elbow, then my
shoulder . . .

LOPAKHIN: Not my lucky day.

(*Everyone laughs.*)

So, Charlotta Ivanovna, show us a trick!

410 LYUBOV ANDREEVNA: Yes, Charlotta, show us a trick!

CHARLOTTA: I don't want to. I wish to sleep. (*Exits.*)

LOPAKHIN: We'll see each other again in three weeks. (*Kisses*
LYUBOV ANDREEVNA'*s hand.*) Farewell for now. Time to
go. (*To* GAEV.) A very good-bye to you. (*Kisses* PISHCHIK.)
415 And to you. (*Shakes hands with* VARYA, *then with* FIRS *and*
YASHA.) I don't feel like going. (*To* LYUBOV ANDREEVNA.)
If you make up your mind about the summer homes, if
you decide to proceed, just let me know, I'll lend you
50,000. Think about it, seriously.

420 VARYA: (*Angrily.*) So go, then!

LOPAKHIN: I'm going, I'm going. . . . (*Exits.*)

GAEV: What a boor. Oh, wait, "pardon" . . . Our Varya's going
to marry him. That's our Varya's fiancé.

VARYA: Don't talk so much, Uncle.

425 LYUBOV ANDREEVNA: Why not, Varya, I'd be so pleased. He's
a good man.

PISHCHIK: And a most worthy man, as they say, truth be
told . . . Now my Dashenka . . . she also says, that . . . well,
she says a variety of things. (*Snores, then suddenly awakes*
430 *with a start.*) Nevertheless, dearest lady, oblige me, would

you, please . . . lend me two hundred and forty rubles . . .
tomorrow I must pay off the interest on my mortgage.

VARYA: (*Startled.*) We have no money! None!

LYUBOV ANDREEVNA: As a matter of fact, I don't, I have nothing, really.   435

PISHCHIK: Some will turn up, you'll see! (*Bursts out laughing.*)
I never lose hope. There, I say to myself, all is lost, all is
ruined, and then suddenly, what do you know—they
build a railroad right through my land, and . . . they pay
me for it! So just wait and see, something will happen, if 440
not today, then tomorrow. My Dashenka is going to win
200,000 . . . she has a lottery ticket.

LYUBOV ANDREEVNA: The coffee's finished, now we can go
to bed.

FIRS: (*Brushes* GAEV'*s clothes, scolding him.*) And you've gone 445
and put on the wrong trousers again. What I am going to
do with you?

VARYA: (*Softly.*) Anya's sleeping. (*Quietly opens the window.*)
The sun is up now, it isn't cold any more. Look,
Mamochka: what glorious trees! My God, the air! And the 450
starlings are singing!

GAEV: (*Opens another window.*) The orchard is all in white. You
haven't forgotten, Lyuba, have you? Look—that long row
of trees stretching on and on, like a silver cord, on and on,
do you remember, how it gleams on moonlit nights? You 455
haven't forgotten, have you?

LYUBOV ANDREEVNA: (*Looks out the window onto the orchard.*)
O, my childhood, my innocence! Once I slept in this very
nursery, I'd look out on the orchard, right from here, and
happiness would awaken with me, every morning, every 460
morning, and look, it's all the same, nothing has changed.
(*Laughs with joy.*) White, all white! O, my orchard! After
the dark, dreary autumn, the cold winter, you're young
again, blooming with joy, the heavenly angels have not
forsaken you . . . If only this terrible weight could be lifted 465
from my soul, if only I could forget my past!

GAEV: Yes, and the orchard will be sold to pay off our debts,
strange, isn't it . . .

LYUBOV ANDREEVNA: Look, there's my mother, walking
through the orchard . . . all in white! (*Laughs with joy.*) 470
There she is.

GAEV: Where?

VARYA: God bless you, Mamochka.

LYUBOV ANDREEVNA: There's no one there, I only dreamed
it . . . Look, to the right, on the way to the summer-house, 475
a white sapling, bowing low, I thought it was a woman . . .

(TROFIMOV *enters, wearing a shabby, threadbare student's uniform,
and spectacles.*)

What an astonishing orchard! Masses of white blossoms,
radiant blue sky . . .

TROFIMOV: Lyubov Andreevna!

(*She turns and looks at him.*)

I only came to pay my respects, I'll go, right away. (*Kisses* 480
her hand passionately.) They told me I had to wait till morning, but I couldn't bear it any longer . . .

(LYUBOV ANDREEVNA *looks at him with bewilderment.*)

VARYA: (*In tears.*) It's Petya Trofimov . . .

TROFIMOV: Petya Trofimov, former tutor to your Grisha . . .
485   Have I really changed that much?

(LYUBOV ANDREEVNA *embraces him and weeps softly.*)

GAEV: (*Embarrassed.*) Now, now, Lyuba.

VARYA: (*Weeps.*) You see, Petya, didn't I tell you to wait till tomorrow.

LYUBOV ANDREEVNA: My Grisha . . . my little boy . . .
490   Grisha . . . son . . .

VARYA: But what can we do, Mamochka. It's God's will.

TROFIMOV: (*Gently, in tears.*) There, there . . .

LYUBOV ANDREEVNA: (*Weeps softly.*) My little boy . . . lost . . . drowned . . . Why? Why, my friend? (*Softer.*) Anya's sleep-
495   ing, and here I am, raising my voice . . . carrying on . . . So, now, Petya, tell me! Why have you grown so ugly? And so old, too!

TROFIMOV: There was an old peasant woman on the train once, she called me "a shabby-looking gentleman."

500 LYUBOV ANDREEVNA: You were just a boy then, a sweet, young student, and now look at you, you're hair's gotten thin, you wear glasses . . . Don't tell me you're still a student? (*Goes to the door.*)

TROFIMOV: And I shall be an eternal student, so it seems.

505 LYUBOV ANDREEVNA: (*Kisses her brother, then* VARYA.) Better go to bed now . . . You've gotten old, too, Leonid.

PISHCHIK: (*Follows her.*) Yes, time for bed . . . Ach, this gout of mine . . . I'll stay the night with you . . . Lyubov An-dreevna, lovely lady, tomorrow morning, if only you
510   would . . . two hundred and forty rubles . . .

GAEV: He never gives up.

PISHCHIK: Two hundred and forty rubles . . . to pay the inter-est on the mortgage.

LYUBOV ANDREEVNA: But I don't have any money, really, my
515   sweet, I don't.

PISHCHIK: I'll pay you back, charming lady . . . Such a small amount . . .

LYUBOV ANDREEVNA: Oh, all right, Leonid will give it to you . . . Give it to him, Leonid.

520 GAEV: I should give it to him? Don't hold your pockets open.

LYUBOV ANDREEVNA: Give it to him, what else can we do . . . He needs it . . . He'll pay it back.

(*Exeunt* LYUBOV ANDREEVNA, TROFIMOV, PISHCHIK, *and* FIRS, GAEV, VARYA, *and* YASHA *remain.*)

GAEV: My sister just can't seem to hold on to her money. (*To* YASHA.) Move away, good fellow, you smell like a chicken
525   coop.

YASHA: (*With a grin.*) And you, Leonid Andreich, you haven't changed a bit.

GAEV: Beg pardon? (*To* VARYA.) What did he say?

VARYA: (*To* YASHA.) Your mother's come from the village to
530   see you, she's been waiting since yesterday in the servants' quarters . . .

YASHA: Good for her!

VARYA: Shame on you!

YASHA: Who needs her? She could have waited till tomorrow
535   to come. (*Exits.*)

VARYA: Mamochka's the same as she's always been, she hasn't changed at all. If she could, she'd give away everything.

GAEV: Yes . . .

(*Pause.*)

If there are many remedies offered for a disease, then that means the disease is incurable. Now, I've been thinking, 540 wracking my brain, and I've got lots of remedies, oh yes, lots and lots of remedies, and you know what that means, don't you, in essence, that means I don't have any. Wouldn't it be nice, for example, if we received a large inheritance from somebody or other, wouldn't it be nice to marry our 545 Anya off to a very rich fellow, wouldn't it be nice to go to Yaroslavl and try and get some money from our aunt, the countess. Our aunty's very very rich, you know.

VARYA: (*Weeps.*) If only God would help us.

GAEV: Stop weeping. The old lady's very rich, it's true, but 550 the fact is, she doesn't like us. For one thing, my dear sis-ter went off and married a lawyer, and not a gentleman . . .

(ANYA *appears in the doorway.*)

She didn't marry a gentleman, and you can't really say she's led a particularly conventional life. I mean, she's a good, kind person, a splendid person, and I love her very 555 very much, of course, but, whatever the extenuating cir-cumstances may have been, let's face it, she hasn't exactly been the model of virtue. Why, you can sense it in every-thing about her, her slightest gesture, her movements.

VARYA: (*In a whisper.*) Anya's standing in the doorway. 560

GAEV: Beg pardon?

(*Pause.*)

Amazing, there's something in my right eye . . . I can't see a thing. And on Thursday, when I was at the circuit court . . .

(ANYA *enters.*)

VARYA: Why aren't you in bed, Anya?

ANYA: I can't fall asleep. I just can't. 565

GAEV: My little one. (*Kisses* ANYA's *face, hands.*) My child . . . (*In tears.*) You're not my niece, you're my angel, you're everything to me. Believe me, believe me . . .

ANYA: I believe you, Uncle, I do. Everyone loves you, every-one reveres you . . . but, darling Uncle, you must try to be 570 quiet, really, just be quiet. What were you saying just now about my Mama, about your own sister? Why would you say such a thing?

GAEV: Yes, yes . . . (*Covers his face with her hand.*) As a matter of fact, it's terrible! My God! My God, save me! And today, I 575 made a speech before a bookcase . . . how foolish of me! And it was only after I'd finished, that I realized how fool-ish it was.

VARYA: It's true, Uncle dear, you should try to be quiet. Just be very quiet, that's all. 580

ANYA: And if you're quiet, you'll feel much better, really.

GAEV: I'll be quiet. (*Kisses* ANYA's *and* VARYA's *hands.*) I'll be quiet. Just one small matter. On Thursday I was at the cir-cuit court, and, well, some people got together and started talking, you know, about this, that, the other thing, and so 585 on and so on, and one thing led to another, and so it seems that a loan might be arranged, to pay off the interest to the bank.

VARYA: God willing!

590 GAEV: And, on Tuesday, I'm going to have another little talk with them again. (*To* VARYA.) Stop weeping. (*To* ANYA.) Your mama will have a word with Lopakhin; he won't refuse her, of course . . . As for you, as soon as you've had your rest, off you'll go to Yaroslavl to see the countess,
595 your great-aunt. So that way, we'll mount a three-pronged attack—and presto! it's in the bag. We'll pay off that interest, I'm sure of it . . . (*Pops a fruit drop into his mouth.*) On my honor, I swear to you, if you like, this estate will not be sold! (*Excited.*) I swear on my happiness! I give you my
600 hand, call me a worthless good-for-nothing, a dishonorable fellow, if I allow it to go up for auction! I swear on my entire being!

ANYA: (*She regains her composure: she is happy.*) How good you are, Uncle, how wise! (*Embraces her uncle.*) Now I'm con-
605 tent! I'm content! I'm happy, now!

(*Enter* FIRS.)

FIRS: (*Reproachfully.*) Leonid Andreich, have you no fear of God in you? When are you going to bed?

GAEV: In a minute, in a minute. Go on, Firs. Yes, it's all right, I'm quite capable of undressing myself. So, children dear,
610 night-night . . . Details tomorrow, but now, it's time for bed. (*Kisses* ANYA *and* VARYA.) I am a man of the eighties . . . These are not laudable times, but nevertheless, I can say that I've suffered greatly for my convictions in this life. It's not without reason that the peasants love me. One must
615 give the peasant his due! Give him his due, for . . .

ANYA: You're off again, Uncle!

VARYA: Uncle, be quiet!

FIRS: (*Angrily.*) Leonid Andreich!

GAEV: I'm coming, I'm coming . . . And so, to bed. "Off two
620 cushions into the middle. Pocket the white . . . clean shot." (*Exits, with* FIRS *shuffling behind him.*)

ANYA: Now, I'm content. I don't want to go to Yaroslavl, not really, I don't like my great-aunt that much, but, all the same, I'm content. Thanks to Uncle. (*Sits.*)

625 VARYA: We must get to bed. I know I'm going to . . . Oh, an awful thing happened here while you were gone. You remember the old servants' quarters, well, only the old ones live there now: you know, Yefimyushka, Polya, Yevstigney, oh, and don't forget Karp . . . Anyway, they started letting
630 some homeless folks stay the night with them—I didn't say anything at first. But then, I hear, they're spreading this rumor, that I'd been giving orders to feed them nothing but dried peas. Because I was being stingy, you see . . . And all this coming from Yevstigney . . . So I say to myself, fine.
635 If that's the way you want it, I say, just you wait and see. So I call for Yevstigney . . . (*Yawns.*) And he comes in . . . And I say to him, how dare you, Yevstigney . . . you're such a fool . . . (*Looks at* ANYA.) Anechka!

(*Pause.*)

She's asleep! (*Takes* ANYA *by the arm.*) Come to bed . . .
640 Come ! . . . (*Leads her.*) My darling's sleeping! Come . . .

(*They go.*)

(*Far beyond the orchard, a shepherd plays on a pipe.* TROFIMOV *enters, crosses the stage, and, seeing* VARYA *and* ANYA, *stops.*)

VARYA: Shh . . . She's asleep . . . fast asleep . . . Come, my precious.

ANYA: (*Softly, half-asleep.*) I'm so tired . . . do you hear the bells . . . Dearest Uncle . . . Mama and Uncle . . .

VARYA: Come, my precious, come . . . (*Exits into* ANYA's *room.*) 645

TROFIMOV: (*Tenderly.*) My sunlight! My springtime!

ACT TWO

A field. There is a small, dilapidated old chapel, long deserted, and beside it, a well, an old bench, and several large stones, once apparently gravestones. The road to GAEV's *country estate is visible. To the side, towering poplar trees loom darkly, where the cherry orchard begins. In the distance, there is a row of telegraph poles, and far beyond that, on the horizon, is the indistinct outline of a large town, visible only in very clear, fine weather. Soon, it will be sunset.* CHARLOTTA, YASHA, *and* DUNYASHA *sit on the bench;* YEPIKHODOV *stands nearby and plays the guitar; all are lost in thought.* CHARLOTTA *is wearing an old, peaked military cap; she removes the rifle from her shoulder and adjusts the buckle on the rifle sling.*

CHARLOTTA: (*Deep in thought.*) I have no passport, no real one . . . no one ever told me how old I was, not really . . . but I always have this feeling that I'm still very young. When I was a little girl, Papa and Mama traveled in a circus, they were acrobats, good ones. And I performed the 5 "salto-mortale," the dive of death, and all kinds of tricks. And when Papa and Mama died, a German lady took me in, she raised me, gave me lessons. "Gut." I grew up, I became a governess. But where I am from, and who I am— I don't know . . . Who were my parents, were they ever 10 married . . . I don't know. (*Takes a cucumber out of her pocket and eats it.*) I don't know anything.

(*Pause.*)

So now I feel like talking, but to whom . . . I have no one to talk to.

YEPIKHODOV: (*Plays guitar and sings.*) "What care I for worldly 15 woe, / What care I for friend and foe . . ." How pleasant it is to play upon the mandolin!

DUNYASHA: That's a guitar, not a mandolin. (*Looks in a little mirror and powders her nose.*)

YEPIKHODOV: For the man, who is mad with love, it's a man- 20 dolin. (*Sings.*) "If my true love were requited, / It would set my heart aglow . . ."

(YASHA *joins in, harmonizing.*)

CHARLOTTA: These people sing terribly . . . Phooey! Like jackals.

DUNYASHA: (*To* YASHA.) How blissful, to have been abroad. 25

YASHA: Well, of course. I'm not going to disagree with you on that one. (*Yawns, then lights a cigar.*)

YEPIKHODOV: But we know that already. Everything abroad is very well organized, and has been so for a long long time.

YASHA: Right. 30

YEPIKHODOV: I am a man of the world. I am. I read many many remarkable books. But, speaking for myself, personally, I have no clue, no clue as to what direction I, personally, want my life to take, I mean: Do I want to live, or do I want to shoot myself, in the head . . . So just in case, I 35 always carry a revolver around with me. Here it is . . . (*Shows them a revolver.*)

CHARLOTTA: I'm finished. And now, I'm leaving. (*Puts on the rifle.*) You, Yepikhodov, you are a very intelligent man and
40   also a very dangerous one; women must be mad for you. Brrr! (*Starts to leave.*) These clever people, they're all such fools, no one for me to talk to . . . Alone, all alone, I have no one . . . and who I am, why I am on this earth, no one knows . . . (*Exits, without hurrying.*)
45 YEPIKHODOV: Now. Speaking for myself, personally, again, putting all else aside, that is, if I may, when it comes to me, I mean, personally, again, I ask myself: Does fate care? No, fate doesn't care, very much as a terrible storm doesn't care about a tiny boat upon the sea. Now. Let us assume I am
50   wrong in this regard, so then, tell me, would you, please, why is it that this morning, yes, this morning, I wake up, just to give you an example, I look up, and there, sitting right on my chest, is this huge and terrifying spider . . . About 'so' big. (*Indicates with both hands.*) And then, to give
55   you yet another example, I go to pick up a glass of kvass, you know, to drink it, I look inside it, and what do I see? Possibly the most offensive species on the face of this earth—like a cockroach.

(*Pause.*)

Have you ever read Buckle?

(*Pause.*)

60   May I trouble you, Avdotya Fyodorovna, for a word or two.
DUNYASHA: Speak.
YEPIKHODOV: It would be far more desirable to speak to you in private . . . (*Sighs.*)
DUNYASHA: (*Embarrassed.*) Oh, all right . . . only first, bring
65   me my cloak . . . I left it near the cupboard . . . it's a bit chilly out . . .
YEPIKHODOV: Of course . . . Right away . . . Of course. Now I know what to do with my revolver . . . (*Takes the guitar and exits, strumming.*)
70 YASHA: Mister Disaster! He's hopeless, just between you and me. (*Yawns.*)
DUNYASHA: God forbid he should shoot himself.

(*Pause.*)

I'm so nervous, I worry all the time. I was just a girl when they took me in, you know, I'm not used to the simple life
75   any more, look at my hands, how lily-white they are, like a young lady's. Can't you see, I've become so delicate, so fragile, so . . . so sensitive, every little thing upsets me . . . It's just awful. And if you deceive me, Yasha, I just don't know what will happen to my nerves.
80 YASHA: (*Kisses her.*) My little cucumber! Of course, a girl should know how to behave, I can't stand a girl who doesn't know how to behave.
DUNYASHA: I've fallen madly in love with you, you are so refined, you can talk about anything.

(*Pause.*)

85 YASHA: (*Yawns.*) Right! . . . Now, in my opinion, if a girl falls in love, that means she's immoral.

(*Pause.*)

Nice, isn't it, to smoke a cigar in the fresh, open air . . . (*Listens.*) Someone's coming . . . It's the ladies and gentlemen . . .

(DUNYASHA *embraces him impetuously.*)

Go home, pretend you've gone for a swim in the river, 90 take that path there, or else they'll run into you and think I arranged this little rendezvous. I can't have that.
DUNYASHA: (*Coughs quietly.*) I've got a headache from all this cigar smoke . . . (*Exits.*)

(YASHA *remains; he sits by the chapel. Enter* LYUBOV ANDREEVNA, GAEV, *and* LOPAKHIN.)

LOPAKHIN: You must decide, once and for all—time waits for 95 no one. The question's quite simple, you know. Will you or won't you agree to lease your land for conversion into summer homes? Answer in one word: yes or no? One word, that's all!
LYUBOV ANDREEVNA: Who has been smoking those disgust- 100 ing cigars here . . . (*Sits.*)
GAEV: Since they've built the railroad, it's all become so convenient. (*Sits down.*) We took a little ride into town, we had our lunch . . . "yellow into the middle pocket!" Now, if only I'd gone home first, and played one little game . . . 105
LYUBOV ANDREEVNA: You'll have plenty of time.
LOPAHKIN: One word, that's all! (*Entreating.*) Give me your answer!
GAEV: (*Yawns.*) Beg pardon?
LYUBOV ANDREEVNA: (*Looks in her purse.*) Yesterday I had so 110 much money, and today I have hardly any at all. My poor, thrifty Varya feeds everyone milk soup, the old folks in the kitchen get nothing but dried peas to eat, and I manage to let money slip right through my fingers. (*Drops her purse, gold coins scatter.*) There, you see, now I've gone and spilled 115 it. . . (*She is annoyed.*)
YASHA: I'll get them, allow me. (*Collects the coins.*)
LYUBOV ANDREEVNA: Please do, Yasha. And why on earth did I go out to lunch . . . That ridiculous restaurant of yours with the music, and the tablecloths that smell of soap . . . And why 120 drink so much, Lyonya? Why eat so much? Why talk so much? Today in the restaurant you went on and on again, on and on . . . About the seventies, about the decadents. And to whom? Talking to the waiters about the decadents!
LOPAKHIN: Yes. 125
GAEV: (*Waves his hand.*) I'm incorrigible, it's obvious . . . (*Irritably, to* YASHA.) What is it with you, you're always disturbing my line of vision . . .
YASHA: (*Laughs.*) I can't hear the sound of your voice without laughing. 130
GAEV: (*To his sister.*) It's either him or me . . .
LYUBOV ANDREEVNA: Go away, Yasha, go on . . .
YASHA: (*Gives* LYUBOV ANDREEVNA *her purse.*) Right away. (*Barely contains his laughter.*) At once . . . (*Exits.*)
LOPAKHIN: Your estate is going to be bought by that million- 135 aire, Deriganov. He's coming to the auction himself, they say, in person.
LYUBOV ANDREEVNA: And where did you hear that?
LOPAKHIN: They were talking about it in town.

140 GAEV: Our aunty from Yaroslavl promised to send us something, but when and how much she will send, who knows . . .

LOPAKHIN: How much is she sending? One hundred thousand? Two hundred thousand?

LYUBOV ANDREEVNA: Oh, well, . . . ten–fifteen thousand, at
145 most, and that much we can be thankful for . . .

LOPAKHIN: Forgive me, but such frivolous people as you, my friends, such strange, impractical people, I have never before met in my entire life. I'm speaking to you in the Russian language, I'm telling you that your estate is about
150 to be sold, and you simply don't understand.

LYUBOV ANDREEVNA: But what on earth are we to do? Tell us, what?

LOPAKHIN: Every day I've been telling you. Every day I've been repeating the same thing, over and over again. The
155 cherry orchard and the land must be leased for summer homes, it must be done immediately, as soon as possible—the auction is imminent! Do you understand! As soon as you decide, once and for all, about the summer homes, you'll have as much money as you'll ever want, and then
160 you will be saved.

LYUBOV ANDREEVNA: Summer homes, summer people—forgive me, please, it all sounds so vulgar.

GAEV: I agree with you, absolutely.

LOPAKHIN: Either I'm going to burst out sobbing, or scream-
165 ing, or else I'm going to fall on the ground, right here in front of you. I can't stand it any more! You're driving me mad! (*To* GAEV.) And you, you act like an old woman!

GAEV: Beg pardon?

LOPAKHIN: An old woman! (*Wants to leave.*)
170 LYUBOV ANDREEVNA: (*Frightened.*) No, don't go, please, stay, dearest. I beg of you. Who knows, perhaps we'll think of something!

LOPAKHIN: What's there to think of!

LYUBOV ANDREEVNA: Don't go, I beg of you. It's so much
175 more cheerful when you're here . . .

(*Pause.*)

I keep waiting for something to happen, as if the house were going to tumble down on top of us.

GAEV: (*Deep in thought.*) "Double into the corner pocket . . . Croisé into the middle . . ."
180 LYUBOV ANDREEVNA: How we have sinned . . .

LOPAKHIN: What are you talking about, what sins . . .

GAEV: (*Pops a fruit drop in his mouth.*) They say I've squandered a entire fortune on fruit drops . . . (*Laughs.*)

LYUBOV ANDREEVNA: O my sins, my sins . . . I've always
185 thrown money around, uncontrollably, like a madwoman, and I married a man, who did nothing but keep us in debt. My husband died from too much champagne—he drank himself to death,—then, for my next misfortune, I fell in love with another man, I began living with him . . . and just
190 at that time, there came my first great punishment, and what a blow it dealt me—right here in this river. . . my little boy drowned, and so I fled, abroad, I simply fled, never to return, never to see this river again . . . I closed my eyes and I ran, not knowing where I was going, what I was do-
195 ing, and *he* following after . . . ruthlessly, relentlessly. I bought a dacha near Menton, *he* had fallen ill there, and for three years I knew no rest, neither day nor night; his illness exhausted me, wasted me, my soul withered away. And then last year, when the dacha was sold to pay off the debts,
200 I fled again, to Paris, and there he robbed me, he left me for another woman, I tried to poison myself . . . How stupid, how shameful . . . And suddenly I felt drawn again to Russia, to my homeland, to my daughter . . . (*Wipes away her tears.*) Dear God, dear God, be merciful, forgive me my sins!
205 Don't punish me any longer! (*Pulls a telegram from her pocket.*) Today, I received this from Paris . . . He begs my forgiveness, beseeches me to return . . . (*Rips up the telegram.*) There's music playing, somewhere. (*Listens.*)

GAEV: It's our celebrated Jewish orchestra. Don't you remem-
210 ber, four violins, flute, and contrabass.

LYUBOV ANDREEVNA: Does it still exist? We ought to invite them sometime, plan a little soirée.

LOPAKHIN: (*Listens.*) I don't hear anything. (*Hums softly.*)

> An enterprising man, the Prussian,
> He'll make a Frenchman from a Russian! 215

(*Laughs.*) What a play I saw at the theatre last night, it was very funny, really.

LYUBOV ANDREEVNA: There probably wasn't anything funny about it. Why go to the theatre to see a play! Better to see
220 yourselves more often. How grey your lives are, how endlessly you talk.

LOPAKHIN: It's the truth. And the truth must be told, our lives are foolish . . .

(*Pause.*)

My papa was a peasant, an ignorant fool, he understood
225 nothing, taught me nothing, he only beat me when he was drunk, and always with a stick. And the fact of the matter is, I'm the same kind of ignorant fool that he was. I never learned anything, I'm ashamed of my own handwriting, it's not even human, it's more like a hoof-mark than a signature.

LYUBOV ANDREEVNA: You ought to get married, my friend. 230

LOPAKHIN: Yes . . . It's the truth.

LYUBOV ANDREEVNA: Why not to our Varya? She's a good girl.

LOPAKHIN: Yes.

LYUBOV ANDREEVNA: She's of simple origin, she works all
235 day long, but the important thing is, she loves you. And you've been fond of her for a long time now.

LOPAKHIN: Well . . . I have nothing against it . . . She's a good girl.

(*Pause.*)

GAEV: They've offered me a job at the bank. 6,000 a year . . .
240 Have you heard?

LYUBOV ANDREEVNA: You, in a bank! Stay where you are . . .

(FIRS *enters; he is carrying a coat.*)

FIRS: (*To* GAEV.) Please, sir, better put this on . . . it's chilly out.

GAEV: (*Puts on the coat.*) You get on my nerves, old man.

FIRS: Now, there's no need for that . . . You went out this
245 morning, without telling anyone. (*Looks him over.*)

LYUBOV ANDREEVNA: How old you've grown, Firs!

FIRS: Yes, what may I do for you?

LOPAKHIN: She said: How old you've grown!

FIRS: Well, I've lived a long time. They were marrying me off, and your papa wasn't even in this world yet . . . 250

(*Laughs.*) Then, when the emancipation came, I was already head valet . . . I didn't want my freedom, so I stayed with my masters . . .

(*Pause.*)

255 I remember how glad everyone was, but what they were glad about, they didn't even know themselves.
LOPAKHIN: Ah yes, the good old days. At least there was flogging.
FIRS: (*Not hearing.*) I'll say. The servants belonged to the masters, the masters belonged to the servants, but now everything's all mixed up, you can't tell one from the other.
260 GAEV: Hush, Firs. Tomorrow I've got to go to town. They've promised to introduce me to some general, he might give us a loan on a promissory note.
LOPAKHIN: Nothing will come of it. And you won't pay off
265 the interest, rest assured.
LYUBOV ANDREEVNA: He's delirious. There are no generals, they don't exist.

(*Enter* TROFIMOV, ANYA, *and* VARYA.)

GAEV: Ah, here they come.
ANYA: Here's Mama.
270 LYUBOV ANDREEVNA: (*Tenderly.*) Come, come . . . My darling children . . . (*Embraces* ANYA *and* VARYA.) If only you knew how much I love you both. Sit here, right next to me.

(*They all get settled.*)

LOPAKHIN: Our eternal student is always in the company of the young ladies.
275 TROFIMOV: Mind your own business.
LOPAKHIN: And when he's fifty, he'll still be a student.
TROFIMOV: Stop your foolish joking.
LOPAKHIN: You're such a peculiar fellow! Why are you so angry with me, anyway?
280 TROFIMOV: Because you won't stop bothering me.
LOPAKHIN: (*Laughs.*) Permit me to ask you, if I may, what do you think of me?
TROFIMOV: Here is what I think of you, Yermolai Alekseich: You are a rich man, soon you'll be a millionaire. So, in the
285 general scheme of things, that is, according to the laws of nature, we need you, we need predatory beasts, who devour everything which stands in their path, so in that sense you are a necessary evil.

(*All laugh.*)

VARYA: Petya, you do better when you talk about astronomy.
290 LYUBOV ANDREEVNA: No, let's continue yesterday's conversation.
TROFIMOV: What about?
GAEV: About pride. Pride in man.
TROFIMOV: That. We talked about that forever, but we did not come to any conclusion. According to your way of
295 thinking, there is something mystical about the proud man, an aura, almost. Perhaps you are correct in your beliefs, but if you analyze the issue clearly, without complicating things, then why does this pride even exist, what reason can there be for pride, if a man is not physically dis-
300 tinguished, if the vast majority of mankind is coarse, stu-

pid, or profoundly miserable. There is no time for the admiration of self. There is only time for work.
GAEV: We're all going to die, anyway, so what difference does it make?
TROFIMOV: Who knows? And what does it really mean—to 305 die? For all we know, man is endowed with a hundred sensibilities, and when he dies, only the five known to us perish along with him, while the other ninety-five remain alive.
LYUBOV ANDREEVNA: How intelligent you are, Petya! . . . 310
LOPAKHIN: (*Ironically.*) Yes, terribly!
TROFIMOV: Mankind marches onward, ever onward, strengthening his skills, his capacities. All that has up until now been beyond his reach may one day be attainable, only he must work, indeed, he must do everything in his power to help 315 those who seek the truth. In Russia, however, very few people actually do work. The vast majority of the intelligentsia, as I know them, do nothing, pursue nothing, and, meanwhile, have no predisposition whatsoever to work, they're completely incapable of it. They call themselves 'the intelli- 320 gentsia,' and yet they address their servants with disrespect, they treat the peasants as if they were animals, they're dismal students, they're poorly educated, they never read serious literature, they're absolutely idle, they don't do a thing except sit around talking about science and art, about which 325 they know nothing at all. And they're all so grim looking, they have tense, taut faces, they only talk about 'important things,' they spend all their time philosophizing, and meanwhile, right before their very eyes, the workers live atrociously, eat abominably, sleep without bedding, thirty-forty 330 to a room, together with bedbugs, stench, dankness, depravity . . . And so it seems that all this lofty talk is simply meant to conceal the truth from themselves and others. Show me, please, where are the day nurseries, about which they speak so much and so often, where are the public reading rooms? 335 They only write about them in novels, they never become a reality, never. There is only filth, vulgarity, barbarism . . . I dread their serious countenances, their serious conversations, I despise them. Better to be silent!
LOPAKHIN: You know, I get up before five every morning, I 340 work from dawn until night, I deal with money, constantly, mine and others, and yes, I see how people really are. You only have to try to get something done to realize how few honest, decent people there are in this world. Sometimes, when I can't fall asleep, I lie there thinking: 345 "Dear Lord, you have given us the vast forests, the boundless plains, the endless horizons, and we who live here on this earth, we should be true giants . . ."
LYUBOV ANDREEVNA: What good are giants . . . They're very nice in fairy tales, you know, but in true life, they're terri- 350 fying.

(YEPIKHODOV *crosses upstage, playing the guitar.*)

(*Pensively.*) There goes Yepikhodov.

ANYA: (*Pensively.*) There goes Yepikhodov.
GAEV: The sun has set, ladies and gentlemen.
TROFIMOV: Yes. 355
GAEV: (*Softly, as if reciting.*) O nature, wondrous nature, you shine on, radiant and eternal, beauteous and indifferent,

you whom we call mother, you embody birth and death, you create and you destroy, you . . .

360 VARYA: (*Imploring.*) Uncle, dear!

ANYA: Not again, Uncle!

TROFIMOV: You're better off "pocketing the yellow . . ."

GAEV: I'll be quiet, I'll be quiet.

(*All sit, deep in thought. Silence. Only* FIRS'*s muttering can be heard. Suddenly from far, far away, a sound is heard, as if coming from the sky, the sound of a breaking string, dying away in the distance, a mournful sound.*)

LYUBOV ANDREEVNA: What was that?

365 LOPAKHIN: Don't know. Somewhere far away, deep in the mines, a bucket broke loose and fell . . . But somewhere very far away.

GAEV: Or a bird of some kind . . . a heron, perhaps.

TROFIMOV: Or an owl . . .

370 LYUBOV ANDREEVNA: (*Shudders.*) Disturbing, somehow.

(*Pause.*)

FIRS: Right before the time of trouble, it was the same thing: The owl screeched, and the samovar hissed, it never stopped.

GAEV: What time of trouble?

FIRS: Why, before the emancipation of the serfs.

(*Pause.*)

375 LYUBOV ANDREEVNA: Let's go, dear friends, shall we, it's getting dark. (*To* ANYA.) You've got tears in your eyes . . . What is it, my pet? (*Embraces her.*)

ANYA: I'm fine, Mama. It's nothing.

TROFIMOV: Someone's coming.

(*A* PASSERBY *appears in a shabby, white cap and a coat; he is slightly drunk.*)

380 PASSERBY: Permit me to inquire, may I pass through here to get to the train station?

GAEV: You may. Go down that road.

PASSERBY: I'm deeply grateful. (*Coughs.*) What superb weather we're having . . . (*Recites.*) "My brother, my suffering
385 brother . . . Come down to the Volga, whose moan . . ." (*To* VARYA.) Mademoiselle, please, give a poor starving Russian thirty kopeks. . .

(VARYA *cries out in fear.*)

LOPAKHIN: (*Angrily.*) This has gone too far!

LYUBOV ANDREEVNA: (*Stunned.*) Here . . . take this . . .
390 (*Searches in her purse.*) I have no silver . . . Never mind, here's a gold piece . . .

PASSERBY: I'm deeply grateful! (*Exits.*)

(*Laughter.*)

VARYA: (*Frightened.*) I'm leaving . . . I'm leaving . . . Oh, Mamochka, the servants at home have nothing to eat, and
395 you gave him a gold piece.

LYUBOV ANDREEVNA: What are you going to do with me, I'm such a silly fool! I'll give you everything I have. Yermolai Alekseich, please, lend me some more money! . . .

LOPAKHIN: Yes, madam.

LYUBOV ANDREEVNA: Come, ladies and gentlemen, time to 400 go. Oh, yes, Varya, we've just made a match for you. Congratulations.

VARYA: (*In tears.*) Mama, you musn't joke about that.

LOPAKHIN: "Oh-phel-i-a, get thee to a nunnery . . ."

GAEV: It's been so long since I've played a game of billiards, 405 my hands are shaking.

LOPAKHIN: "Oh-phel-i-a, o nymph, remember me in thy prayers!"

LYUBOV ANDREEVNA: Come, ladies and gentlemen. It's almost suppertime. 410

VARYA: How he frightened me. My heart is pounding.

LOPAKHIN: May I remind you, ladies and gentlemen: On the twenty-second of August, the cherry orchard will be sold. Think about it! Think! . . .

(*They all leave, except* TROFIMOV *and* ANYA.)

ANYA: (*Laughing.*) The stranger frightened Varya off, thank 415 goodness, now we're alone.

TROFIMOV: Varya's afraid we'll fall madly in love, she hasn't let us out of her sight for days. She's so narrow-minded, she can't understand we're above love. To overcome all obstacles, real and imagined, which stand in the path of free- 420 dom and happiness,—that is our quest in life. Onward! We set forth, undaunted, toward that star, burning bright in the distance! Onward! Don't fall behind, my friends!

ANYA: (*Clasps her hands.*) How beautifully you talk!

(*Pause.*)

It's glorious here today! 425

TROFIMOV: Yes, the weather is amazing.

ANYA: What have you done to me, Petya, why don't I love the cherry orchard, as I did, once? I loved it so tenderly, I couldn't imagine any other place on earth more lovely than our orchard. 430

TROFIMOV: All Russia is our orchard. The land is vast and beautiful, there are many marvelous places in it.

(*Pause.*)

Just think, Anya: Your grandfather, your great-grandfather, and his forefathers before him, all were serf-owners, they all owned living souls, so isn't it possible, then, that in every 435 blossom, every leaf, every tree trunk in the orchard, a human soul now gazes down upon us, can't you hear their voices . . . To own human souls—can't you see how this has transformed each and every one of us, those who have lived before and those who live today, so that you, your mother, 440 your uncle, all of you, are no longer aware that you are alive at the expense of others, at the expense of those whom you would not even permit beyond your front hall . . . We have fallen behind, by two hundred years or so, at least, we have nothing left, absolutely nothing, no clear understanding of 445 the past, we only philosophize, complain about our boredom, or drink vodka. And it's all so clear, can't you see, that to begin a new life, to live in the present, we must first redeem our past, put an end to it, and redeem it we shall, but only with suffering, only with extraordinary, everlasting toil 450 and suffering. You must understand this, Anya.

ANYA: The house, in which we live, is no longer our house, and I shall leave it, I give you my word.

TROFIMOV: If you have the key, throw it in the well and run, run far, far away. Be free, like the wind.

ANYA: (*Ecstatic.*) How wonderfully you say it!

TROFIMOV: Believe me, Anya, believe me! I'm not even thirty yet, I'm young, I'm still a student, and yet, I've endured so much! Come winter, I'm hungry, sick, anxiety-ridden, poverty-stricken, like a beggar, and wherever fate carries me, there I shall be! And yet, all the while, every waking moment, day and night, my soul is filled with an indescribable premonition, a vision. A vision of happiness, Anya, I can see it now . . .

ANYA: (*Pensively.*) The moon is rising.

(YEPIKHODOV *is heard playing the guitar, the same melancholy song as before. The moon is rising. Somewhere near the poplars,* VARYA *is looking for* ANYA *and calling:* "Anya! Where are you?")

TROFIMOV: Yes, the moon is rising.

(*Pause.*)

Here comes happiness, here it comes, closer and closer, I can already hear its footsteps. And if we don't see it, if we don't recognize it, then what does it matter? Others will!

(VARYA'*s voice:* "Anya! Where are you?")

Varya, again! (*Angrily.*) It's disgraceful!

ANYA: I know! Let's go down to the river. It's lovely there.

TROFIMOV: Let's go.

(*They go.*)

(VARYA'*s voice:* "Anya! Anya!")

ACT THREE

The drawing room, separated from the ballroom by an archway. A chandelier burns brightly. A Jewish orchestra, the same one referred to in Act Two, is heard playing in the entrance hall. It is evening. In the ballroom, the crowd is dancing the 'grand-rond.' The voice of SIMEONOV-PISHCHIK *is heard:* "Promenade à une paire!" *The couples dance through the drawing room, as follows: first* PISHCHIK *and* CHARLOTTA IVANOVNA; *then* TROFIMOV *and* LYUBOV ANDREEVNA; *then* ANYA *and the* POST OFFICE CLERK; *then* VARYA *and the* STATIONMASTER, *and so on.* VARYA *is weeping quietly and wipes away her tears as she dances.* DUNYASHA *is in the last couple. They dance around the drawing room.* PISHCHIK *calls out:* "Grand-rond, balancez!" *and* "Les cavaliers à genoux et remerciez vos dames!"

FIRS, *wearing a tailcoat, carries a tray with seltzer water.* PISHCHIK *and* TROFIMOV *enter the drawing room.*

PISHCHIK: I have high blood pressure, I've had two strokes already, it's difficult for me to dance, but, you know what they say: "If you run in a pack, whether you bark or not, you'd better wag your tail." Never you mind, I'm as healthy as a horse. My dear departed father, joker that he was, God rest his soul, always used to say, on the subject of our ancestry, that the Simeonov-Pishchiks are descended from the same horse that Caligula appointed to the Senate . . . (*Sits.*) The only trouble is: We don't have any

money! And you know what they say: "A hungry dog believes only in meat . . ." (*Snores and suddenly wakes up.*) And that's my problem . . . all I ever dream about is money . . .

TROFIMOV: As a matter of fact, you do bear some resemblance to a horse.

PISHCHIK: And why not . . . a horse is a good animal . . . you can get a very good price for a horse, you know . . .

(*In the next room, the sound of a billiard game is heard.* VARYA *appears in the archway to the ballroom.*)

TROFIMOV: (*Teasing.*) Madame Lopakhina! Madame Lopakhina! . . .

VARYA: (*Angrily.*) The shabby-looking gentleman!

TROFIMOV: Yes, I'm a shabby-looking gentleman, and proud of it!

VARYA: (*Bitterly.*) We've gone and hired the musicians, now how are we going to pay for them? (*Exits.*)

TROFIMOV: (*To* PISHCHIK.) Think about it: The energy you've wasted your whole life through in search of money to pay off the interest on your debts, if only you'd spent that energy elsewhere, then, no doubt, you could have changed the world.

PISHCHIK: Nietzsche . . . the philosopher . . . the supreme, the exalted . . . a man of the greatest genius, this man once said, in his own writings, that it's all right to forge banknotes.

TROFIMOV: Have you ever read Nietzsche?

PISHCHIK: Well . . . Dashenka told me that one. And anyway, given my situation, even if I could forge banknotes . . . Day after tomorrow, I owe a payment of three hundred and ten rubles . . . I've already scraped up one hundred and thirty so far . . . (*Searches in his pockets, anxiously.*) My money's gone! I've lost my money! (*In tears.*) Where is my money! (*Overjoyed.*) Here it is, in the lining . . . Look, I even broke into a swear . . .

(*Enter* LYUBOV ANDREEVNA *and* CHARLOTTA IVANOVNA.)

LYUBOV ANDREEVNA: (*Humming the 'lezginka.'*) Why has Leonid been gone so long? What is he doing in town? (*To* DUNYASHA.) Dunyasha, offer the musicians some tea . . .

TROFIMOV: The auction didn't take place, in all probability.

LYUBOV ANDREEVNA: And of all times to invite the musicians and give a ball . . . Oh well, never mind . . . (*Sits and hums softly.*)

CHARLOTTA: (*Gives* PISHCHIK *a deck of cards.*) Here is a deck of cards, think of a card, any card.

PISHCHIK: I've got one.

CHARLOTTA: Now shuffle the deck. Very good. Give it to me, oh my dear Mr. Pishchik, Eins, zwei, drei! Now go look, it's in your side pocket . . .

PISHCHIK: (*Takes a card from his side pocket.*) The eight of spades, you're absolutely right! (*Amazed.*) Imagine that!

CHARLOTTA: (*Holds out the deck of cards in her palm to* TROFIMOV.) Tell me, quickly, which card is the top card?

TROFIMOV: What? Oh, the queen of spades.

CHARLOTTA: Right! (*To* PISHCHIK.) So? Which card is the top card?

PISHCHIK: The ace of hearts.

CHARLOTTA: Right! (*Claps her hands, and the deck of cards disappears.*) My, what lovely weather we're having today!

(*A mysterious female voice answers her as if coming from underneath the floor: "Oh yes, the weather is splendid, dear lady."*)

You are the image of perfection . . .

(*Voice: "And you I like very much too, dear lady."*)

65 STATIONMASTER: (*Applauds.*) Madame Ventriloquist, bravo!

PISHCHIK: (*Amazed.*) Imagine that! Most enchanting Charlotta Ivanovna . . . I'm head-over-heels in love . . .

CHARLOTTA: In love? (*Shrugs her shoulders.*) How could you possibly be in love? "Guter Mensch, aber schlechter Musikant."

70 TROFIMOV: (*Claps* PISHCHIK *on the shoulder.*) Well done, old horse . . .

CHARLOTTA: Your attention please, for one more trick. (*Gets a lap robe from a chair.*) Here is a very lovely lap robe, I wish to sell it . . . (*Shakes it.*) Doesn't anyone wish to buy it?

75 PISHCHIK: (*Amazed.*) Imagine that!

CHARLOTTA: Eins, zwei, drei! (*Quickly lifts the lap robe.*)

(ANYA *appears behind the lap robe; she curtsies, runs to her mother, embraces her, and runs out into the ballroom, amidst general delight.*)

LYUBOV ANDREEVNA: (*Applauds.*) Bravo, bravo! . . .

CHARLOTTA: Once more! Eins, zwei, drei! (*Lifts the lap robe.*)

(VARYA *appears behind the lap robe; she bows.*)

PISHCHIK: (*Amazed.*) Imagine that!

80 CHARLOTTA: The end! (*Throws the lap robe over* PISHCHIK, *curtsies, and runs out into the ballroom.*)

PISHCHIK: (*Hurries after her.*) Sorceress . . . how did you do it? How? (*Exits.*)

LYUBOV ANDREEVNA: And Leonid is still not back. What can
85 he be doing in town this long, I don't understand it! Surely everything is over by now, either the estate has been sold or else the auction never took place, one or the other, so why must we be kept in the dark forever!

VARYA: (*Attempting to console her.*) Uncle has bought it, I'm
90 sure of it.

TROFIMOV: (*Sarcastically.*) Yes.

VARYA: Great-aunt sent him power of attorney to buy the estate in her name and transfer the mortgage to her. She did it for Anya. And Uncle will buy it, with God's help, I'm sure of it.

95 LYUBOV ANDREEVNA: Great-aunt in Yaroslavl sent 50,000 to buy the estate in her name because she doesn't trust us— and that wasn't even enough to pay the interest. (*Covers her face with her hands.*) Today my destiny will be decided, my destiny . . .

100 TROFIMOV: (*Teasing* VARYA.) Madame Lopakhina!

VARYA: (*Angrily.*) The eternal student! Twice you've been expelled from the university.

LYUBOV ANDREEVNA: Why are you so angry, Varya? He's teasing you about Lopakhin, but what does it matter? If you
105 want to—marry Lopakhin, he's a fine man, a fascinating man. And if you don't want to—don't; no one is forcing you to, darling . . .

VARYA: I take this matter very seriously, Mamochka, I must tell you. He is a good man, I like him, I do.

110 LYUBOV ANDREEVNA: Then marry him. What are you waiting for, I don't understand!

VARYA: But Mamochka, I can't propose to him myself. For two years now everyone's been talking to me about him, every-

one, and either he says nothing, or else he jokes about it. I
115 understand. He's busy getting rich, he's preoccupied with his affairs, he has no time for me. Oh, if only I had money, only a little, a hundred rubles even, I'd give up everything, I'd run away as far as I could. I'd enter a convent.

TROFIMOV: Blessings on you!

120 VARYA: (*To* TROFIMOV.) A student's supposed to be intelligent! (*Gently, in tears.*) How ugly you've grown, Petya, and how old, too! (*To* LYUBOV ANDREEVNA, *no longer crying.*) I simply can't live without work, Mamochka. I must be doing something, every minute.

(*Enter* YASHA.)

YASHA: (*Hardly able to contain his laughter.*) Yepikhodov has
125 broken a billiard cue! . . . (*Exits.*)

VARYA: Why is Yepikhodov here? Who allowed him to play billiards? I don't understand these people . . . (*Exits.*)

LYUBOV ANDREEVNA: Don't tease her, Petya, can't you see how miserable she is.
130

TROFIMOV: She's overbearing, that's what she is . . . always poking her nose into other people's business. She hasn't given Anya and me a moment's peace all summer, she's afraid we might fall in love. What business is it of hers, anyway? And how could she even think that of me, I'm far
135 beyond such vulgarity. We are above love!

LYUBOV ANDREEVNA: And I suppose that means I must be beneath love. (*Tremendously agitated.*) Why isn't Leonid back yet? I only want to know: Is the estate sold or isn't it? This terrible business has gone too far, I don't know
140 what to think any more, I'm at my wits' end . . . I might scream any minute . . . I might do something foolish. Save me, Petya. Say something, anything . . .

TROFIMOV: Whether the estate is sold today or not—does it really matter? It's over, it's been so for a long time, there's no
145 turning back again, that path is long overgrown. Face it, dear friend. You mustn't delude yourself any longer, for once in your life you must look the truth straight in the eye.

LYUBOV ANDREEVNA: What truth? Oh, yes, of course, you see what is true and what is not true, while I have lost my vi-
150 sion, I see nothing. You boldly solve all the problems of the world, don't you, but tell me, my darling, isn't that because you're still so young, because you haven't even suffered through one of life's problems yet, not even one? You boldly look to the future, but isn't that because you see
155 nothing so terrible lying ahead, because life is still safely hidden from your young eyes? You have more courage, more character, more honesty than any of us, so then why not have compassion, find it, somewhere in a corner of your heart, have mercy on me. I was born here, my mother
160 and father lived here, my grandfather, too, I love this house, I can't comprehend a life without the cherry orchard, and if it must be sold, then sell me with it . . . (*Embraces* TROFIMOV, *kisses him on the forehead.*) My son drowned here . . . (*Weeps.*) Have pity on me, my good, kind fellow.
165

TROFIMOV: You know I do, with all my heart.

LYUBOV ANDREEVNA: Yes, but there must be another way to say it, another way . . . (*Takes out a handkerchief, a telegram falls on the floor.*) My soul is so heavy today, you can't possibly imagine. There is such a din here, I'm trembling
170 with each and every sound, trembling all over, but I can't

be alone, the silence would be terrifying. Don't judge me, Petya . . . I love you, as if you were my own child. And I'd gladly let you marry Anya, I would, I swear to you, only
175 first you must finish your education, darling, get your degree. You don't do a thing, you just let fate carry you from place to place, and that's such a strange way to live . . . Isn't it? Well? And you simply must do something about that beard, to make it grow, somehow . . . (*Bursts out laughing.*)
180 How funny-looking you are!

TROFIMOV: (*Picks up the telegram.*) I don't wish to be handsome.

LYUBOV ANDREEVNA: It's a telegram from Paris. Every day I receive one. Yesterday, and today, too. That terrible man is ill again, he's in trouble again . . . He begs my forgiveness,
185 he beseeches me to return to him, I really ought to be going to Paris, to be near him. You should see your face now, Petya, so severe, so judgmental, but, really, what am I to do, darling, tell me, what can I do, he's ill, he's alone, unhappy, and who will take care of him, who will keep him
190 from harm, who will nurse him through his illness? Oh, why hide it, why keep silent, I love him, it's the truth. I love him, I love him . . . He is the stone around my neck, and I shall sink with him to the bottom, and how I love this stone, I can't live without it! (*Presses* TROFIMOV'S
195 *hand.*) Don't think ill of me, Petya, and don't speak, please, not a word . . .

TROFIMOV: (*In tears.*) Forgive me for saying it, but for God's sake: This man robbed you, he cleaned you out!

LYUBOV ANDREEVNA: No, no, no, you mustn't talk like that . . .
200 (*Covers her ears.*)

TROFIMOV: He's an absolute scoundrel, and you're the only one who doesn't know it! A petty thief, a good-for-nothing . . .

LYUBOV ANDREEVNA: (*With controlled anger.*) And you're twenty-six or twenty-seven years old, and still a schoolboy!
205 TROFIMOV: So be it!

LYUBOV ANDREEVNA: You're supposed to be a man, at your age you're supposed to understand how lovers behave. Why don't you know this by now . . . why haven't you fallen in love yourself? (*Angrily.*) Yes, yes! You and all your
210 talk about purity . . . why, you're nothing but a prude, that's what you are, an eccentric, a freak . . .

TROFIMOV: (*Horrified.*) What is she saying!

LYUBOV ANDREEVNA: "I am above love." You're not above love, no, as Firs says, you're pathetic! At your age, not to
215 have a lover! . . .

TROFIMOV: (*Horrified.*) This is terrible! What is she saying?! (*Rushes out into the ballroom, holding his head.*) This is terrible . . . I can't bear it, I'm leaving . . . (*Exits, but returns again immediately.*) It's all over between us! (*Exits into the front
220 hall.*)

LYUBOV ANDREEVNA: (*Calls after him.*) Petya, wait! Don't be silly, I was only joking! Petya!

(*In the front hall, someone is heard dashing down the stairs, and suddenly falling the rest of the way with a crash.* ANYA *and* VARYA *cry out, but then, almost immediately, laughter is heard.*)

What happened?

(ANYA *runs in.*)

ANYA: (*Laughing.*) Petya fell down the stairs! (*Runs out.*)
225 LYUBOV ANDREEVNA: What a peculiar fellow that Petya is . . .

(*The* STATIONMASTER *stands in the middle of the ballroom, and starts to recite a poem: 'The Fallen Woman' by Alexey Konstantinovich Tolstoy. Everyone stops to listen, but after a few lines, the strains of a waltz are heard coming from the front hall, and the recitation is interrupted. Everyone dances.* TROFIMOV, ANYA, VARYA, *and* LYUBOV ANDREEVNA *pass through from the entrance hall.*)

Petya . . . my pure Petya . . . I beg your forgiveness . . . Come, dance with me . . . (*Dances with him.*)

(ANYA *and* VARYA *dance together.* FIRS *enters, and places his cane near the side door.* YASHA *also enters, and watches the dancing.*)

YASHA: So, what's new, grandpa?

FIRS: I don't feel very well. In the old days, we used to have generals, barons, admirals dancing at our balls; nowadays 230 we have to send for the postal clerk and the stationmaster, and even they come reluctantly. And I'm getting weaker, somehow. In the old days, when anyone of us fell ill, my old master—that would be their grandfather—he would treat us all with sealing wax. I've taken a dose of sealing 235 wax every day for twenty years now, even more, who knows; perhaps that's why I'm still alive.

YASHA: You get on my nerves, grandpa. (*Yawns.*) Maybe it's time for you to kick the bucket.

FIRS: And you're a pathetic fool, that's what you are. (*Mumbles.*) 240

(TROFIMOV *and* LYUBOV ANDREEVNA *dance in the ballroom, and then in the drawing room.*)

LYUBOV ANDREEVNA: "Merci." Let me sit down . . . (*Sits.*) I'm exhausted.

(*Enter* ANYA.)

ANYA: (*Agitated.*) There's a man out in the kitchen, he was just saying that the cherry orchard was sold today.

LYUBOV ANDREEVNA: To whom? 245

ANYA: He didn't say. He left. (*Dances with* TROFIMOV.)

(*Both exit into the ballroom.*)

YASHA: Some old fellow jabbering, that's all. A stranger.

FIRS: And Leonid Andreich is still not here, he's still not back yet. All he has on is a lightweight overcoat, one for in-between seasons, he's bound to catch cold. Oh, these 250 young people nowadays!

LYUBOV ANDREEVNA: I think I'm going to die. Go, Yasha, hurry, find out to whom it was sold.

YASHA: Oh, he left a long time ago, that old fellow. (*Laughs.*)

LYUBOV ANDREEVNA: (*Slightly annoyed.*) And what are you 255 laughing about? What's so funny?

YASHA: That Yepikhodov, he's a clown. The man is pitiful. "Mister Disaster."

LYUBOV ANDREEVNA: Firs, if the estate is sold, where will you go? 260

FIRS: Wherever you tell me, that's where I'll go.

LYUBOV ANDREEVNA: Why do you look like that? Are you ill? You should be in bed, you know . . .

FIRS: Yes . . . (*With a grin.*) I'll go to bed, and who will serve, who will manage everything? Hm? One servant for the 265 whole household.

YASHA: (*To* LYUBOV ANDREEVNA.) Lyubov Andreevna! One small request, allow me, please! If you go to Paris again, take

270 me with you, I beg of you. I can't stay here any more, it's absolutely impossible. (*Looks around, in a low voice.*) What can I say, you see for yourself, this is an ignorant country, the people are immoral, and anyway, life here is boring, the food they give you in the kitchen is disgusting, and you have Firs wandering around everywhere, muttering all 275 kinds of nonsense. Take me with you, I beg of you!

(*Enter* PISHCHIK.)

PISHCHIK: May I have the pleasure . . . a little waltz, most charming lady . . .

(LYUBOV ANDREEVNA *joins him.*)

But, don't forget, one hundred eighty rubles, enchanting lady . . . That, I'll take . . . (*They dance.*) One hundred and 280 eighty sweet little rubles . . .

(*They cross into the ballroom.*)

YASHA: (*Sings softly.*) "O, do you know how my heart is yearning . . ."

(*In the ballroom, a figure in a grey top hat and checkered trousers waves her hands and jumps up and down; there are cries of: "Bravo, Charlotta Ivanovna!"*)

DUNYASHA: (*Stops to powder her face.*) The mistress told me to dance—too many gentlemen, too few ladies,—but now my 285 head is spinning from too much waltzing, my heart is pounding, and, do you know what else, Firs Nikolaevich, the postmaster just told me something that took my breath away.

(*The music dies down.*)

FIRS: What did he say?
DUNYASHA: "You," he said, "are like a little flower."
290 YASHA: (*Yawns.*) What ignorance . . . (*Exits.*)
DUNYASHA: "A little flower" . . . I'm such a sensitive young woman, you know, I adore a few tender words.
FIRS: You'll get yourself into a lot of trouble.

(*Enter* YEPIKHODOV.)

YEPIKHODOV: Avdotya Fyodorovna, you keep avoiding me . . .
295 what am I, some sort of insect? (*Sighs.*) Ach, life!
DUNYASHA: Yes, what may I do for you?
YEPIKHODOV: And no doubt, probably, you're right. Of course. (*Sighs.*) Who can blame you. And yet, look at it from my point, of view, I mean, if I may say so myself, and 300 I shall, so excuse me, but you have reduced me to a complete state of mind. Now I know my destiny in life, every day some new disaster befalls me, and have I accepted this?—yes, I have, I look upon my fate with a smile. You have given me your word, and though . . .
305 DUNYASHA: Can we have our little talk later, please. Leave me alone now. I'm in a fantasy. (*Plays with her fan.*)
YEPIKHODOV: A new day, a new disaster, and excuse me, I just keep smiling, I even laugh, sometimes.

(*Enter* VARYA *from the ballroom.*)

VARYA: You still haven't left yet, Semyon? Who do you think 310 you are, really. (*To* DUNYASHA.) Get out of here, Dunyasha.

(*To* YEPIKHODOV.) First you play billiards and you break a cue, then you parade around the drawing room like a guest.
YEPIKHIDOV: You should not reprimand me. Excuse me.
VARYA: I'm not reprimanding you, I'm telling you. All you do 315 is float from one place to the next, you don't do a blessed bit of work. Why we keep you as clerk, God only knows.
YEPIKHODOV: (*Offended.*) Whether I work, or float, or eat, or play billiards, for that matter, excuse me, but that's a subject of discussion only for our elders.
VARYA: How dare you speak to me like that! (*Enraged.*) How 320 dare you? Do you mean to tell me I don't know what I'm doing? Get out of here! This minute!
YEPIKHODOV: (*Cowering.*) Excuse me, may I ask that you express yourself in a more delicate fashion?
VARYA: (*Beside herself.*) Get out, this minute! Out! 325

(*He goes to the door, she follows him.*)

"Mister Disaster!" Never set foot in here again, do you hear! I never want to lay eyes on you!

(YEPIKHODOV *has exited; from behind the door, his voice is heard: "I am going to file a complaint against you."*)

So, you're think you're coming back, eh? (*Grabs the cane, which* FIRS *has left by the door.*) Come on . . . come on . . . come on, I'll show you . . . So, are you coming back? Are 330 you? This is for you, then . . . (*Swings the cane.*)

(*Just at this moment* LOPAKHIN *enters.*)

LOPAKHIN: I humbly thank you.
VARYA: (*Angrily and sarcastically.*) Sorry!
LOPAKHIN: Please, it's nothing. I'm most grateful for the warm reception. 335
VARYA: Don't mention it. (*She turns to go, then looks around and asks, meekly.*) I didn't hurt you, did I?
LOPAKHIN: No, of course not, it's nothing. Just a bump, an enormous one, that's all.

(*Voices in the ballroom: "Lopakhin has returned! Yermolai Alekseich!"*)

PISHCHIK: Well, well, well, and speaking of the devil! . . . 340 (*Kisses* LOPAKHIN.) I smell a touch of brandy, my dear, good fellow, yes, I do! And we've been celebrating here, too!

(*Enter* LYUBOV ANDREEVNA.)

LYUBOV ANDREEVNA: Yermolai Alekseich, you're back. Why did it take you so long? Where is Leonid? 345
LOPAKHIN: Leonid Andreich returned with me, he's coming . . .
LYUBOV ANDREEVNA: (*Upset.*) So? Was there an auction? Tell me!
LOPAKHIN: (*Disconcerted, afraid to reveal his excitement.*) The auction was over at four o'clock . . . We missed the train, we had to wait till nine-thirty. (*Sighs heavily.*) Oh! My 350 head is spinning . . .

(*Enter* GAEV. *In his right hand he carries some packages; he wipes away the tears with his left hand.*)

LYUBOV ANDREEVNA: Lyonya, what is it? Lyonya? (*Impatiently, in tears.*) Tell me, quickly, for God's sake . . .

355 GAEV: (*Doesn't answer her, simply waves his hands; weeping, to* FIRS.) Here, take it . . . anchovies, and some kerch herring . . . I haven't had a thing to eat all day . . . What I have lived through!

(*The door to the billiard room is open; the clicking of billiard balls is heard, and* YASHA's *voice: "Seven and eighteen!"* GAEV's *expression changes; he is no longer crying.*)

I'm terribly tired. Help me change my clothes, Firs. (*Exits through the ballroom to his room,* FIRS *follows behind.*)

360 PISHCHIK: What happened at the auction? Tell us! Please!

LYUBOV ANDREEVNA: Is the cherry orchard sold?

LOPAKHIN: It is sold.

LYUBOV ANDREEVNA: Who bought it?

LOPAKHIN: I bought it.

(*Pause.* LYUBOV ANDREEVNA *is stunned; she might have fallen, were she not standing near an armchair and table.* VARYA *takes the keys off her belt, throws them on the floor in the middle of the drawing room, and exits.*)

365 I bought it! Wait, ladies and gentlemen, bear with me, please, my head is spinning, I can't speak . . . (*Laughs.*) We arrived at the auction, and Deriganov was already there. Leonid Andreich only had 15,000, so right away Deriganov bid 30,000 over and above the debt on the mortgage.
370 I saw how it was going, so I decided to take him on, I bid forty. And he bid forty-five. Then I bid fifty-five. You see—he'd raise it by five, I'd raise it by ten . . . And then, it was all over. I bid ninety over and above the debt, and that was it, it went to me. And now, the cherry orchard is mine!
375 Mine! (*Roars with laughter.*) My God, ladies and gentlemen, the cherry orchard is mine! Tell me that I'm drunk, that I'm out of my mind, that I've made it all up . . . (*Stamps his feet.*) Don't you laugh at me! If only my father and my grandfather could get up from their graves and witness all these
380 events, how their Yermolai, their ignorant little Yermolai, the one who was beaten, the one who ran barefoot in the bitter winter, how this same little Yermolai bought the estate, the most beautiful estate in the world. I bought the estate, where my grandfather and my father were slaves,
385 where they were forbidden to set foot in the kitchen. No, I'm dreaming, I'm hallucinating, it's only an illusion . . . a figment of the imagination, shrouded in a cloak of mystery . . . (*Picks up the keys, smiles tenderly.*) She threw down the keys, she's saying she's not the mistress of the house any
390 more . . . (*Jingles the keys.*) Ah, well, what does it matter.

(*The orchestra can be heard tuning up.*)

Eh, musicians, play, I want to hear you play! Everyone, come and see, how Yermolai Lopakhin will take an axe out into the cherry orchard, and all the trees will come crashing to the ground! And we'll build summer homes,
395 and our grandchildren and great grandchildren will see a new life . . . Let's have music, play!

(*The music plays.* LYUBOV ANDREEVNA *lowers herself into a chair and weeps bitterly.*)

(*Reproachfully.*) Why, why didn't you listen to me? My, poor, dear friend, you'll never get it back now, never. (*In*

tears.) Oh, the sooner all this is behind us, the sooner we can change our chaotic lives, our absurd, unhappy lives. 400

PISHCHIK: (*Takes him by the hand, in a low voice.*) She is weeping. Come into the ballroom, let's leave her alone . . . Come . . . (*Takes him by the hand and leads him into the ballroom.*)

LOPAKHIN: What's going on here? Let there be music! Loud, the way I want it! Let everything be the way I want it! 405 (*With irony.*) Here comes the new master, the owner of the cherry orchard! (*Accidentally shoves against a table, almost turning over a candelabrum.*) I can pay for it all, for everything! (*Exits with* PISHCHIK.)

(*There is no one left in the ballroom or the drawing room, except* LYUBOV ANDREEVNA, *who is sitting, huddled over weeping bitterly. The music plays softly.* ANYA *and* TROFIMOV *rush in.* ANYA *goes to her mother and kneels before her.* TROFIMOV *stays at the entrance to the ballroom.*)

ANYA: Mama! . . . Mama, are you crying? My dear, good, kind 410 Mama, my beautiful Mama, I love you . . . I bless you. The cherry orchard is sold, it's gone, it's true, it's true, but don't cry, Mama, you still have your whole life before you to live, and your pure and beautiful soul . . . Come with me, come, my darling, away from here, come! . . . We'll plant 415 a new orchard, more glorious than this one, you'll see, you'll understand, and joy, a deep, peaceful, gentle joy will settle into your soul, like the warm, evening sun, and you will smile, Mama! Come, darling! Come! . . .

ACT FOUR

The same setting as Act One. There are no curtains on the windows, no pictures on the walls; only a few pieces of furniture remain, stacked in a corner, as if for sale. There is a feeling of emptiness. There are suitcases, travel bags, etc. piled high upstage by the door leading to the outside. The door to stage left is open, from which the voices of VARYA *and* ANYA *can be heard.* LOPAKHIN *stands there, waiting.* YASHA *holds a tray of glasses, filled with champagne. In the entrance hall,* YEPIKHODOV *is packing a case. Offstage, voices are heard—the peasants have come to say good-bye.* GAEV's *voice is heard: "Thank you, my friends, I thank you."*

YASHA: The peasants have come to say good-bye. Now here's my opinion on that subject, Yermolai Alekseich: The people are good, but what do *they* know.

(*The noise dies down.* LYUBOV ANDREEVNA *and* GAEV *enter through the entrance hall; she is no longer crying, but she is very pale: she is trembling, and it is difficult for her to speak.*)

GAEV: You gave them everything in your purse, Lyuba. No! You mustn't do that! 5

LYUBOV ANDREEVNA: I couldn't help it! I couldn't help it!

(*Both exit.*)

LOPAKHIN: (*At the door, following after them.*) Please, I humbly beg you! A farewell toast! I didn't think to bring any from town . . . and I could only find one bottle at the station. Please! 10

(*Pause.*)

So, my friends! You don't want any? (*Steps away from the door.*) If I'd known, I wouldn't have bought it. Never mind, I won't have any, either.

(YASHA *carefully places the tray on the table.*)

Drink up, Yasha, why don't you.

15 YASHA: To those who are leaving! And to those who are staying behind! (*Drinks.*) This isn't real champagne, that much I can tell you.

LOPAKHIN: Eight rubles a bottle.

(*Pause.*)

Wickedly cold in here, isn't it.

20 YASHA: They didn't stoke up the stoves today, what's the point, everybody's leaving. (*Laughs.*)

LOPAKHIN: What are you laughing about?

YASHA: I'm happy.

LOPAKHIN: It's October, but outside it's sunny and mild, like
25 summertime. Good weather for construction. (*Looks at his watch, at the door.*) Ladies and gentlemen, bear in mind, only forty-six minutes left until the train departs! That means we have to leave for the station in twenty minutes. Hurry, everyone!

(TROFIMOV *enters from the outside, wearing a coat.*)

30 TROFIMOV: I think it's time to go now. They've already brought the horses around. Where are my galoshes, damn it! They've disappeared. (*At the door.*) Anya, my galoshes aren't here! I can't find them!

LOPAKHIN: And I've got to get to Kharkov. I'll go with you as
35 far as the station. I'm going to spend the winter in Kharkov. Yes. Here I am, standing around, talking to you, I'm lost when I'm not working. I can't live without work, I don't know what to do with my hands; isn't it strange, look, they're hanging there, as if they belonged to someone else.

40 TROFIMOV: We'll be leaving momentarily, and you'll return to all your worthy enterprises.

LOPAKHIN: Have a glass with me.

TROFIMOV: I can't.

LOPAKHIN: So, it's off to Moscow, then?

45 TROFIMOV: Yes, that's right, I'll go with them into town, and tomorrow, it's off to Moscow.

LOPAKHIN: Yes . . . Well, the professors haven't started their lectures yet, no doubt they're all waiting for you!

TROFIMOV: That's none of your business.

50 LOPAKHIN: How many years is it, then, since you've been at the university?

TROFIMOV: Think up something new, why don't you? That's a stale and feeble joke, it's not funny any more. (*Searches for his galoshes.*) It's very likely we may never see each other again,
55 you know, so allow me, please, to give you some parting advice: Don't wave your arms around so much! Try to get out of the habit of waving your arms when you talk, if you can. All this planning of yours, you know, building summer houses, creating a new generation of independent landown-
60 ers, and so on and so forth,—why, that's just another form of waving your arms . . . Oh, well, never mind, all things considered, I like you . . . I do. You have delicate, sensitive fingers, the fingers of an artist . . . you have a delicate, sensitive soul . . .

LOPAKHIN: (*Embraces him.*) Good-bye, my friend. Thanks for
65 everything. Just in case, here, take some money for the journey.

TROFIMOV: Why should I? I don't need it.

LOPAKHIN: But you don't have any!

TROFIMOV: Yes, I do, thank you very much. I've just received some money for a translation. Here it is, right here, in my
70 pocket. (*Anxiously.*) Now where are my galoshes!

VARYA: (*From the other room.*) Here, take the filthy things! (*Tosses a pair of rubber galoshes on the stage.*)

TROFIMOV: Why are you so angry, Varya? Hm . . . These are not my galoshes!
75

LOPAKHIN: This spring I planted almost 3,000 acres of poppies, and made a clean profit of 40,000. And when my poppies bloomed, now what a sight that was! So, here's what I'm saying, I've just made 40,000 rubles, and I'm offering you a loan because I can afford to. Why do you look down your
80 nose at me? I'm a peasant . . . what do you expect?

TROFIMOV: Your father was a peasant, mine was a chemist, none of it means a thing.

(LOPAKHIN *takes out his wallet.*)

Stop that, stop . . . Even if you were to give me 200,000, I wouldn't take it. I am a free man. And everything that is
85 so sacred and dear to all of you, rich and poor alike, hasn't the slightest significance to me, it's all dust, adrift in the wind. I can survive without you, I can even surpass you, I am proud and strong. Mankind is on a quest to seek the highest truth, the greatest happiness possible on this earth,
90 and I am in the front ranks!

LOPAKHIN: And will you reach your destination?

TROFIMOV: Yes, I shall.

(*Pause.*)

I shall, or else I'll show others the way.

(*In the distance, the sound is heard of an axe falling on a tree.*)

LOPAKHIN: So, good-bye, my friend. Time to go. Here we are,
95 looking down our noses at one another, and all the while, life goes on, in spite of any of us. When I work, for days on end, without any rest, that's when my thoughts come most clearly, that's when I know why I am on this earth, why I exist. And how many of us are there in Russia, my friend,
100 who still don't know why they exist. Ah well, what does it matter, that's not the point, is it. They say that Leonid Andreich has taken a position at a bank, 6,000 a year . . . He won't be able to keep it, though, he's too lazy . . .

ANYA: (*At the door.*) Mama asks you not to cut down the or-
105 chard till after she's gone.

TROFIMOV: Isn't it possible to show some tact . . . (*Exits through the entrance hall.*)

LOPAKHIN: Yes, yes, right away . . . Really.

ANYA: Have they sent Firs to the hospital yet?
110

YASHA: I told them about it this morning. I'm sure they did.

ANYA: (*To* YEPIKHODOV, *who is walking through the hall.*) Semyon Panteleich, please, go find out, would you, if they've taken Firs to the hospital yet.

YASHA: (*Offended.*) I told Yegor this morning. Why ask the
115 same question over and over!

YEPIKHODOV: The ancient Firs, in my final opinion, is beyond repair; he should return to his forefathers. And I can only envy him. (*Places the suitcase on a hat box, and crushes it.*)
120   Oh, well, of course. I knew it. (*Exits.*)
YASHA: (*Mocking.*) "Mister Disaster" . . .
VARYA: (*From behind the door.*) Have they taken Firs to the hospital?
ANYA: Yes, they have.
125 VARYA: Why didn't they bring the letter to the doctor?
ANYA: We'll just have to send it along . . . (*Exits.*)
VARYA: (*From the adjacent room.*) Where's Yasha? Tell him his mother's here, she wants to say good-bye to him.
YASHA: (*Waves his hand.*) I'm losing my patience.

(*During this,* DUNYASHA *has been busying herself with the luggage; now that* YASHA *is alone, she goes up to him.*)

130 DUNYASHA: Just one last look, Yasha. You're leaving . . . you're abandoning me . . . (*Weeps and throws her arms around his neck.*)
YASHA: What's there to cry about? (*Drinks champagne.*) In six days, I'll be in Paris again. Tomorrow we'll board an ex-
135   press train, and off we'll go, that's the last you'll ever see of us. I just can't believe it. "Vive la France!" . . . This place is not for me, I can't live here . . . and that's all there is to it. I've seen a lot of ignorance—and I've had enough. (*Drinks champagne.*) What's there to cry about? Behave
140   yourself properly, then you won't cry so much.
DUNYASHA: (*Powders her face, looks at herself in the mirror.*) Send me a letter from Paris. You know much I have loved you, Yasha, I have loved you very, very much! I'm a sensitive creature, Yasha!
145 YASHA: They're coming. (*Busies himself with the luggage, hums softly.*)

(*Enter* LYUBOV ANDREEVNA, GAEV, ANYA, *and* CHARLOTTA IVANOVNA.)

GAEV: We really ought to be going. There's hardly any time left. (*Looks at* YASHA.) Who smells of herring in here?
LYUBOV ANDREEVNA: In ten minutes time we'll be getting
150   into the carriages . . . (*Glances around the room.*) Good-bye, beloved home, home of my forefathers. Winter will pass, spring will come, and you'll no longer be here, they will have destroyed you. How much these walls have seen! (*Kisses her daughter passionately.*) My treasure, you're radi-
155   ant, your eyes are sparkling, like two diamonds. Are you happy? Very happy?
ANYA: Very! We're starting a new life, Mama!
GAEV: (*Cheerfully.*) Everything's turned out quite well, as a matter of fact, yes, indeed. Before the cherry orchard was sold,
160   we were all upset, we suffered a great deal, but then, when everything was settled, once and for all, finally and irrevocably, we all calmed down, we were even glad . . . And now I'm a bank official, a financier . . . "yellow into the middle pocket," and you, Lyuba, for all that we've been through,
165   you're looking better than ever, no doubt about it.
LYUBOV ANDREEVNA: Yes, I'm calmer, it's true.

(*She is given her hat and coat.*)

I can sleep better now. Take my things out, Yasha. It's time. (*To* ANYA.) My darling child, we shall see each other again,
soon . . . I am going to Paris, I shall live there on the money your great-aunt from Yaroslavl sent to buy the estate—God 170 bless great-aunt!—but that money won't last very long.
ANYA: You'll come home soon, Mama, soon . . . won't you? And I'll study, take my examinations, and then I'll work, I'll take care of you. And we'll read all sorts of marvelous books together, Mama . . . Won't we? (*Kisses her mother's* 175 *hands.*) We'll read through the long autumn evenings, we'll read so many books, and a wonderful new world will open before us . . . (*Dreaming.*) Come home, Mama . . .
LYUBOV ANDREEVNA: I'll come, my jewel. (*Embraces her daughter.*)

(*Enter* LOPAKHIN, *and* CHARLOTTA, *who is softly humming a tune.*)

GAEV: Charlotta is happy: she's singing! 180
CHARLOTTA: (*Picks up a bundle, resembling an infant in swaddling clothes.*) "My sweet little baby, 'bye, 'bye . . ."

(*The child's cry: "Wa, wa! . . ." can be heard.*)

"Hushabye, baby, my sweet little boy."

(*The child's cry: "Wa! . . . wa! . . ."*)

Poor baby! I feel so sorry for you! (*Throws the bundle down.*) Now, please, find me another job. I can't go on like this. 185
LOPAKHIN: We shall, Charlotta Ivanovna, don't worry.
GAEV: We're all being cast out, Varya's going away . . . suddenly no one needs us any more.
CHARLOTTA: There's nowhere for me to live in town. I must go away . . . (*Hums.*) It doesn't matter . . . 190

(*Enter* PISHCHIK.)

LOPAKHIN: One of nature's wonders! . . .
PISHCHIK: (*Out of breath.*) Oy, let me catch my breath . . . I'm all worn out . . . Most honorable friends . . . Give me some water . . .
GAEV: Looking for money, by any chance? I remain your 195 humble servant, but, forgive me, I really must avoid the temptation . . . (*Exits.*)
PISHCHIK: I haven't been here in such a long, long, time . . . loveliest lady . . . (*To* LOPAKHIN.) And you are here, too . . . so good to see you . . . a man of the highest intelligence . . . 200 here, take it . . . it's yours . . . (*Gives* LOPAKHIN *some money.*) Four hundred rubles . . . I still owe you eight hundred and forty . . .
LOPAKHIN: (*Shrugs his shoulders in amazement.*) I must be dreaming . . . Where on earth did you get this? 205
PISHCHIK: Wait . . . So hot . . . Most extraordinary circumstances. Some Englishmen came to visit my estate, and what do you know, they found white clay in the earth . . . whatever that is . . . (*To* LYUBOV ANDREEVNA.) And here's four hundred for you . . . elegant, exquisite lady . . . (*Gives* 210 *her some money.*) The rest will come later. (*Drinks the water.*) Just now, a young man on the train was telling us about this great philosopher . . . how he's advising everyone to jump off the roof . . . "Jump!" he says, and that will solve everything. (*Amazed.*) Imagine that! Water! . . . 215
LOPAKHIN: What Englishmen are you talking about?
PISHCHIK: I leased them a plot of the land with the white clay for twenty-four years . . . But now, forgive me, please, I've run out of time . . . a long ride ahead . . . I'm going to the

220 Znoykovs . . . to the Kardamonovs . . . I owe everybody . . . (*Drinks.*) Good day to you all . . . I'll drop by again on Thursday . . .

LYUBOV ANDREEVNA: We're just moving into town now, and tomorrow I'm going abroad . . .

225 PISHCHIK: What? (*Anxiously.*) Why to town? What's this I see . . . furniture . . . suitcases . . . Well, never mind . . . (*In tears.*) Never mind . . . Very very smart people, these Englishmen . . . people of the highest intelligence . . . Never mind . . . I wish you happiness . . . God will watch over you . . .

230 Never mind . . . Everything on this earth must come to an end . . . (*Kisses* LYUBOV ANDREEVNA*s hand.*) And when you hear the news that my own end has come, remember this good old horse, won't you, and say: "Once upon a time there lived an old so-and-so . . . Simeonov-Pishchik . . .

235 God rest his soul" . . . Magnificent weather we're having . . . Yes . . . (*Exits in great confusion, and immediately returns and speaks from the doorway.*) Dashenka sends her regards! (*Exits.*)

LYUBOV ANDREEVNA: And now we can go. But I'm leaving
240 with two worries. The first is Firs—he's ill. (*Looks at her watch.*) We still have five minutes . . .

ANYA: Mama, they've already sent Firs to the hospital. Yasha sent him this morning.

LYUBOV ANDREEVNA: My second sorrow is Varya. She's used
245 to getting up early and working, and now, without work, she's like a fish out of water. She's grown thin and pale, she weeps all the time, poor thing . . .

(*Pause.*)

You know very well, Yermolai Alekseich, I have dreamed . . . that one day she would marry you, in fact, it was ob-
250 vious to everyone that you would be married. (*She whispers to* ANYA, *who motions to* CHARLOTTA, *and both exit.*) She loves you, you seem to be fond of her, and I don't know why, I simply don't know why it is that you go out of your way to avoid one other. I don't understand it!

255 LOPAKHIN: I don't understand it myself, to tell the truth. It's all so strange, somehow . . . If there's still time, then I'm ready to do it now . . . Basta! Let's settle it once and for all; without you here, I don't think I could possibly propose to her.

LYUBOV ANDREEVNA: Excellent. It only takes a minute, you
260 know. I'll call her in right away . . .

LOPAKHIN: Oh yes, and there's champagne, too. (*Looks at glasses.*) It's empty, someone drank it all up.

(YASHA *coughs.*)

Or, should I say, lapped it all up . . .

LYUBOV ANDREEVNA: (*Excited.*) Splendid. We're leaving . . .
265 Yasha, "allez"! I'll call her . . . (*At the door.*) Varya, stop what you're doing, and come here. Come! (*Exits with* YASHA.)

LOPAKHIN: (*Looks at his watch.*) Yes . . .

(*Pause.*)

(*Muffled laughter and whispering is heard from behind the door; finally,* VARYA *enters.*)

VARYA: (*In a lengthy search for something.*) That's strange, I can't find it anywhere . . .

270 LOPAKHIN: What are you looking for?

VARYA: I put it away myself, I can't remember where.

(*Pause.*)

LOPAKHIN: So where will you go now, Varvara Mikhailovna?

VARYA: Me? To the Ragulins' . . . I've agreed to work for them . . . you know . . . as a housekeeper.

LOPAKHIN: Aren't they in Yashnevo? That's about forty-five 275 miles from here.

(*Pause.*)

And so, life has come to an end in this house . . .

VARYA: (*Searching among the things.*) Where can it be . . . Perhaps I put it in the trunk . . . Yes, life has come to an end in this house . . . and will be no more . . . 280

LOPAKHIN: And I'm off to Kharkov now . . . on the same train. I've got a lot of business there. But I'm leaving Yepikhodov here to look after things . . . I've hired him, you know.

VARYA: Really!

LOPAKHIN: Last year at this time it was already snowing, if you 285 remember, and now it's so sunny and calm. Only it's quite cold . . . Three degrees of frost, almost.

VARYA: I hadn't noticed.

(*Pause.*)

Anyway, our thermometer's broken . . .

(*Pause.*)

(*A voice is heard calling from outside:* "Yermolai Alekseich! . . .")

LOPAKHIN: (*As if he'd long been waiting for this call.*) Coming! 290 (*He hurries out.*)

(VARYA *sits on the floor, puts her head on a bundle of clothing, and sobs quietly. The door opens, and* LYUBOV ANDREEVNA *enters cautiously.*)

LYUBOV ANDREEVNA: So?

(*Pause.*)

We'd better go.

VARYA: (*No longer weeping, wipes her eyes.*) Yes, Mamochka, it's time. If I don't miss the train, I might even get to the Rag- 295 ulins' today . . .

LYUBOV ANDREEVNA: (*At the door.*) Anya, put your coat on!

(*Enter* ANYA, *then* GAEV, CHARLOTTA IVANOVNA. GAEV *is wearing a warm coat with a hood. The* SERVANTS *and* CARRIAGE DRIVERS *assemble.* YEPIKHODOV *is busy with the luggage.*)

Now, we can be on our way.

ANYA: (*Overjoyed.*) We're on our way!

GAEV: My friends, my dear, kind friends! Upon leaving this 300 house forever, how can I be silent, how can I refrain, upon this our departure, from expressing those feelings, which now fill my very being . . .

ANYA: (*Imploring.*) Uncle!

VARYA: Uncle, must you! 305

GAEV: (*Dejected.*) "Double the yellow into the middle . . ." I'll be quiet . . .

(*Enter* TROFIMOV, *then* LOPAKHIN.)

TROFIMOV: All right, ladies and gentlemen, time to depart!

LOPAKHIN: Yepikhodov, my coat!

310 LYUBOV ANDREEVNA: I want to sit for just one minute longer. I never really noticed before, what walls this house has, what ceilings, and now I look at them with such longing, with such tender love . . .

GAEV: I remember, when I was six, on Trinity Sunday, I sat at
315 this window and watched my father walking to church . . .

LYUBOV ANDREEVNA: Have they taken everything out?

LOPAKHIN: I think so. (*To* YEPIKHODOV, *who is putting on his coat.*) Yepikhodov, see to it that everything's been taken care of.

YEPIKHODOV: (*Speaking in a hoarse voice.*) Don't you worry,
320 Yermolai Alekseich.

LOPAKHIN: What's the matter with your voice?

YEPIKHODOV: I just drank some water, and I must have swallowed something.

YASHA: (*Contemptuously.*) What ignorance . . .

325 LYUBOV ANDREEVNA: We're leaving—and not a soul will be left here . . .

LOPAKHIN: Until springtime.

VARYA: (*Pulls an umbrella out of a bundle—it appears as if she were about to strike someone;* LOPAKHIN *pretends to be frightened.*)
330 What's wrong with you? . . . I wouldn't think of it . . .

TROFIMOV: Ladies and gentlemen, please, let's get into the carriages now . . . It's time to go! The train will arrive any minute!

VARYA: Petya, here they are, your galoshes, beside the suitcase.
335 (*In tears.*) Look how old and muddy they are . . .

TROFIMOV: (*Putting on the galoshes.*) We're off, ladies and gentlemen!

GAEV: (*Very confused, afraid of bursting into tears.*) Train . . . station . . . "Croisé into the middle pocket, Double the white
340 into the corner . . ."

LYUBOV ANDREEVNA: We're off!

LOPAKHIN: Is everyone here? No one left behind? (*Locks the side door stage left.*) There are some things stored in here, better lock up. We're off!

345 ANYA: Good-bye, house! Good-bye, old life!

TROFIMOV: Hello, new life . . . (*Exits with* ANYA.)

(VARYA *glances around the room and exits without hurrying. Exit* YASHA, *and* CHARLOTTA, *with the little dog.*)

LOPAKHIN: And so, until springtime. Come now, ladies and gentlemen, we'd better be going . . . Once more, a very good-bye!! . . . (*Exits.*)

(LYUBOV ANDREEVNA *and* GAEV *are left alone together. It is as if they have been waiting for this moment; they throw themselves into each others' arms and sob quietly, with restraint, fearing they might be heard.*)

GAEV: (*In despair.*) My sister, my sister . . .   350

LYUBOV ANDREEVNA: O my precious orchard, my sweet, lovely orchard! . . . My life, my youth, my happiness, farewell! . . . Farewell! . . .

(ANYA's *voice calls out, merrily:* "Mama! . . .")

(TROFIMOV's *voice calls out, gaily, excitedly:* "A-oo! . . .")

LYUBOV ANDREEVNA: For the last time, let me look at these walls, these windows . . . how my mother loved to walk   355 about this room . . .

GAEV: My sister, my sister! . . .

(ANYA's *voice:* "Mama! . . .")

(TROFIMOV's *voice:* "A-oo . . .")

LYUBOV ANDREEVNA: We're off! . . .

(*They exit.*)

(*The stage is empty. There is the sound of all the doors being locked, and then of the carriages pulling away. It grows very still. Through the stillness comes the remote sound of the axe falling on a tree, a lonely, melancholy sound. Footsteps are heard.* FIRS *appears at the door, stage right. He is dressed, as always, in a jacket and a white waistcoat, with slippers on his feet. He is ill.*)

FIRS: (*Goes to the door, tries the handle.*) Locked. They've gone . . . (*Sits on the sofa.*) They've forgotten about me . . . Never   360 mind . . . I'll sit here for a just a bit . . . And Leonid Andreich, most likely, didn't put his fur coat on, went off wearing his light one . . . (*Sighs, anxiously.*) Just slipped my notice . . . These young people nowadays! (*Mutters something incomprehensible.*) And life has passed by, somehow, as   365 if I never lived it at all. (*Lies down.*) I'll lie down for just a bit . . . Don't have too much strength left, now, do you, no, not much, not much at all . . . You pathetic old fool, you! . . . (*Lies there, immobile.*)

(*A distant sound is heard, as if coming from the sky, the sound of a breaking string, dying away, a mournful sound. Silence falls, and all that is heard, far off in the orchard, is the sound of the axe falling on a tree.*)

PRONUNCIATION GUIDE TO RUSSIAN NAMES

Cast of Characters

Lyubov (*Lyuba*) *Andreevna Ranevskaya*, Lyoo-bof´ (Lyoo´-ba) An-drey´-ev-na Ra-nyef´-ska-ya
("drey" rhymes with the English word "grey")

Anya (*Anechka*), An´-ya (An´-yech-ka)

Varya (*Varvara Mikhailovna*), Va´-rya (Var-var´-a Mee-khai´-lov-na)
("khai" rhymes with the word "why")

Leonid (*Lyonya*) *Andreevich* (*Andreich*) *Gaev*, Le-o-need´ (Lyon´-ya) Andrey´-e-veech (An-drey´-eech) Ga´-yef

Yermolai Alekseevich (*Alekseich*) *Lopakhin*, Yer-mo-lai´ A-lek-syey´-e-veech (A-lek-sey´-eech) Lo-pa´-kheen
("lai" in "Yermolai" rhymes with the word "why")
("syey" rhymes with the word "grey")

Pyotr (*Petya*) *Sergeevich* (*Sergeich*) *Trofimov*, Pyo´-tr (Pye´-tya) Syer-gey´-e-veech (Syer-gey´-eech) Tro-fee´-mof

Boris Borisovich Simeonov-Pishchik, Bo-rees´ Bo-rees´-o-veech See-myon´-of-Peesh´-cheek

Charlotta Ivanovna, Shar-lo´-ta Ee-van´-ov-na

Semyon Panteleevich (Panteleich) Yepikhodov, Se-myon´ Pan-te-lyey´-e-veech (Pan-te-lyey´-eech) Ye-pee-khod´-of ("lyey" rhymes with the word "grey")

Dunyasha (Avdotya Fyodorovna), Doon-ya´-sha (Av-do´-tya Fyo´-do-rov-na)

Firs Nikolaevich, Feers Nee-ko-la´-ye-veech

Yasha, Ya´-sha

Other Russian Names Appearing in the Text

Anastasy, A-na-sta´-see
Dashenka, Da´-shen-ka
Deriganov, Dye-ree-ga´-nof
Grisha, Gree´-sha
Kardamonov, Kar-da-mo´-nof
Karp, Karp
Kharkov, Khar´-kof
Kozoedov (Fyodor), Ko-zo-ye´-dof (Fyo´-dor)
Lopakhina, Lo-pa´-khee-na
Mama (Mamochka), Ma´-ma (Ma´-moch-ka)
Papa, Pa´-pa

Petrushka, Pye-troosh´-ka
Polya, Po´-lya
Ragulin, Ra-goo´-leen
Yaroslavl, Ya-ro-slavl´
Yashnevo, Yash´-nye-vo
Yefimyushka, Ye-fee´-myoosh-ka
Yegor, Ye-gor´
Yevstigney, Yev-steeg-nyey´ ("nyey" rhymes with the word "grey")
Znoykov, Znoy´-kof

Elizabeth Robins

Elizabeth Robins (1862–1952) was a radical reformer on two fronts. A significant actress, one of the first female actor-managers in England, a significant force in the Ibsen movement in the 1890s, friend of Henry James, Bernard Shaw, and Harley Granville Barker, Robins played a critical role in politicizing theater and theatrical performance. Moreover, Robins was also an important figure in the woman suffrage movement in England. Robins wrote the stage play *Votes for Women!* (1907) and then expanded it into the novel *The Convert* (1907). She helped to organize the Actresses' Franchise League in 1908, recruiting the most important actresses (and some actors) of the era—Ellen Terry, Mrs. Patrick Campbell, among others—to the cause; she gathered a series of lectures on women, politics, and the vote in *Way Stations* (1913); and she wrote an important investigation of the social and philosophical construction of gender relations in society, *Ancilla's Share: An Indictment of Sex Antagonism* (1924).

Robins was born in Kentucky and studied at Putnam Female Seminary before being sent to Vassar College to study medicine; she soon left Vassar for the stage and toured the United States as an actress. In Boston, she married an actor, George Richmond Parkes, but refused to give up acting; he committed suicide shortly thereafter, pitching himself into the Charles River in a suit of stage armor. In the 1880s, she traveled to Norway with the widow of the violinist Ole Bull. When she arrived in London late in the decade, she played a variety of theatrical roles to support herself while organizing a company to produce Ibsen's plays. A woman with a mission, Robins quickly gained the—by no means unequivocal—support of William Archer, Henry James, Bernard Shaw and others; she brought *Hedda Gabler* and *The Master Builder* to England, creating Hedda and Hilde Wangel on the London stage.

In *Ibsen and the Actress* (1924), Robins recounted her struggle both to bring Ibsen to the English theater and to gain financial and institutional power in a theatrical system entirely governed by men. Her suffrage play *Votes for Women!* marks in many ways Robins's entrance onto a new phase of her life, as an important figure in the British suffrage movement. Robins was early converted to the militant program of Emmeline Pankhurst and her daughter Christabel and the Women's Social and Political Union (formed in Manchester in 1903). The Pankhursts orchestrated demonstrations, besieged members of Parliament, and developed hunger strikes among imprisoned suffragettes as a mode of agitating for the vote. Robins's skills as a propagandist and speaker were invaluable, and her career on the stage became important in other respects: she donated the profits from *Votes for Women!* and *The Convert* to buy a farm, which was initially used as a rest home for suffragettes who had been force fed during imprisonment, and was later used to house women studying medicine. Throughout the rest of her career—as polemicist, essayist, and novelist—Robins remained committed to the cause of women's equality.

VOTES FOR WOMEN!

Although the Actresses' Franchise League would eventually produce plays on women and suffrage, when Robins wrote *Votes for Women!,* the League had yet to be founded. She produced the play at the Court Theatre in 1907, where, given the prominence of the Court's repertoire under the Barker-Vedrenne management, its politics were certain to make a keen impact on the theater going public.

To audiences in 1907, the outlines of Robins's plot—suffrage aside—would have marked the play as part of a familiar theatrical type: the "problem play." Part of a genre that includes plays from Arthur Wing Pinero's *The Second Mrs. Tanqueray* (1892) (and Bernard Shaw's send-up of 1893, *Mrs. Warren's Profession*) to John Galsworthy's *The Skin Game*

(1920), this drama uses the heroine's sexuality to motivate the narrative. Some "secret" sexual encounter or relationship is revealed in the play, and usually becomes the cause of the heroine's demise: Paula Tanqueray shoots herself when her stepdaughter falls in love with one of Paula's former lovers; Galsworthy's Chloe throws herself into a gravel pit when her own "past" is revealed to her family.

In *Votes for Women!*, however, Robins appropriates this design as a means of empowering her heroine, not destroying her. For Vida Levering has a "past" of her own, the deeply-coded story of how she had been involved with a man who would not marry her, became pregnant, and escaped to the country for an abortion. But when her "past"—in the person of the new Member of Parliament, Geoffrey Stonor—returns to her life, Vida is galvanized into action. Her "experience" becomes the force behind her political awakening, rather than the cause of a sentimental suicide. Despite a horror of "publicity," she takes the stage at a suffrage rally in Trafalgar square, and speaks so movingly of women's sexual exploitation in male-dominated society that Stonor's fiancée Jean guesses that Stonor was the man involved. In act 3, Jean and Vida combine to persuade Stonor to press for women's suffrage in Parliament.

Robins modeled Vida Levering on the charismatic Christabel Pankhurst, and reviewers of the 1907 production were unanimous in finding the central rally scene in Trafalgar Square a theatrical masterpiece. This is, of course, the scene in which Vida Levering finally takes the stage, moving from the protected sphere of domestic life into the public sphere of politics. Speaking to the audience onstage, Vida also speaks directly to the audience in the theater; Vida Levering is, perhaps, the best image of Robins's lifelong effort to fuse her two voices: the voice of the actress and the voice of the activist.

VOTES FOR WOMEN!

Elizabeth Robins

CHARACTERS

LORD JOHN WYNNSTAY
LADY JOHN WYNNSTAY, *his wife*
MRS HERIOT, *sister of Lady John*
MISS JEAN DUNBARTON, *niece to Lady John and Mrs Heriot*
THE HON. GEOFFREY STONOR, *Unionist M.P. affianced to Jean Dunbarton*
MR ST JOHN GREATOREX, *Liberal M.P.*
THE HON. RICHARD FARNBOROUGH
MR FREDDY TUNBRIDGE
MRS FREDDY TUNBRIDGE

MR ALLEN TRENT
MISS ERNESTINE BLUNT, *a Suffragette*
MR PILCHER, *a working man*
A WORKING WOMAN
MISS VIDA LEVERING
PERSONS IN THE CROWD
SERVANTS IN THE TWO HOUSES

The Entire Action of the Play takes place between Sunday noon and six o'clock in the evening of the same day.

ACT ONE

Hall of Wynnstay House.

Twelve o'clock, Sunday morning, end of June. With the rising of the curtain, enter the BUTLER. *As he is going, with majestic port, to answer the door, enter briskly from the garden, by the lower French window,* LADY JOHN WYNNSTAY, *flushed, and flapping a garden hat to fan herself. She is a pink-cheeked woman of fifty-four, who has plainly been a beauty, keeps her complexion, but is "gone to fat."*

LADY JOHN: Has Miss Levering come down yet?
BUTLER: (*pausing*) I haven't seen her, m'lady.
LADY JOHN: (*almost sharply as* BUTLER *turns*) I won't have her disturbed if she's resting. (*To herself as she goes to the writing*
5 *table.*) She certainly needs it.
BUTLER: Yes, m'lady.
LADY JOHN: (*sitting at the writing table, her back to the front door*) But I want her to know the moment she comes down that the new plans arrived by the morning post.
10 BUTLER: (*pausing nearly at the door*) Plans, m'la—
LADY JOHN: She'll understand. There they are. (*Glancing at the clock.*) It's very important she should have them in time to look over before she goes—

(BUTLER *opens the door.*)

(*Over her shoulder.*) Is that Miss Levering?
15 BUTLER: No, m'lady. Mr Farnborough.

(*Exit* BUTLER.)

(*Enter the* HON. R. FARNBOROUGH. *He is twenty-six; reddish hair, high-coloured, sanguine, self-important.*)

FARNBOROUGH: I'm afraid I'm scandalously early. It didn't take me nearly as long to motor over as Lord John said.
LADY JOHN: (*shaking hands*) I'm afraid my husband is no au-
20 thority on motoring—and he's not home yet from church.
FARNBOROUGH: It's the greatest luck finding *you*. I thought Miss Levering was the only person under this roof who was ever allowed to observe Sunday as a real Day of Rest.
LADY JOHN: If you've come to see Miss Levering—
FARNBOROUGH: Is she here? I give you my word I didn't
25 know it.

LADY JOHN: (*unconvinced*) Oh?
FARNBOROUGH: Does she come every weekend?
LADY JOHN: Whenever we can get her to. But we've only known her a couple of months.
FARNBOROUGH: And I have only known her three weeks! 30 Lady John, I've come to ask you to help me.
LADY JOHN: (*quickly*) With Miss Levering? I can't do it!
FARNBOROUGH: No, no—all that's no good. She only laughs.
LADY JOHN: (*relieved*) Ah!—she looks upon you as a boy.
FARNBOROUGH: (*firing up*) Such rot! What do you think she 35 said to me in London the other day?
LADY JOHN: That she was four years older than you?
FARNBOROUGH: Oh, I knew that. No. She said she knew she was all the charming things I'd been saying, but there was only one way to prove it—and that was to marry some one 40 young enough to be her son. She'd noticed that was what the *most* attractive women did—and she named names.
LADY JOHN: (*laughing*) You were too old!
FARNBOROUGH: (*nods*) Her future husband, she said, was probably just entering Eton. 45
LADY JOHN: Just like her!
FARNBOROUGH: (*waving the subject away*) No. I wanted to see you about the Secretaryship.
LADY JOHN: You didn't get it, then?
FARNBOROUGH: No. It's the grief of my life. 50
LADY JOHN: Oh, if you don't get one you'll get another.
FARNBOROUGH: But there is only one.
LADY JOHN: Only one vacancy?
FARNBOROUGH: Only one man I'd give my ears to work for.
LADY JOHN: (*smiling*) I remember. 55
FARNBOROUGH: (*quickly*) Do I always talk about Stonor? Well, it's a habit people have got into.
LADY JOHN: I forget, do you know Mr Stonor personally, or (*smiling*) are you just dazzled from afar?
FARNBOROUGH: Oh, I know him. The trouble is he doesn't 60 know me. If he did he'd realise he can't be sure of winning his election without my valuable services.
LADY JOHN: Geoffrey Stonor's re-election is always a foregone conclusion.
FARNBOROUGH: That the great man shares that opinion is 65 precisely his weak point. (*Smiling.*) His only one.
LADY JOHN: You think because the Liberals swept the country the last time—

FARNBOROUGH: How can we be sure any Conservative seat
70   is safe after—(*As* LADY JOHN *smiles and turns to her papers:*)
Forgive me, I know you're not interested in politics *qua*
politics. But this concerns Geoffrey Stonor.

LADY JOHN: And you count on my being interested in him
like all the rest of my sex.

75 FARNBOROUGH: (*leans forward*) Lady John, I've heard the news.

LADY JOHN: What news?

FARNBOROUGH: That your little niece—the Scotch heiress—
is going to become Mrs Geoffrey Stonor.

LADY JOHN: Who told you that?

80 FARNBOROUGH: Please don't mind my knowing.

LADY JOHN: (*visibly perturbed*) She had set her heart upon having a few days with just her family in the secret, before the
flood of congratulations breaks loose.

FARNBOROUGH: Oh, that's all right. I always hear things be-
85   fore other people.

LADY JOHN: Well, I must ask you to be good enough to be
very circumspect. I wouldn't have my niece think that I—

FARNBOROUGH: Oh, of course not.

LADY JOHN: She will be here in an hour.

90 FARNBOROUGH: (*jumping up delighted*) What? Today? The future Mrs Stonor!

LADY JOHN: (*harassed*) Yes. Unfortunately we had one or two
people already asked for the weekend—

FARNBOROUGH: And I go and invite myself to luncheon!
95   Lady John, you can buy me off. I'll promise to remove
myself in five minutes if you'll—

LADY JOHN: No, the penalty is you shall stay and keep the
others amused between church and luncheon, and so
leave me free. (*Takes up the plan.*) Only *remember*—

100 FARNBOROUGH: Wild horses won't get a hint out of me! I
only mentioned it to you because—since we've come
back to live in this part of the world you've been so awfully kind—I thought, I hoped maybe you—you'd put in
a word for me.

105 LADY JOHN: With—?

FARNBOROUGH: With your nephew that is to be. Though I'm
not the slavish satellite people make out, you can't doubt—

LADY JOHN: Oh, I don't doubt. But you know Mr Stonor inspires a similar enthusiasm in a good many young—

110 FARNBOROUGH: They haven't studied the situation as I have.
They don't know what's at stake. They don't go to that
hole Dutfield as I did just to hear his Friday speech.

LADY JOHN: Ah! But you were rewarded. Jean—my niece—
wrote me it was "glorious."

115 FARNBOROUGH: (*judicially*) Well, you know, *I* was disappointed. He's too content just to criticise, just to make his
delicate pungent fun of the men who are grappling—very
inadequately, of course—still *grappling* with the big questions. There's a carrying power (*gets up and faces an imagi-*
120   *nary audience*)—some of Stonor's friends ought to point it
out—there's a driving power in the poorest constructive
policy that makes the most brilliant criticism look barren.

LADY JOHN: (*with good-humoured malice*) Who told you that?

FARNBOROUGH: You think there's nothing in it because *I* say
125   it. But now that he's coming into the family, Lord John or
somebody really ought to point out—Stonor's overdoing
his rôle of magnificent security.

LADY JOHN: I don't see even Lord John offering to instruct
Mr Stonor.

FARNBOROUGH: Believe me, that's just Stonor's danger! No- 130
body saying a word, everybody hoping he's on the point
of adopting some definite line, something strong and
original that's going to fire the public imagination and
bring the Tories back into power.

LADY JOHN: So he will. 135

FARNBOROUGH: (*hotly*) Not if he disappoints meetings—goes
calmly up to town—and leaves the field to the Liberals.

LADY JOHN: When did he do anything like that?

FARNBOROUGH: Yesterday! (*With a harassed air.*) And now that
he's got this other preoccupation— 140

LADY JOHN: You mean—

FARNBOROUGH: Yes, your niece—that spoilt child of Fortune. Of course! (*Stopping suddenly.*) She kept him from
the meeting last night. Well! (*Sits down.*) If that's the effect
she's going to have it's pretty serious! 145

LADY JOHN: (*smiling*) You are!

FARNBOROUGH: I can assure you the election agent's more
so. He's simply tearing his hair.

LADY JOHN: (*more gravely and coming nearer*) How do you
know? 150

FARNBOROUGH: He told me so himself—yesterday. I scraped
acquaintance with the agent just to see if—if—

LADY JOHN: It's not only here that you manœuvre for that
Secretaryship!

FARNBOROUGH: (*confidentially*) You can never tell when your 155
chance might come! That election chap's promised to
keep me posted.

(*The door flies open and* JEAN DUNBARTON *rushes in.*)

JEAN: Aunt Ellen—here I—

LADY JOHN: (*astonished*) My dear child!

(*They embrace. Enter* LORD JOHN *from the garden—a benevolent,*
silver-haired despot of sixty-two.)

LORD JOHN: I thought that was you running up the avenue. 160

(JEAN *greets her uncle warmly, but all the time she and her aunt talk to-*
gether. "How did you get here so early?" "I knew you'd be surprised—
wasn't it clever of me to manage it? I don't deserve all the credit." "But
there isn't any train between—" "Yes, wait till I tell you." "You
walked in the broiling sun—" "No, no." "You must be dead. Why
didn't you telegraph? I ordered the carriage to meet the 1.10. Didn't
you say the 1.10? Yes, I'm sure you did—here's your letter.")

LORD JOHN: (*has shaken hands with* FARNBOROUGH *and speaks*
through the torrent) Now they'll tell each other for ten minutes that she's an hour earlier than we expected.

(LORD JOHN *leads* FARNBOROUGH *towards the garden.*)

FARNBOROUGH: The Freddy Tunbridges said *they* were coming to you this week. 165

LORD JOHN: Yes, they're dawdling through the park with the
Church Brigade.

FARNBOROUGH: Oh! (*With a glance back at* JEAN.) I'll go and
meet them.

(*Exit* FARNBOROUGH.)

LORD JOHN: (*as he turns back*) That discreet young man will 170
get on.

LADY JOHN: (*to* JEAN) But *how* did you get here?

JEAN: (*breathless*) "He" motored me down.

LADY JOHN: Geoffrey Stonor? (JEAN *nods.*) Why, where is he,
175   then?

JEAN: He dropped me at the end of the avenue and went on
  to see a supporter about something.

LORD JOHN: You let him go off like that without—

LADY JOHN: (*taking* JEAN's *two hands*) Just tell me, my child, is
180   it all right?

JEAN: My engagement? (*Radiantly.*) Yes, absolutely.

LADY JOHN: Geoffrey Stonor isn't going to be—a little too
  old for you?

JEAN: (*laughing*) Bless me, am I such a chicken?

185 LADY JOHN: Twenty-four used not to be so young—but it's
  become so.

JEAN: Yes, we don't grow up so quick. (*Gaily.*) But on the
  other hand we *stay* up longer.

LORD JOHN: You've got what's vulgarly called "looks," my
190   dear, and that will help to *keep* you up!

JEAN: (*smiling*) I know what Uncle John's thinking. But I'm
  not the only girl who's been left "what's vulgarly called"
  money.

LORD JOHN: You're the only one of our immediate circle
195   who's been left so beautifully much.

JEAN: Ah, but remember Geoffrey could—everybody *knows*
  he could have married any one in England.

LADY JOHN: (*faintly ironic*) I'm afraid everybody does know
  it—not excepting Mr Stonor.

200 LORD JOHN: Well, how spoilt is the great man?

JEAN: Not the least little bit in the world. You'll see! He so
  wants to know my best-loved relations better. (*Another em-*
  brace.) An orphan has so few belongings, she has to make
  the most of them.

205 LORD JOHN: (*smiling*) Let us hope he'll approve of us on more
  intimate acquaintance.

JEAN: (*firmly*) He will. He's an angel. Why, he gets on with my
  grandfather!

LADY JOHN: *Does* he? (*Teasing.*) You mean to say Mr Geoffrey
210   Stonor isn't just a tiny bit—"superior" about Dissenters.

JEAN: (*stoutly*) Not half as much as Uncle John and all the rest
  of you! My grandfather's been ill again, you know, and
  rather difficult—bless him! (*Radiantly.*) But Geoffrey—
  (*Clasps her hands.*)

215 LADY JOHN: He must have powers of persuasion!—to get that
  old Covenanter to let you come in an abhorred motor
  car—on Sunday, too!

JEAN: (*half whispering*) Grandfather didn't know!

LADY JOHN: Didn't know?

220 JEAN: I honestly meant to come by train. Geoffrey met me on
  my way to the station. We had the most glorious run. Oh,
  Aunt Ellen, we're so happy! (*Embracing her.*) I've so looked
  forward to having you to myself the whole day just to talk
  to you about—

225 LORD JOHN: (*turning away with affected displeasure*) Oh, very
  well—

JEAN: (*catches him affectionately by the arm*) You'd find it dreffly
  dull to hear me talk about Geoffrey the whole blessed day!

LADY JOHN: Well, till luncheon, my dear, you mustn't mind if
230   I—(*To* LORD JOHN, *as she goes to the writing table.*) Miss
  Levering wasn't only tired last night, she was ill.

LORD JOHN: I thought she looked very white.

JEAN: Who is Miss—You don't mean to say there are other
  people?

LADY JOHN: One or two. Your uncle's responsible for asking 235
  that old cynic. St. John Greatorex, and I—

JEAN: (*gravely*) Mr. Greatorex—he's a Radical, isn't he?

LORD JOHN: (*laughing*) Jean! Beginning to "think in parties"!

LADY JOHN: It's very natural now that she should—

JEAN: I only meant it was odd he should be here. Naturally 240
  at my grandfather's—

LORD JOHN: It's all right, my child. Of course we expect now
  that you'll begin to think like Geoffrey Stonor, and to feel
  like Geoffrey Stonor, and to talk like Geoffrey Stonor. And
  quite proper too. 245

JEAN: (*smiling*) Well, if I do think with my husband and feel
  with him—as, of course, I shall—it will surprise me if I
  ever find myself talking a tenth as well—(*Following her un-*
  cle to the French window.) You should have heard him at
  Dutfield—(*Stopping short, delighted.*) Oh! The Freddy Tun- 250
  bridges. What? Not Aunt Lydia! Oh-h! (*Looking back re-*
  proachfully at LADY JOHN, *who makes a discreet motion "I*
  couldn't help it.")

(*Enter the* TUNBRIDGES. MR FREDDY, *of no profession and of inde-*
pendent means. Well-groomed, pleasant-looking; of few words. A "nice
man" who likes "nice women," and has married one of them. MRS
FREDDY *is thirty. An attractive figure, delicate face, intelligent grey*
eyes, over-sensitive mouth, and naturally curling dust-coloured hair.)

MRS FREDDY: What a delightful surprise!

JEAN: (*shaking hands warmly*) I'm so glad. How d'ye do, Mr 255
  Freddy?

(*Enter* LADY JOHN's *sister,* MRS HERIOT—*smart, pompous, fifty*—
followed by FARNBOROUGH.)

MRS HERIOT: My dear Jean! My darling child!

JEAN: How do you do, aunt?

MRS HERIOT: (*sotto voce*) I wasn't surprised. I always prophesied— 260

JEAN: Sh! *Please!*

FARNBOROUGH: We haven't met since you were in short
  skirts. I'm Dick Farnborough.

JEAN: Oh, I remember.

(*They shake hands.*)

MRS FREDDY: (*looking round*) Not down yet—the Elusive 265
  One?

JEAN: Who is the Elusive One?

MRS FREDDY: Lady John's new friend.

LORD JOHN: (*to* JEAN) Oh, I forgot you hadn't seen Miss Levering; such a nice creature! (*To* MRS FREDDY.)—don't you 270
  think?

MRS FREDDY: Of course I do. You're lucky to get her to come
  so often. She won't go to other people.

LADY JOHN: She knows she can rest here.

FREDDY: (*who has joined* LADY JOHN *near the writing table*) What 275
  does she do to tire her?

LADY JOHN: She's been helping my sister and me with a
  scheme of ours.

MRS HERIOT: She certainly knows how to inveigle money
  out of the men. 280

LADY JOHN: It would sound less equivocal, Lydia, if you added that the money is to build baths in our Shelter for Homeless Women.

MRS FREDDY: Homeless women?

285 LADY JOHN: Yes, in the most insanitary part of Soho.

FREDDY: Oh—a—really.

FARNBOROUGH: It doesn't sound quite in Miss Levering's line!

LADY JOHN: My dear boy, you know as little about what's in a woman's line as most men.

290 FREDDY: (*laughing*) Oh, I say!

LORD JOHN: (*indulgently to* MR FREDDY *and* FARNBOROUGH) Philanthropy in a woman like Miss Levering is a form of restlessness. But she's a *nice* creature; all she needs is to get some "nice" fella to marry her.

295 MRS FREDDY: (*laughing as she hangs on her husband's arm*) Yes, a woman needs a balance wheel—if only to keep her from flying back to town on a hot day like this.

LORD JOHN: Who's proposing anything so—

MRS FREDDY: The Elusive One.

300 LORD JOHN: Not Miss—

MRS FREDDY: Yes, before luncheon!

(*Exit* FARNBOROUGH *to the garden.*)

LADY JOHN: She must be in London by this afternoon, she says.

LORD JOHN: What for in the name of—

LADY JOHN: Well, *that* I didn't ask her. But (*consults her watch*)

305 I think I'll just go up and see if she's changed her plans.

(*Exit* LADY JOHN.)

LORD JOHN: Oh, she must be *made* to. Such a nice creature! All she needs—

(*Voices outside. Enter fussily, talking and gesticulating,* ST JOHN GREATOREX, *followed by* MISS LEVERING *and* FARNBOROUGH. GREATOREX *is sixty, wealthy, a county magnate, and Liberal MP. He is square, thick-set, square-bearded. His shining bald pate has two strands of coal-black hair trained across his crown from left ear to right and securely pasted there. He has small, twinkling eyes and a reputation for telling good stories after dinner when ladies have left the room. He is carrying a little book for* MISS LEVERING. *She (parasol over shoulder), an attractive, essentially feminine, and rather "smart" woman of thirty-two, with a somewhat foreign grace; the kind of whom men and women alike say, "What's her story? Why doesn't she marry?"*)

GREATOREX: I protest! Good Lord! what are the women of this country coming to? I *protest* against Miss Levering be-

310 ing carried off to discuss anything so revolting. Bless my soul! what can a woman like you *know* about it?

MISS LEVERING: (*smiling*) Little enough. Good morning.

GREATOREX: (*relieved*) I should think so indeed!

LORD JOHN: (*aside*) You aren't serious about going—

315 GREATOREX: (*waggishly breaking in*) We were so happy out there in the summer-house, weren't we?

MISS LEVERING: Ideally.

GREATOREX: And to be haled out to talk about Public *Sanitation* forsooth! (*Hurries after* MISS LEVERING *as she advances*

320 *to speak to the* FREDDYS *& co.*) Why, God bless my soul, do you realise that's *drains?*

MISS LEVERING: I'm dreadfully afraid it is! (*Holds out her hand for the small book* GREATOREX *is carrying.*)

GREATOREX *returns* MISS LEVERING's *book open; he has been keeping the place with his finger. She opens it and shuts her handkerchief in.*)

GREATOREX: And we in the act of discussing Italian literature! Perhaps you'll tell me that isn't a more savoury topic for a 325 lady.

MISS LEVERING: But for the tramp population less conducive to savouriness, don't you think, than—baths?

GREATOREX: No, I can't understand this morbid interest in vagrants. *You're* much too—leave it to the others. 330

JEAN: What others?

GREATOREX: (*with smiling impertinence*) Oh, the sort of woman who smells of indiarubber. The typical English spinster. (*To* MISS LEVERING.) *You* know—Italy's full of her. She never goes anywhere without a mackintosh and a collapsible 335 bath—rubber. When you look at her, it's borne in upon you that she doesn't only smell of rubber. *She's* rubber too.

LORD JOHN: (*laughing*) This is my niece, Miss Jean Dunbarton, Miss Levering.

JEAN: How do you do? (*They shake hands.*) 340

GREATOREX: (*to* JEAN) I'm sure *you* agree with me.

JEAN: About Miss Levering being too—

GREATOREX: For that sort of thing—*much* too—

MISS LEVERING: What a pity you've exhausted the more eloquent adjectives. 345

GREATOREX: But I haven't!

MISS LEVERING: Well, you can't say to me as you did to Mrs Freddy: "You're too young and too happily married—and too—"(*Glances round smiling at* MRS FREDDY, *who, oblivious, is laughing and talking to her husband and* 350 MRS HERIOT.)

JEAN: For what was Mrs Freddy too happily married and all the rest?

MISS LEVERING: (*lightly*) Mr Greatorex was repudiating the horrid rumour that Mrs Freddy had been speaking in 355 public; about Women's Trade Unions—wasn't that what you said, Mrs Heriot?

LORD JOHN: (*chuckling*) Yes, it isn't made up as carefully as your aunt's parties usually are. Here we've got Greatorex (*takes his arm*) who hates political women, and we've got 360 in that mild and inoffensive looking little lady—(*Motion over his shoulder towards* MRS FREDDY.)

GREATOREX: (*shrinking down stage in comic terror*) You don't mean she's *really*—

JEAN: (*simultaneously and gaily rising*) Oh, and you've got me! 365

LORD JOHN: (*with genial affection*) My dear child, he doesn't hate the charming wives and sweethearts who help to win seats.

(JEAN *makes her uncle a discreet little signal of warning.*)

MISS LEVERING: Mr Greatorex objects only to the unsexed creatures who—a— 370

LORD JOHN: (*hastily to cover up his slip*) Yes, yes, who want to act independently of men.

MISS LEVERING: Vote, and do silly things of that sort.

LORD JOHN: (*with enthusiasm*) Exactly.

375 MRS HERIOT: It will be a long time before we hear any more of *that* nonsense.

JEAN: You mean that rowdy scene in the House of Commons?

MRS HERIOT: Yes. No decent woman will be able to say "Suffrage" without blushing for another generation, thank
380 Heaven!

MISS LEVERING: (*smiling*) Oh? I understood that so little I almost imagined people were more stirred up about it than they'd ever been before.

GREATOREX: (*with a quizzical affectation of gallantry*) Not peo-
385 ple like you.

MISS LEVERING: (*teasingly*) How do you know?

GREATOREX: (*with a start*) God bless my soul!

LORD JOHN: She's saying that only to get a rise out of you.

GREATOREX: Ah, yes, your frocks aren't serious enough.

390 MISS LEVERING: I'm told it's an exploded notion that the Suffrage women are all dowdy and dull.

GREATOREX: Don't you believe it!

MISS LEVERING: Well, of course we know you've been an authority on the subject for—let's see, how many years is it
395 you've kept the House in roars whenever Woman's Rights are mentioned?

GREATOREX: (*flattered but not entirely comfortable*) Oh, as long as I've known anything about politics there have been a few discontented old maids and hungry widows—

400 MISS LEVERING: "A few!" That's really rather forbearing of you, Mr Greatorex. I'm afraid the number of the discontented and the hungry was 96,000—among the mill operatives alone. (*Hastily.*) At least the papers said so, didn't they?

GREATOREX: Oh, don't ask me; that kind of woman doesn't
405 interest me, I'm afraid. Only I am able to point out to the people who lose their heads and seem inclined to treat the phenomenon seriously that there's absolutely nothing new in it. There have been women for the last forty years who haven't had anything more pressing to do than peti-
410 tion Parliament.

MISS LEVERING: (*reflectively*) And that's as far as they've got.

LORD JOHN: (*turning on his heel*) It's as far as they'll ever get.

(*Meets the group coming down.*)

MISS LEVERING: (*chaffing* GREATOREX) Let me see, wasn't a deputation sent to you not long ago? (*Sits*)
415 GREATOREX: H'm! (*Irritably.*) Yes, yes.

MISS LEVERING: (*as though she has just recalled the circumstances*) Oh, yes, I remember. I thought at the time, in my modest way, it was nothing short of heroic of them to go asking audience of their arch opponent.
420 GREATOREX: (*stoutly*) It didn't come off.

MISS LEVERING: (*innocently*) Oh! I thought they insisted on bearding the lion in his den.

GREATOREX: Of course I wasn't going to be bothered with a lot of—
425 MISS LEVERING: You don't mean you refused to go out and face them!

GREATOREX: (*with a comic look of terror*) I wouldn't have done it for worlds. But a friend of mine went and had a look at 'em.
430 MISS LEVERING: (*smiling*) Well, did he get back alive?

GREATOREX: Yes, but he advised me not to go. "You're quite right," he said. "Don't you think of bothering," he said.

"I've looked over the lot," he said, "and there isn't a week-ender among 'em."

JEAN: (*gaily precipitates herself into the conversation*) You remem- 435 ber Mrs Freddy's friend who came to tea here in the winter? (*To* GREATOREX.) He was a member of Parliament too—quite a little young one—he said women would never be respected till they had the vote!

(GREATOREX *snorts, the other men smile and all the women except* MRS HERIOT.)

MRS HERIOT: (*sniffing*) I remember telling him that he was 440 too young to know what he was talking about.

LORD JOHN: Yes, I'm afraid you all sat on the poor gentleman.

LADY JOHN: (*entering*) Oh, *there* you are! (*Greets* MISS LEVER-ING.)

JEAN: It was such fun. He was flat as a pancake when we'd 445 done with him. Aunt Ellen told him with her most distinguished air she didn't want to be "respected."

MRS FREDDY: (*with a laugh of remonstrance*) My *dear* Lady John!

FARNBOROUGH: Quite right! Awful idea to think you're re- 450 *spected!*

MISS LEVERING: (*smiling*) Simply revolting.

LADY JOHN: (*at writing-table*) Now, you frivolous people, go away. We've only got a few minutes to talk over the terms of the late Mr Soper's munificence before the carriage 455 comes for Miss Levering—

MRS FREDDY: (*to* FARNBOROUGH) Did you know she'd got that old horror to give Lady John £8,000 for her charity before he died?

MRS FREDDY: Who got him to? 460

LADY JOHN: Miss Levering. He wouldn't do it for me, but she brought him round.

FREDDY: Yes. Bah-ee Jove! I expect so.

MRS FREDDY: (*turning enthusiastically to her husband*) Isn't she wonderful? 465

LORD JOHN: (*aside*) Nice creature. All she needs is—

(MR *and* MRS FREDDY *and* FARNBOROUGH *stroll off to the garden.* LADY JOHN *is on the far side of the writing-table.* MRS HERIOT *is at the top.* JEAN *and* LORD JOHN *on the left.*)

GREATOREX: (*on divan centre, aside to* MISS LEVERING) Too "wonderful" to waste your time on the wrong people.

MISS LEVERING: I shall waste less of my time after this.

GREATOREX: I'm relieved to hear it. I can't see you wheedling 470 money for shelters and rot of that sort out of retired grocers.

MISS LEVERING: You see, you call it rot. We couldn't have got £8,000 out of *you.*

GREATOREX: (*very low*) I'm not sure.

(MISS LEVERING *looks at him.*)

GREATOREX: If I gave you that much—for your little pro- 475 jects—what would you give me?

MISS LEVERING: (*speaking quietly*) *Soper didn't ask that.*

GREATOREX: (*horrified*) Soper! I should think not!

LORD JOHN: (*turning to* MISS LEVERING) Soper? You, two still talking Soper? How flattered the old beggar'd be! 480

LORD JOHN: (*lower*) Did you hear what Mrs Heriot said about him? "So kind; so munificent—so *vulgar*, poor soul, we couldn't know him in London—*but we shall meet him in heaven.*"

(GREATOREX *and* LORD JOHN *go off laughing.*)

485 LADY JOHN: (*to* MISS LEVERING) Sit over there, my dear. (*Indicating chair in front of the writing table.*) You needn't stay, Jean. This won't interest you.

MISS LEVERING: (*in the tone of one agreeing*) It's only an effort to meet the greatest evil in the world.

490 JEAN: (*pausing as she's following the others*) What do you call the greatest evil in the world?

(*Looks pass between* MRS HERIOT *and* LADY JOHN.)

MISS LEVERING: (*without emphasis*) The helplessness of women.

(JEAN *stands still.*)

LADY JOHN: (*rising and putting her arm about the girl's shoulder*)
495 Jean, darling, I know you can think of nothing but (*aside*) *him*—so just go and—

JEAN: (*brightly*) Indeed, indeed, I can think of everything better than I ever did before. He has lit up everything for me—made everything vivider, more—more significant.

500 MISS LEVERING: (*turning round*) Who has?

JEAN: Oh, yes, I don't care about other things less but a thousand times more.

LADY JOHN: You *are* in love.

MISS LEVERING: Oh, that's it! (*Smiling at* JEAN.) I congratulate
505 you.

LADY JOHN: (*returning to the outspread plan*) Well—*this,* you see, obviates the difficulty you raised.

MISS LEVERING: Yes, quite.

MRS HERIOT: But it's going to cost a great deal more.

510 MISS LEVERING: It's worth it.

MRS HERIOT: We'll have nothing left for the organ at St Pilgrim's.

LADY JOHN: My dear Lydia, we're putting the organ aside.

MRS HERIOT: (*with asperity*) We can't afford to "put aside" the
515 elevating effect of music.

LADY JOHN: What we must make for, first, is the cheap and humanely conducted lodging-house.

MRS HERIOT: There are several of those already, but poor St Pilgrim's—

520 MISS LEVERING: There are none for the poorest women.

LADY JOHN: No, even the excellent Soper was for multiplying Rowton Houses. You can never get men to realise—you can't always get women—

MISS LEVERING: It's the work least able to wait.

525 MRS HERIOT: I don't agree with you, and I happen to have spent a great deal of my life in works of charity.

MISS LEVERING: Ah, then you'll be interested in the girl I saw dying in a Tramp Ward a little while ago. *Glad* her cough was worse—only she mustn't die before her father. Two
530 reasons. Nobody but her to keep the old man out of the workhouse—and "father is so proud." If she died first, he would starve; worst of all he might hear what had happened up in London to his girl.

MRS HERIOT: She didn't say, I suppose, how she happened to
535 fall so low.

MISS LEVERING: Yes, she had been in service. She lost the train back one Sunday night and was too terrified of her employer to dare ring him up after hours. The wrong person found her crying on the platform.

540 MRS HERIOT: She should have gone to one of the Friendly Societies.

MISS LEVERING: At eleven at night?

MRS HERIOT: And there are the Rescue Leagues. I myself have been connected with one for twenty years—

545 MISS LEVERING: (*reflectively*) "Twenty years!" Always arriving "after the train's gone"—after the girl and the Wrong Person have got to the journey's end.

(MRS HERIOT's *eyes flash.*)

JEAN: Where is she now?

LADY JOHN: Never mind.

550 MISS LEVERING: Two nights ago she was waiting at a street corner in the rain.

MRS HERIOT: Near a public-house, I suppose.

MISS LEVERING: Yes, a sort of "public-house." She was plainly dying—she was told she shouldn't be out in the rain. "I
555 mustn't go in yet," she said. "*This* is what he gave me," and she began to cry. In her hand were two pennies silvered over to look like half-crowns.

MRS HERIOT: I don't believe that story. It's just the sort of thing some sensation-monger trumps up—now, who tells
560 you such—

MISS LEVERING: Several credible people. I didn't believe them till—

JEAN: Till—?

MISS LEVERING: Till last week I saw for myself.

565 LADY JOHN: *Saw?* Where?

MISS LEVERING: In a low lodging-house not a hundred yards from the church you want a new organ for.

MRS HERIOT: How did *you* happen to be there?

MISS LEVERING: I was on a pilgrimage.

570 JEAN: A pilgrimage?

MISS LEVERING: Into the Underworld.

LADY JOHN: *You* went?

JEAN: How *could* you?

MISS LEVERING: I put on an old gown and a tawdry hat—
575 (*Turns to* LADY JOHN.) You'll never know how many things are hidden from a woman in good clothes. The bold, free look of a man at a woman he believes to be destitute—you must *feel* that look on you before you can understand—a good half of history.

580 MRS HERIOT: (*rises*) Jean!—

JEAN: But where did you go—dressed like that?

MISS LEVERING: Down among the homeless women—on a wet night looking for shelter.

LADY JOHN: (*hastily*) No wonder you've been ill.

585 JEAN: (*under her breath*) And it's like that?

MISS LEVERING: No.

JEAN: No?

MISS LEVERING: It's so much worse I dare not tell about it—even if you weren't here I couldn't.

590 MRS HERIOT: (*to* JEAN) You needn't suppose, darling, that those wretched creatures feel it as we would.

MISS LEVERING: The girls who need shelter and work aren't all serving-maids.

MRS HERIOT: (*with an involuntary flash*) We know that all the
595 women who—*make mistakes* aren't.
MISS LEVERING: (*steadily*) That is why *every* woman ought to
take an interest in this—every girl too.
JEAN: Yes—oh, yes!
LADY JOHN: (*simultaneously*)   No. This is a matter for
600 us older—
MRS HERIOT: (*with an air of sly challenge*) Or for a person who
has some special knowledge. (*Significantly.*) We can't pretend to have access to such sources of information as Miss
Levering.
605 MISS LEVERING: (*meeting* MRS HERIOT's *eye steadily*) Yes, for I
can give you access. As you seem to think, I have some
firsthand knowledge about homeless girls.
LADY JOHN: (*cheerfully turning it aside*) Well, my dear, it will all
come in convenient. (*Tapping the plan.*)
610 MISS LEVERING: It once happened to me to take offence at an
ugly thing that was going on under my father's roof. Oh,
years ago! I was an impulsive girl. I turned my back on my
father's house—
LADY JOHN: (*for* JEAN's *benefit*) That was ill-advised.
615 MRS HERIOT: Of course, if a girl does *that*—
MISS LEVERING: That was what all my relations said (*with a
glance at* JEAN), and I couldn't explain.
JEAN: Not to your mother?
MISS LEVERING: She was dead. I went to London to a small
620 hotel and tried to find employment. I wandered about all
day and every day from agency to agency. I was supposed
to be educated. I'd been brought up partly in Paris; I could
play several instruments, and sing little songs in four different tongues. (*Slight pause.*)
625 JEAN: Did nobody want you to teach French or sing the little songs?
MISS LEVERING: The heads of schools thought me too young.
There were people ready to listen to my singing, but the
terms—they were too hard. Soon my money was gone. I
630 began to pawn my trinkets. *They* went.
JEAN: And still no work?
MISS LEVERING: No; but by that time I had some real educa-
tion—an unpaid hotel bill, and not a shilling in the world.
(*Slight pause.*) Some girls think it hardship to have to earn
635 their living. The horror is not to be allowed to—
JEAN: (*bending forward*) What happened?
LADY JOHN: (*rises*) My dear (*to* MISS LEVERING) have your
things been sent down? Are you quite ready?
MISS LEVERING: Yes, all but my hat.
640 JEAN: Well?
MISS LEVERING: Well, by chance I met a friend of my family.
JEAN: That was lucky.
MISS LEVERING: I thought so. He was nearly ten years older
than I. He said he wanted to help me. (*Pause.*)
645 JEAN: And didn't he?

(LADY JOHN *lays her hand on* MISS LEVERING's *shoulder.*)

MISS LEVERING: Perhaps after all he did. (*With sudden change of
tone.*) Why do I waste time over myself? I belonged to the
little class of armed women. My body wasn't born weak,
and my spirit wasn't broken by the *habit* of slavery. But, as
650 Mrs Heriot was kind enough to hint, I do know something
about the possible fate of homeless girls. I found there were

pleasant parks, museums, free libraries in our great rich
London—and not one single place where destitute women
can be sure of work that isn't killing or food that isn't worse
than prison fare. That's why women ought not to sleep o' 655
nights till this Shelter stands spreading out wide arms.
JEAN: No, no—
MRS HERIOT: (*gathering up her gloves, fan, prayer-book, etc.*) Even
when it's built—you'll see! Many of those creatures will
prefer the life they lead. They *like* it.   660
MISS LEVERING: A woman told me—one of the sort that
knows—told me many of them "like it" so much that they
are indifferent to the risk of being sent to prison. "*It gives
them a rest,*" she said.
LADY JOHN: A rest!   665

(MISS LEVERING *glances at the clock as she rises to go upstairs.*)

(LADY JOHN *and* MRS HERIOT *bend their heads over the plan,
covertly talking.*)

JEAN: (*intercepting* MISS LEVERING) I want to begin to understand something of—I'm horribly ignorant.
MISS LEVERING: (*Looks at her searchingly*) I'm a rather busy
person—
JEAN: (*interrupting*) I have quite a special reason for wanting 670
not to be ignorant. (*Impulsively.*) I'll go to town tomorrow,
if you'll come and lunch with me.
MISS LEVERING: Thank you—I (*catches* MRS HERIOT's *eye*)—I
must go and put my hat on.

(*Exit upstairs.*)

MRS HERIOT: (*aside*) How little she minds all these horrors!   675
LADY JOHN: They turn me cold. Ugh! (*Rising, harassed.*) I
wonder if she's signed the visitors' book!
MRS HERIOT: For all her Shelter schemes, she's a hard woman.
JEAN: Miss Levering is?
MRS HERIOT: Oh, of course *you* won't think so. She has an- 680
gled very adroitly for your sympathy.
JEAN: She doesn't look hard.
LADY JOHN: (*glancing at* JEAN *and taking alarm*) I'm not sure
but what she does. Her mouth—always like this . . . as if
she were holding back something by main force!   685
MRS HERIOT: (*half under her breath*) Well, so she is.

(*Exit* LADY JOHN *into the lobby to look at the visitors' book.*)

JEAN: Why haven't I seen her before?
MRS HERIOT: Oh, she's lived abroad. (*Debating with herself.*)
You don't know about her, I suppose?
JEAN: I don't know how Aunt Ellen came to know her.   690
MRS HERIOT: That was my doing. But I didn't bargain for her
being introduced to you.
JEAN: She seems to go everywhere. And why shouldn't she?
MRS HERIOT: (*quickly*) You mustn't ask her to Eaton Square.
JEAN: I have.   695
MRS HERIOT: Then you'll have to get out of it.
JEAN: (*with a stubborn look*) I must have a reason. And a very
good reason.
MRS HERIOT: Well, it's not a thing I should have preferred to
tell you, but I know how difficult you are to guide . . . so 700
I suppose you'll have to know. (*Lowering her voice.*) It was

ten or twelve years ago. I found her horribly ill in a lonely Welsh farmhouse. We had taken the Manor for that August. The farmer's wife was frightened, and begged me to
705 go and see what I thought. I soon saw how it was—I thought she was dying.

JEAN: *Dying!* What was the—

MRS HERIOT: I got no more out of her than the farmer's wife did. She had had no letters. There had been no one to see
710 her except a man down from London, a shady-looking doctor—nameless, of course. And then this result. The farmer and his wife, highly respectable people, were incensed. They were for turning the girl out.

JEAN: Oh! but—

715 MRS HERIOT: Yes. Pitiless some of these people are! I insisted they should treat the girl humanely, and we became friends . . . that is, "sort of." In spite of all I did for her—

JEAN: What did you do?

MRS HERIOT: I—I've told you, and I lent her money. No
720 small sum either.

JEAN: Has she never paid it back?

MRS HERIOT: Oh, yes, after a time. But I *always* kept her secret—as much as I knew of it.

JEAN: But you've been telling me!

725 MRS HERIOT: That was my duty—and I *never* had her full confidence.

JEAN: Wasn't it natural she—

MRS HERIOT: Well, all things considered, she might have wanted to tell me who was responsible.

730 JEAN: Oh! Aunt Lydia!

MRS HERIOT: All she ever said was that she was ashamed— (*losing her temper and her fine feeling for the innocence of her auditor*)— ashamed that she "hadn't had the courage to resist"—not the original temptation but the pressure brought to bear on her
735 "not to go through with it," as she said.

JEAN: (*wrinkling her brows*) You are being so delicate—I'm not sure I understand.

MRS HERIOT: (*irritably*) The only thing you need understand is that she's not a desirable companion for a young girl.

(*Pause.*)

740 JEAN: When did you see her after—after—

MRS HERIOT: (*with a slight grimace*) I met her last winter at the Bishop's. (*Hurriedly.*) She's a connection of his wife's. They'd got her to help with some of their work. Then she took hold of ours. Your aunt and uncle are quite foolish
745 about her, and I'm debarred from taking any steps, at least till the Shelter is out of hand.

JEAN: I do rather wonder she can bring herself to talk about— the unfortunate women of the world.

MRS HERIOT: The effrontery of it!

750 JEAN: Or . . . the courage! (*Puts her hand up to her throat as if the sentence had caught there.*)

MRS HERIOT: Even presumes to set *me* right! Of course I don't *mind* in the least, poor soul . . . but I feel I owe it to your dead mother to tell you about her, especially as
755 you're old enough now to know something about life—

JEAN: (*slowly*) —and since a girl needn't be very old to suffer for her ignorance. (*Moves a little away.*) I *felt* she was rather wonderful.

MRS HERIOT: Wonderful!

JEAN: (*pausing*) . . . To have lived through *that* when she was 760 . . . how old?

MRS HERIOT: (*rising*) Oh, nineteen or thereabouts.

JEAN: Five years younger than I. To be abandoned and to come out of it like this!

MRS HERIOT: (*laying her hand on the girl's shoulder*) It was too 765 bad to have to tell you such a sordid story today of all days.

JEAN: It is a very terrible story, but this wasn't a bad time. I feel very sorry today for women who aren't happy.

(*Motor horn heard faintly.*)

(*Jumping up.*) That's Geoffrey!

MRS HERIOT: Mr Stonor! What makes you think . . .? 770

JEAN: Yes, yes. I'm sure, I'm sure—

(*Checks herself as she is flying off. Turns and sees* LORD JOHN *entering from the garden.*)

(*Motor horn louder.*)

LORD JOHN: Who do you think is motoring up the drive?

JEAN: (*catching hold of him*) Oh, dear! How am I ever going to be able to behave like a girl who isn't engaged to the only man in the world worth marrying? 775

MRS HERIOT: You were expecting Mr Stonor all the time!

JEAN: He promised he'd come to luncheon if it was humanly possible; but I was afraid to tell you for fear he'd be prevented.

LORD JOHN: (*laughing as he crosses to the lobby*) You felt we 780 couldn't have borne the disappointment.

JEAN: I felt I couldn't.

(*The lobby door opens.* LADY JOHN *appears radiant, followed by a tall figure in a dustcoat, etc., no goggles. He has straight, firm features, a little blunt; fair skin, high coloured; fine, straight hair, very fair; grey eyes, set somewhat prominently and heavy when not interested; lips full, but firmly moulded.* GEOFFREY STONOR *is heavier than a man of forty should be, but otherwise in the pink of physical condition. The* FOOTMAN *stands waiting to help him off with his motor coat.*)

LADY JOHN: Here's an agreeable surprise!

(JEAN *has gone forward only a step, and stands smiling at the approaching figure.*)

LORD JOHN: How do you do? (*As he comes between them and briskly shakes hands with* STONOR.) 785

(FARNBOROUGH *appears at the French window.*)

FARNBOROUGH: Yes, by Jove! (*Turning to the others clustered round the window.*) What gigantic luck!

(*Those outside crane and glance, and then elaborately turn their backs and pretend to be talking among themselves, but betray as far as manners permit the enormous sensation the arrival has created.*)

STONOR: How do you do?

(*Shakes hands with* MRS HERIOT, *who has rushed up to him with both hers outstretched. He crosses to* JEAN, *who meets him half way; they shake hands, smiling into each other's eyes.*)

JEAN: Such a long time since we met!

790 LORD JOHN: (*to* STONOR) You're growing very enterprising. I could hardly believe my ears when I heard you'd motored all the way from town to see a supporter on Sunday.

STONOR: I don't know how we covered the ground in the old days. (*To* LADY JOHN.) It's no use to stand for your bor-
795 ough any more. The American, you know, he "runs" for Congress. By and by we shall all be flying after the thing we want. (*Smiles at* JEAN.)

JEAN: Sh! (*Smiles and then glances over her shoulder and speaks low.*) All sorts of irrelevant people here.

800 FARNBOROUGH: (*unable to resist the temptation, comes forward*) How do you do, Mr Stonor?

STONOR: Oh—how d'you do.

FARNBOROUGH: Some of them were arguing in the smoking-room last night whether it didn't hurt a man's chances go-
805 ing about in a motor.

LORD JOHN: Yes, we've been hearing a lot of stories about the unpopularity of motor cars—among the class that hasn't got 'em, of course. What do you say?

LADY JOHN: I'm sure you gain more votes by being able to
810 reach so many more of your constituency than we used—

STONOR: Well, I don't know—I've sometimes wondered whether the charm of our presence wasn't counterbalanced by the way we tear about smothering our fellow-beings in dust and running down their pigs and chickens,
815 not to speak of their children.

LORD JOHN: (*anxiously*) What on the whole are the prospects?

(FARNBOROUGH *cranes forward.*)

STONOR: (*gravely*) We shall have to work harder than we realised.

FARNBOROUGH: Ah! (*Retires towards group.*)

820 JEAN: (*in a half-aside as she slips her arm in her uncle's and smiles at* GEOFFREY) He says he believes I'll be able to make a real difference to his chances. Isn't it angelic of him?

STONOR: (*in a jocular tone*) Angelic? Macchiavelian. I pin all my hopes on your being able to counteract the pernicious
825 influence of my opponent's glib wife.

JEAN: You want me to have a *real* share in it all, don't you, Geoffrey?

STONOR: (*smiling into her eyes*) Of course I do.

(FARNBOROUGH *drops down again on pretence of talking to* MRS HERIOT.)

LORD JOHN: I don't gather you're altogether sanguine. Any
830 complication?

(JEAN *and* LADY JOHN *stand close together, the girl radiant, following* STONOR *with her eyes and whispering to the sympathetic elder woman.*)

STONOR: Well, (*taking Sunday paper out of pocket*) there's this agitation about the Woman Question. Oddly enough, it seems likely to affect the issue.

LORD JOHN: Why should it? Can't you do what the other
835 four hundred have done?

STONOR: (*laughs*) Easily. But, you see, the mere fact that four hundred and twenty members have been worried into promising support—and then once in the House have let the matter severely alone—

840 LORD JOHN: (*to* STONOR) Let it alone! Bless my soul, I should think so indeed.

STONOR: Of course. Only it's a device that's somewhat worn.

(*Enter* MISS LEVERING, *with hat on; gloves and veil in her hand.*)

LORD JOHN: Still if they think they're getting a future Cabinet Minister on their side—

STONOR: . . . it will be sufficiently embarassing for the Cabi-
845 net Minister.

(STONOR *turns to speak to* JEAN. *He stops dead seeing* MISS LEVERING.)

JEAN: (*smiling*) You know one another?

MISS LEVERING: (*looking at* STONOR *with intentness but quite calmly*) Everybody in this part of the world knows Mr Stonor, but he doesn't know me. 850

LORD JOHN: Miss Levering.

(*They bow.*)

(*Enter* GREATOREX, *sidling in with an air of giving* MRS FREDDY *a wide berth.*)

JEAN: (*to* MISS LEVERING *with artless enthusiasm*) Oh, have you been hearing him speak?

MISS LEVERING: Yes, I was visiting some relations near Dut-field. They took me to hear you. 855

STONOR: Oh—the night the Suffragettes made their customary row.

MISS LEVERING: The night they asked you—

STONOR: (*flying at the first chance of distraction, shakes hands with* MRS FREDDY) Well, Mrs Freddy, what do you think of your 860 friends now?

MRS FREDDY: My friends?

STONOR: (*offering her the Sunday paper*) Yes, the disorderly women.

MRS FREDDY: (*with dignity*) They are not my friends, but I 865 don't think you must call them—

STONOR: Why not? (*Laughs.*) I can forgive them for worrying the late Government. But they *are* disorderly.

MISS LEVERING: (*quietly*) Isn't the phrase consecrated to a different class? 870

GREATOREX: (*who has got hold of the Sunday paper*) He's perfectly right. How do you do? Disorderly women! That's what they are!

FARNBOROUGH: (*reading over his shoulder*) Ought to be locked up! Every one of 'em. 875

GREATOREX: (*assenting angrily*) Public nuisances! Going about with dog whips and spitting in policemen's faces.

FREDDY: (*with a harassed air*) I wonder if they did spit?

GREATOREX: (*exulting*) Of course they did.

MRS FREDDY: (*turns on him*) You're no authority on what they 880 do. *You* run away.

GREATOREX: (*trying to turn the laugh*) Run away? Yes. (*Backing a few paces.*) And if ever I muster up courage to come back, it will be to vote for better manners in public life, not worse than we have already. 885

MRS FREDDY: (*meekly*) So should I. Don't think that *I* defend the Suffragette methods.

JEAN: (*with cheerful curiosity*) Still, you *are* an advocate of the Suffrage, aren't you?

890 MRS FREDDY: *Here?* (*Shrugs.*) I don't beat the air.

GREATOREX: (*mocking*) Only policemen.

MRS FREDDY: (*plaintively*) If you cared to know the attitude of the real workers in the reform, you might have noticed in any paper last week we lost no time in dissociating our-

895 selves from the little group of hysterical—(*Catches her husband's eye, and instantly checks her flow of words.*)

MRS HERIOT: They have lowered the whole sex in the eyes of the entire world.

JEAN: (*joining* GEOFFREY STONOR) I can't quite see what they

900 want—those Suffragettes.

GREATOREX: Notoriety.

FARNBOROUGH: What they want? A good thrashin'—that's what I'd give 'em.

MRS HERIOT: (*murmurs*) Spirited fellow!

905 LORD JOHN: Well, there's one sure thing—they've dished their goose. (GREATOREX *chuckles, still reading the account.*) I believe these silly scenes are a pure joy to you.

GREATOREX: Final death-blow to the whole silly business!

JEAN: (*mystified, looking from one to the other*) The Suffragettes

910 don't seem to *know* they're dead.

GREATOREX: They still keep up a sort of death-rattle. But they've done for themselves.

JEAN: (*clasping her hands with fervour*) Oh, I hope they'll last till the election's over.

915 FARNBOROUGH: (*stares*) Why?

JEAN: Oh, we want them to get the working man to—(*stumbling and a little confused*)—to vote for . . . the Conservative candidate. Isn't that so?

(*Looking round for help. General laughter.*)

LORD JOHN: Fancy, Jean—!

920 GREATOREX: The working man's a good deal of an ass, but even he won't listen to—

JEAN: (*again appealing to the silent* STONOR) But he *does* listen like anything! I asked why there were so few at the Long Mitcham meeting, and I was told, 'Oh, they've all gone to

925 hear Miss—'

STONOR: Just for a lark, that was.

LORD JOHN: It has no real effect on the vote.

GREATOREX: Not the smallest.

JEAN: (*wide-eyed to* STONOR) Why, I thought you said—

930 STONOR: (*hastily, rubbing his hand over the lower part of his face and speaking quickly*) I've a notion a little soap and water wouldn't do me any harm.

LORD JOHN: I'll take you up. You know Freddy Tunbridge.

(STONOR *pauses to shake hands. Exeunt all three.*)

JEAN: (*perplexed, as* STONOR *turns away, says to* GREATOREX)

935 Well, if women are of no importance in politics, it isn't for the reason you gave. There is now and then a weekender among them.

GREATOREX: (*shuffles about uneasily*) Hm—Hm. (*Finds himself near* MRS FREDDY.) Lord! The perils that beset the feet of

940 man! (*With an air of comic caution, moves away, left.*)

JEAN: (*to* FARNBOROUGH, *aside, laughing*) Why does he behave like that?

FARNBOROUGH: His moral sense is shocked.

JEAN: Why, I saw him and Mrs Freddy together at the French

945 Play the other night—as thick as thieves.

MISS LEVERING: Ah, that was before he knew her revolting views.

JEAN: What revolting views?

GREATOREX: Sh! Sunday.

(*As* GREATOREX *sidles cautiously further away.*)

JEAN: (*laughing in spite of herself*) I can't believe women are so 950 helpless when I see men so afraid of them.

GREATOREX: The great mistake was in teaching them to read and write.

JEAN: (*over* MISS LEVERING'*s shoulder, whispers*) Say something.

MISS LEVERING: (*to* GREATOREX, *smiling*) Oh no, that wasn't 955 the worst mistake.

GREATOREX: Yes, it was.

MISS LEVERING: No. Believe me. The mistake was in letting women learn to talk.

GREATOREX: Ah! (*Wheels about with sudden rapture.*) I see now 960 what's to be the next great reform.

MISS LEVERING: (*holding up the little volume*) When women are all dumb, no more discussions of the 'Paradiso.'

GREATOREX: (*with a gesture of mock rapture*) The thing itself! (*Aside.*) That's a great deal better than talking about it, as 965 I'm sure *you* know.

MISS LEVERING: Why do you think I know?

GREATOREX: Only the plain women are in any doubt.

(JEAN *joins* MISS LEVERING.)

GREATOREX: Wait for me, Farnborough. I cannot go about unprotected. 970

(*Exeunt* FARNBOROUGH *and* GREATOREX.)

MRS FREDDY: It's true what that old cynic says. The scene in the House has put back the reform a generation.

JEAN: I wish I'd been there.

MRS FREDDY: I *was.*

JEAN: Oh, was it like the papers said? 975

MRS FREDDY: Worse. I've never been so moved in public. No tragedy, no great opera ever gripped an audience as the situation in the House did that night. There we all sat breathless—with everything more favourable to us than it had been within the memory of women. Another five 980 minutes and the Resolution would have passed. Then . . . all in a moment—

LORD JOHN: (*to* MRS HERIOT) Listen—they're talking about the female hooligans.

MRS HERIOT: No, thank you! (*Sits apart with the "Church* 985 *Times."*)

MRS FREDDY: (*excitedly*) All in a moment a horrible dingy little flag was poked through the grille of the Woman's Gallery—cries—insults—scuffling—the police—the ig-nominious turning out of the women—*us* as well as the— 990 Oh, I can't *think* of it without—(*Jumps up and walks to and fro. Pauses.*) Then the next morning! The people gloating. Our friends antagonised—people who were wavering—nearly won over—all thrown back—heart breaking! Even my husband! Freddy's been an angel about letting me take 995 my share when I felt I must—but of course I've always known he doesn't really like it. It makes him shy. I'm sure it gives him a horrid twist inside when he sees my name

among the speakers on the placards. But he's always been
an angel about it before this. After the disgraceful scene he
said, "It just shows how unfit women are for any sort of
coherent thinking or concerted action."

JEAN: To think that it should be women who've given the
Cause the worst blow it ever had!

MRS FREDDY: The work of forty years destroyed in five minutes!

JEAN: They must have felt pretty sick when they woke up the
next morning—the Suffragettes.

MRS FREDDY: I don't waste any sympathy on *them*. I'm thinking of the penalty *all* women have to pay because a handful of hysterical—

JEAN: Still I think I'm sorry for them. It must be dreadful to
find you've done such a lot of harm to the thing you care
most about in the world.

MISS LEVERING: Do you picture the Suffragettes sitting in
sackcloth?

MRS FREDDY: Well, they can't help realising *now* what they've
done.

MISS LEVERING: (*quietly*) Isn't it just possible they realise
they've waked up interest in the Woman Question so that
it's advertised in every paper and discussed in every house
from Land's End to John O'Groats? Don't you think *they*
know there's been more said and written about it in these
ten days since the scene, than in the ten years before it?

MRS FREDDY: You aren't saying you think it was a good way
to get what they wanted?

MISS LEVERING: (*shrugs*) I'm only pointing out that it seems
not such a bad way to get it known they *do* want something—and (*smiling*) "want it bad."

JEAN: (*getting up*) Didn't Mr Greatorex say women had been
politely petitioning Parliament for forty years?

MISS LEVERING: And men have only laughed.

JEAN: But they'd come round. (*She looks from one to the other.*)
Mrs Tunbridge says, before that horrid scene, everything
was favourable at last.

MISS LEVERING: At last? Hadn't it been just as "favourable"
before?

MRS FREDDY: No. We'd never had so many members pledged
to our side.

MISS LEVERING: I thought I'd heard somebody say the Bill
had got as far as that, time and time again.

JEAN: Oh no. Surely not—

MRS FREDDY: (*reluctantly*) Y—yes. This was only a Resolution.
The Bill passed a second reading thirty-seven years ago.

JEAN: (*with wide eyes*) And what difference did it make?

MISS LEVERING: The men laughed rather louder.

MRS FREDDY: Oh, it's got as far as a second reading several
times—but we never had so many friends in the House
before—

MISS LEVERING: (*with a faint smile*) "Friends!"

JEAN: Why do you say it like that?

MISS LEVERING: Perhaps because I was thinking of a funny
story—he said it was funny—a Liberal Whip told me the
other day. A Radical Member went out of the House after
his speech in favour of the Woman's Bill, and as he
came back half an hour later, he heard some Members
talking in the Lobby about the astonishing number who
were going to vote for the measure. And the Friend of
Woman dropped his jaw and clutched the man next to

him: "My God!" he said, "you don't mean to say they're
going to give it to them!"

JEAN: Oh!

MRS FREDDY: You don't think all men in Parliament are like
that!

MISS LEVERING: I don't think all men are burglars, but I lock
my doors.

JEAN: (*below her breath*) You think that night of the scene—
you think the men didn't *mean* to play fair?

MISS LEVERING: (*her coolness in contrast to the excitement of the
others*) Didn't the women sit quiet till ten minutes to closing time?

JEAN: Ten minutes to settle a question like that!

MISS LEVERING: (*quietly to* MRS FREDDY) Couldn't you see the
men were at their old game?

LADY JOHN: (*coming forward*) You think they were just putting
off the issue till it was too late?

MISS LEVERING: (*in a detached tone*) I wasn't there, but I haven't
heard anybody deny that the women waited till ten minutes to eleven. Then they discovered the policeman who'd
been sent up at the psychological moment to the back of
the gallery. Then, I'm told, when the women saw they
were betrayed once more, they utilised the few minutes
left, to impress on the country at large the fact of their demands—did it in the only way left them. (*Sits leaning forward reflectively smiling, chin in hand.*) It does rather look to
the outsider as if the well-behaved women had worked for
forty years and made less impression on the world then
those fiery young women made in five minutes.

MRS FREDDY: Oh, come, be fair!

MISS LEVERING: Well, you must admit that, next day, every
newspaper reader in Europe and America knew there
were women in England in such dead earnest about the
Suffrage that the men had stopped laughing at last, and
turned them out of the House. Men even advertised how
little they appreciated the fun by sending the women to
gaol in pretty sober earnest. And all the world was talking
about it.

(MRS HERIOT *lays down the "Church Times" and joins the others.*)

LADY JOHN: I have noticed, whenever the men aren't there,
the women sit and discuss that scene.

JEAN: (*cheerfully*) *I* shan't have to wait till the men are gone.
(*Leans over* LADY JOHN's *shoulder and says half aside*) He's in
sympathy.

LADY JOHN: How do you know?

JEAN: He told the interrupting women so.

(MRS FREDDY *looks mystified. The others smile.*)

LADY JOHN: Oh!

(MR FREDDY *and* LORD JOHN *appear by the door they went out
of. They stop to talk.*)

MRS FREDDY: Here's Freddy! (*Lower, hastily to* MISS LEVERING)
You're judging from the outside. Those of us who have
been working for years—we all realise it was a perfectly
lunatic proceeding. Why, *think!* The only chance of our
getting what we want is by *winning over* the men. (*Her
watchful eye, leaving her husband for a moment, catches* MISS
LEVERING's *little involuntary gesture.*) What's the matter?

MISS LEVERING: "Winning over the men" has been the woman's way for centuries. Do you think the result should make us proud of our policy? Yes? Then go and walk in Piccadilly at midnight. (*The older women glance at* JEAN.) No, I forgot—

MRS HERIOT: (*with majesty*) Yes, it's not the first time you've forgotten.

MISS LEVERING: I forgot the magistrate's ruling. He said no decent woman had any business to be in London's main thoroughfare at night unless she has *a man with her.* I heard that in Nine Elms, too. "You're obliged to take up with a chap!" was what the woman said.

MRS HERIOT: (*rising*) Jean! Come!

(*She takes* JEAN *by her arm and draws her to the window, where she signals* GREATOREX *and* FARNBOROUGH. MRS FREDDY *joins her husband and* LORD JOHN.)

LADY JOHN: (*kindly, aside to* MISS LEVERING) My dear, I think Lydia Heriot's right. We oughtn't to do anything or *say* anything to encourage this ferment of feminism, and I'll tell you why: it's likely to bring a very terrible thing in its train.

MISS LEVERING: What terrible thing?

LADY JOHN: Sex antagonism.

MISS LEVERING: (*rising*) It's here.

LADY JOHN: (*very gravely*) Don't say that.

(JEAN *has quietly disengaged herself from* MRS HERIOT, *and the group at the window returns and stands behind* LADY JOHN, *looking up into* MISS LEVERING'*s face.*)

MISS LEVERING: (*to* LADY JOHN) You're so conscious it's here, you're afraid to have it mentioned.

LADY JOHN: (*turning and seeing* JEAN. *Rising hastily*) If it's here, it is the fault of those women agitators.

MISS LEVERING: (*gently*) No woman *begins* that way. (*Leans forward with clasped hands looking into vacancy.*) Every woman's in a state of natural subjection (*smiles at* JEAN)— no, I'd rather say allegiance to her idea of romance and her hope of motherhood. They're embodied for her in man. They're the strongest things in life—till man kills them. (*Rousing herself and looking into* LADY JOHN'*s face.*) Let's be fair. Each woman knows why that allegiance died.

(LADY JOHN *turns hastily, sees* LORD JOHN *coming down with* MR FREDDY *and meets them at the foot of the stairs.* MISS LEVERING *has turned to the table looking for her gloves, etc., among the papers; unconsciously drops the handkerchief she had in her little book.*)

JEAN: (*in a low voice to* MISS LEVERING) All this talk against the wicked Suffragettes—it makes me want to go and hear what they've got to say for themselves.

MISS LEVERING: (*smiling with a noncommittal air as she finds the veil she's been searching for*) Well, they're holding a meeting in Trafalgar Square at three o'clock.

JEAN: This afternoon? But that's no use to people out of town—Unless I could invent some excuse . . .

LORD JOHN: (*benevolently*) Still talking over the Shelter plans?

MISS LEVERING: No. We left the Shelter some time ago.

LORD JOHN: (*to* JEAN) Then what's all the chatterment about?

(JEAN, *a little confused, looks at* MISS LEVERING.)

MISS LEVERING: The latest thing in veils. (*Ties hers round her hat.*)

GREATOREX: The invincible frivolity of woman!

LORD JOHN: (*genially*) Don't scold them. It's a very proper tonic.

MISS LEVERING: (*whimsically*) Oh, I was afraid you'd despise us for it.

BOTH MEN: (*with condescension*) Not at all—not at all.

JEAN: (*to* MISS LEVERING *as* FOOTMAN *appears*) Oh, they're coming for you. Don't forget your book. (FOOTMAN *holds out a salver with a telegram on it for* JEAN.) Why, it's for me!

MISS LEVERING: But it's time I was—

(*She crosses to the table.*)

JEAN: (*opening the telegram*) May I? (*Reads, and glances over the paper at* MISS LEVERING.) I've got your book. (*Crosses to* MISS LEVERING, *and, looking at the back of the volume*) Dante! Whereabouts are you? (*Opening at the marker.*) Oh, the "Inferno."

MISS LEVERING: No; I'm in a worse place.

JEAN: I didn't know there was a worse.

MISS LEVERING: Yes; it's worse with the Vigliacchi.

JEAN: I forget. Were they Guelf or Ghibelline?

MISS LEVERING: (*smiling*) They weren't either, and that was why Dante couldn't stand them. (*More gravely.*) He said there was not place in Heaven nor in Purgatory—not even a corner in Hell—for the souls who had stood aloof from strife. (*Looking steadily into the girl's eyes.*) He called them "wretches who never lived," Dante did, because they'd never felt the pangs of partizanship. And so they wander homeless on the skirts of limbo among the abortions and off-scourings of Creation.

JEAN: (*a long breath after a long look. When* MISS LEVERING *has turned away to make her leisurely adieux* JEAN'*s eyes fall on the open telegram*) Aunt Ellen, I've got to go to London.

(STONOR, *re-entering, hears this, but pretends to talk to* MR FREDDY, *etc.*)

LADY JOHN: My dear child!

MRS HERIOT: Nonsense! Is your grandfather worse?

JEAN: (*folding the telegram*) No-o. I don't think so. But it's necessary I should go, all the same.

MRS HERIOT: Go away when Mr Stonor—

JEAN: He said he'd have to leave directly after luncheon.

LADY JOHN: I'll just see Miss Levering off, and then I'll come back and talk about it.

LORD JOHN: (*to* MISS LEVERING) Why are you saying goodbye as if you were never coming back?

MISS LEVERING: (*smiling*) One never knows. Maybe I shan't come back. (*To* STONOR.) Goodbye.

(STONOR *bows ceremoniously. The others go up laughing.* STONOR *comes down.*)

JEAN: (*impulsively*) There mayn't be another train! Miss Levering—

STONOR: (*standing in front of her*) What if there isn't? I'll take you back in the motor.

JEAN: (*rapturously*) Will you? (*Inadvertently drops the telegram.*) I must be there by three!

STONOR: (*picks up the telegram and a handkerchief lying near,*
1210   *glances at the message*) Why, it's only an invitation to dine—
        Wednesday!
JEAN: Sh! (*Takes the telegram and puts it in her pocket.*)
STONOR: Oh, I see! (*Lower, smiling.*) It's rather dear of you to
        arrange our going off like that. You *are* a clever little girl!
1215 JEAN: It's not that I was arranging. I want to hear those
        women in Trafalgar Square—the Suffragettes.
STONOR: (*incredulous, but smiling*) How perfectly absurd!
        (*Looking after* LADY JOHN.) Besides, I expect she wouldn't
        like my carrying you off like that.
1220 JEAN: Then she'll have to make an excuse and come too.
STONOR: Ah, it wouldn't be quite the same—
JEAN: (*rapidly thinking it out*) We could get back here in time
        for dinner.

(GEOFFREY STONOR *glances down at the handkerchief still in his
hand, and turns it half mechanically from corner to corner.*)

JEAN: (*absent-mindedly*) Mine?
1225 STONOR: (*hastily, without reflection*) No. (*He hands it to* MISS
        LEVERING *as she passes*): Yours.

(MISS LEVERING, *on her way to the lobby with* LORD JOHN *seems
not to notice.*)

JEAN: (*takes the handkerchief to give it to her, glancing down at the
        embroidered corner; stops*) But that's not an L! It's Vi—!

(GEOFFREY STONOR *suddenly turns his back and takes up the
newspaper.*)

LADY JOHN: (*from the lobby*) Come, Vida, since you will go.
1230 MISS LEVERING: Yes; I'm coming.

(*Exit* MISS LEVERING.)

JEAN: *I* didn't know her name was Vida; how did you?

(STONOR *stares silently over the top of his paper.*)

ACT TWO

SCENE: *The north side of the Nelson Column in Trafalgar Square.
The Curtain rises on an uproar. The crowd, which momentarily increases, is composed chiefly of weedy youths and wastrel old men.
There are a few decent artisans; three of four "beery" out-o'-works;
three or four young women of the domestic servant or Strand restaurant cashier class; one aged woman in rusty black peering with
faded, wondering eyes, consulting the faces of men and laughing nervously and apologetically from time to time; one or two quiet-
looking, businesslike women, thirty to forty; two middle-class men,
who stare and whisper and smile. A quiet old man with a lot of un-
sold Sunday papers under one arm stands in an attitude of rapt attention, with the free hand round his deaf ear. A brisk-looking
woman of forty-five or so, wearing pince-nez, goes round with a pile
of propagandist literature on her arm. Many of the men smoking
cigarettes—the old ones pipes. On the outskirts of this crowd, of several hundred, a couple of smart men in tall shining hats hover a few
moments, single eyeglass up, and then saunter off. Against the middle
of the Column, where it rises above the stone platform, is a great red
banner, one supporting pole upheld by a grimy sandwichman, the*
other by a small, dirty boy of eight. If practicable only the lower portion of the banner need be seen, bearing the final words of the
legend— "VOTES FOR WOMEN!" in immense white letters. It will
be well to get, to the full, the effect of the height above the crowd of
the straggling group of speakers on the pedestal platform. These are,
as the Curtain rises, a working-class woman who is waving her
arms and talking very earnestly, her voice for the moment blurred in
the uproar. She is dressed in brown serge and looks pinched and sallow. At her side is the CHAIRMAN urging that she be given a fair
hearing. ALLEN TRENT is a tall, slim, brown-haired man of twenty-
eight, with a slight stoop, an agreeable aspect, well-bred voice, and
the gleaming brown eye of the visionary. Behind these two, looking
on or talking among themselves, are several other carelessly dressed
women; one, better turned out than the rest, is quite young, very
slight and gracefully built, with round, very pink cheeks, full, scarlet
lips, naturally waving brown hair, and an air of childish gravity. She
looks at the unruly mob with imperturbable calm. The CHAIRMAN's
voice is drowned.*

WORKING WOMAN: (*with lean, brown finger out and voice raised
        shriller now above the tumult*) I've got boys o' me own and
        we laugh at all sorts o' things, but I should be ashymed and
        so would they if ever they was to be'yve as you're doin'
        to-d'y.   5

(*In laughter the noise dies.*)

People 'ave been sayin' this is a middle-class woman's move-
        ment. It's a libel. I'm a workin' woman myself, the wife of
        a working man. (*Voice:* "Pore devil!") I'm a Poor Law
        Guardian and a—
NOISY YOUNG MAN: Think of that, now—gracious me!   10

(*Laughter and interruption.*)

OLD NEWSVENDOR: (*to the noisy young man near him*) Oh, shut
        up, cawn't yer?
NOISY YOUNG MAN: Not fur *you!*
VOICE: Go 'ome and darn yer old man's stockens!
VOICE: Just clean yer *own* doorstep!   15
WORKING WOMAN: It's a pore sort of 'ousekeeper' that leaves
        'er doorstep till Sunday afternoon. Maybe that's when you
        would do *your* doorstep. I do mine in the mornin' before
        you men are awake.
OLD NEWSVENDOR: It's true, wot she says!—every word.   20
WORKING WOMAN: You say we women 'ave got no business
        servin' on boards and thinkin' about politics. Wot's *politics?*

(*A derisive roar.*)

It's just 'ousekeepin' on a big scyle. 'Oo among you [workin']
        men 'as the most comfortable 'omes? Those of you that
        gives yer wives yer wyges.   25

(*Loud laughter and jeers.*)

VOICES: { That's it!
         { Wantin' our money.
         { Lord 'Igh 'Ousekeeper of England.
WORKING WOMAN: If it wus only to use fur *our* comfort, d'ye
        think many o' you workin' men would be found turnin'   30
        over their wyges to their wives? No! Wot's the reason

thousands do—and the best and the soberest? Because the workin' man knows that wot's a pound to 'im is twenty shillin's to 'is wife. And she'll myke every penny in every one o' them shillin's *tell*. She gets more fur '*im* out of 'is wyges than wot 'e can! Some o' you know wot the 'omes is like where the men don't let the women manage. Well, the Poor Laws and the 'ole Government is just in the same muddle because the men 'ave tried to do the national 'ousekeepin' without the women.

(*Roars.*)

But, like I told you before, it's a libel to say it's only the well-off women wot's wantin' the vote. Wot about the 96,000 textile workers? Wot about the Yorkshire tailoresses? I can tell you wot plenty o' the poor women think about it. I'm one of them, and I can tell you we see there's reforms needed. *We ought to 'ave the vote (jeers),* and we know 'ow to appreciate the other women 'oo go to prison fur tryin' to get it fur us!

(*With a little final bob of emphasis and a glance over shoulder at the old woman and the young one behind her, she seems about to retire, but pauses as the murmur in the crowd grows into distinct phrases. "They get their 'air cut free." "Naow they don't, that's only us!" "Silly Suffragettes!" "Stop at 'ome!" "['Inderin'] policemen— mykin' rows in the streets!"*)

VOICE: (*louder than the others*) They sees yer ain't fit t'ave—

OTHER VOICES: "Ha, ha!" "Shut up." "Keep quiet, cawn't yer." (*General uproar.*)

CHAIRMAN: You evidently don't know what had to be done by *men* before the extension of the Suffrage in '67. If it hadn't been for demonstrations of violence. (*His voice is drowned.*)

WORKING WOMAN: (*coming forward again, her shrill note rising clear*) You s'y woman's plyce is 'ome! Don't you know there's a third of the women o' this country can't afford the luxury of stayin' in their 'omes? They *got* to go out and 'elp make money to p'y the rent and keep the 'ome from bein' sold up. Then there's all the women that 'aven't got even miseerable 'omes. They 'aven't got any 'omes *at all*.

NOISY YOUNG MAN: You said *you* got one. W'y don't you stop in it?

WORKING WOMAN: Yes, that's like a man. If one o' you is all right, he thinks the rest don't matter. We women—

NOISY YOUNG MAN: The lydies! God bless 'em!

(*Voices drown her and the* CHAIRMAN.)

OLD NEWSVENDOR: (*to* NOISY YOUNG MAN) Oh, take that extra 'alf pint 'ome and *sleep it off!*

WORKING WOMAN: P'r'aps *your* 'omes are all right. P'r'aps you aren't livin', old and young, married and single, in one room. I come from a plyce where many fam'lies 'ave to live like that if they're to go on livin' *at all*. If you don't believe me, come and let me show you! (*She spreads out her lean arms.*) Come with me to Canning Town!—come with me to Bromley—come to Poplar and to Bow! No. You won't even *think* about the overworked women and the underfed children and the 'ovels they live in. And you want that we shouldn't think neither—

A VAGRANT: We'll do the thinkin'. You go 'ome and nuss the byby.

WORKING WOMAN: I do nurse my byby! I've nursed seven. What 'ave you done for yours? P'r'aps your children never goes 'ungry, and maybe you're satisfied—though I must say I wouldn't a' thought it from the *look* o' you.

VOICE: Oh, I s'y!

WORKING WOMAN: But we women are not satisfied. We don't only want better things for our own children. We want better things for all. *Every* child is our child. We know in our 'earts we oughtn't to rest till we've mothered 'em every one.

VOICE: "Women"—"children"—wot about the *men?* Are *they* all 'appy?"

(*Derisive laughter and "No! no!" "Not precisely." "'Appy? Lord!"*)

WORKING WOMAN: No, there's lots o' you men I'm sorry for (*Shrill Voice: "Thanks awfully."*), an' we'll 'elp you if you let us.

VOICE: 'Elp us? You tyke the bread out of our mouths. You women are blackleggin' the men!

WORKING WOMAN: *W'y* does any woman tyke less wyges than a man for the same work? Only because we can't get anything better. That's part the reason w'y we're yere to-d'y. Do you reely think we tyke them there low wyges because we got a *lykin'* for low wyges? No. We're just like you. We want as much as ever we can get. (*"'Ear! 'Ear!" and laughter.*). We got a gryte deal to do with our wyges, we women has. We got the children to think about. And w'en we got our rights, a woman's flesh and blood won't be so cheaper than a man's that employers can get rich on keepin' you out o' work, and sweatin' us. If you men only could see it, we got the *syme* cause, and if you 'elped us you'd be 'elpin yerselves.

VOICES: "Rot!" "Drivel."

OLD NEWSVENDOR: True as gospel!

(*She retires against the banner with the others. There is some applause.*)

A MAN: (*patronisingly*) Well, now, that wusn't so bad—fur a woman.

ANOTHER: Nnaw. *Not fur a woman.*

CHAIRMAN: (*speaking through this last*) Miss Ernestine Blunt will now address you.

(*Applause, chiefly ironic, laughter, a general moving closer and knitting up of attention.* ERNESTINE BLUNT *is about twenty-four, but looks younger. She is very downright, not to say pugnacious—the something amusing and attractive about her is there, as it were, against her will, and the more fetching for that. She has no conventional gestures, and none of any sort at first. As she warms to her work she uses her slim hands to enforce her emphasis, but as though unconsciously. Her manner of speech is less monotonous than that of the average woman-speaker, but she, too, has a fashion of leaning all her weight on the end of the sentence. She brings out the final word or two with an effort of underscoring, and makes a forward motion of the slim body as if the better to drive the last nail in. She evidently means to be immensely practical—the kind who is pleased to think she hasn't a grain of sentimentality in her composition, and whose feeling, when it does all but master her, communicates itself magnetically to others.*)

MISS ERNESTINE BLUNT: Perhaps I'd better begin by explaining a little about our "tactics."

(*Cries of "Tactics! We know!" "My kin'trouble!" "Public scandal!"*)

120   To make you understand what we've done, I must remind you of what others have done. Perhaps you don't know that women first petitioned Parliament for the Franchise as long ago as 1866.
VOICE: How do *you* know?

(*She pauses a moment, taken off her guard by the suddenness of the attack.*)

125   VOICE: You wasn't there!
VOICE: That was the trouble. Haw! haw!
MISS ERNESTINE BLUNT: And the petition was presented—
VOICE: Give 'er a 'earin' now she 'as got out of 'er crydle.
MISS ERNESTINE BLUNT: —presented to the House of Com-
130   mons by that great Liberal, John Stuart Mill. (*Voice:* "Mill? Who is he when he's at home?") Bills or Resolutions have been before the House on and off for the last thirty-six years. That, roughly, is our history. We found ourselves, to-wards the close of the year 1905, with no assurance that if
135   we went on in the same way any girl born into the world in this generation would live to exercise the rights of citizenship, though she lived to be a hundred. So we said all this has been in vain. We must try some other way. How did the working man get the Suffrage, we asked ourselves?
140   Well, we turned up the records, and we *saw*—
VOICES: "Not by scratching people's faces!" . . . "Disraeli give it 'em!" "Dizzy? Get out!" "Cahnty Cahncil scholarships!" "Oh, Lord, this education." "Chartists riots, she's thinkin' of!" (*Noise in the crowd.*)
145   MISS ERNESTINE BLUNT: But we don't *want* to follow such a violent example. We would much rather *not*—but if that's the only way we can make the country see we're in earnest, we are prepared to show them.
VOICE: An' they'll show you!—Give you another month 'ard.
150   MISS ERNESTINE BLUNT: Don't think that going to prison has any fears for us. We'd go *for life* if by doing that we could get freedom for the rest of the women.
VOICES: "Hear, hear!" "Rot!" "W'ye don't the men 'elp ye to get your rights?"
155   MISS ERNESTINE BLUNT: Here's some one asking why the men don't help. It's partly they don't understand yet—they *will* before we've done! (*Laughter.*) Partly they don't understand yet what's at stake—
RESPECTABLE OLD MAN: (*chuckling*) Lord, they're a 'educatin'
160   of us!
VOICE: Wot next?
MISS ERNESTINE BLUNT: —and partly that the bravest man is afraid of ridicule. Oh, yes; we've heard a great deal all our lives about the timidity and the sensitiveness of women.
165   And it's true. We *are* sensitive. But I tell you, ridicule crumples a man up. It steels a woman. We've come to know the value of ridicule. We've educated ourselves so that we welcome ridicule. We owe our sincerest thanks to the comic writers. The cartoonist is our unconscious
170   friend. Who cartoons people who are of no importance? What advertisement is so sure of being remembered?
POETIC YOUNG MAN: I admit that.

MISS ERNESTINE BLUNT: If we didn't know it by any other sign, the comic papers would tell us *we've arrived!* But our greatest debt of gratitude we owe, to the man who called   175 us female hooligans.

(*The crowd bursts into laughter.*)

We aren't hooligans, but we hope the fact will be over-looked. If everybody said we were nice, well-behaved women, who'd come to hear us? *Not the men.*

(*Roars.*)

Men tell us it isn't womanly for us to care about politics.   180 How do they know what's womanly? It's for women to decide that. Let the men attend to being manly. It will take them all their time.
VOICE: Are we down-'earted? Oh no!
MISS ERNESTINE BLUNT: And they say it would be dreadful if   185 we got the vote, because then we'd be pitted against men in the economic struggle. But that's come about already. Do you know that out of every hundred women in this country eighty-two are wage-earning women? It used to be thought unfeminine for women to be students and to   190 aspire to the arts—that bring fame and fortune. But no-body has ever said it was unfeminine for women to do the heavy drudgery that's badly paid. That kind of work had to be done by *some*body—and the men didn't hanker af-ter it. Oh, no.   195

(*Laughter and interruption.*)

A MAN ON THE OUTER FRINGE: She can talk—the little one can.
ANOTHER: Oh, they can all "talk."
A BEERY, DIRTY FELLOW OF FIFTY: I wouldn't like to be 'er 'usban'. Think o' comin' 'ome to *that!*   200
HIS PAL: I'd soon learn 'er!
MISS ERNESTINE BLUNT: (*speaking through the noise*) Oh, no! *Let* the women scrub and cook and wash. That's all right! But if they want to try their hand at the better paid work of the liberal professions—oh, very unfeminine indeed!   205 Then there's another thing. Now I want you to listen to this, because it's *very* important. Men say if we persist in competing with them for the bigger prizes, they're dread-fully afraid we'd lose the beautiful protecting chivalry that—Yes, I don't wonder you laugh. *We* laugh. (*Bending*   210 *forward with lit eyes.*) But the women I found at the Ferry Tin Works working for five shillings a week—I didn't see them laughing. The beautiful chivalry of the employers of women doesn't prevent them from paying women ten-pence a day for sorting coal and loading and unloading   215 carts—doesn't prevent them from forcing women to earn bread in ways worse still. So we won't talk about chivalry. It's being over-sarcastic. We'll just let this poor ghost of chivalry go—in exchange for a little plain justice.
VOICE: If the House of Commons won't give you justice,   220 why don't you go to the House of Lords?
MISS ERNESTINE BLUNT: What?
VOICE: Better 'urry up. Case of early closin'.

(*Laughter. A man at the back asks the speaker something.*)

MISS ERNESTINE BLUNT: (*unable to hear*) You'll be allowed to
225   ask any question you like at the end of the meeting.
NEWCOMER: (*boy of eighteen*) Oh, is it question time? I s'y,
Miss, 'oo killed cock robin?

(*She is about to resume, but above the general noise the voice of a
man at the back reaches her indistinct but insistent. She leans forward trying to catch what he says. While the indistinguishable murmur has been going on* GEOFFREY STONOR *has appeared on the
edge of the crowd, followed by* JEAN *and* LADY JOHN *in motor veils.*)

JEAN: (*pressing forward eagerly and raising her veil*) Is she one of
them? That little thing!
230   STONOR: (*doubtfully*) I—I suppose so.
JEAN: Oh, ask some one, Geoffrey. I'm so disappointed. I did
so hope we'd hear one of the—the worst.
MISS ERNESTINE BLUNT: (*to the interrupter—on the other side*)
What? What do you say? (*She screws up her eyes with the ef-
235   fort to hear, and puts a hand up to her ear. A few indistinguishable words between her and the man.*)
LADY JOHN: (*who has been studying the figures on the platform
through her lorgnon, turns to a working man beside her*) Can
you tell me, my man, which are the ones that—a—that
240   make the disturbances?
WORKING MAN: Don't you be took in, Miss.
MISS ERNESTINE BLUNT: Oh, yes—I see. There's a man over
here asking—
A YOUNG MAN: *I've* got a question, too. Are—you—married?
245   ANOTHER: (*sniggering*) Quick! There's yer chawnce. 'E's a
bachelor.

(*Laughter.*)

MISS ERNESTINE BLUNT: (*goes straight on as if she had not heard*)
—man asking: if the women get full citizenship, and a war
is declared, will the women fight?
250   POETIC YOUNG MAN: No, really—no, really, now!

(*The Crowd:* "Haw! Haw!" "Yes!" "Yes, how about that?")

MISS ERNESTINE BLUNT: (*smiling*) Well, you know, some people say the whole trouble about us is that we *do* fight. But
it is only hard necessity makes us do that. We don't *want*
to fight—as men seem to—just for fighting's sake. Women
255   are for peace.
VOICE: Hear, hear.
MISS ERNESTINE BLUNT: And when we have a share in public affairs there'll be less likelihood of war. But that's not
to say women can't fight. The Boer women did. The
260   Russian women face conflicts worse than any battlefield
can show. (*Her voice shakes a little, and the eyes fill, but she
controls her emotion gallantly, and dashes on.*) But we women
know all that is evil, and we're for peace. Our part—we're
proud to remember it—our part has been to go about af-
265   ter you men in war time, and—*pick up the pieces!*

(*A great shout.*)

Yes—seems funny, doesn't it? You men blow them to bits,
and then we come along and put them together again. If
you know anything about military nursing, you know a
good deal of our work has been done in the face of dan-
270   ger—but it's always been done.

OLD NEWSVENDOR: That's so. That's so.
MISS ERNESTINE BLUNT: You complain that more and more
we're taking away from you men the work that's always
been yours. You can't any longer keep women out of the
industries. The only question is upon what terms shall she   275
continue to be in? As long as she's in on bad terms, she's
not only hurting herself—she's hurting you. But if you're
feeling discouraged about our competing with you, we're
willing to leave you your trade in war. *Let* the men take
life! We *give* life! (*Her voice is once more moved and proud.*)   280
No one will pretend ours isn't one of the dangerous trades
either. I won't say any more to you now, because we've got
others to speak to you, and a new woman helper that I
want you to hear.

(*She retires to the sound of clapping. There's a hurried consultation
between her and the* CHAIRMAN. *Voices in the Crowd:* "The little
'un's all right" "Ernestine's a corker," *etc.*)

JEAN: (*looking at* STONOR *to see how he's taken it*) Well?   285
STONOR: (*smiling down at her*) Well—
JEAN: Nothing reprehensible in what *she* said, was there?
STONOR: (*shrugs*) Oh, reprehensible!
JEAN: It makes me rather miserable all the same.
STONOR: (*draws her hand protectingly through his arm*) You   290
mustn't take it as much to heart as all that.
JEAN: I can't help it—I can't indeed, Geoffrey. I shall *never* be
able to make a speech like that!
STONOR: (*taken aback*) I hope not, indeed.
JEAN: Why, I thought you said you wanted me—?   295
STONOR: (*smiling*) To make nice little speeches with compo-
sure—so I did! So I—(*Seems to lose his thread as he looks at
her.*)
JEAN: (*with a little frown*) You *said*—
STONOR: That you have very pink cheeks? Well, I stick to   300
that.
JEAN: (*smiling*) Sh! Don't tell everybody.
STONOR: And you're the only female creature I ever saw who
didn't look a fright in motor things.
JEAN: (*melted and smiling*) I'm glad you don't think me a   305
fright.
CHAIRMAN: I will now ask (*name indistinguishable*) to address
the meeting.
JEAN: (*as she sees* LADY JOHN: *moving to one side*) Oh, don't go
yet, Aunt Ellen!   310
LADY JOHN: Go? Certainly not. I want to hear another.
(*Craning her neck.*) I can't believe, you know, she was really
one of the worst.

(*A big, sallow Cockney has come forward. His scanty hair grows in
wisps on a great bony skull.*)

VOICE: That's Pilcher.
ANOTHER: 'Oo's Pilcher?   315
ANOTHER: If you can't afford a bottle of Tatcho, w'y don't
you get yer 'air cut.
MR. PILCHER: (*not in the least discomposed*) I've been addressin'
a big meetin' at 'Ammersmith this morning, and w'en I
told 'em I was comin' 'ere this awfternoon to speak fur   320
the women—well—then the usual thing began!

(*An appreciative roar from the crowd.*)

In these times if you want peace and quiet at a public meetin'—

(*The crowd fills in the hiatus with laughter.*)

325 There was a man at 'Ammersmith, too, talkin' about women's sphere bein' 'ome. '*Ome* do you call it? You've got a kennel w'ere you can munch your tommy. You've got a corner w'ere you can curl up fur a few hours till you go out to work again. No, my man, there's too many of you ain't able to *give* the women 'omes—fit to live in, too many of
330 you in that fix fur you to go on jawin' at those o' the women 'oo want to myke the 'omes a little decenter.

VOICE: If the vote ain't done us any good, 'ow'll it do the women any good?

MR. PILCHER: Looke 'ere! Any men here belongin' to the
335 Labour Party?

(*Shouts and applause.*)

Well, I don't need to tell these men the vote 'as done us *some* good. They know it. And it'll do us a lot more good w'en you know 'ow to use the power you got in your 'and.

VOICE: Power! It's those fellers at the bottom o' the street
340 that's got the power.

MR. PILCHER: It's you, and men like you, that gave it to 'em. You carried the Liberals into Parliament Street on your own shoulders.

(*Complacent applause.*)

You believed all their fine words. You never asked your-
345 selves, "Wot's a Liberal, anyw'y?"

A VOICE: He's a jolly good fellow.

(*Cheers and booing.*)

MR. PILCHER: No, 'e ain't, or if 'e is jolly, it's only because 'e thinks you're such silly codfish you'll go swellin' his majority again. (*Laughter, in which* STONOR *joins.*) Its enough
350 to make any Liberal jolly to see sheep like you lookin' on, proud and 'appy, while you see Liberal leaders desertin' Liberal principles.

(*Voices in agreement and protest.*)

You show me a Liberal, and I'll show you a Mr Fycing-both-W'ys. Yuss.

(STONOR *moves closer with an amused look.*)

355 'E sheds the light of 'is warm and 'andsome smile on the working man, and round on the other side 'e's tippin' a wink to the great landowners. That's to let 'em know 'e's standin' between them and the Socialists. Huh! Socialists. Yuss, *Socialists!*

(*General laughter, in which* STONOR *joins.*)

360 The Liberal, 'e's the judicial sort o'chap that sits in the middle—

VOICE: On the fence!

MR. PILCHER: Tories one side—Socialists the other. Well it ain't always so comfortable in the middle. You're like to get

squeezed. Now, I s'y to the women, the Conservatives 365 don't promise you much but what they promise they *do!*

STONOR: (*to* JEAN) This fellow isn't half bad.

MR. PILCHER: The Liberals—they'll promise you the earth, and give yer . . . the whole o' nothing.

(*Roars of approval.*)

JEAN: *Isn't* it fun? Now, aren't you glad I brought you?   370

STONOR: (*laughing*) This chap's rather amusing!

MR. PILCHER: We men 'ave seen it 'appen over and over. But the women can tyke a 'int quicker 'n what we can. They won't stand the nonsense men do. Only they 'aven't got a fair chawnce even to agitate fur their rights. As I wus 375 comin' up 'ere I 'eard a man sayin', "Look at this big crowd." W'y, we're all *men!* If the women want the vote w'y ain't they 'ere to s'y so? Well, I'll tell you w'y. It's because they've 'ad to get the dinner fur you and me, and now they're washin' up the dishes.   380

A VOICE: D'you think *we* ought to st'y 'ome and wash the dishes?

MR. PILCHER: (*laughs good-naturedly*) If they'd leave it to us once or twice per'aps we'd understand a little more about the Woman Question. I know w'y *my* wife isn't here. It's be- 385 cause she *knows* I ain't much use round the 'ouse, and she's 'opin' I can talk to some purpose. Maybe she's mistaken. Any'ow, here I am to vote for her and all the other women.

VOICES: "Hear! hear!", "Oh-h!"

MR. PILCHER: And to tell you men what improvements you 390 can expect to see when women 'as the share in public affairs they *ought* to 'ave!

VOICE: What do you know about it? You can't even talk grammar.

MR. PILCHER: (*is dashed a fraction of a moment, for the first and* 395 *only time*) I'm not 'ere to talk grammar but to talk Reform. I ain't defendin' my grammar—but I'll say in pawssing that if my mother 'ad 'ad 'er rights, maybe my grammar would have been better.

(STONOR *and* JEAN *exchange smiles. He takes her arm again and bends his head to whisper something in her ear. She listens with lowered eyes and happy face. The discreet love-making goes on during the next few sentences. Interruption. One voice insistent but not clear. The speaker waits only a second and then resumes. "Yes, if the women," but he cannot instantly make himself heard. The boyish* CHAIRMAN *looks harassed and anxious.* MISS ERNESTINE BLUNT *alert, watchful.*)

MR. PILCHER: Wait a bit—'arf a minute, my man!   400

VOICE: 'Oo yer talkin' to? I ain't your man.

MR. PILCHER: Lucky for me! There seems to be a *gentleman* 'ere who doesn't think women ought to 'ave the vote.

VOICE: *One?* Oh-h!

(*Laughter.*)

MR. PILCHER: Per'aps 'e doesn't know much about women?   405

(*Indistinguishable repartee.*)

Oh, the gentleman says 'e's married. Well, then, fur the syke of 'is wife we mustn't be too sorry 'e's 'ere. No doubt

she's s'ying: "'Eaven by prysed those women are mykin' a Demonstrytion in Trafalgar Square, and I'll 'ave a little
410   peace and quiet at 'ome for one Sunday in my life."

(*The crowd laughs and there are jeers for the interruptor—and at the speaker.*)

(*Pointing.*) Why, *you're* like the man at 'Ammersmith this morning. 'E was awskin' me: "'Ow would you like men to st'y at 'ome and do the family washin'?"

(*Laughter.*)

I told 'im I wouldn't advise it. I 'ave too much respect fur
415   —me clo'es.

VAGRANT: It's their place—the women ought to do the washin'.

MR PILCHER: I'm not sure you ain't right. For a good many o' you fellas, from the look o' you—you cawn't even wash
420   yerselves.

(*Laughter.*)

VOICE: (*threatening*) 'Oo are you talkin' to?

(CHAIRMAN *more anxious than before—movement in the crowd.*)

THREATENING VOICE: Which of us d'you mean?

MR PILCHER: (*coolly looking down*) Well, it takes about ten of your sort to myke a man, so you may take it I mean the
425   lot of you.

(*Angry indistinguishable retorts and the crowd sways.* MISS ERNESTINE BLUNT, *who has been watching the fray with serious face, turns suddenly, catching sight of someone just arrived at the end of the platform.* MISS BLUNT *goes right with alacrity, saying audibly to* PILCHER *as she passes,* "Here she is," *and proceeds to offer her hand helping some one to get up the improvised steps. Laughter and interruption in the crowd.*)

LADY JOHN: Now, there's another woman going to speak.

JEAN: Oh, is she? Who? Which? I do hope she'll be one of the wild ones.

MR PILCHER: (*speaking through this last. Glancing at the new arrival whose hat appears above the platform.*) That's all right,
430   then. (*Turns to the left.*) When I've attended to this microbe that's vitiating the air on my right—

(*Laughter and interruptions from the crowd.*)

(STONOR *stares, one dazed instant, at the face of the new arrival; his own changes.*)

(JEAN *withdraws her arm from his and quite suddenly presses a shade nearer the platform.* STONOR *moves forward and takes her by the arm.*)

STONOR: We're going now.

JEAN: Not yet—oh, please not yet. (*Breathless, looking back.*)
435   Why I—I do believe—

STONOR: (*to* LADY JOHN, *with decision*) I'm going to take Jean out of this mob. Will you come?

LADY JOHN: What? Oh yes, if you think—(*Another look through her glasses.*) But isn't that—*surely* it's—!!!

(VIDA LEVERING *comes forward. She wears a long, plain, dark green dustcloak. Stands talking to* ERNESTINE BLUNT *and glancing a little apprehensively at the crowd.*)

JEAN: Geoffrey!   440
STONOR: (*trying to draw* JEAN *away*) Lady John's tired—
JEAN: But you don't see who it is, Geoffrey—! (*Looks into his face, and is arrested by the look she finds there.*)

(LADY JOHN *has pushed in front of them amazed, transfixed, with glass up.* GEOFFREY STONOR *restrains a gesture of annoyance, and withdraws behind two big policemen.* JEAN *from time to time turns to look at him with a face of perplexity.*)

MR PILCHER: (*resuming through a fire of indistinct interruption*) I'll come down and attend to that microbe while a lady   445 will say a few words to you (*raises his voice*)—if she can myke 'erself 'eard.

(PILCHER *retires in the midst of booing and cheers.*)

CHAIRMAN: (*harassed and trying to creat a diversion*) Some one suggests—and it's such a good idea I'd like you to listen to it—   450

(*Noise dies down.*)

that a clause shall be inserted in the next Suffrage Bill that shall expressly reserve to each Cabinet Minister, and to any respectable man, the power to prevent the Franchise being given to the female members of his family on his public declaration of their lack of sufficient intelligence to   455 entitle them to vote.

VOICES: Oh! oh.
CHAIRMAN: Now, I ask you to listen, as quietly as you can, to a lady who is not accustomed to speaking—a—in Trafalgar Square—or a . . . as a matter of fact, at all.   460
VOICES: "A dumb lady!" "Hooray!" "Three cheers for the dumb lady!"
CHAIRMAN: A lady who, as I've said, will tell you, if you'll behave yourselves, her impressions of the administration of police court justice in this country.   465

(JEAN *looks wondering at* STONOR*'s sphinx-like face as* VIDA LEVERING *comes to the edge of the platform.*)

MISS LEVERING: Mr Chairman, men and women—
VOICES: (*off*) Speak up.

(MISS LEVERING: *flushes, comes quite to the edge of the platform and raises her voice a little.*)

MISS LEVERING: I just wanted to tell you that I was—I was—present in the police court when the women were charged for creating a disturbance.   470
VOICE: Y' oughtn't t' get mixed up in wot didn't concern you.
MISS LEVERING: I—I—(*Stumbles and stops.*)

(*Talking and laughing increases.* "Wot's 'er name?" . . . "Mrs or Miss?" "Ain't seen this one before.")

CHAIRMAN: (*anxiously*) Now, see here, men; don't interrupt—
A GIRL: (*shrilly*) I don't like this one's 'at. Ye can see she ain't one of 'em.   475

MISS LEVERING: (*trying to recommence*) I—

VOICE: They're a disgrace—them women be'ind yer.

A MAN WITH A FATHERLY AIR: It's the w'y they goes on as mykes the Government keep ye from gettin' yer rights.

480 CHAIRMAN: (*losing his temper*) It's the way *you* go on that—

(*Noise increases.* CHAIRMAN *drowned, waves his arms and moves his lips.* MISS LEVERING *discouraged, turns and looks at* ERNESTINE BLUNT *and pantomimes "It's no good. I can't go on."* ERNESTINE BLUNT *comes forward, says a word to the* CHAIRMAN, *who ceases gyrating, and nods.*)

MISS ERNESTINE BLUNT: (*facing the crowd*) Look here. If the Government withhold the vote because they don't like the way some of us ask for it—*let them give it to the Quiet Ones.* Does the Government want to punish *all* women

485 because they don't like the manners of a handful? Perhaps that's you men's notion of justice. It isn't women's.

VOICES: Haw! haw!

MISS LEVERING: Yes. Thi—this is the first time I've ever 'gone on,' as you call it, but they never gave me a vote.

490 MISS ERNESTINE BLUNT: (*with energy*) No! And there are one—two—three—four women on this platform. Now, we all want the vote, as you know. Well, we'd agree to be disfranchised all our lives, if they'd give the vote to all the other women.

495 VOICE: Look here, you made one speech, give the lady a chawnce.

MISS ERNESTINE BLUNT: (*retires smiling*) That's *just* what I wanted *you* to do!

MISS LEVERING: Perhaps you—you don't know—you don't

500 know—

VOICE: (*sarcastic*) 'Ow 're we goin' to know if you can't tell us?

MISS LEVERING: (*flushing and smiling*) Thank you for that. We couldn't have a better motto. How *are* you to know if we can't somehow manage to tell you? (*With a visible effort she*

505 *goes on.*) Well, I certainly didn't know before that the sergeants and policemen are instructed to deceive the people as to the time such cases are heard. You ask, and you're sent to Marlborough Police Court instead of to Marylebone.

510 VOICE: They ought ter sent yer to 'Olloway—do y' good.

OLD NEWSVENDOR: You go on, Miss, don't mind 'im.

VOICE: Wot d'you expect from a pig but a grunt?

MISS LEVERING: You're told the case will be at two o'clock, and it's really called for eleven. Well, I took a great deal of

515 trouble, and I didn't believe what I was told—

(*Warming a little to her task.*)

Yes, that's almost the first thing we have to learn—to get over our touching faith that, because a man tells us something, it's true. I got to the right court, and I was so anxious not to be late, I was too early. The case before the

520 women's was just coming on. I heard a noise. At the door I saw the helmets of two policemen, and I said to myself: "What sort of crime shall I have to sit and hear about? Is this a burglar coming along between the two big policemen, or will it be a murderer? What sort of felon is to

525 stand in the dock before the women whose crime is they ask for the vote?" But, try as I would, I couldn't see the prisoner. My heart misgave me. Is it a woman, I won-

dered? Then the policemen got nearer, and I saw—(*she waits an instant*)—a little, thin, half-starved boy. What do you think he was charged with? Stealing. What had he 530 been stealing—that small criminal? *Milk.* It seemed to me as I sat there looking on, that the men who had the affairs of the world in their hands from the beginning, and who've made so poor a business of it—

VOICES: Oh! oh! Pore benighted man! Are we down-'earted? 535 *Oh,* no!

MISS LEVERING: —so poor a business of it as to have the poor and the unemployed in the condition they're in today—when your only remedy for a starving child is to hale him off to the police court—because he had managed to get a 540 little milk—well, I *did* wonder that the men refuse to be helped with a problem they've so notoriously failed at. I began to say to myself: "Isn't it time the women lent a hand?"

A VOICE: Would you have women magistrates?   545

(*She is stumped by the suddenness of the demand.*)

VOICES: Haw! Haw! Magistrates!

ANOTHER: Women! Let 'em prove first they deserve—

A SHABBY ART STUDENT: (*his hair longish, soft hat, and flowing tie*) They study music by thousands; where's their Beethoven? Where's their Plato? Where's the woman 550 Shakespeare?

ANOTHER: Yes—what 'a' they ever *done?*

(*The speaker clenches her hands, and is recovering her presence of mind, so that by the time the* CHAIRMAN *can make himself heard with, "Now men, give this lady a fair hearing—don't interrupt"—she, with the slightest of gestures, waves him aside with a low "It's all right.")*

MISS LEVERING: (*steadying and raising her voice*) These questions are quite proper! They are often asked elsewhere; and I would like to ask in return: Since when was human soci- 555 ety held to exist for its handful of geniuses? How many Platos are there here in this crowd?

A VOICE: (*very loud and shrill*) Divil a wan!

(*Laughter.*)

MISS LEVERING: Not one. Yet that doesn't keep you men off the register. How many Shakespeares are there in all Eng- 560 land today? Not one. Yet the State doesn't tumble to pieces. Railroads and ships are built—homes are kept go- ing, and babies are born. The world goes on! (*Bending over the crowd.*) It goes on *by virtue of its common people.*

VOICES: (*subdued*) Hear! hear!   565

MISS LEVERING: I am not concerned that you should think we women can paint great pictures, or compose immor- tal music, or write good books. I am content that we should be classed with the common people—who keep the world going. But (*Straightening up and taking a fresh* 570 *start.*) I'd like the world to go a great deal better. We were talking about justice. I have been inquiring into the kind of lodging the poorest class of homeless women can get in this town of London. I find that only the men of that class are provided for. Some measure to establish Rowton 575 Houses for women has been before the London County

Council. They looked into the question "very carefully," so their apologists say. And what did they decide? They decided that *they could do nothing.*

580 LADY JOHN: (*having forced her way to* STONOR's *side*) Is that true?

STONOR: (*speaking through* MISS LEVERING's *next words*) I don't know.

MISS LEVERING: Why could that great, all-powerful body do
585 nothing? Because, if these cheap and decent houses were opened, they said, the homeless women in the streets would make use of them! You'll think I'm not in earnest. But that was actually the decision and the reason given for it. Women that the bitter struggle for existence has forced
590 into a life of horror—

STONOR: (*sternly to* LADY JOHN) You think this is the kind of thing—(*A motion of the head towards* JEAN.)

MISS LEVERING:—the outcast women might take advantage of the shelter these decent, cheap places offered. But the
595 *men,* I said! Are all who avail themselves of Lord Rowton's hostels, are *they* all angels? Or does wrong-doing in a man not matter? Yet women are recommended to depend on the chivalry of men.

(*The two policemen, who at first had been strolling about, have stood during this scene in front of* GEOFFREY STONOR. *They turn now and walk away, leaving* STONOR *exposed. He, embarrassed, moves uneasily, and* VIDA LEVERING's *eye falls upon his big figure. He still has the collar of his motor coat turned up to his ears. A change passes over her face, and her nerve fails her an instant.*)

MISS LEVERING: Justice and chivalry!! (*She steadies her voice and*
600 *hurries on.*) —they both remind me of what those of you who read the police court news—(I have begun only lately to do that)—but you've seen the accounts of the girl who's been tried in Manchester lately for the murder of her child. Not pleasant reading. Even if we'd noticed it, we
605 wouldn't speak of it in my world. A few months ago I should have turned away my eyes and forgotten even the headline as quickly as I could. But since that morning in the police court, I read these things. This, as you'll remember, was about a little working girl—an orphan of
610 eighteen—who crawled with the dead body of her new born child to her master's back door, and left the baby there. She dragged herself a little way off and fainted. A few days later she found herself in court, being tried for the murder of her child. Her master—a married man—
615 had of course reported the "find" at his back door to the police, and he had been summoned to give evidence. The girl cried out to him in the open court, "You are the father!" He couldn't deny it. The Coroner at the jury's request censured the man, and regretted that the law didn't
620 make him responsible. But he went scot-free. And that girl is now serving her sentence in Strangeways Gaol.

(*Murmuring and scraps of indistinguishable comment in the crowd, through which only* JEAN's *voice is clear.*)

JEAN: (*who has wormed her way to* STONOR's *side*) Why do you dislike her so?

STONOR: I? Why should you think—
625 JEAN: (*With a vaguely frightened air*) I never saw you look as you did—as you do.

CHAIRMAN: Order, please—give the lady a fair—

MISS LEVERING: (*signing to him "It's all right"*) Men make boast that an English citizen is tried by his peers. What woman is tried by hers? 630

(*A sombre passion strengthens her voice and hurries her on.*)

A woman is arrested by a man, brought before a man judge, tried by a jury of men, condemned by men, taken to prison by a man, and by a man she's hanged! Where in all this were *her* "peers"? Why did men so long ago insist 635 on trial by "a jury of their peers"? So that justice shouldn't miscarry—wasn't it? A man's peers would best understand his circumstances, his temptation, the degree of his guilt. Yet there's no such unlikeness between different classes of men as exists between man and woman. What man has the 640 knowledge that makes him a fit judge of woman's deeds at that time of anguish—that hour—(*lowers her voice and bends over the crowd*)—that hour that some woman struggled through to put each man here into the world. I noticed when a previous speaker quoted the Labour Party 645 you applauded. Some of you here—I gather—call yourselves Labour men. Every woman who has borne a child is a Labour woman. No man among you can judge what she goes through in her hour of darkness—

JEAN: (*with frightened eyes on her lover's set, white face, whispers*) Geoffrey— 650

MISS LEVERING: (*catching her fluttering breath, goes on very low*) —in that great agony when, even under the best conditions that money and devotion can buy, many a woman falls into temporary mania, and not a few go down to death. In the case of this poor little abandoned working 655 girl, what man can be the fit judge of her deeds in that awful moment of half-crazed temptation? Women know of these things as those know burning who have walked through fire.

(STONOR *makes a motion towards* JEAN *and she turns away fronting the audience. Her hands go up to her throat as though she suffered a choking sensation. It is in her face that she "knows."* MISS LEVERING *leans over the platform and speaks with a low and thrilling earnestness.*)

I would say in conclusion to the women here, it's not 660 enough to be sorry for these unfortunate sisters. We must get the conditions of life made fairer. We women must organise. We must learn to work together. We have all (rich and poor, happy and unhappy) worked so long and so exclusively for *men,* we hardly know how to work for one 665 another. But we must learn. Those who can, may give money—

VOICES: (*grumbling*) Oh, yes—Money! Money!

MISS LEVERING: Those who haven't pennies to give—even those people aren't so poor they can't give some part of 670 their labour—some share of their sympathy and support. (*Turns to hear something the* CHAIRMAN *is whispering to her.*)

JEAN: (*low to* LADY JOHN) Oh, I'm glad I've got power!

LADY JOHN: (*bewildered*) Power!—you? 675

JEAN: Yes, all that money—

(LADY JOHN *tries to make her way to* STONOR.)

MISS LEVERING: (*suddenly turning from the* CHAIRMAN *to the crowd*) Oh, yes, I hope you'll all join the Union. Come up after the meeting and give your names.

680 LOUD VOICE: You won't get many men.

MISS LEVERING: (*with fire*) Then it's to the women I appeal!

(*She is about to retire when, with a sudden gleam in her lit eyes, she turns for the last time to the crowd, silencing the general murmur and holding the people by the sudden concentration of passion in her face.*)

I don't mean to say it wouldn't be better if men and women did this work together—shoulder to shoulder. But the mass of men won't have it so. I only hope they'll re-
685 alise in time the good they've renounced and the spirit they've aroused. For I know as well as any man could tell me, it would be a bad day for England if all women felt about all men *as I do.*

(*She retires in a tumult. The others on the platform close about her. The* CHAIRMAN *tries in vain to get a hearing from the excited crowd.*

JEAN *tries to make her way through the knot of people surging round her.*)

STONOR: (*calls*) Here—Follow me!

690 JEAN: No—no—I—

STONOR: You're going the wrong way.

JEAN: *This* is the way I must go.

STONOR: You can get out quicker on this side.

JEAN: I don't *want* to get out.

695 STONOR: What! Where are you going?

JEAN: To ask that woman to let me have the honour of working with her.

(*She disappears in the crowd. Curtain.*)

ACT THREE

SCENE: *The drawing room at old* MR DUNBARTON's *house in Eaton Square. Six o'clock the same evening. As the Curtain rises the door opens and* JEAN *appears on the threshold. She looks back into her own sitting room, then crosses the drawing room, treading softly on the parquet spaces between the rugs. She goes to the window and is in the act of parting the lace curtains when the folding doors are opened by the* BUTLER.

JEAN: (*to the Servant*) Sh!

(*She goes softly back to the door she has left open and closes it care-fully. When she turns, the* BUTLER *has stepped aside to admit* GEOFFREY STONOR, *and departed, shutting the folding doors.* STONOR *comes rapidly forward.*)

(*Before he gets a word out.*) Speak low, please.

STONOR: (*angrily*) I waited about a whole hour for you to come back.

(JEAN *turns away as though vaguely looking for the nearest chair.*)

5   If you don't mind leaving *me* like that you might have considered Lady John.

JEAN: (*pausing*) Is she here with you?

STONOR: No. My place was nearer than this, and she was very tired. I left her to get some tea. We couldn't tell whether you'd be here, or *what* had become of you.   10

JEAN: Mr Trent got us a hansom.

STONOR: Trent?

JEAN: The Chairman of the meeting.

STONOR: "Got us—"?

JEAN: Miss Levering and me.   15

STONOR: (*incensed*) MISS L—

BUTLER: (*opens the door and announces*) Mr Farnborough.

(*Enter* MR RICHARD FARNBOROUGH—*more flurried than ever.*)

FARNBOROUGH: (*seeing* STONOR) At last! You'll forgive this incursion, Miss Dunbarton, when you hear—(*Turns abruptly back to* STONOR.) They've been telegraphing you 20 all over London. In despair they set me on your track.

STONOR: Who did? What's up.

FARNBOROUGH: (*lays down his hat and fumbles agitatedly in his breast pocket*) There was the devil to pay at Dutfield last night. The Liberal chap tore down from London and took 25 over your meeting!

STONOR: Oh?—Nothing about it in the Sunday paper *I* saw.

FARNBOROUGH: Wait till you see the Press tomorrow morn-ing! There was a great rally and the beggar made a rous-ing speech.   30

STONOR: What about?

FARNBOROUGH: Abolition of the Upper House—

STONOR: They were at that when I was at Eton!

FARNBOROUGH: Yes. But this new man has got a way of putting things!—the people went mad. (*Pompously.*) The 35 Liberal platform as defined at Dutfield is going to make a big difference.

STONOR: (*drily*) You think so.

FARNBOROUGH: Well, your agent says as much. (*Opens telegram.*)   40

STONOR: My—(*Taking telegram.*) "Try find Stonor"—Hm! Hm!

FARNBOROUGH: (*pointing*)—"tremendous effect of last night's Liberal manifesto ought to be counteracted in tomorrow's papers." (*Very earnestly.*) You see, Mr. Stonor, it's a battle cry 45 we want.

STONOR: (*turns on his heel*) Claptrap!

FARNBOROUGH: (*a little dashed*) Well, they've been saying we have nothing to offer but personal popularity. No practi-cal reform. No—   50

STONOR: No truckling to the masses. I suppose. (*Walks impa-tiently away.*)

FARNBOROUGH: (*snubbed*) Well, in these democratic days—(*Turns to* JEAN *for countenance.*) I hope you'll forgive my bursting in like this. (*Struck by her face.*) But I can see you 55 realise the gravity—(*Lowering his voice with an air of speaking for her ear alone.*) It isn't as if he were going to be a mere pri-vate member. Everybody knows he'll be in the Cabinet.

STONOR: (*drily*) It may be a Liberal Cabinet.

FARNBOROUGH: Nobody thought so up to last night. Why, 60 even your brother—but I am afraid I'm seeming officious. (*Takes up his hat.*)

STONOR: (*coldly*) What about my brother?

FARNBOROUGH: I met Lord Windlesham as I rushed out of the Carlton.   65

STONOR: Did he say anything?

FARNBOROUGH: I told him the Dutfield news.

STONOR: (*impatiently*) Well?

FARNBOROUGH: He said it only confirmed his fears.

70 STONOR: (*half under his breath*) Said that, did he?

FARNBOROUGH: Yes. Defeat is inevitable, he thinks, unless—
(*Pause.*)

(GEOFFREY STONOR *who has been pacing the floor, stops but doesn't raise his eyes.*)

unless you can "manufacture some political dynamite
75   within the next few hours." Those were his words.

STONOR: (*resumes his walking to and fro, raises his head and catches sight of* JEAN*'s white, drawn face. Stops short*) You are very tired.

JEAN: No. No.

80 STONOR: (*to* FARNBOROUGH) I'm obliged to you for taking so much trouble. (*Shakes hands by way of dismissing* FARNBOROUGH.) I'll see what can be done.

FARNBOROUGH: (*offering the reply-paid form*) If you'd like to wire I'll take it.

85 STONOR: (*faintly amused*) You don't understand, my young friend. Moves of this kind are not rushed at by responsible politicians. I must have time for consideration.

FARNBOROUGH: (*disappointed*) Oh, well, I only hope someone else won't jump into the breach before you—(*Watch*
90   *in hand.*) I tell you. (*To* JEAN.) I'll find out what time the newspapers go to press on Sunday. Goodbye (*To* STONOR.) I'll be at the Club just *in case* I can be of any use.

STONOR: (*firmly*) No, don't do that. If I should have anything new to say—

95 FARNBOROUGH: (*feverishly*) B-b-but with our party, as your brother said—"heading straight for a vast electoral disaster—"

STONOR: If I decide on a counterblast I shall simply telegraph to headquarters. Goodbye.

100 FARNBOROUGH: Oh—a—g-goodbye. (*A gesture of "The country's going to the dogs."*)

(JEAN *rings the bell. Exit* FARNBOROUGH.)

STONOR: (*studying the carpet*) "Political dynamite," eh? (*Pause.*) After all . . . women are much more conservative than men—aren't they?

(JEAN *looks straight in front of her, making no attempt to reply.*)

105 Especially the women the property qualification would bring in. (*He glances at* JEAN *as though for the first time conscious of her silence.*) You see now (*He throws himself into the chair by the table.*) one reason why I've encouraged you to take an interest in public affairs. Because people like us don't go
110   screaming about it, is no sign we don't (some of us) see what's on the way. However little they want to, women of our class will have to come into line. All the best things in the world—everything that civilisation has won will be in danger if—when this change comes—the only women
115   who have practical political training are the women of the lower classes. Women of the lower classes, and (*His brows knit heavily.*)—women inoculated by the Socialist virus.

JEAN: Geoffrey.

STONOR: (*draws the telegraph form towards him*) Let us see, how we shall put it—when the time comes—shall we? (*He de-* 120 *taches a pencil from his watch chain and bends over the paper, writing.*)

(JEAN *opens her lips to speak, moves a shade nearer the table and then falls back upon her silent, half-incredulous misery.*)

STONOR: (*holds the paper off, smiling*) Enough dynamite in that! Rather too much, isn't there, little girl?

JEAN: Geoffrey, I know her story. 125

STONOR: Whose story?

JEAN: Miss Levering's

STONOR: *Whose?*

JEAN: Vida Levering's

(STONOR *stares speechless. Slight pause.*)

(*The words escaping from her in a miserable cry.*) Why did you 130 desert her?

STONOR: (*staggered*) I! *I?*

JEAN: Oh, why did you do it?

STONOR: (*bewildered*) What in the name of—What has she been saying to you? 135

JEAN: Someone else told me part. Then the way you looked when you saw her at Aunt Ellen's—Miss Levering's saying you didn't know her—then your letting out that you knew even the curious name on the handkerchief—Oh, I pieced it together— 140

STONOR: (*with recovered self-possession*) Your ingenuity is undeniable!

JEAN: —and then, when she said that at the meeting about "the dark hour" and I looked at your face—it flashed over me—Oh, *why* did you desert her? 145

STONOR: I *didn't* desert her.

JEAN: Ah-h! (*Puts her hands before her eyes.*)

(STONOR *makes a passionate motion towards her, is checked by her muffled voice saying.*)

I'm glad—I'm glad!

(*He stares bewildered.* JEAN *drops her hands in her lap and steadies her voice.*)

She went away from you, then?

STONOR: You don't expect me to enter into— 150

JEAN: She went away from you?

STONOR: (*with a look of almost uncontrollable anger*) Yes!

JEAN: Was that because you wouldn't marry her?

STONOR: I couldn't marry her—and she knew it.

JEAN: Did you want to? 155

STONOR: (*an instant's angry scrutiny and then turning away his eyes*) I thought I did—*then*. It's a long time ago.

JEAN: And why "couldn't" you?

STONOR: (*a movement of strong irritation cut short*) Why are you catechising me? It's a matter that concerns another woman. 160

JEAN: If you're saying that it doesn't concern me, you're saying—(*her lip trembles*)—that *you* don't concern me.

STONOR: (*commanding his temper with difficulty*) In those days I—I was absolutely dependent on my father.

JEAN: Why, you must have been thirty, Geoffrey. 165

STONOR: (*slight pause*) What? Oh—thereabouts.

JEAN: And everybody says you're so clever.

STONOR: Well, everybody's mistaken.

JEAN: (*drawing nearer*) It must have been terribly hard—

(STONOR *turns towards her.*)

170   for you both—

(*He arrests his movement and stands stonily.*)

that a man like you shouldn't have had the freedom that even the lowest seem to have.

STONOR: Freedom?

JEAN: To marry the woman they choose.

175 STONOR: She didn't break off our relations because I couldn't marry her.

JEAN: Why was it, then?

STONOR: You're too young to discuss such a story. (*Half turns away.*)

180 JEAN: I'm not so young as she was when—

STONOR: (*wheeling upon her*) Very well, then, if you will have it! The truth is, it didn't seem to weigh upon her, as it seems to on you, that I wasn't able to marry her.

JEAN: Why are you so sure of that?

185 STONOR: Because she didn't so much as hint such a thing when she wrote that she meant to break off the—the—

JEAN: What made her write like that?

STONOR: (*with suppressed rage*) Why *will* you go on talking of what's so long over and ended?

190 JEAN: What reason did she give?

STONOR: If your curiosity has so got the upper hand—*ask her.*

JEAN: (*her eyes upon him*) You're afraid to tell me.

STONOR: (*putting pressure on himself to answer quietly*) I still
195 hoped—at *that* time—to win my father over. She blamed me because (*goes to the window and looks blindly out and speaks in a low tone.*) if the child had lived it wouldn't have been possible to get my father to—to overlook it.

JEAN: (*faintly*) You wanted it *overlooked?* I don't underst—

200 STONOR: (*turning passionately back to her*) Of course you don't. (*He seizes her hand and tries to draw her to him.*) If you did, you wouldn't be the beautiful, tender, innocent child you are—

JEAN: (*has withdrawn her hand and shrunk from him with an im-
205 pulse—slight as is its expression—so tragically eloquent, that fear for the first time catches hold of him*) I am glad you didn't mean to desert her, Geoffrey. It wasn't your fault after all—only some misunderstanding that can be cleared up.

STONOR: *Cleared up?*

210 JEAN: Yes. Cleared up.

STONOR: (*aghast*) You aren't thinking that this miserable old affair I'd as good as forgotten—

JEAN: (*in a horror struck whisper, with a glance at the door which he doesn't see*) Forgotten!

215 STONOR: No, no. I don't mean exactly forgotten. But you're torturing me so I don't know what I'm saying. (*He goes closer.*) You aren't—Jean! you—you aren't going to let it come between you and me!

JEAN: (*presses her handkerchief to her lips, and then, taking it away,
220 answers steadily*) I can't make or unmake what's past. But I'm glad, at least, that you didn't *mean* to desert her in her

trouble. You'll remind her of that first of all, won't you? (*Moves to the door.*)

STONOR: Where are you going? (*Raising his voice.*) Why should I remind anybody of what I want only to forget? 225

JEAN: (*finger on lip*) Sh!

STONOR: (*with eyes on the door*) You don't mean that *she's*—

JEAN: Yes. I left her to get a little rest.

(*He recoils in an access of uncontrollable rage. She follows him. Speechless, he goes to get his hat.*)

Geoffrey, don't go before you hear me. I don't know if what I think matters to you now—but I hope it does. 230 (*With tears.*) You can still make me think of you without shrinking—if you will.

STONOR: (*fixes her a moment with his eyes. Then sternly*) What is it you are asking of me?

JEAN: To make amends, Geoffrey. 235

STONOR: (*with an outburst*) You poor little innocent!

JEAN: I'm poor enough. But (*locking her hands together.*) I'm not so innocent but what I know you must right that old wrong now, if you're ever to right it.

STONOR: You aren't insane enough to think I would turn 240 round in these few hours and go back to something that ten years ago was ended for ever! Why, it's stark, staring madness!

JEAN: No. (*Catching on his arm*) What you did ten years ago—*that* was mad. This is paying a debt. 245

STONOR: Look here, Jean, you're dreadfully wrought up and excited—tired too—

JEAN: No, not tired—though I've travelled so far today. I know you smile at sudden conversions. You think they're hysterical—worse—vulgar. But people must get their rev- 250 elation how they can. And, Geoffrey, if I can't make you see this one of mine—I shall know your love could never mean strength to me. Only weakness. And I shall be afraid. So afraid I'll never dare to give you the *chance* of making me loathe myself. I shall never see you again. 255

STONOR: How right *I* was to be afraid of that vein of fanaticism in you. (*Moves towards the door.*)

JEAN: Certainly you couldn't make a greater mistake than to go away now and think it any good ever to come back. (*He turns.*) Even if I came to feel different, I couldn't *do* 260 anything different. I should know all this couldn't be forgotten. I should know that it would poison my life in the end. Yours too.

STONOR: (*with suppressed fury*) She has made good use of her time? (*With a sudden thought.*) What has changed her? Has 265 *she* been seeing visions too?

JEAN: What do you mean?

STONOR: Why is she intriguing to get hold of a man that, ten years ago, she flatly refused to see, or hold any communication with? 270

JEAN: "Intriguing to get hold of." She hasn't mentioned you!

STONOR: *What!* Then how in the name of Heaven do you know—that she wants—what you ask?

JEAN: (*firmly*) There can't be any doubt about that.

STONOR: (*with immense relief*) You absurd, ridiculous child! 275 Then all this is just your own unaided invention. Well—I could thank God! (*Falls into the nearest chair and passes his handkerchief over his face.*)

JEAN: (*perplexed, uneasy*) For what are you thanking God?

280 STONOR: (*trying to think out his plan of action*) Suppose, (I'm not going to risk it)—but suppose—(*He looks up and at the sight of* JEAN's *face a new tenderness comes into his own. He rises suddenly.*) Whether I deserve to suffer or not—it's quite certain you don't. Don't cry, dear one. It never was the real

285 thing. I had to wait till I knew you before I understood.

JEAN: (*lifts her eyes brimming*) Oh, is that true? (*Checks her movement towards him.*) Loving you has made things clear to me I didn't dream of before. If I could think that be- cause of me you were able to do this—

290 STONOR: (*seizes her by the shoulders and says hoarsely*) Look here! Do you seriously ask me to give up the girl I love— to go and offer to marry a woman that even to think of—

JEAN: You cared for her once. You'll care about her again. She is beautiful and brilliant—everything. I've heard she could

295 win any man she set herself to—

STONOR: (*pushing* JEAN *from him*) She's bewitched you!

JEAN: Geoffrey, Geoffrey, you aren't going away like that. This isn't *the end!*

STONOR: (*darkly—hesitating*) I suppose even if she refused me,

300 you'd—

JEAN: She won't refuse you.

STONOR: She did once.

JEAN: She didn't refuse to *marry* you—

(JEAN *is going to the door.*)

STONOR: (*catches her by the arm*) Wait!—a—(*Hunting for some*

305 *means of gaining time.*) Lady John is waiting all this while for the car to go back with a message.

JEAN: *That's* not a matter of life and death—

STONOR: All the same—I'll go down and give the order.

JEAN: (*stopping quite still on a sudden*) Very well. (*Sits.*) You'll

310 come back if you're the man I pray you are. (*Breaks into a flood of silent tears, her elbows on the table, her face in her hands.*)

STONOR: (*returns, bends over her, about to take her in his arms*) Dearest of all the world—

(*Door opens softly and* VIDA LEVERING *appears. She is arrested at the sight of* STONOR, *and is in the act of drawing back when, upon the slight noise,* STONOR *looks round. His face darkens, he stands staring at her and then with a look of speechless anger goes silently out.* JEAN, *hearing him shut the door, drops her head on the table with a sob.* VIDA LEVERING *crosses slowly to her and stands a moment silent at the girl's side.*)

MISS LEVERING: What is the matter?

315 JEAN: (*lifting her head and drying her eyes*) I—I've been seeing Geoffrey.

MISS LEVERING: (*with an attempt at lightness*) Is this the effect seeing Geoffrey has?

JEAN: You see, I know now (*as* MISS LEVERING *looks quite un-*

320 *comprehending*)—how he (*drops her eyes*)—how he spoiled some one else's life.

MISS LEVERING: (*quickly*) Who tells you that?

JEAN: Several people have told me.

MISS LEVERING: Well, you should be very careful how you

325 believe what you hear.

JEAN: (*passionately*) You *know* it's true.

MISS LEVERING: I know that it's possible to be mistaken.

JEAN: I see! You're trying to shield him—

MISS LEVERING: Why should I—what is it to me?

JEAN: (*with tears*) Oh-h, how you must love him! 330

MISS LEVERING: Listen to me—

JEAN: (*rising*) What's the use of your going on denying it? (MISS LEVERING, *about to break in, is silenced.*) *Geoffrey doesn't.*

(JEAN, *struggling to command her feelings, goes to window.* VIDA LEV- ERING *relinquishes an impulse to follow, and sits left centre.* JEAN *comes slowly back with her eyes bent on the floor, does not lift them till she is quite near* VIDA. *Then the girl's self-absorbed face changes.*)

Oh, don't look like that! I shall bring him back to you! 335 (*Drops on her knees beside the other's chair.*)

MISS LEVERING: You would be impertinent (*softening*) if you weren't a romantic child. You can't bring him back.

JEAN: Yes, he—

MISS LEVERING: But there's something you *can* do— 340

JEAN: What?

MISS LEVERING: Bring him to the point where he recognises that he's in our debt.

JEAN: In *our* debt?

MISS LEVERING: In debt to women. He can't repay the one 345 he robbed—

JEAN: (*wincing and rising from her knees*) Yes, yes.

MISS LEVERING: (*sternly*) No, he can't repay the dead. But there are the living. There are the thousands with hope still in their hearts and youth in their blood. Let him help 350 them. Let him be a Friend to Women.

JEAN: (*rising on a wave of enthusiasm*) Yes, yes—I understand. That too!

(*The door opens. As* STONOR *enters with* LADY JOHN, *he makes a slight gesture towards the two as much as to say, "You see."*)

JEAN: (*catching sight of him*) Thank you!

LADY JOHN: (*in a clear, commonplace tone to* JEAN) Well, you 355 rather gave us the slip. Vida, I believe Mr. Stonor wants to see you for a few minutes (*glances at watch*)—but I'd like a word with you first, as I must get back. (*To* STONOR.) Do you think the car—your man said something about re- charging. 360

STONOR: (*hastily*) Oh, did he? I'll see about it.

(*As* STONOR *is going out he encounters the* BUTLER. *Exit* STONOR.)

BUTLER: Mr Trent has called, Miss, to take Miss Levering to the meeting.

JEAN: Bring Mr Trent into my sitting room. I'll tell him—you can't go tonight. 365

(*Exeunt* BUTLER *centre,* JEAN *left.*)

LADY JOHN: (*hurriedly*) I know, my dear, *you're* not aware of what that impulsive girl wants to insist on.

MISS LEVERING: Yes, I am aware of it.

LADY JOHN: But it isn't with your sanction, surely, that she goes on making this extraordinary demand. 370

MISS LEVERING: (*slowly*) I didn't sanction it at first, but I've been thinking it over.

LADY JOHN: Then all I can say is I am greatly disappointed in you. You threw this man over years ago for reasons— whatever they were—that seemed to you good and suffi- 375 cient. And now you come between him and a younger woman—just to play Nemesis, so far as I can make out!

MISS LEVERING: Is that what he says?

LADY JOHN: He says nothing that isn't fair and considerate.

380 MISS LEVERING: I can see he's changed.

LADY JOHN: And you're unchanged—is that it?

MISS LEVERING: I've changed even more than he.

LADY JOHN: But (*pity and annoyance blended in her tone*)—you care about him still, Vida?

385 MISS LEVERING: No.

LADY JOHN: I see. It's just that you wish to marry somebody—

MISS LEVERING: Oh, Lady John, there are no men listening.

LADY JOHN: (*surprised*) No, I didn't suppose there were.

390 MISS LEVERING: Then why keep up that old pretence?

LADY JOHN: What pre—

MISS LEVERING: That to marry *at all costs* is every woman's dearest ambition till the grave closes over her. You and I *know* it isn't true.

395 LADY JOHN: Well, but—Oh! it was just the unexpected sight of him bringing it back—*That* was what fired you this afternoon! (*With an honest attempt at sympathetic understanding.*) Of course. The memory of a thing like that can never die—can never even be dimmed—*for the woman.*

400 MISS LEVERING: I mean her to think so.

LADY JOHN: (*bewildered*) Jean!

(MISS LEVERING *nods.*)

LADY JOHN: And it *isn't so?*

MISS LEVERING: You don't seriously believe a woman with anything else to think about, comes to the end of ten years

405 still *absorbed* in a memory of that sort?

LADY JOHN: (*astonished*) You've got over it, then!

MISS LEVERING: If the newspapers didn't remind me I shouldn't remember once a twelvemonth that there was ever such a person as Geoffrey Stonor in the world.

410 LADY JOHN: (*with unconscious rapture*) Oh, I'm *so* glad!

MISS LEVERING: (*smiles grimly*) Yes. I'm glad too.

LADY JOHN: And if Geoffrey Stonor offered you—what's called 'reparation'—you'd refuse it?

MISS LEVERING: (*smiles a little contemptuously*) Geoffrey

415 Stonor! For me he's simply one of the far back links in a chain of evidence. It's certain I think a hundred times of other women's present unhappiness, to once that I remember that old unhappiness of mine that's past. I think of the nail and chain makers of Cradley Heath. The

420 sweated girls of the slums. I think of the army of ill-used women whose very existence I mustn't mention—

LADY JOHN: (*interrupting hurriedly*) Then why in Heaven's name do you let poor Jean imagine—

MISS LEVERING: (*bending forward*) Look—I'll trust you, Lady

425 John. I don't suffer from that old wrong as Jean thinks I do, but I shall coin her sympathy into gold for a greater cause than mine.

LADY JOHN: I don't understand you.

MISS LEVERING: Jean isn't old enough to be able to care as

430 much about a principle as about a person. But if my half-forgotten pain can turn her generosity into the common treasury—

LADY JOHN: What do you propose she shall do, poor child?

MISS LEVERING: Use her hold over Geoffrey Stonor to make him help us!   435

LADY JOHN: Help you?

MISS LEVERING: The man who served one woman—God knows how many more—very ill, shall serve hundreds of thousands well. Geoffrey Stonor shall make it harder for his son, harder still for his grandson, to treat any woman 440 as he treated me.

LADY JOHN: How will he do that?

MISS LEVERING: By putting an end to the helplessness of women.

LADY JOHN: (*ironically*) You must think he has a great deal of 445 power—

MISS LEVERING: Power? Yes, men have too much over penniless and frightened women.

LADY JOHN: (*impatiently*) What nonsense! You talk as though the women hadn't their share of human nature. *We* aren't 450 made of ice any more than the men.

MISS LEVERING: No, but all the same we have more self-control.

LADY JOHN: Than men?

MISS LEVERING: You know we have.   455

LADY JOHN: (*shrewdly*) I know we mustn't admit it.

MISS LEVERING: For fear they'd call us fishes!

LADY JOHN: (*evasively*) They talk of our lack of self-control—but it's the last thing they *want* women to have.

MISS LEVERING: Oh, we know what they want us to have. So 460 we make shift to have it. If we don't, we go without hope—sometimes we go without bread.

LADY JOHN: (*shocked*) Vida—do you mean to say that you—

MISS LEVERING: I mean to say that men's vanity won't let them see it, but the thing's largely a question of economics. 465

LADY JOHN: (*shocked*) You *never* loved him, then!

MISS LEVERING: Oh yes. I loved him—*once*. It was my helplessness turned the best thing life can bring, into a curse for both of us.

LADY JOHN: I don't understand you—   470

MISS LEVERING: Oh, being "understood!"—that's too much to expect. When people come to know I've joined the Union—

LADY JOHN: But you won't—

MISS LEVERING: —who is there who will resist the tempta- 475 tion to say, "Poor Vida Levering! What a pity she hasn't got a husband and a baby to keep her quiet"? The few who know about me, they'll be equally sure that it's not the larger view of life I've gained—my own poor little story is responsible for my new departure. (*Leans forward and* 480 *looks into* LADY JOHN's *face.*) My best friend, she will be surest of all, that it's a private sense of loss, or, lower yet, a grudge—! But I tell you the only difference between me and thousands of women with husbands and babies is that I'm free to say what I think. *They aren't.*   485

LADY JOHN: (*rising and looking at her watch*) I must get back—my poor ill-used guests.

MISS LEVERING: (*rising*) I won't ring. I think you'll find Mr Stonor downstairs waiting for you.

LADY JOHN: (*embarrassed*) Oh—a—he will have left word 490 about the car in any case.

(MISS LEVERING *has opened the door.* ALLEN TRENT *is in the act of saying goodbye to* JEAN *in the hall.*)

MISS LEVERING: Well, Mr Trent, I didn't expect to see you this evening.

TRENT: (*comes and stands in the doorway*) Why not? Have I ever
495   failed?

MISS LEVERING: Lady John, this is one of our allies. He is good enough to squire me through the rabble from time to time.

LADY JOHN: Well, I think it's very handsome of you, after
500   what she said today about men. (*Shakes hands.*)

TRENT: I've no great opinion of most men myself. I might add—or of most women.

LADY JOHN: Oh! Well, at any rate I shall go away relieved to think that Miss Levering's plain speaking hasn't alienated
505   *all* masculine regard.

TRENT: Why should it?

LADY JOHN: That's right, Mr Trent! Don't believe all she says in the heat of propaganda.

TRENT: I do believe all she says. But I'm not cast down.

510 LADY JOHN: (*smiling*) Not when she says—

TRENT: (*interrupting*) Was there never a misogynist of my sex who ended by deciding to make an exception?

LADY JOHN: (*smiling significantly*) Oh, if *that's* what you build on!

515 TRENT: Well, why shouldn't a man-hater on your side prove equally open to reason?

MISS LEVERING: That part of the question doesn't concern me. I've come to a place where I realise that the first battles of this new campaign must be fought by women
520   alone. The only effective help men could give—amendment of the law—they refuse. The rest is nothing.

LADY JOHN: Don't be ungrateful, Vida. Here's Mr Trent ready to face criticism in publicly championing you.

MISS LEVERING: It's an illusion that I as an individual need Mr
525   Trent. I am quite safe in the crowd. Please don't wait for me, and don't come for me again.

TRENT: (*flushes*) Of course if you'd rather—

MISS LEVERING: And that reminds me. I was asked to thank you and to tell you, too, that they—the women of the
530   Union—they won't need your chairmanship any more—though that, I beg you to believe, has nothing to with any feeling of mine.

TRENT: (*hurt*) Of course. I know there must be other men ready—better known men—

535 MISS LEVERING: It isn't that. It's simply that they find a man can't keep a rowdy meeting in order as well as a woman.

(*He stares.*)

LADY JOHN: You aren't serious?

MISS LEVERING: (*to* TRENT) Haven't you noticed that all their worst disturbances come when men are in charge?

540 TRENT: Well—a—(*laughs a little ruefully as he moves to the door.*) I hadn't connected the two ideas. Goodbye.

MISS LEVERING: Goodbye.

(JEAN *takes him downstairs, right centre.*)

LADY JOHN: (*as* TRENT *disappears*) That nice boy's in love with you.

(MISS LEVERING *simply looks at her.*)

Goodbye. (*They shake hands.*) I wish you hadn't been so 545 unkind to that nice boy!

MISS LEVERING: Do you?

LADY JOHN: Yes, for then I would be more certain of your telling Geoffrey Stonor that intelligent women don't nurse their wrongs and lie in wait to punish them. 550

MISS LEVERING: You are *not* certain?

LADY JOHN: (*goes close up to* VIDA) Are you?

(VIDA *stands with her eyes on the ground, silent, motionless.* LADY JOHN, *with a nervous glance at her watch and a gesture of extreme perturbation, goes hurriedly out.* VIDA *shuts the door. She comes slowly back, sits down and covers her face with her hands. She rises and begins to walk up and down, obviously trying to master her agitation. Enter* GEOFFREY STONOR.)

MISS LEVERING: Well, have they primed you? Have you got your lesson (*with a little broken laugh*) by heart at last?

STONOR: (*looking at her from immeasurable distance*) I am not 555 sure I understand you. (*Pause.*) However unpropitious your mood may be—I shall discharge my errand. (*Pause. Her silence irritates him.*) I have promised to offer you what I believe is called "amends."

MISS LEVERING: (*quickly*) You've come to realise, then—after 560 all these years—that you owed me something?

STONOR: (*on the brink of protest, checks himself*) I am not here to deny it.

MISS LEVERING: (*fiercely*) Pay, then—*pay*.

STONOR: (*a moment's dread as he looks at her, his lips set. Then* 565 *stonily*) I have promised that, if you exact it, I will.

MISS LEVERING: Ah! If I insist you'll "make it all good"! (*Quite low.*) Then don't you know you must pay me in kind?

STONOR: What do you mean. 570

MISS LEVERING: Give me back what you took from me: my old faith. Give me that.

STONOR: Oh, if you mean to make phrases—(*A gesture of scant patience.*)

MISS LEVERING: (*going closer*) Or give me back mere kind- 575 ness—or even tolerance. Oh, I don't mean *your* tolerance! Give me back the power to think fairly of my brothers—not as mockers—thieves.

STONOR: I have not mocked you. And I have asked you—

MISS LEVERING: Something you knew I should refuse! Or 580 (*her eyes blaze*) did you dare to be afraid I wouldn't?

STONOR: I suppose, if we set our teeth, we could—

MISS LEVERING: I couldn't—not even if I set my teeth. And you wouldn't dream of asking me, if you thought there was the smallest chance. 585

STONOR: I can do no more than make you an offer of such reparation as is in my power. If you don't accept it—(*He turns with an air of "That's done."*)

MISS LEVERING: Accept it? No! . . . Go away and live in debt! Pay and pay and pay—and find yourself still in debt!—for 590 a thing you'll never be able to give me back. (*Lower.*) And when you come to die, say to yourself. "I paid all creditors but one."

STONOR: I'm rather tired, you know, of this talk of debt. If I hear that you persist in it I shall have to— 595

MISS LEVERING: What? (*She faces him.*)

STONOR: No. I'll keep to my resolution. (*Turning to the door.*)

MISS LEVERING: (*intercepting him*) What resolution?

STONOR: I came here, under considerable pressure, to speak
600   of the future—not to re-open the past.

MISS LEVERING: The Future and the Past are one.

STONOR: You talk as if that old madness was mine alone. It is
the woman's way.

MISS LEVERING: I know. And it's not fair. Men suffer as well
605   as we by the woman's starting wrong. We are taught to
think the man a sort of demigod. If he tells her: "go down
into Hell"—down into Hell she goes.

STONOR: Make no mistake. Not the woman alone. *They go
down together.*

610 MISS LEVERING: Yes, they go down together, but the man
comes up alone. As a rule. It is more convenient so—for
him. And for the Other Woman.

(*The eyes of both go to* JEAN's *door.*)

STONOR: (*angrily*) My conscience is clear. I know—and so do
you—that most men in my position wouldn't have trou-
615   bled themselves. I gave myself endless trouble.

MISS LEVERING: (*with wondering eyes*) So you've gone about all
these years feeling that you'd discharged every obligation.

STONOR: Not only that. I stood by you with a fidelity that
was nothing short of Quixotic. If, woman like, you *must*
620   recall the Past—I insist on your recalling it correctly.

MISS LEVERING: (*very low*) You think I don't recall it correctly?

STONOR: Not when you make—other people believe that I
deserted you. (*With gathering wrath.*) It's a curious enough
charge when you stop to consider—(*Checks himself, and
625   with a gesture of impatience sweeps the whole thing out of his
way.*)

MISS LEVERING: Well, when we *do*—just for five minutes out
of ten years—when we do stop to consider—

STONOR: We remember it was *you* who did the deserting!
630   Since you had to rake the story up, you might have had
the fairness to tell the facts.

MISS LEVERING: You think "the facts" would have excused
you! (*She sits.*)

STONOR: No doubt you've forgotten them, since Lady John
635   tells me you wouldn't remember my existence once a year
if the newspapers didn't—

MISS LEVERING: Ah, you minded that!

STONOR: (*with manly spirit*) I minded your giving false impressions. (*She is about to speak, he advances on her.*) Do you
640   deny that you returned my letters unopened?

MISS LEVERING: (*quietly*) No.

STONOR: Do you deny that you refused to see me—and that,
when I persisted, you vanished?

MISS LEVERING: I don't deny any of those things.

645 STONOR: Why, I had no trace of you for years!

MISS LEVERING: I suppose not.

STONOR: Very well, then. What *could* I do?

MISS LEVERING: Nothing. It was too late to do anything.

STONOR: It wasn't too late! You knew—since you "read the
650   papers"—that my father died that same year. There was no
longer any barrier between us.

MISS LEVERING: Oh yes, there was a barrier.

STONOR: Of your own making, then.

MISS LEVERING: I had my guilty share in it—but the barrier
655   (*her voice trembles*)—the barrier was your invention.

STONOR: It was no "invention." If you had ever known my
father—

MISS LEVERING: Oh, the echoes! The echoes! How often you
used to say, if I "knew your father!" But you said, too,
(*lower*)—you called the greatest barrier by another name.   660

STONOR: What name?

MISS LEVERING: (*very low*) The child that was to come.

STONOR: (*hastily*) That was before my father died. While I still
hoped to get his consent.

MISS LEVERING: (*nods*) How the thought of that all-powerful   665
personage used to terrorise me! What chance had a little
unborn child against "the last of the great feudal lords," as
you called him.

STONOR: You *know* the child would have stood between you
and me!   670

MISS LEVERING: I know the child *did* stand—

STONOR: (*with vague uneasiness*) It *did* stand—

MISS LEVERING: Happy mothers teach their children. Mine
had to teach me.

STONOR: You talk as if—   675

MISS LEVERING: —teach me that a woman may do a thing for
love's sake that shall kill love.

(*A silence.*)

STONOR: (*fearing and putting from him fuller comprehension, rises
with an air of finality*) You certainly made it plain you had
no love left for me.   680

MISS LEVERING: I had need of it all for the child.

STONOR: (*stares—comes closer, speaks hurriedly and very low*) Do
you mean then that, after all—it lived?

MISS LEVERING: No; I mean that it was sacrificed. But it
showed me no barrier is so impassable as the one a little   685
child can raise.

STONOR: (*a light dawning*) Was that why you . . . was *that* why?

MISS LEVERING: (*nods, speechless a moment*) Day and night
there it was!—between my thought of you and me. (*He
sits again, staring at her.*) When I was most unhappy I would   690
wake, thinking I heard it cry. It was my own crying I
heard, but I seemed to have it in my arms. I suppose I was
mad. I used to lie there in that lonely farmhouse pretending to hush it. It was so I hushed myself.

STONOR: I never knew—   695

MISS LEVERING: I didn't blame you. You couldn't risk being
with me.

STONOR: You agreed that for both our sakes—

MISS LEVERING: Yes, you had to be very circumspect. You
were so well known. Your autocratic father—your brilliant   700
political future—

STONOR: Be fair. *Our* future—as I saw it then.

MISS LEVERING: Yes, it all hung on concealment. It must have
looked quite simple to you. You didn't know that the ghost
of a child that had never seen the light, the frail thing you   705
meant to sweep aside and forget—*have* swept aside and forgotten—you didn't know it was strong enough to push
you out of my life. (*Lower with an added intensity.*) It can do
more. (*Leans over him and whispers.*) It can push that girl out.
(*STONOR's face changes.*) It can do more still.   710

STONOR: Are you threatening me?

MISS LEVERING: No. I am preparing you.

STONOR: For what?

MISS LEVERING: For the work that must be done. Either with
715   *your help*—or *that girl's.*

(STONOR *lifts his eyes a moment.*)

One of two things. Either her life, and all she has, given to
this new service—or a Ransom, if I give her up to you.
STONOR: I see. A price. Well—?
MISS LEVERING: (*looks searchingly in his face, hesitates and shakes*
720   *her head*) Even if I could trust you to pay—no, it would be
a poor bargain to give her up for anything you could do.
STONOR: (*rising*) In spite of your assumption—she may not
be your tool.
MISS LEVERING: You are horribly afraid she is! But you are
725   wrong. Don't think it's merely I that have got hold of Jean
Dumbarton.
STONOR: (*angrily*) Who else?
MISS LEVERING: The New Spirit that's abroad.

(STONOR *turns away with an exclamation and begins to pace,*
sentinel-like, up and down before JEAN'*s door.*)

How else should that inexperienced girl have felt the new
730   loyalty and responded as she did?
STONOR: (*under his breath*) "New" indeed—however little
loyal.
MISS LEVERING: Loyal above all. But no newer than electricity was when it first lit up the world. It had been there
735   since the world began—waiting to do away with the dark.
So has the thing you're fighting.
STONOR: (*his voice held down to its lowest register*) The thing I'm
fighting is nothing more than one person's hold on a
highly sensitive imagination. I consented to this interview
740   with the hope—(*A gesture of impotence.*) It only remains for
me to show her your true motive is revenge.
MISS LEVERING: Once say that to her and you are lost!

(STONOR *motionless; his look is the look of a man who sees happi-*
ness slipping away.)

I know what it is that men fear. It even seems as if it must
be through fear that your enlightenment will come. That
745   is why I see a value in Jean Dumbarton far beyond her
fortune.

(STONOR *lifts his eyes dully and fixes them on* VIDA'*s face.*)

More than any girl I know—if I keep her from you—that
gentle, inflexible creature could rouse in men the old half-
superstitious fear—
750   STONOR: "Fear?" I believe you are mad.
MISS LEVERING: "Mad." "Unsexed." These are the words of
today. In the Middle Ages men cried out "Witch!" and
burnt her—the woman who served no man's bed or
board.
765   STONOR: You want to make that poor child believe—
MISS LEVERING: She sees for herself we've come to a place
where we find there's a value men see in them. You teach
us not to look to you for some of the things we need
most. If women must be freed by women, we have need
770   of such as—(*Her eyes go to* JEAN'*s door.*)—who knows? She
may be the new Joan of Arc.
STONOR: (*aghast*) That *she* should be the sacrifice!

MISS LEVERING: You have taught us to look very calmly on
the sacrifice of women. Men tell us in every tongue it's "a
necessary evil."   775

(STONOR *stands rooted, staring at the ground.*)

One girl's happiness—against a thing nobler than happiness for thousands—who can hesitate?—*Not Jean.*
STONOR: Good God! Can't you see that this crazed campaign
you'd start her on—even if it's successful, it can only be so
through the help of men? What excuse shall you make   780
your own soul for not going straight to the goal?
MISS LEVERING: You think we wouldn't be glad to go straight
to the goal?
STONOR: I do. I see you'd much rather punish me and see her
revel in a morbid self-sacrifice.   785
MISS LEVERING: You say I want to punish you only because,
like most men, you won't take the trouble to understand
what we do want—or how determined we are to have it.
You can't kill this new spirit among women. (*Going*
nearer.) And you couldn't make a greater mistake than to   790
think it finds a home only in the exceptional, or the unhappy. It's so strange, Geoffrey, to see a man like you as
much deluded as the Hyde Park loafers who say to Ernestine Blunt, "Who's hurt *your* feelings?" Why not realise
(*Going quite close to him.*) this is a thing that goes deeper   795
than personal experience? And yet (*Lowering her voice and*
glancing at the door.) if you take only the narrowest personal
view, a good deal depends on what you and I agree upon
in the next five minutes.
STONOR: (*bringing her farther away from the door*) You recom-   800
mend my realising the larger issues. But in your ambition
to attach that girl to the chariot wheels of "Progress," you
quite ignore the fact that people fitter for such work—the
men you look to enlist in the end—are ready waiting to
give the thing a chance.   805
MISS LEVERING: Men are ready! What men?
STONOR: (*avoiding her eyes, picking his words*) Women have
themselves to blame that the question has grown so delicate that responsible people shrink—for the moment—
from being implicated in it.   810
MISS LEVERING: We have seen the "shrinking."
STONOR: Without quoting any one else, I might point out
that the New Antagonism seems to have blinded you to
the small fact that I, for one, am not an opponent.
MISS LEVERING: The phrase *has* a familiar ring. We have heard   815
it from four hundred and twenty others.
STONOR: I spoke, if I may say so, of some one who would
count. Some one who can carry his party along with
him—or risk a seat in the Cabinet.
MISS LEVERING: (*quickly*) Did you mean you are ready to do   820
that?
STONOR: An hour ago I was.
MISS LEVERING: Ah! . . . an hour ago.
STONOR: Exactly. You don't understand men. They can be
led. They can't be driven. Ten minutes before you came   825
into the room I was ready to say I would throw in my po-
litical lot with this Reform.
MISS LEVERING: And now . . .?
STONOR: Now you block my way by an attempt at coercion.
By forcing my hand you give my adherence an air of   830

bargain-driving for a personal end. Exactly the mistake of the ignorant agitators of your "Union," as you call it. You have a great deal to learn. This movement will go forward, not because of the agitation, but in spite of it. There are 835 men in Parliament who would have been actively serving the Reform today . . . as actively as so vast a constitutional change—

MISS LEVERING: (*smiles faintly*) And they haven't done it because—

840 STONOR: Because it would have put a premium on breaches of decent behaviour. (*He takes a crumpled piece of paper out of his pocket.*) Look here!

MISS LEVERING: (*flushes with excitement as she reads the telegram*) This is very good. I see only one objection.

845 STONOR: Objection!

MISS LEVERING: You haven't sent it.

STONOR: *That* is your fault.

MISS LEVERING: When did you write this?

STONOR: Just before you came in—when—(*He glances at the* 850 *door.*)

MISS LEVERING: Ah! It must have pleased Jean—that message. (*Offers him back the paper.*)

(STONOR *astonished at her yielding it up so lightly, and remembering* JEAN *had not so much as read it. He throws himself heavily into a chair and drops his head in his hands.*)

I could drive a hard-and-fast bargain with you, but I think I won't. If *both* love and ambition urge you on, perhaps— 855 (*She gazes at the slack, hopeless figure with its sudden look of age—goes over silently and stands by his side.*) After all, life hasn't been quite fair to you—

(*He raises his heavy eyes.*)

You fall out of one ardent woman's dreams into another's.

STONOR: You may as well tell me—do you mean to—?

860 MISS LEVERING: To keep you and her apart? No.

STONOR: (*for the first time tears come into his eyes. After a moment he holds out his hand*) What can I do for you?

(MISS LEVERING *shakes her head—speechless.*)

For the real you. Not the Reformer, or the would-be politician—for the woman I so unwillingly hurt. (*As she* 865 *turns away, struggling with her feelings, he lays a detaining hand on her arm.*) You may not believe it, but now that I understand, there is almost nothing I wouldn't do to right that old wrong.

MISS LEVERING: There's nothing to be done. You can never 870 give me back my child.

STONOR: (*at the anguish in* VIDA's *face his own has changed*) Will that ghost give you no rest?

MISS LEVERING: Yes, oh, yes. I see life is nobler than I knew. There is work to do.

875 STONOR: (*stopping her as she goes towards the folding doors*) Why should you think that it's only you, these ten years have

taught something to? Why not give even a man credit for a willingness to learn something of life, and for being sorry—profoundly sorry—for the pain his instruction has cost others? You seem to think I've taken it all quite 880 lightly. That's not fair. All my life, ever since you disappeared, the thought of you has hurt. I would give anything I possess to know you—were happy again.

MISS LEVERING: Oh, happiness!

STONOR: (*significantly*) Why shouldn't you find it still. 885

MISS LEVERING: (*stares an instant*) I see! She couldn't help telling about Allen Trent—Lady John couldn't.

STONOR: You're one of the people the years have not taken from, but given more to. You are more than ever . . . You haven't lost your beauty. 890

MISS LEVERING: The gods saw it was so little effectual, it wasn't worth taking away. (*She stands looking out into the void.*) One woman's mishap?—what is that? A thing as trivial to the great world as it's sordid in most eyes. But the time has come when a woman may look about her, and 895 say, "What general significance has my secret pain? Does it 'join on' to anything?" And I find it does. I'm no longer merely a woman who has stumbled on the way. I'm one (*She controls with difficulty the shake in her voice.*) who has got up bruised and bleeding, wiped the dust from her hands 900 and the tears from her face, and said to herself not merely, "Here's one luckless woman! but—here is a stone of stumbling to many. Let's see if it can't be moved out of other women's way." And she calls people to come and help. No mortal man, let alone a woman, *by herself,* can 905 move that rock of offence. But (*with a sudden sombre flame of enthusiasm*) if many help, Geoffrey, the thing can be done.

STONOR: (*looks at her with wondering pity*) Lord! how you care!

MISS LEVERING: (*touched by his moved faced*) Don't be so sad. 910 Shall I tell you a secret? Jean's ardent dreams needn't frighten you, if she has a child. *That*—from the beginning, it was not the strong arm—it was the weakest—the little, little arms that subdued the fiercest of us.

(STONOR *puts out a pitying hand uncertainly towards her. She does not take it, but speaks with great gentleness.*)

You will have other children, Geoffrey—for me there was 915 to be only one. Well, well—(*She brushes her tears away.*)— since men alone have tried and failed to make a decent world for the little children to live in—it's as well some of us are childless. (*Quietly taking up her hat and cloak.*) Yes, *we* are the ones who have no excuse for standing aloof from 920 the fight.

STONOR: Vida!

MISS LEVERING: What?

STONOR: You've forgotten something. (*As she looks back he is signing the message.*) This.

(*She goes out silently with the "political dynamite" in her hand.*)

(*Curtain.*)

Bernard Shaw

George Bernard Shaw (1856–1950) was a man of wide-ranging passions and huge abilities (Shaw disliked the name "George" and never used it, preferring "Bernard" or simply "G.B.S."). By his fortieth birthday he had written five novels, three volumes of classic music criticism, and three volumes of incendiary theater reviews; he had become visible in the influential socialist political organization, the **FABIAN SOCIETY;** he had written the first books in English on Wagner's operas and on Ibsen's plays; and he had just started his career as a dramatist, a career that would eventually include more than fifty plays.

Shaw was born in Dublin. Like Jonathan Swift and Richard Brinsley Sheridan before him, Shaw retained the satiric perspective of the Irish outsider in England. His mother was a music teacher and his sister was a promising singer when they left for London while Shaw was in his teens. He followed them to London in 1876. A shy and self-effacing young man, Shaw took a variety of jobs that brought him into contact with the public, and he used the opportunity of lecturing for the Fabian Society to develop the brilliantly articulate persona we recognize today as "G.B.S." Throughout the 1880s, Shaw worked with the Fabians, adopting their plan of gradual social reform in place of a more rigorously Marxist call for social revolution. The Fabians strove to change society through a strategy of permeation, working to get their members elected into prominent offices, where their educational and social reforms might be put into effect. Shaw was deeply influenced by the Fabians' gradualist scheme for social improvement—a scheme that underlies the utopian project of his greatest plays—for Fabian gradualism synchronized with Shaw's other passion, Creative Evolution. Appalled by what he regarded as the mindless mechanism of Darwinian natural selection, Shaw resisted the notion that human evolution followed a random and inevitable process. He urged instead that humanity take command of its future by willing itself to evolve in certain humane directions, and he advocated eugenics, capital punishment, and other ideas in the interest of the development of the species. Shaw attempted an uneasy synthesis of the Fabian socialist project of gradual social evolution with the individualist metaphysics of Creative Evolution: the improvement of society through the improvement of each of its members.

Shaw's friend William Archer once described seeing Shaw in the British Museum reading room simultaneously reading Marx's *Das Kapital* and the score of Wagner's *Ring of the Niebelung* cycle. The blending of political substance with a rich and deeply harmonized verbal music became a constant feature of Shaw's drama. Writing as a theater critic in the 1890s, Shaw became the champion of Ibsen in England. Vowing to lay siege to the conventions of the nineteenth-century theater, he touted Ibsen's plays and lambasted the corny tearjerkers, simplistic melodramas, and overstuffed Shakespearean productions that were the theater's common fare. Not incidentally, he worked to create a taste for his own plays, an operatic drama of the intellectual passions.

Shaw's career as a playwright falls into three main phases. Shaw's earliest plays—*Widowers' Houses* (1892) and *Mrs. Warren's Profession* (1893)—attacked specific social problems, like slum landlords and international prostitution. But Shaw more often linked social ills to the smug pieties of conventional morality. His plays generally work to disillusion his main characters—and his audience—from the ready acceptance of bourgeois ideology as a natural "reality." This process of disillusionment informs Shaw's lighter comedies of the 1890s, plays like *Arms and the Man* (1894), *Candida* (1894), and *Caesar and Cleopatra* (1898). After the turn of the century, however, Shaw entered on his maturity as a playwright, undertaking a series of major comedies that place this process of disillusionment directly in conflict with society's most important institutions: marriage and sexuality in *Man and Superman* (1903); British imperialism in Ireland in *John Bull's Other Island* (1904); salvation, damnation, and raw power in *Major Barbara* (1905); medicine in *The Doctor's Dilemma* (1906); language and class in *Pygmalion* (1912). Several of these plays were first produced at the Court Theater, under the management of Shaw's close friend Harley Granville Barker, who originated the part of Cusins in *Major Barbara* and other Shavian roles. Under Barker and his partner J.E. Vedrenne, the Court Theater in 1904–1907 became the most influential theater in London before World War I. Through its efforts, and Shaw's own energy as playwright, director, and advisor, the Court made Shaw's reputation as a major dramatist. With the coming of World War I, and the violent waste of civilization it brought with it, Shaw's confidence in the eventual perfection of humanity was deeply shaken, and the plays of his final half-century are much bleaker, more uncertain in tone: his magnificent "fantasia in the Russian manner on English themes," *Heartbreak House* (1919), modeled on Chekhov's *The Cherry Orchard; Saint Joan* (1923), perhaps his best-loved play; his five-play quintet on the origin and future of the species, *Back to Methuselah* (1921); and many others. In contrast to the confidence of Shaw's earlier plays, the later dramas generally seem to ask the question that Shaw gave to his Saint Joan: "O God that madest this beautiful earth, when will it be ready to receive Thy saints? How long, O Lord, how long?"

Shaw was born before the publication of Darwin's *Origin of Species* in 1859, and he died after the dropping of the atomic bomb on Hiroshima. His major plays, like *Major Barbara,* treat the problems of the twentieth century in the dramatic vocabulary of Edwardian COMEDY OF MANNERS. *Major Barbara* is typical of the dialectical process of Shaw's plays. From the

MAJOR BARBARA

Adolphus Cusins beats the big drum in the finale of Act 2 of Bernard Shaw's *Major Barbara*.

outset—when Stephen learns that his income is derived from his father's munitions empire—Shaw forces the audience and his characters to question the nature of their values, particularly the sense that good and evil, morality and economics, the power to save and the power to destroy can be easily or conveniently distinguished from one another. As a result, the play forces a deeply ironic experience on its characters and on the audience. For Shaw is interested in salvation, not simply the moralizing salvation promised by the Salvation Army, but a Nietzschean transvaluation of values, a salvation beyond the conventional abstractions of good and evil that he regards as necessary to the transformation of English society.

The play is structured dialectically, progressing from thesis, to antithesis, to a problematic synthesis. The "thesis" of act 1 concerns the values of Wilton Crescent: the comfortable morality of the English upper classes. As the scene proceeds, though, Shaw suggests that conventional morality, the innate knowledge of right and wrong, is in fact supported by Undershaft's money and gunpowder. The "antithesis" of act 2 offers the unconventional morality of the Salvation Army; Barbara's shelter in West Ham claims to provide true salvation by requiring a more sincere form of religious conviction. However, as it turns out, both Wilton Crescent and West Ham are equally in the grip of Bodger and Undershaft. The distiller and the munitions-maker determine the material realities on which society erects its illusory social "ideals" and calls them "reality." The Dionysian sacrifice of Barbara at the end of act 2— with its echoes of Christ's crucifixion as well—prepares us for her resurrection in the "synthesis" offered by act 3; in Perivale St Andrews, the spiritual Barbara and the intellectual Cusins are married with the blessing of the explosive Undershaft. We might be troubled, though, by the "synthesis" offered by the utopian factory town, for Undershaft's utopia hardly seems revolutionary. In many ways, Perivale St Andrews largely duplicates turn-of-the-century English class society and industrial capitalism, with the poverty and dirt cleaned up. The play's last act is often said to be unconvincing, and we might wonder whether that is in fact part of Shaw's purpose in *Major Barbara*. Once Shaw instructs us in the process of dialectical criticism, perhaps he invites us to scrutinize even Undershaft's bourgeois utopia, to see Perivale St Andrews as itself in need of further (r)evolution.

Shaw made Andrew Undershaft a magnificently melodramatic, attractive, amoral munitions-maker, whose creative ability is harnessed to the power to destroy. Moreover, Shaw drew a parallel between Undershaft and a crucial dramatic precursor, the Dionysus of Euripides' *The Bacchae*. The character of Cusins was modeled on Shaw's friend, the well-known classical scholar Gilbert Murray, and in the original production, Cusins was even played to resemble Murray. In act 2, Cusins quotes a brief passage adapted from Murray's translation of *The Bacchae*, part of the choral speech delivered just before Pentheus is led out to spy on the Bacchae and be killed. We might take this invocation of Dionysus as a final clue to the play's attitude. Much like Euripides, Shaw prevents his audience from sympathizing entirely with his hero, from readily accepting the terrible power necessary to change the world. Although the play ends with a ceremonial marriage characteristic of **ROMANTIC COMEDY**—symbolizing the union of intellect, spirit, and power—the fact that Dionysus Undershaft presides over this union should give us pause. Can the power he wields really be harnessed for our salvation?

Shaw, not surprisingly, had a systematic but unconventional approach to English spelling and punctuation, and insisted that publisher's observe it when printing his plays; this edition of *Major Barbara* accordingly preserves Shaw's style.

MAJOR BARBARA
Bernard Shaw

CHARACTERS

STEPHEN UNDERSHAFT   CHARLES LOMAX
LADY BRITOMART   RUMMY MITCHENS
BARBARA UNDERSHAFT   SNOBBY PRICE
SARAH UNDERSHAFT   PETER SHIRLEY
ANDREW UNDERSHAFT   BILTON
JENNY HILL   MRS BAINES
BILL WALKER   ADOLPHUS CUSINS
MORRISON

ACT ONE

It is after dinner in January 1906, in the library in LADY BRITO-
MART UNDERSHAFT'*s house in Wilton Crescent. A large and comfortable settee is in the middle of the room, upholstered in dark
leather. A person sitting on it (it is vacant at present) would have,
on his right,* LADY BRITOMART'*s writing table, with the lady herself
busy at it; a smaller writing table behind him on his left; the door behind him on* LADY BRITOMART'*s side; and a window with a window seat directly on his left. Near the window is an armchair.*

LADY BRITOMART *is a woman of fifty or thereabouts, well dressed
and yet careless of her dress, well bred and quite reckless of her breeding, well mannered and yet appallingly outspoken and indifferent to
the opinion of her interlocutors, amiable and yet peremptory, arbitrary,
and high-tempered to the last bearable degree, and withal a very typical managing matron of the upper class, treated as a naughty child until she grew into a scolding mother, and finally settling down with
plenty of practical ability and worldly experience, limited in the oddest way with domestic and class limitations, conceiving the universe exactly as if it were a large house in Wilton Crescent, though handling
her corner of it very effectively on that assumption, and being quite enlightened and liberal as to the books in the library, the pictures on the
walls, the music in the portfolios, and the articles in the papers.*

Her son, STEPHEN, *comes in. He is a gravely correct young man under 25, taking himself very seriously, but still in some awe of his
mother, from childish habit and bachelor shyness rather than from any
weakness of character.*

STEPHEN: Whats the matter?
LADY BRITOMART: Presently, Stephen.

(STEPHEN *submissively walks to the settee and sits down. He takes
up a Liberal weekly called* The Speaker.)

LADY BRITOMART: Dont begin to read, Stephen. I shall require all your attention.
5   STEPHEN: It was only while I was waiting—
LADY BRITOMART: Dont make excuses, Stephen. (*He puts down*
   The Speaker.) Now! (*She finishes her writing; rises; and comes
   to the settee.*) I have not kept you waiting very long, I think.
STEPHEN: Not at all, mother.
10   LADY BRITOMART: Bring me my cushion. (*He takes the cushion from the chair at the desk and arranges it for her as she sits
   down on the settee.*) Sit down. (*He sits down and fingers his tie
   nervously.*) Dont fiddle with your tie, Stephen: there is
   nothing the matter with it.
STEPHEN: I beg your pardon. (*He fiddles with his watch chain in-*   15
   stead.*)
LADY BRITOMART: Now are you attending to me, Stephen?
STEPHEN: Of course, mother.
LADY BRITOMART: No: it's not of course. I want something
   much more than your everyday matter-of-course atten-   20
   tion. I am going to speak to you very seriously, Stephen. I
   wish you would let that chain alone.
STEPHEN: (*Hastily relinquishing the chain.*) Have I done anything
   to annoy you, mother? If so, it was quite unintentional.
LADY BRITOMART: (*Astonished.*) Nonsense! (*With some re-*   25
   morse.) My poor boy, did you think I was angry with you?
STEPHEN: What is it, then, mother? You are making me very
   uneasy.
LADY BRITOMART: (*Squaring herself at him rather aggressively.*)
   Stephen: may I ask how soon you intend to realize that   30
   you are a grown-up man, and that I am only a woman?
STEPHEN: (*Amazed.*) Only a—
LADY BRITOMART: Dont repeat my words, please: it is a most
   aggravating habit. You must learn to face life seriously,
   Stephen. I really cannot bear the whole burden of our   35
   family affairs any longer. You must advise me: you must
   assume the responsibility.
STEPHEN: I!
LADY BRITOMART: Yes, you, of course. You were 24 last June.
   Youve been at Harrow and Cambridge. Youve been to In-   40
   dia and Japan. You must know a lot of things, now; unless you
   have wasted your time most scandalously. Well, advise me.
STEPHEN: (*Much perplexed.*) You know I have never interfered
   in the household—
LADY BRITOMART: No: I should think not. I dont want you   45
   to order the dinner.
STEPHEN: I mean in our family affairs.
LADY BRITOMART: Well, you must interfere now; for they are
   getting quite beyond me.
STEPHEN: (*Troubled.*) I have thought sometimes that perhaps I   50
   ought; but really, mother, I know so little about them; and
   what I do know is so painful! it is so impossible to men-
   tion some things to you—(*He stops, ashamed.*)
LADY BRITOMART: I suppose you mean your father.
STEPHEN: (*Almost inaudibly.*) Yes.   55
LADY BRITOMART: My dear: we cant go on all our lives not
   mentioning him. Of course you were quite right not to

open the subject until I asked you to; but you are old enough now to be taken into my confidence, and to help me to deal with him about the girls.

60 STEPHEN: But the girls are all right. They are engaged.

LADY BRITOMART: (*Complacently.*) Yes: I have made a very good match for Sarah. Charles Lomax will be a millionaire at 35. But that is ten years ahead; and in the meantime his trustees cannot under the terms of his father's will allow him more than £800 a year.

65 STEPHEN: But the will says also that if he increases his income by his own exertions, they may double the increase.

LADY BRITOMART: Charles Lomax's exertions are much more likely to decrease his income than to increase it. Sarah will have to find at least another £800 a year for the next ten years; and even then they will be as poor as church mice. And what about Barbara? I thought Barbara was going to make the most brilliant career of all of you. And what does she do? Joins the Salvation Army; discharges her maid; lives on a pound a week and walks in one evening with a professor of Greek whom she has picked up in the street, and who pretends to be a Salvationist, and actually plays the big drum for her in public because he has fallen head over ears in love with her.

80 STEPHEN: I was certainly rather taken aback when I heard they were engaged. Cusins is a very nice fellow, certainly: nobody would ever guess that he was born in Australia; but—

LADY BRITOMART: Oh, Adolphus Cusins will make a very good husband. After all, nobody can say a word against Greek: it stamps a man at once as an educated gentleman. And my family, thank Heaven, is not a pig-headed Tory one. We are Whigs, and believe in liberty. Let snobbish people say what they please: Barbara shall marry, not the man they like, but the man *I* like.

90 STEPHEN: Of course I was thinking only of his income. However, he is not likely to be extravagant.

LADY BRITOMART: Dont be too sure of that, Stephen. I know your quiet, simple, refined, poetic people like Adolphus: quite content with the best of everything! They cost more than your extravagant people, who are always as mean as they are second rate. No: Barbara will need at least £2000 a year. You see it means two additional households. Besides, my dear, you must marry soon. I dont approve of the present fashion of philandering bachelors and late marriages; and I am trying to arrange something for you.

STEPHEN: It's very good of you, mother; but perhaps I had better arrange that for myself.

105 LADY BRITOMART: Nonsense! you are much too young to begin matchmaking: you would be taken in by some pretty little nobody. Of course I dont mean that you are not to be consulted: you know that as well as I do. (STEPHEN *closes his lips and is silent.*) Now dont sulk, Stephen.

STEPHEN: I am not sulking, mother. What has all this got to do with—with—with my father?

LADY BRITOMART: My dear Stephen: where is the money to come from? It is easy enough for you and the other children to live on my income as long as we are in the same house; but I cant keep four families in four separate houses. You know how poor my father is: he has barely seven thousand a year now; and really, if he were not the Earl of Stevenage, he would have to give up society. He can do nothing for us. He says, naturally enough, that it is absurd that he should be asked to provide for the children of a man who is rolling in money. You see, Stephen, your 120 father must be fabulously wealthy, because there is always a war going on somewhere.

STEPHEN: You need not remind me of that, mother. I have hardly ever opened a newspaper in my life without seeing our name in it. The Undershaft torpedo! The Undershaft 125 quick firers! The Undershaft ten inch! the Undershaft disappearing rampart gun! the Undershaft submarine! and now the Undershaft aerial battleship! At Harrow they called me the Woolwich Infant. At Cambridge it was the same. A little brute at King's who was always trying to get 130 up revivals, spoilt my Bible—your first birthday present to me—by writing under my name, "Son and heir to Undershaft and Lazarus, Death and Destruction Dealers: address Christendom and Judea." But that was not so bad as the way I was kowtowed to everywhere because my father 135 was making millions by selling cannons.

LADY BRITOMART: It is not only the cannons, but the war loans that Lazarus arranges under cover of giving credit for the cannons. You know, Stephen, it's perfectly scandalous. Those two men, Andrew Undershaft and Lazarus, positively 140 have Europe under their thumbs. That is why your father is able to behave as he does. He is above the law. Do you think Bismarck or Gladstone or Disraeli could have openly defied every social and moral obligation all their lives as your father has? They simply wouldnt have dared. I asked Glad- 145 stone to take it up. I asked The Times to take it up. I asked the Lord Chamberlain to take it up. But it was just like asking them to declare war on the Sultan. They wouldnt. They said they couldnt touch him. I believe they were afraid.

STEPHEN: What could they do? He does not actually break 150 the law.

LADY BRITOMART: Not break the law! He is always breaking the law. He broke the law when he was born: his parents were not married.

STEPHEN: Mother! Is that true? 155

LADY BRITOMART: Of course it's true: that was why we separated.

STEPHEN: He married without letting you know that!

LADY BRITOMART: (*Rather taken aback by this inference.*) Oh no. To do Andrew justice, that was not the sort of thing he did. Besides, you know the Undershaft motto: Unashamed. 160 Everybody knew.

STEPHEN: But you said that was why you separated.

LADY BRITOMART: Yes, because he was not content with being a foundling himself: he wanted to disinherit you for another foundling. That was what I couldnt stand. 165

STEPHEN: (*Ashamed.*) Do you mean for—for—for—

LADY BRITOMART: Dont stammer, Stephen. Speak distinctly.

STEPHEN: But this is so frightful to me, mother. To have to speak to you about such things!

LADY BRITOMART: It's not pleasant for me, either, especially 170 if you are still so childish that you must make it worse by a display of embarrassment. It is only in the middle classes, Stephen, that people get into a state of dumb helpless horror when they find that there are wicked people in the world. In our class, we have to decide what is to be done 175 with wicked people; and nothing should disturb our selfpossession. Now ask your question properly.

STEPHEN: Mother: have you no consideration for me? For Heaven's sake either treat me as a child, as you always do, and tell me nothing at all or tell me everything and let me 180 take it as best I can.

LADY BRITOMART: Treat you as a child! What do you mean? It is most unkind and ungrateful of you to say such a thing. You know I have never treated any of you as chil-
185 dren. I have always made you my companions and friends, and allowed you perfect freedom to do and say whatever you like, so long as you liked what I could approve of.

STEPHEN: (*Desperately.*) I daresay we have been the very imperfect children of a very perfect mother; but I do beg you to
190 let me alone for once, and tell me about this horrible business of my father wanting to set me aside for another son.

LADY BRITOMART: (*Amazed.*) Another son! I never said anything of the kind. I never dreamt of such a thing. This is what comes of interrupting me.

195 STEPHEN: But you said—

LADY BRITOMART: (*Cutting him short.*) Now be a good boy, Stephen, and listen to me patiently. The Undershafts are descended from a foundling in the parish of St Andrew Undershaft in the city. That was long ago, in the reign of
200 James the First. Well, this foundling was adopted by an armorer and gun-maker. In the course of time the foundling succeeded to the business; and from some notion of gratitude, or some vow or something, he adopted another foundling, and left the business to him. And that
205 foundling did the same. Ever since that, the cannon business has always been left to an adopted foundling named Andrew Undershaft.

STEPHEN: But did they never marry? Were there no legitimate sons?

210 LADY BRITOMART: Oh yes: they married just as your father did; and they were rich enough to buy land for their own children and leave them well provided for. But they always adopted and trained some foundling to succeed them in the business; and of course they always quarrelled with
215 their wives furiously over it. Your father was adopted in that way; and he pretends to consider himself bound to keep up the tradition and adopt somebody to leave the business to. Of course I was not going to stand that. There may have been some reason for it when the Undershafts
220 could only marry women in their own class, whose sons were not fit to govern great estates. But there could be no excuse for passing over my son.

STEPHEN: (*Dubiously.*) I am afraid I should make a poor hand of managing a cannon foundry.

225 LADY BRITOMART: Nonsense! you could easily get a manager and pay him a salary.

STEPHEN: My father evidently had no great opinion of my capacity.

LADY BRITOMART: Stuff, child! you were only a baby: it had
230 nothing to do with your capacity. Andrew did it on principle, just as he did every perverse and wicked thing on principle. When my father remonstrated, Andrew actually told him to his face that history tells us of only two successful institutions: one the Undershaft firm, and the other the Ro-
235 man Empire under the Antonines. That was because the Antonine emperors all adopted their successors. Such rubbish! The Stevenages are as good as the Antonines, I hope; and you are a Stevenage. But that was Andrew all over. There you have the man! Always clever and unanswerable when he
240 was defending nonsense and wickedness: always awkward and sullen when he had to behave sensibly and decently!

STEPHEN: Then it was on my account that your home life was broken up, mother. I am sorry.

LADY BRITOMART: Well, dear, there were other differences. I really cannot bear an immoral man. I am not a Pharisee, I 245 hope; and I should not have minded his merely doing wrong things: we are none of us perfect. But your father didnt exactly do wrong things: he said them and thought them: that was what was so dreadful. He really had a sort of religion of wrongness. Just as one doesnt mind men 250 practising immorality so long as they own that they are in the wrong by preaching morality; so I couldnt forgive Andrew for preaching immorality while he practised morality. You would all have grown up without principles, without any knowledge of right and wrong, if he had 255 been in the house. You know, my dear, your father was a very attractive man in some ways. Children did not dislike him; and he took advantage of it to put the wickedest ideas into their heads, and make them quite unmanageable. I did not dislike him myself: very far from it; but 260 nothing can bridge over moral disagreement.

STEPHEN: All this simply bewilders me, mother. People may differ about matters of opinion, or even about religion; but how can they differ about right and wrong? Right is right; and wrong is wrong; and if a man cannot distinguish 265 them properly, he is either a fool or a rascal: thats all.

LADY BRITOMART: (*Touched.*) Thats my own boy! (*She pats his cheek.*) Your father never could answer that: he used to laugh and get out of it under cover of some affectionate nonsense. And now that you understand the situation, 270 what do you advise me to do?

STEPHEN: Well, what can you do?

LADY BRITOMART: I must get the money somehow.

STEPHEN: We cannot take money from him. I had rather go and live in some cheap place like Bedford Square or even 275 Hampstead than take a farthing of his money.

LADY BRITOMART: But after all, Stephen, our present income comes from Andrew.

STEPHEN: (*Shocked.*) I never knew that.

LADY BRITOMART: Well, you surely didnt suppose your 280 grandfather had anything to give me. The Stevenages could not do everything for you. We gave you social position. Andrew had to contribute something. He had a very good bargain, I think.

STEPHEN: (*Bitterly.*) We are utterly dependent on him and his 285 cannons, then?

LADY BRITOMART: Certainly not: the money is settled. But he provided it. So you see it is not a question of taking money from him or not: it is simply a question of how much. I dont want any more for myself. 290

STEPHEN: Nor do I.

LADY BRITOMART: But Sarah does; and Barbara does. That is, Charles Lomax and Adolphus Cusins will cost them more. So I must put my pride in my pocket and ask for it, I suppose. That is your advice, Stephen, is it not? 295

STEPHEN: No.

LADY BRITOMART: (*Sharply.*) Stephen!

STEPHEN: Of course if you are determined—

LADY BRITOMART: I am not determined: I ask your advice; and I am waiting for it. I will not have all the responsibil- 300 ity thrown on my shoulders.

STEPHEN: (*Obstinately.*) I would die sooner than ask him for another penny.

LADY BRITOMART: (*Resignedly.*) You mean that I must ask him. Very well, Stephen: it shall be as you wish. You will be glad 305 to know that your grandfather concurs. But he thinks I ought to ask Andrew to come here and see the girls. After all, he must have some natural affection for them.

STEPHEN: Ask him here!!!

310 LADY BRITOMART: Do not repeat my words, Stephen. Where else can I ask him?

STEPHEN: I never expected you to ask him at all.

LADY BRITOMART: Now dont tease, Stephen. Come! you see that it is necessary that he should pay us a visit, dont you?

315 STEPHEN: (*Reluctantly.*) I suppose so, if the girls cannot do without his money.

LADY BRITOMART: Thank you, Stephen: I knew you would give me the right advice when it was properly explained to you. I have asked your father to come this evening. (STEPHEN

320 *bounds from his seat.*) Dont jump, Stephen: it fidgets me.

STEPHEN: (*In utter consternation.*) Do you mean to say that my father is coming here tonight—that he may be here at any moment?

LADY BRITOMART: (*Looking at her watch.*) I said nine. (*He gasps.*

325 *She rises.*) Ring the bell, please. (STEPHEN *goes to the smaller writing table; presses a button on it; and sits at it with his elbows on the table and his head in his hands, outwitted and overwhelmed.*) It is ten minutes to nine yet; and I have to prepare the girls. I asked Charles Lomax and Adolphus to dinner on purpose

330 that they might be here. Andrew had better see them in case he should cherish any delusions as to their being capable of supporting their wives. (*The butler enters:* LADY BRITOMART *goes behind the settee to speak to him.*) Morrison: go up to the drawing room and tell everybody to come down here at

335 once. (MORRISON *withdraws.* LADY BRITOMART *turns to* STEPHEN.) Now remember, Stephen: I shall need all your countenance and authority. (*He rises and tries to recover some vestige of these attributes.*) Give me a chair, dear. (*He pushes a chair forward from the wall to where she stands, near the smaller*

340 *writing table. She sits down; and he goes to the armchair, into which he throws himself.*) I dont know how Barbara will take it. Ever since they made her a major in the Salvation Army she has developed a propensity to have her own way and order people about which quite cows me sometimes. It's not ladylike:

345 I'm sure I dont know where she picked it up. Anyhow, Barbara shant bully me; but still it's just as well that your father should be here before she has time to refuse to meet him or make a fuss. Dont look nervous, Stephen: it will only encourage Barbara to make difficulties. I am nervous enough,

350 goodness knows; but I dont shew it.

(SARAH *and* BARBARA *come in with their respective young men,* CHARLES LOMAX *and* ADOLPHUS CUSINS. SARAH *is slender, bored, and mundane.* BARBARA *is robuster, jollier, much more energetic.* SARAH *is fashionably dressed:* BARBARA *is in Salvation Army uniform.* LOMAX, *a young man about town, is like many other young men about town. He is afflicted with a frivolous sense of humor which plunges him at the most inopportune moments into paroxysms of imperfectly suppressed laughter.* CUSINS *is a spectacled student, slight, thin haired, and sweet voiced, with a more complex form of* LOMAX's *complaint. His sense of humor is intellectual and subtle, and is complicated by an appalling temper. The lifelong struggle of a benevolent temperament and a high conscience against impulses of inhuman ridicule and fierce impatience has set up a chronic strain which has visibly wrecked his constitution. He is a most implacable, determined, tenacious, intolerant person who by mere force of character presents*

himself as—and indeed actually is—considerate, gentle, explanatory, even mild and apologetic, capable possibly of murder, but not of cruelty or coarseness. By the operation of some instinct which is not merciful enough to blind him with the illusions of love, he is obstinately bent on marrying BARBARA. LOMAX *likes* SARAH *and thinks it will be rather a lark to marry her. Consequently he has not attempted to resist* LADY BRITOMART's *arrangements to that end.*)

(*All four look as if they had been having a good deal of fun in the drawing room. The girls enter first, leaving the swains outside.* SARAH *comes to the settee.* BARBARA *comes in after her and stops at the door.*)

BARBARA: Are Cholly and Dolly to come in?

LADY BRITOMART: (*Forcibly.*) Barbara: I will not have Charles called Cholly: the vulgarity of it positively makes me ill.

BARBARA: It's all right, mother: Cholly is quite correct nowadays. Are they to come in? 355

LADY BRITOMART: Yes, if they will behave themselves.

BARBARA: (*Through the door.*) Come in, Dolly; and behave yourself.

(BARBARA *comes to her mother's writing table.* CUSINS *enters smiling, and wanders towards* LADY BRITOMART.)

SARAH: (*Calling.*) Come in, Cholly. (LOMAX *enters, controlling his features very imperfectly, and places himself vaguely between* 360 SARAH *and* BARBARA.)

LADY BRITOMART: (*Peremptorily.*) Sit down, all of you. (*They sit.* CUSINS *crosses to the window and seats himself there.* LOMAX *takes a chair.* BARBARA *sits at the writing table and* SARAH *on the settee.*) I dont in the least know what you are 365 laughing at, Adolphus. I am surprised at you, though I expected nothing better from Charles Lomax.

CUSINS: (*In a remarkably gentle voice.*) Barbara has been trying to teach me the West Ham Salvation March.

LADY BRITOMART: I see nothing to laugh at in that; nor 370 should you if you are really converted.

CUSINS: (*Sweetly.*) You were not present. It was really funny, I believe.

LOMAX: Ripping.

LADY BRITOMART: Be quiet, Charles. Now listen to me, chil- 375 dren. Your father is coming here this evening.

(*General stupefaction.* LOMAX, SARAH, *and* BARBARA *rise:* SARAH *scared, and* BARBARA *amused and expectant.*)

LOMAX: (*Remonstrating.*) Oh I say!

LADY BRITOMART: You are not called on to say anything, Charles.

SARAH: Are you serious, mother? 380

LADY BRITOMART: Of course I am serious. It is on your account, Sarah, and also on Charles's. (*Silence.* SARAH *sits, with a shrug.* CHARLES *looks painfully unworthy.*) I hope you are not going to object, Barbara.

BARBARA: I! why should I? My father has a soul to be saved 385 like anybody else. He's quite welcome as far as I am concerned. (*She sits on the table, and softly whistles 'Onward, Christian Soldiers.'*)

LOMAX: (*Still remonstrant.*) But really, dont you know! Oh I say!

LADY BRITOMART: (*Frigidly.*) What do you wish to convey, 390 Charles?

LOMAX: Well, you must admit that this is a bit thick.

LADY BRITOMART: (*Turning with ominous suavity to* CUSINS.) Adolphus: you are a professor of Greek. Can you translate
395 Charles Lomax's remarks into reputable English for us?

CUSINS: (*Cautiously.*) If I may say so, Lady Brit, I think Charles has rather happily expressed what we all feel. Homer, speaking of Autolycus, uses the same phrase. πυκινὸν δόμον ελθεῖν means a bit thick.

400 LOMAX: (*Handsomely.*) Not that I mind, you know, if Sarah dont. (*He sits.*)

LADY BRITOMART: (*Crushingly.*) Thank you. Have I your permission, Adolphus, to invite my own husband to my own house?

405 CUSINS: (*Gallantly.*) You have my unhesitating support in everything you do.

LADY BRITOMART: Tush! Sarah: have you nothing to say?

SARAH: Do you mean that he is coming regularly to live here?

LADY BRITOMART: Certainly not. The spare room is ready
410 for him if he likes to stay for a day or two and see a little more of you; but there are limits.

SARAH: Well, he cant eat us, I suppose. *I* dont mind.

LOMAX: (*Chuckling.*) I wonder how the old man will take it.

LADY BRITOMART: Much as the old woman will, no doubt,
415 Charles.

LOMAX: (*Abashed.*) I didnt mean—at least—

LADY BRITOMART: You didnt think, Charles. You never do; and the result is, you never mean anything. And now please attend to me, children. Your father will be quite a
420 stranger to us.

LOMAX: I suppose he hasnt seen Sarah since she was a little kid.

LADY BRITOMART: Not since she was a little kid, Charles, as you express it with that elegance of diction and refinement of thought that seem never to desert you. Accordingly—
425 er—(*Impatiently.*) Now I have forgotten what I was going to say. That comes of your provoking me to be sarcastic, Charles. Adolphus: will you kindly tell me where I was.

CUSINS: (*Sweetly.*) You were saying that as Mr Undershaft has not seen his children since they were babies, he will form
430 his opinion of the way you have brought them up from their behavior tonight, and that therefore you wish us all to be particularly careful to conduct ourselves well, especially Charles.

LADY BRITOMART: (*With emphatic approval.*) Precisely.
435 LOMAX: Look here, Dolly: Lady Brit didnt say that.

LADY BRITOMART: (*Vehemently.*) I did, Charles. Adolphus's recollection is perfectly correct. It is most important that you should be good; and I do beg you for once not to pair off into opposite corners and giggle and whisper while I
440 am speaking to your father.

BARBARA: All right, mother. We'll do you credit. (*She comes off the table, and sits in her chair with ladylike elegance.*)

LADY BRITOMART: Remember, Charles, that Sarah will want to feel proud of you instead of ashamed of you.
445 LOMAX: Oh I say! theres nothing to be exactly proud of, dont you know.

LADY BRITOMART: Well, try and look as if there was.

(MORRISON, *pale and dismayed, breaks into the room in unconcealed disorder.*)

MORRISON: Might I speak a word to you, my lady?

LADY BRITOMART: Nonsense! Shew him up.

MORRISON: Yes, my lady. (*He goes.*)

LOMAX: Does Morrison know who it is?   450

LADY BRITOMART: Of course. Morrison has always been with us.

LOMAX: It must be a regular corker for him, dont you know.

LADY BRITOMART: Is this a moment to get on my nerves, Charles, with your outrageous expressions?

LOMAX: But this is something out of the ordinary, really—   455

MORRISON: (*At the door.*) The—er—Mr Undershaft. (*He retreats in confusion.*)

(ANDREW UNDERSHAFT *comes in. All rise.* LADY BRITOMART *meets him in the middle of the room behind the settee.*)

(ANDREW *is, on the surface, a stoutish, easygoing elderly man, with kindly patient manners, and an engaging simplicity of character. But he has a watchful, deliberate, waiting, listening face, and formidable reserves of power, both bodily and mental, in his capacious chest and long head. His gentleness is partly that of a strong man who has learnt by experience that his natural grip hurts ordinary people unless he handles them very carefully, and partly the mellowness of age and success. He is also a little shy in his present very delicate situation.*)

LADY BRITOMART: Good evening, Andrew.

UNDERSHAFT: How d'ye do, my dear.   460

LADY BRITOMART: You look a good deal older.

UNDERSHAFT: (*Apologetically.*) I am somewhat older. (*Taking her hand with a touch of courtship.*) Time has stood still with you.

LADY BRITOMART: (*Throwing away his hand.*) Rubbish! This is your family.   465

UNDERSHAFT: (*Surprised.*) Is it so large? I am sorry to say my memory is failing very badly in some things. (*He offers his hand with paternal kindness to* LOMAX.)

LOMAX: (*Jerkily shaking his hand.*) Ahdedoo.

UNDERSHAFT: I can see you are my eldest. I am very glad to   470
meet you again, my boy.

LOMAX: (*Remonstrating.*) No, but look here dont you know—(*Overcome.*) Oh I say!

LADY BRITOMART: (*Recovering from momentary speechlessness.*) Andrew: do you mean to say that you dont remember   475
how many children you have?

UNDERSHAFT: Well, I am afraid I—. They have grown so much—er. Am I making any ridiculous mistake? I may as well confess: I recollect only one son. But so many things have happened since, of course—er—   480

LADY BRITOMART: (*Decisively.*) Andrew: you are talking nonsense. Of course you have only one son.

UNDERSHAFT: Perhaps you will be good enough to introduce me, my dear.

LADY BRITOMART: That is Charles Lomax, who is engaged to   485
Sarah.

UNDERSHAFT: My dear sir, I beg your pardon.

LOMAX: Notatall. Delighted, I assure you.

LADY BRITOMART: This is Stephen.

UNDERSHAFT: (*Bowing.*) Happy to make your acquaintance,   490
Mr Stephen. Then (*Going to* CUSINS.) you must be my son. (*Taking* CUSINS' *hands in his.*) How are you, my young friend? (*To* LADY BRITOMART.) He is very like you, my love.

CUSINS: You flatter me, Mr Undershaft. My name is Cusins: engaged to Barbara. (*Very explicitly.*) That is Major Barbara   495
Undershaft, of the Salvation Army. That is Sarah, your second daughter. This is Stephen Undershaft, your son.

UNDERSHAFT: My dear Stephen, I beg your pardon.

STEPHEN: Not at all.

500 UNDERSHAFT: Mr Cusins: I am much indebted to you for ex-plaining so precisely. (*Turning to* SARAH.) Barbara, my dear—

SARAH: (*Prompting him.*) Sarah.

UNDERSHAFT: Sarah, of course. (*They shake hands. He goes over*
505 *to* BARBARA.) Barbara—I am right this time, I hope?

BARBARA: Quite right. (*They shake hands.*)

LADY BRITOMART: (*Resuming command.*) Sit down, all of you. Sit down, Andrew. (*She comes forward and sits on the settee.* CUSINS *also brings his chair forward on her left.* BARBARA *and*
510 STEPHEN *resume their seats.* LOMAX *gives his chair to* SARAH *and goes for another.*)

UNDERSHAFT: Thank you, my love.

LOMAX: (*Conversationally, as he brings a chair forward between the writing table and the settee, and offers it to* UNDERSHAFT.) Takes
515 you some time to find out exactly where you are, dont it?

UNDERSHAFT: (*Accepting the chair, but remaining standing.*) That is not what embarrasses me, Mr Lomax. My difficulty is that if I play the part of a father, I shall produce the effect of an intrusive stranger; and if I play the part of a discreet
520 stranger, I may appear a callous father.

LADY BRITOMART: There is no need for you to play any part at all, Andrew. You had much better be sincere and natural.

UNDERSHAFT: (*Submissively.*) Yes, my dear: I daresay that will be best. (*He sits down comfortably.*) Well, here I am. Now
525 what can I do for you all?

LADY BRITOMART: You need not do anything, Andrew. You are one of the family. You can sit with us and enjoy yourself.

(*A painfully conscious pause.* BARBARA *makes a face at* LOMAX, *whose too long suppressed mirth immediately explodes in agonized neighings.*)

LADY BRITOMART: (*Outraged.*) Charles Lomax: if you can be-have yourself, behave yourself. If not, leave the room.

530 LOMAX: I'm awfully sorry, Lady Brit; but really you know, upon my soul! (*He sits on the settee between* LADY BRITO-MART *and* UNDERSHAFT, *quite overcome.*)

BARBARA: Why dont you laugh if you want to, Cholly? It's good for your inside.

535 LADY BRITOMART: Barbara: you have had the education of a lady. Please let your father see that; and dont talk like a street girl.

UNDERSHAFT: Never mind me, my dear. As you know, I am not a gentleman; and I was never educated.

540 LOMAX: (*Encouragingly.*) Nobody'd know it, I assure you. You look all right, you know.

CUSINS: Let me advise you to study Greek, Mr Undershaft. Greek scholars are privileged men. Few of them know Greek; and none of them know anything else; but their
545 position is unchallengeable. Other languages are the qual-ifications of waiters and commercial travellers: Greek is to a man of position what the hallmark is to silver.

BARBARA: Dolly: dont be insincere. Cholly: fetch your con-certina and play something for us.

550 LOMAX: (*Jumps up eagerly, but checks himself to remark doubtfully to* UNDERSHAFT.) Perhaps that sort of thing isnt in your line, eh?

UNDERSHAFT: I am particularly fond of music.

LOMAX: (*Delighted.*) Are you? Then I'll get it. (*He goes upstairs for the instrument.*)

555 UNDERSHAFT: Do you play, Barbara?

BARBARA: Only the tambourine. But Cholly's teaching me the concertina.

UNDERSHAFT: Is Cholly also a member of the Salvation Army?

BARBARA: No: he says it's bad form to be a dissenter. But I dont
560 despair of Cholly. I made him come yesterday to a meeting at the dock gates, and take the collection in his hat.

UNDERSHAFT: (*Looks whimsically at his wife.*)!!

LADY BRITOMART: It is not my doing, Andrew. Barbara is old enough to take her own way. She has no father to advise her.

565 BARBARA: Oh yes she has. There are no orphans in the Sal-vation Army.

UNDERSHAFT: Your father there has a great many children and plenty of experience, eh?

BARBARA: (*Looking at him with quick interest and nodding.*) Just
570 so. How did you come to understand that? (LOMAX *is heard at the door trying the concertina.*)

LADY BRITOMART: Come in, Charles. Play us something at once.

LOMAX: Righto! (*He sits down in his former place, and preludes.*)

UNDERSHAFT: One moment, Mr Lomax. I am rather inter-
575 ested in the Salvation Army. Its motto might be my own: Blood and Fire.

LOMAX: (*Shocked.*) But not your sort of blood and fire, you know.

UNDERSHAFT: My sort of blood cleanses: my sort of fire purifies.

580 BARBARA: So do ours. Come down tomorrow to my shel-ter—the West Ham shelter—and see what we're doing. We're going to march to a great meeting in the Assembly Hall at Mile End. Come and see the shelter and then march with us: it will do you a lot of good. Can you play anything?

585 UNDERSHAFT: In my youth I earned pennies, and even shillings occasionally, in the streets and in public house parlors by my natural talent for stepdancing. Later on, I became a member of the Undershaft orchestral society, and performed passably on the tenor trombone.

590 LOMAX: (*Scandalized—putting down the concertina.*) Oh I say!

BARBARA: Many a sinner has played himself into heaven on the trombone, thanks to the Army.

LOMAX: (*To* BARBARA, *still rather shocked.*) Yes; but what about the cannon business, dont you know? (*To* UNDERSHAFT.) Getting into heaven is not exactly in your line, is it?

595 LADY BRITOMART: Charles!!!

LOMAX: Well; but it stands to reason, dont it? The cannon business may be necessary and all that: we cant get on without cannons; but it isnt right, you know. On the other hand, there may be a certain amount of tosh about the
600 Salvation Army—I belong to the Established Church myself—but still you cant deny that it's religion; and you cant go against religion, can you? At least unless youre downright immoral, dont you know.

605 UNDERSHAFT: You hardly appreciate my position, Mr Lomax—

LOMAX: (*Hastily.*) I'm not saying anything against you personally—

UNDERSHAFT: Quite so, quite so. But consider for a moment. Here I am, a profiteer in mutilation and murder. I find
610 myself in a specially amiable humor just now because, this morning, down at the foundry, we blew twenty-seven dummy soldiers into fragments with a gun which for-merly destroyed only thirteen.

615 LOMAX: (*Leniently.*) Well, the more destructive war becomes, the sooner it will be abolished, eh?

UNDERSHAFT: Not at all. The more destructive war becomes the more fascinating we find it. No, Mr Lomax: I am obliged to you for making the usual excuse for my trade; but I am not ashamed of it. I am not one of those men who keep their morals and their business in watertight compartments. All the spare money my trade rivals spend on hospitals, cathedrals, and other receptacles for conscience money, I devote to experiments and researches in improved methods of destroying life and property. I have always done so; and I always shall. Therefore your Christmas card moralities of peace on earth and goodwill among men are of no use to me. Your Christianity, which enjoins you to resist not evil, and to turn the other cheek, would make me a bankrupt. My morality—my religion—must have a place for cannons and torpedoes in it.

STEPHEN: (*Coldly—almost sullenly.*) You speak as if there were half a dozen moralities and religions to choose from, instead of one true morality and one true religion.

UNDERSHAFT: For me there is only one true morality; but it might not fit you, as you do not manufacture aerial battleships. There is only one true morality for every man; but every man has not the same true morality.

LOMAX: (*Overtaxed.*) Would you mind saying that again? I didnt quite follow it.

CUSINS: It's quite simple. As Euripides says, one man's meat is another man's poison morally as well as physically.

UNDERSHAFT: Precisely.

LOMAX: Oh, that! Yes, yes, yes. True. True.

STEPHEN: In other words, some men are honest and some are scoundrels.

BARBARA: Bosh! There are no scoundrels.

UNDERSHAFT: Indeed? Are there any good men?

BARBARA: No. Not one. There are neither good men nor scoundrels: there are just children of one Father; and the sooner they stop calling one another names the better. You neednt talk to me: I know them. I've had scores of them through my hands: scoundrels, criminals, infidels, philanthropists, missionaries, county councillors, all sorts. Theyre all just the same sort of sinner; and theres the same salvation ready for them all.

UNDERSHAFT: May I ask have you ever saved a maker of cannons?

BARBARA: No. Will you let me try?

UNDERSHAFT: Well, I will make a bargain with you. If I go to see you tomorrow in your Salvation Shelter, will you come the day after to see me in my cannon works?

BARBARA: Take care. It may end in your giving up the cannons for the sake of the Salvation Army.

UNDERSHAFT: Are you sure it will not end in your giving up the Salvation Army for the sake of the cannons?

BARBARA: I will take my chance of that.

UNDERSHAFT: And I will take my chance of the other. (*They shake hands on it.*) Where is your shelter?

BARBARA: In West Ham. At the sign of the cross. Ask anybody in Canning Town. Where are your works?

UNDERSHAFT: In Perivale St Andrews. At the sign of the sword. Ask anybody in Europe.

LOMAX: Hadnt I better play something?

BARBARA: Yes. Give us 'Onward, Christian Soldiers.'

LOMAX: Well, thats rather a strong order to begin with, dont you know. Suppose I sing 'Thourt passing hence, my brother.' It's much the same tune.

BARBARA: It's too melancholy. You get saved, Cholly; and youll pass hence, my brother, without making such a fuss about it.

LADY BRITOMART: Really, Barbara, you go on as if religion were a pleasant subject. Do have some sense of propriety.

UNDERSHAFT: I do not find it an unpleasant subject, my dear. It is the only one that capable people really care for.

LADY BRITOMART: (*Looking at her watch.*) Well, if you are determined to have it, I insist on having it in a proper and respectable way. Charles: ring for prayers.

(*General amazement.* STEPHEN *rises in dismay.*)

LOMAX: (*Rising.*) Oh I say!

UNDERSHAFT: (*Rising.*) I am afraid I must be going.

LADY BRITOMART: You cannot go now, Andrew: it would be most improper. Sit down. What will the servants think?

UNDERSHAFT: My dear: I have conscientious scruples. May I suggest a compromise? If Barbara will conduct a little service in the drawing room, with Mr Lomax as organist, I will attend it willingly. I will even take part, if a trombone can be procured.

LADY BRITOMART: Dont mock, Andrew.

UNDERSHAFT: (*Shocked—to* BARBARA.) You dont think I am mocking, my love, I hope.

BARBARA: No, of course not; and it wouldnt matter if you were: half the Army came to their first meeting for a lark. (*Rising.*) Come along. (*She throws her arm round her father and sweeps him out, calling to the others from the threshold.*) Come, Dolly. Come, Cholly.

(CUSINS *rises.*)

LADY BRITOMART: I will not be disobeyed by everybody. Adolphus: sit down. (*He does not.*) Charles: you may go. You are not fit for prayers: you cannot keep your countenance.

LOMAX: Oh I say! (*He goes out.*)

LADY BRITOMART: (*Continuing.*) But you, Adolphus, can behave yourself if you choose to. I insist on your staying.

CUSINS: My dear Lady Brit: there are things in the family prayer book that I couldnt bear to hear you say.

LADY BRITOMART: What things, pray?

CUSINS: Well, you would have to say before all the servants that we have done things we ought not to have done, and left undone things we ought to have done, and that there is no health in us. I cannot bear to hear you doing yourself such an injustice, and Barbara such an injustice. As for myself, I flatly deny it: I have done my best. I shouldnt dare to marry Barbara—I couldnt look you in the face—if it were true. So I must go to the drawing room.

LADY BRITOMART: (*Offended.*) Well, go. (*He starts for the door.*) And remember this, Adolphus (*He turns to listen.*): I have a very strong suspicion that you went to the Salvation Army to worship Barbara and nothing else. And I quite appreciate the very clever way in which you systematically humbug me. I have found you out. Take care Barbara doesnt. Thats all.

CUSINS: (*With unruffled sweetness.*) Dont tell on me. (*He steals out.*)

LADY BRITOMART: Sarah: if you want to go, go. Anything's better than to sit there as if you wished you were a thousand miles away.

SARAH: (*Languidly.*) Very well, mamma. (*She goes.*)

735 (LADY BRITOMART, *with a sudden flounce, gives way to a little gust of tears.*)

STEPHEN: (*Going to her.*) Mother: whats the matter?

740 LADY BRITOMART: (*Swishing away her tears with her handkerchief.*) Nothing. Foolishness. You can go with him, too, if you like, and leave me with the servants.

STEPHEN: Oh, you mustnt think that, mother. I—I dont like him.

745 LADY BRITOMART: The others do. That is the injustice of a woman's lot. A woman has to bring up her children; and that means to restrain them, to deny them things they want, to set them tasks, to punish them when they do wrong, to do all the unpleasant things. And then the father, who has nothing to do but pet them and spoil them, comes in when 750 all her work is done and steals their affection from her.

STEPHEN: He has not stolen our affection from you. It is only curiosity.

LADY BRITOMART: (*Violently.*) I wont be consoled, Stephen. There is nothing the matter with me. (*She rises and goes to-* 755 *wards the door.*)

STEPHEN: Where are you going, mother?

LADY BRITOMART: To the drawing room, of course. (*She goes out. 'Onward, Christian Soldiers,' on the concertina, with tambourine accompaniment, is heard when the door opens.*) Are you coming, Stephen?

STEPHEN: No. Certainly not. (*She goes. He sits down on the settee, with compressed lips and an expression of strong dislike.*)

ACT TWO

The yard of the West Ham shelter of the Salvation Army is a cold place on a January morning. The building itself, an old warehouse, is newly whitewashed. Its gabled end projects into the yard in the middle, with a door on the ground floor, and another in the loft above it without any balcony or ladder, but with a pulley rigged over it for hoisting sacks. Those who come from this central gable end into the yard have the gateway leading to the street on their left, with a stone horse-trough just beyond it, and, on the right, a penthouse shielding a table from the weather. There are forms at the table; and on them are seated a man and a woman, both much down on their luck, finishing a meal of bread (one thick slice each, with margarine and golden syrup) and diluted milk.

The man, a workman out of employment, is young, agile, a talker, a poser, sharp enough to be capable of anything in reason except honesty or altruistic considerations of any kind. The woman is a commonplace old bundle of poverty and hard-worn humanity. She looks sixty and probably is forty-five. If they were rich people, gloved and muffed and well wrapped up in furs and overcoats, they would be numbed and miserable; for it is a grindingly cold raw January day; and a glance at the background of grimy warehouses and leaden sky visible over the whitewashed walls of the yard would drive any idle rich person straight to the Mediterranean. But these two, being no more troubled with visions of the Mediterranean than of the moon, and being compelled to keep more of their clothes in the pawnshop, and less on their persons, in winter than in summer, are not depressed by the cold: rather are they stung into vivacity, to which their meal has just now given an almost jolly turn. The man takes a pull at his mug, and then gets up and moves about the yard with his hands deep in his pockets, occasionally breaking into a stepdance.

THE WOMAN: Feel better arter your meal, sir?

THE MAN: No. Call that a meal! Good enough for you, praps; but wot is it to me, an intelligent workin man.

THE WOMAN: Workin man! Wot are you?

THE MAN: Painter. 5

THE WOMAN: (*Sceptically.*) Yus, I dessay.

THE MAN: Yus, you dessay! I know. Every loafer that cant do nothink calls isself a painter. Well, I'm a real painter: grainer, finisher, thirty-eight bob a week when I can get it.

THE WOMAN: Then why dont you go and get it? 10

THE MAN: I'll tell you why. Fust: I'm intelligent—fffff! it's rotten cold here (*He dances a step or two.*)—yes: intelligent beyond the station o life into which it has pleased the capitalists to call me; and they dont like a man that sees through em. Second, an intelligent bein needs a doo share 15 of appiness; so I drink somethink cruel when I get the chawnce. Third, I stand by my class and do as little as I can so's to leave arf the job for me fellow workers. Fourth, I'm fly enough to know wots inside the law and wots outside it; and inside it I do as the capitalists do: pinch wot I can 20 lay me ands on. In a proper state of society I am sober, industrious and honest: in Rome, so to speak, I do as the Romans do. Wots the consequence? When trade is bad— and it's rotten bad just now—and the employers az to sack arf their men, they generally start on me. 25

THE WOMAN: Whats your name?

THE MAN: Price. Bronterre O'Brien Price. Usually called Snobby Price, for short.

THE WOMAN: Snobby's a carpenter, aint it? You said you was a painter. 30

PRICE: Not that kind of snob, but the genteel sort. I'm too uppish, owing to my intelligence, and my father being a Chartist and a reading, thinking man: a stationer, too. I'm none of your common hewers of wood and drawers of water; and dont you forget it. (*He returns to his seat at the* 35 *table, and takes up his mug.*) Wots your name?

THE WOMAN: Rummy Mitchens, sir.

PRICE: (*Quaffing the remains of his milk to her.*) Your elth, Miss Mitchens.

RUMMY: (*Correcting him.*) Missis Mitchens. 40

PRICE: Wot! Oh Rummy, Rummy! Respectable married woman, Rummy, gittin rescued by the Salvation Army by pretendin to be a bad un. Same old game!

RUMMY: What am I to do? I cant starve. Them Salvation lasses is dear good girls; but the better you are, the worse they 45 likes to think you were before they rescued you. Why shouldnt they av a bit o credit, poor loves? theyre worn to rags by their work. And where would they get the money to rescue us if we was to let on we're no worse than other people? You know what ladies and gentlemen are. 50

PRICE: Thievin swine! Wish I ad their job, Rummy, all the same. Wot does Rummy stand for? Pet name praps?

RUMMY: Short for Romola.

PRICE: For wot!?

RUMMY: Romola. It was out of a new book. Somebody me 55 mother wanted me to grow up like.

PRICE: We're companions in misfortune, Rummy. Both on us got names that nobody cawnt pronounce. Consequently I'm Snobby and youre Rummy because Bill and Sally wasnt good enough for our parents. Such is life! 60

RUMMY: Who saved you, Mr Price? Was it Major Barbara?

PRICE: No: I come here on my own. I'm going to be Bronterre O'Brien Price, the converted painter. I know wot they like. I'll tell em how I blasphemed and gambled and
65 wopped my poor old mother—
RUMMY: (*Shocked.*) Used you to beat your mother?
PRICE: Not likely. She used to beat me. No matter: you come and listen to the converted painter, and youll hear how she was a pious woman that taught me me prayers at er knee,
70 an how I used to come home drunk and drag her out o bed be er snow white airs, an lam into er with the poker.
RUMMY: Thats whats so unfair to us women. Your confessions is just as big lies as ours: you dont tell what you really done no more than us; but you men can tell your lies
75 right out at the meetins and be made much of for it; while the sort o confessions we az to make az to be wispered to one lady at a time. It aint right, spite of all their piety.
PRICE: Right! Do you spose the Army'd be allowed if it went and did right? Not much. It combs our air and makes us
80 good little blokes to be robbed and put upon. But I'll play the game as good as any of em. I'll see somebody struck by lightnin, or hear a voice sayin 'Snobby Price: where will you spend eternity?' I'll av a time of it, I tell you.
RUMMY: You wont be let drink, though.
85 PRICE: I'll take it out in gorspellin, then. I dont want to drink if I can get fun enough any other way.

(JENNY HILL, *a pale, overwrought, pretty Salvation lass of 18, comes in through the yard gate, leading* PETER SHIRLEY, *a half hardened, half worn-out elderly man, weak with hunger.*)

JENNY: (*Supporting him.*) Come! pluck up. I'll get you something to eat. Youll be all right then.
PRICE: (*Rising and hurrying officiously to take the old man off*
90 JENNY's *hands.*) Poor old man! Cheer up, brother; youll find rest and peace and appiness ere. Hurry up with the food, miss: e's fair done. (JENNY *hurries into the shelter.*) Ere, buck up, daddy! she's fetchin y'a thick slice o breadn treacle, an a mug o skyblue. (*He seats him at the corner of the table.*)
95 RUMMY: (*Gaily.*) Keep up your old art! Never say die!
SHIRLEY: I'm not an old man. I'm only 46. I'm as good as ever I was. The grey patch come in my hair before I was thirty. All it wants is three pennorth o hair dye: am I to be turned on the streets to starve for it? Holy God! I've worked ten to
100 twelve hours a day since I was thirteen, and paid my way all through; and now am I to be thrown into the gutter and my job given to a young man that can do it no better than me because Ive black hair that goes white at the first change?
PRICE: (*Cheerfully.*) No good jawrin about it. Youre only a
105 jumped-up, jerked-off, orspittle-turned-out incurable of an ole workin man: who cares about you? Eh? Make the thievin swine give you a meal: theyve stole many a one from you. Get a bit o your own back. (JENNY *returns with the usual meal.*) There you are, brother. Awsk a blessin an
110 tuck that into you.
SHIRLEY: (*Looking at it ravenously but not touching it, and crying like a child.*) I never took anything before.
JENNY: (*Petting him.*) Come, come! the Lord sends it to you: he wasnt above taking bread from his friends; and why
115 should you be? Besides, when we find you a job you can pay us for it if you like.

SHIRLEY: (*Eagerly.*) Yes, yes: thats true. I can pay you back: it's only a loan. (*Shivering.*) O Lord! oh Lord! (*He turns to the table and attacks the meal ravenously.*)
JENNY: Well, Rummy, are you more comfortable now? 120
RUMMY: God bless you, lovey! youve fed my body and saved my soul, havnt you? (JENNY, *touched, kisses her.*) Sit down and rest a bit: you must be ready to drop.
JENNY: Ive been going hard since morning. But theres more work than we can do. I mustnt stop. 125
RUMMY: Try a prayer for just two minutes. Youll work all the better after.
JENNY: (*Her eyes lighting up.*) Oh isnt it wonderful how a few minutes prayer revives you! I was quite lightheaded at twelve o'clock, I was so tired; but Major Barbara just sent 130 me to pray for five minutes; and I was able to go on as if I had only just begun. (*To* PRICE.) Did you have a piece of bread?
PRICE: (*With unction.*) Yes, miss; but Ive got the piece that I value more; and thats the peace that passeth hall hanner- 135 stennin.
RUMMY: (*Fervently.*) Glory Hallelujah!

(BILL WALKER, *a rough customer of about 25, appears at the yard gate and looks malevolently at* JENNY.)

JENNY: That makes me so happy. When you say that, I feel wicked for loitering here. I must get to work again.

(*She is hurrying to the shelter, when the new-comer moves quickly up to the door and intercepts her. His manner is so threatening that she retreats as he comes at her truculently, driving her down the yard.*)

BILL: Aw knaow you. Youre the one that took awy maw girl. 140 Youre the one that set er agen me. Well, I'm gowin to ev er aht. Not that Aw care a carse for er or you: see? Bat Aw'll let er knaow; and Aw'll let you knaow. Aw'm gowing to give her a doin thatll teach er to cat awy from me. Nah in wiv you and tell er to cam aht afore Aw cam in 145 and kick er aht. Tell er Bill Walker wants er. She'll knaow wot thet means; and if she keeps me witin itll be worse. You stop to jawr beck at me; and Aw'll stawt on you: d'ye eah? Theres your wy. In you gow. (*He takes her by the arm and slings her towards the door of the shelter. She falls on her 150 hand and knee.* RUMMY *helps her up again.*)
PRICE: (*Rising, and venturing irresolutely towards* BILL.) Easy there, mate. She aint doin you no arm.
BILL: Oo are you callin mite? (*Standing over him threateningly.*) Youre gowin to stend ap for er, aw yer? Put ap your ends. 155
RUMMY: (*Running indignantly to him to scold him.*) Oh, you great brute—(*He instantly swings his left hand back against her face. She screams and reels back to the trough, where she sits down, covering her bruised face with her hands and rocking herself and moaning with pain.*) 160
JENNY: (*Going to her.*) Oh, God forgive you! How could you strike an old woman like that?
BILL: (*Seizing her by the hair so violently that she also screams, and tearing her away from the old woman.*) You Gawd forgimme again an Aw'll Gawd forgive you one on the jawr thetll 165 stop you pryin for a week. (*Holding her and turning fiercely on* PRICE.) Ev you ennything to sy agen it?
PRICE: (*Intimidated.*) No, matey: she aint anything to do with me.

170 BILL: Good job for you! Aw'd pat two meals into you and fawt you with one finger arter, you stawved cur. (*To* JENNY.) Nah are you gowin to fetch aht Mog Ebbijem; or em Aw to knock your fice off you and fetch her meself?

JENNY: (*Writhing in his grasp.*) Oh please someone go in and

175 tell Major Barbara—(*She screams again as he wrenches her head down; and* PRICE *and* RUMMY *flee into the shelter.*)

BILL: You want to gow in and tell your Mijor of me, do you?

JENNY: Oh please dont drag my hair. Let me go.

BILL: Do you or downt you? (*She stifles a scream.*) Yus or nao?

180 JENNY: God give me strength—

BILL: (*Striking her with his fist in the face.*) Gow an shaow her thet, and tell her if she wants one lawk it to cam and interfere with me. (JENNY, *crying with pain, goes into the shed. He goes to the form and addresses the old man.*) Eah: finish

185 your mess; an git aht o maw wy.

SHIRLEY: (*Springing up and facing him fiercely, with the mug in his hand.*) You take a liberty with me, and I'll smash you over the face with the mug and cut your eye out. Aint you satisfied—young whelps like you—with takin the bread out

190 o the mouths of your elders that have brought you up and slaved for you, but you must come shovin and cheekin and bullyin in here, where the bread o charity is sickenin in our stummicks?

BILL: (*Contemptuously, but backing a little.*) Wot good are you,

195 you aold palsy mag? Wot good are you?

SHIRLEY: As good as you and better. I'll do a day's work agen you or any fat young soaker of your age. Go and take my job at Horrockses, where I worked for ten year. They want young men there: they cant afford to keep men over

200 forty-five. Theyre very sorry—give you a character and happy to help you to get anything suited to your years—sure a steady man wont be long out of a job. Well, let em try you. Theyll find the differ. What do you know? Not as much as how to beeyave yourself—layin your dirty fist

205 across the mouth of a respectable woman!

BILL: Downt provowk me to ly it acrost yours: d'ye eah?

SHIRLEY: (*With blighting contempt.*) Yes: you like an old man to hit, dont you, when youve finished with the women. I aint seen you hit a young one yet.

210 BILL: (*Stung.*) You loy, you aold soupkitchener, you. There was a yang menn eah. Did Aw offer to itt him or did Aw not?

SHIRLEY: Was he starvin or was he not? Was he a man or only a crosseyed thief an a loafer? Would you hit my son-in-law's brother?

215 BILL: Oo's ee?

SHIRLEY: Todger Fairmile o Balls Pond. Him that won £20 off the Japanese wrastler at the music hall by standin out 17 minutes 4 seconds agen him.

BILL: (*Sullenly.*) Aw'm nao music awl wrastler. Ken he box?

220 SHIRLEY: Yes: an you cant.

BILL: Wot! Aw cawnt, cawnt Aw? Wots thet you sy (*Threatening him.*)?

SHIRLEY: (*Not budging an inch.*) Will you box Todger Fairmile if I put him on to you? Say the word.

225 BILL: (*Subsiding with a slouch.*) Aw'll stend ap to enny menn alawv, if he was ten Todger Fairmawls. But Aw dont set ap to be a perfeshnal.

SHIRLEY: (*Looking down on him with unfathomable disdain.*) You box! Slap an old woman with the back o your hand! You

230 hadnt even the sense to hit her where a magistrate couldnt see the mark of it, you silly young lump of conceit and ig-

norance. Hit a girl in the jaw and ony make her cry! If Todger Fairmile'd done it, she wouldnt a got up inside o ten minutes, no more than you would if he got on to you. Yah! I'd set about you myself if I had a week's feedin in 235 me instead o two months' starvation. (*He turns his back on him and sits down moodily at the table.*)

BILL: (*Following him and stooping over him to drive the taunt in.*) You loy! youve the bread and treacle in you that you cam eah to beg. 240

SHIRLEY: (*Bursting into tears.*) Oh God! it's true: I'm only an old pauper on the scrap heap. (*Furiously.*) But youll come to it yourself; and then youll know. Youll come to it sooner than a teetotaller like me, fillin yourself with gin at this hour o the mornin! 245

BILL: Aw'm nao gin drinker, you oald lawr; bat wen Aw want to give my girl a bloomin good awdin Aw lawk to ev a bit o devil in me: see? An eah Aw emm, talkin to a rotten aold blawter like you sted o givin her wot for. (*Working himself into a rage.*) Aw'm gowin in there to fetch her aht. (*He* 250 *makes vengefully for the shelter door.*)

SHIRLEY: Youre going to the station on a stretcher, more likely; and theyll take the gin and the devil out of you there when they get you inside. You mind what youre about: the major here is the Earl o Stevenage's granddaughter. 255

BILL: (*Checked.*) Garn!

SHIRLEY: Youll see.

BILL: (*His resolution oozing.*) Well, Aw aint dan nathin to er.

SHIRLEY: Spose she said you did! who'd believe you?

BILL: (*Very uneasy, skulking back to the corner of the penthouse.*) 260 Gawd! theres no jastice in this cantry. To think wot them people can do! Aw'm as good as er.

SHIRLEY: Tell her so. It's just what a fool like you would do.

(BARBARA, *brisk and businesslike, comes from the shelter with a note book, and addresses herself to* SHIRLEY. BILL, *cowed, sits down in the corner on a form, and turns his back on them.*)

BARBARA: Good morning.

SHIRLEY: (*Standing up and taking off his hat.*) Good morning, 265 miss.

BARBARA: Sit down: make yourself at home. (*He hesitates; but she puts a friendly hand on his shoulder and makes him obey.*) Now then! since youve made friends with us, we want to know all about you. Names and addresses and trades. 270

SHIRLEY: Peter Shirley. Fitter. Chucked out two months ago because I was too old.

BARBARA: (*Not at all surprised.*) Youd pass still. Why didnt you dye your hair?

SHIRLEY: I did. Me age come out at a coroner's inquest on 275 me daughter.

BARBARA: Steady?

SHIRLEY: Teetotaller. Never out of a job before. Good worker. And sent to the knackers like an old horse!

BARBARA: No matter: if you did your part God will do his. 280

SHIRLEY: (*Suddenly stubborn.*) My religion's no concern of anybody but myself.

BARBARA: (*Guessing.*) I know. Secularist?

SHIRLEY: (*Hotly.*) Did I offer to deny it?

BARBARA: Why should you? My own father's a Secularist, I 285 think. Our Father—yours and mine—fulfils himself in many ways; and I daresay he knew what he was about when he made a Secularist of you. So buck up, Peter! we

can always find a job for a steady man like you. (SHIRLEY,
290   *disarmed and a little bewildered, touches his hat. She turns from
him to* BILL.) Whats your name?

BILL: (*Insolently.*) Wots thet to you?

BARBARA: (*Calmly making a note.*) Afraid to give his name.
Any trade?

295   BILL: Oo's afride to give is nime? (*Doggedly, with a sense of heroically defying the House of Lords in the person of Lord Stevenage.*) If you want to bring a chawge agen me, bring it.
(*She waits, unruffled.*) Moy nime's Bill Walker.

BARBARA: (*As if the name were familiar: trying to remember how.*)
300   Bill Walker? (*Recollecting.*) Oh, I know: you're the man that
Jenny Hill was praying for inside just now. (*She enters his
name in her note book.*)

BILL: Oo's Jenny Ill? And wot call as she to pry for me?

BARBARA: I dont know. Perhaps it was you that cut her lip.

305   BILL: (*Defiantly.*) Yus, it was me that cat her lip. Aw aint afride
o you.

BARBARA: How could you be, since youre not afraid of God?
Youre a brave man, Mr Walker. It takes some pluck to do
our work here; but none of us dare lift our hand against a
310   girl like that, for fear of her father in heaven.

BILL: (*Sullenly.*) I want nan o your kentin jawr. I spowse you think
Aw cam eah to beg from you, like this demmiged lot eah. Not
me. Aw downt want your bread and scripe and ketlep. Aw
dont blieve in your Gawd, no more than you do yourself.

315   BARBARA: (*Sunnily apologetic and ladylike, as on a new footing
with him.*) Oh, I beg your pardon for putting your name
down, Mr Walker. I didnt understand. I'll strike it out.

BILL: (*Taking this as a slight, and deeply wounded by it.*) Eah! you
let maw nime alown. Aint it good enaff to be in your book?

320   BARBARA: (*Considering.*) Well, you see, theres no use putting
down your name unless I can do something for you, is
there? Whats your trade?

BILL: (*Still smarting.*) Thets nao concern o yours.

BARBARA: Just so. (*Very businesslike.*) I'll put you down as
325   (*Writing.*) the man who—struck—poor little Jenny Hill—
in the mouth.

BILL: (*Rising threateningly.*) See eah. Awve ed enaff o this.

BARBARA: (*Quite sunny and fearless.*) What did you come to us
for?

330   BILL: Aw cam for maw gel, see? Aw cam to tike her aht o this
and to brike er jawr for er.

BARBARA: (*Complacently.*) You see I was right about your
trade. (BILL, *on the point of retorting furiously, finds himself, to
his great shame and terror, in danger of crying instead. He sits
335   down again suddenly.*) Whats her name?

BILL: (*Dogged.*) Er nime's Mog Ebbijem: thets wot her nime is.

BARBARA: Mog Habbijam! Oh, she's gone to Canning Town,
to our barracks there.

BILL: (*Fortified by his resentment of Mog's perfidy.*) Is she? (*Vin-
340   dictively.*) Then Aw'm gowin to Kennintahn arter her. (*He
crosses to the gate; hesitates; finally comes back at* BARBARA.)
Are you loyin to me to git shat o me?

BARBARA: I dont want to get shut of you. I want to keep you
here and save your soul. Youd better stay: youre going to
345   have a bad time today, Bill.

BILL: Oo's gowin to give it to me? You, preps?

BARBARA: Someone you dont believe in. But youll be glad
afterwards.

BILL: (*Slinking off.*) Aw'll gow to Kennintahn to be aht o reach
350   o your tangue. (*Suddenly turning on her with intense malice.*)

And if Aw downt fawnd Mog there, Aw'll cam beck and
do two years for you, selp me Gawd if Aw downt!

BARBARA: (*A shade kindlier, if possible.*) It's no use, Bill. She's
got another bloke.

BILL: Wot!   355

BARBARA: One of her own converts. He fell in love with her
when he saw her with her soul saved, and her face clean,
and her hair washed.

BILL: (*Surprised.*) Wottud she wash it for, the carroty slat? It's
red.   360

BARBARA: It's quite lovely now, because she wears a new look
in her eyes with it. It's a pity youre too late. The new
bloke has put your nose out of joint, Bill.

BILL: Aw'll put his nowse aht o joint for him. Not that Aw
care a carse for er, mawnd thet. But Aw'll teach her to   365
drop me as if Aw was dirt. And Aw'll teach him to meddle with maw judy. Wots iz bleedin nime?

BARBARA: Sergeant Todger Fairmile.

SHIRLEY: (*Rising with grim joy.*) I'll go with him, miss. I want
to see them two meet. I'll take him to the infirmary when   370
it's over.

BILL: (*To* SHIRLEY, *with undissembled misgiving.*) Is thet im you
was speakin on?

SHIRLEY: Thats him.

BILL: Im that wrastled in the music awl?   375

SHIRLEY: The competitions at the National Sportin Club was
worth nigh a hundred a year to him. He's gev em up now
for religion; so he's a bit fresh for want of the exercise he
was accustomed to. He'll be glad to see you. Come along.

BILL: Wots is wight?   380

SHIRLEY: Thirteen four. (BILL's *last hope expires.*)

BARBARA: Go and talk to him, Bill. He'll convert you.

SHIRLEY: He'll convert your head into a mashed potato.

BILL: (*Sullenly.*) Aw aint afride of im. Aw aint afride of ennybody. Bat e can lick me. She's dan me. (*He sits down mood-   385
ily on the edge of the horse trough.*)

SHIRLEY: You aint going. I thought not. (*He resumes his seat.*)

BARBARA: (*Calling.*) Jenny!

JENNY: (*Appearing at the shelter door with a plaster on the corner
of her mouth.*) Yes, Major.   390

BARBARA: Send Rummy Mitchens out to clear away here.

JENNY: I think she's afraid.

BARBARA: (*Her resemblance to her mother flashing out for a moment.*) Nonsense! she must do as she's told.

JENNY: (*Calling into the shelter.*) Rummy: the Major says you   395
must come.

(JENNY *comes to* BARBARA, *purposely keeping on the side next to*
BILL, *lest he should suppose that she shrank from him or bore malice.*)

BARBARA: Poor little Jenny! Are you tired? (*Looking at the
wounded cheek.*) Does it hurt?

JENNY: No: it's all right now. It was nothing.

BARBARA: (*Critically.*) It was as hard as he could hit, I expect.   400
Poor Bill! You dont feel angry with him, do you?

JENNY: Oh no, no, no: indeed I dont, Major, bless his poor
heart! (BARBARA *kisses her; and she runs away merrily into the
shelter.* BILL *writhes with an agonizing return of his new and
alarming symptoms, but says nothing.* RUMMY MITCHENS *comes   405
from the shelter.*)

BARBARA: (*Going to meet* RUMMY.) Now Rummy, bustle.
Take in those mugs and plates to be washed; and throw
the crumbs about for the birds.

(RUMMY *takes the three plates and mugs; but* SHIRLEY *takes back his mug from her, as there is still some milk left in it.*)

410 RUMMY: There aint any crumbs. This aint a time to waste good bread on birds.

PRICE: (*Appearing at the shelter door.*) Gentleman come to see the shelter, Major. Says he's your father.

BARBARA: All right. Coming. (SNOBBY [PRICE] *goes back into*
415 *the shelter, followed by* BARBARA.)

RUMMY: (*Stealing across to* BILL *and addressing him in a subdued voice, but with intense conviction.*) I'd av the lor of you, you flat eared pignosed potwalloper, if she'd let me. Youre no gentleman, to hit a lady in the face. (BILL, *with greater things*
420 *moving in him, takes no notice.*)

SHIRLEY: (*Following her.*) Here! in with you and dont get yourself into more trouble by talking.

RUMMY: (*With hauteur.*) I aint ad the pleasure o being hintro- duced to you, as I can remember. (*She goes into the shelter*
425 *with the plates.*)

SHIRLEY: Thats the—

BILL: (*Savagely.*) Downt you talk to me, d'ye eah? You lea me alown, or Aw'll do you a mischief. Aw'm not dirt under your feet, ennywy.

430 SHIRLEY: (*Calmly.*) Dont you be afeerd. You aint such prime company that you need expect to be sought after. (*He is about to go into the shelter when* BARBARA *comes out, with* UNDERSHAFT *on her right.*)

BARBARA: Oh, there you are, Mr Shirley! (*Between them.*) This
435 is my father: I told you he was a Secularist, didnt I? Per- haps youll be able to comfort one another.

UNDERSHAFT: (*Startled.*) A Secularist! Not the least in the world: on the contrary, a confirmed mystic.

BARBARA: Sorry, I'm sure. By the way, papa, what is your re-
440 ligion? in case I have to introduce you again.

UNDERSHAFT: My religion? Well, my dear, I am a Millionaire. That is my religion.

BARBARA: Then I'm afraid you and Mr Shirley wont be able to comfort one another after all. Youre not a Millionaire,
445 are you, Peter?

SHIRLEY: No; and proud of it.

UNDERSHAFT: (*Gravely.*) Poverty, my friend, is not a thing to be proud of.

SHIRLEY: (*Angrily.*) Who made your millions for you? Me and
450 my like. Whats kep us poor? Keepin you rich. I wouldnt have your conscience, not for all your income.

UNDERSHAFT: I wouldnt have your income, not for all your conscience, Mr Shirley. (*He goes to the penthouse and sits down on a form.*)

455 BARBARA: (*Stopping* SHIRLEY *adroitly as he is about to retort.*) You wouldnt think he was my father, would you, Peter? Will you go into the shelter and lend the lasses a hand for a while: we're worked off our feet.

SHIRLEY: (*Bitterly.*) Yes: I'm in their debt for a meal, aint I?

460 BARBARA: Oh, not because youre in their debt, but for love of them, Peter, for love of them. (*He cannot understand, and is rather scandalized.*) There! dont stare at me. In with you; and give that conscience of yours a holiday (*Bustling him into the shelter.*)

465 SHIRLEY: (*As he goes in.*) Ah! it's a pity you never was trained to use your reason, miss. Youd have been a very taking lecturer on Secularism.

(BARBARA *turns to her father.*)

UNDERSHAFT: Never mind me, my dear. Go about your work; and let me watch it for a while.

BARBARA: All right. 470

UNDERSHAFT: For instance, whats the matter with that out- patient over there?

BARBARA: (*Looking at* BILL, *whose attitude has never changed, and whose expression of brooding wrath has deepened.*) Oh, we shall cure him in no time. Just watch. (*She goes over to* BILL *and* 475 *waits. He glances up at her and casts his eyes down again, un- easy, but grimmer than ever.*) It would be nice to just stamp on Mog Habbijam's face, wouldnt it, Bill?

BILL: (*Starting up from the trough in consternation.*) It's a loy: Aw never said so. (*She shakes her head.*) Oo taold you wot was 480 in moy mawnd?

BARBARA: Only your new friend.

BILL: Wot new friend?

BARBARA: The devil, Bill. When he gets round people they get miserable, just like you. 485

BILL: (*With a heartbreaking attempt at devil-may-care cheerfulness.*) Aw aint miserable. (*He sits down again, and stretches his legs in an attempt to seem indifferent.*)

BARBARA: Well, if youre happy, why dont you look happy, as we do? 490

BILL: (*His legs curling back in spite of him.*) Aw'm eppy enaff, Aw tell you. Woy cawnt you lea me alown? Wot ev I dan to you? Aw aint smashed your fice, ev Aw?

BARBARA: (*Softly: wooing his soul.*) It's not me thats getting at you, Bill. 495

BILL: Oo else is it?

BARBARA: Somebody that doesnt intend you to smash women's faces, I suppose. Somebody or something that wants to make a man of you.

BILL: (*Blustering.*) Mike a menn o me! Aint Aw a menn? eh? 500 Oo sez Aw'm not a menn?

BARBARA: Theres a man in you somewhere, I suppose. But why did he let you hit poor little Jenny Hill? That wasnt very manly of him, was it?

BILL: (*Tormented.*) Ev dan wiv it, Aw tell you. Chack it. Aw'm 505 sick o your Jenny Ill and er silly little fice.

BARBARA: Then why do you keep thinking about it? Why does it keep coming up against you in your mind? Youre not getting converted, are you?

BILL: (*With conviction.*) Not ME. Not lawkly. 510

BARBARA: Thats right, Bill. Hold out against it. Put out your strength. Dont lets get you cheap. Todger Fairmile said he wrestled for three nights against his salvation harder than he ever wrestled with the Jap at the music hall. He gave in to the Jap when his arm was going to break. But he didnt 515 give in to his salvation until his heart was going to break. Perhaps youll escape that. You havnt any heart, have you?

BILL: Wot d'ye mean? Woy aint Aw got a awt the sime as en- nybody else?

BARBARA: A man with a heart wouldnt have bashed poor lit- 520 tle Jenny's face, would he?

BILL: (*Almost crying.*) Ow, will you lea me alown? Ev Aw ever offered to meddle with you, that you cam neggin and provowkin me lawk this? (*He writhes convulsively from his eyes to his toes.*) 525

BARBARA: (*With a steady soothing hand on his arm and a gentle voice that never lets him go.*) It's your soul thats hurting you, Bill, and not me. Weve been through it all ourselves. Come with us, Bill. (*He looks wildly round.*) To brave man-

530 hood on earth and eternal glory in heaven. (*He is on the point of breaking down.*) Come. (*A drum is heard in the shelter; and* BILL, *with a gasp, escapes from the spell as* BARBARA *turns quickly.* ADOLPHUS [CUSINS] *enters from the shelter with a big drum.*) Oh! there you are, Dolly. Let me introduce a

535 new friend of mine, Mr Bill Walker. This is my bloke, Bill: Mr Cusins. (CUSINS *salutes with his drumstick.*)

BILL: Gowin to merry im?

BARBARA: Yes.

BILL: (*Fervently.*) Gawd elp im! Gaw-aw-aw-awd elp im!

540 BARBARA: Why? Do you think he wont be happy with me?

BILL: Awve aony ed to stend it for a mawnin: e'll ev to stend it for a lawftawm.

CUSINS: That is a frightful reflection, Mr Walker. But I cant tear myself away from her.

545 BILL: Well, Aw ken. (*To* BARBARA.) Eah! do you knaow where Aw'm gowin to, and wot Aw'm gowin to do?

BARBARA: Yes: youre going to heaven; and youre coming back here before the week's out to tell me so.

BILL: You loy. Aw'm gowin to Kennintahn, to spit in Todger

550 Fairmawl's eye. Aw beshed Jenny Ill's fice; an nar Aw'll git me aown fice beshed and cam beck and shaow it to er. Ee'll itt me ardern Aw itt her. Thatll mike us square. (*To* ADOLPHUS [CUSINS].) Is thet fair or is it not? Youre a genlmn: you oughter knaow.

555 BARBARA: Two black eyes wont make one white one, Bill.

BILL: Aw didnt awst you. Cawnt you never keep your mahth shat? Oy awst the genlmn.

CUSINS: (*Reflectively.*) Yes: I think youre right, Mr Walker. Yes: I should do it. It's curious: it's exactly what an ancient

560 Greek would have done.

BARBARA: But what good will it do?

CUSINS: Well, it will give Mr Fairmile some exercise; and it will satisfy Mr Walker's soul.

BILL: Rot! there aint nao such a thing as a saoul. Ah kin you

565 tell wevver Awve a saoul or not? You never seen it.

BARBARA: Ive seen it hurting you when you went against it.

BILL: (*With compressed aggravation.*) If you was maw gel and took the word aht o me mahth lawk thet, Aw'd give you sathink youd feel urtin, Aw would. (*To* CUSINS.) You tike

570 maw tip, mite. Stop er jawr; or youll doy afoah your tawm (*With intense expression.*) Wore aht: thets wot youll be: wore aht. (*He goes away through the gate.*)

CUSINS: (*Looking after him.*) I wonder!

BARBARA: Dolly! (*Indignant, in her mother's manner.*)

575 CUSINS: Yes, my dear, it's very wearing to be in love with you. If it lasts, I quite think I shall die young.

BARBARA: Should you mind?

CUSINS: Not at all. (*He is suddenly softened, and kisses her over the drum, evidently not for the first time, as people cannot kiss*

580 *over a big drum without practice.* UNDERSHAFT *coughs.*)

BARBARA: It's all right, papa, weve not forgotten you. Dolly: explain the place to papa: I havnt time. (*She goes busily into the shelter.*)

(UNDERSHAFT *and* ADOLPHUS [CUSINS] *now have the yard to themselves.* UNDERSHAFT, *seated on a form, and still keenly attentive, looks hard at* ADOLPHUS [CUSINS]. ADOLPHUS [CUSINS] *looks hard at him.*)

UNDERSHAFT: I fancy you guess something of what is in my

585 mind, Mr Cusins. (CUSINS *flourishes his drumsticks as if in the*

act of beating a lively rataplan, but makes no sound.) Exactly so. But suppose Barbara finds you out!

CUSINS: You know, I do not admit that I am imposing on Barbara. I am quite genuinely interested in the views of the Salvation Army. The fact is, I am a sort of collector of 590 religions; and the curious thing is that I find I can believe them all. By the way, have you any religion?

UNDERSHAFT: Yes.

CUSINS: Anything out of the common?

UNDERSHAFT: Only that there are two things necessary to 595 Salvation.

CUSINS: (*Disappointed, but polite.*) Ah, the Church Catechism. Charles Lomax also belongs to the Established Church.

UNDERSHAFT: The two things are—

CUSINS: Baptism and— 600

UNDERSHAFT: No. Money and gunpowder.

CUSINS: (*Surprised, but interested.*) That is the general opinion of our governing classes. The novelty is in hearing any man confess it.

UNDERSHAFT: Just so. 605

CUSINS: Excuse me: is there any place in your religion for honor, justice, truth, love, mercy and so forth?

UNDERSHAFT: Yes: they are the graces and luxuries of a rich, strong, and safe life.

CUSINS: Suppose one is forced to choose between them and 610 money or gunpowder?

UNDERSHAFT: Choose money and gunpowder; for without enough of both you cannot afford the others.

CUSINS: That is your religion?

UNDERSHAFT: Yes. 615

(*The cadence of this reply makes a full close in the conversation,* CUSINS *twists his face dubiously and contemplates* UNDERSHAFT. UNDERSHAFT *contemplates him.*)

CUSINS: Barbara wont stand that. You will have to choose between your religion and Barbara.

UNDERSHAFT: So will you, my friend. She will find out that that drum of yours is hollow.

CUSINS: Father Undershaft: you are mistaken: I am a sincere 620 Salvationist. You do not understand the Salvation Army. It is the army of joy, of love, of courage: it has banished the fear and remorse and despair of the old hell-ridden evangelical sects: it marches to fight the devil with trumpet and drum, with music and dancing, with banner and palm, as 625 becomes a sally from heaven by its happy garrison. It picks the waster out of the public house and makes a man of him: it finds a worm wriggling in a back kitchen, and lo! a woman! Men and women of rank too, sons and daughters of the Highest. It takes the poor professor of Greek, 630 the most artificial and self-suppressed of human creatures, from his meal of roots, and lets loose the rhapsodist in him; reveals the true worship of Dionysos to him; sends him down the public street drumming dithyrambs (*He plays a thundering flourish on the drum.*) 635

UNDERSHAFT: You will alarm the shelter.

CUSINS: Oh, they are accustomed to these sudden ecstasies. However, if the drum worries you—(*He pockets the drumsticks; unhooks the drum; and stands it on the ground opposite the gateway.*) 640

UNDERSHAFT: Thank you.

CUSINS: You remember what Euripides says about your money and gunpowder?

UNDERSHAFT: No.

645 CUSINS: (*Declaiming.*)

> One and another
> In money and guns may outpass his brother;
> And men in their millions float and flow
> And seethe with a million hopes as leaven;
650 And they win their will; or they miss their will;
> And their hopes are dead or are pined for still;
> But who'er can know
> As the long days go
> That to live is happy, has found his heaven.

655 My translation: what do you think of it?

UNDERSHAFT: I think, my friend, that if you wish to know, as the long days go, that to live is happy, you must first acquire money enough for a decent life, and power enough to be your own master.

660 CUSINS: You are damnably discouraging. (*He resumes his declamation.*)

> Is it so hard a thing to see
> That the spirit of God—whate'er it be—
> The law that abides and changes not, ages long,
665 The Eternal and Nature-born: these things be strong?
> What else is Wisdom? What of Man's endeavor,
> Or God's high grace so lovely and so great?
> To stand from fear set free? to breathe and wait?
> To hold a hand uplifted over Fate?
670 And shall not Barbara be loved for ever?

UNDERSHAFT: Euripides mentions Barbara, does he?

CUSINS: It is a fair translation. The word means Loveliness.

UNDERSHAFT: May I ask—as Barbara's father—how much a year she is to be loved for ever on?

675 CUSINS: As for Barbara's father, that is more your affair than mine. I can feed her by teaching Greek: that is about all.

UNDERSHAFT: Do you consider it a good match for her?

CUSINS: (*With polite obstinacy.*) Mr Undershaft: I am in many ways a weak, timid, ineffectual person; and my health is far 680 from satisfactory. But whenever I feel that I must have anything, I get it, sooner or later. I feel that way about Barbara. I dont like marriage: I feel intensely afraid of it; and I dont know what I shall do with Barbara or what she will do with me. But I feel that I and nobody else must marry 685 her. Please regard that as settled.—Not that I wish to be arbitrary; but why should I waste your time in discussing what is inevitable?

UNDERSHAFT: You mean that you will stick at nothing: not even the conversion of the Salvation Army to the worship 690 of Dionysos.

CUSINS: The business of the Salvation Army is to save, not to wrangle about the name of the pathfinder. Dionysos or another: what does it matter?

UNDERSHAFT: (*Rising and approaching him.*) Professor Cusins: 695 you are a young man after my own heart.

CUSINS: Mr Undershaft: you are, as far as I am able to gather, a most infernal old rascal; but you appeal very strongly to my sense of ironic humor.

(UNDERSHAFT *mutely offers his hand. They shake.*)

UNDERSHAFT: (*Suddenly concentrating himself.*) And now to business. 700

CUSINS: Pardon me. We are discussing religion. Why go back to such an uninteresting and unimportant subject as business?

UNDERSHAFT: Religion is our business at present, because it is through religion alone that we can win Barbara.

CUSINS: Have you, too, fallen in love with Barbara? 705

UNDERSHAFT: Yes, with a father's love.

CUSINS: A father's love for a grown-up daughter is the most dangerous of all infatuations. I apologize for mentioning my own pale, coy, mistrustful fancy in the same breath with it.

UNDERSHAFT: Keep to the point. We have to win her; and 710 we are neither of us Methodists.

CUSINS: That doesnt matter. The power Barbara wields here—the power that wields Barbara herself—is not Calvinism, not Presbyterianism, not Methodism—

UNDERSHAFT: Not Greek Paganism either, eh? 715

CUSINS: I admit that. Barbara is quite original in her religion.

UNDERSHAFT: (*Triumphantly.*) Aha! Barbara Undershaft would be. Her inspiration comes from within herself.

CUSINS: How do you suppose it got there?

UNDERSHAFT: (*In towering excitement.*) It is the Undershaft in- 720 heritance. I shall hand on my torch to my daughter. She shall make my converts and preach my gospel—

CUSINS: What! Money and gunpowder!

UNDERSHAFT: Yes, money and gunpowder. Freedom and power. Command of life and command of death. 725

CUSINS: (*Urbanely: trying to bring him down to earth.*) This is extremely interesting, Mr Undershaft. Of course you know that you are mad.

UNDERSHAFT: (*With redoubled force.*) And you?

CUSINS: Oh, mad as a hatter. You are welcome to my secret 730 since I have discovered yours. But I am astonished. Can a madman make cannons?

UNDERSHAFT: Would anyone else than a madman make them? And now (*With surging energy.*) question for question. Can a sane man translate Euripides? 735

CUSINS: No.

UNDERSHAFT: (*Seizing him by the shoulder.*) Can a sane woman make a man of a waster or a woman of a worm?

CUSINS: (*Reeling before the storm.*) Father Colossus—Mammoth Millionaire— 740

UNDERSHAFT: (*Pressing him.*) Are there two mad people or three in this Salvation shelter today?

CUSINS: You mean Barbara is as mad as we are?

UNDERSHAFT: (*Pushing him lightly off and resuming his equanimity suddenly and completely.*) Pooh, Professor! let us call 745 things by their proper names. I am a millionaire; you are a poet; Barbara is a savior of souls. What have we three to do with the common mob of slaves and idolators? (*He sits down again with a shrug of contempt for the mob.*)

CUSINS: Take care! Barbara is in love with the common peo- 750 ple. So am I. Have you never felt the romance of that love?

UNDERSHAFT: (*Cold and sardonic.*) Have you ever been in love with Poverty, like St Francis? Have you ever been in love with Dirt, like St Simeon! Have you ever been in love with disease and suffering, like our nurses and philanthropists? 755 Such passions are not virtues, but the most unnatural of all the vices. This love of the common people may please an earl's granddaughter and a university professor; but I have been a common man and a poor man; and it has no ro-

760 mance for me. Leave it to the poor to pretend that poverty is a blessing: leave it to the coward to make a religion of his cowardice by preaching humility: we know better than that. We three must stand together above the common people: how else can we help their children to climb up beside

765 us? Barbara must belong to us, not to the Salvation Army.

CUSINS: Well, I can only say that if you think you will get her away from the Salvation Army by talking to her as you have been talking to me, you dont know Barbara.

UNDERSHAFT: My friend: I never ask for what I can buy.

770 CUSINS: (*In a white fury.*) Do I understand you to imply that you can buy Barbara?

UNDERSHAFT: No; but I can buy the Salvation Army.

CUSINS: Quite impossible.

UNDERSHAFT: You shall see. All religious organizations exist

775 by selling themselves to the rich.

CUSINS: Not the Army. That is the Church of the poor.

UNDERSHAFT: All the more reason for buying it.

CUSINS: I dont think you quite know what the Army does for the poor.

780 UNDERSHAFT: Oh yes I do. It draws their teeth: that is enough for me as a man of business.

CUSINS: Nonsense! It makes them sober—

UNDERSHAFT: I prefer sober workmen. The profits are larger.

CUSINS: —honest—

785 UNDERSHAFT: Honest workmen are the most economical.

CUSINS: —attached to their homes—

UNDERSHAFT: So much the better: they will put up with anything sooner than change their shop.

CUSINS: —happy—

790 UNDERSHAFT: An invaluable safeguard against revolution.

CUSINS: —unselfish—

UNDERSHAFT: Indifferent to their own interests, which suits me exactly.

CUSINS: —with their thoughts on heavenly things—

795 UNDERSHAFT: (*Rising.*) And not on Trade Unionism nor Socialism. Excellent.

CUSINS: (*Revolted.*) You really are an infernal old rascal.

UNDERSHAFT: (*Indicating* PETER SHIRLEY, *who has just come from the shelter and strolled dejectedly down the yard between*

800 *them.*) And this is an honest man!

SHIRLEY: Yes; and what av I got by it? (*He passes on bitterly and sits on the form, in the corner of the penthouse.*)

(SNOBBY PRICE, *beaming sanctimoniously, and* JENNY HILL, *with a tambourine full of coppers, come from the shelter and go to the drum, on which* JENNY *begins to count the money.*)

UNDERSHAFT: (*Replying to* SHIRLEY.) Oh, your employers

805 must have got a good deal by it from first to last. (*He sits on the table, with one foot on the side form,* CUSINS, *overwhelmed, sits down on the same form nearer the shelter.* BARBARA *comes from the shelter to the middle of the yard. She is excited and a little overwrought.*)

BARBARA: Weve just had a splendid experience meeting at the

810 other gate in Cripps's lane. Ive hardly ever seen them so much moved as they were by your confession, Mr Price.

PRICE: I could almost be glad of my past wickedness if I could believe that it would elp to keep hathers stright.

BARBARA: So it will, Snobby. How much, Jenny?

JENNY: Four and tenpence, Major.   815

BARBARA: Oh Snobby, if you had given your poor mother just one more kick, we should have got the whole five shillings!

PRICE: If she heard you say that, miss, she'd be sorry I didnt. But I'm glad. Oh what a joy it will be to her when she hears I'm saved!   820

UNDERSHAFT: Shall I contribute the odd twopence, Barbara? The millionaire's mite, eh? (*He takes a couple of pennies from his pocket.*)

BARBARA: How did you make that twopence?

UNDERSHAFT: As usual. By selling cannons, torpedoes, sub-   825 marines, and my new patent Grand Duke hand grenade.

BARBARA: Put it back in your pocket. You cant buy your salvation here for twopence: you must work it out.

UNDERSHAFT: Is twopence not enough? I can afford a little more, if you press me.   830

BARBARA: Two million millions would not be enough. There is bad blood on your hands; and nothing but good blood can cleanse them. Money is no use. Take it away. (*She turns to* CUSINS.) Dolly: you must write another letter for me to the papers. (*He makes a wry face.*) Yes: I know you dont like   835 it; but it must be done. The starvation this winter is beating us: everybody is unemployed. The General says we must close this shelter if we cant get more money. I force the collections at the meetings until I am ashamed: dont I, Snobby?   840

PRICE: It's a fair treat to see you work it, miss. The way you got them up from three-and-six to four-and-ten with that hymn, penny by penny and verse by verse, was a caution. Not a Cheap Jack on Mile End Waste could touch you at it.

BARBARA: Yes; but I wish we could do without it. I am getting   845 at last to think more of the collection than of the people's souls. And what are those hatfuls of pence and halfpence? We want thousands! tens of thousands! hundreds of thousands! I want to convert people, not to be always begging for the Army in a way I'd die sooner than beg for myself.   850

UNDERSHAFT: (*In profound irony.*) Genuine unselfishness is capable of anything, my dear.

BARBARA: (*Unsuspectingly, as she turns away to take the money from the drum and put it in a cash bag she carries.*) Yes, isnt it? (UNDERSHAFT *looks sardonically at* CUSINS.)   855

CUSINS: (*Aside to* UNDERSHAFT.) Mephistopheles! Machiavelli!

BARBARA: (*Tears coming into her eyes as she ties the bag and pockets it.*) How are we to feed them? I cant talk religion to a man with bodily hunger in his eyes. (*Almost breaking down.*) It's frightful.   860

JENNY: (*Running to her.*) Major, dear—

BARBARA: (*Rebounding.*) No: dont comfort me. It will be all right. We shall get the money.

UNDERSHAFT: How?

JENNY: By praying for it, of course. Mrs Baines says she prayed   865 for it last night; and she has never prayed for it in vain: never once. (*She goes to the gate and looks out into the street.*)

BARBARA: (*Who has dried her eyes and regained her composure.*) By the way, dad, Mrs Baines has come to march with us to our big meeting this afternoon; and she is very anxious to meet   870 you, for some reason or other. Perhaps she'll convert you.

UNDERSHAFT: I shall be delighted, my dear.

JENNY: (*At the gate: excitedly.*) Major! Major! heres that man back again.

BARBARA: What man?   875

JENNY: The man that hit me. Oh, I hope he's coming back to join us.

(BILL WALKER, *with frost on his jacket, comes through the gate, his hands deep in his pockets and his chin sunk between his shoulders, like a cleaned-out gambler. He halts between* BARBARA *and the drum.*)

BARBARA: Hullo, Bill! Back already!

BILL: (*Nagging at her.*) Bin talkin ever sence, ev you?

880 BARBARA: Pretty nearly. Well, has Todger paid you out for poor Jenny's jaw?

BILL: Nao e aint.

BARBARA: I thought your jacket looked a bit snowy.

BILL: Sao it is snaowy. You want to knaow where the snaow
885 cam from, downt you?

BARBARA: Yes.

BILL: Well, it cam from orf the grahnd in Pawkinses Corner in Kennintahn. It got rabbed orf be maw shaoulders: see?

BARBARA: Pity you didnt rub some off with your knees, Bill!
890 That would have done you a lot of good.

BILL: (*With sour mirthless humor.*) Aw was sivin another menn's knees at the tawm. E was kneelin on moy ed, e was.

JENNY: Who was kneeling on your head?

BILL: Todger was. E was pryin for me: pryin camfortable wiv
895 me as a cawpet. Sow was Mog. Sao was the aol bloomin meetin. Mog she sez 'Ow Lawd brike is stabborn sperrit; bat downt urt is dear art.' Thet was wot she said. 'Downt urt is dear art'! An er blowk—thirteen stun four!— kneelin wiv all is wight on me. Fanny, aint it?

900 JENNY: Oh no. We're so sorry, Mr Walker.

BARBARA: (*Enjoying it frankly.*) Nonsense! of course it's funny. Served you right, Bill! You must have done something to him first.

BILL: (*Doggedly.*) Aw did wot Aw said Aw'd do. Aw spit in is eye.
905 E looks ap at the skoy and sez, 'Ow that Aw should be fahnd worthy to be spit upon for the gospel's sike!' e sez; an Mog sez 'Glaory Allelloolier!'; an then e called me Braddher, an dahned me as if Aw was a kid and e was me mather worshin me a Setterda nawt. Aw ednt jast nao shaow wiv im at all.
910 Arf the street pryed; an the tather arf larfed fit to split their-selves. (*To* BARBARA.) There! are you settisfawd nah?

BARBARA: (*Her eyes dancing.*) Wish I'd been there, Bill.

BILL: Yus: youd a got in a hextra bit o talk on me, wouldnt you?

JENNY: I'm so sorry, Mr Walker.

915 BILL: (*Fiercely.*) Downt you gow being sorry for me: youve no call. Listen eah. Aw browk your jawr.

JENNY: No, it didn't hurt me: indeed it didnt, except for a moment. It was only that I was frightened.

BILL: Aw downt want to be forgive be you, or be ennybody.
920 Wot Aw did Aw'll py for. Aw trawd to gat me aown jawr browk to settisfaw you—

JENNY: (*Distressed.*) Oh no—

BILL: (*Impatiently.*) Tell y' Aw did: cawnt you listen to wots bein taold you? All Aw got be it was bein mide a sawt of
925 in the pablic street for me pines. Well, if Aw cawnt settis-faw you one wy, Aw ken another. Listen eah! Aw ed two quid sived agen the frost; an Awve a pahnd of it left. A mite o mawn last week ed words with the judy e's gow-ing to merry. E give er wot-for; an e's bin fawnd fifteen
930 bob. E ed a rawt to itt er cause they was gowin to be mer-

rid; but Aw ednt nao rawt to itt you; sao put anather fawv bob on an call it a pahnd's worth. (*He produces a sovereign.*) Eahs the manney. Tike it; and lets ev no more o your for-givin an prying and your Mijor jawrin me. Let wot Aw dan be dan an pide for; and let there be a end of it. 935

JENNY: Oh, I couldnt take it, Mr Walker. But if you would give a shilling or two to poor Rummy Mitchens! you re-ally did hurt her; and she's old.

BILL: (*Contemptuously.*) Not lawkly. Aw'd give her anather as soon as look at er. Let her ev the lawr o me as she threat- 940 ened! She aint forgiven me: not mach. Wot Aw dan to er is not on me mawnd—wot she (*Indicating* BARBARA.) mawt call on me conscience—no more than stickin a pig. It's this Christian gime o yours that Aw wownt ev plyed agen me: this bloomin forgivin an neggin an jawrin that 945 mikes a menn thet sore that iz lawf's a burdn to im. Aw wownt ev it, Aw tell you; sao tike your manney and stop thraowin your silly beshed fice hap agen me.

JENNY: Major: may I take a little of it for the Army?

BARBARA: No: the Army is not to be bought. We want your 950 soul, Bill; and we'll take nothing less.

BILL: (*Bitterly.*) Aw knaow. Me an maw few shillins is not good enaff for you. Youre a earl's grendorter, you are. Na-think less than a andered pahnd for you.

UNDERSHAFT: Come, Barbara! you could do a great deal of 955 good with a hundred pounds. If you will set this gentle-man's mind at ease by taking his pound, I will give the other ninety-nine.

(BILL, *dazed by such opulence, instinctively touches his cap.*)

BARBARA: Oh, youre too extravagant, papa. Bill offers twenty pieces of silver. All you need offer is the other ten. That 960 will make the standard price to buy anybody who's for sale. I'm not; and the Army's not. (*To* BILL.) Youll never have another quiet moment, Bill, until you come round to us. You cant stand out against your salvation.

BILL: (*Sullenly.*) Aw cawnt stend aht agen music awl wrastlers 965 and awtful tangued women. Awve offered to py. Aw can do no more. Tike it or leave it. There it is. (*He throws the sovereign on the drum, and sits down on the horse-trough. The coin fascinates* SNOBBY PRICE, *who takes an early opportunity of dropping his cap on it.*) 970

(MRS BAINES *comes from the shelter. She is dressed as a Salvation Army Commissioner. She is an earnest looking woman of about 40, with a caressing, urgent voice, and an appealing manner.*)

BARBARA: This is my father, Mrs Baines. (UNDERSHAFT *comes from the table, taking his hat off with marked civility.*) Try what you can do with him. He wont listen to me, because he remembers what a fool I was when I was a baby. (*She leaves them together and chats with* JENNY.) 975

MRS BAINES: Have you been shewn over the shelter, Mr Un-dershaft? You know the work we're doing, of course.

UNDERSHAFT: (*Very civilly.*) The whole nation knows it, Mrs Baines.

MRS BAINES: No, sir: the whole nation does not know it, or 980 we should not be crippled as we are for want of money to carry our work through the length and breadth of the land. Let me tell you that there would have been rioting this winter in London but for us.

985 UNDERSHAFT: You really think so?

MRS BAINES: I know it. I remember 1886, when you rich gentlemen hardened your hearts against the cry of the poor. They broke the windows of your clubs in Pall Mall.

UNDERSHAFT: (*Gleaming with approval of their method.*) And
990 the Mansion House Fund went up next day from thirty thousand pounds to seventy-nine thousand! I remember quite well.

MRS BAINES: Well, wont you help me to get at the people? They wont break windows then. Come here, Price. Let
995 me shew you to this gentleman (PRICE *comes to be inspected.*) Do you remember the window breaking?

PRICE: My ole father thought it was the revolution, maam.

MRS BAINES: Would you break windows now?

PRICE: Oh no, maam. The windows of eaven av bin opened to
1000 me. I know now that the rich man is a sinner like myself.

RUMMY: (*Appearing above at the loft door.*) Snobby Price!

SNOBBY: Wot is it?

RUMMY: Your mother's askin for you at the other gate in Cripps's Lane. She's heard about your confession (PRICE *turns pale.*)

1005 MRS BAINES: Go, Mr Price; and pray with her.

JENNY: You can go through the shelter, Snobby.

PRICE: (*To* MRS BAINES.) I couldnt face her now, maam, with all the weight of my sins fresh on me. Tell her she'll find her son at ome, waitin for her in prayer. (*He skulks off*
1010 *through the gate, incidentally stealing the sovereign on his way out by picking up his cap from the drum.*)

MRS BAINES: (*With swimming eyes.*) You see how we take the anger and the bitterness against you out of their hearts, Mr Undershaft.

1015 UNDERSHAFT: It is certainly most convenient and gratifying to all large employers of labor, Mrs Baines.

MRS BAINES: Barbara: Jenny: I have good news: most wonderful news. (JENNY *runs to her.*) My prayers have been answered. I told you they would, Jenny, didnt I?

1020 JENNY: Yes, yes.

BARBARA: (*Moving nearer to the drum.*) Have we got money enough to keep the shelter open?

MRS BAINES: I hope we shall have enough to keep all the shelters open. Lord Saxmundham has promised us five
1025 thousand pounds—

BARBARA: Hooray!

JENNY: Glory!

MRS BAINES: —if—

BARBARA: 'If!' If what?

1030 MRS BAINES: —if five other gentlemen will give a thousand each to make it up to ten thousand.

BARBARA: Who is Lord Saxmundham? I never heard of him.

UNDERSHAFT: (*Who has pricked up his ears at the peer's name, and is now watching* BARBARA *curiously.*) A new creation, my
1035 dear. You have heard of Sir Horace Bodger?

BARBARA: Bodger! Do you mean the distiller? Bodger's whisky!

UNDERSHAFT: That is the man. He is one of the greatest of our public benefactors. He restored the cathedral at Hakington. They made him a baronet for that. He gave half a million to
1040 the funds of his party: they made him a baron for that.

SHIRLEY: What will they give him for the five thousand?

UNDERSHAFT: There is nothing left to give him. So the five thousand, I should think, is to save his soul.

MRS BAINES: Heaven grant it may! Oh Mr Undershaft, you
1045 have some very rich friends. Cant you help us towards the other five thousand? We are going to hold a great meeting this afternoon at the Assembly Hall in the Mile End Road. If I could only announce that one gentleman had come forward to support Lord Saxmundham, others would follow. Dont you know somebody? couldnt you? 1050 wouldnt you? (*Her eyes fill with tears.*) oh, think of those poor people, Mr Undershaft: think of how much it means to them, and how little to a great man like you.

UNDERSHAFT: (*Sardonically gallant.*) Mrs Baines: you are irresistible. I cant disappoint you; and I cant deny myself the 1055 satisfaction of making Bodger pay up. You shall have your five thousand pounds.

MRS BAINES: Thank God!

UNDERSHAFT: You dont thank me?

MRS BAINES: Oh sir, dont try to be cynical: dont be ashamed 1060 of being a good man. The Lord will bless you abundantly; and our prayers will be like a strong fortification round you all the days of your life. (*With a touch of caution.*) You will let me have the cheque to shew at the meeting, wont you? Jenny: go in and fetch a pen and ink. (JENNY *runs to* 1065 *the shelter door.*)

UNDERSHAFT: Do not disturb Miss Hill: I have a fountain pen. (JENNY *halts. He sits at the table and writes the cheque.* CUSINS *rises to make room for him. They all watch him silently.*)

BILL: (*Cynically, aside to* BARBARA, *his voice and accent horribly* 1070 *debased.*) Wot prawce selvytion nah?

BARBARA: Stop. (UNDERSHAFT *stops writing: they all turn to her in surprise.*) Mrs Baines: are you really going to take this money?

MRS BAINES: (*Astonished.*) Why not, dear? 1075

BARBARA: Why not! Do you know what my father is? Have you forgotten that Lord Saxmundham is Bodger the whisky man? Do you remember how we implored the County Council to stop him from writing Bodger's Whisky in letters of fire against the sky; so that the poor drink- 1080 ruined creatures on the Embankment could not wake up from their snatches of sleep without being reminded of their deadly thirst by that wicked sky sign? Do you know that the worst thing I have had to fight here is not the devil, but Bodger, Bodger, Bodger, with his whisky, his distilleries, 1085 and his tied houses? Are you going to make our shelter another tied house for him, and ask me to keep it?

BILL: Rotten dranken whisky it is too.

MRS BAINES: Dear Barbara: Lord Saxmundham has a soul to be saved like any of us. If heaven has found the way to 1090 make a good use of his money, are we to set ourselves up against the answer to our prayers?

BARBARA: I know he has a soul to be saved. Let him come down here; and I'll do my best to help him to his salvation. But he wants to send his cheque down to buy us, and 1095 go on being as wicked as ever.

UNDERSHAFT: (*With a reasonableness which* CUSINS *alone perceives to be ironical.*) My dear Barbara: alcohol is a very necessary article. It heals the sick—

BARBARA: It does nothing of the sort. 1100

UNDERSHAFT: Well, it assists the doctor: that is perhaps a less questionable way of putting it. It makes life bearable to millions of people who could not endure their existence if they were quite sober. It enables Parliament to do things at eleven at night that no sane person would do at eleven in 1105 the morning. Is it Bodger's fault that this inestimable gift is deplorably abused by less than one per cent of the poor? (*He turns again to the table; signs the cheque; and crosses it.*)

MRS BAINES: Barbara: will there be less drinking or more if
1110 all those poor souls we are saving come tomorrow and find the doors of our shelters shut in their faces? Lord Saxmundham gives us the money to stop drinking—to take his own business from him.

CUSINS: (*Impishly.*) Pure self-sacrifice on Bodger's part,
1115 clearly! Bless dear Bodger! (BARBARA *almost breaks down as* ADOLPHUS, *too, fails her.*)

UNDERSHAFT: (*Tearing out the cheque and pocketing the book as he rises and goes past* CUSINS *to* MRS BAINES.) I also, Mrs Baines, may claim a little disinterestedness. Think of my business!
1120 think of the widows and orphans! the men and lads torn to pieces with shrapnel and poisoned with lyddite! (MRS BAINES *shrinks; but he goes on remorselessly.*) the oceans of blood, not one drop of which is shed in a really just cause! the ravaged crops! the peaceful peasants forced, women and
1125 men, to till their fields under the fire of opposing armies on pain of starvation! the bad blood of the fierce little cowards at home who egg on others to fight for the gratification of their national vanity! All this makes money for me: I am never richer, never busier than when the papers are full of
1130 it. Well, it is your work to preach peace on earth and good will to men. (MRS BAINES's *face lights up again.*) Every convert you make is a vote against war. (*Her lips move in prayer.*) Yet I give you this money to help you to hasten my own commercial ruin. (*He gives her the cheque.*)

1135 CUSINS: (*Mounting the form in an ecstasy of mischief.*) The millennium will be inaugurated by the unselfishness of Undershaft and Bodger. Oh be joyful! (*He takes the drum-sticks from his pocket and flourishes them.*)

MRS BAINES: (*Taking the cheque.*) The longer I live the more
1140 proof I see that there is an Infinite Goodness that turns everything to the work of salvation sooner or later. Who would have thought that any good could have come out of war and drink? And yet their profits are brought today to the feet of salvation to do its blessed work. (*She is af-*
1145 *fected to tears.*)

JENNY: (*Running to* MRS BAINES *and throwing her arms round her.*) Oh dear! how blessed, how glorious it all is!

CUSINS: (*In a convulsion of irony.*) Let us seize this unspeakable moment. Let us march to the great meeting at once. Ex-
1150 cuse me just an instant. (*He rushes into the shelter.* JENNY *takes her tambourine from the drum head.*)

MRS BAINES: Mr Undershaft: have you ever seen a thousand people fall on their knees with one impulse and pray? Come with us to the meeting. Barbara shall tell them that
1155 the Army is saved, and saved through you.

CUSINS: (*Returning impetuously from the shelter with a flag and a trombone, and coming between* MRS BAINES *and* UNDERSHAFT.) You shall carry the flag down the first street, Mrs Baines. (*He gives her the flag.*) Mr Undershaft is a gifted
1160 trombonist: he shall intone an Olympian diapason to the West Ham Salvation March. (*Aside to* UNDERSHAFT, *as he forces the trombone on him.*) Blow, Machiavelli, blow.

UNDERSHAFT: (*Aside to him, as he takes the trombone.*) The trumpet in Zion! (CUSINS *rushes to the drum, which he takes*
1165 *up and puts on.* UNDERSHAFT *continues, aloud.*) I will do my best. I could vamp a bass if I knew the tune.

CUSINS: It is a wedding chorus from one of Donizetti's operas; but we have converted it. We convert everything to good here, including Bodger. You remember the chorus. 'For thee immense rejoicing—immenso giubilo—immenso 1170 giubilo.' (*With drum obbligato.*) Rum tum ti tum tum, tum tum ti ta—

BARBARA: Dolly: you are breaking my heart.

CUSINS: What is a broken heart more or less here? Dionysos Undershaft has descended. I am possessed. 1175

MRS BAINES: Come, Barbara: I must have my dear Major to carry the flag with me.

JENNY: Yes, yes, Major darling.

(CUSINS *snatches the tambourine out of* JENNY's *hand and mutely offers it to* BARBARA.)

BARBARA: (*Coming forward a little as she puts the offer behind her with a shudder, whilst* CUSINS *recklessly tosses the tambourine* 1180 *back to* JENNY *and goes to the gate.*) I cant come.

JENNY: Not come!

MRS BAINES: (*With tears in her eyes.*) Barbara: do you think I am wrong to take the money?

BARBARA: (*Impulsively going to her and kissing her.*) No, no: God 1185 help you, dear, you must: you are saving the Army. Go; and may you have a great meeting!

JENNY: But arnt you coming?

BARBARA: No. (*She begins taking off the silver S brooch from her collar.*) 1190

MRS BAINES: Barbara: what are you doing?

JENNY: Why are you taking your badge off? You cant be going to leave us, Major.

BARBARA: (*Quietly.*) Father: come here.

UNDERSHAFT: (*Coming to her.*) My dear! (*Seeing that she is go-* 1195 *ing to pin the badge on his collar, he retreats to the penthouse in some alarm.*)

BARBARA: (*Following him.*) Dont be frightened. (*She pins the badge on and steps back towards the table, shewing him to the others.*) There! It's not much for £5000, is it? 1200

MRS BAINES: Barbara: if you wont come and pray with us, promise me you will pray for us.

BARBARA: I cant pray now. Perhaps I shall never pray again.

MRS BAINES: Barbara!

JENNY: Major! 1205

BARBARA: (*Almost delirious.*) I cant bear any more. Quick march!

CUSINS: (*Calling to the procession in the street outside.*) Off we go. Play up, there! Immenso giubilo. (*He gives the time with his drum; and the band strikes up the march, which rapidly be-* 1210 *comes more distant as the procession moves briskly away.*)

MRS BAINES: I must go, dear. Youre overworked: you will be all right tomorrow. We'll never lose you. Now Jenny: step out with the old flag. Blood and Fire! (*She marches out through the gate with her flag.*) 1215

JENNY: Glory Hallelujah! (*Flourishing her tambourine and marching.*)

UNDERSHAFT: (*To* CUSINS, *as he marches out past him easing the slide of his trombone.*) 'My ducats and my daughter'!

CUSINS: (*Following him out.*) Money and gunpowder! 1220

BARBARA: Drunkenness and Murder! My God: why hast thou forsaken me?

(She sinks on the form with her face buried in her hands. The march passes away into silence. BILL WALKER *steals across to her.)*

BILL: *(Taunting.)* Wot prawce selvytion nah?

SHIRLEY: Dont you hit her when she's down.

1225 BILL: She itt me wen aw wiz dahn. Waw shouldnt Aw git a bit o me aown beck?

BARBARA: *(Raising her head.)* I didnt take your money, Bill. *(She crosses the yard to the gate and turns her back on the two men to hide her face from them.)*

1230 BILL: *(Sneering after her.)* Naow, it warnt enaff for you. *(Turning to the drum, he misses the money.)* Ellow! If you aint took it sammun else ez. Weres it gorn? Bly me if Jenny Ill didnt tike it after all!

RUMMY: *(Screaming at him from the loft.)* You lie, you dirty black-
1235 guard! Snobby Price pinched it off the drum when he took up his cap. I was up here all the time an see im do it.

BILL: Wot! Stowl maw manney! Waw didnt you call thief on him, you silly aold macker you?

RUMMY: To serve you aht for ittin me across the fice. It's cost
1240 y'pahnd, that az. *(Raising a pæan of squalid triumph.)* I done you. I'm even with you. Uve ad it aht o y—(BILL *snatches up* SHIRLEY's *mug and hurls it at her. She slams the loft door and vanishes. The mug smashes against the door and falls in fragments.)*

1245 BILL: *(Beginning to chuckle.)* Tell us, aol menn, wot o'clock this mawnin was it wen im as they call Snobby Prawce was sived?

BARBARA: *(Turning to him more composedly, and with unspoiled sweetness.)* About half past twelve, Bill. And he pinched
1250 your pound at a quarter to two. *I* know. Well, you cant afford to lose it. I'll send it to you.

BILL: *(His voice and accent suddenly improving.)* Not if Aw wiz to stawve for it. Aw aint to be bought.

SHIRLEY: Aint you? Youd sell yourself to the devil for a pint
1255 o beer; only there aint no devil to make the offer.

BILL: *(Unashamed.)* Sao Aw would, mite, and often ev, cheerful. But she cawnt baw me. *(Approaching* BARBARA.) You wanted maw saoul, did you? Well, you aint got it.

BARBARA: I nearly got it, Bill. But weve sold it back to you
1260 for ten thousand pounds.

SHIRLEY: And dear at the money!

BARBARA: No, Peter: it was worth more than money.

BILL: *(Salvationproof.)* It's nao good: you cawnt get rahnd me nah. Aw downt blieve in it; and Awve seen tody that Aw
1265 was rawt. *(Going.)* Sao long, aol soupkitchener! Ta, ta, Mijor Earl's Grendorter! *(Turning at the gate.)* Wot prawce selvytion nah? Snobby Prawce! Ha! ha!

BARBARA: *(Offering her hand.)* Goodbye, Bill.

BILL: *(Taken aback, half plucks his cap off; then shoves it on again
1270 defiantly.)* Git aht. *(*BARBARA *drops his hand, discouraged. He has a twinge of remorse.)* But thets aw rawt, you knaow. Nathink pasnl. Naow mellice. Sao long, Judy. *(He goes.)*

BARBARA: No malice. So long, Bill.

SHIRLEY: *(Shaking his head.)* You make too much of him, miss,
1275 in your innocence.

BARBARA: *(Going to him.)* Peter: I'm like you now. Cleaned out, and lost my job.

SHIRLEY: Youve youth an hope. Thats two better than me.

BARBARA: I'll get you a job, Peter. Thats hope for you: the youth will have to be enough for me. *(She counts her money.)* 1280 I have just enough left for two teas at Lockharts, a Rowton doss for you, and my tram and bus home. *(He frowns and rises with offended pride. She takes his arm.)* Dont be proud, Peter: it's sharing between friends. And promise me youll talk to me and not let me cry. *(She draws him towards the gate.)* 1285

SHIRLEY: Well, I'm not accustomed to talk to the like of you—

BARBARA: *(Urgently.)* Yes, yes: you must talk to me. Tell me about Tom Paine's books and Bradlaugh's lectures. Come along.

SHIRLEY: Ah, if you would only read Tom Paine in the proper 1290 spirit, miss! *(They go out through the gate together.)*

ACT THREE

Next day after lunch LADY BRITOMART *is writing in the library in Wilton Crescent.* SARAH *is reading in the armchair near the window.* BARBARA, *in ordinary fashionable dress, pale and brooding, is on the settee.* CHARLES LOMAX *enters. He starts on seeing* BARBARA *fashionably attired and in low spirits.*

LOMAX: Youve left off your uniform!

*(*BARBARA *says nothing; but an expression of pain passes over her face.)*

LADY BRITOMART: *(Warning him in low tones to be careful.)* Charles!

LOMAX: *(Much concerned, coming behind the settee and bending sympathetically over* BARBARA.) I'm awfully sorry, Barbara. 5 You know I helped you all I could with the concertina and so forth. *(Momentously.)* Still, I have never shut my eyes to the fact that there is a certain amount of tosh about the Salvation Army. Now the claims of the Church of England—

LADY BRITOMART: Thats enough, Charles. Speak of some- 10 thing suited to your mental capacity.

LOMAX: But surely the Church of England is suited to all our capacities.

BARBARA: *(Pressing his hand.)* Thank you for your sympathy, Cholly. Now go and spoon with Sarah. 15

LOMAX: *(Dragging a chair from the writing table and seating himself affectionately by* SARAH's *side.)* How is my ownest today?

SARAH: I wish you wouldnt tell Cholly to do things, Barbara. He always comes straight and does them. Cholly: we're going to the works this afternoon. 20

LOMAX: What works?

SARAH: The cannon works.

LOMAX: What? your governor's shop!

SARAH: Yes.

LOMAX: Oh I say! 25

*(*CUSINS *enters in poor condition. He also starts visibly when he sees* BARBARA *without her uniform.)*

BARBARA: I expected you this morning, Dolly. Didnt you guess that?

CUSINS: *(Sitting down beside her.)* I'm sorry. I have only just breakfasted.

SARAH: But weve just finished lunch. 30

BARBARA: Have you had one of your bad nights?

CUSINS: No: I had rather a good night: in fact, one of the most remarkable nights I have ever passed.

BARBARA: The meeting?

35 CUSINS: No: after the meeting.

LADY BRITOMART: You should have gone to bed after the meeting. What were you doing?

CUSINS: Drinking.

LADY BRITOMART: Adolphus!

40 SARAH: Dolly!

BARBARA: Dolly!

LOMAX: Oh I say!

LADY BRITOMART: What were you drinking, may I ask?

CUSINS: A most devilish kind of Spanish burgundy, warranted

45 free from added alcohol: a Temperance burgundy in fact. Its richness in natural alcohol made any addition superfluous.

BARBARA: Are you joking, Dolly?

CUSINS: (*Patiently.*) No. I have been making a night of it with the nominal head of this household: that is all.

50 LADY BRITOMART: Andrew made you drunk!

CUSINS: No: he only provided the wine. I think it was Dionysos who made me drunk. (*To* BARBARA.) I told you I was possessed.

LADY BRITOMART: Youre not sober yet. Go home to bed at

55 once.

CUSINS: I have never before ventured to reproach you, Lady Brit; but how could you marry the Prince of Darkness?

LADY BRITOMART: It was much more excusable to marry him than to get drunk with him. That is a new accom-

60 plishment of Andrew's, by the way. He usent to drink.

CUSINS: He doesnt now. He only sat there and completed the wreck of my moral basis, the rout of my convictions, the purchase of my soul. He cares for you, Barbara. That is what makes him so dangerous to me.

65 BARBARA: That has nothing to do with it, Dolly. There are larger loves and diviner dreams than the fireside ones. You know that, dont you?

CUSINS: Yes: that is our understanding. I know it. I hold to it. Unless he can win me on that holier ground he may amuse me

70 for a while; but he can get no deeper hold, strong as he is.

BARBARA: Keep to that; and the end will be right. Now tell me what happened at the meeting.

CUSINS: It was an amazing meeting. Mrs Baines almost died of emotion. Jenny Hill simply gibbered with hysteria. The

75 Prince of Darkness played his trombone like a madman: its brazen roarings were like the laughter of the damned. 117 conversions took place then and there. They prayed with the most touching sincerity and gratitude for Bodger, and for the anonymous donor of the £5000. Your

80 father would not let his name be given.

LOMAX: That was rather fine of the old man, you know. Most chaps would have wanted the advertisement.

CUSINS: He said all the charitable institutions would be down on him like kites on a battle-field if he gave his name.

85 LADY BRITOMART: Thats Andrew all over. He never does a proper thing without giving an improper reason for it.

CUSINS: He convinced me that I have all my life been doing improper things for proper reasons.

LADY BRITOMART: Adolphus: now that Barbara has left the

90 Salvation Army, you had better leave it too. I will not have you playing that drum in the streets.

CUSINS: Your orders are already obeyed, Lady Brit.

BARBARA: Dolly: were you ever really in earnest about it? Would you have joined if you had never seen me?

95 CUSINS: (*Disingenuously.*) Well—er—well, possibly, as a collector of religions—

LOMAX: (*Cunningly.*) Not as a drummer, though, you know. You are a very clearheaded brainy chap, Dolly; and it must have been apparent to you that there is a certain amount

100 of tosh about—

LADY BRITOMART: Charles: if you must drivel, drivel like a grown-up man and not like a schoolboy.

LOMAX: (*Out of countenance.*) Well, drivel is drivel, dont you know, whatever a man's age.

105 LADY BRITOMART: In good society in England, Charles, men drivel at all ages by repeating silly formulas with an air of wisdom. Schoolboys make their own formulas out of slang, like you. When they reach your age, and get political private secretaryships and things of that sort, they drop

110 slang and get their formulas out of the *Spectator* or *The Times.* You had better confine yourself to *The Times.* You will find that there is a certain amount of tosh about *The Times;* but at least its language is reputable.

LOMAX: (*Overwhelmed.*) You are so awfully strong-minded,

115 Lady Brit—

LADY BRITOMART: Rubbish! (MORRISON *comes in.*) What is it?

MORRISON: If you please, my lady, Mr Undershaft has just drove up to the door.

LADY BRITOMART: Well, let him in. (MORRISON *hesitates.*)

120 Whats the matter with you?

MORRISON: Shall I announce him, my lady; or is he at home here, so to speak, my lady?

LADY BRITOMART: Announce him.

MORRISON: Thank you, my lady. You wont mind my asking, I

125 hope. The occasion is in a manner of speaking new to me.

LADY BRITOMART: Quite right. Go and let him in.

MORRISON: Thank you, my lady. (*He withdraws.*)

LADY BRITOMART: Children: go and get ready. (SARAH *and* BARBARA *go upstairs for their out-of-door wraps.*) Charles: go

130 and tell Stephen to come down here in five minutes: you will find him in the drawing room. (CHARLES *goes.*) Adolphus: tell them to send round the carriage in about fifteen minutes. (ADOLPHUS [CUSINS] *goes.*)

MORRISON: (*At the door.*) Mr Undershaft.

(UNDERSHAFT *comes in.* MORRISON *goes out.*)

135 UNDERSHAFT: Alone! How fortunate!

LADY BRITOMART: (*Rising.*) Dont be sentimental, Andrew. Sit down. (*She sits on the settee: he sits beside her, on her left. She comes to the point before he has time to breathe.*) Sarah must have £800 a year until Charles Lomax comes into his

140 property. Barbara will need more, and need it permanently, because Adolphus hasnt any property.

UNDERSHAFT: (*Resignedly.*) Yes, my dear: I will see to it. Anything else? for yourself, for instance?

LADY BRITOMART: I want to talk to you about Stephen.

145 UNDERSHAFT: (*Rather wearily.*) Dont, my dear. Stephen doesnt interest me.

LADY BRITOMART: He does interest me. He is our son.

UNDERSHAFT: Do you really think so? He has induced us to bring him into the world; but he chose his parents very

150 incongruously, I think. I see nothing of myself in him, and less of you.

LADY BRITOMART: Andrew: Stephen is an excellent son, and a most steady, capable, highminded young man. You are simply trying to find an excuse for disinheriting him.

155 UNDERSHAFT: My dear Biddy: the Undershaft tradition disinherits him. It would be dishonest of me to leave the cannon foundry to my son.

LADY BRITOMART: It would be most unnatural and improper of you to leave it to anyone else, Andrew. Do you suppose
160 this wicked and immoral tradition can be kept up for ever? Do you pretend that Stephen could not carry on the foundry just as well as all the other sons of the big business houses?

UNDERSHAFT: Yes: he could learn the office routine without
165 understanding the business, like all the other sons; and the firm would go on by its own momentum until the real Undershaft—probably an Italian or a German—would invent a new method and cut him out.

LADY BRITOMART: There is nothing that any Italian or Ger-
170 man could do that Stephen could not do. And Stephen at least has breeding.

UNDERSHAFT: The son of a foundling! Nonsense!

LADY BRITOMART: My son, Andrew! And even you may have good blood in your veins for all you know.

175 UNDERSHAFT: True. Probably I have. That is another argument in favour of a foundling.

LADY BRITOMART: Andrew: dont be aggravating. And dont be wicked. At present you are both.

UNDERSHAFT: This conversation is part of the Undershaft tra-
180 dition, Biddy. Every Undershaft's wife has treated him to it ever since the house was founded. It is mere waste of breath. If the tradition be ever broken it will be for an abler man than Stephen.

LADY BRITOMART: (*Pouting.*) Then go away.

185 UNDERSHAFT: (*Deprecatory.*) Go away!

LADY BRITOMART: Yes: go away. If you will do nothing for Stephen, you are not wanted here. Go to your foundling, whoever he is; and look after him.

UNDERSHAFT: The fact is, Biddy—

190 LADY BRITOMART: Dont call me Biddy. I dont call you Andy.

UNDERSHAFT: I will not call my wife Britomart: it is not good sense. Seriously, my love, the Undershaft tradition has landed me in a difficulty. I am getting on in years; and my partner Lazarus has at last made a stand and insisted that the succes-
195 sion must be settled one way or the other; and of course he is quite right. You see, I havent found a fit successor yet.

LADY BRITOMART: (*Obstinately.*) There is Stephen.

UNDERSHAFT: Thats just it: all the foundlings I can find are exactly like Stephen.

200 LADY BRITOMART: Andrew!!

UNDERSHAFT: I want a man with no relations and no schooling: that is, a man who would be out of the running altogether if he were not a strong man. And I cant find him. Every blessed foundling nowadays is snapped up in his in-
205 fancy by Barnardo homes, or School Board officers, or Boards of Guardians; and if he shews the least ability he is fastened on by schoolmasters; trained to win scholarships like a racehorse; crammed with secondhand ideas; drilled and disciplined in docility and what they call good taste;
210 and lamed for life so that he is fit for nothing but teaching. If you want to keep the foundry in the family, you had better find an eligible foundling and marry him to Barbara.

LADY BRITOMART: Ah! Barbara! Your pet! You would sacrifice Stephen to Barbara.

215 UNDERSHAFT: Cheerfully. And you, my dear, would boil Barbara to make soup for Stephen.

LADY BRITOMART: Andrew: this is not a question of our likings and dislikings: it is a question of duty. It is your duty to make Stephen your successor.

220 UNDERSHAFT: Just as much as it is your duty to submit to your husband. Come, Biddy! these tricks of the governing class are of no use with me. I am one of the governing class myself; and it is waste of time giving tracts to a missionary. I have the power in this matter; and I am not to
225 be hum-bugged into using it for your purposes.

LADY BRITOMART: Andrew: you can talk my head off; but you cant change wrong into right. And your tie is all on one side. Put it straight.

UNDERSHAFT: (*Disconcerted.*) It wont stay unless it's pinned
230 (*He fumbles at it with childish grimaces.*)—

(STEPHEN *comes in.*)

STEPHEN: (*At the door.*) I beg your pardon. (*About to retire.*)

LADY BRITOMART: No: come in, Stephen. (STEPHEN *comes forward to his mother's writing table.*)

UNDERSHAFT: (*Not very cordially.*) Good afternoon.

235 STEPHEN: (*Coldly.*) Good afternoon.

UNDERSHAFT: (*To* LADY BRITOMART.) He knows all about the tradition, I suppose?

LADY BRITOMART: Yes. (*To* STEPHEN.) It is what I told you last night, Stephen.

240 UNDERSHAFT: (*Sulkily.*) I understand you want to come into the cannon business.

STEPHEN: *I* go into trade! Certainly not.

UNDERSHAFT: (*Opening his eyes, greatly eased in mind and manner.*) Oh! in that case—

245 LADY BRITOMART: Cannons are not trade, Stephen. They are enterprise.

STEPHEN: I have no intention of becoming a man of business in any sense. I have no capacity for business and no taste for it. I intend to devote myself to politics.

250 UNDERSHAFT: (*Rising.*) My dear boy: this is an immense relief to me. And I trust it may prove an equally good thing for the country. I was afraid you would consider yourself disparaged and slighted. (*He moves towards* STEPHEN *as if to shake hands with him.*)

255 LADY BRITOMART: (*Rising and interposing.*) Stephen: I cannot allow you to throw away an enormous property like this.

STEPHEN: (*Stiffly.*) Mother: there must be an end of treating me as a child, if you please. (LADY BRITOMART *recoils, deeply wounded by his tone.*) Until last night I did not take your
260 attitude seriously, because I did not think you meant it seriously. But I find now that you left me in the dark as to matters which you should have explained to me years ago. I am extremely hurt and offended. Any further discussion of my intentions had better take place with my father, as
265 between one man and another.

LADY BRITOMART: Stephen! (*She sits down again, her eyes filling with tears.*)

UNDERSHAFT: (*With grave compassion.*) You see, my dear, it is only the big men who can be treated as children.

270 STEPHEN: I am sorry, mother, that you have forced me—

UNDERSHAFT: (*Stopping him.*) Yes, yes, yes, yes: thats all right, Stephen. She wont interfere with you any more: your independence is achieved: you have won your latchkey. Dont rub it in; and above all, dont apologize. (*He resumes his seat.*) Now what about your future, as between one man and another—I beg your pardon, Biddy: as between two men and a woman.

LADY BRITOMART: (*Who has pulled herself together strongly.*) I quite understand, Stephen. By all means go your own way if you feel strong enough. (STEPHEN *sits down magisterially in the chair at the writing table with an air of affirming his majority.*)

UNDERSHAFT: It is settled that you do not ask for the succession to the cannon business.

STEPHEN: I hope it is settled that I repudiate the cannon business.

285 UNDERSHAFT: Come, come! dont be so devilishly sulky: it's boyish. Freedom should be generous. Besides, I owe you a fair start in life in exchange for disinheriting you. You cant become prime minister all at once. Havnt you a turn for something? What about literature, art, and so forth?

290 STEPHEN: I have nothing of the artist about me, either in faculty or character, thank Heaven!

UNDERSHAFT: A philosopher, perhaps? Eh?

STEPHEN: I make no such ridiculous pretension.

UNDERSHAFT: Just so. Well, there is the army, the navy, the Church, the Bar. The Bar requires some ability. What about the Bar?

STEPHEN: I have not studied law. And I am afraid I have not the necessary push—I believe that is the name barristers give to their vulgarity—for success in pleading.

300 UNDERSHAFT: Rather a difficult case, Stephen. Hardly anything left but the stage, is there? (STEPHEN *makes an impatient movement.*) Well, come! is there anything you know or care for?

STEPHEN: (*Rising and looking at him steadily.*) I know the difference between right and wrong.

305 UNDERSHAFT: (*Hugely tickled.*) You dont say so! What! no capacity for business, no knowledge of law, no sympathy with art, no pretension to philosophy; only a simple knowledge of the secret that has puzzled all the philosophers, baffled all the lawyers, muddled all the men of business, and ruined most of the artists: the secret of right and wrong. Why, man, youre a genius, a master of masters, a god! At twentyfour, too!

STEPHEN: (*Keeping his temper with difficulty.*) You are pleased to be facetious. I pretend to nothing more than any honorable English gentleman claims as his birthright (*He sits down angrily.*)

UNDERSHAFT: Oh, thats everybody's birthright. Look at poor little Jenny Hill, the Salvation lassie! she would think you were laughing at her if you asked her to stand up in the street and teach grammar or geography or mathematics or even drawing room dancing; but it never occurs to her to doubt that she can teach morals and religion. You are all alike, you respectable people. You cant tell me the bursting strain of a ten-inch gun, which is a very simple matter; but you all think you can tell me the bursting strain of a man under temptation. You darent handle high explosives; but youre all ready to handle honesty and truth and justice and the whole duty of man, and kill one another at that game. What a country! What a world!

330 LADY BRITOMART: (*Uneasily.*) What do you think he had better do, Andrew?

UNDERSHAFT: Oh, just what he wants to do. He knows nothing and he thinks he knows everything. That points clearly to a political career. Get him a private secretaryship to someone who can get him an Under Secretaryship; and then leave him alone. He will find his natural and proper place in the end on the Treasury Bench.

STEPHEN: (*Springing up again.*) I am sorry, sir, that you force me to forget the respect due to you as my father. I am an Englishman and I will not hear the Government of my country insulted. (*He thrusts his hands in his pockets, and walks angrily across to the window.*)

UNDERSHAFT: (*With a touch of brutality.*) The government of your country! I am the government of your country: I, and Lazarus. Do you suppose that you and half a dozen amateurs like you, sitting in a row in that foolish gabble shop, can govern Undershaft and Lazarus? No, my friend: you will do what pays us. You will make war when it suits us, and keep peace when it doesnt. You will find out that trade requires certain measures when we have decided on those measures. When I want anything to keep my dividends up, you will discover that my want is a national need. When other people want something to keep my dividends down, you will call out the police and military. And in return you shall have the support and applause of my newspapers, and the delight of imagining that you are a great statesman. Government of your country! Be off with you, my boy, and play with your caucuses and leading articles and historic parties and great leaders and burning questions and the rest of your toys. *I* am going back to my counting-house to pay the piper and call the tune.

STEPHEN: (*Actually smiling, and putting his hand on his father's shoulder with indulgent patronage.*) Really, my dear father, it is impossible to be angry with you. You dont know how absurd all this sounds to me. You are very properly proud of having been industrious enough to make money; and it is greatly to your credit that you have made so much of it. But it has kept you in circles where you are valued for your money and deferred to for it, instead of in the doubtless very old-fashioned and behind-the-times public school and university where I formed my habits of mind. It is natural for you to think that money governs England; but you must allow me to think I know better.

UNDERSHAFT: And what does govern England, pray?

STEPHEN: Character, father, character.

UNDERSHAFT: Whose character? Yours or mine?

STEPHEN: Neither yours nor mine, father, but the best elements in the English national character.

UNDERSHAFT: Stephen: Ive found your profession for you. Youre a born journalist. I'll start you with a high-toned weekly review. There!

(*Before* STEPHEN *can reply,* SARAH, BARBARA, LOMAX, *and* CUSINS *come in ready for walking.* BARBARA *crosses the room to the window and looks out.* CUSINS *drifts amiably to the armchair.* LOMAX *remains near the door, whilst* SARAH *comes to her mother.*)

(STEPHEN *goes to the smaller writing table and busies himself with his letters.*)

SARAH: Go and get ready, mamma: the carriage is waiting. (LADY BRITOMART *leaves the room.*)

UNDERSHAFT: (*To* SARAH.) Good day, my dear. Good afternoon, Mr Lomax.

LOMAX: (*Vaguely.*) Ahdedoo.

UNDERSHAFT: (*To* CUSINS.) Quite well after last night, Euripides, eh?

CUSINS: As well as can be expected.

390 UNDERSHAFT: Thats right. (*To* BARBARA.) So you are coming to see my death and devastation factory, Barbara?

BARBARA: (*At the window.*) You came yesterday to see my salvation factory. I promised you a return visit.

LOMAX: (*Coming forward between* SARAH *and* UNDERSHAFT.)
395   Youll find it awfully interesting. Ive been through the Woolwich Arsenal; and it gives you a ripping feeling of security, you know, to think of the lot of beggars we could kill if it came to fighting. (*To* UNDERSHAFT, *with sudden solemnity.*) Still, it must be rather an awful reflection for
400   you, from the religious point of view as it were. Youre getting on, you know, and all that.

SARAH: You dont mind Cholly's imbecility, papa, do you?

LOMAX: (*Much taken aback.*) Oh I say!

UNDERSHAFT: Mr Lomax looks at the matter in a very proper
405   spirit, my dear.

LOMAX: Just so. Thats all I meant, I assure you.

SARAH: Are you coming, Stephen?

STEPHEN: Well, I am rather busy—er—(*Magnanimously.*) Oh well, yes: I'll come. That is, if there is room for me.

410 UNDERSHAFT: I can take two with me in a little motor I am experimenting with for field use. You wont mind its being rather unfashionable. It's not painted yet; but it's bullet proof.

LOMAX: (*Appalled at the prospect of confronting Wilton Crescent in*
415   *an unpainted motor.*) Oh I say!

SARAH: The carriage for me, thank you. Barbara doesnt mind what she's seen in.

LOMAX: I say, Dolly, old chap: do you really mind the car being a guy? Because of course if you do I'll go in it. Still—

420 CUSINS: I prefer it.

LOMAX: Thanks awfully, old man. Come, my ownest. (*He hurries out to secure his seat in the carriage.* SARAH *follows him.*)

CUSINS: (*Moodily walking across to* LADY BRITOMART's *writing table.*) Why are we two coming to this Works Department
425   of Hell? that is what I ask myself.

BARBARA: I have always thought of it as a sort of pit where lost creatures with blackened faces stirred up smoky fires and were driven and tormented by my father? Is it like that, dad?

UNDERSHAFT: (*Scandalized.*) My dear! It is a spotlessly clean
430   and beautiful hillside town.

CUSINS: With a Methodist chapel? Oh do say theres a Methodist chapel.

UNDERSHAFT: There are two: a Primitive one and a sophisticated one. There is even an Ethical Society; but it is not
435   much patronized, as my men are all strongly religious. In the High Explosives Sheds they object to the presence of Agnostics as unsafe.

CUSINS: And yet they dont object to you!

BARBARA: Do they obey all your orders?

440 UNDERSHAFT: I never give them any orders. When I speak to one of them it is 'Well, Jones, is the baby doing well? and has Mrs Jones made a good recovery?' 'Nicely, thank you, sir.' And thats all.

CUSINS: But Jones has to be kept in order. How do you main-
445   tain discipline among your men?

UNDERSHAFT: I dont. They do. You see, the one thing Jones wont stand is any rebellion from the man under him, or any

assertion of social equality between the wife of the man with 4 shillings a week less than himself, and Mrs Jones! Of course they all rebel against me, theoretically. Practically, 450 every man of them keeps the man just below him in his place. I never meddle with them. I never bully them. I dont even bully Lazarus. I say that certain things are to be done; but I dont order anybody to do them. I dont say, mind you, that there is no ordering about and snubbing and even bul- 455 lying. The men snub the boys and order them about; the carmen snub the sweepers; the artisans snub the unskilled laborers; the foremen drive and bully both the laborers and artisans; the assistant engineers find fault with the foremen; the chief engineers drop on the assistants; the departmen- 460 tal managers worry the chiefs; and the clerks have tall hats and hymnbooks and keep up the social tone by refusing to associate on equal terms with anybody. The result is a colossal profit, which comes to me.

CUSINS: (*Revolted.*) You really are a—well, what I was saying 465 yesterday.

BARBARA: What was he saying yesterday?

UNDERSHAFT: Never mind, my dear. He thinks I have made you unhappy. Have I?

BARBARA: Do you think I can be happy in this vulgar silly 470 dress? I! who have worn the uniform. Do you understand what you have done to me? Yesterday I had a man's soul in my hand. I set him in the way of life with his face to salvation. But when we took your money he turned back to drunkenness and derision. (*With intense conviction.*) I 475 will never forgive you that. If I had a child, and you destroyed its body with your explosives—if you murdered Dolly with your horrible guns—I could forgive you if my forgiveness would open the gates of heaven to you. But to take a human soul from me, and turn it into the soul of a 480 wolf! that is worse than any murder.

UNDERSHAFT: Does my daughter despair so easily? Can you strike a man to the heart and leave no mark on him?

BARBARA: (*Her face lighting up.*) Oh, you are right: he can never be lost now: where was my faith? 485

CUSINS: Oh, clever clever devil!

BARBARA: You may be a devil; but God speaks through you sometimes. (*She takes her father's hands and kisses them.*) You have given me back my happiness: I feel it deep down now, though my spirit is troubled. 490

UNDERSHAFT: You have learnt something. That always feels at first as if you had lost something.

BARBARA: Well, take me to the factory of death; and let me learn something more. There must be some truth or other behind all this frightful irony. Come, Dolly. (*She goes out.*) 495

CUSINS: My guardian angel! (*To* UNDERSHAFT.) Avaunt! (*He follows* BARBARA.)

STEPHEN: (*Quietly, at the writing table.*) You must not mind Cusins, father. He is a very amiable good fellow; but he is a Greek scholar and naturally a little eccentric. 500

UNDERSHAFT: Ah, quite so. Thank you, Stephen. Thank you. (*He goes out.*)

(STEPHEN *smiles patronizingly; buttons his coat responsibly; and crosses the room to the door.* LADY BRITOMART, *dressed for out-of-doors, opens it before he reaches it. She looks round for others; looks at* STEPHEN; *and turns to go without a word.*)

STEPHEN: (*Embarrassed.*) Mother—

505 LADY BRITOMART: Dont be apologetic, Stephen. And dont forget that you have outgrown your mother. (*She goes out.*)

(*Perivale St Andrews lies between two Middlesex hills, half climbing the northern one. It is an almost smokeless town of white walls, roofs of narrow green slates or red tiles, tall trees, domes, campaniles, and slender chimney shafts, beautifully situated and beautiful in itself. The best view of it is obtained from the crest of a slope about half a mile to the east, where the high explosives are dealt with. The foundry lies hidden in the depths between, the tops of its chimneys sprouting like huge skittles into the middle distance. Across the crest runs an emplacement of concrete, with a firestep, and a parapet which suggests a fortification, because there is a huge cannon of the obsolete Woolwich Infant pattern peering across it at the town. The cannon is mounted on an experimental gun carriage: possibly the original model of the Undershaft disappearing rampart gun alluded to by* STEPHEN. *The firestep, being a convenient place to sit, is furnished here and there with straw disc cushions; and at one place there is the additional luxury of a fur rug.*)

(BARBARA *is standing on the firestep, looking over the parapet towards the town. On her right is the cannon; on her left the end of a shed raised on piles, with a ladder of three or four steps up to the door, which opens outwards and has a little wooden landing at the threshold, with a fire bucket in the corner of the landing. Several dummy soldiers more or less mutilated, with straw protruding from their gashes, have been shoved out of the way under the landing. A few others are nearly upright against the shed; and one has fallen forward and lies, like a grotesque corpse, on the emplacement. The parapet stops short of the shed, leaving a gap which is the beginning of the path down the hill through the foundry to the town. The rug is on the firestep near this gap. Down on the emplacement behind the cannon is a trolley carrying a huge conical bombshell with a red band painted on it. Further to the right is the door of an office, which, like the sheds, is of the lightest possible construction.*)

(CUSINS *arrives by the path from the town.*)

BARBARA: Well?
CUSINS: Not a ray of hope. Everything perfect! wonderful! real! It only needs a cathedral to be a heavenly city instead of a hellish one.
510 BARBARA: Have you found out whether they have done anything for old Peter Shirley?
CUSINS: They have found him a job as gatekeeper and timekeeper. He's frightfully miserable. He calls the timekeeping brainwork, and says he isnt used to it; and his gate
515 lodge is so splendid that he's ashamed to use the rooms, and skulks in the scullery.
BARBARA: Poor Peter!

(STEPHEN *arrives from the town. He carries a fieldglass.*)

STEPHEN: (*Enthusiastically.*) Have you two seen the place? Why did you leave us?
520 CUSINS: I wanted to see everything I was not intended to see; and Barbara wanted to make the men talk.
STEPHEN: Have you found anything discreditable?
CUSINS: No. They call him Dandy Andy and are proud of his being a cunning old rascal; but it's all horribly, frightfully,
525 immorally, unanswerably perfect.

(SARAH *arrives.*)

SARAH: Heavens! what a place! (*She crosses to the trolley.*) Did you see the nursing home!? (*She sits down on the shell.*)
STEPHEN: Did you see the libraries and schools!?
SARAH: Did you see the ball room and the banqueting chamber in the Town Hall!? 530
STEPHEN: Have you gone into the insurance fund, the pension fund, the building society, the various applications of cooperation!?

(UNDERSHAFT *comes from the office, with a sheaf of telegrams in his hand.*)

UNDERSHAFT: Well, have you seen everything? I'm sorry I was called away. (*Indicating the telegrams.*) Good news from 535 Manchuria.
STEPHEN: Another Japanese victory?
UNDERSHAFT: Oh, I dont know. Which side wins does not concern us here. No: the good news is that the aerial battleship is a tremendous success. At the first trial it has 540 wiped out a fort with three hundred soldiers in it.
CUSINS: (*From the platform.*) Dummy soldiers?
UNDERSHAFT: (*Striding across to* STEPHEN *and kicking the prostrate dummy brutally out of his way.*) No: the real thing.

(CUSINS *and* BARBARA *exchange glances. Then* CUSINS *sits on the step and buries his face in his hands.* BARBARA *gravely lays her hand on his shoulder. He looks up at her in whimsical desperation.*)

UNDERSHAFT: Well, Stephen, what do you think of the place? 545
STEPHEN: Oh, magnificent. A perfect triumph of modern industry. Frankly, my dear father, I have been a fool: I had no idea of what it all meant: of the wonderful forethought, the power of organization, the administrative capacity, the financial genius, the colossal capital it represents. I have 550 been repeating to myself as I came through your streets 'Peace hath her victories no less renowned than War.' I have only one misgiving about it all.
UNDERSHAFT: Out with it.
STEPHEN: Well, I cannot help thinking that all this provision 555 for every want of your workmen may sap their independence and weaken their sense of responsibility. And greatly as we enjoyed our tea at that splendid restaurant— how they gave us all that luxury and cake and jam and cream for threepence I really cannot imagine!—still you 560 must remember that restaurants break up home life. Look at the continent, for instance! Are you sure so much pampering is really good for the men's characters?
UNDERSHAFT: Well you see, my dear boy, when you are organizing civilization you have to make up your mind 565 whether trouble and anxiety are good things or not. If you decide that they are, then, I take it, you simply dont organize civilization; and there you are, with trouble and anxiety enough to make us all angels! But if you decide the other way, you may as well go through with it. However, 570 Stephen, our characters are safe here. A sufficient dose of anxiety is always provided by the fact that we may be blown to smithereens at any moment.
SARAH: By the way, papa, where do you make the explosives?

575 UNDERSHAFT: In separate little sheds, like that one. When one of them blows up, it costs very little; and only the people quite close to it are killed.

(STEPHEN, *who is quite close to it, looks at it rather scaredly, and moves away quickly to the cannon. At the same moment the door of the shed is thrown abruptly open; and a foreman in overalls and list slippers comes out on the little landing and holds the door for* LOMAX, *who appears in the doorway.*)

LOMAX: (*With studied coolness.*) My good fellow: you neednt get into a state of nerves. Nothing's going to happen to
580 you; and I suppose it wouldnt be the end of the world if anything did. A little bit of British pluck is what you want, old chap. (*He descends and strolls across to* SARAH.)
UNDERSHAFT: (*To the foreman.*) Anything wrong, Bilton?
BILTON: (*With ironic calm.*) Gentleman walked into the high
585 explosives shed and lit a cigaret, sir: thats all.
UNDERSHAFT: Ah, quite so. (*Going over to* LOMAX.) Do you happen to remember what you did with the match?
LOMAX: Oh come! I'm not a fool. I took jolly good care to blow it out before I chucked it away.
590 BILTON: The top of it was red hot inside, sir.
LOMAX: Well, suppose it was! I didnt chuck it into any of your messes.
UNDERSHAFT: Think no more of it, Mr Lomax. By the way, would you mind lending me your matches.
595 LOMAX: (*Offering his box.*) Certainly.
UNDERSHAFT: Thanks. (*He pockets the matches.*)
LOMAX: (*Lecturing to the company generally.*) You know, these high explosives dont go off like gunpowder, except when theyre in a gun. When theyre spread loose, you can put a
600 match to them without the least risk: they just burn quietly like a bit of paper. (*Warming to the scientific interest of the subject.*) Did you know that, Undershaft? Have you ever tried?
UNDERSHAFT: Not on a large scale, Mr Lomax. Bilton will
605 give you a sample of gun cotton when you are leaving if you ask him. You can experiment with it at home. (BILTON *looks puzzled.*)
SARAH: Bilton will do nothing of the sort, papa. I suppose it's your business to blow up the Russians and Japs; but you
610 might really stop short of blowing up poor Cholly. (BILTON *gives it up and retires into the shed.*)
LOMAX: My ownest, there is no danger. (*He sits beside her on the shell.*)

(LADY BRITOMART *arrives from the town with a bouquet.*)

LADY BRITOMART: (*Impetuously.*) Andrew: you shouldnt have
615 let me see this place.
UNDERSHAFT: Why, my dear?
LADY BRITOMART: Never mind why: you shouldnt have: thats all. To think of all that (*Indicating the town.*) being yours! and that you have kept it to yourself all these years!
620 UNDERSHAFT: It does not belong to me. I belong to it. It is the Undershaft inheritance.
LADY BRITOMART: It is not. Your ridiculous cannons and that noisy banging foundry may be the Undershaft inheritance; but all that plate and linen, all that furniture and those
625 houses and orchards and gardens belong to us. They be-

long to me: they are not a man's business. I wont give them up. You must be out of your senses to throw them all away; and if you persist in such folly, I will call in a doctor.
UNDERSHAFT: (*Stooping to smell the bouquet.*) Where did you get the flowers, my dear? 630
LADY BRITOMART: Your men presented them to me in your William Morris Labor Church.
CUSINS: Oh! It needed only that. A Labor Church! (*He mounts the firestep distractedly, and leans with his elbows on the parapet, turning his back to them.*) 635
LADY BRITOMART: Yes, with Morris's words in mosaic letters ten feet high round the dome. NO MAN IS GOOD ENOUGH TO BE ANOTHER MAN'S MASTER. The cynicism of it!
UNDERSHAFT: It shocked the men at first, I am afraid. But now they take no more notice of it than of the ten com- 640
mandments in church.
LADY BRITOMART: Andrew: you are trying to put me off the subject of the inheritance by profane jokes. Well, you shant. I dont ask it any longer for Stephen: he has inherited far too much of your perversity to be fit for it. But Barbara has rights 645
as well as Stephen. Why should not Adolphus succeed to the inheritance? I could manage the town for him; and he can look after the cannons, if they are really necessary.
UNDERSHAFT: I should ask nothing better if Adolphus were a foundling. He is exactly the sort of new blood that is 650
wanted in English business. But he's not a foundling; and theres an end of it. (*He makes for the office door.*)
CUSINS: (*Turning to them.*) Not quite. (*They all turn and stare at him.*) I think—Mind! I am not committing myself in any way as to my future course—but I think the foundling dif- 655
ficulty can be got over. (*He jumps down to the emplacement.*)
UNDERSHAFT: (*Coming back to him.*) What do you mean?
CUSINS: Well, I have something to say which is in the nature of a confession.
SARAH: ⎫   660
LADY BRITOMART: ⎪
BARBARA: ⎬ Confession!
STEPHEN: ⎭
LOMAX: Oh I say!
CUSINS: Yes, a confession. Listen, all. Until I met Barbara I 665
thought myself in the main an honorable, truthful man, because I wanted the approval of my conscience more than I wanted anything else. But the moment I saw Barbara, I wanted her far more than the approval of my conscience. 670
LADY BRITOMART: Adolphus!
CUSINS: It is true. You accused me yourself, Lady Brit, of joining the Army to worship Barbara; and so I did. She bought my soul like a flower at a street corner; but she bought it for herself. 675
UNDERSHAFT: What! Not for Dionysos or another?
CUSINS: Dionysos and all the others are in herself. I adored what was divine in her, and was therefore a true worshipper. But I was romantic about her too. I thought she was a woman of the people, and that a marriage with a professor of Greek 680
would be far beyond the wildest social ambitions of her rank.
LADY BRITOMART: Adolphus!!
LOMAX: Oh I say!!!
CUSINS: When I learnt the horrible truth—
LADY BRITOMART: What do you mean by the horrible truth, 685
pray?

CUSINS: That she was enormously rich; that her grandfather was an earl; that her father was the Prince of Darkness—

UNDERSHAFT: Chut!

690 CUSINS: —and that I was only an adventurer trying to catch a rich wife, then I stooped to deceive her about my birth.

BARBARA: (*Rising.*) Dolly!

LADY BRITOMART: Your birth! Now Adolphus, dont dare to make up a wicked story for the sake of these wretched
695 cannons. Remember: I have seen photographs of your parents; and the Agent General for South Western Australia knows them personally and has assured me that they are most respectable married people.

CUSINS: So they are in Australia; but here they are outcasts.
700 Their marriage is legal in Australia, but not in England. My mother is my father's deceased wife's sister; and in this island I am consequently a foundling. (*Sensation.*)

BARBARA: Silly! (*She climbs to the cannon, and leans, listening, in the angle it makes with the parapet.*)

705 CUSINS: Is the subterfuge good enough, Machiavelli?

UNDERSHAFT: (*Thoughtfully.*) Biddy: this may be a way out of the difficulty.

LADY BRITOMART: Stuff! A man cant make cannons any the better for being his own cousin instead of his proper self
710 (*She sits down on the rug with a bounce that expresses her downright contempt for their casuistry.*)

UNDERSHAFT: (*To* CUSINS.) You are an educated man. That is against the tradition.

CUSINS: Once in ten thousand times it happens that the
715 schoolboy is a born master of what they try to teach him. Greek has not destroyed my mind: it has nourished it. Besides, I did not learn it at an English public school.

UNDERSHAFT: Hm! Well, I cannot afford to be too particular: you have cornered the foundling market. Let it pass. You
720 are eligible, Euripides: you are eligible.

BARBARA: Dolly: yesterday morning, when Stephen told us all about the tradition, you became very silent; and you have been strange and excited ever since. Were you thinking of your birth then?

725 CUSINS: When the finger of Destiny suddenly points at a man in the middle of his breakfast, it makes him thoughtful.

UNDERSHAFT: Aha! You have had your eye on the business, my young friend, have you?

CUSINS: Take care! There is an abyss of moral horror between
730 me and your accursed aerial battleships.

UNDERSHAFT: Never mind the abyss for the present. Let us settle the practical details and leave your final decision open. You know that you will have to change your name. Do you object to that?

735 CUSINS: Would any man named Adolphus—any man called Dolly!—object to be called something else?

UNDERSHAFT: Good. Now, as to money! I propose to treat you handsomely from the beginning. You shall start at a thousand a year.

740 CUSINS: (*With sudden heat, his spectacles twinkling with mischief.*) A thousand! You dare offer a miserable thousand to the son-in-law of a millionaire! No, by Heavens, Machiavelli! you shall not cheat me. You cannot do without me; and I can do without you. I must have two thousand five hun-
745 dred a year for two years. At the end of that time, if I am a failure, I go. But if I am a success, and stay on, you must give me the other five thousand.

UNDERSHAFT: What other five thousand?

CUSINS: To make the two years up to five thousand a year. The two thousand five hundred is only half pay in case I 750 should turn out a failure. The third year I must have ten per cent on the profits.

UNDERSHAFT: (*Taken aback.*) Ten per cent! Why, man, do you know what my profits are?

CUSINS: Enormous, I hope: otherwise I shall require twenty- 755 five per cent.

UNDERSHAFT: But, Mr Cusins, this is a serious matter of business. You are not bringing any capital into the concern.

CUSINS: What! no capital! Is my mastery of Greek no capital? Is my access to the subtlest thought, the loftiest poetry yet 760 attained by humanity, no capital? My character! my intellect! my life! my career! what Barbara calls my soul! are these no capital? Say another word; and I double my salary.

UNDERSHAFT: Be reasonable—

CUSINS: (*Peremptorily.*) Mr Undershaft: you have my terms. 765 Take them or leave them.

UNDERSHAFT: (*Recovering himself.*) Very well. I note your terms; and I offer you half.

CUSINS: (*Disgusted.*) Half!

UNDERSHAFT: (*Firmly.*) Half. 770

CUSINS: You call yourself a gentleman; and you offer me half!!

UNDERSHAFT: I do not call myself a gentleman; but I offer you half.

CUSINS: This to your future partner! your successor! your son-in-law! 775

BARBARA: You are selling your own soul, Dolly, not mine. Leave me out of the bargain, please.

UNDERSHAFT: Come! I will go a step further for Barbara's sake. I will give you three fifths; but that is my last word.

CUSINS: Done! 780

LOMAX: Done in the eye! Why, *I* get only eight hundred, you know.

CUSINS: By the way, Mac, I am a classical scholar, not an arithmetical one. Is three fifths more than half or less?

UNDERSHAFT: More, of course. 785

CUSINS: I would have taken two hundred and fifty. How you can succeed in business when you are willing to pay all that money to a University don who is obviously not worth a junior clerk's wages!—well! What will Lazarus say?

UNDERSHAFT: Lazarus is a gentle romantic Jew who cares for 790 nothing but string quartets and stalls at fashionable theatres. He will be blamed for your rapacity in money matters, poor fellow! as he has hitherto been blamed for mine. You are a shark of the first order, Euripides. So much the better for the firm! 795

BARBARA: Is the bargain closed, Dolly? Does your soul belong to him now?

CUSINS: No: the price is settled: that is all. The real tug of war is still to come. What about the moral question?

LADY BRITOMART: There is no moral question in the matter 800 at all, Adolphus. You must simply sell cannons and weapons to people whose cause is right and just, and refuse them to foreigners and criminals.

UNDERSHAFT: (*Determinedly.*) No: none of that. You must keep the true faith of an Armorer, or you dont come in here. 805

CUSINS: What on earth is the true faith of an Armorer?

UNDERSHAFT: To give arms to all men who offer an honest price for them, without respect of persons or principles: to aristocrat and republican, to Nihilist and Tsar, to Capitalist and Socialist, to Protestant and Catholic, to burglar and policeman, to black man, white man and yellow man, to all sorts and conditions, all nationalities, all faiths, all follies, all causes and all crimes. The first Undershaft wrote up in his shop IF GOD GAVE THE HAND, LET NOT MAN WITHHOLD THE SWORD. The second wrote up ALL HAVE THE RIGHT TO FIGHT: NONE HAVE THE RIGHT TO JUDGE. The third wrote up TO MAN THE WEAPON: TO HEAVEN THE VICTORY. The fourth had no literary turn; so he did not write up anything; but he sold cannons to Napoleon under the nose of George the Third. The fifth wrote up PEACE SHALL NOT PREVAIL SAVE WITH A SWORD IN HER HAND. The sixth, my master, was the best of all. He wrote up NOTHING IS EVER DONE IN THIS WORLD UNTIL MEN ARE PREPARED TO KILL ONE ANOTHER IF IT IS NOT DONE. After that, there was nothing left for the seventh to say. So he wrote up, simply, UNASHAMED.

CUSINS: My good Machiavelli, I shall certainly write something up on the wall; only, as I shall write it in Greek, you wont be able to read it. But as to your Armorer's faith, if I take my neck out of the noose of my own morality I am not going to put it into the noose of yours. I shall sell cannons to whom I please and refuse them to whom I please. So there!

UNDERSHAFT: From the moment when you become Andrew Undershaft, you will never do as you please again. Dont come here lusting for power, young man.

CUSINS: If power were my aim I should not come here for it. You have no power.

UNDERSHAFT: None of my own, certainly.

CUSINS: I have more power than you, more will. You do not drive this place: it drives you. And what drives the place?

UNDERSHAFT: (*Enigmatically.*) A will of which I am a part.

BARBARA: (*Startled.*) Father! Do you know what you are saying; or are you laying a snare for my soul?

CUSINS: Dont listen to his metaphysics, Barbara. The place is driven by the most rascally part of society, the money hunters, the pleasure hunters, the military promotion hunters; and he is their slave.

UNDERSHAFT: Not necessarily. Remember the Armorer's Faith. I will take an order from a good man as cheerfully as from a bad one. If you good people prefer preaching and shirking to buying my weapons and fighting the rascals, dont blame me. I can make cannons: I cannot make courage and conviction. Bah! you tire me, Euripides, with your morality mongering. Ask Barbara: she understands. (*He suddenly reaches up and takes* BARBARA'*s hands, looking powerfully into her eyes.*) Tell him, my love, what power really means.

BARBARA: (*Hypnotized.*) Before I joined the Salvation Army, I was in my own power; and the consequence was that I never knew what to do with myself. When I joined it, I had not time enough for all the things I had to do.

UNDERSHAFT: (*Approvingly.*) Just so. And why was that, do you suppose?

BARBARA: Yesterday I should have said, because I was in the power of God. (*She resumes her self-possession, withdrawing her hands from his with a power equal to his own.*) But you came and shewed me that I was in the power of Bodger and Undershaft. Today I feel—oh! how can I put it into words? Sarah: do you remember the earthquake at Cannes, when we were little children?—how little the surprise of the first shock mattered compared to the dread and horror of waiting for the second? That is how I feel in this place today. I stood on the rock I thought eternal; and without a word of warning it reeled and crumbled under me. I was safe with an infinite wisdom watching me, an army marching to Salvation with me; and in a moment, at a stroke of your pen in a cheque book, I stood alone; and the heavens were empty. That was the first shock of the earthquake: I am waiting for the second.

UNDERSHAFT: Come, come, my daughter! dont make too much of your little tinpot tragedy. What do we do here when we spend years of work and thought and thousands of pounds of solid cash on a new gun or an aerial battleship that turns out just a hairsbreadth wrong after all? Scrap it. Scrap it without wasting another hour or another pound on it. Well, you have made for yourself something that you call a morality or a religion or what not. It doesnt fit the facts. Well, scrap it. Scrap it and get one that does fit. That is what is wrong with the world at present. It scraps its obsolete steam engines and dynamos; but it wont scrap its old prejudices and its old moralities and its old religions and its old political constitutions. Whats the result? In machinery it does very well; but in morals and religion and politics it is working at a loss that brings it nearer bankruptcy every year. Dont persist in that folly. If your old religion broke down yesterday, get a newer and a better one for tomorrow.

BARBARA: Oh how gladly I would take a better one to my soul! But you offer me a worse one. (*Turning on him with sudden vehemence.*) Justify yourself: shew me some light through the darkness of this dreadful place, with its beautifully clean workshops, and respectable workmen, and model homes.

UNDERSHAFT: Cleanliness and respectability do not need justification, Barbara: they justify themselves. I see no darkness here, no dreadfulness. In your Salvation shelter I saw poverty, misery, cold and hunger. You gave them bread and treacle and dreams of heaven. I give from thirty shillings a week to twelve thousand a year. They find their own dreams; but I look after the drainage.

BARBARA: And their souls?

UNDERSHAFT: I save their souls just as I saved yours.

BARBARA: (*Revolted.*) You saved my soul! What do you mean?

UNDERSHAFT: I fed you and clothed you and housed you. I took care that you should have money enough to live handsomely—more than enough; so that you could be wasteful, careless, generous. That saved your soul from the seven deadly sins.

BARBARA: (*Bewildered.*) The seven deadly sins!

UNDERSHAFT: Yes, the deadly seven. (*Counting on his fingers.*) Food, clothing, firing, rent, taxes, respectability and children. Nothing can lift those seven millstones from Man's neck but money; and the spirit cannot soar until the millstones are lifted. I lifted them from your spirit. I enabled Barbara to become Major Barbara; and I saved her from the crime of poverty.

CUSINS: Do you call poverty a crime?

UNDERSHAFT: The worst of crimes. All the other crimes are virtues beside it: all the other dishonors are chivalry itself by comparison. Poverty blights whole cities; spreads horrible pestilences; strikes dead the very souls of all who come within sight, sound, or smell of it. What you call crime is nothing: a murder here and a theft there, a blow now and a curse then: what do they matter? they are only the accidents

and illnesses of life: there are not fifty genuine professional criminals in London. But there are millions of poor people, abject people, dirty people, ill fed, ill clothed people. They poison us morally and physically: they kill the happiness of
935 society: they force us to do away with our own liberties and to organize unnatural cruelties for fear they should rise against us and drag us down into their abyss. Only fools fear crime: we all fear poverty. Pah! (*Turning on* BARBARA.) you talk of your halfsaved ruffian in West Ham: you accuse me of
940 dragging his soul back to perdition. Well, bring him to me here; and I will drag his soul back again to salvation for you. Not by words and dreams; but by thirty-eight shillings a week, a sound house in a handsome street, and a permanent job. In three weeks he will have a fancy waistcoat; in three
945 months a tall hat and a chapel sitting; before the end of the year he will shake hands with a duchess at a Primrose League meeting, and join the Conservative Party.

BARBARA: And will he be the better for that?

UNDERSHAFT: You know he will. Dont be a hypocrite, Barbara.
950 He will be better fed, better housed, better clothed, better behaved; and his children will be pounds heavier and bigger. That will be better than an American cloth mattress in a shelter, chopping firewood, eating bread and treacle, and being forced to kneel down from time to time to thank heaven
955 for it: knee drill, I think you call it. It is cheap work converting starving men with a Bible in one hand and a slice of bread in the other. I will undertake to convert West Ham to Mahometanism on the same terms. Try your hand on my men: their souls are hungry because their bodies are full.

960 BARBARA: And leave the east end to starve?

UNDERSHAFT: (*His energetic tone dropping into one of bitter and brooding remembrance.*) I was an east ender. I moralized and starved until one day I swore that I would be a full-fed free man at all costs; that nothing should stop me except
965 a bullet, neither reason nor morals nor the lives of other men. I said 'Thou shalt starve ere I starve'; and with that word I became free and great. I was a dangerous man until I had my will: now I am a useful, beneficent, kindly person. That is the history of most self-made millionaires,
970 I fancy. When it is the history of every Englishman we shall have an England worth living in.

LADY BRITOMART: Stop making speeches, Andrew. This is not the place for them.

UNDERSHAFT: (*Punctured.*) My dear: I have no other means of
975 conveying my ideas.

LADY BRITOMART: Your ideas are nonsense. You got on because you were selfish and unscrupulous.

UNDERSHAFT: Not at all. I had the strongest scruples about poverty and starvation. Your moralists are quite unscrupu-
980 lous about both: they make virtues of them. I had rather be a thief than a pauper. I had rather be a murderer than a slave. I dont want to be either; but if you force the alternative on me, then, by Heaven, I'll choose the braver and more moral one. I hate poverty and slavery worse than any other crimes
985 whatsoever. And let me tell you this. Poverty and slavery have stood up for centuries to your sermons and leading articles: they will not stand up to my machine guns. Dont preach at them: dont reason with them. Kill them.

BARBARA: Killing. Is that your remedy for everything?

990 UNDERSHAFT: It is the final test of conviction, the only lever strong enough to overturn a social system, the only way of saying Must. Let six hundred and seventy fools loose in the streets; and three policemen can scatter them. But huddle them together in a certain house in Westminster; and let them go through certain ceremonies and call themselves 995 certain names until at last they get the courage to kill; and your six hundred and seventy fools become a government. Your pious mob fills up ballot papers and imagines it is governing its masters; but the ballot paper that really governs is the paper that has a bullet wrapped up in it. 1000

CUSINS: That is perhaps why, like most intelligent people, I never vote.

UNDERSHAFT: Vote! Bah! When you vote, you only change the names of the cabinet. When you shoot, you pull down governments, inaugurate new epochs, abolish old orders 1005 and set up new. Is that historically true, Mr Learned Man, or is it not?

CUSINS: It is historically true. I loathe having to admit it. I repudiate your sentiments. I abhor your nature. I defy you in every possible way. Still, it is true. But it ought not to be true. 1010

UNDERSHAFT: Ought! ought! ought! ought! ought! Are you going to spend your life saying ought, like the rest of our moralists? Turn your oughts into shalls, man. Come and make explosives with me. Whatever can blow men up can blow society up. The history of the world is the history of 1015 those who had courage enough to embrace this truth. Have you the courage to embrace it, Barbara?

LADY BRITOMART: Barbara: I positively forbid you to listen to your father's abominable wickedness. And you, Adolphus, ought to know better than to go about saying that wrong 1020 things are true. What does it matter whether they are true if they are wrong?

UNDERSHAFT: What does it matter whether they are wrong if they are true?

LADY BRITOMART: (*Rising.*) Children: come home instantly. 1025 Andrew: I am exceedingly sorry I allowed you to call on us. You are wickeder than ever. Come at once.

BARBARA: (*Shaking her head.*) It's no use running away from wicked people, mamma.

LADY BRITOMART: It is every use. It shews your disapproba- 1030 tion of them.

BARBARA: It does not save them.

LADY BRITOMART: I can see that you are going to disobey me. Sarah: are you coming home or are you not?

SARAH: I daresay it's very wicked of papa to make cannons; 1035 but I dont think I shall cut him on that account.

LOMAX: (*Pouring oil on the troubled waters.*) The fact is, you know, there is a certain amount of tosh about this notion of wickedness. It doesnt work. You must look at facts. Not that I would say a word in favor of anything wrong; 1040 but then, you see, all sorts of chaps are always doing all sorts of things; and we have to fit them in somehow, dont you know. What I mean is that you cant go cutting everybody; and thats about what it comes to. (*Their rapt attention to his eloquence makes him nervous.*) Perhaps I dont make 1045 myself clear.

LADY BRITOMART: You are lucidity itself, Charles. Because Andrew is successful and has plenty of money to give to Sarah, you will flatter him and encourage him in his wickedness.

LOMAX: (*Unruffled.*) Well, where the carcase is, there will the 1050 eagles be gathered, dont you know. (*To* UNDERSHAFT.) Eh? What?

UNDERSHAFT: Precisely. By the way, may I call you Charles?

LOMAX: Delighted. Cholly is the usual ticket.

1055 UNDERSHAFT: (*To* LADY BRITOMART.) Biddy—

LADY BRITOMART: (*Violently.*) Dont dare call me Biddy. Charles Lomax: you are a fool. Adolphus Cusins: you are a Jesuit. Stephen: you are a prig. Barbara: you are a lunatic.
1060 Andrew: you are a vulgar tradesman. Now you all know my opinion; and my conscience is clear, at all events. (*She sits down with a vehemence that the rug fortunately softens.*)

UNDERSHAFT: My dear: you are the incarnation of morality. (*She snorts.*) Your conscience is clear and your duty done when you have called everybody names. Come, Euripides! it is getting
1065 late; and we all want to go home. Make up your mind.

CUSINS: Understand this, you old demon—

LADY BRITOMART: Adolphus!

UNDERSHAFT: Let him alone, Biddy. Proceed, Euripides.

CUSINS: You have me in a horrible dilemma. I want Barbara.

1070 UNDERSHAFT: Like all young men, you greatly exaggerate the difference between one young woman and another.

BARBARA: Quite true, Dolly.

CUSINS: I also want to avoid being a rascal.

UNDERSHAFT: (*With biting contempt.*) You lust for personal
1075 righteousness, for self-approval, for what you call a good conscience, for what Barbara calls salvation, for what I call patronizing people who are not so lucky as yourself.

CUSINS: I do not: all the poet in me recoils from being a good man. But there are things in me that I must reckon with. Pity—

1080 UNDERSHAFT: Pity! The scavenger of misery.

CUSINS: Well, love.

UNDERSHAFT: I know. You love the needy and the outcast: you love the oppressed races, the negro, the Indian ryot, the underdog everywhere. Do you love the Japanese? Do
1085 you love the French? Do you love the English?

CUSINS: No. Every true Englishman detests the English. We are the wickedest nation on earth; and our success is a moral horror.

UNDERSHAFT: That is what comes of your gospel of love, is it?

1090 CUSINS: May I not love even my father-in-law?

UNDERSHAFT: Who wants your love, man? By what right do you take the liberty of offering it to me? I will have your due heed and respect, or I will kill you. But your love! Damn your impertinence!

1095 CUSINS: (*Grinning.*) I may not be able to control my affections, Mac.

UNDERSHAFT: You are fencing, Euripides. You are weakening: your grip is slipping. Come! try your last weapon. Pity and love have broken in your hand: forgiveness is still left.

1100 CUSINS: No: forgiveness is a beggar's refuge. I am with you there: we must pay our debts.

UNDERSHAFT: Well said. Come! you will suit me. Remember the words of Plato.

CUSINS: (*Starting.*) Plato! You dare quote Plato to me!

1105 UNDERSHAFT: Plato says, my friend, that society cannot be saved until either the Professors of Greek take to making gunpowder, or else the makers of gunpowder become Professors of Greek.

CUSINS: Oh, tempter, cunning tempter!

1110 UNDERSHAFT: Come! choose, man, choose.

CUSINS: But perhaps Barbara will not marry me if I make the wrong choice.

BARBARA: Perhaps not.

CUSINS: (*Desperately perplexed.*) You hear!

BARBARA: Father: do you love nobody? 1115

UNDERSHAFT: I love my best friend.

LADY BRITOMART: And who is that, pray?

UNDERSHAFT: My bravest enemy. That is the man who keeps me up to the mark.

CUSINS: You know, the creature is really a sort of poet in his 1120 way. Suppose he is a great man, after all!

UNDERSHAFT: Suppose you stop talking and make up your mind, my young friend.

CUSINS: But you are driving me against my nature. I hate war.

UNDERSHAFT: Hatred is the coward's revenge for being in- 1125 timidated. Dare you make war on war? Here are the means: my friend Mr Lomax is sitting on them.

LOMAX: (*Springing up.*) Oh I say! You dont mean that this thing is loaded, do you? My ownest: come off it.

SARAH: (*Sitting placidly on the shell.*) If I am to be blown up, the 1130 more thoroughly it is done the better. Dont fuss, Cholly.

LOMAX: (*To* UNDERSHAFT, *strongly remonstrant.*) Your own daughter, you know!

UNDERSHAFT: So I see! (*To* CUSINS.) Well, my friend, may we expect you here at six tomorrow morning? 1135

CUSINS: (*Firmly.*) Not on any account. I will see the whole establishment blown up with its own dynamite before I will get up at five. My hours are healthy, rational hours: eleven to five.

UNDERSHAFT: Come when you please: before a week you will 1140 come at six and stay until I turn you out for the sake of your health. (*Calling.*) Bilton! (*He turns to* LADY BRITO-MART, *who rises.*) My dear: let us leave these two young people to themselves for a moment. (BILTON *comes from the shed.*) I am going to take you through the gun cotton shed. 1145

BILTON: (*Barring the way.*) You cant take anything explosive in here, sir.

LADY BRITOMART: What do you mean? Are you alluding to me?

BILTON: (*Unmoved.*) No, maam. Mr Undershaft has the other gentleman's matches in his pocket. 1150

LADY BRITOMART: (*Abruptly.*) Oh! I beg your pardon. (*She goes into the shed.*)

UNDERSHAFT: Quite right, Bilton, quite right: here you are. (*He gives* BILTON *the box of matches.*) Come, Stephen. Come, Charles. Bring Sarah. (*He passes into the shed.*) 1155

(BILTON *opens the box and deliberately drops the matches into the fire-bucket.*)

LOMAX: Oh! I say (BILTON *stolidly hands him the empty box.*) Infernal nonsense! Pure scientific ignorance! (*He goes in.*)

SARAH: Am I all right, Bilton?

BILTON: Youll have to put on list slippers, miss: thats all. Weve got em inside. (*She goes in.*) 1160

STEPHEN: (*Very seriously to* CUSINS.) Dolly, old fellow, think. Think before you decide. Do you feel that you are a suf- ficiently practical man? It is a huge undertaking, an enor- mous responsibility. All this mass of business will be Greek to you. 1165

CUSINS: Oh, I think it will be much less difficult than Greek.

STEPHEN: Well, I just want to say this before I leave you to your- selves. Dont let anything I have said about right and wrong prejudice you against this great chance in life. I have satisfied myself that the business is one of the highest character and a 1170 credit to our country. (*Emotionally.*) I am very proud of my father. I—(*Unable to proceed, he presses* CUSINS' *hand and goes hastily into the shed, followed by* BILTON.)

(BARBARA *and* CUSINS, *left alone together, look at one another silently.*)

CUSINS: Barbara: I am going to accept this offer.

1175 BARBARA: I thought you would.

CUSINS: You understand, dont you, that I had to decide without consulting you. If I had thrown the burden of the choice on you, you would sooner or later have despised me for it.

BARBARA: Yes: I did not want you to sell your soul for me any
1180 more than for this inheritance.

CUSINS: It is not the sale of my soul that troubles me: I have sold it too often to care about that. I have sold it for a professorship. I have sold it for an income. I have sold it to escape being imprisoned for refusing to pay taxes for
1185 hangmen's ropes and unjust wars and things that I abhor. What is all human conduct but the daily and hourly sale of our souls for trifles? What I am now selling it for is neither money nor position nor comfort, but for reality and for power.

1190 BARBARA: You know that you will have no power, and that he has none.

CUSINS: I know. It is not for myself alone. I want to make power for the world.

BARBARA: I want to make power for the world too; but it
1195 must be spiritual power.

CUSINS: I think all power is spiritual: these cannons will not go off by themselves. I have tried to make spiritual power by teaching Greek. But the world can never be really touched by a dead language and a dead civilization. The people
1200 must have power; and the people cannot have Greek. Now the power that is made here can be wielded by all men.

BARBARA: Power to burn women's houses down and kill their sons and tear their husbands to pieces.

CUSINS: You cannot have power for good without having
1205 power for evil too. Even mother's milk nourishes murderers as well as heroes. This power which only tears men's bodies to pieces has never been so horribly abused as the intellectual power, the imaginative power, the poetic, religious power that can enslave men's souls. As a teacher of
1210 Greek I gave the intellectual man weapons against the common man. I now want to give the common man weapons against the intellectual man. I love the common people. I want to arm them against the lawyers, the doctors, the priests, the literary men, the professors, the artists,
1215 and the politicians, who, once in authority, are more disastrous and tyrannical than all the fools, rascals, and impostors. I want a power simple enough for common men to use, yet strong enough to force the intellectual oligarchy to use its genius for the general good.

1220 BARBARA: Is there no higher power than that? (*Pointing to the shell.*)

CUSINS: Yes; but that power can destroy the higher powers just as a tiger can destroy a man: therefore Man must master that power first. I admitted this when the Turks and
1225 Greeks were last at war. My best pupil went out to fight for Hellas. My parting gift to him was not a copy of Plato's Republic, but a revolver and a hundred Undershaft cartridges. The blood of every Turk he shot—if he shot any—is on my head as well as on Undershaft's. That act committed me to this place for ever. Your father's chal- 1230 lenge has beaten me. Dare I make war on war? I must. I will. And now, is it all over between us?

BARBARA: (*Touched by his evident dread of her answer.*) Silly baby Dolly! How could it be!

CUSINS: (*Overjoyed.*) Then you—you—you—Oh for my 1235 drum! (*He flourishes imaginary drumsticks.*)

BARBARA: (*Angered by his levity.*) Take care, Dolly, take care. Oh, if only I could get away from you and from father and from it all! if I could have the wings of a dove and fly away to heaven! 1240

CUSINS: And leave me!

BARBARA: Yes, you, and all the other naughty mischievous children of men. But I cant. I was happy in the Salvation Army for a moment. I escaped from the world into a paradise of enthusiasm and prayer and soul saving; but the 1245 moment our money ran short, it all came back to Bodger: it was he who saved our people: he, and the Prince of Darkness, my papa. Undershaft and Bodger: their hands stretch everywhere: when we feed a starving fellow creature, it is with their bread, because there is no other bread; 1250 when we tend the sick, it is in the hospitals they endow; if we turn from the churches they build, we must kneel on the stones of the streets they pave. As long as that lasts, there is no getting away from them. Turning our backs on Bodger and Undershaft is turning our backs on life. 1255

CUSINS: I thought you were determined to turn your back on the wicked side of life.

BARBARA: There is no wicked side: life is all one. And I never wanted to shirk my share in whatever evil must be endured, whether it be sin or suffering. I wish I could cure 1260 you of middle-class ideas, Dolly.

CUSINS: (*Gasping.*) Middle cl——! A snub! A social snub to me! from the daughter of a foundling!

BARBARA: That is why I have no class, Dolly: I come straight out of the heart of the whole people. If I were middle- 1265 class I should turn my back on my father's business; and we should both live in an artistic drawing room, with you reading the reviews in one corner, and I in the other at the piano, playing Schumann: both very superior persons, and neither of us a bit of use. Sooner than that, I would 1270 sweep out the guncotton shed, or be one of Bodger's barmaids. Do you know what would have happened if you had refused papa's offer?

CUSINS: I wonder!

BARBARA: I should have given you up and married the man 1275 who accepted it. After all, my dear old mother has more sense than any of you. I felt like her when I saw this place— felt that I must have it—that never, never, never could I let it go; only she thought it was the houses and the kitchen ranges and the linen and china, when it was really all the 1280 human souls to be saved: not weak souls in starved bodies, sobbing with gratitude for a scrap of bread and treacle, but fullfed, quarrelsome, snobbish, uppish creatures, all standing on their little rights and dignities, and thinking that my father ought to be greatly obliged to them for making so 1285 much money for him—and so he ought. That is where salvation is really wanted. My father shall never throw it in my teeth again that my converts were bribed with bread. (*She is transfigured.*) I have got rid of the bribe of bread. I have got rid of the bribe of heaven. Let God's work be done for its own sake: the work he had to create us to do because it cannot be done except by living men and women. When I die, let him be in my debt, not I in his; and let me forgive him as becomes a woman of my rank.

CUSINS: Then the way of life lies through the factory of death?

BARBARA: Yes, through the raising of hell to heaven and of man to God, through the unveiling of an eternal light in the Valley of The Shadow. (*Seizing him with both hands.*) Oh, did you think my courage would never come back? did you believe that I was a deserter? that I, who have stood in the streets, and taken my people to my heart, and talked of the holiest and greatest things with them, could ever turn back and chatter foolishly to fashionable people about nothing in a drawing room? Never, never, never, never: Major Barbara will die with the colors. Oh! and I have my dear little Dolly boy still; and he has found me my place and my work. Glory Hallelujah! (*She kisses him.*)

CUSINS: My dearest: consider my delicate health. I cannot stand as much happiness as you can.

BARBARA: Yes: it is not easy work being in love with me, is it? But it's good for you. (*She runs to the shed, and calls, childlike.*) Mamma! Mamma! (BILTON *comes out of the shed, followed by* UNDERSHAFT.) I want Mamma.

UNDERSHAFT: She is taking off her list slippers, dear. (*He passes on to* CUSINS.) Well? What does she say?

CUSINS: She has gone right up into the skies.

LADY BRITOMART: (*Coming from the shed and stopping on the steps, obstructing* SARAH, *who follows with* LOMAX. BARBARA *clutches like a baby at her mother's skirt.*) Barbara: when will you learn to be independent and to act and think for yourself? I know as well as possible what that cry of 'Mamma, Mamma,' means. Always running to me!

SARAH: (*Touching* LADY BRITOMART'*s ribs with her finger tips and imitating a bicycle horn.*) Pip! pip!

LADY BRITOMART: (*Highly indignant.*) How dare you say Pip! pip! to me, Sarah? You are both very naughty children. What do you want, Barbara?

BARBARA: I want a house in the village to live in with Dolly. (*Dragging at the skirt.*) Come and tell me which one to take.

UNDERSHAFT: (*To* CUSINS.) Six o'clock tomorrow morning, Euripides.

Luigi Pirandello

Luigi Pirandello (1867–1936) created a diverse and influential body of plays, but his work is now most often associated with the preoccupations of his *Six Characters in Search of an Author*. Like *Six Characters*, Pirandello's plays use METATHEATER—roleplaying, plays-within-plays, and a flexible sense of the limits of stage illusion—to examine a highly theatricalized vision of identity. Can any of us be certain of our identity when others hold radically different perspectives on our actions, on who we are?

Pirandello was born in Sicily. He studied language and literature and received his doctoral degree in 1891 from the University of Rome. He then married the daughter of his father's business partner, but the collapse of the business forced him into a career as a writer. He wrote hundreds of stories in the 1890s and in the first decades of the twentieth century, as well as critical and scholarly articles. Pirandello's dramatic interest in the uncertainty of identity can be traced partly to his troubled marriage. His wife suffered a long mental illness and constantly accused him of adultery, despite his careful and constant attention to her health. In a sense, Pirandello was caught between his own sense of himself and the role he was given in this domestic tragedy.

Pirandello's use of the theater as a metaphor for representing this conflict pervades his mature plays: *Six Characters in Search of an Author* (1921; extensively revised 1925), *Enrico IV* (1922), *Each in His Own Way* (1924), and *Tonight We Improvise* (1930). In these plays, the struggle to discover and maintain identity is subjected to the pressure of performance in the world, performance that renders the "self" a kind of fiction. Yet while all behavior seems to verge on mere "acting," undermining our confidence in the authority or reality of a "self," Pirandello's plays do not seem nostalgic for the fixed and determined characters of realistic drama. For in Pirandello's drama, the "self" can also become a kind of prison, a role that traps the individual in a single and confining performance. This is the tragedy that the nameless hero of *Enrico IV* discovers at the close of that play, much as the hero—a famous author like Pirandello himself—of *When One Is Somebody* (1933) is gradually transformed from a man into a statue by the force of his admirers' adulation.

Pirandello became the director of his own company, the Art Theater of Rome, in 1924, and his major plays entered the world repertoire almost immediately. Pirandello's company toured throughout Europe and the Americas, influencing a generation of playwrights with the power of his theatrical conception of modern life. In addition to his short stories and criticism, Pirandello wrote over forty plays. He was awarded the Nobel Prize in 1934 in recognition of his achievement in the modern theater.

SIX CHARACTERS IN SEARCH OF AN AUTHOR

Six Characters seems at first to elaborate a simple and striking idea. What would happen if a cast of dramatic "characters" confronted the actors who gave them life on the stage? Pirandello had toyed with the idea for some time and had sketched it out as a short story. Onstage, though, the story develops a new and challenging dimension, for the confrontation between the Characters and Actors explores the nature of theatrical representation itself. As the play proceeds, it becomes clear that the Actors and Characters represent opposed versions of reality and of the theater, and their contest calls our understanding of the difference between them into question. The Characters need completion. Their melodramatic incest drama has defined each of them in an imprisoning role, as though the climactic moment of their unfinished play—when the Father nearly (or does he?) procures the Stepdaughter in Madame Pace's brothel—was definitive of the identity of each character. That is, Pirandello questions our fundamental notions of how dramatic characters represent the lives of real people, how they represent the rich complexity of a "life" through a short series of a few typical deeds. As the Father asks at one point, who of us would want his or her life summed up in one moment, one act?

The Father tells the story of the Characters standing in profile just upstage in Luigi Pirandello's *Six Characters in Search of an Author*.

The Actors, on the other hand, seem even less real than the Characters. Although the Characters are "fixed" by the design of their common story, that very consistency gives them a coherence and weight that the flighty Actors seem to lack. The Actors are entirely absorbed in the conventions of their lines of business and the petty jealousies of working together; the Leading Actor must always be "acting" the "Leading Actor," whether he is onstage or not, and so on through the rest of the cast. Oddly enough, then, *Six Characters* does not seem to allow us to choose between the Actors or Characters, to decide which kind of representation—narrative or stage performance—provides a more accurate depiction of "reality." The drama of *Six Characters* arises from the unresolved collision between these two perspectives. In the theater, the process of *Six Characters* insistently disorients its audience from the stable categories of "reality" and "illusion," which is perhaps why audiences rioted when the play was first produced. The Characters are, of course, played by actors, while the Actors are clearly "characters" to the audience. Are we, in the audience, any more "real?" Are we outside the play looking in, or has Pirandello managed to place us onstage, showing the audience also to be playing a role in the endless roleplaying of the theater? For this reason, when reading the play we should resist locating its "meanings" in the Father's philosophical monologues, those moments of *pirandellismo* that seem to sum up the play's confrontation between illusion and reality. The play's meaning arises through the entire process of its action, the baffling, inconclusive, and frustrating confrontation between Characters, Actors, and audience, a confrontation that finally prevents the Characters' drama from ever taking the stage.

Students should note that this version of *Six Characters* represents Pirandello's 1925 revision of the play and that it differs in several ways—especially in the play's brilliant finale—from the earlier 1921 version. Also, this translation was first performed in England, where the role of "Producer" is what Americans generally call the "Director."

SIX CHARACTERS IN SEARCH OF AN AUTHOR

Luigi Pirandello

TRANSLATED BY JOHN LINSTRUM

CHARACTERS

THE FATHER
THE MOTHER
THE STEPDAUGHTER
THE SON

THE BOY (*non-speaking*)
THE LITTLE GIRL (*non-speaking*)
MADAME PACE

ACTORS

THE PRODUCER
THE LEADING ACTRESS
THE LEADING ACTOR
THE SECOND ACTRESS
THE YOUNG ACTRESS
THE JUVENILE LEAD
OTHER ACTORS AND
ACTRESSES (*a variable
    number*)

THE STAGE MANAGER
THE PROMPTER
THE PROPERTY MAN
THE STAGE HAND
THE PRODUCER'S SECRETARY
THE DOORKEEPER
OTHER THEATRE STAFF

The action of the play takes place on the stage of a theatre. There are no act or scene divisions, but there are two interruptions: when the PRODUCER *and the* CHARACTERS *go to the office to write the scenario, giving the* ACTORS *a break in rehearsal, and when a* STAGE HAND *lowers the front curtain by mistake.*

References to 'prompt-box,' 'curtains' and 'letting down trees' will need to be altered if they are not appropriate to the theatre where the performance is taking place.

ACT ONE

When the audience enters, the curtain is already up and the stage is just as it would be during the day. There is no set; it is empty, in almost total darkness. This is so that from the beginning the audience will have the feeling of being present, not at a performance of a properly rehearsed play, but at a performance of a play that happens spontaneously. Two small sets of steps, one on the right and one on the left, lead up to the stage from the auditorium. On the stage, the top is off the PROMPTER'S *box and is lying next to it. Downstage, there is a small table and a chair with arms for the* PRODUCER: *it is turned with its back to the audience.*

Also downstage there are two small tables, one a little bigger than the other, and several chairs, ready for the rehearsal if needed. There are more chairs scattered on both left and right for the ACTORS: *to one side at the back and nearly hidden is a piano.*

When the houselights go down, the STAGE HAND *comes on through the back door. He is in blue overalls and carries a tool bag. He brings some pieces of wood on, comes to the front, kneels down and starts to nail them together.*

The STAGE MANAGER *rushes on from the wings.*

STAGE MANAGER: Hey! What are you doing?
STAGE HAND: What do you think I'm doing? I'm banging nails in.
STAGE MANAGER: Now? (*He looks at his watch.*) It's half-past ten
5   already. The Producer will be here in a moment to rehearse.
STAGE HAND: I've got to do my work some time, you know.
STAGE MANAGER: Right—but not now.
STAGE HAND: When?
STAGE MANAGER: When the rehearsal's finished. Come on,
10   get all this out of the way and let me set for the second act of 'The Rules of the Game.'

(*The* STAGE HAND *picks up his tools and wood and goes off, grumbling and muttering. The* ACTORS *of the company come in through the door, men and women, first one then another, then two together and so on: there will be nine or ten, enough for the parts for the rehearsal of a play by Pirandello, 'The Rules of the Game,' today's rehearsal. They come in, say their 'Good-mornings' to the* STAGE MANAGER *and each other. Some go off to the dressing-rooms; others, among them the* PROMPTER *with the text rolled up under his arm, scatter about the stage waiting for the* PRODUCER *to start the rehearsal. Meanwhile, sitting or standing in groups, they chat together; some smoke, one complains about his part, another one loudly reads something from 'The Stage.' It would be as well if the* ACTORS *and* ACTRESSES *were dressed in colourful clothes, and this first scene should be improvised naturally and vivaciously. After a while somebody might sit down at the piano and play a song; the younger* ACTORS *and* ACTRESSES *start dancing.*)

STAGE MANAGER: (*Clapping his hands to call their attention.*)
    Come on everybody! Quiet please. The Producer's here.

(*The piano and the dancing both stop. The* ACTORS *turn to look out into the theatre and through the door at the back comes the* PRODUCER; *he walks down the gangway between the seats and, calling 'Good-morning' to the* ACTORS, *climbs up one of the sets of stairs onto the stage. The* SECRETARY *gives him the post, a few magazines, a script. The* ACTORS *move to one side of the stage.*)

PRODUCER: Any letters?
SECRETARY: No. That's all the post there is. (*Giving him the* 15
    script.)
PRODUCER: Put it in the office. (*Then looking round and turning to the* STAGE MANAGER.) I can't see a thing here. Let's have some lights please.
STAGE MANAGER: Right. (*Calling.*) Workers please!   20

(*In a few seconds the side of the stage where the* ACTORS *are standing is brilliantly lit with white light. The* PROMPTER *has gone into his box and spread out his script.*)

PRODUCER: Good. (*Clapping hands.*) Well then, let's get started. Anybody missing?

STAGE MANAGER: (*Heavily ironic.*) Our leading lady.

PRODUCER: Not again! (*Looking at his watch.*) We're ten min-
25 utes late already. Send her a note to come and see me. It might teach her to be on time for rehearsals. (*Almost before he has finished, the* LEADING ACTRESS's *voice is heard from the auditorium.*)

LEADING ACTRESS: Morning everybody. Sorry I'm late. (*She
30 is very expensively dressed and is carrying a lap-dog. She comes down the aisle and goes up on to the stage.*)

PRODUCER: You're determined to keep us waiting, aren't you?

LEADING ACTRESS: I'm sorry. I just couldn't find a taxi any-
35 where. But you haven't started yet and I'm not on at the opening anyhow. (*Calling the* STAGE MANAGER, *she gives him the dog.*) Put him in my dressing-room for me will you?

PRODUCER: And she's even brought her lap-dog with her! As if we haven't enough lap-dogs here already. (*Clapping his hands and turning to the* PROMPTER.) Right then, the sec-
40 ond act of 'The Rules of the Game.' (*Sits in his arm-chair.*) Quiet please! Who's on?

(*The* ACTORS *clear from the front of the stage and sit to one side, except for three who are ready to start the scene—and the* LEADING ACTRESS. *She has ignored the* PRODUCER *and is sitting at one of the little tables.*)

PRODUCER: Are you in this scene, then?

LEADING ACTRESS: No—I've just told you.

PRODUCER: (*Annoyed.*) Then get off, for God's sake. (*The
45 LEADING ACTRESS goes and sits with the others. To the* PROMPTER.) Come on then, let's get going.

PROMPTER: (*Reading his script.*) 'The house of Leone Gala. A peculiar room, both dining-room and study.'

PRODUCER: (*To the* STAGE MANAGER.) We'll use the red set.
50 STAGE MANAGER: (*Making a note.*) The red set—right.

PROMPTER: (*Still reading.*) 'The table is laid and there is a desk with books and papers. Bookcases full of books and china cabinets full of valuable china. An exit at the back leads to Leone's bedroom. An exit to the left leads to the kitchen.
55 The main entrance is on the right.'

PRODUCER: Right. Listen carefully everybody: there, the main entrance, there, the kitchen. (*To the* LEADING ACTOR *who plays Socrates.*) Your entrances and exits will be from there. (*To the* STAGE MANAGER.) We'll have the French
60 windows there and put the curtains on them.

STAGE MANAGER: (*Making a note.*) Right.

PROMPTER: (*Reading.*) 'Scene One. Leone Gala, Guido Venanzi, and Filippo, who is called Socrates.' (*To* PRODUCER.) Have I to read the directions as well?
65 PRODUCER: Yes, you have! I've told you a hundred times!

PROMPTER: (*Reading.*) 'When the curtain rises, Leone Gala, in a cook's hat and apron, is beating an egg in a dish with a little wooden spoon. Filippo is beating another and he is dressed as a cook too. Guido Venanzi is sitting listening.'
70 LEADING ACTOR: Look, do I really have to wear a cook's hat?

PRODUCER: (*Annoyed by the question.*) I expect so! That's what it says in the script. (*Pointing to the script.*)

LEADING ACTOR: If you ask me it's ridiculous.

PRODUCER: (*Leaping to his feet furiously.*) Ridiculous? It's ridiculous, is it? What do you expect me to do if nobody 75
writes good plays any more and we're reduced to putting on plays by Pirandello? And if you can understand them you must be very clever. He writes them on purpose so nobody enjoys them, neither actors nor critics nor audience. (*The* ACTORS *laugh. Then crosses to* LEADING ACTOR *and shouts at* 80
him.) A cook's hat and you beat eggs. But don't run away with the idea that that's all you are doing—beating eggs. You must be joking! You have to be symbolic of the shells of the eggs you are beating. (*The* ACTORS *laugh again and start making ironical comments to each other.*) Be quiet! Listen care- 85
fully while I explain. (*Turns back to* LEADING ACTOR.) Yes, the shells, because they are symbolic of the empty form of reason, without its content, blind instinct! You are reason and your wife is instinct: you are playing a game where you have been given parts and in which you are not just yourself but 90
the puppet of yourself. Do you see?

LEADING ACTOR: (*Spreading his hands.*) Me? No.

PRODUCER: (*Going back to his chair.*) Neither do I! Come on, let's get going; you wait till you see the end! You haven't seen anything yet! (*Confidentially.*) By the way, I should 95
turn almost to face the audience if I were you, about three-quarters face. Well, what with the obscure dialogue and the audience not being able to hear you properly in any case, the whole lot'll go to hell. (*Clapping hands again.*) Come on. Let's get going! 100

PROMPTER: Excuse me, can I put the top back on the prompt-box? There's a bit of a draught.

PRODUCER: Yes, yes, of course. Get on with it.

(*The* STAGE DOORKEEPER, *in a braided cap, has come into the auditorium, and he comes all the way down the aisle to the stage to tell the* PRODUCER *the* SIX CHARACTERS *have come, who, having come in after him, look about them a little puzzled and dismayed. Every effort must be made to create the effect that the* SIX CHARACTERS *are very different from the* ACTORS *of the company. The placings of the two groups, indicated in the directions, once the* CHARACTERS *are on the stage, will help this; so will using different coloured lights. But the most effective idea is to use masks for the* CHARACTERS, *masks specially made of a material that will not go limp with perspiration and light enough not to worry the actors who wear them: they should be made so that the eyes, the nose and the mouth are all free. This is the way to bring out the deep significance of the play. The* CHARACTERS *should not appear as ghosts, but as created realities, timeless creations of the imagination, and so more real and consistent than the changeable realities of the* ACTORS. *The masks are designed to give the impression of figures constructed by art, each one fixed forever in its own fundamental emotion; that is, Remorse for the* FATHER, *Revenge for the* STEPDAUGHTER, *Scorn for the* SON, *Sorrow for the* MOTHER. *Her mask should have wax tears in the corners of the eyes and down the cheeks like the sculptured or painted weeping Madonna in a church. Her dress should be of a plain material, in stiff folds, looking almost as if it were carved and not of an ordinary material you can buy in a shop and have made up by a dressmaker.*)

(*The* FATHER *is about fifty: his reddish hair is thinning at the temples, but he is not bald: he has a full moustache that almost covers his young-looking mouth, which often opens in an uncertain and empty smile. He is pale, with a high forehead: he has blue oval eyes, clear and sharp: he is dressed in light trousers and a dark jacket: his voice is sometimes rich, at other times harsh and loud.*)

(*The* MOTHER *appears crushed by an intolerable weight of shame and humiliation. She is wearing a thick black veil and is dressed simply in black; when she raises her veil she shows a face like wax, but not suffering, with her eyes turned down humbly.*)

(*The* STEPDAUGHTER, *who is eighteen years old, is defiant, even insolent. She is very beautiful, dressed in mourning as well, but with striking elegance. She is scornful of the timid, suffering, dejected air of her young brother, a grubby little* BOY *of fourteen, also dressed in black; she is full of a warm tenderness, on the other hand, for the* LITTLE SISTER, *a girl of about four, dressed in white with a black silk sash round her waist.*)

(*The* SON *is twenty-two, tall, almost frozen in an air of scorn for the* FATHER *and indifference to the* MOTHER: *he is wearing a mauve overcoat and a long green scarf round his neck.*)

DOORMAN: Excuse me, sir.
105 PRODUCER: (*Angrily.*) What the hell is it now?
DOORMAN: There are some people here—they say they want to see you, sir.

(*The* PRODUCER *and the* ACTORS *are astonished and turn to look out into the auditorium.*)

PRODUCER: But I'm rehearsing! You know perfectly well that no-one's allowed in during rehearsals. (*Turning to face out*
110 *front.*) Who are you? What do you want?
FATHER: (*Coming forward, followed by the others, to the foot of one of the sets of steps.*) We're looking for an author.
PRODUCER: (*Angry and astonished.*) An author? Which author?
FATHER: Any author will do, sir.
115 PRODUCER: But there isn't an author here because we're not rehearsing a new play.
STEPDAUGHTER: (*Excitedly as she rushes up the steps.*) That's better still, better still! We can be your new play.
ACTORS: (*Lively comments and laughter from the* ACTORS.) Oh,
120 listen to that, etc.
FATHER: (*Going up on the stage after the* STEPDAUGHTER.) Maybe, but if there isn't an author here . . . (*To the* PRODUCER.) Unless you'd like to be . . .

(*Hand in hand, the* MOTHER *and the* LITTLE GIRL, *followed by the little* BOY, *go up on the stage and wait. The* SON *stays sullenly behind.*)

PRODUCER: Is this some kind of joke?
125 FATHER: Now, how can you think that? On the contrary, we are bringing you a story of anguish.
STEPDAUGHTER: We might make your fortune for you!
PRODUCER: Do me a favour, will you? Go away. We haven't time to waste on idiots.
130 FATHER: (*Hurt but answering gently.*) You know very well, as a man of the theatre, that life is full of all sorts of odd things which have no need at all to pretend to be real because they are actually true.
PRODUCER: What the devil are you talking about?
135 FATHER: What I'm saying is that you really must be mad to do things the opposite way round: to create situations that

obviously aren't true and try to make them seem to be really happening. But then I suppose that sort of madness is the only reason for your profession.

(*The* ACTORS *are indignant.*)

PRODUCER: (*Getting up and glaring at him.*) Oh, yes? So ours 140 is a profession of madmen, is it?
FATHER: Well, if you try to make something look true when it obviously isn't, especially if you're not forced to do it, but do it for a game . . . Isn't it your job to give life on the stage to imaginary people? 145
PRODUCER: (*Quickly answering him and speaking for the* ACTORS *who are growing more indignant.*) I should like you to know, sir, that the actor's profession is one of great distinction. Even if nowadays the new writers only give us dull plays to act and puppets to present instead of men, I'd have you 150 know that it is our boast that we have given life, here on this stage, to immortal works.

(*The* ACTORS, *satisfied, agree with and applaud the* PRODUCER.)

FATHER: (*Cutting in and following hard on his argument.*) There! You see? Good! You've given life! You've created living beings with more genuine life than people have who 155 breathe and wear clothes! Less real, perhaps, but nearer the truth. We are both saying the same thing.

(*The* ACTORS *look at each other, astonished.*)

PRODUCER: But just a moment! You said before . . .
FATHER: I'm sorry, but I said that before, about acting for fun, because you shouted at us and said you'd no time to waste 160 on idiots, but you must know better than anyone that Nature uses human imagination to lift her work of creation to even higher levels.
PRODUCER: All right then: but where does all this get us?
FATHER: Nowhere. I want to try to show that one can be 165 thrust into life in many ways, in many forms: as a tree or a stone, as water or a butterfly—or as a woman. It might even be as a character in a play.
PRODUCER: (*Ironic, pretending to be annoyed.*) And you, and these other people here, were thrust into life, as you put 170 it, as characters in a play?
FATHER: Exactly! And alive, as you can see.

(*The* PRODUCER *and the* ACTORS *burst into laughter as if at a joke.*)

FATHER: I'm sorry you laugh like that, because we carry in us, as I said before, a story of terrible anguish as you can guess from this woman dressed in black. 175

(*Saying this, he offers his hand to the* MOTHER *and helps her up the last steps and, holding her still by the hand, leads her with a sense of tragic solemnity across the stage which is suddenly lit by a fantastic light.*)

(*The* LITTLE GIRL *and the* BOY *follow the* MOTHER: *then the* SON *comes up and stands to one side in the background: then the* STEPDAUGHTER *follows and leans against the proscenium arch: the*

ACTORS *are astonished at first, but then, full of admiration for the 'entrance,' they burst into applause—just as if it were a performance specially for them.*)

PRODUCER: (*At first astonished and then indignant.*) My God! Be quiet all of you. (*Turns to the* CHARACTERS.) And you lot get out! Clear off! (*To the* STAGE MANAGER.) Jesus! Get them out of here.

180 STAGE MANAGER: (*Comes forward but stops short as if held back by something strange.*) Go on out! Get out!

FATHER: (*To* PRODUCER.) Oh no, please, you see, we . . .

PRODUCER: (*Shouting.*) We came here to work, you know.

LEADING ACTOR: We really can't be messed about like this.

185 FATHER: (*Resolutely, coming forward.*) I'm astonished! Why don't you believe me? Perhaps you are not used to seeing the characters created by an author spring into life up here on the stage face to face with each other. Perhaps it's because we're not in a script? (*He points to the* PROMPTER*'s box.*)

190 STEPDAUGHTER: (*Coming down to the* PRODUCER, *smiling and persuasive.*) Believe me, sir, we really are six of the most fascinating characters. But we've been neglected.

FATHER: Yes, that's right, we've been neglected. In the sense that the author who created us, living in his mind, wouldn't

195 or couldn't make us live in a written play for the world of art. And that really is a crime sir, because whoever has the luck to be born a character can laugh even at death. Because a character will never die! A man will die, a writer, the instrument of creation: but what he has created will

200 never die! And to be able to live for ever you don't need to have extraordinary gifts or be able to do miracles. Who was Sancho Panza? Who was Prospero? But they will live for ever because—living seeds—they had the luck to find a fruitful soil, an imagination which knew how to grow

205 them and feed them, so that they will live for ever.

PRODUCER: This is all very well! But what do you want here?

FATHER: We want to live, sir.

PRODUCER: (*Ironically.*) For ever!

FATHER: No, no: only for a few moments—in you.

210 AN ACTOR: Listen to that!

LEADING ACTRESS: They want to live in us!

YOUNG ACTOR: (*Pointing to the* STEPDAUGHTER.) I don't mind . . . so long as I get her.

FATHER: Listen, listen: the play is all ready to be put together

215 and if you and your actors would like to, we can work it out now between us.

PRODUCER: (*Annoyed.*) But what exactly do you want to do? We don't make up plays like that here! We present comedies and tragedies here.

220 FATHER: That's right, we know that of course. That's why we've come.

PRODUCER: And where's the script?

FATHER: It's in us, sir. (*The* ACTORS *laugh.*) The play is in us: we are the play and we are impatient to show it to you:

225 the passion inside us is driving us on.

STEPDAUGHTER: (*Scornfully, with the tantalising charm of deliberate impudence.*) My passion, if only you knew! My passion for him! (*She points at the* FATHER *and suggests that she is going to embrace him: but stops and bursts into a screeching laugh.*)

230 FATHER: (*With sudden anger.*) You keep out of this for the moment! And stop laughing like that!

STEPDAUGHTER: Really? Then with your permission, ladies and gentlemen; even though it's only two months since I became an orphan, just watch how I can sing and dance.

(*The* ACTORS, *especially the younger, seem strangely attracted to her while she sings and dances and they edge closer and reach out their hands to catch hold of her. She eludes them, and when the* ACTORS *applaud her and the* PRODUCER *speaks sharply to her she stays still quite removed from them all.*)

AN ACTOR: Very good! etc.   235

PRODUCER: (*Angrily.*) Be quiet! Do you think this is a nightclub? (*Turns to* FATHER *and asks with some concern.*) Is she a bit mad?

FATHER: Mad? Oh no—it's worse than that.

STEPDAUGHTER: (*Suddenly running to the* PRODUCER.) Yes. It's 240 worse, much worse! Listen please! Let's put this play on at once, because you'll see that at a particular point I—when this darling little girl here—(*Taking the* LITTLE GIRL *by the hand from next to the* MOTHER *and crossing with her to the* PRODUCER.) Isn't she pretty? (*Takes her in her arms.*) Darling! 245 Darling! (*Puts her down again and adds, moved very deeply but almost without wanting to.*) Well, this lovely little girl here, when God suddenly takes her from this poor Mother: and this little idiot here (*Turning to the* LITTLE BOY *and seizing him roughly by the sleeve.*) does the most stupid thing, like the 250 half-wit he is,—then you will see me run away! Yes, you'll see me rush away! But not yet, not yet! Because, after all the intimate things there have been between him and me (*In the direction of the* FATHER, *with a horrible vulgar wink.*) I can't stay with them any longer, to watch the insult to this 255 mother through that supercilious cretin over there. (*Pointing to the* SON.) Look at him! Look at him! Condescending, standoffish, because he's the legitimate son, him! Full of contempt for me, for the boy and for the little girl: because we are bastards. Do you understand? Bastards. (*Running to* 260 *the* MOTHER *and embracing her.*) And this poor mother— she—who is the mother of all of us—he doesn't want to recognise her as his own mother—and he looks down on her, he does, as if she were only the mother of the three of us who are bastards—the traitor. (*She says all this quickly,* 265 *with great excitement, and after having raised her voice on the word 'bastards' she speaks quietly, half-spitting the word 'traitor.'*)

MOTHER: (*With deep anguish to the* PRODUCER.) Sir, in the name of these two little ones, I beg you . . . (*Feels herself grow faint and sways.*) Oh, my God.   270

FATHER: (*Rushing to support her with almost all the* ACTORS *bewildered and concerned.*) Get a chair someone . . . quick, get a chair for this poor widow.

(*One of the* ACTORS *offers a chair: the others press urgently around. The* MOTHER, *seated now, tries to stop the* FATHER *lifting her veil.*)

ACTORS: Is it real? Has she really fainted? etc.

FATHER: Look at her, everybody, look at her.   275

MOTHER: No, for God's sake, stop it.

FATHER: Let them look!

MOTHER: (*Lifting her hands and covering her face, desperately.*) Oh, please, I beg you, stop him from doing what he is trying to do; it's hateful.   280

PRODUCER: (*Overwhelmed, astounded.*) It's no use, I don't understand this any more. (*To the* FATHER.) Is this woman your wife?

FATHER: (*At once.*) That's right, she is my wife.

285 PRODUCER: How is she a widow, then, if you're still alive?

(*The* ACTORS *are bewildered too and find relief in a loud laugh.*)

FATHER: (*Wounded, with rising resentment.*) Don't laugh! Please don't laugh like that! That's just the point, that's her own drama. You see, she had another man. Another man who ought to be here.

290 MOTHER: No, no! (*Crying out.*)

STEPDAUGHTER: Luckily for him he died. Two months ago, as I told you: we are in mourning for him, as you can see.

FATHER: Yes, he's dead: but that's not the reason he isn't here. He isn't here because—well just look at her, please, and
295 you'll understand at once—hers is not a passionate drama of the love of two men, because she was incapable of love, she could feel nothing—except, perhaps a little gratitude (but not to me, to him). She's not a woman; she's a mother. And her drama—and, believe me, it's a powerful
300 one—her drama is focused completely on these four children of the two men she had.

MOTHER: I had them? How dare you say that I had them, as if I wanted them myself? It was him, sir! He forced the other man on me. He made me go away with him!

305 STEPDAUGHTER: (*Leaping up, indignantly.*) It isn't true!

MOTHER: (*Bewildered.*) How isn't it true?

STEPDAUGHTER: It isn't true, it just isn't true.

MOTHER: What do you know about it?

STEPDAUGHTER: It isn't true. (*To the* PRODUCER.) Don't be-
310 lieve it! Do you know why she said that? She said it because of him, over there. (*Pointing to the* SON.) She tortures herself, she exhausts herself with worry and all because of the indifference of that son of hers. She wants to make him believe that she abandoned him when he was two
315 years old because the Father made her do it.

MOTHER: (*Passionately.*) He did! He made me! God's my witness. (*To the* PRODUCER.) Ask him if it isn't true. (*Pointing to the* FATHER.) Make him tell our son it's true. (*Turning to the* STEPDAUGHTER.) You don't know anything about it.

320 STEPDAUGHTER: I know that when my father was alive you were always happy and contented. You can't deny it.

MOTHER: No, I can't deny it.

STEPDAUGHTER: He was always full of love and care for you. (*Turning to the* LITTLE BOY *with anger.*) Isn't it true? Admit
325 it. Why don't you say something, you little idiot?

MOTHER: Leave the poor boy alone! Why do you want to make me appear ungrateful? You're my daughter. I don't in the least want to offend your father's memory. I've already told him that it wasn't my fault or even to please
330 myself that I left his house and my son.

FATHER: It's quite true. It was my fault.

LEADING ACTOR: (*To other actors.*) Look at this. What a show!

LEADING ACTRESS: And we're the audience.

YOUNG ACTOR: For a change.

335 PRODUCER: (*Beginning to be very interested.*) Let's listen to them! Quiet! Listen!

(*He goes down the steps into the auditorium and stands there as if to get an idea of what the scene will look like from the audience's viewpoint.*)

SON: (*Without moving, coldly, quietly, ironically.*) Yes, listen to his little scrap of philosophy. He's going to tell you all about the Daemon of Experiment.

FATHER: You're a cynical idiot, and I've told you so a hundred 340 times. (*To the* PRODUCER *who is now in the stalls.*) He sneers at me because of this expression I've found to defend myself.

SON: Words, words.

FATHER: Yes words, words! When we're faced by something we don't understand, by a sense of evil that seems as if it's 345 going to swallow us, don't we all find comfort in a word that tells us nothing but that calms us?

STEPDAUGHTER: And dulls your sense of remorse, too. That more than anything.

FATHER: Remorse? No, that's not true. It'd take more than 350 words to dull the sense of remorse in me.

STEPDAUGHTER: It's taken a little money too, just a little money. The money that he was going to offer as payment, gentlemen.

(*The* ACTORS *are horrified.*)

SON: (*Contemptuously to his stepsister.*) That's a filthy trick. 355

STEPDAUGHTER: A filthy trick? There it was in a pale blue envelope on the little mahogany table in the room behind the shop at Madam Pace's. You know Madame Pace, don't you? One of those Madames who sell 'Robes et Manteaux' so that they can attract poor girls like me from de- 360 cent families into their workroom.

SON: And she's bought the right to tyrannise over the whole lot of us with that money—with what he was going to pay her: and luckily—now listen carefully—he had no reason to pay it to her. 365

STEPDAUGHTER: But it was close!

MOTHER: (*Rising up angrily.*) Shame on you, daughter! Shame!

STEPDAUGHTER: Shame? Not shame, revenge! I'm desperate, desperate to live that scene! The room . . . over here the showcase of coats, there the divan, there the mirror, and 370 the screen, and over there in front of the window, that little mahogany table with the pale blue envelope and the money in it. I can see it all quite clearly. I could pick it up! But you should turn your faces away, gentlemen: because I'm nearly naked! I'm not blushing any longer—I leave 375 that to him. (*Pointing at the* FATHER.) But I tell you he was very pale, very pale then. (*To the* PRODUCER.) Believe me.

PRODUCER: I don't understand any more.

FATHER: I'm not surprised when you're attacked like that! Why don't you put your foot down and let me have my 380 say before you believe all these horrible slanders she's so viciously telling about me.

STEPDAUGHTER: We don't want to hear any of your long-winded fairy-stories.

FATHER: I'm not going to tell any fairy-stories! I want to ex- 385 plain things to him.

STEPDAUGHTER: I'm sure you do. Oh, yes! In your own special way.

(*The* PRODUCER *comes back up on stage to take control.*)

FATHER: But isn't that the cause of all the trouble? Words! We
390   all have a world of things inside ourselves and each one of
us has his own private world. How can we understand each
other if the words I use have the sense and the value that I
expect them to have, but whoever is listening to me inevitably thinks that those same words have a different sense
395   and value, because of the private world he has inside himself too. We think we understand each other: but we never
do. Look! All my pity, all my compassion for this woman
(*Pointing to the* MOTHER.) she sees as ferocious cruelty.

MOTHER: But he turned me out of the house!

400   FATHER: There, do you hear? I turned her out! She really believed that I had turned her out.

MOTHER: You know how to talk. I don't . . . But believe me,
sir, (*Turning to the* PRODUCER.) after he married me . . . I
can't think why! I was a poor, simple woman.

405   FATHER: But that was the reason! I married you for your simplicity, that's what I loved in you, believing—(*He stops because she is making gestures of contradiction. Then, seeing the
impossibility of making her understand, he throws his arms wide
in a gesture of desperation and turns back to the* PRODUCER.)

410   No, do you see? She says no! It's terrifying, sir, believe me,
terrifying, her deafness, her mental deafness. (*He taps his
forehead.*) Affection for her children, oh yes. But deaf,
mentally deaf, deaf, sir, to the point of desperation.

STEPDAUGHTER: Yes, but make him tell you what good all his
415   cleverness has brought us.

FATHER: If only we could see in advance all the harm that can
come from the good we think we are doing.

(*The* LEADING ACTRESS, *who has been growing angry watching the*
LEADING ACTOR *flirting with the* STEPDAUGHTER, *comes forward
and snaps at the* PRODUCER.)

LEADING ACTRESS: Excuse me, are we going to go on with
420   our rehearsal?

PRODUCER: Yes, of course. But I want to listen to this first.

YOUNG ACTOR: It's such a new idea.

YOUNG ACTRESS: It's fascinating.

LEADING ACTRESS: For those who are interested. (*She looks
meaningfully at the* LEADING ACTOR.)

425   PRODUCER: (*To the* FATHER.) Look here, you must explain
yourself more clearly. (*He sits down.*)

FATHER: Listen then. You see, there was a rather poor fellow
working for me as my assistant and secretary, very loyal: he
understood her in everything. (*Pointing to the* MOTHER.)

430   But without a hint of deceit, you must believe that: he was
good and simple, like her: neither of them was capable
even of thinking anything wrong, let alone doing it.

STEPDAUGHTER: So instead he thought of it for them and did
it too!

435   FATHER: It's not true! What I did was for their good—oh yes
and mine too, I admit it! The time had come when I
couldn't say a word to either of them without there immediately flashing between them a sympathetic look: each
one caught the other's eye for advice, about how to take
440   what I had said, how not to make me angry. Well, that was
enough, as I'm sure you'll understand, to put me in a bad
temper all the time, in a state of intolerable exasperation.

PRODUCER: Then why didn't you sack this secretary of yours?

FATHER: Right! In the end I did sack him! But then I had to
watch this poor woman wandering about in the house on   445
her own, forlorn, like a stray animal you take in out of pity.

MOTHER: It's quite true.

FATHER: (*Suddenly, turning to her, as if to stop her.*) And what
about the boy? Is that true as well?

MOTHER: But first he tore my son from me, sir.   450

FATHER: But not out of cruelty! It was so that he could grow
up healthy and strong, in touch with the earth.

STEPDAUGHTER: (*Pointing to the* SON *jeeringly.*) And look at the
result!

FATHER: (*Quickly.*) And is it my fault, too, that he's grown up   455
like this? I took him to a nurse in the country, a peasant,
because his mother didn't seem strong enough to me, although she is from a humble family herself. In fact that
was what made me marry her. Perhaps it was superstitious
of me; but what was I to do? I've always had this dreadful   460
longing for a kind of sound moral healthiness.

(*The* STEPDAUGHTER *breaks out again into noisy laughter.*)

Make her stop that! It's unbearable.

PRODUCER: Stop it will you? Let me listen, for God's sake.

(*When the* PRODUCER *has spoken to her, she resumes her previous
position . . . absorbed and distant, a half-smile on her lips. The*
PRODUCER *comes down into the auditorium again to see how it
looks from there.*)

FATHER: I couldn't bear the sight of this woman near me.
(*Pointing to the* MOTHER.) Not so much because of the an-   465
noyance she caused me, you see, or even the feeling of being stifled, being suffocated that I got from her, as for the
sorrow, the painful sorrow that I felt for her.

MOTHER: And he sent me away.

FATHER: With everything you needed, to the other man, to   470
set her free from me.

MOTHER: And to set yourself free!

FATHER: Oh, yes, I admit it. And what terrible things came
out of it. But I did it for the best, and more for her than
for me: I swear it! (*Folds his arms: then turns suddenly to the*   475
MOTHER.) I never lost sight of you did I? Until that fellow, without my knowing it, suddenly took you off to another town one day. He was idiotically suspicious of my
interest in them, a genuine interest, I assure you, without
any ulterior motive at all. I watched the new little family   480
growing up round her with unbelievable tenderness, she'll
confirm that. (*He points to the* STEPDAUGHTER.)

STEPDAUGHTER: Oh yes, I can indeed. I was a pretty little girl,
you know, with plaits down to my shoulders and my little
frilly knickers showing under my dress—so pretty—he   485
used to watch me coming out of school. He came to see
how I was maturing.

FATHER: That's shameful! It's monstrous.

STEPDAUGHTER: No it isn't! Why do you say it is?

FATHER: It's monstrous! Monstrous. (*He turns excitedly to the*   490
PRODUCER *and goes on in explanation.*) After she'd gone
away (*Pointing to the* MOTHER.), my house seemed empty.
She'd been like a weight on my spirit but she'd filled the

house with her presence. Alone in the empty rooms I wan-
495 dered about like a lost soul. This boy here, (*Indicating the*
SON.) growing up away from home—whenever he came
back to the home—I don't know—but he didn't seem to
be mine any more. We needed the mother between us, to
link us together, and so he grew up by himself, apart, with
500 no connection to me either through intellect or love. And
then—it must seem odd, but it's true—first I was curious
about and then strongly attracted to the little family that
had come about because of what I'd done. And the
thought of them began to fill all the emptiness that I felt
505 around me. I needed, I really needed to believe that she was
happy, wrapped up in the simple cares of her life, lucky because she was better off away from the complicated torments of a soul like mine. And to prove it, I used to watch
that child coming out of school.
510 STEPDAUGHTER: Listen to him! He used to follow me along the
street; he used to smile at me and when we came near the
house he'd wave his hand—like this! I watched him, wide-
eyed, puzzled. I didn't know who he was. I told my mother
about him and she knew at once who it must be. (MOTHER
515 *nods agreement.*) At first, she didn't let me go to school again,
at any rate for a few days. But when I did go back, I saw him
standing near the door again—looking ridiculous—with a
brown paper bag in his hand. He came close and petted me:
then he opened the bag and took out a beautiful straw hat
520 with a hoop of rosebuds round it—for me!
PRODUCER: All this is off the point, you know.
SON: (*Contemptuously.*) Yes . . . literature, literature.
FATHER: What do you mean, literature? This is real life: real
passions.
525 PRODUCER: That may be! But you can't put it on the stage
just like that.
FATHER: That's right you can't. Because all this is only leading up to the main action. I'm not suggesting that this part
should be put on the stage. In any case, you can see for
530 yourself, (*Pointing at the* STEPDAUGHTER.) she isn't a pretty
little girl any longer with plaits down to her shoulders.
STEPDAUGHTER: —and with frilly knickers showing under
her frock.
FATHER: The drama begins now: and it's new and complex.
535 STEPDAUGHTER: (*Coming forward, fierce and brooding.*) As soon
as my father died . . .
FATHER: (*Quickly, not giving her time to speak.*) They were so
miserable. They came back here, but I didn't know about
it because of the Mother's stubbornness. (*Pointing to the*
540 MOTHER.) She can't really write you know; but she could
have got her daughter to write, or the boy, or tell me that
they needed help.
MOTHER: But tell me, sir, how could I have known how he felt?
FATHER: And hasn't that always been your fault? You've never
545 known anything about how I felt.
MOTHER: After all the years away from him and after all that
had happened.
FATHER: And was it my fault if that fellow took you so far
away? (*Turning back to the* PRODUCER.) Suddenly,
550 overnight, I tell you, he'd found a job away from here without my knowing anything about it. I couldn't possibly trace
them; and then, naturally I suppose, my interest in them

grew less over the years. The drama broke out, unexpected
and violent, when they came back: when I was driven in
misery by the needs of my flesh, still alive with desire . . . 555
and it is misery, you know, unspeakable misery for the man
who lives alone and who detests sordid, casual affairs; not
old enough to do without women, but not young enough
to be able to go and look for one without shame! Misery?
Is that what I called it. It's horrible, it's revolting, because 560
there isn't a woman who will give her love to him any
more. And when he realises this, he should do without . . .
It's easy to say though. Each of us, face to face with other
men, is clothed with some sort of dignity, but we know
only too well all the unspeakable things that go on in the 565
heart. We surrender, we given in to temptation: but afterwards we rise up out of it very quickly, in a desperate hurry
to rebuild our dignity, whole and firm as if it were a grave-
stone that would cover every sign and memory of our
shame, and hide it from even our own eyes. Everyone's like 570
that, only some of us haven't the courage to talk about it.
STEPDAUGHTER: But they've all got the courage to do it!
FATHER: Yes! But only in secret! That's why it takes more
courage to talk about it. Because if a man does talk about
it—what happens then?—everybody says he's a cynic. 575
And it's simply not true; he's just like everybody else; only
better perhaps, because he's not afraid to use his intelligence to point out the blushing shame of human bestiality, that man, the beast, shuts his eyes to, trying to pretend
it doesn't exist. And what about woman—what is she 580
like? She looks at you invitingly, teasingly. You take her in
your arms. But as soon as she feels your arms round her
she closes her eyes. It's the sign of her mission, the sign by
which she says to a man, 'Blind yourself—I'm blind!'
STEPDAUGHTER: And when she doesn't close her eyes any 585
more? What then? When she doesn't feel the need to hide
from herself any more, to shut her eyes and hide her own
shame. When she can see instead, dispassionately and dry-
eyed this blushing shame of a man who has blinded himself, who is without love. What then? Oh, then what 590
disgust, what utter disgust she feels for all these intellectual complications, for all this philosophy that points to
the bestiality of man and then tries to defend him, to excuse him . . . I can't listen to him, sir. Because when a man
says he needs to 'simplify' life like this—reducing it to 595
bestiality—and throws away every human scrap of innocent desire, genuine feeling, idealism, duty, modesty,
shame, then there's nothing more contemptible and nau-
seating than his remorse—crocodile tears!
PRODUCER: Let's get to the point, let's get to the point. This 600
is all chat.
FATHER: Right then! But a fact is like a sack—it won't stand up
if it's empty. To make it stand up, first you have to put in it all
the reasons and feelings that caused it in the first place. I
couldn't possibly have known that when that fellow died 605
they'd come back here, that they were desperately poor and
that the Mother had gone out to work as a dressmaker, nor
that she'd gone to work for Madame Pace, of all people.
STEPDAUGHTER: She's a very high-class dressmaker—you
must understand that. She apparently has only high-class 610
customers, but she has arranged things carefully so that

these high-class customers in fact serve her—they give her a respectable front . . . without spoiling things for the other ladies at the shop, who are not quite so high-class at all.

615 MOTHER: Believe me, sir, the idea never entered my head that the old hag gave me work because she had an eye on my daughter . . .

STEPDAUGHTER: Poor Mummy! Do you know what that woman would do when I took back the work that my
620 mother had been doing? She would point out how the dress had been ruined by giving it to my mother to sew: she bargained, she grumbled. So, you see, I paid for it, while this poor woman here thought she was sacrificing herself for me and these two children, sewing dresses all night for Madame Pace.

(*The* ACTORS *make gestures and noises of disgust.*)

625 PRODUCER: (*Quickly.*) And there one day, you met . . .

STEPDAUGHTER: (*Pointing at the* FATHER.) Yes, him. Oh, he was an old customer of hers! What a scene that's going to be, superb!

FATHER: With her, the mother, arriving—

STEPDAUGHTER: (*Quickly, viciously.*)—Almost in time!

630 FATHER: (*Crying out.*)—No, just in time, just in time! Because, luckily, I found out who she was in time. And I took them all back to my house, sir. Can you imagine the situation now, for the two of us living in the same house? She, just as you see her here: and I, not able to look her in the face.

635 STEPDAUGHTER: It's so absurd! Do you think it's possible for me, sir, after what happened at Madame Pace's, to pretend that I'm a modest little miss, well brought up and virtuous just so that I can fit in with his damned pretensions to a 'sound moral healthiness'?

640 FATHER: This is the real drama for me; the belief that we all, you see, think of ourselves as one single person: but it's not true: each of us is several different people, and all these people live inside us. With one person we seem like this and with another we seem very different. But we always
645 have the illusion of being the same person for everybody and of always being the same person in everything we do. But it's not true! It's not true! We find this out for ourselves very clearly when by some terrible chance we're suddenly stopped in the middle of doing something and we're left dangling there, suspended. We realise then, that
650 every part of us was not involved in what we'd been doing and that it would be a dreadful injustice of other people to judge us only by this one action as we dangle there, hanging in chains, fixed for all eternity, as if the whole of one's personality were summed up in that single, inter-
655 rupted action. Now do you understand this girl's treachery? She accidentally found me somewhere I shouldn't have been, doing something I shouldn't have been doing! She discovered a part of me that shouldn't have existed for
660 her: and now she wants to fix on me a reality that I should never have had to assume for her: it came from a single brief and shameful moment in my life. This is what hurts me most of all. And you'll see that the play will make a tremendous impact from this idea of mine. But then,
665 there's the position of the others. His . . .

(*Pointing to the* SON.)

SON: (*Shrugging his shoulders scornfully.*) Leave me out of it. I don't come into this.

FATHER: Why don't you come into this?

SON: I don't come into it and I don't want to come into it, because you know perfectly well that I wasn't intended to 670 be mixed up with you lot.

STEPDAUGHTER: We're vulgar, common people, you see! He's a fine gentleman. But you've probably noticed that every now and then I look at him contemptuously, and when I do, he lowers his eyes—he knows the harm he's done me. 675

SON: (*Not looking at her.*) I have?

STEPDAUGHTER: Yes, you. It's your fault, dearie, that I went on the streets! Your fault! (*Movement of horror from the* ACTORS.) Did you or didn't you, with your attitude, deny us—I won't say the intimacy of your home—but that simple hospital- 680 ity that makes guests feel comfortable? We were intruders who had come to invade the country of your 'legitimacy'! (*Turning to the* PRODUCER.) I'd like you to have seen some of the little scenes that went on between him and me, sir. He says that I tyrannised over everyone. But don't you see? 685 It was because of the way he treated us. He called it 'vile' that I should insist on the right we had to move into his house with my mother—and she's his mother too. And I went into the house as its mistress.

SON: (*Slowly coming forward.*) They're really enjoying them- 690 selves, aren't they, sir? It's easy when they all gang up against me. But try to imagine what happened: one fine day, there is a son sitting quietly at home and he sees arrive as bold as brass, a young woman like this, who cheekily asks for his father, and heaven knows what business she 695 has with him. Then he sees her come back with the same brazen look in her eye accompanied by that little girl there: and he sees her treat his father—without knowing why—in a most ambiguous and insolent way—asking him for money in a tone that leads one to suppose he re- 700 ally ought to give it, because he is obliged to do so.

FATHER: But I was obliged to do so: I owed it to your mother.

SON: And how was I to know that? When had I ever seen her before? When had I ever heard her mentioned? Then one day I see her come in with her (*Pointing to the* STEP- 705 DAUGHTER.), that boy and that little girl: they say to me, 'Oh, didn't you know? This is your mother, too.' Little by little I began to understand, mostly from her attitude (*Points to* STEPDAUGHTER.) why they'd come to live in the house so suddenly. I can't and I won't say what I feel, and 710 what I think. I wouldn't even like to confess it to myself. So I can't take any active part in this. Believe me, sir, I am a character who has not been fully developed dramatically, and I feel uncomfortable, most uncomfortable, in their company. So please leave me out of it. 715

FATHER: What! But it's precisely because you feel like this . . .

SON: (*Violently exasperated.*) How do you know what I feel? When have you ever bothered yourself about me?

FATHER: All right! I admit it! But isn't that a situation in itself? This withdrawing of yourself, it's cruel to me and to your 720 mother: when she came back to the house, seeing you almost for the first time, not recognising you, but knowing that you're her own son . . . (*Turning to point out the* MOTHER *to the* PRODUCER.) There, look at her: she's weeping.

725 STEPDAUGHTER: (*Angrily, stamping her foot.*) Like the fool she is!
FATHER: (*Quickly pointing at the* STEPDAUGHTER *to the* PRO-DUCER.) She can't stand that young man, you know. (*Turning and referring to the* SON.) He says that he doesn't come into it, but he's really the pivot of the action! Look here at this lit-
730 tle boy, who clings to his mother all the time, frightened, humiliated. And it's because of him over there! Perhaps this little boy's problem is the worst of all: he feels an outsider, more than the others do; he feels so mortified, so humiliated
735 just being in the house,—because it's charity, you see. (*Quietly.*) He's like his father: timid; he doesn't say anything . . .
PRODUCER: It's not a good idea at all, using him: you don't know what a nuisance children are on the stage.
FATHER: He won't need to be on the stage for long. Nor will the little girl—she's the first to go.
740 PRODUCER: That's good! Yes. I tell you all this interests me—it interests me very much. I'm sure we've the material here for a good play.
STEPDAUGHTER: (*Trying to push herself in.*) With a character like me you have!
745 FATHER: (*Driving her off, wanting to hear what the* PRODUCER *has decided.*) You stay out of it!
PRODUCER: (*Going on, ignoring the interruption.*) It's new, yes.
FATHER: Oh, it's absolutely new!
PRODUCER: You've got a nerve, though, haven't you, coming
750 here and throwing it at me like this?
FATHER: I'm sure you understand. Born as we are for the stage . . .
PRODUCER: Are you amateur actors?
FATHER: No! I say we are born for the stage because . . .
755 PRODUCER: Come on now! You're an old hand at this, at acting!
FATHER: No I'm not. I only act, as everyone does, the part in life that he's chosen for himself, or that others have chosen for him. And you can see that sometimes my own passion gets a bit out of hand, a bit theatrical, as it does with all of us.
760 PRODUCER: Maybe, maybe . . . But you do see, don't you, that without an author . . . I could give you someone's address . . .
FATHER: Oh no! Look here! You do it.
PRODUCER: Me? What are you talking about?
FATHER: Yes, you. Why not?
765 PRODUCER: Because I've never written anything!
FATHER: Well, why not start now, if you don't mind my suggesting it? There's nothing to it. Everybody's doing it. And your job is even easier, because we're here, all of us, alive before you.
770 PRODUCER: That's not enough.
FATHER: Why isn't it enough? When you've seen us live our drama . . .
PRODUCER: Perhaps so. But we'll still need someone to write it.
FATHER: Only to write it down, perhaps, while it happens in
775 front of him—live—scene by scene. It'll be enough to sketch it out simply first and then run through it.
PRODUCER: (*Coming back up, tempted by the idea.*) Do you know I'm almost tempted . . . just for fun . . . it might work.
FATHER: Of course it will. You'll see what wonderful scenes
780 will come right out of it! I could tell you what they will be!
PRODUCER: You tempt me . . . you tempt me! We'll give it a chance. Come with me to the office. (*Turning to the* ACTORS.) Take a break: but don't go far away. Be back in a quarter of an hour or twenty minutes. (*To the* FATHER.) Let's see, let's try
785 it out. Something extraordinary might come out of this.

FATHER: Of course it will! Don't you think it'd be better if the others came too? (*Indicating the other* CHARACTERS.)
PRODUCER: Yes, come on, come on. (*Going, then turning to speak to the* ACTORS.) Don't forget: don't be late: back in a quarter of an hour.   790

(*The* PRODUCER *and the* SIX CHARACTERS *cross the stage and go. The* ACTORS *look at each other in astonishment.*)

LEADING ACTOR: Is he serious? What's he going to do?
YOUNG ACTOR: I think he's gone round the bend.
ANOTHER ACTOR: Does he expect to make up a play in five minutes?
YOUNG ACTOR: Yes, like the old actors in the commedia   795
del'arte!
LEADING ACTRESS: Well if he thinks I'm going to appear in that sort of nonsense . . .
YOUNG ACTOR: Nor me!
FOURTH ACTOR: I should like to know who they are.   800
THIRD ACTOR: Who do you think? They're probably escaped lunatics—or crooks.
YOUNG ACTOR: And is he taking them seriously?
YOUNG ACTRESS: It's vanity. The vanity of seeing himself as an author.   805
LEADING ACTOR: I've never heard of such a thing! If the theatre, ladies and gentlemen, is reduced to this . . .
FIFTH ACTOR: I'm enjoying it!
THIRD ACTOR: Really? We shall have to wait and see what happens next I suppose.   810

(*Talking, they leave the stage. Some go out through the back door, some to the dressing-rooms.*)

(*The Curtain stays up.*)

(*The interval lasts twenty minutes.*)

ACT TWO

The theatre warning-bell sounds to call the audience back. From the dressing-rooms, the door at the back and even from the auditorium, the ACTORS, *the* STAGE MANAGER, *the* STAGE HANDS, *the* PROMPTER, *the* PROPERTY MAN *and the* PRODUCER, *accompanied by the* SIX CHARACTERS *all come back on to the stage.*

The house lights go out and the stage lights come on again.

PRODUCER: Come on, everybody! Are we all here? Quiet now! Listen! Let's get started! Stage manager?
STAGE MANAGER: Yes, I'm here.
PRODUCER: Give me that little parlour setting, will you? A couple of plain flats and a door flat will do. Hurry up with it!   5

(*The* STAGE MANAGER *runs off to order someone to do this immediately and at the same time the* PRODUCER *is making arrangements with the* PROPERTY MAN, *the* PROMPTER, *and the* ACTORS: *the two flats and the door flat are painted in pink and gold stripes.*)

PRODUCER: (*To* PROPERTY MAN.) Go see if we have a sofa in stock.
PROPERTY MAN: Yes, there's that green one.
STEPDAUGHTER: No, no, not a green one! It was yellow, yellow velvet with flowers on it: it was enormous! And so   10
comfortable!

PROPERTY MAN: We haven't got one like that.

PRODUCER: It doesn't matter! Give me whatever there is.

STEPDAUGHTER: What do you mean, it doesn't matter? It was Mme. Pace's famous sofa.

PRODUCER: It's only for a rehearsal! Please, don't interfere. (*To the* STAGE MANAGER.) Oh, and see if there's a shop window, will you—preferably a long, low one.

STEPDAUGHTER: And a little table, a little mahogany table for the blue envelope.

STAGE MANAGER: (*To the* PRODUCER.) There's that little gold one.

PRODUCER: That'll do—bring it.

FATHER: A mirror!

STEPDAUGHTER: And a screen! A screen, please, or I won't be able to manage, will I?

STAGE MANAGER: All right. We've lots of big screens, don't you worry.

PRODUCER: (*To* STEPDAUGHTER.) Then don't you want some coat-hangers and some clothes racks.

STEPDAUGHTER: Yes, lots of them, lots of them.

PRODUCER: (*To the* STAGE MANAGER.) See how many there are and have them brought up.

STAGE MANAGER: Right, I'll see to it.

(*The* STAGE MANAGER *goes off to do it: and while the* PRODUCER *is talking to the* PROMPTER, *the* CHARACTERS *and the* ACTORS, *the* STAGE MANAGER *is telling the* SCENE SHIFTERS *where to set up the furniture they have brought.*)

PRODUCER: (*To the* PROMPTER.) Now you, go sit down, will you? Look, this is an outline of the play, act by act. (*He hands him several sheets of paper.*) But you'll need to be on your toes.

PROMPTER: Shorthand?

PRODUCER: (*Pleasantly surprised.*) Oh, good! You know shorthand?

PROMPTER: I don't know much about prompting, but I do know about shorthand.

PRODUCER: Thank God for that anyway! (*He turns to a* STAGE HAND.) Go fetch me some paper from my office—lots of it—as much as you can find!

(*The* STAGE HAND *goes running off and then comes back shortly with a bundle of paper that he gives to the* PROMPTER.)

PRODUCER: (*Crossing to the* PROMPTER.) Follow the scenes, one after another, as they are played and try to get the lines down . . . at least the most important ones. (*Then turning to the* ACTORS.) Get out of the way everybody! Here, go over to the prompt side (*Pointing to stage left.*) and pay attention!

LEADING ACTRESS: But, excuse me, we . . .

PRODUCER: (*Anticipating her.*) You won't be expected to improvise, don't worry!

LEADING ACTOR: Then what are we expected to do?

PRODUCER: Nothing! Just go over there, listen and watch. You'll all be given your parts later written out. Right now we're going to rehearse, as well as we can. And they will be doing the rehearsal. (*He points to the* CHARACTERS.)

FATHER: (*Rather bewildered, as if he had fallen from the clouds into the middle of the confusion on the stage.*) We are? Excuse me, but what do you mean, a rehearsal?

PRODUCER: I mean a rehearsal—a rehearsal for the benefit of the actors. (*Pointing to the* ACTORS.)

FATHER: But if we are the characters . . .

PRODUCER: That's right, you're the 'characters': but characters don't act here, my dear chap. It's actors who act here. The characters are there in the script—(*Pointing to the* PROMPTER.) that's when there is a script.

FATHER: That's the point! Since there isn't one and you have the luck to have the characters alive in front of you . . .

PRODUCER: Great! You want to do everything yourselves, do you? To act your own play, to produce your own play!

FATHER: Well yes, just as we are.

PRODUCER: That would be an experience for us, I can tell you!

LEADING ACTOR: And what about us? What would we be doing then?

PRODUCER: Don't tell me you think you know how to act! Don't make me laugh! (*The* ACTORS *in fact laugh.*) There you are, you see, you've made them laugh. (*Then remembering.*) But let's get back to the point! We need to cast the play. Well, that's easy: it almost casts itself. (*To the* SECOND ACTRESS.) You, the mother. (*To the* FATHER.) You'll need to give her a name.

FATHER: Amalia.

PRODUCER: But that's the real name of your wife isn't it? We can't use her real name.

FATHER: But why not? That is her name . . . But perhaps if this lady is to play the part . . . (*Indicating the* SECOND ACTRESS *vaguely with a wave of his hand.*) I think of her as Amalia . . . (*Pointing to the* MOTHER.) But do as you like . . . (*A little confused.*) I don't know what to say . . . I'm already starting to . . . how can I explain it . . . to sound false, my own words sound like someone else's.

PRODUCER: Now don't worry yourself about it, don't worry about it at all. We'll work out the right tone of voice. As for the name, if you want it to be Amalia, then Amalia it shall be: or we can find another. For the moment we'll refer to the characters like this: (*To the* YOUNG ACTOR, *the juvenile lead.*) you are The Son. (*To the* LEADING ACTRESS.) You, of course, are The Stepdaughter.

STEPDAUGHTER: (*Excitedly.*) What did you say? That woman is me? (*Bursts into laughter.*)

PRODUCER: (*Angrily.*) What are you laughing at?

LEADING ACTRESS: (*Indignantly.*) Nobody has ever dared to laugh at me before! Either you treat me with respect or I'm walking out! (*Starting to go.*)

STEPDAUGHTER: I'm sorry. I wasn't really laughing at you.

PRODUCER: (*To the* STEPDAUGHTER.) You should feel proud to be played by . . .

LEADING ACTRESS: (*Quickly, scornfully.*) . . . that woman!

STEPDAUGHTER: But I wasn't thinking about her, honestly. I was thinking about me: I can't see myself in you at all . . . you're not a bit like me!

FATHER: Yes, that's right: you see, our meaning . . .

PRODUCER: What are you talking about, 'our meaning'? Do you think you have exclusive rights to what you represent? Do you think it can only exist inside you? Not a bit of it!

FATHER: What? Don't we even have our own meaning?

PRODUCER: Not a bit of it! Whatever you mean is only material here, to which the actors give form and body, voice and gesture, and who, through their art, have given expression to much better material than what you have to offer: yours is really very trivial and if it stands up on the stage, the credit, believe me, will all be due to my actors.

125 FATHER: I don't dare to contradict you. But you for your part, must believe me—it doesn't seem trivial to us. We are suffering terribly now, with these bodies, these faces . . .

PRODUCER: (*Interrupting impatiently.*) Yes, well, the make-up will change that, make-up will change that, at least as far as the faces are concerned.

130 FATHER: Yes, but the voices, the gestures . . .

PRODUCER: That's enough! You can't come on the stage here as yourselves. It is our actors who will represent you here: and let that be the end of it!

135 FATHER: I understand that. But now I think I see why our author who saw us alive as we are here now, didn't want to put us on the stage. I don't want to offend your actors. God forbid that I should! But I think that if I saw myself represented . . . by I don't know whom . . .

140 LEADING ACTOR: (*Rising majestically and coming forward, followed by a laughing group of* YOUNG ACTRESSES.) By me, if you don't object.

FATHER: (*Respectfully, smoothly.*) I shall be honoured, sir. (*He bows.*) But I think, that no matter how hard this gentleman

145 works with all his will and all his art to identify himself with me . . . (*He stops, confused.*)

LEADING ACTOR: Yes, go on.

FATHER: Well, I was saying the performance he will give, even if he is made up to look like me . . . I mean with the dif-

150 ference in our appearance . . . (*All the* ACTORS *laugh.*) it will be difficult for it to be a performance of me as I really am. It will be more like—well, not just because of his figure—it will be more an interpretation of what I am, what he believes me to be, and not how I know myself to

155 be. And it seems to me that this should be taken into account by those who are going to comment on us.

PRODUCER: So you are already worrying about what the critics will say, are you? And I'm still waiting to get this thing started! The critics can say what they like: and we'll

160 worry about putting on the play. If we can! (*Stepping out of the group and looking around.*) Come on, come on! Is the scene set for us yet? (*To the* ACTORS *and* CHARACTERS.) Out of the way! Let's have a look at it. (*Climbing down off the stage.*) Don't let's waste any more time. (*To the* STEP-

165 DAUGHTER.) Does it look all right to you?

STEPDAUGHTER: What? That? I don't recognise it at all.

PRODUCER: Good God! Did you expect us to reconstruct the room at the back of Mme. Pace's shop here on the stage? (*To the* FATHER.) Did you say the room had flowered wallpaper?

170 FATHER: White, yes.

PRODUCER: Well it's not white: it's striped. That sort of thing doesn't matter at all! As for furniture, it looks to me as if we have nearly everything we need. Move that little table a bit further downstage. (*A* STAGE HAND *does it. To the*

175 PROPERTY MAN.) Go and fetch an envelope, pale blue if you can find one, and give it to that gentleman there. (*Pointing to the* FATHER.)

STAGE HAND: An envelope for letters?

PRODUCER: }
FATHER: } Yes, an envelope for letters!

180 STAGE HAND: Right. (*He goes off.*)

PRODUCER: Now then, come on! The first scene is the young lady's. (*The* LEADING ACTRESS *comes to the centre.*) No, no, not yet. I said the young lady's. (*He points to the* STEP-DAUGHTER.) You stay there and watch.

STEPDAUGHTER: (*Adding quickly.*) . . . how I bring it to life. 185

LEADING ACTRESS: (*Resenting this.*) I shall know how to bring it to life, don't you worry, when I am allowed to.

PRODUCER: (*His head in his hands.*) Ladies, please, no more arguments! Now then. The first scene is between the young lady and Mme. Pace. Oh! (*Worried, turning round and look-* 190 *ing out into the auditorium.*) Where is Mme. Pace?

FATHER: She isn't here with us.

PRODUCER: So what do we do now?

FATHER: But she is real. She's real too!

PRODUCER: All right. So where is she? 195

FATHER: May I deal with this? (*Turns to the* ACTRESSES.) Would each of you ladies be kind enough to lend me a hat, a coat, a scarf or something?

ACTRESSES: (*Some are surprised or amused.*) What? My scarf? A coat? What's he want my hat for? What are you wanting 200 to do with them? (*All the* ACTRESSES *are laughing.*)

FATHER: Oh, nothing much, just hang them up here on the racks for a minute or two. Perhaps someone would be kind enough to lend me a coat?

ACTORS: Just a coat? Come on, more! The man must be mad. 205

AN ACTRESS: What for? Only my coat?

FATHER: Yes, to hang up here, just for a moment. I'm very grateful to you. Do you mind?

ACTRESSES: (*Taking off various hats, coats, scarves, laughing and go-ing to hang them on the racks.*) Why not? Here you are. I re- 210 ally think it's crazy. Is it to dress the set?

FATHER: Yes, exactly. It's to dress the set.

PRODUCER: Would you mind telling me what you are doing?

FATHER: Yes, of course: perhaps, if we dress the set better, she will be drawn by the articles of her trade and, who knows, 215 she may even come to join us . . . (*He invites them to watch the door at the back of the set.*) Look! Look!

(*The door at the back opens and* MME. PACE *takes a few steps down-stage: she is a gross old harridan wearing a ludicrous carroty-coloured wig with a single red rose stuck in at one side, Spanish fashion: garishly made-up: in a vulgar but stylish red silk dress, holding an ostrich-feather fan in one hand and a cigarette between two fingers in the other. At the sight of this Apparition, the* ACTORS *and the* PRODUCER *im-mediately jump off the stage with cries of fear, leaping down into the au-ditorium and up the aisles. The* STEPDAUGHTER, *however, runs across to* MME. PACE, *and greets her respectfully, as if she were the mistress.*)

STEPDAUGHTER: (*Running across to her.*) Here she is! Here she is!

FATHER: (*Smiling broadly.*) It's her! What did I tell you? Here she is! 220

PRODUCER: (*Recovering from his shock, indignantly.*) What sort of trick is this?

LEADING ACTOR: (*Almost at the same time as the others.*) What the hell is happening?

JUVENILE LEAD: Where on earth did they get that extra from? 225

YOUNG ACTRESS: They were keeping her hidden!

LEADING ACTRESS: It's a game, a conjuring trick!

FATHER: Wait a minute! Why do you want to spoil a miracle by being factual. Can't you see this is a miracle of reality, that is born, brought to life, lured here, reproduced, just 230 for the sake of this scene, with more right to be alive here than you have? Perhaps it has more truth than you have yourselves. Which actress can improve on Mme. Pace there? Well? That is the real Mme. Pace. You must admit

235　that the actress who plays her will be less true than she is herself—and there she is in person! Look! My daughter recognised her straight away and went to meet her. Now watch—just watch this scene.

(*Hesitantly, the* PRODUCER *and the* ACTORS *move back to their original places on the stage.*)

(*But the scene between the* STEPDAUGHTER *and* MME. PACE *has already begun while the* ACTORS *were protesting and the* FATHER *explaining: it is being played under their breaths, very quietly, very naturally, in a way that is obviously impossible on stage. So when the* ACTORS' *attention is recalled by the* FATHER *they turn and see that* MME. PACE *has just put her hand under the* STEPDAUGHTER's *chin to make her lift her head up: they also hear her speak in a way that is unintelligible to them. They watch and listen hard for a few moments, then they start to make fun of them.*)

PRODUCER: Well?
240　LEADING ACTOR: What's she saying?
　　　LEADING ACTRESS: Can't hear a thing!
　　　JUVENILE LEAD: Louder! Speak up!
　　　STEPDAUGHTER: (*Leaving* MME. PACE *who has an astonishing smile on her face, and coming down to the* ACTORS.) Louder?
245　What do you mean, 'Louder'? What we're talking about you can't talk about loudly. I could shout about it a moment ago to embarrass him (*Pointing to the* FATHER.) to shame him and to get my own back on him! But it's a different matter for Mme. Pace. It would mean prison for her.
250　PRODUCER: What the hell are you on about? Here in the theatre you have to make yourself heard! Don't you see that? We can't hear you even from here, and we're on the stage with you! Imagine what it would be like with an audience out front! You need to make the scene go! And after all,
255　you would speak normally to each other when you're alone, and you will be, because we shan't be here anyway. I mean we're only here because it's a rehearsal. So just imagine that there you are in the room at the back of the shop, and there's no one to hear you.

(*The* STEPDAUGHTER, *with a knowing smile, wags her finger and her head rather elegantly, as if to say no.*)

260　PRODUCER: Why not?
　　　STEPDAUGHTER: (*Mysteriously, whispering loudly.*) Because there is someone who will hear if she speaks normally. (*Pointing to* MME. PACE.)
　　　PRODUCER: (*Anxiously.*) You're not going to make someone
265　else appear are you?

(*The* ACTORS *get ready to dive off the stage again.*)

　　　FATHER: No, no. She means me. I ought to be over there, waiting behind the door: and Mme. Pace knows I'm there, so excuse me will you: I'll go there now so that I shall be ready for my entrance.

(*He goes towards the back of the stage.*)

270　PRODUCER: (*Stopping him.*) No, no wait a minute! You must remember the stage conventions! Before you can go on to that part . . .

STEPDAUGHTER: (*Interrupts him.*) Oh yes, let's get on with that part. Now! Now! I'm dying to do that scene. If he wants to go through it now, I'm ready!　275
PRODUCER: (*Shouting.*) But before that we must have, clearly stated, the scene between you and her. (*Pointing to* MME. PACE.) Do you see?
STEPDAUGHTER: Oh God! She's only told me what you already know, that my mother's needlework is badly done 280 again, the dress is spoilt and that I shall have to be patient if I want her to go on helping us out of our mess.
MME. PACE: (*Coming forward, with a great air of importance.*) Ah, yes, sir, for that I do not wish to make a profit, to make advantage.　285
PRODUCER: (*Half frightened.*) What? Does she really speak like that?

(*All the* ACTORS *burst out laughing.*)

STEPDAUGHTER: (*Laughing too.*) Yes, she speaks like that, half in Spanish, in the silliest way imaginable!
MME. PACE: Ah it is not good manners that you laugh at me 290 when I make myself to speak, as I can, English, señor.
PRODUCER: No, no, you're right! Speak like that, please speak like that, madam. It'll be marvellous. Couldn't be better! It'll add a little touch of comedy to a rather crude situation. Speak like that! It'll be great!　295
STEPDAUGHTER: Great! Why not? When you hear a proposition made in that sort of accent, it'll almost seem like a joke, won't it? Perhaps you'll want to laugh when you hear that there's an 'old señor' who wants to 'amuse himself with me'—isn't that right, Madame?　300
MME. PACE: Not so old . . . but not quite young, no? But if he is not to your taste . . . he is, how you say, discreet!

(*The* MOTHER *leaps up, to the astonishment and dismay of the* ACTORS *who had not been paying any attention to her, so that when she shouts out they are startled and then smilingly restrain her: however she has already snatched off* MME. PACE's *wig and flung it on the floor.*)

MOTHER: You witch! Witch! Murderess! Oh, my daughter!
STEPDAUGHTER: (*Running across and taking hold of the* MOTHER.) No! No! Mother! Please!　305
FATHER: (*Running across to her as well.*) Calm yourself, calm yourself! Come and sit down.
MOTHER: Get her away from here!
STEPDAUGHTER: (*To the* PRODUCER *who has also crossed to her.*) My mother can't bear to be in the same place with her.　310
FATHER: (*Also speaking quietly to the* PRODUCER.) They can't possibly be in the same place! That's why she wasn't with us when we first came, do you see! If they meet, everything's given away from the very beginning.
PRODUCER: It's not important, that's not important! This is 315 only a first run-through at the moment! It's all useful stuff, even if it is confused. I'll sort it all out later. (*Turning to the* MOTHER *and taking her to sit down on her chair.*) Come on my dear, take it easy, take it easy: come and sit down again.
STEPDAUGHTER: Go on, Mme. Pace.　320
MME. PACE: (*Offended.*) Oh no, thank-you! I no longer do nothing here with your mother present.
STEPDAUGHTER: Get on with it, bring in this 'old señor' who wants to 'amuse himself with me'! (*Turning majestically to*

325   *the others.*) You see, this next scene has got to be played out—we must do it now. (*To* MME. PACE.) Oh, you can go!

MME. PACE: Ah, I go, I go—I go! Most probably I go!

(*She leaves banging her wig back into place, glaring furiously at the* ACTORS *who applaud her exit, laughing loudly.*)

STEPDAUGHTER: (*To the* FATHER.) Now you come on! No, you don't need to go off again! Come back! Pretend
330   you've just come in! Look, I'm standing here with my eyes on the ground, modestly—well, come on, speak up! Use that special sort of voice, like somebody who has just come in. 'Good afternoon, my dear.'

PRODUCER: (*Off the stage by now.*) Look here, who's the direc-
335   tor here, you or me? (*To the* FATHER *who looks uncertain and bewildered.*) Go on, do as she says: go upstage—no, no don't bother to make an entrance. Then come down stage again.

(*The* FATHER *does as he is told, half mesmerised. He is very pale but already involved in the reality of his recreated life, smiles as he draws near the back of the stage, almost if he genuinely is not aware of the drama that is about to sweep over him. The* ACTORS *are immediately intent on the scene that is beginning now.*)

THE SCENE

FATHER: (*Coming forward with a new note in his voice.*) Good afternoon, my dear.

STEPDAUGHTER: (*Her head down trying to hide her fright.*) Good afternoon.

5   FATHER: (*Studying her a little under the brim of her hat which partly hides her face from him and seeing that she is very young, he exclaims to himself a little complacently and a little guardedly because of the danger of being compromised in a risky adventure.*) Ah . . . but . . . tell me, this won't be the first time, will it?
10   The first time you've been here?

STEPDAUGHTER: No, sir.

FATHER: You've been here before? (*And after the* STEPDAUGH-TER *has nodded an answer.*) More than once? (*He waits for her reply: tries again to look at her under the brim of her hat,*
15   *smiles, then says.*) Well then . . . it shouldn't be too . . . May I take off your hat?

STEPDAUGHTER: (*Quickly, to stop him, unable to conceal her shudder of fear and disgust.*) No, don't! I'll do it!

(*She takes it off unsteadily.*)

(*The* MOTHER *watches the scene intently with the* SON *and the two smaller children who cling close to her all the time: they make a group on one side of the stage opposite the* ACTORS. *She follows the words and actions of the* FATHER *and the* STEPDAUGHTER *in this scene with a variety of expressions on her face—sadness, dismay, anxiety, horror: sometimes she turns her face away and sobs.*)

MOTHER: Oh God! Oh God!

20   FATHER: (*He stops as if turned to stone by the sobbing: then he goes on in the same tone of voice.*) Here, give it to me. I'll hang it up for you. (*He takes the hat in his hand.*) But such a pretty, dear little head like yours should have a much smarter hat than this! Would you like to help me choose one, then,
25   from these hats of Madame's hanging up here? Would you?

YOUNG ACTRESS: (*Interrupting.*) Be careful! Those are our hats!

PRODUCER: (*Quickly and angrily.*) For God's sake, shut up! Don't try to be funny! We're rehearsing! (*Turns back to the* STEPDAUGHTER.) Please go on, will you, from where you
30   were interrupted.

STEPDAUGHTER: (*Going on.*) No, thank you, sir.

FATHER: Oh, don't say no to me please! Say you'll have one—to please me. Isn't this a pretty one—look! And then it will please Madame too, you know. She's put them out here on
35   purpose, of course.

STEPDAUGHTER: No, look, I could never wear it.

FATHER: Are you thinking of what they would say at home when you went in wearing a new hat? Goodness me! Don't you know what to do? Shall I tell you what to say at home?

STEPDAUGHTER: (*Furiously, nearly exploding.*) That's not why! I
40   couldn't wear it because . . . as you can see: you should have noticed it before. (*Indicating her black dress.*)

FATHER: You're in mourning! Oh, forgive me. You're right, I see that now. Please forgive me. Believe me, I'm really very
45   sorry.

STEPDAUGHTER: (*Gathering all her strength and making herself overcome her contempt and revulsion.*) That's enough. Don't go on, that's enough. I ought to be thanking you and not letting you blame yourself and get upset. Don't think any
50   more about what I told you, please. And I should do the same. (*Forcing herself to smile and adding.*) I should try to forget that I'm dressed like this.

PRODUCER: (*Interrupting, turning to the* PROMPTER *in the box and jumping up on the stage again.*) Hold it, hold it! Don't put that last line down, leave it out. (*Turning to the* FATHER
55   *and the* STEPDAUGHTER.) It's going well! It's going well! (*Then to the* FATHER *alone.*) Then we'll put in there the bit that we talked about. (*To the* ACTORS.) That scene with the hats is good, isn't it?

STEPDAUGHTER: But the best bit is coming now! Why can't
60   we get on with it?

PRODUCER: Just be patient, wait a minute. (*Turning and moving across to the* ACTORS.) Of course, it'll all have to be made a lot more light-hearted.

LEADING ACTOR: We shall have to play it a lot quicker, I think.
65

LEADING ACTRESS: Of course: there's nothing particularly difficult in it. (*To the* LEADING ACTOR.) Shall we run through it now?

LEADING ACTOR: Yes right . . . Shall we take it from my entrance? (*He goes to his position behind the door upstage.*)
70

PRODUCER: (*To the* LEADING ACTRESS.) Now then, listen, imagine the scene between you and Mme. Pace is finished. I'll write it up myself properly later on. You ought to be over here I think—(*She goes the opposite way.*) Where are you going now?
75

LEADING ACTRESS: Just a minute, I want to get my hat—(*She crosses to take her hat from the stand.*)

PRODUCER: Right, good, ready now? You are standing here with your head down.

STEPDAUGHTER: (*Very amused.*) But she's not dressed in black!
80

LEADING ACTRESS: Oh, but I shall be, and I'll look a lot better than you do, darling.

PRODUCER: (*To the* STEPDAUGHTER.) Shut up, will you! Go over there and watch! You might learn something! (*Clapping his hands.*) Right! Come on! Quiet please! Take it
85   from his entrance.

(*He climbs off stage so that he can see better. The door opens at the back of the set and the* LEADING ACTOR *enters with the lively, knowing air of an ageing roué. The playing of the following scene by the* ACTORS *must seem from the very beginning to be something quite different from the earlier scene, but without having the faintest air of parody in it.*)

(*Naturally the* STEPDAUGHTER *and the* FATHER, *unable to see themselves in the* LEADING ACTOR *and* LEADING ACTRESS, *hearing their words said by them, express their reactions in different ways, by gestures, or smiles or obvious protests so that we are aware of their suffering, their astonishment, their disbelief.*)

(*The* PROMPTER's *voice is heard clearly between every line in the scene, telling the* ACTORS *what to say next.*)

LEADING ACTOR: Good afternoon, my dear.
FATHER: (*Immediately, unable to restrain himself.*) Oh, no!

(*The* STEPDAUGHTER, *watching the* LEADING ACTOR *enter this way, bursts into laughter.*)

PRODUCER: (*Furious.*) Shut up, for God's sake! And don't you
90   dare laugh like that! We're never going to get anywhere at this rate.
STEPDAUGHTER: (*Coming to the front.*) I'm sorry, I can't help it! The lady stands exactly where you told her to stand and she never moved. But if it were me and I heard someone
95   say good afternoon to me in that way and with a voice like that I should burst out laughing—so I did.
FATHER: (*Coming down a little too.*) Yes, she's right, the whole manner, the voice . . .
PRODUCER: To hell with the manner and the voice! Get out
100   of the way, will you, and let me watch the rehearsal!
LEADING ACTOR: (*Coming down stage.*) If I have to play an old man who has come to a knocking shop—
PRODUCER: Take no notice, ignore them. Go on please! It's going well, it's going well! (*He waits for the* ACTOR *to begin*
105   *again.*) Right, again!
LEADING ACTOR: Good afternoon, my dear.
LEADING ACTRESS: Good afternoon.
LEADING ACTOR: (*Copying the gestures of the* FATHER, *looking under the brim of the hat, but expressing distinctly the two emo-*
110   *tions, first, complacent satisfaction and then anxiety.*) Ah! But tell me . . . this won't be the first time I hope.
FATHER: (*Instinctively correcting him.*) Not 'I hope'—'will it,' 'will it.'
PRODUCER: Say 'will it'—and it's a question.
115   LEADING ACTOR: (*Glaring at the* PROMPTER.) I distinctly heard him say 'I hope.'
PRODUCER: So what? It's all the same, 'I hope' or 'isn't it.' It doesn't make any difference. Carry on, carry on. But perhaps it should still be a little bit lighter; I'll show you—
120   watch me! (*He climbs up on the stage again, and going back to the entrance, he does it himself.*) Good afternoon, my dear.
LEADING ACTRESS: Good afternoon.
PRODUCER: Ah, tell me . . . (*He turns to the* LEADING ACTOR *to make sure that he has seen the way he has demonstrated of look-*
125   *ing under the brim of the hat.*) You see—surprise . . . anxiety and self-satisfaction. (*Then, starting again, he turns to the* LEADING ACTRESS.) This won't be the first time, will it? The first time you've been here? (*Again turns to the* LEADING

ACTOR, *questioningly.*) Right? (*To the* LEADING ACTRESS.) And then she says, 'No, sir.' (*Again to* LEADING ACTOR.) See   130
what I mean? More subtlety. (*And he climbs off the stage.*)
LEADING ACTRESS: No, sir.
LEADING ACTOR: You've been here before? More than once?
PRODUCER: No, no, no! Wait for it, wait for it. Let her answer first. 'You've been here before?'   135

(*The* LEADING ACTRESS *lifts her head a little, her eyes closed in pain and disgust, and when the* PRODUCER *says 'Now' she nods her head twice.*)

STEPDAUGHTER: (*Involuntarily.*) Oh, my God! (*And she immediately claps her hand over her mouth to stifle her laughter.*)
PRODUCER: What now?
STEPDAUGHTER: (*Quickly.*) Nothing, nothing!
PRODUCER: (*To* LEADING ACTOR.) Come on, then, now it's you.   140
LEADING ACTOR: More than once? Well then, it shouldn't be too . . . May I take off your hat?

(*The* LEADING ACTOR *says this last line in such a way and adds to it such a gesture that the* STEPDAUGHTER, *even with her hand over her mouth trying to stop herself laughing, can't prevent a noisy burst of laughter.*)

LEADING ACTRESS: (*Indignantly turning.*) I'm not staying any longer to be laughed at by that woman!
LEADING ACTOR: Nor am I! That's the end—no more!   145
PRODUCER: (*To* STEPDAUGHTER, *shouting.*) Once and for all, will you shut up! Shut up!
STEPDAUGHTER: Yes, I'm sorry . . . I'm sorry.
PRODUCER: You're an ill-mannered little bitch! That's what you are! And you've gone too far this time!   150
FATHER: (*Trying to interrupt.*) Yes, you're right, she went too far, but please forgive her . . .
PRODUCER: (*Jumping on the stage.*) Why should I forgive her? Her behaviour is intolerable!
FATHER: Yes, it is, but the scene made such a peculiar impact   155
on us . . .
PRODUCER: Peculiar? What do you mean peculiar? Why peculiar?
FATHER: I'm full of admiration for your actors, for this gentleman (*To the* LEADING ACTOR.) and this lady. (*To the*   160
LEADING ACTRESS.) But, you see, well . . . they're not us!
PRODUCER: Right! They're not! They're actors!
FATHER: That's just the point—they're actors. And they are acting our parts very well, both of them. But that's what's different. However much they want to be the same as us,   165
they're not.
PRODUCER: But why aren't they? What is it now?
FATHER: It's something to do with . . . being themselves, I suppose, not being us.
PRODUCER: Well we can't do anything about that! I've told   170
you already. You can't play the parts yourselves.
FATHER: Yes, I know, I know . . .
PRODUCER: Right then. That's enough of that. (*Turning back to the* ACTORS.) We'll rehearse this later on our own, as we usually do. It's always a bad idea to have rehearsals with   175
authors there! They're never satisfied. (*Turns back to the* FATHER *and the* STEPDAUGHTER.) Come on, let's get on with it; and let's see if it's possible to do it without laughing.

STEPDAUGHTER: I won't laugh any more, I won't really. My best bit's coming up now, you wait and see!

PRODUCER: Right: when you say 'Don't think any more about what I told you, please. And I should do the same.' (*Turning to the* FATHER.) then you come in immediately with the line 'I understand, ah yes, I understand' and then you ask …

STEPDAUGHTER: (*Interrupting.*) Ask what? What does he ask?

PRODUCER: Why you're in mourning.

STEPDAUGHTER: No! No! That's not right! Look: when I said that I should try not to think about the way I was dressed, do you know what he said? 'Well then, let's take it off, we'll take it off at once, shall we, your little black dress.'

PRODUCER: That's great! That'll be wonderful! That'll bring the house down!

STEPDAUGHTER: But it's the truth!

PRODUCER: The truth! Do me a favour will you? This is the theatre you know! Truth's all very well up to a point but …

STEPDAUGHTER: What do you want to do then?

PRODUCER: You'll see! You'll see! Leave it all to me.

STEPDAUGHTER: No. No I won't. I know what you want to do! Out of my feeling of revulsion, out of all the vile and sordid reasons why I am what I am, you want to make a sugary little sentimental romance. You want him to ask me why I'm in mourning and you want me to reply with the tears running down my face that it is only two months since my father died. No. No. I won't have it! He must say to me what he really did say. 'Well then, let's take it off, we'll take it off at once, shall we, your little black dress.' And I, with my heart still grieving for my father's death only two months before, I went behind there, do you see? Behind that screen and with my fingers trembling with shame and loathing I took off the dress, unfastened my bra …

PRODUCER: (*His head in his hands.*) For God's sake! What are you saying!

STEPDAUGHTER: (*Shouting excitedly.*) The truth! I'm telling you the truth!

PRODUCER: All right then. Now listen to me. I'm not denying it's the truth. Right. And believe me I understand your horror, but you must see that we can't really put a scene like that on the stage.

STEPDAUGHTER: You can't? Then thanks very much. I'm not stopping here.

PRODUCER: No, listen …

STEPDAUGHTER: No, I'm going. I'm not stopping. The pair of you have worked it all out together, haven't you, what to put in the scene. Well, thank you very much! I understand everything now! He wants to get to the scene where he can talk about his spiritual torments but I want to show you my drama! Mine!

PRODUCER: (*Shaking with anger.*) Now we're getting to the real truth of it, aren't we? Your drama—yours! But it's not only yours, you know. It's drama for the other people as well! For him (*Pointing to the* FATHER.) and for your mother! You can't have one character coming on like you're doing, trampling over the others, taking over the play. Everything needs to be balanced and in harmony so that we can show what has to be shown! I know perfectly well that we've all got a life inside us and that we all want to parade it in front of other people. But that's the difficulty, how to present only the bits that are necessary in relation to the other characters: and in the small amount we show, to hint at all the rest of the inner life of the character! I agree, it would be so much simpler, if each character, in a soliloquy or in a lecture could pour out to the audience what's bubbling away inside him. But that's not the way we work. (*In an indulgent, placating tone.*) You must restrain yourself, you see. And believe me, it's in your own interests: because you could so easily make a bad impression, with all this uncontrollable anger, this disgust and exasperation. That seems a bit odd, if you don't mind my saying so, when you've admitted that you'd been with other men at Mme. Pace's and more than once.

STEPDAUGHTER: I suppose that's true. But you know, all the other men were all him as far as I was concerned.

PRODUCER: (*Not understanding.*) Uum—? What? What are you talking about?

STEPDAUGHTER: If someone falls into evil ways, isn't the responsibility for all the evil which follows to be laid at the door of the person who caused the first mistake? And in my case, it's him, from before I was even born. Look at him: see if it isn't true.

PRODUCER: Right then! What about the weight of remorse he's carrying? Isn't that important? Then, give him the chance to show it to us.

STEPDAUGHTER: But how? How on earth can he show all his long-suffering remorse, all his moral torments as he calls them, if you don't let him show his horror when he finds me in his arms one fine day, after he had asked me to take my dress off, a black dress for my father who had just died: and he finds that I'm the child he used to go and watch as she came out of school, me, a woman now, and a woman he could buy. (*She says these last words in a voice trembling with emotion.*)

(*The* MOTHER, *hearing her say this, is overcome and at first gives way to stifled sobs: but then she bursts out into uncontrollable crying. Everyone is deeply moved. There is a long pause.*)

STEPDAUGHTER: (*As soon as the* MOTHER *has quietened herself she goes on, firmly and thoughtfully.*) At the moment we are here on our own and the public doesn't know about us. But tomorrow you will present us and our story in whatever way you choose, I suppose. But wouldn't you like to see the real drama? Wouldn't you like to see it explode into life, as it really did?

PRODUCER: Of course, nothing I'd like better, then I can use as much of it as possible.

STEPDAUGHTER: Then persuade my mother to leave.

MOTHER: (*Rising and her quiet weeping changing to a loud cry.*) No! No! Don't let her! Don't let her do it!

PRODUCER: But they're only doing it for me to watch—only for me, do you see?

MOTHER: I can't bear it, I can't bear it!

PRODUCER: But if it's already happened, I can't see what's the objection.

MOTHER: No! It's happening now, as well: it's happening all the time. I'm not acting my suffering! Can't you understand that? I'm alive and here now but I can never forget that terrible moment of agony, that repeats itself endlessly and vividly in my mind. And these two little children here,

you've never heard them speak have you? That's because
they don't speak any more, not now. They just cling to me
295 all the time: they help to keep my grief alive, but they don't
really exist for themselves any more, not for themselves.
And she (*Indicating the* STEPDAUGHTER.) . . . she has gone
away, left me completely, she's lost to me, lost . . . you see her
here for one reason only: to keep perpetually before me, al-
300 ways real, the anguish and the torment I've suffered on her
account.

FATHER: The eternal moment, as I told you, sir. She is here
(*Indicating the* STEPDAUGHTER.) to keep me too in that
moment, trapped for all eternity, chained and suspended
305 in that one fleeting shameful moment of my life. She can't
give up her role and you cannot rescue me from it.

PRODUCER: But I'm not saying that we won't present that
bit. Not at all! It will be the climax of the first act, when
she (*He points to the* MOTHER.) surprises you.

310 FATHER: That's right, because that is the moment when I am
sentenced: all our suffering should reach a climax in her
cry. (*Again indicating the* MOTHER.)

STEPDAUGHTER: I can still hear it ringing in my ears! It
was that cry that sent me mad! You can have me played
315 just as you like: it doesn't matter! Dressed, too, if you
want, so long as I can have at least an arm—only an
arm—bare, because, you see, as I was standing like this
(*She moves across to the* FATHER *and leans her head on his
chest.*) with my head like this and my arms round his
320 neck, I saw a vein, here in my arm, throbbing: and then
it was almost as if that throbbing vein filled me with
a shivering fear, and I shut my eyes tightly like this,
like this and buried my head in his chest. (*Turning to
the* MOTHER.) Scream, Mummy, scream. (*She buries her
325 head in the* FATHER's *chest, and with her shoulders raised as
if to try not to hear the scream, she speaks with a voice tense
with suffering.*) Scream, as you screamed then!

MOTHER: (*Coming forward to pull them apart.*) No! She's my
daughter! My daughter! (*Tearing her from him.*) You brute,
330 you animal, she's my daughter! Can't you see she's my
daughter?

PRODUCER: (*Retreating as far as the footlights while the* ACTORS
are full of dismay.) Marvellous! Yes, that's great! And then
curtain, curtain!

335 FATHER: (*Running downstage to him, excitedly.*) That's it, that's it!
Because it really was like that!

PRODUCER: (*Full of admiration and enthusiasm.*) Yes, yes, that's
got to be the curtain line! Curtain! Curtain!

(*At the repeated calls of the* PRODUCER, *the* STAGE MANAGER *lowers the curtain, leaving on the apron in front, the* PRODUCER *and
the* FATHER.)

PRODUCER: (*Looking up to heaven with his arms raised.*) The id-
340 iots! I didn't mean now! The bloody idiots—dropping it
in on us like that! (*To the* FATHER, *and lifting up a corner of
the curtain.*) That's marvellous! Really marvellous! A terrific effect! We'll end the act like that! It's the best tag line
I've heard for ages. What a First Act ending! I couldn't
345 have done better if I'd written it myself!

(*They go through the curtain together.*)

ACT THREE

When the curtain goes up we see that the STAGE MANAGER *and*
STAGE HANDS *have struck the first scene and have set another, a
small garden fountain.*

From one side of the stage the ACTORS *come on and from the other
the* CHARACTERS. *The* PRODUCER *is standing in the middle of the
stage with his hand over his mouth, thinking.*

PRODUCER: (*After a short pause, shrugging his shoulders.*) Well,
then: let's get on to the second act! Leave it all to me, and
everything will work out properly.

STEPDAUGHTER: This is where we go to live at his house
(*Pointing to the* FATHER.) in spite of the objections of him 5
over there. (*Pointing to the* SON.)

PRODUCER: (*Getting impatient.*) All right, all right! But leave
it all to me, will you?

STEPDAUGHTER: Provided that you make it clear that he objected! 10

MOTHER: (*From the corner, shaking her head.*) That doesn't matter! The worse it was for us, the more he suffered from remorse.

PRODUCER: (*Impatiently.*) I know, I know! I'll take it all into
account. Don't worry! 15

MOTHER: (*Pleading.*) To set my mind at rest, sir, please do
make sure it's clear that I tried all I could—

STEPDAUGHTER: (*Interrupting her scornfully and going on.*)—to
pacify me, to persuade me that this despicable creature
wasn't worth making trouble about! (*To the* PRODUCER.) 20
Go on, set her mind at rest, because it's true, she tried very
hard. I'm having a whale of a time now! You can see, can't
you, that the meeker she was and the more she tried to
worm her way into his heart, the more lofty and distant
he became! How's that for a dramatic situation! 25

PRODUCER: Do you think that we can actually begin the
Second Act?

STEPDAUGHTER: I won't say another word! But you'll see that
it won't be possible to play everything in the garden, like
you want to do. 30

PRODUCER: Why not?

STEPDAUGHTER: (*Pointing to the* SON.) Because to start with,
he stays shut up in his room in the house all the time! And
then all the scenes for this poor little devil of a boy happen in the house. I've told you once. 35

PRODUCER: Yes, I know that! But on the other hand we can't
put up a notice to tell the audience where the scene is taking place, or change the set three or four times in each Act.

LEADING ACTOR: That's what they used to do in the good old
days. 40

PRODUCER: Yes, when the audience was about as bright as
that little girl over there!

LEADING ACTRESS: And it makes it easier to create an illusion.

FATHER: (*Leaping up.*) An illusion? For pity's sake don't talk
about illusions! Don't use that word, it's especially hurtful 45
to us!

PRODUCER: (*Astonished.*) And why, for God's sake?

FATHER: It's so hurtful, so cruel! You ought to have realised
that!

50 PRODUCER: What else should we call it? That's what we do here—create an illusion for the audience . . .

LEADING ACTOR: With our performance . . .

PRODUCER: A perfect illusion of reality!

FATHER: Yes, I know that, I understand. But on the other
55 hand, perhaps you don't understand us yet. I'm sorry! But you see, for you and for your actors what goes on here on the stage is, quite rightly, well, it's only a game.

LEADING ACTRESS: (*Interrupting indignantly.*) A game! How dare you! We're not children! What happens here is serious!

60 FATHER: I'm not saying that it isn't serious. And I mean, really, not just a game but an art, that tries, as you've just said, to create the perfect illusion of reality.

PRODUCER: That's right!

FATHER: Now try to imagine that we, as you see us here, (*He
65 indicates himself and the other* CHARACTERS.) that we have no other reality outside this illusion.

PRODUCER: (*Astonished and looking at the* ACTORS *with the same sense of bewilderment as they feel themselves.*) What the hell are you talking about now?

70 FATHER: (*After a short pause as he looks at them, with a faint smile.*) Isn't it obvious? What other reality is there for us? What for you is an illusion you create, for us is our only reality. (*Brief pause. He moves towards the* PRODUCER *and goes on.*) But it's not only true for us, it's true for others as well,
75 you know. Just think about it. (*He looks intently into the* PRODUCER's *eyes.*) Do you really know who you are? (*He stands pointing at the* PRODUCER.)

PRODUCER: (*A little disturbed but with a half smile.*) What? Who I am? I am me!

80 FATHER: What if I told you that that wasn't true: what if I told you that you were me?

PRODUCER: I would tell you that you were mad!

(*The* ACTORS *laugh.*)

FATHER: That's right, laugh! Because everything here is a game! (*To the* PRODUCER.) And yet you object when I say that it is
85 only for a game that the gentleman there (*Pointing to the* LEADING ACTOR.) who is 'himself' has to be 'me,' who, on the contrary, am 'myself.' You see, I've caught you in a trap.

(*The* ACTORS *start to laugh.*)

PRODUCER: Not again! We've heard all about this a little while ago.

90 FATHER: No, no. I didn't really want to talk about this. I'd like you to forget about your game, (*Looking at the* LEADING ACTRESS *as if to anticipate what she will say.*) I'm sorry—your artistry! Your art!—that you usually pursue here with your actors; and I am going to ask you again in all seri-
95 ousness, who are you?

PRODUCER: (*Turning with a mixture of amazement and annoyance, to the* ACTORS.) Of all the bloody nerve! A fellow who claims he is only a character comes and asks me who I am!

FATHER: (*With dignity but without annoyance.*) A character, my
100 dear sir, can always ask a man who he is, because a character really has a life of his own, a life full of his own specific qualities, and because of these he is always 'someone.' While a man—I'm not speaking about you personally, of course, but man in general—well, he can be an absolute
105 'nobody.'

PRODUCER: All right, all right! Well, since you've asked me, I'm the Director, the Producer—I'm in charge! Do you understand?

FATHER: (*Half smiling, but gently and politely.*) I'm only asking to
110 try to find out if you really see yourself now in the same way that you saw yourself, for instance, once upon a time in the past, with all the illusions you had then, with everything inside and outside yourself as it seemed then—and not only seemed, but really was! Well then, look back on those illu-
115 sions, those ideas that you don't have any more, on all those things that no longer seem the same to you. Don't you feel that not only this stage is falling away from under your feet but so is the earth itself, and that all these realities of today are going to seem tomorrow as if they had been an illusion?

120 PRODUCER: So? What does that prove?

FATHER: Oh, nothing much. I only want to make you see that if we (*Pointing to himself and the other* CHARACTERS.) have no other reality outside our own illusion, perhaps you ought to distrust your own sense of reality: because what-
125 ever is a reality today, whatever you touch and believe in and that seems real for you today, is going to be—like the reality of yesterday—an illusion tomorrow.

PRODUCER: (*Deciding to make fun of him.*) Very good! So now you're saying that you as well as this play you're going to
130 show me here, are more real than I am?

FATHER: (*Very seriously.*) There's no doubt about that at all.

PRODUCER: Is that so?

FATHER: I thought you'd realised that from the beginning.

PRODUCER: More real than I am?

135 FATHER: If your reality can change between today and tomorrow—

PRODUCER: But everybody knows that it can change, don't they? It's always changing! Just like everybody else's!

FATHER: (*Crying out.*) But ours doesn't change! Do you see?
140 That's the difference! Ours doesn't change, it can't change, it can never be different, never, because it is already determined, like this, for ever, that's what's so terrible! We are an eternal reality. That should make you shudder to come near us.

PRODUCER: (*Jumping up, suddenly struck by an idea, and standing
145 directly in front of the* FATHER.) Then I should like to know when anyone saw a character step out of his part and make a speech like you've done, proposing things, explaining things. Tell me when, will you? I've never seen it before.

FATHER: You've never seen it because an author usually hides
150 all the difficulties of creating. When the characters are alive, really alive and standing in front of their author, he has only to follow their words, the actions that they suggest to him: and he must want them to be what they want to be: and it's his bad luck if he doesn't do what they want!
155 When a character is born he immediately assumes such an independence even of his own author that everyone can imagine him in scores of situations that his author hadn't even thought of putting him in, and he sometimes acquires a meaning that his author never dreamed of giving him.

160 PRODUCER: Of course I know all that.

FATHER: Well, then. Why are you surprised by us? Imagine what a disaster it is for a character to be born in the imagination of an author who then refuses to give him life in a written script. Tell me if a character, left like this, sus-
165 pended, created but without a final life, isn't right to do what we are doing now, here in front of you. We spent

such a long time, such a very long time, believe me, urging our author, persuading him, first me, then her, (*Pointing to the* STEPDAUGHTER.) then this poor Mother . . .

170 STEPDAUGHTER: (*Coming down the stage as if in a dream.*) It's true, I would go, would go and tempt him, time after time, in his gloomy study just as it was growing dark, when he was sitting quietly in an armchair not even bothering to switch a light on but leaving the shadows to fill the room:
175 the shadows were swarming with us, we had come to tempt him. (*As if she could see herself there in the study and is annoyed by the presence of the* ACTORS.) Go away will you! Leave us alone! Mother there, with that son of hers—me with the little girl—that poor little kid always on his
180 own—and then me with him (*Pointing to the* FATHER.) and then at last, just me, on my own, all on my own, in the shadows. (*She turns quickly as if she wants to cling on to the vision she has of herself, in the shadows.*) Ah, what scenes, what scenes we suggested to him! What a life I could have
185 had! I tempted him more than the others!

FATHER: Oh yes, you did! And it was probably all your fault that he did nothing about it! You were so insistent, you made too many demands.

STEPDAUGHTER: But he wanted me to be like that! (*She comes*
190 *closer to the* PRODUCER *to speak to him in confidence.*) I think it's more likely that he felt discouraged about the theatre and even despised it because the public only wants to see . . .

PRODUCER: Let's get on, for God's sake, let's get on. Come to the point will you?

195 STEPDAUGHTER: I'm sorry, but if you ask me, we've got too much happening already, just with our entry into his house. (*Pointing to the* FATHER.) You said that we couldn't put up a notice or change the set every five minutes.

PRODUCER: Right! Of course we can't! We must combine
200 things, group them together in one continuous flowing action: not the way you've been wanting, first of all seeing your little brother come home from school and wander about the house like a lost soul, hiding behind the doors and brooding on some plan or other that would—what
205 did you say it would do?

STEPDAUGHTER: Wither him . . . shrivel him up completely.

PRODUCER: That's good! That's a good expression. And then you 'can see it there in his eyes, getting stronger all the time'—isn't that what you said?

210 STEPDAUGHTER: Yes, that's right. Look at him! (*Pointing to him as he stands next to his* MOTHER.)

PRODUCER: Yes, great! And then, at the same time, you want to show the little girl playing in the garden, all innocence. One in the house and the other in the garden—we can't
215 do it, don't you see that?

STEPDAUGHTER: Yes, playing in the sun, so happy! It's the only pleasure I have left, her happiness, her delight in playing in the garden: away from the misery, the squalor of that sordid flat where all four of us slept and where she slept with
220 me—with me! Just think of it! My vile, contaminated body close to hers, with her little arms wrapped tightly round my neck, so lovingly, so innocently. In the garden, whenever she saw me, she would run and take my hand. She never wanted to show me the big flowers, she would
225 run about looking for the 'little weeny' ones, so that she could show them to me; she was so happy, so thrilled! (*As she says this, tortured by the memory, she breaks out into a long*

desperate cry, dropping her head on her arms that rest on a little table. Everybody is very affected by her. The PRODUCER comes to her almost paternally and speaks to her in a soothing voice.*) 230

PRODUCER: We'll have the garden scene, we'll have it, don't worry: and you'll see, you'll be very pleased with what we do! We'll play all the scenes in the garden! (*He calls out to a* STAGE HAND *by name.*) Hey . . . . , let down a few bits of tree, will you? A couple of cypresses will do, in front of the 235 fountain. (*Someone drops in the two cypresses and a* STAGE HAND *secures them with a couple of braces and weights.*)

PRODUCER: (*To the* STEPDAUGHTER.) That'll do for now, won't it? It'll just give us an idea. (*Calling out to a* STAGE HAND *by name again.*) Hey, ... give me something for the sky will you? 240

STAGE HAND: What's that?

PRODUCER: Something for the sky! A small cloth to come in behind the fountain. (*A white cloth is dropped from the flies.*) Not white! I asked for a sky! Never mind: leave it! I'll do something with it. (*Calling out.*) Hey lights! Kill everything 245 will you? Give me a bit of moonlight—the blues in the batten and a blue spot on the cloth . . . (*They do.*) That's it! That'll do! (*Now on the scene there is the light he asked for, a mysterious blue light that makes the* ACTORS *speak and move as if in the garden in the evening under a moon. To the* STEPDAUGHTER.) Look 250 here now: the little boy can come out here in the garden and hide among the trees instead of hiding behind the doors in the house. But it's going to be difficult to find a little girl to play the scene with you where she shows you the flowers. (*Turning to the* LITTLE BOY.) Come on, come on, son, come 255 across here. Let's see what it'll look like. (*But the* BOY *doesn't move.*) Come on will you, come on. (*Then he pulls him forward and tries to make him hold his head up, but every time it falls down again on his chest.*) There's something very odd about this lad . . . What's wrong with him? My God, he'll have to 260 say something sometime! (*He comes over to him again, puts his hand on his shoulder and pushes him between the trees.*) Come a bit nearer: let's have a look. Can you hide a bit more? That's it. Now pop your head out and look round. (*He moves away to look at the effect and as the* BOY *does what he has been told to do,* 265 *the* ACTORS *watch impressed and a little disturbed.*) Ahh, that's good, very good . . . (*He turns to the* STEPDAUGHTER.) How about having the little girl, surprised to see him there, run across. Wouldn't that make him say something?

STEPDAUGHTER: (*Getting up.*) It's no use hoping he'll speak, 270 not as long as that creature's there. (*Pointing to the* SON.) You'll have to get him out of the way first.

SON: (*Moving determinedly to one of the sets of steps leading off the stage.*) With pleasure! I'll go now! Nothing will please me better!

PRODUCER: (*Stopping him immediately.*) Hey, no! Where are 275 you going? Hang on!

(*The* MOTHER *gets up, anxious at the idea that he is really going and instinctively raising her arms as if to hold him back, but without moving from where she is.*)

SON: (*At the footlights, to the* PRODUCER *who is restraining him there.*) There's no reason why I should be here! Let me go will you? Let me go!

PRODUCER: What do you mean there's no reason for you to 280 be here?

STEPDAUGHTER: (*Calmly, ironically.*) Don't bother to stop him. He won't go!

FATHER: You have to play that terrible scene in the garden
285   with your mother.

SON: (*Quickly, angry and determined.*) I'm not going to play
anything! I've said that all along! (*To the* PRODUCER.) Let
me go will you?

STEPDAUGHTER: (*Crossing to the* PRODUCER.) It's all right. Let
290   him go. (*She moves the* PRODUCER's *hand from the* SON. *Then
she turns to the* SON *and says.*) Well, go on then! Off you go!

(*The* SON *stays near the steps but as if pulled by some strange force
he is quite unable to go down them: then to the astonishment and
even the dismay of the* ACTORS, *he moves along the front of the stage
towards the other set of steps down into the auditorium: but having
got there, he again stays near and doesn't actually go down them.
The* STEPDAUGHTER *who has watched him scornfully but very intently, bursts into laughter.*)

STEPDAUGHTER: He can't, you see? He can't! He's got to stay
here! He must. He's chained to us for ever! No, I'm the
295   one who goes, when what must happen does happen, and
I run away, because I hate him, because I can't bear the
sight of him any longer. Do you think it's possible for him
to run away? He has to stay here with that wonderful father of his and his mother there. She doesn't think she has
any other son but him. (*She turns to the* MOTHER.) Come
300   on, come on, Mummy, come on! (*Turning back to the* PRO-
DUCER *to point her out to him.*) Look, she's going to try to
stop him . . . (*To the* MOTHER, *half compelling her, as if by
some magic power.*) Come on, come on. (*Then to the* PRO-
DUCER *again.*) Imagine how she must feel at showing her
305   affection for him in front of your actors! But her longing
to be near him is so strong that—look! She's going to go
through that scene with him again! (*The* MOTHER *has now
actually come close to the* SON *as the* STEPDAUGHTER *says the
last line: she gestures to show that she agrees to go on.*)

310   SON: (*Quickly.*) But I'm not! I'm not! If I can't get away then
I suppose I shall have to stay here; but I repeat that I will
not have any part in it.

FATHER: (*To the* PRODUCER, *excitedly.*) You must make him!

SON: Nobody's going to make me do anything!

315   FATHER: I'll make you!

STEPDAUGHTER: Wait! Just a minute! Before that, the little girl
has to go to the fountain. (*She turns to take the* LITTLE GIRL,
*drops on her knees in front of her and takes her face between her
hands.*) My poor little darling, those beautiful eyes, they look
320   so bewildered. You're wondering where you are, aren't
you? Well, we're on a stage, my darling! What's a stage? Well,
it's a place where you pretend to be serious. They put on
plays here. And now we're going to put on a play. Seriously!
Oh, yes! Even you . . . (*She hugs her tightly and rocks her gently
325   for a moment.*) Oh, my little one, my little darling, what a terrible play it is for you! What horrible things have been
planned for you! The garden, the fountain . . . Oh, yes, it's
only a pretend fountain, that's right. That's part of the game,
my pretty darling: everything is pretends here. Perhaps
330   you'll like a pretends fountain better than a real one: you can
play here then. But it's only a game for the others; not for
you, I'm afraid, it's real for you, my darling, and your game is
in a real fountain, a big beautiful green fountain with bam-

boos casting shadows, looking at your own reflection, with
lots of baby ducks paddling about, shattering the reflec-   335
tions. You want to stroke one! (*With a scream that electrifies
and terrifies everybody.*) No, Rosetta, no! Your mummy isn't
watching you, she's over there with that selfish bastard! Oh,
God, I feel as if all the devils in hell were tearing me apart
inside . . . And you . . . (*Leaving the* LITTLE GIRL *and turning to*   340
the LITTLE BOY *in the usual way.*) What are you doing here,
hanging about like a beggar? It'll be your fault too, if that little girl drowns; you're always like this, as if I wasn't paying
the price for getting all of you into this house. (*Shaking his
arm to make him take his hand out of his pocket.*) What have you   345
got there? What are you hiding? Take it out, take your hand
out! (*She drags his hand out of his pocket and to everyone's horror
he is holding a revolver. She looks at him for a moment, almost with
satisfaction: then she says, grimly.*) Where on earth did you get
that? (*The* BOY, *looking frightened, with his eyes wide and empty,*   350
doesn't answer.) You idiot, if I'd been you, instead of killing
myself, I'd have killed one of those two: either or both, the
father and the son. (*She pushes him towards the cypress trees
where he then stands watching: then she takes the* LITTLE GIRL
and helps her to climb in to the fountain, making her lie so that she   355
*is hidden: after that she kneels down and puts her head and arms on
the rim of the fountain.*)

PRODUCER: That's good! It's good! (*Turning to the* STEP-
DAUGHTER.) And at the same time . . .

SON: (*Scornfully.*) What do you mean, at the same time? There   360
was nothing at the same time! There wasn't any scene between her and me. (*Pointing to the* MOTHER.) She'll tell
you the same thing herself, she'll tell you what happened.

(*The* SECOND ACTRESS *and the* JUVENILE LEAD *have left the
group of* ACTORS *and have come to stand nearer the* MOTHER *and
the* SON *as if to study them so as to play their parts.*)

MOTHER: Yes, it's true. I'd gone to his room . . .

SON: Room, do you hear? Not the garden!   365

PRODUCER: It's not important! We've got to reorganise the
events anyway. I've told you that already.

SON: (*Glaring at the* JUVENILE LEAD *and the* SECOND ACTRESS.)
What do you want?

JUVENILE LEAD: Nothing. I'm just watching.   370

SON: (*Turning to the* SECOND ACTRESS.) You as well! Getting
ready to play her part are you? (*Pointing to the* MOTHER.)

PRODUCER: That's it. And I think you should be grateful—
they're paying you a lot of attention.

SON: Oh, yes, thank you! But haven't you realised yet that   375
you'll never be able to do this play? There's nothing of us
inside you and you actors are only looking at us from the
outside. Do you think we could go on living with a mirror held up in front of us that didn't only freeze our reflection for ever, but froze us in a reflection that laughed   380
back at us with an expression that we didn't even recognise as our own?

FATHER: That's right! That's right!

PRODUCER: (*To* JUVENILE LEAD *and* SECOND ACTRESS.) Okay.
Go back to the others.   385

SON: It's quite useless. I'm not prepared to do anything.

PRODUCER: Oh, shut up, will you, and let me listen to your mother. (*To the* MOTHER.) Well, you'd gone to his room, you said.

390 MOTHER: Yes, to his room. I couldn't bear it any longer. I wanted to empty my heart to him, tell him about all the agony that was crushing me. But as soon as he saw me come in . . .

SON: Nothing happened. I got away! I wasn't going to get involved. I never have been involved. Do you understand?

395 MOTHER: It's true! That's right!

PRODUCER: But we must make up the scene between you, then. It's vital!

MOTHER: I'm ready to do it! If only I had the chance to talk to him for a moment, to pour out all my troubles to him.

400 FATHER: (*Going to the* SON *and speaking violently.*) You'll do it! For your Mother! For your Mother!

SON: (*More than ever determined.*) I'm doing nothing!

FATHER: (*Taking hold of his coat collar and shaking him.*) For God's sake, do as I tell you! Do as I tell you! Do you hear

405 what she's saying? Haven't you any feelings for her?

SON: (*Taking hold of his* FATHER.) No I haven't! I haven't! Let that be the end of it!

(*There is a general uproar. The* MOTHER *frightened out of her wits, tries to get between them and separate them.*)

MOTHER: Please stop it! Please!

FATHER: (*Hanging on.*) Do as I tell you! Do as I tell you!

410 SON: (*Wrestling with him and finally throwing him to the ground near the steps. Everyone is horrified.*) What's come over you? Why are you so frantic? Do you want to parade our disgrace in front of everybody? Well, I'm having nothing to do with it! Nothing! And I'm doing what our author

415 wanted as well—he never wanted to put us on the stage.

PRODUCER: Then why the hell did you come here?

SON: (*Pointing to the* FATHER.) He wanted to, I didn't.

PRODUCER: And aren't you here now?

SON: He was the one who wanted to come and he dragged

420 all of us here with him and agreed with you in there about what to put in the play: and that meant not only what had really happened, as if that wasn't bad enough, but what hadn't happened as well.

PRODUCER: All right, then, you tell me what happened. You tell

425 me! Did you rush out of your room without saying anything?

SON: (*After a moment's hesitation.*) Without saying anything. I didn't want to make a scene.

PRODUCER: (*Needling him.*) What then? What did you do then?

SON: (*He is now the centre of everyone's agonised attention and he

430 crosses the stage.*) Nothing . . . I went across the garden . . . (*He breaks off gloomy and absorbed.*)

PRODUCER: (*Urging him to say more, impressed by his reluctance to speak.*) Well? What then? You crossed the garden?

SON: (*Exasperated, putting his face into the crook of his arm.*) Why

435 do you want me to talk about it? It's horrible! (*The* MOTHER *is trembling with stifled sobs and looking towards the fountain.*)

PRODUCER: (*Quietly, seeing where she is looking and turning to the* SON *with growing apprehension.*) The little girl?

SON: (*Looking straight in front, out to the audience.*) There, in the

440 fountain . . .

FATHER: (*On the floor still, pointing with pity at the* MOTHER.) She was trailing after him!

PRODUCER: (*To the* SON, *anxiously.*) What did you do then?

SON: (*Still looking out front and speaking slowly.*) I dashed across. I was going to jump in and pull her out . . . But something 445 else caught my eye: I saw something behind the tree that made my blood run cold: the little boy, he was standing there with a mad look in his eyes: he was standing looking into the fountain at his little sister, floating there, drowned.

(*The* STEPDAUGHTER *is still bent at the fountain hiding the* LITTLE GIRL, *and she sobs pathetically, her sobs sounding like an echo.*)

(*There is a pause.*)

SON: (*Continued.*) I made a move towards him: but then . . . 450

(*From behind the trees where the little* BOY *is standing there is the sound of a shot.*)

MOTHER: (*With a terrible cry she runs along with the* SON *and all the* ACTORS *in the midst of a great general confusion.*) My son! My son! (*And then from out of the confusion and crying her voice comes out.*) Help! Help me!

PRODUCER: (*Amidst the shouting he tries to clear a space whilst the* 455 *little* BOY *is carried by his feet and shoulders behind the white skycloth.*) Is he wounded? Really wounded? (*Everybody except the* PRODUCER *and the* FATHER *who is still on the floor by the steps, has gone behind the skycloth and stays there talking anxiously. Then independently the* ACTORS *start to come back* 460 *into view.*)

LEADING ACTRESS: (*Coming from the right, very upset.*) He's dead! The poor boy! He's dead! What a terrible thing!

LEADING ACTOR: (*Coming back from the left and smiling.*) What do you mean, dead? It's all make-believe. It's a sham! He's 465 not dead. Don't you believe it!

OTHER ACTORS FROM THE RIGHT: Make-believe? It's real! Real! He's dead!

OTHER ACTORS FROM THE LEFT: No, he isn't. He's pretending! It's all make-believe. 470

FATHER: (*Running off and shouting at them as he goes.*) What do you mean, make-believe? It's real! It's real, ladies and gentlemen! It's reality! (*And with desperation on his face he too goes behind the skycloth.*)

PRODUCER: (*Not caring any more.*) Make-believe?! Reality?! 475 Oh, go to hell the lot of you! Lights! Lights! Lights!

(*At once all the stage and auditorium is flooded with light. The* PRODUCER *heaves a sigh of relief as if he has been relieved of a terrible weight and they all look at each other in distress and with uncertainty.*)

PRODUCER: God! I've never known anything like this! And we've lost a whole day's work! (*He looks at the clock.*) Get off with you, all of you! We can't do anything now! It's too late to start a rehearsal. (*When the* ACTORS *have gone,* 480 *he calls out.*) Hey, lights! Kill everything! (*As soon as he has said this, all the lights go out completely and leave him in the pitch dark.*) For God's sake!! You might have left the workers! I can't see where I'm going!

(*Suddenly, behind the skycloth, as if because of a bad connection, a green light comes up to throw on the cloth a huge sharp shadow of the* CHARACTERS, *but without the little* BOY *and the* LITTLE GIRL. *The* PRODUCER, *seeing this, jumps off the stage, terrified. At the same time the flood of light on them is switched off and the stage is again bathed in the same blue light as before. Slowly the* SON *comes on from the right, followed by the* MOTHER *with her arms raised towards him. Then from the left, the* FATHER *enters.*)

(*They come together in the middle of the stage and stand there as if transfixed. Finally from the left the* STEPDAUGHTER *comes on and moves towards the steps at the front: on the top step she pauses for a moment to look back at the other three and then bursts out in a raucous laugh, dashes down the steps and turns to look at the three figures still on the stage. Then she runs out of the auditorium and we can still hear her manic laughter out into the foyer and beyond.*)

(*After a pause the curtain falls slowly.*)

Bertolt Brecht

Bertolt Brecht (1898–1956) changed the course of the modern European theater—and theater around the world—more than any playwright since Ibsen. However, Brecht's sphere of influence extends beyond his career as a playwright. As a dramatist, he wrote an unsurpassed body of plays; as a theoretician, Brecht's conception of "alienation" in the epic theater opened the way for sweeping innovation in our understanding of the possibilities of the stage; as a director, Brecht's work with his company, the Berliner Ensemble, made it the most influential and important theater in postwar Europe. The challenge of understanding Brecht is to understand the dialectical interplay between theory and practice that informs his assault on stage realism, and on the bourgeois theater itself.

Eugen Berthold Brecht (he later changed his name to Bertolt) was born in Augsburg, Bavaria, in 1898 to a prosperous family. In 1917, he enrolled at Munich University in the natural sciences and worked as a drama critic on the side. He also began work on several plays, including *Baal* (1917). In 1918 he was conscripted into military service for the remainder of World War I and worked in a military hospital. He returned briefly to the university after the war, but soon turned his attention full time to the theater. He moved to Berlin—Germany's theatrical capital at the time—and had the good fortune to work with two influential directors, Max Reinhardt and Erwin Piscator. Piscator advocated the use of new technologies in the theater, as a way of developing a kind of performance more responsive to the mechanized and accelerated routines of modern life. Brecht acknowledged that many of his own staging techniques were derived from his work with Piscator in the 1920s. Throughout the 1920s and early 1930s, Brecht wrote a series of plays that brought him notoriety, largely for their satire of the bourgeois establishment: *Drums in the Night* (1919), *In the Jungle of Cities* (1921), *Man Is Man* (1926), and the musical plays he wrote in collaboration with the composer Kurt Weill, *The Threepenny Opera* (1928) and *The Rise and Fall of the City of Mahagonny* (1930). In the 1920s, Brecht also began to collaborate with Margarete Steffin, one of several women—including Elisabeth Hauptmann, Hella Wuolijoki, and Ruth Berlau—with whom he collaborated as playwright.

Brecht also began his serious reading of Marx in the 1920s, and it was his application of Marxist dialectic to the process of theater that gave rise to his most powerful and original ideas for the stage. From Marx, Brecht adopted a revolutionary posture, not only toward the class struggle, but toward the stage of bourgeois "realism." To Brecht, the realistic theater was not an unbiased window on social reality. Instead, Brecht argued that realistic theater presented a particular political vision, a view of society as inevitably determined by history and evolution, and therefore not susceptible to change. In order to displace "realism," and to demonstrate these hidden politics, Brecht redefined Marx's conception of "alienation" as a theatrical practice. In *Das Kapital*, Marx argues that the division of labor in modern industrial production has altered the relationship between mankind and the world. In modern industry, workers sell their labor in order to produce commodities. These commodities, Marx contends, then seem "alien" in that they appear to have arisen magically. Capitalist production conceals the signs of how they were produced, so that commodities come to have a "natural" life of their own. Yet, even as commodities seem to come alive, the workers become dehumanized, incorporated into the machinery of production. In the world of capital, where everything is for sale, all human relations, lives, and desires become commodified. The prevailing view of the world—in which commodities confront workers as something natural and entirely separate from their makers—is, to Marx, a *false* view, perpetuated within the bourgeois social order to the political advantage of the ruling classes.

Brecht's theater works to provide its audience with ways of regarding bourgeois reality—including realistic theater and drama—as "unnatural," as a political vision, as an ideological view of the world produced in the interest of profit. Brecht's theater, that is, works to "alienate" or "estrange" the audience from the commonplace "realities" of daily life—which we have unreflectively come to regard as "natural" and "inevitable"—in order to train us to question the world made by modern capitalism and the society it sustains. As he wrote in "The Modern Theater Is the Epic Theater," his theater is based on a "radical separation of the elements" of production, rather than on the scenic unity typical of realism. The seamless illusion of the realistic stage is that theater's most seductive commodity: it constantly and subliminally urges the audience to accept its "picture" of reality as a natural, apolitical image of the world as it is. Brecht's theater, in contrast, always shows both the dramatic illusion (the character, the setting, the action) and the process of its making (the work of the actor, the machinery of the theater, the activities of the stage). Brecht works to show the "means of production" in his theater, as a way of suggesting that stage realism, like social reality outside the theater, is *made*, not given.

Brecht called this theater by a variety of names, including **EPIC THEATER,** the term now generally used for Brecht's body of theory and technique. Brecht's plays tend to be episodic, a disconnected, open-ended **MONTAGE** of scenes: The audience must arrive at its own understanding of how the events are linked together, rather than being given an apparently inevitable narrative. Brecht generally left the stage bare in his productions, as a way of preventing the audience from seeing a complete illusion of some fictional dramatic locale. He exposed the lights above the stage, so the audience could see how lights influence the mood of the scene and so influence the audience's judgment. Brecht fragmented the "realistic" unity of the setting in other ways, too. Films could be projected on screens above the stage, forcing the audience to hold the drama in counterpoint to more recent events; placards onstage described the action to take place before the scene began. Finally, Brecht also urged his actors not to empathize entirely with the characters they played, but to strike a balance between a Stanislavskian identification with the character (being "in character," acting the character entirely from his or her point of view) and a more demonstrative attitude, one that enables the actor to represent the character from a variety of perspectives. Through these means, Brecht worked to involve the audience in the process of the play's production. Rather than being seduced by a commodified illusion of reality, the audience of epic theater is invited to consider, and enjoy, how the theater makes its fictions—as a way of teaching the audience to adopt a more critical, "alienated" way of seeing life outside the theater.

Brecht used many of these devices in *The Threepenny Opera* and in the series of plays he wrote in exile. Forced to flee Germany by Nazi purges of left-wing writers in 1933, Brecht spent the greater part of his creative life on the run, living briefly in Sweden, in Finland, and finally in Santa Monica, California, from 1941 to 1947. Although he had drafted *Life of Galileo* in 1938, Brecht continued to work on the play in California, collaborating on an English version with the actor Charles Laughton. He was also questioned by the House Un-American Activities Committee in 1947, as part of its infamous investigation of communism in the entertainment industry. Brecht was not charged and left the United States the following day to return to Europe and Germany. Living in exile, with no theater and little support, Brecht wrote his major plays: *Life of Galileo* (1938), *The Good Person of Szechwan* (1939), *Mother Courage and Her Children* (1939), and *The Caucasian Chalk Circle* (1944). He also wrote his most important theoretical essays, including *A Short Organum for the Theater,* written in Zurich, Switzerland in 1947, but published in 1948 after Brecht returned to Germany.

Brecht returned to East Berlin in 1947 and established his company, the Berliner Ensemble. Brecht's antirealist plays had long been the source of conflict with the **SOCIAL RE-ALISM** advocated by the Communist Party, and even after the war Brecht had to work with a wary eye on the East German authorities. Nonetheless, the Berliner Ensemble—under Brecht's guidance and with the talents of his wife, Helene Weigel—became the leading European production company of the 1950s, sowing the seeds of innovation in every country they visited. Brecht died in August of 1956, just before the Berliner Ensemble's stunning visit to London, but the influence of his conception of theater has become worldwide, visible in plays from Luis Valdez's *Los Vendidos* to Caryl Churchill's *Cloud Nine* to Tony Kushner's *Angels in America* to Maishe Maponya's *Gangsters*.

MOTHER COURAGE AND HER CHILDREN

Mother Courage and Her Children is typical of Brecht's innovative approach to theater and to "political theater" as well. Rather than presenting a thesis, the play works to question the audience's attitudes about a variety of social institutions: warfare, business, motherhood, morality. In a parable-like series of scenes reminiscent both of expressionist theater and of morality drama, *Mother Courage and Her Children* invites the audience to estrange, and so reconsider, its ways of mapping the world.

In his model-book of the play, Brecht wrote that he wanted to show that "war, which is a continuation of business by other means, makes the human virtues fatal to their possessors." The play considers this problem in a variety of challenging ways. Although it is perhaps tempting to see Courage—Why is she called Courage? Was she courageous?—as a tragic heroine, the play relentlessly questions her "heroic" survival, and our own attitudes about the distinctions between war, business, and morality. As Scene I demonstrates, war and business create an all-embracing market in which everything is commodified, that is, for sale. Mother Courage sells a belt buckle and loses a son as part of the same transaction.

Much of the play's power onstage arises through its use of physical space and a few significant properties. The wagon—Courage's home, her means of survival, her mode of production—becomes in a sense the play's central "character." Placing it on a turntable, most productions convey the sense that the wagon is almost always in motion, yet never actually getting anywhere, much as Courage herself enters the play and leaves it singing the same song. Courage's fortunes are emblematized by the wagon as well. Loaded with goods and pulled by her two strong sons in the first scene, it is battered, barren, and empty in the last,

Mother Courage and Kattrin harness themselves to the wagon in Bertolt Brecht's *Mother Courage and Her Children*.

pulled by Mother Courage herself as she struggles to catch up with the army. Brecht was attracted to the idea of using the wagon, the play's economic and material "base," so to speak, to elucidate some of the play's symbolic or moral themes. He used Courage's wash-line to link the wagon to the cannon at the opening of scene 3, tying warfare, the economy, and the domestic sphere together. He raised the harness-poles to form a kind of crucifix after the death of her son Swiss Cheese. Many of the most ironic moments of the Berliner Ensemble production of the play were Weigel's invention: as Mother Courage, she bit the coin in Scene I and slowly measured her pennies out of her purse when she paid the peasants to bury Kattrin at the end of the play. This is the kind of moment that Brecht worked— in theory, as a playwright, in directing productions—to make happen in the theater, a moment when a single gesture forces the audience to consider the scene in a new light, to question the relationship between its ideas of identity and morality and the society that gives them shape and meaning.

MOTHER COURAGE AND HER CHILDREN
A CHRONICLE OF THE THIRTY YEARS' WAR

Bertolt Brecht

TRANSLATED BY JOHN WILLETT

CHARACTERS

MOTHER COURAGE	A CLERK
KATTRIN, *her dumb daughter*	A YOUNG SOLDIER
EILIF, *the elder son*	AN OLDER SOLDIER
SWISS CHEESE, *the younger son*	A PEASANT
THE RECRUITER	THE PEASANT'S WIFE
THE SERGEANT	THE YOUNG MAN
THE COOK	THE OLD WOMAN
THE GENERAL	ANOTHER PEASANT
THE CHAPLAIN	HIS WIFE
THE ARMOURER	THE YOUNG PEASANT
YVETTE POTTIER	THE ENSIGN
THE MAN WITH THE PATCH	SOLDIERS
ANOTHER SERGEANT	A VOICE
THE ANCIENT COLONEL	

SCENE ONE

Spring 1624. The Swedish Commander-in-Chief Count Oxenstierna is raising troops in Dalecarlia for the Polish campaign. The canteen woman Anna Fierling, known under the name of Mother Courage, loses one son.

Country road near a town.

A SERGEANT *and a* RECRUITER *stand shivering.*

RECRUITER: How can you muster a unit in a place like this? I've been thinking about suicide, sergeant. Here am I, got to find our commander four companies before the twelfth of the month, and people round here are so nasty I can't
5 sleep nights. S'pose I get hold of some bloke and shut my eye to his pigeon chest and varicose veins, I get him proper drunk, he signs on the line, I'm just settling up, he goes for a piss, I follow him to the door because I smell a rat; bob's your uncle, he's off like a flea with the itch. No notion of
10 word of honour, loyalty, faith, sense of duty. This place has shattered my confidence in the human race, sergeant.

SERGEANT: It's too long since they had a war here; stands to reason. Where's their sense of morality to come from? Peace—that's just a mess; takes a war to restore order.
15 Peacetime, the human race runs wild. People and cattle get buggered about, who cares? Everyone eats just as he feels inclined, a hunk of cheese on top of his nice white bread, and a slice of fat on top of the cheese. How many young blokes and good horses in that town there, nobody knows;
20 they never thought of counting. I been in places ain't seen a war for nigh seventy years: folks hadn't got names to them, couldn't tell one another apart. Takes a war to get proper nominal rolls and inventories—shoes in bundles and corn in bags, and man and beast properly numbered
25 and carted off, cause it stands to reason: no order, no war.

RECRUITER: Too true.

SERGEANT: Same with all good things, it's a job to get a war going. But once it's blossomed out there's no holding it; folk start fighting shy of peace like punters what can't stop for fear of having to tot up what they lost. Before that it's 30 war they're fighting shy of. It's something new to them.

RECRUITER: Hey, here's a cart coming. Two tarts with two young fellows. Stop her, sergeant. If this one's a flop I'm not standing around in your spring winds any longer, I can tell you. 35

(Sound of a jew's-harp. Drawn by two young fellows, a covered cart rolls in. On it sit MOTHER COURAGE *and her dumb daughter* KATTRIN.)

MOTHER COURAGE: Morning, sergeant.
SERGEANT: *(Blocking the way.)* Morning, all. And who are you?
MOTHER COURAGE: Business folk. *(Sings.)*

> You captains, tell the drums to slacken
> And give your infanteers a break: 40
> It's Mother Courage with her waggon
> Full of the finest boots they make.
> With crawling lice and looted cattle
> With lumbering guns and straggling kit—
> How can you flog them into battle 45
> Unless you get them boots that fit?
>   The new year's come. The watchmen shout.
>   The thaw sets in. The dead remain.
>   Whatever life has not died out
>   It staggers to its feet again. 50
>
> Captains, how can you make them face it—
> Marching to death without a brew?
> Courage has rum with which to lace it
> And boil their souls and bodies through.
> Their musket primed, their stomach hollow— 55
> Captains, your men don't look so well.
> So feed them up and let them follow

While you command them into hell.
The new year's come. The watchmen shout.
60 The thaw sets in. The dead remain.
Wherever life has not died out
It staggers to its feet again.

SERGEANT: Halt! Who are you with, you trash?

THE ELDER SON: Second Finnish Regiment.

65 SERGEANT: Where's your papers?

MOTHER COURAGE: Papers?

THE YOUNGER SON: What, mean to say you don't know Mother Courage?

SERGEANT: Never heard of her. What's she called Courage for?

70 MOTHER COURAGE: Courage is the name they gave me because I was scared of going broke, sergeant, so I drove me cart right through the bombardment of Riga with fifty loaves of bread aboard. They were going mouldy, it was high time, hadn't any choice really.

75 SERGEANT: Don't be funny with me. Your papers.

MOTHER COURAGE: (*Pulling a bundle of papers from a tin box and climbing down off the cart.*) That's all my papers, sergeant. You'll find a whole big missal from Altötting in Bavaria for wrapping gherkins in, and a road map of Moravia, the Lord
80 knows when I'll ever get there, might as well chuck it away, and here's a stamped certificate that my horse hasn't got foot-and-mouth, only he's dead worse luck, cost fifteen florins he did—not me luckily. That enough paper for you?

SERGEANT: You pulling my leg? I'll knock that sauce out of
85 you. S'pose you know you got to have a licence.

MOTHER COURAGE: Talk proper to me, do you mind, and don't you dare say I'm pulling your leg in front of my unsullied children, 'tain't decent, I got no time for you. My honest face, that's me licence with the Second Regiment,
90 and if it's too difficult for you to read there's nowt I can do about it. Nobody's putting a stamp on that.

RECRUITER: Sergeant, methinks I smell insubordination in this individual. What's needed in our camp is obedience.

MOTHER COURAGE: Sausage, if you ask me.

95 SERGEANT: Name.

MOTHER COURAGE: Anna Fierling.

SERGEANT: You all called Fierling then?

MOTHER COURAGE: What d'you mean? It's me's called Fierling, not them.

100 SERGEANT: Aren't all this lot your children?

MOTHER COURAGE: You bet they are, but why should they all have to be called the same, eh? (*Pointing to her elder son.*) For instance, that one's called Eilif Nojocki—Why? his father always claimed he was called Kojocki or Mojocki or some-
105 thing. The boy remembers him clearly, except that the one he remembers was someone else, a Frenchie with a little beard. Aside from that he's got his father's wits; that man knew how to snitch a peasant's pants off his bum without him noticing. This way each of us has his own name, see.

110 SERGEANT: What, each one different?

MOTHER COURAGE: Don't tell me you ain't never come across that.

SERGEANT: So I s'pose he's a Chinaman? (*Pointing to the younger son.*)

115 MOTHER COURAGE: Wrong. Swiss.

SERGEANT: After the Frenchman?

MOTHER COURAGE: What Frenchman? I never heard tell of no Frenchman. You keep muddling things up, we'll be hanging around here till dark. A Swiss, but called Fejos, and the name has nowt to do with his father. He was
120 called something quite different and was a fortifications engineer, only drunk all the time.

(SWISS CHEESE *beams and nods; dumb* KATTRIN *too is amused.*)

SERGEANT: How in hell can he be called Fejos?

MOTHER COURAGE: I don't like to be rude, sergeant, but you ain't got much imagination, have you? Course he's called
125 Fejos, because when he arrived I was with a Hungarian, very decent fellow, had terrible kidney trouble though he never touched a drop. The boy takes after him.

SERGEANT: But he wasn't his father . . .

MOTHER COURAGE: Took after him just the same. I call him
130 Swiss Cheese. (*Pointing to her daughter.*) And that's Kattrin Haupt, she's half German.

SERGEANT: Nice family, I must say.

MOTHER COURAGE: Aye, me cart and me have seen the world.

SERGEANT: I'm writing all this down. (*He writes.*) And you're
135 from Bamberg in Bavaria; how d'you come to be here?

MOTHER COURAGE: Can't wait till war chooses to visit Bamberg, can I?

RECRUITER: (*To* EILIF.) You two should be called Jacob Ox and Esau Ox, pulling the cart like that. I s'pose you never
140 get out of harness?

EILIF: Ma, can I clobber him one? I wouldn't half like to.

MOTHER COURAGE: And I says you can't; just you stop where you are. And now two fine officers like you, I bet you could use a good pistol, or a belt buckle, yours is on its last
145 legs, sergeant.

SERGEANT: I could use something else. Those boys are healthy as young birch trees, I observe: chests like barrels, solid leg muscles. So why are they dodging their military service, may I ask?
150

MOTHER COURAGE: (*Quickly.*) Nowt doing, sergeant. Yours is no trade for my kids.

RECRUITER: But why not? There's good money in it, glory too. Flogging boots is women's work. (*To* EILIF.) Come here, let's see if you've muscles in you or if you're a chicken.
155

MOTHER COURAGE: He's a chicken. Give him a fierce look, he'll fall over.

RECRUITER: Killing a young bull that happens to be in his way. (*Wants to lead him off.*)

MOTHER COURAGE: Let him alone, will you? He's nowt for
160 you folk.

RECRUITER: He was crudely offensive and talked about clobbering me. The two of us are going to step into that field and settle it man to man.

EILIF: Don't you worry, mum, I'll fix him.
165

MOTHER COURAGE: Stop there! You varmint! I know you, nowt but fights. There's a knife down his boot. A slasher, that's what he is.

RECRUITER: I'll draw it out of him like a milk-tooth. Come along, sonny.
170

MOTHER COURAGE: Sergeant, I'll tell the colonel. He'll have you both in irons. The lieutenant's going out with my daughter.

SERGEANT: No rough stuff, chum. (*To* MOTHER COURAGE.)
175   What you got against military service? Wasn't his own father a soldier? Died a soldier's death, too? Said it yourself.
MOTHER COURAGE: He's nowt but a child. You want to take
him off to slaughterhouse, I know you lot. They'll give
you five florins for him.
180 RECRUITER: First he's going to get a smart cap and boots, eh?
EILIF: Not from you.
MOTHER COURAGE: Let's both go fishing, said angler to
worm. (*To* SWISS CHEESE.) Run off, call out they're trying
to kidnap your brother. (*She pulls a knife.*) Go on, you kid-
185   nap him, just try. I'll slit you open, trash. I'll teach you to
make war with him. We're doing an honest trade in ham
and linen, and we're peaceable folk.
SERGEANT: Peaceable I don't think; look at your knife. You
should be ashamed of yourself; put that knife away, you
190   old harridan. A minute back you were admitting you live
off the war, how else should you live, what from? But
how's anyone to have war without soldiers?
MOTHER COURAGE: No need for it to be my kids.
SERGEANT: Oh, you'd like war to eat the pips but spit out the
195   apple? It's to fatten up your kids, but you won't invest in
it. Got to look after itself, eh? And you called Courage,
fancy that. Scared of the war that keeps you going? Your
sons aren't scared of it, I can see that.
EILIF: Take more than a war to scare me.
200 SERGEANT: And why? Look at me: has army life done all that
badly by me? Joined up at seventeen.
MOTHER COURAGE: Still got to reach seventy.
SERGEANT: I don't mind waiting.
MOTHER COURAGE: Under the sod, eh?
205 SERGEANT: You trying to insult me, saying I'll die?
MOTHER COURAGE: S'pose it's true? S'pose I can see the mark's
on you? S'pose you look like a corpse on leave to me? Eh?
SWISS CHEESE: She's got second sight, Mother has.
RECRUITER: Go ahead, tell the sergeant's fortune, might
210   amuse him.
MOTHER COURAGE: Gimme helmet. (*He gives it to her.*)
SERGEANT: It don't mean a bloody sausage. Anything for a
laugh though.
MOTHER COURAGE: (*Taking out a sheet of parchment and tearing it
215   up.*) Eilif, Swiss Cheese and Kattrin, may all of us be torn apart
like this if we lets ourselves get too mixed up in the war. (*To
the* SERGEANT.) Just for you I'm doing it for free. Black's for
death. I'm putting a big black cross on this slip of paper.
SWISS CHEESE: Leaving the other one blank, see?
220 MOTHER COURAGE: Then I fold them across and shake them.
All of us is jumbled together like this from our mother's
womb, and now draw a slip and you'll know. (*The
SERGEANT hesitates.*)
RECRUITER: (*To* EILIF.) I don't take just anybody, they all know
225   I'm choosey, but you got the kind of fire I like to see.
SERGEANT: (*Fishing in the helmet.*) Too silly. Load of eyewash.
SWISS CHEESE: Drawn a black cross, he has. Write him off.
RECRUITER: They're having you on; not everybody's name's
on a bullet.
230 SERGEANT: (*Hoarsely.*) You've put me in the shit.
MOTHER COURAGE: Did that yourself the day you became a
soldier. Come along, let's move on now. 'Tain't every day
we have a war, I got to get stirring.

SERGEANT: God damn it, you can't kid me. We're taking that
bastard of yours for a soldier.   235
EILIF: Swiss Cheese'd like to be a soldier too.
MOTHER COURAGE: First I've heard of that. You'll have to
draw too, all three of you. (*She goes to the rear to mark crosses
on further slips.*)
RECRUITER: (*To* EILIF.) One of the things they say against us is 240
that it's all holy-holy in the Swedish camp; but that's a malicious rumour to do us down. There's no hymn-singing but
Sundays, just a single verse, and then only for those got voices.
MOTHER COURAGE: (*Coming back with the slips, which she drops
into the* SERGEANT'*s helmet.*) Trying to get away from their 245
ma, the devils, off to war like calves to salt-lick. But I'm
making you draw lots, and that'll show you the world is no
vale of joys with 'Come along, son, we need a few more
generals'. Sergeant, I'm so scared they won't get through
the war. Such dreadful characters, all three of them. (*She 250
hands the helmet to* EILIF.) Hey, come on, fish out your slip.
(*He fishes one out, unfolds it. She snatches it from him.*) There
you are, it's a cross. Oh, wretched mother that I am, o pain-
racked giver of birth! Shall he die? Aye, in the springtime
of life he is doomed. If he becomes a soldier he shall bite 255
the dust, it's plain to see. He is too foolhardy, like his dad
was. And if he ain't sensible he'll go the way of all flesh, his
slip proves it. (*Shouts at him.*) You going to be sensible?
EILIF: Why not?
MOTHER COURAGE: Sensible thing is stay with your mother, 260
never mind if they poke fun at you and call you chicken,
just you laugh.
RECRUITER: If you're pissing in your pants I'll make do with
your brother.
MOTHER COURAGE: I told you laugh. Go on, laugh. Now you 265
draw, Swiss Cheese. I'm not so scared on your account,
you're honest. (*He fishes in the helmet.*) Oh, why look at
your slip in that strange way? It's got to be a blank. There
can't be any cross on it. Surely I'm not going to lose *you*.
(*She takes the slip.*) A cross? What, you too? Is that because 270
you're so simple, perhaps? O Swiss Cheese, you too will
be sunk if you don't stay utterly honest all the while, like
I taught you from childhood when you brought the
change back from the baker's. Else you can't save yourself.
Look, sergeant, that's a black cross, ain't it?   275
SERGEANT: A cross, that's right. Can't think how I come to
get one. I always stay in the rear. (*To the* RECRUITER.)
There's no catch. Her own family get it too.
SWISS CHEESE: I get it too. But I listen to what I'm told.
MOTHER COURAGE: (*To* KATTRIN.) And now you're the only 280
one I know's all right, you're a cross yourself; got a kind
heart you have. (*Holds the helmet up to her on the cart, but
takes the slip out herself.*) No, that's too much. That can't be
right; must have made a mistake shuffling. Don't be too
kindhearted, Kattrin, you'll have to give it up, there's a 285
cross above your path too. Lie doggo, girl, it can't be that
hard once you're born dumb. Right, all of you know now.
Look out for yourselves, you'll need to. And now up we
get and on we go. (*She climbs on to the cart.*)
RECRUITER: (*To the* SERGEANT.) Do something.   290
SERGEANT: I don't feel very well.
RECRUITER: Must of caught a chill taking your helmet off in
that wind. Involve her in a deal. (*Aloud.*) Might as well

have a look at that belt-buckle, sergeant. After all, our
friends here have to live by their business. Hey, you people, the sergeant wants to buy that belt-buckle.

MOTHER COURAGE: Half a florin. Two florins is what a belt
like that's worth. (*Climbs down again.*)

SERGEANT: 'Tain't new. Let me get out of this damned wind and
have a proper look at it. (*Goes behind the cart with the buckle.*)

MOTHER COURAGE: Ain't what I call windy.

SERGEANT: I s'pose it might be worth half a florin, it's silver.

MOTHER COURAGE: (*Joining him behind the cart.*) It's six solid
ounces.

RECRUITER: (*To* EILIF.) And then we men'll have one together. Got your bounty money here, come along. (EILIF
stands undecided.)

MOTHER COURAGE: Half a florin it is.

SERGEANT: It beats me. I'm always at the rear. Sergeant's the
safest job there is. You can send the others up front, cover
themselves with glory. Me dinner hour's properly spoiled.
Shan't be able to hold nowt down, I know.

MOTHER COURAGE: Mustn't let it prey on you so's you can't
eat. Just stay at the rear. Here, take a swig of brandy, man.
(*Gives him a drink.*)

RECRUITER: (*Has taken* EILIF *by the arm and is leading him away
up stage.*) Ten florins bounty money, then you're a gallant
fellow fighting for the king and women'll be after you like
flies. And you can clobber me for free for insulting you.

(*Exeunt both.*)

(*Dumb* KATTRIN *leans down from the cart and makes hoarse noises.*)

MOTHER COURAGE: All right, Kattrin, all right. Sergeant's just
paying. (*Bites the half-florin.*) I got no faith in any kind of
money. Burnt child, that's me, sergeant. This coin's good,
though. And now let's get moving. Where's Eilif?

SWISS CHEESE: Went off with the recruiter.

MOTHER COURAGE: (*Stands quite still, then.*) You simpleton.
(*To* KATTRIN.) 'Tain't your fault, you can't speak, I know.

SERGEANT: Could do with a swig yourself, ma. That's life.
Plenty worse things than being a soldier. Want to live off
war, but keep yourself and family out of it, eh?

MOTHER COURAGE: You'll have to help your brother pull
now, Kattrin.

(*Brother and sister hitch themselves to the cart and start pulling.*
MOTHER COURAGE *walks alongside. The cart rolls on.*)

SERGEANT: (*Looking after them.*)
Like the war to nourish you?
Have to feed it something too.

SCENE TWO

In the years 1625 and 1626 Mother Courage crosses
Poland in the train of the Swedish armies. Before the
fortress of Wallhof she meets her son again. Successful
sale of a capon and heyday of her dashing son.

The GENERAL'S *tent.*

Beside it, his kitchen. Thunder of cannon. The COOK *is arguing
with* MOTHER COURAGE, *who wants to sell him a capon.*

THE COOK: Sixty hellers for a miserable bird like that?

MOTHER COURAGE: Miserable bird? This fat brute? Mean to
say some greedy old general—and watch your step if you
got nowt for his dinner—can't afford sixty hellers for him?

THE COOK: I can get a dozen like that for ten hellers just
down the road.

MOTHER COURAGE: What, a capon like this you can get just
down the road? In time of siege, which means hunger that
tears your guts. A rat you might get: 'might' I say because
they're all being gobbled up, five men spending best part
of day chasing one hungry rat. Fifty hellers for a giant
capon in time of siege!

THE COOK: But it ain't us having the siege, it's t'other side.
We're conducting the siege, can't you get that in your head?

MOTHER COURAGE: But we got nowt to eat too, even worse
than them in the town. Took it with them, didn't they?
They're having a high old time, everyone says. And look
at us! I been to the peasants, there's nowt there.

THE COOK: There's plenty. They're sitting on it.

MOTHER COURAGE: (*Triumphantly.*) They ain't. They're bust,
that's what they are. Just about starving. I saw some, were
grubbing up roots from sheer hunger, licking their fingers
after they boiled some old leather strap. That's way it is.
And me got a capon here and supposed to take forty
hellers for it.

THE COOK: Thirty, not forty. I said thirty.

MOTHER COURAGE: Here, this ain't just any old capon. It was
such a gifted beast, I been told, it could only eat to music,
had a military march of its own. It could count, it was that
intelligent. And you say forty hellers is too much? General
will make mincemeat of you if there's nowt on his table.

THE COOK: See what I'm doing? (*He takes a piece of beef and
puts his knife to it.*) Here I got a bit of beef, I'm going to
roast it. Make up your mind quick.

MOTHER COURAGE: Go on, roast it. It's last year's.

THE COOK: Last night's. That animal was still alive and kicking, I saw him myself.

MOTHER COURAGE: Alive and stinking, you mean.

THE COOK: I'll cook him five hours if need be. I'll just see if
he's still tough. (*He cuts into it.*)

MOTHER COURAGE: Put plenty of pepper on it so his lordship the general don't smell the pong.

(*The* GENERAL, *a* CHAPLAIN *and* EILIF *enter the tent.*)

THE GENERAL: (*Slapping* EILIF *on the shoulder.*) Now then, Eilif
my son, into your general's tent with you and sit thou at
my right hand. For you accomplished a deed of heroism,
like a pious cavalier; and doing what you did for God, and
in a war of religion at that, is something I commend in
you most highly, you shall have a gold bracelet as soon as
we've taken this town. Here we are, come to save their
souls for them, and what do those insolent dung-
encrusted yokels go and do? Drive their beef away from
us. They stuff it into those priests of theirs all right, back
and front, but you taught 'em manners, ha! So here's a pot
of red wine for you, the two of us'll knock it back at one
gulp. (*They do so.*) Piss all for the chaplain, the old bigot.
And now, what would you like for dinner, my darling?

EILIF: A bit of meat, why not?

THE GENERAL: Cook! Meat!

THE COOK: And then he goes and brings guests when there's
60   nowt there.

(MOTHER COURAGE *silences him so she can listen.*)

EILIF: Hungry job cutting down peasants.
MOTHER COURAGE: Jesus Christ, it's my Eilif.
THE COOK: Your what?
MOTHER COURAGE: My eldest boy. It's two years since I lost
65   sight of him, they pinched him from me on the road, must
think well of him if the general's asking him to dinner, and
what kind of a dinner can you offer? Nowt. You heard
what the visitor wishes to eat: meat. Take my tip, you set-
tle for the capon, it'll be a florin.
70 THE GENERAL: (*Has sat down with* EILIF, *and bellows.*) Food,
Lamb, you foul cook, or I'll have your hide.
THE COOK: Give it over, dammit, this is blackmail.
MOTHER COURAGE: Didn't someone say it was a miserable bird?
THE COOK: Miserable; give it over, and a criminal price, fifty
75   hellers.
MOTHER COURAGE: A florin, I said. For my eldest boy, the
general's guest, no expense is too great for me.
THE COOK: (*Gives her the money.*) You might at least pluck it
while I see to the fire.
80 MOTHER COURAGE: (*Sits down to pluck the fowl.*) He won't
half be surprised to see me. He's my dashing clever son.
Then I got a stupid one too, he's honest though. The girl's
nowt. One good thing, she don't talk.
THE GENERAL: Drink up, my son, this is my best Falernian;
85   only got a barrel or two left, but that's nothing to pay for
a sign that's there's still true faith to be found in my army.
As for that shepherd of souls he can just look on, because
all he does is preach, without the least idea how it's to be
carried out. And now, my son Eilif, tell us more about the
90   neat way you smashed those yokels and captured the
twenty oxen. Let's hope they get here soon.
EILIF: A day or two at most.
MOTHER COURAGE: Thoughtful of our Eilif not to bring the
oxen in till tomorrow, else you lot wouldn't have looked
95   twice at my capon.
EILIF: Well, it was like this, see. I'd heard peasants had been
driving the oxen they'd hidden, out of the forest into one
particular wood, on the sly and mostly by night. That's
where people from the town were s'posed to come and
100   pick them up. So I holds off and lets them drive their oxen
together, reckoning they'd be better than me at finding
'em. I had my blokes slavering after the meat, cut their
emergency rations even further for a couple of days till
their mouths was watering at the least sound of any word
105   beginning with 'me-', like 'measles' say.
THE GENERAL: Very clever of you.
EILIF: Possibly. The rest was a piece of cake. Except that the
peasants had cudgels and outnumbered us three to one
and made a murderous attack on us. Four of 'em shoved
110   me into a thicket, knocked my sword from my hand and
bawled out 'Surrender!' What's the answer, I wondered;
they're going to make mincemeat of me.
THE GENERAL: What did you do?
EILIF: I laughed.
115 THE GENERAL: You did what?
EILIF: Laughed. So we got talking. I put it on a business footing from the start, told them 'Twenty florins a head's too

much. I'll give you fifteen'. As if I was meaning to pay.
That threw them, and they began scratching their heads.
In a flash I'd picked up my sword and was hacking 'em to 120
pieces. Necessity's the mother of invention, eh, sir?
THE GENERAL: What is your view, pastor of souls?
THE CHAPLAIN: That phrase is not strictly speaking in the
Bible, but when Our Lord turned the five loaves into five
hundred there was no war on and he could tell people to 125
love their neighbours as they'd had enough to eat. Today
it's another story.
THE GENERAL: (*Laughs.*) Quite another story. You can have a
swig after all for that, you old Pharisee. (*To* EILIF.) Hacked
'em to pieces, did you, so my gallant lads can get a proper 130
bite to eat? What do the Scriptures say? 'Whatsoever thou
doest for the least of my brethren, thou doest for me'. And
what did you do for them? Got them a good square meal
of beef, because they're not accustomed to mouldy bread,
the old way was to fix a cold meal of rolls and wine in 135
your helmet before you went out to fight for God.
EILIF: Aye, in a flash I'd picked up my sword and was hacking
them to pieces.
THE GENERAL: You've the makings of a young Caesar. You
ought to see the King. 140
EILIF: I have from a distance. He kind of glows. I'd like to
model myself on him.
THE GENERAL: You've got something in common already. I
appreciate soldiers like you, Eilif, men of courage. Somebody like that I treat as I would my own son. (*He leads him* 145
over to the map.) Have a look at the situation, Eilif; it's a
long haul still.
MOTHER COURAGE: (*Who has been listening and now angrily*
plucks the fowl.) That must be a rotten general.
THE COOK: He's ravenous all right, but why rotten? 150
MOTHER COURAGE: Because he's got to have men of courage,
that's why. If he knew how to plan a proper campaign what
would he be needing men of courage for? Ordinary ones
would do. It's always the same; whenever there's a load of
special virtues around it means something stinks. 155
THE COOK: I thought it meant things is all right.
MOTHER COURAGE: No, that they stink. Look, s'pose some
general or king is bone stupid and leads his men up shit
creek, then those men've got to be fearless, there's another
virtue for you. S'pose he's stingy and hires too few soldiers, 160
then they got to be a crowd of Hercules's. And s'pose he's
slapdash and don't give a bugger, then they got to be clever
as monkeys else their number's up. Same way they got to
show exceptional loyalty each time he gives them impossible jobs. Nowt but virtues no proper country and no decent 165
king or general would ever need. In decent countries folk
don't have to have virtues, the whole lot can be perfectly ordinary, average intelligence, and for all I know cowards.
THE GENERAL: I'll wager your father was a soldier.
EILIF: A great soldier, I been told. My mother warned me 170
about it. There's a song I know.
THE GENERAL: Sing it to us. (*Roars.*) When's that dinner coming?
EILIF: It's called The Song of the Girl and the Soldier. (*He*
sings it, dancing a war dance with his sabre.)

The guns blaze away, and the bay'nit'll slay 175
And the water can't hardly be colder.
What's the answer to ice? Keep off's my advice!

That's what the girl told the soldier.
Next thing the soldier, wiv' a round up the spout
180 Hears the band playing and gives a great shout:
Why, it's marching what makes you a soldier!
So it's down to the south and then northwards once more:
See him catching that bay'nit in his naked paw!
That's what his comrades done told her.

185 Oh, do not despise the advice of the wise
Learn wisdom from those that are older
And don't try for things that are out of your reach—
That's what the girl told the soldier.
Next thing the soldier, his bay'nit in place
190 Wades into the river and laughs in her face
Though the water comes up to his shoulder.
When the shingle roof glints in the light o' the moon
We'll be wiv' you again, not a moment too soon!
That's what his comrades done told her.

195 MOTHER COURAGE: (*Takes up the song in the kitchen, beating on a pot with her spoon.*)

You'll go out like a light! And the sun'll take flight
For your courage just makes us feel colder.
Oh, that vanishing light! May God see that it's right!—
200 That's what the girl told the soldier.

EILIF: What's that?
MOTHER COURAGE: (*Continues singing.*)

Next thing the soldier, his bay'nit in place
Was caught by the current and went down without trace
205 And the water couldn't hardly be colder.
Then the shingle roof froze in the light o' the moon
As both soldier and ice drifted down to their doom—
And d'you know what his comrades done told her?

He went out like a light. And the sunshine took flight
210 For his courage just made 'em feel colder.
Oh, do not despise the advice of the wise!
That's what the girl told the soldier.

THE GENERAL: The things they get up to in my kitchen these days.
215 EILIF: (*Has gone into the kitchen. He flings his arms round his mother.*) Fancy seeing you again, ma! Where's the others?
MOTHER COURAGE: (*In his arms.*) Snug as a bug in a rug. They made Swiss Cheese paymaster of the Second Finnish; any road he'll stay out of fighting that way, I
220 couldn't keep him out altogether.
EILIF: How's the old feet?
MOTHER COURAGE: Bit tricky getting me shoes on of a morning.
THE GENERAL: (*Has joined them.*) So you're his mother, I hope you've got plenty more sons for me like this one.
225 EILIF: Ain't it my lucky day? You sitting out there in the kitchen, ma, hearing your son commended . . .
MOTHER COURAGE: You bet I heard. (*Slaps his face.*)
EILIF: (*Holding his cheek.*) What's that for? Taking the oxen?
MOTHER COURAGE: No. Not surrendering when those four
230 went for you and wanted to make mincemeat of you. Didn't I say you should look after yourself? You Finnish devil!

(*The* GENERAL *and the* CHAPLAIN *stand in the doorway laughing.*)

SCENE THREE

Three years later Mother Courage is taken prisoner along with elements of a Finnish regiment. She manages to save her daughter, likewise her covered cart, but her honest son is killed.

Military camp.

Afternoon. A flagpole with the regimental flag. From her cart, festooned now with all kinds of goods, MOTHER COURAGE *has stretched a washing line to a large cannon, across which she and* KATTRIN *are folding the washing. She is bargaining at the same time with an* ARMOURER *over a sack of shot.* SWISS CHEESE, *now wearing a paymaster's uniform, is looking on.*

A comely person, YVETTE POTTIER, *is sewing a gaily coloured hat, a glass of brandy before her. She is in her stockinged feet, having laid aside her red high-heeled boots.*

THE ARMOURER: I'll let you have that shot for a couple of florins. It's cheap at the price, I got to have the money because the colonel's been boozing with his officers since two days back, and the drink's run out.
MOTHER COURAGE: That's troops' munitions. They catch me 5 with that, I'm for court-martial. You crooks flog the shot, and troops got nowt to fire at enemy.
THE ARMOURER: Have a heart, can't you; you scratch my back and I'll scratch yours.
MOTHER COURAGE: I'm not taking army property. Not at 10 that price.
THE ARMOURER: You can sell it on the q.t. tonight to the Fourth Regiment's armourer for five florins, eight even, if you let him have a receipt for twelve. He's right out of ammunition. 15
MOTHER COURAGE: Why not you do it?
THE ARMOURER: I don't trust him, he's a pal of mine.
MOTHER COURAGE: (*Takes the sack.*) Gimme. (*To* KATTRIN.) Take it away and pay him a florin and a half. (*The* ARMOURER *protests.*) I said a florin and a half. (KATTRIN *drags* 20 *the sack upstage, the* ARMOURER *following her* MOTHER COURAGE *addresses* SWISS CHEESE.) Here's your woollies, now look after them, it's October and autumn may set in any time. I ain't saying it's got to, cause I've learned nowt's got to come when you think it will, not even seasons of 25 the year. But your regimental accounts got to add up right, come what may. Do they add up right?
SWISS CHEESE: Yes, mother.
MOTHER COURAGE: Don't you forget they made you paymaster cause you was honest, not dashing like your 30 brother, and above all so stupid I bet you ain't even thought of clearing off with it, no not you. That's a big consolation to me. And don't lose those woollies.
SWISS CHEESE: No, mother, I'll put them under my mattress. (*Begins to go.*) 35
THE ARMOURER: I'll go along with you, paymaster.
MOTHER COURAGE: And don't you start learning him none of your tricks.

(*The* ARMOURER *leaves with* SWISS CHEESE *without any farewell gesture.*)

YVETTE: (*Waving to him.*) No reason not to say goodbye, ar-
40   mourer.
MOTHER COURAGE: (*To* YVETTE.) I don't like to see them to-
     gether. He's wrong company for our Swiss Cheese. Oh
     well, war's off to a good start. Easily take four, five years
     before all countries are in. A bit of foresight, don't do
45   nothing silly, and business'll flourish. Don't you know you
     ain't s'posed to drink before midday with your complaint?
YVETTE: Complaint, who says so, it's a libel.
MOTHER COURAGE: They all say so.
YVETTE: Because they're all telling lies, Mother Courage, and
50   me at my wits' end cause they're all avoiding me like
     something the cat brought in thanks to those lies, what
     the hell am I remodelling my hat for? (*She throws it away.*)
     That's why I drink before midday. Never used to, gives
     you crows' feet, but now what the hell? All the Second
55   Finnish know me. Ought to have stayed at home when
     my first fellow did me wrong. No good our sort being
     proud. Eat shit, that's what you got to do, or down you go.
MOTHER COURAGE: Now don't you start up again about that
60   Pieter of yours and how it all happened, in front of my in-
     nocent daughter too.
YVETTE: She's the one should hear it, put her off love.
MOTHER COURAGE: Nobody can put 'em off that.
YVETTE: Then I'll go on, get it off my chest. It all starts with
     yours truly growing up in lovely Flanders, else I'd never of
65   seen him and wouldn't be stuck here now in Poland, cause
     he was an army cook, fair-haired, a Dutchman but thin for
     once. Kattrin, watch out for the thin ones, only in those
     days I didn't know that, or that he'd got a girl already, or
     that they all called him Puffing Piet cause he never took his
70   pipe out of his mouth when he was on the job, it meant
     that little to him. (*She sings the Song of Fraternisation.*)

       When I was only sixteen
       The foe came into our land.
       He laid aside his sabre
75   And with a smile he took my hand.
       After the May parade
       The May light starts to fade.
       The regiment dressed by the right
       The drums were beaten, that's the drill.
80   The foe took us behind the hill
       And fraternised all night.

       There were so many foes then
       But mine worked in the mess.
       I loathed him in the daytime.
85   At night I loved him none the less.
       After the May parade
       The May light starts to fade.
       The regiment dressed by the right
       The drums were beaten, that's the drill.
90   The foe took us behind the hill
       And fraternised all night.

       The love which came upon me
       Was wished on me by fate.
       My friends could never grasp why
95   I found it hard to share their hate.
       The fields were wet with dew
       When sorrow first I knew.

       The regiment dressed by the right
       The drums were beaten, that's the drill.
       And then the foe, my lover still   100
       Went marching out of sight.

I followed him, fool that I was, but I never found him, and
that was five years back. (*She walks unsteadily behind the cart.*)
MOTHER COURAGE: You left your hat here.
YVETTE: Anyone wants it can have it.   105
MOTHER COURAGE: Let that be a lesson, Kattrin. Don't you
     start anything with them soldiers. Love makes the world
     go round, I'm warning you. Even with fellows not in the
     army it's no bed of roses. He says he'd like to kiss the
     ground your feet walk on—reminds me, did you wash   110
     them yesterday?—and after that you're his skivvy. Be
     thankful you're dumb, then you can't contradict yourself
     and won't be wanting to bite your tongue off for speak-
     ing the truth; it's a godsend, being dumb is. And here
     comes the general's cook, now what's he after?   115

(*Enter the* COOK *and the* CHAPLAIN.)

THE CHAPLAIN: I have a message for you from your son Eilif,
     and the cook has come along because you made such a
     profound impression on him.
THE COOK: I just came along to get a bit of air.
MOTHER COURAGE: That you can always do here if you be-   120
     have yourself, and if you don't I can deal with you. What
     does he want? I got no spare cash.
THE CHAPLAIN: Actually I had a message for his brother the
     paymaster.
MOTHER COURAGE: He ain't here now nor anywhere else   125
     neither. He ain't his brother's paymaster. He's not to lead
     him into temptation nor be clever at his expense. (*Giving
     him money from the purse slung round her.*) Give him this, it's
     a sin, he's banking on mother's love and ought to be
     ashamed of himself.   130
THE COOK: Not for long, he'll have to be moving off with
     the regiment, might be to his death. Give him a bit extra,
     you'll be sorry later. You women are tough, then later on
     you're sorry. A little glass of brandy wouldn't have been a
     problem, but it wasn't offered and, who knows, a bloke 135
     may lie beneath the green sod and none of you people
     will ever be able to dig him up again.
THE CHAPLAIN: Don't give way to your feelings, cook. To fall
     in battle is a blessing, not an inconvenience, and why? It is
     a war of faith. None of your common wars but a special 140
     one, fought for the faith and therefore pleasing to God.
THE COOK: Very true. It's a war all right in one sense, what
     with requisitioning, murder and looting and the odd bit of
     rape thrown in, but different from all the other wars be-
     cause it's a war of faith; stands to reason. But it's thirsty 145
     work at that, you must admit.
THE CHAPLAIN: (*To* MOTHER COURAGE, *indicating the* COOK.)
     I tried to stop him, but he says he's taken a shine to you,
     you figure in his dreams.
THE COOK: (*Lighting a stumpy pipe.*) Just want a glass of   150
     brandy from a fair hand, what harm in that? Only I'm
     groggy already cause the chaplain here's been telling such
     jokes all the way along you bet I'm still blushing.

MOTHER COURAGE: Him a clergyman too. I'd best give the
pair of you a drink or you'll start making me immoral
suggestions cause you've nowt else to do.

THE CHAPLAIN: Behold a temptation, said the court preacher,
and fell. (*Turning back to look at* KATTRIN *as he leaves.*) And
who is this entrancing young person?

MOTHER COURAGE: That ain't an entrancing but a decent
young person. (*The* CHAPLAIN *and the* COOK *go behind the
cart with* MOTHER COURAGE. KATTRIN *looks after them, then
walks away from her washing towards the hat. She picks it up
and sits down, pulling the red boots towards her.* MOTHER
COURAGE *can be heard in the background talking politics with
the* CHAPLAIN *and the* COOK.)

MOTHER COURAGE: Those Poles here in Poland had no business sticking their noses in. Right, our king moved in on
them, horse and foot, but did they keep the peace? no, went
and stuck their noses into their own affairs, they did, and fell
on king just as he was quietly clearing off. They committed
a breach of peace, that's what, so blood's on their own head.

THE CHAPLAIN: All our king minded about was freedom. The
emperor had made slaves of them all, Poles and Germans
alike, and the king had to liberate them.

THE COOK: Just what I say, your brandy's first rate, I weren't
mistaken in your face, but talk of the king, it cost the king
dear trying to give freedom to Germany, what with giving Sweden the salt tax, what cost the poor folk a bit, so
I've heard, on top of which he had to have the Germans
locked up and drawn and quartered cause they wanted to
carry on slaving for the emperor. Course the king took a
serious view when anybody didn't want to be free. He set
out by just trying to protect Poland against bad people,
particularly the emperor, then it started to become a habit
till he ended up protecting the whole of Germany. They
didn't half kick. So the poor old king's had nowt but trouble for all his kindness and expenses, and that's something
he had to make up for by taxes of course, which caused
bad blood, not that he'd let a little matter like that depress
him. One thing he had on his side, God's word, that was a
help. Because otherwise folk would of been saying he
done it all for himself and to make a bit on the side. So
he's always had a good conscience, which was the main
point.

MOTHER COURAGE: Anyone can see you're no Swede or you
wouldn't be talking that way about the Hero King.

THE CHAPLAIN: After all he provides the bread you eat.

THE COOK: I don't eat it, I bake it.

MOTHER COURAGE: They'll never beat him, and why, his men
got faith in him. (*Seriously.*) To go by what the big shots
say, they're waging war for almighty God and in the name
of everything that's good and lovely. But look closer, they
ain't so silly, they're waging it for what they can get. Else
little folk like me wouldn't be in it at all.

THE COOK: That's the way it is.

THE CHAPLAIN: As a Dutchman you'd do better to glance at
the flag above your head before venting your opinions
here in Poland.

MOTHER COURAGE: All good Lutherans here. Prosit!

(KATTRIN *has put on* YVETTE's *hat and begun strutting around in
imitation of her way of walking.*)

(*Suddenly there is a noise of cannon fire and shooting. Drums.*
MOTHER COURAGE, *the* COOK *and the* CHAPLAIN *rush out from
behind the cart, the two last-named still carrying their glasses. The*
ARMOURER *and another* SOLDIER *run up to the cannon and try to
push it away.*)

MOTHER COURAGE: What's happening? Wait till I've taken my
washing down, you louts! (*She tries to rescue her washing.*)

THE ARMOURER: The Catholics! Broken through. Don't
know if we'll get out of here. (*To the* SOLDIER.) Get that
gun shifted! (*Runs on.*)

THE COOK: God, I must find the general. Courage, I'll drop
by in a day or two for another talk.

MOTHER COURAGE: Wait, you forgot your pipe.

THE COOK: (*In the distance.*) Keep it for me. I'll be needing it.

MOTHER COURAGE: Would happen just as we're making a bit
of money.

THE CHAPLAIN: Ah well, I'll be going too. Indeed, if the enemy is so close as that it might be dangerous. Blessèd are
the peacemakers is the motto in wartime. If only I had a
cloak to cover me.

MOTHER COURAGE: I ain't lending no cloaks, not on your
life. I been had too often.

THE CHAPLAIN: But my faith makes it particularly dangerous
for me.

MOTHER COURAGE: (*Gets him a cloak.*) Goes against my conscience, this does. Now you run along.

THE CHAPLAIN: Thank you, dear lady, that's very generous of
you, but I think it might be wiser for me to remain seated
here; it could arouse suspicion and bring the enemy down
on me if I were seen to run.

MOTHER COURAGE: (*To the* SOLDIER.) Leave it, you fool,
who's going to pay you for that? I'll look after it for you,
you're risking your neck.

THE SOLDIER: (*Running away.*) You can tell 'em I tried.

MOTHER COURAGE: Cross my heart. (*Sees her daughter with the
hat.*) What you doing with that strumpet's hat? Take that
lid off, you gone crazy? And the enemy arriving any
minute! (*Pulls the hat off* KATTRIN's *head.*) Want 'em to pick
you up and make a prostitute of you? And she's gone and
put those boots on, whore of Babylon! Off with those
boots! (*Tries to tug them off her.*) Jesus Christ, chaplain,
gimme a hand, get those boots off her, I'll be right back.
(*Runs to the cart.*)

YVETTE: (*Arrives, powdering her face.*) Fancy that, the Catholics
are coming. Where's my hat? Who's been kicking it
around? I can't go about looking like this if the Catholics
are coming. What'll they think of me? No mirror either.
(*To the* CHAPLAIN.) How do I look? Too much powder?

THE CHAPLAIN: Exactly right.

YVETTE: And where are them red boots? (*Fails to find them as*
KATTRIN *hides her feet under her skirt.*) I left them here all
right. Now I'll have to get to me tent barefoot. It's an outrage.

(*Exit.*)

(SWISS CHEESE *runs in carrying in a small box.*)

MOTHER COURAGE: (*Arrives with her hands full of ashes. To*
KATTRIN.) Here some ashes. (*To* SWISS CHEESE.) What's
that you're carrying?

SWISS CHEESE: Regimental cash box.

MOTHER COURAGE: Chuck it away. No more paymastering for you.

265 SWISS CHEESE: I'm responsible. (*He goes to the rear.*)

MOTHER COURAGE: (*To the* CHAPLAIN.) Take your clerical togs off, padre, or they'll spot you under that cloak. (*She rubs* KATTRIN's *face with ash.*) Keep still, will you? There you are, a bit of muck and you'll be safe. What a disaster.
270 Sentries were drunk. Hide your light under a bushel, it says. Take a soldier, specially a Catholic one, add a clean face, and there's your instant whore. For weeks they get nowt to eat, then soon as they manage to get it by looting they're falling on anything in skirts. That ought to do.
275 Let's have a look. Not bad. Looks like you been grubbing in muckheap. Stop trembling. Nothing'll happen to you like that. (*To* SWISS CHEESE.) Where d'you leave cash box?

SWISS CHEESE: Thought I'd put it in cart.

MOTHER COURAGE: (*Horrified.*) What, my cart? Sheer crimi-
280 nal idiocy. Only take me eyes off you one instant. Hang us all three, they will.

SWISS CHEESE: I'll put it somewhere else then, or clear out with it.

MOTHER COURAGE: You sit on it, it's too late now.

285 THE CHAPLAIN: (*Who is changing his clothes downstage.*) For heaven's sake, the flag!

MOTHER COURAGE: (*Hauls down the regimental flag.*) Bozhe moi! I'd given up noticing it were there. Twenty-five years I've had it.

(*The thunder of cannon intensifies.*)

(*A morning three days later. The cannon has gone.* MOTHER COURAGE, KATTRIN, *the* CHAPLAIN *and* SWISS CHEESE *are sitting gloomily over a meal.*)

290 SWISS CHEESE: That's three days I been sitting around with nowt to do, and sergeant's always been kind to me but any moment now he'll start asking where's Swiss Cheese with the pay box?

MOTHER COURAGE: You thank your stars they ain't after you.

295 THE CHAPLAIN: What can I say? I can't even hold a service here, it might make trouble for me. Whosoever hath a full heart, his tongue runneth over, it says, but heaven help me if mine starts running over.

MOTHER COURAGE: That's how it goes. Here they sit, one
300 with his faith and the other with his cash box. Dunno which is more dangerous.

THE CHAPLAIN: We are all of us in God's hands.

MOTHER COURAGE: Oh, I don't think it's as bad as that yet, though I must say I can't sleep nights. If it weren't for you,
305 Swiss Cheese, things'd be easier. I think I got meself cleared. I told 'em I didn't hold with Antichrist, the Swedish one with horns on, and I'd observed left horn was a bit unserviceable. Half way through their interrogation I asked where I could get church candles not too dear. I knows the
310 lingo cause Swiss Cheese's dad were Catholic, often used to make jokes about it, he did. They didn't believe me all that much, but they ain't got no regimental canteen lady. So they're winking an eye. Could turn out for the best, you know. We're prisoners, but same like fleas on dog.

THE CHAPLAIN: That's good milk. But we'll need to cut down 315 our Swedish appetites a bit. After all, we've been defeated.

MOTHER COURAGE: Who's been defeated? Look, victory and defeat ain't bound to be same for the big shots up top as for them below, not by no means. Can be times the bottom lot find a defeat really pays them. Honour's lost, nowt else. I re- 320 member once up in Livonia our general took such a beating from enemy I got a horse off our baggage train in the confusion, pulled me cart seven months, he did, before we won and they checked up. As a rule you can say victory and defeat both come expensive to us ordinary folk. Best thing for us is when 325 politics get bogged down solid. (*To* SWISS CHEESE.) Eat up.

SWISS CHEESE: Got no appetite for it. What's sergeant to do when pay day comes round?

MOTHER COURAGE: They don't have pay days on a retreat.

SWISS CHEESE: It's their right, though. They needn't retreat if 330 they don't get paid. Needn't stir a foot.

MOTHER COURAGE: Swiss Cheese, you're that conscientious it makes me quite nervous. I brought you up to be honest, you not being clever, but you got to know where to stop. Chaplain and me, we're off now to buy Catholic flag 335 and some meat. Dunno anyone so good at sniffing meat, like sleepwalking it is, straight to target. I'd say he can pick out a good piece by the way his mouth starts watering. Well, thank goodness they're letting me go on trading. You don't ask tradespeople their faith but their prices. 340 And Lutheran trousers keep cold out too.

THE CHAPLAIN: What did the mendicant say when he heard the Lutherans were going to turn everything in town and country topsy-turvy? 'They'll always need beggars'. (MOTHER COURAGE *disappears into the cart.*) So she's still 345 worried about the cash box. So far they've taken us all for granted as part of the cart, but how long for?

SWISS CHEESE: I can get rid of it.

THE CHAPLAIN: That's almost more dangerous. Suppose you're seen. They have spies. Yesterday a fellow popped 350 up out of the ditch in front of me just as I was relieving myself first thing. I was so scared I only just suppressed an ejaculatory prayer. That would have given me away all right. I think what they'd like best is to go sniffing people's excrement to see if they're Protestants. The spy was 355 a little runt with a patch over one eye.

MOTHER COURAGE: (*Clambering out of the cart with a basket.*) What have I found, you shameless creature? (*She holds up the red boots in triumph.*) Yvette's red high-heeled boots! Coolly went and pinched them, she did. Cause you put it in her 360 head she was an enchanting young person. (*She lays them in the basket.*) I'm giving them back. Stealing Yvette's boots! She's wrecking herself for money. That's understandable. But you'd do it for nothing, for pleasure. What did I tell you: you're to wait till it's peace. No soldiers for you. You're 365 not to start exhibiting yourself till it's peacetime.

THE CHAPLAIN: I don't find she exhibits herself.

MOTHER COURAGE: Too much for my liking. Let her be like a stone in Dalecarlia, where there's nowt else, so folk say 'Can't see that cripple', that's how I'd lief have her. Then 370 nowt'll happen to her. (*To* SWISS CHEESE.) You leave that box where it is, d'you hear? And keep an eye on your sister, she needs it. The pair of you'll have me in grave yet. Sooner be minding a bagful of fleas.

(*She leaves with the* CHAPLAIN. KATTRIN *clears away the dishes.*)

375 SWISS CHEESE: Won't be able to sit out in the sun in shirt-sleeves much longer. (KATTRIN *points at a tree.*) Aye, leaves turning yellow. (KATTRIN *asks by gestures if he wants a drink.*) Don't want no drink. I'm thinking. (*Pause.*) Said she can't sleep. Best if I got rid of that box, found a good
380 place for it. All right, let's have a glass. (KATTRIN *goes behind the cart.*) I'll stuff it down the rat-hole by the river for the time being. Probably pick it up tonight before first light and take it to Regiment. How far can they have retreated in three days? Bet sergeant's surprised. I'm agree-
385 ably disappointed in you, Swiss Cheese, he'll say. I make you responsible for the cash, and you go and bring it back.

(*As* KATTRIN *emerges from behind the cart with a full glass in her hand, two men confront her. One is a* SERGEANT, *the other doffs his hat to her. He has a patch over one eye.*)

THE MAN WITH THE PATCH: God be with you, mistress. Have you seen anyone round here from Second Finnish Regimental Headquarters?

(KATTRIN, *badly frightened, runs downstage, spilling the brandy. The two men look at one another, then withdraw on seeing* SWISS CHEESE *sitting there.*)

390 SWISS CHEESE: (*Interrupted in his thoughts.*) You spilt half of it. What are those faces for? Jabbed yourself in eye? I don't get it. And I'll have to be off, I've thought it over, it's the only way. (*He gets up. She does everything possible to make him realise the danger. He only shrugs her off.*) Wish I knew what
395 you're trying to say. Sure you mean well, poor creature, just can't get words out. What's it matter your spilling my brandy, I'll drink plenty more glasses yet, what's one more or less? (*He gets the box from the cart and takes it under his tunic.*) Be back in a moment. Don't hold me up now, or I'll
400 be angry. I know you mean well. Too bad you can't speak.

(*As she tries to hold him back he kisses her and tears himself away. Exit. She is desperate, running hither and thither uttering little noises. The* CHAPLAIN *and* MOTHER COURAGE *return.* KATTRIN *rushes to her mother.*)

MOTHER COURAGE: What's all this? Pull yourself together, love. They done something to you? Where's Swiss Cheese? Tell it me step by step, Kattrin. Mother understands you. What, so that bastard did take the box? I'll
405 wrap it round his ears, the little hypocrite. Take your time and don't gabble, use your hands, I don't like it when you howl like a dog, what'll his reverence say? Makes him uncomfortable. What, a one-eyed man came along?

THE CHAPLAIN: That one-eyed man is a spy. Have they ar-
410 rested Swiss Cheese? (KATTRIN *shakes her head, shrugs her shoulders.*) We're done for.

MOTHER COURAGE: (*Fishes in her basket and brings out a Catholic flag, which the* CHAPLAIN *fixes to the mast.*) Better hoist new flag.

415 THE CHAPLAIN: (*Bitterly.*) All good Catholics here.

(*Voices are heard from the rear. The two men bring in* SWISS CHEESE.)

SWISS CHEESE: Let me go, I got nowt. Don't twist my shoulder, I'm innocent.

SERGEANT: Here's where he came from. You know each other.

MOTHER COURAGE: Us? How?

SWISS CHEESE: I don't know her. Got no idea who she is, had 420 nowt to do with them. I bought me dinner here, ten hellers it cost. You might have seen me sitting here, it was too salty.

SERGEANT: Who are you people, eh?

MOTHER COURAGE: We're law-abiding folk. That's right, he 425 bought a dinner. Said it was too salty.

SERGEANT: Trying to pretend you don't know each other, that it?

MOTHER COURAGE: Why should I know him? Can't know everyone. I don't go asking 'em what they're called and are 430 they a heretic; if he pays he ain't a heretic. You a heretic?

SWISS CHEESE: Go on.

THE CHAPLAIN: He sat there very properly, never opening his mouth except when eating. Then he had to.

SERGEANT: And who are you? 435

MOTHER COURAGE: He's just my potboy. Now I expect you gentlemen are thirsty, I'll get you a glass of brandy, you must be hot and tired with running.

SERGEANT: No brandy on duty. (*To* SWISS CHEESE.) You were carrying something. Must have hidden it by the river. Was 440 a bulge in your tunic when you left here.

MOTHER COURAGE: You sure it was him?

SWISS CHEESE: You must be thinking of someone else. I saw someone bounding off with a bulge in his tunic. I'm the wrong man. 445

MOTHER COURAGE: I'd say it was a misunderstanding too, such things happen. I'm a good judge of people, I'm Courage, you heard of me, everyone knows me, and I tell you that's an honest face he has.

SERGEANT: We're on the track of the Second Finnish Regi- 450 ment's cash box. We got the description of the fellow responsible for it. Been trailing him two days. It's you.

SWISS CHEESE: It's not me.

SERGEANT: And you better cough it up, or you're a goner, you know. Where is it? 455

MOTHER COURAGE: (*Urgently.*) Of course he'd give it over rather than be a goner. Right out he'd say: I got it, here it is, you're too strong. He ain't all that stupid. Speak up, stupid idiot, here's the sergeant giving you a chance.

SWISS CHEESE: S'pose I ain't got it. 460

SERGEANT: Then come along. We'll get it out of you. (*They lead him off.*)

MOTHER COURAGE: (*Calls after them.*) He'd tell you. He's not that stupid. And don't you twist his shoulder! (*Runs after them.*) 465

(*Evening of the same day. The* CHAPLAIN *and dumb* KATTRIN *are cleaning glasses and polishing knives.*)

THE CHAPLAIN: Cases like that, where somebody gets caught, are not unknown in religious history. It reminds me of the Passion of Our Lord and Saviour. There's an old song about that. (*He sings the Song of the Hours.*)

---

469 **Song of the Hours** translated by Ralph Manheim

470 In the first hour Jesus mild
Who had prayed since even
Was betrayed and led before
Pontius the heathen.

Pilate found him innocent
475 Free from fault and error
Therefore, having washed his hands
Sent him to King Herod.

In the third hour he was scourged
480 Stripped and clad in scarlet
And a plaited crown of thorns
Set upon his forehead.

On the Son of Man they spat
Mocked him and made merry.
Then the cross of death was brought
485 Given him to carry.

At the sixth hour with two thieves
To the cross they nailed him
And the people and the thieves
Mocked him and reviled him.

490 This is Jesus King of Jews
Cried they in derision
Till the sun withdrew its light
From that awful vision.

At the ninth hour Jesus wailed
495 Why hast thou me forsaken?
Soldiers brought him vinegar
Which he left untaken.

Then he yielded up the ghost
And the earth was shaken.
500 Rended was the temple's veil
And the saints were wakened.

Soldiers broke the two thieves' legs
As the night descended.
Thrust a spear in Jesus' side
505 When his life had ended.

Still they mocked, as from his wound
Flowed the blood and water
And blasphemed the Son of Man
With their cruel laughter.

510 MOTHER COURAGE: (*Entering excitedly.*) It's touch and go. They say sergeant's open to reason though. Only we mustn't let on it's Swiss Cheese else they'll say we helped him. It's a matter of money, that's all. But where's money to come from? Hasn't Yvette been round? I ran into her, she's got her hooks on
515 some colonel, maybe he'd buy her a canteen business.

THE CHAPLAIN: Do you really wish to sell?

MOTHER COURAGE: Where's money for sergeant to come from?

THE CHAPLAIN: What'll you live on, then?

MOTHER COURAGE: That's just it.

(YVETTE POTTIER *arrives with an extremely ancient* COLONEL.)

520 YVETTE: (*Embracing* MOTHER COURAGE.) My dear Courage, fancy seeing you so soon. (*Whispers.*) He's not unwilling. (*Aloud.*) This is my good friend who advises me in busi-

ness matters. I happened to hear you wanted to sell your cart on account of circumstances. I'll think it over.

MOTHER COURAGE: Pledge it, not sell, just not too much 525 hurry, 'tain't every day you find a cart like this in wartime.

YVETTE: (*Disappointed.*) Oh, pledge. I thought it was for sale. I'm not so sure I'm interested. (*To the* COLONEL.) How do you feel about it?

THE COLONEL: Just as you feel, pet. 530

MOTHER COURAGE: I'm only pledging it.

YVETTE: I thought you'd got to have the money.

MOTHER COURAGE: (*Firmly.*) I got to have it, but sooner run myself ragged looking for a bidder than sell outright. And why? The cart's our livelihood. It's a chance for you, 535 Yvette; who knows when you'll get another like it and have a special friend to advise you, am I right?

YVETTE: Yes, my friend thinks I should clinch it, but I'm not sure. If it's only a pledge . . . so you agree we ought to buy outright? 540

THE COLONEL: I agree, pet.

MOTHER COURAGE: Best look and see if you can find anything for sale then; maybe you will if you don't rush it, take your friend along with you, say a week or fortnight, might find something suits you. 545

YVETTE: Then let's go looking. I adore going around looking for things, I adore going around with you, Poldi, it's such fun, isn't it? No matter if it takes a fortnight. How soon would you pay the money back if you got it?

MOTHER COURAGE: I'd pay back in two weeks, maybe one. 550

YVETTE: I can't make up my mind, Poldi chéri, you advise me. (*Takes the* COLONEL *aside.*) She's got to sell, I know, no problem there. And there's that ensign, you know, the fair-haired one, he'd be glad to lend me the money. He's crazy about me, says there's someone I remind him of. What do 555 you advise?

THE COLONEL: You steer clear of him. He's no good. He's only making use of you. I said I'd buy you something, didn't I, pussykins?

YVETTE: I oughtn't to let you. Of course if you think the ensign 560 might try to take advantage . . . Poldi, I'll accept it from you.

THE COLONEL: That's how I feel too.

YVETTE: Is that your advice?

THE COLONEL: That is my advice.

YVETTE: (*To* COURAGE *once more.*) My friend's advice would 565 be to accept. Make me out a receipt saying the cart's mine once two weeks are up, with all its contents, we'll check it now, I'll bring the two hundred florins later. (*To the* COLONEL.) You go back to the camp, I'll follow, I got to check it all and see there's nothing missing from my cart. 570 (*She kisses him. He leaves. She climbs up on the cart.*) Not all that many boots, are there?

MOTHER COURAGE: Yvette, it's no time for checking your cart, s'posing it is yours. You promised you'd talk to sergeant about Swiss Cheese, there ain't a minute to lose, 575 they say in an hour he'll be courtmartialled.

YVETTE: Just let me count the shirts.

MOTHER COURAGE: (*Pulling her down by the skirt.*) You bloody vampire. Swiss Cheese's life's at stake. And not a word about who's making the offer, for God's sake, pretend it's your 580 friend, else we're all done for cause we looked after him.

YVETTE: I fixed to meet that one-eyed fellow in the copse, he should be there by now.

THE CHAPLAIN: It doesn't have to be the whole two hundred
585   either, I'd go up to a hundred and fifty, that may be enough.
MOTHER COURAGE: Since when has it been your money? You kindly keep out of this. You'll get your hotpot all right, don't worry. Hurry up and don't haggle, it's life or death. (*Pushes* YVETTE *off*.)
590   THE CHAPLAIN: Far be it from me to interfere, but what are we going to live on? You're saddled with a daughter who can't earn her keep.
MOTHER COURAGE: I'm counting on regimental cash box, Mr. Clever. They'll allow it as his expenses.
595   THE CHAPLAIN: But will she get the message right?
MOTHER COURAGE: It's her interest I should spend her two hundred so she gets the cart. She's set on that, God knows how long that colonel of hers'll last. Kattrin, polish the knives, there's the pumice. And you, stop hanging round
600   like Jesus on Mount of Olives, get moving, wash them glasses, we'll have fifty or more of cavalry in tonight and I don't want to hear a lot of 'I'm not accustomed to having to run about, oh my poor feet, we never ran in church'. Thank the Lord they're corruptible. After all, they ain't
605   wolves, just humans out for money. Corruption in humans is same as compassion in God. Corruption's our only hope. Long as we have it there'll be lenient sentences and even an innocent man'll have a chance of being let off.
YVETTE: (*Comes in panting.*) They'll do it for two hundred.
610   But it's got to be quick. Soon be out of their hands. Best thing is I go right away to my colonel with the one-eyed man. He's admitted he had the box, they put the thumb-screws on him. But he chucked it in the river soon as he saw they were on his track. The box is a write-off. I'll go
615   and get the money from my colonel, shall I?
MOTHER COURAGE: Box is a write-off? How'm I to pay back two hundred then?
YVETTE: Oh, you thought you'd get it from the box, did you? And I was to be Joe Soap I suppose? Better not count on
620   that. You'll have to pay up if you want Swiss Cheese back, or would you sooner I dropped the whole thing so's you can keep your cart?
MOTHER COURAGE: That's something I didn't allow for. Don't worry, you'll get your cart, I've said goodbye to it, had it
625   seventeen years, I have. I just need a moment to think, it's bit sudden, what'm I to do, two hundred's too much for me, pity you didn't beat 'em down. Must keep a bit back, else any Tom, Dick and Harry'll be able to shove me in ditch. Go and tell them I'll pay hundred and twenty florins,
630   else it's all off, either way I'm losing me cart.
YVETTE: They won't do it. That one-eyed man's impatient already, keeps looking over his shoulder, he's so worked up. Hadn't I best pay them the whole two hundred?
MOTHER COURAGE: (*In despair.*) I can't pay that. Thirty years
635   I been working. She's twenty-five already, and no husband. I got her to think of too. Don't push me, I know what I'm doing. Say a hundred and twenty, or it's off.
YVETTE: It's up to you. (*Rushes off.*)

(*Without looking at either the* CHAPLAIN *or her daughter,* MOTHER COURAGE *sits down to help* KATTRIN *polish knives.*)

MOTHER COURAGE: Don't smash them glasses, they ain't ours
640   now. Watch what you're doing, you'll cut yourself. Swiss Cheese'll be back, I'll pay two hundred if it comes to the pinch. You'll get your brother, love. For eighty florins we could fill a pack with goods and start again. Plenty of folk has to make do.
THE CHAPLAIN: The Lord will provide, it says.   645
MOTHER COURAGE: See they're properly dry. (*She cleans knives in silence.* KATTRIN *suddenly runs behind the cart, sobbing.*)
YVETTE: (*Comes running in.*) They won't do it. I told you so. The one-eyed man wanted to leave right away, said there was no point. He says he's just waiting for the drum-roll;   650
that means sentence has been pronounced. I offered a hundred and fifty. He didn't even blink. I had to convince him to stay there so's I could have another word with you.
MOTHER COURAGE: Tell him I'll pay the two hundred. Hurry! (YVETTE *runs off. They sit in silence. The* CHAPLAIN *has stopped*   655
polishing the glasses.) I reckon I bargained too long.

(*In the distance drumming is heard. The* CHAPLAIN *gets up and goes to the rear.* MOTHER COURAGE *remains seated. It grows dark. The drumming stops. It grows light once more.* MOTHER COURAGE *is sitting exactly as before.*)

YVETTE: (*Arrives, very pale.*) Well, you got what you asked for, with your haggling and trying to keep your cart. Eleven bullets they gave him, that's all. You don't deserve I should bother any more about you. But I did hear they don't be-   660
lieve the box really is in the river. They've an idea it's here and anyhow that you're connected with him. They're going to bring him here, see if you gives yourself away when you sees him. Thought I'd better warn you so's you don't recognise him, else you'll all be for it. They're right on my   665
heels, best tell you quick. Shall I keep Kattrin away? (MOTHER COURAGE *shakes her head.*) Does she know? She mayn't have heard the drumming or know what it meant.
MOTHER COURAGE: She knows. Get her.

(YVETTE *fetches* KATTRIN, *who goes to her mother and stands beside her.* MOTHER COURAGE *takes her hand. Two lansequenets come carrying a stretcher with something lying on it covered by a sheet. The* SERGEANT *marches beside them. They set down the stretcher.*)

SERGEANT: Here's somebody we dunno the name of. It's got to   670
be listed, though, so everything's shipshape. He had a meal here. Have a look, see if you know him. (*He removes the sheet.*) Know him? (MOTHER COURAGE *shakes her head.*) What, never see him before he had that meal here? (MOTHER COURAGE *shakes her head.*) Pick him up. Chuck him in the   675
pit. He's got nobody knows him. (*They carry him away.*)

SCENE FOUR

Mother Courage sings the Song of the Grand Capitulation.

Outside an officer's tent.

MOTHER COURAGE *is waiting. A* CLERK *looks out of the tent.*

THE CLERK: I know you. You had a paymaster from the Lutherans with you, what was in hiding. I'd not complain if I were you.
MOTHER COURAGE: But I got a complaint to make. I'm innocent, would look as how I'd a bad conscience if I let this   5

pass. Slashed everything in me cart to pieces with their sabres, they did, then wanted I should pay five taler fine for nowt, I tell you, nowt.

THE CLERK: Take my tip, better shut up. We're short of can- 10 teens, so we let you go on trading, specially if you got a bad conscience and pay a fine now and then.

MOTHER COURAGE: I got a complaint.

THE CLERK: Have it your own way. Then you must wait till the captain's free. (*Withdraws inside the tent.*)

15 YOUNG SOLDIER: (*Enters aggressively.*) Bouque la Madonne! Where's that bleeding pig of a captain what's took my reward money to swig with his tarts? I'll do him.

OLDER SOLDIER: (*Running after him.*) Shut up. They'll put you in irons.

20 YOUNG SOLDIER: Out of there, you thief! I'll slice you into pork chops, I will. Pocketing my prize money after I'd swum the river, only one in the whole squadron, and now I can't even buy meself a beer. I'm not standing for that. Come on out there so I can cut you up!

25 OLDER SOLDIER: Blessed Mother of God, he's asking for trouble.

MOTHER COURAGE: Is it some reward he weren't paid?

YOUNG SOLDIER: Lemme go, I'll slash you too while I'm at it.

OLDER SOLDIER: He rescued the colonel's horse and got no 30 reward for it. He's young yet, still wet behind the ears.

MOTHER COURAGE: Let him go, he ain't a dog you got to chain up. Wanting your reward is good sound sense. Why be a hero otherwise?

YOUNG SOLDIER: So's he can sit in there and booze. You're 35 shit-scared, the lot of you. I done something special and I want my reward.

MOTHER COURAGE: Don't you shout at me, young fellow. Got me own worries, I have; any road you should spare your voice, be needing it when captain comes, else there he'll be 40 and you too hoarse to make a sound, which'll make it hard for him to clap you in irons till you turn blue. People what shouts like that can't keep it up ever; half an hour, and they have to be rocked to sleep, they're so tired.

YOUNG SOLDIER: I ain't tired and to hell with sleep. I'm hun- 45 gry. They make our bread from acorns and hemp-seed, and they even skimp on that. He's whoring away my re- ward and I'm hungry. I'll do him.

MOTHER COURAGE: Oh I see, you're hungry. Last year that general of yours ordered you all off roads and across fields 50 so corn should be trampled flat; I could've got ten florins for a pair of boots s'pose I'd had boots and s'pose anyone'd been able to pay ten florins. Thought he'd be well away from that area this year, he did, but here he is, still there, and hunger is great. I see what you're angry about.

55 YOUNG SOLDIER: I won't have it, don't talk to me, it ain't fair and I'm not standing for that.

MOTHER COURAGE: And you're right; but how long? How long you not standing for unfairness? One hour, two hours? Didn't ask yourself that, did you, but it's the whole 60 point, and why, once you're in irons it's too bad if you sud- denly finds you can put up with unfairness after all.

YOUNG SOLDIER: What am I listening to you for, I'd like to know? Bouque la Madonne, where's that captain?

MOTHER COURAGE: You been listening to me because you 65 knows it's like what I say, your anger has gone up in smoke already, it was just a short one and you needed a long one, but where you going to get it from?

YOUNG SOLDIER: Are you trying to tell me asking for my re- ward is wrong?

MOTHER COURAGE: Not a bit. I'm just telling you your anger 70 ain't long enough, it's good for nowt, pity. If you'd a long one I'd be trying to prod you on. Cut him up, the swine, would be my advice to you in that case; but how about if you don't cut him up cause you feels your tail going be- tween your legs? Then I'd look silly and captain'd take it 75 out on me.

OLDER SOLDIER: You're perfectly right, he's just a bit crazy.

YOUNG SOLDIER: Very well, let's see if I don't cut him up. (*Draws his sword.*) When he arrives I'm going to cut him up.

THE CLERK: (*Looks out.*) The captain'll be here in one minute. 80 Sit down.

(*The* YOUNG SOLDIER *sits down.*)

MOTHER COURAGE: He's sitting now. See, what did I say? You're sitting now. Ah, how well they know us, no one need tell 'em how to go about it. Sit down! and, bingo, we're sitting. And sitting and sedition don't mix. Don't try 85 to stand up, you won't stand the way you was standing be- fore. I shouldn't worry about what I think; I'm no better, not one moment. Bought up all our fighting spirit, they have. Eh? S'pose I kick back, might be bad for business. Let me tell you a thing or two about the Grand Capitu- 90 lation. (*She sings the Song of the Grand Capitulation.*)

Back when I was young, I was brought to realise
What a very special person I must be
(Not just any old cottager's daughter, what with my looks
    and my talents and my urge towards Higher Things)
And insisted that my soup should have no hairs in it. 95
No one makes a sucker out of me!
(All or nothing, only the best is good enough, each man
    for himself, nobody's telling *me* what to do.)
Then I heard a tit
Chirp: Wait a bit!
    And you'll be marching with the band 100
    In step, responding to command
    And striking up your little dance:
    Now we advance.
    And now: parade, form square!
    Then men swear God's there— 105
    Not the faintest chance!

In no time at all anyone who looked could see
That I'd learned to take my medicine with good grace.
(Two kids on my hands and look at the price of bread,
    and things they expect of you!)
When they finally came to feel that they were through 110
    with me
They'd got me grovelling on my face.
(Takes all sorts to make a world, you scratch my back
    and I'll scratch yours, no good banging your head
    against a brick wall.)
Then I heard that tit
Chirp: Wait a bit!
    And you'll be marching with the band 115
    In step, responding to command
    And striking up your little dance:
    Now they advance.
    And now: parade, form square!

120   Then men swear God's there—
    Not the faintest chance!

    I've known people tried to storm the summits:
    There's no star too bright or seems too far away.
    (Dogged does it, where there's a will there's a way, by
        hook or by crook.)
125   As each peak disclosed fresh peaks to come, it's
    Strange how much a plain straw hat could weigh.
    (You have to cut your coat according to your cloth.)
    Then I hear the tit
    Chirp: Wait a bit!
130   And they'll be marching with the band
        In step, responding to command
        And striking up their little dance:
        Now they advance
        And now: parade, form square!
135   Then men swear God's there—
    Not the faintest chance!

MOTHER COURAGE: (*To the* YOUNG SOLDIER.) That's why I reckon you should stay there with your sword drawn if you're truly set on it and your anger's big enough, because
140 you got grounds, I agree, but if your anger's a short one best leave right away.

YOUNG SOLDIER: Oh stuff it. (*He staggers off with the* OLDER SOLDIER *following.*)

THE CLERK: (*Sticks his head out.*) Captain's here now. You can
145 make your complaint.

MOTHER COURAGE: I changed me mind. I ain't complaining. (*Exit.*)

SCENE FIVE

Two years have gone by. The war is spreading to new areas. Ceaselessly on the move, Courage's little cart crosses Poland, Moravia, Bavaria, Italy, then Bavaria again. 1631. Tilly's victory at Magdeburg costs Mother Courage four officers' shirts.

MOTHER COURAGE's *cart has stopped in a badly shot-up village. Thin military music in the distance. Two* SOLDIERS *at the bar being served by* KATTRIN *and* MOTHER COURAGE. *One of them has a lady's fur coat over his shoulders.*

MOTHER COURAGE: Can't pay, that it? No money, no schnapps. They give us victory parades, but catch them giving men their pay.

FIRST SOLDIER: I want my schnapps. I missed the looting.
5   That double-crossing general only allowed an hour's looting in the town. He ain't an inhuman monster, he said. Town must of paid him.

THE CHAPLAIN: (*Stumbles in.*) There are people still lying in that yard. The peasant's family. Somebody give me a hand.
10   I need linen.

(*The* SECOND SOLDIER *goes off with him.* KATTRIN *becomes very excited and tries to make her mother produce linen.*)

MOTHER COURAGE: I got none. All my bandages was sold to regiment. I ain't tearing up my officer's shirts for that lot.

THE CHAPLAIN: (*Calling back.*) I need linen, I tell you.

MOTHER COURAGE: (*Blocking* KATTRIN's *way into the cart by sitting on the step.*) I'm giving nowt. They'll never pay, and 15 why, nowt to pay with.

THE CHAPLAIN: (*Bending over a woman he has carried in.*) Why d'you stay around during the gunfire?

PEASANT WOMAN: (*Feebly.*) Farm.

MOTHER COURAGE: Catch them abandoning anything. But 20 now I'm s'posed to foot the bill. I won't do it.

FIRST SOLDIER: Those are Protestants. What they have to be Protestants for?

MOTHER COURAGE: They ain't bothering about faith. They lost their farm. 25

SECOND SOLDIER: They're no Protestants. They're Catholics like us.

FIRST SOLDIER: No way of sorting 'em out in a bombardment.

A PEASANT: (*Brought in by the* CHAPLAIN.) My arm's gone.

THE CHAPLAIN: Where's that linen? 30

MOTHER COURAGE: I can't give nowt. What with expenses, taxes, loan interest and bribes. (*Making guttural noises,* KATTRIN *raises a plank and threatens her mother with it.*) You gone plain crazy? Put that plank away or I'll paste you one, you cow. I'm giving nowt, don't want to, got to think 35 of meself. (*The* CHAPLAIN *lifts her off the steps and sets her on the ground, then starts pulling out shirts and tearing them into strips.*) My officers' shirts! Half a florin apiece! I'm ruined. (*From the house comes the cry of a child in pain.*)

THE PEASANT: The baby's in there still. (KATTRIN *dashes in.*) 40

THE CHAPLAIN: (*To the woman.*) Don't move. They'll get it out.

MOTHER COURAGE: Stop her, roof may fall in.

THE CHAPLAIN: I'm not going back in there.

MOTHER COURAGE: (*Torn both ways.*) Don't waste my precious linen. 45

(KATTRIN *brings a baby out of the ruins.*)

MOTHER COURAGE: How nice, found another baby to cart around? Give it to its ma this instant, unless you'd have me fighting for hours to get it off you, like last time, d'you hear? (*To the* SECOND SOLDIER.) Don't stand there gawping, you go back and tell them cut out that music, we can 50 see it's a victory with our own eyes. All your victories mean to me is losses.

THE CHAPLAIN: (*Tying a bandage.*) Blood's coming through.

(KATTRIN *is rocking the baby and making lullaby noises.*)

MOTHER COURAGE: Look at her, happy as a queen in all this misery; give it back at once, its mother's coming round. (*She* 55 *catches the* FIRST SOLDIER, *who has been attacking the drinks and is trying to make off with one of the bottles.*) Psia krew! Thought you'd score another victory, you animal? Now pay.

FIRST SOLDIER: I got nowt.

MOTHER COURAGE: (*Pulling the fur coat off his back.*) Then 60 leave that coat, it's stolen any road.

THE CHAPLAIN: There's still someone under there.

SCENE SIX

Outside the Bavarian town of Ingolstadt Courage participates in the funeral of the late Imperial commander Tilly. Discussions are held about war heroes and the war's duration. The Chaplain complains that his talents are lying fallow, and dumb Kattrin gets the red boots. The year is 1632.

Inside a canteen tent.

It has a bar towards the rear. Rain. Sound of drums and Funeral music. The CHAPLAIN *and the regimental* CLERK *are playing a board game.* MOTHER COURAGE *and her daughter are stocktaking.*

THE CHAPLAIN: Now the funeral procession will be moving off.

MOTHER COURAGE: Too bad about commander in chief—twenty-two pairs those socks—he fell by accident, they say. Mist over fields, that was the trouble. General had just
5 been haranguing a regiment saying they must fight to last man and last round, he was riding back when mist made him lose direction so he was up front and a bullet got him in midst of battle—only four hurricane lamps left. (*A whistle from the rear. She goes to the bar.*) You scrimshankers,
10 dodging your commander in chief's funeral, scandal I call it. (*Pours drinks.*)

THE CLERK: They should never of paid troops out before the funeral. Instead of going now they're all getting pissed.

THE CHAPLAIN: (*To the* CLERK.) Aren't you supposed to go to
15 the funeral?

THE CLERK: Dodged it cause of the rain.

MOTHER COURAGE: It's different with you, your uniform might get wet. I heard they wanted to toll bells for funeral as usual, except it turned out all churches had been blown
20 to smithereens by his orders, so poor old commander in chief won't be hearing no bells as they let the coffin down. They're going to let off three salvoes instead to cheer things up—seventeen belts.

SHOUTS: (*From the bar.*) Hey, Missis, a brandy!
25 MOTHER COURAGE: Let's see your money. No, I ain't having you in my tent with your disgusting boots. You can drink outside, rain or no rain. (*To the* CLERK.) I'm only letting in sergeants and up. Commander in chief had been having his worries, they say. S'posed to have been trouble with
30 Second Regiment cause he stopped their pay, said it was a war of faith and they should do it for free. (*Funeral march. All look to the rear.*)

THE CHAPLAIN: Now they'll be filing past the noble corpse.

MOTHER COURAGE: Can't help feeling sorry for those gener-
35 als and emperors, there they are maybe thinking they're doing something extra special what folk'll talk about in years to come, and earning a public monument, like conquering the world for instance, that's a fine ambition for a general, how's he to know any better? I mean, he plagues
40 hisself to death, then it all breaks down on account of ordinary folk what just wants their beer and bit of a chat, nowt higher. Finest plans get bolloxed up by the pettiness of them as should be carrying them out, because emperors can't do nowt themselves, they just counts on soldiers
45 and people to back 'em up whatever happens, am I right?

THE CHAPLAIN: (*Laughs.*) Courage, you're right, aside from the soldiers. They do their best. Give me that lot outside there, for instance, drinking their brandy in the rain, and I'd guarantee to make you one war after another for a hundred years if need be, and I'm no trained general. 50

MOTHER COURAGE: You don't think war might end, then?

THE CHAPLAIN: What, because the commander in chief's gone? Don't be childish. They're two a penny, no shortage of heroes.

MOTHER COURAGE: Ee, I'm not asking for fun of it, but because I'm thinking whether to stock up, prices are low 55 now, but if war's going to end it's money down the drain.

THE CHAPLAIN: I realise it's a serious question. There've always been people going round saying 'the war can't go on for ever'. I tell you there's nothing to stop it going on for ever. Of course there can be a bit of a breathing space. The war 60 may need to get its second wind, it may even have an accident so to speak. There's no guarantee against that; nothing's perfect on this earth of ours. A perfect war, the sort you might say couldn't be improved on, that's something we shall probably never see. It can suddenly come to a 65 standstill for some quite unforeseen reason, you can't allow for everything. A slight case of negligence, and it's bogged down up to the axles. And then it's a matter of hauling the war out of the mud again. But emperor and kings and popes will come to its rescue. So on the whole it has noth- 70 ing serious to worry about, and will live to a ripe old age.

A SOLDIER: (*Sings at the bar.*)

> A schnapps, landlord, you're late!
> A soldier cannot wait
> To do his emperor's orders. 75

Make it a double, this is a holiday.

MOTHER COURAGE: S'pose I went by what you say . . .

THE CHAPLAIN: Think it out for yourself. What's to compete with the war?

THE SOLDIER: (*At the rear.*) 80

> Your breast, my girl, you're late!
> A soldier cannot wait
> To ride across the borders.

THE CLERK: (*Unexpectedly.*) And what about peace? I'm from Bohemia and I'd like to go home some day. 85

THE CHAPLAIN: Would you indeed? Ah, peace. Where is the hole once the cheese has been eaten?

THE SOLDIER: (*At the rear.*)

> Lead trumps, my friend, you're late!
> A soldier cannot wait. 90
> His emperor needs him badly.

> Your blessing, priest, you're late!
> A soldier cannot wait.
> Must lay his life down gladly.

THE CLERK: In the long run life's impossible if there's no peace. 95

THE CHAPLAIN: I'd say there's peace in war too; it has its peaceful moments. Because war satisfies all requirements, peaceable ones included, they're catered for, and it would simply fizzle out if they weren't. In war you can do a crap like in the depths of peacetime, then between one battle 100 and the next you can have a beer, then even when you're moving up you can lay your head on your arms and have a bit of shuteye in the ditch, it's entirely possible. During a charge you can't play cards maybe, but nor can you in the

105 depths of peacetime when you're ploughing, and after a victory there are various openings. You may get a leg blown off, then you start by making a lot of fuss as though it were serious, but afterwards you calm down or get given a schnapps, and you end up hopping around and the war's
110 no worse off than before. And what's to stop you being fruitful and multiplying in the middle of all the butchery, behind a barn or something, in the long run you can't be held back from it, and then the war will have your progeny and can use them to carry on with. No, the war will always
115 find an outlet, mark my words. Why should it ever stop?

(KATTRIN *has ceased working and is staring at the* CHAPLAIN.)

MOTHER COURAGE: I'll buy fresh stock then. If you say so. (KATTRIN *suddenly flings a basket full of bottles to the ground and runs off.*) Kattrin! (*Laughs.*) Damn me if she weren't waiting for peace. I promised her she'd get a husband soon
120 as peace came. (*Hurries after her.*)
THE CLERK: (*Standing up.*) I won. You been talking too much. Pay up.
MOTHER COURAGE: (*Returning with* KATTRIN.) Don't be silly, war'll go on a bit longer, and we'll make a bit more
125 money, and peacetime'll be all the nicer for it. Now you go into town, that's ten minutes' walk at most, fetch things from Golden Lion, the expensive ones, we can fetch rest in cart later, it's all arranged, regimental clerk here will go with you. Nearly everybody's attending commander in
130 chief's funeral, nowt can happen to you. Careful now, don't let them steal nowt, think of your dowry.

(KATTRIN *puts a cloth over her head and leaves with the* CLERK.)

THE CHAPLAIN: Is that all right to let her go with the clerk?
MOTHER COURAGE: She's not that pretty they'd want to ruin her.
THE CHAPLAIN: I admire the way you run your business and
135 always win through. I see why they called you Courage.
MOTHER COURAGE: Poor folk got to have courage. Why, they're lost. Simply getting up in morning takes some doing in their situation. Or ploughing a field, and in a war at that. Mere fact they bring kids into world shows they got
140 courage, cause there's no hope for them. They have to hang one another and slaughter one another, so just looking each other in face must call for courage. Being able to put up with emperor and pope shows supernatural courage, cause those two cost 'em their lives. (*She sits down, takes a little pipe from
145 her purse and smokes.*) You might chop us a bit of kindling.
THE CHAPLAIN: (*Reluctantly removing his coat and preparing to chop up sticks.*) I happen to be a pastor of souls, not a woodcutter.
MOTHER COURAGE: I got no soul, you see. Need firewood, though.
150 THE CHAPLAIN: Where's that stumpy pipe from?
MOTHER COURAGE: Just a pipe.
THE CHAPLAIN: What d'you mean, 'just', it's a quite particular pipe, that.
MOTHER COURAGE: Aha?
155 THE CHAPLAIN: That stumpy pipe belongs to the Oxenstierna Regiment's cook.
MOTHER COURAGE: If you know that already why ask, Mr Clever?
THE CHAPLAIN: Because I didn't know if you were aware
160 what you're smoking. You might just have been rummag-

ing around in your things, come across some old pipe or other, and used it out of sheer absence of mind.
MOTHER COURAGE: And why not?
THE CHAPLAIN: Because you didn't. You're smoking that de-
165 liberately.
MOTHER COURAGE: And why shouldn't I?
THE CHAPLAIN: Courage, I'm warning you. It's my duty. Probably you'll never clap eyes on the gentleman again, and that's no loss but your good fortune. He didn't make
170 at all a reliable impression on me. Quite the opposite.
MOTHER COURAGE: Really? Nice fellow that.
THE CHAPLAIN: So he's what you would call a nice fellow? I wouldn't. Far be it from me to bear him the least ill-will, but nice is not what I would call him. More like one of
175 those Don Juans, a slippery one. Have a look at that pipe if you don't believe me. You must admit it tells you a good deal about his character.
MOTHER COURAGE: Nowt that I can see. Worn out, I'd call it.
THE CHAPLAIN: Practically bitten through, you mean. A man
180 of wrath. That is the pipe of an unscrupulous man of wrath; you must see that if you have any discrimination left.
MOTHER COURAGE: Don't chop my chopping block in two.
THE CHAPLAIN: I told you I'm not a woodcutter by trade. I studied to be a pastor of souls. My talent and abilities are
185 being abused in this place, by manual labour. My God-given endowments are denied expression. It's a sin. You have never heard me preach. One sermon of mine can put a regiment in such a frame of mind it'll treat the enemy like a flock of sheep. Life to them is a smelly old foot-
190 cloth which they fling away in a vision of final victory. God has given me the gift of speech. I can preach so you'll lose all sense of sight and hearing.
MOTHER COURAGE: I don't wish to lose my sense of sight and hearing. Where'd that leave me?
195 THE CHAPLAIN: Courage, I have often thought that your dry way of talking conceals more than just a warm heart. You too are human and need warmth.
MOTHER COURAGE: Best way for us to get this tent warm is have plenty of firewood.
200 THE CHAPLAIN: Don't change the subject. Seriously, Courage, I sometimes ask myself what it would be like if our relationship were to become somewhat closer. I mean, given that the whirlwind of war has so strangely whirled us together.
MOTHER COURAGE: I'd say it was close enough. I cook meals
205 for you and you run around and chop firewood for instance.
THE CHAPLAIN: (*Coming closer.*) You know what I mean by closer; it's not a relationship founded on meals and wood-chopping and other such base necessities. Let your head speak, harden thyself not.
210 MOTHER COURAGE: Don't you come at me with that axe. That'd be too close a relationship.
THE CHAPLAIN: You shouldn't make a joke of it. I'm a serious person and I've thought about what I'm saying.
MOTHER COURAGE: Be sensible, padre. I like you. I don't want
215 to row you. All I'm after is get myself and children through all this with my cart. I don't see it as mine, and I ain't in the mood for private affairs. Right now I'm taking a gamble, buying stores just when commander in chief's fallen and all the talk's of peace. Where d'you reckon you'd turn if I'm
220 ruined? Don't know, do you? You chop us some kindling wood, then we can keep warm at night, that's quite some-

thing these times. What's this? (*She gets up. Enter* KATTRIN, *out of breath, with a wound above her eye. She is carrying a variety of stuff: parcels, leather goods, a drum and so on.*)

225 MOTHER COURAGE: What happened, someone assault you? On way back? She was assaulted on her way back. Bet it was that trooper was getting drunk here. I shouldn't have let you go, love. Drop that stuff. Not too bad, just a flesh wound you got. I'll bandage it and in a week it'll be all right. Worse than
230 wild beasts, they are. (*She ties up the wound.*)

THE CHAPLAIN: It's not them I blame. They never went raping back home. The fault lies with those that start wars, it brings humanity's lowest instincts to the surface.

MOTHER COURAGE: Calm down. Didn't clerk come back
235 with you? That's because you're respectable, they don't bother. Wound ain't a deep one, won't leave no mark. There you are, all bandaged up. You'll get something, love, keep calm. Something I put aside for you, wait till you see. (*She delves into a sack and brings out* YVETTE's *red high-heeled*
240 *boots.*) Made you open your eyes, eh? Something you always wanted. They're yours. Put 'em on quick, before I change me mind. Won't leave no mark, and what if it does? Ones I'm really sorry for's the ones they fancy. Drag them around till they're worn out, they do. Those they
245 don't care for they leaves alive. I seen girls before now had pretty faces, then in no time looking fit to frighten a hyaena. Can't even go behind a bush without risking trouble, horrible life they lead. Same like with trees, straight well-shaped ones get chopped down to make beams for
250 houses and crooked ones live happily ever after. So it's a stroke of luck for you really. Them boots'll be all right, I greased them before putting them away.

(KATTRIN *leaves the boots where they are and crawls into the cart.*)

THE CHAPLAIN: Let's hope she's not disfigured.

MOTHER COURAGE: She'll have a scar. No use her waiting for peacetime now.
255 THE CHAPLAIN: She didn't let them steal the things.

MOTHER COURAGE: Maybe I shouldn't have dinned that into her so. Wish I knew what went on in that head of hers. Just once she stayed out all night, once in all those years. Afterwards she went around like before, except she
260 worked harder. Couldn't get her to tell what had happened. Worried me quite a while, that did. (*She collects the articles brought by* KATTRIN, *and sorts them angrily.*) That's war for you. Nice way to get a living!

(*Sound of cannon fire.*)

265 THE CHAPLAIN: Now they'll be burying the commander in chief. This is a historic moment.

MOTHER COURAGE: What I call a historic moment is them bashing my daughter over the eye. She's half wrecked already, won't get no husband now, and her so crazy about
270 kids; any road she's only dumb from war, soldier stuffed something in her mouth when she was little. As for Swiss Cheese I'll never see him again, and where Eilif is God alone knows. War be damned.

SCENE SEVEN

| Mother Courage at the peak of her business career. |

High road.

The CHAPLAIN, MOTHER COURAGE *and* KATTRIN *are pulling the cart, which is hung with new wares.* MOTHER COURAGE *is wearing a necklace of silver coins.*

MOTHER COURAGE: I won't have you folk spoiling my war for me. I'm told it kills off the weak, but they're write-off in peacetime too. And war gives its people a better deal. (*She sings.*)

> And if you feel your forces fading   5
> You won't be there to share the fruits.
> But what is war but private trading
> That deals in blood instead of boots?

And what's the use of settling down? Them as does are first to go. (*Sings.*)   10

> Some people think to live by looting
> The goods some others haven't got.
> You think it's just a line they're shooting
> Until you hear they have been shot.

> And some I saw dig six feet under   15
> In haste to lie down and pass out.
> Now they're at rest perhaps they wonder
> Just what was all their haste about.

(*They pull it further.*)

SCENE EIGHT

| The same year sees the death of the Swedish king Gustavus Adolphus at the battle of Lützen. Peace threatens to ruin Mother Courage's business. Courage's dashing son performs one heroic deed too many and comes to a sticky end. |

Camp.

A summer morning. In front of the cart stand an OLD WOMAN *and her son. The son* [YOUNG MAN] *carries a large sack of bedding.*

MOTHER COURAGE'S VOICE: (*From inside the cart.*) Does it need to be this ungodly hour?

THE YOUNG MAN: We walked twenty miles in the night and got to be back today.

MOTHER COURAGE'S VOICE: What am I to do with bedding? 5 Folk've got no houses.

THE YOUNG MAN: Best have a look first.

THE OLD WOMAN: This place is no good either. Come on.

THE YOUNG MAN: What, and have them sell the roof over our head for taxes? She might pay three florins if you throw 10 in the bracelet. (*Bells start ringing.*) Listen, mother.

VOICES: (*From the rear.*) Peace! Swedish king's been killed.

MOTHER COURAGE: (*Sticks her head out of the cart. She has not yet done her hair.*) What's that bell-ringing about in mid-week?

THE CHAPLAIN: (*Crawling out from under the cart.*) What are 15 they shouting? Peace?

MOTHER COURAGE: Don't tell me peace has broken out just after I laid in new stock.

THE CHAPLAIN: (*Calling to the rear.*) That true? Peace?

20 VOICES: Three weeks ago, they say, only no one told us.

THE CHAPLAIN: (*To* COURAGE.) What else would they be ringing the bells for?

VOICES: A whole lot of Lutherans have driven into town, they brought the news.

25 THE YOUNG MAN: Mother, it's peace. What's the matter?

(*The* OLD WOMAN *has collapsed.*)

MOTHER COURAGE: (*Speaking into the cart.*) Holy cow! Kattrin, peace! Put your black dress on, we're going to church. Least we can do for Swiss Cheese. Is it true, though?

THE YOUNG MAN: The people here say so. They've made
30 peace. Can you get up? (*The* OLD WOMAN *stands up dumbfounded.*) I'll get the saddlery going again, I promise. It'll all work out. Father will get his bedding back. Can you walk? (*To the* CHAPLAIN.) She came over queer. It's the news. She never thought there'd be peace again. Father al-
35 ways said so. We're going straight home. (*They go off.*)

MOTHER COURAGE'S VOICE: Give her a schnapps.

THE CHAPLAIN: They've already gone.

MOTHER COURAGE'S VOICE: What's up in camp?

THE CHAPLAIN: They're assembling. I'll go on over. Shouldn't
40 I put on my clerical garb?

MOTHER COURAGE'S VOICE: Best check up before parading yourself as heretic. I'm glad about peace, never mind if I'm ruined. Any road I'll have got two of me children through the war. Be seeing Eilif again now.

45 THE CHAPLAIN: And who's that walking down the lines? Bless me, the army commander's cook.

THE COOK: (*Somewhat bedraggled and carrying a bundle.*) What do I behold? The padre!

THE CHAPLAIN: Courage, we've got company.

(MOTHER COURAGE *clambers out.*)

50 THE COOK: I promised I'd drop over for a little talk soon as I had the time. I've not forgotten your brandy, Mrs Fierling.

MOTHER COURAGE: Good grief, the general's cook! After all these years! Where's my eldest boy Eilif?

THE COOK: Hasn't he got here? He left before me, he was on
55 his way to see you too.

THE CHAPLAIN: I shall don my clerical garb, just a moment.

(*Goes off behind the cart.*)

MOTHER COURAGE: Then he may be here any minute. (*Calls into the cart.*) Kattrin, Eilif's on his way. Get cook a glass of brandy, Kattrin! (KATTRIN *does not appear.*) Drag your hair
60 down over it, that's all right. Mr Lamb's no stranger. (*Fetches the brandy herself.*) She don't like to come out, peace means nowt to her. Took too long coming, it did. They gave her a crack over one eye, you barely notice it now but she thinks folks are staring at her.

65 THE COOK: Ah yes. War. (*He and* MOTHER COURAGE *sit down.*)

MOTHER COURAGE: Cooky, you caught me at bad moment. I'm ruined.

THE COOK: What? That's hard.

MOTHER COURAGE: Peace'll wring my neck. I went and took Chaplain's advice, laid in fresh stocks only t'other day. And 70 now they're going to demobilise and I'll be left sitting on me wares.

THE COOK: What d'you want to go and listen to padre for? If I hadn't been in such a hurry that time, the Catholics arriving so quickly and all, I'd warned you against that man. All piss 75 and wind, he is. So he's the authority around here, eh?

MOTHER COURAGE: He's been doing washing-up for me and helping pull.

THE COOK: Him pull! I bet he told you some of those jokes of his too, I know him, got a very unhealthy view of 80 women, he has, all my good influence on him went for nowt. He ain't steady.

MOTHER COURAGE: You steady then?

THE COOK: Whatever else I ain't, I'm steady. Mud in your eye!

MOTHER COURAGE: Steady, that's nowt. I only had one steady 85 fellow, thank God. Hardest I ever had to work in me life; he flogged the kids' blankets soon as autumn came, and he called me mouth-organ an unchristian instrument. Ask me, you ain't saying much for yourself admitting you're steady.

THE COOK: Still tough as nails, I see; but that's what I like 90 about you.

MOTHER COURAGE: Now don't tell me you been dreaming of me nails.

THE COOK: Well, well, here we are, along with armistice bells and your brandy like what nobody else ever serves, it's fa- 95 mous, that is.

MOTHER COURAGE: I don't give two pins for your armistice bells just now. Can't see 'em handing out all the back pay what's owing, so where does that leave me with my famous brandy? Had your pay yet? 100

THE COOK: (*Hesitantly.*) Not exactly. That's why we all shoved off. If that's how it is, I thought, I'll go and visit friends. So here I am sitting with you.

MOTHER COURAGE: Other words you got nowt.

THE COOK: High time they stopped that bloody clanging. 105 Wouldn't mind getting into some sort of trade. I'm fed up being cook to that lot. I'm s'posed to rustle them up meals out of tree roots and old bootsoles, then they fling the hot soup in my face. Cook these days is a dog's life. Sooner do war service, only of course it's peacetime now. (*He sees the* 110 CHAPLAIN *reappearing in his old garments.*) More about that later.

THE CHAPLAIN: It's still all right, only had a few moths in it.

THE COOK: Can't see why you bother. You won't get your old job back, who are you to inspire now to earn his pay hon- 115 ourably and lay down his life? What's more I got a bone to pick with you, cause you advised this lady to buy a lot of unnecessary goods saying war would go on for ever.

THE CHAPLAIN: (*Heatedly.*) I'd like to know what concern that is of yours. 120

THE COOK: Because it's unscrupulous, that sort of thing is. How dare you meddle in other folks' business arrangements with your unwanted advice?

THE CHAPLAIN: Who's meddling? (*To* COURAGE.) I never knew this gentleman was such an intimate you had to ac- 125 count to him for everything.

MOTHER COURAGE: Keep your hair on, cook's only giving his personal opinion and you can't deny your war was a flop.

THE CHAPLAIN: You should not blaspheme against peace,
130　Courage. You are a hyaena of the battlefield.
MOTHER COURAGE: I'm what?
THE COOK: If you're going to insult this lady you'll have to
settle with me.
THE CHAPLAIN: It's not you I'm talking to. Your intentions
135　are only too transparent. (*To* COURAGE.) But when I see
you picking up peace betwixt your finger and your thumb
like some dirty old snot-rag, then my humanity feels outraged; for then I see that you don't want peace but war,
because you profit from it; in which case you shouldn't
140　forget the ancient saying that whosoever sups with the
devil needs a long spoon.
MOTHER COURAGE: I got no use for war, and war ain't got
much use for me. But I'm not being called no hyaena, you
and me's through.
145　THE CHAPLAIN: Then why grumble about peace when everybody's breathing sighs of relief? Because of some old junk
in your cart?
MOTHER COURAGE: My goods ain't old junk but what I lives
by, and you too up to now.
150　THE CHAPLAIN: Off war, in other words. Aha.
THE COOK: (*To the* CHAPLAIN.) You're old enough to know
it's always a mistake offering advice. (*To* COURAGE.) Way
things are, your best bet's to get rid of certain goods quick
as you can before prices hit rock-bottom. Dress yourself
155　and get moving, not a moment to lose.
MOTHER COURAGE: That ain't bad advice. I'll do that, I guess.
THE CHAPLAIN: Because cooky says it.
MOTHER COURAGE: Why couldn't you say it? He's right, I'd
best go off to market. (*Goes inside the cart.*)
160　THE COOK: That's one to me, padre. You got no presence of
mind. What you should of said was: what, me offer advice,
all I done was discuss politics. Better not take me on.
Cock-fighting don't suit that get-up.
THE CHAPLAIN: If you don't stop your gob I'll murder you,
165　get-up or no get-up.
THE COOK: (*Pulling off his boots and unwrapping his foot-cloths.*)
Pity the war made such a godless shit of you, else you'd
easily get another parsonage now it's peacetime. Cooks
won't be needed, there's nowt to cook, but faith goes on
170　just the same, nowt changed in that direction.
THE CHAPLAIN: Mr Lamb, I'm asking you not to elbow me
out. Since I came down in the world I've become a better person. I couldn't preach to anyone now.

(*Enter* YVETTE POTTIER *in black, dressed up to the nines, carrying
a cane. She is much older and fatter, and heavily powdered. She is
followed by a manservant.*)

YVETTE: Hullo there, everybody. Is this Mother Courage's es-
175　tablishment?
THE CHAPLAIN: It is. And with whom have we the honour …?
YVETTE: With the Countess Starhemberg, my good man.
Where's Courage?
THE CHAPLAIN: (*Calls into the cart.*) The Countess Starhem-
180　berg wishes to speak to you.
MOTHER COURAGE'S VOICE: Just coming.
YVETTE: It's Yvette.
MOTHER COURAGE'S VOICE: Oh, Yvette!

YVETTE: Come to see how you are. (*Sees the* COOK *turn round
aghast.*) Pieter!　　185
THE COOK: Yvette!
YVETTE: Well I never! How d'you come to be here?
THE COOK: Got a lift.
THE CHAPLAIN: You know each other then? Intimately?
YVETTE: I should think so. (*She looks the* COOK *over.*) Fat.　190
THE COOK: Not all that skinny yourself.
YVETTE: All the same I'm glad to see you, you shit. Gives me
a chance to say what I think of you.
THE CHAPLAIN: You say it, in full; but don't start till Courage
is out here.　　195
MOTHER COURAGE: (*Coming out with all kinds of goods.*)
Yvette! (*They embrace.*) But what are you in mourning for?
YVETTE: Suits me, don't it? My husband the colonel died a
few years back.
MOTHER COURAGE: That old fellow what nearly bought the cart?　200
YVETTE: His elder brother.
MOTHER COURAGE: Then you're sitting pretty. Nice to find
somebody what's made it in this war.
YVETTE: Up and down and up again, that's the way it went.
MOTHER COURAGE: I'm not hearing a word against colonels,　205
they make a mint of money.
THE CHAPLAIN: I would put my boots back on if I were you.
(*To* YVETTE.) You promised you would say what you think
of the gentleman.
THE COOK: Don't kick up a stink here, Yvette.　210
MOTHER COURAGE: Yvette, this is a friend of mine.
YVETTE: That's old Puffing Piet.
THE COOK: Let's drop the nicknames. I'm called Lamb.
MOTHER COURAGE: (*Laughs.*) Puffing Piet! Him as made all the
women crazy! Here, I been looking after your pipe for you.　215
THE CHAPLAIN: Smoking it, too.
YVETTE: What luck I can warn you against him. Worst of the
lot, he was, rampaging along the whole Flanders coastline.
Got more girls in trouble than he has fingers.
THE COOK: That's all a long while ago. 'Tain't true anyhow.　220
YVETTE: Stand up when a lady brings you into the conversa-
tion! How I loved this man! All the time he had a little
dark girl with bandy legs, got her in trouble too of course.
THE COOK: Got you into high society more like, far as I can see.
YVETTE: Shut your trap, you pathetic remnant! Better watch　225
out for him, though; fellows like that are still dangerous
even when on their last legs.
MOTHER COURAGE: (*To* YVETTE.) Come along, got to get rid
of my stuff afore prices start dropping. You might be able
to put a word in for me at regiment, with your connec-　230
tions. (*Calls into the cart.*) Kattrin, church is off, I'm going
to market instead. When Eilif turns up, one of you give
him a drink. (*Exit with* YVETTE.)
YVETTE: (*As she leaves.*) Fancy a creature like that ever making me leave the straight and narrow path. Thank my　235
lucky stars I managed to reach the top all the same. But
I've cooked your goose, Puffing Piet, and that's something
that'll be credited to me one day in the world to come.
THE CHAPLAIN: I would like to take as a text for our little talk
'The mills of God grind slowly'. Weren't you complain-　240
ing about my jokes?
THE COOK: Dead out of luck, I am. It's like this, you see: I
thought I might get a hot meal. Here am I starving, and

245 now they'll be talking about me and she'll get quite a wrong picture. I think I'll clear out before she's back.

THE CHAPLAIN: I think so too.

THE COOK: Padre, I'm fed up already with this bloody peace. Human race has to go through fire and sword cause it's sinful from the cradle up. I wish I could be roasting a fat
250 capon once again for the general, wherever he's got to, in mustard sauce with a carrot or two.

THE CHAPLAIN: Red cabbage. Red cabbage for a capon.

THE COOK: You're right, but carrots was what he had to have.

THE CHAPLAIN: No sense of what's fitting.

255 THE COOK: Not that it stopped you guzzling your share.

THE CHAPLAIN: With misgivings.

THE COOK: Anyway you must admit those were the days.

THE CHAPLAIN: I might admit it if pressed.

THE COOK: Now you've called her a hyaena your days here
260 are finished. What you staring at?

THE CHAPLAIN: Eilif! (EILIF *arrives, followed by* SOLDIERS *with pikes. His hands are fettered. His face is chalky-white.*) What's wrong?

EILIF: Where's mother?

265 THE CHAPLAIN: Gone into town.

EILIF: I heard she was around. They've allowed me to come and see her.

THE COOK: (*To the* SOLDIERS.) What you doing with him?

A SOLDIER: Something not nice.

270 THE CHAPLAIN: What's he been up to?

THE SOLDIER: Broke into a peasant's place. The wife's dead.

THE CHAPLAIN: How could you do a thing like that?

EILIF: It's what I did last time, ain't it?

THE COOK: Aye, but it's peace now.

275 EILIF: Shut up. All right if I sit down till she comes?

THE SOLDIER: We've no time.

THE CHAPLAIN: In wartime they recommended him for that, sat him at the general's right hand. Dashing, it was, in those days. Any chance of a word with the provost-marshal?

280 THE SOLDIER: Wouldn't do no good. Taking some peasant's cattle, what's dashing about that?

THE COOK: Dumb, I call it.

EILIF: If I'd been dumb you'd of starved, clever bugger.

THE COOK: But as you were clever you're going to be shot.

285 THE CHAPLAIN: We'd better fetch Kattrin out anyhow.

EILIF: Sooner have a glass of schnapps, could do with that.

THE SOLDIER: No time, come along.

THE CHAPLAIN: And what shall we tell your mother?

EILIF: Tell her it wasn't any different, tell her it was the same
290 thing. Or tell her nowt. (*The* SOLDIERS *propel him away.*)

THE CHAPLAIN: I'll accompany you on your grievous journey.

EILIF: Don't need any bloody parsons.

THE CHAPLAIN: Wait and see. (*Follows him.*)

THE COOK: (*Calls after them.*) I'll have to tell her, she'll want
295 to see him.

THE CHAPLAIN: I wouldn't tell her anything. At most that he was here and will come again, maybe tomorrow. By then I'll be back and can break it to her. (*Hurries off.*)

(*The* COOK *looks after him, shaking his head, then walks restlessly around. Finally he comes up to the cart.*)

THE COOK: Hoy! Don't you want to come out? I can under-
300 stand you hiding away from peace. Like to do the same myself. Remember me, I'm general's cook? I was won-dering if you'd a bit of something to eat while I wait for your mum. I don't half feel like a bit of pork, or bread even, just to fill the time. (*Peers inside.*) Head under blan-
305 ket. (*Sound of gunfire off.*)

MOTHER COURAGE: (*Runs in, out of breath and with all her goods still.*) Cooky, peacetime's over. War's been on again three days now. Heard news before selling me stuff, thank God. They're having a shooting match with Lutherans in town.
310 We must get cart away at once. Kattrin, pack up! What you in the dumps for? What's wrong?

THE COOK: Nowt.

MOTHER COURAGE: Something is. I see it way you look.

THE COOK: Cause war's starting up again, I s'pose. Looks as if
315 it'll be tomorrow night before I get next hot food inside me.

MOTHER COURAGE: You're lying, cooky.

THE COOK: Eilif was here. Had to leave almost at once, though.

MOTHER COURAGE: Was he now? Then we'll be seeing him on march. I'm joining our side this time. How's he look?

320 THE COOK: Same as usual.

MOTHER COURAGE: Oh, he'll never change. Take more than war to steal him from me. Clever, he is. You going to help me get packed? (*Begins to pack up.*) What's his news? Still in general's good books? Say anything about his deeds of
325 valour?

THE COOK: (*Glumly.*) Repeated one of them, I'm told.

MOTHER COURAGE: Tell it me later, we got to move off. (KAT-TRIN *appears.*) Kattrin, peacetime's finished now. We're moving on. (*To the* COOK.) How about you?

330 THE COOK: Have to join up again.

MOTHER COURAGE: Why don't you . . . Where's padre?

THE COOK: Went into town with Eilif.

MOTHER COURAGE: Then you come along with us a way. Need somebody to help me.

335 THE COOK: That business with Yvette, you know . . .

MOTHER COURAGE: Done you no harm in my eyes. Oppo-site. Where there's smoke there's fire, they say. You com-ing along?

THE COOK: I won't say no.

340 MOTHER COURAGE: The Twelfth moved off already. Take the shaft. Here's a bit of bread. We must get round behind to Lutherans. Might even be seeing Eilif tonight. He's my favourite one. Short peace, wasn't it? Now we're off again. (*She sings as the* COOK *and* KATTRIN *harness themselves up.*)

345 From Ulm to Metz, from Metz to Munich
Courage will see the war gets fed.
The war will show a well-filled tunic
Given its daily shot of lead.
But lead alone can hardly nourish
350 It must have soldiers to subsist.
It's you it needs to make it flourish.
The war's still hungry. So enlist!

SCENE NINE

It is the seventeenth year of the great war of faith. Ger-many has lost more than half her inhabitants. Those who survive the bloodbath are killed off by terrible epidemics. Once fertile areas are ravaged by famine, wolves roam the burnt-out towns. In autumn 1634 we find Courage in the Fichtelgebirge, off the main axis of the Swedish armies. The winter this year is early and harsh. Business is bad, so that there is nothing to do but beg. The cook gets a letter from Utrecht and is sent packing.

Outside a semi-dilapidated parsonage.

Grey morning in early winter. Gusts of wind. MOTHER COURAGE *and the* COOK *in shabby sheepskins, drawing the cart.*

THE COOK: It's all dark, nobody up yet.
MOTHER COURAGE: Except it's parson's house. Have to crawl out of bed to ring bells. Then he'll have hot soup.
THE COOK: What from when whole village is burnt, we
5   seen it.
MOTHER COURAGE: It's lived in, though, dog was barking.
THE COOK: S'pose parson's got, he'll give nowt.
MOTHER COURAGE: Maybe if we sing. . . .
THE COOK: I've had enough. (*Abruptly.*) Got a letter from
10   Utrecht saying mother died of cholera and inn's mine. Here's letter if you don't believe me. No business of yours the way aunty goes on about my mode of existence, but have a look.
MOTHER COURAGE: (*Reads the letter.*) Lamb, I'm tired too of
15   always being on the go. I feel like butcher's dog, dragging meat round customers and getting nowt off it. I got nowt left to sell, and folk got nowt left to buy nowt with. Saxony a fellow in rags tried landing me a stack of old books for two eggs, Württemberg they wanted to swap their
20   plough for a titchy bag of salt. What's to plough for? Nowt growing no more, just brambles. In Pomerania villages are s'posed to have started in eating the younger kids, and nuns have been caught sticking folk up.
THE COOK: World's dying out.
25 MOTHER COURAGE: Sometimes I sees meself driving through hell with me cart selling brimstone, or across heaven with packed lunches for hungry souls. Give me my kids what's left, let's find some place they ain't shooting, and I'd like a few more years undisturbed.
30 THE COOK: You and me could get that inn going, Courage, think it over. Made up me mind in the night, I did: back to Utrecht with or without you, and starting today.
MOTHER COURAGE: Have to talk to Kattrin. That's a bit quick for me; I'm against making decisions all freezing cold and
35   nowt inside you. Kattrin! (KATTRIN *climbs out of the cart.*) Kattrin, got something to tell you. Cook and I want to go to Utrecht. He's been left an inn there. That'd be a settled place for you, let you meet a few people. Lots of 'em respect somebody mature, looks ain't everything. I'd like it
40   too. I get on with cook. Say one thing for him, got a head for business. We'd have our meals for sure, not bad, eh? And your own bed too; like that, wouldn't you? Road's no life really. God knows how you might finish up. Lousy already, you are. Have to make up our minds, see, we could move
45   with the Swedes, up north, they're somewhere up that way. (*She points to the left.*) Reckon that's fixed, Kattrin.
THE COOK: Anna, I got something private to say to you.
MOTHER COURAGE: Get back in cart, Kattrin.

(KATTRIN *climbs back.*)

THE COOK: I had to interrupt, cause you don't understand, far as I can see. I didn't think there was need to say it, 50 sticks out a mile. But if it don't, then let me tell you straight, no question of taking her along, not on your life. You get me, eh.

(KATTRIN *sticks her head out of the cart behind them and listens.*)

MOTHER COURAGE: You mean I'm to leave Kattrin back here?
THE COOK: Use your imagination. Inn's got no room. It ain't 55 one of the sort got three bar parlours. Put our backs in it we two'll get a living, but not three, no chance of that. She can keep cart.
MOTHER COURAGE: Thought she might find husband in Utrecht. 60
THE COOK: Go on, make me laugh. Find a husband, how? Dumb and that scar on top of it. And at her age?
MOTHER COURAGE: Don't talk so loud.
THE COOK: Loud or soft, no getting over facts. And that's another reason why I can't have her in the inn. Customers 65 don't want to be looking at that all the time. Can't blame them.
MOTHER COURAGE: Shut your big mouth. I said not so loud.
THE COOK: Light's on in parson's house. We can try singing.
MOTHER COURAGE: Cooky, how's she to pull the cart on her 70 own? War scares her. She'll never stand it. The dreams she must have . . . I hear her nights groaning. Mostly after a battle. What's she seeing in those dreams, I'd like to know. She's got a soft heart. Lately I found she'd got another hedgehog tucked away what we'd run over. 75
THE COOK: Inn's too small. (*Calls out.*) Ladies and gentlemen, domestic staff and other residents! We are now going to give you a song concerning Solomon, Julius Caesar and other famous personages what had bad luck. So's you can see we're respectable folk, which makes it difficult to carry 80 on, particularly in winter. (*They sing.*)

> You saw sagacious Solomon
> You know what came of him.
> To him complexities seemed plain.
> He cursed the hour that gave birth to him 85
> And saw that everything was vain.
> How great and wise was Solomon!
> The world however didn't wait
> But soon observed what followed on.
> It's wisdom that had brought him to this state— 90
> How fortunate the man with none!

Yes, the virtues are dangerous stuff in this world, as this fine song proves, better not to have them and have a pleasant life and breakfast instead, hot soup for instance. Look at me: I haven't any but I'd like some. I'm a serving soldier 95 but what good did my courage do me in all them battles, nowt, here I am starving and better have been shit-scared and stayed at home. For why?

> You saw courageous Caesar next
> You know what he became. 100
> They deified him in his life
> Then had him murdered just the same.
> And as they raised the fatal knife
> How loud he cried: You too, my son!

105 The world however didn't wait
But soon observed what followed on.
It's courage that had brought him to that state.
How fortunate the man with none!

110 (*Sotto voce.*) Don't even look out. (*Aloud.*) Ladies and gentlemen, domestic staff and other inmates! All right, you may say, gallantry never cooked a man's dinner, what about trying honesty? You can eat all you want then, or anyhow not stay sober. How about it?

115 You heard of honest Socrates
The man who never lied:
They weren't so grateful as you'd think
Instead the rulers fixed to have him tried
And handed him the poisoned drink.
How honest was the people's noble son!
120 The world however didn't wait
But soon observed what followed on.
It's honesty that brought him to that state.
How fortunate the man with none!

125 Ah yes, they say, be unselfish and share what you've got, but how about if you got nowt? It's all very well to say the dogooders have a hard time, but you still got to have something. Aye, unselfishness is a rare virtue, cause it just don't pay.

130 Saint Martin couldn't bear to see
His fellows in distress.
He met a poor man in the snow
And shared his cloak with him, we know.
Both of them therefore froze to death.
His place in Heaven was surely won!
135 The world however didn't wait
But soon observed what followed on.
Unselfishness had brought him to that state.
How fortunate the man with none!

140 That's how it is with us. We're respectable folk, stick together, don't steal, don't murder, don't burn places down. And all the time you might say we're sinking lower and lower, and it's true what the song says, and soup is few and far between, and if we weren't like this but thieves and murderers I dare say we'd be eating our fill. For virtues
145 aren't their own reward, only wickednesses are, that's how the world goes and it didn't ought to.

Here you can see respectable folk
Keeping to God's own laws.
So far he hasn't taken heed.
150 You who sit safe and warm indoors
Help to relieve our bitter need!
How virtuously we had begun!
The world however didn't wait
But soon observed what followed on.
155 It's fear of God that brought us to that state.
How fortunate the man with none!

VOICE: (*From above.*) Hey, you there! Come on up! There's hot soup if you want.
160 MOTHER COURAGE: Lamb, me stomach won't stand nowt. 'Tain't that it ain't sensible, what you say, but is that your last word? We got on all right.

THE COOK: Last word. Think it over.
MOTHER COURAGE: I've nowt to think. I'm not leaving her here.
THE COOK: That's proper senseless, nothing I can do about it though. I'm not a brute, just the inn's a small one. So now 165 we better get on up, or there'll be nowt here either and wasted time singing in the cold.
MOTHER COURAGE: I'll get Kattrin.
THE COOK: Better bring a bit back for her. Scare them if they sees three of us coming. (*Exeunt both.*) 170

(KATTRIN *climbs out of the cart with a bundle. She looks around to see if the other two have gone. Then she takes an old pair of trousers of the* COOK's *and a skirt of her mother's, and lays them side by side on one of the wheels, so that they are easily seen. She has finished and is picking up her bundle to go, when* MOTHER COURAGE *comes back from the house.*)

MOTHER COURAGE: (*With a plate of soup.*) Kattrin! Will you stop there? Kattrin! Where you off to with that bundle? Has devil himself taken you over? (*She examines the bundle.*) She's packed her things. You been listening? I told him nowt doing, Utrecht, his rotten inn, what'd we be up to there? You 175 me and me, inn's no place for us. Still plenty to be got out of war. (*She sees the trousers and the skirt.*) You're plain stupid. S'pose I'd seen that, and you gone away? (*She holds* KATTRIN *back as she tries to break away.*) Don't you start thinking it's on your account I given him the push. It was cart, that's it. 180 Catch me leaving my cart I'm used to, it ain't you, it's for cart. We'll go off in t'other direction, and we'll throw cook's stuff out so he finds it, silly man. (*She climbs in and throws out a few other articles in the direction of the trousers.*) There, he's out of our business now, and I ain't having nobody else in, ever. 185 You and me'll carry on now. This winter will pass, same as all the others. Get hitched up, it looks like snow.

(*They both harness themselves to the cart, then wheel it round and drag it off. When the* COOK *arrives he looks blankly at his kit.*)

SCENE TEN

During the whole of 1635 Mother Courage and her daughter Kattrin travel over the highroads of central Germany, in the wake of the increasingly bedraggled armies.

High road.

MOTHER COURAGE *and* KATTRIN *are pulling the cart. They pass a* PEASANT's *house inside which there is a voice singing.*

THE VOICE: The roses in our arbour
Delight us with their show:
They have such lovely flowers
Repaying all our labour
After the summer showers.
Happy are those with gardens now: 5
They have such lovely flowers.

When winter winds are freezing
As through the woods they blow
Our home is warm and pleasing.
We fixed the thatch above it 10

With straw and moss we wove it.
Happy are those with shelter now
When winter winds are freezing.

(MOTHER COURAGE *and* KATTRIN *pause to listen, then continue pulling.*)

SCENE ELEVEN

January 1636. The emperor's troops are threatening the Protestant town of Halle. The stone begins to speak. Mother Courage loses her daughter and trudges on alone. The war is a long way from being over.

The cart is standing, much the worse for wear, alongside a PEASANT's *house with a huge thatched roof, backing on a wall of rock. It is night.*

An ENSIGN *and* THREE SOLDIERS *in heavy armour step out of the wood.*

THE ENSIGN: I want no noise now. Anyone shouts, shove your pike into him.

FIRST SOLDIER: Have to knock them up, though, if we're to find a guide.

5 THE ENSIGN: Knocking sounds natural. Could be a cow bumping the stable wall.

(*The* SOLDIERS *knock on the door of the house. The* PEASANT's *wife opens it. They stop her mouth.* TWO SOLDIERS *go in.*)

MAN'S VOICE: (*Within.*) What is it?

(*The* SOLDIERS *bring out the* PEASANT *and his son* [THE YOUNG PEASANT].)

THE ENSIGN: (*Pointing at the cart, where* KATTRIN's *head has appeared.*) There's another one. (*A* SOLDIER *drags her out.*)
10   Anyone else live here beside you lot?

THE PEASANTS: This is our son. And she's dumb. Her mother's gone into town to buy stuff. For their business, cause so many people's getting out and selling things cheap. They're just passing through. Canteen folk.

15 THE ENSIGN: I'm warning you, keep quiet, or if there's the least noise you get a pike across your nut. Now I want someone to come with us and show us the path to the town. (*Points to the* YOUNG PEASANT.) Here, you.

THE YOUNG PEASANT: I don't know no path.

20 SECOND SOLDIER: (*Grinning.*) He don't know no path.

THE YOUNG PEASANT: I ain't helping Catholics.

THE ENSIGN: (*To the* SECOND SOLDIER.) Stick your pike in his ribs.

THE YOUNG PEASANT: (*Forced to his knees, with the pike threat-*
25   *ening him.*) I won't do it, not to save my life.

FIRST SOLDIER: I know what'll change his mind. (*Goes towards the stable.*) Two cows and an ox. Listen, you: if you're not reasonable I'll chop up your cattle.

THE YOUNG PEASANT: No, not that!

30 THE PEASANT'S WIFE: (*Weeps.*) Please spare our cattle, captain, it'd be starving us to death.

THE ENSIGN: They're dead if he goes on being obstinate.

FIRST SOLDIER: I'm taking the ox first.

THE YOUNG PEASANT: (*To his father.*) Have I got to? (*The* WIFE *nods.*) Right.   35

THE PEASANT'S WIFE: And thank you kindly, captain, for sparing us, for ever and ever, Amen.

(*The* PEASANT *stops his* WIFE *from further expressions of gratitude.*)

FIRST SOLDIER: I knew the ox was what they minded about most, was I right?

(*Guided by the* YOUNG PEASANT, *the* ENSIGN *and his* SOLDIERS *continue on their way.*)

THE PEASANT: What are they up to, I'd like to know. Nowt good.   40

THE PEASANT'S WIFE: Perhaps they're just scouting. What you doing?

THE PEASANT: (*Putting a ladder against the roof and climbing up it.*) Seeing if they're on their own. (*From the top.*) Something moving in the wood. Can see something down by   45
the quarry. And there are men in armour in the clearing. And a gun. That's at least a regiment. God's mercy on the town and everyone in it!

THE PEASANT'S WIFE: Any lights in the town?

THE PEASANT: No. They'll all be asleep. (*Climbs down.*) If   50
those people get in they'll butcher the lot.

THE PEASANT'S WIFE: Sentries're bound to spot them first.

THE PEASANT: Sentry in the tower up the hill must have been killed, or he'd have blown his bugle.

THE PEASANT'S WIFE: If only there were more of us.   55

THE PEASANT: Just you and me and that cripple.

THE PEASANT'S WIFE: Nowt we can do, you'd say. . . .

THE PEASANT: Nowt.

THE PEASANT'S WIFE: Can't possibly run down there in the blackness.   60

THE PEASANT: Whole hillside's crawling with 'em. We could give a signal.

THE PEASANT'S WIFE: What, and have them butcher us too?

THE PEASANT: You're right, nowt we can do.

THE PEASANT'S WIFE: (*To* KATTRIN.) Pray, poor creature, pray!   65
Nowt we can do to stop bloodshed. You can't talk, maybe, but at least you can pray. He'll hear you if no one else can. I'll help you. (*All kneel,* KATTRIN *behind the two* PEASANTS.)
Our Father, which art in Heaven, hear Thou our prayer, let not the town be destroyed with all what's in it sound   70
asleep and suspecting nowt. Arouse Thou them that they may get up and go to the walls and see how the enemy approacheth with picks and guns in the blackness across fields below the slope. (*Turning to* KATTRIN.) Guard Thou our mother and ensure that the watchman sleepeth not   75
but wakes up, or it will be too late. Succour our brother-in-law also, he is inside there with his four children, spare Thou them, they are innocent and know nowt. (*To* KATTRIN, *who gives a groan.*) One of them's not two yet, the eldest's seven. (KATTRIN *stands up distractedly.*) Our Father,   80
hear us, for only Thou canst help; we look to be doomed, for why, we are weak and have no pike and nowt and can risk nowt and are in Thy hand along with our cattle and all the farm, and same with the town, it too is in Thy hand and the enemy is before the walls in great strength.   85

(*Unobserved,* KATTRIN *has slipped away to the cart and taken from it something which she hides beneath her apron; then she climbs up the ladder on to the stable roof.*)

THE PEASANT'S WIFE: Forget not the children, what are in danger, the littlest ones especially, the old folk what can't move, and every living creature.

THE PEASANT: And forgive us our trespasses as we forgive
90 them that trespass against us. Amen.

(*Sitting on the roof,* KATTRIN *begins to beat the drum which she has pulled out from under her apron.*)

THE PEASANT'S WIFE: Jesus Christ, what's she doing?
THE PEASANT: She's out of her mind.
THE PEASANT'S WIFE: Quick, get her down.

(*The* PEASANT *hurries to the ladder, but* KATTRIN *pulls it up on to the roof.*)

THE PEASANT'S WIFE: She'll do us in.
95 THE PEASANT: Stop drumming at once, you cripple!
THE PEASANT'S WIFE: Bringing the Catholics down on us!
THE PEASANT: (*Looking for stones to throw.*) I'll stone you.
THE PEASANT'S WIFE: Where's your feelings? Where's your heart? We're done for if they come down on us. Slit our
100 throats, they will.

(KATTRIN *stares into the distance towards the town and carries on drumming.*)

THE PEASANT'S WIFE: (*To her husband.*) I told you we shouldn't have allowed those vagabonds on to farm. What do they care if our last cows are taken?
THE ENSIGN: (*Runs in with his* SOLDIERS *and the* YOUNG PEAS-
105 ANT.) I'll cut you to ribbons, all of you!
THE PEASANT'S WIFE: Please, sir, it's not our fault, we couldn't help it. It was her sneaked up there. A foreigner.
THE ENSIGN: Where's the ladder?
THE PEASANT: There.
110 THE ENSIGN: (*Calls up.*) I order you, throw that drum down.

(KATTRIN *goes on drumming.*)

THE ENSIGN: You're all in this together. It'll be the end of you.
THE PEASANT: They been cutting pine trees in that wood. How about if we got one of the trunks and poked her off....
FIRST SOLDIER: (*To the* ENSIGN.) Permission to make a sug-
115 gestion, sir! (*He whispers something in the* ENSIGN's *ear.*) Listen, we got a suggestion could help you. Get down off there and come into town with us right away. Show us which your mother is and we'll see she ain't harmed.

(KATTRIN *goes on drumming.*)

THE ENSIGN: (*Pushes him roughly aside.*) She doesn't trust you;
120 with a mug like yours it's not surprising. (*Calls up.*) Suppose I gave you my word? I can give my word of honour as an officer.

(KATTRIN *drums harder.*)

THE ENSIGN: Is nothing sacred to her?
THE YOUNG PEASANT: There's more than her mother involved, sir.
125 FIRST SOLDIER: This can't go on much longer. They're bound to hear in the town.
THE ENSIGN: We'll somehow to make a noise that's louder than her drumming. What can we make a noise with?

FIRST SOLDIER: Thought we weren't s'posed to make no noise.
THE ENSIGN: A harmless one, you fool. A peaceful one.   130
THE PEASANT: I could chop wood with my axe.
THE ENSIGN: Good: you chop. (*The* PEASANT *fetches his axe and attacks a tree-trunk.*) Chop harder! Harder! You're chopping for your life.

(KATTRIN *has been listening, drumming less loudly the while. She now looks wildly round, and goes on drumming.*)

THE ENSIGN: Not loud enough. (*To the* FIRST SOLDIER.) You   135
chop too.
THE PEASANT: Only got the one axe. (*Stops chopping.*)
THE ENSIGN: We'll have to set the farm on fire. Smoke her out, that's it.
THE PEASANT: It wouldn't help, captain. If the townspeople   140
see a fire here they'll know what's up.

(KATTRIN *has again been listening as she drums. At this point she laughs.*)

THE ENSIGN: Look at her laughing at us. I'm not having that. I'll shoot her down, and damn the consequences. Fetch the harquebus.

(THREE SOLDIERS *hurry off.* KATTRIN *goes on drumming.*)

THE PEASANT'S WIFE: I got it, captain. That's their cart. If we   145
smash it up she'll stop. Cart's all they got.
THE ENSIGN: (*To the* YOUNG PEASANT.) Smash it up. (*Calls up.*) We're going to smash up your cart if you don't stop drumming. (*The* YOUNG PEASANT *gives the cart a few feeble blows.*)
THE PEASANT'S WIFE: Stop it, you animal!   150

(*Desperately looking towards the cart,* KATTRIN *emits pitiful noises. But she goes on drumming.*)

THE ENSIGN: Where are those clodhoppers with the harquebus?
FIRST SOLDIER: Can't have heard nowt in town yet, else we'd be hearing their guns.
THE ENSIGN: (*Calls up.*) They can't hear you at all. And now we're going to shoot you down. For the last time: throw   155
down that drum!
THE YOUNG PEASANT: (*Suddenly flings away his plank.*) Go on drumming! Or they'll all be killed! Go on, go on....

(*The* FIRST SOLDIER *knocks him down and beats him with his pike.* KATTRIN *starts to cry, but she goes on drumming.*)

THE PEASANT'S WIFE: Don't strike his back! For God's sake, you're beating him to death!   160

(*The* SOLDIERS *hurry in with the arquebus.*)

SECOND SOLDIER: Colonel's frothing at the mouth, sir. We're all for court-martial.
THE ENSIGN: Set it up! Set it up! (*Calls up while the gun is being erected.*) For the very last time: stop drumming! (KATTRIN, *in tears, drums as loud as she can.*) Fire! (*The* SOLDIERS *fire.* KAT-   165
TRIN *is hit, gives a few more drumbeats and then slowly crumples.*)
THE ENSIGN: That's the end of that.

(*But* KATTRIN's *last drumbeats are taken up by the town's cannon. In the distance can be heard a confused noise of tocsins and gunfire.*)

FIRST SOLDIER: She's made it.

SCENE TWELVE

Before first light. Sound of the fifes and drums of troops marching off into the distance.

In front of the cart MOTHER COURAGE *is squatting by her daughter. The peasant family are standing near her.*

THE PEASANTS: (*With hostility.*) You must go, missis. There's only one more regiment behind that one. You can't go on your own.

MOTHER COURAGE: I think she's going to sleep. (*She sings.*)

5   Lullaby baby
       What's that in the hay?
       Neighbours' kids grizzle
       But my kids are gay.
       Neighbours' are in tatters
10   And you're dressed in lawn
       Cut down from the raiment an
       Angel has worn.
       Neighbours' kids go hungry
       And you shall eat cake
15   Suppose it's too crumbly
       You've only to speak.
       Lullaby baby
       What's that in the hay?
       The one lies in Poland
20   The other—who can say?

Better if you'd not told her nowt about your brother-in-law's kids.

THE PEASANT: If you'd not gone into town to get your cut it might never of happened.

25 MOTHER COURAGE: Now she's asleep.

THE PEASANT'S WIFE: She ain't asleep. Can't you see she's passed over?

THE PEASANT: And it's high time you got away yourself. There are wolves around and, what's worse, marauders.

MOTHER COURAGE: Aye.   30

(*She goes and gets a tarpaulin to cover the dead girl with.*)

THE PEASANT'S WIFE: Ain't you got nobody else? What you could go to?

MOTHER COURAGE: Aye, one left. Eilif.

THE PEASANT: (*As* MOTHER COURAGE *covers the dead girl.*) Best look for him, then. We'll mind her, see she gets 35 proper burial. Don't you worry about that.

MOTHER COURAGE: Here's money for expenses.

(*She counts out coins into the* PEASANT's *hands. The* PEASANT *and his* SON *shake hands with her and carry* KATTRIN *away.*)

THE PEASANT'S WIFE: (*As she leaves.*) I'd hurry.

MOTHER COURAGE: (*Harnessing herself to the cart.*) Hope I can pull cart all right by meself. Be all right, nowt much in- 40 side it. Got to get back in business again.

(*Another regiment with its fifes and drums marches past in the background.*)

MOTHER COURAGE: (*Tugging the cart.*) Take me along!

(*Singing is heard from offstage.*)

       With all its luck and all its danger
       The war is dragging on a bit
       Another hundred years or longer   45
       The common man won't benefit.
       Filthy his food, no soap to shave him
       The regiment steals half his pay.
       But still a miracle may save him:
       Tomorrow is another day!   50
          The new year's come. The watchmen shout.
          The thaw sets in. The dead remain.
          Wherever life has not died out
          It staggers to its feet again.

Samuel Beckett

Samuel Beckett (1906–1989) is the most influential European dramatist of the postwar period. Born near Dublin, Ireland, Beckett was educated at Trinity College, Dublin, where he studied modern languages. Taking his B.A. in 1928, Beckett received an appointment as *lecteur* at l'École Normale Supérieure in Paris. While in Paris, Beckett met the Irish novelist James Joyce. Beckett assisted Joyce (who was nearly blind) in a variety of ways and became a close friend. Joyce also exerted a profound influence on Beckett's writing. In 1929, Beckett contributed an essay entitled "Dante . . . Bruno . Vico . . Joyce" to a volume on Joyce's *Finnegans Wake*. Throughout the 1930s, Beckett was associated with Joyce and with a variety of avant-garde movements in Paris. He wrote a series of poems—including the prize-winning "Whoroscope"—as well as a study of Proust (1931), the volume of short stories *More Pricks than Kicks* (1934), and the novel *Murphy* (1938). Although Beckett returned briefly to Ireland on a few occasions, he had settled permanently in Paris. During World War II, Beckett served in the French Resistance. He was discovered by the Nazis and forced to flee Paris in 1942. He worked in the unoccupied zone of southern France for the remainder of the war, where he wrote the novel *Watt* (1953). After the war, Beckett received the Croix de Guerre and the Médaille de la Résistance for his services. He began to write exclusively in French, starting work on a major trilogy of novels—*Molloy* (1951), *Malone Dies* (1951), and *The Unnameable* (1953).

Beckett had experimented with drama during the 1930s and 1940s, but his first staged play, *Waiting for Godot* (first written in French, as *En attendant Godot*), produced at the tiny Théâtre de Babylone in January of 1953, impelled him in a new direction. Although Beckett continued to write fiction—including *From an Abandoned Work* (1956), *How It Is* (1964), *Imagination Dead Imagine* (1965), and *Company* (1979)—his major writing of the 1960s, 1970s, and 1980s was for the theater. His second play, *Endgame*, also written in French, was produced in 1957 and was followed by a series of challenging works for the stage: *Krapp's Last Tape* (1958), *Happy Days* (1962), *Play* (1963), *Not I* (1972), *Footfalls* (1975), *Rockaby* (1981), and *Catastrophe* (1982). For his extraordinarily diverse and influential body of work, Beckett won the Nobel Prize for Literature in 1970. Beckett also wrote several plays for radio and television, as well as a film starring Buster Keaton, *Film* (1965). Beginning in the mid-1960s, Beckett directed productions of his plays, and several productions he directed in France and in Germany now have the status of classics—something like Elia Kazan's productions of Tennessee Williams's plays, or Stanislavski's productions of Chekhov.

Beckett's impact on the contemporary theater can hardly be overestimated and can be seen in the work of Sam Shepard, Harold Pinter, and many others. *Waiting for Godot* signaled new possibilities for stage action—or inaction—and developed the implications of Chekhov's static stage in a more symbolic direction. Each of Beckett's plays explores the nature and limitations of its medium in new and challenging ways. *Endgame* refigures the claustral box of realistic drama, for its characters are trapped in a room of endless—or possibly ending—routine. In *Play*, Beckett puts three urns onstage, from which three heads emerge to deliver, more or less simultaneously, a jarring, repetitive monologue of seduction and betrayal. Once the play has finished, Beckett directs his performers—and his audience—to "Repeat play," and so calls the relationship between actors and spectators, theater and reality into question: If we cannot leave the theater when the play is over, is it possible that there is no way out of the purgatory on the stage and in the auditorium? This sense that the self is always in flight is the theme of several of Beckett's later plays. In *Not I,* for instance, all that the audience sees is a Mouth eight feet above the stage, reciting an endless narrative in which she avoids claiming the speech as her own. In *Ohio Impromptu* (1981), an identical reader and listener relate a painful narrative of loss, in which it is unclear whether they are two individuals or parts of a single person. The power of Beckett's spare, minimalist theater, the beauty of his sculptural use of actors and stage space, and the harsh exigency of the action of his plays have transformed the stage of our time.

Endgame is Beckett's second full-length play to reach the stage; although its simplicity and repetitiveness are in some ways reminiscent of *Waiting for Godot,* the tone of *Endgame* is bleaker, harsher. As Beckett wrote to Alan Schneider, the play's first American director, *Endgame*'s power is "the power of the text to claw."

The "endgame" of a chess match is the final portion of the game, at which either a checkmate or a stalemate has become inevitable. In *Endgame,* Beckett literalizes the uncertainty of the endgame—will the tortuous nothingness of the characters' lives continue indefinitely, move after move, or will it somehow end? Although some critics have taken the "shelter" and the empty landscape outside as an indication that the play takes place in a bomb shelter after a nuclear bombing, *Endgame* seems to present a microcosm of postmodern life, in which the futile search for fugitive "meanings" raises the despairing feeling that our lives are meaningless, "absurd" after all. Hamm is a kind of ham actor and recalls Shakespeare's Richard III ("My kingdom for a nightman") and Prospero ("Our revels now are ended"), as well as perhaps King Lear and Hamlet in his performance. Hamm is perhaps the first **POSTMODERN** dramatic hero, less a full "character" than a *pastiche* of dramatic roles and possibilities, which exist now only in bits and pieces, recollected fragments (on **PASTICHE,** see Fredric Jameson's essay). Hamm's blindness also recalls both Oedipus—who also struggled with his father—and Ham the son of Noah, who was blinded when he saw his father naked. Hamm continually reminds us that his performance—it's full of asides, a "last soliloquy," and many self-regarding comments on Hamm's success or failure—is an attempt to impose meaning on the process of the play's action. This recollection of the dramatic and literary tradition also points to the problematic place—or absence—of history in *Endgame.* If there is a kind of past ("Once!") in *Endgame,* it is recalled most clearly by Hamm's parents: Nagg and Nell, legless in their garbage cans, describe an earlier, more sentimental or

Nagg and Nell in their ashbins in Samuel Beckett's *Endgame,* in the 2000 Rude Mechanicals Theater Company production.

romantic era, when couples rode tandems in the Ardennes and rowed on Lake Como. Overall, though, time seems to be an endless present moment in *Endgame,* a moment disconnected from the past that once gave it meaning, and from the future which gave it closure. It may be that the play is postnuclear (although Beckett's draft manuscripts suggest that the inspiration was really a war hospital), but this setting is less important than the sense of time that this tiny world contains. For *Endgame* is finally about time and its passing, the painfully slow passage of moment to moment, and its finality once it is past.

Endgame was originally written in French as *Fin de partie* and was rewritten into English by Beckett himself; there are several small differences in dialogue and action between the two versions.

ENDGAME

Samuel Beckett

CHARACTERS

NAGG	HAMM
NELL	CLOV

Bare interior.

Grey light.

Left and right back, high up, two small windows, curtains drawn.

Front right, a door. Hanging near door, its face to wall, a picture.

Front left, touching each other, covered with an old sheet, two ashbins.

Center, in an armchair on castors, covered with an old sheet, HAMM.

Motionless by the door, his eyes fixed on HAMM, CLOV. *Very red face.*

Brief tableau.

CLOV *goes and stands under window left. Stiff, staggering walk. He looks up at window left. He turns and looks at window right. He goes and stands under window right. He looks up at window right. He turns and looks at window left. He goes out, comes back immediately with a small step-ladder, carries it over and sets it down under window left, gets up on it, draws back curtain. He gets down, takes six steps (for example) towards window right, goes back for ladder, carries it over and sets it down under window right, gets up on it, draws back curtain. He gets down, takes three steps towards window left, goes back for ladder, carries it over and sets it down under window left, gets up on it, looks out of window. Brief laugh. He gets down, takes one step towards window right, goes back for ladder, carries it over and sets it down under window right, gets up on it, looks out of window. Brief laugh. He gets down, goes with ladder towards ashbins, halts, turns, carries back ladder and sets it down under window right, goes to ashbins, removes sheet covering them, folds it over his arm. He raises one lid, stoops and looks into bin. Brief laugh. He closes lid. Same with other bin. He goes to* HAMM, *removes sheet covering him, folds it over his arm. In a dressing-gown, a stiff toque on his head, a large blood-stained handkerchief over his face, a whistle hanging from his neck, a rug over his knees, thick socks on his feet,* HAMM *seems to be asleep.* CLOV *looks him over. Brief laugh. He goes to door, halts, turns towards auditorium.*

CLOV: (*Fixed gaze, tonelessly.*) Finished, it's finished, nearly finished, it must be nearly finished.

(*Pause.*)

Grain upon grain, one by one, and one day, suddenly, there's a heap, a little heap, the impossible heap.

(*Pause.*)

5   I can't be punished any more.

(*Pause.*)

I'll go now to my kitchen, ten feet by ten feet by ten feet, and wait for him to whistle me.

(*Pause.*)

Nice dimensions, nice proportions, I'll lean on the table, and look at the wall, and wait for him to whistle me.

(*He remains a moment motionless, then goes out. He comes back immediately, goes to window right, takes up the ladder and carries it out. Pause.* HAMM *stirs. He yawns under the handkerchief. He removes the handkerchief from his face. Very red face. Black glasses.*)

HAMM: Me—   10

(*He yawns.*)

—to play.

(*He holds the handkerchief spread out before him.*)

Old stancher!

(*He takes off his glasses, wipes his eyes, his face, the glasses, puts them on again, folds the handkerchief and puts it back neatly in the breast-pocket of his dressing-gown. He clears his throat, joins the tips of his fingers.*)

Can there be misery—

(*He yawns.*)

—loftier than mine? No doubt. Formerly. But now?

(*Pause.*)

My father?   15

(*Pause.*)

My mother?

(*Pause.*)

My . . . dog?

(*Pause.*)

Oh I am willing to believe they suffer as much as such creatures can suffer. But does that mean their sufferings equal mine? No doubt.   20

(*Pause.*)

No, all is a—

(*He yawns.*)

—bsolute,

(*Proudly.*)

the bigger a man is the fuller he is.

(*Pause. Gloomily.*)

And the emptier.

(*He sniffs.*)

Clov!   25

(*Pause.*)

No, alone.

(*Pause.*)

What dreams! Those forests!

(*Pause.*)

Enough, it's time it ended, in the shelter too.

(*Pause.*)

And yet I hesitate, I hesitate to . . . to end. Yes, there it is, it's time it ended and yet I hesitate to—   30

(*He yawns.*)

—to end.

(*Yawns.*)

God, I'm tired, I'd be better off in bed.

(*He whistles. Enter* CLOV *immediately. He halts beside the chair.*)

    You pollute the air!

(*Pause.*)

    Get me ready, I'm going to bed.

35 CLOV: I've just got you up.

    HAMM: And what of it?

    CLOV: I can't be getting you up and putting you to bed every five minutes, I have things to do.

(*Pause.*)

    HAMM: Did you ever see my eyes?

40 CLOV: No.

    HAMM: Did you never have the curiosity, while I was sleeping, to take off my glasses and look at my eyes?

    CLOV: Pulling back the lids?

(*Pause.*)

    No.

45 HAMM: One of these days I'll show them to you.

(*Pause.*)

    It seems they've gone all white.

(*Pause.*)

    What time is it?

    CLOV: The same as usual.

    HAMM: (*Gesture towards window right.*) Have you looked?

50 CLOV: Yes.

    HAMM: Well?

    CLOV: Zero.

    HAMM: It'd need to rain.

    CLOV: It won't rain.

(*Pause.*)

55 HAMM: Apart from that, how do you feel?

    CLOV: I don't complain.

    HAMM: You feel normal?

    CLOV: (*Irritably.*) I tell you I don't complain.

    HAMM: I feel a little queer.

(*Pause.*)

60   Clov!

    CLOV: Yes.

    HAMM: Have you not had enough?

    CLOV: Yes!

(*Pause.*)

    Of what?

65 HAMM: Of this . . . this . . . thing.

    CLOV: I always had.

(*Pause.*)

    Not you?

    HAMM: (*Gloomily.*) Then there's no reason for it to change.

    CLOV: It may end.

(*Pause.*)

70   All life long the same questions, the same answers.

    HAMM: Get me ready.

(CLOV *does not move.*)

    Go and get the sheet.

(CLOV *does not move.*)

    Clov!

    CLOV: Yes.

75 HAMM: I'll give you nothing more to eat.

    CLOV: Then we'll die.

    HAMM: I'll give you just enough to keep you from dying. You'll be hungry all the time.

    CLOV: Then we won't die.

(*Pause.*)

    I'll go and get the sheet.   80

(*He goes towards the door.*)

    HAMM: No!

(CLOV *halts.*)

    I'll give you one biscuit per day.

(*Pause.*)

    One and a half.

(*Pause.*)

    Why do you stay with me?

    CLOV: Why do you keep me?   85

    HAMM: There's no one else.

    CLOV: There's nowhere else.

(*Pause.*)

    HAMM: You're leaving me all the same.

    CLOV: I'm trying.

    HAMM: You don't love me.   90

    CLOV: No.

    HAMM: You loved me once.

    CLOV: Once!

    HAMM: I've made you suffer too much.

(*Pause.*)

    Haven't I?   95

    CLOV: It's not that.

    HAMM: (*Shocked.*) I haven't made you suffer too much?

    CLOV: Yes!

    HAMM: (*Relieved.*) Ah you gave me a fright!

(*Pause. Coldly.*)

    Forgive me.   100

(*Pause. Louder.*)

    I said, Forgive me.

    CLOV: I heard you.

(*Pause.*)

    Have you bled?

    HAMM: Less.

(*Pause.*)

    Is it not time for my pain-killer?   105

    CLOV: No.

(*Pause.*)

    HAMM: How are your eyes?

    CLOV: Bad.

    HAMM: How are your legs?

    CLOV: Bad.   110

    HAMM: But you can move.

    CLOV: Yes.

    HAMM: (*Violently.*) Then move!

(CLOV *goes to back wall, leans against it with his forehead and hands.*)

    Where are you?

    CLOV: Here.   115

    HAMM: Come back!

(CLOV *returns to his place beside the chair.*)

    Where are you?

    CLOV: Here.

    HAMM: Why don't you kill me?

120 CLOV: I don't know the combination of the cupboard.

(*Pause.*)

HAMM: Go and get two bicycle-wheels.
CLOV: There are no more bicycle-wheels.
HAMM: What have you done with your bicycle?
CLOV: I never had a bicycle.
125 HAMM: The thing is impossible.
CLOV: When there were still bicycles I wept to have one. I
      crawled at your feet. You told me to go to hell. Now there
      are none.
HAMM: And your rounds? When you inspected my paupers.
130   Always on foot?
CLOV: Sometimes on horse.
(*The lid of one of the bins lifts and the hands of* NAGG *appear, grip-
ping the rim. Then his head emerges. Nightcap. Very white face.*
NAGG *yawns, then listens.*)
      I'll leave you, I have things to do.
HAMM: In your kitchen?
CLOV: Yes.
135 HAMM: Outside of here it's death.
(*Pause.*)
      All right, be off.
(*Exit* CLOV. *Pause.*)
      We're getting on.
NAGG: Me pap!
HAMM: Accursed progenitor!
140 NAGG: Me pap!
HAMM: The old folks at home! No decency left! Guzzle, guz-
      zle, that's all they think of.
(*He whistles. Enter* CLOV. *He halts beside the chair.*)
      Well! I thought you were leaving me.
CLOV: Oh not just yet, not just yet.
145 NAGG: Me pap!
HAMM: Give him his pap.
CLOV: There's no more pap.
HAMM: (*To* NAGG.) Do you hear that? There's no more pap.
      You'll never get any more pap.
150 NAGG: I want me pap!
HAMM: Give him a biscuit.
(*Exit* CLOV.)
      Accursed fornicator! How are your stumps?
NAGG: Never mind me stumps.

(*Enter* CLOV *with biscuit.*)

CLOV: I'm back again, with the biscuit.

(*He gives biscuit to* NAGG *who fingers it, sniffs it.*)

155 NAGG: (*Plaintively.*) What is it?
CLOV: Spratt's medium.
NAGG: (*As before.*) It's hard! I can't!
HAMM: Bottle him!

(CLOV *pushes* NAGG *back into the bin, closes the lid.*)

CLOV: (*Returning to his place beside the chair.*) If age but knew!
160 HAMM: Sit on him!
CLOV: I can't sit.
HAMM: True. And I can't stand.
CLOV: So it is.

HAMM: Every man his speciality.
(*Pause.*)
      No phone calls?   165
(*Pause.*)
      Don't we laugh?
CLOV: (*After reflection.*) I don't feel like it.
HAMM: (*After reflection.*) Nor I.
(*Pause.*)
      Clov!
CLOV: Yes.   170
HAMM: Nature has forgotten us.
CLOV: There's no more nature.
HAMM: No more nature! You exaggerate.
CLOV: In the vicinity.
HAMM: But we breathe, we change! We lose our hair, our 175
      teeth! Our bloom! Our ideals!
CLOV: Then she hasn't forgotten us.
HAMM: But you say there is none.
CLOV: (*Sadly.*) No one that ever lived ever thought so
      crooked as we.   180
HAMM: We do what we can.
CLOV: We shouldn't.

(*Pause.*)

HAMM: You're a bit of all right, aren't you?
CLOV: A smithereen.

(*Pause.*)

HAMM: This is slow work.   185
(*Pause.*)
      Is it not time for my pain-killer?
CLOV: No.
(*Pause.*)
      I'll leave you, I have things to do.
HAMM: In your kitchen?
CLOV: Yes.   190
HAMM: What, I'd like to know.
CLOV: I look at the wall.
HAMM: The wall! And what do you see on your wall? Mene,
      mene? Naked bodies?
CLOV: I see my light dying.   195
HAMM: Your light dying! Listen to that! Well, it can die just as
      well here, *your* light. Take a look at me and then come
      back and tell me what you think of *your* light.

(*Pause.*)

CLOV: You shouldn't speak to me like that.

(*Pause.*)

HAMM: (*Coldly.*) Forgive me.   200
(*Pause. Louder.*)
      I said, Forgive me.
CLOV: I heard you.

(*The lid of* NAGG's *bin lifts. His hands appear, gripping the rim.
Then his head emerges. In his mouth the biscuit. He listens.*)

HAMM: Did your seeds come up?
CLOV: No.

205 HAMM: Did you scratch round them to see if they had sprouted?
CLOV: They haven't sprouted.
HAMM: Perhaps it's still too early.
CLOV: If they were going to sprout they would have sprouted.
(*Violently.*)
   They'll never sprout!

(*Pause.* NAGG *takes biscuit in his hand.*)

210 HAMM: This is not much fun.
(*Pause.*)
   But that's always the way at the end of the day, isn't it,
   Clov?
CLOV: Always.
HAMM: It's the end of the day like any other day, isn't it, Clov?
215 CLOV: Looks like it.

(*Pause.*)

HAMM: (*Anguished.*) What's happening, what's happening?
CLOV: Something is taking its course.

(*Pause.*)

HAMM: All right, be off.
(*He leans back in his chair, remains motionless.* CLOV *does not move,
heaves a great groaning sigh.* HAMM *sits up.*)
   I thought I told you to be off.
220 CLOV: I'm trying.
(*He goes to door, halts.*)
   Ever since I was whelped.

(*Exit* CLOV.)

HAMM: We're getting on.

(*He leans back in his chair, remains motionless.* NAGG *knocks on the
lid of the other bin. Pause. He knocks harder. The lid lifts and the
hands of* NELL *appear, gripping the rim. Then her head emerges.
Lace cap. Very white face.*)

NELL: What is it, my pet?
(*Pause.*)
   Time for love?
225 NAGG: Were you asleep?
NELL: Oh no!
NAGG: Kiss me.
NELL: We can't.
NAGG: Try.

(*Their heads strain towards each other, fail to meet, fall apart again.*)

230 NELL: Why this farce, day after day?

(*Pause.*)

NAGG: I've lost me tooth.
NELL: When?
NAGG: I had it yesterday.
NELL: (*Elegiac.*) Ah yesterday!

(*They turn painfully towards each other.*)

235 NAGG: Can you see me?
NELL: Hardly. And you?

NAGG: What?
NELL: Can you see me?
NAGG: Hardly.
NELL: So much the better, so much the better. 240
NAGG: Don't say that.
(*Pause.*)
   Our sight has failed.
NELL: Yes.

(*Pause. They turn away from each other.*)

NAGG: Can you hear me?
NELL: Yes. And you? 245
NAGG: Yes.
(*Pause.*)
   Our hearing hasn't failed.
NELL: Our what?
NAGG: Our hearing.
NELL: No. 250
(*Pause.*)
   Have you anything else to say to me?
NAGG: Do you remember—
NELL: No.
NAGG: When we crashed on our tandem and lost our shanks.

(*They laugh heartily.*)

NELL: It was in the Ardennes. 255

(*They laugh less heartily.*)

NAGG: On the road to Sedan.
(*They laugh still less heartily.*)
   Are you cold?
NELL: Yes, perished. And you?
NAGG: (*Pause.*) I'm freezing.
(*Pause.*)
   Do you want to go in? 260
NELL: Yes.
NAGG: Then go in.
(NELL *does not move.*)
   Why don't you go in?
NELL: I don't know.

(*Pause.*)

NAGG: Has he changed your sawdust? 265
NELL: It isn't sawdust.
(*Pause. Wearily.*)
   Can you not be a little accurate, Nagg?
NAGG: Your sand then. It's not important.
NELL: It is important.

(*Pause.*)

NAGG: It was sawdust once. 270
NELL: Once!
NAGG: And now it's sand.
(*Pause.*)
   From the shore.
(*Pause. Impatiently.*)
   Now it's sand he fetches from the shore.
NELL: Now it's sand. 275

NAGG: Has he changed yours?

NELL: No.

NAGG: Nor mine.

(*Pause.*)

I won't have it!

(*Pause. Holding up the biscuit.*)

280 Do you want a bit?

NELL: No.

(*Pause.*)

Of what?

NAGG: Biscuit. I've kept you half.

(*He looks at the biscuit. Proudly.*)

Three quarters. For you. Here.

(*He proffers the biscuit.*)

285 No?

(*Pause.*)

Do you not feel well?

HAMM: (*Wearily.*) Quiet, quiet, you're keeping me awake.

(*Pause.*)

Talk softer.

(*Pause.*)

If I could sleep I might make love. I'd go into the woods.

290 My eyes would see . . . the sky, the earth. I'd run, run, they wouldn't catch me.

(*Pause.*)

Nature!

(*Pause.*)

There's something dripping in my head.

(*Pause.*)

A heart, a heart in my head.

(*Pause.*)

295 NAGG: (*Soft.*) Do you hear him? A heart in his head!

(*He chuckles cautiously.*)

NELL: One mustn't laugh at those things, Nagg. Why must you always laugh at them?

NAGG: Not so loud!

NELL: (*Without lowering her voice.*) Nothing is funnier than un-

300 happiness, I grant you that. But—

NAGG: (*Shocked.*) Oh!

NELL: Yes, yes, it's the most comical thing in the world. And we laugh, we laugh, with a will, in the beginning. But it's always the same thing. Yes, it's like the funny story we

305 have heard too often, we still find it funny, but we don't laugh any more.

(*Pause.*)

Have you anything else to say to me?

NAGG: No.

NELL: Are you quite sure?

(*Pause.*)

310 Then I'll leave you.

NAGG: Do you not want your biscuit?

(*Pause.*)

I'll keep it for you.

(*Pause.*)

I thought you were going to leave me.

NELL: I am going to leave you.

315 NAGG: Could you give me a scratch before you go?

NELL: No.

(*Pause.*)

Where?

NAGG: In the back.

NELL: No.

(*Pause.*)

Rub yourself against the rim. 320

NAGG: It's lower down. In the hollow.

NELL: What hollow?

NAGG: The hollow!

(*Pause.*)

Could you not?

(*Pause.*)

Yesterday you scratched me there. 325

NELL: (*Elegiac.*) Ah yesterday!

NAGG: Could you not?

(*Pause.*)

Would you like me to scratch you?

(*Pause.*)

Are you crying again?

NELL: I was trying. 330

(*Pause.*)

HAMM: Perhaps it's a little vein.

(*Pause.*)

NAGG: What was that he said?

NELL: Perhaps it's a little vein.

NAGG: What does that mean?

(*Pause.*)

That means nothing. 335

(*Pause.*)

Will I tell you the story of the tailor?

NELL: No.

(*Pause.*)

What for?

NAGG: To cheer you up.

NELL: It's not funny. 340

NAGG: It always made you laugh.

(*Pause.*)

The first time I thought you'd die.

NELL: It was on Lake Como.

(*Pause.*)

One April afternoon.

(*Pause.*)

Can you believe it? 345

NAGG: What?

NELL: That we once went out rowing on Lake Como.

(*Pause.*)

One April afternoon.

NAGG: We had got engaged the day before.

NELL: Engaged! 350

NAGG: You were in such fits that we capsized. By rights we should have been drowned.

NELL: It was because I felt happy.

NAGG: (*Indignant.*) It was not, it was not, it was my story and nothing else. Happy! Don't you laugh at it still? Every 355 time I tell it. Happy!

NELL: It was deep, deep. And you could see down to the bottom. So white. So clean.

NAGG: Let me tell it again.

(*Raconteur's voice.*)

360   An Englishman, needing a pair of striped trousers in a hurry for the New Year festivities, goes to his tailor who takes his measurements.

(*Tailor's voice.*)

"That's the lot, come back in four days, I'll have it ready." Good. Four days later.

(*Tailor's voice.*)

365   "So sorry, come back in a week, I've made a mess of the seat." Good, that's all right, a neat seat can be very ticklish. A week later.

(*Tailor's voice.*)

"Frightfully sorry, come back in ten days, I've made a hash of the crotch." Good, can't be helped, a snug crotch is al-

370   ways a teaser. Ten days later.

(*Tailor's voice.*)

"Dreadfully sorry, come back in a fortnight, I've made a balls of the fly." Good, at a pinch, a smart fly is a stiff proposition.

(*Pause. Normal voice.*)

I never told it worse.

(*Pause. Gloomy.*)

I tell this story worse and worse.

(*Pause. Raconteur's voice.*)

375   Well, to make it short, the bluebells are blowing and he ballockses the buttonholes.

(*Customer's voice.*)

"God damn you to hell, Sir, no, it's indecent, there are lim-its! In six days, do you hear me, six days, God made the world. Yes Sir, no less Sir, the WORLD! And you are not

380   bloody well capable of making me a pair of trousers in three months!"

(*Tailor's voice, scandalized.*)

"But my dear Sir, my dear Sir, look—

(*Disdainful gesture, disgustedly.*)

—at the world—

(*Pause.*)

and look—

(*Loving gesture, proudly.*)

385   —at my TROUSERS!"

(*Pause. He looks at* NELL *who has remained impassive, her eyes un-seeing, breaks into a high forced laugh, cuts it short, pokes his head towards* NELL, *launches his laugh again.*)

HAMM: Silence!

(NAGG *starts, cuts short his laugh.*)

NELL: You could see down to the bottom.

HAMM: (*Exasperated.*) Have you not finished? Will you never finish?

(*With sudden fury.*)

390   Will this never finish?

(NAGG *disappears into his bin, closes the lid behind him.* NELL *does not move. Frenziedly.*)

My kingdom for a nightman!

(*He whistles. Enter* CLOV.)

Clear away this muck! Chuck it in the sea!

(CLOV *goes to bins, halts.*)

NELL: So white.

HAMM: What? What's she blathering about?

(CLOV *stoops, takes* NELL's *hand, feels her pulse.*)

NELL: (*To* CLOV.) Desert!   395

(CLOV *lets go her hand, pushes her back in the bin, closes the lid.*)

CLOV: (*Returning to his place beside the chair.*) She has no pulse.

HAMM: What was she drivelling about?

CLOV: She told me to go away, into the desert.

HAMM: Damn busybody! Is that all?

CLOV: No.   400

HAMM: What else?

CLOV: I didn't understand.

HAMM: Have you bottled her?

CLOV: Yes.

HAMM: Are they both bottled?   405

CLOV: Yes.

HAMM: Screw down the lids.

(CLOV *goes towards door.*)

Time enough.

(CLOV *halts.*)

My anger subsides, I'd like to pee.

CLOV: (*With alacrity.*) I'll go and get the catheter.   410

(*He goes towards door.*)

HAMM: Time enough.

(CLOV *halts.*)

Give me my pain-killer.

CLOV: It's too soon.

(*Pause.*)

It's too soon on top of your tonic, it wouldn't act.

HAMM: In the morning they brace you up and in the evening   415
they calm you down. Unless it's the other way round.

(*Pause.*)

That old doctor, he's dead naturally?

CLOV: He wasn't old.

HAMM: But he's dead?

CLOV: Naturally.   420

(*Pause.*)

You ask me that?

(*Pause.*)

HAMM: Take me for a little turn.

(CLOV *goes behind the chair and pushes it forward.*)

Not too fast!

(CLOV *pushes chair.*)

Right round the world!

(CLOV *pushes chair.*)

Hug the walls, then back to the center again.   425

(CLOV *pushes chair.*)

I was right in the center, wasn't I?

CLOV: (*Pushing.*) Yes.

HAMM: We'd need a proper wheel-chair. With big wheels. Bicycle wheels!

(*Pause.*)

Are you hugging?   430

CLOV: (*Pushing.*) Yes.

HAMM: (*Groping for wall.*) It's a lie! Why do you lie to me?

CLOV: (*Bearing closer to wall.*) There! There!

HAMM: Stop!

(CLOV *stops chair close to back wall.* HAMM *lays his hand against wall.*)

435   Old wall!

(*Pause.*)

Beyond is the . . . other hell.

(*Pause. Violently.*)

Closer! Closer! Up against!

CLOV: Take away your hand.

(HAMM *withdraws his hand.* CLOV *rams chair against wall.*)

There!

(HAMM *leans towards wall, applies his ear to it.*)

440   HAMM: Do you hear?

(*He strikes the wall with his knuckles.*)

Do you hear? Hollow bricks!

(*He strikes again.*)

All that's hollow!

(*Pause. He straightens up. Violently.*)

That's enough. Back!

CLOV: We haven't done the round.

445   HAMM: Back to my place!

(CLOV *pushes chair back to center.*)

Is that my place?

CLOV: Yes, that's your place.

HAMM: Am I right in the center?

CLOV: I'll measure it.

450   HAMM: More or less! More or less!

CLOV: (*Moving chair slightly.*) There!

HAMM: I'm more or less in the center?

CLOV: I'd say so.

HAMM: You'd say so! Put me right in the center!

455   CLOV: I'll go and get the tape.

HAMM: Roughly! Roughly!

(CLOV *moves chair slightly.*)

Bang in the center!

CLOV: There!

(*Pause.*)

HAMM: I feel a little too far to the left.

(CLOV *moves chair slightly.*)

460   Now I feel a little too far to the right.

(CLOV *moves chair slightly.*)

I feel a little too far forward.

(CLOV *moves chair slightly.*)

Now I feel a little too far back.

(CLOV *moves chair slightly.*)

Don't stay there,

(*i.e., Behind the chair.*)

you give me the shivers.

(CLOV *returns to his place beside the chair.*)

465   CLOV: If I could kill him I'd die happy.

(*Pause.*)

HAMM: What's the weather like?

CLOV: As usual.

HAMM: Look at the earth.

CLOV: I've looked.

HAMM: With the glass?   470

CLOV: No need of the glass.

HAMM: Look at it with the glass.

CLOV: I'll go and get the glass.

(*Exit* CLOV.)

HAMM: No need of the glass!

(*Enter* CLOV *with telescope.*)

CLOV: I'm back again, with the glass.   475

(*He goes to window right, looks up at it.*)

I need the steps.

HAMM: Why? Have you shrunk?

(*Exit* CLOV *with telescope.*)

I don't like that, I don't like that.

(*Enter* CLOV *with ladder, but without telescope.*)

CLOV: I'm back again, with the steps.

(*He sets down ladder under window right, gets up on it, realizes he has not the telescope, gets down.*)

I need the glass.   480

(*He goes towards door.*)

HAMM: (*Violently.*) But you have the glass!

CLOV: (*Halting, violently.*) No, I haven't the glass!

(*Exit* CLOV.)

HAMM: This is deadly.

(*Enter* CLOV *with telescope. He goes towards ladder.*)

CLOV: Things are livening up.

(*He gets up on ladder, raises the telescope, lets it fall.*)

I did it on purpose.   485

(*He gets down, picks up the telescope, turns it on auditorium.*)

I see . . . a multitude . . . in transports . . . of joy.

(*Pause.*)

That's what I call a magnifier.

(*He lowers the telescope, turns towards* HAMM.)

Well? Don't we laugh?

HAMM: (*After reflection.*) I don't.

CLOV: (*After reflection.*) Nor I.   490

(*He gets up on ladder, turns the telescope on the without.*)

Let's see.

(*He looks, moving the telescope.*)

Zero . . .

(*He looks.*)

. . . zero . . .

(*He looks.*)

. . . and zero.

HAMM: Nothing stirs. All is—   495

CLOV: Zer—

HAMM: (*Violently.*) Wait till you're spoken to!

(*Normal voice.*)

All is . . . all is . . . all is what?

(*Violently.*)

All is what?

CLOV: What all is? In a word? Is that what you want to know?   500

Just a moment.

(*He turns the telescope on the without, looks, lowers the telescope, turns towards* HAMM.)

    Corpsed.

(*Pause.*)

    Well? Content?

HAMM: Look at the sea.

505 CLOV: It's the same.

HAMM: Look at the ocean!

(CLOV *gets down, takes a few steps towards window left, goes back for ladder, carries it over and sets it down under window left, gets up on it, turns the telescope on the without, looks at length. He starts, lowers the telescope, examines it, turns it again on the without.*)

CLOV: Never seen anything like that!

HAMM: (*Anxious.*) What? A sail? A fin? Smoke?

CLOV: (*Looking.*) The light is sunk.

510 HAMM: (*Relieved.*) Pah! We all knew that.

CLOV: (*Looking.*) There was a bit left.

HAMM: The base.

CLOV: (*Looking.*) Yes.

HAMM: And now?

515 CLOV: (*Looking.*) All gone.

HAMM: No gulls?

CLOV: (*Looking.*) Gulls!

HAMM: And the horizon? Nothing on the horizon?

CLOV: (*Lowering the telescope, turning towards* HAMM, *exasperated.*) What in God's name could there be on the horizon?

(*Pause.*)

520 HAMM: The waves, how are the waves?

CLOV: The waves?

(*He turns the telescope on the waves.*)

    Lead.

HAMM: And the sun?

CLOV: (*Looking.*) Zero.

525 HAMM: But it should be sinking. Look again.

CLOV: (*Looking.*) Damn the sun.

HAMM: Is it night already then?

CLOV: (*Looking.*) No.

HAMM: Then what is it?

530 CLOV: (*Looking.*) Gray.

(*Lowering the telescope, turning towards* HAMM, *louder.*)

    Gray!

(*Pause. Still louder.*)

    GRRAY!

(*Pause. He gets down, approaches* HAMM *from behind, whispers in his ear.*)

HAMM: (*Starting.*) Gray! Did I hear you say gray?

CLOV: Light black. From pole to pole.

535 HAMM: You exaggerate.

(*Pause.*)

    Don't stay there, you give me the shivers.

(CLOV *returns to his place beside the chair.*)

CLOV: Why this farce, day after day?

HAMM: Routine. One never knows.

(*Pause.*)

    Last night I saw inside my breast. There was a big sore.

CLOV: Pah! You saw your heart. 540

HAMM: No, it was living.

(*Pause. Anguished.*)

    Clov!

CLOV: Yes.

HAMM: What's happening?

CLOV: Something is taking its course. 545

(*Pause.*)

HAMM: Clov!

CLOV: (*Impatiently.*) What is it?

HAMM: We're not beginning to . . . to . . . mean something?

CLOV: Mean something! You and I, mean something!

(*Brief laugh.*)

    Ah that's a good one! 550

HAMM: I wonder.

(*Pause.*)

    Imagine if a rational being came back to earth, wouldn't he be liable to get ideas into his head if he observed us long enough.

(*Voice of rational being.*)

    Ah, good, now I see what it is, yes, now I understand what 555 they're at!

(CLOV *starts, drops the telescope and begins to scratch his belly with both hands. Normal voice.*)

    And without going so far as that, we ourselves . . .

(*With emotion.*)

    . . . we ourselves . . . at certain moments . . .

(*Vehemently.*)

    To think perhaps it won't all have been for nothing!

CLOV: (*Anguished, scratching himself.*) I have a flea! 560

HAMM: A flea! Are there still fleas?

CLOV: On me there's one.

(*Scratching.*)

    Unless it's a crablouse.

HAMM: (*Very perturbed.*) But humanity might start from there all over again! Catch him, for the love of God! 565

CLOV: I'll go and get the powder.

(*Exit* CLOV.)

HAMM: A flea! This is awful! What a day!

(*Enter* CLOV *with a sprinkling-tin.*)

CLOV: I'm back again, with the insecticide.

HAMM: Let him have it!

(CLOV *loosens the top of his trousers, pulls it forward and shakes powder into the aperture. He stoops, looks, waits, starts, frenziedly shakes more powder, stoops, looks, waits.*)

CLOV: The bastard! 570

HAMM: Did you get him?

CLOV: Looks like it.

(*He drops the tin and adjusts his trousers.*)

    Unless he's laying doggo.

HAMM: Laying! Lying you mean. Unless he's *lying* doggo.

CLOV: Ah? One says lying? One doesn't say laying? 575

HAMM: Use your head, can't you. If he was laying we'd be bitched.

CLOV: Ah.

(*Pause.*)

What about that pee?

580 HAMM: I'm having it.

CLOV: Ah that's the spirit, that's the spirit!

(*Pause.*)

HAMM: (*With ardour.*) Let's go from here, the two of us! South! You can make a raft and the currents will carry us away, far away, to other . . . mammals!

585 CLOV: God forbid!

HAMM: Alone, I'll embark alone! Get working on that raft immediately. Tomorrow I'll be gone for ever.

CLOV: (*Hastening towards door.*) I'll start straight away.

HAMM: Wait!

(CLOV *halts.*)

590 Will there be sharks, do you think?

CLOV: Sharks? I don't know. If there are there will be.

(*He goes towards door.*)

HAMM: Wait!

(CLOV *halts.*)

Is it not yet time for my pain-killer?

CLOV: (*Violently.*) No!

(*He goes towards door.*)

595 HAMM: Wait!

(CLOV *halts.*)

How are your eyes?

CLOV: Bad.

HAMM: But you can see.

CLOV: All I want.

600 HAMM: How are your legs?

CLOV: Bad.

HAMM: But you can walk.

CLOV: I come . . . and go.

HAMM: In my house.

(*Pause. With prophetic relish.*)

605 One day you'll be blind, like me. You'll be sitting there, a speck in the void, in the dark, for ever, like me.

(*Pause.*)

One day you'll say to yourself, I'm tired, I'll sit down, and you'll go and sit down. Then you'll say, I'm hungry, I'll get up and get something to eat. But you won't get up. You'll

610 say, I shouldn't have sat down, but since I have I'll sit on a little longer, then I'll get up and get something to eat. But you won't get up and you won't get anything to eat.

(*Pause.*)

You'll look at the wall a while, then you'll say, I'll close my eyes, perhaps have a little sleep, after that I'll feel better, and you'll close them. And when you open them again there'll be no wall any more.

(*Pause.*)

Infinite emptiness will be all around you, all the resur-rected dead of all the ages wouldn't fill it, and there you'll be like a little bit of grit in the middle of the steppe.

(*Pause.*)

620 Yes, one day you'll know what it is, you'll be like me, ex-cept that you won't have anyone with you, because you won't have had pity on anyone and because there won't be anyone left to have pity on.

(*Pause.*)

CLOV: It's not certain.

(*Pause.*)

And there's one thing you forget. 625

HAMM: Ah?

CLOV: I can't sit down.

HAMM: (*Impatiently.*) Well you'll lie down then, what the hell! Or you'll come to a standstill, simply stop and stand still, the way you are now. One day you'll say, I'm tired, I'll 630 stop. What does the attitude matter?

(*Pause.*)

CLOV: So you all want me to leave you.

HAMM: Naturally.

CLOV: Then I'll leave you.

HAMM: You can't leave us. 635

CLOV: Then I won't leave you.

(*Pause.*)

HAMM: Why don't you finish us?

(*Pause.*)

I'll tell you the combination of the cupboard if you promise to finish me.

CLOV: I couldn't finish you. 640

HAMM: Then you won't finish me.

(*Pause.*)

CLOV: I'll leave you, I have things to do.

HAMM: Do you remember when you came here?

CLOV: No. Too small, you told me.

HAMM: Do you remember your father. 645

CLOV: (*Wearily.*) Same answer.

(*Pause.*)

You've asked me these questions millions of times.

HAMM: I love the old questions.

(*With fervour.*)

Ah the old questions, the old answers, there's nothing like them! 650

(*Pause.*)

It was I was a father to you.

CLOV: Yes.

(*He looks at* HAMM *fixedly.*)

You were that to me.

HAMM: My house a home for you.

CLOV: Yes. 655

(*He looks about him.*)

This was that for me.

HAMM: (*Proudly.*) But for me,

(*Gesture towards himself.*)

no father. But for Hamm,

(*Gesture towards surroundings.*)

no home.

(*Pause.*)

CLOV: I'll leave you. 660

HAMM: Did you ever think of one thing?
CLOV: Never.
HAMM: That here we're down in a hole.
(*Pause.*)
    But beyond the hills? Eh? Perhaps it's still green. Eh?
(*Pause.*)
665   Flora! Pomona!
(*Ecstatically.*)
    Ceres!
(*Pause.*)
    Perhaps you won't need to go very far.
CLOV: I can't go very far.
(*Pause.*)
    I'll leave you.
670   HAMM: Is my dog ready?
CLOV: He lacks a leg.
HAMM: Is he silky?
CLOV: He's a kind of Pomeranian.
HAMM: Go and get him.
675   CLOV: He lacks a leg.
HAMM: Go and get him!
(*Exit* CLOV.)
    We're getting on.

(*Enter* CLOV *holding by one of its three legs a black toy dog.*)

CLOV: Your dogs are here.

(*He hands the dog to* HAMM *who feels it, fondles it.*)

HAMM: He's white, isn't he?
680   CLOV: Nearly.
    HAMM: What do you mean, nearly? Is he white or isn't he?
CLOV: He isn't.

(*Pause.*)

HAMM: You've forgotten the sex.
CLOV: (*Vexed.*) But he isn't finished. The sex goes on at the end.

(*Pause.*)

685   HAMM: You haven't put on his ribbon.
    CLOV: (*Angrily.*) But he isn't finished, I tell you! First you fin-
    ish your dog and then you put on his ribbon!

(*Pause.*)

HAMM: Can he stand?
CLOV: I don't know.
690   HAMM: Try.
(*He hands the dog to* CLOV *who places it on the ground.*)
    Well?
CLOV: Wait!

(*He squats down and tries to get the dog to stand on its three legs,
fails, lets it go. The dog falls on its side.*)

    HAMM: (*Impatiently.*) Well?
    CLOV: He's standing.
695   HAMM: (*Groping for the dog.*) Where? Where is he?

(CLOV *holds up the dog in a standing position.*)

CLOV: There.

(*He takes* HAMM'*s hand and guides it towards the dog's head.*)

HAMM: (*His hand on the dog's head.*) Is he gazing at me?
CLOV: Yes.
HAMM: (*Proudly.*) As if he were asking me to take him for a
    walk?   700
CLOV: If you like.
HAMM: (*As before.*) Or as if he were begging me for a bone.
(*He withdraws his hand.*)
    Leave him like that, standing there imploring me.

(CLOV *straightens up. The dog falls on its side.*)

CLOV: I'll leave you.
HAMM: Have you had your visions?   705
CLOV: Less.
HAMM: Is Mother Pegg's light on?
CLOV: Light! How could anyone's light be on?
HAMM: Extinguished!
CLOV: Naturally it's extinguished. If it's not on it's extin-   710
    guished.
HAMM: No, I mean Mother Pegg.
CLOV: But naturally she's extinguished!
(*Pause.*)
    What's the matter with you today?
HAMM: I'm taking my course.   715
(*Pause.*)
    Is she buried?
CLOV: Buried! Who would have buried her?
HAMM: You.
CLOV: Me! Haven't I enough to do without burying people?
HAMM: But you'll bury me.   720
CLOV: No I won't bury you.

(*Pause.*)

HAMM: She was bonny once, like a flower of the field.
(*With reminiscent leer.*)
    And a great one for the men!
CLOV: We too were bonny—once. It's a rare thing not to have
    been bonny—once.   725

(*Pause.*)

HAMM: Go and get the gaff.

(CLOV *goes to door, halts.*)

CLOV: Do this, do that, and I do it. I never refuse. Why?
HAMM: You're not able to.
CLOV: Soon I won't do it any more.
HAMM: You won't be able to any more.   730
(*Exit* CLOV.)
    Ah the creatures, the creatures, everything has to be ex-
    plained to them.

(*Enter* CLOV *with gaff.*)

CLOV: Here's your gaff. Stick it up.

(*He gives the gaff to* HAMM *who, wielding it like a puntpole, tries to move his chair.*)

HAMM: Did I move?

735 CLOV: No.

(HAMM *throws down the gaff.*)

HAMM: Go and get the oilcan.
CLOV: What for?
HAMM: To oil the castors.
CLOV: I oiled them yesterday.
740 HAMM: Yesterday! What does that mean? Yesterday!
CLOV: (*Violently.*) That means that bloody awful day, long ago, before this bloody awful day. I use the words you taught me. If they don't mean anything any more, teach me others. Or let me be silent.

(*Pause.*)

745 HAMM: I once knew a madman who thought the end of the world had come. He was a painter—and engraver. I had a great fondness for him. I used to go and see him, in the asylum. I'd take him by the hand and drag him to the window. Look! There! All that rising corn! And there! Look!
750 The sails of the herring fleet! All that loveliness!
(*Pause.*)
He'd snatch away his hand and go back into his corner. Appalled. All he had seen was ashes.
(*Pause.*)
He alone had been spared.
(*Pause.*)
Forgotten.
(*Pause.*)
755 It appears the case is . . . was not so . . . so unusual.
CLOV: A madman? When was that?
HAMM: Oh way back, way back, you weren't in the land of the living.
CLOV: God be with the days!

(*Pause.* HAMM *raises his toque.*)

760 HAMM: I had a great fondness for him.
(*Pause. He puts on his toque again.*)
He was a painter—and engraver.
CLOV: There are so many terrible things.
HAMM: No, no, there are not so many now.
(*Pause.*)
Clov!
765 CLOV: Yes.
HAMM: Do you not think this has gone on long enough?
CLOV: Yes!
(*Pause.*)
What?
HAMM: This . . . this . . . thing.
770 CLOV: I've always thought so.
(*Pause.*)
You not?
HAMM: (*Gloomily.*) Then it's a day like any other day.
CLOV: As long as it lasts.
(*Pause.*)

All life long the same inanities.
HAMM: I can't leave you.   775
CLOV: I know. And you can't follow me.

(*Pause.*)

HAMM: If you leave me how shall I know?
CLOV: (*Briskly.*) Well you simply whistle me and if I don't come running it means I've left you.

(*Pause.*)

HAMM: You won't come and kiss me goodbye?   780
CLOV: Oh I shouldn't think so.

(*Pause.*)

HAMM: But you might be merely dead in your kitchen.
CLOV: The result would be the same.
HAMM: Yes, but how would I know, if you were merely dead in your kitchen?   785
CLOV: Well . . . sooner or later I'd start to stink.
HAMM: You stink already. The whole place stinks of corpses.
CLOV: The whole universe.
HAMM: (*Angrily.*) To hell with the universe.
(*Pause.*)
Think of something.   790
CLOV: What?
HAMM: An idea, have an idea.
(*Angrily.*)
A bright idea!
CLOV: Ah good.
(*He starts pacing to and fro, his eyes fixed on the ground, his hands behind his back. He halts.*)
The pains in my legs! It's unbelievable! Soon I won't be 795
able to think any more.
HAMM: You won't be able to leave me.
(CLOV *resumes his pacing.*)
What are you doing?
CLOV: Having an idea.
(*He paces.*)
Ah!   800

(*He halts.*)

HAMM: What a brain!
(*Pause.*)
Well?
CLOV: Wait!
(*He meditates. Not very convinced.*)
Yes . . .
(*Pause. More convinced.*)
Yes!   805
(*He raises his head.*)
I have it! I set the alarm.

(*Pause.*)

HAMM: This is perhaps not one of my bright days, but frankly—
CLOV: You whistle me. I don't come. The alarm rings. I'm gone. It doesn't ring. I'm dead.   810

(*Pause.*)

HAMM: Is it working?
(*Pause. Impatiently.*)
    The alarm, is it working?
CLOV: Why wouldn't it be working?
HAMM: Because it's worked too much.
815 CLOV: But it's hardly worked at all.
HAMM: (*Angrily.*) Then because it's worked too little!
CLOV: I'll go and see.
(*Exit* CLOV. *Brief ring of alarm off. Enter* CLOV *with alarm-clock. He holds it against* HAMM'*s ear and releases alarm. They listen to it ringing to the end. Pause.*)
    Fit to wake the dead! Did you hear it?
HAMM: Vaguely.
820 CLOV: The end is terrific!
HAMM: I prefer the middle.
(*Pause.*)
    Is it not time for my pain-killer?
CLOV: No!
(*He goes to door, turns.*)
    I'll leave you.
825 HAMM: It's time for my story. Do you want to listen to my story.
CLOV: No.
HAMM: Ask my father if he wants to listen to my story.

(CLOV *goes to bins, raises the lid of* NAGG'*s, stoops, looks into it. Pause. He straightens up.*)

CLOV: He's asleep.
830 HAMM: Wake him.

(CLOV *stoops, wakes* NAGG *with the alarm. Unintelligible words.* CLOV *straightens up.*)

CLOV: He doesn't want to listen to your story.
HAMM: I'll give him a bon-bon.

(CLOV *stoops. As before.*)

CLOV: He wants a sugar-plum.
HAMM: He'll get a sugar-plum.

(CLOV *stoops. As before.*)

835 CLOV: It's a deal.
(*He goes towards door.* NAGG'*s hands appear, gripping the rim. Then the head emerges.* CLOV *reaches door, turns.*)
    Do you believe in the life to come?
HAMM: Mine was always that.
(*Exit* CLOV.)
    Got him that time!
NAGG: I'm listening.
840 HAMM: Scoundrel! Why did you engender me?
NAGG: I didn't know.
HAMM: What? What didn't you know?
NAGG: That it'd be you.
(*Pause.*)
    You'll give me a sugar-plum?
845 HAMM: After the audition.

NAGG: You swear?
HAMM: Yes.
NAGG: On what?
HAMM: My honor.

(*Pause. They laugh heartily.*)

NAGG: Two.   850
HAMM: One.
NAGG: One for me and one for—
HAMM: One! Silence!
(*Pause.*)
    Where was I?
(*Pause. Gloomily.*)
    It's finished, we're finished.   855
(*Pause.*)
    Nearly finished.
(*Pause.*)
    There'll be no more speech.
(*Pause.*)
    Something dripping in my head, ever since the fontanelles.
(*Stifled hilarity of* NAGG.)
    Splash, splash, always on the same spot.
(*Pause.*)
    Perhaps it's a little vein.   860
(*Pause.*)
    A little artery.
(*Pause. More animated.*)
    Enough of that, it's story time, where was I?
(*Pause. Narrative tone.*)
    The man came crawling towards me, on his belly. Pale, wonderfully pale and thin, he seemed on the point of—
(*Pause. Normal tone.*)
    No, I've done that bit.   865
(*Pause. Narrative tone.*)
    I calmly filled my pipe—the meerschaum, lit it with . . . let us say a vesta, drew a few puffs. Aah!
(*Pause.*)
    Well, what is it *you* want?
(*Pause.*)
    It was an extra-ordinarily bitter day, I remember, zero by the thermometer. But considering it was Christmas Eve   870 there was nothing . . . extra-ordinary about that. Season-able weather, for once in a way.
(*Pause.*)
    Well, what ill wind blows you my way? He raised his face to me, black with mingled dirt and tears.
(*Pause. Normal tone.*)
    That should do it.   875
(*Narrative tone.*)
    No no, don't look at me, don't look at me. He dropped his eyes and mumbled something, apologies I presume.
(*Pause.*)
    I'm a busy man, you know, the final touches, before the festivities, you know what it is.
(*Pause. Forcibly.*)
    Come on now, what is the object of this invasion?   880
(*Pause.*)
    It was a glorious bright day, I remember, fifty by the he-liometer, but already the sun was sinking down into the . . . down among the dead.

(Normal tone.)
Nicely put, that.
(Narrative tone.)
885 Come on now, come on, present your petition and let me
resume my labors.
(Pause. Normal tone.)
There's English for you. Ah well . . .
(Narrative tone.)
It was then he took the plunge. It's my little one, he said.
Tsstss, a little one, that's bad. My little boy, he said, as if the
890 sex mattered. Where did he come from? He named the
hole. A good half-day, on horse. What are you insinuating? That the place is still inhabited? No no, not a soul, except himself and the child—assuming he existed. Good. I
enquired about the situation at Kov, beyond the gulf. Not
895 a sinner. Good. And you expect me to believe you have
left your little one back there, all alone, and alive into the
bargain? Come now!
(Pause.)
It was a howling wild day, I remember, a hundred by the
anenometer. The wind was tearing up the dead pines and
900 sweeping them . . . away.
(Pause. Normal tone.)
A bit feeble, that.
(Narrative tone.)
Come on, man, speak up, what is it you want from me, I
have to put up my holly.
(Pause.)
Well to make it short it finally transpired that what he wanted
905 from me was . . . bread for his brat? Bread? But I have no bread,
it doesn't agree with me. Good. Then perhaps a little corn?
(Pause. Normal tone.)
That should do it.
(Narrative tone.)
Corn, yes, I have corn, it's true, in my granaries. But use
your head. I give you some corn, a pound, a pound and a
910 half, you bring it back to your child and you make him—
if he's still alive—a nice pot of porridge,
*(*NAGG* reacts.)*
a nice pot and a half of porridge, full of nourishment.
Good. The colors come back into his little cheeks—per-
haps. And then?
(Pause.)
915 I lost patience.
(Violently.)
Use your head, can't you, use your head, you're on earth,
there's no cure for that!
(Pause.)
It was an exceedingly dry day, I remember, zero by the hy-
grometer. Ideal weather, for my lumbago.
(Pause. Violently.)
920 But what in God's name do you imagine? That the earth
will awake in spring? That the rivers and seas will run with
fish again? That there's manna in heaven still for imbeciles
like you?
(Pause.)
Gradually I cooled down, sufficiently at least to ask him how
925 long he had taken on the way. Three whole days. Good. In
what condition he had left the child. Deep in sleep.
(Forcibly.)
But deep in what sleep, deep in what sleep already?

(Pause.)
Well to make it short I finally offered to take him into my
service. He had touched a chord. And then I imagined al-
ready that I wasn't much longer for this world. 930
(He laughs. Pause.)
Well?
(Pause.)
Well? Here if you were careful you might die a nice nat-
ural death, in peace and comfort.
(Pause.)
Well?
(Pause.)
In the end he asked me would I consent to take in the 935
child as well—if he were still alive.
(Pause.)
It was the moment I was waiting for.
(Pause.)
Would I consent to take in the child . . .
(Pause.)
I can see him still, down on his knees, his hands flat on the
ground, glaring at me with his mad eyes, in defiance of my 940
wishes.
(Pause. Normal tone.)
I'll soon have finished with this story.
(Pause.)
Unless I bring in other characters.
(Pause.)
But where would I find them?
(Pause.)
Where would I look for them? 945
(Pause. He whistles. Enter CLOV.)*
Let us pray to God.
NAGG: Me sugar-plum!
CLOV: There's a rat in the kitchen!
HAMM: A rat! Are there still rats?
CLOV: In the kitchen there's one. 950
HAMM: And you haven't exterminated him?
CLOV: Half. You disturbed us.
HAMM: He can't get away?
CLOV: No.
HAMM: You'll finish him later. Let us pray to God. 955
CLOV: Again!
NAGG: Me sugar-plum!
HAMM: God first!
(Pause.)
Are you right?
CLOV: *(Resigned.)* Off we go. 960
HAMM: *(To* NAGG.) And you?
NAGG: *(Clasping his hands, closing his eyes, in a gabble.)* Our Fa-
ther which art—
HAMM: Silence! In silence! Where are your manners?
(Pause.)
Off we go. 965
(Attitudes of prayer. Silence. Abandoning his attitude, discouraged.)
Well?
CLOV: *(Abandoning his attitude.)* What a hope! And you?
HAMM: Sweet damn all!
(To NAGG.)
And you?
NAGG: Wait! 970
(Pause. Abandoning his attitude.)

Nothing doing!

HAMM: The bastard! He doesn't exist!

CLOV: Not yet.

NAGG: Me sugar-plum!

975 HAMM: There are no more sugar-plums!

(*Pause.*)

NAGG: It's natural. After all I'm your father. It's true if it hadn't been me it would have been someone else. But that's no excuse.

(*Pause.*)

980 Turkish Delight, for example, which no longer exists, we all know that, there is nothing in the world I love more. And one day I'll ask you for some, in return for a kindness, and you'll promise it to me. One must live with the times.

(*Pause.*)

Whom did you call when you were a tiny boy, and were frightened, in the dark? Your mother? No. Me. We let you

985 cry. Then we moved you out of earshot, so that we might sleep in peace.

(*Pause.*)

I was asleep, as happy as a king, and you woke me up to have me listen to you. It wasn't indispensable, you didn't really need to have me listen to you.

(*Pause.*)

990 I hope the day will come when you'll really need to have me listen to you, and need to hear my voice, any voice.

(*Pause.*)

Yes, I hope I'll live till then, to hear you calling me like when you were a tiny boy, and were frightened, in the dark, and I was your only hope.

(*Pause.* NAGG *knocks on lid of* NELL's *bin. Pause.*)

995 Nell!

(*Pause. He knocks louder. Pause. Louder.*)

Nell!

(*Pause.* NAGG *sinks back into his bin, closes the lid behind him. Pause.*)

HAMM: Our revels now are ended.

(*He gropes for the dog.*)

The dog's gone.

CLOV: He's not a real dog, he can't go.

1000 HAMM: (*Groping.*) He's not there.

CLOV: He's lain down.

HAMM: Give him up to me.

(CLOV *picks up the dog and gives it to* HAMM. HAMM *holds it in his arms. Pause.* HAMM *throws away the dog.*)

Dirty brute!

(CLOV *begins to pick up the objects lying on the ground.*)

What are you doing?

1005 CLOV: Putting things in order.

(*He straightens up. Fervently.*)

I'm going to clear everything away!

(*He starts picking up again.*)

HAMM: Order!

CLOV: (*Straightening up.*) I love order. It's my dream. A world where all would be silent and still and each thing in its last

1010 place, under the last dust.

(*He starts picking up again.*)

HAMM: (*Exasperated.*) What in God's name do you think you are doing?

CLOV: (*Straightening up.*) I'm doing my best to create a little order.

HAMM: Drop it!   1015

(CLOV *drops the objects he has picked up.*)

CLOV: After all, there or elsewhere.

(*He goes towards door.*)

HAMM: (*Irritably.*) What's wrong with your feet?

CLOV: My feet?

HAMM: Tramp! Tramp!

CLOV: I must have put on my boots.   1020

HAMM: Your slippers were hurting you?

(*Pause.*)

CLOV: I'll leave you.

HAMM: No!

CLOV: What is there to keep me here?

HAMM: The dialogue.   1025

(*Pause.*)

I've got on with my story.

(*Pause.*)

I've got on with it well.

(*Pause. Irritably.*)

Ask me where I've got to.

CLOV: Oh, by the way, your story?

HAMM: (*Surprised.*) What story?   1030

CLOV: The one you've been telling yourself all your days.

HAMM: Ah you mean my chronicle?

CLOV: That's the one.

(*Pause.*)

HAMM: (*Angrily.*) Keep going, can't you, keep going!

CLOV: You've got on with it, I hope.   1035

HAMM: (*Modestly.*) Oh not very far, not very far.

(*He sighs.*)

There are days like that, one isn't inspired.

(*Pause.*)

Nothing you can do about it, just wait for it to come.

(*Pause.*)

No forcing, no forcing, it's fatal.

(*Pause.*)

I've got on with it a little all the same.   1040

(*Pause.*)

Technique, you know.

(*Pause. Irritably.*)

I say I've got on with it a little all the same.

CLOV: (*Admiringly.*) Well I never! In spite of everything you were able to get on with it!

HAMM: (*Modestly.*) Oh not very far, you know, not very far,   1045 but nevertheless, better than nothing.

CLOV: Better than nothing! Is it possible?

HAMM: I'll tell you how it goes. He comes crawling on his belly—

1050 CLOV: Who?
HAMM: What?
CLOV: Who do you mean, he?
HAMM: Who do I mean! Yet another.
CLOV: Ah him! I wasn't sure.
1055 HAMM: Crawling on his belly, whining for bread for his brat.
He's offered a job as gardener. Before—
(CLOV *bursts out laughing.*)
What is there so funny about that?
CLOV: A job as gardener!
HAMM: Is that what tickles you?
1060 CLOV: It must be that.
HAMM: It wouldn't be the bread?
CLOV: Or the brat.

(*Pause.*)

HAMM: The whole thing is comical, I grant you that. What
about having a good guffaw the two of us together?
1065 CLOV: (*After reflection.*) I couldn't guffaw again today.
HAMM: (*After reflection.*) Nor I.
(*Pause.*)
I continue then. Before accepting with gratitude he asks if
he may have his little boy with him.
CLOV: What age?
1070 HAMM: Oh tiny.
CLOV: He would have climbed the trees.
HAMM: All the little odd jobs.
CLOV: And then he would have grown up.
HAMM: Very likely.

(*Pause.*)

1075 CLOV: Keep going, can't you, keep going!
HAMM: That's all. I stopped there.

(*Pause.*)

CLOV: Do you see how it goes on.
HAMM: More or less.
CLOV: Will it not soon be the end?
1080 HAMM: I'm afraid it will.
CLOV: Pah! You'll make up another.
HAMM: I don't know.
(*Pause.*)
I feel rather drained.
(*Pause.*)
The prolonged creative effort.
(*Pause.*)
1085 If I could drag myself down to the sea! I'd make a pillow
of sand for my head and the tide would come.
CLOV: There's no more tide.

(*Pause.*)

HAMM: Go and see is she dead.

(CLOV *goes to bins, raises the lid of* NELL'*s, stoops, looks into it.
Pause.*)

CLOV: Looks like it.

(*He closes the lid, straightens up.* HAMM *raises his toque. Pause. He
puts it on again.*)

HAMM: (*With his hand to his toque.*) And Nagg?   1090

(CLOV *raises lid of* NAGG'*s bin, stoops, looks into it. Pause.*)

CLOV: Doesn't look like it.

(*He closes the lid, straightens up.*)

HAMM: (*Letting go his toque.*) What's he doing?

(CLOV *raises lid of* NAGG'*s bin, stoops, looks into it. Pause.*)

CLOV: He's crying.

(*He closes lid, straightens up.*)

HAMM: Then he's living.
(*Pause.*)
Did you ever have an instant of happiness?   1095
CLOV: Not to my knowledge.

(*Pause.*)

HAMM: Bring me under the window.
(CLOV *goes towards chair.*)
I want to feel the light on my face.
(CLOV *pushes chair.*)
Do you remember, in the beginning, when you took me
for a turn? You used to hold the chair too high. At every 1100
step you nearly tipped me out.
(*With senile quaver.*)
Ah great fun, we had, the two of us, great fun.
(*Gloomily.*)
And then we got into the way of it.
(CLOV *stops the chair under window right.*)
There already?
(*Pause. He tilts back his head.*)
Is it light?   1105
CLOV: It isn't dark.
HAMM: (*Angrily.*) I'm asking you is it light.
CLOV: Yes.

(*Pause.*)

HAMM: The curtain isn't closed?
CLOV: No.   1110
HAMM: What window is it?
CLOV: The earth.
HAMM: I knew it!
(*Angrily.*)
But there's no light there! The other!
(CLOV *pushes chair towards window left.*)
The earth!   1115
(CLOV *stops the chair under window left.* HAMM *tilts back his head.*)
That's what I call light!
(*Pause.*)
Feels like a ray of sunshine.
(*Pause.*)

No?
CLOV: No.
1120   HAMM: It isn't a ray of sunshine I feel on my face?
CLOV: No.

(*Pause.*)

HAMM: Am I very white?
(*Pause. Angrily.*)
    I'm asking you am I very white!
CLOV: Not more so than usual.

(*Pause.*)

1125   HAMM: Open the window.
CLOV: What for?
HAMM: I want to hear the sea.
CLOV: You wouldn't hear it.
HAMM: Even if you opened the window?
1130   CLOV: No.
HAMM: Then it's not worth while opening it?
CLOV: No.
HAMM: (*Violently.*) Then open it!
(CLOV *gets up on the ladder, opens the window. Pause.*)
    Have you opened it?
1135   CLOV: Yes.

(*Pause.*)

HAMM: You swear you've opened it?
CLOV: Yes.

(*Pause.*)

HAMM: Well . . . !
(*Pause.*)
    It must be very calm.
(*Pause. Violently.*)
1140   I'm asking you is it very calm!
CLOV: Yes.
HAMM: It's because there are no more navigators.
(*Pause.*)
    You haven't much conversation all of a sudden. Do you
    not feel well?
1145   CLOV: I'm cold.
HAMM: What month are we?
(*Pause.*)
    Close the window, we're going back.
(CLOV *closes the window, gets down, pushes the chair back to its place, remains standing behind it, head bowed.*)
    Don't stay there, you give me the shivers!
(CLOV *returns to his place beside the chair.*)
    Father!
(*Pause. Louder.*)
1150   Father!
(*Pause.*)
    Go and see did he hear me.

(CLOV *goes to* NAGG's *bin, raises the lid, stoops. Unintelligible words.* CLOV *straightens up.*)

CLOV: Yes.
HAMM: Both times?

(CLOV *stoops. As before.*)

CLOV: Once only.
HAMM: The first time or the second?   1155

(CLOV *stoops. As before.*)

CLOV: He doesn't know.
HAMM: It must have been the second.
CLOV: We'll never know.

(*He closes lid.*)

HAMM: Is he still crying?
CLOV: No.   1160
HAMM: The dead go fast.
(*Pause.*)
    What's he doing?
CLOV: Sucking his biscuit.
HAMM: Life goes on.
(CLOV *returns to his place beside the chair.*)
    Give me a rug, I'm freezing.   1165
CLOV: There are no more rugs.

(*Pause.*)

HAMM: Kiss me.
(*Pause.*)
    Will you not kiss me?
CLOV: No.
HAMM: On the forehead.   1170
CLOV: I won't kiss you anywhere.

(*Pause.*)

HAMM: (*Holding out his hand.*) Give me your hand at least.
(*Pause.*)
    Will you not give me your hand?
CLOV: I won't touch you.

(*Pause.*)

HAMM: Give me the dog.   1175
(CLOV *looks round for the dog.*)
    No!
CLOV: Do you not want your dog?
HAMM: No.
CLOV: Then I'll leave you.
HAMM: (*Head bowed, absently.*) That's right.   1180

(CLOV *goes to door, turns.*)

CLOV: If I don't kill that rat he'll die.
HAMM: (*As before.*) That's right.
(*Exit* CLOV. *Pause.*)
    Me to play.
(*He takes out his handkerchief, unfolds it, holds it spread out before him.*)
    We're getting on.
(*Pause.*)
    You weep, and weep, for nothing, so as not to laugh, and   1185
    little by little . . . you begin to grieve.
(*He folds the handkerchief, puts it back in his pocket, raises his head.*)
    All those I might have helped.

(*Pause.*)
Helped!
(*Pause.*)
Saved.
(*Pause.*)
1190 Saved!
(*Pause.*)
The place was crawling with them!
(*Pause. Violently.*)
Use your head, can't you, use your head, you're on earth, there's no cure for that!
(*Pause.*)
Get out of here and love one another! Lick your neigh-
1195 bor as yourself!
(*Pause. Calmer.*)
When it wasn't bread they wanted it was crumpets.
(*Pause. Violently.*)
Out of my sight and back to your petting parties!
(*Pause.*)
All that, all that!
(*Pause.*)
Not even a real dog!
(*Calmer.*)
1200 The end is in the beginning and yet you go on.
(*Pause.*)
Perhaps I could go on with my story, end it and begin another.
(*Pause.*)
Perhaps I could throw myself out on the floor.
(*He pushes himself painfully off his seat, falls back again.*)
Dig my nails into the cracks and drag myself forward with
1205 my fingers.
(*Pause.*)
It will be the end and there I'll be, wondering what can have brought it on and wondering what can have . . .
(*He hesitates.*)
. . . why it was so long coming.
(*Pause.*)
There I'll be, in the old shelter, alone against the silence
1210 and . . .
(*He hesitates.*)
. . . the stillness. If I can hold my peace, and sit quiet, it will be all over with sound, and motion, all over and done with.
(*Pause.*)
I'll have called my father and I'll have called my . . .
(*He hesitates.*)
. . . my son. And even twice, or three times, in case they
1215 shouldn't have heard me, the first time, or the second.
(*Pause.*)
I'll say to myself, He'll come back.
(*Pause.*)
And then?
(*Pause.*)
And then?
(*Pause.*)
He couldn't, he has gone too far.
(*Pause.*)
1220 And then?
(*Pause. Very agitated.*)
All kinds of fantasies! That I'm being watched! A rat! Steps! Breath held and then . . .

(*He breathes out.*)
Then babble, babble, words, like the solitary child who turns himself into children, two, three, so as to be together, and whisper together, in the dark. 1225
(*Pause.*)
Moment upon moment, pattering down, like the millet grains of . . .
(*He hesitates.*)
. . . that old Greek, and all life long you wait for that to mount up to a life.
(*Pause. He opens his mouth to continue, renounces.*)
Ah let's get it over! 1230
(*He whistles. Enter* CLOV *with alarm-clock. He halts beside the chair.*)
What? Neither gone nor dead?
CLOV: In spirit only.
HAMM: Which?
CLOV: Both.
HAMM: Gone from me you'd be dead. 1235
CLOV: And vice versa.
HAMM: Outside of here it's death!
(*Pause.*)
And the rat?
CLOV: He's got away.
HAMM: He can't go far. 1240
(*Pause. Anxious.*)
Eh?
CLOV: He doesn't need to go far.

(*Pause.*)

HAMM: Is it not time for my pain-killer?
CLOV: Yes.
HAMM: Ah! At last! Give it to me! Quick! 1245

(*Pause.*)

CLOV: There's no more pain-killer.

(*Pause.*)

HAMM: (*Appalled.*) Good . . . !
(*Pause.*)
No more pain-killer!
CLOV: No more pain-killer. You'll never get any more pain-killer. 1250

(*Pause.*)

HAMM: But the little round box. It was full!
CLOV: Yes. But now it's empty.

(*Pause.* CLOV *starts to move about the room. He is looking for a place to put down the alarm-clock.*)

HAMM: (*Soft.*) What'll I do?
(*Pause. In a scream.*)
What'll I do?
(CLOV *sees the picture, takes it down, stands it on the floor with its face to the wall, hangs up the alarm-clock in its place.*)
What are you doing? 1255
CLOV: Winding up.
HAMM: Look at the earth.

CLOV: Again!

HAMM: Since it's calling to you.

1260 CLOV: Is your throat sore?

(*Pause.*)

Would you like a lozenge?

(*Pause.*)

No.

(*Pause.*)

Pity.

(CLOV *goes, humming, towards window right, halts before it, looks up at it.*)

HAMM: Don't sing.

1265 CLOV: (*Turning towards* HAMM.) One hasn't the right to sing any more?

HAMM: No.

CLOV: Then how can it end?

HAMM: You want it to end?

1270 CLOV: I want to sing.

HAMM: I can't prevent you.

(*Pause.* CLOV *turns towards window right.*)

CLOV: What did I do with that steps?

(*He looks around for ladder.*)

You didn't see that steps?

(*He sees it.*)

Ah, about time.

(*He goes towards window left.*)

1275 Sometimes I wonder if I'm in my right mind. Then it passes over and I'm as lucid as before.

(*He gets up on ladder, looks out of window.*)

Christ, she's under water!

(*He looks.*)

How can that be?

(*He pokes forward his head, his hand above his eyes.*)

It hasn't rained.

(*He wipes the pane, looks. Pause.*)

1280 Ah what a fool I am! I'm on the wrong side!

(*He gets down, takes a few steps towards window right.*)

Under water!

(*He goes back for ladder.*)

What a fool I am!

(*He carries ladder towards window right.*)

Sometimes I wonder if I'm in my right senses. Then it passes off and I'm as intelligent as ever.

(*He sets down ladder under window right, gets up on it, looks out of window. He turns towards* HAMM.)

1285 Any particular sector you fancy? Or merely the whole thing?

HAMM: Whole thing.

CLOV: The general effect? Just a moment.

(*He looks out of window. Pause.*)

HAMM: Clov.

1290 CLOV: (*Absorbed.*) Mmm.

HAMM: Do you know what it is?

CLOV: (*As before.*) Mmm.

HAMM: I was never there.

(*Pause.*)

Clov!

CLOV: (*Turning towards* HAMM, *exasperated.*) What is it?   1295

HAMM: I was never there.

CLOV: Lucky for you.

(*He looks out of window.*)

HAMM: Absent, always. It all happened without me. I don't know what's happened.

(*Pause.*)

Do you know what's happened?   1300

(*Pause.*)

Clov!

CLOV: (*Turning towards* HAMM, *exasperated.*) Do you want me to look at this muckheap, yes or no?

HAMM: Answer me first.

CLOV: What?   1305

HAMM: Do you know what's happened?

CLOV: When? Where?

HAMM: (*Violently.*) When! What's happened? Use your head, can't you! What has happened?

CLOV: What for Christ's sake does it matter?   1310

(*He looks out of window.*)

HAMM: I don't know.

(*Pause.* CLOV *turns towards* HAMM.)

CLOV: (*Harshly.*) When old Mother Pegg asked you for oil for her lamp and you told her to get out to hell, you knew what was happening then, no?

(*Pause.*)

You know what she died of, Mother Pegg? Of darkness.   1315

HAMM: (*Feebly.*) I hadn't any.

CLOV: (*As before.*) Yes, you had.

(*Pause.*)

HAMM: Have you the glass?

CLOV: No, it's clear enough as it is.

HAMM: Go and get it.   1320

(*Pause.* CLOV *casts up his eyes, brandishes his fists. He loses balance, clutches on to the ladder. He starts to get down, halts.*)

CLOV: There's one thing I'll never understand.

(*He gets down.*)

Why I always obey you. Can you explain that to me?

HAMM: No.... Perhaps it's compassion.

(*Pause.*)

A kind of great compassion.

(*Pause.*)

Oh you won't find it easy, you won't find it easy.   1325

(*Pause.* CLOV *begins to move about the room in search of the telescope.*)

CLOV: I'm tired of our goings on, very tired.

(*He searches.*)

You're not sitting on it?

(*He moves the chair, looks at the place where it stood, resumes his search.*)

HAMM: (*Anguished.*) Don't leave me there!
(*Angrily* CLOV *restores the chair to its place.*)
   Am I right in the center?

1330 CLOV: You'd need a microscope to find this—
(*He sees the telescope.*)
   Ah, about time.

(*He picks up the telescope, gets up on the ladder, turns the telescope on the without.*)

HAMM: Give me the dog.
CLOV: (*Looking.*) Quiet!
HAMM: (*Angrily.*) Give me the dog!

(CLOV *drops the telescope, clasps his hands to his head. Pause. He gets down precipitately, looks for the dog, sees it, picks it up, hastens towards* HAMM *and strikes him violently on the head with the dog.*)

1335 CLOV: There's your dog for you!

(*The dog falls to the ground. Pause.*)

HAMM: He hit me!
CLOV: You drive me mad, I'm mad!
HAMM: If you must hit me, hit me with the axe.
(*Pause.*)
   Or with the gaff, hit me with the gaff. Not with the dog.
1340   With the gaff. Or with the axe.

(CLOV *picks up the dog and gives it to* HAMM *who takes it in his arms.*)

CLOV: (*Imploringly.*) Let's stop playing!
HAMM: Never!
(*Pause.*)
   Put me in my coffin.
CLOV: There are no more coffins.
1345 HAMM: Then let it end!
(CLOV *goes towards ladder.*)
   With a bang!
(CLOV *gets up on ladder, gets down again, looks for telescope, sees it, picks it up, gets up ladder, raises telescope.*)
   Of darkness! And me? Did anyone ever have pity on me?
CLOV: (*Lowering the telescope, turning towards* HAMM.) What?
(*Pause.*)
   Is it me you're referring to?
1350 HAMM: (*Angrily.*) An aside, ape! Did you never hear an aside before?
(*Pause.*)
   I'm warming up for my last soliloquy.
CLOV: I warn you. I'm going to look at this filth since it's an order. But it's the last time.
(*He turns the telescope on the without.*)
1355   Let's see.
(*He moves the telescope.*)
   Nothing . . . nothing . . . good . . . good . . . nothing . . . goo—
(*He starts, lowers the telescope, examines it, turns it again on the without. Pause.*)
   Bad luck to it!
HAMM: More complications!
(CLOV *gets down.*)
   Not an underplot, I trust.

(CLOV *moves ladder nearer window, gets up on it, turns telescope on the without.*)

CLOV: (*Dismayed.*) Looks like a small boy!   1360
HAMM: (*Sarcastic.*) A small . . . boy!
CLOV: I'll go and see.
(*He gets down, drops the telescope, goes towards door, turns.*)
   I'll take the gaff.

(*He looks for the gaff, sees it, picks it up, hastens towards door.*)

HAMM: No!

(CLOV *halts.*)

CLOV: No? A potential procreator?   1365
HAMM: If he exists he'll die there or he'll come here. And if he doesn't . . .

(*Pause.*)

CLOV: You don't believe me? You think I'm inventing?

(*Pause.*)

HAMM: It's the end, Clov, we've come to the end. I don't need you any more.   1370

(*Pause.*)

CLOV: Lucky for you.

(*He goes towards door.*)

HAMM: Leave me the gaff.

(CLOV *gives him the gaff, goes towards door, halts, looks at alarm-clock, takes it down, looks round for a better place to put it, goes to bins, puts it on lid of* NAGG's *bin. Pause.*)

CLOV: I'll leave you.

(*He goes towards door.*)

HAMM: Before you go . . .
(CLOV *halts near door.*)
   . . . say something.   1375
CLOV: There is nothing to say.
HAMM: A few words . . . to ponder . . . in my heart.
CLOV: Your heart!
HAMM: Yes.
(*Pause. Forcibly.*)
   Yes!   1380
(*Pause.*)
   With the rest, in the end, the shadows, the murmurs, all the trouble, to end up with.
(*Pause.*)
   Clov. . . . He never spoke to me. Then, in the end, before he went, without my having asked him, he spoke to me. He said . . .   1385
CLOV: (*Despairingly.*) Ah . . . !
HAMM: Something . . . from your heart.
CLOV: My heart!
HAMM: A few words . . . from your heart.

(*Pause.*)

1390   CLOV: (*Fixed gaze, tonelessly, towards auditorium.*) They said to me, That's love, yes, yes, not a doubt, now you see how—

HAMM: Articulate!

CLOV: (*As before.*) How easy it is. They said to me, That's friendship, yes, yes, no question, you've found it. They said

1395   to me, Here's the place, stop, raise your head and look at all that beauty. That order! They said to me, Come now, you're not a brute beast, think upon these things and you'll see how all becomes clear. And simple! They said to me, What skilled attention they get, all these dying of their wounds.

1400   HAMM: Enough!

CLOV: (*As before.*) I say to myself—sometimes, Clov, you must learn to suffer better than that if you want them to weary of punishing you—one day. I say to myself—sometimes, Clov, you must be there better than that if you want them

1405   to let you go—one day. But I feel too old, and too far, to form new habits. Good, it'll never end, I'll never go.

(*Pause.*)

Then one day, suddenly, it ends, it changes, I don't understand, it dies, or it's me, I don't understand, that either. I ask the words that remain—sleeping, waking, morning,

1410   evening. They have nothing to say.

(*Pause.*)

I open the door of the cell and go. I am so bowed I only see my feet, if I open my eyes, and between my legs a little trail of black dust. I say to myself that the earth is extinguished, though I never saw it lit.

(*Pause.*)

1415   It's easy going.

(*Pause.*)

When I fall I'll weep for happiness.

(*Pause. He goes towards door.*)

HAMM: Clov!

(CLOV *halts, without turning.*)

Nothing.

(CLOV *moves on.*)

Clov!

(CLOV *halts, without turning.*)

1420   CLOV: This is what we call making an exit.

HAMM: I'm obliged to you, Clov. For your services.

CLOV: (*Turning, sharply.*) Ah pardon, it's I am obliged to you.

HAMM: It's we are obliged to each other.

(*Pause.* CLOV *goes towards door.*)

One thing more.

(CLOV *halts.*)

1425   A last favor.

(*Exit* CLOV.)

Cover me with the sheet.

(*Long pause.*)

No? Good.

(*Pause.*)

Me to play.

(*Pause. Wearily.*)

Old endgame lost of old, play and lose and have done

1430   with losing.

(*Pause. More animated.*)

Let me see.

(*Pause.*)

Ah yes!

(*He tries to move the chair, using the gaff as before. Enter* CLOV, *dressed for the road. Panama hat, tweed coat, raincoat over his arm, umbrella, bag. He halts by the door and stands there, impassive and motionless, his eyes fixed on* HAMM, *till the end.* HAMM *gives up.*)

Good.

(*Pause.*)

Discard.

(*He throws away the gaff, makes to throw away the dog, thinks better of it.*)

Take it easy.   1435

(*Pause.*)

And now?

(*Pause.*)

Raise hat.

(*He raises his toque.*)

Peace to our . . . arses.

(*Pause.*)

And put on again.

(*He puts on his toque.*)

Deuce.   1440

(*Pause. He takes off his glasses.*)

Wipe.

(*He takes out his handkerchief and, without unfolding it, wipes his glasses.*)

And put on again.

(*He puts on his glasses, puts back the handkerchief in his pocket.*)

We're coming. A few more squirms like that and I'll call.

(*Pause.*)

A little poetry.

(*Pause.*)

You prayed—   1445

(*Pause. He corrects himself.*)

You CRIED for night; it comes—

(*Pause. He corrects himself.*)

It FALLS: now cry in darkness.

(*He repeats, chanting.*)

You cried for night; it falls: now cry in darkness.

(*Pause.*)

Nicely put, that.

(*Pause.*)

And now?   1450

(*Pause.*)

Moments for nothing, now as always, time was never and time is over, reckoning closed and story ended.

(*Pause. Narrative tone.*)

If he could have his child with him. . . .

(*Pause.*)

It was the moment I was waiting for.

(*Pause.*)

You don't want to abandon him? You want him to bloom   1455
while you are withering? Be there to solace your last million last moments?

(*Pause.*)

He doesn't realize, all he knows is hunger, and cold, and death to crown it all. But you! You ought to know what the earth is like, nowadays. Oh I put him before his re-   1460
sponsibilities!

(*Pause. Normal tone.*)

Well, there we are, there I am, that's enough.
(*He raises the whistle to his lips, hesitates, drops it. Pause.*)
Yes, truly!
(*He whistles. Pause. Louder. Pause.*)
Good.
(*Pause.*)
1465   Father!
(*Pause. Louder.*)
Father!
(*Pause.*)
Good.
(*Pause.*)
We're coming.
(*Pause.*)
And to end up with?
(*Pause.*)
1470   Discard.
(*He throws away the dog. He tears the whistle from his neck.*)
With my compliments.
(*He throws whistle towards auditorium. Pause. He sniffs. Soft.*)

Clov!
(*Long pause.*)
No? Good.
(*He takes out the handkerchief.*)
Since that's the way we're playing it . . .
(*He unfolds handkerchief.*)
. . . let's play it that way . . .   1475
(*He unfolds.*)
. . . and speak no more about it . . .
(*He finishes unfolding.*)
. . . speak no more.
(*He holds handkerchief spread out before him.*)
Old stancher!
(*Pause.*)
You . . . remain.
(*Pause. He covers his face with handkerchief, lowers his arms to arm-rests, remains motionless.*)

(*Brief tableau.*)

Harold Pinter

Harold Pinter (b. 1930) has had an extensive career as an actor, playwright, and screenwriter, but is best-known for his strikingly disorienting stage plays. Pinter was born and raised in Hackney, a working-class neighborhood just beyond London's East End. He studied briefly at the Royal Academy of Dramatic Art and pursued a career as a stage and radio actor in the early 1950s before becoming a playwright. His early plays—notably *The Room* (1957), *The Birthday Party* (1958), and *The Dumb Waiter* (1960)—are inflected by the theater of the absurd in the indirect, often menacing, and finally inexplicable quality of their action. However, Pinter's drama is set in a much more recognizable locale than are many of Beckett's or Ionesco's plays; his plays often work by frustrating our "realistic" expectations of characters and their stage world. This is particularly true of Pinter's two major successes of the 1960s, *The Caretaker* (1960) and *The Homecoming* (1965). In both of these plays, a visitor disturbs the delicate balance of relations that bind a family together. What is characteristically "Pinteresque" about the action is the way that Pinter's spare and oblique dialogue makes the characters' motives and intentions nearly unreadable, often despite the violence with which they are expressed. If the poverty of language in most realistic drama tends to imply the emptiness of the characters, in Pinter's drama it seems most often to imply their explosive potential to erupt.

Pinter went through a period of profound writer's block in the late 1960s, writing only the short plays *Landscape* (1969) and *Silence* (1969). In the 1970s, though, he wrote a series of major dramas: *Old Times* (1971), *No Man's Land* (1975), and *Betrayal* (1978). These plays take memory and the past as their subject, examining how, in the words of Anna in *Old Times,* "There are things I remember which may never have happened but as I recall them so they take place." More recently, Pinter has written *A Kind of Alaska* (1982), a play based on Oliver Sachs's *Awakenings,* and several plays, sometimes on more political subjects: *One for the Road* (1984), *Mountain Language* (1988), *Party Time* (1990), *Moonlight* (1993), *Ashes to Ashes* (1996), and *Celebration* (2000). Pinter also has written a number of screenplays, both for his own plays, such as *Betrayal,* and for other projects, including *The French Lieutenant's Woman* and *Turtle Diary.*

THE HOMECOMING

The Homecoming is typical of Pinter's earlier drama in that it provides us with a recognizable situation—Teddy, an American college professor, returns home to London with his wife Ruth to visit his family—that immediately twists in new and surprising directions. For much like the room onstage, with its missing upstage wall, something is missing in this family that determines the structure of their relationships. The most obvious missing element of family life here is the absent mother, Jessie, whose absence informs the relationships between the men of the play: Max, who does the cleaning and cooking, to everyone's ridicule; Sam, who is accused of homosexual prostitution; Lenny, the pimp; Joey, the macho boxer. When Ruth appears in this scenario, she seems suddenly to take the role vacated by Jessie, becoming the controlling figure in the house of crippled men. Ruth assumes the two roles attributed to Jessie—mother and whore. The question, as Max asks at the end, is will she prove "adaptable" to the men's fantasies or will she—as Ruth's independence suggests—adapt the men to her own designs?

The Homecoming clearly plays with the formalities and conventions of realistic drama. The secret that often motivates the action of an Ibsen play (Nora's forgery in *A Doll House,* for example) seems to be disclosed in the play by Sam—"MacGregor had Jessie in the back of my cab as I drove them along"—but finally this "secret" loses its power to explain. It is either already known or finally irrelevant to the characters. Indeed, the past in *The Home-*

Sam "dies" in Harold Pinter's *The Homecoming,* staged by the American Repertory Theatre.

coming seems to be largely improvised or invented. The characters frequently seem to make up stories of the "past" that function more as maneuverings in the present than as reliable accounts of something that actually happened. Lenny's story of beating up a prostitute underneath an arch in act 1, for instance, seems not really to have happened. It is instead an effort to intimidate the seductive Ruth, also a woman standing underneath an arch in the living room. The past in *The Homecoming* is one that the characters invent and reinvent as the action progresses. The past becomes a fantasy that the characters work to re-create in the present action of the play.

THE HOMECOMING

Harold Pinter

CHARACTERS

MAX, *a man of seventy*
LENNY, *a man in his early thirties*
SAM, *a man of sixty-three*
JOEY, *a man in his middle twenties*
TEDDY, *a man in his middle thirties*
RUTH, *a woman in her early thirties*

Summer: An old house in North London.

A large room, extending the width of the stage.

The back wall, which contained the door, has been removed. A square arch shape remains. Beyond it, the hall. In the hall a staircase, ascending upstage left, well in view. The front door upstage right. A coatstand, hooks, etc.

In the room a window, right. Odd tables, chairs. Two large armchairs. A large sofa, left. Against right wall a large sideboard, the upper half of which contains a mirror. Upstage left, a radiogram.

ACT ONE

Evening.

LENNY *is sitting on the sofa with a newspaper, a pencil in his hand. He wears a dark suit. He makes occasional marks on the back page.*

MAX *comes in, from the direction of the kitchen. He goes to sideboard, opens top drawer, rummages in it, closes it.*

He wears an old cardigan and a cap, and carries a stick.

He walks downstage, stands, looks about the room.

MAX: What have you done with the scissors?

(Pause.)

I said I'm looking for the scissors. What have you done with them?

(Pause.)

Did you hear me? I want to cut something out of the paper.
5 LENNY: I'm reading the paper.
MAX: Not that paper. I haven't even read that paper. I'm talking about last Sunday's paper. I was just having a look at it in the kitchen.

(Pause.)

Do you hear what I'm saying? I'm talking to you! Where's
10 the scissors?
LENNY: (*Looking up, quietly.*) Why don't you shut up, you daft prat?

(MAX *lifts his stick and points it at him.*)

MAX: Don't you talk to me like that. I'm warning you.

(He sits in large armchair.)

There's an advertisement in the paper about flannel vests.
15 Cut price. Navy surplus. I could do with a few of them.

(Pause.)

I think I'll have a fag. Give me a fag.

(Pause.)

I just asked you to give me a cigarette.

(Pause.)

Look what I'm lumbered with.

(He takes a crumpled cigarette from his pocket.)

I'm getting old, my word of honour.

(He lights it.)

You think I wasn't a tearaway? I could have taken care of you, 20 twice over. I'm still strong. You ask your Uncle Sam what I was. But at the same time I always had a kind heart. Always.

(Pause.)

I used to knock about with a man called MacGregor. I called him Mac. You remember Mac? Eh?

(Pause.)

Huhh! We were two of the worst hated men in the West 25 End of London. I tell you, I still got the scars. We'd walk into a place, the whole room'd stand up, they'd make way to let us pass. You never heard such silence. Mind you, he was a big man, he was over six foot tall. His family were all MacGregors, they came all the way from Aberdeen, but 30 he was the only one they called Mac.

(Pause.)

He was very fond of your mother, Mac was. Very fond. He always had a good word for her.

(Pause.)

Mind you, she wasn't such a bad woman. Even though it made me sick just to look at her rotten stinking face, she 35 wasn't such a bad bitch. I gave her the best bleeding years of my life, anyway.
LENNY: Plug it, will you, you stupid sod, I'm trying to read the paper.

40 MAX: Listen! I'll chop your spine off, you talk to me like that! You understand? Talking to your lousy filthy father like that!

LENNY: You know what, you're getting demented.

(*Pause.*)

What do you think of Second Wind for the three-thirty?

45 MAX: Where?

LENNY: Sandown Park.

MAX: Don't stand a chance.

LENNY: Sure he does.

MAX: Not a chance.

50 LENNY: He's the winner.

(LENNY *ticks the paper.*)

MAX: He talks to me about horses.

(*Pause.*)

I used to live on the course. One of the loves of my life. Epsom? I knew it like the back of my hand. I was one of the best-known faces down at the paddock. What a mar-
55 vellous open-air life.

(*Pause.*)

He talks to me about horses. You only read their names in the papers. But I've stroked their manes, I've held them, I've calmed them down before a big race. I was the one they used to call for. Max, they'd say, there's a horse here, he's
60 highly strung, you're the only man on the course who can calm him. It was true. I had a . . . I had an instinctive un-derstanding of animals. I should have been a trainer. Many times I was offered the job—you know, a proper post, by the Duke of . . . I forget his name . . . one of the Dukes. But
65 I had family obligations, my family needed me at home.

(*Pause.*)

The times I've watched those animals thundering past the post. What an experience. Mind you, I didn't lose, I made a few bob out of it, and you know why? Because I always had the smell of a good horse. I could smell him. And not
70 only the colts but the fillies. Because the fillies are more highly strung than the colts, they're more unreliable, did you know that? No, what do you know? Nothing. But I was always able to tell a good filly by one particular trick. I'd look her in the eye. You see? I'd stand in front of her
75 and look her straight in the eye, it was a kind of hypno-tism, and by the look deep down in her eye I could tell whether she was a stayer or not. It was a gift. I had a gift.

(*Pause.*)

And he talks to me about horses.

LENNY: Dad, do you mind if I change the subject?

(*Pause.*)

80 I want to ask you something. That dinner we had before, what was the name of it? What do you call it?

(*Pause.*)

Why don't you buy a dog? You're a dog cook. Honest. You think you're cooking for a lot of dogs.

MAX: If you don't like it get out.

LENNY: I am going out. I'm going out to buy myself a proper 85 dinner.

MAX: Well, get out! What are you waiting for?

(LENNY *looks at him.*)

LENNY: What did you say?

MAX: I said shove off out of it, that's what I said.

LENNY: You'll go before me, Dad, if you talk to me in that 90 tone of voice.

MAX: Will I, you bitch?

(MAX *grips his stick.*)

LENNY: Oh, Daddy, you're not going to use your stick on me, are you? Eh? Don't use your stick on me, Daddy. No, please. It wasn't my fault, it was one of the others. I haven't 95 done anything wrong, Dad, honest. Don't clout me with that stick, Dad.

(*Silence.*)

(MAX *sits hunched.* LENNY *reads the paper.*)

(SAM *comes in the front door. He wears a chauffeur's uniform. He hangs his hat on a hook in the hall and comes into the room. He goes to a chair, sits in it and sighs.*)

Hullo, Uncle Sam.

SAM: Hullo.

LENNY: How are you, Uncle? 100

SAM: Not bad. A bit tired.

LENNY: Tired? I bet you're tired. Where you been?

SAM: I've been to London Airport.

LENNY: All the way up to London Airport? What, right up the M4? 105

SAM: Yes, all the way up there.

LENNY: Tch, tch, tch. Well, I think you're entitled to be tired, Uncle.

SAM: Well, it's the drivers.

LENNY: I know. That's what I'm talking about. I'm talking 110 about the drivers.

SAM: Knocks you out.

(*Pause.*)

MAX: I'm here, too, you know.

(SAM *looks at him.*)

I said I'm here, too. I'm sitting here.

SAM: I know you're here. 115

(*Pause.*)

SAM: I took a Yankee out there today . . . to the Airport.

LENNY: Oh, a Yankee, was it?

SAM: Yes, I been with him all day. Picked him up at the Savoy at half past twelve, took him to the Caprice for his lunch. After lunch I picked him up again, took him down to a 120 house in Eaton Square—he had to pay a visit to a friend there—and then round about tea-time I took him right the way out to the Airport.

LENNY: Had to catch a plane there, did he?

125 SAM: Yes. Look what he gave me. He gave me a box of cigars.

(SAM *takes a box of cigars from his pocket.*)

MAX: Come here. Let's have a look at them.

(SAM *shows* MAX *the cigars.* MAX *takes one from the box, pinches it and sniffs it.*)

It's a fair cigar.

SAM: Want to try one?

(MAX *and* SAM *light cigars.*)

You know what he said to me? He told me I was the best

130 chauffeur he'd ever had. The best one.

MAX: From what point of view?

SAM: Eh?

MAX: From what point of view?

LENNY: From the point of view of his driving, Dad, and his

135 general sense of courtesy, I should say.

MAX: Thought you were a good driver, did he, Sam? Well, he gave you a first-class cigar.

SAM: Yes, he thought I was the best he'd ever had. They all say that, you know. They won't have anyone else, they only ask

140 for me. They say I'm the best chauffeur in the firm.

LENNY: I bet the other drivers tend to get jealous, don't they, Uncle?

SAM: They do get jealous. They get very jealous.

MAX: Why?

(*Pause.*)

145 SAM: I just told you.

MAX: No, I just can't get it clear, Sam. Why do the other drivers get jealous?

SAM: Because (a) I'm the best driver, and because . . . (b) I don't take liberties.

(*Pause.*)

150 I don't press myself on people, you see. These big businessmen, men of affairs, they don't want the driver jawing all the time, they like to sit in the back, have a bit of peace and quiet. After all, they're sitting in a Humber Super Snipe, they can afford to relax. At the same time, though,

155 this is what really makes me special . . . I do know how to pass the time of day when required.

(*Pause.*)

For instance, I told this man today I was in the second world war. Not the first. I told him I was too young for the first. But I told him I fought in the second.

(*Pause.*)

160 So did he, it turned out.

(LENNY *stands, goes to the mirror and straightens his tie.*)

LENNY: He was probably a colonel, or something, in the American Air Force.

SAM: Yes.

LENNY: Probably a navigator, or something like that, in a Flying Fortress. Now he's most likely a high executive in a 165 worldwide group of aeronautical engineers.

SAM: Yes.

LENNY: Yes, I know the kind of man you're talking about.

(LENNY *goes out, turning to his right.*)

SAM: After all, I'm experienced. I was driving a dust cart at the age of nineteen. Then I was in long-distance haulage. 170 I had ten years as a taxi-driver and I've had five as a private chauffeur.

MAX: It's funny you never got married, isn't it? A man with all your gifts.

(*Pause.*)

Isn't it? A man like you? 175

SAM: There's still time.

MAX: Is there?

(*Pause.*)

SAM: You'd be surprised.

MAX: What you been doing, banging away at your lady customers, have you? 180

SAM: Not me.

MAX: In the back of the Snipe? Been having a few crafty reefs in a layby, have you?

SAM: Not me.

MAX: On the back seat? What about the armrest, was it up or 185 down?

SAM: I've never done that kind of thing in my car.

MAX: Above all that kind of thing, are you, Sam?

SAM: Too true.

MAX: Above having a good bang on the back seat, are you? 190

SAM: Yes, I leave that to others.

MAX: You leave it to others? What others? You paralysed prat!

SAM: I don't mess up my car! Or my . . . my boss's car! Like other people.

MAX: Other people? What other people? 195

(*Pause.*)

What other people?

(*Pause.*)

SAM: Other people.

(*Pause.*)

MAX: When you find the right girl, Sam, let your family know, don't forget, we'll give you a number one send-off, I promise you. You can bring her to live here, she can 200 keep us all happy. We'd take it in turns to give her a walk around the park.

SAM: I wouldn't bring her here.

MAX: Sam, it's your decision. You're welcome to bring your bride here, to the place where you live, or on the other hand 205 you can take a suite at the Dorchester. It's entirely up to you.

SAM: I haven't got a bride.

(SAM *stands, goes to the sideboard, takes an apple from the bowl, bites into it.*)

Getting a bit peckish.

(*He looks out of the window.*)

210   Never get a bride like you had, anyway. Nothing like your bride . . . going about these days. Like Jessie.

(*Pause.*)

After all, I escorted her once or twice, didn't I? Drove her round once or twice in my cab. She was a charming woman.

(*Pause.*)

215   All the same, she was your wife. But still . . . they were some of the most delightful evenings I've ever had. Used to just drive her about. It was my pleasure.
MAX: (*Softly, closing his eyes.*) Christ.
SAM: I used to pull up at a stall and buy her a cup of coffee. She was a very nice companion to be with.

(*Silence.*)

(JOEY *comes in the front door. He walks into the room, takes his jacket off, throws it on a chair and stands.*)

(*Silence.*)

JOEY: Feel a bit hungry.
220   SAM: Me, too.
MAX: Who do you think I am, your mother? Eh? Honest. They walk in here every time of the day and night like bloody animals. Go and find yourself a mother.

(LENNY *walks into the room, stands.*)

JOEY: I've been training down at the gym.
225   SAM: Yes, the boy's been working all day and training all night.
MAX: What do you want, you bitch? You spend all the day sitting on your arse at London Airport, buy yourself a jam-roll. You expect me to sit here waiting to rush into the kitchen the moment you step in the door? You've been
230   living sixty-three years, why don't you learn to cook?
SAM: I can cook.
MAX: Well, go and cook!

(*Pause.*)

LENNY: What the boys want, Dad, is your own special brand of cooking, Dad. That's what the boys look forward to. The
235   special understanding of food, you know, that you've got.
MAX: Stop calling me Dad. Just stop all that calling me Dad, do you understand?
LENNY: But I'm your son. You used to tuck me up in bed every night. He tucked you up, too, didn't he, Joey?

(*Pause.*)

240   He used to like tucking up his sons.

(LENNY *turns and goes towards the front door.*)

MAX: Lenny.
LENNY: (*Turning.*) What?
MAX: I'll give you a proper tuck up one of these nights, son. You mark my word.

(*They look at each other.*)

(LENNY *opens the front door and goes out.*)

(*Silence.*)

JOEY: I've been training with Bobby Dodd.   245

(*Pause.*)

And I had a good go at the bag as well.

(*Pause.*)

I wasn't in bad trim.
MAX: Boxing's a gentleman's game.

(*Pause.*)

I'll tell you what you've got to do. What you've got to do is you've got to learn how to defend yourself, and you've   250
got to learn how to attack. That's your only trouble as a boxer. You don't know how to defend yourself, and you don't know how to attack.

(*Pause.*)

Once you've mastered those arts you can go straight to the top.   255

(*Pause.*)

JOEY: I've got a pretty good idea . . . of how to do that.

(JOEY *looks round for his jacket, picks it up, goes out of the room and up the stairs.*)

(*Pause.*)

MAX: Sam . . . why don't you go, too, eh? Why don't you just go upstairs? Leave me quiet. Leave me alone.
SAM: I want to make something clear about Jessie, Max. I want to. I do. When I took her out in the cab, round the   260
town, I was taking care of her, for you. I was looking after her for you, when you were busy, wasn't I? I was showing her the West End.

(*Pause.*)

You wouldn't have trusted any of your other brothers. You wouldn't have trusted Mac, would you? But you   265
trusted me. I want to remind you.

(*Pause.*)

Old Mac died a few years ago, didn't he? Isn't he dead?

(*Pause.*)

He was a lousy stinking rotten loudmouth. A bastard uncouth sodding runt. Mind you, he was a good friend of yours.   270

(*Pause.*)

MAX: Eh, Sam . . .

SAM: What?

MAX: Why do I keep you here? You're just an old grub.

SAM: Am I?

275 MAX: You're a maggot.

SAM: Oh yes?

MAX: As soon as you stop paying your way here, I mean when you're too old to pay your way, you know what I'm going to do? I'm going to give you the boot.

280 SAM: You are, eh?

MAX: Sure. I mean, bring in the money and I'll put up with you. But when the firm gets rid of you—you can flake off.

SAM: This is my house as well, you know. This was our mother's house.

285 MAX: One lot after the other. One mess after the other.

SAM: Our father's house.

MAX: Look what I'm lumbered with. One cast-iron bunch of crap after another. One flow of stinking pus after another.

(*Pause.*)

Our father? I remember him. Don't worry. You kid your-
290 self. He used to come over to me and look down at me. My old man did. He'd bend right over me, then he'd pick me up. I was only that big. Then he'd dandle me. Give me the bottle. Wipe me clean. Give me a smile. Pat me on the bum. Pass me around, pass me from hand to hand. Toss me
295 up in the air. Catch me coming down. I remember my father.

(*Blackout.*)

(*Lights up. Night.* TEDDY *and* RUTH *stand at the threshold of the room.*)

(*They are both well dressed in light summer suits and light raincoats. Two suitcases are by their side.*)

(*They look at the room.* TEDDY *tosses the key in his hand, smiles.*)

TEDDY: Well, the key worked.

(*Pause.*)

They haven't changed the lock.

(*Pause.*)

RUTH: No one's here.

300 TEDDY: (*Looking up.*) They're asleep.

(*Pause.*)

RUTH: Can I sit down?

TEDDY: Of course.

RUTH: I'm tired.

(*Pause.*)

TEDDY: Then sit down.

(*She does not move.*)

That's my father's chair. 305

RUTH: That one?

TEDDY: (*Smiling.*) Yes, that's it. Shall I go up and see if my room's still there?

RUTH: It can't have moved.

TEDDY: No, I mean if my bed's still there. 310

RUTH: Someone might be in it.

TEDDY: No. They've got their own beds.

(*Pause.*)

RUTH: Shouldn't you wake someone up? Tell them you're here?

TEDDY: Not at this time of night. It's too late.

(*Pause.*)

Shall I go up? 315

(*He goes into the hall, looks up the stairs, comes back.*)

Why don't you sit down?

(*Pause.*)

I'll just go up . . . have a look.

(*He goes up the stairs, stealthily.*)

(RUTH *stands, then slowly walks across the room.*)

(TEDDY *returns.*)

It's still there. My room. Empty. The bed's there. What are you doing?

(*She looks at him.*)

Blankets, no sheets. I'll find some sheets. I could hear 320
snores. Really. They're all still here, I think. They're all snoring up there. Are you cold?

RUTH: No.

TEDDY: I'll make something to drink, if you like. Something hot. 325

RUTH: No, I don't want anything.

(TEDDY *walks about.*)

TEDDY: What do you think of the room? Big, isn't it? It's a big house. I mean, it's a fine room, don't you think? Actually there was a wall, across there . . . with a door. We knocked it down . . . years ago . . . to make an open living area. The 330
structure wasn't affected, you see. My mother was dead.

(RUTH *sits.*)

Tired?

RUTH: Just a little.

TEDDY: We can go to bed if you like. No point in waking anyone up now. Just go to bed. See them all in the morn- 335
ing . . . see my father in the morning . . .

(*Pause.*)

RUTH: Do you want to stay?

TEDDY: Stay?

(*Pause.*)

We've come to stay. We're bound to stay . . . for a few days.
340 RUTH: I think . . . the children . . . might be missing us.
TEDDY: Don't be silly.
RUTH: They might.
TEDDY: Look, we'll be back in a few days, won't we?

(*He walks about the room.*)

Nothing's changed. Still the same.

(*Pause.*)

345   Still, he'll get a surprise in the morning, won't he? The old
man. I think you'll like him very much. Honestly. He's
a . . . well, he's old, of course. Getting on.

(*Pause.*)

I was born here, do you realize that?
RUTH: I know.

(*Pause.*)

350 TEDDY: Why don't you go to bed? I'll find some sheets. I
feel . . . wide awake, isn't it odd? I think I'll stay up for a
bit. Are you tired?
RUTH: No.
TEDDY: Go to bed. I'll show you the room.
355 RUTH: No, I don't want to.
TEDDY: You'll be perfectly all right up there without me. Really you will. I mean, I won't be long. Look, it's just up
there. It's the first door on the landing. The bathroom's
right next door. You . . . need some rest, you know.

(*Pause.*)

360   I just want to . . . walk about for a few minutes. Do you
mind?
RUTH: Of course I don't.
TEDDY: Well . . . Shall I show you the room?
RUTH: No, I'm happy at the moment.
365 TEDDY: You don't have to go to bed. I'm not saying you have
to. I mean, you can stay up with me. Perhaps I'll make a cup
of tea or something. The only thing is we don't want to
make too much noise, we don't want to wake anyone up.
RUTH: I'm not making any noise.
370 TEDDY: I know you're not.

(*He goes to her.*)

(*Gently.*) Look, it's all right, really. I'm here. I mean . . . I'm
with you. There's no need to be nervous. Are you nervous?
RUTH: No.
TEDDY: There's no need to be.

(*Pause.*)

375   They're very warm people, really. Very warm. They're my
family. They're not ogres.

(*Pause.*)

Well, perhaps we should go to bed. After all, we have to
be up early, see Dad. Wouldn't be quite right if he found
us in bed, I think. (*He chuckles.*) Have to be up before six,
come down, say hullo.   380

(*Pause.*)

RUTH: I think I'll have a breath of air.
TEDDY: Air?

(*Pause.*)

What do you mean?
RUTH: (*Standing.*) Just a stroll.
TEDDY: At this time of night? But we've . . . only just got here.   385
We've got to go to bed.
RUTH: I just feel like some air.
TEDDY: But I'm going to bed.
RUTH: That's all right.
TEDDY: But what am I going to do?   390

(*Pause.*)

The last thing I want is a breath of air. Why do you want
a breath of air?
RUTH: I just do.
TEDDY: But it's late.
RUTH: I won't go far. I'll come back.   395

(*Pause.*)

TEDDY: I'll wait up for you.
RUTH: Why?
TEDDY: I'm not going to bed without you.
RUTH: Can I have the key?

(*He gives it to her.*)

Why don't you go to bed?   400

(*He puts his arms on her shoulders and kisses her.*)

(*They look at each other, briefly. She smiles.*)

I won't be long.

(*She goes out of the front door.*)

(TEDDY *goes to the window, peers out after her, half turns from the*
window, stands, suddenly chews his knuckles.)

(LENNY *walks into the room from upstage left. He stands. He wears*
pyjamas and dressing-gown. He watches TEDDY.)

(TEDDY *turns and sees him.*)

(*Silence.*)

TEDDY: Hullo, Lenny.
LENNY: Hullo, Teddy.

(*Pause.*)

TEDDY: I didn't hear you come down the stairs.
LENNY: I didn't.   405

(*Pause.*)

    I sleep down here now. Next door. I've got a kind of study, workroom cum bedroom next door now, you see.
TEDDY: Oh. Did I . . . wake you up?
LENNY: No. I just had an early night tonight. You know how 410   it is. Can't sleep. Keep waking up.

(*Pause.*)

TEDDY: How are you?
LENNY: Well, just sleeping a bit restlessly, that's all. Tonight, anyway.
TEDDY: Bad dreams?
415 LENNY: No, I wouldn't say I was dreaming. It's not exactly a dream. It's just that something keeps waking me up. Some kind of tick.
TEDDY: A tick?
LENNY: Yes.
420 TEDDY: Well, what is it?
LENNY: I don't know.

(*Pause.*)

TEDDY: Have you got a clock in your room?
LENNY: Yes.
TEDDY: Well, maybe it's the clock.
425 LENNY: Yes, could be, I suppose.

(*Pause.*)

    Well, if it's the clock I'd better do something about it. Stifle it in some way, or something.

(*Pause.*)

TEDDY: I've . . . just come back for a few days.
LENNY: Oh yes? Have you?

(*Pause.*)

430 TEDDY: How's the old man?
LENNY: He's in the pink.

(*Pause.*)

TEDDY: I've been keeping well.
LENNY: Oh, have you?

(*Pause.*)

    Staying the night then, are you?
435 TEDDY: Yes.
LENNY: Well, you can sleep in your old room.
TEDDY: Yes, I've been up.
LENNY: Yes, you can sleep there.

(LENNY *yawns.*)

    Oh well.
440 TEDDY: I'm going to bed.
LENNY: Are you?
TEDDY: Yes, I'll get some sleep.
LENNY: Yes, I'm going to bed, too.

(TEDDY *picks up the cases.*)

    I'll give you a hand.
TEDDY: No, they're not heavy. 445

(TEDDY *goes into the hall with the cases.* LENNY *turns out the light in the room.*)

(*The light in the hall remains on.*)

(LENNY *follows into the hall.*)

LENNY: Nothing you want?
TEDDY: Mmmm?
LENNY: Nothing you might want, for the night? Glass of water, anything like that?
TEDDY: Any sheets anywhere? 450
LENNY: In the sideboard in your room.
TEDDY: Oh, good.
LENNY: Friends of mine occasionally stay there, you know, in your room, when they're passing through this part of the world. 455

(LENNY *turns out the hall light and turns on the first landing light.*)

(TEDDY *begins to walk up the stairs.*)

TEDDY: Well, I'll see you at breakfast, then.
LENNY: Yes, that's it. Ta-ta.

(TEDDY *goes upstairs.*)

(LENNY *goes off left.*)

(*Silence.*)

(*The landing light goes out. Slight night light in the hall and room.*)

(LENNY *comes back into the room, goes to the window and looks out.*)

(*He leaves the window and turns on a lamp. He is holding a small clock.*)

(*He sits, places the clock in front of him, lights a cigarette and sits.* RUTH *comes in the front door.*)

(*She stands still.* LENNY *turns his head, smiles. She walks slowly into the room.*)

LENNY: Good evening.
RUTH: Morning, I think.
LENNY: You're right there. 460

(*Pause.*)

    My name's Lenny. What's yours?
RUTH: Ruth.

(*She sits, puts her coat collar around her.*)

LENNY: Cold?
RUTH: No.
LENNY: It's been a wonderful summer, hasn't it? Remarkable. 465

(*Pause.*)

Would you like something? Refreshment of some kind? An aperitif, anything like that?

RUTH: No, thanks.

LENNY: I'm glad you said that. We haven't got a drink in the
470   house. Mind you, I'd soon get some in, if we had a party or something like that. Some kind of celebration . . . you know.

(*Pause.*)

You must be connected with my brother in some way. The one who's been abroad.

475 RUTH: I'm his wife.

LENNY: Eh listen, I wonder if you can advise me. I've been having a bit of a rough time with this clock. The tick's been keeping me up. The trouble is I'm not all that convinced it was the clock. I mean there are lots of things which tick in
480   the night, don't you find that? All sorts of objects, which, in the day, you wouldn't call anything else but commonplace. They give you no trouble. But in the night any given one of a number of them is liable to start letting out a bit of a tick. Whereas you look at these objects in the day and they're just
485   commonplace. They're as quiet as mice during the daytime. So . . . all things being equal . . . this question of me saying it was the clock that woke me up, well, that could very easily prove something of a false hypothesis.

(*He goes to the sideboard, pours from a jug into a glass, takes the glass to* RUTH.)

Here you are. I bet you could do with this.

490 RUTH: What is it?

LENNY: Water.

(*She takes it, sips, places the glass on a small table by her chair.*)

(LENNY *watches her.*)

Isn't it funny? I've got my pyjamas on and you're fully dressed?

(*He goes to the sideboard and pours another glass of water.*)

Mind if I have one? Yes, it's funny seeing my old brother
495   again after all these years. It's just the sort of tonic my Dad needs, you know. He'll be chuffed to his bollocks in the morning, when he sees his eldest son. I was surprised myself when I saw Teddy, you know. Old Ted. I thought he was in America.

500 RUTH: We're on a visit to Europe.

LENNY: What, both of you?

RUTH: Yes.

LENNY: What, you sort of live with him over there, do you?

RUTH: We're married.

505 LENNY: On a visit to Europe, eh? Seen much of it?

RUTH: We've just come from Italy.

LENNY: Oh, you went to Italy first, did you? And then he brought you over here to meet the family, did he? Well, the old man'll be pleased to see you, I can tell you.

510 RUTH: Good.

LENNY: What did you say?

RUTH: Good.

(*Pause.*)

LENNY: Where'd you go to in Italy?

RUTH: Venice.

LENNY: Not dear old Venice? Eh? That's funny. You know, 515
I've always had a feeling that if I'd been a soldier in the last war—say in the Italian campaign—I'd probably have found myself in Venice. I've always had that feeling. The trouble was I was too young to serve, you see. I was only a child, I was too small, otherwise I've got a pretty shrewd 520 idea I'd probably have gone through Venice. Yes, I'd almost certainly have gone through it with my battalion. Do you mind if I hold your hand?

RUTH: Why?

LENNY: Just a touch.   525

(*He stands and goes to her.*)

Just a tickle.

RUTH: Why?

(*He looks down at her.*)

LENNY: I'll tell you why.

(*Slight pause.*)

One night, not too long ago, one night down by the docks, I was standing alone under an arch, watching all the men 530 jibbing the boom, out in the harbour, and playing about with the yardarm, when a certain lady came up to me and made me a certain proposal. This lady had been searching for me for days. She'd lost track of my whereabouts. However, the fact was she eventually caught up with me, and 535 when she caught up with me she made me this certain proposal. Well, this proposal wasn't entirely out of order and normally I would have subscribed to it. I mean I would have subscribed to it in the normal course of events. The only trouble was she was falling apart with the pox. So I 540 turned it down. Well, this lady was very insistent and started taking liberties with me down under this arch, liberties which by any criterion I couldn't be expected to tolerate, the facts being what they were, so I clumped her one. It was on my mind at the time to do away with her, you 545 know, to kill her, and the fact is, that as killings go, it would have been a simple matter, nothing to it. Her chauffeur, who had located me for her, he'd popped around the corner to have a drink, which just left this lady and myself, you see, alone, standing underneath this arch, watching all the 550 steamers steaming up, no one about, all quiet on the Western Front, and there she was up against the wall—well, just sliding down the wall, following the blow I'd given her. Well, to sum up, everything was in my favour, for a killing. Don't worry about the chauffeur. The chauffeur would 555 never have spoken. He was an old friend of the family. But . . . in the end I thought . . . Aaah, why go to all the bother . . . you know, getting rid of the corpse and all that, getting yourself into a state of tension. So I just gave her another belt in the nose and a couple of turns of the boot and sort 560 of left it at that.

RUTH: How did you know she was diseased?

LENNY: How did I know?

(*Pause.*)

I decided she was.

(*Silence.*)

565   You and my brother are newly-weds, are you?

RUTH: We've been married six years.

LENNY: He's always been my favourite brother, old Teddy. Do you know that? And my goodness we are proud of him here, I can tell you. Doctor of Philosophy and all that . . . leaves
570   quite an impression. Of course, he's a very sensitive man, isn't he? Ted. Very. I've often wished I was as sensitive as he is.

RUTH: Have you?

LENNY: Oh yes. Oh yes, very much so. I mean, I'm not saying I'm not sensitive. I am. I could just be a bit more so,
575   that's all.

RUTH: Could you?

LENNY: Yes, just a bit more so, that's all.

(*Pause.*)

I mean, I am very sensitive to atmosphere, but I tend to get desensitized, if you know what I mean, when people make
580   unreasonable demands on me. For instance, last Christmas I decided to do a bit of snow-clearing for the Borough Council, because we had a heavy snow over here that year in Europe. I didn't have to do this snow-clearing—I mean I wasn't financially embarrassed in any way—it just ap-
585   pealed to me, it appealed to something inside me. What I anticipated with a good deal of pleasure was the brisk cold bite in the air in the early morning. And I was right. I had to get my snowboots on and I had to stand on a corner, at about five-thirty in the morning, to wait for the lorry to
590   pick me up, to take me to the allotted area. Bloody freezing. Well, the lorry came, I jumped on the tailboard, headlights on, dipped, and off we went. Got there, shovels up, fags on, and off we went, deep into the December snow, hours be-fore cockcrow. Well, that morning, while I was
595   having my mid-morning cup of tea in a neighboring cafe, the shovel standing by my chair, an old lady approached me and asked me if I would give her a hand with her iron mangle. Her brother-in-law, she said, had left it for her, but he'd left it in the wrong room, he'd left it in the front room.
600   Well, naturally, she wanted it in the back room. It was a present he'd given her, you see, a mangle, to iron out the washing. But he'd left it in the wrong room, he'd left it in the front room, well that was a silly place to leave it, it couldn't stay there. So I took time off to give her a hand. She only
605   lived up the road. Well, the only trouble was when I got there I couldn't move this mangle. It must have weighed about half a ton. How this brother-in-law got it up there in the first place I can't even begin to envisage. So there I was, doing a bit of shoulders on with the mangle, risking a
610   rupture, and this old lady just standing there, waving me on, not even lifting a little finger to give me a helping hand. So after a few minutes I said to her, now look here, why don't you stuff this iron mangle up your arse? Anyway, I said, they're out of date, you want to get a spin drier. I had
615   a good mind to give her a workover there and then, but as I was feeling jubilant with the snow-clearing I just gave her

a short-arm jab to the belly and jumped on a bus outside. Excuse me, shall I take this ashtray out of your way?

RUTH: It's not in my way.

LENNY: It seems to be in the way of your glass. The glass was   620
about to fall. Or the ashtray. I'm rather worried about the carpet. It's not me, it's my father. He's obsessed with order and clarity. He doesn't like mess. So, as I don't believe you're smoking at the moment, I'm sure you won't object if I move the ashtray.   625

(*He does so.*)

And now perhaps I'll relieve you of your glass.

RUTH: I haven't quite finished.

LENNY: You've consumed quite enough, in my opinion.

RUTH: No, I haven't.

LENNY: Quite sufficient, in my own opinion.   630

RUTH: Not in mine, Leonard.

(*Pause.*)

LENNY: Don't call me that, please.

RUTH: Why not?

LENNY: That's the name my mother gave me.

(*Pause.*)

Just give me the glass.   635

RUTH: No.

(*Pause.*)

LENNY: I'll take it, then.

RUTH: If you take the glass . . . I'll take you.

(*Pause.*)

LENNY: How about me taking the glass without you taking me?   640

RUTH: Why don't I just take you?

(*Pause.*)

LENNY: You're joking.

(*Pause.*)

You're in love, anyway, with another man. You've had a secret liaison with another man. His family didn't even know. Then you come here without a word of warning   645
and start to make trouble.

(*She picks up the glass and lifts it towards him.*)

RUTH: Have a sip. Go on. Have a sip from my glass.

(*He is still.*)

Sit on my lap. Take a long cool sip.

(*She pats her lap.*)

(*Pause. She stands, moves to him with the glass.*)

Put your head back and open your mouth.

LENNY: Take that glass away from me.
RUTH: Lie on the floor. Go on. I'll pour it down your throat.
LENNY: What are you doing, making me some kind of proposal?

(She laughs shortly, drains the glass.)

RUTH: Oh, I was thirsty.

(She smiles at him, puts the glass down, goes into the hall and up the stairs.)

(He follows into the hall and shouts up the stairs.)

LENNY: What was that supposed to be? Some kind of proposal?

(Silence.)

(He comes back into the room, goes to his own glass, drains it.)

(A door slams upstairs. The landing light goes on.)

(MAX comes down the stairs, in pyjamas and cap. He comes into the room.)

MAX: What's going on here? You drunk?

(He stares at LENNY.)

What are you shouting about? You gone mad?

(LENNY pours another glass of water.)

Prancing about in the middle of the night shouting your head off. What are you, a raving lunatic?
LENNY: I was thinking aloud.
MAX: Is Joey down here? You been shouting at Joey?
LENNY: Didn't you hear what I said, Dad? I said I was thinking aloud.
MAX: You were thinking so loud you got me out of bed.
LENNY: Look, why don't you just . . . pop off, eh?
MAX: Pop off? He wakes me up in the middle of the night, I think we got burglars here, I think he's got a knife stuck in him, I come down here, he tells me to pop off.

(LENNY sits down.)

He was talking to someone. Who could he have been talking to? They're all asleep. He was having a conversation with someone. He won't tell me who it was. He pretends he was thinking aloud. What are you doing, hiding someone here?
LENNY: I was sleepwalking. Get out of it, leave me alone, will you?
MAX: I want an explanation, you understand? I asked you who you got hiding here.

(Pause.)

LENNY: I'll tell you what, Dad, since you're in the mood for a bit of a . . . chat, I'll ask you a question. It's a question I've been meaning to ask you for some time. That night . . . you know . . . the night you got me . . . that night with Mum, what was it like? Eh? When I was just a glint in your eye. What was it like? What was the background to it? I mean, I want to know the real facts about my background. I mean, for instance, is it a fact that you had me in mind all the time, or is it a fact that I was the last thing you had in mind?

(Pause.)

I'm only asking this in a spirit of inquiry, you understand that, don't you? I'm curious. And there's lots of people of my age share that curiosity, you know that, Dad? They often ruminate, sometimes singly, sometimes in groups, about the true facts of that particular night—the night they were made in the image of those two people at it. It's a question long overdue, from my point of view, but as we happen to be passing the time of day here tonight I thought I'd pop it to you.

(Pause.)

MAX: You'll drown in your own blood.
LENNY: If you prefer to answer the question in writing I've got no objection.

(MAX stands.)

I should have asked my dear mother. Why didn't I ask my dear mother? Now it's too late. She's passed over to the other side.

(MAX spits at him.)

(LENNY looks down at the carpet.)

Now look what you've done. I'll have to Hoover that in the morning, you know.

(MAX turns and walks up the stairs.)

(LENNY sits still.)

(Blackout.)

(Lights up.)

(Morning.)

(JOEY in front of the mirror. He is doing some slow limbering-up exercises. He stops, combs his hair, carefully. He then shadowboxes, heavily, watching himself in the mirror.)

(MAX comes in from upstage left.)

(Both MAX and JOEY are dressed. MAX watches JOEY in silence. JOEY stops shadowboxing, picks up a newspaper and sits.)

(Silence.)

MAX: I hate this room.

(Pause.)

It's the kitchen I like. It's nice in there. It's cosy.

(Pause.)

But I can't stay in there. You know why? Because he's always washing up in there, scraping the plates, driving me out of the kitchen, that's why.

710 JOEY: Why don't you bring your tea in here?

MAX: I don't want to bring my tea in here. I hate it here. I want to drink my tea in there.

(*He goes into the hall and looks towards the kitchen.*)

What's he doing in there?

(*He returns.*)

What's the time?

715 JOEY: Half past six.

MAX: Half past six.

(*Pause.*)

I'm going to see a game of football this afternoon. You want to come?

(*Pause.*)

I'm talking to you.

720 JOEY: I'm training this afternoon. I'm doing six rounds with Blackie.

MAX: That's not till five o'clock. You've got time to see a game of football before five o'clock. It's the first game of the season.

725 JOEY: No, I'm not going.

MAX: Why not?

(*Pause.*)

(MAX *goes into the hall.*)

Sam! Come here!

(MAX *comes back into the room.*)

(SAM *enters with a cloth.*)

SAM: What?

MAX: What are you doing in there?

730 SAM: Washing up.

MAX: What else?

SAM: Getting rid of your leavings.

MAX: Putting them in the bin, eh?

SAM: Right in.

735 MAX: What point you trying to prove?

SAM: No point.

MAX: Oh yes, you are. You resent making my breakfast, that's what it is, isn't it? That's why you bang round the kitchen like that, scraping the frying-pan, scraping all the leavings

740 into the bin, scraping all the plates, scraping all the tea out of the teapot . . . that's why you do that, every single stinking morning. I know. Listen, Sam. I want to say something to you. From my heart.

(*He moves closer.*)

I want you to get rid of these feelings of resentment

745 you've got towards me. I wish I could understand them.

Honestly, have I ever given you cause? Never. When Dad died he said to me, Max, look after your brothers. That's exactly what he said to me.

SAM: How could he say that when he was dead?

MAX: What? 750

SAM: How could he speak if he was dead?

(*Pause.*)

MAX: Before he died, Sam. Just before. They were his last words. His last sacred words, Sammy. A split second after he said those words . . . he was a dead man. You think I'm joking? You think when my father spoke—on his death-bed— 755 I wouldn't obey his words to the last letter? You hear that, Joey? He'll stop at nothing. He's even prepared to spit on the memory of our Dad. What kind of a son were you, you wet wick? You spent half your time doing crossword puzzles! We took you into the butcher's shop, you couldn't even 760 sweep the dust off the floor. We took MacGregor into the shop, he could run the place by the end of a week. Well, I'll tell you one thing. I respected my father not only as a man but as a number one butcher! And to prove it I followed him into the shop. I learned to carve a carcass at his knee. I com- 765 memorated his name in blood. I gave birth to three grown men! All on my own bat. What have you done?

(*Pause.*)

What have you done? You tit!

SAM: Do you want to finish the washing up? Look, here's the cloth. 770

MAX: So try to get rid of these feelings of resentment, Sam. After all, we are brothers.

SAM: Do you want the cloth? Here you are. Take it.

(TEDDY *and* RUTH *come down the stairs. They walk across the hall and stop just inside the room.*)

(*The others turn and look at them.* JOEY *stands.*)

(TEDDY *and* RUTH *are wearing dressing-gowns.*)

(*Silence.*)

(TEDDY *smiles.*)

TEDDY: Hullo . . . Dad . . . We overslept.

(*Pause.*)

What's for breakfast? 775

(*Silence.*)

(TEDDY *chuckles.*)

Huh. We overslept.

(MAX *turns to* SAM.)

MAX: Did you know he was here?

SAM: No.

(MAX *turns to* JOEY.)

MAX: Did you know he was here?

(*Pause.*)

780   I asked you if you knew he was here.
JOEY: No.
MAX: Then who knew?

(*Pause.*)

Who knew?

(*Pause.*)

I didn't know.
785 TEDDY: I was going to come down, Dad, I was going to . . .
be here, when you came down.

(*Pause.*)

How are you?

(*Pause.*)

Uh . . . look, I'd . . . like you to meet . . .
MAX: How long you been in this house?
790 TEDDY: All night.
MAX: All night? I'm a laughing-stock. How did you get in?
TEDDY: I had my key.

(MAX *whistles and laughs.*)

MAX: Who's this?
TEDDY: I was just going to introduce you.
795 MAX: Who asked you to bring tarts in here?
TEDDY: Tarts?
MAX: Who asked you to bring dirty tarts into this house?
TEDDY: Listen, don't be silly—
MAX: You been here all night?
800 TEDDY: Yes, we arrived from Venice—
MAX: We've had a smelly scrubber in my house all night.
We've had a stinking pox-ridden slut in my house all night.
TEDDY: Stop it! What are you talking about?
MAX: I haven't seen the bitch for six years, he comes home
805   without a word, he brings a filthy scrubber off the street,
he shacks up in my house!
TEDDY: She's my wife! We're married!

(*Pause.*)

MAX: I've never had a whore under this roof before. Ever since
your mother died. My word of honour. (*To* JOEY.) Have you
810   ever had a whore here? Has Lenny ever had a whore here?
They come back from America, they bring the slopbucket
with them. They bring the bedpan with them. (*To* TEDDY.)
Take that disease away from me. Get her away from me.
TEDDY: She's my wife.
815 MAX: (*To* JOEY.) Chuck them out.

(*Pause.*)

A Doctor of Philosophy. Sam, you want to meet a Doctor
of Philosophy? (*To* JOEY.) I said chuck them out.

(*Pause.*)

What's the matter? You deaf?
JOEY: You're an old man. (*To* TEDDY.) He's an old man.

(LENNY *walks into the room, in a dressing-gown.*)

(*He stops.*)

(*They all look round.* MAX *turns back, hits* JOEY *in the stomach
with all his might.*)

(JOEY *contorts, staggers across the stage.* MAX, *with the exertion of
the blow, begins to collapse. His knees buckle. He clutches his stick.*)

(SAM *moves forward to help him.*)

(MAX *hits him across the head with his stick.*)

(SAM *sits, head in hands.*)

(JOEY, *hands pressed to his stomach, sinks down at the feet of*
RUTH.)

(*She looks down at him.* LENNY *and* TEDDY *are still.*)

(JOEY *slowly stands. He is close to* RUTH. *He turns from* RUTH,
looks round at MAX.)

(SAM *clutches his head.* MAX *breathes heavily, very slowly gets to his
feet.* JOEY *moves to him.*)

(*They look at each other.*)

(*Silence.*)

(MAX *moves past* JOEY, *walks towards* RUTH. *He gestures with his
stick.*)

MAX: Miss.   820

(RUTH *walks toward him.*)

RUTH: Yes?

(*He looks at her.*)

MAX: You a mother?
RUTH: Yes.
MAX: How many you got?
RUTH: Three.   825

(*He turns to* TEDDY.)

MAX: All yours, Ted?

(*Pause.*)

Teddy, why don't we have a nice cuddle and kiss, eh? Like
the old days? What about a nice cuddle and kiss, eh?
TEDDY: Come on, then.

(*Pause.*)

MAX: You want to kiss your old father? Want a cuddle with   830
your old father?
TEDDY: Come on, then.

(TEDDY *moves a step towards him.*)

Come on.

(*Pause.*)

MAX: You still love your old Dad, eh?

(*They face each other.*)

835 TEDDY: Come on, Dad. I'm ready for the cuddle.

(MAX *begins to chuckle, gurgling.*)

(*He turns to the family and addresses them.*)

MAX: He still loves his father!

(*Curtain.*)

ACT TWO

Afternoon.

MAX, TEDDY, LENNY *and* SAM *are about the stage, lighting cigars.*

JOEY *comes in from upstage left with a coffee tray, followed by* RUTH. *He puts the tray down.* RUTH *hands coffee to all the men. She sits with her cup.* MAX *smiles at her.*

RUTH: That was a very good lunch.
MAX: I'm glad you liked it. (*To the others.*) Did you hear that? (*To* RUTH.) Well, I put my heart and soul into it, I can tell you. (*He sips.*) And this is a lovely cup of coffee.
5 RUTH: I'm glad.

(*Pause.*)

MAX: I've got the feeling you're a first-rate cook.
RUTH: I'm not bad.
MAX: No, I've got the feeling you're a number one cook. Am I right, Teddy?
10 TEDDY: Yes, she's a very good cook.

(*Pause.*)

MAX: Well, it's a long time since the whole family was together, eh? If only your mother was alive. Eh, what do you say, Sam? What would Jessie say if she was alive? Sitting here with her three sons. Three fine grown-up lads. And
15 a lovely daughter-in-law. The only shame is her grandchildren aren't here. She'd have petted them and cooed over them, wouldn't she, Sam? She'd have fussed over them and played with them, told them stories, tickled them—I tell you she'd have been hysterical. (*To* RUTH.)
20 Mind you, she taught those boys everything they know. She taught them all the morality they know. I'm telling you. Every single bit of the moral code they live by—was taught to them by their mother. And she had a heart to go with it. What a heart. Eh, Sam? Listen, what's the use
25 of beating round the bush? That woman was the backbone to this family. I mean, I was busy working twenty-four hours a day in the shop, I was going all over the country to find meat, I was making my way in the world, but I left a woman at home with a will of iron, a heart of
30 gold and a mind. Right, Sam?

(*Pause.*)

What a mind.

(*Pause.*)

Mind you, I was a generous man to her. I never left her short of a few bob. I remember one year I entered into negotiations with a top-class group of butchers with continental connections. I was going into association with 35 them. I remember the night I came home, I kept quiet. First of all I gave Lenny a bath, then Teddy a bath, then Joey a bath. What fun we used to have in the bath, eh, boys? Then I came downstairs and I made Jessie put her feet up on a pouffe—what happened to that pouffe, I 40 haven't seen it for years—she put her feet up on the pouffe and I said to her, Jessie, I think our ship is going to come home, I'm going to treat you to a couple of items, I'm going to buy you a dress in pale corded blue silk, heavily encrusted in pearls, and for casual wear, a pair of 45 pantaloons in lilac flowered taffeta. Then I gave her a drop of cherry brandy. I remember the boys came down, in their pyjamas, all their hair shining, their faces pink, it was before they started shaving, and they knelt down at our feet, Jessie's and mine. I tell you, it was like Christmas. 50

(*Pause.*)

RUTH: What happened to the group of butchers?
MAX: The group? They turned out to be a bunch of criminals like everyone else.

(*Pause.*)

This is a lousy cigar.

(*He stubs it out.*)

(*He turns to* SAM.)

What time you going to work? 55
SAM: Soon.
MAX: You've got a job on this afternoon, haven't you?
SAM: Yes, I know.
MAX: What do you mean, you know? You'll be late. You'll lose your job? What are you trying to do, humiliate me? 60
SAM: Don't worry about me.
MAX: It makes the bile come up in my mouth. The bile— you understand. (*To* RUTH.) I worked as a butcher all my life, using the chopper and the slab, the slab, you know what I mean, the chopper and the slab! To keep my fam- 65 ily in luxury. Two families! My mother was bedridden, my brothers were all invalids. I had to earn the money for the leading psychiatrists. I had to read books! I had to study the disease, so that I could cope with an emergency at every stage. A crippled family, three bastard sons, a slut- 70 bitch of a wife—don't talk to me about the pain of childbirth—I suffered the pain, I've still got the pangs—when I give a little cough my back collapses— and here I've got a lazy idle bugger of a brother won't even get to work on time. The best chauffeur in the world. All his life he's sat 75 in the front seat giving lovely hand signals. You call that work? This man doesn't know his gearbox from his arse!

SAM: You go and ask my customers! I'm the only one they ever ask for.

80 MAX: What do the other drivers do, sleep all day?

SAM: I can only drive one car. They can't all have me at the same time.

MAX: Anyone could have you at the same time. You'd bend over for half a dollar on Blackfriars Bridge.

85 SAM: Me!

MAX: For two bob and a toffee apple.

SAM: He's insulting me. He's insulting his brother. I'm driving a man to Hampton Court at four forty-five.

MAX: Do you want to know who could drive? MacGregor!

90 MacGregor was a driver.

SAM: Don't you believe it.

(MAX *points his stick at* SAM.)

MAX: He didn't even fight in the war. This man didn't even fight in the bloody war!

SAM: I did!

95 MAX: Who did you kill?

(*Silence.*)

(SAM *gets up, goes to* RUTH, *shakes her hand and goes out of the front door.*)

(MAX *turns to* TEDDY.)

Well, how you been keeping, son?

TEDDY: I've been keeping very well, Dad.

MAX: It's nice to have you with us, son.

TEDDY: It's nice to be back, Dad.

(*Pause.*)

100 MAX: You should have told me you were married, Teddy. I'd have sent you a present. Where was the wedding, in America?

TEDDY: No. Here. The day before we left.

MAX: Did you have a big function?

TEDDY: No, there was no one there.

105 MAX: You're mad. I'd have given you a white wedding. We'd have had the cream of the cream here. I'd have been only too glad to bear the expense, my word of honour.

(*Pause.*)

TEDDY: You were busy at the time. I didn't want to bother you.

MAX: But you're my own flesh and blood. You're my first

110 born. I'd have dropped everything. Sam would have driven you to the reception in the Snipe, Lenny would have been your best man, and then we'd have all seen you off on the boat. I mean, you don't think I disapprove of marriage, do you? Don't be daft. (*To* RUTH.) I've been begging my two

115 youngsters for years to find a nice feminine girl with proper credentials—it makes life worth living. (*To* TEDDY.) Anyway, what's the difference, you did it, you made a wonderful choice, you've got a wonderful family, a marvellous career . . . so why don't we let bygones be bygones?

(*Pause.*)

120 You know what I'm saying? I want you both to know that you have my blessing.

TEDDY: Thank you.

MAX: Don't mention it. How many other houses in the district have got a Doctor of Philosophy sitting down drinking a cup of coffee?   125

(*Pause.*)

RUTH: I'm sure Teddy's very happy . . . to know that you're pleased with me.

(*Pause.*)

I think he wondered whether you would be pleased with me.

MAX: But you're a charming woman.   130

(*Pause.*)

RUTH: I was . . .

MAX: What?

(*Pause.*)

What she say?

(*They all look at her.*)

RUTH: I was . . . different . . . when I met Teddy . . . first.

TEDDY: No you weren't. You were the same.   135

RUTH: I wasn't.

MAX: Who cares? Listen, live in the present, what are you worrying about? I mean, don't forget the earth's about five thousand million years old, at least. Who can afford to live in the past?   140

(*Pause.*)

TEDDY: She's a great help to me over there. She's a wonderful wife and mother. She's a very popular woman. She's got lots of friends. It's a great life, at the University . . . you know . . . it's a very good life. We've got a lovely house . . . we've got all . . . we've got everything we want. It's a very   145
stimulating environment.

(*Pause.*)

My department . . . is highly successful.

(*Pause.*)

We've got three boys, you know.

MAX: All boys? Isn't that funny, eh? You've got three, I've got three. You've got three nephews, Joey. Joey! You're an un-   150
cle, do you hear? You could teach them how to box.

(*Pause.*)

JOEY: (*To* RUTH.) I'm a boxer. In the evenings, after work. I'm in demolition in the daytime.

RUTH: Oh?

JOEY: Yes. I hope to be full time, when I get more bouts.   155

MAX: (*To* LENNY.) He speaks so easily to his sister-in-law, do you notice? That's because she's an intelligent and sympathetic woman.

(*He leans to her.*)

160   Eh, tell me, do you think the children are missing their mother?

(*She looks at him.*)

TEDDY: Of course they are. They love her. We'll be seeing them soon.

(*Pause.*)

LENNY: (*To* TEDDY.) Your cigar's gone out.
TEDDY: Oh, yes.
165   LENNY: Want a light?
TEDDY: No. No.

(*Pause.*)

So has yours.
LENNY: Oh, yes.

(*Pause.*)

Eh, Teddy, you haven't told us much about your Doctor-
170   ship of Philosophy. What do you teach?
TEDDY: Philosophy.
LENNY: Well, I want to ask you something. Do you detect a certain logical incoherence in the central affirmations of Christian theism?
175   TEDDY: That question doesn't fall within my province.
LENNY: Well, look at it this way . . . you don't mind my asking you some questions, do you?
TEDDY: If they're within my province.
LENNY: Well, look at it this way. How can the unknown merit
180   reverence? In other words, how can you revere that of which you're ignorant? At the same time, it would be ridiculous to propose that what we *know* merits reverence. What we know merits any one of a number of things, but it stands to reason reverence isn't one of them. In other words,
185   apart from the known and the unknown, what else is there?

(*Pause.*)

TEDDY: I'm afraid I'm the wrong person to ask.
LENNY: But you're a philosopher. Come on, be frank. What do you make of all this business of being and not-being?
TEDDY: What do you make of it?
190   LENNY: Well, for instance, take a table. Philosophically speaking. What is it?
TEDDY: A table.
LENNY: Ah. You mean it's nothing else but a table. Well, some people would envy your certainty, wouldn't they, Joey?
195   For instance, I've got a couple of friends of mine, we often sit round the Ritz Bar having a few liqueurs, and they're always saying things like that, you know, things like: Take a table, take it. All right, I say, *take* it, *take* a table, but once you've taken it, what you going to do with it?
200   Once you've got hold of it, where you going to take it?
MAX: You'd probably sell it.
LENNY: You wouldn't get much for it.
JOEY: Chop it up for firewood.

(LENNY *looks at him and laughs.*)

RUTH: Don't be too sure though. You've forgotten something. Look at me. I . . . move my leg. That's all it is. But   205
I wear . . . underwear . . . which moves with me . . . it . . .
captures your attention. Perhaps you misinterpret. The action is simple. It's a leg . . . moving. My lips move. Why
don't you restrict . . . your observations to that? Perhaps
the fact that they move is more significant . . . than the   210
words which come through them. You must bear that . . .
possibility . . . in mind.

(*Silence.*)

(TEDDY *stands.*)

I was born quite near here.

(*Pause.*)

Then . . . six years ago, I went to America.

(*Pause.*)

It's all rock. And sand. It stretches . . . so far . . . everywhere   215
you look. And there's lots of insects there.

(*Pause.*)

And there's lots of insects there.

(*Silence.*)

(*She is still.*)

(MAX *stands.*)

MAX: Well, it's time to go to the gym. Time for your work-
out, Joey.
LENNY: (*Standing.*) I'll come with you.   220

(JOEY *sits looking at* RUTH.)

MAX: Joe.

(JOEY *stands. The three go out.*)

(TEDDY *sits by* RUTH, *holds her hand. She smiles at him.*)

(*Pause.*)

TEDDY: I think we'll go back. Mmnn?

(*Pause.*)

Shall we go home?
RUTH: Why?
TEDDY: Well, we were only here for a few days, weren't we?   225
We might as well . . . cut it short, I think.
RUTH: Why? Don't you like it here?
TEDDY: Of course I do. But I'd like to go back and see the
boys now.

(*Pause.*)

RUTH: Don't you like your family?   230
TEDDY: Which family?
RUTH: Your family here.

TEDDY: Of course I like them. What are you talking about?

(*Pause.*)

RUTH: You don't like them as much as you thought you did?

235 TEDDY: Of course I do. Of course I . . . like them. I don't know what you're talking about.

(*Pause.*)

Listen. You know what time of the day it is there now, do you?

RUTH: What?

240 TEDDY: It's morning. It's about eleven o'clock.

RUTH: Is it?

TEDDY: Yes, they're about six hours behind us . . . I mean . . . behind the time here. The boys'll be at the pool . . . now . . . swimming. Think of it. Morning over there. Sun. We'll

245 go anyway, mmnn? It's so clean there.

RUTH: Clean.

TEDDY: Yes.

RUTH: Is it dirty here?

TEDDY: No, of course not. But it's cleaner there.

(*Pause.*)

250 Look, I just brought you back to meet the family, didn't I? You've met them, we can go. The fall semester will be starting soon.

RUTH: You find it dirty here?

TEDDY: I didn't say I found it dirty here.

(*Pause.*)

255 I didn't say that.

(*Pause.*)

Look. I'll go and pack. You rest for a while. Will you? They won't be back for at least an hour. You can sleep. Rest. Please.

(*She looks at him.*)

You can help me with my lectures when we get back. I'd
260 love that. I'd be so grateful for it, really. We can bathe till October. You know that. Here, there's nowhere to bathe, except the swimming bath down the road. You know what it's like? It's like a urinal. A filthy urinal!

(*Pause.*)

You liked Venice, didn't you? It was lovely, wasn't it? You
265 had a good week. I mean . . . I took you there. I can speak Italian.

RUTH: But if I'd been a nurse in the Italian campaign I would have been there before.

(*Pause.*)

TEDDY: You just rest. I'll go and pack.

(TEDDY *goes out and up the stairs.*)

(*She closes her eyes.*)

(LENNY *appears from upstage left. He walks into the room and sits near her.*)

(*She opens her eyes.*)

(*Silence.*)

LENNY: Well, the evenings are drawing in.   270
RUTH: Yes, it's getting dark.

(*Pause.*)

LENNY: Winter'll soon be upon us. Time to renew one's wardrobe.

(*Pause.*)

RUTH: That's a good thing to do.
LENNY: What?   275

(*Pause.*)

RUTH: I always . . .

(*Pause.*)

Do you like clothes?
LENNY: Oh, yes. Very fond of clothes.

(*Pause.*)

RUTH: I'm fond . . .

(*Pause.*)

What do you think of my shoes?   280
LENNY: They're very nice.
RUTH: No, I can't get the ones I want over there.
LENNY: Can't get them over there, eh?
RUTH: No . . . you don't get them there.

(*Pause.*)

I was a model before I went away.   285
LENNY: Hats?

(*Pause.*)

I bought a girl a hat once. We saw it in a glass case, in a shop. I tell you what it had. It had a bunch of daffodils on it, tied with a black satin bow, and then it was covered with a cloche of black veiling. A cloche. I'm telling you.   290
She was made for it.
RUTH: No . . . I was a model for the body. A photographic model for the body.
LENNY: Indoor work?
RUTH: That was before I had . . . all my children.   295

(*Pause.*)

No, not always indoors.

(*Pause.*)

Once or twice we went to a place in the country, by train. Oh, six or seven times. We used to pass a . . . a large white

300 water tower. This place . . . this house . . . was very big . . . the trees . . . there was a lake, you see . . . we used to change and walk down towards the lake . . . we went down a path . . . on stones . . . there were . . . on this path. Oh, just . . . wait . . . yes . . . when we changed in the house we had a drink. There was a cold buffet.

(*Pause.*)

305 Sometimes we stayed in the house but . . . most often . . . we walked down to the lake . . . and did our modelling there.

(*Pause.*)

Just before we went to America I went down there. I walked from the station to the gate and then I walked up the drive. There were lights on . . . I stood in the drive . . . the house was very light.

310

(*TEDDY comes down the stairs with the cases. He puts them down, looks at* LENNY.)

TEDDY: What have you been saying to her?

(*He goes to* RUTH.)

Here's your coat.

(LENNY *goes to the radiogram and puts on a record of slow jazz.*)

Ruth. Come on. Put it on.
315 LENNY: (*To* RUTH.) What about one dance before you go?
TEDDY: We're going.
LENNY: Just one.
TEDDY: No. We're going.
LENNY: Just one dance, with her brother-in-law, before she
320 goes.

(LENNY *bends to her.*)

Madam?

(RUTH *stands. They dance, slowly.*)

(TEDDY *stands, with* RUTH's *coat.*)

(MAX *and* JOEY *come in the front door and into the room. They stand.*)

(LENNY *kisses* RUTH. *They stand, kissing.*)

JOEY: Christ, she's wide open. Dad, look at that.

(*Pause.*)

She's a tart.

(*Pause.*)

Old Lenny's got a tart in here.

(JOEY *goes to them. He takes* RUTH's *arm. He smiles at* LENNY. *He sits with* RUTH *on the sofa, embraces and kisses her.*)

(*He looks up at* LENNY.)

Just up my street. 325

(*He leans her back until she lies beneath him. He kisses her. He looks up at* TEDDY *and* MAX.)

It's better than a rubdown, this.

(LENNY *sits on the arm of the sofa. He caresses* RUTH's *hair as* JOEY *embraces her.*)

(MAX *comes forward, looks at the cases.*)

MAX: You going, Teddy? Already?

(*Pause.*)

Well, when you coming over again, eh? Look, next time you come over, don't forget to let us know beforehand whether you're married or not. I'll always be glad to meet 330 the wife. Honest. I'm telling you.

(JOEY *lies heavily on* RUTH.)

(*They are almost still.*)

(LENNY *caresses her hair.*)

Listen, you think I don't know why you didn't tell me you were married? I know why. You were ashamed. You thought I'd be annoyed because you married a woman beneath you. You should have known me better. I'm 335 broadminded. I'm a broadminded man.

(*He peers to see* RUTH's *face under* JOEY, *turns back to* TEDDY.)

Mind you, she's a lovely girl. A beautiful woman. And a mother too. A mother of three. You've made a happy woman out of her. It's something to be proud of. I mean, we're talking about a woman of quality. We're talking 340 about a woman of feeling.

(JOEY *and* RUTH *roll off the sofa on to the floor.*)

(JOEY *clasps her.* LENNY *moves to stand above them. He looks down on them. He touches* RUTH *gently with his foot.*)

(RUTH *suddenly pushes* JOEY *away.*)

(*She stands up.* JOEY *gets to his feet, stares at her.*)

RUTH: I'd like something to eat. (*To* LENNY.) I'd like a drink. Did you get any drink?
LENNY: We've got drink.
RUTH: I'd like one, please. 345
LENNY: What drink?
RUTH: Whisky.
LENNY: I've got it.

(*Pause.*)

RUTH: Well, get it.

(LENNY *goes to the sideboard, takes out bottle and glasses.*)

(JOEY *moves towards her.*)

Put the record off. 350

(*He looks at her, turns, puts the record off.*)

I want something to eat.

(*Pause.*)

JOEY: I can't cook. (*Pointing to* MAX.) He's the cook.

(LENNY *brings her a glass of whisky.*)

LENNY: Soda on the side?
RUTH: What's this glass? I can't drink out of this. Haven't you
355   got a tumbler?
LENNY: Yes.
RUTH: Well, put it in a tumbler.

(*He takes the glass back, pours whisky into a tumbler, brings it to her.*)

LENNY: On the rocks? Or as it comes?
RUTH: Rocks? What do you know about rocks?
360 LENNY: We've got rocks. But they're frozen stiff in the fridge.

(RUTH *drinks.*)

(LENNY *looks round at the others.*)

Drinks all round?

(*He goes to the sideboard and pours drinks.*)

(JOEY *moves closer to* RUTH.)

JOEY: What food do you want?

(RUTH *walks round the room.*)

RUTH: (*To* TEDDY.) Have your family read your critical works?
MAX: That's one thing I've never done. I've never read one of
365 his critical works.
TEDDY: You wouldn't understand them.

(LENNY *hands drinks all round.*)

JOEY: What sort of food do you want? I'm not the cook, anyway.
LENNY: Soda, Ted? Or as it comes?
370 TEDDY: You wouldn't understand my works. You wouldn't have
the faintest idea of what they were about. You wouldn't appreciate the points of reference. You're way behind. All of
you. There's no point in my sending you my works. You'd
be lost. It's nothing to do with the question of intelligence.
375 It's a way of being able to look at the world. It's a question of
how far you can operate on things and not in things. I mean
it's a question of your capacity to ally the two, to relate the
two, to balance the two. To see, to be able to see! I'm the one
who can see. That's why I can write my critical works.
380 Might do you good . . . have a look at them . . . see how certain people can view . . . things . . . how certain people can
maintain . . . intellectual equilibrium. Intellectual equilibrium. You're just objects. You just . . . move about. I can observe it. I can see what you do. It's the same as I do. But you're
385 lost in it. You won't get me being . . . I won't be lost in it.

(*Blackout.*)

(*Lights up.*)

(*Evening.*)

(TEDDY *sitting, in his coat, the cases by him.* SAM.)

(*Pause.*)

SAM: Do you remember MacGregor, Teddy?
TEDDY: Mac?
SAM: Yes.
TEDDY: Of course I do.
SAM: What did you think of him? Did you take to him?   390
TEDDY: Yes. I liked him. Why?

(*Pause.*)

SAM: You know, you were always my favourite, of the lads. Always.

(*Pause.*)

When you wrote to me from America I was very
touched, you know. I mean you'd written to your father a   395
few times but you'd never written to me. But then, when
I got that letter from you . . . well, I was very touched. I
never told him. I never told him I'd heard from you.

(*Pause.*)

(*Whispering.*) Teddy, shall I tell you something? You were
always your mother's favourite. She told me. It's true. You   400
were always the . . . you were always the main object of
her love.

(*Pause.*)

Why don't you stay for a couple more weeks, eh? We
could have a few laughs.

(LENNY *comes in the front door and into the room.*)

LENNY: Still here, Ted? You'll be late for your first seminar.   405

(*He goes to the sideboard, opens it, peers in it, to the right and the left, stands.*)

Where's my cheese-roll?

(*Pause.*)

Someone's taken my cheese-roll. I left it there. (*To* SAM.)
You been thieving?
TEDDY: I took your cheese-roll, Lenny.

(*Silence.*)

(SAM *looks at them, picks up his hat and goes out of the front door.*)

(*Silence.*)

LENNY: You took my cheese-roll?   410
TEDDY: Yes.
LENNY: I made that roll myself. I cut it and put the butter on.
I sliced a piece of cheese and put it in between. I put it on

a plate and I put it in the sideboard. I did all that before I
415 went out. Now I come back and you've eaten it.
TEDDY: Well, what are you going to do about it?
LENNY: I'm waiting for you to apologize.
TEDDY: But I took it deliberately, Lenny.
LENNY: You mean you didn't stumble on it by mistake?
420 TEDDY: No, I saw you put it there. I was hungry, so I ate it.

(*Pause.*)

LENNY: Barefaced audacity.

(*Pause.*)

What led you to be so . . . vindictive against your own
brother? I'm bowled over.

(*Pause.*)

Well, Ted, I would say this is something approaching the
425 naked truth, isn't it? It's a real cards on the table stunt. I
mean, we're in the land of no holds barred now. Well, how
else can you interpret it? To pinch your younger brother's
specially made cheese-roll when he's out doing a spot of
work, that's not equivocal, it's unequivocal.

(*Pause.*)

430 Mind you, I will say you do seem to have grown a bit sulky
during the last six years. A bit sulky. A bit inner. A bit less
forthcoming. It's funny, because I'd have thought that in the
United States of America, I mean with the sun and all that,
the open spaces, on the old campus, in your position, lectur-
435 ing, in the centre of all the intellectual life out there, on the
old campus, all the social whirl, all the stimulation of it all, all
your kids and all that, to have fun with, down by the pool,
the Greyhound buses and all that, tons of iced water, all the
comfort of those Bermuda shorts and all that, on the old
440 campus, no time of the day or night you can't get a cup of
coffee or a Dutch gin, I'd have thought you'd have grown
more forthcoming, not less. Because I want you to know
that you set a standard for us, Teddy. Your family looks up to
you, boy, and you know what it does? It does its best to fol-
445 low the example you set. Because you're a great source of
pride to us. That's why we were so glad to see you come
back, to welcome you back to your birthplace. That's why.

(*Pause.*)

No, listen, Ted, there's no question that we live a less rich
life here than you do over there. We live a closer life. We're
450 busy, of course. Joey's busy with his boxing, I'm busy with
my occupation, Dad still plays a good game of poker, and
he does the cooking as well, well up to his old standard, and
Uncle Sam's the best chauffeur in the firm. But nevertheless we do make up a unit, Teddy, and you're an integral part
455 of it. When we all sit round the backyard having a quiet
gander at the night sky, there's always an empty chair standing in the circle, which is in fact yours. And so when you
at length return to us, we do expect a bit of grace, a bit of
je ne sais quoi, a bit of generosity of mind, a bit of liberal-
460 ity of spirit, to reassure us. We do expect that. But do we
get it? Have we got it? Is that what you've given us?

(*Pause.*)

TEDDY: Yes.

(JOEY *comes down the stairs and into the room, with a newspaper.*)

LENNY: (*To* JOEY.) How'd you get on?
JOEY: Er . . . not bad.
LENNY: What do you mean? 465

(*Pause.*)

What do you mean?
JOEY: Not bad.
LENNY: I want to know what you mean—by not bad.
JOEY: What's it got to do with you?
LENNY: Joey, you tell your brother everything. 470

(*Pause.*)

JOEY: I didn't get all the way.
LENNY: You didn't get all the way?

(*Pause.*)

(*With emphasis.*) You didn't get all the way?
But you've had her up there for two hours.
JOEY: Well? 475
LENNY: You didn't get all the way and you've had her up there
for two hours!
JOEY: What about it?

(LENNY *moves closer to him.*)

LENNY: What are you telling me?
JOEY: What do you mean? 480
LENNY: Are you telling me she's a tease?

(*Pause.*)

She's a tease!

(*Pause.*)

What do you think of that, Ted? Your wife turns out to be
a tease. He's had her up there for two hours and he didn't
go the whole hog. 485
JOEY: I didn't say she was a tease.
LENNY: Are you joking? It sounds like a tease to me, don't it
to you, Ted?
TEDDY: Perhaps he hasn't got the right touch.
LENNY: Joey? Not the right touch? Don't be ridiculous. He's 490
had more dolly than you've had cream cakes. He's irresistible. He's one of the few and far between. Tell him
about the last bird you had, Joey.

(*Pause.*)

JOEY: What bird?
LENNY: The last bird! When we stopped the car . . . 495
JOEY: Oh, that . . . yes . . . well, we were in Lenny's car one
night last week . . .
LENNY: The Alfa.
JOEY: And er . . . bowling down the road . . .

500 LENNY: Up near the Scrubs.
JOEY: Yes, up over by the Scrubs . . .
LENNY: We were doing a little survey of North Paddington.
JOEY: And er . . . it was pretty late, wasn't it?
LENNY: Yes, it was late. Well?

(*Pause.*)

505 JOEY: And then we . . . well, by the kerb, we saw this parked
car . . . with a couple of girls in it.
LENNY: And their escorts.
JOEY: Yes, there were two geezers in it. Anyway . . .

(*Pause.*)

What we do then?
510 LENNY: We stopped the car and got out!
JOEY: Yes . . . we got out . . . and we told the . . . two escorts
. . . to go away . . . which they did . . . and then we . . . got
the girls out of the car . . .
LENNY: We didn't take them over the Scrubs.
515 JOEY: Oh, no. Not over the Scrubs. Well, the police would
have noticed us there . . . you see. We took them over a
bombed site.
LENNY: Rubble. In the rubble.
JOEY: Yes, plenty of rubble.

(*Pause.*)

520 Well . . . you know . . . then we had them.
LENNY: You've missed out the best bit. He's missed out the
best bit!
JOEY: What bit?
LENNY: (*To* TEDDY.) His bird says to him, I don't mind, she
525 says, but I've got to have some protection. I've got to have
some contraceptive protection. I haven't got any contraceptive protection, old Joey says to her. In that case I won't
do it, she says. Yes you will says Joey, never mind about the
contraceptive protection.

(LENNY *laughs.*)

530 Even my bird laughed when she heard that. Yes, even she
gave out a bit of a laugh. So you can't say old Joey isn't a
bit of a knockout when he gets going, can you? And here
he is upstairs with your wife for two hours and he hasn't
even been the whole hog. Well, your wife sounds like a
535 bit of a tease to me, Ted. What do you make of it, Joey?
You satisfied? Don't tell me you're satisfied without going
the whole hog?

(*Pause.*)

JOEY: I've been the whole hog plenty of times. Sometimes . . .
you can be happy . . . and not go the whole hog. Now and
540 again . . . you can be happy . . . without going any hog.

(LENNY *stares at him.*)

(MAX *and* SAM *come in the front door and into the room.*)

MAX: Where's the whore? Still in bed? She'll make us all animals.

LENNY: The girl's a tease.
MAX: What?
LENNY: She's had Joey on a string.   545
MAX: What do you mean?
TEDDY: He had her up there for two hours and he didn't go
the whole hog.

(*Pause.*)

MAX: My Joey? She did that to my boy?

(*Pause.*)

To my youngest son? Tch, tch, tch, tch. How you feeling, 550
son? Are you all right?
JOEY: Sure I'm all right.
MAX: (*To* TEDDY.) Does she do that to you, too?
TEDDY: No.
LENNY: He gets the gravy.   555
MAX: You think so?
JOEY: No he don't.

(*Pause.*)

SAM: He's her lawful husband. She's his lawful wife.
JOEY: No he don't! He don't get no gravy! I'm telling you.
I'm telling all of you. I'll kill the next man who says he 560
gets the gravy.
MAX: Joey . . . what are you getting so excited about? (*To*
LENNY.) It's because he's frustrated. You see what happens?
JOEY: Who is?
MAX: Joey. No one's saying you're wrong. In fact, everyone's 565
saying you're right.

(*Pause.*)

(MAX *turns to the others.*)

You know something? Perhaps it's not a bad idea to have
a woman in the house. Perhaps it's a good thing. Who
knows? Maybe we should keep her.

(*Pause.*)

Maybe we'll ask her if she wants to stay.   570

(*Pause.*)

TEDDY: I'm afraid not, Dad. She's not well, and we've got to
get home to the children.
MAX: Not well? I told you, I'm used to looking after people
who are not so well. Don't worry about that. Perhaps we'll
keep her here.   575

(*Pause.*)

SAM: Don't be silly.
MAX: What's silly?
SAM: You're talking rubbish.
MAX: Me?
SAM: She's got three children.   580
MAX: She can have more! Here. If she's so keen.
TEDDY: She doesn't want any more.
MAX: What do you know about what she wants, eh, Ted?

TEDDY: (*Smiling.*) The best thing for her is to come home
585   with me, Dad. Really. We're married, you know.

(MAX *walks about the room, clicks his fingers.*)

MAX: We'd have to pay her, of course. You realize that? We
    can't leave her walking about without any pocket money.
    She'll have to have a little allowance.
JOEY: Of course we'll pay her. She's got to have some money
590   in her pocket.
MAX: That's what I'm saying. You can't expect a woman to
    walk about without a few bob to spend on a pair of stock-
    ings.

(*Pause.*)

LENNY: Where's the money going to come from?
595 MAX: Well, how much is she worth? What we talking about,
    three figures?
LENNY: I asked you where the money's going to come from.
    It'll be an extra mouth to feed. It'll be an extra body to
    clothe. You realize that?
600 JOEY: I'll buy her clothes.
LENNY: What with?
JOEY: I'll put in a certain amount out of my wages.
MAX: That's it. We'll pass the hat round. We'll make a dona-
    tion. We're all grown-up people, we've got a sense of re-
605   sponsibility. We'll all put a little in the hat. It's democratic.
LENNY: It'll come to a few quid, Dad.

(*Pause.*)

    I mean, she's not a woman who likes walking around in
    second-hand goods. She's up to the latest fashion. You
    wouldn't want her walking about in clothes which don't
610   show her off at her best, would you?
MAX: Lenny, do you mind if I make a little comment? It's not
    meant to be critical. But I think you're concentrating too
    much on the economic considerations. There are other
    considerations. There are the human considerations. You
615   understand what I mean? There are the human consider-
    ations. Don't forget them.
LENNY: I won't.
MAX: Well don't.

(*Pause.*)

    Listen, we're bound to treat her in something approxi-
620   mating, at least, to the manner in which she's accustomed.
    After all, she's not someone off the street, she's my
    daughter-in-law!
JOEY: That's right.
MAX: There you are, you see. Joey'll donate, Sam'll donate. . . .

(SAM *looks at him.*)

625   I'll put in a few bob out of my pension, Lenny'll cough
    up. We're laughing. What about you, Ted? How much
    you going to put in the kitty?
TEDDY: I'm not putting anything in the kitty.
MAX: What? You won't even help to support your own wife?
630   I thought he was a son of mine. You lousy stinkpig. Your
    mother would drop dead if she heard you take that attitude.

LENNY: Eh, Dad.

(LENNY *walks forward.*)

    I've got a better idea.
MAX: What?
LENNY: There's no need for us to go to all this expense. I   635
    know these women. Once they get started they ruin your
    budget. I've got a better idea. Why don't I take her up
    with me to Greek Street?

(*Pause.*)

MAX: You mean put her on the game?

(*Pause.*)

    We'll put her on the game. That's a stroke of genius, that's   640
    a marvellous idea. You mean she can earn the money
    herself—on her back?
LENNY: Yes.
MAX: Wonderful. The only thing is, it'll have to be short
    hours. We don't want her out of the house all night.   645
LENNY: I can limit the hours.
MAX: How many?
LENNY: Four hours a night.
MAX: (*Dubiously.*) Is that enough?
LENNY: She'll bring in a good sum for four hours a night.   650
MAX: Well, you should know. After all, it's true, the last thing
    we want to do is wear the girl out. She's going to have her
    obligations this end as well. Where you going to put her
    in Greek Street?
LENNY: It doesn't have to be right in Greek Street, Dad. I've   655
    got a number of flats all around that area.
MAX: You have? Well, what about me? Why don't you give
    me one?
LENNY: You're sexless.
JOEY: Eh, wait a minute, what's all this?   660
MAX: I know what Lenny's saying. Lenny's saying she can pay
    her own way. What do you think, Teddy? That'll solve all
    our problems.
JOEY: Eh, wait a minute. I don't want to share her.
MAX: What did you say?   665
JOEY: I don't want to share her with a lot of yobs!
MAX: Yobs! You arrogant git! What arrogance. (*To* LENNY.)
    Will you be supplying her with yobs?
LENNY: I've got a very distinguished clientèle, Joey. They're
    more distinguished than you'll ever be.   670
MAX: So you can count yourself lucky we're including you in.
JOEY: I didn't think I was going to have to share her!
MAX: Well, you *are* going to have to share her! Otherwise she
    goes straight back to America. You understand?

(*Pause.*)

    It's tricky enough as it is, without you shoving your oar   675
    in. But there's something worrying me. Perhaps she's not
    so up to the mark. Eh? Teddy, you're the best judge. Do
    you think she'd be up to the mark?

(*Pause.*)

    I mean what about all this teasing? Is she going to make a
    habit of it? That'll get us nowhere.   680

(*Pause.*)

TEDDY: It was just love play . . . I suppose . . . that's all I suppose it was.

MAX: Love play? Two bleeding hours? That's a bloody long time for love play!

685 LENNY: I don't think we've got anything to worry about on that score, Dad.

MAX: How do you know?

LENNY: I'm giving you a professional opinion.

(LENNY *goes to* TEDDY.)

LENNY: Listen, Teddy, you could help us, actually. If I were to
690 send you some cards, over to America . . . you know, very nice ones, with a name on, and a telephone number, very discreet, well, you could distribute them . . . to various parties, who might be making a trip over here. Of course, you'd get a little percentage out of it.

695 MAX: I mean, you needn't tell them she's your wife.

LENNY: No, we'd call her something else. Dolores, or something.

MAX: Or Spanish Jacky.

LENNY: No, you've got to be reserved about it, Dad. We could
700 call her something nice . . . like Cynthia . . . or Gillian.

(*Pause.*)

JOEY: Gillian.

(*Pause.*)

LENNY: No, what I mean, Teddy, you must know lots of professors, heads of departments, men like that. They pop
705 over here for a week at the Savoy, they need somewhere they can go to have a nice quiet poke. And of course you'd be in a position to give them inside information.

MAX: Sure. You can give them proper data. You know, the kind of thing she's willing to do. How far she'd be prepared to go with their little whims and fancies. Eh, Lenny? To what ex-
710 tent she's various. I mean if you don't know who does?

(*Pause.*)

I bet you before two months we'd have a waiting list.

LENNY: You could be our representative in the States.

MAX: Of course. We're talking in international terms! By the time we've finished Pan-American'll give us a discount.

(*Pause.*)

715 TEDDY: She'd get old . . . very quickly.

MAX: No . . . not in this day and age! With the health service? Old! How could she get old? She'll have the time of her life.

(RUTH *comes down the stairs, dressed.*)

(*She comes into the room.*)

(*She smiles at the gathering, and sits.*)

(*Silence.*)

TEDDY: Ruth . . . the family have invited you to stay, for a little while longer. As a . . . as a kind of guest. If you like the

idea I don't mind. We can manage very easily at home . . .   720
until you come back.

RUTH: How very nice of them.

(*Pause.*)

MAX: It's an offer from our heart.

RUTH: It's very sweet of you.

MAX: Listen . . . it would be our pleasure.   725

(*Pause.*)

RUTH: I think I'd be too much trouble.

MAX: Trouble? What are you talking about? What trouble? Listen, I'll tell you something. Since poor Jessie died, eh, Sam? we haven't had a woman in the house. Not one. Inside this house. And I'll tell you why. Because their   730
mother's image was so dear any other woman would have . . . tarnished it. But you . . . Ruth . . . you're not only lovely and beautiful, but you're kin. You're kin. You belong here.

(*Pause.*)

RUTH: I'm very touched.

MAX: Of course you're touched. I'm touched.   735

(*Pause.*)

TEDDY: But Ruth, I should tell you . . . that you'll have to pull your weight a little, if you stay. Financially. My father isn't very well off.

RUTH: (*To* MAX.) Oh, I'm sorry.

MAX: No, you'd just have to bring in a little, that's all. A few   740
pennies. Nothing much. It's just that we're waiting for Joey to hit the top as a boxer. When Joey hits the top . . . well . . .

(*Pause.*)

TEDDY: Or you can come home with me.

LENNY: We'd get you a flat.   745

(*Pause.*)

RUTH: A flat?

LENNY: Yes.

RUTH: Where?

LENNY: In town.

(*Pause.*)

But you'd live here, with us.   750

MAX: Of course you would. This would be your home. In the bosom of the family.

LENNY: You'd just pop up to the flat a couple of hours a night, that's all.

MAX: Just a couple of hours, that's all. That's all.   755

LENNY: And you make enough money to keep you going here.

(*Pause.*)

RUTH: How many rooms would this flat have?

LENNY: Not many.

RUTH: I would want at least three rooms and a bathroom.

760 LENNY: You wouldn't need three rooms and a bathroom.
MAX: She'd need a bathroom.
LENNY: But not three rooms.

(*Pause.*)

RUTH: Oh, I would. Really.
LENNY: Two would do.
765 RUTH: No. Two wouldn't be enough.

(*Pause.*)

I'd want a dressing-room, a rest-room, and a bedroom.

(*Pause.*)

LENNY: All right, we'll get you a flat with three rooms and a bathroom.
RUTH: With what kind of conveniences?
770 LENNY: All conveniences.
RUTH: A personal maid?
LENNY: Of course.

(*Pause.*)

We'd finance you, to begin with, and then, when you were established, you could pay us back, in instalments.
775 RUTH: Oh, no, I wouldn't agree to that.
LENNY: Oh, why not?
RUTH: You would have to regard your original outlay simply as a capital investment.

(*Pause.*)

LENNY: I see. All right.
780 RUTH: You'd supply my wardrobe, of course?
LENNY: We'd supply everything. Everything you need.
RUTH: I'd need an awful lot. Otherwise I wouldn't be content.
LENNY: You'd have everything.
RUTH: I would naturally want to draw up an inventory of
785 everything I would need, which would require your signatures in the presence of witnesses.
LENNY: Naturally.
RUTH: All aspects of the agreement and conditions of employment would have to be clarified to our mutual satis-
790 faction before we finalized the contract.
LENNY: Of course.

(*Pause.*)

RUTH: Well, it might prove a workable arrangement.
LENNY: I think so.
MAX: And you'd have the whole of your daytime free, of
795 course. You could do a bit of cooking here if you wanted to.
LENNY: Make the beds.
MAX: Scrub the place out a bit.
TEDDY: Keep everyone company.

(SAM *comes forward.*)

SAM: (*In one breath.*) MacGregor had Jessie in the back of my
800 cab as I drove them along.

(*He croaks and collapses.*)

(*He lies still.*)

(*They look at him.*)

MAX: What's he done? Dropped dead?
LENNY: Yes.
MAX: A corpse? A corpse on my floor? Get him out of here! Clear him out of here!

(JOEY *bends over* SAM.)

JOEY: He's not dead.   805
LENNY: He probably was dead, for about thirty seconds.
MAX: He's not even dead!

(LENNY *looks down at* SAM.)

LENNY: Yes, there's still some breath there.
MAX: (*Pointing at* SAM.) You know what that man had?
LENNY: Has.   810
MAX: Has! A diseased imagination.

(*Pause.*)

RUTH: Yes, it sounds a very attractive idea.
MAX: Do you want to shake on it now, or do you want to leave it till later?
RUTH: Oh, we'll leave it till later.   815

(TEDDY *stands.*)

(*He looks down at* SAM.)

TEDDY: I was going to ask him to drive me to London Airport.

(*He goes to the cases, picks one up.*)

Well, I'll leave your case, Ruth. I'll just go up the road to the Underground.
MAX: Listen, if you go the other way, first left, first right, you remember, you might find a cab passing there.   820
TEDDY: Yes, I might do that.
MAX: Or you can take the tube to Piccadilly Circus, won't take you ten minutes, and pick up a cab from there out to the Airport.
TEDDY: Yes, I'll probably do that.   825
MAX: Mind you, they'll charge you double fare. They'll charge you for the return trip. It's over the six-mile limit.
TEDDY: Yes. Well, bye-bye, Dad. Look after yourself.

(*They shake hands.*)

MAX: Thanks, son. Listen. I want to tell you something. It's been wonderful to see you.   830

(*Pause.*)

TEDDY: It's been wonderful to see you.
MAX: Do your boys know about me? Eh? Would they like to see a photo, do you think, of their grandfather?
TEDDY: I know they would.

(MAX *brings out his wallet.*)

MAX: I've got one on me. I've got one here. Just a minute. 835
Here you are. Will they like that one?

TEDDY: (*Taking it.*) They'll be thrilled.

(*He turns to* LENNY.)

   Good-bye, Lenny.

(*They shake hands.*)

LENNY: Ta-ta, Ted. Good to see you. Have a good trip.
840 TEDDY: Bye-bye, Joey.

(JOEY *does not move.*)

JOEY: Ta-ta.

(TEDDY *goes to the front door.*)

RUTH: Eddie.

(TEDDY *turns.*)

(*Pause.*)

   Don't become a stranger.

(TEDDY *goes, shuts the front door.*)

(*Silence.*)

(*The three men stand.*)

(RUTH *sits relaxed in her chair.* SAM *lies still.*)

(JOEY *walks slowly across the room. He kneels at her chair.*)

(*She touches his head, lightly.*)

(*He puts his head in her lap.*)

(MAX *begins to move above them, backwards and forwards.*)

(LENNY *stands still.* MAX *turns to* LENNY.)

MAX: I'm too old, I suppose. She thinks I'm an old man.

(*Pause.*)

845   I'm not such an old man.

(*Pause.*)

   (*To* RUTH.) You think I'm too old for you?

(*Pause.*)

Listen. You think you're just going to get that big slag all
the time? You think you're just going to have him . . . you're
going to just have him all the time? You're going to have to
work! You'll have to take them on, you understand?   850

(*Pause.*)

   Does she realize that?

(*Pause.*)

   Lenny, do you think she understands . . .

(*He begins to stammer.*)

   What . . . what . . . what . . . we're getting at? What . . .
we've got in mind? Do you think she's got it clear?

(*Pause.*)

   I don't think she's got it clear.   855

(*Pause.*)

   You understand what I mean? Listen, I've got a funny idea
she'll do the dirty on us, you want to bet? She'll use us,
she'll make use of us, I can tell you! I can smell it! You
want to bet?

(*Pause.*)

   She won't . . . be adaptable!   860

(*He falls to his knees, whimpers, begins to moan and sob. He stops
sobbing, crawls past* SAM's *body round her chair, to the other side of
her.*)

   I'm not an old man.

(*He looks up at her.*)

   Do you hear me?

(*He raises his face to her.*)

   Kiss me.

(*She continues to touch* JOEY's *head, lightly.*)

(LENNY *stands, watching.*)

(*Curtain.*)

Marguerite Duras

Born in 1914, Marguerite Duras was raised in Indochina (now Vietnam) during the period of French colonial rule; although she visited France occasionally, much of her youth was spent in Vietnam which would later provide the setting for her most powerful novels. After completing school in Saigon, Duras went to Paris in 1932, and took degrees in law and political science in 1935. She became a secretary in the Department of Colonies, and began to write as well; her first novel, *The Impudent Ones,* was published in 1943. Much of Duras's fiction involves her sense of the exploitation and poverty of the Vietnam of her youth, which provides the background for an intense exploration of personal relationships; this is particularly true of *The Sea Wall* (1950) and *The Lover* (1984); other novels, such as *Moderato Cantabile* (1958) and *The Vice-Consul* (1965), are set elsewhere in Asia and also confront the depredations of colonial exploitation.

Duras's drama similarly centers on interpersonal conflict, in short plays like *The Square* (1956), the murder-thriller, *The Viaduct* (1963), *Water and Forests* (1965), *La Musica* (1966), and in her first full-length play, *Days In the Trees* (1966). Duras's evocative sense of the visual is explored in other genres as well; her powerful film *Hiroshima Mon Amour* (1959), directed by Alain Resnais, won the International Critics' Prize at the Cannes Film Festival in 1959. In the 1960s, Duras's experiments with non-linear narrative led her to other cinematic projects: she directed the filming of her own *Days in the Trees* (1976), wrote two other films, *Aurélia Steiner* (1979) and *The Atlantic Man* (1982), and experimented with a simultaneous film/fiction version of the same work, *Destroy, She Said* (1969). *India Song* (1972), commissioned by Peter Hall for the opening of the Lyttleton Theater of London's National Theatre, is part of Duras's efforts to transgress the boundaries of genre. Based on her novel *The Vice-Consul*, it is at once a play and a film scenario. Duras produced and directed the film version of *India Song* in 1975.

INDIA SONG

In an interview published in 1987, Duras remarked on her interest in a theater in which language and acting would be held separate from one another, in which the voice alone would register the drama: "No need to gesticulate to show how the body is suffering because of the words being uttered: the whole drama resides in the words themselves and the body remains unmoved" (see *Practicalities,* Trans. Barbara Bray, New York: Grove Weidenfeld, 1990, p. 9). This special sense of the different registers of representation that can be achieved by the voice and the body stands at the center of Duras's play *India Song.* As she suggests in her "General Remarks" to the play, she has drawn characters from her novel *The Vice-Consul* and projected them "into new narrative regions." There are, nonetheless, a number of stylistic and narrative similarities between the two works. Both centrally concern Anne-Marie Stretter and the various colonial officials and businessmen who surround her—her husband, the Young Attaché (named Charles Rossett in the novel), Michael Richardson, and the mysterious Vice-Consul, waiting in disgrace in Calcutta after wildly shooting at lepers in the Shalimar Gardens of Lahore. And in both the novel and the play the Europeans, the "whites," live in a constant state of mental oppression, as the heat, the poverty, the futility of India seem to drive them to the brink of madness—and possibly beyond it. Finally, in both works, Anne-Marie—originally from Venice, mysteriously married, perhaps rescued by marriage in Savannakhet, Laos—is paired with the beggar woman, abandoned as a child, living on scraps of food from the Embassy and fish she catches and eats raw from the Ganges, a woman whose vitality, suffering, degradation, and dignity make her a kind of alter-ego to Stretter herself.

While both works have an extraordinary lyricism, *India Song* deploys that lyricism onstage in effective and original ways. *India Song* is centrally about desire, the desire that circulates around, and largely objectifies its central character, Anne-Marie Stretter. The play

Anne-Marie Stretter and the Vice-Consul in the 1999 Dutch company Het Zuidelijk Toneel's production of Marguerite Duras's *India Song*.

opens with Anne-Marie lying dead onstage and closes with her suicide; it is centrally occupied with how she is desired: by the male characters in the play, and, more powerfully, by the voices, male and female, that narrate the action. For in many ways *India Song* is less about the narrative, the "plot" of the interinvolved love affairs that the play brings together, than about how "Anne-Marie Stretter" is positioned as an object of desire, both in the narrative past and in the theatrical present. Much as the play's voices produce Anne-Marie, they also fetishize her, and the play systematically forces its audience into a similar position of voyeurism, where the desire for narrative closure becomes inseparable from the desire for Stretter herself. This dimension of the play becomes clear early in the action, where Stretter, the "*white of the naked body*" visible onstage "*freezes. Head thrown back. Gasping for air. Touching grace of the thin, fragile body. Stays like that, upright, exposed. Offered to the voices. (The voices are slow, stifled, a prey to desire—through this motionless body).*" The voices are prey to desire, but Stretter is also their victim; more important, the scene laminates the audience to the voices, suggesting that narration, the desire to tell the story, is inseparable from spectating, the desire to see Stretter there, powerless before our gaze on the stage. In *India Song,* the off-stage voices are unable to achieve a kind of narrative closure, to complete the story; what they are able to do is to evoke their dependence, their realization through the story they narrate. In this sense, Duras forges an explicit critique of theater in *India Song,* which suggests that the stage necessarily animates desire, renders it visible.

INDIA SONG

Marguerite Duras

TRANSLATED BY BARBARA BRAY

GENERAL REMARKS

The names of Indian towns, rivers, states, and seas are used here primarily in a musical sense.

All references to physical, human, or political geography are incorrect:

You can't drive from Calcutta to the estuary of the Ganges in an afternoon. Nor to Nepal.

The "Prince of Wales" hotel is not on an island in the Delta, but in Colombo.

And New Delhi, not Calcutta, is the administrative capital of India.

And so on.

The characters in the story have been taken out of a book called *The Vice-Consul* and projected into new narrative regions. So it is not possible to relate them back to the book and see *India Song* as a film or theatre adaptation of *The Vice-Consul*. Even where a whole episode is taken over from the book, its insertion into the new narrative means that it has to be read, seen, differently.

In fact, *India Song* follows on from *The Woman of the Ganges*. If *The Woman of the Ganges* hadn't been written, neither would *India Song*. The fact that it goes into and reveals an unexplored area of *The Vice-Consul* wouldn't have been a sufficient reason.

What was a sufficient reason was the discovery, in *The Woman of the Ganges*, of the *means* of exploration, revelation: the voices external to the narrative. This discovery made it possible to let the narrative be forgotten and put at the disposal of memories other than that of the author: memories which might remember, in the same way, any other love story. Memories that distort. That create.

Some voices from *The Woman of the Ganges* have been used here. And even some of their words.

That is about all that can be said.

As far as I know, no "India Song" yet exists. When it has been written, the author will make it available and it should be used for all performances of *India Song* in France and elsewhere.

If by any chance *India Song* were performed in France, there should be no public dress rehearsal. This does not apply to other countries.

ONE

NOTES ON VOICES 1 AND 2

VOICES 1 and 2 are women's voices. Young.

They are linked together by a love story.

Sometimes they speak of this love, their own. Most of the time they speak of another love, another story. But this other story leads us back to theirs. And vice versa.

Unlike the men's voices—VOICES 3 and 4, which don't come in until the end of the narrative—the women's voices are tinged with madness. Their sweetness is pernicious. Their memory of the love story is illogical, anarchic. Most of the time they are in a state of transport, a delirium, at once calm and feverish. VOICE 1 is consumed with the story of ANNE-MARIE STRETTER. VOICE 2 is consumed with its passion for VOICE 1.

They should always be heard with perfect clarity, but the level varies according to what they are saying. They are most immediately present when they veer toward their own story—that is, when, in the course of a perpetual shifting process, the love story of *India Song* is juxtaposed with their own. But there is a distinction. When they speak of the story we see unfolding before us, they rediscover it at the same time we do, and so are frightened and perhaps moved by it in the same way we are. But when they speak of their own story, they are always shot through with desire, and we should feel the difference between their two passions. Above all, we should feel the terror of VOICE 2 at the fascination the resuscitated story exerts over VOICE 1. VOICE 1 is in danger of being "lost" in the story of *India Song,* which is in the past, legendary, a model. VOICE 1 is in danger of departing its own life.

The voices are never raised, and their sweetness remains constant.

Blackout.

A tune from between the two wars, "India Song," is played slowly on the piano.

It is played right through, to cover the time—always long—that it takes the audience, or the reader, to emerge from the ordinary world they are in when the performance, or the book, begins.

"India Song" still.

Still.

And now it ends.

Now it is repeated, "farther away" than the first time, as if it were being played elsewhere.

Now it is played at its usual rhythm—blues.

The darkness begins to lighten.

As the dark slowly disperses, suddenly there are voices. Others besides ourselves were watching, hearing, what we thought we alone were watching and hearing. They are women. The voices are slow, sweet. Very close, enclosed like us in this place. And intangible, inaccessible.

VOICE 1: He followed her to India.
VOICE 2: Yes.

(Pause.)

VOICE 2: For he left everything.
   Overnight.
VOICE 1: The night of the dance?
VOICE 2: Yes.

5

(The light continues to grow. We still hear "India Song." The voices are silent for some time. Then they begin again:)

VOICE 1: Was it she who played the piano?
VOICE 2: *(hesitating)* Yes . . . but he played too . . . It was he who used sometimes, in the evening, to play the tune they
10   played in S. Thala . . .

(Silence.)
(A house in India. Huge. A "white people's" house. Divans. Armchairs.)
(Furniture of the period of "India Song.")
(A ceiling fan is working, but at nightmare slowness.)
(Net screens over the windows. Beyond, the paths of a large tropical garden. Oleanders. Palm trees.)
(Complete stillness. No wind outside. Inside, dense shadow. Is it the evening? We don't know. Space. Gilt. A piano. Unlit chandeliers. Indoor plants. Nothing moves, nothing except the fan, which moves with nightmare "unreality.")
(The slowness of the voices goes with the very slow growth of the light; their sweetness matches the poignancy of the setting.)

VOICE 1: *(as if reading)* "Michael Richardson was engaged to a girl from S. Thala. Lola Valérie Stein.
They were to have been married in the autumn.
Then there was the dance.
15   The dance at S. Thala . . ."

(Silence.)

VOICE 2: She arrived at the dance late . . . in the middle of the night . . .
VOICE 1: Yes . . . *dressed in black* . . .
What love, at the dance . . .
20   What desire . . .

(Silence.)
(As the light grows we see, set in this colonial décor, presences. There were people there all the time.)
(They are behind either a row of plants, or a fine net screen, or a transparent blind, or smoke from perfume burners—something which makes the second part of the space explored less easily visible.)
(Lying on a divan, long, slender, almost thin, is a woman dressed in black.)
(Sitting close to her is a man, also dressed in black.)
(Away from the lovers there is another man in black. [One of the men is smoking a cigarette—is that what made us sense there were people there?])
(VOICE 1 discovers—after we do—the presence of the woman in black.)

VOICE 1: *(tense, low)* Anne-Marie Stretter . . .

(It is as if VOICE 2 had not heard.)

VOICE 2: *(low)* How pale you are . . . what are you frightened of . . .

(No answer.)
(Silence.)
(The three people seem struck by a deathly stillness. "India Song" has stopped.)
(The voices grow lower, to match the deathliness of the scene.)

VOICE 2: After she died, he left India . . .

(Silence.)
(That was said all in one breath, as if recited slowly. So the woman in black, there in front of us, is dead. The light is now steady, somber.)
(Silence everywhere.)
(Near and far.)
(The voices are full of pain. Their memory, which was gone, is coming back. But they are as sweet, as gentle as before.)

VOICE 2: She's buried in the English cemetery . . .   25

(Pause.)

VOICE 1: . . . she died there?
VOICE 2: In the islands. *(Hesitates.)* One night. Found dead.

(Silence.)
("India Song" again, slow, far away.)
(At first we don't see the movement, the beginnings of movement. But it begins exactly on the first note of "India Song.")
(The woman in black and the man sitting near her begin to stir. Emerge from death. Their footsteps make no sound.)
(They are standing up.)
(They are close together.)
(What are they doing?)
(They are dancing.)
(Dancing. We only realize it when they are already dancing.)
(They go on, slowly, dancing.)
(When VOICE 1 speaks they have been dancing for some time.)
(VOICE 1 is gradually remembering.)

VOICE 1: The French Embassy in India . . .
VOICE 2: Yes.

(Pause.)

VOICE 1: That murmur? The Ganges?   30
VOICE 2: Yes.

(Pause.)

VOICE 1: That light?
VOICE 2: The monsoon.
VOICE 1: . . . no wind . . .
VOICE 2: *(continues)* . . . it will break over Bengal . . .   35
VOICE 1: The dust?
VOICE 2: The middle of Calcutta.

(Silence.)

VOICE 1: Isn't there a smell of flowers?
VOICE 2: Leprosy.

Silence.)
(They are still dancing to "India Song.")
(They are dancing. But it needs to be said.)
([As if otherwise it weren't sure. And so that the image and the voices coincide, touch.])

VOICE 2: They're dancing.   40

(Silence.)

VOICE 2: In the evening they used to dance.

(*Silence.*)
(*They dance.*)
(*So close they are one.*)
(*"India Song" fades in the distance.*)
(*They are merged together in the dance, almost motionless.*)
(*Now quite motionless.*)

VOICE 2: Why are you crying?

(*No answer.*)
(*Silence.*)
(*No more music.*)
(*A murmur in the distance. Then it stops. Other murmurs.*)
(*They, the man and woman, are still motionless in the silence hemmed in by sound.*)
(*Fixed. Arrested.*)
(*It lasts a long while.*)
(*Over the fixed couple:*)

VOICE 2: I love you so much I can't see any more, can't hear . . .
45   . . . can't live . . .

(*No answer.*)
(*Silence.*)
(*"India Song" comes back from far away. Slowly the couple unfreeze, come back to life.*)
(*Sound increases behind the music: the sound of Calcutta: a loud, a great murmur. All around, various other sounds. The regular cries of merchants. Dogs. Shouts in the distance.*)
(*As the sound outside increases, the sky in the garden becomes overcast. Murky light. No wind.*)
(*Silence.*)
(*The couple separate and turn toward the garden. They look out at it, motionless.*)
(*The second man sitting there also begins to look out at the garden.*)
(*The light grows still murkier.*)
(*The sound of Calcutta ceases.*)
(*Waiting.*)
(*Waiting. It is almost dark.*)
(*Suddenly the waiting is over:*)
(*The noise of the rain.*)
(*A cool, slaking noise.*)
(*It is raining over Bengal.*)
(*The rain cannot be seen. Only heard. As if it were raining everywhere except in the garden, deleted from life.*)
(*Everyone looks at the sound of the rain.*)

VOICE 2: (*scarcely voiced*) It's raining over Bengal . . .
VOICE 1: An ocean . . .

(*Silence.*)
(*Cries in the distance, of joy, shouts in Hindustani, the unknown language.*)
(*The light gradually returns.*)
(*The rain, the noise, very loud for a few seconds.*)
(*It grows less. Isolated shouts and laughter are heard more clearly through the sound of the rain.*)
(*The light continues to grow stronger.*)
(*Suddenly, clearer, nearer cries—a woman's. Her laughter.*)

VOICE 1: Someone's shouting . . . a woman . . .
VOICE 2: What?
VOICE 1: Disconnected words. She's laughing.   50
VOICE 2: A beggar.

(*Pause.*)

VOICE 1: Mad?
VOICE 2: Yes . . .

(*In the garden paths, sun after the rain. Moving sunlight. Patches of light, gray, pale.*)
(*Still the shouting and laughter of the* BEGGAR WOMAN.)

VOICE 1: Oh yes . . . I remember. She goes by the banks of the rivers . . . is she from Burma?   55
VOICE 2: Yes.

(*While the voices speak of the beggar, the three people move, leave the room by side doors.*)

VOICE 2: She's not Indian.
She comes from Savannakhet.
Born there.
VOICE 1: Ah yes . . . yes . . .   60
One day . . . she's been walking ten years, and one day, there in front of her, the Ganges?
VOICE 2: Yes.
And there she stops.
VOICE 1: Yes . . .   65

(*The three people have disappeared. The place is empty.*)
(*Someone speaking, almost shouting, in the distance, in a soft-sounding language, Laotian.*)

VOICE 1: (*after a pause*) Twelve children die while she's walking to Bengal . . . ?
VOICE 2: Yes. She leaves them. Sells them. Forgets them. (*Pause.*) On the way to Bengal, becomes barren.

(*The three people reach the garden and stroll slowly through the cool after the rain, moving through the patches of sunlight. In the distance, the shouting of the* BEGGAR WOMAN, *still. Suddenly, in the shouting, the word* SAVANNAKHET.)
(*The voices halt briefly. Then resume:*)

VOICE 1: Savannakhet—Laos?   70
VOICE 2: Yes. (*Pause.*) Seventeen . . . she's pregnant, she's seventeen . . . (*Pause.*) She's turned out by her mother, goes away. (*Pause.*) She asks the way to get lost. Remember? No one knows.
VOICE 1: (*pause*) Yes.   75
One day, she's been walking ten years, and one day: Calcutta, there in front of her.
She stays.

(*Silence.*)

VOICE 2: She's there on the banks of the Ganges, under the trees. She has forgotten.   80

(*Silence.*)
(*The three people go out of the garden.*)

(Movements of light, monsoon, in the empty garden.)
(The song of the beggar— "song of Savannakhet"—in the distance.)
*([*VOICE 2 *is informative, calm, gentle.])*

VOICE 2: Lepers burst like sacks of dust, you know.
VOICE 1: Don't suffer?
VOICE 2: No. Not a thing.
  Laugh.

(Silence.)

85 VOICE 2: They were there together, in Calcutta. The white
    woman and the other. During the same years.

(The voices are silent.)
*(A distant part of the garden, so far very dark, as if neglected by the
lighting, gradually becomes visible. It is revealed by spotlights—ex-
tremely slowly, but regularly, mathematically.)*
*(Far away, the song of Savannakhet—coming, going. Sound of Cal-
cutta, in the distance.)*
*(The wire netting round a tennis court emerges from the darkness.
Against the wire a woman's bicycle—red.)*
(The place is deserted.)
(The voices recognize these things and are afraid:)

VOICE 1: *(smothered exclamation of fear)* The tennis courts, de-
    serted . . .
VOICE 2: *(the same)* . . . Anne-Marie Stretter's red bicycle . . .

(Silence.)
*(A man has come into the garden. Tall, thin, dressed in white. He
walks slowly. His footsteps make no sound.)*
*(He gazes around him at the stillness everywhere. Gazes for some
time. Tries to see into the house: no one there.)*
*(Now what is he looking at? We don't know at first. Then it becomes
clear: he's looking at* ANNE-MARIE STRETTER*'s red bicycle by the
deserted tennis courts.)*
*(He goes over to the bicycle. Stops. Hesitates. Doesn't go any nearer.
Looks, stares at it. [The voices are low, scared.])*

90 VOICE 2: . . . he comes every night . . .

(Pause.)

VOICE 1: The French Vice-Consul in Lahore . . .
VOICE 2: Yes.
    . . . in Calcutta in disgrace . . .

(Silence.)
*(Slowly, the man in white moves. He walks. He goes along a path.
He goes away.)*
(Disappears.)
(After he has disappeared, everything remains in suspense.)
(Silence. Fear.)
(The song of Savannakhet, in the distance, innocent.)
(Then, two shots.)
(The first makes the light go dim.)
(The second makes it go out.)
(Silence.)
(Blackout.)
*(The song of Savannakhet stopped when the shots were fired. As if
they had been aimed at it.)*
(Silence.)

(Blackout.)
(The voices are very quiet, terrified.)

VOICE 2: Someone fired a gun under the trees . . . on the
    banks of the Ganges . . .   95

(Silence.)

VOICE 1: It was a song of Savannakhet . . . ?
VOICE 2: Yes.

(Silence.)
*(By a strictly symmetrical inversion, and without passing through
any intermediate stages, the light becomes the same as it was when
the first shot made it go dim.)*
(This stands for night.)
(It is night.)
(The place, the stage, is still empty.)
(The only movement—that of the nightmare fan.)
(Time passes over the empty place.)
(Silence.)
*(A Hindu servant dressed in white goes by, passing through the
drawing rooms of the French Embassy.)*
(He has gone. Emptiness again.)
(Far away, the song of Savannakhet begins again: the BEGGAR
WOMAN *wasn't killed.)*
(The voices are still low, frightened.)

VOICE 1: . . . she's not dead . . .
VOICE 2: Can't die.
VOICE 1: *(scarcely heard)* No . . .   100

(Silence.)

VOICE 2: She goes hunting at night beside the Ganges. For
    food . . .

(No answer.)
(Silence.)

VOICE 1: Where's the one dressed in black?
VOICE 2: Out. Every evening.
    She comes back when it's dark   105

(Silence.)
*(A servant enters, lights a lamp, very faint, in a corner of the room.
Does various things.)*
(Goes away [but remains visible].)
(Comes back.)
(Opens a window.)
*(Perhaps he lights some sticks of incense against the mosquitoes—in
which case the audience will be able to smell it.)*
(Empties ashtrays.)

VOICE 2: She's back.
    The Embassy's black Lancia has just come through the
    gates.

(Silence.)
(The servant goes out.)
*(The place remains empty for a few more seconds, and then the
woman in black enters the darkness. She is barefoot. Her hair is
loose. She is wearing a short wrap of loose black cotton.)*

(*The scene is very long and slow.*)
(*Slowly she goes and stands under the nightmare fan. Stays there.*)
(*Puts up her hands and thrusts her hair away from her body in a gesture of exhaustion—someone stifling from the heat. Then lets her arms fall down by her sides.*)
(*Through the opening of the wrap, the white of the naked body.*)
(*She freezes. Head thrown back. Gasping for air. Trying to escape out of the heat.*)
(*Touching grace of the thin, fragile body.*)
(*Stays like that, upright, exposed. Offered to the voices.*)
([*The voices are slow, stifled, a prey to desire—through this motionless body.*])

VOICE 2: (*smothered outburst*) How lovely you look dressed in
110   white . . .

(*Pause.*)

VOICE 1: I'd like to go and visit the woman of the Ganges . . .

(*Held pause.*)

VOICE 1: . . . the white woman . . .
VOICE 2: (*pause*) The one who . . . ?
VOICE 1: Her . . .
115   VOICE 2: . . . dead in the islands . . .
VOICE 1: Eyes dead, blinded with light.
VOICE 2: Yes.
     There under the stone.
     In a bend in the Ganges.

(*Silence.*)
(*Still motionless before us, the dead woman of the Ganges.*)
(*The voices are a song so quiet it does not awaken her death.*)
(*Apparently nothing changes, nothing happens. But suddenly, fear.*)

120   VOICE 1: (*low, frightened*) What is it?

(*No answer.*)

VOICE 1: (*as before*) What time is it?
VOICE 2: (*pause*) Four o'clock.
     Black night.

(*Pause.*)

VOICE 1: No one can sleep?
125   VOICE 2: No.

(*Silence.*)
(*Tears on the woman's face.*)
(*The features remain unmoving.*)
(*She is weeping. Without suffering.*)
(*A state of tears.*)
(*The voices speak of the heat, they speak of desire—as if the voices were issuing from the weeping body.*)

VOICE 1: The heat
     Impossible
     Terrible

(*Pause.*)

VOICE 2: Another storm . . .
130   Approaching Bengal . . .

VOICE 1: (*pause*) Coming from the islands . . .
VOICE 2: (*pause*) The estuaries.
     Inexhaustible . . .

(*Silence.*)

VOICE 1: What's that sound?
VOICE 2: (*pause*) Her weeping.   135

(*Silence.*)

VOICE 1: Doesn't suffer, does she . . . ?
VOICE 2: She neither.
     A leper, of the heart.

(*Silence.*)

VOICE 1: Can't bear it . . . ?
VOICE 2: No.   140
     Can't bear it.
     Can't bear India.

(*Silence.*)
(*A man enters through the door on the left. He too is wearing a black wrap.*)
(*He halts, looks at her.*)
(*Then slowly goes over to her, a statue in her tears, under the fan, asleep.*)
(*He looks at her—asleep standing up. Goes right up to her.*)
(*Passes lightly over her face a hand outspread in a caress. Takes his hand away, looks at it: it is wet from the tears.*)

VOICE 2: (*very low*) She's asleep.

(*With infinite precaution, the man takes up the weeping woman and lays her down on the floor.*)
(*He's the man we have already seen, the man she danced with at the dance in S. Thala:* MICHAEL RICHARDSON.)
(*He sits down beside the outstretched body.*)
(*Looks at it.*)
(*Uncovers the body so that it is better exposed to the cool—imaginary—from the fan.*)
(*Strokes her forehead. Wipes away the tears, the sweat. Caresses the sleeping body.*)
(*Doesn't go close. Stays there watching over her sleep.*)
(*The voices slow down to the rhythm of the man's movements, taking up again in a sort of sung complaint the themes adjacent to the main story.*)

VOICE 1: He loved her more than anything in the world.
VOICE 2: (*pause*) More even than that . . .   145

(*Silence.*)
(VOICE 2 *spoke as if of its own love.*)

VOICE 1: Where was the girl from S. Thala?

(*No answer.*)

VOICE 1: (*as if reading*) "From behind the indoor plants in the
     bar, she watches them. (*Pause.*) It was only at dawn . . .
     (*Stops.*) . . . when the lovers were going toward the door
     of the ballroom that Lola Valérie Stein uttered a cry."   150

(Silence.)
(In the distance, a regular cry in Hindustani. Someone selling something again.)
(It stops.)
(Quiet.)

VOICE 2: At four in the morning, sometimes, sleep comes.

(Silence.)
(The lover is still beside the sleeping body.)
(He looks at it.)
(Takes the hands, touches them. Looks at them. They fall back, dead.)
(Silence.)

VOICE 1: She never got over it, the girl from S. Thala?
VOICE 2: Never.
VOICE 1: They didn't hear her cry out?
155 VOICE 2: No.
    Couldn't hear any more.
    Couldn't see.

(Pause.)

VOICE 1: *(pause)* They abandoned her? *(Pause.)* Killed her?
VOICE 2: Yes.

(Pause.)

160 VOICE 1: And with this crime behind them . . .
VOICE 2: *(scarcely heard)* Yes.

(Silence.)

VOICE 1: What did the girl from S. Thala want?
VOICE 2: To go with them
    See them
165   The lovers of the Ganges: to see them.

(Silence.)
(That is what we are doing: seeing.)
(Slowly the man lies down beside the sleeping body. His hand goes on caressing the face, the body.)
(Far away, distant sounds, oars, water. Then laughter, a zither, fading in the distance.)
(Then it stops.)

VOICE 2: Listen . . .
    Ganges fishermen . . .
    Musicians . . .

(Silence again.)
(The voices speak of the heat again. Of their desire.)

VOICE 2: *(very slow)* What darkness
170   What heat
    Unmitigated
    Deathly

(Silence.)
(A voice that is clear, implacable, terrifying:)

VOICE 2: I love you with a desire that is absolute.

(No answer.)
(Silence.)
(The hand of MICHAEL RICHARDSON—*the lover—immediately stops caressing the body, as if arrested by what* VOICE 2 *has just said.)*
(It lies there where it is on the body.)
(Silence.)
(A second man enters the room. He stands in the doorway for a moment, looking at the lovers.)
*(*MICHAEL RICHARDSON's *hand starts to move again, caressing the uncovered body.)*
(The man goes over to them.)
(Like the lover, he sits down beside her.)
(The lover's hand now moves more slowly.)
(Then it stops.)
(The newcomer does not caress the woman's body.)
(He lies down too.)
(All three lie motionless under the fan.)
(Silence.)
(Rain.)
(Another storm over Bengal.)
(The sound of rain over sleep.)
(The voices are like breaths of coolness, gentle murmurs.)

VOICE 1: . . . rain . . .
VOICE 2: . . . yes . . .   175

(Pause.)

VOICE 1: . . . cool . . .

(Silence.)
(The sky gets lighter, but it is still night.)
(Gradually, music: Beethoven's 14th Variation on a Theme of Diabelli. Piano, very distant.)
(The rain slackens.)
(In its place, a white light. Patches of moonlight on the garden paths. No wind.)
(The three bodies, their eyes closed, sleep.)
(The voices, interwoven, in a climax of sweetness, are about to sing the legend of ANNE-MARIE STRETTER. *A slow recitative made up of scraps of memory. Out of it, every so often, a phrase emerges, intact, from oblivion.)*

VOICE 1: Venice.
    She was from Venice . . .
VOICE 2: Yes. The music was in Venice.
    A hope in music . . .   180
VOICE 1: *(pause)* She never gave up playing?
VOICE 2: No.

(Silence.)

VOICE 1: *(very slow)* Anna Maria Guardi . . .
VOICE 2: Yes.

(Silence.)

VOICE 1: The first marriage, the first post . . . ?   185
VOICE 2: Savannakhet, Laos.
    She's married to a French colonial official.
    She's eighteen.

VOICE 1: (*remembering*) Ah yes . . . a river . . .
190   . . . she's sitting by a river. Already . . .
   Looking at it.
VOICE 2: The Mekong.
VOICE 1: (*pause*) She's silent?
   Crying?
195 VOICE 2: Yes. They say: "She can't get acclimatized. She'll have to be sent back to Europe."

(*Pause.*)

VOICE 1: Couldn't bear it. Even then.
VOICE 2: Even then.

(*Silence.*)

VOICE 1: (*visionary*) Those walls all round her?
200 VOICE 2: The grounds of the chancellery.
VOICE 1: (*as before*) The sentries?
VOICE 2: Official.
VOICE 1: Even then . . .
VOICE 2: Yes.
205 VOICE 1: Even then, couldn't bear it.
VOICE 2: No.

(*Silence.*)

VOICE 2: One day a government launch calls. Monsieur Stretter is inspecting the posts on the Mekong.
VOICE 1: (*pause*) He takes her away from Savannakhet?
210 VOICE 2: Yes. Takes her with him.
   Takes her with him for seventeen years through the capitals of Asia.

(*Pause.*)

VOICE 2: You find her in Peking.
   Then in Mandalay.
215   In Bangkok.
   Rangoon. Sydney.
   Lahore.
   Seventeen years.
   You find her in Calcutta.
220   In Calcutta:
   She dies.

(*Silence.*)
(*The tall thin man dressed in white enters the garden.*)
(*The voices haven't seen him.*)
(*He stops. Looks through the screens on the windows at the three sleeping forms.*)
(*Stops, looking at her, the woman.*)
(*The voices still haven't seen him.*)

VOICE 1: Michael Richardson used to go to S. Thala in the summer.
VOICE 2: Yes.
225   She didn't go often.
   But that summer . . .
VOICE 1: He was English, Michael Richardson?
VOICE 2: Yes. (*Pause. As if reading:*) "Michael Richardson started a marine insurance company in Bengal, so that he
230   could stay in India."

VOICE 1: Near her.
VOICE 2: Yes.

(*The man goes away. We see him, from behind, going slowly along the path toward the deserted tennis courts.*)

VOICE 1: The other man who's sleeping?
VOICE 2: Passing through. A friend of the Stretters'.
   She belongs to whoever wants her.   235
   Gives her to whoever will have her.
VOICE 1: (*pause, pain*) Prostitution in Calcutta.
VOICE 2: Yes.
   She's a Christian without God.
   Splendor.   240
VOICE 1: (*very low*) Love.
VOICE 2: (*scarcely heard*) Yes . . .

(*Silence.*)
(*The thin man goes toward the red bicycle propped against the wire around the deserted tennis courts.*)
(*The voices have seen him.*)
(*They resume very softly, in fear.*)

VOICE 1: He's back in the garden.
VOICE 2: Yes . . . Every night . . .
   Looks at her . . .   245

(*Silence.*)
(*The man hesitates. Then goes up to* ANNE-MARIE STRETTER'*s bicycle.*)

VOICE 1: He never spoke to her . . .
VOICE 2: No.
   Never went near . . .

(*Halt.*)

VOICE 1: The male virgin of Lahore . . .
VOICE 2: Yes . . .   250

(*The man is beside the bicycle.*)
(*Puts out his hands. Hesitates.*)
(*Then touches it.*)
(*Strokes it.*)
(*Leans forward and holds it in his arms.*)
(*Stays clasping* ANNE-MARIE STRETTER'*s bicycle—frozen in this gesture of desire.*)
(*Silence.*)
(*Almost imperceptibly, a movement over by the sleeping bodies. It is she.*)
(*As he bends over the bicycle, she, by a converse movement, sits up. In the same slow rhythm she sits up and turns toward the garden.*)
(ANNE-MARIE STRETTER *looks at the man in white with his arms around her bicycle.*)
(*Silence.*)
(*Suddenly the man lets go of the bicycle. Remains with his arms hanging by his sides, his hands open, in an attitude of passion and despair.*)
(*Sound of a man sobbing [the only sound heard directly].*)
(*The woman still looks, sitting with her hands flat on the ground.*)
(*The sobs cease.*)
(*The man gets up.*)

(He stands facing the bicycle.)
(Then slowly turns around.)
(Sees her.)
(The woman doesn't move.)
(Silence.)
(They look at each other.)
(This lasts several seconds.)
(Silence.)
(It is the man who stops looking.)
(First he turns his face away. Then his body moves.)
(He walks away.)
(She, still sitting, watches him walk away.)
(Then, after he has slowly disappeared from sight, she takes up her former position, asleep under the nightmare fan.)
(Silence.)
(Stillness.)
(Sobs of the VICE-CONSUL *in the distance.)*
(Silence again.)
(In the garden the light grows dim again, murky.)
(No wind in the deserted garden.)

VOICE 2: *(afraid, very low)* The sound of your heart frightens me . . .

(Silence.)
(Another stirring in the still mass of the three sleeping bodies: MICHAEL RICHARDSON'S *hand reaches out to the woman's body, caresses it, stays there.)*
*(*MICHAEL RICHARDSON *was not asleep.)*
(The light gets dimmer still.)
*(*VOICE 2 *is full of desire and terror.)*

VOICE 2: Your heart, so young, a child's . . .

(No answer.)
(Silence.)

VOICE 2: Where are you?

(No answer.)
(Silence.)
(Shouts in the distance: the VICE-CONSUL. *Cries of despair. Heart-rending, obscene.)*

255 VOICE 1: *(distant)* What's he shouting?
  VOICE 2: The name she used to have in Venice, in the desert of Calcutta.

(Silence.)
(The cries fade in the distance.)
(Disappear.)
*(*VOICE 2, *all in one breath, in fear, tells the story of the crime, the crime committed in Lahore:)*

VOICE 2: *(low)* "He fired a gun. One night, from his balcony in Lahore, he fired on the lepers in the Shalimar gardens."

(Silence.)
*(*VOICE 1 *is gentle—calm and gentle:)*

260 VOICE 1: Couldn't bear it.
  VOICE 2: No.
  VOICE 1: India—couldn't bear India?

VOICE 2: No.
VOICE 1: What couldn't he bear about it?
VOICE 2: The idea.   265

(Silence.)
(It is getting darker. The bodies grow less and less distinguishable. Above them the fan goes on turning, the blades gleaming slowly.)
(You can no longer tell one body from another.)
(Silence.)

VOICE 1: A black Lancia is speeding along the road to Chandernagor . . .

(No answer.)

VOICE 1: *(continuing)* . . . It was there . . . there that she first . . .

(The voice stops.)

VOICE 2: Yes.
  Brought back by ambulance.   270
  They talked about an accident . . .

(Pause.)

VOICE 1: She's been thin ever since.
VOICE 2: *(scarcely heard)* Yes.

(Beethoven's 14th Variation on a Theme of Diabelli. Distant.)
(Total blackout.)
(Then, beyond the garden, gleams in the sky. Either day or fire—rust-colored fire.)
(The voice is slow: a calm declaration.)

VOICE 1: Those gleams over there?
VOICE 2: The burning-ghats.   275
VOICE 1: Burning people who've starved to death?
VOICE 2: Yes.
  It will soon be daylight.

(Silence.)
(The 14th Variation is heard till the end, over the gleams from the burning-ghats.)
(Blackout.)

TWO

We are in the same place as before.

The only difference is that the right side of it is now revealed, as if the angle of vision had been changed. Doors opening on the reception rooms on one side, and on the other on the garden.

(As if these rooms were in a wing of the Embassy.)

Bright light everywhere. Chandeliers.

Chinese lanterns in the garden.

Silence.

It is as if the French Embassy were quite empty.

Nothing can be seen of the reception rooms except the light coming out of the doors and illuminating the garden.

All remains empty for a few seconds.

Then, *without a sound, a servant passes through.*

Carrying a tray with glasses of champagne, he goes through and out toward the right.

Silence again. Emptiness again.

Waiting.

Then, suddenly, noise.

The noise of the reception begins quite suddenly, full volume. The party is triggered off as if by some mechanism: the noise bursts forth instantaneously from behind the walls, through the open doors.

A woman is singing "The Merry Widow," accompanied by a piano and two violins.

Behind the music:

The sound of many conversations all merging into one.

The sound of glasses, crockery, etc.

But the feet of the dancers make no sound.

No conversation will take place on the stage, or be seen. It will never be the actors on the stage who are speaking.

The only exception to this rule is that the sobs of the French VICE-CONSUL *are both seen and heard.*

When the conversations recorded here take place, the sound of the reception grows fainter.

Often it almost stops: for example, during the conversations between the YOUNG ATTACHÉ *and* ANNE-MARIE STRETTER, *and between her and the French* VICE-CONSUL. *It is as if the guests at the reception, intrigued, watched them talking instead of talking themselves. So the fading of the sound is not arbitrary.*

All the conversations, whether private or not, whether they make the guests around them go quiet or not, should give the impression that only the spectators hear them clearly—not the guests.

So the sound of the reception should be heard, however faintly, behind all the conversations. The fact that these conversations are now and again mingled with conversations on other subjects should prove that the private conversations are not audible, or hardly, to the guests. So also the fact that some of what is overheard is sometimes repeated, but always more or less wrongly—with slight mistakes which show that only the spectators hear the private conversations properly.

The sound of the reception should come from the right and from the stage, and from the auditorium, as if the reception were taking place beyond the walls of the auditorium, too.

ANNE-MARIE STRETTER *wears a black dress—the one she wore at the dance in S. Thala—the one described in* Le Ravissement de Lol. V. Stein.

The men wear black dinner jackets, with the exception of the French VICE-CONSUL *in Lahore, who wears a white one.*

The other women at the reception wear long dresses, colored.

The reception overflows, all the time it lasts, either into the garden or into the place we already know: ANNE-MARIE STRETTER'*s private drawing room.*

From the point of view of sound, the image, the stage, plays the part of an echo chamber. Passing through that space, the voices should sound, to the spectator, like his own "internal rending" voice.

The set should seem accidental—stolen from a "whole" that is by its nature inaccessible, that is, the reception.

The diction should in general be extremely precise. It should not seem completely natural. During rehearsals some slight defect should be settled on, common to all the voices.

One ought to get the impression of a reading, but one which is reported, that is, one which has been performed before. That is what is meant by a "reading-to-himself voice."

To repeat: not a single word is uttered on the stage.

(*"Heure exquise" sung by a woman. Then repeated by the orchestra.*)

(*A waltzing couple cross a corner of the garden.*)

Some women are talking: (*quite close*)
——This is the last reception before the monsoon.
——What? Do you mean to say the monsoon hasn't begun?
——Not really. It'll be at its height in a fortnight. No sun for six months . . . You'll see . . . No one can sleep . . . They just wait for the storms to break . . .   5

(*An Indian servant passes through, on his way to the reception. He carries a tray with brimming glasses of champagne.*)
(*Two couples go through, waltzing. Slowly. Disappear.*)

Some women are talking: (*farther away*)
——She invited the French Vice-Consul in Lahore . . .
——Yes. At the last minute she sent him a card: "Come." The Ambassador didn't say anything.

(*A young man arrives. He stops and looks around. Clearly he isn't familiar with this part of the Embassy. He looks tired, as if he wants to get away from the reception. He looks out toward the deserted tennis courts.*)
(*As he looks, a couple dance across a corner of the garden and disappear.*)

Some men are talking: (*about the young man*)
——Who is he?
——The new Attaché . . . Only been out here a month . . .   10 He can't get used to it.
——It's the first time he's been here.

(*Pause.*)

——He'll be back. He'll be invited, he'll go to the islands . . . The Ambassador asks people to stay there. For her—for his wife.   15

(*Pause.*)

——What makes you think *he'll* be asked?

(Pause.)

——He looks so troubled . . . She doesn't like people who
  get used to it.
——Are there any?
20 ——Some . . .
——Clubs, to keep India out, that's the answer . . . isn't it?
——Yes.

(The YOUNG ATTACHÉ *goes on looking around. Then he turns to-
ward the dancing, watches the reception. And goes back to it.)*
("Heure exquise" ends.)
(There is a moment without music.)
*(Only the sound of the reception. No laughter. A sort of general de-
jection.)*
(Some women go by in the garden, looking curiously toward ANNE-
MARIE STRETTER'*s drawing room. They fan themselves with big
white fans. They are gone.)*

A man speaks (the Ambassador):
——I think my wife may have mentioned it . . . we'd be very
  glad if you'd join us some time in the islands . . . There are
25 some newcomers one feels specially attracted to . . . And
  the rules governing ordinary society don't apply here . . .
  We don't choose . . . *(A smile in the voice.)* You will? The
  residency looks out on the Indian Ocean, it dates from the
  days of the Company, it's worth seeing. And the islands are
30 very healthy, especially the main one, it's the biggest island
  in the Delta.

(Silence.)

Men talking:
——He used to write, the Ambassador . . . Did you know?
  I've read a little volume of his poems . . .
——So I've heard . . . They say it's because of her he gave it
35 up . . .

("Heure exquise" has been followed by a tango.)
(The French VICE-CONSUL *in Lahore has come into the garden. He
is wearing a white dinner jacket. He is alone. No one seems to have
noticed him yet.)*

Two conversations (1 and 2) between men and women:
No. 1
——She might have spared us the embarrassment . . .

(Pause.)

——What exactly did he do? I never know what goes on . . .
——The worst possible thing . . . How can I explain . . . ?
——The worst . . . ?

(Silence.)

No. 2
40 ——An intriguing woman. No one really knows how she
  spends her time . . . What does she do? She must do something . . .
——She must read . . . Between her siesta and when it's time
  to go out, what else could she do . . .
45 ——Parcels of books come for her from Venice . . . And she
  spends some time with her daughters . . . In the dry sea-

son they play tennis—you see all three of them going by
the office, dressed in white . . .

(Pause.)

——The fact that one wonders what she does, that's what's
strangest of all.   50

(Silence.)

No. 1 *(continued)*
——Did he kill somebody?
——He used to fire shots at the Shalimar gardens at night . . .
  You knew that . . . ? But bullets were found in the mirrors
  of his own residence in Lahore . . .
——He was shooting at himself . . . *(Little laugh.)*   55

(No answer.)

——It's difficult to tell which are the lepers . . .
——You see, you do know: you talk about the lepers . . .

(Silence.)

No. 2 *(continued)*
——She goes cycling too, very early in the morning, in the
  grounds. Not during the monsoon, of course . . .
No. 1 *(continued)*
——What's the official version?   60
——His nerves gave way . . . Often happens.

(Pause.)

——Funny, he forces you to think about him . . .

*(*MICHAEL RICHARDSON *has entered. He is not wearing a dinner
jacket. He sits down. He smokes a cigarette. He doesn't look toward
the garden.)*
(In the garden, the VICE-CONSUL: *he looks at* MICHAEL
RICHARDSON.*)*
(Two women enter on the right, and stop. They have seen MICHAEL
RICHARDSON *and look at him with curiosity. He doesn't see them.)*
(A servant goes by with glasses of champagne. He offers one to
MICHAEL RICHARDSON, *and goes.)*
(The tango, as if in the distance.)
*(*MICHAEL RICHARDSON *gets up, begins to go toward the reception,
looks at it from some distance, then turns around: sees the* VICE-
CONSUL *in the garden.)*
(Then the women see him too and draw back.)

Women speaking: (low)
——Look . . . Michael Richardson . . .

(Pause.)

——Yes . . . He doesn't attend receptions?
——No, only at the end, toward the middle of the night.   65
  When there's just a few friends left . . .

(Pause.)

——What a business . . . what love . . . They say he gave up
  everything to be with her . . .
——Everything. He was engaged to be married. Everything.
  Overnight . . .   70

(*Silence.*)
(MICHAEL RICHARDSON *makes a movement toward the* VICE-CONSUL—*toward the gate into the garden.*)
(*The* VICE-CONSUL *turns away.*)
(MICHAEL RICHARDSON *stops.*)
(*The two women watch.*)

Women talking: (*low, afraid*)
——Look in the garden . . .
——Is that him?
——Yes.
——So thin . . . and the face . . . as if it were grafted on . . .
75   so pale. . .

(*Silence.*)
(MICHAEL RICHARDSON *turns back toward the reception.*)
(*The watching women disappear.*)

Women: (*continued*)
——Do they know each other?
——Evidently not . . .

(*Silence.*)
(*The* VICE-CONSUL *looks at the reception.* MICHAEL RICHARDSON *looks again at him. The* VICE-CONSUL *seems absorbed, and does not notice him.*)

Men talking:
——He used to fire shots at night from his balcony.
——Yes. He used to shout too. Half naked.
80 ——What?
——Disconnected words. He used to laugh.

(*Pause.*)

——And no woman was ever close enough to him, in Lahore, to be able to say anything . . . ?
——No. Never.
85 ——How is that possible?
——His house, no one ever went to his house in Lahore . . .
——It's terrifying . . . Such abstinence . . . Terrible . . .

(*Silence.*)
(MICHAEL RICHARDSON *turns toward the reception, tries to make out what the* VICE-CONSUL *can be watching so avidly.*)

Men and women:
——Did you hear? The Ambassador said to the Young Attaché: "People avoid him, I know . . . he frightens them . . .
90   But I'd be grateful if you'd go and have a word with him."

(*Pause.*)

——What's known about his background? his childhood?
——His father was a bank manager in Neuilly. An only child. The mother's supposed to have left the father. Expelled from several schools for bad behavior. Brilliant at
95   his work, but after high school . . . That's all . . .
——So they don't know anything about him really?
——Nothing.

(*Pause.*)

——Isn't there in all of us . . . how shall I put it . . . ? a chance in a thousand we might be like him . . . I mean . . . (*Pause.*)
100   I'm only asking . . .

(*No answer.*)
(*Silence.*)
(*A couple come to the edge of the garden. They see the* VICE-CONSUL, *and don't go any farther.* MICHAEL RICHARDSON *looks at them. They hesitate. Turn away. Go back to the reception.*)
(*The* VICE-CONSUL *looks at the reception and laughs.*)
(*Some women go through the garden fanning themselves. They don't see the* VICE-CONSUL. *They stop and look at the reception from a distance: something catches their attention:*)

Women:
——Who's she dancing with?
——The Ambassador.
——You knew he took her away from some official in the wilds of French Indochina . . . I can't quite remember where . . . Laos, I think . . .   105
——Savannakhet?
——That's it . . .
——Don't you remember? ". . . slow launch with awnings, slow journey up the Mekong to Savannakhet . . . wide expanse of water between virgin forest, gray paddyfields . . .   110
and in the evening, clusters of mosquitoes clinging to the mosquito nets . . ."
——What a memory! (*Little laugh.*)

(*Silence.*)

——Seventeen years they've been wandering around Asia.

(*Silence.*)
(*They all look toward the reception, toward the Ambassador dancing with his wife.*)
(*The* VICE-CONSUL *laughs silently.*)

Men:
——Has he ever talked to anyone about Lahore?   115
——Never.
——About anything else?
——I don't think so . . . He gets letters from France. An elderly aunt . . . The letters were intercepted . . . Apparently . . . he told the Secretary of the European Club he was in   120
a reformatory . . . when he was fifteen . . . in the North . . .
——He talks to him, then? That drunk?
——Well . . . the other one's asleep, so really he's talking to himself . . . (*Little laugh.*)
——So he doesn't talk to anyone then . . .   125
——That's right . . . (*Little laugh.*)
——What did he find in India to set him off? Didn't he know about it before? Did he actually have to see it? It's not so difficult to find out . . .
Women:
——There are moments when he seems happy. Look . . . As   130
if he were suddenly madly happy . . .

(*Pause.*)

——Perhaps when she dances . . .
——What an idea . . .
——I've only just noticed . . .

(*Silence.*)

——Who mentioned Bombay?   135

——He did, to the Secretary at the Club. He saw himself being photographed beside the Sea of Oman on a chaise lounge . . . (*Little laugh.*)
——He doesn't talk about it any more, apparently.

(*Silence.*)
(*The* YOUNG ATTACHÉ *has now entered the garden. He goes toward the French* VICE-CONSUL, *slowly, as if not to frighten him. The* VICE-CONSUL *makes as if to run away. The* YOUNG ATTACHÉ *hesitates, then takes him by the arm. The* VICE-CONSUL *doesn't attempt to run away any more.*)
(*The* YOUNG ATTACHÉ *signs to the* VICE-CONSUL *to go with him.*)
(*They go toward the reception. Go in.* MICHAEL RICHARDSON *has seen them—he is the only one not watching* ANNE-MARIE STRETTER *dancing with her husband.*)

Women:
140 ——Did you see . . . ?

(*Pause.*)

——Yes, it's her he's looking at . . .

(*Pause.*)

——If you ask me, Bombay's too popular, they'll send him somewhere else . . .

(*Silence.*)

——Tell me about Madame Stretter.
145 ——Irreproachable. Outside the kitchens you'll see big jars of cold water put out for the beggars . . . It's she who . . .
——. . . Irreproachable . . . (*Little laugh.*)
Come, come . . .
——Nothing that shows. That's what we mean here by irre-
150 proachable.

(*Several people go into the garden and look toward the reception. Women fan themselves. [It is to be remembered that it's never those who are seen that speak.]*)

A man and a woman:
——She looks . . . imprisoned in a kind of suffering. But . . . a very old suffering . . . too old to make her sad any more . . .

(*Pause.*)

——And yet she cries . . . People have seen her . . . in the gar-
155 den . . . sometimes . . .
——The light perhaps, it's so harsh . . . and her eyes are so pale . . .
——Perhaps . . . What grace . . . Look
——Yes . . .
160 ——Frightening . . . don't you think?

(*Silence.*)
(MICHAEL RICHARDSON *has sat down on the left side of the room. He looks as if he is waiting. He doesn't look toward the reception. He is clearly visible. Very handsome. Younger than* ANNE-MARIE STRETTER. *Obviously shy.*)
(*He is smoking. He is tense, absorbed.*)

(*Several conversations take place between people, some of whom have and some of whom have not seen the* VICE-CONSUL *go into the reception.*)

Women:
——The roses are sent direct from Nepal . . .
——She gives them away when the dance is over.
——(*Low*) Look . . . there he is . . .

(*Silence.*)

——He doesn't notice everyone is looking at him . . .
——You can hardly see his eyes . . .   165
——His face looks dead . . . Don't you think so? . . . Frightening . . .
——Yes. The laugh looks . . . stuck on . . . (*Pause.*) What's he laughing at?
——Who knows?   170

(*Pause.*)

——In the gardens, on the way to the office, he whistles "India Song."
——What work does he do?
——Filing . . . nothing much . . . just to keep him occupied . . .   175

(*Silence.*)

Men:
——It's strange—most women in India have very white skins . . .
——They live out of the sun. Closed shutters . . . they're recluses . . .
——And they don't do anything out here . . . they're waited on.   180
——Yes, they just rest.

(*Silence.*)

——I admit I have a look when she and her daughters go by on their way to play tennis . . . In shorts . . . Women's legs seem so beautiful here . . . walking through all that horror . . . (*Pause, then a start.*) But look . . .   185

(*Silence.*)

Women:
——The first thing to see is the islands . . .
——They're so beautiful . . . I don't know what we'd do here without them.
——That's what we'll miss about India—the islands in the Indian Ocean . . .   190

(*Silence.*)

Isolated woman's voice:
——The best thing during the monsoon . . . did you know? . . . hot green tea, the way the Chinese make it . . .

(*Silence.*)

Women:
——Do you see? The Young Attaché's talking to the Vice Consul from Lahore . . .

(Silence.)

195   ——The voice . . . listen to the voice . . . how blank it is . . .

(Silence.)
(Almost total silence. Everyone looks at the YOUNG ATTACHÉ *and the* VICE-CONSUL.*)*
([The VICE-CONSUL's *voice is harsh, almost strident. The* YOUNG ATTACHÉ's *voice is low and soft.])*

Young Attaché and Vice-Consul:
V.–CONSUL: Yes, it's difficult, of course. But what is it with you, exactly?
Y. ATTACHÉ: The heat, naturally. But also the monotony . . . the light . . . no color . . . I don't know if I shall ever get
200   used to it.
V.–CONSUL: As bad as that?
Y. ATTACHÉ: Well . . . I wasn't prejudiced before I left France . . . What about you? before Lahore? would you have preferred somewhere else?
205   V.–CONSUL: No. Lahore was what I wanted.

(Silence.)
(Then "India Song.")

Man and woman: (low)
——Did you hear?
——Not very clearly. I thought he said: "Lahore was what I desired". . .
——I heard: "what I . . . what I'd . . ."
210   ——And what does it mean? Nothing . . .
——*(In one breath.)* The report said people used to see him at night through his bedroom window, walking up and down as if it was broad daylight . . . and talking . . . always to himself . . .
215   ——. . . At night . . . as if it was broad daylight . . .
——Yes. . .

(Silence.)
(One man's voice is heard dominating all the others.)

Man (George Crawn):
——Come over to the bar. Allow me to introduce myself. An old friend of Anne-Marie Stretter's. George Crawn . . . Serve yourselves . . . there isn't a bartender . . .

(Hubbub for a few seconds—people going over to the bar.)

Woman:
220   ——He said that to distract people's attention . . .

(The noise dies down.)

Y. ATTACHÉ: Come over to the bar. *(Pause.)* What are you afraid of?

(No answer.)

Y. ATTACHÉ: They say you'd like to go to Bombay?
V.–CONSUL: Won't they let me stay in Calcutta?
225   Y. ATTACHÉ: No.
V.–CONSUL: In that case I leave it to the authorities. They can send me where they like.

Y. ATTACHÉ: Bombay's not so crowded, the climate's better, and it's pleasant to be by the sea.

(Silence.)

Isolated man's voice:
——It's as if he didn't hear when you speak to him.   230
Y. ATTACHÉ: What are you doing? Come along . . .
V.–CONSUL: I'm listening to "India Song." *(Pause.)* I came to India because of it.

(Silence.)
*(*ANNE-MARIE STRETTER *appears on the stage for the first time in Act II. She has come from the reception. She smiles at* MICHAEL RICHARDSON. *He stands, and watches her coming. He doesn't smile. No one sees them [everyone is watching the* VICE-CONSUL *and the* YOUNG ATTACHÉ]. *It was she whom* MICHAEL RICHARDSON *was waiting for.)*
*(*ANNE-MARIE STRETTER *and* MICHAEL RICHARDSON *look at each other.)*
(He puts his arms around her.)
(They dance in a corner of the room, alone.)
(We hear the public voice of the VICE-CONSUL.*)*

V.–CONSUL: That tune makes me want to love. I never have.

(No answer.)
(Silence.)
(The last speech was delivered while we could see the couple dancing.)
(The couple disappear, left.)
("India Song" still.)

V.–CONSUL: I'm sorry.   235
I didn't ask to see my file. But you know it. What do they say?
Y. ATTACHÉ: They say Lahore . . . What you did in Lahore . . . People can't understand it, no one can, no matter how they try . . .   240
V.–CONSUL: *(pause)* No one?

(No answer.)
(Silence.)
(The BEGGAR WOMAN *appears in the garden.)*
(She hides behind a bush.)
(Stays there.)

Men:
——He said it was impossible for him to give a convincing explanation of what he did in Lahore.
——. . . convincing . . . ?
——I was particularly struck by the word.   245

*(*ANNE-MARIE STRETTER *comes back, from the left side of the room. Slowly. She stops. She looks toward the garden: the two women of the Ganges look at each other.)*
(The BEGGAR WOMAN, *unafraid, sticks her bald head out, then hides again.)*
*(*ANNE-MARIE STRETTER *walks away, with the same slow step.)*

Women:
——She goes to the islands alone. The Ambassador goes hunting in Nepal.
——Alone . . . well . . .

——With him—Michael Richardson. And others . . .
250 ——They say her lovers are Englishmen, foreigners from the
    embassies . . . They say the Ambassador knows . . .
——It's only what he expected when he met her . . . he's
    older than she is . . .

(*Pause.*)

——There's a friendship between them now that's proof
255   against anything . . .

(*Silence.*)
(ANNE-MARIE STRETTER *has gone into the reception.*)
("*India Song*" *ends.*)
(*The* VICE-CONSUL *goes back into the garden.*)
(*He is near the* BEGGAR WOMAN, *but they don't see each other.*)
(*A blues.*)

Men and women:
——Protocol requires everyone to have one dance with the
    Ambassador's wife . . .
——Look . . . He's left the Young Attaché . . . He's gone back
    into the garden . . .
260 ——Again . . . Ever since the beginning of the evening he's
    kept going back there . . .
——As if he was on the point of running away.
——And yet at the same time . . .

(*Silence.*)
(*The* VICE-CONSUL *stands motionless, staring at the reception with
all his might.*)

Men and women (continued):
——What's he looking at?
265 ——The Ambassador's wife dancing with the Young Attaché.

(*Silence.*)
(*The* YOUNG ATTACHÉ *and* ANNE-MARIE STRETTER *dance into
the room, then back to the reception. They too create a silence around
them.*)

Women: (low)
——Did you hear? (*Pause.*) She said to him: "I wish I were
    you, arriving in India for the first time during the sum-
    mer monsoon." (*Pause.*) They're too far away . . . I can't
    hear any more . . .

(*Conversation between Anne-Marie Stretter (voice marvelous in its
sweetness] and the Young Attaché:*)

270 A.-M. S.: (*deliberate repetition with slight error*) I wish I were you,
    coming here for the first time in the rains. (*Pause.*) You're
    not bored? What do you do? In the evenings? On Sun-
    days?
    Y. ATTACHÉ: I read . . . I sleep . . . I don't really know . . .
275 A.-M. S.: (*pause*) Boredom is a personal thing, of course. One
    doesn't know what to advise.
    Y. ATTACHÉ: I don't think I'm bored.

(*Pause.*)

A.-M. S.: And then . . . (*stops*) . . . perhaps it's not so important
    as people make out . . . Thank you for the parcels of books,
280   you send them on from the office so quickly . . .

Y. ATTACHÉ: A pleasure . . .

(*Silence.*)
(*The noise gradually starts up around them again, faintly.*)

Men: (in the silence of the preceding conversation)
——What an intriguing woman. All those books. Those
    sleepless nights in the residency in the Delta . . .
——Yes . . . What can be behind that sweetness . . . ?
——Nearly every smile is enough to break your heart . . .   285

(*Silence.*)

A.-M. S.: One might say practically nothing is . . . one can do
    practically nothing in India . . .
Y. ATTACHÉ: (*gentle*) You mean . . . ?
A.-M. S.: Oh . . . nothing . . . the general despondency . . .
    (*There is a smile in her voice.*)
Men and women:
——They say she sometimes has had . . . attacks . . .   290
——(*Low*) You mean . . . the trip to Chandernagor?
——Yes. And something else . . . sometimes she shuts herself
    up in her room . . . No one can see her . . .
——Except him, Michael Richardson . . .
——Yes, of course . . .   295
A.-M. S.: It's neither painful nor pleasant living in India. Nei-
    ther easy nor difficult. It's nothing, really . . . nothing . . .
Y. ATTACHÉ: (*pause*) You mean it's impossible?
A.-M. S.: Well . . . (*Charming frivolity in her voice.*) . . . yes . . .
    perhaps . . . (*Smile in her voice.*) But that's probably an over- 300
    simplification . . .
Men and women:
——She used to give concerts in Venice . . . She was one of
    the hopes of European music.
——Was she very young when she left Venice?
——Yes. She went away with a French civil servant that she 305
    left for Stretter.

(*Silence.*)

Y. ATTACHÉ: They say you're a Venetian.
A.-M. S.: My father was French. My mother . . . yes, she was
    from Venice.

(*Silence.*)

Men and women: (continued)
——She plays nearly every evening. In the dry season, that is. 310
    (*Pause.*) During the monsoon it's so damp pianos get out
    of tune overnight . . .

(*Silence.*)

Y. ATTACHÉ: The first time I saw you I thought you were
    English.
A.-M. S.: That does sometimes happen.   315

(*Pause.*)

Y. ATTACHÉ: Are there any who never get used to it?
A.-M.S.: (*slowly*) Nearly everyone gets used to it.

(*Silence.*)

Y. ATTACHÉ: (*suddenly crisp*) The French Vice-Consul in Lahore is looking at you.

(*No answer.*)

320 Y. ATTACHÉ: He's been looking at you all evening.

(*No answer.*)

Y. ATTACHÉ: Haven't you noticed?

(*She avoids answering.*)

A.-M. S.: Where is he hoping to be posted, do you know?
Y. ATTACHÉ: (*he knows*) Here in Calcutta.
A.-M. S.: Really . . .
325 Y. ATTACHÉ: I imagined you knew.

(*No answer.*)
(*Silence.*)
(*Servants pass through.*)
(*Dances follow one another: blues, tangos, foxtrots.*)

A.-M. S.: Did my husband tell you? We'd like to invite you to
the islands.
Y. ATTACHÉ: I'll be very pleased to come.

(*Silence.*)

Man and woman:
——If you listen closely, the voice has certain Italian inflec-
330   tions . . .

(*Pause.*)

——Yes . . . Perhaps it's that . . . the foreign origin . . . that
makes her seem . . . far away?
——Perhaps . . .
A.-M. S.: You write, I believe?
335 Y. ATTACHÉ: (*Pause.*) I once thought I could. Before. (*Pause.*)
Did someone tell you?
A.-M. S.: Yes, but I'd probably have guessed . . . (*Smile in the
voice.*) From your way of being silent . . .
Y. ATTACHÉ: (*smiling*) I gave it up. (*Pause.*) Monsieur Stretter
340   used to write too?
A.-M. S.: Yes, it did happen, to him too. And then . . . (*She
stops.*)
Y. ATTACHÉ: (*pause*) And you?
A.-M. S.: I've never tried . . .
345 Y. ATTACHÉ: (*crisply*) You think it's not worth it, don't you . . .?
A.-M. S.: (*smile*) Well . . . (*She stops.*) Well, yes, if you like . . .

(*Pause.*)

Y. ATTACHÉ: You play.
A.-M. S.: Sometimes. (*Pause.*) Not so much, the last few years . . .
Y. ATTACHÉ: (*gently; love already*) Why?
350 A.-M. S.: (*slowly*) It's hard to put it into words . . .

(*Long pause.*)

Y. ATTACHÉ: Tell me.
A.-M. S.: For me . . . for some time . . . there's been a kind of
pain . . . associated with music . . .

(*No answer.*)
(*Silence.*)
(*The* VICE-CONSUL *moves from where he was standing in the gar-
den and goes into the reception. The people still going back and forth
between the garden and the reception watch him.*)
(*A certain commotion. Some stifled exclamations.*)
(*Then two or three couples come into the garden, as if they were run-
ning away from the man from Lahore.*)

Woman:
——What's happening?
——The Vice-Consul from Lahore has asked the wife of the   355
First Secretary at the Spanish Embassy to dance . . .

(*Pause.*)

——Poor woman . . . But what are people afraid of?
——They're not afraid . . . It's more a sort of . . . repulsion . . .
But it's . . . involuntary . . . you can't analyze it . . .

(*Silence.*)

Y. ATTACHÉ: Will you have to dance with him?   360
A.-M.S.: I don't have to do anything, but . . . (*Smile in the voice.*)

(*Pause.*)

Y. ATTACHÉ: Last night he was in the garden. By the tennis
courts.

(*The answer comes slowly.*)

A.-M. S.: I think he sleeps badly.

(*Pause.*)

Y. ATTACHÉ: He's still looking at you.   365

(*Silence.*)

Isolated woman's voice:
——Poor woman . . . and on top of that she feels obliged to
talk to him . . .

(*Silence.*)

Y. ATTACHÉ: Repulsion is a feeling you know nothing about?

(*Pause.*)

A.-M. S.: I don't understand . . . How could one know nothing about it?   370
Y. ATTACHÉ: (*low*) The horror . . .

(*No answer.*)
(*Silence.*)

Y. ATTACHÉ: (*very clear and distinct*) They're talking about leprosy.

(*Silence.*)
(*The* YOUNG ATTACHÉ *was referring to the conversation between
the* VICE-CONSUL *and the wife* [Spanish] *of the Secretary at the
Spanish Embassy.*)

Vice-Consul and Spanish Woman:

SPANISH WOMAN: (*accent*) . . . the wife of one of our secretaries
375   was going mad, thinking she'd caught it . . . impossible to
       get the idea out of her head . . . she had to be sent back to
       Madrid . . .
V.–CONSUL: She had leprosy?
SPANISH WOMAN: (*astonished*) Of course not! . . . accidents are
380   very rare . . . in three years I only know of a ballboy at the
       Club . . . all the staff are examined regularly . . . most thor-
       ough . . . I shouldn't have mentioned it . . . I don't know
       how it happened . . .
V.–CONSUL: But I'm not frightened of leprosy.
385 SPANISH WOMAN: Just as well, because . . . Of course, there are
       worse places . . . Take Singapore . . .
V.–CONSUL: (*interrupting*) Don't you understand? I want to
       catch it.

(*Slight commotion.*)
(*Then silence.*)

Man and woman:
——She left him in the middle of the dance . . . What hap-
390   pened?
——He must have said something . . . something that fright-
       ened her . . .

(*Silence.*)
(*Some guests leave the garden and go back into the reception.*)
(*The* BEGGAR WOMAN *sticks her bald head out and watches—like
an owl. Then hides again. The* YOUNG ATTACHÉ *must have seen
her.*)

Y. ATTACHÉ: There's a beggar woman in the garden.
A.-M. S.: I know . . . She's the one who sings—didn't you
395   know? Of course, you've only just arrived in Calcutta . . .
       I think she sings a song from Savannakhet . . . That's in
       Laos . . . She intrigues us . . . I tell myself I must be mis-
       taken, it's not possible, we're thousands of miles from In-
       dochina here . . . How could she have done it?
400 Y. ATTACHÉ: (*pause*) I've heard her in the street, early in the
       morning . . . It's a cheerful song.
A.-M. S.: The children sing it in Laos . . . She must have come
       down through the river valleys. But how did she cross the
       mountains—the Cardamon Hills?
405 Y. ATTACHÉ: She's quite mad.
A.-M. S.: Yes, but you see . . . she's alive. Sometimes she comes
       to the islands. How? No one knows.
Y. ATTACHÉ: Perhaps she follows you. Follows white people?
A.-M. S.: That happens. Food.

(*Some guests leave the reception. Slight fear.*)

Men and women:
410 ——Where is he?
——Over by the bar . . . He drinks too much, that fellow. It'll
       end badly.
——There's something . . . impossible . . . about him.
——Yes.
415 ——And no one invited him anywhere in Lahore either?
——No.
——He went through hell in Lahore.
——Yes, but . . . How can one overcome this . . . this
       disgust . . . ?

Men:
——He's anger personified.   420
——Against whom? Against what?

(*No answer.*)
(*Silence.*)

Women:
——He used to call down death on Lahore, fire and death.
——Perhaps he drank?
——No, no . . . Out here, drinking affects us all in the
       same way—we talk about going home . . . No, he wasn't   425
       drunk . . .

(*Two women have come into the room. They are hot, they fan them-
selves. They look around.*)
(*A blues.*)
(*They look at the reception.*)
(*Suddenly they stop fanning themselves: they've just seen something.*)
(*Blues.*)

Isolated woman's voice:
——It was bound to happen. Look . . . The Vice-Consul from
       Lahore is going over to Madame Stretter . . .

(*Silence.*)

Men:
——Have you noticed? Out here the white people talk
       about nothing but themselves . . . The rest . . . And yet the   430
       time when most Europeans commit suicide is during
       famines . . .
——. . . which don't cause them any suffering . . . (*Little
       laugh.*)

(*Silence.*)
(*The two women watch with intense curiosity as the* VICE-CONSUL
goes over toward Madame Stretter.)
(*The sound of the reception ceases almost completely for a few sec-
onds.*)
(*Then it begins again, faintly. Politely stifled exclamations.*)
Men and women (*conversations 1 and 2*):

No. 1
——Did you see? The Ambassador . . . ? How cleverly he got   435
his wife out of it . . .

(*Silence.*)

——Where are they going?
——Into the other drawing room . . . Of course, the Ambas-
       sador would have had to talk to him sooner or later . . .
       so . . .   440

(*Silence.*)

No. 2
——Did you see? What diplomacy . . . everyone saw.
——Where are they going?
——Into the other drawing room . . . (*Pause.*) A servant's
       bringing them some champagne . . .

(*Silence.*)

No. 1

445 ——Why doesn't he go? Asking to be humiliated like that . . .

No. 2

——He said something to the Club Secretary that keeps coming back to me . . . "At home, in Neuilly, in a drawing room, there's a big black piano—closed . . . On the music rest there's the score of "India Song." My mother
450 used to play it. I could hear it from my bedroom. It's been there ever since she died . . ."

——What is it you find so striking?

——The image.

(*Silence.*)

(*Silence. Blues.*)

(MADAME STRETTER *and the* YOUNG ATTACHÉ *are walking through the gardens.*)

Ambassador and Vice-Consul:

AMBASSADOR: If I've got it right, my dear fellow, you'd pre-
455 fer Bombay? But you wouldn't be given the same job there as you had in . . . (*He hesitates.*) Lahore. It's too soon yet . . . Whereas if you stay here . . . people will forget . . . India is a gulf of indifference, really . . . If you like, I'll keep you on in Calcutta . . . Would you like me to?

V.–CONSUL: Yes.

(*Silence.*)

Women: (*low*)
460 ——He told her he wanted to catch leprosy.

——Mad . . .

(*Silence.*)

AMBASSADOR: Funny things, careers. The more you want one the less you make one. You can't just make a career. There are a thousand different ways of being a French Vice-
465 Consul . . . If you forget Lahore other people will forget it too . . .

V.–CONSUL: (*pause*) I don't forget Lahore.

(*Silence.*)

Isolated man's voice:

——Only one person has anything to do with him. The Secretary at the European Club. A drunk.
470 AMBASSADOR: You can't get used to Calcutta? (*No answer.*) People put that sort of thing down to their nerves. There are remedies, you know.

V.–CONSUL: No.

(*Silence.*)

Woman and man: (*low*)

——And what are they talking about?
475 ——The reformatory in Arras. Childhood. And . . . (*Stops.*)

——And . . . ?

——Her . . . the French Ambassador's wife . . .

(*Silence.*)

AMBASSADOR: At first everyone's like that. I remember I was, myself. You either go home or you stay. If you stay, you

have to find . . . or rather invent . . . a way of looking at 480 things . . . of enduring Lahore . . .

V.–CONSUL: I couldn't.

(*Silence.*)

Isolated woman's voice: (*low*)

——She's gone into the garden with the Young Attaché. (*Pause.*) I told you.

(*Silence.*)

AMBASSADOR: Take my advice . . . weigh up the pros and cons 485 . . . and if you're not . . . sure of yourself, go back to Paris . . .

V.–CONSUL: No.

(*Silence.*)

AMBASSADOR: In that case . . . how do you see the future?

V.–CONSUL: I see nothing.

(*Silence.*)

Women: (*low*)

——After every reception the leftovers are given to the poor. 490 Her idea. (*Lower.*) She's coming back . . .

(*Silence.*)

——Oh, I see! The garden's full of beggars . . . crowds of them all around the kitchens . . .

——The sentries have been told to let them through.

(*Silence.*)

(ANNE-MARIE STRETTER *and the* YOUNG ATTACHÉ *come in again* [*from the left*]. *They go toward the reception.*)

(*The blues is over. Another takes up the theme of "India Song."*)

(*Before entering the reception* ANNE-MARIE STRETTER *halts, as does the* YOUNG ATTACHÉ. *They wait.*)

(*For there, on the other side of the room, is the man from Lahore. Distraught, he comes toward her. Stops. Bows. Pale.*)

(*The* YOUNG ATTACHÉ *makes a gesture as if to stop* ANNE-MARIE STRETTER *from accepting.*)

(*She hesitates, but only for a second, and then accepts the man from Lahore's invitation to dance.*)

(*"India Song" becomes very distant. All conversations grow faint, become intermittent murmurs. Almost total silence.*)

(*At first, the* VICE-CONSUL *and* ANNE-MARIE STRETTER *dance in the room.*)

(*The* YOUNG ATTACHÉ *watches them.*)

(*Then they move toward the reception.*)

(*The* YOUNG ATTACHÉ *moves forward, still watching them.*)

(*Other people move toward the garden. They all look toward the reception.*)

Conversation between A.–M. S. *and the Vice-Consul, low but violent, very slow:*

(*Long silence, before the conversation begins.*)

V.–CONSUL: I didn't know that you existed.   495

(*No answer.*)

V.-CONSUL: Calcutta has become a form of hope for me.

(*Silence.*)

A.-M. S.: I love Michael Richardson. I'm not free of that love.
V.-CONSUL: I know.
I love you like that, in that love.
500   It doesn't matter to me.

(*No answer.*)

V.-CONSUL: My voice sounds odd. Can you hear?
It frightens them.
A.-M. S.: Yes.
V.-CONSUL: Whose voice is it?

(*No answer.*)

505   V.-CONSUL: I shot at myself in Lahore, but I didn't die.
Other people separate me from Lahore. I don't separate myself.
Lahore is me. Do you understand too?

(*Pause. Gently.*)

A.-M. S.: Yes. Don't shout.
510   V.-CONSUL: No.

(*Silence.*)

V.-CONSUL: You are with me about Lahore. I know. You are in me. I'll carry you inside me. (*Terrible brief laugh.*) And you'll shoot the Shalimar lepers with me. What can you do about it?

(*Silence.*)

515   V.-CONSUL: I didn't need to dance with you to know you.
You know that.
A.-M. S.: Yes.

(*Pause.*)

V.-CONSUL: There's no need for us to go any further, you and I. (*Terrible brief laugh.*) We haven't anything to say to each
520   other. We are the same.

(*Pause.*)

A.-M. S.: I believe you.

(*Pause.*)

V.-CONSUL: Love affairs you have with others. We don't need that.

(*Silence.*)
(*The* VICE-CONSUL's *voice is broken by a sob. It is no longer under his control*).

V.-CONSUL: I wanted to know the smell of your hair—that's
525   why I . . . (*He stops. A sob.*)

(*Silence.*)
(*His voice returns to normal—almost.*)

V.-CONSUL: After the reception your friends stay on.
I'd like to stay with you for once.
A.-M. S.: You haven't a chance.

(*Pause.*)

V.-CONSUL: They'd throw me out.   530
A.-M. S.: Yes.
You're someone they have to forget.

(*Pause.*)

V.-CONSUL: Like Lahore.
A.-M. S.: Yes.

(*Silence.*)

V.-CONSUL: What will become of me?
A.-M. S.: You'll be posted somewhere a long way from Cal-   535
cutta.

(*Pause.*)

V.-CONSUL: That's what you want.
A.-M. S.: Yes.

(*Pause.*)

V.-CONSUL: Very well. And when will it end?
A.-M. S.: When you die, I believe.   540

(*Silence.*)

V.-CONSUL: (*heart-rending*) What's this pain? Mine?

(*Pause.*)

A.-M. S.: Knowledge.
V.-CONSUL: (*terrible laugh*) Of you?

(*No answer.*)
(*Silence.*)

V.-CONSUL: I'm going to shout. I'm going to ask them to let
me stay tonight.   545

(*Pause.*)

A.-M. S.: (*pause*) Do as you like.
V.-CONSUL: So that something should happen between us. In public. Shouting is all I know. Let them at least find out a love can be shouted.

(*No answer.*)

V.-CONSUL: They'll feel uncomfortable for half an hour. Then 550
they'll start talking again.

(*No answer.*)

V.-CONSUL: I even know you won't tell anyone you agreed.

(*No answer.*)
(*Silence.*)
(*"India Song" ends.*)

(It is replaced by "Heure exquise," sung.)
(The sky grows pale.)
(Two men, drunk, stagger in and collapse into armchairs.)
(Over "Heure exquise," mingled with it, the VICE-CONSUL's *first cry.)*

V.–CONSUL: Let me stay!

(Silence.)
(Guests shrink back toward the garden. The two drunk men laugh. The others are horrified.)

V.–CONSUL: I'm going to stay here tonight, with her, for
555   once, with her! Do you hear?

(Silence.)

Isolated woman's voice:
——How awful . . .
Isolated voice of Young Attaché:
——You really ought to go home, you've had too much to
    drink . . . come along . . .

("Heure exquise" still.)
(The VICE-CONSUL *shrieks.)*

V.–CONSUL: I'm going to stay! In the French Embassy!
560   I'm going to the islands with her!
    Please! Please! Let me stay!

(Silence.)

Isolated woman's voice: (anguished)
——She looks as if she didn't hear . . .
Another: (the same)
——This is terrible . . .

(Silence.)

V.–CONSUL: *(shrieking)* Once! Just once! I've never loved any-
565   one but her!

(Silence.)

Isolated man's voice, to Vice-Consul:
——We're sorry, but you're the sort of person who only in-
    terests us when you're not there.

(Silence.)

Isolated woman's voice:
——How cruel . . . It's terrible . . . horrible . . .

(The VICE-CONSUL *sobs. Unrestrained. All dignity swept away.)*
(Everyone suddenly turns aside.)

Isolated woman's voice:
——I can't bear to see it . . .

(The VICE-CONSUL *appears, shaken with sobs. We see and hear them.)*
(A man, a stranger, leads him by the arm toward the entrance of the Embassy. The VICE-CONSUL *resists at first, then lets himself be led away.)*
(They disappear.)

(Everyone stands looking after them.)

Isolated woman's voice:
——He's gone. *(Long pause.)* They're shutting the gate.   570

(In the distance, the same cries: the VICE-CONSUL *has started to shout again.)*

Isolated woman's voice:
——He was laughing and crying at the same time. Did you
    see?

(Silence.)
("Heure exquise" continues imperturbably to the end, while every-one stands looking away from the reception and toward the VICE-CONSUL.*)*
(The cries still go on.)

Isolated man's voice:
——He's trying to break down the gate.

(Silence.)
("Heure exquise" ends.)
(The cries get farther away.)

Isolated voice:
——The beggars are frightened . . .
Isolated voice, the last:
——He's gone.   575

(Silence. A few seconds of it, then:)
(Blackout.)
(Darkness gradually blots out the picture as, in the far distance, the silhouette of the BEGGAR WOMAN *passes by, then disappears.)*
(Silence.)
(Then suddenly, on the piano, Beethoven's 14th Variation on a Theme of Diabelli.)
(Blackout.)

THREE

NOTES ON VOICES 3 AND 4

VOICES 3 and 4 are men's voices. The only thing that connects them is the fascination exerted on them by the story of the lovers of the Ganges, especially, once again, by that of ANNE-MARIE STRETTER.

VOICE 3 can remember almost nothing of the chronology of the story. It questions VOICE 4, and VOICE 4 answers.

Of all the voices, VOICE 4 is the one which has forgotten the story the least. It knows almost all of it.

But VOICE 3, although it has forgotten almost everything, recognizes things as VOICE 4 relates them. VOICE 4 doesn't tell it anything it didn't know before, at a time when it too knew the story very well.

The difference between VOICES 3 and 4, between forget-fulness on the one hand and remembrance on the other, arises from the same cause—the fascination the story exerts on the two voices. VOICE 3 has rejected the fascination, VOICE 4 has tolerated it.

The story of the lovers of the Ganges is *in* both voices—latent in the one, manifest in the other. About to survive or revive.

The difference—between the tolerable and the intolera-ble—should be reflected in the sensibilities of the two voices.

It is not without apprehension that VOICE 4 informs VOICE 3. VOICE 4 often hesitates. For VOICE 3 is exposed to the danger, not of madness, like VOICE 1, but of suffering.

We are in the same part of the Embassy as before. There are five people there in the darkness, which slowly disappears:

ANNE-MARIE STRETTER, MICHAEL RICHARDSON, *the* YOUNG ATTACHÉ, *the* GUEST *(friend of the Stretters), and an old friend, an Englishman,* GEORGE CRAWN.

The drunk journalists have gone. The rest are by themselves, in an intimacy in which each of them feels alone. It is late, they are separated by fatigue.

They are waiting. Their chairs—except for those of ANNE-MARIE STRETTER *and* MICHAEL RICHARDSON*—are too far apart for conversation.*

The YOUNG ATTACHÉ *and the Stretters'* GUEST *look exhausted, also, by the events of the evening.*

We don't know what they are waiting for: perhaps for it to be light, so that they can leave for the islands. Probably.

We still hear Beethoven's 14th Variation on a Theme by Diabelli. Through the music, the sounds of Calcutta grow stronger with the light.

ANNE-MARIE STRETTER *sits with her head flung back and to one side over the arm of a chair. She might seem to be asleep if it weren't for the fact that her eyes are open.*

MICHAEL RICHARDSON *is near her, half lying on a low chair.*

The YOUNG ATTACHÉ *is sitting up straight, smoking. He looks as if he is listening to the noises of Calcutta, through which one suddenly recognizes the cries, the last spasms of the calls to love of the* VICE-CONSUL *from Lahore. The* YOUNG ATTACHÉ *obviously finds them hard to bear. The others do not.*

The Stretters' GUEST*, standing, looks around at the others: these people of India whom he thought he knew, but whom he scarcely recognizes after the night of the reception. He too listens to the cries of the* VICE-CONSUL.

GEORGE CRAWN *listens to the Beethoven: he is entirely absorbed by the music.*

VOICE 4: As usual after a reception, some people stayed on.
VOICE 3: *(low)* Is he the one sitting near her—Michael Richardson?
VOICE 4: Yes.
5 VOICE 3: *(hesitating)* Did they ever find out . . . ?
VOICE 4: *(hesitating)* After she died he left India.

(Silence.)

VOICE 4: *(continuing)* The one standing up is the Young Attaché.
VOICE 3: And the elderly Englishman?
10 VOICE 4: George Crawn. He knew her in Peking.

(Pause.)

VOICE 3: And the one looking at them?
VOICE 4: Someone passing through. Stretter's guest.

(Silence.)

VOICE 3: Is that the French Vice-Consul shouting?
VOICE 4: Yes. Still.

(Silence.)

VOICE 4: All trace of him disappears in 1938. *(Pause.)* He re- 15
signs from the consular service. The resignation is the last thing on the file.
VOICE 3: *(hesitating)* Very soon afterwards . . .
VOICE 4: A few days.

(Silence. Cries.)

VOICE 3: What's he shouting?   20
VOICE 4: Her name.

(Pause.)

VOICE 3: *(slowly)* Anna Maria Guardi.
VOICE 4: Yes. All night, all through Calcutta, he's been shouting that name.

(Silence.)
(The women's voices [from Act I] now arrive. They too speak of the VICE-CONSUL.*)*

VOICE 2: *(as if exhausted)* He walks along by the Ganges.   25
He comes on the lepers asleep.
Someone else is shouting on the other bank.

(Pause.)

VOICE 1: Yes.

(Silence.)

VOICE 2: Can you see him?
VOICE 1: *(distant)* Yes. I'm watching.   30
I see.

(Silence.)

VOICE 2: *(slow)* Is he looking for something? . . . Or walking at random? . . . Aimlessly?

(No answer.)

VOICE 2: Is he looking for something he's lost?

(No answer.)

VOICE 2: Something in common that he's lost too?   35

(No answer.)

VOICE 2: The love of her?
VOICE 1: Love. Yes.

(Silence.)

VOICE 2: (*yearning, desire*) How far away you are . . . from me . . .

(*No answer.*)
(*Silence.*)
(*A servant goes through with trays piled with glasses, ashtrays, etc. He passes them as though he didn't see them.*)
(*Gleams in the sky. The burning-ghats.*)

40   VOICE 1: (*slow*) It will soon be day.

(*Silence.*)

VOICE 1: (*very slow*) Dawn is breaking here, all around. And there.
    The air smells of mud. And leprosy. And burning.
VOICE 2: Not a breath.
45   VOICE 1: No. Slow stirrings, slow movements, smells.

(*Silence.*)

VOICE 2: Can't I hear music?
VOICE 1: No.
VOICE 2: That sound of wings, of birds.
VOICE 1: The fan. Forgotten.

(*Silence.*)
(*The men's voices mingle with the women's.*)

50   VOICE 3: Those gleams.
VOICE 4: Day.
    The first zone is the zone of leprosy and dogs. They are on the banks of the Ganges, under the trees. No strength left. No pain.
55   VOICE 3: And those who have died of hunger?
VOICE 4: Farther away, in the density of the North. The last zone.

(*Pause.*)

VOICE 4: Day. The sun.

(*Pause.*)

VOICE 3: The light. Terrible.

(*Silence.*)

60   VOICE 1: The light. Of exile.
VOICE 2: Is she asleep?
VOICE 1: Which one?
VOICE 2: The white woman.
VOICE 1: No. Resting.

(*Silence.*)

65   VOICE 2: (*mournfully*) How far away you are. Quite absent.

(*No answer.*)
(*Silence.*)
(MICHAEL RICHARDSON *slowly turns his head toward* ANNE-MARIE STRETTER. *Looks at her.*)

VOICE 3: (*startled*) Voices near us suddenly? Did you hear?
VOICE 4: (*pause*) No . . .

VOICE 3: Young voices . . . women's?
VOICE 4: (*pause*) I don't hear anything. (*Pause.*) Silence.

(*Silence.*)

VOICE 4: He's looking at her.   70
VOICE 3: Yes.
    She is far away. Quite absent.

(*Silence.*)

VOICE 4: (*in one breath*) People said one day they'd both be found dead in a brothel in Calcutta they used to go to sometimes during the monsoon.   75

(*Silence.*)

VOICE 3: Not a breath. The heat is the color of rust. Above, the smoke.
VOICE 4: The factories. The middle zone.

(*Silence.*)
(*Very slowly* ANNE-MARIE STRETTER *has inclined her head toward* MICHAEL RICHARDSON. *They look at each other.*)

VOICE 3: That overhanging mass . . . ?
VOICE 4: The monsoon.   80
    Below, Bengal.
VOICE 3: And farther away . . . lower . . . under the clouds . . . ? Look. . .

(*No answer.*)

VOICE 3: That white patch . . . in a bend in the Ganges . . . ? There . . . ?   85
VOICE 4: (*hesitating*) The English cemetery.

(*Silence.*)
(*The stranger and the* YOUNG ATTACHÉ *begin to look at* ANNE-MARIE STRETTER.)

VOICE 1: Is she a leper?
VOICE 2: Which one?
VOICE 1: The beggar.
VOICE 2: She sleeps in leprosy, and every morning . . . No.   90
    (*Pause.*) No.

(*Silence.*)

VOICE 1: And the white woman?
VOICE 2: A false alarm ten years ago. But no, she neither.
    (*Pause.*) Listen . . .

(*Sound of a machine and of water.*)

VOICE 1: The water sprinklers in the English quarter.   95

(*Silence.*)
(*The men turn their eyes away from* ANNE-MARIE STRETTER *and look at the ground.*)
(*The stage gradually gets lighter.*)

VOICE 1: A car is speeding along the straight roads. Beside the Ganges.
VOICE 2: Black?

VOICE 1: Yes.
100 VOICE 2: They've left for the islands.

(*Silence.*)
(*The fires of the ghats are out. It is daylight. Pale daylight.*)
(*They lie there, in the same deathly attitude, as the voices describe the journey.*)

VOICE 4: The French Embassy's black Lancia has started out for the Delta.

(*Long silence.*)

VOICE 3: (*as if reciting a lesson*) The granary of northern India . . . The frontier of the waters. The Delta.
105 VOICE 4: Yes, the mingling of the waters. The sweet and the salt.
VOICE 3: After the deluge, before the light . . .

(*Pause.*)

VOICE 3: And those junks?
VOICE 4: Rice.
110   Sailing down to Coromandel.

(*Pause.*)

VOICE 3: Those dark patches on the banks?
VOICE 4: People.
        The highest density in the world.

(*Silence.*)

VOICE 3: Those thousands of dark mirrors?
115 VOICE 4: The paddy fields of India.

(*Silence.*)

VOICE 4: They're asleep.
        She's lying close to him.

(*Silence.*)

VOICE 3: She used to wake up late during the monsoon?
VOICE 4: Yes. Didn't go out till after dark.

(*Silence.*)

120 VOICE 3: The black Lancia has stopped.
VOICE 4: The rain. The roads are blocked.
        They took shelter in a rest house. (*As if reading.*) It was there the Young Attaché said: "I saw the Vice-Consul again before I left. He was still shouting in the streets. He
125   asked me if I was going to the islands. I said no, I was going to Nepal with the Ambassador."

(*Pause.*)

VOICE 3: Did she approve of the Young Attaché's lie?
VOICE 4: She practically never mentioned the man from Lahore.

(*Silence.*)

130 VOICE 3: That patch of green? it's getting bigger . . .
VOICE 4: The sea.

(*Silence.*)
(*Blackout.*)
(*The voices speak in the dark.*)

VOICE 4: The islands.
VOICE 3: Which one?
VOICE 4: The biggest, the middle one. They're there.

(*Silence.*)

VOICE 3: That big white building . . . ?   135
VOICE 4: A big international hotel. The "Prince of Wales." The sea is rough. There's been a storm.

(*Blackout ends.*)

FOUR

The same as before, but it has become a lounge in the "Prince of Wales."

They are not here.

A bright, greenish light instead of that of the monsoon.

The servants in white gloves are putting up green canvas blinds over the screened windows.

We do not recognize the garden. It has exploded into a violent green light—the garden of the "Prince of Wales." All that remains of the garden in Calcutta are some clumps of foliage.

The sound of the sea gradually spreads, increasing every second, until it invades everything. Then it remains stable.

The wind makes the blinds flap.

Sound of launches' sirens in the distance.

Close, the cheeping of birds.

The fan is still there, going around at the same nightmare speed.

In the distance, a dance: an orchestra is playing "India Song."

The sounds occur one after the other. For example:

1. *The wind.*
2. *The sea.*
3. *Sirens.*
4. *Birds.*
5. *Dance.*

As the two servants put up the blinds, thus creating the set for the "Prince of Wales," VOICES 3 *and* 4 *speak to each other.*

(VOICE 4 *remains the same throughout.*)
(VOICE 3 *changes as the end of the story approaches. It becomes either more pressing or, conversely, less eager to question. When it speaks of* ANNE-MARIE STRETTER *it gets lower, with silences between words and phrases.*)

VOICE 4: In front, the landing stages. The boats go to and from the South Pacific.
        Behind, there's a yachting harbor.

(*Silence.*)

VOICE 3: Beyond the palms, the same flat horizon.
5 VOICE 4: They're alluvial islands, formed by the Ganges mud.

(*Silence.*)

VOICE 3: Where's the French residency?
VOICE 4: The other side of the hotel, looking out to sea.

(*The servants go out. They have "finished" the set for the "Prince of Wales." When they have gone the sound of the dance is heard in the distance.*)
(*They are playing "India Song."*)

VOICE 4: At this time of the day, people used to start to drink at all the tables in the "Prince of Wales." On the sideboards
10   there are French grapes. In the showcases, perfumes. Roses are sent every day from Nepal.
VOICE 3: Who lives in this hotel?
VOICE 4: White India.

(*Silence.*)

VOICE 3: (*almost shouting*) What's that sudden smell of death?
15 VOICE 4: Incense.

(*The smell of incense should pervade the auditorium.*)
(*Silence.*)

VOICE 3: She wanted to go for a swim when they got here?
VOICE 4: Yes. It was late, the sea was rough, it was impossible to swim. Just let the warm waves break over you. She and he both went in.

(*Silence.*)

20 VOICE 3: (*afraid*) All those screens in the sea?
VOICE 4: Protection against the sharks.
VOICE 3: Oh.

(*Silence.*)

VOICE 3: Where is she?
VOICE 4: She'll come.

(*Silence.*)

25 VOICE 4: Here she is.
VOICE 3: (*hesitating; lower, more slowly*) Was she like that that night . . . ?
VOICE 4: (*pause*) Smiling.
     Dressed in white.

(*Silence.*)
(*These last two phrases should be felt as terrifying:* ANNE-MARIE STRETTER*'s smile, the whiteness of her dress.*)
(*In the green light,* ANNE-MARIE STRETTER *enters.*)
(*Smiling, dressed in white.*)
(*She goes and looks at the sea, beyond the garden. The four men enter, also dressed in white, from different parts of the hotel.*)
(*They all go toward the garden and look out at the sea.*)
(MICHAEL RICHARDSON *turns and gazes at* ANNE-MARIE STRETTER.)

(*She doesn't look at him any more.*)
(*In the distance, a voice over a loudspeaker.*)

LOUDSPEAKER: The last boat tonight leaves at seven o'clock. 30
VOICE 4: That's for the tourists who want to get back. There's a storm threatening.

(*Ships' sirens. Then silence.*)

VOICE 4: The last launch has just arrived. The one that brings supplies.

(*Silence.*)
(*A head waiter comes and bows to the five people. Their table is ready. They go off toward the left. Still the distant airport music.*)

VOICE 4: (*pause*) Their table's ready. The food here is excel- 35
lent.
     Michael Richardson used to say that once you knew the "Prince of Wales" you were never really satisfied anywhere else in the world.
VOICE 3: (*low*) I can't quite remember . . . isn't she going to 40
the French residency?
VOICE 4: She only used to sleep there.
     She used to dine at the "Prince of Wales" when she stayed on the islands. (*Hesitates.*)
     She'd had the servants at the residency sent back to 45
Calcutta.

(*Pause.*)
(*Fear.*)

VOICE 3: (*low*) How long ago?
VOICE 4: A few weeks.

(*Bird cries, so loud they are almost unbearable.*)

VOICE 3: The birds . . . thousands of them.
VOICE 4: Prisoners on the islands. They couldn't fly back to 50
the coast because of the storm.
VOICE 3: It's as if they were right inside the hotel . . .
VOICE 4: They're in the mango trees. They strip them. They'll fly away when it's light.

(*Noise of birds swamps everything else.*)
(*Silence.*)

VOICE 3: There's dancing at the other end of the lounge. 55
VOICE 4: Tourists from Ceylon.

(*Silence.*)

VOICE 4: During dinner . . . she asked them to raise the blind.
     She wants to see the sea, the sky, above the estuaries. They scarcely speak, they're very tired from last night.

(*Silence.*)

VOICE 3: She's not eating anything. 60
VOICE 4: Hardly anything. She's looking out of the window.
VOICE 3: I remember . . . A wall of mist is sweeping toward the islands . . .
VOICE 4: Yes. She's saying something about Venice. (*Effort of memory.*) Venice in the winter . . . yes, that's right . . . 65

(*Pause.*)

VOICE 3: Venice . . .
VOICE 4: Yes. Perhaps, some winter evenings in Venice, the same kind of mist . . .
VOICE 3: . . . she's saying the name of . . . (*stops*) of a color . . .
70   VOICE 4: Purple. The color of the mist in the Delta . . .

(*Silence.*)
(*Beyond the green windows of the hotel, disheveled, exhausted, his features contorted, still wearing his white dinner jacket, appears the French* VICE-CONSUL. *He goes through the garden of the hotel, searching.*)
(*Disappears.*)
(*Then reappears almost at once on the stage, now the lounge of the "Prince of Wales," walks across the room, looks toward the left, stops short.*)
(*He has seen her.*)
(*He stands there looking at her.*)

VOICE 3: He came over by the last boat.
VOICE 4: Yes. The seven-o'clock.

(*Pause.*)

He hadn't been home all day. (*Pause.*) He never went back to Calcutta.

(*Silence.*)
(*The tune of "India Song" is played loudly for a few seconds, then fades.*)

75   VOICE 3: "India Song" . . .
VOICE 4: Yes.

(*Silence.*)

VOICE 4: Now that the mist has come the wind has dropped.

(*Silence.*)
(*Some tourists go by in the garden beyond the green windows. One can make out women fanning themselves with white fans. Light-colored dresses.*)

VOICE 4: They're talking about the beggar woman.

(*No answer.*)
(*Silence.*)

VOICE 4: George Crawn and the Stretters' guest are talking
80   about the beggar woman.

(*Silence.*)
(FIRST VERSION: The conversation between GEORGE CRAWN and the Stretters' GUEST is heard as from some distance. [Very light and ordinary.])

G. CRAWN: She doesn't know a word of Hindustani.
GUEST: Not a word. If she's from Savannakhet she must have come through Laos, Cambodia, Siam, and Burma, and then probably down through the Irrawaddy Valley . . .
85   Mandalay . . . Prome . . . Bassein . . .
G. CRAWN: It must have been not just one journey, as we might think, but hundreds, thousands, every day, each one

the last . . . Hunger always driving her on, farther and farther . . . She must have followed roads, railways, boats . . . but what's strange is that she always went toward the sun-   90
set . . .
GUEST: . . . I suppose she traveled at night, and faced toward the light . . . She's bald . . . Because of hunger, do you think?
G. CRAWN: Yes.   95

(*Pause.*)

G. CRAWN: Sometimes she comes to the islands. Following the whites, probably: food . . . In Calcutta she lives by the Ganges, under the trees. She gets up at night and goes through the English quarter. Apparently she hunts for food at night along the Ganges.   100

(*Pause.*)

GUEST: And what's left of her in Calcutta? Not much . . . The song of Savannakhet, the laugh . . . and her native language is still there of course, but there's no use for it. The madness was there when she arrived . . . already too far gone . . .

(*Pause.*)

G. CRAWN: Why Calcutta? Why did her journey stop there?   105
GUEST: Perhaps because she can lose herself there. She's always been trying to lose herself, really, ever since her life began . . .

(*Pause.*)

G. CRAWN: She too.
GUEST: Yes . . .

(*Silence.*)
(SECOND VERSION: (VOICES 3 and 4 relate the conversation between GEORGE CRAWN and the STRETTERS' GUEST. [VOICE 4 is the one that hears it.])

VOICE 4: They've seen her.   110
    She must have crossed the Delta on the roof of a bus. She stowed away on the last boat.
    They met her by the lagoon, a few hundred yards from the French residency.

(*Pause.*)

VOICE 3: She must have been following Anne-Marie Stret-   115
ter . . .
VOICE 4: The guest says she followed him to the gate.
    She frightened him.
    He said: "That eternal smile is frightening . . ."
VOICE 3: That too . . .   120
VOICE 4: Yes. (*Pause.*) You remember?
    The first attempt . . . (*stops*) at Savannakhet, because of a dead child . . .
VOICE 3: . . . sold by its mother, a beggar from the North . . . very young . . . ?   125
VOICE 4: Yes. Seventeen . . . (*Pause.*) A few days before Stretter arrived.

(*Silence.*)

(*Suddenly the* VICE-CONSUL *goes toward the right, and disappears: he has seen them.*)
(*Here they are, coming out from dinner. There are now only three of them:* ANNE-MARIE STRETTER, MICHAEL RICHARDSON, *the* YOUNG ATTACHÉ.)
(*They walk across the lounge, making for the garden through the middle door.*)
(*In the garden they separate.*)
(ANNE-MARIE STRETTER *goes to the right.*)
(*The others go straight on through the garden and disappear.*)
(*The* VICE-CONSUL *begins to go after* ANNE-MARIE STRETTER.)
(*He halts.*)
(*She has stopped too.*)
(*She looks around her at the sea, the palms.*)
(*She hasn't seen the* VICE-CONSUL.)

VOICE 4: She wanted to walk back on her own.

(*Silence.*)

VOICE 4: The other two went for a sail. . .

(*Silence.*)

130   VOICE 4: The Young Attaché and Michael Richardson went back to the French residency the other way, along the beach.

(*Pause.*)

VOICE 4: It was as hot again as it had been in Calcutta.

(ANNE-MARIE STRETTER *walks slowly away.*)
(*Behind her, the* VICE-CONSUL. *He is following her. They disappear.*)
(*Blackout.*)
(*During the blackout, the 14th Beethoven-Diabelli Variation in the distance.*)
(*Blackout fades.*)

FIVE

The same as before, but it is now the French residency.

The light is different. It seems to come from outside. It is blue, like moonlight.

The fan is still there. Still going around.

The garden of the Embassy and the garden of the hotel have both gone. There is just an empty space. A path, and at the end of it a white gate.

Everything is enveloped in endless, fathomless emptiness. But it has a sound: the sea.

After a while, MICHAEL RICHARDSON *and the* YOUNG ATTACHÉ *come in through the white gate.*

Simultaneously, she enters, from the left of the house.

She is barefoot. Her hair is loose. She wears the short black cotton wrap.

She joins them on the path, they go toward one another, meet in the half-light.

They look at the sea.

VOICE 4: She's supposed to have said she was worried about George Crawn and the Guest. The sea was rough.

(*Sound of a rowing boat in the distance. They all look toward something out at sea.*)

VOICE 4: She didn't have to worry any more. George Crawn and the Guest went straight back to the hotel without calling in at the residency.   5

(*Silence.*)
(*They slowly walk back into the house.*)

VOICE 3: (*pause; stricken*) She didn't say anything that evening that might have made anyone think . . . (*Stops.*)
VOICE 4: No. Nothing.

(*Terrific tension. But nothing breaks the quiet spell of death.*)
(MICHAEL RICHARDSON *goes over to the piano.*)
(*She goes out of the room.*)
(*The two men are left there alone. They look at each other.*)
(*Outside, in the distance, at the end of the path, the white shape of the* VICE-CONSUL *comes through the open gate.*)
(*They don't see him.*)
(*She comes back, bringing glasses and champagne. She smiles at them.*)
(*She puts the bottle and glasses down on a low table and pours out the champagne.*)
(*She takes it to them.*)
(*They drink.*)
(*She sits down on a sofa.*)
(*There is still the fixed smile on* ANNE-MARIE STRETTER'S *face.*)
(*Outside, the* VICE-CONSUL *watches.*)
(MICHAEL RICHARDSON *plays.*)
(*He plays the 14th Beethoven-Diabelli Variation. Complete stillness.*)
(*Suddenly the stillness is shattered:*)
(*The* YOUNG ATTACHÉ *goes over to* ANNE-MARIE STRETTER, *puts his arms around her, then falls at her feet, and stays there with his arms around her legs.*)
(*He stays there, riveted to her.*)
(*She doesn't prevent him.*)
(*Strokes his hair.*)
(*Still the smile. The fixed smile.*)
(*He gets up. Draws her to her feet, flings his arms around her body, naked under the wrap. A gesture of supplication. Vain.*)
(*They kiss. A long kiss.*)
(MICHAEL RICHARDSON *watches. Plays the piano and watches them. His face is as we have always known it.*)
(*The white shape from Lahore gazes in avidly from outside.*)
(*The* YOUNG ATTACHÉ *roughly releases* ANNE-MARIE STRETTER, *staggers over to the piano and leans on it with his head in his hands. The Beethoven continues:* MICHAEL RICHARDSON *goes on playing. Stillness. Stillness enveloped in music.*)
(*The* YOUNG ATTACHÉ *remains leaning on the piano, motionless. The attitude of despair itself.*)
(*For the last time, one of the women's voices:*)

VOICE 2: (*terrified*) Where are you? (*Waits. No answer.*) You're
so far away ... I'm frightened ...

(VOICE 1 *doesn't answer any more.*)

(*Silence.*)
(ANNE-MARIE STRETTER *turns toward outside, toward the sea.*)
(*Shows no surprise when she sees the* VICE-CONSUL.)
(*He doesn't move, makes no attempt to conceal himself. Gazes fixedly at her.*)
(*She turns and bares her body to the fan.*)
(*Perhaps her naked body is visible to everyone.*)
(*To the* VICE-CONSUL *also—the body already separate from her.*)
(*She stands there motionless under the fan.*)
(*Silence.*)

VOICE 3: (*low, almost a murmur*) Michael Richardson left her alone that evening?
VOICE 4: (*hesitating*) It had been agreed between the lovers of the Ganges that they'd leave each other free if ever either of them decided ... (*Stops.*)

(*Silence.*)

VOICE 3: (*suffering, terror*) But he doesn't know, it isn't possible ...

(*No answer.*)

VOICE 3: What does he know?
VOICE 4: (*pause*) Ever since the servants were sent away, Michael Richardson had been living with this possibility.

(*Silence.*)
(ANNE-MARIE STRETTER *has lain down under the fan.*)
(*She has closed her eyes.*)
(MICHAEL RICHARDSON *and the* YOUNG ATTACHÉ *slowly tear themselves away, as if she had actually ordered them to leave her alone there.*)
(*They cross the empty space outside. Shadows.*)
(*The* VICE-CONSUL *is there. He doesn't hide as they go past.*)
(*It is as if they do not see him.*)
(*They disappear from sight.*)
(ANNE-MARIE STRETTER *and the* VICE-CONSUL *from Lahore are the only ones left in the French residency.*)
(*Silence.*)
(*She gets up, goes out, slowly walks through the empty space toward the white gate.*)
(*It is as if she doesn't see anything. She doesn't see the* VICE-CONSUL.)
(*And he makes not the slightest gesture toward her.*)

VOICE 3: (*scarcely breathed*) Is he the only one who saw ...?
VOICE 4: He didn't say.
VOICE 3: (*as before*) ... he didn't do anything to stop ...

(*No answer.*)

VOICE 4: The Young Attaché came back to the residency in the course of the night. He saw her.

She was lying on the path, resting on her elbow.
He said: "She laid her arm out straight and leaned her head on it. The Vice-Consul from Lahore was sitting ten yards away. They didn't speak to each other."

(*Silence.*)
(*What has just been related is what* ANNE-MARIE STRETTER *does. She lays her face on her arm. Stays like that. The* VICE-CONSUL *looks at her, riveted to the distance between them.*)

VOICE 4: She must have stayed there a long while, till day-light—and then she must have gone along the path ... (*Stops.*) They found the wrap on the beach.

(*Silence.*)
(*The fan stops.*)
(*Rest a few seconds on the stopping of the fan.*)
(*Blackout.*)

SUMMARY

This summary is the only one which should accompany productions of *India Song*.

This is the story of a love affair which takes place in India in the thirties, in an overpopulated city on the banks of the Ganges. Two days in this love story are presented. It is the season of the summer monsoon.

Four voices—faceless—speak of the story. Two of the voices are those of young women, two are men's.

The voices do not address the spectator or reader. They are totally independent. They speak among themselves, and do not know they are being heard.

The voices have known or read of this love story long ago. Some of them remember it better than others. But none of them remembers it completely. And none of them has completely forgotten it.

We never know who the voices are. But just by the way each of them has forgotten or remembers, we get to know them more deeply than through their identity.

The story is a love story immobilized in the culmination of passion. Around it is another story, a story of horror—famine and leprosy mingled in the pestilential humidity of the monsoon—which is also immobilized, in a daily paroxysm.

The woman, Anne-Marie Stretter, wife of a French Ambassador to India and now dead—her grave is in the English cemetery in Calcutta—might be said to be born of this horror. She stands in the midst of it with a grace which engulfs everything, in unfailing silence—a grace which the voices try to see again, a grace which is porous and dangerous, dangerous also for some of them.

Besides the woman, in the same city, there is a man, the French Vice-Consul in Lahore, in Calcutta in disgrace. It is by anger and murder that he is connected to the horror of India.

There is a reception at the French Embassy, in the course of which the outcast Vice-Consul cries out his love to Anne-Marie Stretter, as white India looks on.

After the reception she drives along the straight roads of the Delta to the islands in the estuary.

Heiner Müller

Since the 1970s, Heiner Müller (1929–1996) has been widely considered the most provocative playwright in Germany, East or West. Müller was born in 1929 and spent his youth watching the Weimar Republic give way to the rise of Nazism in Germany. He was drafted into the German army in 1945 and taken prisoner by the U.S. forces, but escaped into the Soviet-controlled zone near Neubrandenberg. Müller and his family settled after the war in East Germany, where his father briefly worked as a political functionary but then defected to the West in 1952. Müller, however, remained in East Germany, where he finished school and—under the influence of Brecht's Berliner Ensemble—began to pursue a career as a playwright. He wrote two short plays at this time, *The Battle* (1949) and *Tractor* (1949), before becoming closely involved with the journal *New German Literature* and the League of German Writers. Never an apologist for the Communist party, Müller was nonetheless a deeply committed socialist playwright. In the 1950s he wrote a series of "Productionsstücke," plays set in farms or factories dealing with the daily problems of workers' lives and the difficulties of achieving a truly socialist state.

His first full-length play to be staged was a dramatization of John Reed's *Ten Days That Shook the World* (1957), which was followed by *The Wage Cutter* and *The Correction* (1958). In 1964, Müller adapted Erik Neutsch's novel *The Construction Project* for the stage, a play about the sacrifices required of workers in rebuilding East Germany. The Communist party attacked the play as subversive, and Müller's plays were officially banned from 1965 to 1969; Müller suffered the suicide of his wife, Ingeborg Schwenker, in 1965 as well. At this time, Müller concentrated on a series of brilliant translations and adaptations, of Sophocles' *Oedipus the King* (1967), an adaptation of *Philoctetes* written in 1966 but not permitted to be staged in East Germany until 1979, and a translation of Aeschylus' *Prometheus* (1969). In 1969, Müller was officially "rehabilitated," and was invited to serve as dramaturg for the Berliner Ensemble. Working with the Berliner Ensemble—and Erich Honecker's lifting of some of the restrictions on writers—spurred Müller's most productive period in the theater: *Cement* (1973), *Germania Death in Berlin* (1977), *Mauser* (written while visiting at the University of Texas–Austin in 1978), *The Farmers* (1978), *Hamletmachine* (1978), *Quartett* (1981), *Ruined Shoreline—Medea-Material—Landscape with Argonauts* (1983). Many of these plays deal with the challenges both of patriotism and of finding a true form of revolution; given the fact that Müller's dramatic style in this period became more dense, elliptical, and poetic, it is perhaps not surprising that he continued to have difficulties with the party, and many of his plays—including *Hamletmachine*—continued to be banned in East Germany until the fall of the Berlin Wall in 1989. Müller's drama now receives as much attention in Germany as in the rest of the West, and the idiom of his work—its imagistic and fragmentary quality, as well as its glancing engagement with "history"—has come to define the possibilities of postmodern theater. Müller died in 1996.

HAMLETMACHINE

Hamletmachine is one of the most celebrated performance "texts" of the 1970s and 1980s. Originally drafted under the working title "Shakespeare's Factory," *Hamletmachine* has been produced in both Europe and the United States, notably in a 1986 production at New York University designed by Robert Wilson. Both as a dramatic text and in performance, *Hamletmachine* is a brilliant instance of one way postmodern "pastiche" operates in the theater. As a text, the play invokes, "quotes," and distorts a variety of texts from the history of literature and culture. It opens with the actor declaring "I was Hamlet," and is structured around five confrontations between Hamlet and Ophelia. Shakespeare, Marx, and other writers are invoked throughout. Müller closes the play by laminating Ophelia to Electra to the radical

Heiner Müller's *Hamletmachine*, directed by Robert Wilson at the Thalia Theater in Hamburg, Germany (1989).

terrorist Ulrike Meinhoff and to the would-be assassin of President Gerald Ford, Squeaky Fromm. In performance, this dense and elliptical script intersects with the other "languages" of the stage: Ophelia appears with a clock in her heart; the actor playing Hamlet declares "I'm not Hamlet" and proceeds to tear up photographs of the author; the visual field of the stage is distributed among live action, film, and video; three naked women speak the words of Marx, Lenin, and Mao, then have their heads split by Hamlet; scenes include an "*Ice Age*" and "*The deep sea.* OPHELIA *in a wheelchair. Fish, debris, dead bodies and limbs drift by.*"

Hamletmachine is divided into five sections; in each, Hamlet and Ophelia—or, more accurately, voices identified with Hamlet's famous indecision and Ophelia's innocent victimization—confront the necessity of acting, and the impossibility of acting among the contemporary "ruins of Europe." Müller's densely imagistic imagination resists summary, but it is clear that *Hamletmachine* is at once about the incoherence of modern life and about the specific political failures of socialism in Eastern Europe, where "SOMETHING IS ROTTEN IN THIS AGE OF HOPE." Hamlet, for instance, is haunted by "the ghost who made me," a ghost whose armor he assumes at the end of the play to destroy the icons of Marxist history, Marx, Lenin, Mao; in section 4, "PEST IN BUDA/BATTLE FOR GREENLAND," Hamlet seems to confront and criticize the failed Hungarian revolt of 1956. He seems specifically alienated from a world in which the possibility of revolution has become merely theatrical: "I don't take part any more. My words have nothing to tell me any more. My thoughts suck the blood out of the images. My drama doesn't happen anymore. Behind me a set is put up. By people who aren't interested in my drama, for people to whom it means nothing." This vision of a "world without mothers," where we "could butcher each other in peace and quiet" is complemented by Ophelia's function in the play, for Ophelia becomes a figure for the metaphysical evacuation of a world without ideals, where to "walk into the street clothed in my blood" is the only form of resistance left. In her final speech,

HAMLETMACHINE

Heiner Müller

TRANSLATED BY CARL WEBER

I FAMILY SCRAPBOOK

I was Hamlet. I stood at the shore and talked with the surf
BLABLA, the ruins of Europe in back of me. The bells
tolled the state-funeral, murderer and widow a couple, the
councillors goose-stepping behind the highranking car-
5 cass' coffin, bawling with badly paid grief WHO IS THE
CORPSE IN THE HEARSE / ABOUT WHOM
THERE'S SUCH A HUE AND CRY / 'TIS THE
CORPSE OF A GREAT / GIVER OF ALMS the lane
formed by the populace, creation of his statecraft HE WAS
10 A MAN HE TOOK THEM ALL FOR ALL. I stopped
the funeral procession, I pried open the coffin with my
sword, the blade broke, yet with the blunt reminder I succeeded, and I dispensed my dead procreator FLESH
LIKES TO KEEP THE COMPANY OF FLESH among
15 the bums around me. The mourning turned into rejoic-
ing, the rejoicing into lip-smacking, on top of the empty
coffin the murderer humped the widow LET ME HELP
YOU UP, UNCLE, OPEN YOUR LEGS, MAMA. I laid
down on the ground and listened to the world doing its
20 turns in step with the putrefaction.
I'M GOOD HAMLET GI'ME A CAUSE FOR GRIEF★
AH THE WHOLE GLOBE FOR A REAL SORROW★
RICHARD THE THIRD I THE PRINCE-KILLING
KING★
25 OH MY PEOPLE WHAT HAVE I DONE UNTO THEE★
I'M LUGGING MY OVERWEIGHT BRAIN LIKE A
HUNCHBACK
CLOWN NUMBER TWO IN THE SPRING OF
COMMUNISM
30 SOMETHING IS ROTTEN IN THIS AGE OF HOPE★
LET'S DELVE IN EARTH AND BLOW HER AT THE
MOON★
Here comes the ghost who made me, the ax still in his
skull. Keep your hat on, I know you've got one hole too
35 many. I would my mother had one less when you were
still of flesh: I would have been spared myself. Women
should be sewed up—a world without mothers. We could
butcher each other in peace and quiet, and with some
confidence, if life gets too long for us or our throats too
40 tight for our screams. What do you want of me? Is one
state-funeral not enough for you? You old sponger. Is
there no blood on your shoes? What's your corpse to me?
Be glad the handle is sticking out, maybe you'll go to
heaven. What are you waiting for? All the cocks have been
45 butchered. Tomorrow morning has been cancelled.
SHALL I
AS IS THE CUSTOM STICK A PIECE OF IRON INTO
THE NEAREST FLESH OR THE SECOND BEST
TO LATCH UNTO IT SINCE THE WORLD IS
50 SPINNING

★The lines with an asterisk are in English in the German text.

LORD BREAK MY NECK WHILE I'M FALLING
FROM AN
ALEHOUSE BENCH

Enters Horatio. Confidant of my thoughts so full of blood
since the morning is curtained by the empty sky. 55
YOU'LL BE TOO LATE MY FRIEND FOR YOUR
PAY-CHECK / NO PART FOR YOU IN THIS MY
TRAGEDY. Horatio, do you know me? Are you my
friend, Horatio? If you know me how can you be my
friend? Do you want to play Polonius who wants to sleep 60
with his daughter, the delightful Ophelia, here she enters
right on cue, look how she shakes her ass, a tragic character. Horatio Polonius. I knew you're an actor. I am too, I'm
playing Hamlet. Denmark is a prison, a wall is growing
between the two of us. Look what's growing from that 65
wall. Exit Polonius. My mother the bride. Her breasts a
rosebed, her womb the snakepit. Have you forgotten your
lines, Mama. I'll prompt you. WASH THE MURDER
OFF YOUR FACE MY PRINCE / AND OFFER THE
NEW DENMARK YOUR GLAD EYE. I'll change you 70
back into a virgin mother, so your king will have a blood-
wedding. A MOTHER'S WOMB IS NOT A ONE-
WAY STREET. Now, I tie your hands on your back with
your bridal veil since I'm sick of your embrace. Now, I
tear the wedding dress. Now, I smear the shreds of the 75
wedding dress with the dust my father turned into, and
with the soiled shreds your face your belly your breasts.
Now, I take you, my mother, in his, my father's invisible
tracks. I stifle your scream with my lips. Do you recognize
the fruit of your womb? Now go to your wedding, whore, 80
in the broad Danish sunlight which shines on the living
and the dead. I want to cram the corpse down the latrine
so the palace will choke in royal shit. Then let me eat your
heart, Ophelia, which weeps my tears.

II THE EUROPE OF WOMEN

Enormous room.★ OPHELIA. *Her heart is a clock.*

OPHELIA (CHORUS/HAMLET): I am Ophelia. The one the 85
river didn't keep. The woman dangling from the rope.
The woman with her arteries cut open. The woman with
the overdose. SNOW ON HER LIPS. The woman with
her head in the gas stove. Yesterday I stopped killing myself. I'm alone with my breasts my thighs my womb. I 90
smash the tools of my captivity, the chair the table the bed.
I destroy the battlefield that was my home. I fling open the
doors so the wind gets in and the scream of the world. I
smash the window. With my bleeding hands I tear the
photos of the men I loved and who used me on the bed 95
on the table on the chair on the ground. I set fire to my
prison. I throw my clothes into the fire. I wrench the
clock that was my heart out of my breast. I walk into the
street clothed in my blood.

III SCHERZO

The university of the dead. Whispering and muttering. From their gravestones (lecterns), the dead philosophers throw their books at HAMLET. *Gallery (ballet) of the dead women. The woman dangling from the rope. The woman with her arteries cut open, etc. . . .* HAMLET *views them with the attitude of a visitor in a museum (theatre). The dead women tear his clothes off his body. Out of an upended coffin, labeled HAMLET 1 step* CLAUDIUS *and* OPHELIA, *the latter dressed and made up like a whore. Striptease by* OPHELIA.

100 OPHELIA: Do you want to eat my heart, Hamlet? (*Laughs.*)
HAMLET: (*Face in his hands.*) I want to be a woman.

(HAMLET *dresses in* OPHELIA's *clothes,* OPHELIA *puts the make-up of a whore on his face,* CLAUDIUS—*now* HAMLET's *father—laughs without uttering a sound,* OPHELIA *blows* HAMLET *a kiss and steps with* CLAUDIUS/HAMLET's FATHER *back into the coffin.* HAMLET *poses as a whore. An* ANGEL, *his face at the back of his head:* HORATIO. *He dances with* HAMLET.)

VOICES: (*From the coffin.*) What thou killed thou shalt love.

(*The dance grows faster and wilder. Laughter from the coffin. On a swing, the madonna with breast cancer.* HORATIO *opens an umbrella, embraces* HAMLET. *They freeze under the umbrella, embracing. The breast cancer radiates like a sun.*)

IV PEST IN BUDA / BATTLE FOR GREENLAND

Space 2, as destroyed by OPHELIA. *An empty armor, an ax stuck in the helmet.*

HAMLET: The stove is smoking in quarrelsome October
A BAD COLD HE HAD OF IT JUST THE WORST
TIME★
105 JUST THE WORST TIME OF THE YEAR FOR A
REVOLUTION★
Cement in bloom walks through the slums
Doctor Zhivago weeps
For his wolves
SOMETIMES IN WINTER THEY CAME INTO
THE VILLAGE
110 AND TORE APART A PEASANT

(*He takes off make-up and costume.*)

THE ACTOR PLAYING HAMLET: I'm not Hamlet. I don't take part any more. My words have nothing to tell me anymore. My thoughts suck the blood out of the images. My drama doesn't happen anymore. Behind me the set is put up. By
115 people who aren't interested in my drama, for people to whom it means nothing. I'm not interested in it anymore either. I won't play along anymore. (*Unnoticed by the* ACTOR PLAYING HAMLET, STAGEHANDS *place a refrigerator and three TV-sets on the stage. Humming of the refrigerator. Three TV-*
120 *channels without sound.*) The set is a monument. It presents a man who made history, enlarged a hundred times. The petrification of a hope. His name is interchangeable, the hope has not been fulfilled. The monument is toppled into the dust, razed by those who succeeded him in power three

years after the state funeral of the hated and most honored 125 leader. The stone is inhabited. In the spacy nostrils and auditory canals, in the creases of skin and uniform of the demolished monument, the poorer inhabitants of the capital are dwelling. After an appropriate period, the uprising follows the toppling of the monument. My drama, if it still 130 would happen, would happen in the time of the uprising. The uprising starts with a stroll. Against the traffic rules, during the working hours. The street belongs to the pedestrians. Here and there, a car is turned over. Nightmare of a knife thrower: Slowly driving down a one-way street 135 towards an irrevocable parking space surrounded by armed pedestrians. Policemen, if in the way, are swept to the curb. When the procession approaches the government district it is stopped by a police line. People form groups, speakers arise from them. On the balcony of a government build- 140 ing, a man in badly fitting mufti appears and begins to speak too. When the first stone hits him, he retreats behind the double doors of bullet-proof glass. The call for more freedom turns into the cry for the overthrow of the government. People begin to disarm the policemen, to storm 145 two, three buildings, a prison a police precinct an office of the secret police, they string up a dozen henchmen of the rulers by their heels, the government brings in troops, tanks. My place, if my drama would still happen, would be on both sides of the front, between the frontlines, over and 150 above them. I stand in the stench of the crowd and hurl stones at policemen soldiers tanks bullet-proof glass. I look through the double doors of bullet-proof glass at the crowd pressing forward and smell the sweat of my fear. Choking with nausea, I shake my fist at myself who stands behind 155 the bullet-proof glass. Shaking with fear and contempt, I see myself in the crowd pressing forward, foaming at the mouth, shaking my fist at myself. I string up my uniformed flesh by my own heels. I am the soldier in the gun turret, my head is empty under the helmet, the stifled scream un- 160 der the tracks. I am the typewriter. I tie the noose when the ringleaders are strung up, I pull the stool from under their feet, I break my own neck. I am my own prisoner. I feed my own data into the computers. My parts are the spittle and the spittoon the knife and the wound the fang and the 165 throat the neck and the rope. I am the data bank. Bleeding in the crowd. Breathing again behind the double doors. Oozing wordslime in my soundproof blurb over and above the battle. My drama didn't happen. The script has been lost. The actors put their faces on the rack in the dressing 170 room. In his box, the prompter is rotting. The stuffed corpses in the house don't stir a hand. I go home and kill the time, at one with my undivided self.

Television The daily nausea Nausea
Of prefabricated babble Of decreed cheerfulness   175
How do you spell GEMÜTLICHKEIT
Give us this day our daily murder
Since thine is nothingness Nausea
Of the lies which are believed
By the liars and nobody else   180
Nausea
Of the lies which are believed Nausea
Of the mugs of the manipulators marked
By their struggle for positions votes bank accounts

185 Nausea A chariot armed with scythes sparkling with
    punchlines
I walk through street stores Faces
Scarred by the consumers battle Poverty
Without dignity Poverty without the dignity
Of the knife the knuckleduster the clenched fist
190 The humiliated bodies of women
Hope of generations
Stifled in blood cowardice stupidity
Laughter from dead bellies
Hail Coca Cola
195 A kingdom
For a murderer
I WAS MACBETH
THE KING HAD OFFERED HIS THIRD MISTRESS
TO ME
200 I KNEW EVERY MOLE ON HER HIPS
RASKOLNIKOV CLOSE TO THE
HEART UNDER THE ONLY COAT THE AX FOR
THE
ONLY
205 SKULL OF THE PAWNBROKER
In the solitude of airports
I breathe again I am
A privileged person My nausea
Is a privilege
210 Protected by torture
Barbed wire Prisons

(*Photograph of the author.*)

I don't want to eat drink breathe love a woman a man a
child an animal anymore. I don't want to die anymore. I
don't want to kill anymore.

(*Tearing of the author's photograph.*)

215 I force open my sealed flesh. I want to dwell in my veins,
in the marrow of my bones, in the maze of my skull. I retreat into my entrails. I take my seat in my shit, in my blood.
Somewhere bodies are torn apart so I can dwell in my shit.

Somewhere bodies are opened so I can be alone with my
blood. My thoughts are lesions in my brain. My brain is a 220
scar. I want to be a machine. Arms for grabbing Legs to
walk on, no pain no thoughts.

(*TV screens go black. Blood oozes from the refrigerator. Three naked
women:* MARX, LENIN, MAO. *They speak simultaneously, each one
in his own language, the text:*)

    THE MAIN POINT IS TO OVERTHROW ALL
    EXISTING CONDITIONS . . .*

(*The* ACTOR OF HAMLET *puts on make-up and costume.*)

    HAMLET THE DANE PRINCE AND MAGGOT'S   225
    FODDER STUMBLING FROM HOLE TO HOLE
    TOWARDS THE FINAL HOLE LISTLESS IN HIS
    BACK THE GHOST THAT ONCE MADE HIM
    GREEN LIKE OPHELIA'S FLESH IN CHILDBED
    AND SHORTLY ERE THE THIRD COCK'S   230
    CROW A CLOWN WILL TEAR THE FOOL'S CAP
    OFF THE PHILOSOPHER A BLOATED BLOOD-
    HOUND'LL CRAWL INTO THE ARMOR

(*He steps into the armor, splits with the ax the heads of* MARX,
LENIN, MAO. *Snow. Ice Age.*)

V FIERCELY ENDURING MILLENIUMS IN THE FEARFUL ARMOR

The deep sea. OPHELIA *in a wheelchair. Fish, debris, dead bodies and
limbs drift by.*

OPHELIA: (*While two* MEN *in white smocks wrap gauze around her
and the wheelchair, from bottom to top.*) This is Electra speak- 235
ing. In the heart of darkness. Under the sun of torture. To
the capitals of the world. In the name of the victims. I
eject all the sperm I have received. I turn the milk of my
breasts into lethal poison. I take back the world I gave
birth to. I choke between my thighs the world I gave birth 240
to. I bury it in my womb. Down with the happiness of
submission. Long live hate and contempt, rebellion and
death. When she walks through your bedrooms carrying
butcher knives you'll know the truth.

(*The men exit.* OPHELIA *remains on stage, motionless in her white
wrappings.*)

---

*English-language productions could use the entire quote from
Karl Marx: Introduction to *Critique of Hegel's Philosophy of Law.*

Caryl Churchill

Caryl Churchill (b. 1938) was born in England and began her education in Canada during World War II; she returned to study at Oxford University, taking her B.A. in 1960. At Oxford, Churchill began her career as a playwright, producing several plays: *Downstairs* (1958), *Having a Wonderful Time* (1960), and *Early Death* (1962). During the 1960s, she wrote a series of brilliant radio plays. She also studied radical politics and returned to the theater in the 1970s with a series of striking political dramas: *Owners* (1972), *Objections to Sex and Violence* (1975), and *A Light Shining in Buckinghamshire* (1976). In the mid-1970s, Churchill began to work more closely with experimental theater companies, collaborating with actors and directors in the writing of her plays. Working with the feminist theater company Monstrous Regiment (the name alludes to the Calvinist preacher John Knox's 1558 diatribe against Queen Mary of England, "The First Blast of the Trumpet against the Monstrous Regiment of Women"), she wrote *Vinegar Tom* (1976), a play about witchcraft and sexual politics in seventeenth-century England. With the Joint Stock company, she investigated the politics of sexuality more extensively in *Cloud Nine* (1979), a pastiche of melodrama, Gilbert and Sullivan operetta, and modern realistic theater that uses CROSS-DRESSING and ROLE-DOUBLING to explore the relationship between colonial and sexual oppression in the nineteenth century and today. The history of gender oppression and the options for contemporary women are the subject of *Top Girls* (1982), and Churchill has continued to write challenging plays on the relationship between class, race, and gender in British social life, including *Fen* (1983), *Serious Money* (1987), and *Three More Sleepless Nights* (1995). *Mad Forest* (1990) concerns the revolution in Rumania and *Skryker* (1994) was developed from Lancashire folktales; *Blue Heart* (1997) was written after Churchill collaborated on several music-theater pieces, including *Lives of the Great Poisoners* (1993) and *Hotel* (1997). Her most recent plays represent a new stylistic and political departure for Churchill: *Far Away* (2001), considers the problems of political resistance in the allegorical mode of magical realism; *A Number* (2002), interrogates the ethics of cloning.

CLOUD NINE

Onstage, the most exciting and interesting device in *Cloud Nine* is its use of CROSS-DRESSING and ROLE-DOUBLING. In the first act, for instance, Betty must be played by a man, Joshua by a white man, and Edward by a woman. By "alienating" actors from the characters they play, Churchill clearly intends to raise the questions of gender, sexual orientation, and race as ideological issues, for in each of these cases the difference between the performer and the role marks what Clive wants to see as real. Betty is played by a man because Clive—and his patriarchal society—cannot envision women's identity; women are constructed on the model of male attitudes. Joshua is played by a white man because imperial and racist culture reduces African identity to the construction of white, European attitudes. Edward is played by a woman to express the impossibility of Edward's conforming to Clive's heterosexual standards. In all three cases, the "identity" of the character is compromised or even erased, to be filled in and embodied by the attitudes that Clive and his society want them to hold. This performative dimension of the play's politics is echoed by the play's doubling of parts—each of the actors in act 1 takes a part in act 2, inviting the audience to draw comparisons between the two characters. Although other doubling patterns are possible, Churchill has suggested doubling Harry Bagley, the explorer, with Martin, the superficially liberated man; Clive, the father, with Cathy, the child; Betty with Edward; and so on. Doubling and cross-dressing are familiar conventions in the theater, but in *Cloud Nine* they have a specific dramatic purpose in developing the themes of the play. By denaturalizing the categories of gender, race, and sexuality, *Cloud Nine* undertakes a typically postmodern inquiry into the construction of social reality, asking

Danny Scheie as Betty, waving to Harry Bagley in Caryl Churchill's *Cloud Nine*, produced by the Trinity Repertory Theatre.

what meanings are created by these categories, and how they work to structure the relationship between self and society.

Author's Note

Cloud Nine was written for Joint Stock Theatre Group in 1978–1979. The company's usual work method is to set up a workshop in which the writer, director and actors research a particular subject. The writer then goes away to write the play, before returning to the company for a rehearsal and rewrite period. In the case of *Cloud Nine* the workshop lasted for three weeks, the writing period for twelve, and the rehearsal for six.

The workshop for *Cloud Nine* was about sexual politics. This meant that the starting point for our research was to talk about ourselves and share our very different attitudes and experiences. We also explored stereotypes and role reversals in games and improvisations, read books and talked to other people. Though the play's situations and characters were not developed in the workshop, it draws deeply on this material, and I wouldn't have written the same play without it.

When I came to write the play, I returned to an idea that had been touched on briefly in the workshop—the parallel between colonial and sexual oppression, which Genet calls "the colonial or feminine mentality of interiorised repression." So the first act of *Cloud Nine* takes place in Victorian Africa, where Clive, the white man, imposes his ideals on his family and the natives. Betty, Clive's wife, is played by a man because she wants to be what men want her to be, and, in the same way, Joshua, the black servant, is played by a white man because he wants to be what whites want him to be. Betty does not value herself as a woman, nor does Joshua value himself as a black. Edward, Clive's son, is played by a woman for a different reason—partly to do with the stage convention of having boys played by women (Peter Pan, radio plays, etc.) and partly with highlighting the way Clive tries to impose traditional male behaviour on him. Clive struggles throughout the act to maintain the world he wants to see—a faithful wife, a manly son. Harry's homosexuality is reviled, Ellen's is invisible. Rehearsing the play for the first time, we were initially taken by how funny the first act was and then by the painfulness of the relationships—which then became more funny than when they had seemed purely farcical.

The second act is set in London in 1979—this is where I wanted the play to end up, in the changing sexuality of our own time. Betty is middle-aged, Edward and Victoria have grown up. A hundred years have passed, but for the characters only twenty-five years. There were two reasons for this. I felt the first act would be stronger set in Victorian times, at the height of colonialism, rather than in Africa during the 1950s. And when the company talked about their childhoods and the attitudes to sex and marriage that they had been given when they were young, everyone felt that they had received very conventional, almost Victorian expectations and that they had made great changes and discoveries in their lifetimes.

The first act, like the society it shows, is male dominated and firmly structured. In the second act, more energy comes from the women and the gays. The uncertainties and changes of society, and a more feminine and less authoritarian feeling, are reflected in the looser structure of the act. Betty, Edward and Victoria all change from the rigid positions they had been left in by the first act, partly because of their encounters with Gerry and Lin.

In fact, all the characters in this act change a little for the better. If men are finding it hard to keep control in the first act, they are finding it hard to let go in the second: Martin dominates Victoria, despite his declarations of sympathy for feminism, and the bitter end of colonialism is apparent in Lin's soldier brother, who dies in Northern Ireland. Betty is now played by a woman, as she gradually becomes real to herself. Cathy is played by a man, partly as a simple reversal of Edward being played by a woman, partly because the size and presence of a man on stage seemed appropriate to the emotional force of young children, and partly, as with Edward, to show more clearly the issues involved in learning what is considered correct behaviour for a girl.

It is essential for Joshua to be played by a white, Betty (I) by a man, Edward (I) by a woman, and Cathy by a man. The soldier should be played by the actor who plays Cathy. The doubling of Mrs Saunders and Ellen is not intended to make a point so much as for sheer fun—and of course to keep the company to seven in each act. The doubling can be done in any way that seems right for any particular production. The first production went Clive-Cathy, Betty-Edward, Edward-Betty, Maud-Victoria, Mrs Saunders/Ellen-Lin, Joshua-Gerry, Harry-Martin. When we did the play again, at the Royal Court in 1980, we decided to try a different doubling: Clive-Edward, Betty-Gerry, Edward-Victoria, Maud-Lin, Mrs Saunders/Ellen-Betty, Joshua-Cathy, Harry-Martin. I've a slight preference for the first way because I like seeing Clive become Cathy, and enjoy the Edward-Betty connections. Some doublings aren't practicable, but any way of doing the doubling seems to set up some interesting resonances between the two acts.

C.C. 1983

THE TEXT

The first edition of *Cloud Nine* (Pluto/Joint Stock 1979) went to press before the end of rehearsal. Further changes were made within the first week or two of production, and these were incorporated in the Pluto/Joint Stock/Royal Court edition (1980). This edition also went to press during rehearsal, so although it may include some small changes made for that production, others don't turn up till the Pluto Plays edition (1983), which also includes a few changes from the American production, a few lines cut here or reinstated there. Other changes for the American production can be found in French's American acting edition—the main ones are the position of Betty's monologue and some lines of the 'ghosts'. For the

Fireside Bookclub and Methuen Inc. (1984) in America I did another brushing up, not very different from Pluto '83, and I have kept almost the same text for this edition. The scenes I tinker with most are the flogging scene and Edward's and Gerry's last scene—I no longer know what's the final version except by looking at the text.

There's a problem with the Maud and Ellen reappearances in Act Two. If Ellen is doubled with Betty, obviously only Maud can appear. Equally Maud-Betty would mean only Ellen could, though that seems a dull doubling. This text gives both Maud and Ellen. In the production at the Court in 1981 only Maud appeared and she has some extra lines so she can talk about sex as well as work; they can be found in Pluto (1983).

C.C. 1984

CLOUD NINE

Caryl Churchill

CHARACTERS

ACT ONE

CLIVE, *a colonial administrator*
BETTY, *his wife, played by a man*
JOSHUA, *his black servant, played by a white*
EDWARD, *his son, played by a woman*
VICTORIA, *his daughter, a dummy*
MAUD, *his mother-in-law*
ELLEN, *Edward's governess*
HARRY BAGLEY, *an explorer*
MRS SAUNDERS, *a widow*

ACT TWO

BETTY
EDWARD, *her son*

VICTORIA, *her daughter*
MARTIN, *Victoria's husband*
LIN
CATHY, *Lin's daughter, age 5, played by a man*
GERRY, *Edward's lover*

Except for CATHY, characters in Act Two are played by actors of their own sex.

Act One takes place in a British colony in Africa in Victorian times.

Act Two takes place in London in 1979. But for the characters it is twenty-five years later.

ACT ONE

SCENE I

Low bright sun. Verandah. Flagpole with union jack. The Family—
CLIVE, BETTY, EDWARD, VICTORIA, MAUD, ELLEN, JOSHUA.

ALL: (*Sing.*)

> Come gather, sons of England, come gather in your pride.
> Now meet the world united, now face it side by side;
> Ye who the earth's wide corners, from veldt to prairie, roam.
> From bush and jungle muster all who call old England "home."
> 5 Then gather round for England,
> Rally to the flag,
> From North and South and East and West
> Come one and all for England!

CLIVE: This is my family. Though far from home
10 We serve the Queen wherever we may roam
I am a father to the natives here,
And father to my family so dear.

(*He presents* BETTY. *She is played by a man.*)

> My wife is all I dreamt a wife should be,
> And everything she is she owes to me.
15 BETTY: I live for Clive. The whole aim of my life
> Is to be what he looks for in a wife.
> I am a man's creation as you see,
> And what men want is what I want to be.

(CLIVE *presents* JOSHUA. *He is played by a white.*)

CLIVE: My boy's a jewel. Really has the knack.
20 You'd hardly notice that the fellow's black.
JOSHUA: My skin is black but oh my soul is white.
I hate my tribe. My master is my light.
I only live for him. As you can see,
What white men want is what I want to be.

(CLIVE *presents* EDWARD. *He is played by a woman.*)

CLIVE: My son is young. I'm doing all I can   25
To teach him to grow up to be a man.
EDWARD: What father wants I'd dearly like to be.
I find it rather hard as you can see.

(CLIVE *presents* VICTORIA, *who is a dummy*, MAUD, *and* ELLEN.)

CLIVE: No need for any speeches by the rest.
My daughter, mother-in-law, and governess.   30
ALL: (*Sing.*)

> O'er countless numbers she, our Queen,
> Victoria reigns supreme;
> O'er Africa's sunny plains, and o'er
> Canadian frozen stream;
> The forge of war shall weld the chains of brotherhood   35
> secure;
> So to all time in ev'ry clime our Empire shall endure.
> Then gather round for England,
> Rally to the flag,
> From North and South and East and West
> Come one and all for England!   40

(*All go except* BETTY. CLIVE *comes.*)

BETTY: Clive?
CLIVE: Betty. Joshua!

(JOSHUA *comes with a drink for* CLIVE.)

BETTY: I thought you would never come. The day's so long
without you.
CLIVE: Long ride in the bush.   45
BETTY: Is anything wrong? I heard drums.
CLIVE: Nothing serious. Beauty is a damned good mare. I
must get some new boots sent from home. These ones
have never been right. I have a blister.
BETTY: My poor dear foot.   50
CLIVE: It's nothing.
BETTY: Oh but it's sore.

CLIVE: We are not in this country to enjoy ourselves. Must have ridden fifty miles. Spoke to three different headmen
55   who would all gladly chop off each other's heads and wear them round their waists.

BETTY: Clive!

CLIVE: Don't be squeamish, Betty, let me have my joke. And what has my little dove done today?

60   BETTY: I've read a little.

CLIVE: Good. Is it good?

BETTY: It's poetry.

CLIVE: You're so delicate and sensitive.

BETTY: And I played the piano. Shall I send for the children?

65   CLIVE: Yes, in a minute. I've a piece of news for you.

BETTY: Good news?

CLIVE: You'll certainly think it's good. A visitor.

BETTY: From home?

CLIVE: No. Well of course originally from home.

70   BETTY: Man or woman?

CLIVE: Man.

BETTY: I can't imagine.

CLIVE: Something of an explorer. Bit of a poet. Odd chap but brave as a lion. And a great admirer of yours.

75   BETTY: What do you mean? Whoever can it be?

CLIVE: With an H and a B. And does conjuring tricks for little Edward.

BETTY: That sounds like Mr Bagley.

CLIVE: Harry Bagley.

80   BETTY: He certainly doesn't admire me, Clive, what a thing to say. How could I possibly guess from that. He's hardly explored anything at all, he's just been up a river, he's done nothing at all compared to what you do. You should have said a heavy drinker and a bit of a bore.

85   CLIVE: But you like him well enough. You don't mind him coming?

BETTY: Anyone at all to break the monotony.

CLIVE: But you have your mother. You have Ellen.

BETTY: Ellen is a governess. My mother is my mother.

90   CLIVE: I hoped when she came to visit she would be company for you.

BETTY: I don't think mother is on a visit. I think she lives with us.

CLIVE: I think she does.

95   BETTY: Clive you are so good.

CLIVE: But are you bored my love?

BETTY: It's just that I miss you when you're away. We're not in this country to enjoy ourselves. If I lack society that is my form of service.

100   CLIVE: That's a brave girl. So today has been all right? No fainting? No hysteria?

BETTY: I have been very tranquil.

CLIVE: Ah what a haven of peace to come home to. The coolth, the calm, the beauty.

105   BETTY: There is one thing, Clive, if you don't mind.

CLIVE: What can I do for you, my dear?

BETTY: It's about Joshua.

CLIVE: I wouldn't leave you alone here with a quiet mind if it weren't for Joshua.

110   BETTY: Joshua doesn't like me.

CLIVE: Joshua has been my boy for eight years. He has saved my life. I have saved his life. He is devoted to me and to mine. I have said this before.

BETTY: He is rude to me. He doesn't do what I say. Speak to him.

CLIVE: Tell me what happened.   115

BETTY: He said something improper.

CLIVE: Well, what?

BETTY: I don't like to repeat it.

CLIVE: I must insist.

BETTY: I had left my book inside on the piano. I was in the   120
hammock. I asked him to fetch it.

CLIVE: And did he not fetch it?

BETTY: Yes, he did eventually.

CLIVE: And what did he say?

BETTY: Clive—   125

CLIVE: Betty.

BETTY: He said Fetch it yourself. You've got legs under that dress.

CLIVE: Joshua!

(JOSHUA *comes.*)

Joshua, madam says you spoke impolitely to her this afternoon.   130

JOSHUA: Sir?

CLIVE: When she asked you to pass her book from the piano.

JOSHUA: She has the book, sir.

BETTY: I have the book now, but when I told you—

CLIVE: Betty, please, let me handle this. You didn't pass it at   135
once?

JOSHUA: No sir, I made a joke first.

CLIVE: What was that?

JOSHUA: I said my legs were tired, sir. That was funny because the book was very near, it would not make my legs tired   140
to get it.

BETTY: That's not true.

JOSHUA: Did madam hear me wrong?

CLIVE: She heard something else.

JOSHUA: What was that, madam?   145

BETTY: Never mind.

CLIVE: Now Joshua, it won't do you know. Madam doesn't like that kind of joke. You must do what madam says, just do what she says and don't answer back. You know your place, Joshua. I don't have to say any more.   150

JOSHUA: No sir.

BETTY: I expect an apology.

JOSHUA: I apologise, madam.

CLIVE: There now. It won't happen again, my dear. I'm very shocked Joshua, very shocked.   155

(CLIVE *winks at* JOSHUA, *unseen by* BETTY. JOSHUA *goes.*)

CLIVE: I think another drink, and send for the children, and isn't that Harry riding down the hill? Wave, wave. Just in time before dark. Cuts it fine, the blighter. Always a hothead, Harry.

BETTY: Can he see us?   160

CLIVE: Stand further forward. He'll see your white dress. There, he waved back.

BETTY: Do you think so? I wonder what he saw. Sometimes sunset is so terrifying I can't bear to look.

CLIVE: It makes me proud. Elsewhere in the empire the sun   165
is rising.

BETTY: Harry looks so small on the hillside.

(ELLEN *comes.*)

ELLEN: Shall I bring the children?
BETTY: Shall Ellen bring the children?
170 CLIVE: Delightful.
BETTY: Yes, Ellen, make sure they're warm. The night air is deceptive. Victoria was looking pale yesterday.
CLIVE: My love.

(MAUD *comes from inside the house.*)

MAUD: Are you warm enough Betty?
175 BETTY: Perfectly.
MAUD: The night air is deceptive.
BETTY: I'm quite warm. I'm too warm.
MAUD: You're not getting a fever, I hope? She's not strong, you know, Clive. I don't know how long you'll keep her
180 in this climate.
CLIVE: I look after Her Majesty's domains. I think you can trust me to look after my wife.

(ELLEN *comes carrying* VICTORIA, *age 2.* EDWARD, *age 9, lags behind.*)

BETTY: Victoria, my pet, say good evening to papa.

(CLIVE *takes* VICTORIA *on his knee.*)

CLIVE: There's my sweet little Vicky. What have we done today?
185 BETTY: She wore Ellen's hat.
CLIVE: Did she wear Ellen's big hat like a lady? What a pretty.
BETTY: And Joshua gave her a piggy back. Tell papa. Horsy with Joshy?
ELLEN: She's tired.
190 CLIVE: Nice Joshy played horsy. What a big strong Joshy. Did you have a gallop? Did you make him stop and go? Not very chatty tonight are we?
BETTY: Edward, say good evening to papa.
CLIVE: Edward my boy. Have you done your lessons well?
195 EDWARD: Yes papa.
CLIVE: Did you go riding?
EDWARD: Yes papa.
CLIVE: What's that you're holding?
BETTY: It's Victoria's doll. What are you doing with it, Edward?
200 EDWARD: Minding her.
BETTY: Well I should give it to Ellen quickly. You don't want papa to see you with a doll.
CLIVE: No, we had you with Victoria's doll once before, Edward.
ELLEN: He's minding it for Vicky. He's not playing with it.
205 BETTY: He's not playing with it, Clive. He's minding it for Vicky.
CLIVE: Ellen minds Victoria, let Ellen mind the doll.
ELLEN: Come, give it to me.

(ELLEN *takes the doll.*)

EDWARD: Don't pull her about. Vicky's very fond of her. She
210 likes me to have her.
BETTY: He's a very good brother.
CLIVE: Yes, it's manly of you Edward, to take care of your little sister. We'll say no more about it. Tomorrow I'll take you riding with me and Harry Bagley. Would you like that?
215 EDWARD: Is he here?
CLIVE: He's just arrived. There Betty, take Victoria now. I must go and welcome Harry.

(CLIVE *tosses* VICTORIA *to* BETTY, *who gives her to* ELLEN.)

EDWARD: Can I come, papa?
BETTY: Is he warm enough?
EDWARD: Am I warm enough?
220
CLIVE: Never mind the women, Ned. Come and meet Harry.

(*They go. The women are left. There is a silence.*)

MAUD: I daresay Mr Bagley will be out all day and we'll see nothing of him.
BETTY: He plays the piano. Surely he will sometimes stay at home with us.
225
MAUD: We can't expect it. The men have their duties and we have ours.
BETTY: He won't have seen a piano for a year. He lives a very rough life.
ELLEN: Will it be exciting for you, Betty?
230
MAUD: Whatever do you mean, Ellen?
ELLEN: We don't have very much society.
BETTY: Clive is my society.
MAUD: It's time Victoria went to bed.
ELLEN: She'd like to stay up and see Mr Bagley.
235
MAUD: Mr Bagley can see her tomorrow.

(ELLEN *goes.*)

MAUD: You let that girl forget her place, Betty.
BETTY: Mother, she is governess to my son. I know what her place is. I think my friendship does her good. She is not very happy.
240
MAUD: Young women are never happy.
BETTY: Mother, what a thing to say.
MAUD: Then when they're older they look back and see that comparatively speaking they were ecstatic.
BETTY: I'm perfectly happy.
245
MAUD: You are looking very pretty tonight. You were such a success as a young girl. You have made a most fortunate marriage. I'm sure you will be an excellent hostess to Mr Bagley.
BETTY: I feel quite nervous at the thought of entertaining.
250
MAUD: I can always advise you if I'm asked.
BETTY: What a long time they're taking. I always seem to be waiting for the men.
MAUD: Betty you have to learn to be patient. I am patient. My mama was very patient.
255

(CLIVE *approaches, supporting* CAROLINE SAUNDERS.)

CLIVE: It is a pleasure. It is an honour. It is positively your duty to seek my help. I would be hurt, I would be insulted by any show of independence. Your husband would have been one of my dearest friends if he had lived. Betty, look who has come, Mrs Saunders. She has ridden here all
260
alone, amazing spirit. What will you have? Tea or something stronger? Let her lie down, she is overcome. Betty, you will know what to do.

(MRS SAUNDERS *lies down.*)

MAUD: I knew it. I heard drums. We'll be killed in our beds.
CLIVE: Now, please, calm yourself.
265

MAUD: I am perfectly calm. I am just outspoken. If it comes to being killed I shall take it as calmly as anyone.

CLIVE: There is no cause for alarm. Mrs Saunders has been alone since her husband died last year, amazing spirit. Not
270 surprisingly, the strain has told. She has come to us as her nearest neighbours.

MAUD: What happened to make her come?

CLIVE: This is not an easy country for a woman.

MAUD: Clive, I heard drums. We are not children.

275 CLIVE: Of course you heard drums. The tribes are constantly at war, if the term is not too grand to grace their squabbles. Not unnaturally Mrs Saunders would like the company of white women. The piano. Poetry.

BETTY: We are not her nearest neighbours.

280 CLIVE: We are among her nearest neighbours and I was a dear friend of her late husband. She knows that she will find a welcome here. She will not be disappointed. She will be cared for.

MAUD: Of course we will care for her.

285 BETTY: Victoria is in bed. I must go and say goodnight. Mother, please, you look after Mrs Saunders.

CLIVE: Harry will be here at once.

(BETTY *goes*.)

MAUD: How rash to go out after dark without a shawl.

CLIVE: Amazing spirit. Drink this.

290 MRS SAUNDERS: Where am I?

MAUD: You are quite safe.

MRS SAUNDERS: Clive? Clive? Thank God. This is very kind. How do you do? I am sorry to be a nuisance. Charmed. Have you a gun? I have a gun.

295 CLIVE: There is no need for guns I hope. We are all friends here.

MRS SAUNDERS: I think I will lie down again.

(HARRY BAGLEY *and* EDWARD *have approached*.)

MAUD: Ah, here is Mr Bagley.

EDWARD: I gave his horse some water.

CLIVE: You don't know Mrs Saunders, do you Harry? She has at
300 present collapsed, but she is recovering thanks to the good offices of my wife's mother who I think you've met before. Betty will be along in a minute. Edward will go home to school shortly. He is quite a young man since you saw him.

HARRY: I hardly knew him.

305 MAUD: What news have you for us, Mr Bagley?

CLIVE: Do you know Mrs Saunders, Harry? Amazing spirit.

EDWARD: Did you hardly know me?

HARRY: Of course I knew you. I mean you have grown.

EDWARD: What do you expect?

310 HARRY: That's quite right, people don't get smaller.

MAUD: Edward. You should be in bed.

EDWARD: No, I'm not tired, I'm not tired am I Uncle Harry?

HARRY: I don't think he's tired.

CLIVE: He is overtired. It is past his bedtime. Say goodnight.

315 EDWARD: Goodnight, sir.

CLIVE: And to your grandmother.

EDWARD: Goodnight, grandmother.

(EDWARD *goes*.)

MAUD: Shall I help Mrs Saunders indoors? I'm afraid she may get a chill.

CLIVE: Shall I give her an arm?   320

MAUD: How kind of you, Clive. I think I am strong enough.

(MAUD *helps* MRS SAUNDERS *into the house*.)

CLIVE: Not a word to alarm the women.

HARRY: Absolutely.

CLIVE: I did some good today I think. Kept up some alliances. There's a lot of affection there.   325

HARRY: They're affectionate people. They can be very cruel of course.

CLIVE: Well they are savages.

HARRY: Very beautiful people many of them.

CLIVE: Joshua! (*To* HARRY.) I think we should sleep with guns. 330

HARRY: I haven't slept in a house for six months. It seems extremely safe.

(JOSHUA *comes*.)

CLIVE: Joshua, you will have gathered there's a spot of bother. Rumours of this and that. You should be armed I think.

JOSHUA: There are many bad men, sir. I pray about it. Jesus 335 will protect us.

CLIVE: He will indeed and I'll also get you a weapon. Betty, come and keep Harry company. Look in the barn, Joshua, every night.

(CLIVE *and* JOSHUA *go*. BETTY *comes*.)

HARRY: I wondered where you were.   340

BETTY: I was singing lullabies.

HARRY: When I think of you I always think of you with Edward in your lap.

BETTY: Do you think of me sometimes then?

HARRY: You have been thought of where no white woman 345 has ever been thought of before.

BETTY: It's one way of having adventures. I suppose I will never go in person.

HARRY: That's up to you.

BETTY: Of course it's not. I have duties.   350

HARRY: Are you happy, Betty?

BETTY: Where have you been?

HARRY: Built a raft and went up the river. Stayed with some people. The king is always very good to me. They have a lot of skulls around the place but not white men's I think. 355 I made up a poem one night. If I should die in this forsaken spot, There is a loving heart without a blot, Where I will live—and so on.

BETTY: When I'm near you it's like going out into the jungle. It's like going up the river on a raft. It's like going out 360 in the dark.

HARRY: And you are safety and light and peace and home.

BETTY: But I want to be dangerous.

HARRY: Clive is my friend.

BETTY: I am your friend.   365

HARRY: I don't like dangerous women.

BETTY: Is Mrs Saunders dangerous?

HARRY: Not to me. She's a bit of an old boot.

(JOSHUA *comes, unobserved*.)

BETTY: Am I dangerous?

370 HARRY: You are rather.
BETTY: Please like me.
HARRY: I worship you.
BETTY: Please want me.
HARRY: I don't want to want you. Of course I want you.
375 BETTY: What are we going to do?
HARRY: I should have stayed on the river. The hell with it.

(*He goes to take her in his arms, she runs away into the house.* HARRY *stays where he is. He becomes aware of* JOSHUA.)

HARRY: Who's there?
JOSHUA: Only me sir.
HARRY: Got a gun now have you?
380 JOSHUA: Yes sir.
HARRY: Where's Clive?
JOSHUA: Going round the boundaries sir.
HARRY: Have you checked there's nobody in the barns?
JOSHUA: Yes sir.
385 HARRY: Shall we go in a barn and fuck? It's not an order.
JOSHUA: That's all right, yes.

(*They go off.*)

SCENE II

An open space some distance from the house. MRS SAUNDERS *alone, breathless. She is carrying a riding crop.* CLIVE *arrives.*

CLIVE: Why? Why?
MRS SAUNDERS: Don't fuss, Clive, it makes you sweat.
CLIVE: Why ride off now? Sweat, you would sweat if you
    were in love with somebody as disgustingly capricious as
5   you are. You will be shot with poisoned arrows. You will
    miss the picnic. Somebody will notice I came after you.
MRS SAUNDERS: I didn't want you to come after me. I wanted
    to be alone.
CLIVE: You will be raped by cannibals.
10 MRS SAUNDERS: I just wanted to get out of your house.
CLIVE: My God, what women put us through. Cruel, cruel. I
    think you are the sort of woman who would enjoy whip-
    ping somebody. I've never met one before.
MRS SAUNDERS: Can I tell you something, Clive?
15 CLIVE: Let me tell you something first. Since you came to the
    house I have had an erection twenty-four hours a day ex-
    cept for ten minutes after the time we had intercourse.
MRS SAUNDERS: I don't think that's physically possible.
CLIVE: You are causing me appalling physical suffering. Is this
20   the way to treat a benefactor?
MRS SAUNDERS: Clive, when I came to your house the other
    night I came because I was afraid. The cook was going to
    let his whole tribe in through the window.
CLIVE: I know that, my poor sweet. Amazing—
25 MRS SAUNDERS: I came to you although you are not my
    nearest neighbour—
CLIVE: Rather than to the old major of seventy-two.
MRS SAUNDERS: Because the last time he came to visit me I
    had to defend myself with a shotgun and I thought you
30   would take no for an answer.
CLIVE: But you've already answered yes.
MRS SAUNDERS: I answered yes once. Sometimes I want to
    say no.

CLIVE: Women, my God. Look the picnic will start, I have to
    go to the picnic. Please Caroline—   35
MRS SAUNDERS: I think I will have to go back to my own house.
CLIVE: Caroline, if you were shot with poisoned arrows do
    you know what I'd do? I'd fuck your dead body and poi-
    son myself. Caroline, you smell amazing. You terrify me.
    You are dark like this continent. Mysterious. Treacherous.   40
    When you rode to me through the night. When you
    fainted in my arms. When I came to you in your bed,
    when I lifted the mosquito netting, when I said let me in,
    let me in. Oh don't shut me out, Caroline, let me in.

(*He has been caressing her feet and legs. He disappears completely under her skirt.*)

MRS SAUNDERS: Please stop. I can't concentrate. I want to go   45
    home. I wish I didn't enjoy the sensation because I don't
    like you, Clive. I do like living in your house where there's
    plenty of guns. But I don't like you at all. But I do like the
    sensation. Well I'll have it then. I'll have it, I'll have it—

(*Voices are heard singing The First Noël.*)

Don't stop. Don't stop.   50

(CLIVE *comes out from under her skirt.*)

CLIVE: The Christmas picnic. I came.
MRS SAUNDERS: I didn't.
CLIVE: I'm all sticky.
MRS SAUNDERS: What about me? Wait.
CLIVE: All right, are you? Come on. We mustn't be found.   55
MRS SAUNDERS: Don't go now.
CLIVE: Caroline, you are so voracious. Do let go. Tidy your-
    self up. There's a hair in my mouth.

(CLIVE *and* MRS SAUNDERS *go off.* BETTY *and* MAUD *come, with* JOSHUA *carrying hamper.*)

MAUD: I never would have thought a guinea fowl could taste
    so like a turkey.   60
BETTY: I had to explain to the cook three times.
MAUD: You did very well dear.

(JOSHUA *sits apart with gun.* EDWARD *and* HARRY *with* VICTORIA *on his shoulder, singing The First Noël.* MAUD *and* BETTY *are un-packing the hamper.* CLIVE *arrives separately.*)

MAUD: This tablecloth was one of my mama's.
BETTY: Uncle Harry playing horsy.
EDWARD: Crackers crackers.   65
BETTY: Not yet, Edward.
CLIVE: And now the moment we have all been waiting for.

(CLIVE *opens champagne. General acclaim.*)

CLIVE: Oh dear, stained my trousers, never mind.
EDWARD: Can I have some?
MAUD: Oh no Edward, not for you.   70
CLIVE: Give him half a glass.
MAUD: If your father says so.
CLIVE: All rise please. To Her Majesty Queen Victoria, God
    bless her, and her husband and all her dear children.

75   ALL: The Queen.
EDWARD: Crackers crackers.

(*General cracker pulling, hats.* CLIVE *and* HARRY *discuss champagne.*)

HARRY: Excellent, Clive, wherever did you get it?
CLIVE: I know a chap in French Equatorial Africa.
EDWARD: I won, I won mama.

(ELLEN *arrives.*)

80   BETTY: Give a hat to Joshua, he'd like it.

(EDWARD *takes hat to* JOSHUA. BETTY *takes a ball from the hamper and plays catch with* ELLEN. *Murmurs of surprise and congratulations from the men whenever they catch the ball.*)

EDWARD: Mama, don't play. You know you can't catch a ball.
BETTY: He's perfectly right. I can't throw either.

(BETTY *sits down.* ELLEN *has the ball.*)

EDWARD: Ellen, don't you play either. You're no good. You
       spoil it.

(EDWARD *takes* VICTORIA *from* HARRY *and gives her to* ELLEN. *He takes the ball and throws it to* HARRY. HARRY, CLIVE *and* EDWARD *play ball.*)

85   BETTY: Ellen come and sit with me. We'll be spectators and
       clap.

(EDWARD *misses the ball.*)

CLIVE: Butterfingers.
EDWARD: I'm not.
HARRY: Throw straight now.
90   EDWARD: I did, I did.
CLIVE: Keep your eye on the ball.
EDWARD: You can't throw.
CLIVE: Don't be a baby.
EDWARD: I'm not, throw a hard one, throw a hard one—
95   CLIVE: Butterfingers. What will Uncle Harry think of you?
EDWARD: It's your fault. You can't throw. I hate you.

(*He throws the ball wildly in the direction of* JOSHUA.)

CLIVE: Now you've lost the ball. He's lost the ball.
EDWARD: It's Joshua's fault. Joshua's butterfingers.
CLIVE: I don't think I want to play any more. Joshua, find the
100   ball will you?
EDWARD: Yes, please play. I'll find the ball. Please play.
CLIVE: You're so silly and you can't catch. You'll be no good
       at cricket.
MAUD: Why don't we play hide and seek?
105 EDWARD: Because it's a baby game.
BETTY: You've hurt Edward's feelings.
CLIVE: A boy has no business having feelings.
HARRY: Hide and seek. I'll be it. Everybody must hide. This
       is the base, you have to get home to base.
110 EDWARD: Hide and seek, hide and seek.
HARRY: Can we persuade the ladies to join us?
MAUD: I'm playing. I love games.

BETTY: I always get found straight away.
ELLEN: Come on, Betty, do. Vicky wants to play.
EDWARD: You won't find me ever.   115

(*They all go except* CLIVE, HARRY, JOSHUA.)

HARRY: It is safe, I suppose?
CLIVE: They won't go far. This is very much my territory and
       it's broad daylight. Joshua will keep an open eye.
HARRY: Well I must give them a hundred. You don't know
       what this means to me, Clive. A chap can only go on so   120
       long alone. I can climb mountains and go down rivers, but
       what's it for? For Christmas and England and games and
       women singing. This is the empire, Clive. It's not me
       putting a flag in new lands. It's you. The empire is one big
       family. I'm one of its black sheep, Clive. And I know you   125
       think my life is rather dashing. But I want you to know I
       admire you. This is the empire, Clive, and I serve it. With
       all my heart.
CLIVE: I think that's about a hundred.
HARRY: Ready or not, here I come!   130

(*He goes.*)

CLIVE: Harry Bagley is a fine man, Joshua. You should be
       proud to know him. He will be in history books.
JOSHUA: Sir, while we are alone.
CLIVE: Joshua of course, what is it? You always have my ear.
       Any time.   135
JOSHUA: Sir, I have some information. The stable boys are not
       to be trusted. They whisper. They go out at night. They
       visit their people. Their people are not my people. I do
       not visit my people.
CLIVE: Thank you, Joshua. They certainly look after Beauty.   140
       I'll be sorry to have to replace them.
JOSHUA: They carry knives.
CLIVE: Thank you, Joshua.
JOSHUA: And, sir.
CLIVE: I appreciate this, Joshua, very much.   145
JOSHUA: Your wife.
CLIVE: Ah, yes?
JOSHUA: She also thinks Harry Bagley is a fine man.
CLIVE: Thank you, Joshua.
JOSHUA: Are you going to hide?   150
CLIVE: Yes, yes I am. Thank you. Keep your eyes open Joshua.
JOSHUA: I do, sir.

(CLIVE *goes.* JOSHUA *goes.* HARRY *and* BETTY *race back to base.*)

BETTY: I can't run, I can't run at all.
HARRY: There, I've caught you.
BETTY: Harry, what are we going to do?   155
HARRY: It's impossible, Betty.
BETTY: Shall we run away together?

(MAUD *comes.*)

MAUD: I give up. Don't catch me. I have been stung.
HARRY: Nothing serious I hope.
MAUD: I have ointment in my bag. I always carry ointment. I   160
       shall just sit down and rest. I am too old for all this fun.
       Hadn't you better be seeking, Harry?

(HARRY *goes.* MAUD *and* BETTY *are alone for some time. They don't speak.* HARRY *and* EDWARD *race back.*)

EDWARD: I won, I won, you didn't catch me.
HARRY: Yes I did.
165 EDWARD: Mama, who was first?
BETTY: I wasn't watching. I think it was Harry.
EDWARD: It wasn't Harry. You're no good at judging. I won, didn't I grandma?
MAUD: I expect so, since it's Christmas.
170 EDWARD: I won, Uncle Harry. I'm better than you.
BETTY: Why don't you help Uncle Harry look for the others?
EDWARD: Shall I?
HARRY: Yes, of course.
BETTY: Run along then. He's just coming.

(EDWARD *goes.*)

175   Harry, I shall scream.
HARRY: Ready or not, here I come.

(HARRY *runs off.*)

BETTY: Why don't you go back to the house, mother, and rest your insect-bite?
MAUD: Betty, my duty is here. I don't like what I see. Clive
180   wouldn't like it, Betty. I am your mother.
BETTY: Clive gives you a home because you are my mother.

(HARRY *comes back.*)

HARRY: I can't find anyone else. I'm getting quite hot.
BETTY: Sit down a minute.
HARRY: I can't do that. I'm he. How's your sting?
185 MAUD: It seems to be swelling up.
BETTY: Why don't you go home and rest? Joshua will go with you. Joshua!
HARRY: I could take you back.
MAUD: That would be charming.
190 BETTY: You can't go. You're he.

(JOSHUA *comes.*)

   Joshua, my mother wants to go back to the house. Will you go with her please.
JOSHUA: Sir told me I have to keep an eye.
BETTY: I am telling you to go back to the house. Then you
195   can come back here and keep an eye.
MAUD: Thank you Betty. I know we have our little differences, but I always want what is best for you.

(JOSHUA *and* MAUD *go.*)

HARRY: Don't give way. Keep calm.
BETTY: I shall kill myself.
200 HARRY: Betty, you are a star in my sky. Without you I would have no sense of direction. I need you, and I need you where you are, I need you to be Clive's wife. I need to go up rivers and know you are sitting here thinking of me.
BETTY: I want more than that. Is that wicked of me?
205 HARRY: Not wicked, Betty. Silly.

(EDWARD *calls in the distance.*)

EDWARD: Uncle Harry, where are you?
BETTY: Can't we ever be alone?
HARRY: You are a mother. And a daughter. And a wife.
BETTY: I think I shall go and hide again.

(BETTY *goes.* HARRY *goes.* CLIVE *chases* MRS SAUNDERS *across the stage.* EDWARD *and* HARRY *call in the distance.*)

EDWARD: Uncle Harry!   210
HARRY: Edward!

(EDWARD *comes.*)

EDWARD: Uncle Harry!

(HARRY *comes.*)

   There you are. I haven't found anyone have you?
HARRY: I wonder where they all are.
EDWARD: Perhaps they're lost forever. Perhaps they're dead. 215   There's trouble going on isn't there, and nobody says because of not frightening the women and children.
HARRY: Yes, that's right.
EDWARD: Do you think we'll be killed in our beds?
HARRY: Not very likely.   220
EDWARD: I can't sleep at night. Can you?
HARRY: I'm not used to sleeping in a house.
EDWARD: If I'm awake at night can I come and see you? I won't wake you up. I'll only come in if you're awake.
HARRY: You should try to sleep.   225
EDWARD: I don't mind being awake because I make up adventures. Once we were on a raft going down to the rapids. We've lost the paddles because we used them to fight off the crocodiles. A crocodile comes at me and I stab it again and again and the blood is everywhere and it tips up the raft and 230   it has you by the leg and it's biting your leg right off and I take my knife and stab it in the throat and rip open its stomach and it lets go of you but it bites my hand but it's dead. And I drag you onto the river bank and I'm almost fainting with pain and we lie there in each other's arms.   235
HARRY: Have I lost my leg?
EDWARD: I forgot about the leg by then.
HARRY: Hadn't we better look for the others?
EDWARD: Wait. I've got something for you. It was in mama's box but she never wears it.   240

(EDWARD *gives* HARRY *a necklace.*)

   You don't have to wear it either but you might like it to look at.
HARRY: It's beautiful. But you'll have to put it back.
EDWARD: I wanted to give it to you.
HARRY: You did. It can go back in the box. You still gave it 245   to me. Come on now, we have to find the others.
EDWARD: Harry, I love you.
HARRY: Yes I know. I love you too.
EDWARD: You know what we did when you were here before. I want to do it again. I think about it all the time. I try to do it 250   to myself but it's not as good. Don't you want to any more?
HARRY: I do, but it's a sin and a crime and it's also wrong.
EDWARD: But we'll do it anyway won't we?
HARRY: Yes of course.

255 EDWARD: I wish the others would all be killed. Take it out
       now and let me see it.
    HARRY: No.
    EDWARD: Is it big now?
    HARRY: Yes.
260 EDWARD: Let me touch it.
    HARRY: No.
    EDWARD: Just hold me.
    HARRY: When you can't sleep.
    EDWARD: We'd better find the others then. Come on.
265 HARRY: Ready or not, here we come.

(*They go out with whoops and shouts.* BETTY *and* ELLEN *come.*)

    BETTY: Ellen, I don't want to play any more.
    ELLEN: Nor do I, Betty.
    BETTY: Come and sit here with me. Oh Ellen, what will be-
       come of me?
270 ELLEN: Betty, are you crying? Are you laughing?
    BETTY: Tell me what you think of Harry Bagley.
    ELLEN: He's a very fine man.
    BETTY: No, Ellen, what you really think.
    ELLEN: I think you think he's very handsome.
275 BETTY: And don't you think he is? Oh Ellen, you're so good
       and I'm so wicked.
    ELLEN: I'm not so good as you think.

(EDWARD *comes.*)

    EDWARD: I've found you.
    ELLEN: We're not hiding Edward.
280 EDWARD: But I found you.
    ELLEN: We're not playing, Edward, now run along.
    EDWARD: Come on, Ellen, do play. Come on, mama.
    ELLEN: Edward, don't pull your mama like that.
    BETTY: Edward, you must do what your governess says. Go
285   and play with Uncle Harry.
    EDWARD: Uncle Harry!

(EDWARD *goes.*)

    BETTY: Ellen, can you keep a secret?
    ELLEN: Oh yes, yes please.
    BETTY: I love Harry Bagley. I want to go away with him.
290   There, I've said it, it's true.
    ELLEN: How do you know you love him?
    BETTY: I kissed him.
    ELLEN: Betty.
    BETTY: He held my hand like this. Oh I want him to do it
295   again. I want him to stroke my hair.
    ELLEN: Your lovely hair. Like this, Betty?
    BETTY: I want him to put his arm around my waist.
    ELLEN: Like this, Betty?
    BETTY: Yes, oh I want him to kiss me again.
300 ELLEN: Like this Betty?

(ELLEN *kisses* BETTY.)

    BETTY: Ellen, whatever are you doing? It's not a joke.
    ELLEN: I'm sorry, Betty. You're so pretty. Harry Bagley doesn't
       deserve you. You wouldn't really go away with him?
    BETTY: Oh Ellen, you don't know what I suffer. You don't
305   know what love is. Everyone will hate me, but it's worth
       it for Harry's love.

    ELLEN: I don't hate you, Betty, I love you.
    BETTY: Harry says we shouldn't go away. But he says he wor-
       ships me.
    ELLEN: I worship you Betty.   310
    BETTY: Oh Ellen, you are my only friend.

(*They embrace. The others have all gathered together.* MAUD *has re-
joined the party, and* JOSHUA.)

    CLIVE: Come along everyone, you mustn't miss Harry's con-
       juring trick.

(BETTY *and* ELLEN *go to join the others.*)

    MAUD: I didn't want to spoil the fun by not being here.
    HARRY: What is it that flies all over the world and is up my   315
       sleeve?

(HARRY *produces a union jack from up his sleeve. General acclaim.*)

    CLIVE: I think we should have some singing now. Ladies, I
       rely on you to lead the way.
    ELLEN: We have a surprise for you. I have taught Joshua a
       Christmas carol. He has been singing it at the piano but   320
       I'm sure he can sing it unaccompanied, can't you, Joshua?
    JOSHUA: In the deep midwinter
                  Frosty wind made moan,
                  Earth stood hard as iron,
                  Water like a stone.   325
                  Snow had fallen snow on snow
                  Snow on snow,
                  In the deep midwinter
                  Long long ago.

                  What can I give him   330
                  Poor as I am?
                  If I were a shepherd
                  I would bring a lamb.
                  If I were a wise man
                  I would do my part   335
                  What can I give him,
                  Give my heart.

SCENE III

Inside the house. BETTY, MRS SAUNDERS, MAUD *with* VICTORIA.
*The blinds are down so the light isn't bright though it is day out-
side.* CLIVE *looks in.*

    CLIVE: Everything all right? Nothing to be frightened of.

(CLIVE *goes. Silence.*)

    MAUD: Clap hands, daddy comes, with his pockets full of
       plums. All for Vicky.

(*Silence.*)

    MRS SAUNDERS: Who actually does the flogging?
    MAUD: I don't think we want to imagine.   5
    MRS SAUNDERS: I imagine Joshua.
    BETTY: Yes I think it would be Joshua. Or would Clive do it
       himself?
    MRS SAUNDERS: Well we can ask them afterwards.

10 MAUD: I don't like the way you speak of it, Mrs Saunders.

MRS SAUNDERS: How should I speak of it?

MAUD: The men will do it in the proper way, whatever it is. We have our own part to play.

MRS SAUNDERS: Harry Bagley says they should just be sent
15   away. I don't think he likes to see them beaten.

BETTY: Harry is so tender hearted. Perhaps he is right.

MAUD: Harry Bagley is not altogether—He has lived in this country a long time without any responsibilities. It is part of his charm but it hasn't improved his judgment. If the
20   boys were just sent away they would go back to the village and make more trouble.

MRS SAUNDERS: And what will they say about us in the village if they've been flogged?

BETTY: Perhaps Clive should keep them here.

25 MRS SAUNDERS: That is never wise.

BETTY: Whatever shall we do?

MAUD: I don't think it is up to us to wonder. The men don't tell us what is going on among the tribes, so how can we possibly make a judgment?

30 MRS SAUNDERS: I know a little of what is going on.

BETTY: Tell me what you know. Clive tells me nothing.

MAUD: You would not want to be told about it, Betty. It is enough for you that Clive knows what is happening. Clive will know what to do. Your father always knew what to do.

35 BETTY: Are you saying you would do something different, Caroline?

MRS SAUNDERS: I would do what I did at my own home. I left. I can't see any way out except to leave. I will leave here. I will keep leaving everywhere I suppose.

40 MAUD: Luckily this household has a head. I am squeamish myself. But luckily Clive is not.

BETTY: You are leaving here then, Caroline?

MRS SAUNDERS: Not immediately. I'm sorry.

(*Silence.*)

MRS SAUNDERS: I wonder if it's over.

(EDWARD *comes in.*)

45 BETTY: Shouldn't you be with the men, Edward?

EDWARD: I didn't want to see any more. They got what they deserved. Uncle Harry said I could come in.

MRS SAUNDERS: I never allowed the servants to be beaten in my own house. I'm going to find out what's happening.

(MRS SAUNDERS *goes out.*)

50 BETTY: Will she go and look?

MAUD: Let Mrs Saunders be a warning to you, Betty. She is alone in the world. You are not, thank God. Since your father died, I know what it is to be unprotected. Vicky is such a pretty little girl. Clap hands, daddy comes, with his
55   pockets full of plums. All for Vicky.

(EDWARD, *meanwhile, has found the doll and is playing clap hands with her.*)

BETTY: Edward, what have you got there?

EDWARD: I'm minding her.

BETTY: Edward, I've told you before, dolls are for girls.

MAUD: Where is Ellen? She should be looking after Edward. (*She goes to the door.*) Ellen! Betty, why do you let that girl 60
mope about in her own room? That's not what she's come to Africa for.

BETTY: You must never let the boys at school know you like dolls. Never, never. No one will talk to you, you won't be on the cricket team, you won't grow up to be a man like 65
your papa.

EDWARD: I don't want to be like papa. I hate papa.

MAUD: Edward! Edward!

BETTY: You're a horrid wicked boy and papa will beat you. Of course you don't hate him, you love him. Now give 70
Victoria her doll at once.

EDWARD: She's not Victoria's doll, she's my doll. She doesn't love Victoria and Victoria doesn't love her. Victoria never even plays with her.

MAUD: Victoria will learn to play with her. 75

EDWARD: She's mine and she loves me and she won't be happy if you take her away, she'll cry, she'll cry, she'll cry.

(BETTY *takes the doll away, slaps him, bursts into tears.* ELLEN *comes in.*)

BETTY: Ellen, look what you've done. Edward's got the doll again. Now, Ellen, will you please do your job.

ELLEN: Edward, you are a wicked boy. I am going to lock you 80
in the nursery until supper time. Now go upstairs this minute.

(*She slaps* EDWARD, *who bursts into tears and goes out.*)

I do try to do what you want. I'm so sorry.

(ELLEN *bursts into tears and goes out.*)

MAUD: There now, Vicky's got her baby back. Where did Vicky's naughty baby go? Shall we smack her? Just a little 85
smack. (MAUD *smacks the doll hard.*) There, now she's a good baby. Clap hands, daddy comes, with his pockets full of plums. All for Vicky's baby. When I was a child we honoured our parents. My mama was an angel.

(JOSHUA *comes in. He stands without speaking.*)

BETTY: Joshua? 90

JOSHUA: Madam?

BETTY: Did you want something?

JOSHUA: Sent to see the ladies are all right, madam.

(MRS SAUNDERS *comes in.*)

MRS SAUNDERS: We're very well thank you, Joshua, and how are you? 95

JOSHUA: Very well thank you, Mrs Saunders.

MRS SAUNDERS: And the stable boys?

JOSHUA: They have had justice, madam.

MRS SAUNDERS: So I saw. And does your arm ache?

MAUD: This is not a proper conversation, Mrs Saunders. 100

MRS SAUNDERS: You don't mind beating your own people?

JOSHUA: Not my people, madam.

MRS SAUNDERS: A different tribe?

JOSHUA: Bad people.

(HARRY *and* CLIVE *come in.*)

105 CLIVE: Well this is all very gloomy and solemn. Can we have the shutters open? The heat of the day has gone, we could have some light, I think. And cool drinks on the verandah, Joshua. Have some lemonade yourself. It is most refreshing.

(*Sunlight floods in as the shutters are opened.* EDWARD *comes.*)

EDWARD: Papa, papa, Ellen tried to lock me in the nursery.
110 Mama is going to tell you of me. I'd rather tell you myself. I was playing with Vicky's doll again and I know it's very bad of me. And I said I didn't want to be like you and I said I hated you. And it's not true and I'm sorry, I'm sorry and please beat me and forgive me.

115 CLIVE: Well there's a brave boy to own up. You should always respect and love me, Edward, not for myself, I may not deserve it, but as I respected and loved my own father, because he was my father. Through our father we love our Queen and our God, Edward. Do you understand? It is
120 something men understand.

EDWARD: Yes papa.

CLIVE: Then I forgive you and shake you by the hand. You spend too much time with the women. You may spend more time with me and Uncle Harry, little man.

125 EDWARD: I don't like women. I don't like dolls. I love you, papa, and I love you, Uncle Harry.

CLIVE: There's a fine fellow. Let us go out onto the verandah.

(*They all start to go.* EDWARD *takes* HARRY'*s hand and goes with him.* CLIVE *draws* BETTY *back. They embrace.*)

BETTY: Poor Clive.

CLIVE: It was my duty to have them flogged. For you and Ed-
130 ward and Victoria, to keep you safe.

BETTY: It is terrible to feel betrayed.

CLIVE: You can tame a wild animal only so far. They revert to their true nature and savage your hand. Sometimes I feel the natives are the enemy. I know that is wrong. I know I
135 have a responsibility towards them, to care for them and bring them all to be like Joshua. But there is something dangerous. Implacable. This whole continent is my enemy. I am pitching my whole mind and will and reason and spirit against it to tame it, and I sometimes feel it will
140 break over me and swallow me up.

BETTY: Clive, Clive, I am here. I have faith in you.

CLIVE: Yes, I can show you my moments of weakness, Betty, because you are my wife and because I trust you. I trust you, Betty, and it would break my heart if you did not de-
145 serve that trust. Harry Bagley is my friend. It would break my heart if he did not deserve my trust.

BETTY: I'm sorry, I'm sorry. Forgive me. It is not Harry's fault, it is all mine. Harry is noble. He has rejected me. It is my wickedness, I get bored, I get restless, I imagine things.
150 There is something so wicked in me, Clive.

CLIVE: I have never thought of you having the weakness of your sex, only the good qualities.

BETTY: I am bad, bad, bad—

CLIVE: You are thoughtless, Betty, that's all. Women can be
155 treacherous and evil. They are darker and more dangerous than men. The family protects us from that, you protect me

from that. You are not that sort of woman. You are not unfaithful to me, Betty. I can't believe you are. It would hurt me so much to cast you off. That would be my duty.

BETTY: No, no, no.   160

CLIVE: Joshua has seen you kissing.

BETTY: Forgive me.

CLIVE: But I don't want to know about it. I don't want to know. I wonder of course, I wonder constantly. If Harry Bagley was not my friend I would shoot him. If I shot you 165 every British man and woman would applaud me. But no. It was a moment of passion such as women are too weak to resist. But you must resist it, Betty, or it will destroy us. We must fight against it. We must resist this dark female lust, Betty, or it will swallow us up.   170

BETTY: I do, I do resist. Help me. Forgive me.

CLIVE: Yes I do forgive you. But I can't feel the same about you as I did. You are still my wife and we still have duties to the household.

(*They go out arm in arm. As soon as they have gone* EDWARD *sneaks back to get the doll, which has been dropped on the floor. He picks it up and comforts it.* JOSHUA *comes through with a tray of drinks.*)

JOSHUA: Baby. Sissy. Girly.   175

(JOSHUA *goes.* BETTY *calls from off.*)

BETTY: Edward?

(BETTY *comes in.*)

BETTY: There you are, my darling. Come, papa wants us all to be together. Uncle Harry is going to tell how he caught a crocodile. Mama's sorry she smacked you.

(*They embrace.* JOSHUA *comes in again, passing through.*)

BETTY: Joshua, fetch me some blue thread from my sewing 180 box. It is on the piano.

JOSHUA: You've got legs under that skirt.

BETTY: Joshua.

JOSHUA: And more than legs.

BETTY: Edward, are you going to stand there and let a servant 185 insult your mother?

EDWARD: Joshua, get my mother's thread.

JOSHUA: Oh little Eddy, playing at master. It's only a joke.

EDWARD: Don't speak to my mother like that again.

JOSHUA: Ladies have no sense of humour. You like a joke 190 with Joshua.

EDWARD: You fetch her sewing at once, do you hear me? You move when I speak to you, boy.

JOSHUA: Yes sir, master Edward sir.

(JOSHUA *goes.*)

BETTY: Edward, you were wonderful.   195

(*She goes to embrace him but he moves away.*)

EDWARD: Don't touch me.

Song

A BOY'S BEST FRIEND

ALL: While plodding on our way, the toilsome road of life,
How few the friends that daily there we meet.
Not many will stand in trouble and in strife,
200   With counsel and affection ever sweet.
But there is one whose smile will ever on us beam,
Whose love is dearer far than any other;
And wherever we may turn
This lesson we will learn
205   A boy's best friend is his mother.

Then cherish her with care
And smooth her silv'ry hair,
When gone you will never get another.
And wherever we may turn
210   This lesson we shall learn,
A boy's best friend is his mother.

SCENE IV

The verandah as in Scene One. Early morning. Nobody there.
JOSHUA *comes out of the house slowly and stands for some time doing nothing.* EDWARD *comes out.*

EDWARD: Tell me another bad story, Joshua. Nobody else is
even awake yet.

JOSHUA: First there was nothing and then there was the great
goddess. She was very large and she had golden eyes and
5   she made the stars and the sun and the earth. But soon she
was miserable and lonely and she cried like a great waterfall and her tears made all the rivers in the world. So the
great spirit sent a terrible monster, a tree with hundreds of
eyes and a long green tongue, and it came chasing after
10   her and she jumped into a lake and the tree jumped in after her, and she jumped right up into the sky. And the tree
couldn't follow, he was stuck in the mud. So he picked up
a big handful of mud and he threw it at her, up among the
stars, and it hit her on the head. And she fell down onto
15   the earth into his arms and the ball of mud is the moon
in the sky. And then they had children which is all of us.

EDWARD: It's not true, though.

JOSHUA: Of course it's not true. It's a bad story. Adam and Eve is
true. God made man white like him and gave him the bad
20   woman who liked the snake and gave us all this trouble.

(CLIVE *and* HARRY *come out.*)

CLIVE: Run along now, Edward. No, you may stay. You
mustn't repeat anything you hear to your mother or your
grandmother or Ellen.

EDWARD: Or Mrs Saunders?

25   CLIVE: Mrs Saunders is an unusual woman and does not require protection in the same way. Harry, there was trouble
last night where we expected it. But it's all over now.
Everything is under control but nobody should leave the
house today I think.

30   HARRY: Casualties?

CLIVE: No, none of the soldiers hurt thank God. We did a certain amount of damage, set a village on fire and so forth.

HARRY: Was that necessary?

CLIVE: Obviously, it was necessary, Harry, or it wouldn't have
happened. The army will come and visit, no doubt. You'll   35
like that, eh, Joshua, to see the British army? And a treat
for you, Edward, to see the soldiers. Would you like to be
a soldier?

EDWARD: I'd rather be an explorer.

CLIVE: Ah, Harry, like you, you see. I didn't know an explorer   40
at his age. Breakfast, I think, Joshua.

(CLIVE *and* JOSHUA *go in.* HARRY *is following.*)

EDWARD: Uncle.

(HARRY *stops.*)

EDWARD: Harry, why won't you talk to me?

HARRY: Of course I'll talk to you.

EDWARD: If you won't be nice to me I'll tell father.   45

HARRY: Edward, no, not a word, never, not to your mother,
nobody, please. Edward, do you understand? Please.

EDWARD: I won't tell. I promise I'll never tell. I've cut my finger and sworn.

HARRY: There's no need to get so excited Edward. We can't   50
be together all the time. I will have to leave soon anyway,
and go back to the river.

EDWARD: You can't, you can't go. Take me with you.

ELLEN: Edward!

HARRY: I have my duty to the Empire.   55

(HARRY *goes in.* ELLEN *comes out.*)

ELLEN: Edward, breakfast time. Edward.

EDWARD: I'm not hungry.

ELLEN: Betty, please come and speak to Edward.

(BETTY *comes.*)

BETTY: Why what's the matter?

ELLEN: He won't come in for breakfast.   60

BETTY: Edward, I shall call your father.

EDWARD: You can't make me eat.

(*He goes in.* BETTY *is about to follow.*)

ELLEN: Betty.

(BETTY *stops.*)

ELLEN: Betty, when Edward goes to school will I have to leave?

BETTY: Never mind, Ellen dear, you'll get another place. I'll   65
give you an excellent reference.

ELLEN: I don't want another place, Betty. I want to stay with
you forever.

BETTY: If you go back to England you might get married,
Ellen. You're quite pretty, you shouldn't despair of getting   70
a husband.

ELLEN: I don't want a husband. I want you.

BETTY: Children of your own, Ellen, think.

ELLEN: I don't want children, I don't like children. I just want
to be alone with you, Betty, and sing for you and kiss you   75
because I love you, Betty.

BETTY: I love you too, Ellen. But women have their duty as
soldiers have. You must be a mother if you can.

ELLEN: Betty, Betty, I love you so much. I want to stay with
80   you forever, my love for you is eternal, stronger than
     death. I'd rather die than leave you, Betty.
BETTY: No you wouldn't, Ellen, don't be silly. Come, don't
     cry. You don't feel what you think you do. It's the loneli-
     ness here and the climate is very confusing. Come and
85   have breakfast, Ellen dear, and I'll forget all about it.

(ELLEN *goes,* CLIVE *comes.*)

BETTY: Clive, please forgive me.
CLIVE: Will you leave me alone?

(BETTY *goes back into the house.* HARRY *comes.*)

CLIVE: Women, Harry. I envy you going into the jungle, a
     man's life.
90   HARRY: I envy you.
CLIVE: Harry, I know you do. I have spoken to Betty.
HARRY: I assure you, Clive—
CLIVE: Please say nothing about it.
HARRY: My friendship for you—
95   CLIVE: Absolutely. I know the friendship between us, Harry,
     is not something that could be spoiled by the weaker sex.
     Friendship between men is a fine thing. It is the noblest
     form of relationship.
HARRY: I agree with you.
100 CLIVE: There is the necessity of reproduction. The family is
     all important. And there is the pleasure. But what we put
     ourselves through to get that pleasure, Harry. When I
     heard about our fine fellows last night fighting those sav-
     ages to protect us I thought yes, that is what I aspire to. I
105 tell you Harry, in confidence, I suddenly got out of Mrs
     Saunders' bed and came out here on the verandah and
     looked at the stars.
HARRY: I couldn't sleep last night either.
CLIVE: There is something dark about women, that threatens
110 what is best in us. Between men that light burns brightly.
HARRY: I didn't know you felt like that.
CLIVE: Women are irrational, demanding, inconsistent,
     treacherous, lustful, and they smell different from us.
HARRY: Clive—
115 CLIVE: Think of the comradeship of men, Harry, sharing ad-
     ventures, sharing danger, risking their lives together.

(HARRY *takes hold of* CLIVE.)

CLIVE: What are you doing?
HARRY: Well, you said—
CLIVE: I said what?
120 HARRY: Between men.

(CLIVE *is speechless.*)

     I'm sorry, I misunderstood, I would never have dreamt, I
     thought—
CLIVE: My God, Harry, how disgusting.
HARRY: You will not betray my confidence.
125 CLIVE: I feel contaminated.
HARRY: I struggle against it. You cannot imagine the shame.
     I have tried everything to save myself.
CLIVE: The most revolting perversion. Rome fell, Harry, and
     this sin can destroy an empire.

HARRY: It is not a sin, it is a disease.   130
CLIVE: A disease more dangerous than diphtheria. Effeminacy
     is contagious. How I have been deceived. Your face does
     not look degenerate. Oh Harry, how did you sink to this?
HARRY: Clive, help me, what am I to do?
CLIVE: You have been away from England too long.   135
HARRY: Where can I go except into the jungle to hide?
CLIVE: You don't do it with the natives, Harry? My God, what
     a betrayal of the Queen.
HARRY: Clive, I am like a man born crippled. Please help me.
CLIVE: You must repent.   140
HARRY: I have thought of killing myself.
CLIVE: That is a sin too.
HARRY: There is no way out. Clive, I beg of you, do not be-
     tray my confidence.
CLIVE: I cannot keep a secret like this. Rivers will be named after 145
     you, it's unthinkable. You must save yourself from depravity.
     You must get married. You are not unattractive to women.
     What a relief that you and Betty were not after all—good
     God, how disgusting. Now Mrs Saunders. She's a woman of
     spirit, she could go with you on your expeditions.   150
HARRY: I suppose getting married wouldn't be any worse
     than killing myself.
CLIVE: Mrs Saunders! Mrs Saunders! Ask her now, Harry.
     Think of England.

(MRS SAUNDERS *comes.* CLIVE *withdraws.* HARRY *goes up to* MRS
SAUNDERS.)

HARRY: Mrs Saunders, will you marry me?   155
MRS SAUNDERS: Why?
HARRY: We are both alone.
MRS SAUNDERS: I choose to be alone, Mr Bagley. If I can look
     after myself, I'm sure you can. Clive, I have something im-
     portant to tell you. I've just found Joshua putting earth on 160
     his head. He tells me his parents were killed last night by
     the British soldiers. I think you owe him an apology on
     behalf of the Queen.
CLIVE: Joshua! Joshua!
MRS SAUNDERS: Mr Bagley, I could never be a wife again.   165
     There is only one thing about marriage that I like.

(JOSHUA *comes.*)

CLIVE: Joshua, I am horrified to hear what has happened.
     Good God!
MRS SAUNDERS: His father was shot. His mother died in the
     blaze.   170

(MRS SAUNDERS *goes.*)

CLIVE: Joshua, do you want a day off? Do you want to go to
     your people?
JOSHUA: Not my people, sir.
CLIVE: But you want to go to your parents' funeral?
JOSHUA: No sir.   175
CLIVE: Yes, Joshua, yes, your father and mother. I'm sure they
     were loyal to the crown. I'm sure it was all a terrible mistake.
JOSHUA: My mother and father were bad people.
CLIVE: Joshua, no.
JOSHUA: You are my father and mother.   180

CLIVE: Well really. I don't know what to say. That's very decent of you. Are you sure there's nothing I can do? You can have the day off you know.

(BETTY *comes out followed by* EDWARD.)

BETTY: What's the matter? What's happening?

185 CLIVE: Something terrible has happened. No, I mean some relatives of Joshua's met with an accident.

JOSHUA: May I go sir?

CLIVE: Yes, yes of course. Good God, what a terrible thing. Bring us a drink will you Joshua?

(JOSHUA *goes.*)

190 EDWARD: What? What?

BETTY: Edward, go and do your lessons.

EDWARD: What is it, Uncle Harry?

HARRY: Go and do your lessons.

ELLEN: Edward, come in here at once.

195 EDWARD: What's happened, Uncle Harry?

(HARRY *has moved aside,* EDWARD *follows him.* ELLEN *comes out.*)

HARRY: Go away. Go inside. Ellen!

ELLEN: Go inside, Edward. I shall tell your mother.

BETTY: Go inside, Edward at once. I shall tell your father.

CLIVE: Go inside, Edward. And Betty you go inside too.

(BETTY, EDWARD *and* ELLEN *go.* MAUD *comes out.*)

200 CLIVE: Go inside. And Ellen, you come outside.

(ELLEN *comes out.*)

Mr Bagley has something to say to you.

HARRY: Ellen. I don't suppose you would marry me?

ELLEN: What if I said yes?

CLIVE: Run along now, you two want to be alone.

(HARRY *and* ELLEN *go out.* JOSHUA *brings* CLIVE *a drink.*)

205 JOSHUA: The governess and your wife, sir.

CLIVE: What's that, Joshua?

JOSHUA: She talks of love to your wife, sir. I have seen them. Bad women.

CLIVE: Joshua, you go too far. Get out of my sight.

SCENE V

The verandah. A table with a white cloth. A wedding cake and a large knife. Bottles and glasses. JOSHUA *is putting things on the table.* EDWARD *has the doll.* JOSHUA *sees him with it. He holds out his hand.* EDWARD *gives him the doll.* JOSHUA *takes the knife and cuts the doll open and shakes the sawdust out of it.* JOSHUA *throws the doll under the table.*

MAUD: Come along Edward, this is such fun.

(*Everyone enters, triumphal arch for* HARRY *and* ELLEN.)

MAUD: Your mama's wedding was a splendid occasion, Edward. I cried and cried.

(ELLEN *and* BETTY *go aside.*)

ELLEN: Betty, what happens with a man? I don't know what to do. 5

BETTY: You just keep still.

ELLEN: And what does he do?

BETTY: Harry will know what to do.

ELLEN: And is it enjoyable?

BETTY: Ellen, you're not getting married to enjoy yourself. 10

ELLEN: Don't forget me, Betty.

(ELLEN *goes.*)

BETTY: I think my necklace has been stolen Clive. I did so want to wear it at the wedding.

EDWARD: It was Joshua. Joshua took it.

CLIVE: Joshua? 15

EDWARD: He did, he did, I saw him with it.

HARRY: Edward, that's not true.

EDWARD: It is, it is.

HARRY: Edward, I'm afraid you took it yourself.

EDWARD: I did not. 20

HARRY: I have seen him with it.

CLIVE: Edward, is that true? Where is it? Did you take your mother's necklace? And to try and blame Joshua, good God.

(EDWARD *runs off.*)

BETTY: Edward, come back. Have you got my necklace?

HARRY: I should leave him alone. He'll bring it back. 25

BETTY: I wanted to wear it. I wanted to look my best at your wedding.

HARRY: You always look your best to me.

BETTY: I shall get drunk.

(MRS SAUNDERS *comes.*)

MRS SAUNDERS: The sale of my property is completed. I shall 30 leave tomorrow.

CLIVE: That's just as well. Whose protection will you seek this time?

MRS SAUNDERS: I shall go to England and buy a farm there. I shall introduce threshing machines. 35

CLIVE: Amazing spirit.

(*He kisses her.* BETTY *launches herself on* MRS SAUNDERS. *They fall to the ground.*)

CLIVE: Betty—Caroline—I don't deserve this—Harry, Harry.

(HARRY *and* CLIVE *separate them.* HARRY *holding* MRS SAUNDERS, CLIVE, BETTY.)

CLIVE: Mrs Saunders, how can you abuse my hospitality? How dare you touch my wife? You must leave here at once.

BETTY: Go away, go away. You are a wicked woman. 40

MAUD: Mrs Saunders, I am shocked. This is your hostess.

CLIVE: Pack your bags and leave the house this instant.

MRS SAUNDERS: I was leaving anyway. There's no place for me here. I have made arrangements to leave tomorrow, and tomorrow is when I will leave. I wish you joy, Mr Bagley. 45

(MRS SAUNDERS *goes.*)

CLIVE: No place for her anywhere I should think. Shocking behaviour.

BETTY: Oh Clive, forgive me, and love me like you used to.
CLIVE: Were you jealous my dove? My own dear wife!
50 MAUD: Ah, Mr Bagley, one flesh, you see.

(EDWARD *comes back with the necklace.*)

CLIVE: Good God, Edward, it's true.
EDWARD: I was minding it for mama because of the troubles.
CLIVE: Well done, Edward, that was very manly of you. See
     Betty? Edward was protecting his mama's jewels from the
55   rebels. What a hysterical fuss over nothing. Well done, lit-
     tle man. It is quite safe now. The bad men are dead.
     Edward, you may do up the necklace for mama.

(EDWARD *does up* BETTY*'s necklace, supervised by* CLIVE, JOSHUA
is drinking steadily. ELLEN *comes back.*)

MAUD: Ah, here's the bride. Come along, Ellen, you don't cry
     at your own wedding, only at other people's.
60 CLIVE: Now, speeches, speeches. Who is going to make a
     speech? Harry, make a speech.
HARRY: I'm no speaker. You're the one for that.
ALL: Speech, speech.
HARRY: My dear friends—what can I say—the empire—the
65   family—the married state to which I have always
     aspired—your shining example of domestic bliss—my
     great good fortune in winning Ellen's love—happiest day
     of my life.

(*Applause.*)

CLIVE: Cut the cake, cut the cake.

(HARRY *and* ELLEN *take the knife to cut the cake.* HARRY *steps on
the doll under the table.*)

70 HARRY: What's this?
ELLEN: Oh look.
BETTY: Edward.
EDWARD: It was Joshua. It was Joshua. I saw him.
CLIVE: Don't tell lies again.

(*He hits* EDWARD *across the side of the head.*)

75   Unaccustomed as I am to public speaking—

(*Cheers.*)

     Harry, my friend. So brave and strong and supple.
     Ellen, from neath her veil so shyly peeking.
     I wish you joy. A toast—the happy couple.
     Dangers are past. Our enemies are killed.
80   —Put your arm round her, Harry, have a kiss—
     All murmuring of discontent is stilled.
     Long may you live in peace and joy and bliss.

(*While he is speaking* JOSHUA *raises his gun to shoot* CLIVE. *Only*
EDWARD *sees. He does nothing to warn the others. He puts his
hands over his ears.*)

(*Black.*)

ACT TWO

SCENE I

*Winter afternoon. Inside the hut of a one o'clock club, a children's
playcentre in a park,* VICTORIA *and* LIN, *mothers.* CATHY, LIN*'s
daughter, age 5, played by a man, clinging to* LIN. VICTORIA *reading a book.*

CATHY: Yum yum bubblegum.
     Stick it up your mother's bum.
     When it's brown
     Pull it down
     Yum yum bubblegum.   5
LIN: Like your shoes, Victoria.
CATHY: Jack be nimble, Jack be quick,
     Jack jump over the candlestick.
     Silly Jack, he should jump higher,
     Goodness gracious, great balls of fire.   10
LIN: Cathy, do stop. Do a painting.
CATHY: You do a painting.
LIN: You do a painting.
CATHY: What shall I paint?
LIN: Paint a house.   15
CATHY: No.
LIN: Princess.
CATHY: No.
LIN: Pirates.
CATHY: Already done that.   20
LIN: Spacemen.
CATHY: I never paint spacemen. You know I never.
LIN: Paint a car crash and blood everywhere.
CATHY: No, don't tell me. I know what to paint.
LIN: Go on then. You need an apron, where's an apron. Here.   25
CATHY: Don't want an apron.
LIN: Lift up your arms. There's a good girl.
CATHY: I don't want to paint.
LIN: Don't paint. Don't paint.
CATHY: What shall I do? You paint. What shall I do mum?   30
VICTORIA: There's nobody on the big bike, Cathy, quick.

(CATHY *goes out.* VICTORIA *is watching the children playing outside.*)

VICTORIA: Tommy, it's Jimmy's gun. Let him have it. What
     the hell.

(*She goes on reading. She reads while she talks.*)

LIN: I don't know how you can concentrate.
VICTORIA: You have to or you never do anything.   35
LIN: Yeh, well. It's really warm in here, that's one thing. It's
     better than standing out there. I got chilblains last winter.
VICTORIA: It is warm.
LIN: I suppose Tommy doesn't let you read much. I expect he
     talks to you while you're reading.   40
VICTORIA: Yes, he does.
LIN: I didn't get very far with that book you lent me.
VICTORIA: That's all right.
LIN: I was glad to have it, though. I sit with it on my lap while
     I'm watching telly. Well, Cathy's off. She's frightened I'm 45
     going to leave her. It's the babyminder didn't work out
     when she was two, she still remembers. You can't get

them used to other people if you're by yourself. It's no good blaming me. She clings round my knees every morning up the nursery and they don't say anything but they make you feel you're making her do it. But I'm desperate for her to go to school. I did cry when I left her the first day. You wouldn't, you're too fucking sensible. You'll call the teacher by her first name. I really fancy you.

VICTORIA: What?

LIN: Put your book down will you for five minutes. You didn't hear a word I said.

VICTORIA: I don't get much time to myself.

LIN: Do you ever go to the movies?

VICTORIA: Tommy's very funny who he's left with. My mother babysits sometimes.

LIN: Your husband could babysit.

VICTORIA: But then we couldn't go to the movies.

LIN: You could go to the movies with me.

VICTORIA: Oh I see.

LIN: Couldn't you?

VICTORIA: Well yes, I could.

LIN: Friday night?

VICTORIA: What film are we talking about?

LIN: Does it matter what film?

VICTORIA: Of course it does.

LIN: You choose then. Friday night.

(CATHY *comes in with gun, shoots them saying Kiou kiou kiou, and runs off again.*)

Not in a foreign language, ok. You don't go in the movies to read.

(LIN *watches the children playing outside.*)

Don't hit him, Cathy, kill him. Point the gun, kiou, kiou, kiou. That's the way.

VICTORIA: They've just banned war toys in Sweden.

LIN: The kids'll just hit each other more.

VICTORIA: Well, psychologists do differ in their opinions as to whether or not aggression is innate.

LIN: Yeh?

VICTORIA: I'm afraid I do let Tommy play with guns and just hope he'll get it out of his system and not end up in the army.

LIN: I've got a brother in the army.

VICTORIA: Oh I'm sorry. Whereabouts is he stationed?

LIN: Belfast.

VICTORIA: Oh dear.

LIN: I've got a friend who's Irish and we went on a Troops Out march. Now my dad won't speak to me.

VICTORIA: I don't get on too well with my father either.

LIN: And your husband? How do you get on with him?

VICTORIA: Oh, fine. Up and down. You know. Very well. He helps with the washing up and everything.

LIN: I left mine two years ago. He let me keep Cathy and I'm grateful for that.

VICTORIA: You shouldn't be grateful.

LIN: I'm a lesbian.

VICTORIA: You still shouldn't be grateful.

LIN: I'm grateful he didn't hit me harder than he did.

VICTORIA: I suppose I'm very lucky with Martin.

LIN: Don't get at me about how I bring up Cathy, ok?

VICTORIA: I didn't.

LIN: Yes you did. War toys. I'll give her a rifle for Christmas and blast Tommy's pretty head off for a start.

(VICTORIA *goes back to her book.*)

LIN: I hate men.

VICTORIA: You have to look at it in a historical perspective in terms of learnt behaviour since the industrial revolution.

LIN: I just hate the bastards.

VICTORIA: Well it's a point of view.

(*By now* CATHY *has come back in and started painting in many colours, without an apron.* EDWARD *comes in.*)

EDWARD: Victoria, mother's in the park. She's walking round all the paths very fast.

VICTORIA: By herself?

EDWARD: I told her you were here.

VICTORIA: Thanks.

EDWARD: Come on.

VICTORIA: Ten minutes talking to my mother and I have to spend two hours in a hot bath.

(VICTORIA *goes out.*)

LIN: Shit, Cathy, what about an apron. I don't mind you having paint on your frock but if it doesn't wash off just don't tell me you can't wear your frock with paint on, ok?

CATHY: Ok.

LIN: You're gay, aren't you?

EDWARD: I beg your pardon?

LIN: I really fancy your sister. I thought you'd understand. You do but you can go on pretending you don't, I don't mind. That's lovely Cathy, I like the green bit.

EDWARD: Don't go around saying that. I might lose my job.

LIN: The last gardener was ever so straight. He used to flash at all the little girls.

EDWARD: I wish you hadn't said that about me. It's not true.

LIN: It's not true and I never said it and I never thought it and I never will think it again.

EDWARD: Someone might have heard you.

LIN: Shut up about it then.

(BETTY *and* VICTORIA *come up.*)

BETTY: It's quite a nasty bump.

VICTORIA: He's not even crying.

BETTY: I think that's very worrying. You and Edward always cried. Perhaps he's got concussion.

VICTORIA: Of course he hasn't mummy.

BETTY: That other little boy was very rough. Should you speak to somebody about him?

VICTORIA: Tommy was hitting him with a spade.

BETTY: Well he's a real little boy. And so brave not to cry. You must watch him for signs of drowsiness. And nausea. If he's sick in the night, phone an ambulance. Well, you're looking very well darling, a bit tired, a bit peaky. I think the fresh air agrees with Edward. He likes the open air life because of growing up in Africa. He misses the sunshine, don't you, darling? We'll soon have Edward back on his feet. What fun it is here.

VICTORIA: This is Lin. And Cathy.

BETTY: Oh Cathy what a lovely painting. What is it? Well I
think it's a house on fire. I think all that red is a fire. Is that
right? Or do I see legs, is it a horse? Can I have the lovely
155　painting or is it for mummy? Children have such imagination, it makes them so exhausting. (*To* LIN.) I'm sure
you're wonderful, just like Victoria. I had help with my
children. One does need help. That was in Africa of
course so there wasn't the servant problem. This is my son
160　Edward. This is—
EDWARD: Lin.
BETTY: Lin, this is Lin. Edward is doing something such fun,
he's working in the park as a gardener. He does look exactly like a gardener.
165　EDWARD: I am a gardener.
BETTY: He's certainly making a stab at it. Well it will be a story
to tell. I expect he will write a novel about it, or perhaps a
television series. Well what a pretty child Cathy is. Victoria was a pretty child just like a little doll—you can't be cer-
170　tain how they'll grow up. I think Victoria's very pretty but
she doesn't make the most of herself, do you darling, it's not
the fashion I'm told but there are still women who dress
out of *Vogue,* well we hope that's not what Martin looks
for, though in many ways I wish it was, I don't know what
175　it is Martin looks for and nor does he I'm afraid poor Martin. Well I am rattling on. I like your skirt dear but your
shoes won't do at all. Well do they have lady gardeners, Edward, because I'm going to leave your father and I think I
might need to get a job, not a gardener really of course. I
180　haven't got green fingers I'm afraid, everything I touch
shrivels straight up. Vicky gave me a poinsettia last Christmas and the leaves all fell off on Boxing Day. Well good
heavens, look what's happened to that lovely painting.

(CATHY *has slowly and carefully been going over the whole sheet
with black paint. She has almost finished.*)

LIN: What you do that for silly? It was nice.
185　CATHY: I like your earrings.
VICTORIA: Did you say you're leaving Daddy?
BETTY: Do you darling? Shall I put them on you? My ears
aren't pierced, I never wanted that, they just clip on the lobe.
LIN: She'll get paint on you, mind.
190　BETTY: There's a pretty girl. It doesn't hurt does it. Well you'll
grow up to know you have to suffer a little bit for beauty.
CATHY: Look mum I'm pretty, I'm pretty, I'm pretty.
LIN: Stop showing off Cathy.
VICTORIA: It's time we went home. Tommy, time to go
195　home. Last go then, all right.
EDWARD: Mum did I hear you right just now?
CATHY: I want my ears pierced.
BETTY: Ooh, not till you're big.
CATHY: I know a girl got her ears pierced and she's three.
200　She's got real gold.
BETTY: I don't expect she's English, darling. Can I give her a
sweety? I know they're not very good for the teeth, Vicky
gets terribly cross with me. What does mummy say?
LIN: Just one, thank you very much.
205　CATHY: I like your beads.
BETTY: Yes they are pretty. Here you are.

(*It is the necklace from Act One.*)

CATHY: Look at me, look at me. Vicky, Vicky, Vicky look at me.
LIN: You look lovely, come on now.
CATHY: And your hat, and your hat.
LIN: No, that's enough.　　　　　　　　　　　　　　　　　210
BETTY: Of course she can have my hat.
CATHY: Yes, yes, hat, hat. Look look look.
LIN: That's enough, please, stop it now. Hat off, bye bye hat.
CATHY: Give me my hat.
LIN: Bye bye beads.　　　　　　　　　　　　　　　　　　215
BETTY: It's just fun.
LIN: It's very nice of you.
CATHY: I want my beads.
LIN: Where's the other earring?
CATHY: I want my beads.　　　　　　　　　　　　　　　220

(CATHY *has the other earring in her hand. Meanwhile* VICTORIA
and EDWARD *look for it.*)

EDWARD: Is it on the floor?
VICTORIA: Don't step on it.
EDWARD: Where?
CATHY: I want my beads. I want my beads.
LIN: You'll have a smack.　　　　　　　　　　　　　　　225

(LIN *gets the earring from* CATHY.)

CATHY: I want my beads.
BETTY: Oh dear oh dear. Have you got the earring? Thank
you darling.
CATHY: I want my beads, you're horrid, I hate you, mum, you
smell.　　　　　　　　　　　　　　　　　　　　　　230
BETTY: This is the point you see where one had help. Well it's
been lovely seeing you dears and I'll be off again on my
little walk.
VICTORIA: You're leaving him? Really?
BETTY: Yes you hear alright, Vicky, yes. I'm finding a little flat,　235
that will be fun.

(BETTY *goes.*)

Bye bye Tommy, granny's going now. Tommy don't hit
that little girl, say goodbye to granny.
VICTORIA: Fucking hell.
EDWARD: Puking Jesus.　　　　　　　　　　　　　　　240
LIN: That was news was it, leaving your father?
EDWARD: They're going to want so much attention.
VICTORIA: Does everybody hate their mothers?
EDWARD: Mind you, I wouldn't live with him.
LIN: Stop snivelling, pigface. Where's your coat? Be quiet　245
now and we'll have doughnuts for tea and if you keep on
we'll have dogshit on toast.

(CATHY *laughs so much she lies on the floor.*)

VICTORIA: Tommy, you've had two last goes. Last last last go.
LIN: Not that funny, come on, coat on.
EDWARD: Can I have your painting?　　　　　　　　　250
CATHY: What for?
EDWARD: For a friend of mine.
CATHY: What's his name?
EDWARD: Gerry.
CATHY: How old is he?　　　　　　　　　　　　　　　255
EDWARD: Thirty-two.

CATHY: You can if you like. I don't care. Kiou kiou kiou kiou.

(CATHY *goes out*. EDWARD *takes the painting and goes out*.)

LIN: Will you have sex with me?
VICTORIA: I don't know what Martin would say. Does it
260   count as adultery with a woman?
LIN: You'd enjoy it.

SCENE II

Spring. Swing, bench, pond nearby. EDWARD *is gardening.* GERRY *sitting on a bench.*

EDWARD: I sometimes pretend we don't know each other. And you've come to the park to eat your sandwiches and look at me.
GERRY: That would be more interesting, yes. Come and sit
5   down.
EDWARD: If the superintendent comes I'll be in trouble. It's not my dinner time yet. Where were you last night? I think you owe me an explanation. We always do tell each other everything.
10   GERRY: Is that a rule?
EDWARD: It's what we agreed.
GERRY: It's a habit we've got into. Look, I was drunk. I woke up at 4 o'clock on somebody's floor. I was sick. I hadn't any money for a cab. I went back to sleep.
15   EDWARD: You could have phoned.
GERRY: There wasn't a phone.
EDWARD: Sorry.
GERRY: There was a phone and I didn't phone you. Leave it alone, Eddy, I'm warning you.
20   EDWARD: What are you going to do to me, then?
GERRY: I'm going to the pub.
EDWARD: I'll join you in ten minutes.
GERRY: I didn't ask you to come. (EDWARD *goes*.) Two years I've been with Edward. You have to get away sometimes or you
25   lose sight of yourself. The train from Victoria to Clapham still has those compartments without a corridor. As soon as I got on the platform I saw who I wanted. Slim hips, tense shoulders, trying not to look at anyone. I put my hand on my packet just long enough so that he couldn't miss it.
30   The train came in. You don't want to get in too fast or some straight dumbo might get in with you. I sat by the window. I couldn't see where the fuck he'd got to. Then just as the whistle went he got in. Great. It's a six-minute journey so you can't start anything you can't finish. I stared
35   at him and he unzipped his flies. Then he stopped. So I stood up and took my cock out. He took me in his mouth and shut his eyes tight. He was sort of mumbling it about as if he wasn't sure what to do, so I said, 'A bit tighter son' and he said 'Sorry' and then got on with it. He was jerking
40   off with his left hand, and I could see he'd got a fairsized one. I wished he'd keep still so I could see his watch. I was getting really turned on. What if we pulled into Clapham Junction now. Of course by the time we sat down again the train was just slowing up. I felt wonderful. Then he started
45   talking. It's better if nothing is said. Once you find he's a librarian in Walthamstow with a special interest in science fiction and lives with his aunt, then forget it. He said I hope you don't think I do this all the time. I said I hope you will

from now on. He said he would if I was on the train, but
50   why don't we go out for a meal? I opened the door before the train stopped. I told him I live with somebody, I don't want to know. He was jogging sideways to keep up. He said 'What's your phone number, you're my ideal physical type, what sign of the zodiac are you? Where do you live? Where
55   are you going now?' It's not fair, I saw him at Victoria a couple of months later and I went straight down to the end of the platform and I picked up somebody really great who never said a word, just smiled.

(CATHY *is on the swing*.)

CATHY: Batman and Robin
        Had a batmobile.   60
        Robin done a fart
        And paralysed the wheel.
        The wheel couldn't take it,
        The engine fell apart,
        All because of Robin   65
        And his supersonic fart.

(CATHY *goes*. MARTIN, VICTORIA *and* BETTY *walking slowly*.)

MARTIN: Tom!
BETTY: He'll fall in.
VICTORIA: No he won't.
MARTIN: Don't go too near the edge Tom. Throw the bread   70
    from there. The ducks can get it.
BETTY: I'll never be able to manage. If I can't even walk down the street by myself. Everything looks so fierce.
VICTORIA: Just watch Tommy feeding the ducks.
BETTY: He's going to fall in. Make Martin make him move back. 75
VICTORIA: He's not going to fall in.
BETTY: It's since I left your father.
VICTORIA: Mummy, it really was the right decision.
BETTY: Everything comes at me from all directions. Martin despises me.   80
VICTORIA: Of course he doesn't, mummy.
BETTY: Of course he does.
MARTIN: Throw the bread. That's the way. The duck can get it. Quack quack quack quack quack.
BETTY: I don't want to take pills. Lin says you can't trust doctors. 85
VICTORIA: You're not taking pills. You're doing very well.
BETTY: But I'm so frightened.
VICTORIA: What are you frightened of?
BETTY: Victoria, you always ask that as if there was suddenly going to be an answer.   90
VICTORIA: Are you all right sitting there?
BETTY: Yes, yes. Go and be with Martin.

(VICTORIA *joins* MARTIN, BETTY *stays sitting on the bench*.)

MARTIN: You take the job, you go to Manchester. You turn it down, you stay in London. People are making decisions like this every day of the week. It needn't be for more than 95
a year. You get long vacations. Our relationship might well stand the strain of that, and if it doesn't we're better out of it. I don't want to put any pressure on you. I'd just like to know so we can sell the house. I think we're moving into an entirely different way of life if you go to Man- 100
chester because it won't end there. We could keep the

house as security for Tommy but he might as well get used to the fact that life nowadays is insecure. You should ask your mother what she thinks and then do the opposite. I 105 could just take that room in Barbara's house, and then we could babysit for each other. You think that means I want to fuck Barbara. I don't. Well, I do, but I won't. And even if I did, what's a fuck between friends? What are we meant to do it with, strangers? Whatever you want to do, I'll be 110 delighted. If you could just let me know what it is I'm to be delighted about. Don't cry again, Vicky, I'm not the sort of man who makes women cry.

(LIN *has come in and sat down with* BETTY, CATHY *joins them. She is wearing a pink dress and carrying a rifle.*)

LIN: I've bought her three new frocks. She won't wear jeans to school any more because Tracy and Mandy called her a boy.
115 CATHY: Tracy's got a perm.
LIN: You should have shot them.
CATHY: They're coming to tea and we've got to have trifle. Not trifle you make, trifle out of a packet. And you've got to wear a skirt. And tights.
120 LIN: Tracy's mum wears jeans.
CATHY: She does not. She wears velvet.
BETTY: Well I think you look very pretty. And if that gun has caps in it please take it a long way away.
CATHY: It's got red caps. They're louder.
125 MARTIN: Do you think you're well enough to do this job? You don't have to do it. No one's going to think any the less of you if you stay here with me. There's no point being so liberated you make yourself cry all the time. You stay and we'll get everything sorted out. What it is about sex, when
130 we talk while it's happening I get to feel it's like a driving lesson. Left, right, a little faster, carry on, slow down—

(CATHY *shoots* VICTORIA.)

CATHY: You're dead Vicky.
VICTORIA: Aaaargh.
CATHY: Fall over.
135 VICTORIA: I'm not falling over, the ground's wet.
CATHY: You're dead.
VICTORIA: Yes, I'm dead.
CATHY: The Dead Hand Gang fall over. They said I had to fall over in the mud or I can't play. That duck's a mandarin.
140 MARTIN: Which one? Look, Tommy.
CATHY: That's a diver. It's got a yellow eye and it dives. That's a goose. Tommy doesn't know it's a goose, he thinks it's a duck. The babies get eaten by weasels. Kiou kiou.

(CATHY *goes.*)

MARTIN: So I lost my erection last night not because I'm not
145 prepared to talk, it's just that taking in technical information is a different part of the brain and also I don't like to feel that you do it better to yourself. I have read the Hite report. I do know that women have to learn to get their pleasure despite our clumsy attempts at expressing undying
150 devotion and ecstasy, and that what we spent our adolescence thinking was an animal urge we had to suppress is in fact a fine art we have to acquire. I'm not like whatever percentage of American men have become impotent as a

direct result of women's liberation, which I am totally in favour of, more I sometimes think than you are yourself. 155 Nor am I one of your villains who sticks it in, bangs away, and falls asleep. My one aim is to give you pleasure. My one aim is to give you rolling orgasms like I do other women. So why the hell don't you have them? My analysis for what it's worth is that despite all my efforts you still feel domi- 160 nated by me. I in fact think it's very sad that you don't feel able to take that job. It makes me feel very guilty. I don't want you to do it just because I encourage you to do it. But don't you think you'd feel better if you did take the job? You're the one who's talked about freedom. You're the one 165 who's experimenting with bisexuality, and I don't stop you, I think women have something to give each other. You seem to need the mutual support. You find me too overwhelming. So follow it through, go away, leave me and Tommy alone for a bit, we can manage perfectly well with- 170 out you. I'm not putting any pressure on you but I don't think you're being a whole person. God knows I do everything I can to make you stand on your own two feet. Just be yourself. You don't seem to realise how insulting it is to me that you can't get yourself together. 175

(MARTIN *and* VICTORIA *go.*)

BETTY: You must be very lonely yourself with no husband. You don't miss him?
LIN: Not really, no.
BETTY: Maybe you like being on your own.
LIN: I'm seeing quite a lot of Vicky. I don't live alone. I live 180 with Cathy.
BETTY: I would have been frightened when I was your age. I thought, the poor children, their mother all alone.
LIN: I've a lot of friends.
BETTY: I find when I'm making tea I put out two cups. It's 185 strange not having a man in the house. You don't know who to do things for.
LIN: Yourself.
BETTY: Oh, that's very selfish.
LIN: Have you any women friends? 190
BETTY: I've never been so short of men's company that I've had to bother with women.
LIN: Don't you like women?
BETTY: They don't have such interesting conversations as men. There has never been a woman composer of genius. 195 They don't have a sense of humour. They spoil things for themselves with their emotions. I can't say I do like women very much, no.
LIN: But you're a woman.
BETTY: There's nothing says you have to like yourself. 200
LIN: Do you like me?
BETTY: There's no need to take it personally, Lin.

(MARTIN *and* VICTORIA *come back.*)

MARTIN: Did you know if you put cocaine on your prick you can keep it up all night? The only thing is of course it goes numb so you don't feel anything. But you would, that's 205 the main thing. I just want to make you happy.
BETTY: Vicky, I'd like to go home.
VICTORIA: Yes, mummy, of course.
BETTY: I'm sorry, dear.

210 VICTORIA: I think Tommy would like to stay out a bit longer.

LIN: Hello, Martin. We do keep out of each other's way.

MARTIN: I think that's the best thing to do.

BETTY: Perhaps you'd walk home with me, Martin. I do feel safer with a man. The park is so large the grass seems to tilt.

215 MARTIN: Yes, I'd like to go home and do some work. I'm writing a novel about women from the women's point of view.

(MARTIN *and* BETTY *go.* LIN *and* VICTORIA *are alone. They embrace.*)

VICTORIA: Why the hell can't he just be a wife and come with me? Why does Martin make me tie myself in knots? No wonder we can't just have a simple fuck. No, not Mar-
220 tin, why do I make myself tie myself in knots. It's got to stop, Lin. I'm not like that with you. Would you love me if I went to Manchester?

LIN: Yes.

VICTORIA: Would you love me if I went on a climbing expe-
225 dition in the Andes mountains?

LIN: Yes.

VICTORIA: Would you love me if my teeth fell out?

LIN: Yes.

VICTORIA: Would you love me if I loved ten other people?

230 LIN: And me?

VICTORIA: Yes.

LIN: Yes.

VICTORIA: And I feel apologetic for not being quite so subordi-nate as I was. I am more intelligent than him. I am brilliant.

235 LIN: Leave him Vic. Come and live with me.

VICTORIA: Don't be silly.

LIN: Silly, Christ, don't then. I'm not asking because I need to live with someone. I'd enjoy it, that's all, we'd both enjoy it. Fuck you. Cathy, for fuck's sake stop throwing stones at
240 the ducks. The man's going to get you.

VICTORIA: What man? Do you need a man to frighten your child with?

LIN: My mother said it.

VICTORIA: You're so inconsistent, Lin.

245 LIN: I've changed who I sleep with, I can't change everything.

VICTORIA: Like when I had to stop you getting a job in a boutique and collaborating with sexist consumerism.

LIN: I should have got that job, Cathy would have liked it. Why shouldn't I have some decent clothes? I'm sick of dressing
250 like a boy, why can't I look sexy, wouldn't you love me?

VICTORIA: Lin, you've no analysis.

LIN: No but I'm good at kissing aren't I? I give Cathy guns, my mum didn't give me guns. I dress her in jeans, she wants to wear dresses. I don't know. I can't work it out, I
255 don't want to. You read too many books, you get at me all the time, you're worse to me than Martin is to you, you piss me off, my brother's been killed. I'm sorry to win the argument that way but there it is.

VICTORIA: What do you mean win the argument?

260 LIN: I mean be nice to me.

VICTORIA: In Belfast?

LIN: I heard this morning. Don't don't start. I've hardly seen him for two years. I rung my father. You'd think I'd shot myself. He doesn't want me to go to the funeral.

(CATHY *approaches.*)

VICTORIA: What will you do?   265

LIN: Go of course.

CATHY: What is it? Who's killed? What?

LIN: It's Bill. Your uncle. In the army. Bill that gave you the blue teddy.

CATHY: Can I have his gun?   270

LIN: It's time we went home. Time you went to bed.

CATHY: No it's not.

LIN: We go home and you have tea and you have a bath and you go to bed.

CATHY: Fuck off.   275

LIN: Cathy, shut up.

VICTORIA: It's only half past five, why don't we—

LIN: I'll tell you why she has to go to bed—

VICTORIA: She can come home with me.

LIN: Because I want her out of the fucking way.   280

VICTORIA: She can come home with me.

CATHY: I'm not going to bed.

LIN: I want her home with me not home with you, I want her in bed, I want today over.

CATHY: I'm not going to bed.   285

(LIN *hits* CATHY, CATHY *cries.*)

LIN: And shut up or I'll give you something to cry for.

CATHY: I'm not going to bed.

VICTORIA: Cathy—

LIN: You keep out of it.

VICTORIA: Lin for God's sake.   290

(*They are all shouting.* CATHY *runs off.* LIN *and* VICTORIA *are silent. Then they laugh and embrace.*)

LIN: Where's Tommy?

VICTORIA: What? Didn't he go with Martin?

LIN: Did he?

VICTORIA: God oh God.

LIN: Cathy! Cathy!   295

VICTORIA: I haven't thought about him. How could I not think about him? Tommy!

LIN: Cathy! Come on, quick, I want some help.

VICTORIA: Tommy! Tommy!

(CATHY *comes back.*)

LIN: Where's Tommy? Have you seen him? Did he go with   300
Martin? Do you know where he is?

CATHY: I showed him the goose. We went in the bushes.

LIN: Then what?

CATHY: I came back on the swing.

VICTORIA: And Tommy? Where was Tommy?   305

CATHY: He fed the ducks.

LIN: No that was before.

CATHY: He did a pee in the bushes. I helped him with his trousers.

VICTORIA: And after that?   310

CATHY: He fed the ducks.

VICTORIA: No no.

CATHY: He liked the ducks. I expect he fell in.

LIN: Did you see him fall in?

VICTORIA: Tommy! Tommy!   315

LIN: What's the last time you saw him?

CATHY: He did a pee.

VICTORIA: Mummy said he would fall in. Oh God, Tommy!

320 LIN: We'll go round the pond. We'll go opposite ways round the pond.

ALL: (*Shout.*) *Tommy!*

(VICTORIA *and* LIN *go off opposite sides.* CATHY *climbs the bench.*)

CATHY: Georgie Best, superstar
    Walks like a woman and wears a bra.
      There he is! I see him! Mum! Vicky! There he is! He's
325   in the bushes.

(LIN *comes back.*)

LIN: Come on Cathy love, let's go home.

CATHY: Vicky's got him.

LIN: Come on.

CATHY: Is she cross?

330 LIN: No. Come on.

CATHY: I found him.

LIN: Yes. Come on.

(CATHY *gets off the bench.* CATHY *and* LIN *hug.*)

CATHY: I'm watching telly.

LIN: Ok.

335 CATHY: After the news.

LIN: Ok.

CATHY: I'm not going to bed.

LIN: Yes you are.

CATHY: I'm not going to bed now.

340 LIN: Not now but early.

CATHY: How early?

LIN: Not late.

CATHY: How not late?

LIN: Early.

345 CATHY: How early?

LIN: Not late.

(*They go off together.* GERRY *comes on. He waits.* EDWARD *comes.*)

EDWARD: I've got some fish for dinner. I thought I'd make a cheese sauce.

GERRY: I won't be in.

350 EDWARD: Where are you going?

GERRY: For a start I'm going to a sauna. Then I'll see.

EDWARD: All right. What time will you be back? We'll eat then.

GERRY: You're getting like a wife.

355 EDWARD: I don't mind that.

GERRY: Why don't I do the cooking sometime?

EDWARD: You can if you like. You're just not so good at it that's all. Do it tonight.

GERRY: I won't be in tonight.

360 EDWARD: Do it tomorrow. If we can't eat it we can always go to a restaurant.

GERRY: Stop it.

EDWARD: Stop what?

GERRY: Just be yourself.

365 EDWARD: I don't know what you mean. Everyone's always tried to stop me being feminine and now you are too.

GERRY: You're putting it on.

EDWARD: I like doing the cooking. I like being fucked. You do like me like this really.

GERRY: I'm bored, Eddy. 370

EDWARD: Go to the sauna.

GERRY: And you'll stay home and wait up for me.

EDWARD: No, I'll go to bed and read a book.

GERRY: Or knit. You could knit me a pair of socks.

EDWARD: I might knit. I like knitting. 375

GERRY: I don't mind if you knit. I don't want to be married.

EDWARD: I do.

GERRY: Well I'm divorcing you.

EDWARD: I wouldn't want to keep a man who wants his freedom. 380

GERRY: Eddy, do stop playing the injured wife, it's not funny.

EDWARD: I'm not playing. It's true.

GERRY: I'm not the husband so you can't be the wife.

EDWARD: I'll always be here, Gerry, if you want to come back. I know you men like to go off by yourselves. I don't 385 think I could love deeply more than once. But I don't think I can face life on my own so don't leave it too long or it may be too late.

GERRY: What are you trying to turn me into?

EDWARD: A monster, darling, which is what you are. 390

GERRY: I'll collect my stuff from the flat in the morning.

(GERRY *goes.* EDWARD *sits on the bench. It gets darker.* VICTORIA *comes.*)

VICTORIA: Tommy dropped a toy car somewhere, you haven't seen it? It's red. He says it's his best one. Oh the hell with it. Martin's reading him a story. There, isn't it quiet?

(*They sit on the bench, holding hands.*)

EDWARD: I like women. 395

VICTORIA: That should please mother.

EDWARD: No listen Vicky. I'd rather be a woman. I wish I had breasts like that, I think they're beautiful. Can I touch them?

VICTORIA: What, pretending they're yours? 400

EDWARD: No, I know it's you.

VICTORIA: I think I should warn you I'm enjoying this.

EDWARD: I'm sick of men.

VICTORIA: I'm sick of men.

EDWARD: I think I'm a lesbian. 405

SCENE III

The park. Summer night. VICTORIA, LIN *and* EDWARD *drunk.*

LIN: Where are you?

VICTORIA: Come on.

EDWARD: Do we sit in a circle?

VICTORIA: Sit in a triangle.

EDWARD: You're good at mathematics. She's good at mathe- 5
matics.

VICTORIA: Give me your hand. We all hold hands.

EDWARD: Do you know what to do?

LIN: She's making it up.

VICTORIA: We start off by being quiet. 10

EDWARD: What?

LIN: Hush.

EDWARD: Will something appear?

VICTORIA: It was your idea.

15 EDWARD: It wasn't my idea. It was your book.

LIN: You said call up the goddess.

EDWARD: I don't remember saying that.

LIN: We could have called her on the telephone.

EDWARD: Don't be so silly, this is meant to be frightening.

20 LIN: Kiss me.

VICTORIA: Are we going to do it?

LIN: We're doing it.

VICTORIA: A ceremony.

LIN: It's very sexy, you said it is. You said the women were
25   priests in the temples and fucked all the time. I'm just
      helping.

VICTORIA: As long as it's sacred.

LIN: It's very sacred.

VICTORIA: Innin, Innana, Nana, Nut, Anat, Anahita, Istar, Isis.

30 LIN: I can't remember all that.

VICTORIA: Lin! Innin, Innana, Nana, Nut, Anat, Anahita, Istar,
      Isis.

(LIN *and* EDWARD *join in and continue the chant under* VICTORIA'S
speech.)

      Goddess of many names, oldest of the old, who walked in
      chaos and created life, hear us calling you back through
35   time, before Jehovah, before Christ, before men drove you
      out and burnt your temples, hear us, Lady, give us back
      what we were, give us the history we haven't had, make us
      the women we can't be.

ALL: Innin, Innana, Nana, Nut, Anat, Anahita, Istar, Isis.

(*Chant continues under other speeches.*)

40 LIN: Come back, goddess.

VICTORIA: Goddess of the sun and the moon her brother, lit-
      tle goddess of Crete with snakes in your hands.

LIN: Goddess of breasts.

VICTORIA: Goddess of cunts.

45 LIN: Goddess of fat bellies and babies. And blood blood blood.

(*Chant continues.*)

      I see her.

EDWARD: What?

(*They stop chanting.*)

LIN: I see her. Very tall. Snakes in her hands. Light light
      light—look out! Did I give you a fright?

50 EDWARD: I was terrified.

VICTORIA: Don't spoil it Lin.

LIN: It's all out of a book.

VICTORIA: Innin Innana—I can't do it now. I was really en-
      joying myself.

55 LIN: She won't appear with a man here.

VICTORIA: They had men, they had sons and lovers.

EDWARD: They had eunuchs.

LIN: Don't give us ideas.

VICTORIA: There's Attis and Tammuz, they're torn to pieces.

60 EDWARD: Tear me to pieces, Lin.

VICTORIA: The priestess chose a lover for a year and he was
      king because she chose him and then he was killed at the
      end of the year.

EDWARD: Hurray.

VICTORIA: And the women had the children and nobody 65
      knew it was done by fucking so they didn't know about
      fathers and nobody cared who the father was and the
      property was passed down through the maternal line—

LIN: Don't turn it into a lecture, Vicky, it's meant to be an orgy.

VICTORIA: It never hurts to understand the theoretical back- 70
      ground. You can't separate fucking and economics.

LIN: Give us a kiss.

EDWARD: Shut up, listen.

LIN: What?

EDWARD: There's somebody there.   75

LIN: Where?

EDWARD: There.

VICTORIA: The priestesses used to make love to total strangers.

LIN: Go on then, I dare you.

EDWARD: Go on, Vicky.   80

VICTORIA: He won't know it's a sacred rite in honour of the
      goddess.

EDWARD: We'll know.

LIN: We can tell him.

EDWARD: It's not what he thinks, it's what we think.   85

LIN: Don't tell him till after, he'll run a mile.

VICTORIA: Hello. We're having an orgy. Do you want me to
      suck your cock?

(*The stranger approaches. It is* MARTIN.)

MARTIN: There you are. I've been looking everywhere. What
      the hell are you doing? Do you know what the time is? 90
      You're all pissed out of your minds.

(*They leap on* MARTIN, *pull him down and start to make love to
him.*)

MARTIN: Well that's all right. If all we're talking about is hav-
      ing a lot of sex there's no problem. I was all for the sixties
      when liberation just meant fucking.

(*Another stranger approaches.*)

LIN: Hey you, come here. Come and have sex with us.   95

VICTORIA: Who is it?

(*The stranger is a soldier.*)

LIN: It's my brother.

EDWARD: Lin, don't.

LIN: It's my brother.

VICTORIA: It's her sense of humour, you get used to it.   100

LIN: Shut up Vicky, it's my brother. Isn't it? Bill?

SOLDIER: Yes it's me.

LIN: And you are dead.

SOLDIER: Fucking dead all right yeh.

LIN: Have you come back to tell us something?   105

SOLDIER: No I've come for a fuck. That was the worst thing in
      the fucking army. Never fucking let out. Can't fucking talk
      to Irish girls. Fucking bored out of my fucking head. That
      or shit scared. For five minutes I'd be glad I wasn't bored,
      then I was fucking scared. Then we'd come in and I'd be 110

glad I wasn't scared and then I was fucking bored. Spent the day reading fucking porn and the fucking night wanking. Man's fucking life in the fucking army? No fun when the fucking kids hate you. I got so I fucking wanted to kill
115   someone and I got fucking killed myself and I want a fuck.
LIN: I miss you. Bill. Bill.

(LIN *collapses.* SOLDIER *goes.* VICTORIA *comforts* LIN.)

EDWARD: Let's go home.
LIN: Victoria, come home with us. Victoria's coming to live with me and Edward.
120 MARTIN: Tell me about it in the morning.
LIN: It's true.
VICTORIA: It is true.
MARTIN: Tell me when you're sober.

(EDWARD, LIN, VICTORIA *go off together.* MARTIN *goes off alone.* GERRY *comes on.*)

GERRY: I come here sometimes at night and pick somebody up.
125   Sometimes I come here at night and don't pick anybody up. I do also enjoy walking about at night. There's never any trouble finding someone. I can have sex any time. You might not find the type you most fancy every day of the week, but there's plenty of people about who just enjoy having a good
130   time. I quite like living alone. If I live with someone I get annoyed with them. Edward always put on Capital radio when he got up. The silence gets wasted. I wake up at four o'clock sometimes. Birds. Silence. If I bring somebody home I never let them stay the night. Edward! Edward!

(EDWARD *from Act One comes on.*)

135 EDWARD: Gerry I love you.
GERRY: Yes, I know. I love you, too.
EDWARD: You know what we did? I want to do it again. I think about it all the time. Don't you want to any more?
GERRY: Yes, of course.

Song
CLOUD NINE

140 ALL: It'll be fine when you reach Cloud Nine.

Mist was rising and the night was dark.
Me and my baby took a walk in the park.
He said Be mine and you're on Cloud Nine.

Better watch out when you're on Cloud Nine.

145   Smoked some dope on the playground swings
Higher and higher on true love's wings
He said Be mine and you're on Cloud Nine.

Twenty-five years on the same Cloud Nine.

Who did she meet on her first blind date?
150   The guys were no surprise but the lady was great
They were women in love, they were on Cloud Nine.

Two the same, they were on Cloud Nine.

The bride was sixty-five, the groom was seventeen,
They fucked in the back of the black limousine.
155   It was divine in their silver Cloud Nine.

Simply divine in their silver Cloud Nine.

The wife's lover's children and my lover's wife,
Cooking in my kitchen, confusing my life.
And it's upside down when you reach Cloud Nine.

Upside down when you reach Cloud Nine.   160

SCENE IV

The park. Afternoon in late summer. MARTIN, CATHY, EDWARD.

CATHY: Under the bramble bushes,
Under the sea boom boom boom,
True love for you my darling,
True love for me my darling,
When we are married,   5
We'll raise a family.
Boy for you, girl for me,
Boom tiddley oom boom
SEXY.
EDWARD: You'll have Tommy and Cathy tonight then ok? 10
Tommy's still on antibiotics, do make him finish the bottle, he takes it in Ribena. It's no good in orange, he spits it out. Remind me to give you Cathy's swimming things.
CATHY: I did six strokes, didn't I Martin? Did I do a width? How many strokes is a length? How many miles is a 15
swimming pool? I'm going to take my bronze and silver and gold and diamond.
MARTIN: Is Tommy still wetting the bed?
EDWARD: Don't get angry with him about it.
MARTIN: I just need to go to the launderette so I've got a 20
spare sheet. Of course I don't get fucking angry, Eddy, for God's sake. I don't like to say he is my son but he is my son. I'm surprised I'm not wetting the bed myself.
CATHY: I don't wet the bed ever. Do you wet the bed Martin?
MARTIN: No.   25
CATHY: You said you did.

(BETTY *comes.*)

BETTY: I do miss the sun living in England but today couldn't be more beautiful. You appreciate the weekend when you're working. Betty's been at work this week, Cathy. It's terrible tiring, Martin, I don't know how you've done it 30
all these years. And the money, I feel like a child with the money, Clive always paid everything but I do understand it perfectly well. Look Cathy let me show you my money.
CATHY: I'll count it. Let me count it. What's that?
BETTY: Five pounds, Five and five is—   35
CATHY: One two three—
BETTY: Five and five is ten, and five—
CATHY: If I get it right can I have one?
EDWARD: No you can't.

(CATHY *goes on counting the money.*)

BETTY: I never like to say anything, Martin, or you'll think 40
I'm being a mother-in-law.
EDWARD: Which you are.
BETTY: Thank you, Edward, I'm not talking to you. Martin, I think you're being wonderful. Vicky will come back. Just let her stay with Lin till she sorts herself out. It's very nice 45

for a girl to have a friend; I had friends at school, that was very nice. But I'm sure Lin and Edward don't want her with them all the time. I'm not at all shocked that Lin and Edward aren't married and she already has a child, we all know first marriages don't always work out. But really Vicky must be in the way. And poor little Tommy. I hear he doesn't sleep properly and he's had a cough.

MARTIN: No, he's fine, Betty, thank you.

CATHY: My bed's horrible. I want to sleep in the big bed with Lin and Vicky and Eddy and I do get in if I've got a bad dream, and my bed's got a bump right in my back. I want to sleep in a tent.

BETTY: Well Tommy has got a nasty cough, Martin, whatever you say.

EDWARD: He's over that. He's got some medicine.

MARTIN: He takes it in Ribena.

BETTY: Well I'm glad to hear it. Look what a lot of money, Cathy, and I sit behind a desk of my own and I answer the telephone and keep the doctor's appointment book and it really is great fun.

CATHY: Can we go camping, Martin, in a tent? We could take the Dead Hand Gang.

BETTY: Not those big boys, Cathy? They're far too big and rough for you. They climb back into the park after dark. I'm sure mummy doesn't let you play with them, does she Edward? Well I don't know.

(*Ice cream bells.*)

CATHY: Ice cream. Martin you promised. I'll have a double ninety-nine. No I'll have a shandy lolly. Betty, you have a shandy lolly and I'll have a lick. No, you have a double ninety-nine and I'll have the chocolate.

(MARTIN, CATHY *and* BETTY *go, leaving* EDWARD. GERRY *comes.*)

GERRY: Hello, Eddy. Thought I might find you here.

EDWARD: Gerry.

GERRY: Not working today then?

EDWARD: I don't work here any more.

GERRY: Your mum got you into a dark suit?

EDWARD: No of course not. I'm on the dole. I am working, though, I do housework.

GERRY: Whose wife are you now then?

EDWARD: Nobody's. I don't think like that any more. I'm living with some women.

GERRY: What women?

EDWARD: It's my sister, Vic, and her lover. They go out to work and I look after the kids.

GERRY: I thought for a moment you said you were living with women.

EDWARD: We do sleep together, yes.

GERRY: I was passing the park anyway so I thought I'd look in. I was in the sauna the other night and I saw someone who looked like you but it wasn't. I had sex with him anyway.

EDWARD: I do go to the sauna sometimes.

(CATHY *comes, gives* EDWARD *an ice cream, goes.*)

GERRY: I don't think I'd like living with children. They make a lot of noise don't they?

EDWARD: I tell them to shut up and they shut up. I wouldn't want to leave them at the moment.

GERRY: Look why don't we go for a meal sometime?

EDWARD: Yes I'd like that. Where are you living now?

GERRY: Same place.

EDWARD: I'll come round for you tomorrow night about 7:30.

GERRY: Great.

(EDWARD *goes.* HARRY *comes.* HARRY *and* GERRY *pick each other up. They go off.* BETTY *comes back.*)

BETTY: No, the ice cream was my treat, Martin. Off you go. I'm going to have a quiet sit in the sun.

(MAUD *comes.*)

MAUD: Let Mrs Saunders be a warning to you, Betty. I know what it is to be unprotected.

BETTY: But mother, I have a job. I earn money.

MAUD: I know we have our little differences but I always want what is best for you.

(ELLEN *comes.*)

ELLEN: Betty, what happens with a man?

BETTY: You just keep still.

ELLEN: And is it enjoyable? Don't forget me, Betty.

(MAUD *and* ELLEN *go.*)

BETTY: I used to think Clive was the one who liked sex. But then I found I missed it. I used to touch myself when I was very little, I thought I'd invented something wonderful. I used to do it to go to sleep with or to cheer myself up, and one day it was raining and I was under the kitchen table, and my mother saw me with my hand under my dress rubbing away, and she dragged me out so quickly I hit my head and it bled and I was sick, and nothing was said, and I never did it again till this year. I thought if Clive wasn't looking at me there wasn't a person there. And one night in bed in my flat I was so frightened I started touching myself. I thought my hand might go through space. I touched my face, it was there, my arm, my breast, and my hand went down where I thought it shouldn't, and I thought well there is somebody there. It felt very sweet, it was a feeling from very long ago, it was very soft, just barely touching, and I felt myself gathering together more and more and I felt angry with Clive and angry with my mother and I went on and on defying them, and there was this vast feeling growing in me and all round me and they couldn't stop me and no one could stop me and I was there and coming and coming. Afterwards I thought I'd betrayed Clive. My mother would kill me. But I felt triumphant because I was a separate person from them. And I cried because I didn't want to be. But I don't cry about it any more. Sometimes I do it three times in one night and it really is great fun.

(VICTORIA *and* LIN *come in.*)

VICTORIA: So I said to the professor, I don't think this is an occasion for invoking the concept of structural causality—oh hello mummy.

BETTY: I'm going to ask you a question, both of you. I have
145 a little money from your grandmother. And the three of
you are living in that tiny flat with two children. I wonder if we could get a house and all live in it together? It
would give you more room.
VICTORIA: But I'm going to Manchester anyway.
150 LIN: We'd have a garden, Vicky.
BETTY: You do seem to have such fun all of you.
VICTORIA: I don't want to.
BETTY: I didn't think you would.
LIN: Come on, Vicky, she knows we sleep together, and Eddy.
155 BETTY: I think I've known for quite a while but I'm not sure.
I don't usually think about it, so I don't know if I know
about it or not.
VICTORIA: I don't want to live with my mother.
LIN: Don't think of her as your mother, think of her as Betty.
160 VICTORIA: But she thinks of herself as my mother.
BETTY: I am your mother.
VICTORIA: But mummy we don't even like each other.
BETTY: We might begin to.

(CATHY *comes on howling with a nosebleed.*)

LIN: Oh Cathy what happened?
165 BETTY: She's been assaulted.
VICTORIA: It's a nosebleed.
CATHY: Took my ice cream.
LIN: Who did?
CATHY: Took my money.

(MARTIN *comes.*)

170 MARTIN: Is everything all right?
LIN: I thought you were looking after her.
CATHY: They hit me. I can't play. They said I'm a girl.
BETTY: Those dreadful boys, the gang, the Dead Hand.
MARTIN: What do you mean you thought I was looking after her?
175 LIN: Last I saw her she was with you getting an ice cream. It's
your afternoon.
MARTIN: Then she went off to play. She goes off to play. You
don't keep an eye on her every minute.
LIN: She doesn't get beaten up when I'm looking after her.
180 CATHY: Took my money.
MARTIN: Why the hell should I look after your child anyway?
I just want Tommy. Why should he live with you and
Vicky all week?
LIN: I don't mind if you don't want to look after her but don't
185 say you will and then this happens.
VICTORIA: When I get to Manchester everything's going to be
different anyway, Lin's staying here, and you're staying here,
we're all going to have to sit down and talk it through.
MARTIN: I'd really enjoy that.
190 CATHY: Hit me on the face.
LIN: You were the one looking after her and look at her now,
that's all.
MARTIN: I've had enough of you telling me.
LIN: Yes you know it all.
195 MARTIN: Now stop it. I work very hard at not being like this,
I could do with some credit.

LIN: Ok you're quite nice, try and enjoy it. Don't make me
sorry for you, Martin, it's hard for me too. We've better
things to do than quarrel. I've got to go and sort those little bastards out for a start. Where are they, Cathy?   200
CATHY: Don't kill them, mum, hit them. Give them a nose-
bleed, mum.

(LIN *goes.*)

VICTORIA: Tommy's asleep in the pushchair. We'd better
wake him up or he won't sleep tonight.
MARTIN: Sometimes I keep him up watching television till he   205
falls asleep on the sofa so I can hold him. Come on, Cathy,
we'll get another ice cream.
CATHY: Chocolate sauce and nuts.
VICTORIA: Betty, would you like an ice cream?
BETTY: No thank you, the cold hurts my teeth, but what a   210
nice thought, Vicky, thank you.

(VICTORIA *goes.* BETTY *alone.* GERRY *comes.*)

BETTY: I think you used to be Edward's flatmate.
GERRY: You're his mother. He's talked about you.
BETTY: Well never mind. Children are always wrong about
their parents. It's a great problem knowing where to live   215
and who to share with. I live by myself just now.
GERRY: Good, So do I. You can do what you like.
BETTY: I don't really know what I like.
GERRY: You'll soon find out.
BETTY: What do you like?   220
GERRY: Waking up at four in the morning.
BETTY: I like listening to music in bed and sometimes for supper I just have a big piece of bread and dip it in very hot
lime pickle. So you don't get lonely by yourself? Perhaps
you have a lot of visitors. I've been thinking I should have 225
some visitors, I could give a little dinner party. Would you
come? There wouldn't just be bread and lime pickle.
GERRY: Thank you very much.
BETTY: Or don't wait to be asked to dinner. Just drop in in-
formally. I'll give you the address shall I? I don't usually   230
give strange men my address but then you're not a strange
man, you're a friend of Edward's. I suppose I seem a different generation to you but you are older than Edward. I
was married for so many years it's quite hard to know how
to get acquainted. But if there isn't a right way to do   235
things you have to invent one. I always thought my
mother was far too old to be attractive but when you get
to an age yourself it feels quite different.
GERRY: I think you could be quite attractive.
BETTY: If what?   240
GERRY: If you stop worrying.
BETTY: I think when I do more about things I worry about
them less. So perhaps you could help me do more.
GERRY: I might be going to live with Edward again.
BETTY: That's nice, but I'm rather surprised if he wants to   245
share a flat. He's rather involved with a young woman he
lives with, or two young women, I don't understand Ed-
ward but never mind.
GERRY: I'm very involved with him.

250   BETTY: I think Edward did try to tell me once but I didn't listen. So what I'm being told now is that Edward is 'gay' is that right? And you are too. And I've been making rather a fool of myself. But Edward does also sleep with women.

GERRY: He does, yes, I don't.

255   BETTY: Well people always say it's the mother's fault but I don't intend to start blaming myself. He seems perfectly happy.

GERRY: I could still come and see you.

BETTY: So you could, yes. I'd like that. I've never tried to pick up a man before.

260   GERRY: Not everyone's gay.

BETTY: No, that's lucky isn't it.

(GERRY *goes.* CLIVE *comes.*)

CLIVE: You are not that sort of woman, Betty. I can't believe you are. I can't feel the same about you as I did. And Africa is to be communist I suppose. I used to be proud to be British. There was a high ideal. I came out onto the 265 verandah and looked at the stars.

(CLIVE *goes.* BETTY *from Act One comes.* BETTY *and* BETTY *embrace.*)

David Edgar

David Edgar (b. 1948), is one of the most prolific and celebrated of living British playwrights. Raised in a theatrical family—his parents were both actors and stage managers at the Birmingham Repertory Theatre—Edgar studied drama and Manchester University, and worked briefly as a journalist before taking up a full-time playwriting career in 1972. Edgar's work in the theater spans a range of genres, from his Vietnam-war/Richard Nixon/Richard III satire, *Dick Deterred* (1974), to *Wreckers*, written for the radical 7:84 Theatre Company (1977), to the moving realism of *Mary Barnes* (1977). In the 1970s and 1980s he wrote a series of important plays for the Royal Shakespeare Company which he characterizes as "social realism"—plays that interrogate the working of contemporary society: an adaptation of *The Jail Diary of Albie Sachs* (1978), his brilliant indictment of the rise of the conservative right in England, *Destiny* (1977), and an incisive critique of the failure of the political left, *Maydays* (1983); he also wrote a celebrated and widely-toured adaptation of Charles Dickens's *Nicholas Nickelby* (1980), Edgar has worked with smaller companies (*Teendreams,* produced by Monstrous Regiment, 1979), and with major companies like the Royal National Theatre, which staged *The Shape of the Table* (1990) and *Albert Speer* (2000). His most recent plays—including *Pentecost* (1994) and *The Prisoner's Dilemma* (2001)—continue Edgar's frank interest in the use of theater as a form of political inquiry, here trained on the problems of nationalism and cultural identity facing the new, unified Europe. Edgar is also a prominent writer for film and television; and writes widely about contemporary politics. In the course of his distinguished career, he has served as resident playwright for the Birmingham Rep, and as literary consultant for the Royal Shakespeare Company; he also founded the playwriting program at the University of Birmingham. Edgar has just completed a two-play cycle, *Continental Divide* (2003), on American electoral politics; the play was produced by the Oregon Shakespeare Festival and the Berkeley Repertory Theater.

PENTECOST

Pentecost is in many ways a play about the problems of the New Europe. First produced in 1994, as Europe was moving toward the political and monetary cooperation of the European Union, *Pentecost* raises the question of a European identity from several perspectives. The play is set in an unnamed Eastern European country, one regarded (dismissively, and incorrectly) as a cultural backwater both by the visiting British art historian Oliver Davenport and by his American colleague Leo Katz. Yet as the play demonstrates, the notion of European identity is framed by Europe's border with the East, a border that has always been permeable. In the central conceit of the play, Oliver Davenport has been invited to inspect a medieval fresco, one that has recently been discovered in an abandoned church, a building that has, in the course of the twentieth-century, served the purposes of its occupiers (much like this unnamed country). When the fresco is uncovered, it bears a strikingly close resemblance to one of the foundational works of European art, Giotto's scene of the Lamentation in the Arena Chapel in Padua, Italy. Begun in 1305, this fresco—and indeed, the entire series of brilliant frescoes with which Giotto decorated this small chapel—is taken to mark a decisive innovation in European painting, and one that marks a decisive innovation in how Europeans were able to conceptualize themselves: single-point perspective. As Leo summarizes it in act 2:

> And thus doubtless won't need telling that about the beginning of the 14th century there was a mighty change nay turnaround in the way that western painters chose to address the world around them. Which, although it technically consisted of a number of devices to render the effect of three dimensions on a flat plane, was essentially a key step in the growing understanding, or belief, that not God but Man is the measure of all things. That his point of vision is *the* point of vision. That

there is no outside authority defining or pre-empting what he sees, with his own restless, quest-ing, yearning, endlessly inquisitive two eyes. . . . And it has been argued that the starting point of that, the first leg of the race from God to Man, was run by this guy, Giotto di Bonedone, in 1300-ish in Northern Italy.

Giotto's ability to transform the flat surface of the wall into a surface containing the ap-pearance of depth, his ability to place the figures of the Christian narrative into a naturalis-tic environment, not only presented a new kind of technical accomplishment; it signaled—and indeed, helped to create—a different way of representing, and understanding, the world.

But what would it mean if this decisive moment in the fashioning of "European" hu-manity did not take place in Europe? That is, what if Giotto's painting were, in effect, a copy of an earlier painting, one not located at the wellspring of European culture—Italy—but farther to the east, in a territory at best on the periphery—and more probably across the pe-riphery—of Europe's self-imagined space? This is the central question of *Pentecost,* a ques-tion that Edgar brilliantly deepens, elaborates, and complicates. For works of art don't arise in a vacuum: they are fashioned in a dense context of social life. Much as Oliver, Leo, and Gabriella struggle over the provenance and meaning of the fresco, they do so against the backdrop of contemporary Europe's struggles: the war in Bosnia is in the immediate back-ground of the play; Western Europe's efforts to deal with massive immigration from the south and east—the former Soviet republics, the Middle East, Central and South Asia, Africa; and the struggles of this small country both to confront its own recent history, and its centuries of its struggles on the frontier between Europe and the East. What does it mean to see *this* place as the center and source of European identity, a place so unimaginable that Oliver can only understand it as "Illyria"—the fictitious landscape of Shakespeare's *Twelfth Night?* Transforming this romantic nowhere into a real part of European identity proves challenging in a number of ways: the British and American experts are hardly able to com-

The refugees invade the chapel and take hostages in David Edgar's *Pentecost* at the Yale Repertory Theatre.

prehend their own condescension and misunderstanding of the place they are visiting; the local officials—artistic and political—have a keen sense of the fragility of their own newly nationalist enterprise; and, of course, the rag-tag band of illegal immigrants who come to occupy the church embody another kind of challenge, a challenge to the notion—or myth—of origin as determining identity.

Pentecost is a deeply "conceptual" play, a play that attempts to use the medium of dramatic performance to think through, in the immediate terms that performance offers, the intractable problems of contemporary Europe. It offers no easy answers, and certainly no romantic truths. Instead, *Pentecost* deftly uses the relationships between its principal characters to chart the tensions between Western and Eastern Europe, between Europe and its defining periphery, between the emerging, globalized European Union and the very different globalization of migration, of rootless nomads. Readers should note that while Edgar often provides translations in the text for the various non-English languages spoken by his characters, these translations are mainly for the actors' benefit: in the theater, the audience is—like the refugees in this sense—forced to negotiate the meaning of events.

PENTECOST

David Edgar

CHARACTERS

GABRIELLA PECS, *art curator*
OLIVER DAVENPORT, *art historian*
FATHER SERGEI BOJOVIC, *Orthodox*
FATHER PETR KAROLYI, *Catholic*
MIKHAIL CZABA, *minister*
PUSBAS, *leader of Heritage*
LEO KATZ, *art historian*
ANNA JEDLIKOVA, *former dissident*
TONI NEWSOME, *TV hostess*
A TEENAGE GIRL
A SWEDISH MAN
FIRST SOLDIER
SECOND SOLDIER
CZABA'S SECRETARY
A RESTORER
A POLICEWOMAN
A DRIVER
FIRST COMMANDO
SECOND COMMANDO
YASMIN, *Palestinian Kuwaiti*
RAIF, *Azeri*
ANTONIO, *Mozambican*
AMIRA, *Bosnian*
MARINA, *Russian*
GRIGORI, *Ukrainian*
ABDUL, *Afghan*
TUNU, *Sri Lankan*
NICO, *'Bosnian' Roma*
CLEOPATRA, *'Bosnian' Roma*
FATIMA, *Kurd*
RESTORERS, SOLDIERS, COMMANDOS

LOCATION: *The play is set in an abandoned church of the Romanesque period in an unnamed south-east European country. The large main door is to one side; facing us is an imposing wall, on which a large heroic revolutionary mural has been painted. There is also a high window through which it is possible to monitor the approach to the main door. There is at the beginning a stage spotlight,* a stepladder covered in curtaining, and other debris attesting to the church's chequered history.

The fresco that is discovered behind the mural is only seen in total at the very end: in Scene One a small section is revealed, in Scene Two it is in the process of being cleaned, in Scene Three it is being covered with a gauze and canvas facing, a procedure completed by Scene Four. In the second act, the facing is removed but the painting remains largely in darkness until the beginning of Scene Seven. We do however see reproductions and outlines of sections of the painting, and the whole in a blown up photograph.

Although stylistically Byzantine, the painting is compositionally clearly very similar to Giotto's Lamentation in the Arena Chapel, Padua (the main iconographic differences are described in the text). It is important that the section revealed in Scene One includes foreshortening, elements of perspective and clearly solid figures.

LANGUAGE: *All characters speak the languages they know, whether their own or indeed English. For information, I have identified the languages and given English translations of the non-English speeches (printed in square brackets and not intended to be spoken).*

In this text, the non-Roman script languages are phonetically transliterated, as is the Polish (in round brackets between the correctly-spelt speech and the English translation). The language of 'our country' is in fact Bulgarian, though Bulgaria is not 'our country'.

The transliteration is intended to render the languages in a form that will be accessible to actors, to convey the equivalent sounds of the letters rather than their correct orthography.

In the case of the Arabic and Turkic speeches, there are a number of vowels and consonants which have no direct equivalent in English. Thus 'aa', 'ee' and 'oo' are long (as in far, been and pool); 'o' is like the vowel in third, 'u' is like the tu in French, and the vowel 'ı' is like the 'er' in father. 'kh' is like the 'ch' in loch, 'H' is a strongly aspirated 'h', 'gh' like the French 'r' in Paris, 'q' is similar to a hard C, ''' is a glottal stop, and 'c' is a kind of choke, with no equivalent in English.

ACT ONE

The primary purpose of the painter is to
make a plane surface display a body
in relief, detached from the plane,
and he who in that art most surpasses
others deserves most praise.

Leonardo da Vinci

What determines and characterises European culture? Europe is formed by the community of nations which are largely characterised by the inherited civilisation whose most important sources are: the Judao-Christian religion, the Greek-Hellenistic ideas in the field of government, philosophy, arts and science, and finally, the Roman views concerning law.

Mr M. Mourik, Dutch ambassador
for International Cultural Cooperation, 1987

For more than a generation we have been bombarded with jingles and ditties about 'whiter than white' laundry, sparkling pots and pans, glistening floors, glowing toilet bowls. It is the same with our bodies: our hair, shimmering, dyed a designer-selected colour, our teeth capped pearly white. We must be scrubbed and caressed with chemicals, and covered again with fragrances and Fomblin-like oils, our faces lifted and lumpy cellulite made to disappear with miraculous products.

The treatment of art was not immune to this obsession with perfection. For if clean is beautiful, dirty is ugly, dirty is poor and dirty is bad. Get it off, get it all off. Brush a chemical on, let it work and wipe it away. That is how Easy-off gets the grime from the stove, and that is how AB57 works. No ring around the collar, no telltale stains . . .

As I stand against pollution of our world so do I oppose the risky restoration of the Sistine ceiling.

James Beck, art historian, in Art Restoration

All I know is that it's about three sides and this cleansing thing.

Samantha Fox, on a visit to Bosnia, 7 July 1993

SCENE I

Autumn. The church at night. Shafts of moonlight through high windows; the arc of car headlamps from a nearby motorway curl through the open door. An Englishman between 40 and 50 stands amid the debris. Nearby is a Woman with a torch, in her 30s, a native of this country. They are both dressed smartly, though not formally, for dinner; they both wear overcoats and scarves. He is OLIVER DAVENPORT, *an art historian; she is* GABRIELLA PECS, *of the National Museum.*

OLIVER: So this is it?

*(*GABRIELLA *nods.)*

This is the place?

*(*GABRIELLA *nods.)*

Where are we?
GABRIELLA: Okeydoke.

(She goes to shut the main door, blocking most of the light from the cars and the traffic noise.)

5   Hang on one moment.
OLIVER: *(to himself)* 'Okeydoke'.

(Seeing her shut the door, glancing at his watch.)

I do—you know, I have this dinner.
GABRIELLA: Yeah, yeah. I attend it.
OLIVER: I address it. May I ask—

*(*GABRIELLA *finds the light and turns it on.)*

10 GABRIELLA: Voilà.

(The light illuminates the grand heroic revolutionary picture on the wall.)

OLIVER: Good lord. The heroic revolutionary masses.
GABRIELLA: Plus naturally allies in cooperative peasantry and forward-viewing technical intelligensia.

*(*GABRIELLA *takes the curtaining off the ladder in order to climb up the wall.)*

OLIVER: Presumably that's 'forward-looking'.

GABRIELLA: Towards radiant future in which everybody's 15 quite as primitive and backwards clods as everybody else.
OLIVER: Now look, I really ought to—
GABRIELLA: Illyich.

(Slight pause.)

OLIVER: I'm sorry?
GABRIELLA: You ask where we are. Answer: filthy little village, 20 20 kilometres off capital, and 17 off border.
OLIVER: Illyich?
GABRIELLA: It is Lenin's father's name.
OLIVER: I know. I wondered why they hadn't changed it back. 25
GABRIELLA: Smart question. Unfortunately villagers cannot agree new name. Historic name, for Hungarians is Cholovar, for Saxons Klozendorf, for rest of people Clop.

*(*OLIVER *laughs.)*

This is amusing?
OLIVER: No. No, I was only thinking: just one vowel shift, 30 and I'd be stranded miles from anywhere, about to miss a professionally vital dinner in the presence of your Minister of Culture and His Excellency the Ambassador, in the abandoned Church of St Pulcheria the Pious, Clap.
GABRIELLA: It is church of St John Climacus, actually. And he 35 is now called Minister for Restoration of our National Monuments. And what is so desperately funny about a village means 'applause'?
OLIVER: Well, nothing, obviously. It's just that, as it happens, um, colloquially . . . 40
GABRIELLA: Yes?
OLIVER: 'Clap' means VD. Venereal,—uh, sexual disease.

(Slight pause.)

GABRIELLA: I see.
OLIVER: In fact, 'clop' means a—the sound of horse's hooves.
GABRIELLA: *(trying it out)* Clop, clop. 45
OLIVER: Clip clop.
GABRIELLA: *(affecting 'all the difference')* Clip clop.
OLIVER: Yes.

*(*GABRIELLA *climbs up the ladder.)*

GABRIELLA: As it happens you're not stranded. You will be back for your important dinner in good time. 50
OLIVER: That's a relief.
GABRIELLA: But now dear Dr Davenport five minutes please.

(Pause.)

OLIVER: It took the best part of an—
GABRIELLA: I drive roundabout. Will you take bricks please?

(Pause.)

Five minutes only. Please. 55

*(*OLIVER *can't not help as* GABRIELLA *begins to take bricks out of the cooperative peasantry.)*

OLIVER: Okeydoke.

(GABRIELLA *handing bricks down.*)

GABRIELLA: All righty, one abandoned church. As well as warehouse, church is used by heroic peasantry for store potatoes. *Pile* bricks please. And before potatoes, Museum
60 of Atheism and Progressive People's Culture. And before museum, prison.
OLIVER: Prison?

(OLIVER *is taking the bricks.* GABRIELLA *is revealing a section of dirty whitewashed wall with scribbled words on it.*)

GABRIELLA: 'Transit Centre'. German Army. You can still see signatures of prisoners on wall. You note also wall is
65 whitewash with clear mark of nail where Catholics hang pictures, how you say it, Via Dolorosa.
OLIVER: Stations of the Cross.
GABRIELLA: And underneath whitewash, pictures of our saints of orthodox religion.

(*A little along, she is revealing heads of saints.*)

70   Pretty bloody dull, I think.
OLIVER: So this place was orthodox before?
GABRIELLA: When we are Hungary, it Catholic, when we are holy Slavic people, Orthodox. When we have our friendly Turkish visitor who drop by for few hundred years, for
75 while is mosque. When Napoleon pass through, is house for horses.
OLIVER: Stable.
GABRIELLA: Stable, yes. Clip clop.
OLIVER: But presumably it's built—
80 GABRIELLA: At turn of thirteen century. So can you guess now why I bring you here?

(*Pause.* OLIVER *looks at his watch.*)

OLIVER: Now, look. Look, really, Mrs—Pesh—
GABRIELLA: Is 'Pecs'. Okeydoke. I tell you. Pronto.
OLIVER: (*as a statement of fact*) I am in your hands.

(*During the following,* GABRIELLA *takes bricks out of a different section of the wall.*)

85 GABRIELLA: Now in 1989 we have great turnaround.
OLIVER: Agreed.
GABRIELLA: And everything is opened up. Including naturally files of secret police.

(*Slight pause.* OLIVER *waves her on.*)

And most of it is—recent, time of communists. But as se-
90 cret police is very systematic in our country, files go way way back. For several hundred years. Some even in old Nagolitic language, before it become capital offence to speak it.
OLIVER: (*to speed* GABRIELLA *along*) And so?
100 GABRIELLA: And so, cops pass on files to us at National Museum. And then guess what, I find in 1425, when we are vassal state of Ottomans, report of trial of so-called Italian merchant, Leonello Vegni, who come here from Padua and is tried as spy of Holy Roman Empire, found guilty
105 and deheaded.

OLIVER: Or indeed 'beheaded'.
GABRIELLA: Or beheaded, yes.
OLIVER: And this report is in Old Nagolitic?
GABRIELLA: No I should coco. I tell you, capital offence, no-
110 body speak it after thirteen hundred. Though it is interesting to note, since turnaround, some old words creeping back—

(OLIVER *looks pointedly at his watch.*)

GABRIELLA: But point is, in summary of trial, in nice new Slavic language, they explain how Signor Vegni's way of
115 spying is to pose as connoisseur and report back to his master on all grand sight he sees. But actually, of course, he is really connoisseur, as well as really spy, and mixes truth and false. So it is hard to tell if when he writes he see 'octagonal basilica with fresco of our Holy Mother
120 with dead Christ' is actually code for barrack with brigade of horse or . . . just what it says.

(OLIVER *looks at* GABRIELLA.)

As he say: 'A painting so akin to nature you might think it real'. To be compared to glorious work of his own Giotto di Bondone, hitherto unequal in all world.
125 OLIVER: I see. And what makes you think it's not a troop of cavalry?
GABRIELLA: Smart question.
OLIVER: Speedy answer?
GABRIELLA: Sure, like billyo. Now it is no surprise I think to find our country has great national patriotic poem.
130
OLIVER: None at all.
GABRIELLA: And in fourth canto famous legend about traveller journeying to Persia, who arrive in little village twenty league from Zabocz. And traveller made captive—
135 what in old Nagolitic called 'involuntary guest'—and he is threaten even that he will be quite beheaded. But when sword is raise he promise if he will be spared he give to village gift much greater than his life. And to prove he take up brush and paint on church wall painting of Christ's fol-
140 lowers and Virgin mourning Christ so natural and real its figures seem to live and breathe. And so they say he keep his bargain and they let him go. And everyone is most content, except for wise old man who say—neighbours, I fear this painting prove great price for us, that it prophecy
145 of many miseries which fate inflicts on us throughout all centuries, that every mother looks on Virgin with dead son will one day mourn their own.
OLIVER: And was he right?
GABRIELLA: Well. It always said that painting was in Valley of Seven Churches.
150
OLIVER: Which is where?
GABRIELLA: Which lie indeed bit near Zabocz.
OLIVER: And which—
GABRIELLA: And which is laid waste by Turks in 1392.

(*Slight pause.*)

OLIVER: But I take it you're persuaded that the painting was
155 elsewhere.
GABRIELLA: You forgive please: 'take it'?
OLIVER: I—presume.

GABRIELLA: Old Nagolitic too has its peculiarities.

160 OLIVER: You stagger me.

GABRIELLA: Words for 'to' and 'from' are actually inter-changable.

OLIVER: This would explain the taxis.

GABRIELLA: But only if cab driver speak Old Nagolitic.

165 OLIVER: Which has been a capital offence since— . . .

GABRIELLA: —blah-di-blah.

(GABRIELLA *is clearly waiting for* OLIVER *to guess where she's going.*)

OLIVER: In Hindi, as I understand it, the words for 'tomor-row' and 'yesterday' are the same.

GABRIELLA: Well, blow me down.

(OLIVER *decides to catch up.*)

170 OLIVER: And so . . . you are—presumably—persuaded that the painting in the poem might not have been laid waste by Turks, but could have been the Lamentation Vegni may have seen in fourteen blah-di-blah. And if it was, then it's just about conceivable—though hardly likely, surely—it
175 could still exist. And if it might have been few kilometres *to* Zabocz instead of *from*—depending naturally where you started—

GABRIELLA: Bingo. And so, I go round churches in 20 kilo-metre—circle?

180 OLIVER: Radius.

(*Now she is handing bricks down again.*)

GABRIELLA: Of Zabocz. And I tell my friends I am—mending country cottage?

OLIVER: Well, 'repairing' . . .

GABRIELLA: Good, so I can borrow tools and I tap away on
185 walls and scrub at whitewash and I chip away at plaster and I pull out brick . . . And it is some time but eventu-ally I find—voilà.

(GABRIELLA *has uncovered a section of whitewash, in the middle of which a rough oval has been cleaned away. In the oval is the face of the Virgin holding Christ's naked body, partially obscured by a solid-looking rock in the foreground It is clear there is a good stab at per-spective, a bent arm is foreshortened, and the Virgin's face betrays great emotion.*)

I guess I go that way and I find St John.

(*She is climbing down.*)

I think—single point perspective. Kind of. Figures occupy
190 real space. Foreshortening. Individualised emotion. So, in short—

(GABRIELLA *is down. Pause.*)

OLIVER: In short, your Italian knew his cipolle.

GABRIELLA: Forgive please?

OLIVER: Onions. In that it's very like a Giotto.

195 GABRIELLA: Yes.

OLIVER: But you're not suggesting that it is a Giotto.

GABRIELLA: No.

OLIVER: Completed on a hitherto undocumented Balkan holiday.

GABRIELLA: Ha ha.   200

OLIVER: But a kind of—copy. By a follower. Hm. Interesting.

GABRIELLA: Not exactly.

OLIVER: Not exactly interesting?

GABRIELLA: Not exactly—copy.

(*Slight pause.*)

OLIVER: Mrs Pecs, I'm sorry. But this does appear—thus far   205
at least—to be, well, shall we say, akin, to Giotto's Lamen-tation in the Arena Chapel, Padua.

GABRIELLA: Yes.

OLIVER: So either it's by Giotto, or it's the most remarkable coincidence in the history of art, or it's a copy.   210

GABRIELLA: Copy? You think that this is copy?

OLIVER: Well, I'd need to see the rest of it.

GABRIELLA: A. But this is not possible.

OLIVER: I must assure you, it happens all the time.

GABRIELLA: Or only possible in Hindi. If tomorrow really   215
yesterday.

(*Pause.*)

OLIVER: When was—your national patriotic—thing, com-posed?

GABRIELLA: In early portion of twelve hundreds.

OLIVER: Giotto started painting the Arena in 1305.   220

GABRIELLA: Or thereabout. I know.

(*She holds the ladder, as an invitation for* OLIVER *to climb.*)

You want close butchers now?

OLIVER: Mrs Pecs, why did you bring me here?

GABRIELLA: Because if I am right that painting with perspec-tive even kind of painted before Giotto born, then I think   225
I make pretty damn substantial finding here.

OLIVER: To put it mildly.

GABRIELLA: So naturally I want just little bit to know if it will be true. And if so how best I proceed.

(*She gestures at the ladder.* OLIVER *climbs far enough to see the sur-face of the painting.*)

OLIVER: What solvent did you use on this?   230

GABRIELLA: (*proudly*) Hydrogen peroxide.

OLIVER: What?

GABRIELLA: My sister is hairdresser. Most effective.

OLIVER: So it would appear.

GABRIELLA: This is not good?   235

(OLIVER *turns from the painting.*)

OLIVER: And does—does your museum know about this?

GABRIELLA: No-one knows about this. Present company ex-cluded.

(OLIVER *comes down the ladder.*)

OLIVER: Should you not tell them?

GABRIELLA: I tell you.   240

OLIVER: You see, I'm sure, that you have, in this country, many expert—

GABRIELLA: You know that's bullshit.

OLIVER: And really, honestly, it's not my field—

245 GABRIELLA: Forgive please? Senior Professor, Ruskin Institute?

OLIVER: Just senior fellow, I'm afraid. In the Department of Contemporary Art Theory. So, actually, you see—

GABRIELLA: Okeydoke. Alrighty. Leave it to our great Na-
250 tional Museum. After all, it is our painting. And we are responsible, grown-up democracy. And either it is hogwash
and we are laughing stock or it right and we try to clean
with hairdye and we are clumsy clods, destroying priceless
work of art.

255 OLIVER: I didn't—for a moment—

GABRIELLA: You think we don't know what you say? East Europe. Where even crooks don't know what icons worth.
Where you pick up masterpiece for string of beads. Where
everything is ugly and pathetic. Where they botch up so-
260 cialism and make even bigger botch of market system too.

OLIVER: Well, I must assure you, back at home—

GABRIELLA: And what we spend on meal for you is tip. And
you can buy our whole machine tool industry for thirty
second ad on NBC. And sure we have funny language
265 and we all have names which sound like horse's feet and
sexual disease.

(*Slight pause.*)

OLIVER: I'm sorry. I—

GABRIELLA: So *here?* We have great genius painting which
change history of art? What, here? In such a country make
270 such botch of everything it touch? Well, I should bloody
coco.

(*Pause.*)

OLIVER: Yes.

(*Slight pause.*)

I'm sorry. It's just basic British insularity. It's suddenly the
papers are all full of places one had always vaguely thought
275 to be made up.

(*Slight pause.*)

If not Slovenia, then certainly Slavonia. And then suddenly
concentration camps start springing up all over pastoral
Shakespearian locations.

GABRIELLA: And now I guess we drive back to your grand
280 important meal presumably.

(*A car screeches to a halt outside.* GABRIELLA *goes quickly to put out
the spotlight.*)

OLIVER: What's this?

GABRIELLA: Shh. Shh.

OLIVER: (*whispers*) The police?

GABRIELLA: (*whispers*) Perhaps. Or . . . we are very near main
285 autoroute.

OLIVER: Which means—

(*The door of the church is opened. A mid-teenage* GIRL *enters with
a middle-aged* SWEDISH MAN. *They don't see* GABRIELLA *or*
OLIVER, *who move back into shadow.*)

GIRL: (*speaking in the language of our country*) Tova e myastoto.
Bezopasno e, nikoy ne idva took. [This is the place. It's
safe, nobody comes here.]

(*The* GIRL *goes and gathers up the curtaining, to fold it over as a
makeshift mattress.*)

SWEDISH MAN: Do you have English?   290
GIRL: Ne. [No.]
SWEDISH MAN: (*in German*) Oder Deutsch? [Or German?]
GIRL: (*German*) Ein bisschen. [Little bit.]
SWEDISH MAN: Wir machen es hier? [We do it here?]
GIRL: Richtig. [That's right.]   295

(*The* GIRL *has made the 'bed.'*)

OLIVER: (*whispers*) What's happening?
GABRIELLA: (*whispers*). What d'you think?
GIRL: Es ist zwanzig Mark. [It's 20 deutschmark.]
SWEDISH MAN: (*opening his wallet*) Ich habe Krone. Es ist so
egal wie Deutschmark. [I have Swedish krona. It's as good 300
as Deutschmark.]
GIRL: Nein. Es muss Deutschmark sein. [No. It must be
Deutschmark.]
SWEDISH MAN: Dollars?
GIRL: Ja. Fünf Dollars ist gut. [Yes, five dollars is OK.]   305

(*She waits for the* SWEDISH MAN *to hand over the dollar bill, but
he folds the note and puts it in his own outside pocket for payment
later. The* GIRL *shrugs and lies down on her back.*)

OLIVER: (*whispers*) He's German?
GABRIELLA: (*whispers*) Swedish I think.
SWEDISH MAN: Um—Darf ich von hinten? [Um—can I have
it from the back?]
GABRIELLA: (*whispers*) He wants it from behind.   310
GIRL: Es ist mir gleich. [All right by me.]
GABRIELLA: (*whispers*). She doesn't mind

(*The* GIRL *goes on all fours.*)

SWEDISH MAN: Verstehst? Ich will Arsch ficken. [You under-
stand—I want anal sex.]
GABRIELLA: (*whispers*) Does she understand, he is wanting   315
anal sex.
GIRL: Es ist mir gleich. [It doesn't matter]
GABRIELLA: (*whispers*) She doesn't mind.

(*The* MAN *kneels behind the* GIRL.)

SWEDISH MAN: Ich habe kein Gummi. [I don't have a con-
dom.]   320
GABRIELLA: (*whispers*) He doesn't have protective.
GIRL: Es ist OK. [It's OK.]
GABRIELLA: (*whispers*) She doesn't mind.

(*The* MAN *is pulling up the* GIRL's *skirt when* OLIVER *speaks loud
enough for him to hear.*)

OLIVER: St John the Who?

(*The* MAN *and the* GIRL *freeze.*)

GABRIELLA: Forgive please.   325

OLIVER: You said, the Church was dedicated to St John some-one. St John who?

GABRIELLA: Originally, St John Climacus. Catholics call it af-ter St John Evangelist. I don't know what they call when
330 mosque.

(*The* MAN *stands, and runs out. The* GIRL *jumps up, but she's missed him.*)

OLIVER: Please—forgive?

(*We hear the car door slam and see the arc of the headlamps as it turns and drives away. The* GIRL *turns to* OLIVER *and* GABRIELLA.)

GIRL: Cocksuckers.

(*She marches furiously out. Pause.*)

GABRIELLA: Why do you ask?

(*Slight pause.*)

OLIVER: Because we still don't know for sure this was the
335 Lamentation Vegni saw. And one way to nail it would be if his letter named the church.

GABRIELLA: But we don't have letter. Just report in trial.

OLIVER: In which case, it's a fair bet that he sent it. And it pre-sumably arrived.

(*Slight pause.*)

340 GABRIELLA: So then, you'll help me?

OLIVER: Yes.

GABRIELLA: Well. Blimey.

(OLIVER *looks at his watch.*)

OLIVER: That is, as long as—

GABRIELLA: Yes. of course.

(*She is going to put the bricks back.*)

345   May I ask why?

(OLIVER *looks at the scrumpled curtaining on the floor.*)

OLIVER: Because . . . because . . . This is Illyria, lady.

(*Lights fade.*)

SCENE II

Scaffolding has been erected in front of the painting. There is a plat-form at the bottom of the painting itself, about six feet above the ground, and a ladder going up and down. Bricks have been removed most of the plaster and some of the whitewash. So we can sense the outline of the Lamentation. Also on the platform there are cleaning materials and boxes of electronic equipment, some of them opened. At ground level there are more boxes, a computer console (the computer is on and flashing), a telephone (with modem) and a nearly empty noticeboard.

At ground level, there are two PRIESTS: *the Orthodox, middle-aged and bearded Father Sergei* BOJOVIC *and the younger Catholic Father Petr* KAROLYI. *They have brief cases and—as do most peo-*

ple—their car radios. There is also a SOLDIER *near the computer con-sole, with an automatic weapon. A* SECOND SOLDIER *stands 'guard-ing' the equipment.*

GABRIELLA *sits on the platform, her feet dangling over the edge.* OLIVER, *who is standing, moves to take a close look at a section of the painting. The* SOLDIER *notices.*

FIRST SOLDIER: (*waving his gun at* OLIVER) Ay!   5

(*Furious,* OLIVER *goes to* GABRIELLA.)

OLIVER: Vandalism.

GABRIELLA: Well, I tell you.

OLIVER: But *vandalism.*

(*The* SECOND SOLDIER, *bored, looks inside one of the open boxes.*)

GABRIELLA: I tell you. It just what they say.

OLIVER: It's what I've been accused of.   10

GABRIELLA: It—it just way they say in legal code. You know, like if you are dissident they call you 'hooligan' or 'para-site'.

OLIVER: I thought all that had changed.

(GABRIELLA *shrugs as* OLIVER *notices the* SECOND SOLDIER.)

OLIVER: (*to the* SECOND SOLDIER) Excuse me. *Excuse* me.   15

(*The* SECOND SOLDIER *looks questioningly at* GABRIELLA, *who gestures that he should leave the equipment alone. He does, with a contemptuous shrug.* OLIVER, *gesturing at the* PRIESTS.)

OLIVER: And who the hell are they?

(*Slight pause.*)

GABRIELLA: Well, one with beard obviously East Rite Church. What you say Orthodox. One with clean shave usually Catholic.

OLIVER: Well, let no-one say you're spiritually stuck for   20 choice.

GABRIELLA: Oh not so much choice. Basically, historical and geographic. It all depend, who is most long in charge.

OLIVER: You mean, which party?

GABRIELLA: No, which country. In south, where maybe peo-   25 ple bit more backward, longest under Turk. And Turk bit happier with Orthodox. In north, for more time more Hungarian, and so more people Catholic, and naturally most civilised and up-to-date. Which all persist up to our present day.   30

(OLIVER *has seen the* FIRST SOLDIER, *on ground level, playing with the computer.*)

OLIVER: Indeed. Please forgive me, for a moment.

(OLIVER *shins down the ladder.*)

   I wonder, could you stop that, please?

(*The* FIRST SOLDIER *carries on tapping at the keyboard.*)

FIRST SOLDIER: I think—

OLIVER: This is actually not your property.   35

FIRST SOLDIER: I think—you have message.

OLIVER: Just—don't touch.

FIRST SOLDIER: You have message, via modem.

OLIVER: Please. Just leave it.

(*The* SOLDIER *does, shrugging.* OLIVER *tries to switch the computer off, but fails. The* FIRST SOLDIER, *automatically, moves in to help.*)

40   OLIVER: *Leave* it.

(*The* FIRST SOLDIER *shrugs again.* OLIVER *looks up to* GABRIELLA, *who pats the platform next to her, to request him to return. Breathing deeply,* OLIVER *climbs up and joins* GABRIELLA *once more.*)

OLIVER: Speaking of hooligans.

(*Slight pause.* OLIVER *looks at his watch.*)

And it is half past ten. And the Minister was due at nine.

GABRIELLA: I notice, you always glancing at your watch. Do you never throw caution to four winds and take it off?

(OLIVER *looks balefully at* GABRIELLA.)

45   OLIVER: Perhaps, faced with the prospect of our project being—aquisitioned by the Pastorate of St Goliathos the Sensitive, and despite my naturally notorious sang-froid, stiff-upper arse and consequent tight lip, I am unable quite to emulate your enviably icy Balkan calm.

(*Slight pause.*)

50   Also this is not the first time I have been stood up by your Minister.

GABRIELLA: And in this you not so much unique. Put mildly.

(OLIVER *looks at her.*)

GABRIELLA: Hey. My arse it not so stiff. I do not want our fresco kissed and rubbed and bashed about with bells and
55   smeared with candle grease. But I learn in time that anger finite quantity one should not squander needlessly. And softly softly often best way catch your monkey.

OLIVER: (*mollified*) To coin a phrase.

(*Slight pause.*)

So where do you fit in?

60   GABRIELLA: To what?

OLIVER: To the great historical divide.

GABRIELLA: Oh, I think is pretty childish by and large. I do not pay these matters much attention. I am European.

OLIVER: Isn't everyone?

(*An impressive car slam causes everyone to look towards the door. A middle-aged man in a black leather coat enters, carrying a car radio. The man—whose name is* PUSBAS—*turns to* KAROLYI.)

65   PUSBAS: (*in the language of our country*) Pristigna li ministurut? [Has the Minister arrived?]

KAROLYI: (*glancing at his watch*) Oshte ne. [Not yet.]

(PUSBAS *sees* BOJOVIC, *marches over to him, gesturing towards* OLIVER.)

PUSBAS: Tova li e groopata razboynitsi? [This is the group of vandals?]

BOJOVIC: Khorata na izkoostvoto, da. Ministurut pristigna.   70
[The art people, yes. The Minister is coming.]

PUSBAS: Choodo e, che sa gi poosnali dotook. [It's a mystery they've been allowed in here.]

OLIVER: Is that the Minister?

GABRIELLA: No fear. That is group called 'Nasledstvo'. They   75
march about and dig up body of people killed in period of negative phenomena and think everything is plot of international masonry.

OLIVER: Nas—ledso?

GABRIELLA: 'Stvo'. I guess you will say 'Heritage'.   80

(*Enter Mikhail* CZABA, *the Minister. He is in his late 20s, dressed in fashionably baggy clothes, and carries a car radio. He is followed by his dazzlingly beautiful female* SECRETARY *into the centre of the church.*)

CZABA: (*seeing the assemblage of people, to himself*) Well, holy shit.

GABRIELLA: Now that is Minister.

OLIVER: Well, blimey.

CZABA: (*in our country's language*) E, gospoda, kakvo e tova?   85
[Well, gentlemen, what's this?]

(BOJOVIC, KAROLYI *and* PUSBAS *move in on* CZABA, *gesturing with their car radios, and speaking more or less simultaneously. The* SOLDIERS *smarten up,* OLIVER *and* GABRIELLA *stand.*)

BOJOVIC: Uvazhaemi gospodin ministur, vizhdate kakvo stava Tozi chovek oonishtozhava tsurkvata. [Esteemed Minister. You can see what's happening. This man is destroying the church.]

(*Overlapping with:*)

KAROLYI: Iskut za sobstvenost na pravoslavnata tsurkva e   90
yavno nevaliden. [The claim by the Orthodox church to ownership is obviously false.]

(*Overlapping with.*)

PUSBAS: Nie ot Nasledstvo nastoyavame tezi choozhdentsi da budut izgoneni! [We in Tradition demand that these foreigners be expelled!]   95

CZABA: Ta znachi tova e rabotata? [And this is the work being done up here?]

(CZABA *hands his radio to his* SECRETARY—*who puts it in her shoulder bag—and starts to climb the ladder up on to the platform.*)

BOJOVIC: Te veche oonishtozhikha beztsenno izkoostvoto s dookhovno stoinost. [They have already destroyed an artwork of great spiritual value.]   100

KAROLYI: Me interesoova dali sudut e oovedomen i, kakvo vie predlagate da se napravi po vuprosa. [My concern is whether or not the courts have been informed and what action you propose to take.]

PUSBAS: Koi e naredil tezi khorata da budut dopoosnati took?   105
Po chiya zapoved sa vneseni tezi su'orozheniya? [On whose instructions have these people been allowed here? On what authority was this equipment imported?]

(CZABA *has reached* OLIVER *and* GABRIELLA *on the platform.*)

110 CZABA: Dobro ootro, kazvam se Mikhail Czaba. [Good morning, I am Mikhail Czaba.]

GABRIELLA: Kazvam se Gabriella Pecs. [They call me Gabriella Pecs.] And this is Dr Oliver Davenport, of Ruskin Institute in London.

CZABA: Dobur den. [Good day to you.] (*English, with Ameri-*
115 *can inflection.*) Hi there I'm glad—

PUSBAS: (*interrupts*) Gospodin ministur, nastoyavam da popi-tate tozi chovek—[Mr Minister, I must insist you ask this man—]

CZABA: (*raising his finger*) Now, out of courtesy to our distin-
120 guished guest, does anyone have problem that we speak in English?

PUSBAS: I certainly have problem.

CZABA: Surely not.

PUSBAS: In principle.

125 CZABA: But clearly not in practice. So, we can all be good Eu-ropeans, speaking in American. Now, listen up. I'm run-ning kind of late, so we have ten minutes only I'm afraid. Professor Davenport, you must forgive me, since three weeks ago I am supposed to be at dinner with you. Sadly,
130 our currency is choosing that night to make bungee-jump, and I am otherwise engaged. My name is Czaba, I am Minister for Conservation of the National Monu-ments.

OLIVER: I thought that it was 'restoration'.

135 CZABA: (*he tries the our country word*) 'Zapazvane'. Too close to call.

OLIVER: Depending I suppose on what you thought of what had happened to your national culture recently.

CZABA: Well, yes, sure. But our difficulty as I understand that
140 in our country we have now law of Restitution, intend-ing to return all property expropriated by state since 1940 to its rightful owner.

BOJOVIC: Which depend I must say naturally which state.

CZABA: So maybe you see problem.

145 BOJOVIC: As I must say for example this church is built in na-tional faith.

KAROLYI: But its most recent use of course is Catholic.

CZABA: It is same with factories and country homes.

BOJOVIC: It is more recent Catholic because in 1940 Roman
150 Church in thrall to aristocratic-military regime who are themselves in thrall to Nazis. Hence Catholic Bishop hands it to SS for special centre.

PUSBAS: I have to state that Iron Legion is in thrall to noone.

CZABA: Sad to say.

155 KAROLYI: In fact, of course, as Father Bojovic is well aware, it was not handed over but expropriated. For three weeks. Whereas for the last 40 years, as the whole world knows, the Orthodox obedience has demonstrated amply why it is so called.

160 BOJOVIC: I must say this easier to say from London than from here.

CZABA: Now, guys . . .

KAROLYI: All of which has little bearing on Professor Daven-port's discovery, which is in fact we gather now agreed to
165 be a work completed in the early 13th Century—

BOJOVIC: In fact is not agreed at all.

KAROLYI: —by an itinerant Italian on a journey east—

BOJOVIC: Or equally by unknown national artist of a late Byzantine time—

KAROLYI: —and in considerable advance of other paintings of 170 its period—

BOJOVIC: —with element of earlier Italian style.

PUSBAS: Oh of course if it is national artist then it must be copy.

BOJOVIC: In fact I do not think I say—   175

PUSBAS: Or if advance it must be foreigner.

OLIVER: Whereas, in fact, whatever may turn out to be its his-tory, this painting is not my 'discovery'. I am here purely in an advisory capacity, assisting Mrs Pecs, who is Deputy Chief Curator of the Early Modern section of the na-   180 tional Museum.

BOJOVIC: Acting Deputy Chief Curator, I must say.

OLIVER: Who through a quite remarkable combination of detection, application and frankly vision, has discovered a piece of work in the Giottan manner that may prove—to   185 put it no more dramatically—to be of considerable inter-est to art historians.

(*Slight pause.*)

So if acting, acting pretty bloody well.

CZABA: I'm sorry—Gottan?

OLIVER: Giottan. As in Giotto.   190

(CZABA *looks blank.*)

OLIVER: The Trecento—14th century—Italian master.

CZABA: And you reckon this thing painted earlier than 14 century?

OLIVER: It is still a matter of dispute.

CZABA: Well, holy—smoke.   195

OLIVER: But if I am asked my opinion about the future of the building . . .

CZABA: Please.

OLIVER: I would say it should revert to its most recent func-tion. As a secular museum.   200

BOJOVIC: I think most recently it dump.

OLIVER: In which Mrs Pecs' potentially priceless find can be properly conserved, and studied, and appreciated.

KAROLYI: Mr Czaba, as is surely obvious to everyone—

OLIVER: Or at least that's what I thought till I became aware   205 of the extent of passion in this case.

PUSBAS: What's this?

(GABRIELLA *waves at* OLIVER *in alarm.*)

OLIVER: For certainly our sponsors would be most unhappy to be seen to be infringing anybody's legal rights. Partic-ularly religious rights. To a degree which might well   210 threaten their involvement.

(*Slight pause.*)

Our Italian, and—German sponsors.

(*Pause.*)

CZABA: Professor Davenport, what say we take five here.

(CZABA *to the head of the ladder.*)

BOJOVIC: In privacy?
215   CZABA: That's right.

(He invites KAROLYI, BOJOVIC, PUSBAS *to ascend, and* OLIVER *to descend.)*

Maybe during we are gone Mrs Pecs may tell you all about this painting. And bring you up to speed on why and whether it is painted when and where. Oh, and naturally by whom.

(Now CZABA, OLIVER *and the* SECRETARY *are at ground level, with* KAROLYI, BOJOVIC, PUSBAS *and* GABRIELLA *above.)*

220   CZABA: Babel's Stairway.
OLIVER: Sorry?
CZABA: Is it not Babel, where God invent all different language, to stop mankind build stairway to heaven?
OLIVER: I think it's, in fact it's Babel's Tower.
225   CZABA: Of course. I am thinking of Led Zeppelin.

*(*OLIVER *doesn't get this but acknowledges anyway.)*

OLIVER: Now, look—
CZABA: And now maybe we cut crap and come clean with our bottom line here.
OLIVER: Sorry?
230   CZABA: I mean, it obvious what our black-suited comrades want. They want they own building with priceless painting on wall. You too, I guess.
OLIVER: I—just want to find the truth.
CZABA: Sure. Me also. And as great Lenin teaches, often best
235   way to find out truth to ask whose interests are served.
OLIVER: I'm surprised you learn from Lenin.
CZABA: But of course. But with opposite effect. To me, to serve your interest is good. And frankly dear Professor I see through I think this flim-flam about 'considerable in-
240   terest'. In fact I think that if this painting will be what you say, you find great hot-shit art discovery?

(Slight pause.)

OLIVER: In fact it's—not Professor. Merely Doctor.
CZABA: Well not so merely I dare say.
OLIVER: But yes. You're right. If the fresco predates Giotto
245   then it could be viewed as the starting point of 600 years of western art.
CZABA: And it found by you and Mrs Pecs. And you clean it and you put up light and you unveil it at grand ceremony and you write big book and you go round campuses with
250   talk and you go down in history as people who make biggest art find since King Tut or maybe even digging up Pompeii. And this for love of Mike not in your interest?
OLIVER: It isn't—*merely* in my interest.
CZABA: Oh sure. Interest also of truth beauty and universal
255   European values.

(Slight pause.)

Listen. I know. You pick it up I don't know who your great painter is. You think—this man who has not heard of great Italian master, he is Minister of Culture, whatever

fancy name they use. And you recall those past days—maybe you are visitor—and you lecture on your work at   260
our great University and you think how nice it is that everybody speak good English and know so much more about your subject than your students back at home. And you go on peanut-costing tram and you see pretty girls with nice dress and nice hair and they are reading Tolstoy   265
or Turgenev and you think in England they are dressed like tramp and reading garbage pail. And of course it's sad you come back and you find—yes, when they have choice, Turgenev goes in trashcan and instead it's video of Star Trek if not Terminator Two. And sure, I take your   270
point. But I tell you, Doctor, it is price worth paying.
OLIVER: Really?
CZABA: Oh you bet your sweet boots Dr Davenport.

(Slight pause.)

This shocks you?
OLIVER: No.   275
CZABA: Fess up.
OLIVER: No, truly. As it happens, I've never seen a firm distinction between art and artefact. I certainly don't think a work's devalued if it operates within a market. I think that Star Trek works, for what it is, as well as Pride and Preju-   280
dice. Or even that up there.
CZABA: Well, whop that thing.
OLIVER: It's just that that was done—may have been done—the best part of a hundred years before we thought it was. Which is why it is in both our interests—as well as of our   285
sponsors and your Ministry of Tourism—not to mention naturally your foreign currency reserves—if it is removed from here and remounted in your National Museum.
CZABA: Removed?
OLIVER: That's right.   290
CZABA: You can do that?
OLIVER: Sure. You stick a canvas and gauze facing on it, soaked in rabbit skin glue, let it dry, and yank it off. They used to do it all the time.
CZABA: They used to?   295
OLIVER: It's become, like many things, somewhat unfashionable among the current, minimalist tendency of fine art restoration. I'm sorry, conservation. But however out of favour, it would mean one set of clergy gets the church, your national museum gets the painting, and you get the   300
biggest tourist trap since the Chinese terracotta army. So everybody's happy. Even Lenin.
CZABA: How long do you need?
OLIVER: A month?
CZABA: I give it my best shot.   305

(As he turns to go back up he ladder, CZABA *notices the flashing message on the computer.)*

I think that you have message.

(As OLIVER *turns to the screen, he catches the* FIRST SOLDIER*'s eye.* CZABA *is climbing the ladder.)*

OLIVER: Um . . .
CZABA: I guess you access it and then you print it. It's like fax, only it come straight on to your hard disk.

(*He nods to the* SECRETARY, *to come to* OLIVER's *aid. She moves in.*)

SECRETARY: Excuse me?
310 OLIVER: Thank you, yes.

(*The* SECRETARY *is not sure about the first step on the keyboard.*)

FIRST SOLDIER: Mislya, che tryabva da vlezete v 'action menu'. [I think you need to get into the Action Menu.]
SECRETARY: Yasno. [Right]

(*By this time,* CZABA *has arrived on the platform.*)

KAROLYI: E, Ministre? [Well, Minister?]
315 CZABA: Gospoda, izvinyavam se, gospozho i gospoda. Sama sudut mozhe da reshi vuprosa za sobstvenostta na sgradata. Mislya, che tryabva da pozvolim na doktor Davenport da produlzhi sledstvieto moo. [Gentlemen, I'm sorry, lady and gentlemen. Only the courts can decide about the
320 ownership of the building. I think we must allow Dr Davenport to continue his investigation.]
BOJOVIC: Oovazhaemi gospodin ministur, oomolyavam vi da prerazgledate reshenieto si. [Esteemed Minister, I must beg you to reconsider.]
325 KAROLYI: Tova e bezobrazie! Az protestiram nai-kategorichno! [This is outrageous! I must protest in the strongest terms!]
PUSBAS: Predooprezhdavam vi, che moyata organizatsiya nyama de se ogranichi samo s protesti! [I must tell you, there will be more than mere protests from my organisa-
330 tion!]

(*As soon as the above is established:*)

SECRETARY: OK.
OLIVER: Is—can you get it?

(*The printer bursts into life.*)

SECRETARY: Is grass green?
OLIVER: Well done.

(*They go to the printer,* OLIVER *once again catching the* SOLDIER's *eye.*)

335 SECRETARY: In fact, I am not so too much use to IBM compatible.
OLIVER: It's supposed to be—state of the art.

(OLIVER *joins her watching the fearsomely fast printout. Above,* CZABA *continues his pitch.*)

CZABA: Razberete, che sum s vurzani rutse. Neshtata ostavat vuv vlastta na sudut. [You must understand my hands are
340 tied. The matter rests with the court.]
BOJOVIC: Ami ako ima oshte shteti? [But what if there is further damage?]
CZABA: Az opredeleno smyatam, che sgradata e v sigurni rutse. A sega tryabva da vurvya. [I really think the building
345 is in safe hands. Now, really, I must go.]

(CZABA *goes to descend the ladder, followed by* BOJOVIC, KAROLYI, PUSBAS, *and* GABRIELLA.)

SECRETARY: Hot money is on AppleMac to clean up east of Oder.

(*She tears off the message, and hands it to* OLIVER.)

OLIVER: Is that so.

(CZABA *arrives in the workstation area.*)

CZABA: Dr Davenport. You get your message?
OLIVER: Yes . . .   350

(*With a preoccupied nod to the* SECRETARY.)

Yes, thank you very much . . .
CZABA: (*filling in*) All Ministers get drop dead gorgeous secretaries. But mine has wordprocessing and one hundred word per minute shorthand also. So no surprise I am envy of whole cabinet.   355

(*Most of the* PRIESTS *have arrived:*)

I have told our friends that you have our permission to continue with your investigation, pending final ruling by our court. On understanding naturally there is no substantial alteration to building's fabric.
OLIVER: (*quietly*) The paint layer is a millimetre thick.   360
CZABA: (*quietly*) Well, you don't say.

(*Louder, to cover:*)

You know, I have theory that big problem with high culture is it makes you think too much of past. You go to opera, see painting, all time they are reminding you of dreadful precedent, how everything goes wrong before.   365
Which is why if you want real change, you put barbarians in charge. People who don't know about how walls will all fall down. Who don't know history of Tower of Babel.

(OLIVER *looks quizzical.* CZABA *drops his voice again.*)

CZABA: I'd say, you have two weeks.

(CZABA *turns and goes, followed by his* SECRETARY.)

PUSBAS: (*to* OLIVER) Don't worry. We'll be back.   370

(PUSBAS *and* KAROLYI *go out. The* FIRST SOLDIER *gestures to the* SECOND. *The* SECOND SOLDIER *leaves, but the* FIRST *decides to wait by the church door.*)

BOJOVIC: Dear Dr Davenport, there is something you must understand about this country. It will always prove last barrier. To Russia from above, to Muslim from below. As   375
has always been, way back into Byzantine days. You stand on Europe's battlement. Take care.

(BOJOVIC *turns and goes towards the church door. As he reaches it, the* FIRST SOLDIER *buttonholes him, gesturing back to* OLIVER *and they go out together, the* FIRST SOLDIER *talking. Meanwhile.*)

GABRIELLA: Well? *Well?*
OLIVER: What does 'Climacus' mean?
GABRIELLA: Forgive please?   380
OLIVER: As in St John. The patron of this church.
GABRIELLA: What, literally?
OLIVER: Literally.

GABRIELLA: It mean ladder. St John is monk who writes most
385   famous book called Ladder of Divine Ascent. Each chap-
        ter is called—what is this thing?
OLIVER: Rung.

(*Slight pause.* BOJOVIC *and the* SOLDIER *have gone.*)

GABRIELLA: It come you see from Greek word for 'ladder'.
        Which in fact is Klimax.

(*Slight pause.*)

390   Which of course in English means 'Big Finish'. And has
        sex meaning too I think.
OLIVER: Yes. Yes, it does.

(*He looks at the letter.* GABRIELLA *looks inquiringly at* OLIVER.)

        And you were right. Softly softly did catch monkey. He
        will let us take it down.
395 GABRIELLA: What, take off wall?
OLIVER: That's right. And remount it in the national musuem.
GABRIELLA: And this is good?
OLIVER: Well, only if we're right.

(GABRIELLA *realises the significance of the printout in* OLIVER's
hand.)

400 GABRIELLA: And are we?

(*Pause.*)

OLIVER: Well, they did find the letter. It was in an archive that
        had not been opened since the death of Emperor Maxi-
        milian the First. And there was indeed a description of the
        painting, which was quite detailed, and included both a
405   foreground rock and the fact that St John's right arm was
        outstretched towards the Virgin, as if perhaps to comfort
        her. And while Vegni doesn't make any direct comparison
        with Giotto's Lamentation, he does note the similarity be-
        tween the painter and 'our great Italian masters of last
410   century'. Which is as he himself points out all the more
        remarkable, in view of the painting being mentioned—
        celebrated, even—in a noted national epic poem com-
        posed no later than 1220.

(*Slight pause.*)

        Oh, and he names the church. It's San Giovanni della
415   Scala. 'Scala' means 'ladder', in Italian.

(*He starts to climb the ladder to the platform.*)

        So it looks like, you were wrong. You didn't botch it. You
        have great genius painting after all. The starting pistol for
        the next 600 years. Here of all places. The frontier be-
        tween the mediaeval and the modern world.

(*He reaches the platform and looks down at* GABRIELLA.)

420   Mrs Pecs, it seems you've made the biggest art find since
        the unearthing of Pompeii. What say we take a butchers at
        the rest of it?

SCENE III

Two weeks later. On the platform, RESTORERS *in white dungarees
are preparing the painting for removal from the wall. This involves
painting a layer of glue on sections of the painting and then affixing
40 by 40cm pieces of loose cotton gauze—themselves steeped in
glue—on the surface, stretched out gently by hand. This procedure
starts from the bottom of the painting and moves upwards. As they
work, the* RESTORERS *are listening to music on walkmans.*

*The workstation area below has also developed There are some new
creature comforts: an armchair, a coffee machine. There are also mi-
croscopic machines now unpacked and in operation, and a big noticeboard on which a black-and-white, sectioned photograph of the
painting is displayed, along with other lists and data, and reproductions of other Lamentations (including Giotto's at Padua). The computer is on and the screen is presently showing an outline of a section
of the painting.*

Suddenly the door opens and LEO KATZ, *an American in his 30s,
marches in followed by two* SOLDIERS. LEO *has come straight from the
airport with his luggage and duty free bag. The* SOLDIERS *do not need
to be same as in the last scene. The* FIRST SOLDIER *is smoking.*

FIRST SOLDIER: Ne, ne. Not passport. Propoosk. Pass.
LEO: Look, I don't have a pass.

(*The* FIRST SOLDIER *looks at the* SECOND SOLDIER.)

FIRST SOLDIER: (*to the* SECOND SOLDIER) No pass.
LEO: You see, I've come straight from the airport.
FIRST SOLDIER: Eh?   5
LEO: I use the word 'straight' loosely.
FIRST SOLDIER: So you want go airport?
LEO: Never again.
FIRST SOLDIER: No pass, no entry.
LEO: Hey. Is Dr Davenport around?   10

(*The* FIRST SOLDIER *looks at the* SECOND SOLDIER, *who stands.*)

SECOND SOLDIER: Dr Davenport not here. He is come back
        at twelve o'clock.
LEO: Well, hey, that's my appointment.
SECOND SOLDIER: What?
LEO: Twelve o'clock. He is come back to see me.   15

(*The* SOLDIERS *look at each other.*)

        It is ten of already. Can I not wait?

(*The* SOLDIERS *look at each other. the* FIRST SOLDIER *decides to
angle for a bribe.*)

FIRST SOLDIER: Duty free.
LEO: That's right.
FIRST SOLDIER: Jack Daniels.
LEO: Correct.   20
FIRST SOLDIER: And cigarette?
LEO: No, I don't smoke.

(*He picks up his bags.*)

        And no more should you.

(*As he carries his bags over to the workstation area.*)

It is a fucking house of worship, for Christ's sake.

(*The* SOLDIERS *decide it's too much trouble to make an issue of this.*)

25 FIRST SOLDIER: (*in the language of our country*) Abe, kazval li e anglichaninut, che ima sreshta s nyakovo? [Did the Englishman say someone was coming to see him?]

SECOND SOLDIER: Ne. No toi yavno govori istinata. [No. But he is obviously right.]

30 FIRST SOLDIER: Da, znam. Mean bastard!

(LEO, *who knows exactly what he is doing, smiles to himself as he puts down his bags. He notes that the work on the painting is going on above him. He looks round the workstation area, noting the telephone. He takes a letter from his pocket and goes and picks up the phone. He tries to make sense of it.*)

LEO: Now is this a busy or a dial tone.

(*Slight pause.*)

Hallo?

(OLIVER *and* GABRIELLA *enter the church.* GABRIELLA *has her car radio. The* FIRST SOLDIER *is about to tell* OLIVER *about his visitor, but decides against it, as the conversation is in full flow.* OLIVER *and* GABRIELLA *are getting on well with the task in hand and each other, and are in an excellent mood.*)

OLIVER: No, my contention is not that national stereotypes are true, but that if they aren't true they aren't true in
35   spades.

(LEO *puts the telephone down, and quickly moves his luggage somewhere inconspicuous.*)

GABRIELLA: Forgive please? Spades?

OLIVER: To the opposite extreme. So there is nothing *less* efficient than an inefficient German. No-one *less* frugal than a spendthrift Scot.

(LEO *goes up the ladder.*)

40 GABRIELLA: Nothing less miserable than cheery Russian.

OLIVER: Right. And no-one more engaging than an interesting Belgian. No-one ruder than a discourteous Japanese.

(LEO *looks at the painting and the work going on. He is noticed after a moment by a female* RESTORER. GABRIELLA *puts down her car radio.*)

GABRIELLA: Nothing meaner maybe than ungenerous American.

45 OLIVER: Your experience has clearly been quite different from mine.

(OLIVER *and* GABRIELLA *are taking their overcoats and jackets off, and changing into white coats.* LEO *is looking closely at the painting as yet uncovered.*)

RESTORER: Dobur den. Good morning.

LEO: Morning.

OLIVER: Nothing quieter than a restrained Italian.

50 RESTORER: Can I help you?

LEO: No, I'm fine.

OLIVER: Nothing more prosaic than an unromantic Pole.

LEO: Just carry on as if I wasn't here.

GABRIELLA: And English?

(*The* RESTORER *returns to her work.*)

OLIVER: What do you think?   55

GABRIELLA: Nothing as—loose-lipped—

OLIVER: Or indeed loose-arsed . . . as an—

(GABRIELLA *touches his lips with her finger, just a moment longer than is necessary for the demonstration:*)

GABRIELLA: It is impossibility to conceive.

(*A moment between them.*)

OLIVER: I am told that the South Ibo word for—'arse', is in North Ibo the first person pronoun singular.   60

(*Slight pause.*)

GABRIELLA: Big deal. Old Nagolitic word for—ladies' place, new language word for 'flute'.

OLIVER: Leading no doubt to all kinds of droll misunderstandings in the orchestra.

(LEO *is descending the ladder.*)

LEO: I am reliably informed by people paid to know these   65
things that the Finnish word for 'fart' is the Swedish for 'speed'.

(OLIVER *and* GABRIELLA *look at each other and the new arrival.*)

LEO: As of course the British for 'apartment' is the American for 'puncture'.

GABRIELLA: You forgive please?   70

LEO: Flat.

OLIVER: Uh, may I ask—

LEO: Pretty neat set-up you got up there. You're going for a strappo?

OLIVER: Stacco.   75

LEO: No kidding. Coletta or a resin?

OLIVER: Um—coletta.

LEO: So you reckon it's all painted wet?

OLIVER: Uh—

LEO: (*to* GABRIELLA) Coletta's a water-based adhesive. It dis-   80
solves medium—paint—applied to a dry surface.

OLIVER: Yes, Mrs Pecs knows that. And no, it's mostly but not all buon fresco. So we're using polyvinal acetate to fix the secco.

(*Now* LEO*'s going to the computer.*)

LEO: State of the art. Now this is Getty software, right?   85

OLIVER: Now, look, are you a journalist?

LEO: Kind of. Now how d'you get the palette on this thing?

(OLIVER *takes over. He is now more adept at using this machine and gets a print-out almost immediately.*)

OLIVER: I'm told it's more or less what you'd expect. Lime white, red and yellow ochre, burnt sienna, ultramarine—

90   LEO: You're told?
      OLIVER: By people paid to know these things.
      LEO: (*to* GABRIELLA) And the reflectography and photogram-
          metry and all that stuff checked out?
      GABRIELLA: Yes, thank you. Hunkydorily.
95   LEO: But you're basically dating on the provenance? Some . . .
          poem.

(OLIVER *leaves the computer. He wishes he knew* LEO's *game.* LEO *himself takes the print-out of the palette and pockets it.*)

      GABRIELLA: Our great national poem. Which is composed at
          latest by twelve hundred twenty-five.
      LEO: That early. Boy.
100   OLIVER: No earlier than Magna Carta.
      LEO: But I'm right, to date the thing that soon, you need to
          to tack the poem to, some letter, from some envoy?
      OLIVER: Spy.
      LEO: Hey, I bet you guys are praying that you got it right.

(*Pause.*)

105   OLIVER: What do you mean?
      LEO: Because without the poem, it's a copy of the Giotto
          Lamentation in the Arena Chapel, Padua.

(LEO *takes a postcard of the Padua Lamentation from his pocket and hands it to* OLIVER. *He goes to the photograph of our painting and points out the differences.*)

      I mean, one arm is headed forward, and the old girl's
      turned into a rock, and instead of angels you got stars . . .
110   But all the kind of errors you'd commit if you were draw-
      ing from a drawing. Or from memory.
      OLIVER: There is no problem with the provenance.
      LEO: Well, fingers crossed. But, hey. It's always scary, wanting
          anything so badly to be true.

(*Pause.*)

115   OLIVER: Who are you?
      LEO: Oh, I'm sorry.

(*He makes a bit of a meal of searching for his card in his wallet.*)

      OLIVER: I am H.O. Davenport.
      LEO: That's Dr, Senior Fellow, Ruskin Institute.
      OLIVER: And this is Mrs Gabriella Pecs, of the National Mu-
120   seum.
      LEO: (*handing his card to* GABRIELLA) Ah, and you're the folks
          who get the fresco, right?
      GABRIELLA: How do you do?
      LEO: Oh, hunkydorily.

(GABRIELLA *hands the card to* OLIVER.)

125   But I do need a phone.

(*He is already there and using it.* OLIVER *has read the card and closes his eyes.*)

      GABRIELLA: You dial eight and then number.
      LEO: *Eight.*

(*He dials, taking the number from the letter.*)

      OLIVER: You're Leonard Katz.
      LEO: But my chums all call me Leo.

(*Down phone:*)

      Hi, this is Professor Katz.   130
      OLIVER: Well, let's not rush to judgement.
      LEO: English?

(*Slight pause.*)

      Hey, is that 27612? It's Professor Katz from Cornell Uni-
      versity.
      GABRIELLA: What is he?   135
      OLIVER: He's an art historian.
      GABRIELLA: Not journalist?
      OLIVER: In the sense that Pol Pot was an urban redeveloper.

(LEO's *got the right person on the telephone.*)

      LEO: Ah, hi. Yuh, sure, no problem. Took the pretty way.
      GABRIELLA: So he is presumably bad news?   140
      OLIVER: Spot on.

(LEO *suddenly asks* GABRIELLA.)

      LEO: Hey, when d'you pull?
      GABRIELLA: When dry. Tomorrow.
      OLIVER: Why d'you ask?
      LEO: (*down phone*) It's tomorrow so you'll have to shift. Move   145
          quickly. Sure. Bye bye.

(*He puts the phone down.*)

      OLIVER: Now, Profesor Katz, I have to make it plain —
      LEO: Me too. Four points. First of all, to 'make it plain' that
          thus far I have not had a good day. Due to some error of
          judgement, Mrs Pecs, I flew your national airline, which is   150
          to civil aviation what Van Gogh was to cosmetic surgery.
          Then, two, this may turn out to be five points, at passport
          control the guy reads out my name—which is Leonard
          Aaron Katz—and quips, 'Israeli passport, no?'

(OLIVER *looks at* GABRIELLA, *who bites her lip.*)

      And we haven't even gotten *in* the taxi.   155
      GABRIELLA: (*to lighten the atmosphere*) In fact, in our old lan-
          guage, 'to' and 'from' are only distinguishable by context.
      LEO: I beg your pardon?
      GABRIELLA: This significant pecularity accounting maybe for
          some shortcoming of taxicabs.   160

(*It hasn't worked.*)

      LEO: Mrs Pecs, I know a little of your country's history. I am
          aware for instance of your enviable record under German
          occupation. Only 80,000 of your Jews deported to the
          camps in Poland. This heartening statistic is accounted for
          however by the fact that by the time the Germans got   165
          round to deporting them, there weren't that many more
          than 80,000 left. So, three, I think it's probably unlikely
          that we're going to get along.

OLIVER: Now, I naturally haven't asked, but I would guess
170 that Mrs Pecs is at the very outside 35—
LEO: And it is no surprise to me, point four, that having found
a dubiously provenanced but interesting fresco all of two
hours from the airport even driving straight, you plan to
rip it off its wall and shove it into a collection whose ma-
175 jor works consist of portraits of the Mighty Leader pinning medals on Young Pioneers and blessing tractors.
GABRIELLA: This is not true. We have Gentile Fabriano and
young Brueghel.
LEO: You have a copy of a school of Fabriano and your
180 Brueghel is at best a distant cousin. You should also know
you've a section of St Nicodemus' drapery as verdigris in
secco which it obviously can't be as it's fugitive and at a
quick glance two protruding nails.
OLIVER: This is a travesty.
185 LEO: The nails? I must assure you, buddy—
OLIVER: Your description of our aims and purpose in this
transfer.
LEO: Oh, which are?
OLIVER: Well, the main intention, obviously, is the protection
190 of the work from the considerable environmental risks—
LEO: What, 'to save the village it was necessary to destroy it'?
OLIVER: Sorry?
LEO: General Westmoreland in Vietnam.
GABRIELLA: What has this to do with Vietnam?
195 OLIVER: Smart question. You see, Gabriella, Professor Katz has
made something of a career of bowling round the world
attacking restoration beg their pardon conservation projects on the grounds that Michelangelo took 500 years of
candlegrease and overpainting into full account when he
200 did the Sistene ceiling, and thus actually intended it
should turn dark brown—
LEO: Now this *is* a travesty.
OLIVER: Whereas, in fact, for all this guff about 'acknowledging the painting's history', what it comes down to for Pro-
205 fessor Katz and ilk is that they want their art—and more
crucially their artists—to be ancient, brooding and mysterious. So that we're rendered totally dependent on the insight of historians to explain their tortured genius to us.
Whereas—
210 LEO: Whereas the problem with the scrapers,—Gabby, is that
for all their spritz about the artist's original intentions,
they too have prejudices, which is for things that look as
bright and bland and squeaky clean as television. And if as
they believe there's no real difference between a quattro-
215 cento Venus and a pin-up, and the Sistene back wall's just
a billboard, then why not strip 'em down and make 'em
look that way?
GABRIELLA: But presumably no-one takes seriously this—
OLIVER: As opposed that is to the Professor, who does not see
220 painters as the makers of material objects in the context
of their place and time at all—
GABRIELLA: But decidedly it is not possible for serious art
critic—
OLIVER:—but rather as essentially no more than tubes through
225 which God pours unique and universal truths upon the
world.
GABRIELLA: But this is surely actually true.

(*Pause.* OLIVER *is forced to turn to* GABRIELLA.)

OLIVER: Look. Look. I have no problem with the notion of
good painters. I just don't think they're fundamentally different from other kinds of maker of other kinds of thing. 230
GABRIELLA: So presumably if Leonardo will be alive today, he
directs advert for Pizza Hut?
LEO: That is exactly what he thinks.
OLIVER: That is a—grotesque parody of what I think.
GABRIELLA: I am pleased because that utter bullshit to my 235
mind.

(LEO *laughs.*)

GABRIELLA: And if you have last 40 years as we have, you will
see how it bullshit too.

(*Pause.*)

OLIVER: What do you mean?
GABRIELLA: I mean, during 40 years we are having no great 240
artists and all social and historic context, and this means
our museums full of children's crayon drawings and old
quilts and bits of painted cart because naturally we must
combat petit-bourgeois formalism and acknowledge art
of heroic revolutionary masses quite as good as Michelan- 245
gelo. So I tell you what I think. I think there is great painting and there is also less great and there is pretty bloody
bad as well.

(*To* LEO:)

And I don't know if it come from God or love or what
you have for breakfast. But if something great and beauti- 250
ful defaced, and made ugly and pathetic, then we must
scrape clean, and restore to what it was before.
LEO: But surely, you shouldn't wipe out all that history?
GABRIELLA: No? Whyever not?
LEO: 'Cos it'll be forgotten. 255
GABRIELLA: Maybe some things best forgotten.
OLIVER: (*gently*) So there was no value in the last 40 years?
GABRIELLA: No. There was no value absolutely in last 40
years.

(*Father* BOJOVIC *enters with a young* POLICEWOMAN *carrying a
document case and a car radio.*)

BOJOVIC: Professor Katz? I'm Father Bojovic. 260
LEO: Ah. How do you do.
BOJOVIC: I truly please to see you I must say.
LEO: I'm—pleased to be here.
BOJOVIC: And you will be meeting Dr Davenport and Mrs
Pecs? 265
LEO: Yes, I surely have.
OLIVER: Forgive me, what is this?
LEO: Oh, did I not explain? I am here at the invitation of
Father Bojovic. As an expert witness in the suit he's bring-
ing to prevent the—the removal of this most intriguing 270
artwork from this wall.
BOJOVIC: Suit which bring forward till tomorrow. I must say,
in nick of time, it seem.

(BOJOVIC *nods to the* POLICEWOMAN *who hands a document to*
OLIVER.)

BOJOVIC: This order for you to be at court. What I think you
275 call subpoena.

(OLIVER *looks at the document.*)

It in our language I'm afraid.

(OLIVER *hands the document to* GABRIELLA.)

Also it forbidding naturally from you take artwork down.
LEO: Well, hey. The US Cavalry.

(GABRIELLA *nods to confirm the content of the document.* OLIVER *breathes deeply.*)

OLIVER: This is—too ridiculous for words. I will have to fax
280 Milan. And Munich.

(BOJOVIC *looks impassive.* OLIVER *glances at the computer. He decides against risking failure.*)

Gabriella, can I take the car?

(GABRIELLA *hands him the keys.*)

GABRIELLA: I will check out all these nails and naturally remove them.

(*She goes up the ladder to join the* RESTORERS. OLIVER *goes briskly out. The* POLICEWOMAN *gestures to* BOJOVIC *to go.*)

(BOJOVIC *gestures that he'd like to stay a little.*)

BOJOVIC: So Professor, do you have good flight?
285 LEO: Oh, um, you know.
BOJOVIC: You fly Lufthansa, I assume?
LEO: No, not exactly.
BOJOVIC: Ah. And may I enquire, if you have time yet to form opinion?
290 LEO: What about the fresco?
BOJOVIC: Yes of course.

(*Slight pause.*)

LEO: Well, it's a hard shot. Their dating seems improbable, to say the least. But it could be right. It's tough to call.

(*Pause.*)

BOJOVIC: I must say, it is refreshing to hear scholar who con-
295 fess he does not know.
LEO: Well, we've hardly anything to go on. Only one percent of Byzantine paintings have come down to us. So we're thrown back on the documents, which are themselves fragmentary, subject to misquotation, mistranslation, printing
300 errors . . .
BOJOVIC: Ah, yes. Sometime I think I must say if this gift of writing is so wonderful. When Catholics come to liberate from Mongol yoke, they ban not books but language. It no surprise I think great national poetry and song—work
305 which stretch out to embrace a people's soul—is pass on not by eye but ear. So it great comfort I must say that with all this—

(*Gesturing to the equipment.*)

—it is still hard shot to call.
LEO: I am naturally pleased to be a comfort.
BOJOVIC: On other hand . . . It in our interest, still, that you
say 'no'. 310

(*Pause.*)

LEO: Father, that's how I earn my living.
BOJOVIC: Saying 'no'?
LEO: Saying to those who would abuse these fragile objects: 'let them be'.

(BOJOVIC *smiles. The* POLICEWOMAN *is pointedly looking at her watch.*)

BOJOVIC: But now our lift maybe is grown impatient. 315
LEO: Our lift?
BOJOVIC: The police kindly offer you quick run to Hyatt Regency.
LEO: Can't wait.
BOJOVIC: (*to* POLICEWOMAN) Tryabva da si vurvim. [We must 320
go.]

(LEO *goes to pick up his bags. A thought strikes him.*)

LEO: Um, father. Your great national poem.
BOJOVIC: Yes?
LEO: It was orally transmitted? Mouth to ear?
BOJOVIC: Of course. Indeed, it is not poem really, more na- 325
tional song. It is sung to gusle, our great national instru-
ment, by mediaeval troubadour.
LEO: I see.

(BOJOVIC *turns to go.*)

LEO: So when was it first written down?

SCENE IV

The next day. Outside, it is pouring with rain. The canvas and gauze facing of the painting has been completed. Anna JEDLIKOVA, *who is 50 and soberly dressed, stands on the platform looking at the now concealed painting, slightly bemused. In the workstation area below, Father* KAROLYI *stands with his umbrella looking at the photograph of the painting. After a moment,* JEDLIKOVA *shrugs and starts to climb down the ladder.* KAROLYI *recognises her.*

KAROLYI: (*in our country's language*) Tova ne e li Anna Jed-
likova? [It is not, Anna Jedlikova?]
JEDLIKOVA: Ami, da, tya e. Sreshtali li sme? [Well, yes, it is.
Have we met?]
KAROLYI: Ne, no se radvam da se zapoznaem. Kazvam se Petr 5
Karolyi. [No, but I'm pleased to do so. My name's Petr
Karolyi]

(*He puts his hand out.*)

JEDLIKOVA: Proshtavaite, da ne bi da ste sinut na Tomaz
Karolyi? [I'm sorry, not the son of Tomaz Karolyi?]
KAROLYI: Da. [Yes.] 10
JEDLIKOVA: Kakva neochakvana sreshta. [Well, how unex-
pected.] Well, father, maybe we should speak in your
adopted language.

(*Slight pause.*)

KAROLYI: At home in London we spoke our mother tongue.

15 JEDLIKOVA: Since you return no doubt you hear great change.

KAROLYI: Well, yes—

JEDLIKOVA: We shake off language of international working class and take on speech of middle ages.

(KAROLYI *smiles uncertainly.*)

KAROLYI: Is this so bad?

20 JEDLIKOVA: Well, I am not so sure we fight since all these years to stop our neighbours share our word for postage stamp or petrol station or umbrella.

(KAROLYI *shrugs.*)

So I am happy with all chances to brush up my English. Now I may use it for more thing than 'do you hear news 25 from Moscow' and 'careful here come guard'.

KAROLYI: I'm sorry?

JEDLIKOVA: Having learnt it not in harsh English school but delightful second category camp in Bejec.

(KAROLYI *gets it.*)

KAROLYI: In fact, it's not so harsh.

30 JEDLIKOVA: Oh no? I thought in English system it is sitting dumb in rows and if you speak they hit your bottom with long stick.

KAROLYI: No. this is by no means accurate. In fact, it is well understood today, that children may do anything they like, 35 as long as they are wearing the right shoes.

JEDLIKOVA: While in Bejec this is hardly option.

KAROLYI: No.

(*Pause.* KAROLYI *decides not to pick up on* JEDLIKOVA*'s tone.*)

In fact, my only problem is my father changed his name from Karolyi to Karol. Unfortunately no-one tells us 40 'Carol' is a girl's name. A little trying, for a young boy in an English school.

JEDLIKOVA: Oh, well. To change your name is surely price of exile. Didn't Trotsky take his jailor's?

(LEO *enters, shaking the rain from his coat.* KAROLYI *decides he can't ignore* JEDLIKOVA*'s acid tone.*)

KAROLYI: So it is true.

45 JEDLIKOVA: What's true?

KAROLYI: You do resent us.

JEDLIKOVA: Who?

KAROLYI: The people who got out.

JEDLIKOVA: You are then no more than twelve years old I 50 guess.

KAROLYI: Well, then, my father?

(*Slight pause.*)

JEDLIKOVA: Well, maybe.

(*Pause.*)

KAROLYI: It is a little harsh, perhaps. In a society which, as everyone accepts, offered the choice of being hangman,

victim or accomplice. To say: you cannot choose to get out 55 if you get the chance.

JEDLIKOVA: Except of course there are some people who do not accept such choice. And pay the price. As your father knows full well.

(KAROLYI *shrugs and turns to go.* LEO *is about to make himself known to* JEDLIKOVA. *But then she collars* KAROLYI.)

JEDLIKOVA: OK. I tell you what I think. You leave, you stop 60 to be a witness. Worst story that I ever hear, in second world war, Serb children are transport to camp at Jaseno-vac, and they are so hungry that they eat cardboard tags around their neck. Which is their family, their age, their name. They eat their history. They die, and nobody re- 65 member them.

(*Slight pause.*)

And now, already, here, our past is being erased. And exiles with new names come back, and restore old names of streets and squares and towns. But in fact you cannot wipe it all away, like a cosmetic. Because for 40 years it is not 70 normal here. And so we must remember. We must not eat our names. Otherwise, like Trotsky, we might end up with our jailor's.

(JEDLIKOVA *turns to* LEO.)

Yes?

LEO: Your honour? My name's Leo Katz. I'm an—expert 75 witness.

JEDLIKOVA: Ah. How do you do.

(*They shake hands.*)

KAROLYI: Your honour?

JEDLIKOVA: Oh, forgive me. I presume you know. For my sins, I am presiding magistrate. 80

(KAROLYI *didn't know.*)

JEDLIKOVA: Yes. I am jailor now.

(OLIVER *and* GABRIELLA *hurry in,* GABRIELLA *pumping the rain off her umbrella.*)

GABRIELLA: (*to* JEDLIKOVA) Izvinyavaite, dvizhenieto po aootostrada beshe uzhasno. [I am so sorry, the traffic on the autoroute is terrible.]

JEDLIKOVA: Molya vi. Na men mi beshe priyatno da ostana za 85 malko sama. [Please, I was happy to have a moment or two on my own.]

(*To* OLIVER.)

I'm afraid some thing do not yet change. Black Cosmo passes, and all traffic light go green. So where is Father Bojovic? 90

OLIVER: He was—I think we overtook him on the motorway.

GABRIELLA: In his 1980 Laika.

(KAROLYI, JEDLIKOVA *and* KAROLYI *all know the significance of this.*)

JEDLIKOVA: (*to* OLIVER) Hey. Perhaps you don't know difference between Laika and Jehovah's Witness?
95 OLIVER: No.
JEDLIKOVA: You can shut door on Jehovah's Witness.
LEO: You have Jehovah's Witnesses already?

(*Slight pause.*)

JEDLIKOVA: Oh, yes. And we have also Sunday Coming people, glamour contests, ice-dispensers. All mod cons. I think
100 we wait five minutes. Then we must begin.

(JEDLIKOVA *withdraws to set out chairs in a rough semicircle.*
GABRIELLA, OLIVER, LEO *and* KAROLYI *are left uncomfortably together. After a pause.*)

OLIVER: How's the hotel?
LEO: It's fine. The clientele consists almost entirely of Amer-
icans with names that end with yitch and yuck who have
come back to reclaim estates their grandfathers aban-
105 doned 40 years ago.
GABRIELLA: I think not so much abandoned.
LEO: One guy from Michigan is now proud owner of the
paediatric wing of the International Friendship Hospital.
The plan is for a hotshot nite-spot, with showgirls drawn
110 exclusively from the Olympics women gymnast's team.
GABRIELLA: This to coin phrase is grotesque parody.
LEO: And tell me, does it bother anyone that as the opera
houses close, the synagogues are being desecrated? That
Vietnamese and gypsies—and Ukrainians—are beaten up
115 by skinheads on the streets and everyone applauds? That as
the walls fall in the west, there's new ones rising just as
high the other side?

(*Slight pause.*)

I mean, I merely ask.
GABRIELLA: Oh yes. You 'merely' ask. Well, I should bloody
120 coco.

(*She is very angry.*)

You have—you know that you have no idea. You have—
actually—no idea.

(LEO *and* OLIVER *are a little taken aback.* GABRIELLA *moves to
stalk away, then turns back.*)

GABRIELLA: And in answer to mere question, no. I don't see
just because of war, we have to be trashcan for world mis-
125 fits. Or Ellis Island for all huddled masses en route to wild
west. OK, so bad things happen. Very bad. But that is since
50 years ago now actually. Why should we be world transit camp? Why should we get rid of Russian army and get
Russian dregs and scum in place? To coin phrase, in
130 spades?
OLIVER: So, um, a huddled mass is a heroic mass without a
visa?
GABRIELLA: Oh, ha bloody ha.

(*Slight pause.*)

No, actually, it poem carve on Statue of Liberty New York.
135 'Give me your huddled masses, wanting to breathe free'.

LEO: It's 'yearning'. 'Yearning to breathe free'.
GABRIELLA: Well, tallyho.

(*Now she does stride off to the side.* KAROLYI *smiles dryly and goes
to look at the photographs on the noticeboard. Pause.*)

LEO: Um, is she always—
OLIVER: No.

(*Pause.*)

LEO: So, um, is there a Mr Pecs?   140
OLIVER: No longer.
LEO: (*'That explains it'*) Ah.

(OLIVER *looks dangerously at* LEO *as a dripping Father* BOJOVIC
enters.)

JEDLIKOVA: Ah. Father Bojovic.
BOJOVIC: Oovazhaema gospozho sudya. Kolata mi se schoopi.
Zakusukh na aootostrada—[Esteemed madam magistrate. 145
My car broke down. I was stranded on the autoroute—]
JEDLIKOVA: It is no matter. Now maybe we begin. Please,
everybody, take a pew.

(EVERYONE *sits. As they do so,* OLIVER *hands* GABRIELLA *a document.*)

OLIVER: Are you all right.
GABRIELLA: Just hunkydory, thank you.   150
OLIVER: Okeydoke.
JEDLIKOVA: Right now, gentlemen and lady. This afternoon is
most informal. We are concerned entirely with request for
taking down of painting. Our task today does not concern
at all with ownership of building and I will not discuss 155
that matter at this time. And in support of international
understanding, we will all speak English.
BOJOVIC: Respected magistrate, I must object.
JEDLIKOVA: Already?

(KAROLYI *gestures to* BOJOVIC *not to push this at this stage.*)

BOJOVIC: Very well. Withdrawn.   160

(LEO *looks a little quizzical.* JEDLIKOVA *picks this up.*)

JEDLIKOVA: Our western guests will please forgive us. But we
are all infants in this business. Of real trials with real out-
comes.

(*Pause. She opens a file.*)

Now, Dr Davenport. You drag us all out here so we ap-
preciate full situation, and I must say I am mildly disap- 165
pointed to find painting is wrapped up in bandage.
OLIVER: Well, it can all be readily explained.
JEDLIKOVA: Well, please proceed.
OLIVER: By Mrs Pecs, the Director of the project.

(JEDLIKOVA *and* OTHERS *had expected* OLIVER *to lead off.* OLIVER
gives GABRIELLA *a good luck wink. She is working from the notes
prepared with and handed to her by* OLIVER; *she is nervous but determined.*)

170 GABRIELLA: Um—Respected magistrate. We drag you here today for two—three reasons. First to show how this procedure to transfer painting—which you may hear accused to be a yanking off or ripping off or skinning off or flaying—is actually technique developed in middle ages and

175   used to great effect for all time since.

(*She looks at* LEO, *challengingly.*)

JEDLIKOVA: Professor Katz?
LEO: Yes?
JEDLIKOVA: Do you wish to comment on this at all?
LEO: No. No, this is all fine.

(*Slight Pause.*)

180 JEDLIKOVA: (*to* GABRIELLA) Please carry on.
GABRIELLA: However, we also want show you *reason* for transferral. For though painting has survive so many century of candlegrease and sprinkling of holy water, shaking cause by bells—

185 KAROLYI: Well, it is a religious painting.
GABRIELLA: What may be it cannot endure so well is to end up half way from zinc smelting works to major international autoroute. Particularly as painting faces back on autoroute and has one layer of brick remove.

190 KAROLYI: By you.
OLIVER: Yes of course by us.
BOJOVIC: And not just layer of brick I ought to stress.
JEDLIKOVA: Yes, yes. Professor Katz, this is all OK with you?
LEO: Oh, sure. Just hunkydory.

(*Slight pause.* GABRIELLA *is alarmed by* LEO's *silence but decides to plough gamely on.*)

195 GABRIELLA: So, question obviously remain as to why this painting matter. It unheard of. Anonymous. As you see from photo, not in excellent condition. But there is quite enough to tell that very similar to fresco of Italian master Giotto, painted in thirteen hundred five. With main dif-

200   ference that lady from behind is rock, and St John instead of throwing arm back in gesture of despair, leans one arm forward as if to comfort Virgin in her grief. And this is naturally all kind of error you must make if you are drawing from a drawing, or else out of memory.

(LEO *recognises the quotation from his own remark.*)

GABRIELLA: Except. Except we think that it is not this look like Giotto but that Giotto look like this. And if we are right, then it—fountainhead of next 600 years. To coin

205   phrase, starting shot of great race to change Europe out from state of childish mediaeval superstition into modern rational universal man.

(*Slight pause.*)

And you know such progress can seem less big deal, if you go through your renaissance and enlightenment, if you have your Michelangelo and Mozart and Voltaire. Maybe if you reach to journey's end then it bit more easy to say,

210   actually, this being grown up maybe not so hunkydory after all. But, for us, it is maybe bit different. For us, being

child not so far back. For those who stand on Europe's battlements since all of last 600 years.

(*Pause.*)

And yes it probably was painted here by foreigner. But maybe too you understand what it is meaning to us if de- 215 spite all Turkish occupation, despite Mongol yoke, still this painting made, and wanted, asked for, and appreciated here. Maybe then we may feel bit more universal, bit more grown up, maybe even bit more European.

(*Pause. There is a moment between* OLIVER *and* GABRIELLA. *Then she sits.*)

JEDLIKOVA: Well. Thank you. Now— 220
BOJOVIC: Respected magistrate, to my opinion all of this is most instructive, but I must say not of relevance to question of removing painting at this time.
KAROLYI: Absolutely. There is surely no necessary connection between the painting's age and where it's ultimately 225 housed. For otherwise—
LEO: Oh, but there is.

(*They turn to* LEO. *Pause.*)

JEDLIKOVA: Aha. Professor Katz.
LEO: For three—for several reasons.

(JEDLIKOVA *gestures to* LEO *to proceed. He in turn gestures to the computer equipment.*)

LEO: First being, you can understand how all these folks 230 might get kinda jumpy, spending all this cash on evidence that frankly wouldn't stand up in a court of law in No Hope Idaho.
OLIVER: There is nothing suspect with the provenance.
LEO: Oh no? The letter of a spy, reporting home in code? 235
OLIVER: All Vegni's letter does is to confirm the National—
LEO: —the National Patriotic Poem.
OLIVER: Yes.
LEO: AKA Great National Patriotic Song.
OLIVER: Indeed. 240
LEO: Remind me. Which edition did you use?

(*Pause.*)

OLIVER: I'm sorry. Which *edition*?
LEO: Or rather, which *transcription*?
OLIVER: Which *transcription*?

(OLIVER *turns to* GABRIELLA, *who remains looking steadfastly away.* BOJOVIC *looks smug.*)

LEO: OK. Let's run this through. The thing is apparently first 245 actually written down, by monks, in 1350. Intriguingly, not in the language of its composition, the use of which becomes a capital offence in twelve hundred eighty-five. So what we have here, people, is a plan to stick—not wrap— but stick a canvas bandage on the painting, hammer it all 250 over with a rubber mallet, then force metal bars around the edges and then lever all or some of it away—
OLIVER: This is absurd—

LEO: —that's what they haven't scrubbed off yet with
255   bleach—

(OLIVER *looks bleakly at* GABRIELLA, *who chooses not to look back*.)

LEO: —On the basis of the absolute reliability of a transcription and translation of a memorially reported song, as to the existence and description of a work of art completed, what? a hundred fifty years before? And with oodles of re-
260   spect, it seems to me around conceivable that a mediaeval monk can embellish the description of a painting, with reference to one he may have seen himself. Shortly after it had been so ably copied, from the Italian original, in the charming church of St John Something, Cholovar.

(*Pause.*)

265   OLIVER: It is—I suppose, a possible interpretation—
LEO: *Possible?*
OLIVER: It hardly proves—
LEO: Spot on. What *proves* it, Olly, is right here.

(*He takes the pallette print-out from his pocket.*)

OLIVER: What's this?
270   LEO: Ultramarine? In, what, 1195?

(*Pause.*)

JEDLIKOVA: Would someone please explain?
LEO: Ultramarine is powdered lapis lazuli, a semi-precious stone found only in what's now north-east Afghanistan. It has very high infra-red reflectance, so on Dr Davenport's
275   machine it shows up nearly white, on what's left of the Virgin's robe, St Nicodemus' mantle and the sky. And the general opinion is against its use in mediaeval Europe before at the earliest the middle of the 13th century.

(*Pause.*)

OLIVER: Look. Yes. But, look. It still, it doesn't absolutely—
280   LEO: No. Not absolutely, sure. But let's put it at its mildest. If you're trying to revolutionise the history of western art, it doesn't help.

(*Pause.*)

GABRIELLA: Is this right?

(*Slight pause.*)

OLIVER: I'm sorry. I did tell you. Not my field.

(*Slight pause.*)

285   Oh damn.

(*Pause.*)

JEDLIKOVA: So do I understand that painting is no longer what you say?
OLIVER: It seems—less likely.
JEDLIKOVA: And so then, presumably—

LEO: And so then, sure, presumably, Deutschelectronic and   290
Peruzzi fold their tents and steal away. But before they go, your honour, I think it's worth enquiring why they came.

(*Pause.* OLIVER *rises.*)

OLIVER: What do you mean?

(LEO *shrugs, smiling.*)

LEO: Hey, come on, Olly. You know what I mean.

(*Slight pause.*)

OLIVER: No, I'm afraid I don't.   295
JEDLIKOVA: And nor do I.

(*Attention is back on* LEO. OLIVER *sits. Affecting reluctance*, LEO *continues.*)

LEO: OK. It's simple. What this operation does is to make the painting mobile. And sure, right now, it's only booked in for one trip. But does anybody really reckon that'd be the end of it?   300

(LEO *gestures round the equipment.*)

You really think, Peruzzi and Deutschelectronic, after all of this, would transport you to the National Museum, assist you with the heavy lifting, and then slope off home?

(GABRIELLA *did.*)

Come on. It'd be—hey, we got the big bang here, you can't keep it to yourself, what say we take it on a little   305
tour? Just think of all that currency. Or rather, while you guys are sorting out security, maybe more like an extended loan? Or even, now we come to think of it, wouldn't it be actually much happier, and much more accessible to doctors and professors and their ilk, in a nice   310
new hi-tech California gallery with state-of-the-art air conditioning and three gold trowels from Architecture Quarterly? Hey, come on, Olly, wasn't that the deal?

(GABRIELLA *is appalled.*)

OLIVER: This is—this is an absolute—
LEO: 'Cos that's what happens, Gabriella. That's what paint-   315
ings are. They're stars, of the Hollywood variety. With tours. And fans. And franchised merchandise. And—entourage. And as such, they are, they must be, universal and eternal. Not allowed to change. Most surely, not allowed to fade. To crumble, or grow old. And of course, they'll   320
never die.

(*Slight pause.*)

But paintings do grow old. Their history is written on their faces, just like it is on ours. And like the history of people, or of peoples, either you acknowledge it, and try to understand it, or you say it never happened, nothing's   325
changed, and you end up doing it again.

(LEO *looks directly at* JEDLIKOVA.)

Hey, do you know, there were names here on the wall, from when it was a torture chamber, which they scraped away?

(JEDLIKOVA *stands.*)

330 JEDLIKOVA: I see no reason to delay my ruling. This procedure must now cease. The painting must remain, here in church. This facing can be taken off?

LEO: Sure. It comes off with water. And a little tender loving care.

335 JEDLIKOVA: Then please, Dr Davenport and Mrs Pecs, re-move it.

(*She gathers up her papers and goes quickly out.* GABRIELLA, *furious and upset, throws down her notes and climbs the ladder to the platform.* KAROLYI *goes quickly to* LEO.)

KAROLYI: Well done Professor.
LEO: Well. Well, I—

(KAROLYI *senses the approaching* BOJOVIC, *smiles, turns and goes.* OLIVER *follows* GABRIELLA *up the ladder.* BOJOVIC *to* LEO.)

BOJOVIC: We have saying that best doctor is one who leave
340 you no closer to your deathbed than before.
LEO: We have a saying, too. If it ain't broke, don't fix it. Please forgive me for a moment.
BOJOVIC: Naturally.

(LEO *climbs the ladder. On the platform,* GABRIELLA *stands, apart from* OLIVER *still angry.*)

LEO: Well, I told you, people. Wanting it so much.
345 GABRIELLA: (*turns to* LEO) You shit. You cocksucker.
LEO: Hey now, chill out—
GABRIELLA: I say you have no idea. But it is me. I have no idea of how few you scumbags really comprehend.
LEO: Now loosen up here—
350 GABRIELLA: No, not me. You listen up. You know why this church turn to torture chamber? Because when Nazi come all Catholic are out in street with little flags waving like billyo, because now they get their hands on Jewish businesses and stores.
355 LEO: Hey. I have absolutely no relationship—
GABRIELLA: No, no, of course. You are brought here by our great national church. Which is indeed call Orthodox for no bad reason looking at last 40 years. And you say that being Jew is pretty bad in 1941–45. You bet. But is not too
360 hunkydory actually since 1948 put mildly. And that is not to mention Mr Pusbas and his bald boys who think all this basically part of international Zionist conspiracy.

(*She looks defiantly at* LEO.)

And these people on your side. And up your arse. You cocksucker.

(*She jabs* LEO *in the chest and turns away.* OLIVER *goes to her and puts his arm on hers.* GABRIELLA *flings it aside.*)

365 GABRIELLA: No no.

(OLIVER *turns to* LEO.)

LEO: To coin a phrase. This is a travesty.
OLIVER: (*indicating that* LEO *should leave*) But nonetheless, per-haps it's best, if you—
GABRIELLA: (*turns to* OLIVER) And you.
OLIVER: I'm sorry?   370
GABRIELLA: Perhaps it best 'if you' as well.
OLIVER: What's this?
GABRIELLA: (*heavily sarcastic*) I mean, must you not call up chums in Munich and Milan? And explain how you fail to get your mitts on big star painting? How you miss to 375
clinch your deal?
OLIVER: Now that, that was—
GABRIELLA: Oh, yes. Big travesty. *I trusted you.*

(*Slight pause.*)

OLIVER: And you were right—
GABRIELLA: And I am thinking during all these days how 380
everybody judge our painting. How for Catholic is spread of European culture, for national church expression of our holy Slavic soul. And for great Western intellectuals is ei-ther not so quite good photograph or megaphone of God. But even I do not think actually is international currency. 385
OLIVER: No more do I.
GABRIELLA: Whereas for me I must say painting very simple. It is like our poem beg its pardon song explain. How our country through all history will be betrayed. By occupying oh so sorry by protecting power. By our own High Priest 390
and screaming mob. By seeming friend. And now by you.

(*She looks defiantly at* OLIVER *and* LEO, *who gestures at the painting.*)

LEO: OK. Let's cut the crap. You want to know what this is actually about?
OLIVER: Um, Leo—
LEO: 'Cos I frankly couldn't give a shit how old this is, who 395
got what first and least of all how much it's worth.

(*A moment, then:*)

GABRIELLA: (*defiantly*) Yes please?
LEO: 'Cos what *I* see's a guy who tells a story of a man who's actually a God who's put to death before his mother like a common criminal. And although he's heard it told a 400
thousand times, he brings to it that innocence, that fresh-ness and that rage we all feel when we hear a story first time round.

(*We begin to hear the approach of a noisy diesel engine through the speech.*)

Which I appreciate may not go down a storm round here. Where you had a chance to make the world anew, you 405
built a prison camp.

(*The screech of a lorry braking, the slam of a door.* BOJOVIC'S *head turns towards it.*)

And now the walls are down, you shut out all the other voices in the world—in all their rich variety—you throw up the portcullis and you sell yourself to fucking Disney-land. So, don't you—   410

(*The church door flies open. A long-haired Azeri with a metal leg enters, turns back, and calls:*)

RAIF: (*speaking in Russian*) OK. Zdyes padaidyot. [OK. This will do.]

(RAIF *is followed in by a Mozambican student and a middle-aged gypsy man. They are called* ANTONIO *and* NICO. ANTONIO *has an automatic weapon.*)

GABRIELLA: (*our country*) Ay-bogoo. Kakvo stava? [My God, what's happening?]

415   OLIVER: What's this—?

LEO: Hey. Christ.

BOJOVIC: Kakvo e tova? [What is this?]

RAIF: (*speaking in Russian, to* BOJOVIC) Atyets, miy ishchem oobezhishche. [Father. We wish sanctuary.]

(BOJOVIC *sees that* RAIF, ANTONIO *and* NICO *are being quickly followed in by a motley group of* REFUGEES, *all of whom are dripping wet from the storm. They are an armed Afghan,* ABDUL, *who holds a gagged Englishman* DEREK, *a Palestinian woman,* YASMIN, *who is pushing in a young English woman* TONI—*also gagged and bound—followed by the middle-aged Bosnian* AMIRA, *who carries her cello in its case, a middle-aged Russian,* MARINA, *a young Kurdish woman,* FATIMA, *a young Sri Lankan woman,* TUNU, *a 30-something Russian called* GRIGORI, *and a teenage gyspy girl,* CLEOPATRA, *who pushes a pram. Many of the* REFUGEES *carry luggage, equipment, provisions and tools of various kinds, including two big cans of petrol.*)

420   BOJOVIC: Az . . . ne . . . ne. Tova ne e tsurkva. [I—No. No. This is not a church.]

(BOJOVIC *is moving to the door.*)

RAIF: (*Russian*) Mi bezhentsiy. Miy trebooyem, shtobiy viy predastavili nam oobyezhishche. [We are refugees. We demand you give us sanctuary.]

425   BOJOVIC: Ne vi razbiram. [I'm sorry. I don't understand.]

LEO: What are they saying?

GABRIELLA: They're demanding sanctuary.

BOJOVIC: Samo posetitel. [Just a visitor.]

(*He has managed to get to the door, and slips out.*)

OLIVER: Sanctuary?

430   GABRIELLA: You know, asylum.

ANTONIO: (*Russian, shouting after* BOJOVIC) Eta zhe tserkof, svolach! [Isn't this a church, you bastard!]

(RAIF *has drawn a handgun.*)

RAIF: Miy dolzhniy ostatsa zdyes. [Well, we must stay here!]

OLIVER: They have a gun.

435   RAIF: (*Azeri, to* YASMIN) Burada galmalıyız yokh? [Shouldn't we stay here?]

(YASMIN *shrugs.*)

ABDUL: (*Arabic, to* YASMIN) baddu yaᶜraf iza badna nibga hown. [He wants to know if we should stay.]

YASMIN: (*Arabic*) shoo badna nsawi gheir heik? [What else are we to do?]

440

ANTONIO: (*Russian, pointing at* OLIVER *and* GABRIELLA) A kak biyt setimi lyoodmi? [What about this people?]

(KAROLYI *enters the church.*)

KAROLYI: (*our country*) Kakvo iskate? [What do you want?] What do you want?

ANTONIO: (*Russian*) Oobyezhishche. [Refuge.]   445

GRIGORI: Asylum.

KAROLYI: (*Russian*) Eta nye tserkof. [This is not a church.] This is not a church.

(*Ineffectively, to* LEO, OLIVER *and* GABRIELLA.)

Run! You must run!

(*As* EVERYONE's *attention turns to* OLIVER, LEO *and* GABRIELLA, DEREK *makes a dash for it and escapes with* KAROLYI.)

RAIF: (*Russian*) Da astanovitye zhe yivo! [Stop him!]   450

YASMIN: (*Arabic*) ni'fil il-abwaab. Shoofoo iza feeh makhraj taani. [We shut the doors. See if there are other exits.]

ANTONIO: (*pointing again at* OLIVER *and* GABRIELLA) A kak biyt setimi lyoodmi? [What about this people?]

RAIF: (*Russian*) Zastav ikh slyezt. [Make them come down.]   455

(*The doors are closed and locked.*)

ABDUL: (*Turkish*) Qapıyı qapattım. Girilmez. [I have closed the door. It cannot be entered.]

RAIF: (*To* NICO, *in Russian*) Viykhadiy. [Exits.]

(RAIF *and* NICO *go and look for other exits.*)

ANTONIO: (*Russian*) Ladno. Slyeztye. Postepyenno, slyezaitye. [OK. Come down. Come slowly down.]   460

OLIVER: What's this?

GABRIELLA: It kind of Russian. He say we must come down.

ANTONIO: (*Russian*) Postepyenno! [Slowly!]

GABRIELLA: Slowly.

LEO: Fine by me.   465

(*As* LEO, GABRIELLA *and* OLIVER *climb down,* RAIF *and* NICO *return.*)

RAIF: (*Russian*) Droogikh viykhodov nyetoo. [No other exits.]

ANTONIO: (*Russian, to* RAIF) Miy zaderzhim etikh lyoodyei zalozhnikami? [Shall we hold these people as hostages?]

YASMIN: (*to* ABDUL, *in Arabic*) 'ul-luh laazim niHtijiz an-nas haadool. [Tell him we should hold these people.]   470

OLIVER: What are they saying?

ABDUL: (*Turkish, to* RAIF) Bunlar rehin olduklarını, diyerler gibi tutmalarını gerekhtiyini söylüyor. [She says they're hostages. We should hold them like the others.]

RAIF: (*Azeri*) Yakhshı. [Good.] (*To* ANTONIO, *in Russian*)   475   Zaderzhim. [We hold them.]

YASMIN: (*Arabic*) Naᶜam. [Yes.]

RAIF: (*Russian*) Miy zaderzhali etikh lyoodyei! Ani zalozhniki! Na kalyeni, na kalyeni! [We keep these people! They are hostages! On their knees, on their knees!]   480

(OLIVER, LEO *and* GABRIELLA *are pushed over to join* TONI. *Equipment is being brought from the door into the body of the church.*)

OLIVER: (*to* TONI) Who are they?

TONI: Who knows. Asylum seekers. We were ambushed at the border.

LEO: We?

485 TONI: (*with heavy irony*) Mercy convoy. Humanitarian relief.

(LEO *sees the cans being moved.*)

LEO: What the hell's that?

TONI: Petrol.

RAIF: (*Russian, to* ANTONIO) Ta dvyer zaperta? [Is that door secure?]

490 ANTONIO: (*Russian*) Da, zaperta. [Yes, it's secure.]

TONI: *One* be observant, *two* try to rest, *three* advise of medical needs.

LEO: Beg pardon?

TONI: I once went to the Middle East. They show this video.

495 Three do's and don'ts if you get taken as a hostage.

LEO: Let's run through the 'don'ts'.

TONI: It's *one* don't argue, *three* don't draw attention to yourself—and *two* I can't remember—

LEO: Try.

500 YASMIN: Yes please. That would be very helpful.

(*The* HOSTAGES *look round at* YASMIN. *Pause.*)

Well, perhaps a little later. Now, do you have passport please?

(OLIVER *finds a card:*)

OLIVER: In the hotel. Please do have my card.

TONI: Mine's in the lorry.

505 GABRIELLA: (*hands over her ID card*) ID.

LEO: (*hands over as insouciantly as possible*) Passport.

(YASMIN *reads* LEO's *passport.*)

YASMIN: Well. Leonard. Aaron. Katz. What a distinctive name.

(*She looks at* LEO. LEO *looks at her.* YASMIN *goes and pulls forward* ABDUL, RAIF, AMIRA *and* FATIMA.)

But now you change clothes. So if anyone burst in, you are a little less distinctive.

(*The* HOSTAGES *look blank.*)

510 YASMIN: You give your clothes to these people. And then they give you theirs.

ABDUL: (*Turkish*) Ne oluyor? [What's happening?]

RAIF: (*Azeri, to* ABDUL) Elbise deyishtirmemizi gerekhiyor gaaliba. [I think she is saying we must change clothes.]

515 ANTONIO: (*Russian*) Razdyevaityes pazhalsta. [Take off your clothes!]

(*To* TONI.)

Take clothes off please.

LEO: Don't 'one'.

(*The* HOSTAGES *begin to undress.* ABDUL, RAIF *and* AMIRA *start to undress too.* TONI *is aware of the* MEN *looking at her.*)

TONI: I spend five years trying to get out of doing this.

YASMIN: Now your names are Raif, and—   520

(*To* ABDUL *in Arabic.*)

—eysh ismak? [What's your name?]

ABDUL: Abdul.

YASMIN: Abdul, and—

AMIRA: Amira.

FATIMA: Fatima.   525

YASMIN: You are now—Azeri, Kurdish?

ABDUL: (*Turkish*) Afghanee. [Afghan.]

(*Pointing to* FATIMA.)

hiyya kurdeeya [She is Kurdish.]

YASMIN: Afghan, Bosnian?

(AMIRA *nods.*)

And Kurd.   530

(OLIVER *stops undressing.*)

OLIVER: In fact—you should know, that I'm actually diabetic—

(YASMIN *looks at* OLIVER.)

YASMIN: In fact, you should know—you are a different people now.

(FATIMA *goes upstage to change behind a blanket.* OLIVER, GABRIELLA, LEO *and* TONI *continue to undress. Their* CAPTORS *stand watching. A* LOUDSPEAKER *breaks in suddenly from outside as the lights fade to blackout.*)

LOUDSPEAKER: (*in the language of our country*) Politsiya! Govori 535 politsiyata! Nie sme mnogo! Narushavate zakona! Khvuriete oruzhiata i izlezte, sega! Povtoryavam: Nie sme mnogo! Narushavate zakona! Khvuriete oruzhiata i izlezte, sega! . . . [Police! This is the police! We are present in large numbers! You are breaking the law! Put down any weapons and 540 come out now! I repeat: We are present in large numbers! You are trespassing in this church! Put down any weapons and come out now! . . .]

(*End of Act One*)

ACT TWO

To call nationalism 'atavistic' or to proclaim
an anti-nationalist crusade is like proclaiming
a crusade against hydrogen in water.
The point is not to overcome nationalism
but to understand it.

Neil Ascherson,
Independent on Sunday, 31 January 1993

The new Serbia should include the existing republic of Serbia, as well as Vojvodina, Kosovo, Bosnia-Hercegovina, Macedonia, Montenegro and the parts of Croatia where Serbs live. Croatia should consist of what you can see from the top of Zagreb Cathedral.

Vojslav Sesilj, Serbian leader, August 1991

People all over Eastern Europe are refusing to be governed by those who do not speak their language.

Norman Tebbit, Newsnight, 10 December 1991

In Ivo Andric's novel, *The Bridge over the Drina*, a nineteenth-century Muslim shopkeeper tries to explain God's creation of Bosnia. 'When Allah the Merciful and Compassionate created this world', he says, 'the earth was smooth and even as a finely engraved plate. That displeased the devil who envied man this gift of God. And while the earth was still just as it had come from God's hands, damp and soft as unbaked clay, he stole up and scratched the face of God's earth with his nails as much and as deeply as he could. Therefore, deep rivers and ravines were formed which divided one district from another and kept men apart. And Allah felt pity when he saw what the Accursed One had done, so he sent his angels to spread their wings above those places and men learnt from the angels of God how to build bridges, and therefore the greatest blessing is to build a bridge and the greatest sin to interfere with it . . .'

Quoted in the Independent on Sunday,
19 June 1994

I am not willing to risk the lives of German soldiers for countries whose names we cannot spell properly.

Volker Ruhe, German defence minister,
December 1992

SCENE V

The afternoon of the following day. A routine has been established, and little clumps of REFUGEES *have established themselves and their possessions around the church. They have been eating packaged food taken from the van when they arrived.*

The HOSTAGES *are sitting together, their hands tied behind their backs, wearing their unfamiliar clothes.* OLIVER *is presently absent,* GABRIELLA *sits near* TONI; LEO *sits a little way apart.* FATIMA *is nursing* CLEOPATRA's *baby.* CLEOPATRA *is sitting near the* HOSTAGES *with a notebook, in which she makes the occasional note.*

A ladder has been set up to a window through which the REFUGEES *can monitor the approach to the church door. At present,* ANTONIO *is up the ladder, looking out. He calls down to* RAIF. YASMIN *is standing beside him.* GRIGORI *is nearby.*

RAIF: (*Russian*) Tebye shto niboot vidna? [Can you see anything?]
ANTONIO: (*Russian*) Nyet. Anee vsyo oobrali. [No. They've moved everything back.]
5   RAIF: (*Russian*) Vubshche nichevo? [Nothing at all?]
ANTONIO: (*Russian*) A da. Kriysha, pokhozhe bolshovovo groozovika. Na nyei taryelka. [Oh, yes. There's the top of what looks like a big van. It's got a dish on it.]
RAIF: (*Russian*) Eto dalzhno biyt . . . satellite. [That must be a
10   satellite.]
ANTONIO: (*Russian*) Shto tiy dumayesh? Politsiya? [What, you think police?]

GRIGORI: (*Russian*) Nyet, skuryaiye vsyevo. Say-N-N. [No, more likely CNN.]
YASMIN: What does he say?   15

(ANTONIO *is descending.*)

GRIGORI: He says they move everything back. He think he see TV van.
YASMIN: No police? No helicopters?
ANTONIO: Not that I can see.
GRIGORI: Quiet. Damn quiet. Too quiet.   20

(YASMIN *looks questioningly at* GRIGORI.)

GRIGORI: (*explaining*) Cowboy. Red Indian.
YASMIN: Well, they have twenty minutes. Till our deadline.

(*She moves away: a little later* RAIF *will descend. Now* ABDUL *brings* OLIVER *in, clearly from some makeshift toiletry arrangement.* ABDUL *has the pistol and feels the need to pull the hand-tied* OLIVER *back to his place.*)

OLIVER: All right. All right.

(ABDUL *'helps'* OLIVER *sit down, shrugs, and moves a little apart.*)

GABRIELLA: How are facilities?
OLIVER: (*slightly snappy*) Well, they've not *demonstrably* im-   25
proved since lunchtime.

(GABRIELLA *calls.*)

GABRIELLA: Maybe quite soon they send in insulin! Before you will become in coma!

(OLIVER *swallows.* ABDUL *and* RAIF *look round.*)

LEO: (*sarcastic*) Three. 'Don't draw attention to yourself'.
OLIVER: (*angry*) Well, doesn't that depend on the alternative?   30

(*This spat has attracted* YASMIN's *and* ANTONIO's *attention as well.* LEO *smiles to himself, humourlessly.* GABRIELLA *covers.*)

GABRIELLA: Which is that we make best of it we can. And Toni tell us how things bottom out when she take good butchers at her sophisticated but essentially empty life as nationally-famous Third Page Girl and concludes well sod this for a game of soldiers.   35
OLIVER: Sorry?
GABRIELLA: Which is that she plan to lengthen profile—
TONI: Broaden.
GABRIELLA: And record this disc which called—
TONI: Which I'm talked into calling Heavy Petting.   40
GABRIELLA: And which bomb.

(*To* OLIVER.)

And 'bomb' I think is bad.
TONI: And 'bomb' is terrible.
GABRIELLA: (*to* TONI) So not like 'go a bomb'.
TONI: Hey. No.   45
GABRIELLA: And then—
TONI: OK, and then I gets took up by this arsehole with a blow-wave who assures me if I keep my boobs in from

henceforward—which is fine by *me*—I'm due some seri-
50 ously basic repositioning. And so I ends up and-the-first-
prize-is-this-Satsasuma-Microwaveing on a gameshow
called Fame Sex and Match.

GABRIELLA: Which also bomb?

TONI: As does Atlantic City and the caper movie. So he says,
55 look, doll, had you ever thought of dedicating your talents
to the needs of others, and I says no way I'm doing skinhead retards in Romania or kids on drips in Sarajevo 'cos
I'm sorry but I'm just not good with children, dogs or
blood. And *he* says you should read the papers and I ends
60 up mascot of a mercy dash to somewhere unpronounca-
ble and we're in a lay-by half way up a border queue when
we're hijacked by the Munsters, forced at gunpoint
through a railway tunnel—backwards—and the rest is
fucking history.

(*She remembers where she is, bites her lip and crosses herself.*)

65   Oops.

OLIVER: I'm sorry, did you say 'Fame Sex and Match'?

TONI: That's right.

OLIVER: And this is or was a British television programme?

TONI: Sure. Kind of a—raunchy remix of Blind Date.

70 OLIVER: Blind Date?

TONI: Blind Date.

(*Slight pause.*)

The television show.

(*Slight pause.*)

GABRIELLA: You know, sometime it quite hard to believe you
two coming from same country.

(*Pause.* OLIVER *laughs.*)

75 OLIVER: Two nations divided by a common language.

GABRIELLA: Please?

OLIVER: Conventionally attributed to Bernard Shaw. He said
it about Americans and Brits but—I was thinking of
Disraeli.

80 GABRIELLA: Who?

TONI: Benjamin Disraeli. 18-oh-something to 1881. British
Conservative Prime Minister. Later first Earl of Beacons-
field. Author of Sybil the Two Nations. Yup?

(OLIVER *looks at* TONI *in some surprise.*)

America is named after the Italian explorer Amerigo
85 Vespucci. Words not in Dr Samuel Johnson's famous dictionary include 'euphemism', 'irritable' and 'anus'. And
there are more nude boobs in the National Gallery in
Washington than in a year's supply of Playboy Magazine.
So don't *you* give me a hard time.

(*Slight pause.*)

90 LEO: In fact, Dr Davenport is of the view—

OLIVER: In fact, Dr Davenport agrees. You can't cut high art
off from the culture that surrounds it.

TONI: Well, there you go.

(*During this,* YASMIN *and* ANTONIO *approach.*)

OLIVER: And, sure, if the quintessence of renaissance man is
Michelangelo and his Risen Christ emerging shamelessly 95
stark bollock naked from the tomb, then maybe now, yuh,
it's a gameshow or a caper movie or a Playboy centrefold.

YASMIN: Ah. Michelangelo and Playboy magazine. The great art
critic taking solace in the triumphs of western civilisation.

(OLIVER *doesn't reply.*)

YASMIN: Are you all right?   100

OLIVER: For now.

YASMIN: And when do you get ill?

OLIVER: Well, this doesn't happen very often. But—as I remember—it's not much more than a day. I mean—I'm already starting—to be thirsty, and to—need to use the 105
lavatory.

YASMIN: Your friends outside who know all this presumably.
Don't seem to care too much about you.

OLIVER: They wouldn't need to, if I wasn't kept a prisoner
here.   110

YASMIN: That too is easily resolved.

OLIVER: You think so?

YASMIN: Surely. You are 300 million people in the European
Community. I think you can squeeze in a dozen more.

OLIVER: You know that's not the point.   115

YASMIN: No, the point is that this country wants to join the
Western Club, and you won't let them in unless their eastern border is made watertight. So we are chased by dogs
and helicopters, and you are in your present—situation, so
she can enter European Union. Is this not true?   120

LEO: Hey. You know what I resent?

(*Pause.* YASMIN *turns to* LEO.)

YASMIN: No. What do you resent?

LEO: Two things.

YASMIN: Do please proceed.

LEO: First thing, is all this 'you'. I'm not the European com- 125
munity. I am not even the government of the United
States.

YASMIN: Well, this is true.

LEO: And second thing—I'm sorry, three things—second is
that although I'm not my government, I would point out 130
that in the last two centuries it's generally agreed that government has been pretty damned hospitable to strangers
from beyond its shores. To other country's—huddled
masses, yearning to breathe free.

(*Pause.*)

YASMIN: So, yes?   135

LEO: It's a poem, carved on the Statue of Liberty in New York
harbour.

YASMIN: Yes, I know. I was waiting for the third thing.

LEO: Oh, yes. Third, you know, it would be nice also if we
knew your names. Like, you know ours. You changed 140
them, as you may recall. To those of a Pakistani, an Azeri
and a Kurd. Which I know is something of a habit in this
region. Wasn't it Bulgaria made their Turks change not just
their own names, but their fathers'? Posthumously?

ANTONIO: What, like the Americans gave their slaves names 145
like 'Witherspoon' and 'Pettigrew'?

LEO: So now I'm a slave-owner?

YASMIN: And, actually, Abdul is Afghan. But do you know what *I* resent? About the western intellectuals?

(*Slight pause.*)

150 LEO: Do please proceed.

YASMIN: It is not those who say the west does nothing wrong, because that is so self-evidently absurd. No, it is liberals who say that west alone *knows* it does wrong. And when Bulgarians oppress their Turks, or Turks their Kurds,

155 it's because they are but infants and the grown-up west must fatherly forgive them for they know not what they do. That it is only western countries who have reached the age of criminal responsibility. The western European tradition as world superego. The universal moral measure of

160 all things.

LEO: Well there you go again.

YASMIN: Where do I go?

LEO: I'm not a western European. I'm an American of mixed Polish and Lithuanian descent.

165 YASMIN: So do you speak it? Polish? Lithuanian?

LEO: No of course I don't.

YASMIN: Or Hebrew?

LEO: I live in Ithaca, New York. Hebrew is the language of a country in the middle east.

170 YASMIN: Or for that matter any language but your own?

(*Slight pause.*)

LEO: Yuh, as it happens, I do speak a little Spanish. The third world language in our hemisphere.

YASMIN: Doubtless enough to say 'please make up the spare room'.

175 LEO: Oh please.

YASMIN: But you know the most delicious irony? That it is the west itself exposes its own ignorance and hypocrisy for everyone to see. In the time of the crusades, the Muslim armies exchanged Christian prisoners for Christian

180 books. Because, perhaps, they realised it is preferable to know your enemy than to hold him. And indeed from then to now, by all the means whereby you have invaded us—from the star of Bethlehem to satellite TV—you have taught us oh so much much more of you than you will

185 ever take the pains to learn of us.

(*Slight pause.*)

LEO: Well, sure, I take the point—

(*The telephone rings. The Russian* MARINA, *who is nearest, answers.*)

MARINA: (*Russian*) Da? Nye veshayete troobkoo. [Yes? Hold on please.]

(*She holds out the phone to* YASMIN. YASMIN *to the* HOSTAGES *as she goes to take the call.*)

YASMIN: My name is Yasmin. I am a stateless Palestinian. Be-

190 fore that I had residency in Kuwait, but then 'you' came to rescue us. Fair exchange?

(*She goes and takes the phone.*)

Hello?

(*Slight pause.*)

No I'm sorry. There is no-one speaks your language. You will have to talk in English.

(*Slight pause.*)

We will both speak slowly. That is fine.   195

(OLIVER *to* LEO.)

OLIVER: Well done.

LEO: What for?

OLIVER: Your little aria. Well, fingers crossed they may decide not to kill us after all.

YASMIN: Yes, 'Oliver' is fine.   200

LEO: Oh please.

YASMIN: Yes, and 'Gabriella, Toni, and Leonard' are just fine as well.

(YASMIN *continues to converse. During this,* CLEOPATRA *approaches the* HOSTAGES, *with her notebook.*)

OLIVER: Remind me. What was it Gabriella wasn't to shut out? 'All the other voices in the world—in all their rich   205 variety'?

LEO: Yuh, sure, the irony did not escape me.

YASMIN: So, now, we have exhausted all the social pleasantries, maybe we can proceed to our demands?

GABRIELLA: (*to* OLIVER) Hey, you are wrong. We are not pris-   210 oners.

OLIVER: Oh, no?

GABRIELLA: You remember poem? We are 'involuntary guests'.

OLIVER: (*wryly*) If not, 'involuntary hosts'.

CLEOPATRA: Excuse please. Is this how maybe you write   215 down 'damnosspitable'?

(*The* HOSTAGES *turn to* CLEOPATRA. YASMIN *has been talking both down the phone and, via* ABDUL, *to* RAIF.)

TONI: Beg pardon?

(CLEOPATRA *shows her book to* GABRIELLA.)

CLEOPATRA: See, I write down word. For good vocabulary in English. Take good care vocabulary, grammar she will look behind herself.   220

GABRIELLA: In fact, it is two word. And I think one 's'. And 'hemisphere' also. But 'Princess' I think two.

(YASMIN *has finished her call and is talking to* ABDUL *and* RAIF.)

CLEOPATRA: Pop call my infant word for 'Princess'. So we must learn to say so in America.

(GABRIELLA *has been affected by the book. So* OLIVER *responds.*)

OLIVER: And what's your name?   225

CLEOPATRA: Is change. First Juanita for my mom. Then Rosa when we are travel much from Hungary. Now pop has gave me new name. Cleopatra.

OLIVER: Blimey.

(*To prove it,* CLEOPATRA *turns her book to the title page.*)

230 CLEOPATRA: No. Is true. Look here.

(RAIF *issue orders:* ANTONIO *moves up the ladder, the* WOMEN
HOSTAGE-TAKERS *secure the* HOSTAGES *and put hands over their
mouths,* ABDUL *leaves* GRIGORI *with the rifle and the armed* RAIF
and ABDUL *place themselves at the door.*)

RAIF: (*Russian*) Kharasho. Ani poslali kovo-to. Fsyem pa
myestam! [OK. They're sending someone. Everybody to
position.]

235 YASMIN: (*Arabic*) kull waaHıd ᶜala makaanuh. [Everybody to
the agreed position.]
ABDUL: (*Turkish*) Yerlerinize! Susun! [To positions! Silence!]
ANTONIO: (*Russian*) Vot on. On i saldat! [He's coming! Him
and a soldier!]

240 RAIF: (*Russian*) Oo nyivo zavyazani glaza? [Is he blindfold?]
ANTONIO: (*Russian*) Da, zavyazani. Yivo vyedyot saldat. [Yes,
he's blindfold. The soldier's leading him.]
YASMIN: What's happening?
ANTONIO: He's with a soldier. The soldier's going back now.
245 He's alone. (*Russian*) Soldat ookhodit. [The soldier's going
back now!].

(*There is a knock at the door.* RAIF *looks over to* YASMIN.)

YASMIN: (*Arabic*) iftaH al-baab. [Open the door.]
ABDUL: (*Turkish*) Icheriye gelsin. [Let's admit him.]

(*The door is opened.* BOJOVIC *enters, blindfold, with a small package. The door is quickly closed behind him.*)

BOJOVIC: (*in the language of our country*) Kazvam se Otets Bo-
250 jovic. Nosya lekarstvoto. [I am Father Bojovic. I have
brought medication.]
RAIF: (*Russian*) Pa-rooski gavaritye? [Do you speak Russian?]
BOJOVIC: English is better. I am Father Bojovic. I have medication for Dr Oliver Davenport.
255 YASMIN: Do you have the answer to our demands?
BOJOVIC: I have—statement. but first I must speak with Dr
Davenport. And Mrs Pecs and Miss—uh, um . . . and Professor Katz.
YASMIN: This is the medication?
260 BOJOVIC: Yes. Where is Dr Davenport?

(YASMIN *nods to* FATIMA. *The hands are taken off the* HOSTAGES'
mouths. This dialogue is translated into Russian by GRIGORI *and*
AMIRA.)

OLIVER: Uh, here I am.
BOJOVIC: Are you all right?
OLIVER: Well . . .
GABRIELLA: You have his medication?
265 BOJOVIC: Yes, of course. I must say, there is shortage of all
medication in our country. We must fly from Rimini. So
instructions I'm so sorry in Italian.

(*Meanwhile* GRIGORI *has been translating to* NICO.)

GRIGORI: (*Russian*) On prinyos lekarstva dlya Doctora Dav-
enporta. [He has brought the medicine for Dr Daven-
270 port.]

BOJOVIC: But presumably you are used as well—
OLIVER: Oh yes.
BOJOVIC: So here it is.

(*He doesn't know where* OLIVER *is.* YASMIN *gestures to* ABDUL *not
to let* OLIVER *step forward. She tries to take the package.*)

YASMIN: Thank you.
BOJOVIC: I'm sorry. I must give this package direct to Dr 275
Davenport.

(GRIGORI *continues to whisper in Russian.*)

GRIGORI: On dolzhen atdat pakyet doktoroo Davenportoo.
[He must give the package to Dr Davenport.]
YASMIN: You give it to me.
BOJOVIC: But I must say this is not arranged. 280
GRIGORI: (*to* NICO) On gavarit shto ab etom nye dagavarilis.
[He says this was not arranged.]
YASMIN: Oh I am so sorry. Perhaps if you permit us to call
out as well as you call in our arrangements might prove
more equitable. 285

(RAIF *gestures to* YASMIN *not to lose her temper.*)

YASMIN: We have no time for games. You give the package to
the hostage after you respond to our demands.

(BOJOVIC *senses* REFUGEES *gathering and is getting flustered.*)

BOJOVIC: I—um, I am empowered only—
ANTONIO: (*impatient*) Food. Transport. Permit.
BOJOVIC: Yes, when Dr Davenport, there will be food— 290
ABDUL: (*Arabic*) tosreeH ᶜamal? [Work permit?]
YASMIN: And work permit.
BOJOVIC: And also I am safe return of course—
YASMIN: Of course.
BOJOVIC: And you tell what food you want— 295
ANTONIO: But main demand. Transport. Work permits.
GRIGORI: (*to* NICO, *whispering in Russian*) Antonio tryebooyet
yediy, transporta, dakoomyentaf. [Antonio's demanding
food, transport and documents.]
BOJOVIC: Yes. On—main demand— 300
YASMIN: They do, they tell you what to say?
BOJOVIC: Yes. yes. But you must understand. I am not lawyer.
I am simple priest. You are demanding priest in blindfold.
Here I am.

(*Pause.* AMIRA *intervenes.*)

AMIRA: Please, father. Take your time. 305
BOJOVIC: I must ask. I must hear voice of Mrs Pecs and Pro-
fessor Katz. And um, Miss Um.
YASMIN: Feel free.

(*As the* HOSTAGES *reply,* AMIRA *tells* MARINA *what's been happening:*)

AMIRA: (*Russian*) On prinyos lekarstva dlya Doktora Daven-
porta. Antonio tryebooyet yediy, transporta i dokoomenta. 310
On nye yoorist. Prastoi svyashchennik. [He's brought medication for Dr Davenport. Antonio demanded food, transport and documents. He says he isn't a lawyer, simply a
priest.]

(Meanwhile:)

315 GABRIELLA: *(in the language of our country)* Kazvam se Gabriella Pecs. [I am Gabriella Pecs.]

BOJOVIC: I dobre ste? [And you're all right?]

GABRIELLA: Oh, hunkydory.

BOJOVIC: Professor Katz?

320 LEO: OK. As Olly said.

BOJOVIC: And Miss—

TONI: Miss Newsome. Fine. I'd just like to thank my agent and please send my best to all at Number 32. And I'd murder for a bacon lettuce and tomato sandwich.

(This expression is slightly mystifying to some people.)

325 BOJOVIC: Thank you.

(BOJOVIC has regained composure.)

You demand one that all asylum seekers grant asylum and work permit in country of their choice.

GRIGORI: *(translates quietly to NICO)* Miy fsye tryebooyem oobyezhishcha i razresheniya na rabotoo. [We are all asking for asylum and work permits.]

330

(Meanwhile.)

YASMIN: Yes?

BOJOVIC: I must say this hard demand for government of this one country to concede I think.

ANTONIO: I don't believe this.

335 AMIRA: *(whispers to MARINA)* On gavarit shto eta trebovaniye ochen seryoznoye. [He is saying this is a very serious demand.]

YASMIN: You have had a whole day to consult the governments of other countries.

340 BOJOVIC: Also this country and all governments of western countries signing international convention on asylum seekers, which lay down procedure for consideration of these problems.

ABDUL: *(Arabic)* weysh yagool? [What is he saying?]

345 YASMIN: This cannot be serious.

BOJOVIC: However.

(Slight pause.)

There are provisions also of—of 1950-something international law on refugee. Which if—a person prove he risk political or race or religious persecution, he can stay in country.

350 GRIGORI: *(translates to NICO)* Yest myezhdoonarodniy zakon . . . [There is an international law . . .]

YASMIN: I think that is 1952.

AMIRA: *(translates to MARINA)* No, yest myezhdoonarodniy zakon . . . [There is an international law . . .]

355 BOJOVIC: So what I must ask you, for list of all identity, your country, reason for departing, and country of your choice to enter. Oh, and passport number. And this matter then will be resolve as quickly as maybe.

360 GRIGORI: *(translates)* Miy dalzhniy skazat yemoo, familii, grazhdanstvo, prichiny viyyezda. On gavarit, shto vapros boodyet reshon, pa vazmozhnasti biystra . . . [We must tell him our names, country, reason for departing, then he says the matter will be resolved as quickly as possible.]

ANTONIO: Names? 365

RAIF: Passport?

YASMIN: This is not possible.

BOJOVIC: You make demand you want work permit in country of your choice. Sooner or later, you must choose I think. 370

(Pause as YASMIN whispers via ABDUL to RAIF and to ANTONIO; and AMIRA to the Russian speakers.)

AMIRA: *(whispers to MARINA)* Miy dalzhni skazat yemoo prichiny viyyezda i stranoo kooda miy khatim viyyekhat. [We must tell him our reason for departing and the country we wish to enter.]

(Meanwhile, GRIGORI is grabbed by NICO:)

NICO: *(kind of Polish)* Nazywam sie Nico. To jest moja córka, 375 Kleopatra, a to jej dziecko. Jesteśmy z Bośni. Nie mamy paszportów. (Nazyvam shem Nico. To yest moya tchurka Cleopatra, a to yey djetsko. Yesteshmee zzz Boshnee. Niye mamee pashportuv.) [My name is Nico. This is my daughter Cleopatra and her baby. We are from Bosnia. We have 380 no passports.]

(Meanwhile, ANTONIO to BOJOVIC.)

ANTONIO: Not everyone has passport.

BOJOVIC: Well, I guess ID.

YASMIN: Even ID.

ANTONIO: And we are not arrested? 385

BOJOVIC: No. No, there is amnesty.

ABDUL: *(Turkish, to RAIF)* Aff çıkhtığını mı söyledi? [Did he say, there was an amnesty.]

(Another brief moment of consultation. AMIRA has continued to speak to MARINA:)

AMIRA: *(whispers)* On gavarit shto vapros boodyet reshon pa vazmozhnosti biystra. [He says the matter will be settled as 390 quickly as possible.]

(Meanwhile NICO has continued to brief GRIGORI, including:)

NICO: Najprzót Serbowie, a potem Węgrzy dali nam papiery, ale my wyrzucilismy je. Jesteśmy cyganami, starym narodę. A teraz jesteśmy ofiarami oczyszczenia etnicznego przez Kroatów. (Nighpshrut Serboviye, a pottem Vengzhry dali 395 nam papiery, alleh mi vyshuchillishmy yay. Yesteshme tzyganamee, starhim naroden. A teraz yesteshme offyarami ochchischenia etnichnego pshez Kroatov.) [We have no passports. The Serbs gave us papers, and then the Hungarians, but we threw them away. Now we are victim of ethnic 400 cleansing by Croats.]

(Meanwhile:)

BOJOVIC: Please what happens now?

YASMIN: All right. We make a list. No names, just initials. No passport numbers. But we will all write down the name of our country, what has driven us to leave it and where we 405 want to go.

(*Somewhat unwillingly,* GRIGORI *is pushed forward by* NICO.)

GRIGORI: This man. He is call Nico and his daughter Cleopatra and her baby.

410 NICO: Jesteśmy z Bośni. (Yesteshmee zzzBoshnee.) [We are Bosnian.]

GRIGORI: They say they Bosnian. They have no passport. They are give Serb passport. This they throw away.

(AMIRA *translates:*)

AMIRA: (*whispers to* MARINA) On abyasnyayet shto sloochilas. [He's explaining what happened.]

(NICO *prompts* GRIGORI:)

415 NICO: Papiery wyrzucilismy. (Papiery vyshuchillishmy.) [Papers thrown away.]

GRIGORI: Then they are give Hungarian ID, but they are not Hungarians. Why should they have this paper? So they throw away too.

420 NICO: Jesteśmy cyganami, starym narodę. (Yesteshme tzyganamee, starhim naroden.) [We are gypsies, an ancient people.]

(*More prompting from* NICO. GRIGORI *continues, unconvincingly.*)

GRIGORI: This family gypsy. They most ancient people. They come from ancient time in India, they travel all of world.

425 NICO: Flamenco.

GRIGORI: Yes, they invent flamenco dance and pots found they bring from England to Bulgaria.

NICO: Flamenco.

GRIGORI: I say flamenco already.

430 NICO: Za Hitlera. (Za Heetlera.)

GRIGORI: They many of thousands killed by Hitler but they give no compensation like Israelis.

NICO: Jesteśmy z Bośni. (Yesteshmee zzzBoshnee.) [We are Bosnian.]

(NICO *goes to fetch* CLEOPATRA. GRIGORI, *lowering his voice:*)

435 GRIGORI: They say they Bosnia and ethnic cleaned by Serb.

NICO: Ne, Kroaty! (Nye, Kroatov!)

GRIGORI: No, sorry, Croat. They speak I think a kind of Polish. I think they are usari gyspy. But they say Bosnia.

(NICO *returns with* CLEOPATRA *and the baby.*)

NICO: Sprzedać dziecko za dobrą cenę. (Spshedach dietsko za
440 dobrom tsenen.) [Sell baby for good price.]

GRIGORI: (*unhappily*) Oh, and they prepare to sell small baby to good family in western country. With good price. So they do not come with hollow hand to Germany.

AMIRA: (*whispers to* MARINA) On gavarit shto on khochet pra-
445 dat rebyonka. [He says he wants to sell the baby.]

OLIVER: (*whispers*) Usari?

GABRIELLA: (*whispers*) Scum.

TONI: (*whispers*) She says she'll sell her baby?

YASMIN: Right. We make a list. No names. No papers.

(*Arabic, to* FATIMA:)

450 utliqee yadeyh aHsan. [You'd better untie his hands.]

(*She takes* BOJOVIC'*s arm and leads him to* OLIVER.)

Now, here is Dr Davenport.

BOJOVIC: He is here?

OLIVER: Yes, I'm here.

(BOJOVIC *gives him the package.*)

Thank you. That's a great relief.

(*He gestures to the effect that he can't give the injection unless they untie his hands.*)

YASMIN: (*Arabic, to* ABDUL) khud hal-wara'a wuktub ᶜaleyha   455
tafaaseelak ash-shakhseeya. [Here is some paper for you to write down your details.]

(*As* ABDUL *unties* OLIVER'*s hands, the* REFUGEES *huddle round drawing up their histories. They are writing on computer paper from the workstation.* FATIMA *will call upon* ABDUL *and* YASMIN'*s help to draw up her submission.*)

TONI: Why don't they have fucking passports, for Christ's sake? If they're trying to emigrate?

LEO: Well, I guess that some of them come from countries   460
where they don't issue them to everybody.

GABRIELLA: Also, I think, if you will arrive in west illegally, it will be better with no passport, so nowhere deport you to.

(OLIVER *is immersed in the instructions in the package, which contains a phial of insulin and a hypodermic.* NICO *is convinced he is being overlooked by others, as if it's an exam. He summons* CLEOPATRA *to go further afield. They go out to another corner of the church.* GRIGORI, *with his completed 'form', has approached* BOJOVIC. *He speaks quietly:*)

GRIGORI: Father. I must explain. My name is Grigori   465
Kolorenko. I from Ukraine. But by birth I am German.

BOJOVIC: Yes?

GRIGORI: Yes, you see, my mother she of German ancestry. My real name not Grigori but Gyor.

(GRIGORI *turns to see* ANTONIO *watching him suspiciously. He lowers his voice but carries on lobbying* BOJOVIC.)

LEO: What's that guy saying?   470

GABRIELLA: He claim he German.

LEO: And that helps?

GABRIELLA: Not half. Everybody German can go back. No matter if they leave in fifteen century. Just like Israel.

(GRIGORI *has finished his pitch.*)

BOJOVIC: I do my best.   475

GRIGORI: Thank you, father.

(*He moves away.*)

LEO: In the war, the judge was saying, there were kids, being transported to some camp or other, so starved they ate their name tags. For the cardboard.

GABRIELLA: In Hermitage, art gallery in Leningrad, where   480
you know they have siege for two winters, curators live on jelly made from restoration glue.

(NICO *appears from the gloom of the rest of the church, and gives a big 'psst' to* AMIRA, *who follows him back out.*)

GABRIELLA: But this does not mean I think they have therefore right of entry to nice country of their choice for all
485 time since.
OLIVER: (*reading*) Forgive me?

(YASMIN *and* RAIF *have collected the 'forms' and are passing the* HOSTAGES *en route to* BOJOVIC. YASMIN *notices that* OLIVER *has not taken his shot.*)

YASMIN: So is this not OK?
OLIVER: It's fine.
YASMIN: It is the right stuff?
490 OLIVER: Yes. I'm just putting off the evil moment.

(*Slight pause.*)

  Ever since I was a boy.

(YASMIN *shakes her head dismissively. They turn to go to* BOJOVIC. ANTONIO *is watching* OLIVER *closely;* GRIGORI *among the* REFUGEES *listening.*)

YASMIN: All done. OK.
LEO: Good luck.
YASMIN: You wish us 'Good luck'?
495 LEO: Yuh. Is that a shock to you?

(YASMIN *turns away, perhaps moving a little towards* BOJOVIC *before she suddenly turns back, waving the applications.*)

YASMIN: OK. You wish to know these people. Fine.

(*She is turning the pages of the sheaf of applications.*)

  This is—A.R., the Bosnian, she plays the cello in the orchestra in Banja Luka, but due to—changing circumstances she decides for safety to move down to Sarajevo.
500 And—what's this?
RAIF: (*reading the Russian*) Marina. Uh—Riga.
YASMIN: Oh, yes. This woman, who as I gather lives in Lithuania or Latvia since half her life but is denied the vote because she's Russian. And this is, AA?
505 ANTONIO: Me.
YASMIN: Of course, Antonio, who is student at Patrice Lumumba University in Moscow. And once upon a time he
  lives in a . . .

(*She can't read the writing.*)

ANTONIO: A dormitory.
510 YASMIN: Aha, with fifty other Africans and they are besieged
  by fellow students—good heroic Russian international-
  ists—and he decides to emigrate to western Europe, and
  ends up in a—squatter camp? just outside Paris which the
  police break up because they need the land to build the
515 National Library. And so heyho he is deported back, not
  in fact to Russia but to—
ANTONIO: Poland.
YASMIN: Where he enters into an 'indeterminate condition'
  where he remains until today. While—T—is—Sri
520 Lankan? who is, goes as maid to—ah, Kuwait—where the

citizens are not known themselves to lift anything heavier
than money. Where she is beaten and from which she presumably escapes to . . . be a 'disco dancer' in the Hot Banana Club in Cyprus. Limassol.

(*She notes missing forms. To* RAIF, *in Arabic:*)

  weyn al-ghajar? [Where are the gypsies?] (*English.*) Gypsies?   525
RAIF: (*Azeri*) Gidib bakhajaaım. [I'll go and look.]

(RAIF *goes.* YASMIN *gestures with his form, which is next.*)

YASMIN: And that is Raif, who is Azeri and also has a tale to
  tell. First, he loses his right leg doing his internationalist
  duty and fighting mediaeval obscurantism in Afghanistan.
  Then he's demobilised and earns his living taking flowers 530
  from Baku to sell in Moscow till he is threatened so much
  by the Chechen mafia he returns home to Azerbaijan, just
  in time to find his father, exactly as the Armenians had left
  him, surrounded by his luggage, at the entrance to his village and without his face.   535
LEO: I'm sorry?
YASMIN: You know, like Red Indians?
LEO: Jesus Christ.
YASMIN: Oh, and that is Abdul, who may well be himself a
  mediaeval obscurantist, but who doubtless feels that al-   540
  most anywhere is preferable to contemporary Kabul. So,
  do you know enough?

(RAIF *reappears from his search, and shrugs.*)

YASMIN: (*Arabic*) laazim hown weyn makaan hummi. [They
  must be somewhere.]

(GRIGORI *takes the opportunity for a confidential word with* OLIVER.)

GRIGORI: It is not true.   545
OLIVER: What?
GRIGORI: There are no massacre of Azeri villages. Is Muslim
  propaganda.

(YASMIN *has come across another piece of paper.*)

YASMIN: Oh, now you look there. While you are busy making Kuwait safe for democracy and freedom. It is in Eng- 550
  lish. We help her write it down.

(*She hands the paper to* OLIVER, *then takes the other papers to* BOJOVIC *as* OLIVER *looks at the paper. Its contents disturb him.*)

GABRIELLA: What does it say?
OLIVER: She's a Kurd. She is born in would you credit Batman Turkey but her family moves south to avoid the persecution. Having moved, her father and her aunt are   555
  gassed and killed at—Halabja?—in 1988. In 1989 her husband emigrates to Austria and leaves her with their child.
  Her brother is conscripted to the Iraqi army and refuses.
  He is taken to a camp and three months later he turns up
  a half-wit with one eye. She is by this time in the moun- 560
  tains but decides to take her brother back to—Qala Diza?
  where her mother now lives with her son. When they arrive. When they arrive.

(Slight pause.)

She finds . . .

(He hands the paper to TONI. *Pause.)*

565   I think. I can give myself a small injection.

(He looks up at ANTONIO *who is watching;* OLIVER *thinks because of the Kurdish paper. As* TONI *looks at the paper,* OLIVER *tries to find a vein.)*

TONI: I'm wearing her clothes.

*(*OLIVER *slips and stabs himself.)*

OLIVER: Ow.
ANTONIO: You OK?
OLIVER: Yes. I'm sorry, I—
570   ANTONIO: You sorry? Why? Whatever for?

*(*ANTONIO *goes and picks up* OLIVER*'s package of equipment.)*

So you are diabetes, right?
OLIVER: That's right
ANTONIO: And so you do this everyday?

*(*OLIVER *nods.* ANTONIO *is looking at the printed instructions.)*

ANTONIO: What is the phrase—'preferring you to me'?
575   OLIVER: Um—'rather you than me'.
ANTONIO: Oh, yes. And you speak Italian?
OLIVER: They send—they have to send—
ANTONIO: But still—you speak Italian.

(Slight pause. REFUGEES *are beginning to gather round this quiet interrogation.)*

OLIVER: Yup.
580   ANTONIO: What does this say?
OLIVER: Oh, you know. The usual chemist's—pharmacist's, instructions.
ANTONIO: Yes?
OLIVER: So many—dosage. Keep from children, all that stuff.
585   ANTONIO: *(pointing to a particular sentence)* What is this saying?
OLIVER: It says—'not to be taken orally'. That means, by the mouth.
ANTONIO: Which is the word for 'orally'?

(Pause. OLIVER *can't keep it up. He closes his eyes.)*

ANTONIO: What does it really say?

(Pause.)

590   OLIVER: It says, the insulin is a harmless salt solution. And it tells us—sforzo, that all *efforts* are being made for our release, negotiations are proceeding, we must stay—composto? oh, composed. Collected. And they—plan to cut the lights and the water and the heat at nightfall. Oh, and
595   they ask if you know about the painting.

*(*OLIVER *hands the 'instructions' back to* ANTONIO, *who looks inquisitive.)*

That's the painting up there on the wall. Covered by the bandage.
ANTONIO: *(pointing to another section)* And this? What does this say?

(Slight pause.)

OLIVER: 'The bug is in the spare cartridge'.
LEO: Oh, Jesus.   600
ANTONIO: *(Russian)* Yest padslooshka. [There's a bug.]

(Immediate reaction from the REFUGEES. BOJOVIC *too works out the implications of this discovery.* RAIF *takes the cartridge from* OLIVER, *and looks at it.)*

BOJOVIC: I think now, I will like to go.

(This draws general attention to him.)

I must say I know naturally nothing of all this.

(Pause.)

I am safe return. Then I think that naturally food must be sent in quickly.   605

(Slight pause. AMIRA *has reappeared with* NICO *and* CLEOPATRA.)*

AMIRA: No need. Look what my friends maybe of Bosnia are finding here.

*(*NICO *and* CLEOPATRA *carry armfuls of potatoes, bags of dried fish and rice, pulses and firewood. The* GYPSIES *dump their treasures, with a huge clatter, in the centre of the church.* NICO *marches over to present his application to* BOJOVIC.)*

NICO: *(kind of Polish)* Prosze księdza, tu są nasze papiery. Prosze zrozumiec ze jesteśmy z Bozni-Hercegowinji. (Proshe kshienndza, tu sown nashe papyery. Proshe zro- 610
zoomyiyech ze yesteshmi zzzBoshnee-Hertsegoveenee.) [Father. Here are our forms. Please understand we are from Bosnia Hercegovina.]

(He kisses BOJOVIC*'s hand.* BOJOVIC *has realised the discovery of the food has revoked his passport.)*

BOJOVIC: Now I must say—I insist—
YASMIN: Oh yes. Please go. We have no desire to harm one 615
hair of the head of a Minister of the Holy One True Church.

(She goes and takes FATIMA*'s form from* TONI *and gives it to* BOJOVIC.)*

ANTONIO: *(Russian)* Fsyem pa myestam. (Everybody into position.)

*(*ANTONIO *goes up the ladder,* ABDUL *to the door. The* HOSTAGES *are being held and silenced in preparation for the door being opened.)*

YASMIN: But I'm afraid you are the last. We wish no more 620
nice friendly visitors with little secrets up their sleeves. And you will please inform your friends—we need a guarantee that everyone will be admitted to the country

625 of their choice. And if we have no such guarantee by—six o'clock tomorrow morning, we will kill a hostage. Most likely it will be the Zionist Professor Katz. So get him out of here.

LEO: (*bleakly*) Hey. Look—

(*A hand is slapped over his mouth.* RAIF *escorts* BOJOVIC—*none too gently*—*to the door.*)

630 ABDUL: (*to* YASMIN, *joking, in Arabic*) mish laazim tudkhulee-hum illa, iza hum caryaaneen. [You should admit them naked.]

YASMIN: Oh, yes, why not?

(YASMIN *speaks straight into* BOJOVIC'*s face.*)

635 There is one exception to the rule. We will admit you. Or another Priest of the Holy One True Church. But only without sleeves. Like the Risen Christ of Michelangelo. Stark bollock naked.

(*Laughter, and perhaps a little more, as this is translated.* ANTONIO *signals the all clear to* RAIF *who opens the door for* BOJOVIC *to be pushed through by* RAIF. *The door is closed and locked.* YASMIN *turns back to the* HOSTAGES. *Hands are removed from their mouths. A long silence.*)

YASMIN: Or maybe the first will be Dr Diabetic Davenport with his distressing ailments and fluent technical Italian.

(YASMIN *marches over to* OLIVER. *To* ABDUL, *Arabic.*)

640 huwwa kassar jihaaz attasonnut? [Did he destroy the bug?]
ABDUL: (*to* RAIF, *Turkish*) O dinleme jihaazı qırdın mı? [Did you destroy the bug?]
RAIF: (*Azeri*) Haalaa gırajaaım onu. [No, but I will.]

(RAIF *takes the cartridge, finds a hammer, and gets smashing.*)

YASMIN: Who having kindly told us all about his friends out there and their nice plans for us—
645 OLIVER: They're not—
YASMIN: —will now explain please all about this painting. The one they ask you if we know about. Raif!

(*She takes the revolver from* RAIF.)

Which now—I think—we will.

(YASMIN *is pointing the revolver at* OLIVER. *He is scared.*)

OLIVER: Um, look—look, please—
650 YASMIN: I mean, one must imagine it is something fairly special, for two great art historians to come all this way, with all this magnificent technology.
OLIVER: Well, actually, in fact—
YASMIN: But now I think we should know quite how special.
655 Or perhaps, to show that we mean business—
OLIVER: Please—
GABRIELLA: (*quickly*) In fact, it actually not so special.

(YASMIN *looks to* GABRIELLA.)

GABRIELLA: In fact, it just ordinary church painting.

(YASMIN *gestures witheringly at the equipment.*)

GABRIELLA: Which we think at first is maybe painted very long ago, and is first of its kind in all world, and therefore 660 yes a little bit damn special. But, actually, we find that it turn out—
LEO: —to be exactly what you thought it was.

(GABRIELLA *looks at* LEO *in horror.*)

LEO: I mean, come on, let's not try to pull one over on these people. 665
GABRIELLA: Leo—
LEO: I mean, they'll understand why this painting is so valuable. Knowing, as they do, so much more of us than we will ever take the pains to learn of them.

(*Pause.* GABRIELLA *looks desperately at* OLIVER, *who can't do anything.*)

YASMIN: Please do proceed. 670
LEO: (*gesturing with his tied hands*) Sure. If you'd be so kind.

(YASMIN *gives a curt nod.* GRIGORI *unties* LEO'*s hands.*)

LEO: And thus doubtless won't need telling that about the beginning of the 14th century there was a mighty change nay turnaround in the way that western painters chose to address the world around them. Which, although it techni- 675 cally consisted of a number of devices to render the effect of three dimensions on a flat plane, was essentially a key step in the growing understanding, or belief, that not God but Man is the measure of all things. That his point of vision is *the* point of vision. That there is no outside author- 680 ity defining or pre-empting what he sees, with his own restless, questing, yearning, endlessly inquisitive two eyes.

(*He's at the photograph of the Giotto Lamentation.*)

And it has been argued that the starting point of that, the first leg of the race from God to Man, was run by this guy, Giotto di Bondone, in 1300-ish in Northern Italy. But 685 what these guys have discovered is that in fact by then the first lap was already run. Right here. Up there. So people, what you have here is not just the most valuable art-find of the century, but, to coin a phrase, the birth of universal European man. 690

(*He looks questioningly at* GABRIELLA.)

GABRIELLA: I think I say of modern rational universal man.
LEO: Well you do too. Which is of course the *most* delicious irony. That the folks out there, who want so badly to be universal Europeans, to be part of that, are much more in- terested in that than they are in you, or even us. So they'll 695 bar their gates to you, and risk our lives, to keep the art. For Christ's sake: 'Do they know about the painting?'. And it's not the first time. As Dubrovnik burns, western intellectuals write polite letters to the papers protesting the destruction of the architecture. Mitterand destroys a 700 squatter camp to build a library. The camp guards at Auschwitz spend their evenings listening to Mozart on the gramophone.

(*Pause.*)

And of course, it can be argued that you shouldn't blame
705 the art. But on the other hand . . . there is a view, that
somewhere in all that remorseless questioning—there is—
as you point out—a kind of arrogance. That somehow it's
always Western man who's doing the inquisiting, and
everybody else who's quisited. So maybe, yuh, there *is*
710 some line, if not from Beethoven to Buchenwald, then at
least to the World Bank, the IMF and NATO.

(*Slight pause. Half to* OLIVER *and* GABRIELLA.)

Which is a view I find increasingly persuasive. Actually.

(*A moment. Then:*)

So hey. You know what I'd do? I would write a statement,
addressing this—this intriguing double standard. And I'd
715 insist it gets put out on the radio. And I'd say that if it isn't,
then you'll douse that S.O.B. in gasoline and fry it off the
wall.

(*Slight pause. As if an afterthought:*)

Hey, even better. As you say, there's a tradition of exchanging prisoners for books. Well, we're not nearly so
720 valuable to you as that is. So, hell, why not underline the
irony. And set your—huddled masses free.

(*There is a silence.*)

AMIRA: This is painting here?
LEO: That's right. Under the canvas. In fact, before they cut
the water off, you could remove the facing. Take a look at
725 what you got.

(*A moment.* AMIRA *goes up the ladder, to the painting. She touches it.*)

AMIRA: How do you take this off?
LEO: With water. And a little—tender loving care.

(YASMIN *quickly to* ABDUL *and* RAIF.)

YASMIN: (*Arabic*) ᶜul-luh hannaaqish kalaam az-zalami. [Tell
him we'll discuss what he said.]
730 ABDUL: (*Turkish*) Söylediklerini tartışhmak istiyor. [She
wants to discuss what he said.]
ANTONIO: (*to* GRIGORI, *Russian*) Atvyedi yivo. [Take him
back.]

(YASMIN, RAIF, ABDUL *and* ANTONIO *go into a huddle.* AMIRA
looks at the covered painting. GRIGORI *brings* LEO *back to the other*
HOSTAGES. LEO *puts his hands behind his back for tying.* GRIGORI
*shrugs and gestures for him to sit. He does so, his hands untied, with
a smile on his face.* GRIGORI *like the others is keener on the* HUD-
DLE *than the* HOSTAGES.)

GABRIELLA: What are you doing?
735 LEO: I am trying to get us out of here.
GABRIELLA: But you put at risk our painting.
LEO: Which if it means anything at all, must surely rate the
needs and rights of living human beings higher than what
you described—acutely—as a form of currency.

(GABRIELLA *shrugs.*)

Oh, but I'm sorry. You can't be dumping ground for dregs. 740
GABRIELLA: Oh, please.
LEO: (*to* OLIVER) And of course, all that is based on the idea
that works of art might contain some kind of universal
moral truth. Well, hush my mouth.
OLIVER: No. Actually, I think you may be right. 745

(*Slight pause.*)

LEO: I'm sorry?
OLIVER: Perhaps there are universal human values which we
should protect. From those who threaten them.

(LEO *picks up the hypodermic package and gestures with it towards
the door of the church.*)

LEO: Olly, those fuckers nearly got us killed.

(OLIVER *gestures towards the* HOSTAGE-TAKERS.)

OLIVER: Oh no. Those fuckers nearly killed us. And still may. 750

(*The huddle has split:* RAIF *has commandeered* GRIGORI *and is calling down* AMIRA *to start writing a statement.* YASMIN *arrives at*
HOSTAGES, *with* ANTONIO.)

YASMIN: OK. We have reached a decision. We will issue a
statement, as you so helpfully suggest.

(LEO *looks to* OLIVER, *then nods graciously to* YASMIN.)

YASMIN: And to underline your irony, sure, we will make a
humanitarian gesture. We will let the women go.

(*Pause. The* HOSTAGES *react—or attempt to disguise—their reactions to this news.*)

TONI: What, now? 755
YASMIN: Yes, now.

(*Slight pause.*)

TONI: Well, great. Thanks.

(*To* LEO:)

And—uh, thanks. I'm— 760
LEO: (*to stop her*) Please.
YASMIN: (*Arabic, to* ABDUL, *turning to go*) khalleehum jaahzeen.
[Get them ready.]
GABRIELLA: Um—forgive me please. 765

(YASMIN *turns back.*)

YASMIN: Yes? What?
GABRIELLA: If I will say I stay, will you let one of men go?
OLIVER: What?

(YASMIN *quick eye contact with* ANTONIO.)

YASMIN: No. No I'm sorry. It is you or no-one.

(*Again, she turns to go upstage.*)

770   GABRIELLA: Well. So be it.

(YASMIN *turns back.*)

YASMIN: You—you want to stay?

(*Slight pause.*)

GABRIELLA: Not want. I will.
YASMIN: You're sure?
GABRIELLA: (*with a shrug*) Voilà.

(*Pause.*)

775   YASMIN: So be it.

(*To* ABDUL, *in Arabic:*)

shoof iza kull shee tamaam. [Check if everything's OK.]

(ABDUL *goes up the ladder.* ANTONIO *goes to take* TONI *to the door.*)

TONI: (*to* GABRIELLA) Hey, have you gone crazy?
GABRIELLA: No.
TONI: Right.
780   ANTONIO: (*to* TONI) Hey. You want your pretty clothe?

(*He gestures to* FATIMA. TONI *looks longingly at her clothes.*)

TONI: Well, p'raps . . .

(*Slight pause.*)

No. Let her keep 'em.

(*To* OLIVER *and* LEO, *but also, perhaps, to* FATIMA:*)

And good luck.
YASMIN: You tell them. They call up on the telephone for a
785   statement in—in half an hour.
TONI: Yuh. Sure.

(TONI *seems almost unwilling to go.*)

TONI: Hey, guys. I've just remembered number two.
OLIVER: What was it?
TONI: 'Don't make helpful suggestions'.

(ABDUL *nods the all clear from the ladder.* ANTONIO *takes* TONI *to the door. Quickly the door is opened,* TONI *is pushed through, and it's locked again. Meanwhile,* GRIGORI *has come forward, with the beginnings of a draft statement in his hands.*)

790   GRIGORI: Excuse. We have Paris library and concentration
camp. There was a third example, no?
LEO: Dubrovnik.
GRIGORI: (*turning to go*) Thank you.
LEO: So could you use some help?

(*Pause.*)

795   YASMIN: Yes. We could use some help.

(*He goes back upstage.* LEO *making to follow:*)

OLIVER: Leo. You heard.

(*A moment.* LEO *goes upstage to join the drafting group. There is a moment between* OLIVER *and* GABRIELLA *before* OLIVER *speaks.*)

OLIVER: Gabri—
GABRIELLA: For three reasons. One is whatever painting really worth, still it is my discovery, and I don't want to see
it fry off wall.   800
OLIVER: But still, you—
GABRIELLA: Two. If it not what we first think, then likely
painter from our country. And so I should coco I run out
and leave it here.

(*Slight pause.*)

As after all said and done, I am curator there if only of   805
Brueghel second cousin. And now of Giotto copy in late
Byzantine style.

(*Pause.*)

And three: to show that scumbag, even after forty year of
botch-ups, forty year of fail to build one wall of new
Jerusalem, still we worthless folks can behave—well, little   810
bitty better—braver—than he think we do.

(*Pause.*)

OLIVER: I should have been more brave. That stupid business
with the cartridge.
GABRIELLA: Hey come on.

(*Pause.*)

OLIVER: You know, it was your passion.   815
GABRIELLA: Sorry?
OLIVER: Why I changed my mind, that evening. And I remember thinking, even then. How pathetically unserious,
our—discourse must appear to you.

(*Slight pause.* GABRIELLA *looks at* OLIVER.)

How easy it must seem—it is—from the portals of the   820
Ruskin Institute, to claim it's more or less a toss-up between Pride and Prejudice and Police Academy.

(*Slight pause.*)

To those who do our dirty work. Who have stood on Europe's battlements for all those years.

(*Pause.* GABRIELLA *takes* OLIVER's *hands.*)

GABRIELLA: Okeydoke. Fourth reason. If I cannot leave here   825
painting, how do you presume I can leave you?

SCENE VI

*Shortly before dawn. The church is lit with candles and the dying fires
on which food has been cooked and round which* HOSTAGES *and*
REFUGEES *are sat to keep warm. The facing of the painting has been
removed, but in the darkness we can see little of it. There is some ner-
vousness in the air.* YASMIN *is playing with a set of keys.* AMIRA *has*

taken her cello from its case. ABDUL *is with* RAIF. *There is tension between* LEO, OLIVER *and* GABRIELLA, *which* LEO *resolves to address.*

LEO: 'God bless Vespuccia'.
OLIVER: I beg your pardon?

(TUNU *is coming to the* HOSTAGES *to collect their plates.* GRIGORI *starts to listen to the conversation.*)

LEO: An idle speculation. Whether things might have gone differently, had they chosen our beloved founder's surname rather than his first name.

(*Slight pause.*)

OLIVER: 'Vespuccia the Beautiful'.
LEO: Well, exactly.
GABRIELLA: 'As Vespuccian as apple pie'.
LEO: 'The House Un-Vespuccian Activities Committee'.
OLIVER: Promoting naturally 'life, liberty and the Vespuccian way'.
GRIGORI: Hey. Or maybe. 'All-Vespuccian Girl'.

(*Slight pause.*)

LEO: Hey. Right.

(TUNU *takes the plates.* OLIVER *calls after her.*)

OLIVER: Excuse me, what's the time?

(TUNU *looks to* YASMIN, *who shakes her head.*)

GRIGORI: Actually—
YASMIN: No.

(GRIGORI *shrugs.* YASMIN *goes a little way apart.*)

OLIVER: Just, it would be nice to know. How long we have before they take up your suggestion. And fry our painting off the wall.
LEO: Hey. Olly.

(AMIRA *doesn't see why the* HOSTAGES *shouldn't know the time. She puts down her cello and comes down to them.*)

OLIVER: Hello.
AMIRA: Hello.

(*Slight pause.*)

  Your painting. Look like window.
OLIVER: Yes.
AMIRA: So many star.

(*Slight pause.*)

  Is good word 'star'. Our word is 'zvezda'. Ugly word I think.
GABRIELLA. Is same for us.

(*Slight pause* AMIRA *takes out some photographs from her wallet to show to the* HOSTAGES.)

AMIRA: This my mother.

(*A moment, then* GABRIELLA *takes the picture to look at it.*)

AMIRA: This my father with my sister. This string section of our orchestra, in trip to Prague. Our big night out.

(*The* HOSTAGES *look at* AMIRA's *pictures.*)

OLIVER: Perhaps—you'll play for us.

(AMIRA *is shaking her head as* YASMIN *appears.* ABDUL *and* RAIF *are sharing a joke.*)

YASMIN: What's going on?
LEO: We were asking if she'd play for us.

(AMIRA *shrugs and shakes her head.*)

YASMIN: And what are these?
GABRIELLA: Just photographs.
AMIRA: Of better days.

(*She is gathering her pictures up.*)

LEO: So why d'you leave?

(*Slight pause.*)

AMIRA: Terrible things.

(*She stands.*)

GABRIELLA: 'Lora'. In our old language word for star is 'lora'.
AMIRA: It is ten minutes before five.

(AMIRA *goes upstage.*)

OLIVER: An hour to go.

(*We hear* RAIF *finishing his joke.*)

RAIF: (*Azeri*) Adam da dedi ki, bakh, daha shimdiden bazaarlıkh yapıyorsun. [And so the man said, see, you're haggling already.]

(YASMIN, *angry, strides to* RAIF *and* ABDUL.)

YASMIN: What is this? (*Arabic.*) rijaa'an, eysh biseer hown? [What is going on please?]
ABDUL: (*Arabic.*) huwwa yimzaH faqat. [It's just a joke.]
YASMIN: (*Arabic.*) irweelna fa'izan, salleena kullna. [You tell it please? Amuse us all?]
ABDUL: (*Arabic.*) yagool innoo maafee moomisaat fee . . . [It is about there being no prostitutes . . .] (*English.*) OK. No hooker in USSR . . .
YASMIN: I see.

(ANTONIO *gestures to* YASMIN *to cool it.*)

GRIGORI: (*Russian*) Ya shootkoo znayoo. [I know a joke.]
AMIRA: (*gesturing that he should include the* HOSTAGES) Grigori.
GRIGORI: (*in English*) I know great joke. In village remote corner of Siberia, where they see pig for first time. One say is overfeeding rat. Another say, is starving cow. Third say, maybe rat who strive that he develop into cow.

(*There's something not quite right about the joke.*)

Or she.

(*That hasn't cracked it.*)

It is joke how peasant backwardness counter by revolutionary optimism. Now maybe bit more irony. Sorry.

(*Pause.*)

ANTONIO: Hey. Like—violonchel?

65 AMIRA: Cello.

ANTONIO: Like guitar who want to grow up to be double bass.

(*Laughter.*)

So where you play? Jazz band?

(AMIRA *shakes her head.*)

ANTONIO: (*Russian, to* RAIF) Djaz-banda nyetoo. [No jazz
70   band.]

RAIF: Maybe rock and roll.

ANTONIO: One for money, two for show. Three to get ready—

RAIF: (*sings*) Three to get ready now Blue Suede Shoes.

(ANTONIO *is moving to the cello to hand it to* AMIRA.)

75 AMIRA: No, no.

(*To change the subject.*)

But I tell joke. No, story. Once there was and there was not a Padisah—great ruler, who must go off to battle, leaving three lovely daughters back behind.

(CLEOPATRA *is translating to* NICO, *who becomes increasingly agitated.*)

AMIRA: And he tell them, while that he is gone, they may go
80   anywhere in all the palace and its gardens, but they are
         forbid to enter one room at the very back and on right
         hand side. Else there will be great harm.

CLEOPATRA: Excuse excuse.

AMIRA: Yes please?

85 NICO: (*kind of Polish*) Historia nie tak idzie. (Historiya nye tak
         idzhe.) [The story is wrong.]

CLEOPATRA: Is not right story.

AMIRA: Oh?

NICO: (*waving at* GRIGORI *to translate*) W prawdziwej historji
90   jest syn i corką i—fudhopp (Y pravdiviy historiyi yest syn
         i tchurka i—fudhopp.) [In the real story it is a son and
         daughter and a woodcutter.]

GRIGORI: In real story, apparently, it one daughter and one
         son of—fudhopp?

95 NICO: (*miming vigorously*) Fudhopp.

GRIGORI: (*realising it's the English word*) Oh, woodchopper.

(AMIRA *allows* NICO *to take over the story.*)

NICO: Fudhopp. I wysyła córkę przez lasu z trzema rozka-
         zami. (I visiwa tchurkan pshes lassu z chrema rozkazami.)
         [And he sends his daughter out across the forest with three
100   rules.]

GRIGORI: And he send out daughter with three rule.

NICO: Pierwszy rozkaz; nie rozmawjaj z obcymi ludzmi. (Py-
         ervishi rozkazi; nye rozmayvi z obtsimi ludjmi.) [One—
         talk to no stranger.]

GRIGORI: Talk to no stranger—one.   105

NICO: Drugi rozkaz: trzymaj się ścieżki . Trzeci rozkaz:
         nie jeść jedzenia z lasu. (Drugi rozkaz: trzhimay shen
         shcheshki. Chrechi rozkaz: nye yesht yedzeniya z lassu.)
         [Two: keep to the path. Three: do not eat food of the
         forest.]   110

GRIGORI: Keep all of way to path, two, and three, she forbid
         from pick up food of forest.

NICO: Eat.

GRIGORI: Forbid from eating food of forest.

NICO: A po trzech godzinakh nie wróćiła. (A po chrekh god- 115
         jinakh nye vroochiwa.) [And three hours later she had not
         returned.

GRIGORI: And three hour later she not return.

NICO: I wysyła syna poszukać. (I visiwa siyna poshukach.)
         [And he sends the son to look.]   120

GRIGORI: And so father send off son to look for her.

NICO: I syn znajduję v lasu . . . (I siyn znayduyen v lassu . . .)
         [And the son finds in the forest . . .]

GRIGORI: And the son finds in the forest . . .

NICO: (*graphically*) . . . Kupę pociętych ramją i nóg i kawałki 125
         ciała—(Koopen pochentikh ramyan i nog i kavawki
         chowa—) [. . . a pile of bits of dismembered limbs and cut
         up arms and bits of body—]

GRIGORI: Hey actually you know I don't think this so good.

(*Very slight pause.*)

AMIRA: OK. I hear it differently. I hear it not ordinary wood- 130
         chopper. But king. And not ordinary son, but hero.

MARINA: (*Russian*) Shto praiskhodit? [What's happening?]

NICO: (*Polish*) Królewcz wyjeżda w daleką podrósz. (Kroole-
         vich viyezhdzha v dalekan podroozh.) [There is a king's
         son going on a journey.]   135

MARINA: (*enthusiastically*) Ah. Tsaryevich.

AMIRA: Yes, good, he set out on a journey—

NICO: Wielka wyprawa . . . (Vyelka viprava . . .) [A great ex-
         pedition . . .]

AMIRA: Or why not, yes, there set out hero with great 140
         army—

GRIGORI: Expedition . . .

NICO: . . . przez drogi mlecznę . . . (. . . pshes drogi mlechnen
         . . .) [. . . through the galaxies . . .]

AMIRA: Which together journey through the . . .   145

NICO: . . . żeby przelecic przez ostateczn granicę . . . . (. . .
         rshebi pshelechich pshez ostatechnan granitsen . . .) [. . . to
         cross the final frontier . . .]

AMIRA: Crossing last border . . .

NICO: Smialę lecic tam gdzie nikogo jeszcze nie było, w— 150
         (Smayale lechich tam gdzhe nikogo yeshche nye biwo
         v—) [. . . boldly going where no man had gone before
         in—]

GRIGORI: I think he say—

NICO: —Starship Enterprise.   155

AMIRA: (*dismissively*) It Starship. Dr Spock. Boldly going
         where no man is gone before.

NICO: Space—the final frontier.

RAIF: Hey. Beam me up Scotty.

160 NICO: Da.

(*To* ANTONIO:)

Uhura.

ANTONIO: OK. No starship. But small village, central Africa.
And it is World War Two and an aircraft officer, let us say
from England, is shot down and parachutes down in the
165 village. And he is naturally captured by the tribesmen who
have never seen a white man and they prepare their
grandest pot to cook him in. And as spear is raised to slice
him up, he say: now look here chaps if you will save my
life I will tell you all the story of my military exploits don-
170 chaknow. And the villagers who hadn't understood said,
oh are you a warrior? And he said, yes, well, you might say
so. And they were warriors so they jumped up and down.
And they asked, is your side winning in the war? And he
said, yes, I think we can say more or less that all in all we're
175 winning. And the Africans throw up their spears in joy.
And how many of the other side d'you kill? And he answered, well now actually you come to mention it I have
personally done in thirty of the blighters wizard show.
And the savages jump up and down and throw their spears
180 in huge delight. Dear fellow, thirty done in single-handed,
what a feast you must have had! And the officer says: gentlemen, I am from Europe, cradle of world civilisation. We
don't eat people where I come from. 'Oh', say the Africans
in puzzlement. 'So why d'you kill them?'

(*He turns to* RAIF *and* ABDUL, *who has picked up the essence of the
story from the gestures.*)

185 ABDUL: Hey not spear. Kalashinikov.

(ANTONIO *wants to involve* RAIF *and* ABDUL *in the game. So he
shouts to them:*)

ANTONIO: Who dare win.
RAIF: Hasta La Vista, baby.

(*Running to kick an imaginary ball at* RAIF *and* ANTONIO:)

ANTONIO: Go—o—oal!

(ABDUL *goes into what might be a kind of sword dance if he had a
sword, with* RAIF *accompanying, beating out the rhythm on a petrol
drum. Then* NICO *enters the circle with an impressive Romany dancing turn, involving first* MARINA, *then* AMIRA *and eventually*
CLEOPATRA *in a swirling fandango. All the* REFUGEES *except* YAS-
MIN, FATIMA *and* TUNU *become caught up in the dance. Then*
TUNU *comes forward with her story.*)

TUNU: OK. (*Sinhalese*) mama kathandarayak kiyannang. [I'll
190 tell you a story.]

(TUNU'*s story is initially incomprehensible as no-one but her speaks
her language. But gradually, through a kind of collective reading of
the story, supplemented by* TUNU'*s own hints, confirmations, corrections and echoes of the other* STORYTELLERS' *gestural language—
for 'king', 'expedition', 'capture', going into a forest, giving a gift and
so on—the story emerges and becomes clear.*)

TUNU: Ékamath éka rataka, hitiya Dhasharartha kiyala hungak balasampanne rajathunék. [Once upon a time there
lived a very powerful king called Dhasharartha.]

GRIGORI: King.

TUNU: Unwahanséta hitiya bisawak, mé bisawa hungak 195
papuru, ahankara ganiyek. [His highness had a wife, who
was a cruel and conceited woman.]

MARINA: Tsarevna.

AMIRA: (*Russian*) Zhestokaya. [Malicious.]

TUNU: Unwahanséta thawath hitiya puthék. Puthagé name 200
Rama. Ishwara déviyangé dunne bindala Rama, Sita dina-
gaththa. Mé atharathuré Dhasharartha rajathuma thamangé rajakama Rama kumarayate pavaranne kalpana
kéruwa. [He also had a son, and the son's name was Rama.
Prince Rama proved his great strength by snapping Lord 205
Ishawara's bow in two and won the beautiful Princess Sita.
In the meantime, King Dhasharartha decided to hand over
his kingdom to Rama.]

MARINA: (*to* GRIGORI) Atkazatsa of prestola? [Abdicate?]

TUNU: Namuth unwahanségé napuru bisawate mégana irisiya 210
hithila Rama kumarayawe awrudu dhahahatharakate
vanantharayate pituwahal kérewwa. [But in jealousy his
cruel queen had Rama banished to the woods for fourteen years.]

GRIGORI: Execution? 215

YASMIN: Exile.

TUNU: Ithin, Rama Sita kumariya samaga vanagatha vuna.
Vanantharayé dakke thapasayék Rama kumarayate vidya
balaya athi eethalayak dunna. [So Rama sets off into the
woods with Sita. A hermit they meet in the forest gives 220
Rama a magic arrow.]

YASMIN: (*to* CLEOPATRA) Holy man.

TUNU: Mé atharathure Ravana— [In the meantime Ravana—]

GRIGORI: This Rama still? 225

TUNU: Ravana.

GRIGORI: Sorry.

TUNU: Ravana kiyana rakus raja Sita kumariya dake, Sitawe
labaganne kalpanakéruwa. Ithin Rama gethara hitiya nathi
velawake, Ravana balahathkarayén Sita kumariyawe tha- 230
mangé dupathate paharegenagiya. Ithin Rama visala ham-
udavak raskaragéna thamangé raté indala Ravana rajugé
dupathate palamák hadanne theeranaya kela. [Ravana the
Demon king claps eyes on Sita and decides he must have
her. So at a moment when Rama is not about, Ravanna 235
abducts Sita and carries her across the seas to his island. So
Rama gathers himself an enormous army and starts building a bridge from his homeland to Ravana's island.]

AMIRA: He—make boat? Build bridge? to Sita.

TUNU: Visala yuddhayakate pasuwe Rama saha Ravana 240
moonate moona hambawuna. Namuth éka oluwak angin
wénwénakota thavath oluwak Ravana rajugé kandin
mathuwénawa. Anthimata, Rama éyayge vidya balaya athi
eethalaya aragéna Ravana rajuwe marumuwate pathkela.
Yuddayen pasuwa Rama saha Sita navatha ekathuvuna. 245
[After a terrible and bloody battle, Rama and Ravana finally engage in mortal combat. But, to his dismay, Rama
finds that every time he manages to lop one of Ravana's
many heads off another grows in its place. But then Rama
remembers his magic arrow—and shoots Ravana dead. 250
And after the battle Rama and Sita are reunited.]

(MOST PEOPLE *respond as if this was the end; a smattering of applause.*)

TUNU: Namuth, Rama, Sita ayagé pathivatha rekagéna hitiyé nè kiyala sèka pahalakéruwa. [But Rama doubts Sita's faith.]

(*The* LISTENERS *look blank, and whisper questions to each other.*)

255 MARINA: (*Russian*) Shto ana gavarit? [What is she saying?]
GRIGORI: (*Russian*) Ya nye znayoo. [I don't know.]
TUNU: Sita mégana dukwéla, visala ginimaleyak gahala ginnata pènna. Namuth aya pichchune nè. Mokadha, aya
260 thamungé pathivatha rèkagéna hitapu nisa. [Sita, hugely saddened by his distrust of her, makes herself a pyre and throws herself upon it. But because she has been faithful she doesn't burn.]
AMIRA: I think—Rama doubt if Sita faithful during her captivity.

(TUNU *nods.*)

265 AMIRA: And so to prove she build great fire and throw herself within. But she suffers no harm.

(TUNU *nods.*)

TUNU: Ithin anthimata, Rama saha Sita, thamangé ratate gos hondin rajakamkela. [And so in the end Rama and Sita return to claim their kingdom and live happily for all eter-
270 nity.]
YASMIN: (*trying to be harsher than she feels*) Oh yes, of course. And they live happily for ever afterwards.

(OLIVER, *caught up in the story, whispers to* GABRIELLA.)

OLIVER: Or as we might more readily remember it: a God forbids his child the forest fruit . . .

(OLIVER *realises he is being heard by the* HOSTAGE-TAKERS. *He decides to tell his story; perhaps he too echoing the gestures of proscription, banishment, capture and death:*)

275 OLIVER: Or as we might remember it: a God forbids his child the forest fruit. The child of disobedience is banished and his children are condemned to wander through the earth. But finally the God in pity sends his only son for their redemption. Who teaches them through parables and tales.
280 Who rides unrecognised into the holy city. Prophesies his capture and his death. But promises his followers that nonetheless, in three days' time he'll prove himself the thing he claims to be.

(*Slight pause.* AMIRA *steps towards* OLIVER.)

AMIRA: And then? And then?

(OLIVER *is being invited into the circle to finish his story. Suddenly,* FATIMA *bursts into the circle. She is furious.*)

285 FATIMA: (*Turkish*) Ama bu, bu olmamalı. Biz bu insanlarla oturup masal anlatıyoruz. Onlar emperyalistler ishkenjejiler. Onlar bizim eseerlerimiz, onlara göz kulak olmalıyız. Onlar öldürmekle tehdeed ettik. Shimdi onları nasıl öldürürüz

sonra? Bizim hakkımızda ne düshünejekler? [This is—this must not happen. We are sitting here telling infant's stories, 290 with these people. They are imperialists and torturers. They are our captives and we must keep them secure. We have threatened to kill them. How can we kill them now? What will they think of us?]

(*Slight pause.*)

Elleri, ayakları baalanmalı ve aaızları tıkanmalı! Onlarla 295 hich konushmamalıyız! [They must be bound and gagged! We mustn't speak to them!]

(*She storms off to the side.* AMIRA *feels she must explain* FATIMA's *outburst to the* HOSTAGES.)

AMIRA: She was with the PKK. They are kind of army, fighting for Kurdistan. Her brother turn up, he is driven crazy. She take him home to where her mother keep her son. 300 She is deserter. They kill her if they catch her. And there she find . . .
OLIVER: Yes. Yes, I know.

(*Slight pause.*)

I wonder. How you grieve. When you find that. How you lament. 305

(*The baby begins to cry.* CLEOPATRA *and* TUNU *go to fetch the baby. She is brought in, and comforted. The baby becomes a focus:* PEOPLE *group round. The beginnings of a lullaby.* YASMIN *jangles her keys at the baby.* YASMIN *catches* AMIRA's *eye.*)

YASMIN: It is—my house keys. From Kuwait City. It is crazy that I keep them.

(*Slight pause.*)

It is like your photos I suppose.

(AMIRA *goes to the* HOSTAGES.)

AMIRA: OK. It is like this. I have a cousin. Who is Muslim sure but sophisticated European woman. She is taken from 310 her house by lorry to an iron ore plant. Then they transfer her to what had been a tile factory. Then the men are separated out and they go 'shopping'. While the women are transported to an elementary school. For what is called 'exchange'. 315

(*Gesturing to* FATIMA.)

She is Muslim. In Koran, it say: 'Whoever is removed from fire and admitted unto paradise, shall win great victory'. 'The present life is but delusion'. 'We all belong to God and to Him we shall return'.
OLIVER: What does that mean? 320
AMIRA: It means that only Muslim true believer of the resurrection. It is for them great blasphemy, to despair at a loved one being called to God.
LEO: For 'them'? Is all of this about a 'them'. Or you?

(AMIRA *can't answer. She goes to sit with her cello.*)

YASMIN: So. Not so much a fairy tale. 325

(Slight pause. She approaches the HOSTAGES, *pointing at* FATIMA.)

When she came back at first it looked quite normal. And as it was the morning it was no surprise to find the door was open, and the door down to the cellar also. The neighbours came and shouted at her not to go. Down the steps 330 the first thing that she notices was the care with which the sheet was laid out on the ground. Just the faintest outline of a child's shape. As if maybe he was asleep beneath it. Or even for a moment that he wasn't there.

(Suddenly, the deep, long, sad tone of a cello. AMIRA *has started to play. Singing begins, over the cello. It's a kind of lament. It swells and fades. And then, as the first shafts of light appear through the high windows and across the painting, there is a sudden heavy drumming on the door.)*

SCENE VII

It is dawn. Shafts of light through the high windows catch the painting: the star in the sky and St John's arm stretched out towards the Virgin; we can just see the rock in the foreground. EVERYONE *stands still, silenced by the knocking.* YASMIN, *who is nearest, shins up the ladder. She looks out, and turns. To* RAIF:

YASMIN: *(Arabic)* iftaH al-baab. [Open the door.]

(As YASMIN *descends,* RAIF *and* ABDUL *open the door. Father* KAROLYI *enters, naked, holding up a piece of paper. He walks into the centre of the nave. No-one moves.)*

KAROLYI: You said. I understood. You would admit only a naked priest. I am Father Petr Karolyi.

(With the paper:)

I have the answer to your demands.

(Pause.)

5   Can I please have—something to cover me?

*(*AMIRA *finds him a coat.* KAROLYI *puts the paper in his teeth and puts on the coat. Then he takes the paper from his mouth.)*

AMIRA: Is this your church, Father?
KAROLYI: It is your church. As is surely clear to everyone.
YASMIN: So we will have our answer please. Or do you want us to fulfil our promise?
10   KAROLYI: Promise?
YASMIN: Threat.

(Slight pause.)

KAROLYI: I am so sorry. Yes, of course.

(Addressing the paper:)

First of all, of course, the national authorities must make clear that in considering your requests—
15   RAIF: Demands!
KAROLYI: —they cannot accede to threats of violence.

*(*YASMIN *gestures dismissively.)*

KAROLYI: On the other hand, as a gesture of humanitarianism, your 'demands' have been passed on to the internal ministries of concerned countries. And have been considered. In as—generous a light as possible. In accordance 20 naturally with United Nations Convention on Refugees of 1951 . . .

(He senses impatience.)

Etcetera. So, first of all. And on condition as you must expect that all the hostages are released unharmed . . . the following is the result. 25

(He goes through the list:)

The woman T, of Sri Lankan origin. A religious charity in Savonlinna, Finland, has agreed to sponsor. So she is admitted there. RH—Azerbaijan—is deemed to be at risk of persecution living in territory presently Armenian. So he is OK for Germany. The Bosnian family N, C and baby P 30 are granted emergency asylum on the grounds of the baby and their residence in Bosnia.

*(*GRIGORI *snorts.)*

MNN, originally of Latvia, has been subject to political discrimination—persecution—and has been invited by an American foundation to make a new life in Pittsburg, 35 Pennsylvania. And finally YA, former Kuwait resident, is stateless clearly. And is offered refuge under regulation for emergency humanitarian admission in Holland, Canada or Denmark. So, some choice there.

(He has finished, and folds the paper.)

YASMIN: That's it?   40
KAROLYI: That's it.
GRIGORI: And what about about the rest of us?
KAROLYI: I must guess your applications—your demands— were unsuccessful.
GRIGORI: This fantasy. These not Bosnian. They Polish, if any- 45 thing at all.
KAROLYI: I'm so sorry.
GRIGORI: Look, I explain. I am ethnic German. I say in application. I explain.
KAROLYI: I am just a messenger.   50
YASMIN: *(to* ANTONIO*)* This is transparent.
ANTONIO: But you are OK.
ABDUL: *(Turkish)* Meni sokhajakhlar? [Well? Am I to be admitted?]
RAIF: *(to* ABDUL, *in Azeri)* Chokh üzüldüm, meni sokhtular, 55 seni degil. [I am so sorry. They let me in, but not you.]
ABDUL: *(Turkish)* Ne? [What?]
GRIGORI: You let in gypsies, but not hard worker.
ABDUL: *(Turkish, to* RAIF*)* Roosee oldugun ichin sokhtular seni. [They let you in, because you are Russian!] 60
RAIF: *(Azeri)* Men Roosee deyilim. [I am not Russian.]
GRIGORI: You admit Muslims but not Christian people.
KAROLYI: 'I' am doing nothing.
GRIGORI: You admit this woman who lives forty years in Latvia— 65
MARINA: *(Russian)* Shto on gavareet? [What is he saying?]

GRIGORI: —and in all that time does not learn word for bread.

MARINA: (*Russian*) Minya razreshen v'yezd? [Have I been admitted?]

KAROLYI: I am most sorry, but—

GRIGORI: You let in Muslim, let in gypsy—

LEO: What is the situation with the Kurd?

(*Slight pause.*)

MARINA: (*Russian, to* ANTONIO) Pazhalsta, minya poostili? [Please, am I admitted?]

LEO: Please.

ANTONIO: (*Russian, bleakly*) Da, poostili. Pazdravlyayoo. [Yes, you are admitted. Congratulations.]

LEO: What please is the position of this woman here?

(*Pause.*)

KAROLYI: I'm sorry?

(LEO *points to* FATIMA, *who is still with* GABRIELLA. *Pause.*)

LEO: By what conceivable criteria of selection. Can this woman be excluded from the list of people threatened by political and religious persecution?

KAROLYI: Oh, Professor Katz. In this part of Europe, it is a little arbitrary sometimes, whether one is cast as victim or accomplice. An invader or a liberator. The object of unjust persecution or a voluntary exile.

GRIGORI: And so what happens to the rest of us? Those not 'selected'?

KAROLYI: There is a bus in half an hour.

AMIRA: To take us where?

KAROLYI: Well, naturally, the border.

ANTONIO: Which? Which border?

KAROLYI: The one you crossed two days ago. As you must surely have expected.

ABDUL: (*Turkish*) Ne diyor? [What does he say?] (*Russian*) Shto on gavarit? [What does he say?]

RAIF: Shto praiskhodit? [What's going on?]

FATIMA: (*Turkish*) Ne oluyor? Ne diyorlar? [What's happening? What are they saying?]

ABDUL: (*Turkish*) Bizi laade etmekh istiyorlar gaaliba. [They want to send us back.]

MARINA: (*Russian*) Shto praiskhodit? [What is going on?]

ANTONIO: (*Russian*) On gavarit shto nas viyshloot abratna. [He says that we will be deported back.]

KAROLYI: It is as you must acknowledge generous. There are no arrests, no charges. If you go.

(AMIRA *stands, buttons her coat, picks up her cello and walks to the door. She sits.* KAROLYI *looks at his list.*)

AMIRA: AR. From Sarajevo. But now not so chic.

KAROLYI: So now everybody must I think decide.

(ANTONIO *assembles* ABDUL *and* GRIGORI *to confer.*)

ANTONIO: (*Russian*) Nam biy nado ab etom pagavarit. [Now we must talk about this.]

GRIGORI: (*Russian*) Eta zhe prosta byezooiye. [This is crazy.]

(YASMIN *wants to join but is excluded.* RAIF *is clearly unwelcome too. In the background,* FATIMA *and* ABDUL *confer.*)

LEO: So what's the game?

KAROLYI: There is no game.

OLIVER: And all of this is true?

(*The phone rings.* YASMIN *beats* ANTONIO *to answer it.*)

YASMIN: Hallo? Hallo.

(*Slight pause.*)

No it is not. Do you speak English?

(ANTONIO *has his hand out for the phone.* YASMIN, *impatient:*)

Hold on. Hold on.

(*She has no choice but to hand the phone to* ANTONIO. *To cover:*)

It seems the English-speaking man is only days.

ANTONIO: (*Russian*) Viy pa-rooski gavaritye? [Do you speak Russian?]

(*Slight pause.*)

Da, on zdyes, ya payidoo za nim. [Yes, he is here. I'll get him for you.]

(*To* KAROLYI:)

It's for you.

(KAROLYI *comes to the phone. As he takes it,* ANTONIO *looks coldly at* YASMIN.)

KAROLYI: (*down the phone, speaking in the language of our country*) Obazhda se Karolyi. Obsuzhdat predlozhenieto. [It's Karolyi. They are considering the offer.]

LEO: What's he saying?

GABRIELLA: (*shrugs*) That they considering.

KAROLYI: Da, da. Kakvo? Kolko? [Yes, yes. What? How many?]

(*Slight pause.*)

Da, shte im kazha. Da. [Yes, I'll tell them. Yes.]

(*Still holding the phone, he turns to* YASMIN.)

YASMIN: Well?

KAROLYI: I'm afraid there is a complication.

YASMIN: Oh, I see.

KAROLYI: It is not in my hands. Nor those of the authorities.

YASMIN: No, no. Of course not.

ANTONIO: Please, go on.

KAROLYI: It is that apparently a crowd—well, more a mob, is forming—

GRIGORI: A mob?

KAROLYI: —of people, you know, close-cropped—skinheads. And they are demanding that the police will storm the building. Or else they threaten they'll do it themselves.

(*He hears words from the phone and lifts it to his ear. He listens, then, in our country's language:*)

145   Razbira se. [Of course.]

(*To* YASMIN:)

And the police are fearful that unless we can evacuate the
building soon—
ANTONIO: How many people?
KAROLYI: They say at least a hundred.
150 YASMIN: Armed?
KAROLYI: (*down phone*) Pitat dali sa vu'oruzheni. [They are
asking, are they armed?]

(*Slight pause.*)

Giob'yo? Kakvi giob'yo? [Rocks? What sort of rocks?]

(*To the* REFUGEES:)

As yet they do not seem, the people who are there, to have
155   firearms. Yet. Just sticks and rocks. So the police will bring
the bus up to the church in a quarter of an hour.
OLIVER: Did you say 'rocks'?
KAROLYI: Yes, only rocks. So far.

(*Now* TUNU *gathers her possessions and moves to the exit, followed
by* MARINA. GRIGORI *looks fearfully to* ANTONIO.)

YASMIN: Give me that phone.

(*She snatches the telephone from* KAROLYI. *Down phone:*)

160   Now we know why fascists were so welcome in your
country!

(*She slams the phone down.*)

KAROLYI: That will not I think be very helpful.
RAIF: (*Azeri*) Ne yapıyorsun? [What are you doing?] (*English*)
What this you do?
165 YASMIN: Oh, come on. Do you believe this for a moment?
They will take you into Germany? This is all bullshit.
KAROLYI: This is not bullshit.
OLIVER: Um, excuse me—
YASMIN: OK, now. No more shit. We demand—now—we are
170   taken, in a bloc . . .
OLIVER: Excuse me . . .

(NICO *picks up his release is threatened.*)

YASMIN: . . . in a single bloc . . . .
OLIVER: Excuse me, what word did you use?
YASMIN: . . . to and *across* the German border . . .
175 KAROLYI: I'm afraid that I say 'bullshit'.
YASMIN: . . . . where we are given all EC work permits . . .
OLIVER: No, I meant, before.
KAROLYI: (*to* YASMIN) Now, please, you surely understand—
YASMIN: And we will take—two hostages with us. As *you* will
180   surely understand.
OLIVER: The word for rock.
YASMIN: And unless we have transport for that purpose here
in a quarter of an hour . . .

(YASMIN *goes and picks up one of the petrol cans.*)

OLIVER: (*to* GABRIELLA) The word he used for rock.

GABRIELLA: (*offhand*) He say 'giob'yo'. It is old word.   185
YASMIN: . . . then we fulfil our threat.

(*She gestures to* ABDUL *to get the other can as she climbs on to the
platform.*)

OLIVER: Old word?
GABRIELLA: Old language word. I tell you. Oliver—
YASMIN: And in Professor Katz's telling phrase we fry this
greatest artfind of the century right off the wall.   190

(*From the platform; defiantly, to* KAROLYI:)

OK? You understand me now?
KAROLYI: But, I'm afraid that this is not correct.

(*Slight pause.*)

YASMIN: You do, you read our statement?
KAROLYI: Yes, of course. But I'm afraid that you are misinformed. The painting is of very little value.   195

(*Slight pause.*)

YASMIN: Sorry?
KAROLYI: It was thought at one time that it was painted in
the early thirteenth century and thus of great value as you
say. But despite all efforts by these most distinguished art
historians, it has not been proved. It is a matter of regret 200
to many of us. But the painting has no real worth. To this
place, this country. Or to you. So now, maybe, you are
ready for the bus?

(*Pause.* YASMIN *turns to* LEO.)

YASMIN: Oh, oh. Professor Katz.
GABRIELLA: Please, Father—   205
YASMIN: Lies. And more lies.

(*To* RAIF *and* ANTONIO, *as she descends the ladder.*)

Hold him!
LEO: Hey—
YASMIN: We can believe no-one.

(*To* GRIGORI:)

YASMIN: You want to get to Germany? You hold him.   210

(GRIGORI *takes* LEO.)

LEO: Hey, what is this.
YASMIN: And then I think at least we are believed. That hav-
ing killed one, we will kill another.
LEO: Jesus Christ—
YASMIN: (*to* ANTONIO) Give me the pistol.   215
KAROLYI: Please, no, this is madness.
RAIF: (*with a step towards* YASMIN, *in Azeri*) Sus, heyejanlanma
. . . [Quiet, don't get excited . . .]
YASMIN: Antonio. give me the gun. Give it to me.

(OLIVER *steps between* ANTONIO *and* YASMIN.)

OLIVER: No, don't.   220
YASMIN: Oh, come now, please. The gun.

OLIVER: For one—because, he's right. It's madness. If anyone is killed. You'll none of you get anywhere.

(ANTONIO *is not moving.*)

For two, yes, sure, he lied. But wouldn't you?
225 KAROLYI: Dr Davenport—
OLIVER: For three—because—it could be—he was right.
ANTONIO: What's right?
OLIVER: The painting. It is—it may well be—your lifeline after all.
230 YASMIN: Oh yes? And why is this?
OLIVER: Because the word for rock in the old language of this country, is 'gobbyo'. As 'lora' is the word for star.
ABDUL: (*Arabic*) eysh yagool. [What is he saying?]
YASMIN: (*Arabic*) yabdoo innoo injann iz-zalami. [I think he's
235 gone berserk.]
OLIVER: Which if you give me just three minutes, I'll explain.

(*Pause.* ANTONIO *lowers his gun.* YASMIN *shrugs.* OLIVER *points up at the painting.*)

OLIVER: For where this painting has ten stars, or 'lora', Giotto's has ten wildly grieving angels. And where this has a boulder, Giotto has a second woman painted from be-
240 hind. In a kind of huddled, sort of, humpy shouldered pose. And 'gobbo' is, in fact. Is as it happens. The Italian for 'hunchback'. As 'dolore' is for 'grief'.

(*Pause.* GRIGORI *leaves* LEO. ABDUL *too moves a little apart.*)

And of course this could be easily explained by someone misdescribing Giotto's fresco to a painter here . . . But for
245 the fact that by the time that Giotto painted what he painted, describing anything in your old language was to put it mildly ill-advised.

(*Slight pause.*)

ANTONIO: Now this most interesting—
YASMIN: (*looks at her watch*) This is shit—
250 OLIVER: No. This is proof that we were right.

(*He is on the ladder up to the painting.*)

You see, the problem is. We have this mindset, still, about the mediaeval period. That everybody knows their places, no-one travels, no-one moves. To each his own walled garden. Whereas actually mediaeval Europe was a chaos of di-
255 aspora. Every frontier teeming, every crossroads thronged. So it is frankly more than possible that a painter could have set off in the early years of the thirteenth century. From what perils we cannot imagine. And coming to this place, and being taken captive, and offering for his release to paint
260 a picture, here, so akin to nature that its figures seem to live and breathe . . .

(AMIRA *stands and moves closer to look at the painting.*)

And employing for that purpose a particularly vital but as yet unknown deep blue. For the simple reason—that he brought it with him.
265 LEO: Sorry?
GABRIELLA: Like taxis.

LEO: Taxis?
OLIVER: Yes. Not going to the east, but coming from. Boldly going where no painter went before.

(GABRIELLA *doesn't understand.*)

GABRIELLA: What you mean, he is—Italian explorer?   270
OLIVER: No I mean, I think he was an Arab.

(*Pause.*)

LEO: (*delicately*) An Arab Figurative Painter? Early thirteenth century?

(*Now* OLIVER *is on the platform in front of the painting.*)

OLIVER: Yes. Absolutely and precisely so. An Arab colourist, who learns his fresco in the monasteries of Serbia or Mace- 275
donia. Who sees the great mosaics of the mighty churches of Constantinople. And who thinks, like any artist, I could do that too. And having thought some more, that he could do it better. But his huge advantage over almost everybody else is not just that he has the classic geometry the Arabs 280
kept alive for the best part of 800 years, nor yet again the optics they hypothesised around the first millennium, but the fact that nobody's explained to him that painters aren't supposed to use them. So he has two eyes, and they tell him things have three dimensions, and he paints the world that 285
way. With all that innocence, that freshness and that rage, we bring to things when we come up against them for the very first—first time.

(GABRIELLA *moves near the bottom of the ladder.*)

GABRIELLA: Because, for him—it is.
OLIVER: Exactly.   290
GABRIELLA: And so they tell him this strange story.
OLIVER: Of a woman who has see her son die on a tree.
LEO: Shortly after he had told her and his followers—
GABRIELLA: That he will die—
OLIVER: But rise again in three days' time.   295
LEO: So for him the story's not about her weight of grief—
GABRIELLA: But actually—
OLIVER: —her want of faith.

(*He's at St John.*)

He's not reaching out to comfort her at all. He's reaching out to warn her. It' an act of admonition.   300

(*To* AMIRA:)

Because he know, and like the man who painted him, believed, if you are taken from the fire, you gain a mighty victory.
LEO: Our present life is but delusion.
GABRIELLA: That we all belong to God and to Him we shall 305
return.
OLIVER: And should you not believe that even more, if your son has promised you there is eternal life, and in three days' time he'll rise again, and prove it?

(*Pause. It sinks in.*)

GABRIELLA: So then it true.
OLIVER: It's true.
GABRIELLA: Well—tallyho.

(*Pause.* AMIRA *is looking up in wonder at the painting.*)

AMIRA: Well. Glory be.
OLIVER: Well glory be indeed.

(*Pause.*)

315   YASMIN: So, then. We need not kill Professor Katz to show
that we mean business.

(LEO *looks bleakly at* YASMIN.)

LEO: Well. Good.
YASMIN: We need only to destroy this painting.

(YASMIN *pushes past* GABRIELLA *and climbs up the ladder.*)

GABRIELLA: No.
320   YASMIN: (*calling behind her, in Arabic*) haat al-banzeen. [Bring
the petrol.]

(*Turning to see no-one move:*)

That is, if anybody wishes to get out of here.

(ABDUL, *shrugging, picks up the second petrol can.*)

OLIVER: Now surely, you can't think of—
YASMIN: Try me.
325   GABRIELLA: But don't you see—it is your painting.

(*The telephone rings.* ABDUL *to the ladder.*)

YASMIN: Aha. The telephone.

(KAROLYI *goes to the telephone.* ABDUL *is nearly at the platform
with his can.*)

YASMIN: (*to* KAROLYI) You can tell them what is happening.
AMIRA: (*Russian, to* ANTONIO) Eto prosta byezoomiye. Da astanavi zhe yeyo. [This is insane, please stop her.]
330   YASMIN: Secure the hostages!
KAROLYI: (*down phone*) Allo? Karolyi.
ABDUL: (*shouts behind him, to* RAIF, *in Turkish*) Rehinlere göz
qulaq ol, onları qachırmayın! [Keep an eye on the
hostages, don't let them escape!] Grigori!

(ABDUL *hands* GRIGORI *the gun.* RAIF *and* ANTONIO, *a little uncertainly, move in on* LEO *and* GABRIELLA.)

LEO: Now this is *really* crazy.
335   KAROLYI: (*our country*) Kato che li igrata zagroobyava. [Things
are getting ugly.]
YASMIN: (*to* ABDUL, *Arabic*) khalleek jaahiz inta wal-banzeen.
[OK, be sure the petrol's ready.]

(*She hurries down the ladder as* ABDUL *prepares to douse the painting with petrol.* GRIGORI *has a weapon.* RAIF *shouts at* MARINA:)

40   RAIF: (*Russian*) Von at dvyeri! Von at dvyeri! [Get away from
the door!]

GABRIELLA: Don't let this happen.
OLIVER: (*to* ABDUL) Please. Please, I beg you—
KAROLYI: (*our country*) Da mislya che sega. [Yes I think now.]
AMIRA: (*to* ANTONIO *in Russian*) Astanavi eto, prashoo vas! 340
[Stop this! Please!]
YASMIN: (*to* KAROLYI) OK. Now, tell them. That they have ex-
actly five—

(ABDUL *is about to douse the painting. There is a sudden explosion.
It is not immediately clear where from. Engines rev, sirens wail.
Smoke billows. Armed* COMMANDOES *in black uniforms and bala-
clavas burst through a gaping hole that has appeared in the painting,
on to the platform. They see* OLIVER *there.*)

FIRST COMMANDO: Terrorist? Terrorist?
OLIVER: Uh—   345

(OLIVER *of course looks like a refugee. The* COMMANDO *shoots him
dead. Neither* ANTONIO, GRIGORI *nor* RAIF *can fire.* YASMIN *grabs*
GRIGORI'S *weapon.*)

YASMIN: (*Arabic*) aacteeni iyyaah. [Give that to me.]

(*The* FIRST COMMANDO *shoots* YASMIN *dead.* ABDUL *dives to the
deck.* RAIF *raises his weapon and the* SECOND COMMANDO *shoots
him dead.* ANTONIO *drops his weapon, but he is shot by the* SEC-
OND COMMANDO. TUNU *makes a run for it, but the* FIRST COM-
MANDO *shoots her. The* SECOND COMMANDO *has* LEO *and*
GABRIELLA *on the floor.*)

SECOND COMMANDO: Tu est terroriste? Tu est terroriste?
LEO: No I'm not a fucking terrorist. I'm a fucking art historian.

(CLEOPATRA *grabs her pram and makes a dash for the door.*)

CLEOPATRA: My infant. Infant, infant, infant! Tallyho!   350

(CLEOPATRA *makes it through the door.*)

SECOND COMMANDO: (*to* GABRIELLA) You terrorist?
LEO: And so is she.
FIRST COMMANDO: Jemand getroffen? [Has anybody scored?]
SECOND COMMANDO: (*shouts back*) Zwei hier! [Two here!]
FIRST COMMANDO: (*shouts*) Nieder halten. Alle fichen nieder! 355
[Everyone down. Everyone fucking keep down!] (*English*)
Keep fucking down!

(*The smoke is clearing; the sirens and the engines beginning to die.*)

SCENE VIII

*A few hours later. On the floor are red plastic flags with attached la-
bels, marking where the dead* REFUGEES (*and* OLIVER) *lay.* LEO
stands with Mikhail CZABA *and Anna* JEDLIKOVA. LEO *has returned from debriefing ostensibly to fetch his files. He holds* AMIRA'S
broken cello in his hands. He's very angry.

LEO: So you were there throughout?
CZABA: You bet. I am Minister for Preservation of our National Monuments. And Mrs Jedlikova is observer from
our Ministry of Law and Order.
LEO: (*looking round, bitterly*) Preservation.   5

JEDLIKOVA: Certainly of law.

(LEO *looks at the little red flags.*)

CZABA: It most sophisticated. First you limit access of world outside. Move everything from field of vision. Don't give phone number so they must always wait for you to call. Change over guy on phone so different languages. Then slowly build up their routine. You order mealtime. Control all aspect of environment. Heat, light. And gradually they are turn to child.
LEO: I'm sorry?
CZABA: All part of softly softly catch your monkey.
LEO: (*waving round at the scene*) Though not—in this case—with *demonstrable* success.

(*Pause.*)

CZABA: Well, no. Agreed.

(*Slight pause.*)

In fact, there big dispute. Between all European counter-terrorist, who say, negotiate, you get through first two days, out of long grass. But also wiseguys from America, who say, if you don't clean up in two day, you send in US cavalry. So they prepare two gameplan. One if Karolyi will succeed. And one if plan go belly up. And unfortunately belly up she go. And so—bouf—Pax Vespucciana.

(LEO *looks to* CZABA.)

JEDLIKOVA: I think it not so much 'unfortunate'. I think there is big risk hostages are killed.
CZABA: Beg pardon. Your friend's joke I think.
LEO: So then you heard it all.

(*Pause.*)

CZABA: Of course.
LEO: They bust the bug.
CZABA: Ah, wonders of your English language.
LEO: *What?*
CZABA: They bust *a* bug. *The* bug was in *the* syringe.
LEO: And presumably, they were supposed to?
CZABA: (*smiling*) Sure. Presumably.
LEO: And you hear everything?
CZABA: (*smiling*) Hey. Talk of fucking Tower of Babel.

(CZABA *realises* LEO *is concerned.*)

Hey, listen up. They say, you will be bound to bond. In fact, it whole idea. No-one hold one word you say against you.

(GABRIELLA *stands in doorway. She has a borrrowed overcoat and* CLEOPATRA'*s pram.*)

GABRIELLA: Well, that I must say great relief.

(LEO, CZABA *and* JEDLIKOVA *look over to* GABRIELLA *who gently pushes the pram over towards them. We see that a swastika has been spray-painted on the side.* EVERYONE *takes this in. Then:*)

GABRIELLA: Voilà.

(*Slight pause.* CZABA *to* LEO:)

CZABA: Look. We are young poor country. Our industry is junkyard and our currency confetti. So, no, we cannot be dumping ground for everybody's rejects.

(*To* GABRIELLA:)

Of course I so choked about your friend. And this. And that. But still. So sorry. No.

(*He goes out. Pause.*)

LEO: Uh, d'you know, if she, if they . . .
GABRIELLA: Have no idea.

(*Slight pause.*)

Well, if she survive. Maybe her father will not sell her baby now.
JEDLIKOVA: Yes. Yes, we hear this. Terrible.
GABRIELLA: You hear?
LEO: They heard it all.

(*Slight pause.*)

GABRIELLA: So they know that painting real.
JEDLIKOVA: I think—by this time—no-one very much is listening.
LEO: Yuh, sure. Shoot first, ask questions later. Ausländer verboten. Welcome to the West.

(*Pause.* JEDLIKOVA *feels she must respond.*)

JEDLIKOVA: Look. I know how it appear. What happen in this country since great turnaround.

(*Slight pause.*)

But you must understand what we are losing during all this century. How communism strip away all culture from our past, and clothe us all instead in uniform. And when we throw it off we think, hey, we have been through all so much, we are new kind of people, we will build new life.

(*Slight pause.*)

But we find that we are not so special. Even those of us who suffer very much. And so yes, we turn from proletcult to Rambo, or pornography. And you know, is maybe best we march to next millennium in silly national costume. When alternative is dress of Arnold Schwarzenegger, or wearing nothing very much at all.

(*Slight pause.*)

It is, apparently, the weakest wall.

(*She goes out.* LEO *and* GABRIELLA *are left together.*)

GABRIELLA: Well. Church. Mosque. Stable. Torture centre. Foodstore. Fortress. Cemetery.

(*Slight pause.*)

Middle Europe theme park? Sure.
LEO: Hey. Gab. I am—so sorry.

(*Slight pause.* GABRIELLA *takes* CLEOPATRA's *notebook from the pram. She opens it and reads.*)

GABRIELLA: (*reads*) Roadblock. Closed-circuit. Permit.
80 LEO: But hey. Hey.
GABRIELLA: Shrapnel. Tarpaulin. Yes?
LEO: You must hang on to one thing.
GABRIELLA: Checkpoint. What?
LEO: That he was right.

(*Pause.* GABRIELLA *looks up to* LEO.)

85   That basically, we are the sum of all the people who've invaded us. We are, involuntarily, each other's guests.

(*Pause.*)

GABRIELLA: Transfer. Exchanges. School.

(LEO *takes the book.*)

LEO: Mercy mission.

(*Pause.*)

GABRIELLA: Ambush.
LEO: Convoy. Baggage handler.   90
GABRIELLA: Backlog.
LEO: Buffer. Buffet.
GABRIELLA: Quota.
LEO: Flight.

(*Slight pause.*)

Chevrolet. Milkshake.   95

(*Slight pause.*)

Diaper. Princess.

(GABRIELLA *isn't going. He turns the pages.*)

Huddled.
GABRIELLA: Yearning?
LEO: Free.

(*And the lights slowly fade.*)
(*End of play.*)

CRITICAL CONTEXTS

FRIEDRICH NIETZSCHE (1844–1900)

from *The Birth of Tragedy* (1872)
TRANSLATED BY WALTER KAUFMANN

*Throughout his career, the German philosopher and poet Friedrich Nietzsche criticized the limitations of modern conceptual and moral categories. This revolutionary subversion of the premises of philosophy forms the core of his most famous works—*The Gay Science *(1882),* Also Spoke Zarathustra *(1883–92), and* Beyond Good and Evil *(1886). In* The Birth of Tragedy *(1872), Nietzsche argues that Greek tragedy arose from the collision between Athenian rationalism—symbolized by Apollo, Socrates, and Euripides—and an earlier, irrational mysticism, symbolized by Dionysus. Although Nietzsche's reading of Greek history has been generally discredited, the essay offers a powerful and influential reading of the tension between the rational and irrational informing Greek drama. Nietzsche was admired by several modern playwrights represented in this volume, including Bernard Shaw, August Strindberg, and Eugene O'Neill.*

Despite its symbolic contours, Nietzsche's representation of tragedy shares in the dialectical imagination that also drives other major theorists of tragic drama, including Aristotle. In what ways are the Appollinian and the Dionysian complicit in one another? What are the aspects of tragic experience that Nietzsche means to capture in these two images? Why do you think the full title of the essay is The Birth of Tragedy from the Spirit of Music?

SECTION 1

We shall have gained much for the science of aesthetics, once we perceive not merely by logical inference, but with the immediate certainty of vision, that the continuous development of art is bound up with the *Apollinian* and *Dionysian* duality—just as procreation depends on the duality of the sexes, involving perpetual strife with only periodically intervening reconciliations. The terms Dionysian and Apollinian we borrow from the Greeks, who disclose to the discerning mind the profound mysteries of their view of art, not, to be sure, in concepts, but in the intensely clear figures of their gods. Through Apollo and Dionysus, the two art deities of the Greeks, we come to recognize that in the Greek world there existed a tremendous opposition, in origin and aims, between the Apollinian art of sculpture, and the nonimagistic, Dionysian art of music. These two different tendencies run parallel to each other, for the most part openly at variance; and they continually incite each other to new and more powerful births, which perpetuate an antagonism, only superficially reconciled by the common term "art"; till eventually, by a metaphysical miracle of the Hellenic "will," they appear coupled with each other and through this coupling ultimately generate an equally Dionysian and Apollinian form of art—Attic tragedy.

In order to grasp these two tendencies, let us first conceive of them as the separate art worlds of *dreams* and *intoxication*. These physiological phenomena present a contrast analogous to that existing between the Apollinian and the Dionysian. It was in dreams, says Lucretius, that the glorious divine figures first appeared to the souls of men; in dreams the great shaper beheld the splendid bodies of superhuman beings; and the Hellenic poet, if questioned about the mysteries of poetic inspiration, would likewise have suggested dreams and he might have given an explanation like that of Hans Sachs in the *Meistersinger:*

> The poet's task is this, my friend,
> to read his dreams and comprehend.
> The truest human fancy seems
> to be revealed to us in dreams:
> all poems and versification
> are but true dreams' interpretation.

The beautiful illusion of the dream worlds, in the creation of which every man is truly an artist, is the prerequisite of all plastic art, and, as we shall see, of an important part of poetry also. In our dreams we delight in the immediate understanding of figures; all forms speak to us; there is nothing unimportant or superfluous. But even when this dream reality is most intense, we still have, glimmering through it, the sensation that it is *mere appearance:* at least this is my experience, and for its frequency—indeed, normality—I could adduce many proofs, including the sayings of the poets.

Philosophical men even have a presentiment that the reality in which we live and have our being is also mere appearance, and that another, quite different reality lies beneath it. Schopenhauer actually indicates as the criterion of philosophical ability the occasional ability to view men and things as mere phantoms or dream images. Thus the aesthetically sensitive man stands in the same relation to the reality of dreams as the philosopher does to the reality of existence; he is a close and willing observer, for these images afford him an interpretation of life, and by reflecting on these processes he trains himself for life.

It is not only the agreeable and friendly images that he experiences as something universally intelligible: the serious, the troubled, the sad, the gloomy, the sudden restraints, the tricks of accident, anxious expectations, in short, the whole divine comedy of life, including the inferno, also pass before him, not like mere shadows on a wall—for he lives and suffers with these scenes—and yet not without that fleeting sensation of illusion. And perhaps many will, like myself, recall how amid the dangers and terrors of dreams they have occasionally said to themselves in self-encouragement, and not without success: "It is a dream! I will dream on!" I have likewise heard of people who were able to continue one and the same dream for three and even more successive nights—facts which indicate clearly how our innermost being, our common ground, experiences dreams with profound delight and a joyous necessity.

This joyous necessity of the dream experience has been embodied by the Greeks in their Apollo: Apollo, the god of all plastic energies, is at the same time the soothsaying god. He, who (as the etymology of the name indicates) is the "shining one," the deity of light, is also ruler over the beautiful illusion of the inner world of fantasy. The higher truth, the perfection of these states in contrast to the incompletely intelligible everyday world, this deep consciousness of nature, healing and helping in sleep and dreams, is at the same time the symbolical analogue of the soothsaying faculty and of the arts generally, which make life possible and worth living. But we must also include in our image of Apollo that delicate boundary which the dream image must not overstep lest it have a pathological effect (in which case mere appearance would deceive us as if it were crude reality). We must keep in mind that measured restraint, that freedom from the wilder emotions, that calm of the sculptor god. His eye must be "sunlike," as befits his origin; even when it is angry and distempered it is still hallowed by beautiful illusion. And so, in one sense, we might apply to Apollo the words of Schopenhauer when he speaks of the man wrapped in the veil of *māyā* [illusion]: "Just as in a stormy sea that, unbounded in all directions, raises and drops mountainous waves, howling, a sailor sits in a boat and trusts in his frail bark: so in the midst of a world of torments the individual human being sits quietly, supported by and trusting in the *principium individuationis*." In fact, we might say of Apollo that in him the unshaken faith in this *principium* and the calm repose of the man wrapped up in it receive their most sublime expression; and we might call Apollo himself the glorious divine image of

the *principium individuationis*, through whose gestures and eyes all the joy and wisdom of "illusion," together with its beauty, speak to us.

In the same work Schopenhauer has depicted for us the tremendous terror which seizes man when he is suddenly dumbfounded by the cognitive form of phenomena because the principle of sufficient reason, in some one of its manifestations, seems to suffer an exception. If we add to this terror the blissful ecstasy that wells from the innermost depths of man, indeed of nature, at this collapse of the *principium individuationis*, we steal a glimpse into the nature of the *Dionysian*, which is brought home to us most intimately by the analogy of intoxication.

Either under the influence of the narcotic draught, of which the songs of all primitive men and peoples speak, or with the potent coming of spring that penetrates all nature with joy, these Dionysian emotions awake, and as they grow in intensity everything subjective vanishes into complete self-forgetfulness. In the German Middle Ages, too, singing and dancing crowds, ever increasing in number, whirled themselves from place to place under this same Dionysian impulse. In these dancers of St. John and St. Vitus, we rediscover the Bacchic choruses of the Greeks, with their prehistory in Asia Minor, as far back as Babylon and the orgiastic Sacaea. There are some who, from obtuseness or lack of experience, turn away from such phenomena as from "folk-diseases," with contempt or pity born of the consciousness of their own "healthy-mindedness." But of course such poor wretches have no idea how corpselike and ghostly their so-called "healthy-mindedness" looks when the glowing life of the Dionysian revelers roars past them.

Under the charm of the Dionysian not only is the union between man and man reaffirmed, but nature which has become alienated, hostile, or subjugated, celebrates once more her reconciliation with her lost son, man. Freely, earth proffers her gifts, and peacefully the beasts of prey of the rocks and desert approach. The chariot of Dionysus is covered with flowers and garlands; panthers and tigers walk under its yoke. Transform Beethoven's "Hymn to Joy" into a painting; let your imagination conceive the multitudes bowing to the dust, awestruck—then you will approach the Dionysian. Now the slave is a free man; now all the rigid, hostile barriers that necessity, caprice, or "impudent convention" have fixed between man and man are broken. Now, the gospel of universal harmony, each one feels himself not only united, reconciled, and fused with his neighbor, but as one with him, as if the veil of *māyā* had been torn aside and were now merely fluttering in tatters before the mysterious primordial unity.

In song and in dance man expresses himself as a member of a higher community; he has forgotten how to walk and speak and is on the way toward flying into the air, dancing. His very gestures express enchantment. Just as the animals now talk, and the earth yields milk and honey, supernatural sounds emanate from him, too: he feels himself a god, he himself now walks about enchanted, in ecstasy, like the gods he saw walking in his dreams. He is no longer an artist, he has become a work of art: in these paroxysms of intoxication the artistic power of all nature reveals itself to the highest gratification of the primordial unity. The noblest clay, the most costly marble, man, is here kneaded and cut, and to the sound of the chisel stokes of the Dionysian world-artist rings out the cry of the Eleusinian mysteries: "Do you prostrate yourselves, millions? Do you sense your Maker, world?" . . .

SECTION 10

The tradition is undisputed that Greek tragedy in its earliest form had for its sole theme the sufferings of Dionysus and that for a long time the only stage hero was Dionysus himself. But it may be claimed with equal confidence that until Euripides, Dionysus never ceased to be the tragic hero; that all the celebrated figures of the Greek stage—Prometheus. Oedipus, etc.—are mere masks of this original hero, Dionysus. That behind all these masks there is a deity, that is one essential reason for the typical "ideality" of these famous figures which has caused so much astonishment. Somebody, I do not know who, has claimed that all individuals, taken as individuals, are comic and hence untragic—from which it would follow that the Greeks simply *could* not suffer individuals on the tragic stage. In fact, this is what they seem to have felt; and the Platonic distinction and evaluation of the "idea" and the "idol," the mere image, is very deeply rooted in the Hellenic character.

Using Plato's terms we should have to speak of the tragic figures of the Hellenic stage somewhat as follows: the one truly real Dionysus appears in a variety of forms, in the mask of a fighting hero, and entangled, as it were, in the net of the individual will. The god who appears talks and acts so as to resemble an erring, striving, suffering individual. That he *appears* at all with such epic precision and clarity is the work of the dream-interpreter, Apollo, who through this symbolic appearance interprets to the chorus its Dionysian state. In truth, however, the hero is the suffering Dionysus of the Mysteries, the god experiencing in himself the agonies of individuation, of whom wonderful myths tell that as a boy he was torn to pieces by the Titans and now is worshiped in this state as Zagreus. Thus it is intimated that this dismemberment, the properly Dionysian *suffering,* is like a transformation into air, water, earth, and fire, that we are therefore to regard the state of individuation as the origin and primal cause of all suffering, as something objectionable in itself. From the

smile of this Dionysus sprang the Olympian gods, from his tears sprang man. In this existence as a dismembered god, Dionysus possesses the dual nature of a cruel, barbarized demon and a mild, gentle ruler. But the hope of the epopts [initiates] looked toward a rebirth of Dionysus, which we must now dimly conceive as the end of individuation. It was for this coming third Dionysus that the epopts' roaring hymns of joy resounded. And it is this hope alone that casts a gleam of joy upon the features of a world torn asunder and shattered into individuals; this is symbolized in the myth of Demeter, sunk in eternal sorrow, who *rejoices* again for the first time when told that she may *once more* give birth to Dionysus. This view of things already provides us with all the elements of a profound and pessimistic view of the world, together with the *mystery doctrine of tragedy:* the fundamental knowledge of the oneness of everything existent, the conception of individuation as the primal cause of evil, and of art as the joyous hope that the spell of individuation may be broken in augury of a restored oneness.

We have already suggested that the Homeric epos is the poem of Olympian culture, in which this culture has sung its own song of victory over the terrors of the war of the Titans. Under the predominating influence of tragic poetry, these Homeric myths are now born anew; and this metempsychosis reveals that in the meantime the Olympian culture also has been conquered by a still more profound view of the world. The defiant Titan Prometheus has announced to his Olympian tormentor that some day the greatest danger will menace his rule, unless Zeus should enter into an alliance with him in time. In Aeschylus we recognize how the terrified Zeus, fearful of his end, allies himself with the Titan. Thus the former age of the Titans is once more recovered from Tartarus and brought to the light.

The philosophy of wild and naked nature beholds with the frank, undissembling gaze of truth the myths of the Homeric world as they dance past: they turn pale, they tremble under the piercing glance of this goddess—till the powerful fist of the Dionysian artist forces them into the service of the new deity. Dionysian truth takes over the entire domain of myth as the symbolism of *its* knowledge which it makes known partly in the public cult of tragedy and partly in the secret celebrations of dramatic mysteries, but always in the old mythical garb.

What power was it that freed Prometheus from his vultures and transformed the myth into a vehicle of Dionysian wisdom? It is the Heraclean power of music: having reached its highest manifestation in tragedy, it can invest myths with a new and most profound significance. This we have already characterized as the most powerful function of music. For it is the fate of every myth to creep by degrees into the narrow limits of some alleged historical reality, and to be treated by some later generation as a unique fact with historical claims: and the Greeks were already fairly on the way toward re-stamping the whole of their mythical juvenile dream saga-ciously and arbitrarily into a historico-pragmatical *juvenile history*. For this is the way in which religions are wont to die out: under the stern, intelligent eyes of an orthodox dogma-tism, the mythical premises of a religion are systematized as a sum total of historical events; one begins apprehensively to defend the credibility of the myths, while at the same time one opposes any continuation of their natural vitality and growth; the feeling for myth perishes, and its place is taken by the claim of religion to historical foundations. This dying myth was now seized by the new-born genius of Dionysian music; and in these hands it flourished once more with colors such as it had never yet displayed, with a fragrance that awak-ened a longing anticipation of a metaphysical world. After this final effulgence it collapses, its leaves wither, and soon the mocking Lucians of antiquity catch at the discolored and faded flowers carried away by the four winds. Through tragedy the myth attains its most profound content, its most expres-sive form; it rises once more like a wounded hero, and its whole excess of strength, together with the philosophic calm of the dying, burns in its eyes with a last powerful gleam.

What did you want, sacrilegious Euripides, when you sought to compel this dying myth to serve you once more? It died under your violent hands—and then you needed a copied, masked myth that, like the ape of Heracles, merely knew how to deck itself out in the ancient pomp. And just as the myth died on you, the genius of music died on you, too. Though with greedy hands you plundered all the gardens of music, you still managed only copied, masked music. And be-cause you had abandoned Dionysus, Apollo abandoned you: rouse all the passions from their resting places and conjure them into your circle, sharpen and whet a sophistical dialec-tic for the speeches of your heroes—your heroes, too, have only copied, masked passions and speak only copied, masked speeches. . . .

ÉMILE ZOLA (1840–1902)

from *Naturalism in the Theatre* (1878)
TRANSLATED BY ALBERT BERMEL

An influential novelist, playwright, and literary theorist, Zola became the spokesman for naturalism in the theater in a series of articles he wrote in the 1870s, collected as Naturalism in the Theatre *in 1878. In these essays, Zola urged the theater to adopt an attitude of scientific objectivity, an attitude reflected in the development of a new dramatic style. The naturalistic theater asserted such objectivity through its choice of subject matter (middle-class life), its treatment of characters (driven by "physiological" motives, not by "metaphysical" passions), its use of a prosaic, antiliterary language, and by the importance attached to the material environment. Zola's energy in summoning a new form of theatrical representation is evident here: what will be the signs of that new theatre onstage? What is the value that Zola ascribes to life-like representation, and how will it become visible onstage? How will this new theater be distinguished from the classical and romantic past?*

It seems impossible that the movement of inquiry and analy-sis, which is precisely the movement of the nineteenth cen-tury, can have revolutionized all the sciences and arts and left dramatic art to one side, as if isolated. The natural sci-ences date from the end of the last century; chemistry and physics are less than a hundred years old; history and criti-cism have been renovated, virtually re-created since the Rev-olution; an entire world has arisen; it has sent us back to the study of documents, to experience, made us realize that to start afresh we must first take things back to the beginning, become familiar with man and nature, verify what is. Thence-forward, the great naturalistic school, which has spread se-cretly, irrevocably, often making its way in darkness but always advancing, can finally come out triumphantly into the light of day. To trace the history of this movement, with the misunderstandings that might have impeded it and the mul-tiple causes that have thrust it forward or slowed it down, would be to trace the history of the century itself. An irre-sistible current carries our society towards the study of real-ity. In the novel Balzac has been the bold and mighty innovator who has replaced the observation of the scholar with the imagination of the poet. But in the theatre the evo-lution seems slower. No eminent writer has yet formulated the new idea with any clarity.

I certainly do not say that some excellent works have not been produced, with characters in them who are ingeniously examined and bold truths taken right on to the stage. Let me, for instance, cite certain plays by M. Dumas *fils*, whose talent I scarcely admire, and M. Émile Augier, the most hu-mane and powerful of all. Still, they are midgets beside

Balzac; they lack the genius to lay down the formula. It must be said that one can never tell quite when a movement is getting under way; generally its source is remote and lost in the earlier movement from which it emerged. In a manner of speaking, the naturalistic current has always existed. It brings with it nothing absolutely novel. But it has finally flowed into a period favourable to it; it is succeeding and expanding because the human mind has attained the necessary maturity. I do not, therefore, deny the past; I affirm the present. The strength of naturalism is precisely that it has deep roots in our national literature which contains plenty of wisdom. It comes from the very entrails of humanity; it is that much the stronger because it has taken longer to grow and is found in a greater number of our masterpieces.

Certain things have come to pass and I point them out. Can we believe that *L'Ami Fritz* would have been applauded at the Comédie-Française twenty years ago? Definitely not! This play, in which people eat all the time and the lover talks in such homely language, would have disgusted both the classicists and the romantics. To explain its success we must concede that as the years have gone by a secret fermentation has been at work. Lifelike paintings, which used to repel the public, today attract them. The majority has been won over and the stage is open to every experiment. This is the only conclusion to draw.

So that is where we stand. To explain my point better—am not afraid of repeating myself—I will sum up what I have said. Looking closely at the history of our dramatic literature, one can detect several clearly separated periods. First, there was the infancy of the art, farces and the mystery plays of the Middle Ages, the reciting of simple dialogues which developed as part of a naïve convention, with primitive staging and sets. Gradually, the plays became more complex but in a crude fashion. When Corneille appeared he was acclaimed most of all for his status as an innovator, for refining the dramatic formula of the time, and for hallowing it by means of his genius. It would be very interesting to study the pertinent documents and discover how our classical formula came to be created. It corresponded to the social spirit of the period. Nothing is solid that is not built on necessity. Tragedy reigned for two centuries because it satisfied the exact requirements of those centuries. Geniuses of differing temperaments had buttressed it with their masterpieces. And it continued to impose itself long afterwards, even when second-rate talents were producing inferior work. It acquired a momentum. It persisted also as the literary expression of that society, and nothing would have overthrown it if the society, had not itself disappeared. After the Revolution, after that profound disturbance that was meant to transform everything and give birth to a new world, tragedy struggled

to stay alive for a few more years. Then the formula cracked and romanticism broke through. A new formula asserted itself. We must look back at the first half of the century to understand the meaning of this cry for liberty. The young society was in the tremor of its infancy. The excited, bewildered, violently unleashed people were still racked by a dangerous fever; and in the first flush of their new liberty they yearned for prodigious adventures and superhuman love affairs. They gaped at the stars; some committed suicide, a very curious reaction to the social enfranchisement which had just been declared at the cost of so much blood. Turning specifically to dramatic literature, I maintain that romanticism in the theatre was an uncomplicated revolt, the invasion by a victorious group who took over the stage violently with drums beating and flags flying. In these early moments the combatants dreamed of making their imprint with a new form; to one rhetoric they opposed another: the Middle Ages to Antiquity, the exalting of passion to the exalting of duty. And that was all, for only the scenic conventions were altered. The characters remained marionettes in new clothing. Only the exterior aspect and the language were modified. But for the period that was enough. Romanticism had taken possession of the theatre in the name of literary freedom and it carried out its revolutionary task with incomparable bravura. But who does not see today that its role could extend no farther than that? Does romanticism have anything whatever to say about our present society? Does it meet one of our requirements? Obviously not. It is as outmoded as a jargon we no longer follow. It confidently expected to replace classical literature which had lasted for two centuries because it was based on social conditions. But romanticism was based on nothing but the fantasy of a few poets or, if you will, on the passing malady of minds overwhelmed by historical events; it was bound to disappear with the malady. It provided the occasion for a magnificent flowering of lyricism; that will be its eternal glory. Today, however, with the evolution accomplished, it is plain that romanticism was no more than the necessary link between classicism and naturalism. The struggle is over; now we must found a secure state. Naturalism flows out of classical art, just as our present society has arisen from the wreckage of the old society. Naturalism alone corresponds to our social needs; it alone has deep roots in the spirit of our times; and it alone can provide a living, durable formula for our art, because this formula will express the nature of our contemporary intelligence. There may be fashions and passing fantasies that exist outside naturalism but they will not survive for long. I say again, naturalism is the expression of our century and it will not die until a new upheaval transforms our democratic world.

Only one thing is needed now: men of genius who can fix the naturalistic formula. Balzac has done it for the novel and the novel is established. When will our Corneilles, Molières and Racines appear to establish our new theatre? We must hope and wait.

• • •

The period when romantic drama ruled now seems distant. In Paris five or six of its playhouses prospered. The demolition of the old theatres along the Boulevard du Temple was a catastrophe of the first order. The theatres became separated from one another, the public changed, different fashions arose. But the discredit into which the drama has fallen proceeds mostly from the exhaustion of the genre—ridiculous, boring plays have gradually taken over from the potent works of 1830.

To this enfeeblement we must add the absolute lack of new actors who understand and can interpret these kinds of plays, for every dramatic formula that vanishes carries away its interpreters with it. Today the drama, hunted from stage to stage, has only two houses that really belong to it, the Ambigu and the Théâtre-Historique. Even at the Saint-Martin the drama is lucky to win a brief showing for itself, between one great spectacle and the next.

An occasional success may renew its courage. But its decline is inevitable; romantic drama is sliding into oblivion, and if it seems sometimes to check its descent, it does so only to roll even lower afterwards. Naturally, there are loud complaints. The tail-end romanticists are desperately unhappy. They swear that except in the drama—meaning their kind of drama—there is no salvation for dramatic literature. I believe, on the contrary, that we must find a new formula that will transform the drama, just as the writers in the first half of the century transformed tragedy. That is the essence of the matter. Today the battle is between romantic drama and naturalistic drama. By romantic drama I mean every play that mocks truthfulness in its incidents and characterization, that struts about in its puppet-box, stuffed to the belly with noises that flounder, for some idealistic reason or other, in pastiches of Shakespeare and Hugo. Every period has its formula; ours is certainly not that of 1830. We are an age of method, of experimental science; our primary need is for precise analysis. We hardly understand the liberty we have won if we use it only to imprison ourselves in a new tradition. The way is open: we can now return to man and nature.

Finally, there have been great efforts to revive the historical drama. Nothing could be better. A critic cannot roundly condemn the choice of historical subjects, even if his own preferences are entirely for subjects that are modern. It is simply that I am full of distrust. The manager one gives this sort of play to frightens me in advance. It is a question of how history is treated, what unusual characters are presented bearing the names of kings, great captains or great artists, and what awful sauce they are served up in to make the history palatable. As soon as the authors of these concoctions move into the past they think everything is permitted: improbabilities, cardboard dolls, monumental idiocies, the hysterical scribblings that falsely represent local colour. And what strange dialogue—François I talking like a haberdasher straight out of the Rue Saint-Denis, Richelieu using the words of a criminal from the Boulevard du Crime, Charlotte Corday with the weeping sentimentalities of a factory girl.

What astounds me is that our playwrights do not seem to suspect for a moment that the historical genre is unavoidably the least rewarding, the one that calls most strongly for research, integrity, a consummate gift of intuition, a talent for reconstruction. I am all for historical drama when it is in the hands of poets of genius or men of exceptional knowledge who are capable of making the public see an epoch come alive with its special quality, its manners, its civilization. In that case we have a work of prophecy or of profoundly interesting criticism.

But unfortunately I know what it is these partisans of historical drama want to revive: the swaggering and swordplay, the big spectacle with big words, the play of lies that shows off in front of the crowd, the gross exhibition that saddens honest minds. Hence my distrust. I think that all this antiquated business is better left in our museum of dramatic history under a pious layer of dust.

There are, undeniably, great obstacles to original experiments: we run up against the hypocrisies of criticism and the long education in idiocies that has been foisted on the public. This public, which titters at every childishness in melodramas, nevertheless lets itself be carried away by outbursts of fine sentiment. But the public is changing. Shakespeare's public and Molière's are no longer ours. We must reckon with shifts in outlook, with the need for reality which is everywhere getting more insistent. The last few romantics vainly repeat that the public wants this and the public wants that; the day is coming when the public will want the truth.

• • •

The old formulas, classical and romantic, were based on the rearrangement and systematic amputation of the truth. They determined on principle that the truth is not good enough; they tried to draw out of it an essence, a 'poetry', on the pretext that nature must be expurgated and magnified. Up to the present the different literary schools disputed only over the question of the best way to disguise the truth so that it might not look too brazen to the public. The classicists adopted the toga; the romantics fought a revolution to impose the coat of mail and the doublet. Essentially the change of dress made little difference; the counterfeiting of nature went on. But today the naturalistic thinkers are telling us that the truth does not need clothing; it can walk naked. That, I repeat, is the quarrel.

Writers with any sense understand perfectly that tragedy and romantic drama are dead. The majority, though, are badly troubled when they turn their minds to the as-yet-unclear formula of tomorrow. Does the truth seriously ask them to give up the grandeur, the poetry, the traditional epic effects that their ambition tells them to put into their plays? Does naturalism demand that they shrink their horizons and risk not one flight into fantasy?

I will try to reply. But first we must determine the methods used by the idealists to lift their works into poetry. They begin by placing their chosen subject in a distant time. That provides them with costumes and makes the framework of the story vague enough to give them full scope for lying. Next, they generalize instead of particularizing; their characters are no longer living people but sentiments, arguments, passions that have been induced by reasoning. This false framework calls for heroes of marble or cardboard. A man of flesh and bone with his own originality would jar in such a legendary setting. Moreover, when we see the characters in romantic drama or tragedy walking about they are stiffened into an attitude, one representing duty, another patriotism, a third superstition, a fourth maternal love; thus, all the abstract ideas file by. Never the thorough analysis of an organism, never a character whose muscles and brain function as in nature.

These, then, are the mannerisms that writers with epic inclinations do not want to give up. For them poetry resides in the past and in abstraction, in the idealizing of facts and characters. As soon as one confronts them with daily life, with the people who fill our streets, they blink, they stammer, they are afraid; they no longer see clearly; they find everything ugly and not good enough for art. According to them, a subject must enter the lies of legend, men must harden and turn to stone like statues before the artist can accept them and make them fit the disguises he has prepared.

Now, it is at this point that the naturalistic movement comes along and says squarely that poetry is everywhere, in everything, even more in the present and the real than in the past and the abstract. Each event at each moment has its poetic, superb aspect. We brush up against heroes who are great and powerful in different respects from the puppets of the epic-makers. Not one playwright in this century has brought to life figures as lofty as Baron Hulot, Old Grandet, César Birotteau, and all the other characters of Balzac, who are so individual and so alive. Beside these real, giant creations Greek and Roman heroes quake; the heroes of the Middle Ages fall flat on their faces like lead soldiers.

With the superior works being produced in these times by the naturalistic school—works of high endeavour, pulsing with life—it is ridiculous and false to park our poetry in some antiquated temple and bury it in cobwebs. Poetry flows at its full force through everything that exists; the truer to life, the greater it becomes. And I mean to give the word poetry its widest definition, not to pin it down exclusively to the cadence of two rhymes, nor to burn it in a narrow coterie of dreamers, but to restore its real human significance which concerns the expansion and encouragement of every kind of truth.

Take our present environment, then, and try to make men live in it: you will write great works. It will undoubtedly call for some effort; it means sifting out of the confusion of life the simple formula of naturalism. Therein lies the difficulty: to do great things with the subjects and characters that our eyes, accustomed to the spectacle of the daily round, have come to see as small. I am aware that it is more convenient to present a marionette to the public and name it Charlemagne and puff it up with such tirades that the public believes it is watching a colossus; it is more convenient than taking a bourgeois of our time, a grotesque, unsightly man, and drawing sublime poetry out of him, making him, for example, Père Goriot, the father who gives his guts for his daughters, a figure so gigantic with truth and love that no other literature can offer his equal.

Nothing is as easy as persuading the managers with known formulas; and heroes in the classical or romantic taste cost so little labour that they are manufactured by the dozen, and have become standardized articles that clutter up our literature. But it takes hard work to create a real hero, intelligently analysed, alive and performing. That is probably why naturalism terrifies those authors who are used to fishing up great men from the troubled waters of history. They would have to burrow too deeply into humanity, learn about life, go straight for the greatness of reality and make it function with all their power. And let nobody gainsay this true poetry of humanity; it has been sifted out in the novel and can be in the theatre; only the method of adaptation remains to be found.

I am troubled by a comparison; it has been haunting me and I will now free myself of it. For two long months a play called *Les Danicheff* has been running at the Odéon. It takes place in Russia. It has been very successful here, but is apparently so dishonest, so packed with gross improbabilities, that the author, a Russian, has not even dared to show it in his country. What can you think of this work which is applauded in Paris and would be booed in St Petersburg? Well, imagine for a moment that the Romans could come back to life and see a performance of *Rome vaincue*. Can you hear their roars of laughter? Do you think the play would complete one performance? It would strike them as a parody; it would sink under the weight of mockery. And is there one historical play that could be performed before the society it claims to portray? A strange theatre, this, which is plausible only among foreigners, is based on the disappearance of the generations it deals with, and is made up of so much misinformation that it is good only for the ignorant!

The future is with naturalism. The formula will be found; it will be proved that there is more poetry in the little apartment of a bourgeois than in all the empty, worm-eaten palaces of history; in the end we will see that everything meets in the real: lovely fantasies that are free of capriciousness and whimsy, and idylls, and comedies, and dramas. Once the soil has been turned over, the task that seems alarming and unfeasible today will become easy.

I am not qualified to pronounce on the form that tomorrow's drama will take; that must be left to the voice of some genius to come. But I will allow myself to indicate the path I consider our theatre will follow.

First, the romantic drama must be abandoned. It would be disastrous for us to take over its outrageous acting, its rhetoric, its inherent thesis of action at the expense of character analysis. The finest models of the genre are, as has been said, mere operas with big effects. I believe, then, that we must go back to tragedy—not, heaven forbid, to borrow more of its rhetoric, its system of confidants, its declaiming, its endless speeches, but to return to its simplicity of action and its unique psychological and physiological study of the characters. Thus understood, the tragic framework is excellent; one deed unwinds in all its reality, and moves the characters to passions and feelings, the exact analysis of which constitutes the sole interest of the play—and in a contemporary environment, with the people who surround us.

My constant concern, my anxious vigil, has made me wonder which of us will have the strength to raise himself to the pitch of genius. If the naturalistic drama must come into being, only a genius can give birth to it. Corneille and Racine made tragedy. Victor Hugo made romantic drama. Where is the as-yet-unknown author who must make the naturalistic drama? In recent years experiments have not been wanting. But either because the public was not ready or because none of the beginners had the necessary staying-power, not one of these attempts has had decisive results.

In battles of this kind, small victories mean nothing; we need triumphs that overwhelm the adversary and win the

public to the cause. Audiences would give way before the onslaught of a really strong man. This man would come with the expected word, the solution to the problem, the formula for a real life on stage, combining it with the illusions necessary in the theatre. He would have what the newcomers have as yet lacked: the cleverness or the might to impose himself and to remain so close to truth that his cleverness could not lead him into lies.

And what an immense place this innovator would occupy in our dramatic literature! He would be at the peak. He would build his monument in the middle of the desert of mediocrity that we are crossing, among the jerry-built houses strewn about our most illustrious stages. He would put everything in question and remake everything, scour the boards, create a world whose elements he would lift from life, from outside our traditions. Surely there is no more ambitious dream that a writer of our time could fulfil. The domain of the novel is crowded; the domain of the theatre is free. At this time in France an imperishable glory awaits the man of genius who takes up the work of Molière and finds in the reality of living comedy the full, true drama of modern society.

• • •

PHYSIOLOGICAL MAN

. . . In effect, the great naturalistic evolution, which comes down directly from the fifteenth century to ours has everything to do with the gradual substitution of physiological man for metaphysical man. In tragedy metaphysical man, man according to dogma and logic, reigned absolutely. The body did not count; the soul was regarded as the only interesting piece of human machinery; drama took place in the air, in pure mind. Consequently, what use was the tangible world? Why worry about the place where the action was located? Why be surprised at a baroque costume or false declaiming? Why notice that Queen Dido was a boy whose budding beard forced him to wear a mask? None of that mattered; these trifles were not worth stooping to; the play was heard out as if it were a school essay or a law case; it was on a higher plane than man, in the world of ideas, so far away from real man that any intrusion of reality would have spoiled the show.

Such is the point of departure—in Mystery plays, the religious point; the philosophical point in tragedy. And from that beginning natural man, stifling under the rhetoric and dogma, struggled secretly, tried to break free, made lengthy, futile efforts, and in the end asserted himself, limb by limb. The whole history of our theatre is in this conquest by the physiological man, who emerged more clearly in each period from behind the dummy of religious and philosophical idealism. Corneille, Molière, Racine, Voltaire, Beaumarchais and, in our day, Victor Hugo, Émile Augier, Alexandre Dumas *fils*, even Sardou, have had only one task, even when they were not completely aware of it: to increase the reality of our corpus of drama, to progress towards truth, to sift out more and more of the natural man and impose him on the public. And inevitably, the evolution will not end with them. It continues; it will continue forever. Mankind is very young. . . .

COSTUME, STAGE DESIGN, SPEECH

Modern clothes make a poor spectacle. If we depart from bourgeois tragedy, shut in between its four walls, and wish to use the breadth of larger stages for crowd scenes we are embarrassed and constrained by the monotony and the uniformly funereal look of the extras. In this case, I think, we should take advantage of the variety of garb offered by the different classes and occupations. To elaborate: I can imagine an author setting one act in the main marketplace of les Halles in Paris. The setting would be superb, with its bustling life and bold possibilities. In this immense setting we could have a very picturesque ensemble by displaying the porters wearing their large hats, the saleswomen with their white aprons and vividly-coloured scarves, the customers dressed in silk or wool or cotton prints, from the ladies accompanied by their maids to the female beggars on the prowl for anything they can pick up off the street. For inspiration it would be enough to go to les Halles and look about. Nothing is gaudier or more interesting. All of Paris would enjoy seeing this set if it were realized with the necessary accuracy and amplitude.

And how many other settings for popular drama there are for the taking! Inside a factory, the interior of a mine, the gingerbread market, a railway station, flower stalls, a racetrack, and so on. All the activities of modern life can take place in them. It will be said that such sets have already been tried. Unquestionably we have seen factories and railway stations in fantasy plays; but these were fantasy stations and factories. I mean, these sets were thrown together to create an illusion that was at best incomplete. What we need is detailed reproduction: costumes supplied by tradespeople, not sumptuous but adequate for the purposes of truth and for the interest of the scenes. Since everybody mourns the death of the drama our playwrights certainly ought to make a try at this type of popular, contemporary drama. At one stroke they could satisfy the public hunger for spectacle and the need for exact studies which grows more pressing every day. Let us hope, though, that the playwrights will show us real people and not those whining members of the working class who play such strange roles in boulevard melodrama.

As M. Adolphe Jullien has said—and I will never be tired of repeating it—everything is interdependent in the theatre. Lifelike costumes look wrong if the sets, the diction, the plays themselves are not lifelike. They must all march in step along the naturalistic road. When costume becomes more accurate, so do sets; actors free themselves from bombastic declaiming; plays study reality more closely and their characters are more true to life. I could make the same observations about sets I have just made about costume. With them too, we may seem to have reached the highest possible degree of truth, but we still have long strides to take. Most of all we would need to intensify the illusion in reconstructing the environments, less for their picturesque quality than for dramatic utility. The environment must determine the character. When a set is planned so as to give the lively impression of a description by Balzac; when, as the curtain rises, one catches the first glimpse of the characters, their personalities and behaviour, if only to see the actual locale in which they move, the importance of exact reproduction in the decor will be appreciated. Obviously, that is the way we are going. Environment, the study of which has transformed science and literature, will have to take a large role in the theatre. And here I may mention again the question of metaphysical man, the abstraction who had to be satisfied with his three walls in tragedy—whereas the physiological man in our modern works is asking more and more compellingly to be determined by his setting, by the environment that produced him. We see then that the road to progress is still long, for sets as well as costume. We are coming upon the truth but we can hardly stammer it out.

Another very serious matter is diction. True, we have got away from the chanting, the plainsong, of the seventeenth century. But we now have a "theatre voice," a false recitation that is very obtrusive and very annoying. Everything that is wrong with it comes from the fixed traditional code set up by the majority of critics. They found the theatre in a certain state and, instead of looking to the future, and judging the progress we are making and the progress we shall make by the progress we have already made, they stubbornly defend the relics of the old conventions, swearing that these relics must be preserved. Ask them why, make them see how far we have travelled; they will give you no logical reason. They will reply with assertions based on a set of conditions that are disappearing.

In diction the errors come from what the critics call "theatre language." Their theory is that on stage you must not speak as you do in everyday life. To support this viewpoint they pick examples from traditional practices, from what was happening yesterday—and is happening still—without taking account of the naturalistic movement, the phases of which have been established for us by M. Jullien's book.[1] Let us realize that there is no such thing as "theatre language." There

---

[1] Adolphe Jullien 1845–1932, writer on music and the theatre. The book Zola cites is *Histoire du costume au théâtre*, 1880.

has been a rhetoric which grew more and more feeble and is now dying out. Those are the facts. If you compare the declaiming of actors under Louis XIV with that of Lekain, and if you compare Lekain's with that of our own artists today, you will clearly distinguish the phases from tragic chanting down to our search for the natural, precise tone, the cry of truth. It follows that "theatre language," that language of booming sonority, is vanishing. We are moving towards simplicity, the exact word spoken without emphasis, quite naturally. How many examples I could give if I had unlimited space! Consider the powerful effect that Geoffroy has on the public; all his talent comes from his natural personality. He holds the public because he speaks on stage as he does at home. When a sentence sounds outlandish he cannot pronounce it; the author has to find another one. That is the fundamental criticism of so-called "theatre language." Again, follow the diction of a talented actor and at the same time watch the public; the cheers go up, the house is in raptures when a truthful accent gives the words the exact value they must have. All the great successes of the stage are triumphs over convention.

Alas, yes, there is a "theatre language." It is the clichés, the resounding platitudes, the hollow words that roll about like empty barrels, all that intolerable rhetoric of our vaude-villes and dramas, which is beginning to make us smile. It would be very interesting to study the style of such talented authors as MM. Augier, Dumas and Sardou. I could find much to criticize, especially in the last two with their conventional language, a language of their own that they put into the mouths of all their characters, men, women, children, old folk, both sexes and all ages. This irritates me, for each character has his own language, and to create living people you must give them to the public not merely in accurate dress and in the environments that have made them what they are, but with their individual ways of thinking and expressing themselves. I repeat that that is the obvious aim of our theatre. There is no theatre language regulated by such a code as "cadenced sentences" or sonority. There is simply a kind of dialogue that is growing more precise and is following—or rather, leading—sets and costumes towards naturalistic progress. When plays are more truthful, the actors' diction will gain enormously in simplicity and naturalness.

To conclude, I will repeat that the battle of the conventions is far from being finished, and that it will no doubt last forever. Today we are beginning to see clearly where we are going, but our steps are still impeded by the melting slush of rhetoric and metaphysics.

MARTIN ESSLIN

from *The Theatre of the Absurd* (1961)

In his seminal study of the postwar theater of Eugène Ionesco, Samuel Beckett, Harold Pinter, and other playwrights, Martin Esslin (d. 2002) coined the phrase "theater of the absurd" to describe the disorienting quality of their plays. The book has been widely influential and provided the first generation of postwar theatergoers with a way of understanding the new drama. Esslin wrote several books on modern drama and theater, including Brecht: A Choice of Evils *(1959),* Pinter: A Study of His Plays *(1976), and* An Anatomy of Drama *(1976). He also worked for the British Broadcasting Corporation and taught drama at Stanford University and elsewhere.*

On 19 November 1957, a group of worried actors were preparing to face their audience. The actors were members of the company of the San Francisco Actors' Workshop. The audience consisted of fourteen hundred convicts at the San Quentin penitentiary. No live play had been performed at San Quentin since Sarah Bernhardt appeared there in 1913. Now, forty-four years later, the play that had been chosen, largely because no woman appeared in it, was Samuel Beckett's *Waiting for Godot*.

No wonder the actors and Herbert Blau, the director, were apprehensive. How were they to face one of the toughest audiences in the world with a highly obscure, intellectual play that had produced near riots among a good many highly sophisticated audiences in Western Europe? Herbert Blau de-cided to prepare the San Quentin audience for what was to come. He stepped on to the stage and addressed the packed, darkened North Dining Hall—a sea of flickering matches that the convicts tossed over their shoulders after lighting their cigarettes. Blau compared the play to a piece of jazz music "to which one must listen for whatever one may find in it." In the same way, he hoped, there would be some meaning, some personal significance for each member of the audience in *Waiting for Godot*.

The curtain parted. The play began. And what had bewildered the sophisticated audiences of Paris, London, and New York was immediately grasped by an audience of convicts. As the writer of "Memos of a first-nighter" put it in the columns of the prison paper, the *San Quentin News*:

The trio of muscle-men, biceps overflowing, . . . parked all 642 lbs on the aisle and waited for the girls and funny stuff. When this didn't appear they audibly fumed and audibly decided to wait until the house lights dimmed before escaping. They made one error. They listened and looked two minutes too long and stayed. Left at the end. All shook . . .[1]

Or as the writer of the lead story of the same paper reported, under the headline, "San Francisco Group Leaves S.Q. Audience Waiting for Godot":

From the moment Robin Wagner's thoughtful and limbo-like set was dressed with light, until the last futile and expectant handclasp was hesitantly activated between the two searching vagrants, the San Francisco company had its audience of captives in its collective hand. . . . Those that had felt a less controversial vehicle should be attempted as a first play here had their fears allayed a short five minutes after the Samuel Beckett piece began to unfold.[2]

A reporter from the San Francisco *Chronicle* who was present noted that the convicts did not find it difficult to understand the play. One prisoner told him, "Godot is society." Said another: "He's the outside."[3] A teacher at the prison was quoted as saying, "They know what is meant by waiting . . . and they knew if Godot finally came, he would only be a disappointment."[4] The leading article of the prison paper showed how clearly the writer had understood the meaning of the play:

It was an expression, symbolic in order to avoid all personal error, by an author who expected each member of his audience to draw his own conclusions, make his own errors. It asked nothing in point, it forced no dramatized moral on the viewer, it held out no specific hope. . . . We're still waiting for Godot, and shall continue to wait. When the scenery gets too drab and the action too slow, we'll call each other names and swear to part forever—but then, there's no place to go![5]

It is said that Godot himself, as well as turns of phrase and characters from the play, have since become a permanent part of the private language, the institutional mythology of San Quentin.

Why did a play of the supposedly esoteric avant-garde make so immediate and so deep an impact on an audience of convicts? Because it confronted them with a situation in some ways analogous to their own? Perhaps. Or perhaps because they were unsophisticated enough to come to the theatre without any preconceived notions and ready-made expecta-

tions, so that they avoided the mistake that trapped so many established critics who condemned the play for its lack of plot, development, characterization, suspense, or plain common sense. Certainly the prisoners of San Quentin could not be suspected of the sin of intellectual snobbery, for which a sizeable proportion of the audiences of *Waiting for Godot* have often been reproached; of pretending to like a play they did not even begin to understand, just to appear in the know.

The reception of *Waiting for Godot* at San Quentin, and the wide acclaim given to plays by Ionesco, Adamov, Pinter, and others, testify that these plays, which are so often superciliously dismissed as nonsense or mystification, have something to say and can be understood. Most of the incomprehension with which plays of this type are still being received by critics and theatrical reviewers, most of the bewilderment they have caused and to which they still give rise, come from the fact that they are part of a new, and still developing stage convention that has not yet been generally understood and has hardly ever been defined. Inevitably, plays written in this new convention will, when judged by the standards and criteria of another, be regarded as impertinent and outrageous impostures. If a good play must have a cleverly constructed story, these have no story or plot to speak of; if a good play is judged by subtlety of characterization and motivation, these are often without recognizable characters and present the audience with almost mechanical puppets; if a good play has to have a fully explained theme, which is neatly exposed and finally solved, these often have neither a beginning nor an end; if a good play is to hold the mirror up to nature and portray the manners and mannerisms of the age in finely observed sketches, these seem often to be reflections of dreams and nightmares; if a good play relies on witty repartee and pointed dialogue, these often consists of incoherent babblings.

But the plays we are concerned with here pursue ends quite different from those of the conventional play and therefore use quite different methods. They can be judged only by the standards of the Theatre of the Absurd. . . .

It must be stressed, however, that the dramatists whose work is here discussed do not form part of any self-proclaimed or self-conscious school or movement. On the contrary, each of the writers in question is an individual who regards himself as a lone outsider, cut off and isolated in his private world. Each has his own personal approach to both subject- matter and form; his own roots, sources, and background. If they also, very clearly and in spite of themselves, have a good deal in common, it is because their work most sensitively mirrors and reflects the preoccupations and anxieties, the emotions and thinking of many of their contemporaries in the Western world.

[1] *San Quentin News*, San Quentin, Calif., 28 November 1957.

[2] Ibid.

[3] *Theatre Arts*, New York, July 1958.

[4] Ibid.

[5] *San Quentin News*, 28 November 1957.

This is not to say that their works are representative of mass attitudes. It is an oversimplification to assume that any age presents a homogeneous pattern. Ours being, more than most others, an age of transition, it displays a bewilderingly stratified picture: medieval beliefs still held and overlaid by eighteenth-century rationalism and mid-nineteenth-century Marxism, rocked by sudden volcanic eruptions of prehistoric fanaticisms and primitive tribal cults. Each of these components of the cultural pattern of the age finds its own artistic expression. The Theatre of the Absurd, however, can be seen as the reflection of what seems to be the attitude most genuinely representative of our own time.

The hallmark of this attitude is its sense that the certitudes and unshakable basic assumptions of former ages have been swept away, that they have been tested and found wanting, that they have been discredited as cheap and somewhat childish illusions. The decline of religious faith was masked until the end of the Second World War by the substitute religions of faith in progress, nationalism, and various totalitarian fallacies. All this was shattered by the war. By 1942, Albert Camus was calmly putting the question why, since life had lost all meaning, man should not seek escape in suicide. In one of the great, seminal heart-searchings of our time, *The Myth of Sisyphus,* Camus tried to diagnose the human situation in a world of shattered beliefs:

> A world that can be explained by reasoning, however faulty, is a familiar world. But in a universe that is suddenly deprived of illusions and of light, man feels a stranger. His is an irremediable exile, because he is deprived of memories of a lost homeland as much as he lacks the hope of a promised land to come. This divorce between man and his life, the actor and his setting, truly constitutes the feeling of Absurdity.[6]

"Absurd" originally means "out of harmony," in a musical context. Hence its dictionary definition: "out of harmony with reason or propriety; incongruous, unreasonable, illogical." In common usage, "absurd" may simply mean "ridiculous," but this is not the sense in which Camus uses the word, and in which it is used when we speak of the Theatre of the Absurd. In an essay on Kafka, Ionesco defined his understanding of the term as follows: "Absurd is that which is devoid of purpose. . . . Cut off from his religious, metaphysical, and transcendental roots, man is lost; all his actions become senseless, absurd, useless."[7]

---

[6]Albert Camus, *Le Mythe de Sisyphe* (Paris: Gallimard, 1942), p. 18.

[7]Eugène Ionesco, "Dans les armes de la ville," *Cahiers de la Compagnie Madeleine Renaud-Jean-Louis Barrault,* Paris, no. 20, October 1957.

This sense of metaphysical anguish at the absurdity of the human condition is, broadly speaking, the theme of the plays of Beckett, Adamov, Ionesco, Genet, and the other writers. . . . But it is not merely the subject-matter that defines what is here called the Theatre of the Absurd. A similar sense of the senselessness of life, of the inevitable devaluation of ideals, purity, and purpose, is also the theme of much of the work of dramatists like Giraudoux, Anouilh, Salacrou, Sartre, and Camus himself. Yet these writers differ from the dramatists of the Absurd in an important respect: they present their sense of the irrationality of the human condition in the form of highly lucid and logically constructed reasoning, while the Theatre of the Absurd strives to express its sense of the senselessness of the human condition and the inadequacy of the rational approach by the open abandonment of rational devices and discursive thought. While Sartre or Camus express the new content in the old convention, the Theatre of the Absurd goes a step further in trying to achieve a unity between its basic assumptions and the form in which these are expressed. In some senses, the *theatre* of Sartre and Camus is less adequate as an expression of the *philosophy* of Sartre and Camus—in artistic, as distinct from philosophic, terms—than the Theatre of the Absurd.

If Camus argued that in our disillusioned age the world has ceased to make sense, he did so in the elegantly rationalistic and discursive style of an eighteenth-century moralist, in well-constructed and polished plays. If Sartre argues that existence comes before essence and that human personality can be reduced to pure potentiality and the freedom to choose itself anew at any moment, he presents his ideas in plays based on brilliantly drawn characters who remain wholly consistent and thus reflect the old convention that each human being has a core of immutable, unchanging essence—in fact, an immortal soul. And the beautiful phrasing and argumentative brilliance of both Sartre and Camus in their relentless probing still, by implication, proclaim a tacit conviction that logical discourse can offer valid solutions, that the analysis of language will lead to the uncovering of basic concepts—Platonic ideas.

This is an inner contradiction that the dramatists of the Absurd are trying, by instinct and intuition rather than by conscious effort, to overcome and resolve. The Theatre of the Absurd has renounced arguing *about* the absurdity of the human condition; it merely *presents* it in being—that is, in terms of concrete stage images. This is the difference between the approach of the philosopher and that of the poet; the difference, to take an example from another sphere, between the *idea* of God in the works of Thomas Aquinas or Spinoza and the *intuition* of God in those of St John of the Cross or Meister Eckhart—the difference between theory and experience.

It is this striving for an integration between the subject-matter and the form in which it is expressed that separates the Theatre of the Absurd from the Existentialist theatre.

It must also be distinguished from another important, and parallel, trend in the contemporary French theatre, which is equally preoccupied with the absurdity and uncertainty of the human condition: the "poetic avant-garde" theatre of dramatists like Michel de Ghelderode, Jacques Audiberti, Georges Neveux, and, in the younger generation, Georges Schehadé, Henri Pichette, and Jean Vauthier, to name only some of its most important exponents. This is an even more difficult dividing line to draw, for the two approaches overlap a good deal. The "poetic avant-garde" relies on fantasy and dream reality as much as the Theatre of the Absurd does; it also disregards such traditional axioms as that of the basic unity and consistency of each character or the need for a plot. Yet basically the "poetic avant-garde" represents a different mood; it is more lyrical, and far less violent and grotesque. Even more important is its different attitude toward language: the "poetic avant-garde" relies to a far greater extent on consciously "poetic" speech; it aspires to plays that are in effect poems, images composed of a rich web of verbal associations.

The Theatre of the Absurd, on the other hand, tends toward a radical devaluation of language, toward a poetry that is to emerge from the concrete and objectified images of the stage itself. The element of language still plays an important part in this conception, but what *happens* on the stage transcends, and often contradicts, the *words* spoken by the characters. In Ionesco's *The Chairs,* for example, the poetic content of a powerfully poetic play does not lie in the banal words that are uttered but in the fact that they are spoken to an ever-growing number of empty chairs.

The Theatre of the Absurd is thus part of the "anti-literary" movement of our time, which has found its expression in abstract painting, with its rejection of "literary" elements in pictures; or in the "new novel" in France, with its reliance on the description of objects and its rejection of empathy and anthropomorphism. It is no coincidence that, like all these movements and so many of the efforts to create new forms of expression in all the arts, the Theatre of the Absurd should be centred in Paris. . . .

FREDRIC JAMESON
from "Postmodernism and Consumer Society" (1983)

Fredric Jameson is probably the most prominent Marxist cultural critic writing in the United States today and is the author of several important books, including Marxism and Form *(1971),* The Prison-House of Language *(1972),* The Political Unconscious *(1988), and* Postmodernism, or, The Cultural Logic of Late Capitalism *(1991). This section is from one of Jameson's many essays on postmodern art, culture, and society. Jameson uses the term* pastiche *to characterize the problematic ways contemporary arts invoke the imagery and style of earlier historical eras, paradoxically erasing "history" in the process. How does Jameson identify pastiche as both a feature of a work's style and as an index of its broader political, social, and cultural meaning? How does the movement from parody to pastiche epitomize the movement from modernism to postmodernism?*

PASTICHE ECLIPSES PARODY

One of the most significant features or practices in postmodernism today is pastiche. I must first explain this term, which people generally tend to confuse with or assimilate to that related verbal phenomenon called parody. Both pastiche and parody involve the imitation or, better still, the mimicry of other styles and particularly of the mannerisms and stylistic twitches of other styles. It is obvious that modern literature in general offers a very rich field for parody, since the great modern writers have all been defined by the invention or production of rather unique styles: think of the Faulknerian long sentence or of D.H. Lawrence's characteristic nature imagery; think of Wallace Stevens's peculiar way of using abstractions; think also of the mannerisms of the philosophers, of Heidegger for example, or Sartre; think of the musical styles of Mahler or Prokofiev. All of these styles, however different from each other, are comparable in this: each is quite unmistakable; once one is learned, it is not likely to be confused with something else.

Now parody capitalizes on the uniqueness of these styles and seizes on their idiosyncrasies and eccentricities to produce an imitation which mocks the original. I won't say that the satiric impulse is conscious in all forms of parody. In any case, a good or great parodist has to have some secret sympathy for the original, just as a great mimic has to have the capacity to put himself/herself in the place of the person imitated. Still, the general effect of parody is—whether in sympathy or with malice—to cast ridicule on the private nature of these stylistic mannerisms and their excessiveness and eccentricity with respect to the way people normally speak or write. So there remains somewhere behind all parody the feeling that there is a linguistic norm in contrast to which the styles of the great modernists can be mocked.

But what would happen if one no longer believed in the existence of normal language, of ordinary speech, of the linguistic norm (the kind of clarity and communicative power celebrated by Orwell in his famous essay, say)? One could think of it in this way; perhaps the immense fragmentation and privatization of modern literature—its explosion into a host of distinct private styles and mannerisms—foreshadows deeper and more general tendencies in social life as a whole. Supposing that modern art and modernism—far from being a kind of specialized aesthetic curiosity—actually anticipated social developments along these lines; supposing that in the decades since the emergence of the great modern styles society has itself begun to fragment in this way, each group coming to speak a curious private language of its own, each profession developing its private code or idiolect, and finally each individual coming to be a kind of linguistic island, separated from everyone else? But then in that case, the very possibility of any linguistic norm in terms of which one could ridicule private languages and idiosyncratic styles would vanish, and we would have nothing but stylistic diversity and heterogeneity.

That is the moment at which pastiche appears and parody has become impossible. Pastiche is, like parody, the imitation of a peculiar or unique style, the wearing of a stylistic mask, speech in a dead language: but it is a neutral practice of such mimicry, without parody's ulterior motive, without the satirical impulse, without laughter, without that still latent feeling that there exists something *normal* compared to which what is being imitated is rather comic. Pastiche is blank parody, parody that has lost its sense of humor: pastiche is to parody what that curious thing, the modern practice of a kind of blank irony, is to what Wayne Booth calls the stable and comic ironies of, say, the eighteenth century.

THE DEATH OF THE SUBJECT

But now we need to introduce a new piece into this puzzle, which may help to explain why classical modernism is a thing of the past and why postmodernism should have taken its place. This new component is what is generally called the 'death of the subject' or, to say it in more conventional language, the end of individualism as such. The great modernisms were, as we have said, predicated on the invention of a personal, private style, as unmistakable as your fingerprint, as incomparable as your own body. But this means that the modernist aesthetic is in some way organically linked to the conception of a unique self and private identity, a unique personality and individuality, which can be expected to generate its own unique vision of the world and to forge its own unique, unmistakable style.

Yet today, from any number of distinct perspectives, the social theorists, the psychoanalysts, even the linguists, not to speak of those of us who work in the area of culture and cultural and formal change, are all exploring the notion that that kind of individualism and personal identity is a thing of the past; that the old individual or individualist subject is 'dead'; and that one might even describe the concept of the unique individual and the theoretical basis of individualism as ideological. There are in fact two positions on all this, one of which is more radical than the other. The first one is content to say: yes, once upon a time, in the classic age of competitive capitalism, in the heyday of the nuclear family and the emergence of the bourgeoisie as the hegemonic social class, there was such a thing as individualism, as individual subjects. But today, in the age of corporate capitalism, of the so-called organization man, of bureaucracies in business as well as in the state, of demographic explosion—today, that older bourgeois individual subject no longer exists.

Then there is a second position, the more radical of the two, what one might call the poststructuralist position. It adds: not only is the bourgeois individual subject a thing of the past, it is also a myth: it *never* really existed in the first place; there have never been autonomous subjects of that type. Rather, this construct is merely a philosophical and cultural mystification which sought to persuade people that they 'had' individual subjects and possessed this unique personal identity.

For our purposes, it is not particularly important to decide which of these positions is correct (or rather, which is more interesting and productive). What we have to retain from all this is rather an aesthetic dilemma: because if the experience and the ideology of the unique self, an experience and ideology which informed the stylistic practice of classical modernism, is over and done with, then it is no longer clear what the artists and writers of the present period are supposed to be doing. What is clear is merely that the older models—Picasso, Proust, T. S. Eliot—do not work any more (or are positively harmful), since nobody has that kind of unique private world and style to express any longer. And this is perhaps not merely a 'psychological' matter: we also have to take into account the immense weight of seventy or eighty years of classical modernism itself. There is another sense in which the writers and artists of the present day will no longer be able to invent new styles and worlds—they've already been invented; only a limited number of combinations are possible; the unique ones have been thought of already. So the weight of the whole modernist aesthetic tradition—now dead—also 'weighs like a nightmare on the brains of the living,' as Marx said in another context.

Hence, once again, pastiche: in a world in which stylistic innovation is no longer possible, all that is left is to imitate dead styles, to speak through the masks and with the voices of the styles in the imaginary museum. But this means that contemporary or postmodernist art is going to be about art itself in a new kind of way: even more, it means that one of its essential messages will involve the necessary failure of art and the aesthetic, the failure of the new, the imprisonment in the past.

THE NOSTALGIA MODE

As this may seem very abstract, I want to give a few examples, one of which is so omnipresent that we rarely link it with the kinds of developments in high art discussed here. This particular practice of pastiche is not high-cultural but very much within mass culture, and it is generally known as the 'nostalgia film' (what the French neatly call *la mode rétro*—retrospective styling). We must conceive of this category in the broadest way: narrowly, no doubt, it consists merely of films about the past and about specific generational moments of that past. Thus, one of the inaugural films in this new 'genre' (if that's what it is) was Lucas's *American Graffiti*, which in 1973 set out to recapture all the atmosphere and stylistic peculiarities of the 1950s United States, the United States of the Eisenhower era. Polanski's great film *Chinatown* does something similar for the 1930s, as does Bertolucci's *The Conformist* for the Italian and European context of the same period, the fascist era in Italy; and so forth. We could go on listing these films for some time: why call them pastiche? Are they not rather work in the more traditional genre known as the historical film—work which can more simply be theorized by extrapolating that other well-known form which is the historical novel?

I have my reasons for thinking that we need new categories for such films. But let me first add some anomalies: supposing I suggested that *Star Wars* is also a nostalgia film. What could that mean? I presume we can agree that this is not a historical film about our own intergalactic past. Let me put it somewhat differently: one of the most important cultural experiences of the generations that grew up from the 1930s to the 1950s was the Saturday afternoon serial of the Buck Rogers type—alien villains, true American heroes, heroines in distress, the death ray or the doomsday box, and the cliffhanger at the end whose miraculous resolution was to be witnessed next Saturday afternoon. *Star Wars* reinvents this experience in the form of a pastiche: that is, there is no longer any point to a parody of such serials since they are long extinct. *Star Wars,* far from being a pointless satire of such now dead forms, satisfies a deep (might I even say repressed?) longing to experience them again: it is a complex object in which on some first level children and adolescents can take the adventures straight, while the adult public is able to gratify a deeper and more properly nostalgic desire to return to that older period and to live its strange old aesthetic artifacts through once again. This film is thus *metonymically* a historical or nostalgia film: unlike *American Graffiti*, it does not reinvent a picture of the past in its lived totality; rather, by reinventing the feel and shape of characteristic art objects of an older period (the serials), it seeks to reawaken a sense of the past associated with those objects. *Raiders of the Lost Ark,* meanwhile, occupies an intermediary position here: on some level it is about the 1930s and 1940s, but in reality it too conveys that period metonymically through its own characteristic adventure stories (which are no longer ours).

Now let me discuss another interesting anomaly which may take us further towards understanding nostalgia film in particular and pastiche generally. This one involves a recent film called *Body Heat,* which, as has abundantly been pointed out by the critics, is a kind of distant remake of *The Postman Always Rings Twice* or *Double Indemnity.* (The allusive and elusive plagiarism of older plots is, of course, also a feature of pastiche.) Now *Body Heat* is technically not a nostalgia film, since it takes place in a contemporary setting, in a little Florida village near Miami. On the other hand, this technical contemporaneity is most ambiguous indeed: the credits—always our first cue—are lettered and scripted in a 1930s Art-Deco style which cannot but trigger nostalgic reactions (first to *Chinatown,* no doubt, and then beyond it to some more historical referent). Then the very style of the hero himself is ambiguous: William Hurt is a new star but has nothing of the distinctive style of the preceding generation of male superstars like Steve McQueen or even Jack Nicholson, or rather, his persona here is a kind of mix of their characteristics with an older role of the type generally associated with Clark Gable. So here too there is a faintly archaic feel to all this. The spectator begins to wonder why this story, which could have been situated anywhere, is set in a small Florida town, in spite of its contemporary reference. One begins to realize after a while that the small town setting has a crucial strategic function: it allows the film to do without most of the signals and references which we might associate with the contemporary world, with consumer society—the appliances and artifacts, the high rises, the object world of late capitalism. Technically, then, its objects (its cars, for instance) are 1980s products, but everything in the film conspires to blur that immediate contemporary reference and to make it possible to receive this too as nostalgia work—as a narrative set in some indefinable nostalgic past, an eternal 1930s, say, beyond history. It seems to me exceedingly symptomatic to find the very style of nostalgia films invading and colonizing even those movies today which have contemporary settings: as though, for some reason, we were unable today to focus our own present, as though we have become incapable of achieving aesthetic representations of our own current experience. But if that is so, then it is a terrible indictment of consumer capitalism itself—or, at the very least, an alarming and pathological symptom of a society that has become incapable of dealing with time and history.

So now we come back to the question of why nostalgia film or pastiche is to be considered different from the older historical novel or film. (I should also include in this discussion the major literary example of all this, to my mind: the novels of E.L. Doctorow—*Ragtime*, with its turn-of-the-century atmosphere, and *Loon Lake*, for the most part about our 1930s. But these are, in my opinion, historical novels in appearance only. Doctorow is a serious artist and one of the few genuinely left or radical novelists at work today. It is no disservice to him, however, to suggest that his narratives do not represent our historical past so much as they represent our ideas or cultural stereotypes about that past.) Cultural production has been driven back inside the mind, within the monadic subject: it can no longer look directly out of its eyes at the real world for the referent but must, as in Plato's cave, trace its mental images of the world on its confining walls. If there is any realism left here, it is a 'realism' which springs from the shock of grasping that confinement and of realizing that, for whatever peculiar reasons, we seem condemned to seek the historical past through our own pop images and stereotypes about that past, which itself remains forever out of reach.

PERFORMANCE IN HISTORY

CONSTANTIN STANISLAVSKI (1863–1938)
"Direction and Acting" (1947)

One of the founders of the Moscow Art Theater, Stanislavski developed a systematic approach to acting that involved working both on the actor's psychological and on his or her physical portrayal of character. In this article, originally written for the Encyclopedia Britannica, *Stanislavski outlines some of the central features of his "system": public solitude, concentration, internal technique.*

Theatrical art has always been collective, arising only where poetical-dramatic talent was actively combined with the actor's. The basis of a play is always a dramatic conception; a general artistic sense is imparted to the theatrical action by the unifying, creative genius of the actor. Thus the actor's dramatic activity begins at the foundation of the play. In the first place, each actor, either independently or through the theatre manager, must probe for the fundamental motive in the finished play—the creative idea that is characteristic of the author and that reveals itself as the germ from which his work grows organically. The motive of the play always keeps the character developing before the spectator; each personality in the work takes a part conforming to his own character; the work, then developing in the appointed direction, flows on to the final point conceived by the author. The first stage in the work of the actor and theatre manager is to probe for the germ of the play, investigating the fundamental line of action that traverses all of its episodes and is therefore called by the writer its transparent effect or action. In contrast to some theatrical directors, who consider every play only as material for theatrical repetition, the writer believes that in the production of every important drama the director and actor must go straight for the most exact and profound conception of the mind and ideal of the dramatist, and must not change that ideal for their own. The interpretation of the play and the character of its artistic incarnation inevitably appear in a certain measure subjective, and bear the mark of the individual peculiarities of the manager and actors; but only by profound attention to the artistic individuality of the author and to his ideal and mentality, which have been disclosed as the creative germ of the play, can the theatre realize all its artistic depth and transmit, as in a poetical production, completeness and harmony of composition. Every part of the future spectacle is then unified in it by its own artistic work; each part, in the measure of its own genius, will flow on to the artistic realization aimed at by the dramatist.

The actor's task, then, begins with the search for the play's artistic seed. All artistic action—organic action, as in every constructive operation of nature—starts from this seed at the moment when it is conveyed to the mind. On reaching the actor's mind, the seed must wander around, germinate, put out roots, drinking in the juices of the soil in which it is planted, grow and eventually bring forth a lively flowering plant. Artistic process must in all cases flow very rapidly, but usually, in order that it may preserve the character of the true organic action and may lead to the creation of life, of a clear truly artistic theatrical image, and not of a trade substitute, it demands much more time than is allotted to it in the best European theatres. That is why in the writer's theatre every dramatization passes through eight to ten revisions, as is also done in Germany by the famous theatre manager and theorist, K. Hagemann. Sometimes even more than ten revisions are needed, occasionally extending over several months. But even under these conditions, the creative genius of the actor does not appear so freely as does, for instance, the creative genius of the dramatist. Bound by the strict obligations of his *collectif,* the actor must not postpone his work to the moment when his physical and psychic condition appears propitious for creative genius. Meanwhile, his exacting and capricious artistic nature is prompted by aspirations of his artistic intuition, and in the absence of creative genius is not reached by any effort of his will. He is not aided in that respect by outward technique—his skill in making use of his body, his vocal equipment and his powers of speech.

THE ARTISTIC CONDITION

But is it really impossible? Are there no means, no processes that sensibly would help us, and spontaneously lead to that artistic condition which is born of genius without any effort on its part? If that capacity is unattainable all at once, by some process or other, it may, perhaps, be acquired in parts, and through progressive stages may perfect those elements out of which the artistic condition is composed, and which are subject to our will. Of course the general run of acting does not come into being from this genius, but cannot such acting, in some measure, be brought by it near to what is evidence of genius? These are the problems which presented themselves to the writer about 20 years ago, when reflecting on the external obstacles that hamper actors' artistic genius, and partly compel substitution of the crude outward marks of the actor's profession for its results. They drove him to the rediscovery of processes of external technique, i.e., methods proceeding form consciousness to subconsciousness, in which domain flow nine-tenths of all real artistic processes. Observations both upon himself and other actors with whom he happened to rehearse, but chiefly upon growing theatrical skill in Russia and abroad, allowed him to do some generalizing, which thereupon he verified in practice.

The first is that, in an artistic condition, full freedom of body plays a principal rôle; i.e., the freedom from that muscular strain which, without our knowing it, fetters us not only on the stage but also in ordinary life, hindering us from being obedient conductors of our psychic action. This muscular strain, reaching its maximum at those times when the actor is called upon to perform something especially difficult in his theatrical work, swallows up the bulk of this external energy, diverting him from activity of the higher centres. This teaches us the possibility of availing ourselves of the muscular energy of our limbs only as necessity demands, and in exact conformity with our creative efforts.

PUBLIC SOLITUDE

The second observation is that the flow of the actor's artistic force is considerably retarded by the visual auditorium and the public, whose presence may hamper his outward freedom of movement, and powerfully hinder his concentration on his own artistic taste. It is almost unnecessary to remark that the artistic achievement of great actors is always bound by the concentration of attention to the action of their own performance, and that when in that condition, i.e., just when the actor's attention is taken away from the spectator, he gains a particular power over the audience, grips it, and compels it to take an active share in his artistic existence. This does not mean, of course, that the actor must altogether cease to feel the public; but the public is concerned only in so far as it neither exerts pressure on him nor diverts him unnecessarily from the artistic demands of the moment, which last might happen to him even while knowing how to regulate his attention. The actor suitably disciplined must automatically restrict the sphere of his attention, concentrating on what comes within this sphere, and only half consciously seizing on what comes within its aura. If need be, he must restrict that sphere to such an extent that it reaches a condition that may be called *public solitude*. But as a rule this sphere of attention is elastic, it expands or contracts for the actor, with regard to the course of his theatrical actions. Within the boundary of this sphere, as one of the actual aspects of the play, there is also the actor's immediate central *object of attention*, the object on which, somehow or other, his will is concentrated at the moment with which, in the course of the play, he is in inward communication. This theatrical sympathy with the object can only be complete when the actor has trained himself by long practice to surrender himself in his own impressions, and also in his reactions to those impressions, with maximum intensity: only so does theatrical action attain the necessary force, only so is created between the actual aspects of the play, i.e., between the actors, that link, that living bond, which is essential for the carrying through of the play to its goal, with the general maintenance of the rhythm and time of each performance.

CONCENTRATION

But whatever may be the sphere of the actor's attention, whether it confines him at some moments to public solitude, or whether it grips the faces of all those before the stage, dramatic artistic genius, as in the preparation of the part so in its repeated performance, requires a full concentration of all the mental and physical talents of the actor, and the participation of the whole of his physical and psychic capacity. It takes hold of his sight and hearing, all his external senses; it draws out not only the periphery but also the essential depth of his existence, and it evokes to activity his memory, imagination, emotions, intelligence and will. The whole mental and physical being of the actor must be directed to that which is derived from his facial expression. At the moment of inspiration, of the involuntary use of all the actor's qualities, at that moment he actually exists. On the other hand, in the absence of this employment of his qualities, the actor is gradually led astray along the road leading to time-honored theatrical traditions; he begins to "produce" wherever he sees them, or, glancing at his own image, imitates the inward manifestations of his emotions, or tries to draw from himself the emotions of the perfected part, to "inspire" them within himself. But when forcing such an image by his own psychic equipment, with its unchanging organic laws, he by no means attains that desired result of artistic genius; he must present only the rough counterfeit of emotion, because emotions do not come to order. By no effort of conscious will can one awake them in oneself at a moment, nor can they ever be of use for creative genius striving to bring this about by searching the depths of its mind. A fundamental axiom, therefore, for the actor who wishes to be a real artist on the stage, may be stated thus: he must not play to produce emotions, and he must not involuntarily evoke them in himself.

ACTIVITY OF IMAGINATION

Considerations on the nature of artistically gifted people, however, inevitably open up the road to the possession of the emotion of the part. This road traverses activity of imagination, which in most of its stages is subject to the action of consciousness. One must not suddenly begin to operate on emotion; one must put oneself in motion in the direction of artistic imagination, but imagination—as is also shown by observations of scientific psychology—disturbs our aberrant memory, and, luring from the hidden recesses beyond the boundaries of its sense of harmony whatever elements there may be of proved emotions, organizes them afresh in sympathy with those that have arisen in our imagery. So surrounded within our figures of imagination, without effort on our part, the answer to our aberrant memory is found and the sounds of sympathetic emotion are called out from us. This is why the creative imagination presents itself afresh, the indispensable gift of the actor. Without a well developed, mobile imagination, creative faculty is by no means possible, not by instinct nor intuition nor the aid of external technique. In the acquiring of it, that which has lain dormant in the mind of the artist is, when immersed in his sphere of unconscious imagery and emotion, completely harmonized within him.

This practical method for the artistic education of the actor, directed by means of his imagination to the storing up of affective memory, is sufficiently enlarged upon; his individual emotional experience, by its limits, actually leads to the restriction of the sphere of his creative genius, and does not allow him to play parts dissimilar to those of his psychic harmony. This opinion is fundamental for the clearing away of misunderstandings of those elements of reality from which are produced fictitious creations of imagination; these are also derived from organic experience, but a wealth and variety of these creations are only obtained by combinations drawn from a trial of elements. The musical scale has only its basic notes, the solar spectrum its radical colors, but the combination of sounds in music and of colors in painting are

infinite. One can in the same way speak of radical emotions preserved in imaginative memory, just as the reception in imagination of outward harmony remains in the intellectual memory; the sum of these radical emotions in the inner experience of each person is limited, but the shades and combinations are as infinite as the combinations that create activity of imagination out of the elements of inward experience.

Certainly, but the actor's outward experience—i.e., his sphere of vital sensations and reflections—must always be elastic, for only in that condition can the actor enlarge the sphere of his creative faculty. On the other hand, he must judiciously develop his imagination, harnessing it again and again to new propositions. But, in order that that imaginary union which is the actor's very foundation, produced by the creative genius of the dramatist, should take hold of him emotionally and lead him on to theatrical action, it is necessary that the actor should "swing toward" that union, as toward something as real as the union of reality surrounding him.

THE EMOTION OF TRUTH

This does not mean that the actor must surrender himself on the stage to some such hallucination as that when playing he should lose the sense of reality around him, to take scenery for real trees, etc. On the contrary, some part of his senses must remain free from the grip of the play to control everything that he attempts and achieves as the performer of his part. He does not forget that surrounding him on the stage are decorations, scenery, etc., but they have no meaning for him. He says to himself, as it were: "I know that all around me on the stage is a rough counterfeit of reality. It is false. But if all should be real, see how I might be carried away to some such scene; then I would act." And at that instant, when there arises in his mind that artistic "suppose," encircling his real life, he loses interest in it, and is transported to another plane, created for him, of imaginary life. Restored to real life again, the actor must perforce modify the truth, as in the actual construction of his invention, so also in the survivals connected to it. His invention can be shown to be illogical, wide of the truth—and then he ceases to believe it. Emotion rises in him with invention; i.e., his outward regard for imagined circumstances may be shown as "determined" without relation to the individual nature of a given emotion. Finally, in the expression of the outward life of his part, the actor, as a living complex emotion, never making use of sufficient perfection of all his bodily equipment, may give an untrue intonation, may not keep the artistic mean in gesticulation and may through the temptation of cheap effect drift into mannerism or awkwardness.

Only by a strongly developed sense of truth may he achieve a single inward beauty in which, unlike the conventional theatrical gestures and poses, the true condition of the character is expressed in every one of his attitudes and outward gestures.

INTERNAL TECHNIQUE

The combination of all the above-named procedure and habits also composes the actor's external technique. Parallel with its development must go also the development of internal technique—the perfecting of that bodily equipment which serves for the incarnation of the theatrical image created by the actor, and the exact, clear expression of his external consciousness. With this aim in view the actor must work out within himself not only the ordinary flexibility and mobility of action, but also the particular consciousness that directs all his groups of muscles, and the ability to feel the energy transfused within him, which, arising from his highest creative centres, forms in a definite manner his mimicry and gestures, and, radiating from him, brings into the circle of its influence his partners on the stage and in the auditorium. The same growth of consciousness and fineness of internal feelings must be worked out by the actor in relation to his vocal equipment. Ordinary speech—as in life, so on the stage—is prosaic and monotonous; in it words sound disjointed, without any harmonious stringing together in a vocal melody as continuous as that of a violin, which by the hand of a master violinist can become fuller, deeper, finer and more transparent, and can without difficulty run from the higher to the lower notes and vice versa, and can alternate from pianissimo to forte. To counteract the wearisome monotony of reading, actors often elaborate, especially when declaiming poetry, with those artificial vocal *fioritures,* cadences and sudden raising and lowering of the voice, which are so characteristic of the conventional, pompous declamation, and which are not influenced by the corresponding emotion of the part, and therefore impress the more sensitive auditors with a feeling of unreality.

But there exists another natural musical sonorousness of speech, which we may see in great actors at the moment of their own true artistic elation, and which is closely knit to the internal sonorousness of their rôle. The actor must develop within himself this natural musical speech by practising his voice with due regard to his sense of reality, almost as much as a singer. At the same time he must perfect his elocution. It is possible to have a strong, flexible, impressive voice, and still distort speech, on the one hand by incorrect pronunciation, on the other by neglect of those almost imperceptible pauses and emphasis through which are attained the exact transmission of the sense of the sentence, and also its particular emotional coloring. In the perfect production of the dramatist, every word, every letter, every punctuation mark has its part in transmitting his inward reality; the actor in his interpretation of the play, according to his intelligence, introduces into each sentence his individual nuances, which must be transmitted not only by the motions of his body, but also by artistically developed speech. He must bear this in mind, that every sound which goes to make a word appears as a separate note, which has its part in the harmonious sound of the word, and which is the expression of one or other particle of the soul drawn out through the word. The perfecting, therefore, of the phonetics of speech cannot be limited to mechanical exercise of the vocal equipment, but must also be directed in such a way that the actor learns to feel each separate sound in a word as an instrument of artistic expression. But in regard to the musical tone of the voice, freedom, elasticity, rhythm of movement and generally all external technique of dramatic art, to say nothing of internal technique, the present day actor is still on a low rung of the ladder of artistic culture, still far behind in this respect, from many causes, the masters of music, poetry and painting, with an almost infinite road of development to travel.

It is evident that under these conditions, the staging of a play, which will satisfy highly artistic demands, cannot be achieved at the speed that economic factors unfortunately make necessary in most theatres. This creative process, which every actor must go through, from his conception of the part to its artistic incarnation, is essentially very complicated, and is hampered by lack of perfection of outward and inward technique. It is also much hindered by the necessity of fitting in the actors one with another—the adjustment of their artistic individualities into an artistic whole.

PRODUCTION

Responsibility for bringing about this accord, and the artistic integrity and expression of the performance rests with the theatre manager. During the period when the manager exercised a despotic rule in the theatre, a period starting with the Meiningen players and still in force even in many of the foremost theatres, the manager worked out in advance all the plans for staging a play, and, while certainly having regard to the existing cast, indicated to the actors the general outlines of the scenic effects, and the *mise-en-scène*. The writer also adhered to this system, but now he has come to the conclusion that the creative work of the manager must be done in collaboration with the actor's work, neither ignoring nor confirming it. To encourage the actor's creative genius, to control and adjust it, ensuring that this creative genius grows out of the unique artistic germ of the drama, as much as the external building up of the performance—that in the opinion of the writer is the problem of the theatre director to-day.

The joint work of the director and actor begins with the analysis of the drama and the discovery of its artistic germ, and with the investigation of its *transparent effect*. The next step is the discovery of the transparent effect of individual parts—of that fundamental will direction of each individual actor, which, organically derived from his character, determines his place in the general action of the play. If the actor cannot at once secure this transparent effect, then it must be traced bit by bit with the manager's aid—by dividing the part into sections corresponding to the separate stages of the life of the particular actor—from the separate problems developing before him in his struggle for the attainment of his goal. Each such section of a part of each problem, can, if necessary, be subjected to further psychological analysis, and subdivided into problems even more detailed, corresponding to those separate mind actions of the performer out of which stage life is summed up. The actor must catch the *mind axes* of the emotions and temperaments, but not the emotions and temperaments that give color to these sections of the part. In other words, when studying each portion of his part, he must ask himself what he wants, what he requires as a performer of the play and which definite partial problem he is putting before himself at a given moment. The answer to this question should not be in the form of a noun, but rather of a verb: "I wish to obtain possession of the heart of this lady"— "I wish to enter her house"—"I wish to push aside the servants who are protecting her," etc. Formulated in this manner, the mind problem, of which the object and setting, thanks to the working of his creative imagination, are forming a brighter and clearer picture for the actor, begins to grip him and to excite him, extracting from the recesses of his working memory the combinations of emotions necessary to the part, of emotions that have an active character and mould themselves into dramatic action. In this way the different sections of the actor's part grow more lively and richer by degrees, owing to the involuntary play of the complicated organic survivals. By joining together and grafting these sections, the *score of the part* is formed; the scores of the separate parts, after the continual joint work of the actors during rehearsals and by the necessary adjustment of them one with another, are summed up in a single *score of the performance*.

THE SCORE CONDENSED

Nevertheless, the work of the actors and manager is still unfinished. The actor is studying and living in the part and the play deeper and deeper still, finding their deeper artistic motives; so he lives in the score of his part still more profoundly. But the score of the part itself and of the play are actually subject by degrees during the work to further alterations. As in a perfect poetical production there are no superfluous words but only those necessary to the poet's artistic scheme, so in a score of the part there must not be a single superfluous emotion but only emotions necessary for the *transparent effect*. The score of each part must be condensed, as also the form of its transmitting, and bright, simple and compelling forms of its incarnation must be found. Only then, when in each actor every part not only organically ripens and comes to life but also all emotions are stripped of the superfluous, when they all crystallize and sum up into a live contact, when they harmonize amongst themselves in the general tune, rhythm and time of the performance, then the play may be presented to the public.

During repeated presentations the theatrical score of the play and each part remains in general unaltered. But that does not mean that from the moment the performance is shown to the public the actor's creative process is to be considered ended, and that there remains for him only the mechanical repetition of his achievement at the first presentation. On the contrary, every performance imposes on him creative conditions; all his psychical forces must take part in it, because only in these conditions can they creatively adapt the score of the part to those capricious changes which may develop in them from hour to hour, as in all living nervous creatures influencing one another by their emotions, and only then can they transmit to the spectator that invisible something, inexpressible in words, which forms the spiritual content of the play. And that is the whole origin of the substance of dramatic art.

As regards the outward arrangements of the play— scenery, theatrical properties, etc.—all are of value in so far as they correspond to the expression of dramatic action, i.e., to the actors' talents; in no case may they claim to have an independent artistic importance in the theatre, although up to now they have been so considered by many great scene painters. The art of scene painting, as well as the music included in the play, is on the stage only an auxiliary art, and the manager's duty is to get from each what is necessary for the illumination of the play performed before an audience, while subordinating each to the problems of the actors.

BERTOLT BRECHT (1898–1956)

"Theatre for Pleasure or Theatre for Instruction" (1935–1936)

TRANSLATED BY JOHN WILLETT

In this essay, Brecht attacks the bourgeois notion that the theater can be divided into two kinds of art, as though drama were either instructive or entertaining. As he does in his plays, Brecht dialecticizes these categories, showing that they define one another and therefore exist within one another. Realistic plays, after all, not only entertain their audiences, but also offer an image of the world, a kind of instruction. On the other hand, intellectual or critical activity is not only pleasurable in itself, but it also can lead to a lively kind of theater as well, as Brecht's plays illustrate. This essay was unpublished in Brecht's lifetime: John Willett dates it from 1935 or 1936. He notes that Brecht uses the word Entfremdung *here for "alienation," the same word used by Marx and Hegel. Brecht later coined his own word* Verfremdungseffekt *for "alienation effect."* defamiliarize

A few years back, anybody talking about the modern theatre meant the theatre in Moscow, New York and Berlin. He might have thrown in a mention of one of Jouvet's productions in Paris or Cochran's in London, or *The Dybbuk* as given by the Habima (which is to all intents and purposes part of the Russian theatre, since Vakhtangov was its director). But broadly speaking there were only three capitals so far as modern theatre was concerned.

Russian, American and German theatres differed widely from one another, but were alike in being modern, that is to say in introducing technical and artistic innovations. In a sense they even achieved a certain stylistic resemblance, probably because technology is international (not just that part which is directly applied to the stage but also that which influences it, the film for instance), and because large progressive cities in large industrial countries are involved. Among the older capitalist countries it is the Berlin theatre that seemed of late to be in the lead. For a period all that is common to the modern theatre received its strongest and (so far) maturest expression there.

The Berlin theatre's last phase was the so-called epic theatre, and it showed the modern theatre's trend of development in its purest form. Whatever was labelled '*Zeitstück*' or '*Piscatorbühne*' or '*Lehrstück*' belongs to the epic theatre.

THE EPIC THEATRE

Many people imagine that the term 'epic theatre' is self-contradictory, as the epic and dramatic ways of narrating a story are held, following Aristotle, to be basically distinct. The difference between the two forms was never thought simply to lie in the fact that the one is performed by living beings while the other operates via the written word; epic works such as those of Homer and the medieval singers were at the same time theatrical performances, while dramas like Goethe's *Faust* and Byron's *Manfred* are agreed to have been

more effective as books. Thus even by Aristotle's definition the difference between the dramatic and epic forms was attributed to their different methods of construction, whose laws were dealt with by two different branches of aesthetics. The method of construction depended on the different way of presenting the work to the public, sometimes via the stage, sometimes through a book; and independently of that there was the 'dramatic element' in epic works and the 'epic element' in dramatic. The bourgeois novel in the last century developed much that was 'dramatic,' by which was meant the strong centralization of the story, a momentum that drew the separate parts into a common relationship. A particular passion of utterance, a certain emphasis on the clash of forces are hallmarks of the 'dramatic'. The epic writer Döblin provided an excellent criterion when he said that with an epic work, as opposed to a dramatic, one can as it were take a pair of scissors and cut it into individual pieces, which remain fully capable of life.

This is no place to explain how the opposition of epic and dramatic lost its rigidity after having long been held to be irreconcilable. Let us just point out that the technical advances alone were enough to permit the stage to incorporate an element of narrative in its dramatic productions. The possibility of projections, the greater adaptability of the stage due to mechanization, the film, all completed the theatre's equipment, and did so at a point where the most important transactions between people could no longer be shown simply by personifying the motive forces or subjecting the characters to invisible metaphysical powers.

To make these transactions intelligible the environment in which the people lived had to be brought to bear in a big and 'significant' way.

This environment had of course been shown in the existing drama, but only as seen from the central figure's point of view, and not as an independent element. It was defined by the hero's reactions to it. It was seen as a storm can be seen when one sees the ships on a sheet of water unfolding their sails, and the sails filling out. In the epic theatre it was to appear standing on its own.

The stage began to tell a story. The narrator was no longer missing, along with the fourth wall. Not only did the background adopt an attitude to the events on the stage—by big screens recalling other simultaneous events elsewhere, by projecting documents which confirmed or contradicted what the characters said, by concrete and intelligible figures to accompany abstract conversations, by figures and sentences to support mimed transactions whose sense was unclear—but the actors too refrained from going over wholly into their role, remaining detached from the character they were playing and clearly inviting criticism of him.

The spectator was no longer in any way allowed to submit to an experience uncritically (and without practical consequences) by means of simple empathy with the characters in a play. The production took the subject-matter and the incidents shown and put them through a process of alienation: the alienation that is necessary to all understanding. When something seems 'the most obvious thing in the world' it means that any attempt to understand the world has been given up.

What is 'natural' must have the force of what is startling. This is the only way to expose the laws of cause and effect. People's activity must simultaneously be so and be capable of being different.

It was all a great change.

The dramatic theatre's spectator says: Yes, I have felt like that too—Just like me—It's only natural—It'll never change—The sufferings of this man appal me, because they are inescapable—That's great art; it all seems the most obvious thing in the world—I weep when they weep, I laugh when they laugh.

The epic theatre's spectator says: I'd never have thought it—That's not the way—That's extraordinary, hardly believable—It's got to stop—The sufferings of this man appal me, because they are unnecessary—That's great art: nothing obvious in it—I laugh when they weep, I weep when they laugh.

THE INSTRUCTIVE THEATRE

The stage began to be instructive.

Oil, inflation, war, social struggles, the family, religion, wheat, the meat market, all became subjects for theatrical representation. Choruses enlightened the spectator about facts unknown to him. Films showed a montage of events from all over the world. Projections added statistical material. And as the 'background' came to the front of the stage so people's activity was subjected to criticism. Right and wrong courses of action were shown. People were shown who knew what they were doing, and others who did not. The theatre became an affair for philosophers, but only for such philosophers as wished not just to explain the world but also to change it. So we had philosophy, and we had instruction. And where was the amusement in all that? Were they sending us back to school, teaching us to read and write? Were we supposed to pass exams, work for diplomas?

Generally there is felt to be a very sharp distinction between learning and amusing oneself. The first may be useful, but only the second is pleasant. So we have to defend the epic theatre against the suspicion that it is a highly disagreeable, humourless, indeed strenuous affair.

Well: all that can be said is that the contrast between learning and amusing oneself is not laid down by divine rule; it is not one that has always been and must continue to be.

Undoubtedly there is much that is tedious about the kind of learning familiar to us from school, from our professional training, etc. But it must be remembered under what conditions and to what end that takes place.

It is really a commercial transaction. Knowledge is just a commodity. It is acquired in order to be resold. All those who have grown out of going to school have to do their learning virtually in secret, for anyone who admits that he still has something to learn devalues himself as a man whose knowledge is inadequate. Moreover the usefulness of learning is very much limited by factors outside the learner's control. There is unemployment, for instance, against which no knowledge can protect one. There is the division of labour, which makes generalized knowledge unnecessary and impossible. Learning is often among the concerns of those whom no amount of concern will get any forwarder. There is not much knowledge that leads to power, but plenty of knowledge to which only power can lead.

Learning has a very different function for different social strata. There are strata who cannot imagine any improvement in conditions: they find the conditions good enough for them. Whatever happens to oil they will benefit from it. And: they feel the years beginning to tell. There can't be all that many years more. What is the point of learning a lot now? They have said their final word: a grunt. But there are also strata 'waiting their turn' who are discontented with conditions, have a vast interest in the practical side of learning, want at all costs to find out where they stand, and know that they are lost without learning; these are the best and keenest learners. Similar differences apply to countries and peoples. Thus the pleasure of learning depends on all sorts of things; but none the less there is such a thing as pleasurable learning, cheerful and militant learning.

If there were not such amusement to be had from learning the theatre's whole structure would unfit it for teaching.

Theatre remains theatre even when it is instructive theatre, and in so far as it is good theatre it will amuse.

THEATRE AND KNOWLEDGE

But what has knowledge got to do with art? We know that knowledge can be amusing, but not everything that is amusing belongs in the theatre.

I have often been told, when pointing out the invaluable services that modern knowledge and science, if properly applied, can perform for art and specially for the theatre, that art and knowledge are two estimable but wholly distinct fields of human activity. This is a fearful truism, of course, and it is as well to agree quickly that, like most truisms, it is perfectly true. Art and science work in quite different ways: agreed. But, bad as it may sound, I have to admit that I cannot get along as an artist without the use of one or two sciences. This may well arouse serious doubts as to my artistic capacities. People are used to seeing poets as unique and slightly unnatural beings who reveal with a truly godlike assurance things that other people can only recognize after much sweat and toil. It is naturally distasteful to have to admit that one does not belong to this select band. All the same, it must be admitted. It must at the same time be made clear that the scientific occupations just confessed to are not pardonable side interests, pursued on days off after a good week's work. We all know how Goethe was interested in natural history, Schiller in history: as a kind of hobby, it is charitable to assume. I have no wish promptly to accuse these two of having needed these sciences for their poetic activity; I am not trying to shelter behind them; but I must say that I do need the sciences. I have to admit, however, that I look askance at all sorts of people who I know do not operate on the level of scientific understanding: that is to say, who sing as the birds sing, or as people imagine the birds to sing. I don't mean by that that I would reject a charming poem about the taste of fried fish or the delights of a boating party just because the writer had not studied gastronomy or navigation. But in my view the great and complicated things that go on in the world cannot be adequately recognized by people who do not use every possible aid to understanding.

Let us suppose that great passions or great events have to be shown which influence the fate of nations. The lust for power is nowadays held to be such a passion. Given that a poet 'feels' this lust and wants to have someone strive for power, how is he to show the exceedingly complicated machinery within which the struggle for power nowadays takes place? If his hero is a politician, how do politics work? If he is a business man, how does business work? And yet there are writers who find business and politics nothing like so passionately interesting as the individual's lust for power. How are they to acquire the necessary knowledge? They are scarcely likely to learn enough by going round and keeping their eyes open, though even then it is more than they would get by just rolling their eyes in an exalted frenzy. The foundation of a paper like the *Völkischer Beobachter* or a business like Standard Oil is a pretty complicated affair, and such things cannot be conveyed just like that. One important field for the playwright is psychology. It is taken for granted that a poet, if not an ordinary man, must be able without further instruction to discover the motives that lead a man to commit murder; he must be able to give a picture of a murderer's mental state 'from within himself.' It is taken for granted that one only has to look inside oneself in such a case; and then there's always one's imagination. . . . There are various reasons why I can no longer surrender to this agreeable hope of getting a result quite so simply. I can no longer find in myself all those motives which the press or scientific reports show to have been observed in people. Like the average judge when pronouncing sentence, I cannot without further ado conjure up an adequate picture of a murderer's mental state. Modern psychology, from psychoanalysis to behaviourism, acquaints me with facts that lead me to judge the case quite differently, especially if I bear in mind the findings of sociology and do not overlook economics and history. You will say: but that's getting complicated. I have to answer that it *is* complicated. Even if you let yourself be convinced, and agree with me that a large slice of literature is exceedingly primitive, you may still ask with profound concern: won't an evening in such a theatre be a most alarming affair? The answer to that is: no.

Whatever knowledge is embodied in a piece of poetic writing has to be wholly transmuted into poetry. Its utilization fulfils the very pleasure that the poetic element provokes. If it does not at the same time fulfil that which is fulfilled by the scientific element, none the less in an age of great discoveries and inventions one must have a certain inclination to penetrate deeper into things—a desire to make the world controllable—if one is to be sure of enjoying its poetry.

IS THE EPIC THEATRE SOME KIND OF 'MORAL INSTITUTION'?

According to Friedrich Schiller the theatre is supposed to be a moral institution. In making this demand it hardly occurred to Schiller that by moralizing from the stage he might drive the audience out of the theatre. Audiences had no objection to moralizing in his day. It was only later that Friedrich Nietzsche attacked him for blowing a moral trumpet. To Nietzsche any concern with morality was a depressing affair; to Schiller it seemed thoroughly enjoyable. He knew of nothing that could give greater amusement and satisfaction than the propagation of ideas. The bourgeoisie was setting about forming the ideas of the nation.

Putting one's house in order, patting oneself on the back, submitting one's account, is something highly agreeable. But describing the collapse of one's house, having pains in the back, paying one's account, is indeed a depressing affair, and that was how Friedrich Nietzsche saw things a century later. He was poorly disposed towards morality, and thus towards the previous Friedrich too.

The epic theatre was likewise often objected to as moralizing too much. Yet in the epic theatre moral arguments only took second place. Its aim was less to moralize than to observe. That is to say it observed, and then the thick end of the wedge followed: the story's moral. Of course we cannot pretend that we started our observations out of a pure passion for observing and without any more practical motive, only to be completely staggered by their results. Undoubtedly there were some painful discrepancies in our environment, circumstances that were barely tolerable, and this not merely on account of moral considerations. It is not only moral considerations that make hunger, cold and oppression hard to bear. Similarly, the object of our inquiries was not just to arouse moral objections to such circumstances (even though they could easily be felt—though not by all the audience alike; such objections were seldom for instance felt by those who profited by the circumstances in question) but to discover means for their elimination. We were not in fact speaking in the name of morality but in that of the victims. These truly are two distinct matters, for the victims are often told that they ought to be contented with their lot, for moral reasons. Moralists of this sort see man as existing for morality, not morality for man. At least it should be possible to gather from the above to what degree and in what sense the epic theatre is a moral institution.

CAN EPIC THEATRE BE PLAYED ANYWHERE?

Stylistically speaking, there is nothing all that new about the epic theatre. Its expository character and its emphasis on virtuosity bring it close to the old Asiatic theatre. Didactic tendencies are to be found in the medieval mystery plays and the classical Spanish theatre, and also in the theatre of the Jesuits.

These theatrical forms corresponded to particular trends of their time, and vanished with them. Similarly the modern epic theatre is linked with certain trends. It cannot by any means be practised universally. Most of the great nations today are not disposed to use the theatre for ventilating their problems. London, Paris, Tokyo and Rome maintain their theatres for quite different purposes. Up to now favourable circumstances for an epic and didactic theatre have only been found in a few places and for a short period of time. In Berlin Fascism put a very definite stop to the development of such a theatre.

It demands not only a certain technological level but a powerful movement in society which is interested to see vital questions freely aired with a view to their solution, and can defend this interest against every contrary trend.

The epic theatre is the broadest and most far-reaching attempt at large-scale modern theatre, and it has all those immense difficulties to overcome that always confront the vital forces in the sphere of politics, philosophy, science and art.

ANTONIN ARTAUD (1896–1948)
from *The Theater and Its Double* (1938)
TRANSLATED BY MARY CAROLINE RICHARDS

An early member of the surrealist movement in Paris, Antonin Artaud was well-known between the wars as an actor, playwright, and essayist of the avant-garde theater, and he is one of the formative influences on the modern European theater. Artaud is most often associated with the "theater of cruelty," his label for a theater that would assault the representational dynamics of traditional theater and break the boundaries between actor and audience, stage and spectacle. Artaud was declared insane and committed to a mental hospital in 1937. He remained institutionalized for most of the remainder of his life.

THE THEATER AND CULTURE

Never before, when it is life itself that is in question, has there been so much talk of civilization and culture. And there is a curious parallel between this generalized collapse of life at the root of our present demoralization and our concern for a culture which has never been coincident with life, which in fact has been devised to tyrannize over life.

Before speaking further about culture, I must remark that the world is hungry and not concerned with culture, and that the attempt to orient toward culture thoughts turned only toward hunger is a purely artificial expedient.

What is most important, it seems to me, is not so much to defend a culture whose existence has never kept a man from going hungry, as to extract, from what is called culture, ideas whose compelling force is identical with that of hunger.

We need to live first of all; to believe in what makes us live and that something *makes* us live—to believe that whatever is produced from the mysterious depths of ourselves need not forever haunt us as an exclusively digestive concern.

I mean that if it is important for us to eat first of all, it is even more important for us not to waste in the sole concern for eating our simple power of being hungry.

If confusion is the sign of the times, I see at the root of this confusion a rupture between things and words, between things and the ideas and signs that are their representation.

Not, of course, for lack of philosophical systems; their number and contradictions characterize our old French and European culture: but where can it be shown that life, our life, has ever been affected by these systems? I will not say that philosophical systems must be applied directly and immediately: but of the following alternatives, one must be true:

Either these systems are within us and permeate our being to the point of supporting life itself (and if this is the case, what use are books?), or they do *not* permeate us and therefore do not have the capacity to support life (and in this case what does their disappearance matter?).

We must insist upon the idea of culture-in-action, of culture growing within us like a new organ, a sort of second breath; and on civilization as an applied culture controlling even our subtlest actions, a *presence of mind;* the distinction between culture and civilization is an artificial one, providing two words to signify an identical function.

A civilized man judges and is judged according to his behavior, but even the term "civilized" leads to confusion: a cultivated "civilized" man is regarded as a person instructed in systems, a person who thinks in forms, signs, representations—a monster whose faculty of deriving thoughts from acts, instead of identifying acts with thoughts, is developed to an absurdity.

If our life lacks brimstone, i.e., a constant magic, it is because we choose to observe our acts and lose ourselves in considerations of their imagined form instead of being impelled by their force.

And this faculty is an exclusively human one. I would even say that it is this infection of the human which contaminates ideas that should have remained divine; for far from believing that man invented the supernatural and the divine, I think it is man's age-old intervention which has ultimately corrupted the divine within him.

All our ideas about life must be revised in a period when nothing any longer adheres to life; it is this painful cleavage which is responsible for the revenge of *things;* the poetry which is no longer within us and which we no longer succeed in finding in things suddenly appears on their wrong side: consider the unprecedented number of crimes whose perverse gratuitousness is explained only by our powerlessness to take complete possession of life.

If the theater has been created as an outlet for our repressions, the agonized poetry expressed in its bizarre corruptions of the facts of life demonstrates that life's intensity is still intact and asks only to be better directed.

But no matter how loudly we clamor for magic in our lives, we are really afraid of pursuing an existence entirely under its influence and sign.

Hence our confirmed lack of culture is astonished by certain grandiose anomalies; for example, on an island without any contact with modern civilization, the mere passage of a ship carrying only healthy passengers may provoke the sudden outbreak of diseases unknown on that island but a specialty of nations like our own: shingles, influenza, grippe, rheumatism, sinusitis, polyneuritis, etc.

Similarly, if we think Negroes smell bad, we are ignorant of the fact that anywhere but in Europe it is we whites who "smell bad." And I would even say that we give off an odor as white as the gathering of pus in an infected wound.

As iron can be heated until it turns white, so it can be said that everything excessive is white; for Asiatics white has become the mark of extreme decomposition.

This said, we can begin to form an idea of culture, an idea which is first of all a protest.

A protest against the senseless constraint imposed upon the idea of culture by reducing it to a sort of inconceivable Pantheon, producing an idolatry no different from the image-worship of those religions which relegate their gods to Pantheons.

A protest against the idea of culture as distinct from life—as if there were culture on one side and life on the other, as if true culture were not a refined means of understanding and *exercising* life.

The library at Alexandria can be burnt down. There are forces above and beyond papyrus: we may temporarily be deprived of our ability to discover these forces, but their energy will not be suppressed. It is good that our excessive facilities are no longer available, that forms fall into oblivion: a culture without space or time, restrained only by the capacity of our own nerves, will reappear with all the more energy. It is right that from time to time cataclysms occur which compel us to return to nature, i.e., to rediscover life. The old totemism of animals, stones, objects capable of discharging thunderbolts, costumes impregnated with bestial essences—everything, in short, that might determine, disclose, and direct the secret forces of the universe—is for us a dead thing, from which we derive nothing but static and aesthetic profit, the profit of an audience, not of an actor.

Yet totemism is an actor, for it moves, and has been created in behalf of actors; all true culture relies upon the barbaric and primitive means of totemism whose savage, i.e., entirely spontaneous, life I wish to worship.

What has lost us culture is our Occidental idea of art and the profits we seek to derive from it. Art and culture cannot be considered together, contrary to the treatment universally accorded them!

True culture operates by exaltation and force, while the European ideal of art attempts to cast the mind into an attitude distinct from force but addicted to exaltation. It is a lazy, unserviceable notion which engenders an imminent death. If the Serpent Quetzalcoatl's multiple twists and turns are harmonious, it is because they express the equilibrium and fluctuations of a sleeping force; the intensity of the forms is there only to seduce and direct a force which, in music, would produce an insupportable range of sound.

The gods that sleep in museums: the god of fire with his incense burner that resembles an Inquisition tripod; Tlaloc, one of the manifold Gods of the Waters, on his wall of green granite; the Mother Goddess of Waters, the Mother Goddess of Flowers; the immutable expression, echoing from beneath many layers of water, of the Goddess robed in green jade; the enraptured, blissful expression, features crackling with incense, where atoms of sunlight circle—the countenance of the Mother Goddess of Flowers; this world of obligatory servitude in which a stone comes alive when it has been properly carved, the world of organically civilized men whose vital organs too awaken from their slumber, this human world enters into us, participating in the dance of the gods without turning round or looking back, on pain of becoming, like ourselves, crumbled pillars of salt.

In Mexico, since we are talking about Mexico, there is no art: things are made for use. And the world is in perpetual exaltation.

To our disinterested and inert idea of art an authentic culture opposes a violently egoistic and magical, i.e., *interested* idea. For the Mexicans seek contact with the *Manas*, forces latent in every form, unreleased by contemplation of the forms for themselves, but springing to life by magic identification with these forms. And the old Totems are there to hasten the communication.

How hard it is, when everything encourages us to sleep, though we may look about us with conscious, clinging eyes, to wake and yet look about us as in a dream, with eyes that no longer know their function and whose gaze is turned inward.

This is how our strange idea of disinterested action originated, though it is action nonetheless, and all the more violent for skirting the temptation of repose.

Every real effigy has a shadow which is its double; and art must falter and fail from the moment the sculptor believes he has liberated the kind of shadow whose very existence will destroy his repose.

Like all magic cultures expressed by appropriate hieroglyphs, the true theater has its shadows too, and, of all languages and all arts, the theater is the only one left whose shadows have shattered their limitations. From the beginning, one might say its shadows did not tolerate limitations.

Our petrified idea of the theater is connected with our petrified idea of a culture without shadows, where, no matter which way it turns, our mind *(esprit)* encounters only emptiness, though space is full.

But the true theater, because it moves and makes use of living instruments, continues to stir up shadows where life has never ceased to grope its way. The actor does not make the same gestures twice, but he makes gestures, he moves; and although he brutalizes forms, nevertheless behind them and through their destruction he rejoins that which outlives forms and produces their continuation.

The theater, which is in *no thing,* but makes use of everything—gestures, sounds, words, screams, light, darkness—rediscovers itself at precisely the point where the mind requires a language to express its manifestations.

And the fixation of the theater in one language—written words, music, lights, noises—betokens its imminent ruin, the choice of any one language betraying a taste for the special effects of that language; and the dessication of the language accompanies its limitation.

For the theater as for culture, it remains a question of naming and directing shadows: and the theater, not confined to a fixed language and form, not only destroys false shadows but prepares the way for a new generation of shadows, around which assembles the true spectacle of life.

To break through language in order to touch life is to create or recreate the theater; the essential thing is not to believe that this act must remain sacred, i.e., set apart—the essential thing is to believe that not just anyone can create it, and that there must be a preparation.

This leads to the rejection of the usual limitations of man and man's powers, and infinitely extends the frontiers of what is called reality.

We must believe in a sense of life renewed by the theater, a sense of life in which man fearlessly makes himself master of what does not yet exist, and brings it into being. And everything that has not been born can still be brought to life if we are not satisfied to remain mere recording organisms.

Furthermore, when we speak the word "life," it must be understood we are not referring to life as we know it from its surface of fact, but to that fragile, fluctuating center which forms never reach. And if there is still one hellish, truly accursed thing in our time, it is our artistic dallying with forms, instead of being like victims burnt at the stake, signaling through the flames.

• • •

NO MORE MASTERPIECES

One of the reasons for the asphyxiating atmosphere in which we live without possible escape or remedy—and in which we all share, even the most revolutionary among us—is our respect for what has been written, formulated, or painted, what has been given form, as if all expression were not at last exhausted, were not at a point where things must break apart if they are to start anew and begin fresh.

We must have done with this idea of masterpieces reserved for a self-styled elite and not understood by the general public; the mind has no such restricted districts as those so often used for clandestine sexual encounters.

Masterpieces of the past are good for the past: they are not good for us. We have the right to say what has been said and even what has not been said in a way that belongs to us, a way that is immediate and direct, corresponding to present modes of feeling, and understandable to everyone.

It is idiotic to reproach the masses for having no sense of the sublime, when the sublime is confused with one or another of its formal manifestations, which are moreover always defunct manifestations. And if for example a contemporary public does not understand *Oedipus Rex,* I shall make bold to say that it is the fault of *Oedipus Rex* and not of the public.

In *Oedipus Rex* there is the theme of incest and the idea that nature mocks at morality and that there are certain unspecified powers at large which we would do well to beware of, call them *destiny* or anything you choose.

There is in addition the presence of a plague epidemic which is a physical incarnation of these powers. But the whole in a manner and language that have lost all touch with the rude and epileptic rhythm of our time. Sophocles speaks grandly perhaps, but in a style that is no longer timely. His language is too refined for this age. It is as if he were speaking beside the point.

However, a public that shudders at train wrecks, that is familiar with earthquakes, plagues, revolutions, wars; that is sensitive to the disordered anguish of love, can be affected by all these grand notions and asks only to become aware of them, but on condition that it is addressed in its own language, and that its knowledge of these things does not come to it through adulterated trappings and speech that belong to extinct eras which will never live again.

Today as yesterday, the public is greedy for mystery: it asks only to become aware of the laws according to which destiny manifests itself, and to divine perhaps the secret of its apparitions.

Let us leave textual criticism to graduate students, formal criticism to esthetes, and recognize that what has been said is not still to be said; that an expression does not have the same value twice, does not live two lives; that all words, once spoken, are dead and function only at the moment when they are uttered, that a form, once it has served, cannot be used again and asks only to be replaced by another, and that the theater is the only place in the world where a gesture, once made, can never be made the same way twice.

If the public does not frequent our literary masterpieces, it is because those masterpieces are literary, that is to say, fixed; and fixed in forms that no longer respond to the needs of the time.

Far from blaming the public, we ought to blame the formal screen we interpose between ourselves and the public, and this new form of idolatry, the idolatry of fixed masterpieces which is one of the aspects of bourgeois conformism.

This conformism makes us confuse sublimity, ideas, and things with the forms they have taken in time and in our minds—in our snobbish, precious, aesthetic mentalities which the public does not understand.

How pointless in such matters to accuse the public of bad taste because it relishes insanities, so long as the public is not shown a valid spectacle; and I defy anyone to show me *here* a spectacle valid—valid in the supreme sense of the theater—since the last great romantic melodramas, i.e., since a hundred years ago.

The public, which takes the false for the true, has the sense of the true and always responds to it when it is manifested. However it is not upon the stage that the true is to be sought nowadays, but in the street; and if the crowd in the street is offered an occasion to show its human dignity, it will always do so.

If people are out of the habit of going to the theater, if we have all finally come to think of theater as an inferior art, a means of popular distraction, and to use it as an outlet for our worst instincts, it is because we have learned too well what the theater has been, namely, falsehood and illusion. It is because we have been accustomed for four hundred years, that is since the Renaissance, to a purely descriptive and narrative theater—storytelling psychology; it is because every possible ingenuity has been exerted in bringing to life on the stage plausible but detached beings, with the spectacle on one side, the public on the other—and because the public is no longer shown anything but the mirror of itself.

Shakespeare himself is responsible for this aberration and decline, this disinterested idea of the theater which wishes a theatrical performance to leave the public intact, without setting off one image that will shake the organism to its foundations and leave an ineffaceable scar.

If, in Shakespeare, a man is sometimes preoccupied with what transcends him, it is always in order to determine the ultimate consequences of this preoccupation within him, i.e., psychology.

Psychology, which works relentlessly to reduce the unknown to the known, to the quotidian and the ordinary, is the cause of the theater's abasement and its fearful loss of energy, which seems to me to have reached its lowest point. And I think both the theater and we ourselves have had enough of psychology.

I believe furthermore that we can all agree on this matter sufficiently so that there is no need to descend to the repugnant level of the modern and French theater to condemn the theater of psychology.

Stories about money, worry over money, social careerism, the pangs of love unspoiled by altruism, sexuality sugar-coated with an eroticism that has lost its mystery have nothing to do with the theater, even if they do belong to psychology. These torments, seductions, and lusts before which we are nothing but Peeping Toms gratifying our cravings, tend to go bad, and their rot turns to revolution: we must take this into account.

But this is not our most serious concern.

If Shakespeare and his imitators have gradually insinuated the idea of art for art's sake, with art on one side and life on the other, we can rest on this feeble and lazy idea only as long as the life outside endures. But there are too many signs that everything that used to sustain our lives no longer does so, that we are all mad, desperate, and sick. And I call for us to react.

This idea of a detached art, of poetry as a charm which exists only to distract our leisure, is a decadent idea and an unmistakable symptom of our power to castrate.

Our literary admiration for Rimbaud, Jarry, Lautréamont, and a few others, which has driven two men to suicide, but turned into café gossip for the rest, belongs to this idea of literary poetry, of detached art, of neutral spiritual activity which creates nothing and produces nothing; and I can bear witness that at the very moment when that kind of personal poetry which involves only the man who creates it and only at the moment he creates it broke out in its most abusive fashion, the theater was scorned more than ever before by poets

who have never had the sense of direct and concerted action, nor of efficacity, nor of danger.

We must get rid of our superstitious valuation of texts and *written* poetry. Written poetry is worth reading once, and then should be destroyed. Let the dead poets make way for others. Then we might even come to see that it is our veneration for what has already been created, however beautiful and valid it may be, that petrifies us, deadens our responses, and prevents us from making contact with that underlying power, call it thought-energy, the life force, the determinism of change, lunar menses, or anything you like. Beneath the poetry of the texts, there is the actual poetry, without form and without text. And just as the efficacity of masks in the magic practices of certain tribes is exhausted—and these masks are no longer good for anything except museums—so the poetic efficacity of a text is exhausted; yet the poetry and the efficacity of the theater are exhausted least quickly of all, since they permit the *action* of what is gesticulated and pronounced, and which is never made the same way twice.

It is a question of knowing what we want. If we are prepared for war, plague, famine, and slaughter we do not even need to say so, we have only to continue as we are; continue behaving like snobs, rushing en masse to hear such and such a singer, to see such and such an admirable performance which never transcends the realm of art (and even the Russian ballet at the height of its splendor never transcended the realm of art), to marvel at such and such an exhibition of painting in which exciting shapes explode here and there but at random and without any genuine consciousness of the forces they could rouse.

This empiricism, randomness, individualism, and anarchy must cease.

Enough of personal poems, benefitting those who create them much more than those who read them.

Once and for all, enough of this closed, egoistic, and personal art.

Our spiritual anarchy and intellectual disorder is a function of the anarchy of everything else—or rather, everything else is a function of this anarchy.

I am not one of those who believe that civilization has to change in order for the theater to change; but I do believe that the theater, utilized in the highest and most difficult sense possible, has the power to influence the aspect and formation of things: and the encounter upon the stage of two passionate manifestations, two living centers, two nervous magnetisms is something as entire, true, even decisive, as, in life, the encounter of one epidermis with another in a timeless debauchery.

That is why I propose a theater of cruelty.—With this mania we all have for depreciating everything, as soon as I have said "cruelty," everybody will at once take it to mean "blood." But *theater of cruelty*" means a theater difficult and cruel for myself first of all. And, on the level of performance, it is not the cruelty we can exercise upon each other by hacking at each other's bodies, carving up our personal anatomies, or, like Assyrian emperors, sending parcels of human ears, noses, or neatly detached nostrils through the mail, but the much more terrible and necessary cruelty which things can exercise against us. We are not free. And the sky can still fall on our heads. And the theater has been created to teach us that first of all.

Either we will be capable of returning by present-day means to this superior idea of poetry and poetry-through-theater which underlies the Myths told by the great ancient tragedians, capable once more of entertaining a religious idea of the theater (without meditation, useless contemplation, and vague dreams), capable of attaining awareness and a possession of certain dominant forces, of certain notions that control all others, and (since ideas, when they are effective, carry their energy with them) capable of recovering within ourselves those energies which ultimately create order and increase the value of life, or else we might as well abandon ourselves now, without protest, and recognize that we are no longer good for anything but disorder, famine, blood, war, and epidemics.

Either we restore all the arts to a central attitude and necessity, finding an analogy between a gesture made in painting or the theater, and a gesture made by lava in a volcanic explosion, or we must stop painting, babbling, writing, or doing whatever it is we do.

I propose to bring back into the theater this elementary magical idea, taken up by modern psychoanalysis, which consists in effecting a patient's cure by making him assume the apparent and exterior attitudes of the desired condition.

I propose to renounce our empiricism of imagery, in which the unconscious furnishes images at random, and which the poet arranges at random too, calling them poetic and hence hermetic images, as if the kind of trance that poetry provides did not have its reverberations throughout the whole sensibility, in every nerve, and as if poetry were some vague force whose movements were invariable.

I propose to return through the theater to an idea of the physical knowledge of images and the means of inducing trances, as in Chinese medicine which knows, over the entire extent of the human anatomy, at what points to puncture in order to regulate the subtlest functions.

Those who have forgotten the communicative power and magical mimesis of a gesture, the theater can reinstruct, because a gesture carries its energy with it, and there are still human beings in the theater to manifest the force of the gesture made.

To create art is to deprive a gesture of its reverberation in the organism, whereas this reverberation, if the gesture is made in the conditions and with the force required, incites the organism and, through it, the entire individuality, to take attitudes in harmony with the gesture.

The theater is the only place in the world, the last general means we still possess of directly affecting the organism and, in periods of neurosis and petty sensuality like the one in which we are immersed, of attacking this sensuality by physical means it cannot withstand.

If music affects snakes, it is not on account of the spiritual notions it offers them, but because snakes are long and coil their length upon the earth, because their bodies touch the earth at almost every point; and because the musical vibrations which are communicated to the earth affect them like a very subtle, very long massage; and I propose to treat the spectators like the snakecharmer's subjects and conduct them *by means of their organisms* to an apprehension of the subtlest notions.

At first by crude means, which will gradually be refined. These immediate crude means will hold their attention at the start.

That is why in the "theater of cruelty" the spectator is in the center and the spectacle surrounds him.

In this spectacle the sonorisation is constant: sounds, noises, cries are chosen first for their vibratory quality, then for what they represent.

Among these gradually refined means light is interposed in its turn. Light which is not created merely to add color or to brighten, and which brings its power, influence, suggestions with it. And the light of a green cavern does not sensually dispose the organism like the light of a windy day.

After sound and light there is action, and the dynamism of action: here the theater, far from copying life, puts itself whenever possible in communication with pure forces. And whether you accept or deny them, there is nevertheless a way of speaking which gives the name of "forces" to whatever brings to birth images of energy in the unconscious, and gratuitous crime on the surface.

A violent and concentrated action is a kind of lyricism: it summons up supernatural images, a bloodstream of images, a bleeding spurt of images in the poet's head and in the spectator's as well.

Whatever the conflicts that haunt the mind of a given period, I defy any spectator to whom such violent scenes will have transferred their blood, who will have felt in himself the transit of a superior action, who will have seen the extraordinary and essential movements of his thought illuminated in extraordinary deeds—the violence and blood having been placed at the service of the violence of the thought—I defy that spectator to give himself up, once outside the theater, to ideas of war, riot, and blatant murder.

So expressed, this idea seems dangerous and sophomoric. It will be claimed that example breeds example, that if the attitude of cure induces cure, the attitude of murder will induce murder. Everything depends upon the manner and the purity with which the thing is done. There is a risk. But let it not be forgotten that though a theatrical gesture is violent, it is disinterested; and that the theater teaches precisely the uselessness of the action which, once done, is not to be done, and the superior use of the state unused by the action and which, *restored,* produces a purification.

I propose then a theater in which violent physical images crush and hypnotize the sensibility of the spectator seized by the theater as by a whirlwind of higher forces.

A theater which, abandoning psychology, recounts the extraordinary, stages natural conflicts, natural and subtle forces, and presents itself first of all as an exceptional power of redirection. A theater that induces trance, as the dances of Dervishes induce trance, and that addresses itself to the organism by precise instruments, by the same means as those of certain tribal music cures which we admire on records but are incapable of originating among ourselves.

There is a risk involved, but in the present circumstances I believe it is a risk worth running. I do not believe we have managed to revitalize the world we live in, and I do not believe it is worth the trouble of clinging to; but I do propose something to get us out of our marasmus, instead of continuing to complain about it, and about the boredom, inertia, and stupidity of everything.

UNA CHAUDHURI

from *Staging Place: The Geography of Modern Drama* (1995)
THE POLITICS OF HOME AND THE POETICS OF EXILE

Una Chaudhuri has written widely on modern drama and performance, and is the author of a well-known book on Genet, as well as of Staging Place. *In this selection from the opening chapter of* Staging Place, *Chaudhuri explores the many places of modern drama, elaborating the relationship between the ongoing thematics of home and exile.*

I think that it is at least empirically arguable that our daily life, our psychic experience, our cultural languages, are today dominated by categories of space rather than categories of time, as in the period of high modernism.
—Fredric Jameson, *Postmodernism, or The Cultural Logic of Late Capitalism*

The prevalence of space-based studies in the social sciences and in cultural studies is a response to an increasingly complex cultural experience of space and place,[1] one that has decisively displaced the older paradigms of spatial intelligibility not only in the realm of art but also, thanks to the mass media, in that of public culture, and hence in contemporary consciousness. Therefore, the conceptual horizon for considering the theater's use of space and the drama's discourse on place is an ever-changing one, reflecting changes in the cultural, technological, and even the theoretical processing of space.

For example: during the time this book was being written, an inescapable element of the American popular culture scene was an ad campaign for Pepsi-Cola. The original TV commercials featured Ray Charles accompanied by three gorgeous female backup singers (the Raylettes) in short, shiny, skintight dresses. The main lyric asserted that Pepsi-Cola was "the right one, Baby," to which Ray, supported by the Raylettes, added an enthusiastic (and cinematographically punched-in) "Uh-huh." The commercial became (or was made, through the efforts of the ad agency) so popular that T-shirts and other consumer goods appeared bearing the legend "Uh-huh!" A news item in the *Wall Street Journal* reported that executives at the rival company, Coca-Cola, were going around trying to avoid using the expression "uh-huh" in their conversations! As time went on, the original commercial was expanded and extended and varied in a number of highly effective ways. One of these showed other famous people, including Jerry Lewis, Charo, and Tiny Tim, "auditioning" for Ray's role, doing hilariously bad renditions of the by now famous lyric.

One quite extraordinary installment, for which much anticipation was whipped up by the ad company, and which first aired during the half-time period of the Super Bowl, extended the range of jingle singers far beyond the American pop-cultural scene. This lengthy commercial showed huge gatherings of people in foreign lands—China, India, Japan—singing the jingle in their own various stereotypical ways, with a variety of accents and music styles. One of the scenes showed a group of Buddhist monks sitting cross-legged on the ground in formal rows in a monastery, intoning "uh-huh, uh-huh" in deep and solemn tones, as if it were a mantra or prayer.

The technical brilliance of this commercial, as well as its appropriation of the seductive and stereotypical images often used by the airline and tourist industries of the world, was partly responsible for the pleasure it gave. But there was another, less benign, element in its success as well. Under its cheery good humor and its apparently generous sharing of the pleasures of Pepsi with the peoples of the world, the ad was a blatant inscription of American economic imperialism, and it revealed quite precisely what the semiological—that is, the ideological, aesthetic, and psychological—terms of this imperialism are. In this semiotic, which is also the semiotic of Walt Disney World's World Showcase, parts of the world are isolated and double coded as different and yet the same, their difference being a matter of spectacle, while their sameness is a matter of desire. The spectacular Other, whose otherness is contained within—and figured purely as—superficial *style* (of clothes, architecture, music, etc.) is the necessary foundation for a figuration of universal consumerist desire.

How successful this figuration has been in material terms is now depressingly well known. The triumph of American consumerism goes beyond its undeniable monuments—the McDonald's in Moscow, the Disneyland near Paris, the Pizza Hut in Calcutta, and so on—to the realm of representation itself. The full import of the Pepsi commercial as universalizing discourse did not become clear to me until I saw, on a trip to India, the Indian version of the commercial. Gone were Ray and the Raylettes; in their place a number of Indian actors in different situations sang the same jingle, while the aforementioned Buddhist monks (on loan from the American version of the ad?) intoned their solemn "uh-huhs."

The West's construction of otherness takes a dizzying turn when, supported by the power of multinational capital, it dictates the self-construction of non-Western identities. This spiral of misrepresentation and self-misrepresentation—which has its origins in the orientalist discourse of the earliest colonialisms—is now well established. The logic it obeys is similar to the traditional logic of gender difference, according to which the best woman is a man, because (as Song Liling says in *M. Butterfly*) "only a man knows how a woman is supposed to act." Unlike gender, however, national and ethnic identities are often derived from or directed toward a *geography*; there is a *location* of identity based on race, nation, ethnicity, language—in short, all the elements that together or in part designate the notion of a culture—that is often absent from the discourse of gender. To put it bluntly, the construction of cultural otherness is also a *mapping of the world,* a fact that contributes powerfully to the literalization of accounts of ethnic difference.

A book on place and the representation of place such as this one cannot avoid acknowledging the discourse of the Pepsi commercial as one of its horizons; no contemporary inquiry into the nature of place can ignore the placement and displacement wrought by the global mass media operating in support of a global consumer economy. The images of otherness set to the music of Ray Charles are simply the quintessential summarizing of the current state of the category of place, a category this century has seen beset by extraordinary challenges and changes. As Brecht's astonishing prologue to *The Caucasian Chalk Circle* makes clear, the *meaning* (not merely the ownership) of place has given this century its politics; we should not be surprised to find, as this book argues, that it has also given it its theater, and that a complex engagement with the significance, determinations, and potentialities of place courses through the body of modern drama.

Besides the mass media's capture of otherness—within a web of implied sameness disguised as difference—the second major source of the gradual reinscription of place in the late twentieth century is the revolution in electronic communications. In the modern world of computerized data management and instantaneous information dispersal, a person's basic mode of location is altered. Instead of experiencing life from a fixed point in space and time, the subject of the electronic society is, as Mark Poster writes, "multiplied by databases, dispersed by computer messaging and conferencing, decontextualized and reidentified by TV ads, dissolved and materialized continuously in the electronic transmission of symbols." So thoroughgoing and ubiquitous is this dispersal of subjective experience over multiple electronic channels that human beings can be said to be returning to a nomadic form of existence, wandering over vast global distances daily as they change channels, fax letters, leave messages on answering machines, and have the facts of their socioeconomic lives gathered, stored, and analyzed by myriad marketing concerns.

As Mark Poster puts it, the new version of "who am I?" is firmly anchored in a new form of "*where* am I?"

> If I can speak directly to a friend in Paris while sitting in California, if I can witness political and cultural events as they occur across the globe without leaving my home, if a database at a remote location contains my profile and informs government agencies which make the decisions that affect my life without any knowledge on my part of these events, if I can shop in my home using my TV or computer, then where am I and who am I? In these circumstances, I cannot consider myself centered in my rational, autonomous subjectivity or bordered by a defined ego, but I am disrupted, subverted, and dispersed across social space.

The erasure of spatial particularity, one of the hallmarks of post-modernism, is represented in drama (and elsewhere) through the figure of America. As we shall see in a later chapter, the America of the modern theater's imagination is a principle of dispersal, of dissolution. This America, which we shall meet in various guises throughout this book, is a complex and ultimately redemptive figure, for it is the hinge, the turning point in a more than century-long neglect of the very principle that it seems to erase: space. The rise in the nineteenth century of what Edward Soja calls a "destabilizing historicism" had, by the twentieth, deprivileged space to the point of denying it any explanatory or theoretical force whatsoever. Michel Foucault summarized the situation, asking, "Did it start with Bergson or before? Space was treated as the dead, the fixed, the undialectical, the immobile. Time, on the contrary, was richness, fecundity, life."

The category of space reenters the field of critical and social theory, as Soja has argued, through the works of Foucault, through structuralism, and through the writings of Henri Lefebvre. The formulation of a "postmodern critical geography" to counter and complement the rigid historicism of twentieth-century thought is a vast and vital project, of which one of the crucial goals is the recovery of *place*. It is in this area that the figure of America functions as a hinge, for it both *reproduces* and *displaces* the dominant theoretical bias against space. Through its alliance with the principles of progress and of homogeneity, the figure of America first signified a kind of ultimate placelessness, a guarantee of the absolute *un*meaning of place as a component of human experience. But the very success of this figuration—what one might call the hyperbole of American utopianism—proved to be its undoing. In the late twentieth century the figure of America has begun to be required, increasingly, to make good its utopian claims, and the principle of placelessness is confronted by the multivoiced demand for new *placements*. The movement known generally as multiculturalism is in fact a call for America to be reimagined: not, this time, as a utopia, but as what Foucault would call a "heterotopia," a place capable of containing within it many different, even incompatible, places.

As Soja explains it, Foucault's move was to navigate beyond several already ongoing efforts to respatialize social theory:

> Foucault outlined his notion of "heterotopias" as the characteristic spaces of the modern world, superseding the hierarchic "ensemble of places" of the Middle Ages and the enveloping "space of emplacement" opened up by Galileo into an early-modern, infinitely folding, "space of extension" and measurement. Moving away from both the "internal space" of Bachelard's brilliant poetics . . . and the intentional regional descriptions of the phenomenologists, Foucault focused our attention on another spatiality of social life, an "external space," the actually lived (and socially produced) space of sites and the relations between them.

This other spatiality is actually (to apply a neologism) a new *platiality,* a recognition of the signifying power and political potential of *specific places*.

In the theater (to return to the place that concerns me here) the encounter between this new platiality and the figure of America occurs most memorably in the drama of immigration and multiculturalism, which is the subject of the latter part of this book. But before this recent drama can replace the old accounts of space, place, and identity, the drama that supported those accounts must be thoroughly understood, which is to say, in terms of theatrical practice: deconstructed. The figure (or idea, or image, or myth) of America, then, is frequently used in contemporary drama as the vehicle for a critique, an engagement with and finally a revisioning of place. The figure of America is able to serve in this way—that is, in the deconstruction of place as traditionally conceived—because the discourse this figure disrupts most decisively is one that has structured—and continues to structure—traditional dramatic paradigms of place and identity most profoundly: the discourse of home.[2]

The privileged setting of modern drama is the family home.[3] The domestic interior contains the history of a process, begun in the nineteenth century and still unconcluded as the twentieth century nears its end, of a locational stage practice, a way of filling the signifying space of theater with an *environment*. This kind of environmentalism, which enters the drama through realism and naturalism (and which is intimately related to the figure of home), relies on and propagates a very special account of space and place. According to (and then thanks to) this environmentalism, placement becomes available to rational understanding and explanation. That is to say, place enters the positivist project as a factor of knowledge and a code of representation.

The first sign of this new coding of place is the ready divisibility of the world into what Philip Fisher calls "a spectrum of environments," a set of discrete economic zones each with "its local features, types, common languages, heroes and catastrophes."[4] The theater responds to this new view of space by developing a stage practice based on the principle of spatial intelligibility, on the idea that *where* an action unfolds goes a long way toward explaining it. The name of this stage practice is, of course, naturalism, but (as Raymond Williams argued in what remains the most sophisticated discussion of theatrical naturalism) it is not only as *stage* practice but also as a dramatic discourse that naturalism engages and revisions the category of space: "In high naturalism," writes Williams, "the lives of the characters have soaked into their environment. . . . Moreover, the environment has soaked into their lives."

Recognizing that this environmentalism determines dramatic discourse at a deep structural level, Williams singles out a plot device that will become central to the evolving discourse of modern drama: escape, or, more generally, creative displacement. For Williams, naturalism marks only the exhaustion or contradiction of this device. "The pre-naturalist conventions of providential escape or of resolution through recognition," he writes, "fall away in the face of this sombre assessment of the weight of the world: not a world which is background, nor an illustrative setting; but one which has entwined itself in the deepest layers of the personality." But the figure of escape is not so quickly depleted. From the late nineteenth century on, the image or idea of escape, of creative displacement, develops into a full-blown poetics of exile, from which the drama of the later twentieth century is still seeking to free itself.

THE POLITICS OF HOME

That there is a politics to simply being at home is no longer an unfamiliar idea: in terms of recent cultural practice, we saw one aspect of that politics in the transformation of the word *housewife* into the word *homemaker,* a substitution that played out a whole reconceptualization of the power relations between women and domesticity. The historical backgrounds of this shift and its far-reaching theoretical implications are being charted by feminist scholars today.[5] In the area that concerns me directly here, that of theatrical representation, a similar political thematic of home has prevailed. Indeed, as far as the stage is concerned, the ideology we recognize as modern humanism was inaugurated by a decision not to remain in a home as artificial and stifling as a doll's house.

However, as both these examples show, there has long been a certain reductive literalness in this conceptualization of home, one that, for all its desire to liberate or liberalize, will inevitably produce only a limited and ultimately reactionary account of identity. One of the cleverest (and earliest) schemas of this mode of self-production, as well as its disastrous consequences, is to be found in Poe's story "The Fall of the House of Usher," which suggests that the figure of home has long involved a denial of difference. The story shows the damage that unchecked literalism can do, as it forces an unwanted equivalence on several distinct entities: two individuals, a family, a family history, and a house. Poe's account of destruction by sheer reductiveness—all the Ushers collapse together into one undifferentiated heap—is also a deconstruction of the grotesque late-Romantic politics of singular identity, identity that feels itself too securely "housed" in a place where it can no longer be at home.

The theatrical version of the literalized home is to be found in realism, which from its inception has staged both the deterministic power as well as the crisis of this concept. One sign of the crisis is the violent ambiguity, in realism, of spatial signs. Ibsen's famous interactive architectural symbols—his climbable towers, slammable doors, and burnable buildings—help to construct domestic space as a problematic: both the *condition for* and the *obstacle to* psychological coherence. Again and again in Ibsen, the crisis of the concept of home appears as the collision therein of two incommensurable desires: the desire for a stable container for identity and the desire to deterritorialize the self.[6]

The figure of home lends itself to one of the basic impulses of realism—the attempt to locate a space of personal experimentation: experimentation with the definition of persons, and with selfhood. This project dovetails nicely with the sense we have, from the nuclear family setups of the twentieth century, that home is a space of obligatory self-fashioning. As James Ellenwood expressed it in 1939, when the bourgeois discourse of home was at its most unreflective and unproblematized:

> Because, and this is basic, we learn by doing, . . . the home is the one ideal place for working things out realistically. It is the laboratory where most experiments are tried. Other agencies lecture and teach us about good living, but here we are up against life itself. . . . In a home one HAS to work out problems and relationships that, elsewhere, are only theorized over. Here you have to make good.

But Ellenwood also isolates a few other characteristics of the figure of home that play into the increasingly paradoxical discourse of realism. Home is both a site of *difference* ("It would take no less than a genius to interest all the members of a family in many common programs," says Ellenwood) and a site of *compulsion* ("It is the place where you have to go when there is no other place you can or want to go. . . . Only rarely does one run away or resign. The normal home is a long sentence"). As we shall see in chapter 2, this contradictory conditionality of the figure of home—its status as both shelter and prison, security and as entrapment—is crucial to its dramatic meaning.

The theatrical conventions of the realist drama made their own contribution to the practice of deriving identity from environment. Under realism's rich re-creation of actual environments lay an attempted closure of fictionality, a will to close the gap between the world of the stage and the world of the spectator (the same will that led, later, to the hyperinclusive theatrology of environmental theater; see chap. 1). Several of the practices of the early naturalists sought to erase the difference between the public nature of theater and the private world of experience.[7] André Antoine, founder of the Théâtre-Libre, recalls that "For our second production, we decided to emphasize that this is no public playhouse, but a special private society, by sending out announcements folded in the form of wedding invitations" (quoted by Waxman). Antoine also had Strindberg's preface to *Miss Julie* translated and distributed to his audiences. As Samuel Waxman notes, "It was another step forward toward the twentieth century 'little' theatre that has become almost universal."

Needless to say, the public was not always ready to be drawn into the imagined intimacy dreamed of by the theater practitioners. Nemirovich-Danchenko, writing on the need to regulate late arrivals, exposes this conflict with spectators, reading so trivial a fact as lateness as a deliberate attempt on the spectator's part "to violate my will." He asserts that he "can't allow it," calling one such spectator a "bourgeois of the first water," and when the problem persists after the Russian Revolution, that kind of spectator is an "imbecile" who thinks "that the revolution gave him the right to do as he liked." He concludes by insisting that "our attitude to the public" is not the attitude of a "master," but that the spectator should be happy and grateful for the privilege of entering. The audience should behave like "charming guests," or "we [will] force it to submit to rules essential for the artistic unity of the spectacle."

The realist stage installed a logic of representation to which the spectator was, essentially, an obstacle, a hindrance, an inconvenience. As I will show in my discussion of *Miss Julie* in chapter 1, the paradox of this drama—the paradox of shared (i.e., public) private experience—involved the spectator in an impossible displacement, where s/he was asked to play the role of ultimate hermeneutic authority while being reminded simultaneously of the authorizing but invisible presence of the omnipotent puppet master/playwright, creator of all meaning.

Certainly the most significant intervention that realism made into the developing discourse on space was through its commitment to what we could now call a platiality of the stage, an emphasis on the particularity and materiality of each dramatic environment. How great a revolution this was is memorably expressed by Nemirovich-Danchenko in the following detailed account of what had been the scenic norm before realism:

> every play must have its own setting. . . . At present in every theatre of the Soviet Union this is commonly accepted as the ABC of the business, but then it seemed like a revolution. The old theatre had its "garden," its "wood"—as the officials themselves contended, "of the most approved verdure"; it had a reception room with soft-lined chairs and a tall lamp in the corner with a yellow shade eminently suited for a comfortable love passage; a large reception room with pillars, painted of course; a middle-class room with red mahogany furniture. In the storeroom of decorations there were "Gothic" and "Renaissance" properties for "classical" plays, as all costume-plays were called by the director,

even though they were written by contemporary authors. They had, correspondingly, chairs with high backs, a black carved table, and a curule chair, which the director stubbornly persisted in calling the "culture" chair. All these properties were used now in one play, now in its successor.

The fully iconic, single-set, middle-class living room of realism produced so closed and so *complete* a stage world that it supported the new and powerful fantasy of the stage not as a place to pretend in or to perform on but a place to *be*, a fully existential arena. We tend to associate this fantasy primarily with acting theory, and specifically with Stanislavsky, but its effects can also be seen in the new structural emphasis, in realist drama, on arrivals and departures. So literally global is the signification of the stage-home of realism, that simply to enter or leave it becomes a decisive—perhaps *the* decisive—dramatic act.

This is precisely what Chekhov ironizes in his drama. In Chekhov's plays as in Ibsen's, arrivals and departures are used as macrostructural devices, but Chekhov's arrivals and departures, unlike Ibsen's, are marked by a certain comic-pathetic arbitrariness. In historical terms, they look forward to the random wanderings of absurdist characters, led famously by Beckett's vagabonds Didi and Gogo. They initiate a figure of motiveless meandering that gains, much later, a political meaning when it is associated with such overpowering external determinants of movement as governments and technologies: thus, in David Rabe's *Streamers,* the soldiers waiting in boot camp to be shipped off to Vietnam express the meaninglessness of arrivals and departures:

> BILLY: How long you think we got?
> ROGER: What do you mean?
> BILLY: Till they pack us up, man, ship us out.
> ROGER: To the war, you mean? To Disneyland? Man, I dunno; that up to them IBMs. Them machines is figurin' that. Maybe tomorrow, maybe next week, maybe never.

The surprising intrusion of Disneyland into this account of a malevolent and absurd exilic condition is not the merely decorative flourish it might appear to be: as we shall see later, the figure of the artificial environment, of which Disneyland is the most powerful and complex exemplar, haunts the imagination of modern drama from *The Wild Duck* onward, marking the sense of an increasingly catastrophic dispossession of nature, which is the end point and inevitable outcome of that crisis of place we are tracking through the discourse of home.[8]

But already in Chekhov, the act of displacement, shorn of its decisiveness, ceases to be a strategy for the formulation of a stable identity and becomes instead a symptom of its loss. In the legendary dispute between Chekhov and Stanislavsky what was being contested, in part, was the whole politics of deriving individual identities from environments, of grounding in a stage-home characters who were essentially homeless. By contrast, the more stylized, less realistic stagings of Chekhov's plays by contemporary directors like Andre Serban and Peter Brook recover the problematic of identity that naturalism tends to bracket out. To the degree that the stage-home is deliteralized, it reveals itself as a complex and contradictory thematic, precisely an *idea* of home—not a place but a discursive field laid out in such a way as to guarantee its inhabitants a certain psychological homelessness.

In Chekhov's drama, the discourse of home is deconstructed to produce the image of a *static* exilic consciousness, experienced by the characters as a feeling of being homesick while at home. Here the sentimental image of home—as an actual place correlated with a strong and desirable emotional experience (the sense of "belonging")—unravels as the logic linking belonging with exile is revealed to be not a logic of opposition but rather one of supplementarity: the emotional structure that is most familiar, most habitual and homelike, to these characters is the feeling of being displaced from somewhere else. They are not exiled *from* where they belong but exiled *to* where they belong.

However, the literalistic and domestic space of naturalism contained Chekhov's deconstruction and stopped it short of any ideological reformulation of the politics of identity. Exilic consciousness, read either as upper-class malaise or as universal tragic alienation, was ultimately something the spectator could be *at home* with. Once situated in terms of an already well coded "milieu and moment," the contradiction embodied by these characters is easily absorbed into a modernist account of psychological fragmentation and alienation, the same account, indeed, that has made exile itself a privileged poetic figure.

The realist discourse of home relies on a long-standing conceptual structure in which two figures are balanced—and constructed—as opposites: the figures of belonging and exile. The home as house (and, behind it, the home as homeland) is the site of a claim to affiliation whose incontestability has been established by a thick web of economic, juridical, and scientific discourses—which also construct the meaning of exile. It is a usefully ambivalent meaning: on the one hand, exile is branded by the negatives of loss and separation; on the other, it is distinguished by distance, detachment, perspective. For the individual (and exile is a decidedly individualistic figure) the poetics of exile offers a mechanism whereby suffering is exchanged for a certain moral authority, personal rupture for aesthetic rapture, as heard, for example, in Nabokov's reflection that "the break in my destiny affords me in retrospect a syncopal kick that I would not have missed for worlds."

The conjunction of naturalism and certain proxemic compulsions—exile, homelessness—inhabits one of the originary moments of the myth of dramatic modernism, the story of the first production of André Antoine's Théâtre-Libre. As is well known, one of the plays to be presented on the first evening, March 30, 1887, was *Jacques Damour*, adapted by M. Leon Hennique from a novel by Emile Zola. For his part, Antoine regarded this association with the name of the controversial father of naturalism not only as the aesthetic and ideological cornerstone of his theater-to-be, but also as a badge of artistic relevance, if not revolutionary correctness: "I realized instantly," he claims, "that Zola's name on our program would guarantee us the attention of [the influential critic] Sarcey." The amateur group with whom Antoine performed, however, felt differently: "Zola's name was already causing some misgivings in our society. Certain of the members were disturbed by the notoriety I was gaining. Finally, the club's name and meeting place were both refused me for such a presentation."

In a sense, then, the Théâtre-Libre is created out of an experience of loss, disenfranchisement, *homelessness*. Certainly that is how it seemed to Antoine himself, who frames his narrative with the image of dispossession. The story of the Théâtre-Libre, as its founder tells it, begins with this first exile and ends with another, more literal one:

> Here ends the odyssey of the Thèâtre-Libre. Having set out seven years ago from my garret in the Rue de Dunkerque with forty sous in my pocket, to rehearse our first production in the little wine shop in the Rue des Abesses, I at last find myself in Rome, with almost the same sum in my pocket, surrounded by fifteen companions as dejected as myself, with a hundred thousand francs of debts awaiting me in Paris, and with no idea of what we will do tomorrow.

Antoine's memoir reproduces a characteristic association of modern dramatic thought: spatial specificity is combined with figures of exile and displacement, street and city names mark the *loss* of place. Of course, spatial specificity, indeed literalism, is one of the things the Théâtre-Libre is famous for, and Antoine is justly celebrated for his attention to the details of the spaces his stage re-created. At this level too, an originary moment from the Théâtre-Libre legend links the stage with the discourse of home. Three days before the opening of the first production, Antoine writes: "I had a lot of trouble this morning finding the furniture and properties, since I scarcely had the means to rent them. I spoke to my mother about it, and she allowed me to take the furniture from her dining room—chairs and table—for the room behind the shop in *Jacques Damour*." Thus the first production of Antoine's theater involves him in a literal re-creation of home; later on the situation is reversed, and the stage becomes the site of a "creative" homelessness: "I no longer have a cent or a home; for the time being, I will sleep on a small cot which is folded up during the day and passes for a property."

Homelessness is only the most graphic version of the many displacements that constitute the insistent and pervasive challenges to home, transforming this apparently simple figure into a powerful irreality, something on the order of a fantasy, fable, myth, or impossible dream. Other displacements, all of which will be discussed in the following pages and all of which are complex figures, even whole discourses, are exile, immigration, and refugeehood. Of these exile is certainly the most fully theorized and poeticized concept, having become nothing short of a symbol for modern culture itself. According to George Steiner, the literature of the twentieth century is best understood as an "extraterritorial" art, expressing the universal experience of exile and refugeehood: "It seems proper that those who create art in a civilization of quasi-barbarism, which has made so many homeless, should themselves be poets unhoused and wanderers across language. Eccentric, aloof, nostalgic, deliberately untimely" (quoted by Said). The names of Conrad, Joyce, Kafka, and Nabokov are sufficient to evoke the principle of a potent exilic consciousness as the shaping force of modern literature. The history of drama supplies its own names: Ibsen, Strindberg, Chekhov, Beckett, Brecht—all experienced and were marked by exile or other displacements; all made dislocation one of the central themes of their drama.

But, as Edward Said points out in his essay "Reflections on Exile," the unparalleled scale of contemporary displacements removes the figure of exile from its earlier status as literary and cultural motif, signifying heightened consciousness and privileged perspective:

> But the difference between earlier exiles and those of our own times is, it bears stressing, scale: our age with its modern warfare, imperialism and quasi-theological ambitions of totalitarian rulers—is indeed the age of the refugee, the displaced person, mass immigration. . . . On the twentieth-century scale, exile is neither aesthetically nor humanistically comprehensible: at most the literature about exile objectifies an anguish and a predicament most people rarely experience at first hand. . . . Is it not true that the views of exile in literature and, moreover, in religion obscure what is truly horrendous: that exile is irremediably secular and unbearably historical; that it is produced by human beings for other human beings; and that, like death but without death's ultimate mercy, it has torn millions of people from the nourishment of tradition, family and geography?

This terrible truth of actual exile makes its way into Western drama quite late, but when it does, it illuminates the terms of a century-long struggle with the problem of place. This struggle, to which I have given the label geopathology,

unfolds as an incessant dialogue between belonging and exile, home and homelessness. At midcentury, a new discourse enters the dialogue and changes the established terms of the drama's engagement with place, displacing as well the dramatic structures that had served the geopathic model. The new discourse centers upon the figure of America, explicating it, first, as a *betrayal* of place, and then finding in it a muted celebration of placelessness. Out of this celebration there emerges, finally, a kind of solution—or at least the beginnings of a new formulation that might redirect, if not entirely overcome, that painful politics of place I am calling geopathology. In the emerging drama of multiculturalism, it seems to me, are the outlines of a new *heterotopic* account of the relationship between persons and places. This account begins by creatively confronting the problem of place, regarding it as a challenge and an invitation rather than as a tragic impasse.

A work that exemplifies this evolving new attitude toward place is Laurie Anderson's epic piece, *United States*. As Henry Sayre points out, Anderson uses performance to realize the postmodern experience of what Gilles Deleuze, describing the logic of Nietzsche's texts, has called "nomadism":

> The only conceivable key [to these texts], perhaps, would be in the concept of "embarkation." . . . We embark, then, in a kind of raft of "the Medusa"; bombs fall all around the raft as it drifts towards icy subterranean streams—or towards torrid rivers, the Orinoco, the Amazon; the passengers row together. They are not supposed to like one another, they fight with one another, they eat one another. To row together is to share, to share something beyond law, contract or institution. It is a period of drifting, of "deterritorialization."

According to Sayre, Anderson "manages to 'deterritorialize' the United States, to give her audience a sense that they are in some measure *outside*—or wanderers within—the very place they live."

Employing two tropes that have been involved in the figuration of place from the beginning of the modern period—the tropes of dislocation and of the technologies of representation—Anderson in effect completes what has been a halting but nevertheless progressive reinscription of the figure of home, as well as of the general category of place. That process, begun in midcentury (when it was figured as the failure of homecoming), concludes when, in Sayre's words, "we recognize in [Anderson's] wanderings our own homelessness." Her lavish use of technology—technologies for manipulating sound, image, and even voice—is the extreme realization of a century-long rebellion against the naturalistic theater's dream of total visibility (the inner logic of that dream and the theatrical functioning it dictates are discussed in chap. 1). One playful passage in *United States* encapsulates the whole complex relation between *seeing* and *place:*

> Over the river
> And through the woods
> Whose woods these are
> Long time no see
> Long time no see[9]

The multiple experiences of place invoked here—as home and origin (Grandmother's house), as property (whose woods these are), as travel (miles to go before I sleep)—the copresence of high and low culture (Robert Frost and Little Red Riding Hood), as well as, finally, the muted reference to the dispossession of nature (the river and woods no longer seen): all these are part of the gradually evolving postgeopathological drama of the past two decades. Among the many aspects of geopathic drama that are revisioned in the contemporary theater is one that Anderson (like most other avant-garde practitioners of theater) deeply engages, the problematic of visibility. As Sayre articulates it: "Are we meeting someone we have not seen for a long time, or have we been, for a long time, blind?"

The chapters that follow describe a development that is also, at every "stage," a forecast and a memory. The conventionality of dramatic discourse—dictated by both its public nature as well as its material contextualization in an ongoing theater culture—makes the drama powerfully intertextual. This book traces that intertextuality by tracking not only the figures of home, homelessness, exile, and immigration, but also an apparently unconnected collection of recurring figures that insistently accompany the dramatic discourse of place: addiction, photography, performance, and burial.

Chapter 1, "Plays and Place," presents a theoretical model for the relationship of theatrical space and dramatic place by considering the habitual—and, I argue, false—opposition between naturalism and the experimental stage practice known as environmental theater. An exploration of the theoretics of naturalism as refracted through *Miss Julie* and Strindberg's preface to the play leads to a recognition that naturalism rested on a fantasy of total visibility, of the impossible translation of private experience into public expression. This problematic of a public privacy survives long after naturalism, persisting into environmental theater, where its presence is occluded by new spatial arrangements designed to create "shared experiences" (shared, that is, between the audience and the actors). These spatial arrangements, I argue, are deceptive, and the ideology sustaining them is the subject of Jim Cartwright's play *Road.* As I read it, *Road* stages the politics of place that link environmentalism to its supposed opposite, naturalism, and these

politics are intimately connected to the dramatic discourse of home.

Chapter 2, "Geopathology," lays out the terms and consequences of a foundational semiology of place based on the idea of ill placement. Several of the themes and motifs that enter the drama through this semiology persist long into the future; among these, the figures of photography and of performance surface with interesting variations even after the discourse of home has been thoroughly revised through what I have called the "multicultural imagination," the topic of my final chapter. In the last play that I examine in that chapter, Ping Chong's *Nuit Blanche,* the figures of photography and performance are fused into the play's basic expressive strategy, its combination of slides and live action. In this play also, one of the most vibrant undercurrents running through the whole history of this thematic, namely, an ecological current, is brought to the surface. The relation between ecology and geopathology, discovered as early as Ibsen's *Wild Duck,* emerges as crucial to the deterritorialized theatrology of postmodernism.

Before the drama of multiculturalism can reconfigure place, the terms of geopathology have to be confronted. Chapter 3, "America and the Limits of Homecoming," traces the effects of the figure of America on the unraveling discourse of home. Focusing on two transatlantic pairs of plays—first Pinter's *The Homecoming* and Shepard's *Buried Child* and then Caryl Churchill's *Ice Cream* and George C. Wolfe's *The Colored Museum*—this chapter presents an encapsulated history of the dramatic discourse of home, its past and future condensed into the figure of failed homecoming and the dramaturgy of the hidden (and now worthless) secret.

From this analysis, an unexpected image, the image of the buried child, emerges as a privileged—even obsessional—device of the modern dramatic imagination. The figure of the buried child occurs again and again in modern drama, tempting one to turn to psychoanalysis for an explanation. I have preferred simply to track the fate of this strange figure in the evolving postgeopathic platial discourse of modern drama and to link it, finally, to a peculiar figure in the discourse of what Harold Bloom calls "the American religion." According to Bloom, America's obsession with the unborn child marks this culture's unacknowledged commitment to an essentially Gnostic belief system, whereby the essential self is as old as God himself and, like God, no part of the creation. George Bush's apparently contradictory concern for fetuses and unconcern for unwanted infants make a kind of sense from this point of view, valuing the uncreated—or precreated—divine being over the unwanted child who "is sadly fallen away from freedom": "One sees why the fetus and the flag are one; the baby is not alone, and will drain the pious taxpayer, but the fetus can wave over the land of the free, whose Fundamentalists will remain solitary and god-like, poised always *before* the Creation."

Bloom's reading of the American obsession with the unborn child helps to explain the painful contradiction this figure registers when brought into line with another powerful American mythology, America's view of itself as a *place* of exceptional potentiality, a land of unimagined progress and plenty. Bloom's reading would suggest that, for George Bush and his unwitting Gnostic constituency, this land—like the unwanted starving infant over whom the innocent fetus takes precedence—is part of the fallen creation and as such of little intrinsic concern to those whose minds and hearts are turned to the Hereafter. For them, as for Joseph Smith, the Mormon prophet, America is merely the ancient burial ground of a truth awaiting revelation. (The Book of Mormon was said to have lain buried for centuries in upstate New York until the Angel Moroni led Joseph Smith to it.) But another imagination of America, one that celebrates the land itself, its majestic landscapes and its vast spaces, contests this religious vision, substituting another, perhaps secular, faith, whose greatest manifestation has been American ecological thinking. The desecration of America, figured time and time again through the imagery of waste and garbage—the all-American figure of *junk*—provokes a reconsideration of the figure of the buried child. In this ongoing reformulation, the buried child is precious not for its links to a divinity that pre-exists creation but for its figuration of *recovery*: the hope, however hopeless, that what has been lost or destroyed by industrialization, technology, modernism can somehow be reclaimed, "dug up," revived, and acknowledged for the precious gift it always was.

Once again, it is Laurie Anderson's *United States* that seems to summarize the contradictory logic of the figure of the buried child and its relation to America, to the present, and (if our luck as a species holds out) to the future. In a section entitled "Song for Two Jims," Anderson tells of visiting a family in Kentucky, two parents and four children:

> One day Mrs Taylor told me that she used to have another
> kid, but that he had apparently fallen down one of the holes.
> Her description was very abstract. Nobody tried to rescue him.
> He just fell down the hole. She said: "Well one
> day I saw him out there
> and I was watching
> and then I didn't see him out there no more."

The abstraction of the mother's description of this extraordinary event is the key to its meaning. It is not only, as Sayre says, that "the 'meaning' of the narrative lies in the very meaninglessness of the Taylors' lives," but also that their defective access to meaning (and hence to affect, to

feeling) takes the form of—precisely—a sudden invisibility. The buried child of modern drama is the unseen and unseeable force of circumstance; and circumstance, as we shall see, has long been understood as place, or rather as ill placement. In Anderson's text, however, a very precise characterization is given to the traditionally abstract discourse of geopathology, and we should not be surprised to find that that characterization consists of the two major unacknowledged or unconscious themes of geopathic drama: technology and ecology. The hole into which the "kid" falls is one of many deep holes drilled in the shale surrounding the Taylor household—by Standard Oil. The buried child is the covictim—with the land, with the earth itself—of unbridled technological progress.

The midcentury drama of failed homecoming is also the drama in which the figure of the buried child, and the related dramaturgy of discovery, begins to unravel and betray its hitherto invisible functioning. The process is completed in Laurie Anderson's piece, where the buried child finally speaks and, speaking, exposes the logic of its invisibility, naming that which is destroying, erasing, "burying" it:

> So hold me, Mom, in your long arms,
> in your automatic arms,
> your electronic arms . . .
> your petrochemical arms,
> your military arms,
> in your electronic arms.

After the failure of homecoming, the drama embarks on a quest for new places, and language is among the privileged sites of this exploration. Chapter 4, "The Places of Language," looks at the idea of language as place in three plays that also extend the dramatic discourse on America. Eric Overmyer's *On the Verge* links language, place, and the future, a connection that is then reengaged in a more material and historical mode by Caryl Churchill's *Mad Forest* and in a more apocalyptic and ecological mode by Maria Irene Fornes's *The Danube*. The newly awakened desire for a new platiality to replace the geopathic idealization of ill placement moves beyond language in the plays of immigration and multiculturalism that are the subjects of chapters 5 and 6, respectively. In the plays discussed in these chapters, the discourse of place begins to shift—more or less decisively—toward a recognition of the power of actual and specific places, although the old figuration of America as the principle of placelessness is never far away, never finally overcome.

The figures of home and exile have developed, in the course of this century, far beyond the scope of the literary figures with which they were first associated. The massive and agonizing dislocations of the modern age have left the poetics of exile far behind. The question I finally ask, in the epilogue of this book but also from the beginning, is this: How is the experience of dislocation making its voice heard in the theatrical language of the West? Two recent plays serve to outline an answer: Tony Kushner's monumental (and hugely successful) *Angels in America* and Suzan-Lori Parks's fragile (and largely unheralded) *The America Play* allow for a tentative formulation of where the journey beyond geopathology has led us. That both plays focus their reflections on the fig-

ure of America suggests that the modern drama's discourse of place has now transmuted itself into something quite site-specific. Both plays' meditations on the approaching millennium, their shared irony toward the morbid seductions of closure, their playful refusal of the logic of last words—all this makes them the ideal vehicle for what a book like this one must seek: a non-ending, an "other" place from which the otherness of place can continue to be explored and enjoyed.

A DIRECTOR'S PERSPECTIVE

A Director's Approach: An Interview with Peter Hall on his Production of *The Homecoming*
INTERVIEWED BY IRVING WARDLE

Sir Peter Hall is one of England's most celebrated directors, the founder of the Royal Shakespeare Company, and later head of the Royal National Theatre. He is widely known for landmark productions of Aeschylus, Shakespeare, Beckett, and other playwrights. He directed the premiere of Harold Pinter's The Homecoming *at the Aldwych Theatre in 1965. In this interview, Hall outlines his working methods for that production, and implies some of the ways that Pinter's innovative dramatic style confronted the typical practices of actors and directors.*

IW: How did the play strike you when you first read it?

PH: I remember having received the script of *The Homecoming* through the post with a letter from Harold Pinter saying: "Dear Peter, here it is. Yours ever. . . ." I mention that because I think it's important. What it was was what it was. And although my views of it changed in emphasis as we worked, it seemed to me such a complete play on first reading and my responses changed very little. I think during our working time we cut maybe twelve or fifteen lines, not more. The play was there as a complete thing in its own right. I thought at the time it came that this play looks unblinkingly at life in the human jungle. It's not a pleasant play. It's not a play which is comfortable. It's abrasive and uncomfortable.

IW: Did the jungle image occur to you right away?

PH: Yes, right away. There's something deeply animalistic about the people's reactions to each other and the way they treat each other. So if we want a word, that was my reaction. A jungle. I remember Harold had warned me. All he'd said about the play was, "I'm writing a play about a man coming home who's secretly married; and it's going to be quite something. And it's going to present you with great difficulties." Because it came to me just after we'd done *Marat/Sade* and *Afore Night Come*—and there'd been a great scream from a minority of people in London about us doing dirty plays—Harold had warned me jokingly that another piece of dirt was arriving. I did not classify it or the other plays as "dirt." I merely warned my board that the controversy might continue. It didn't.

I must explain that when I read a play, I read it straight through. I've always found that at the end of that one reading I know whether I ought to direct it or not. I couldn't for the life of me at the end of a first reading be interviewed and say what it was about or *why* I wanted to direct it. But I know whether I can do it or not. And one has to trust the instinct in this way, because if I finish a play and think, "Well I don't think so," and read it a second, third, fourth, fifth, sixth time—by the sixth

time, I bet you any money that I'll be directing it, because I see that there are problems that will be interesting to solve . . . that is if it's of any standard at all. I get fascinated by how to get over the problems. So I have to have just that first reading. And I didn't then study *The Homecoming* very closely. I just knew I had to do it.

IW: Did you arrive at any conceptual idea of the play before starting rehearsal?

PH: I read the text so often that I more or less knew it by heart. I'd also worked hard with John Bury [the designer] and with Harold Pinter on what the thing should look like. Pinter wrote this play for the Aldwych and he says in his stage directions, "A large room." This is partly because we'd worked together on two of his other plays at the Aldwych and he'd been rather preoccupied, and rightly, by the fact that the Aldwych is a very large stage. And he said to me, "I think properly speaking that this is a large play that needs a large room, and it'll go on a large stage." His stage directions are minimal—I think any good playwright's are—if you can't pick up what it's like and where it is and what the whole tone of the thing is about from actually reading the text, then no amount of descriptive passages are going to help you. I suppose before we started I had a set which was simple, antiseptic, gray, dead—I mean it reminded me of an old butcher who used to be covered in blood and is now in a sterile world.

IW: You accept Max's biographical credentials?

PH: Yes, I take him on trust as an old butcher. I would, though, hesitate to argue with you if you said he isn't a butcher—for purposes of this discussion, he is butcher enough. It's a sterile world from which women have been excluded; the set has to mirror that.

This is my process of work before I begin rehearsal: I jot down every physical or atmospheric thing that I pick up from the text which seems worth exploring in the design. I can't remember how I briefed John Bury, but I would certainly have talked about the antiseptic and the sterile, the unfeminine.

IW: The impression of the set was monumental.

PH: Yes. That was part of Pinter's idea. Because the back wall has been knocked down "to make an open living area." Within this place of horror a larger space has been made, an emptier space for the figures to confront each other in. "Living area" is an ironic term for this jungle. Although one begins to work with the designer and tries all sorts of ways of mirroring the actual function of the play, more than anything else I think you have to have a subjective image of what kind of play it is and what impression, what atmosphere you want to create, and make sure that that is secure enough so that the set doesn't contradict it as you work. One of the most ghastly things in the theater is designing the set before you begin rehearsals. In an ideal world I would like to work with the actors for a month and then design the production. But that never happens except with the Berliner Ensemble where they have enormous rehearsal time. In this case, though, I knew my Pinter, I already had a close working relationship with him, and I liked very much his form of theater. Pinter's ambiguity in technical terms is that he makes silence speak by defining silence by the noise around it. He equally well makes movements and action unbearably meaningful by the stillness on either side of them. Therefore a Pinter set has to be stripped to its absolute essential so that a movement means the thing it ought to mean. You can't litter a Pinter set, or Pinter staging, or Pinter performances with any kind of naturalism that tries to kid the audience that they're not in a theater. So certainly my brief to John Bury—this I do remember—said, "We will have nothing on the stage except what is necessary," because what is necessary will speak that much more eloquently. So we took everything away except a few pieces of furniture.

IW: Is there any special relationship between character and environment in *The Homecoming?*

PH: I think all of Harold's work relates to a confined space where people confront each other in often very ugly terms. Territorial rights? It hadn't occurred to me. But it's patriarchal with the boss figure, and everyone's trying to castrate the boss in one way or another. So certainly I would accept this, after the event, as part of an analysis. You see, in everything I say I want to emphasize this very very strongly. Harold always refuses to say what his plays *mean,* and I think quite rightly. I don't think one can literally define metaphor. A metaphor reverberates and has many meanings to many people, and that's why it's a metaphor. In the same way I don't think I as a director can say why I consciously did this or that, because I don't work like that. I can only tell you, as far as

I can remember, what the processes were behind it, but I didn't sit in a corner and say, Jungle—therefore the linoleum should have green tones in it. Or, Space—therefore let's put the walls like this. Perhaps half the time I couldn't have explained in my work with John Bury why we were going in the direction we were. And I remember the first model we presented to Pinter—I remember him being very concerned about the pillar that ran across the top of the set, which is where the wall had been knocked down. In our first model it was very rough hewn; it was very obvious that a wall had been knocked down, and a large beam had been put in to keep the house up. Harold quite rightly said, "Yes, that's right, but it's too explicit." When they talk about the wall being knocked down and the audience looks, *then* they should understand why the wall is like it is; but when the curtain goes up they shouldn't look and say, "Ah, a wall has been knocked down and a beam has been put in."

Perhaps this is a suitable moment for saying how I work with Pinter. We had and still have a very close working relationship and I think our terms of reference are very clear. He can say whatever he likes to me about the way I'm directing his play, but I remain the final arbiter of what is done in the production. And I can say whatever I like about his text, but he remains the final arbiter of what is in and what is out. That sounds very simple, and it's always worked with us over quite a long and complex period. And we said those things equally to each other *in front of the cast,* which is enough to make some actors run screaming from the theater. But in this case, it didn't. We had six actors who had a sufficiently rich relationship with each other and with us for it to be a totally acceptable working form. So we were able to be quite frank, and I think this is terribly important. If an actor's not big enough to be told why he's doing it wrongly, or a dramatist's not big enough to be told why the line is not working, or a director's not big enough to be told that the scene is all wrong, then nothing can actually come out. I don't believe in pride in the theater. But you can only collaborate in this way when everybody is secure. Which means working in a company. And this is precisely how I tried to make the Royal Shakespeare Company.

I think why Harold and I have worked well together is that finally we do coalesce into one person in terms of the production. We have a complete reaction on each other. So if you said to me, "Could you have done that production without Harold Pinter?" I would certainly say, "No, I couldn't." I would have done a production which would have been in some ways very similar, but it wouldn't have been like that. And I think he would say exactly the same. But he didn't direct it, and I didn't write it.

IW: Did you work on *The Homecoming* with the same musical values that apply to his previous plays?

PH: Ultimately yes. But musical values only come from meaning. What did impress me about the play was its ugly brutality. I think that the writing is as meticulous and formed as ever. But underneath the writing there is a pressure of emotion and an ugliness of motive which I think is a new note in his work—because he's dealt in the past with menace and with violence, but in a rather cool and sophisticated way. In this play there seemed to be something unleashed which gave the work to me—and I choose my words very carefully—brutal and epic proportions. I think this is the biggest play he's written. It has the largest size; it's the most painful, and deals with the rawest emotions; although it continues to express them for a lot of the time in terms of ambiguity and mockery. The phrase always on our lips when we were doing this play was "Taking the piss." It's a cockney phrase meaning getting the better of your opponent by mockery. This play doesn't take the piss in a light or flippant way. It takes the piss in a cruel and bitter way. The characters are all doing this to each other. They take the piss—this cockneyism is central to the play. But of course one of the great factors about taking the piss is that if you're taking the piss satisfactorily the person whose piss is being taken must not be sure whether or not it is being taken! And this was the first problem for the actors.

I always like to present actors at the beginning of rehearsals with an image we can refer to later. It may be modified—it must be modified, and will change—but in general, I try to state why I want to do the play and what it's about without being over-literal. In this sense I did talk about the jungle and destructiveness and the unfeminine society, that hatred of women which informs this society. The resentment of the male animal, that he is born of woman and needs woman in order to create more people. But I didn't give them a sentence which said "This is what the play *says.*"

IW: How did the two absent figures of MacGregor and the dead wife color the production?

PH: We talked about them a great deal. In our work they were living characters. We gradually knew what kind of a bastard MacGregor was, and what kind of a rapacious bitch-like lady Jessie was. But these two figures only colored the production in relation to each character's views of them. If you said to me now, "What was MacGregor like?" I could only tell you what he or she was like to the person in the play that I was discussing it with. And there are

certain contradictions, because Pinter is writing a play that takes cognizance of the fact that everybody's view of everybody else is slightly different and that there are many more than two sides to every question.

In the early stages of the work we always circumscribed ourselves by saying, "Let's not move physically in the staging at all unless it's absolutely necessary." Perhaps I can expand that a little bit more. In the early stages of work, when an actor is still learning his lines and still exploring motives, there is a great tendency to move around the stage or to physicalize motives as an alibi, for want of something better to do. In the old days you always went and took a drink from the cocktail cabinet or you lit a cigarette. I think that Pinter's concentrated form of theater means that *nothing* must happen on the stage when it is not relevant, *ever*. If a man lights a cigarette it mustn't just be that he happens to light a cigarette. It's got to contribute.

So I encouraged the actors in this very sparse, spare unfurnished room just to sit around and talk to each other and not to try and move. But at the same time we explored all kinds of naturalistic behavior, naturalistic motives. In Pinter, as in Beckett, you need to start with naturalistic exploration. And the process would apply to another great stylist, Edward Albee. You should examine all the naturalistic motives only for one reason: Pinter (or Beckett) is a highly formed and in my view poetic dramatist, and the actor's task is already heavily circumscribed. He can only say what is written, and not an approximation. Therefore he has an exterior formula given to him, a very highly stylized form of utterance, even. And unless you give him the rein to naturalize it and let free his own emotions and instincts, it could be a puppetlike performance. I was very aware of this in *The Homecoming*, and I think, if I may say so, one of the achievements of the production is that it sailed dangerously near to a puppetlike production without being one. And out of that tension was born what I believe it had to be.

I think that is true of any poetic drama. That was the main stylistic task. I made them learn the lines with meticulous accuracy. And it's not generally, perhaps, understood, how slovenly actors are about text. A lot of texts they work on are so imprecise that the actors might just as well be slovenly; an "and" instead of a "but" doesn't make much difference. In Shakespeare it's amazing what gets by because actors learn lazily and they *have* to learn meticulously. I think the problem is exactly like that of an opera singer. No opera singer would think of not learning a Mozart aria with the most meticulous regard for the notes. The problem of then making them true and human is a later problem. And that's what we did with *The Homecoming*. I not only asked them to learn the words, but I asked them to be absolutely aware of Harold's shorthand. He has this technique (which again he shares with Sam Beckett): If there is a pause in the proceedings, for a small pause he puts three dots; for a large pause he puts "Pause"; for a very, very long pause he puts "Silence." Now of course it's not just enough to do that; because you have to *fill* those indications. But if one analyzes the scene, every time one of those three things happens there is a bridge which dramatists of the past have always verbalized. Now, Harold writes in silence as much as he does in words; he defines silence by the noise on either side of it and the literal communication on either side of it. So you have to discover what goes on through that. It's very easy in learning to miss this. And if as a director one doesn't keep one's eye on the text during rehearsal all the time, you forget that Harold has said, "There is a bridge here which you've got to find." Remember, Shakespeare only used silence this way once. Coriolanus answers his mother's great plea not to burn Rome with a stage direction: "Holds her by the hand, silent."

IW: Did you hold special rehearsals for silences?

PH: I did once have a dot and pause rehearsal. It drove the actors absolutely mad. I said, "You don't remember the phrases." Exactly as if an actor in Shakespeare had learned his text without knowing where the ends of the lines are, which is the whole phrasing unit. If you run the line on in Shakespeare, which you must once in ten, you still must *know* where the end of the line is. So I said, "We will now sit down and have a word rehearsal, sitting where we are, and each of you will tell me where your dots are and where your pauses are and where your silences are." And we went right through it. It only happened once. It was just to try and make the actors understand that we were dealing with something which was highly formed and highly wrought. And our first responsibility was to know what it was.

IW: Was there any metrical timing?

PH: No. That would be like conducting a piece of music with a metronome. I wouldn't do that with Shakespeare either. In the case of a concert, the rehearsed phrasing happens slightly differently because of the human dynamic of the conductor. In the case of a theater performance, the phrasing which has been set happens slightly differently because of the actor and the audience response. And any attempt to say, "Hold this for four seconds" is as bad as saying to an actor, "Walk four steps to the left or four steps to the right," which I would never do. I think people who hear that I held a dot and pause rehearsal per-

haps misunderstand its purpose. It wasn't done to imprison the actor, but to add to his knowledge of the text.

But after the period of naturalistic exploration we took away everything which didn't relate. And who was the arbiter of that? Well, me—with Harold at my side making comments when he wanted. I seem to remember in the early days there was much more carry-on with Joey coming home with his coat and his boxing bag, much more naturalism, and all he had to do was come in with his bag and stand still. I seem to remember that there was a great deal more cigarette smoking on the part of Max to keep him comfortable sitting in that central chair. I remember that there was a lot more walking around the room, particularly on the part of Sam the chauffeur-brother. And gradually we whittled these away to give the thing a kind of strength, so that a move was a positive shock. Or the glass of water was an object, which was horrifyingly real because it was so isolated. And that was a very difficult time for the actors because all their props were removed.

IW: How far were actors allowed to rely on given biography?

PH: Completely, unless there is textual evidence that there are two sides to the question. The given biographies are used during the first process of naturalistic exploration. For instance, what does Joey the construction man feel like coming home to go straight down to the gym? We decided all sorts of things: that Joey, having to keep up as a boxer and all the rest was pretty shagged out most of the time. But finally that wasn't at all significant; it didn't mean anything. It's the kind of thing that we explored and cast aside. Didn't help. I think in the selecting stage that it is extremely hard, and important in Pinter, to try and keep every situation open ended. I *did* say to the company that the play was like a diamond which presented many facets to an audience. Well, what the actors had to do was not select a facet to be presented, but to show many facets at once. So that it was almost like something being moved around. But it always had to be logical to the actor himself from moment to moment. And of course one of the fatal things to do in that jungle is to be honest or to be candid or sincere, because if you do you immediately become vulnerable. The characters destroy any sign of actual truth in each other. It was very hard indeed to find a coherence which an audience could understand. And as you know, some people didn't. Maybe they thought too much instead of feeling it.

IW: Was there any attempt to implant any unspoken sense of what the characters really want?

PH: No, because I think that the play is so complex that to give any simple solution really reduces it to an anecdote.

You have to see it from each character's point of view, and they all judge it differently, in different terms; you have to shift from one to another and see how it works for each of them in turn. Gradually you piece together this very complicated structure, and I found the play's complexity as it moved toward its end of rehearsals, grew greater. It was clearer, yet *more* complex.

IW: Is it part of the director's job to resolve ambiguities?

PH: In the case of Harold Pinter it's not his job at all. It is his job to present the contradictions clearly. Also I think worthwhile theater always deals in ambiguity. The only kind of theater that's really interesting is something which is, in the proper sense of the term, poetic, which is produced by the clash of opposites and reverberates beyond its literal meaning. Well, if you say, I've got an interpretation of *The Homecoming*—and many were advanced to me, as they were years ago about *Godot* when I did it—you then have a simple literal meaning which is not a metaphor.

IW: What about the production groupings? For instance, when Max hits Joey, is this something you consciously attempted?

PH: I didn't think anything as we did them. I did not say, "Let's do that because it will show. . . ." I built it up as a situation and it seemed inevitable finally. It went through many stages before it did seem inevitable. There were many times when it went wrong. I don't think you consciously think up a bit of business to express something. Business evolves, you suggest certain things, you create an atmosphere in which the actors create something with you, and you then relate that to your central instinct about the play and either discard it or keep it. I think it's for other people to say, "That expressed this for me." I do remember many years ago Harold Hobson [*Sunday Times* of London] writing a long piece about a moment of Christian clarification in *Godot* when Vladimir took off his hat and said, "Christ have mercy upon us." That, quite rightly, had not been in any of our minds when we did it; the actor had wanted to take his hat off. It seemed to me the right place. I'm not saying that Harold Hobson was wrong, but it wasn't in our minds when we did it. And I think if it *had* been in our minds, everybody would have found it acutely embarrassing and literal.

IW: Was the stylistic finesse of the production (e.g., the cigarette-lighting group opening up like a flower) an answer to the brutality of the material? The more brutal the contents, the finer the shell?

PH: That's not my solution to Pinter; that's Pinter's solution to Pinter. The bestiality of the play is encased in the very elegant shell of the writing, which is extremely meticulous, formed, and rhythmic, and certainly has—in some areas you've mentioned, I agree—a vigor and crudity which is a new quality in him; but it still has this extraordinary finesse. Harold Pinter's style as a playwright led me to do the things I did in physical form. This production was a culmination of the experiences we'd had together.

IW: What was the reason for the Teddy change in America?

PH: Teddy was only changed because Michael Bryant, who played it in England, couldn't go. So we got Michael Craig to play it. A new personality brought new problems and new qualities, which was good. I think it was actually a great help to the production—to the other five—that there was a new factor. I can't compare the two performances; I thought they were both brilliant. Michael Bryant was so much the campus intellectual who'd opted out of any kind of responsibility in human terms, wanted to keep his hands clean. He did that absolutely beautifully. Michael Craig got some of that, but he also had something else which in some ways made the play even more horrific. He was the biggest bastard of the lot, as well as being the withdrawn intellectual. He really was. So when he went at the end, leaving his wife, he was not in any way a victim or a martyr. He was the biggest shit of all. He was leaving them with their deserts. He was leaving her with her deserts. And he was the worst of the lot.

IW: At what point does the production indicate Teddy's decision to abandon her?

PH: I think he brings her back—now I am intellectualizing, which I didn't do until after I'd done the play—he brings his wife back to the jungle to have her tested by the laws of the jungle, and makes one vow: that he will not lift a finger to alter the outcome of the test, one way or the other.

IW: Is Teddy still a part of the jungle himself?

PH: He's produced by the jungle, so this is the necessary place he must bring his wife to. But I don't think he goes out a defeated man, or a saddened man, or a martyred man. He goes back, in a way, confirmed in the family's hatred of women. In that sense, he's victorious. Because Lenny can't break him. Joey actually having his wife can't break him. He apparently is unbreakable. And if she wants to stay, she can stay. But of course he plays it all so cool it could look as though he doesn't care at all. He does care, but he's not going to be involved in any action about that caring.

If I had made the speech I have just made to you about Teddy to the actor playing Teddy, I think he would have been incapable of playing the last scene. Because he would have had a very crude and simple objective, which is, I'm not going to lift a finger to do anything about this. And it is much more complex that that, because Teddy's motives change almost from second to second. The amount of force he has to apply to keeping uninvolved—that's the main thing, and that I would discuss with the actor: How do you manage to sit there, how? Can you imagine this situation? How can you keep control? But you mustn't ever produce an actor by giving him the results, because then he acts results. You can ask him the right questions. You can hint at a path he can follow. You can't tell him what the audience should see. I suppose I could have said what I've said about Teddy while I was doing the play to an outsider, but I wouldn't have it said to the actor. One can only go on what is said in the text. When you're dealing with Pinter, you're not dealing with seven types of ambiguity, but an infinite number of ambiguities. Because any proposition we draw from one side of the play we can contradict or modify by a proposition from some other side.

IW: Are there any types of human material which an actor could legitimately bring to another playwright but not to Pinter?

PH: An actor must bring his own instincts and his own responses to any play. Paul Rogers certainly brought to Max his understanding of aggression; all the ideas of a family life being an opportunity to release aggression; the hatred of his sons because they were younger than him. Each one of the actors drew on themselves. They always must. And the background, I think, is terribly important: the building site, the pimp, the intellectual, the campus figure, that girl who was some kind of call-girl or model, or was she? These have to be investigated and lived and understood by the actor; they have to bring the problem to themselves, because otherwise one would get an entirely arid experience. I would say that the personal involvement of the actor in Pinter has to be deeper and more passionate and more instinctive at a certain time in rehearsal, and then one has to cool it. In the jungle it is dangerous to show one's feelings. The process still goes on. But we had some rehearsals in which we tried to explore the dangers. We didn't have improvisations as such, but we did say: Actor A—If you see an opening, a vulnerability, a commitment, a sincerity, anything that you could get back on in the other man, say it. So that everyone was *guarded*. And this really raised the whole thing to fever pitch. What I'm saying is that all the characters are feeling passionate, ugly, instinctive, destructive, and they can't even show those things. To shout in that house is a weakness. You have to contain every-

thing. Now the minute the actors started to say, "Well if we're going to contain everything, hide everything, then why bother to feel it?" the play went dead. So it was a passionate and violent and instinctive exercise for them in which their fellow actors on the stage had to be used as people from whom they hid these feelings; but they had to undergo them at each performance. Otherwise it became pastel and totally enigmatic. So the part played by the instinct of the actor, I think, is greater in a way because Pinter is a very passionate dramatist in that sense and *demands* passion from his actor. And if you just play the surface of Pinter it is apparently incoherent. One has seen productions of Pinter where the actors just said the words, or naturalized them, and they don't mean anything at all.

IW: What about the rehearsal period?

PH: We rehearsed it for six weeks, which was our normal period at that time. We went on tour though and worked on it a bit on tour; then we worked on it again before we took it to New York. Walter Kerr didn't like it, and at that point New York's opinion of a play was apparently only his. Alexander Cohen, who'd brought us over, said, "You'll be off in a fortnight." I said, "Is that a definite promise, because I need these actors at home." And he was very cross. They say it doesn't matter if you succeed or fail; but in fact there's still this belief on Broadway that if you fail you ought to feel punished. But then he fought for the play and it won all the Tony awards and became a great success. I do appreciate the fight he made for the play, which made it a success. I think the production was at its best in New York; by that time, it had really been fined down to a cutting edge.

IW: In what areas is Pinter most flexible as a collaborator?

PH: He's an actor, and a director, and a man of the theater: I think he's extremely flexible. He has his opinions, and so he bloody well should with the genius he's got. But he respects other people's opinions and is never arbitrary. As a director, if you question a scene or a speech or a word, he never *collects* his genius around him like a protective cloak and says, "That's my business." He is open. That's all I can say. He's entirely flexible; finally, if he's in the right and believes he's in the right, he says he's in the right; and it's my job as the director to bow to him. Actually I don't remember that there was an author dispute or a director dispute left on the stage by the time we'd finished.

IW: Will you tell me more about the set?

PH: The set took its final form before we began rehearsals. But the exact placement of the furniture and exactly *what* it was, did not. I remember I staged the first scene in a totally different way to begin with; then I changed it and it stayed the way it is now.

IW: What about the images, Lenny on the threshold, etc.?

PH: Yes. I never said to Ian Holm, "Lenny's always on the threshold, let's see if we can work that in." It's just that in our investigation of the play, Lenny was often on the threshold. I can see it now . . . the images were arrived at by work. If you give an actor a move, it's no good. If the process of work dictates the move, it's a good move. I think this is where Pinter's stage directions are splendid, because they leave open the investigation of these things. As soon as a dramatist says, "Max hits Sam across the head with an upraised stick, having the air of a man who is frustrated," the actor reads that, the director reads that, well, that's it! Finish! It'll never express that; it won't even express what's been described. Pinter never makes that mistake.

In a lot of the appreciations of the production there was a lot of talk about its stylistic qualities, that it had a stylized form. I would just like to make clear that it wasn't a conscious decision before the work was done, and it wasn't a style that I was aiming at, because I don't think one can work that way. I don't know what my style is;

that's for other people to say, if I have one. Anyway, my style has to be altered, changed, modified by the dictates of the particular play. So the style was dictated very much by the play, I hope, and is produced by the work process. Style is doing within the premise of the play. I am very much in sympathy with the idea of doing nothing and having nothing on the stage unless it means something; but there are other plays that one can think of which require a great deal of naturalistic bolstering—obviously the plays of the naturalistic revolution which you have to think of, at least at first, in those terms. But it wasn't a stylistic exercise, this production. And I think, thanks to Pinter the playwright and his collaboration with me as a director, it's one of the few productions I've done in my life in which what was on the stage, if I may say this, was better than my first concept of it. I think that's happened to me four times in my life, and usually it's the other way round.

IW: Is that the benefit of working with your own company?

PH: Absolutely. I could not have put an ad hoc group through that needling and meticulous process. They would have felt that they were in corsets.

PERFORMANCE REVIEW

A Doll's House Again

BERNARD SHAW
Review of *A Doll's House*

GLOBE THEATRE, LONDON, 10 MAY 1897.

Bernard Shaw was one of the first champions of Henrik Ibsen's plays in England, and as the theater reviewer for The Saturday Review, *he had a pulpit from which not only to advance the cause of the new drama, but to excoriate actors, managers, and playwrights who seemed wedded to the values and traditions of the past. In this review, Shaw compares this revival to the original 1889 English première, noting in particular the ways time has changed the performance of Janet Achurch. Although the play is commonly translated into English as* A Doll's House, *Rolf Fjelde—who translated the play in* The Heinle Anthology—*explains that "a doll house" is a more accurate translation, conveying Ibsen's emphasis on the imprisoning qualities of Nora's "house."*

At last I am beginning to understand anti-Ibsenism. It must be that I am growing old and weak and sentimental and foolish; for I cannot stand up to reality as I did once. Eight years ago, when Mr. Charrington, with "A Doll's House," struck the decisive blow for Ibsen—perhaps the only one that has really got home in England as yet—I rejoiced in it, and watched the ruin and havoc it made among the idols and temples of the idealists as a young war correspondent watches the bombardment of the unhealthy quarters of a city. But now I understand better what it means to the unhappy wretches who can conceive no other life as possible to them except the Doll's House life. The master of the Doll's House may endure and even admire himself as long as he is called King Arthur and prodigiously flattered; but to paint a Torvald Helmer for him, and leave his conscience and his ever-gnawing secret diffidence to whisper "Thou art the man" when he has perhaps outlived all chance of being any other sort of man, must be bitter and dreadful to him. Dr. Rank, too, with his rickets and his scrofula, no longer an example, like Herod, of the wrath of God, or a curiosity to be stared at as villagers stare at a sheep with two heads, but a matter-of-fact completion of the typical picture of family life by one of the inevitable congenital invalids, or drunkards, or lunatics whose teeth are set on edge because their fathers have eaten sour grapes: this also is a horror against which an agony of protest may well be excused.

It will be remarked that I no longer dwell on the awakening of the woman, which was once the central point of the controversy as it is the central point of the drama. Why should I? The play solves that problem just as it is being solved in real life. The woman's eyes are opened; and instantly her doll's dress is thrown off and her husband left staring at her, helpless, bound thenceforth either to do without her (an alternative which makes short work of his fancied independence) or else treat her as a human being like himself, fully recognizing that he is not a creature of one superior species, Man, living with a creature of another and inferior species, Woman, but that Mankind is male and female, like other kinds, and that the inequality of the sexes is literally a cock and bull story, certain to end in such an unbearable humiliation as that which our suburban King Arthurs suffer at the hands of Ibsen. The ending of the play is not on the face of it particularly tragic: the alleged "note of interrogation" is a sentimental fancy; for it is clear that Helmer is brought to his senses, and that Nora's departure is no claptrap "Farewell forever," but a journey in search of self-respect and apprenticeship to life. Yet there is an underlying solemnity caused by a fact that the popular instinct has divined: to wit, that Nora's revolt is the end of a chapter of human history. The slam of the door behind her is more momentous than the cannon of Waterloo or Sedan, because when she comes back, it will not be to the old home; for when the patriarch no longer rules, and the "breadwinner" acknowledges his dependence, there is an end of the old order; and an institution upon which so much human affection and suffering have been lavished, and about which so much experience of the holiest right and bitterest wrong has gathered, cannot fall without moving even its destroyers, much more those who believe that its extirpation is a mortal wound to society. This moment of awe and remorse in "A Doll's House" was at first lightened by the mere Women's Rights question. Now that this no longer distracts us, we feel the full weight of the unsolved destiny of our Helmers, our Krogstads, our Ranks and our Rank ancestors, whom we cannot, like the Heavenly Twin, dispose of by breaking their noses and saying, "Take that, you father of a speckled toad."

It may be, however, that this difference between the impression made by the famous performance in 1889 and the present revival is due partly to artistic conditions. On Monday last Mr. Courtenay Thorpe accomplished the remarkable feat of playing Helmer in the afternoon and the Ghost in "Hamlet" in the evening, and doing both better than we have seen them done before. Mr. Waring, our original Helmer, realized the importance of this most unflattering part, and sacrificed himself to play it. But he could not bring himself to confess to it wholly. He played it critically, and realized it by a process of intentional self-stultification. The resultant performance, excellently convincing up to fully nineteen-twentieths, was, as regards the remaining twentieth, obviously a piece of acting in which a line was drawn, as a matter of self-respect, between Mr. Waring and Mr. Helmer. Nevertheless, it was badly missed when Mr. Charrington tried the part later on and achieved a record as the very worst Helmer in the world through sheer incompatibility of temperament. But Mr. Courtenay Thorpe obliterates both records. He plays Helmer with passion. It is the first time we have seen this done; and the effect is overwhelming. We no longer study an object lesson in lord-of-creationism, appealing to our sociological interest only. We see a fellow-creature blindly wrecking his happiness and losing his "love life," and are touched dramatically. There were slips and blunders, it is true. Mr. Courtenay Thorpe did not know his dialogue thoroughly; and when the words did not come unsought he said anything that came into his head (stark nonsense sometimes) sooner than go out of his part to look for them. And he succumbed to the temptation to utter the two or three most fatuously conceited of Helmer's utterances as "points," thereby destroying the naturalness that could alone make them really credible and effective. But it did not matter: the success was beyond being undone by trifles. Ibsen has in this case repeated his old feat of making an actor's reputation.

Miss Achurch's Nora is an old story by this time; and I leave its celebration to the young critics who saw it on Monday for the first time. It still seems to me to place her far ahead of any living English actress of her generation in this class of work—the only class, let me add, which now presents any difficulty to actresses who bring some personal charm to the aid of quite commonplace attainments. Here and there we have had some bits of new-fashioned work on the stage—for instance, Mrs. Kendal's extraordinarily fine and finished performance in "The Greatest of These," and Miss Winifred Emery's last serious feat of acting in "The Benefit of the Doubt." These show that Miss Achurch's monopoly is not one of executive skill, but of the modernity of culture, the mental power and quickness of vision to recognize the enormous value of the opportunity she has seized. In the eight years since 1889 she has gained in strength and art; and her performance is more powerful, more surely gripped, and more expertly carried out than it used to be; but it has losses to show as well as gains. In the old days Nora's first scene with Krogstad had a wonderful naïveté: her youthfully unsympathetic contempt for him, her certainty that his effort to make a serious business of the forgery was mere vulgarity, her utter repudiation of the notion that there could be any comparison between his case and hers, were expressed to perfection. And in the first half of the renowned final scene the chill "clearness and certainty" of the disillusion, the quite new tone of intellectual seriousness, announcing by its freshness and coolness a complete change in her as she calls her husband to account with her eyes wide open for the first time: all this, so vitally necessary to the novel truth of the scene and the convincing effect of the statement that she no longer loves him, came with lifegiving naturalness. But these two scenes have now become unmistakably stale to Miss Achurch. In the Krogstad one she plays as if the danger of penal servitude were the whole point of it; and she agonizes over the cool opening of the explanation with Helmer with all the conventional pangs of parting in full play from the first. This ages her Nora perceptibly. Physically she is youthful enough: Helmer's "squirrel" still dances blithely, sings unmercifully, and wears reckless garments at which the modish occupants of the stalls stare in scandal and consternation (and which, by the way, are impossible for a snobbish bank manager's wife). But Miss Achurch can no longer content herself with a girl's allowance of passion and sympathy. She fills the cup and drains it; and consequently, though Nora has all her old vitality and originality, and more than her old hold of the audience, she is less girlish and more sophisticated with the passions of the stage than she was at the Novelty when she first captivated us.

Mr. Charrington's Rank, always an admirable performance, is now better than ever. But it is also sterner and harder to bear. He has very perceptibly increased the horror of the part by a few touches which bring and keep his despair and doom more vividly before the audience; and he no longer softens his final exit by the sentimental business of snatching Nora's handkerchief.

The effect of a performance of the "Doll's House" with the three most important parts very well played, and the economy of the mounting—which involves a disembowelled sofa—got over by intelligent stage management and a little judicious hiring and borrowing, is almost painfully strong. It is mitigated by the earnest but mistaken efforts of Mr. Charles Fulton and Miss Vane Featherstone as Krogstad and Mrs. Linden. Mr. Fulton, invaluable at the Adelphi, struggles with his part like a blacksmith mending a watch; and the style of play which makes Miss Vane Featherstone so useful and attractive in the unrealistic drama produces, in a realistic part, exactly the effect that might have been expected. The flattering notion, still current in the profession, that anybody can play Ibsen, is hardly bearing the test of experience. Happily, the elements of strength in the performance triumph over all drawbacks. If "The Wild Duck" next week is as good as "A Doll's House," the Independent Theatre (for which, as a small shareholder, I have a certain partiality) will have done very well. . . .

The Doll *from London Brings Down the House*

BEN BRANTLEY
Review of *A Doll's House*

DIRECTED BY ANTHONY PAGE, AT THE BELASCO THEATER, NEW YORK, 3 APRIL 1997.

Ben Brantley's review of the New York opening of A Doll's House *for the* New York Times *testifies to the play's ongoing vitality. This production not only featured a script adapted by the Irish playwright Frank McGuinness, but also a series of stunning performances, particularly by Janet McTeer as Nora. It's clear from Brantley's review that McTeer strove throughout the production to make her Nora a strong, erotically powerful woman; what's surprising—and clearly effective—is the way she also managed to register her love for Helmer. Brantley suggests that this production has worked hard to make Helmer—played by Owen Teale—equally imposing, an energetic and attractive man whose life falls to pieces when his illusions about marriage are broken.*

It just doesn't happen that often, and when it does, you sit there, open-mouthed, grateful, admiring and shaken, and think, "This is why I love the theater."

It's the response that comes when a dramatic performance is so completely and richly realized that you find yourself truly living through the character portrayed on stage, even when you want to pull back to a comfortable spectator's distance. The pulse quickens, the eyes well. And there is somehow the sense that ordinary life has been heightened to the bursting point.

The occasion for this revelation is the new production of Ibsen's "Doll's House," a London import that opened last night at the Belasco Theater. The name of the revelation is Janet McTeer, an actress, little known in America, whose apparition on Broadway suggests the theater's timely answer to the Hale-Bopp comet.

What Ms. McTeer achieves, with the magnificent support of the director Anthony Page and a flawless supporting cast, is the sense that the landmark, century-old role of Ibsen's Nora Helmer, the childlike housewife who comes so painfully of age, was only just written, and written specifically for her. You may think you know "A Doll's House" inside out. This production is guaranteed to prove you wrong.

The 1879 classic, with its iconoclastic portrayal of a woman who leaves her marriage to find herself, assumed an instant, thundering social significance and that has clouded perceptions of the play. There was a theory, starting with George Bernard Shaw, that the drama's greatness was more historical than artistic, and that, like most things searingly topical, it was destined to become a fossil.

Still the play has never left the international repertory with great actresses repeatedly drawn to Nora like the proverbial moths to the flame. Very often, they have indeed been burned, provoking criticism that Nora's conversion from domestic plaything to proto-feminist requires radical jumps in psychological continuity, accompanied by the creaking of a mechanical, agenda-driven plot.

Not a single creak is heard in Mr. Page's production, Ms. McTeer's performance or Frank McGuinness's wonderfully loose-limbed adaptation. They never impose on Ibsen's text but instead mine it for an emotional consistency and logic that is very definitely there. And marvel of marvels, the most stirring part of this interpretation comes in its last 20 minutes, when Nora speaks the lines that, out of context, have become feminist rallying cries.

Ms. McTeer's Nora, confronting her husband, Torvald (the masterly Owen Teale), with the failure of their marriage, is no coolly articulate visionary, for whom a light has suddenly been turned on after a lifetime of benightedness. She is still fumbling in the dark, still struggling to find words to match her growing belief that something is very, very wrong. She seems surprised, in fact, by her own perceptions, as if they were only just taking form in her consciousness.

The entire evening builds carefully to this moment in ways you are aware of only after you've arrived there.

From the outset, Ms. McTeer's performance has suggested a struggle between willful self-delusion and a subterranean uneasiness that Nora reflexively works to suppress. She's a hardworking actress who doesn't even know she's playing a part or how tired she has grown of it.

Ms. McTeer starts off with a mannered intensity some audience members may at first find grating. There's a glow of fever about Nora as she busily trims her comfortably appointed living room for Christmas. The laughter with which she punctuates her speech has a loon-like quality; she tries on different, silly voices like an eager-to-please comedian; she flaps her wrists in a way that dismisses what she's saying even as she calls attention to it.

It is a brave, risky conception that even comes across as grotesque at moments, a feeling underscored by the fact that Ms. McTeer is no doll-size ingenue but a woman of towering height and erotic presence. (She compliantly bends her knees for her long, frequent kisses with Torvald.) She's a fluttery geisha in overdrive, on call to entertain and make merry whenever her husband chooses to appear from his invincible fortress of a study.

What cannot be doubted is that Nora behaves like this out of love for the man she married. It's the same impulse that drove her to commit the criminal act—the forging of her father's signature when she needed to borrow money to take her ailing husband to Italy—that provides the play with its plot. And this production ingeniously melds Nora's apprehension about being exposed by the embittered money lender Nils Krogstad (Peter Gowen) with the encroaching awareness that her love for Torvald, the center of her existence, is built on sand.

There are moments throughout, especially in Nora's scenes with her childhood friend Kristine Linde (Jan Maxwell) and her cynical admirer, Dr. Rank (John Carlisle), when shafts of light break into the doll's house, a sense of how hard and unfair the world can be and of the imbalance in the Helmers' marriage.

The scene when, in conversation with Dr. Rank, Nora realizes that her relationship with her husband is like that she had with her doting father, is remarkable both for how the perception astonishes her and for how she seems to brush it away. So when the play reaches its climax, it feels less like an abrupt turn than the inevitable end of a single, well-paved road.

Mr. Page, best known here for his productions of "Heartbreak House" (with Rex Harrison and Rosemary Harris) and "Inadmissible Evidence" (with Nicol Williamson), reminds you of the virtues of pure naturalism in theater. There's a ripe physicality to the production, an awareness of the comforts of the warmth of home and clothing (deliciously embodied by Deirdre Clancy's set and costumes) and of the literal coldness outside. (This is the first production of "A Doll's House" I've seen in which, when Nora makes her famous final exit, I worried whether she was dressed warmly enough.)

There is a definite sensual heat as well. It's apparent in the coded, tantalizing body language between Nora and Helmer; the hungry kisses stolen by Kristine and Nils after they declare their love for each other; in Nora's mischievously displaying her silk stockings to the terminally ill Dr. Rank, an act that registers as one of infinite, if misplaced, kindness to a dying man; and, above all, in Ms. McTeer's dancing the tarantella as a giddy, erotic collapse into nervous exhaustion.

It is also hard to imagine a more persuasively balanced ensemble. Mr. Carlisle's flinty, troubled doctor; Ms. Maxwell's sober, pragmatic Kristine (a perfect foil to Ms. McTeer's agitation); Mr. Gowen's all-too-human, self-preserving desperation; these performances remind you that Ibsen did indeed create complete characters who are always waiting to be rediscovered.

As Torvald, the handsome, imposingly centered Mr. Teale couldn't be better. For once, you understand the magnetic hold this husband has over his wife, as well as why he is destined to lose her. His blunt air of authority is so compelling that when it finally shatters, the effect is devastating.

Nora leaves this broken man less in anger than in sorrow, a fitting conclusion to an evening infused not with polemical rage but with a sad compassion for the mess people make of their lives. The "something glorious" that Nora so ravenously craves, a heroic act from her husband that would redeem their marriage, doesn't happen, of course. But thanks to Ms. McTeer and company, something glorious is very definitely occurring at the Belasco.

The United States

Jeffrey Wright as Lincoln and Don Cheadle as Booth in the 2002 Joseph Papp Public Theater production of Suzan-Lori Parks's play, *Topdog/Underdog*.

Social and technological change transformed the world in the late nineteenth and early twentieth centuries. Between 1860 and today, the United States emerged from a crippling civil war, two world wars, and the anxieties of the Cold War to become a dominant global power. However, despite the nation's emergence as a major player on the world stage, the arts in the United States were shaped by divided and contradictory impulses. The desire to imitate European models competed with a desire to bring distinctively American arts into being. Even as the Civil War threatened to destroy the nation itself, writers such as Walt Whitman, Ralph Waldo Emerson, Henry David Thoreau, and others gave voice to a national literature that both incorporated and redefined European traditions. With the global expansion of U.S. influence, especially after World War I, the question of an "American culture" became a pressing one; after World War II, certain forms of culture became one of the United States' most significant exports, exports at once assimilated, resisted, and redefined in the contemporary era of globalized culture.

In the theater, the modern era has brought with it the search for a quintessentially "American" drama in which theme, setting, and characterization explore American experience, often by invoking and then discarding styles and attitudes derived from the European stage. In a sense, American drama in the twentieth century translated the idea of American political freedom into more abstract, metaphorical, even Romantic terms, as a conflict between individual freedom and the pressures of confining social realities, such as economic hardship, social class, gender, and race. The search for an American idiom in the theater absorbs the stylistic experiments of European modernism and reshapes them, bending the formal innovation of the European theater to American issues and concerns.

"THE" AMERICAN THEATER?

The democratic experience and populist rhetoric of American public life has generally resisted the idea of a national culture emanating from a single center like New York City or Washington, D.C. For this reason, perhaps, the dream of a national theater has repeatedly failed. In the nineteenth century, westward expansion brought theater from New York, Philadelphia, and Boston to the Midwestern cities of Chicago, St. Louis, and Kansas City, and then to Los Angeles and San Francisco, and to scores of smaller towns between the Mississippi River and the Pacific Ocean. The theater was a widely dispersed local affair. Towns often boasted theaters that could be used for opera, drama, or vaudeville and that supported local companies while also catering to touring shows with stars drawn from New York and Europe. Although a lively local theater thrived throughout the country, offering melodrama, classical plays, comedies, and other entertainments, the appetite for touring shows created a demand for organizations capable of handling scheduling problems for local theaters and regional booking agencies.

In 1896 a group of theatrical entrepreneurs headed by Charles Frohman formed a nationwide organization of booking agents called the **SYNDICATE.** In a sense, they created the first model of how a national theater might work in the United States. The Syndicate offered theater managers a full season of touring shows—provided that the manager contracted to deal only with the Syndicate. By gaining exclusive control over theaters on key travel routes, the Syndicate thwarted competition from other touring producers and often even denied local companies the use of local theaters. At its height, the Syndicate had exclusive rights to more than 700 theaters. It could blackball non-Syndicate performers from working by threatening producers who hired them, and it could withdraw Syndicate support from any manager who booked non-Syndicate shows or performers.

The effects of the Syndicate were profound and shaped the American theater for the next half-century. The Syndicate's grip on the theater effectively extinguished major professional theater outside New York as a source of new plays and productions; it also influenced playwriting, since the Syndicate developed plays only as commercial properties that could be successfully marketed to a general audience coast-to-coast. Although the Syndicate's power was resisted by a few famous actors and powerful producers, its approach was imitated by other groups. The parochial interests of the New York stage—where the shows of such organizations originated—became in practice the interests of the American theater, and New York became the center of theatrical production and theatrical investment. The revival of significant, professional "regional" theaters as centers of new productions—Margo Jones's Theater 47 in Dallas, the Alley Theater of Houston, the Arena Stage in Washington, D.C., the Actors Workshop of San Francisco, the Guthrie Theater in Minneapolis—had to wait until the 1940s and 1950s. The Syndicate's fortunes also point out the fallacy inherent in the notion of *an* American theater. Throughout its history, the American theater has embraced a range of dynamic and contradictory attitudes toward the stage and its place in society: New York versus the "provinces," mainstream versus elite, conventional versus experimental, commercial versus artistic. Theatrical innovation has been spurred primarily by theaters outside the commercial mainstream, especially by small, amateur "little theaters," by university and college theaters, by community theaters, and by ethnic theaters.

EUROPEAN INFLUENCE AND AMERICAN INNOVATION

The growth of American drama and theater was decisively shaped by the commercial climate of the stage and also by the United States' isolation from the energetic traditions of European theater. While there had long been a homegrown playwriting tradition, many of the most successful plays in nineteenth-century America were—in an era before copyright protection was extended to dramatic authors—productions, adaptations, or piracies of European novels and plays, as well as of American classics like Harriet Beecher Stowe's *Uncle Tom's Cabin*. Moreover, given the lucrative opportunities of touring, British and European actor/managers frequently brought shows to the United States, and some—notably the prolific playwright and actor Dion Boucicault, whose plays *The Poor of New York* (1857) and *The Octoroon* (1859) were written and successfully staged in the United States—developed plays on American themes. Although turn-of-the-century Broadway developed a homegrown version of theatrical realism—epitomized by writer/producer David Belasco's *The Governor's Lady* (1912), which reproduced the interior of a familiar theater district restaurant onstage— European experimentation made its impact on America in more indirect ways, usually only after those experiments had crystallized into a body of theatrical practices and conventions. Many major companies toured the United States. The Abbey Theater came with John Millington Synge's *The Playboy of the Western World* in 1911–1912, and the German producer Max Reinhardt brought his spectacular productions to the United States in 1912, 1914, 1924, and 1927–1928. The British director Harley Granville Barker, who sponsored Shaw's plays and had gained fame as an innovative director of Shakespeare, directed in New York in 1915; the Ballets Russes toured in 1916; and the Moscow Art Theater, whose disciples Richard Boleslavsky and Maria Ouspenskaya founded the American Laboratory Theater in 1923, performed in 1923–1924.

Many of these companies, the Abbey and the Moscow Art Theater in particular, had begun as small, independent, amateur theaters, and their work was most directly implemented in the United States by similar groups. Some innovation came from the new college and university programs in drama: George Pierce Baker's famous playwriting course at Harvard University in the first decades of the century (taken by Eugene O'Neill, among many others) and Montgomery T. Gregory's program for black writers and performers at Howard University in the 1920s were only the beginning of a concerted effort to bring theater and drama into the university curriculum and to develop a greater awareness of progressive theater. However, it largely fell to the **LITTLE THEATER MOVEMENT** to assimilate this new work and redirect it toward particularly American concerns. Innovation in the American theater came largely from these small companies, committed to mounting new and uncommercial work. The Chicago Little Theater, the Toy Theater of Boston, the Neighborhood Playhouse and the Washington Square Playhouse of New York, and Detroit's Arts and Crafts Theater were all in operation by 1917, and the Little Negro Theater Movement was producing plays in Harlem and Washington, D.C., as well.

The Provincetown Playhouse provides a model of the "little theaters" and their fortunes in the early twentieth century. Founded in 1915 in Provincetown, Massachusetts—an artists' retreat at the tip of Cape Cod—the company was initially a group of young amateurs intent on theater, including the playwright Susan Glaspell; her husband, George Cram Cook; and, later, Eugene O'Neill. In the first year, the players produced plays in their summer homes. In 1916 they converted an old wharf building into a small theater and produced, among other plays, O'Neill's *Bound East for Cardiff.* In the autumn, the players returned to New York and opened a small theater in Greenwich Village. The company could hardly afford complex and expensive sets and turned its efforts instead toward a simple and realistic kind of performance. Eugene O'Neill's early plays were produced by the Provincetown company, and after he became a successful Broadway playwright, he continued to open many of his plays there. Like all of the "little theaters," the Provincetown had difficulty managing the transition from a small amateur company to the larger demands of a self-sustaining professional company. It went through a series of transformations before closing in 1929, having introduced O'Neill to the stage and having staged plays by John Reed, Edna St. Vincent Millay, Susan Glaspell, Djuna Barnes, Edmund Wilson, Paul Green, Wallace Stevens, Theodore Dreiser, August Strindberg, and many others.

In the United States, the freedom to make theater has always been qualified by the need to make it pay. The trials of sustaining artistic ambition in the commercial environment of the theater is the central narrative of the most innovative theatrical companies of the modern era. The ideal of an American theater remained tantalizing yet elusive and was often pursued in several ways, usually by developing a distinctive repertoire of plays, or by trying to define a typically American performance idiom. "Little theaters" like the Provincetown emphasized the production of American drama. Other theaters tried to produce American drama, the new European drama, and the classics for a larger audience than the "little theaters" could reach. The Theater Guild, for example, was organized in 1919 in New York as a subscription company specifically for the purpose of producing noncommercial plays. In the course of the next decade, the Guild staged plays by Shaw, Pirandello, Ibsen, and Strindberg, as well as plays by Americans like O'Neill and Elmer Rice. The Guild succeeded in incorporating American plays like O'Neill's *Strange Interlude* (1928) and Rice's *The Adding Machine* (1923) into the repertoire of serious modern drama and in bringing it to a significant public. However, following the stock market crash of 1929 and the economic depression that ensued, the Guild invested in a less adventuresome repertoire in the hopes of drawing a larger audience and so lost its original mission.

Although it sponsored an innovative selection of plays, the Theater Guild did not develop an original style of production. In 1931, several Guild members began a spin-off company—called simply the Group—for the purpose of investigating different kinds of drama and different approaches to performance. Eventually including Harold Clurman, Cheryl Crawford, Lee Strasberg, Elia Kazan, Sanford Meisner, and many others, the Group at first worked on plays examining the social ferment of the 1930s and the hardship of the Great Depression. Much as Chekhov became the centerpiece of Stanislavski's Moscow Art Theater, so the plays of Clifford Odets became the Group's standards: *Awake and Sing!, Waiting for Lefty,* and *Golden Boy.* However, the Group's most extensive contribution to the American theater was its systematic importation of Stanislavskian acting techniques. In the Group, and later in the Actors Studio, actors were trained in Stanislavski's approach to **EMOTION MEMORY** and **GIVEN CIRCUMSTANCES,** laying the groundwork for what became a distinctly "American" style of acting, acting that was emotionally spontaneous, grounded in subtext, psychologically realistic and nuanced. Nonetheless, the Group, the Studio, and the training they devised produced a generation of actors ready to meet the challenges of the burgeoning American drama of the 1940s and 1950s: Marlon Brando, Ben Gazzara, Karl Malden, Geraldine Page, Kim Stanley, Maureen Stapleton, and many others.

The impact of this acting can be seen in the great stage productions of the post-war period. The 1940s and early 1950s saw the development of a distinctively American approach to stage realism, balancing nuanced characterization with a concern for the social environment. Arthur Miller's *Death of a Salesman* and *The Crucible,* Tennessee Williams's *A Streetcar Named Desire* and *The Glass Menagerie,* and Eugene O'Neill's *The Iceman Cometh* and *Long Day's Journey into Night* demanded the subtle realism that became the hallmark of American acting and of American drama in the world repertoire. These plays—and their descendants, like the plays of Beth Henley, David Mamet, Maria Irene Fornes, August Wilson, or Sam Shepard—succeeded by criticizing American ideals and institutions while at the same time exploring the psyche of the American character. Indeed, in these plays the American character often seems to be thwarted precisely by the process of American society. The fragile beauty of Tennessee Williams's Southern belles is usually crushed by the sordid realities of modern urban life; in Shepard's *True West,* the American West becomes a mythic battleground, where a yuppie and a drifter shoot it out for control of the image.

POSTWAR EXPERIMENTS

After World War II, the most significant innovations in American theater have come from small "experimental" theater companies. In part through the influence of Antonin Artaud's conception of a **THEATER OF CRUELTY** (see Unit V), and the several tours of Jerzy Grotowski's Lab Theater of Poland, experimental theater in the 1960s and 1970s tended to reject the esthetic of stage realism in favor of producing an immediate, quintessentially *theatrical* experience for its audiences. As a result, many productions in the 1960s and 1970s—the Living Theater's *Paradise Now,* the Performance Group's *Dionysus in 69,* the Open Theater's *The Serpent,* the work of the Bread and Puppet Theater, of the San Francisco Mime Troup, of Mabou Mines, and many others—incorporated the audience as participants in the action. Many of these experiments also led to new forms of playwriting, in which classical notions of representation also were broken down. Moreover, these experiments not only led to the incorporation of a more immediate, physical esthetic into American drama (visible, too, in performance art), but also to the exploration of Brechtian epic theater: experiments with narrative (Fornes's *Fefu and Her Friends*), with an episodic epic form (Kushner's *Angels in America*), or with a more politicized performance of "character" (Anna Deavere Smith's monologues).

Indeed, American drama continued to strike a compromise with the innovations of the European theater after World War II. Eric Bentley—a brilliant scholar, director, playwright, and translator—worked indefatigably to bring Bertolt Brecht to the attention of the American theater. Brecht became particularly important in the United States as the Vietnam War and widespread civil and social discontent spurred the theater in more agitational, political directions. Feminist theater, ethnic theater, and gay and lesbian theater have all at times availed themselves of Brecht's theater theory and practice. The work of Luis Valdez and El Teatro Campesino in California in the 1960s and 1970s is a direct extension of Brecht's sense of theater. Bringing a flatbed truck to farmworkers' strikes, Teatro Campesino produced its short, political dramas to an active, involved audience and became part of the process of social change. "Absurdist" playwrights like Samuel Beckett, Harold Pinter, and Eugène Ionesco were also both produced and imitated in the United States, influencing the work of American playwrights like Edward Albee, Maria Irene Fornes, Jack Gelber, Adrienne Kennedy, David Mamet, and Sam Shepard. Indeed, in plays like Amiri Baraka's *Dutch-*

man or Sam Shepard's *True West,* we can see the inflections of **THEATER OF THE ABSURD** in plays that are recognizably "American" in style and subject matter.

In 1935, an act of Congress established the Federal Theater Project, as a way to employ workers left unemployed by the Depression (see Aside box). The Federal Theater Project also sponsored a Negro Unit, directed by John Houseman and Orson Welles, which operated in ten cities around the United States; two of its productions, an all-black *Macbeth* and *The Swing Mikado,* were among the Federal Theater's most successful productions. The fact of a separate Negro Unit points to a different crisis in the idea of an American theater. How could a theater largely in the hands of the white, Anglo, male, middle class adequately represent the diversity of the nation's experience, particularly the experience of the oppressed? As the poet and playwright Langston Hughes observed in "Notes on Commercial Theater," published in 1940, the stage had in many ways appropriated African-American culture, systematically absorbing it into its own dominant values:

> *Yep, you done taken my blues and gone.*
> *You also took my spirituals and gone.*
> *You put me in Macbeth and Carmen Jones*
> *And all kinds of Swing Mikados*
> *And in everything but what's about me—*
> *But someday somebody'll*
> *Stand up and talk about me,*
> *And write about me—*
> *Black and beautiful—*

Far from representing authentic black experience in America, such theater more often confirmed the discriminatory fantasies already prominent on the stage and in society. Such stereotypes as the boozy Irishman, the dull Swede, the sunny and/or murderous Italian, and the greedy Jew—appearing even in "realistic" plays like Rice's *Street Scene* (1929), and dating back through the stereotyped slaves and Indians of Boucicault's *Octoroon*—work to reinforce the "normative" perspective of dominant culture, reflecting the attitudes, behavior, and social practices that oppress such groups in the world outside the theater. It is not surprising, then, that throughout the history of the United States, ethnic theaters have played a prominent part in maintaining the cultural identity of America's minority populations: the Yiddish theater of New York, Polish theaters in Chicago, Scandinavian theaters throughout the Midwest, a thriving circuit of Spanish-language theaters shared by Mexico and Southwestern states from Texas to California, Cuban-influenced theater in Florida, and Puerto Rican theater in New York. Some of these theaters produced versions of classic European plays in their own accents, but most developed their own dramatic forms, as ways of maintaining themselves in the face of a brutally exclusive "American" culture.

The experience of slavery places African Americans in a different position vis-à-vis the culture of the United States, and the black theater has had a profound impact on the course of the American stage. Although an African Theater Company was founded in New York in 1821—sponsoring, among others, the brilliant Shakespearean actor Ira Aldridge (1807–1867) who left the United States for a distinguished career in Europe—in the main, African Americans had little direct access to the theater before the twentieth century. Black characters had long figured as stage villains and comic buffoons in American drama. Played by white actors in blackface makeup, these abusive types literally enacted white attitudes toward racial difference. "Jim Crow" was first popularized by the white song-and-dance man T. D. Rice in the 1830s, and more "sympathetic" characters, like Tom in the hugely popular stage adaptations of Harriet Beecher Stowe's *Uncle Tom's Cabin* (1832), were devised by white authors and played by white actors. The minstrel troupes that became popular after the Civil

If the Group Theater and the Actors Studio created an identifiably "American" approach to acting, the Federal Theater Project succeeded—briefly—in creating a truly national theater. An act of Congress established the Federal Theater Project in 1935 under the Works Projects Administration, with Hallie Flanagan Davis (1890–1969) as director. Like other WPA projects, the Federal Theater was designed both to employ workers idled by the Depression and to provide service to the community. It was an enormous undertaking; in New York City alone, half the theaters were closed by 1933 and half its population of actors unemployed. Given the mission of providing employment by hiring large casts and supporting personnel, and a commitment to dramatizing contemporary social issues, the Federal Theater developed its most notable genre, the Living Newspaper. Living Newspapers incorporated dialogue taken from newspapers and other public media into a series of vignettes, readings, films, and other techniques to a problem in current national and world affairs: the farm crisis in *Triple A Plowed Under* (1936), housing in *One-Third of a Nation* (1938), rural electrification in *Power* (1937). At its height, the Federal Theater had branches in forty states; these branches staged productions devised by the project's directors, using their own local resources, and often developed their own material. In 1936, for instance, a stage adaptation of Sinclair Lewis's *It Can't Happen Here* opened simultaneously in twenty-one theaters around the country, including black-cast and Yiddish productions. The Federal Theater ran for four full seasons before being terminated by Congress in 1939: it financed 1,200 productions of 830 major works, at times employing more than ten thousand people, most of whom had been unemployed. Admission to its shows was inexpensive, and in an average week 500,000 people saw its productions; over its four years of production, its audiences numbered more than 30 million people. In New York alone, more than 12 million people saw its productions. However, in an era of labor unrest and the pervasive fear of outside agitation, the Newspapers were seen by the Project's enemies in government—many of whom opposed the WPA altogether—as too left-wing for government support.

Despite its demise, the United State's' only truly national theater had significant influence on the course of American theater and drama. Not only did the Federal Theater have huge audiences, but it brought new audiences into the theater: 65 percent of its audiences were seeing a stage play for the first time. The Living Newspapers developed a home-grown adaptation of the techniques of European experimental theater (including Brechtian epic theater) in the United States. In this sense, the Federal Theater inspired the work of several distinguished theater companies that survived its demise, notably John Houseman's (1915–1985) Mercury Theater, which produced Mark Blitzstein's *The Cradle Will Rock,* and a distinguished series of productions of modern and classic plays—by Shaw, Büchner, Shakespeare, and others. In addition, the Negro Units of the Federal Theater operated in Seattle, Hartford, Philadelphia, Newark, Los Angeles, Boston, Birmingham, Raleigh, San Francisco, and Chicago, employing more than 800 people and staging seventy-five productions in the project's four years of operation. Most importantly, the Federal Theater enabled a generation of actors, designers, directors, and playwrights to survive the Depression, and it brought the theater powerfully into the national scene.

LIVING NEWSPAPER

The Federal Theater Project dramatizes news events in the New York production of 1935.

War for depicting romanticized vignettes of plantation life were also first performed by white actors. Later, black performers—in minstrel troupes, or in the newly popular "Negro musicals"—often had little choice other than to enact these stereotypes themselves, for such roles were the only openings available on the stage (even black theaters were usually financed and operated by white entrepreneurs). Despite small inroads like the Lafayette Theater (founded in Harlem in 1915), representing black experience to America at large was almost exclusively the prerogative of white actors, producers, playwrights, and performers. In this regard, the theater—like the institutions of literature, the press, the legal system, and state and federal government—denied African Americans their own voice.

Spurred in part by successful plays by white dramatists that self-consciously attempted to "humanize" black characters for white audiences—O'Neill's *The Emperor Jones* (1920) and *All God's Chillun Got Wings* (1924), Marc Connelly's *The Green Pastures* (1930), Paul Green's *In Abraham's Bosom* (1926), and Dubose and Dorothy Heyward's *Porgy* (1920; transformed into the Gershwin musical *Porgy and Bess* in 1935)—black actors and writers became galvanized to "stand up and talk" about themselves. Throughout the 1920s the **LITTLE NEGRO THEATER MOVEMENT** sponsored plays of black life largely for black audiences. The Lafayette Theater, for example, opened Willis Richardson's *The Chipwoman's Fortune* in 1923; it later became the first play by a black playwright to reach Broadway. In the 1920s and 1930s, black drama increasingly addressed the politics of racism in the United States, while also depicting the effect of racism in daily life. Several organizations worked to sponsor African-American drama and theater. W.E.B. DuBois, a founder of the National Association for the Advancement of Colored People (NAACP), used his *Crisis* magazine—in collaboration with the National Urban League's *Opportunity*—to give a series of prizes to promising African American playwrights; winners included Eulalie Spence's *Foreign Mail* (1926), Zora Neale Hurston's *Colorstruck* and *Spears* (1925), and Georgia Douglas Johnson's *Blue Blood* (1926). The NAACP also sponsored the production of plays, including Angelina Weld Grimké's influential drama of a young woman's reaction to the lynching of her father and brother, *Rachel* (1916). *Rachel* was one of the first of a series of plays about lynching. How this important genre of black theater—and a crucial element of black experience in the United States—was both overlooked and distorted by white theater is the subject of Alice Childress's brilliant play *Trouble in Mind,* which opened off-Broadway in 1955. Finally, black colleges, universities, and even high schools also became centers for a new dramatic repertoire. In 1921, Montgomery T. Gregory formed a department of Dramatic Arts at Howard University in Washington, D.C., and with Alain Locke developed an influential program in acting, playwriting, and theatrical production, offering the first institutionalized training for black writers and performers in the United States.

In a 1926 playbill for Harlem's Krigwa Players, W.E.B. DuBois described the goals of a black theater:

> The plays of a real Negro theater must be: *One: About us.* That is, they must have plots which reveal Negro life as it is. *Two: By us.* That is, they must be written by Negro authors who understand from birth and continual association just what it means to be a Negro today. *Three: For us.* That is, the theater must cater primarily to Negro audiences and be supported and sustained by their entertainment and approval. *Fourth: Near us.* The theater must be in a Negro neighborhood near the mass of ordinary Negro people.

Throughout the 1930s and 1940s, African American playwrights and actors came into increasing national prominence, both by developing DuBois's agenda and by working to bring an authentic black drama to a wider audience. Langston Hughes wrote a number of plays in the 1930s, including the well-known *Mulatto* (1935); the Federal Theater Project produced W.E.B. DuBois's *Haiti* at the Lafayette Theater; and playwrights trained at Howard were produced in New York and elsewhere. The founding of the companies like the American Negro Theater in 1939, the Negro Playwrights Company in 1940, and the Negro Ensemble Company in 1957 began to meet DuBois's charge, developing the actors, the production experience, and the financing that would sustain the explosive growth of black American drama after World War II. When Lorraine Hansberry's *A Raisin in the Sun* opened in 1959, it was the first play written by a black woman to reach Broadway, the first directed by a black director (Lloyd Richards), and the first financed predominantly by African Americans. The success of *Raisin* foretold the success of black theater in the coming decades, as black playwrights—Amiri Baraka, Adrienne Kennedy, Charles Gordone, Ed Bullins, Charles Fuller, Ntozake Shange, August Wilson, Anna Deavere Smith, Suzan-Lori Parks, and many others—came to shape the American theater.

POPULAR THEATER AND MASS CULTURE

The tension between commercial viability and dramatic achievement is perhaps best symbolized by Broadway itself, the American theater's "magnificent invalid," where even the greatest American plays can hardly compare in terms of commercial and popular success with Broadway's most uniquely American genre: the musical. Musical theater has a long history in the United States, and in many respects its fortunes parallel those of the dramatic theater. Musical theater also witnessed the tyranny of national producing syndicates, the impact of European innovation, and the powerful contributions of black and ethnic cultures. However, the integration of song and dance, orchestral music, and (usually) a romantic plot characteristic of the Broadway musical really dates to the period of World War II, probably to Richard Rodgers and Oscar Hammerstein's *Oklahoma!* (1943), which ran for 2,248 performances (*Death of a Salesman,* in contrast, ran for 742). *Oklahoma!* provided the model not only for other Rodgers and Hammerstein hits—*Carousel* (1945), *South Pacific* (1949), *The King and I* (1951)—but for other musicals as well: Alan Jay Lerner and Frederick Loewe's updating of Shaw's *Pygmalion* in *My Fair Lady* (1956), Frank Loesser's *Guys and Dolls* (1950), and Leonard Bernstein, Stephen Sondheim, and Arthur Laurents's *West Side Story* (1957). Although the form of the Broadway musical underwent significant changes in the 1970s and 1980s, its popularity points to one of the ways that the theater has sought to recapture an audience from film and television: by emphasizing the unique excitement of a dazzling live spectacle. This is as true of recent Broadway hits like *High Society* (1997), which used the Cole Porter music from the 1956 film of the same name, as it is of several musicals adapted from animated films—notably *The Lion King* (1997). The musical theater also points to the fundamental conditions of the Broadway theatrical economy as well. Musicals remain popular with producers because the huge financial investment required to mount a musical can repay much larger returns for investors than any "straight" play.

Throughout the history of the stage in the West, important theaters have succeeded both in creating innovative drama and in creating a public. However, the American theater—if there is *an* American theater—is a different entity altogether from the citizens' theater of classical Athens, the courtly theater of Racine and Molière, or even the educated circle of subscribers to Shaw's Court Theater. In a sense, this difference can be traced to the fact that the American theater first came into force only in the twentieth century, at just the moment when other dramatic media—film and television—began to compete with it. The American theater has had to define itself in the environment of modern mass culture. Not only are film and television more accessible to most people, but the technology and distribution of such mass media have fundamentally altered our understanding both of drama and performance, and of what an audience *is*. "The American theater" has always been a critical fiction, homogenizing the diversity of stage activity in the United States, writing some forms of drama—chiefly American realistic plays—into history, and writing others out of it. Today, it may be equally artificial to separate live theater from other forms of dramatic production, forms that have massively changed the terrain where dramatic performance takes place.

With the global expansion of the United States in the first two thirds of the twentieth century, the development of new modes of commerce and trade in the 1960s and 1970s (notably the multinational corporation), and especially with the breakup of the Soviet Union and its satellite states symbolized by the fall of the Berlin Wall in 1989, "American" culture has become a widely exported commodity. Much as American culture has absorbed both immigrant and conquered cultures as part of the development of the United States, so now the image of "America" is projected around the world, on T-shirts, in cartoons, in the imagery of Mickey Mouse and Michael Jordan, in television programs, in films.

Drama and theater are also part of that projected image, and American drama has rapidly become part of a global canon of modern theater: plays such as *Death of a Salesman* and *Fences* have been performed in the People's Republic of China; *Angels in America* was produced in London before it opened in New York, and has since been produced around the world. One of the most challenging aspects of American theater, however, is what might be called its *diversity,* the way different playwrights have worked to challenge a monolithic notion of "American" culture, and the values—white, masculinist, heterosexual, middle-class, English-speaking—it asserts as definitive. This diversity emerges in several ways, not only through a writer's or a company's decision to make their own alternative perspective *count*—as Luis Valdez and El Teatro Campesino do in *Los Vendidos*—but to use theatrical production to mark, make visible, "alienate" in Brecht's sense the ways the normative values of "American" culture are produced, and the kinds of work those values do.

For this reason, while there remains a large "mainstream" of stage style, much of the most adventurous work in the American theater has experimented with new, alternative ways of representing drama on the stage, and new ways of engaging its audience. The "rep and rev" of Suzan-Lori Parks's plays, the ways they "repeat and revise" a single gesture in order to highlight the *constructedness* of the body and the ways it represents itself culturally is one of these techniques; Anna Deavere Smith's effort to imitate the gestural conventions of her interview subjects does a similar kind of work, implying that those gestures are part of a common cultural repertoire, an individual act of expression that uses social means. This "alienating" of the ways "identity" is produced onstage extends to a wide range of contemporary performance. In 1983, for example, the Wooster Group's *L.S.D.—Just the High Points* set portions of Arthur Miller's *The Crucible* as a trial, literalizing the parallel with the McCarthy hearings that the play was widely thought to allegorize; in *Routes 1 & 9,* the company integrated scenes from Thornton Wilder's *Our Town* into a blackface minstrel show, in effect staging the racist attitudes that "our town"—white America in this case—has both produced and disowned.

This use of the stage to expose dominant or oppressive attitudes that are concealed within the monuments of American culture is also characteristic of performance works like Coco Fusco and Guillermo Gómez-Peña's *Two Undiscovered Amerindians Visit . . . ,* (which has been filmed as *The Couple in the Cage*). In the early 1990s, Gómez-Peña (a performance artist born in Mexico) and Fusco (a Cuban-American) devised a performance in which they portrayed "native" or "indigenous" inhabitants of the (fictitious) Carribean island of Guatinaui. Wearing deeply layered costumes—basketball sneakers, feathered headdresses, sunglasses, bottle-cap–studded vests—Fusco and Gómez-Peña were displayed in a cage, as anthropological "discoveries." During the course of the performance, which was produced in several art museums around the United States, as well as in the Field Museum of Natural History in Chicago, and on a plaza in Madrid, Gómez-Peña and Fusco exhibited behavior: they watched TV, they ate, for a fee they had their photo taken with spectators, or danced, and so on. The purpose of the production, however, was less to portray an exoticized native "other," than it was to *stage* the attitudes of their audiences to the spectacle of these imprisoned, displayed people. Although we might think this an extreme or at least a special case, it might be said that what Gómez-Peña and Fusco did here—stage the audience—is a task that stretches back to Valdez's work in the 1960s, and has become one of the principal innovations of contemporary American performance.

PERFORMANCE ART

Since the mid-1960s, a variety of non-dramatic performance modes have developed in Western theater that are commonly known by the generic label of "performance art." Although it is difficult to generalize about this wide range of performances, most performance-art works share certain features: many (though certainly not all) are solo works, in which a performer (or performers) relates directly to an audience; the performer(s) may be working from a plan or script, but the performance is not a traditional "drama," enacting a fictitious narrative of the deeds of a fictitious "character" through "acting." Instead, in performance art, the performer uses a variety of means—monologue, physical performance, music, dance—to produce a spectacle that is "really happening" between himself or herself and the spectators.

Many performance-art works of the 1970s and 1980s used the performers' bodies to explore the limits of "theater." Chris Burden, for example, staged several events in which he wounded himself before an audience: in one 1970 work, he shot himself in the arm with a pistol; in another, he was crucified on top of a Volkswagen. In one of Carolee Schneeman's works, she unwinds a long scroll from her vagina, reading it to the audience. Annie Sprinkle, once a pornographic film star, openly objectifies her body onstage for a visible audience of men (and women), as she had once done in the more covert and coercive scene of pornography; in one performance, she invites the audience onstage while she conducts her own cervical examination. Many performance art works take place outside theatrical venues, so that the performance becomes part of the everyday "performance" of street life. Linda Montano spent one year connected by a short rope to Teching

Tsieh; the artists' lack of privacy was constantly on display in the streets of New York. In one of her early performances, Laurie Anderson stood on a large block of ice on a New York City street, playing her violin until the ice melted.

Several performance artists have become well-known for their monologue-performances, which range widely in technique and strategy. Anna Deavere Smith's works—such as *Fires in the Mirror: Crown Heights, Brooklyn and Other Identities* and *Twilight—Los Angeles, 1992*—differ from many performance art monologues in that Smith impersonates and represents a range of speakers; yet both in the brilliance of her individual performance and in her effort to perform the speakers faithfully (rather than "act" them in a theatrical sense), Smith's work touches on the "authentic" aspect of performance art. This emphasis on the "authentic," the "real," enables several performance artists to explore the relationship between identity politics and performance. In *Memory Tricks*, Marga Gomez, daughter of a Cuban theater impresario and a Puerto Rican "exotic dancer," recalls her family and childhood to interrogate the formation of Latina identity in the United States. David Drake's *The Night Larry Kramer Kissed Me* dramatizes the performer's understanding and exploration of his gay sexuality from the time of his sixth birthday, on the night of the 1969 Stonewall Riots in New York's Greenwich Village—in which gay men and lesbians protested abusive treatment by the police—through the AIDS crisis of the 1980s and 1990s.

Many artists use performance to foreground and criticize the everyday racist, sexist, and/or homophobic "performance" commonly accepted as "normal behavior" in U.S. society, and to bring into view other ways of performing identity. Adrian Piper, a light-skinned African American woman, sometimes hands out business cards to people who "ignore" her race:

I am black. I am sure that you did not realize this when you made / laughed at / agreed with that racist remark. In the past, I have attempted to alert white people to my racial identity in advance. Unfortunately, this invariably causes them to react to me as pushy, manipulative, or socially inappropriate. Therefore, my policy is to assume that white people do not make these remarks, even when they believe there are no black people present, and to distribute this card when they do. I regret any discomfort my presence is causing you, just as I am sure you regret the discomfort your racism is causing me.

Lesbian playwright Holly Hughes had written several plays—notably *The Well of Horniness, The Lady Dick,* and *Dress Suits for Hire,* which was performed by Peggy Shaw and Lois Weaver at the WOW Cafe—before developing her well-known performance piece *World Without End* in 1989. In *My Queer Body,* Tim Miller narrates the history of his sexual experience and the formation of his identity as a gay man; he undresses during the performance and performs part of *My Queer Body* in the nude, sometimes moving about the audience. Karen Finley's performances often express her outrage at the implicit and explicit violence against women in American culture; in monologues like *Constant State of Desire* and *We Keep Our Victims Ready,* she uses her body to enact and physicalize the "obscenity" of such violence. In a section of *We Keep Our Victims Ready* entitled "St. Valentine's Massacre," Finley examines the way patriarchal culture encodes a subtle hatred of women, one that women can self-destructively internalize. In performance, while Finley monologues, "My life is worth nothing but shit," she smears her naked body with chocolate pudding and studs it with spermlike bean sprouts, a stunning and physical image of the sexualization of violence.

As the performance continues, though, she layers herself with tinsel and red candies, transforming her abjection into a strange beauty. Such performances purposefully transgress the boundaries of decorous social behavior, in part to dramatize the kind of oppression that lurks in "everyday" performance. By all accounts, audiences who have seen Finley's or Miller's performances have found them powerful and moving; but to some critics (who often proudly claim that they have not seen the performance), such performance verges on "obscenity." In 1990, conservative politicians led by Senator Jesse Helms (R–North Carolina) pressured the National Endowment for the Arts to withdraw funding from four performance artists who had been recommended by the peer-review process for support. Not only were Tim Miller, Karen Finley, Holly Hughes, and John Fleck denied funding, but the Endowment's head, John Frohnmayer, subsequently resigned, and a "general standards of decency" restriction of dubious constitutionality was required of subsequent recipients of NEA support.

Perhaps the best-known autobiographical performer, however, is Spalding Gray. Gray began his career with The Performance Group, an avant-garde company working with **ENVIRONMENTAL THEATER** in the late 1960s and 1970s. With Elizabeth LeCompte and other members of the group, Gray collaborated on a series of performances, collectively called *The Rhode Island Trilogy*—*Sakonnet Point* (1975), *Rumstick Road* (1977), and *Nyatt School* (1978), followed by an epilogue, *Point Judith* (1979). The Performance Group was committed to authentic "performance" (in which the actors behave as themselves, rather than "acting" in a theatrical sense), and Gray found a sequence of *Rumstick Road*—in which he narrated events of his life to the audience—to be a particularly fertile ground for continued exploration. In the course of the next several years, Gray developed a se-

PERFORMANCE ART

Anna Deavere Smith portrays Angela King at the world premier of Smith's *Twilight—Los Angeles, 1992.*

ries of autobiographical performances. In some of these works, Gray structures a certain degree of randomness in the performance: in *India and After (America)* (1979), for example, he randomly chooses words from a dictionary to key part of his monologue; in *A Personal History of the American Theatre* (1980), he shuffles a collection of index cards with play titles on them and uses the series to direct his performance. Gray's more recent work has been made into films, and so has become known to a wider audience. The film versions of *Swimming to Cambodia* (1984) and *Monster in a Box* (1990) preserve much of the ambience of Gray's performance. In the opening sequence of *Swimming to Cambodia,* for example, we see Gray walking through the streets of the Village, entering the Performance Garage, seating himself onstage at a long table, and opening the notebook that seems to provide the score for his performance. Gray addresses the camera and, as in his stage performances, seems to occupy a startling and fascinating middle ground between acting and being: he is clearly shaping the story, representing and constructing the narrative of his life as a kind of fiction, while at the same time claiming that quasi-fictive narrative as his own, as himself. Like other postmodern art forms, performance art evocatively explores the edge between representation and "reality," refusing to demarcate a fixed difference between them.

One of the most challenging aspects of research into the history of drama and theater has to do with evaluating the public documentary record that surrounds a production. Angelina Weld Grimké's play *Rachel* was performed by the drama committee of the Washington, D.C. branch of the NAACP and almost immediately led to controversy, particularly the charge that Grimké's play advocated a form of "race suicide." In 1920, *Competitor* published this essay, "*Rachel*—The Play of the Month: The Reason and Synopsis by the Author," in which Grimké outlines her purposes in the play.

With the rise of print, it has become increasingly common for playwrights to be interviewed on the subject of their work, or indeed to write essays—as Arthur Miller did in writing "Tragedy and the Common Man"—explaining, and even justifying, their plays. But such writing cannot be taken as replacing the work of the play itself, either as a literary text or in theatrical production. How can we position Grimké's essay alongside *Rachel?* In what way does Grimké seem to take into account the complexity of her play, and in what ways does the essay present a narrowing of interpretive possibilities? How does Grimké see *Rachel* to resist and redefine the representation of African Americans on the stage? Does the play justify this reading? Does the play specify this reading in interesting or surprising ways? How effectively do you think Grimké defends the play against the charge of "race suicide?" Are there ways in which you think a theatrical production of the play might work to confirm and extend Grimké's understanding of her play? Are there ways a stage production—acting, direction, design—might develop new possibilities in the play? Would Grimké's essay change how *you* might think about the play's action, or how you might think about directing or acting in the play?

ANGELINA WELD GRIMKÉ

from "Rachel—The Play of the Month: The Reason and Synopsis by the Author" (1920)

REPRINTED FROM THE *COMPETITOR* 1 (JAN. 1920):51–52.

First printed in Competitor *in January 1920, Angelina Weld Grimké's description of* Rachel *outlines several of her goals in writing the play, particularly her sense of Rachel's complex refusal of motherhood in the play's finale.*

Since it has been understood that "Rachel" preaches race suicide, I would emphasize that that was not my intention. To the contrary, the appeal is not primarily to the colored people, but to the whites.

Because of environment and certain inherent qualities each of us reacts correspondingly and logically to the various forces about us. For example, if these forces be of love we react with love, and if of hate with hate. Very naturally all of us will not react as strongly or in the same manner—that is impossible.

Now the colored people in this country form what may be called the "submerged tenth." From morning until night, week in week out, year in year out, until death ends all, they never know what it means to draw one clean, deep breath free from the contamination of the poison of that enveloping force which we call race prejudice. Of necessity they react to it. Some are embittered, made resentful, belligerent, even dangerous; some are made hopeless, indifferent, submissive, lacking in initiative; some again go to any extreme in a search for temporary pleasures to drown their memory, thought, etc.

Now the purpose was to show how a refined, sensitive, highly-strung girl, a dreamer and an idealist, the strongest instinct in whose nature is a love for children and a desire some day to be a mother herself—how this girl would react to this force.

The majority of women, everywhere, although they are beginning to awaken, form one of the most conservative elements of society. They are, therefore, opposed to changes. For this reason and for sex reasons the white women of this country are about the worst enemies with which the colored race has to contend. My belief was, then, that if a vulnerable point in their armor could be found, if their hearts could be active or passive enemies, they might become, at least, less inimical and possibly friendly.

Did they have a vulnerable point and, if so, what was it? I believed it to be motherhood. Certainly all the noblest, finest, most sacred things in their lives converge about this. If anything can make all women sisters underneath their skins it is motherhood. If, then, the white women of this country could see, feel, understand just what effect their prejudice and the prejudice of their fathers, brothers, husbands, sons were having on the souls of the colored mothers everywhere, and upon the mothers that are to be, a great power to affect public opinion would be set free and the battle would be half won.

This was the main purpose. There is a subsidiary one as well. Whenever you say "colored person" to a white man he immediately, either through an ignorance that is deliberate or stupid, conjures up in his mind the picture of what he calls "the darkey." In other words, he believes, or says he does, that all colored people are a grinning, white-toothed, shiftless, carefree set, given to chicken-stealing, watermelon-eating, always, under all circumstances, properly obsequious to a white skin and always amusing. Now, it is possible that this type is to be found among the colored people; but if the white man is honest and observant he will have to acknowledge that the same type can be duplicated in his own race. Human nature, after all, is the same. And if the white man only cared to find out he would know that, type for type, he could find the same in both races. Certainly colored people are living in homes that are clean, well-kept with many evidences of taste and refinement about them. They are many of them well educated, cultivated and cultured; they are well-mannered and,

in many instances, more moral than the whites; they love beauty; they have ideals and ambitions, and they do not talk—this educated type—in the Negro dialect. All the joys and sorrows and emotions the white people feel they feel; their feelings are as sensitive; they can be hurt as easily; they are as proud. I drew my characters, then, from the best type of colored people.

Now as to the play itself. In the first act Rachel, loving, young, joyous and vital, caring more to be a mother than anything else in the world, comes suddenly and terribly face to face with what motherhood means to the colored woman in the South. Four years elapse between the first and second acts. Rachel has learned much. She is saddened, disillusioned and embittered. She knows now that organized society in the North has decreed that if a colored man or woman is to be an economic factor, then he or she must, with comparatively few exceptions, remain in the menial class. This has been taught her by her own experience, by the experience of her brother, Tom, and by the experience of John Strong, the man she loves. She has learned that she may not go to a theater for an evening's entertainment without having it spoiled for her since, because of her color she must sit as an outcast, a pariah in a segregated section. And yet in spite of all this youth in her dies hard and hope and the desire for motherhood. She loves children, if anything, more than ever. It is in this act that she feels certain, for the first time, that John Strong loves her. She is made very happy by this knowledge, but in the midst of her joy there comes a knocking at the door. And very terribly and swiftly again it is brought home to her what motherhood means, this time to the colored

woman in the North. The lesson comes to her through a little black girl and her own little adopted son, Jimmy. Not content with maiming and marring the lives of colored men and women she learns this baneful thing, race prejudice, strikes at the souls of little colored children. In her anguish and despair at the knowledge she turns against God, believing that He has been mocking at her by implanting in her breast this desire for motherhood, and she swears by the most solemn oath of which she can think never to bring a child here to have its life blighted and ruined.

A week elapses between Acts II and III. During the time Rachel has been very ill, not in body, but in mind and soul. She is up and about again, but is in a highly overwrought, nervous state. John Strong, whom she has not seen since she has been sick, comes to see her. She knows what his coming means and tries unsuccessfully to ward off his proposal. He pleads so well that, although she feels she is doing a wicked thing she finally yields. Just at the moment of her surrender, however, the sound of little Jimmy's heartbreaking weeping comes to her ears. She changes immediately and leaves him to go to Jimmy. Every night since Jimmy has undergone that searing experience in the previous act he has dreamed of it and awakens weeping. With that sound in her ears and soul she finds that she cannot break her oath. She returns and tells John Strong she cannot marry him. He is inclined, at first, not to take her seriously; but she shows him that this time her answer is final. Although her heart is breaking she sends him away. The play ends in blackness and with the inconsolable sounds of little Jimmy weeping.

The conflict in Sam Shepard's *True West* escalates when Austin (Gary Sinise) confronts Lee (John Malkovitch) after a night of stealing toasters.

The Angel appears above Prior Walter in Tony Kushner's *Angels in America, Part I: Millennium Approaches.*

This scene from August Wilson's *Fences* shows how Wilson's attention to the play's social environment has been translated into a detailed mise-en-scène; here, James Earl Jones plays the role of Troy Maxon.

Dion Boucicault

Dion Boucicault (1822–1890) was one of the most prominent and successful playwrights of the nineteenth-century English-speaking world. Born Dionysus Lardner Boursiquot in Dublin, Boucicault was first educated there, and later in England, after his family moved to London in 1828 or 1829. The family was accompanied by Dr. Dionysus Lardner, who remained with and supported Boucicault's mother Anne and her children after Boucicault's father Samuel returned to Dublin; he was probably her lover as well. Although Boucicault was apprenticed as an engineer to Lardner, he fled to the theater where he pursued a long and successful career as playwright, actor, and manager. Boucicault, like most of his contemporaries, was an inventive adapter, and many of his 230 plays are based on the novels and French plays he was paid to bring to the English stage. But he was also a shrewd and original playwright. His first real success as a writer, *London Assurance,* was one of the most popular plays of the century, and was innovative in several respects: staged by Madame Vestris in 1841, it used a **BOX SET,** with practical doors and real furniture onstage, creating a new level of naturalism in the theater. He adapted the durable *Corsican Brothers* for the stage in 1852, providing a great success for the actor/manager Charles Kean, and later for Henry Irving. In 1852 he also met the actress Agnes Robertson—who became his lover and had several children with Boucicault—and left England with her for his first American tour.

Although Boucicault was not an American, many of his most important plays were written and produced in the United States, and take American social issues as their subject. Living in the United States in the 1850s, Boucicault wrote *The Poor of New York* (1857); the play was hugely popular, and Boucicault later adapted it to play in whatever city he was visiting (later versions included *The Poor of Liverpool, The Poor of London,* and so on). He also wrote (and acted in, alongside Agnes) *The Octoroon* in 1859, as well as one of the first of his important Irish melodramas, *The Colleen Bawn,* in 1860. Returning to England, Boucicault capitalized on the vogue of sensation melodrama with *Arrah-na-Pogue* in 1864 and writing, starring in, and touring the United States in *The Shaughraun* in 1874.

Boucicault was involved in all aspects of theater as playwright, actor, and manager (in the era before the rise of the stage director, the actor/manager was typically in charge of assembling the company and of directing the play). Moreover, he was centrally involved in changing the financing of play-production, insisting that the playwright should be granted a percentage of a play's profit onstage, rather than being paid a straight fee or receiving the "benefit" of receipts of a single night's performance; and while he had often been involved in pirating work for the stage, he also pressed for copyright protection for playwrights, whose writing was not protected by copyright legislation. An efficient master of popular theater, Boucicault nonetheless adapted those forms—especially **MELODRAMA**—to original purposes. Although Boucicault's drama slipped into obscurity in the later nineteenth century, several of his plays—especially his American and Irish melodramas—are seen to deploy the conventions of popular theater toward a critique of social injustice.

THE OCTOROON

Adapted from Mayne Reid's novel, *The Quadroon,* and performed on the eve of the American Civil War, *The Octoroon* addresses the "American problem"—slavery—in the sentimental accents of nineteenth-century melodrama. Following the lead of Harriet Beecher Stowe's massively popular novel, *Uncle Tom's Cabin*—a novel that was widely adapted to the stage, and helped to turn popular feeling against slavery—Boucicault develops the standard devices of melodrama: a strong and sensational plot; a central conflict between a malevolent villain and his virtuous and vulnerable victims; and a highly-colored emotional palette. Boucicault's mastery of the form can be seen most easily in the structure of the play: each scene ends with a striking **TABLEAU,** a highly charged scene that focuses on a change in the plot and that usually involves some elaborate stage effects—McClosky discovering the error in Zoe's manumission papers and vowing to own the Octoroon himself; McClosky murdering Paul and seizing the fateful letter that would save Terrebone Plantation (and Zoe) from sale to creditors; McClosky fleeing in his canoe, pursued by the relentless Indian Wahnotee.

Much of Boucicault's skill as a dramatist lies in his ingenious adaptation of the character stereotypes of melodrama, which are given a clearly "American" spin in *The Octoroon*. The heroine of the play—Zoe, played by Agnes Robertson—is an octoroon, one eighth African American, and so is by law susceptible to enslavement and prohibited from marrying a white man (in this case, the play's virtuous hero, George Peyton). Although raised in the Peyton family as a white woman, she is Judge Peyton's "natural"—i.e., illegitimate—daughter by one of his "quadroon" slaves, and so is treated much less formally than the other women; several of the characters—McClosky in particular—order her about much as they would order a household servant, despite her evident refinement. George Peyton arrives at the outset of the play to assume his inheritance: the Terrebone Plantation, which has suffered from years of mismanagement, and is now facing sale to its creditors. Educated in Paris, George has developed both the effete manners and the cultivated sensibilities of a European: while George is the only character onstage to notice—and object to—the way Zoe is treated by others, he has to learn "American" directness in the course of the play. If Zoe and George adapt the conventional heroine and hero of melodrama to the American grain, Boucicault adapts a quintessentially American character-type—the Yankee—to the conventions of melodrama. There are two Yankee types in the play: the current overseer Scudder, a kindly inventor whose good intentions are partly responsible for the collapse of the plantation, and McClosky, the murderous villain of the piece (who, as the previous overseer, took advantage of Judge Peyton and gradually acquired part of the plantation himself). Boucicault's use of "American" stereotypes extends, of course, to characters prominent on the nineteenth-century stage: slaves and Indians. Here, it is a measure of Boucicault's larger aims that the slaves (played in blackface by white actors) are consistently represented as virtuous, loving, and beloved members of the Peyton extended family (this doesn't prevent Boucicault from portraying them as simple, fun-loving, and often lazy), and the Indian Wahnotee—played by Boucicault himself—as the implacable agent of justice (if, again playing to a familiar stereotype, addicted to rum).

Written by an Irishman whose Irish plays reveal a canny critique of British oppression, *The Octoroon* frames the central issue of American history—slavery—in the forms of popular theater. Not surprisingly, then, the ethical and sentimental axes of the play often seem conflicted. Like many melodramas, *The Octoroon* is a "rent-day" play: the tragedy is framed as the virtuous family's loss of their property, the Terrebone Plantation and its slaves. Yet while Boucicault amply visualizes the tragedies associated with slavery onstage—splitting up slave families in the auction scene in act 3, the legal barriers to Zoe's marriage to George, McClosky's purchase of Zoe to be his mistress—the play is not finally able to mount a political critique of the tragedy of slavery itself. Zoe's reluctance to be sold to McClosky is figured in the play in both sentimental terms (she is in love with another man) and in class terms (she is much more refined than the low-class McClosky); she barely mentions the institution of slavery itself, and Boucicault goes out of his way to show her loving sense of gratitude to the deceased Judge Peyton for taking her into his home (the fact that her mother, a "quadroon" slave owned by the Peytons, was probably raped by the Judge, is bypassed in the play). Indeed, the theme of "justice" that runs through the play—How should Zoe be treated by white society? Who owns the plantation? Should McClosky be given the rough justice of a lynching when the murder is discovered? Should George be allowed to marry Zoe?—never quite touches on the fundamental injustice of slavery itself.

Given the political and social context of 1859—the play opened during John Brown's raid on Harper's Ferry, one of the ignition points of the Civil War—it is perhaps not surprising that Zoe kills herself at the end of the play. Although we understand that the Plantation may be saved by the discovery of McClosky's deception (he found and concealed the letter from Liverpool that would have bailed the plantation out of debt, murdering little Paul to get it), no playwright, and no theater, could risk staging miscegenation positively onstage, as the marriage—or even the plausible romance—of George and Zoe would have required. Miscegenation figures in the play, of course, in the mixed-race "problem" posed by Zoe herself, a problem the play is finally unwilling to confront by proposing a "legitimate" marriage between the play's sentimental hero and heroine.

When he brought the play to England, however, Boucicault rewrote the ending of the play. Instead of showing Zoe stealing to the plantation's slave quarters and taking poison, the new version ends the play with the capture of McClosky, revealed in his crime—spectacularly enough—by the photographic plate showing his murderous triumph over the body of Paul. In this version, as the steamship explodes in fire in the background and Wahnotee struggles with and finally kills McClosky, George carries the prostrate body of Zoe—dead? or simply fainted?—ambiguously onstage.

THE OCTOROON

Dion Boucicault

CHARACTERS

GEORGE PEYTON

SALEM SCUDDER

MR SUNNYSIDE

JACOB M'CLOSKY

WAHNOTEE

LAFOUCHE

CAPTAIN RATTS

COLONEL POINTDEXTER

JULES THIBODEAUX

JUDGE CAILLOU

JACKSON

OLD PETE

PAUL, *a boy slave*

SOLON

MRS PEYTON

ZOE

DORA SUNNYSIDE

GRACE

MINNIE

DIDO

ACT ONE

The scene opens on a view of the Plantation Terrebonne, in Louisiana. A branch of the Mississippi is seen winding through the estate. A low-built but extensive planter's dwelling, surrounded with a veranda, and raised a few feet from the ground, occupies the left side. On the right stand a table and chairs. GRACE *is discovered sitting at breakfast-table with the Negro children.*

SOLON: (*Enters, from the house.*) Yah! you bomn'ble fry—git out—a gen'leman can't pass for you.

GRACE: (*Seizing a fly whisk.*) Hee!—ha git out! (*She drives the children away. In escaping, they tumble against* SOLON, *who falls* 5 *with the tray; the children steal the bananas and rolls that fall about.*)

PETE: (*Who is lame, enters; he carries a mop and pail.*) Hey! laws a massey! why, clar out! drop dat banana! I'll murder this yer crowd. (*He chases children about; they leap over railing at* 10 *back.*)

(*Exit* SOLON.)

Dem little niggers is a judgment upon dis generation.

GEORGE: (*Enters, from the house.*) What's the matter, Pete?

PETE: It's dem black trash, Mas'r George; dis ere property wants claring; dem's getting too numerous round: when I 15 gets time I'll kill some on 'em, sure!

GEORGE: They don't seem to be scared by the threat.

PETE: Stop, you varmin! stop till I get enough of you in one place!

GEORGE: Were they all born on this estate?

20 PETE: Guess they nebber was born—dem tings! what, dem?— get away! Born here—dem darkies? What, on Terrebonne! Don't b'lieve it, Mas'r George; dem black tings never was born at all; dey swarmed one mornin' on a sassafras tree in the swamp; I cotched 'em; dey ain't no 'count. Don't be- 25 lieve dey'll turn out niggers when dey're growed; dey'll come out sunthin' else.

GRACE: Yes, Mas'r George, dey was born here; and old Pete is fonder on 'em dan he is of his fiddle on a Sunday.

PETE: What? dem tings—dem? get away. (*Makes blow at the* 30 *children.*) Born here! dem darkies! What, on Terrebonne! Don't b'lieve it, Mas'r George—no. One morning dey swarmed on a sassafras tree in de swamp, and I cotched

'em all in a sieve—dat's how dey come on top of dis yearth—git out, you—ya, ya! (*Laughs.*)

(*Exit* GRACE.)

MRS PEYTON: (*Enters from the house.*) So, Pete, you are spoil- 35 ing those children as usual!

PETE: Dat's right, missus! gib it to ole Pete! he's allers in for it! Git away dere! Ya! if dey ain't all lighted, like coons, on dat snake fence, just out of shot. Look dar! Ya, ya! Dem de- bils. Ya! 40

MRS PEYTON: Pete, do you hear?

PETE: Git down dar! I'm arter you! (*Hobbles off.*)

MRS PEYTON: You are out early this morning, George.

GEORGE: I was up before daylight. We got the horses saddled, and galloped down the shell road over the Piney Patch; 45 then coasting the Bayou Lake, we crossed the long swamps, by Paul's Path, and so came home again.

MRS PEYTON: (*Laughing.*) You seem already familiar with the names of every spot on the estate.

(*Enter* PETE, *who arranges breakfast.*)

GEORGE: Just one month ago I quitted Paris. I left that siren 50 city as I would have left a beloved woman.

MISS PEYTON: No wonder! I dare say you left at least a dozen beloved women there, at the same time.

GEORGE: I feel that I departed amid universal and sincere re- gret. I left my loves and my creditors equally inconsolable. 55

MRS PEYTON: George, you are incorrigible. Ah! you remind me so much of your uncle, the judge.

GEORGE: Bless his dear old handwriting, it's all I ever saw of him. For ten years his letters came every quarter-day, with a remittance and a word of advice in his formal cavalier style; 60 and then a joke in the postscript, that upset the dignity of the foregoing. Aunt, when he died, two years ago, I read over those letters of his, and if I didn't cry like a baby—

MRS PEYTON: No, George; say you wept like a man. And so you really kept those foolish letters? 65

GEORGE: Yes; I kept the letters, and squandered the money.

MRS PEYTON: (*Embracing him.*) Ah! why were you not my son—you are so like my dear husband.

SCUDDER: (*Enters.*) Ain't he! Yes—when I saw him and Miss Zoe galloping through the green sugar crop, and doing 70 ten dollars' worth of damage at every stride, says I, how like his old uncle he do make the dirt fly.

GEORGE: O, aunt! what a bright, gay creature she is!

SCUDDER: What, Zoe! Guess that you didn't leave anything
75 female in Europe that can lift an eyelash beside that gal. When she goes along, she just leaves a streak of love behind her. It's a good drink to see her come into the cotton fields—the niggers get fresh on the sight of her. If she ain't worth her weight in sunshine you may take one of
80 my fingers off, and choose which you like.

MRS PEYTON: She need not keep us waiting breakfast, though. Pete, tell Miss Zoe that we are waiting.

PETE: Yes, missus. Why, Minnie, why don't you run when you hear, you lazy crittur?

(MINNIE *runs off.*)

85 Dat's de laziest nigger on dis yere property. (*Sitting down.*) Don't do nuffin.

MRS PEYTON: My dear George, you are left in your uncle's will heir to this estate.

GEORGE: Subject to your life interest and an annuity to Zoe,
90 is it not so?

MRS PEYTON: I fear that the property is so involved that the strictest economy will scarcely recover it. My dear husband never kept any accounts, and we scarcely know in what condition the estate really is.

95 SCUDDER: Yes, we do, ma'am; it's in a darned bad condition. Ten years ago the judge took as overseer a bit of Connecticut hardware called M'Closky. The judge didn't understand accounts—the overseer did. For a year or two all went fine. The judge drew money like Bourbon whisky from a bar-
100 rel, and never turned off the tap. But out it flew, free for everybody or anybody to beg, borrow, or steal. So it went, till one day the judge found the tap wouldn't run. He looked in to see what stopped it, and pulled out a big mortgage. 'Sign that,' says the overseer; 'it's only a formality.' 'All
105 right,' says the judge, and away went a thousand acres; so at the end of eight years, Jacob M'Closky, Esquire, finds himself proprietor of the richest half of Terrebonne—

GEORGE: But the other half is free.

SCUDDER: No, it ain't; because, just then, what does the judge
110 do, but hire another overseer—a Yankee—a Yankee named Salem Scudder.

MRS PEYTON: O, no, it was—

SCUDDER: Hold on, now! I'm going to straighten this account clear out. What was this here Scudder? Well, he
115 lived in New York by sittin' with his heels up in front of French's Hotel, and inventin'—

GEORGE: Inventing what?

SCUDDER: Improvements—anything, from a stay-lace to a fire-engine. Well, he cut that for the photographing line.
120 He and his apparatus arrived here, took the judge's likeness and his fancy, who made him overseer right off. Well, sir, what does this Scudder do but introduces his inventions and improvements on this estate. His new cotton gins broke down, the steam sugarmills burst up, until he
125 finished off with his folly what Mr M'Closky with his knavery began.

MRS PEYTON: O, Salem! how can you say so? Haven't you worked like a horse?

SCUDDER: No, ma'am, I worked like an ass—an honest one,
130 and that's all. Now, Mr George, between the two overseers, you and that good lady have come to the ground; that is the state of things, just as near as I can fix it.

(ZOE *sings without.*)

GEORGE: 'Tis Zoe.

SCUDDER: O, I have not spoiled that anyhow. I can't introduce any darned improvement there. Ain't that a cure for
135 old age; it kinder lifts the heart up, don't it?

MRS PEYTON: Poor child! what will become of her when I am gone? If you haven't spoiled her, I fear I have. She has had the education of a lady.

GEORGE: I have remarked that she is treated by the neighbours
140 with a kind of familiar condescension that annoyed me.

SCUDDER: Don't you know that she is the natural daughter of the judge, your uncle, and that old lady thar just adored anything her husband cared for; and this girl, that another woman would 'a' hated, she loves as if she'd been her own
145 child.

GEORGE: Aunt, I am prouder and happier to be your nephew and heir to the ruins of Terrebonne, than I would have been to have had half Louisiana without you.

ZOE: (*Enters from the house.*) Am I late? Ah! Mr Scudder, good
150 morning.

SCUDDER: Thank'ye. I'm from fair to middlin', like a bamboo cane, much the same all the year round.

ZOE: No; like a sugar cane; so dry outside, one would never think there was so much sweetness within.
155
SCUDDER: Look here: I can't stand that gal! if I stop here, I shall hug her right off. (*He sees* PETE, *who has set his pail down up stage, and gone to sleep on it.*) If that old nigger ain't asleep, I'm blamed. Hillo! (*He kicks pail from under* PETE, *and lets him down. Exit.*)
160
PETE: Hi! Debbel's in de pail! Whar's breakfass?

(*Enter* SOLON *and* DIDO *with coffeepot and dishes.*)

DIDO: Bless'ee, Missey Zoe, here it be. Dere's a dish of penpans—jess taste, Mas'r George—and here's fried bananas; smell 'em do, sa glosh.

PETE: Hole yer tongue, Dido. Whar's de coffee? (*He pours it*
165 *out.*) If it don't stain de cup, your wicked ole life's in danger, sure! dat right! black as nigger; clar as ice. You may drink dat, Mas'r George. (*Looks off.*) Yah! here's Mas'r Sunnyside, and Missey Dora, jist drove up. Some of you niggers run and hole de hosses; and take dis, Dido. (*He gives her cof-*
170 *feepot to hold, and hobbles off, followed by* SOLON *and* DIDO.)

(*Enter* SUNNYSIDE *and* DORA.)

SUNNYSIDE: Good day, ma'am. (*He shakes hands with George.*) I see we are just in time for breakfast. (*He sits.*)

DORA: O, none for me; I never eat. (*She sits.*)

GEORGE: (*Aside.*) They do not notice Zoe. (*Aloud.*) You don't
175 see Zoe, Mr Sunnyside.

SUNNYSIDE: Ah! Zoe, girl; are you there?

DORA: Take my shawl, Zoe. (ZOE *helps her.*) What a good creature she is.

SUNNYSIDE: I dare say, now, that in Europe you have never
180 met any lady more beautiful in person, or more polished in manners, than that girl.

GEORGE: You are right, sir; though I shrank from expressing that opinion in her presence, so bluntly.

185 SUNNYSIDE: Why so?

GEORGE: It may be considered offensive.

SUNNYSIDE: (*Astonished.*) What? I say, Zoe, do you hear that?

DORA: Mr Peyton is joking.

MRS PEYTON: My nephew is not acquainted with our cus-
190 toms in Louisiana, but he will soon understand.

GEORGE: Never, Aunt! I shall never understand how to wound the feelings of any lady; and, if that is the custom here, I shall never acquire it.

DORA: Zoe, my dear, what does he mean?

195 ZOE: I don't know.

GEORGE: Excuse me, I'll light a cigar. (*He goes up.*)

DORA: (*Aside to* ZOE.) Isn't he sweet! O, dear, Zoe, is he in love with anybody?

ZOE: How can I tell?

200 DORA: Ask him, I want to know; don't say I told you to in-
quire, but find out. Minnie, fan me, it is so nice—and his clothes are French, ain't they?

ZOE: I think so; shall I ask him that too?

DORA: No, dear. I wish he would make love to me. When he
205 speaks to one he does it so easy, so gentle; it isn't bar-room style; love lined with drinks, sighs tinged with tobacco— and they say all the women in Paris were in love with him, which I feel *I* shall be. Stop fanning me; what nice boots he wears.

210 SUNNYSIDE: (*To* MRS PEYTON.) Yes, ma'am, I hold a mortgage over Terrebonne; mine's a ninth, and pretty near covers all the property, except the slaves. I believe Mr M'Closky has a bill of sale on them. O, here he is.

(*Enter* M'CLOSKY.)

SUNNYSIDE: Good morning. Mr M'Closky.

215 M'CLOSKY: Good morning, Mr Sunnyside; Miss Dora, your servant.

DORA: (*Seated.*) Fan me, Minnie.— (*Aside.*) I don't like that man.

M'CLOSKY: (*Aside.*) Insolent as usual.—(*Aloud.*) You begged
220 me to call this morning. I hope I'm not intruding.

MRS PEYTON: My nephew, Mr Peyton.

M'CLOSKY: O, how d'ye do, sir? (*He offers his hand,* GEORGE *bows coldly. Aside.*) A puppy—if he brings any of his European airs here we'll fix him.—(*Aloud.*) Zoe, tell Pete to
225 give my mare a feed, will ye?

GEORGE: (*Angrily.*) Sir!

M'CLOSKY: Hillo! did I tread on ye?

MRS PEYTON: What is the matter with George?

ZOE: (*Takes fan from* MINNIE.) Go, Minnie, tell Pete; run! (*Exit*
230 MINNIE.)

MRS PEYTON: Grace, attend to Mr M'Closky.

M'CLOSKY: A julep, gal, that's my breakfast, and a bit of cheese.

GEORGE: (*Aside to* MRS PEYTON.) How can you ask that vul-
235 gar ruffian to your table!

MRS PEYTON: Hospitality in Europe is a courtesy: here, it is an obligation. We tender food to a stranger, not because he is a gentleman, but because he is hungry.

GEORGE: Aunt, I will take my rifle down to the Atchafalaya.
240 Paul has promised me a bear and a deer or two. I see my

little Nimrod yonder, with his Indian companion. Excuse me, ladies. Ho! Paul! (*He enters house.*)

PAUL: (*Outside.*) I'ss, Mas'r George.

(*Enter* PAUL *with the Indian.*)

SUNNYSIDE: It's a shame to allow that young cub to run over the swamps and woods, hunting and fishing his life away 245 instead of hoeing cane.

MRS PEYTON: The child was a favourite of the judge, who encouraged his gambols. I couldn't bear to see him put to work.

GEORGE: (*Returning with rifle.*) Come, Paul, are you ready? 250

PAUL: I'ss Mas'r George. O, golly! ain't that a pooty gun.

M'CLOSKY: See here, you imp; if I catch you, and your redskin yonder, gunning in my swamps, I'll give you rats, mind. Them vagabonds, when the game's about, shoot my pigs.

(GEORGE *goes into house.*)

PAUL: You gib me rattan, Mas'r Clostry, but I guess you take a 255 berry long stick to Wahnotee. Ugh, he make bacon of you.

M'CLOSKY: Make bacon of me, you young whelp! Do you mean that I'm a pig? Hold on a bit. (*He seizes whip and holds* PAUL.)

ZOE: O, sir! don't, pray, don't. 260

M'CLOSKY: (*Slowly lowering his whip.*) Darn you, redskin, I'll pay you off some day, both of ye. (*He returns to table and drinks.*)

SUNNYSIDE: That Indian is a nuisance. Why don't he return to his nation out West? 265

M'CLOSKY: He's too fond of thieving and whiskey.

ZOE: No; Wahnotee is a gentle, honest creature, and remains here because he loves that boy with the tenderness of a woman. When Paul was taken down with the swamp fever the Indian sat outside the hut, and neither ate, slept, 270 nor spoke for five days, till the child could recognise and call him to his bedside. He who can love so well is honest—don't speak ill of poor Wahnotee.

MRS PEYTON: Wahnotee, will you go back to your people?

WAHNOTEE: Sleugh. 275

PAUL: He don't understand; he speaks a mash-up of Indian and Mexican. Wahnotee Patira na sepau assa wigiran?

WAHNOTEE: Weal Omenee.

PAUL: Says he'll go if I'll go with him. He calls me Omenee, the Pigeon, and Miss Zoe is Ninemoosha, the Sweetheart. 280

WAHNOTEE: (*Pointing to* ZOE.) Ninemoosha.

ZOE: No, Wahnotee, we can't spare Paul.

PAUL: If Omenee remain, Wahnotee will die in Terrebonne.

(*During the dialogue,* WAHNOTEE *has taken* GEORGE's *gun.*)

GEORGE: (*Enters.*) Now I'm ready. (GEORGE *tries to regain his gun;* WAHNOTEE *refuses to give it up;* PAUL *quietly takes it from* 285 *him and remonstrates with him.*)

DORA: Zoe, he's going; I want him to stay and make love to me, that's what I came for today.

MRS PEYTON: George, I can't spare Paul for an hour or two; he must run over to the landing; the steamer from New 290 Orleans passed up the river last night, and if there's a mail they have thrown it ashore.

SUNNYSIDE: I saw the mailbags lying in the shed this morning.

MRS PEYTON: I expect an important letter from Liverpool; away with you, Paul; bring the mailbags here.

295 PAUL: I'm 'most afraid to take Wahnotee to the shed, there's rum there.

WAHNOTEE: Rum!

PAUL: Come, then, but if I catch you drinkin', O, laws a mussey, you'll get snakes! I'll gib it you! now mind. (*Exits*
300 *with Indian.*)

GEORGE: Come, Miss Dora, let me offer you my arm.

DORA: Mr George, I am afraid, if all we hear is true, you have led a dreadful life in Europe.

GEORGE: That's a challenge to begin a description of my fem-
305 inine adventures.

DORA: You have been in love, then?

GEORGE: Two hundred and forty-nine times! Let me relate you the worst cases.

DORA: No! no!

310 GEORGE: I'll put the naughty parts in French.

DORA: I won't hear a word! O, you horrible man! go on.
(GEORGE *and* DORA *go into the house.*)

M'CLOSKY: Now, ma'am, I'd like a little business, if agreeable. I bring you news; your banker, old Lafouche, of New Or-
315 leans, is dead; the executors are winding up his affairs, and have foreclosed on all overdue mortgages, so Terrebonne is for sale. Here's the *Picayune* (*Producing paper.*) with the advertisement.

ZOE: Terrebonne for sale!

320 MRS PEYTON: Terrebonne for sale, and you, sir, will doubtless become its purchaser.

M'CLOSKY: Well, ma'am, I s'pose there's no law agin my bidding for it. The more bidders, the better for you. You'll take care, I guess, it don't go too cheap.

325 MRS PEYTON: O, sir, I don't value the place for its price, but for the many happy days I've spent here; that landscape, flat and uninteresting though it may be, is full of charm for me, those poor people, born around me, growing up about my heart, have bounded my view of life; and now
330 to lose that homely scene, lose their black, ungainly faces! O, sir, perhaps you should be as old as I am, to feel as I do, when my past life is torn away from me.

M'CLOSKY: I'd be darned glad if somebody would tear my past life away from *me*. Sorry I can't help you, but the fact
335 is, you're in such an all-fired mess that you couldn't be pulled out without a derrick.

MRS PEYTON: Yes, there is a hope left yet, and I cling to it. The house of Mason Brothers, of Liverpool, failed some twenty years ago in my husband's debt.

340 M'CLOSKY: They owed him over fifty thousand dollars.

MRS PEYTON: I cannot find the entry in my husband's accounts; but you, Mr M'Closky, can doubtless detect it. Zoe, bring here the judge's old desk; it is in the library.

(*Exit* ZOE *to the house.*)

M'CLOSKY: You don't expect to recover any of this old debt,
345 do you?

MRS PEYTON: Yes; the firm has recovered itself, and I received a notice two months ago that some settlement might be anticipated.

SUNNYSIDE: Why, with principal and interest this debt has
350 been more than doubled in twenty years.

MRS PEYTON: But it may be years yet before it will be paid off, if ever.

SUNNYSIDE: If there's a chance of it, there's not a planter round here who wouldn't lend you the whole cash, to keep your name and blood amongst us. Come, cheer up, 355 old friend.

MRS PEYTON: Ah! Sunnyside, how good you are; so like my poor Peyton. (*Exit* MRS PEYTON *and* SUNNYSIDE *to the house.*)

M'CLOSKY: Curse their old families—they cut me—a bilious, 360 conceited, thin lot of dried-up aristocracy. I hate 'em. Just because my grandfather wasn't some broken-down Virginia transplant, or a stingy old Creole, I ain't fit to sit down to the same meat with them. It makes my blood so hot I feel my heart hiss. I'll sweep these Peytons from this section 365 of the country. Their presence keeps alive the reproach against me that I ruined them. Yet, if this money should come! Bah! There's no chance of it. Then, if they go, they'll take Zoe—she'll follow them. Darn that girl; she makes me quiver when I think of her; she's took me for all I'm worth. 370

(*Enter* ZOE *from house, with the desk.*)

M'CLOSKY: O, here, do you know what the annuity the old judge left you is worth today? Not a picayune.

ZOE: It is surely worth the love that dictated it: here are the papers and accounts. (*Putting the desk on the table.*)

M'CLOSKY: Stop, Zoe; come here! How would you like to 375 rule the house of the richest planter on Atchafalaya—eh? or say the word, and I'll buy this old barrack, and you shall be mistress of Terrebonne.

ZOE: O, sir, do not speak so to me!

M'CLOSKY: Why not! look here, these Peytons are bust; cut 380 'em; I am rich, jine me; I'll set you up grand, and we'll give these first families here our dust, until you'll see their white skins shrivel up with hate and rage; what d'ey say?

ZOE: Let me pass! O, pray, let me go!

M'CLOSKY: What, you won't, won't ye? If young George Pey- 385 ton was to make you the same offer, you'd jump at it pretty darned quick, I guess. Come, Zoe, don't be a fool; I'd marry you if I could, but you know I can't; so just say what you want. Here, then, I'll put back these Peytons in Terrebonne, and they shall know you done it; yes, they'll 390 have you to thank for saving them from ruin.

ZOE: Do you think they would live here on such terms?

M'CLOSKY: Why not? We'll hire out our slaves, and live on their wages.

ZOE: But I'm not a slave. 395

M'CLOSKY: No; if you were I'd buy you, if you cost all I'm worth.

ZOE: Let me pass!

M'CLOSKY: Stop.

SCUDDER: (*Enters.*) Let her pass. 400

M'CLOSKY: Eh?

SCUDDER: Let her pass! (*He takes out his knife. Exit* ZOE *to house.*)

M'CLOSKY: Is that you, Mr Overseer? (*He examines paper.*)

SCUDDER: Yes, I'm here, somewhere, interferin'. 405

M'CLOSKY: (*Sitting.*) A pretty mess you've got this estate in—

SCUDDER: Yes—me and Co.— we done it; but, as you were senior partner in the concern, I reckon you got the big lick.

M'CLOSKY: What d'ye mean?

410 SCUDDER: Let me proceed by illustration. (*Sits.*) Look thar! (*Points with his knife off.*) D'ye see that tree?—it's called a live oak, and is a native here; beside it grows a creeper; year after year that creeper twines its long arms round and round the tree—sucking the earth dry all about its roots—
415 living on its life—overrunning its branches, until at last the live oak withers and dies out. Do you know what the niggers round here call that sight? they call it the Yankee hugging the Creole.

M'CLOSKY: Mr. Scudder, I've listened to a great many of your
420 insinuations, and now I'd like to come to an understanding what they mean. If you want a quarrel!—

SCUDDER: No, I'm the skurriest crittur at a fight you ever see; my legs have been too well brought up to stand and see my body abused; I take good care of myself, I can tell you.

425 M'CLOSKY: Because I heard that you had traduced my character.

SCUDDER: Traduced! Whoever said so lied. I always said you were the darndest thief that ever escaped a white jail to misrepresent the North to the South.

430 M'CLOSKY: (*Raises hand to back of his neck.*) What!

SCUDDER: Take your hand down—take it down.(M'CLOSKY *lowers his hand.*) Whenever I gets into company like yours, I always start with the advantage on my side.

M'CLOSKY: What d'ye mean?

435 SCUDDER: I mean that before you could draw that bowie knife, you wear down your back, I'd cut you into shingles. Keep quiet, and let's talk sense. You wanted to come to an understanding, and I'm coming thar as quick as I can. Now, Jacob M'Closky, you despise me because you think
440 I'm a fool; I despise you because I know you to be a knave. Between us we've ruined these Peytons; you fired the judge, and I finished off the widow. Now, I feel bad about my share in the business. I'd give half the balance of my life to wipe out my part of the work. Many a night
445 I've laid awake and thought how to pull them through, till I've cried like a child over the sum I couldn't do; and you know how darned hard 'tis to make a Yankee cry.

M'CLOSKY: Well, what's that to me?

SCUDDER: Hold on, Jacob, I'm coming to that—I tell ye, I'm
450 such a fool—I can't bear the feeling, it keeps at me like a skin complaint, and if this family is sold up—

M'CLOSKY: What then?

SCUDDER: (*Rising.*) I'd cut my throat—or yours—yours I'd prefer.

455 M'CLOSKY: Would you now? why don't you do it?

SCUDDER: 'Cos I's skeered to try! I never killed a man in my life—and civilisation is so strong in me I guess I couldn't do it—I'd like to, though!

M'CLOSKY: And all for the sake of that old woman and that
460 young puppy—eh? No other cause to hate—to envy me—to be jealous of me—eh?

SCUDDER: Jealous? what for?

M'CLOSKY: Ask the colour in your face: d'ye think I can't read you, like a book? With your New England hypocrisy, you
465 would persuade yourself that it was this family alone you cared for; it ain't—you know it ain't—'t is the 'Octoroon'; and you love her as I do; and you hate me because I'm your rival—that's where the tears come from, Salem Scudder, if you ever shed any—that's where the shoe pinches.

470 SCUDDER: Wal, I do like the gal; she's a—

M'CLOSKY: She's in love with young Peyton; it make me curse whar it made you cry, as it does now; I see the tears on your cheeks now.

SCUDDER: Look at 'em Jacob, for they are honest water from
475 the well of truth. I ain't ashamed of it—I do love the gal; but I ain't jealous of you, because I believe the only sincere feeling about you is your love for Zoe, and it does your heart good to have her image thar; but I believe you put it thar to spile. By fair means I don't think you can get
480 her, and don't you try foul with her, 'cause if you do, Jacob, civilisation be darned, I'm on you like a painter, and when I'm drawed out I'm pizin.

(*Exit* SCUDDER *to house.*)

M'CLOSKY: Fair or foul, I'll have her—take that home with you! (*He opens desk.*) What's here—judgment? yes, plenty
485 of 'em; bill of costs; account with Citizens' Bank—what's this? "Judgment, $40,000, 'Thibodeaux against Peyton,'"—surely, that is the judgment under which this estate is now advertised for sale—(*He takes up paper and examines it.*) yes, 'Thibodeaux against Peyton, 1838.' Hold
490 on! whew! this is worth taking to—in this desk the judge used to keep one paper I want—this should be it. (*Reads.*) 'The free papers of my daughter Zoe, registered February 4th, 1841.' Why, Judge, wasn't you lawyer enough to know that while a judgment stood against you it was a lien on
495 your slaves? Zoe is your child by a quadroon slave, and you didn't free her; blood! if this is so, she's mine! this old Liverpool debt—that may cross me—if it only arrive too late—if it don't come by this mail—Hold on! this letter the old lady expects—that's it; let me only head off that
500 letter, and Terrebonne will be sold before they can recover it. That boy and the Indian have gone down to the landing for the post-bags; they'll idle on the way as usual? my mare will take me across the swamp, and before they can reach the shed, I'll have purified them bags—ne'er a let-
505 ter shall show this mail. Ha, ha!—(*Calls.*) Pete, you old turkey-buzzard, saddle my mare. Then, if I sink every dollar I'm worth in her purchase, I'll own that Octoroon.

ACT TWO

The wharf with goods, boxes, and bales scattered about—a camera on a stand; DORA *being photographed by* SCUDDER, *who is arranging photographic apparatus,* GEORGE *and* PAUL *looking on at back.*

SCUDDER: Just turn your face a leetle this way—fix your— let's see—look here.

DORA: So?

SCUDDER: That's right. (*Putting his head under the darkening apron.*) It's such a long time since I did this sort of thing, and this old machine has got so dirty and stiff, I'm afraid
5 it won't operate. That's about right. Now don't stir.

PAUL: Ugh! she looks as though she war gwine to have a tooth drawed!

SCUDDER: I've got four plates ready, in case we miss the first shot. One of them is prepared with a self-developing liq-
10 uid that I've invented. I hope it will turn out better than most of my notions. Now fix yourself. Are you ready?

DORA: Ready!

SCUDDER: Fire!—one, two, three. (SCUDDER *takes out watch.*)

15 PAUL: Now it's cooking; laws mussey? I feel it all inside, as if I was at a lottery.

SCUDDER: So! (*Throws down apron.*) That's enough. (*Withdrawing slide, turns and sees* PAUL.) What! what are you doing there, you young varmint! Ain't you took them bags

20 to the house yet?

PAUL: Now, it ain't no use trying to get mad, Mas'r Scudder. I'm gwine! I only come back to find Wahnotee; whar is dat ign'ant Injiun?

SCUDDER: You'll find him scenting round the rum store,

25 hitched up by the nose. (*Goes into the room.*)

PAUL: (*Calling at the door.*) Say, Mas'r Scudder, take me in dat telescope?

SCUDDER: (*Inside the room.*) Get out, you cub! clar out!

PAUL: You got four of dem dishes ready. Gosh, wouldn't I like

30 to hab myself took! What's de charge, Mas'r Scudder? (*He runs off.*)

SCUDDER: (*Enters from the room.*) Job had none of them critters on his plantation, else he'd never ha' stood through so many chapters. Well, that has come out clear, ain't it?

35 (*Showing the plate.*)

DORA: O, beautiful! Look, Mr Peyton.

GEORGE: (*Looking.*) Yes, very fine!

SCUDDER: The apparatus can't mistake. When I traveled round with this machine, the homely folks used to sing

40 out, 'Hillo, mister, this ain't like me!' 'Ma'am,' says I, 'the apparatus can't mistake.' 'But, mister, that ain't my nose.' 'Ma'am, your nose drawed it. The machine can't err—you may mistake your phiz but the apparatus don't.' 'But, sir, it ain't agreeable.' 'No, ma'am, the truth seldom is.'

45 PETE: (*Enters, puffing.*) Mas'r Scudder! Mas'r Scudder!

SCUDDER: Hillo! what are you blowing about like a steamboat with one wheel for?

PETE: *You* blow, Mas'r Scudder, when I tole you: dere's a man from Noo Aleens just arriv'd at de house, and he's

50 stuck up two papers on de gates: 'For sale—dis yer property,' and a heap of oder tings—an he seen missus, and arter he shown some papers she burst out crying— I yelled; den de corious of little niggers dey set up, den de hull plantation children—de live stock reared up and

55 created a purpiration of lamentation as did de ole heart good to har.

DORA: What's the matter?

SCUDDER: He's come.

PETE: Dass it—I saw 'm!

60 SCUDDER: The sheriff from New Orleans has taken possession—Terrebonne is in the hands of the law.

ZOE: (*Enters.*) O, Mr Scudder! Dora! Mr Peyton! come home—there are strangers in the house.

DORA: Stay, Mr Peyton: Zoe, a word! (*She leads her forward—*

65 *aside.*) Zoe, the more I see of George Peyton the better I like him; but he is too modest—that is a very impertinent virtue in a man.

ZOE: I'm no judge, dear.

DORA: Of course not, you little fool; no one ever made love

70 to you, and you can't understand; I mean, that George knows I am an heiress; my fortune would release this estate from debt.

ZOE: O, I see!

DORA: If he would only propose to marry me I would accept

75 him, but he don't know that, and he will go on fooling, in his slow European way, until it is too late.

ZOE: What's to be done?

DORA: You tell him.

ZOE: What? that he isn't to go on fooling in his slow—

80 DORA: No, you goose! twit him on his silence and abstraction—I'm sure it's plain enough, for he has not spoken two words to me all the day; then joke round the subject, and at last speak out.

SCUDDER: Pete, as you came here, did you pass Paul and the

85 Indian with the letter-bags?

PETE: No, sar; but dem vagabonds neber take the 'specable straight road, dey goes by de swamp. (*Exits up the path.*)

SCUDDER: Come, sir!

DORA: (*To* ZOE.) Now's your time.—(*Aloud.*) Mr Scudder,

90 take us with you—Mr Peyton is so slow, there's no getting him on.

(*Exit* DORA *and* SCUDDER.)

ZOE: They are gone!—(*Glancing at* GEORGE.) Poor fellow, he has lost all.

GEORGE: Poor child! how sad she looks now she has no re-

95 source.

ZOE: How shall I ask him to stay?

GEORGE: Zoe, will you remain here? I wish to speak to you.

ZOE: (*Aside.*) Well, that saves trouble.

GEORGE: By our ruin you lose all.

ZOE: O, I'm nothing; think of yourself.

100 GEORGE: I can think of nothing but the image that remains face to face with me; so beautiful, so simple, so confiding, that I dare not express the feelings that have grown up so rapidly in my heart.

ZOE: (*Aside.*) He means Dora.

105 GEORGE: If I dared to speak!

ZOE: That's just what you must do, and do it at once, or it will be too late.

GEORGE: Has my love been divined?

ZOE: It has been more than suspected.

110 GEORGE: Zoe, listen to me, then. I shall see this estate pass from me without a sigh, for it possesses no charm for me; the wealth I covet is the love of those around me—eyes that are rich in fond looks, lips that breathe endearing words; the only estate I value is the heart of one true

115 woman, and the slaves I'd have are her thoughts.

ZOE: George, George, your words take away my breath!

GEORGE: The world, Zoe, the free struggle of minds and hands is before me; the education bestowed on me by my dear uncle is a noble heritage which no sheriff can seize;

120 with that I can build up a fortune, spread a roof over the heads I love, and place before them the food I have earned; I will work—

ZOE: Work! I thought none but coloured people worked.

GEORGE: Work, Zoe, is the salt that gives savour to life.

125 ZOE: Dora said you were slow; if she could hear you now—

GEORGE: Zoe, you are young; your mirror must have told you that you are beautiful. Is your heart free?

ZOE: Free? of course it is!

GEORGE: We have known each other but a few days, but to

130 me those days have been worth all the rest of my life. Zoe,

you have suspected the feeling that now commands an utterance—you have seen that I love you.

ZOE: Me! you love *me?*

135 GEORGE: As my wife—the sharer of my hopes, my ambitions,
and my sorrows; under the shelter of your love I could
watch the storms of fortune pass unheeded by.

ZOE: *My* love! *My* love? George, you know not what you say!
I the sharer of your sorrows—your wife! Do you know
140 what I am?

GEORGE: Your birth—I know it. Has not my dear aunt forgotten it—she who had the most right to remember it?
You are illegitimate, but love knows no prejudice.

ZOE: (*Aside.*) Alas! he does not know, he does not know! and
145 will despise me, spurn me, loathe me, when he learns who,
what, he has so loved—(*Aloud.*) George, O, forgive me!
Yes, I love you—I did not know it until your words
showed me what has been in my heart; each of them
awoke a new sense, and now I know how unhappy—how
150 very unhappy I am.

GEORGE: Zoe, what have I said to wound you?

ZOE: Nothing; but you must learn what I thought you already knew. George you cannot marry me; the laws forbid it!

155 GEORGE: Forbid it?

ZOE: There is a gulf between us, as wide as your love, as deep
as my despair; but, O, tell me, say you will pity me! that
you will not throw me from you like a poisoned thing!

GEORGE: Zoe, explain yourself—your language fills me with
160 shapeless fears.

ZOE: And what shall I say?—I—my mother was—no, no—
not her! Why should I refer the blame to her? George, do
you see that hand you hold? look at these fingers; do you
see the nails are of a bluish tinge?

165 GEORGE: Yes, near the quick there is a faint blue mark.

ZOE: Look in my eyes; is not the same colour in the white?

GEORGE: It is their beauty.

ZOE: Could you see the roots of my hair you would see the
same dark, fatal mark. Do you know what that is?

170 GEORGE: No.

ZOE: That is the ineffaceable curse of Cain. Of the blood that
feeds my heart, one drop in eight is black—bright red as
the rest may be, that one drop poisons all the flood; those
seven bright drops give me love like yours—hope like
175 yours—ambition like yours—life hung with passions like
dewdrops on the morning flowers; but the one black drop
gives me despair, for I'm an unclean thing—forbidden by
the laws—I'm an Octoroon!

GEORGE: Zoe, I love you none the less; this knowledge brings
180 no revolt to my heart, and I can overcome the obstacle.

ZOE: But *I* cannot.

GEORGE: We can leave this country, and go far away where
none can know.

ZOE: And you mother, she who from infancy treated me with
185 such fondness, she who, as you said, has most reason to
spurn me, can she forget what I am? Will she gladly see
you wedded to the child of her husband's slave? No! she
would revolt from it, as all but you would; and if I consented to hear the cries of my heart, if I did not crush out
190 my infant love, what would she say to the poor girl on
whom she had bestowed so much? No, no!

GEORGE: Zoe, must we immolate our lives on her prejudice?

ZOE: Yes, for I'd rather be black than ungrateful! Ah, George,
our race has at least one virtue—it knows how to suffer!

GEORGE: Each word you utter makes my love sink deeper 195
into my heart.

ZOE: And I remained here to induce you to offer that heart
to Dora!

GEORGE: If you bid me do so I will obey you—

ZOE: No, no! if you cannot be mine, O, let me not blush 200
when I think of you.

GEORGE: Dearest Zoe! (*Exit* GEORGE *and* ZOE. *As they exit,*
M'CLOSKY *rises from behind a rock and looks after them.*)

M'CLOSKY: She loves him! I felt it—and how she can love!
(*Advances.*) That one black drop of blood burns in her 205
veins and lights up her heart like a foggy sun. O, how I
lapped up her words, like a thirsty bloodhound! I'll have
her, if it costs me my life! Yonder the boy still lurks with
those mail-bags; the devil still keeps him here to tempt
me, darn his yellow skin! I arrived just too late, he had 210
grabbed the prize as I came up. Hillo! he's coming this
way, fighting with his Injiun. (*Conceals himself.*)

PAUL: (*Enters, wrestling with* WAHNOTEE.) It ain't no use now:
you got to gib it up!

WAHNOTEE: Ugh!   215

PAUL: It won't do! You got dat bottle of rum hid under your
blanket—gib it up now, you—Yar! (*Wrenching it from him.*)
You nasty, lying Injiun! It's no use you putting on airs; I
ain't gwine to sit up wid you all night and you drunk.
Hillo! war's de crowd gone? And dar's de 'paratus—O, 220
gosh, if I could take a likeness ob dis child! Uh—uh, let's
have a peep. (*Looking through camera.*) O, golly! yar, you
Wahnotee! you stan' dar, I see you. Ta demine usti. (*He
looks at* WAHNOTEE *through the camera;* WAHNOTEE *springs
back with an expression of alarm.*)   225

WAHNOTEE: No tue Wahnotee.

PAUL: Ha, ha! he tinks it's a gun. You ign'ant Injiun, it can't
hurt you! Stop, here's dem dishes—plates—dat's what he
call 'em, all fix: I see Mas'r Scudder do it often—tink I can
take likeness—stay dere, Wahnotee.   230

WAHNOTEE: No, carabine tue.

PAUL: I must operate and take my own likeness too—how
debbel I do dat? Can't be ober dar an' here too—I ain't
twins. Ugh! ach! 'Top; you look, you Wahnotee; you see
dis rag, eh? Well when I say go, den lift dis rag like dis, see! 235
den run to dat pine tree up dar (*Points.*) and back ag'in,
and den pull down de rag so, d'ye see?

WAHNOTEE: Hugh!

PAUL: Den you hab glass ob rum.

WAHNOTEE: Rum!   240

PAUL: Dat wakes him up. Coute, Wahnotee in omenee dit go
Wahnotee, poina la fa, comb a pine tree, la revieut sala,
la fa.

WAHNOTEE: Firewater!

PAUL: Yes, den a glass ob firewater; now den. (*Throwing mail-* 245
bags down and sitting on them.) Pret, now den go.

(WAHNOTEE *raises the apron and runs off.* PAUL *sits for his pic-*
*ture—*M'CLOSKY *appears.*)

M'CLOSKY: Where are they? Ah, yonder goes the Indian!

PAUL: De time he gone just 'bout enough to cook dat dish
plate.

250 M'CLOSKY: Yonder is the boy—now is my time! What's he
doing; is he asleep? (*Advancing.*) He is sitting on my prize!
darn his carcass! I'll clear him off there—he'll never know
what stunned him. (*He takes Indian's tomahawk and steals to*
PAUL.)

255 PAUL: Dam dat Injiun! is dat him creeping dar? I daren't move
fear to spile myself. (M'CLOSKY *strikes him on the head—he*
falls dead.)

M'CLOSKY: Horraw; the bags are mine—now for it!—(*Open-*
ing the mail-bags.) What's here? Sunnyside, Pointdexter,
260 Jackson, Peyton; here it is—the Liverpool postmark, sure
enough!—(*Opening letter—reads.*) 'Madam, we are instructed by the firm of Mason and Co., to inform you that
a dividend of forty per cent is payable on the first prox-
imo, this amount in consideration of position, they send
265 herewith, and you will find enclosed by draft to your order, on the Bank of Louisiana, which please acknowledge—the balance will be paid in full, with interest, in
three, six, and nine months—your drafts on Mason Brothers at those dates will be accepted by La Palisse and Com-
270 pagnie, N. O., so that you may command immediate use
of the whole amount at once, if required. Yours, etc.,
James Brown.' What a find! this infernal letter would have
saved all. (*During the reading of the letter, he remains nearly mo-*
tionless under the focus of the camera.) But now I guess it will
275 arrive too late—these darned U.S. mails are to blame. The
Injiun! he must not see me. (*Exits rapidly.*)

(WAHNOTEE *runs on, and pulls down the apron. He sees* PAUL, *ly-*
ing on the ground, and speaks to him, thinking that he is shamming
sleep. He gesticulates and jabbers to him and moves him with his
feet, then kneels down to rouse him. To his horror he finds him dead.
Expressing great grief he raises his eyes and they fall upon the cam-
era. Rising with a savage growl, he seizes the tomahawk and smashes
the camera to pieces. Going to PAUL *he expresses in pantomime grief,*
sorrow, and fondness, and takes him in his arms to carry him away.)

ACT THREE

A room in MRS PEYTON'*s house showing the entrance on which an*
auction bill is pasted. SOLON *and* GRACE *are there.*

PETE: (*Outside.*) Dis way—dis way.

(*Enter* PETE, POINTDEXTER, JACKSON, LAFOUCHE, *and* CAIL-
LOU.)

PETE: Dis way, gen'l'men; now, Solon—Grace—dey's hot and
tirsty—sangaree, brandy, rum.
JACKSON: Well, what d'ye say, Lafouche—d'ye smile?

(*Enter* THIBODEAUX *and* SUNNYSIDE.)

5 THIBODEAUX: I hope we don't intrude on the family.
PETE: You see dat hole in dar, sar? I was raised on dis yar plantation—nebber see no door in it—always open, sar, for
stranger to walk in.
SUNNYSIDE: And for substance to walk out.
10 RATTS: (*Enters.*) Fine southern style that, eh!
LAFOUCHE: (*Reading the bill.*) 'A fine, well-built old family
mansion, replete with every comfort.'
RATTS: There's one name on the list of slaves scratched, I see.

LAFOUCHE: Yes; No. 49, Paul, a quadroon boy, aged thirteen.
SUNNYSIDE: He's missing.   15
POINTDEXTER: Run away, I suppose.
PETE: (*Indignantly.*) No, sar; nigger nebber cut stick on Terre-
bonne; dat boy's dead, sure.
RATTS: What, Picayune Paul, as we called him, that used to
come abroad my boat?—poor little darkey, I hope not;   20
many a picayune he picked up for his dance and nigger
songs, and he supplied our table with fish and game from
the Bayous.
PETE: Nebber supply no more, sar—nebber dance again.
Mas'r Ratts, you hard him sing about de place where de   25
good niggers go, de last time.
RATTS: Well!
PETE: Well, he gone dar hisself; why I tink so—'cause we
missed Paul for some days, but nebber tout nothin' till one
night dat Injiun Wahnotee suddenly stood right dar   30
'mongst us—was in his war paint, and mighty cold and
grave—he sit down by de fire. 'Whar's Paul?' I say—he
smoke and smoke, but nebber look out ob de fire; well
knowing dem critters, I wait a long time—den he say,
'Wahnotee great chief'; den I say nothing—smoke anoder 35
time—last, rising to go, he turn round at door, and say
berry low—O, like a woman's voice he say, 'Omenee
Pangeuk'—dat is, Paul is dead—nebber see him since.
RATTS: That redskin killed him.
SUNNYSIDE: So we believe; and so mad are the folks around, 40
if they catch the redskin they'll lynch him sure.
RATTS: Lynch him! Darn his copper carcass, I've got a set of
Irish deck-hands abroad that just loved that child; and af-
ter I tell them this, let them get a sight of the redskin, I
believe they would eat him, tomahawk and all. Poor little 45
Paul!
THIBODEAUX: What was he worth?
RATTS: Well, near on five hundred dollars.
PETE: (*Scandalised.*) What, sar! You p'tend to be sorry for Paul,
and prize him like dat! Five hundred dollars! (*To* THI-   50
BODEAUX.) T'ousand dollars, Massa Thibodeau.
SCUDDER: (*Enters.*) Gentlemen, the sale takes place at three.
Good morning, Colonel. It's near that now, and there's still
the sugarhouses to be inspected. Good day, Mr Thibo-
deaux—shall we drive down that way? Mr Lafouche, why, 55
how do you do, sir? you're looking well.
LAFOUCHE: Sorry I can't return the compliment.
RATTS: Salem's looking a kinder hollowed out.
SCUDDER: What, Mr Ratts, are you going to invest in
swamps?   60
RATTS: No; I want a nigger.
SCUDDER: Hush.
PETE: Eh! wass dat?
SCUDDER: Mr Sunnyside, I can't do this job of showin' round
the folks; my stomach goes agin it. I want Pete here a   65
minute.
SUNNYSIDE: I'll accompany them certainly.
SCUDDER: (*Eagerly.*) Will ye? Thank ye; thank ye.
SUNNYSIDE: We must excuse Scudder, friends. I'll see you
round the estate.   70

(*Enter* GEORGE *and* MRS PEYTON.)

LAFOUCHE: Good morning, Mrs Peyton.

(*All salute.*)

SUNNYSIDE: This way, gentlemen.

RATTS: (*Aside to* SUNNYSIDE.). I say, I'd like to say summit soft to the old woman; perhaps it wouldn't go well, would it?

75 THIBODEAUX: No; leave it alone.

RATTS: Darn it, when I see a woman in trouble, I feel like selling the skin off my back.

(*Exit* THIBODEAUX, SUNNYSIDE, RATTS, POINTDEXTER, GRACE, JACKSON, LAFOUCHE, CAILLOU, SOLON.)

SCUDDER: (*Aside to* PETE.) Go outside there; listen to what you hear, then go down to the quarters and tell the boys,

80 for I can't do it. O, get out.

PETE: He said 'I want a nigger.' Laws, a mussey! What am goin' to cum ob us! (*Exits slowly, as if trying to conceal himself.*)

GEORGE: My dear aunt, why do you not move from this

85 painful scene? Go with Dora to Sunnyside.

MRS PEYTON: No, George; your uncle said to me with his dying breath, 'Nellie, never leave Terrebonne,' and I never *will* leave it, till the law compels me.

SCUDDER: Mr George, I'm going to say somethin' that has

90 been chokin' me for some time. I know you'll excuse it. Thar's Miss Dora—that girl's in love with you; yes, sir, her eyes are startin' out of her head with it: now her fortune would redeem a good part of this estate.

MRS PEYTON: Why, George, I never suspected this!

95 GEORGE: I did, Aunt, I confess but—

MRS PEYTON: And you hesitated from motives of delicacy?

SCUDDER: No, ma'am; here's the plan of it. Mr George is in love with Zoe.

GEORGE: Scudder!

100 MRS PEYTON: George!

SCUDDER: Hold on, now! things have got so jammed in on top of us, we ain't got time to put kid gloves on to handle them. He loves Zoe, and has found out that she loves him. (*Sighing.*) Well, that's all right; but as he can't marry

105 her, and as Miss Dora would jump at him—

MRS PEYTON: Why didn't you mention this before?

SCUDDER: Why, because *I* love Zoe, too, and I couldn't take that young feller from her; and she's jist living on the sight of him, as I saw her do; and they so happy in spite of this

110 yer misery around them, and they reproachin' themselves with not feeling as they ought. I've seen it, I tell you; and darn it, ma'am, can't you see that's what's been a hollowing me out so—I beg your pardon.

MRS PEYTON: O, George—my son, let me call you—I do not

115 speak for my own sake, nor for the loss of the estate, but for the poor people here: they will be sold, divided, and taken away—they have been born here. Heaven has denied me children; so all the strings of my heart have grown around and amongst them, like the fibres and roots of an

120 old tree in its native earth. O, let all go, but save them! With them around us, if we have not wealth, we shall at least have the home that they alone can make—

GEORGE: My dear mother—Mr Scudder—you teach me what I ought to do; if Miss Sunnyside will accept me as I

125 am, Terrebonne shall be saved: I will sell myself, but the slaves shall be protected.

MRS PEYTON: *Sell* yourself, George! Is not Dora worth any man's—

SCUDDER: Don't say that, ma'am; don't say that to a man that loves another gal. He's going to do an heroic act; don't 130 spile it.

MRS PEYTON: But Zoe is only an Octoroon.

SCUDDER: She's won this race agin the white, anyhow; it's too late now to start her pedigree. (*As* DORA *enters.*) Come, Mrs Peyton, take my arm. Hush! here's the other one: 135 she's a little too thoroughbred— too much of the greyhound; but the heart's there, I believe.

(*Exeunt* SCUDDER *and* MRS PEYTON.)

DORA: Poor Mrs Peyton.

GEORGE: Miss Sunnyside, permit me a word: a feeling of delicacy has suspended upon my lips an avowal, which— 140

DORA: (*Aside.*) O, dear, has he suddenly come to his senses?

(*Enter* ZOE, *stopping at back.*)

GEORGE: In a word, I have seen and admired you!

DORA: (*Aside.*) He has a strange way of showing it. European, I suppose.

GEORGE: If you would pardon the abruptness of the question, 145 I would ask you. Do you think the sincere devotion of my life to make yours happy would succeed?

DORA: (*Aside.*) Well, he has the oddest way of making love.

GEORGE: You are silent?

DORA: Mr Peyton, I presume you have hesitated to make this 150 avowal because you feared, in the present condition of affairs here, your object might be misconstrued, and that your attention was rather to my fortune than myself. (*A pause.*) Why don't he speak?—I mean, you feared I might not give you credit for sincere and pure feelings. Well, you 155 wrong me. I don't think you capable of anything else but—

GEORGE: No, I hesitated because an attachment I had formed before I had the pleasure of seeing you had not altogether died out. 160

DORA: (*Smiling.*) Some of those sirens of Paris, I presume. (*Pausing.*) I shall endeavour not to be jealous of the past; perhaps I have no right to be. (*Pausing.*) But now that vagrant love is—eh, faded—is it not? Why don't you speak, sir? 165

GEORGE: Because, Miss Sunnyside, I have not learned to lie.

DORA: Good gracious—who wants you to?

GEORGE: I do, but I can't do it. No, the love I speak of is not such as you suppose—it is a passion that has grown up here since I arrived; but it is a hopeless, mad, wild feeling, 170 that must perish.

DORA: Here! since you arrived! Impossible: you have seen no one; whom can you mean?

ZOE: (*Advancing.*) Me.

GEORGE: Zoe! 175

DORA: You!

ZOE: Forgive him, Dora; for he knew no better until I told him. Dora, you are right. He is incapable of any but sincere and pure feelings—so are you. He loves me—what of that? You know you can't be jealous of a poor creature like 180 me. If he caught the fever, were stung by a snake, or possessed of any other poisonous or unclean thing, you could

pity, tend, love him through it, and for your gentle care he
would love you in return. Well, is he not thus afflicted
185   now? I am his love—he loves an Octoroon.

GEORGE: O, Zoe, you break my heart!

DORA: At college they said I was a fool—I must be. At New
Orleans, they said, 'She's pretty, very pretty, but no brains.'
I'm afraid they must be right; I can't understand a word of
190   all this.

ZOE: Dear Dora, try to understand it with your heart. You
love George; you love him dearly; I know it; and you deserve to be loved by him. He will love you—he must. His
love for me will pass away—it shall. You heard him say it
195   was hopeless. O, forgive him and me!

DORA: (*Weeping*.) O, why did he speak to me at all then?
You've made me cry, then, and I hate you both! (*Exits
through room*.)

(*Enter* MRS PEYTON *and* SCUDDER, M'CLOSKY *and* POINTDEX-
TER.)

M'CLOSKY: I'm sorry to intrude, but the business I came
200   upon will excuse me.

MRS PEYTON: Here is my nephew, sir.

ZOE: Perhaps I had better go.

M'CLOSKY: Wal, as it consarns you, perhaps you better had.

SCUDDER: Consarns Zoe?

205   M'CLOSKY: I don't know; she may as well hear the hull of it.
Go on, Colonel—Colonel Pointdexter, ma'am—the
mortgagee, auctioneer, and general agent.

POINTDEXTER: Pardon me, madam, but do you know these
papers? (*He hands the papers to* MRS PEYTON.)

210   MRS PEYTON: (*Taking them*.) Yes, sir; they were the free papers
of the girl Zoe; but they were in my husband's secretary.
How came they in your possession?

M'CLOSKY: I—I found them.

GEORGE: And you purloined them?

215   M'CLOSKY: Hold on, you'll see. Go on, Colonel.

POINTDEXTER: The list of your slaves is incomplete—it wants
one.

SCUDDER: The boy Paul—we know it.

POINTDEXTER: No, sir, you have omitted the Octoroon girl,
220   Zoe.

MRS PEYTON: } Zoe!
ZOE: } Me!

POINTDEXTER: At the time the judge executed those free papers to his infant slave, a judgment stood recorded against
225   him; while that was on record he had no right to make
away with his property. That judgment still exists: under
it and others this estate is sold today. Those free papers
ain't worth the paper that's on 'em.

MRS PEYTON: Zoe a slave! It is impossible!

230   POINTDEXTER: It is certain, madam: the judge was negligent,
and doubtless forgot this small formality.

SCUDDER: But the creditors will not claim the gal?

M'CLOSKY: Excuse me; one of the principal mortgagees has
made the demand.

(*Exeunt* M'CLOSKY *and* POINTDEXTER.)

235   SCUDDER: Hold on yere, George Peyton; you sit down there.
You're trembling so, you'll fall down directly. This blow
has staggered me some.

MRS PEYTON: O, Zoe, my child! don't think too hard of your
poor father.

ZOE: I shall do so if you weep. See, I'm calm.   240

SCUDDER: Calm as a tombstone, and with about as much life.
I see it in your face.

GEORGE: It cannot be! It shall not be!

SCUDDER: Hold your tongue—it must. Be calm—darn the
things; the proceeds of this sale won't cover the debts of   245
the estate. Consarn those Liverpool English fellers, why
couldn't they send something by the last mail? Even a letter, promising something—such is the feeling round
amongst the planters. Darn me, if I couldn't raise thirty
thousand on the envelope alone, and ten thousand more   250
on the postmark.

GEORGE: Zoe, they shall not take you from us while I live.

SCUDDER: Don't be a fool; they'd kill you, and then take her,
just as soon as—stop: old Sunnyside, he'll buy her; that'll
save her.   255

ZOE: No, it won't; we have confessed to Dora that we love
each other. How can she then ask her father to free me?

SCUDDER: What in thunder made you do that?

ZOE: Because it was the truth, and I had rather be a slave with
a free soul, than remain free with a slavish, deceitful heart.   260
My father gives me freedom—at least he thought so. May
Heaven bless him for the thought, bless him for the happiness he spread around my life. You say the proceeds of
the sale will not cover his debts. Let me be sold then, that
I may free his name. I give him back the liberty he be-   265
stowed upon me; for I can never repay him the love he
bore his poor Octoroon child, on whose breast his last
sigh was drawn, into whose eyes he looked with the last
gaze of affection.

MRS PEYTON: O, my husband! I thank Heaven you have not   270
lived to see this day.

ZOE: George, leave me! I would be alone a little while.

GEORGE: Zoe! (*Turns away, overpowered*.)

ZOE: Do not weep, George. Dear George, you now see what
a miserable thing I am.   275

GEORGE: Zoe!

SCUDDER: I wish they could sell *me*! I brought half this ruin on
this family, with my all-fired improvements. I deserve to be
a nigger this day—I feel like one, inside. (*Exit* SCUDDER.)

ZOE: Go now, George—leave me—take her with you.   280

(*Exit* MRS PEYTON *and* GEORGE.)

A slave! a slave! Is this a dream—for my brain reels with
the blow? He said so. What! then I shall be sold—sold!
and my master—O! (*She falls on her knees, with her face in
her hands*.) No—no master but one. George—George—
hush—they come! save me! No, (*Looks off*.) 't is Pete and   285
the servants—they come this way. (*Enters the inner room*.)

(*Enter* PETE, GRACE, MINNIE, SOLON, DIDO, *and all the* NE-
GROES.)

PETE: Cum yer now—stand round, 'cause I've got to talk to
you darkies—keep dem chil'n quiet—don't make no
noise, de missus up dar har us.

SOLON: Go on, Pete.   290

PETE: Gen'l'men, my coloured frens and ladies, dar's mighty
bad news gone round. Dis yer prop'ty to be sold—old

Terrebonne—whar we all been raised, is gwine—dey's gwine to tak it away—can't stop here nohow.

295 ALL: O-o!—O-o!

PETE: Hold quiet, you trash o' niggers! Tink anybody wants you to cry? Who's you to set up screeching?—Be quiet! But dis ain't all. Now, my culled brethren, gird up your lines, and listen—hold on yer bref—it's a comin'. We

300 t'ought dat de niggers would belong to de ole missus, and if she lost Terrebonne, we must live dere allers, and we would hire out, and bring our wages to ole Missus Peyton.

ALL: Ya! ya! Well—

PETE: Hush! I tell ye, 't ain't so—we can't do it—we've got to

305 be sold—

ALL: Sold!

PETE: Will you hush? she will har you. Yes! I listen dar jess now—dar was ole lady cryin'—Mas'r George—ah! you seen dem big tears in his eyes. O, Mas'r Scudder, he didn't

310 cry zackly; both ob his eyes and cheek look like de bad Bayou in low season—so dry dat I cry for him. (Raising his voice.) Den say de missus, "T ain't for de land I keer, but for dem poor niggers—dey'll be sold—dat wot stagger me.' 'No,' say Mas'r George, 'I'd rather sell myself fuss; but

315 dey shan't suffer, nohow—I see 'em dam fuss.'

ALL: O, bless 'um! Bless Mas'r George.

PETE: Hole yer tongues. Yes, for you, for me, for dem little ones, dem folks cried. Now, den, if Grace dere wid her chil'n were all sold, she'll begin screechin' like a cat. She

320 didn't mind how kind old judge was to her; and Solon, too, he'll holler, and break de ole lady's heart.

GRACE: No, Pete; no, I won't. I'll bear it.

PETE: I don't tink you will any more, but dis here will; 'cause de family spile Dido, dey has. She nebber was worth much

325 a' dat nigger.

DIDO: How dar you say dat, you black nigger, you? I fetch as much as any odder cook in Louisiana.

PETE: What's de use of your takin' it kind, and comfortin' de missus' heart, if Minnie dere, and Louise, and Marie, and

330 Julie is to spile it?

MINNIE: We won't, Pete; we won't.

PETE: (To the men.) Dar, do ye hear dat, ye mis'able darkies; dem gals is worth a boat load of kinder men dem is. Cum, for de pride of de family, let every darky look his best for

335 the judge's sake—dat ole man so good to us, and dat ole woman—so dem strangers from New Orleans shall say, dem's happy darkies, dem's a fine set of niggers; every one say when he's sold, 'Lor' bless dis yer family I'm gwine out of, and send me as good a home.'

340 ALL: We'll do it, Pete; we'll do it.

PETE: Hush! hark! I tell ye dar's somebody in dar. Who is it?

GRACE: It's Missy Zoe. See! see!

PETE: Come along; she har what we say, and she's cryin' for us. None o' ye ign'rant niggers could cry for yerselves like

345 dat. Come here quiet: now quiet.

(Exeunt PETE and all the NEGROES, slowly.)

ZOE: (Who is supposed to have overheard the last scene, enters.) O! must I learn from these poor wretches how much I owe, and how I ought to pay the debt? Have I slept upon the benefits I received, and never saw, never felt, never knew

350 that I was forgetful and ungrateful? O, my father! my dear, dear father! forgive your poor child. You made her life too happy, and now these tears will flow. Let me hide them till I teach my heart. O, my—my heart! (Exits, with a low, wailing, suffocating cry.)

(Enter M'CLOSKY, LAFOUCHE, JACKSON, SUNNYSIDE, and POINTDEXTER.)

POINTDEXTER: (Looking at his watch.) Come, the hour is past. 355 I think we may begin business. Where is Mr Scudder?

JACKSON: I want to get to Ophelensis tonight.

DORA: (Enters.) Father, come here.

SUNNYSIDE: Why, Dora, what's the matter? Your eyes are red.

DORA: Are they? Thank you. I don't care, they were blue this 360 morning, but it don't signify now.

SUNNYSIDE: My darling! Who has been teasing you?

DORA: Never mind. I want you to buy Terrebonne.

SUNNYSIDE: Buy Terrebonne! What for?

DORA: No matter—buy it! 365

SUNNYSIDE: It will cost me all I'm worth. This is folly, Dora.

DORA: Is my plantation at Comptableau worth this?

SUNNYSIDE: Nearly—perhaps.

DORA: Sell it, then, and buy this.

SUNNYSIDE: Are you mad, my love? 370

DORA: Do you want me to stop here and bid for it?

SUNNYSIDE: Good gracious, no!

DORA: Then I'll do it if you don't.

SUNNYSIDE: I will! I will! But for Heaven's sake go—here comes the crowd. (Exit DORA.) What on earth does that 375 child mean or want?

(Enter SCUDDER, GEORGE, RATTS, CAILLOU, PETE, GRACE, MINNIE, and all the NEGROES. A large table is in the centre of the background. POINTDEXTER mounts the table with his hammer, his clerk sitting at his feet. The Negro mounts the table from behind. The rest sit down.)

POINTDEXTER: Now, gentlemen, we shall proceed to business. It ain't necessary for me to dilate, describe or enumerate; Terrebonne is known to you as one of the richest bits of sile in Louisiana, and its condition reflects credit on them 380 as had to keep it. I'll trouble you for that piece of baccy, Judge—thank you—so, gentlemen, as life is short, we'll start right off. The first lot on here is the estate in block, with its sugar-houses, stock, machines, implements, good dwelling-houses and furniture. If there is no bid for the es- 385 tate and stuff, we'll sell it in smaller lots. Come, Mr Thibodeaux, a man has a chance once in his life—here's yours.

THIBODEAUX: Go on. What's the reserve bid?

POINTDEXTER: The first mortgagee bids forty thousand dollars.

THIBODEAUX: Forty-five thousand. 390

SUNNYSIDE: Fifty thousand.

POINTDEXTER: When you have done joking, gentlemen, you'll say one hundred and twenty thousand. It carried that easy on mortgage.

LAFOUCHE: Then why don't you buy it yourself, Colonel? 395

POINTDEXTER: I'm waiting on your fifty thousand bid.

CAILLOU: Eighty thousand.

POINTDEXTER: Don't be afraid: it ain't going for that, Judge.

SUNNYSIDE: Ninety thousand.

POINTDEXTER: We're getting on. 400

THIBODEAUX: One hundred—

POINTDEXTER: One hundred thousand bid for this mag—

CAILLOU: One hundred and ten thousand—

POINTDEXTER: Good again—one hundred and—

405 SUNNYSIDE: Twenty.

POINTDEXTER: And twenty thousand bid. Squire Sunnyside is going to sell this at fifty thousand advance tomorrow. (*Looking round.*) Where's that man from Mobile that wanted to give one hundred and eighty thousand?

410 THIBODEAUX: I guess he ain't left home yet, Colonel.

POINTDEXTER: I shall knock it down to the Squire—going—gone—for one hundred and twenty thousand dollars. (*Raising hammer.*) Judge, you can raise the hull on mortgage—going for half its value. (*Knocking on the table.*)

415 Squire Sunnyside, you've got a pretty bit o' land, Squire. Hillo, darkey, hand me a smash dar.

SUNNYSIDE: I got more than I can work now.

POINTDEXTER: Then buy the hands along with the property. Now, gentlemen, I'm proud to submit to you the finest lot

420 of field hands and house servants that was ever offered for competition: they speak for themselves, and do credit to their owners. (*Reading.*) 'No. 1, Solon, a guest boy, and a good waiter.'

PETE: That's my son—buy him, Mas'r Ratts; he's sure to sarve

425 you well.

POINTDEXTER: Hold your tongue!

RATTS: Let the old darkey alone—eight hundred for that boy.

CAILLOU: Nine.

RATTS: A thousand.

430 SOLON: Thank you, Mas'r Ratts: I die for you sar; hold up for me, sar.

RATTS: Look here, the boy knows and likes me, Judge; let him come my way?

CAILLOU: Go on—I'm dumb.

435 POINTDEXTER: One thousand bid. He's yours, Captain Ratts, *Magnolia* steamer.

(SOLON *goes and stands behind* RATTS.)

'No. 2, the yellow girl, Grace, with two children—Saul, aged four, and Victoria, five.' (*They get on table.*)

SCUDDER: That's Solon's wife and children, Judge.

440 GRACE: (*To* RATTS.) Buy me, Mas'r Ratts, do buy me, sar?

RATTS: What in thunder should I do with you and those devils on board my boat?

GRACE: Wash, sar—cook, sar—anyting.

RATTS: Eight hundred agin, then—I'll go it.

445 JACKSON: Nine.

RATTS: I'm broke, Solon—I can't stop the Judge.

THIBODEAUX: What's the matter, Ratts? I'll lend you all you want. Go it, if you're a mind to.

RATTS: Eleven.

450 JACKSON: Twelve.

SUNNYSIDE: O, O!

SCUDDER: (*To* JACKSON.) Judge, my friend. The Judge is a little deaf. Hello! (*Speaking in his ear trumpet.*) This gal and them children belong to that boy Solon there. You're bid-

455 ding to separate them, Judge.

JACKSON: The devil I am! (*Rising.*) I'll take back my bid, Colonel.

POINTDEXTER: All right, Judge; I thought there was a mistake. I must keep you, Captain, to the eleven hundred.

RATTS: Go it. 460

POINTDEXTER: Eleven hundred—going—going—sold! 'No. 3, Pete, a house servant.'

PETE: Dat's me—yer, I'm comin'—stand around dar. (*Tumbles upon the table.*)

POINTDEXTER: Aged seventy-two. 465

PETE: What's dat? A mistake, sar—forty-six.

POINTDEXTER: Lame.

PETE: But don't mount to nuffin—kin work cannel. Come, Judge, pick up. Now's your time, sar.

JACKSON: One hundred dollars. 470

PETE: What, sar? me! for me!—look ye here! (*He dances.*)

GEORGE: Five hundred.

PETE: Mas'r George—ah, no, sar—don't buy me—keep your money for some udder dat is to be sold. I ain't no 'count, sar.

POINTDEXTER: Five hundred bid—it's a good price. He's 475 yours, Mr George Peyton. (PETE *goes down.*) 'No. 4, the Octoroon girl, Zoe.'

(*Enter* ZOE, *very pale, and stands on table.* M'CLOSKY *who hitherto has taken no interest in the sale, now turns his chair.*)

SUNNYSIDE: (*Rising.*) Gentlemen, we are all acquainted with the circumstances of this girl's position, and I feel sure that no one here will oppose the family who desires to redeem 480 the child of our esteemed and noble friend, the late Judge Peyton.

ALL: Hear! bravo! hear!

POINTDEXTER: While the proceeds of this sale promises to realise less than the debts upon it, it is my duty to prevent 485 any collusion for the depreciation of the property.

RATTS: Darn ye! You're a man as well as an auctioneer, ain't ye?

POINTDEXTER: What is offered for the slave?

SUNNYSIDE: One thousand dollars.

M'CLOSKY: Two thousand. 490

SUNNYSIDE: Three thousand.

M'CLOSKY: Five thousand.

GEORGE: Demon!

SUNNYSIDE: I bid seven thousand, which is the last dollar this family possesses. 495

M'CLOSKY: Eight.

THIBODEAUX: Nine.

ALL: Bravo!

M'CLOSKY: Ten. It's no use, Squire.

SCUDDER: Jacob M'Closky, you shan't have that girl. Now, 500 take care what you do. Twelve thousand.

M'CLOSKY: Shan't I! Fifteen thousand. Beat that any of ye.

POINTDEXTER: Fifteen thousand bid for the Octoroon.

DORA: (*Enters.*) Twenty thousand.

ALL: Bravo! 505

M'CLOSKY: Twenty-five thousand.

ALL: (*Groan.*) O! O!

GEORGE: Yelping hound—take that. (*He rushes on* M'CLOSKY. M'CLOSKY *draws his knife.*)

SCUDDER: (*Darting between them.*) Hold on, George Peyton— 510 stand back. This is your own house; we are under your uncle's roof; recollect yourself. And, strangers, ain't we forgetting there's a lady present? (*The knives disappear.*) If we can't behave like Christians, let's try and act like gentlemen. Go on, Colonel. 515

LAFOUCHE: He didn't ought to bid against a lady.

M'CLOSKY: O, that's it, is it? Then I'd like to hire a lady to go to auction and buy my hands.

POINTDEXTER: Gentlemen, I believe none of us have two feelings about the conduct of that man; but he has the law on his side—we may regret, but we must respect it. Mr M'Closky has bid twenty-five thousand dollars for the Octoroon. Is there any other bid? For the first time, twenty-five thousand—last time! (*Brings hammer down.*) To Jacob M'Closky, the Octoroon girl, Zoe, twenty-five thousand dollars.

ACT FOUR

The wharf. The steamer, Magnolia, *alongside a bluff rock.* RATTS *discovered, superintending the loading of ship. Enter* LAFOUCHE *and* JACKSON.

JACKSON: How long before we start, captain?

RATTS: Just as soon as we put this cotton on board.

(*Enter* PETE, *with a lantern, and* SCUDDER, *with notebook.*)

SCUDDER: One hundred and forty-nine bales. Can you take any more?

5 RATTS: Not a bale. I've got engaged eight hundred bales at the next landing, and one hundred hogsheads of sugar at Patten's Slide—that'll take my guards under—hurry up thar.

VOICE: (*Outside.*) Wood's aboard.

10 RATTS: All aboard then.

(*Enter* M'CLOSKY.)

SCUDDER: Sign that receipt, Captain, and save me going up to the clerk.

M'CLOSKY: See here—there's a small freight of turpentine in the fore hold there, and one of the barrels leaks; a spark

15 from your engines might set the ship on fire, and you'll go with it.

RATTS: You be darned! Go and try it, if you've a mind to.

LAFOUCHE: Captain, you've loaded up here until the boat is sunk so deep in the mud she won't float.

20 RATTS: (*Calling off.*) Wood up thar, you Pollo—hang on to the safety valve—guess she'll crawl off on her paddles. (*Shouts heard.*)

JACKSON: What's the matter?

SOLON: (*Enters.*) We got him!

25 SCUDDER: Who?

SOLON: The Injiun!

SCUDDER: Wahnotee? Where is he? D'ye call running away from a fellow catching him?

RATTS: Here he comes.

30 ALL: Where? Where?

(*Enter* WAHNOTEE. *They are all about to rush on him.*)

SCUDDER: Hold on! stan' round thar! no violence—the crittur don't know what we mean.

JACKSON: Let him answer for the boy then.

M'CLOSKY: Down with him—lynch him.

35 ALL: Lynch him!

(*Exit* LAFOUCHE.)

SCUDDER: Stan' back, I say! I'll nip the first that lays a finger on him. Pete, speak to the redskin.

PETE: Whar's Paul, Wahnotee? What's come ob de child?

WAHNOTEE: Paul wunce—Paul pangeuk.

PETE: Pangeuk—dead! 40

WAHNOTEE: Mort!

M'CLOSKY: And you killed him? (*They approach him.*)

SCUDDER: Hold on!

PETE: Um, Paul reste?

WAHNOTEE: Hugh vieu. (*Goes.*) Paul reste ci! 45

SCUDDER: Here, stay! (*Examines the ground.*) The earth has been stirred here lately.

WAHNOTEE: Weenee Paul. (*He points down, and shows by pantomime how he buried* PAUL.)

SCUDDER: The Injiun means that he buried him there! Stop! 50 here's a bit of leather. (*Drawing out the mail-bags.*) The mailbags that were lost! (*Sees the tomahawk in* WAHNOTEE's *belt—draws it out and examines it.*) Look! here are marks of blood—look thar, redskin, what's that?

WAHNOTEE: Paul! (*Makes a sign that* PAUL *was killed by a blow* 55 *on the head.*)

M'CLOSKY: He confesses it; the Indian got drunk, quarreled with him, and killed him.

LAFOUCHE: (*Re-enters with smashed apparatus.*) Here are evidences of the crime; this rum-bottle half emptied—this 60 photographic apparatus smashed—and there are marks of blood and footsteps around the shed.

M'CLOSKY: What more d'ye want—ain't that proof enough? Lynch him!

ALL: Lynch him! Lynch him! 65

SCUDDER: Stan' back, boys! He's an Injiun—fair play.

JACKSON: Try him, then—try him on the spot of his crime.

ALL: Try him! Try him!

LAFOUCHE: Don't let him escape!

RATTS: I'll see to that. (*Drawing revolver.*) If he stirs, I'll put a 70 bullet through his skull, mighty quick.

M'CLOSKY: Come, form a court then, choose a jury—we'll fix this varmin.

(*Enter* THIBODEAUX *and* CAILLOU.)

THIBODEAUX: What's the matter?

LAFOUCHE: We've caught this murdering Injiun, and are go- 75 ing to try him.

(WAHNOTEE *sits, rolled in blanket.*)

PETE: Poor little Paul—poor little nigger!

SCUDDER: This business goes agin me, Ratts—'t ain't right.

LAFOUCHE: We're ready; the jury's impanelled—go ahead— who'll be accuser? 80

RATTS: M'Closky.

M'CLOSKY: Me?

RATTS: Yes; you was the first to hail Judge Lynch.

M'CLOSKY: Well, what's the use of argument whar guilt sticks out so plain; the boy and Injiun were alone when last 85 seen.

SCUDDER: Who says that?

M'CLOSKY: Everybody—that is, I heard so.

SCUDDER: Say what you know—not what you heard.

M'CLOSKY: I know then that the boy was killed with that 90 tomahawk—the redskin owns it—the signs of violence are all round the shed—this apparatus smashed—ain't it plain that in a drunken fit he slew the boy, and when sober concealed the body yonder?

95   ALL: That's it—that's it.

RATTS: Who defends the Injiun?

SCUDDER: I will; for it is agin my natur' to b'lieve him guilty; and if he be, this ain't the place, nor you the authority to try him. How are we sure the boy is dead at all? There are

100   no witnesses but a rum bottle and an old machine. Is it on such evidence you'd hang a human being?

RATTS: His own confession.

SCUDDER: I appeal against your usurped authority. This lynch law is a wild and lawless proceeding. Here's a pic-

105   tur' for a civilised community to afford; yonder, a poor, ignorant savage, and round him a circle of hearts, white with revenge and hate, thirsting for his blood: you call yourselves judges—you ain't—you're a jury of executioners. It is such scenes as these that bring disgrace upon our West-

110   ern life.

M'CLOSKY: Evidence! Evidence! Give us evidence. We've had talk enough; now for proof.

ALL: Yes, yes! Proof, proof!

SCUDDER: Where am I to get it? The proof is here, in my

115   heart.

PETE: (*Who has been looking about the camera.*) 'Top, sar! 'Top a bit! O, laws-a-mussey, see dis! here's a pictur' I found stickin' in that yar telescope machine, sar! look, sar!

SCUDDER: A photographic plate.

(PETE *holds his lantern up.*)

120   What's this, eh! two forms! The child—'t is he! dead—and above him—Ah! ah! Jacob M'Closky, 't was you murdered that boy!

M'CLOSKY: Me?

SCUDDER: You! You slew him with that tomahawk; and as you

125   stood over his body with the letter in your hand, you thought that no witness saw the deed, that no eye was on you—but there was, Jacob M'Closky, there was. The eye of the Eternal was on you—the blessed sun in heaven, that, looking down, struck upon this plate the image of

130   the deed. Here you are, in the very attitude of your crime!

M'CLOSKY: 'T is false!

SCUDDER: 'T is true! the apparatus can't lie. Look there, jurymen. (*Showing plate to jury.*) Look there. O, you wanted evidence—you called for proof—Heaven has answered

135   and convicted you.

M'CLOSKY: What court of law would receive such evidence? (*Going.*)

RATTS: Stop! *This* would! You called it yourself; you wanted to make us murder that Injiun; and since we've got our

140   hands in for justice, we'll try it on *you.* What say ye? shall we have one law for the redskin and another for the white?

ALL: Try him! Try him!

RATTS: Who'll be accuser?

145   SCUDDER: I will! Fellow citizens, you are convened and assembled here under a higher power than the law. What's the law? When the ship's abroad on the ocean, when the army is before the enemy, where in thunder's the law? It is in the hearts of brave men, who can tell right from

wrong, and from whom justice can't be bought. So it is   150 here, in the wilds of the West, where our hatred of crime is measured by the speed of our executions—where necessity is law! I say, then, air you honest men? air you true? Put your hands on your naked breasts, and let every man as don't feel a real American heart there, bustin' up with   155 freedom, truth, and right, let that man step out—that's the oath I put to ye—and then say, Darn ye, go it!

ALL: Go on! Go on!

SCUDDER: No! I won't go on; that man's down. I won't strike him, even with words. Jacob, your accuser is that picter of   160 the crime—let that speak—defend yourself.

M'CLOSKY: (*Drawing knife.*) I will, quicker than lightning.

RATTS: Seize him, then!

(*They rush on* M'CLOSKY*, and disarm him.*)

He can fight though he's a painter: claws all over.

SCUDDER: Stop! Search him, we may find more evidence.   165

M'CLOSKY: Would you rob me first, and murder me afterwards?

RATTS: (*Searching him.*) That's his programme—here's a pocketbook.

SCUDDER: (*Opening it.*) What's here? Letters! Hello! To 'Mrs   170 Peyton, Terrebonne, Louisiana, United States.' Liverpool postmark. Ho! I've got hold of the tail of a rat—come out. (*Reads.*) What's this? A draft for eighty-five thousand dollars, and credit on Palisse and Co., of New Orleans, for the balance. Hi! the rat's out. You killed the boy to steal this   175 letter from the mail-bags—you stole this letter, that the money should not arrive in time to save the Octoroon; had it done so, the lien on the estate would have ceased, and Zoe be free.

ALL: Lynch him! Lynch him! Down with him!   180

SCUDDER: Silence in the court: stand back, let the gentlemen of the jury retire, consult, and return their verdict.

RATTS: I'm responsible for the crittur—go on.

PETE: (*To* WAHNOTEE.) See, Injiun; look dar, (*Showing him the plate.*) see dat innocent; look, dar's de murderer of poor   185 Paul.

WAHNOTEE: Ugh! (*Examining the plate.*)

PETE: Ya! as he? Closky tue Paul—kill de child with your tomahawk dar: 't wasn't you, no—ole Pete allus say so. Poor Injiun lub our little Paul.   190

(WAHNOTEE *rises and looks at* M'CLOSKY—*he is in his war paint and fully armed.*)

SCUDDER: What say ye, gentlemen? Is the prisoner guilty, or is he not guilty?

ALL: Guilty!

SCUDDER: And what is to be his punishment?   195

ALL: Death! (*All advance.*)

WAHNOTEE: (*Crosses to* M'CLOSKY). Ugh!

SCUDDER: No, Injiun; we deal out justice here, not revenge. 'T ain't you he has injured, 't is the white man, whose laws he has offended.   200

RATTS: Away with him—put him down the aft hatch, till we rig his funeral.

M'CLOSKY: Fifty against one! O! if I had you one by one alone in the swamp, I'd rip ye all. (*He is borne off in boat, struggling.*)   205

SCUDDER: Now, then, to business.

PETE: (*Re-enters from boat.*) O, law, sir, dat debil Closky, he tore hisself from de gen'lam, knock me down, take my light, and trows it on de turpentine barrels, and de shed's all afire!

(*Fire seen.*)

210 JACKSON: (*Re-entering.*) We are catching fire forward: quick, cut free from the shore.

RATTS: All hands aboard there—cut the starn ropes—give her headway!

ALL: Ay, ay!

(*Cry of 'Fire' heard—engine bells heard—steam whistle noise.*)

215 RATTS: Cut all away, for'ard—overboard with every bale afire.

(*The steamer moves off with the fire still blazing.*)

M'CLOSKY: (*Re-enters, swimming.*) Ha! have I fixed ye? Burn! burn! that's right. You thought you had cornered me, did ye? As I swam down, I thought I heard something in the water, as if pursuing me—one of them darned alligators, I

220 suppose—they swarm hereabout—may they crunch every limb of ye. (*Exits.*)

(WAHNOTEE *is seen swimming. He finds trail and follows* M'CLOSKY. *The steamer floats on at back, burning.*)

ACT FIVE

SCENE I

Negroes' quarters.

ZOE: (*Enters.*) It wants an hour yet to daylight—here is Pete's hut—(*Knocks.*) He sleeps—no: I see a light.

DIDO: (*Enters from hut.*) Who dat?

ZOE: Hush, Aunty 'T is I—Zoe.

5 DIDO: Miss Zoe? Why you out in de swamp dis time ob night; you catch de fever sure—you is all wet.

ZOE: Where's Pete?

DIDO: He gone down to de landing last night wid Mas'r Scudder; not come back since—kint make it out.

10 ZOE: Aunty, there is sickness up at the house; I have been up all night beside one who suffers, and I remembered that when I had the fever you gave me a drink, a bitter drink, that made me sleep—do you remember it?

DIDO: Didn't I? Dem doctors ain't no 'count; dey don't know

15 nuffin.

ZOE: No; but you, Aunty, you are wise—you know every plant, don't you, and what it is good for?

DIDO: Dat you drink is fust rate for red fever. Is de folks' head bad?

20 ZOE: Very bad, Aunty; and the heart aches worse, so they can get no rest.

DIDO: Hold on a bit, I get you de bottle. (*Exits.*)

ZOE: In a few hours that man, my master, will come for me: he has paid my price, and he only consented to let me re-

25 main here this one night, because Mrs Peyton promised to give me up to him today.

DIDO: (*Re-enters with phial.*) Here 't is—now you give one timble-full—dat's nuff.

ZOE: All there is there would kill one, wouldn't it?

DIDO: Guess it kill a dozen—nebber try. 30

ZOE: It's not a painful death, Aunty, is it? You told me it produced a long, long sleep.

DIDO: Why you tremble so? Why you speak so wild? What you's gwine to do, missey?

ZOE: Give me the drink. 35

DIDO: No. Who dat sick at de house?

ZOE: Give it to me.

DIDO: No. You want to hurt yourself. O, Miss Zoe, why you ask old Dido for dis pizen?

ZOE: Listen to me. I love one who is here, and he loves me— 40 George. I sat outside his door all night—I heard his sighs—his agony—torn from him by my coming fate; and he said, 'I'd rather see her dead than his!'

DIDO: Dead!

ZOE: He said so—then I rose up, and stole from the house, 45 and ran down to the bayou: but its cold, black, silent stream terrified me—drowning must be so horrible a death. I could not do it. Then, as I knelt there, weeping for courage, a snake rattled beside me. I shrunk from it and fled. Death was there beside me, and I dared not take it. 50 O! I'm afraid to die; yet I am more afraid to live.

DORA: Die!

ZOE: So I came here to you; to you, my own dear nurse; to you, who so often hushed me to sleep when I was a child; who dried my eyes and put your little Zoe to rest. Ah! 55 give me the rest that no master but One can disturb—the sleep from which I shall awake free! You can protect me from that man—do let me die without pain.

DIDO: No, no—life is good for young t'ing like you.

ZOE: O! good, good nurse: you will you, will. 60

DIDO: No— g' way.

ZOE: Then I shall never leave Terrebonne—the drink, nurse; the drink; that I may never leave my home—my dear, dear home. You will not give me to that man? Your own Zoe, that loves you, Aunty, so much, so much. (*She gets the* 65 *phial.*) Ah! I have it.

DIDO: No, missey. O! no—don't.

ZOE: Hush! (*Runs off.*)

DIDO: Here, Solon, Minnie, Grace.

(*They enter.*)

ALL: Was de matter? 70

DIDO: Miss Zoe got de pizen. (*Exits.*)

ALL: O! O! (*Exeunt.*)

SCENE II

In a canebrake bayou, on a bank, with a canoe nearby, M'CLOSKY *is seen asleep.*

M'CLOSKY: Burn, burn! blaze away! How the flames crack. I'm not guilty; would ye murder me? Cut, cut the rope— I choke—choke—Ah! (*Wakes.*) Hello! where am I? Why, I was dreaming—curse it! I can never sleep now without dreaming. Hush! I thought I heard the sound of a paddle 5 in the water. All night, as I fled through the canebrake, I heard footsteps behind me. I lost them in the cedar swamp—again they haunted my path down the bayou,

moving as I moved, resting when I rested—hush! there
again!—no; it was only the wind over the canes. The sun
is rising. I must launch my dug-out, and put for the bay,
and in a few hours I shall be safe from pursuit on board of
one of the coasting schooners that run from Galveston to
Matagorda. In a little time this darned business will blow
over, and I can show again. Hark! there's that noise again!
If it was the ghost of that murdered boy haunting me!
Well—I didn't mean to kill him, did I? Well, then, what
has my all-cowardly heart got to skeer me so far? (*He gets
in canoe and rows off.* WAHNOTEE *appears in another canoe. He
gets out and finds trail and paddles off after* M'CLOSKY.)

SCENE III

A cedar swamp. Enter SCUDDER *and* PETE.

SCUDDER: Come on, Pete, we shan't reach the house before
midday.
PETE: Nebber mind, sa, we bring good news—it won't spile
for de keeping.
SCUDDER: Ten miles we've had to walk, because some blamed
varmin onhitched our dug-out. I left it last night all safe.
PETE: P'r'aps it floated away itself.
SCUDDER: No; the hitching line was cut with a knife.
PETE: Say, Mas'r Scudder, s'pose we go in round by de quar-
ters and raise de darkies, den dey cum long wid us, and we
'proach dat ole house like Gin'ral Jackson when he took
London out dar.
SCUDDER: Hello, Pete, I never heard of that affair.
PETE: I tell you, sa—hush!
SCUDDER: What?
PETE: Was dat?—a cry out dar in the swamp—dar again!
SCUDDER: So it is. Something forcing its way through the
undergrowth—it comes this way—it's either a bear or a
runaway nigger. (*He draws a pistol.* M'CLOSKY *rushes on, and
falls at* SCUDDER's *feet.*)
SCUDDER: Stand off—what are ye?
PETE: Mas'r Clusky.
M'CLOSKY: Save me—save me! I can go no farther. I heard
voices.
SCUDDER: Who's after you?
M'CLOSKY: I don't know, but I feel it's death! In some form,
human, or wild best, or ghost, it has tracked me through
the night. I fled; it followed. Hark! there it comes—it
comes—don't you hear a footstep on the dry leaves!
SCUDDER: Your crime has driven you mad.
M'CLOSKY: D'ye hear it—nearer—nearer—ah!

(WAHNOTEE *rushes on, and attacks* M'CLOSKY.)

SCUDDER: The Injiun! By thunder.
PETE: You'se a dead man, Mas'r Clusky—you got to b'lieve
dat.
M'CLOSKY: No—no. If I must die, give me up to the law; but
save me from the tomahawk. You are a white man; you'll
not leave one of your own blood to be butchered by the
redskin?
SCUDDER: Hold on now, Jacob; we've got to figure on that—
let us look straight at the thing. Here we are on the sel-
vage of civilisation. It ain't our side, I believe, rightly; but

Nature has said that where the white man sets his foot, the
red man and the black man shall up sticks and stand
around. But what do we pay for that possession? In cash?
No—in kind—that is, in protection, forbearance, gentleness, in all them goods that show the critters the difference between the Christian and the savage. Now, what
have you done to show them the distinction? For, darn
me, if I can find out.
M'CLOSKY: For what I have done, let me be tried.
SCUDDER: You have been tried—honestly tried and convicted. Providence has chosen your executioner. I shan't
interfere.
PETE: O, no; Mas'r Scudder, don't leave Mas'r Closky like
dat—don't, sa—'t ain't what good Christian should do.
SCUDDER: D'ye hear that, Jacob? This old nigger, the grandfather of the boy you murdered, speaks for you—don't that
go through you? D'ye feel it? Go on, Pete, you've waked
up the Christian here, and the old hoss responds. (*He throws
bowie knife to* M'CLOSKY.) Take that, and defend yourself.

(*Exeunt* SCUDDER *and* PETE. WAHNOTEE *faces him. They fight,*
M'CLOSKY *runs off,* WAHNOTEE *follows him.—Screams outside.*)

SCENE IV

Parlour at Terrebonne.

ZOE: (*Enters.*) My home, my home! I must see you no more.
Those little flowers can live, but I cannot. Tomorrow they'll
bloom the same—all will be here as now, and I shall be cold.
O! my life, my happy life; why has it been so bright?

(*Enter* MRS PEYTON *and* DORA.)

DORA: Zoe, where have you been?
MRS PEYTON: We felt quite uneasy about you.
ZOE: I've been to the Negro quarters. I suppose I shall go be-
fore long, and I wished to visit all the places, once again,
to see the poor people.
MRS PEYTON: Zoe, dear, I'm glad to see you more calm this
morning.
DORA: But how pale she looks, and she trembles so.
ZOE: Do I? (*Enter* GEORGE.) Ah! he is here.
DORA: George, here she is.
ZOE: I have come to say good bye, sir; two hard words—so
hard, they might break many a heart; mightn't they?
GEORGE: O, Zoe! can you smile at this moment?
ZOE: You see how easily I have become reconciled to my
fate—so it will be with you. You will not forget poor
Zoe! but her image will pass away like a little cloud that
obscured your happiness a while—you will love each
other? you are both too good not to join your hearts.
Brightness will return amongst you. Dora, I once made
you weep; those were the only tears I caused anybody.
Will you forgive me?
DORA: Forgive you—(*Kisses her.*)
GEORGE: Zoe, you are pale. Zoe!—she faints!
ZOE: No; a weakness, that's all—a little water. (DORA *gets some
water.*) I have a restorative here—will you pour it in the
glass? (DORA *attempts to take it.*) No; not you—George.
(GEORGE *pours the contents of the phial into glass.*) Now, give
it to me. George, dear George, do you love me?

GEORGE: Do you doubt it, Zoe?

ZOE: No! (*She drinks.*)

35 DORA: Zoe, if all I possess would buy your freedom, I would gladly give it.

ZOE: I am free! I had but one Master on earth, and he has given me my freedom!

DORA: Alas! but the deed that freed you was not lawful.

40 ZOE: Not lawful—no—but I am going to where there is no law—where there is only justice.

GEORGE: Zoe, you are suffering—your lips are white—your cheeks are flushed.

ZOE: I must be going—it is late. Farewell, Dora. (*Retires.*)

45 PETE: (*Outside.*) Whar's Missus—whar's Mas'r George?

GEORGE: They come.

SCUDDER: (*Enters.*) Stand around and let me pass—room thar! I feel so big with joy, creation ain't wide enough to hold me. Mrs Peyton, George Peyton, Terrebonne is

50 yours. It was that rascal M'Closky—but he got rats, I swow—he killed the boy, Paul, to rob this letter from the mail-bags—the letter from Liverpool you know—he sot fire to the shed—that was how the steamboat got burned up.

55 MRS PEYTON: What d' ye mean?

SCUDDER: Read—read that. (*He gives letter to them.*)

GEORGE: Explain yourself.

SUNNYSIDE: (*Enters.*) Is it true?

SCUDDER: Every word of it, Squire. Here, you tell it, since

60 you know it. If I was to try, I'd bust.

MRS PEYTON: Read, George. Terrebonne is yours.

(*Enter* PETE, DIDO, SOLON, MINNIE, *and* GRACE.)

PETE: War is she—war is Miss Zoe?

SCUDDER: What's the matter?

PETE: Don't ax me. Whar's de gal? I say.

65 SCUDDER: Here she is—Zoe!—water—she faints.

PETE: No—no. 'T ain't no faint—she's a dying, sa: she got pizon from old Dido here, this mornin'.

GEORGE: Zoe!

SCUDDER: Zoe! is this true?—no, it ain't—darn it, say it ain't.

70 Look here, you're free, you know; nary a master to hurt you now: you will stop here as long as you're a mind to, only don't look so.

DORA: Her eyes have changed colour.

PETE: Dat's what her soul's gwine to do. It's going up dar,

75 whar dere's no line atween folks.

GEORGE: She revives.

ZOE: (*On the sofa.*) George—where—where—

GEORGE: O, Zoe! what have you done?

ZOE: Last night I overheard you weeping in your room, and

80 you said, 'I'd rather see her dead than so!'

GEORGE: Have I then prompted you to this?

ZOE: No; but I loved you so, I could not bear my fate; and then I stood between your heart and hers. When I am dead she will not be jealous of your love for me,

85 no laws will stand between us. Lift me; so—(GEORGE *raises her head.*)—let me look at you, that your face may be the last I see of this world. O! George, you may, without a blush, confess your love for the Octoroon. (*She dies.* GEORGE *lowers her head gently and kneels beside*

90 *her.*)

The English Happy Ending

ACT FOUR

SCENE: *The wharf.—The Steamer 'Magnolia' alongside, L.—A bluff rock, R.U.E.* RATTS *discovered, superintending the loading of ship. Enter* LAFOUCHE *and* JACKSON, L.

JACKSON: How long before we start, captain?

RATTS: Just as soon as we put this cotton on board.

(*Enter* PETE, *with lantern, and* SCUDDER, *with notebook.* R.)

SCUDDER: One hundred and forty-nine bales. Can you take any more?

RATTS: Not a bale. I've got engaged eight hundred bales at the next landing, and one hundred hogsheads of sugar at Patten's Slide—that'll take my guards under—hurry up thar!   5

VOICE: (*Outside.*) Wood's aboard.

RATTS: All aboard then.

(*Enter* M'CLOSKY, R.)

SCUDDER: Sign that receipt, captain, and save me going up to the clerk.

M'CLOSKY: See here—there's a small freight of turpentine in   10 the fore-hold there, and one of the barrels leaks; a spark from your engines might set the ship on fire, and you'd go with it.

RATTS: You be darned! Go and try if you've a mind to.

LAFOUCHE: Captain, you've loaded up here until the boat is   15 sunk so deep in the mud she won't float.

RATTS: (*Calls off.*) Wood up thar, you Pollo—hang on to the safety valve—guess she'll crawl off on her paddles. (*Shouts heard,* R.)

JACKSON: What's the matter?   20

(*Enter* SOLON, R.)

SOLON: We got him!

SCUDDER: Who?

SOLON: The Inginn!

SCUDDER: Wahnotee? where is he? d'ye call running away from a fellow catching him?   25

RATTS: Here he comes.

OMNES: Where? where?

(*Enter* WAHNOTEE, R., *they are all about to rush on him.*)

SCUDDER: Hold on! stan' round thar! no violence—the critter don't know what we mean.

JACKSON: Let him answer for the boy then.   30

M'CLOSKY: Down with him—lynch him.

OMNES: Lynch him!

(*Exit* LAFOUCHE, R.)

SCUDDER: Stan' back, I say! I'll nip the first that lays a finger on him. Pete, speak to the redskin.

PETE: Whar's Paul, Wahnotee? What's come ob de child?   35

WAHNOTEE: Paul wunce—Paul pangeuk.

PETE: Pangeuk—dead.

WAHNOTEE: Mort!

M'CLOSKY: And you killed him? (*They approach again.*)

40 SCUDDER: Hold on!

PETE: Um, Paul reste?

WAHNOTEE: Hugh vieu—(*Goes L.*)—Paul reste ci!

SCUDDER: Here, stay! (*Examines the ground.*) The earth has been stirred here lately.

45 WAHNOTEE: Weenee Paul. (*Points down and shows by pantomime how he buried* PAUL.)

SCUDDER: The Inginn means that he buried him there! Stop, here's a bit of leather. (*Draws out mail-bags.*) The mail-bags that were lost! (*Sees tomahawk in* WAHNOTEE's *belt—draws*

50 *it out and examines it.*) Look! here are marks of blood—look thar, red-skin, what's that?

WAHNOTEE: Paul! (*Makes sign that* PAUL *was killed by a blow on the head.*)

M'CLOSKY: He confesses it; the Indian got drunk, quarreled

55 with him, and killed him.

(*Re-enter* LAFOUCHE, R., *with smashed apparatus.*)

LAFOUCHE: Here are evidences of the crime; this rum bottle half emptied—this photographic apparatus smashed—and there are marks of blood and footsteps around the shed.

M'CLOSKY: What more d'ye want—ain't that proof enough?

60 Lynch him!

OMNES: Lynch him! Lynch him!

SCUDDER: Stan' back, boys! he's an Inginn—fair play.

JACKSON: Try him then— try him on the spot of his crime.

OMNES: Try him! try him!

65 LAFOUCHE: Don't let him escape!

RATTS: I'll see to that. (*Draws revolver.*) If he stirs, I'll put a bullet through his skull, mighty quick.

M'CLOSKY: Come—form a court, then, choose a jury—we'll fix this varmin.

(*Enter* THIBODEAUX *and* CAILLOU, L.)

70 THIBODEAUX: What's the matter?

LAFOUCHE: We've caught this murdering Inginn, and are going to try him.

(WAHNOTEE *sits L., rollen in blanket.*)

PETE: Poor little Paul—poor little nigger!

SCUDDER: This business goes agin me, Ratts—'taint right.

75 LAFOUCHE: We're ready, the jury is empannelled—go ahead—who'll be accuser?

RATTS: M'Closky.

M'CLOSKY: Me!

RATTS: Yes; you was the first to hail Judge Lynch.

80 M'CLOSKY: (R.) Well, what's the use of argument, whar guilt sticks out so plain; the boy and Inginn were alone when last seen.

SCUDDER: (L. C.) Who says that?

M'CLOSKY: Everybody—that is, I heard so.

85 SCUDDER: Say what you know—not what you heard.

M'CLOSKY: I know then, that the boy was killed with that tomahawk—the redskin owns it—the signs of violence are all round the shed—this apparatus smashed—ain't it plain that in a drunken fit he slew the boy, and when sober

90 concealed the body yonder?

OMNES: That's it—that's it.

RATTS: Who defends the Indian?

SCUDDER: I will; for it's agin my natur' to b'lieve him guilty; and if he be, this ain't the place, nor you the authority, to try him. How are we sure the boy is dead at all? There are 95 no witnesses but a rum-bottle and an old machine. Is it on such evidence you'd hang a human being?

RATTS: His own confession.

SCUDDER: I appeal against your usurped authority; this lynch law is a wild and lawless proceeding. Here's a picture for a 100 civilised community to afford; yonder, a poor ignorant savage, and round him a circle of hearts, white with revenge and hate, thirsting for his blood; you call yourselves judges—you ain't—you're a jury of executioners. It is such scenes as these that bring disgrace upon our Western life. 105

M'CLOSKY: Evidence! Evidence! give us evidence, we've had talk enough; now for proof.

OMNES: Yes, yes! Proof, proof!

SCUDDER: Where am I to get it? the proof is here, in my heart! 110

PETE: (*Who has been looking about the camera.*) Top sar! top a bit! Oh, laws-a-mussey, see dis, here's a pictur' I found sticking in that yar telescope machine, sar! look, sar!

SCUDDER: A photographic plate. (PETE *holds lantern up.*) What's this, eh? two forms! the child—'tis he! dead—and 115 above him—Ah, ah! Jacob M'Closky—'twas you murdered the boy!

M'CLOSKY: Me?

SCUDDER: You! You slew him with that tomahawk, and as you stood over his body with the letter in your hand, you 120 thought that no witness saw the deed, that no eye was on you; but there was, Jacob M'Closky, there was—the eye of the Eternal was on you—the blessed sun in heaven, that, looking down, struck upon this plate the image of the deed. Here you are, in the very attitude of your crime! 125

M'CLOSKY: 'Tis false!

SCUDDER: 'Tis true! the apparatus can't lie. Look there, jurymen—(*shows plate to jury*)—look there. Oh, you wanted evidence—you called for proof—heaven has answered and convicted you. 130

M'CLOSKY: What court of law would receive such evidence? (*Going.*)

RATTS: Stop, *this* would—you called it yourself; you wanted to make us murder that Inginn, and since we've got our hands in for justice, we'll try it on you. What say ye? Shall we 135 have one law for the redskin and another for the white?

OMNES: Try him! try him!

RATTS: Who'll be accuser?

SCUDDER: I will! Fellow citizens, you have convened and assembled here under a higher power than the law. What's 140 the law? When the ship's abroad on the ocean—when the army is before the enemy—where in thunder's the law? It is in the hearts of brave men who can tell right from wrong, and from whom justice can't be bought. So it is here, in the Wilds of the West, where out hatred of crime 145 is measured by the speed of our executions—where necessity is law!—I say, then, air you honest men? air you true? put your hands on your naked breasts, and let every man as don't feel a real American heart there, bustin' up with freedom, truth and right, let that man step out— 150 that's the oath I put to ye—and then say, darn ye, go it!

OMNES: Go on—Go on.

SCUDDER: No! I won't go on, that man's down, I won't strike him even with words. Jacob, your accuser is that picter of
155   the crime—let that speak—defend yourself.

M'CLOSKY: (*Draws knife.*) I will, quicker than lightning.

RATTS: Seize him, then! (*They rush on* M'CLOSKY *and disarm him.*) He can fight though—he's a painter, claws all over.

SCUDDER: Stop! Search him, we may find more evidence.

160   M'CLOSKY: Would you rob me first, and murder me afterwards?

RATTS: (*Searching him.*) That's his programme—here's a pocketbook.

SCUDDER: (*Opens it.*) What's here? Letters! Hello! to 'Mrs Pey-
165   ton, Terrebonne, Louisiana, United States' Liverpool post mark. Ho! I've got hold of the tail of a rat—come out. (*Reads.*) What's this?—a draft for 85,000 dollars and credit on Palisse and Co., of New Orleans, for the balance. Hi! the rat's out—you killed the boy to steal this letter from the
170   mail-bags—you stole this letter that the money should not arrive in time to save the Octoroon; had it done so, the lien on the estate would have ceased, and Zoe be free.

OMNES: Lynch him!—lynch him!—down with him!

SCUDDER: Silence in the court—stand back, let the gentle-
175   men of the jury retire, consult, and return their verdict.

RATTS: I'm responsible for the crittur—go on.

PETE: (*To* WAHNOTEE.) See, Inginn, look dar. (*Shows him plate.*) See dat innocent, look, dare's the murderer of poor Paul.

WAHNOTEE: Ugh! (*Examines plate.*)

180   PETE: Ya! as he? Closky tue Paul—kill de child with your tomahawk dar, 'twasn't you, no—ole Pete allus say so. Poor Inginn lub our little Paul.

(WAHNOTEE *rises and looks at* M'CLOSKY—*he is in his war paint and fully armed.*)

SCUDDER: What say ye, gentlemen? Is the prisoner guilty, or is he not guilty?

185   OMNES: Guilty!

SCUDDER: And what is to be his punishment?

OMNES: Death!

WAHNOTEE: (*Crosses to* M'CLOSKY.) Ugh!

SCUDDER: The Inginn, by thunder!

190   PETE: (*To* M'CLOSKY.) You's a dead man, mas'r; you've got to b'lieve dat.

M'CLOSKY: No! If I must die, give me up to the laws, but save me from the tomahawk of the savage; you are a white man, you'll not leave one of your own blood to be
195   butchered by the scalping knife of the redskin.

SCUDDER: Hold on now, Jacob, we've got to figure that out; let us look straight at the thing. Here we are on the confines of civilisation; it ain't our sile, I believe, rightly; Natur' has said that where the white man sets his foot the
200   red man and the black man shall up sticks and stan' round. Now, what do we pay for that possession? In cash? No—in kind—that is, in protection and forbearance, in gentleness, and in all them goods that show the critturs the difference between the Christian and the Savage. Now what
205   have you done to show 'em the distinction? for darn me if I can find out.

M'CLOSKY: For what I've done let me be tried.

SCUDDER: Oh, you have been fairly and honestly tried, and convicted: Providence has chosen your executioner—I
210   shan't interfere.

PETE: Oh! sar! hi, Mas'r Scudder, don't leave Mas'r 'Closky like date—don't, sar—tain't what a good Christian would do.

SCUDDER: D'ye hear that, Jacob?—this old nigger, the grandfather of the boy you murdered, speaks for you—don't that go through ye—d'ye feel it? Go on, Pete, you've   215
woke up the Christian here, and the old hoss responds.

WAHNOTEE: (*Placing his hand on* M'CLOSKY'S *head.*) Wahnotee!

SCUDDER: No, Inginn, we deal justice here, not revenge; tain't you he has injured, 'tis the white man, whose laws he has offended.   220

RATTS: Away with him! put him down the hatch till we rig his funeral.

M'CLOSKY: Fifty against one! Oh! if you were alone—if I had ye one by one in the swamp, I'd rip ye all.

PETE: (*Lighting him off,* R.) Dis way, Mas'r 'Closky, take care, sar.   225

(*Exit with* M'CLOSKY *and* JACKSON *to steamer.*)

LAFOUCHE: Off with him quick—here comes the ladies.

(*Enter* MRS CLAIBORNE, R 1 E.)

MRS CLAIBORNE: Shall we soon start, Captain?

RATTS: Yes, ma'am; we've only got a—Take my hand, ma'am, to steady you—a little account to square, and we're off.

MRS CLAIBORNE: A fog is rising.   230

RATTS: Swamp mist; soon clear off. (*Hands her to steamer.*)

MRS CLAIBORNE: Good night.

RATTS: Good night, ma'am—good night.

SCUDDER: Now to business.

(PETE *appears on deck.*)

PETE: Oh! law, sar. Dat debbel, 'Closky—he tore hisself from   235
de gentleman—knock me down—take away my light, and throwed it on de turpentine barrels—de ship's on fire!

(*All hurry off to ship—alarm bell rings—loud shouts; a hatch in the deck is opened—a glare of red—and* M'CLOSKY *emerges from the aperture; he is without his coat, and carries a bowie knife; he rushes down—*WAHNOTEE *alone is watching him from R. U. E.*).

M'CLOSKY: Ha, ha ha! I've given them something to remember how they treated Jacob M'Closky. Made my way from one end of the vessel to the other, and now the road to es-   240
cape is clear before me—and thus to secure it! (*He goes to R. C., and is met by* WAHNOTEE, *who silently confronts him.*)

WAHNOTEE: Paul.

M'CLOSKY: Devils!—you here!—stand clear!

WAHNOTEE: Paul.   245

M'CLOSKY: You won't—die, fool!

(*Thrusts at him—*WAHNOTEE, *with his tomahawk, strikes the knife out of his hand;* M'CLOSKY *starts back;* WAHNOTEE *throws off his blanket, and strikes at* M'CLOSKY *several times, who avoids him; at last he catches his arm, and struggles for the tomahawk, which falls; a violent struggle and fight takes place, ending with the triumph of* WAHNOTEE, *who drags* M'CLOSKY *along the ground, takes up the knife and stabs him repeatedly;* GEORGE *enters, bearing* ZOE *in his arms—all the* CHARACTERS *rush on—noise increasing—The steam vessel blows up—grand Tableau, and*

(*Curtain.*)

Susan Glaspell

Susan Glaspell (1882–1948) was born in Iowa, studied at Drake University in Des Moines and at the University of Chicago, and then briefly pursued a career as a journalist. With her husband, George Cram Cook, she founded the Provincetown Playhouse and wrote many of the plays it produced: *Suppressed Desires* (1914, written with Cook), a spoof of the vogue for psychoanalysis among New York's intellectual elite; *Trifles* (1916); *Close the Book* (1917); *A Woman's Honor* (1918); and *Tickless Time* (1918, again written with Cook). After the reorganization of the Provincetown in 1921, Glaspell wrote a series of full-length, often experimental, plays: *Inheritors* (1920), *The Verge* (1921), and *Alison's House* (1930). *Alison's House,* based loosely on the life of Emily Dickinson and her family, won Glaspell the Pulitzer Prize in 1930. Glaspell then retired from playwriting and largely from the theater as well, returning briefly to serve as the director of the Mid-West Play Bureau for the Federal Theater Project.

Trifles is an important play in the development of American realism. It poses a distinct contrast to Eugene O'Neill's early plays, with which it shared the Provincetown stage. O'Neill's realistic plays attempt to filter an abstract, metaphysical longing into the drab world of his down-and-out drifters and sailors. Glaspell's drama more directly examines the values and behavior of the society she brings to the stage. In *Trifles*—and in the short story "A Jury of Her Peers," which she adapted from the play the following year—Glaspell considers the relationship between truth, power, and gender. The play is a murder mystery. A local man, John Wright, has been found dead, and his wife, Minnie, is suspected of killing him. Called to investigate, County Attorney George Henderson, Sheriff Henry Peters, and neighbor Lewis Hale readily assume a masculine prerogative to discover the truth of John Wright's murder, telling their wives to remain in the kitchen out of the way. How-

TRIFLES

The Provincetown Players' 1917 production of Susan Glaspell's *Trifles*.

ever, the truth of the crime is in fact concealed *in* the kitchen, and only the women are able to discover it. Glaspell shows the audience that the "trifles" of the women's world are the signs of a reality wholly unreadable to the men, precisely because it is a world they regard as feminine, and therefore unimportant and uninteresting. *Trifles,* that is, works to subvert our notions of reality and truth by suggesting how such ideas are constructed within a specific social order—the masculine order of modern society.

TRIFLES

A PLAY IN ONE ACT

Susan Glaspell

CHARACTERS

COUNTY ATTORNEY, *George Henderson*
SHERIFF, *Henry Peters*
LEWIS HALE, *a neighboring farmer*
MRS. PETERS

MRS. HALE

THE SETTING: *The kitchen in the now abandoned farmhouse of John Wright*

SCENE: *The kitchen in the now abandoned farmhouse of John Wright, a gloomy kitchen, and left without having been put in order—unwashed pans under the sink, a loaf of bread outside the breadbox, a dish towel on the table—other signs of incompleted work. At the rear the outer door opens and the* SHERIFF *comes in followed by the* COUNTY ATTORNEY *and* HALE. *The* SHERIFF *and* HALE *are men in middle life, the* COUNTY ATTORNEY *is a young man; all are much bundled up and go at once to the stove. They are followed by the two women—the* SHERIFF's *wife first; she is a slight wiry woman, a thin nervous face.* MRS. HALE *is larger and would ordinarily be called more comfortable looking, but she is disturbed now and looks fearfully about as she enters. The women have come in slowly, and stand close together near the door.*

COUNTY ATTORNEY: (*Rubbing his hands.*) This feels good. Come up to the fire, ladies.

MRS. PETERS: (*After taking a step forward.*) I'm not—cold.

SHERIFF: (*Unbuttoning his overcoat and stepping away from the*
5   *stove as if to mark the beginning of official business.*) Now, Mr. Hale, before we move things about, you explain to Mr. Henderson just what you saw when you came here yesterday morning.

COUNTY ATTORNEY: By the way, has anything been moved?
10   Are things just as you left them yesterday?

SHERIFF: (*Looking about.*) It's just the same. When it dropped below zero last night I thought I'd better send Frank out this morning to make a fire for us—no use getting pneumonia with a big case on, but I told him not to touch any-
15   thing except the stove—and you know Frank.

COUNTY ATTORNEY: Somebody should have been left here yesterday.

SHERIFF: Oh—yesterday. When I had to send Frank to Morris Center for that man who went crazy—I want you to
20   know I had my hands full yesterday, I knew you could get back from Omaha by today and as long as I went over everything here myself—

COUNTY ATTORNEY: Well, Mr. Hale, tell just what happened when you came here yesterday morning.

25   HALE: Harry and I had started to town with a load of potatoes. We came along the road from my place and as I got here I said, "I'm going to see if I can't get John Wright to go in with me on a party telephone." I spoke to Wright about it once before and he put me off, saying folks talked too
30   much anyway, and all he asked was peace and quiet—I guess you know about how much he talked himself; but I thought maybe if I went to the house and talked about it before his wife, though I said to Harry that I didn't know as what his wife wanted made much difference to John—

COUNTY ATTORNEY: Let's talk about that later, Mr. Hale. I do   35
want to talk about that, but tell now just what happened when you got to the house.

HALE: I didn't hear or see anything; I knocked at the door, and still it was all quiet inside. I knew they must be up, it was past eight o'clock. So I knocked again, and I thought   40
I heard somebody say, "Come in." I wasn't sure, I'm not sure yet, but I opened the door—this door (*Indicating the door by which the two women are still standing.*) and there in that rocker—(*Pointing to it.*) sat Mrs. Wright.

(*They all look at the rocker.*)

COUNTY ATTORNEY: What—was she doing?   45

HALE: She was rockin' back and forth. She had her apron in her hand and was kind of—pleating it.

COUNTY ATTORNEY: And how did she—look?

HALE: Well, she looked queer.

COUNTY ATTORNEY: How do you mean—queer?   50

HALE: Well, as if she didn't know what she was going to do next. And kind of done up.

COUNTY ATTORNEY: How did she seem to feel about your coming?

HALE: Why, I don't think she minded—one way or other. She didn't pay much attention. I said, "How do, Mrs. Wright,   55
it's cold, ain't it?" And she said, "Is it?"—and went on kind of pleating at her apron. Well, I was surprised; she didn't ask me to come up to the stove, or to set down, but just sat there, not even looking at me, so I said, "I want to see John." And then she—laughed. I guess you would call it a   60
laugh. I thought of Harry and the team outside, so I said a little sharp: "Can't I see John?" "No," she says, kind o' dull like. "Ain't he home?" says I. "Yes," says she, "he's home." "Then why can't I see him?" I asked her, out of patience. "'Cause he's dead," says she. "*Dead?*" says I. She just   65
nodded her head, not getting a bit excited, but rockin' back and forth. "Why—where is he?" says I, not knowing what to say. She just pointed upstairs—like that (*Himself pointing to the room above.*) I got up, with the idea of going up there. I walked from there to here—then I says, "Why,   70
what did he die of?" "He died of a rope round his neck," says she, and just went on pleatin' at her apron. Well, I went out and called Harry. I thought I might—need help. We went upstairs and there he was lyin'—

COUNTY ATTORNEY: I think I'd rather have you go into that   75
upstairs, where you can point it all out. Just go on now with the rest of the story.

HALE: Well, my first thought was to get that rope off. It looked
. . . (*Stops, his face twitches.*) . . . but Harry, he went up to him,

80 and he said, "No, he's dead all right, and we'd better not touch anything." So we went back down stairs. She was still sitting that same way. "Has anybody been notified?" I asked. "No," says she, unconcerned. "Who did this, Mrs.
Wright?" said Harry. He said it businesslike—and she
85 stopped pleatin' of her apron. "I don't know," she says. "You don't *know?*" says Harry. "No," says she. "Weren't you sleepin' in the bed with him?" says Harry. "Yes," says she, "but I was on the inside." "Somebody slipped a rope round his neck and strangled him and you didn't wake up?" says
90 Harry. "I didn't wake up," she said after him. We must 'a looked as if we didn't see how that could be, for after a minute she said, "I sleep sound." Harry was going to ask her more questions but I said maybe we ought to let her tell her story first to the coroner, or the sheriff, so Harry went fast as
95 he could to Rivers' place, where there's a telephone.
COUNTY ATTORNEY: And what did Mrs. Wright do when she knew that you had gone for the coroner?
HALE: She moved from that chair to this one over here (*Pointing to a small chair in the corner.*) and just sat there with her
100 hands held together and looking down. I got a feeling that I ought to make some conversation, so I said I had come in to see if John wanted to put in a telephone, and at that she started to laugh, and then she stopped and looked at me—scared. (*The* COUNTY ATTORNEY, *who has had his*
105 *notebook out, makes a note.*) I dunno, maybe it wasn't scared. I wouldn't like to say it was. Soon Harry got back, and then Dr. Lloyd came, and you, Mr. Peters, and so I guess that's all I know that you don't.
COUNTY ATTORNEY: (*Looking around.*) I guess we'll go up-
110 stairs first—and then out to the barn and around there. (*To the* SHERIFF.) You're convinced that there was nothing important here—nothing that would point to any motive.
SHERIFF: Nothing here but kitchen things.

(*The* COUNTY ATTORNEY *after again looking around the kitchen, opens the door of a cupboard closet. He gets up on a chair and looks on a shelf. Pulls his hand away, sticky.*)

COUNTY ATTORNEY: Here's a nice mess.

(*The women draw nearer.*)

115 MRS. PETERS: (*To the other woman.*) Oh, her fruit; it did freeze. (*To the* COUNTY ATTORNEY.) She worried about that when it turned so cold. She said the fire'd go out and her jars would break.
SHERIFF: Well, can you beat the women! Held for murder and
120 worryin' about her preserves.
COUNTY ATTORNEY: I guess before we're through she may have something more serious than preserves to worry about.
HALE: Well, women are used to worrying over trifles.

(*The two women move a little closer together.*)

COUNTY ATTORNEY: (*With the gallantry of a young politician.*)
125 And yet, for all their worries, what would we do without the ladies? (*The women do not unbend. He goes to the sink, takes a dipperful of water from the pail and pouring it into a basin, washes his hands. Starts to wipe them on the roller towel, turns it for a cleaner place.*) Dirty towels! (*Kicks his foot against*

the pans under the sink.) Not much of a housekeeper, would 130 you say, ladies?
MRS. HALE: (*Stiffly.*) There's a great deal of work to be done on a farm.
COUNTY ATTORNEY: To be sure. And yet (*With a little bow to her.*) I know there are some Dickson county farmhouses 135 which do not have such roller towels.

(*He gives it a pull to expose its full length again.*)

MRS. HALE: Those towels get dirty awful quick. Men's hands aren't always as clean as they might be.
COUNTY ATTORNEY: Ah, loyal to your sex, I see. But you and Mrs. Wright were neighbors. I suppose you were friends, 140 too.
MRS. HALE: (*Shaking her head.*) I've not seen much of her of late years. I've not been in this house—it's more than a year.
COUNTY ATTORNEY: And why was that? You didn't like her?
MRS. HALE: I liked her all well enough. Farmers' wives have 145 their hands full, Mr. Henderson. And then—
COUNTY ATTORNEY: Yes—?
MRS. HALE: (*Looking about.*) It never seemed a very cheerful place.
COUNTY ATTORNEY: No—it's not cheerful. I shouldn't say she had the homemaking instinct. 150
MRS. HALE: Well, I don't know as Wright had, either.
COUNTY ATTORNEY: You mean that they didn't get on very well?
MRS. HALE: No, I don't mean anything. But I don't think a place'd be any cheerfuller for John Wright's being in it.
COUNTY ATTORNEY: I'd like to talk more of that a little later. 155 I want to get the lay of things upstairs now.

(*He goes to the left, where three steps lead to a stair door.*)

SHERIFF: I suppose anything Mrs. Peters does'll be all right. She was to take in some clothes for her, you know, and a few little things. We left in such a hurry yesterday.
COUNTY ATTORNEY: Yes, but I would like to see what you 160 take, Mrs. Peters, and keep an eye out for anything that might be of use to us.
MRS. PETERS: Yes, Mr. Henderson.

(*The women listen to the men's steps on the stairs, then look about the kitchen.*)

MRS. HALE: I'd hate to have men coming into my kitchen, snooping around and criticising. 165

(*She arranges the pans under sink which the* COUNTY ATTORNEY *had shoved out of place.*)

MRS. PETERS: Of course it's no more than their duty.
MRS. HALE: Duty's all right, but I guess that deputy sheriff that came out to make the fire might have got a little of this on. (*Gives the roller towel a pull.*) Wish I'd thought of that sooner. Seems mean to talk about her for not having things slicked 170 up when she had to come away in such a hurry.
MRS. PETERS: (*Who has gone to a small table in the left rear corner of the room, and lifted one end of a towel that covers a pan.*) She had bread set.

(*Stands still.*)

175 MRS. HALE: (*Eyes fixed on a loaf of bread beside the breadbox, which is on a low shelf at the other side of the room. Moves slowly toward it.*) She was going to put this in there. (*Picks up loaf, then abruptly drops it. In a manner of returning to familiar things.*) It's a shame about her fruit. I wonder if it's all gone. (*Gets*
180 *up on the chair and looks.*) I think there's some here that's all right, Mrs. Peters. Yes—here; (*Holding it toward the window.*) this is cherries, too. (*Looking again.*) I declare I believe that's the only one. (*Gets down, bottle in her hand. Goes to the sink and wipes it off on the outside.*) She'll feel awful bad after all
185 her hard work in the hot weather. I remember the afternoon I put up my cherries last summer.

(*She puts the bottle on the big kitchen table, center of the room. With a sigh, is about to sit down in the rocking-chair. Before she is seated realizes what chair it is; with a slow look at it, steps back. The chair which she has touched rocks back and forth.*)

MRS. PETERS: Well, I must get those things from the front room closet. (*She goes to the door at the right, but after looking into the other room, steps back.*) You coming with me,
190 Mrs. Hale? You could help me carry them.

(*They go in the other room; reappear,* MRS. PETERS *carrying a dress and skirt,* MRS. HALE *following with a pair of shoes.*)

MRS. PETERS: My, it's cold in there.

(*She puts the clothes on the big table, and hurries to the stove.*)

MRS. HALE: (*Examining the skirt.*) Wright was close. I think maybe that's why she kept so much to herself. She didn't even belong to the Ladies Aid. I suppose she felt she
195 couldn't do her part, and then you don't enjoy things when you feel shabby. She used to wear pretty clothes and be lively, when she was Minnie Foster, one of the town girls singing in the choir. But that—oh, that was thirty years ago. This all you was to take in?
200 MRS. PETERS: She said she wanted an apron. Funny thing to want, for there isn't much to get you dirty in jail, goodness knows. But I suppose just to make her feel more natural. She said they was in the top drawer in this cupboard. Yes, here. And then her little shawl that always hung be-
205 hind the door. (*Opens stair door and looks.*) Yes, here it is.

(*Quickly shuts door leading upstairs.*)

MRS. HALE: (*Abruptly moving toward her.*) Mrs. Peters?
MRS. PETERS: Yes, Mrs. Hale?
MRS. HALE: Do you think she did it?
MRS. PETERS: (*In a frightened voice.*) Oh, I don't know.
210 MRS. HALE: Well, I don't think she did. Asking for an apron and her little shawl. Worrying about her fruit.
MRS. PETERS: (*Starts to speak, glances up, where footsteps are heard in the room above. In a low voice.*) Mr. Peters says it looks bad for her. Mr. Henderson is awful sarcastic in a speech and
215 he'll make fun of her sayin' she didn't wake up.
MRS. HALE: Well, I guess John Wright didn't wake when they was slipping that rope under his neck.
MRS. PETERS: No, it's strange. It must have been done awful crafty and still. They say it was such a—funny way to kill
220 a man, rigging it all up like that.

MRS. HALE: That's just what Mr. Hale said. There was a gun in the house. He says that's what he can't understand.
MRS. PETERS: Mr. Henderson said coming out that what was needed for the case was a motive; something to show anger, or—sudden feeling. 225
MRS. HALE: (*Who is standing by the table.*) Well, I don't see any signs of anger around here. (*She puts her hand on the dish towel which lies on the table, stands looking down at table, one half of which is clean, the other half messy.*) It's wiped to here. (*Makes a move as if to finish work, then turns and looks at loaf* 230 *of bread outside the breadbox. Drops towel. In that voice of coming back to familiar things.*) Wonder how they are finding things upstairs. I hope she had it a little more red-up up there. You know, it seems kind of *sneaking.* Locking her up in town and then coming out here and trying to get her 235 own house to turn against her!
MRS. PETERS: But Mrs. Hale, the law is the law.
MRS. HALE: I s'pose 'tis. (*Unbuttoning her coat.*) Better loosen up your things, Mrs. Peters. You won't feel them when you go out. 240

(MRS. PETERS *takes off her fur tippet, goes to hang it on hook at back of room, stands looking at the under part of the small corner table.*)

MRS. PETERS: She was piecing a quilt.

(*She brings the large sewing basket and they look at the bright pieces.*)

MRS. HALE: It's log cabin pattern. Pretty, isn't it? I wonder if she was goin' to quilt it or just knot it?

(*Footsteps have been heard coming down the stairs. The* SHERIFF *enters followed by* HALE *and the* COUNTY ATTORNEY.)

SHERIFF: They wonder if she was going to quilt it or just knot it!

(*The men laugh; the women look abashed.*)

COUNTY ATTORNEY: (*Rubbing his hands over the stove.*) Frank's 245 fire didn't do much up there, did it? Well, let's go out to the barn and get that cleared up.

(*The men go outside.*)

MRS. HALE: (*Resentfully.*) I don't know as there's anything so strange, our takin' up our time with little things while we're waiting for them to get the evidence. (*She sits down* 250 *at the big table smoothing out a block with decision.*) I don't see as it's anything to laugh about.
MRS. PETERS: (*Apologetically.*) Of course they've got awful important things on their minds.

(*Pulls up a chair and joins* MRS. HALE *at the table.*)

MRS. HALE: (*Examining another block.*) Mrs. Peters, look at this 255 one. Here, this is the one she was working on, and look at that sewing! All the rest of it has been so nice and even. And look at this! It's all over the place! Why, it looks as if she didn't know what she was about!

(*After she has said this they look at each other, then start to glance back at the door. After an instant* MRS. HALE *has pulled at a knot and ripped the sewing.*)

260 MRS. PETERS: Oh, what are you doing, Mrs. Hale?
MRS. HALE: (*Mildly.*) Just pulling out a stitch or two that's not sewed very good. (*Threading a needle.*) Bad sewing always made me fidgety.
MRS. PETERS: (*Nervously.*) I don't think we ought to touch things.
265 MRS. HALE: I'll just finish up this end. (*Suddenly stopping and leaning forward.*) Mrs. Peters?
MRS. PETERS: Yes, Mrs. Hale?
MRS. HALE: What do you suppose she was so nervous about?
MRS. PETERS: Oh—I don't know. I don't know as she was
270 nervous. I sometimes sew awful queer when I'm just tired. (MRS. HALE *starts to say something, looks at* MRS. PETERS, *then goes on sewing.*) Well, I must get these things wrapped up. They may be through sooner than we think. (*Putting apron and other things together.*) I wonder where I can find a piece
275 of paper, and string.
MRS. HALE: In that cupboard, maybe.
MRS. PETERS: (*Looking in cupboard.*) Why, here's a birdcage. (*Holds it up.*) Did she have a bird, Mrs. Hale?
MRS. HALE: Why, I don't know whether she did or not—I've
280 not been here for so long. There was a man around last year selling canaries cheap, but I don't know as she took one; maybe she did. She used to sing real pretty herself.
MRS. PETERS: (*Glancing around.*) Seems funny to think of a bird here. But she must have had one, or why would she
285 have a cage? I wonder what happened to it.
MRS. HALE: I s'pose maybe the cat got it.
MRS. PETERS: No, she didn't have a cat. She's got that feeling some people have about cats—being afraid of them. My cat got in her room and she was real upset and asked me to take it out.
290 MRS. HALE: My sister Bessie was like that. Queer, ain't it?
MRS. PETERS: (*Examining the cage.*) Why, look at this door. It's broke. One hinge is pulled apart.
MRS. HALE: (*Looking too.*) Looks as if someone must have been rough with it.
295 MRS. PETERS: Why, yes.

(*She brings the cage forward and puts it on the table.*)

MRS. HALE: I wish if they're going to find any evidence they'd be about it. I don't like this place.
MRS. PETERS: But I'm awful glad you came with me, Mrs. Hale. It would be lonesome for me sitting here alone.
300 MRS. HALE: It would, wouldn't it? (*Dropping her sewing.*) But I tell you what I do wish, Mrs. Peters. I wish I had come over sometimes when *she* was here. I—(*Looking around the room.*)— wish I had.
MRS. PETERS: But of course you were awful busy, Mrs.
305 Hale— your house and your children.
MRS. HALE: I could've come. I stayed away because it weren't cheerful—and that's why I ought to have come. I—I've never liked this place. Maybe because it's down in a hollow and you don't see the road. I dunno what it is, but it's
310 a lonesome place and always was. I wish I had come over to see Minnie Foster sometimes. I can see now—

(*Shakes her head.*)

MRS. PETERS: Well you mustn't reproach yourself, Mrs. Hale. Somehow we just don't see how it is with other folks until—something comes up.

315 MRS. HALE: Not having children makes less work—but it makes a quiet house, and Wright out to work all day, and no company when he did come in. Did you know John Wright, Mrs. Peters?
MRS. PETERS: Not to know him; I've seen him in town. They
320 say he was a good man.
MRS. HALE: Yes—good; he didn't drink, and kept his word as well as most, I guess, and paid his debts. But he was a hard man, Mrs. Peters. Just to pass the time of day with him— (*Shivers.*) Like a raw wind that gets to the bone. (*Pauses, her eye falling on the cage.*) I should think she would 'a wanted
325 a bird. But what do you suppose went with it?
MRS. PETERS: I don't know, unless it got sick and died.

(*She reaches over and swings the broken door, swings it again. Both women watch it.*)

MRS. HALE: You weren't raised round here, were you? (MRS. PETERS *shakes her head.*) You didn't know—her?
330 MRS. PETERS: Not till they brought her yesterday.
MRS. HALE: She—come to think of it, she was kind of like a bird herself—real sweet and pretty, but kind of timid and— fluttery. How—she—did—change. (*Silence; then as if struck by a happy thought and relieved to get back to every day
things.*) Tell you what, Mrs. Peters, why don't you take the
335 quilt in with you? It might take up her mind.
MRS. PETERS: Why, I think that's a real nice idea, Mrs. Hale. There couldn't possibly be any objection to it, could there? Now, just what would I take? I wonder if her patches are in here—and her things.
340

(*They look in the sewing basket.*)

MRS. HALE: Here's some red. I expect this has got sewing things in it. (*Brings out a fancy box.*) What a pretty box. Looks like something somebody would give you. Maybe her scissors are in here. (*Opens box. Suddenly puts her hand to her nose.*) Why—(MRS. PETERS *bends nearer, then turns her face
345 away.*) There's something wrapped up in this piece of silk.
MRS. PETERS: Why, this isn't her scissors.
MRS. HALE: (*Lifting the silk.*) Oh, Mrs. Peters—its—

(MRS. PETERS *bends closer.*)

MRS. PETERS: It's the bird.
350 MRS. HALE: (*Jumping up.*) But, Mrs. Peters—look at it! Its neck! Look at its neck! It's all—other side *to.*
MRS. PETERS: Somebody—wrung—its—neck.

(*Their eyes meet. A look of growing comprehension, of horror. Steps are heard outside.* MRS. HALE *slips box under quilt pieces, and sinks into her chair. Enter* SHERIFF *and* COUNTY ATTORNEY. MRS. PETERS *rises.*)

COUNTY ATTORNEY: (*As one turning from serious things to little pleasantries.*) Well, ladies, have you decided whether she was going to quilt it or knot it?
355
MRS. PETERS: We think she was going to—knot it.
COUNTY ATTORNEY: Well, that's interesting, I'm sure. (*Seeing the birdcage.*) Has the bird flown?
MRS. HALE: (*Putting more quilt pieces over the box.*) We think the—cat got it.
360

COUNTY ATTORNEY: (*Preoccupied.*) Is there a cat?

(MRS. HALE *glances in a quick covert way at* MRS. PETERS.)

MRS. PETERS: Well, not now. They're superstitious, you know. They leave.

COUNTY ATTORNEY: (*To* SHERIFF PETERS, *continuing an interrupted conversation.*) No sign at all of anyone having come from the outside. Their own rope. Now let's go up again and go over it piece by piece. (*They start upstairs.*) It would have to have been someone who knew just the—

365

(MRS. PETERS *sits down. The two women sit there not looking at one another, but as if peering into something and at the same time holding back. When they talk now it is in the manner of feeling their way over strange ground, as if afraid of what they are saying, but as if they cannot help saying it.*)

MRS. HALE: She liked the bird. She was going to bury it in that pretty box.

370

MRS. PETERS: (*In a whisper.*) When I was a girl—my kitten—there was a boy took a hatchet, and before my eyes—and before I could get there—(*Covers her face an instant.*) If they hadn't held me back I would have—(*Catches herself, looks upstairs where steps are heard, falters weakly.*)—hurt him.

375

MRS. HALE: (*With a slow look around her.*) I wonder how it would seem never to have had any children around. (*Pause.*) No, Wright wouldn't like the bird—a thing that sang. She used to sing. He killed that, too.

MRS. PETERS: (*Moving uneasily.*) We don't know who killed the bird.

380

MRS. HALE: I knew John Wright.

MRS. PETERS: It was an awful thing was done in this house that night, Mrs. Hale. Killing a man while he slept, slipping a rope around his neck that choked the life out of him.

385

MRS. HALE: His neck. Choked the life out of him.

(*Her hand goes out and rests on the birdcage.*)

MRS. PETERS: (*With rising voice.*) We don't know who killed him. We don't know.

MRS. HALE: (*Her own feeling not interrupted.*) If there'd been years and years of nothing, then a bird to sing to you, it would be awful—still, after the bird was still.

390

MRS. PETERS: (*Something within her speaking.*) I know what stillness is. When we homesteaded in Dakota, and my first baby died—after he was two years old, and me with no other then—

395

MRS. HALE: (*Moving.*) How soon do you suppose they'll be through, looking for the evidence?

MRS. PETERS: I know what stillness is. (*Pulling herself back.*) The law has got to punish crime, Mrs. Hale.

MRS. HALE: (*Not as if answering that.*) I wish you'd seen Minnie Foster when she wore a white dress with blue ribbons and stood up there in the choir and sang. (*A look around the room.*) Oh, I wish I'd come over here once in a while! That was a crime! That was a crime! Who's going to punish that?

400

MRS. PETERS: (*Looking upstairs.*) We mustn't—take on.

405

MRS. HALE: I might have known she needed help! I know how things can be—for women. I tell you, it's queer, Mrs. Peters. We live close together and we live far apart. We all go through the same things—it's all just a different kind of the same thing. (*Brushes her eyes; noticing the bottle of fruit, reaches out for it.*) If I was you I wouldn't tell her her fruit was gone. Tell her it ain't. Tell her it's all right. Take this in to her. She—she may never know whether it was broke or not.

410

MRS. PETERS: (*Takes the bottle, looks about for something to wrap it in, takes petticoat from the clothes brought from the other room, very nervously begins winding this around the bottle. In a false voice.*) My, it's a good thing the men couldn't hear us. Wouldn't they just laugh! Getting all stirred up over a little thing like a—dead canary. As if that could have anything to do with—with—wouldn't they *laugh!*

415

420

(*The men are heard coming down stairs.*)

MRS. HALE: (*Under her breath.*) Maybe they would—maybe they wouldn't.

COUNTY ATTORNEY: No, Peters, it's all perfectly clear except a reason for doing it. But you know juries when it comes to women. If there was some definite thing. Something to show—something to make a story about—a thing that would connect up with this strange way of doing it—

425

(*The women's eyes meet for an instant. Enter* HALE *from outer door.*)

HALE: Well, I've got the team around. Pretty cold out there.

COUNTY ATTORNEY: I'm going to stay here a while by myself. (*To the* SHERIFF.) You can send Frank out for me, can't you? I want to go over everything. I'm not satisfied that we can't do better.

430

SHERIFF: Do you want to see what Mrs. Peters is going to take in?

(*The* COUNTY ATTORNEY *goes to the table, picks up the apron, laughs.*)

COUNTY ATTORNEY: Oh, I guess they're not very dangerous things the ladies have picked out. (*Moves a few things about, disturbing the quilt pieces which cover the box. Steps back.*) No, Mrs. Peters doesn't need supervising. For that matter, a sheriff's wife is married to the law. Ever think of it that way, Mrs. Peters?

435

MRS. PETERS: Not—just that way.

SHERIFF: (*Chuckling.*) Married to the law. (*Moves toward the other room.*) I just want you to come in here a minute, George. We ought to take a look at these windows.

440

COUNTY ATTORNEY: (*Scoffingly.*) Oh, windows!

SHERIFF: We'll be right out, Mr. Hale.

(HALE *goes outside. The* SHERIFF *follows the* COUNTY ATTORNEY *into the other room. Then* MRS. HALE *rises, hands tight together, looking intensely at* MRS. PETERS, *whose eyes make a slow turn, finally meeting* MRS. HALE's. *A moment* MRS. HALE *holds her, then her own eyes point the way to where the box is concealed. Suddenly* MRS. PETERS *throws back quilt pieces and tries to put the box in the bag she is wearing. It is too big. She opens box, starts to take bird out, cannot touch it, goes to pieces, stands there helpless. Sound of a knob turning in the other room.* MRS. HALE *snatches the box and puts it in the pocket of her big coat. Enter* COUNTY ATTORNEY *and* SHERIFF.)

COUNTY ATTORNEY: (*Facetiously.*) Well, Henry, at least we found out that she was not going to quilt it. She was going to—what is it you call it, ladies?

445

MRS. HALE: (*Her hand against her pocket.*) We call it—knot it, Mr. Henderson.

Angelina Weld Grimké

Angelina Weld Grimké (1880–1958) was an important African American poet, essayist, and writer of short fiction in the early decades of the twentieth century. Her only play, *Rachel* (1916), is one of the earliest American plays to address the subject of lynching and the more general oppression of African Americans. Grimké was born and largely raised in the Boston area. Her father, Archibald Grimké, was the illegitimate, black son of a white South Carolina slaveholder, Henry Grimké, and his slave Nancy Weston. Her mother, who was white, left the Grimké family soon after Angelina was born, and Grimké was raised mainly by her father.

Educated at the Fairmount Grammar School in Hyde Park, Massachusetts, Carleton Academy in Minnesota, and at the Cushing Academy and the Girls' Latin School in Massachusetts, Grimké took her degree in physical education from the Boston Normal School of Gymnastics in 1902. She pursued a teaching career, first at the Armstrong Manual Training School in Washington, D.C., and then at the M Street High School, later renamed Dunbar High School, before retiring and moving to New York City in 1926.

Grimké's writing dates mainly from the 1910s and 1920s. Although *Rachel* is the only work she published in book form, her poetry, essays, and stories were printed frequently in magazines, journals, and anthologies during her lifetime. Grimké was a lesbian and appears to have recognized her sexual orientation early in life; many of her love poems are openly addressed to women. Her fiction and nonfiction prose is more concerned with the themes of racism in the United States, and stories like "The Closing Door" and "Blackness"—later revised as "Goldie"—directly condemn the lynchings of African Americans common in the United States in the first third of the twentieth century.

Like many African American women writers—Zora Neale Hurston is perhaps the best example—Grimké was well known in her lifetime, but her works were not readily assimilated to the canon of American literature. *The Selected Works of Angelina Weld Grimké* was published in 1991 as a part of the Schomburg Library of Nineteenth-Century Black Women Writers series. This excellent collection, edited by Carolivia Herron, is the first collection to bring Grimké's important body of writing together for modern readers.

RACHEL

Rachel (1916) is an important play in the canon of American drama, in part because it links a critique of overt racism—the lynching that killed Rachel's father and half-brother, the taunts of "nigger" that follow her brother Tom and her adopted son Jimmy—with an account of the more subtle racism that oppresses the Loving family in other ways.

From the outset, Grimké establishes the Loving family as honest, hard-working, and upwardly mobile. Much as in Ibsen's plays, Grimké layers the class and the aspirations of the Lovings into their domestic environment. When the curtain rises, the audience sees a spare, unprepossessing room decorated with the ornaments of middle-class respectability: prints of famous artwork (Millais, Burne-Jones, Raphael), a full and well-used bookcase, a piano. Although Mrs. Loving supports them on her meager wages as a seamstress, her children seem bursting with vitality and potential. Yet in the course of act 1, Mrs. Loving reveals the cause of her distracted behavior: ten years earlier, on this date, her husband and their stepbrother had been seized and lynched outside their home in the South. Grimké makes it plain that such lynchings are both commonplace and supported by the majority of whites. The men who lynched Loving and seven-year-old George were not aberrant criminals; they were "all church members in good standing—the best people" of the community.

The violence of the South is, in *Rachel,* only a more explicit version of the institutionalized racism that pervades American culture as a whole, North and South. Even in act 1, Tom reports being called a "nigger" by his white rival for quarterback, and that a white girl—once apparently his girl friend—has begun to ignore him, now that she has become friends with two girls recently moved from the South. Finally, John Strong, a polite, college-educated family friend, has been able to find work only as a waiter—"He had the tremendous handicap of being colored," as Mrs. Loving reminds her children.

"We sing a song at school, I believe," Rachel remarks, "about 'The land of the free and the home of the brave.' What an amusing nation it is." But the "amusing nation" is clearly a nation of real freedom only for its white citizens. Its black citizens can by lynched with impunity in this "white Christian nation," and men like Tom and John Strong face equally certain discrimination; despite talent, effort, and education, they are able to find only relatively menial employment. As Tom says, "In the South, they make it as impossible as they can for us to get an education. . . . In the North, they make a pretence of liberality: they give us the ballot and a good education, and then—snuff us out." And as the play shows, the schools themselves are where the lessons of racism are both taught and learned.

Writing the play, Grimké had toyed with calling it *The Pervert, The Daughter,* and *Blessed Are the Barren* before deciding on *Rachel.* These draft titles point to the most difficult dimension of Grimké's play for modern readers: that Rachel's act of resistance in the play is to refuse to bear children, to refuse to bring more black children into a world in which they will be systematically oppressed. As a strategy of resistance, Rachel's act implies a kind of autogenocide oddly complicit with the racism she wants to oppose. Yet as Grimké suggests in her article on the play (see "Reading the Material Theater," p. 962), Rachel's refusal is meant to signify the extent to which white, racist culture is itself unnatural. By making Rachel refuse the life she seems so naturally to desire—the life of wife and mother—Grimké hopes to make "the white women of this country . . . see, feel, understand just what effect their prejudice and the prejudice of their fathers, brothers, husbands, sons were having on the sons of colored mothers everywhere."

Grimké, that is, attempts to forge a "natural" union among women—black and white—to oppose the unnatural, racist culture of the United States. Throughout *Rachel,* Grimké urgently resists the dramatic stereotypes applied by white authors to African American characters onstage. While Grimké deftly shows notions of "race" to be socially constructed, though, her assumptions about gender remain more deeply rooted in her sense of an "essential" nature distinguishing men from women. Grimké uses Rachel in something like the way Elizabeth Robins uses Vida Levering in her play *Votes for Women!:* she brings Rachel's "natural" feminine experience into conflict with the dominant (white, male) social order, in order to expose the unnatural ways in which that order deforms and destroys women. It will remain for later playwrights—Caryl Churchill in *Cloud Nine* and Anna Deavere Smith in *Fires in the Mirror,* for example—to suggest that notions of both "race" and "gender" are ideologically conditioned ways of representing a particular social order, and a particular structure of social power.

RACHEL

A PLAY IN THREE ACTS

Angelina Weld Grimké

CHARACTERS

MRS. MARY LOVING, *a widow*
RACHEL LOVING, *her daughter*
THOMAS LOVING, *her son*
JIMMY MASON, *a small boy*
JOHN STRONG, *a friend of the family*
MRS LANE, *a caller*
ETHEL LANE, *her daughter*
MARY
NANCY
EDITH
JENNY   } *little friends of Rachel*
LOUISE
MARTHA

TIME: *The first decade of the Twentieth Century.*

Act I.   October 16th.
Act II.   October 16th, four years later.
Act III. One week later.

PLACE: *A northern city. The living room in the small apartment of Mrs. Loving.*

All of the characters are colored.

ACT ONE

The scene is a room scrupulously neat and clean and plainly furnished. The walls are painted green, the woodwork, white. In the rear at the left an open doorway leads into a hall. Its bare, green wall and white baseboard are all that can be seen of it. It leads into the other rooms of the flat. In the centre of the rear wall of the room is a window. It is shut. The white sash curtains are pushed to right and left as far as they will go. The green shade is rolled up to the top. Through the window can be seen the red bricks of a house wall, and the tops of a couple of trees moving now and then in the wind. Within the window, and just below the sill, is a shelf upon which are a few potted plants. Between the window and the door is a bookcase full of books and above it, hanging on the wall, a simply framed, inexpensive copy of Millet's "The Reapers." There is a run extending from the right center to just below the right upper entrance. It is the vestibule of the flat. Its open doorway faces the left wall. In the right wall near the front is another window. Here the sash curtains are drawn together and the green shade is partly lowered. The window is up from the bottom. Through it street noises can be heard. In front of this window is an open, threaded sewing-machine. Some frail, white fabric is lying upon it. There is a chair in front of the machine and at the machine's left a small table covered with a green cloth. In the rear of the left wall and directly opposite to the entrance to the flat is the doorway leading into the kitchenette, dishes on shelves can be seen behind glass doors.

In the center of the left wall is a fireplace with a grate in it for coals; over this is a wooden mantel painted white. In the center is a small clock. A pair of vases, green and white in coloring, one at each end, complete the ornaments. Over the mantel is a narrow mirror; and over this, hanging on the wall, Burne-Jones' "Golden Stairs," simply framed. Against the front end of the left wall is an upright piano with a stool in front of it. On top is music neatly piled. Hanging over the piano is Raphael's "Sistine Madonna." In the center of the floor is a green rug, and in the center of this, a rectangular dining-room table, the long side facing front. It is covered with a green table-cloth. Three dining-room chairs are at the table, one at either end and one at the rear facing front. Above the table is a chandelier with four gas jets enclosed by glass globes. At the right front center is a rather shabby arm-chair upholstered in green.

Left and right from the spectator's point of view.

Before the sewing-machine, MRS. LOVING is seated. She looks worried. She is sewing swiftly and deftly by hand upon a waist in her lap. It is a white, beautiful thing and she sews upon it delicately. It is about half-past four in the afternoon; and the light is failing. MRS. LOVING pauses in her sewing, rises and lets the window-shade near her go up to the top. She pushes the sash-curtains to either side, the corner of a red brick house wall being thus brought into view. She shivers slightly, then pushes the window down at the bottom and lowers it a trifle from the top. The street noises become less distinct. She takes off her thimble, rubs her hands gently, puts the thimble on again, and looks at the clock on the mantel. She then reseats herself, with her chair as close to the window as possible and begins to sew. Presently a key is heard, and the door opens and shuts noisily. RACHEL comes in from the vestibule. In her left arm she carries four or five books strapped together; under her right, a roll of music. Her hat is twisted over her left ear and her hair is falling in tendrils about her face. She brings into the room with her the spirit of abounding life, health, joy, youth. MRS. LOVING pauses, needle in hand, as soon as she hears the turning key and the banging door. There is a smile on her face. For a second, mother and daughter smile at each other. Then RACHEL throws her books upon the dining-room table, places the music there also, but with care, and rushing to her mother, gives her a bear hug and a kiss.

RACHEL: Ma dear! dear, old Ma dear!
MRS. LOVING: Look out for the needle, Rachel! The waist! Oh, Rachel!
RACHEL: (*On her knees and shaking her finger directly under her mother's nose.*) You old, old fraud! You know you adore being hugged. I've a good mind . . .   5
MRS. LOVING: Now, Rachel, please! Besides, I know your tricks. You think you can make me forget you are late. What time is it?
RACHEL: (*Looking at the clock and expressing surprise.*) Jiminy   10 Xmas! (*Whistles.*) Why, it's five o'clock!

MRS. LOVING: (*Severely.*) Well!

RACHEL: (*Plaintively.*) Now, Ma dear, you're going to be horrid and cross.

15 MRS. LOVING: (*Laughing.*) Really, Rachel, that expression is not particularly affecting, when your hat is over your ear, and you look, with your hair over your eyes, exactly like some one's pet poodle. I wonder if you are ever going to grow up and be ladylike.

20 RACHEL: Oh! Ma dear, I hope not, not for the longest time, two long, long years at least. I just want to be silly and irresponsible, and have you to love and torment, and, of course, Tom, too.

MRS. LOVING: (*Smiling down at* RACHEL.) You'll not make me
25 forget, young lady. Why are you late, Rachel?

RACHEL: Well, Ma dear, I'm your pet poodle, and my hat is over my ear, and I'm late, for the loveliest reason.

MRS. LOVING: Don't be silly, Rachel.

RACHEL: That may sound silly, but it isn't. And please don't
30 "Rachel" me so much. It was honestly one whole hour ago when I opened the front door down stairs. I know it was, because I heard the postman telling some one it was four o'clock. Well, I climbed the first flight, and was just starting up the second, when a little shrill voice said,
35 "'Lo!" I raised my eyes, and there, half-way up the stairs, sitting in the middle of a step, was just the dearest, cutest, darlingest little brown baby boy you ever saw. "'Lo! yourself," I said. "What are you doing, and who are you anyway?" "I'm Jimmy; and I'm widing to New York on the
40 choo-choo tars." As he looked entirely too young to be going such a distance by himself, I asked him if I might go too. For a minute or two he considered the question and me very seriously, and then he said, "'Es," and made room for me on the step beside him. We've been everywhere:
45 New York, Chicago, Boston, London, Paris and Oshkosh. I wish you could have heard him say that last place. I suggested going there just to hear him. Now, Ma dear, is it any wonder I am late? See all the places we have been in just one "teeny, weeny" hour? We would have been trav-
50 eling yet, but his horrid, little mother came out and called him in. They're in the flat below, the new people. But before he went, Ma dear, he said the "cunningest" thing. He said, "Will you tum out an' p'ay wif me aden in two minutes?" I nearly hugged him to death, and it's a wonder my
55 hat is on my head at all. Hats are such unimportant nuisances anyway!

MRS. LOVING: Unimportant nuisances! What ridiculous language you do use, Rachel! Well, I'm no prophet, but I see very distinctly what is going to happen. This little brown
60 baby will be living here night and day. You're not happy unless some child is trailing along in your rear.

RACHEL: (*Mischievously.*) Now, Ma dear, whose a hypocrite? What? I suppose you don't like children! I can tell you one thing, though, it won't be my fault if he isn't here
65 night and day. Oh, I wish he were all mine, every bit of him! Ma dear, do you suppose that "she woman" he calls mother would let him come up here until it is time for him to go to bed? I'm going down there this minute. (*Rises impetuously.*)

70 MRS. LOVING: Rachel, for Heaven's sake! No! I am entirely too busy and tired today without being bothered with a child romping around in here.

RACHEL: (*Reluctantly and a trifle petulantly.*) Very well, then. (*For several moments she watches her mother, who has begun to sew again. The displeasure vanishes from her face.*) Ma dear! 75

MRS. LOVING: Well.

RACHEL: Is there anything wrong today?

MRS. LOVING: I'm just tired, chickabiddy, that's all.

RACHEL: (*Moves over to the table. Mechanically takes off her hat and coat and carries them out into the entryway of the flat. She* 80 *returns and goes to the looking glass over the fireplace and tucks in the tendrils of her hair in rather a preoccupied manner. The electric doorbell rings. She returns to the speaking tube in the vestibule. Her voice is heard answering.*) Yes!—Yes!—No, I'm not Mrs. Loving. She's here, yes!—What? Oh! come right 85 up! (*Appearing in the doorway.*) Ma dear, it's some man, who is coming for Mrs. Strong's waist.

MRS. LOVING: (*Pausing and looking at Rachel.*) It is probably her son. She said she would send for it this afternoon. (RACHEL *disappears. A door is heard opening and closing. There* 90 *is the sound of a man's voice.* RACHEL *ushers in* MR JOHN STRONG.)

STRONG: (*Bowing pleasantly to* MRS. LOVING.) Mrs Loving? (MRS. LOVING *bows, puts down her sewing, rises and goes toward* STRONG..) My name is Strong. My mother asked me to 95 come by and get her waist this afternoon. She hoped it would be finished.

MRS. LOVING: Yes, Mr. Strong, it is all ready. If you'll sit down a minute, I'll wrap it up for you. (*She goes into hallway leading to other rooms in flat.*) 100

RACHEL: (*Manifestly ill at ease at being left alone with a stranger; attempting, however, to be the polite hostess.*) Do sit down, Mr. Strong. (*They both sit.*)

RACHEL: (*Nervously after a pause.*) It's a very pleasant day, isn't it, Mr. Strong? 105

STRONG: Yes, very. (*He leans back composedly, his hat on his knee, the faintest expression of amusement in his eyes.*)

RACHEL: (*After a pause.*) It's quite a climb up to our flat, don't you think?

STRONG: Why, no! It didn't strike me so. I'm not old enough 110 yet to mind stairs.

RACHEL: (*Nervously.*) Oh! I didn't mean that you are old! Anyone can see you are quite young, that is, of course, not too young, but,—(*Strong laughs quietly.*) There! I don't blame you for laughing. I'm always clumsy just like that. 115

MRS. LOVING: (*Calling from the other room.*) Rachel, bring me a needle and the sixty cotton, please.

RACHEL: All right. Ma dear! (*Rummages for the cotton in the machine drawer, and upsets several spools upon the floor. To* STRONG.) You see! I can't even get a spool of cotton with- 120 out spilling things all over the floor. (STRONG *smiles,* RACHEL *picks up the spools and finally gets the cotton and needle.*) Excuse me! (*Goes out door leading to other rooms.* STRONG *left to himself, looks around casually. The "Golden Stairs" interests him and the "Sistine Madonna.".*) 125

RACHEL: (*Reenters, evidently continuing her function of hostess.*) We were talking about the climb to our flat, weren't we? You see, when you're poor, you have to live in a top flat. There is always a compensation, though: we have bully— I mean nice air, better light, a lovely view, and nobody 130 "thud-thudding" up and down over our heads night and day. The people below have our "thud-thudding," and it must be something *awful*, especially when Tom and I play

"Ivanhoe" and have a tournament up here. We're entirely
135 too old, but we still play. Ma dear rather dreads the climb
up three flights, so Tom and I do all the errands. We don't
mind climbing the stairs, particularly when we go up two
or three at a time,—that is—Tom still does. I can't. Ma
dear stopped me. (*Sighs.*) I've got to grow up it seems.
140 STRONG: (*Evidently amused.*) It is rather hard being a girl,
isn't it?
RACHEL: Oh, no! It's not hard at all. That's the trouble; they
won't let me be a girl. I'd love to be.
MRS. LOVING: (*Reentering with parcel. She smiles.*) My chatter-
145 box, I see, is entertaining you, Mr. Strong. I'm sorry to
have kept you waiting, but I forgot, I found, to sew the
ruching in the neck. I hope everything is satisfactory. If it
isn't, I'll be glad to make any changes.
STRONG: (*Who has risen upon her entrance.*) Thank you, Mrs.
150 Loving, I'm sure everything is all right. (*He takes the package and bows to her and* RACHEL. *He moves towards the
vestibule.* MRS. LOVING *following him. She passes through the
doorway first. Before leaving,* STRONG *turns for a second and
looks back quietly at* RACHEL. *He goes out too.* RACHEL *returns
155 to the mirror, looks at her face for a second, and then begins to
touch and pat her hair lightly and delicately here and there.* MRS.
LOVING *returns.*)
RACHEL: (*Still at the glass.*) He *was* rather nice, wasn't he, Ma
dear?—for a man? (*Laughs.*) I guess my reason's a vain
160 one,—he let me do all the talking. (*Pauses.*) Strong? Strong?
Ma dear, is his mother the little woman with the sad, black
eyes?
MRS. LOVING: (*Resuming her sewing; sitting before the machine.*)
Yes. I was rather curious, I confess, to see this son of hers.
165 The whole time I'm fitting her she talks of nothing else.
She worships him. (*Pauses.*) It's rather a sad case, I believe.
She is a widow. Her husband was a doctor and left her a
little money. She came up from the South to educate this
boy. Both of them worked hard and the boy got through
170 college. Three months he hunted for work that a college
man might expect to get. You see he had the tremendous
handicap of being colored. As the two of them had to
live, one day, without her knowing it, he hired himself out
as a waiter. He has been one now for two years. He is ev-
175 idently goodness itself to his mother.
RACHEL: (*Slowly and thoughtfully.*) Just because he is *colored!*
(*Pauses.*) We sing a song at school. I believe, about "The
land of the free and the home of the brave." What an
amusing nation it is.
180 MRS. LOVING: (*Watching* RACHEL *anxiously.*) Come, Rachel,
you haven't time for "amusing nations." Remember, you
haven't practised any this afternoon. And put your books
away; don't leave them on the table. You didn't practise
any this morning either, did you?
185 RACHEL: No, Ma dear.—didn't wake up in time. (*Goes to the
table and in an abstracted manner puts books on the bookcase: returns to the table; picks up the roll of sheet music she has brought
home with her; brightens: impulsively.*) Ma dear, just listen to
this lullaby. It's the sweetest thing. I was so "daffy" over it,
190 one of the girls at school lent it to me. (*She rushes to the piano with the music and plays the accompaniment through softly
and then sings, still softly and with great expression. Jessie
Gaynor's "Slumber Boat"*—

Baby's boat the silver moon;
Sailing in the sky.   195
Sailing o'er the sea of sleep.
While the clouds float by.

Sail, baby, sail.
Out upon that sea,
Only don't forget to sail   200
Back again to me.

Baby's fishing for a dream,
Fishing near and far.
His line a silver moonbeam is,
His bait a silver star.   205

Sail, baby, sail, etc.

Listen. Ma dear, right here. Isn't it lovely? (*Plays and sings
very softly and slowly.*)

"Only don't forget to sail
Back again to me."   210

(*Pauses: in hushed tones.*) Ma dear, it's so beautiful—it—it
hurts.
MRS. LOVING: (*Quietly.*) Yes, dear, it is pretty.
RACHEL: (*For several minutes watches her mother's profile from the
piano stool. Her expression is rather wistful.*) Ma dear!   215
MRS. LOVING: Yes, Rachel.
RACHEL: What's the matter?
MRS. LOVING: (*Without turning.*) Matter! What do you mean?
RACHEL: I don't know. I just *feel* something is not quite right
with you.   220
MRS. LOVING: I'm only tired—that's all.
RACHEL: Perhaps. But—(*Watches her mother a moment or two
longer; shakes her head: turns back to the piano. She is thoughtful: looks at her hands in her lap.*) Ma dear, wouldn't it be
nice if we could keep all the babies in the world—always 225
little babies? Then they'd be always little, and cunning, and
lovable; and they could never grow up, then, and—and—
be bad. I'm so sorry for mothers, whose little babies—
grow up—and—and—are bad.
MRS. LOVING: (*Startled; controlling herself, looks at* RACHEL *anx-* 230
iously, perplexedly. RACHEL's *eyes are still on her hands. Attempting a light tone.*) Come, Rachel, what experience have
you had with mothers whose babies have grown up to be
bad? You—you talk like an old, old woman.
RACHEL: (*Without raising her eyes, quietly.*) I know I'm not old; 235
but, just the same I know that is true. (*Softly.*) And I'm so
sorry for the mothers.
MRS. LOVING: (*With a forced laugh.*) Well, Miss Methuselah,
how do you happen to know all this? Mothers whose babies grow up to be bad don't, as a rule, parade their faults 240
before the world.
RACHEL: That's just it—that's *how* you know. They don't talk
at all.
MRS. LOVING: (*Involuntarily.*) Oh! (*Ceases to sew; looks at
RACHEL sharply: she is plainly worried. There is a long silence.* 245
Presently RACHEL *raises her eyes to Raphael's "Madonna" over
the piano. Her expression becomes rapt: then, very softly, her eyes
still on the picture, she plays and sings Nevin's "Mighty Lak A
Rose".*)—

250   Sweetest li'l feller,
    Ev'rybody knows:
    Dunno what to call him.
    But he mighty lak' a rose!
    Lookin' at his Mammy
255   Wid eyes so shiny blue,
    Mek' you think that heav'n
    Is comin' clost ter you!

    W'en [he's] dar a sleepin'
    In his li'l place
260   Think I see de angels
    Lookin' thro' de lace:
    W'en de dark is fallin',
    W'en de shadders creep.
    Den dey comes on tip-toe,
265   Ter kiss him in his sleep.

    Sweetest li'l feller, etc.

(*With head still raised, after she has finished, she closes her eyes. Half to herself and slowly.*) I think the loveliest thing of all the lovely things in this world is just (*Almost in a whisper.*)
270 being a mother!

MRS. LOVING: (*Turns and laughs.*) Well, of all the startling children, Rachel! I am getting to feel, when you're around as though I'm shut up with dynamite. What next? (RACHEL *rises, goes slowly to her mother, and kneels*
275 *down beside her. She does not touch her mother.*) Why so serious, chickabiddy?

RACHEL: (*Slowly and quietly.*) It is not kind to laugh at scared things. When you laughed, it was as though you laughed—at God!

280 MRS. LOVING: (*Startled.*) Rachel!

RACHEL: (*Still quietly.*) It's true. It was the best in me that said that—it was God! (*Pauses.*) And, Ma dear, if I believed that I should grow up and not be a mother, I'd pray to die now. I've thought about it a lot, Ma dear, and once I
285 dreamed, and a voice said to me—oh! it was so real— "Rachel, you are to be a mother to little children." Wasn't that beautiful? Ever since I have known how Mary felt at the "Annunciation." (*Almost in a whisper.*) *God spoke to me through some one, and I believe.* And it has
290 explained so much to me. I know now why I just can't resist any child. I have to love it—it calls me—it—draws me. I want to take care of it, wash it, dress it, live for it. I want the feel of its little warm body against me, its breath on my neck, its hands against my face. (*Pauses thoughtfully*
295 *for a few moments.*) Ma dear, here's something I don't understand: I love the little black and brown babies best of all. There is something about them that—that—clutches at my heart. Why—why—should they be—oh!— pathetic? I don't understand. It's dim. More than the
300 other babies, I feel that I must protect them. They're in danger, but from what? I don't know. I've tried so hard to understand, but I can't. (*Her face radiant and beautiful.*) Ma dear, I think their white teeth and the clear whites of their big black eyes and their dimples everywhere—are—
305 are (*Breaks off.*) And, Ma dear, because I love them best, I pray God every night to give me, when I grow up, little black and brown babies—to protect and guard. (*Wist-*

fully.) Now, Ma dear, don't you see why you must never laugh at me again? Dear, dear, Ma dear? (*Buries her head in her mother's lap and sobs.*)
310

MRS. LOVING: (*For a few seconds, sits as though dazed, and then instinctively begins to caress the head in her lap. To herself.*) And I suppose my experience is every mother's. Sooner or later—of a sudden she finds her own child a stranger to her. (*To* RACHEL, *very tenderly.*) Poor little girl! Poor little 315 chickabiddy!

RACHEL: (*Raising her head.*) Why do you say, "Poor little girl," like that? I don't understand. Why, Ma dear. I never saw tears in your eyes before. Is it—is it—because you know the things I do not understand? Oh! it *is* that. 320

MRS. LOVING: (*Simply.*) Yes, Rachel, and I cannot save you.

RACHEL: Ma dear, you frighten me. Save me from *what*?

MRS. LOVING: Just life, my little chickabiddy!

RACHEL: Is life so terrible? I had found it mostly beautiful. How can life be terrible, when the world is full of little 325 children?

MRS. LOVING: (*Very sadly.*) Oh, Rachel! Rachel!

RACHEL: Ma dear, what have I said?

MRS. LOVING: (*Forcing a smile.*) Why, the truth, of course, 330 Rachel. Life is not terrible when there are little children— and you—and Tom—and a roof over our heads—and work—and food—and clothes—and sleep at night. (*Pauses.*) Rachel, I am not myself today. I'm tired. Forget what I've said. Come, chickabiddy, wipe your eyes and smile. That's only an imitation smile, but it's better than 335 none. Jump up now, and light the lamp for me, will you? Tom's late, isn't he? I shall want you to go, too, for the rolls and pie for supper.

RACHEL: (*Rises rather wearily and goes into the kitchenette. While she is out of the room* MRS. LOVING *does not move. She sits star-* 340 *ing in front of her. The room for some time has been growing dark.* MRS. LOVING *can just be seen when* RACHEL *reenters with the lamp. She places it on the small table near her mother, adjusts it, so the light falls on her mother's work, and then lowers the window shades at the windows. She still droops.* MRS. LOVING, 345 *while* RACHEL *is in the room, is industrious.* RACHEL *puts on her hat and coat listlessly. She does not look in the glass.*) Where is the money, Ma dear? I'm ready.

MRS. LOVING: Before you go, Rachel, just give a look at the meat and see if it is cooking all right, will you, dearie? 350

RACHEL: (*Goes out into the kitchenette and presently returns.*) It's all right, Ma dear.

MRS. LOVING: (*While* RACHEL *is out of the room, she takes her pocket-book out of the machine-drawer, opens it, takes out money and gives it to* RACHEL *upon her return.*) A dozen brown rolls, 355 Rachel. Be sure they're brown! And, I guess,—an apple pie. As you and Tom never seem to get enough apple pie, get the largest she has. And here is a quarter. Get some candy—any kind *you* like. Chickabiddy. Let's have a party tonight, I feel extravagant. Why, Rachel! why are you crying? 360

RACHEL: Nothing, dear Ma dear. I'll be all right when I get in the air. Goodbye! (*Rushes out of the flat.* MRS. LOVING *sits idle. Presently the outer door of the flat opens and shuts with a bang, and* TOM *appears.* MRS. LOVING *begins to work as soon as she hears the banging door.*) 365

TOM: 'Lo, Ma! Where's Sis.—out? The door's off the latch. (*Kisses his mother and hangs hat in entryway.*)

MRS. LOVING: (*Greeting him with the same beautiful smile with which she greeted* RACHEL.) Rachel just went after the rolls and pie. She'll be back in a few minutes. You're late, Tommy.

TOM: No, Ma—you forget—it's pay day. (*With decided shyness and awkwardness he hands her his wages.*) Here, Ma!

MRS. LOVING: (*Proudly counting it.*) But, Tommy, this is every bit of it. You'll need some.

TOM: Not yet! (*Constrainedly.*) I only wish—. Say, Ma, I hate to see you work so hard. (*Fiercely.*) Some day—some day—. (*Breaks off.*)

MRS. LOVING: Son, I'm as proud as though you had given me a million dollars.

TOM: (*Emphatically.*) I may some day,—you see. (*Abruptly changing the subject.*) Gee! Ma, I'm hungry. What's for dinner? Smell's good.

MRS. LOVING: Lamb and dumplings and rice.

TOM: Gee! I'm glad I'm living—and a pie too?

MRS. LOVING: Apple pie, Tommy.

TOM: Say, Ma, don't wake me up. And shall "muzzer's" own little boy set the table?

MRS. LOVING: Thank you, Son.

TOM: (*Folds the green cloth, hangs it over the back of the armchair, gets white table-cloth from kitchenette and sets the table. The whole time he is whistling blithely a popular air. He lights one of the gas jets over the table.*) Ma!

MRS. LOVING: Yes, Son.

TOM: I made "squad" today—I'm quarterback. Five other fellows tried to make it. We'll all have to buy new hats, now.

MRS. LOVING: (*With surprise.*) Buy new hats! Why?

TOM: (*Makes a ridiculous gesture to show that his head and hers are both swelling.*) Honest, Ma, I had to carry my hat in my hand tonight,—couldn't even get it to perch aloft.

MRS. LOVING: (*Smiling.*) Well, I for one, Son, am not going to say anything to make you more conceited.

TOM: You don't *have* to say anything. Why, Ma, ever since I told you, you can almost look down your own back your head is so high. What? (MRS. LOVING *laughs. The outer door of the flat opens and shuts.* RACHEL's *voice is heard.*)

RACHEL: (*Without.*) My! that was a "drefful" climb, wasn't it? Ma. I've got something here for you. (*Appears in the doorway carrying packages and leading a little boy by the hand. The little fellow is shy but smiling.*) Hello, Tommy! Here, take these things for me. This is Jimmy. Isn't he a dear? Come Jimmy. (TOM *carries the packages into the kitchenette.* RACHEL *leads* JIMMY *to* MRS. LOVING.) Ma dear, this is my brown baby. I'm going to take him right down stairs again. His mother is as sweet as can be, and let me bring him up just to see you. Jimmy, this is Ma dear. (MRS. LOVING *turns expectantly to see the child. Standing before her, he raises his face to hers with an engaging smile. Suddenly, without word or warning, her body stiffens: her hands grip her sewing convulsively; her eyes stare. She makes no sound.*)

RACHEL: (*Frightened.*) Ma dear! What is the matter? Tom! Quick! (TOM *reenters and goes to them.*)

MRS. LOVING: (*Controlling herself with an effort and breathing hard.*) Nothing, dears, nothing. I must be—I am—nervous tonight. (*With a forced smile.*) How do-you-do, Jimmy? Now, Rachel—perhaps—don't you think—you had better take him back to his mother? Good-night, Jimmy! (*Eyes the child in a fascinated way the whole time he is in the*

room. RACHEL, *very much perturbed, takes the child out.*) Tom, open that window, please! There! That's better! (*Still breathing deeply.*) What a fool I am!

TOM: (*Patting his mother awkwardly on the back.*) You're all pegged out, that's the trouble—working entirely too hard. Can't you stop for the night and go to bed right after supper?

MRS. LOVING: I'll see, Tommy dear. Now, I must look after the supper.

TOM: Huh! Well, I guess not. How old do you think Rachel and I are anyway? I see; you think we'll break some of this beau-ti-ful Hav-i-land china, we bought at the "Five and Ten Cent Store." (*To* RACHEL *who has just reentered wearing a puzzled and worried expression. She is without hat and coat.*) Say, Rachel, do you think you're old enough?

RACHEL: Old enough for what, Tommy?

TOM: To dish up the supper for Ma.

RACHEL: (*With attempted sprightliness.*) Ma dear thinks nothing can go on in this little flat unless she does it. Let's show her a thing or two. (*They bring in the dinner.* MRS. LOVING *with trembling hands tries to sew.* TOM *and* RACHEL *watch her covertly. Presently she gets up.*)

MRS. LOVING: I'll be back in a minute, children. (*Goes out the door that leads to the other rooms of the flat.* TOM *and* RACHEL *look at each other.*)

RACHEL: (*In a low voice keeping her eyes on the door.*) Why do you suppose she acted so strangely about Jimmy?

TOM: Don't know—nervous. I guess,—worn out. I wish— (*Breaks off.*)

RACHEL: (*Slowly.*) It may be that: but she hasn't been herself this afternoon. I wonder—. Look out! Here she comes!

TOM: (*In a whisper.*) Liven her up. (RACHEL *nods.* MRS. LOVING *reenters. Both rush to her and lead her to her place at the right end of the table. She smiles and tries to appear cheerful. They sit down,* TOM *opposite* MRS. LOVING *and* RACHEL *at the side facing front.* MRS. LOVING *asks grace. Her voice trembles. She helps the children bountifully, herself sparingly. Every once in a while she stops eating and stares blankly into her plate; then, remembering where she is suddenly, looks around with a start and goes on eating.* TOM *and* RACHEL *appear not to notice her.*)

TOM: Ma's "some" cook, isn't she?

RACHEL: Is she! Delmonico's isn't in it.

TOM: (*Presently.*) Say, Rachel, do you remember that Reynolds boy in the fourth year?

RACHEL: Yes. You mean the one who is flat-nosed, freckled, and who squints and sneers?

TOM: (*Looking at* RACHEL *admiringly.*) The same.

RACHEL: (*Vehemently.*) I hate him!

MRS. LOVING: Rachel, you do use such violent language. Why hate him?

RACHEL: I do—that's all.

TOM: Ma, if you saw him just once, you'd understand. No one likes him. But, then, what can you expect? His father's in "quod" doing time for something. I don't know just what. One of the fellows says he has a real decent mother, though. She never mentions him in any way, shape or form, he says. Hard on her, isn't it? Bet I'd keep my head shut too;—you'd never get a yap out of me. (RACHEL *looks up quickly at her mother;* MRS. LOVING *stiffens perceptibly, but keeps her eyes on her plate.* RACHEL *catches* TOM's *eye; silently draws his attention to their mother; and shakes her head warningly at him.*)

490 TOM: (*Continuing hastily and clumsily.*) Well, anyway, he called me "Nigger" today. If his face isn't black, his eye is.

RACHEL: Good! Oh! Why did you let the other one go?

TOM: (*Grinning.*) I knew he said things behind my back; but today he was hopping mad, because I made quarterback.
495 He didn't!

RACHEL: Oh, Tommy! How lovely! Ma dear, did you hear that? (*Chants.*) Our Tommy's on the team! Our Tommy's on the team!

TOM: (*Trying not to appear pleased.*) Ma dear, what did I say
500 about er—er "capital" enlargements?

MRS. LOVING: (*Smiling.*) You're right, Son.

TOM: I hope you got that "capital," Rachel. How's that for Latin knowledge? Eh?

RACHEL: I don't think much of your knowledge, Tommy
505 dear: but (*continuing to chant.*) Our Tommy's on the team! Our Tommy's on the team! Our—(*Breaks off.*) I've a good mind to kiss you.

TOM: (*Threateningly.*) Don't you dare.

RACHEL: (*Rising and going toward him.*) I will! I will! I will!
510 TOM: (*Rising, too, and dodging her.*) No, you don't, young lady. (*A tremendous tussle and scuffle ensues.*)

MRS. LOVING: (*Laughing.*) For Heaven's sake! children, do stop playing and eat your supper. (*They nod brightly at each other behind her back and return smiling to the table.*)
515 RACHEL: (*Sticking out her tongue at* TOM.) I will!

TOM: (*Mimicking her.*) You won't!

MRS. LOVING: Children! (*They eat for a time in silence.*)

RACHEL: Ma dear, have you noticed Mary Shaw doesn't come here much these days?
520 MRS. LOVING: Why, that's so, she doesn't. Have you two quarreled?

RACHEL: No, Ma dear. (*Uncomfortably.*) I—think I know the reason—but I don't like to say, unless I'm certain.

TOM: Well, I know. I've seen her lately with those two girls
525 who have just come from the South. Twice she bowed stiffly, and the last time made believe she didn't see me.

RACHEL: Then you think—? Oh! I was afraid it was that.

TOM: (*Bitterly.*) Yes—we're "niggers"—that's why.

MRS. LOVING: (*Slowly and sadly.*) Rachel, that's one of the
530 things I can't save you from. I worried considerably about Mary, at first—you do take your friendships so seriously. I knew exactly how it would end. (*Pauses.*) And then I saw that if Mary Shaw didn't teach you the lesson—some one else would. They don't want you, dearies, when you and
535 they grow up. You may have everything in your favor—but they don't *dare* to like you.

RACHEL: I know all that is generally true—but I had hoped that Mary—(*Breaks off.*)

TOM: Well, I guess we can still go on living even if people don't
540 speak to us. I'll never bow to *her* again—that's certain.

MRS. LOVING: But, Son, that wouldn't be polite, if she bowed to you first.

TOM: Can't help it. I guess I can be blind, too.

MRS. LOVING: (*Wearily.*) Well—perhaps you are right—I
545 don't know. It's the way I feel about it too—but—but I wish my son always to be a *gentleman*.

TOM: If being a *gentleman* means not being a *man*—I don't wish to be one.

RACHEL: Oh! well, perhaps we're wrong about Mary—I hope
550 we are. (*Sighs.*) Anyway, let's forget it. Tommy guess what

I've got. (*Rises, goes out into entryway swiftly, and returns holding up a small bag.*) Ma dear treated. Guess!

TOM: Ma, you're a thoroughbred. Well, let's see—it's—a dozen dill pickles?

RACHEL: Oh! stop fooling.   555

TOM: I'm not. Tripe?

RACHEL: Silly!

TOM: Hog's jowl?

RACHEL: Ugh! Give it up—quarter-back.

TOM: Pig's feet?   560

RACHEL: (*In pretended disgust.*) Oh! Ma dear—send him from the table. It's CANDY!

TOM: Candy? Funny, I never thought of that! And I was just about to say some nice, delicious chitlings. Candy! Well! Well! (RACHEL *disdainfully carries the candy to her mother, returns* 565 *to her own seat with the bag and helps herself. She ignores* TOM.)

TOM: (*In an aggrieved voice.*) You see, Ma, how she treats me. (*In affected tones.*) I have a good mind, young lady to punish you, er—er corporeally speaking. Tut! Tut! I have a mind to master thee—I mean—you. Methinks that if I 570 should advance upon you, apply, perchance, two or three digits to your glossy locks and extract—aha!—say, a strand—you would no more defy me. (*He starts to rise.*)

MRS. LOVING: (*Quickly and sharply.*) Rachel! give Tom the candy and stop playing. (RACHEL *obeys. They eat in silence.* 575 *The old depression returns. When the candy is all gone,* RACHEL *pushes her chair back, and is just about to rise, when her mother, who is very evidently nerving herself for something, stops her.*) Just a moment, Rachel. (*Pauses, continuing slowly and very seriously.*) Tom and Rachel! I have been trying to make up 580 my mind for some time whether a certain thing is my duty or not. Today—I have decided it is. You are old enough, now,—and I see you ought to be told. Do you know what day this is? (*Both* TOM *and* RACHEL *have been watching their mother intently.*) It's the sixteenth of October. 585 Does that mean anything to either of you?

TOM *and* RACHEL: (*Wonderingly.*) No.

MRS. LOVING: (*Looking at both of them thoughtfully, half to herself.*) No—I don't know why it should. (*Slowly.*) Ten years ago—today—your father and your half-brother died. 590

TOM: I do remember, now, that you told us it was in October.

RACHEL: (*With a sigh.*) That explains—today.

MRS. LOVING: Yes, Rachel. (*Pauses.*) Do you know—how they—died?

TOM *and* RACHEL: Why, no.   595

MRS. LOVING: Did it ever strike you as strange—that they—died—the same day?

TOM: Well, yes.

RACHEL: We often wondered, Tom and I: but—but somehow we never quite dared to ask you. You—you—always re- 600 fused to talk about them, you know, Ma dear.

MRS. LOVING: Did you think—that—perhaps—the reason—I—I—wouldn't talk about them—was—because, because—I was ashamed—of them? (TOM *and* RACHEL *look uncomfortable.*)   605

RACHEL: Well, Ma dear—we—we—did—wonder.

MISS LOVING: (*Questioningly.*) And you thought?

RACHEL: (*Haltingly.*) W-e-l-l—

MRS. LOVING: (*Sharply.*) Yes?

TOM: Oh! come, now, Rachel, you know we haven't both- 610 ered about it at all. Why should we? We've been happy.

MRS. LOVING: But when you have thought—you've been ashamed? (*Intensely.*) Have you?

TOM: Now, Ma, aren't you making a lot out of nothing?

615 MRS. LOVING: (*Slowly.*) No. (*Half to herself.*) You evade—both—of you. You *have* been ashamed. And I never dreamed until today you *could* take it this way. How blind—how almost criminally blind, I have been.

RACHEL: (*Tremulously.*) Oh! Ma dear, don't! (TOM *and* RACHEL

620 *watch their mother anxiously and uncomfortably.* MRS. LOVING *is very evidently nerving herself for something.*)

MRS. LOVING: (*Very slowly, with restrained emotion.*) Tom—and Rachel!

TOM: Ma!

625 RACHEL: Ma dear! (*A tense, breathless pause.*)

MRS. LOVING: (*Bracing herself.*) They—they—were lynched!!

TOM *and* RACHEL: (*In a whisper.*) Lynched!

MRS. LOVING: (*Slowly, laboring under strong but restrained emotion.*) Yes—by Christian people—in a Christian land. We

630 found out afterwards they were all church members in good standing—the best people. (*A silence.*) Your father was a man among men. He was a fanatic. He was a Saint!

TOM: (*Breathing with difficulty.*) Ma—can you—will you—tell us—about it?

635 MRS. LOVING: I believe it to be my duty. (*A silence.*) When I married your father I was a widow. My little George was seven years old. From the very beginning he worshiped your father. He followed him around—just like a little dog. All children were like that with him. I myself have never

640 seen anybody like him. "Big" seems to fit him better than any other word. He was big-bodied—big-souled. His loves were big and his hates. You can imagine, then, how the wrongs of the Negro—ate into his soul. (*Pauses.*) He was utterly fearless. (*A silence.*) He edited and owned, for several

645 years, a small negro paper. In it he said a great many daring things. I used to plead with him to be more careful. I was always afraid for him. For a long time, nothing happened—he was too important to the community. And then—one night—ten years ago—a mob made up of the respectable

650 people in the town lynched an innocent black man—and what was worse—they knew him to be innocent. A white man was guilty. I never saw your father so wrought up over anything: he couldn't eat; he couldn't sleep; he brooded night and day over it. And then—realizing fully the great

655 risk he was running, although I begged him not to—and all his friends also—he deliberately and calmly went to work and published a most terrific denunciation of that mob. The old prophets in the Bible were not more terrible than he. A day or two later, he received an anonymous

660 letter, very evidently from an educated man, calling upon him to retract his words in the next issue. If he refused his life was threatened. The next week's issue contained an arraignment as frightful, if not more so, than the previous one. Each word was white-hot, searing. That night, some

665 dozen masked men came to our house.

RACHEL: (*Moaning.*) O, Ma dear! Ma dear!

MRS. LOVING: (*Too absorbed to hear.*) We were not asleep—your father and I. They broke down the front door and made their way to our bedroom. Your father kissed me—

670 and took up his revolver. It was always loaded. They broke down the door. (*A silence. She continues slowly and quietly.*) I tried to shut my eyes—I could not. Four masked men

fell—they did not move any more—after a little. (*Pauses.*) Your father was finally overpowered and dragged out. In the hall—my little seventeen-year-old George tried to 675 rescue him. Your father begged him not to interfere. He paid no attention. It ended in their dragging them both out. (*Pauses.*) My little George—was—a man! (*Controls herself with an effort.*) He never made an outcry. His last words to me were: "Ma, I am glad to go with Father." I 680 could only nod to him. (*Pauses.*) While they were dragging them down the steps, I crept into the room where you were. You were both asleep. Rachel, I remember, was smiling. I knelt down by you—and covered my ears with my hands—and waited. I could not pray—I couldn't for a 685 long time—afterwards. (*A silence.*) It was very still when I finally uncovered my ears. The only sounds were the faint rustle of leaves and the "tap-tapping of the twig of a tree" against the window. I hear it still—sometimes in my dreams. *It was the tree—where they were.* (*A silence.*) While I 690 had knelt there waiting—I had made up my mind what to do. I dressed myself and then I woke you both up and dressed you. (*Pauses.*) We set forth. It was a black, still night. Alternately dragging you along and carrying you—I walked five miles to the house of some friends. They 695 took us in, and we remained there until I had seen my dead laid comfortably at rest. They lent me money to come North—I couldn't bring you up—in the South. (*A silence.*) Always remember this: There never lived anywhere—or at any time—any two whiter or more beauti- 700 ful souls. God gave me one for a husband and one for a son and I am proud. (*Brokenly.*) You—must—be—proud—too. (*A long silence.* MRS. LOVING *bows her head in her hands.* TOM *controls himself with an effort.* RACHEL *creeps softly to her mother, kneels beside her and lifts the hem of her* 705 *dress to her lips. She does not dare touch her. She adores her with her eyes.*)

MRS. LOVING: (*Presently raising her head and glancing at the clock.*) Tom, it's time, now, for you to go to work. Rachel and I will finish up here. 710

TOM: (*Still laboring under great emotion goes out into the entryway and comes back and stands in the doorway with his cap. He twirls it around and around nervously.*) I want you to know, Ma, before I go—how—how proud I am. Why, I didn't believe two people could be like that—and live. And then 715 to find out that one—was your own father—and one—your own brother.—It's wonderful! I'm—not much yet, Ma, but—I've—I've just got to be something now. (*Breaks off.*) (*His face becomes distorted with passion and hatred.*) When I think—when I think—of those devils with white 720 skins—living somewhere today—living and happy—I—see—red! I—I—goodbye! (*Rushes out, the door bangs.*)

MRS. LOVING: (*Half to herself.*) I was afraid—of just that. I wonder—if I did the wise thing—after all.

RACHEL: (*With a gesture infinitely tender, puts her arms around her* 725 *mother.*) Yes, Ma dear, you did. And, hereafter, Tom and I share and share alike with you. To think, Ma dear, of ten years of this—all alone. It's wicked! (*A short silence.*)

MRS. LOVING: And, Rachel, about that dear, little boy, Jimmy.

RACHEL: Now, Ma dear, tell me tomorrow. You've stood 730 enough for one day.

MRS. LOVING: No, it's better over and done with—all at once. If I had seen that dear child suddenly any other day than

735 this—I might have borne it better. When he lifted his little face to me—and smiled—for a moment—I thought it
was the end—of all things. Rachel, he is the image of my
boy—my George!

RACHEL: Ma dear!

MRS. LOVING: And, Rachel—it will hurt—to see him again.

740 RACHEL: I understand, Ma dear. (*A silence. Suddenly.*) Ma dear,
I am beginning to see—to understand—so much. (*Slowly
and thoughtfully.*) Ten years ago, all things being equal,
Jimmy might have been—George? Isn't that so?

MRS. LOVING: Why—yes, if I understand you.

745 RACHEL: I guess that doesn't sound very clear. It's only getting clear to me, little by little. Do you mind my thinking
out loud to you?

MRS. LOVING: No, chickabiddy.

RACHEL: If Jimmy went South now—and grew up—he

750 might be—a George?

MRS. LOVING: Yes.

RACHEL: Then, the South is full of tens, hundreds, thousands
of little boys, who, one day may be—and some of them
with certainty—Georges?

755 MRS. LOVING: Yes, Rachel.

RACHEL: And the little babies, the dear, little, helpless babies,
being born today—now—and those who will be, tomorrow, and all the tomorrows to come—have *that* sooner or
later to look forward to? They will laugh and play and sing

760 and be happy and grow up, perhaps, and be ambitious—
just for *that*!

MRS. LOVING: Yes, Rachel.

RACHEL: Then, everywhere, everywhere, throughout the
South, there are hundreds of dark mothers who live in fear,

765 terrible, suffocating fear, whose rest by night is broken, and
whose joy by day in their babies on their hearts is three
parts—pain. Oh, I know this is true—for this is the way I
should feel, if I were little Jimmy's mother. How horrible!
Why—it would be more merciful—to strangle the little

770 things at birth. And so this nation—this white Christian
nation—has deliberately set its curse upon the most beautiful—the most holy thing in life—motherhood! Why—
it—makes—you doubt—God!

MRS. LOVING: Oh, hush! little girl. Hush!

775 RACHEL: (*Suddenly with a great cry.*) Why, Ma dear, *you know.
You* were *a mother, George's mother.* So, this is what it means.
Oh, Ma dear! Ma dear! (*Faints in her mother's arms.*)

ACT TWO

TIME: *October sixteenth, four years later: seven o'clock in the
morning.*

SCENE: *The same room. There have been very evident improvements made. The room is not so bare: it is cosier. On the shelf, before each window, are potted red geraniums. At the windows are
green denim drapery curtains covering fresh white dotted Swiss inner curtains. At each doorway are green denim portieres. On the
wall between the kitchenette and the entrance to the outer rooms of
the flat, a new picture is hanging, Millet's "The Man With the
Hoe." Hanging against the side of the run that faces front is
Watts's "Hope." There is another easy-chair at the left front. The
table in the center is covered with a white table-cloth. A small asparagus fern is in the middle of this. When the curtain rises there is
the clatter of dishes in the kitchenette. Presently* RACHEL *enters
with dishes and silver in her hands. She is clad in a bungalow
apron. She is noticeable all of four years older. She frowns as she
sets the table. There is a set expression about the mouth. A child's
voice is heard from the rooms within.*

JIMMY: (*Still unseen.*) Ma Rachel!

RACHEL: (*Pauses and smiles.*) What is it, Jimmy boy?

JIMMY: (*Appearing in rear doorway, half-dressed, breathless, and
tremendously excited over something. Rushes toward* RACHEL.)
Three guesses! Three guesses! Ma Rachel!   5

RACHEL: (*Her whole face softening.*) Well, let's see—maybe there
is a circus in town.

JIMMY: No siree! (*In a sing-song.*) You're not right! You're not
right!

RACHEL: Well, maybe Ma Loving's going to take you some-   10
where.

JIMMY: No! (*Vigorously shaking his head.*) It's—

RACHEL: (*Interrupting quickly.*) You said I could have three
guesses, honey. I've only had two.

JIMMY: I thought you had three. How many are three?   15

RACHEL: (*Counting on her fingers.*) One! Two! Three! I've only
had one! two!—See? Perhaps Uncle Tom is going to give
you some candy.

JIMMY: (*Dancing up and down.*) No! No! No! (*Catches his
breath.*) I leaned over the bath-tub, way over, and got hold   20
of the chain with the button on the end, and dropped it
into the little round place in the bottom. And then I
runned lots and lots of water in the tub and climbed over
and fell in splash! just like a big stone: (*Loudly.*) and took
a bath all by myself alone.   25

RACHEL: (*Laughing and hugging him.*) All by yourself, honey?
You ran the water, too, boy, not "runned" it. What I want
to know is, where was Ma Loving all this time?

JIMMY: I stole in "creepy-creep" and looked at Ma Loving and
she was awful fast asleep. (*Proudly.*) Ma Rachel, I'm a "naw-   30
ful," big boy now, aren't I? I are almost a man, aren't I?

RACHEL: Oh! Boy. I'm getting tired of correcting you—"I am
almost a man, am I not?" Jimmy, boy, what will Ma Rachel
do, if you grow up? Why, I won't have a little boy any
more! Honey, you mustn't grow up, do you hear? You   35
mustn't.

JIMMY: Oh, yes. I must; and you'll have me just the same, Ma
Rachel. I'm going to be a policeman and make lots of
money for you and Ma Loving and Uncle Tom, and I'm
going to buy you some trains and fire-engines, and little,   40
cunning ponies, and some rabbits, and some great 'nor-
mous banks full of money—lots of it. And then, we are going to live in a great, big castle and eat lots of ice cream, all
the time, and drink lots and lots of nice pink lemonade.

RACHEL: What a generous Jimmy boy! (*Hugs him.*) Before I   45
give you "morning kiss," I must see how clean my boy is.
(*Inspects teeth, ears and neck.*) Jimmy, you're sweet and clean
enough to eat. (*Kisses him; he tries to strangle her with hugs.*)
Now the hands. Oh! Jimmy, look at those nails! Oh!
Jimmy! (JIMMY *wriggles and tries to get his hands away.*)   50
Honey, get my file off of my bureau and go to Ma Loving; she must be awake by this time. Why, honey, what's
the matter with your feet?

JIMMY: I don't know. I thought they looked kind of queer,
myself. What's the matter with them?   55

RACHEL: (*Laughing.*) You have your shoes on the wrong feet.

JIMMY: (*Bursts out laughing.*) Isn't that most 'normously funny? I'm a case, aren't I—(*Pauses thoughtfully.*) I mean—am I not, Ma Rachel?

60   RACHEL: Yes, honey, a great big case of molasses. Come, you must hurry now, and get dressed. You don't want to be late for school, you know.

JIMMY: Ma Rachel! (*Shyly.*) I—I have been making something for you all the morning—ever since I waked up. It's

65   awful nice. It's—stoop down, Ma Rachel, please—a great, big (*Puts both arms about her neck and gives her a noisy kiss.* RACHEL *kisses him in return, then pushes his head back. For a long moment they look at each other; and, then, laughing joyously, he makes believe he is a horse, and goes prancing out of the*

70   *room.* RACHEL, *with a softer, gentler expression, continues setting the table. Presently,* MRS. LOVING, *bent and worn-looking, appears in the doorway in the rear. She limps a trifle.*)

MRS. LOVING: Good morning, dearie. How's my little girl, this morning? (*Looks around the room.*) Why, where's Tom?

75   I was certain I heard him running the water in the tub, sometime ago. (*Limps into the room.*)

RACHEL: (*Laughing.*) Tom isn't up yet. Have you seen Jimmy?

MRS. LOVING: Jimmy? No. I didn't know he was awake, even.

RACHEL: (*Going to her mother and kissing her.*) Well! What do

80   you think of that! I sent the young gentleman to you, a few minutes ago, for help with his nails. He is very much grown up this morning, so I suppose that explains why he didn't come to you. Yesterday, all day, you know, he was a puppy. No one knows what he will be tomorrow. All of

85   this, Ma dear, is preliminary to telling you that Jimmy boy has stolen a march on you, this morning.

MRS. LOVING: Stolen a march! How?

RACHEL: It appears that he took his bath all by himself and, as a result, he is so conceited, peacocks aren't in it with

90   him.

MRS. LOVING: I heard the water running and thought, of course, it was Tom. Why, the little rascal! I must go and see how he has left things. I was just about to wake him up.

RACHEL: Rheumatism's not much better this morning, Ma

95   dear. (*Confronting her mother.*) Tell me the truth, now, did you or did you not try that liniment I bought you yesterday?

MRS. LOVING: (*Guiltily.*) Well, Rachel, you see—it was this way. I was—I was so tired, last night.—I—I really forgot it.

RACHEL: I thought as much. Shame on you!

100 MRS. LOVING: As soon as I walk around a bit it will be all right. It always is. It's bad, when I first get up—that's all. I'll be spry enough in a few minutes. (*Limps to the door; pauses.*) Rachel, I don't know why the thought should strike me, but how very strangely things turn out. If any

105 one had told me four years ago that Jimmy would be living with us, I should have laughed at him. Then it hurt to see him: now it would hurt not to. (*Softly.*) Rachel, sometimes—I wonder—if, perhaps, God—hasn't relented a little—and given me back my boy,—my George.

110 RACHEL: The whole thing was strange, wasn't it?

MRS. LOVING: Yes. God's ways are strange and often very beautiful; perhaps all would be beautiful—if we only understood.

RACHEL: God's ways are certainly very mysterious. Why, of

115 all the people in this apartment-house, should Jimmy's father and mother be the only two to take the smallpox, and the only two to die! It's queer!

MRS. LOVING: It doesn't seem like two years ago, does it?

RACHEL: Two years. Ma dear! Why it's three the third of January.   120

MRS. LOVING: Are you sure, Rachel?

RACHEL: (*Gently.*) I don't believe I could ever forget that, Ma dear.

MRS. LOVING: No, I suppose not. That is one of the differences between youth and old age—youth attaches   125 tremendous importance to dates.—old age does not.

RACHEL: (*Quickly.*) Ma dear, don't talk like that. You're not old.

MRS. LOVING: Oh! yes, I am, dearie. It's sixty long years since I was born; and I am much older than that, much older. 130

RACHEL: Please, Ma dear, please!

MRS. LOVING: (*Smiling.*) Very well, dearie. I won't say it any more. (*A pause.*) By the way,—how—does Tom strike you, these days?

RACHEL: (*Avoiding her mother's eye.*) The same old, bantering, 135 cheerful Tom. Why?

MRS. LOVING: I know he's all that, dearie, but it isn't possible for him to be really cheerful. (*Pauses; goes on wistfully.*) When you are little, we mothers can kiss away all the trouble, but when you grow up—and go out—into the 140 world—and get hurt—we are helpless. There is nothing we can do.

RACHEL: Don't worry about Tom, Ma dear, he's game. He doesn't show the white feather.

MRS. LOVING: Did you see him, when he came in, last night? 145

RACHEL: Yes.

MRS. LOVING: Had he had—any luck?

RACHEL: No. (*Firmly.*) Ma dear, we may as well face it—it's hopeless, I'm afraid.

MRS. LOVING: I'm afraid—you are right. (*Shakes her head* 150 *sadly.*) Well, I'll go and see how Jimmy has left things and wake up Tom, if he isn't awake yet. It's the waking up in the mornings that's hard. (*Goes limping out rear door.* RACHEL *frowns as she continues going back and forth between the kitchenette and the table. Presently* TOM *appears in the door* 155 *at the rear. He watches* RACHEL *several moments before he speaks or enters.* RACHEL *looks grim enough.*)

TOM: (*Entering and smiling.*) Good-morning. "Merry Sunshine"! Have you, perhaps, been taking a—er—prolonged draught of that very delightful beverage—vinegar? 160 (RACHEL, *with a knife in her hand, looks up unsmiling. In pretended fright.*) I take it all back, I'm sure. May I request, humbly, that before I press my chaste, morning salute upon your forbidding lips, that you—that you—that you—er—in some way rid yourself of that—er—knife? (*Bows as* 165 RACHEL *puts it down.*) I thank you. (*He comes to her and tips her head back: gently.*) What's the matter with my little Sis?

RACHEL: (*Her face softening.*) Tommy dear, don't mind me. I'm getting wicked. I guess. At present I feel just like—like curdled milk. Once upon a time, I used to have quite a 170 nice disposition, didn't I, Tommy?

TOM: (*Smiling.*) Did you, indeed! I'm not going to flatter you. Well, brace yourself, old lady. Ready, One! Two! Three! Go! (*Kisses her, then puts his hands on either side of her face, and raising it, looks down into it.*) You're a pretty, decent lit- 175 tle sister, Sis, that's what T. Loving thinks about it; and he knows a thing or two. (*Abruptly looking around.*) Has the paper come yet?

RACHEL: I haven't looked, it must have, though, by this time.
180 (TOM, *hands in his pockets, goes into the vestibule. He whistles. The outer door opens and closes, and presently he saunters back, newspaper in hand. He lounges carelessly in the arm-chair and looks at* RACHEL.)
TOM: May T. Loving be of any service to you?
185 RACHEL: Service! How?
TOM: May he run, say, any errands, set the table, cook the breakfast? Anything?
RACHEL: (*Watching the lazy figure.*) You look like working.
TOM: (*Grinning.*) It's at least—polite—to offer.
190 RACHEL: You can't do anything: I don't trust you to do it right. You may just sit there, and read your paper—and try to behave yourself.
TOM: (*In affectedly meek tones.*) Thank you, ma'am. (*Opens the paper, but does not read.* JIMMY *presently enters riding around the*
195 *table on a cane.* RACHEL *peeps in from the kitchenette and smiles.* TOM *puts down his paper.*) 'Lo! Big Fellow, what's this?
JIMMY: (*Disgustedly.*) How can I hear? I'm miles and miles away yet. (*Prances around and around the room; presently stops near* TOM, *attempting a gruff voice.*) Good-morning!
200 TOM: (*Lowering his paper again.*) Bless my stars! Who's this? Well, if it isn't Mr. Mason! How-do-you-do, Mr. Mason? That's a beautiful horse you have there. He limps a trifle in his left, hind, front foot, though.
JIMMY: He doesn't.
205 TOM: He does!
JIMMY: (*Fiercely.*) He doesn't!
TOM: (*As fiercely.*) I say he does!
MRS. LOVING: (*Appearing in the doorway in the rear.*) For Heaven's sake! What is this? Good-morning, Tommy.
210 TOM: (*Rising and going toward his mother,* JIMMY *following astride of the cane in his rear.*) Good-morning, Ma. (*Kisses her; lays his head on her shoulder and makes believe he is crying: in a high falsetto.*) Ma! Jimmy says his horse doesn't limp in his hind, front right leg, and I say he does.
215 JIMMY: (*Throws his cane aside, rolls on the floor and kicks up his heels. He roars with laughter.*) I think Uncle Tom is funnier than any clown in the "Kickus."
TOM: (*Raising his head and looking down at* JIMMY: RACHEL *stands in the kitchenette doorway.*) In the *what*, Jimmy?
220 JIMMY: In the "kickus," of course.
TOM: "Kickus"! "Kickus"! Oh, Lordy! (TOM *and* RACHEL *shriek with laughter:* MRS. LOVING *looks amused:* JIMMY, *very much affronted, gets upon his feet again.* TOM *leans over and swings* JIMMY *high in the air.*) Boy, you'll be the death of me
225 yet. Circus, son! Circus!
JIMMY: (*From on high, soberly and with injured dignity.*) Well, I thinks "Kickus" and circus are very much alike. Please put me down.
RACHEL: (*From the doorway.*) We laugh, honey, because we
230 love you so much.
JIMMY: (*Somewhat mollified, to* TOM.) Is that so, Uncle Tom?
TOM: Surest thing in the world! (*Severely.*) Come, get down, young man. Don't you know you'll wear my arms out? Besides, there is something in my lower vest pocket, that's
235 just dying to come to you. Get down, I say.
JIMMY: (*Laughing.*) How can I get down? (*Wriggles around.*)
TOM: How should I know? Just get down, of course. (*Very suddenly puts* JIMMY *down on his feet.* JIMMY *tries to climb up over him.*)

JIMMY: Please sit down, Uncle Tom. 240
TOM: (*In feigned surprise.*) Sit down! What for?
JIMMY: (*Pummeling him with his little fists, loudly.*) Why, you said there was something for me in your pocket.
TOM: (*Sitting down.*) So I did. How forgetful I am!
JIMMY: (*Finding a bright, shiny penny, shrieks.*) Oh! Oh! Oh! 245 (*Climbs up and kisses* TOM *noisily.*)
TOM: Why, Jimmy! You embarrass me. My! My!
JIMMY: What is 'barrass?
TOM: You make me blush.
JIMMY: What's that? 250
MISS LOVING: Come, come, children! Rachel has the breakfast on the table. (TOM *sits in* JIMMY'S *place and* JIMMY *tries to drag him out.*)
TOM: What's the matter, now?
JIMMY: You're in *my* place. 255
TOM: Well, can't you sit in mine?
JIMMY: (*Wistfully.*) I wants to sit by my Ma Rachel.
TOM: Well, so do I.
RACHEL: Tom, stop teasing Jimmy. Honey, don't you let him bother you: ask him please prettily. 260
JIMMY: Please prettily, Uncle Tom.
TOM: Oh! well then. (*Gets up and takes his own place. They sit as they did in Act I, only* JIMMY *sits between* TOM, *at the end, and* RACHEL.)
JIMMY: (*Loudly.*) Oh, goody! goody! goody! We've got sau- 265 sages.
MRS. LOVING: Sh!
JIMMY: (*Silenced for a few moments;* RACHEL *ties a big napkin around his neck, and prepares his breakfast. He breaks forth again suddenly and excitedly.*) Uncle Tom! 270
TOM: Sir?
JIMMY: I took a bath this morning, all by myself alone, in the bath-tub, and I ranned, no (*Doubtfully.*) I runned. I think—the water all in it, and got in it all by myself; and Ma Loving thought it was you; but it was *me*. 275
TOM: (*In feignedly severe tones.*) See here, young man, this won't do. Don't you know I'm the only one who is allowed to do that here? It's a perfect waste of water—that's what it is.
JIMMY: (*Undaunted.*) Oh! no, you're not the only one, 'cause 280 Ma Loving and Ma Rachel and me—all takes baths every single morning. So there!
TOM: You 'barrass me. (JIMMY *opens his mouth to ask a question:* TOM *quickly.*) Young gentleman, your mouth is open. Close it, sir; close it. 285
MRS. LOVING: Tom, you're as big a child exactly as Jimmy.
TOM: (*Bowing to right and left.*) You compliment me. I thank you, I am sure.

(*They finish in silence.*)

JIMMY: (*Sighing with contentment.*) I'm through, Ma Rachel.
MRS. LOVING: Jimmy, you're a big boy, now, aren't you? 290 (JIMMY *nods his head vigorously and looks proud.*) I wonder if you're big enough to wash your own hands, this morning?
JIMMY: (*Shrilly.*) Yes, ma'am.
MRS. LOVING: Well, if they're beautifully clean, I'll give you another penny. 295
JIMMY: (*Excitedly to* RACHEL.) Please untie my napkin, Ma Rachel! (RACHEL *does so.*) "Excoose" me, please.

MRS. LOVING *and* RACHEL: Certainly. (JIMMY *climbs down and rushes out at the rear doorway.*)

300 MRS. LOVING: (*Solemnly and slowly: breaking the silence.*) Rachel, do you know what day this is?

RACHEL: (*Looking at her plate: slowly.*) Yes, Ma dear.

MRS. LOVING: Tom.

TOM: (*Grimly and slowly.*) Yes, Ma.

(*A silence.*)

305 MRS. LOVING: (*Impressively.*) We must never—as long—as we live—forget this day.

RACHEL: No, Ma dear.

TOM: No, Ma.

(*Another silence.*)

TOM: (*Slowly; as though thinking aloud.*) I hear people talk about
310 God's justice—and I wonder. There, are you, Ma. There isn't a sacrifice—that you haven't made. You're still working your fingers to the bone—sewing—just so all of us may keep on living. Rachel is a graduate in Domestic Science; she was high in her class; most of the girls below her in rank
315 have positions in the schools. I'm an electrical engineer—and I've tried steadily for several months—to practice my profession. It seems our educations aren't of much use to us: we aren't allowed to make good—because our skins are dark. (*Pauses.*) And, in the South today, there are white
320 men—(*Controls himself.*) They have everything; they're well-dressed, well-fed, well-housed; they're prosperous in business; they're important politically; they're pillars in the church. I know all this is true—I've inquired. Their children (our ages, some of them) are growing up around them;
325 and they are having a square deal handed out to them—college, position, wealth, and best of all, freedom, without galling restrictions, to work out their own salvations. With ability, they may become—anything; and all this will be true of their children's children after them. (*A pause.*) Look at
330 us—and look at them. We are destined to failure—they, to success. Their children shall grow up in hope; ours, in despair. Our hands are clean;—theirs are red with blood—red with the blood of a noble man—and a boy. They're nothing but low, cowardly, bestial murderers. The scum of the earth
335 shall succeed.—God's justice, I suppose.

MRS. LOVING: (*Rising and going to* TOM: *brokenly.*) Tom, promise me—one thing.

TOM: (*Rises gently.*) What is it, Ma?

MRS. LOVING: That—you'll try—not to lose faith—in God.
340 I've been where you are now—and it's black. Tom, we don't understand God's ways. My son, I know, now—He is beautiful. Tom, won't you try to believe, again?

TOM: (*Slowly, but not convincingly.*) I'll try, Ma.

MRS. LOVING: (*Sighs.*) Each one, I suppose, has to work out
345 his own salvation. (*After a pause.*) Rachel, if you'll get Jimmy ready, I'll take him to school. I've got to go down town shopping for a customer, this morning. (RACHEL *rises and goes out the rear doorway;* MRS. LOVING, *limping very slightly now, follows. She turns and looks back yearningly at*
350 TOM, *who has seated himself again, and is staring unseeingly at his plate. She goes out.* TOM *sits without moving until he hears* MRS. LOVING'*s voice within and* RACHEL'*s faintly; then he gets the paper, sits in the arm-chair and pretends to read.*)

MRS. LOVING: (*From within.*) A yard, you say, Rachel? You're
sure that will be enough. Oh! you've measured it. Any- 355
thing else?—What?—Oh! all right. I'll be back by one
o'clock, anyway. Good-bye. (*Enters with* JIMMY. *Both are
dressed for the street.* TOM *looks up brightly at* JIMMY.)

TOM: Hello! Big Fellow, where are you taking *my* mother, I'd
like to know? This is a pretty kettle of fish. 360

JIMMY: (*Laughing.*) Aren't you funny, Uncle Tom! Why, I'm
not taking her anywhere. She's taking me. (*Importantly.*)
I'm going to school.

TOM: Big Fellow, come here. (JIMMY *comes with a rush.*) Now,
where's that penny I gave you? No, I don't want to see it. 365
All right. Did Ma Loving give you another? (*Vigorous nod-
dings of the head from* JIMMY.) I wish you to promise me
solemnly—Now, listen! Here, don't wriggle so! not to
buy—Listen! too many pints of ice-cream with my penny.
Understand? 370

JIMMY: (*Very seriously.*) Yes. Uncle Tom, cross my "tummy"! I
promise.

TOM: Well, then, you may go. I guess that will be all for the
present. (JIMMY *loiters around looking up wistfully into his
face.*) Well? 375

JIMMY: Haven't you—aren't you—isn't you—forgetting
something?

TOM: (*Grabbing at his pockets.*) Bless my stars! what now?

JIMMY: If you could kind of lean over this way. (TOM *leans forward.*) No, not that way. (TOM *leans toward the side away from* 380
JIMMY.) No, this way, this way! (*Laughs and pummels him
with his little fists.*) This way!

TOM: (*Leaning toward* JIMMY.) Well, why didn't you say so, at
first?

JIMMY: (*Puts his arms around* TOM'*s neck and kisses him.*) Good- 385
bye, dear old Uncle Tom. (TOM *catches him and hugs him
hard.*) I likes to be hugged like that—I can taste—sau-sa-
ges.

TOM: You 'barrass me, son. Here, Ma, take your boy. Now remember all I told you, Jimmy. 390

JIMMY: I 'members.

MRS. LOVING: God bless you, Tom Good luck.

JIMMY: (*To* TOM.) God bless you, Uncle Tom. Good luck!

TOM: (*Much affected, but with restraint, rising.*) Thank you—
Good-bye. (MRS. LOVING *and* JIMMY *go out through the* 395
vestibule. TOM *lights a cigarette and tries to read the paper. He
soon sinks into a brown study. Presently* RACHEL *enters humming.* TOM *relights his cigarette; and* RACHEL *proceeds to clear
the table. In the midst of this, the bell rings three distinct
times.*) 400

RACHEL *and* TOM: John!

TOM: I wonder what's up—It's rather early for him.—I'll go.
(*Rises leisurely and goes out into the vestibule. The outer door
opens and shuts. Men's voices are heard.* TOM *and* JOHN
STRONG *enter. During the ensuing conversation* RACHEL *fin-* 405
*ishes clearing the table, takes the fern off, puts on the green table-
cloth, places a doily carefully in the centre, and replaces the fern.
She apparently pays no attention to the conversation between her
brother and* STRONG. *After she has finished, she goes to the
kitchenette. The rattle of dishes can be heard now and then.*) 410

RACHEL: (*Brightly.*) Well, stranger, how does it happen you're
out so early in the morning?

STRONG: I hadn't seen any of you for a week, and I thought
I'd come by, on my way to work, and find out how things

415   are going. There is no need of asking how you are, Rachel. And the mother and the boy?

RACHEL: Ma dear's rheumatism still holds on.—Jimmy's fine.

STRONG: I'm sorry to hear that your mother is not well. There isn't a remedy going that my mother doesn't know
420   about. I'll get her advice and let you know. (*Turning to* TOM.) Well, Tom, how goes it? (STRONG *and* TOM *sit*.)

TOM: (*Smiling grimly*.) There's plenty of "go," but no "git there."

STRONG: I was hoping for better news.

425 TOM: If I remember rightly, not so many years ago, you tried—and failed. Then, a colored man had hardly a ghost of a show;—now he hasn't even the ghost of a ghost.

(RACHEL *has finished and goes into the kitchenette*.)

STRONG: That's true enough. (*A pause*.) What are you going to do?
430 TOM: (*Slowly*.) I'll do this little "going act" of mine the rest of the week; (*pauses*.) and then, I'll do anything I can get to do. If necessary, I suppose, I can be a "White-wing."

STRONG: Tom, I came— (*Breaks off; continuing slowly*.) Six years ago, I found I was up against a stone wall—your ex-
435   perience, you see, to the letter. I couldn't let my mother starve, so I became a waiter. (*Pauses*.) I studied waiting; I made a science of it, an art. In a comparatively short time, I'm a head-waiter and I'm up against another stonewall. I've reached my limit. I'm thirty-two now, and I'll die a
440   head-waiter. (*A pause*.) College friends, so-called, and acquaintances used to come into the restaurant. One or two at first—attempted to commiserate with me. They didn't do it again. I waited upon them—I did my best. Many of them tipped me. (*Pauses and smiles grimly*.) I can remember
445   my first tip, still. They come in yet; many of them are already powers, not only in this city, but in the country. Some of them make a personal request that I wait upon them. I am an artist, now, in my proper sphere. They tip me well, extremely well—the larger the tip, the more
450   pleased they are with me. Because of me, in their own eyes, they're philanthropists. Amusing, isn't it? I can stand their attitude now. My philosophy—learned hard, is to make the best of everything you can, and go on. At best, life isn't so very long. You're wondering why I'm telling
455   you all this. I wish you to see things exactly as they are. There are many disadvantages and some advantages in being a waiter. My mother can live comfortably; I am able, even, to see that she gets some of the luxuries. Tom, it's this way—I can always get you a job as a waiter; I'll teach
460   you the art. If you care to begin the end of the week—all right. And remember this, as long as I keep my job—this offer holds good.

TOM: I—I— (*Breaks off*.) Thank you. (*A pause; then smiling wryly*.) I guess it's safe enough to say, you'll see me at the
465   end of the week. John you're— (*Breaking off again. A silence interrupted presently by the sound of much vigorous rapping on the outer door of the flat.* RACHEL *appears and crosses over to the vestibule*.) Hear the racket! My kiddies gently begging for admittance. It's about twenty minutes of nine, isn't it?
470 (TOM *nods*.) I thought so. (*Goes into the entryway; presently reappears with a group of six little girls ranging in age from five to about nine. All are fighting to be close to her; and all are talk-*

ing at once. There is one exception; the smallest tot is self-possessed and self-sufficient. She carries a red geranium in her hand and gives it her full attention*.) 475

LITTLE MARY: It's my turn to get "Morning kiss" first, this morning, Miss Rachel. You kissed Louise first yesterday. You said you'd kiss us "alphabetically." (*Ending in a shriek*.) You promised! (RACHEL *kisses* MARY, *who subsides*.)

LITTLE MARY: (*Imperiously*.) Now, me. (RACHEL *kisses her, and* 480 *then amid shrieks, recriminations, pulling of hair, jostling, etc., she kisses the rest. The small tot is still oblivious to everything that is going on*.)

RACHEL: (*Laughing*.) You children will pull me limb from limb; and then I'll be all dead; and you'll be sorry—see, if 485 you aren't. (*They fall back immediately.* TOM *and* JOHN *watch in amused silence.* RACHEL *loses all self-consciousness, and seems to bloom in the children's midst.*) Edith! come here this minute, and let me tie your hair ribbon again. Nancy, I'm ashamed of you. I saw you trying to pull it off. (NANCY 490 *looks abashed but mischievous*.) Louise, you look as sweet as sweet, this morning; and Jenny, where did you get the pretty, pretty dress?

LITTLE JENNY: (*Snuffling, but proud*.) My mother made it. (*Pauses with more snuffles*.) My mother says I have a very 495 bad cold. (*There is a brief silence interrupted by the small tot with the geranium*.)

LITTLE MARTHA: (*In a sweet, little voice*.) I—have—a—pitty—'ittle flower.

RACHEL: Honey, it's beautiful. Don't you want "Morning 500 kiss" too?

LITTLE MARTHA: Yes, I do.

RACHEL: Come, honey. (RACHEL *kisses her*.) Are you going to give the pretty flower to Jenny's teacher? (*Vigorous shakings of the head in denial*.) It is for—mother? (*More shakings of* 505 *the head*.) Is it for—let's see—Daddy? (*More shakings of the head*.) I give up. To whom are you going to give the pretty flower, honey?

LITTLE MARTHA: (*Shyly*.) "Oo."

RACHEL: You, darling! 510

LITTLE MARTHA: Muzzer and I picked it—for "oo." Here 't is. (*Puts her finger in her mouth, and gives it shyly*.)

RACHEL: Well, I'm going to pay you with three big kisses. One! Two! Three!

LITTLE MARTHA: I can count. One! Two! Free! Tan't I? I am 515 going to school soon; and I wants to put the flower in your hair.

RACHEL: (*Kneels*.) All right, baby. (LITTLE MARTHA *fumbles and* RACHEL *helps her*.)

LITTLE MARTHA: (*Dreamily*.) Miss Rachel, the 'ittle flower 520 loves you. It told me so. It said it wanted to lie in your hair. It is going to tell you a pitty 'ittle secret. You listen awful hard—and you'll hear. I wish I were a fairy and had a little wand, I'd turn everything into flowers. Wouldn't that be nice, Miss Rachel? 525

RACHEL: Lovely, honey!

LITTLE JENNY: (*Snuffling loudly*.) If I were a fairy and had a wand, I'd turn you, Miss Rachel, into a queen—and then I'd always be near you and see that you were happy.

RACHEL: Honey, how beautiful! 530

LITTLE LOUISE: I'd make my mother happy—if I were a fairy. She cries all the time. My father can't get anything to do.

LITTLE NANCY: If I were a fairy, I'd turn a boy in my school
into a spider. I hate him.

RACHEL: Honey, why?

LITTLE NANCY: I'll tell you sometime—I hate him.

LITTLE EDITH: Where's Jimmy, Miss Rachel?

RACHEL: He went long ago; and chickies, you'll have to clear
out, all of you, now, or you'll be late. Shoo! Shoo! (*She
drives them out prettily before her. They laugh merrily. They all
go into the vestibule.*)

TOM: (*Slowly.*) Does it ever strike you—how pathetic and
tragic a thing—a little colored child is?

STRONG: Yes.

TOM: Today, we colored men and women, everywhere—are
up against it. Every year, we are having a harder time of it.
In the South, they make it as impossible as they can for us
to get an education. We're hemmed in on all sides. Our
one safeguard—the ballot—in most states, is taken away
already, or is being taken away. Economically, in a few
lines, we have a slight show—but at what a cost! In the
North, they make a pretence of liberality; they give us the
ballot and a good education, and then—snuff us out. Each
year, the problem just to live, gets more difficult to solve.
How about these children—if we're fools enough to have
any? (RACHEL *reenters. Her face is drawn and pale. She returns
to the kitchenette.*)

STRONG: (*Slowly, with emphasis.*) That part—is damnable! (*A
silence.*)

TOM: (*Suddenly looking at the clock.*) It's later than I thought.
I'll have to be pulling out of here now, if you don't mind.
(*Raising his voice.*) Rachel! (RACHEL *still drawn and pale, appears in the doorway of the kitchenette. She is without her
apron.*) I've got to go now, Sis. I leave John in your hands.

STRONG: I've got to go, myself, in a few minutes.

TOM: Nonsense, man! Sit still. I'll begin to think, in a minute,
you're afraid of the ladies.

STRONG: I am.

TOM: What! And not ashamed to acknowledge it?

STRONG: No.

TOM: You're lots wiser than I dreamed. So long! (*Gets hat out
in the entry-way and returns; smiles wryly.*) "Morituri Saluta-
mus." (*They nod at him*—RACHEL *wistfully. He goes out.
There is the sound of an opening and closing door.* RACHEL *sits
down. A rather uncomfortable silence, on the part of* RACHEL,
ensues. STRONG *is imperturbable.*)

RACHEL: (*Nervously.*) John!

STRONG: Well?

RACHEL: I—I listened.

STRONG: Listened! To what?

RACHEL: To you and Tom.

STRONG: Well,—what of it?

RACHEL: I didn't think it was quite fair not to tell you. It—it
seemed, well, like eavesdropping.

STRONG: Don't worry about it. Nonsense!

RACHEL: I'm glad—I want to thank you for what you did for
Tom. He needs you, and will need you. You'll help him?

STRONG: (*Thoughtfully.*) Rachel, each one—has his own little
battles. I'll do what I can. After all, an outsider doesn't
help much.

RACHEL: But friendship—just friendship—helps.

STRONG: Yes. (*A silence.*) Rachel, do you hear anything encouraging from the schools? Any hope for you yet?

RACHEL: No, nor ever will be. I know that now. There's no
more chance for me than there is for Tom,—or than there
was for you—or for any of us with dark skins. It's lucky
for me that I love to keep house, and cook, and sew. I'll
never get anything else. Ma dear's sewing, the little work
Tom has been able to get, and the little sewing I sometimes get to do—keeps us from the poorhouse. We live.
According to your philosophy, I suppose, make the best of
it—it might be worse.

STRONG: (*Quietly.*) You don't want to get morbid over these
things, you know.

RACHEL: (*Scornfully.*) That's it. If you see things as they are,
you're either pessimistic or morbid.

STRONG: In the long run, do you believe, that attitude of
mind—will be—beneficial to you? I'm ten years older
than you. I tried your way. I know. Mine is the only sane
one. (*Goes over to her slowly; deliberately puts his hands on her
hair, and tips her head back. He looks down into her face quietly
without saying anything.*)

RACHEL: (*Nervous and startled.*) Why, John, don't! (*He pays no
attention, but continues to look down into her face.*)

STRONG: (*Half to himself.*) Perhaps—if you had—a little more
fun in your life, your point of view would be—more normal. I'll arrange it so I can take you to some theatre, one
night, this week.

RACHEL: (*Irritably.*) You talk as though I were a—a jellyfish.
You'll take me, how do you know *I'll* go?

STRONG: You will.

RACHEL: (*Sarcastically.*) Indeed! (STRONG *makes no reply.*) I
wonder if you know how—how—maddening you are.
Why, you talk as though my will counts for nothing. It's
as if you're trying to master me. I think a domineering
man is detestable.

STRONG: (*Softly.*) If he's, perhaps, *the* man?

RACHEL: (*Hurriedly, as though she had not heard.*) Besides, some
of these theatres put you off by yourself as though you had
leprosy. I'm not going.

STRONG: (*Smiling at her.*) You know I wouldn't ask you to go,
under those circumstances. (*A silence.*) Well, I must be going now. (*He takes her hand, and looks at it reverently.*
RACHEL, *at first resists; but he refuses to let go. When she finds
it useless, she ceases to resist. He turns his head and smiles down
into her face.*) Rachel, I am coming back to see you, this
evening.

RACHEL: I'm sure *we'll* all be very glad to see you.

STRONG: (*Looking at her calmly.*) I said—you. (*Very deliberately,
he turns her hand palm upwards, leans over and kisses it; then he
puts it back into her lap. He touches her cheek lightly.*) Good-
bye—little Rachel. (*Turns in the vestibule door and looks
back, smiling.*) Until tonight. (*He goes out.* RACHEL *sits for
some time without moving. She is lost in a beautiful day-dream.
Presently she sighs happily, and after looking furtively around the
room, lifts the palm* JOHN *has kissed to her lips. She laughs shyly
and jumping up, begins to hum. She opens the window at the
rear of the room and then commences to thread the sewing-
machine. She hums happily the whole time. A light rapping is
heard at the outer door.* RACHEL *listens. It stops, and begins
again. There is something insistent, and yet hopeless in the
sound.* RACHEL *looking puzzled, goes out into the vestibule . . .
The door closes.* RACHEL, *a black woman, poorly dressed, and a
little ugly, black child come in. There is the stoniness of despair*

in the woman's face. The child is thin, nervous, suspicious, frightened.)

MRS. LANE: (*In a sharp, but toneless voice.*) May I sit down? I'm tired.

660 RACHEL: (*Puzzled, but gracious; draws up a chair for her.*) Why, certainly.

MRS. LANE: No, you don't know me—never even heard of me—nor I of you. I was looking at the vacant flat on this floor—and saw your name—on your door,—"Loving!"

665 It's a strange name to come across—in this world.—I thought, perhaps, you might give me some information. (*The child hides behind her mother and looks around at* RACHEL *in a frightened way.*)

RACHEL: (*Smiling at the woman and child in a kindly manner.*) I'll

670 be glad to tell you anything, I am able Mrs.—

MRS. LANE: Lane. What I want to know is, how do they treat the colored children in the school I noticed around the corner? (*The child clutches at her mother's dress.*)

RACHEL: (*Perplexed.*) Very well—I'm sure.

675 MRS. LANE: (*Bluntly.*) What reason have you for being sure?

RACHEL: Why, the little boy I've adopted goes there; and he's very happy. All the children in this apartment-house go there too; and I know they're happy.

MRS. LANE: Do you know how many colored children there

680 are in the school?

RACHEL: Why, I should guess around thirty.

MRS. LANE: I see. (*Pauses.*) What color is this little adopted boy of yours?

RACHEL: (*Gently.*) Why—he's brown.

685 MRS. LANE: Any black children there?

RACHEL: (*Nervously.*) Why—yes.

MRS. LANE: Do you mind if I send Ethel over by the piano to sit?

RACHEL: N—no, certainly not. (*Places a chair by the piano and

690 goes to the little girl holding out her hand. She smiles beautifully. The child gets farther behind her mother.*)

MRS. LANE: She won't go to you—she's afraid of everybody now but her father and me. Come Ethel. (MRS. LANE *takes the little girl by the hand and leads her to the chair. In a gentler

695 voice.*) Sit down, Ethel. (ETHEL *obeys. When her mother starts back again toward* RACHEL, *she holds out her hands pitifully. She makes no sound.*) I'm not going to leave you, Ethel. I'll be right over here. You can see me. (*The look of agony on the child's face, as her mother leaves her, makes* RACHEL *shud-

700 der.*) Do you mind if we sit over here by the sewing-machine? Thank you. (*They move their chairs.*)

RACHEL: (*Looking at the little, pitiful figure watching its mother almost unblinkingly.*) Does Ethel like apples, Mrs. Lane?

MRS. LANE: Yes.

705 RACHEL: Do you mind if I give her one?

MRS. LANE: No. Thank you, very much.

RACHEL: (*Goes into the kitchenette and returns with a fringed napkin, a plate, and a big, red apple, cut into quarters. She goes to the little girl, who cowers away from her; very gently.*) Here,

710 dear, little girl, is a beautiful apple for you. (*The gentle tones have no appeal for the trembling child before her.*)

MRS. LANE: (*Coming forward.*) I'm sorry, but I'm afraid she won't take it from you. Ethel, the kind lady has given you an apple. Thank her nicely. Here! I'll spread the napkin for

715 you, and put the plate in your lap. Thank the lady like a good little girl.

ETHEL: (*Very low.*) Thank you. (*They return to their seats.* ETHEL *with difficulty holds the plate in her lap. During the rest of the interview between* RACHEL *and her mother, she divides her attention between the apple on the plate and her mother's face. She* 720 *makes no attempt to eat the apple, but holds the plate in her lap with a care that is painful to watch. Often, too, she looks over her shoulder fearfully. The conversation between* RACHEL *and her mother is carried on in low tones.*)

MRS. LANE: I've got to move— it's *Ethel.* 725

RACHEL: What is the matter with that child? It's—it's heart-breaking to see her.

MRS. LANE: I understand how you feel,—I don't feel anything, myself, any more. (*A pause.*) My husband and I are poor, and we're ugly and we're black. Ethel looks like her 730 father more than she does like me. We live in 55th Street—near the railroad. It's a poor neighborhood, but the rent's cheap. My husband is a porter in a store; and, to help out, I'm a caretaker. (*Pauses.*) I don't know why I'm tell you all this. We had a nice little home—and the three 735 of us were happy. Now we've got to move.

RACHEL: Move! Why?

MRS. LANE: It's Ethel. I put her in school this September. She stayed two weeks. (*Pointing to* ETHEL.) That's the result.

RACHEL: (*In horror.*) You mean—that just two weeks—in 740 school—did that?

MRS. LANE: Yes. Ethel never had a sick day in her life—before. (*A brief pause.*) I took her to the doctor at the end of the two weeks. He says she's a nervous wreck.

RACHEL: But what could they have done to her? 745

MRS. LANE: (*Laughs grimly and mirthlessly.*) I'll tell you what they did the first day. Ethel is naturally sensitive and backward. She's not assertive. The teacher saw that, and, after I had left, told her to sit in a seat in the rear of the class. She was alone there—in a corner. The children, immediately 750 feeling there was something wrong with Ethel because of the teacher's attitude, turned and stared at her. When the teacher's back was turned they whispered about her, pointed their fingers at her and tittered. The teacher divided the class into two parts, divisions, I believe, they are 755 called. She forgot all about Ethel, of course, until the last minute, and then, looking back, said sharply: "That little girl there may join this division," meaning the group of pupils standing around her. Ethel naturally moved slowly. The teacher called her sulky and told her to lose a part of 760 her recess. When Ethel came up—the children drew away from her in every direction. She was left standing alone. The teacher then proceeded to give a lesson about kindness to animals. Funny, isn't it, *kindness to animals?* The children forgot Ethel in the excitement of talking about 765 their pets. Presently, the teacher turned to Ethel and said disagreeably: "Have you a pet?" Ethel said, "Yes," very low. "Come, speak up, you sulky child, what is it?" Ethel said: "A blind puppy." They all laughed, the teacher and all. Strange, isn't it, but Ethel loves that puppy. She spoke up: 770 "It's mean to laugh at a little blind puppy. I'm glad he's blind." This remark brought forth more laughter. "Why are you glad," the teacher asked curiously. Ethel refused to say. (*Pauses.*) When I asked her why, do you know what she told me? "If he saw me, he might not love me any 775 more." (*A pause.*) Did I tell you that Ethel is only seven years old?

RACHEL: (*Drawing her breath sharply.*) Oh! I didn't believe any one could be as cruel as that—to a little child.

780 MRS. LANE: It isn't very pleasant, is it? When the teacher found out that Ethel wouldn't answer, she said severely: "Take your seat!" At recess, all the children went out. Ethel could hear them playing and laughing and shrieking. Even the teacher went too. She was made to sit there all alone—
785 in that big room—because God made her ugly—and black. (*Pauses.*) When the recess was half over the teacher came back. "You may go now," she said coldly. Ethel didn't stir. "Did you hear me?" "Yes'm." "Why don't you obey?" "I don't want to go out, please." "You don't, don't you, you
790 stubborn child! Go immediately!" Ethel went. She stood by the school steps. No one spoke to her. The children near her moved away in every direction. They stopped playing, many of them, and watched her. They stared as only children can stare. Some began whispering about
795 her. Presently one child came up and ran her hand roughly over Ethel's face. She looked at her hand and Ethel's face and ran screaming back to the others, "It won't come off! See!" Other children followed the first child's example. Then one boy spoke up loudly: "I know
800 what she is, she's a nigger!" Many took up the cry. God or the devil interfered—the bell rang. The children filed in. One boy boldly called her "Nigger!" before the teacher. She said, "That isn't nice,"—but she smiled at the boy. Things went on about the same for the rest of the day. At
805 the end of school, Ethel put on her hat and coat—the teacher made her hang them at a distance from the other pupil's wraps; and started for home. Quite a crowd escorted her. They called her "Nigger!" all the way. I *made* Ethel go the next day. I complained to the authorities.
810 They treated me lightly. I was determined not to let them force my child out of school. At the end of two weeks—I had to take her out.

RACHEL: (*Brokenly.*) Why,—I never—in all my life—heard anything—so—pitiful.

815 MRS. LANE: Did you ever go to school here?

RACHEL: Yes. I was made to feel my color—but I never had an experience like that.

MRS. LANE: How many years ago were you in the graded schools?

820 RACHEL: Oh!—around ten.

MRS. LANE: (*Laughs grimly.*) Ten years! Every year things are getting worse. Last year wasn't as bad as this. (*Pauses.*) So they treat the children all right in this school?

RACHEL: Yes! Yes! I know that.

825 MRS. LANE: I can't afford to take this flat here, but I'll take it. I'm going to have Ethel educated. Although, when you think of it,—it's all rather useless—this education! What are our children going to do with it, when they get it? We strive and save and sacrifice to educate them—and the
830 whole time—down underneath, we know—they'll have no chance.

RACHEL: (*Sadly.*) Yes, that's true, all right.—God seems to have forgotten us.

MRS. LANE: God! It's all a lie about God. I know.—This fall I
835 sent Ethel to a white Sunday-school near us. She received the same treatment there she did in the day school. Her being there, nearly broke up the school. At the end, the superintendent called her to him and asked her if she

didn't know of some nice colored Sunday-school. He told her she must feel out of place, and uncomfortable there. 840 That's your Church of God!

RACHEL: Oh! how unspeakably brutal. (*Controls herself with an effort; after a pause.*) Have you any other children?

MRS. LANE: (*Dryly.*) Hardly! If I had another—I'd kill it. It's kinder. (*Rising presently.*) Well, I must go, now. Thank you, 845 for your information—and for listening. (*Suddenly.*) You aren't married, are you?

RACHEL: No.

MRS. LANE: Don't marry—that's my advice. Come, Ethel. (ETHEL *gets up and puts down the things in her lap, carefully* 850 *upon her chair. She goes in a hurried, timid way to her mother and clutches her hand.*) Say good-bye to the lady.

ETHEL: (*Faintly.*) Good-bye.

RACHEL: (*Kneeling by the little girl—a beautiful smile on her face.*) Dear little girl, won't you let me kiss you good-bye? I love 855 little girls. (*The child hides behind her mother; continuing brokenly.*) Oh!—no child—ever did—that to me—before!

MRS. LANE: (*In a gentler voice.*) Perhaps, when we move in here, the first of the month, things may be better. Thank you, again. Good-morning! You don't belie your name. 860 (*All three go into the vestibule. The outside door opens and closes.* RACHEL *as though dazed and stricken returns. She sits in a chair, leans forward, and clasping her hands loosely between her knees, stares at the chair with the apple on it where* ETHEL LANE *has sat. She does not move for some time. Then she gets up and* 865 *goes to the window in the rear center and sits there. She breathes in the air deeply and then goes to the sewing-machine and begins to sew on something she is making. Presently her feet slow down on the pedals; she stops; and begins brooding again. After a short pause, she gets up and begins to pace up and down slowly, me-* 870 *chanically, her head bent forward. The sharp ringing of the electric bell breaks in upon this.* RACHEL *starts and goes slowly into the vestibule. She is heard speaking dully through the tube.*)

RACHEL: Yes!—All right! Bring it up! (*Presently she returns with a long flower box. She opens it listlessly at the table. Within are* 875 *six, beautiful crimson rosebuds with long stems.* RACHEL *looks at the name on the card. She sinks down slowly on her knees and leans her head against the table. She sighs wearily.*) Oh! John! John!—What are we to do?—I'm—I'm—afraid! Everywhere—it is the same thing. My mother! My little 880 brother! Little, black, crushed Ethel! (*In a whisper.*) Oh! God! You who I have been taught to believe are so good, so beautiful how could—You permit—these—things? (*Pauses, raises her head and sees the rosebuds. Her face softens and grows beautiful, very sweetly.*) Dear little rosebuds— 885 you—make me think—of sleeping, curled up, happy babies. Dear beautiful, little rosebuds! (*Pauses; goes on thoughtfully to the rosebuds.*) When—I look—at you—I believe—God is beautiful. He who can make a little exquisite thing like this, and this can't be cruel. Oh! He can't mean me— 890 to give up—love—and the hope of little children. (*There is the sound of a small hand knocking at the outer door.* RACHEL *smiles.*) My Jimmy! It must be twelve o'clock. (*Rises.*) I didn't dream it was so late. (*Starts for the vestibule.*) Oh! the world can't be so bad. I don't believe it. I won't. I *must* for- 895 get that little girl. My little Jimmy is happy—and today John—sent me beautiful rosebuds. Oh, there are lovely things, yet. (*Goes into the vestibule. A child's eager cry is heard; and* RACHEL *carrying* JIMMY *in her arms comes in. He has both*

900   *arms about her neck and is hugging her. With him in her arms,*
she sits down in the armchair at the right front.)

RACHEL: Well, honey, how was school today?

JIMMY: (*Sobering a trifle.*) All right, Ma Rachel. (*Suddenly sees
the roses.*) Oh! look at the pretty flowers. Why, Ma Rachel,
905   you forgot to put them in water. They'll die.

RACHEL: Well, so they will. Hop down this minute, and I'll
put them in right away. (*Gathers up box and flowers and goes
into the kitchenette.* JIMMY *climbs back into the chair. He looks
thoughtful and serious.* RACHEL *comes back with the buds in a*
910   *tall, glass vase. She puts the fern on top of the piano, and places
the vase in the centre of the table.*) There, honey, that's better,
isn't it? Aren't they lovely?

JIMMY: Yes, that's lots better. Now they won't die, will they?
Rosebuds are just like little "chilyun," aren't they, Ma
915   Rachel? If you are good to them, they'll grow up into
lovely roses, won't they? And if you hurt them, they'll die.
Ma Rachel do you think all peoples are kind to little rosebuds?

RACHEL: (*Watching* JIMMY *shortly.*) Why, of course. Who could
920   hurt little children? Who would have the heart to do such
a thing?

JIMMY: If you hurt them, it would be lots kinder, wouldn't it,
to kill them all at once, and not a little bit and a little bit?

RACHEL: (*Sharply.*) Why, honey boy, why are you talking like
925   this?

JIMMY: Ma Rachel, what is a "Nigger"?

(RACHEL *recoils as though she has been struck.*)

RACHEL: Honey boy, why—why do you ask that?

JIMMY: Some big boys called me that when I came out of
school just now. They said: "Look at the little nigger!"
930   And they laughed. One of them runned, no ranned, after
me and threw stones; and they all kept calling "Nigger!
Nigger! Nigger!" One stone struck me hard in the back,
and it hurt awful bad; but I didn't cry, Ma Rachel. I
wouldn't let them make me cry. The stone hurts me
935   there, Ma Rachel; but what they called me hurts and hurts
here. What is a "Nigger," Ma Rachel?

RACHEL: (*Controlling herself with a tremendous effort. At last she
sweeps down upon him and hugs and kisses him.*) Why, honey
boy, those boys didn't mean anything. Silly, little, honey
940   boy! They're rough, that's all. How *could* they mean anything?

JIMMY: You're only saying that, Ma Rachel, so I won't be
hurt. I know. It wouldn't ache here like it does—if they
didn't mean something.

945   RACHEL: (*Abruptly.*) Where's Mary, honey?

JIMMY: She's in her flat. She came in just after I did.

RACHEL: Well, honey, I'm going to give you two big cookies
and two to take to Mary, and you may stay in there and play
with her, till I get your lunch ready. Won't that be jolly?

950   JIMMY: (*Brightening a little.*) Why, you never give me but one
at a time. You'll give me two?—One? Two? (RACHEL *gets
the cookies and brings them to him.* JIMMY *climbs down from the
chair.*) Shoo! now, little honey boy. See how many laughs
you can make for me, before I come after you. Hear? Have
955   a good time, now. (JIMMY *starts for the door quickly; but he begins to slow down. His face gets long and serious again.* RACHEL
watches him.)

RACHEL: (*Jumping at him.*) Shoo! Shoo! Get out of here
quickly, little chicken. (*She follows him out. The outer door
opens and shuts. Presently she returns. She looks old and worn and* 960
grey: calmly. Pauses.) First, it's little, black Ethel—and then's
it's Jimmy. Tomorrow, it will be some other little child. The
blight—sooner or later—strikes all. My little Jimmy, only
seven years old poisoned! (*Through the open window comes
the laughter of little children at play.* RACHEL, *shuddering, covers* 965
her ears.) And once I said, centuries ago, it must have been:
"How can life be so terrible, when there are little children
in the world?" Terrible! Terrible! (*In a whisper, slowly.*) That's
the reason it *is* so terrible. (*The laughter reaches her again; this
time she listens.*) And, suddenly, some day, from out of the 970
black, the blight shall descend, and shall still forever—the
laughter on those little lips, and in those little hearts. (*Pauses
thoughtfully.*) And the loveliest thing—almost, that ever
happened to me, that beautiful voice, in my dream, those
beautiful words: "Rachel, you are to be the mother to lit- 975
tle children." (*Pauses, then slowly and with dawning surprise.*)
Why, God, you were making a mock of me; you were
laughing at me. I didn't believe God could laugh at our sufferings, but He can. We are accursed, accursed! We have
nothing, absolutely nothing. (STRONG's *rosebuds attract her* 980
*attention. She goes over to them, puts her hand out as if to touch
them, and then shakes her head, very sweetly.*) No, little rosebuds, I may not touch you. Dear, little, baby rosebuds,—I
am accursed. (*Gradually her whole form stiffens, she breathes
deeply: at last slowly.*) You God!—You terrible, laughing 985
God! Listen! I swear—and may my soul be damned to all
eternity, if I do break this oath—I swear—that no child of
mine shall ever lie upon my breast, for I will not have it rise
up, in the terrible days that are to be—and call me cursed.
(*A pause, very wistfully; questioningly.*) Never to know the 990
loveliest thing in all the world—the feel of a little head, the
touch of little hands, the beautiful utter dependence—of a
little child? (*With sudden frenzy.*) You can laugh. Oh God!
Well, so can I. (*Bursts into terrible, racking laughter.*) But I can
be kinder than You. (*Fiercely she snatches the rosebuds from the* 995
*vase, grasps them roughly, tears each head from the stem, and
grinds it under her feet. The vase goes over with a crash; the water drips unheeded over the table-cloth and floor.*) If I kill, You
Mighty God, I kill at once—I do not torture. (*Falls face
downward on the floor. The laughter of the children shrills loudly* 1000
through the window.)

ACT THREE

TIME: *Seven o'clock in the evening, one week later.*

PLACE: *The same room. There is a coal fire in the grate. The curtains are drawn. A lighted oil lamp with a dark green porcelain
shade is in the center of the table.* MRS. LOVING *and* TOM *are sitting by the table.* MRS. LOVING *sewing,* TOM *reading. There is the
sound of much laughter and the shrill screaming of a child from the
bedrooms. Presently* JIMMY *clad in a flannelet sleeping suit, covering all of him but his head and hands, chases a pillow, which has
come flying through the doorway at the rear. He struggles with it,
finally gets it in his arms, and rushes as fast as he can through the
doorway again.* RACHEL *jumps at him with a cry. He drops the
pillow and shrieks. There is a tussle for possession of it, and they
disappear. The noise grows louder and merrier.* TOM *puts down his
paper and grins. He looks at his mother.*

TOM: Well, who's the giddy one in this family now?

MRS. LOVING: (*Shaking her head in a troubled manner.*) I don't like it. It worries me. Rachel—(*Breaks off.*)

TOM: Have you found out, yet—

5 MRS. LOVING: (*Turning and looking toward the rear doorway, quickly interrupting him.*) Sh! (RACHEL, *laughing, her hair tumbling over her shoulders, comes rushing into the room.* JIMMY *is in close pursuit. He tries to catch her, but she dodges him. They are both breathless.*)

10 MRS. LOVING: (*Deprecatingly.*) Really, Rachel, Jimmy will be so excited he won't be able to sleep. It's after his bedtime, now. Don't you think you had better stop?

RACHEL: All right, Ma dear. Come on, Jimmy; let's play "Old Folks" and sit by the fire. (*She begins to push the big armchair*
15 *over to the fire.* TOM *jumps up, moves her aside, and pushes it himself.* JIMMY *renders assistance.*)

TOM: Thanks, Big Fellow, you are "sure some" strong. I'll remember you when these people around here come for me to move pianos and such things around. Shake! (*They*
20 *shake hands.*)

JIMMY: (*Proudly.*) I am awful strong, am I not?

TOM: You "sure" are a Hercules. (*Hurriedly, as* JIMMY'*s mouth and eyes open wide.*) And see here! don't ask me tonight who that was. I'll tell you the first thing tomorrow morn-
25 ing. Hear? (*Returns to his chair and paper.*)

RACHEL: (*Sitting down.*) Come on, honey boy, and sit in my lap.

JIMMY: (*Doubtfully.*) I thought we were going to play "Old Folks."

30 RACHEL: We are.

JIMMY: Do old folks sit in each other's laps?

RACHEL: Old folks do anything. Come on.

JIMMY: (*Hesitatingly climbs into her lap, but presently snuggles down and sighs audibly from sheer content;* RACHEL *starts to*
35 *bind up her hair.*) Ma Rachel, don't please! I like your hair like that. You're—you're pretty. I like to feel of it; and it smells like—like—oh!—like a barn.

RACHEL: My! how complimentary! I like that. Like a barn, indeed!

40 JIMMY: What's "complimentary"?

RACHEL: Oh! saying nice things about me. (*Pinching his cheek and laughing.*) That my hair is like a barn, for instance.

JIMMY: (*Stoutly.*) Well, that is "complimentary." It smells like hay—like the hay in the barn you took me to, one day, last
45 summer. 'Member?

RACHEL: Yes honey.

JIMMY: (*After a brief pause.*) Ma Rachel!

RACHEL: Well?

JIMMY: Tell me a story, please. It's "story-time," now, isn't it?

50 RACHEL: Well, let's see. (*They both look into the fire for a space; beginning softly.*) Once upon a time, there were two, dear, little boys, and they were all alone in the world. They lived with a cruel, old man and woman, who made them work hard, very hard—all day, and beat them when they did not move
55 fast enough, and always, every night, before they went to bed. They slept in an attic on a rickety, narrow bed, that went screech! screech! whenever they moved. And, in summer, they nearly died with the heat up there, and in winter, with the cold. One wintry night, when they were both
60 weeping very bitterly after a particularly hard beating, they suddenly heard a pleasant voice saying: "Why are you cry-

ing, little boys?" They looked up, and there, in the moonlight, by their bed, was the dearest, little old lady. She was dressed all in gray, from the peak of her little pointed hat to her little, buckled shoes. She held a black cane much taller 65 than her little self. Her hair fell about her ears in tiny, grey corkscrew curls, and they bobbed about as she moved. Her eyes were black and bright—as bright as—well, as that lovely, white light there. No, there! And her cheeks were as red as the apple I gave you yesterday. Do you remember? 70

JIMMY: (*Dreamily.*) Yes.

RACHEL: "Why are you crying, little boys?" she asked again, in a lovely, low, little voice. "Because we are tired and sore and hungry and cold; and we are all alone in the world; and we don't know how to laugh any more. We should so like to 75 laugh again." "Why, that's easy," she said, "it's just like this." And she laughed a little, joyous, musical laugh. "Try!" she commanded. They tried, but their laughing boxes were very rusty, and they made horrid sounds. "Well," she said, "I advise you to pack up, and go away, as soon as you can, 80 to the Land of Laughter. You'll soon learn there, I can tell you." "Is there such a land?" they asked doubtfully. "To be sure there is," she answered the least bit sharply. "We never heard of it," they said. "Well, I'm sure there must be plenty of things you never heard about," she said just the "leastest" 85 bit more sharply. "In a moment you'll be telling me flowers don't talk together, and the birds." "We never heard of such a thing," they said in surprise, their eyes like saucers. "There!" she said, bobbing her little curls. "What did I tell you? You have much to learn." "How do you get to the 90 Land of Laughter?" they asked. "You go out of the eastern gate of the town, just as the sun is rising; and you take the highway there, and follow it; and if you go with it long enough, it will bring you to the very gates of the Land of Laughter. It's a long, long way from here; and it will take 95 you many days." The words had scarcely left her mouth, when, lo! the little lady disappeared, and where she had stood was the white square of moonlight—nothing else. And without more ado these two little boys put their arms around each other and fell fast asleep. And in the grey, just 100 before daybreak, they awoke and dressed; and, putting on their ragged caps and mittens, for it was a wintry day, they stole out of the house and made for the eastern gate. And just as they reached it, and passed through, the whole east leapt into fire. All day they walked, and many days there- 105 after, and kindly people, by the way, took them in and gave them food and drink and sometimes a bed at night. Often they slept by the roadside, but they didn't mind that for the climate was delightful—not too hot, and not too cold. They soon threw away their ragged little mittens. They 110 walked for many days, and there was no Land of Laughter. Once they met an old man, richly dressed, with shining jewels on his fingers, and he stopped them and asked: "Where are you going so fast, little boys?" "We are going to the Land of Laughter," they said together gravely. "That," 115 said the old man, "is a very foolish thing to do. Come with me, and I will take you to the Land of Riches. I will cover you with garments of beauty, and give you jewels and a castle to live in and servants and horses and many things besides." And they said to him: "No, we wish to learn how to 120 laugh again; we have forgotten how, and we are going to the Land of Laughter." "You will regret not going with me.

See, if you don't," he said; and he left them in quite a huff. And they walked again, many days, and again they met an old man. He was tall and imposing-looking and very dignified. And he said: "Where are you going so fast, little boys?" "We are going to the Land of Laughter," they said together very seriously. "What!" he said, "that is an extremely foolish thing to do. Come with me, and I will give you power. I will make you great men: generals, kings, emperors. Whatever you desire to accomplish will be permitted you." And they smiled politely: "Thank you very much, but we have forgotten how to laugh, and we are going there to learn how." He looked upon them haughtily, without speaking, and disappeared. And they walked and walked more days; and they met another old man. And he was clad in rags, and his face was thin, and his eyes were unhappy. And he whispered to them: "Where are you going so fast, little boys?" "We are going to the Land of Laughter," they answered, without a smile. "Laughter! Laughter! that is useless. Come with me and I will show you the beauty of life through sacrifice, suffering for others. That is the only life. I come from the Land of Sacrifice." And they thanked him kindly, but said: "We have suffered long enough. We have forgotten how to laugh. We would learn again." And they went on; and he looked after them very wistfully. They walked more days, and at last they came to the Land of Laughter. And how do you suppose they knew this? Because they could hear, over the wall, the sound of joyous laughter,—the laughter of men, women, and children. And one sat guarding the gate, and they went to her. "We have come a long, long distance; and we would enter the Land of Laughter." "Let me see you smile, first," she said gently. "I sit at the gate; and no one who does not know how to smile may enter the Land of Laughter." And they tried to smile, but could not. "Go away and practice," she said kindly, "and come back tomorrow." And they went away, and practiced all night how to smile; and in the morning they returned, and the gentle lady at the gate said: "Dear little boys, have you learned how to smile?" And they said: "We have tried. How is this?" "Better," she said, "much better. Practice some more, and come back tomorrow." And they went away obediently and practiced. And they came the third day. And she said: "Now try again." And tears of delight came into her lovely eyes. "Those were very beautiful smiles," she said. "Now, you may enter." And she unlocked the gate, and kissed them both, and they entered the Land—the beautiful Land of Laughter. Never had they seen such blue skies, such green trees and grass; never had they heard such birds songs. And people, men, women and children, laughing softly, came to meet them, and took them in, and made them as home; and soon, very soon, they learned to sleep. And they grew up here, and married, and had laughing, happy children. And sometimes they thought of the Land of Riches, and said: "Ah! well!" and sometimes of the Land of Power, and sighed a little; and sometimes of the Land of Sacrifice—and their eyes were wistful. But they soon forgot, and laughed again. And they grew old, laughing. And then when they died—a laugh was on their lips. Thus are things in the beautiful Land of Laughter. (*There is a long pause.*)

JIMMY: I like that story, Ma Rachel. It's nice to laugh, isn't it? Is there such a land?

RACHEL: (*Softly.*) What do you think, honey?

JIMMY: I thinks it would be awful nice if there was. Don't you?

RACHEL: (*Wistfully.*) If there only were! If there only were!

JIMMY: Ma Rachel.

RACHEL: Well?

JIMMY: It makes you think—kind of—doesn't it—of sunshine medicine?

RACHEL: Yes, honey,—but it isn't medicine there. It's always there—just like—well—like our air here. It's *always* sunshine there.

JIMMY: Always sunshine? Never any dark?

RACHEL: No, honey.

JIMMY: You'd—never—be—afraid there, then, would you? Never afraid of nothing?

RACHEL: No, honey.

JIMMY: (*With a big sigh.*) Oh!—Oh! I *wish* it was here—not there. (*Puts his hand up to* RACHEL'*s face; suddenly sits up and looks at her.*) Why, Ma Rachel dear, you're crying. Your face is all wet. Why! Don't cry! Don't cry!

RACHEL: (*Gently.*) Do you remember that I told you the lady at the gate had tears of joy in her eyes, when the two, dear, little boys smiled that beautiful smile?

JIMMY: Yes.

RACHEL: Well, these are tears of joy, honey, that's all—tears of joy.

JIMMY: It must be awful queer to have tears of joy, 'cause you're happy. I never did. (*With a sigh.*) But, if you say they are, dear Ma Rachel, they must be. You knows everything, don't you?

RACHEL: (*Sadly.*) Some things, honey, some things. (*A silence.*)

JIMMY: (*Sighing happily.*) This is the beautiful-est night I ever knew. If you would do just one more thing, it would be lots more beautiful. Will you, Ma Rachel?

RACHEL: Well, what, honey?

JIMMY: Will you sing—at the piano, I mean, it's lots prettier that way—the little song you used to rock me to sleep by? You know, the one about the "Slumber Boat"?

RACHEL: Oh! honey, not tonight. You're too tired. It's bed-time now.

JIMMY: (*Patting her face with his little hand; wheedlingly.*) Please! Ma Rachel, please! pretty please!

RACHEL: Well, honey boy, this once, then. Tonight, you shall have the little song—I used to sing you to sleep by (*half to herself.*) perhaps, for the last time.

JIMMY: Why, Ma Rachel, why the last time?

RACHEL: (*Shaking her head sadly, goes to the piano; in a whisper.*) The last time. (*She twists up her hair into a knot at the back of her head and looks at the keys for a few moments; then she plays the accompaniment of the "Slumber Boat" through softly, and, after a moment, sings. Her voice is full of pent-up longing, and heartbreak, and hopelessness. She ends in a little sob, but attempts to cover it by singing, lightly and daintily, the chorus of "The Owl and the Moon" . . . Then softly and with infinite tenderness, almost against her will, she plays and sings again the refrain of the "Slumber Boat".*)

> "Sail, baby, sail
> Out from that sea.
> Only don't forget to sail
> Back again to me."

245 (*Presently she rises and goes to* JIMMY, *who is lolling back happily in the big chair. During the singing,* TOM *and* MRS. LOVING *apparently do not listen; when she sobs, however,* TOM'S *hand on his paper tightens;* MRS. LOVING'S *needle poises for a moment in mid-air. Neither looks at* RACHEL. JIMMY *evidently has not noticed the sob.*)

250 RACHEL: (*Kneeling by* JIMMY.) Well, honey, how did you like it?

JIMMY: (*Proceeding to pull down her hair from the twist.*) It was lovely, Ma Rachel. (*Yawns audibly.*) Now, Ma Rachel, I'm just beautifully sleepy. (*Dreamily.*) I think that p'r'aps I'll go to the Land of Laughter tonight in my dreams. I'll go in 255 the "Slumber Boat" and come back in the morning and tell you all about it. Shall I?

RACHEL: Yes, honey. (*Whispers.*)

"Only don't forget to sail
Back again to me."

260 TOM: (*Suddenly.*) Rachel! (RACHEL *starts slightly.*) I nearly forgot. John is coming here tonight to see how you are. He told me to tell you so.

RACHEL: (*Stiffens perceptibly, then in different tones.*) Very well. Thank you. (*Suddenly with a little cry she puts her arms* 265 *around* JIMMY.) Jimmy! honey! don't go tonight. Don't go without Ma Rachel. Wait for me, honey. I do so wish to go, too, to the Land of Laughter. Think of it, Jimmy; nothing but birds always singing, and flowers always blooming, and skies always blue—and people, all of them, always 270 laughing, laughing. You'll wait for Ma Rachel, won't you honey?

JIMMY: Is there really and truly, Ma Rachel, a Land of Laughter?

RACHEL: Oh! Jimmy, let's hope so; let's pray so.

JIMMY: (*Frowns.*) I've been thinking— (*Pauses.*) You have to 275 smile at the gate, don't you, to get in?

RACHEL: Yes, honey.

JIMMY: Well, I guess I couldn't smile if my Ma Rachel wasn't somewhere close to me. So I couldn't get in after all, could I? Tonight, I'll go somewhere else, and tell you all about it. 280 And then, some day, we'll go together, won't we?

RACHEL: (*Sadly.*) Yes, honey, some day—some day. (*A short silence.*) Well, this isn't going to "sleepy-sleep," is it? Go, now, and say good-night to Ma Loving and Uncle Tom.

JIMMY: (*Gets down obediently, and goes first to* MRS. LOVING. *She* 285 *leans over, and he puts his little arms around her neck. They kiss; very sweetly.*) Sweet dreams! God keep you all the night!

MRS. LOVING: The sweetest of sweet dreams to you, dear little boy! Good-night. (RACHEL *watches, unwatched, the scene.* 290 *Her eyes are full of yearning.*)

JIMMY: (*Going to* TOM, *who makes believe he does not see him.*) Uncle Tom!

TOM: (*Jumps as though tremendously startled;* JIMMY *laughs.*) My! how you frightened me. You'll put my gizzard out of 295 commission, if you do that often. Well, sir, what can I do for you?

JIMMY: I came to say good-night.

TOM: (*Gathering* JIMMY *up in his arms and kissing him; gently and with emotion.*) Good-night, dear little Big Fellow! Good-300 night!

JIMMY: Sweet dreams! God keep you all the night! (*Goes sedately to* RACHEL, *and holds out his little hand.*) I'm ready, Ma Rachel. (*Yawns.*) I'm so nice and sleepy.

305 RACHEL: (*With* JIMMY's *hand in hers, she hesitates a moment, and then approaches* TOM *slowly. For a short time she stands looking down at him; suddenly leaning over him.*) Why, Tom, what a pretty tie! Is it new?

TOM: Well, no, not exactly. I've had it about a month. It is rather a beauty, isn't it?

310 RACHEL: Why, I never remember seeing it.

TOM: (*Laughing.*) I guess not. I saw to that.

RACHEL: Stingy!

TOM: Well, I am—where my ties are concerned. I've had experience.

315 RACHEL: (*Tentatively.*) Tom!

TOM: Well?

RACHEL: (*Nervously and wistfully.*) Are you—will you—I mean, won't you be home this evening?

TOM: You've got a long memory, Sis. I've that engagement, 320 you know. Why?

RACHEL: (*Slowly.*) I forgot; so you have.

TOM: Why?

RACHEL: (*Hastily.*) Oh! nothing—nothing. Come on, Jimmy boy, you can hardly keep those little peepers open, can you? Come on, honey. (RACHEL *and* JIMMY *go out the rear* 325 *doorway. There is a silence.*)

MRS. LOVING: (*Slowly, as though thinking aloud.*) I try to make out what could have happened; but it's no use—I can't. Those four days, she lay in bed hardly moving, scarcely speaking. Only her eyes seemed alive. I never saw such a 330 wide, tragic look in my life. It was as though her soul had been mortally wounded. But how? how? What could have happened?

TOM: (*Quietly.*) I don't know. She generally tells me everything; but she avoids me now. If we are alone in a room— 335 she gets out. I don't know what it means.

MRS. LOVING: She will hardly let Jimmy out of her sight. While he's at school, she's nervous and excited. She seems always to be listening, but for what? When he returns, she nearly devours him. And she always asks him in a fright- 340 ened sort of way, her face as pale and tense as can be: "Well, honey boy, how was school today?" And he always answers, "Fine, Ma Rachel, fine! I learned—"; and then he goes on to tell her everything that has happened. And when he has finished, she says in an uneasy sort of way: 345 "Is—is that all?" And when he says "Yes," she relaxes and becomes limp. After a little while she becomes feverishly happy. She plays with Jimmy and the children more than ever she did—and she played a good deal, as you know. They're here, or she's with them. Yesterday, I said in rem- 350 onstrance, when she came in, her face pale and haggard and black hollows under her eyes: "Rachel, remember you're just out of a sickbed. You're not well enough to go on like this." "I know," was all she would say, "but I've got to. I can't help myself. This part of their little lives must 355 be happy—it just must be." (*Pauses.*) The last couple of nights, Jimmy has awakened and cried most pitifully. She wouldn't let me go to him; said I had enough trouble, and she could quiet him. She never will let me know why he cries; but she stays with him, and soothes him until at last, 360 he falls asleep again. Every time she has come out like a rag; and her face is like a dead woman's. Strange isn't it, this is the first time we have ever been able to talk it over? Tom, what could have happened?

365 TOM: I don't know, Ma, but I feel, as you do; something terrible and sudden has hurt her soul; and, poor little thing, she's trying bravely to readjust herself to life again. (*Pauses, looks at his watch and then rises, and goes to her. He pats her back awkwardly.*) Well, Ma, I'm going now. Don't worry too

370 much. Youth, you know, gets over things finally. It takes them hard, that's all—. At least, that's what the older heads tell us. (*Gets his hat and stands in the vestibule doorway.*) Ma, you know, I begin with John tomorrow. (*With emotion.*) I don't believe we'll ever forget John. Good-night! (*Exit.*

375 MRS. LOVING *continues to sew.* RACHEL, *her hair arranged, reenters through the rear doorway. She is humming.*)

RACHEL: He's sleeping like a top. Aren't little children, Ma dear, the sweetest things, when they're all helpless and asleep? One little hand is under his cheek; and he's smil-

380 ing. (*Stops suddenly, biting her lips. A pause.*) Where's Tom?

MRS. LOVING: He went out a few minutes ago.

RACHEL: (*Sitting in* TOM'*s chair and pickin up his paper. She is exceedingly nervous. She looks the paper over rapidly; presently trying to make her tone casual.*) Ma,—you—you—aren't going

385 anywhere tonight, are you?

MRS. LOVING: I've got to go out for a short time about half-past eight. Mrs. Jordan, you know, I'll not be gone very long, though. Why?

RACHEL: Oh! nothing particular. I just thought it would be

390 cosy if we could sit here together the rest of the evening. Can't you—can't you go tomorrow?

MRS. LOVING: Why, I don't see how I can. I've made the engagement. It's about a new reception gown; and she's exceedingly exacting, as you know. I can't afford to lose her.

395 RACHEL: No. I suppose not. All right, Ma dear. (*Presently, paper in hand, she laughs, but not quite naturally.*) Look! Ma dear! How is that for fashion, anyway? Isn't it the "limit"? (*Rises and shows her mother a picture in the paper. As she is in the act, the bell rings. With a startled cry.*) Oh! (*Drops the pa-*

400 *per, and grips her mother's hand.*)

MRS. LOVING: (*Anxiously.*) Rachel, your nerves are right on edge; and your hand feels like fire. I'll have to see a doctor about you; and that's all there is to it.

RACHEL: (*Laughing nervously, and moving toward the vestibule.*)

405 Nonsense, Ma dear! Just because I let out a whoop now and then, and have nice warm hands? (*Goes out, is heard talking through the tube.*) Yes! (*Her voice emitting tremendous relief.*) Oh! bring it right up! (*Appearing in the doorway.*) Ma dear, did you buy anything at Goddard's today?

410 MISS LOVING: Yes; and I've been wondering why they were so late in delivering it. I bought it early this morning. (RACHEL *goes out again. A door opens and shuts. She reappears with a bundle.*)

MRS. LOVING: Put it on my bed, Rachel, please. (*Exit* RACHEL

415 *rear doorway; presently returns empty-handed; sits down again at the table with the paper between herself and mother; sinks in a deep revery. Suddenly there is the sound of many loud knocks made by numerous small fists.* RACHEL *drops the paper, and comes to a sitting posture, tense again. Her mother looks at her,*

420 *but says nothing. Almost immediately* RACHEL *relaxes.*)

RACHEL: My kiddies! They're late, this evening. (*Goes out into the vestibule. A door opens and shuts. There is the shrill, excited sound of childish voices.* RACHEL *comes in surrounded by the children, all trying to say something to her at once.* RACHEL *puts*

425 *her finger on her lip and points toward the doorway in the rear.*

They all quiet down. She sits on the floor in the front of the stage, and the children all cluster around her. Their conversation takes place in a half-whisper. As they enter they nod brightly at MRS. LOVING, *who smiles in return.*) Why so late, kiddies? It's long past "sleepy-time." 430

LITTLE NANCY: We've been playing "Hide and Seek," and having the mostest fun. We promised, all of us, that if we could play until half-past seven tonight we wouldn't make any fuss about going to bed at seven o'clock the rest of the week. It's awful hard to go. I *hate* to go to bed! 435

LITTLE MARY, LOUISE and EDITH: So do I! So do I! So do I!

LITTLE MARTHA: I don't. I love bed. My bed, after my muzzer tucks me all in, is like a nice warm bag. I just stick my nose out. When I lifts my head up I can see the light from the dining-room come in the door. I can hear my muzzer and 440 fazzer talking nice and low; and then, before I know it, I'm fast asleep, and I dream pretty things, and in about a minute it's morning again. I love my little bed, and I love to dream.

LITTLE MARY: (*Aggressively.*) Well, I guess I love to dream too. 445 I wish I could dream, though, without going to bed.

LITTLE NANCY: When I grow up, I'm never going to bed at night! (*Darkly.*) You see.

LITTLE LOUISE: "Grown-ups" just love to poke their heads out of windows and cry, "Child'run, it's time for bed 450 now; and you'd better hurry, too. I can tell you." They "sure" are queer, for sometimes when I wake up, it must be about twelve o'clock, I can hear by big sister giggling and talking to some silly man. If it's good for me to go to bed early—I should think— 455

RACHEL: (*Interrupting suddenly.*) Why, where is my little Jenny? Excuse me, Louise dear.

LITTLE MARTHA: Her cold is awful bad. She coughs like this (*giving a distressing imitation.*) and snuffles all the time. She can't talk out loud, and she can't go to sleep. Muzzer says 460 she's fev'rish—I thinks that's what she says. Jenny says she knows she could go to sleep, if you would come and sit with her a little while.

RACHEL: I certainly will. I'll go when you do, honey.

LITTLE MARTHA: (*Softly stroking* RACHEL'*s arm.*) You're the 465 very nicest "grown-up," (*loyally.*) except my muzzer, of course, I ever knew. You knows all about little chil'run and you can be one, although you're all grown up. I think you would make a lovely muzzer. (*To the rest of the children.*) Don't you? 470

ALL: (*In excited whispers.*) Yes, I do.

RACHEL: (*Winces, then says gently.*) Come, kiddies, you must go now, or your mothers will blame me for keeping you. (*Rises, as do the rest.* LITTLE MARTHA *puts her hand into* RACHEL'*s.*) Ma dear, I'm going down to sit a little while 475 with Jenny. I'll be back before you go, though. Come, kiddies, say good-night to my mother.

ALL: (*Gravely.*) Good-night! Sweet dreams! God keep you all the night.

MRS. LOVING: Good-night dears! Sweet dreams, all! 480

(*Exeunt* RACHEL *and the children.* MRS. LOVING *continues to sew. The bell presently rings three distinct times. In a few moments,* MRS. LOVING *gets up and goes out into the vestibule. A door opens and closes.* MRS. LOVING *and* JOHN STRONG *come in. He is a trifle pale but his imperturbable self.* MRS. LOVING, *somewhat nervous, takes her seat and resumes her sewing. She motions* STRONG *to a chair. He returns to the vestibule, leaves his hat, returns, and sits down.*)

STRONG: Well, how is everything?

MRS. LOVING: Oh! about the same, I guess. Tom's out. John, we'll never forget you—and your kindness.

STRONG: That was nothing. And Rachel?

485 MRS. LOVING: She'll be back presently. She went to sit with a sick child for a little while.

STRONG: And how is she?

MRS. LOVING: She's not herself yet, but I think she is better.

STRONG: (*After a short pause.*) Well, what *did* happen—exactly.

490 MRS. LOVING: That's just what I don't know.

STRONG: When you came home—you couldn't get in—was that it?

MRS. LOVING: Yes. (*Pauses.*) It was just a week ago today. I was down town all the morning. It was about one o'clock when 495 I got back. I had forgotten my key. I rapped on the door and then called. There was no answer. A window was open, and I could feel the air under the door, and I could hear it as the draught sucked it through. There was no other sound. Presently I made such a noise the people began to come out 500 into the hall. Jimmy was in one of the flats playing with a little girl named Mary. He told me he had left Rachel here a short time before. She had given him four cookies, two for him and two for Mary, and had told him he could play with her until she came to tell him his lunch was ready. I saw he 505 was getting frightened, so I got the little girl and her mother to keep him in their flat. Then, as no man was at home, I sent out for help. Three men broke the door down. (*Pauses.*) We found Rachel unconscious, lying on her face. For a few minutes I thought she was dead. (*Pauses.*) A vase had fallen 510 over on the table and the water had dripped through the cloth onto the floor. There had been flowers in it. When I left, there were no flowers here. What she could have done to them, I can't say. The long stems were lying everywhere, and the flowers had been ground into the floor. I could tell 515 that they must have been roses from the stems. After we had put her to bed and called the doctor, and she had finally regained consciousness, I very naturally asked her what had happened. All she would say was, "Ma dear, I'm too— tired—please." For four days she lay in bed scarcely moving, 520 speaking only when spoken to. That first day, when Jimmy came to see her, she shrank away from him. We had to take him out, and comfort him as best we could. We kept him away, almost by force, until she got up. And, then, she was utterly miserable when he was out of her sight. What hap- 525 pened, I don't know. She avoids Tom, and she won't tell me. (*Pauses.*) Tom and I both believe her soul has been hurt. The trouble isn't with her body. You'll find her highly nervous. Sometimes she is very much depressed; again she is fever- ishly gay—almost reckless. What do you think about it, 530 John?

STRONG: (*Who has listened quietly.*) Had anybody been here, do you know?

MRS. LOVING: No, I don't. I don't like to ask Rachel; and I can't ask the neighbors.

535 STRONG: No, of course not. (*Pauses.*) You say there were some flowers?

MRS. LOVING: Yes.

STRONG: And the flowers were ground into the carpet?

MRS. LOVING: Yes.

STRONG: Did you happen to notice the box? They must have 540 come in a box, don't you think?

MRS. LOVING: Yes, there was a box in the kitchenette. It was from "Marcy's." I saw no card.

STRONG: (*Slowly.*) It is rather strange. (*A long silence, during which the outer door opens and shuts.* RACHEL *is heard singing.* 545 *She stops abruptly. In a second or two she appears in the door. There is an air of suppressed excitement about her.*)

RACHEL: Hello! John. (STRONG *rises, nods at her, and brings forward for her the big arm-chair near the fire.*) I thought that was your hat in the hall. It's brand new, I know—but it 550 looks—"Johnlike." How are you? Ma! Jenny went to sleep like a little lamb. I don't like her breathing, though. (*Looks from one to the other; flippantly.*) Who's dead? (*Nods her thanks to* STRONG *for the chair and sits down.*)

MRS. LOVING: Dead, Rachel? 555

RACHEL: Yes. The atmosphere here is so funereal,—it's posi- tively "crapey."

STRONG: I don't know why it should be—I was just asking how you are.

RACHEL: Heavens! Does the mere inquiry into my health 560 precipitate such an atmosphere? Your two faces were as long, as long—(*Breaks off.*) Kind sir, let me assure you, I am in the very best of health. And how are you, John?

STRONG: Oh! I'm always well. (*Sits down.*)

MRS. LOVING: Rachel, I'll have to get ready to go now. John, 565 don't hurry. I'll be back shortly, probably in three-quarters of an hour—maybe less.

RACHEL: And maybe more, if I remember Mrs. Jordan. How- ever, Ma dear, I'll do the best I can—while you are away. I'll try to be a credit to your training. (MRS. LOVING *smiles* 570 *and goes out the rear doorway.*) Now, let's see—in the books of etiquette, I believe, the properly reared young lady, al- ways asks the young gentleman caller—you're young enough, aren't you, to be classed still as a "young gentle- man caller?" (*No answer.*) Well, anyway, she always asks the 575 young gentleman caller sweetly something about the weather. (*Primly.*) This has been an exceedingly beautiful day, hasn't it, Mr. Strong? (*No answer from* STRONG, *who, with his head resting against the back of the chair, and his knees crossed is watching her in an amused, quizzical manner.*) Well, 580 really, every properly brought up young gentleman, I'm sure, ought to know, that it's exceedingly rude not to an- swer a civil question.

STRONG: (*Lazily.*) Tell me what to answer, Rachel.

RACHEL: Say, "Yes, very"; and look interested and pleased 585 when you say it.

STRONG: (*With a half-smile.*) Yes, very.

RACHEL: Well, I certainly wouldn't characterize that as a par- ticularly animated remark. Besides, when you look at me through half-closed lids like that—and kind of smile— 590 what are you thinking? (*No answer.*) John Strong, are you deaf or—just plain stupid?

STRONG: Plain stupid, I guess.

RACHEL: (*In wheedling tones.*) What were you thinking, John?

STRONG: (*Slowly.*) I was thinking—(*Breaks off.*) 595

RACHEL: (*Irritably.*) Well?

STRONG: I've changed my mind.

RACHEL: You're not going to tell me?

STRONG: No.

(MRS. LOVING *dressed for the street comes in.*)

600 MRS. LOVING: Goodbye, children. Rachel, don't quarrel so much with John. Let me see—if I have my key. (*Feels in her bag.*) Yes, I have it. I'll be back shortly. Good-bye. (STRONG *and* RACHEL *rise. He bows.*)

RACHEL: Good-bye, Ma dear. Hurry back as soon as you can,
605 won't you? (*Exit* MRS. LOVING *through the vestibule.* STRONG *leans back again in his chair, and watches* RACHEL *through half-closed eyes.* RACHEL *sits in her chair nervously.*)

STRONG: Do you mind, if I smoke?

RACHEL: You know I don't.

610 STRONG: I am trying to behave like—Reginald—"the properly reared young gentleman caller." (*Lights a cigar; goes over to the fire, and throws his match away.* RACHEL *goes into the kitchenette, and brings him a saucer for his ashes. She places it on the table near him.*) Thank you. (*They both sit again,* STRONG
615 *very evidently enjoying his cigar and* RACHEL.) Now this is what I call cosy.

RACHEL: Cosy! Why?

STRONG: A nice warm room—shut in—curtains drawn—a cheerful fire crackling at my back—a lamp, not an electric
620 or gas one, but one of your plain, old-fashioned kerosene ones—

RACHEL: (*Interrupting.*) Ma dear would like to catch you, I am sure, talking about *her* lamp like that. "Old-fashioned! plain!"—You have nerve.

625 STRONG: (*Continuing as though he had not been interrupted.*) A comfortable chair—a good cigar—and not very far away, a little lady, who is looking charming, so near, that if I reached over, I could touch her. You there—and I here.— It's living.

630 RACHEL: Well! of all things! A compliment—and from *you!* How did it slip out, pray? (*No answer.*) I suppose that you realize that a conversation between two persons is absolutely impossible, if one has to do her share all alone. Soon my ingenuity for introducing interesting subjects
635 will be exhausted; and then will follow what, I believe, the story books call, "an uncomfortable silence."

STRONG: (*Slowly.*) Silence—between friends—isn't such a bad thing.

RACHEL: Thanks awfully. (*Leans back; cups her cheek in her hand,*
640 *and makes no pretense at further conversation. The old look of introspection returns to her eyes. She does not move.*)

STRONG: (*Quietly.*) Rachel! (RACHEL *starts perceptibly.*) You must remember I'm here. I don't like looking into your soul—when you forget you're not alone.

645 RACHEL: I hadn't forgotten.

STRONG: Wouldn't it be easier for you, little girl, if you could tell—some one?

RACHEL: No. (*A silence.*)

STRONG: Rachel,—you're fond of flowers,—aren't you?
650 RACHEL: Yes.

STRONG: Rosebuds—red rosebuds—particularly?

RACHEL: (*Nervously.*) Yes.

STRONG: Did you—dislike—the giver?

RACHEL: (*More nervously; bracing herself.*) No, of course not.
655 STRONG: Rachel,—why—why—did you—kill the roses— then?

RACHEL: (*Twisting her hands.*) Oh, John! I'm so sorry, Ma dear told you that. She didn't know, you sent them.

STRONG: So I gathered. (*Pauses and then leans forward; quietly.*)
Rachel, little girl, why—did you kill them?   660

RACHEL: (*Breathing quickly.*) Don't you believe—it—a—a— kindness—sometimes—to kill?

STRONG: (*After a pause.*) You—considered—it—a—kind- ness—to kill them?

RACHEL: Yes. (*Another pause.*)   665

STRONG: Do you mean—just—the roses?

RACHEL: (*Breathing more quickly.*) John!—Oh! must I say?

STRONG: Yes, little Rachel.

RACHEL: (*In a whisper.*) No. (*There is a long pause.* RACHEL *leans back limply, and closes her eyes. Presently* STRONG *rises, and*   670 *moves his chair very close to hers. She does not stir. He puts his cigar on the saucer.*)

STRONG: (*Leaning forward; very gently.*) Little girl, little girl, can't you tell me why?

RACHEL: (*Wearily.*) I can't—It hurts—too much—to talk   675 about it yet.—please.

STRONG: (*Takes her hand; looks at it a few minutes and then at her quietly.*) You—don't—care, then? (*She winces.*) Rachel!—Look at me, little girl! (*As if against her will, she looks at him. Her eyes are fearful, hunted. She tries to look away,*   680 *to draw away her hand; but he holds her gaze and her hand steadily.*) Do you?

RACHEL: (*Almost sobbing.*) John! John! don't ask me. You are drawing my very soul out of my body with your eyes. You must not talk this way. You mustn't look—John, don't!   685 (*Tries to shield her eyes.*)

STRONG: (*Quietly takes both of her hands, and kisses the backs and the palms slowly. A look of horror creeps into her face. He delib- erately raises his eyes and looks at her mouth. She recoils as though she expected him to strike her. He resumes slowly.*) If—   690 you—do—care, and I know now—that you do—nothing else, *nothing* should count.

RACHEL: (*Wrenching herself from his grasp and rising. She covers her ears; she breathes rapidly.*) No! No! No!—You *must* stop. (*Laughs nervously; continues feverishly.*) I'm not behaving   695 very well as a hostess, am I? Let's see. What shall I do? I'll play you something, John. How will that do? Or I'll sing to you. You used to like to hear me sing; you said my voice, I remember, was sympathetic, didn't you? (*Moves quickly to the piano.*) I'll sing you a pretty song. I think   700 it's beautiful. You've never heard it, I know. I've never sung it to you before. It's Nevin's "At Twilight." (*Pauses, looks down, before she begins, then turns toward him and says quietly and sweetly.*) Sometimes—in the coming years—I want—you to remember—I sang you this little song.—   705 Will you?—I think it will make it easier for me—when I—when I—(*Breaks off and begins the first chords.* STRONG *goes slowly to the piano. He leans there watching intently.* RACHEL *sings.*)

"The roses of yester-year   710
Were all of the white and red;
It fills my heart with silent fear
To find all their beauty fled.

The roses of white are sere,
All faded the roses red,   715
And one who loves me is not here
And one that I love is dead."

(*A long pause. Then* STRONG *goes to her and lifts her from the piano-stool. He puts one arm around her very tenderly and pushes her head back so he can look into her eyes. She shuts them, but is passive.*)

STRONG: (*Gently.*) Little girl, little girl, don't you know that suggestions—suggestions—like those you are sending
720 yourself constantly—are wicked things? You, who are so gentle, so loving, so warm—(*Breaks off and crushes her to him. He kisses her many times. She does not resist, but in the midst of his caresses she breaks suddenly into convulsive laughter. He tries to hush the terrible sound with his mouth; then bro-*
725 *kenly.*) Little girl—don't laugh—like that.
RACHEL: (*Interrupted throughout by her laughter.*) I have to.— God is laughing.—We're his puppets.—He pulls the wires,—and we're so funny to Him.—I'm laughing too— because I can hear—my little children—weeping. They
730 come to me generally while I'm asleep,—but I can hear them now.—They've begged me—do you understand?— begged me—not to bring them here;—and I've promised them—not to.—I've promised. I can't stand the sound of their crying.—I have to laugh—Oh! John! laugh!—laugh
735 too!—I can't drown their weeping.

(STRONG *picks her up bodily and carries her to the armchair.*)

STRONG: (*Harshly.*) Now, stop that!
740 RACHEL: (*In sheer surprise.*) W-h-a-t?
STRONG: (*Still harshly.*) Stop that!—You've lost your self-control.—Find yourself again!

(*He leaves her and goes over to the fireplace, and stands looking down into it for some little time.* RACHEL, *little by little, becomes*
745 *calmer.* STRONG *returns and sits beside her again. She doesn't move. He smoothes her hair back gently, and kisses her forehead—and then, slowly, her mouth. She does not resist; simply sits there, with shut eyes, inert, limp.*)

750 STRONG: Rachel!—(*Pauses.*) There is a little flat on 43rd Street. It faces south and overlooks a little park. Do you remember it?—it's on the top floor?—Once I remember your saying—you liked it. That was over a year ago. That same day—I rented it. I've never lived there. No one
755 knows about it—not even my mother. It's completely furnished now—and waiting—do you know for whom? Every single thing in it, I've bought myself—even to the pins on the little bird's-eye maple dresser. It has been the happiest year I have ever known. I furnished it—one
760 room at a time. It's the prettiest, the most homelike little flat I've ever seen. (*Very low.*) Everything there—breathes love. Do you know for whom it is waiting? On the sitting-room floor is a beautiful, Turkish rug—red, and blue and gold. It's soft—and rich—and do you know for
765 whose little feet it is waiting? There are delicate curtains at the windows and a bookcase full of friendly, eager, little books.—Do you know for whom they are waiting? There are comfortable leather chairs, just the right size, and a beautiful piano—that I leave open—sometimes, and
770 lovely pictures of Madonnas. Do you know for whom they are waiting? There is an open fireplace with logs of wood, all carefully piled on gleaming andirons—and waiting. There is a bellows and a pair of shining tongs— waiting. And in the kitchenette painted blue and white,

and smelling sweet with paint is everything: bright pots 775 and pans and kettles, and blue and white enamel-ware, and all kinds of knives and forks and spoons—and on the door—a roller-towel. Little girl, do you know for whom they are all waiting? And somewhere—there's a big, strong man—with broad shoulders. And he's willing and anxious 780 to do anything—everything, and he's waiting very patiently. Little girl, is it to be—yes or no?
RACHEL: (*During* STRONG's *speech life has come flooding back to her. Her eyes are shining; her face, eager. For a moment she is beautifully happy.*) Oh! you're too good to me and mine, 785 John. I—didn't dream any one—could be—so good. (*Leans forward and puts his big hand against her cheek and kisses it shyly.*)
STRONG: (*Quietly.*) Is it—yes—or no, little girl?
RACHEL: (*Feverishly, gripping his hands.*) Oh, yes! yes! yes! and 790 take me quickly, John. Take me before I can think any more. You mustn't let me think, John. And you'll be good to me, won't you? Every second of every minute, of every hour, of every day, you'll have me in your thoughts, won't you? And you'll be with me every minute that you can? 795 And, John. John!—you'll keep away the weeping of my little children. You won't let me hear it, will you? You'll make me forget everything everything—won't you?— Life is so short, John. (*Shivers and then fearfully and slowly.*) And eternity so—long. (*Feverishly again.*) And, John, after 800 I am dead—promise me, promise me you'll love me more. (*Shivers again.*) I'll need love then. Oh! I'll need it. (*Suddenly there comes to their ears the sound of a child's weeping. It is monotonous, hopeless, terribly afraid.* RACHEL *recoils.*) Oh! John!—Listen!—It's my boy, again.—I—John—I'll be 805 back in a little while. (*Goes swiftly to the door in the rear, pauses and looks back. The weeping continues. Her eyes are tragic. Slowly she kisses her hand to him and disappears.* JOHN *stands where she has left him looking down. The weeping stops. Presently* RACHEL *appears in the doorway. She is haggard, and* 810 *grey. She does not enter the room. She speaks as one dead might speak—tonelessly, slowly.*)
RACHEL: Do you wish to know why Jimmy is crying?
STRONG: Yes.
RACHEL: I am twenty-two—and I'm old; you're thirty-two— 815 and you're old; Tom's twenty-three—and he is old. Ma dear's sixty—and she said once she is much older than that. She is. We are all blighted; we are all accursed—all of us—, everywhere, we whose skins are dark—our lives blasted by the white man's prejudice. (*Pauses.*) And my lit- 820 tle Jimmy—seven years old, that's all—is blighted too. In a year or two, at best, he will be made old by suffering. (*Pauses.*) One week ago, today, some white boys, older and larger than my little Jimmy, as he was leaving the school— called him "Nigger"! They chased him through the streets 825 calling him, "Nigger! Nigger! Nigger!" One boy threw stones at him. There is still a bruise on his little back where one struck him. That will get well; but they bruised his soul—and that—will never—get well. He asked me what "Nigger" meant. I made light of the whole 830 thing, laughed it off. He went to his little playmates, and very naturally asked them. The oldest of them is nine!— and they knew, poor little things—and they told him. (*Pauses.*) For the last couple of nights he has been dream- ing—about these boys. And he always awakes—in the 835

dark—afraid—afraid—of the now—and the future—I have seen that look of deadly fear—in the eyes—of other little children. I know what it is myself.—I was twelve—when some big boys chased me and called me names.—I

840 never left the house afterwards—without being afraid. I was afraid, in the streets—in the school—in the church, everywhere, always, afraid of being hurt. And I—was not—afraid in vain. (*The weeping begins again.*) He's only a baby—and he's blighted. (*To* JIMMY.) Honey, I'm right

845 here. I'm coming in just a minute. Don't cry. (*To* STRONG.) If it nearly kills me to hear my Jimmy's crying, do you think I could stand it, when my own child, flesh of my flesh, blood of my blood—learned the same reason for weeping? Do you? (*Pauses.*) Ever since I fell here—a week

850 ago—I am afraid—to go—to sleep, for every time I do—my children come—and beg me—weeping—not to—bring them here—to suffer. Tonight, they came—when I was awake. (*Pauses.*) I have promised them again, now—by Jimmy's bed. (*In a whisper.*) I have damned—my soul to

855 all eternity—if I do. (*To* JIMMY.) Honey, don't! I'm coming. (*To* STRONG.) And John.—dear John—you see—it can never be—all the beautiful, beautiful things—you have—told me about. (*Wistfully.*) No—they—can never be—now. (STRONG *comes toward her.*) No.—John dear,—

860 you—must not—touch me—any more. (*Pauses.*) Dear, this—is—"Good-bye."

STRONG: (*Quietly.*) It's not fair—to you, Rachel, to take you—at your word—tonight. You're sick; you've brooded so long, so continuously,—you've lost—your perspective.

865 Don't answer, yet. Think it over for another week and I'll come back.

RACHEL: (*Wearily.*) No.—I can't think—any more.

STRONG: You realize—fully—you're sending me—for always?

RACHEL: Yes.

870 STRONG: And you care?

RACHEL: Yes.

STRONG: It's settled, then for all time—"Good-bye!"

RACHEL: (*After a pause.*) Yes.

STRONG: (*Stands looking at her steadily a long time, and then moves to the door and turns, facing her with infinite tenderness.*) 875 Good-bye, dear, little Rachel—God bless you.

RACHEL: Good-bye, John! (STRONG *goes out. A door opens and shuts. There is finality in the sound. The weeping continues. Suddenly, with a great cry.*) John! John! (*Runs out into the vestibule. She presently returns. She is calm again. Slowly.*) No! 880 No! John. Not for us. (*A pause with infinite warning.*) Oh! John.—if it only—if it only—(*Breaks off, controls herself. Slowly again; thoughtfully.*) No—No sunshine—no laughter—always, always—darkness. That is it. Even our little flat— (*In a whisper.*) John's and mine—the little flat—that 885 calls, calls us—through darkness. It shall wait—and wait—in—vain—in darkness. Oh, John! (*Pauses.*) And my little children! my little children! (*The weeping ceases; pauses.*) I shall never—see—you—now. Your little, brown, beautiful bodies—I shall never see.—Your dimples—everywhere— 890 your laughter—your tears—the beautiful, lovely feel of you here. (*Puts her hands against her heart.*) Never—never—to be. (*A pause, fiercely.*) But you are somewhere—and wherever you are you are mine! You are mine! All of you! Every bit of you! Even God can't take you away. (*A pause;* 895 *very sweetly; pathetically.*) Little children!—My little children!—No more need you come to me—weeping—weeping. You may be happy now—you are safe. Little weeping, voices, hush! hush! (*The weeping begins again. To* JIMMY, *her whole soul in her voice.*) Jimmy! My little Jimmy! 900 Honey! I'm coming.—Ma Rachel loves you so. (*Sobs and goes blindly, unsteadily to the rear doorway; she leans her head there one second against the door; and then stumbles through and disappears. The light in the lamp flickers and goes out. . . . It is black. The terrible, heartbreaking weeping continues.*) 1000

THE END

Eugene O'Neill

Born the son of the famous turn-of-the-century actor James O'Neill, Eugene O'Neill (1888–1953) became America's greatest dramatist. Much of O'Neill's younger life is described in his late play, *Long Day's Journey into Night:* how he spent his first several years touring with his family following his father's career on the stage; his stints in boarding school and at Princeton; some time spent working on ships sailing to South America and Africa, and bumming around in Buenos Aires and New York; a serious bout with tuberculosis. In the play, O'Neill leaves the future of his young poet-hero uncertain, but in fact illness provided O'Neill with the time to begin writing seriously. When he recovered, O'Neill attended George Pierce Baker's playwriting classes at Harvard. He worked briefly in Greenwich Village and then joined the Provincetown Playhouse company on Cape Cod in 1916, where his first plays were produced.

O'Neill had a long and tumultuous career in the theater. An admirer of Strindberg's drama, and widely read in Nietzsche, Freud, and Jung, O'Neill experimented in a variety of different theatrical styles, always searching for new ways to reveal the complex working of a character's psychology. He wrote a series of short realistic plays that were produced at the Provincetown and other "little theaters," the best of which concern life at sea: *Bound East for Cardiff* (1916), *Fog* (1917), *In the Zone* (1917), *The Long Voyage Home* (1917), and *The Moon of the Caribbees* (1918). His first Broadway production, *Beyond the Horizon* (1920) won him the first of four Pulitzer Prizes; he later won for *Anna Christie* (1921), *Strange Interlude* (1928), and *Long Day's Journey into Night* (awarded posthumously in 1956). Throughout the 1920s, the period of his greatest success in the theater, O'Neill both wrote realistic plays like *Desire Under the Elms* (1924) and experimented in a variety of other modes. He tried expressionistic techniques in *The Hairy Ape* (1922) and *The Emperor Jones* (1920); masks in *The Great God Brown* (1926); and revealing "asides" in *Strange Interlude,* in which characters speak their unspoken "thoughts" directly to the audience. He also took a chance with comedy in *Ah, Wilderness!* (1932), something of a study for *Long Day's Journey.*

O'Neill's decade of success was followed by a series of impressive failures. Some of these plays are nonetheless fascinating. Although it played well in 1928, the asides and length (more than eight hours) of *Strange Interlude* have militated against many revivals; the parallels between Aeschylus' *Oresteia* and O'Neill's *Mourning Becomes Electra* (1931) still attract comment and discussion. Much of O'Neill's work from the late 1920s and 1930s is inflated and bombastic, and plays like *Lazarus Laughed* (1928), *Marco Millions* (1929), *Dynamo* (1929), and *Days Without End* (1934) seemed to mark his flagging powers as a writer. When O'Neill won the Nobel Prize in 1936, his career was widely regarded as finished. His plays had become empty and grandiose, and he suffered from Parkinson's disease, which made it increasingly difficult for him to write. Throughout the 1930s and 1940s, though, O'Neill planned a massive cycle of plays concerning the fortunes of an American family, called *A Tale of Possessors Self-dispossessed;* of these he completed only *A Touch of the Poet* (written 1935–1942) and a draft of *More Stately Mansions* (1935–1940). However, in the 1940s, O'Neill also wrote his greatest plays, realistic dramas based for the most part on his family's history and on his own life. These hard-won plays may have been out of keeping with the national mood in the aftermath of World War II: when *The Iceman Cometh* opened in 1946, it ran for only 136 performances, and *A Moon for the Misbegotten* (1947) closed in Ohio before reaching New York. Yet when *Iceman* was revived in 1956, directed by Jose Quintero, it was a huge success and prompted a widespread reevaluation of O'Neill's drama.

Since O'Neill was raised on his father's melodramatic portrayal of *The Count of Monte Cristo,* it is not surprising that he was at times also infected with the spirit of melodrama. O'Neill's plays often recall melodrama's emphasis on the passions of the characters, its striking moments of stage action, its penchant for the romantic and the sentimental. O'Neill's experimentation and sure sense of the stage enabled him to achieve an unparalleled body of work and to define the course of drama in the United States in the first half of the twenti-eth century.

THE HAIRY APE

Although O'Neill is today most often remembered for the realistic plays he wrote late in his career, *The Hairy Ape* testifies to his ongoing experiments with the form and purpose of the-atrical representation. O'Neill was an admirer of Strindberg's drama, and throughout his ca-reer experimented with various **EXPRESSIONIST THEATER** techniques, ways of expressing a character's state of mind directly in the setting: the offstage drumming that's heard in *Moon of the Caribbees,* the Little Formless Fears in *The Emperor Jones,* the convention that lets char-acters speak their "real" thoughts directly to the audience as asides in *Strange Interlude.* In *The Hairy Ape,* O'Neill develops another aspect of expressionist theater, its use of a morality-play structure and a distorted stage set to allegorize the predicament of "modern man." But while later plays—Elmer Rice's *The Adding Machine* or Sophie Treadwell's *Machinal*—take the plight of the faceless, routinized office worker as their model, O'Neill locates the prob-lem of identity in modern culture in an industrial worker, the coal-stoker Yank. *The Hairy Ape* begins by showing Yank in his element, the ship's forecastle, and O'Neill emphasizes the play's evocation of Yank's perspective in his stage directions. Much as the play will show the vital Yank to be hemmed in on every side by imprisoning social conventions, so here in the ship, *"The lines of bunks, the uprights supporting them, cross each other like the steel framework of a cage. The ceiling crushes down upon the men's heads."* From the outset, Yank is the creature of industrial society, a man transformed into a kind of machine, breathing the smoke of the stokehole, reveling in its heat: "Hell, sure, dat's my fav'rite climate. I eat it up! I git fat on it!

Willem Dafoe as Yank in the 1996 production of Eugene O'Neill's *The Hairy Ape* by The Wooster Group.

It's me makes it hot! It's me makes it roar! It's me makes it move!" In the scenes that follow, however, Yank goes on a kind of pilgrimage: when Mildred is brought to the stokehole in scene 3, Yank is insulted, and vows to "show her who's a ape!"; in the subsequent scenes he leaves the ship, encounters the riches of Fifth Avenue, is thrown in jail and firehosed, is attacked and beaten by labor organizers who take him for a spy, and winds up at the gorilla cage in the zoo. The language of industrial protest—indeed, of a Marxist industrial proletariat—suffuses the play, and O'Neill takes Yank's predicament to represent both a social and a kind of existential crisis; like Charlie Chaplin in his film *Modern Times*—but with a harder, less sentimental edge—O'Neill sees modern industrial culture as a new form of social production: a social order that requires the destruction of its Yanks even as it depends on their creation.

Although some readers may find O'Neill's language here quaint or off-putting—both in its stagey imitation of a 1920s dialect and in its accurate use of racist epithets—the play has had a continuing vitality on the stage; it was recently produced by the avant-garde Wooster Group company and starred Willem Dafoe as Yank.

THE HAIRY APE

A COMEDY OF ANCIENT AND MODERN LIFE IN EIGHT SCENES

Eugene O'Neill

CHARACTERS

ROBERT SMITH, "YANK"
PADDY
LONG
MILDRED DOUGLAS
HER AUNT
SECOND ENGINEER
FOURTH ENGINEER
A GUARD
A SECRETARY OF AN ORGANIZATION
STOKERS, LADIES, GENTLEMEN, ETC.

SCENE ONE

SCENE: *The firemen's forecastle of a transatlantic liner an hour after sailing from New York for the voyage across. Tiers of narrow, steel bunks, three deep, on all sides. An entrance in rear. Benches on the floor before the bunks. The room is crowded with men, shouting, cursing, laughing, singing—a confused, inchoate uproar swelling into a sort of unity, a meaning—the bewildered, furious, baffled defiance of a beast in a cage. Nearly all the men are drunk. Many bottles are passed from hand to hand. All are dressed in dungaree pants, heavy ugly shoes. Some wear singlets, but the majority are stripped to the waist.*

The treatment of this scene, or of any other scene in the play, should by no means be naturalistic. The effect sought after is a cramped space in the bowels of a ship, imprisoned by white steel. The lines of bunks, the uprights supporting them, cross each other like the steel framework of a cage. The ceiling crushes down upon the men's heads. They cannot stand upright. This accentuates the natural stooping posture which shoveling coal and the resultant overdevelopment of back and shoulder muscles have given them. The men themselves should resemble those pictures in which the appearance of Neanderthal Man is guessed at. All are hairy-chested, with long arms of tremendous power, and low, receding brows above their small, fierce, resentful eyes. All the civilized white races are represented, but except for the slight differentiation in color of hair, skin, eyes, all these men are alike.

The curtain rises on a tumult of sound. YANK *is seated in the foreground. He seems broader, fiercer, more truculent, more powerful, more sure of himself than the rest. They respect his superior strength—the grudging respect of fear. Then, too, he represents to them a self-expression, the very last word in what they are, their most highly developed individual.*

VOICES: Gif me trink dere, you!
  'Ave a wet!
  Salute!
  Gesundheit!
5 Skoal!
  Drunk as a lord, God stiffen you!
  Here's how!
  Luck!
  Pass back that bottle, damn you!
  Pourin' it down his neck!   10
  Ho, Froggy! Where the devil have you been?
  La Touraine.
  I hit him smash in yaw, py Gott!
  Jenkins the First he's a rotten swine—
  And the coppers nabbed him—and I run—   15
  I like peer better. It don't pig head gif you.
  A slut, I'm sayin'. She robbed me aslape—
  To hell with 'em all!
  You're a bloody liar!
  Say dot again! (*Commotion. Two men about to fight are*   20
    pulled apart.)
  No scrappin' now!
  Tonight—
  See who's the best man!
  Bloody Dutchman!
  Tonight on the for'ard square.   25
  I'll bet on Dutchy.
  He packa da wallop, I tell you!
  Shut up, Wop!
  No fightin', maties. We're all chums, ain't we?

(*A voice starts bawling a song.*)

  Beer, beer, glorious beer!   30
  Fill yourselves right up to here.

YANK: (*For the first time seeming to take notice of the uproar about him, turns around threateningly—in a tone of contemptuous authority.*) Choke off dat noise! Where d'yuh get dat beer stuff? Beer, hell! Beer's for goils—and Dutchmen. Me for 35
  somep'n wit a kick to it! Gimme a drink, one of youse guys. (*Several bottles are eagerly offered. He takes a tremendous gulp at one of them; then, keeping the bottle in his hand, glares belligerently at the owner, who hastens to acquiesce in this robbery by saying.*) All righto, Yank. Keep it and have another. 40
  (YANK *contemptuously turns his back on the crowd again. For a second there is an embarrassed silence. Then—.*)
VOICES: We must be passing the Hook.
  She's beginning to roll to it.

45   Six days in hell—and then Southampton.
        Py Yesus, I vish somepody take my first vatch for me!
        Gittin' seasick, Square-head?
        Drink up and forget it!
        What's in your bottle?
50   Gin.
        Dot's a nigger trink.
        Absinthe? It's doped. You'll go off your chump, Froggy!
        Cochon!
        Whisky, that's the ticket!
55   Where's Paddy?
        Going asleep.
        Sing us that whisky song, Paddy.

(*They all turn to an old, wizened Irishman who is dozing, very drunk, on the benches forward. His face is extremely monkey-like with all the sad, patient pathos of that animal in his small eyes.*)

        Singa da song, Caruso Pat!
        He's gettin' old. The drink is too much for him.
60   He's too drunk.
        PADDY: (*Blinking about him, starts to his feet resentfully, swaying, holding on to the edge of a bunk.*) I'm never too drunk to sing. 'Tis only when I'm dead to the world I'd be wishful to sing at all. (*With a sort of sad contempt.*) "Whisky
65   Johnny," ye want? A chanty, ye want? Now that's a queer wish from the ugly like of you. God help you. But no mather, (*He starts to sing in a thin, nasal, doleful tone.*)

            Oh, whisky is the life of man!
                Whisky! O Johnny! (*They all join in on this.*)
70   Oh, whisky is the life of man!
                Whisky for my Johnny! (*Again chorus.*)
            Oh, whisky drove my old man mad!
                Whisky! O Johnny!
            Oh, whisky drove my old man mad!
75   Whisky for my Johnny!

        YANK: (*Again turning around scornfully.*) Aw hell! Nix on dat old sailing ship stuff! All dat bull's dead, see? And you're dead, too, yuh damned old Harp, on'y yuh don't know it. Take it easy, see. Give us a rest. Nix on de loud noise.
80   (*With a cynical grin.*) Can't youse see I'm tryin' to t'ink?
        ALL: (*Repeating the word after him as one with the same cynical amused mockery.*) Think! (*The choroused word has a brazen metallic quality as if their throats were phonograph horns. It is followed by a general uproar of hard, barking laughter.*)
85   VOICES: Don't be cracking your head wit ut, Yank.
        You gat headache, py yingo!
        One thing about it—it rhymes with drink!
        Ha, ha, ha!
        Drink, don't think!
90   Drink, don't think!
        Drink, don't think! (*A whole chorus of voices has taken up this refrain, stamping on the floor, pounding on the benches with fists.*)
        YANK: (*Taking a gulp from his bottle—good-naturedly.*) Aw right. Can de noise. I got yuh de foist time. (*The uproar subsides. A very drunken sentimental tenor begins to sing.*)

95   Far away in Canada,
                Far across the sea,
            There's a lass who fondly waits
                Making a home for me—

YANK: (*Fiercely contemptuous.*) Shut up, yuh lousy boob! Where d'yuh get dat tripe? Home? Home, hell! I'll make a home   100 for yuh! I'll knock yuh dead. Home! T'hell wit home! Where d'yuh get dat tripe? Dis is home, see? What d'yuh want wit home? (*Proudly.*) I runned away from mine when I was a kid. On'y too glad to beat it, dat was me. Home was lickings for me, dat's all. But yuh can bet your shoit no one   105 ain't never licked me since! Wanter try it, any of youse? Huh! I guess not. (*In a more placated but still contemptuous tone.*) Goils waitin' for yuh, huh? Aw, hell! Dat's all tripe. Dey don't wait for no one. Dey'd double-cross yuh for a nickel. Dey're all tarts, get me? Treat 'em rough, dat's me.   110 To hell wit 'em. Tarts, dat's what, de whole bunch of 'em.
LONG: (*Very drunk, jumps on a bench excitedly, gesticulating with a bottle in his hand.*) Listen 'ere, Comrades. Yank 'ere is right. 'E says this 'ere stinkin' ship is our 'ome. And 'e says as 'ome is 'ell. And 'e's right! This is 'ell. We lives in 'ell,   115 Comrades—and right enough we'll die in it. (*Raging.*) And who's ter blame, I arsks yer? We ain't. We wasn't born this rotten way. All men is born free and ekal. That's in the bleedin' Bible, maties. But what d'they care for the Bible—them lazy, bloated swine what travels first cabin?   120 Them's the ones. They dragged us down 'til we're on'y wage slaves in the bowels of a bloody ship, sweatin', burnin' up, eatin' coal dust! Hit's them's ter blame—the damned Capitalist clarss! (*There had been a gradual murmur of contemptuous resentment rising among the men until now he   125 is interrupted by a storm of catcalls, hisses, boos, hard laughter.*)
VOICES: Turn it off!
        Shut up!
        Sit down!
        Closa da face!   130
        Tamn fool! (*Etc.*)
YANK: (*Standing up and glaring at* LONG.) Sit down before I knock yuh down! (LONG *makes haste to efface himself.* YANK *goes on contemptuously.*) De Bible, huh? De Cap'tlist class, huh? Aw nix on dat Salvation Army–Socialist bull. Git a   135 soapbox! Hire a hall! Come and be saved, huh? Jerk us to Jesus, huh? Aw g'wan! I've listened to lots of guys like you, see. Yuh're all wrong. Wanter know what I t'ink? Yuh ain't no good for no one. Yuh're de bunk. Yuh ain't got no noive, get me? Yuh're yellow, dat's what. Yellow, dat's you.   140 Say! What's dem slobs in de foist cabin got to do wit us? We're better men dan dey are, ain't we? Sure! One of us guys could clean up de whole mob wit one mit. Put one of 'em down here for one watch in de stokehole, what'd happen? Dey'd carry him off on a stretcher. Dem boids   145 don't amount to nothin'. Dey're just baggage. Who makes dis old tub run? Ain't it us guys? Well den, we belong, don't we? We belong and dey don't. Dat's all. (*A loud chorus of approval.* YANK *goes on.*) As for dis bein' hell—aw, nuts! Yuh lost your noive, dat's what. Dis is a man's job, get   150 me? It belongs. It runs dis tub. No stiffs need apply. But yuh're a stiff, see? Yuh're yellow, dat's you.
VOICES: (*With a great hard pride in them.*)
        Righto!
        A man's job!   155
        Talk is cheap, Long.
        He never could hold up his end.
        Divil take him!
        Yank's right. We make it go.
        Py Gott, Yank say right ting!   160

We don't need no one cryin' over us.
Makin' speeches.
Throw him out!
Yellow!
165 Chuck him overboard!
I'll break his jaw for him!

(*They crowd around* LONG *threateningly.*)

YANK: (*Half good-natured again—contemptuously.*) Aw, take it
easy. Leave him alone. He ain't woith a punch. Drink up.
Here's how, whoever owns dis. (*He takes a long swallow from
170 his bottle. All drink with him. In a flash all is hilarious ami-
ability again, back-slapping, loud talk, etc.*)

PADDY: (*Who has been sitting in a blinking, melancholy daze—
suddenly cries out in a voice full of old sorrow.*) We belong to
this, you're saying? We make the ship to go, you're saying?
175 Yerra then, that Almighty God have pity on us! (*His voice
runs into the wail of a keen, he rocks back and forth on his bench.
The men stare at him, startled and impressed in spite of themselves.*)—Oh, to be back in the fine days of my youth,
ochone! Oh, there was fine beautiful ships them days—
180 clippers wid tall masts touching the sky—fine strong men
in them—men that was sons of the sea as if 'twas the
mother that bore them. Oh, the clean skins of them, and the
clear eyes, the straight backs and full chests of them! Brave
men they was, and bold men surely! We'd be sailing out,
185 bound down round the Horn maybe. We'd be making sail
in the dawn, with a fair breeze, singing a chanty song wid
no care to it. And astern the land would be sinking low
and dying out, but we'd give it no heed but a laugh, and
never a look behind. For the day that was, was enough, for
190 we was free men—and I'm thinking 'tis only slaves do be
giving heed to the day that's gone or the day to come—
until they're old like me. (*With a sort of religious exaltation.*)
Oh, to be scudding south again wid the power of the
Trade Wind driving her on steady through the nights and
195 the days! Full sail on her! Nights and days! Nights when
the foam of the wake would be flaming wid fire, when the
sky'd be blazing and winking wid stars. Or the full of
the moon maybe. Then you'd see her driving through the
gray night, her sails stretching aloft all silver and white, not
200 a sound on the deck, the lot of us dreaming dreams, till
you'd believe 'twas no real ship at all you was on but a
ghost ship like the *Flying Dutchman* they say does be roaming the seas forevermore widout touching a port. And
there was the days, too. A warm sun on the clean decks.
205 Sun warming the blood of you, and wind over the miles
of shiny green ocean like strong drink to your lungs.
Work—aye, hard work—but who'd mind that at all? Sure,
you worked under the sky and 'twas work wid skill and
daring to it. And wid the day done, in the dog watch,
210 smoking me pipe at ease, the lookout would be raising
land maybe, and we'd see the mountains of South Amer-
icy wid the red fire of the setting sun painting their white
tops and the clouds floating by them! (*His tone of exaltation ceases. He goes on mournfully.*) Yerra, what's the use of
215 talking? 'Tis a dead man's whisper. (*To* YANK *resentfully.*)
'Twas them days men belonged to ships, not now. 'Twas
them days a ship was part of the sea, and a man was part
of a ship, and the sea joined all together and made it one.
(*Scornfully.*) Is it one wid this you'd be, Yank—black smoke

from the funnels smudging the sea, smudging the decks— 220
the bloody engines pounding and throbbing and shaking-
wid—divil a sight of sun or a breath of clean air—choking
our lungs wid coal dust—breaking our backs and hearts in
the hell of the stokehole—feeding the bloody furnace—
feeding our lives along wid the coal, I'm thinking—caged 225
in by steel from a sight of the sky like bloody apes in the
Zoo! (*With a harsh laugh.*) Ho-ho, divil mend you! Is it to
belong to that you're wishing? Is it a flesh and blood
wheel of the engines you'd be?

YANK: (*Who has been listening with a contemptuous sneer, barks 230
out the answer.*) Sure ting! Dat's me. What about it?

PADDY: (*As if to himself—with great sorrow.*) Me time is past
due. That a great wave wid sun in the heart of it may
sweep me over the side sometime I'd be dreaming of the
days that's gone! 235

YANK: Aw, yuh crazy Mick! (*He springs to his feet and advances on
PADDY threateningly—then stops, fighting some queer struggle
within himself—lets his hands fall to his sides—contemptuously.*)
Aw, take it easy. Yuh're aw right, at dat. Yuh're bugs, dat's
all—nutty as a cuckoo. All dat tripe yuh been pullin'—Aw, 240
dat's all right. On'y it's dead, get me? Yuh don't belong no
more, see. Yuh don't get de stuff. Yuh're too old. (*Disgustedly.*) But aw say, come up for air onct in a while, can't yuh?
See what's happened since yuh croaked. (*He suddenly bursts
forth vehemently, growing more and more excited.*) Say! Sure! 245
Sure I meant it! What de hell—Say, lemme talk! Hey! Hey,
you old Harp! Hey, youse guys! Say, listen to me—wait a
moment—I gotta talk, see. I belong and he don't. He's dead
but I'm livin'. Listen to me! Sure I'm part of de engines!
Why de hell not? Dey move, don't dey? Dey're speed, ain't 250
dey? Dey smash trou, don't dey? Twenty-five knots a hour!
Dat's goin' some! Dat's new stuff! Dat belongs! But him, he's
too old. He gets dizzy. Say, listen. All dat crazy tripe about
nights and days; all dat crazy tripe about stars and moons; all
dat crazy tripe about suns and winds, fresh air and de rest of 255
it—Aw hell, dat's all a dope dream! Hittin' de pipe of de
past, dat's what he's doin'. He's old and don't belong no
more. But me, I'm young! I'm in de pink! I move wit it! It,
get me! I mean de ting dat's de guts of all dis. It ploughs trou
all de tripe he's been sayin'. It blows dat up! It knocks dat 260
dead! It slams dat offen de face of de oith! It, get me! De engines and de coal and de smoke and all de rest of it! He can't
breathe and swallow coal dust, but I kin, see? Dat's fresh air
for me! Dat's food for me! I'm new, get me? Hell in de
stokehole? Sure! It takes a man to work in hell. Hell, sure, 265
dat's my fav'rite climate. I eat it up! I git fat on it! It's me
makes it hot! It's me makes it roar! It's me makes it move!
Sure, on'y for me everyting stops. It all goes dead, get me?
De noise and smoke and all de engines movin' de woild, dey
stop. Dere ain't nothin' no more! Dat's what I'm sayin'. 270
Everything else dat makes de woild move, somep'n makes it
move. It can't move witout somep'n else, see? Den yuh get
down to me. I'm at de bottom, get me! Dere ain't nothin'
foither. I'm de end! I'm de start! I start somep'n and de
woild moves! It—dat's me!—de new dat's moiderin' de old! 275
I'm de ting in coal dat makes it boin; I'm steam and oil for
de engines; I'm de ting in noise dat makes yuh hear it; I'm
smoke and express trains and steamers and factory whistles;
I'm de ting in gold dat makes money! And I'm what makes
iron into steel! Steel, dat stands for de whole ting! And I'm 280
steel—steel—steel! I'm de muscles in steel, de punch

behind it. (*As he says this he pounds with his fist against the steel bunks. All the men, roused to a pitch of frenzied self-glorification by his speech, do likewise. There is a deafening metallic roar, through which* YANK'*s voice can be heard bellowing.*) Slaves, hell! We run de whole woiks. All de rich guys dat tink dey're somep'n, dey ain't nothin'! Dey don't belong. But us guys, we're in de move, we're at de bottom, de whole ting is us! (PADDY *from the start of* YANK'*s speech has been taking one gulp after another from his bottle, at first frightenedly, as if he were afraid to listen, then desperately, as if to drown his senses, but finally has achieved complete indifferent, even amused, drunkenness.* YANK *sees his lips moving. He quells the uproar with a shout.*) Hey, youse guys, take it easy! Wait a moment! De nutty Harp is sayin' somep'n.

PADDY: (*Is heard now—throws his head back with a mocking burst of laughter.*) Ho-ho-ho-ho-ho—

YANK: (*Drawing back his fist, with a snarl.*) Aw! Look out who yuh're givin' the bark!

PADDY: (*Begins to sing "The Miller of Dee" with enormous good nature.*)

I care for nobody, no, not I,
And nobody cares for me.

YANK: (*Good-natured himself in a flash, interrupts* PADDY *with a slap on the bare back like a report.*) Dat's de stuff! Now yuh're gettin' wise to somep'n. Care for nobody, dat's de dope! To hell wit 'em all! And nix on nobody else carin'. I kin care for myself, get me! (*Eight bells sound; muffled, vibrating through the steel walls as if some enormous brazen gong were imbedded in the heart of the ship. All the men jump up mechanically, file through the door silently close upon each other's heels in what is very like a prisoners' lockstep.* YANK *slaps* PADDY *on the back.*) Our watch, yuh old Harp! (*Mockingly.*) Come on down in hell. Eat up de coal dust. Drink in de heat. It's it, see! Act like yuh like it, yuh better—or croak yuhself.

PADDY: (*With jovial defiance.*) To the divil wid it! I'll not report this watch. Let them log me and be damned. I'm no slave the like of you. I'll be sittin' here at me ease, and drinking, and thinking, and dreaming dreams.

YANK: (*Contemptuously.*) Tinkin' and dreamin', what'll that get yuh? What's tinkin' got to do wit it? We move, don't we? Speed, ain't it? Fog, dat's all you stand for. But we drive trou dat, don't we? We split dat up and smash trou—twenty-five knots a hour! (*Turns his back on* PADDY *scornfully.*) Aw, yuh make me sick! Yuh don't belong! (*He strides out the door in rear.* PADDY *hums to himself, blinking drowsily.*)

(*The curtain falls.*)

SCENE TWO

SCENE: *Two days out. A section of the promenade deck.* MILDRED DOUGLAS *and her* AUNT *are discovered reclining in deck chairs. The former is a girl of twenty, slender, delicate, with a pale, pretty face marred by a self-conscious expression of disdainful superiority. She looks fretful, nervous and discontented, bored by her own anemia.* HER AUNT *is a pompous and proud—and fat—old lady. She is a type even to the point of a double chin and lorgnettes. She is dressed pretentiously, as if afraid her face alone would never indicate her position in life.* MILDRED *is dressed all in white.*

The impression to be conveyed by this scene is one of the beautiful, vivid life of the sea all about—sunshine on the deck in a great flood, the fresh sea wind blowing across it. In the midst of this, these two incongruous, artificial figures, inert and disharmonious, the elder like a gray lump of dough touched up with rouge, the younger looking as if the vitality of her stock had been sapped before she was conceived, so that she is the expression not of its life energy but merely of the artificialities that energy had won for itself in the spending.

MILDRED: (*Looking up with affected dreaminess.*) How the black smoke swirls back against the sky! Is it not beautiful?

AUNT: (*Without looking up.*) I dislike smoke of any kind.

MILDRED: My great-grandmother smoked a pipe—a clay pipe.

AUNT: (*Ruffling.*) Vulgar!

MILDRED: She was too distant a relative to be vulgar. Time mellows pipes.

AUNT: (*Pretending boredom but irritated.*) Did the sociology you took up at college teach you that—to play the ghoul on every possible occasion, excavating old bones? Why not let your great-grandmother rest in her grave?

MILDRED: (*Dreamily.*) With her pipe beside her—puffing in Paradise.

AUNT: (*With spite.*) Yes, you are a natural born ghoul. You are even getting to look like one, my dear.

MILDRED: (*In a passionless tone.*) I detest you, Aunt. (*Looking at her critically.*) Do you know what you remind me of? Of a cold pork pudding against a background of linoleum tablecloth in the kitchen of a—but the possibilities are wearisome. (*She closes her eyes.*)

AUNT: (*With a bitter laugh.*) Merci for your candor. But since I am and must be your chaperon—in appearance—at least—let us patch up some sort of armed truce. For my part you are quite free to indulge any pose of eccentricity that beguiles you—as long as you observe the amenities

MILDRED: (*Drawling.*) The inanities?

AUNT: (*Going on as if she hadn't heard.*) After exhausting the morbid thrills of social service work on New York's East Side—how they must have hated you, by the way, the poor that you made so much poorer in their own eyes!— you are now bent on making your slumming international. Well, I hope Whitechapel will provide the needed nerve tonic. Do not ask me to chaperon you there, however. I told your father I would not. I loathe deformity. We will hire an army of detectives and you may investigate everything—they allow you to see.

MILDRED: (*Protesting with a trace of genuine, earnestness.*) Please do not mock at my attempts to discover how the other half lives. Give me credit for some sort of groping sincerity in that at least. I would like to help them. I would like to be of some use in the world. Is it my fault I don't know how? I would like to be sincere, to touch life somewhere. (*With weary bitterness.*) But I'm afraid I have neither the vitality nor integrity. All that was burnt out in our stock before I was born. Grandfather's blast furnaces, flaming to the sky, melting steel, making millions—then father keeping those home fires burning, making more millions—and little me at the tail-end of it all. I'm a waste product in the Bessemer process—like the millions. Or rather, I inherit the acquired trait of the by-product, wealth, but none of the energy, none of the strength of the steel that made it. I am sired by gold and damned by it, as they say at the race track—damned in more ways than one. (*She laughs mirthlessly.*)

55 AUNT: (*Unimpressed—superciliously.*) You seem to be going in for sincerity today. It isn't becoming to you, really—except as an obvious pose. Be as artificial as you are, I advise. There's a sort of sincerity in that, you know. And, after all, you must confess you like that better.

MILDRED: (*Again affected and bored.*) Yes, I suppose I do. Par-
60 don me for my outburst. When a leopard complains of its spots, it must sound rather grotesque. (*In a mocking tone.*) Purr, little leopard. Purr, scratch, tear, kill, gorge yourself and be happy—only stay in the jungle, where your spots are camouflage. In a cage they make you conspicuous.

65 AUNT: I don't know what you are talking about.

MILDRED: It would be rude to talk about anything to you. Let's just talk. (*She looks at her wrist watch.*) Well, thank goodness, it's about time for them to come for me. That ought to give me a new thrill, Aunt.

70 AUNT: (*Affectedly troubled.*) You don't mean to say you're going? The dirt—the heat must be frightful—

MILDRED: Grandfather started as a puddler. I should have inherited an immunity to heat that would make a salamander shiver. It will be fun to put it to the test.

75 AUNT: But don't you have to have the captain's—or someone's—permission to visit the stokehole?

MILDRED: (*With a triumphant smile.*) I have it—both his and the chief engineer's. Oh, they didn't want to at first, in spite of my social service credentials. They didn't seem a bit anx-
80 ious that I should investigate how the other half lives and works on a ship. So I had to tell them that my father, the president of Nazareth Steel, chairman of the board of directors of this line, had told me it would be all right.

AUNT: He didn't.

85 MILDRED: How naïve age makes one! But I said he did, Aunt. I even said he had given me a letter to them—which I had lost. And they were afraid to take the chance that I might be lying. (*Excitedly.*) So it's ho! for the stokehole. The second engineer is to escort me. (*Looking at her watch again.*)
90 It's time. And here he comes, I think. (*The* SECOND ENGINEER *enters. He is a husky, fine-looking man of thirty-five or so. He stops before the two and tips his cap, visibly embarrassed and ill-at-ease.*)

SECOND ENGINEER: Miss Douglas?

95 MILDRED: Yes. (*Throwing off her rugs and getting to her feet.*) Are we all ready to start?

SECOND ENGINEER: In just a second, ma'am. I'm waiting for the Fourth. He's coming along.

MILDRED: (*With a scornful smile.*) You don't care to shoulder
100 this responsibility alone, is that it?

SECOND ENGINEER: (*Forcing a smile.*) Two are better than one. (*Disturbed by her eyes, glances out to sea—blurts out.*) A fine day we're having.

MILDRED: Is it?

105 SECOND ENGINEER: A nice warm breeze—

MILDRED: It feels cold to me.

SECOND ENGINEER: But it's hot enough in the sun—

MILDRED: Not hot enough for me. I don't like Nature. I was never athletic.

110 SECOND ENGINEER: (*Forcing a smile.*) Well, you'll find it hot enough where you're going.

MILDRED: Do you mean hell?

SECOND ENGINEER: (*Flabbergasted, decides to laugh.*) Ho-ho! No, I mean the stokehole.

115 MILDRED: My grandfather was a puddler. He played with boiling steel.

SECOND ENGINEER: (*All at sea—uneasily.*) Is that so? Hum, you'll excuse me, ma'am, but are you intending to wear that dress?

120 MILDRED: Why not?

SECOND ENGINEER: You'll likely rub against oil and dirt. It can't be helped.

MILDRED: It doesn't matter. I have lots of white dresses.

SECOND ENGINEER: I have an old coat you might throw over—

125 MILDRED: I have fifty dresses like this. I will throw this one into the sea when I come back. That ought to wash it clean, don't you think?

SECOND ENGINEER: (*Doggedly.*) There's ladders to climb down that are none too clean—and dark alleyways—

130 MILDRED: I will wear this very dress and none other.

SECOND ENGINEER: No offense meant. It's none of my business. I was only warning you—

MILDRED: Warning? That sounds thrilling.

SECOND ENGINEER: (*Looking down the deck—with a sigh of relief.*) There's the Fourth now. He's waiting for us. If you'll
135 come—

MILDRED: Go on. I'll follow you. (*He goes.* MILDRED *turns a mocking smile on her* AUNT.) An oaf—but a handsome, virile oaf.

AUNT: (*Scornfully.*) Poser!

MILDRED: Take care. He said there were dark alleyways—
140 AUNT: (*In the same tone.*) Poser!

MILDRED: (*Biting her lips angrily.*) You are right. But would that my millions were not so anemically chaste!

AUNT: Yes, for a fresh pose I have no doubt you would drag the name of Douglas in the gutter!
145 MILDRED: From which it sprang. Good-by, Aunt. Don't pray too hard that I may fall into the fiery furnace.

AUNT: Poser!

MILDRED: (*Viciously.*) Old hag! (*She slaps her* AUNT *insultingly across the face and walks off, laughing gaily.*)
150 AUNT: (*Screams after her.*) I said poser!

(*The curtain falls.*)

SCENE THREE

SCENE: *The stokehole. In the rear, the dimly-out-lined bulks of the furnaces and boilers. High overhead one hanging electric bulb sheds just enough light through the murky air laden with coal dust to pile up masses of shadows everywhere. A line of men, stripped to the waist, is before the furnace doors. They bend over, looking neither to right nor left, handling their shovels as if they were part of their bodies, with a strange, awkward, swinging rhythm. They use the shovels to throw open the furnace doors. Then from these fiery round holes in the black a flood of terrific light and heat pours full upon the men who are outlined in silhouette in the crouching, inhuman attitudes of chained gorillas. The men shovel with a rhythmic motion, swinging as on a pivot from the coal which lies in heaps on the floor behind to hurl it into the flaming mouths before them. There is a tumult of noise—the brazen clang of the furnace doors as they are flung open or slammed shut, the grating, teeth-gritting grind of steel against steel, of crunching coal. This clash of sounds stuns one's ears with its rending dissonance. But there is order in it, rhythm, a mechanical regulated recurrence, a tempo. And rising above all, making the air hum with the quiver of liberated energy, the roar of leaping flames in the furnaces, the monotonous throbbing beat of the engines.*

As the curtain rises, the furnace doors are shut. The men are taking a breathing spell. One or two are arranging the coal behind them, pulling it into more accessible heaps. The others can be dimly made out leaning on their shovels in relaxed attitudes of exhaustion.

PADDY: (*From somewhere in the line—plaintively.*) Yerra, will this divil's own watch nivir end? Me back is broke. I'm destroyed entirely.

5 YANK: (*From the center of the line—with exuberant scorn.*) Aw, yuh make me sick! Lie down and croak, why don't yuh? Always beefin', dat's you! Say, dis is a cinch! Dis was made for me! It's my meat, get me! (*A whistle is blown—a thin, shrill note from somewhere overhead in the darkness.* YANK *curses without resentment.*) Dere's de damn engineer crackin' de
10 whip. He tinks we're loafin'.

PADDY: (*Vindictively.*) God stiffen him!

YANK: (*In an exultant tone of command.*) Come on, youse guys! Git into de game! She's gettin' hungry! Pile some grub in her. Trow it into her belly! Come on now, all of youse!
15 Open her up! (*At this last all the men, who have followed his movements of getting into position, throw open their furnace doors with a deafening clang. The fiery light floods over their shoulders as they bend round for the coal. Rivulets of sooty sweat have traced maps on their backs. The enlarged muscles form bunches of*
20 *high light and shadow.*)

YANK: (*Chanting a count as he shovels without seeming effort.*) One—two—tree—(*His voice rising exultantly in the joy of battle.*) Dat's de stuff! Let her have it! All togedder now! Sling it into her! Let her ride! Shoot de piece now! Call
25 de toin on her! Drive her into it! Feel her move. Watch her smoke! Speed, dat's her middle name! Give her coal, youse guys! Coal, dat's her booze! Drink it up, baby! Let's see yuh sprint! Dig in and gain a lap! Dere she go-o-es. (*This last in the chanting formula of the galley gods at the six-*
30 *day bike race. He slams his furnace door shut. The others do like-wise with as much unison as their wearied bodies will permit. The effect is of one fiery eye after another being blotted out with a series of accompanying bangs.*)

PADDY: (*Groaning.*) Me back is broke. I'm bate out—bate—
35 (*There is a pause. Then the inexorable whistle sounds again from the dim regions above, the electric light. There is a growl of cursing rage from all sides.*)

YANK: (*Shaking his fist upward—contemptuously.*) Take it easy dere, you! Who d'yuh tinks runnin' dis game, me or you?
40 When I git ready, we move. Not before! When I git ready, get me!

VOICES: (*Approvingly.*)
That's the stuff!
Yank tal him, py golly!
45 Yank ain't afeerd.
Goot poy, Yank!
Give him hell!
Tell'im 'e's a bloody swine!
Bloody slave-driver!
50 YANK: (*Contemptuously.*) He ain't got no noive. He's yellow, get me? All de engineers is yellow. Dey got streaks a mile wide. Aw, to hell with him! Let's move, youse guys. We

had a rest. Come on, she needs it! Give her pep! It ain't for him. Him and his whistle, dey don't belong. But we belong, see! We gotter feed de baby! Come on! (*He turns* 55 *and flings his furnace door open. They all follow his lead. At this instant the* SECOND *and* FOURTH ENGINEERS *enter from the darkness on the left with* MILDRED *between them. She starts, turns paler, her pose is crumbling, she shivers with fright in spite of the blazing heat, but forces herself to leave the* ENGINEERS *and* 60 *take a few steps near the men. She is right behind* YANK. *All this happens quickly while the men have their backs turned.*)

YANK: Come on, youse guys! (*He is turning to get coal when the whistle sounds again in a peremptory, irritating note. This drives* YANK *into a sudden fury. While the other men have turned full* 65 *around and stopped dumbfounded by the spectacle of* MILDRED *standing there in her white dress,* YANK *does not turn far enough to see her. Besides, his head is thrown back, he blinks upward through the murk trying to find the owner of the whistle, he bran-dishes his shovel murderously over his head in one hand, pound-* 70 *ing on his chest, gorilla-like, with the other, shouting.*) Toin off dat whistle! Come down outa dere, yuh yellow, brass-buttoned, Belfast bum, yuh! Come down and I'll knock yer brains out! Yuh lousy, stinkin, yellow mut of a Catholic-moiderin' bastard! Come down and I'll moider yuh! 75 Pullin' dat whistle on me, huh? I'll show yuh! I'll crash yer skull in! I'll drive yer teet' down yer troat! I'll slam yer nose trou de back of yer head! I'll cut yer guts out for a nickel, yuh lousy boob, yuh dirty, crummy, muck-eatin' son of a— (*Suddenly he becomes conscious of all the other men staring at* 80 *something directly behind his back. He whirls defensively with a snarling, murderous growl, crouching to spring, his lips drawn back over his teeth, his small eyes gleaming ferociously. He sees* MIL-DRED, *like a white apparition in the full light from the open fur-nace doors. He glares into her eyes, turned to stone. As for her,* 85 *during his speech she has listened, paralyzed with horror, terror, her whole personality crushed, beaten in, collapsed, by the terrific im-pact of this unknown, abysmal brutality, naked and shameless. As she looks at his gorilla face, as his eyes bore into hers, she utters a low, choking cry and shrinks away from him, putting both hands* 90 *up before her eyes to shut out the sight of his face, to protect her own. This startles* YANK *to a reaction. His mouth falls open, his eyes grow bewildered.*)

MILDRED: (*About to faint—to the* ENGINEERS, *who now have her one by each arm—whimperingly.*) Take me away! Oh, the 95 filthy beast! (*She faints. They carry her quickly back, disap-pearing in the darkness at the left, rear. An iron door clangs shut. Rage and bewildered fury rush back on* YANK. *He feels himself insulted in some unknown fashion in the very heart of his pride. He roars.*) God damn yuh! (*And hurls his shovel after them at* 100 *the door which has just closed. It hits the steel bulkhead with a clang and falls clattering on the steel floor. From overhead the whistle sounds again in a long, angry, insistent command.*)

(*The curtain falls.*)

SCENE FOUR

SCENE: *The firemen's forecastle.* YANK'S *watch has just come off duty and had dinner. Their faces and bodies shine from a soap and water scrubbing but around their eyes, where a hasty dousing does not touch, the coal dust sticks like black make-up, giving them a queer, sinister expression.* YANK *has not washed either face or body. He stands out in contrast to them, a blackened, brooding figure. He is seated forward on a bench in the exact attitude of Rodin's "The Thinker." The others, most of them smoking pipes, are staring at* YANK *half-apprehensively, as if fearing an outburst; half-amusedly, as if they saw a joke somewhere that tickled them.*

VOICES: He ain't ate nothin'.
　　Py golly, a fallar gat to gat grub in him.
　　Divil a lie.
　　Yank feeda da fire, no feeda da face.
5　Ha-ha.
　　He ain't even washed hisself.
　　He's forgot.
　　Hey, Yank, you forgot to wash.
YANK: (*Sullenly.*) Forgot nothin'! To hell wit washin'.
10　VOICES: It'll stick to you.
　　It'll get under your skin.
　　Give yer the bleedin' itch, that's wot.
　　It makes spots on you—like a leopard.
　　Like a piebald nigger, you mean.
15　Better wash up, Yank.
　　You sleep better.
　　Wash up, Yank.
　　Wash up! Wash up!
YANK: (*Resentfully.*) Aw say, youse guys. Lemme alone. Can't
20　youse see I'm tryin' to tink?
ALL: (*Repeating the word after him as one with cynical mockery.*) Think! (*The word has a brazen, metallic quality as if their throats were phonograph horns. It is followed by a chorus of hard, barking, laughter.*)
25　YANK: (*Springing to his feet and glaring at them belligerently.*) Yes, tink! Tink, dat's what I said! What about it? (*They are silent, puzzled by his sudden resentment at what used to be one of his jokes.* YANK *sits down again in the same attitude of "The Thinker."*)
30　VOICES: Leave him alone.
　　He's got a grouch on.
　　Why wouldn't he?
PADDY: (*With a wink at the others.*) Sure I know what's the matther. 'Tis aisy to see. He's fallen in love, I'm telling you.
35　ALL: (*Repeating the word after him as one with cynical mockery.*) Love! (*The word has a brazen, metallic quality as if their throats were phonograph horns. It is followed by a chorus of hard, barking laughter.*)
YANK: (*With a contemptuous snort.*) Love, hell! Hate, dat's what.
40　I've fallen in hate, get me?
PADDY: (*Philosophically.*) 'Twould take a wise man to tell one from the other. (*With a bitter, ironical scorn, increasing as he goes on.*) But I'm telling you it's love that's in it. Sure what else but love for us poor bastes in the stokehole would be
45　bringing a fine lady, dressed like a white quane, down a mile of ladders and steps to be havin' a look at us? (*A growl of anger goes up from all sides.*)
LONG: (*Jumping on a bench—hecticly.*) Hinsultin' us! Hinsultin' us, the bloody cow! And them bloody engineers! What
50　right 'as they got to be exhibitin' us 's if we was bleedin' monkeys in a menagerie? Did we sign for hinsults to our dignity as 'onest workers? Is that in the ship's articles? You kin bloody well bet it ain't! But I knows why they done it. I arsked a deck steward 'o she was and 'e told me. 'Er
55　old man's a bleedin' millionaire, a bloody Capitalist! 'E's

got enuf bloody gold to sink this bleedin' ship! 'E makes arf the bloody steel in the world! 'E owns this bloody boat! And you and me, Comrades, we're 'is slaves! And the skipper and mates and engineers, they're 'is slaves! And
60　she's 'is bloody daughter and we're all 'er slaves, too! And she gives 'er orders as 'ow she wants to see the bloody animals below decks and down they take 'er! (*There is a roar of rage from all sides.*)
YANK: (*Blinking at him bewilderedly.*) Say! Wait a moment! Is all
65　dat straight goods?
LONG: Straight as string! The bleedin' steward as waits on 'em, 'e told me about 'er. And what're we goin' ter do, I arsks yer? 'Ave we got ter swaller 'er hinsults like dogs? It ain't in the ship's articles. I tell yer we got a case. We kin
70　go to law—
YANK: (*With abysmal contempt.*) Hell! Law!
ALL: (*Repeating the word after him as one with cynical mockery.*) Law! (*The word has a brazen metallic quality as if their throats were phonograph horns. It is followed by a chorus of hard, bark-
75　ing laughter.*)
LONG: (*Feeling the ground slipping from under his feet—desperately.*) As voters and citizens we kin force the bloody governments—
YANK: (*With abysmal contempt.*) Hell! Governments!
ALL: (*Repeating the word after him as one with cynical mockery.*)
80　Governments! (*The word has a brazen metallic quality as if their throats were phonograph horns. It is followed by a chorus of hard, barking laughter.*)
LONG: (*Hysterically.*) We're free and equal in the sight of God—
YANK: (*With abysmal contempt.*) Hell! God!
85　ALL: (*Repeating the word after him as one with cynical mockery.*) God! (*The word has a brazen metallic quality as if their throats were phonograph horns. It is followed by a chorus of hard, barking, laughter.*)
YANK: (*Witheringly.*) Aw, join de Salvation Army!
90　ALL: Sit down! Shut up! Damn fool! Sea-lawyer! (LONG *slinks back out of sight.*)
PADDY: (*Continuing the trend of his thoughts as if he had never been interrupted—bitterly.*) And there she was standing behind us, and the Second pointing at us like a man you'd
95　hear in a circus would be saying: In this cage is a queerer kind of baboon than ever you'd find in darkest Africy. We roast them in their own sweat—and be damned if you won't hear some of thim saying they like it! (*He glances scornfully at* YANK.)
100　YANK: (*With a bewildered uncertain growl.*) Aw!
PADDY: And there was Yank roarin' curses and turning round wid his shovel to brain her—and she looked at him, and him at her—
YANK: (*Slowly.*) She was all white. I thought she was a ghost.
105　Sure.
PADDY: (*With heavy, biting sarcasm.*) 'Twas love at first sight, divil a doubt of it! If you'd seen the endearin' look on her pale mug when she shriveled away with her hands over her eyes to shut out the sight of him! Sure, 'twas as if she'd
110　seen a great hairy ape escaped from the Zoo!
YANK: (*Stung—with a growl of rage.*) Aw!
PADDY: And the loving way Yank heaved his shovel at the skull of her, only she was out the door! (*A grin breaking over his face.*) 'Twas touching, I'm telling you! It put the touch of home, swate home in the stokehole. (*There is a roar of
115　laughter from all.*)

YANK: (*Glaring at* PADDY *menacingly.*) Aw, choke dat off, see!

PADDY: (*Not heeding him—to the others.*) And her grabbin' at the Second's arm for protection. (*With a grotesque imitation of a woman's voice.*) Kiss me, Engineer, dear, for it's dark down here and me old man's in Wall Street making money! Hug me tight, darlin', for I'm afeerd in the dark and me mother's on deck makin' eyes at the skipper! (*Another roar of laughter.*)

YANK: (*Threateningly.*) Say! What yuh tryin' to do, kid me, yuh old Harp?

PADDY: Divil a bit! Ain't I wishin' myself you'd brained her?

YANK: (*Fiercely.*) I'll brain her! I'll brain her yet, wait 'n' see! (*Coming over to* PADDY *slowly.*) Say, is dat what she called me—a hairy ape?

PADDY: She looked it at you if she didn't say the word itself.

YANK: (*Grinning horribly.*) Hairy ape, huh? Sure! Dat's de way she looked at me, aw right. Hairy ape! So dat's me, huh? (*Bursting into rage—as if she were still in front of him.*) Yuh skinny tart! Yuh white-faced bum, yuh! I'll show yuh who's a ape! (*Turning to the others, bewilderment seizing him again.*) Say, youse guys. I was bawlin' him out for pullin' de whistle on us. You heard me. And den I seen youse lookin' at somep'n and I tought he'd sneaked down to come up in back of me, and I hopped round to knock him dead wit de shovel. And dere she was wit de light on her! Christ, yuh coulda pushed me over with a finger! I was scared, get me? Sure! I tought she was a ghost, see? She was all in white like dey wrap around stiffs. You seen her. Kin yuh blame me? She didn't belong, dat's what. And den when I come to and seen it was a real skoit and seen de way she was lookin' at me—like Paddy said—Christ, I was sore, get me? I don't stand for dat stuff from nobody. And I flung de shovel—on'y she'd beat it. (*Furiously.*) I wished it'd banged her! I wished it'd knocked her block off!

LONG: And be 'anged for murder or 'lectrocuted? She ain't bleedin' well worth it.

YANK: I don't give a damn what! I'd be square wit her, wouldn't I? Tink I wanter let her put somep'n over on me? Tink I'm goin' to let her git away wit dat stuff? Yuh don't know me! No one ain't never put nothin' over on me and got away wit it, see!—not dat kind of stuff—no guy and no skoit neither! I'll fix her! Maybe she'll come down again—

VOICE: No chance, Yank. You scared her out of a year's growth.

YANK: I scared her? Why de hell should I scare her? Who de hell is she? Ain't she de same as me? Hairy ape, huh? (*With his old confident bravado.*) I'll show her I'm better'n her, if she on'y knew it. I belong and she don't, see! I move and she's dead! Twenty-five knots a hour, dat's me! Dat carries her but I make dat. She's on'y baggage. Sure! (*Again bewilderedly.*) But, Christ, she was funny lookin'! Did yuh pipe her hands? White and skinny. Yuh could see de bones through 'em. And her mush, dat was dead white, too. And her eyes, dey was like dey'd seen a ghost. Me, dat was! Sure! Hairy ape! Ghost, huh? Look at dat arm! (*He extends his right arm, swelling out the great muscles.*) I coulda took her wit dat, wit' just my little finger even, and broke her in two. (*Again bewilderedly.*) Say, who is dat skoit, huh? What is she? What's she come from? Who made her? Who give her de noive to look at me like dat? Dis ting's got my goat right. I don't get her. She's new to me. What does a skoit like her mean, huh? She don't belong, get me! I can't see her. (*With growing anger.*) But one ting I'm wise to, aw right, aw right! Youse all kin bet your shoits I'll git even wit her. I'll show her if she tinks she—She grinds de organ and I'm on de string, huh? I'll fix her! Let her come down again and I'll fling her in de furnace! She'll move den! She won't shiver at nothin' den! Speed, dat'll be her! She'll belong den! (*He grins horribly.*)

PADDY: She'll never come. She's had her bellyfull, I'm telling you. She'll be in bed now, I'm thinking, wid ten doctors and nurses feedin' her salts to clean the fear out of her.

YANK: (*Enraged.*) Yuh tink I made her sick, too, do yuh? Just lookin' at me, huh? Hairy ape, huh? (*In a frenzy of rage.*) I'll fix her! I'll tell her where to git off! She'll git down on her knees and take it back or I'll bust de face offen her! (*Shaking one fist upward and beating on his chest with the other.*) I'll find yuh! I'm comin', d'yuh hear? I'll fix yuh, God damn yuh! (*He makes a rush for the door.*)

VOICES: Stop him!
   He'll get shot!
   He'll murder her!
   Trip him up!
   Hold him!
   He's gone crazy!
   Gott, he's strong!
   Hold him down!
   Look out for a kick!
   Pin his arms!

(*They have all piled on him and, after a fierce struggle, by sheer weight of numbers have borne him to the floor just inside the door.*)

PADDY: (*Who has remained detached.*) Kape him down till he's cooled off. (*Scornfully.*) Yerra, Yank, you're a great fool. Is it payin' attention at all you are to the like of that skinny sow widout one drop of rale blood in her?

YANK: (*Frenziedly, from the bottom of the heap.*) She's done me doit! She done me doit, didn't she? I'll git square wit her! I'll get her some way! Git offen me, youse guys! Lemme up! I'll show her who's a ape!

(*The curtain falls.*)

SCENE FIVE

SCENE: *Three weeks later. A corner of Fifth Avenue in the Fifties on a fine Sunday morning. A general atmosphere of clean, well-tidied, wide street; a flood of mellow, tempered sunshine; gentle, genteel breezes. In the rear, the show windows of two shops, a jewelry establishment on the corner, a furrier's next to it. Here the adornments of extreme wealth are tantalizingly displayed. The jeweler's window is gaudy with glittering diamonds, emeralds, rubies, pearls, etc., fashioned in ornate tiaras, crowns, necklaces, collars, etc. From each piece hangs an enormous tag from which a dollar sign and numerals in intermittent electric lights wink out the incredible prices. The same in the furrier's. Rich furs of all varieties hang there bathed in a downpour of artificial light. The general effect is of a background of magnificence cheapened and made grotesque by commercialism, a background in tawdry disharmony with the clear light and sunshine on the street itself.*

Up the side street YANK *and* LONG *come swaggering.* LONG *is dressed in shore clothes, wears a black Windsor tie, cloth cap.* YANK *is in his dirty dungarees. A fireman's cap with black peak is cocked defiantly on the side of his head. He has not shaved for days and around his fierce, resentful eyes—as around those of* LONG *to a lesser degree—the black smudge of coal dust still sticks like make-up. They hesitate and stand together at the corner, swaggering, looking about them with a forced, defiant contempt.*

LONG: (*Indicating it all with an oratorical gesture.*) Well, 'ere we are. Fif' Avenoo. This 'ere's their bleedin' private lane, as yer might say. (*Bitterly.*) We're trespassers 'ere. Proletarians keep orf the grass!

5 YANK: (*Dully.*) I don't see no grass, yuh boob. (*Staring at the sidewalk.*) Clean, ain't it? Yuh could eat a fried egg offen it. The white wings got some job sweepin' dis up. (*Looking up and down the avenue—surlily.*) Where's all de white-collar stiffs yuh said was here—and de skoits—*her* kind?

10 LONG: In church, blarst 'em! Arskin' Jesus to give 'em more money.

YANK: Choich, huh? I useter go to choich onct—sure—when I was a kid. Me old man and woman, dey made me. Dey never went demselves, dough. Always got too big a head on
15 Sunday mornin', dat was dem. (*With a grin.*) Dey was scrappers for fair, bot' of dem. On Satiday nights when dey bot' got a skinful dey could put up a bout oughter been staged at de Garden. When dey got trough dere wasn't a chair or table with a leg under it. Or else dey bot' jumped on me for
20 somep'n. Dat was where I loined to take punishment. (*With a grin and a swagger.*) I'm a chip offen de old block, get me?

LONG: Did yer old man follow the sea?

YANK: Naw. Worked along shore. I runned away when me old lady croaked with de tremens. I helped at truckin' and
25 in de market. Den I shipped in de stokehole. Sure. Dat belongs. De rest was nothin'. (*Looking around him.*) I ain't never seen dis before. De Brooklyn waterfront, dat was where I was dragged up. (*Taking a deep breath.*) Dis ain't so bad at dat, huh?

30 LONG: Not bad? Well, we pays for it wiv our bloody sweat, if yer wants to know!

YANK: (*With sudden angry disgust.*) Aw, hell! I don't see no one, see—like her. All dis gives me a pain. It don't belong. Say, ain't dere a back room around dis dump? Let's go shoot a
35 ball. All dis is too clean and quiet and dolled-up, get me? It gives me a pain.

LONG: Wait and yer'll bloody well see—

YANK: I don't wait for no one. I keep on de move. Say, what yuh drag me up here for, anyway? Tryin' to kid me, yuh
40 simp, yuh?

LONG: Yer wants to get back at 'er, don't yer? That's what yer been sayin' every bloomin' hour since she hinsulted yer.

YANK: (*Vehemently.*) Sure ting I do! Didn't I try to get even wit her in Southampton? Didn't I sneak on de dock and wait
45 for her by de gangplank? I was goin' to spit in her pale mug, see! Sure, right in her pop-eyes! Dat woulda made me even, see? But no chanct. Dere was a whole army of plain-clothes bulls around. Dey spotted me and gimme de bum's rush. I never seen her. But I'll git square wit her yet, you
50 watch! (*Furiously.*) De lousy tart! She tink she kin get away with moider—but not wit me! I'll fix her! I'll tink of a way!

LONG: (*As disgusted as he dares to be.*) Ain't that why I brought yer up 'ere—to show yer? Yer been lookin' at this 'ere 'ole affair wrong. Yer been actin' an' talkin' 's if it was all a
55 bleedin' personal matter between yer and that bloody cow.

I wants to convince yer she was on'y a representative of 'er clarss. I wants to awaken yer bloody clarss consciousness. Then yer'll see it's 'er clarss yer've got to fight, not 'er alone. There's a 'ole mob of 'em like 'er, Gawd blind 'em!

60 YANK: (*Spitting on his hands—belligerently.*) De more de merrier when I gits started. Bring on de gang!

LONG: Yer'll see 'em in arf a mo', when that church lets out. (*He turns and sees the window display in the two stores for the first time.*) Blimey! Look at that, will yer? (*They both walk back and stand looking in the jeweler's.* LONG *flies into a fury.*) Just look at
65 this 'ere bloomin' mess! Just look at it! Look at the bleedin' prices on 'em—more'n our 'ole bloody stokehole makes in ten voyages sweatin' in 'ell! And they—'er and 'er bloody clarss—buys 'em for toys to dangle on 'em! One of these
70 'ere, would buy scoff for a starvin' family for a year!

YANK: Aw, cut de sob stuff! T' hell wit de starvin' family! Yuh'll be passin' de hat to me next. (*With naïve admiration.*) Say, dem tings is pretty, huh? Bet yuh dey'd hock for a piece of change aw right. (*Then turning away, bored.*) But
75 aw hell, what good are dey? Let 'er have 'em. Dey don't belong no more'n she does. (*With a gesture of sweeping the jewelers into oblivion.*) All dat don't count, get me?

LONG: (*Who has moved to the furrier's—indignantly.*) And I s'pose this 'ere don't count neither—skins of poor, 'arm-
80 less animals slaughtered so as 'er and 'ers can keep their bleedin' noses warm!

YANK: (*Who has been staring at something inside—with queer excitement.*) Take a slant at dat! Give it de once-over! Monkey fur—two t'ousand bucks! (*Bewilderedly.*) Is dat straight
85 goods—monkey fur? What de hell—?

LONG: (*Bitterly.*) It's straight enuf. (*With grim humor.*) They wouldn't bloody well pay that for 'airy ape's skin—no, nor for the 'ole livin' ape with all 'is 'ead, and body, and soul thrown in!

90 YANK: (*Clenching his fists, his face growing pale with rage as if the skin in the window were a personal insult.*) Trowin' it up in my face! Christ! I'll fix her!

LONG: (*Excitedly.*) Church is out. 'Ere they come, the bleedin' swine. (*After a glance at* YANK'S *lowering face—uneasily.*) Easy
95 goes, Comrade. Keep yer bloomin' temper. Remember force defeats itself. It ain't our weapon. We must impress our demands through peaceful means—the votes of the on-marching proletarians of the bloody world!

YANK: (*With abysmal contempt.*) Votes, hell! Votes is a joke, see.
100 Votes for women! Let dem do it!

LONG: (*Still more uneasily.*) Calm, now. Treat 'em wiv the proper contempt. Observe the bleedin' parasites but 'old yer 'orses.

YANK: (*Angrily.*) Git away from me! Yuh're yellow, dat's what. Force, dat's me! De punch, dat's me every time, see! (*The
105 crowd from church enter from the right, sauntering slowly and affectedly, their heads held stiffly up, looking neither to right nor left, talking in toneless, simpering voices. The women are rouged, calcimined, dyed, overdressed to the nth degree. The men are in Prince Alberts, high hats, spats, canes, etc. A procession of gaudy mari-
110 onettes, yet with something of the relentless horror of Frankenstein monsters in their detached, mechanical unawareness.*)

VOICES: Dear Doctor Caiaphas! He is so sincere!

   What was the sermon? I dozed off.

   About the radicals, my dear—and the false doctrines that are being preached.

115 We must organize a hundred per cent American bazaar.

And let everyone contribute one one-hundredth per cent
of their income tax.
What an original idea!
We can devote the proceeds to rehabilitating the veil of
the temple.
But that has been done so many times.

120 YANK: (*Glaring from one to the other of them—with an insulting
snort of scorn.*) Huh! Huh! (*Without seeming to see him, they
make wide detours to avoid the spot where he stands in the middle of the sidewalk.*)

LONG: (*Frightenedly.*) Keep yer bloomin' mouth shut, I tells yer.

125 YANK: (*Viciously.*) G'wan! Tell it to Sweeney! (*He swaggers
away and deliberately lurches into a top-hatted gentleman, then
glares at him pugnaciously.*) Say, who d'yuh tink yuh're
bumpin'? Tink yuh own de oith?

GENTLEMAN: (*Coldly and affectedly.*) I beg your pardon. (*He has
130 not looked at* YANK *and passes on without a glance, leaving him
bewildered.*)

LONG: (*Rushing up and grabbing* YANK's *arm.*) 'Ere! Come
away! This wasn't what I meant. Yer'll 'ave the bloody
coppers down on us.

135 YANK: (*Savagely—giving him a push that sends him sprawling.*)
G'wan!

LONG: (*Picks himself up—hysterically.*) I'll pop orf then. This
ain't what I meant. And whatever 'appens yer can't blame
me. (*He slinks off left.*)

140 YANK: T' hell wit youse! (*He approaches a lady—with a vicious
grin and a smirking wink.*) Hello, Kiddo. How's every little
ting? Got anyting on for tonight? I know an old boiler
down to de docks we kin crawl into. (*The lady stalks by without a look, without a change of pace.* YANK *turns to others—
145 insultingly.*) Holy smokes, what a mug! Go hide yuhself
before de horses shy at yuh. Gee, pipe de heine on dat one!
Say, youse, yuh look like de stoin of a ferryboat. Paint and
powder! All dolled up to kill! Yuh look like stiffs laid out for
de boneyard! Aw, g'wan, de lot of youse! Yuh give me de
150 eyeache. Yuh don't belong, get me! Look at me, why don't
youse dare? I belong, dat's me! (*Pointing to skyscraper across
the street which is in process of construction—with bravado.*) See
dat building goin' up dere? See de steel work? Steel, dat's
me! Youse guys live on it and tink yuh're somep'n. But I'm
155 in it, see I'm de-hoistin' engine dat makes it go up! I'm it—
de inside and bottom of it! Sure! I'm steel and steam and
smoke and de rest of it! It moves—speed—twenty-five stories up—and me at de top and bottom—movin'! Youse
simps don't move. Yuh're on'y dolls I winds up to see 'm
160 spin. Yuh're de garbage, get me—de leavins—der ashes we
dump over de side! Now, what's 'a' yuh gotta say? (*But as
they seem neither to see nor hear him, he flies into a fury.*) Bums!
Pigs! Tarts! Bitches! (*He turns in rage on the men, bumping viciously into them but not jarring them the least bit. Rather it is he
165 who recoils after each collision. He keeps growling.*) Git off de
oith! G'wan, yuh bum! Look where yuh're goin', can't
yuh? Git outa here! Fight, why don't yuh? Put up yer mits!
Don't be a dog! Fight or I'll knock yuh dead! (*But, without
seeming to see him, they all answer with mechanical affected po-
170 liteness.*) I beg your pardon. (*Then at a cry from one of the
women they all scurry to the furrier's window.*)

THE WOMAN: (*Ecstatically, with a gasp of delight.*) Monkey fur!
(*The whole crowd of men and women chorus after her in the
same tone of affected delight.*) Monkey fur!

175 YANK: (*With a jerk of his head back on his shoulders, as if he had received a punch full in the face—raging.*) I see yuh, all in white!
I see yuh, yuh white-faced tart, yuh! Hairy ape, huh? I'll
hairy ape yuh! (*He bends down and grips at the street curbing as
if to pluck it out and hurl it. Foiled in this, snarling with passion,
180 he leaps to the lamppost on the corner and tries to pull it up for a
club. Just at that moment a bus is heard rumbling up. A fat, high-
hatted, spatted gentleman runs out from the side street. He calls
out plaintively.*) Bus! Bus! Stop there! (*And runs full tilt into
the bending straining* YANK, *who is bowled off his balance.*)

185 YANK: (*Seeing a fight—with a roar of joy as he springs to his feet.*)
At last! Bus, huh! I'll bust yuh! (*He lets drive a terrific swing,
his fist landing full on the fat gentleman's face. But the gentleman stands unmoved as if nothing had happened.*)

GENTLEMAN: I beg your pardon. (*Then irritably.*) You have
190 made me lose my bus. (*He claps his hands and begins to
scream.*) Officer! Officer! (*Many police whistles shrill out on
the instant and a whole platoon of policemen rush in on* YANK
*from all sides. He tries to fight but is clubbed to the pavement and
fallen upon. The crowd at the window have not moved or noticed
195 this disturbance. The clanging gong of the patrol wagon approaches with a clamoring din.*)

(*The curtain falls.*)

SCENE SIX

SCENE: *Night of the following day. A row of cells in the prison on
Blackwell's Island. The cells extend back diagonally from right front
to left rear. They do not stop, but disappear in the dark background
as if they ran on, numberless, into infinity. One electric bulb from the
low ceiling of the narrow corridor sheds its light through the heavy
steel bars of the cell at the extreme front and reveals part of the interior.* YANK *can be seen within, crouched on the edge of his cot in
the attitude of Rodin's "The Thinker." His face is spotted with black
and blue bruises. A blood-stained bandage is wrapped around his
head.*

YANK: (*Suddenly starting as if awakening from a dream, reaches out
and shakes the bars—aloud to himself, wonderingly.*) Steel. Dis
is de Zoo, huh? (*A burst of hard barking laughter comes from
the unseen occupants of the cells, runs back down the tier, and
abruptly ceases.*)   5

VOICES: (*Mockingly.*) The Zoo? That's a new name for this
coop—a damn good name!
Steel, eh? You said a mouthful. This is the old iron
house.
Who is that boob talkin'?
He's the bloke they brung in out of his head. The bulls
had beat him up fierce.

YANK: (*Dully.*) I musta been dreamin'. I tought I was in a cage   10
at de Zoo—but de apes don't talk, do dey?

VOICES: (*With mocking laughter.*) You're in a cage aw right.
A coop!
A pen!
A sty!
A kennel! (*Hard laughter—a pause.*)   15
Say, guy! Who are you? No, never mind lying. What are
you?

Yes, tell us your sad story. What's your game?

What did they jug yuh for?

YANK: (*Dully.*) I was a fireman—stokin' on de liners. (*Then with*
20   *sudden rage, rattling his cell bars.*) I'm a hairy ape, get me? And
I'll bust youse all in de jaw if yuh don't lay off kiddin' me.

VOICES: Huh! You're a hard-boiled duck, ain't you!

When you spit, it bounces! (*Laughter.*)

Aw, can it. He's a regular guy. Ain't you?
25   What did he say he was—a ape?

YANK: (*Defiantly.*) Sure ting! Ain't dat what youse all are—
apes? (*A silence. Then a furious rattling of bars from down the
corridor.*)

A VOICE: (*Thick with rage.*) I'll show yuh who's a ape, yuh bum!
30 VOICES: Ssshh! Nix!

Can de noise!

Piano!

You'll have the guard down on us!

YANK: (*Scornfully.*) De guard? Yuh mean de keeper don't yuh?
35   (*Angry exclamations from all the cells.*)

VOICE: (*Placatingly.*) Aw, don't pay no attention to him. He's off
his nut from the beatin'-up he got. Say, you guy! We're waitin'
to hear what they landed you for—or ain't yuh tellin'?

YANK: Sure, I'll tell youse. Sure! Why de hell not? On'y—
40   youse won't get me. Nobody gets me but me, see? I
started to tell de Judge and all he says was: "Toity days to
tink it over." Tink it over! Christ, dat's all I been doin' for
weeks! (*After a pause.*) I was tryin' to git even with someone, see?—someone dat done me doit.

45 VOICES: (*Cynically.*) De old stuff, I bet. Your goil, huh?

Give yuh the double-cross, huh?

That's them every time!

Did yuh beat up de odder guy?

YANK: (*Disgustedly.*) Aw, yuh're all wrong! Sure dere was a skoit
50   in it—but not what youse mean, not dat old tripe. Dis was
a new kind of skoit. She was dolled up all in white—in de
stokehole. I tought she was a ghost. Sure. (*A pause.*)

VOICES: (*Whispering.*) Gee, he's still nutty.

Let him rave. It's fun listenin'.

55 YANK: (*Unheeding—groping in his thoughts.*) Her hands—dey
was skinny and white like dey wasn't real but painted on
somep'n. Dere was a million miles from me to her—
twenty-five knots an hour. She was like some dead ting de
cat brung in. Sure, dat's what. She didn't belong. She be-
60   longed in de window of a toy store, or on de top of a
garbage can, see! Sure! (*He breaks out angrily.*) But would
yuh believe it, she had de noive to do me doit. She lamped
me like she was seein' somep'n broke loose from de
menagerie. Christ, yuh'd oughter seen her eyes! (*He rattles*
65   *the bars of his cell furiously.*) But I'll get back at her yet, you
watch! And if I can't find her I'll take it out on de gang
she runs wit. I'm wise to where dey hangs out now. I'll
show her who belongs! I'll show her who's in de move
and who ain't. You watch my smoke!
70 VOICES: (*Serious and joking.*) Dat's de talkin'!

Take her for all she's got!

What was this dame, anyway? Who was she, eh?

YANK: I dunno. First cabin stiff. Her old man's a millionaire,
dey says—name of Douglas.

75 VOICES: Douglas? That's the president of the Steel Trust, I bet.

Sure. I seen his mug in de papers.

He's filthy with dough.

VOICE: Hey, feller, take a tip from me. If you want to get back
at that dame, you better join the Wobblies. You'll get some
action, then.   80

YANK: Wobblies? What de hell's dat?

VOICE: Ain't you ever heard of the I. W. W.?

YANK: Naw. What is it?

VOICE: A gang of blokes—a tough gang. I been readin' about
'em today in the paper. The guard give me the *Sunday Times.*   85
There's a long spiel about 'em. It's from a speech made in the
Senate by a guy named Senator Queen. (*He is in the cell next
to* YANK*'s. There is a rustling of paper.*) Wait'll I see if I got light
enough and I'll read you. Listen. (*He reads.*) "There is a menace existing in this country today which threatens the vitals   90
of our fair Republic—as foul a menace against the very life-
blood of the American Eagle as was the foul conspiracy of
Cataline against the eagles of ancient Rome!"

VOICE: (*Disgustedly.*) Aw, hell! Tell him to salt de tail of dat
eagle!   95

VOICE: (*Reading.*) "I refer to that devil's brew of rascals, jail-
birds, murderers and cutthroats who libel all honest working men by calling themselves the Industrial Workers of
the World; but in the light of their nefarious plots, I call
them the Industrious Wreckers of the World!"   100

YANK: (*With vengeful satisfaction.*) Wreckers, dat's de right
dope! Dat belongs! Me for dem!

VOICE: Ssshh! (*Reading.*) "This fiendish organization is a foul
ulcer on the fair body of our Democracy—"

VOICE: Democracy, hell! Give him de boid, fellers—the rasp-   105
berry! (*They do.*)

VOICE: Ssshh! (*Reading.*) "Like Cato I say to this Senate, the I.
W. W. must be destroyed! For they represent an ever-
present dagger pointed at the heart of the greatest nation
the world has ever known, where all men are born free and   110
equal, with equal opportunities to all, where the Founding
Fathers have guaranteed to each one happiness, where
Truth, Honor, Liberty, Justice, and the Brotherhood of
Man are a religion absorbed with one's mother's milk,
taught at our father's knee, sealed, signed, and stamped   115
upon in the glorious Constitution of these United States!"
(*A perfect storm of hisses, catcalls, boos, and hard laughter.*)

VOICES: (*Scornfully.*) Hurrah for de Fort' of July!

Pass de hat!

Liberty!   120

Justice!

Honor!

Opportunity!

Brotherhood!

ALL: (*With abysmal scorn.*) Aw, hell!   125

VOICE: Give that Queen Senator guy the bark! All togedder
now— one—two—tree—(*A terrific chorus of barking and yapping.*)

GUARD: (*From a distance.*) Quiet, there, youse—or I'll get the
hose. (*The noise subsides.*)   130

YANK: (*With growling rage.*) I'd like to catch dat senator guy
alone for a second. I'd loin him some trute!

VOICE: Ssshh! Here's where he gits down to cases on the Wobblies. (*Reads.*) "They plot with fire in one hand and dynamite in the other. They stop not before murder to gain   135
their ends, nor at the outraging of defenseless womanhood.
They would tear down society, put the lowest scum in the
seats of the mighty, turn Almighty God's revealed plan for

140 the world topsy-turvy, and make of our sweet and lovely
civilization a shambles, a desolation where man, God's masterpiece, would soon degenerate back to the ape!"

VOICE: (*To* YANK.) Hey, you guy. There's your ape stuff again.

YANK: (*With a growl of fury.*) I got him. So dey blow up tings,
145 do dey? Dey turn tings round, do dey? Hey, lend me dat
paper, will yuh?

VOICE: Sure. Give it to him. On'y keep it to yourself, see. We
don't wanter listen to no more of that slop.

VOICE: Here you are. Hide it under your mattress.

YANK: (*Reaching out.*) Tanks. I can't read much but I kin man-
150 age. (*He sits, the paper in the hand at his side, in the attitude of
Rodin's "The Thinker." A pause. Several snores from down the
corridor. Suddenly* YANK *jumps to his feet with a furious groan as
if some appalling thought had crashed on him—bewilderedly.*)
Sure—her old man—president of de Steel Trust—makes
155 half de steel in de world—steel—where I tought I belonged—drivin' trou—movin'—in dat—to make *her*—
and cage me in for her to spit on! Christ! (*He shakes the bars
of his cell door till the whole tier trembles. Irritated, protesting exclamations from those awakened or trying to get to sleep.*) He
160 made dis—dis cage! Steel! *It* don't belong, dat's what!
Cages, cells, locks, bolts, bars—dat's what it means!—
holdin' me down wit him at de top! But I'll manage trou!
Fire, dat melts it! I'll be fire—under de heap—fire dat
never goes out—hot as hell—breakin' out in de night—
165 (*While he has been saying this last he has shaken his cell door to
a clanging accompaniment. As he comes to the "breakin' out" he
seizes one bar with both hands and, putting his two feet up against
the others so that his position is parallel to the floor like a monkey's, he gives a great wrench backwards. The bar bends like a
170 licorice stick under his tremendous strength. Just at this moment
the* PRISON GUARD *rushes in dragging a hose behind him.*)

GUARD: (*Angrily.*) I'll loin youse bums to wake me up! (*Sees*
YANK.) Hello, it's you, huh? Got the D.Ts., hey? Well, I'll cure
'em. I'll drown your snakes for yuh! (*Noticing the bar.*) Hell,
175 look at dat bar bended! On'y a bug is strong enough for dat!

YANK: (*Glaring at him.*) Or a hairy ape, yuh big yellow bum!
Look out! Here I come! (*He grabs another bar.*)

GUARD: (*Scared now—yelling off left.*) Toin de hose on, Ben!—
full pressure! And call de others—and a straitjacket! (*The
180 curtain is falling. As it hides* YANK *from view, there is a splatter-
ing smash as the stream of water hits the steel of* YANK's *cell.*)

(*The curtain falls.*)

SCENE SEVEN

SCENE: *Nearly a month later. An I. W. W. local near the waterfront,
showing the interior of a front room on the ground floor, and the
street outside. Moonlight on the narrow street, buildings massed in
black shadow. The interior of the room, which is general assembly
room, office; and reading room, resembles some dingy settlement boys'
club. A desk and high stool are in one corner. A table with papers,
stacks of pamphlets, chairs about it, is at center. The whole is decidedly cheap, banal, commonplace and unmysterious as a room could
well be. The Secretary is perched on the stool making entries in a
large ledger. And eye shade casts his face into shadows. Eight or ten
men, longshoremen, iron workers, and the like are grouped about the*
table. *Two are playing checkers. One is writing a letter. Most of them
are smoking pipes. A big signboard is on the wall at the rear, "Industrial Workers of the World—Local No. 57."*

YANK: (*Comes down the street outside. He is dressed as in Scene
Five. He moves cautiously, mysteriously. He comes to a point opposite the door; tiptoes softly up to it, listens, is impressed by the
silence within, knocks carefully, as if he were guessing at the password to some secret rite. Listens. No answer. Knocks again a bit 5
louder. No answer. Knocks impatiently, much louder.*)

SECRETARY: (*Turning around on his stool.*) What the hell is
that—someone knocking? (*Shouts.*) Come in, why don't
you? (*All the men in the room look up.* YANK *opens the door
slowly, gingerly, as if afraid of an ambush. He looks around for 10
secret doors, mystery, is taken aback by the commonplaceness of
the room and the men in it, thinks he may have gotten in the
wrong place, then sees the signboard on the wall and is reassured.*)

YANK: (*Blurts out.*) Hello.

MEN: (*Reservedly.*) Hello. 15

YANK: (*More easily.*) I tought I'd bumped into de wrong dump.

SECRETARY: (*Scrutinizing him carefully.*) Maybe you have. Are
you a member?

YANK: Naw, not yet. Dat's what I come for—to join.

SECRETARY: That's easy. What's your job—long-shore? 20

YANK: Naw. Fireman—stoker on de liners.

SECRETARY: (*With satisfaction.*) Welcome to our city. Glad to
know you people are waking up at last. We haven't got
many members in your line.

YANK: Naw. Dey're all dead to de woild. 25

SECRETARY: Well, you can help to wake 'em. What's your
name? I'll make out your card.

YANK: (*Confused.*) Name? Lemme tink.

SECRETARY: (*Sharply.*) Don't you know your own name?

YANK: Sure; but I been just Yank for so long—Bob, dat's it— 30
Bob Smith.

SECRETARY: (*Writing.*) Robert Smith. (*Fills out the rest of the
card.*) Here you are. Cost you half a dollar.

YANK: Is dat all—four bits? Dat's easy. (*Gives the* SECRETARY
the money.) 35

SECRETARY: (*Throwing it in drawer.*) Thanks. Well, make yourself at home. No introductions needed. There's literature
on the table. Take some of those pamphlets with you to
distribute aboard ship. They may bring results. Sow the
seed, only go about it right. Don't get caught and fired. 40
We got plenty out of work. What we need is men who
can hold their jobs—and work for us at the same time.

YANK: Sure. (*But he still stands, embarrassed and uneasy.*)

SECRETARY: (*Looking at him—curiously.*) What did you knock
for? Think we had a coon in uniform to open doors? 45

YANK: Naw. I tought it was locked—and dat yuh'd wanter
give me the once-over trou a peephole or somep'n to see
if I was right.

SECRETARY: (*Alert and suspicious but with an easy laugh.*) Think
we were running a crap game? 50
That door is never locked. What put that in your nut?

YANK: (*With a knowing grin, convinced that this is all camouflage,
a part of the secrecy.*) Dis burg is full of bulls, ain't it?

SECRETARY: (*Sharply.*) What have the cops got to do with us?
We're breaking no laws. 55

YANK: (*With a knowing wink.*) Sure. Youse wouldn't for woilds. Sure. I'm wise to dat.

SECRETARY: You seem to be wise to a lot of stuff none of us knows about.

60 YANK: (*With another wink.*) Aw, dat's aw right, see. (*Then made a bit resentful by the suspicious glances from all sides.*) Aw, can it! Youse needn't put me trou de toid degree. Can't youse see I belong? Sure! I'm reg'lar. I'll stick, get me? I'll shoot de woiks for youse. Dat's why I wanted to join in.

65 SECRETARY: (*Breezily, feeling him out.*) That's the right spirit. Only are you sure you understand what you've joined? It's all plain and aboveboard; still, some guys get a wrong slant on us. (*Sharply.*) What's your notion of the purpose of the I.W.W.?

70 YANK: Aw, I know all about it.

SECRETARY: (*Sarcastically.*) Well, give us some of your valuable information.

YANK: (*Cunningly.*) I know enough not to speak outa my toin. (*Then resentfully again.*) Aw, say! I'm reg'lar. I'm wise to de
75 game. I know yuh got to watch your step wit a stranger. For all youse know, I might be a plain-clothes dick, or somep'n, dat's what yuh're tinkin', huh? Aw, forget it! I belong, see? Ask any guy down to de docks if I don't.

SECRETARY: Who said you didn't?

80 YANK: After I'm 'nitiated, I'll show yuh.

SECRETARY: (*Astounded.*) Initiated? There's no initiation.

YANK: (*Disappointed.*) Ain't there no password—no grip nor nothin'?

SECRETARY: What'd you think this is—the Elks—or the
85 Black Hand?

YANK: De Elks, hell! De Black Hand, dey're a lot of yellow backstickin' Ginees. Naw. Dis is a man's gang, ain't it?

SECRETARY: You said it! That's why we stand on our two feet in the open. We got no secrets.

90 YANK: (*Surprised but admiringly.*) Yuh mean to say yuh always run wide open—like dis?

SECRETARY: Exactly.

YANK: Den yuh sure got your noive wit youse!

SECRETARY: (*Sharply.*) Just what was it made you want to join
95 us? Come out with that straight.

YANK: Yuh call me? Well, I got noive, too! Here's my hand. Yuh wanter blow tings up, don't yuh? Well, dat's me! I belong!

SECRETARY: (*With pretended carelessness.*) You mean change the
100 unequal conditions of society by legitimate direct action—or with dynamite?

YANK: Dynamite! Blow it offen de oith—steel—all de cages—all de factories, steamers, buildings, jails—de Steel Trust and all dat makes it go.

105 SECRETARY: So—that's your idea, eh? And did you have any special job in that line you wanted to propose to us? (*He makes a sign to the men, who get up cautiously one by one and group behind* YANK.)

YANK: (*Boldly.*) Sure, I'll come out wit it. I'll show youse I'm
110 one of de gang. Dere's dat millionaire guy, Douglas—

SECRETARY: President of the Steel Trust, you mean? Do you want to assassinate him?

YANK: Naw, dat don't get yuh nothin'. I mean blow up de factory, de woiks, where he makes de steel. Dat's what I'm
115 after—to blow up de steel, knock all de steel in de woild up to de moon. Dat'll fix tings! (*Exactly, with a touch of bravado.*) I'll do it by me lonesome! I'll show yuh! Tell me where his woiks is, how to git there, all de dope. Gimme de stuff, de old butter—and watch me do de rest! Watch
120 de smoke and see it move! I don't give a damn if dey nab me—long as it's done! I'll soive life for it—and give 'em de laugh! (*Half to himself.*) And I'll write her a letter and tell her de hairy ape done it. Dat'll square tings.

SECRETARY: (*Stepping away from* YANK.) Very interesting. (*He
125 gives a signal. The men, huskies all, throw themselves on* YANK *and before he knows it they have his legs and arms pinioned. But he is too flabbergasted to make a struggle, anyway. They feel him over for weapons.*)

MAN: No gat, no knife. Shall we give him what's what and
130 put the boots to him?

SECRETARY: No. He isn't worth the trouble we'd get into. He's too stupid. (*He comes closer and laughs mockingly in* YANK's *face.*) Ho-ho! By God, this is the biggest joke they've put up on us yet. Hey, you Joke! Who sent you—
135 Burns or Pinkerton? No, by God, you're such a bonehead I'll bet you're in the Secret Service! Well, you dirty spy, you rotten agent provocator, you can go back and tell whatever skunk is paying you blood-money for betraying your brothers that he's wasting his coin. You couldn't
140 catch a cold. And tell him that all he'll ever get on us, or ever has got, is just his own sneaking plots that he's framed up to put us in jail. We are what our manifesto says we are, neither more nor less—and we'll give him a copy of that any time he calls. And as for you—(*He glares scornfully
145 at* YANK, *who is sunk in an oblivious stupor.*) Oh, hell, what's the use of talking? You're a brainless ape.

YANK: (*Aroused by the word to fierce but futile struggles.*) What's dat, yuh Sheeny bum, yuh!

SECRETARY: Throw him out, boys. (*In spite of his struggles, this
150 is done with gusto and éclat. Propelled by several parting kicks,* YANK *lands sprawling in the middle of the narrow cobbled street. With a growl he starts to get up and storm the closed door, but stops bewildered by the confusion in his brain, pathetically impotent. He sits there, brooding, in as near to the attitude of Rodin's
155 "Thinker" as he can get in his position.*)

YANK: (*Bitterly.*) So dem boids don't tink I belong, neider. Aw, to hell wit 'em! Dey're in de wrong pew—de same old bull—soapboxes and Salvation Army—no guts! Cut out an hour offen de job a day and make me happy! Gimme a dollar more a day and make me happy! Tree
160 square a day, and cauliflowers in de front yard—ekal rights—a woman and kids—a lousy vote—and I'm all fixed for Jesus, huh? Aw, hell! What does dat get yuh? Dis ting's in your inside, but it ain't your belly. Feedin' your face—sinkers and coffee—dat don't touch it. It's way
165 down—at de bottom. Yuh can't grab it, and yuh can't stop it. It moves, and everything moves. It stops and de whole woild stops. Dat's me now—I don't tick, see?—I'm a busted Ingersoll, dat's what. Steel was me, and I owned de woild. Now I ain't steel, and de woild owns me. Aw, hell!
170 I can't see—it's all dark, get me? It's all wrong! (*He turns a bitter mocking face up like an ape gibbering at the moon.*) Say, youse up dere, Man in de Moon, yuh look so wise, gimme

175 de answer, huh? Slip me de inside dope, de information right from de stable—where do I get off at, huh?

A POLICEMAN: (*Who has come up the street in time to hear this last with grim humor.*) You'll get off at the station, you boob, if you don't get up out of that and keep movin'.

YANK: (*Looking up at him—with a hard, bitter laugh.*) Sure!
180 Lock me up! Put me in a cage! Dat's de on'y answer yuh know. G'wan, lock me up!

POLICEMAN: What you been doin'?

YANK: Enuf to gimme life for! I was born, see? Sure, dat's de charge. Write it in de blotter. I was born, get me?

185 POLICEMAN: (*Jocosely.*) God pity your old woman! (*Then matter-of-fact.*) But I've no time for kidding. You're soused. I'd run you in but it's too long a walk to the station. Come on now, get up, or I'll fan your ears with this club. Beat it now! (*He hauls* YANK *to his feet.*)

190 YANK: (*In a vague mocking tone.*) Say, where do I go from here?

POLICEMAN: (*Giving him a push—with a grin, indifferently.*) Go to hell.

(*The curtain falls.*)

SCENE EIGHT

SCENE: *Twilight of the next day. The monkey house at the Zoo. One spot of clear gray light falls on the front of one cage so that the interior can be seen. The other cages are vague, shrouded in shadow from which chatterings pitched in a conversational tone can be heard. On the one cage a sign from which the word "gorilla" stands out. The gigantic animal himself is seen squatting on his haunches on a bench in much the same attitude as Rodin's "Thinker."* YANK *enters from the left. Immediately a chorus of angry chattering and screeching breaks out. The gorilla turns his eyes but makes no sound or move.*

YANK: (*With a hard, bitter laugh.*) Welcome to your city, huh? Hail, hail, de gang's all here! (*At the sound of his voice the chattering dies away into an attentive silence.* YANK *walks up to the gorilla's cage and, leaning over the railing, stares in at its occupant,*
5 *who stares back at him, silent and motionless. There is a pause of dead stillness. Then* YANK *begins to talk in a friendly confidential tone, half-mockingly, but with a deep undercurrent of sympathy.*) Say, yuh're some hard-lookin' guy, ain't yuh? I seen lots of tough nuts dat de gang called gorillas, but yuh're de foist
10 real one I ever seen. Some chest yuh got, and shoulders, and dem arms and mits! I bet yuh got a punch in eider fist dat'd knock 'em all silly. (*This with genuine admiration. The gorilla, as if he understood, stands upright, swelling out his chest and pounding on it with his fist.* YANK *grins sympathetically.*)
15 Sure, I get yuh. Yuh challenge de whole woild, huh? Yuh got what I was sayin' even if yuh muffed de woids. (*Then bitterness creeping in.*) And why wouldn't yuh get me? Ain't we both members of de same club—de Hairy Apes? (*They stare at each other—a pause—then* YANK *goes on slowly and bit-*
20 *terly.*) So yuh're what she seen when she looked at me, de white-faced tart! I was you to her, get me? On'y outa de cage—broke out—free to moider her, see? Sure! Dat's what she tought. She wasn't wise dat I was in a cage, too—worser'n yours—sure—a damn sight—'cause you got
25 some chanct to bust loose—but me—(*He grows confused.*) Aw, hell! It's all wrong, ain't it? (*A pause.*) I s'pose yuh wan-

ter know what I'm doin' here, huh? I been warmin' a bench down to de Battery—ever since last night. Sure. I seen de sun come up. Dat was pretty, too—all red and pink and green. I was lookin' at de skyscrapers—steel—and all
30 de ships comin' in, sailin' out, all over de oith—and dey was steel, too. De sun was warm, dey wasn't no clouds, and dere was a breeze blowin'. Sure, it was great stuff. I got it aw right—what Paddy said about dat bein' de right dope—on'y I couldn't get *in* it, see? I couldn't belong in dat. It was
35 over my head. And I kept tinkin'—and den I beat it up here to see what youse was like. And I waited till dey was all gone to git yuh alone. Say, how d'yuh feel sittin' in dat pen all de time, havin' to stand for 'em comin' and starin' at yuh—de white-faced, skinny tarts and de boobs what
40 marry 'em—makin' fun of yuh, laughin' at yuh, gittin' scared of yuh—damn 'em! (*He pounds on the rail with his fist. The gorilla rattles the bars of his cage and snarls. All the other monkeys set up an angry chattering in the darkness.* YANK *goes on excitedly.*) Sure! Dat's de way it hits me, too. On'y yuh're
45 lucky, see? Yuh don't belong with 'em and you know it. But me, I belong wit 'em—but I don't, see? Dey don't belong wit me, dat's what. Get me? Tinkin' is hard—(*He passes one hand across his forehead with a painful gesture. The gorilla growls impatiently.* YANK *goes on gropingly.*) It's dis way, what I'm dri-*
50 vin' at. Youse can sit and dope dream in de past, green woods, de jungle and de rest of it. Den yuh belong and dey don't. Den yuh kin laugh at 'em, see? Yuh're de champ of de woild. But me—I ain't got no past to tink in, nor nothin' dat's comin', on'y what's now—and dat don't be-
55 long. Sure, you're de best off! Yuh can't tink, can yuh? Yuh can't talk neider. But I kin make a bluff at talkin' and tin-kin'—a'most git away wit it—a'most!—and dat's where de joker comes in. (*He laughs.*) I ain't on oith and I ain't in heaven, get me? I'm in de middle tryin' to separate 'em,
60 takin' all de woist punches from bot' of 'em. Maybe dat's what dey call hell, huh? But you, yuh're at de bottom. You belong! Sure! Yuh're de on'y one in de woild dat does, yuh lucky stiff! (*The gorilla growls proudly.*) And dat's why dey gotter put yuh in a cage, see? (*The gorilla roars angrily.*) Sure!
65 Yuh get me. It beats it when you try to tink it or talk it—it's way down—deep—behind—you 'n' me we feel it. Sure! Bot' members of dis club! (*He laughs—then in a sav-age tone.*) What de hell! T' hell wit it! A little action, dat's our meat! Dat belongs! Knock 'em down and keep bustin' 'em
70 till dey croaks yuh wit a gat—wit steel! Sure! Are yuh game? Dey've looked at youse, ain't dey—in a cage? Wan-ter get even? Wanter wind up like a sport 'stead of croakin' slow in dere? (*The gorilla roars an emphatic affirmative.* YANK *goes on with a sort of furious exaltation.*) Sure! Yuh're de reg'lar!
75 Yuh'll stick to de finish! Me 'n' you, huh?—bot' members of this club! We'll put up one last star bout dat'll knock 'em offen deir seats! Dey'll have to make de cages stronger af-ter we're trou! (*The gorilla is straining at his bars, growling, hop-ping from one foot to the other.* YANK *takes a jimmy from under*
80 *his coat and forces the lock on the cage door. He throws this open.*) Pardon from de governor! Step out and shake hands! I'll take yuh for a walk down Fif' Avenoo. We'll knock 'em of-fen de oith and croak wit de band playin'. Come on, Brother. (*The gorilla scrambles gingerly out of his cage. Goes to*
85 YANK *and stands looking at him.* YANK *keeps his mocking tone—holds out his hand.*) Shake—de secret grip of our order.

(*Something, the tone of mockery, perhaps, suddenly enrages the animal. With a spring he wraps his huge arms around* YANK *in a*
90   *murderous hug. There is a crackling snap of crushed ribs—a gasping cry, still mocking, from* YANK.) Hey, I didn't say kiss me!
(*The gorilla lets the crushed body slip to the floor; stands over it uncertainly, considering; then picks it up, throws it in the cage, shuts the door, and shuffles off menacingly into the darkness at left.*
95   *A great uproar of frightened chattering and whimpering comes from the other cages. Then* YANK *moves, groaning, opening his eyes, and there is silence. He mutters painfully.*) Say—dey oughter match him—wit Zybszko. He got me, aw right. I'm trou. Even him didn't tink I belonged. (*Then, with sudden passionate despair.*) Christ, where do I get off at? Where
100
do I fit in? (*Checking himself as suddenly.*) Aw, what de hell! No squawkin', see! No quittin', get me! Croak wit your boots on! (*He grabs hold of the bars of the cage and hauls himself painfully to his feet—looks around him bewilderedly—forces a mocking laugh.*) In de cage, huh? (*In the strident tones of a* 105 *circus barker.*) Ladies and gents, step forward and take a slant at de one and only—(*His voice weakened.*)—one and original—Hairy Ape from de wilds of—(*He slips in a heap on the floor and dies. The monkeys set up a chattering, whimpering wail. And, perhaps, the Hairy Ape at last belongs.*) 110

(*The curtain falls.*)

Tennessee Williams

Like Amanda Wingfield in *The Glass Menagerie,* Tennessee Williams (1911–1983) regarded himself as a product of the Old South and its genteel, rural, and—finally—obsolete traditions. Born Thomas Lanier Williams to a traveling shoe salesman and his wife, Williams was raised in Mississippi before moving to the tenements of St. Louis. As a child, Williams contracted diphtheria, which briefly paralyzed his legs and left him frail and homebound for some time. During his convalescence, Williams read and wrote avidly and published his first story at the age of sixteen. After high school, he briefly attended the University of Missouri, but withdrew when his poor health prevented him from passing the ROTC course. He then worked for three years in a shoe factory, then tried Washington University in St. Louis, but again dropped out. He finally took his degree in playwriting from the University of Iowa in 1938, when he changed his name to "Tennessee." In the 1930s, Williams's embattled relation to the world was deepened by the "loss" of his beloved sister Rose. Rose became chronically depressed, and Williams's mother, unable to cope with her erratic and wild behavior, consented to having a lobotomy performed. Rose was left docile but inert and became the prototype of several of Williams's most memorable dramatic characters, women whose inner beauty is too delicate to be disclosed to the world. At this time Williams also recognized his own homosexuality, a recognition that deepened his sense of the threatening conformity imposed by mainstream American society.

Coming of age in the Great Depression was formative for Williams's drama, particularly the range of themes associated with his mature work: a sexual tension surging beneath the surface of the characters' lives, the collapse of a sustaining family and social order, the attraction of misfits destroyed by a world that will not accept them. Williams wrote several now-lost plays in the late 1930s, and *Battle of Angels* (1940; later revised as *Orpheus Descending* in 1957) was produced by the Theater Guild in Boston, where it failed. Williams scored a major success with his next play, *The Glass Menagerie* (1944). He continued his success with a series of important dramas: *Summer and Smoke* (1947), *A Streetcar Named Desire* (1947), *The Rose Tattoo* (1951), *Camino Real* (1953), *Cat on a Hot Tin Roof* (1955), *Sweet Bird of Youth* (1959), and *Night of the Iguana* (1961). In his later years, Williams's drama became increasingly gothic and sensational, and his personal life suffered as well; Williams became an alcoholic and was institutionalized on several occasions. He continued to write plays to the end of his life, developing his characteristic strengths: a feel for the nuances of character, and a flair for dramatizing the victims of an unfeeling world.

THE GLASS MENAGERIE

First performed in 1944, *The Glass Menagerie* looks back to the 1930s. Its characters are reminiscent of Williams and his family, and their grinding poverty recalls the depression-era plays of Elmer Rice and Clifford Odets. In many ways, *The Glass Menagerie* is a play in the realistic tradition. Laura's menagerie recalls how Ibsen, Chekhov, and Strindberg used stage objects (Nora's Christmas tree in *A Doll House,* the cherry orchard in Chekhov's play) to evoke and symbolize the characters' motives and sensibilities. However, Williams also uses the device of the "memory play" to disrupt the linearity of realistic drama. Tom constructs the scene and the characters for the audience, and slide projections of phrases and images often illustrate the action as it takes place. These devices lend *The Glass Menagerie* the flavor of symbolist theater. Moreover, Tom's anticipation of the Spanish Civil War and World War II sets the play in a larger social and political context that looms forebodingly over the fragile and self-absorbed characters. Amanda and Laura seem doomed never to escape the drab apartment, and even Tom, wandering the world, finally cannot escape it either. Deeply personal (Williams's given name was Tom), *The Glass Menagerie* also provides a kind of study

Tom, Laura, Jim, and Amanda in Tennessee Williams's *The Glass Menagerie* at the Williamstown Theatre Festival.

for Williams's later plays, for it includes a typical panoply of Williams's characters: the blunt, sexually aggressive, emotionally stunted Jim; Amanda, the faded Southern belle; Laura, more crippled emotionally than physically; and Tom, who falls in love with long distance yet never succeeds in escaping his past or in finding his future.

Production Notes

Being a "memory play," *The Glass Menagerie* can be presented with unusual freedom of convention. Because of its considerably delicate or tenuous material, atmospheric touches and subtleties of direction play a particularly important part. Expressionism and all other unconventional techniques in drama have only one valid aim, and that is a closer approach to truth. When a play employs unconventional techniques, it is not, or certainly shouldn't be, trying to escape its responsibility of dealing with reality, or interpreting experience, but is actually or should be attempting to find a closer approach, a more penetrating and vivid expression of things as they are. The straight realistic play with its genuine Frigidaire and authentic ice-cubes, its characters who speak exactly as its audience speaks, corresponds to the academic landscape and has the same virtue of a photographic likeness. Everyone should know nowadays the unimportance of the photographic in art: that truth, life, or reality is an organic thing which the poetic imagination can represent or suggest, in essence, only through transformation, through changing into other forms than those which were merely present in appearance.

These remarks are not meant as a preface only to this particular play. They have to do with a conception of a new, plastic theatre which must take the place of the exhausted theatre of realistic conventions if the theatre is to resume vitality as a part of our culture.

THE SCREEN DEVICE

There is *only one important difference between the original and the acting version of the play* and that is the *omission* in the latter of the device that I tentatively included in my *original* script. This device was the use of a screen on which were projected magic-lantern slides bearing images or titles. I do not regret the omission of this device from the original Broadway production. The extraordinary power of Miss Taylor's performance made it suitable to have the utmost simplicity in the physical production. But I think it may be interesting to some readers to see how this device was conceived. So I am putting it into the published manuscript. These images and legends, projected from behind, were cast on a section of wall between the front-room and dining-room areas, which should be indistinguishable from the rest when not in use.

The purpose of this will probably be apparent. It is to give accent to certain values in each scene. Each scene contains a particular point (or several) which is structurally the most important. In an episodic play, such as this, the basic structure or narrative line may be obscured from the audience; the effect may seem fragmentary rather than architectural. This may not be the fault of the play so much as a lack of attention in the audience. The legend or image upon the screen will strengthen the effect of what is merely allusion in the writing and allow the primary point to be made more simply and lightly than if the entire responsibility were on the spoken lines. Aside from this structural value, I think the screen will have a definite emotional appeal, less definable but just as important. An imaginative producer or director may invent many other uses for this device than those indicated in the present script. In fact the possibilities of the device seem much larger to me than the instance of this play can possibly utilize.

THE MUSIC

Another extra-literary accent in this play is provided by the use of music. A single recurring tune, "The Glass Menagerie," is used to give emotional emphasis to suitable passages. This tune is like circus music, not when you are on the grounds or in the immediate vicinity of the parade, but when you are at some distance and very likely thinking of something else. It seems under those circumstances to continue almost interminably and it weaves in and out of your preoccupied consciousness; then it is the lightest, most delicate music in the world and perhaps the saddest. It expresses the surface vivacity of life with the underlying strain of immutable and inexpressible sorrow. When you look at a piece of delicately spun glass you think of two things: how beautiful it is and how easily it can be broken. Both of those ideas should be woven into the recurring tune, which dips in and out of the play as if it were carried on a wind that changes. It serves as a thread of connection and allusion between the narrator with his separate point in time and space and the subject of his story. Between each episode it returns as reference to the emotion, nostalgia, which is the first condition of the play. It is primarily Laura's music and therefore comes out most clearly when the play focuses upon her and the lovely fragility of glass which is her image.

THE LIGHTING

The lighting in the play is not realistic. In keeping with the atmosphere of memory, the stage is dim. Shafts of light are focused on selected areas or actors, sometimes in contradistinction to what is the apparent center. For instance, in the quarrel scene between Tom and Amanda, in which Laura has no active part, the clearest pool of light is on her figure. This is also true of the supper scene, when her silent figure on the sofa should remain the visual center. The light upon Laura should be distinct from the others, having a peculiar pristine clarity such as light used in early religious portraits of female saints or madonnas. A certain correspondence to light in religious paintings, such as El Greco's, where the figures are radiant in atmosphere that is relatively dusky, could be effectively used throughout the play. (It will also permit a more effective use of the screen.) A free, imaginative use of light can be of enormous value in giving a mobile, plastic quality to plays of a more or less static nature.

Tennessee Williams

THE GLASS MENAGERIE

Tennessee Williams

CHARACTERS

AMANDA WINGFIELD (*the mother*), *a little woman of great but confused vitality clinging frantically to another time and place. Her characterization must be carefully created, not copied from type. She is not paranoiac, but her life is paranoia. There is much to admire in Amanda, and as much to love and pity as there is to laugh at. Certainly she has endurance and a kind of heroism, and though her foolishness makes her unwittingly cruel at times, there is tenderness in her slight person.*

LAURA WINGFIELD (*her daughter*), *Amanda, having failed to establish contact with reality, continues to live vitally in her illusions, but Laura's situation is even graver. A childhood illness has left her crippled, one leg slightly shorter than the other, and held in a brace. This defect need not be more than suggested on the stage. Stemming from this, Laura's separation increases till she is like a piece of her own glass collection, too exquisitely fragile to move from the shelf.*

TOM WINGFIELD (*her son*), *and the narrator of the play. A poet with a job in a warehouse. His nature is not remorseless, but to escape from a trap he has to act without pity.*

JIM O'CONNOR (*the gentleman caller*), *a nice, ordinary, young man.*

SCENE: *An Alley in St. Louis*

Part I   Preparation for a Gentleman Caller.

Part II The Gentlemen calls.

TIME: *Now and the Past*

SCENE ONE

The Wingfield apartment is in the rear of the building, one of those vast hive-like conglomerations of the cellular living-units that flower as warty growths in overcrowded urban centers of lower middle-class population and are symptomatic of the impulse of this largest and fundamentally enslaved section of American society to avoid fluidity and differentiation and to exist and function as one interfused mass of automatism.

The apartment faces an alley and is entered by a fire escape, a structure whose name is a touch of accidental poetic truth, for all of these huge buildings are always burning with the slow and implacable fires of human desperation. The fire escape is part of what we see—that is, the landing of it and steps descending from it.

The scene is memory and is therefore nonrealistic. Memory takes a lot of poetic license. It omits some details; others are exaggerated, according to the emotional value of the articles it touches, for memory is seated predominantly in the heart. The interior is therefore rather dim and poetic.

At the rise of the curtain, the audience is faced with the dark, grim rear wall of the Wingfield tenement. This building is flanked on both sides by dark, narrow alleys which run into murky canyons of tangled clotheslines, garbage cans, and the sinister latticework of neighboring fire escapes. It is up and down these side alleys that exterior entrances and exits are made during the play. At the end of TOM's opening commentary, the dark tenement wall slowly becomes transparent and reveals the interior of the ground-floor Wingfield apartment.

Nearest the audience is the living room, which also serves as a sleeping room for LAURA, the sofa unfolding to make her bed. Just beyond, separated from the living room by a wide arch or second proscenium with transparent faded portieres (or second curtain), is the dining room. In an old-fashioned whatnot in the living room are seen scores of transparent glass animals. A blown-up photograph of the father hangs on the wall of the living room, to the left of the archway. It is the face of a very handsome young man in a doughboy's First World War cap. He is gallantly smiling, ineluctably smiling, as if to say "I will be smiling forever."

Also hanging on the wall, near the photograph, are a typewriter keyboard chart and a Gregg shorthand diagram. An upright typewriter on a small table stands beneath the charts.

The audience hears and sees the opening scene in the dining room through both the transparent fourth wall of the building and the transparent gauze portieres of the dining-room arch. It is during this revealing scene that the fourth wall slowly ascends, out of sight. This transparent exterior wall is not brought down again until the very end of the play, during TOM's final speech.

The narrator is an undisguised convention of the play. He takes whatever license with dramatic convention is convenient to his purposes.

TOM *enters, dressed as a merchant sailor, and strolls across to the fire escape. There he stops and lights a cigarette. He addresses the audience.*

TOM: Yes, I have tricks in my pocket, I have things up my sleeve. But I am the opposite of a stage magician. He gives you illusion that has the appearance of truth. I give you truth in the pleasant disguise of illusion.

    To begin with, I turn back time. I reverse it to that 5
quaint period, the thirties, when the huge middle class of America was matriculating in a school for the blind. Their eyes had failed them, or they had failed their eyes, and so they were having their fingers pressed forcibly down on the fiery Braille alphabet of a dissolving economy. 10

    In Spain there was revolution. Here there was only shouting and confusion. In Spain there was Guernica. Here there were disturbances of labor, sometimes pretty violent, in otherwise peaceful cities such as Chicago, Cleveland, Saint Louis . . . This is the social background of the play. 15

(Music begins to play.)

    The play is memory. Being a memory play, it is dimly lighted, it is sentimental, it is not realistic. In memory everything seems to happen to music. That explains the fiddle in the wings.

    I am the narrator of the play, and also a character in it. 20
The other characters are my mother, Amanda, my sister, Laura, and a gentleman caller who appears in the final

scenes. He is the most realistic character in the play, being an
emissary from a world of reality that we were somehow set
25 apart from. But since I have a poet's weakness for symbols, I
am using this character also as a symbol; he is the long-
delayed but always expected something that we live for.

There is a fifth character in the play who doesn't appear except in this larger-than-life-size photograph over
30 the mantel. This is our father who left us a long time ago.
He was a telephone man who fell in love with long distances; he gave up his job with the telephone company
and skipped the light fantastic out of town . . .

The last we heard of him was a picture postcard from
35 Mazatlan, on the Pacific coast of Mexico, containing a
message of two words: "Hello—Goodbye!" and no address.

I think the rest of the play will explain itself. . . .

(AMANDA's voice becomes audible through the portieres.)

(Legend on screen: "Ou sont les neiges.")

(TOM divides the portieres and enters the dining room. AMANDA and
LAURA are seated at a drop-leaf table. Eating is indicated by gestures
without food or utensils. AMANDA faces the audience. TOM and
LAURA are seated in profile. The interior has lit up softly and
through the scrim we see AMANDA and LAURA seated at the table.)

AMANDA: (Calling.) Tom?
TOM: Yes, Mother.
40 AMANDA: We can't say grace until you come to the table!
TOM: Coming, Mother. (He bows slightly and withdraws, reappearing a few moments later in his place at the table.)
AMANDA: (To her son.) Honey, don't push with your fingers. If
you have to push with something, the thing to push with
45 is a crust of bread. And chew—chew! Animals have se-
cretions in their stomachs which enable them to digest
food without mastication, but human beings are supposed
to chew their food before they swallow it down. Eat food
leisurely, son, and really enjoy it. A well-cooked meal has
50 lots of delicate flavors that have to be held in the mouth
for appreciation. So chew your food and give your salivary
glands a chance to function!

(TOM deliberately lays his imaginary fork down and pushes his chair
back from the table.)

TOM: I haven't enjoyed one bite of this dinner because of your
constant directions on how to eat it. It's you that make me
55 rush through meals with your hawklike attention to every
bite I take. Sickening—spoils my appetite—all this discussion of—animals' secretion—salivary glands—mastication!
AMANDA: (Lightly.) Temperament like a Metropolitan star!

(TOM rises and walks toward the living room.)

You're not excused from the table.
60 TOM: I'm getting a cigarette.
AMANDA: You smoke too much.

(LAURA rises.)

LAURA: I'll bring in the blanc mange.

(TOM remains standing with his cigarette by the portieres.)

AMANDA: (Rising.) No, sister, no, sister—you be the lady this
time and I'll be the darky.
LAURA: I'm already up. 65
AMANDA: Resume your seat, little sister—I want you to stay
fresh and pretty—for gentlemen callers!
LAURA: (Sitting down.) I'm not expecting any gentlemen callers.
AMANDA: (Crossing out to the kitchenette, airily.) Sometimes
they come when they are least expected! Why, I remem- 70
ber one Sunday afternoon in Blue Mountain—

(She enters the kitchenette.)

TOM: I know what's coming!
LAURA: Yes. But let her tell it.
TOM: Again?
LAURA: She loves to tell it. 75

(AMANDA returns with a bowl of dessert.)

AMANDA: One Sunday afternoon in Blue Mountain—your
mother received—seventeen!—gentlemen callers! Why,
sometimes there weren't chairs enough to accommodate
them all. We had to send the nigger over to bring in folding chairs from the parish house. 80
TOM: (Remaining at the portieres.) How did you entertain those
gentlemen callers?
AMANDA: I understood the art of conversation!
TOM: I bet you could talk.
AMANDA: Girls in those days knew how to talk, I can tell you. 85
TOM: Yes?

(Image on screen: AMANDA as a girl on a porch, greeting callers.)

AMANDA: They knew how to entertain their gentlemen
callers. It wasn't enough for a girl to be possessed of a
pretty face and a graceful figure—although I wasn't
slighted in either respect. She also needed to have a nim- 90
ble wit and a tongue to meet all occasions.
TOM: What did you talk about?
AMANDA: Things of importance going on in the world!
Never anything coarse or common or vulgar.

(She addresses TOM as though he were seated in the vacant chair at
the table though he remains by the portieres. He plays this scene as
though reading from a script.)

My callers were gentlemen—all! Among my callers were 95
some of the most prominent young planters of the Mississippi Delta—planters and sons of planters!

(TOM motions for music and a spot of light on AMANDA. Her eyes
lift, her face glows, her voice becomes rich and elegiac.)

(Screen legend: "Ou sont les neiges d'antan?")

There was young Champ Laughlin who later became
vice-president of the Delta Planters Bank. Hadley Steven-
son who was drowned in Moon Lake and left his widow 100
one hundred and fifty thousand in Government bonds.
There were the Cutrere brothers, Wesley and Bates. Bates
was one of my bright particular beaux! He got in a quarrel with that wild Wainwright boy. They shot it out on the
floor of Moon Lake Casino. Bates was shot through the 105

stomach. Died in the ambulance on his way to Memphis.
His widow was also well provided-for, came into eight or
ten thousand acres, that's all. She married him on the
rebound—never loved her—carried my picture on him
110 the night he died! And there was that boy that every girl
in the Delta had set her cap for! That beautiful, brilliant
young Fitzhugh boy from Greene County!

TOM: What did he leave his widow?

AMANDA: He never married! Gracious, you talk as though all
115 of my old admirers had turned up their toes to the daisies!

TOM: Isn't this the first you've mentioned that still survives?

AMANDA: That Fitzhugh boy went North and made a
fortune—came to be known as the Wolf of Wall Street!
He had the Midas touch, whatever he touched turned to
120 gold! And I could have been Mrs. Duncan J. Fitzhugh,
mind you! But—I picked your *father!*

LAURA: (*Rising.*) Mother, let me clear the table.

AMANDA: No, dear, you go in front and study your typewriter
chart. Or practice your shorthand a little. Stay fresh and
125 pretty!—It's almost time for our gentlemen callers to start arriving. (*She flounces girlishly toward the kitchenette.*) How many
do you suppose we're going to entertain this afternoon?

(TOM *throws down the paper and jumps up with a groan.*)

LAURA: (*Alone in the dining room.*) I don't believe we're going
to receive any, Mother.

130 AMANDA: (*Reappearing, airily.*) What? No one—not one? You
must be joking!

(LAURA *nervously echoes her laugh. She slips in a fugitive manner
through the half-open portieres and draws them gently behind her. A
shaft of very clear light is thrown on her face against the faded tapestry of the curtains. Faintly the music of "The Glass Menagerie"
is heard as she continues, lightly.*)

Not one gentleman caller? It can't be true! There must be
a flood, there must have been a tornado!

LAURA: It isn't a flood, it's not a tornado, Mother. I'm just not
135 popular like you were in Blue Mountain. . . .

(TOM *utters another groan.* LAURA *glances at him with a faint,
apologetic smile. Her voice catches a little.*)

Mother's afraid I'm going to be an old maid.

(*The scene dims out with the "Glass Menagerie" music.*)

SCENE TWO

*On the dark stage the screen is lighted with the image of blue roses.
Gradually* LAURA's *figure becomes apparent and the screen goes out.
The music subsides.*

LAURA *is seated in the delicate ivory chair at the small claw-foot
table. She wears a dress of soft violet material for a kimono—her hair
is tied back from her forehead with a ribbon. She is washing and polishing her collection of glass.* AMANDA *appears on the fire escape
steps. At the sound of her ascent,* LAURA *catches her breath, thrusts
the bowl of ornaments away, and seats herself stiffly before the diagram of the typewriter keyboard as though it held her spellbound.
Something has happened to* AMANDA. *It is written in her face as she
climbs to the landing: a look that is grim and hopeless and a little*

*absurd. She has on one of those cheap or imitation velvety-looking
cloth coats with imitation fur collar. Her hat is five or six years old,
one of those dreadful cloche hats that were worn in the late Twenties,
and she is clutching an enormous black patent-leather pocketbook
with nickel clasps and initials. This is her full-dress outfit, the one
she usually wears to the D.A.R. Before entering she looks through
the door. She purses her lips, opens her eyes very wide, rolls them upward and shakes her head. Then she slowly lets herself in the door.
Seeing her mother's expression* LAURA *touches her lips with a nervous gesture.*

LAURA: Hello, Mother, I was—(*She makes a nervous gesture toward the chart on the wall.* AMANDA *leans against the shut door
and stares at* LAURA *with a martyred look.*)

AMANDA: Deception? Deception? (*She slowly removes her hat
and gloves, continuing the sweet suffering stare. She lets the hat 5
and gloves fall on the floor—a bit of acting.*)

LAURA: (*Shakily.*) How was the D.A.R. meeting?

(AMANDA *slowly opens her purse and removes a dainty white handkerchief which she shakes out delicately and delicately touches to her
lips and nostrils.*)

Didn't you go to the D.A.R. meeting, Mother?

AMANDA: (*Faintly, almost inaudibly.*) —No.—No. (*Then more
forcibly.*) I did not have the strength—to go to the D.A.R. 10
In fact, I did not have the courage! I wanted to find a hole
in the ground and hide myself in it forever! (*She crosses
slowly to the wall and removes the diagram of the typewriter keyboard. She holds it in front of her for a second, staring at it sweetly
and sorrowfully—then bites her lips and tears it into two pieces.*) 15

LAURA: (*Faintly.*) Why did you do that, Mother?

(AMANDA *repeats the same procedure with the chart of the Gregg
Alphabet.*)

Why are you—

AMANDA: Why? Why? How old are you, Laura?

LAURA: Mother, you know my age.

AMANDA: I thought that you were an adult; it seems that I was 20
mistaken. (*She crosses slowly to the sofa and sinks down and
stares at* LAURA.)

LAURA: Please don't stare at me, Mother.

(AMANDA *closes her eyes and lowers her head. There is a ten-second
pause.*)

AMANDA: What are we going to do, what is going to become
of us, what is the future?   25

(*There is another pause.*)

LAURA: Has something happened, Mother?

(AMANDA *draws a long breath, takes out the handkerchief again,
goes through the dabbing process.*)

Mother, has—something happened?

AMANDA: I'll be all right in a minute, I'm just bewildered—
(*She hesitates.*)—by life. . . .

LAURA: Mother, I wish that you would tell me what's happened! 30

AMANDA: As you know, I was supposed to be inducted into
my office at the D.A.R. this afternoon.

(*Screen image:* A swarm of typewriters.)

But I stopped off at Rubicam's Business College to speak
to your teachers about your having a cold and ask them
35   what progress they thought you were making down there.

LAURA: Oh . . . .

AMANDA: I went to the typing instructor and introduced myself as your mother. She didn't know who you were.
"Wingfield," she said, "We don't have any such student
40   enrolled at the school!"

I assured her she did, that you had been going to classes
since early in January.

"I wonder," she said, "If you could be talking about
that terribly shy little girl who dropped out of school af-
45   ter only a few days' attendance?"

"No," I said, "Laura, my daughter, has been going to
school every day for the past six weeks!"

"Excuse me," she said. She took the attendance book
out and there was your name, unmistakably printed, and
50   all the dates you were absent until they decided that you
had dropped out of school.

I still said, "No, there must have been some mistake!
There must have been some mix-up in the records!"

And she said, "No—I remember her perfectly now.
55   Her hands shook so that she couldn't hit the right keys!
The first time we gave a speed test, she broke down completely—was sick at the stomach and almost had to be
carried into the wash room! After that morning she never
showed up any more. We phoned the house but never got
60   any answer"—While I was working at Famous-Barr, I
suppose, demonstrating those—

(*She indicates a brassiere with her hands.*)

Oh! I felt so weak I could barely keep on my feet! I had to sit
down while they got me a glass of water! Fifty dollars' tu-
ition, all of our plans—my hopes and ambitions for you—
65   just gone up the spout, just gone up the spout like that.

(LAURA *draws a long breath and gets awkwardly to her feet. She
crosses to the Victrola and winds it up.*)

What are you doing?

LAURA: Oh! (*She releases the handle and returns to her seat.*)

AMANDA: Laura, where have you been going when you've gone
out pretending that you were going to business college?

70   LAURA: I've just been going out walking.

AMANDA: That's not true.

LAURA: It is. I just went walking.

AMANDA: Walking? Walking? In winter? Deliberately courting
pneumonia in that light coat? Where did you walk to, Laura?

75   LAURA: All sorts of places—mostly in the park.

AMANDA: Even after you'd started catching that cold?

LAURA: It was the lesser of two evils, Mother.

(*Screen image:* Winter scene in a park.)

I couldn't go back there. I—threw up—on the floor!

AMANDA: From half past seven till after five every day you
80   mean to tell me you walked around in the park, because
you wanted to make me think that you were still going to
Rubicam's Business College?

LAURA: It wasn't as bad as it sounds. I went inside places to
get warmed up.

AMANDA: Inside where?   85

LAURA: I went in the art museum and the bird houses at the
Zoo. I visited the penguins every day! Sometimes I did
without lunch and went to the movies. Lately I've been
spending most of my afternoons in the Jewel Box, that big
glass house where they raise the tropical flowers.   90

AMANDA: You did all this to deceive me, just for deception?
(LAURA *looks down.*) Why?

LAURA: Mother, when you're disappointed, you get that awful suffering look on your face, like the picture of Jesus'
mother in the museum!   95

AMANDA: Hush!

LAURA: I couldn't face it.

(*There is a pause. A whisper of strings is heard. Legend on screen:*
"The Crust of Humility.")

AMANDA: (*Hopelessly fingering the huge pocketbook.*) So what are
we going to do the rest of our lives? Stay home and watch
the parades go by? Amuse ourselves with the glass   100
menagerie, darling? Eternally play those worn-out phonograph records your father left as a painful reminder of him?
We won't have a business career—we've given that up because it gave us nervous indigestion! (*She laughs wearily.*)
What is there left but dependency all our lives? I know so   105
well what becomes of unmarried women who aren't prepared to occupy a position. I've seen such pitiful cases in
the South—barely tolerated spinsters living upon the
grudging patronage of sister's husband or brother's wife!—
stuck away in some little mousetrap of a room—encour-   110
aged by one in-law to visit another—little birdlike women
without any nest—eating the crust of humility all their life!

Is that the future that we've mapped out for ourselves?
I swear it's the only alternative I can think of! (*She pauses.*)
It isn't a very pleasant alternative, is it? (*She pauses again.*)   115
Of course—some girls *do marry.*

(LAURA *twists her hands nervously.*)

Haven't you ever liked some boy?

LAURA: Yes. I liked one once. (*She rises.*) I came across his picture a while ago.

AMANDA: (*With some interest.*) He gave you his picture?   120

LAURA: No, it's in the yearbook.

AMANDA: (*Disappointed.*) Oh—a high school boy.

(*Screen image:* JIM as the high school hero bearing a silver cup.)

LAURA: Yes. His name was Jim. (*She lifts the heavy annual from
the claw-foot table.*) Here he is in *The Pirates of Penzance.*

AMANDA: (*Absently.*) The what?   125

LAURA: The operetta the senior class put on. He had a wonderful voice and we sat across the aisle from each other
Mondays, Wednesdays and Fridays in the Aud. Here he is
with the silver cup for debating! See his grin?

AMANDA: (*Absently.*) He must have had a jolly disposition.   130

LAURA: He used to call me—Blue Roses.

(*Screen image:* Blue roses.)

AMANDA: Why did he call you such a name as that?

LAURA: When I had that attack of pleurosis—he asked me what was the matter when I came back. I said pleurosis—
135 he thought that I said Blue Roses! So that's what he always called me after that. Whenever he saw me, he'd holler, "Hello, Blue Roses!" I didn't care for the girl that he went out with. Emily Meisenbach. Emily was the best-dressed girl at Soldan. She never struck me, though, as being sin-
140 cere . . . It says in the Personal Section—they're engaged. That's—six years ago! They must be married by now.

AMANDA: Girls that aren't cut out for business careers usually wind up married to some nice man. (*She gets up with a spark of revival.*) Sister, that's what you'll do!

(LAURA *utters a startled, doubtful laugh. She reaches quickly for a piece of glass.*)

145 LAURA: But, Mother—

AMANDA: Yes? (*She goes over to the photograph.*)

LAURA: (*In a tone of frightened apology.*) I'm—crippled!

AMANDA: Nonsense! Laura, I've told you never, never to use that word. Why, you're not crippled, you just have a little
150 defect—hardly noticeable, even! When people have some slight disadvantage like that, they cultivate other things to make up for it—develop charm—and vivacity—and— *charm!* That's all you have to do! (*She turns again to the photograph.*) One thing your father had *plenty of*—was charm!

(*The scene fades out with music.*)

SCENE THREE

Legend on screen: "After the fiasco—"

TOM *speaks from the fire escape landing.*

TOM: After the fiasco at Rubicam's Business College, the idea of getting a gentleman caller for Laura began to play a more and more important part in Mother's calculations. It became an obsession. Like some archetype of the univer-
5 sal unconscious, the image of the gentleman caller haunted our small apartment. . . .

(*Screen image:* A young man at the door of a house with flowers.)

An evening at home rarely passed without some allu-sion to this image, this specter, this hope . . . Even when he wasn't mentioned, his presence hung in Mother's preoccu-
10 pied look and in my sister's frightened, apologetic man-ner—hung like a sentence passed upon the Wingfields!

Mother was a woman of action as well as words. She began to take logical steps in the planned direction. Late that winter and in the early spring—realizing that extra
15 money would be needed to properly feather the nest and plume the bird—she conducted a vigorous campaign on the telephone, roping in subscribers to one of those mag-azines for matrons called *The Homemaker's Companion,* the type of journal that features the serialized sublimations of
20 ladies of letters who think in terms of delicate cuplike breasts, slim, tapering waists, rich, creamy thighs, eyes like wood smoke in autumn, fingers that soothe and caress like strains of music, bodies as powerful as Etruscan sculpture.

(*Screen image:* The cover of a glamor magazine.)

(AMANDA *enters with the telephone on a long extension cord. She is spotlighted in the dim stage.*)

AMANDA: Ida Scott? This is Amanda Wingfield! We missed you at the D.A.R. last Monday! I said to myself: She's 25 probably suffering with that sinus condition! How is that sinus condition?

Horrors! Heaven have mercy!—You're a Christian martyr, yes, that's what you are, a Christian martyr!

Well, I just now happened to notice that your subscrip- 30 tion to the *Companion's* about to expire! Yes, it expires with the next issue, honey!—just when that wonderful new serial by Bessie Mae Hopper is getting off to such an exciting start. Oh, honey, it's something that you can't miss! You remember how *Gone with the Wind* took everybody by storm? You sim- 35 ply couldn't go out if you hadn't read it. All everybody *talked* was Scarlett O'Hara. Well, this is a book that critics already compare to *Gone with the Wind.* It's the *Gone with the Wind* of the post–World War generation!—What?—Burning?— Oh, honey, don't let them burn, go take a look in the oven 40 and I'll hold the wire! Heavens—I think she's hung up!

(*The scene dims out.*)

(*Legend on screen:* "You think I'm in love with Continental Shoemakers?"*)

(*Before the lights come up again, the violent voices of* TOM *and* AMANDA *are heard. They are quarreling behind the portieres. In front of them stands* LAURA *with clenched hands and panicky ex-pression. A clear pool of light is on her figure throughout this scene.*)

TOM: What in Christ's name am I—

AMANDA: (*Shrilly.*) Don't you use that—

TOM: —supposed to do!

AMANDA: —expression! Not in my— 45

TOM: Ohhh!

AMANDA: —presence! Have you gone out of your senses?

TOM: I have, that's true, *driven* out!

AMANDA: What is the matter with you, you—big—big— IDIOT! 50

TOM: Look!—I've got *no thing,* no single thing—

AMANDA: Lower your voice!

TOM: —in my life here that I can call my OWN! Everything is—

AMANDA: Stop that shouting!

TOM: Yesterday you confiscated my books! You had the nerve 55 to—

AMANDA: I took that horrible novel back to the library—yes! That hideous book by that insane Mr. Lawrence.

(TOM *laughs wildly.*)

I cannot control the output of diseased minds or people who cater to them— 60

(TOM *laughs still more wildly.*)

BUT I WON'T ALLOW SUCH FILTH BROUGHT INTO MY HOUSE! No, no, no, no, no!

TOM: House, house! Who pays rent on it, who makes a slave of himself to—

65 AMANDA: (*Fairly screeching.*) Don't you DARE to—
TOM: No, no, *I* mustn't say things! *I've* got to just—
AMANDA: Let me tell you—
TOM: I don't want to hear any more!

(*He tears the portieres open. The dining-room area is lit with a turgid smoky red glow. Now we see* AMANDA; *her hair is in metal curlers and she is wearing a very old bathrobe, much too large for her slight figure, a relic of the faithless Mr. Wingfield. The upright typewriter now stands on the drop-leaf table, along with a wild disarray of manuscripts. The quarrel was probably precipitated by* AMANDA's *interruption of* TOM's *creative labor. A chair lies overthrown on the floor. Their gesticulating shadows are cast on the ceiling by the fiery glow.*)

AMANDA: You *will* hear more, you—
70 TOM: No, I won't hear more, I'm going out!
AMANDA: You come right back in—
TOM: Out, out, out! Because I'm—
AMANDA: Come back here, Tom Wingfield! I'm not through talking to you!
75 TOM: Oh, go—
LAURA: (*Desperately.*)—Tom!
AMANDA: You're going to listen, and no more insolence from you! I'm at the end of my patience!

(*He comes back toward her.*)

TOM: What do you think I'm at? Aren't I supposed to have
80 any patience to reach the end of, Mother? I know, I know. It seems unimportant to you, what I'm *doing*—what I *want* to do—having a little *difference* between them! You don't think that—
AMANDA: I think you've been doing things that you're
85 ashamed of. That's why you act like this. I don't believe that you go every night to the movies. Nobody goes to the movies night after night. Nobody in their right minds goes to the movies as often as you pretend to. People don't go to the movies at nearly midnight, and movies don't let
90 out at two A.M. Come in stumbling. Muttering to yourself like a maniac! You get three hours' sleep and then go to work. Oh, I can picture the way you're doing down there. Moping, doping, because you're in no condition.
TOM: (*Wildly.*) No, I'm in no condition!
95 AMANDA: What right have you got to jeopardize your job? Jeopardize the security of us all? How do you think we'd manage if you were—
TOM: Listen! You think I'm crazy about the *warehouse?* (*He bends fiercely toward her slight figure.*) You think I'm in love
100 with the Continental Shoemakers? You think I want to spend fifty-five years down there in that—*celotex interior!* with—*fluorescent*—*tubes!* Look! I'd rather somebody picked up a crowbar and battered out my brains—than go back mornings! I *go!* Every time you come in yelling that
105 Goddamn *"Rise and Shine!" "Rise and Shine!"* I say to myself, "How *lucky dead* people are!" But I get up. I *go!* For sixty-five dollars a month I give up all that I dream of doing and being *ever!* And you say self—*self's* all I ever think of. Why, listen, if self is what I thought of, Mother, I'd be
110 where he is—GONE! (*He points to his father's picture.*) As far as the system of transportation reaches! (*He starts past her. She grabs his arm.*) Don't grab at me, Mother!
AMANDA: Where are you going?

TOM: I'm going to the *movies!*
AMANDA: I don't believe that lie! 115

(TOM *crouches toward her, overtowering her tiny figure. She backs away, gasping.*)

TOM: I'm going to opium dens! Yes, opium dens, dens of vice and criminals' hangouts, Mother. I've joined the Hogan Gang, I'm a hired assassin, I carry a tommy gun in a violin case! I run a string of cat houses in the Valley! They call me Killer, Killer Wingfield, I'm leading a double-life, a simple, 120 honest warehouse worker by day, by night a dynamic *czar* of the *underworld, Mother.* I go to gambling casinos, I spin away fortunes on the roulette table! I wear a patch over one eye and a false mustache, sometimes I put on green whiskers. On those occasions they call me—*El Diablo!* Oh, I could 125 tell you many things to make you sleepless! My enemies plan to dynamite this place. They're going to blow us all sky-high some night! I'll be glad, very happy, and so will you! You'll go up, up on a broomstick, over Blue Mountain with seventeen gentlemen callers! You ugly—babbling 130 old—witch . . . (*He goes through a series of violent, clumsy movements, seizing his overcoat, lunging to the door, pulling it fiercely open. The women watch him, aghast. His arm catches in the sleeve of the coat as he struggles to pull it on. For a moment he is pinioned by the bulky garment. With an outraged groan he tears the coat off* 135 *again, splitting the shoulder of it, and hurls it across the room. It strikes against the shelf of* LAURA's *glass collection, and there is a tinkle of shattering glass.* LAURA *cries out as if wounded.*)

(*Music.*)

(*Screen legend:* "The Glass Menagerie.")

LAURA: (*Shrilly.*) My glass!—menagerie . . . (*She covers her face and turns away.*) 140

(*But* AMANDA *is still stunned and stupefied by the "ugly witch" so that she barely notices this occurrence. Now she recovers her speech.*)

AMANDA: (*In an awful voice.*) I won't speak to you—until you apologize!

(*She crosses through the portieres and draws them together behind her.* TOM *is left with* LAURA. LAURA *clings weakly to the mantel with her face averted.* TOM *stares at her stupidly for a moment. Then he crosses to the shelf. He drops awkwardly on his knees to collect the fallen glass, glancing at* LAURA *as if he would speak but couldn't.*)

(*"The Glass Menagerie" music steals in as the scene dims out.*)

SCENE FOUR

The interior of the apartment is dark. There is a faint light in the alley. A deep-voiced bell in a church is tolling the hour of five.

TOM *appears at the top of the alley. After each solemn boom of the bell in the tower, he shakes a little noisemaker or rattle as if to express the tiny spasm of man in contrast to the sustained power and dignity of the Almighty. This and the unsteadiness of his advance make it evident that he has been drinking. As he climbs the few steps to the fire escape landing light steals up inside.* LAURA *appears in the front room in a nightdress. She notices that* TOM's *bed is empty.* TOM *fishes in his pockets for his door key, removing a motley assortment of articles in the search, including a shower of movie ticket stubs and an empty bottle. At last he finds the key, but just as he is about to insert it, it slips from his fingers. He strikes a match and crouches below the door.*

TOM: (*Bitterly.*) One crack—and it falls through!

(LAURA *opens the door.*)

LAURA: Tom! Tom, what are you doing?
TOM: Looking for a door key.
LAURA: Where have you been all this time?
5 TOM: I have been to the movies.
LAURA: All this time at the movies?
TOM: There was a very long program. There was a Garbo picture and a Mickey Mouse and a travelogue and a news-reel and a preview of coming attractions. And there was
10 an organ solo and a collection for the Milk Fund—simultaneously—which ended up in a terrible fight between a fat lady and an usher!
LAURA: (*Innocently.*) Did you have to stay through everything?
TOM: Of course! And, oh, I forgot! There was a big stage
15 show! The headliner on this stage show was Malvolio the Magician. He performed wonderful tricks, many of them, such as pouring water back and forth between pitchers. First it turned to wine and then it turned to beer and then it turned to whisky. I know it was whisky it finally turned
20 into because he needed somebody to come up out of the audience to help him, and I came up—both shows! It was Kentucky Straight Bourbon. A very generous fellow, he gave souvenirs. (*He pulls from his back pocket a shimmering rainbow-colored scarf.*) He gave me this. This is his magic
25 scarf. You can have it, Laura. You wave it over a canary cage and you get a bowl of goldfish. You wave it over the goldfish bowl and they fly away canaries . . . But the wonderfullest trick of all was the coffin trick. We nailed him into a coffin and he got out of the coffin without remov-
30 ing one nail. (*He has come inside.*) There is a trick that would come in handy for me—get me out of this two-by-four situation! (*He flops onto the bed and starts removing his shoes.*)
LAURA: Tom—shhh!
35 TOM: What're you shushing me for?
LAURA: You'll wake up Mother.
TOM: Goody, goody! Pay 'er back for all those "Rise an' Shines." (*He lies down, groaning.*) You know it don't take much intelligence to get yourself into a nailed-up coffin,
40 Laura. But who in hell ever got himself out of one without removing one nail?

(*As if in answer, the father's grinning photograph lights up. The scene dims out.*)

(*Immediately following, the church bell is heard striking six. At the sixth stroke the alarm clock goes off in* AMANDA'S *room, and after a few moments we hear her calling: "Rise and Shine! Rise and Shine!* LAURA, *go tell your brother to rise and shine!"*)

TOM: (*Sitting up slowly.*) I'll rise—but I won't shine.

(*The light increases.*)

AMANDA: Laura, tell your brother his coffee is ready.

(LAURA *slips into the front room.*)

LAURA: Tom!—It's nearly seven. Don't make Mother nervous.

(*He stares at her stupidly.*)

(*Beseechingly.*) Tom, speak to Mother this morning. Make 45
up with her, apologize, speak to her!
TOM: She won't to me. It's her that started not speaking.
LAURA: If you just say you're sorry she'll start speaking.
TOM: Her not speaking—is that such a tragedy?
LAURA: Please—please! 50
AMANDA: (*Calling from the kitchenette.*) Laura, are you going to do what I asked you to do, or do I have to get dressed and go out myself?
LAURA: Going, going—soon as I get on my coat!

(*She pulls on a shapeless felt hat with a nervous, jerky movement, pleadingly glancing at* TOM. *She rushes awkwardly for her coat. The coat is one of* AMANDA'S, *inaccurately made-over, the sleeves too short for* LAURA.)

Butter and what else? 55
AMANDA: (*Entering from the kitchenette.*) Just butter. Tell them to charge it.
LAURA: Mother, they make such faces when I do that.
AMANDA: Sticks and stones can break our bones, but the expression on Mr. Garfinkel's face won't harm us! Tell your 60
brother his coffee is getting cold.
LAURA: (*At the door.*) Do what I asked you, will you, will you, Tom?

(*He looks sullenly away.*)

AMANDA: Laura, go now or just don't go at all!
LAURA: (*Rushing out.*) Going—going! 65

(*A second later she cries out.* TOM *springs up and crosses to the door.* TOM *opens the door.*)

TOM: Laura?
LAURA: I'm all right. I slipped, but I'm all right.
AMANDA: (*Peering anxiously after her.*) If anyone breaks a leg on those fire-escape steps, the landlord ought to be sued for every cent he possesses! (*She shuts the door. Now she remem-* 70
bers she isn't speaking to TOM *and returns to the other room.*)

(*As* TOM *comes listlessly for his coffee, she turns her back to him and stands rigidly facing the window on the gloomy gray vault of the areaway. Its light on her face with its aged but childish features is cruelly sharp, satirical as a Daumier print.*)

(*The music of "Ave Maria" is heard softly.*)

(TOM *glances sheepishly but sullenly at her averted figure and slumps at the table. The coffee is scalding hot; he sips it and gasps and spits it back in the cup. At his gasp,* AMANDA *catches her breath and half turns. Then she catches herself and turns back to the window.* TOM *blows on his coffee, glancing sidewise at his mother. She clears her throat.* TOM *clears his. He starts to rise, sinks back down again, scratches his head, clears his throat again.* AMANDA *coughs.* TOM *raises his cup in both hands to blow on it, his eyes staring over the rim of it at his mother for several moments. Then he slowly sets the cup down and awkwardly and hesitantly rises from the chair.*)

TOM: (*Hoarsely.*) Mother. I—I apologize, Mother.

(AMANDA *draws a quick, shuddering breath. Her face works grotesquely. She breaks into childlike tears.*)

I'm sorry for what I said, for everything that I said, I didn't mean it.

75 AMANDA: (*Sobbingly.*) My devotion has made me a witch and so I make myself hateful to my children!

TOM: *No, you don't.*

AMANDA: I worry so much, don't sleep, it makes me nervous!

TOM: (*Gently.*) I understand that.

80 AMANDA: I've had to put up a solitary battle all these years. But you're my right-hand bower! Don't fall down, don't fail!

TOM: (*Gently.*) I try, Mother.

AMANDA: (*With great enthusiasm.*) Try and you will *succeed!* (*The notion makes her breathless.*) Why, you—you're just *full*

85 of natural endowments! Both of my children—they're *unusual* children! Don't you think I know it? I'm so—*proud!* Happy and—feel I've—so much to be thankful for but—promise me one thing, son!

TOM: What, Mother?

90 AMANDA: Promise, son, you'll—never be a drunkard!

TOM: (*Turns to her grinning.*) I will never be a drunkard, Mother.

AMANDA: That's what frightened me so, that you'd be drinking! Eat a bowl of Purina!

TOM: Just coffee, Mother.

95 AMANDA: Shredded wheat biscuit?

TOM: No. No, Mother, just coffee.

AMANDA: You can't put in a day's work on an empty stomach. You've got ten minutes—don't gulp! Drinking too-hot liquids makes cancer of the stomach . . . Put cream in.

100 TOM: No, thank you.

AMANDA: To cool it.

TOM: No! No, thank you, I want it black.

AMANDA: I know, but it's not good for you. We have to do all that we can to build ourselves up. In these trying times

105 we live in, all that we have to cling to is—each other . . . That's why it's so important to—Tom, I—sent out your sister so I could discuss something with you. If you hadn't spoken I would have spoken to you. (*She sits down.*)

TOM: (*Gently.*) What is it, Mother, that you want to discuss?

110 AMANDA: *Laura!*

(TOM *puts his cup down slowly.*)

(*Legend on screen:* "Laura." *Music:* "The Glass Menagerie.")

TOM: —Oh.—Laura . . .

AMANDA: (*Touching his sleeve.*) You know how Laura is. So quiet but—still water runs deep! She notices things and I think she—broods about them.

(TOM *looks up.*)

115   A few days ago I came in and she was crying.

TOM: What about?

AMANDA: You.

TOM: Me?

AMANDA: She has an idea that you're not happy here.

120 TOM: What gave her that idea?

AMANDA: What gives her any idea? However, you do act strangely. I—I'm not criticizing, understand *that!* I know

your ambitions do not lie in the warehouse, that like everybody in the whole wide world—you've had to— make sacrifices, but—Tom—Tom—life's not easy, it calls 125 for—Spartan endurance! There's so many things in my heart that I cannot describe to you! I've never told you but I—*loved* your father. . . .

TOM: (*Gently.*) I know that, Mother.

AMANDA: And you—when I see you taking after his ways! 130 Staying out late—and—well, you *had* been drinking the night you were in that—terrifying condition! Laura says that you hate the apartment and that you go out nights to get away from it! Is that true, Tom?

TOM: No. You say there's so much in your heart that you 135 can't describe to me. That's true of me, too. There's so much in my heart that I can't describe to *you!* So let's respect each other's—

AMANDA: But, why—*why*, Tom—are you always so *restless?* Where do you *go* to, nights? 140

TOM: I—go to the movies.

AMANDA: Why do you go to the movies so much, Tom?

TOM: I go to the movies because—I like adventure. Adventure is something I don't have much of at work, so I go to the movies. 145

AMANDA: But, Tom, you go to the movies *entirely* too *much!*

TOM: I like a lot of adventure.

(AMANDA *looks baffled, then hurt. As the familiar inquisition resumes,* TOM *becomes hard and impatient again.* AMANDA *slips back into her querulous attitude toward him.*)

(*Image on screen:* A sailing vessel with Jolly Roger.)

AMANDA: Most young men find adventure in their careers.

TOM: Then most young men are not employed in a warehouse.

AMANDA: The world is full of young men employed in ware- 150 houses and offices and factories.

TOM: Do all of them find adventure in their careers?

AMANDA: They do or they do without it! Not everybody has a craze for adventure.

TOM: Man is by instinct a lover, a hunter, a fighter, and none 155 of those instincts are given much play at the warehouse!

AMANDA: Man is by instinct! Don't quote instinct to me! Instinct is something that people have got away from! It belongs to animals! Christian adults don't want it!

TOM: What do Christian adults want, then, Mother? 160

AMANDA: Superior things! Things of the mind and the spirit! Only animals have to satisfy instincts! Surely your aims are somewhat higher than theirs! Than monkeys—pigs—

TOM: I reckon they're not.

AMANDA: You're joking. However, that isn't what I wanted to 165 discuss.

TOM: (*Rising.*) I haven't much time.

AMANDA: (*Pushing his shoulders.*) Sit down.

TOM: You want me to punch in red at the warehouse, Mother?

AMANDA: You have five minutes. I want to talk about Laura. 170

(*Screen legend:* "Plans and Provisions.")

TOM: All right! What about Laura?

AMANDA: We have to be making some plans and provisions for her. She's older than you, two years, and nothing has

175 happened. She just drifts along doing nothing. It frightens
me terribly how she just drifts along.

TOM: I guess she's the type that people call home girls.

AMANDA: There's no such type, and if there is, it's a pity! That
is unless the home is hers, with a husband!

TOM: What?

180 AMANDA: Oh, I can see the handwriting on the wall as plain as I
see the nose in front of my face! It's terrifying! More and
more you remind me of your father! He was out all hours
without explanation!—Then *left! Goodbye!* And me with
the bag to hold. I saw that letter you got from the Merchant

185 Marine. I know what you're dreaming of. I'm not standing
here blindfolded. (*She pauses.*) Very well, then. Then do it!
But not till there's somebody to take your place.

TOM: What do you mean?

AMANDA: I mean that as soon as Laura has got somebody to

190 take care of her, married, a home of her own, independent—why, then you'll be free to go wherever you please,
on land, on sea, whichever way the wind blows you! But
until that time you've got to look out for your sister. I
don't say me because I'm old and don't matter! I say for

195 your sister be-cause she's young and dependent.

I put her in business college—a dismal failure! Frightened her so it made her sick at the stomach. I took her over
to the Young People's League at the church. Another fiasco.
She spoke to nobody, nobody spoke to her. Now all she

200 does is fool with those pieces of glass and play those worn-
out records. What kind of a life is that for a girl to lead?

TOM: What can I do about it?

AMANDA: Overcome selfishness! Self, self, self is all that you
ever think of!

(TOM *springs up and crosses to get his coat. It is ugly and bulky. He
pulls on a cap with earmuffs.*)

205 Where is your muffler? Put your wool muffler on!

(*He snatches it angrily from the closet, tosses it around his neck and
pulls both ends tight.*)

Tom! I haven't said what I had in mind to ask you.

TOM: I'm too late to—

AMANDA: (*Catching his arm—very importunately; then shyly.*)
Down at the warehouse, aren't there some—nice young

210 men?

TOM: No!

AMANDA: There *must* be—some. . . .

TOM: Mother—(*He gestures.*)

AMANDA: Find out one that's clean-living—doesn't drink and

215 ask him out for sister!

TOM: What?

AMANDA: For *sister!* To *meet! Get acquainted!*

TOM: (*Stamping to the door.*) Oh, my go-osh!

AMANDA: Will you?

(*He opens the door. She says, imploringly:*)

220 Will you?

(*He starts down the fire escape.*)

Will you? *Will* you, dear?

TOM: (*Calling back.*) Yes!

(AMANDA *closes the door hesitantly and with a troubled but faintly
hopeful expression.*)

(*Screen image:* The cover of a glamor magazine.)

(*The spotlight picks up* AMANDA *at the phone.*)

AMANDA: Ella Cartwright? This is Amanda Wingfield!
How are you, honey?
How is that kidney condition?   225

(*There is a five-second pause.*)

Horrors!

(*There is another pause.*)

You're a Christian martyr, yes, honey, that's what you are, a
Christian martyr! Well, I just now happened to notice in my
little red book that your subscription to the *Companion* has
just run out! I knew that you wouldn't want to miss out on 230
the wonderful serial starting in this new issue. It's by Bessie
Mae Hopper, the first thing she's written since *Honeymoon
for Three.* Wasn't that a strange and interesting story? Well,
this one is even lovelier, I believe. It has a sophisticated, society background. It's all about the horsey set on Long Island! 235

(*The light fades out.*)

SCENE FIVE

Legend on the screen: "Annunciation."

Music is heard as the light slowly comes on.

*It is early dusk of a spring evening. Supper has just been finished in
the Wingfield apartment.* AMANDA *and* LAURA, *in light-colored
dresses, are removing dishes from the table in the dining room, which
is shadowy, their movements formalized almost as a dance or ritual,
their moving forms as pale and silent as moths.* TOM, *in white shirt
and trousers, rises from the table and crosses toward the fire escape.*

AMANDA: (*As he passes her.*) Son, will you do me a favor?

TOM: What?

AMANDA: Comb your hair! You look so pretty when your
hair is combed!

(TOM *slouches on the sofa with the evening paper. Its enormous
headline reads:* "Franco Triumphs.")

There is only one respect in which I would like you to   5
emulate your father.

TOM: What respect is that?

AMANDA: The care he always took of his appearance. He
never allowed himself to look untidy.

(*He throws down the paper and crosses to the fire escape.*)

Where are you going?   10

TOM: I'm going out to smoke.

AMANDA: You smoke too much. A pack a day at fifteen cents a
pack. How much would that amount to in a month? Thirty
times fifteen is how much, Tom? Figure it out and you will
be astounded at what you could save. Enough to give you a 15

night-school course in accounting at Washington U! Just think what a wonderful thing that would be for you, son!

(TOM *is unmoved by the thought.*)

TOM: I'd rather smoke. (*He steps out on the landing, letting the screen door slam.*)

20 AMANDA: (*Sharply.*) I know! That's the tragedy of it.... (*Alone, she turns to look at her husband's picture.*)

(*Dance music:* "The World Is Waiting for the Sunrise!")

TOM: (*To the audience.*) Across the alley from us was the Paradise Dance-hall. On evenings in spring the windows and doors were open and the music came outdoors. Sometimes the

25 lights were turned out except for a large glass sphere that hung from the ceiling. It would turn slowly about and filter the dusk with delicate rainbow colors. Then the orchestra played a waltz or a tango, something that had a slow and sensuous rhythm. Couples would come outside, to the rela-

30 tive privacy of the alley. You could see them kissing behind ash pits and telephone poles. This was the compensation for lives that passed like mine, without any change or adventure. Adventure and change were imminent in this year. They were waiting around the corner for all these kids. Sus-

35 pended in the mist over Berchtesgaden, caught in the folds of Chamberlain's umbrella. In Spain there was Guernica! But here there was only hot swing music and liquor, dance-halls, bars, and movies, and sex that hung in the gloom like a chandelier and flooded the world with brief, deceptive

40 rainbows.... All the world was waiting for bombardments!

(AMANDA *turns from the picture and comes outside.*)

AMANDA: (*Sighing.*) A fire escape landing's a poor excuse for a porch. (*She spreads a newspaper on a step and sits down, gracefully and demurely as if she were settling into a swing on a Mississippi veranda.*) What are you looking at?

45 TOM: The moon.
AMANDA: Is there a moon this evening?
TOM: It's rising over Garfinkel's Delicatessen.
AMANDA: So it is! A little silver slipper of a moon. Have you made a wish on it yet?

50 TOM: Um-hum.
AMANDA: What did you wish for?
TOM: That's a secret.
AMANDA: A secret, huh? Well, I won't tell mine either. I will be just as mysterious as you.

55 TOM: I bet I can guess what yours is.
AMANDA: Is my head so transparent?
TOM: You're not a sphinx.
AMANDA: No, I don't have secrets. I'll tell you what I wished for on the moon. Success and happiness for my precious

60 children! I wish for that whenever there's a moon, and when there isn't a moon, I wish for it, too.
TOM: I thought perhaps you wished for a gentleman caller.
AMANDA: Why do you say that?
TOM: Don't you remember asking me to fetch one?

65 AMANDA: I remember suggesting that it would be nice for your sister if you brought home some nice young man from the warehouse. I think that I've made that suggestion more than once.

TOM: Yes, you have made it repeatedly.
AMANDA: Well? 70
TOM: We are going to have one.
AMANDA: *What?*
TOM: A gentleman caller!

(*The annunciation is celebrated with music.*)

(AMANDA *rises.*)

(*Image on screen:* A caller with a bouquet.)

AMANDA: You mean you have asked some nice young man to come over? 75
TOM: Yep. I've asked him to dinner.
AMANDA: You really did?
TOM: I did!
AMANDA: You did, and did he—*accept?*
TOM: He did! 80
AMANDA: Well, well—well, well! That's—lovely!
TOM: I thought that you would be pleased.
AMANDA: It's definite then?
TOM: Very definite.
AMANDA: Soon? 85
TOM: Very soon.
AMANDA: For heaven's sake, stop putting on and tell me some things, will you?
TOM: What things do you want me to tell you?
AMANDA: *Naturally* I would like to know when he's coming! 90
TOM: He's coming tomorrow.
AMANDA: *Tomorrow?*
TOM: Yep. Tomorrow.
AMANDA: But, Tom!
TOM: Yes, Mother? 95
AMANDA: Tomorrow gives me no time!
TOM: Time for what?
AMANDA: Preparations! Why didn't you phone me at once, as soon as you asked him, the minute that he accepted? Then don't you see, I could have been getting ready! 100
TOM: You don't have to make any fuss.
AMANDA: Oh, Tom, Tom, Tom, of course I have to make a fuss! I want things nice, not sloppy! Not thrown together. I'll certainly have to do some fast thinking, won't I?
TOM: I don't see why you have to think at all. 105
AMANDA: You just don't know. We can't have a gentleman caller in a pigsty! All my wedding silver has to be polished, the monogrammed table linen ought to be laundered! The windows have to be washed and fresh curtains put up. And how about clothes? We have to *wear* something, don't we? 110
TOM: Mother, this boy is no one to make a fuss over!
AMANDA: Do you realize he's the first young man we've introduced to your sister? It's terrible, dreadful, disgraceful that poor little sister has never received a single gentleman caller! Tom, come inside! (*She opens the screen door.*) 115
TOM: What for?
AMANDA: I want to ask you some things.
TOM: If you're going to make such a fuss, I'll call it off, I'll tell him not to come!
AMANDA: You certainly won't do anything of the kind. Noth- 120
ing offends people worse than broken engagements. It simply means I'll have to work like a Turk! We won't be brilliant, but we will pass inspection. Come on inside.

(TOM *follows her inside, groaning.*)

Sit down.

125 TOM: Any particular place you would like me to sit?

AMANDA: Thank heavens I've got that new sofa! I'm also making payments on a floor lamp I'll have sent out! And put the chintz covers on, they'll brighten things up! Of course I'd hoped to have these walls re-papered. . . . What

130 is the young man's name?

TOM: His name is O'Connor.

AMANDA: That, of course, means fish—tomorrow is Friday! I'll have that salmon loaf—with Durkee's dressing! What does he do? He works at the warehouse?

135 TOM: Of course! How else would I—

AMANDA: Tom, he—doesn't drink?

TOM: Why do you ask me that?

AMANDA: Your father *did!*

TOM: Don't get started on that!

140 AMANDA: He *does* drink, then?

TOM: Not that I know of!

AMANDA: Make sure, be certain! The last thing I want for my daughter's a boy who drinks!

TOM: Aren't you being a little bit premature? Mr. O'Connor

145 has not yet appeared on the scene!

AMANDA: But will tomorrow. To meet your sister, and what do I know about his character? Nothing! Old maids are better off than wives of drunkards!

TOM: Oh, my God!

150 AMANDA: Be still!

TOM: (*Leaning forward to whisper.*) Lots of fellows meet girls whom they don't marry!

AMANDA: Oh, talk sensibly, Tom—and don't be sarcastic! (*She has gotten a hairbrush.*)

155 TOM: What are you doing?

AMANDA: I'm brushing that cowlick down! (*She attacks his hair with the brush.*) What is this young man's position at the warehouse?

TOM: (*Submitting grimly to the brush and the interrogation.*) This

160 young man's position is that of a shipping clerk, Mother.

AMANDA: Sounds to me like a fairly responsible job, the sort of a job *you* would be in if you just had more *get-up.* What is his salary? Have you any idea?

TOM: I would judge it to be approximately eighty-five dol-

165 lars a month.

AMANDA: Well—not princely, but—

TOM: Twenty more than I make.

AMANDA: Yes, how well I know! But for a family man, eighty-five dollars a month is not much more than you can just

170 get by on. . . .

TOM: Yes, but Mr. O'Connor is not a family man.

AMANDA: He might be, mightn't he? Some time in the future?

TOM: I see. Plans and provisions.

AMANDA: You are the only young man that I know of who

175 ignores the fact that the future becomes the present, the present the past, and the past turns into everlasting regret if you don't plan for it!

TOM: I will think that over and see what I can make of it.

AMANDA: Don't be supercilious with your mother! Tell me

180 some more about this—what do you call him?

TOM: James D. O'Connor. The D. is for Delaney.

AMANDA: Irish on *both* sides! *Gracious!* And doesn't drink?

TOM: Shall I call him up and ask him right this minute?

AMANDA: The only way to find out about those things is to make discreet inquiries at the proper moment. When I was 185 a girl in Blue Mountain and it was suspected that a young man drank, the girl whose attentions he had been receiving, if any girl *was,* would sometimes speak to the minister of his church, or rather her father would if her father was living, and sort of feel him out on the young man's charac- 190 ter. That is the way such things are discreetly handled to keep a young woman from making a tragic mistake!

TOM: Then how did you happen to make a tragic mistake?

AMANDA: That innocent look of your father's had everyone fooled! He *smiled*—the world was *enchanted!* No girl can do 195 worse than put herself at the mercy of a handsome appearance! I hope that Mr. O'Connor is not too good-looking.

TOM: No, he's not too good-looking. He's covered with freckles and hasn't too much of a nose.

AMANDA: He's not right-down homely, though? 200

TOM: Not right-down homely. Just medium homely, I'd say.

AMANDA: Character's what to look for in a man.

TOM: That's what I've always said, Mother.

AMANDA: You've never said anything of the kind and I suspect you would never give it a thought. 205

TOM: Don't be so suspicious of me.

AMANDA: At least I hope he's the type that's up and coming.

TOM: I think he really goes in for self-improvement.

AMANDA: What reason have you to think so?

TOM: He goes to night school. 210

AMANDA: (*Beaming.*) Splendid! What does he do, I mean study?

TOM: Radio engineering and public speaking!

AMANDA: Then he has visions of being advanced in the world! Any young man who studies public speaking is aiming to have an executive job some day! And radio en- 215 gineering? A thing for the future! Both of these facts are very illuminating. Those are the sort of things that a mother should know concerning any young man who comes to call on her daughter. Seriously or—not.

TOM: One little warning. He doesn't know about Laura. I 220 didn't let on that we had dark ulterior motives. I just said, why don't you come and have dinner with us? He said okay and that was the whole conversation.

AMANDA: I bet it was! You're eloquent as an oyster. However, he'll know about Laura when he gets here. When he sees 225 how lovely and sweet and pretty she is, he'll thank his lucky stars he was asked to dinner.

TOM: Mother, you mustn't expect too much of Laura.

AMANDA: What do you mean?

TOM: Laura seems all those things to you and me because 230 she's ours and we love her. We don't even notice she's crippled any more.

AMANDA: Don't say crippled! You know that I never allow that word to be used!

TOM: But face facts, Mother. She is and—that's not all— 235

AMANDA: What do you mean "not all"?

TOM: Laura is very different from other girls.

AMANDA: I think the difference is all to her advantage.

TOM: Not quite all—in the eyes of others—strangers—she's terribly shy and lives in a world of her own and those things 240 make her seem a little peculiar to people outside the house.

AMANDA: Don't say peculiar.

TOM: Face the facts. She is.

(*The dance-hall music changes to a tango that has a minor and somewhat ominous tone.*)

AMANDA: In what way is she peculiar—may I ask?

245 TOM: (*Gently.*) She lives in a world of her own—a world of little glass ornaments, Mother. . . .

(*He gets up.* AMANDA *remains holding the brush, looking at him, troubled.*)

She plays old phonograph records and—that's about all— (*He glances at himself in the mirror and crosses to the door.*)

AMANDA: (*Sharply.*) Where are you going?

250 TOM: I'm going to the movies. (*He goes out the screen door.*)

AMANDA: Not to the movies, every night to the movies! (*She follows quickly to the screen door.*) I don't believe you always go to the movies!

(*He is gone.* AMANDA *looks worriedly after him for a moment. Then vitality and optimism return and she turns from the door, crossing to the portieres.*)

Laura! Laura!

(LAURA *answers from the kitchenette.*)

255 LAURA: Yes, Mother.

AMANDA: Let those dishes go and come in front!

(LAURA *appears with a dish towel.* AMANDA *speaks to her gaily.*)

Laura, come here and make a wish on the moon!

(*Screen image:* The Moon.)

LAURA: (*Entering.*) Moon—moon?

AMANDA: A little silver slipper of a moon. Look over your left

260 shoulder, Laura, and make a wish!

(LAURA *looks faintly puzzled as if called out of sleep.* AMANDA *seizes her shoulders and turns her at an angle by the door.*)

Now! Now, darling, *wish!*

LAURA: What shall I wish for, Mother?

AMANDA: (*Her voice trembling and her eyes suddenly filling with tears.*) Happiness! Good fortune!

(*The sound of the violin rises and the stage dims out.*)

SCENE SIX

The light comes up on the fire escape landing. TOM *is leaning against the grill, smoking.*

Screen image: The high school hero.

TOM: And so the following evening I brought Jim home to dinner. I had known Jim slightly in high school. In high school Jim was a hero. He had tremendous Irish good nature and vitality with the scrubbed and polished look of

5   white chinaware. He seemed to move in a continual spotlight. He was a star in basketball, captain of the debating club, president of the senior class and the glee club and he sang the male lead in the annual light operas. He was al-

ways running or bounding, never just walking. He seemed always at the point of defeating the law of gravity. He was 10 shooting with such velocity through his adolescence that you would logically expect him to arrive at nothing short of the White House by the time he was thirty. But Jim apparently ran into more interference after his graduation from Soldan. His speed had definitely slowed. Six years af- 15 ter he left high school he was holding a job that wasn't much better than mine.

(*Screen image:* The Clerk.)

He was the only one at the warehouse with whom I was on friendly terms. I was valuable to him as someone who could remember his former glory, who had seen him win 20 basketball games and the silver cup in debating. He knew of my secret practice of retiring to a cabinet of the washroom to work on poems when business was slack in the warehouse. He called me Shakespeare. And while the other boys in the warehouse regarded me with suspicious hostil- 25 ity, Jim took a humorous attitude toward me. Gradually his attitude affected the others, their hostility wore off and they also began to smile at me as people smile at an oddly fashioned dog who trots across their path at some distance.

I knew that Jim and Laura had known each other at Sol- 30 dan, and I had heard Laura speak admiringly of his voice. I didn't know if Jim remembered her or not. In high school Laura had been as unobtrusive as Jim had been astonishing. If he did remember Laura, it was not as my sister, for when I asked him to dinner, he grinned and said, "You know, 35 Shakespeare, I never thought of you as having folks!"

He was about to discover that I did. . . .

(*Legend on screen:* "The accent of a coming foot.")

(*The light dims out on* TOM *and comes up in the Wingfield living room—a delicate lemony light. It is about five on a Friday evening of late spring which comes "scattering poems in the sky."*)

(AMANDA *has worked like a Turk in preparation for the gentleman caller. The results are astonishing. The new floor lamp with its rose silk shade is in place, a colored paper lantern conceals the broken light fixture in the ceiling, new billowing white curtains are at the windows, chintz covers are on the chairs and sofa, a pair of new sofa pillows make their initial appearance. Open boxes and tissue paper are scattered on the floor.*)

(LAURA *stands in the middle of the room with lifted arms while* AMANDA *crouches before her, adjusting the hem of a new dress, devout and ritualistic. The dress is colored and designed by memory. The arrangement of* LAURA's *hair is changed; it is softer and more becoming. A fragile, unearthly prettiness has come out in* LAURA: *she is like a piece of translucent glass touched by light, given a momentary radiance, not actual, not lasting.*)

AMANDA: (*Impatiently.*) Why are you trembling?

LAURA: Mother, you've made me so nervous!

AMANDA: How have I made you nervous? 40

LAURA: By all this fuss! You make it seem so important!

AMANDA: I don't understand you, Laura. You couldn't be satisfied with just sitting home, and yet whenever I try to arrange something for you, you seem to resist it. (*She gets*

45   *up.*) Now take a look at yourself. No, wait! Wait just a mo-
      ment—I have an idea!
      LAURA: What is it now?

(AMANDA *produces two powder puffs which she wraps in handkerchiefs and stuffs in* LAURA's *bosom.*)

      LAURA: Mother, what are you doing?
      AMANDA: They call them "Gay Deceivers"!
50   LAURA: I won't wear them!
      AMANDA: You will!
      LAURA: Why should I?
      AMANDA: Because, to be painfully honest, your chest is flat.
      LAURA: You make it seem like we were setting a trap.
55   AMANDA: All pretty girls are a trap, a pretty trap, and men ex-
      pect them to be.

(*Legend on screen:* "A pretty trap.")

      Now look at yourself, young lady. This is the prettiest you
      will ever be! (*She stands back to admire* LAURA.) I've got to
      fix myself now! You're going to be surprised by your
60   mother's appearance!

(AMANDA *crosses through the portieres, humming gaily.* LAURA
*moves slowly to the long mirror and stares solemnly at herself. A
wind blows the white curtains inward in a slow, graceful motion and
with a faint, sorrowful sighing.*)

      AMANDA: (*From somewhere behind the portieres.*) It isn't dark
      enough yet.

(LAURA *turns slowly before the mirror with a troubled look.*)

(*Legend on screen:* "This is my sister: Celebrate her with
strings!" *Music plays.*)

      AMANDA: (*Laughing, still not visible.*) I'm going to show you
      something. I'm going to make a spectacular appearance!
65   LAURA: What is it, Mother?
      AMANDA: Possess your soul in patience—you will see! Some-
      thing I've resurrected from that old trunk! Styles haven't
      changed so terribly much after all.... (*She parts the portieres.*)
      Now just look at your mother! (*She wears a girlish frock of
70   yellowed voile with a blue silk sash. She carries a bunch of jon-
      quils—the legend of her youth is nearly revived. Now she speaks
      feverishly.*) This is the dress in which I led the cotillion. Won
      the cakewalk twice at Sunset Hill, wore one Spring to the
      Governor's Ball in Jackson! See how I sashayed around the
75   ballroom, Laura? (*She raises her skirt and does a mincing step
      around the room.*) I wore it on Sundays for my gentlemen
      callers! I had it on the day I met your father. . . . I had
      malaria fever all that Spring. The change of climate from
      East Tennessee to the Delta—weakened resistance. I had a
80   little temperature all the time—not enough to be seri-
      ous—just enough to make me restless and giddy! Invita-
      tions poured in—parties all over the Delta! "Stay in bed,"
      said Mother, "you have a fever!"—but I just wouldn't. I
      took quinine but kept on going, going! Evenings, dances!
85   Afternoons, long, long rides! Picnics—lovely! So lovely,
      that country in May—all lacy with dogwood, literally
      flooded with jonquils! That was the spring I had the craze
      for jonquils. Jonquils became an absolute obsession.

Mother said, "Honey, there's no more room for jonquils."
And still I kept on bringing in more jonquils. Whenever,   90
wherever I saw them, I'd say "Stop! Stop! I see jonquils!" I
made the young men help me gather the jonquils! It was a
joke, Amanda and her jonquils. Finally there were no more
vases to hold them, every available space was filled with
jonquils. No vases to hold them? All right, I'll hold them   95
myself! And then I—(*She stops in front of the picture. Music
plays.*) met your father! Malaria fever and jonquils and
then—this—boy. . . . (*She switches on the rose-colored lamp.*) I
hope they get here before it starts to rain. (*She crosses the
room and places the jonquils in a bowl on the table.*) I gave your   100
brother a little extra change so he and Mr. O'Connor could
take the service car home.
      LAURA: (*With an altered look.*) What did you say his name was?
      AMANDA: O'Connor.
      LAURA: What is his first name?   105
      AMANDA: I don't remember. Oh, yes, I do. It was—Jim!

(LAURA *sways slightly and catches hold of a chair.*)

(*Legend on screen:* "Not Jim!")

      LAURA: (*Faintly.*) Not—Jim!
      AMANDA: Yes, that was it, it was Jim! I've never known a Jim
      that wasn't nice!

(*The music becomes ominous.*)

      LAURA: Are you sure his name is Jim O'Connor?   110
      AMANDA: Yes. Why?
      LAURA: Is he the one that Tom used to know in high school?
      AMANDA: He didn't say so. I think he just got to know him
      at the warehouse.
      LAURA: There was a Jim O'Connor we both knew in high   115
      school—(*Then, with effort.*) If that is the one that Tom is
      bringing to dinner—you'll have to excuse me, I won't
      come to the table.
      AMANDA: What sort of nonsense is this?
      LAURA: You asked me once if I'd ever liked a boy. Don't you   120
      remember I showed you this boy's picture?
      AMANDA: You mean the boy you showed me in the yearbook?
      LAURA: Yes, that boy.
      AMANDA: Laura, Laura, were you in love with that boy?
      LAURA: I don't know, Mother. All I know is I couldn't sit at   125
      the table if it was him!
      AMANDA: It won't be him! It isn't the least bit likely. But
      whether it is or not, you will come to the table. You will
      not be excused.
      LAURA: I'll have to be, Mother.   130
      AMANDA: I don't intend to humor your silliness, Laura. I've had
      too much from you and your brother, both! So just sit down
      and compose yourself till they come. Tom has forgotten his
      key so you'll have to let them in, when they arrive.
      LAURA: (*Panicky.*) Oh, Mother—*you* answer the door!   135
      AMANDA: (*Lightly.*) I'll be in the kitchen—busy!
      LAURA: Oh, Mother, please answer the door, don't make me
      do it!
      AMANDA: (*Crossing into the kitchenette.*) I've got to fix the dress-
      ing for the salmon. Fuss, fuss—silliness!—over a gentle-   140
      man caller!

(*The door swings shut.* LAURA *is left alone.*)

(*Legend on screen:* "Terror!")

(*She utters a low moan and turns off the lamp—sits stiffly on the edge of the sofa, knotting her fingers together.*)

(*Legend on screen:* "The Opening of a Door!")

(TOM *and* JIM *appear on the fire escape steps and climb to the landing. Hearing their approach, laura rises with a panicky gesture. She retreats to the portieres. The doorbell rings.* LAURA *catches her breath and touches her throat. Low drums sound.*)

AMANDA: (*Calling.*) Laura, sweetheart! The door!

(LAURA *stares at it without moving.*)

JIM: I think we just beat the rain.
TOM: Uh-huh. (*He rings again, nervously.* JIM *whistles and fishes for a cigarette.*)
145
AMANDA: (*Very, very gaily.*) Laura, that is your brother and Mr. O'Connor! Will you let them in, darling?

(LAURA *crosses toward the kitchenette door.*)

LAURA: (*Breathlessly.*) Mother—you go to the door!

(AMANDA *steps out of the kitchenette and stares furiously at* LAURA. *She points imperiously at the door.*)

LAURA: Please, please!
150 AMANDA: (*In a fierce whisper.*) What is the matter with you, you silly thing?
LAURA: (*Desperately.*) Please, you answer it, *please!*
AMANDA: I told you I wasn't going to humor you, Laura. Why have you chosen this moment to lose your mind?
155 LAURA: Please, please, please, you go!
AMANDA: You'll have to go to the door because I can't!
LAURA: (*Despairingly.*) I can't either!
AMANDA: *Why?*
LAURA: I'm *sick!*
160 AMANDA: I'm sick, too—of your nonsense! Why can't you and your brother be normal people? Fantastic whims and behavior!

(TOM *gives a long ring.*)

Preposterous goings on! Can you give me one reason—(*She calls out lyrically.*) Coming! Just one second!—why you
165 should be afraid to open a door? Now you answer it, Laura!
LAURA: Oh, oh, oh . . . (*She returns through the portieres, darts to the Victrola, winds it frantically and turns it on.*)
AMANDA: Laura Wingfield, you march right to that door!
LAURA: *Yes—yes, Mother!*

(*A faraway, scratchy rendition of "Dardanella" softens the air and gives her strength to move through it. She slips to the door and draws it cautiously open.* TOM *enters with the caller,* JIM O'CONNOR.)

170 TOM: Laura, this is Jim. Jim, this is my sister, Laura.
JIM: (*Stepping inside.*) I didn't know that Shakespeare had a sister!

LAURA: (*Retreating, stiff and trembling, from the door.*) How—how do you do?
JIM: (*Heartily, extending his hand.*) Okay!

(LAURA *touches it hesitantly with hers.*)

JIM: Your hand's *cold,* Laura!   175
LAURA: Yes, well—I've been playing the Victrola. . . .
JIM: Must have been playing classical music on it! You ought to play a little hot swing music to warm you up!
LAURA: Excuse me—I haven't finished playing the Victrola . . . (*She turns awkwardly and hurries into the front room. She* 180 *pauses a second by the Victrola. Then she catches her breath and darts through the portieres like a frightened deer.*)
JIM: (*Grinning.*) What was the matter?
TOM: Oh—with Laura? Laura is—terribly shy.
JIM: Shy, huh? It's unusual to meet a shy girl nowadays. I don't 185 believe you ever mentioned you had a sister.
TOM: Well, now you know. I have one. Here is the *Post Dispatch.* You want a piece of it?
JIM: Uh-huh.
TOM: What piece? The comics?   190
JIM: Sports! (*He glances at it.*) Ole Dizzy Dean is on his bad behavior.
TOM: (*Uninterested.*) Yeah? (*He lights a cigarette and goes over to the fire-escape door.*)
JIM: Where are *you* going?   195
TOM: I'm going out on the terrace.
JIM: (*Going after him.*) You know, Shakespeare—I'm going to sell you a bill of goods!
TOM: What goods?
JIM: A course I'm taking.   200
TOM: Huh?
JIM: In public speaking! You and me, we're not the warehouse type.
TOM: Thanks—that's good news. But what has public speaking got to do with it?   205
JIM: It fits you for—executive positions!
TOM: Awww.
JIM: I tell you it's done a helluva lot for me.

(*Image on screen:* Executive at his desk.)

TOM: In what respect?
JIM: In every! Ask yourself what is the difference between 210 you an' me and men in the office down front? Brains?—No!— Ability?—No! Then what? Just one little thing—
TOM: What is that one little thing?
JIM: Primarily it amounts to—social poise! Being able to square up to people and hold your own on any social level! 215
AMANDA: (*From the kitchenette.*) Tom?
TOM: Yes, Mother?
AMANDA: Is that you and Mr. O'Connor?
TOM: Yes, Mother.
AMANDA: Well, you just make yourselves comfortable in there. 220
TOM: Yes, Mother.
AMANDA: Ask Mr. O'Connor if he would like to wash his hands.
JIM: Aw, no—no—thank you—I took care of that at the warehouse. Tom—   225
TOM: Yes?
JIM: Mr. Mendoza was speaking to me about you.

TOM: Favorably?

JIM: What do you think?

230 TOM: Well—

JIM: You're going to be out of a job if you don't wake up.

TOM: I am waking up—

JIM: You show no signs.

TOM: The signs are interior.

(*Image on screen:* The sailing vessel with the Jolly Roger again.)

235 TOM: I'm planning to change. (*He leans over the fire-escape rail, speaking with quiet exhilaration. The incandescent marquees and signs of the first-run movie houses light his face from across the alley. He looks like a voyager.*) I'm right at the point of committing myself to a future that doesn't include the ware
240 house and Mr. Mendoza or even a night-school course in public speaking.

JIM: What are you gassing about?

TOM: I'm tired of the movies.

JIM: Movies!

245 TOM: Yes, movies! Look at them—(*A wave toward the marvels of Grand Avenue.*) All of those glamorous people—having adventures—hogging it all, gobbling the whole thing up! You know what happens? People go to the *movies* instead of *moving!* Hollywood characters are supposed to have all
250 the adventures for everybody in America, while everybody in America sits in a dark room and watches them have them! Yes, until there's a war. That's when adventure becomes available to the masses! *Everyone's* dish, not only Gable's! Then the people in the dark room come out of
255 the dark room to have some adventures themselves—goody, goody! It's our turn now, to go to the South Sea Island—to make a safari—to be exotic, far-off! But I'm not patient. I don't want to wait till then. I'm tired of the *movies* and I am *about* to move!

260 JIM: (*Incredulously.*) Move?

TOM: Yes.

JIM: When?

TOM: Soon!

JIM: Where? Where?

(*The music seems to answer the question, while* TOM *thinks it over. He searches in his pockets.*)

265 TOM: I'm starting to boil inside. I know I seem dreamy, but inside—well, I'm boiling! Whenever I pick up a shoe, I shudder a little thinking how short life is and what I am doing! Whatever that means, I know it doesn't mean shoes—except as something to wear on a traveler's feet!
270 (*He finds what he has been searching for in his pockets and holds out a paper to Jim.*) Look—

JIM: What?

TOM: I'm a member.

JIM: (*Reading.*) The Union of Merchant Seamen.

275 TOM: I paid my dues this month, instead of the light bill.

JIM: You will regret it when they turn the lights off.

TOM: I won't be here.

JIM: How about your mother?

TOM: I'm like my father. The bastard son of a bastard! Did
280 you notice how he's grinning in his picture in there? And he's been absent going on sixteen years!

JIM: You're just talking, you drip. How does your mother feel about it?

TOM: Shhh! Here comes Mother! Mother is not acquainted with my plans! 285

AMANDA: (*Coming through the portieres.*) Where are you all?

TOM: On the terrace, Mother.

(*They start inside. She advances to them.* TOM *is distinctly shocked at her appearance. Even* JIM *blinks a little. He is making his first contact with girlish Southern vivacity and in spite of the night-school course in public speaking is somewhat thrown off the beam by the unexpected outlay of social charm. Certain responses are attempted by* JIM *but are swept aside by* AMANDA'*s gay laughter and chatter.* TOM *is embarrassed but after the first shock* JIM *reacts very warmly. He grins and chuckles, is altogether won over.*)

(*Image on screen:* AMANDA *as a girl.*)

AMANDA: (*Coyly smiling, shaking her girlish ringlets.*) Well, well, well, so this is Mr. O'Connor. Introductions entirely unnecessary. I've heard so much about you from my boy. I fi 290
nally said to him, Tom—good gracious!—why don't you bring this paragon to supper? I'd like to meet this nice young man at the warehouse!—instead of just hearing him sing your praises so much! I don't know why my son is so stand-offish—that's not Southern behavior! 295
Let's sit down and—I think we could stand a little more air in here! Tom, leave the door open. I felt a nice fresh breeze a moment ago. Where has it gone to? Mmm, so warm already! And not quite summer, even. We're going to burn up when summer really gets started. However, 300
we're having—we're having a very light supper. I think light things are better fo' this time of year. The same as light clothes are. Light clothes an' light food are what warm weather calls fo'. You know our blood gets so thick during th' winter—it takes a while fo' us to *adjust* 305
ou'selves!—when the season changes . . . It's come so quick this year. I wasn't prepared. All of a sudden—heavens! Already summer! I ran to the trunk an' pulled out this light dress—terribly old! Historical almost! But feels so good—so good an' co-ol, y' know. . . . 310

TOM: Mother—

AMANDA: Yes, honey?

TOM: How about—supper?

AMANDA: Honey, you go ask Sister if supper is ready! You know that Sister is in full charge of supper! Tell her you hungry 315
boys are waiting for it. (*To* JIM.) Have you met Laura?

JIM: She—

AMANDA: Let you in? Oh, good, you've met already! It's rare for a girl as sweet an' pretty as Laura to be domestic! But Laura is, thank heavens, not only pretty but also very domestic. I'm 320
not at all. I never was a bit. I never could make a thing but angel-food cake. Well, in the South we had so many servants. Gone, gone, gone. All vestige of gracious living! Gone completely! I wasn't prepared for what the future brought me. All of my gentlemen callers were sons of 325
planters and so of course I assumed that I would be married to one and raise my family on a large piece of land with plenty of servants. But man proposes—and woman accepts the proposal! To vary that old, old saying a little bit—I married no planter! I married a man who worked for the 330

telephone company! That gallantly smiling gentleman over there! (*She points to the picture.*) A telephone man who—fell in love with long-distance! Now he travels and I don't even know where! But what am I going on for about my—tribu-
335 lations? Tell me yours—I hope you don't have any! Tom?
TOM: (*Returning.*) Yes, Mother?
AMANDA: Is supper nearly ready?
TOM: It looks to me like supper is on the table.
AMANDA: Let me look—(*She rises prettily and looks through the*
340 *portieres.*) Oh, lovely! But where is Sister?
TOM: Laura is not feeling well and she says that she thinks she'd better not come to the table.
AMANDA: What? Nonsense! Laura? Oh, Laura!
LAURA: (*From the kitchenette, faintly.*) Yes, Mother.
345 AMANDA: You really must come to the table. We won't be seated until you come to the table! Come in, Mr. O'Connor. You sit over there, and I'll . . . . Laura? Laura Wingfield! You're keeping us waiting, honey! We can't say grace until you come to the table!

(*The kitchenette door is pushed weakly open and LAURA comes in. She is obviously quite faint, her lips trembling, her eyes wide and staring. She moves unsteadily toward the table.*)

(*Screen legend: "Terror!"*)

(*Outside a summer storm is coming on abruptly. The white curtains billow inward at the windows and there is a sorrowful murmur from the deep blue dusk.*)

(*LAURA suddenly stumbles; she catches at a chair with a faint moan.*)

350 TOM: Laura!
AMANDA: Laura!

(*There is a clap of thunder.*)

(*Screen legend: "Ah!"*)

(*Despairingly.*) Why, Laura, you *are* ill, darling! Tom, help your sister into the living room, dear! Sit in the living room, Laura—rest on the sofa. Well! (*To JIM as TOM helps*
355 *his sister to the sofa in the living room.*) Standing over the hot stove made her ill! I told her that it was just too warm this evening, but—

(*TOM comes back to the table.*)

Is Laura all right now?
TOM: Yes.
360 AMANDA: What *is* that? Rain? A nice cool rain has come up! (*She gives JIM a frightened look.*) I think we may—have grace—now . . . (*TOM looks at her stupidly.*) Tom, honey—you say grace!
TOM: Oh . . . "For these and all thy mercies—"

(*They bow their heads, AMANDA stealing a nervous glance at JIM. In the living room LAURA, stretched on the sofa, clenches her hand to her lips, to hold back a shuddering sob.*)

365 God's Holy Name be praised—

(*The scene dims out.*)

SCENE SEVEN

It is half an hour later. Dinner is just being finished in the dining room, LAURA is still huddled upon the sofa, her feet drawn under her, her head resting on a pale blue pillow, her eyes wide and mysteriously watchful. The new floor lamp with its shade of rose-colored silk gives a soft, becoming light to her face, bringing out the fragile, unearthly prettiness which usually escapes attention. From outside there is a steady murmur of rain, but it is slackening and soon stops; the air outside becomes pale and luminous as the moon breaks through the clouds. A moment after the curtain rises, the lights in both rooms flicker and go out.

JIM: Hey, there, Mr. Light Bulb!

(*AMANDA laughs nervously.*)

(*Legend on screen: "Suspension of a public service."*)

AMANDA: Where was Moses when the lights went out? Ha-ha. Do you know the answer to that one, Mr. O'Connor?
JIM: No, Ma'am, what's the answer?
AMANDA: In the dark!   5

(*JIM laughs appreciatively.*)

Everybody sit still. I'll light the candles. Isn't it lucky we have them on the table? Where's a match? Which of you gentlemen can provide a match?
JIM: Here.
AMANDA: Thank you, Sir.   10
JIM: Not at all, Ma'am!
AMANDA: (*As she lights the candles.*) I guess the fuse has burnt out. Mr. O'Connor, can you tell a burnt-out fuse? I know I can't and Tom is a total loss when it comes to mechanics.

(*They rise from the table and go into the kitchenette, from where their voices are heard.*)

Oh, be careful you don't bump into something. We don't   15
want our gentleman caller to break his neck. Now wouldn't that be a fine howdy-do?
JIM: Ha-ha! Where is the fuse-box?
AMANDA: Right here next to the stove. Can you see anything?
JIM: Just a minute.   20
AMANDA: Isn't electricity a mysterious thing? Wasn't it Benjamin Franklin who tied a key to a kite? We live in such a mysterious universe, don't we? Some people say that science clears up all the mysteries for us. In my opinion it only creates more! Have you found it yet?   25
JIM: No, Ma'am. All these fuses look okay to me.
AMANDA: Tom!
TOM: Yes, Mother?
AMANDA: That light bill I gave you several days ago. The one I told you we got the notices about?   30

(*Legend on screen: "Ha!"*)

TOM: Oh—yeah.
AMANDA: You didn't neglect to pay it by any chance?
TOM: Why, I—
AMANDA: Didn't! I might have known it!
JIM: Shakespeare probably wrote a poem on that light bill,   35
Mrs. Wingfield.

AMANDA: I might have known better than to trust him with
   it! There's such a high price for negligence in this world!
JIM: Maybe the poem will win a ten-dollar prize.
40 AMANDA: We'll just have to spend the remainder of the
   evening in the nineteenth century, before Mr. Edison
   made the Mazda lamp!
JIM: Candlelight is my favorite kind of light.
AMANDA: That shows you're romantic! But that's no excuse
45   for Tom. Well, we got through dinner. Very considerate of
   them to let us get through dinner before they plunged us
   into everlasting darkness, wasn't it, Mr. O'Connor?
JIM: Ha-ha!
AMANDA: Tom, as a penalty for your carelessness you can help
50   me with the dishes.
JIM: Let me give you a hand.
AMANDA: Indeed you will not!
JIM: I ought to be good for something.
AMANDA: Good for something? (*Her tone is rhapsodic.*) You?
55   Why, Mr. O'Connor, nobody, *nobody's* given me this much
   entertainment in years—as you have!
JIM: Aw, now, Mrs. Wingfield!
AMANDA: I'm not exaggerating, not one bit! But Sister is all
   by her lonesome. You go keep her company in the par-
60   lor! I'll give you this lovely old candelabrum that used to
   be on the altar at the Church of the Heavenly Rest. It was
   melted a little out of shape when the church burnt down.
   Lightning struck it one spring. Gypsy Jones was holding a
   revival at the time and he intimated that the church was
65   destroyed because the Episcopalians gave card parties.
JIM: Ha-ha.
AMANDA: And how about you coaxing Sister to drink a little
   wine? I think it would be good for her! Can you carry
   both at once?
70 JIM: Sure. I'm Superman!
AMANDA: Now, Thomas, get into this apron!

(JIM *comes into the dining room, carrying the candelabrum, its candles lighted, in one hand and a glass of wine in the other. The door
of the kitchenette swings closed on* AMANDA's *gay laughter; the flickering light approaches the portieres.* LAURA *sits up nervously as* JIM
*enters. She can hardly speak from the almost intolerable strain of be-
ing alone with a stranger.*)

(*Screen legend:* "I don't suppose you remember me at all!")

(*At first, before* JIM's *warmth overcomes her paralyzing shyness,*
LAURA's *voice is thin and breathless, as though she had just run up
a steep flight of stairs.* JIM's *attitude is gently humorous. While the
incident is apparently unimportant, it is to* LAURA *the climax of her
secret life.*)

JIM: Hello there, Laura.
LAURA: (*Faintly.*) Hello.

(*She clears her throat.*)

JIM: How are you feeling now? Better?
75 LAURA: Yes. Yes, thank you.
JIM: This is for you. A little dandelion wine. (*He extends the
   glass toward her with extravagant gallantry.*)
LAURA: Thank you.
JIM: Drink it—but don't get drunk!

(*He laughs heartily.* LAURA *takes the glass uncertainly; she laughs
shyly.*)

Where shall I set the candles?   80
LAURA: Oh—oh, anywhere. . . .
JIM: How about here on the floor? Any objections?
LAURA: No.
JIM: I'll spread a newspaper under to catch the drippings. I
   like to sit on the floor. Mind if I do?   85
LAURA: Oh, no.
JIM: Give me a pillow?
LAURA: What?
JIM: A pillow!
LAURA: Oh . . . (*She hands him one quickly.*)   90
JIM: How about you? Don't you like to sit on the floor?
LAURA: Oh—yes.
JIM: Why don't you, then?
LAURA: I—will.
JIM: Take a pillow!   95
   (LAURA *does. She sits on the floor on the other side of the can-
   delabrum.* JIM *crosses his legs and smiles engagingly at her.*) I
   can't hardly see you sitting way over there.
LAURA: I can—see you.
JIM: I know, but that's not fair, I'm in the limelight.   100

(LAURA *moves her pillow closer.*)

Good! Now I can see you! Comfortable?
LAURA: Yes.
JIM: So am I. Comfortable as a cow! Will you have some gum?
LAURA: No, thank you.
JIM: I think that I will indulge, with your permission. (*He   105
   musingly unwraps a stick of gum and holds it up.*) Think of the
   fortune made by the guy that invented the first piece of
   chewing gum. Amazing, huh? The Wrigley Building is
   one of the sights of Chicago—I saw it when I went up to
   the Century of Progress. Did you take in the Century of 110
   Progress?
LAURA: No, I didn't.
JIM: Well, it was quite a wonderful exposition. What impressed
   me most was the Hall of Science. Gives you an idea of
   what the future will be in America, even more wonderful 115
   than the present time is! (*There is a pause.* JIM *smiles at her.*)
   Your brother tells me you're shy. Is that right, Laura?
LAURA: I—don't know.
JIM: I judge you to be an old-fashioned type of girl. Well, I
   think that's a pretty good type to be. Hope you don't   120
   think I'm being too personal—do you?
LAURA: (*Hastily, out of embarrassment.*) I believe I *will* take a
   piece of gum, if you—don't mind. (*Clearing her throat.*)
   Mr. O'Connor, have you—kept up with your singing?
JIM: Singing? Me?   125
LAURA: Yes. I remember what a beautiful voice you had.
JIM: When did you hear me sing?

(LAURA *does not answer, and in the long pause which follows a
man's voice is heard singing offstage.*)

VOICE: O blow, ye winds, heigh-ho,
                  A-roving I will go!
                  I'm off to my love   130
                     With a boxing glove—
                  Ten thousand miles away!

JIM: You say you've heard me sing?

LAURA: Oh, yes! Yes, very often . . . I—don't suppose—you
135   remember me—at all?

JIM: (*Smiling doubtfully.*) You know I have an idea I've seen
    you before. I had that idea soon as you opened the door.
    It seemed almost like I was about to remember your
    name. But the name that I started to call you—wasn't a
140   name! And so I stopped myself before I said it.

LAURA: Wasn't it—Blue Roses?

JIM: (*Springing up, grinning.*) Blue Roses! My gosh, yes—Blue
    Roses! That's what I had on my tongue when you opened
    the door! Isn't it funny what tricks your memory plays? I
145   didn't connect you with high school somehow or other.
    But that's where it was; it was high school. I didn't even
    know you were Shakespeare's sister! Gosh, I'm sorry.

LAURA: I didn't expect you to. You—barely knew me!

JIM: But we did have a speaking acquaintance, huh?

150 LAURA: Yes, we—spoke to each other.

JIM: When did you recognize me?

LAURA: Oh, right away!

JIM: Soon as I came in the door?

LAURA: When I heard your name I thought it was probably you.
155   I knew that Tom used to know you a little in high school. So
    when you came in the door—well, then I was—sure.

JIM: Why didn't you *say* something, then?

LAURA: (*Breathlessly.*) I didn't know what to say, I was—too
    surprised!

160 JIM: For goodness' sakes! You know, this sure is funny!

LAURA: Yes! Yes, isn't it, though. . . .

JIM: Didn't we have a class in something together?

LAURA: Yes, we did.

JIM: What class was that?

165 LAURA: It was—singing—chorus!

JIM: Aw!

LAURA: I sat across the aisle from you in the Aud.

JIM: Aw.

LAURA: Mondays, Wednesdays, and Fridays.

170 JIM: Now I remember—you always came in late.

LAURA: Yes, it was so hard for me, getting upstairs. I had that
    brace on my leg—it clumped so loud!

JIM: I never heard any clumping.

LAURA: (*Wincing at the recollection.*) To me it sounded like—
175   thunder!

JIM: Well, well, well, I never even noticed.

LAURA: And everybody was seated before I came in. I had to
    walk in front of all those people. My seat was in the back
    row. I had to go clumping all the way up the aisle with
180   everyone watching!

JIM: You shouldn't have been self-conscious.

LAURA: I know, but I was. It was always such a relief when
    the singing started.

JIM: Aw, yes, I've placed you now! I used to call you Blue
185   Roses. How was it that I got started calling you that?

LAURA: I was out of school a little while with pleurosis.
    When I came back you asked me what was the matter. I
    said I had pleurosis—you thought I said *Blue Roses.* That's
    what you always called me after that!

190 JIM: I hope you didn't mind.

LAURA: Oh, no—I liked it. You see, I wasn't acquainted with
    many—people. . . .

JIM: As I remember you sort of stuck by yourself.

LAURA: I—I—never have had much luck at—making friends.

JIM: I don't see why you wouldn't. 195

LAURA: Well, I—started out badly.

JIM: You mean being—

LAURA: Yes, it sort of—stood between me—

JIM: You shouldn't have let it!

LAURA: I know, but it did, and— 200

JIM: You were shy with people!

LAURA: I tried not to be but never could—

JIM: Overcome it?

LAURA: No, I—I never could!

JIM: I guess being shy is something you have to work out of 205
    kind of gradually.

LAURA: (*Sorrowfully.*) Yes—I guess it—

JIM: Takes time!

LAURA: Yes—

JIM: People are not so dreadful when you know them. That's 210
    what you have to remember! And everybody has prob-
    lems, not just you, but practically everybody has got some
    problems. You think of yourself as having the only prob-
    lems, as being the only one who is disappointed. But just
    look around you and you will see lots of people as disap- 215
    pointed as you are. For instance, I hoped when I was go-
    ing to high school that I would be further along at this
    time, six years later, than I am now. You remember that
    wonderful write-up I had in *The Torch?*

LAURA: Yes! (*She rises and crosses to the table.*) 220

JIM: It said I was bound to succeed in anything I went into!

(LAURA *returns with the high school yearbook.*)

Holy Jeez! *The Torch!*

(*He accepts it reverently. They smile across the book with mutual
wonder.* LAURA *crouches beside him and they begin to turn the pages.*
LAURA's *shyness is dissolving in his warmth.*)

LAURA: Here you are in *The Pirates of Penzance!*

JIM: (*Wistfully.*) I sang the baritone lead in that operetta.

LAURA: (*Raptly.*) So—beautifully! 225

JIM: (*Protesting.*) Aw—

LAURA: Yes, yes—beautifully—beautifully!

JIM: You heard me?

LAURA: All three times!

JIM: No! 230

LAURA: Yes!

JIM: All three performances?

LAURA: (*Looking down.*) Yes.

JIM: Why?

LAURA: I—wanted to ask you to—autograph my program. (*She* 235
    takes the program from the back of the yearbook and shows it to him.)

JIM: Why didn't you ask me to?

LAURA: You were always surrounded by your own friends so
    much that I never had a chance to.

JIM: You should have just— 240

LAURA: Well, I—thought you might think I was—

JIM: Thought I might think you was—what?

LAURA: Oh—

JIM: (*With reflective relish.*) I was beleaguered by females in
    those days. 245

LAURA: You were terribly popular!

JIM: Yeah—

LAURA: You had such a—friendly way—

JIM: I was spoiled in high school.

250 LAURA: Everybody—liked you!

JIM: Including you?

LAURA: I—yes, I—did, too—(*She gently closes the book in her lap.*)

JIM: Well, well, well! Give me that program, Laura.

(*She hands it to him. He signs it with a flourish.*)

There you are—better late than never!

255 LAURA: Oh, I—what a—surprise!

JIM: My signature isn't worth very much right now. But some day—maybe—it will increase in value! Being disappointed is one thing and being discouraged is something else. I am disappointed but I am not discouraged. I'm
260　twenty-three years old. How old are you?

LAURA: I'll be twenty-four in June.

JIM: That's not old age!

LAURA: No, but—

JIM: You finished high school?

265 LAURA: (*With difficulty.*) I didn't go back.

JIM: You mean you dropped out?

LAURA: I made bad grades in my final examinations. (*She rises and replaces the book and the program on the table. Her voice is strained.*) How is—Emily Meisenbach getting along?

270 JIM: Oh, that kraut-head!

LAURA: Why do you call her that?

JIM: That's what she was.

LAURA: You're not still—going with her?

JIM: I never see her.

275 LAURA: It said in the "Personal" section that you were—engaged!

JIM: I know, but I wasn't impressed by that—propaganda!

LAURA: It wasn't—the truth?

JIM: Only in Emily's optimistic opinion!

280 LAURA: Oh—

(*Legend:* "What have you done since high school?")

(JIM *lights a cigarette and leans indolently back on his elbows smiling at* LAURA *with a warmth and charm which lights her inwardly with altar candles. She remains by the table, picks up a piece from the glass menagerie collection, and turns it in her hands to cover her tumult.*)

JIM: (*After several reflective puffs on his cigarette.*) What have you done since high school?

(*She seems not to hear him.*)

Huh?

(LAURA *looks up.*)

I said what have you done since high school, Laura?

285 LAURA: Nothing much.

JIM: You must have been doing something these six long years.

LAURA: Yes.

JIM: Well, then, such as what?

LAURA: I took a business course at business college—

JIM: How did that work out?　　　　　　　　　　　　　　290

LAURA: Well, not very—well—I had to drop out, it gave me—indigestion—

(JIM *laughs gently.*)

JIM: What are you doing now?

LAURA: I don't do anything—much. Oh, please don't think I sit around doing nothing! My glass collection takes up a　295　good deal of time. Glass is something you have to take good care of.

JIM: What did you say—about glass?

LAURA: Collection I said—I have one—(*She clears her throat and turns away again, acutely shy.*)　　　　　　　　　300

JIM: (*Abruptly.*) You know what I judge to be the trouble with you? Inferiority complex! Know what that is? That's what they call it when someone low-rates himself! I understand it because I had it, too. Although my case was not so aggravated as yours seems to be. I had it until I took up pub-　305　lic speaking, developed my voice, and learned that I had an aptitude for science. Before that time I never thought of myself as being outstanding in any way whatsoever! Now I've never made a regular study of it, but I have a friend who says I can analyze people better than doctors that　310　make a profession of it. I don't claim that to be necessarily true, but I can sure guess a person's psychology, Laura! (*He takes out his gum.*) Excuse me, Laura. I always take it out when the flavor is gone. I'll use this scrap of paper to wrap it in. I know how it is to get it stuck on a shoe. (*He wraps*　315　*the gum in paper and puts it in his pocket.*) Yep—that's what I judge to be your principal trouble. A lack of confidence in yourself as a person. You don't have the proper amount of faith in yourself. I'm basing that fact on a number of your remarks and also on certain observations I've made. For in-　320　stance that clumping you thought was so awful in high school. You say that you even dreaded to walk into class. You see what you did? You dropped out of school, you gave up an education because of a clump, which as far as I know was practically non-existent! A little physical defect is what　325　you have. Hardly noticeable even! Magnified thousands of times by imagination! You know what my strong advice to you is? Think of yourself as *superior* in some way!

LAURA: In what way would I think?

JIM: Why, man alive, Laura! Just look about you a little. What　330　do you see? A world full of common people! All of 'em born and all of 'em going to die! Which of them has one-tenth of your good points! Or mine! Or anyone else's, as far as that goes—gosh! Everybody excels in some one thing. Some in many! (*He unconsciously glances at himself in*　335　*the mirror.*) All you've got to do is discover in *what!* Take me, for instance. (*He adjusts his tie at the mirror.*) My interest happens to lie in electro-dynamics. I'm taking a course in radio engineering at night school, Laura, on top of a fairly responsible job at the warehouse. I'm taking that　340　course and studying public speaking.

LAURA: Ohhhh.

JIM: Because I believe in the future of television! (*Turning his back to her.*) I wish to be ready to go up right along with it. Therefore I'm planning to get in on the ground floor.　345　In fact I've already made the right connections and all that remains is for the industry itself to get under way! Full steam—(*His eyes are starry.*) Knowledge—Zzzzzp! Money—Zzzzzp!—*Power!* That's the cycle democracy is built on!

(*His attitude is convincingly dynamic.* LAURA *stares at him, even her shyness eclipsed in her absolute wonder. He suddenly grins.*)

350 I guess you think I think a lot of myself!
LAURA: No—o-o-o, I—
JIM: Now how about you? Isn't there something you take more interest in than anything else?
LAURA: Well, I do—as I said—have my—glass collection—

(*A peal of girlish laughter rings from the kitchenette.*)

355 JIM: I'm not right sure I know what you're talking about. What kind of glass is it?
LAURA: Little articles of it, they're ornaments mostly! Most of them are little animals made out of glass, the tiniest little animals in the world. Mother calls them a glass menagerie!
360 Here's an example of one, if you'd like to see it! This one is one of the oldest. It's nearly thirteen.

(*Music:* "The Glass Menagerie.")

(*He stretches out his hand.*)

Oh, be careful—if you breathe, it breaks!
JIM: I'd better not take it. I'm pretty clumsy with things.
LAURA: Go on, I trust you with him! (*She places the piece in his*
365 *palm.*) There now—you're holding him gently! Hold him over the light, he loves the light! You see how the light shines through him?
JIM: It sure does shine!
LAURA: I shouldn't be partial, but he is my favorite one.
370 JIM: What kind of a thing is this one supposed to be?
LAURA: Haven't you noticed the single horn on his forehead?
JIM: A unicorn, huh?
LAURA: Mmmm-hmmm!
JIM: Unicorns—aren't they extinct in the modern world?
375 LAURA: I know!
JIM: Poor little fellow, he must feel sort of lonesome.
LAURA: (*Smiling.*) Well, if he does, he doesn't complain about it. He stays on a shelf with some horses that don't have horns and all of them seem to get along nicely together.
380 JIM: How do you know?
LAURA: (*Lightly.*) I haven't heard any arguments among them!
JIM: (*Grinning.*) No arguments, huh? Well, that's a pretty good sign! Where shall I set him?
LAURA: Put him on the table. They all like a change of
385 scenery once in a while!
JIM: Well, well, well, well—(*He places the glass piece on the table, then raises his arms and stretches.*) Look how big my shadow is when I stretch!
LAURA: Oh, oh, yes—it stretches across the ceiling!
390 JIM: (*Crossing to the door.*) I think it's stopped raining. (*He opens the fire-escape door and the background music changes to a dance tune.*) Where does the music come from?
LAURA: From the Paradise Dance-hall across the alley.
JIM: How about cutting the rug a little, Miss Wingfield?
395 LAURA: Oh, I—

JIM: Or is your program filled up? Let me have a look at it. (*He grasps an imaginary card.*) Why, every dance is taken! I'll just have to scratch some out.

(*Waltz music:* "La Golondrina.")

Ahhh, a waltz! (*He executes some sweeping turns by himself, then holds his arms toward* LAURA.)   400
LAURA: (*Breathlessly.*) I—can't dance!
JIM: There you go, that inferiority stuff!
LAURA: I've never danced in my life!
JIM: Come on, try!
LAURA: Oh, but I'd step on you!   405
JIM: I'm not made out of glass.
LAURA: How—how—how do we start?
JIM: Just leave it to me. You hold your arms out a little.
LAURA: Like this?
JIM: (*Taking her in his arms.*) A little bit higher. Right. Now 410
don't tighten up, that's the main thing about it—relax.
LAURA: (*Laughing breathlessly.*) It's hard not to.
JIM: Okay.
LAURA: I'm afraid you can't budge me.
JIM: What do you bet I can't? (*He swings her into motion.*)   415
LAURA: Goodness, yes, you can!
JIM: Let yourself go, now, Laura, just let yourself go.
LAURA: I'm—
JIM: Come on!
LAURA: —trying!   420
JIM: Not so stiff—easy does it!
LAURA: I know but I'm—
JIM: Loosen th' backbone! There now, that's a lot better.
LAURA: Am I?
JIM: Lots, lots better! (*He moves her about the room in a clumsy 425
waltz.*)
LAURA: Oh, my!
JIM: Ha-ha!
LAURA: Oh, my goodness!
JIM: Ha-ha-ha!   430

(*They suddenly bump into the table, and the glass piece on it falls to the floor.* JIM *stops the dance.*)

What did we hit on?
LAURA: Table.
JIM: Did something fall off it? I think—
LAURA: Yes.
JIM: I hope that it wasn't the little glass horse with the horn! 435
LAURA: Yes. (*She stoops to pick it up.*)
JIM: Aw, aw, aw. Is it broken?
LAURA: Now it is just like all the other horses.
JIM: It's lost its—
LAURA: Horn! It doesn't matter. Maybe it's a blessing in dis- 440
guise.
JIM: You'll never forgive me. I bet that that was your favorite piece of glass.
LAURA: I don't have favorites much. It's no tragedy, Freckles. Glass breaks so easily. No matter how careful you are. The 445
traffic jars the shelves and things fall off them.
JIM: Still I'm awfully sorry that I was the cause.
LAURA: (*Smiling.*) I'll just imagine he had an operation. The horn was removed to make him feel less—freakish!

(*They both laugh.*)

450   Now he will feel more at home with the other horses, the ones that don't have horns. . . .

JIM: Ha-ha, that's very funny! (*Suddenly he is serious.*) I'm glad to see that you have a sense of humor. You know—
455   you're—well—very different! Surprisingly different from anyone else I know! (*His voice becomes soft and hesitant with a genuine feeling.*) Do you mind me telling you that?

(LAURA *is abashed beyond speech.*)

I mean it in a nice way—

(LAURA *nods shyly, looking away.*)

You make me feel sort of—I don't know how to put it! I'm usually pretty good at expressing things, but—this is
460   something that I don't know how to say!

(LAURA *touches her throat and clears it—turns the broken unicorn in her hands. His voice becomes softer.*)

Has anyone ever told you that you were pretty?

(*There is a pause, and the music rises slightly.* LAURA *looks up slowly, with wonder, and shakes her head.*)

Well, you are! In a very different way from anyone else. And all the nicer because of the difference, too.

(*His voice becomes low and husky.* LAURA *turns away, nearly faint with the novelty of her emotions.*)

I wish that you were my sister. I'd teach you to have some
465   confidence in yourself. The different people are not like other people, but being different is nothing to be ashamed of. Because other people are not such wonderful people. They're one hundred times one thousand. You're one times one! They walk all over the earth. You just stay here.
470   They're common as—weeds, but—you—well, you're—*Blue Roses!*

(*Image on screen:* Blue Roses.)

(*The music changes.*)

LAURA: But blue is wrong for—roses. . . .

JIM: It's right for you! You're—pretty!

LAURA: In what respect am I pretty?

475   JIM: In all respects—believe me! Your eyes—your hair—are pretty! Your hands are pretty! (*He catches hold of her hand.*) You think I'm making this up because I'm invited to dinner and have to be nice. Oh, I could do that! I could put on an act for you, Laura, and say lots of things without be-
480   ing very sincere. But this time I am. I'm talking to you sincerely. I happened to notice you had this inferiority complex that keeps you from feeling comfortable with people. Somebody needs to build your confidence up and make you proud instead of shy and turning away and—
485   blushing. Somebody—ought to—*kiss* you, Laura!

(*His hand slips slowly up her arm to her shoulder as the music swells tumultuously. He suddenly turns her about and kisses her on the lips. When he releases her,* LAURA *sinks on the sofa with a bright, dazed look.* JIM *backs away and fishes in his pocket for a cigarette.*)

(*Legend on screen:* "A souvenir.")

Stumblejohn!

(*He lights the cigarette, avoiding her look. There is a peal of girlish laughter from* AMANDA *in the kitchenette.* LAURA *slowly raises and opens her hand. It still contains the little broken glass animal. She looks at it with a tender, bewildered expression.*)

Stumblejohn! I shouldn't have done that—that was way off the beam. You don't smoke, do you?

(*She looks up, smiling, not hearing the question. He sits beside her rather gingerly. She looks at him speechlessly—waiting. He coughs decorously and moves a little farther aside as he considers the situation and senses her feelings, dimly, with perturbation. He speaks gently.*)

Would you—care for a—mint?

(*She doesn't seem to hear him but her look grows brighter even.*)

Peppermint? Life Saver? My pocket's a regular drug-   490
store—wherever I go . . . (*He pops a mint in his mouth. Then he gulps and decides to make a clean breast of it. He speaks slowly and gingerly.*) Laura, you know, if I had a sister like you, I'd do the same thing as Tom. I'd bring out fellows and—introduce her to them. The right type of boys—of   495
a type to—appreciate her. Only—well—he made a mistake about me. Maybe I've got no call to be saying this. That may not have been the idea in having me over. But what if it was? There's nothing wrong about that. The only trouble is that in my case—I'm not in a situation   500
to—do the right thing. I can't take down your number and say I'll phone. I can't call up next week and—ask for a date. I thought I had better explain the situation in case you—misunderstood it and—I hurt your feelings. . . .

(*There is a pause. Slowly, very slowly,* LAURA*'s look changes, her eyes returning slowly from his to the glass figure in her palm.* AMANDA *utters another gay laugh in the kitchenette.*)

LAURA: (*Faintly.*) You—won't—call again?   505

JIM: No, Laura, I can't. (*He rises from the sofa.*) As I was just explaining, I've—got strings on me. Laura, I've—been going steady! I go out all the time with a girl named Betty. She's a home-girl like you, and Catholic, and Irish, and in a great many ways we—get along fine. I met her last sum-   510
mer on a moonlight boat trip up the river to Alton, on the *Majestic.* Well—right away from the start it was—love!

(*Legend:* "Love!")

(LAURA *sways slightly forward and grips the arm of the sofa. He fails to notice, now enrapt in his own comfortable being.*)

Being in love has made a new man of me!

(*Leaning stiffly forward, clutching the arm of the sofa,* LAURA *struggles visibly with her storm. But* JIM *is oblivious; she is a long way off.*)

The power of love is really pretty tremendous! Love is something that—changes the whole world, Laura!   515

(*The storm abates a little and* LAURA *leans back. He notices her again.*)

It happened that Betty's aunt took sick, she got a wire and had to go to Centralia. So Tom—when he asked me to dinner—I naturally just accepted the invitation, not knowing that you—that he—that I—(*He stops awkwardly.*)
520   Huh—I'm a stumblejohn!

(*He flops back on the sofa. The holy candles on the altar of* LAURA's *face have been snuffed out. There is a look of almost infinite desolation.* JIM *glances at her uneasily.*)

I wish that you would—say something.

(*She bites her lip which was trembling and then bravely smiles. She opens her hand again on the broken glass figure. Then she gently takes his hand and raises it level with her own. She carefully places the unicorn in the palm of his hand, then pushes his fingers closed upon it.*)

What are you—doing that for? You want me to have him? Laura?

(*She nods.*)

What for?
525   LAURA: A—souvenir. . . .

(*She rises unsteadily and crouches beside the Victrola to wind it up.*)

(*Legend on screen:* "Things have a way of turning out so badly!" *Or image:* Gentleman caller waving goodbye—gaily.)

(*At this moment* AMANDA *rushes brightly back into the living room. She bears a pitcher of fruit punch in an old-fashioned cut-glass pitcher, and a plate of macaroons. The plate has a gold border and poppies painted on it.*)

AMANDA: Well, well, well! Isn't the air delightful after the shower? I've made you children a little liquid refreshment. (*She turns gaily to* JIM.) Jim, do you know that song about lemonade?
530   "Lemonade, lemonade
              Made in the shade and stirred with a spade—
              Good enough for any old maid!"
JIM: (*Uneasily.*) Ha-ha! No—I never heard it.
AMANDA: Why, Laura! You look so serious!
535   JIM: We were having a serious conversation.
AMANDA: Good! Now you're better acquainted!
JIM: (*Uncertainly.*) Ha-ha! Yes.
AMANDA: You modern young people are much more seriousminded than my generation. I was so gay as a girl!
540   JIM: You haven't changed, Mrs. Wingfield.
AMANDA: Tonight I'm rejuvenated! The gaiety of the occasion, Mr. O'Connor! (*She tosses her head with a peal of laughter, spilling some lemonade.*) Oooo! I'm baptizing myself!
JIM: Here—let me—
545   AMANDA: (*Setting the pitcher down.*) There now. I discovered we had some maraschino cherries. I dumped them in, juice and all!
JIM: You shouldn't have gone to that trouble, Mrs. Wingfield.
AMANDA: Trouble, trouble? Why, it was loads of fun! Didn't
550   you hear me cutting up in the kitchen? I bet your ears were burning! I told Tom how outdone with him I was

for keeping you to himself so long a time! He should have brought you over much, much sooner! Well, now that you've found your way, I want you to be a very frequent caller! Not just occasional but all the time. Oh, we're go-   555
ing to have a lot of gay times together! I see them coming! Mmm, just breathe that air! So fresh, and the moon's so pretty! I'll skip back out—I know where my place is when young folks are having a—serious conversation!
JIM: Oh, don't go out, Mrs. Wingfield. The fact of the mat-   560
ter is I've got to be going.
AMANDA: Going, now? You're joking! Why, it's only the shank of the evening, Mr. O'Connor!
JIM: Well, you know how it is.
AMANDA: You mean you're a young workingman and have to   565
keep workingmen's hours. We'll let you off early tonight. But only on the condition that next time you stay later. What's the best night for you? Isn't Saturday night the best night for you workingmen?
JIM: I have a couple of time-clocks to punch, Mrs. Wingfield.   570
One at morning, another one at night!
AMANDA: My, but you are ambitious! You work at night, too?
JIM: No, Ma'am, not work but—Betty!

(*He crosses deliberately to pick up his hat. The band at the Paradise Dance-hall goes into a tender waltz.*)

AMANDA: Betty? Betty? Who's—Betty!

(*There is an ominous cracking sound in the sky.*)

JIM: Oh, just a girl. The girl I go steady with!   575

(*He smiles charmingly. The sky falls.*)

(*Legend:* "The Sky Falls.")

AMANDA: (*A long-drawn exhalation.*) Ohhhh . . . Is it a serious romance, Mr. O'Connor?
JIM: We're going to be married the second Sunday in June.
AMANDA: Ohhhh—how nice! Tom didn't mention that you were engaged to be married.   580
JIM: The cat's not out of the bag at the warehouse yet. You know how they are. They call you Romeo and stuff like that. (*He stops at the oval mirror to put on his hat. He carefully shapes the brim and the crown to give a discreetly dashing effect.*) It's been a wonderful evening, Mrs. Wingfield. I guess this   585
is what they mean by Southern hospitality.
AMANDA: It really wasn't anything at all.
JIM: I hope it don't seem like I'm rushing off. But I promised Betty I'd pick her up at the Wabash depot, an' by the time I get my jalopy down there her train'll be in. Some   590
women are pretty upset if you keep 'em waiting.
AMANDA: Yes, I know—the tyranny of women! (*She extends her hand.*) Goodbye, Mr. O'Connor. I wish you luck—and happiness—and success! All three of them, and so does Laura! Don't you, Laura?   595
LAURA: Yes!
JIM: (*Taking* LAURA's *hand.*) Goodbye, Laura. I'm certainly going to treasure that souvenir. And don't you forget the good advice I gave you. (*He raises his voice to a cheery shout.*) So long, Shakespeare! Thanks again, ladies. Good night!   600

(He grins and ducks jauntily out. Still bravely grimacing, AMANDA *closes the door on the gentleman caller. Then she turns back to the room with a puzzled expression. She and* LAURA *don't dare to face each other.* LAURA *crouches beside the Victrola to wind it.)*

AMANDA: *(Faintly.)* Things have a way of turning out so badly. I don't believe that I would play the Victrola. Well, well—well! Our gentleman caller was engaged to be married! *(She raises her voice.)* Tom!

605   TOM: *(From the kitchenette.)* Yes, Mother?

AMANDA: Come in here a minute. I want to tell you something awfully funny.

TOM: *(Entering with a macaroon and a glass of the lemonade.)* Has the gentleman caller gotten away already?

610   AMANDA: The gentleman caller has made an early departure. What a wonderful joke you played on us!

TOM: How do you mean?

AMANDA: You didn't mention that he was engaged to be married.

615   TOM: Jim? Engaged?

AMANDA: That's what he just informed us.

TOM: I'll be jiggered! I didn't know about that.

AMANDA: That seems very peculiar.

TOM: What's peculiar about it?

620   AMANDA: Didn't you call him your best friend down at the warehouse?

TOM: He is, but how did I know?

AMANDA: It seems extremely peculiar that you wouldn't know your best friend was going to be married!

625   TOM: The warehouse is where I work, not where I know things about people!

AMANDA: You don't know things anywhere! You live in a dream; you manufacture illusions!

(He crosses to the door.)

Where are you going?

630   TOM: I'm going to the movies.

AMANDA: That's right, now that you've had us make such fools of ourselves. The effort, the preparations, all the expense! The new floor lamp, the rug, the clothes for Laura! All for what? To entertain some other girl's fiancé! Go to

635   the movies, go! Don't think about us, a mother deserted, an unmarried sister who's crippled and has no job! Don't let anything interfere with your selfish pleasure! Just go, go, go—to the movies!

TOM: All right, I will! The more you shout about my selfish-

640   ness to me the quicker I'll go, and I won't go to the movies!

AMANDA: Go, then! Go to the moon—you selfish dreamer!

*(*TOM *smashes his glass on the floor. He plunges out on the fire escape, slamming the door.* LAURA *screams in fright. The dance-hall music becomes louder.* TOM *stands on the fire escape, gripping the rail. The moon breaks through the storm clouds, illuminating his face.)*

(Legend on screen: "And so goodbye . . .")

*(*TOM*'s closing speech is timed with what is happening inside the house. We see, as though through soundproof glass, that* AMANDA *appears to be making a comforting speech to* LAURA, *who is huddled upon the sofa. Now that we cannot hear the mother's speech, her silliness is gone and she has dignity and tragic beauty.* LAURA*'s hair hides her face until, at the end of the speech, she lifts her head to smile at her mother.* AMANDA*'s gestures are slow and graceful, almost dancelike, as she comforts her daughter. At the end of her speech she glances a moment at the father's picture—then withdraws through the portieres. At the close of* TOM*'s speech,* LAURA *blows out the candles, ending the play.)*

TOM: I didn't go to the moon, I went much further—for time is the longest distance between two places. Not long after that I was fired for writing a poem on the lid of a shoe-box. I left Saint Louis. I descended the steps of this fire escape   645 for a last time and followed, from then on, in my father's footsteps, attempting to find in motion what was lost in space. I traveled around a great deal. The cities swept about me like dead leaves, leaves that were brightly colored but torn away from the branches. I would have stopped, but I   650 was pursued by something. It always came upon me unawares, taking me altogether by surprise. Perhaps it was a familiar bit of music. Perhaps it was only a piece of transparent glass. Perhaps I am walking along a street at night, in some strange city, before I have found companions. I pass   655 the lighted window of a shop where perfume is sold. The window is filled with pieces of colored glass, tiny transparent bottles in delicate colors, like bits of a shattered rainbow. Then all at once my sister touches my shoulder. I turn around and look into her eyes. Oh, Laura, Laura, I tried to   660 leave you behind me, but I am more faithful than I intended to be! I reach for a cigarette, I cross the street, I run into the movies or a bar, I buy a drink, I speak to the nearest stranger—anything that can blow your candles out!

*(*LAURA *bends over the candles.)*

For nowadays the world is lit by lightning! Blow out your   665 candles, Laura—and so goodbye. . . .

(She blows the candles out.)

Arthur Miller

Arthur Miller (b. 1915) was born in Harlem and raised in Brooklyn. The son of Jewish immigrants, Miller often takes the milieu of urban New York as the substance of his drama. Like Tennessee Williams, Miller was formed by the Depression. He worked a variety of jobs to help his family make ends meet, and eventually gained provisional admission to the University of Michigan, where he studied playwriting and graduated in 1938. He worked briefly for the Federal Theater Project. Although his first play—*The Man Who Had All the Luck* (1944)—failed, Miller went on to write a series of gritty and powerful plays: *All My Sons* (1947), *Death of a Salesman* (1949), an adaptation of Ibsen's *An Enemy of the People* (1950), and *The Crucible* (1953). In 1955, Miller wrote *A View from the Bridge,* a story of honor and betrayal among New York's Italian immigrants. He also married Marilyn Monroe in that year, and his next play, *After the Fall* (1964), is a lightly disguised account of their stormy marriage and its break-up. In 1964 he also produced *Incident at Vichy,* a play concerning the Nazi persecution of the Jews during World War II, and he returned to the subject in his 1981 screenplay, *Playing for Time.* Miller continues to write and have his plays produced worldwide—including *The Price* (1968), *The Creation of the World and Other Business* (1972—revised as *Up from Paradise* 1974), *The Archbishop's Calling* (1977), *The American Clock* (1980), *Danger: Memory* (1987), *The Ride Down Mount Morgan* (1991), *The Last Yankee* (1993); and *Resurrection Blues* (2002). He has also published a memoir (*Timebends*), a series of collected essays, and an account of the production of *Salesman* in the People's Republic of China during the 1980s. He writes and lectures frequently about his career and about American theater.

DEATH OF A SALESMAN

Something like *Oedipus the King* for the classical theater, or *Hamlet* for the English Renaissance stage, *Death of a Salesman* has become an icon of the American theater: Miller's central characters—Willy Loman, the worn-out, dreaming salesman; his two sons, Biff, the All-American star, who can never quite fit into American society, and Happy, the unhappy younger brother—have entered into the popular lexicon of cultural stereotypes, landmarks for later playwrights. (Think of Troy Maxson in August Wilson's *Fences,* or Lee and Austin in Sam Shepard's *True West,* or even Lincoln and Booth in Suzan-Lori Parks's *Topdog/ Underdog.*) And, again like *Hamlet,* the play provides a dominant central role that has tested generations of actors from Lee J. Cobb, who created Willy Loman onstage, to Dustin Hoffman and Brian Dennehy.

As in classical tragedy (see Miller's essay, "Tragedy and the Common Man," later in this unit), the action of *Death of a Salesman* is impelled by a single, climactic event: Willy is approaching the end of his career, his glad-handing sales contacts are all dead or retired, and he's no longer pulling in business for the company—he's about to be fired. While this is perhaps less sensational than the crimes that prompt Oedipus or Hamlet to tragic action, Miller uses the fluidity of his stage and his remarkable ear for the prosaic poetry of everyday speech to give this event an extraordinary resonance. Blending scenes from Willy's past (the affecting scenes of Willy as a young father; the Woman in Boston and Biff's discovery of Willy's hypocrisy) with the Loman family's present straits, *Death of a Salesman* claims Willy as a representative figure, embodying the contradictions of the American dream. As Linda puts it, "Willy Loman never made alot of money. His name was never in the paper. He's not the finest character that ever lived. But he's a human being, and a terrible thing is happening to him. So attention must be paid." Miller deftly focuses a conflict between the material circumstances of Willy's life, his hard work, his exploitation by the company that finally sends him "to his grave like an old dog," and Willy's nonetheless eager belief in the system, in the salesman's ethic that has sustained and destroyed him. *Death of a Salesman* stages a double perspective on deadly mythology of America: Willy at once believes, and teaches his two sons to believe, that to be "well liked" is more important, more critical than ability or achievement; at the same time, he turns aside from the life represented by his uncle Ben, remaining with his good job and steady income instead of pursuing the intangible fortunes of Alaska like his pioneering father. Although the play stages many of the turning points in Willy's life, the opportunities missed to take a new direction, the central "cause" of the play's action took place years earlier, when Willy met an aging salesman and decided to pursue his career rather than light out for the frontier. What most impressed Willy about *that* salesman was his funeral: he died the "death of a salesman, in his green velvet slippers in the smoker of the New York, New Haven and Hartford, going into Boston—when he died, hundreds of salesmen and buyers were at his funeral." Part of Miller's genius in *Death of a Salesman* lies in the reach he gives to this figure and in the central conflict between the city and the frontier still embodied by the career of the salesman, represented in the play as a kind of Kit Carson or Daniel Boone, a rootless wanderer domesticated and destroyed by his willing acceptance of the demands of business and the society it sustains. As Charlie puts it in the "Requiem" ending the play: "Willy was a salesman. And for a salesman, there is no rock bottom to the life. He don't put a bolt to a nut, he don't tell you the law or give you medicine. He's a man way out there in the blue, riding on a smile and a shoeshine. . . . A salesman is got to dream, boy. It comes with the territory."

Jo Mielziner's celebrated set for the premiere production of Arthur Miller's *Death of a Salesman*, showing the cutaway house and the downstage playing area.

DEATH OF A SALESMAN

Arthur Miller

CHARACTERS

WILLY LOMAN
LINDA
BIFF
HAPPY
BERNARD
THE WOMAN
CHARLEY
UNCLE BEN
HOWARD WAGNER

JENNY
STANLEY
MISS FORSYTHE
LETTA

The action takes place in Willy Loman's house and yard and in various places he visits in the New York and Boston of today.

Throughout the play, in the stage directions, left and right mean stage left and stage right.

ACT ONE

A melody is heard, played upon a flute. It is small and fine, telling of grass and trees and the horizon. The curtain rises.

Before us is the Salesman's house. We are aware of towering, angular shapes behind it, surrounding it on all sides. Only the blue light of the sky falls upon the house and forestage; the surrounding area shows an angry glow of orange. As more light appears, we see a solid vault of apartment houses around the small, fragile-seeming home. An air of the dream clings to the place, a dream rising out of reality. The kitchen at center seems actual enough, for there is a kitchen table with three chairs, and a refrigerator. But no other fixtures are seen. At the back of the kitchen there is a draped entrance, which leads to the living-room. To the right of the kitchen, on a level raised two feet, is a bedroom furnished only with a brass bedstead and a straight chair. On a shelf over the bed a silver athletic trophy stands. A window opens onto the apartment house at the side.

Behind the kitchen, on a level raised six and a half feet, is the boys' bedroom, at present barely visible. Two beds are dimly seen, and at the back of the room a dormer window. (This bedroom is above the unseen living-room.) At the left a stairway curves up to it from the kitchen.

The entire setting is wholly, or, in some places, partially transparent. The roof-line of the house is one-dimensional; under and over it we see the apartment buildings. Before the house lies an apron, curving beyond the forestage into the orchestra. This forward area serves as the back yard as well as the locale of all Willy's imaginings and of his city scenes. Whenever the action is in the present the actors observe the imaginary wall-lines, entering the house only through its door at the left. But in the scenes of the past these boundaries are broken, and characters enter or leave a room by stepping "through" a wall onto the forestage.

From the right, Willy Loman, the Salesman, enters, carrying two large sample cases. The flute plays on. He hears but is not aware of it. He is past sixty years of age, dressed quietly. Even as he crosses the stage to the doorway of the house, his exhaustion is apparent. He unlocks the door, comes into the kitchen, and thankfully lets his burden down, feeling the soreness of his palms. A word-sigh escapes his lips—it might be "Oh, boy, oh, boy." He closes the door, then carries his cases out into the living-room, through the draped kitchen doorway.

Linda, his wife, has stirred in her bed at the right. She gets out and puts on a robe, listening. Most often jovial, she has developed an iron repression of her exceptions to Willy's behavior—she more than loves him, she admires him, as though his mercurial nature, his temper, his massive dreams and little cruelties, served her only as sharp reminders of the turbulent longings within him, longings which she shares but lacks the temperament to utter and follow to their end.

LINDA: (*Hearing* WILLY *outside the bedroom, calls with some trepidation.*) Willy!
WILLY: It's all right. I came back.
LINDA: Why? What happened? (*Slight pause.*) Did something happen, Willy?   5
WILLY: No, nothing happened.
LINDA: You didn't smash the car, did you?
WILLY: (*With casual irritation.*) I said nothing happened. Didn't you hear me?
LINDA: Don't you feel well?   10
WILLY: I'm tired to the death. (*The flute has faded away. He sits on the bed beside her, a little numb.*) I couldn't make it. I just couldn't make it, Linda.
LINDA: (*Very carefully, delicately.*) Where were you all day? You look terrible.   15
WILLY: I got as far as a little above Yonkers. I stopped for a cup of coffee. Maybe it was the coffee.
LINDA: What?
WILLY: (*After a pause.*) I suddenly couldn't drive any more. The car kept going off onto the shoulder, y'know?'   20
LINDA: (*Helpfully.*) Oh. Maybe it was the steering again. I don't think Angelo knows the Studebaker.
WILLY: No, it's me, it's me. Suddenly I realize I'm goin' sixty miles an hour and I don't remember the last five minutes. I'm—I can't seem to—keep my mind to it.   25
LINDA: Maybe it's your glasses. You never went for your new glasses.
WILLY: No, I see everything. I came back ten miles an hour. It took me nearly four hours from Yonkers.
LINDA: (*Resigned.*) Well, you'll just have to take a rest, Willy, 30 you can't continue this way.
WILLY: I just got back from Florida.
LINDA: But you didn't rest your mind. Your mind is overactive, and the mind is what counts, dear.

35 WILLY: I'll start out in the morning. Maybe I'll feel better in the morning. (*She is taking off his shoes.*) These goddam arch supports are killing me.

LINDA: Take an aspirin. Should I get you an aspirin? It'll soothe you.

40 WILLY: (*With wonder.*) I was driving along, you understand? And I was fine. I was even observing the scenery. You can imagine, me looking at scenery, on the road every week of my life. But it's so beautiful up there, Linda, the trees are so thick, and the sun is warm. I opened the windshield

45 and just let the warm air bathe over me. And then all of a sudden I'm goin' off the road! I'm tellin' ya, I absolutely forgot I was driving. If I'd've gone the other way over the white line I might've killed somebody. So I went on again—and five minutes later I'm dreamin' again, and I

50 nearly— (*He presses two fingers against his eyes.*) I have such thoughts, I have such strange thoughts.

LINDA: Willy, dear. Talk to them again. There's no reason why you can't work in New York.

WILLY: They don't need me in New York. I'm the New En-

55 gland man. I'm vital in New England.

LINDA: But you're sixty years old. They can't expect you to keep traveling every week.

WILLY: I'll have to send a wire to Portland. I'm supposed to see Brown and Morrison tomorrow morning at ten

60 o'clock to show the line. Goddammit, I could sell them! (*He starts putting on his jacket.*)

LINDA: (*Taking the jacket from him.*) Why don't you go down to the place tomorrow and tell Howard you've simply got to work in New York? You're too accommodating,

65 dear.

WILLY: If old man Wagner was alive I'd a been in charge of New York now! That man was a prince, he was a masterful man. But that boy of his, that Howard, he don't appreciate. When I went north the first time, the Wagner

70 Company didn't know where New England was!

LINDA: Why don't you tell those things to Howard, dear?

WILLY: (*Encouraged.*) I will, I definitely will. Is there any cheese?

LINDA: I'll make you a sandwich.

75 WILLY: No, go to sleep. I'll take some milk. I'll be up right away. The boys in?

LINDA: They're sleeping. Happy took Biff on a date tonight.

WILLY: (*Interested.*) That so?

LINDA: It was so nice to see them shaving together, one be-

80 hind the other, in the bathroom. And going out together. You notice? The whole house smells of shaving lotion.

WILLY: Figure it out. Work a lifetime to pay off a house. You finally own it, and there's nobody to live in it.

85 LINDA: Well, dear, life is a casting off. It's always that way.

WILLY: No, no, some people—some people accomplish something. Did Biff say anything after I went this morning?

LINDA: You shouldn't have criticized him, Willy, especially after he just got off the train. You mustn't lose your temper

90 with him.

WILLY: When the hell did I lose my temper? I simply asked him if he was making any money. Is that a criticism?

LINDA: But, dear, how could he make any money?

WILLY: (*Worried and angered.*) There's such an undercurrent in him. He became a moody man. Did he apologize when I 95 left this morning?

LINDA: He was crestfallen, Willy. You know how he admires you. I think if he finds himself, then you'll both be happier and not fight any more.

WILLY: How can he find himself on a farm? Is that a life? A 100 farmhand? In the beginning, when he was young, I thought, well, a young man, it's good for him to tramp around, take a lot of different jobs. But it's more than ten years now and he has yet to make thirty-five dollars a week! 105

LINDA: He's finding himself, Willy.

WILLY: Not finding yourself at the age of thirty-four is a disgrace!

LINDA: Shh!

WILLY: The trouble is he's lazy, goddammit! 110

LINDA: Willy, please!

WILLY: Biff is a lazy bum!

LINDA: They're sleeping. Get something to eat. Go on down.

WILLY: Why did he come home? I would like to know what brought him home. 115

LINDA: I don't know. I think he's still lost, Willy. I think he's very lost.

WILLY: Biff Loman is lost. In the greatest country in the world a young man with such—personal attractiveness, gets lost. And such a hard worker. There's one thing about 120 Biff—he's not lazy.

LINDA: Never.

WILLY: (*With pity and resolve.*) I'll see him in the morning; I'll have a nice talk with him. I'll get him a job selling. He could be big in no time. My God! Remember how they 125 used to follow him around in high school? When he smiled at one of them their faces lit up. When he walked down the street. . . (*He loses himself in reminiscences.*)

LINDA: (*Trying to bring him out of it.*) Willy, dear, I got a new kind of American-type cheese today. It's whipped. 130

WILLY: Why do you get American when I like Swiss?

LINDA: I just thought you'd like a change—

WILLY: I don't want a change! I want Swiss cheese. Why am I always being contradicted?

LINDA: (*With a covering laugh.*) I thought it would be a surprise. 135

WILLY: Why don't you open a window in here, for God's sake?

LINDA: (*With infinite patience.*) They're all open, dear.

WILLY: The way they boxed us in here. Bricks and windows, windows and bricks.

LINDA: We should've bought the land next door. 140

WILLY: The street is lined with cars. There's not a breath of fresh air in the neighborhood. The grass don't grow any more, you can't raise a carrot in the back yard. They should've had a law against apartment houses. Remember those two beautiful elm trees out there? When I and Biff 145 hung the swing between them?

LINDA: Yeah, like being a million miles from the city.

WILLY: They should've arrested the builder for cutting those down. They massacred the neighborhood. (*Lost.*) More and more I think of those days, Linda. This time of year 150 it was lilac and wisteria. And then the peonies would come out, and the daffodils. What fragrance in this room!

LINDA: Well, after all, people had to move somewhere.

WILLY: No, there's more people, now.

155 LINDA: I don't think there's more people I think—

WILLY: There's more people! That's what's ruining this country! Population is getting out of control. The competition is maddening! Smell the stink from that apartment house! And another one on the other side ... How can they whip
160 cheese?

(On WILLY's *last line,* BIFF *and* HAPPY *raise themselves up in their beds, listening.)*

LINDA: Go down, try it. And be quiet.

WILLY: *(Turning to* LINDA, *guiltily.)* You're not worried about me, are you, sweetheart?

BIFF: What's the matter?

165 HAPPY: Listen!

LINDA: You've got too much on the ball to worry about.

WILLY: You're my foundation and my support, Linda.

LINDA: Just try to relax, dear. You make mountains out of molehills.

170 WILLY: I won't fight with him any more. If he wants to go back to Texas, let him go.

LINDA: He'll find his way.

WILLY: Sure. Certain men just don't get started till later in life. Like Thomas Edison, I think. Or B. F. Goodrich. One
175 of them was deaf. *(He starts for the bedroom doorway.)* I'll put my money on Biff.

LINDA: And Willy—if it's warm Sunday we'll drive in the country. And we'll open the windshield, and take lunch.

WILLY: No, the windshields don't open on the new cars.

180 LINDA: But you opened it today.

WILLY: Me? I didn't. *(He stops.)* Now isn't that peculiar! Isn't that a remarkable—*(He breaks off in amazement and fright as the flute is heard distantly.)*

LINDA: What, darling?

185 WILLY: That is the most remarkable thing.

LINDA: What, dear?

WILLY: I was thinking of the Chevvy. *(Slight pause.)* Nineteen twenty-eight ... when I had that red Chevvy—*(Breaks off.)* That funny? I coulda sworn I was driving that Chevvy
190 today.

LINDA: Well, that's nothing. Something must've reminded you.

WILLY: Remarkable. Ts. Remember those days? The way Biff used to simonize that car? The dealer refused to believe
195 there was eighty thousand miles on it. *(He shakes his head.)* Heh! *(To* LINDA.) Close your eyes, I'll be right up. *(He walks out of the bedroom.)*

HAPPY *to* BIFF: Jesus, maybe he smashed up the car again!

LINDA: *(Calling after* WILLY.) Be careful on the stairs, dear! The
200 cheese is on the middle shelf! *(She turns, goes over to the bed, takes his jacket, and goes out of the bedroom.)*

(Light has risen on the boys' room. Unseen, WILLY *is heard talking to himself, "Eighty thousand miles," and a little laugh.* BIFF *gets out of bed, comes downstage a bit, and stands attentively.* BIFF *is two years older than his brother* HAPPY, *well built, but in these days bears a worn air and seems less self-assured. He has succeeded less, and his dreams are stronger and less acceptable than* HAPPY's. HAPPY *is tall, powerfully made. Sexuality is like a visible color on him, or a scent that many women have discovered. He, like his brother, is lost, but in*

a different way, for he has never allowed himself to turn his face toward defeat and is thus more confused and hard-skinned, although seemingly more content.

HAPPY: *(Getting out of bed.)* He's going to get his license taken away if he keeps that up. I'm getting nervous about him, y'know, Biff?

BIFF: His eyes are going. 205

HAPPY: No, I've driven with him. He sees all right. He just doesn't keep his mind on it. I drove into the city with him last week. He stops at a green light and then it turns red and he goes. *(He laughs.)*

BIFF: Maybe he's color-blind. 210

HAPPY: Pop? Why he's got the finest eye for color in the business. You know that.

BIFF: *(Sitting down on his bed.)* I'm going to sleep.

HAPPY: You're not still sour on Dad, are you, Biff?

BIFF: He's all right, I guess. 215

WILLY: *(Underneath them, in the living-room.)* Yes, sir, eighty thousand miles—eighty-two thousand!

BIFF: You smoking?

HAPPY: *(Holding out a pack of cigarettes.)* Want one?

BIFF: *(Taking a cigarette.)* I can never sleep when I smell it. 220

WILLY: What a simonizing job, heh!

HAPPY: *(With deep sentiment.)* Funny, Biff, y'know? Us sleeping in here again? The old beds. *(He pats his bed affectionately.)* All the talk that went across those two beds, huh? Our whole lives. 225

BIFF: Yeah. Lotta dreams and plans.

HAPPY: *(With a deep and masculine laugh.)* About five hundred women would like to know what was said in this room.

(They share a soft laugh.)

BIFF: Remember that big Betsy something—what the hell was her name—over on Bushwick Avenue? 230

HAPPY: *(Combing his hair.)* With the collie dog!

BIFF: That's the one. I got you in there, remember?

HAPPY: Yeah, that was my first time—I think. Boy, there was a pig! *(They laugh, almost crudely.)* You taught me everything I know about women. Don't forget that. 235

BIFF: I bet you forgot how bashful you used to be. Especially with girls.

HAPPY: Oh, I still am, Biff.

BIFF: Oh, go on.

HAPPY: I just control it, that's all. I think I got less bashful and 240 you got more so. What happened, Biff? Where's the old humor, the old confidence? *(He shakes* BIFF's *knee.* BIFF *gets up and moves restlessly about the room.)* What's the matter?

BIFF: Why does Dad mock me all the time?

HAPPY: He's not mocking you, he— 245

BIFF: Everything I say there's a twist of mockery on his face. I can't get near him.

HAPPY: He just wants you to make good, that's all. I wanted to talk to you about Dad for a long time, Biff. Something's—happening to him. He—talks to himself. 250

BIFF: I noticed that this morning. But he always mumbled.

HAPPY: But not so noticeable. It got so embarrassing I sent him to Florida. And you know something? Most of the time he's talking to you.

BIFF: What's he say about me? 255

HAPPY: I can't make it out.

BIFF: What's he say about me?

HAPPY: I think the fact that you're not settled, that you're still kind of up in the air . . .

260 BIFF: There's one or two other things depressing him, Happy.

HAPPY: What do you mean?

BIFF: Never mind. Just don't lay it all to me.

HAPPY: But I think if you just got started—I mean—is there any future for you out there?

265 BIFF: I tell ya, Hap, I don't know what the future is. I don't know—what I'm supposed to want.

HAPPY: What do you mean?

BIFF: Well, I spent six or seven years after high school trying to work myself up. Shipping clerk, salesman, business of 270 one kind or another. And it's a measly manner of existence. To get on that subway on the hot mornings in summer. To devote your whole life to keeping stock, or making phone calls, or selling or buying. To suffer fifty weeks of the year for the sake of a two-week vacation, 275 when all you really desire is to be outdoors, with your shirt off. And always to have to get ahead of the next fella. And still—that's how you build a future.

HAPPY: Well, you really enjoy it on a farm? Are you content out there?

280 BIFF: (*With rising agitation.*) Hap, I've had twenty or thirty different kinds of jobs since I left home before the war, and it always turns out the same. I just realized it lately. In Nebraska when I herded cattle, and the Dakotas, and Arizona, and now in Texas. It's why I came home now, I 285 guess, because I realized it. This farm I work on, it's spring there now, see? And they've got about fifteen new colts. There's nothing more inspiring or—beautiful than the sight of a mare and a new colt. And it's cool there now, see? Texas is cool now, and it's spring. And whenever 290 spring comes to where I am, I suddenly get the feeling, my God, I'm not gettin' anywhere! What the hell am I doing, playing around with horses, twenty-eight dollars a week! I'm thirty-four years old, I oughta be makin' my future. That's when I come running home. And now, I get 295 here, and I don't know what to do with myself. (*After a pause.*) I've always made a point of not wasting my life, and everytime I come back here I know that all I've done is to waste my life.

HAPPY: You're a poet, you know that, Biff? You're a—you're 300 an idealist!

BIFF: No, I'm mixed up very bad. Maybe I oughta get married. Maybe I oughta get stuck into something. Maybe that's my trouble. I'm like a boy. I'm not married, I'm not in business, I just—I'm like a boy. Are you content, Hap? 305 You're a success, aren't you? Are you content?

HAPPY: Hell, no!

BIFF: Why? You're making money, aren't you?

HAPPY: (*Moving about with energy, expressiveness.*) All I can do now is wait for the merchandise manager to die. And sup-310 pose I get to be merchandise manager? He's a good friend of mine, and he just built a terrific estate on Long Island. And he lived there about two months and sold it, and now he's building another one. He can't enjoy it once it's finished. And I know that's just what I would do. I don't 315 know what the hell I'm workin' for. Sometimes I sit in my apartment—all alone. And I think of the rent I'm paying. And it's crazy. But then, it's what I always wanted. My own

apartment, a car, and plenty of women. And still, god-dammit, I'm lonely.

BIFF: (*With enthusiasm.*) Listen, why don't you come out West 320 with me?

HAPPY: You and I, heh?

BIFF: Sure, maybe we could buy a ranch. Raise cattle, use our muscles. Men built like we are should be working out in the open. 325

HAPPY: (*Avidly.*) The Loman Brothers, heh?

BIFF: (*With vast affection.*) Sure, we'd be known all over the counties!

HAPPY: (*Enthralled.*) That's what I dream about, Biff. Sometimes I want to just rip my clothes off in the middle of the 330 store and outbox that goddam merchandise manager. I mean I can outbox, outrun, and outlift anybody in that store, and I have to take orders from those common, petty sons-of-bitches till I can't stand it any more.

BIFF: I'm tellin' you, kid, if you were with me I'd be happy 335 out there.

HAPPY: (*Enthused.*) See, Biff, everybody around me is so false that I'm constantly lowering my ideals . . .

BIFF: Baby, together we'd stand up for one another, we'd have someone to trust. 340

HAPPY: If I were around you—

BIFF: Hap, the trouble is we weren't brought up to grub for money. I don't know how to do it.

HAPPY: Neither can I!

BIFF: Then let's go! 345

HAPPY: The only thing is—what can you make out there?

BIFF: But look at your friend. Builds an estate and then hasn't the peace of mind to live in it.

HAPPY: Yeah, but when he walks into the store the waves part in front of him. That's fifty-two thousand dollars a year 350 coming through the revolving door, and I got more in my pinky finger than he's got in his head.

BIFF: Yeah, but you just said—

HAPPY: I gotta show some of those pompous, self-important executives over there that Hap Loman can make the 355 grade. I want to walk into the store the way he walks in. Then I'll go with you, Biff. We'll be together yet, I swear. But take those two we had tonight. Now weren't they gorgeous creatures?

BIFF: Yeah, yeah, most gorgeous I've had in years. 360

HAPPY: I get that any time I want, Biff. Whenever I feel disgusted. The only trouble is, it gets like bowling or something. I just keep knockin' them over and it doesn't mean anything. You still run around a lot?

BIFF: Naa. I'd like to find a girl—steady, somebody with sub-365 stance.

HAPPY: That's what I long for.

BIFF: Go on! You'd never come home.

HAPPY: I would! Somebody with character, with resistance! Like Mom, y'know? You're gonna call me a bastard when I 370 tell you this. That girl Charlotte I was with tonight is engaged to be married in five weeks. (*He tries on his new hat.*)

BIFF: No kiddin'!

HAPPY: Sure, the guy's in line for the vice-presidency of the store. I don't know what gets into me, maybe I just have 375 an overdeveloped sense of competition or something, but I went and ruined her, and furthermore I can't get rid of her. And he's the third executive I've done that

380 to. Isn't that a crummy characteristic? And to top it all, I go to their weddings! (*Indignantly, but laughing.*) Like I'm not supposed to take bribes. Manufacturers offer me a hundred-dollar bill now and then to throw an order their way. You know how honest I am, but it's like this

385 girl, see. I hate myself for it. Because I don't want the girl, and, still, I take it and—I love it!

BIFF: Let's go to sleep.

HAPPY: I guess we didn't settle anything, heh?

BIFF: I just got one idea that I think I'm going to try.

HAPPY: What's that?

390 BIFF: Remember Bill Oliver?

HAPPY: Sure, Oliver is very big now. You want to work for him again?

BIFF: No, but when I quit he said something to me. He put his arm on my shoulder, and he said, "Biff, if you ever

395 need anything, come to me."

HAPPY: I remember that. That sounds good.

BIFF: I think I'll go to see him. If I could get ten thousand or even seven or eight thousand dollars I could buy a beautiful ranch.

400 HAPPY: I bet he'd back you. 'Cause he thought highly of you, Biff. I mean, they all do. You're well liked, Biff. That's why I say to come back here, and we both have the apartment. And I'm tellin' you, Biff, any babe you want . . .

BIFF: No, with a ranch I could do the work I like and still be

405 something. I just wonder though. I wonder if Oliver still thinks I stole that carton of basketballs.

HAPPY: Oh, he probably forgot that long ago. It's almost ten years. You're too sensitive. Anyway, he didn't really fire you.

410 BIFF: Well, I think he was going to. I think that's why I quit. I was never sure whether he knew or not. I know he thought the world of me, though. I was the only one he'd let lock up the place.

WILLY: (*Below.*) You gonna wash the engine, Biff?

415 HAPPY: Shh!

(BIFF *looks at* HAPPY, *who is gazing down, listening.* WILLY *is mumbling in the parlor.*)

HAPPY: You hear that?

(*They listen.* WILLY *laughs warmly.*)

BIFF: (*Growing angry.*) Doesn't he know Mom can hear that?

WILLY: Don't get your sweater dirty, Biff!

(*A look of pain crosses* BIFF'S *face.*)

HAPPY: Isn't that terrible? Don't leave again, will you? You'll

420 find a job here. You gotta stick around. I don't know what to do about him, it's getting embarrassing.

WILLY: What a simonizing job!

BIFF: Mom's hearing that!

WILLY: No kiddin', Biff, you got a date? Wonderful!

425 HAPPY: Go on to sleep. But talk to him in the morning, will you?

BIFF: (*Reluctantly getting into bed.*) With her in the house. Brother!

HAPPY: (*Getting into bed.*) I wish you'd have a good talk with

430 him.

(*The light on their room begins to fade.*)

BIFF: (*To himself in bed.*) That selfish, stupid . . .

HAPPY: Sh . . . Sleep, Biff.

(*Their light is out. Well before they have finished speaking,* WILLY's *form is dimly seen below in the darkened kitchen. He opens the refrigerator, searches in there, and takes out a bottle of milk. The apartment houses are fading out, and the entire house and surroundings become covered with leaves. Music insinuates itself as the leaves appear.*)

WILLY: Just wanna be careful with those girls, Biff, that's all. Don't make any promises. No promises of any kind. Be-

435 cause a girl, y'know, they always believe what you tell 'em, and you're very young, Biff, you're too young to be talking seriously to girls.

(*Light rises on the kitchen.* WILLY, *talking, shuts the refrigerator door and comes downstage to the kitchen table. He pours milk into a glass. He is totally immersed in himself, smiling faintly.*)

WILLY: Too young entirely, Biff. You want to watch your schooling first. Then when you're all set, there'll be plenty

440 of girls for a boy like you. (*He smiles broadly at a kitchen chair.*) That so? The girls pay for you? (*He laughs.*) Boy, you must really be makin' a hit.

(WILLY *is gradually addressing—physically—a point offstage, speaking through the wall of the kitchen, and his voice has been rising in volume to that of a normal conversation.*)

WILLY: I been wondering why you polish the car so careful. Ha! Don't leave the hubcaps, boys. Get the chamois to the

445 hubcaps. Happy, use newspaper on the windows, it's the easiest thing. Show him how to do it, Biff! You see, Happy? Pad it up, use it like a pad. That's it, that's it, good work. You're doin' all right, Hap. (*He pauses, then nods in approbation for a few seconds, then looks upward.*) Biff, first

450 thing we gotta do when we get time is clip that big branch over the house. Afraid it's gonna fall in a storm and hit the roof. Tell you what. We get a rope and sling her around, and then we climb up there with a couple of saws and take her down. Soon as you finish the car, boys, I

455 wanna see ya. I got a surprise for you, boys.

BIFF: (*Offstage.*) Whatta ya got, Dad?

WILLY: No, you finish first. Never leave a job till you're finished—remember that. (*Looking toward the "big trees".*) Biff, up in Albany I saw a beautiful hammock. I think I'll

460 buy it next trip, and we'll hang it right between those two elms. Wouldn't that be something? Just swingin' there under those branches. Boy, that would be . . .

(*Young* BIFF *and* YOUNG HAPPY *appear from the direction* WILLY *was addressing.* HAPPY *carries rags and a pail of water.* BIFF, *wearing a sweater with a block "S," carries a football.*)

BIFF: (*Pointing in the direction of the car offstage.*) How's that, Pop, professional?

WILLY: Terrific. Terrific job, boys. Good work, Biff.

465 HAPPY: Where's the surprise, Pop?

WILLY: In the back seat of the car.

HAPPY: Boy! (*He runs off.*)

BIFF: What is it, Dad? Tell me, what'd you buy?

470 WILLY: (*Laughing, cuffs him.*) Never mind, something I want
      you to have.
   BIFF: (*Turns and starts off.*) What is it, Hap?
   HAPPY: (*Offstage.*) It's a punching bag!
   BIFF: Oh, Pop!
475 WILLY: It's got Gene Tunney's signature on it!

(HAPPY *runs onstage with a punching bag.*)

   BIFF: Gee, how'd you know we wanted a punching bag?
   WILLY: Well, it's the finest thing for the timing.
   HAPPY: (*Lies down on his back and pedals with his feet.*) I'm los-
      ing weight, you notice, Pop?
480 WILLY: (*To* HAPPY.) Jumping rope is good too.
   BIFF: Did you see the new football I got?
   WILLY: (*Examining the ball.*) Where'd you get a new ball?
   BIFF: The coach told me to practice my passing.
   WILLY: That so? And he gave you the ball, heh?
485 BIFF: Well, I borrowed it from the locker room. (*He laughs con-
      fidentially.*)
   WILLY: (*Laughing with him at the theft.*) I want you to return
      that.
   HAPPY: I told you he wouldn't like it!
490 BIFF: (*Angrily.*) Well, I'm bringing it back!
   WILLY: (*Stopping the incipient argument, to* HAPPY.) Sure, he's
      gotta practice with a regulation ball, doesn't he? (*To* BIFF.)
      Coach'll probably congratulate you on your initiative!
   BIFF: Oh, he keeps congratulating my initiative all the time,
495   Pop.
   WILLY: That's because he likes you. If somebody else took that
      ball there'd be an uproar. So what's the report, boys, what's
      the report?
   BIFF: Where'd you go this time, Dad? Gee we were lonesome
500   for you.
   WILLY: (*Pleased, puts an arm around each boy and they come down
      to the apron.*) Lonesome, heh?
   BIFF: Missed you every minute.
   WILLY: Don't say? Tell you a secret, boys. Don't breathe it to
505   a soul. Someday I'll have my own business, and I'll never
      have to leave home any more.
   HAPPY: Like Uncle Charley, heh?
   WILLY: Bigger than Uncle Charley! Because Charley is not—
      liked. He's liked, but he's not—well liked.
510 BIFF: Where'd you go this time, Dad?
   WILLY: Well, I got on the road, and I went north to Provi-
      dence. Met the Mayor.
   BIFF: The Mayor of Providence!
   WILLY: He was sitting in the hotel lobby.
515 BIFF: What'd he say?
   WILLY: He said, "Morning!" And I said, "You got a fine city
      here, Mayor." And then he had coffee with me. And then
      I went to Waterbury. Waterbury is a fine city. Big clock
      city, the famous Waterbury clock. Sold a nice bill there.
520   And then Boston—Boston is the cradle of the Revolu-
      tion. A fine city. And a couple of other towns in Mass.,
      and on to Portland and Bangor and straight home!
   BIFF: Gee, I'd love to go with you sometime, Dad.
   WILLY: Soon as summer comes.
525 HAPPY: Promise?
   WILLY: You and Hap and I, and I'll show you all the towns.
      America is full of beautiful towns and fine, upstanding

people. And they know me, boys, they know me up and
down New England. The finest people. And when I
bring you fellas up, there'll be open sesame for all of us,   530
'cause one thing, boys: I have friends. I can park my car in
any street in New England, and the cops protect it like
their own. This summer, heh?
   BIFF *and* HAPPY: (*Together.*) Yeah! You bet!
   WILLY: We'll take our bathing suits.   535
   HAPPY: We'll carry your bags, Pop!
   WILLY: Oh, won't that be something! Me comin' into the
      Boston stores with you boys carryin' my bags. What a
      sensation!

(BIFF *is prancing around, practicing passing the ball.*)

   WILLY: You nervous, Biff, about the game?   540
   BIFF: Not if you're gonna be there.
   WILLY: What do they say about you in school, now that they
      made you captain?
   HAPPY: There's a crowd of girls behind him everytime the
      classes change.   545
   BIFF: (*Taking* WILLY's *hand.*) This Saturday, Pop, this Satur-
      day—just for you, I'm going to break through for a
      touchdown.
   HAPPY: You're supposed to pass.
   BIFF: I'm takin' one play for Pop. You watch me, Pop, and   550
      when I take off my helmet, that means I'm breakin' out.
      Then you watch me crash through that line!
   WILLY: (*Kisses* BIFF.) Oh, wait'll I tell this in Boston!

(BERNARD *enters in knickers. He is younger than* BIFF, *earnest and
loyal, a worried boy.*)

   BERNARD: Biff, where are you? You're supposed to study with
      me today.   555
   WILLY: Hey, looka Bernard. What're you lookin' so anemic
      about, Bernard?
   BERNARD: He's gotta study, Uncle Willy. He's got Regents
      next week.
   HAPPY: (*Tauntingly, spinning* BERNARD *around.*) Let's box,   560
      Bernard!
   BERNARD: Biff! (*He gets away from* HAPPY.) Listen, Biff, I heard
      Mr. Birnbaum say that if you don't start studyin' math he's
      gonna flunk you, and you won't graduate. I heard him!
   WILLY: You better study with him, Biff. Go ahead now.   565
   BERNARD: I heard him!
   BIFF: Oh, Pop, you didn't see my sneakers! (*He holds up a foot
      for* WILLY *to look at.*)
   WILLY: Hey, that's a beautiful job of printing!
   BERNARD: (*Wiping his glasses.*) Just because he printed Uni-   570
      versity of Virginia on his sneakers doesn't mean they've
      got to graduate him, Uncle Willy!
   WILLY: (*Angrily.*) What're you talking about? With scholar-
      ships to three universities they're gonna flunk him?
   BERNARD: But I heard Mr. Birnbaum say—   575
   WILLY: Don't be a pest, Bernard! (*To his boys.*) What an anemic!
   BERNARD: Okay, I'm waiting for you in my house, Biff.

(BERNARD *goes off. The* LOMANS *laugh.*)

   WILLY: Bernard is not well liked, is he?
   BIFF: He's liked, but he's not well liked.

580 HAPPY: That's right, Pop.

WILLY: That's just what I mean. Bernard can get the best marks in school, y'understand, but when he gets out in the business world, y'understand, you are going to be five times ahead of him. That's why I thank Almighty God you're

585 both built like Adonises. Because the man who makes an appearance in the business world, the man who creates personal interest, is the man who gets ahead. Be liked and you will never want. You take me, for instance. I never have to wait in line to see a buyer. "Willy Loman is here!" That's all

590 they have to know, and I go right through.

BIFF: Did you knock them dead, Pop?

WILLY: Knocked 'em cold in Providence, slaughtered 'em in Boston.

HAPPY: (*On his back, pedaling again.*) I'm losing weight, you

595 notice, Pop?

(LINDA *enters, as of old, a ribbon in her hair, carrying a basket of washing.*)

LINDA: (*With youthful energy.*) Hello, dear!

WILLY: Sweetheart!

LINDA: How'd the Chevvy run?

WILLY: Chevrolet, Linda, is the greatest car ever built. (*To the*

600 *boys.*) Since when do you let your mother carry wash up the stairs?

BIFF: Grab hold there, boy!

HAPPY: Where to, Mom?

LINDA: Hang them up on the line. And you better go down

605 to your friends, Biff. The cellar is full of boys. They don't know what to do with themselves.

BIFF: Ah, when Pop comes home they can wait!

WILLY: (*Laughs appreciatively.*) You better go down and tell them what to do, Biff.

610 BIFF: I think I'll have them sweep out the furnace room.

WILLY: Good work, Biff.

BIFF: (*Goes through wall-line of kitchen to doorway at back and calls down.*) Fellas! Everybody sweep out the furnace room! I'll be right down!

615 VOICES: All right! Okay, Biff.

BIFF: George and Sam and Frank, come out back! We're hangin' up the wash! Come on, Hap, on the double! (*He and* HAPPY *carry out the basket.*)

LINDA: The way they obey him!

620 WILLY: Well, that's training, the training. I'm tellin' you, I was sellin' thousands and thousands, but I had to come home.

LINDA: Oh, the whole block'll be at that game. Did you sell anything?

WILLY: I did five hundred gross in Providence and seven

625 hundred gross in Boston.

LINDA: No! Wait a minute, I've got a pencil. (*She pulls pencil and paper out of her apron pocket.*) That makes your commission . . . Two hundred—my God! Two hundred, and twelve dollars!

630 WILLY: Well, I didn't figure it yet, but . . .

LINDA: How much did you do?

WILLY: Well, I—I did—about a hundred and eighty gross in Providence. Well, no—it came to—roughly two hundred gross on the whole trip.

635 LINDA: (*Without hesitation.*) Two hundred gross. That's . . . (*She figures.*)

WILLY: The trouble was that three of the stores were half closed for inventory in Boston. Otherwise I woulda broke records.

LINDA: Well, it makes seventy dollars and some pennies. 640 That's very good.

WILLY: What do we owe?

LINDA: Well, on the first there's sixteen dollars on the refrigerator—

WILLY: Why sixteen? 645

LINDA: Well, the fan belt broke, so it was a dollar eighty.

WILLY: But it's brand new.

LINDA: Well, the man said that's the way it is. Till they work themselves in, y'know.

(*They move through the wall-line into the kitchen.*)

WILLY: I hope we didn't get stuck on that machine. 650

LINDA: They got the biggest ads of any of them!

WILLY: I know, it's a fine machine. What else?

LINDA: Well, there's nine-sixty for the washing machine. And for the vacuum cleaner there's three and a half due on the fifteenth. Then the roof, you got twenty-one dollars re- 655 maining.

WILLY: It don't leak, does it?

LINDA: No, they did a wonderful job. Then you owe Frank for the carburetor.

WILLY: I'm not going to pay that man! That goddam Chevro- 660 let, they ought to prohibit the manufacture of that car!

LINDA: Well, you owe him three and a half. And odds and ends, comes to around a hundred and twenty dollars by the fifteenth.

WILLY: A hundred and twenty dollars! My God, if business 665 don't pick up I don't know what I'm gonna do!

LINDA: Well, next week you'll do better.

WILLY: Oh, I'll knock 'em dead next week. I'll go to Hartford. I'm very well liked in Hartford. You know, the trouble is, Linda, people don't seem to take to me. 670

(*They move onto the forestage.*)

LINDA: Oh, don't be foolish.

WILLY: I know it when I walk in. They seem to laugh at me.

LINDA: Why? Why would they laugh at you? Don't talk that way, Willy.

(WILLY *moves to the edge of the stage.* LINDA *goes into the kitchen and starts to darn stockings.*)

WILLY: I don't know the reason for it, but they just pass me 675 by. I'm not noticed.

LINDA: But you're doing wonderful, dear. You're making seventy to a hundred dollars a week.

WILLY: But I gotta be at it ten, twelve hours a day. Other men—I don't know—they do it easier. I don't know 680 why—I can't stop myself—I talk too much. A man oughta come in with a few words. One thing about Charley. He's a man of few words, and they respect him.

LINDA: You don't talk too much, you're just lively.

WILLY: (*Smiling.*) Well, I figure, what the hell, life is short, a 685 couple of jokes (*To himself.*) I joke too much! (*The smile goes.*)

LINDA: Why? You're—

WILLY: I'm fat. I'm very—foolish to look at, Linda. I didn't tell
690   you, but Christmas time I happened to be calling on F. H.
      Stewarts, and a salesman I know, as I was going in to see the
      buyer I heard him say something about—walrus. And I—
      I cracked him right across the face. I won't take that. I sim-
      ply will not take that. But they do laugh at me. I know that.
695 LINDA: Darling . . .
      WILLY: I gotta overcome it. I know I gotta overcome it. I'm
      not dressing to advantage, maybe.
      LINDA: Willy, darling, you're the handsomest man in the
      world—
700 WILLY: Oh, no, Linda.
      LINDA: To me you are. (*Slight pause.*) The handsomest.

(*From the darkness is heard the laughter of a woman.* WILLY *doesn't
turn to it, but it continues through* LINDA's *lines.*)

LINDA: And the boys, Willy. Few men are idolized by their
      children the way you are.

(*Music is heard as behind a scrim, to the left of the house,* THE
WOMAN, *dimly seen, is dressing.*)

WILLY: (*With great feeling.*) You're the best there is, Linda,
705   you're a pal, you know that? On the road—on the road I
      want to grab you sometimes and just kiss the life outa you.

(*The laughter is loud now, and he moves into a brightening area at
the left, where* THE WOMAN *has come from behind the scrim and is
standing, putting on her hat, looking into a "mirror" and laughing.*)

WILLY: 'Cause I get so lonely—especially when business is
      bad and there's nobody to talk to. I get the feeling that I'll
      never sell anything again, that I won't making a living for
710   you, or a business, a business for the boys. (*He talks through*
      THE WOMAN's *subsiding laughter;* THE WOMAN *primps at the
      "mirror."*) There's so much I want to make for—
      THE WOMAN: Me? You didn't make me, Willy. I picked you.
      WILLY: (*Pleased.*) You picked me?
715 THE WOMAN: (*Who is quite proper-looking,* WILLY's *age.*) I did.
      I've been sitting at that desk watching all the salesmen go
      by, day in, day out. But you've got such a sense of humor,
      and we do have such a good time together, don't we?
      WILLY: Sure, sure. (*He takes her in his arms.*) Why do you have
720   to go now?
      THE WOMAN: It's two o'clock . . .
      WILLY: No, come on in! (*He pulls her.*)
      THE WOMAN: . . . my sisters'll be scandalized. When'll you be
      back?
725 WILLY: Oh, two weeks about. Will you come up again?
      THE WOMAN: Sure thing. You do make me laugh. It's good
      for me. (*She squeezes his arm, kisses him.*) And I think you're
      a wonderful man.
      WILLY: You picked me, heh?
730 THE WOMAN: Sure. Because you're so sweet. And such a kidder.
      WILLY: Well, I'll see you next time I'm in Boston.
      THE WOMAN: I'll put you right through to the buyers.
      WILLY: (*Slapping her bottom.*) Right. Well, bottoms up!
      THE WOMAN: (*Slaps him gently and laughs.*) You just kill me,
735   Willy. (*He suddenly grabs her and kisses her roughly.*) You kill
      me. And thanks for the stockings. I love a lot of stockings.
      Well, good night.

WILLY: Good night. And keep your pores open!
THE WOMAN: Oh, Willy!

(THE WOMAN *bursts out laughing, and* LINDA's *laughter blends in.*
THE WOMAN *disappears into the dark. Now the area at the kitchen
table brightens.* LINDA *is sitting where she was at the kitchen table,
but now is mending a pair of her silk stockings.*)

LINDA: You are, Willy. The handsomest man. You've got no   740
      reason to feel that—
WILLY: (*Coming out of* THE WOMAN's *dimming area and going
      over to* LINDA.) I'll make it all up to you, Linda, I'll—
LINDA: There's nothing to make up, dear. You're doing fine,
      better than—   745
WILLY: (*Noticing her mending.*) What's that?
LINDA: Just mending my stockings. They're so expensive—
WILLY: (*Angrily, taking them from her.*) I won't have you mend-
      ing stockings in this house! Now throw them out!

(LINDA *puts the stockings in her pocket.*)

BERNARD: (*Entering on the run.*) Where is he? If he doesn't   750
      study!
WILLY: (*Moving to the forestage, with great agitation.*) You'll give
      him the answers!
BERNARD: I do, but I can't on a Regents! That's a state exam!
      They're liable to arrest me!   755
WILLY: Where is he? I'll whip him, I'll whip him!
LINDA: And he'd better give back that football, Willy, it's not
      nice.
WILLY: Biff! Where is he? Why is he taking everything?
LINDA: He's too rough with the girls, Willy. All the mothers   760
      are afraid of him!
WILLY: I'll whip him!
BERNARD: He's driving the car without a license!

(THE WOMAN's *laugh is heard.*)

WILLY: Shut up!
LINDA: All the mothers—   765
WILLY: Shut up!
BERNARD: (*Backing quietly away and out.*) Mr. Birnbaum says
      he's stuck up.
WILLY: Get outa here!
BERNARD: If he doesn't buckle down he'll flunk math! (*He   770
      goes off.*)
LINDA: He's right, Willy, you've gotta—
WILLY: (*Exploding at her.*) There's nothing the matter with
      him! You want him to be a worm like Bernard? He's got
      spirit, personality . . .   775

(*As he speaks,* LINDA, *almost in tears, exits into the living-room.*
WILLY *is alone in the kitchen, wilting and staring. The leaves are gone.
It is night again, and the apartment houses look down from behind.*)

WILLY: Loaded with it. Loaded! What is he stealing? He's giv-
      ing it back, isn't he? Why is he stealing? What did I tell him?
      I never in my life told him anything but decent things.

(HAPPY *in pajamas has come down the stairs;* WILLY *suddenly becomes aware of* HAPPY's *presence.*)

HAPPY: Let's go now, come on.

780   WILLY: (*Sitting down at the kitchen table.*) Huh! Why did she have to wax the floors herself? Everytime she waxes the floors she keels over. She knows that!

HAPPY: Shh! Take it easy. What brought you back tonight?

WILLY: I got an awful scare. Nearly hit a kid in Yonkers. God! 785 Why didn't I go to Alaska with my brother Ben that time! Ben! That man was a genius, that man was success incarnate! What a mistake! He begged me to go.

HAPPY: Well, there's no use in—

WILLY: You guys! There was a man started with the clothes on 790 his back and ended up with diamond mines!

HAPPY: Boy, someday I'd like to know how he did it.

WILLY: What's the mystery? The man knew what he wanted and went out and got it! Walked into a jungle, and comes out, the age of twenty-one, and he's rich! The world is an 795 oyster, but you don't crack it open on a mattress!

HAPPY: Pop, I told you I'm gonna retire you for life.

WILLY: You'll retire me for life on seventy goddam dollars a week? And your women and your car and your apartment, and you'll retire me for life! Christ's sake, I couldn't 800 get past Yonkers today! Where are you guys, where are you? The woods are burning! I can't drive a car!

(CHARLEY *has appeared in the doorway. He is a large man, slow of speech, laconic, immovable. In all he says, despite what he says, there is pity, and, now, trepidation. He has a robe over pajamas, slippers on his feet. He enters the kitchen.*)

CHARLEY: Everything all right?

HAPPY: Yeah, Charley, everything's . . .

WILLY: What's the matter?

805 CHARLEY: I heard some noise. I thought something happened. Can't we do something about the walls? You sneeze in here, and in my house hats blow off.

HAPPY: Let's go to bed, Dad. Come on.

(CHARLEY *signals to* HAPPY *to go.*)

WILLY: You go ahead, I'm not tired at the moment.

810 HAPPY: (*To* WILLY.) Take it easy, huh? (*He exits.*)

WILLY: What're you doin' up?.

CHARLEY: (*Sitting down at the kitchen table opposite* WILLY.) Couldn't sleep good. I had a heartburn.

WILLY: Well, you don't know how to eat.

815 CHARLEY: I eat with my mouth.

WILLY: No, you're ignorant. You gotta know about vitamins and things like that.

CHARLEY: Come on, let's shoot. Tire you out a little.

WILLY: (*Hesitantly.*) All right. You got cards?

820 CHARLEY: (*Taking a deck from his pocket.*) Yeah, I got them. Someplace. What is it with those vitamins?

WILLY: (*Dealing.*) They build up your bones. Chemistry.

CHARLEY: Yeah, but there's no bones in a heartburn.

WILLY: What are you talkin' about? Do you know the first 825 thing about it?

CHARLEY: Don't get insulted.

WILLY: Don't talk about something you don't know anything about.

(*They are playing. Pause.*)

CHARLEY: What're you doin' home?

WILLY: A little trouble with the car. 830

CHARLEY: Oh. (*Pause.*) I'd like to take a trip to California.

WILLY: Don't say.

CHARLEY: You want a job?

WILLY: I got a job, I told you that. (*After a slight pause.*) What the hell are you offering me a job for? 835

CHARLEY: Don't get insulted.

WILLY: Don't insult me.

CHARLEY: I don't see no sense in it. You don't have to go on this way.

WILLY: I got a good job. (*Slight pause.*) What do you keep 840 comin' in here for?

CHARLEY: You want me to go?

WILLY: (*After a pause, withering.*) I can't understand it. He's going back to Texas again. What the hell is that?

CHARLEY: Let him go. 845

WILLY: I got nothin' to give him, Charley, I'm clean, I'm clean.

CHARLEY: He won't starve. None a them starve. Forget about him.

WILLY: Then what have I got to remember? 850

CHARLEY: You take it too hard. To hell with it. When a deposit bottle is broken you don't get your nickel back.

WILLY: That's easy enough for you to say.

CHARLEY: That ain't easy for me to say.

WILLY: Did you see the ceiling I put up in the living-room? 855

CHARLEY: Yeah, that's a piece of work. To put up a ceiling is a mystery to me. How do you do it?

WILLY: What's the difference?

CHARLEY: Well, talk about it.

WILLY: You gonna put up a ceiling? 860

CHARLEY: How could I put up a ceiling?

WILLY: Then what the hell are you bothering me for?

CHARLEY: You're insulted again.

WILLY: A man who can't handle tools is not a man. You're disgusting. 865

CHARLEY: Don't call me disgusting, Willy.

(UNCLE BEN, *carrying a valise and an umbrella, enters the forestage from around the right corner of the house. He is a stolid man, in his sixties, with a mustache and an authoritative air. He is utterly certain of his destiny, and there is an aura of far places about him. He enters exactly as* WILLY *speaks.*)

WILLY: I'm getting awfully tired, Ben.

(BEN's *music is heard.* BEN *looks around at everything.*)

CHARLEY: Good, keep playing; you'll sleep better. Did you call me Ben?

(BEN *looks at his watch.*)

WILLY: That's funny. For a second there you reminded me of 870 my brother Ben.

BEN: I only have a few minutes. (*He strolls, inspecting the place.* WILLY *and* CHARLEY *continue playing.*)

CHARLEY: You never heard from him again, heh? Since that time? 875

WILLY: Didn't Linda tell you? Couple of weeks ago we got a letter from his wife in Africa. He died.

CHARLEY: That so.

BEN: (*Chuckling.*) So this is Brooklyn, eh?

880 CHARLEY: Maybe you're in for some of his money.

WILLY: Naa, he had seven sons. There's just one opportunity I had with that man . . .

BEN: I must make a train, William. There are several properties I'm looking at in Alaska.

885 WILLY: Sure, sure! If I'd gone with him to Alaska that time, everything would've been totally different.

CHARLEY: Go on, you'd froze to death up there.

WILLY: What're you talking about?

BEN: Opportunity is tremendous in Alaska, William. Surprised you're not up there.

890 WILLY: Sure, tremendous.

CHARLEY: Heh?

WILLY: There was the only man I ever met who knew the answers.

895 CHARLEY: Who?

BEN: How are you all?

WILLY: (*Taking a pot, smiling.*) Fine, fine.

CHARLEY: Pretty sharp tonight.

BEN: Is Mother living with you?

900 WILLY: No, she died a long time ago.

CHARLEY: Who?

BEN: That's too bad. Fine specimen of a lady, Mother.

WILLY: (*To* CHARLEY.) Heh?

BEN: I'd hoped to see the old girl.

905 CHARLEY: Who died?

BEN: Heard anything from Father, have you?

WILLY: (*Unnerved.*) What do you mean, who died?

CHARLEY: (*Taking a pot.*) What're you talkin' about?

BEN: (*Looking at his watch.*) William, it's half-past eight!

910 WILLY: (*As though to dispel his confusion he angrily stops* CHARLEY's *hand.*) That's my build!

CHARLEY: I put the ace—

WILLY: If you don't know how to play the game I'm not gonna throw my money away on you!

915 CHARLEY: (*Rising.*) It was my ace, for God's sake!

WILLY: I'm through, I'm through!

BEN: When did Mother die?

WILLY: Long ago. Since the beginning you never knew how to play cards.

920 CHARLEY: (*Picks up the cards and goes to the door.*) All right! Next time I'll bring a deck with five aces.

WILLY: I don't play that kind of game!

CHARLEY: (*Turning to him.*) You ought to be ashamed of yourself!

925 WILLY: Yeah?

CHARLEY: Yeah! (*He goes out.*)

WILLY: (*Slamming the door after him.*) Ignoramus!

BEN: (*As* WILLY *comes toward him through the wall-line of the kitchen.*) So you're William.

930 WILLY: (*Shaking* BEN's *hand.*) Ben! I've been waiting for you so long! What's the answer? How did you do it?

BEN: Oh, there's a story in that.

(LINDA *enters the forestage, as of old, carrying the wash basket.*)

LINDA: Is this Ben?

BEN: (*Gallantly.*) How do you do, my dear.

935 LINDA: Where've you been all these years? Willy's always wondered why you—

WILLY: (*Pulling* BEN *away from her impatiently.*) Where is Dad? Didn't you follow him? How did you get started?

BEN: Well, I don't know how much you remember.

WILLY: Well, I was just a baby, of course, only three or four 940 years old—

BEN: Three years and eleven months.

WILLY: What a memory, Ben!

BEN: I have many enterprises, William, and I have never kept books. 945

WILLY: I remember I was sitting under the wagon in—was it Nebraska?

BEN: It was South Dakota, and I gave you a bunch of wild-flowers.

WILLY: I remember you walking away down some open road. 950

BEN: (*Laughing.*) I was going to find Father in Alaska.

WILLY: Where is he?

BEN: At that age I had a very faulty view of geography, William. I discovered after a few days that I was heading due south, so instead of Alaska, I ended up in Africa. 955

LINDA: Africa!

WILLY: The Gold Coast!

BEN: Principally diamond mines.

LINDA: Diamond mines!

BEN: Yes, my dear. But I've only a few minutes— 960

WILLY: No! Boys! Boys! (YOUNG BIFF *and* HAPPY *appear.*) Listen to this. This is your Uncle Ben, a great man! Tell, my boys, Ben!

BEN: Why, boys, when I was seventeen I walked into the jungle, and when I was twenty-one I walked out. (*He laughs.*) 965 And by God I was rich.

WILLY: (*To the boys.*) You see what I been talking about? The greatest things can happen!

BEN: (*Glancing at his watch.*) I have an appointment in Ketchikan Tuesday week. 970

WILLY: No, Ben! Please tell about Dad. I want my boys to hear. I want them to know the kind of stock they spring from. All I remember is a man with a big beard, and I was in Mamma's lap, sitting around a fire, and some kind of high music. 975

BEN: His flute. He played the flute.

WILLY: Sure, the flute, that's right?

(*New music is heard, a high, rollicking tune.*)

BEN: Father was a very great and a very wild-hearted man. We would start in Boston, and he'd toss the whole family into the wagon, and then he'd drive the team right across 980 the country; through Ohio, and Indiana, Michigan, Illinois, and all the Western states. And we'd stop in the towns and sell the flutes that he'd made on the way. Great inventor, Father. With one gadget he made more in a week than a man like you could make in a lifetime. 985

WILLY: That's just the way I'm bringing them up, Ben—rugged, well liked, all-around.

BEN: Yeah? (*To* BIFF.) Hit that, boy—hard as you can. (*He pounds his stomach.*)

BIFF: Oh, no, sir! 990

BEN: (*Taking boxing stance.*) Come on, get to me! (*He laughs.*)

WILLY: Go to it, Biff! Go ahead, show him!

BIFF: Okay! (*He cocks his fists and starts in.*)

LINDA: (*To* WILLY.) Why must he fight, dear?

995   BEN: (*Sparring with* BIFF.) Good boy! Good boy!
WILLY: How's that, Ben, heh?
HAPPY: Give him the left, Biff!
LINDA: Why are you fighting?
BEN: Good boy! (*Suddenly comes in, trips* BIFF, *and stands over*
1000   *him, the point of his umbrella poised over* BIFF's *eye.*)
LINDA: Look out, Biff!
BIFF: Gee!
BEN: (*Patting* BIFF's *knee.*) Never fight fair with a stranger, boy.
You'll never get out of the jungle that way. Taking LINDA's
1005   *hand and bowing.*) It was an honor and a pleasure to meet
you, Linda.
LINDA: (*Withdrawing her hand coldly, frightened.*) Have a nice—
trip.
BEN: (*To* WILLY.) And good luck with your—what do you do?
1010   WILLY: Selling.
BEN: Yes. Well . . . (*He raises his hand in farewell to all.*)
WILLY: No, Ben, I don't want you to think . . . (*He takes* BEN's
arm to show him.) It's Brooklyn, I know, but we hunt too.
BEN: Really, now.
1015   WILLY: Oh, sure, there's snakes and rabbits and—that's why I
moved out here. Why, Biff can fell any one of these trees
in no time! Boys! Go right over to where they're building
the apartment house and get some sand. We're gonna rebuild the entire front stoop right now! Watch this Ben!
1020   BIFF: Yes, sir! On the double, Hap!
HAPPY: (*As he and* BIFF *run off.*) I lost weight, Pop, you notice?

(CHARLEY *enters in knickers, even before the boys are gone.*)

CHARLEY: Listen, if they steal any more from that building
the watchman'll put the cops on them!
LINDA: (*To* WILLY.) Don't let Biff . . .

(BEN *laughs lustily.*)

1025   WILLY: You shoulda seen the lumber they brought home last
week. At least a dozen six-by-tens worth all kinds a
money.
CHARLEY: Listen, if that watchman—
WILLY: I gave them hell, understand. But I got a couple of
1030   fearless characters there.
CHARLEY: Willy, the jails are full of fearless characters.
BEN: (*Clapping* WILLY *on the back, with a laugh at* CHARLEY.)
And the stock exchange, friend!
WILLY: (*Joining in* BEN's *laughter.*) Where are the rest of your
1035   pants?
CHARLEY: My wife bought them.
WILLY: Now all you need is a golf club and you can go up-
stairs and go to sleep. (*To* BEN.) Great athlete! Between
him and his son Bernard they can't hammer a nail!
1040   BERNARD: (*Rushing in.*) The watchman's chasing Biff!
WILLY: (*Angrily.*) Shut up! He's not stealing anything!
LINDA: (*Alarmed, hurrying off left.*) Where is he? Biff, dear! (*She
exits.*)
WILLY: (*Moving toward the left, away from* BEN.) There's noth-
1045   ing wrong. What's the matter with you?
BEN: Nervy boy. Good!
WILLY: (*Laughing.*) Oh, nerves of iron, that Biff!
CHARLEY: Don't know what it is. My New England man
comes back and he's bleedin', they murdered him up there.
1050   WILLY: It's contacts, Charley, I got important contacts!

CHARLEY: (*Sarcastically.*) Glad to hear it, Willy. Come in later,
we'll shoot a little casino. I'll take some of your Portland
money. (*He laughs at* WILLY *and exits.*)
WILLY: (*Turning to* BEN.) Business is bad, it's murderous. But
not for me, of course.   1055
BEN: I'll stop by on my way back to Africa.
WILLY: (*Longingly.*) Can't you stay a few days? You're just what
I need, Ben, because I—I have a fine position here, but
I—well, Dad left when I was such a baby and I never had
a chance to talk to him and I still feel—kind of temporary   1060
about myself.
BEN: I'll be late for my train.

(*They are at opposite ends of the stage.*)

WILLY: Ben, my boys—can't we talk? They'd go into the jaws
of hell for me, see, but I—
BEN: William, you're being first-rate with your boys. Out-   1065
standing, manly chaps!
WILLY: (*Hanging on to his words.*) Oh, Ben, that's good to hear!
Because sometimes I'm afraid that I'm not teaching them
the right kind of—Ben, how should I teach them?
BEN: (*Giving great weight to each word, and with a certain vicious*   1070
audacity.) William, when I walked into the jungle, I was
seventeen. When I walked out I was twenty-one. And, by
God, I was rich! (*He goes off into the darkness around the right
corner of the house.*)
WILLY: . . . was rich! That's just the spirit I want to imbue   1075
them with! To walk into a jungle! I was right! I was right!
I was right!

(BEN *is gone, but* WILLY *is still speaking to him as* LINDA, *in nightgown and robe, enters the kitchen, glances around for* WILLY, *then
goes to the door of the house, looks out and sees him. Comes down
to his left. He looks at her.*)

LINDA: Willy, dear? Willy?
WILLY: I was right!
LINDA: Did you have some cheese? (*He can't answer.*) It's very   1080
late, darling. Come to bed, heh?
WILLY: (*Looking straight up.*) Gotta break your neck to see a
star in this yard.
LINDA: You coming in?
WILLY: Whatever happened to that diamond watch fob? Re-   1085
member? When Ben came from Africa that time? Didn't
he give me a watch fob with a diamond in it?
LINDA: You pawned it, dear. Twelve, thirteen years ago. For
Biff's radio correspondence course.
WILLY: Gee, that was a beautiful thing. I'll take a walk.   1090
LINDA: But you're in your slippers.
WILLY: (*Starting to go around the house at the left.*) I was right! I
was! (*Half to* LINDA, *as he goes, shaking his head.*) What a
man! There was a man worth talking to. I was right!
LINDA: (*Calling after* WILLY.) But in your slippers, Willy!   1095

(WILLY *is almost gone when* BIFF, *in his pajamas, comes down the
stairs an enters the kitchen.*)

BIFF: What is he doing out there?
LINDA: Sh!
BIFF: God Almighty, Mom, how long has he been doing this?
LINDA: Don't, he'll hear you.

1100 BIFF: What the hell is the matter with him?

LINDA: It'll pass by morning.

BIFF: Shouldn't we do anything?

LINDA: Oh, my dear, you should do a lot of things, but there's nothing to do, so go to sleep.

(HAPPY *comes down the stair and sits on the steps.*)

1105 HAPPY: I never heard him so loud, Mom.

LINDA: Well, come around more often; you'll hear him. (*She sits down at the table and mends the lining of* WILLY'*s jacket.*)

BIFF: Why didn't you ever write me about this, Mom?

LINDA: How would I write to you? For over three months

1110 you had no address.

BIFF: I was on the move. But you know I thought of you all the time. You know that, don't you, pal?

LINDA: I know, dear, I know. But he likes to have a letter. Just to know that there's still a possibility for better things.

1115 BIFF: He's not like this all the time, is he?

LINDA: It's when you come home he's always the worst.

BIFF: When I come home?

LINDA: When you write you're coming, he's all smiles, and talks about the future, and—he's just wonderful. And then

1120 the closer you seem to come, the more shaky he gets, and then, by the time you get here, he's arguing, and he seems angry at you. I think it's just that maybe he can't bring himself to—to open up to you. Why are you so hateful to each other? Why is that?

1125 BIFF: (*Evasively.*) I'm not hateful, Mom.

LINDA: But you no sooner come in the door than you're fighting!

BIFF: I don't know why. I mean to change. I'm tryin', Mom, you understand?

1130 LINDA: Are you home to stay now?

BIFF: I don't know. I want to look around, see what's doin'.

LINDA: Biff, you can't look around all your life, can you?

BIFF: I just can't take hold, Mom. I can't take hold of some kind of a life.

1135 LINDA: Biff, a man is not a bird, to come and go with the springtime.

BIFF: Your hair . . . (*He touches her hair.*) Your hair got so gray.

LINDA: Oh, it's been gray since you were in high school. I just stopped dyeing it, that's all.

1140 BIFF: Dye it again, will ya? I don't want my pal looking old. (*He smiles.*)

LINDA: You're such a boy! You think you can go away for a year and . . . You've got to get it into your head now that one day you'll knock on this door and there'll be strange

1145 people here—

BIFF: What are you talking about? You're not even sixty, Mom.

LINDA: But what about your father?

BIFF: (*Lamely.*) Well, I meant him too.

1150 HAPPY: He admires Pop.

LINDA: Biff, dear, if you don't have any feeling for him, then you can't have any feeling for me.

BIFF: Sure I can, Mom.

LINDA: No. You can't just come to see me, because I love

1155 him. (*With a threat, but only a threat, of tears.*) He's the dearest man in the world to me, and I won't have anyone making him feel unwanted and low and blue. You've got to

make up your mind now, darling, there's no leeway any more. Either he's your father and you pay him that re-

1160 spect, or else you're not to come here. I know he's not easy to get along with—nobody knows that better than me—but . . .

WILLY: (*From the left, with a laugh.*) Hey, hey, Biffo!

BIFF: (*Starting to go out after* WILLY.) What the hell is the mat-

1165 ter with him? (HAPPY *stops him.*)

LINDA: Don't—don't go near him!

BIFF: Stop making excuses for him! He always, always wiped the floor with you. Never had an ounce of respect for you.

1170 HAPPY: He's always had respect for—

BIFF: What the hell do you know about it?

HAPPY: (*Surlily.*) Just don't call him crazy!

BIFF: He's got no character—Charley wouldn't do this. Not in his own house—spewing out that vomit from his mind.

1175 HAPPY: Charley never had to cope with what he's got to.

BIFF: People are worse off than Willy Loman. Believe me, I've seen them!

LINDA: Then make Charley your father, Biff. You can't do that, can you? I don't say he's a great man. Willy Loman

1180 never made a lot of money. His name was never in the paper. He's not the finest character that ever lived. But he's a human being, and a terrible thing is happening to him. So attention must be paid. He's not to be allowed to fall into his grave like an old dog. Attention, attention must

1185 finally be paid to such a person. You called him crazy—

BIFF: I didn't mean—

LINDA: No, a lot of people think he's lost his—balance. But you don't have to be very smart to know what his trouble is. The man is exhausted.

1190 HAPPY: Sure!

LINDA: A small man can be just as exhausted as a great man. He works for a company thirty-six years this March, opens up unheard-of territories to their trademark, and now in his old age they take his salary away.

1195 HAPPY: (*Indignantly.*) I didn't know that, Mom.

LINDA: You never asked, my dear! Now that you get your spending money someplace else you don't trouble your mind with him.

HAPPY: But I gave you money last—

1200 LINDA: Christmas time, fifty dollars! To fix the hot water it cost ninety-seven fifty! For five weeks he's been on straight commission, like a beginner, an unknown!

BIFF: Those ungrateful bastards!

LINDA: Are they any worse than his sons? When he brought

1205 them business, when he was young, they were glad to see him. But now his old friends, the old buyers that loved him so and always found some order to hand him in a pinch—they're all dead, retired. He used to be able to make six, seven calls a day in Boston. Now he takes his valises out of

1210 the car and puts them back and takes them out again and he's exhausted. Instead of walking he talks now. He drives seven hundred miles, and when he gets there no one knows him any more, no one welcomes him. And what goes through a man's mind, driving seven hundred miles home

1215 without having earned a cent? Why shouldn't he talk to himself? Why? When he has to go to Charley and borrow fifty dollars a week and pretend to me that it's his pay? How long can that go on? How long? You see what I'm sitting

1220 here and waiting for? And you tell me he has no character? The man who never worked a day but for your benefit? When does he get the medal for that? Is this his reward—to turn around at the age of sixty-three and find his sons, who he loved better than his life, one a philandering bum—

HAPPY: Mom!

1225 LINDA: That's all you are, my baby! (*To* BIFF.) And you! What happened to the love you had for him? You were such pals! How you used to talk to him on the phone every night! How lonely he was till he could come home to you!

BIFF: All right, Mom. I'll live here in my room, and I'll get a

1230 job. I'll keep away from him, that's all.

LINDA: No, Biff. You can't stay here and fight all the time.

BIFF: He threw me out of this house, remember that.

LINDA: Why did he do that? I never knew why.

BIFF: Because I know he's a fake and he doesn't like anybody

1235 around who knows!

LINDA: Why a fake? In what way? What do you mean?

BIFF: Just don't lay it all at my feet. It's between me and him—that's all I have to say. I'll chip in from now on. He'll settle for half my pay check. He'll be all right. I'm going to

1240 bed. (*He starts for the stairs.*)

LINDA: He won't be all right.

BIFF: (*Turning on the stairs, furiously.*) I hate this city and I'll stay here. Now what do you want?

LINDA: He's dying, Biff.

(HAPPY *turns quickly to her, shocked.*)

1245 BIFF: (*After a pause.*) Why is he dying?

LINDA: He's been trying to kill himself.

BIFF: (*With great horror.*) How?

LINDA: I live from day to day.

BIFF: What're you talking about?

1250 LINDA: Remember I wrote you that he smashed up the car again? In February?

BIFF: Well?

LINDA: The insurance inspector came. He said that they have evidence. That all these accidents in the last year—

1255 weren't—weren't—accidents.

HAPPY: How can they tell that? That's a lie.

LINDA: It seems there's a woman . . . (*She takes a breath as*

⌠ BIFF: (*Sharply but contained.*) What woman?

⌡ LINDA: (*Simultaneously.*) . . . and this woman . . .

1260 LINDA: What?

BIFF: Nothing. Go ahead.

LINDA: What did you say?

BIFF: Nothing. I just said what woman?

HAPPY: What about her?

1265 LINDA: Well, it seems she was walking down the road and saw his car. She says that he wasn't driving fast at all, and that he didn't skid. She says he came to that little bridge, and then deliberately smashed into the railing, and it was only the shallowness of the water that saved him.

1270 BIFF: Oh, no, he probably just fell asleep again.

LINDA: I don't think he fell asleep.

BIFF: Why not?

LINDA: Last month . . . (*With great difficulty.*) Oh, boys, it's so hard to say a thing like this! He's just a big stupid man to

1275 you, but I tell you there's more good in him than in many other people. (*She chokes, wipes her eyes.*) I was looking for

a fuse. The lights blew out, and I went down the cellar. And behind the fuse box—it happened to fall out—was a length of rubber pipe—just short.

HAPPY: No kidding? 1280

LINDA: There's a little attachment on the end of it. I knew right away. And sure enough, on the bottom of the water heater there's a new little nipple on the gas pipe.

HAPPY: (*Angrily.*) That—jerk.

BIFF: Did you have it taken off? 1285

LINDA: I'm—I'm ashamed to. How can I mention it to him? Every day I go down and take away that little rubber pipe. But, when he comes home, I put it back where it was. How can I insult him that way? I don't know what to do. I live from day to day, boys. I tell you, I know every 1290 thought in his mind. It sounds so old-fashioned and silly, but I tell you he put his whole life into you and you've turned your backs on him. (*She is bent over in the chair, weeping, her face in her hands.*) Biff, I swear to God! Biff, his life is in your hands! 1295

HAPPY: (*To* BIFF.) How do you like that damned fool!

BIFF: (*Kissing her.*) All right, pal, all right. It's all settled now. I've been remiss. I know that, Mom. But now I'll stay, and I swear to you, I'll apply myself. (*Kneeling in front of her, in a fever of self-reproach.*) It's just—you see, Mom, I don't fit in 1300 business. Not that I won't try. I'll try, and I'll make good.

HAPPY: Sure you will. The trouble with you in business was you never tried to please people.

BIFF: I know, I—

HAPPY: Like when you worked for Harrison's. Bob Harrison 1305 said you were tops, and then you go and do some damn fool thing like whistling whole songs in the elevator like a comedian.

BIFF: (*Against* HAPPY.) So what? I like to whistle sometimes.

HAPPY: You don't raise a guy to a responsible job who whis- 1310 tles in the elevator!

LINDA: Well, don't argue about it now.

HAPPY: Like when you'd go off and swim in the middle of the day instead of taking the line around.

BIFF: (*His resentment rising.*) Well, don't you run off? You take 1315 off sometimes, don't you? On a nice summer day?

HAPPY: Yeah, but I cover myself!

LINDA: Boys!

HAPPY: If I'm going to take a fade the boss can call any number where I'm supposed to be and they'll swear to him 1320 that I just left. I'll tell you something that I hate to say, Biff, but in the business world some of them think you're crazy.

BIFF: (*Angered.*) Screw the business world!

HAPPY: All right, screw it! Great, but cover yourself!

LINDA: Hap, Hap! 1325

BIFF: I don't care what they think! They've laughed at Dad for years, and you know why? Because we don't belong in this nuthouse of a city! We should be mixing cement on some open plain, or—or carpenters. A carpenter is allowed to whistle! 1330

(WILLY *walks in from the entrance of the house, at left.*)

WILLY: Even your grandfather was better than a carpenter. (*Pause. They watch him.*) You never grew up. Bernard does not whistle in the elevator, I assure you.

BIFF: (*As though to laugh* WILLY *out of it.*) Yeah, but you do, Pop.

1335 WILLY: I never in my life whistled in an elevator! And who in the business world thinks I'm crazy?

BIFF: I didn't mean it like that, Pop. Now don't make a whole thing out of it, will ya?

WILLY: Go back to the West! Be a carpenter, a cowboy, enjoy
1340 yourself!

LINDA: Willy, he was just saying—

WILLY: I heard what he said!

HAPPY: (*Trying to quiet* WILLY.) Hey, Pop, come on now . . .

WILLY: (*Continuing over* HAPPY's *line.*) They laugh at me, heh?
1345 Go to Filene's, go to the Hub, go to Slattery's, Boston. Call out the name Willy Loman and see what happens! Big shot!

BIFF: All right, Pop.

WILLY: Big!

1350 BIFF: All right!

WILLY: Why do you always insult me?

BIFF: I didn't say a word. (*To* LINDA.) Did I say a word?

LINDA: He didn't say anything, Willy.

WILLY: (*Going to the doorway of the living-room.*) All right, good
1355 night, good night.

LINDA: Willy, dear, he just decided . . .

WILLY: (*To* BIFF.) If you get tired hanging around tomorrow, paint the ceiling I put up in the living-room.

BIFF: I'm leaving early tomorrow.

1360 HAPPY: He's going to see Bill Oliver, Pop.

WILLY: (*Interestedly.*) Oliver? For what?

BIFF: (*With reserve, but trying, trying.*) He always said he'd stake me. I'd like to go into business, so maybe I can take him up on it.

1365 LINDA: Isn't that wonderful?

WILLY: Don't interrupt. What's wonderful about it? There's fifty men in the City of New York who'd stake him. (*To* BIFF.) Sporting goods?

BIFF: I guess so. I know something about it and—

1370 WILLY: He knows something about it! You know sporting goods better than Spalding, for God's sake! How much he giving you?

BIFF: I don't know, I didn't even see him yet, but—

WILLY: Then what're you talkin' about?

1375 BIFF: (*Getting angry.*) Well, all I said was I'm gonna see him, that's all!

WILLY: (*Turning away.*) Ah, you're counting your chickens again.

BIFF: (*Starting left for the stairs.*) Oh, Jesus, I'm going to sleep!

1380 WILLY: (*Calling after him.*) Don't curse in this house!

BIFF: (*Turning.*) Since when did you get so clean?

HAPPY: (*Trying to stop them.*) Wait a . . .

WILLY: Don't use that language to me! I won't have it!

HAPPY: (*Grabbing* BIFF, *shouts.*) Wait a minute! I got an idea. I
1385 got a feasible idea. Come here, Biff, let's talk this over now, let's talk some sense here. When I was down in Florida last time, I thought of a great idea to sell sporting goods. It just came back to me. You and I, Biff—we have a line, the Loman Line. We train a couple of weeks, and put on
1390 a couple of exhibitions, see?

WILLY: That's an idea!

HAPPY: Wait! We form two basketball teams, see? Two water-polo teams. We play each other. It's a million dollars' worth of publicity. Two brothers, see? The Loman Broth-
1395 ers. Displays in the Royal Palms—all the hotels. And ban-ners over the ring and the basketball court: "Loman Brothers." Baby, we could sell sporting goods!

WILLY: That is a one-million-dollar idea!

LINDA: Marvelous!

BIFF: I'm in great shape as far as that's concerned.   1400

HAPPY: And the beauty of it is, Biff, it wouldn't be like a business. We'd be out playin' ball again.

BIFF: (*Enthused.*) Yeah, that's . . .

WILLY: Million-dollar . . .

HAPPY: And you wouldn't get fed up with it, Biff. It'd be the 1405
family again. There'd be the old honor, and comradeship, and if you wanted to go off for a swim or somethin'—well, you'd do it! Without some smart cooky gettin' up ahead of you!

WILLY: Lick the world! You guys together could absolutely 1410
lick the civilized world.

BIFF: I'll see Oliver tomorrow. Hap, if we could work that out . . .

LINDA: Maybe things are beginning to—

WILLY: (*Wildly enthused, to* LINDA.) Stop interrupting! (*To* BIFF.) 1415
But don't wear sport jacket and slacks when you see Oliver.

BIFF: No, I'll—

WILLY: A business suit, and talk as little as possible, and don't crack any jokes.

BIFF: He did like me. Always liked me.   1420

LINDA: He loved you!

WILLY: (*To* LINDA.) Will you stop! (*To* BIFF.) Walk in very se-rious. You are not applying for a boy's job. Money is to pass. Be quiet, fine, and serious. Everybody likes a kidder, but nobody lends him money.   1425

HAPPY: I'll try to get some myself, Biff. I'm sure I can.

WILLY: I see great things for you kids, I think your troubles are over. But remember, start big and you'll end big. Ask for fifteen. How much you gonna ask for?

BIFF: Gee, I don't know—   1430

WILLY: And don't say "Gee." "Gee" is a boy's word. A man walking in for fifteen thousand dollars does not say "Gee!"

BIFF: Ten, I think, would be top though.

WILLY: Don't be so modest. You always started too low. Walk in with a big laugh. Don't look worried. Start off with a 1435
couple of your good stories to lighten things up. It's not what you say, it's how you say it—because personality al-ways wins the day.

LINDA: Oliver always thought the highest of him—

WILLY: Will you let me talk?   1440

BIFF: Don't yell at her, Pop, will ya?

WILLY: (*Angrily.*) I was talking, wasn't I?

BIFF: I don't like you yelling at her all the time, and I'm tellin' you, that's all.

WILLY: What're you, takin' over this house?   1445

LINDA: Willy—

WILLY: (*Turning on her.*) Don't take his side all the time, god-dammit!

BIFF: (*Furiously.*) Stop yelling at her!

WILLY: (*Suddenly pulling on his cheek, beaten down, guilt ridden.*) 1450
Give my best to Bill Oliver—he may remember me. (*He exits through the living-room doorway.*)

LINDA: (*Her voice subdued.*) What'd you have to start that for? (BIFF *turns away.*) You see how sweet he was as soon as you talked hopefully? (*She goes over to* BIFF.) Come up and say 1455
good night to him. Don't let him go to bed that way.

HAPPY: Come on, Biff, let's buck him up.

LINDA: Please, dear. Just say good night. It takes so little to make him happy. Come. (*She goes through the living-room doorway, calling upstairs from within the living-room.*) Your pajamas are hanging in the bathroom, Willy!

HAPPY: (*Looking toward where* LINDA *went out.*) What a woman! They broke the mold when they made her. You know that, Biff?

BIFF: He's off salary. My God, working on commission!

HAPPY: Well, let's face it: he's no hot-shot selling man. Except that sometimes, you have to admit, he's a sweet personality.

BIFF: (*Deciding.*) Lend me ten bucks, will ya? I want to buy some new ties.

HAPPY: I'll take you to a place I know. Beautiful stuff. Wear one of my striped shirts tomorrow.

BIFF: She got gray. Mom got awful old. Gee, I'm gonna go in to Oliver tomorrow and knock him for a—

HAPPY: Come on up. Tell that to Dad. Let's give him a whirl. Come on.

BIFF: (*Steamed up.*) You know, with ten thousand bucks, boy!

HAPPY: (*As they go into the living-room.*) That's the talk, Biff, that's the first time I've heard the old confidence out of you! (*From within the living-room, fading off.*) You gonna live with me, kid, and any babe you want just say the word . . . (*The last lines are hardly heard. They are mounting the stairs to their parents' bedroom.*)

LINDA: (*Entering her bedroom and addressing* WILLY, *who is in the bathroom. She is straightening the bed for him.*) Can you do anything about the shower? It drips.

WILLY: (*From the bathroom.*) All of a sudden everything falls to pieces! Goddam plumbing, oughta be sued, those people. I hardly finished putting it in and the thing . . . (*His words rumble off.*)

LINDA: I'm just wondering if Oliver will remember him. You think he might?

WILLY: (*Coming out of the bathroom in his pajamas.*) Remember him? What's the matter with you, you crazy? If he'd've stayed with Oliver he'd be on top by now! Wait'll Oliver gets a look at him. You don't know the average caliber any more. The average young man today—(*He is getting into bed.*)—is got a caliber of zero. Greatest thing in the world for him was to bum around.

(BIFF *and* HAPPY *enter the bedroom. Slight pause.*)

WILLY: (*Stops short, looking at* BIFF.) Glad to hear it, boy.

HAPPY: He wanted to say good night to you, sport.

WILLY: (*To* BIFF.) Yeah. Knock him dead, boy. What'd you want to tell me?

BIFF: Just take it easy, Pop. Good night. (*He turns to go.*)

WILLY: (*Unable to resist.*) And if anything falls off the desk while you're talking to him—like a package or something—don't you pick it up. They have office boys for that.

LINDA: I'll make a big breakfast—

WILLY: Will you let me finish? (*To* BIFF.) Tell him you were in the business in the West. Not farm work.

BIFF: All right, Dad.

LINDA: I think everything—

WILLY: (*Going right through her speech.*) And don't undersell yourself. No less than fifteen thousand dollars.

BIFF: (*Unable to bear him.*) Okay. Good night, Mom. (*He starts moving.*)

WILLY: Because you got a greatness in you, Biff, remember that. You got all kinds a greatness . . . (*He lies back, exhausted.* BIFF *walks out.*)

LINDA: (*Calling after* BIFF.) Sleep well, darling!

HAPPY: I'm gonna get married, Mom. I wanted to tell you.

LINDA: Go to sleep, dear.

HAPPY: (*Going.*) I just wanted to tell you.

WILLY: Keep up the good work. (HAPPY *exits.*) God . . . remember that Ebbets Field game? The championship of the city?

LINDA: Just rest. Should I sing to you?

WILLY: Yeah. Sing to me. (LINDA *hums a soft lullaby.*) When that team came out—he was the tallest, remember?

LINDA: Oh, yes. And in gold.

(BIFF *enters the darkened kitchen, takes a cigarette, and leaves the house. He comes downstage into a golden pool of light. He smokes, staring at the night.*)

WILLY: Like a young god. Hercules—something like that. And the sun, the sun all around him. Remember how he waved to me? Right up from the field, with the representatives of three colleges standing by? And the buyers I brought, and the cheers when he came out—Loman, Loman, Loman! God Almighty, he'll be great yet. A star like that, magnificent, can never really fade away!

(*The light on* WILLY *is fading. The gas heater begins to glow through the kitchen wall, near the stairs, a blue flame beneath red coils.*)

LINDA: (*Timidly.*) Willy dear, what has he got against you?

WILLY: I'm so tired. Don't talk any more.

(BIFF *slowly returns to the kitchen. He stops, stares toward the heater.*)

LINDA: Will you ask Howard to let you work in New York?

WILLY: First thing in the morning. Everything'll be all right.

(BIFF *reaches behind the heater and draws out a length of rubber tubing. He is horrified and turns his head toward* WILLY's *room, still dimly lit, from which the strains of* LINDA's *desperate but monotonous humming rise.*)

WILLY: (*Staring through the window into the moonlight.*) Gee, look at the moon moving between the buildings!

(BIFF *wraps the tubing around his hand and quickly goes up the stairs.*)

(*Curtain.*)

ACT TWO

Music is heard, gay and bright. The curtain rises as the music fades away. WILLY, *in shirt sleeves, is sitting at the kitchen table, sipping coffee, his hat in his lap.* LINDA *is filling his cup when she can.*

WILLY: Wonderful coffee. Meal in itself.

LINDA: Can I make you some eggs?

WILLY: No. Take a breath.

LINDA: You look so rested, dear.

5 WILLY: I slept like a dead one. First time in months. Image, sleeping till ten on a Tuesday morning. Boys left nice and early, heh?

LINDA: They were out of here by eight o'clock.

WILLY: Good work!

10 LINDA: It was so thrilling to see them leaving together. I can't get over the shaving lotion in this house!

WILLY: (*Smiling.*) Mmm—

LINDA: Biff was very changed this morning. His whole attitude seemed to be hopeful. He couldn't wait to get down-

15   town to see Oliver.

WILLY: He's heading for a change. There's no question, there simply are certain men that take longer to get—solidified. How did he dress?

LINDA: His blue suit. He's so handsome in that suit. He could

20   be a—anything in that suit!

(WILLY *gets up from the table.* LINDA *holds his jacket for him.*)

WILLY: There's no question, no question at all. Gee, on the way home tonight I'd like to buy some seeds.

LINDA: (*Laughing.*) That'd be wonderful. But not enough sun gets back there. Nothing'll grow any more.

25 WILLY: You wait, kid, before it's all over we're gonna get a little place out in the country, and I'll raise some vegetables, a couple of chickens . . .

LINDA: You'll do it yet, dear.

(WILLY *walks out of his jacket.* LINDA *follows him.*)

WILLY: And they'll get married, and come for a weekend. I'd

30   build a little guest house. 'Cause I got so many fine tools, all I'd need would be a little lumber and some peace of mind.

LINDA: (*Joyfully.*) I sewed the lining . . .

WILLY: I could build two guest houses, so they'd both come.

35   Did he decide how much he's going to ask Oliver for?

LINDA: (*Getting him into the jacket.*) He didn't mention it, but I imagine ten or fifteen thousand. You going to talk to Howard today?

WILLY: Yeah. I'll put it to him straight and simple. He'll just

40   have to take me off the road.

LINDA: And Willy, don't forget to ask for a little advance, because we've got the insurance premium. It's the grace period now.

WILLY: That's a hundred . . .?

45 LINDA: A hundred and eight, sixty-eight. Because we're a little short again.

WILLY: Why are we short?

LINDA: Well, you had the motor job on the car . . .

WILLY: That goddam Studebaker!

50 LINDA: And you got one more payment on the refrigerator . . .

WILLY: But it just broke again!

LINDA: Well, it's old, dear.

WILLY: I told you we should've bought a well-advertised machine. Charley bought a General Electric and it's twenty

55   years old and it's still good, that son-of-a-bitch.

LINDA: But, Willy—

WILLY: Whoever heard of a Hastings refrigerator? Once in my life I would like to own something outright before it's broken! I'm always in a race with the junkyard! I just fin-

60   ished paying for the car and it's on its last legs. The refrigerator consumes belts like a goddam maniac. They time those things. They time them so when you finally paid for them, they're used up.

LINDA: (*Buttoning up his jacket as he unbuttons it.*) All told, about two hundred dollars would carry us, dear. But that

65   includes the last payment on the mortgage. After this payment, Willy, the house belongs to us.

WILLY: It's twenty-five years!

LINDA: Biff was nine years old when we bought it.

WILLY: Well, that's a great thing. To weather a twenty-five

70   year mortgage is—

LINDA: It's an accomplishment.

WILLY: All the cement, the lumber, the reconstruction I put in this house! There ain't a crack to be found in it any

75   more.

LINDA: Well, it served its purpose.

WILLY: What purpose? Some stranger'll come along, move in, and that's that. If only Biff would take this house, and raise a family . . . (*He starts to go.*) Good-by, I'm late.

80 LINDA: (*Suddenly remembering.*) Oh, I forgot! You're supposed to meet them for dinner.

WILLY: Me?

LINDA: At Frank's Chop House on Forty-eighth near Sixth Avenue.

85 WILLY: Is that so! How about you?

LINDA: No, just the three of you. They're gonna blow you to a big meal!

WILLY: Don't say! Who thought of that?

LINDA: Biff came to me this morning, Willy, and he said, "Tell

90   Dad, we want to blow him to a big meal." Be there six o'clock. You and your two boys are going to have dinner.

WILLY: Gee whiz! That's really somethin'. I'm gonna knock Howard for a loop, kid. I'll get an advance, and I'll come home with a New York job. Goddammit, now I'm gonna

95   do it!

LINDA: Oh, that's the spirit, Willy!

WILLY: I will never get behind a wheel the rest of my life!

LINDA: It's changing, Willy, I can feel it changing!

WILLY: Beyond a question. G'by, I'm late. (*He starts to go*

100 *again.*)

LINDA: (*Calling after him as she runs to the kitchen table for a handkerchief.*) You got your glasses?

WILLY: (*Feels for them, then comes back in.*) Yeah, yeah, got my glasses.

105 LINDA: (*Giving him the handkerchief.*) And a handkerchief.

WILLY: Yeah, handkerchief.

LINDA: And your saccharine?

WILLY: Yeah, my saccharine.

LINDA: Be careful on the subway stairs.

(*She kisses him, and a silk stocking is seen hanging from her hand.* WILLY *notices it.*)

110 WILLY: Will you stop mending stockings? At least while I'm in the house. It gets me nervous. I can't tell you. Please.

(LINDA *hides the stocking in her hand as she follows* WILLY *across the forestage in front of the house.*)

LINDA: Remember, Frank's Chop House.
WILLY: (*Passing the apron.*) Maybe beets would grow out there.
115 LINDA: (*Laughing.*) But you tried so many times.
WILLY: Yeah. Well, don't work hard today. (*He disappears around the right corner of the house.*)
LINDA: Be careful!

(*As* WILLY *vanishes,* LINDA *waves to him. Suddenly the phone rings. She runs across the stage and into the kitchen and lifts it.*)

120 LINDA: Hello? Oh, Biff! I'm so glad you called, I just . . . Yes, sure, I just told him. Yes, he'll be there for dinner at six o'clock, I didn't forget. Listen, I was just dying to tell you. You know that little rubber pipe I told you about? That he connected to the gas heater? I finally decided to go
125 down the cellar this morning and take it away and destroy it. But it's gone! Imagine? He took it away himself, it isn't there! (*She listens.*) When? Oh, then you took it. Oh—nothing, it's just that I'd hoped he'd taken it away himself. Oh, I'm not worried, darling, because this morn-
130 ing he left in such high spirits, it was like the old days! I'm not afraid any more. Did Mr. Oliver see you? . . . Well, you wait there then. And make a nice impression on him, dar-ling. Just don't perspire too much before you see him. And have a nice time with Dad. He may have big news
135 too! . . . That's right, a New York job. And be sweet to him tonight, dear. Be loving to him. Because he's only a little boat looking for a harbor. (*She is trembling with sorrow and joy.*) Oh, that's wonderful, Biff, you'll save his life. Thanks, darling. Just put your arm around him when he comes
140 into the restaurant. Give him a smile. That's the boy . . . Good-by, dear, . . . You got your comb? . . . That's fine. Good-by, Biff dear.

(*In the middle of her speech,* HOWARD WAGNER, *thirty-six, wheels on a small typewriter table on which is a wire-recording machine and proceeds to plug it in. This is on the left forestage. Light slowly fades on* LINDA *as it rises on* HOWARD. HOWARD *is intent on threading the machine and only glances over his shoulder as* WILLY *appears.*)

WILLY: Pst! Pst!
HOWARD: Hello, Willy, come in.
145 WILLY: Like to have a little talk with you, Howard.
HOWARD: Sorry to keep you waiting. I'll be with you in a minute.
WILLY: What's that, Howard?
HOWARD: Didn't you ever see one of these? Wire recorder.
150 WILLY: Oh. Can we talk a minute?
HOWARD: Records things. Just got delivery yesterday. Been driving me crazy, the most terrific machine I ever saw in my life. I was up all night with it.
WILLY: What do you do with it.
155 HOWARD: I bought it for dictation, but you can do anything with it. Listen to this. I had it home last night. Listen to what I picked up. The first one is my daughter. Get this. (*He flicks the switch and "Roll out the Barrel" is heard being whistled.*) Listen to that kid whistle.
160 WILLY: That is lifelike, isn't it?
HOWARD: Seven years old. Get that tone.
WILLY: Ts, ts. Like to ask a little favor if you . . .

(*The whistling breaks off, and the voice of* HOWARD's *daughter is heard.*)

HIS DAUGHTER: "Now you, Daddy."
HOWARD: She's crazy for me! (*Again the same song is whistled.*) That's me! Ha! (*He winks.*) 165
WILLY: You're very good!

(*The whistling breaks off again. The machine runs silent a moment.*)

HOWARD: Sh! Get this now, this is my son.
HIS SON: "The capital of Alabama is Montgomery; the capi-tal of Arizona is Phoenix; the capital of Arkansas is Little Rock; the capital of California is Sacramento . . . (*And on,* 170 *and on.*)
HOWARD: (*Holding up five fingers.*) Five years old, Willy!
WILLY: He'll make an announcer some day!
HIS SON: (*Continuing.*) "The capital . . ."
HOWARD: Get that—alphabetical order! (*The machine breaks* 175 *off suddenly.*) Wait a minute. The maid kicked the plug out.
WILLY: It certainly is a—
HOWARD: Sh, for God's sake!
HIS SON: "It's nine o'clock, Bulova watch time. So I have to go to sleep." 180
WILLY: That really is—
HOWARD: Wait a minute! The next is my wife.

(*They wait.*)

HOWARD's VOICE: "Go on, say something." (*Pause.*) "Well, you gonna talk?"
HIS WIFE: "I can't think of anything." 185
HOWARD's VOICE: "Well, talk—it's turning."
HIS WIFE: (*Shyly, beaten.*) "Hello." (*Silence.*) "Oh, Howard, I can't talk into this . . ."
HOWARD: (*Snapping the machine off.*) That was my wife.
WILLY: That is a wonderful machine. Can we— 190
HOWARD: I tell you, Willy, I'm gonna take my camera, and my bandsaw, and all my hobbies, and out they go. This is the most fascinating relaxation I ever found.
WILLY: I think I'll get one myself.
HOWARD: Sure, they're only a hundred and a half. You can't 195 do without it. Supposing you wanna hear Jack Benny, see? But you can't be at home at that hour. So you tell the maid to turn the radio on when Jack Benny comes on, and this automatically goes on with the radio . . .
WILLY: And when you come home you . . . 200
HOWARD: You can come home twelve o'clock, one o'clock, any time you like, and you get yourself a Coke and sit yourself down, throw the switch, and there's Jack Benny's program in the middle of the night!
WILLY: I'm definitely going to get one. Because lots of time 205 I'm on the road, and I think to myself, what I must be missing on the radio!
HOWARD: Don't you have a radio in the car?
WILLY: Well, yeah, but who ever thinks of turning it on?
HOWARD: Say, aren't you supposed to be in Boston? 210
WILLY: That's what I want to talk to you about, Howard. You got a minute? (*He draws a chair in from the wing.*)
HOWARD: What happened? What're you doing here?
WILLY: Well . . .
HOWARD: You didn't crack up again, did you? 215

WILLY: Oh, no. No . . .

HOWARD: Geez, you had me worried there for a minute. What's the trouble?

WILLY: Well, tell you the truth, Howard. I've come to the de-
220   cision that I'd rather not travel any more.

HOWARD: Not travel! Well, what'll you do?

WILLY: Remember, Christmas time, when you had the party here? You said you'd try to think of some spot for me here in town.

225 HOWARD: With us?

WILLY: Well, sure.

HOWARD: Oh, yeah, yeah. I remember. Well, I couldn't think of anything for you, Willy.

WILLY: I tell ya, Howard. The kids are all grown up, y'know.
230   I don't need much any more. If I could take home—well, sixty-five dollars a week, I could swing it.

HOWARD: Yeah, but Willy, see I—

WILLY: I tell ya why, Howard. Speaking frankly and between the two of us, y'know—I'm just a little tired.

235 HOWARD: Oh, I could understand that, Willy. But you're a road man, Willy, and we do a road business. We've only got a half-dozen salesmen on the floor here.

WILLY: God knows, Howard, I never asked a favor of any man. But I was with the firm when your father used to
240   carry you in here in his arms.

HOWARD: I know that, Willy, but—

WILLY: Your father came to me the day you were born and asked me what I thought of the name of Howard, may he rest in peace.

245 HOWARD: I appreciate that, Willy, but there just is no spot here for you. If I had a spot I'd slam you right in, but I just don't have a single solitary spot.

(*He looks for his lighter.* WILLY *has picked it up and gives it to him. Pause.*)

WILLY: (*With increasing anger.*) Howard, all I need to set my
250   table is fifty dollars a week.

HOWARD: But where am I going to put you, kid?

WILLY: Look, it isn't a question of whether I can sell merchandise, is it?

HOWARD: No, but it's a business, kid, and everybody's gotta
255   pull his own weight.

WILLY: (*Desperately.*) Just let me tell you a story, Howard—

HOWARD: 'Cause you gotta admit, business is business.

WILLY: (*Angrily.*) Business is definitely business, but just listen for a minute. You don't understand this. When I was a
260   boy—eighteen, nineteen—I was already on the road. And there was a question in my mind as to whether selling had a future for me. Because in those days I had a yearning to go to Alaska. See, there were three gold strikes in one month in Alaska, and I felt like going out. Just for the ride
265   you might say.

HOWARD: (*Barely interested.*) Don't say.

WILLY: Oh, yeah, my father lived many years in Alaska. He was an adventurous man. We've got quite a little streak of self-reliance in our family. I thought I'd go out with my older
270   brother and try to locate him, and maybe settle in the North with the old man. And I was almost decided to go, when I met a salesman in the Parker House. His name was Dave Singleman. And he was eighty-four years old, and

he'd drummed merchandise in thirty-one states. And old Dave, he'd go up to his room, y'understand, put on his   275
green velvet slippers—I'll never forget—and pick up his phone and call the buyers, and without ever leaving his room, at the age of eighty-four, he made his living. And when I saw that, I realized that selling was the greatest career a man could want. 'Cause what could be more satisfy-   280
ing than to be able to go, at the age of eighty-four, into twenty or thirty different cities, and pick up a phone, and be remembered and loved and helped by so many different people? Do you know? when he died—and by the way he died the death of a salesman, in his green velvet slippers in   285
the smoker of the New York, New Haven and Hartford, going into Boston—when he died, hundreds of salesmen and buyers were at his funeral. Things were sad on a lotta trains for months after that. (*He stands up.* HOWARD *has not looked at him.*) In those days there was personality in it,   290
Howard. There was respect, and comradeship, and gratitude in it. Today, it's all cut and dried, and there's no chance for bringing friendship to bear—or personality. You see what I mean? They don't know me any more.

HOWARD: (*Moving away, to the right.*) That's just the thing,   295
Willy.

WILLY: If I had forty dollars a week—that's all I'd need. Forty dollars, Howard.

HOWARD: Kid, I can't take blood from a stone, I—

WILLY: (*Desperation is on him now.*) Howard, the year Al Smith   300
was nominated, your father came to me and—

HOWARD: (*Starting to go off.*) I've got to see some people, kid.

WILLY: (*Stopping him.*) I'm talking about your father! There were promises made across this desk! You mustn't tell me you've got people to see—I put thirty-four years into this   305
firm, Howard, and now I can't pay my insurance! You can't eat the orange and throw the peel away—a man is not a piece of fruit! (*After a pause.*) Now pay attention. Your father—in 1928 I had a big year. I averaged a hundred and seventy dollars a week in commissions.   310

HOWARD: (*Impatiently.*) Now, Willy, you never averaged—

WILLY: (*Banging his hand on the desk.*) I averaged a hundred and seventy dollars a week in the year of 1928! And your father came to me—or rather, I was in the office here—it was right over this desk—and he put his hand on my   315
shoulder—

HOWARD: (*Getting up.*) You'll have to excuse me, Willy, I gotta see some people. Pull yourself together. (*Going out.*) I'll be back in a little while.

(*On* HOWARD's *exit, the light on his chair grows very bright and strange.*)

WILLY: Pull myself together! What the hell did I say to him?   320
My God, I was yelling at him! How could I! (WILLY *breaks off, staring at the light, which occupies the chair, animating it. He approaches this chair, standing across the desk from it.*) Frank, Frank, don't you remember what you told me that time? How you put your hand on my shoulder, and Frank . . .   325
(*He leans on the desk and as he speaks the dead man's name he accidentally switches on the recorder, and instantly.*)

HOWARD'S SON: ". . . of New York is Albany. The capital of Ohio is Cincinnati, the capital of Rhode Island is . . ." (*The recitation continues.*)   330

WILLY: (*Leaping away with fright, shouting.*) Ha! Howard! Howard! Howard!

HOWARD: (*Rushing in.*) What happened?

340 WILLY: (*Pointing at the machine, which continues nasally, childishly, with the capital cities.*) Shut it off! Shut it off!

HOWARD: (*Pulling the plug out.*) Look, Willy . . .

WILLY: (*Pressing his hands to his eyes.*) I gotta get myself some coffee. I'll get some coffee . . .

(WILLY *starts to walk out.* HOWARD *stops him.*)

HOWARD: (*Rolling up the cord.*) Willy, look . . .

345 WILLY: I'll go to Boston.

HOWARD: Willy, you can't go to Boston for us.

WILLY: Why can't I go?

HOWARD: I don't want you to represent us. I've been meaning to tell you for a long time now.

350 WILLY: Howard, are you firing me?

HOWARD: I think you need a good long rest, Willy.

WILLY: Howard—

HOWARD: And when you feel better, come back, and we'll see if we can work something out.

355 WILLY: But I gotta earn money, Howard. I'm in no position to—

HOWARD: Where are your sons? Why don't your sons give you a hand?

WILLY: They're working on a very big deal.

360 HOWARD: This is no time for false pride, Willy. You go to your sons and you tell them that you're tired. You've got two great boys, haven't you?

WILLY: Oh, no question, no question, but in the meantime . . .

HOWARD: Then that's that, heh?

365 WILLY: All right, I'll go to Boston tomorrow.

HOWARD: No, no.

WILLY: I can't throw myself on my sons. I'm not a cripple!

HOWARD: Look, kid, I'm busy this morning.

WILLY: (*Grasping* HOWARD's *arm.*) Howard, you've got to let

370 me go to Boston!

HOWARD: (*Hard, keeping himself under control.*) I've got a line of people to see this morning. Sit down, take five minutes, and pull yourself together, and then go home, will ya? I need the office, Willy. (*He starts to go, turns, remembering the*

375 *recorder, starts to push off the table holding the recorder.*) Oh, yeah. Whenever you can this week, stop by and drop off the samples. You'll feel better, Willy, and then come back and we'll talk. Pull yourself together, kid, there's people outside.

(HOWARD *exits, pushing the table off left.* WILLY *stares into space, exhausted. Now the music is heard*—BEN's *music—first distantly, then closer, closer. As* WILLY *speaks,* BEN *enters from the right. He carries valise and umbrella.*)

380 WILLY: Oh, Ben, how did you do it? What is the answer? Did you wind up the Alaska deal already?

BEN: Doesn't take much time if you know what you're doing. Just a short business trip. Boarding ship in an hour. Wanted to say good-by.

385 WILLY: Ben, I've got to talk to you.

BEN: (*Glancing at his watch.*) Haven't the time, William.

WILLY: (*Crossing the apron to Ben.*) Ben, nothing's working out. I don't know what to do.

BEN: Now, look here, William. I've bought timberland in Alaska and I need a man to look after things for me.   390

WILLY: God, timberland! Me and my boys in those grand outdoors!

BEN: You've a new continent at your doorstep, William. Get out of these cities, they're full of talk and time payments and courts of law. Screw on your fists and you can fight   395 for a fortune up there.

WILLY: Yes, yes! Linda, Linda!

(LINDA *enters as of old, with the wash.*)

LINDA: Oh, you're back?

BEN: I haven't much time.

WILLY: No, wait! Linda, he's got a proposition for me in   400 Alaska.

LINDA: But you've got— (*To* BEN.) He's got a beautiful job here.

WILLY: But in Alaska, kid, I could—

LINDA: You're doing well enough, Willy!   405

BEN: (*To* LINDA.) Enough for what, my dear?

LINDA: (*Frightened of* BEN *and angry at him.*) Don't say those things to him! Enough to be happy right here, right now. (*To* WILLY, *while* BEN *laughs.*) Why must everybody conquer the world? You're well liked, and the boys love you,   410 and someday—(*To* BEN.)—why, old man Wagner told him just the other day that if he keeps it up he'll be a member of the firm, didn't he, Willy?

WILLY: Sure, sure. I am building something with this firm, Ben, and if a man is building something he must be on the   415 right track, mustn't he?

BEN: What are you building? Lay your hand on it. Where is it?

WILLY: (*Hesitantly.*) That's true, Linda, there's nothing.

LINDA: Why? (*To* BEN.) There's a man eighty-four years old—

WILLY: That's right, Ben, that's right. When I look at that man   420 I say, what is there to worry about?

BEN: Bah!

WILLY: It's true, Ben. All he has to do is go into any city, pick up the phone, and he's making his living and you know why?   425

BEN: (*Picking up his valise.*) I've got to go.

WILLY: (*Holding* BEN *back.*) Look at this boy!

(BIFF, *in his high school sweater, enters carrying suitcase.* HAPPY *carries* BIFF's *shoulder guards, gold helmet, and football pants.*)

WILLY: Without a penny to his name, three great universities are begging for him, and from there the sky's the limit, because it's not what you do, Ben. It's who you know and   430 the smile on your face! It's contacts, Ben, contacts! The whole wealth of Alaska passes over the lunch table at the Commodore Hotel, and that's the wonder, the wonder of this country, that a man can end with diamonds here on the basis of being liked! (*He turns to* BIFF.) And that's why   435 when you get out on that field today it's important. Because thousands of people will be rooting for you and loving you. (*To* BEN, *who has again begun to leave.*) And Ben! when he walks into a business office his name will sound out like a bell and all the doors will open to him! I've seen   440 it, Ben, I've seen it a thousand times! You can't feel it with your hand like timber, but it's there!

BEN: Good-by, William.

WILLY: Ben, am I right? Don't you think I'm right? I value
445   your advice.
BEN: There's a new continent at your doorstep, William. You
      could walk out rich. Rich! (*He is gone.*)
WILLY: We'll do it here, Ben! You hear me? We're gonna do it
      here!

(*Young* BERNARD *rushes in. The gay music of the Boys is heard.*)

450 BERNARD: Oh, gee, I was afraid you left already!
WILLY: Why? What time is it?
BERNARD: It's half-past one!
WILLY: Well, come on, everybody! Ebbets Field next stop!
      Where's the pennants? (*He rushes through the wall-line of the*
455   *kitchen and out into the living-room.*)
LINDA: (*To* BIFF.) Did you pack fresh underwear?
BIFF: (*Who has been limbering up.*) I want to go!
BERNARD: Biff, I'm carrying your helmet, ain't I?
HAPPY: No, I'm carrying the helmet.
460 BERNARD: Oh, Biff, you promised me.
HAPPY: I'm carrying the helmet.
BERNARD: How am I going to get in the locker room?
LINDA: Let him carry the shoulder guards. (*She puts her coat*
      and hat on in the kitchen.)
465 BERNARD: Can I, Biff? 'Cause I told everybody I'm going to
      be in the locker room.
HAPPY: In Ebbets Field it's the clubhouse.
BERNARD: I meant the clubhouse. Biff!
HAPPY: Biff!
470 BIFF: (*Grandly, after a slight pause.*) Let him carry the shoulder
      guards.
HAPPY: (*As he gives* BERNARD *the shoulder guards.*) Stay close to
      us now.

(WILLY *rushes in with the pennants.*)

WILLY: (*Handing them out.*) Everybody wave when Biff comes
475   out on the field. (HAPPY *and* BERNARD *run off.*) You set
      now, boy?

(*The music has died away.*)

BIFF: Ready to go, Pop. Every muscle is ready.
WILLY: (*At the edge of the apron.*) You realize what this means?
BIFF: That's right, Pop.
480 WILLY: (*Feeling* BIFF's *muscles.*) You're comin' home this after-
      noon captain of the All-Scholastic Championship Team of
      the City of New York.
BIFF: I got it, Pop. And remember, pal, when I take off my
      helmet, that touchdown is for you.
485 WILLY: Let's go! (*He is starting out, with his arm around* BIFF,
      when CHARLEY *enters, as of old, in knickers.*) I got no room
      for you, Charley.
CHARLEY: Room? For what?
WILLY: In the car.
490 CHARLEY: You goin' for a ride? I wanted to shoot some
      casino.
WILLY: (*Furiously.*) Casino! (*Incredulously.*) Don't you realize
      what today is?
LINDA: Oh, he knows, Willy. He's just kidding you.
495 WILLY: That's nothing to kid about!
CHARLEY: No. Linda, what's goin' on?

LINDA: He's playing in Ebbets Field.
CHARLEY: Baseball in this weather?
WILLY: Don't talk to him. Come on, come on! (*He is pushing*
      them out.)   500
CHARLEY: Wait a minute, didn't you hear the news?
WILLY: What?
CHARLEY: Don't you listen to the radio? Ebbets Field just
      blew up.
WILLY: You go to hell! (CHARLEY *laughs. Pushing them out.*)   505
      Come on, come on! We're late.
CHARLEY: (*As they go.*) Knock a homer, Biff, knock a homer!
WILLY: (*The last to leave, turning to* CHARLEY.) I don't think
      that was funny, Charley. This is the greatest day of his life.
CHARLEY: Willy, when are you going to grow up?   510
WILLY: Yeah, heh? When this game is over, Charley, you'll be
      laughing out of the other side of your face. They'll be call-
      ing him another Red Grange. Twenty-five thousand a year.
CHARLEY: (*Kidding.*) Is that so?
WILLY: Yeah, that's so.   515
CHARLEY: Well, then, I'm sorry, Willy. But tell me something.
WILLY: What?
CHARLEY: Who is Red Grange?
WILLY: Put up your hands. Goddam you, put up your hands!

(CHARLEY, *chuckling, shakes his head and walks away, around the*
left corner of the stage. WILLY *follows him. The music rises to a*
mocking frenzy.)

WILLY: Who the hell do you think you are, better than every- 520
      body else? You don't know everything, you big, ignorant,
      stupid . . . Put up your hands!

(*Light rises, on the right side of the forestage, on a small table in the*
reception room of CHARLEY's *office. Traffic sounds are heard.*
BERNARD, *now mature, sits whistling to himself. A pair of tennis*
rackets and an overnight bag are on the floor beside him.)

WILLY: (*Offstage.*) What are you walking away for? Don't walk
      away! If you're going to say something say it to my face! I
      know you laugh at me behind my back. You'll laugh out   525
      of the other side of your goddam face after this game.
      Touchdown! Touchdown! Eighty thousand people!
      Touchdown! Right between the goal posts.

(BERNARD *is a quiet, earnest, but self-assured young man.* WILLY's
voice is coming from right upstage now. BERNARD *lowers his feet off*
the table and listens. JENNY, *his father's secretary, enters.*)

JENNY: (*Distressed.*) Say, Bernard, will you go out in the hall?
BERNARD: What is that noise? Who is it?   530
JENNY: Mr. Loman. He just got off the elevator.
BERNARD: (*Getting up.*) Who's he arguing with?
JENNY: Nobody. There's nobody with him. I can't deal with
      him any more, and your father gets all upset everytime he
      comes. I've got a lot of typing to do, and your father's   535
      waiting to sign it. Will you see him?
WILLY: (*Entering.*) Touchdown! Touch— (*He sees* JENNY.)
      Jenny, Jenny, good to see you. How're ya? Workin'? Or still
      honest?
JENNY: Fine. How've you been feeling?   540
WILLY: Not much any more, Jenny. Ha, ha! (*He is surprised to*
      see the rackets.)

BERNARD: Hello, Uncle Willy.

WILLY: (*Almost shocked.*) Bernard! Well, look who's here! (*He comes quickly, guiltily, to* BERNARD *and warmly shakes his hand.*)

BERNARD: How are you? Good to see you.

WILLY: What are you doing here?

BERNARD: Oh, just stopped by to see Pop. Get off my feet till my train leaves. I'm going to Washington in a few minutes.

WILLY: Is he in?

BERNARD: Yes, he's in his office with the accountant. Sit down.

WILLY: (*Sitting down.*) What're you going to do in Washington?

BERNARD: Oh, just a case I've got there, Willy.

WILLY: That so? (*Indicating the rackets.*) You going to play tennis there?

BERNARD: I'm staying with a friend who's got a court.

WILLY: Don't say. His own tennis court. Must be fine people, I bet.

BERNARD: They are, very nice. Dad tells me Biff's in town.

WILLY: (*With a big smile.*) Yeah, Biff's in. Working on a very big deal, Bernard.

BERNARD: What's Biff doing?

WILLY: Well, he's been doing very big things in the West. But he decided to establish himself here. Very big. We're having dinner. Did I hear your wife had a boy?

BERNARD: That's right. Our second.

WILLY: Two boys! What do you know!

BERNARD: What kind of a deal has Biff got?

WILLY: Well, Bill Oliver—very big sporting-goods man—he wants Biff very badly. Called him in from the West. Long distance, carte blanche, special deliveries. Your friends have their own private tennis court?

BERNARD: You still with the old firm, Willy?

WILLY: (*After a pause.*) I'm—I'm overjoyed to see how you made the grade, Bernard, overjoyed. It's an encouraging thing to see a young man really—really— Looks very good for Biff—very— (*He breaks off, then.*) Bernard— (*He is so full of emotion, he breaks off again.*)

BERNARD: What is it, Willy?

WILLY: (*Small and alone.*) What—what's the secret?

BERNARD: What secret?

WILLY: How—how did you? Why didn't he ever catch on?

BERNARD: I wouldn't know that, Willy.

WILLY: (*Confidentially, desperately.*) You were his friend, his boyhood friend. There's something I don't understand about it. His life ended after that Ebbets Field game. From the age of seventeen nothing good ever happened to him.

BERNARD: He never trained himself for anything.

WILLY: But he did, he did. After high school he took so many correspondence courses. Radio mechanics; television; God knows what, and never made the slightest mark.

BERNARD: (*Taking off his glasses.*) Willy, do you want to talk candidly?

WILLY: (*Rising, faces* BERNARD.) I regard you as a very brilliant man, Bernard. I value your advice.

BERNARD: Oh, the hell with the advice, Willy. I couldn't advise you. There's just one thing I've always wanted to ask you. When he was supposed to graduate, and the math teacher flunked him—

WILLY: Oh, that son-of-a-bitch ruined his life.

BERNARD: Yeah, but, Willy, all he had to do was go to summer school and make up that subject.

WILLY: That's right, that's right.

BERNARD: Did you tell him not to go to summer school?

WILLY: Me? I begged him to go. I ordered him to go!

BERNARD: Then why wouldn't he go?

WILLY: Why? Why! Bernard, that question has been trailing me like a ghost for the last fifteen years. He flunked the subject, and laid down and died like a hammer hit him!

BERNARD: Take it easy, kid.

WILLY: Let me talk to you—I got nobody to talk to. Bernard, Bernard, was it my fault? Y'see? It keeps going around in my mind, maybe I did something to him. I got nothing to give him.

BERNARD: Don't take it so hard.

WILLY: Why did he lay down? What is the story there? You were his friend!

BERNARD: Willy, I remember, it was June, and our grades came out. And he'd flunked math.

WILLY: That son-of-a-bitch!

BERNARD: No, it wasn't right then. Biff just got very angry, I remember, and he was ready to enroll in summer school.

WILLY: (*Surprised.*) He was?

BERNARD: He wasn't beaten by it at all. But then, Willy, he disappeared from the block for almost a month. And I got the idea that he'd gone up to New England to see you. Did he have a talk with you then?

(WILLY *stares in silence.*)

BERNARD: Willy?

WILLY: (*With a strong edge of resentment in his voice.*) Yeah, he came to Boston. What about it?

BERNARD: Well, just that when he came back—I'll never forget this, it always mystifies me. Because I'd thought so well of Biff, even though he'd always taken advantage of me. I loved him, Willy, y'know? And he came back after that month and took his sneakers—remember those sneakers with "University of Virginia" printed on them? He was so proud of those, wore them every day. And he took them down in the cellar, and burned them up in the furnace. We had a fist fight. It lasted at least half an hour. Just the two of us, punching each other down thee cellar, and crying right through it. I've often thought of how strange it was that I knew he'd given up his life. What happened in Boston, Willy?

(WILLY *looks at him as at an intruder.*)

BERNARD: I just bring it up because you asked me.

WILLY: (*Angrily.*) Nothing. What do you mean, "What happened?" What's that got to do with anything?

BERNARD: Well, don't get sore.

WILLY: What are you trying to do, blame it on me? If a boy lays down is that my fault?

BERNARD: Now, Willy, don't get—

WILLY: Well, don't—don't talk to me that way! What does that mean, "What happened?"

(CHARLEY *enters. He is in his vest, and he carries a bottle of bourbon.*)

CHARLEY: Hey, you're going to miss that train. (*He waves the bottle.*)

660 BERNARD: Yeah, I'm going. (*He takes the bottle.*) Thanks, Pop. (*He picks up his rackets and bag.*) Good-by, Willy, and don't worry about it. You know, "If at first you don't succeed . . ."

WILLY: Yes, I believe in that.

BERNARD: But sometimes, Willy, it's better for a man just to
665 walk away.

WILLY: Walk away?

BERNARD: That's right.

WILLY: But if you can't walk away?

BERNARD: (*After a slight pause.*) I guess that's when it's tough.
670 (*Extending his hand.*) Good-by, Willy.

WILLY: (*Shaking* BERNARD's *hand.*) Good-by, boy.

CHARLEY: (*An arm on* BERNARD's *shoulder.*) How do you like this kid? Gonna argue a case in front of the Supreme Court.

675 BERNARD: (*Protesting.*) Pop!

WILLY: (*Genuinely shocked, pained, and happy.*) No! The Supreme Court!

BERNARD: I gotta run. 'By, Dad!

CHARLEY: Knock 'em dead, Bernard!

(BERNARD *goes off.*)

680 WILLY: (*As* CHARLEY *takes out his wallet.*) The Supreme Court! And he didn't even mention it!

CHARLEY: (*Counting out money on the desk.*) He don't have to—he's gonna do it.

WILLY: And you never told him what to do, did you? You
685 never took any interest in him.

CHARLEY: My salvation is that I never took any interest in anything. There's some money—fifty dollars. I got an accountant inside.

WILLY: Charley, look . . . (*With difficulty.*) I got my insurance
690 to pay. If you can manage it—I need a hundred and ten dollars.

(CHARLEY *doesn't reply for a moment; merely stops moving.*)

WILLY: I'd draw it from my bank but Linda would know, and I . . .

CHARLEY: Sit down, Willy.

695 WILLY: (*Moving toward the chair.*) I'm keeping an account of everything, remember. I'll pay every penny back. (*He sits.*)

CHARLEY: Now listen to me, Willy.

WILLY: I want you to know I appreciate . . .

CHARLEY: (*Sitting down on the table.*) Willy, what're you doin'?
700 What the hell is goin' on in your head?

WILLY: Why? I'm simply . . .

CHARLEY: I offered you a job. You can make fifty dollars a week. And I won't send you on the road.

WILLY: I've got a job.

705 CHARLEY: Without pay? What kind of a job is a job without pay? (*He rises.*) Now, look, kid, enough is enough. I'm no genius but I know when I'm being insulted.

WILLY: Insulted!

CHARLEY: Why don't you want to work for me?

710 WILLY: What's the matter with you? I've got a job.

CHARLEY: Then what're you walkin' in here every week for?

WILLY: (*Getting up.*) Well, if you don't want me to walk in here—

CHARLEY: I am offering you a job.

WILLY: I don't want your goddam job!   715

CHARLEY: When the hell are you going to grow up?

WILLY: (*Furiously.*) You big ignoramus, if you say that to me again I'll rap you one! I don't care how big you are! (*He's ready to fight.*)

(*Pause.*)

CHARLEY: (*Kindly, going to him.*) How much do you need,   720
Willy?

WILLY: Charley, I'm strapped, I'm strapped. I don't know what to do. I was just fired.

CHARLEY: Howard fired you?

WILLY: That snotnose. Imagine that? I named him. I named   725
him Howard.

CHARLEY: Willy, when're you gonna realize that them things don't mean anything? You named him Howard, but you can't sell that. The only thing you got in this world is what you can sell. And the funny thing is that you're a   730
salesman, and you don't know that.

WILLY: I've always tried to think otherwise, I guess. I always felt that if a man was impressive, and well liked, that nothing—

CHARLEY: Why must everybody like you? Who liked J. P. Morgan? Was he impressive? In a Turkish bath he'd look   735
like a butcher. But with his pockets on he was very well liked. Now listen, Willy, I know you don't like me, and nobody can say I'm in love with you, but I'll give you a job because—just for the hell of it, put it that way. Now what do you say?   740

WILLY: I—I just can't work for you, Charley.

CHARLEY: What're you, jealous of me?

WILLY: I can't work for you, that's all, don't ask me why.

CHARLEY: (*Angered, takes out more bills.*) You been jealous of me all your life, you damned fool! Here, pay your insur-   745
ance. (*He puts the money in* WILLY's *hand.*)

WILLY: I'm keeping strict accounts.

CHARLEY: I've got some work to do. Take care of yourself. And pay your insurance:

WILLY: (*Moving to the right.*) Funny, y'know? After all the   750
highways, and the trains, and the appointments, and the years, you end up worth more dead than alive.

CHARLEY: Willy, nobody's worth nothin' dead. (*After a slight pause.*) Did you hear what I said?

(WILLY *stands still, dreaming.*)

CHARLEY: Willy!   755

WILLY: Apologize to Bernard for me when you see him. I didn't mean to argue with him. He's a fine boy. They're all fine boys, and they'll end up big—all of them. Someday they'll all play tennis together. Wish me luck, Charley. He saw Bill Oliver today.   760

CHARLEY: Good luck.

WILLY: (*On the verge of tears.*) Charley, you're the only friend I got. Isn't that a remarkable thing? (*He goes out.*)

CHARLEY: Jesus!

(CHARLEY *stares after him a moment and follows. All light blacks out. Suddenly raucous music is heard, and a red glow rises behind the screen at right.* STANLEY, *a young waiter, appears, carrying a table, followed by* HAPPY, *who is carrying two chairs.*)

765 STANLEY: (*Putting the table down.*) That's all right, Mr. Loman, I can handle it myself. (*He turns and takes the chairs from* HAPPY *and places them at the table.*)

HAPPY: (*Glancing around.*) Oh, this is better.

770 STANLEY: Sure, in the front there you're in the middle of all kinds a noise. Whenever you got a party, Mr. Loman, you just tell me and I'll put you back here. Y'know, there's a lotta people they don't like it private, because when they go out they like to see a lotta action around them because they're sick and tired to stay in the house by theirself. But 775 I know you, you ain't from Hackensack. You know what I mean?

HAPPY: (*Sitting down.*) So how's it coming, Stanley?

STANLEY: Ah, it's a dog's life. I only wish during the war they'd a took me in the Army. I coulda been dead by now.

780 HAPPY: My brother's back, Stanley.

STANLEY: Oh, he come back, heh? From the Far West.

HAPPY: Yeah, big cattle man, my brother, so treat him right. And my father's coming too.

STANLEY: Oh, your father too!

785 HAPPY: You got a couple of nice lobsters?

STANLEY: Hundred per cent, big.

HAPPY: I want them with the claws.

STANLEY: Don't worry, I don't give you no mice. (HAPPY *laughs.*) How about some wine? It'll put a head on the 790 meal.

HAPPY: No. You remember, Stanley, that recipe I brought you from overseas? With the champagne in it?

STANLEY: Oh, yeah, sure. I still got it tacked up yet in the kitchen. But that'll have to cost a buck apiece anyways.

795 HAPPY: That's all right.

STANLEY: What'd you, hit a number or somethin'?

HAPPY: No, it's a little celebration. My brother is—I think he pulled off a big deal today. I think we're going into business together.

800 STANLEY: Great! That's the best for you. Because a family business, you know what I mean?—that's the best.

HAPPY: That's what I think.

STANLEY: 'Cause what's the difference? Somebody steals? It's in the family. Know what I mean? (*Sotto voce.*) Like this 805 bartender here. The boss is goin' crazy what kinda leak he's got in the cash register. You put it in but it don't come out.

HAPPY: (*Raising his head.*) Sh!

STANLEY: What?

810 HAPPY: You notice I wasn't lookin' right or left, was I?

STANLEY: No.

HAPPY: And my eyes are closed.

STANLEY: So what's the—?

HAPPY: Strudel's comin'.

815 STANLEY: (*Catching on, looks around.*) Ah, no, there's no—

(*He breaks off as a furred, lavishly dressed girl enters and sits at the next table. Both follow her with their eyes.*)

STANLEY: Geez, how'd ya know?

HAPPY: I got radar or something. (*Staring directly at her profile.*) Oooooooo . . . Stanley.

STANLEY: I think that's for you, Mr. Loman.

820 HAPPY: Look at that mouth. Oh, God. And the binoculars.

STANLEY: Geez, you got a life, Mr. Loman.

HAPPY: Wait on her.

STANLEY: (*Going to the girl's table.*) Would you like a menu, ma'am?

GIRL: I'm expecting someone, but I'd like a—   825

HAPPY: Why don't you bring her—excuse me, miss, do you mind? I sell champagne, and I'd like you to try my brand. Bring her a champagne, Stanley.

GIRL: That's awfully nice of you.

HAPPY: Don't mention it. It's all company money. (*He laughs.*)   830

GIRL: That's a charming product to be selling, isn't it?

HAPPY: Oh, gets to be like everything else. Selling is selling, y'know.

GIRL: I suppose.

HAPPY: You don't happen to sell, do you?   835

GIRL: No, I don't sell.

HAPPY: Would you object to a compliment from a stranger? You ought to be on a magazine cover.

GIRL: (*Looking at him a little archly.*) I have been.

(STANLEY *comes in with a glass of champagne.*)

HAPPY: What'd I say before, Stanley? You see? She's a cover   840 girl.

STANLEY: Oh, I could see, I could see.

HAPPY: (*To the* GIRL.) What magazine?

GIRL: Oh, a lot of them. (*She takes the drink.*) Thank you.

HAPPY: You know what they say in France, don't you?   845 "Champagne is the drink of the complexion"—Hya Biff!

(BIFF *has entered and sits with* HAPPY.)

BIFF: Hello, kid. Sorry I'm late.

HAPPY: I just got here. Uh, Miss—?

GIRL: Forsythe.

HAPPY: Miss Forsythe, this is my brother.   850

BIFF: Is Dad here?

HAPPY: His name is Biff. You might've heard of him. Great football player.

GIRL: Really? What team?

HAPPY: Are you familiar with football?   855

GIRL: No, I'm afraid I'm not.

HAPPY: Biff is quarterback with the New York Giants.

GIRL: Well, that is nice, isn't it? (*She drinks.*)

HAPPY: Good health.

GIRL: I'm happy to meet you.   860

HAPPY: That's my name. Hap. It's really Harold, but at West Point they called me Happy.

GIRL: (*Now really impressed.*) Oh, I see. How do you do? (*She turns her profile.*)

BIFF: Isn't Dad coming?   865

HAPPY: You want her?

BIFF: Oh, I could never make that.

HAPPY: I remember the time that idea would never come into your head. Where's the old confidence, Biff?

BIFF: I just saw Oliver—   870

HAPPY: Wait a minute, I've got to see that old confidence again. Do you want her? She's on call.

BIFF: Oh, no. (*He turns to look at the* GIRL.)

HAPPY: I'm telling you. Watch this. (*Turning to the* GIRL.) Honey? (*She turns to him.*) Are you busy?   875

GIRL: Well, I am . . . but I could make a phone call.

HAPPY: Do that, will you, honey? And see if you can get a
   friend. We'll be here for a while. Biff is one of the greatest football players in the country.
880 GIRL: (*Standing up.*) Well, I'm certainly happy to meet you.
HAPPY: Come back soon.
GIRL: I'll try.
HAPPY: Don't try, honey, try hard.

(*The* GIRL *exits.* STANLEY *follows, shaking his head in bewildered
admiration.*)

HAPPY: Isn't that a shame now? A beautiful girl like that?
885   That's why I can't get married. There's not a good woman
   in a thousand. New York is loaded with them, kid!
BIFF: Hap, look—
HAPPY: I told you she was on call!
BIFF: (*Strangely unnerved.*) Cut it out, will ya? I want to say
890   something to you.
HAPPY: Did you see Oliver?
BIFF: I saw him all right. Now look, I want to tell Dad a couple of things and I want you to help me.
HAPPY: What? Is he going to back you?
895 BIFF: Are you crazy? You're out of your goddam head, you
   know that?
HAPPY: Why? What happened?
BIFF: (*Breathlessly.*) I did a terrible thing today, Hap. It's been
   the strangest day I ever went through. I'm all numb, I swear.
900 HAPPY: You mean he wouldn't see you?
BIFF: Well, I waited six hours for him, see? All day. Kept sending my name in. Even tried to date his secretary so she'd
   get me to him, but no soap.
HAPPY: Because you're not showin' the old confidence, Biff.
905   He remembered you, didn't he?
BIFF: (*Stopping* HAPPY *with a gesture.*) Finally, about five
   o'clock, he comes out. Didn't remember who I was or anything. I felt like such an idiot, Hap.
HAPPY: Did you tell him my Florida idea?
910 BIFF: He walked away. I saw him for one minute. I got so mad
   I could've torn the walls down! How the hell did I ever
   get the idea I was a salesman there? I even believed myself
   that I'd been a salesman for him! And then he gave me one
   look and—I realized what a ridiculous lie my whole life
915   has been! We've been talking in a dream for fifteen years.
   I was a shipping clerk.
HAPPY: What'd you do?
BIFF: (*With great tension and wonder.*) Well, he left, see. And the
   secretary went out. I was all alone in the waiting-room. I
920   don't know what came over me, Hap. The next thing I
   know I'm in his office—paneled walls, everything. I can't
   explain it. I—Hap, I took his fountain pen.
HAPPY: Geez, did he catch you?
BIFF: I ran out. I ran down all eleven flights. I ran and ran and
925   ran.
HAPPY: That was an awful dumb—what'd you do that for?
BIFF: (*Agonized.*) I don't know, I just—wanted to take something, I don't know. You gotta help me, Hap, I'm gonna
   tell Pop.
930 HAPPY: You crazy? What for?
BIFF: Hap, he's got to understand that I'm not the man somebody lends that kind of money to. He thinks I've been
   spiting him all these years and it's eating him up.

HAPPY: That's just it. You tell him something nice.
BIFF: I can't.   935
HAPPY: Say you got a lunch date with Oliver tomorrow.
BIFF: So what do I do tomorrow?
HAPPY: You leave the house tomorrow and come back at
   night and say Oliver is thinking it over. And he thinks it
   over for a couple of weeks, and gradually it fades away   940
   and nobody's the worse.
BIFF: But it'll go on forever!
HAPPY: Dad is never so happy as when he's looking forward
   to something!

(WILLY *enters.*)

HAPPY: Hello, scout!   945
WILLY: Gee, I haven't been here in years!

(STANLEY *has followed* WILLY *in and sets a chair for him.* STANLEY
starts off but HAPPY *stops him.*)

HAPPY: Stanley!

(STANLEY *stands by, waiting for an order.*)

BIFF: (*Going to* WILLY *with guilt, as to an invalid.*) Sit down, Pop.
   You want a drink?
WILLY: Sure, I don't mind.   950
BIFF: Let's get a load on.
WILLY: You look worried.
BIFF: N-no. (*To* STANLEY.) Scotch all around. Make it doubles.
STANLEY: Doubles, right. (*He goes.*)
WILLY: You had a couple already, didn't you?   955
BIFF: Just a couple, yeah.
WILLY: Well, what happened, boy? (*Nodding affirmatively, with
   a smile.*) Everything go all right?
BIFF: (*Takes a breath, then reaches out and grasps* WILLY's *hand.*)
   Pal . . . (*He is smiling bravely, and* WILLY *is smiling too*). I had 960
   an experience today.
HAPPY: Terrific, Pop.
WILLY: That so? What happened?
BIFF: (*High, slightly alcoholic, above the earth.*) I'm going to tell
   you everything from first to last. It's been a strange day.   965
   (*Silence. He looks around, composes himself as best he can, but
   his breath keeps breaking the rhythm of his voice.*) I had to wait
   quite a while for him, and—
WILLY: Oliver?
BIFF: Yeah, Oliver. All day, as a matter of cold fact. And a lot 970
   of—instances—facts, Pop, facts about my life came back to
   me. Who was it, Pop? Who ever said I was a salesman with
   Oliver?
WILLY: Well, you were.
BIFF: No, Dad, I was a shipping clerk.   975
WILLY: But you were practically—
BIFF: (*With determination.*) Dad, I don't know who said it first,
   but I was never a salesman for Bill Oliver.
WILLY: What're you talking about?
BIFF: Let's hold onto the facts tonight, Pop. We're not going 980
   to get anywhere bullin' around. I was a shipping clerk.
WILLY: (*Angrily.*) All right, now listen to me—
BIFF: Why don't you let me finish?
WILLY: I'm not interested in stories about the past or any crap
   of that kind because the woods are burning, boys, you   985

understand? There's a big blaze going on all around. I was fired today.

BIFF: (*Shocked.*) How could you be?

990 WILLY: I was fired, and I'm looking for a little good news to tell your mother, because the woman has waited and the woman has suffered. The gist of it is that I haven't got a story left in my head, Biff. So don't give me a lecture about facts and aspects. I am not interested. Now what've you got to say to me?

(STANLEY *enters with three drinks. They wait until he leaves.*)

995 WILLY: Did you see Oliver?

BIFF: Jesus, Dad!

WILLY: You mean you didn't go up there?

HAPPY: Sure he went up there.

BIFF: I did. I—saw him. How could they fire you?

1000 WILLY: (*On the edge of his chair.*) What kind of a welcome did he give you?

BIFF: He won't even let you work on commission?

WILLY: I'm out! (*Driving.*) So tell me, he gave you a warm welcome?

1005 HAPPY: Sure, Pop, sure!

BIFF: (*Driven.*) Well, it was kind of—

WILLY: I was wondering if he'd remember you. (*To* HAPPY.) Imagine, man doesn't see him for ten, twelve years and gives him that kind of a welcome!

1010 HAPPY: Damn right!

BIFF: (*Trying to return to the offensive.*) Pop, look—

WILLY: You know why he remembered you, don't you? Because you impressed him in those days.

BIFF: Let's talk quietly and get this down to the facts, huh?

1015 WILLY: (*As though* BIFF *had been interrupting.*) Well, what happened? It's great news, Biff. Did he take you into his office or'd you talk in the waiting-room?

BIFF: Well, he came in, see, and—

WILLY: (*With a big smile.*) What'd he say? Betcha he threw his arm around you.

1020

BIFF: Well, he kinda—

WILLY: He's a fine man. (*To* HAPPY.) Very hard man to see, y'know.

HAPPY: (*Agreeing.*) Oh, I know.

1025 WILLY: (*To* BIFF.) Is that where you had the drinks?

BIFF: Yeah, he gave me a couple of—no, no!

HAPPY: (*Cutting in.*) He told him my Florida idea.

WILLY: Don't interrupt. (*To* BIFF.) How'd he react to the Florida idea?

1030 BIFF: Dad, will you give me a minute to explain?

WILLY: I've been waiting for you to explain since I sat down here! What happened? He took you into his office and what?

BIFF: Well—I talked. And—and he listened, see.

1035 WILLY: Famous for the way he listens, y'know. What was his answer?

BIFF: His answer was— (*He breaks off, suddenly angry.*) Dad, you're not letting me tell you what I want to tell you!

WILLY: (*Accusing, angered.*) You didn't see him, did you?

1040 BIFF: I did see him!

WILLY: What'd you insult him or something? You insulted him didn't you?

BIFF: Listen, will you let me out of it, will you just let me out of it!

HAPPY: What the hell! 1045

WILLY: Tell me what happened!

BIFF: (*To* HAPPY.) I can't talk to him!

(*A single trumpet note jars the ear. The light of green leaves stains the house, which holds the air of night and a dream* YOUNG BERNARD *enters and knocks on the door of the house.*)

YOUNG BERNARD: (*Frantically.*) Mrs. Loman, Mrs. Loman!

HAPPY: Tell him what happened!

BIFF: (*To* HAPPY.) Shut up and leave me alone! 1050

WILLY: No, no! You had to go and flunk math!

BIFF: What math? What're you talking about?

YOUNG BERNARD: Mrs. Loman, Mrs. Loman!

(LINDA *appears in the house, as of old.*)

WILLY: (*Wildly.*) Math, math, math!

BIFF: Take it easy, Pop! 1055

YOUNG BERNARD: Mrs. Loman!

WILLY: (*Furiously.*) If you hadn't flunked you'd've been set by now!

BIFF: Now, look, I'm gonna tell you what happened, and you're going to listen to me. 1060

YOUNG BERNARD: Mrs. Loman!

BIFF: I waited six hours—

HAPPY: What the hell are you saying?

BIFF: I kept sending in my name but he wouldn't see me. So finally he . . . (*He continues unheard as light fades low on the* 1065 *restaurant.*)

YOUNG BERNARD: Biff flunked math!

LINDA: No!

YOUNG BERNARD: Birnbaum flunked him! They won't graduate him! 1070

LINDA: But they have to. He's gotta go to the university. Where is he? Biff! Biff!

YOUNG BERNARD: No, he left. He went to Grand Central.

LINDA: Grand—You mean he went to Boston!

YOUNG BERNARD: Is Uncle Willy in Boston? 1075

LINDA: Oh, maybe Willy can talk to the teacher. Oh, the poor, poor boy!

(*Light on house area snaps out.*)

BIFF: (*At the table, now audible, holding up a gold fountain pen.*) . . . so I'm washed up with Oliver, you understand? Are you listening to me? 1080

WILLY: (*At a loss.*) Yeah, sure. If you hadn't flunked—

BIFF: Flunked what? What're you talking about?

WILLY: Don't blame everything on me! I didn't flunk math— you did! What pen?

HAPPY: That was awful dumb, Biff, a pen like that is worth— 1085

WILLY: (*Seeing the pen for the first time.*) You took Oliver's pen?

BIFF: (*Weakening.*) Dad, I just explained it to you.

WILLY: You stole Bill Oliver's fountain pen!

BIFF: I didn't exactly steal it! That's just what I've been explaining to you! 1090

HAPPY: He had it in his hand and just then Oliver walked in, so he got nervous and stuck it in his pocket!

WILLY: My God, Biff!

BIFF: I never intended to do it, Dad!

1095 OPERATOR'S VOICE: Standish Arms, good evening!

WILLY: (*Shouting.*) I'm not in my room!

BIFF: (*Frightened.*) Dad, what's the matter? (*He and* HAPPY *stand up.*)

OPERATOR: Ringing Mr. Loman for you!

1100 WILLY: I'm not there, stop it!

BIFF: (*Horrified, gets down on one knee before* WILLY.) Dad, I'll make good, I'll make good. (WILLY *tries to get to his feet.* BIFF *holds him down.*) Sit down now.

WILLY: No, you're no good, you're no good for anything.

1105 BIFF: I am, Dad, I'll find something else, you understand? Now don't worry about anything. (*He holds up* WILLY's *face.*) Talk to me, Dad.

OPERATOR: Mr. Loman does not answer. Shall I page him?

WILLY: (*Attempting to stand, as though to rush and silence the*
1110 OPERATOR.) No, no, no!

HAPPY: He'll strike something, Pop.

WILLY: No, no . . .

BIFF: (*Desperately, standing over* WILLY.) Pop, listen! Listen to me! I'm telling you something good. Oliver talked to his
1115 partner about the Florida idea. You listening? He—he talked to his partner, and he came to me . . . I'm going to be all right, you hear? Dad, listen to me, he said it was just a question of the amount!

WILLY: Then you . . . got it?

1120 HAPPY: He's gonna be terrific, Pop!

WILLY: (*Trying to stand.*) Then you got it, haven't you? You got it! You got it!

BIFF: (*Agonized, holds* WILLY *down.*) No, no. Look, Pop. I'm supposed to have lunch with them tomorrow. I'm just
1125 telling you this so you'll know that I can still make an impression, Pop. And I'll make good somewhere, but I can't go tomorrow, see?

WILLY: Why not? You simply—

BIFF: But the pen, Pop!

1130 WILLY: You give it to him and tell him it was an oversight!

HAPPY: Sure, have lunch tomorrow!

BIFF: I can't say that—

WILLY: You were doing a crosswood puzzle and accidentally used his pen!

1135 BIFF: Listen, kid, I took those balls years ago, now I walk in with his fountain pen? That clinches it, don't you see? I can't face him like that! I'll try elsewhere.

PAGE'S VOICE: Paging Mr. Loman!

WILLY: Don't you want to be anything?

1140 BIFF: Pop, how can I go back?

WILLY: You don't want to be anything, is that what's behind it?

BIFF: (*Now angry at* WILLY *for not crediting his sympathy.*) Don't take it that way! You think it was easy walking into that office after what I'd done to him? A team of horses
1145 couldn't have dragged me back to Bill Oliver!

WILLY: Then why'd you go?

BIFF: Why did I go? Why did I go! Look at you! Look at what's become of you!

(*Off left,* THE WOMAN *laughs.*)

WILLY: Biff, you're going to go to that lunch tomorrow, or—

BIFF: I can't go. I've got no appointment!   1150

HAPPY: Biff, for . . .!

WILLY: Are you spiting me?

BIFF: Don't take it that way! Goddammit!

WILLY: (*Strikes* BIFF *and falters away from the table.*) You rotten little louse! Are you spiting me?   1155

THE WOMAN: Someone's at the door, Willy!

BIFF: I'm no good, can't you see what I am?

HAPPY: (*Separating them.*) Hey, you're in a restaurant! Now cut it out, both of you! (*The girls enter.*) Hello, girls, sit down.

(THE WOMAN *laughs, off left.*)

MISS FORSYTHE: I guess we might as well. This is Letta.   1160

THE WOMAN: Willy, are you going to wake up?

BIFF: (*Ignoring* WILLY.) How're ya, miss, sit down. What do you drink?

MISS FORSYTHE: Letta might not be able to stay long.

LETTA: I gotta get up very early tomorrow. I got jury duty.   1165
I'm so excited! Were you fellows ever on a jury?

BIFF: No, but I been in front of them! (*The girls laugh.*) This is my father.

LETTA: Isn't he cute? Sit down with us, Pop.

HAPPY: Sit him down, Biff!   1170

BIFF: (*Going to him.*) Come on, slugger, drink us under the table. To hell with it! Come on, sit down, pal.

(*On* BIFF's *last insistence,* WILLY *is about to sit.*)

THE WOMAN: (*Now urgently.*) Willy, are you going to answer the door!

(*The* WOMAN's *call pulls* WILLY *back. He starts right, befuddled.*)

BIFF: Hey, where are you going?   1175

WILLY: Open the door.

BIFF: The door?

WILLY: The washroom . . . the door . . . where's the door?

BIFF: (*Leading* WILLY *to the left.*) Just go straight down.

(WILLY *moves left.*)

THE WOMAN: Willy, Willy, are you going to get up, get up, get   1180
up, get up?

(WILLY *exits left.*)

LETTA: I think it's sweet you bring your daddy along.

MISS FORSYTHE: Oh, he isn't really your father!

BIFF: (*At left, turning to her resentfully.*) Miss Forsythe, you've just seen a prince walk by. A fine, troubled prince. A hard-   1185
working, unappreciated prince. A pal, you understand? A good companion. Always for his boys.

LETTA: That's so sweet.

HAPPY: Well, girls, what's the program? We're wasting time. Come on, Biff. Gather round. Where would you like to go?   1190

BIFF: Why don't you do something for him?

HAPPY: Me!

BIFF: Don't you give a damn for him, Hap?

HAPPY: What're you talking about? I'm the one who—

BIFF: I sense it, you don't give a good goddam about him. (*He*   1195
takes the rolled-up hose from his pocket and puts it on the table

in front of HAPPY.) Look what I found in the cellar, for Christ's sake. How can you bear to let it go on?

HAPPY: Me? Who goes away? Who runs off and—

1200 BIFF: Yeah, but he doesn't mean anything to you. You could help him—I can't! Don't you understand what I'm talking about? He's going to kill himself, don't you know that?

HAPPY: Don't I know it! Me!

1205 BIFF: Hap, help him! Jesus . . . help him . . . Help me, help me, I can't bear to look at his face! (*Ready to weep, he hurries out, up right.*)

HAPPY: (*Starting after him.*) Where are you going?

MISS FORSYTHE: What's he so mad about?

1210 HAPPY: Come on, girls, we'll catch up with him.

MISS FORSYTHE: (*As* HAPPY *pushes her out.*) Say, I don't like that temper of his!

HAPPY: He's just a little overstrung, he'll be all right!

WILLY: (*Off left, as* THE WOMAN *laughs.*) Don't answer! Don't

1215 answer!

LETTA: Don't you want to tell your father—

HAPPY: No, that's not my father. He's just a guy. Come on, we'll catch Biff, and, honey, we're going to paint this town! Stanley, where's the check! Hey, Stanley!

(*They exit.* STANLEY *looks toward left.*)

1220 STANLEY: (*Calling to* HAPPY *indignantly.*) Mr. Loman! Mr. Loman!

(STANLEY *picks up a chair and follows them off. Knocking is heard off left.* THE WOMAN *enters, laughing.* WILLY *follows her. She is in a black slip; he is buttoning his shirt. Raw, sensuous music accompanies their speech.*)

WILLY: Will you stop laughing? Will you stop?

THE WOMAN: Aren't you going to answer the door? He'll wake the whole hotel.

1225 WILLY: I'm not expecting anybody.

THE WOMAN: Whyn't you have another drink, honey, and stop being so damn self-centered?

WILLY: I'm so lonely.

THE WOMAN: You know you ruined me, Willy? From now

1230 on, whenever you come to the office, I'll see that you go right through to the buyers. No waiting at my desk any more, Willy. You ruined me.

WILLY: That's nice of you to say that.

THE WOMAN: Gee, you are self-centered! Why so sad? You are

1235 the saddest, self-centeredest soul I ever did see-saw. (*She laughs. He kisses her.*) Come on inside, drummer boy. It's silly to be dressing in the middle of the night. (*As knocking is heard.*) Aren't you going to answer the door?

WILLY: They're knocking on the wrong door.

1240 THE WOMAN: But I felt the knocking. And he heard us talking in here. Maybe the hotel's on fire!

WILLY: (*His terror rising.*) It's a mistake.

THE WOMAN: Then tell him to go away!

WILLY: There's nobody there.

1245 THE WOMAN: It's getting on my nerves, Willy. There's somebody standing out there and it's getting on my nerves!

WILLY: (*Pushing her away from him.*) All right, stay in the bathroom here, and don't come out. I think there's a law in Massachusetts about it, so don't come out. It may be that

new room clerk. He looked very mean. So don't come 1250 out. It's a mistake, there's no fire.

(*The knocking is heard again. He takes a few steps away from her, and she vanishes into the wing. The light follows him, and now he is facing* YOUNG BIFF, *who carries a suitcase.* BIFF *steps toward him. The music is gone.*)

BIFF: Why didn't you answer?

WILLY: Biff! What are you doing in Boston?

BIFF: Why didn't you answer? I've been knocking for five minutes, I called you on the phone— 1255

WILLY: I just heard you. I was in the bathroom and had the door shut. Did anything happen home?

BIFF: Dad—I let you down.

WILLY: What do you mean?

BIFF: Dad . . . 1260

WILLY: Biffo, what's this about? (*Putting his arm around* BIFF.) Come on, let's go downstairs and get you a malted.

BIFF: Dad, I flunked math.

WILLY: Not for the term?

BIFF: The term. I haven't got enough credits to graduate. 1265

WILLY: You mean to say Bernard wouldn't give you the answers?

BIFF: He did, he tried, but I only got a sixty-one.

WILLY: And they wouldn't give you four points?

BIFF: Birnbaum refused absolutely. I begged him, Pop, but he 1270 won't give me those points. You gotta talk to him before they close the school. Because if he saw the kind of man you are, and you just talked to him in your way, I'm sure he'd come through for me. The class came right before practice, see, and I didn't go enough. Would you talk to 1275 him? He'd like you, Pop. You know the way you could talk.

WILLY: You're on. We'll drive right back.

BIFF: Oh, Dad, good work! I'm sure he'll change it for you!

WILLY: Go downstairs and tell the clerk I'm checkin' out. Go 1280 right down.

BIFF: Yes, sir! See, the reason he hates me, Pop—one day he was late for class so I got up at the blackboard and imitated him. I crossed my eyes and talked with a lithp.

WILLY: (*Laughing.*) You did? The kids like it? 1285

BIFF: They nearly died laughing!

WILLY: Yeah? What'd you do?

BIFF: The thquare root of thixty twee is . . . (WILLY *bursts out laughing;* BIFF *joins him.*) And in the middle of it he walked in!

(WILLY *laughs and* THE WOMAN *joins in offstage.*)

WILLY: (*Without hesitation.*) Hurry downstairs and— 1290

BIFF: Somebody in there?

WILLY: No, that was next door.

(THE WOMAN *laughs offstage.*)

BIFF: Somebody got in your bathroom!

WILLY: No, it's the next room, there's a party—

THE WOMAN: (*Enters, laughing. She lisps this.*) Can I come in? 1295 There's something in the bathtub, Willy, and it's moving!

(WILLY *looks at* BIFF, *who is staring open-mouthed and horrified at* THE WOMAN.)

WILLY: Ah—you better go back to your room. They must be finished painting by now. They're painting her room so I let her take a shower here. Go back, go back . . . (*He pushes her.*)

1300

THE WOMAN: (*Resisting.*) But I've got to get dressed, Willy, I can't—

WILLY: Get out of here! Go back, go back . . . (*Suddenly striving for the ordinary.*) This is Miss Francis, Biff, she's a buyer.

1305 They're painting her room. Go back, Miss Francis, go back . . .

THE WOMAN: But my clothes, I can't go out naked in the hall!

WILLY: (*Pushing her offstage.*) Get outa here! Go back, go back!

(BIFF *slowly sits down on his suitcase as the argument continues offstage.*)

THE WOMAN: Where's my stockings? You promised me stock-

1310 ings, Willy!

WILLY: I have no stockings here!

THE WOMAN: You had two boxes of size nine sheers for me, and I want them!

WILLY: Here, for God's sake, will you get outa here!

1315 THE WOMAN: (*Enters holding a box of stockings.*) I just hope there's nobody in the hall. That's all I hope. (*To* BIFF.) Are you football or baseball?

BIFF: Football.

THE WOMAN: (*Angry, humiliated.*) That's me too. G'night. (*She*

1320 *snatches her clothes from* WILLY, *and walks out.*)

WILLY: (*After a pause.*) Well, better get going. I want to get to the school first thing in the morning. Get my suits out of the closet. I'll get my valise. (BIFF *doesn't move.*) What's the matter? (BIFF *remains motionless, tears falling.*) She's a buyer.

1325 Buys for J.H. Simmons. She lives down the hall—they're painting. You don't imagine—(*He breaks off. After a pause.*) Now listen, pal, she's just a buyer. She sees merchandise in her room and they have to keep it looking just so . . . (*Pause. Assuming command.*) All right, get my suits. (BIFF

1330 *doesn't move.*) Now stop crying and do as I say. I gave you an order. Biff, I gave you an order! Is that what you do when I give you an order? How dare you cry! (*Putting his arm around* BIFF.) Now look, Biff, when you grow up you'll understand about these things. You mustn't—you

1335 mustn't overemphasize a thing like this. I'll see Birnbaum first thing in the morning.

BIFF: Never mind.

WILLY: (*Getting down beside* BIFF.) Never mind! He's going to give you those points. I'll see to it.

1340 BIFF: He wouldn't listen to you.

WILLY: He certainly will listen to me. You need those points for the U. of Virginia.

BIFF: I'm not going there.

WILLY: Heh? If I can't get him to change that mark you'll

1345 make it up in summer school. You've got all summer to—

BIFF: (*His weeping breaking from him.*) Dad . . .

WILLY: (*Infected by it.*) Oh, my boy . . .

BIFF: Dad . . .

WILLY: She's nothing to me, Biff. I was lonely, I was terribly

1350 lonely.

BIFF: You—you gave her Mama's stockings! (*His tears break through and he rises to go.*)

WILLY: (*Grabbing for* BIFF.) I gave you an order!

BIFF: Don't touch me, you—liar!

WILLY: Apologize for that!   1355

BIFF: You fake! You phony little fake! You fake! (*Overcome, he turns quickly and weeping fully goes out with his suitcase.* WILLY *is left on the floor on his knees.*)

WILLY: I gave you an order! Biff, come back here or I'll beat you! Come back here! I'll whip you!   1360

(STANLEY *comes quickly in from the right and stands in front of* WILLY.)

WILLY: (*Shouts at* STANLEY.) I gave you an order . . .

STANLEY: Hey, let's pick it up, pick it up, Mr. Loman. (*He helps* WILLY *to his feet.*) Your boys left with the chippies. They said they'll see you home.

(*A second waiter watches some distance away.*)

WILLY: But we were supposed to have dinner together.   1365

(*Music is heard,* WILLY'S *theme.*)

STANLEY: Can you make it?

WILLY: I'll—sure, I can make it. (*Suddenly concerned about his clothes.*) Do I—I look all right?

STANLEY: Sure, you look all right. (*He flicks a speck off* WILLY'S *lapel.*)   1370

WILLY: Here—here's a dollar.

STANLEY: Oh, your son paid me. It's all right.

WILLY: (*Putting it in* STANLEY'S *hand.*) No, take it. You're a good, boy.

STANLEY: Oh, no, you don't have to . . .   1375

WILLY: Here—here's some more, I don't need it any more. (*After a slight pause.*) Tell me—is there a seed store in the neighborhood?

STANLEY: Seeds? You mean like to plant?

(*As* WILLY *turns,* STANLEY *slips the money back into his jacket pocket.*)

WILLY: Yes. Carrots, peas . . .   1380

STANLEY: Well, there's hardware stores on Sixth Avenue, but it may be too late now.

WILLY: (*Anxiously.*) Oh, I'd better hurry. I've got to get some seeds. (*He starts off to the right.*) I've got to get some seeds, right away. Nothing's planted. I don't have a thing in the 1385 ground.

(WILLY *hurries out as the light goes down.* STANLEY *moves over to the right after him, watches him off. The other waiter has been staring at* WILLY.)

STANLEY: (*To the waiter.*) Well, whatta you looking at?

(*The waiter picks up the chairs and moves off right.* STANLEY *takes the table and follows him. The light fades on this area. There is a long pause, the sound of the flute coming over. The light gradually rises on the kitchen, which is empty.* HAPPY *appears at the door of the house, followed by* BIFF. HAPPY *is carrying a large bunch of long-stemmed roses. He enters the kitchen, looks around for* LINDA. *Not seeing her, he turns to* BIFF, *who is just outside the house door, and makes a gesture with his hands, indicating "Not here, I guess." He looks into the living-room and freezes. Inside,* LINDA, *unseen, is seated,* WILLY's *coat on her lap. She rises ominously and quietly and moves toward* HAPPY, *who backs up into the kitchen, afraid.*)

HAPPY: Hey, what're you doing up? (LINDA *says nothing but moves toward him implacably.*) Where's Pop? (*He keeps backing to the right, and now* LINDA *is in full view in the doorway to the living-room.*) Is he sleeping?

LINDA: Where were you?

HAPPY: (*Trying to laugh it off.*) We met two girls, Mom, very fine types. Here, we brought you some flowers. (*Offering them to her.*) Put them in your room, Ma.

(*She knocks them to the floor at* BIFF's *feet. He has now come inside and closed the door behind him. She stares at* BIFF, *silent.*)

HAPPY: Now what'd you do that for? Mom, I want you to have some flowers—

LINDA: (*Cutting* HAPPY *off, violently to* BIFF.) Don't you care whether he lives or dies?

HAPPY: (*Going to the stairs.*) Come upstairs, Biff.

BIFF: (*With a flare of disgust, to* HAPPY.) Go away from me! (*To* LINDA.) What do you mean, lives or dies? Nobody's dying around here, pal.

LINDA: Get out of my sight! Get out of here!

BIFF: I wanna see the boss.

LINDA: You're not going near him!

BIFF: Where is he? (*He moves into the living-room and* LINDA *follows.*)

LINDA: (*Shouting after* BIFF.) You invite him for dinner. He looks forward to it all day—(BIFF *appears in his parents' bedroom, looks around, and exits.*)—and then you desert him there. There's no stranger you'd do that to!

HAPPY: Why? He had a swell time with us. Listen, when I—(LINDA *comes back into the kitchen.*)—desert him I hope I don't outlive the day!

LINDA: Get out of here!

HAPPY: Now look, Mom . . .

LINDA: Did you have to go to women tonight? You and your lousy rotten whores!

(BIFF *re-enters the kitchen.*)

HAPPY: Mom, all we did was follow Biff around trying to cheer him up! (*To* BIFF.) Boy, what a night you gave me!

LINDA: Get out of here, both of you, and don't come back! I don't want you tormenting him any more. Go on now, get your things together! (*To* BIFF.) You can sleep in his apartment. (*She starts to pick up the flowers and stops herself.*) Pick up this stuff, I'm not your maid any more. Pick it up, you bum, you!

(HAPPY *turns his back to her in refusal.* BIFF *slowly moves over and gets down on his knees, picking up the flowers.*)

LINDA: You're a pair of animals! Not one, not another living soul would have had the cruelty to walk out on that man in a restaurant!

BIFF: (*Not looking at her.*) Is that what he said?

LINDA: He didn't have to say anything. He was so humiliated he nearly limped when he came in.

HAPPY: But, Mom, he had a great time with us—

BIFF: (*Cutting him off violently.*) Shut up!

(*Without another word,* HAPPY *goes upstairs.*)

LINDA: You! You didn't even go in to see if he was all right!

BIFF: (*Still on the floor in front of* LINDA, *the flowers in his hand; with self-loathing.*) No. Didn't. Didn't do a damned thing. How do you like that, heh? Left him babbling in a toilet.

LINDA: You louse. You . . .

BIFF: Now you hit it on the nose! (*He gets up, throws the flowers in the wastebasket.*) The scum of the earth, and you're looking at him!

LINDA: Get out of here!

BIFF: I gotta talk to the boss, Mom. Where is he?

LINDA: You're not going near him. Get out of this house!

BIFF: (*With absolute assurance, determination.*) No. We're gonna have an abrupt conversation, him and me.

LINDA: You're not talking to him!

(*Hammering is heard from outside the house, off right.* BIFF *turns toward the noise.*)

LINDA: (*Suddenly pleading.*) Will you please leave him alone?

BIFF: What's he doing out there?

LINDA: He's planting the garden!

BIFF: (*Quietly.*) Now? Oh, my God!

(BIFF *moves outside,* LINDA *following. The light dies down on them and comes up on the center of the apron as* WILLY *walks into it. He is carrying a flashlight, a hoe, and a handful of seed packets. He raps the top of the hoe sharply to fix it firmly, and then moves to the left, measuring off the distance with his foot. He holds the flashlight to look at the seed packets, reading off the instructions. He is in the blue of night.*)

WILLY: Carrots . . . quarter-inch apart. Rows . . . one-foot rows. (*He measures it off.*) One foot. (*He puts down a package and measures off.*) Beets. (*He puts down another package and measures again.*) Lettuce. (*He reads the package, puts it down.*) One foot—(*He breaks off as* BEN *appears at the right and moves slowly down to him.*) What a proposition, ts, ts. Terrific, terrific. 'Cause she's suffered, Ben, the woman has suffered. You understand me? A man can't go out the way he came in, Ben, a man has got to add up to something. You can't, you can't—(BEN *moves toward him as though to interrupt.*) You gotta consider, now. Don't answer so quick. Remember, it's a guaranteed twenty-thousand-dollar proposition. Now look, Ben, I want you to go through the ins and outs of this thing with me. I've got nobody to talk to, Ben, and the woman has suffered, you hear me?

BEN: (*Standing still, considering.*) What's the proposition?

WILLY: It's twenty thousand dollars on the barrelhead. Guaranteed, gilt-edged, you understand?

BEN: You don't want to make a fool of yourself. They might not honor the policy.

WILLY: How can they dare refuse? Didn't I work like a coolie to meet every premium on the nose? And now they don't pay off? Impossible!

BEN: It's called a cowardly thing, William.

WILLY: Why? Does it take more guts to stand here the rest of my life ringing up a zero?

BEN: (*Yielding.*) That's a point, William. (*He moves, thinking, turns.*) And twenty thousand—that *is* something one can feel with the hand, it is there.

WILLY: (*Now assured, with rising power.*) Oh, Ben, that's the whole beauty of it! I see it like a diamond, shining in the dark, hard and rough, that I can pick up and touch in my hand. Not like—like an appointment! This would not be another damned-fool appointment, Ben, and it changes all the aspects. Because he thinks I'm nothing, see, and so he spites me. But the funeral— (*Straightening up.*) Ben, that funeral will be massive! They'll come from Maine, Massachusetts, Vermont, New Hampshire! All the old-timers with the strange license plates—that boy will be thunderstruck, Ben, because he never realized—I am known! Rhode Island, New York, New Jersey—I am known, Ben, and he'll see it with his eyes once and for all. He'll see what I am, Ben! He's in for a shock, that boy!

BEN: (*Coming down to the edge of the garden.*) He'll call you a coward.

WILLY: (*Suddenly fearful.*) No, that would be terrible.

BEN: Yes. And a damned fool.

WILLY: No, no, he mustn't, I won't have that! (*He is broken and desperate.*)

BEN: He'll hate you, William.

(*The gay music of the Boys is heard.*)

WILLY: Oh, Ben, how do we get back to all the great times? Used to be so full of light, and comradeship, the sleigh-riding in winter, and the ruddiness on his cheeks. And always some kind of good news coming up, always something nice coming up ahead. And never even let me carry the valises in the house, and simonizing, simonizing that little red car! Why, why can't I give him something and not have him hate me?

BEN: Let me think about it. (*He glances at his watch.*) I still have a little time. Remarkable proposition, but you've got to be sure you're not making a fool of yourself.

(BEN *drifts off upstage and goes out of sight.* BIFF *comes down from the left.*)

WILLY: (*Suddenly conscious of* BIFF, *turns and looks up at him, then begins picking up the packages of seeds in confusion.*) Where the hell is that seed? (*Indignantly.*) You can't see nothing out here! They boxed in the whole goddam neighborhood!

BIFF: There are people all around here. Don't you realize that?

WILLY: I'm busy. Don't bother me.

BIFF: (*Taking the hoe from* WILLY.) I'm saying good-by to you, Pop. (WILLY *looks at him, silent, unable to move.*) I'm not coming back any more.

WILLY: You're not going to see Oliver tomorrow?

BIFF: I've got no appointment, Dad.

WILLY: He put his arm around you, and you've got no appointment?

BIFF: Pop, get this now, will you? Everytime I've left it's been a fight that sent me out of here. Today I realized something about myself and I tried to explain it to you and I—I think I'm just not smart enough to make any sense out of it for you. To hell with whose fault it is or anything like that. (*He takes* WILLY's *arm.*) Let's just wrap it up, heh? Come on in, we'll tell Mom. (*He gently tries to pull* WILLY *to left.*)

WILLY: (*Frozen, immobile, with guilt in his voice.*) No, I don't want to see her.

BIFF: Come on! (*He pulls again, and* WILLY *tries to pull away.*)

WILLY: (*Highly nervous.*) No, no, I don't want to see her.

BIFF: (*Tries to look into* WILLY's *face, as if to find the answer there.*) Why don't you want to see her?

WILLY: (*More harshly now.*) Don't bother me, will you?

BIFF: What do you mean, you don't want to see her? You don't want them calling you yellow, do you? This isn't your fault; it's me, I'm a bum. Now come inside! (WILLY *strains to get away.*) Did you hear what I said to you?

(WILLY *pulls away and quickly goes by himself into the house.* BIFF *follows.*)

LINDA: (*To* WILLY). Did you plant, dear?

BIFF: (*At the door, to* LINDA.) All right, we had it out. I'm going and I'm not writing any more.

LINDA: (*Going to* WILLY *in the kitchen.*) I think that's the best way, dear. 'Cause there's no use drawing it out, you'll just never get along.

(WILLY *doesn't respond.*)

BIFF: People ask where I am and what I'm doing, you don't know, and you don't care. That way it'll be off your mind and you can start brightening up again. All right? That clears it, doesn't it? (WILLY *is silent, and* BIFF *goes to him.*) You gonna wish me luck, scout? (*He extends his hand.*) What do you say?

LINDA: Shake his hand, Willy.

WILLY: (*Turning to her, seething with hurt.*) There's no necessity to mention the pen at all, y'know.

BIFF: (*Gently.*) I've got no appointment, Dad.

WILLY: (*Erupting fiercely.*) He put his arm around . . . ?

BIFF: Dad, you're never going to see what I am, so what's the use of arguing? If I strike oil I'll send you a check. Meantime forget I'm alive.

WILLY: (*To* LINDA.) Spite, see?

BIFF: Shake hands, Dad.

WILLY: Not my hand.

BIFF: I was hoping not to go this way.

WILLY: Well, this is the way you're going. Good-by.

(BIFF *looks at him a moment, then turns sharply and goes to the stairs.*)

WILLY: (*Stops him with.*) May you rot in hell if you leave this house!

BIFF: (*Turning.*) Exactly what is it that you want from me?

WILLY: I want you to know, on the train, in the mountains, in the valleys, wherever you go, that you cut down your life for spite!

BIFF: No, no.

WILLY: Spite, spite, is the word of your undoing! And when you're down and out, remember what did it. When you're rotting somewhere beside the railroad tracks, remember, and don't you dare blame it on me!

BIFF: I'm not blaming it on you!

WILLY: I won't take the rap for this, you hear?

(HAPPY *comes down the stairs and stands on the bottom step, watching.*)

BIFF: That's just what I'm telling you!

1585   WILLY: (*Sinking into a chair at the table, with full accusation.*) You're trying to put a knife in me—don't think I don't know what you're doing!

BIFF: All right, phony! Then let's lay it on the line. (*He whips the rubber tube out of his pocket and puts it on the table.*)

1590   HAPPY: You crazy—

LINDA: Biff! (*She moves to grab the hose, but BIFF holds it down with his hand.*)

BIFF: Leave it there! Don't move it!

WILLY: (*Not looking at it.*) What is that?

1595   BIFF: You know goddam well what that is.

WILLY: (*Caged, wanting to escape.*) I never saw that.

BIFF: You saw it. The mice didn't bring it into the cellar! What is this supposed to do, make a hero out of you? This supposed to make me sorry for you?

1600   WILLY: Never heard of it.

BIFF: There'll be no pity for you, you hear it? No pity!

WILLY: (*To LINDA.*) You hear the spite!

BIFF: No, you're going to hear the truth—what you are and what I am!

1605   LINDA: Stop it!

WILLY: Spite!

HAPPY: (*Coming down toward BIFF.*) You cut it now!

BIFF: (*To HAPPY.*) The man don't know who we are! The man is gonna know! (*To WILLY.*) We never told the truth for ten

1610   minutes in this house!

HAPPY: We always told the truth!

BIFF: (*Turning on him.*) You big blow, are you the assistant buyer? You're one of the two assistants to the assistant, aren't you?

1615   HAPPY: Well, I'm practically—

BIFF: You're practically full of it! We all are! And I'm through with it. (*To WILLY.*) Now hear this, Willy, this is me

WILLY: I know you!

BIFF: You know why I had no address for three months? I

1620   stole a suit in Kansas City and I was in jail. (*To LINDA, who is sobbing.*) Stop crying. I'm through with it.

(LINDA *turns away from them, her hands covering her face.*)

WILLY: I suppose that's my fault!

BIFF: I stole myself out of every good job since high school!

WILLY: And whose fault is that?

1625   BIFF: And I never got anywhere because you blew me so full of hot air I could never stand taking orders from anybody! That's whose fault it is!

WILLY: I hear that!

LINDA: Don't, Biff!

1630   BIFF: It's goddam time you heard that! I had to be boss big shot in two weeks, and I'm through with it!

WILLY: Then hang yourself! For spite, hang yourself!

BIFF: No! Nobody's hanging himself, Willy! I ran down eleven flights with a pen in my hand today. And suddenly I

1635   stopped, you hear me? And in the middle of that office building, do you hear this? I stopped in the middle of that building and I saw—the sky. I saw the things that I love in this world. The work and the food and time to sit and smoke. And I looked at the pen and said to myself, what

1640   the hell am I grabbing this for? Why am I trying to become what I don't want to be? What am I doing in an office, making a contemptuous, begging fool of myself, when all

I want is out there, waiting for me the minute I say I know who I am! Why can't I say that, Willy? (*He tries to make WILLY face him, but WILLY pulls away and moves to the left.*)   1645

WILLY: (*With hatred, threateningly.*) The door of your life is wide open!

BIFF: Pop! I'm a dime a dozen, and so are you!

WILLY: (*Turning on him now in an uncontrolled outburst.*) I am not a dime a dozen! I am Willy Loman, and you are Biff   1650 Loman!

(BIFF *starts for WILLY, but is blocked by HAPPY. In his fury, BIFF seems on the verge of attacking his father.*)

BIFF: I am not a leader of men, Willy, and neither are you. You were never anything but a hard-working drummer who landed in the ash can like all the rest of them! I'm one dollar an hour, Willy! I tried seven states and couldn't   1655 raise it. A buck an hour! Do you gather my meaning? I'm not bringing home any prizes any more, and you're going to stop waiting for me to bring them home!

WILLY: (*Directly to BIFF.*) You vengeful, spiteful mut!

(BIFF *breaks from HAPPY. WILLY, in fright, starts up the stairs. BIFF grabs him.*)

BIFF: (*At the peak of his fury.*) Pop, I'm nothing! I'm nothing,   1660 Pop. Can't you understand that? There's no spite in it any more. I'm just what I am, that's all.

(BIFF's *fury has spent itself, and he breaks down, sobbing, holding on to WILLY, who dumbly fumbles for BIFF's face.*)

WILLY: (*Astonished.*) What're you doing? What're you doing? (*To LINDA.*) Why is he crying?

BIFF: (*Crying, broken.*) Will you let me go, for Christ's sake?   1665 Will you take that phony dream and burn it before something happens? (*Struggling to contain himself, he pulls away and moves to the stairs.*) I'll go in the morning. Put him— put him to bed. (*Exhausted, BIFF moves up the stairs to his room.*)   1670

WILLY: (*After a long pause, astonished, elevated.*) Isn't that—isn't that remarkable? Biff—he likes me!

LINDA: He loves you, Willy!

HAPPY: (*Deeply moved.*) Always did, Pop.

WILLY: Oh, Biff! (*Staring wildly.*) He cried! Cried to me. (*He   1675 is choking with his love, and now cries out his promise.*) That boy—that boy is going to be magnificent!

(BEN *appears in the light just outside the kitchen.*)

BEN: Yes, outstanding, with twenty thousand behind him.

LINDA: (*Sensing the racing of his mind, fearfully, carefully.*) Now come to bed, Willy. It's all settled now.   1680

WILLY: (*Finding it difficult not to rush out of the house.*) Yes, we'll sleep. Come on. Go to sleep, Hap.

BEN: And it does take a great kind of a man to crack the jungle.

(*In accents of dread,* BEN's *idyllic music starts up.*)

HAPPY: (*His arm around LINDA.*) I'm getting married, Pop, don't forget it. I'm changing everything. I'm gonna run   1685 that department before the year is up. You'll see, Mom. (*He kisses her.*)

BEN: The jungle is dark but full of diamonds, Willy.

(WILLY *turns, moves, listening to* BEN.)

1690 LINDA: Be good. You're both good boys, just act that way, that's all.

HAPPY: 'Night, Pop. (*He goes upstairs.*)

LINDA: (*To* WILLY). Come, dear.

BEN: (*With greater force.*) One must go in to fetch a diamond out.

1695 WILLY: (*To* LINDA, *as he moves slowly along the edge of the kitchen, toward the door.*) I just want to get settled down, Linda. Let me sit alone for a little.

LINDA: (*Almost uttering her fear.*) I want you upstairs.

WILLY: (*Taking her in his arms.*) In a few minutes, Linda. I

1600 couldn't sleep right now. Go on, you look awful tired. (*He kisses her.*)

BEN: Not like an appointment at all. A diamond is rough and hard to the touch.

WILLY: Go on now. I'll be right up.

1705 LINDA: I think this is the only way, Willy.

WILLY: Sure, it's the best thing.

BEN: Best thing!

WILLY: The only way. Everything is gonna be—go on, kid, get to bed. You look so tired.

1710 LINDA: Come right up.

WILLY: Two minutes.

(LINDA *goes into the living-room, then reappears in her bedroom.* WILLY *moves just outside the kitchen door.*)

WILLY: Loves me. (*Wonderingly.*) Always loved me. Isn't that a remarkable thing? Ben, he'll worship me, for it!

BEN: (*With promise.*) It's dark there, but full of diamonds.

1715 WILLY: Can you imagine that magnificence with twenty thousand dollars in his pocket?

LINDA: (*Calling from her room.*) Willy! Come up!

WILLY: (*Calling into the kitchen.*) Yes! Yes. Coming! It's very smart, you realize that, don't you, sweetheart? Even Ben

1720 sees it. I gotta go, baby. 'By! 'By! (*Going over to* BEN, *almost dancing.*) Imagine? When the mail comes he'll be ahead of Bernard again!

BEN: A perfect proposition all around.

WILLY: Did you see how he cried to me? Oh, if I could kiss

1725 him, Ben!

BEN: Time, William, time!

WILLY: Oh, Ben, I always knew one way or another we were gonna make it, Biff and I!

BEN: (*Looking at his watch.*) The boat. We'll be late. (*He moves*

1730 *slowly off into the darkness.*)

WILLY: (*Elegiacally, turning to the house.*) Now when you kick off, boy, I want a seventy-yard boot, and get right down the field under the ball, and when you hit, hit low and hit hard, because it's important, boy. (*He swings around and faces*

1735 *the audience.*) There's all kinds of important people in the stands, and the first thing you know . . . (*Suddenly realizing he is alone.*) Ben! Ben, where do I . . . ? (*He makes a sudden movement of search.*) Ben, how do I . . . ?

LINDA: (*Calling.*) Willy, you coming up?

1740 WILLY: (*Uttering a gasp of fear, whirling about as if to quiet her.*) Sh! (*He turns around as if to find his way; sounds, faces, voices, seem to be swarming in upon him and he flicks at them, crying.*)

Sh! Sh! (*Suddenly music, faint and high, stops him. It rises in intensity, almost to an unbearable scream. He goes up and down on his toes, and rushes off around the house.*) Shhh!   1745

LINDA: Willy?

(*There is no answer.* LINDA *waits.* BIFF *gets up off his bed He is still in his clothes.* HAPPY *sits up.* BIFF *stands listening.*)

LINDA: (*With real fear.*) Willy, answer me! Willy!

(*There is the sound of a car starting and moving away at full speed.*)

LINDA: No!

BIFF: (*Rushing down the stairs.*) Pop!

(*As the car speeds off, the music crashes down in a frenzy of sound, which becomes the soft pulsation of a single cello string.* BIFF *slowly returns to his bedroom. He and* HAPPY *gravely don their jackets.* LINDA *slowly walks out of her room. The music has developed into a dead march. The leaves of day are appearing over everything.* CHARLEY *and* BERNARD, *somberly dressed, appear and knock on the kitchen door.* BIFF *and* HAPPY *slowly descend the stairs to the kitchen as* CHARLEY *and* BERNARD *enter. All stop a moment when* LINDA, *in clothes of mourning, bearing a little bunch of roses, comes through the draped doorway into the kitchen. She goes to* CHARLEY *and takes his arm. Now all move toward the audience, through the wall-line of the kitchen. At the limit of the apron,* LINDA *lays down the flowers, kneels, and sits back on her heels. All stare down at the grave.*)

REQUIEM

CHARLEY: It's getting dark, Linda.

(LINDA *doesn't react. She stares at the grave.*)

BIFF: How about it, Mom? Better get some rest, heh? They'll be closing the gate soon.

(LINDA *makes no move. Pause.*)

HAPPY: (*Deeply angered.*) He had no right to do that. There was no necessity for it. We would've helped him.   5

CHARLEY: (*Grunting.*) Hmmm.

BIFF: Come along, Mom.

LINDA: Why didn't anybody come?

CHARLEY: It was a very nice funeral.

LINDA: But where are all the people he knew? Maybe they   10 blame him.

CHARLEY: Naa. It's a rough world, Linda. They wouldn't blame him.

LINDA: I can't understand it. At this time especially. First time in thirty-five years we were just about free and clear. He   15 only needed a little salary. He was even finished with the dentist.

CHARLEY: No man only needs a little salary.

LINDA: I can't understand it.

BIFF: There were a lot of nice days. When he'd come home   20 from a trip; or on Sundays, making the stoop; finishing the cellar; putting on the new porch; when he built the extra bathroom; and put up the garage. You know something, Charley, there's more of him in that front stoop than in all the sales he ever made.   25

CHARLEY: Yeah. He was a happy man with a batch of cement.

LINDA: He was so wonderful with his hands.

BIFF: He had the wrong dreams. All, all, wrong.

HAPPY: (*Almost ready to fight* BIFF.) Don't say that!

30 BIFF: He never knew who he was.

CHARLEY: (*Stopping* HAPPY*'s movement and reply. To* BIFF.) Nobody dast blame this man. You don't understand: Willy was a salesman. And for a salesman, there is no rock bottom to the life. He don't put a bolt to a nut, he don't tell

35 you the law or give you medicine. He's a man way out there in the blue, riding on a smile and a shoeshine. And when they start not smiling back—that's an earthquake. And then you get yourself a couple of spots on your hat, and you're finished. Nobody dast blame this man. A sales-

40 man is got to dream, boy. It comes with the territory.

BIFF: Charley, the man didn't know who he was.

HAPPY: (*Infuriated.*) Don't say that!

BIFF: Why don't you come with me, Happy?

HAPPY: I'm not licked that easily. I'm staying right in this city,

45 and I'm gonna beat this racket! (*He looks at* BIFF, *his chin set.*) The Loman Brothers!

BIFF: I know who I am, kid.

HAPPY: All right, boy. I'm gonna show you and everybody else that Willy Loman did not die in vain. He had a good

50 dream. It's the only dream you can have—to come out number-one man. He fought it out here, and this is where I'm gonna win it for him.

BIFF: (*With a hopeless glance at* HAPPY, *bends toward his mother.*) Let's go, Mom.

LINDA: I'll be with you in a minute. Go on, Charley. (*He hes-* 55 *itates.*) I want to, just for a minute. I never had a chance to say good-by.

(CHARLEY *moves away, followed by* HAPPY. BIFF *remains a slight distance up and left of* LINDA. *She sits there, summoning herself. The flute begins, not far away, playing behind her speech.*)

LINDA: Forgive me, dear. I can't cry. I don't know what it is, but I can't cry. I don't understand it. Why did you ever do that? Help me, Willy, I can't cry. It seems to me that you're 60 just on another trip. I keep expecting you. Willy, dear, I can't cry. Why did you do it? I search and search and I search, and I can't understand it, Willy. I made the last payment on the house today. Today, dear. And there'll be nobody home. (*A sob rises in her throat.*) We're free and clear. 65 (*Sobbing more fully, released.*) We're free. (BIFF *comes slowly toward her.*) We're free . . . We're free . . .

BIFF *lifts her to her feet and moves out up right with her in his arms.* LINDA *sobs quietly.* BERNARD *and* CHARLEY *come together and follow them, followed by* HAPPY. *Only the music of the flute is left on the darkening stage as over the house the hard towers of the apartment buildings rise into sharp focus, and*

The Curtain Falls

Amiri Baraka / LeRoi Jones

Born Everett LeRoi Jones in Newark, New Jersey, in 1934, Amiri Baraka has become the most important revolutionary voice in contemporary black theater in the United States. He attended Rutgers University and Howard University, taking his B.A. from Howard in 1954. Baraka later said that his education at Howard was too involved with "learning to be white." He served in the United States Air Force before returning to New York in 1958. Living in Greenwich Village, he studied at Columbia University, married his first wife—an interracial marriage, lightly disguised in his play *The Slave*—and worked to develop his talents as a writer. Jones worked everywhere to develop a black esthetic, in his own poetry (in the mode of the Beat poets Gregory Corso and Allen Ginsberg), in essays, and in magazines that he founded and edited. In 1960, Jones was part of a delegation of black Americans invited to Cuba to celebrate Fidel Castro's revolution. That visit had a profound impact on Jones, sharpening his sense of the need both for a distinctive black esthetic and culture, and for a social revolution to eradicate the injustices of white-dominated American society. His plays of the 1960s are, in fact, often directly concerned with this issue and with how white liberalism—ostensibly the ally of black power—finally becomes an obstacle to the more fundamental revolution needed to bring black identity, culture, and power into being. In 1964, three of his plays opened in New York: *The Eighth Ditch, The Baptism,* and *Dutchman,* which won the Obie award for the best American play of the season. He then wrote a series of plays examining black activism and revolution in American life: *The Slave* (1964) and *The Toilet* (1964), *Experimental Death Unit #1* (1965), and *J-e-l-l-o* (1965). The assassination of Malcolm X in 1965 and the Watts riots in Los Angeles also drove Jones toward a more militant position, as articulated in plays like *A Black Mass* (1966), *Slave Ship* (1966), *The Great Goodness of Life* (*A Coon Show*) (1967), *Home on the Range* (1968), and *The Death of Malcolm X* (1969), and later in *The*

Clay strangles Lula in the subway at the climax of Amiri Baraka/LeRoi Jones's *Dutchman,* produced by the Hartford Stage in 2000.

Motion of History (1977) and *Money* (1988). In 1964 Jones established the Black Arts Repertory Theater and School in Harlem and began a program of cultural nationalism there, which he has pursued subsequently in several other organizations and described in several collections of essays. He has been deeply involved in developing a theater that would serve the need for cultural and political revolution in the black community.

As part of his commitment to forging a sustaining system of values for the African American community, Jones became a Kawaidi Muslim minister in 1968, adopting the title Imamu (spiritual leader) and the name Amiri Baraka at that time. Throughout the 1970s and 1980s, Baraka articulated and solidified the claims of cultural nationalism, frequently in a fiercely revolutionary, Marxist rhetoric. Baraka continues to be involved in a variety of political and social activities in the black community.

DUTCHMAN

Dutchman is one of Baraka's most powerful plays, both in its indictment of racist culture and in its straightforward confrontation between Lula and Clay. The title alludes to the legendary *Flying Dutchman*, the ship of the dead said to haunt the high seas. The subway car of the play is at once a ghost ship—where the young black man Clay is murdered—and a ghostly incarnation of racist fantasies. At the beginning of the play, Lula seems attracted to the middle-class Clay, but as the play develops it becomes clear that, to seduce Clay, Lula must transform him into something else, a fantasy figure of the white imagination. When Clay refuses to play along, delivering instead an impassioned statement of his own black identity, Lula murders him, with the implied consent of the white riders of the subway. *Dutchman* is a powerful parable of the problems of black identity in white culture.

DUTCHMAN

Amiri Baraka/Leroi Jones

CHARACTERS

CLAY, *twenty-year-old Negro*
LULA, *thirty-year-old white woman*
RIDERS OF COACH, *white and black*
YOUNG NEGRO
CONDUCTOR

In the flying underbelly of the city. Steaming hot, and summer on top, outside. Underground. The subway heaped in modern myth.

Opening scene is a man sitting in a subway seat, holding a magazine but looking vacantly just above its wilting pages. Occasionally he looks blankly toward the window on his right. Dim lights and darkness whistling by against the glass. (Or paste the lights, as admitted props, right on the subway windows. Have them move, even dim and flicker. But give the sense of speed. Also stations, whether the train is stopped or the glitter and activity of these stations merely flashes by the windows.)

The man is sitting alone. That is, only his seat is visible, though the rest of the car is outfitted as a complete subway car. But only

his seat is shown. There might be, for a time, as the play begins, a loud scream of the actual train. And it can recur throughout the play, or continue on a lower key once the dialogue starts.

The train slows after a time, pulling to a brief stop at one of the stations. The man looks idly up, until he sees a woman's face staring at him through the window; when it realizes that the man has noticed the face, it begins very premeditatedly to smile. The man smiles too, for a moment, without a trace of self-consciousness. Almost an instinctive though undesirable response. Then a kind of awkwardness or embarrassment sets in, and the man makes to look away, is further embarrassed, so he brings back his eyes to where the face was, but by now the train is moving again, and the face would seem to be left behind by the way the man turns his head to look back through the other windows at the slowly fading platform. He smiles then; more comfortably confident, hoping perhaps that his memory of this brief encounter will be pleasant. And then he is idle again.

SCENE ONE

Train roars. Lights flash outside the windows.

LULA *enters from the rear of the car in bright, skimpy summer clothes and sandals. She carries a net bag full of paper books, fruit, and other anonymous articles. She is wearing sunglasses, which she pushes up on her forehead from time to time.* LULA *is a tall, slender, beautiful woman with long red hair hanging straight down her back, wearing only loud lipstick in somebody's good taste. She is eating an apple, very daintily. Coming down the car toward* CLAY.

She stops beside CLAY's *seat and hangs languidly from the strap, still managing to eat the apple. It is apparent that she is going to sit in the seat next to* CLAY, *and that she is only waiting for him to notice her before she sits.*

CLAY *sits as before, looking just beyond his magazine, now and again pulling the magazine slowly back and forth in front of his face in a hopeless effort to fan himself. Then he sees the woman hanging there beside him and he looks up into her face, smiling quizzically.*

LULA: Hello.
CLAY: Uh, hi're you?
LULA: I'm going to sit down. . . . O.K.?
CLAY: Sure.
5 LULA:

(Swings down onto the seat, pushing her legs straight out as if she is very weary.)

Oooof! Too much weight.
CLAY: Ha, doesn't look like much to me.

(Leaning back against the window, a little surprised and maybe stiff.)

LULA: It's so anyway.

(And she moves her toes in the sandals, then pulls her right leg up on the left knee, better to inspect the bottoms of the sandals and the back of her heel. She appears for a second not to notice that CLAY *is sitting next to her or that she has spoken to him just a second before.* CLAY *looks at the magazine, then out the black window. As he does this, she turns very quickly toward him.)*

Weren't you staring at me through the window?
CLAY: 10

(Wheeling around and very much stiffened.)

What?
LULA: Weren't you staring at me through the window? At the last stop?
CLAY: Staring at you? What do you mean?
LULA: Don't you know what staring means?   15
CLAY: I saw you through the window . . . if that's what it means. I don't know if I was staring. Seems to me you were staring through the window at me.
LULA: I was. But only after I'd turned around and saw you staring through that window down in the vicinity of my 20 ass and legs.
CLAY: Really?
LULA: Really. I guess you were just taking those idle potshots. Nothing else to do. Run your mind over people's flesh.
CLAY: Oh boy. Wow, now I admit I was looking in your di- 25 rection. But the rest of that weight is yours.
LULA: I suppose.
CLAY: Staring through train windows is weird business. Much weirder than staring very sedately at abstract asses.
LULA: That's why I came looking through the window . . . so 30 you'd have more than that to go on. I even smiled at you.
CLAY: That's right.
LULA: I even got into this train, going some other way than mine. Walked down the aisle . . . searching you out.

35 CLAY: Really? That's pretty funny.
    LULA: That's pretty funny. . . . God, you're dull.
    CLAY: Well, I'm sorry, lady, but I really wasn't prepared for party talk.
    LULA: No, you're not. What are you prepared for?

    (*Wrapping the apple core in a Kleenex and dropping it on the floor.*)

40 CLAY:

    (*Takes her conversation as pure sex talk. He turns to confront her squarely with this idea.*)

    I'm prepared for anything. How about you?
    LULA:

    (*Laughing loudly and cutting it off abruptly.*)

    What do you think you're doing?
    CLAY: What?
45 LULA: You think I want to pick you up, get you to take me somewhere and screw me, huh?
    CLAY: Is that the way I look?
    LULA: You look like you been trying to grow a beard. That's exactly what you look like. You look like you live in New
50   Jersey with your parents and are trying to grow a beard. That's what. You look like you've been reading Chinese poetry and drinking lukewarm sugarless tea.

    (*Laughs, uncrossing and recrossing her legs.*)

    You look like death eating a soda cracker.
    CLAY:

    (*Cocking his head from one side to the other, embarrassed and trying to make some comeback, but also intrigued by what the woman is saying . . . even the sharp city coarseness of her voice, which is still a kind of gentle sidewalk throb.*)

55 Really? I look like all that?
    LULA: Not all of it.

    (*She feigns a seriousness to cover an actual somber tone.*)

    I lie a lot.

    (*Smiling.*)

    It helps me control the world.
    CLAY:

    (*Relieved and laughing louder than the humor.*)

60 Yeah, I bet.
    LULA: But it's true, most of it, right? Jersey? Your bumpy neck?
    CLAY: How'd you know all that? Huh? Really. I mean about Jersey . . . and even the beard. I met you before? You know Warren Enright?
65 LULA: You tried to make it with your sister when you were ten.

    (CLAY *leans back hard against the back of the seat, his eyes opening now, still trying to look amused.*)

    But I succeeded a few weeks ago.

    (*She starts to laugh again.*)

    CLAY: What're you talking about? Warren tell you that? You're a friend of Georgia's?
    LULA: I told you I lie. I don't know your sister. I don't know Warren Enright.   70
    CLAY: You mean you're just picking these things out of the air?
    LULA: Is Warren Enright a tall skinny black black boy with a phony English accent?
    CLAY: I figured you knew him.
    LULA: But I don't. I just figured you would know somebody 75
        like that.

    (*Laughs.*)

    CLAY: Yeah, yeah.
    LULA: You're probably on your way to his house now.
    CLAY: That's right.
    LULA: 80

    (*Putting her hand on* CLAY*'s closer knee, drawing it from the knee up to the thigh's hinge, then removing it, watching his face very closely, and continuing to laugh, perhaps more gently than before.*)

    Dull, dull, dull. I bet you think I'm exciting.
    CLAY: You're O.K.
    LULA: Am I exciting you now?
    CLAY: Right. That's not what's supposed to happen?
    LULA: How do I know?   85

    (*She returns her hand, without moving it, then takes it away and plunges it in her bag to draw out an apple.*)

    You want this?
    CLAY: Sure.
    LULA:

    (*She gets one out of the bag for herself.*)

    Eating apples together is always the first step. Or walking up uninhabited Seventh Avenue in the twenties on weekends.   90

    (*Bites and giggles, glancing at* CLAY *and speaking in loose singsong.*)

    Can get you involved . . . boy! Get us involved. Um-huh.

    (*Mock seriousness.*)

    Would you like to get involved with me, Mister Man?
    CLAY:

    (*Trying to be as flippant as* LULA, *whacking happily at the apple.*)

    Sure. Why not? A beautiful woman like you. Huh, I'd be a fool not to.   95
    LULA: And I bet you're sure you know what you're talking about.

    (*Taking him a little roughly by the wrist, so he cannot eat the apple, then shaking the wrist.*)

    I bet you're sure of almost everything anybody ever asked you about . . . right?

(Shakes his wrist harder.)

100   Right?
       CLAY: Yeah, right. . . . Wow, you're pretty strong, you know? Whatta you, a lady wrestler or something?
       LULA: What's wrong with lady wrestlers? And don't answer because you never knew any. Huh.

(Cynically.)

105   That's for sure. They don't have any lady wrestlers in that part of Jersey. That's for sure.
       CLAY: Hey, you still haven't tole me how you know so much about me.
       LULA: I told you I didn't know anything about *you* . . . you're
110   a well-known type.
       CLAY: Really?
       LULA: Or at least I know the type very well. And your skinny English friend too.
       CLAY: Anonymously?
115   LULA:

(Settles back in seat, single-mindedly finishing her apple and humming snatches of rhythm and blues song.)

       What?
       CLAY: Without knowing us specifically?
       LULA: Oh boy.

(Looking quickly at CLAY.)

       What a face. You know, you could be a handsome man.
120   CLAY: I can't argue with you.
       LULA:

(Vague, off-center response.)

       What?
       CLAY:

(Raising his voice, thinking the train noise has drowned part of his sentence.)

       I can't argue with you.
125   LULA: My hair is turning gray. A gray hair for each year and type I've come through.
       CLAY: Why do you want to sound so old?
       LULA: But it's always gentle when it starts.

(Attention drifting.)

       Hugged against tenements, day or night.
130   CLAY: What?
       LULA:

(Refocusing.)

       Hey, why don't you take me to that party you're going to?
       LULA: You must be a friend of Warren's to know about the party.
135   LULA: Wouldn't you like to take me to the party?

(Imitates clinging vine.)

       Oh, come on, ask me to your party.
       CLAY: Of course I'll ask you to come with me to the party. And I'll bet you're a friend of Warren's.
       LULA: Why not be a friend of Warren's? Why not?

(Taking his arm.)

       Have you asked me yet?   140
       CLAY: How can I ask you when I don't know your name?
       LULA: Are you talking to my name?
       CLAY: What is it, a secret?
       LULA: I'm Lena the Hyena.
       CLAY: The famous woman poet?   145
       LULA: Poetess! The same!
       CLAY: Well, you know so much about me . . . what's my name?
       LULA: Morris the Hyena.
       CLAY: The famous woman poet?
       LULA: The same.   150

(Laughing and going into her bag.)

       You want another apple?
       CLAY: Can't make it, lady. I only have to keep one doctor away a day.
       LULA: I bet your name is . . . something like . . . uh, Gerald or Walter. Huh?   155
       CLAY: God, no.
       LULA: Lloyd, Norman? One of those hopeless colored names creeping out of New Jersey. Leonard? Gag. . . .
       CLAY: Like Warren?
       LULA: Definitely. Just exactly like Warren. Or Everett.   160
       CLAY: Gag. . . .
       LULA: Well, for sure, it's not Willie.
       CLAY: It's Clay.
       LULA: Clay? Really? Clay what?
       CLAY: Take your pick. Jackson, Johnson, or Williams.   165
       LULA: Oh, really? Good for you. But it's got to be Williams. You're too pretentious to be a Jackson or Johnson.
       CLAY: Thass right.
       LULA: But Clay's O.K.
       CLAY: So's Lena.   170
       LULA: It's Lula.
       CLAY: Oh?
       LULA: Lula the Hyena.
       CLAY: Very good.
       LULA: 175

(Starts laughing again.)

       Now you say to me, "Lula, Lula, why don't you go to this party with me tonight?" It's your turn, and let those be your lines.
       CLAY: Lula, why don't you go to this party with me tonight, Huh?
       LULA: Say my name twice before you ask, and no huh's.   180
       CLAY: Lula, Lula, why don't you go to this party with me tonight?
       LULA: I'd like to go, Clay, but how can you ask me to go when you barely know me?
       CLAY: That is strange, isn't it?   185
       LULA: What kind of reaction is that? You're supposed to say, "Aw, come on, we'll get to know each other better at the party."

CLAY: That's pretty corny.
LULA: What are you into anyway?

(*Looking at him half sullenly but still amused.*)

190   What thing are you playing at, Mister? Mister Clay Williams?

(*Grabs his thigh, up near the crotch.*)

What are you thinking about?
CLAY: Watch it now, you're gonna excite me for real.
LULA:

(*Taking her hand away and throwing her apple core through the window.*)

195   I bet.

(*She slumps in the seat and is heavily silent.*)

CLAY: I thought you knew everything about me? What happened?

(LULA *looks at him, then looks slowly away, then over where the other aisle would be. Noise of the train. She reaches in her bag and pulls out one of the paper books. She puts it on her leg and thumbs the pages listlessly.* CLAY *cocks his head to see the title of the book. Noise of the train.* LULA *flips pages and her eyes drift. Both remain silent.*)

Are you going to the party with me, Lula?
LULA:

(*Bored and not even looking.*)

I don't even know you.
200   CLAY: You said you know my type.
LULA:

(*Strangely irritated.*)

Don't get smart with me, Buster. I know you like the palm of my hand.
CLAY: The one you eat the apples with?
205   LULA: Yeh. And the one I open doors late Saturday evening with. That's my door. Up at the top of the stairs. Five flights. Above a lot of Italians and lying Americans. And scrape carrots with. Also . . .

(*Looks at him.*)

the same hand I unbutton my dress with, or let my skirt
210   fall down. Same hand. Lover.
CLAY: Are you angry about anything? Did I say something wrong?
LULA: Everything you say is wrong.

(*Mock smile.*)

That's what makes you so attractive. Ha. In that funny-book jacket with all the buttons.

(*More animate, taking hold of his jacket.*)

215   What've you got the jacket and tie on in all this heat for? And why're you wearing a jacket and tie like that? Did your people ever burn witches or start revolutions over the price of tea? Boy, those narrow-shoulder clothes come from a tradition you ought to feel oppressed by. A three-button suit. What right do you have to be wearing a 220 three-button suit and striped tie? Your grandfather was a slave, he didn't go to Harvard.
CLAY: My grandfather was a night watchman.
LULA: And you went to a colored college where everybody thought they were Averell Harriman. 225
CLAY: All except me.
LULA: And who did you think you were? Who do you think you are now?
CLAY:

(*Laughs as if to make light of the whole trend of the conversation.*)

Well, in college I thought I was Baudelaire. But I've 230 slowed down since.
LULA: I bet you never once thought you were a black nigger.

(*Mock serious, then she howls with laughter.* CLAY *is stunned but after initial reaction, he quickly tries to appreciate the humor.* LULA *almost shrieks.*)

A black Baudelaire.
CLAY: That's right.
LULA: Boy, are you corny. I take back what I said before. 235 Everything you say is not wrong. It's perfect. You should be on television.
CLAY: You act like you're on television already.
LULA: That's because I'm an actress.
CLAY: I thought so. 240
LULA: Well, you're wrong. I'm no actress. I told you I always lie. I'm nothing, honey, and don't you ever forget it.

(*Lighter.*)

Although my mother was a Communist. The only person in my family ever to amount to anything.
CLAY: My mother was a Republican. 245
LULA: And your father voted for the man rather than the party.
CLAY: Right!
LULA: Yea for him. Yea, yea for him.
CLAY: Yea!
LULA: And yea for America where he is free to vote for the 250 mediocrity of his choice! Yea!
CLAY: Yea!
LULA: And yea for both your parents who even though they differ about so crucial a matter as the body politic still forged a union of love and sacrifice that was destined to flower at the 255 birth of the noble Clay . . . what's your middle name?
CLAY: Clay.
LULA: A union of love and sacrifice that was destined to flower at the birth of the noble Clay Clay Williams. Yea! And most of all yea yea for you. Clay Clay. The Black Baudelaire! Yes! 260

(*And with knifelike cynicism.*)

My Christ. My Christ.
CLAY: Thank you, ma'am.
LULA: May the people accept you as a ghost of the future. And love you, that you might not kill them when you can.
CLAY: What? 265

LULA: You're a murderer, Clay, and you know it.

(*Her voice darkening with significance.*)

You know goddamn well what I mean.

CLAY: I do?

LULA: So we'll pretend the air is light and full of perfume.

270 CLAY:

(*Sniffing at her blouse.*)

It is.

LULA: And we'll pretend the people cannot see you. That is, the citizens. And that you are free of your own history. And I am free of my history. We'll pretend that we are both anonymous beauties smashing along through the city's entrails.

(*She yells as loud as she can.*)

GROOVE!

(*Black.*)

SCENE TWO

Scene is the same as before, though now there are other seats visible in the car. And throughout the scene other people get on the subway. There are maybe one or two seated in the car as the scene opens, though neither CLAY *nor* LULA *notices them.* CLAY's *tie is open.* LULA *is hugging his arm.*

CLAY: The party!

LULA: I know it'll be something good. You can come in with me, looking casual and significant. I'll be strange, haughty, and silent, and walk with long slow strides.

5 CLAY: Right.

LULA: When you get drunk, pat me once, very lovingly on the flanks, and I'll look at you cryptically, licking my lips.

CLAY: It sounds like something we can do.

LULA: You'll go around talking to young men about your

10   mind, and to old men about your plans. If you meet a very close friend who is also with someone like me, we can stand together, sipping our drinks and exchanging codes of lust. The atmosphere will be slithering in love and half-love and very open moral decision.

15 CLAY: Great. Great.

LULA: And everyone will pretend they don't know your name, and then . . .

(*She pauses heavily.*)

later, when they have to, they'll claim a friendship that denies your sterling character.

20 CLAY:

(*Kissing her neck and fingers.*)

And then what?

LULA: Then? Well, then we'll go down the street, late night, eating apples and winding very deliberately toward my house.

25 CLAY: Deliberately?

LULA: I mean, we'll look in all the shop windows, and make fun of the queers. Maybe we'll meet a Jewish Buddhist and flatten his conceits over some pretentious coffee.

CLAY: In honor of whose God?

LULA: Mine.   30

CLAY: Who is . . . ?

LULA: Me . . . and you.

CLAY: A corporate Godhead.

LULA: Exactly. Exactly.

(*Notices one of the other people entering.*)

CLAY: Go on with the chronicle. Then what happens to us? 35

LULA:

(*A mild depression, but she still makes her description triumphant and increasingly direct.*)

To my house, of course.

CLAY: Of course.

LULA: And up the narrow steps of the tenement.

CLAY: You live in a tenement?   40

LULA: Wouldn't live anywhere else. Reminds me specifically of my novel form of insanity.

CLAY: Up the tenement stairs.

LULA: And with my apple-eating hand I push open the door and lead you, my tender big-eyed prey, into my . . . God, 45 what can I call it . . . into my hovel.

CLAY: Then what happens?

LULA: After the dancing and games, after the long drinks and long walks, the real fun begins.

CLAY: Ah, the real fun.   50

(*Embarrassed, in spite of himself.*)

Which is . . . ?

LULA:

(*Laughs at him.*)

Real fun in the dark house. Hah! Real fun in the dark house, high up above the street and the ignorant cowboys. I lead you in, holding your wet hand gently in my hand . . . 55

CLAY: Which is not wet?

LULA: Which is dry as ashes.

CLAY: And cold?

LULA: Don't think you'll get out of your responsibility that way. It's not cold at all. You Fascist! Into my dark living 60 room. Where we'll sit and talk endlessly, endlessly.

CLAY: About what?

LULA: About what? About your manhood, what do you think? What do you think we've been talking about all this time?

CLAY: Well, I didn't know it was that. That's for sure. Every 65 other thing in the world but that.

(*Notices another person entering, looks quickly, almost involuntarily, up and down the car, seeing the other people in the car.*)

Hey, I didn't even notice when those people got on.

LULA: Yeah, I know.

CLAY: Man, this subway is slow.

LULA: Yeah, I know.   70

CLAY: Well, go on. We were talking about my manhood.

LULA: We still are. All the time.

CLAY: We were in your living room.

LULA: My dark living room. Talking endlessly.

75 CLAY: About my manhood.

LULA: I'll make you a map of it. Just as soon as we get to my house.

CLAY: Well, that's great.

LULA: One of the things we do while we talk. And screw.

CLAY:

(*Trying to make his smile broader and less shaky.*)

80   We finally got there.

LULA: And you'll call my rooms black as a grave. You'll say, "This place is like Juliet's tomb."

CLAY:

(*Laughs.*)

    I might.

85 LULA: I know. You've probably said it before.

CLAY: And is that all? The whole grand tour?

LULA: Not all. You'll say to me very close to my face, many, many times, you'll say, even whisper, that you love me.

CLAY: Maybe I will.

90 LULA: And you'll be lying.

CLAY: I wouldn't lie about something like that.

LULA: Hah. It's the only kind of thing you will lie about. Especially if you think it'll keep me alive.

CLAY: Keep you alive? I don't understand.

95 LULA:

(*Bursting out laughing, but too shrilly.*)

    Don't understand? Well, don't look at me. It's the path I take, that's all. Where both feet take me when I set them down. One in front of the other.

CLAY: Morbid. Morbid. You sure you're not an actress? All 100   that self-aggrandizement.

LULA: Well, I told you I wasn't an actress . . . but I also told you I lie all the time. Draw your own conclusions.

CLAY: And is that all of our lives together you've described? There's no more?

105 LULA: I've told you all I know. Or almost all.

CLAY: There's no funny parts?

LULA: I thought it was all funny.

CLAY: But you mean peculiar, not ha-ha.

LULA: You don't know what I mean.

110 CLAY: Well, tell me the almost part then. You said almost all. What else? I want the whole story.

LULA:

(*Searching aimlessly through her bag. She begins to talk breathlessly, with a light and silly tone.*)

    All stories are whole stories. All of 'em. Our whole story . . . nothing but change. How could things go on like that 115   forever? Huh?

(*Slaps him on the shoulder, begins finding things in her bag, taking them out and throwing them over her shoulder into the aisle.*)

    Except I do go on as I do. Apples and long walks with deathless intelligent lovers. But you mix it up. Look out

the window, all the time. Turning pages. Change change change. Till, shit, I don't know you. Wouldn't, for that mat- ter. You're too serious. I bet you're even too serious to be 120 psychoanalyzed. Like all those Jewish poets from Yonkers, who leave their mothers looking for other mothers, or others' mothers, on whose baggy tits they lay their fum- bling heads. Their poems are always funny, and all about sex. 125

CLAY: They sound great. Like movies.

LULA: But you change.

(*Blankly.*)

    And things work on you till you hate them.

(*More people come into the train. They come closer to the couple, some of them not sitting, but swinging drearily on the straps, staring at the two with uncertain interest.*)

CLAY: Wow. All these people, so suddenly. They must all come from the same place. 130

LULA: Right. That they do.

CLAY: Oh? You know about them too?

LULA: Oh yeah. About them more than I know about you. Do they frighten you?

CLAY: Frighten me? Why should they frighten me? 135

LULA: 'Cause you're an escaped nigger.

CLAY: Yeah?

LULA: 'Cause you crawled through the wire and made tracks to my side.

CLAY: Wire? 140

LULA: Don't they have wire around plantations?

CLAY: You must be Jewish. All you can think about is wire. Plantations didn't have any wire. Plantations were big open whitewashed places like heaven, and everybody on 'em was grooved to be there. Just strummin' and hummin' 145 all day.

LULA: Yes, yes.

CLAY: And that's how the blues was born.

LULA: Yes, yes. And that's how the blues was born.

(*Begins to make up a song that becomes quickly hysterical. As she sings she rises from her seat, still throwing things out of her bag into the aisle, beginning a rhythmical shudder and twistlike wiggle, which she continues up and down the aisle, bumping into many of the standing people and tripping over the feet of those sitting. Each time she runs into a person she lets out a very vicious piece of profanity, wiggling and stepping all the time.*)

    And that's how the blues was born. Yes. Yes. Son of a 150 bitch, get out of the way. Yes. Quack. Yes. Yes. And that's how the blues was born. Ten little niggers sitting on a limb, but none of them ever looked like him.

(*Points to* CLAY, *returns toward the seat, with her hands extended for him to rise and dance with her.*)

    And that's how blues was born. Yes. Come on. Clay. Let's do the nasty. Rub bellies. Rub bellies. 155

CLAY:

(*Waves his hands to refuse. He is embarrassed, but determined to get a kick out of the proceedings.*)

Hey, what was in those apples? Mirror, mirror on the wall, who's the fairest one of all? Snow White, baby, and don't you forget it.

160 LULA:

(*Grabbing for his hands, which he draws away.*)

Come on, Clay. Let's rub bellies on the train. The nasty. The nasty. Do the gritty grind, like your ol' rag-head mammy. Grind till you lose your mind. Shake it, shake it, shake it, shake it! OOOOweeee! Come on, Clay. Let's do

165 the choo-choo train shuffle, the navel scratcher.

CLAY: Hey, you coming on like the lady who smoked up her grass skirt.

LULA:

(*Becoming annoyed that he will not dance, and becoming more animated as if to embarrass him still further.*)

Come on, Clay . . . let's do the thing. Uhh! Uhh! Clay!

170 Clay! You middle-class black bastard. Forget your social-working mother for a few seconds and let's knock stomachs. Clay, you liver-lipped white man. You would-be Christian. You ain't no nigger, you're just a dirty white man. Get up, Clay. Dance with me, Clay.

175 CLAY: Lula! Sit down, now. Be cool.

LULA:

(*Mocking him, in wild dance.*)

Be cool. Be cool. That's all you know . . . shaking the wild-root cream-oil on your knotty head, jackets buttoning up to your chin, so full of white man's words. Christ!

180 God! Get up and scream at these people. Like scream meaningless shit in these hopeless faces.

(*She screams at people in train, still dancing.*)

Red trains cough Jewish underwear for keeps! Expanding smells of silence. Gravy snot whistling like sea birds. Clay. Clay, you got to break out. Don't sit there dying the way

185 they want you to die. Get up.

CLAY: Oh, sit the fuck down.

(*He moves to restrain her.*)

Sit down, goddamn it.

LULA:

(*Twisting out of his reach.*)

Screw yourself, Uncle Tom. Thomas Woolly-Head.

(*Begins to dance a kind of jig, mocking* CLAY *with loud forced humor.*)

190 There is Uncle Tom . . . I mean, Uncle Thomas Woolly-Head. With old white matted mane. He hobbles on his wooden cane. Old Tom. Old Tom. Let the white man hump his ol' mama, and he jes' shuffle off in the woods and hide his gentle gray head. Ol' Thomas Woolly-Head.

(*Some of the other riders are laughing now. A drunk gets up and joins* LULA *in her dance, singing, as best he can, her "song."* CLAY *gets up out of his seat and visibly scans the faces of the other riders.*)

CLAY: Lula! Lula!   195

(*She is dancing and turning, still shouting as loud as she can. The drunk too is shouting, and waving his hands wildly.*)

Lula . . . you dumb bitch. Why don't you stop it?

(*He rushes half stumbling from his seat, and grabs one of her flailing arms.*)

LULA: Let me go! You black son of a bitch.

(*She struggles against him.*)

Let me go! Help!

(CLAY *is dragging her towards her seat, and the drunk seeks to interfere. He grabs* CLAY *around the shoulders and begins wrestling with him.* CLAY *clubs the drunk to the floor without releasing* LULA, *who is still screaming.* CLAY *finally gets her to the seat and throws her into it.*)

CLAY: Now you shut the hell up.

(*Grabbing her shoulders.*)

Just shut up. You don't know what you're talking about.   200
You don't know anything. So just keep your stupid mouth closed.

LULA: You're afraid of white people. And your father was. Uncle Tom Big Lip!

CLAY: 205

(*Slaps her as hard as he can, across the mouth.* LULA's *head bangs against the back of the seat. When she raises it again,* CLAY *slaps her again.*)

Now shut up and let me talk.

(*He turns toward the other riders, some of whom are sitting on the edge of their seats. The drunk is on one knee, rubbing his head, and singing softly the same song. He shuts up too when he sees* CLAY *watching him. The others go back to newspapers or stare out the windows.*)

Shit, you don't have any sense, Lula, nor feelings either. I could murder you now. Such a tiny ugly throat. I could squeeze it flat, and watch you turn blue, on a humble. For dull kicks. And all these weak-faced ofays squatting   210
around here, staring over their papers at me. Murder them too. Even if they expected it. That man there . . .

(*Points to well-dressed man.*)

I could rip that *Times* right out of his hand, as skinny and middle-classed as I am, I could rip that paper out of his hand and just as easily rip out his throat. It takes no great   215
effort. For what? To kill you soft idiots? You don't understand anything but luxury.

LULA: You fool!

CLAY:

(*Pushing her against the seat.*)

I'm not telling you again, Tallulah Bankhead! Luxury. In your   220
face and your fingers. You telling me what I ought to do.

(Sudden scream frightening the whole coach.)

Well, don't! Don't you tell me anything! If I'm a middle-class fake white man . . . let me be. And let me be in the way I want.

(Through his teeth.)

225 I'll rip your lousy breasts off! Let me be who I feel like being. Uncle Tom. Thomas. Whoever. It's none of your business. You don't know anything except what's there for you to see. An act. Lies. Device. Not the pure heart, the pumping black heart. You don't ever know that. And I sit here,
230 in this buttoned-up suit, to keep myself from cutting all your throats. I mean wantonly. You great liberated whore! You fuck some black man, and right away you're an expert on black people. What a lotta shit that is. The only thing you know is that you come if he bangs you hard enough.
235 And that's all. The belly rub? You wanted to do the belly rub? Shit, you don't even know how. You don't know how. That ol' dipty-dip shit you do, rolling your ass like an elephant. That's not my kind of belly rub. Belly rub is not Queens. Belly rub is dark places, with big hats and over-
240 coats held up with one arm. Belly rub hates you. Old bald-headed four-eyed ofays popping their fingers . . . and don't know yet what they're doing. They say, "I love Bessie Smith." And don't even understand that Bessie Smith is saying, "Kiss my ass, kiss my black unruly ass." Before love,
245 suffering, desire, anything you can explain, she's saying, and very plainly, "Kiss my black ass." And if you don't know that, it's you that's doing the kissing.
Charlie Parker? Charlie Parker. All the hip white boys scream for Bird. And Bird saying, "Up your ass, feeble-
250 minded ofay! Up your ass." And they sit there talking about the tortured genius of Charlie Parker. Bird would've played not a note of music if he just walked up to East Sixty-seventh Street and killed the first ten white people he saw. Not a note! And I'm the great would-be poet. Yes.
255 That's right! Poet. Some kind of bastard literature . . . all it needs is a simple knife thrust. Just let me bleed you, you loud whore, and one poem vanished. A whole people of neurotics, struggling to keep from being sane. And the only thing that would cure the neurosis would be your
260 murder. Simple as that. I mean if I murdered you, then other white people would begin to understand me. You understand? No. I guess not. If Bessie Smith had killed some white people she wouldn't have needed that music. She could have talked very straight and plain about the
265 world. No metaphors. No grunts. No wiggles in the dark of her soul. Just straight two and two are four. Money. Power. Luxury. Like that. All of them. Crazy niggers turning their backs on sanity. When all it needs is that simple act. Murder. Just murder! Would make us all sane.

(Suddenly weary.)

270 Ahhh. Shit. But who needs it? I'd rather be a fool. Insane. Safe with my words, and no deaths, and clean, hard thoughts, urging me to new conquests. My people's madness. Hah! That's a laugh. My people. They don't need me to claim them. They got legs and arms of their own. Per-
275 sonal insanities. Mirrors. They don't need all those words.

They don't need any defense. But listen, though, one more thing. And you tell this to your father, who's probably the kind of man who needs to know at once. So he can plan ahead. Tell him not to preach so much rationalism and cold logic to these niggers. Let them alone. Let them sing curses 280 at you in code and see your filth as simple lack of style. Don't make the mistake, through some irresponsible surge of Christian charity, of talking too much about the advantages of Western rationalism, or the great intellectual legacy of the white man, or maybe they'll begin to listen. And then, 285 maybe one day, you'll find they actually do understand exactly what you are talking about, all these fantasy people. All these blues people. And on that day, as sure as shit, when you really believe you can "accept" them into your fold, as half-white trusties late of the subject peoples. With no more 290 blues, except the very old ones, and not a watermelon in sight, the great missionary heart will have triumphed, and all of those ex-coons will be stand-up Western men, with eyes for clean hard useful lives, sober, pious and sane, and they'll murder you. They'll murder you, and have very ra- 295 tional explanations. Very much like your own. They'll cut your throats, and drag you out to the edge of your cities so the flesh can fall away from your bones, in sanitary isolation.

LULA:

(Her voice takes on a different, more businesslike quality.)

I've heard enough. 300

CLAY:

(Reaching for his books.)

I bet you have. I guess I better collect my stuff and get off this train. Looks like we won't be acting out that little pageant you outlined before.

LULA: No. We won't. You're right about that, at least. 305

(She turns to look quickly around the rest of the car.)

All right!

(The others respond.)

CLAY:

(Bending across the girl to retrieve his belongings.)

Sorry, baby, I don't think we could make it.

(As he is bending over her, the girl brings up a small knife and plunges it into CLAY's chest. Twice. He slumps across her knees, his mouth working stupidly.)

LULA: Sorry is right.

(Turning to the others in the car who have already gotten up from their seats.)

Sorry is the rightest thing you've said. Get this man off 310 me! Hurry, now!

(The others come and drag CLAY's body down the aisle.)

Open the door and throw his body out.

(They throw him off.)

And all of you get off at the next stop.

(LULA busies herself straightening her things. Getting everything in order. She takes out a notebook and makes a quick scribbling note. Drops it in her bag. The train apparently stops and all the others get off, leaving her alone in the coach. Very soon a YOUNG NEGRO *of about twenty comes into the coach, with a couple of books under his arm. He sits a few seats in back of* LULA. *When he is seated she turns and gives him a long slow look. He looks up from his book and drops the book on his lap. Then an old Negro* CONDUCTOR *comes into the car, doing a sort of restrained soft shoe, and half mumbling the words of some song. He looks at the young man, briefly, with a quick greeting.)*

CONDUCTOR: Hey, brother!
YOUNG NEGRO: Hey.   315

(The CONDUCTOR *continues down the aisle with his little dance and the mumbled song.* LULA *turns to stare at him and follows his movements down the aisle. The* CONDUCTOR *tips his hat when he reaches her seat, and continues out the car.)*

Luis Valdez and El Teatro Campesino

Luis Valdez (b. 1940) was born and raised the son of farmworkers in Delano, California. He majored in drama at San Jose State College, taking his B.A. in 1964, and then joined the San Francisco Mime Troup, an important experimental theater company. In 1965, when farm workers at the Delano grape plantations went on strike, Valdez formed El Teatro Campesino ("The Farmworkers' Theater"). Valdez and Teatro Campesino devised two dramatic forms: *ACTOS,* short, satirical plays dramatizing the oppression of the fieldworkers, and *MITOS,* poetic, lyrical plays on Chicano life. *Actos* were improvised by members of El Teatro Campesino playing "stock" characters (the farmworker, the boss, and so on); because they were improvised for each production and each community, *actos* varied considerably from performance to performance. The final versions published by Valdez were written down much later. El Teatro Campesino became one of several important Chicano theater companies that performed throughout the Southwest and in urban areas of the Midwest and Northeast, drawing on both American and European dramatic traditions, as well as traditions of Mexican and Spanish-language theater in the United States that date to the seventeenth century. In the late 1960s and 1970s, Teatro Campesino toured the United States and Europe and gained an international reputation. Valdez's other *actos* with El Teatro Campesino include *Las Dos Caras del Patroncito* (1965), *No Saco Nada de la Escuela* (1969), *Vietnam Campesino* (1970), and *Los Vendidos* (1970). Valdez wrote the stage play *Zoot Suit* in 1979, and it was released as a film in 1981. In 1980, Valdez transformed El Teatro Campesino into a production company, a marked shift from its collaborative and activist origins. This version of El Teatro Campesino hired "professional" actors, abandoning the collective esthetic characteristic of the company's earlier work. Valdez developed several new projects in connection with the company's new theater in San Juan Bautista (built in 1981), notably *Bandido!* (1981), *Corridos* (1992), and *I Don't Have to Show You No Stinking Badges* (1990). His film *La Bamba* was released in 1987, and Valdez filmed *Pastorelas* for PBS television in 1990. Valdez has held academic appointments at the University of California, Berkeley, and at the University of California, Santa Cruz. He is teaching at the new campus of the California State University at Monterey.

LOS VENDIDOS

One of Teatro Campesino's best and most popular *actos, Los Vendidos*—"The Sellouts"—is reminiscent both of Brechtian political theater and more generally of popular satire. In its brief sketch of Honest Sancho's Used Mexican Lot, the play dramatizes a range of stereotypes applied by Anglo culture (represented by the Anglicized Mexican American, Miss JIM-enez) to Chicano experience: farmworkers, Johnny Pachuco, the *revolucionario,* and the "new 1970 Mexican-American" yuppie. In the play's surprising finale, though, the yuppie turns on Miss JIM-enez, and the "used Mexicans" turn out to run the shop: Honest Sancho is their front.

The play clearly engages conflicting attitudes toward social experience, as emblematized by its title. For the title can mean both "those who are sold"—like the "used Mexicans" on Sancho's lot—and "the sellouts," presumably Honest Sancho and Miss JIM-enez. This duplicity is also inflected by the play's language, its mixture of Spanish and English, the two languages Chicano culture uses to define itself and to engage the Anglo world. The play works at the border between two cultures, where language is part of the complex social and political negotiation that characterizes Mexican American life today.

LOS VENDIDOS

Luis Valdez and El Teatro Campesino

CHARACTERS

HONEST SANCHO
SECRETARY
FARM WORKER
JOHNNY
REVOLUCIONARIO
MEXICAN–AMERICAN

SCENE: *Honest Sancho's Used Mexican Lot and Mexican Curio Shop. Three models are on display in Honest Sancho's shop: to the right, there is a* REVOLUCIONARIO, *complete with sombrero, carrilleras, and carabina 30–30. At center, on the floor, there is the* FARM WORKER, *under a broad straw sombrero. At stage left is* JOHNNY, *the Pachuco, filero in hand.*

HONEST SANCHO *is moving among his models, dusting them off and preparing for another day of business.*

SANCHO: Bueno, bueno, mis monos, vamos a ver a quien vendemos ahora, ¿no? (*To audience.*) ¡Quihubo! I'm Honest Sancho and this is my shop. Antes fui contratista pero ahora logré tener mi negocito. All I need now is a cus-
5 tomer. (*A bell rings offstage.*) Ay, a customer!
SECRETARY: (*Entering.*) Good morning, I'm Miss Jiménez from—
SANCHO: ¡Ah, una chicana! Welcome, welcome Señorita Jiménez.
10 SECRETARY: (*Anglo pronunciation.*) JIM-enez.
SANCHO: ¿Qué?
SECRETARY: My name is Miss JIM-enez. Don't you speak English? What's wrong with you?
SANCHO: Oh, nothing, Señorita JIM-enez. I'm here to help you.
15 SECRETARY: That's better. As I was starting to say, I'm a secretary from Governor Reagan's office, and we're looking for a Mexican type for the administration.
SANCHO: Well, you come to the right place, lady. This is Honest Sancho's Used Mexican lot, and we got all types
20 here. Any particular type you want?
SECRETARY: Yes, we were looking for somebody suave—
SANCHO: Suave.
SECRETARY: Debonair.
SANCHO: De buen aire.
25 SECRETARY: Dark.
SANCHO: Prieto.
SECRETARY: But of course not too dark.
SANCHO: No muy prieto.
SECRETARY: Perhaps, beige.
30 SANCHO: Beige, just the tone. Así como cafecito con leche, ¿no?
SECRETARY: One more thing. He must be hard-working.
SANCHO: That could only be one model. Step right over here to the center of the shop, lady. (*They cross to the* FARM WORKER.) This is our standard farm worker model. As you
35 can see, in the words of our beloved Senator George Murphy, he is "built close to the ground." Also take special no-

---

Scene **carrilleras** literally chin straps, but may refer to cartridge belts **Pachuco** Chicano slang for 1940s zoot suiter **filero** blade 1–2 **Bueno, bueno, . . . Quihubo** "Good, good, my cute ones, let's see who we can sell now, O.K.?" 3–4 **Antes fui . . . negocito** "I used to be a contractor, but now I've succeeded in having my little business." 30 **Así como . . . leche** like coffee with milk

---

tice of his four-ply Goodyear huaraches, made from the rain tire. This wide-brimmed sombrero is an extra added feature—keeps off the sun, rain, and dust.
40 SECRETARY: Yes, it does look durable.
SANCHO: And our farm worker model is friendly. Muy amable. Watch. (*Snaps his fingers.*)
FARM WORKER: (*Lifts up head.*) Buenos días, señorita. (*His head drops.*)
45 SECRETARY: My, he's friendly.
SANCHO: Didn't I tell you? Loves his patrones! But his most attractive feature is that he's hard-working. Let me show you. (*Snaps fingers.* FARM WORKER *stands.*)
FARM WORKER: ¡El jale! (*He begins to work.*)
50 SANCHO: As you can see, he is cutting grapes.
SECRETARY: Oh, I wouldn't know.
SANCHO: He also picks cotton. (*Snap.* FARM WORKER *begins to pick cotton.*)
SECRETARY: Versatile isn't he?
55 SANCHO: He also picks melons. (*Snap.* FARM WORKER *picks melons.*) That's his slow speed for late in the season. Here's his fast speed. (*Snap.* FARM WORKER *picks faster.*)
SECRETARY: ¡Chihuahua! . . . I mean, goodness, he sure is a hard worker.
60 SANCHO: (*Pulls the* FARM WORKER *to his feet.*) And that isn't the half of it. Do you see these little holes on his arms that appear to be pores? During those hot sluggish days in the field, when the vines or the branches get so entangled, it's almost impossible to move; these holes emit a certain
65 grease that allow our model to slip and slide right through the crop with no trouble at all.
SECRETARY: Wonderful. But is he economical?
SANCHO: Economical? Señorita, you are looking at the Volkswagen of Mexicans. Pennies a day is all it takes. One plate of beans and tortillas will keep him going all day. That, and
70 chile. Plenty of chile. Chile jalapenos, chile verde, chile colorado. But, of course, if you do give him chile (*Snap.* FARM WORKER *turns left face. Snap.* FARM WORKER *bends over.*) then you have to change his oil filter once a week.
75 SECRETARY: What about storage?
SANCHO: No problem. You know these new farm labor camps our Honorable Governor Reagan has built out by Parlier or Raisin City? They were designed with our model in mind. Five, six, seven, even ten in one of those
80 shacks will give you no trouble at all. You can also put him in old barns, old cars, river banks. You can even leave him out in the field overnight with no worry!

---

41 **Muy amable** very friendly   49 **El jale** the job

SECRETARY: Remarkable.

SANCHO: And here's an added feature: Every year at the end of the season, this model goes back to Mexico and doesn't return, automatically, until next Spring.

SECRETARY: How about that. But tell me: does he speak English?

SANCHO: Another outstanding feature is that last year this model was programmed to go out on STRIKE! (*Snap.*)

FARM WORKER: ¡HUELGA! ¡HUELGA! Hermanos, sálganse de esos files. (*Snap. He stops.*)

SECRETARY: No! Oh no, we can't strike in the State Capitol.

SANCHO: Well, he also scabs. (*Snap.*)

FARM WORKER: Me vendo barato, ¿y qué? (*Snap.*)

SECRETARY: That's much better, but you didn't answer my question. Does he speak English?

SANCHO: Bueno . . . no pero he has other—

SECRETARY: No.

SANCHO: Other features.

SECRETARY: NO! He just won't do!

SANCHO: Okay, okay pues. We have other models.

SECRETARY: I hope so. What we need is something a little more sophisticated.

SANCHO: Sophisti—¿qué?

SECRETARY: An urban model.

SANCHO: Ah, from the city! Step right back. Over here in this corner of the shop is exactly what you're looking for. Introducing our new 1969 JOHNNY PACHUCO model! This is our fast-back model. Streamlined. Built for speed, low-riding, city life. Take a look at some of these features. Mag shoes, dual exhausts, green chartreuse paint-job, dark-tint windshield, a little poof on top. Let me just turn him on. (*Snap.* JOHNNY *walks to stage center with a pachuco bounce.*)

SECRETARY: What was that?

SANCHO: That, señorita, was the Chicano shuffle.

SECRETARY: Okay, what does he do?

SANCHO: Anything and everything necessary for city life. For instance, survival: He knife fights. (*Snap.* JOHNNY *pulls out switch blade and swings at secretary.*)

(SECRETARY *screams.*)

SANCHO: He dances. (*Snap.*)

JOHNNY: (*Singing.*) "Angel Baby, my Angel Baby . . ." (*Snap.*)

SANCHO: And here's a feature no city model can be without. He gets arrested, but not without resisting, of course. (*Snap.*)

JOHNNY: ¡En la madre, la placa! I didn't do it! I didn't do it! (JOHNNY *turns and stands up against an imaginary wall, legs spread out, arms behind his back.*)

SECRETARY: Oh no, we can't have arrests! We must maintain law and order.

SANCHO: But he's bilingual!

SECRETARY: Bilingual?

SANCHO: Simón que yes. He speaks English! Johnny, give us some English. (*Snap.*)

JOHNNY: (*Comes downstage.*) Fuck-you!

90–91 **¡HUELGA! ¡HUELGA! . . . esos files** "Strike! Strike! Brothers, leave those rows."   94 **Me vendo . . . qué** "I come cheap, so what?"   97 **Bueno . . . no pero** "Well, no, but . . ."   124 **En la . . . placa** "Wow, the police!"   131 **Simón . . . yes** yeah, sure

SECRETARY: (*Gasps.*) Oh! I've never been so insulted in my whole life!

SANCHO: Well, he learned it in your school.

SECRETARY: I don't care where he learned it.

SANCHO: But he's economical!

SECRETARY: Economical?

SANCHO: Nickels and dimes. You can keep JOHNNY running on hamburgers, Taco Bell tacos, Lucky Lager beer, Thunderbird wine, yesca—

SECRETARY: Yesca?

SANCHO: Mota.

SECRETARY: Mota?

SANCHO: Leños . . . Marijuana. (*Snap.* JOHNNY *inhales on an imaginary joint.*)

SECRETARY: That's against the law!

JOHNNY: (*Big smile, holding his breath.*) Yeah.

SANCHO: He also sniffs glue. (*Snap.* JOHNNY *inhales glue, big smile.*)

JOHNNY: Tha's too much man, ése.

SECRETARY: No, Mr. Sancho, I don't think this—

SANCHO: Wait a minute, he has other qualities I know you'll love. For example, an inferiority complex. (*Snap.*)

JOHNNY: (*To* SANCHO.) You think you're better than me, huh ése? (*Swings switch blade.*)

SANCHO: He can also be beaten and he bruises, cut him and he bleeds; kick him and he—(*He beats, bruises and kicks* PACHUCO.) would you like to try it?

SECRETARY: Oh, I couldn't.

SANCHO: Be my guest. He's a great scapegoat.

SECRETARY: No, really.

SANCHO: Please.

SECRETARY: Well, all right. Just once. (*She kicks* PACHUCO.) Oh, he's so soft.

SANCHO: Wasn't that good? Try again.

SECRETARY: (*Kicks* PACHUCO.) Oh, he's so wonderful! (*She kicks him again.*)

SANCHO: Okay, that's enough, lady. You ruin the merchandise. Yes, our Johnny Pachuco model can give you many hours of pleasure. Why, the L.A.P.D. just bought twenty of these to train their rookie cops on. And talk about maintenance. Señorita, you are looking at an entirely self-supporting machine. You're never going to find our Johnny Pachuco model on the relief rolls. No, sir, this model knows how to liberate.

SECRETARY: Liberate?

SANCHO: He steals. (*Snap.* JOHNNY *rushes the secretary and steals her purse.*)

JOHNNY: ¡Dame esa bolsa, vieja! (*He grabs the purse and runs. Snap by* SANCHO. *He stops.*)

(SECRETARY *runs after* JOHNNY *and grabs purse away from him, kicking him as she goes.*)

SECRETARY: No, no, no! We can't have any *more* thieves in the State Administration. Put him back.

SANCHO: Okay, we still got other models. Come on, Johnny, we'll sell you to some old lady. (SANCHO *takes johnny back to his place.*)

---

146 **Leños** "joints" of marijuana   181 **Dame esa . . . , vieja** "Gimme that bag, old lady!"

SECRETARY: Mr. Sancho, I don't think you quite understand what we need. What we need is something that will attract the women voters. Something more traditional, more romantic.

SANCHO: Ah, a lover. (*He smiles meaningfully.*) Step right over here, señorita. Introducing our standard Revolucionario and/or Early California Bandit type. As you can see he is well-built, sturdy, durable. This is the International Harvester of Mexicans.

SECRETARY: What does he do?

SANCHO: You name it, he does it. He rides horses, stays in the mountains, crosses deserts, plains, rivers, leads revolutions, follows revolutions, kills, can be killed, serves as a martyr, hero, movie star—did I say movie star? Did you ever see *Viva Zapata? Viva Villa? Villa Rides? Pancho Villa Returns? Pancho Villa Goes Back? Pancho Villa Meets Abbot and Costello*—

SECRETARY: I've never seen any of those.

SANCHO: Well, he was in all of them. Listen to this. (*Snap.*)

REVOLUCIONARIO: (*Scream.*) ¡VIVA VILLAAAAA!

SECRETARY: That's awfully loud.

SANCHO: He has a volume control. (*He adjusts volume. Snap.*)

REVOLUCIONARIO: (*Mousey voice.*) ¡Viva Villa!

SECRETARY: That's better.

SANCHO: And even if you didn't see him in the movies, perhaps you saw him on TV. He makes commercials. (*Snap.*)

REVOLUCIONARIO: Is there a Frito Bandito in your house?

SECRETARY: Oh yes, I've seen that one!

SANCHO: Another feature about this one is that he is economical. He runs on raw horsemeat and tequila!

SECRETARY: Isn't that rather savage?

SANCHO: Al contrario, it makes him a lover. (*Snap.*)

REVOLUCIONARIO: (*To* SECRETARY.) ¡Ay, mamasota, cochota, ven pa'ca! (*He grabs* SECRETARY *and folds her back—Latin-lover style.*)

SANCHO: (*Snap.* REVOLUCIONARIO *goes back upright.*) Now wasn't that nice?

SECRETARY: Well, it was rather nice.

SANCHO: And finally, there is one outstanding feature about this model I KNOW the ladies are going to love: He's a GENUINE antique! He was made in Mexico in 1910!

SECRETARY: Made in Mexico?

SANCHO: That's right. Once in Tijuana, twice in Guadalajara, three times in Cuernavaca.

SECRETARY: Mr. Sancho, I thought he was an American product.

SANCHO: No, but—

SECRETARY: No, I'm sorry. We can't buy anything but American-made products. He just won't do.

SANCHO: But he's an antique!

SECRETARY: I don't care. You still don't understand what we need. It's true we need Mexican models such as these, but it's more important that he be *American*.

SANCHO: American?

SECRETARY: That's right, and judging from what you've shown me, I don't think you have what we want. Well, my lunch hour's almost over; I better—

SANCHO: Wait a minute! Mexican but American?

SECRETARY: That's correct.

SANCHO: Mexican but . . . (*A sudden flash.*) AMERICAN! Yeah, I think we've got exactly what you want. He just came in today! Give me a minute. (*He exits. Talks from backstage.*) Here he is in the shop. Let me just get some pa-

216 **Al contrario** on the contrary

pers off. There. Introducing our new 1970 Mexican-American! Ta-ra-ra-ra-ra-ra-ra-RA-RAAA!

(SANCHO *brings out the* MEXICAN–AMERICAN *model, a clean-shaven middle-class type in business suit, with glasses.*)

SECRETARY: (*Impressed.*) Where have you been hiding this one?

SANCHO: He just came in this morning. Ain't he a beauty? Feast your eyes on him! Sturdy US Steel frame, streamlined, modern. As a matter of fact, he is built exactly like our Anglo models except that he comes in a variety of darker shades: naugahyde, leather, or leatherette.

SECRETARY: Naugahyde.

SANCHO: Well, we'll just write that down. Yes, señorita, this model represents the apex of American engineering! He is bilingual, college educated, ambitious! Say the word "acculturate" and he accelerates. He is intelligent, well-mannered, clean—did I say clean? (*Snap.* MEXICAN–AMERICAN *raises his arm.*) Smell.

SECRETARY: (*Smells.*) Old Sobaco, my favorite.

SANCHO: (*Snap.* MEXICAN–AMERICAN *turns toward sancho.*) Eric! (*To* SECRETARY.) We call him Eric Garcia. (*To* ERIC.) I want you to meet Miss JIM-enez, Eric.

MEXICAN–AMERICAN: Miss JIM-enez, I am delighted to make your acquaintance. (*He kisses her hand.*)

SECRETARY: Oh, my, how charming!

SANCHO: Did you feel the suction? He has seven especially engineered suction cups right behind his lips. He's a charmer all right!

SECRETARY: How about boards? Does he function on boards?

SANCHO: You name them, he is on them. Parole boards, draft boards, school boards, taco quality control boards, surf boards, two-by-fours.

SECRETARY: Does he function in politics?

SANCHO: Señorita, you are looking at a political MACHINE. Have you ever heard of the OEO, EOC, COD, WAR ON POVERTY? That's our model! Not only that, he makes political speeches.

SECRETARY: May I hear one?

SANCHO: With pleasure. (*Snap.*) Eric, give us a speech.

MEXICAN–AMERICAN: Mr. Congressman, Mr. Chairman, members of the board, honored guests, ladies and gentlemen. (SANCHO *and* SECRETARY *applaud.*) Please, please, I come before you as a Mexican-American to tell you about the problems of the Mexican. The problems of the Mexican stem from one thing and one thing alone: He's stupid. He's uneducated. He needs to stay in school. He needs to be ambitious, forward-looking, harder-working. He needs to think American, American, American, AMERICAN, AMERICAN, AMERICAN. GOD BLESS AMERICA! GOD BLESS AMERICA!! (*He goes out of control.*)

(SANCHO *snaps frantically and the* MEXICAN–AMERICAN *finally slumps forward, bending at the waist.*)

SECRETARY: Oh my, he's patriotic too!

SANCHO: Sí, señorita, he loves his country. Let me just make a little adjustment here. (*Stands* MEXICAN–AMERICAN *up.*)

SECRETARY: What about upkeep? Is he economical?

SANCHO: Well, no, I won't lie to you. The Mexican-American costs a little bit more, but you get what you pay for. He's worth every extra cent. You can keep him running on dry martinis, Langendorf bread.

300 SECRETARY: Apple pie?

SANCHO: Only Mom's. Of course, he's also programmed to eat Mexican food on ceremonial functions, but I must warn you: an overdose of beans will plug up his exhaust.

SECRETARY: Fine! There's just one more question: How much
305 do you want for him?

SANCHO: Well, I tell you what I'm gonna do. Today and to-day only, because you've been so sweet, I'm gonna let you steal this model from me! I'm gonna let you drive him off the lot for the simple price of—let's see taxes and license
310 included— $15,000.

SECRETARY: Fifteen thousand DOLLARS? For a MEXICAN!

SANCHO: Mexican? What are you talking, lady? This is a Mexican-AMERICAN! We had to melt down two pachucos, a farm worker and three gabachos to make this
315 model! You want quality, but you gotta pay for it! This is no cheap run-about. He's got class!

SECRETARY: Okay, I'll take him.

SANCHO: You will?

SECRETARY: Here's your money.

320 SANCHO: You mind if I count it?

SECRETARY: Go right ahead.

SANCHO: Well, you'll get your pink slip in the mail. Oh, do you want me to wrap him up for you? We have a box in the back.

SECRETARY: No, thank you. The Governor is having a lun-
325 cheon this afternoon, and we need a brown face in the crowd. How do I drive him?

SANCHO: Just snap your fingers. He'll do anything you want.

(SECRETARY *snaps.* MEXICAN–AMERICAN *steps forward.*)

MEXICAN-AMERICAN: RAZA QUERIDA, ¡VAMOS LEV-ANTANDO ARMAS PARA LIBERARNOS DE ES-
330 TOS DESGRACIADOS GABACHOS QUE NOS EXPLOTAN! VAMOS.

SECRETARY: What did he say?

SANCHO: Something about lifting arms, killing white people, etc.

SECRETARY: But he's not supposed to say that!

335 SANCHO: Look, lady, don't blame me for bugs from the fac-tory. He's your Mexican-American; you bought him, now drive him off the lot!

SECRETARY: But he's broken!

SANCHO: Try snapping another finger.

(SECRETARY *snaps.* MEXICAN–AMERICAN *comes to life again.*)

340 MEXICAN-AMERICAN: ¡ESTA GRAN HUMANIDAD HA DICHO BASTA! Y SE HA PUESTO EN MARCHA! ¡BASTA! ¡BASTA! ¡VIVA LA RAZA! ¡VIVA LA CAUSA! ¡VIVA LA HUELGA! ¡VIVAN LOS BROWN BERETS! ¡VIVAN LOS ESTUDIANTES! ¡CHICANO POWER!

329–332 **RAZA QUERIDA, . . . VAMOS** "Beloved Raza, let's pick up arms to liberate ourselves from those damned whites that exploit us! Let's go."   340–344 **ESTA GRAN . . . CHI-CANO POWER** "This great mass of humanity has said enough! And it begins to march! Enough! Enough! Long live La Raza! Long live the Cause! Long live the strike! Long live the Brown Berets! Long live the students! Chicano Power!"

(*The* MEXICAN-AMERICAN *turns toward the* SECRETARY, *who gasps and backs up. He keeps turning toward the* PACHUCO, FARM WORKER, *and* REVOLUCIONARIO, *snapping his fingers and turn-ing each of them on, one by one.*)

PACHUCO: (*Snap. To* SECRETARY.) I'm going to get you, baby! 345 ¡Viva La Raza!

FARM WORKER: (*Snap. To* SECRETARY.) ¡Viva la huelga! ¡Viva la Huelga! ¡VIVA LA HUELGA!

REVOLUCIONARIO: (*Snap. To* SECRETARY.) ¡Viva la revolu-ción! ¡VIVA LA REVOLUCIÓN! 350

REVOLUCIONARIO: (*Snap. To* SECRETARY.) ¡Viva la revolu-ción! ¡VIVA LA REVOLUCIÓN!

(*The three models join together and advance toward the* SECRETARY *who backs up and runs out of the shop screaming.* SANCHO *is at the other end of the shop holding his money in his hand. All freeze. After a few seconds of silence, the* PACHUCO *moves and stretches, shaking his arms and loosening up. The* FARM WORKER *and* REVOLUCIONARIO *do the same.* SANCHO *stays where he is, frozen to his spot.*)

JOHNNY: Man, that was a long one, ése. (*Others agree with him.*)

FARM WORKER: How did we do?

JOHNNY: Perty good, look all that lana, man! (*He goes over to* 355 SANCHO *and removes the money from his hand.* SANCHO *stays where he is.*)

REVOLUCIONARIO: En la madre, look at all the money.

JOHNNY: We keep this up, we're going to be rich.

FARM WORKER: They think we're machines. 360

REVOLUCIONARIO: Burros.

JOHNNY: Puppets.

MEXICAN-AMERICAN: The only thing I don't like is—how come I always got to play the goddamn Mexican-American?

JOHNNY: That's what you get for finishing high school. 365

FARM WORKER: How about our wages, ése?

JOHNNY: Here it comes right now. $3,000 for you, $3,000 for you, $3,000 for you, and $3,000 for me. The rest we put back into the business.

MEXICAN-AMERICAN: Too much, man. Heh, where you vatos 370 going tonight?

FARM WORKER: I'm going over to Concha's. There's a party.

JOHNNY: Wait a minute, vatos. What about our salesman? I think he needs an oil job.

REVOLUCIONARIO: Leave him to me. 375

(*The* PACHUCO, FARM WORKER, *and* MEXICAN-AMERICAN *exit, talking loudly about their plans for the night. The* REVOLU-CIONARIO *goes over to* SANCHO, *removes his derby hat and cigar, lifts him up and throws him over his shoulder.* SANCHO *hangs loose, lifeless.*)

REVOLUCIONARIO: (*To audience.*) He's the best model we got! ¡Ajúa! (*Exit.*)

Maria Irene Fornes

Maria Irene Fornes was born in Cuba in 1930 and emigrated to the United States in 1943. She toured Europe in the mid-1950s, studying to be a painter, and in Paris saw Roger Blin's production of Samuel Beckett's *Waiting for Godot*. Fornes was impressed both by its power and by its severe visual imagery onstage. She returned to the United States in 1957 as a textile designer, but three years later had the idea for her first play, *Tango Palace*. Fornes has had a distinguished career in the avant-garde theater, experimenting in a variety of theatrical modes; she has produced brilliant absurdist plays like *There! You Died* (1963, revised as *Tango Palace* in 1964) and *Dr. Kheal* (1968), a successful musical, *Promenade* (1968, with music by Al Carmines), and a moving, ritual-participatory play, *A Vietnamese Wedding* (1967). More recently, her plays have taken a serious—though no less experimental—turn, examining women's identity in *Fefu and her Friends* (1977) and *Abingdon Square* (1988), the relationship between politics, language, and love in *The Danube* (1982), and between military and sexual oppression in *The Conduct of Life* (1985). In 1986, she wrote another musical, with Tito Puente, *Lovers and Keepers,* and her most recent plays include *What of the Night?* (1993). Fornes has won several prestigious awards, including an Obie for Sustained Achievement in the Theater in 1982.

FEFU AND HER FRIENDS

Fefu and Her Friends is one of Fornes's most-performed plays; it was originally written to be performed as a piece of **ENVIRONMENTAL THEATER** in a SoHo loft, and has since been produced in conventional theaters as well as in "home" performance-spaces. The play is set in 1935 and takes place in Fefu's home. She has invited a group of women to rehearse a series of skits for a charity benefit; the women are introduced to the audience in the first scene, and seem to know each other well—some were friends in college, two are lovers, or ex-lovers. In several ways, though, the action of the play centers on Julia, who is in a wheelchair as the result of a mysterious hunting accident: although the bullet missed her, she is nonetheless paralyzed, and haunted by mysterious male voices, the "judges" who torment her in Part 2.

On several occasions, Fornes has argued that *Fefu* is not a specifically "feminist" play; while this may be true, the play certainly raises the question of the relations of power that structure women's lives in the world of the play. From Fefu's opening line ("My husband married me to have a constant reminder of how loathsome women are") to Emma's question in Part 2 ("Do you think about genitals all the time?") to Julia's extraordinary monologue, in which she seems to give voice to the unconscious and oppressive voice of the patriarchy itself ("The human being is of the masculine gender"), the play seems to turn on how the women's sense of themselves is deformed. The women seem, that is, to have internalized a male vision of themselves, a vision of their inferiority and powerlessness, that they are able to combat only in indirect ways—like the game Fefu plays with her husband Phillip, in which she shoots a gun at him not knowing whether it's loaded with live ammunition or blanks. And yet despite the horror of Julia's suffering, *Fefu* is in many ways a comedy; though Julia dies—again, she is hit by a bullet that seems to have missed her—the play seems to confirm the survival of Fefu and her friends.

One of the most striking features of *Fefu and Her Friends* is Fornes's brilliant manipulation of the conventions of realistic theater and of realistic performance. In one sense, *Fefu* is deeply indebted to the formal traditions of American realism: it is a domestic play that is so "realistic" that it invites the audience into Fefu's home, and encourages them to follow the characters around the house in Part 2. Yet by inviting the audience into the performance space, Fornes subtly reshapes the dynamics of realistic representation; the audience is no

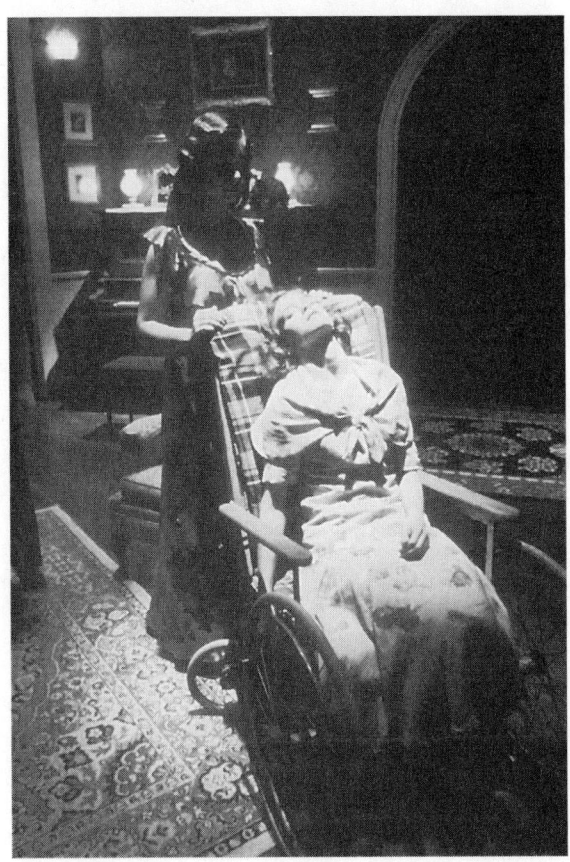

Julia confronts her invisible "judges" in Maria Irene Fornes's *Fefu and Her Friends*.

longer a privileged observer, looking "scientifically" or "objectively" through the fourth-wall window into the secret lives of the characters. Instead, Fornes unseats the audience, divides it into four groups, and in the second section of the play each group sees each of the four scenes in a different order. The effect of this device is striking; the audience members (in small groups) are usually much closer to the performers, sharing their space; whether the "Kitchen Scene" is performed in an offstage area of a theater or in an actual kitchen, the actors play the scene in an intimate relation to the audience, one that enables their performance to be much more low-key, much more like everyday behavior. Moreover, throughout Part 2, the audience is aware that all four scenes are being played simultaneously (and repeated four times). While one group is watching the "Lawn Scene," for instance, it may well hear Julia's screams in the "Bedroom Scene."

By bringing her audience into the scene, Fornes works to break down the traditional logic of realistic theater; we see the characters from inside their world, and have a different position of "judgment" in relation to them—especially after Julia's monologue, in which the audience "stands in" for the invisible "judges." Part 2 also breaks down the logic of realistic drama, in that the audience is made aware that it doesn't share a single perspective on the events, the omniscient viewpoint of the absent spectator of realism. We know, even as we take different seats in Part 3 than we had in 1, that at least *four* plays have been seen by the audience, and that how we interpret the action depends not only on the order in which we have witnessed the scenes, but perhaps on where we sit as well. This multiplication of perspective is complemented by Fornes's brilliant and elliptical strategy of characterization in the play. For Fornes's dialogue is at once familiar and surprising; the language seems both to obey the conventional superficiality of realistic dialogue and suddenly to swerve into other registers of feeling and experience. In the expressionist theater of the early twentieth century, characters often were able to speak their "thoughts" to an audience, and the Shakespearean soliloquy usually enables a character to reveal or explore some inner question. But Fornes's strategy here is much more subtle, much more unstable, for the boundary between "inner" and "outer" discourse is often blurry and uncertain. Much as she does by blurring the boundary between actors and audience in Part 2, Fornes presents her characters as more flexible and elastic, capable of giving voice to emotions, anxieties, and desires that are usually concealed from view, hidden as much behind the conventions of realistic representation as they are behind the façade with which the women confront the masculine world around them.

FEFU AND HER FRIENDS

Maria Irene Fornes

CHARACTERS

FEFU
CINDY
CHRISTINA
JULIA
EMMA
PAULA
SUE
CECILIA

New England, Spring 1935.

Part I: Noon. The living room. The entire audience watches from the main auditorium.

Part II: Afternoon. The lawn, the study, the bedroom, the kitchen. The audience is divided into four groups. Each group is led to the spaces. These scenes are performed simultaneously. When the scenes are completed the audience moves to the next space and the scenes are performed again. This is re-peated four times until each group has seen all four scenes. Then the audience is led back to the main auditorium.

Part III: Evening. The living room. The entire audience watches from the main auditorium.

Author's Note: Fefu is pronounced Feh-foo.

PART I

The living room of a country house in New England. The decor is a tasteful mixture of styles. To the right is the foyer and the main door. To the left, French doors leading to a terrace, the lawn and a pond. At the rear, there are stairs that lead to the upper floor, the en-trance to the kitchen, and the entrance to other rooms on the ground floor. A couch faces the audience. There is a coffee table, two chairs on each side of the table. Upstage right there is a piano. Against the right wall there is an open liquor cabinet. Besides bottles of liquor there are glasses, an ice bucket, and a seltzer bottle. A double barrel shotgun leans on the wall near the French doors. On the table there is a dish with chocolates. On the couch there is a throw. FEFU *stands on the landing.* CINDY *lies on the couch.* CHRISTINA *sits on the chair to the right.*

FEFU: My husband married me to have a constant reminder of how loathsome women are.

CINDY: What?

FEFU: Yup.

5 CINDY: That's just awful.

FEFU: No, it isn't.

CINDY: It isn't awful?

FEFU: No.

CINDY: I don't think anyone would marry for that reason.

10 FEFU: He did.

CINDY: Did he say so?

FEFU: He tells me constantly.

CINDY: Oh, dear.

FEFU: I don't mind. I laugh when he tells me.

15 CINDY: You laugh?

FEFU: I do.

CINDY: How can you?

FEFU: It's funny.—And it's true. That's why I laugh.

CINDY: What is true?

20 FEFU: That women are loathsome.

CINDY: . . . Fefu!

FEFU: That shocks you.

CINDY: It does. I don't feel loathsome.

FEFU: I don't mean that you are loathsome.

CINDY: You don't mean that I'm loathsome. 25

FEFU: No . . . It's something to think about. It's a thought.

CINDY: It's a hideous thought.

FEFU: I take it all back.

CINDY: Isn't she incredible?

FEFU: Cindy, I'm not talking about anyone in particular. It's 30
something to think about.

CINDY: No one in particular, just women.

FEFU: Yes.

CINDY: In that case I am relieved. I thought you were referring to us. 35

FEFU: (*Affectionately.*) You are being stupid.

CINDY: Stupid and loathsome. (*To* CHRISTINA.) Have you ever
heard anything so outrageous.

CHRISTINA: I am speechless.

FEFU: Why are you speechless? 40

CHRISTINA: I think you are outrageous.

FEFU: Don't be offended. I don't take enough care to be tactful. I know I don't. But don't be offended. Cindy is not
offended. She pretends to be, but she isn't really. She understands what I mean. 45

CINDY: I do not.

FEFU: Yes, you do.—I like exciting ideas. They give me energy.

CHRISTINA: And how is women being loathsome an exciting
idea? 50

FEFU: (*With mischief.*) It revolts me.

CHRISTINA: You find revulsion exciting?

FEFU: Don't you?

CHRISTINA: No.

FEFU: I do. It's something to grapple with.—What do you do 55
with revulsion?

CHRISTINA: I avoid anything that's revolting to me.

FEFU: Hmmm. (*To* CINDY.) You too?

CINDY: Yes.

FEFU: Hmm. Have you ever turned a stone over in damp soil? 60

CHRISTINA: Ahm.

FEFU: And when you turn it there are worms crawling on it?

1119

CHRISTINA: Ahm.

FEFU: And it's damp and full of fungus?

65 CHRISTINA: Ahm.

FEFU: Were you revolted?

CHRISTINA: Yes.

FEFU: Were you fascinated?

CHRISTINA: I was.

70 FEFU: There you have it! You too are fascinated with revulsion.

CHRISTINA: Hmm.

FEFU: You see, that which is exposed to the exterior . . . is smooth and dry and clean. That which is not . . . under-
75 neath, is slimy and filled with fungus and crawling with worms. It is another life that is parallel to the one we manifest. It's there. The way worms are underneath the stone. If you don't recognize it . . . (*Whispering.*) it eats you. That is my opinion. Well, who is ready for lunch?

80 CINDY: I'll have some fried worms with lots of pepper.

FEFU: (*To* CHRISTINA.) You?

CHRISTINA: I'll have mine in a sandwich with mayonnaise.

FEFU: And to drink?

CHRISTINA: Just some dirty dishwater in a tall glass with ice.

(FEFU *looks at* CINDY.)

85 CINDY: That sounds fine.

FEFU: I'll go dig them up. (FEFU *walks to the French doors. Beckoning* CHRISTINA.) Pst! (FEFU *gets the gun as* CHRISTINA *goes to the French doors.*) You haven't met Phillip. Have you?

CHRISTINA: No.

90 FEFU: That's him.

CHRISTINA: Which one?

FEFU: (*Aims and shoots.*) That one!

(CHRISTINA *and* CINDY *scream.* FEFU *smiles proudly. She blows on the mouth of the barrel. She puts down the gun and looks out again.*)

CINDY: Christ, Fefu.

FEFU: There he goes. He's up. It's a game we play. I shoot and
95 he falls. Whenever he hears the blast he falls. No matter where he is, he falls. One time he fell in a puddle of mud and his clothes were a mess. (*She looks out.*) It's not too bad. He's just dusting off some stuff. (*She waves to* PHILLIP *and starts to go upstairs.*) He's all right. Look.

100 CINDY: A drink?

CHRISTINA: Yes.

(CINDY *goes to the liquor cabinet.*)

CINDY: What would you like?

CHRISTINA: Bourbon and soda . . . (CINDY *puts ice and bourbon in a glass. As she starts to squirt the soda . . .*) lots of soda. Just
105 soda. (CINDY *starts with a fresh glass. She starts to squirt soda just as* CHRISTINA *speaks.*) Wait. (CINDY *stops squirting, but not soon enough.*) I'll have an ice cube with a few drops of bourbon. (CINDY *starts with a fresh glass.*)

CINDY: One or two ice cubes?

110 CHRISTINA: One. Something to suck on.

CINDY: She's unique. There's no one like her.

CHRISTINA: Thank God.

(CINDY *gives the drink to* CHRISTINA.)

CINDY: But she is lovely you know. She really is.

CHRISTINA: She's crazy.

CINDY: A little. She has a strange marriage.   115

CHRISTINA: Strange? It's revolting.—What is he like?

CINDY: He's crazy too. They drive each other crazy. They are not crazy really. They drive each other crazy.

CHRISTINA: Why do they stay together?

CINDY: They love each other.   120

CHRISTINA: Love?

CINDY: It's love.

CHRISTINA: Who are the other two men?

CINDY: Fefu's younger brother, John. And the gardener. His name is Tom.—The gun is not loaded.   125

CHRISTINA: How do you know?

CINDY: It's not. Why should it be loaded?

CHRISTINA: It seemed to be loaded a moment ago.

CINDY: That was just a blank.

CHRISTINA: It sounded like a cannon shot.   130

CINDY: That was just gun powder. There's no bullet in a blank.

CHRISTINA: The blast alone could kill you. One can die of fright, you know.

CINDY: True.   135

CHRISTINA: My heart is still beating.

CINDY: That's just fright. You're being a scaredy cat.

CHRISTINA: Of course it's just fright. It's fright.

CINDY: I mean, you were just scared. You didn't get hurt.

CHRISTINA: Just scared. I guess I was lucky I didn't get shot. 140

CINDY: Fefu won't shoot you. She only shoots Phillip.

CHRISTINA: That's nice of her. Put the gun away, I don't like looking at it.

FEFU: (*As she appears on the landing.*) I just fixed the toilet in your bathroom.   145

CINDY: You did?

FEFU: I did. The water stopper didn't work. It drained. I adjusted it. I'm waiting for the tank to fill up. Make sure it all works.

CHRISTINA: You do your own plumbing?   150

FEFU: I just had to bend the metal that supports the rubber stopper so it falls right over the hole. What happened was it fell to the side so the water wouldn't stop running into the bowl. (FEFU *sits near* CINDY.) He scared me this time, you know. He looked like he was really hurt.   155

CINDY: I thought the guns were not loaded.

FEFU: I'm never sure.

CHRISTINA: What?

CINDY: Fefu, what do you mean?

FEFU: He told me one day he'll put real bullets in the guns.   160
He likes to make me nervous. (*There is a moment's silence.*) I have upset you . . . I don't mean to upset you. That's the way we are with each other. We always go to extremes but it's not anything to be upset about.

CHRISTINA: You scare me.   165

FEFU: That's all right. I scare myself too, sometimes. But there's nothing wrong with being scared . . . it makes you stronger.—It does me.—He won't put real bullets in the guns.—It suits our relationship . . . the game, I mean. If I didn't shoot him with blanks, I might shoot him for real. 170
Do you see the sense of it?

CHRISTINA: I think you're crazy.

FEFU: I'm not. I'm sane.

CHRISTINA: (*Gently.*) You're very stupid.

175 FEFU: I'm not. I'm very bright.

CHRISTINA: (*Gently.*) You depress me.

FEFU: Don't be depressed. Laugh at me if you don't agree with me. Say I'm ridiculous. I know I'm ridiculous. Come on, laugh. I hate to think I'm depressing to you.

180 CHRISTINA: All right. I'll laugh.

FEFU: I'll make you a drink.

CHRISTINA: No, I'm just sucking on the ice.

FEFU: Don't you feel well?

CHRISTINA: I'm all right.

185 FEFU: What are you drinking?

CHRISTINA: Bourbon.

FEFU: (*Getting* CHRISTINA's *glass and going to the liquor cabinet.*) Would you like some more? I'll get you some.

CHRISTINA: Just a drop.

190 FEFU: (*With great care pours a single drop of bourbon on the ice cube.*) Like that?

CHRISTINA: Yes, thank you.

FEFU: (*Gives* CHRISTINA *the drink and watches her put the cube to her lips.*) That's the cutest thing I've ever seen. It's cold.

195 (CHRISTINA *nods.*) You need a stick in the ice, like a popsicle stick. You hold the stick and your fingers won't get cold. I have some sticks. I'll do some for you.

CHRISTINA: Don't trouble yourself.

FEFU: It won't be any trouble. You might want some later.—

200 I'm strange, Christina. But I am fortunate in that I don't mind being strange. It's hard on others sometimes. But not that hard. Is it, Cindy? Those who love me, love me precisely because I am the way I am. (*To* CINDY.) Isn't that so? (CINDY *smiles and nods.*)

205 CINDY: I would love you even if you weren't the way you are.

FEFU: You wouldn't know it was me if I weren't the way I am.

CINDY: I would still know it was you underneath.

FEFU: (*To* CHRISTINA.) You see?—There are some good things about me.—I'm never angry, for example.

210 CHRISTINA: But you make everyone else angry.

(FEFU *thinks a moment.*)

FEFU: No.

CHRISTINA: You've made me furious.

FEFU: I know. And I might make you angry again. Still I would like it if you liked me.—You think it's unlikely.

215 CHRISTINA: I don't know.

FEFU: . . . We'll see. (FEFU *goes to the doors. She stands there briefly and speaks reflectively.*) I still like men better than women.— I envy them. I like being like a man. Thinking like a man. Feeling like a man.—They are well together. Women are

220 not. Look at them. They are checking the new grass mower. . . . Out in the fresh air and the sun, while we sit here in the dark. . . . Men have natural strength. Women have to find their strength, and when they do find it, it comes forth with bitterness and it's erratic. . . . Women are

225 restless with each other. They are like live wires . . . either chattering to keep themselves from making contact, or else, if they don't chatter, they avert their eyes . . . like Orpheus . . . as if a god once said "and if they shall recognize each other, the world will be blown apart." They are always

230 eager for the men to arrive. When they do, they can put themselves at rest, tranquilized and in a mild stupor. With

the men they feel safe. The danger is gone. That's the closest they can be to feeling wholesome. Men are muscle that cover the raw nerve. They are the insulators. The danger is gone, but the price is the mind and the spirit. . . . High 235 price.—I've never understood it. Why?—What is feared?—Hmm. Well . . .—Do you know? Perhaps the heavens would fall.—Have I offended you again?

CHRISTINA: No. I too have wished for that trust men have for each other. The faith the world puts in them and they in 240 turn put in the world. I know I don't have it.

FEFU: Hmm. Well, I have to see how my toilet is doing. (FEFU *goes to the landing and exits. She puts her head out. She smiles.*) Plumbing is more important than you think.

(CHRISTINA *falls off her chair in a mock faint.* CINDY *goes to her.*)

CINDY: What do you think? 245

CHRISTINA: Think? I hurt. I'm all shreds inside.

CINDY: Anything I can do?

CHRISTINA: Sing.

(CINDY *sings* "Winter Wonderland." CHRISTINA *harmonizes. There is the sound of a horn.* FEFU *enters.*)

FEFU: It's Julia. (*To* CHRISTINA, *who is on the floor.*) Are you all right? 250

CHRISTINA: Yes. (FEFU *exits through the foyer.*) Darn it! (CHRISTINA *starts to stand.*)

FEFU: (*Off-stage.*) Julia . . . let me help you.

JULIA: I can manage. I'm much stronger now.

FEFU: There you go. 255

JULIA: You have my bag.

FEFU: Yes.

(JULIA *and* FEFU *enter.* JULIA *is in a wheelchair.*)

JULIA: Hello Cindy.

CINDY: Hello darling. How are you?

JULIA: I'm very well now. I'm driving now. You must see my 260 car. It's very clever the way they worked it all out. You might want to drive it. It's not hard at all. (*Turning to* CHRISTINA.) Christina.

CHRISTINA: Hello Julia.

JULIA: I'm glad to see you. 265

FEFU: I'll take this to your room. You're down here, if you want to wash up.

(FEFU *exits through the upstage exit.* JULIA *follows her.*)

CINDY: I can't get used to it.

CHRISTINA: She's better. Isn't she?

CINDY: Not really. 270

CHRISTINA: Was she actually hit by the bullet?

CINDY: No . . . I was with her.

CHRISTINA: I know.

CINDY: I thought the bullet hit her, but it didn't.—How do you know if a person is hit by a bullet? 275

CHRISTINA: Cindy . . . there's a wound and . . . there's a bullet.

CINDY: Well, the hunter aimed . . . at the deer. He shot.

CHRISTINA: He?

CINDY: Yes.

CHRISTINA: (*Pointing in the direction of* FEFU.) It wasn't . . . ? 280

CINDY: Fefu? . . . No. She wasn't even there. She used to hunt but she doesn't hunt any more. She loves animals.
CHRISTINA: Go on.
CINDY: He shot. Julia and the deer fell. The deer was dead . . . dying. Julia was unconscious. She had convulsions . . . like the deer. He died and she didn't. I screamed for help and the hunter came and examined Julia. He said, "She is not hurt." Julia's forehead was bleeding. He said, "It is a surface wound. I didn't hurt her." I know it wasn't he who hurt her. It was someone else. He went for help and Julia started talking. She was delirious.—Apparently there was a spinal nerve injury. She hit her head and she suffered a concussion. She blanks out and that is caused by the blow on the head. It's a scar in the brain. It's called the petit mal.

(FEFU enters.)

CHRISTINA: What was it she said?
CINDY: Hmm? . . .
CHRISTINA: When she was delirious.
CINDY: When she was delirious? That she was persecuted.— That they tortured her. . . . That they had tried her and that the shot was her execution. That she recanted because she wanted to live. . . . That if she talked about it . . . to anyone . . . she would be tortured further and killed. And I have not mentioned this before because . . . I fear for her.
CHRISTINA: It doesn't make any sense, Cindy.
CINDY: It makes sense to me. You heard? (FEFU goes to CINDY and holds her.)
FEFU: Who hurt her?
CINDY: I don't know.
FEFU: (To CHRISTINA.) Did you know her?
CHRISTINA: I met her once years ago.
FEFU: You remember her then as she was. . . . She was afraid of nothing. . . . Have you ever met anyone like that? . . . She knew so much. She was so young and yet she knew so much. . . . How did she learn all that? . . . (To CINDY.) Did you ever wonder? Well, I still haven't checked my toilet. Can you believe that. I still haven't checked it. (FEFU goes upstairs.)
CHRISTINA: How long ago was the accident?
CINDY: A year . . . a little over a year.
CHRISTINA: Is she in pain?
CINDY: I don't think so.
CHRISTINA: We are made of putty. Aren't we?

(There is the sound of a car. Car doors opening and closing. A house window opening.)

FEFU: (Off-stage.) Emma! What is that you're wearing. You look marvelous.
EMMA: (Off-stage.) I got it in Turkey.
FEFU: Hi Paula, Sue.
PAULA: Hi.
SUE: Hi.

(CINDY goes out to greet them. JULIA enters. She wheels herself to the downstage area.)

FEFU: I'll be right down! Hey, my toilet works.
EMMA: Stephany. Mine does too.

FEFU: Don't be funny.
EMMA: Come down.

(FEFU enters as EMMA, SUE, and PAULA enter. EMMA and FEFU embrace.)

FEFU: How are you?
EMMA: Good . . . good . . . good . . . (Still embracing FEFU, EMMA sees JULIA.) Julia! (She runs to JULIA and sits on her lap.)
FEFU: Emma!
JULIA: It's all right.
EMMA: Take me for a ride. (JULIA wheels the chair in a circle. EMMA waves as they ride.) Hi, Cindy, Paula, Sue, Fefu.
JULIA: Do you know Christina?
EMMA: How do you do.
CHRISTINA: How do you do.
EMMA: (Pointing.) Sue . . . Paula . . .
SUE: Hello.
PAULA: Hello.
CHRISTINA: Hello.
PAULA: (To FEFU.) I liked your talk at Flossie Crit.
FEFU: Oh god, don't remind me. I thought I was awful. Come, I'll show you your rooms. (She starts to go up.)
PAULA: I thought you weren't. I found it very stimulating.
EMMA: When was that? . . . What was it on?
FEFU: Aviation.
PAULA: It wasn't on aviation. It was on Voltairine de Cleyre.
JULIA: I wish I had known.
FEFU: It wasn't important.
JULIA: I would have gone, Fefu.
FEFU: Really, it wasn't worth the trouble.
EMMA: Now you'll have to tell Julia and me all about Voltairine de Cleyre.
FEFU: You know all about Voltairine de Cleyre.
EMMA: I don't.
FEFU: I'll tell you at lunch.
EMMA: I had lunch.
JULIA: You can sit and listen while we eat.
EMMA: I will. When do we start our meeting?
FEFU: After lunch. We'll have something to eat and then we'll have our meeting. Who's ready for lunch?

(The following lines are said almost simultaneously.)

CINDY: I am.
JULIA: I'm not really hungry.
CHRISTINA: I could eat now.
PAULA: I'm ready.
SUE: I'd rather wait.
EMMA: I'll have coffee.
FEFU: . . . Well . . . we'll take a vote later.
CINDY: What are we doing exactly?
FEFU: About lunch?
CINDY: That too, but I meant the agenda.
SUE: Well, I thought we should first discuss what each of us is going to talk about, so we don't duplicate what someone else is saying, and then we have a review of it, a sort of rehearsal, so we know in what order we should speak and how long it's going to take.
EMMA: We should do a rehearsal in costume. What color should each wear. It matters. Do you know what you're wearing?

PAULA: I haven't thought about it. What color should I wear?

EMMA: Red.

PAULA: Red!

EMMA: Cherry red or white.

390 SUE: And I?

EMMA: Dark green.

CINDY: The treasurer should wear green.

EMMA: It suits her too.

SUE: And then we'll speak in order of color.

395 EMMA: Right. Who else wants to know? (CINDY and JULIA *raise their hands. To* CINDY.) For you lavender. (*To* JULIA.) Purpurra. (FEFU *raises her hand.*) For you, all the gold in Persia.

FEFU: There is no gold in Persia.

400 EMMA: In Peru. I brought my costume. I'll put it on later.

FEFU: You're not in costume?

EMMA: No. This is just a dress. My costume is . . . dramatic. I won't tell you any more about it. You'll see it.

SUE: I had no idea we were going to do theatre.

405 EMMA: Life is theatre. Theatre is life. If we're showing what life is, can be, we must do theatre.

SUE: Will I have to act?

EMMA: It's not acting. It's being. It's springing forth with the powers of the spirit. It's breathing.

410 JULIA: I'll do a dance.

EMMA: I'll stage a dance for you.

JULIA: Sitting?

EMMA: On a settee.

JULIA: I'm game.

415 EMMA: (*Takes a deep breath and walks through the French doors.*) Phillip! What are you doing?—Hello.—Hello, John.— What? I'm staging a dance for Julia!

FEFU: We'll never see her again.—Come.

(FEFU, PAULA, *and* SUE *go upstairs.* JULIA *goes to the gun, takes it and smells the mouth of the barrel. She looks at* CINDY.)

CINDY: It's a blank.

(JULIA *takes the remaining slug out of the gun. She lets it fall on the floor.*)

420 JULIA: She's hurting herself. (JULIA *looks blank and is motionless.* CINDY *picks up the slug. She notices* JULIA'S *condition.*)

CINDY: Julia. (*To* CHRISTINA.) She's absent.

CHRISTINA: What do we do?

CINDY: Nothing, she'll be all right in a moment. (*She takes the* 425 *gun from* JULIA. JULIA *comes to.*)

JULIA: It's a blank . . .

CINDY: It is.

JULIA: She's hurting herself. (JULIA *lets out a strange whimper. She goes to the coffee table, takes a piece of chocolate, puts it in* 430 *her mouth and goes toward her room. After she crosses the threshold, she stops.*) I must lie down a while.

CINDY: Call me if you need anything.

JULIA: I will. (*She exits.* CINDY *tries to put the slug in the rifle. There is the sound of a car, a car door opening, closing.*)

435 CINDY: Do you know how to do this?

CHRISTINA: Of course not.

(CINDY *succeeds in putting the slug in the gun.* CECILIA *stands in the threshold of the foyer.*)

CECILIA: I am Cecilia Johnson. Do I have the right place?

CINDY: Yes.

(CINDY *locks the gun. Lights fade all around* CECILIA. *Only her head is lit. The light fades.*)

PART II

ON THE LAWN

There is a bench or a tree stump. FEFU *and* EMMA *bring boxes of potatoes, carrots, beets, winter squash, and other vegetables from a root cellar and put them in a small wagon.* FEFU *wears a hat and gardening gloves.*

EMMA: (*Re-enters carrying a box as* FEFU *exits.*) Do you think about genitals all the time?

FEFU: Genitals? No, I don't think about genitals all the time.

EMMA: (*Starting to exit.*) I do, and it drives me crazy. Each person I see in the street, anywhere at all . . . I keep thinking 5 of their genitals, what they look like, what position they are in. I think it's odd that everyone has them. Don't you?

FEFU: (*Crossing* EMMA.) No, I think it'd be odder if they didn't have them.

(EMMA *laughs.* FEFU *re-enters.*)

EMMA: I mean, people act as if they don't have genitals.   10

FEFU: How do people with genitals act?

EMMA: I mean, how can business men and women stand in a room and discuss business without even one reference to their genitals. I mean everybody has them. They just pretend they don't.   15

FEFU: I see. (*Shifting her glance from left to right with a fiendish look.*) You mean they should do this all the time.

(EMMA *laughs.*)

EMMA: No, I don't mean that. Think of it. Don't you think I'm right?

FEFU: Yes, I think you're right. (FEFU *sits.*) Oh, Emma, Emma 20 EmmaEmma.

EMMA: That's m'name.—Well, you see, it's generally believed that you go to heaven if you are good. If you are bad you go to hell. That is correct. However, in heaven they don't judge goodness the way we think. They don't. They have 25 a divine registry of sexual performance. In that registry they mark down every little sexual activity in your life. If your faith is not entirely in it, if you just perform as an obligation and you don't feel the most profound devotion, if your spirit, your heart, and your flesh is not religiously 30 delivered to it, you are condemned. They put you down in the black list and you don't go to heaven. Heaven is populated with divine lovers. And in hell live the duds.

FEFU: That's probably true.

EMMA: I knew you'd see it that way.   35

FEFU: Oh, I do. I do. You see, on earth we are judged by public acts, and sex is a private act. The partner cannot be said to be the public, since both partners are engaged. So naturally, it stands to reason that it's angels who judge our sexual life.   40

EMMA: Naturally.

(*Pause.*)

FEFU: You always bring joy to me.

EMMA: Thank you.

FEFU: I thank you. (FEFU *becomes distressed. She sits.*) I am in
45   constant pain. I don't want to give in to it. If I do I am
    afraid I will never recover. . . . It's not physical, and it's not
    sorrow. It's very strange Emma, I can't describe it, and it's
    very frightening. . . . It is as if normally there is a lubricant
    . . . not in the body . . . a spiritual lubricant . . . it's hard to
50   describe . . . and without it, life is a nightmare, and every-
    thing is distorted.—A black cat started coming to my
    kitchen. He's awfully mangled and big. He is missing an
    eye and his skin is diseased. At first I was repelled by him,
    but then, I thought, this is a monster that has been sent to
55   me and I must feed him. And I fed him. One day he came
    and shat all over my kitchen. Foul diarrhea. He still comes
    and I still feed him.—I am afraid of him. (EMMA *kisses*
    FEFU.) How about a little lemonade?

EMMA: Yes.

60 FEFU: How about a game of croquet?

EMMA: Fine.

(FEFU *exits.* EMMA *improvises an effigy of* FEFU. *She puts* FEFU's
hat and gloves on it.)

    Not from the stars do I my judgment pluck.
    And yet methinks I have astronomy;
    But not to tell of good or evil luck,
65   Of plagues, of dearths, or seasons' quality;
    Nor can I fortune to brief minutes tell,
    Pointing to each his thunder, rain, and wind,
    Or say with princes if it shall go well
    By oft predict that I in heaven find.
70   But from thine eyes my knowledge I derive.
    And, constant stars, in them I read such art
    As truth and beauty shall together thrive
    If from thyself to store thou wouldst convert:
        Or else of thee this I prognosticate,
75   Thy end is truth's and beauty's doom and date.

(*If* FEFU's *entrance is delayed,* EMMA *will sing a popular song of the
period.* FEFU *re-enters with a pitcher and two glasses.*)

IN THE STUDY

*There are books on the walls, a desk, Victorian chairs, a rug on the
floor.* CHRISTINA *sits behind the desk. She reads a French text book.
She mumbles French sentences.* CINDY *sits to the left of the desk
with her feet up on a chair. She looks at a magazine. A few moments pass.*

CHRISTINA: (*Practicing.*) Etes-vous externe ou demi-pension-
    naire? La cuisine de votre cantine est-elle bonne, passable
    ou mauvaise? (*She continues reading almost inaudibly. A mo-
    ment passes.*)

5 CINDY: (*Reading.*) A lady in Africa divorced her husband be-
    cause he was a cheetah.

CHRISTINA: Oh, dear. (*They laugh. They go back to their read-
    ing. A moment passes.*) Est-ce que votre professeur inter-
    roge souvant les eleves? (*They go back to their reading. A
10   moment passes.*)

CINDY: I suppose . . . when a person is swept off their feet . . .
    the feet remain and the person goes off . . . with the
    broom.

CHRISTINA: No . . . when a person is swept off their feet . . .
    there is no broom.   15

CINDY: What does the sweeping?

CHRISTINA: An emotion . . . a feeling.

CINDY: Then emotions have bristles?

CHRISTINA: Yes.

CINDY: Now I understand. Do the feet remain?   20

CHRISTINA: No, the feet fly also . . . but separate from the
    body. At the end of the leap, just before the landing, they
    join the ankles and one is complete again.

CINDY: Oh, that sounds nice.

CHRISTINA: It is. Being swept off your feet is nice. Anything   25
    else?

CINDY: Not for now. (*They go back to their reading. A moment
    passes.*) Are you having a good time?

CHRISTINA: Yes, I'm very glad I came.

CINDY: Do you like everybody?   30

CHRISTINA: Yes.

CINDY: Do you like Fefu?

CHRISTINA: I do . . . She confuses me a little.—I try to be hon-
    est . . . and I wonder if she is . . . I don't mean that she doesn't
    tell the truth. I know she does. I mean a kind of integrity.   35
    I know she has integrity too. . . . But I don't know if she's
    careful with life . . . something bigger than the self . . . I sup-
    pose I don't mean with life but more with convention. I
    think she is an adventurer in a way. Her mind is adventur-
    ous. I don't know if there is dishonesty in that. But in ad-   40
    venture there is taking chances and risks, and then one has
    to, somehow, have less regard or respect for things as they
    are. That is, regard for a kind of convention, I suppose. I am
    probably ultimately a conformist, I think. And I suppose I
    do hold back for fear of being disrespectful or destroying   45
    something—and I admire those who are not. But I also feel
    they are dangerous to me. I don't think they are dangerous
    to the world; they are more useful than I am, more impor-
    tant, but I feel some of my life is endangered by their way
    of thinking. Do you understand?   50

CINDY: Yes, I do.

CHRISTINA: I guess I am proud and I don't like thinking that
    I am thoughtful of things that have no value.—I like her.

CINDY: I had a terrible dream last night.

CHRISTINA: What was it?   55

CINDY: I was at a dance. And there was a young doctor I had
    seen in connection with my health. We all danced in a cir-
    cle and he identified himself and said that he had spoken to
    Mike about me, but that it was all right, that he had put it
    so that it was all right. I was puzzled as to why Mike would   60
    mind and why he had spoken to him. Then, suddenly
    everybody sat down on the floor and pretended they were
    having singing lessons and one person was practicing Ital-
    ian. The singing professor was being tested by two secret
    policemen. They were having him correct the voice of   65
    someone they had brought. He apparently didn't know
    how to do it. Then, one of the policemen put his hands on
    his vocal cords and kicked him out the door. Then he
    grabbed me and felt my throat from behind with his
    thumbs while he rubbed my nipples with his pinkies.   70
    Then, he pushed me out the door. Then, the young doctor

started cursing me. His mouth moved like the mouth of a horse. I was on an upper level with a railing and I said to him, "Stop and listen to me." I said it so strongly that he 75 stopped. Everybody turned to me in admiration because I had made him stop. Then, I said to him, "Restrain yourself." I wanted to say respect me. I wasn't sure whether the words coming out of my mouth were what I wanted to say. I turned to ask my sister. The young man was bending over 80 and trembling in mad rage. Another man told me to run before the young man tried to kill me. Meg and I ran downstairs. She asked me if I wanted to go to her place. We grabbed a taxi, but before the taxi got enough speed he came out and ran to the taxi and was on the verge of open- 85 ing the door when I woke up.

(The door opens. FEFU *looks in. Her entrance may interrupt* CINDY*'s speech at any point according to how long it takes her to reach the kitchen.)*

FEFU: Who's for a game of croquet?
CINDY: In a little while.
FEFU: See you outside.
CHRISTINA: That was quite a dream.
90 CINDY: What do you think it means?
CHRISTINA: I think it means you should go to a different doctor.
CINDY: He's not my doctor. I never saw him before.
CHRISTINA: Well good. I'm sure he's not a good doctor.

(At the end of the fourth repeat, when FEFU *invites them for croquet,* CINDY *says, "Oh let's play croquet" and they follow* FEFU*.)*

IN THE BEDROOM

A plain unpainted room. Perhaps a room that was used for storage and was set up as a sleeping place for JULIA. *There is a mattress on the floor. To the right of the mattress there is a small table, to the left is* JULIA*'s wheelchair. There is a sink on the wall. There are dry leaves on the floor although the time is not fall. The sheets are linen.* JULIA *lies in bed covered to her shoulders. She wears a white hospital gown.* JULIA *hallucinates. However, her behavior should not be the usual behavior attributed to a mad person. It should be rather still and luminous. There will be aspects of her hallucination that frighten her, but hallucinating itself does not.*

JULIA: They clubbed me. They broke my head. They broke my will. They broke my hands. They tore my eyes out. They took my voice away. They didn't do anything to my heart because I didn't bring my heart with me. They 5 clubbed me again, but my head did not fall off in pieces. That was because they were so good and they felt sorry for me. The judges. You didn't know the judges?—I was good and quiet. I never dropped my smile. I smiled to everyone. If I stopped smiling I would get clubbed be- 10 cause they love me. They say they love me. I go along with that because if I don't . . .

(With her finger she indicates her throat being cut and makes the sound that usually accompanies that gesture.)

I told them the stinking parts of the body are the important ones: the genitals, the anus, the mouth, the armpit. All important parts except the armpits. And who knows,

maybe the armpits are important too. That's what I said. 15 *(Her voice becomes gravelly and tight in imitation of the judges.)* He said that all those parts must be kept clean and put away. He said that women's entrails are heavier than anything on earth and to see a woman running creates a disparate and incongruous image in the mind. It's antiaesthetic. There- 20 fore women should not run. Instead they should strike positions that take into account the weight of their entrails. Only if they do, can they be aesthetic. He said, for example, Goya's Maja. He said Ruben's women are not aesthetic. Flesh. He said that a woman's bottom should be in a cush- 25 ion, otherwise it's revolting. He said there are exceptions. Ballet dancers are exceptions. They can run and lift their legs because they have no entrails. Isadora Duncan had entrails, that's why she should not have danced. But she danced and for this reason became crazy. *(Her voice is back* 30 *to normal.)* She wasn't crazy.

(She moves her hand as if guarding from a blow.)

She was. He said that I had to be punished because I was getting too smart. I'm not smart. I never was. Neither is Fefu smart. They are after her too. Well, she's still walking!

(She guards from a blow. Her eyes close.)

Wait! I'll say my prayers. I'm saying it.   35

(She mumbles. She opens her eye with caution.)

You don't think I'm going to argue with them, do you? I repented. I told them exactly what they wanted to hear. They killed me. I was dead. The bullet didn't hit me. It hit the deer. But I died. He didn't. Then I repented and the deer died and I lived. *(With a gravelly voice.)* They said, 40 "Live but crippled. And if you tell . . ."

(She repeats the throat cutting gesture.)

Why do you have to kill Fefu, for she's only a joker? *(With a gravelly voice.)* "Not kill, cure. Cure her." Will it hurt?

(She whimpers.)

Oh, dear, dear, my dear, they want your light. Your light my dear. Your precious light. Oh dear, my dear.   45

(Her head moves as if slapped.)

Not cry. I'll say my prayer. I'll say it. Right now. Look.

(She sits up as if pulled by an invisible force.)

The human being is of the masculine gender. The human being is a boy as a child and grown up he is a man. Everything on earth is for the human being, which is man. To nourish him.—There are evil things on earth, and nox- 50 ious things. Evil and noxious things are on earth for man also. For him to fight with, and conquer and turn its evil into good. So that it too can nourish him.—There are Evil Plants, Evil Animals, Evil Minerals, and Women are Evil.—Woman is not a human being. She is: 1—A mys- 55 tery. 2—Another species. 3—As yet undefined. 4— Unpredictable; therefore wicked and gentle and evil and good which is evil.—If a man commits an evil act, he must be pitied. The evil comes from outside him, through him and into the act. Woman generates the evil herself.— God gave man no other mate but woman. The oxen is good but it is not a mate for man. The sheep is good but it is not a mate for man. The mate for man is woman and that is the cross man must bear.—Man is not spiritually sexual, he therefore can enjoy sexuality. His sexuality is physical which means his spirit is pure. Women's spirit is sexual. That is why after coitus they dwell in nefarious feelings. Because that is their natural habitat. That is why it is difficult for them to return to the human world. Their sexual feelings remain with them till they die. And they take those feelings with them to the afterlife where they corrupt the heavens, and they are sent to hell where through suffering they may shed those feelings and return to earth as man.

(Her head moves as if slapped.)

Don't hit me. Didn't I just say my prayer?

(A smaller slap.)

I believe it.

(She lies back.)

They say when I believe the prayer I will forget the judges. And when I forget the judges I will believe the prayer. They say both happen at once. And all women have done it. Why can't I?

(SUE enters with a bowl of soup on a tray.)

SUE: Julia, are you asleep?

(Short pause.)

JULIA: No.
SUE: I brought your soup.
JULIA: Put it down. I'm getting up in a moment.

(SUE puts the soup down.)

SUE: Do you want me to help you?
JULIA: No, I can manage. Thank you, Sue.

(SUE goes to the door.)

SUE: You're all right?
JULIA: Yes.
SUE: I'll see you later.
JULIA: Thank you, Sue.

(SUE exits. JULIA closes her eyes. As soon as each audience group leaves, the tray is removed, if possible through a back door.)

IN THE KITCHEN

A fully equipped kitchen. There is a table and chairs and a high cutting table. On a counter next to the stove there is a tray with a soup dish and a spoon. There is also a ladle. On the cutting table there are two empty glasses. Soup is heating on a burner. A kettle with water sits on an unlit burner. In the refrigerator there is an ice tray with wooden sticks in each cube. The sticks should rest on the edge of the tray forming two parallel rows, like a caterpillar lying on its back. In the refrigerator there are also two pitchers, one with water, one with lemonade. PAULA sits at the table. She is writing on a pad. SUE waits for the soup to heat.

PAULA: I have it all figured out.
SUE: What?
PAULA: A love affair lasts seven years and three months.
SUE: It does?
PAULA: *(Reading.)* 3 months of love. 1 year saying: It's all right. This is just a passing disturbance. 1 year trying to understand what's wrong. 2 years knowing the end had come. 1 year finding the way to end it. After the separation, 2 years trying to understand what happened. 7 years, 3 months. *(No longer reading.)* At any point the sequence might be interrupted by another love affair that has the same sequence. That is, it's not really interrupted, the new love affair relegates the first one to a second plane and both continue their sequence at the same time.

(SUE looks over PAULA's shoulder.)

SUE: You really added it up.
PAULA: Sure.
SUE: What do you want to drink?
PAULA: Water. The old love affair may fade, so you are not aware the process goes on. A year later it may surface and you might find yourself figuring out what's wrong with the new one while trying to end the old one.
SUE: So how do you solve the problem?
PAULA: Celibacy?
SUE: *(Going to the refrigerator.)* Celibacy doesn't solve anything.
PAULA: That's true.
SUE: *(Taking out the ice tray with the sticks.)* What's this? *(PAULA shakes her head.)* Dessert. *(PAULA shrugs her shoulders. SUE takes an ice cube and places it against her forehead.)* For a headache. *(She takes another cube and moves her arms in a Judo style.)* Eskimo wrestling. *(She places one stick behind her ear.)* Brain cooler. That's when you're thinking too much. You could use one. *(She tries to put the ice cube behind PAULA's ear. They wrestle and laugh. She puts the stick in her own mouth. She takes it out to speak.)* This is when you want to keep chaste. No one will kiss you. *(She puts it back in to demonstrate. Then takes it out.)* That's good for celibacy. If you walk around with one of these in your mouth for seven years you can keep all your sequences straight. Finish one before you start the other. *(She puts the ice cube in the tray and looks at it.)* A frozen caterpillar. *(She puts the tray away.)*
PAULA: You're leaving that ice cube in there?
SUE: I'm clean. *(Looking at the soup.)* So what else do you have on love? *(SUE places a bowl and spoon on the table and sits as she waits for the soup to heat.)*
PAULA: Well, the break-up takes place in parts. The brain, the heart, the body, mutual things, shared things. The mind leaves but the heart is still there. The heart has left but the body wants to stay. The body leaves but the things are still at the apartment. You must come back. You move everything out of the apartment but the mind stays behind. Memory lingers in the place. Seven years later, perhaps

seven years later, it doesn't matter any more. Perhaps it takes longer. Perhaps it never ends.

SUE: It depends.

55 PAULA: Yup. It depends.

SUE: (*Pouring soup in the bowl.*) Something's bothering you.

PAULA: No.

SUE: (*Taking the trail.*) I'm going to take this to Julia.

PAULA: Go ahead.

(*As* SUE *exits,* CECILIA *enters.*)

60 CECILIA: May I come in?

PAULA: Yes . . . Would you like something to eat?

CECILIA: No, I ate lunch.

PAULA: I didn't eat lunch. I wasn't very hungry.

CECILIA: I know.

65 PAULA: Would you like some coffee?

CECILIA: I'll have tea.

PAULA: I'll make some.

CECILIA: No, you sit. I'll make it. (CECILIA *looks for tea.*)

PAULA: Here it is. (*She gets the tea and gives it to* CECILIA.)

70 CECILIA: (*As she lights the burner.*) I've been meaning to call you.

PAULA: It doesn't matter. I know you're busy.

CECILIA: Still I would have called you but I really didn't find the time.

75 PAULA: Don't worry.

CECILIA: I wanted to see you again. I want to see you often.

PAULA: There's no hurry. Now we know we can see each other.

CECILIA: Yes, I'm glad we can.

80 PAULA: I have thought a great deal about my life since I saw you. I have questioned my life. I can't help doing that. It's been many years and I wondered how you see me now.

CECILIA: You're the same.

PAULA: I felt small in your presence . . . I haven't done all that

85 I could have. All I wanted to do. Our lives have gone in such different directions I cannot help but review what those years have been for me. I gave up, almost gave up. I missed you in my life. . . . I became lazy. I lost the drive. You abandoned me and I kept going. But after a while I

90 didn't know how to. I didn't know how to go on. I knew why when I was with you. To give you pleasure. So we could laugh together. So we could rejoice together. To bring beauty to the world. . . . Now we look at each other like strangers. We are guarded. I speak and you don't un-

95 derstand my words. I remember every day.

(FEFU *enters. She takes the lemonade pitcher from the refrigerator and two glasses from the top of the refrigerator.*)

FEFU: Emma and I are going to play croquet. You want to join us? . . . No. You're having a serious conversation.

PAULA: Very serious. (PAULA *smiles at* CECILIA *in a conciliatory manner.*) Too serious.

100 FEFU: (*As she exits.*) Come.

PAULA: I'm sorry. Let's go play croquet.—I'm not reproaching you.

CECILIA: (*Reaching for* PAULA'*s hand.*) I know. I've missed you too.

(*They exit. As soon as the audience leaves the props are reset.*)

PART III

The living room. It is dusk. As the audience enters, two or three of the women are around the piano playing and singing Schubert's "Who Is Silvia." They exit. EMMA *enters, checks the lights in the room on her hand, looks around the room and goes upstairs. The rest enter through the rear.* CECILIA *enters speaking.*

CECILIA: Well, we each have our own system of receiving information, placing it, responding to it. (*She sits in the center of the couch; the rest sit around her.*) That system can function with such a bias that it could take any situation and translate it into one formula. That is, I think, the main 5 reason for stupidity or even madness, not being able to tell the difference between things.

SUE: Like?

CECILIA: Like . . . this person is screaming at me. He's a bully. I don't like being screamed at. Another person or the 10 same person screams in a different situation. But you know you have done something that provokes him to scream. He has a good reason. They are two different things, the screaming of one and the screaming of the other. Often that distinction is not made. We cannot sur- 15 vive in a vacuum. We must be part of a community, perhaps 10, 100, 1000. It depends on how strong you are. But even the strongest will need a dozen, three, even one who sees, thinks, and feels as he does. The greater the need for that kind of reassurance, the greater the number that he 20 needs to identify with. Some need to identify with the whole nation. Then, the greater the number the more limited the number of responses and thoughts. A common denominator must be reached. Thoughts, emotions that fit all, have to be limited to a small number. That is, 25 I feel, the concern of the educator—to teach how to be sensitive to the differences in ourselves as well as outside ourselves, not to supervise the memorization of facts. (EMMA'*s head appears in the doorway to the stairs.*) Otherwise the unusual in us will perish. As we grow we feel we are 30 strange and fear any thought that is not shared with everyone.

JULIA: As I feel I am perishing. My hallucinations are madness, of course, but I wish I could be with others who hallucinate also. I would still know I am mad but I would not 35 feel so isolated.—Hallucinations are real, you know. They are not like dreams. They are as real as all of you here. I have actually asked to be hospitalized so I could be with other nuts. But the doctors don't want to. They can't diagnose me. That makes me even more isolated. (*There is a* 40 *moment's silence.*) You see, right now, it's an awful moment because you don't know what to say or do. If I were with other people who hallucinate, they would say, "Oh yeah. Sure. It's awful. Those dummies, they don't see anything." (*The others begin to relax.*) It's not so bad, really. I can laugh 45 at it. . . . Emma is ready. We should start. (*The others are hesitant.* JULIA *speaks to* FEFU.) Come on.

FEFU: Sure. (FEFU *begins to move the table. Others help move the table and enough furniture to clear a space in the center. They sit in a semicircle downstage on the floor facing upstage.* CECILIA 50 *sits on a chair to the left of the semicircle.*) All right. I start. Right?

CINDY: Right.

(FEFU *goes to center and faces the others.* EMMA *sits on the steps. Only her head and legs are visible.*)

FEFU: I talk about the stifling conditions of primary school
55   education, etc. . . . etc. . . . The project . . . I know what
I'm going to say but I don't want to bore you with it. We
all know it by heart. Blah blah blah blah. And so on and
so on. And so on and so on. Then I introduce Emma . . .
And now Miss Emma Blake. (*They applaud.* EMMA *shakes*
60   *her head.*) What.
EMMA: Paula goes next.
FEFU: Does it matter?
EMMA: Of course it matters. Dra-ma-tics. It has to build. I'm
in costume.
65   FEFU: Oh. And now, ladies and gentlemen, Miss Paula Cori
will speak on Art as a Tool for Learning. And I tell them
the work you have done at the Institute, community centers, essays, etc. Miss Paula Cori.

(*They applaud.* PAULA *goes to center.*)

PAULA: Ladies and gentlemen, I, like my fellow educator and
70   colleague, Stephany Beckmann . . .
FEFU: I am not an educator.
PAULA: What are you?
FEFU: . . . a do gooder, a girl scout.
PAULA: Well, I, like my fellow girl scout Stephany Beckmann
75   say blah blah blah blah, blab blah blah and I offer the jewels of my wisdom and experience, which I will write
down and memorize, otherwise I would just stand there
and stammer and go blank. And even after I memorize it
I'm sure I will just stand there and stammer and go blank.
80   EMMA: I'll work with you on it.
PAULA: However, after our other colleague Miss Emma Blake
works with me on it . . . (*In imitation of* EMMA *she brings her
hands together and opens her arms as she moves her head back
and speaks.*) My impulses will burst forth through a sym-
85   phony of eloquence.
EMMA: Breathe . . . in . . . (PAULA *inhales slowly.*) And bow.
(PAULA *bows. They applaud.*)
PAULA: (*Coming up from the bow.*) Oh, I liked that. (*She sits.*)
EMMA: Good . . .

(*They applaud.*)

90   FEFU: And now, ladies and gentlemen, the one and only, the
incomparable, our precious, dear Emma Blake.

(EMMA *walks to center. She wears a robe which hangs from her arms
to the floor.*)

EMMA: From the prologue to "The Science of Educational
Dramatics" by Emma Sheridan Fry. (*She takes a dramatic
pose and starts. The whole speech is dramatized by interpretive
95   gestures and movements that cover the stage area.*)
Environment knocks at the gateway of the senses. A
rain of summons beats upon us day and night. . . . We do

93 **Emma Sheridan Fry** taught acting to children at The Educational Alliance in New York from 1903 to 1909. In 1917, her
book *Educational Dramatics* was published by Lloyd Adams
Noble. The text of Emma's speech is taken from the prologue.

not answer. Everything around us shouts against our deafness, struggles with our unwillingness, batters our walls,
flashes into our blindness, strives to sieve through us at   100
every pore, begging, fighting, insisting. It shouts, "Where
are you? Where are you?" But we are deaf. The signals do
not reach us.
Society restricts us, school straight jackets us, civilization submerges us, privation wrings us, luxury feather-   105
beds us. The Divine Urge is checked. The Winged Horse
balks on the road, and we, discouraged, defeated, dismount
and burrow into ourselves. The gates are closed and Divine Urge is imprisoned at Center. Thus we are taken by
indifference that is death. Environment finding the gates   110
closed tries to break in. Turned away, it comes another
way. Kept back, it stretches its hands to us. Always scheming to reach us. Never was suitor more insistent than Environment, seeking admission, claiming recognition,
signaling to be seen, shouting to be heard. And through   115
the ages we sit inside ourselves deaf, dumb and blind, and
will not stir. . . .
. . . Maybe you are not deaf. . . . Perhaps signals reach
you. Maybe you stir. . . . The gates give. . . . Eternal Urge
pushes through the stupor of our senses, making paths to   120
meet the challenging suitor, windows through which to
see him, ears through which to hear him. Environment
shouting, "Where are you?" and Center battering at the
inner side of the wall crying, "Here I am," and dragging
down bars, wrenching gates, prying at port-holes. Listen-   125
ing at cracks, reaching everywhere, and demanding that
sense gates be flung open. The gates are open! Eternal
Urge stands at the threshold signaling with venturous flag.
An imperious instinct lets us know that "all" is ours, and
that whatever anyone has ever known, or may ever have   130
or know, we will call and claim. A sense of life universal
surges through our life individual. We attack the feast of
this table with an insatiable appetite that cries for all.
What are we? A creation of God's consciousness coming now slowly and painfully into recognition of our-   135
selves.
What is Personality? A small part of us. The whole of
us is behind that hungry rush at the gates of Senses.
What is Civilization? A circumscribed order in which
the whole has not entered.   140
What is Environment? Our mate, our true mate that
clamors for our reunion.
We will meet him. We will seize all, learn all, know all
here, that we may fare further on the great quest! The task
of Now is only a step toward the task of the Whole! Let   145
us then seek the laws governing real life forces, that coming into their own, they may create, develop and reconstruct. Let us awaken life dormant! Let us, boldly, seizing
the star of our intent, lift it as the lantern of our necessity,
and let it shine over the darkness of our compliance.   150
Come! The light shines. Come! It brightens our way.
Come! Don't let its glorious light pass you by! Come! The
day has come!
(EMMA *throws herself on the couch.* PAULA *embraces her.*)
Oh, it's so beautiful.   155
JULIA: It is, Emma. It is.

(*They applaud.*)

CINDY: Encore! Encore!

(EMMA *stands.*)

EMMA: Environment knocks at the gateway . . . (*She laughs and joins the others in the semi-circle.* PAULA *remains seated on the*
160   *couch.*) What's next.
FEFU: (*Going center.*) I introduce Cecilia. I don't think I should introduce Cecilia. She should just come after Emma. Now things don't need introduction. (*Imitating* EMMA *as she goes to her seat.*) They are happening.
165 EMMA: Right!

(CECILIA *goes to center.*)

CECILIA: Well, as we say in the business, that's a very hard act to follow.
EMMA: Not *very* hard. It's a hard act to follow.
CECILIA: Right. I should say my name first.
170 FEFU: Yes.
CECILIA: I should breathe too. (*She takes a breath. All except* PAULA *start singing "Cecilia."* CECILIA *is perplexed and walks backwards till she sits on the couch. She is next to* PAULA. *Un-aware of who she is next to, she puts her hand on* PAULA's *leg.*
175   *At the end of the song* CECILIA *realizes she is next to* PAULA *and stands.*) I should go before Emma. I don't think anyone should speak after Emma.
CINDY: Right. It should be Fefu, Paula, Cecilia, then Emma, and then Sue explaining the finances and asking for
180   pledges. And the money should roll in. It's very good. (*They applaud.*) Sue . . . (SUE *goes to center.*)
SUE: Yes, blahblahblahblah, pledges and money. (*She does a few balletic moves and bows. They applaud.*)
FEFU: (*As* SUE *returns to her seat.*) Who's ready for coffee?
185 CINDY: (*As she stands.*) And dishes.
CHRISTINA: (*As she stands.*) I'll help.
EMMA: (*As she stands.*) Me too.
FEFU: Don't all come. Sit. Sit. You have done enough, relax.

(*They put the furniture back as* EMMA *and* SUE *jump over the couch making loud warlike sounds. As they exit to the kitchen,* SUE *tries to get ahead of* EMMA. EMMA *speeds ahead of her. All except* JULIA *jump over the couch. All except* CINDY *and* JULIA *exit.*)

JULIA: I should go do the dishes. I haven't done anything.
190 CINDY: You can do them tomorrow.
JULIA: True.—So how have you been?
CINDY: Hmm.
JULIA: Let me see. I can tell by looking at your face. Not so bad.
195 CINDY: Not so bad.

(*There is the sound of laughter from the kitchen.* CHRISTINA *runs in.*)

CHRISTINA: They're having a water fight over who's going to do the dishes.
CINDY: Emma?
CHRISTINA: And Paula, and Sue, all of them. Fefu was getting
200   into it when I left. Cecilia got out the back door.

(CHRISTINA *walks back to the kitchen with some caution. She runs back and lies on the couch covering her head with the throw.* EMMA

enters with a pan of water in her hand. She is wet. CINDY *and* JU-LIA *point to the lawn.* EMMA *runs to the lawn. There is the sound of knocking from upstairs. While the following conversation goes on,* EMMA, SUE, CINDY, *and* JULIA *engage in water fights in and out of the living room. The screams, laughter, and water splashing may drown the words.*)

PAULA: Open up.
FEFU: There's no one here.
PAULA: Open up you coward.
FEFU: I can't. I'm busy.   205
PAULA: What are you doing?
FEFU: I have a man here. Ah ah ah ah ah.
PAULA: O.K. I'll wait. Take your time.
FEFU: It's going to take quite a while.
PAULA: It's all right. I'll wait.   210
FEFU: Do me a favor?
PAULA: Sure. Open up and I'll do you a favor.

(*There is the sound of a pot falling, a door slamming.*)

FEFU: Fill it up for me.
PAULA: O.K.
FEFU: Thank you.   215
PAULA: Here's water. Open up.
FEFU: Leave it there. I'll come out in a minute.
PAULA: O.K. Here it is. I'm leaving now.

(*Loud steps.* PAULA *comes down with a filled pan.* EMMA *hides by the entrance to the steps.* EMMA *splashes water on* PAULA. PAULA *splashes water on* EMMA. SUE *appears with a full pan.*)

PAULA: Truce!
SUE: Who's the winner?   220
PAULA: You are. You do the dishes.
SUE: I'm the winner. You do the dishes.
FEFU: (*From the landing.*) Line up!
SUE: Psst. (PAULA *and* EMMA *look.* SUE *splashes water on them.*)
    Gotcha!   225
EMMA: Please don't.
PAULA: Truce. Truce.
FEFU: O.K. Line up. (*Pointing to the kitchen.*) Get in there! (*They all go to the kitchen.*) Start doing those dishes. (*There is a moment's pause.*)   230
JULIA: It's over.
CINDY: We're safe.
JULIA: (*To* CHRISTINA.) You can come up now. (CHRISTINA *stays down.*) You rather wait a while.

(CHRISTINA *nods.*)

CHRISTINA: (*Playful.*) I feel danger lurking.   235
CINDY: She's been hiding all day.

(FEFU *enters. She is wet.*)

FEFU: I won. I got them working.
JULIA: I thought the fight was over who'd do the dishes.
FEFU: Yes. (*Starting to go.*) I have to change. I'm soaked.
CHRISTINA: They forgot what the fight was about.   240
FEFU: We did?
JULIA: That's usually the way it is.

FEFU: (*Going to* CHRISTINA *and lifting the cover from her face.*) Are you ready for an ice cube?

(FEFU *exits upstairs.* CHRISTINA *runs upstairs. There is silence.*)

245 CINDY: So.—And how have you been?
JULIA: All right. I've been taking care of myself.
CINDY: You look well.
JULIA: I do not. . . . Have you seen Mike?
CINDY: No, not since Christmas.
250 JULIA: I'm sorry.
CINDY: I'm O.K.—And how's your love life?
JULIA: Far away. . . . I have no need for it.
CINDY: I'm sorry.
JULIA: Don't be. I'm very morbid these days. I think of death
255 all the time.
PAULA: (*Standing in the doorway.*) Anyone for coffee? (*They raise their hands.*) Anyone take milk? (*They raise their hands.*)
JULIA: Should be go in?
PAULA: I'll bring it out. (PAULA *exits.*)
260 JULIA: I feel we are constantly threatened by death, every second, every instant, it's there. And every moment something rescues us. Something rescues us from death every moment of our lives. For every moment we live we have to thank something. We have to be grateful to something
265 that fights for us and saves us. I have felt lifeless and in the face of death. Death is not anything. It's being lifeless and I have felt lifeless sometimes for a brief moment, but I have been rescued by these . . . guardians. I am not sure who these guardians are. I only know they exist because I
270 have felt their absence. I think we have come to know them as life, and we have become familiar with certain forms they take. Our sight is a form they take. That is why we take pleasure in seeing things, and we find some things beautiful. The sun is a guardian. Those things we take
275 pleasure in are usually guardians. We enjoy looking at the sunlight when it comes through the window. Don't we? We, as people, are guardians to each other when we give love. And then of course we have white cells and antibodies protecting us. Those moments when I feel lifeless
280 have occurred, and I am afraid one day the guardians won't come in time and I will be defenseless. I will die . . . for no apparent reason.

(*Pause.* PAULA *stands in the doorway with a bottle of milk.*)

PAULA: (*In a low-keyed manner.*) Anyone take rotten milk? (*Pause.*) I'm kidding. This one is no good but there's more
285 in there . . . (*Remaining in good spirits.*) Forget it. It's not a good joke.
JULIA: It's good.
PAULA: In there it seemed funny but here it isn't. (*As she exits and shrugging her shoulders.*) It's a kitchen joke. Bye.
290 JULIA: (*After her.*) It is funny, Paula. (*To* CINDY.) It was funny.
CINDY: It's all right, Paula doesn't mind.
JULIA: I'm sure she minds. I'll go see . . . (JULIA *starts to go.* PAULA *appears in the doorway.*)
PAULA: (*In a low-keyed manner.*) Hey, who was that lady I saw
295 you with?—That was no lady. That was my rotten wife. That one wasn't good either, was it? (*Exiting.*) Emma. . . . That one was no good either.

(SUE *starts to enter carrying a tray with sugar, milk, and two cups of coffee. She stops at the doorway to look at* PAULA *and* EMMA *who are behind the wall.*)

SUE: (*Whispering.*) What are you doing?—What?—O.K., O.K. (*She enters whispering.* SUE *puts the tray down.*) They're plotting something. 300

(PAULA *appears in the doorway.*)

PAULA: (*In a low-keyed manner.*) Ladies and gentlemen. Ladies, since our material is too shocking and avant-garde, we have decided to uplift our subject matter so it's more palatable to the sensitive public. (PAULA *takes a pose.* EMMA *enters. She lifts an imaginary camera to her face.*) 305
EMMA: Say cheese.
PAULA: Cheese. (*They both turn front and smile. The others applaud.*) Ah, success, success. Make it clean and you'll succeed.—Coffee's in the kitchen.
SUE: Oh, I brought theirs out. 310
PAULA: Oh, shall we have it here?
JULIA: We can all go in the kitchen. (*They each take their coffee and go to the kitchen.* SUE *takes the tray to the kitchen. The sugar remains on the table.*)
PAULA: Either here or there. (*She sits on the couch.*) I'm ex- 315 hausted.

(CECILIA *enters from the lawn.*)

CECILIA: Is the war over?
PAULA: Yes.
CECILIA: It's nice out. (PAULA *nods in agreement.*) Where's everybody? 320
PAULA: In the kitchen, having coffee.
CECILIA: We must talk. (PAULA *starts to speak.*) Not now. I'll call you. (CECILIA *starts to go.*)
PAULA: When?
CECILIA: I don't know. 325
PAULA: I don't want you, you know.
CECILIA: I know.
PAULA: No, you don't. I'm not lusting after you.
CECILIA: I know that. (*She starts to go.*) I'll call you.
PAULA: When? 330
CECILIA: As soon as I can.
PAULA: I won't be home then.
CECILIA: When will you be home?
PAULA: I'll check my book and let you know.
CECILIA: Do that.—I'll be leaving after coffee. I'll say good- 335 bye now.
PAULA: Goodbye. (CECILIA *goes towards the kitchen.* PAULA *starts towards the steps.* FEFU *comes down the steps.*)
FEFU: You're still wet.
PAULA: I'm going to change now. 340
FEFU: Do you need anything?
PAULA: No, I have something I can change to. Thank you.

(PAULA *goes upstairs.* FEFU *stands by the steps. She is downcast. As the lights shift to an eerie tone,* JULIA *enters in slow motion, walking. She goes to the coffee table, gets the sugar bowl, lifts it in* FEFU's *direction, takes the cover off, puts it back on and walks to the kitchen. As soon as* JULIA *exits,* SUE's *voice is heard speaking the following lines. Immediately after,* JULIA *re-enters wheeled by* SUE. CINDY,

CHRISTINA, EMMA, *and* CECILIA *are with them. On the arms of the wheelchair rests a tray with a coffee pot and cups. As they reach the couch and chairs they sit.* SUE *puts the tray on the table.* FEFU *stares at* JULIA.)

SUE: I was terribly exhausted and run down. I lived on coffee so I could stay up all night and do my work. And they
345   used to give us these medical check-ups all the time. But
all they did was ask how we felt and we'd say "Fine," and
they'd check us out. In the meantime I looked like a
ghost. I was all bones. Remember Susan Austin? She was
very naive and when they asked her how she felt, she said
350   she was nervous and she wasn't sleeping well. So she had
to see a psychiatrist from then on.
EMMA: Well, she was crazy.

(FEFU *exits.*)

SUE: No, she wasn't.—Oh god, those were awful days. . . . Remember Julie Brooks?
355   EMMA: Sure
SUE: She was a beautiful girl.
EMMA: Ah yes, she was gorgeous.

(PAULA *comes down the stairs as soon as she has changed. She sits
on the steps half way down.*)

SUE: At the end of the first semester they called her in because she had been out with 28 men and they thought
360   that was awful. And the worst thing was that after that, she
thought there was something wrong with her.
CINDY: (*Jokingly.*) She was a nymphomaniac, that's all.
SUE: She was not. She was just very beautiful so all the boys
wanted to go out with her. And if a boy asked her to go
365   have a cup of coffee she'd sign out and write in the name
of the boy. None of us did of course. All she did was go
for coffee or go to a movie. She was really very innocent.
EMMA: And Gloria Schuman? She wrote a psychology paper
the faculty decided she didn't write and they called her in
370   to try to make her admit she hadn't written it. She insisted
she wrote it and they sent her to a psychiatrist also.
JULIA: Everybody ended going to the psychiatrist.

(FEFU *enters through the foyer.*)

EMMA: After a few visits the psychiatrist said: Don't you think
you know me well enough now that you can tell me the
375   truth about the paper? He almost drove her crazy. They
just couldn't believe she was so smart.
SUE: Those were difficult times.
PAULA: We were young. That's why it was difficult. On my first
year I thought you were all very happy. I had been so de-
380   prived in my childhood that I believed the rich were all
happy. During the summer you spent your vacations in Europe or the Orient. I went to work and I resented that. But
then I realized that many lives are ruined by poverty and
many lives are ruined by wealth. I was always able to man-
385   age. And I think I enjoyed myself as much when I went to
Revere Beach on my day off as you did when you visited
the Taj Mahal. (CECILIA *enters from the foyer. She stands there
and listens.* PAULA *doesn't acknowledge her.*) Then, when I
stopped feeling envy, I started noticing the waste. I began

feeling contempt for those who, having everything a per-   390
son can ask for, make such a mess of it. I resented them because they were not better than the poor. If you have all
you need you should be generous. If you can afford to go
to school your mind should be better. If you didn't have to
fight for your place on earth you should be nobler. But I   395
saw them cheating and grabbing like the kids in the slums,
or wasting away with self-indulgence. And I saw them be
plain stupid. If there is a reason why some are rich while
others starve it must be so they put everything they have at
the service of others. They should take the responsibility   400
of everything that happens in the world. They are the only
ones who can influence things. The poor don't have the
power to change things. I think we should teach the poor
and let the rich take care of themselves. I'm sorry, I know
that's what we're doing. That's what Emma has been do-   405
ing. I'm sorry . . . I guess I feel it's not enough. (PAULA *sobs.*)
I'll wash my face. I'll be right back. (*She starts to go towards
the kitchen.*) I think highly of all of you.

(CECILIA *follows her.* PAULA *turns.* CECILIA *opens her arms and puts
them around* PAULA, *engulfing her. She kisses* PAULA *on the lips.*
PAULA *steps back. She is fearful.* CECILIA *follows her.* FEFU *enters
from the lawn.*)

FEFU: Have you been out? The sky if full of stars.   410

(EMMA, SUE, CHRISTINA, *and* CINDY *exit.*)

JULIA: What's the matter?

(FEFU *shakes her head.* JULIA *starts to go toward the door.*)

FEFU: Stay a moment, will you?
JULIA: Of course.
FEFU: Did you have enough coffee?
JULIA: Yes.   415
FEFU: Did you find the sugar?
JULIA: Yes. There was sugar in the kitchen. What's the matter?
FEFU: Can you walk? (JULIA *is hurt. She opens her arms imply-
ing she hides nothing.*) I am sorry, my dear.
JULIA: What is the matter?   420
FEFU: I don't know, Julia. Every breath is painful for me. I
don't know. (FEFU *turns* JULIA's *head to look into her eyes.*) I
think you know.

(JULIA *breaks away from* FEFU.)

JULIA: (*Avoiding* FEFU's *glance.*) No, I don't know. I haven't
seen much of you lately. I have thought of you a great   425
deal. I always think of you. Cindy tells me how you are. I
always ask her. How is Phillip? Things are not well with
Phillip?
FEFU: No.
JULIA: What's wrong?   430
FEFU: A lot is wrong.
JULIA: He loves you.
FEFU: He can't stand me.
JULIA: He loves you.
FEFU: He's left me. His body is here but the rest is gone. I ex-   435
haust him. I torment him and I torment myself. I need
him, Julia.
JULIA: I know you do.

FEFU: I need his touch. I need his kiss. I need the person he
440   is. I can't give him up. (*She looks into* JULIA's *eyes.*) I look
into your eyes and I know what you see. (JULIA *closes her
eyes.*) It's death. (JULIA *shakes her head.*) Fight!
JULIA: I can't.
FEFU: I saw you walking.
445   JULIA: No. I can't walk.
FEFU: You came for sugar, Julia. You came for sugar. Walk!
JULIA: You know I can't walk.
FEFU: Why not? Try! Get up! Stand up!
JULIA: What is wrong with you?
450   FEFU: You have given up!
JULIA: I get tired! I get exhausted! I am exhausted!
FEFU: What is it you see? (JULIA *doesn't answer.*) What is it you
see! Where is it you go that tires you so?
JULIA: I can't spend time with others! I get tired!
455   FEFU: What is it you see!
JULIA: You want to see it too?
FEFU: No, I don't. You're nuts, and willingly so.
JULIA: You know I'm not.
FEFU: And you're contagious. I'm going mad too.
460   JULIA: I try to keep away from you.
FEFU: Why?
JULIA: I might be harmful to you.
FEFU: Why?
JULIA: I am contagious. I can't be what I used to be.
465   FEFU: You have no courage.
JULIA: You're being cruel.
FEFU: I want to rest, Julia. How does a person rest. I want to
put my mind at rest. I am frightened. (JULIA *looks at* FEFU.)
Don't look at me. (*She covers* JULIA's *eyes with her hand.*) I
470   lose my courage when you look at me.
JULIA: May no harm come to your head.
FEFU: Fight!
JULIA: May no harm come to your will.
FEFU: Fight, Julia!

(FEFU *starts shaking the wheelchair and pulling* JULIA *off the wheelchair.*)

475   JULIA: I have no life left.
FEFU: Fight, Julia!
JULIA: May no harm come to your hands.
FEFU: I need you to fight.
JULIA: May no harm come to your eyes.
480   FEFU: Fight with me!
JULIA: May no harm come to your voice.

FEFU: Fight with me!
JULIA: May no harm come to your heart.

(CHRISTINA *enters.* FEFU *sees* CHRISTINA, *releases* JULIA. *To*
CHRISTINA.)

FEFU: Now I have done it. Haven't I. You think I'm a monster. (*She turns to* JULIA *and speaks to her with kindness.*) For-   485
give me if you can. (JULIA *nods.*)
JULIA: I forgive you.

(FEFU *gets the gun.*)

CHRISTINA: What in the word are you doing with that gun!
FEFU: I'm going to clean it!
CHRISTINA: I think you better not!   490
FEFU: You're silly!

(CECILIA *appears on the landing.*)

CHRISTINA: I don't care if you shoot yourself! I just don't like
the mess you're making!

(FEFU *starts to go to the lawn and turns.*)

FEFU: I enjoy betting it won't be a real bullet! You want to
bet!   495
CHRISTINA: No! (FEFU *exits.* CHRISTINA *goes to* JULIA.) Are you
all right?
JULIA: Yes.
CHRISTINA: Can I get you anything?
JULIA: Water. (CECILIA *goes to the liquor cabinet for water.*) Put   500
some sugar in it. Could I have a damp cloth for my fore-
head? (CHRISTINA *goes toward the kitchen.* JULIA *speaks front.*)
I didn't tell her anything. Did I? I didn't.
CECILIA: (*Going to* JULIA *with the water.*) About what?
JULIA: She knew.   505

(*There is the sound of a shot.* CHRISTINA *and* CECILIA *run out.*
JULIA *puts her hand to her forehead. Her hand goes down slowly.
There is blood on her forehead. Her head falls back.* FEFU *enters
holding a dead rabbit.*)

FEFU: I killed it . . . I just shot . . . and killed it. . . . Julia . . .

(*Dropping the rabbit,* FEFU *walks to* JULIA *and stands behind the
chair as she looks at* JULIA. SUE *and* CINDY *enter from the foyer,*
EMMA *and* PAULA *from the kitchen,* CHRISTINA *and* CECILIA *from
the lawn. They surround* JULIA. *The lights fade.*)

Sam Shepard

Sam Shepard (b. 1943) is probably the best-known American playwright of his generation. Born Samuel Shepard Rogers to a military family stationed in Illinois, Shepard spent his youth moving from base to base, until his father retired and settled the family in southern California. Shepard was an indifferent student and left college for New York City in 1963. He took a job busing tables at the Village Gate jazz club and began to write plays for off-Broadway, including *Cowboys* (1964), *Red Cross* (1966), *La Turista* (1966), *The Unseen Hand* (1970), *Cowboy Mouth* (1971), and *Tooth of Crime* (1972). In these plays, Shepard invented what became his characteristic idiom: a search for the "West" of myth, an image both fascinating and elusive, somehow undiscoverable amid the consumer trash of suburban society. He also developed a sense of split and fragmented characters, relying on his typically jazzy use of language. This is particularly true of *Tooth of Crime*, in which a kind of shoot-out between the old rock 'n' roll star, Hoss, and the Keith Richards–like Crow is conducted in an invented language of rock music, drugs, cars, gangsters, and old movies. Shepard won six Obie awards between 1964 and 1970, but his work took a great step forward in the major plays of the late 1970s and 1980s: *Curse of the Starving Class* (1978), *Buried Child* (Pulitzer Prize, 1979), *True West* (1980), *Fool for Love* (1982), *A Lie of the Mind* (1985), *States of Shock* (1991), *Simpatico* (1994), and *Eyes for Consuela* (1998). Shepard also has written the screenplay for the Wim Wenders film, *Paris, Texas,* and has starred in several films himself, notably as Chuck Yeager in *The Right Stuff* (1983) and as the Ghost of Old Hamlet in Michael Almereyda's *Hamlet* (2000).

Gary Sinise as Austin and John Malkovitch as Lee in the 1980 Steppenwolf Theater production of Sam Shepard's *True West*.

TRUE WEST   *True West* is the leanest, most elemental of Shepard's plays and brings the question of identity—individual and cultural—into sharp focus. The play concerns two brothers: Austin, a yuppie screenwriter, and his derelict brother, Lee, a petty thief who spends much of his time in the desert. In the course of the play, however, Austin and Lee subtly change roles and identities: Lee swings a deal to write the screenplay for a Western movie, while Austin seems to abandon the desire to be a writer, working to prove himself to Lee by stealing toasters from the suburban neighbors. *True West* is a kind of Western, though the brothers don't fight it out for any actual piece of territory, since there is no Dodge City, no True West to fight over. What the brothers finally duel for is a mythic terrain, the terrain of their father, of the desert, of Westerns: the "West" of the imagination.

TRUE WEST

Sam Shepard

CHARACTERS

AUSTIN, *early thirties, light blue sports shirt, light tan cardigan sweater, clean blue jeans, white tennis shoes*

LEE, *his older brother, early forties, filthy white t-shirt, tattered brown overcoat covered with dust, dark blue baggy suit pants from the Salvation Army, pink suede belt, pointed black forties dress shoes scuffed up, holes in the soles, no socks, no hat, long pronounced sideburns, "Gene Vincent" hairdo, two days' growth of beard, bad teeth*

SAUL KIMMER, *late forties, Hollywood producer, pink and white flower print sports shirt, white sports coat with matching polyester slacks, black and white loafers*

MOM, *early sixties, mother of the brothers, small woman, conservative white skirt and matching jacket, red shoulder bag, two pieces of matching red luggage*

SCENE: *All nine scenes take place on the same set; a kitchen and adjoining alcove of an older home in a Southern California suburb, about 40 miles east of Los Angeles. The kitchen takes up most of the playing area to stage left. The kitchen consists of a sink, upstage center, surrounded by counter space, a wall telephone, cupboards, and a small window just above it bordered by neat yellow curtains. Stage left of sink is a stove. Stage right, a refrigerator. The alcove adjoins the kitchen to stage right. There is no wall division or door to the alcove. It is open and easily accessible from the kitchen and defined only by the objects in it: a small round glass breakfast table mounted on white iron legs, two matching white iron chairs set across from each other. The two exterior walls of the alcove which prescribe a corner in the upstage right are composed of many small windows, beginning from a solid wall about three feet high and extending to the ceiling. The windows look out to bushes and citrus trees. The alcove is filled with all sorts of house plants in various pots, mostly Boston ferns hanging in planters at different levels. The floor of the alcove is composed of green synthetic grass.*

All entrances and exits are made stage left from the kitchen. There is no door. The actors simply go off and come onto the playing area.

NOTE ON SET AND COSTUME: *The set should be constructed realistically with no attempt to distort its dimensions, shapes, objects, or colors. No objects should be introduced which might draw special attention to themselves other than the props demanded by the script. If a stylistic "concept" is grafted onto the set design it will only serve to confuse the evolution of the characters' situation, which is the most important focus of the play.*

Likewise, the costumes should be exactly representative of who the characters are and not added onto for the sake of making a point to the audience.

NOTE ON SOUND: *The Coyote of Southern California has a distinct yapping, dog-like bark, similar to a Hyena. This yapping grows more intense and maniacal as the pack grows in numbers, which is usually the case when they lure and kill pets from suburban yards. The sense of growing frenzy in the pack should be felt in the background, particularly in Scenes 7 and 8. In any case, these Coyotes never make the long, mournful, solitary howl of the Hollywood stereotype.*

The sound of Crickets can speak for itself.

These sounds should also be treated realistically even though they sometimes grow in volume and numbers.

ACT ONE

SCENE 1

Night. Sound of crickets in dark. Candlelight appears in alcove, illuminating AUSTIN, seated at glass table hunched over a writing notebook, pen in hand, cigarette burning in ashtray, cup of coffee, typewriter on table, stacks of paper, candle burning on table.

Soft moonlight fills kitchen illuminating LEE, beer in hand, six-pack on counter behind him. He's leaning against the sink, mildly drunk; takes a slug of beer.

LEE: So, Mom took off for Alaska, huh?

AUSTIN: Yeah.

LEE: Sorta' left you in charge.

AUSTIN: Well, she knew I was coming down here so she of-
5   fered me the place.

LEE: You keepin' the plants watered?

AUSTIN: Yeah.

LEE: Keepin' the sink clean? She don't like even a single tea leaf in the sink ya' know.

10 AUSTIN: (*Trying to concentrate on writing.*) Yeah, I know.

(Pause.)

LEE: She gonna' be up there a long time?

AUSTIN: I don't know.

LEE: Kinda' nice for you, huh? Whole place to yourself.

AUSTIN: Yeah, it's great.

LEE: Ya' got crickets anyway. Tons a' crickets out there. (*Looks*   15
    around kitchen.) Ya' got groceries? Coffee?

AUSTIN: (*Looking up from writing.*) What?

LEE: You got coffee?

AUSTIN: Yeah.

LEE: At's good. (*Short pause.*) Real coffee? From the bean?   20

AUSTIN: Yeah. You want some?

LEE: Naw. I brought some uh—(*Motions to beer.*)

AUSTIN: Help yourself to whatever's—(*Motions to refrigerator.*)

LEE: I will. Don't worry about me. I'm not the one to worry
    about. I mean I can uh—(*Pause.*) You always work by can-   25
    dlelight?

AUSTIN: No—uh—Not always.

LEE: Just sometimes?

AUSTIN: (*Puts pen down, rubs his eyes.*) Yeah. Sometimes it's
    soothing.   30

LEE: Isn't that what the old guys did?

AUSTIN: What old guys?

LEE: The Forefathers. You know.

AUSTIN: Forefathers?

35 LEE: Isn't that what they did? Candlelight burning into the night? Cabins in the wilderness.

AUSTIN: (*Rubs hand through his hair.*) I suppose.

LEE: I'm not botherin' you am I? I mean I don't wanna break into yer uh—concentration or nothin'.

40 AUSTIN: No, it's all right.

LEE: That's good. I mean I realize that yer line a' work demands a lota' concentration.

AUSTIN: It's okay.

LEE: You probably think that I'm not fully able to compre-

45 hend somethin' like that, huh?

AUSTIN: Like what?

LEE: That stuff yer doin'. That art. You know. Whatever you call it.

AUSTIN: It's just a little research.

50 LEE: You may not know it but I did a little art myself once.

AUSTIN: You did?

LEE: Yeah! I did some a' that. I fooled around with it. No future in it.

AUSTIN: What'd you do?

55 LEE: Never mind what I did! Just never mind about that. (*Pause.*) It was ahead of its time.

(*Pause.*)

AUSTIN: So, you went out to see the old man, huh?

LEE: Yeah, I seen him.

AUSTIN: How's he doing?

60 LEE: Same. He's doin' just about the same.

AUSTIN: I was down there too, you know.

LEE: What d'ya' want, an award? You want some kinda' medal? You were down there. He told me all about you.

AUSTIN: What'd he say?

65 LEE: He told me. Don't worry.

(*Pause.*)

AUSTIN: Well—

LEE: You don't have to say nothin'.

AUSTIN: I wasn't.

LEE: Yeah, you were gonna' make somethin' up. Somethin'

70   brilliant.

(*Pause.*)

AUSTIN: You going to be down here very long, Lee?

LEE: Might be. Depends on a few things.

AUSTIN: You got some friends down here?

LEE: (*Laughs.*) I know a few people. Yeah.

75 AUSTIN: Well, you can stay here as long as I'm here.

LEE: I don't need your permission do I?

AUSTIN: No.

LEE: I mean she's my mother too, right?

AUSTIN: Right.

80 LEE: She might've just as easily asked me to take care of her place as you.

AUSTIN: That's right.

LEE: I mean I know how to water plants.

(*Long pause.*)

AUSTIN: So you don't know how long you'll be staying then?

LEE: Depends mostly on houses, ya' know.   85

AUSTIN: Houses?

LEE: Yeah. Houses. Electric devices. Stuff like that. I gotta' make a little tour first.

(*Short pause.*)

AUSTIN: Lee, why don't you just try another neighborhood, all right?   90

LEE: (*Laughs.*) What'sa' matter with this neighborhood? This is a great neighborhood. Lush. Good class a' people. Not many dogs.

AUSTIN: Well, our uh—Our mother just happens to live here. That's all.   95

LEE: Nobody's gonna' know. All they know is somethin's missing. That's all. She'll never even hear about it. Nobody's gonna' know.

AUSTIN: You're going to get picked up if you start walking around here at night.   100

LEE: Me? I'm gonna' git picked up? What about you? You stick out like a sore thumb. Look at you. You think yer regular lookin'?

AUSTIN: I've got too much to deal with here to be worrying about—   105

LEE: Yer not gonna' have to worry about me! I've been doin' all right without you. I haven't been anywhere near you for five years! Now isn't that true?

AUSTIN: Yeah.

LEE: So you don't have to worry about me. I'm a free agent.   110

AUSTIN: All right.

LEE: Now all I wanna' do is borrow yer car.

AUSTIN: No!

LEE: Just fer a day. One day.

AUSTIN: No!   115

LEE: I won't take it outside a twenty mile radius. I promise ya'. You can check the speedometer.

AUSTIN: You're not borrowing my car! That's all there is to it.

(*Pause.*)

LEE: Then I'll just take the damn thing.

AUSTIN: Lee, look—I don't want any trouble, all right?   120

LEE: That's a dumb line. That is a dumb fuckin' line. You git paid fer dreamin' up a line like that?

AUSTIN: Look, I can give you some money if you need money.

(LEE *suddenly lunges at* AUSTIN, *grabs him violently by the shirt and shakes him with tremendous power.*)

LEE: Don't you say that to me! Don't you ever say that to me! (*Just as suddenly he turns him loose, pushes him away and backs* 125 *off.*) You may be able to git away with that with the Old Man. Git him tanked up for a week! Buy him off with yer Hollywood blood money, but not me! I can git my own money my own way. Big money!

AUSTIN: I was just making an offer.   130

LEE: Yeah, well keep it to yourself!

(*Long pause.*)

Those are the most monotonous fuckin' crickets I ever heard in my life.

AUSTIN: I kinda' like the sound.

135 LEE: Yeah. Supposed to be able to tell the temperature by the number a' pulses. You believe that?

AUSTIN: The temperature?

LEE: Yeah. The air. How hot it is.

AUSTIN: How do you do that?

140 LEE: I don't know. Some woman told me that. She was a Botanist. So I believed her.

AUSTIN: Where'd you meet her?

LEE: What?

AUSTIN: The woman Botanist?

145 LEE: I met her on the desert. I been spendin' a lota' time on the desert.

AUSTIN: What were you doing out there?

LEE: (*Pause, stares in space.*) I forgit. Had me a Pit Bull there for a while but I lost him.

150 AUSTIN: Pit Bull?

LEE: Fightin' dog. Damn I made some good money off that little dog. Real good money.

(*Pause.*)

AUSTIN: You could come up north with me, you know.

LEE: What's up there?

155 AUSTIN: My family.

LEE: Oh, that's right, you got the wife and kiddies now don't ya'. The house, the car, the whole slam. That's right.

AUSTIN: You could spend a couple days. See how you like it. I've got an extra room.

160 LEE: Too cold up there.

(*Pause.*)

AUSTIN: You want to sleep for a while?

LEE: (*Pause, stares at* AUSTIN.) I don't sleep.

(*Lights to black.*)

SCENE 2

Morning. AUSTIN *is watering plants with a vaporizer,* LEE *sits at glass table in alcove drinking beer.*

LEE: I never realized the old lady was so security-minded.

AUSTIN: How do you mean?

LEE: Made a little tour this morning. She's got locks on every-thing. Locks and double-locks and chain locks and—

5   What's she got that's so valuable?

AUSTIN: Antiques I guess. I don't know.

LEE: Antiques? Brought everything with her from the old place, huh. Just the same crap we always had around. Plates and spoons.

10 AUSTIN: I guess they have personal value to her.

LEE: Personal value. Yeah. Just a lota' junk. Most of it's phony anyway. Idaho decals. Now who in the hell wants to eat offa' plate with the State of Idaho starin' ya' in the face. Every time ya' take a bite ya' get to see a little bit more.

15 AUSTIN: Well it must mean something to her or she wouldn't save it.

LEE: Yeah, well personally I don't wann' be invaded by Idaho when I'm eatin'. When I'm eatin' I'm home. Ya' know

what I'm sayin? I'm not driftin', I'm home. I don't need my thoughts swept off to Idaho. I don't need that!   20

(*Pause.*)

AUSTIN: Did you go out last night?

LEE: Why?

AUSTIN: I thought I heard you go out.

LEE: Yeah, I went out. What about it?

AUSTIN: Just wondered.   25

LEE: Damn coyotes kept me awake.

AUSTIN: Oh yeah, I heard them. They must've killed some-body's dog or something.

LEE: Yappin' their fool heads off. They don't yap like that on the desert. They howl. These are city coyotes here.   30

AUSTIN: Well, you don't sleep anyway do you?

(*Pause,* LEE *stares at him.*)

LEE: You're pretty smart aren't ya?

AUSTIN: How do you mean?

LEE: I mean you never had any more on the ball than I did. But here you are gettin' invited into prominent people's   35 houses. Sittin' around talkin' like you know somethin'.

AUSTIN: They're not so prominent.

LEE: They're a helluva' lot more prominent than the houses I get invited into.

AUSTIN: Well you invite yourself.   40

LEE: That's right. I do. In fact I probably got a wider range a' choices than you do, come to think of it.

AUSTIN: I wouldn't doubt it.

LEE: In fact I been inside some pretty classy places in my time. And I never even went to an Ivy League school either.   45

AUSTIN: You want some breakfast or something?

LEE: Breakfast?

AUSTIN: Yeah. Don't you eat breakfast?

LEE: Look, don't worry about me pal. I can take care a' myself. You just go ahead as though I wasn't even here, all right?   50

(AUSTIN *goes into kitchen, makes coffee.*)

AUSTIN: Where'd you walk to last night?

(*Pause.*)

LEE: I went up in the foothills there. Up in the San Gabriels. Heat was drivin' me crazy.

AUSTIN: Well, wasn't it hot out on the desert?

LEE: Different kinda' heat. Out there it's clean. Cools off at   55 night. There's a nice little breeze.

AUSTIN: Where were you, the Mojave?

LEE: Yeah. The Mojave. That's right.

AUSTIN: I haven't been out there in years.

LEE: Out past Needles there.   60

AUSTIN: Oh yeah.

LEE: Up here it's different. This country's real different.

AUSTIN: Well, it's been built up.

LEE: Built up? Wiped out is more like it. I don't even hardly recognize it.   65

AUSTIN: Yeah. Foothills are the same though, aren't they?

LEE: Pretty much. It's funny goin' up in there. The smells and everything. Used to catch snakes up there, remember?

AUSTIN: You caught snakes.

70 LEE: Yeah. And you'd pretend you were Geronimo or some damn thing. You used to go right out to lunch.

AUSTIN: I enjoyed my imagination.

LEE: That what you call it? Looks like yer still enjoyin' it.

AUSTIN: So you just wandered around up there, huh?

75 LEE: Yeah. With a purpose.

AUSTIN: See any houses?

(*Pause.*)

LEE: Couple. Couple a' real nice ones. One of 'em didn't even have a dog. Walked right up and stuck my head in the window. Not a peep. Just a sweet kinda' suburban silence.

80 AUSTIN: What kind of a place was it?

LEE: Like a paradise. Kinda' place that sorta' kills ya' inside. Warm yellow lights. Mexican tile all around. Copper pots hangin' over the stove. Ya' know like they got in the magazines. Blonde people movin' in and outa' the rooms,

85 talkin' to each other. (*Pause.*) Kinda' place you wish you sorta' grew up in, ya' know.

AUSTIN: That's the kind of place you wish you'd grown up in?

LEE: Yeah, why not?

AUSTIN: I thought you hated that kind of stuff.

90 LEE: Yeah, well you never knew too much about me did ya'?

(*Pause.*)

AUSTIN: Why'd you go out to the desert in the first place?

LEE: I was on my way to see the old man.

AUSTIN: You mean you just passed through there?

LEE: Yeah. That's right. Three months of passin' through.

95 AUSTIN: Three months?

LEE: Somethin' like that. Maybe more. Why?

AUSTIN: You lived on the Mojave for three months?

LEE: Yeah. What'sa' matter with that?

AUSTIN: By yourself?

100 LEE: Mostly. Had a couple a' visitors. Had that dog for a while.

AUSTIN: Didn't you miss people?

LEE: (*Laughs.*) People?

AUSTIN: Yeah. I mean I go crazy if I have to spend three nights in a motel by myself.

105 LEE: Yer not in a motel now.

AUSTIN: No, I know. But sometimes I have to stay in motels.

LEE: Well, they got people in motels don't they?

AUSTIN: Strangers.

LEE: Yer friendly aren't ya'? Aren't you the friendly type?

(*Pause.*)

110 AUSTIN: I'm going to have somebody coming by here later, Lee.

LEE: Ah! Lady friend?

AUSTIN: No, a producer.

LEE: Aha! What's he produce?

AUSTIN: Film. Movies. You know.

115 LEE: Oh, movies. Motion Pictures! A Big Wig huh?

AUSTIN: Yeah.

LEE: What's he comin' by here for?

AUSTIN: We have to talk about a project.

LEE: Whadya' mean, "a project"? What's a "project"?

120 AUSTIN: A script.

LEE: Oh. That's what yer doin' with all these papers?

AUSTIN: Yeah.

LEE: Well, what's the project about?

AUSTIN: We're uh—it's a period piece.

LEE: What's "a period piece"?   125

AUSTIN: Look, it doesn't matter. The main thing is we need to discuss this alone. I mean—

LEE: Oh, I get it. You want me outa' the picture.

AUSTIN: Not exactly. I just need to be alone with him for a couple of hours. So we can talk.   130

LEE: Yer afraid I'll embarrass ya' huh?

AUSTIN: I'm not afraid you'll embarrass me!

LEE: Well, I tell ya' what—Why don't you just gimme the keys to yer car and I'll be back here around six o'clock or so. That give ya' enough time?   135

AUSTIN: I'm not loaning you my car, Lee.

LEE: You want me to just git lost huh? Take a hike? Is that it? Pound the pavement for a few hours while you bullshit yer way into a million bucks.

AUSTIN: Look, it's going to be hard enough for me to face   140 this character on my own without—

LEE: You don't know this guy?

AUSTIN: No I don't know—He's a producer. I mean I've been meeting with him for months but you never get to know a producer.   145

LEE: Yer tryin' to hustle him? Is that it?

AUSTIN: I'm not trying to hustle him! I'm trying to work out a deal! It's not easy.

LEE: What kinda' deal?

AUSTIN: Convince him it's a worthwhile story.   150

LEE: He's not convinced? How come he's comin' over here if he's not convinced? I'll convince him for ya'.

AUSTIN: You don't understand the way things work down here.

LEE: How do things work down here?

(*Pause.*)

AUSTIN: Look, if I loan you my car will you have it back here   155 by six?

LEE: On the button. With a full tank a' gas.

AUSTIN: (*Digging in his pocket for keys.*) Forget about the gas.

LEE: Hey, these days gas is gold, old buddy.

(AUSTIN *hands the keys to* LEE.)

You remember that car I used to loan you?   160

AUSTIN: Yeah.

LEE: Forty Ford. Flathead.

AUSTIN: Yeah.

LEE: Sucker hauled ass didn't it?

AUSTIN: Lee, it's not that I don't want to loan you my car—   165

LEE: You are loanin' me yer car.

(LEE *gives* AUSTIN *a pat on the shoulder, pause.*)

AUSTIN: I know. I just wish—

LEE: What? You wish what?

AUSTIN: I don't know. I wish I wasn't—I wish I didn't have to be doing business down here. I'd like to just spend some   170 time with you.

LEE: I thought it was "Art" you were doin'.

(LEE *moves across kitchen toward exit, tosses keys in his hand.*)

AUSTIN: Try to get it back here by six, okay?

175 LEE: No sweat. Hey, ya' know, if that uh—story of yours doesn't go over with the guy—tell him I got a couple a' "projects" he might be interested in. Real commercial. Full a' suspense. True-to-life stuff.

(LEE *exits,* AUSTIN *stares after* LEE *then turns, goes to papers at table, leafs through pages, lights fade to black.*)

SCENE 3

Afternoon. Alcove, SAUL KIMMER *and* AUSTIN *seated across from each other at table.*

SAUL: Well, to tell you the truth Austin, I have never felt so confident about a project in quite a long time.

AUSTIN: Well, that's good to hear, Saul.

5 SAUL: I am absolutely convinced we can get this thing off the ground. I mean we'll have to make a sale to television and that means getting a major star. Somebody bankable. But I think we can do it. I really do.

AUSTIN: Don't you think we need a first draft before we approach a star?

10 SAUL: No, no, not at all. I don't think it's necessary. Maybe a brief synopsis. I don't want you to touch the typewriter until we have some seed money.

AUSTIN: That's fine with me.

SAUL: I mean it's a great story. Just the story alone. You've re-

15 ally managed to capture something this time.

AUSTIN: I'm glad you like it, Saul.

(LEE *enters abruptly into kitchen carrying a stolen television set, short pause.*)

LEE: Aw shit, I'm sorry about that. I am really sorry Austin.

AUSTIN: (*Standing.*) That's all right.

LEE: (*Moving toward them.*) I mean I thought it was way past

20 six already. You said to have it back here by six.

AUSTIN: We were just finishing up. (*To* SAUL.) This is my, uh—brother, Lee.

SAUL: (*Standing.*) Oh, I'm very happy to meet you.

(LEE *sets T.V. on sink counter, shakes hands with* SAUL.)

LEE: I can't tell ya' how happy I am to meet you sir.

25 SAUL: Saul Kimmer.

LEE: Mr. Kipper.

SAUL: Kimmer.

AUSTIN: Lee's been living out on the desert and he just uh—

SAUL: Oh, that's terrific! (*To* LEE.) Palm Springs?

30 LEE: Yeah. Yeah, right. Right around in that area. Near uh— Bob Hope Drive there.

SAUL: Oh I love it out there. I just love it. The air is wonderful.

LEE: Yeah. Sure is. Healthy.

35 SAUL: And the golf. I don't know if you play golf, but the golf is just about the best.

LEE: I play a lota' golf.

SAUL: Is that right?

LEE: Yeah. In fact I was hoping I'd run into somebody out here

40 who played a little golf. I've been lookin' for a partner.

SAUL: Well, I uh—

AUSTIN: Lee's just down for a visit while our mother's in Alaska.

SAUL: Oh, your mother's in Alaska?

AUSTIN: Yes. She went up there on a little vacation. This is

45 her place.

SAUL: I see. Well isn't that something. Alaska.

LEE: What kinda' handicap do ya' have, Mr. Kimmer?

SAUL: Oh I'm just a Sunday duffer really. You know.

LEE: That's good 'cause I haven't swung a club in months.

50 SAUL: Well we ought to get together sometime and have a little game. Austin, do you play?

(SAUL *mimes a Johnny Carson golf swing for* AUSTIN.)

AUSTIN: No. I don't uh—I've watched it on T.V.

LEE: (*To* SAUL.) How 'bout tomorrow morning? Bright and early. We could get out there and put in eighteen holes be-

55 fore breakfast.

SAUL: Well, I've got uh—I have several appointments—

LEE: No, I mean real early. Crack a' dawn. While the dew's still thick on the fairway.

SAUL: Sounds really great.

60 LEE: Austin could be our caddie.

SAUL: Now that's an idea. (*Laughs.*)

AUSTIN: I don't know the first thing about golf.

LEE: There's nothin' to it. Isn't that right, Saul? He'd pick it up in fifteen minutes.

65 SAUL: Sure. Doesn't take long. 'Course you have to play for years to find your true form. (*Chuckles.*)

LEE: (*To* AUSTIN.) We'll give ya' a quick run-down on the club faces. The irons, the woods. Show ya' a couple pointers on the basic swing. Might even let ya' hit the ball a couple

70 times. Whadya' think, Saul?

SAUL: Why not. I think it'd be great. I haven't had any exercise in weeks.

LEE: At's the spirit! We'll have a little orange juice right afterwards.

(*Pause.*)

75 SAUL: Orange juice?

LEE: Yeah! Vitamin C! Nothin' like a shot a' orange juice after a round a' golf. Hot shower. Snappin' towels at each others' privates. Real sense a' fraternity.

SAUL: (*Smiles at* AUSTIN.) Well, you make it sound very invit-

80 ing, I must say. It really does sound great.

LEE: Then it's a date.

SAUL: Well, I'll call the country club and see if I can arrange something.

LEE: Great! Boy, I sure am sorry that I busted in on ya' all in

85 the middle of yer meeting.

SAUL: Oh that's quite all right. We were just about finished anyway.

LEE: I can wait out in the other room if you want.

SAUL: No really—

90 LEE: Just got Austin's color T.V. back from the shop. I can watch a little amateur boxing now.

(LEE *and* AUSTIN *exchange looks.*)

SAUL: Oh—Yes.

LEE: You don't fool around in Television, do you Saul?

95 SAUL: Uh—I have in the past. Produced some T.V. Specials. Network stuff. But it's mainly features now.

LEE: That's where the big money is, huh?

SAUL: Yes. That's right.

AUSTIN: Why don't I call you tomorrow, Saul and we'll get
100   together. We can have lunch or something.

SAUL: That'd be terrific.

LEE: Right after the golf.

(*Pause.*)

SAUL: What?

LEE: You can have lunch right after the golf.
105 SAUL: Oh, right.

LEE: Austin was tellin' me that yer interested in stories.

SAUL: Well, we develop certain projects that we feel have commercial potential.

LEE: What kinda' stuff do ya' go in for?
110 SAUL: Oh, the usual. You know. Good love interest. Lots of action. (*Chuckles at* AUSTIN.)

LEE: Westerns?

SAUL: Sometimes.

AUSTIN: I'll give you a ring, Saul.

(AUSTIN *tries to move* SAUL *across the kitchen but* LEE *blocks their way.*)

115 LEE: I got a Western that'd knock yer lights out.

SAUL: Oh really?

LEE: Yeah. Contemporary Western. Based on a true story. 'Course I'm not a writer like my brother here. I'm not a man of the pen.
120 SAUL: Well—

LEE: I mean I can tell ya' a story off the tongue but I can't put it down on paper. That don't make any difference though does it?

SAUL: No, not really.
125 LEE: I mean plenty a' guys have stories don't they? True-life stories. Musta' been a lota' movies made from real life.

SAUL: Yes. I suppose so.

LEE: I haven't seen a good Western since "Lonely Are the Brave." You remember that movie?
130 SAUL: No, I'm afraid I—

LEE: Kirk Douglas. Helluva' movie. You remember that movie, Austin?

AUSTIN: Yes.

LEE: (*To* SAUL.) The man dies for the love of a horse.
135 SAUL: Is that right?

LEE: Yeah. Ya' hear the horse screamin' at the end of it. Rain's comin' down. Horse is screamin'. Then there's a shot. BLAM! Just a single shot like that. Then nothin' but the sound of rain. And Kirk Douglas is ridin' in the ambu-
140   lance. Ridin' away from the scene of the accident. And when he hears that shot he knows that his horse has died. He knows. And you see his eyes. And his eyes die. Right inside his face. And then his eyes close. And you know that he's died too. You know that Kirk Douglas has died
145   from the death of his horse.

SAUL: (*Eyes* AUSTIN *nervously.*) Well, it sounds like a great movie. I'm sorry I missed it.

LEE: Yeah, you shouldn't a' missed that one.

SAUL: I'll have to try to catch it some time. Arrange a screening or something. Well, Austin, I'll have to hit the freeway before rush hour.   150

AUSTIN: (*Ushers him toward exit.*) It's good seeing you, Saul.

(AUSTIN *and* SAUL *shake hands.*)

LEE: So ya' think there's room for a real Western these days? A true-to-life Western?

SAUL: Well, I don't see why not. Why don't you uh—tell the story to Austin and have him write a little outline.   155

LEE: You'd take a look at it then?

SAUL: Yes. Sure. I'll give it a read-through. Always eager for new material. (*Smiles at* AUSTIN.)

LEE: That's great! You'd really read it then huh?

SAUL: It would just be my opinion of course.   160

LEE: That's all I want. Just an opinion. I happen to think it has a lota' possibilities.

SAUL: Well, it was great meeting you and I'll—

(SAUL *and* LEE *shake.*)

LEE: I'll call you tomorrow about the golf.

SAUL: Oh. Yes, right.   165

LEE: Austin's got your number, right?

SAUL: Yes.

LEE: So long Saul. (*Gives* SAUL *a pat on the back.*)

(SAUL *exits,* AUSTIN *turns to* LEE, *looks at T.V. then back to lee.*)

AUSTIN: Give me the keys.

(AUSTIN *extends his hand toward* LEE, LEE *doesn't move, just stares at* AUSTIN, *smiles, lights to black.*)

SCENE 4

Night. Coyotes in distance, fade, sound of typewriter in dark, crickets, candlelight in alcove, dim light in kitchen, lights reveal AUSTIN *at glass table typing,* LEE *sits across from him, foot on table, drinking beer and whiskey, the T.V. is still on sink counter,* AUSTIN *types for a while, then stops.*

LEE: All right, now read it back to me.

AUSTIN: I'm not reading it back to you, Lee. You can read it when we're finished. I can't spend all night on this.

LEE: You got better things to do?

AUSTIN: Let's just go ahead. Now what happens when he   5
leaves Texas?

LEE: Is he ready to leave Texas yet? I didn't know we were that far along. He's not ready to leave Texas.

AUSTIN: He's right at the border.

LEE: (*Sitting up.*) No, see this is one a' the crucial parts. Right   10
here. (*Taps paper with beer can.*) We can't rush through this. He's not right at the border. He's a good fifty miles from the border. A lot can happen in fifty miles.

AUSTIN: It's only an outline. We're not writing an entire script now.   15

LEE: Well ya' can't leave things out even if it is an outline. It's one a' the most important parts. Ya' can't go leavin' it out.

AUSTIN: Okay, okay. Let's just—get it done.

LEE: All right. Now. He's in the truck and he's got his horse trailer and his horse.   20

AUSTIN: We've already established that.

LEE: And he sees this other guy comin' up behind him in another truck. And that truck is pullin' a gooseneck.

AUSTIN: What's a gooseneck?

25 LEE: Cattle trailer. You know the kind with a gooseneck, goes right down in the bed a' the pick-up.

AUSTIN: Oh. All right. (*Types.*)

LEE: It's important.

AUSTIN: Okay. I got it.

30 LEE: All these details are important.

(AUSTIN *types as they talk.*)

AUSTIN: I've got it.

LEE: And this other guy's got his horse all saddled up in the back a' the gooseneck.

AUSTIN: Right.

35 LEE: So both these guys have got their horses right along with 'em, see.

AUSTIN: I understand.

LEE: Then this first guy suddenly realizes two things.

AUSTIN: The guy in front?

40 LEE: Right. The guy in front realizes two things almost at the same time. Simultaneous.

AUSTIN: What were the two things?

LEE: Number one, he realizes that the guy behind him is the husband of the woman he's been—

(LEE *makes gesture of screwing by pumping his arm.*)

45 AUSTIN: (*Sees* LEE's *gesture.*) Oh. Yeah.

LEE: And number two, he realizes he's in the middle of Tornado Country.

AUSTIN: What's "Tornado Country"?

LEE: Panhandle.

50 AUSTIN: Panhandle?

LEE: Sweetwater. Around in that area. Nothin'. Nowhere. And number three—

AUSTIN: I thought there was only two.

LEE: There's three. There's a third unforeseen realization.

55 AUSTIN: And what's that?

LEE: That he's runnin' outa' gas.

AUSTIN: (*Stops typing.*) Come on, Lee.

(AUSTIN *gets up, moves to kitchen, gets a glass of water.*)

LEE: Whadya' mean, "come on"? That's what it is. Write it down! He's runnin' outa' gas.

60 AUSTIN: It's too—

LEE: What? It's too what? It's too real! That's what ya' mean isn't it? It's too much like real life!

AUSTIN: It's not like real life! It's not enough like real life. Things don't happen like that.

65 LEE: What! Men don't fuck other men's women?

AUSTIN: Yes. But they don't end up chasing each other across the Panhandle. Through "Tornado Country."

LEE: They do in this movie!

AUSTIN: And they don't have horses conveniently along with

70 them when they run out of gas! And they don't run out of gas either!

LEE: These guys run outa' gas! This is my story and one a' these guys runs outa' gas!

AUSTIN: It's just a dumb excuse to get them into a chase scene. It's contrived. 75

LEE: It is a chase scene! It's already a chase scene. They been chasin' each other fer days.

AUSTIN: So now they're supposed to abandon their trucks, climb on their horses and chase each other into the mountains?

LEE: (*Standing suddenly.*) There aren't any mountains in the 80 Panhandle! It's flat!

(LEE *turns violently toward windows in alcove and throws beer can at them.*)

LEE: Goddamn these crickets! (*Yells at crickets.*) Shut up out there! (*Pause, turns back toward table.*) This place is like a fuckin' rest home here. How're you supposed to think!

AUSTIN: You wanna' take a break? 85

LEE: No, I don't wanna' take a break! I wanna' get this done! This is my last chance to get this done.

AUSTIN: (*Moves back into alcove.*) All right. Take it easy.

LEE: I'm gonna' be leavin' this area. I don't have time to mess around here. 90

AUSTIN: Where are you going?

LEE: Never mind where I'm goin'! That's got nothin' to do with you. I just gotta' get this done. I'm not like you. Hangin' around bein' a parasite offa' other fools. I gotta' do this thing and get out. 95

(*Pause.*)

AUSTIN: A parasite? Me?

LEE: Yeah, you!

AUSTIN: After you break into people's houses and take their televisions?

LEE: They don't need their televisions! I'm doin' them a ser- 100 vice.

AUSTIN: Give me back my keys, Lee.

LEE: Not until you write this thing! You're gonna' write this outline thing for me or that car's gonna' wind up in Arizona with a different paint job. 105

AUSTIN: You think you can force me to write this? I was doing you a favor.

LEE: Git off yer high horse will ya'! Favor! Big favor. Handin' down favors from the mountain top.

AUSTIN: Let's just write it, okay? Let's sit down and not get 110 upset and see if we can just get through this.

(AUSTIN *sits at typewriter.*)

(*Long pause.*)

LEE: Yer not gonna' even show it to him, are ya'?

AUSTIN: What?

LEE: This outline. You got no intention of showin' it to him. Yer just doin' this 'cause yer afraid a' me. · 115

AUSTIN: You can show it to him yourself.

LEE: I will, boy! I'm gonna' read it to him on the golf course.

AUSTIN: And I'm not afraid of you either.

LEE: Then how come yer doin' it?

AUSTIN: (*Pause.*) So I can get my keys back. 120

(*Pause as* LEE *takes keys out of his pocket slowly and throws them on table, long pause,* AUSTIN *stares at keys.*)

LEE: There. Now you got yer keys back.

(AUSTIN *looks up at* LEE *but doesn't take keys.*)

LEE: Go ahead. There's yer keys.

(AUSTIN *slowly takes keys off table and puts them back in his own pocket.*)

Now what're you gonna' do? Kick me out?

AUSTIN: I'm not going to kick you out, Lee.

125 LEE: You couldn't kick me out, boy.

AUSTIN: I know.

LEE: So you can't even consider that one. (*Pause.*) You could call the police. That'd be the obvious thing.

AUSTIN: You're my brother.

130 LEE: That don't mean a thing. You go down to the L.A. Police Department there and ask them what kinda' people kill each other the most. What do you think they'd say?

AUSTIN: Who said anything about killing?

LEE: Family people. Brothers. Brothers-in-law. Cousins. Real
135 American-type people. They kill each other in the heat mostly. In the Smog-Alerts. In the Brush Fire Season. Right about this time a' year.

AUSTIN: This isn't the same.

LEE: Oh no? What makes it different?

140 AUSTIN: We're not insane. We're not driven to acts of violence like that. Not over a dumb movie script. Now sit down.

(*Long pause,* LEE *considers which way to go with it.*)

LEE: Maybe not. (*He sits back down at table across from* AUSTIN.) Maybe you're right. Maybe we're too intelligent, huh? (*Pause.*) We got our heads on our shoulders. One of us has
145 even got a Ivy League diploma. Now that means somethin' don't it? Doesn't that mean somethin'?

AUSTIN: Look, I'll write this thing for you, Lee. I don't mind writing it. I just don't want to get all worked up about it. It's not worth it. Now, come on. Let's just get through it, okay?

150 LEE: Nah. I think there's easier money. Lotsa' places I could pick up thousands. Maybe millions. I don't need this shit. I could go up to Sacramento Valley and steal me a diesel. Ten thousand a week dismantling one a' those suckers. Ten thousand a week!

(LEE *opens another beer, puts his foot back up on table.*)

155 AUSTIN: No, really, look, I'll write it out for you. I think it's a great idea.

LEE: Nah, you got yer own work to do. I don't wanna' interfere with yer life.

AUSTIN: I mean it'd be really fantastic if you could sell this.
160 Turn it into a movie. I mean it.

(*Pause.*)

LEE: Ya' think so huh?

AUSTIN: Absolutely. You could really turn your life around, you know. Change things.

LEE: I could get me a house maybe.

165 AUSTIN: Sure you could get a house. You could get a whole ranch if you wanted to.

LEE: (*Laughs.*) A ranch? I could get a ranch?

AUSTIN: 'Course you could. You know what a screenplay sells for these days?

LEE: No. What's it sell for? 170

AUSTIN: A lot. A whole lot of money.

LEE: Thousands?

AUSTIN: Yeah. Thousands.

LEE: Millions?

AUSTIN: Well— 175

LEE: We could get the old man outa' hock then.

AUSTIN: Maybe.

LEE: Maybe? Whadya' mean, maybe?

AUSTIN: I mean it might take more than money.

LEE: You were just tellin' me it'd change my whole life 180
around. Why wouldn't it change his?

AUSTIN: He's different.

LEE: Oh, he's of a different ilk huh?

AUSTIN: He's not gonna' change. Let's leave the old man out
of it. 185

LEE: That's right. He's not gonna' change but I will. I'll just turn myself right inside out. I could be just like you then, huh? Sittin' around dreamin' stuff up. Gettin' paid to dream. Ridin' back and forth on the freeway just dreamin'
my fool head off. 190

AUSTIN: It's not all that easy.

LEE: It's not, huh?

AUSTIN: No. There's a lot of work involved.

LEE: What's the toughest part? Deciding whether to jog or
play tennis? 195

(*Long pause.*)

AUSTIN: Well, look. You can stay here—do whatever you want to. Borrow the car. Come in and out. Doesn't matter to me. It's not my house. I'll help you write this thing or—not. Just let me know what you want. You tell me.

LEE: Oh. So now suddenly you're at my service. Is that it? 200

AUSTIN: What do you want to do Lee?

(*Long pause,* LEE *stares at him then turns and dreams at windows.*)

LEE: I tell ya' what I'd do if I still had that dog. Ya' wanna' know what I'd do?

AUSTIN: What?

LEE: Head out to Ventura. Cook up a little match. God that 205
little dog could bear down. Lota' money in dog fightin'. Big money.

(*Pause.*)

AUSTIN: Why don't we try to see this through, Lee. Just for the hell of it. Maybe you've really got something here.
What do you think? 210

(*Pause,* LEE *considers.*)

LEE: Maybe so. No harm in tryin' I guess. You think it's such a hot idea. Besides, I always wondered what'd be like to be you.

AUSTIN: You did?

LEE: Yeah, sure. I used to picture you walkin' around some campus with yer arms fulla' books. Blondes chasin' after ya'. 215

AUSTIN: Blondes? That's funny.

LEE: What's funny about it?

AUSTIN: Because I always used to picture you somewhere.

LEE: Where'd you picture me?

220 AUSTIN: Oh, I don't know. Different places. Adventures. You were always on some adventure.

LEE: Yeah.

AUSTIN: And I used to say to myself, "Lee's got the right idea. He's out there in the world and here I am. What am I do-

225   ing?"

LEE: Well you were settin' yourself up for somethin'.

AUSTIN: I guess.

LEE: We better get started on this thing then.

AUSTIN: Okay.

(AUSTIN *sits up at typewriter, puts new paper in.*)

230 LEE: Oh. Can I get the keys back before I forget?

(AUSTIN *hesitates.*)

You said I could borrow the car if I wanted, right? Isn't that what you said?

AUSTIN: Yeah. Right.

(AUSTIN *takes keys out of his pocket, sets them on table,* LEE *takes keys slowly, plays with them in his hand.*)

LEE: I could get a ranch, huh?

235 AUSTIN: Yeah. We have to write it first though.

LEE: Okay. Let's write it.

(*Lights start dimming slowly to end as* AUSTIN *types,* LEE *speaks.*)

So they take off after each other straight into an endless black prairie. The sun is just comin' down and they can feel the night on their backs. What they don't know is that each one

240 of 'em is afraid, see. Each one separately thinks that he's the only one that's afraid. And they keep ridin' like that straight into the night. Not knowing. And the one who's chasin' doesn't know where the other one is taking him. And the one who's being chased doesn't know where he's going.

(*Lights to black, typing stops in the dark, crickets fade.*)

ACT TWO

SCENE 5

Morning. LEE *at the table in alcove with a set of golf clubs in a fancy leather bag,* AUSTIN *at sink washing a few dishes.*

AUSTIN: He really liked it, huh?

LEE: He wouldn't a' gave me these clubs if he didn't like it.

AUSTIN: He gave you the clubs?

LEE: Yeah. I told ya' he gave me the clubs. The bag too.

5 AUSTIN: I thought he just loaned them to you.

LEE: He said it was part a' the advance. A little gift like. Gesture of his good faith.

AUSTIN: He's giving you an advance?

LEE: Now what's so amazing about that? I told ya' it was a

10   good story. You even said it was a good story.

AUSTIN: Well that is really incredible Lee. You know how many guys spend their whole lives down here trying to break into this business? Just trying to get in the door?

LEE: (*Pulling clubs out of bag, testing them.*) I got no idea. How many?   15

(*Pause.*)

AUSTIN: How much of an advance is he giving you?

LEE: Plenty. We were talkin' big money out there. Ninth hole is where I sealed the deal.

AUSTIN: He made a firm commitment?

LEE: Absolutely.   20

AUSTIN: Well, I know Saul and he doesn't fool around when he says he likes something.

LEE: I thought you said you didn't know him.

AUSTIN: Well, I'm familiar with his tastes.

LEE: I let him get two up on me goin' into the back nine. He   25 was sure he had me cold. You shoulda' seen his face when I pulled out the old pitching wedge and plopped it pin-high, two feet from the cup. He 'bout shit his pants. "Where'd a guy like you ever learn how to play golf like that?" he says.   30

(LEE *laughs,* AUSTIN *stares at him.*)

AUSTIN: 'Course there's no contract yet. Nothing's final until it's on paper.

LEE: It's final, all right. There's no way he's gonna' back out of it now. We gambled for it.

AUSTIN: Saul, gambled?   35

LEE: Yeah, sure. I mean he liked the outline already so he wasn't risking that much. I just guaranteed it with my short game.

(*Pause.*)

AUSTIN: Well, we should celebrate or something. I think Mom left a bottle of champagne in the refrigerator. We should have a little toast.   40

(AUSTIN *gets glasses from cupboard, goes to refrigerator, pulls out bottle of champagne.*)

LEE: You shouldn't oughta' take her champagne, Austin. She's gonna' miss that.

AUSTIN: Oh, she's not going to mind. She'd be glad we put it to good use. I'll get her another bottle. Besides, it's perfect for the occasion.   45

(*Pause.*)

LEE: Yer gonna' get a nice fee fer writin' the script a' course. Straight fee.

(AUSTIN *stops, stares at* LEE, *puts glasses and bottle on table, pause.*)

AUSTIN: I'm writing the script?

LEE: That's what he said. Said we couldn't hire a better screen-writer in the whole town.   50

AUSTIN: But I'm already working on a script. I've got my own project. I don't have time to write two scripts.

LEE: No, he said he was gonna' drop that other one.

(*Pause.*)

AUSTIN: What? You mean mine? He's going to drop mine and do yours instead?   55

LEE: (*Smiles.*) Now look, Austin, it's jest beginner's luck ya' know. I mean I sank a fifty foot putt for this deal. No hard feelings.

(AUSTIN *goes to phone on wall, grabs it, starts dialing.*)

60   He's not gonna' be in, Austin. Told me he wouldn't be in 'till late this afternoon.

AUSTIN: (*Stays on phone, dialing, listen.*) I can't believe this. I just can't believe it. Are you sure he said that? Why would he drop mine?

LEE: That's what he told me.

65   AUSTIN: He can't do that without telling me first. Without talking to me at least. He wouldn't just make a decision like that without talking to me!

LEE: Well I was kinda' surprised myself. But he was real enthusiastic about my story.

(AUSTIN *hangs up phone violently, paces.*)

70   AUSTIN: What'd he say! Tell me everything he said!

LEE: I been tellin' ya'! He said he liked the story a whole lot. It was the first authentic Western to come along in a decade.

AUSTIN: He liked that story! Your story?

LEE: Yeah! What's so surprisin' about that?

75   AUSTIN: It's stupid! It's the dumbest story I ever heard in my life.

LEE: Hey, hold on! That's my story yer talkin' about!

AUSTIN: It's a bullshit story! It's idiotic. Two lamebrains chasing each other across Texas! Are you kidding? Who do you

80   think's going to go see a film like that?

LEE: It's not a film! It's a movie. There's a big difference. That's somethin' Saul told me.

AUSTIN: Oh he did, huh?

LEE: Yeah, he said, "In this business we make movies, Ameri-

85   can movies. Leave the films to the French."

AUSTIN: So you got real intimate with old Saul huh? He started pouring forth his vast knowledge of Cinema.

LEE: I think he liked me a lot, to tell ya' the truth. I think he felt I was somebody he could confide in.

90   AUSTIN: What'd you do, beat him up or something?

LEE: (*Stands fast.*) Hey, I've about had it with the insults buddy! You think yer the only one in the brain department here? Yer the only one that can sit around and cook things up? There's other people got ideas too, ya' know!

95   AUSTIN: You must've done something. Threatened him or something. Now what'd you do Lee?

LEE: I convinced him!

(LEE *makes sudden menacing lunge toward* AUSTIN, *wielding golf club above his head, stops himself, frozen moment, long pause,* LEE *lowers club.*)

AUSTIN: Oh, Jesus. You didn't hurt him did you?

(*Long silence,* LEE *sits back down at table.*)

Lee! Did you hurt him?

100   LEE: I didn't do nothin' to him! He liked my story. Pure and simple. He said it was the best story he's come across in a long, long time.

AUSTIN: That's what he told me about my story! That's the same thing he said to me.

LEE: Well, he musta' been lyin'. He musta' been lyin' to one   105
of us anyway.

AUSTIN: You can't come into this town and start pushing people around. They're gonna' put you away!

LEE: I never pushed anybody around! I beat him fair and square. (*Pause.*) They can't touch me anyway. They can't   110
put a finger on me. I'm gone. I can come in through the window and go out through the door. They never knew what hit 'em. You, yer stuck. Yer the one that's stuck. Not me. So don't be warnin' me what to do in this town.

(*Pause,* AUSTIN *crosses to table, sits at typewriter, rests.*)

AUSTIN: Lee, come on, level with me will you? It doesn't   115
make any sense that suddenly he'd throw my idea out the window. I've been talking to him for months. I've got too much at stake. Everything's riding on this project.

LEE: What's yer idea?

AUSTIN: It's just a simple love story.   120

LEE: What kinda' love story?

AUSTIN: (*Stands, cross into kitchen.*) I'm not telling you!

LEE: Ha! 'Fraid I'll steal it huh? Competition's gettin' kinda' close to home isn't it?

AUSTIN: Where did Saul say he was going?   125

LEE: He was gonna' take my story to a couple studios.

AUSTIN: That's *my* outline you know! I wrote that outline! You've got no right to be peddling it around.

LEE: You weren't ready to take credit for it last night.

AUSTIN: Give me my keys!   130

LEE: What?

AUSTIN: The keys! I want my keys back!

LEE: Where you goin'?

AUSTIN: Just give me my keys! I gotta' take a drive. I gotta' get out of here for a while.   135

LEE: Where you gonna' go, Austin?

AUSTIN: (*Pause.*) I might just drive out to the desert for a while. I gotta' think.

LEE: You can think here just as good. This is the perfect setup for thinkin'. We got some writin' to do here, boy. Now   140
let's just have us a little toast. Relax. We're partners now.

(LEE *pops the cork of the champagne bottle, pours two drinks as the lights fade to black.*)

SCENE 6

Afternoon. LEE *and* SAUL *in kitchen,* AUSTIN *in alcove.*

LEE: Now you tell him. You tell him, Mr. Kipper.

SAUL: Kimmer.

LEE: Kimmer. You tell him what you told me. He don't believe me.

AUSTIN: I don't want to hear it.   5

SAUL: It's really not a big issue, Austin. I was simply amazed by your brother's story and—

AUSTIN: Amazed? You lost a bet! You gambled with my material!

SAUL: That's really beside the point, Austin. I'm ready to go all the way with your brother's story. I think it has a great   10
deal of merit.

AUSTIN: I don't want to hear about it, okay? Go tell it to the executives! Tell it to somebody who's going to turn it into a package deal or something. A T.V. series. Don't tell it to me.

15 SAUL: But I want to continue with your project too, Austin. It's not as though we can't do both. We're big enough for that aren't we?

AUSTIN: "We"? *I* can't do both! I don't know about "we."

LEE: (*To* SAUL.) See, what'd I tell ya'. He's totally unsympathetic.

20 SAUL: Austin, there's no point in our going to another screenwriter for this. It just doesn't make sense. You're brothers. You know each other. There's a familiarity with the material that just wouldn't be possible otherwise.

AUSTIN: There's no familiarity with the material! None! I

25 don't know what "Tornado Country" is. I don't know what a "gooseneck" is. And I don't want to know! (*Pointing to* LEE.) He's a hustler! He's a bigger hustler than you are! If you can't see that, then—

LEE: (*To* AUSTIN.) Hey, now hold on. I didn't have to bring

30 this bone back to you, boy. I persuaded Saul here that you were the right man for the job. You don't have to go throwin' up favors in my face.

AUSTIN: Favors! I'm the one who wrote the fuckin' outline! You can't even spell.

35 SAUL: (*To* AUSTIN.) Your brother told me about the situation with your father.

(*Pause.*)

AUSTIN: What? (*Looks at* LEE.)

SAUL: That's right. Now we have a clear-cut deal here, Austin. We have big studio money standing behind this thing. Just

40 on the basis of your outline.

AUSTIN: (*To* SAUL.) What'd he tell you about my father?

SAUL: Well—that he's destitute. He needs money.

LEE: That's right. He does.

(AUSTIN *shakes his head, stares at them both.*)

AUSTIN: (*To* LEE.) And this little assignment is supposed to go

45 toward the old man? A charity project? Is that what this is? Did you cook this up on the ninth green too?

SAUL: It's a big slice, Austin.

AUSTIN: (*To* LEE.) I gave him money! I already gave him money. You know that. He drank it all up!

50 LEE: This is a different deal here.

SAUL: We can set up a trust for your father. A large sum of money. It can be doled out to him in parcels so he can't misuse it.

AUSTIN: Yeah, and who's doing the doling?

SAUL: Your brother volunteered.

(AUSTIN *laughs.*)

55 LEE: That's right. I'll make sure he uses it for groceries.

AUSTIN: (*To* SAUL.) I'm not doing this script! I'm not writing this crap for you or anybody else. You can't blackmail me into it. You can't threaten me into it. There's no way I'm doing it. So just give it up. Both of you.

(*Long pause.*)

60 SAUL: Well, that's it then. I mean this is an easy three hundred grand. Just for a first draft. It's incredible, Austin. We've got three different studios all trying to cut each other's throats to get this material. In one morning. That's how hot it is.

AUSTIN: Yeah, well you can afford to give me a percentage on 65 the outline then. And you better get the genius here an agent before he gets burned.

LEE: Saul's gonna' be my agent. Isn't that right, Saul?

SAUL: That's right. (*To* AUSTIN.) Your brother has really got something, Austin. I've been around too long not to rec- 70 ognize it. Raw talent.

AUSTIN: He's got a lota' balls is what he's got. He's taking you right down the river.

SAUL: Three hundred thousand, Austin. Just for a first draft. Now you've never been offered that kind of money before. 75

AUSTIN: I'm not writing it.

(*Pause.*)

SAUL: I see. Well—

LEE: We'll just go to another writer then. Right, Saul? Just hire us somebody with some enthusiasm. Somebody who can recognize the value of a good story. 80

SAUL: I'm sorry about this, Austin.

AUSTIN: Yeah.

SAUL: I mean I was hoping we could continue both things but now I don't see how it's possible.

AUSTIN: So you're dropping my idea altogether. Is that it? Just 85 trade horses in midstream? After all these months of meetings.

SAUL: I wish there was another way.

AUSTIN: I've got everything riding on this, Saul. You know that. It's my only shot. If this falls through— 90

SAUL: I have to go with what my instincts tell me—

AUSTIN: Your instincts!

SAUL: My gut reaction.

AUSTIN: You lost! That's your gut reaction. You lost a gamble. Now you're trying to tell me you like his story? How 95 could you possibly fall for that story? It's as phony as Hopalong Cassidy. What do you see in it? I'm curious.

SAUL: It has the ring of truth, Austin.

AUSTIN: (*Laughs.*) Truth?

LEE: It is true. 100

SAUL: Something about the real West.

AUSTIN: Why? Because it's got horses? Because it's got grown men acting like little boys?

SAUL: Something about the land. Your brother is speaking from experience. 105

AUSTIN: So am I!

SAUL: But nobody's interested in love these days, Austin. Let's face it.

LEE: That's right.

AUSTIN: (*To* SAUL.) He's been camped out on the desert for 110 three months. Talking to cactus. What's he know about what people wanna' see on the screen! I drive on the freeway every day. I swallow the smog. I watch the news in color. I shop in the Safeway. I'm the one who's in touch! Not him!

SAUL: I have to go now, Austin. 115

(SAUL *starts to leave.*)

AUSTIN: There's no such thing as the West anymore! It's a dead issue! It's dried up, Saul, and so are you.

(SAUL *stops and turns to* AUSTIN.)

SAUL: Maybe you're right. But I have to take the gamble, don't I?

120 AUSTIN: You're a fool to do this, Saul.

SAUL: I've always gone on my hunches. Always. And I've never been wrong. (*To* LEE.) I'll talk to you tomorrow, Lee.

LEE: All right, Mr. Kimmer.

125 SAUL: Maybe we could have some lunch.

LEE: Fine with me. (*Smiles at* AUSTIN.)

SAUL: I'll give you a ring.

(SAUL *exits, lights to black as brothers look at each other from a distance.*)

SCENE 7

Night. Coyotes, crickets, sound of typewriter in dark, candlelight up on LEE *at typewriter struggling to type with one finger system,* AUSTIN *sits sprawled out on kitchen floor with whiskey bottle, drunk.*

AUSTIN: (*Singing, from floor.*)

> "Red sails in the sunset
> Way out on the blue
> Please carry my loved one
> 5 Home safely to me
>
> Red sails in the sunset—"

LEE: (*Slams fist on table.*) Hey! Knock it off will ya'! I'm tryin' to concentrate here.

AUSTIN: (*Laughs.*) You're tryin' to concentrate?

10 LEE: Yeah. That's right.

AUSTIN: Now you're tryin' to concentrate.

LEE: Between you, the coyotes and the crickets a thought don't have much of a chance.

AUSTIN: "Between me, the coyotes and the crickets." What a
15 great title.

LEE: I don't need a title! I need a thought.

AUSTIN: (*Laughs.*) A thought! Here's a thought for ya'—

LEE: I'm not askin' fer yer thoughts! I got my own. I can do this thing on my own.

20 AUSTIN: You're going to write an entire script on your own?

LEE: That's right.

(*Pause.*)

AUSTIN: Here's a thought. Saul Kimmer—

LEE: Shut up will ya'!

AUSTIN: He thinks we're the same person.

25 LEE: Don't get cute.

AUSTIN: He does! He's lost his mind. Poor old Saul. (*Giggles.*) Thinks we're one and the same.

LEE: Why don't you ease up on that champagne.

AUSTIN: (*Holding up bottle.*) This isn't champagne anymore.
30 We went through the champagne a long time ago. This is serious stuff. The days of champagne are long gone.

LEE: Well, go outside and drink it.

AUSTIN: I'm enjoying your company, Lee. For the first time since your arrival I am finally enjoying your company.
35 And now you want me to go outside and drink alone?

LEE: That's right.

(LEE *reads through paper in typewriter, makes an erasure.*)

AUSTIN: You think you'll make more progress if you're alone? You might drive yourself crazy.

LEE: I could have this thing done in a night if I had a little si-
40 lence.

AUSTIN: Well you'd still have the crickets to contend with. The coyotes. The sounds of the Police Helicopters prowling above the neighborhood. Slashing their searchlights down through the streets. Hunting for the likes of you.

45 LEE: I'm a screenwriter now! I'm legitimate.

AUSTIN: (*Laughing.*) A screenwriter!

LEE: That's right. I'm on salary. That's more'n I can say for you. I got an advance coming.

AUSTIN: This is true. This is very true. An advance. (*Pause.*)
50 Well, maybe I oughta' go out and try my hand at your trade. Since you're doing so good at mine.

LEE: Ha!

(LEE *attempts to type some more but gets the ribbon tangled up, starts trying to re-thread it as they continue talking.*)

AUSTIN: Well why not? You don't think I've got what it takes to sneak into people's houses and steal their T.V.s?

55 LEE: You couldn't steal a toaster without losin' yer lunch.

(AUSTIN *stands with a struggle, supports himself by the sink.*)

AUSTIN: You don't think I could sneak into somebody's house and steal a toaster?

LEE: Go take a shower or somethin' will ya!

(LEE *gets more tangled up with the typewriter ribbon, pulling it out of the machine as though it was fishing line.*)

AUSTIN: You really don't think I could steal a crumby toaster?
60 How much you wanna' bet I can't steal a toaster! How much? Go ahead! You're a gambler aren't you? Tell me how much yer willing to put on the line. Some part of your big advance? Oh, you haven't got that yet have you. I forgot.

LEE: All right. I'll bet you your car that you can't steal a toaster
65 without gettin' busted.

AUSTIN: You already got my car!

LEE: Okay, your house then.

AUSTIN: What're you gonna' give me! I'm not talkin' about my house and my car, I'm talkin' about what are you gonna' give me. You don't have nothin' to give me.
70

LEE: I'll give you—shared screen credit. How 'bout that? I'll have it put in the contract that this was written by the both of us.

AUSTIN: I don't want my name on that piece of shit! I want something of value. You got anything of value? You got any tidbits from the desert? Any Rattlesnake bones? I'm
75 not a greedy man. Any little personal treasure will suffice.

LEE: I'm gonna' just kick yer ass out in a minute.

AUSTIN: Oh, so now you're gonna' kick me out! Now I'm the intruder. I'm the one who's invading your precious privacy.

LEE: I'm trying to do some screenwriting here!!
80

(LEE *stands, picks up typewriter, slams it down hard on table, pause, silence except for crickets.*)

AUSTIN: Well, you got everything you need. You got plenty a' coffee? Groceries. You got a car. A contract. (*Pause.*)

Might need a new typewriter ribbon but other than that you're pretty well fixed. I'll just leave ya' alone for a while.

(AUSTIN *tries to steady himself to leave,* LEE *makes a move toward him.*)

85 LEE: Where you goin'?
AUSTIN: Don't worry about me. I'm not the one to worry about.

(AUSTIN *weaves toward exit, stops.*)

LEE: What're you gonna' do? Just go wander out into the night?
AUSTIN: I'm gonna' make a little tour.
LEE: Why don't ya' just go to bed for Christ's sake. Yer makin'
90   me sick.
AUSTIN: I can take care a' myself. Don't worry about me.

(AUSTIN *weaves badly in another attempt to exit, he crashes to the floor,* LEE *goes to him but remains standing.*)

LEE: You want me to call your wife for ya' or something?
AUSTIN: (*From floor.*) My wife?
LEE: Yeah. I mean maybe she can help ya' out. Talk to ya' or
95   somethin'.
AUSTIN: (*Struggles to stand again.*) She's five hundred miles away.
       North. North of here. Up in the North country where
       things are calm. I don't need any help. I'm gonna' go outside
       and I'm gonna' steal a toaster. I'm gonna' steal some other
100   stuff too. I might even commit bigger crimes. Bigger than
       you ever dreamed of. Crimes beyond the imagination!

(AUSTIN *manages to get himself vertical, tries to head for exit again.*)

LEE: Just hang on a minute, Austin.
AUSTIN: Why? What for? You don't need my help, right? You
       got a handle on the project. Besides, I'm lookin' forward
105   to the smell of the night. The bushes. Orange blossoms.
       Dust in the driveways. Rain bird sprinklers. Lights in peo-
       ple's houses. You're right about the lights, Lee. Everybody
       else is livin' the life. Indoors. Safe. This is a Paradise down
       here. You know that? We're livin' in a Paradise. We've for-
110   gotten about that.
LEE: You sound just like the old man now.
AUSTIN: Yeah, well we all sound alike when we're sloshed. We
       just sorta' echo each other.
LEE: Maybe if we could work on this together we could bring
115   him back out here. Get him settled down some place.

(AUSTIN *turns violently toward* LEE, *takes a swing at him, misses and crashes to the floor again,* LEE *stays standing.*)

AUSTIN: I don't want him out here! I've had it with him! I
       went all the way out there! I went out of my way. I gave
       him money and all he did was play Al Jolson records and
       spit at me! I gave him money!

(*Pause.*)

120 LEE: Just help me a little with the characters, all right? You
       know how to do it, Austin.
AUSTIN: (*On floor, laughs.*) The characters!
LEE: Yeah. You know. The way they talk and stuff. I can hear
       it in my head but I can't get it down on paper.

AUSTIN: What characters?   125
LEE: The guys. The guys in the story.
AUSTIN: Those aren't characters.
LEE: Whatever you call 'em then. I need to write somethin' out.
AUSTIN: Those are illusions of characters.
LEE: I don't give a damn what ya' call 'em! You know what   130
       I'm talkin' about!
AUSTIN: Those are fantasies of a long lost boyhood.
LEE: I gotta' write somethin' out on paper!!

(*Pause.*)

AUSTIN: What for? Saul's gonna' get you a fancy screenwriter
       isn't he?   135
LEE: I wanna' do it myself!
AUSTIN: Then do it! Yer on your own now, old buddy. You
       bulldogged yer way into contention. Now you gotta' carry
       it through.
LEE: I will but I need some advice. Just a couple a' things.   140
       Come on, Austin. Just help me get 'em talkin' right. It
       won't take much.
AUSTIN: Oh, now you're having a little doubt huh? What
       happened? The pressure's on, boy. This is it. You gotta'
       come up with it now. You don't come up with a winner   145
       on your first time out they just cut your head off. They
       don't give you a second chance ya' know.
LEE: I got a good story! I know it's a good story. I just need
       a little help is all.
AUSTIN: Not from me. Not from yer little old brother. I'm re-   150
       tired.
LEE: You could save this thing for me, Austin. I'd give ya' half the
       money. I would. I only need half anyway. With this kinda'
       money I could be a long time down the road. I'd never
       bother ya' again. I promise. You'd never even see me again.   155
AUSTIN: (*Still on floor.*) You'd disappear?
LEE: I would for sure.
AUSTIN: Where would you disappear to?
LEE: That don't matter. I got plenty a' places.
AUSTIN: Nobody can disappear. The old man tried that.   160
       Look where it got him. He lost his teeth.
LEE: He never had any money.
AUSTIN: I don't mean that. I mean his teeth! His real teeth.
       First he lost his real teeth, then he lost his false teeth. You
       never knew that did ya'? He never confided in you.   165
LEE: Nah, I never knew that.
AUSTIN: You wanna' drink?

(AUSTIN *offers bottle to* LEE, LEE *takes it, sits down on kitchen floor with* AUSTIN, *they share the bottle.*)

Yeah, he lost his real teeth one at a time. Woke up every
       morning with another tooth lying on the mattress. Finally,
       he decides he's gotta' get 'em all pulled out but he doesn't   170
       have any money. Middle of Arizona with no money and
       no insurance and every morning another tooth is lying on
       the mattress. (*Takes a drink.*) So what does he do?
LEE: I dunno'. I never knew about that.
AUSTIN: He begs the government. G.I. Bill or some damn   175
       thing. Some pension plan he remembers in the back of his
       head. And they send him out the money.
LEE: They did?

(They keep trading the bottle between them, taking drinks.)

AUSTIN: Yeah. They send him the money but it's not enough
180   money. Costs a lot to have all yer teeth yanked. They
charge by the individual tooth, ya' know. I mean one
tooth isn't equal to another tooth. Some are more expensive. Like the big ones in the back—
LEE: So what happened?
185 AUSTIN: So he locates a Mexican dentist in Juarez who'll do
the whole thing for a song. And he takes off hitchhiking
to the border.
LEE: Hitchhiking?
AUSTIN: Yeah. So how long you think it takes him to get to
190   the border? A man his age.
LEE: I dunno.
AUSTIN: Eight days it takes him. Eight days in the rain and the
sun and every day he's droppin' teeth on the blacktop nobody'll pick him up 'cause his mouth's full a' blood.

(Pause, they drink.)

195   So finally he stumbles into the dentist. Dentist takes all his
money and all his teeth. And there he is, in Mexico, with
his gums sewed up and his pockets empty.

(Long silence, AUSTIN drinks.)

LEE: That's it?
AUSTIN: Then I go out to see him, see. I go out there and I
200   take him out for a nice Chinese dinner. But he doesn't eat.
All he wants to do is drink Martinis outa' plastic cups.
And he takes his teeth out and lays 'em on the table 'cause
he can't stand the feel of 'em. And we ask the waitress for
one a' those doggie bags to take the Chop Suey home in.
205   So he drops his teeth in the doggie bag along with the
Chop Suey. And then we go out to hit all the bars up and
down the highway. Says he wants to introduce me to all
his buddies. And in one a' those bars, in one a' those bars
up and down the highway, he left that doggie bag with his
210   teeth laying in the Chop Suey.
LEE: You never found it?
AUSTIN: We went back but we never did find it. *(Pause.)* Now
that's a true story. True to life.

(They drink as lights fade to black.)

SCENE 8

*Very early morning, between night and day. No crickets, coyotes yap-
ping feverishly in distance before light comes up, a small fire blazes up
in the dark from alcove area, sound of LEE smashing typewriter with
a golf club, lights coming up, LEE seen smashing typewriter methodically then dropping pages of his script into a burning bowl set on the
floor of alcove, flames leap up, AUSTIN has a whole bunch of stolen
toasters lined up on the sink counter along with LEE's stolen T.V., the
toasters are of a wide variety of models, mostly chrome, AUSTIN goes
up and down the line of toasters, breathing on them and polishing
them with a dish towel, both men are drunk, empty whiskey bottles
and beer cans litter floor of kitchen, they share a half empty bottle on
one of the chairs in the alcove, LEE keeps periodically taking deliberate
ax-chops at the typewriter using a nine-iron as AUSTIN speaks, all of
their mother's house plants are dead and drooping.*

AUSTIN: *(Polishing toasters.)* There's gonna' be a general lack of
toast in the neighborhood this morning. Many, many unhappy, bewildered breakfast faces. I guess it's best not to
even think of the victims. Not to even entertain it. Is that
the right psychology?   5
LEE: *(Pauses.)* What?
AUSTIN: Is that the correct criminal psychology? Not to
think of the victims?
LEE: What victims?

*(LEE takes another swipe at typewriter with nine-iron, adds pages to
the fire.)*

AUSTIN: The victims of crime. Of breaking and entering. I   10
mean is it a prerequisite for a criminal not to have a conscience?
LEE: Ask a criminal.

(Pause, LEE stares at AUSTIN.)

What're you gonna' do with all those toasters? That's the
dumbest thing I ever saw in my life.   15
AUSTIN: I've got hundreds of dollars worth of household ap-
pliances here. You may not realize that.
LEE: Yeah, and how many hundreds of dollars did you walk
right past?
AUSTIN: It was toasters you challenged me to. Only toasters. 20
I ignored every other temptation.
LEE: I never challenged you! That's no challenge. Anybody
can steal a toaster.

(LEE smashes typewriter again.)

AUSTIN: You don't have to take it out on my typewriter ya'
know. It's not the machine's fault that you can't write. It's 25
a sin to do that to a good machine.
LEE: A sin?
AUSTIN: When you consider all the writers who never even
had a machine. Who would have given an eyeball for a
good typewriter. Any typewriter. 30

(LEE smashes typewriter again.)

AUSTIN: *(Polishing toasters.)* All the ones who wrote on match-
book covers. Paper bags. Toilet paper. Who had their
writing destroyed by their jailers. Who persisted beyond
all odds. Those writers would find it hard to understand
your actions. 35

*(LEE comes down on typewriter with one final crushing blow of the
nine-iron then collapses in one of the chairs, takes a drink from bottle, pause.)*

AUSTIN: *(After pause.)* Not to mention demolishing a perfectly good golf club. What about all the struggling
golfers? What about Lee Trevino? What do you think he
would've said when he was batting balls around with
broomsticks at the age of nine. Impoverished. 40

(Pause.)

LEE: What time is it anyway?
AUSTIN: No idea. Time stands still when you're havin' fun.

LEE: Is it too late to call a woman? You know any women?

AUSTIN: I'm a married man.

45 LEE: I mean a local woman.

(AUSTIN *looks out at light through window above sink.*)

AUSTIN: It's either too late or too early. You're the nature enthusiast. Can't you tell the time by the light in the sky? Orient yourself around the North Star or something?

LEE: I can't tell anything.

50 AUSTIN: Maybe you need a little breakfast. Some toast! How 'bout some toast?

(AUSTIN *goes to cupboard, pulls out loaf of bread and starts dropping slices into every toaster,* LEE *stays sitting, drinks, watches* AUSTIN.)

LEE: I don't need toast. I need a woman.

AUSTIN: A woman isn't the answer. Never was.

LEE: I'm not talkin' about permanent. I'm talkin' about temporary.

55

AUSTIN: (*Putting toast in toasters.*) We'll just test the merits of these little demons. See which brands have a tendency to burn. See which one can produce a perfectly golden piece of fluffy toast.

60 LEE: How much gas you got in yer car?

AUSTIN: I haven't driven my car for days now. So I haven't had an opportunity to look at the gas gauge.

LEE: Take a guess. You think there's enough to get me to Bakersfield?

65 AUSTIN: Bakersfield? What's in Bakersfield?

LEE: Just never mind what's in Bakersfield! You think there's enough goddamn gas in the car!

AUSTIN: Sure.

LEE: Sure. You could care less, right. Let me run outa' gas on the Grapevine. You could give a shit.

70

AUSTIN: I'd say there was enough gas to get you just about any-where, Lee. With your determination and guts.

LEE: What the hell time is it anyway?

(LEE *pulls out his wallet, starts going through dozens of small pieces of paper with phone numbers written on them, drops some on the floor, drops others in the fire.*)

AUSTIN: Very early. This is the time of morning when the coyotes kill people's cocker spaniels. Did you hear them? That's what they were doing out there. Luring innocent pets away from their homes.

75

LEE: (*Searching through his papers.*) What's the area code for Bakersfield? You know?

80 AUSTIN: You could always call the operator.

LEE: I can't stand that voice they give ya'.

AUSTIN: What voice?

LEE: That voice that warns you that if you'd only tried harder to find the number in the phone book you wouldn't have to be calling the operator to begin with.

85

(LEE *gets up, holding a slip of paper from his wallet, stumbles toward phone on wall, yanks receiver, starts dialing.*)

AUSTIN: Well I don't understand why you'd want to talk to anybody else anyway. I mean you can talk to me. I'm your brother.

LEE: (*Dialing.*) I wanna' talk to a woman. I haven't heard a woman's voice in a long time.   90

AUSTIN: Not since the Botanist?

LEE: What?

AUSTIN: Nothing. (*Starts singing as he tends toast.*)

> "Red sails in the sunset
> Way out on the blue   95
> Please carry my loved one
> Home safely to me"

LEE: Hey, knock it off will ya'! This is long distance here.

AUSTIN: Bakersfield?

LEE: Yeah, Bakersfield. It's Kern County.   100

AUSTIN: Well, what County are *we* in?

LEE: You better get yourself a 7-Up, boy.

AUSTIN: One County's as good as another.

(AUSTIN *hums "Red Sails" softly as* LEE *talks on phone.*)

LEE: (*To phone.*) Yeah, operator look—first off I wanna' know the area code for Bakersfield. Right. Bakersfield! Okay.   105
Good. Now I wanna' know if you can help me track somebody down. (*Pause.*) No, no I mean a phone number. Just a phone number. Okay. (*Holds a piece of paper up and reads it.*) Okay, the name is Melly Ferguson. Melly. (*Pause.*) I dunno'. Melly. Maybe. Yeah. Maybe Melanie. Yeah. Melanie Fer-   110
guson. Okay. (*Pause.*) What? I can't hear ya' so good. Sounds like yer under the ocean. (*Pause.*) You got ten Melanie Fergusons? How could that be? Ten Melanie Fergusons in Bakersfield? Well gimme all of 'em then. (*Pause.*) What d'ya mean? Gimme all ten Melanie Fergusons! That's right. Just   115
a second. (*To* AUSTIN.) Gimme a pen.

AUSTIN: I don't have a pen.

LEE: Gimme a pencil then!

AUSTIN: I don't have a pencil.

LEE: (*To phone.*) Just a second, operator. (*To* AUSTIN.) Yer a   120
writer and ya' don't have a pen or a pencil!

AUSTIN: I'm not a writer. You're a writer.

LEE: I'm on the phone here! Get me a pen or a pencil.

AUSTIN: I gotta' watch the toast.

LEE: (*To phone.*) Hang on a second, operator.   125

(LEE *lets the phone drop then starts pulling all the drawers in the kitchen out on the floor and dumping the contents, searching for a pencil,* AUSTIN *watches him casually.*)

LEE: (*Crashing through drawers, throwing contents around kitchen.*) This is the last time I try to live with people, boy! I can't believe it. Here I am! Here I am again in a desperate situation! This would never happen out on the desert. I would never be in this kinda' situation out on the desert. Isn't there a pen   130
or a pencil in this house! Who lives in this house anyway!

AUSTIN: Our mother.

LEE: How come she don't have a pen or a pencil! She's a social person isn't she? Doesn't she have to make shopping lists? She's gotta' have a pencil. (*Finds a pencil.*) Aaha! (*He*   135
rushes back to phone, picks up receiver.) All right operator. Operator? Hey! Operator! Goddamnit!

(LEE *rips the phone off the wall and throws it down, goes back to chair and falls into it, drinks, long pause.*)

AUSTIN: She hung up?

LEE: Yeah, she hung up. I knew she was gonna' hang up. I
140   could hear it in her voice.

(LEE *starts going through his slips of paper again.*)

AUSTIN: Well, you're probably better off staying here with me
    anyway. I'll take care of you.
LEE: I don't need takin' care of! Not by you anyway.
AUSTIN: Toast is almost ready.

(AUSTIN *starts buttering all the toast as it pops up.*)

145 LEE: I don't want any toast!

(*Long pause.*)

AUSTIN: You gotta' eat something. Can't just drink. How long
    have we been drinking, anyway?
LEE: (*Looking through slips of paper.*) Maybe it was Fresno.
    What's the area code for Fresno? How could I have lost
150   that number! She was beautiful.

(*Pause.*)

AUSTIN: Why don't you just forget about that, Lee. Forget
    about the woman.
LEE: She had green eyes. You know what green eyes do to me?
AUSTIN: I know but you're not gonna' get it on with her now
155   anyway. It's dawn already. She's in Bakersfield for Christ's
    sake.

(*Long pause,* LEE *considers the situation.*)

LEE: Yeah. (*Looks at windows.*) It's dawn?
AUSTIN: Let's just have some toast and—
LEE: What is this bullshit with the toast anyway! You make it
160   sound like salvation or something. I don't want any god-
    damn toast! How many times I gotta' tell ya'! (LEE *gets up,
    crosses upstage to windows in alcove, looks out,* AUSTIN *butters
    toast.*)
AUSTIN: Well it is like salvation sort of. I mean the smell. I
165   love the smell of toast. And the sun's coming up. It makes
    me feel like anything's possible. Ya' know?
LEE: (*Back to* AUSTIN, *facing windows upstage.*) So go to church
    why don't ya'.
AUSTIN: Like a beginning. I love beginnings.
170 LEE: Oh yeah. I've always been kinda' partial to endings myself.
AUSTIN: What if I come with you, Lee?
LEE: (*Pause as* LEE *turns toward* AUSTIN.) What?
AUSTIN: What if I come with you out to the desert?
LEE: Are you kiddin'?
175 AUSTIN: No. I'd just like to see what it's like.
LEE: You wouldn't last a day out there pal.
AUSTIN: That's what you said about the toasters. You said I
    couldn't steal a toaster either.
LEE: A toaster's got nothin' to do with the desert.
180 AUSTIN: I could make it, Lee. I'm not that helpless. I can cook.
LEE: Cook?
AUSTIN: I can.
LEE: So what! You can cook. Toast.
AUSTIN: I can make fires. I know how to get fresh water from
185   condensation.

(AUSTIN *stacks buttered toast up in a tall stack on plate.*)

(LEE *slams table.*)

LEE: It's not somethin' you learn out of a Boy Scout hand-
    book!
AUSTIN: Well how do you learn it then! How're you supposed
    to learn it!

(*Pause.*)

LEE: Ya' just learn it, that's all. Ya' learn it 'cause ya' have to
    learn it. You don't *have* to learn it.   190
AUSTIN: You could teach me.
LEE: (*Stands.*) What're you, crazy or somethin'? You went to
    college. Here, you are down here, rollin' in bucks. Floatin'
    up and down in elevators. And you wanna' learn how to
    live on the desert!   195
AUSTIN: I do, Lee. I really do. There's nothin' down here for
    me. There never was. When we were kids here it was dif-
    ferent. There was a life here then. But now—I keep
    comin' down here thinkin' it's the fifties or somethin'. I
    keep finding myself getting off the freeway at familiar   200
    landmarks that turn out to be unfamiliar. On the way to
    appointments. Wandering down streets I thought I recog-
    nized that turn out to be replicas of streets I remember.
    Streets I misremember. Streets I can't tell if I lived on or
    saw in a postcard. Fields that don't even exist anymore.   205
LEE: There's no point cryin' about that now.
AUSTIN: There's nothin' real down here, Lee! Least of all me!
LEE: Well I can't save you from that!
AUSTIN: You can let me come with you.
LEE: No dice, pal.   210
AUSTIN: You could let me come with you, Lee!
LEE: Hey, do you actually think I chose to live out in the mid-
    dle a' nowhere? Do ya'? Ya' think it's some kinda' philo-
    sophical decision I took or somethin'? I'm livin' out there
    'cause I can't make it here! And yer bitchin' to me about   215
    all yer success!
AUSTIN: I'd cash it all in in a second. That's the truth.
LEE: (*Pause, shakes his head.*) I can't believe this.
AUSTIN: Let me go with you.
LEE: Stop sayin' that will ya'! Yer worse than a dog.   220

(AUSTIN *offers out the plate of neatly stacked toast to* LEE.)

AUSTIN: You want some toast?

(LEE *suddenly explodes and knocks the plate out of* AUSTIN's *hand,
toast goes flying, long frozen moment where it appears* LEE *might go
all the way this time when austin breaks it by slowly lowering himself to his knees and begins gathering the scattered toast from the floor
and stacking it back on the plate,* LEE *begins to circle* AUSTIN *in a
slow, predatory way, crushing pieces of toast in his wake, no words for
a while,* AUSTIN *keeps gathering toast, even the crushed pieces.*)

LEE: Tell ya' what I'll do, little brother. I might just consider
    makin' you a deal. Little trade. (AUSTIN *continues gathering
    toast as* LEE *circles him through this.*) You write me up this
    screenplay thing just like I tell ya'. I mean you can use all yer   225
    usual tricks and stuff. Yer fancy language. Yer artistic hocus
    pocus. But ya' gotta' write everything like I say. Every move.
    Every time they run outa' gas, they run outa' gas. Every time
    they wanna' jump on a horse, they do just that. If they

230   wanna' stay in Texas, by God they'll stay in Texas! (*Keeps circling.*) And you finish the whole thing up for me. Top to bottom. And you put my name on it. And I own all the rights. And every dime goes in my pocket. You do that and I'll sure enough take ya' with me to the desert. (LEE *stops,*
235   *pause, looks down at* AUSTIN.) How's that sound?

(*Pause as* AUSTIN *stands slowly holding plate of demolished toast, their faces are very close, pause.*)

AUSTIN: It's a deal.

(LEE *stares straight into* AUSTIN'*s eyes, then he slowly takes a piece of toast off the plate, raises it to his mouth and takes a huge crushing bite never taking his eyes off* AUSTIN'*s as* lee *crunches into the toast the lights black out.*)

SCENE 9

Mid-day. No sound, blazing heat, the stage is ravaged; bottles, toasters, smashed typewriter, ripped out telephone, etc. All the debris from previous scene is now starkly visible in intense yellow light, the effect should be like a desert junkyard at high noon, the coolness of the preceding scenes is totally obliterated. AUSTIN *is seated at table in alcove, shirt open, pouring with sweat, hunched over a writing notebook, scribbling notes desperately with a ballpoint pen.* LEE *with no shirt, beer in hand, sweat pouring down his chest, is walking a slow circle around the table, picking his way through the objects, sometimes kicking them aside.*

LEE: (*As he walks.*) All right, read it back to me. Read it back to me!
AUSTIN: (*Scribbling at top speed.*) Just a second.
LEE: Come on, come on! Just read what ya' got.
5   AUSTIN: I can't keep up! It's not the same as if I had a typewriter.
LEE: Just read what we got so far. Forget about the rest.
AUSTIN: All right. Let's see—okay—(*Wipes sweat from his face, reads as* LEE *circles.*) Luke says uh—
LEE: Luke?
10   AUSTIN: Yeah.
LEE: His name's Luke? All right, all right—we can change the names later. What's he say? Come on, come on.
AUSTIN: He says uh—(*Reading.*) "I told ya' you were a fool to follow me in here. I know this prairie like the back a' my
15   hand."
LEE: No, no, no! That's not what I said. I never said that.
AUSTIN: That's what I wrote.
LEE: It's not what I said. I never said "like the back a' my hand." That's stupid. That's one a' those—whadya' call it?
20   Whadya' call that?
AUSTIN: What?
LEE: Whadya' call it when somethin's been said a thousand times before. Whadya' call that?
AUSTIN: Um—a cliché?
25   LEE: Yeah. That's right. Cliché. That's what that is. A cliché. "The back a' my hand." That's stupid.
AUSTIN: That's what you said.
LEE: I never said that! And even if I did, that's where yer supposed to come in. That's where yer supposed to change it
30   to somethin' better.
AUSTIN: Well how am I supposed to do that and write down what you say at the same time?

LEE: Ya' just do, that's all! You hear a stupid line you change it. That's yer job.
AUSTIN: All right. (*Makes more notes.*)   35
LEE: What're you changin' it to?
AUSTIN: I'm not changing it. I'm just trying to catch up.
LEE: Well change it! We gotta' change that, we can't leave that in there like that. ". . . the back a' my hand." That's dumb.
AUSTIN: (*Stops writing, sits back.*) All right.   40
LEE: (*Pacing.*) So what'll we change it to?
AUSTIN: Um—How 'bout—"I'm on intimate terms with this prairie."
LEE: (*To himself considering line as he walks.*) "I'm on intimate terms with this prairie." Intimate terms, intimate terms.   45
Intimate—that means like uh—sexual right?
AUSTIN: Well—yeah—or—
LEE: He's on sexual terms with the prairie? How dya' figure that?
AUSTIN: Well it doesn't necessarily have to mean sexual.
LEE: What's it mean then?   50
AUSTIN: It means uh—close—personal—
LEE: All right. How's it sound? Put it into the uh—the line there. Read it back. Let's see how it sounds. (*To himself.*) "Intimate terms."
AUSTIN: (*Scribbles in notebook.*) Okay. It'd go something like   55
this: (*Reads.*) "I told ya' you were a fool to follow me in here. I'm on intimate terms with this prairie."
LEE: That's good. I like that. That's real good.
AUSTIN: You do?
LEE: Yeah. Don't you?   60
AUSTIN: Sure.
LEE: Sounds original now. "Intimate terms." That's good. Okay. Now we're cookin! That has a real ring to it.

(AUSTIN *makes more notes,* LEE *walks around, pours beer on his arms and rubs it over his chest feeling good about the new progress, as he does this* MOM *enters unobtrusively down left with her luggage, she stops and stares at the scene still holding luggage as the two men continue, unaware of her presence,* AUSTIN *absorbed in his writing,* LEE *cooling himself off with beer.*)

LEE: (*Continues.*) "He's on intimate terms with this prairie." Sounds real mysterious and kinda' threatening at the same   65
time.
AUSTIN: (*Writing rapidly.*) Good.
LEE: Now—(LEE *turns and suddenly sees* MOM, *he stares at her for a while, she stares back,* AUSTIN *keeps writing feverishly, not noticing,* LEE *walks slowly over to* MOM *and takes a closer look, long pause.*)   70
LEE: Mom?

(AUSTIN *looks up suddenly from his writing, sees* MOM, *stands quickly, long pause,* MOM *surveys the damage.*)

AUSTIN: Mom. What're you doing back?
MOM: I'm back.
LEE: Here, lemme take those for ya.

(LEE *sets beer on counter then takes both her bags but doesn't know where to set them down in the sea of junk so he just keeps holding them.*)

AUSTIN: I wasn't expecting you back so soon. I thought uh—   75
How was Alaska?
MOM: Fine.

LEE: See any igloos?

MOM: No. Just glaciers.

80 AUSTIN: Cold huh?

MOM: What?

AUSTIN: It must've been cold up there?

MOM: Not really.

LEE: Musta' been colder than this here. I mean we're havin' a
85   real scorcher here.

MOM: Oh? (*She looks at damage.*)

LEE: Yeah. Must be in the hundreds.

AUSTIN: You wanna' take your coat off, Mom?

MOM: No. (*Pause, she surveys space.*) What happened in here?

90 AUSTIN: Oh um—Me and Lee were just sort of celebrating
     and uh—

MOM: Celebrating?

AUSTIN: Yeah. Uh—Lee sold a screenplay. A story, I mean.

MOM: Lee did?

95 AUSTIN: Yeah.

MOM: Not you?

AUSTIN: No. Him.

MOM: (*To* LEE.) *You sold a screenplay?*

LEE: Yeah. That's right. We're just sorta' finishing it up right
100   now. That's what we're doing here.

AUSTIN: Me and Lee are going out to the desert to live.

MOM: You and Lee?

AUSTIN: Yeah. I'm taking off with Lee.

MOM: (*She looks back and forth at each of them, pause.*) You
105   gonna go live with your father?

AUSTIN: No. We're going to a different desert Mom.

MOM: I see. Well, you'll probably wind up on the same desert
     sooner or later. What're all these toasters doing here?

AUSTIN: Well—we had kind of a contest.

110 MOM: Contest?

LEE: Yeah.

AUSTIN: Lee won.

MOM: Did you win a lot of money, Lee?

LEE: Well not yet. It's comin' in any day now.

115 MOM: (*To* LEE.) What happened to your shirt?

LEE: Oh. I was sweatin' like a pig and I took it off.

(AUSTIN *grabs* LEE's *shirt off the table and tosses it to him,* LEE *sets
down suitcases and puts his shirt on.*)

MOM: Well it's one hell of a mess in here isn't it?

AUSTIN: Yeah, I'll clean it up for you, Mom. I just didn't know
     you were coming back so soon.

120 MOM: I didn't either.

AUSTIN: What happened?

MOM: Nothing. I just started missing all my plants.

(*She notices dead plants.*)

AUSTIN: Oh.

MOM: Oh, they're all dead aren't they. (*She crosses toward them,*
125   *examines them closely.*) You didn't get a chance to water I
     guess.

AUSTIN: I was doing it and then Lee came and—

LEE: Yeah I just distracted him a whole lot here, Mom. It's not
     his fault.

(*Pause, as* MOM *stares at plants.*)

MOM: Oh well, one less thing to take care of I guess. (*Turns*   130
     toward brothers.) Oh, that reminds me—You boys will
     probably never guess who's in town. Try and guess.

(*Long pause, brothers stare at her.*)

AUSTIN: Whadya' mean, Mom?

MOM: Take a guess. Somebody very important has come to
     town. I read it, coming down on the Greyhound.   135

LEE: Somebody very important?

MOM: See if you can guess. You'll never guess.

AUSTIN: Mom—we're trying to uh—(*Points to writing pad.*)

MOM: Picasso. (*Pause.*) Picasso's in town. Isn't that incredible?
     Right now.   140

(*Pause.*)

AUSTIN: Picasso's dead, Mom.

MOM: No, he's not dead. He's visiting the museum. I read it
     on the bus. We have to go down there and see him.

AUSTIN: Mom—

MOM: This is the chance of a lifetime. Can you imagine? We   145
     could all go down and meet him. All three of us.

LEE: Uh—I don't think I'm really up fer meetin' anybody
     right now. I'm uh—What's his name?

MOM: Picasso! Picasso! You've never heard of Picasso? Austin,
     you've heard of Picasso.   150

AUSTIN: Mom, we're not going to have time.

MOM: It won't take long. We'll just hop in the car and go
     down there. An opportunity like this doesn't come along
     every day.

AUSTIN: We're gonna' be leavin' here, Mom!   155

(*Pause.*)

MOM: Oh.

LEE: Yeah.

(*Pause.*)

MOM: You're both leaving?

LEE: (*Looks at* AUSTIN.) Well we were thinkin' about that be-
     fore but now I—   160

AUSTIN: No, we are! We're both leaving. We've got it all
     planned.

MOM: (*To* AUSTIN.) Well you can't leave. You have a family.

AUSTIN: I'm leaving. I'm getting out of here.

LEE: (*To* MOM.) I don't really think Austin's cut out for the   165
     desert do you?

MOM: No. He's not.

AUSTIN: I'm going with you, Lee!

MOM: He's too thin.

LEE: Yeah, he'd just burn up out there.   170

AUSTIN: (*To* LEE.) We just gotta' finish this screenplay and
     then we're gonna' take off. That's the plan. That's what you
     said. Come on, let's get back to work, Lee.

LEE: I can't work under these conditions here. It's too hot.

AUSTIN: Then we'll do it on the desert.   175

LEE: Don't be tellin' me what we're gonna' do!

MOM: Don't shout in the house.

LEE: We're just gonna' have to postpone the whole deal.

AUSTIN: I can't postpone it! It's gone past postponing! I'm
180   doing everything you said. I'm writing down exactly what
       you tell me.
LEE: Yeah, but you were right all along see. It is a dumb story.
       "Two lamebrains chasin' each other across Texas." That's
       what you said, right?
185 AUSTIN: I never said that.

(LEE *sneers in* AUSTIN's *face then turns to* MOM.)

LEE: I'm gonna' just borrow some a' your antiques, Mom. You
       don't mind do ya'? Just a few plates and things. Silverware.

(LEE *starts going through all the cupboards in kitchen pulling out
plates and stacking them on counter as* MOM *and* AUSTIN *watch.*)

MOM: You don't have any utensils on the desert?
LEE: Nah, I'm fresh out.
190 AUSTIN: (*To* LEE.) What're you doing?
MOM: Well some of those are very old. Bone China.
LEE: I'm tired of eatin' outa' my bare hands, ya' know. It's not
       civilized.
AUSTIN: (*To* LEE.) What're you doing? We made a deal!
195 MOM: Couldn't you borrow the plastic ones instead? I have
       plenty of plastic ones.
LEE: (*As he stacks plates.*) It's not the same. Plastic's not the
       same at all. What I need is somethin' authentic. Somethin'
       to keep me in touch. It's easy to get outa' touch out there.
200   Don't worry I'll get 'em back to ya'.

(AUSTIN *rushes up to* LEE, *grabs him by shoulders.*)

AUSTIN: You can't just drop the whole thing, Lee!

(LEE *turns, pushes* AUSTIN *in the chest knocking him backwards into
the alcove,* MOM *watches numbly, lee returns to collecting the plates,
silverware, etc.*)

MOM: You boys shouldn't fight in the house. Go outside and fight.
LEE: I'm not fightin'. I'm leavin'.
MOM: There's been enough damage done already.
205 LEE: (*His back to* AUSTIN *and* MOM, *stacking dishes on counter.*)
       I'm clearin' outa' here once and for all. All this town does
       is drive a man insane. Look what it's done to Austin there.
       I'm not lettin' that happen to me. Sell myself down the
       river. No sir. I'd rather be a hundred miles from nowhere
210   than let that happen to me.

(*During this* AUSTIN *has picked up the ripped-out phone from the
floor and wrapped the cord tightly around both his hands, he lunges
at* LEE *whose back is still to him, wraps the cord around* LEE's *neck,
plants a foot in lee's back and pulls back on the cord, tightening it,*
LEE *chokes desperately, can't speak and can't reach* AUSTIN *with his
arms,* AUSTIN *keeps applying pressure on* LEE's *back with his foot,
bending him into the sink,* MOM *watches.*)

AUSTIN: (*Tightening cord.*) You're not goin' anywhere! You're
       not takin' anything with you. You're not takin' my car!
       You're not takin' the dishes! You're not takin' anything!
       You're stayin' right here!
215 MOM: You'll have to stop fighting in the house. There's plenty
       of room outside to fight. You've got the whole outdoors
       to fight in.

(LEE *tries to tear himself away, he crashes across the stage like an enraged bull dragging* AUSTIN *with him, he snorts and bellows but*
AUSTIN *hangs on and manages to keep clear of* LEE's *attempts to
grab him, they crash into the table, to the floor,* LEE *is face down
thrashing wildly and choking,* AUSTIN *pulls cord tighter, stands with
one foot planted on* LEE's *back and the cord stretched taut.*)

AUSTIN: (*Holding cord.*) Gimme back my keys, Lee! Take the
       keys out! Take 'em out!

(LEE *desperately tries to dig in his pockets, searching for the car keys,*
MOM *moves closer.*)

MOM: (*Calmly to* AUSTIN.) You're not killing him are you?   220
AUSTIN: I don't know. I don't know if I'm killing him. I'm
       stopping him. That's all. I'm just stopping him.

(LEE *thrashes but* AUSTIN *is relentless.*)

MOM: You oughta' let him breathe a little bit.
AUSTIN: Throw the keys out, Lee!

(LEE *finally gets keys out and throws them on floor but out of*
AUSTIN's *reach,* AUSTIN *keeps pressure on cord, pulling* LEE's *neck
back,* LEE *gets one hand to the cord but can't relieve the pressure.*)

       Reach me those keys would ya', Mom.   225
MOM: (*Not moving.*) Why are you doing this to him?
AUSTIN: Reach me the keys!
MOM: Not until you stop choking him.
AUSTIN: I can't stop choking him! He'll kill me if I stop
       choking him!   230
MOM: He won't kill you. He's your brother.
AUSTIN: Just get me the keys would ya'!

(*Pause.* MOM *picks keys up off floor, hands them to* AUSTIN.)

AUSTIN: (*To* MOM.) Thanks.
MOM: Will you let him go now?
AUSTIN: I don't know. He's not gonna' let me get outa' here.   235
MOM: Well you can't kill him.
AUSTIN: I can kill him! I can easily kill him. Right now. Right
       here. All I gotta' do is just tighten up. See? (*He tightens cord,*
       LEE *thrashes wildly.* AUSTIN *releases pressure a little, maintain-
       ing control.*) Ya' see that?   240
MOM: That's a savage thing to do.
AUSTIN: Yeah well we'll don't tell me I can't kill him because I can.
       I can just twist. I can just keep twisting. (AUSTIN *twists the
       cord tighter,* LEE *weakens, his breathing changes to a short rasp.*)
MOM: Austin!   245

(AUSTIN *relieves pressure,* LEE *breathes easier but* AUSTIN *keeps him
under control.*)

AUSTIN: (*Eyes on* LEE, *holding cord.*) I'm goin' to the desert.
       There's nothing stopping me. I'm going by myself to the
       desert.

(MOM *moving toward her luggage.*)

MOM: Well, I'm going to go check into a motel. I can't stand
       this anymore.   250
AUSTIN: Don't go yet!

(MOM *pauses.*)

MOM: I can't stay here. This is worse than being homeless.

AUSTIN: I'll get everything fixed up for you, Mom. I promise. Just stay for a while.

255 MOM: (*Picking up luggage.*) You're going to the desert.

AUSTIN: Just wait!

(LEE *thrashes,* AUSTIN *subdues him,* MOM *watches holding luggage, pause.*)

MOM: It was the worst feeling being up there. In Alaska. Staring out a window. I never felt so desperate before. That's why when I saw that article on Picasso I thought—

260 AUSTIN: Stay here, Mom. This is where you live.

(*She looks around the stage.*)

MOM: I don't recognize it at all.

(*She exits with luggage,* AUSTIN *makes a move toward her but* LEE *starts to struggle and* AUSTIN *subdues him again with cord, pause.*)

AUSTIN: (*Holding cord.*) Lee? I'll make ya' a deal. You let me get outa' here. Just let me get to my car. All right, Lee? Gimme a little headstart and I'll turn you loose. Just gimme a little headstart. All right?   265

(LEE *makes no response,* AUSTIN *slowly releases tension cord, still nothing from* LEE.)

AUSTIN: Lee?

(LEE *is motionless,* AUSTIN *very slowly begins to stand, still keeping a tenuous hold on the cord and his eyes riveted to* LEE *for any sign of movement,* AUSTIN *slowly drops the cord and stands, he stares down at* LEE *who appears to be dead.*)

AUSTIN: (*Whispers.*) Lee?

(*Pause,* AUSTIN *considers, looks toward exit, back to* LEE, *then makes a small movement as if to leave. Instantly* LEE *is on his feet and moves toward exit, blocking austin's escape. They square off to each other, keeping a distance between them. Pause, a single coyote heard in distance, lights fade softly into moonlight, the figures of the brothers now appear to be caught in a vast desert-like landscape, they are very still but watchful for the next move, lights go slowly to black as the after-image of the brothers pulses in the dark, coyote fades.*)

August Wilson

August Wilson was born in 1945 and raised on "The Hill," the black ghetto of Pittsburgh. He dropped out of school in the ninth grade, but supported himself with odd jobs while he continued his self-education, reading and studying; he also began to write poems and stories on the changing problems of race relations in America. He founded a theater in Pittsburgh in the mid-1960s, and then founded Black Horizons Theater Company there in 1968. His first play, *Jitney,* was staged in 1978. Wilson then applied to study playwriting at the Eugene O'Neill Theater Center's National Playwrights' Conference, where he submitted the text of *Ma Rainey's Black Bottom,* which was read by the eminent African American stage director Lloyd Richards, who had brought Lorraine Hansberry's *A Raisin in the Sun* to Broadway in 1959. Richards read the play and produced it at the Yale Repertory Theater in 1984 before bringing it to Broadway. *Ma Rainey's Black Bottom* is the first of several plays examining African American history in the twentieth century, many of them using jazz as a musical idiom; it was followed by *Fences* (1985)—which won the Pulitzer Prize—*Joe Turner's Come and Gone* (1986), *The Piano Lesson* (1987), *Two Trains Running* (1991), *Seven Guitars* (1995), and *King Hedley II* (1999).

FENCES

Set in 1957, the action of *Fences* sits on the brink of the civil rights movement and outlines the challenges facing African Americans whose legal freedoms had yet to become a social reality. The play is—as its final funeral scene implies—deeply reminiscent of Arthur Miller's *Death of a Salesman,* and suggests that realism is in many way still the dominant mode of American theater. Like Miller's play, it is about a hardworking man whose responsibilities to his family fall athwart his dreams of happiness, a conflict that finally costs him both. However, while Miller's Willy Loman is victimized by his belief in the "American Dream," Wilson's Troy Maxson lives his life on the underside of that dream. Thrown out of his home at fourteen by his father, Troy moved north to Pittsburgh; unable to find work, he made a living through petty crime until he was caught and sentenced to fifteen years' imprisonment. On his release, he found his wife and child and began a career in baseball, playing in the Negro Leagues. Integration came to baseball, and by 1957 Jackie Robinson, Hank Aaron, and a young Roberto Clemente are all playing in the major leagues—but it is too late for Troy. He is now working as a trash collector, fighting the company to let African Americans drive the garbage trucks as well as pick up the trash.

Like Willy Loman, Troy too is a family man. The family is Troy's refuge from the racism and defeat of his daily life, and his proudest accomplishment as well: he has forced himself to shoulder the responsibility of providing for his children and of loving his wife, a responsibility that lends his life purpose and direction. As he says to Rose in act 1, "Woman . . . I do the best I can do. . . . We go upstairs in that room at night . . . and I fall down on you and try to blast a hole into forever. I get up Monday morning . . . find my lunch on the table. I go out. Make my way. Find my strength to carry me through to the next Friday." However, as Rose notes, the world is changing around Troy, and these changes threaten the life that he has made. His son Cory is being recruited on a football scholarship. Troy, his own exploitation by the white-dominated sports industry still in mind, forces Cory to quit the team, and so to pass up the scholarship—and the chance to go to college. Nor does Troy shoulder the rest of his family life easily. He cares for his mentally handicapped brother Gabriel, but eventually has him committed to a mental hospital in order to get half of his government pension. Despite his love for and gratitude to Rose, he has an affair with another woman, who dies delivering their daughter. Although family life has been Troy's salvation, it also has hemmed him in—in the dead-end jobs, the constant poverty, the fence he

James Earl Jones reprises his role as Troy in this 1986 Goodman Theatre production of August Wilson's *Fences*.

builds at the end of the play. He risks it all for the chance of some happiness with Alberta and loses; Rose takes in Troy's daughter: "From right now . . . this child got a mother. But you a womanless man." He fights Cory, and much as his own father had thrown him out of the house, he forces his own son to leave as well.

The joyous, mournful conclusion of *Fences*—when Gabriel dances Troy's soul into heaven—perhaps provides the best commentary on the life of Troy Maxson. Suffering the indignities and humiliation of racism throughout his life, Troy built a stable home for himself, a life. As a defense against the world, perhaps, that life was bound to crumble, particularly as pressure of social change forced Troy to deal with a future he had never imagined. In Wilson's final image, however, Troy's life is celebrated, a thing of rough and rugged beauty, demanding our attention and respect.

FENCES

August Wilson

CHARACTERS

TROY MAXSON
IM BONO, *Troy's friend*
ROSE, *Troy's wife*
LYONS, *Troy's oldest son by previous marriage*
GABRIEL, *Troy's brother*
CORY, *Troy and Rose's son*
RAYNELL, *Troy's daughter*

> When the sins of our fathers visit us
> We do not have to play host.
> We can banish them with forgiveness
> As God, in His Largeness and Laws.
> —AUGUST WILSON

SETTING: *The setting is the yard which fronts the only entrance to the Maxson household, an ancient two-story brick house set back off a small alley in a big-city neighborhood. The entrance to the house is gained by two or three steps leading to a wooden porch badly in need of paint.*

A relatively recent addition to the house and running its full width, the porch lacks congruence. It is a sturdy porch with a flat roof. One or two chairs of dubious value sit at one end where the kitchen window opens onto the porch. An old-fashioned icebox stands silent guard at the opposite end.

The yard is a small dirt yard, partially fenced, except for the last scene, with a wooden sawhorse, a pile of lumber, and other fence-building equipment set off to the side. Opposite is a tree from which hangs a ball made of rags. A baseball bat leans against the tree. Two oil drums serve as garbage receptacles and sit near the house at right to complete the setting.

THE PLAY: *Near the turn of the century, the destitute of Europe sprang on the city with tenacious claws and an honest and solid dream. The city devoured them. They swelled its belly until it burst into a thousand furnaces and sewing machines, a thousand butcher shops and bakers' ovens, a thousand churches and hospitals and funeral parlors and moneylenders. The city grew. It nourished itself and offered each man a partnership limited only by his talent, his guile, and his willingness and capacity for hard work. For the immigrants of Europe, a dream dared and won true.*

The descendants of African slaves were offered no such welcome or participation. They came from places called the Carolinas and the Virginias, Georgia, Alabama, Mississippi, and Tennessee. They came strong, eager, searching. The city rejected them and they fled and settled along the riverbanks and under bridges in shallow, ramshackle houses made of sticks and tar-paper. They collected rags and wood. They sold the use of their muscles and their bodies. They cleaned houses and washed clothes, they shined shoes, and in quiet desperation and vengeful pride, they stole, and lived in pursuit of their own dream. That they could breathe free, finally, and stand to meet life with the force of dignity and whatever eloquence the heart could call upon.

By 1957, the hard-won victories of the European immigrants had solidified the industrial might of America. War had been confronted and won with new energies that used loyalty and patriotism as its fuel. Life was rich, full, and flourishing. The Milwaukee Braves won the World Series, and the hot winds of change that would make the sixties a turbulent, racing, dangerous, and provocative decade had not yet begun to blow full.

ACT ONE

SCENE I

It is 1957. TROY *and* BONO *enter the yard, engaged in conversation.* TROY *is fifty-three years old, a large man with thick, heavy hands; it is this largeness that he strives to fill out and make an accommodation with. Together with his blackness, his largeness informs his sensibilities and the choices he has made in his life.*

Of the two men, BONO *is obviously the follower. His commitment to their friendship of thirty-odd years is rooted in his admiration of* TROY'S *honesty, capacity for hard work, and his strength, which* BONO *seeks to emulate.*

It is Friday night, payday, and the one night of the week the two men engage in a ritual of talk and drink. TROY *is usually the most talkative and at times he can be crude and almost vulgar, though he is capable of rising to profound heights of expression. The men carry lunch buckets and wear or carry burlap aprons and are dressed in clothes suitable to their jobs as garbage collectors.*

BONO: Troy, you ought to stop that lying!
TROY: I ain't lying! The nigger had a watermelon this big.

(He indicates with his hands.)

Talking about . . . "What watermelon, Mr. Rand?" I liked to fell out! "What watermelon, Mr. Rand?" . . . And it sitting there big as life. 5
BONO: What did Mr. Rand say?
TROY: Ain't said nothing. Figure if the nigger too dumb to know he carrying a watermelon, he wasn't gonna get much sense out of him. Trying to hide that great big old watermelon under his coat. Afraid to let the white man see him carry it home. 10
BONO: I'm like you . . . I ain't got no time for them kind of people.
TROY: Now what he look like getting mad cause he see the man from the union talking to Mr. Rand?
BONO: He come to me talking about . . . "Maxson gonna get 15 us fired." I told him to get away from me with that. He walked away from me calling you a troublemaker. What Mr. Rand say?
TROY: Ain't said nothing. He told me to go down the Commissioner's office next Friday. They called me down there 20 to see them.
BONO: Well, as long as you got your complaint filed, they can't fire you. That's what one of them white fellows tell me.

TROY: I ain't worried about them firing me. They gonna fire
25   me cause I asked a question? That's all I did. I went to Mr.
Rand and asked him, "Why? Why you got the white mens
driving and the colored lifting?" Told him, "what's the
matter, don't I count? You think only white fellows got
sense enough to drive a truck. That ain't no paper job!
30   Hell, anybody can drive a truck. How come you got all
whites driving and the colored lifting?" He told me "take
it to the union." Well, hell, that's what I done! Now they
wanna come up with this pack of lies.
BONO: I told Brownie if the man come and ask him any
35   questions . . . just tell the truth! It ain't nothing but something they done trumped up on you cause you filed a
complaint on them.
TROY: Brownie don't understand nothing. All I want them to
do is change the job description. Give everybody a chance
40   to drive the truck. Brownie can't see that. He ain't got that
much sense.
BONO: How you figure he be making out with that gal be up
at Taylors' all the time . . . that Alberta gal?
TROY: Same as you and me. Getting just as much as we is.
45 BONO: Which is to say nothing.
BONO: It is, huh? I figure you doing a little better than me
. . . and I ain't saying what I'm doing.
TROY: Aw, nigger, look here . . . I know you. If you had got
anywhere near that gal, twenty minutes later you be look-
50   ing to tell somebody. And the first one you gonna tell . . .
that you gonna want to brag to . . . is gonna be me.
BONO: I ain't saying that. I see where you be eyeing her.
TROY: I eye all the women. I don't miss nothing. Don't never
let nobody tell you Troy Maxson don't eye the women.
55 BONO: You been doing more than eyeing her. You done
bought her a drink or two.
TROY: Hell yeah, I bought her a drink! What that mean? I
bought you one, too. What that mean cause I buy her a
drink? I'm just being polite.
60 BONO: It's alright to buy her one drink. That's what you call
being polite. But when you wanna be buying two or three
. . . that's what you call eyeing her.
TROY: Look here, as long as you known me . . . you ever
known me to chase after women?
65 BONO: Hell yeah! Long as I done known you. You forgetting
I knew you when.
TROY: Naw, I'm talking about since I been married to Rose?
BONO: Oh, not since you been married to Rose. Now, that's
the truth, there. I can say that.
70 TROY: Alright then! Case closed.
BONO: I see you be walking up around Alberta's house. You
supposed to be at Taylors' and you be walking up around
there.
TROY: What you watching where I'm walking for? I ain't
75   watching after you.
BONO: I seen you walking around there more than once.
TROY: Hell, you liable to see me walking anywhere! That don't
mean nothing cause you see me walking around there.
BONO: Where she come from anyway? She just kinda showed
80   up one day.
TROY: Tallahassee. You can look at her and tell she one of
them Florida gals. They got some big healthy women
down there. Grow them right up out the ground. Got a

little bit of Indian in her. Most of them niggers down in
Florida got some Indian in them.   85
BONO: I don't know about that Indian part. But she damn
sure big and healthy. Woman wear some big stockings.
Got them great big old legs and hips as wide as the Mis-
sissippi River.
TROY: Legs don't mean nothing. You don't do nothing but   90
push them out of the way. But them hips cushion the ride!
BONO: Troy, you ain't got no sense.
TROY: It's the truth! Like you riding on Goodyears!

(ROSE *enters from the house. She is ten years younger than* TROY, *her
devotion to him stems from her recognition of the possibilities of her
life without him: a succession of abusive men and their babies, a life of
partying and running the streets, the Church, or aloneness with its attendant pain and frustration. She recognizes* TROY's *spirit as a fine
and illuminating one and she either ignores or forgives his faults, only
some of which she recognizes. Though she doesn't drink, her presence
is an integral part of the Friday night rituals. She alternates between
the porch and the kitchen, where supper preparations are under way.*)

ROSE: What you all out here getting into?
TROY: What you worried about what we getting into for?   95
This is men talk, woman.
ROSE: What I care what you all talking about? Bono, you
gonna stay for supper?
BONO: No, I thank you, Rose. But Lucille say she cooking up
a pot of pigfeet.   100
TROY: Pigfeet! Hell, I'm going home with you! Might even
stay the night if you got some pigfeet. You got something
in there to top them pigfeet, Rose?
ROSE: I'm cooking up some chicken. I got some chicken and
collard greens.   105
TROY: Well, go on back in the house and let me and Bono
finish what we was talking about. This is men talk. I got
some talk for you later. You know what kind of talk I
mean. You go on and powder it up.
ROSE: Troy Maxson, don't you start that now!   110
TROY: (*Puts his arm around her.*) Aw, woman . . . come here. Look
here, Bono . . . when I met this woman . . . I got out that
place, say, "Hitch up my pony, saddle up my mare . . . there's a
woman out there for me somewhere. I looked here. Looked
there. Saw Rose and latched on to her." I latched on to her   115
and told her—I'm gonna tell you the truth—I told her,
"Baby, I don't wanna marry, I just wanna be your man."
Rose told me . . . tell him what you told me, Rose.
ROSE: I told him if he wasn't the marrying kind, then move
out the way so the marrying kind could find me.   120
TROY: That's what she told me. "Nigger, you in my way. You
blocking the view! Move out the way so I can find me a
husband." I thought it over two or three days. Come back—
ROSE: Ain't no two or three days nothing. You was back the
same night.   125
TROY: Come back, told her . . . "Okay, baby . . . but I'm gonna
buy me a banty rooster and put him out there in the backyard . . . and when he sees a stranger come, he'll flap his wings
and crow . . ." Look here, Bono, I could watch the front door
by myself . . . it was that back door I was worried about.   130
ROSE: Troy, you ought not talk like that. Troy ain't doing
nothing but telling a lie.

TROY: Only thing is . . . when we first got married . . . forget the rooster . . . we ain't had no yard!

135 BONO: I hear you tell it. Me and Lucille was staying down there on Logan Street. Had two rooms with the outhouse in the back. I ain't mind the outhouse none. But when that goddamn wind blow through there in the winter . . . that's what I'm talking about! To this day I wonder why in
140 the hell I ever stayed down there for six long years. But see, I didn't know I could do no better. I thought only white folks had inside toilets and things.

ROSE: There's a lot of people don't know they can do no better than they doing now. That's just something you got to
145 learn. A lot of folks still shop at Bella's.

TROY: Ain't nothing wrong with shopping at Bella's. She got fresh food.

ROSE: I ain't said nothing about if she got fresh food. I'm talking about what she charge. She charge ten cents more
150 than the A&P.

TROY: The A&P ain't never done nothing for me. I spends my money where I'm treated right. I go down to Bella, say, "I need a loaf of bread, I'll pay you Friday." She give it to me. What sense that make when I got money to go and spend
155 it somewhere else and ignore the person who done right by me? That ain't in the Bible.

ROSE: We ain't talking about what's in the Bible. What sense it make to shop there when she overcharge?

TROY: You shop where you want to. I'll do my shopping
160 where the people been good to me.

ROSE: Well, I don't think it's right for her to overcharge. That's all I was saying.

BONO: Look here . . . I got to get on. Lucille going be raising all kind of hell.

165 TROY: Where you going, nigger? We ain't finished this pint. Come here, finish this pint.

BONO: Well, hell, I am . . . if you ever turn the bottle loose.

TROY: (*Hands him the bottle.*) The only thing I say about the A&P is I'm glad Cory got that job down there. Help him
170 take care of his school clothes and things. Gabe done moved out and things getting tight around here. He got that job . . . He can start to look out for himself.

ROSE: Cory done went and got recruited by a college football team.

175 TROY: I told that boy about that football stuff. The white man ain't gonna let him get nowhere with that football. I told him when he first come to me with it. Now you come telling me he done went and got more tied up in it. He ought to go and get recruited in how to fix cars or
180 something where he can make a living.

ROSE: He ain't talking about making no living playing football. It's just something the boys in school do. They gonna send a recruiter by to talk to you. He'll tell you he ain't talking about making no living playing football. It's a
185 honor to be recruited.

TROY: It ain't gonna get him nowhere. Bono'll tell you that.

BONO: If he be like you in the sports . . . he's gonna be alright. Ain't but two men ever played baseball as good as you. That's Babe Ruth and Josh Gibson. Them's the only
190 two men ever hit more home runs than you.

TROY: What it ever get me? Ain't got a pot to piss in or a window to throw it out of.

ROSE: Times have changed since you was playing baseball, Troy. That was before the war. Times have changed a lot since then. 195

TROY: How in hell they done changed?

ROSE: They got lots of colored boys playing ball now. Baseball and football.

BONO: You right about that, Rose. Times have changed, Troy. You just come along too early. 200

TROY: There ought not never have been no time called too early! Now you take that fellow . . . what's that fellow they had playing right field for the Yankees back then? You know who I'm talking about, Bono. Used to play right field for the Yankees. 205

ROSE: Selkirk?

TROY: Selkirk! That's it! Man batting .269, understand? .269. What kind of sense that make? I was hitting .432 with thirty-seven home runs! Man batting .269 and playing right field for the Yankees! I saw Josh Gibson's daughter 210 yesterday. She walking around with raggedy shoes on her feet. Now I bet you Selkirk's daughter ain't walking around with raggedy shoes on her feet! I bet you that!

ROSE: They got a lot of colored baseball players now. Jackie Robinson was the first. Folks had to wait for Jackie 215 Robinson.

TROY: I done seen a hundred niggers play baseball better than Jackie Robinson. Hell, I know some teams Jackie Robinson couldn't even make! What you talking about Jackie Robinson. Jackie Robinson wasn't nobody. I'm talking 220 about if you could play ball then they ought to have let you play. Don't care what color you were. Come telling me I come along too early. If you could play . . . then they ought to have let you play.

(TROY *takes a long drink from the bottle.*)

ROSE: You gonna drink yourself to death. You don't need to 225 be drinking like that.

TROY: Death ain't nothing. I done seen him. Done wrassled with him. You can't tell me nothing about death. Death ain't nothing but a fastball on the outside corner. And you know what I'll do to that! Lookee here, Bono . . . am I ly- 230 ing? You get one of them fastballs, about waist high, over the outside corner of the plate where you can get the meat of the bat on it . . . and good god! You can kiss it goodbye. Now, am I lying?

BONO: Naw, you telling the truth there. I seen you do it. 235

TROY: If I'm lying . . . that 450 feet worth of lying!

(*Pause.*)

That's all death is to me. A fastball on the outside corner.

ROSE: I don't know why you want to get on talking about death.

TROY: Ain't nothing wrong with talking about death. That's 240 part of life. Everybody gonna die. You gonna die, I'm gonna die. Bono's gonna die. Hell, we all gonna die.

ROSE: But you ain't got to talk about it. I don't like to talk about it.

TROY: You the one brought it up. Me and Bono was talking 245 about baseball . . . you tell me I'm gonna drink myself to

death. Ain't that right, Bono? You know I don't drink this but one night out of the week. That's Friday night. I'm gonna drink just enough to where I can handle it. Then
250 I cuts it loose. I leave it alone. So don't you worry about me drinking myself to death. 'Cause I ain't worried about Death. I done seen him. I done wrestled with him.

Look here, Bono . . . I looked up one day and Death was marching straight at me. Like Soldiers on Parade! The
255 Army of Death was marching straight at me. The middle of July, 1941. It got real cold just like it be winter. It seem like Death himself reached out and touched me on the shoulder. He touch me just like I touch you. I got cold as ice and Death standing there grinning at me.

260 ROSE: Troy, why don't you hush that talk.

TROY: I say . . . What you want, Mr. Death? You be wanting me? You done brought your army to be getting me? I looked him dead in the eye. I wasn't fearing nothing. I was ready to tangle. Just like I'm ready to tangle now. The
265 Bible say be ever vigilant. That's why I don't get but so drunk. I got to keep watch.

ROSE: Troy was right down there in Mercy Hospital. You remember he had pneumonia? Laying there with a fever talking plumb out of his head.

270 TROY: Death standing there staring at me . . . carrying that sickle in his hand. Finally he say, "You want bound over for another year?" See, just like that . . . "You want bound over for another year?" I told him, "Bound over hell! Let's settle this now!"

275 It seem like he kinda fell back when I said that, and all the cold went out of me. I reached down and grabbed that sickle and threw it just as far as I could throw it . . . and me and him commenced to wrestling.

We wrestled for three days and three nights. I can't say
280 where I found the strength from. Every time it seemed like he was gonna get the best of me, I'd reach way down deep inside myself and find the strength to do him one better.

ROSE: Every time Troy tell that story he find different ways to
285 tell it. Different things to make up about it.

TROY: I ain't making up nothing. I'm telling you the facts of what happened. I wrestled with Death for three days and three nights and I'm standing here to tell you about it.

(Pause.)

Alright. At the end of the third night we done weakened
290 each other to where we can't hardly move. Death stood up, throwed on his robe . . . had him a white robe with a hood on it. He throwed on that robe and went off to look for his sickle. Say, "I'll be back." Just like that. "I'll be back." I told him, say, "Yeah, but . . . you gonna have to find
295 me!" I wasn't no fool. I wasn't going looking for him. Death ain't nothing to play with. And I know he's gonna get me. I know I got to join his army . . . his camp followers. But as long as I keep my strength and see him coming . . . as long as I keep up my vigilance . . . he's gonna
300 have to fight to get me. I ain't going easy.

BONO: Well, look here, since you got to keep up your vigilance . . . let me have the bottle.

TROY: Aw hell, I shouldn't have told you that part. I should have left out that part.

ROSE: Troy be talking that stuff and half the time don't even 305 know what he be talking about.

TROY: Bono know me better than that.

BONO: That's right. I know you. I know you got some Uncle Remus in your blood. You got more stories than the devil got sinners. 310

TROY: Aw hell, I done seen him too! Done talked with the devil.

ROSE: Troy, don't nobody wanna be hearing all that stuff.

(LYONS enters the yard from the street. Thirty-four years old, TROY's son by a previous marriage, he sports a neatly trimmed goatee, sport coat, white shirt, tieless and buttoned at the collar. Though he fancies himself a musician, he is more caught up in the rituals and "idea" of being a musician than in the actual practice of the music. He has come to borrow money from TROY, and while he knows he will be successful, he is uncertain as to what extent his lifestyle will be held up to scrutiny and ridicule.)

LYONS: Hey, Pop.

TROY: What you come "Hey, Popping" me for? 315

LYONS: How you doing, Rose?

(He kisses her.)

Mr. Bono. How you doing?

BONO: Hey, Lyons . . . how you been?

TROY: He must have been doing alright. I ain't seen him around here last week. 320

ROSE: Troy, leave your boy alone. He come by to see you and you wanna start all that nonsense.

TROY: I ain't bothering Lyons.

(Offers him the bottle.)

Here . . . get you a drink. We got an understanding. I know why he come by to see me and he know I know. 325

LYONS: Come on, Pop . . . I just stopped by to say hi . . . see how you was doing.

TROY: You ain't stopped by yesterday.

ROSE: You gonna stay for supper, Lyons? I got some chicken cooking in the oven. 330

LYONS: No, Rose . . . thanks. I was just in then neighborhood and thought I'd stop by for a minute.

TROY: You was in the neighborhood alright, nigger. You telling the truth there. You was in the neighborhood cause it's my payday. 335

LYONS: Well, hell, since you mentioned it . . . let me have ten dollars.

TROY: I'll be damned! I'll die and go to hell and play blackjack with the devil before I give you ten dollars.

BONO: That's what I wanna know about . . . that devil you 340 done seen.

LYONS: What . . . Pop done seen the devil? You too much, Pops.

TROY: Yeah, I done seen him. Talked to him too!

ROSE: You ain't seen no devil. I done told you that man ain't had nothing to do with the devil. Anything you can't un- 345 derstand, you want to call it the devil.

TROY: Look here, Bono . . . I went down to see Hertzberger about some furniture. Got three rooms for two-ninety-eight. That what it say on the radio. "Three rooms . . . two-ninety-eight." Even made up a little song about it. Go 350

down there . . . man tell me I can't get no credit. I'm working every day and can't get no credit. What to do? I got an
empty house with some raggedy furniture in it. Cory ain't
got no bed. He's sleeping on a pile of rags on the floor.
355 Working every day and can't get no credit. Come back
here—Rose'll tell you—madder than hell. Sit down . . . try
to figure what I'm gonna do. Come a knock on the door.
Ain't been living here but three days. Who know I'm here?
Open the door . . . devil standing there bigger than life.
360 White fellow . . . got on good clothes and everything.
Standing there with a clipboard in his hand. I ain't had to
say nothing. First words come out of his mouth was . . . "I
understand you need some furniture and can't get no
credit." I liked to fell over. He say "I'll give you all the credit
365 you want, but you got to pay the interest on it." I told him,
"Give me three rooms worth and charge whatever you
want." Next day a truck pulled up here and two men un-
loaded them three rooms. Man what drove the truck give
me a book. Say send ten dollars, first of every month to the
370 address in the book and everything will be alright. Say if I
miss a payment the devil was coming back and it'll be hell
to pay. That was fifteen years ago. To this day . . . the first
of the month I send my ten dollars, Rose'll tell you.

ROSE: Troy lying.

375 TROY: I ain't never seen that man since. Now you tell me
who else that could have been but the devil? I ain't sold
my soul or nothing like that, you understand. Naw, I
wouldn't have truck with the devil about nothing like
that. I got my furniture and pays my ten dollars the first
380 of the month just like clockwork.

BONO: How long you say you been paying this ten dollars a
month?

TROY: Fifteen years!

BONO: Hell, ain't you finished paying for it yet? How much
385 the man done charged you.

TROY: Aw hell, I done paid for it. I done paid for it ten times
over! The fact is I'm scared to stop paying it.

ROSE: Troy lying. We got that furniture from Mr. Glickman.
He ain't paying no ten dollars a month to nobody.

390 TROY: Aw hell, woman. Bono know I ain't that big a fool.

LYONS: I was just getting ready to say . . . I know where there's
a bridge for sale.

TROY: Look here, I'll tell you this . . . it don't matter to me if
he was the devil. It don't matter if the devil give credit.
395 Somebody has got to give it.

ROSE: It ought to matter. You going around talking about
having truck with the devil . . . God's the one you gonna
have to answer to. He's the one gonna be at the Judgment.

LYONS: Yeah, well, look here, Pop . . . let me have that ten dol-
400 lars. I'll give it back to you. Bonnie got a job working at
the hospital.

TROY: What I tell you, Bono? The only time I see this nigger is
when he wants something. That's the only time I see him.

LYONS: Come on, Pop, Mr. Bono don't want to hear all that.
405 Let me have the ten dollars. I told you Bonnie working.

TROY: What that mean to me? "Bonnie working." I don't care
if she working. Go ask her for the ten dollars if she working. Talking about "Bonnie working." Why ain't you
working?

410 LYONS: Aw, Pop, you know I can't find no decent job. Where
am I gonna get a job at? You know I can't get no job.

TROY: I told you I know some people down there. I can get
you on the rubbish if you want to work. I told you that
the last time you came by here asking me for something.

LYONS: Naw, Pop . . . thanks. That ain't for me. I don't wanna 415
be carrying nobody's rubbish. I don't wanna be punching
nobody's time clock.

TROY: What's the matter, you too good to carry people's rubbish? Where you think that ten dollars you talking about
come from? I'm just supposed to haul people's rubbish and 420
give my money to you cause you too lazy to work. You too
lazy to work and wanna know why you ain't got what I got.

ROSE: What hospital Bonnie working at? Mercy?

LYONS: She's down at Passavant working in the laundry.

TROY: I ain't got nothing as it is. I give you that ten dollars 425
and I got to eat beans the rest of the week. Naw . . . you
ain't getting no ten dollars here.

LYONS: You ain't got to be eating no beans. I don't know why
you wanna say that.

TROY: I ain't got no extra money. Gabe done moved over to 430
Miss Pearl's paying her the rent and things done got tight
around here. I can't afford to be giving you every payday.

LYONS: I ain't asked you to give me nothing. I asked you to
loan me ten dollars. I know you got ten dollars.

TROY: Yeah, I got it. You know why I got it? Cause I don't 435
throw my money away out there in the streets. You living
the fast life . . . wanna be a musician . . . running around
in them clubs and things . . . then, you learn to take care
of yourself. You ain't gonna find me going and asking nobody for nothing. I done spent too many years without. 440

LYONS: You and me is two different people, Pop.

TROY: I done learned my mistake and learned to do what's
right by it. You still trying to get something for nothing.
Life don't owe you nothing. You owe it to yourself. Ask
Bono. He'll tell you I'm right. 445

LYONS: You got your way of dealing with the world . . . I got
mine. The only thing that matters to me is the music.

TROY: Yeah, I can see that! It don't matter how you gonna eat
. . . where your next dollar is coming from. You telling the
truth there. 450

LYONS: I know I got to eat. But I got to live too. I need something that gonna help me to get out of the bed in the
morn-ing. Make me feel like I belong in the world. I don't
bother nobody. I just stay with my music cause that's the
only way I can find to live in the world. Otherwise there 455
ain't no telling what I might do. Now I don't come criticizing you and how you live. I just come by to ask you for
ten dollars. I don't wanna hear all that about how I live.

TROY: Boy, your mama did a hell of a job raising you.

LYONS: You can't change me, Pop. I'm thirty-four years old. If 460
you wanted to change me, you should have been there
when I was growing up. I come by to see you . . . ask for
ten dollars and you want to talk about how I was raised.
You don't know nothing about how I was raised.

ROSE: Let the boy have ten dollars, Troy. 465

TROY: (*To* LYONS.) What the hell you looking at me for? I ain't
got no ten dollars. You know what I do with my money.

(*To* ROSE.)

Give him ten dollars if you want him to have it.

ROSE: I will. Just as soon as you turn it loose.

470 TROY: (*Handing* ROSE *the money.*) There it is. Seventy-six dollars and forty-two cents. You see this, Bono? Now, I ain't gonna get but six of that back.
ROSE: You ought to stop telling that lie. Here, Lyons.

(*She hands him the money.*)

LYONS: Thanks, Rose. Look . . . I got to run . . . I'll see you later.
475 TROY: Wait a minute. You gonna say, "thanks, Rose" and ain't gonna look to see where she got that ten dollars from? See how they do me, Bono?
LYONS: I know she got it from you, Pop. Thanks. I'll give it back to you.
480 TROY: There he go telling another lie. Time I see that ten dollars . . . he'll be owing me thirty more.
LYONS: See you, Mr. Bono.
BONO: Take care, Lyons!
LYONS: Thanks, Pop. I'll see you again.

(LYONS *exits the yard.*)

485 TROY: I don't know why he don't go and get him a decent job and take care of that woman he got.
BONO: He'll be alright, Troy. The boy is still young.
TROY: The *boy* is thirty-four years old.
ROSE: Let's not get off into all that.
490 BONO: Look here . . . I got to be going. I got to be getting on. Lucille gonna be waiting.
TROY: (*Puts his arm around* ROSE.) See this woman, Bono? I love this woman. I love this woman so much it hurts. I love her so much . . . I done run out of ways of loving
495 her. So I got to go back to basics. Don't you come by my house Monday morning talking about time to go to work . . . 'cause I'm still gonna be stroking!
ROSE: Troy! Stop it now!
BONO: I ain't paying him no mind, Rose. That ain't nothing
500 but gin-talk. Go on, Troy. I'll see you Monday.
TROY: Don't you come by my house, nigger! I done told you what I'm gonna be doing.

(*The lights go down to black.*)

SCENE II

The lights come up on ROSE *hanging up clothes. She hums and sings softly to herself. It is the following morning.*

ROSE: (*Sings.*)

Jesus, be a fence all around me every day.
Jesus, I want you to protect me as I travel on my way.
Jesus, be a fence all around me every day.

(TROY *enters from the house.*)

5 ROSE: (*Continues.*)

Jesus, I want you to protect me
As I travel on my way.

(*To* TROY.)

'Morning. You ready for breakfast? I can fix it soon as I finish hanging up these clothes?

TROY: I got the coffee on. That'll be alright. I'll just drink 10 some of that this morning.
ROSE: That 651 hit yesterday. That's the second time this month. Miss Pearl hit for a dollar . . . seem like those that need the least always get lucky. Poor folks can't get nothing.
TROY: Them numbers don't know nobody. I don't know why 15 you fool with them. You and Lyons both.
ROSE: It's something to do.
TROY: You ain't doing nothing but throwing your money away.
ROSE: Troy, you know I don't play foolishly. I just play a nickel here and a nickel there. 20
TROY: That's two nickels you done thrown away.
ROSE: Now I hit sometimes . . . that makes up for it. It always comes in handy when I do hit. I don't hear you complaining then.
TROY: I ain't complaining now. I just say it's foolish. Trying 25 to guess out of six hundred ways which way the number gonna come. If I had all the money niggers, these Negroes, throw away on numbers for one week—just one week—I'd be a rich man.
ROSE: Well, you wishing and calling it foolish ain't gonna stop 30 folks from playing numbers. That's one thing for sure. Besides . . . some good things come from playing numbers. Look where Pope done bought him that restaurant off of numbers.
TROY: I can't stand niggers like that. Man ain't had two dimes 35 to rub together. He walking around with his shoes all run over bumming money for cigarettes. Alright. Got lucky there and hit the numbers . . .
ROSE: Troy, I know all about it.
TROY: Had good sense, I'll say that for him. He ain't throwed 40 his money away. I seen niggers hit the numbers and go through two thousand dollars in four days. Man bought him that restaurant down there . . . fixed it up real nice . . . and then didn't want nobody to come in it! A Negro go in there and can't get no kind of service. I seen a white fellow 45 come in there and order a bowl of stew. Pope picked all the meat out the pot for him. Man ain't had nothing but a bowl of meat! Negro come behind him and ain't got nothing but the potatoes and carrots. Talking about what numbers do for people, you picked a wrong example. Ain't done noth- 50 ing but make a worser fool out of him than he was before.
ROSE: Troy, you ought to stop worrying about what happened at work yesterday.
TROY: I ain't worried. Just told me to be down there at the Commissioner's office on Friday. Everybody think they 55 gonna fire me. I ain't worried about them firing me. You ain't got to worry about that.

(*Pause.*)

Where's Cory? Cory in the house? (*Calls.*) Cory?
ROSE: He gone out.
TROY: Out, huh? He gone out 'cause he know I want him to 60 help me with this fence. I know how he is. That boy scared of work.

(GABRIEL *enters. He comes halfway down the alley and, hearing* TROY's *voice, stops.*)

TROY: (*Continues.*) He ain't done a lick of work in his life.

ROSE: He had to go to football practice. Coach wanted them
65   to get in a little extra practice before the season start.
TROY: I got his practice . . . running out of here before he get
      his chores done.
ROSE: Troy, what is wrong with you this morning? Don't
      nothing set right with you. Go on back in there and go to
70   bed . . . get up on the other side.
TROY: Why something got to be wrong with me? I ain't said
      nothing wrong with me.
ROSE: You got something to say about everything. First it's the
      numbers . . . then it's the way the man runs his restaurant
75   . . . then you done got on Cory. What's it gonna be next?
      Take a look up there and see if the weather suits you . . .
      or is it gonna be how you gonna put up the fence with
      the clothes hanging in the yard.
TROY: You hit the nail on the head then.
80 ROSE: I know you like I know the back of my hand. Go on
      in there and get you some coffee . . . see if that straighten
      you up. 'Cause you ain't right this morning.

(TROY *starts into the house and sees* GABRIEL. GABRIEL *starts
singing.* TROY'*s brother, he is seven years younger than* TROY. *Injured in World War II, he has a metal plate in his head. He carries
an old trumpet tied around his waist and believes with every fiber of
his being that he is the Archangel Gabriel. He carries a chipped basket with an assortment of discarded fruits and vegetables he has
picked up in the strip district and which he attempts to sell.*)

GABRIEL: (*Singing.*)

            Yes, ma'am, I got plums
85   You ask me how I sell them
            Oh ten cents apiece
            Three for a quarter
            Come and buy now
            'Cause I'm here today
90   And tomorrow I'll be gone

(GABRIEL *enters.*)

      Hey, Rose!
ROSE: How you doing, Gabe?
GABRIEL: There's Troy . . . Hey, Troy!
TROY: Hey, Gabe.

(*Exit into kitchen.*)

95 ROSE: (*To* GABRIEL.) What you got there?
GABRIEL: You know what I got, Rose. I got fruits and vegetables.
ROSE: (*Looking in basket.*) Where's all these plums you talking
      about?
GABRIEL: I ain't got no plums today, Rose. I was just singing
100   that. Have some tomorrow. Put me in a big order for
      plums. Have enough plums tomorrow for St. Peter and
      everybody.

(TROY *re-enters from kitchen, crosses to steps.*)

(*To* ROSE.)

      Troy's mad at me.
TROY: I ain't mad at you. What I got to be mad at you about?
105   You ain't done nothing to me.

GABRIEL: I just moved over to Miss Pearl's to keep out from
      in your way. I ain't mean no harm by it.
TROY: Who said anything about that? I ain't said anything
      about that.
GABRIEL: You ain't mad at me, is you?   110
TROY: Naw . . . I ain't mad at you, Gabe. If I was mad at you
      I'd tell you about it.
GABRIEL: Got me two rooms. In the basement. Got my own
      door too. Wanna see my key?

(*He holds up a key.*)

      That's my own key! Ain't nobody else got a key like that. 115
      That's my key! My two rooms!
TROY: Well, that's good, Gabe. You got your own key . . . that's
      good.
ROSE: You hungry, Gabe? I was just fixing to cook Troy his
      breakfast.   120
GABRIEL: I'll take some biscuits. You got some biscuits? Did
      you know when I was in heaven . . . every morning me
      and St. Peter would sit down by the gate and eat some big
      fat biscuits? Oh, yeah! We had us a good time. We'd sit
      there and eat us them biscuits and then St. Peter would go 125
      off to sleep and tell me to wake him up when it's time to
      open the gates for the judgment.
ROSE: Well, come on . . . I'll make up a batch of biscuits.

(ROSE *exits into the house.*)

GABRIEL: Troy . . . St. Peter got your name in the book. I seen
      it. It say . . . Troy Maxson. I say . . . I know him! He got 130
      the same name like what I got. That's my brother!
TROY: How many times you gonna tell me that, Gabe?
GABRIEL: Ain't got my name in the book. Don't have to have
      my name. I done died and went to heaven. He got your
      name though. One morning St. Peter was looking at his 135
      book . . . marking it for the judgment . . . and he let me
      see your name. Got it in there under M. Got Rose's name
      . . . I ain't seen it like I seen yours . . . but I know it's in
      there. He got a great big book. Got everybody's name
      what was ever been born. That's what he told me. But I 140
      seen your name. Seen it with my own eyes.
TROY: Go on in the house there. Rose going to fix you
      something to eat.
GABRIEL: Oh, I ain't hungry. I done had breakfast with Aunt
      Jemimah. She come by and cooked me up a whole mess of 145
      flapjacks. Remember how we used to eat them flapjacks.
TROY: Go on in the house and get you something to eat now.
GABRIEL: I got to go sell my plums. I done sold some toma-
      toes. Got me two quarters. Wanna see?

(*He shows* TROY *his quarters.*)

      I'm gonna save them and buy me a new horn so St. Peter 150
      can hear me when it's time to open the gates.

(GABRIEL *stops suddenly. Listens.*)

      Hear that? That's the hellhounds. I got to chase them out
      of here. Go on get out of here! Get out!

(GABRIEL *exits singing.*)

155
  Better get ready for the judgment
  Better get ready for the judgment
  My Lord is coming down

(ROSE *enters from the house.*)

TROY: He gone off somewhere.
GABRIEL: (*Offstage.*)

160
  Better get ready for the judgment
  Better get ready for the judgment morning
  Better get ready for the judgment
  My God is coming down

ROSE: He ain't eating right. Miss Pearl say she can't get him to eat nothing.
165 TROY: What you want me to do about it, Rose? I done did everything I can for the man. I can't make him get well. Man got half his head blown away . . . what you expect?
ROSE: Seem like something ought to be done to help him.
TROY: Man don't bother nobody. He just mixed up from that
170 metal plate he got in his head. Ain't no sense for him to go back into the hospital.
ROSE: Least he be eating right. They can help him take care of himself.
TROY: Don't nobody wanna be locked up, Rose. What you
175 wanna lock him up for? Man go over there and fight the war . . . messin' around with them Japs, get half his head blown off . . . and they give him a lousy three thousand dollars. And I had to swoop down on that.
ROSE: Is you fixing to go into that again?
180 TROY: That's the only way I got a roof over my head . . . cause of that metal plate.
ROSE: Ain't no sense you blaming yourself for nothing. Gabe wasn't in no condition to manage that money. You done what was right by him. Can't nobody say you ain't done
185 what was right by him. Look how long you took care of him . . . till he wanted to have his own place and moved over there with Miss Pearl.
TROY: That ain't what I'm saying, woman! I'm just stating the facts. If my brother didn't have that metal plate in his head
190 . . . I wouldn't have a pot to piss in or a window to throw it out of. And I'm fifty-three years old. Now see if you can understand that!

(TROY *gets up from the porch and starts to exit the yard.*)

ROSE: Where you going off to? You been running out of here every Saturday for weeks. I thought you was gonna work
195 on this fence?
TROY: I'm gonna walk down to Taylors'. Listen to the ball game. I'll be back in a bit. I'll work on it when I get back.

(He exits the yard. The lights go to black.)

SCENE III

The lights come up on the yard. It is four hours later. ROSE *is taking down the clothes from the line.* CORY *enters carrying his football equipment.*

ROSE: Your daddy like to had a fit with you running out of here this morning without doing your chores.

CORY: I told you I had to go to practice.
ROSE: He say you were supposed to help him with this fence.
CORY: He been saying that the last four or five Saturdays, and 5 then he don't never do nothing, but go down to Taylors'. Did you tell him about the recruiter?
ROSE: Yeah, I told him.
CORY: What he say?
ROSE: He ain't said nothing too much. You get in there and 10 get started on your chores before he gets back. Go on and scrub down them steps before he gets back here hollering and carrying on.
CORY: I'm hungry. What you got to eat, Mama?
ROSE: Go on and get started on your chores. I got some meat 15 loaf in there. Go on and make you a sandwich . . . and don't leave no mess in there.

(CORY *exits into the house.* ROSE *continues to take down the clothes.* TROY *enters the yard and sneaks up and grabs her from behind.*)

  Troy! Go on, now. You liked to scared me to death. What was the score of the game? Lucille had me on the phone and I couldn't keep up with it. 20
TROY: What I care about the game? Come here, woman.

(*He tries to kiss her.*)

ROSE: I thought you went down Taylors' to listen to the game. Go on, Troy! You supposed to be putting up this fence.
TROY: (*Attempting to kiss her again.*) I'll put it up when I finish with what is at hand. 25
ROSE: Go on, Troy. I ain't studying you.
TROY: (*Chasing after her.*) I'm studying you . . . fixing to do my homework!
ROSE: Troy, you better leave me alone.
TROY: Where's Cory? That boy brought his butt home yet? 30
ROSE: He's in the house doing his chores.
TROY: (*Calling.*) Cory! Get your butt out here, boy!

(ROSE *exits into the house with the laundry.* TROY *goes over to the pile of wood, picks up a board, and starts sawing.* CORY *enters from the house.*)

TROY: You just now coming in here from leaving this morning?
CORY: Yeah, I had to go to football practice.
TROY: Yeah, what? 35
CORY: Yessir.
TROY: I ain't but two seconds off you noway. The garbage sitting in there overflowing . . . you ain't done none of your chores . . . and you come in here talking about "Yeah."
CORY: I was just getting ready to do my chores now, Pop . . . 40
TROY: Your first chore is to help me with this fence on Saturday. Everything else come after that. Now get that saw and cut them boards.

(CORY *takes the saw and begins cutting the boards.* TROY *continues working. There is a long pause.*)

CORY: Hey, Pop . . . why don't you buy a TV?
TROY: What I want with a TV? What I want one of them for? 45
CORY: Everybody got one. Earl, Ba Bra . . . Jesse!

TROY: I ain't asked you who had one. I say what I want with one?

CORY: So you can watch it. They got lots of things on TV. Baseball games and everything. We could watch the World Series.

TROY: Yeah . . . and how much this TV cost?

CORY: I don't know. They got them on sale for around two hundred dollars.

TROY: Two hundred dollars, huh?

CORY: That ain't that much, Pop.

TROY: Naw, it's just two hundred dollars. See that roof you got over your head at night? Let me tell you something about that roof. It's been over ten years since that roof was last tarred. See now . . . the snow come this winter and sit up there on that roof like it is . . . and it's gonna seep inside. It's just gonna be a little bit . . . ain't gonna hardly notice it. Then the next thing you know, it's gonna be leaking all over the house. Then the wood rot from all that water and you gonna need a whole new roof. Now, how much you think it cost to get that roof tarred?

CORY: I don't know.

TROY: Two hundred and sixty-four dollars . . . cash money. While you thinking about a TV, I got to be thinking about the roof . . . and whatever else go wrong around here. Now if you had two hundred dollars, what would you do . . . fix the roof or buy a TV?

CORY: I'd buy a TV. Then when the roof started to leak . . . when it needed fixing . . . I'd fix it.

TROY: Where you gonna get the money from? You done spent it for a TV. You gonna sit up and watch the water run all over your brand new TV.

CORY: Aw, Pop. You got money. I know you do.

TROY: Where I got it at, Huh?

CORY: You got it in the bank.

TROY: You wanna see my bankbook? You wanna see that seventy-three dollars and twenty-two cents I got sitting up in there.

CORY: You ain't got to pay for it all at one time. You can put a down payment on it and carry it on home with you.

TROY: Not me. I ain't gonna owe nobody nothing if I can help it. Miss a payment and they come and snatch it right out your house. Then what you got? Now, soon as I get two hundred dollars clear, then I'll buy a TV. Right now, as soon as I get two hundred and sixty-four dollars, I'm gonna have this roof tarred.

CORY: Aw . . . Pop!

TROY: You go on and get you two hundred dollars and buy one if ya want it. I got better things to do with my money.

CORY: I can't get no two hundred dollars. I ain't never seen two hundred dollars.

TROY: I'll tell you what . . . you get you a hundred dollars and I'll put the other hundred with it.

CORY: Alright, I'm gonna show you.

TROY: You gonna show me how you can cut them boards right now.

(CORY *begins to cut the boards. There is a long pause.*)

CORY: The Pirates won today. That makes five in a row.

TROY: I ain't thinking about the Pirates. Got an all-white team. Got that boy . . . that Puerto Rican boy . . .

Clemente. Don't even half-play him. That boy could be something if they give him a chance. Play him one day and sit him on the bench the next.

CORY: He gets a lot of chances to play.

TROY: I'm talking about playing regular. Playing every day so you can get your timing. That's what I'm talking about.

CORY: They got some white guys on the team that don't play every day. You can't play everybody at the same time.

TROY: If they got a white fellow sitting on the bench . . . you can bet your last dollar he can't play! The colored guy got to be twice as good before he get on the team. That's why I don't want you to get all tied up in them sports. Man on the team and what it get him? They got colored on the team and don't use them. Same as not having them. All them teams the same.

CORY: The Braves got Hank Aaron and Wes Covington. Hank Aaron hit two home runs today. That makes forty-three.

TROY: Hank Aaron ain't nobody. That's what you supposed to do. That's how you supposed to play the game. Ain't nothing to it. It's just a matter of timing . . . getting the right follow-through. Hell, I can hit forty-three home runs right now!

CORY: Not off no major-league pitching, you couldn't.

TROY: We had better pitching in the Negro leagues. I hit seven home runs off of Satchel Paige. You can't get no better than that!

CORY: Sandy Koufax. He's leading the league in strikeouts.

TROY: I ain't thinking of no Sandy Koufax.

CORY: You got Warren Spahn and Lew Burdette. I bet you couldn't hit no home runs off of Warren Spahn.

TROY: I'm through with it now. You go on and cut them boards.

(*Pause.*)

Your mama tell me you done got recruited by a college football team? Is that right?

CORY: Yeah. Coach Zellman say the recruiter gonna be coming by to talk to you. Get you to sign the permission papers.

TROY: I thought you supposed to be working down there at the A&P. Ain't you suppose to be working down there after school?

CORY: Mr. Stawicki say he gonna hold my job for me until after the football season. Say starting next week I can work weekends.

TROY: I thought we had an understanding about this football stuff? You suppose to keep up with your chores and hold that job down at the A&P. Ain't been around here all day on a Saturday. Ain't none of your chores done . . . and now you telling me you done quit your job.

CORY: I'm gonna be working weekends.

TROY: You damn right you are! And ain't no need for nobody coming around here to talk to me about signing nothing.

CORY: Hey, Pop . . . you can't do that. He's coming all the way from North Carolina.

TROY: I don't care where he coming from. The white man ain't gonna let you get nowhere with that football noway. You go on and get your book-learning so you can work yourself up in that A&P or learn how to fix cars or build houses or something, get you a trade. That way you have something can't nobody take away from you. You go on and learn how to put your hands to some good use. Besides hauling people's garbage.

165 CORY: I get good grades, Pop. That's why the recruiter wants to talk with you. You got to keep up your grades to get recruited. This way I'll be going to college. I'll get a chance . . .

TROY: First you gonna get your butt down there to the A&P
170 and get your job back.

CORY: Mr. Stawicki done already hired somebody else 'cause I told him I was playing football.

TROY: You a bigger fool than I thought . . . to let somebody take away your job so you can play some football. Where
175 you gonna get your money to take out your girlfriend and whatnot? What kind of foolishness is that to let somebody take away your job?

CORY: I'm still gonna be working weekends.

TROY: Naw . . . naw. You getting your butt out of here and
180 finding you another job.

CORY: Come on, Pop! I got to practice. I can't work after school and play football too. The team needs me. That's what Coach Zellman say . . .

TROY: I don't care what nobody else say. I'm the boss . . . you
185 understand? I'm the boss around here. I do the only saying what counts.

CORY: Come on, Pop!

TROY: I asked you . . . did you understand?

CORY: Yeah . . .

190 TROY: What?!

CORY: Yessir.

TROY: You go on down there to that A&P and see if you can get your job back. If you can't do both . . . then you quit the football team. You've got to take the crookeds with
195 the straights.

CORY: Yessir.

(*Pause.*)

Can I ask you a question?

TROY: What the hell you wanna ask me? Mr. Stawicki the one you got the questions for.

200 CORY: How come you ain't never liked me?

TROY: Liked you? Who the hell say I got to like you? What law is there say I got to like you? Wanna stand up in my face and ask a damn fool-ass question like that. Talking about liking somebody. Come here boy, when I talk to you.

(CORY *comes over to where* TROY *is working. He stands slouched over and* TROY *shoves him on his shoulder.*)

205 Straighten up, goddammit! I asked you a question . . . what law is there say I got to like you?

CORY: None.

TROY: Well, alright then! Don't you eat every day?

(*Pause.*)

Answer me when I talk to you! Don't you eat every day?
210 CORY: Yeah.

TROY: Nigger, as long as you in my house, you put that sir on the end of it when you talk to me!

CORY: Yes . . . sir.

TROY: You eat every day.

215 CORY: Yessir!

TROY: Got a roof over your head.

CORY: Yessir!

TROY: Got clothes on your back.

CORY: Yessir.

220 TROY: Why you think that is?

CORY: Cause of you.

TROY: Aw, hell I know it's 'cause of me . . . but why do you think that is?

CORY: (*Hesitant.*) Cause you like me.

225 TROY: Like you? I go out of here every morning . . . bust my butt . . . putting up with them crackers every day . . . cause I like you? You about the biggest fool I ever saw.

(*Pause.*)

It's my job. It's my responsibility! You understand that? A man got to take care of his family. You live in my house
230 . . . sleep you behind on my bedclothes . . . fill you belly up with my food . . . cause you my son. You my flesh and blood. Not 'cause I like you! Cause it's my duty to take care of you. I owe a responsibility to you! Let's get this straight right here . . . before it go along any further . . . I
235 ain't got to like you. Mr. Rand don't give me my money come payday cause he likes me. He gives me cause he owe me. I done give you everything I had to give you. I gave you your life! Me and your mama worked that out between us. And liking your black ass wasn't part of the bar-
240 gain. Don't you try and go through life worrying about if somebody like you or not. You best be making sure they doing right by you. You understand what I'm saying, boy?

CORY: Yessir.

TROY: Then get the hell out of my face, and get on down to
245 that A&P.

(ROSE *has been standing behind the screen door for much of the scene. She enters as* CORY *exits.*)

ROSE: Why don't you let the boy go ahead and play football, Troy? Ain't no harm in that. He's just trying to be like you with the sports.

TROY: I don't want him to be like me! I want him to move
250 as far away from my life as he can get. You the only decent thing that ever happened to me. I wish him that. But I don't wish him a thing else from my life. I decided seventeen years ago that boy wasn't getting involved in no sports. Not after what they did to me in the sports.

255 ROSE: Troy, why don't you admit you was too old to play in the major leagues? For once . . . why don't you admit that?

TROY: What do you mean too old? Don't come telling me I was too old. I just wasn't the right color. Hell, I'm fifty-three years old and can do better than Selkirk's .269 right now!

260 ROSE: How's was you gonna play ball when you were over forty? Sometimes I can't get no sense out of you.

TROY: I got good sense, woman. I got sense enough not to let my boy get hurt over playing no sports. You been mothering that boy too much. Worried about if people like him.

265 ROSE: Everything that boy do . . . he do for you. He wants you to say "Good job, son." That's all.

TROY: Rose, I ain't got time for that. He's alive. He's healthy. He's got to make his own way. I made mine. Ain't nobody gonna hold his hand when he get out there in that world.

ROSE: Times have changed from when you was young, Troy.
  People change. The world's changing around you and you
  can't even see it.

TROY: (*Slow, methodical.*) Woman . . . I do the best I can do. I
  come in here every Friday. I carry a sack of potatoes and
  a bucket of lard. You all line up at the door with your
  hands out. I give you the lint from my pockets. I give you
  my sweat and my blood. I ain't got no tears. I done spent
  them. We go upstairs in that room at night . . . and I fall
  down on you and try to blast a hole into forever. I get up
  Monday morning . . . find my lunch on the table. I go out.
  Make my way. Find my strength to carry me through to
  the next Friday.

(*Pause.*)

  That's all I got, Rose. That's all I got to give. I can't give
  nothing else.

(TROY *exits into the house. The lights go down to black.*)

SCENE IV

It is Friday. Two weeks later. CORY *starts out of the house with his
football equipment. The phone rings.*

CORY: (*Calling.*) I got it!

(*He answers the phone and stands in the screen door talking.*)

  Hello? Hey, Jesse. Naw . . . I was just getting ready to leave
  now.

ROSE: (*Calling.*) Cory!

CORY: I told you, man, them spikes is all tore up. You can use
  them if you want, but they ain't no good. Earl got some
  spikes.

ROSE: (*Calling.*) Cory!

CORY: (*Calling to* ROSE.) Mam? I'm talking to Jesse.

(*Into phone.*)

  When she say that. (*Pause.*) Aw, you lying, man. I'm gonna
  tell her you said that.

ROSE: (*Calling.*) Cory, don't you go nowhere!

CORY: I got to go to the game, Ma!

(*Into the phone.*)

  Yeah, hey, look, I'll talk to you later. Yeah, I'll meet you
  over Earl's house. Later. Bye, Ma.

(CORY *exits the house and starts out the yard.*)

ROSE: Cory, where you going off to? You got that stuff all
  pulled out and thrown all over your room.

CORY: (*In the yard.*) I was looking for my spikes. Jesse wanted
  to borrow my spikes.

ROSE: Get up there and get that cleaned up before your
  daddy get back in here.

CORY: I got to go to the game! I'll clean it up *when I get back.*

(CORY *exits.*)

ROSE: That's all he need to do is see that room all messed up.

(ROSE *exits into the house.* TROY *and* BONO *enter the yard.* TROY
is dressed in clothes other than his work clothes.)

BONO: He told him the same thing he told you. Take it to
  the union.

TROY: Brownie ain't got that much sense. Man wasn't thinking about nothing. He wait until I confront them on it . . .
  then he wanna come crying seniority.

(*Calls.*)

  Hey, Rose!

BONO: I wish I could have seen Mr. Rand's face when he told
  you.

TROY: He couldn't get it out of his mouth! Liked to bit his
  tongue! When they called me down there to the Commissioner's office . . . he thought they was gonna fire me.
  Like everybody else.

BONO: I didn't think they was gonna fire you. I thought they
  was gonna put you on the warning paper.

TROY: Hey, Rose!

(*To* BONO.)

  Yeah, Mr. Rand like to bit his tongue.

(TROY *breaks the seal on the bottle, takes a drink, and hands it to*
BONO.)

BONO: I see you run right down to Taylors' and told that Alberta gal.

TROY: (*Calling.*) Hey Rose! (*To* BONO.) I told everybody.
  Hey, Rose! I went down there to cash my check.

ROSE: (*Entering from the house.*) Hush all that hollering, man!
  I know you out here. What they say down there at the
  Commissioner's office?

TROY: You supposed to come when I call you, woman.
  Bono'll tell you that.

(*To* BONO.)

  Don't Lucille come when you call her?

ROSE: Man, hush your mouth. I ain't no dog . . . talk about
  "come when you call me."

TROY: (*Puts his arm around* ROSE.) You hear this, Bono? I had
  me an old dog used to get uppity like that. You say,
  "C'mere, Blue!" . . . and he just lay there and look at you.
  End up getting a stick and chasing him away trying to
  make him come.

ROSE: I ain't studying you and your dog. I remember you
  used to sing that old song.

TROY: (*He sings.*) Hear it ring! Hear it ring! I had a dog his
  name was Blue.

ROSE: Don't nobody wanna hear you sing that old song.

TROY: (*Sings.*) You know Blue was mighty true.

ROSE: Used to have Cory running around here singing that song.

BONO: Hell, I remember that song myself.

TROY: (*Sings.*)

  You know Blue was a good old dog.
  Blue treed a possum in a hollow log.

That was my daddy's song. My daddy made up that song.

ROSE: I don't care who made it up. Don't nobody wanna hear
70   you sing it.
TROY: (*Makes a song like calling a dog.*) Come here, woman.
ROSE: You come in here carrying on, I reckon they ain't fired
     you. What they say down there at the Commissioner's office?
TROY: Look here, Rose . . . Mr. Rand called me into his of-
75   fice today when I got back from talking to them people
     down there . . . it come from up top . . . he called me in
     and told me they was making me a driver.
ROSE: Troy, you kidding!
TROY: No I ain't. Ask Bono.
80   ROSE: Well, that's great, Troy. Now you don't have to hassle
     them people no more.

(LYONS *enters from the street.*)

TROY: Aw hell, I wasn't looking to see you today. I thought
     you was in jail. Got it all over the front page of the *Courier*
     about them raiding Sefus' place . . . where you be hanging
85   out with all them thugs?
LYONS: Hey, Pop . . . that ain't got nothing to do with me. I
     don't go down there gambling. I go down there to sit in
     with the band. I ain't got nothing to do with the gambling
     part. They got some good music down there.
90   TROY: They got some rogues . . . is what they got.
LYONS: How you been, Mr. Bono? Hi, Rose.
BONO: I see where you playing down at the Crawford Grill
     tonight.
ROSE: How come you ain't brought Bonnie like I told you.
95   You should have brought Bonnie with you, she ain't been
     over in a month of Sundays.
LYONS: I was just in the neighborhood . . . thought I'd stop by.
TROY: Here he come . . .
BONO: Your daddy got a promotion on the rubbish. He's
100 gonna be the first colored driver. Ain't got to do nothing
     but sit up there and read the paper like them white fellows.
LYONS: Hey, Pop . . . if you knew how to read you'd be alright.
BONO: Naw . . . naw . . . you mean if the nigger knew how
     to *drive* he'd be all right. Been fighting with them people
105 about driving and ain't even got a license. Mr. Rand know
     you ain't got no driver's license?
TROY: Driving ain't nothing. All you do is point the truck
     where you want it to go. Driving ain't nothing.
BONO: Do Mr. Rand know you ain't got no driver's license?
110 That's what I'm talking about. I ain't asked if driving was
     easy. I asked if Mr. Rand know you ain't got no driver's li-
     cense.
TROY: He ain't got to know. The man ain't got to know my busi-
     ness. Time he find out, I have two or three driver's licenses.
115 LYONS: (*Going into his pocket.*) Say, look here, Pop . . .
TROY: I knew it was coming. Didn't I tell you, Bono? I know
     what kind of "Look here, Pop" that was. The nigger fix-
     ing to ask me for some money. It's Friday night. It's my
     payday. All them rogues down there on the avenue . . . the
120 ones that ain't in jail . . . and Lyons is hopping in his shoes
     to get down there with them.
LYONS: See, Pop . . . if you give somebody else a chance to
     talk sometime, you'd see that I was fixing to pay you back
     your ten dollars like I told you. Here . . . I told you I'd pay
125 you when Bonnie got paid.

TROY: Naw . . . you go ahead and keep that ten dollars. Put
     it in the bank. The next time you feel like you wanna
     come by here and ask me for something . . . you go on
     down there and get that.
130 LYONS: Here's your ten dollars, Pop. I told you I don't want you
     to give me nothing. I just wanted to borrow ten dollars.
TROY: Naw . . . you go on and keep that for the next time
     you want to ask me.
LYONS: Come on, Pop . . . here go your ten dollars.
135 ROSE: Why don't you go on and let the boy pay you back, Troy?
LYONS: Here you go, Rose. If you don't take it I'm gonna
     have to hear about it for the next six months.

(*He hands her the money.*)

ROSE: You can hand yours over here too, Troy.
TROY: You see this, Bono. You see how they do me.
140 BONO: Yeah, Lucille do me the same way.

(GABRIEL *is heard singing offstage. He enters.*)

GABRIEL: Better get ready for the Judgment! Better get ready
     for . . . Hey! . . . Hey! . . . There's Troy's boy!
LYONS: How you doing, Uncle Gabe?
GABRIEL: Lyons . . . The King of the Jungle! Rose . . . hey,
145 Rose. Got a flower for you.

(*He takes a rose from his pocket.*)

Picked it myself. That's the same rose like you is!
ROSE: That's right nice of you, Gabe.
LYONS: What you been doing, Uncle Gabe?
GABRIEL: Oh, I been chasing hellhounds and waiting on the
150 time to tell St. Peter to open the gates.
LYONS: You been chasing hellhounds, huh? Well . . . you doing
     the right thing, Uncle Gabe. Somebody got to chase them.
GABRIEL: Oh, yeah . . . I know it. The devil's strong. The devil
     ain't no pushover. Hellhounds snipping at everybody's
155 heels. But I got my trumpet waiting on the judgment time.
LYONS: Waiting on the Battle of Armageddon, huh?
GABRIEL: Ain't gonna be too much of a battle when God get
     to waving that Judgment sword. But the people's gonna
     have a hell of a time trying to get into heaven if them
160 gates ain't open.
LYONS: (*Putting his arm around* GABRIEL.) You hear this, Pop.
     Uncle Gabe, you alright!
GABRIEL: (*Laughing with* LYONS.) Lyons! King of the Jungle.
ROSE: You gonna stay for supper, Gabe. Want me to fix you
165 a plate?
GABRIEL: I'll take a sandwich, Rose. Don't want no plate. Just
     wanna eat with my hands. I'll take a sandwich.
ROSE: How about you, Lyons? You staying? Got some short
     ribs cooking.
170 LYONS: Naw, I won't eat nothing till after we finished playing.

(*Pause.*)

You ought to come down and listen to me play, Pop.
TROY: I don't like that Chinese music. All that noise.
ROSE: Go on in the house and wash up, Gabe . . . I'll fix you
     a sandwich.

175   GABRIEL: (*To* LYONS, *as he exits.*) Troy's mad at me.

LYONS: What you mad at Uncle Gabe for, Pop.

ROSE: He thinks Troy's mad at him cause he moved over to Miss Pearl's.

TROY: I ain't mad at the man. He can live where he want to
180   live at.

LYONS: What he move over there for? Miss Pearl don't like nobody.

ROSE: She don't mind him none. She treats him real nice. She just don't allow all that singing.

185   TROY: She don't mind that rent he be paying . . . that's what she don't mind.

ROSE: Troy, I ain't going through that with you no more. He's over there cause he want to have his own place. He can come and go as he please.

190   TROY: Hell, he could come and go as he please here. I wasn't stopping him. I ain't put no rules on him.

ROSE: It ain't the same thing, Troy. And you know it.

(GABRIEL *comes to the door.*)

Now, that's the last I wanna hear about that. I don't wanna hear nothing else about Gabe and Miss Pearl. And next
195   week . . .

GABRIEL: I'm ready for my sandwich, Rose.

ROSE: And next week . . . when that recruiter come from that school . . . I want you to sign that paper and go on and let Cory play football. Then that'll be the last I have to hear
200   about that.

TROY: (*To* ROSE *as she exits into the house.*) I ain't thinking about Cory nothing.

LYONS: What . . . Cory got recruited? What school he going to?

TROY: That boy walking around here smelling his piss . . .
205   thinking he's grown. Thinking he's gonna do what he want, irrespective of what I say. Look here, Bono . . . I left the Commissioner's office and went down to the A&P . . . that boy ain't working down there. He lying to me. Telling me he got his job back . . . telling me he working
210   weekends . . . telling me he working after school . . . Mr. Stawicki tell me he ain't working down there at all!

LYONS: Cory just growing up. He's just busting at the seams trying to fill out your shoes.

TROY: I don't care what he's doing. When he get to the point
215   where he wanna disobey me . . . then it's time for him to move on. Bono'll tell you that. I bet he ain't never disobeyed his daddy without paying the consequences.

BONO: I ain't never had a chance. My daddy came on through . . . but I ain't never knew him to see him . . . or what he
220   had on his mind or where he went. Just moving on through. Searching out the New Land. That's what the old folks used to call it. See a fellow moving around from place to place . . . woman to woman . . . called it searching out the New Land. I can't say if he ever found it. I come along,
225   didn't want no kids. Didn't know if I was gonna be in one place long enough to fix on them right as their daddy. I figured I was going searching too. As it turned out I been hooked up with Lucille near about as long as your daddy been with Rose. Going on sixteen years.

230   TROY: Sometimes I wish I hadn't known my daddy. He ain't cared nothing about no kids. A kid to him wasn't noth-ing. All he wanted was for you to learn how to walk so he could start you to working. When it come time for eating . . . he ate first. If there was anything left over, that's
235   what you got. Man would sit down and eat two chickens and give you the wing.

LYONS: You ought to stop that, Pop. Everybody feed their kids. No matter how hard times is . . . everybody care about their kids. Make sure they have something to eat.

240   TROY: The only thing my daddy cared about was getting them bales of cotton into Mr. Lubin. That's the only thing that mattered to him. Sometimes I used to wonder why he was living. Wonder why the devil hadn't come and got him. "Get them bales of cotton in to Mr. Lubin" and find
245   out he owe him money . . .

LYONS: He should have just went on and left when he saw he couldn't get nowhere. That's what I would have done.

TROY: How he gonna leave with eleven kids? And where he gonna go? He ain't knew how to do nothing but farm.
250   No, he was trapped and I think he knew it. But I'll say this for him . . . he felt a responsibility toward us. Maybe he ain't treated us the way I felt he should have . . . but without that responsibility he could have walked off and left us . . . made his own way.

255   BONO: A lot of them did. Back in those days what you talk-ing about . . . they walk out their front door and just take on down one road or another and keep on walking.

LYONS: There you go! That's what I'm talking about.

BONO: Just keep on walking till you come to something else.
260   Ain't you never heard of nobody having the walking blues? Well, that's what you call it when you just take off like that.

TROY: My daddy ain't had them walking blues! What you talk-ing about? He stayed right there with his family. But he was just as evil as he could be. My mama couldn't stand
265   him. Couldn't stand that evilness. She run off when I was about eight. She sneaked off one night after he had gone to sleep. Told me she was coming back for me. I ain't never seen her no more. All his women run off and left him. He wasn't good for nobody.

270   When my turn come to head out, I was fourteen and got to sniffing around Joe Canewell's daughter. Had us an old mule we called Greyboy. My daddy sent me out to do some plowing and I tied up Greyboy and went to fooling around with Joe Canewell's daughter. We done found us a nice lit-
275   tle spot, got real cozy with each other. She about thirteen and we done figured we was grown anyway . . . so we down there enjoying ourselves . . . ain't thinking about nothing. We didn't know Greyboy had got loose and wandered back to the house and my daddy was looking for me. We down
280   there by the creek enjoying ourselves when my daddy come up on us. Surprised us. He had them leather straps off the mule and commenced to whupping me like there was no tomorrow. I jumped up, mad and embarrassed. I was scared of my daddy. When he commenced to whupping on
285   me . . . quite naturally I run to get out of the way.

(*Pause.*)

Now I thought he was mad cause I ain't done my work. But I see where he was chasing me off so he could have the gal for himself. When I see what the matter of it was,

290 I lost all fear of my daddy. Right there is where I become a man . . . at fourteen years of age.

(*Pause.*)

Now it was my turn to run him off. I picked up them same reins that he had used on me. I picked up them reins and commenced to whupping on him. The gal jumped up and run off . . . and when my daddy turned to face me, I could
295 see why the devil had never come to get him . . . cause he was the devil himself. I don't know what happened. When I woke up, I was laying right there by the creek, and Blue . . . this old dog we had . . . was licking my face. I thought I was blind. I couldn't see nothing. Both my eyes were
300 swollen shut. I layed there and cried. I didn't know what I was gonna do. The only thing I knew was the time had come for me to leave my daddy's house. And right there the world suddenly got big. And it was a long time before I could cut it down to where I could handle it.

305 Part of that cutting down was when I got to the place where I could feel him kicking in my blood and knew that the only thing that separated us was the matter of a few years.

(GABRIEL *enters from the house with a sandwich.*)

LYONS: What you got there, Uncle Gabe?
GABRIEL: Got me a ham sandwich. Rose gave me a ham
310 sandwich.
TROY: I don't know what happened to him. I done lost touch with everybody except Gabriel. But I hope he's dead. I hope he found some peace.
LYONS: That's a heavy story, Pop. I didn't know you left home
315 when you was fourteen.
TROY: And didn't know nothing. The only part of the world I knew was the forty-two acres of Mr. Lubin's land. That's all I knew about life.
LYONS: Fourteen's kinda young to be out on your own. (*Phone
320 rings.*) I don't even think I was ready to be out on my own at fourteen. I don't know what I would have done.
TROY: I got up from the creek and walked on down to Mobile. I was through with farming. Figured I could do better in the city. So I walked the two hundred miles to Mobile.
325 LYONS: Wait a minute . . . you ain't walked no two hundred miles, Pop. Ain't nobody gonna walk no two hundred miles. You talking about some walking there.
BONO: That's the only way you got anywhere back in them days.
LYONS: Shhh. Damn if I wouldn't have hitched a ride with
330 somebody!
TROY: Who you gonna hitch it with? They ain't had no cars and things like they got now. We talking about 1918.
ROSE: (*Entering.*) What you all out here getting into?
TROY: (*To* ROSE.) I'm telling Lyons how good he got it. He
335 don't know nothing about this I'm talking.
ROSE: Lyons, that was Bonnie on the phone. She say you supposed to pick her up.
LYONS: Yeah, okay, Rose.
TROY: I walked on down to Mobile and hitched up with
340 some of them fellows that was heading this way. Got up here and found out . . . not only couldn't you get a job . . . you couldn't find no place to live. I thought I was in freedom. Shhh. Colored folks living down there on the river-

banks in whatever kind of shelter they could find for themselves. Right down there under the Brady Street 345 Bridge. Living in shacks made of sticks and tarpaper. Messed around there and went from bad to worse. Started stealing. First it was food. Then I figured, hell, if I steal money I can buy me some food. Buy me some shoes too! One thing led to another. Met your mama. I was young 350 and anxious to be a man. Met your mama and had you. What I do that for? Now I got to worry about feeding you and her. Got to steal three times as much. Went out one day looking for somebody to rob . . . that's what I was, a robber. I'll tell you the truth. I'm ashamed of it today. 355 But it's the truth. Went to rob this fellow . . . pulled out my knife . . . and he pulled out a gun. Shot me in the chest. It felt just like somebody had taken a hot branding iron and laid it on me. When he shot me I jumped at him with my knife. They told me I killed him and they put 360 me in the penitentiary and locked me up for fifteen years. That's where I met Bono. That's where I learned how to play baseball. Got out that place and your mama had taken you and went on to make life without me. Fifteen years was a long time for her to wait. But that fifteen years 365 cured me of that robbing stuff. Rose'll tell you. She asked me when I met her if I had gotten all that foolishness out of my system. And I told her, "Baby, it's you and baseball all what count with me." You hear me, Bono? I meant it too. She say, "Which one comes first?" I told her, "Baby, 370 ain't no doubt it's baseball . . . but you stick and get old with me and we'll both outlive this baseball." Am I right, Rose? And it's true.
ROSE: Man, hush your mouth. You ain't said no such thing. Talking about, "Baby, you know you'll always be number 375 one with me." That's what you was talking.
TROY: You hear that, Bono. That's why I love her.
BONO: Rose'll keep you straight. You get off the track, she'll straighten you up.
ROSE: Lyons, you better get on up and get Bonnie. She wait- 380 ing on you.
LYONS: (*Gets up to go.*) Hey, Pop, why don't you come on down to the Grill and hear me play?
TROY: I ain't going down there. I'm too old to be sitting around in them clubs. 385
BONO: You got to be good to play down at the Grill.
LYONS: Come on, Pop . . .
TROY: I got to get up in the morning.
LYONS: You ain't got to stay long.
TROY: Naw, I'm gonna get my supper and go on to bed. 390
LYONS: Well, I got to go. I'll see you again.
TROY: Don't you come around my house on my payday.
ROSE: Pick up the phone and let somebody know you coming. And bring Bonnie with you. You know I'm always glad to see her. 395
LYONS: Yeah, I'll do that, Rose. You take care now. See you, Pop. See you, Mr. Bono. See you, Uncle Gabe.
GABRIEL: Lyons! King of the Jungle!

(LYONS *exits.*)

TROY: Is supper ready, woman? Me and you got some business to take care of. I'm gonna tear it up too. 400

ROSE: Troy, I done told you now!

TROY: (*Puts his arm around* BONO.) Aw hell, woman . . . this is Bono. Bono like family. I done known this nigger since . . . how long I done know you?

405 BONO: It's been a long time.

TROY: I done known this nigger since Skippy was a pup. Me and him done been through some times.

BONO: You sure right about that.

TROY: Hell, I done know him longer than I known you. And 410 we still standing shoulder to shoulder. Hey, look here, Bono . . . a man can't ask for no more than that.

(*Drinks to him.*)

I love you, nigger.

BONO: Hell, I love you too . . . but I got to get home see my woman. You got yours in hand. I got to go get mine.

(BONO *starts to exit as* CORY *enters the yard, dressed in his football uniform. He gives* TROY *a hard, uncompromising look.*)

415 CORY: What you do that for, Pop?

(*He throws his helmet down in the direction of* TROY.)

ROSE: What's the matter? Cory . . . what's the matter?

CORY: Papa done went up to the school and told Coach Zellman I can't play football no more. Wouldn't even let me play the game. Told him to tell the recruiter not to come.

420 ROSE: Troy . . .

TROY: What you Troying me for? Yeah, I did it. And the boy know why I did it.

CORY: Why you wanna do that to me? That was the one chance I had.

425 ROSE: Ain't nothing wrong with Cory playing football, Troy.

TROY: The boy lied to me. I told the nigger if he wanna play football . . . to keep his chores and hold down that job at the A&P. That was the conditions. Stopped down there to see Mr. Stawicki . . .

430 CORY: I can't work after school during the football season, Pop! I tried to tell you that Mr. Stawicki's holding my job for me. You don't never want to listen to nobody. And then you wanna go and do this to me!

TROY: I ain't done nothing to you. You done it to yourself.

435 CORY: Just cause you didn't have a chance! You just scared I'm gonna be better than you, that's all.

TROY: Come here.

ROSE: Troy . . .

(CORY *reluctantly crosses over to* TROY.)

TROY: Alright! See. You done made a mistake.

440 CORY: I didn't even do nothing!

TROY: I'm gonna tell you what your mistake was. See . . . you swung at the ball and didn't hit it. That's strike one. See, you in the batter's box now. You swung and you missed. That's strike one. Don't you strike out!

(*Lights fade to black.*)

ACT TWO

SCENE I

The following morning. CORY *is at the tree hitting the ball with the bat. He tries to mimic* TROY, *but his swing is awkward, less sure.* ROSE *enters from the house.*

ROSE: Cory, I want you to help me with this cupboard.

CORY: I ain't quitting the team. I don't care what Poppa say.

ROSE: I'll talk to him when he gets back. He had to go see about your Uncle Gabe. The police done arrested him. Say he was disturbing the peace. He'll be back directly. Come 5 on in here and help me clean out the top of this cupboard.

(CORY *exits into the house.* ROSE *sees* TROY *and* BONO *coming down the alley.*)

Troy . . . what they say down there?

TROY: Ain't said nothing. I give them fifty dollars and they let him go. I'll talk to you about it. Where's Cory?

ROSE: He's in there helping me clean out these cupboards. 10

TROY: Tell him to get his butt out here.

(TROY *and* BONO *go over to the pile of wood.* BONO *picks up the saw and begins sawing.*)

TROY: (*To* BONO.) All they want is the money. That makes six or seven times I done went down there and got him. See me coming they stick out their hands.

BONO: Yeah. I know what you mean. That's all they care 15 about . . . that money. They don't care about what's right.

(*Pause.*)

Nigger, why you got to go and get some hard wood? You ain't doing nothing but building a little old fence. Get you some soft pine wood. That's all you need.

TROY: I know what I'm doing. This is outside wood. You 20 put pine wood inside the house. Pine wood is inside wood. This here is outside wood. Now you tell me where the fence is gonna be?

BONO: You don't need this wood. You can put it up with pine wood and it's stand as long as you gonna be here 25 looking at it.

TROY: How you know how long I'm gonna be here, nigger? Hell, I might just live forever. Live longer than old man Horsely.

BONO: That's what Magee used to say. 30

TROY: Magee's a damn fool. Now you tell me who you ever heard of gonna pull their own teeth with a pair of rusty pliers.

BONO: The old folks . . . my granddaddy used to pull his teeth with pliers. They ain't had no dentists for the colored 35 folks back then.

TROY: Get clean pliers! You understand? Clean pliers! Sterilize them! Besides we ain't living back then. All Magee had to do was walk over to Doc Goldblums.

BONO: I see where you and that Tallahassee gal . . . that Al- 40 berta . . . I see where you all done got tight.

TROY: What you mean "got tight"?

BONO: I see where you be laughing and joking with her all the time.

45 TROY: I laughs and jokes with all of them, Bono. You know me.
    BONO: That ain't the kind of laughing and joking I'm talking about.

(CORY *enters from the house.*)

    CORY: How you doing, Mr. Bono?
    TROY: Cory? Get that saw from Bono and cut some wood.
50   He talking about the wood's too hard to cut. Stand back there, Jim, and let that young boy show you how it's done.
    BONO: He's sure welcome to it.

(CORY *takes the saw and begins to cut the wood.*)

    Whew-e-e! Look at that. Big old strong boy. Look like Joe Louis. Hell, must be getting old the way I'm watching that
55   boy whip through that wood.
    CORY: I don't see why Mama want a fence around the yard noways.
    TROY: Damn if I know either. What the hell she keeping out with it? She ain't got nothing nobody want.
60 BONO: Some people build fences to keep people out . . . and other people build fences to keep people in. Rose wants to hold on to you all. She loves you.
    TROY: Hell, nigger, I don't need nobody to tell me my wife loves me, Cory . . . go on in the house and see if you can
65   find that other saw.
    CORY: Where's it at?
    TROY: I said find it! Look for it till you find it!

(CORY *exits into the house.*)

    What's that supposed to mean? Wanna keep us in?
    BONO: Troy . . . I done known you seem like damn near my
70   whole life. You and Rose both. I done know both of you all for a long time. I remember when you met Rose. When you was hitting them baseball out the park. A lot of them old gals was after you then. You had the pick of the litter. When you picked Rose, I was happy for you.
75   That was the first time I knew you had any sense. I said . . . My man Troy knows what he's doing . . . I'm gonna follow this nigger . . . he might take me somewhere. I been following you too. I done learned a whole heap of things about life watching you. I done learned how to tell where
80   the shit lies. How to tell it from the alfalfa. You done learned me a lot of things. You showed me how to not make the same mistakes . . . to take life as it comes along and keep putting one foot in front of the other.

(*Pause.*)

    Rose a good woman, Troy.
85 TROY: Hell, nigger, I know she a good woman. I been married to her for eighteen years. What you got on your mind, Bono?
    BONO: I just say she a good woman. Just like I say anything. I ain't got to have nothing on my mind.
    TROY: You just gonna say she a good woman and leave it
90   hanging out there like that? Why you telling me she a good woman?
    BONO: She loves you, Troy. Rose loves you.
    TROY: You saying I don't measure up. That's what you trying to say. I don't measure up cause I'm seeing this other gal.
95   I know what you trying to say.

    BONO: I know what Rose means to you, Troy. I'm just trying to say I don't want to see you mess up.
    TROY: Yeah, I appreciate that, Bono. If you was messing around on Lucille I'd be telling you the same thing.
    BONO: Well, that's all I got to say. I just say that because I love   100 you both.
    TROY: Hell, you know me . . . I wasn't out there looking for nothing. You can't find a better woman than Rose. I know that. But seems like this woman just stuck onto me where I can't shake her loose. I done wrestled with it,   105 tried to throw her off me . . . but she just stuck on tighter. Now she's stuck on for good.
    BONO: You's in control . . . that's what you tell me all the time. You responsible for what you do.
    TROY: I ain't ducking the responsibility of it. As long as it sets   110 right in my heart . . . then I'm okay. Cause that's all I listen to. It'll tell me right from wrong every time. And I ain't talking about doing Rose no bad turn. I love Rose. She done carried me a long ways and I love and respect her for that.   115
    BONO: I know you do. That's why I don't want to see you hurt her. But what you gonna do when she find out? What you got then? If you try and juggle both of them . . . sooner or later you gonna drop one of them. That's common sense.
    TROY: Yeah, I hear what you saying, Bono. I been trying to   120 figure a way to work it out.
    BONO: Work it out right, Troy. I don't want to be getting all up between you and Rose's business . . . but work it so it come out right.
    TROY: Aw hell, I get all up between you and Lucille's business.   125 When you gonna get that woman that refrigerator she been wanting? Don't tell me you ain't got no money now. I know who your banker is. Mellon don't need that money bad as Lucille want that refrigerator. I'll tell you that.
    BONO: Tell you what I'll do . . . when you finish building this   130 fence for Rose . . . I'll buy Lucille that refrigerator.
    TROY: You done stuck your foot in your mouth now!

(TROY *grabs up a board and begins to saw.* BONO *starts to walk out the yard.*)

    Hey, nigger . . . where you going?
    BONO: I'm going home. I know you don't expect me to help you now. I'm protecting my money. I wanna see you put   135 that fence up by yourself. That's what I want to see. You'll be here another six month without me.
    TROY: Nigger, you ain't right.
    BONO: When it comes to my money . . . I'm right as fireworks on the Fourth of July.   140
    TROY: Alright, we gonna see now. You better get out your bankbook.

(BONO *exits, and* TROY *continues to work.* ROSE *enters from the house.*)

    ROSE: What they say down there? What's happening with Gabe?
    TROY: I went down there and got him out. Cost me fifty dol-   145 lars. Say he was disturbing the peace. Judge set up a hearing for him in three weeks. Say to show cause why he shouldn't be re-committed.

ROSE: What was he doing that cause them to arrest him?

150 TROY: Some kids was teasing him and he run them off home. Say he was howling and carrying on. Some folks seen him and called the police. That's all it was.

ROSE: Well, what's you say? What'd you tell the judge?

TROY: Told him I'd look after him. It didn't make no sense to
155 recommit the man. He stuck out his big greasy palm and told me to give him fifty dollars and take him on home.

ROSE: Where's he at now? Where'd he go off to?

TROY: He's gone on about his business. He don't need nobody to hold his hand.

160 ROSE: Well, I don't know. Seem like that would be the best place for him if they did put him into the hospital. I know what you're gonna say. But that's what I think would be best.

TROY: The man done had his life ruined fighting for what?
165 And they wanna take and lock him up. Let him be free. He don't bother nobody.

ROSE: Well, everybody got their own way of looking at it I guess. Come on and get your lunch. I got a bowl of lima beans and some cornbread in the oven. Come on get
170 some-thing to eat. Ain't no sense you fretting over Gabe.

(ROSE *turns to go into the house.*)

TROY: Rose . . . got something to tell you.

ROSE: Well, come on . . . wait till I get this food on the table.

TROY: Rose!

(*She stops and turns around.*)

I don't know how to say this.

(*Pause.*)

175 I can't explain it none. It just sort of grows on you till it gets out of hand. It starts out like a little bush . . . and the next thing you know it's a whole forest.

ROSE: Troy . . . what is you talking about?

TROY: I'm talking, woman, let me talk. I'm trying to find a
180 way to tell you . . . I'm gonna be a daddy. I'm gonna be somebody's daddy.

ROSE: Troy . . . you're not telling me this? You're gonna be . . . what?

TROY: Rose . . . now . . . see . . .

185 ROSE: You telling me you gonna be somebody's daddy? You telling your *wife* this?

(GABRIEL *enters from the street. He carries a rose in his hand.*)

GABRIEL: Hey, Troy! Hey, Rose!

ROSE: I have to wait eighteen years to hear something like this.

GABRIEL: Hey, Rose . . . I got a flower for you.

(*He hands it to her.*)

190 That's a rose. Same rose like you is.

ROSE: Thanks, Gabe.

GABRIEL: Troy, you ain't mad at me is you? Them bad mens come and put me away. You ain't mad at me is you?

TROY: Naw, Gabe, I ain't mad at you.

195 ROSE: Eighteen years and you wanna come with this.

GABRIEL: (*Takes a quarter out of his pocket.*) See what I got? Got a brand new quarter.

TROY: Rose . . . it's just . . .

ROSE: Ain't nothing you can say, Troy. Ain't no way of ex-
200 plaining that.

GABRIEL: Fellow that give me this quarter had a whole mess of them. I'm gonna keep this quarter till it stop shining.

ROSE: Gabe, go on in the house there. I got some watermelon in the frigidaire. Go on and get you a piece.

GABRIEL: Say, Rose . . . you know I was chasing hellhounds 205 and them bad mens come and get me and take me away. Troy helped me. He come down there and told them they better let me go before he beat them up. Yeah, he did!

ROSE: You go on and get you a piece of watermelon, Gabe.
Them bad mens is gone now.   210

GABRIEL: Okay, Rose . . . gonna get me some watermelon. The kind with the stripes on it.

(GABRIEL *exits into the house.*)

ROSE: Why, Troy? Why? After all these years to come dragging this in to me now. It don't make no sense at your age. I could have expected this ten or fifteen years ago, but not 215 now.

TROY: Age ain't got nothing to do with it, Rose.

ROSE: I done tried to be everything a wife should be. Everything a wife could be. Been married eighteen years and I got to live to see the day you tell me you been seeing an- 220 other woman and done fathered a child by her. And you know I ain't never wanted no half nothing in my family. My whole family is half. Everybody got different fathers and mothers . . . my two sisters and my brother. Can't hardly tell who's who. Can't never sit down and talk about 225 Papa and Mama. It's your papa and your mama and my papa and my mama . . .

TROY: Rose . . . stop it now.

ROSE: I ain't never wanted that for none of my children. And now you wanna drag your behind in here and tell me 230 something like this.

TROY: You ought to know. It's time for you to know.

ROSE: Well, I don't want to know, goddamn it!

TROY: I can't just make it go away. It's done now. I can't wish the circumstance of the thing away.   235

ROSE: And you don't want to either. Maybe you want to wish me and my boy away. Maybe that's what you want? Well, you can't wish us away. I've got eighteen years of my life invested in you. You ought to have stayed upstairs in my bed where you belong.   240

TROY: Rose . . . now listen to me . . . we can get a handle on this thing. We can talk this out . . . come to an understanding.

ROSE: All of a sudden it's "we." Where was "we" at when you was down there rolling around with some godforsaken woman? "We" should have come to an understanding be- 245 fore you started making a damn fool of yourself. You're a day late and a dollar short when it comes to an understanding with me.

TROY: It's just . . . She gives me a different idea . . . a different understanding about myself. I can step out of this house 250 and get away from the pressures and problems . . . be a different man. I ain't got to wonder how I'm gonna pay the bills or get the roof fixed. I can just be a part of myself that I ain't never been.

ROSE: What I want to know . . . is do you plan to continue 255 seeing her. That's all you can say to me.

TROY: I can sit up in her house and laugh. Do you understand what I'm saying. I can laugh out loud . . . and it feels good. It reaches all the way down to the bottom of my shoes.

(*Pause.*)

260   Rose, I can't give that up.

ROSE: Maybe you ought to go on and stay down there with her . . . if she a better woman than me.

TROY: It ain't about nobody being a better woman or nothing. Rose, you ain't the blame. A man couldn't ask for no
265   woman to be a better wife than you've been. I'm responsible for it. I done locked myself into a pattern trying to take care of you all that I forgot about myself.

ROSE: What the hell was I there for? That was my job, not somebody else's.

270 TROY: Rose, I done tried all my life to live decent . . . to live a clean . . . hard . . . useful life. I tried to be a good husband to you. In every way I knew how. Maybe I come into the world backwards, I don't know. But . . . you born with two strikes on you before you come to the plate. You got to guard it
275   closely . . . always looking for the curve-ball on the inside corner. You can't afford to let none get past you. You can't afford a call strike. If you going down . . . you going down swinging. Everything lined up against you. What you gonna do. I fooled them, Rose. I bunted. When I found you and
280   Cory and a halfway decent job . . . I was safe. Couldn't nothing touch me. I wasn't gonna strike out no more. I wasn't going back to the penitentiary. I wasn't gonna lay in the streets with a bottle of wine. I was safe. I had me a family. A job. I wasn't gonna get that last strike. I was on first looking
285   for one of them boys to knock me in. To get me home.

ROSE: You should have stayed in my bed, Troy.

TROY: Then when I saw that gal . . . she firmed up my backbone. And I got to thinking that if I tried . . . I just might be able to steal second. Do you understand after eighteen
290   years I wanted to steal second.

ROSE: You should have held me tight. You should have grabbed me and held on.

TROY: I stood on first base for eighteen years and I thought . . . well, goddamn it . . . go on for it!

295 ROSE: We're not talking about baseball! We're talking about you going off to lay in bed with another woman . . . and then bring it home to me. That's what we're talking about. We ain't talking about no baseball.

TROY: Rose, you're not listening to me. I'm trying the best I
300   can to explain it to you. It's not easy for me to admit that I been standing in the same place for eighteen years.

ROSE: I been standing with you! I been right here with you, Troy. I got a life too. I gave eighteen years of my life to stand in the same spot with you. Don't you think I ever wanted
305   other things? Don't you think I had dreams and hopes? What about my life? What about me? Don't you think it ever crossed my mind to want to know other men? That I wanted to lay up somewhere and forget about my responsibilities? That I wanted someone to make me laugh so I
310   could feel good? You not the only one who's got wants and needs. But I held on to you, Troy. I took all my feelings, my wants and needs, my dreams . . . and I buried them inside you. I planted a seed and watched and prayed over it. I planted myself inside you and waited to bloom. And it

didn't take me no eighteen years to find out the soil was   315
hard and rocky and it wasn't never gonna bloom.

       But I held on to you, Troy. I held you tighter. You was
my husband. I owed you everything I had. Every part of
me I could find to give you. And upstairs in that room . . .
with the darkness falling in on me . . . I gave everything I   320
had to try and erase the doubt that you wasn't the finest
man in the world. And wherever you was going . . . I
wanted to be there with you. Cause you was my husband.
Cause that's the only way I was gonna survive as your
wife. You always talking about what you give . . . and what   325
you don't have to give. But you take too. You take . . . and
don't even know nobody's giving!

(ROSE *turns to exit into the house;* TROY *grabs her arm.*)

TROY: You say I take and don't give!

ROSE: Troy! You're hurting me!

TROY: You say I take and don't give.   330

ROSE: Troy . . . you're hurting my arm! Let go!

TROY: I done give you everything I got. Don't you tell that lie on me.

ROSE: Troy!

TROY: Don't you tell that lie on me!   335

(CORY *enters from the house.*)

CORY: Mama!

ROSE: Troy. You're hurting me.

TROY: Don't you tell me about no taking and giving.

(CORY *comes up behind* TROY *and grabs him.* TROY, *surprised, is thrown off balance just as* CORY *throws a glancing blow that catches him on the chest and knocks him down.* TROY *is stunned, as is* CORY.)

ROSE: Troy. Troy. No!

(TROY *gets to his feet and starts at* CORY.)

       Troy . . . no. Please! Troy!   340

(ROSE *pulls on* TROY *to hold him back.* TROY *stops himself.*)

TROY: (*To* CORY.) Alright. That's strike two. You stay away from around me, boy. Don't you strike out. You living with a full count. Don't you strike out.

(TROY *exits out the yard as the lights go down.*)

SCENE II

It is six months later, early afternoon. TROY *enters from the house and starts to exit the yard.* ROSE *enters from the house.*

ROSE: Troy, I want to talk to you.

TROY: All of a sudden, after all this time, you want to talk to me, huh? You ain't wanted to talk to me for months. You ain't wanted to talk to me last night. You ain't wanted no part of me then. What you wanna talk to me about now?   5

ROSE: Tomorrow's Friday.

TROY: I know what day tomorrow is. You think I don't know tomorrow's Friday? My whole life I ain't done nothing but look to see Friday coming and you got to tell me it's Friday.

10 ROSE: I want to know if you're coming home.
   TROY: I always come home, Rose. You know that. There ain't never been a night I ain't come home.
   ROSE: That ain't what I mean . . . and you know it. I want to know if you're coming straight home after work.
15 TROY: I figure I'd cash my check . . . hang out at Taylors' with the boys . . . maybe play a game of checkers . . .
   ROSE: Troy, I can't live like this. I won't live like this. You livin' on borrowed time with me. It's been going on six months now you ain't been coming home.
20 TROY: I be here every night. Every night of the year. That's 365 days.
   ROSE: I want you to come home tomorrow after work.
   TROY: Rose . . . I don't mess up my pay. You know that now. I take my pay and I give it to you. I don't have no money
25 but what you give me back. I just want to have a little time to myself . . . a little time to enjoy life.
   ROSE: What about me? When's my time to enjoy life?
   TROY: I don't know what to tell you, Rose. I'm doing the best I can.
30 ROSE: You ain't been home from work but time enough to change your clothes and run out . . . and you wanna call that the best you can do?
   TROY: I'm going over to the hospital to see Alberta. She went into the hospital this afternoon. Look like she might have
35 the baby early. I won't be gone long.
   ROSE: Well, you ought to know. They went over to Miss Pearl's and got Gabe today. She said you told them to go ahead and lock him up.
   TROY: I ain't said no such thing. Whoever told you that is
40 telling a lie. Pearl ain't doing nothing but telling a big fat lie.
   ROSE: She ain't had to tell me. I read it on the papers.
   TROY: I ain't told them nothing of the kind.
   ROSE: I saw it right there on the papers.
   TROY: What it say, huh?
45 ROSE: It said you told them to take him.
   TROY: Then they screwed that up, just the way they screw up everything. I ain't worried about what they got on the paper.
   ROSE: Say the government send part of his check to the hos-
50 pital and the other part to you.
   TROY: I ain't got nothing to do with that if that's the way it works. I ain't made up the rules about how it work.
   ROSE: You did Gabe just like you did Cory. You wouldn't sign the paper for Cory . . . but you signed for Gabe. You
55 signed that paper.

(The telephone is heard ringing inside the house.)

   TROY: I told you I ain't signed nothing, woman! The only thing I signed was the release form. Hell, I can't read, I don't know what they had on that paper! I ain't signed nothing about sending Gabe away.
60 ROSE: I said send him to the hospital . . . you said let him be free . . . now you done went down there and signed him to the hospital for half his money. You went back on yourself, Troy. You gonna have to answer for that.
   TROY: See now . . . you been over there talking to Miss Pearl.
65 She done got mad cause she ain't getting Gabe's rent money. That's all it is. She's liable to say anything.
   ROSE: Troy, I seen where you signed the paper.

TROY: You ain't seen nothing I signed. What she doing got papers on my brother anyway? Miss Pearl telling a big fat lie. And I'm gonna tell her about it too! You ain't seen 70 nothing I signed. Say . . . you ain't seen nothing I signed.

(ROSE exits into the house to answer the telephone. Presently she returns.)

ROSE: Troy . . . that was the hospital. Alberta had the baby.
TROY: What she have? What is it?
ROSE: It's a girl.
TROY: I better get on down to the hospital to see her. 75
ROSE: Troy . . .
TROY: Rose . . . I got to go see her now. That's only right . . . what's the matter . . . the baby's alright, ain't it?
ROSE: Alberta died having the baby.
TROY: Died . . . you say she's dead? Alberta's dead? 80
ROSE: They said they done all they could. They couldn't do nothing for her.
TROY: The baby? How's the baby?
ROSE: They say it's healthy. I wonder who's gonna bury her.
TROY: She had family, Rose. She wasn't living in the world 85 by herself.
ROSE: I know she wasn't living in the world by herself.
TROY: Next thing you gonna want to know if she had any insurance.
ROSE: Troy, you ain't got to talk like that. 90
TROY: That's the first thing that jumped out your mouth. "Who's gonna bury her?" Like I'm fixing to take on that task for myself.
ROSE: I am your wife. Don't push me away.
TROY: I ain't pushing nobody away. Just give me some space. 95 That's all. Just give me some room to breathe.

(ROSE exits into the house. TROY walks about the yard.)

TROY: *(With a quiet rage that threatens to consume him.)* Alright . . . Mr. Death. See now . . . I'm gonna tell you what I'm gonna do. I'm gonna take and build me a fence around this yard. See? I'm gonna build me a fence around what belongs 100 to me. And then I want you to stay on the other side. See? You stay over there until you're ready for me. Then you come on. Bring your army. Bring your sickle. Bring your wrestling clothes. I ain't gonna fall down on my vigilance this time. You ain't gonna sneak up on me no more. When 105 you ready for me . . . when the top of your list say Troy Maxson . . . that's when you come around here. You come up and knock on the front door. Ain't nobody else got nothing to do with this. This is between you and me. Man to man. You stay on the other side of that fence until you 110 ready for me. Then you come up and knock on the front door. Anytime you want. I'll be ready for you.

(The lights go down to black.)

SCENE III

The lights come up on the porch. It is late evening three days later. ROSE sits listening to the ball game waiting for TROY. The final out of the game is made and ROSE switches off the radio. troy enters the yard carrying an infant wrapped in blankets. He stands back from the house and calls.

ROSE *enters and stands on the porch. There is a long, awkward silence, the weight of which grows heavier with each passing second.*

TROY: Rose . . . I'm standing here with my daughter in my arms. She ain't but a wee bittie little old thing. She don't know nothing about grownups' business. She innocent . . . and she ain't got no mama.

5 ROSE: What you telling me for, Troy?

(She turns and exits into the house.)

TROY: Well . . . I guess we'll just sit out here on the porch.

(He sits down on the porch. There is an awkward indelicateness about the way he handles the baby. His largeness engulfs and seems to swallow it. He speaks loud enough for ROSE to hear.)

A man's got to do what's right for him. I ain't sorry for nothing I done. It felt right in my heart.

(To the baby.)

What you smiling at? Your daddy's a big man. Got these
10 great big old hands. But sometimes he's scared. And right now your daddy's scared cause we sitting out here and ain't got no home. Oh, I been homeless before. I ain't had no little baby with me. But I been homeless. You just be out on the road by your lonesome and you see one of
15 them trains coming and you just kinda go like this . . .

(He sings as a lullaby.)

Please, Mr. Engineer let a man ride the line
Please, Mr. Engineer let a man ride the line
I ain't got no ticket please let me ride the blinds

(ROSE enters from the house. TROY hearing her steps behind him, stands and faces her.)

She's my daughter, Rose. My own flesh and blood. I can't
20 deny her no more than I can deny them boys.

(Pause.)

You and them boys is my family. You and them and this child is all I got in the world. So I guess what I'm saying is . . . I'd appreciate it if you'd help take care of her.

ROSE: Okay, Troy . . . you're right. I'll take care of your baby
25 for you . . . cause . . . like you say . . . she's innocent . . . and you can't visit the sins of the father upon the child. A motherless child has got a hard time.

(She takes the baby from him.)

From right now . . . this child got a mother. But you a womanless man.

(ROSE turns and exits into the house with the baby. Lights go down to black.)

SCENE IV

It is two months later. LYONS *enters from the street. He knocks on the door and calls.*

LYONS: Hey, Rose! *(Pause.)* Rose!

ROSE: *(From inside the house.)* Stop that yelling. You gonna wake up Raynell. I just got her to sleep.

LYONS: I just stopped by to pay Papa this twenty dollars I owe him. Where's Papa at?   5

ROSE: He should be here in a minute. I'm getting ready to go down to the church. Sit down and wait on him.

LYONS: I got to go pick up Bonnie over her mother's house.

ROSE: Well, sit it down there on the table. He'll get it.

LYONS: *(Enters the house and sets the money on the table.)* Tell 10 Papa I said thanks. I'll see you again.

ROSE: Alright, Lyons. We'll see you.

(LYONS starts to exit as CORY enters.)

CORY: Hey, Lyons.

LYONS: What's happening, Cory. Say man, I'm sorry I missed your graduation. You know I had a gig and couldn't get 15 away. Otherwise, I would have been there, man. So what you doing?

CORY: I'm trying to find a job.

LYONS: Yeah I know how that go, man. It's rough out here. Jobs are scarce.   20

CORY: Yeah, I know.

LYONS: Look here, I got to run. Talk to Papa . . . he know some people. He'll be able to help get you a job. Talk to him . . . see what he say.

CORY: Yeah . . . alright, Lyons.   25

LYONS: You take care. I'll talk to you soon. We'll find some time to talk.

(LYONS exits the yard. CORY wanders over to the tree, picks up the bat and assumes a batting stance. He studies an imaginary pitcher and swings. Dissatisfied with the result, he tries again. TROY enters. They eye each other for a beat. CORY puts the bat down and exits the yard. TROY starts into the house as ROSE exits with RAYNELL. She is carrying a cake.)

TROY: I'm coming in and everybody's going out.

ROSE: I'm taking this cake down to the church for the bake-sale. Lyons was by to see you. He stopped by to pay you 30 your twenty dollars. It's laying in there on the table.

TROY: *(Going into his pocket.)* Well . . . here go this money.

ROSE: Put it in there on the table, Troy. I'll get it.

TROY: What time you coming back?

ROSE: Ain't no use in you studying me. It don't matter what 35 time I come back.

TROY: I just asked you a question, woman. What's the matter . . . can't I ask you a question?

ROSE: Troy, I don't want to go into it. Your dinner's in there on the stove. All you got to do is heat it up. And don't you 40 be eating the rest of them cakes in there. I'm coming back for them. We having a bakesale at the church tomorrow.

(ROSE exits the yard. TROY sits down on the steps, takes a pint bottle from his pocket, opens it and drinks. He begins to sing.)

TROY: Hear it ring! Hear it ring!
Had an old dog his name was Blue
You know Blue was mighty true   45
You know Blue as a good old dog
Blue trees a possum in a hollow log
You know from that he was a good old dog.

(BONO *enters the yard.*)

BONO: Hey, Troy.

50 TROY: Hey, what's happening, Bono?

BONO: I just thought I'd stop by to see you.

TROY: What you stop by and see me for? You ain't stopped by in a month of Sundays. Hell, I must owe you money or something.

55 BONO: Since you got your promotion I can't keep up with you. Used to see you everyday. Now I don't even know what route you working.

TROY: They keep switching me around. Got me out in Green-tree now . . . hauling white folks' garbage.

60 BONO: Greentree, huh? You lucky, at least you ain't got to be lifting them barrels. Damn if they ain't getting heavier. I'm gonna put in my two years and call it quits.

TROY: I'm thinking about retiring myself.

BONO: You got it easy. You can *drive* for another five years.

65 TROY: It ain't the same, Bono. It ain't like working the back of the truck. Ain't got nobody to talk to . . . feel like you working by yourself. Naw, I'm thinking about retiring. How's Lucille?

BONO: She alright. Her arthritis get to acting up on her
70 sometime. Saw Rose on my way in. She going down to the church, huh?

TROY: Yeah, she took up going down there. All them preachers looking for somebody to fatten their pockets.

(*Pause.*)

Got some gin here.

75 BONO: Naw, thanks. I just stopped by to say hello.

TROY: Hell, nigger . . . you can take a drink. I ain't never known you to say no to a drink. You ain't got to work tomorrow.

BONO: I just stopped by. I'm fixing to go over to Skinner's.
80 We got us a domino game going over his house every Friday.

TROY: Nigger, you can't play no dominoes. I used to whup you four games out of five.

BONO: Well, that learned me. I'm getting better.

85 TROY: Yeah? Well, that's alright.

BONO: Look here . . . I got to be getting on. Stop by sometime, huh?

TROY: Yeah, I'll do that, Bono. Lucille told Rose you bought her a new refrigerator.

90 BONO: Yeah, Rose told Lucille you had finally built your fence . . . so I figured we'd call it even.

TROY: I knew you would.

BONO: Yeah . . . okay. I'll be talking to you.

TROY: Yeah, take care, Bono. Good to see you. I'm gonna stop
95 over.

BONO: Yeah. Okay, Troy.

(BONO *exits.* TROY *drinks from the bottle.*)

TROY: Old Blue died and I dig his grave
       Let him down with a golden chain
       Every night when I hear old Blue bark
100   I know Blue treed a possum in Noah's Ark.
       Hear it ring! Hear it ring!

(CORY *enters the yard. They eye each other for a beat.* TROY *is sitting in the middle of the steps.* CORY *walks over.*)

CORY: I got to get by.

TROY: Say what? What's you say?

CORY: You in my way. I got to get by.

105 TROY: You got to get by where? This is my house. Bought and paid for. In full. Took me fifteen years. And if you wanna go in my house and I'm sitting on the steps . . . you say excuse me. Like your mama taught you.

CORY: Come on, Pop . . . I got to get by.

(CORY *starts to maneuver his way past* TROY. TROY *grabs his leg and shoves him back.*)

TROY: You just gonna walk over top of me?   110

CORY: I live here too!

TROY: (*Advancing toward him.*) You just gonna walk over top of me in my own house?

CORY: I ain't scared of you.

TROY: I ain't asked if you was scared of me. I asked you if you   115
was fixing to walk over top of me in my own house? That's the question. You ain't gonna say excuse me? You just gonna walk over top of me?

CORY: If you wanna put it like that.

TROY: How else am I gonna put it?   120

CORY: I was walking by you to go into the house cause you sitting on the steps drunk, singing to yourself. You can put it like that.

TROY: Without saying excuse me???

(CORY *doesn't respond.*)

I asked you a question. Without saying excuse me???   125

CORY: I ain't got to say excuse me to you. You don't count around here no more.

TROY: Oh, I see . . . I don't count around here no more. You ain't got to say excuse me to your daddy. All of a sudden you done got so grown that your daddy don't count   130
around here no more . . . Around here in his own house and yard that he done paid for with the sweat of his brow. You done got so grown to where you gonna take over. You gonna take over my house. Is that right? You gonna wear my pants. You gonna go in there and stretch out on   135
my bed. You ain't got to say excuse me cause I don't count around here no more. Is that right?

CORY: That's right. You always talking this dumb stuff. Now, why don't you just get out my way.

TROY: I guess you got someplace to sleep and something to   140
put in your belly. You got that, huh? You got that? That's what you need. You got that, huh?

CORY: You don't know what I got. You ain't got to worry about what I got.

TROY: You right! You one hundred percent right! I done   145
spent the last seventeen years worrying about what you got. Now it's your turn, see? I'll tell you what to do. You grown . . . we done established that. You a man. Now, let's see you act like one. Turn your behind around and walk out this yard. And when you get out there in the alley . . . 150
you can forget about this house. See? Cause this is my house. You go on and be a man and get your own house. You can forget about this. Cause this is mine. You go on and get yours cause I'm through with doing for you.

CORY: You talking about what you did for me . . . what'd you   155
ever give me?

TROY: Them feet and bones! That pumping heart, nigger! I give you more than anybody else is ever gonna give you.

CORY: You ain't never gave me nothing! You ain't never done
160 nothing but hold me back. Afraid I was gonna be better than you. All you ever did was try and make me scared of you. I used to tremble every time you called my name. Every time I heard your footsteps in the house. Wondering all the time . . . what's Papa gonna say if I do this? . . .
165 What's he gonna say if I do that? . . . What's Papa gonna say if I turn on the radio? And Mama, too . . . she tries . . . but she's scared of you.

TROY: You leave your mama out of this. She ain't got nothing to do with this.

170 CORY: I don't know how she stand you . . . after what you did to her.

TROY: I told you to leave your mama out of this!

(He advances toward CORY.*)*

CORY: What you gonna do . . . give me a whupping? You can't whup me no more. You're too old. You just an old man.

175 TROY: *(Shoves him on his shoulder.)* Nigger! That's what you are. You just another nigger on the street to me!

CORY: You crazy! You know that?

TROY: Go on now! You got the devil in you. Get on away from me!

180 CORY: You just a crazy old man . . . talking about I got the devil in me.

TROY: Yeah, I'm crazy! If you don't get on the other side of that yard . . . I'm gonna show you how crazy I am! Go on . . . get the hell out of my yard!

185 CORY: It ain't your yard. You took Uncle Gabe's money he got from the army to buy this house and then you put him out.

TROY: *(TROY advances on* CORY.*)* Get your black ass out of my yard!

(TROY's advance backs CORY *up against the tree.* CORY *grabs up the bat.)*

CORY: I ain't going nowhere! Come on . . . put me out! I ain't
190 scared of you.

TROY: That's my bat!

CORY: Come on!

TROY: Put my bat down!

CORY: Come on, put me out.

(CORY swings at TROY, *who backs across the yard.)*

195 What's the matter? You so bad . . . put me out!

(TROY advances toward CORY.*)*

CORY: *(Backing up.)* Come on! Come on!

TROY: You're gonna have to use it! You wanna draw that bat back on me . . . you're gonna have to use it.

CORY: Come on! . . . Come on!

(CORY swings the bat at TROY *a second time. He misses.* TROY *continues to advance toward him.)*

200 TROY: You're gonna have to kill me! You wanna draw that bat back on me. You're gonna have to kill me.

(CORY, backed up against the tree, can go no farther. TROY *taunts him. He sticks out his head and offers him a target.)*

Come on! Come on!

(CORY is unable to swing the bat. TROY *grabs it.)*

TROY: Then I'll show you.

(CORY and TROY *struggle over the bat. The struggle is fierce and fully engaged.* TROY *ultimately is the stronger, and takes the bat from* CORY *and stands over him ready to swing. He stops himself.)*

Go on and get away from around my house.

(CORY, stung by his defeat, picks himself up, walks slowly out of the yard and up the alley.)

CORY: Tell Mama I'll be back for my things.   205
TROY: They'll be on the other side of that fence.

(CORY exits.)

TROY: I can't taste nothing. Helluljah! I can't taste nothing no more. *(TROY assumes a batting posture and begins to taunt Death, the fastball in the outside corner.)* Come on! It's between you and me now! Come on! Anytime you want!   210
Come on! I be ready for you . . . but I ain't gonna be easy.

(The lights go down on the scene.)

SCENE V

The time is 1965. The lights come up in the yard. It is the morning of TROY's *funeral. A funeral plaque with a light hangs beside the door. There is a small garden plot off to the side. There is noise and activity in the house as* ROSE, LYONS *and* BONO *have gathered. The door opens and* RAYNELL, *seven years old, enters dressed in a flannel nightgown. She crosses to the garden and pokes around with a stick.* ROSE *calls from the house.*

ROSE: Raynell!
RAYNELL: Mam?
ROSE: What you doing out there?
RAYNELL: Nothing.

(ROSE comes to the door.)

ROSE: Girl, get in here and get dressed. What you doing?   5
RAYNELL: Seeing if my garden growed.
ROSE: I told you it ain't gonna grow overnight. You got to wait.
RAYNELL: It don't look like it never gonna grow. Dag!
ROSE: I told you a watched pot never boils. Get in here and get dressed.   10
RAYNELL: This ain't even no pot, Mama.
ROSE: You just have to give it a chance. It'll grow. Now you come on and do what I told you. We got to be getting ready. This ain't no morning to be playing around. You hear me?
RAYNELL: Yes, mam.   15

(ROSE exits into the house. RAYNELL *continues to poke at her garden with a stick.* CORY *enters. He is dressed in a Marine corporal's uniform, and carries a duffel bag. His posture is that of a military man, and his speech has a clipped sternness.)*

CORY: (*To* RAYNELL.) Hi.

(*Pause.*)

I bet your name is Raynell.

RAYNELL: Uh huh.

CORY: Is your mama home?

(RAYNELL *runs up on the porch and calls through the screen door.*)

20 RAYNELL: Mama . . . there's some man out here. Mama?

(ROSE *comes to the door.*)

ROSE: Cory? Lord have mercy! Look here, you all!

(ROSE *and* CORY *embrace in a tearful reunion as* BONO *and* LYONS *enter from the house dressed in funeral clothes.*)

BONO: Aw, looka here . . .

ROSE: Done got all grown up!

CORY: Don't cry, Mama. What you crying about?

25 ROSE: I'm just so glad you made it.

CORY: Hey Lyons. How you doing, Mr. Bono.

(LYONS *goes to embrace* CORY.)

LYONS: Look at you, man. Look at you. Don't he look good,
Rose. Got them Corporal stripes.

ROSE: What took you so long.

30 CORY: You know how the Marines are, Mama. They got to
get all their paperwork straight before they let you do
anything.

ROSE: Well, I'm sure glad you made it. They let Lyons come.
Your Uncle Gabe's still in the hospital. They don't know
35 if they gonna let him out or not. I just talked to them a
little while ago.

LYONS: A Corporal in the United States Marines.

BONO: Your daddy knew you had it in you. He used to tell
me all the time.

40 LYONS: Don't he look good, Mr. Bono?

BONO: Yeah, he remind me of Troy when I first met him.

(*Pause.*)

Say, Rose, Lucille's down at the church with the choir. I'm
gonna go down and get the pallbearers lined up. I'll be
back to get you all.

45 ROSE: Thanks, Jim.

CORY: See you, Mr. Bono.

LYONS: (*With his arm around* RAYNELL.) Cory . . . look at
Raynell. Ain't she precious? She gonna break a whole lot
of hearts.

50 ROSE: Raynell, come and say hello to your brother. This is
your brother, Cory. You remember Cory.

RAYNELL: No, Mam.

CORY: She don't remember me, Mama.

ROSE: Well, we talk about you. She heard us talk about you.
55 (*To* RAYNELL.) This is your brother, Cory. Come on and
say hello.

RAYNELL: Hi.

CORY: Hi. So you're Raynell. Mama told me a lot about you.

ROSE: You all come on into the house and let me fix you
60 some breakfast. Keep up your strength.

CORY: I ain't hungry, Mama.

LYONS: You can fix me something, Rose. I'll be in there in a
minute.

ROSE: Cory, you sure you don't want nothing. I know they
ain't feeding you right.   65

CORY: No, Mama . . . thanks. I don't feel like eating. I'll get
something later.

ROSE: Raynell . . . get on upstairs and get that dress on like I
told you.

(ROSE *and* RAYNELL *exit into the house.*)

LYONS: So . . . I hear you thinking about getting married.   70

CORY: Yeah, I done found the right one, Lyons. It's about time.

LYONS: Me and Bonnie been split up about four years now.
About the time Papa retired. I guess she just got tired of
all them changes I was putting her through.

(*Pause.*)

I always knew you was gonna make something out your-   75
self. Your head was always in the right direction. So . . .
you gonna stay in . . . make it a career . . . put in your
twenty years?

CORY: I don't know. I got six already, I think that's enough.

LYONS: Stick with Uncle Sam and retire early. Ain't nothing   80
out here. I guess Rose told you what happened with me.
They got me down the workhouse. I thought I was being
slick cashing other people's checks.

CORY: How much time you doing?

LYONS: They give me three years. I got that beat now. I ain't 85
got but nine more months. It ain't so bad. You learn to
deal with it like anything else. You got to take the
crookeds with the straights. That's what Papa used to say.
He used to say that when he struck out. I seen him strike
out three times in a row . . . and the next time up he hit   90
the ball over the grandstand. Right out there in Home-
stead Field. He wasn't satisfied hitting in the seats . . . he
want to hit it over everything! After the game he had two
hundred people standing around waiting to shake his
hand. You got to take the crookeds with the straights.   95
Yeah, papa was something else.

CORY: You still playing?

LYONS: Cory . . . you know I'm gonna do that. There's some
fellows down there we got us a band . . . we gonna try and
stay together when we get out . . . but yeah, I'm still play- 100
ing. It still helps me to get out of bed in the morning. As
long as it do that I'm gonna be right there playing and
trying to make some sense out of it.

ROSE: (*Calling.*) Lyons, I got these eggs in the pan.

LYONS: Let me go on and get these eggs, man. Get ready to   105
go bury Papa.

(*Pause.*)

How you doing? You doing alright?

(CORY *nods.* LYONS *touches him on the shoulder and they share a
moment of silent grief.* LYONS *exits into the house.* CORY *wanders
about the yard.* RAYNELL *enters.*)

RAYNELL: Hi.

CORY: Hi.

RAYNELL: Did you used to sleep in my room?

CORY: Yeah . . . that used to be my room.

RAYNELL: That's what Papa call it. "Cory's room." It got your football in the closet.

(ROSE *comes to the door.*)

ROSE: Raynell, get in there and get them good shoes on.

RAYNELL: Mama, can't I wear these. Them other ones hurt my feet.

ROSE: Well, they just gonna have to hurt your feet for a while. You ain't said they hurt your feet when you went down to the store and got them.

RAYNELL: They didn't hurt then. My feet done got bigger.

ROSE: Don't you give me no backtalk now. You get in there and get them shoes on.

(RAYNELL *exits into the house.*)

Ain't too much changed. He still got that piece of rag tied to that tree. He was out here swinging that bat. I was just ready to go back in the house. He swung that bat and then he just fell over. Seem like he swung it and stood there with this grin on his face . . . and then he just fell over. They carried him on down to the hospital, but I knew there wasn't no need . . . why don't you come on in the house?

CORY: Mama . . . I got something to tell you. I don't know how to tell you this . . . but I've got to tell you . . . I'm not going to Papa's funeral.

ROSE: Boy, hush your mouth. That's your daddy you talking about. I don't want hear that kind of talk this morning. I done raised you to come to this? You standing there all healthy and grown talking about you ain't going to your daddy's funeral.

CORY: Mama . . . listen . . .

ROSE: I don't want to hear it, Cory. You just get that thought out of your head.

CORY: I can't drag Papa with me everywhere I go. I've got to say no to him. One time in my life I've got to say no.

ROSE: Don't nobody have to listen to nothing like that. I know you and your daddy ain't seen eye to eye, but I ain't got to listen to that kind of talk this morning. Whatever was between you and your daddy . . . the time has come to put it aside. Just take it and set it over there on the shelf and forget about it. Disrespecting your daddy ain't gonna make you a man, Cory. You got to find a way to come to that on your own. Not going to your daddy's funeral ain't gonna make you a man.

CORY: The whole time I was growing up . . . living in his house . . . Papa was like a shadow that followed you everywhere. It weighed on you and sunk into your flesh. It would wrap around you and lay there until you couldn't tell which one was you anymore. That shadow digging in your flesh. Trying to crawl in. Trying to live through you. Everywhere I looked, Troy Maxson was staring back at me . . . hiding under the bed . . . in the closet. I'm just saying I've got to find a way to get rid of that shadow, Mama.

ROSE: You just like him. You got him in you good.

CORY: Don't tell me that, Mama.

ROSE: You Troy Maxson all over again.

CORY: I don't want to be Troy Maxson. I want to be me.

ROSE: You can't be nobody but who you are, Cory. That shadow wasn't nothing but you growing into yourself. You either got to grow into it or cut it down to fit you. But that's all you got to make life with. That's all you got to measure yourself against that world out there. Your daddy wanted you to be everything he wasn't . . . and at the same time he tried to make you into everything he was. I don't know if he was right or wrong . . . but I do know he meant to do more· good than he meant to do harm. He wasn't always right. Sometimes when he touched he bruised. And sometimes when he took me in his arms he cut.

When I first met your daddy I thought . . . Here is a man I can lay down with and make a baby. That's the first thing I thought when I seen him. I was thirty years old and had done seen my share of men. But when he walked up to me and said, "I can dance a waltz that'll make you dizzy," I thought, Rose Lee, here is a man that you can open yourself up to and be filled to bursting. Here is a man that can fill all them empty spaces you been tipping around the edges of. One of them empty spaces was being somebody's mother.

I married your daddy and settled down to cooking his supper and keeping clean sheets on the bed. When your daddy walked through the house he was so big he filled it up. That was my first mistake. Not to make him leave some room for me. For my part in the matter. But at that time I wanted that. I wanted a house that I could sing in. And that's what your daddy gave me. I didn't know to keep up his strength I had to give up little pieces of mine. I did that. I took on his life as mine and mixed up the pieces so that you couldn't hardly tell which was which anymore. It was my choice. It was my life and I didn't have to live it like that. But that's what life offered me in the way of being a woman and I took it. I grabbed hold of it with both hands.

By the time Raynell came into the house, me and your daddy had done lost touch with one another. I didn't want to make my blessing off of nobody's misfortune . . . but I took on to Raynell like she was all them babies I had wanted and never had.

(*The phone rings.*)

Like I'd been blessed to relive a part of my life. And if the Lord see fit to keep up my strength . . . I'm gonna do her just like your daddy did you . . . I'm gonna give her the best of what's in me.

RAYNELL: (*Entering, still with her old shoes.*) Mama . . . Reverend Tollivier on the phone.

(ROSE *exits into the house.*)

RAYNELL: Hi.

CORY: Hi.

RAYNELL: You in the Army or the Marines?

CORY: Marines.

RAYNELL: Papa said it was the Army. Did you know Blue?

CORY: Blue? Who's Blue?

RAYNELL: Papa's dog what he sing about all the time.

CORY: (*Singing.*)

220   Hear it ring! Hear it ring!
       I had a dog his name was Blue
       You know Blue was mighty true
       You know Blue was a good old dog
       Blue treed a possum in a hollow log
225   You know from that he was a good old dog.
       Hear it ring! Hear it ring!

(RAYNELL *joins in singing.*)

CORY and RAYNELL: Blue treed a possum out on a limb
       Blue looked at me and I looked at him
       Grabbed that possum and put him in a sack
230   Blue stayed there till I came back
       Old Blue's feets was big and round
       Never allowed a possum to touch the ground.
       Old Blue died and I dug his grave
       I dug his grave with a silver spade
235   Let him down with a golden chain
       And every night I call his name
       Go on Blue, you good dog you
       Go on Blue, you good dog you
RAYNELL: Blue laid down and died like a man
240   Blue laid down and died . . .
BOTH: Blue laid down and died like a man
       Now he's treeing possums in the Promised Land
       I'm gonna tell you this to let you know
       Blue's gone where the good dogs go
245   When I hear old Blue bark
       When I hear old Blue bark
       Blue treed a possum in Noah's Ark
       Blue treed a possum in Noah's Ark.

(ROSE *comes to the screen door.*)

ROSE: Cory, we gonna be ready to go in a minute.
250 CORY: (*To* RAYNELL.) You go on in the house and change
       them shoes like Mama told you so we can go to Papa's
       funeral.

RAYNELL: Okay, I'll be back.

(RAYNELL *exits into the house.* CORY *gets up and crosses over to the tree.* ROSE *stands in the screen door watching him.* GABRIEL *enters from the alley.*)

GABRIEL: (*Calling.*) Hey, Rose!
ROSE: Gabe?   255
GABRIEL: I'm here, Rose. Hey Rose, I'm here!

(ROSE *enters from the house.*)

ROSE: Lord . . . Look here, Lyons!
LYONS: See, I told you, Rose . . . I told you they'd let him
       come.
CORY: How you doing, Uncle Gabe?   260
LYONS: How you doing, Uncle Gabe?
GABRIEL: Hey, Rose. It's time. It's time to tell St. Peter to open
       the gates. Troy, you ready? You ready, Troy. I'm gonna tell
       St. Peter to open the gates. You get ready now.

(GABRIEL, *with great fanfare, braces himself to blow. The trumpet is without a mouthpiece. He puts the end of it into his mouth and blows with great force, like a man who has been waiting some* 265 *twenty-odd years for this single moment. No sound comes out of the trumpet. He braces himself and blows again with the same result. A third time he blows. There is a weight of impossible description that falls away and leaves him bare and exposed to a frightful realization. It is a trauma that a sane and normal mind would be unable to withstand. He begins to dance. A slow, strange dance, eerie and lifegiving. A dance of atavistic signature and ritual.* LYONS *attempts to embrace him.* GABRIEL *pushes* LYONS *away. He begins to howl in what is an attempt at song, or perhaps a song turning back into itself in an attempt at speech. He finishes his dance and the gates of heaven stand open as wide as God's closet.*)

       That's the way that go!

(*Blackout.*)

David Henry Hwang

David Henry Hwang was born in Los Angeles in 1957. He graduated with a B.A. in English from Stanford University in 1979 and studied at the Yale School of Drama 1980–1981. In the 1980s, Hwang wrote a series of powerful plays concerning the cultural and political experience of Asian Americans in the United States. His first play, *F.O.B.* ("fresh off the boat"), dramatizes the tensions that arise between Chinese immigrants to the United States and their assimilated friends and relatives. The play won an Obie award in 1980. Hwang addressed similar issues in *The Dance of the Railroad* (1981) and in *Rich Relations* (1986), and he collaborated with composer Philip Glass on *1000 Airplanes on the Roof* (1988). Hwang's Tony Award–winning *M. Butterfly* (1988) is a brilliant critique of Western attitudes toward Asia, epitomized by one of Western culture's most powerful and seductive images of the Orient: Giacomo Puccini's opera, *Madame Butterfly*. His recent plays include *Trying to Find Chinatown* (1996) and *Bondage* (1996); he has also written the book for a revival of Rodgers and Hammerstein's musical, *Flower Drum Song* (2001).

M. BUTTERFLY   In *M. Butterfly,* Hwang traces the relationship between the "Orient" of the Western imagination and the political realities that such images help to foster. The play's central character, the diplomat Gallimard, conducts his relationship with China in terms of Puccini's *Madame Butterfly*. In Puccini's 1904 opera, based on the 1900 play by David Belasco, the

John Lithgow as Gallimard and B.D. Wong as Song Liling in the 1988 Broadway production of David Henry Hwang's *M. Butterfly*.

naval officer Pinkerton marries the Japanese geisha girl Butterfly. He leaves for the United States, promising to return, and Butterfly waits for him, meanwhile bearing his child. When Pinkerton returns with his wife from America to collect his child, Butterfly realizes that he will never return to her. She commits suicide.

As Hwang has remarked, Butterfly has become a cultural stereotype of East-West relations—"speaking of an Asian woman, we would sometimes say, 'She's pulling a Butterfly,' which meant playing the submissive Oriental number." This sexist and racist stereotype, Hwang argues, pervades not only Western men's fantasies about Asian women—as the mail-order business in Asian wives suggests, Western men see Asian women as obedient, submissive, and sexually self-sacrificing—but also conditions the political relationship between Asia and the West as well.

M. Butterfly fuses this erotic and political desire for domination in the character of Gallimard, a French diplomat who falls in love with Song Liling, an opera singer whom he first sees singing the death aria from *Madame Butterfly*. However, the play develops a fascinating twist, for Song is in fact a man, who plays female roles in the Beijing Opera, and who—as a woman—develops a love affair with Gallimard in order to spy for the Chinese government. *M. Butterfly* compacts a complex reading of the politics of race, gender, and sexuality in a brilliantly theatrical drama.

M. BUTTERFLY

David Henry Hwang

CHARACTERS

KUROGO
RENE GALLIMARD
SONG LILING
MARC
MAN 2
CONSUL SHARPLESS
RENEE
WOMAN AT PARTY
PINUP GIRL
COMRADE CHIN

SUZUKI
SHU-FANG
HELGA
M. TOULON
MAN 1
JUDGE

The action of the play takes place in a Paris prison in the present, and in recall, during the decade 1960 to 1970 in Beijing, and from 1966 to the present in Paris.

ACT ONE

SCENE I

M. GALLIMARD*'s prison cell. Paris. Present.*

Lights fade up to reveal RENE GALLIMARD, *65, in a prison cell. He wears a comfortable bathrobe, and looks old and tired. The sparsely furnished cell contains a wooden crate upon which sits a hot plate with a kettle, and a portable tape recorder.* GALLIMARD *sits on the crate staring at the recorder, a sad smile on his face.*

Upstage SONG, *who appears as a beautiful woman in traditional Chinese garb, dances a traditional piece from the Peking Opera, surrounded by the percussive clatter of Chinese music.*

Then, slowly, lights and sound cross-fade; the Chinese opera music dissolves into a Western opera, the "Love Duet" from Puccini's Madame Butterfly. SONG *continues dancing, now to the Western accompaniment. Though her movements are the same, the difference in music now gives them a balletic quality.*

GALLIMARD *rises, and turns upstage towards the figure of* SONG, *who dances without acknowledging him.*

GALLIMARD: Butterfly, Butterfly . . .

(He forces himself to turn away, as the image of SONG *fades out, and talks to us.)*

GALLIMARD: The limits of my cell are as such: four-and-a-half meters by five. There's one window against the far wall; a door, very strong, to protect me from autograph hounds.
5 I'm responsible for the tape recorder, the hot plate, and this charming coffee table.
     When I want to eat, I'm marched off to the dining room—hot, steaming slop appears on my plate. When I want to sleep, the light bulb turns itself off—the work of
10 fairies. It's an enchanted space I occupy. The French—we know how to run a prison.
     But, to be honest, I'm not treated like an ordinary prisoner. Why? Because I'm a celebrity. You see, I make people laugh.
15 I never dreamed this day would arrive. I've never been considered witty or clever. In fact, as a young boy, in an informal poll among my grammar school classmates, I was

voted "least likely to be invited to a party." It's a title I managed to hold onto for many years. Despite some stiff competition.   20
     But now, how the tables turn! Look at me: the life of every social function in Paris. Paris? Why be modest? My fame has spread to Amsterdam, London, New York. Listen to them! In the world's smartest parlors. I'm the one who lifts their spirits!   25

(With a flourish, GALLIMARD *directs our attention to another part of the stage.)*

SCENE II

A party. Present.

Lights go up on a chic-looking parlor, where a well-dressed trio, two men and one woman, make conversation. GALLIMARD *also remains lit; he observes them from his cell.*

WOMAN: And what of Gallimard?
MAN 1: Gallimard?
MAN 2: Gallimard!
GALLIMARD: *(To us.)* You see? They're all determined to say my name, as if it were some new dance.   5
WOMAN: He still claims not to believe the truth.
MAN 1: What? Still? Even since the trial?
WOMAN: Yes. Isn't it mad?
MAN 2: *(Laughing.)* He says . . . it was dark . . . and she was very modest!   10

(The trio break into laughter.)

MAN 1: So—what? He never touched her with his hands?
MAN 2: Perhaps he did, and simply misidentified the equipment. A compelling case for sex education in the schools.
WOMAN: To protect the National Security—the Church can't argue with that.   15
MAN 1: That's impossible! How could he not know?
MAN 2: Simple ignorance.
MAN 1: For twenty years?
MAN 2: Time flies when you're being stupid.
WOMAN: Well, I thought the French were ladies' men.   20
MAN 2: It seems Monsieur Gallimard was overly anxious to live up to his national reputation.

WOMAN: Well, he's not very good-looking.

MAN 1: No, he's not.

25 MAN 2: Certainly not.

WOMAN: Actually, I feel sorry for him.

MAN 2: A toast! To Monsieur Gallimard!

WOMAN: Yes! To Gallimard!

MAN 1: To Gallimard!

30 MAN 2: Vive la différence!

(*They toast, laughing. Lights down on them.*)

SCENE III

M. GALLIMARD's *cell*.

GALLIMARD: (*Smiling.*) You see? They toast me. I've become patron saint of the socially inept. Can they really be so foolish? Men like that—they should be scratching at my door, begging to learn my secrets! For I, Rene Gallimard, you see, I

5 have known, and been loved by ... the Perfect Woman.

Alone in this cell, I sit night after night, watching our story play through my head, always searching for a new ending, one which redeems my honor, where she returns at last to my arms. And I imagine you—my ideal audience—who come

10 to understand and even, perhaps just a little, to envy me.

(*He turns on his tape recorder. Over the house speakers, we hear the opening phrases of* Madame Butterfly.)

GALLIMARD: In order for you to understand what I did and why, I must introduce you to my favorite opera: *Madame Butterfly*. By Giacomo Puccini. First produced at La Scala, Milan, in 1904, it is now beloved throughout the Western world.

(*As* GALLIMARD *describes the opera, the tape segues in and out to sections he may be describing.*)

15 GALLIMARD: And why not? Its heroine, Cio-Cio-San, also known as Butterfly, is a feminine ideal, beautiful and brave. And its hero, the man for whom she gives up everything, is—(*He pulls out a naval officer's cap from under his crate, pops it on his head, and struts about.*)—not very good-

20 looking, not too bright, and pretty much a wimp: Benjamin Franklin Pinkerton of the U.S. Navy. As the curtain rises, he's just closed on two great bargains: one on a house, the other on a woman—call it a package deal.

Pinkerton purchased the rights to Butterfly for one

25 hundred yen—in modern currency, equivalent to about . . . sixty-six cents. So, he's feeling pretty pleased with himself as Sharpless, the American consul, arrives to witness the marriage.

(MARC, *wearing an official cap to designate* SHARPLESS, *enters and plays the character.*)

SHARPLESS/MARC: Pinkerton!

30 PINKERTON/GALLIMARD: Sharpless! How's it hangin'? It's a great day, just great. Between my house, my wife, and the rickshaw ride in from town, I've saved nineteen cents just this morning.

SHARPLESS: Wonderful. I can see the inscription on your

35 tombstone already: "I saved a dollar, here I lie." (*He looks around.*) Nice house.

PINKERTON: It's artistic. Artistic, don't you think? Like the way the shoji screens slide open to reveal the wet bar and disco mirror ball? Classy, huh? Great for impressing the chicks.

SHARPLESS: "Chicks"? Pinkerton, you're going to be a mar- 40 ried man!

PINKERTON: Well, sort of.

SHARPLESS: What do you mean?

PINKERTON: This country—Sharpless, it is okay. You got all these geisha girls running around— 45

SHARPLESS: I know! I live here!

PINKERTON: Then, you know the marriage laws, right? I split for one month, it's annulled!

SHARPLESS: Leave it to you to read the fine print. Who's the lucky girl? 50

PINKERTON: Cio-Cio-San. Her friends call her Butterfly. Sharpless, she eats out of my hand!

SHARPLESS: She's probably very hungry.

PINKERTON: Not like American girls. It's true what they say about Oriental girls. They want to be treated bad! 55

SHARPLESS: Oh, please!

PINKERTON: It's true!

SHARPLESS: Are you serious about this girl?

PINKERTON: I'm marrying her, aren't I?

SHARPLESS: Yes—with generous trade-in terms. 60

PINKERTON: When I leave, she'll know what it's like to have loved a real man. And I'll even buy her a few nylons.

SHARPLESS: You aren't planning to take her with you?

PINKERTON: Huh? Where?

SHARPLESS: Home! 65

PINKERTON: You mean, America? Are you crazy? Can you see her trying to buy rice in St. Louis?

SHARPLESS: So, you're not serious.

(*Pause.*)

PINKERTON/GALLIMARD: (*As* PINKERTON.) Consul, I am a sailor in port. (*As* GALLIMARD.) They then proceed to sing 70 the famous duet, "The Whole World Over."

(*The duet plays on the speakers.* GALLIMARD, *as* PINKERTON, *lip-syncs his lines from the opera.*)

GALLIMARD: To give a rough translation: "The whole world over, the Yankee travels, casting his anchor wherever he wants. Life's not worth living unless he can win the hearts of the fairest maidens, then hotfoot it off the premises 75 ASAP." (*He turns towards* MARC.) In the preceding scene, I played Pinkerton, the womanizing cad, and my friend Marc from school . . . (MARC *bows grandly for our benefit.*) played Sharpless, the sensitive soul of reason. In life, however, our positions were usually—no, always—reversed. 80

SCENE IV

Ecole Nationale. Aix-en-Provence. 1947.

GALLIMARD: No, Marc, I think I'd rather stay home.

MARC: Are you crazy?! We are going to Dad's condo in Marseille! You know what happened last time?

GALLIMARD: Of course I do.

MARC: Of course you don't! You never know. . . . They 5 stripped, Rene!

GALLIMARD: Who stripped?

MARC: The girls!

GALLIMARD: Girls? Who said anything about girls?

10   MARC: Rene, we're a buncha university guys goin' up to the woods. What are we gonna do—talk philosophy?

GALLIMARD: What girls? Where do you get them?

MARC: Who cares? The point is, they come. On trucks. Packed in like sardines. The back flips open, babes hop

15   out, we're ready to roll.

GALLIMARD: You mean, they just—?

MARC: Before you know it, every last one of them—they're stripped and splashing around my pool. There's no moon out, they can't see what's going on, their boobs are flap-

20   ping, right? You close your eyes, reach out—it's grab bag, get it? Doesn't matter whose ass is between whose legs, whose teeth are sinking into who. You're just in there, go-ing at it, eyes closed, on and on for as long as you can stand. (*Pause.*) Some fun, huh?

25   GALLIMARD: What happens in the morning?

MARC: In the morning, you're ready to talk some philosophy. (*Beat.*) So how 'bout it?

GALLIMARD: Marc, I can't . . . I'm afraid they'll say no—the girls. So I never ask.

30   MARC: You don't have to ask! That's the beauty—don't you see? They don't have to say yes. It's perfect for a guy like you, really.

GALLIMARD: You go ahead . . . I may come later.

MARC: Hey, Rene—it doesn't matter that you're clumsy and

35   got zits—they're not looking!

GALLIMARD: Thank you very much.

MARC: Wimp.

(MARC *walks over to the other side of the stage, and starts waving and smiling at women in the audience.*)

GALLIMARD: (*To us.*) We now return to my version of *Madame Butterfly* and the events leading to my recent conviction

40   for treason.

(GALLIMARD *notices* MARC *making lewd gestures.*)

Marc, what are you doing?

MARC: Huh? (*Sotto voce.*) Rene, there're a lotta great babes out there. They're probably lookin' at me and thinking, "What a dangerous guy."

45   GALLIMARD: Yes—how could they help but be impressed by your cool sophistication?

(GALLIMARD *pops the* SHARPLESS *cap on* MARC*'s head, and points him offstage.* MARC *exits, leering.*)

SCENE V

M. GALLIMARD*'s cell.*

GALLIMARD: Next, Butterfly makes her entrance. We learn her age—fifteen . . . but very mature for her years.

(*Lights come up on the area where we saw* SONG *dancing at the top of the play. She appears there again, now dressed as* MADAME BUTTERFLY, *moving to the "Love Duet."* GALLIMARD *turns up-stage slightly to watch, transfixed.*)

GALLIMARD: But as she glides past him, beautiful, laughing softly behind her fan, don't we who are men sigh with hope? We, who are not handsome, nor brave, nor power-   5 ful, yet somehow believe, like Pinkerton, that we deserve a Butterfly. She arrives with all her possessions in the folds of her sleeves, lays them all out, for her man to do with as he pleases. Even her life itself—she bows her head as she whispers that she's not even worth the hundred yen he   10 paid for her. He's already given too much, when we know he's really had to give nothing at all.

(*Music and lights on* SONG *out.* GALLIMARD *sits at his crate.*)

GALLIMARD: In real life, women who put their total worth at less than sixty-six cents are quite hard to find. The closest we come is in the pages of these magazines. (*He reaches into*   15 *his crate, pulls out a stack of girlie magazines, and begins flipping through them.*) Quite a necessity in prison. For three or four dollars, you get seven or eight women.

I first discovered these magazines at my uncle's house. One day, as a boy of twelve. The first time I saw them in   20 his closet . . . all lined up—my body shook. Not with lust—no, with power. Here were women—a shelfful— who would do exactly as I wanted.

(*The "Love Duet" creeps in over the speakers. Special comes up, re-vealing, not* SONG *this time, but a* PINUP GIRL *in a sexy negligee, her back to us.* GALLIMARD *turns upstage and looks at her.*)

GIRL: I know you're watching me.

GALLIMARD: My throat . . . it's dry.   25

GIRL: I leave my blinds open every night before I go to bed.

GALLIMARD: I can't move.

GIRL: I leave my blinds open and the lights on.

GALLIMARD: I'm shaking. My skin is hot, but my penis is soft. Why?   30

GIRL: I stand in front of the window.

GALLIMARD: What is she going to do?

GIRL: I toss my hair, and I let my lips part . . . barely.

GALLIMARD: I shouldn't be seeing this. It's so dirty. I'm so bad.   35

GIRL: Then, slowly, I lift off my nightdress.

GALLIMARD: Oh, god. I can't believe it. I can't—

GIRL: I toss it to the ground.

GALLIMARD: Now, she's going to walk away. She's going to—

GIRL: I stand there, in the light, displaying myself.   40

GALLIMARD: No. She's—why is she naked?

GIRL: To you.

GALLIMARD: In front of a window? This is wrong. No—

GIRL: Without shame.

GALLIMARD: No, she must . . . like it.   45

GIRL: I like it.

GALLIMARD: She . . . she wants me to see.

GIRL: I want you to see.

GALLIMARD: I can't believe it! She's getting excited!

GIRL: I can't see you. You can do whatever you want.   50

GALLIMARD: I can't do a thing. Why?

GIRL: What would you like me to do . . . next?

(*Lights go down on her. Music off. Silence, as* GALLIMARD *puts away his magazines. Then he resumes talking to us.*)

GALLIMARD: Act Two begins with Butterfly staring at the ocean. Pinkerton's been called back to the U.S., and he's
55 given his wife a detailed schedule of his plans. In the column marked "return date," he's written "when the robins nest." This failed to ignite her suspicions. Now, three years have passed without a peep from him. Which brings a response from her faithful servant, Suzuki.

(COMRADE CHIN *enters, playing* SUZUKI.)

60 SUZUKI: Girl, he's a loser. What'd he ever give you? Nineteen cents and those ugly Day-Glo stockings? Look, it's finished! Kaput! Done! And you should be glad! I mean, the guy was a woofer! He tried before, you know—before he met you, he went down to geisha central and plunked
65 down his spare change in front of the usual candidates— everyone else gagged! These are hungry prostitutes, and they were not interested, get the picture? Now, stop slathering when an American ship sails in, and let's make some bucks—I mean, yen! We are broke!
70   Now, what about Yamadori? Hey, hey—don't look away—the man is a prince—figuratively, and, what's even better, literally. He's rich, he's handsome, he says he'll die if you don't marry him—and he's even willing to overlook the little fact that you've been deflowered all over the place
75 by a foreign devil. What do you mean, "But he's Japanese?" You're Japanese! You think you've been touched by the whitey god? He was a sailor with dirty hands!

(SUZUKI *stalks offstage.*)

GALLIMARD: She's also visited by Consul Sharpless, sent by Pinkerton on a minor errand.

(MARC *enters, as* SHARPLESS.)

80 SHARPLESS: I hate this job.
GALLIMARD: This Pinkerton—he doesn't show up personally to tell his wife he's abandoning her. No, he sends a government diplomat . . . at taxpayer's expense.
SHARPLESS: Butterfly? Butterfly? I have some bad—I'm go-
85 ing to be ill. Butterfly, I came to tell you—
GALLIMARD: Butterfly says she knows he'll return and if he doesn't she'll kill herself rather than go back to her own people. (*Beat.*) This causes a lull in the conversation.
SHARPLESS: Let's put it this way . . .
90 GALLIMARD: Butterfly runs into the next room, and returns holding—

(*Sound cue: a baby crying.* SHARPLESS, *"seeing" this, backs away.*)

SHARPLESS: Well, good. Happy to see things going so well. I suppose I'll be going now. Ta ta. Ciao. (*He turns away. Sound cue out.*) I hate this job. (*He exits.*)
95 GALLIMARD: At that moment, Butterfly spots in the harbor an American ship—the *Abramo Lincoln!*

(*Music cue: "The Flower Duet."* SONG, *still dressed as* BUTTERFLY, *changes into a wedding kimono, moving to the music.*)

GALLIMARD: This is the moment that redeems her years of waiting. With Suzuki's help, they cover the room with flowers—

(CHIN, *as* SUZUKI, *trudges onstage and drops a lone flower without much enthusiasm.*)

GALLIMARD: —and she changes into her wedding dress to   100
prepare for Pinkerton's arrival.

(SUZUKI *helps* BUTTERFLY *change.* HELGA *enters, and helps* GALLIMARD *change into a tuxedo.*)

GALLIMARD: I married a woman older than myself—Helga.
HELGA: My father was ambassador to Australia. I grew up among criminals and kangaroos.
GALLIMARD: Hearing that brought me to the altar—   105

(HELGA *exits.*)

GALLIMARD: —where I took a vow renouncing love. No fantasy woman would ever want me, so, yes, I would settle for a quick leap up the career ladder. Passion, I banish, and in its place—practicality!
    But my vows had long since lost their charm by the   110
time we arrived in China. The sad truth is that all men want a beautiful woman, and the uglier the man, the greater the want.

(SUZUKI *makes final adjustments of* BUTTERFLY's *costume, as does* GALLIMARD *of his tuxedo.*)

GALLIMARD: I married late, at age thirty-one. I was faithful to my marriage for eight years. Until the day when, as a   115
junior-level diplomat in puritanical Peking, in a parlor at the German ambassador's house, during the "Reign of a Hundred Flowers," I first saw her . . . singing the death scene from *Madame Butterfly.*

(SUZUKI *runs offstage.*)

SCENE VI

German ambassador's house. Beijing. 1960.

The upstage special area now becomes a stage. Several chairs face upstage, representing seating for some twenty guests in the parlor. A few "diplomats"—RENEE, MARC, TOULON—*in formal dress enter and take seats.*

GALLIMARD *also sits down, but turns towards us and continues to talk. Orchestral accompaniment on the tape is now replaced by a simple piano.* SONG *picks up the death scene from the point where* BUTTERFLY *uncovers the hara-kiri knife.*

GALLIMARD: The ending is pitiful. Pinkerton, in an art of great courage, stays home and sends his American wife to pick up Butterfly's child. The truth, long deferred, has come up to her door.

(SONG, *playing* BUTTERFLY, *sings the lines from the opera in her own voice—which, though not classical, should be decent.*)

SONG: "Con onor muore/ chi non puo serbar/ vita con onore."   5
GALLIMARD: (*Simultaneously.*) "Death with honor / Is better than life / Life with dishonor."

(*The stage is illuminated; we are now completely within an elegant diplomat's residence.* SONG *proceeds to play out an abbreviated death scene. Everyone in the room applauds.* SONG, *shyly, takes her bows. Others in the room rush to congratulate her.* GALLIMARD *remains with us.*)

GALLIMARD: They say in opera the voice is everything. That's probably why I'd never before enjoyed opera. Here . . . here
10 was a Butterfly with little or no voice—but she had the grace, the delicacy . . . I believed this girl. I believed her suffering. I wanted to take her in my arms—so delicate, even I could protect her, take her home, pamper her until she smiled.

(*Over the course of the preceding speech,* SONG *has broken from the upstage crowd and moved directly upstage of* GALLIMARD.)

SONG: Excuse me. Monsieur . . . ?

(GALLIMARD *turns upstage, shocked.*)

15 GALLIMARD: Oh! Gallimard. Mademoiselle . . . ? A beautiful . . .
SONG: Song Liling.
GALLIMARD: A beautiful performance.
SONG: Oh, please.
GALLIMARD: I usually—
20 SONG: You make me blush. I'm no opera singer at all.
GALLIMARD: I usually don't like *Butterfly*.
SONG: I can't blame you in the least.
GALLIMARD: I mean, the story—
SONG: Ridiculous.
25 GALLIMARD: I like the story, but . . . what?
SONG: Oh, you like it?
GALLIMARD: I . . . what I mean is, I've always seen it played by huge women in so much bad makeup.
SONG: Bad makeup is not unique to the West.
30 GALLIMARD: But, who can believe them?
SONG: And you believe me?
GALLIMARD: Absolutely. You were utterly convincing. It's the first time—
SONG: Convincing? As a Japanese woman? The Japanese used
35 hundreds of our people for medical experiments during the war, you know. But I gather such an irony is lost on you.
GALLIMARD: No! I was about to say, it's the first time I've seen the beauty of the story.
SONG: Really?
40 GALLIMARD: Of her death. It's a . . . a pure sacrifice. He's unworthy, but what can she do? She loves him . . . so much. It's a very beautiful story.
SONG: Well, yes, to a Westerner.
GALLIMARD: Excuse me?
45 SONG: It's one of your favorite fantasies, isn't it? The submissive Oriental woman and the cruel white man.
GALLIMARD: Well, I didn't quite mean . . .
SONG: Consider it this way: what would you say if a blonde homecoming queen fell in love with a short Japanese
50 businessman? He treats her cruelly, then goes home for three years, during which time she prays to his picture and turns down marriage from a young Kennedy. Then, when she learns he has remarried, she kills herself. Now, I believe you would consider this girl to be a deranged idiot,
55 correct? But because it's an Oriental who kills herself for a Westerner—ah!—you find it beautiful.

(*Silence.*)

GALLIMARD: Yes . . . well . . . I see your point . . .
SONG: I will never do Butterfly again, Monsieur Gallimard. If you wish to see some real theatre, come to the Peking Opera sometime. Expand your mind.   60

(SONG *walks offstage.*)

GALLIMARD: (*To us.*) So much for protecting her in my big Western arms.

SCENE VII

M. GALLIMARD's *apartment. Beijing. 1960.*

GALLIMARD *changes from his tux into a casual suit.* HELGA *enters.*

GALLIMARD: The Chinese are an incredibly arrogant people.
HELGA: They warned us about that in Paris, remember?
GALLIMARD: Even Parisians consider them arrogant. That's a switch.
HELGA: What is it that Madame Su says? "We are a very old   5
civilization." I never know if she's talking about her country or herself.
GALLIMARD: I walk around here, all I hear every day, everywhere is how *old* this culture is. The fact that "old" may be synonymous with "senile" doesn't occur to them.   10
HELGA: You're not going to change them. "East is east, west is west, and . . ." whatever that guy said.
GALLIMARD: It's just that—silly. I met . . . at Ambassador Koening's tonight—you should've been there.
HELGA: Koening? Oh god, no. Did he enchant you all again   15
with the history of Bavaria?
GALLIMARD: No. I met, I suppose, the Chinese equivalent of a diva. She's a singer in the Chinese opera.
HELGA: They have an opera, too? Do they sing in Chinese? Or maybe—in Italian?   20
GALLIMARD: Tonight, she did sing in Italian.
HELGA: How'd she manage that?
GALLIMARD: She must've been educated in the West before the Revolution. Her French is very good also. Anyway, she sang the death scene from *Madame Butterfly*.   25
HELGA: *Madame Butterfly*! Then I should have come. (*She begins humming, floating around the room as if dragging long kimono sleeves.*) Did she have a nice costume? I think it's a classic piece of music.
GALLIMARD: That's what *I* thought, too. Don't let her hear   30
you say that.
HELGA: What's wrong?
GALLIMARD: Evidently the Chinese hate it.
HELGA: She hated it, but she performed it anyway? Is she perverse?   35
GALLIMARD: They hate it because the white man gets the girl. Sour grapes if you ask me.
HELGA: Politics again? Why can't they just hear it as a piece of beautiful music? So, what's in their opera?
GALLIMARD: I don't know. But, whatever it is, I'm sure it   40
must be *old*.

(HELGA *exits.*)

SCENE VIII

Chinese opera house and the streets of Beijing. 1960.

The sound of gongs clanging fills the stage.

GALLIMARD: My wife's innocent question kept ringing in my ears. I asked around, but no one knew anything about the Chinese opera. It took four weeks, but my curiosity overcame my cowardice. This Chinese diva—this unwilling
5   Butterfly—what did she do to make her so proud?
      The room was hot, and full of smoke. Wrinkled faces, old women, teeth missing—a man with a growth on his neck, like a human toad. All smiling, pipes falling from their mouths, cracking nuts between their teeth, a live
10 chicken pecking at my foot—all looking, screaming, gawking . . . at her.

(*The upstage area is suddenly hit with a harsh white light. It has become the stage for the Chinese opera performance. Two dancers enter, along with* SONG. GALLIMARD *stands apart, watching.* SONG *glides gracefully amidst the two dancers. Drums suddenly slam to a halt.* SONG *strikes a pose, looking straight at* GALLIMARD. *Dancers exit. Light change. Pause, then* SONG *walks right off the stage and straight up to* GALLIMARD.)

SONG: Yes. You. White man. I'm looking straight at you.
GALLIMARD: Me?
SONG: You see any other white men? It was too easy to spot
15   you. How often does a man in my audience come in a tie?

(SONG *starts to remove her costume. Underneath, she wears simple baggy clothes. They are now backstage. The show is over.*)

SONG: So, you are an adventurous imperialist?
GALLIMARD: I . . . thought it would further my education.
SONG: It took you four weeks. Why?
GALLIMARD: I've been busy.
20 SONG: Well, education has always been undervalued in the West, hasn't it?
GALLIMARD: (*Laughing.*) I don't think it's true.
SONG: No, you wouldn't. You're a Westerner. How can you objectively judge your own values?
25 GALLIMARD: I think it's possible to achieve some distance.
SONG: Do you? (*Pause.*) It stinks in here. Let's go.
GALLIMARD: These are the smells of your loyal fans.
SONG: I love them for being my fans, I hate the smell they leave behind. I too can distance myself from my people.
30   (*She looks around, then whispers in his ear.*) "Art for the masses" is a shitty excuse to keep artists poor. (*She pops a cigarette in her mouth.*) Be a gentleman, will you? And light my cigarette.

(GALLIMARD *fumbles for a match.*)

GALLIMARD: I don't . . . smoke.
35 SONG: (*Lighting her own.*) Your loss. Had you lit my cigarette, I might have blown a puff of smoke right between your eyes. Come.

(*They start to walk about the stage. It is a summer night on the Beijing streets. Sounds of the city play on the house speakers.*)

SONG: How I wish there were even a tiny cafe to sit in. With cappuccinos, and men in tuxedos and bad expatriate jazz.
GALLIMARD: If my history serves me correctly, you weren't even   40
allowed into the clubs in Shanghai before the Revolution.
SONG: Your history serves you poorly, Monsieur Gallimard. True, there were signs reading "No dogs and Chinamen." But a woman, especially a delicate Oriental woman—we always go where we please. Could you imagine it other-   45
wise? Clubs in China filled with pasty, big-thighed white women, while thousands of slender lotus blossoms wait just outside the door? Never. The clubs would be empty. (*Beat.*) We have always held a certain fascination for you Caucasian men, have we not?   50
GALLIMARD: But . . . that fascination is imperialist, or so you tell me.
SONG: Do you believe everything I tell you? Yes. It is always imperialist. But sometimes . . . sometimes, it is also mutual. Oh—this is my flat.   55
GALLIMARD: I didn't even—
SONG: Thank you. Come another time and we will further expand your mind.

(SONG *exits.* GALLIMARD *continues roaming the streets as he speaks to us.*)

GALLIMARD: What was that? What did she mean, "Sometimes . . . it is mutual?" Women do not flirt with me. And   60
I normally can't talk to them. But tonight, I held up my end of the conversation.

SCENE IX

GALLIMARD'*s bedroom. Beijing. 1960.*

HELGA *enters.*

HELGA: You didn't tell me you'd be home late.
GALLIMARD: I didn't intend to. Something came up.
HELGA: Oh! Like what?
GALLIMARD: I went to the . . . to the Dutch ambassador's home.
HELGA: Again?   5
GALLIMARD: There was a reception for a visiting scholar. He's writing a six-volume treatise on the Chinese revolution. We all gathered that meant he'd have to live here long enough to actually write six volumes, and we all expressed our deepest sympathies.   10
HELGA: Well, I had a good night too. I went with the ladies to a martial arts demonstration. Some of those men— when they break those thick boards—(*She mimes fanning herself.*) whoo-whoo!

(HELGA *exits. Lights dim.*)

GALLIMARD: I lied to my wife. Why? I've never had any rea-   15
son to lie before. But what reason did I have tonight? I didn't do anything wrong. That night, I had a dream. Other people, I've been told, have dreams where angels appear. Or dragons, or Sophia Loren in a towel. In my dream, Marc from school appeared.   20

(MARC *enters, in a nightshirt and cap.*)

MARC: Rene! You met a girl!

(GALLIMARD *and* MARC *stumble down the Beijing streets. Night sounds over the speakers.*)

GALLIMARD: It's not that amazing, thank you.
MARC: No! It's so monumental, I heard about it halfway around the world in my sleep!
25 GALLIMARD: I've met girls before, you know.
MARC: Name one. I've come across time and space to congratulate you. (*He hands* GALLIMARD *a bottle of wine.*)
GALLIMARD: Marc, this is expensive.
MARC: On those rare occasions when you become a formless
30 spirit, why not steal the best?

(MARC *pops open the bottle, begins to share it with* GALLIMARD.)

GALLIMARD: You embarrass me. She . . . there's no reason to think she likes me.
MARC: "Sometimes, it is mutual"?
GALLIMARD: Oh.
35 MARC: "Mutual"? "Mutual"? What does that mean?
GALLIMARD: You heard!
MARC: It means the money is in the bank, you only have to write the check!
GALLIMARD: I am a married man!
40 MARC: And an excellent one too. I cheated after . . . six months. Then again and again, until now—three hundred girls in twelve years.
GALLIMARD: I don't think we should hold that up as a model.
MARC: Of course not! My life—it is disgusting! Phooey!
45 Phooey! But, you—you are the model husband.
GALLIMARD: Anyway, it's impossible. I'm a foreigner.
MARC: Ah, yes. She cannot love you, it is taboo, but something deep inside her heart . . . she cannot help herself . . . she must surrender to you. It is her destiny.
50 GALLIMARD: How do you imagine all this?
MARC: The same way you do. It's an old story. It's in our blood. They fear us, Rene. Their women fear us. And their men—their men hate us. And, you know something? They are all correct.

(*They spot a light in a window.*)

55 MARC: There! There, Rene!
GALLIMARD: It's her window.
MARC: Late at night—it burns. The light—it burns for you.
GALLIMARD: I won't look. It's not respectful.
MARC: We don't have to be respectful. We're foreign devils.

(*Enter* SONG, *in a sheer robe. The "One Fine Day" aria creeps in over the speakers. With her back to us,* SONG *mimes attending to her toilette. Her robe comes loose, revealing her white shoulders.*)

60 MARC: All your life you've waited for a beautiful girl who would lay down for you. All your life you've smiled like a saint when it's happened to every other man you know. And you see them in magazines and you see them in movies. And you wonder, what's wrong with me? Will
65 anyone beautiful ever want me? As the years pass, your hair thins and you struggle to hold onto even your hopes. Stop struggling, Rene. The wait is over. (*He exits.*)

GALLIMARD: Marc? Marc?

(*At that moment,* SONG, *her back still towards us, drops her robe. A second of her naked back, then a sound cue: a phone ringing, very loud. Blackout, followed in the next beat by a special up on the bedroom area, where a phone now sits.* GALLIMARD *stumbles across the stage and picks up the phone. Sound cue out. Over the course of his conversation, area lights fill in the vicinity of his bed. It is the following morning.*)

GALLIMARD: Yes? Hello?
SONG: (*Offstage.*) Is it very early? 70
GALLIMARD: Why, yes.
SONG: (*Offstage.*) How early?
GALLIMARD: It's . . . it's 5:30. Why are you—?
SONG: (*Offstage.*) But it's light outside. Already.
GALLIMARD: It is. The sun must be in confusion today. 75

(*Over the course of* SONG's *next speech, her upstage special comes up again. She sits in a chair, legs crossed, in a robe, telephone to her ear.*)

SONG: I waited until I saw the sun. That was as much discipline as I could manage for one night. Do you forgive me?
GALLIMARD: Of course . . . for what?
SONG: Then I'll ask you quickly. Are you really interested in the opera? 80
GALLIMARD: Why, yes. Yes I am.
SONG: Then come again next Thursday. I am playing *The Drunken Beauty.* May I count on you?
GALLIMARD: Yes. You may.
SONG: Perfect. Well, I must be getting to bed. I'm exhausted. 85 It's been a very long night for me.

(SONG *hangs up; special on her goes off.* GALLIMARD *begins to dress for work.*)

SCENE X

SONG LILING's *apartment. Beijing. 1960.*

GALLIMARD: I returned to the opera that next week, and the week after that . . . she keeps our meetings so short—perhaps fifteen, twenty minutes at most. So I am left each week with a thirst which is intensified. In this way, fifteen weeks have gone by. I am starting to doubt the words of my 5 friend Marc. But no, not really. In my heart, I know she has . . . an interest in me. I suspect this is her way. She is outwardly bold and outspoken, yet her heart is shy and afraid. It is the Oriental in her at war with her Western education.
SONG: (*Offstage.*) I will be out in an instant. Ask the servant 10 for anything you want.
GALLIMARD: Tonight, I have finally been invited to enter her apartment. Though the idea is almost beyond belief, I believe she is afraid of me.

(GALLIMARD *looks around the room. He picks up a picture in a frame, studies it. Without his noticing,* SONG *enters, dressed elegantly in a black gown from the twenties. She stands in the doorway looking like Anna May Wong.*)

SONG: That is my father. 15
GALLIMARD: (*Surprised.*) Mademoiselle Song . . .

(*She glides up to him, snatches away the picture.*)

SONG: It is very good that he did not live to see the Revolution. They would, no doubt, have made him kneel on broken glass. Not that he didn't deserve such a punishment.
20   But he is my father. I would've hated to see it happen.
GALLIMARD: I'm very honored that you've allowed me to visit your home.

(SONG *curtsys.*)

SONG: Thank you. Oh! Haven't you been poured any tea?
GALLIMARD: I'm really not—
25   SONG: (*To her offstage servant.*) Shu-Fang! Cha! Kwai-lah! (*To GALLIMARD.*) I'm sorry. You want everything to be perfect—
GALLIMARD: Please.
SONG: —and before the evening even begins—
GALLIMARD: I'm really not thirsty.
30   SONG: —it's ruined.
GALLIMARD: (*Sharply.*) Mademoiselle Song!

(SONG *sits down.*)

SONG: I'm sorry.
GALLIMARD: What are you apologizing for now?

(*Pause; SONG starts to giggle.*)

SONG: I don't know!

(GALLIMARD *laughs.*)

35   GALLIMARD: Exactly my point.
SONG: Oh, I am silly. Lightheaded. I promise not to apologize for anything else tonight, do you hear me?
GALLIMARD: That's a good girl!

(SHU-FANG, *a servant girl, comes out with a tea tray and starts to pour.*)

SONG: (*To SHU-FANG.*) No! I'll pour myself for the gentleman!

(SHU-FANG, *staring at GALLIMARD, exits.*)

40   SONG: No, I . . . I don't even know why I invited you up.
GALLIMARD: Well, I'm glad you did.

(SONG *looks around the room.*)

SONG: There is an element of danger to your presence.
GALLIMARD: Oh?
SONG: You must know.
45   GALLIMARD: It doesn't concern me. We both know why I'm here.
SONG: It doesn't concern me either. No . . . well perhaps . . .
GALLIMARD: What?
SONG: Perhaps I am slightly afraid of scandal.
50   GALLIMARD: What are we doing?
SONG: I'm entertaining you. In my parlor.
GALLIMARD: In France, that would hardly—
SONG: France. France is a country living in the modern era. Perhaps even ahead of it. China is a nation whose soul is
55   firmly rooted two thousand years in the past. What I do,

even pouring the tea for you now . . . it has . . . implications. The walls and windows say so. Even my own heart, strapped inside this Western dress . . . even it says things—things I don't care to hear.

(SONG *hands* GALLIMARD *a cup of tea.* GALLIMARD *puts his hand over both the teacup and* SONG's *hand.*)

GALLIMARD: This is a beautiful dress.   60
SONG: Don't.
GALLIMARD: What?
SONG: I don't even know if it looks right on me.
GALLIMARD: Believe me—
SONG: You are from France. You see so many beautiful women. 65
GALLIMARD: France? Since when are the European women—?
SONG: Oh! What am I trying to do, anyway?!

(SONG *runs to the door, composes herself, then turns towards* GALLIMARD.)

SONG: Monsieur Gallimard, perhaps you should go.
GALLIMARD: But . . . why?
SONG: There's something wrong about this.   70
GALLIMARD: I don't see what.
SONG: I feel . . . I am not myself.
GALLIMARD: No. You're nervous.
SONG: Please. Hard as I try to be modern, to speak like a man, to hold a Western woman's strong face up to my own . . . in 75
the end, I fail. A small, frightened heart beats too quickly and gives me away. Monsieur Gallimard, I'm a Chinese girl. I've never . . . never invited a man up to my flat before. The forwardness of my actions makes my skin burn.
GALLIMARD: What are you afraid of? Certainly not me, I hope. 80
SONG: I'm a modest girl.
GALLIMARD: I know. And very beautiful. (*He touches her hair.*)
SONG: Please—go now. The next time you see me, I shall again be myself.
GALLIMARD: I like you the way you are right now.   85
SONG: You are a cad.
GALLIMARD: What do you expect? I'm a foreign devil.

(GALLIMARD *walks downstage.* SONG *exits.*)

GALLIMARD: (*To us.*) Did you hear the way she talked about Western women? Much differently than the first night. She does—she feels inferior to them—and to me.   90

SCENE XI

The French embassy. Beijing. 1960.

GALLIMARD *moves towards a desk.*

GALLIMARD: I determined to try an experiment. In *Madame Butterfly,* Cio-Cio-San fears that the Western man who catches a butterfly will pierce its heart with a needle, then leave it to perish. I began to wonder: had I, too, caught a butterfly who would writhe on a needle?   5

(MARC *enters, dressed as a bureaucrat, holding a stack of papers. As* GALLIMARD *speaks,* MARC *hands papers to him. He peruses, then signs, stamps or rejects them.*)

GALLIMARD: Over the next five weeks, I worked like a dynamo. I stopped going to the opera, I didn't phone or
write her. I knew this little flower was waiting for me to
call, and, as I wickedly refused to do so, I felt for the first
10   time that rush of power—the absolute power of a man.

(MARC *continues acting as the bureaucrat, but he now speaks as
himself.*)

MARC: Rene! It's me!
GALLIMARD: Marc—I hear your voice everywhere now. Even
in the midst of work.
MARC: That's because I'm watching you—all the time.
15 GALLIMARD: You were always the most popular guy in
school.
MARC: Well, there's no guarantee of failure in life like happiness
in high school. Somehow I knew I'd end up in the suburbs
working for Renault and you'd be in the Orient picking
20   exotic women off the trees. And they say there's no justice.
GALLIMARD: That's why you were my friend?
MARC: I gave you a little of my life, so that now you can give
me some of yours. (*Pause.*) Remember Isabelle?
GALLIMARD: Of course I remember! She was my first experience.
25 MARC: We all wanted to ball her. But she only wanted me.
GALLIMARD: I had her.
MARC: Right. You balled her.
GALLIMARD: You were the only one who ever believed me.
MARC: Well, there's a good reason for that. (*Beat.*) C'mon.
30   You must've guessed.
GALLIMARD: You told me to wait in the bushes by the cafe-
teria that night. The next thing I knew, she was on me.
Dress up in the air.
MARC: She never wore underwear.
35 GALLIMARD: My arms were pinned to the dirt.
MARC: She loved the superior position. A girl ahead of her time.
GALLIMARD: I looked up, and there was this woman . . .
bouncing up and down on my loins.
MARC: Screaming, right?
40 GALLIMARD: Screaming, and breaking off the branches all
around me, and pounding my butt up and down into the dirt.
MARC: Huffing and puffing like a locomotive.
GALLIMARD: And in the middle of all this, the leaves were
getting into my mouth, my legs were losing circulation, I
45   thought, "God. So this is *it?*"
MARC: You thought that?
GALLIMARD: Well, I was worried about my legs falling off.
MARC: You didn't have a good time?
GALLIMARD: No, that's not what I—I had a great time!
50 MARC: You're sure?
GALLIMARD: Yeah. Really.
MARC: 'Cuz I wanted you to have a good time.
GALLIMARD: I did.

(*Pause.*)

MARC: Shit. (*Pause.*) When all is said and done, she was kind
55   of a lousy lay, wasn't she? I mean, there was a lot of energy
there, but you never knew what she was doing with it.
Like when she yelled "I'm coming!"—hell, it was so loud,
you wanted to go "Look, it's not that big a deal."
GALLIMARD: I got scared. I thought she meant someone was
60   actually coming. (*Pause.*) But, Marc?

MARC: What?
GALLIMARD: Thanks.
MARC: Oh, don't mention it.
GALLIMARD: It was my first experience.
MARC: Yeah. You got her.   65
GALLIMARD: I got her.
MARC: Wait! Look at that letter again!

(GALLIMARD *picks up one of the papers he's been stamping, and
rereads it.*)

GALLIMARD: (*To us.*) After six weeks, they began to arrive.
The letters.

(*Upstage special on* SONG, *as* MADAME BUTTERFLY. *The scene is
underscored by the "Love Duet."*)

SONG: Did we fight? I do not know. Is the opera no longer   70
of interest to you? Please come—my audiences miss the
white devil in their midst.

(GALLIMARD *looks up from the letter, towards us.*)

GALLIMARD: (*To us.*) A concession, but much too dignified.
(*Beat; he discards the letter.*) I skipped the opera again that
week to complete a position paper on trade.   75

(*The bureaucrat hands him another letter.*)

SONG: Six weeks have passed since last we met. In this your
practice—to leave friends in the lurch? Sometimes I hate
you, sometimes I hate myself, but always I miss you.
GALLIMARD: (*To us.*) Better, but I don't like the way she calls
me "friend." When a woman calls a man her "friend,"   80
she's calling him a eunuch or a homosexual. (*Beat; he discards the letter.*) I was absent from the opera for the seventh
week, feeling a sudden urge to clean out my files.

(*Bureaucrat hands him another letter.*)

SONG: Your rudeness is beyond belief. I don't deserve this cruelty.
Don't bother to call. I'll have you turned away at the door.   85
GALLIMARD: (*To us.*) I didn't. (*He discards the letter; bureaucrat
hands him another.*) And then finally, the letter that con-
cluded my experiment.
SONG: I am out of words. I can hide behind dignity no longer.
What do you want? I have already given you my shame.   90

(GALLIMARD *gives the letter back to* MARC, *slowly. Special on*
SONG *fades out.*)

GALLIMARD: (*To us.*) Reading it, I became suddenly ashamed.
Yes, my experiment had been a success. She was turning
on my needle. But the victory seemed hollow.
MARC: Hollow? Are you crazy?
GALLIMARD: Nothing, Marc. Please go away.   95
MARC: (*Exiting, with papers.*) Haven't I taught you anything?
GALLIMARD: "I have already given you my shame." I had to
attend a reception that evening. On the way, I felt sick. If
there is a God, surely he would punish me now. I had finally gained power over a beautiful woman, only to abuse 100
it cruelly. There must be justice in the world. I had the
strange feeling that the ax would fall this very evening.

SCENE XII

AMBASSADOR TOULON's *residence. Beijing. 1960.*

Sound cue: party noises. Light change. We are now in a spacious residence. TOULON, *the French ambassador, enters and taps* GALLIMARD *on the shoulder.*

TOULON: Gallimard? Can I have a word? Over here.

GALLIMARD: (*To us.*) Manuel Toulon. French ambassador to China. He likes to think of us all as his children. Rather like God.

5   TOULON: Look, Gallimard, there's not much to say. I've liked you. From the day you walked in. You were no leader, but you were tidy and efficient.

GALLIMARD: Thank you, sir.

TOULON: Don't jump the gun. Okay, our needs in China are
10   changing. It's embarrassing that we lost Indochina. Someone just wasn't on the ball there. I don't mean you personally, of course.

GALLIMARD: Thank you, sir.

TOULON: We're going to be doing a lot more information-
15   gathering in the future. The nature of our work here is changing. Some people are just going to have to go. It's nothing personal.

GALLIMARD: Oh.

TOULON: Want to know a secret? Vice-Consul LeBon is be-
20   ing transferred.

GALLIMARD: (*To us.*) My immediate superior!

TOULON: And most of his department.

GALLIMARD: (*To us.*) Just as I feared! God has seen my evil heart—

25   TOULON: But not you.

GALLIMARD: (*To us.*)—and he's taking her away just as . . . (*To* TOULON.) Excuse me, sir?

TOULON: Scare you? I think I did. Cheer up, Gallimard. I want you to replace LeBon as vice-consul.

30   GALLIMARD: You—? Yes, well, thank you, sir.

TOULON: Anytime.

GALLIMARD: I . . . accept with great humility.

TOULON: Humility won't be part of the job. You're going to coordinate the revamped intelligence division. Want to
35   know a secret? A year ago, you would've been out. But the past few months, I don't know how it happened, you've become this new aggressive confident . . . thing. And they also tell me you get along with the Chinese. So I think you're a lucky man, Gallimard. Congratulations.

(*They shake hands.* TOULON *exits. Party noises out.* GALLIMARD *stumbles across a darkened stage.*)

40   GALLIMARD: Vice-consul? Impossible! As I stumbled out of the party, I saw it written across the sky: There is no God. Or, no—say that there is a God. But that God . . . understands. Of course! God who creates Eve to serve Adam, who blesses Solomon with his harem but ties Jezebel to a
45   burning bed—that God is a man. And he understands! At age thirty-nine, I was suddenly initiated into the way of the world.

SCENE XIII

SONG LILING's *apartment. Beijing. 1960.*

SONG *enters, in a sheer dressing gown.*

SONG: Are you crazy?

GALLIMARD: Mademoiselle Song—

SONG: To come here—at this hour? After . . . after eight weeks?

GALLIMARD: It's the most amazing—

SONG: You bang on my door? Scare my servants, scandalize   5
the neighbors?

GALLIMARD: I've been promoted. To vice-consul.

(*Pause.*)

SONG: And what is that supposed to mean to me?

GALLIMARD: Are you my Butterfly?

SONG: What are you saying?   10

GALLIMARD: I've come tonight for an answer: are you my Butterfly?

SONG: Don't you know already?

GALLIMARD: I want you to say it.

SONG: I don't want to say it.   15

GALLIMARD: So, that is your answer?

SONG: You know how I feel about—

GALLIMARD: I do remember one thing.

SONG: What?

GALLIMARD: In the letter I received today.   20

SONG: Don't.

GALLIMARD: "I have already given you my shame."

SONG: It's enough that I even wrote it.

GALLIMARD: Well, then—

SONG: I shouldn't have it splashed across my face.   25

GALLIMARD: —if that's all true—

SONG: Stop!

GALLIMARD: Then what is one more short answer?

SONG: I don't want to!

GALLIMARD: Are you my Butterfly? (*Silence; he crosses the room* 30
and begins to touch her hair.) I want from you honesty.
There should be nothing false between us. No false pride.

(*Pause.*)

SONG: Yes, I am. I am your Butterfly.

GALLIMARD: Then let me be honest with you. It is because of you that I was promoted tonight. You have changed my   35
life forever. My little Butterfly, there should be no more secrets: I love you.

(*He starts to kiss her roughly. She resists slightly.*)

SONG: No . . . no . . . gently . . . please, I've never . . .

GALLIMARD: No?

SONG: I've tried to appear experienced, but . . . the truth   40
is . . . no.

GALLIMARD: Are you cold?

SONG: Yes. Cold.

GALLIMARD: Then we will go very, very slowly.

(*He starts to caress her; her gown begins to open.*)

SONG: No . . . let me . . . keep my clothes . . .   45

GALLIMARD: But . . .

SONG: Please . . . it all frightens me. I'm a modest Chinese girl.

GALLIMARD: My poor little treasure.

SONG: I am your treasure. Though inexperienced, I am not . . .
50 ignorant. They teach us things, our mothers, about pleasing a man.

GALLIMARD: Yes?

SONG: I'll do my best to make you happy. Turn off the lights.

(GALLIMARD *gets up and heads for a lamp.* SONG, *propped up on one elbow, tosses her hair back and smiles.*)

SONG: Monsieur Gallimard?
55 GALLIMARD: Yes, Butterfly?

SONG: "Vieni, vieni!"

GALLIMARD: "Come, darling."

SONG: "Ah! Dolce notte!"

GALLIMARD: "Beautiful night."
60 SONG: "Tutto estatico d'amor ride il ciel!"

GALLIMARD: "All ecstatic with love, the heavens are filled with laughter."

(*He turns off the lamp. Blackout.*)

ACT TWO

SCENE I

M. GALLIMARD's *cell. Paris. Present.*

Lights up on GALLIMARD. *He sits in his cell, reading from a leaflet.*

GALLIMARD: This, from a contemporary critic's commentary on *Madame Butterfly*: "Pinkerton suffers from . . . being an obnoxious bounder whom every man in the audience itches to kick." Bully for us men in the audience! Then, in
5 the same note: "Butterfly is the most irresistibly appealing of Puccini's 'Little Women.' Watching the succession of her humiliations is like watching a child under torture." (*He tosses the pamphlet over his shoulder.*) I suggest that, while we men may all want to kick Pinkerton, very few of us would
10 pass up the opportunity to be Pinkerton.

(GALLIMARD *moves out of his cell.*)

SCENE II

GALLIMARD *and* BUTTERFLY's *flat. Beijing. 1960.*

We are in a simple but well-decorated parlor. GALLIMARD *moves to sit on a sofa, while* SONG, *dressed in a chong sam, enters and curls up at his feet.*

GALLIMARD: (*To us.*) We secured a flat on the outskirts of Peking. Butterfly, as I was calling her now, decorated our "home" with Western furniture and Chinese antiques. And there, on a few stolen afternoons or evenings each
5 week, Butterfly commenced her education.

SONG: The Chinese men—they keep us down.

GALLIMARD: Even in the "New Society"?

SONG: In the "New Society," we are all kept ignorant equally. That's one of the exciting things about loving a Western
10 man. I know you are not threatened by a woman's education.

GALLIMARD: I'm no saint, Butterfly.

SONG: But you come from a progressive society.

GALLIMARD: We're not always reminding each other how "old" we are, if that's what you mean.

SONG: Exactly. We Chinese—once, I suppose, it is true, we 15 ruled the world. But so what? How much more exciting to be part of the society ruling the world today. Tell me— what's happening in Vietnam?

GALLIMARD: Oh, Butterfly—you want me to bring my work home? 20

SONG: I want to know what you know. To be impressed by my man. It's not the particulars so much as the fact that you're making decisions which change the shape of the world.

GALLIMARD: Not the world. At best, a small corner.

(TOULON *enters, and sits at a desk upstage.*)

SCENE III

French embassy. Beijing. 1961.

GALLIMARD *moves downstage, to* TOULON's *desk.* SONG *remains upstage, watching.*

TOULON: And a more troublesome corner is hard to imagine.

GALLIMARD: So, the Americans plan to begin bombing?

TOULON: This is very secret, Gallimard: yes. The Americans don't have an embassy here. They're asking us to be their eyes and ears. Say Jack Kennedy signed an order to bomb 5 North Vietnam, Laos. How would the Chinese react?

GALLIMARD: I think the Chinese will squawk—

TOULON: Uh-huh.

GALLIMARD: —but, in their hearts, they don't even like Ho Chi Minh. 10

(*Pause.*)

TOULON: What a bunch of jerks. Vietnam was *our* colony. Not only didn't the Americans help us fight to keep them, but now, seven years later, they've come back to grab the territory for themselves. It's very irritating.

GALLIMARD: With all due respect, sir, why should the Amer- 15 icans have won our war for us back in '54 if we didn't have the will to win it ourselves?

TOULON: You're kidding, aren't you?

(*Pause.*)

GALLIMARD: The Orientals simply want to be associated with whoever shows the most strength and power. You live with 20 the Chinese, sir. Do you think they like Communism?

TOULON: I live in China. Not with the Chinese.

GALLIMARD: Well, I—

TOULON: *You* live with the Chinese.

GALLIMARD: Excuse me? 25

TOULON: I can't keep a secret.

GALLIMARD: What are you saying?

TOULON: Only that I'm not immune to gossip. So, you're keeping a native mistress. Don't answer. It's none of my business. (*Pause.*) I'm sure she must be gorgeous. 30

GALLIMARD: Well . . .

TOULON: I'm impressed. You have the stamina to go out into the streets and hunt one down. Some of us have to be content with the wives of the expatriate community.

35 GALLIMARD: I do feel . . . fortunate.

TOULON: So, Gallimard, you've got the inside knowledge—what *do* the Chinese think?

GALLIMARD: Deep down, they miss the old days. You know, cappuccinos, men in tuxedos—

40 TOULON: So what do we tell the Americans about Vietnam?

GALLIMARD: Tell them there's a natural affinity between the West and the Orient.

TOULON: And that you speak from experience?

GALLIMARD: The Orientals are people too. They want the good things we can give them. If the Americans demonstrate the will to win, the Vietnamese will welcome them into a mutually beneficial union.

45

TOULON: I don't see how the Vietnamese can stand up to American firepower.

50 GALLIMARD: Orientals will always submit to a greater force.

TOULON: I'll note your opinions in my report. The Americans always love to hear how "welcome" they'll be. (*He starts to exit.*)

GALLIMARD: Sir?

55 TOULON: Mmmm?

GALLIMARD: This . . . rumor you've heard.

TOULON: Uh-huh?

GALLIMARD: How . . . widespread do you think it is?

TOULON: It's only widespread within this embassy. Where nobody talks because everybody is guilty. We were worried about you, Gallimard. We thought you were the only one here without a secret. Now you go and find a lotus blossom . . . and top us all. (*He exits.*)

60

GALLIMARD: (*To us.*) Toulon knows! And he approves! I was learning the benefits of being a man. We form our own clubs, sit behind thick doors, smoke—and celebrate the fact that we're still boys. (*He starts to move downstage, towards* SONG.) So, over the—

65

(*Suddenly* COMRADE CHIN *enters.* GALLIMARD *backs away.*)

GALLIMARD: (*To* SONG.) No! Why does she have to come in?

70 SONG: Rene, be sensible. How can they understand the story without her? Now, don't embarrass yourself.

(GALLIMARD *moves down center.*)

GALLIMARD: (*To us.*) Now, you will see why my story is so amusing to so many people. Why they snicker at parties in disbelief. Please—try to understand it from my point of view. We are all prisoners of our time and place. (*He exits.*)

75

SCENE IV

GALLIMARD *and* BUTTERFLY's *flat. Beijing. 1961.*

SONG: (*To us.*) 1961. The flat Monsieur Gallimard rented for us. An evening after he has gone.

CHIN: Okay, see if you find out when the Americans plan to start bombing Vietnam. If you can find out what cities, even better.

5

SONG: I'll do my best, but I don't want to arouse his suspicions.

CHIN: Yeah, sure, of course. So, what else?

SONG: The Americans will increase troops in Vietnam to 170,000 soldiers with 120,000 militia and 11,000 American advisors.

10

CHIN: (*Writing.*) Wait, wait. 120,000 militia and—

SONG: —11,000 American—

CHIN: —American advisors. (*Beat.*) How do you remember so much?

SONG: I'm an actor.

15

CHIN: Yeah. (*Beat.*) Is that how come you dress like that?

SONG: Like what, Miss Chin?

CHIN: Like that dress! You're wearing a dress. And every time I come here, you're wearing a dress. Is that because you're an actor? Or what?

20

SONG: It's a . . . disguise, Miss Chin.

CHIN: Actors, I think they're all weirdos. My mother tells me actors are like gamblers or prostitutes or —

SONG: It helps me in my assignment.

(*Pause.*)

CHIN: You're not gathering information in any way that violates Communist Party principles, are you?

25

SONG: Why would I do that?

CHIN: Just checking. Remember: when working for the Great Proletarian State, you represent our Chairman Mao in every position you take.

30

SONG: I'll try to imagine the Chairman taking my positions.

CHIN: We all think of him this way. Good-bye, comrade. (*She starts to exit.*) Comrade?

SONG: Yes?

CHIN: Don't forget: there is no homosexuality in China!

35

SONG: Yes, I've heard.

CHIN: Just checking. (*She exits.*)

SONG: (*To us.*) What passes for a woman in modern China.

(GALLIMARD *sticks his head out from the wings.*)

GALLIMARD: Is she gone?

SONG: Yes, Rene. Please continue in your own fashion.

40

SCENE V

Beijing. 1961–63.

GALLIMARD *moves to the couch where* SONG *still sits. He lies down in her lap, and she strokes his forehead.*

GALLIMARD: (*To us.*) And so, over the years 1961, '62, '63, we settled into our routine, Butterfly and I. She would always have prepared a light snack and then, ever so delicately, and only if I agreed, she would start to pleasure me. With her hands, her mouth . . . too many ways to explain, and too sad, given my present situation. But mostly we would talk. About my life. Perhaps there is nothing more rare than to find a woman who passionately listens.

5

(SONG *remains upstage, listening, as* HELGA *enters and plays a scene downstage with* GALLIMARD.)

HELGA: Rene, I visited Dr. Bolleart this morning.

GALLIMARD: Why? Are you ill?

10

HELGA: No, no. You see, I wanted to ask him . . . that question we've been discussing.

GALLIMARD: And I told you, it's only a matter of time. Why did you bring a doctor into this? We just have to keep try-ing—like a crapshoot, actually.

HELGA: I went, I'm sorry. But listen: he says there's nothing wrong with me.

GALLIMARD: You see? Now, will you stop—?

HELGA: Rene, he says he'd like you to go in and take some tests.

GALLIMARD: Why? So he can find there's nothing wrong with both of us?

HELGA: Rene, I don't ask for much. One trip! One visit! And then, whatever you want to do about it—you decide.

GALLIMARD: You're assuming he'll find something defective!

HELGA: No! Of course not! Whatever he finds—if he finds nothing, we decide what to do about nothing! But go!

GALLIMARD: If he finds nothing, we keep trying. Just like we do now.

HELGA: But at least we'll know! (*Pause.*) I'm sorry. (*She starts to exit.*)

GALLIMARD: Do you really want me to see Dr. Bolleart?

HELGA: Only if you want a child, Rene. We have to face the fact that time is running out. Only if you want a child. (*She exits.*)

GALLIMARD: (*To* SONG.) I'm a modern man, Butterfly. And yet, I don't want to go. It's the same old voodoo. I feel like God himself is laughing at me if I can't produce a child.

SONG: You men of the West—you're obsessed by your odd desire for equality. Your wife can't give you a child, and *you're going to the doctor?*

GALLIMARD: Well, you see, she's already gone.

SONG: And because this incompetent can't find the defect, you now have to subject yourself to him? It's unnatural.

GALLIMARD: Well, what is the "natural" solution?

SONG: In Imperial China, when a man found that one wife was inadequate, he turned to another—to give him his son.

GALLIMARD: What do you—? I can't . . . marry you, yet.

SONG: Please. I'm not asking you to be my husband. But I am already your wife.

GALLIMARD: Do you want to . . . have my child?

SONG: I thought you'd never ask.

GALLIMARD: But, your career . . . your—

SONG: Phooey on my career! That's your Western mind, twist-ing itself into strange shapes again. Of course I love my ca-reer. But what would I love most of all? To feel something inside me—day and night—something I know is yours. (*Pause.*) Promise me . . . you won't go to this doctor. Who is this Western quack to set himself as judge over the man I love? I know who is a man, and who is not. (*She exits.*)

GALLIMARD: (*To us.*) Dr. Bolleart? Of course I didn't go. What man would?

SCENE VI

Beijing. 1963.

Party noises over the house speakers. RENEE *enters, wearing a re-vealing gown.*

GALLIMARD: 1963. A party at the Austrian embassy. None of us could remember the Austrian ambassador's name, which seemed somehow appropriate. (*To* RENEE.) So, I tell the Americans, Diem must go. The U.S. wants to be respected by the Vietnamese, and yet they're propping up this nobody seminarian as her president. A man whose claim to fame is his sister-in-law imposing fanatic "moral order" cam-paigns? Oriental women—when they're good, they're very good, but when they're bad, they're Christians.

RENEE: Yeah.

GALLIMARD: And what do you do?

RENEE: I'm a student. My father exports a lot of useless stuff to the Third World.

GALLIMARD: How useless?

RENEE: You know. Squirt guns, confectioner's sugar, hula hoops . . .

GALLIMARD: I'm sure they appreciate the sugar.

RENEE: I'm here for two years to study Chinese.

GALLIMARD: Two years?

RENEE: That's what everybody says.

GALLIMARD: When did you arrive?

RENEE: Three weeks ago.

GALLIMARD: And?

RENEE: I like it. It's primitive, but . . . well, this is the place to learn Chinese, so here I am.

GALLIMARD: Why Chinese?

RENEE: I think it'll be important someday.

GALLIMARD: You do?

RENEE: Don't ask me when, but . . . that's what I think.

GALLIMARD: Well, I agree with you. One hundred percent. That's very farsighted.

RENEE: Yeah. Well of course, my father thinks I'm a complete weirdo.

GALLIMARD: He'll thank you someday.

RENEE: Like when the Chinese start buying hula hoops?

GALLIMARD: There're a billion bellies out there.

RENEE: And if they end up taking over the world—well, then I'll be lucky to know Chinese too, right?

(*Pause.*)

GALLIMARD: At this point, I don't see how the Chinese can possibly take—

RENEE: You know what I *don't* like about China?

GALLIMARD: Excuse me? No—what?

RENEE: Nothing to do at night.

GALLIMARD: You come to parties at embassies like everyone else.

RENEE: Yeah, but they get out at ten. And then what?

GALLIMARD: I'm afraid the Chinese idea of a dance hall is a dirt floor and a man with a flute.

RENEE: Are you married?

GALLIMARD: Yes. Why?

RENEE: You wanna . . . fool around?

(*Pause.*)

GALLIMARD: Sure.

RENEE: I'll wait for you outside. What's your name?

GALLIMARD: Gallimard. Rene.

RENEE: Weird. I'm Renee too. (*She exits.*)

GALLIMARD: (*To us.*) And so, I embarked on my first extra-extramarital affair. Renee was picture perfect. With a body like those girls in the magazines. If I put a tissue pa-per over my eyes, I wouldn't have been able to tell the dif-ference. And it was exciting to be with someone who wasn't afraid to be seen completely naked. But is it possible for a woman to be *too* uninhibited, *too* willing, so as to seem almost too . . . masculine?

(*Chuck Berry blares from the house speakers, then comes down in volume as* RENEE *enters, toweling her hair.*)

RENEE: You have a nice weenie.

65 GALLIMARD: What?

RENEE: Penis. You have a nice penis.

GALLIMARD: Oh. Well, thank you. That's very . . .

RENEE: What—can't take a compliment?

GALLIMARD: No, it's very . . . reassuring.

70 RENEE: But most girls don't come out and say it, huh?

GALLIMARD: And also . . . what did you call it?

RENEE: Oh. Most girls don't call it a "weenie," huh?

GALLIMARD: It sounds very—

RENEE: Small, I know.

75 GALLIMARD: I was going to say, "young."

RENEE: Yeah. Young, small, same thing. Most guys are pretty, uh, sensitive about that. Like, you know, I had a boyfriend back home in Denmark. I got mad at him once and called him a little weeniehead. He got so mad! He said at least I

80 should call him a great big weeniehead.

GALLIMARD: I suppose I just say "penis."

RENEE: Yeah. That's pretty clinical. There's "cock," but that sounds like a chicken. And "prick" is painful, and "dick" is like you're talking about someone who's not in the room.

85 GALLIMARD: Yes. It's a . . . bigger problem than I imagined.

RENEE: I—I think maybe it's because I really don't know what to do with them—that's why I call them "weenies."

GALLIMARD: Well, you did quite well with . . . mine.

RENEE: Thanks, but I mean, really *do* with them. Like, okay,

90 have you ever looked at one? I mean, really?

GALLIMARD: No, I suppose when it's part of you, you sort of take it for granted.

RENEE: I guess. But, like, it just hangs there. This little . . . flap of flesh. And there's so much fuss that we make about it.

95 Like, I think the reason we fight wars is because we wear clothes. Because no one knows—between the men, I mean—who has the bigger . . . weenie. So, if I'm a guy with a small one, I'm going to build a really big building or take over a really big piece of land or write a really long book

100 so the other men don't know, right? But, see, it never really works, that's the problem. I mean, you conquer the country, or whatever, but you're still wearing clothes, so there's no way to prove absolutely whose is bigger or smaller. And that's what we call a civilized society. The whole world run

105 by a bunch of men with pricks the size of pins. (*She exits.*)

GALLIMARD: (*To us.*) This was simply not acceptable.

(*A high-pitched chime rings through the air.* SONG, *dressed as Butterfly, appears in the upstage special. She is obviously distressed. Her body swoons as she attempts to clip the stems of flowers she's arranging in a vase.*)

GALLIMARD: But I kept up our affair, wildly, for several months. Why? I believe because of Butterfly. She knew the secret I was trying to hide. But, unlike a Western

110 woman, she didn't confront me, threaten, even pout. I remembered the words of Puccini's *Butterfly:*

SONG: "Noi siamo gente avvezza / alle piccole cose / umili e silenziose."

GALLIMARD: "I come from a people / Who are accustomed to little / Humble and silent." I saw Pinkerton and Butterfly, and 115 what she would say if he were unfaithful . . . nothing. She would cry, alone, into those wildly soft sleeves, once full of possessions, now empty to collect her tears. It was her tears and her silence that excited me, every time I visited Renee.

TOULON: (*Offstage.*) Gallimard!   120

(TOULON *enters.* GALLIMARD *turns towards him. During the next section,* SONG, *up center, begins to dance with the flowers. It is a drunken dance, where she breaks small pieces off the stems.*)

TOULON: They're killing him.

GALLIMARD: Who? I'm sorry? What?

TOULON: Bother you to come over at this late hour?

GALLIMARD: No . . . of course not.

TOULON: Not after you hear my secret. Champagne?   125

GALLIMARD: Um . . . thank you.

TOULON: You're surprised. There's something that you've wanted, Gallimard. No, not a promotion. Next time. Something in the world. You're not aware of this, but there's an informal gossip circle among intelligence agents.   130 And some of ours heard from some of the Americans—

GALLIMARD: Yes?

TOULON: That the U.S. will allow the Vietnamese generals to stage a coup . . . and assassinate President Diem.

(*The chime rings again.* TOULON *freezes.* GALLIMARD *turns upstage and looks at* SONG, *who slowly and deliberately clips a flower off its stem.* GALLIMARD *turns back towards* TOULON.)

GALLIMARD: I think . . . that's a very wise move!   135

(TOULON *unfreezes.*)

TOULON: It's what you've been advocating. A toast?

GALLIMARD: Sure. I consider this a vindication.

TOULON: Not exactly. "To the test. Let's hope you pass."

(*They drink. The chime rings again.* TOULON *freezes.* GALLIMARD *turns upstage, and* SONG *clips another flower.*)

GALLIMARD: (*To* TOULON.) The test?

TOULON: (*Unfreezing.*) It's a test of everything you've been   140 saying. I personally think the generals probably will stop the Communists. And you'll be a hero. But if anything goes wrong, then your opinions won't be worth a pig's ear. I'm sure that won't happen. But sometimes it's easier when they don't listen to you.   145

GALLIMARD: They're your opinions too, aren't they?

TOULON: Personally, yes.

GALLIMARD: So we agree.

TOULON: But my opinions aren't on that report. Yours are. Cheers.   150

(TOULON *turns away from* GALLIMARD *and raises his glass. At that instant* SONG *picks up the vase and hurls it to the ground. It shatters.* SONG *sinks down amidst the shards of the vase, in a calm, childlike trance. She sings softly, as if reciting a child's nursery rhyme.*)

SONG: (*Repeat as necessary.*) "The whole world over, the white man travels, setting anchor, wherever he likes. Life's not worth living, unless he finds, the finest maidens, of every land . . ."

(GALLIMARD *turns downstage towards us.* SONG *continues singing.*)

155 GALLIMARD: I shook as I left his house. That coward! That worm! To put the burden for his decisions on my shoulders! I started for Renee's. But no, that was all I needed. A schoolgirl who would question the role of the penis in modern society. What I wanted was revenge. A vessel to
160 contain my humiliation. Though I hadn't seen her in several weeks, I headed for Butterfly's.

(GALLIMARD *enters* SONG's *apartment.*)

SONG: Oh! Rene . . . I was dreaming!
GALLIMARD: You've been drinking?
SONG: If I can't sleep, then yes, I drink. But then, it gives me
165 these dreams which—Rene, it's been almost three weeks since you visited me last.
GALLIMARD: I know. There's been a lot going on in the world.
SONG: Fortunately I am drunk. So I can speak freely. It's not the world, it's you and me. And an old problem. Even the
170 softest skin becomes like leather to a man who's touched it too often. I confess I don't know how to stop it. I don't know how to become another woman.
GALLIMARD: I have a request.
SONG: Is this a solution? Or are you ready to give up the flat?
175 GALLIMARD: It may be a solution. But I'm sure you won't like it.
SONG: Oh well, that's very important. "Like it?" Do you think I "like" lying here alone, waiting, always waiting for your return? Please—don't worry about what I may not "like."
GALLIMARD: I want to see you . . . naked.

(*Silence.*)

180 SONG: I thought you understood my modesty. So you want me to—what—strip? Like a big cowboy girl? Shiny pasties on my breasts? Shall I fling my kimono over my head and yell "ya-hoo" in the process? I thought you respected my shame!
185 GALLIMARD: I believe you gave me your shame many years ago.
SONG: Yes—and it is just like a white devil to use it against me. I can't believe it. I thought myself so repulsed by the passive Oriental and the cruel white man. Now I see—we are always most revolted by the things hidden within us.
190 GALLIMARD: I just mean—
SONG: Yes?
GALLIMARD: —that it will remove the only barrier left between us.
SONG: No, Rene. Don't couch your request in sweet words.
195 Be yourself—a cad—and know that my love is enough, that I submit—submit to the worst you can give me. (*Pause.*) Well, come. Strip me. Whatever happens, know that you have willed it. Our love, in your hands. I'm helpless before my man.

(GALLIMARD *starts to cross the room.*)

200 GALLIMARD: Did I not undress her because I knew, somewhere deep down, what I would find? Perhaps. Happiness is so rare that our mind can turn somersaults to protect it.

At the time, I only knew that I was seeing Pinkerton stalking towards his Butterfly, ready to reward her love with his lecherous hands. The image sickened me, pulled 205 me to my knees, so I was crawling towards her like a worm. By the time I reached her, Pinkerton . . . had vanished from my heart. To be replaced by something new, something unnatural, that flew in the face of all I'd learned in the world—something very close to love. 210

(*He grabs her around the waist; she strokes his hair.*)

GALLIMARD: Butterfly, forgive me.
SONG: Rene . . .
GALLIMARD: For everything. From the start.
SONG: I'm . . .
GALLIMARD: I want to— 215
SONG: I'm pregnant. (*Beat.*) I'm pregnant. (*Beat.*) I'm pregnant.

(*Beat.*)

GALLIMARD: I want to marry you!

SCENE VII

GALLIMARD *and* BUTTERFLY's *flat. Beijing. 1963.*

Downstage, SONG *paces as* COMRADE CHIN *reads from her notepad. Upstage,* GALLIMARD *is still kneeling. He remains on his knees throughout the scene, watching it.*

SONG: I need a baby.
CHIN: (*From pad.*) He's been spotted going to a dorm.
SONG: I need a baby.
CHIN: At the Foreign Language Institute.
SONG: I need a baby. 5
CHIN: The room of a Danish girl . . . What do you mean, you need a baby?!
SONG: Tell Comrade Kang—last night, the entire mission, it could've ended.
CHIN: What do you mean? 10
SONG: Tell Kang—he told me to strip.
CHIN: *Strip?!*
SONG: Write!
CHIN: I tell you, I don't understand nothing about this case anymore. Nothing. 15
SONG: He told me to strip, and I took a chance. Oh, we Chinese, we know how to gamble.
CHIN: (*Writing.*) " . . . told him to strip."
SONG: My palms were wet, I had to make a split-second decision.
CHIN: Hey! Can you slow down?! 20

(*Pause.*)

SONG: You write faster, I'm the artist here. Suddenly, it hit me—"All he wants is for her to submit. Once a woman submits, a man is always ready to become 'generous.'"
CHIN: You're just gonna end up with rough notes.
SONG: And it worked! He gave in! Now, if I can just present 25 him with a baby. A Chinese baby with blond hair—he'll be mine for life!
CHIN: Kang will never agree! The trading of babies has to be a counterrevolutionary act.

30 SONG: Sometimes, a counterrevolutionary act is necessary to counter a counterrevolutionary act.

(*Pause.*)

CHIN: Wait.
SONG: I need one . . . in seven months. Make sure it's a boy.
CHIN: This doesn't sound like something the Chairman would
35   do. Maybe you'd better talk to Comrade Kang yourself.
SONG: Good. I will.

(CHIN *gets up to leave.*)

SONG: Miss Chin? Why, in the Peking Opera, are women's roles played by men?
CHIN: I don't know. Maybe, a reactionary remnant of male—
40 SONG: No. (*Beat.*) Because only a man knows how a woman is supposed to act.

(CHIN *exits.* SONG *turns upstage, towards* GALLIMARD.)

GALLIMARD: (*Calling after* CHIN.) Good riddance! (*To* SONG.) I could forget all that betrayal in an instant, you know. If you'd just come back and become Butterfly again.
45 SONG: Fat chance. You're here in prison, rotting in a cell. And I'm on a plane, winging my way back to China. Your President pardoned me of our treason, you know.
GALLIMARD: Yes, I read about that.
SONG: Must make you feel . . . lower than shit.
50 GALLIMARD: But don't you, even a little bit, wish you were here with me?
SONG: I'm an artist, Rene. You were my greatest . . . acting challenge. (*She laughs.*) It doesn't matter how rotten I answer, does it? You still adore me. That's why I love you,
55   Rene. (*She points to us.*) So—you were telling your audience about the night I announced I was pregnant.

(GALLIMARD *puts his arms around* SONG'S *waist. He and* SONG *are in the positions they were in at the end of Scene 6.*)

SCENE VIII

Same.

GALLIMARD: I'll divorce my wife. We'll live together here, and then later in France.
SONG: I feel so . . . ashamed.
GALLIMARD: Why?
5 SONG: I had begun to lose faith. And now, you shame me with your generosity.
GALLIMARD: Generosity? No, I'm proposing for very selfish reasons.
SONG: Your apologies only make me feel more ashamed. My
10   outburst a moment ago!
GALLIMARD: Your outburst? What about my request?!
SONG: You've been very patient dealing with my . . . eccentricities. A Western man, used to women freer with their bodies—
15 GALLIMARD: It was sick! Don't make excuses for me.
SONG: I have to. You don't seem willing to make them for yourself.

(*Pause.*)

GALLIMARD: You're crazy.
SONG: I'm happy. Which often looks like crazy.
GALLIMARD: Then make me crazy. Marry me. 20

(*Pause.*)

SONG: No.
GALLIMARD: What?
SONG: Do I sound silly, a slave, if I say I'm not worthy?
GALLIMARD: Yes. In fact you do. No one has loved me like you.
SONG: Thank you. And no one ever will. I'll see to that. 25
GALLIMARD: So what is the problem?
SONG: Rene, we Chinese are realists. We understand rice, gold, and guns. You are a diplomat. Your career is skyrocketing. Now, what would happen if you divorced your wife to marry a Communist Chinese actress? 30
GALLIMARD: That's not being realistic. That's defeating yourself before you begin.
SONG: We must conserve our strength for the battles we can win.
GALLIMARD: That sounds like a fortune cookie!
SONG: Where do you think fortune cookies come from? 35
GALLIMARD: I don't care.
SONG: You do. So do I. And we should. That is why I say I'm not worthy. I'm worthy to love and even to be loved by you. But I am not worthy to end the career of one of the West's most promising diplomats. 40
GALLIMARD: It's not that great a career! I made it sound like more than it is!
SONG: Modesty will get you nowhere. Flatter yourself, and you flatter me. I'm flattered to decline your offer. (*She exits.*)
GALLIMARD: (*To us.*) Butterfly and I argued all night. And, in 45 the end, I left, knowing I would never be her husband. She went away for several months—to the countryside, like a small animal. Until the night I received her call.

(*A baby's cry from offstage.* SONG *enters, carrying a child.*)

SONG: He looks like you.
GALLIMARD: Oh! (*Beat; he approaches the baby.*) Well, babies are 50 never very attractive at birth.
SONG: Stop!
GALLIMARD: I'm sure he'll grow more beautiful with age. More like his mother.
SONG: "Chi vide mai / a bimbo del Giappon . . ." 55
GALLIMARD: "What baby, I wonder, was ever born in Japan"—or China, for that matter—
SONG: ". . . occhi azzurrini?"
GALLIMARD: "With azure eyes"—they're actually sort of brown, wouldn't you say? 60
SONG: "E il labbro."
GALLIMARD: "And such lips!" (*He kisses* SONG.) And such lips.
SONG: "E i ricciolini d'oro schietto?"
GALLIMARD: "And such a head of golden"—if slightly patchy—"curls?" 65
SONG: I'm going to call him "Peepee."
GALLIMARD: Darling, could you repeat that because I'm sure a rickshaw just flew by overhead.
SONG: You heard me.
GALLIMARD: "Song Peepee"? May I suggest Michael, or 70 Stephan, or Adolph?
SONG: You may, but I won't listen.
GALLIMARD: You can't be serious. Can you imagine the time this child will have in school?

75 SONG: In the West, yes.

GALLIMARD: It's worse than naming him Ping Pong or Long Dong or—

SONG: But he's never going to live in the West, is he?

(*Pause.*)

GALLIMARD: That wasn't my choice.

80 SONG: It is mine. And this is my promise to you: I will raise him, he will be our child, but he will never burden you outside of China.

GALLIMARD: Why do you make these promises? I want to be burdened! I want a scandal to cover the papers!

85 SONG: (*To us.*) Prophetic.

GALLIMARD: I'm serious.

SONG: So am I. His name is as I registered it. And he will never live in the West.

(SONG *exits with the child.*)

GALLIMARD: (*To us.*) It is possible that her stubbornness only
90 made me want her more. That drawing back at the moment of my capitulation was the most brilliant strategy she could have chosen. It is possible. But it is also possible that by this point she could have said, could have done . . . anything, and I would have adored her still.

SCENE IX

Beijing. 1966.

A driving rhythm of Chinese percussion fills the stage.

GALLIMARD: And then, China began to change. Mao became very old, and his cult became very strong. And, like many old men, he entered his second childhood. So he handed over the reins of state to those with minds like his own.
5 And children ruled the Middle Kingdom with complete caprice. The doctrine of the Cultural Revolution implied continuous anarchy. Contact between Chinese and foreigners became impossible. Our flat was confiscated. Her fame and my money now counted against us.

(*Two dancers in Mao suits and red-starred caps enter, and begin crudely mimicking revolutionary violence, in an agitprop fashion.*)

10 GALLIMARD: And somehow the American war went wrong too. Four hundred thousand dollars were being spent for every Viet Cong killed; so General Westmoreland's remark that the Oriental does not value life the way Americans do was oddly accurate. Why weren't the Vietnamese people giving in?
15 Why were they content instead to die and die and die again?

(TOULON *enters.*)

TOULON: Congratulations, Gallimard.

GALLIMARD: Excuse me, sir?

TOULON: Not a promotion. That was last time. You're going home.

20 GALLIMARD: What?

TOULON: Don't say I didn't warn you.

GALLIMARD: I'm being transferred . . . because I was wrong about the American war?

TOULON: Of course not. We don't care about the Americans. We care about your mind. The quality of your analysis. In 25
general, everything you've predicted here in the Orient . . . just hasn't happened.

GALLIMARD: I think that's premature.

TOULON: Don't force me to be blunt. Okay, you said China was ready to open to Western trade. The only thing 30
they're trading out there are Western heads. And, yes, you said the Americans would succeed in Indochina. You were kidding, right?

GALLIMARD: I think the end is in sight.

TOULON: Don't be pathetic. And don't take this personally. 35
You were wrong. It's not your fault.

GALLIMARD: But I'm going home.

TOULON: Right. Could I have the number of your mistress? (*Beat.*) Joke! Joke! Eat a croissant for me.

(TOULON *exits.* SONG, *wearing a Mao suit, is dragged in from the wings as part of the upstage dance. They "beat" her, then lampoon the acrobatics of the Chinese opera, as she is made to kneel onstage.*)

GALLIMARD: (*Simultaneously.*) I don't care to recall how But- 40
terfly and I said our hurried farewell. Perhaps it was better to end our affair before it killed her.

(GALLIMARD *exits.* COMRADE CHIN *walks across the stage with a banner reading: "The Actor Renounces His Decadent Profession!" She reaches the kneeling* SONG. *Percussion stops with a thud. Dancers strike poses.*)

CHIN: Actor-oppressor, for years you have lived above the common people and looked down on their labor. While the farmer ate millet— 45

SONG: I ate pastries from France and sweetmeats from silver trays.

CHIN: And how did you come to live in such an exalted position?

SONG: I was a plaything for the imperialists! 50

CHIN: What did you do?

SONG: I shamed China by allowing myself to be corrupted by a foreigner . . .

CHIN: What does this mean? The People demand a full confession! 55

SONG: I engaged in the lowest perversions with China's enemies!

CHIN: What perversions? Be more clear!

SONG: I let him put it up my ass!

(*Dancers look over, disgusted.*)

CHIN: Aaaa-ya! How can you use such sickening language?!

SONG: My language . . . is only as foul as the crimes I com- 60
mitted . . .

CHIN: Yeah. That's better. So—what do you want to do now?

SONG: I want to serve the people.

(*Percussion starts up, with Chinese strings.*)

CHIN: What?

SONG: I want to serve the people! 65

(*Dancers regain their revolutionary smiles, and begin a dance of victory.*)

CHIN: What?!

SONG: I want to serve the people!

(*Dancers unveil a banner: "The Actor Is Rehabilitated!"* SONG *remains kneeling before* CHIN, *as the dancers bounce around them, then exit. Music out.*)

SCENE X

A commune. Hunan Province. 1970.

CHIN: How you planning to do that?

SONG: I've already worked four years in the fields of Hunan, Comrade Chin.

CHIN: So? Farmers work all their lives. Let me see your hands.

(SONG *holds them out for her inspection.*)

5 CHIN: Goddamn! Still so smooth! How long does it take to turn you actors into good anythings? Hunh. You've just spent too many years in luxury to be any good to the Revolution.

SONG: I served the Revolution.

10 CHIN: Serve the Resolution? Bullshit! You wore dresses! Don't tell me—I was there. I saw you! You and your white vice-consul! Stuck up there in your flat, living off the People's Treasury! Yeah, I knew what was going on! You two . . . homos! Homos! Homos! (*Pause; she composes herself.*) Ah! Well . . . you will serve the people, all right. But not with the Revolution's money. This time, you use your own money.

SONG: I have no money.

CHIN: Shut up! And you won't stink up China anymore with
20 your pervert stuff. You'll pollute the place where pollution begins—the West.

SONG: What do you mean?

CHIN: Shut up! You're going to France. Without a cent in your pocket. You find your consul's house, you make him
25 pay your expenses—

SONG: No.

CHIN: And you give us weekly reports! Useful information!

SONG: That's crazy. It's been four years.

CHIN: Either that, or back to rehabilitation center!

30 SONG: Comrade Chin, he's not going to support me! Not in France! He's a white man! I was just his plaything—

CHIN: Oh yuck! Again with the sickening language. Where's my stick?

SONG: You don't understand the mind of a man.

(*Pause.*)

35 CHIN: Oh no? No I don't? Then how come I'm married, huh? How come I got a man? Five, six years ago, you always tell me those kinds of things, I felt very bad. But not now! Be-cause what does the Chairman say? He tells us *I'm* now the smart one, you're now the nincompoop!
40 *You're* the blackhead, the harebrain, the nitwit! You think you're so smart? You understand "The Mind of a Man"? Good! Then *you* go to France and be a pervert for Chairman Mao!

(CHIN *and* SONG *exit in opposite directions.*)

SCENE XI

Paris. 1968–70.

GALLIMARD *enters.*

GALLIMARD: And what was waiting for me back in Paris? Well, better Chinese food than I'd eaten in China. Friends and relatives. A little accounting, regular schedule, keeping track of traffic violations in the suburbs. . . . And the indignity of students shouting the slogans of Chairman 5
Mao at me—in French.

HELGA: Rene? Rene? (*She enters, soaking wet.*) I've had a . . . a problem. (*She sneezes.*)

GALLIMARD: You're wet.

HELGA: Yes, I . . . coming back from the grocer's. A group of 10
students, waving red flags, they—

(GALLIMARD *fetches a towel.*)

HELGA: —they ran by, I was caught up along with them. Before I knew what was happening—

(GALLIMARD *gives her the towel.*)

HELGA: Thank you. The police started firing water cannons at us. I tried to shout, to tell them I was the wife of a diplo- 15
mat, but—you know how it is . . . (*Pause.*) Needless to say, I lost the groceries. Rene, what's happening to France?

GALLIMARD: What's—? Well, nothing, really.

HELGA: Nothing? The storefronts are in flames, there's glass in the streets, buildings are toppling—and I'm wet! 20

GALLIMARD: Nothing! . . . that I care to think about.

HELGA: And is that why you stay in this room?

GALLIMARD: Yes, in fact.

HELGA: With the incense burning? You know something? I hate incense. It smells so sickly sweet. 25

GALLIMARD: Well, I hate the French. Who just smell—period!

HELGA: And the Chinese were better?

GALLIMARD: Please—don't start.

HELGA: When we left, this exact same thing, the riots—

GALLIMARD: No, no . . . 30

HELGA: Students screaming slogans, smashing down doors—

GALLIMARD: Helga—

HELGA: It was all going on in China, too. Don't you remember?!

GALLIMARD: Helga! Please! (*Pause.*) You have never understood China, have you? You walk in here with these 35
ridiculous ideas, that the West is falling apart, that China was spitting in our faces. You come in, dripping of the streets, and you leave water all over my floor. (*He grabs* HELGA*'s towel, begins mopping up the floor.*)

HELGA: But it's the truth! 40

GALLIMARD: Helga, I want a divorce.

(*Pause;* GALLIMARD *continues, mopping the floor.*)

HELGA: I take it back. China is . . . beautiful. Incense, I like incense.

GALLIMARD: I've had a mistress.

HELGA: So? 45

GALLIMARD: For eight years.

HELGA: I knew you would. I knew you would the day I married you. And now what? You want to marry her?

GALLIMARD: I can't. She's in China.

50 HELGA: I see. You want to leave. For someone who's not here, is that right?

GALLIMARD: That's right.

HELGA: You can't live with her, but still you don't want to live with me.

55 GALLIMARD: That's right.

(*Pause.*)

HELGA: Shit. How terrible that I can figure that out. (*Pause.*) I never thought I'd say it. But, in China, I was happy. I knew, in my own way, I knew that you were not everything you pretended to be. But the pretense—going on your arm to
60 the embassy ball, visiting your office and the guards saying, "Good morning, good morning, Madame Gallimard"— the pretense . . . was very good indeed. (*Pause.*) I hope everyone is mean to you for the rest of your life. (*She exits.*)

GALLIMARD: (*To us.*) Prophetic.

(MARC *enters with two drinks.*)

65 GALLIMARD: (*To* MARC.) In China, I was different from all other men.

MARC: Sure. You were white. Here's your drink.

GALLIMARD: I felt . . . touched.

MARC: In the head? Rene, I don't want to hear about the
70 Oriental love goddess. Okay? One night—can we just drink and throw up without a lot of conversation?

GALLIMARD: You still don't believe me, do you?

MARC: Sure I do. She was the most beautiful, et cetera, et cetera, blasé blasé.

(*Pause.*)

75 GALLIMARD: My life in the West has been such a disappointment.

MARC: Life in the West is like that. You'll get used to it. Look, you're driving me away. I'm leaving. Happy, now? (*He exits, then returns.*) Look, I have a date tomorrow night. You
80 wanna come? I can fix you up with—

GALLIMARD: Of course. I would love to come.

(*Pause.*)

MARC: Uh—on second thought, no. You'd better get ahold of yourself first.

(*He exits;* GALLIMARD *nurses his drink.*)

GALLIMARD: (*To us.*) This is the ultimate cruelty, isn't it? That
85 I can talk and talk and to anyone listening, it's only air— too rich a diet to be swallowed by a mundane world. Why can't anyone understand? That in China, I once loved, and was loved by, very simply, the Perfect Woman.

(SONG *enters, dressed as Butterfly in wedding dress.*)

GALLIMARD: (*To* SONG.) Not again. My imagination is hell.
90 Am I asleep this time? Or did I drink too much?

SONG: Rene?

GALLIMARD: God, it's too painful! That you speak?

SONG: What are you talking about? Rene—touch me.

GALLIMARD: Why?

SONG: I'm real. Take my hand.   95

GALLIMARD: Why? So you can disappear again and leave me clutching at the air? For the entertainment of my neighbors who—?

(SONG *touches* GALLIMARD.)

SONG: Rene?

(GALLIMARD *takes* SONG's *hand. Silence.*)

GALLIMARD: Butterfly? I never doubted you'd return.   100

SONG: You hadn't . . . forgotten—?

GALLIMARD: Yes, actually, I've forgotten everything. My mind, you see—there wasn't enough room in this hard head—not for the world *and* for you. No, there was only room for one. (*Beat.*) Come, look. See? Your bed has been 105
waiting, with the Klimt poster you like, and—see? The xiang lu [incense burner] you gave me?

SONG: I . . . I don't know what to say.

GALLIMARD: There's nothing to say. Not at the end of a long trip. Can I make you some tea?   110

SONG: But where's your wife?

GALLIMARD: She's by my side. She's by my side at last.

(GALLIMARD *reaches to embrace* SONG. SONG *sidesteps, dodging him.*)

GALLIMARD: Why?

SONG: (*To us.*) So I did return to Rene in Paris. Where I found—   115

GALLIMARD: Why do you run away? Can't we show them how we embraced that evening?

SONG: Please. I'm talking.

GALLIMARD: You have to do what I say! I'm conjuring you up in *my* mind!   120

SONG: Rene, I've never done what you've said. Why should it be any different in your mind? Now split—the story moves on, and I must change.

GALLIMARD: I welcomed you into my home! I didn't have to, you know! I could've left you penniless on the streets of 125
Paris! But I took you in!

SONG: Thank you.

GALLIMARD: So . . . please . . . don't change.

SONG: You know I have to. You know I will. And anyway, what difference does it make? No matter what your eyes tell you, 130
you can't ignore the truth. You already know too much.

(GALLIMARD *exits.* SONG *turns to us.*)

SONG: The change I'm going to make requires about five minutes. So I thought you might want to take this opportunity to stretch your legs, enjoy a drink, or listen to the musicians. I'll be here, when you return, right where you 135
left me.

(SONG *goes to a mirror in front of which is a wash basin of water. She starts to remove her makeup as stagelights go to half and houselights come up.*)

ACT THREE

SCENE I

A courthouse in Paris. 1986.

As he promised, SONG *has completed the bulk of his transformation onstage by the time the houselights go down and the stagelights come up full. He removes his wig and kimono, leaving them on the floor. Underneath, he wears a well-cut suit.*

SONG: So I'd done my job better than I had a right to expect. Well, give him some credit, too. He's right—I was in a fix when I arrived in Paris. I walked from the airport into town, then I located, by blind groping, the Chinatown district. Let me make one thing clear: whatever else may be said about the Chinese, they are stingy! I slept in doorways three days until I could find a tailor who would make me this kimono on credit. As it turns out, maybe I didn't even need it. Maybe he would've been happy to see me in a simple shift and mascara. But . . . better safe than sorry.

That was 1970, when I arrived in Paris. For the next fifteen years, yes, I lived in a very comfy life. Some relief, believe me, after four years on a fucking commune in Nowheresville, China. Rene supported the boy and me, and I did some demonstrations around the country as part of my "cultural exchange" cover. And then there was the spying.

*(*SONG *moves upstage, to a chair.* TOULON *enters as a* JUDGE, *wearing the appropriate wig and robes. He sits near* SONG. *It's 1986, and* SONG *is testifying in a courtroom.)*

SONG: Not much at first. Rene had lost all his high-level contacts. Comrade Chin wasn't very interested in parking-ticket statistics. But finally, at my urging, Rene got a job as a courier, handling sensitive documents. He'd photograph them for me, and I'd pass them on to the Chinese embassy.

JUDGE: Did he understand the extent of his activity?

SONG: He didn't ask. He knew that I needed those documents, and that was enough.

JUDGE: But he must've known he was passing classified information.

SONG: I can't say.

JUDGE: He never asked what you were going to do with them?

SONG: Nope.

(Pause.)

JUDGE: There is one thing that the court—indeed, that all of France—would like to know.

SONG: Fire away.

JUDGE: Did Monsieur Gallimard know you were a man?

SONG: Well, he never saw me completely naked. Ever.

JUDGE: But surely, he must've . . . how can I put this?

SONG: Put it however you like. I'm not shy. He must've felt around?

JUDGE: Mmmmm.

SONG: Not really. I did all the work. He just laid back. Of course we did enjoy more . . . complete union, and I suppose he *might* have wondered why I was always on my stomach, but. . . . But what you're thinking is, "Of course a wrist must've brushed . . . a hand hit . . . over twenty years!" Yeah. Well, Your Honor, it was my job to make him think I was a woman. And chew on this: it wasn't all that hard. See, my mother was a prostitute along the Bundt before the Revolution. And, uh, I think it's fair to say she learned a few things about Western men. So I borrowed her knowledge. In service to my country.

JUDGE: Would you care to enlighten the court with this secret knowledge? I'm sure we're all very curious.

SONG: I'm sure you are. *(Pause.)* Okay, Rule One is: Men always believe what they want to hear. So a girl can tell the most obnoxious lies and the guys will believe them every time—"This is my first time"—"That's the biggest I've ever seen"—or *both,* which, if you really think about it, is not possible in a single lifetime. You've maybe heard those phrases a few times in your own life, yes, Your Honor?

JUDGE: It's not my life, Monsieur Song, which is on trial today.

SONG: Okay, okay, just trying to lighten up the proceedings. Tough room.

JUDGE: Go on.

SONG: Rule Two: As soon as a Western man comes into contact with the East—he's already confused. The West has sort of an international rape mentality towards the East. Do you know rape mentality?

JUDGE: Give us your definition, please.

SONG: Basically, "Her mouth says no, but her eyes say yes." The West thinks of itself as masculine—big guns, big industry, big money—so the East is feminine—weak, delicate, poor . . . but good at art, and full of inscrutable wisdom—the feminine mystique.

Her mouth says no, but her eyes say yes. The West believes the East, deep down, *wants* to be dominated—because a woman can't think for herself.

JUDGE: What does this have to do with my question?

SONG: You expect Oriental countries to submit to your guns, and you expect Oriental women to be submissive to your men. That's why you say they make the best wives.

JUDGE: But why would that make it possible for you to fool Monsieur Gallimard? Please—get to the point.

SONG: One, because when he finally met his fantasy woman, he wanted more than anything to believe that she was, in fact, a woman. And second, I am an Oriental. And being an Oriental, I could never be completely a man.

(Pause.)

JUDGE: Your armchair political theory is tenuous, Monsieur Song.

SONG: You think so? That's why you'll lose in all your dealings with the East.

JUDGE: Just answer my question: did he know you were a man?

(Pause.)

SONG: You know, your Honor, I never asked.

SCENE II

Same.

Music from the "Death Scene" from Butterfly *blares over the house speakers. It is the loudest thing we've heard in this play.*

GALLIMARD *enters, crawling towards* SONG's *wig and kimono.*

GALLIMARD: Butterfly? Butterfly?

(SONG *remains a man, in the witness box, delivering a testimony we do not hear.*)

GALLIMARD: (*To us.*) In my moment of greatest shame, here, in this courtroom—with that . . . person up there, telling the world. . . . What strikes me especially is how shallow he is, how glib and obsequious . . . completely . . . without substance! The type that prowls around discos with a gold medallion stinking of garlic. So little like my Butterfly.
    Yet even in this moment my mind remains agile, flip-flopping like a man on a trampoline. Even now, my picture dissolves, and I see that . . . witness . . . talking to me.

(SONG *suddenly stands straight up in his witness box, and looks at* GALLIMARD.)

SONG: Yes. You. White man.

(SONG *steps out of the witness box, and moves downstage towards* GALLIMARD. *Light change.*)

GALLIMARD: (*To* SONG.) Who? Me?
SONG: Do you see any other white men?
GALLIMARD: Yes. There're white men all around. This is a French courtroom.
SONG: So you are an adventurous imperialist. Tell me, why did it take you so long? To come back to this place?
GALLIMARD: What place?
SONG: This theatre in China. Where we met many years ago.
GALLIMARD: (*To us.*) And once again, against my will, I am transported.

(*Chinese opera music comes up on the speakers.* SONG *begins to do opera moves, as he did the night they met.*)

SONG: Do you remember? The night you gave your heart?
GALLIMARD: It was a long time ago.
SONG: Not long enough. A night that turned your world up-side down.
GALLIMARD: Perhaps.
SONG: Oh, be honest with me. What's another bit of flattery when you've already given me twenty years' worth? It's a wonder my head hasn't swollen to the size of China.
GALLIMARD: Who's to say it hasn't?
SONG: Who's to say? And what's the shame? In pride? You think I could've pulled this off if I wasn't already full of pride when we met? No, not just pride. Arrogance. It takes arrogance, really—to believe you can will, with your eyes and your lips, the destiny of another. (*He dances.*) C'mon. Admit it. You still want me. Even in slacks and a button-down collar.
GALLIMARD: I don't see what the point of—
SONG: You don't? Well maybe, Rene, just maybe—I want you.
GALLIMARD: You do?
SONG: Then again, maybe I'm just playing with you. How can you tell? (*Reprising his feminine character, he sidles up to* GALLIMARD.) "How I wish there were even a small cafe to sit in. With men in tuxedos, and cappuccinos, and bad ex-patriate jazz." Now you want to kiss me, don't you?

GALLIMARD: (*Pulling away.*) What makes you—?
SONG: —so sure? See? I take the words from your mouth. Then I wait for you to come and retrieve them. (*He re-clines on the floor.*)
GALLIMARD: Why? Why do you treat me so cruelly?
SONG: Perhaps I *was* treating you cruelly. But now—I'm being nice. Come here, my little one.
GALLIMARD: I'm not your little one!
SONG: My mistake. It's I who am *your* little one, right?
GALLIMARD: Yes, I—
SONG: So come get your little one. If you like. I may even let you strip me.
GALLIMARD: I mean, you were! Before . . . but not like this!
SONG: I was? Then perhaps I still am. If you look hard enough. (*He starts to remove his clothes.*)
GALLIMARD: What—what are you doing?
SONG: Helping you to see through my act.
GALLIMARD: Stop that! I don't want to! I don't—
SONG: Oh, but you asked me to strip, remember?
GALLIMARD: What? That was years ago! And I took it back!
SONG: No. You postponed it. Postponed the inevitable. To-day, the inevitable has come calling.

(*From the speakers, cacophony: Butterfly mixed in with Chinese gongs.*)

GALLIMARD: No! Stop! I don't want to see!
SONG: Then look away.
GALLIMARD: You're only in my mind! All this is in my mind! I order you! To stop!
SONG: To what? To strip? That's just what I'm—
GALLIMARD: No! Stop! I want you—!
SONG: You want me?
GALLIMARD: To stop!
SONG: You know something, Rene? Your mouth says no, but your eyes say yes. Turn them away. I dare you.
GALLIMARD: I don't have to! Every night, you say you're go-ing to strip, but then I beg you and you stop!
SONG: I guess tonight is different.
GALLIMARD: Why? Why should that be?
SONG: Maybe I've become frustrated. Maybe I'm saying "Look at me, you fool!" Or maybe I'm just feeling . . . sexy. (*He is down to his briefs.*)
GALLIMARD: Please. This is unnecessary. I know what you are.
SONG: Do you? What am I?
GALLIMARD: A—a man.
SONG: You don't really believe that.
GALLIMARD: Yes I do! I knew all the time somewhere that my happiness was temporary, my love a deception. But my mind kept the knowledge at bay. To make the wait bearable.
SONG: Monsieur Gallimard—the wait is over.

(SONG *drops his briefs. He is naked. Sound cue out. Slowly, we and* SONG *come to the realization that what we had thought to be* GALLIMARD's *sobbing is actually his laughter.*)

GALLIMARD: Oh god! What an idiot! Of course!
SONG: Rene—what?
GALLIMARD: Look at you! You're a man! (*He bursts into laugh-ter again.*)
SONG: I fail to see what's so funny!

GALLIMARD: "You fail to see—!" I mean, you never did have much of a sense of humor, did you? I just think it's ridiculously funny that I've wasted so much time on just a man!

100 SONG: Wait. I'm not "just a man."

GALLIMARD: No? Isn't that what you've been trying to convince me of?

SONG: Yes, but what I mean—

GALLIMARD: And now, I finally believe you, and you tell me 105 it's not true? I think you must have some kind of identity problem.

SONG: Will you listen to me?

GALLIMARD: Why?! I've been listening to you for twenty years. Don't I deserve a vacation?

110 SONG: I'm not just any man!

GALLIMARD: Then, what exactly are you?

SONG: Rene, how can you ask—? Okay, what about this?

(He picks up Butterfly's robes, starts to dance around. No music.)

GALLIMARD: Yes, that's very nice. I have to admit.

(SONG holds out his arm to GALLIMARD.)

SONG: It's the same skin you've worshiped for years. Touch it.

115 GALLIMARD: Yes, it does feel the same.

SONG: Now—close your eyes.

(SONG covers GALLIMARD's eyes with one hand. With the other, SONG draws GALLIMARD's hand up to his face. GALLIMARD, like a blind man, lets his hands run over SONG's face.)

GALLIMARD: This skin, I remember. The curve of her face, the softness of her cheek, her hair against the back of my hand . . .

120 SONG: I'm your Butterfly. Under the robes, beneath everything, it was always me. Now, open your eyes and admit it— you adore me. *(He removes his hand from GALLIMARD's eyes.)*

GALLIMARD: You, who knew every inch of my desires—how could you, of all people, have made such a mistake?

125 SONG: What?

GALLIMARD: You showed me your true self. When all I loved was the lie. A perfect lie, which you let fall to the ground—and now, it's old and soiled.

130 SONG: So—you never really loved me? Only when I was playing a part?

GALLIMARD: I'm a man who loved a woman created by a man. Everything else—simply falls short.

(Pause.)

SONG: What am I supposed to do now?

135 GALLIMARD: You were a fine spy, Monsieur Song, with an even finer accomplice. But now I believe you should go. Get out of my life!

SONG: Go where? Rene, you can't live without me. Not after twenty years.

140 GALLIMARD: I certainly can't live with you—not after twenty years of betrayal.

SONG: Don't be so stubborn! Where will you go?

GALLIMARD: I have a date . . . with my Butterfly.

SONG: So, throw away your pride. And come . . .

GALLIMARD: Get away from me! Tonight, I've finally learned to tell fantasy from reality. And, knowing the difference, I 145 choose fantasy.

SONG: I'm your fantasy!

GALLIMARD: You? You're as real as hamburger. Now get out! I have a date with my Butterfly and I don't want your body polluting the room! *(He tosses SONG's suit at him.)* 150 Look at these—you dress like a pimp.

SONG: Hey! These are Armani slacks and—! *(He puts on his briefs and slacks.)* Let's just say . . . I'm disappointed in you, Rene. In the crush of your adoration, I thought you'd become something more. More like . . . a woman. 155

But no. Men. You're like the rest of them. It's all in the way we dress, and make up our faces, and bat our eyelashes. You really have so little imagination!

GALLIMARD: You, Monsieur Song? Accuse me of too little imagination? You, if anyone, should know—I am pure 160 imagination. And in imagination I will remain. Now get out!

(GALLIMARD bodily removes SONG from the stage, taking his kimono.)

SONG: Rene! I'll never put on those robes again! You'll be sorry!

GALLIMARD: *(To SONG.)* I'm already sorry! *(Looking at the ki-* 165 *mono in his hands.)* Exactly as sorry . . . as a Butterfly.

SCENE III

M. GALLIMARD's *prison cell. Paris. Present.*

GALLIMARD: I've played out the events of my life night after night, always searching for a new ending to my story, one where I leave this cell and return forever to my Butterfly's arms.

Tonight I realize my search is over. That I've looked all 5 along in the wrong place. And now, to you, I will prove that my love was not in vain—by returning to the world of fantasy where I first met her.

(He picks up the kimono; dancers enter.)

GALLIMARD: There is a vision of the Orient that I have. Of slender women in chong sams and kimonos who die for 10 the love of unworthy foreign devils. Who are born and raised to be the perfect women. Who take whatever punishment we give them, and bounce back, strengthened by love, unconditionally. It is a vision that has become my life.

(Dancers bring the wash basin to him and help him make up his face.)

GALLIMARD: In public, I have continued to deny that Song Lil- 15 ing is a man. This brings me headlines, and is a source of great embarrassment to my French colleagues, who can now be sent into a coughing fit by the mere mention of Chinese food. But alone, in my cell, I have long since faced the truth.

And the truth demands a sacrifice. For mistakes made 20 over the course of a lifetime. My mistakes were simple and absolute—the man I loved was a cad, a bounder. He deserved nothing but a kick in the behind, and instead I gave him . . . all my love.

25   Yes—love. Why not admit it all? That was my undoing, wasn't it? Love warped my judgment, blinded my
eyes, rearranged the very lines on my face . . . until I could
look in the mirror and see nothing but . . . a woman.

(*Dancers help him put on the Butterfly wig.*)

GALLIMARD: I have a vision. Of the Orient. That, deep
30   within its almond eyes, there are still women. Women
willing to sacrifice themselves for the love of a man. Even
a man whose love is completely without worth.

(*Dancers assist* GALLIMARD *in donning the kimono. They hand
him a knife.*)

GALLIMARD: Death with honor is better than life . . . life with
dishonor. (*He sets himself center stage, in a seppuku position.*)
35   The love of a Butterfly can withstand many things—
unfaithfulness, loss, even abandonment. But how can it
face the one sin that implies all others? The devastating
knowledge that, underneath it all, the object of her love
was nothing more, nothing less than . . . a man. (*He sets the
tip of the knife against his body.*) It is 19 . And I have found   40
her at last. In a prison on the outskirts of Paris. My name
is Rene Gallimard—also known as Madame Butterfly.

(GALLIMARD *turns upstage and plunges his knife into his body, as
music from the "Love Duet" blares over the speakers. He collapses
into the arms of the dancers, who lay him reverently on the floor. The
image holds for several beats. Then a tight special up on* SONG, *who
stands as a man, staring at the dead* GALLIMARD. *He smokes a cigarette; the smoke filters up through the lights. Two words leave his
lips.*)

SONG: Butterfly? Butterfly?

(*Smoke rises as lights fade slowly to black.*)

Tony Kushner

Born in 1956, Tony Kushner first came to international prominence with *Angels in America* (1991), a two-part play that was an enormous success both in London and in Los Angeles before moving to New York in 1993. Kushner's "gay fantasia on national themes" is, in a sense, a displaced autobiography: the displaced narrative of his own growing up as a gay man in the American era of Roy Cohn, the decline of the Communist menace, the onset of the AIDS epidemic, and the rise of the conservative political agenda that dominated American politics in the 1980s. Kushner was born in New York, but his family soon moved to New Orleans, where his parents were musicians in the New Orleans Philharmonic. When he was two, the family moved to Lake Charles, Louisiana; his mother, once a prominent New York bassoonist, devoted herself to educating the children in literature, music, and the arts; she also acted in the Lake Charles theater company. Kushner knew that he was gay but concealed it from his parents; when he went to college at Columbia University, he spent some time in psychoanalysis trying to alter his sexual orientation. However, by his mid-twenties, Kushner was able to accept his sexuality and came out. After taking his B.A. at Columbia, he studied theater at New York University. His first play, *A Bright Room Called Day* (1985), was written while he worked as a switchboard operator; it concerns the collapse of the political left and the rise of fascism during the German Weimar Republic; Kushner also adapted a translation of Corneille's play, *The Illusion*. *Angels in America* is his second play. *Slavs* opened in New York in 1994, and an early play, *Hydriotaphia,* opened in 1998. His most recent play, *Homebody/Kabul,* opened in 2001.

The first part of *Angels in America* (the second part is entitled *Perestroika*), *Millennium Approaches* is a complete play in its own right. Kushner began writing the play in 1988 when Oskar Eustis, who had directed his first play for the Eureka Theater Company in San Francisco, asked Kushner for another play. Subtitled "A Gay Fantasia on National Themes," *Millennium*

ANGELS IN AMERICA, PART I: MILLENNIUM APPROACHES

The Angel (Ellen McLaughlin) appears to Prior Walter (Stephen Spinella) at the climax of Tony Kushner's *Angels in America, Part One: Millennium Approaches* in the 1993 Broadway production.

Approaches is at once a deeply personal look at the lives of two couples—Joe and Harper, a young Mormon couple transplanted to New York; Louis and Prior, a gay couple facing (and not facing) the onset of AIDS—and a political "fantasia" in the manner of Shaw's *Heartbreak House* or *The Apple Cart.* Kushner sets the characters' struggles against the background of conservative politics and the increasing power of the conservative right in 1980s America; as Martin remarks in act 2: ". . . we'll get our way on just about everything: abortion, defense, Central America, protecting the family, a live investment climate. . . . It's really the end of Liberalism. The end of New Deal Socialism. The end of ipso facto secular humanism."

While Kushner's play takes aim at the policies of the Republican administration, the play's politics extend deeply into the politics of personal action. The emphasis on individualism, on self-sufficiency, on destroying the liberal consensus, and on eliminating social programs characteristic of the Reagan administration has consequences in the private sphere as well, where freedom looks alternately like selfishness and chaos. Roy Cohn—famous for his anticommunist activities and for prosecuting (and winning) the death sentence for Julius and Ethel Rosenberg for selling secret information to the Soviet Union—in many ways exemplifies this linkage in the play. Unable to give up his view of political power ("the game . . . of being alive"), Cohn refuses to be treated for AIDS because it would mean a public admission that he is gay, something generally known but not acknowledged. Louis, unable to bring himself to care for Prior during his horrifying illness, finds both emptiness and freedom in deserting his lover. Harper, whose valium-induced fantasies summon the cosmic travel agent Mr. Lies (who whisks her off to Antarctica) is in the throes of a nervous breakdown, a literalized response to the decaying world in which she lives, where "everywhere, things are collapsing, lies surfacing, systems of defense giving way."

The hallucinatory style of *Millennium Approaches* enables Kushner to bring this blending of public and private, the grand sweep of history and the narrower compass of individual suffering, into a close juxtaposition. *Millennium Approaches* ends when Prior's ancestors—a medieval monk and a seventeenth-century dandy—appear to announce the coming of a mysterious angel, whose voice is heard intermittently throughout the play. The Angel's arrival is heralded in a number of ways: Prior regards his first lesion of Kaposi's sarcoma as the mark of the angel of death; a feather drops from above and the voice is heard at the end of Harper's/Prior's intertwined dream-hallucination in act 1; Joe alludes to Jacob wrestling with his angel, an image of Joe's fight to recognize and admit his own homosexuality. The Angel is a figure of release and redemption from the isolation in which the characters find themselves.

However, the Angel also has a public, historical significance as well. Kushner has suggested that the Angel alludes to a comment made by the German cultural critic Walter Benjamin. In "Theses on the Philosophy of History," Benjamin makes the following remark on the process of history:

> A Klee painting named "Angelus Novus" shows an angel looking as though he is about to move away from something he is fixedly contemplating. His eyes are staring, his mouth is open, his wings are spread. This is how one pictures the angel of history. His face is turned toward the past. Where we perceive a chain of events, he sees one single catastrophe which keeps piling wreckage upon wreckage and hurls it in front of his feet. The angel would like to stay, awaken the dead, and make whole what has been smashed. But a storm is blowing from Paradise; it has got caught in his wings with such violence that the angel can no longer close them. This storm irresistibly propels him into the future to which his back is turned, while the pile of debris before him grows skyward. This storm is what we call progress.

The Angel is, to Kushner as to Benjamin, a figure for the dialectical force of history, the way that history moves into the future both in antithesis to the past, and yet bearing the past along with it. In *Angels in America,* Tony Kushner provides a sense of how it is we live today, in the midst of this "storm . . . we call progress."

ANGELS IN AMERICA, PART I: MILLENNIUM APPROACHES

Tony Kushner

CHARACTERS

ROY M. COHN, *a successful New York lawyer and unofficial power broker*

JOSEPH (JOE) PORTER PITT, *chief clerk for Justice Theodore Wilson of the Federal Court of Appeals, Second Circuit*

HARPER AMATY PITT, *Joe's wife, an agoraphobic with a mild Valium addiction*

LOUIS IRONSON, *a word processor working for the Second Circuit Court of Appeals*

PRIOR WALTER, *Louis's boyfriend. Occasionally works as a club designer or caterer, otherwise lives very modestly but with great style off a small trust fund*

HANNAH PORTER PITT, *Joe's mother, currently residing in Salt Lake City, living off her deceased husband's army pension*

BELIZE, *a former drag queen and former lover of Prior's: A registered nurse. Belize's name was originally Norman Arriaga; Belize is a drag name that stuck*

THE ANGEL, *four divine emanations, Fluor, Phosphor, Lumen and Candle; manifest in One: the Continental Principality of America. She has magnificent steel-gray wings*

RABBI ISIDOR CHEMELWITZ, *an orthodox Jewish rabbi, played by the actor playing Hannah*

MR. LIES, *Harper's imaginary friend, a travel agent, who in style of dress and speech suggests a jazz musician; he always wears a large lapel badge emblazoned "IOTA" (The International Order of Travel Agents). He is played by the actor playing Belize*

THE MAN IN THE PARK, *played by the actor playing Prior*

THE VOICE, *the voice of The Angel*

HENRY, *Roy's doctor, played by the actor playing Hannah*

EMILY, *a nurse, played by the actor playing The Angel*

MARTIN HELLER, *a Reagan Administration Justice Department flackman, played by the actor playing Harper*

SISTER ELLA CHAPTER, *a Salt Lake City real-estate saleswoman, played by the actor playing The Angel*

PRIOR 1, *the ghost of a dead Prior Walter from the 13th century, played by the actor playing Joe. He is a blunt, gloomy medieval farmer with a gutteral Yorkshire accent*

PRIOR 2, *the ghost of a dead Prior Walter from the 17th century, played by the actor playing Roy. He is a Londoner, sophisticated, with a High British accent*

THE ESKIMO, *played by the actor playing Joe*

THE WOMAN IN THE SOUTH BRONX, *played by the actor playing The Angel*

ETHEL ROSENBERG, *played by the actor playing Hannah*

PLAYWRIGHT'S NOTES

A DISCLAIMER: *Roy M. Cohn, the character, is based on the late Roy M. Cohn (1927–1986), who was all too real; for the most part the acts attributed to the character Roy, such as his illegal conferences with Judge Kaufmann during the trial of Ethel Rosenberg, are to be found in the historical record. But this Roy is a work of dramatic fiction; his words are my invention, and liberties have been taken.*

A NOTE ABOUT THE STAGING: *The play benefits from a pared-down style of presentation, with minimal scenery and scene shifts done rapidly (no blackouts!), employing the cast as well as stagehands—which makes for an actor-driven event, as this must be. The moments of magic—the appearance and disappearance of Mr. Lies and the ghosts, the Book hallucination, and the ending—are to be fully realized, as bits of wonderful theatrical illusion—which means it's OK if the wires show, and maybe it's good that they do, but the magic should at the same time be thoroughly amazing.*

> ... In a murderous time
> the heart breaks and breaks
> and lives by breaking.
>
> —STANLEY KUNITZ
> "THE TESTING-TREE"

ACT ONE

Bad News October–November 1985

SCENE I

The last days of October. RABBI ISODOR CHEMELWITZ *alone on-stage with a small coffin. It is a rough pine box with two wooden pegs, one at the foot and one at the head, holding the lid in place. A prayer shawl embroidered with a Star of David is draped over the lid, and by the head a yarzheit candle is burning.*

RABBI ISIDOR CHEMELWITZ: (*He speaks sonorously, with a heavy Eastern European accent, unapologetically consulting a sheet of notes for the family names.*) Hello and good morning. I am Rabbi Isidor Chemelwitz of the Bronx Home for Aged Hebrews. We are here this morning to pay respects at the passing of Sarah Ironson, devoted wife of Benjamin Ironson, also deceased, loving and caring mother of her sons Morris, Abraham, and Samuel, and her daughters Esther and Rachel; beloved grandmother of Max, Mark, Louis, Lisa, Maria ... uh ... Lesley, Angela, Doris, Luke and Eric. (*Looks more closely at paper.*) Eric? This is a Jewish name? (*Shrugs.*) Eric. A large and loving family. We assemble that we may mourn collectively this good and righteous woman.

(*He looks at the coffin.*)

This woman. I did not know this woman. I cannot accurately describe her attributes, nor do justice to her dimensions. She was. ... Well, in the Bronx Home of Aged Hebrews are many like this, the old, and to many I speak but not to be frank with this one. She preferred silence. So I do not know her and yet I know her. She was . . .

(*He touches the coffin.*)

20   . . . not a person but a whole kind of person, the ones who crossed the ocean, who brought with us to America the villages of Russia and Lithuania—and how we struggled, and how we fought, for the family, for the Jewish home, so that you would not grow up *here,* in this strange
25 place, in the melting pot where nothing melted. Descendants of this immigrant woman, you do not grow up in America, you and your children and their children with the goyische names. You do not live in America. No such place exists. Your clay is the clay of some Litvak shtetl,
30 your air the air of the steppes—because she carried the old world on her back across the ocean, in a boat, and she put it down on Grand Concourse Avenue, or in Flatbush, and she worked that earth into your bones, and you pass it to your children, this ancient, ancient culture and
35 home.

(*Little pause.*)

You can never make that crossing that she made, for such Great Voyages in this world do not any more exist. But every day of your lives the miles that voyage between that place and this one you cross. Every day. You understand
40 me? In you that journey is.

    So . . .

    She was the last of the Mohicans, this one was. Pretty soon . . . all the old will be dead.

SCENE II

Same day. ROY *and* JOE *in* ROY's *office.* ROY *at an impressive desk, bare except for a very elaborate phone system, rows and rows of flashing buttons which bleep and beep and whistle incessantly, making chaotic music underneath* ROY's *conversations.* JOE *is sitting, waiting.* ROY *conducts business with great energy, impatience and sensual abandon: gesticulating, shouting, cajoling, crooning, playing the phone, receiver and hold button with virtuosity and love.*

ROY: (*Hitting a button.*) Hold. (*To* JOE.) I wish I was an octopus, a fucking octopus. Eight loving arms and all those suckers. Know what I mean?

JOE: No, I . . .

5 ROY: (*Gesturing to a deli platter of little sandwiches on his desk.*) You want lunch?

JOE: No, that's OK really I just . . .

ROY: (*Hitting a button.*) Ailene? Roy Cohn. Now what kind of a greeting is. . . . I thought we were friends, Ai. . . . Look
10 Mrs. Soffer you don't have to get. . . . You're upset. You're yelling. You'll aggravate your condition, you shouldn't yell, you'll pop little blood vessels in your face if you yell. . . . No that was a joke, Mrs. Soffer, I was joking. . . . I already apologized sixteen times for that, Mrs. Soffer, you
15 . . . (*While she's fulminating,* ROY *covers the mouthpiece with his hand and talks to* JOE.) This'll take a minute, eat already, what is this tasty sandwich here it's—(*He takes a bite of a sandwich.*) Mmmmm, liver or some. . . . Here.

(*He pitches the sandwich to* JOE, *who catches it and returns it to the platter.*)

ROY: (*Back to Mrs. Soffer.*) Uh huh, uh huh. . . . No, I already told you, it wasn't a vacation, it was business. Mrs. Soffer, 20 I have clients in Haiti, Mrs. Soffer, I. . . . Listen, Ailene, YOU THINK I'M THE ONLY GODDAM LAWYER IN HISTORY EVER MISSED A COURT DATE? Don't make such a big fucking. . . . Hold. (*He hits the hold button.*) You HAG! 25

JOE: If this is a bad time . . .

ROY: *Bad* time? This is a *good* time! (*Button.*) Baby doll, get me. . . . Oh fuck, wait . . . (*Button, button.*) Hello? Yah. Sorry to keep you holding, Judge Hollins, I. . . . Oh *Mrs.* Hollins, sorry dear deep voice you got. Enjoying your visit? (*Hand* 30 *over mouthpiece, to* JOE.) She sounds like a truckdriver and he sounds like Kate Smith, very confusing. Nixon appointed him, all the geeks are Nixon appointees . . . (*To Mrs. Hollins.*) Yeah yeah right good so how many tickets dear? Seven. For what, *Cats, 42nd Street,* what? No you wouldn't like *La* 35 *Cage,* trust me, I know. Oh for godsake. . . . Hold. (*Button, button.*) Baby doll, seven for *Cats* or something, anything hard to get, I don't give a fuck what and neither will they. (*Button; to* JOE.) You see *La Cage?*

JOE: No, I . . . 40

ROY: Fabulous. Best thing on Broadway. Maybe ever. (*Button.*) Who? Aw, Jesus H. Christ, Harry, *no,* Harry, Judge John Francis Grimes, Manhattan Family Court. Do I have to do every goddam thing myself? *Touch* the bastard, Harry, and don't call me on this line again, I told you not to . . . 45

JOE: (*Starting to get up.*) Roy, uh, should I wait outside or . . .

ROY: (*To* JOE.) Oh sit. (*To* HARRY.) You hold. I pay you to hold fuck you Harry you jerk. (*Button.*) Half-wit dickbrain. (*Instantly philosophical.*) I see the universe, Joe, as a kind of sandstorm in outer space with winds of mega- 50 hurricane velocity, but instead of grains of sand it's shards and splinters of glass. You ever feel that way? Ever have one of those days?

JOE: I'm not sure I . . .

ROY: So how's life in Appeals? How's the Judge? 55

JOE: He sends his best.

ROY: He's a good man. Loyal. Not the brightest man on the bench, but he has manners. And a nice head of silver hair.

JOE: He gives me a lot of responsibility.

ROY: Yeah, like writing his decisions and signing his name. 60

JOE: Well . . .

ROY: He's a nice guy. And you cover admirably.

JOE: Well, thanks, Roy, I . . .

ROY: (*Button.*) Who is *this?* Well who the fuck are *you?* Hold—(*Button.*) Harry? Eighty-seven grand, something 65 like that. Fuck him. Eat me. New Jersey, chain of porno film stores in, uh, Weehawken. That's—Harry, that's the beauty of the law. (*Button.*) So, baby doll, what? *Cats?* Bleah. (*Button.*) *Cats!* It's about cats. Singing cats, you'll love it. Eight o'clock, the theatre's always at eight. (*Button.*) 70 Fucking tourists. (*Button, then to* JOE.) Oh live a little, Joe, *eat* something for Christ sake—

JOE: Um, Roy, could you . . .

ROY: What? (*To* HARRY.) Hold a minute. (*Button.*) Mrs. Soffer? Mrs. . . . (*Button.*) God-fucking-dammit to hell, where 75 is . . .

JOE: (*Overlapping.*) Roy, I'd really appreciate it if . . .

ROY: (*Overlapping.*) Well she was here a minute ago, baby doll, see if . . .

(*The phone starts making three different beeping sounds, all at once.*)

80 ROY: (*Smashing buttons.*) Jesus fuck this goddam thing . . .

JOE: (*Overlapping.*) I really wish you wouldn't . . .

ROY: (*Overlapping.*) Baby doll? Ring the *Post* get me Suzy see if . . .

(*The phone starts whistling loudly.*)

ROY: CHRIST!

85 JOE: *Roy.*

ROY: (*Into receiver.*) Hold. (*Button; to* JOE.) What?

JOE: Could you please not take the Lord's name in vain?

(*Pause.*)

I'm sorry. But please. At least while I'm . . .

ROY: (*Laughs, then.*) Right. Sorry. Fuck.

90 Only in America. (*Punches a button.*) Baby doll, tell 'em all to fuck off. Tell 'em I died. You handle Mrs. Soffer. Tell her it's on the way. Tell her I'm schtupping the judge. I'll call her back. I *will* call her. I *know* how much I borrowed. She's got four hundred times that stuffed up her. . . . Yeah,

95 tell her I said that. (*Button. The phone is silent.*)

So, Joe.

JOE: I'm sorry Roy, I just . . .

ROY: No no no no, principles count, I respect principles, I'm not religious but I like God and God likes me. Baptist,

100 Catholic?

JOE: Mormon.

ROY: Mormon. Delectable. Absolutely. Only in America. So, Joe. Whattya think?

JOE: It's . . . well . . .

105 ROY: Crazy life.

JOE: Chaotic.

ROY: Well but God bless chaos. Right?

JOE: Ummm . . .

ROY: Huh. Mormons. I knew Mormons, in, um, Nevada.

110 JOE: Utah, mostly.

ROY: No, these Mormons were in Vegas.

So. So, how'd you like to go to Washington and work for the Justice Department?

JOE: Sorry?

115 ROY: How'd you like to go to Washington and work for the Justice Department? All I gotta do is pick up the phone, talk to Ed, and you're in.

JOE: In . . . what, exactly?

ROY: Associate Assistant Something Big. Internal Affairs, heart

120 of the woods, something nice with clout.

JOE: Ed . . . ?

ROY: Meese. The Attorney General.

JOE: Oh.

ROY: I just have to pick up the phone . . .

125 JOE: I have to think.

ROY: Of course.

(*Pause.*)

It's a great time to be in Washington, Joe.

JOE: Roy, it's incredibly exciting . . .

ROY: And it would mean something to me. You understand?

(*Little pause.*)

JOE: I . . . can't say how much I appreciate this Roy, I'm sort 130 of . . . well, stunned, I mean. . . . Thanks, Roy. But I have to give it some thought. I have to ask my wife.

ROY: Your wife. Of course.

JOE: But I really appreciate . . .

ROY: Of course. Talk to your wife. 135

SCENE III

Later that day. HARPER *at home, alone. She is listening to the radio and talking to herself, as she often does. She speaks to the audience.*

HARPER: People who are lonely, people left alone, sit talking nonsense to the air, imagining . . . beautiful systems dying, old fixed orders spiraling apart . . .

When you look at the ozone layer, from outside, from a spaceship, it looks like a pale blue halo, a gentle, shim- 5 mer-ing aureole encircling the atmosphere encircling the earth. Thirty miles above our heads, a thin layer of three-atom oxygen molecules, product of photosynthesis, which explains the fussy vegetable preference for visible light, its rejection of darker rays and emanations. Danger from 10 without. It's a kind of gift, from God, the crowning touch to the creation of the world: guardian angels, hands linked, make a spherical net, a blue-green nesting orb, a shell of safety for life itself. But everywhere, things are collapsing, lies surfacing, systems of defense giving way. . . . This is 15 why, Joe, this is why I shouldn't be left alone.

(*Little pause.*)

I'd like to go traveling. Leave you behind to worry. I'll send postcards with strange stamps and tantalizing messages on the back. "Later maybe." "Nevermore . . ."

(MR. LIES, *a travel agent, appears.*)

HARPER: Oh! You startled me! 20

MR. LIES: Cash, check or credit card?

HARPER: I remember you. You're from Salt Lake. You sold us the plane tickets when we flew here. What are you doing in Brooklyn?

MR. LIES: You said you wanted to travel . . . 25

HARPER: And here you are. How thoughtful.

MR. LIES: Mr. Lies. Of the International Order of Travel Agents. We mobilize the globe, we set people adrift, we stir the populace and send nomads eddying across the planet. We are adepts of motion, acolytes of the flux. 30 Cash, check or credit card. Name your destination.

HARPER: Antarctica, maybe. I want to see the hole in the ozone. I heard on the radio . . .

MR. LIES: (*He has a computer terminal in his briefcase.*) I can arrange a guided tour. Now? 35

HARPER: Soon. Maybe soon. I'm not safe here you see. Things aren't right with me. Weird stuff happens . . .

MR. LIES: Like?

HARPER: Well, like you, for instance. Just appearing. Or last
40   week . . . well never mind.
       People are like planets, you need a thick skin. Things get
       to me, Joe stays away and now. . . . Well look. My dreams
       are talking back to me.

MR. LIES: It's the price of rootlessness. Motion sickness. The
45   only cure: to keep moving.

HARPER: I'm undecided. I feel . . . that something's going to
       give. It's 1985. Fifteen years till the third millennium.
       Maybe Christ will come again. Maybe seeds will be
       planted, maybe there'll be harvests then, maybe early figs to
50   eat, maybe new life, maybe fresh blood, maybe compan-
       ionship and love and protection, safety from what's outside,
       maybe the door will hold, or maybe . . . maybe the troubles
       will come, and the end will come, and the sky will collapse
       and there will be terrible rains and showers of poison light,
55   or maybe my life is really fine, maybe Joe loves me and I'm
       only crazy thinking otherwise, or maybe not, maybe it's
       even worse than I know, maybe . . . I want to know, maybe
       I don't. The suspense, Mr. Lies, it's killing me.

MR. LIES: I suggest a vacation.

60 HARPER: (Hearing something.) That was the elevator. Oh God,
       I should fix myself up, I . . . . You have to go, you shouldn't
       be here . . . you aren't even real.

MR. LIES: Call me when you decide . . .

HARPER: Go!

(The travel agent [MR. LIES] vanishes as JOE enters.)

65 JOE: Buddy?
       Buddy? Sorry I'm late. I was just . . . out. Walking. Are
       you mad?

HARPER: I got a little anxious.

JOE: Buddy kiss.

(They kiss.)

70   Nothing to get anxious about.
       So. So how'd you like to move to Washington?

SCENE IV

*Same day. LOUIS and PRIOR outside the funeral home, sitting on a
bench, both dressed in funereal finery, talking. The funeral service for
Sarah Ironson has just concluded and LOUIS is about to leave for the
cemetery.*

LOUIS: My grandmother actually saw Emma Goldman speak.
       In Yiddish. But all Grandma could remember was that she
       spoke well and wore a hat.
       What a weird service. That rabbi . . .

5 PRIOR: A definite find. Get his number when you go to the
       graveyard. I want him to bury me.

LOUIS: Better head out there. Everyone gets to put dirt on
       the coffin once it's lowered in.

PRIOR: Oooh. Cemetery fun. Don't want to miss that.

10 LOUIS: It's an old Jewish custom to express love. Here,
       Grandma, have a shovelful. Latecomers run the risk of
       finding the grave completely filled.
       She was pretty crazy. She was up there in that home for
       ten years, talking to herself. I never visited. She looked too
15   much like my mother.

PRIOR: (Hugs him.) Poor Louis. I'm sorry your grandma is
       dead.

LOUIS: Tiny little coffin, huh?
       Sorry I didn't introduce you to. . . . I always get so clos-
       ety at these family things.   20

PRIOR: Butch. You get butch. (Imitating.) "Hi Cousin Doris,
       you don't remember me I'm Lou, Rachel's boy." Lou, not
       Louis, because if you say Louis they'll hear the sibilant S.

LOUIS: I don't have a . . .

PRIOR: I don't blame you, hiding. Bloodlines. Jewish curses are 25
       the worst. I personally would dissolve if anyone ever looked
       me in the eye and said "Feh." Fortunately WASPs don't say
       "Feh." Oh and by the way, darling, cousin Doris is a dyke.

LOUIS: No.
       Really?   30

PRIOR: You don't notice anything. If I hadn't spent the last
       four years fellating you I'd swear you were straight.

LOUIS: You're in a pissy mood. Cat still missing?

(Little pause.)

PRIOR: Not a furball in sight. It's your fault.

LOUIS: It is?   35

PRIOR: I warned you, Louis. Names are important. Call an
       animal "Little Sheba" and you can't expect it to stick
       around. Besides, it's a dog's name.

LOUIS: I wanted a dog in the first place, not a cat. He sprayed
       my books.   40

PRIOR: He was a female cat.

LOUIS: Cats are stupid, high-strung predators. Babylonians
       sealed them up in bricks. Dogs have brains.

PRIOR: Cats have intuition.

LOUIS: A sharp dog is as smart as a really dull two-year-old   45
       child.

PRIOR: Cats know when something's wrong.

LOUIS: Only if you stop feeding them.

PRIOR: They know. That's why Sheba left, because she knew.

LOUIS: Knew what?   50

(Pause.)

PRIOR: I did my best Shirley Booth this morning, floppy slip-
       pers, housecoat, curlers, can of Little Friskies; "Come
       back, little Sheba, come back. . . ." To no avail. Le chat, elle
       ne reviendra jamais, jamais . . .

*(He removes his jacket, rolls up his sleeve, shows LOUIS a dark pur-
ple spot on the underside of his arm near the shoulder.)*

       See.   55

LOUIS: That's just a burst blood vessel.

PRIOR: Not according to the best medical authorities.

LOUIS: What?

(Pause.)

       Tell me.

PRIOR: K.S., baby. Lesion number one. Lookit. The wine-   60
       dark kiss of the angel of death.

LOUIS: (Very softly, holding PRIOR's arm.) Oh please . . .

PRIOR: I'm a lesionnaire. The Foreign Lesion. The American
       Lesion. Lesionnaire's disease.

65 LOUIS: Stop.

PRIOR: My troubles are lesion.

LOUIS: Will you *stop*.

PRIOR: Don't you think I'm handling this well? I'm going to die.

70 LOUIS: Bullshit.

PRIOR: Let go of my arm.

LOUIS: No.

PRIOR: Let go.

LOUIS: (*Grabbing* PRIOR, *embracing him ferociously.*) No.

75 PRIOR: I can't find a way to spare you baby. No wall like the wall of hard scientific fact. K.S. Wham. Bang your head on that.

LOUIS: Fuck you. (*Letting go.*) Fuck you fuck you fuck you.

PRIOR: Now that's what I like to hear. A mature reaction.

80 Let's go see if the cat's come home.
   Louis?

LOUIS: When did you find this?

PRIOR: I couldn't tell you.

LOUIS: Why?

85 PRIOR: I was scared, Lou.

LOUIS: Of what?

PRIOR: That you'll leave me.

LOUIS: Oh.

(*Little pause.*)

PRIOR: Bad timing, funeral and all, but I figured as long as
90 we're on the subject of death . . .

LOUIS: I have to go bury my grandma.

PRIOR: Lou?

(*Pause.*)

   Then you'll come home?

LOUIS: Then I'll come home.

SCENE V

Same day, later on. Split scene: JOE *and* HARPER *at home;* LOUIS *at the cemetery with* RABBI ISIDOR CHEMELWITZ *and the little coffin.*

HARPER: Washington?

JOE: It's an incredible honor, buddy, and . . .

HARPER: I have to think.

JOE: Of course.

5 HARPER: Say no.

JOE: You said you were going to think about it.

HARPER: I don't want to move to Washington.

JOE: Well I do.

HARPER: It's a giant cemetery, huge white graves and mau-
10 soleums everywhere.

JOE: We could live in Maryland. Or Georgetown.

HARPER: We're happy here.

JOE: That's not really true, buddy, we . . .

HARPER: Well happy enough! Pretend-happy. That's better
15 than nothing.

JOE: It's time to make some changes, Harper.

HARPER: No changes. Why?

JOE: I've been chief clerk for four years. I make twenty-nine thousand dollars a year. That's ridiculous. I graduated
20 fourth in my class and I make less than anyone I know.

And I'm . . . I'm tired of being a clerk, I want to go where something good is happening.

HARPER: Nothing good happens in Washington. We'll forget church teachings and buy furniture at . . . at *Conran's* and become yuppies. I have too much to do here. 25

JOE: Like what?

HARPER: I *do* have things . . .

JOE: What things?

HARPER: I have to finish painting the bedroom.

JOE: You've been painting in there for over a year. 30

HARPER: I know, I. . . . It just isn't done because I never get time to finish it.

JOE: Oh that's . . . that doesn't make sense. You have all the time in the world. You could finish it when I'm at work.

HARPER: I'm afraid to go in there alone. 35

JOE: Afraid of what?

HARPER: I heard someone in there. Metal scraping on the wall. A man with a knife, maybe.

JOE: There's no one in the bedroom, Harper.

HARPER: Not now. 40

JOE: Not this morning either.

HARPER: How do you know? You were at work this morn-ing. There's something creepy about this place. Remem-ber *Rosemary's Baby*?

JOE: *Rosemary's Baby*? 45

HARPER: Our apartment looks like that one. Wasn't that apartment in Brooklyn?

JOE: No, it was . . .

HARPER: Well, it looked like this. It did.

JOE: Then let's move. 50

HARPER: Georgetown's worse. *The Exorcist* was in Georgetown.

JOE: The devil, everywhere you turn, huh, buddy.

HARPER: Yeah. Everywhere.

JOE: How many pills today, buddy?

HARPER: None. One. Three. Only three. 55

LOUIS: (*Pointing at the coffin.*) Why are there just two little wooden pegs holding the lid down?

RABBI ISIDOR CHEMELWITZ: So she can get out easier if she wants to.

LOUIS: I hope she stays put. 60
   I pretended for years that she was already dead. When they called to say she had died it was a surprise. I aban-doned her.

RABBI ISIDOR CHEMELWITZ: "Sharfer vi di tson fun a shlang iz an umdankbar kind!" 65

LOUIS: I don't speak Yiddish.

RABBI ISIDOR CHEMELWITZ: Sharper than the serpent's tooth is the ingratitude of children. Shakespeare. *Kenig Lear.*

LOUIS: Rabbi, what does the Holy Writ say about someone who abandons someone he loves at a time of great need? 70

RABBI ISIDOR CHEMELWITZ: Why would a person do such a thing?

LOUIS: Because he has to.
   Maybe because this person's sense of the world, that it will change for the better with struggle, maybe a person 75 who has this neo-Hegelian positivist sense of constant his-torical progress towards happiness or perfection or some-thing, who feels very powerful because he feels connected to these forces, moving uphill all the time . . . maybe that person can't, um, incorporate sickness into this sense of 80 how things are supposed to go. Maybe vomit . . . and sores

and disease . . . really frighten him, maybe . . . he isn't so good with death.

RABBI ISIDOR CHEMELWITZ: The Holy Scriptures have nothing to say about such a person.

85 LOUIS: Rabbi, I'm afraid of the crimes I may commit.

RABBI ISIDOR CHEMELWITZ: Please, mister. I'm a sick old rabbi facing a long drive home to the Bronx. You want to confess, better you should find a priest.

90 LOUIS: But I'm not a Catholic, I'm a Jew.

RABBI ISIDOR CHEMELWITZ: Worse luck for you, bubbulah. Catholics believe in forgiveness. Jews believe in Guilt. (*He pats the coffin tenderly.*)

LOUIS: You just make sure those pegs are in good and tight.

95 RABBI ISIDOR CHEMELWITZ: Don't worry, mister. The life she had, she'll stay put. She's better off.

JOE: Look, I know this is scary for you. But try to understand what it means to me. Will you try?

HARPER: Yes.

100 JOE: Good. Really try.

I think things are starting to change in the world.

HARPER: But I don't want . . .

JOE: Wait. For the good. Change for the good. America has rediscovered itself. Its sacred position among nations. And

105 people aren't ashamed of that like they used to be. This is a great thing. The truth restored. Law restored. That's what President Reagan's done, Harper. He says "Truth exists and can be spoken proudly." And the country responds to him. We become better. More good. I need to be a part of that,

110 I need something big to lift me up. I mean, six years ago the world seemed in decline, horrible, hopeless, full of unsolvable problems and crime and confusion and hunger and . . .

HARPER: But it still seems that way. More now than before. They say the ozone layer is . . .

115 JOE: Harper . . .

HARPER: And today out the window on Atlantic Avenue there was a schizophrenic traffic cop who was making these . . .

JOE: Stop it! I'm trying to make a point.

HARPER: So am I.

120 JOE: You aren't even making sense, you . . .

HARPER: My point is the world seems just as . . .

JOE: It only seems that way to you because you never go out in the world, Harper, and you have emotional problems.

HARPER: I do so get out in the world.

125 JOE: You don't. You stay in all day, fretting about imaginary . . .

HARPER: I get out. I do. You don't know what I do.

JOE: You don't stay in all day.

HARPER: No.

JOE: Well. . . . Yes you do.

130 HARPER: That's what you think.

JOE: Where do you go?

HARPER: Where do *you* go? When you walk.

(*Pause, then angrily.*) And I DO NOT have emotional problems.

135 JOE: I'm sorry.

HARPER: And if I do have emotional problems it's from living with you. Or . . .

JOE: I'm sorry buddy, I didn't mean to . . .

HARPER: Or if you do think I do then you should never have

140 married me. You have all these secrets and lies.

JOE: I want to be married to you, Harper.

HARPER: You shouldn't. You never should.

(*Pause.*)

Hey buddy. Hey buddy.

JOE: Buddy kiss . . .

(*They kiss.*)

HARPER: I heard on the radio how to give a blowjob. 145

JOE: What?

HARPER: You want to try?

JOE: You really shouldn't listen to stuff like that.

HARPER: Mormons can give blowjobs.

JOE: *Harper.* 150

HARPER: (*Imitating his tone.*) *Joe.*

It was a little Jewish lady with a German accent. This is a good time. For me to make a baby.

(*Little pause.* JOE *turns away.*)

HARPER: Then they went on to a program about holes in the ozone layer. Over Antarctica. Skin burns, birds go blind, 155 icebergs melt. The world's coming to an end.

SCENE VI

First week of November. In the men's room of the offices of the Brooklyn Federal Court of Appeals; LOUIS *is crying over the sink;* JOE *enters.*

JOE: Oh, um. . . . Morning.

LOUIS: Good morning, counselor.

JOE: (*He watches* LOUIS *cry.*) Sorry, I . . . I don't know your name.

LOUIS: Don't bother. Word processor. The lowest of the low.

JOE: (*Holding out hand.*) Joe Pitt. I'm with Justice Wilson . . . 5

LOUIS: Oh, I know that. Counselor Pitt. Chief Clerk.

JOE: Were you . . . are you OK?

LOUIS: Oh, yeah. Thanks. What a nice man.

JOE: Not so nice.

LOUIS: What? 10

JOE: Not so nice. Nothing. You sure you're . . .

LOUIS: Life sucks shit. Life . . . just sucks shit.

JOE: What's wrong?

LOUIS: Run in my nylons.

JOE: Sorry . . . ? 15

LOUIS: Forget it. Look, thanks for asking.

JOE: Well . . .

LOUIS: I mean it really is nice of you.

(*He starts crying again.*)

Sorry, sorry, sick friend . . .

JOE: Oh, I'm sorry. 20

LOUIS: Yeah, yeah, well, that's sweet.

Three of your colleagues have preceded you to this baleful sight and you're the first one to ask. The others just opened the door, saw me, and fled. I hope they had to pee real bad. 25

JOE: (*Handing him a wad of toilet paper.*) They just didn't want to intrude.

LOUIS: Hah. Reaganite heartless macho asshole lawyers.

JOE: Oh, that's unfair.

LOUIS: What is? Heartless? Macho? Reaganite? Lawyer? 30

JOE: I voted for Reagan.

LOUIS: You did?

JOE: Twice.

LOUIS: Twice? Well, oh boy. A Gay Republican.

35 JOE: Excuse me?

LOUIS: Nothing.

JOE: I'm not . . .
Forget it.

LOUIS: Republican? Not Republican? Or . . .

40 JOE: What?

LOUIS: What?

JOE: Not gay. I'm not gay.

LOUIS: Oh. Sorry. (*Blows his nose loudly.*) It's just . . .

JOE: Yes?

45 LOUIS: Well, sometimes you can tell from the way a person
sounds that . . . I mean you *sound* like a . . .

JOE: No I don't. Like what?

LOUIS: Like a Republican.

(*Little pause.* JOE *knows he's being teased;* LOUIS *knows he knows.*
JOE *decides to be a little brave.*)

JOE: (*Making sure no one else is around.*) Do I? Sound like a . . .?

50 LOUIS: What? Like a . . .? Republican, or . . .? Do *I*?

JOE: Do you what?

LOUIS: Sound like a . . .?

JOE: Like a . . .?
I'm confused.

55 LOUIS: Yes.
My name is Louis. But all my friends call me Louise. I
work in Word Processing. Thanks for the toilet paper.

(LOUIS *offers* JOE *his hand,* JOE *reaches,* LOUIS *feints and pecks* JOE
on the cheek, then exits.)

SCENE VII

A week later. Mutual dream scene. PRIOR *is at a fantastic makeup
table, having a dream, applying the face.* HARPER *is having a pill-
induced hallucination. She has these from time to time. For some reason,* PRIOR *has appeared in this one. Or* HARPER *has appeared in*
PRIOR's *dream. It is bewildering.*

PRIOR: (*Alone, putting on makeup, then examining the results in
the mirror; to the audience.*) "I'm ready for my closeup, Mr.
DeMille."
5 One wants to move through life with elegance and
grace, blossoming infrequently but with exquisite taste,
and perfect timing, like a rare bloom, a zebra orchid. . . .
One wants. . . . But one so seldom gets what one wants,
does one? No. One does not. One gets fucked. Over. One
. . . dies at thirty, robbed of . . . decades of majesty.
10 Fuck this shit. Fuck this shit.

(*He almost crumbles; he pulls himself together; he studies his handiwork in the mirror.*)

I look like a corpse. A corpsette. Oh my queen; you know
you've hit rock-bottom when even drag is a drag.

(HARPER *appears.*)

HARPER: Are you. . . . Who are you?

PRIOR: Who are you?

HARPER: What are you doing in my hallucination?   15

PRIOR: I'm not in your hallucination. You're in my dream.

HARPER: You're wearing makeup.

PRIOR: So are you.

HARPER: But you're a man.

PRIOR: (*Feigning dismay, shock, he mimes slashing his throat with*   20
his lipstick and dies, fabulously tragic. Then.) The hands and
feet give it away.

HARPER: There must be some mistake here. I don't recognize
you. You're not. . . . Are you my . . . some sort of imaginary friend?   25

PRIOR: No. Aren't you too old to have imaginary friends?

HARPER: I have emotional problems. I took too many pills.
Why are you wearing makeup?

PRIOR: I was in the process of applying the face, trying to
make myself feel better—I swiped the new fall colors at   30
the Clinique counter at Macy's. (*Showing her.*)

HARPER: You stole these?

PRIOR: I was out of cash; it was an emotional emergency!

HARPER: Joe will be so angry. I promised him. No more pills.

PRIOR: These pills you keep alluding to?   35

HARPER: Valium. I take Valium. Lots of Valium.

PRIOR: And you're dancing as fast as you can.

HARPER: I'm not *addicted.* I don't believe in addiction, and I
never . . . well, I *never* drink. And I *never* take drugs.

PRIOR: Well, smell *you,* Nancy Drew.   40

HARPER: Except Valium.

PRIOR: Except Valium; in wee fistfuls.

HARPER: It's terrible. Mormons are not supposed to be addicted to anything. I'm a Mormon.

PRIOR: I'm a homosexual.   45

HARPER: Oh! In my church we don't believe in homosexuals.

PRIOR: In my church we don't believe in Mormons.

HARPER: What church do . . . oh! (*She laughs.*) I get it.
I don't understand this. If I didn't ever see you before
and I don't think I did then I don't think you should be   50
here, in this hallucination, because in my experience the
mind, which is where hallucinations come from, shouldn't
be able to make up anything that wasn't there to start
with, that didn't enter it from experience, from the real
world. Imagination can't create anything new, can it? It   55
only recycles bits and pieces from the world and reassem-
bles them into visions. . . . Am I making sense right now?

PRIOR: Given the circumstances, yes.

HARPER: So when we think we've escaped the unbearable ordinariness and, well, untruthfulness of our lives, it's really   60
only the same old ordinariness and falseness rearranged
into the appearance of novelty and truth. Nothing unknown is knowable. Don't you think it's depressing?

PRIOR: The limitations of the imagination?

HARPER: Yes.   65

PRIOR: It's something you learn after your second theme
party: It's All Been Done Before.

HARPER: The world. Finite. Terribly, terribly. . . . Well . . . This
is the most depressing hallucination I've ever had.

PRIOR: Apologies. I do try to be amusing.   70

HARPER: Oh, well, don't apologize, you. . . . I can't expect
someone who's really sick to entertain me.

PRIOR: How on earth did you know . . .

HARPER: Oh that happens. This is the very threshhold of rev-
75   elation sometimes. You can see things . . . how sick you
  are. Do you see anything about me?
PRIOR: Yes.
HARPER: What?
PRIOR: You are amazingly unhappy.
80 HARPER: Oh big deal. You meet a Valium addict and you fig-
  ure out she's unhappy. That doesn't count. Of course I. . . .
  Something else. Something surprising.
PRIOR: Something surprising.
HARPER: Yes.
85 PRIOR: Your husband's a homo.

(*Pause.*)

HARPER: Oh, ridiculous.

(*Pause, then very quietly.*)

  Really?
PRIOR: (*Shrugs.*) Threshhold of revelation.
HARPER: Well I don't like your revelations. I don't think you
90   intuit well at all. Joe's a very normal man, he . . .
    Oh God. Oh God. He. . . . Do homos take, like, lots of
  long walks?
PRIOR: Yes. We do. In stretch pants with lavender coifs. I just
  looked at you, and there was . . .
95 HARPER: A sort of blue streak of recognition.
PRIOR: Yes.
HARPER: Like you knew me incredibly well.
PRIOR: Yes.
HARPER: Yes.
100   I have to go now, get back, something just . . . fell apart.
  Oh God, I feel so sad . . .
PRIOR: I . . . I'm sorry. I usually say, "Fuck the truth," but
  mostly, the truth fucks you.
HARPER: I see something else about you . . .
105 PRIOR: Oh?
HARPER: Deep inside you, there's a part of you, the most in-
  ner part, entirely free of disease. I can see that.
PRIOR: Is that. . . . That isn't true.
HARPER: Threshhold of revelation.
110   Home . . .

(*She vanishes.*)

PRIOR: People come and go so quickly here . . .
  (*To himself in the mirror.*) I don't think there's any unin-
  fected part of me. My heart is pumping polluted blood. I
  feel dirty.

(*He begins to wipe makeup off with his hands, smearing it around.
A large gray feather falls from up above. PRIOR stops smearing the
makeup and looks at the feather. He goes to it and picks it up.*)

115 THE VOICE: (*It is an incredibly beautiful voice.*) Look up!
PRIOR: (*Looking up, not seeing anyone.*) Hello?
THE VOICE: Look up!
PRIOR: Who is that?
THE VOICE: Prepare the way!
120 PRIOR: I don't see any . . .

(*There is a dramatic change in lighting, from above.*)

A VOICE: Look up, look up,
  prepare the way
  the infinite descent
  A breath in air
  floating down   125
  Glory to . . .

(*Silence.*)

PRIOR: Hello? Is that it? Helloooo!
  What the fuck . . . ? (*He holds himself.*)
  Poor me. Poor poor me. Why me? Why poor poor
  me? Oh I don't feel good right now. I really don't.   130

SCENE VIII

That night. Split scene: HARPER *and* JOE *at home;* PRIOR *and* LOUIS
in bed.

HARPER: Where were you?
JOE: Out.
HARPER: Where?
JOE: Just out. Thinking.
HARPER: It's late.   5
JOE: I had a lot to think about.
HARPER: I burned dinner.
JOE: Sorry.
HARPER: Not my dinner. My dinner was fine. Your dinner. I
  put it back in the oven and turned everything up as high 10
  as it could go and I watched till it burned black. It's still
  hot. Very hot. Want it?
JOE: You didn't have to do that.
HARPER: I know. It just seemed like the kind of thing a mentally
  deranged sex-starved pill-popping housewife would do. 15
JOE: Uh huh.
HARPER: So I did it. Who knows anymore what I have to do?
JOE: How many pills?
HARPER: A bunch. Don't change the subject.
JOE: I won't talk to you when you . . .   20
HARPER: No. No. Don't do that! I'm . . . fine, pills are not the
  problem, not our problem, I WANT TO KNOW
  WHERE YOU'VE BEEN! I WANT TO KNOW
  WHAT'S GOING ON!
JOE: Going on with what? The job?   25
HARPER: Not the job.
JOE: I said I need more time.
HARPER: Not the job!
JOE: Mr. Cohn, I talked to him on the phone, he said I had
  to hurry . . .   30
HARPER: Not the . . .
JOE: But I can't get you to talk sensibly about anything so . . .
HARPER: SHUT UP!
JOE: Then what?
HARPER: Stick to the subject.   35
JOE: I don't know what that is. You have something you want
  to ask me? Ask me. Go.
HARPER: I . . . can't. I'm scared of you.
JOE: I'm tired, I'm going to bed.
HARPER: Tell me without making me ask. Please.   40
JOE: This is crazy, I'm not . . .
HARPER: When you come through the door at night your
  face is never exactly the way I remembered it. I get sur-

prised by something . . . mean and hard about the way you look. Even the weight of you in the bed at night, the way you breathe in your sleep seems unfamiliar.
        You terrify me.
JOE: (*Cold.*) I know who you are.
HARPER: Yes. I'm the enemy. That's easy. That doesn't change. You think you're the only one who hates sex; I do; I hate it with you; I do. I dream that you batter away at me till all my joints come apart, like wax, and I fall into pieces. It's like a punishment. It was wrong of me to marry you. I knew you . . . (*She stops herself.*) It's a sin, and it's killing us both.
JOE: I can always tell when you've taken pills because it makes you red-faced and sweaty and frankly that's very often why I don't want to . . .
HARPER: Because . . .
JOE: Well, you aren't pretty. Not like this.
HARPER: I have something to ask you.
JOE: Then ASK! ASK! What in hell are you . . .
HARPER: Are you a homo?

(*Pause.*)

Are you? If you try to walk out right now I'll put your dinner back in the oven and turn it up so high the whole building will fill with smoke and everyone in it will asphyxiate. So help me God I will.
        Now answer the question.
JOE: What if I . . .

(*Small pause.*)

HARPER: Then tell me, please. And we'll see.
JOE: No. I'm not.
        I don't see what difference it makes.

LOUIS: Jews don't have any clear textual guide to the afterlife; even that it exists. I don't think much about it. I see it as a perpetual rainy Thursday afternoon in March. Dead leaves.
PRIOR: Eeeugh. Very Greco-Roman.
LOUIS: Well for us it's not the verdict that counts, it's the act of judgment. That's why I could never be a lawyer. In court all that matters is the verdict.
PRIOR: You could never be a lawyer because you are oversexed. You're too distracted.
LOUIS: Not distracted, *ab*stracted. I'm trying to make a point:
PRIOR: Namely:
LOUIS: It's the judge in his or her chambers, weighing, books open, pondering the evidence, ranging freely over categories: good, evil, innocent, guilty; the judge in the chamber of circumspection, not the judge on the bench with the gavel. The shaping of the law, not its execution.
PRIOR: The point, dear, the point . . .
LOUIS: That it should be the questions and shape of a life, its total complexity gathered, arranged and considered, which matters in the end, not some stamp of salvation or damnation which disperses all the complexity in some unsatisfying little decision—the balancing of the scales . . .
PRIOR: I like this; very zen; it's . . . reassuringly incomprehensible and useless. We who are about to die thank you.
LOUIS: You are not about to die.
PRIOR: It's not going well, really . . . two new lesions. My leg hurts. There's protein in my urine, the doctor says, but who knows what the fuck that portends. Anyway it shouldn't be there, the protein. My butt is chapped from diarrhea and yesterday I shat blood.
LOUIS: I really hate this. You don't tell me . . .
PRIOR: You get too upset, I wind up comforting you. It's easier . . .
LOUIS: Oh thanks.
PRIOR: If it's bad I'll tell you.
LOUIS: Shitting blood sounds bad to me.
PRIOR: And I'm telling you.
LOUIS: And I'm handling it.
PRIOR: Tell me some more about justice.
LOUIS: I *am* not handling it.
PRIOR: Well Louis you win Trooper of the Month.

(LOUIS *starts to cry.*)

PRIOR: I take it back. You aren't Trooper of the Month. This isn't working . . .
        Tell me some more about justice.
LOUIS: You are not about to die.
PRIOR: Justice . . .
LOUIS: is an immensity, a confusing vastness. Justice is God. Prior?
PRIOR: Hmmm?
LOUIS: You love me.
PRIOR: Yes.
LOUIS: What if I walked out on this?
        Would you hate me forever?

(PRIOR *kisses* LOUIS *on the forehead.*)

PRIOR: Yes.

JOE: I think we ought to pray. Ask God for help. Ask him together . . .
HARPER: God won't talk to me. I have to make up people to talk to me.
JOE: You have to keep asking.
HARPER: I forgot the question.
        Oh yeah. God, is my husband a . . .
JOE: (*Scary.*) Stop it. Stop it. I'm warning you.
        Does it make any difference? That I might be one thing deep within, no matter how wrong or ugly that thing is, so long as I have fought, with everything I have, to kill it. What do you want from me? What do you want from me, Harper? More than that? For God's sake, there's nothing left, I'm a shell. There's nothing left to kill.
        As long as my behavior is what I know it has to be. Decent. Correct. That alone in the eyes of God.
HARPER: No, no, not that, that's Utah talk, Mormon talk, I hate it, Joe, tell me, say it . . .
JOE: All I will say is that I am a very good man who has worked very hard to become good and you want to destroy that. You want to destroy me, but I am not going to let you do that.

(*Pause.*)

HARPER: I'm going to have a baby.
JOE: Liar.
HARPER: You liar.
        A baby born addicted to pills. A baby who does not dream but who hallucinates, who stares up at us with big mirror eyes and who does not know who we are.

(*Pause.*)

JOE: Are you really . . .

HARPER: No. Yes. No. Yes. Get away from me.

155   Now we both have a secret.

PRIOR: One of my ancestors was a ship's captain who made money bringing whale oil to Europe and returning with immigrants—Irish mostly, packed in tight, so many dollars per head. The last ship he captained foundered off the coast
160   of Nova Scotia in a winter tempest and sank to the bottom. He went down with the ship—la Grande Geste—but his crew took seventy women and kids in the ship's only longboat, this big, open rowboat, and when the weather got too rough, and they thought the boat was overcrowded, the
165   crew started lifting people up and hurling them into the sea. Until they got the ballast right. They walked up and down the longboat, eyes to the waterline, and when the boat rode low in the water they'd grab the nearest passenger and throw them into the sea. The boat was leaky, see; seventy
170   people; they arrived in Halifax with nine people on board.

LOUIS: Jesus.

PRIOR: I think about that story a lot now. People in a boat, waiting, terrified, while implacable, unsmiling men, irresistibly strong, seize . . . maybe the person next to you,
175   maybe you, and with no warning at all, with time only for a quick intake of air you are pitched into freezing, turbulent water and salt and darkness to drown.

       I like your cosmology, baby. While time is running out I find myself drawn to anything that's suspended, that lacks
180   an ending—but it seems to me that it lets you off scot-free.

LOUIS: What do you mean?

PRIOR: No judgment, no guilt or responsibility.

LOUIS: For me.

PRIOR: For anyone. It was an editorial "you."

185 LOUIS: Please get better. Please.

       Please don't get any sicker.

SCENE IX

Third week in November. ROY *and* HENRY, *his doctor, in* HENRY's *office.*

HENRY: Nobody knows what causes it. And nobody knows how to cure it. The best theory is that we blame a retrovirus, the Human Immunodeficiency Virus. Its presence is made known to us by the useless antibodies which appear in
5   reaction to its entrance into the bloodstream through a cut, or an orifice. The antibodies are powerless to protect the body against it. Why, we don't know. The body's immune system ceases to function. Sometimes the body even attacks itself. At any rate it's left open to a whole horror house of
10   infections from microbes which it usually defends against.

       Like Kaposi's sarcomas. These lesions. Or your throat problem. Or the glands.

       We think it may also be able to slip past the blood-brain barrier into the brain. Which is of course very bad
15   news. And it's fatal in we don't know what percent of people with suppressed immune responses.

(*Pause*)

ROY: This is very interesting, Mr. Wizard, but why the fuck are you telling me this?

(*Pause.*)

HENRY: Well, I have just removed one of three lesions which biopsy results will probably tell us is a Kaposi's sarcoma le- 20
sion. And you have a pronounced swelling of glands in your neck, groin, and armpits—lymphadenopathy is another sign. And you have oral candidiasis and maybe a little more fungus under the fingernails of two digits on your right hand. So that's why . . . 25

ROY: This disease . . .

HENRY: Syndrome.

ROY: Whatever. It afflicts mostly homosexuals and drug addicts.

HENRY: Mostly. Hemophiliacs are also at risk.

ROY: Homosexuals and drug addicts. So why are you imply- 30
ing that I . . .

(*Pause.*)

       What are you implying, Henry?

HENRY: I don't . . .

ROY: I'm not a drug addict.

HENRY: Oh come on Roy. 35

ROY: What, what, come on Roy what? Do you think I'm a junkie, Henry, do you see tracks?

HENRY: This is absurd.

ROY: Say it.

HENRY: Say what? 40

ROY: Say, "Roy Cohn, you are a . . . "

HENRY: Roy.

ROY: "You are a . . . ." Go on. Not "Roy Cohn you are a drug fiend." "Roy Marcus Cohn, you are a . . . "

       Go on, Henry, it starts with an "H." 45

HENRY: Oh I'm not going to . . .

ROY: *With an "H,"* Henry, and it isn't "Hemophiliac." Come on . . .

HENRY: What are you doing, Roy?

ROY: No, say it. I mean it. Say: "Roy Cohn, you are a homo- 50
sexual."

(*Pause.*)

       And I will proceed, systemically, to destroy your reputation and your practice and your career in New York State, Henry. Which you know I can do.

(*Pause.*)

HENRY: Roy, you have been seeing me since 1958. Apart from 55
the facelifts I have treated you for everything from syphilis . . .

ROY: From a whore in Dallas.

HENRY: From syphilis to venereal warts. In your rectum. Which you may have gotten from a whore in Dallas, but it wasn't a female whore. 60

(*Pause.*)

ROY: So say it.

HENRY: Roy Cohn, you are . . .

       You have had sex with men, many many times, Roy, and one of them, or any number of them, has made you very sick. You have AIDS. 65

ROY: AIDS.

Your problem, Henry, is that you are hung up on words, on labels, that you believe they mean what they seem to mean. AIDS. Homosexual. Gay. Lesbian. You 70 think these are names that tell you who someone sleeps with, but they don't tell you that.

HENRY: No?

ROY: No. Like all labels they tell you one thing and one thing only: where does an individual so identified fit in the food 75 chain, in the pecking order? Not ideology, or sexual taste, but something much simpler: clout. Not who I fuck or who fucks me, but who will pick up the phone when I call, who owes me favors. This is what a label refers to. Now to someone who does not understand this, homosexual is what I am 80 because I have sex with men. But really this is wrong. Homosexuals are not men who sleep with other men. Homosexuals are men who in fifteen years of trying cannot get a pissant antidiscrimination bill through City Council. Homosexuals are men who know nobody and who nobody knows. 85 Who have zero clout. Does this sound like me, Henry?

HENRY: No.

ROY: No. I have clout. A lot. I can pick up this phone, punch fifteen numbers, and you know who will be on the other end in under five minutes, Henry?

90 HENRY: The President.

ROY: Even better, Henry. His wife.

HENRY: I'm impressed.

ROY: I don't want you to be impressed. I want you to understand. This is not sophistry. And this is not hypocrisy. This 95 is reality. I have sex with men. But unlike nearly every other man of whom this is true, I bring the guy I'm screwing to the White House and President Reagan smiles at us and shakes his hand. Because *what* I am is defined entirely by *who* I am. Roy Cohn is not a homosexual. Roy Cohn is a 100 heterosexual man, Henry, who fucks around with guys.

HENRY: OK, Roy.

ROY: And what is my diagnosis, Henry?

HENRY: You have AIDS, Roy.

ROY: No, Henry, no. AIDS is what homosexuals have. I have 105 liver cancer.

(*Pause.*)

HENRY: Well, whatever the fuck you have, Roy, it's very serious, and I haven't got a damn thing for you. The NIH in Bethesda has a new drug called AZT with a two-year waiting list that not even I can get you onto. So get on the 110 phone, Roy, and dial the fifteen numbers, and tell the First Lady you need in on an experimental treatment for liver cancer, because you can call it any damn thing you want, Roy, but what it boils down to is very bad news.

ACT TWO

In Vitro
December 1985–January 1986

SCENE I

Night, the third week in December. PRIOR *alone on the floor of his bedroom; he is much worse.*

PRIOR: Louis, Louis, please wake up, oh God.

(LOUIS *runs in.*)

PRIOR: I think something horrible is wrong with me I can't breathe . . .

LOUIS: (*Starting to exit.*) I'm calling the ambulance.

PRIOR: No, wait, I . . .   5

LOUIS: *Wait?* Are you fucking crazy? Oh God you're on fire, your head is on fire.

PRIOR: It hurts, it hurts . . .

LOUIS: I'm calling the ambulance.

PRIOR: I don't want to go to the hospital, I don't want to go 10 to the hospital please let me lie here, just . . .

LOUIS: No, no, God, Prior, stand up . . .

PRIOR: DON'T TOUCH MY LEG!

LOUIS: We have to . . . oh God this is so crazy.

PRIOR: I'll be OK if I just lie here Lou, really, if I can only 15 sleep a little . . .

(LOUIS *exits.*)

PRIOR: Louis?

NO! NO! Don't call, you'll send me there and I won't come back, please, please Louis I'm begging, baby, please . . . (*Screams.*) LOUIS!!   20

LOUIS: (*From off; hysterical.*) WILL YOU SHUT THE FUCK UP!

PRIOR: (*Trying to stand.*) Aaaah. I have . . . to go to the bathroom. Wait. Wait, just . . . oh. Oh God. (*He shits himself.*)

LOUIS: (*Entering.*) Prior? They'll be here in . . . Oh my God. 25

PRIOR: I'm sorry, I'm sorry.

LOUIS: What did . . . ? What?

PRIOR: I had an accident.

(LOUIS *goes to him.*)

LOUIS: This is blood.

PRIOR: Maybe you shouldn't touch it . . . me. . . . I . . . (*He* 30 *faints.*)

LOUIS: (*Quietly.*) Oh help. Oh help. Oh God oh God oh God help me I can't I can't I can't.

SCENE II

Same night. HARPER *is sitting at home, all alone, with no lights on. We can barely see her.* JOE *enters, but he doesn't turn on the lights.*

JOE: Why are you sitting in the dark? Turn on the light.

HARPER: *No.* I heard the sounds in the bedroom again. I know someone was in there.

JOE: No one was.

HARPER: Maybe actually in the bed, under the covers with a 5 knife.

Oh, boy. Joe. I, um, I'm thinking of going away. By which I mean: I think I'm going off again. You . . . you know what I mean?

JOE: Please don't. Stay. We can fix it. I pray for that. This is 10 my fault, but I can correct it. You have to try too . . .

(*He turns on the light. She turns it off again.*)

HARPER: When you pray, what do you pray for?

JOE: I pray for God to crush me, break me up into little pieces and start all over again.

15 HARPER: Oh. Please. Don't pray for that.

JOE: I had a book of Bible stories when I was a kid. There
was a picture I'd look at twenty times every day: Jacob
wrestles with the angel. I don't really remember the story,
or why the wrestling—just the picture. Jacob is young and
20 very strong. The angel is . . . a beautiful man, with golden
hair and wings, of course. I still dream about it. Many
nights. I'm. . . . It's me. In that struggle. Fierce, and unfair.
The angel is not human, and it holds nothing back, so
how could anyone human win, what kind of a fight is
25 that? It's not just. Losing means your soul thrown down in
the dust, your heart torn out from God's. But you can't
not lose.

HARPER: In the whole entire world, you are the only person,
the only person I love or have ever loved. And I love you
30 terribly. Terribly. That's what's so awfully, irreducibly real.
I can make up anything but I can't dream that away.

JOE: Are you . . . are you really going to have a baby?

HARPER: It's my time and there's no blood. I don't really
know. I suppose it wouldn't be a great thing. Maybe I'm
35 just not bleeding because I take too many pills. Maybe I'll
give birth to a pill. That would give a new meaning to
pill-popping, huh?

I think you should go to Washington. Alone. Change,
like you said.

40 JOE: I'm not going to leave you, Harper.

HARPER: Well maybe not. But I'm going to leave you.

SCENE III

*One A.M., the next morning. LOUIS and a nurse, EMILY, are sitting
in PRIOR's room in the hospital.*

EMILY: He'll be all right now.

LOUIS: No he won't.

EMILY: No. I guess not. I gave him something that makes him
sleep.

5 LOUIS: Deep asleep?

EMILY: Orbiting the moons of Jupiter.

LOUIS: A good place to be.

EMILY: Anyplace better than here. You his . . . uh?

LOUIS: Yes. I'm his uh.

10 EMILY: This must be hell for you.

LOUIS: It is. Hell. The After Life. Which is not at all like a
rainy afternoon in March, by the way, Prior. A lot more
vivid than I'd expected. Dead leaves, but the crunchy
kind. Sharp, dry air. The kind of long, luxurious dying
15 feeling that breaks your heart.

EMILY: Yeah, well we all get to break our hearts on this one.
He seems like a nice guy. Cute.

LOUIS: Not like this.
Yes, he is. Was. Whatever.

20 EMILY: Weird name. Prior Walter. Like, "The Walter before this
one."

LOUIS: Lots of Walters before this one. Prior is an old old family name in an old old family. The Walters go back to the
Mayflower and beyond. Back to the Norman Conquest. He
25 says there's a Prior Walter stitched into the Bayeux tapestry.

EMILY: Is that impressive?

LOUIS: Well, it's old. Very old. Which in some circles equals
impressive.

EMILY: Not in my circle. What's the name of the tapestry?

LOUIS: The Bayeux tapestry. Embroidered by La Reine Mathilde. 30

EMILY: I'll tell my mother. She embroiders. Drives me nuts.

LOUIS: Manual therapy for anxious hands.

EMILY: Maybe you should try it.

LOUIS: Mathilde stitched while William the Conqueror was
off to war. She was capable of . . . more than loyalty. Devo- 35
tion. She waited for him, she stitched for years. And if he
had come back broken and defeated from war, she would
have loved him even more. And if he had returned mutilated, ugly, full of infection and horror, she would still have
loved him; fed by pity, by a sharing of pain, she would love 40
him even more, and even more, and she would never, never
have prayed to God, please let him die if he can't return to
me whole and healthy and able to live a normal life. . . . If
he had died, she would have buried her heart with him.
So what the fuck is the matter with me? 45

(Little pause.)

Will he sleep through the night?

EMILY: At least.

LOUIS: I'm going.

EMILY: It's one A.M. Where do you have to go at . . .

LOUIS: I know what time it is. A walk. Night air, good for 50
the. . . . The park.

EMILY: Be careful.

LOUIS: Yeah. Danger.
Tell him, if he wakes up and you're still on, tell him
goodbye, tell him I had to go. 55

SCENE IV

*An hour later. Split scene: JOE and ROY in a fancy (straight) bar;
LOUIS and a MAN in the Rambles in Central Park. JOE and ROY
are sitting at the bar; the place is brightly lit. JOE has a plate of food
in front of him but he isn't eating. ROY occasionally reaches over the
table and forks small bites off JOE's plate. ROY is drinking heavily,
JOE not at all. LOUIS and the MAN are eyeing each other, each alternating interest and indifference.*

JOE: The pills were something she started when she miscarried
or . . . no, she took some before that. She had a really bad
time at home, when she was a kid, her home was really bad.
I think a lot of drinking and physical stuff. She doesn't talk
about that, instead she talks about . . . the sky falling down, 5
people with knives hiding under sofas. Monsters. Mormons. Everyone thinks Mormons don't come from homes
like that, we aren't supposed to behave that way, but we do.
It's not lying, or being two-faced. Everyone tries very hard
to live up to God's strictures, which are very . . . um . . . 10

ROY: Strict.

JOE: I shouldn't be bothering you with this.

ROY: No, please. Heart to heart. Want another. . . . What is
that, seltzer?

JOE: The failure to measure up hits people very hard. From 15
such a strong desire to be good they feel very far from
goodness when they fail.
What scares me is that maybe what I really love in her
is the part of her that's farthest from the light, from God's
love; maybe I was drawn to that in the first place. And I'm 20
keeping it alive because I need it.

ROY: Why would you need it?

JOE: There are things. . . . I don't know how well we know ourselves. I mean, what if? I know I married her because she . . . because I loved it that she was always wrong, always doing something wrong, like one step out of step. In Salt Lake City that stands out. I never stood out, on the outside, but inside, it was hard for me. To pass.

ROY: Pass?

JOE: Yeah.

ROY: Pass as what?

JOE: Oh. Well. . . . As someone cheerful and strong. Those who love God with an open heart unclouded by secrets and struggles are cheerful; God's easy simple love for them shows in how strong and happy they are. The saints.

ROY: But you had secrets? Secret struggles . . .

JOE: I wanted to be one of the elect, one of the Blessed. You feel you ought to be, that the blemishes are yours by choice, which of course they aren't. Harper's sorrow, that really deep sorrow, she didn't choose that. But it's there.

ROY: You didn't put it there.

JOE: No.

ROY: You sound like you think you did.

JOE: I am responsible for her.

ROY: Because she's your wife.

JOE: That. And I do love her.

ROY: Whatever. She's your wife. And so there are obligations. To her. But also to yourself.

JOE: She'd fall apart in Washington.

ROY: Then let her stay here.

JOE: She'll fall apart if I leave her.

ROY: Then bring her to Washington.

JOE: I just can't, Roy. She needs me.

ROY: Listen, Joe. I'm the best divorce lawyer in the business.

(*Little pause.*)

JOE: Can't Washington wait?

ROY: You do what you need to do, Joe. What you need. You. Let her life go where it wants to go. You'll both be better for that. *Somebody* should get what they want.

MAN: What do you want?

LOUIS: I want you to fuck me, hurt me, make me bleed.

MAN: I want to.

LOUIS: Yeah?

MAN: I want to hurt you.

LOUIS: Fuck me.

MAN: Yeah? You been a bad boy?

(*Pause.* LOUIS *laughs, softly.*)

LOUIS: Very bad. Very bad.

MAN: You need to be punished, boy?

LOUIS: Yes. I do.

MAN: Yes what?

(*Little pause.*)

LOUIS: Um, I . . .

MAN: Yes *what*, boy?

LOUIS: Oh. Yes sir.

MAN: I want you to take me to your place, boy.

LOUIS: No, I can't do that.

MAN: No *what*?

LOUIS: No sir, I can't, I . . .
   I don't live alone, sir.

MAN: Your lover know you're out with a man tonight, boy?

LOUIS: No sir, he . . .
   My lover doesn't know.

MAN: Your lover know you . . .

LOUIS: Let's change the subject, OK? Can we go to your place?

MAN: I live with my parents.

LOUIS: Oh.

ROY: Everyone who makes it in this world makes it because somebody older and more powerful takes an interest. The most precious asset in life, I think, is the ability to be a good son. You have that, Joe. Somebody who can be a good son to a father who pushes them farther than they would otherwise go. I've had many fathers, I owe my life to them, powerful, powerful men. Walter Winchell, Edgar Hoover. Joe McCarthy most of all. He valued me because I am a good lawyer, but he loved me because I was and am a good son. He was a very difficult man, very guarded and cagey; I brought out something tender in him. He would have died for me. And me for him. Does this embarrass you?

JOE: I had a hard time with my father.

ROY: Well sometimes that's the way. Then you have to find other fathers, substitutes, I don't know. The father-son relationship is central to life. Women are for birth, beginning, but the father is continuance. The son offers the father his life as a vessel for carrying forth his father's dream. Your father's living?

JOE: Um, dead.

ROY: He was . . . what? A difficult man?

JOE: He was in the military. He could be very unfair. And cold.

ROY: But he loved you.

JOE: I don't know.

ROY: No, no, Joe, he did, I know this. Sometimes a father's love has to be very, very hard, unfair even, cold to make his son grow strong in a world like this. This isn't a good world.

MAN: Here, then.

LOUIS: I. . . . Do you have a rubber?

MAN: I don't use rubbers.

LOUIS: You should. (*He takes one from his coat pocket.*) Here.

MAN: I don't use them.

LOUIS: Forget it, then. (*He starts to leave.*)

MAN: No, wait.
   Put it on me. Boy.

LOUIS: Forget it, I have to get back. Home. I must be going crazy.

MAN: Oh come on please he won't find out.

LOUIS: It's cold. Too cold.

MAN: It's never too cold, let me warm you up. Please?

(*They begin to fuck.*)

MAN: Relax.

LOUIS: (*A small laugh.*) Not a chance.

MAN: It . . .

LOUIS: What?

MAN: I think it broke. The rubber. You want me to keep going? (*Little pause.*) Pull out? Should I . . .

LOUIS: Keep going.
  Infect me.
  I don't care. I don't care.

(*Pause. The* MAN *pulls out.*)

135 MAN: I . . . um, look, I'm sorry, but I think I want to go.
  LOUIS: Yeah.
    Give my best to mom and dad.

(*The* MAN *slaps him.*)

LOUIS: Ow!

(*They stare at each other.*)

LOUIS: It was a joke.

(*The* MAN *leaves.*)

140 ROY: How long have we known each other?
  JOE: Since 1980.
  ROY: Right. A long time. I feel close to you, Joe. Do I advise you well?
  JOE: You've been an incredible friend, Roy, I . . .
145 ROY: I want to be family. Familia, as my Italian friends call it. La Familia. A lovely word. It's important for me to help you, like I was helped.
  JOE: I owe practically everything to you, Roy.
  ROY: I'm dying, Joe. Cancer.
150 JOE: Oh my God.
  ROY: Please. Let me finish.
    Few people know this and I'm telling you this only because. . . . I'm not afraid of death. What can death bring that I haven't faced? I've lived; life is the worst. (*Gently*
155 *mocking himself.*) Listen to me, I'm a philosopher.
      Joe. You must do this. You must must must. Love; that's a trap. Responsibility; that's a trap too. Like a father to a son I tell you this: Life is full of horror; nobody es-
160 capes, nobody; save yourself. Whatever pulls on you, whatever needs from you, threatens you. Don't be afraid; people are so afraid; don't be afraid to live in the raw wind, naked, alone. . . . Learn at least this: What you are capable of. Let nothing stand in your way.

SCENE V

Three days later. PRIOR *and* BELIZE *in* PRIOR's *hospital room.* PRIOR *is very sick but improving.* BELIZE *has just arrived.*

PRIOR: Miss Thing.
BELIZE: Ma cherie bichette.
PRIOR: Stella.
BELIZE: Stella for star. Let me see. (*Scrutinizing* PRIOR.) You
5   look like shit, why yes indeed you do, comme la merde!
PRIOR: Merci.
BELIZE: (*Taking little plastic bottles from his bag, handing them to* PRIOR.) Not to despair, Belle Reeve. Lookie! Magic goop!
PRIOR: (*Opening a bottle, sniffing.*) Pooh! What kinda crap is that?
10 BELIZE: Beats me. Let's rub it on your poor blistered body and see what it does.
PRIOR: This is not Western medicine, these bottles . . .
BELIZE: Voodoo cream. From the botanica 'round the block.

PRIOR: And you a registered nurse.
BELIZE: (*Sniffing it.*) Beeswax and cheap perfume. Cut with 15 Jergen's Lotion. Full of good vibes and love from some little black Cubana witch in Miami.
PRIOR: Get that trash away from me. I am immune-suppressed.
BELIZE: I *am* a health professional. I *know* what I'm doing.
PRIOR: It stinks. Any word from Louis? 20

(*Pause.* BELIZE *starts giving* PRIOR *a gentle massage.*)

PRIOR: Gone.
BELIZE: He'll be back. I know the type. Likes to keep a girl on edge.
PRIOR: It's been . . .

(*Pause*)

BELIZE: (*Trying to jog his memory.*) How long? 25
PRIOR: I don't remember.
BELIZE: How long have you been here?
PRIOR: (*Getting suddenly upset.*) I don't remember, I don't give a fuck. I want Louis. I want my fucking boyfriend, where the fuck is he? I'm dying, I'm dying, where's Louis? 30
BELIZE: Shhhh, shhh . . .
PRIOR: This is a very strange drug, this drug. Emotional lability, for starters.
BELIZE: Save a tab or two for me.
PRIOR: Oh no, not this drug, ce n'est pas pour la joyeux noël 35 et la bonne année, this drug she is serious poisonous chemistry, ma pauvre bichette.
  And not just disorienting. I hear things. Voices.
BELIZE: Voices.
PRIOR: A voice. 40
BELIZE: Saying what?

(*Pause.*)

PRIOR: I'm not supposed to tell.
BELIZE: You better tell the doctor. Or I will.
PRIOR: No no don't. Please. I want the voice; it's wonderful. It's all that's keeping me alive. I don't want to talk to some 45 intern about it.
  You know what happens? When I hear it, I get hard.
BELIZE: Oh my.
PRIOR: Comme ça. (*He uses his arm to demonstrate.*) And you know I am slow to rise. 50
BELIZE: My jaw aches at the memory.
PRIOR: And would you deny me this little solace—betray my concupiscence to Florence Nightingale's storm troopers?
BELIZE: Perish the thought, ma bébé.
PRIOR: They'd change the drug just to spoil the fun. 55
BELIZE: You and your boner can depend on me.
PRIOR: Je t'adore, ma belle nègre.
BELIZE: All this girl-talk shit is politically incorrect, you know. We should have dropped it back when we gave up drag.
PRIOR: I'm sick, I get to be politically incorrect if it makes 60 me feel better. You sound like Lou.

(*Little pause.*)

  Well, at least I have the satisfaction of knowing he's in anguish somewhere. I loved his anguish. Watching him stick his head up his asshole and eat his guts out over some rel-

65 atively minor moral conundrum—it was the best show in town. But Mother warned me; if they get overwhelmed by the little things . . .

BELIZE: They'll be belly-up bustville when something big comes along.

70 PRIOR: Mother warned me.

BELIZE: And they do come along.

PRIOR: But I didn't listen.

BELIZE: No. (*Doing Hepburn.*) Men are beasts.

PRIOR: (*Also Hepburn.*) The absolute lowest.

75 BELIZE: I have to go. If I want to spend my whole lonely life looking after white people I can get underpaid to do it.

PRIOR: You're just a Christian martyr.

BELIZE: Whatever happens, baby, I will be here for you.

PRIOR: Je t'aime.

80 BELIZE: Je t'aime. Don't go crazy on me, girlfriend, I already got enough crazy queens for one lifetime. For two. I can't be bothering with dementia.

PRIOR: I promise.

BELIZE: (*Touching him; softly.*) Ouch.

85 PRIOR: Ouch. Indeed.

BELIZE: Why'd they have to pick on you?
And eat more, girlfriend, you really do look like shit.

(BELIZE *leaves.*)

PRIOR: (*After waiting a beat.*) He's gone.
Are you still . . .

90 VOICE: I can't stay. I will return.

PRIOR: Are you one of those "Follow me to the other side" voices?

VOICE: No. I am no nightbird. I am a messenger . . .

PRIOR: You have a beautiful voice, it sounds . . . like a viola,
95 like a perfectly tuned, tight string, balanced, the truth. . . .
Stay with me.

THE VOICE: Not now. Soon I will return, I will reveal myself to you; I am glorious, glorious; my heart, my countenance and my message. You must prepare.

100 PRIOR: For what? I don't want to . . .

THE VOICE: No death, no:
A marvelous work and a wonder we undertake, an edifice awry we sink plumb and straighten, a great Lie we abolish, a great error correct, with the rule, sword and
105 broom of Truth!

PRIOR: What are you talking about, I . . .

THE VOICE: I am on my way; when I am manifest, our Work begins;
Prepare for the parting of the air,
110 The breath, the ascent,
Glory to . . .

SCENE VI

The second week of January. MARTIN, ROY *and* JOE *in a fancy Manhattan restaurant.*

MARTIN: It's a revolution in Washington, Joe. We have a new agenda and finally a real leader. They got back the Senate but we have the courts. By the nineties the Supreme Court will be block-solid Republican appointees, and the
5 Federal bench—Republican judges like land mines,

everywhere, everywhere they turn. Affirmative action? Take it to court. Boom! Land mine. And we'll get our way on just about everything: abortion, defense, Central America, family values, a live investment climate. We have the White House locked till the year 2000. And beyond. 10 A permanent fix on the Oval Office? It's possible. By '92 we'll get the Senate back, and in ten years the South is going to give us the House. It's really the end of Liberalism. The end of New Deal Socialism. The end of ipso facto secular humanism. The dawning of a genuinely American 15 political personality. Modeled on Ronald Wilson Reagan.

JOE: It sounds great, Mr. Heller.

MARTIN: Martin. And Justice is the hub. Especially since Ed Meese took over. He doesn't specialize in Fine Points of the Law. He's a flatfoot, a cop. He reminds me of Teddy 20 Roosevelt.

JOE: I can't wait to meet him.

MARTIN: Too bad, Joe, he's been dead for sixty years!

(*There is a little awkwardness.* JOE *doesn't respond.*)

MARTIN: Teddy Roosevelt. You said you wanted to. . . . Little joke. It reminds me of the story about the . . . 25

ROY: (*Smiling, but nasty.*) Aw shut the fuck up Martin.
(*To* JOE.) You see that? Mr. Heller here is one of the mighty, Joseph, in D.C. he sitteth on the right hand of the man who sitteth on the right hand of The Man. And yet I can say "shut the fuck up" and he will take no offense. 30 Loyalty. He . . . Martin?

MARTIN: Yes, Roy?

ROY: Rub my back.

MARTIN: Roy . . .

ROY: No no really, a sore spot, I get them all the time now, 35 these. . . . Rub it for me darling, would you do that for me?

(MARTIN *rubs* ROY's *back. They both look at* JOE.)

ROY: (*To* JOE.) How do you think a handful of Bolsheviks turned St. Petersburg into Leningrad in one afternoon? *Comrades.* Who do for each other. Marx and Engels. Lenin and Trotsky. Josef Stalin and Franklin Delano Roosevelt. 40

(MARTIN *laughs.*)

ROY: *Comrades,* right Martin?

MARTIN: This man, Joe, is a Saint of the Right.

JOE: I know, Mr. Heller, I . . .

ROY: And you see what I mean, Martin? He's special, right?

MARTIN: Don't embarrass him, Roy. 45

ROY: Gravity, decency, smarts! His strength is as the strength of ten because his heart is pure! *And* he's a Royboy, one hundred percent.

MARTIN: We're on the move, Joe. On the move.

JOE: Mr. Heller, I . . . 50

MARTIN: (*Ending backrub.*) We can't wait any longer for an answer.

(*Little pause.*)

JOE: Oh. Um, I . . .

ROY: Joe's a married man, Martin.

MARTIN: Aha. 55

ROY: With a wife. She doesn't care to go to D.C., and so Joe cannot go. And keeps us dangling. We've seen that kind of thing before, haven't we? These men and their wives.

MARTIN: Oh yes. Beware.

60 JOE: I really can't discuss this under . . .

MARTIN: Then *don't* discuss. Say yes, Joe.

ROY: Now.

MARTIN: Say yes I will.

ROY: Now.

65   Now. I'll hold my breath till you do, I'm turning blue waiting. . . . *Now*, goddammit!

MARTIN: Roy, calm down, it's not . . .

ROY: Aw, fuck it. (*He takes a letter from his jacket pocket, hands it to* JOE.)

70   Read. Came today.

(JOE *reads the first paragraph, then looks up.*)

JOE: Roy. This is . . . Roy, this is terrible.

ROY: You're telling me.

   A letter from the New York State Bar Association, Martin. They're gonna try and disbar me.

75 MARTIN: Oh my.

JOE: Why?

ROY: Why, Martin?

MARTIN: Revenge.

ROY: The whole Establishment. Their little rules. Because I

80   know no rules. Because I don't see the Law as a dead and arbitrary collection of antiquated dictums, thou shall, thou shalt not, because, because I know the Law's a pliable, breathing, sweating . . . *organ,* because, because . . .

MARTIN: Because he borrowed half a million from one of his

85   clients.

ROY: Yeah, well, there's that.

MARTIN: *And* he forgot to *return* it.

JOE: Roy, that's. . . . You borrowed money from a client?

ROY: I'm deeply ashamed.

(*Little pause.*)

90 JOE: (*Very sympathetic.*) Roy, you know how much I admire you. Well I mean I know you have unorthodox ways, but I'm sure you only did what you thought at the time you needed to do. And I have faith that . . .

ROY: Not so damp, please. I'll deny it was a loan. She's got no

95   paperwork. Can't prove a fucking thing.

(*Little pause.* MARTIN *studies the menu.*)

JOE: (*Handing back the letter, more official in tone.*) Roy I really appreciate your telling me this, and I'll do whatever I can to help.

ROY: (*Holding up a hand, then, carefully.*) I'll tell you what you

100 can do.

   I'm about to be tried, Joe, by a jury that is not a jury of my peers. The disbarment committee: genteel gentleman Brahmin lawyers, country-club men. I offend them, to these men . . . I'm what, Martin, some sort of filthy lit-

105 tle Jewish troll?

MARTIN: Oh well, I wouldn't go so far as . . .

ROY: Oh well I would.

   Very fancy lawyers, these disbarment committee lawyers, fancy lawyers with fancy corporate clients and complicated cases. Antitrust suits. Deregulation. Environ- 110 mental control. Complex cases like these need Justice Department cooperation like flowers need the sun. Wouldn't you say that's an accurate assessment, Martin?

MARTIN: I'm not here, Roy. I'm not hearing any of this.

ROY: No. Of course not.   115

   Without the light of the sun, Joe, these cases, and the fancy lawyers who represent them, will wither and die.

   A well-placed friend, someone in the Justice Department, say, can turn off the sun. Cast a deep shadow on my behalf. Make them shiver in the cold. If they overstep. 120 They would fear that.

(*Pause.*)

JOE: Roy. I don't understand.

ROY: You do.

(*Pause.*)

JOE: You're not asking me to . . .

ROY: Ssshhhh. Careful.   125

JOE: (*A beat, then.*) Even if I said yes to the job, it would be illegal to interfere. With the hearings. It's unethical. No. I can't.

ROY: Un-ethical.

   Would you excuse us, Martin?   130

MARTIN: Excuse you?

ROY: Take a walk, Martin. For real.

(MARTIN *leaves.*)

ROY: Un-ethical. Are you trying to embarrass me in front of my friend?

JOE: Well it is unethical, I can't . . .   135

ROY: Boy, you are really something. What the fuck do you think this is, Sunday School?

JOE: No, but Roy this is . . .

ROY: This is . . . this is gastric juices churning, this is enzymes and acids, this is intestinal is what this is, bowel movement 140 and blood-red meat—this stinks, this is *politics,* Joe, the game of being alive. And you think you're. . . . What? Above that? Above alive is what? Dead! In the clouds! You're on earth, goddammit! Plant a foot, stay a while.

   I'm sick. They smell I'm weak. They want blood this 145 time. I must have eyes in Justice. In Justice you will protect me.

JOE: Why can't Mr. Heller . . .

ROY: Grow up, Joe. The administration can't get involved.

JOE: But I'd be part of the administration. The same as him.   150

ROY: Not the same. Martin's Ed's man. And Ed's Reagan's man. So Martin's Reagan's man.

   And you're mine.

(*Little pause. He holds up the letter.*)

This will never be. Understand me?

(*He tears the letter up.*)

I'm gonna be a lawyer, Joe, I'm gonna be a lawyer, Joe, I'm 155 gonna be a goddam motherfucking legally licensed member of the bar lawyer, just like my daddy was, till my last bitter day on earth, Joseph, until the day I die.

(MARTIN *returns.*)

ROY: Ah, Martin's back.

160 MARTIN: So are we agreed?

ROY: Joe?

(*Little pause.*)

JOE: I will think about it.
    (*To* ROY.) I will.

ROY: Huh.

165 MARTIN: It's the fear of what comes after the doing that
    makes the doing hard to do.

ROY: Amen.

MARTIN: But you can almost always live with the conse-
    quences.

SCENE VII

That afternoon. On the granite steps outside the Hall of Justice,
Brooklyn. It is cold and sunny. A Sabrett wagon is selling hot dogs.
LOUIS, in a shabby overcoat, is sitting on the steps contemplatively
eating one. JOE enters with three hot dogs and a can of Coke.

JOE: Can I . . . ?

LOUIS: Oh sure. Sure. Crazy cold sun.

JOE: (*Sitting.*) Have to make the best of it.
    How's your friend?

5 LOUIS: My . . . ? Oh. He's worse. My friend is worse.

JOE: I'm sorry.

LOUIS: Yeah, well. Thanks for asking. It's nice. You're nice. I
    can't believe you voted for Reagan.

JOE: I hope he gets better.

10 LOUIS: Reagan?

JOE: Your friend.

LOUIS: He won't. Neither will Reagan.

JOE: Let's not talk politics, OK?

LOUIS: (*Pointing to JOE's lunch.*) You're eating three of those?

15 JOE: Well . . . I'm . . . hungry.

LOUIS: They're really terrible for you. Full of rat-poo and
    beetle legs and wood shavings 'n' shit.

JOE: Huh.

LOUIS: And . . . um . . . irridium, I think. Something toxic.

20 JOE: You're eating one.

LOUIS: Yeah, well, the shape, I can't help myself, plus I'm try-
    ing to commit suicide, what's your excuse?

JOE: I don't have an excuse. I just have Pepto-Bismol.

(JOE *takes a bottle of Pepto-Bismol and chugs it. LOUIS shudders*
audibly.)

JOE: Yeah I know but then I wash it down with Coke.

(*He does this. LOUIS mimes barfing in JOE's lap. JOE pushes LOUIS's*
head away.)

25 JOE: Are you always like this?

LOUIS: I've been worrying a lot about his kids.

JOE: Whose?

LOUIS: Reagan's. Maureen and Mike and little orphan Patti
    and Miss Ron Reagan Jr., the you-should-pardon-the-
30   expression heterosexual.

JOE: Ron Reagan Jr. is *not* . . . You shouldn't just make these
    assumptions about people. How do you know? About
    him? What he is? You don't know.

LOUIS: (*Doing Tallulah.*) Well darling he never sucked *my* cock
    but . . .   35

JOE: Look, if you're going to get vulgar . . .

LOUIS: No no really I mean. . . . What's it like to be the child
    of the Zeitgeist? To have the American Animus as your
    dad? It's not really a *family*, the Reagans, I read *People*, there
    aren't any connections there, no love, they don't ever even   40
    speak to each other except through their agents. So what's
    it like to be Reagan's kid? Enquiring minds want to know.

JOE: You can't believe everything you . . .

LOUIS: (*Looking away.*) But . . . I think we all know what that's
    like. Nowadays. No connections. No responsibilities. All   45
    of us . . . falling through the cracks that separate what we
    owe to our selves and . . . and what we owe to love.

JOE: You just. . . . Whatever you feel like saying or doing, you
    don't care, you just . . . do it.

LOUIS: Do what?   50

JOE: It. Whatever. Whatever it is you want to do.

LOUIS: Are you trying to tell me something?

(*Little pause, sexual. They stare at each other. JOE looks away.*)

JOE: No, I'm just observing that you . . .

LOUIS: Impulsive.

JOE: Yes, I mean it must be scary, you . . .   55

LOUIS: (*Shrugs.*) Land of the free. Home of the brave. Call me
    irresponsible.

JOE: It's kind of terrifying.

LOUIS: Yeah, well, freedom is. Heartless, too.

JOE: Oh you're not heartless.   60

LOUIS: You don't know.
    Finish your weenie.

(*He pats JOE on the knee, starts to leave.*)

JOE: Um . . .

(LOUIS *turns, looks at him. JOE searches for something to say.*)

JOE: Yesterday was Sunday but I've been a little unfocused re-
    cently and I thought it was Monday. So I came here like   65
    I was going to work. And the whole place was empty.
    And at first I couldn't figure out why, and I had this mo-
    ment of incredible . . . fear and also. . . . It just flashed
    through my mind: The whole Hall of Justice, it's empty, it's
    deserted, it's gone out of business. Forever. The people   70
    that make it run have up and abandoned it.

LOUIS: (*Looking at the building.*) Creepy.

JOE: Well yes but. I felt that I was going to scream. Not be-
    cause it was creepy, but because the emptiness felt so *fast*.
    And . . . well, good. A . . . happy scream.   75
    I just wondered what a thing it would be . . . if
    overnight everything you owe anything to, justice, or love,
    had really gone away. Free.
    It would be . . . heartless terror. Yes. Terrible, and . . .
    Very great. To shed your skin, every old skin, one by   80
    one and then walk away, unencumbered, into the morning.

(*Little pause. He looks at the building.*)

I can't go in there today.

LOUIS: Then don't.

JOE: (*Not really hearing* LOUIS.) I can't go in, I need . . .

(*He looks for what he needs. He takes a swig of Pepto-Bismol.*)

85   I can't *be* this anymore. I need . . . a change, I should just . . .

LOUIS: (*Not a come-on, necessarily; he doesn't want to be alone.*) Want some company? For whatever?

(*Pause.* JOE *looks at* LOUIS *and looks away, afraid.* LOUIS *shrugs.*)

LOUIS: Sometimes, even if it scares you to death, you have to be willing to break the law. Know what I mean?

(*Another little pause.*)

90 JOE: Yes.

(*Another little pause.*)

LOUIS: I moved out. I moved out on my . . .
   I haven't been sleeping well.

JOE: Me neither.

(LOUIS *goes up to* JOE, *licks his napkin and dabs at* JOE's *mouth.*)

LOUIS: Antacid moustache.
95   (*Points to the building.*) Maybe the court won't convene. Ever again. Maybe we are free. To do whatever.
   Children of the new morning, criminal minds. Selfish and greedy and loveless and blind. Reagan's children.
   You're scared. So am I. Everybody is in the land of the
100 free.
   God help us all.

SCENE VIII

Late that night. JOE *at a payphone phoning* HANNAH *at home in Salt Lake City.*

JOE: Mom?

HANNAH: Joe?

JOE: Hi.

HANNAH: You're calling from the street. It's . . . it must be four
5   in the morning. What's happened?

JOE: Nothing, nothing, I . . .

HANNAH: It's Harper. Is Harper. . . . Joe? Joe?

JOE: Yeah, hi. No, Harper's fine. Well, no, she's . . . not fine. How are you, Mom?

10 HANNAH: What's happened?

JOE: I just wanted to talk to you. I, uh, wanted to try something out on you.

HANNAH: Joe, you haven't . . . have you been drinking, Joe?

JOE: Yes ma'am. I'm drunk.

15 HANNAH: That isn't like you.

JOE: No. I mean, who's to say?

HANNAH: Why are you out on the street at four A.M.? In that crazy city. It's dangerous.

JOE: Actually, Mom, I'm not on the street. I'm near the
20   boathouse in the park.

HANNAH: What park?

JOE: Central Park.

HANNAH: CENTRAL PARK! Oh my Lord. What on earth are you doing in Central Park at this time of night? Are you . . . Joe, I think you ought to go home right now. Call 25 me from home.

(*Little pause.*)

   Joe?

JOE: I come here to watch, Mom. Sometimes. Just to watch.

HANNAH: Watch what? What's there to watch at four in the . . .

JOE: Mom, did Dad love me? 30

HANNAH: What?

JOE: Did he?

HANNAH: You ought to go home and call from there.

JOE: Answer.

HANNAH: Oh now really. This is maudlin. I don't like this 35 conversation.

JOE: Yeah, well, it gets worse from here on.

(*Pause.*)

HANNAH: Joe?

JOE: Mom. Momma. I'm a homosexual, Momma.
   Boy, did that come out awkward. 40

(*Pause.*)

   Hello? Hello?
     I'm a homosexual.

(*Pause.*)

   Please, Momma, Say something.

HANNAH: You're old enough to understand that your father didn't love you without being ridiculous about it. 45

JOE: What?

HANNAH: You're ridiculous. You're being ridiculous.

JOE: I'm . . .
     What?

HANNAH: You really ought to go home now to your wife. I 50 need to go to bed. This phone call. . . . We will just forget this phone call.

JOE: Mom.

HANNAH: No more talk. Tonight. This . . .
   (*Suddenly very angry.*) Drinking is a sin! A sin! I raised 55 you better than that. (*She hangs up.*)

SCENE IX

The following morning, early. Split scene: HARPER *and* JOE *at home;* LOUIS *and* PRIOR *in* PRIOR's *hospital room.* JOE *and* LOUIS *have just entered. This should be fast and obviously furious; overlapping is fine; the proceedings may be a little confusing but not the final results.*

HARPER: Oh God. Home. The moment of truth has arrived.

JOE: Harper.

LOUIS: I'm going to move out.

PRIOR: The fuck you are.

JOE: Harper. Please listen. I still love you very much. You're 5 still my best buddy; I'm not going to leave you.

HARPER: No, I don't like the sound of this. I'm leaving.

LOUIS: I'm leaving.
   I already have.

10   JOE: Please listen. Stay. This is really hard. We have to talk.

HARPER: We are talking. Aren't we. Now please shut up. OK?

PRIOR: Bastard. Sneaking off while I'm flat out here, that's low. If I could get up now I'd beat the holy shit out of you.

15   JOE: Did you take pills? How many?

HARPER: No pills. Bad for the . . . (*Pats stomach.*)

JOE: You aren't pregnant. I called your gynecologist.

HARPER: I'm seeing a new gynecologist.

PRIOR: You have no right to do this.

20   LOUIS: Oh, that's ridiculous.

PRIOR: No right. It's criminal.

JOE: Forget about that. Just listen. You want the truth. This is the truth.
   I knew this when I married you. I've known this I guess for as long as I've known anything, but . . . I don't

25   know, I thought maybe that with enough effort and will I could change myself . . . but I can't . . .

PRIOR: Criminal.

LOUIS: There oughta be a law.

30   PRIOR: There is a law. You'll see.

JOE: I'm losing ground here, I go walking, you want to know where I walk, I . . . go to the park, or up and down 53rd Street, or places where. . . . And I keep swearing I won't go walking again, but I just can't.

35   LOUIS: I need some privacy.

PRIOR: That's new.

LOUIS: Everything's new, Prior.

JOE: I try to tighten my heart into a knot, a snarl, I try to learn to live dead, just numb, but then I see someone I

40   want, and it's like a nail, like a hot spike right through my chest, and I know I'm losing.

PRIOR: Apartment too small for three? Louis and Prior comfy but not Louis and Prior and Prior's disease?

LOUIS: Something like that.

45   I won't be judged by you. This isn't a crime, just—the inevitable consequence of people who run out of— whose limitations . . .

PRIOR: Bang bang bang. The court will come to order.

LOUIS: I mean let's talk practicalities, schedules; I'll come over

50   if you want, spend nights with you when I can, I can . . .

PRIOR: Has the jury reached a verdict?

LOUIS: I'm doing the best I can.

PRIOR: Pathetic. Who cares?

JOE: My whole life has conspired to bring me to this place,

55   and I can't despise my whole life. I think I believed when I met you I could save you, you at least if not myself, but . . . I don't have any sexual feelings for you, Harper. And I don't think I ever did.

(*Little pause.*)

HARPER: I think you should go.

60   JOE: Where?

HARPER: Washington. Doesn't matter.

JOE: What are you talking about?

HARPER: Without me.
   Without me, Joe. Isn't that what you want to hear?

(*Little pause.*)

JOE: Yes.   65

LOUIS: You can love someone and fail them. You can love someone and not be able to . . .

PRIOR: You *can*, theoretically, yes. A person can, maybe an editorial "you" can love, Louis, but not *you*, specifically you, I don't know, I think you are excluded from that general   70   category.

HARPER: You were going to save me, but the whole time you were spinning a lie. I just don't understand that.

PRIOR: A person could theoretically love and maybe many do but we both know now you can't.   75

LOUIS: I do.

PRIOR: You can't even say it.

LOUIS: I love you, Prior.

PRIOR: I repeat. Who cares?

HARPER: This is so scary, I want this to stop, to go back . . .   80

PRIOR: We have reached a verdict, your honor. This man's heart is deficient. He loves, but his love is worth nothing.

JOE: Harper . . .

HARPER: Mr. Lies, I want to get away from here. Far away. Right now. Before he starts talking again. Please, please . . .   85

JOE: As long as I've known you Harper you've been afraid of . . . of men hiding under the bed, men hiding under the sofa, men with knives.

PRIOR: (*Shattered; almost pleading; trying to reach him.*) I'm dying! You stupid fuck! Do you know what that is! Love! Do   90   you know what love means? We lived together four-and-a-half years, you animal, you idiot.

LOUIS: I have to find some way to save myself.

JOE: Who are these men? I never understood it. Now I know.

HARPER: What?   95

JOE: It's me.

HARPER: It is?

PRIOR: GET OUT OF MY ROOM!

JOE: I'm the man with the knives.

HARPER: You are?   100

PRIOR: If I could get up now I'd kill you. I would. Go away. Go away or I'll scream.

HARPER: Oh God . . .

JOE: I'm sorry . . .

HARPER: It is you.   105

LOUIS: Please don't scream.

PRIOR: Go.

HARPER: I recognize you now.

LOUIS: Please . . .

JOE: Oh. Wait, I. . . . Oh!   110

(*He covers his mouth with his hand, gags, and removes his hand, red with blood.*)

   I'm bleeding.

(PRIOR *screams.*)

HARPER: Mr. Lies.

MR. LIES: (*Appearing, dressed in antarctic explorer's apparel.*) Right here.

HARPER: I want to go away. I can't see him anymore.   115

MR. LIES: Where?

HARPER: Anywhere. Far away.

MR. LIES: Absolutamento.

(HARPER *and* MR. LIES *vanish.* JOE *looks up, sees that she's gone.*)

PRIOR: (*Closing his eyes.*) When I open my eyes you'll be gone.

(LOUIS *leaves.*)

120 JOE: Harper?
PRIOR: (*Opening his eyes.*) Huh. It worked.
JOE: (*Calling.*) Harper?
PRIOR: I hurt all over. I wish I was dead.

SCENE X

The same day, sunset. HANNAH *and* SISTER ELLA CHAPTER, *a real-estate saleswoman,* HANNAH PITT's *closest friend, in front of* HANNAH's *house in Salt Lake City.*

SISTER ELLA CHAPTER: Look at that view! A view of heaven. Like the living city of heaven, isn't it, it just fairly glimmers in the sun.
HANNAH: Glimmers.
5 SISTER ELLA CHAPTER: Even the stone and brick it just glimmers and glitters like heaven in the sunshine. Such a nice view you get, perched up on a canyon rim. Some kind of beautiful place.
HANNAH: It's just Salt Lake, and you're selling the house *for*
10 me, not *to* me.
SISTER ELLA CHAPTER: I like to work up an enthusiasm for my properties.
HANNAH: Just get me a good price.
SISTER ELLA CHAPTER: Well, the market's off.
15 HANNAH: At least fifty.
SISTER ELLA CHAPTER: Forty'd be more like it.
HANNAH: Fifty.
SISTER ELLA CHAPTER: Wish you'd wait a bit.
HANNAH: Well I can't.
20 SISTER ELLA CHAPTER: Wish you would. You're about the only friend I got.
HANNAH: Oh well now.
SISTER ELLA CHAPTER: Know why I decided to like you? I decided to like you 'cause you're the only unfriendly
25 Mormon I ever met.
HANNAH: Your wig is crooked.
SISTER ELLA CHAPTER: Fix it.

(HANNAH *straightens* SISTER ELLA's *wig.*)

SISTER ELLA CHAPTER: New York City. All they got there is tiny rooms.
30   I always thought: People ought to stay put. That's why I got my license to sell real estate. It's a way of saying: Have a house! Stay put! It's a way of saying traveling's no good. Plus I needed the cash. (*She takes a pack of cigarettes out of her purse, lights one, offers pack to* HANNAH.)
35 HANNAH: Not out here, anyone could come by.
    There's been days I've stood at this ledge and thought about stepping over.
    It's a hard place, Salt Lake: baked dry. Abundant energy; not much intelligence. That's a combination that can
40 wear a body out. No harm looking someplace else. I don't need much room.
    My sister-in-law Libby thinks there's radon gas in the basement.

SISTER ELLA CHAPTER: Is there gas in the . . .
HANNAH: Of course not. Libby's a fool.   45
SISTER ELLA CHAPTER: 'Cause I'd have to include that in the description.
HANNAH: There's no gas, Ella. (*Little pause.*) Give a puff. (*She takes a furtive drag of* ELLA's *cigarette.*) Put it away now.
SISTER ELLA CHAPTER: So I guess it's goodbye.   50
HANNAH: You'll be all right, Ella, I wasn't ever much of a friend.
SISTER ELLA CHAPTER: I'll say something but don't laugh, OK? This is the home of saints, the godliest place on earth, they say, and I think they're right. That means there's no evil here? No. Evil's everywhere. Sin's everywhere. But this   55
. . . is the spring of sweet water in the desert, the desert flower. Every step a Believer takes away from here is a step fraught with peril. I fear for you, Hannah Pitt, because you are my friend. Stay put. This is the right home of saints.
HANNAH: Latter-day saints.   60
SISTER ELLA CHAPTER: Only kind left.
HANNAH: But still. Late in the day . . . for saints and everyone. That's all. That's all.
    Fifty thousand dollars for the house, Sister Ella Chapter; don't undersell. It's an impressive view.   65

ACT THREE
Not-Yet-Conscious, Forward Dawning
January 1986

SCENE I

Late night, three days after the end of Act Two. The stage is completely dark. PRIOR *is in bed in his apartment, having a nightmare. He wakes up, sits up and switches on a nightlight. He looks at his clock. Seated by the table near the bed is a man dressed in the clothing of a 13th-century British squire.*

PRIOR: (*Terrified.*) Who are you?
PRIOR 1: My name is Prior Walter.

(*Pause.*)

PRIOR: My name is Prior Walter.
PRIOR 1: I know that.
PRIOR: Explain.   5
PRIOR 1: You're alive. I'm not. We have the same name. What do you want me to explain?
PRIOR: A ghost?
PRIOR 1: An ancestor.
PRIOR: Not *the* Prior Walter? The Bayeux tapestry Prior Walter?   10
PRIOR 1: His great-great grandson. The fifth of the name.
PRIOR: I'm the thirty-fourth, I think.
PRIOR 1: Actually the thirty-second.
PRIOR: Not according to Mother.
PRIOR 1: She's including the two bastards, then; I say leave   15
them out. I say no room for bastards. The little things you swallow . . .
PRIOR: Pills.
PRIOR 1: Pills. For the pestilence. I too . . .
PRIOR: Pestilence. . . . You too what?   20
PRIOR 1: The pestilence in my time was much worse than now. Whole villages of empty houses. You could look outdoors

and see Death walking in the morning, dew dampening the ragged hem of his black robe. Plain as I see you now.

25 PRIOR: You died of the plague.

PRIOR 1: The spotty monster. Like you, alone.

PRIOR: I'm not alone.

PRIOR 1: You have no wife, no children.

PRIOR: I'm gay.

30 PRIOR 1: So? Be gay, dance in your altogether for all I care, what's that to do with not having children?

PRIOR: Gay homosexual, not bonny, blithe and . . . never mind.

PRIOR 1: I had twelve. When I died.

(*The second ghost appears, this one dressed in the clothing of an elegant 17th-century Londoner.*)

PRIOR 1: (*Pointing to* PRIOR 2.) And I was three years younger 35 than him.

(PRIOR *sees the new ghost, screams.*)

PRIOR: Oh God another one.

PRIOR 2: Prior Walter. Prior to you by some seventeen others.

PRIOR 1: He's counting the bastards.

PRIOR: Are we having a convention?

40 PRIOR 2: We've been sent to declare her fabulous incipience. They love a well-paved entrance with lots of heralds, and . . .

PRIOR 1: The messenger come. Prepare the way. The infinite descent, a breath in air . . .

45 PRIOR 2: They chose us, I suspect, because of the mortal affinities. In a family as long-descended as the Walters there are bound to be a few carried off by plague.

PRIOR 1: The spotty monster.

PRIOR 2: Black Jack. Came from a water pump, half the city 50 of London, can you imagine? His came from fleas. Yours, I understand, is the lamentable consequence of venery . . .

PRIOR 1: Fleas on rats, but who knew that?

PRIOR: Am I going to die?

PRIOR 2: We aren't allowed to discuss . . .

55 PRIOR 1: When you do, you don't get ancestors to help you through it. You may be surrounded by children but you die alone.

PRIOR: I'm afraid.

PRIOR 1: You should be. There aren't even torches, and the 60 path's rocky, dark and steep.

PRIOR 2: Don't alarm him. There's good news before there's bad.
    We two come to strew rose petal and palm leaf before the triumphal procession. Prophet. Seer. Revelator. It's a 65 great honor for the family.

PRIOR 1: He hasn't got a family.

PRIOR 2: I meant for the Walters, for the family in the larger sense.

PRIOR: (*Singing.*)

70   All I want is a room somewhere,
      Far away from the cold night air . . .

PRIOR 2: (*Putting a hand on* PRIOR*'s forehead.*) Calm, calm, this is no brain fever . . .

(PRIOR *calms down, but keeps his eyes closed. The lights begin to change. Distant Glorious Music.*)

PRIOR 1: (*Low chant.*) Adonai, Adonai,
    Olam ha-yichud,   75
    Zefirot, Zazahot,
    Ha-adam, ha-gadol
    Daughter of Light,
    Daughter of Splendors,
    Fluor! Phosphor!   80
    Lumen! Candle!

PRIOR 2: (*Simultaneously.*) Even now,
    From the mirror-bright halls of heaven,
    Across the cold and lifeless infinity of space,
    The Messenger comes   85
    Trailing orbs of light,
    Fabulous, incipient,
    Oh Prophet,
    To you . . .

PRIOR 1 and PRIOR 2: Prepare, prepare,   90
    The Infinite Descent,
    A breath, a feather,
    Glory to . . .

(*They vanish.*)

SCENE II

The next day. Split scene: LOUIS *and* BELIZE *in a coffee shop.* PRIOR *is at the outpatient clinic at the hospital with* EMILY, *the nurse; she has him on a pentamidine IV drip.*

LOUIS: Why has democracy succeeded in America? Of course by succeeded I mean comparatively, not literally, not in the present, but what makes for the prospect of some sort of radical democracy spreading outward and growing up? Why does the power that was once so carefully preserved at 5 the top of the pyramid by the original framers of the Constitution seem drawn inexorably downward and outward in spite of the best effort of the Right to stop this? I mean it's the really hard thing about being Left in this country, the American Left can't help but trip over all these petrified lit- 10 tle fetishes: freedom, that's the worst; you know, *Jeane Kirkpatrick* for God's sake will go on and on about freedom and so what does that mean, the word freedom, when she talks about it, or human rights; you have Bush talking about human rights, and so what are these people talking about, they 15 might as well be talking about the mating habits of Venusians, these people don't begin to know what, ontologically, freedom is or human rights, like they see these bourgeois property-based Rights-of-Man-type rights but that's not enfranchisement, not democracy, not what's implicit, what's 20 potential within the idea, not the idea with blood in it. That's just liberalism, the worst kind of liberalism, really, bourgeois tolerance, and what I think is that what AIDS shows us is the limits of tolerance, that it's not enough to be tolerated, because when the shit hits the fan you find out 25 how much tolerance is worth. Nothing. And underneath all the tolerance is intense, passionate hatred.

BELIZE: Uh huh.

LOUIS: Well don't you think that's true?

BELIZE: Uh huh. It is.   30

LOUIS: *Power* is the object, not being tolerated. Fuck assimilation. But I mean in spite of all this the thing about America,

I think, is that ultimately we're different from every other nation on earth, in that, with people here of every race, we can't. . . . Ultimately what defines us isn't race, but politics. Not like any European country where there's an insurmountable fact of a kind of racial, or ethnic, monopoly, or monolith, like all Dutchmen, I mean Dutch people, are well, Dutch, and the Jews of Europe were never Europeans, just a small problem. Facing the monolith. But here there are so many small problems, it's really just a collection of small problems, the monolith is missing. Oh, I mean, of course I suppose there's the monolith of White America. White Straight Male America.

BELIZE: Which is not unimpressive, even among monoliths.

LOUIS: Well, no, but when the race thing gets taken care of, and I don't mean to minimalize how major it is, I mean I know it is, this is a really, really incredibly racist country but it's like, well, the British. I mean, all these blue-eyed pink people. And it's just weird, you know, I mean I'm not all that Jewish-looking, or . . . well, maybe I am but, you know, in New York, everyone is . . . well, not everyone, but so many are but so but in England, in London I walk into bars and I feel like Sid the Yid, you know I mean like Woody Allen in *Annie Hall,* with the payess and the gabardine coat, like never, never anywhere so much—I mean, not actively despised, not like they're Germans, who I think are still terribly anti-Semitic, and racist too, I mean black-racist, they pretend otherwise but, anyway, in London, there's just . . . and at one point I met this black gay guy from Jamaica who talked with a lilt but he said his family'd been living in London since before the Civil War—the American one—and how the English never let him forget for a minute that he wasn't blue-eyed and pink and I said yeah, me too, these people are anti-Semites and he said yeah but the British Jews have the clothing business all sewed up and blacks there can't get a foothold. And it was an incredibly awkward moment of just. . . . I mean here we were, in this bar that was gay but it was a *pub,* you know, the beams and the plaster and those horrible little, like, two-day-old fish and egg sandwiches—and just so British, so *old,* and I felt, well, there's no way out of this because both of us are, right now, too much immersed in this history, hope is dissolved in the sheer age of this place, where race is what counts and there's no real hope of change—it's the racial destiny of the Brits that matters to them, not their political destiny, whereas in America . . .

BELIZE: Here in America race doesn't count.

LOUIS: No, no, that's not. . . . I mean you *can't* be hearing that . . .

BELIZE: I . . .

LOUIS: It's—look, race, yes, but ultimately race here is a political question, right? Racists just try to use race here as a tool in a political struggle. It's not really about race. Like the spiritualists try to use that stuff, are you enlightened, are you centered, channeled, whatever, this reaching out for a spiritual past in a country where no indigenous spirits exist—only the Indians, I mean Native American spirits and we killed them off so now, there are no gods here, no ghosts and spirits in America, there are no angels in America, no spiritual past, no racial past, there's only the political, and the decoys and the ploys to maneuver around the inescapable battle of politics, the shifting downwards and outwards of political power to the people . . .

BELIZE: POWER to the People! AMEN! (*Looking at his watch.*) *OH MY GOODNESS!* Will you look at the time, I gotta . . .

LOUIS: Do you. . . . You think this is, what, racist or naive or something?

BELIZE: Well it's certainly *something.* Look, I just remembered I have an appointment . . .

LOUIS: What? I mean I really don't want to, like, speak from some position of privilege and . . .

BELIZE: I'm sitting here, thinking, eventually he's *got* to run out of steam, so I let you rattle on and on saying about maybe seven or eight things I find really offensive.

LOUIS: What?

BELIZE: But I know you, Louis, and I know the guilt fueling this peculiar tirade is obviously already swollen bigger than your hemorrhoids.

LOUIS: I don't have hemorrhoids.

BELIZE: I hear different. May I finish?

LOUIS: Yes, but I don't have hemorrhoids.

BELIZE: So finally, when I . . .

LOUIS: Prior told you, he's an asshole, he shouldn't have . . .

BELIZE: You promised, Louis. Prior is not a subject.

LOUIS: You brought him up.

BELIZE: I brought up hemorrhoids.

LOUIS: So it's indirect. Passive-aggressive.

BELIZE: Unlike, I suppose, banging me over the head with your theory that America doesn't have a race problem.

LOUIS: Oh be fair I never said that.

BELIZE: Not exactly, but . . .

LOUIS: I said . . .

BELIZE: but it was close enough, because if it'd been that blunt I'd've just walked out and . . .

LOUIS: You deliberately misinterpreted! I . . .

BELIZE: Stop interrupting! I haven't been able to . . .

LOUIS: Just let me . . .

BELIZE: NO! What, *talk*? You've been running your mouth nonstop since I got here, yaddadda yaddadda blah blah blah, up the hill, down the hill, playing with your MONOLITH . . .

LOUIS: (*Overlapping*) Well, you could have joined in at any time instead of . . .

BELIZE: (*Continuing over* LOUIS.) . . . and girlfriend it is truly an awesome spectacle but I got better things to do with my time than sit here listening to this racist bullshit just because I feel sorry for you that . . .

LOUIS: I am not a racist!

BELIZE: Oh come on . . .

LOUIS: So maybe I am a racist but . . .

BELIZE: Oh I really hate that! It's no fun picking on you Louis; you're so guilty, it's like throwing darts at a glob of jello, there's no satisfying hits, just quivering, the darts just blop in and vanish.

LOUIS: I just think when you are discussing lines of oppression it gets very complicated and . . .

BELIZE: Oh is that a fact? You know, we black drag queens have a rather intimate knowledge of the complexity of the lines of . . .

LOUIS: *Ex*-black drag queen.

BELIZE: Actually ex-ex.

LOUIS: You're doing drag again?
BELIZE: I don't. . . . Maybe. I don't have to tell you. Maybe.
155 LOUIS: I think it's sexist.
BELIZE: I didn't ask you.
LOUIS: Well it is. The gay community, I think, has to adopt the same attitude towards drag as black women have to take towards black women blues singers.
160 BELIZE: Oh my we *are* walking dangerous tonight.
LOUIS: Well, it's all internalized oppression, right, I mean the masochism, the stereotypes, the . . .
BELIZE: Louis, are you deliberately trying to make me hate you?
165 LOUIS: No, I . . .
BELIZE: I mean, are you deliberately transforming yourself into an arrogant, sexual-political Stalinist-slash-racist flag-waving thug for my benefit?

(*Pause.*)

LOUIS: You know what I think?
170 BELIZE: What?
LOUIS: You hate me because I'm a Jew.
BELIZE: I'm leaving.
LOUIS: It's true.
BELIZE: You have no basis except your . . .
175   Louis, it's good to know you haven't changed; you are still an honorary citizen of the Twilight Zone, and after your pale, pale white polemics on behalf of racial insensitivity you have a flaming *fuck* of a lot of nerve calling me an anti-Semite. Now I really gotta go.
180 LOUIS: You called me Lou the Jew.
BELIZE: That was a joke.
LOUIS: I didn't think it was funny. It was hostile.
BELIZE: It was three years ago.
LOUIS: So?
185 BELIZE: You just called yourself Sid the Yid.
LOUIS: That's not the same thing.
BELIZE: Sid the Yid is different from Lou the Jew.
LOUIS: Yes.
BELIZE: Someday you'll have to explain that to me, but right
190   now . . .
     You hate me because you hate black people.
LOUIS: I do not. But I do think most black people are anti-Semitic.
BELIZE: "Most black people." *That's* racist, Louis, and *I* think
195   most Jews . . .
LOUIS: Louis Farrakhan.
BELIZE: Ed Koch.
LOUIS: Jesse Jackson.
BELIZE: Jackson. Oh really, Louis, this is . . .
200 LOUIS: Hymietown! Hymietown!
BELIZE: Louis, you voted for Jesse Jackson. You send checks to the Rainbow Coalition.
LOUIS: I'm ambivalent. The checks bounced.
BELIZE: All your checks bounce, Louis; you're ambivalent
205   about everything.
LOUIS: What's that supposed to mean?
BELIZE: You may be dumber than shit but I refuse to believe you can't figure it out. Try.

LOUIS: I was never ambivalent about Prior. I love him. I do. I really do.
210
BELIZE: Nobody said different.
LOUIS: Love and ambivalence are. . . . Real love isn't ambivalent.
BELIZE: "Real love isn't ambivalent." I'd swear that's a line from my favorite bestselling paperback novel, *In Love with* 215 *the Night Mysterious,* except I don't think you ever read it.

(*Pause.*)

LOUIS: I never read it, no.
BELIZE: You ought to. Instead of spending the rest of your life trying to get through *Democracy in America.* It's about this white woman whose Daddy owns a plantation in the 220 Deep South in the years before the Civil War—the American one—and her name is Margaret, and she's in love with her Daddy's number-one slave, and his name is Thaddeus, and she's married but her white slave-owner husband has AIDS: Antebellum Insufficiently Developed 225 Sexorgans. And there's a lot of hot stuff going down when Margaret and Thaddeus can catch a spare torrid ten under the cottonpicking moon, and then of course the Yankees come, and they set the slaves free, and the slaves string up old Daddy, and so on. Historical fiction. Somewhere in 230 there I recall Margaret and Thaddeus find the time to discuss the nature of love; her face is reflecting the flames of the burning plantation—you know, the way white people do—and his black face is dark in the night and she says to him, "Thaddeus, real love isn't ever ambivalent." 235

(*Little pause.* EMILY *enters and turns off IV drip.*)

BELIZE: Thaddeus looks at her; he's contemplating her thesis; and he isn't sure he agrees.
EMILY: (*Removing IV drip from* PRIOR'*s arm.*) Treatment number . . . (*Consulting chart.*) four.
PRIOR: Pharmaceutical miracle. Lazarus breathes again. 240
LOUIS: Is he. . . . How bad is he?
BELIZE: You want the laundry list?
EMILY: Shirt off, let's check the . . .

(PRIOR *takes his shirt off. She examines his lesions.*)

BELIZE: There's the weight problem and the shit problem and the morale problem. 245
EMILY: Only six. That's good. Pants.

(*He drops his pants. He's naked. She examines.*)

BELIZE: And. He thinks he's going crazy.
EMILY: Looking good. What else?
PRIOR: Ankles sore and swollen, but the leg's better. The nausea's mostly gone with the little orange pills. BM's pure 250 liquid but not bloody anymore, for now, my eye doctor says everything's OK, for now, my dentist says "Yuck!" when he sees my fuzzy tongue, and now he wears little condoms on his thumb and forefinger. And a mask. So what? My dermatologist is in Hawaii and my mother . . . 255 well leave my mother out of it. Which is usually where my mother is, out of it. My glands are like walnuts, my

weight's holding steady for week two, and a friend died
two days ago of bird tuberculosis; bird tuberculosis; that
260   scared me and I didn't go to the funeral today because he
was an Irish Catholic and it's probably open casket and
I'm afraid of . . . something, the bird TB or seeing him
or. . . . So I guess I'm doing OK. Except for of course I'm
going nuts.

265   EMILY: We ran the toxoplasmosis series and there's no indication . . .

PRIOR: I know, I know, but I feel like something terrifying is
on its way, you know, like a missile from outer space, and
it's plummeting down towards the earth, and I'm ground
270   zero, and . . . I am generally known where I am known as
one cool, collected queen. And I am ruffled.

EMILY: There's really nothing to worry about. I think that
shochen bamromim hamtzeh menucho nechono al kan-
fey haschino.

275   PRIOR: What?

EMILY: Everything's fine. Bemaalos k'doshim ut'horim kezo-
har horokeea mazhirim . . .

PRIOR: Oh I don't understand what you're . . .

EMILY: Es nishmas Prior sheholoch leolomoh, baavur shen-
280   odvoo z'dokoh b'ad hazkoras nishmosoh.

PRIOR: Why are you doing that?! Stop it! Stop it!

EMILY: Stop what?

PRIOR: You were just . . . weren't you just speaking in Hebrew
or something.

285   EMILY: *Hebrew?* (*Laughs.*) I'm basically Italian-American. No.
I didn't speak in Hebrew.

PRIOR: Oh no, oh God please I really think I . . .

EMILY: Look, I'm sorry, I have a waiting room full of. . . . I
think you're one of the lucky ones, you'll live for years,
290   probably—you're pretty healthy for someone with no immune system. Are you seeing someone? Loneliness is a
danger. A therapist?

PRIOR: No, I don't need to see anyone, I just . . .

EMILY: Well think about it. You aren't going crazy. You're just
295   under a lot of stress. No wonder . . . (*She starts to write in
his chart.*)

(*Suddenly there is an astonishing blaze of light, a huge chord
sounded by a gigantic choir, and a great book with steel pages
mounted atop a molten-red pillar pops up from the stage floor. The
book opens; there is a large Aleph inscribed on its pages, which bursts
into flames. Immediately the book slams shut and disappears instantly under the floor as the lights become normal again.* EMILY *notices none of this, writing.* PRIOR *is agog.*)

EMILY: (*Laughing, exiting.*) Hebrew . . .

(PRIOR *flees.*)

LOUIS: Help me.

BELIZE: I beg your pardon?

300   LOUIS: You're a nurse, give me something, I . . . don't know
what to do anymore, I. . . . Last week at work I screwed
up the Xerox machine like permanently and so I . . . then
I tripped on the subway steps and my glasses broke and I
cut my forehead, here, see, and now I can't see much and
305   my forehead . . . it's like the Mark of Cain, stupid, right,
but it won't heal and every morning I see it and I think,
Biblical things, Mark of Cain, Judas Iscariot and his silver

and his noose, people who . . . in betraying what they
love betray what's truest in themselves, I feel . . . nothing
but cold for myself, just cold, and every night I miss him,   310
I miss him so much but then . . . those sores, and the
smell and . . . where I thought it was going. . . . I could
be . . . I could be sick too, maybe I'm sick too. I don't
know.
Belize. Tell him I love him. Can you do that?   315

BELIZE: I've thought about it for a very long time, and I still
don't understand what love is. Justice is simple. Democracy is simple. Those things are unambivalent. But love is
very hard. And it goes bad for you if you violate the hard
law of love.   320

LOUIS: I'm dying.

BELIZE: He's dying. You just wish you were. Oh cheer up,
Louis. Look at that heavy sky out there.

LOUIS: Purple.

BELIZE: *Purple?* Boy, what kind of a homosexual are you,   325
anyway? That's not purple, Mary, that color up there is
(*Very grand.*) mauve.
All day today it's felt like Thanksgiving. Soon, this . . .
ruination will be blanketed white. You can smell it—can
you smell it?   330

LOUIS: Smell what?

BELIZE: Softness, compliance, forgiveness, grace.

LOUIS: No . . .

BELIZE: I can't help you learn that. I can't help you, Louis.
You're not my business. (*He exits.*)   335

(LOUIS *puts his head in his hands, inadvertently touching his cut
forehead.*)

LOUIS: Ow FUCK! (*He stands slowly, looks towards where*
BELIZE *exited.*) Smell what? (*He looks both ways to be sure no
one is watching, then inhales deeply, and is surprised.*) Huh.
Snow.

SCENE III

Same day. HARPER *in a very white, cold place, with a brilliant blue
sky above; a delicate snowfall. She is dressed in a beautiful snowsuit.
The sound of the sea, faint.*

HARPER: Snow! Ice! Mountains of ice! Where am I? I . . . feel
better, I do, I . . . feel better. There are ice crystals in my
lungs, wonderful and sharp. And the snow smells like cold,
crushed peaches. And there's something . . . some current
of blood in the wind, how strange, it has that iron taste.   5

MR. LIES: Ozone.

HARPER: Ozone! Wow! Where am I?

MR. LIES: The Kingdom of Ice, the bottommost part of the
world.

HARPER: (*Looking around, then realizing.*) Antarctica. This is   10
Antarctica!

MR. LIES: Cold shelter for the shattered. No sorrow here, tears
freeze.

HARPER: Antarctica, Antarctica, oh boy oh boy, LOOK at this,
I. . . . Wow, I must've really snapped the tether, huh?   15

MR. LIES: Apparently . . .

HARPER: That's great. I want to stay here forever. Set up camp.
Build things. Build a city, an enormous city made up of

frontier forts, dark wood and green roofs and high gates
20 made of pointed logs and bonfires burning on every street
corner. I should build by a river. Where are the forests?

MR. LIES: No timber here. Too cold. Ice, no trees.

HARPER: Oh details! I'm sick of details! I'll plant them and
grow them. I'll live off caribou fat, I'll melt it over the
25 bon-fires and drink it from long, curved goat-horn cups.
It'll be great. I want to make a new world here. So that I
never have to go home again.

MR. LIES: As long as it lasts. Ice has a way of melting . . .

HARPER: No. Forever. I can have anything I want here—
30 maybe even companionship, someone who has . . . desire
for me. You, maybe.

MR. LIES: It's against the by-laws of the International Order
of Travel Agents to get involved with clients. Rules are
rules. Anyway, I'm not the one you really want.

35 HARPER: There isn't anyone . . . maybe an Eskimo. Who
could ice-fish for food. And help me build a nest for
when the baby comes.

MR. LIES: There are no Eskimo in Antarctica. And you're not
really pregnant. You made that up.

40 HARPER: Well all of this is made up. So if the snow feels cold
I'm pregnant. Right? Here, I can be pregnant. And I can
have any kind of a baby I want.

MR. LIES: This is a retreat, a vacuum, its virtue is that it lacks
everything; deep-freeze for feelings. You can be numb
45 and safe here, that's what you came for. Respect the delicate ecology of your delusions.

HARPER: You mean like no Eskimo in Antarctica.

MR. LIES: Correcto. Ice and snow, no Eskimo. Even hallucinations have laws.

50 HARPER: Well then who's that?

(*The* ESKIMO *appears.*)

MR. LIES: An Eskimo.

HARPER: An antarctic Eskimo. A fisher of the polar deep.

MR. LIES: There's something wrong with this picture.

(*The* ESKIMO *beckons.*)

HARPER: I'm going to like this place. It's my own National
55 Geo-graphic Special! Oh! Oh! (*She holds her stomach.*) I
think . . . I think I felt her kicking. Maybe I'll give birth
to a baby covered with thick white fur, and that way she
won't be cold. My breasts will be full of hot cocoa so she
doesn't get chilly. And if it gets really cold, she'll have a
60 pouch I can crawl into. Like a marsupial. We'll mend together. That's what we'll do; we'll mend.

SCENE IV

Same day. An abandoned lot in the South Bronx. A homeless
WOMAN *is standing near an oil drum in which a fire is burning.*
Snowfall. Trash around. HANNAH *enters dragging two heavy suit-*
cases.

HANNAH: Excuse me? I said excuse me? Can you tell me
where I am? Is this Brooklyn? Do you know a Pineapple
Street? Is there some sort of bus or train or . . . ?
I'm lost, I just arrived from Salt Lake. City. Utah? I took
5 the bus that I was told to take and I got off—well it was the

very last stop, so I had to get off, and I *asked* the driver was
this Brooklyn, and he nodded yes but he was from one of
those foreign countries where they think it's good manners
to nod at everything even if you have no idea what it is
you're nodding at, and in truth I think he spoke no English 10
at all, which I think would make him ineligible for employment on public transportation. The public being
English-speaking, mostly. Do you speak English?

(*The* WOMAN *nods.*)

HANNAH: I was supposed to be met at the airport by my son.
He didn't show and I don't wait more than three and 15
three-quarters hours for *anyone*. I should have been patient, I guess, I. . . . Is this . . .

WOMAN: Bronx.

HANNAH: Is that. . . . The *Bronx?* Well how in the name of
Heaven did I get to the Bronx when the bus driver said . . . 20

WOMAN: (*Talking to herself.*) Slurp slurp slurp will you STOP
that disgusting slurping! YOU DISGUSTING SLURP-
ING FEEDING ANIMAL! Feeding yourself, just feeding
yourself, what would it matter, to you or to ANYONE, if
you just stopped. Feeding. And DIED? 25

(*Pause.*)

HANNAH: Can you just tell me where I . . .

WOMAN: Why was the Kosciusko Bridge named after a Polack?

HANNAH: I don't know what you're . . .

WOMAN: That was a joke.

HANNAH: Well what's the punchline? 30

WOMAN: I don't know.

HANNAH: (*Looking around desperately.*) Oh for pete's sake, is
there anyone else who . . .

WOMAN: (*Again, to herself.*) Stand further off you fat loathsome whore, you can't have any more of this soup, slurp 35
slurp slurp you animal, and the—I know you'll just go pee
it all away and where will you do that? Behind what bush?
It's FUCKING COLD out here and I . . .
Oh that's right, because it was supposed to have been
a tunnel! 40
That's not very funny.
Have you read the prophecies of Nostradamus?

HANNAH: Who?

WOMAN: Some guy I went out with once somewhere, Nostradamus. Prophet, outcast, eyes like. . . . Scary shit, he . . . 45

HANNAH: Shut up. Please. Now I want you to stop jabbering
for a minute and pull your wits together and tell me how
to get to Brooklyn. Because you know! And you are going to tell me! Because there is no one else around to tell
me and I am wet and cold and I am very angry! So I am 50
sorry you're psychotic but just make the effort—take a
deep breath—DO IT!

(HANNAH *and* WOMAN *breathe together.*)

HANNAH: That's good. Now exhale.

(*They do.*)

HANNAH: Good. Now how do I get to Brooklyn?

WOMAN: Don't know. Never been. Sorry. Want some soup? 55

HANNAH: Manhattan? Maybe you know . . . I don't suppose you know the location of the Mormon Visitor's . . .

WOMAN: 65th and Broadway.

HANNAH: How do you . . .

60 WOMAN: Go there all the time. Free movies. Boring, but you can stay all day.

HANNAH: Well. . . . So how do I . . .

WOMAN: Take the D Train. Next block make a right.

HANNAH: Thank you.

65 WOMAN: Oh yeah. In the new century I think we will all be insane.

SCENE V

Same day. JOE *and* ROY *in the study of* ROY's *brownstone.* ROY *is wearing an elegant bathrobe. He has made a considerable effort to look well. He isn't well, and he hasn't succeeded much in looking it.*

JOE: I can't. The answer's no. I'm sorry.

ROY: Oh, well, apologies . . .

I can't see that there's anyone asking for apologies.

(*Pause.*)

JOE: I'm sorry, Roy.

5 ROY: Oh, well, apologies.

JOE: My wife is missing, Roy. My mother's coming from Salt Lake to . . . to help look, I guess. I'm supposed to be at the airport now, picking her up but. . . . I just spent two days in a hospital, Roy, with a bleeding ulcer, I was spitting up

10 blood.

ROY: Blood, huh? Look, I'm very busy here and . . .

JOE: It's just a job.

ROY: A job? A *job? Washington!* Dumb Utah Mormon hick shit!

15 JOE: Roy . . .

ROY: *WASHINGTON!* When Washington called me I was younger than you, you think I said "Aw fuck no I can't go I got two fingers up my asshole and a little moral nose-bleed to boot!" When Washington calls you my pretty

20 young punk friend you go or you can go fuck yourself sideways 'cause the train has pulled out of the station, and you are *out,* nowhere, out in the cold. Fuck you, Mary Jane, get outta here.

JOE: Just let me . . .

25 ROY: Explain? Ephemera. You broke my heart. Explain that. Explain that.

JOE: I love you. Roy.

There's so much that I want, to be . . . what you see in me, I want to be a participant in the world, in your world,

30 Roy, I want to be capable of that, I've tried, really I have but . . . I can't do this. Not because I don't believe in you, but because I believe in you so much, in what you stand for, at heart, the order, the decency. I would give anything to protect you, but. . . . There are laws I can't break. It's

35 too ingrained. It's not me. There's enough damage I've already done.

Maybe you were right, maybe I'm dead.

ROY: You're not dead, boy, you're a sissy.

You love me; that's moving, I'm moved. It's nice to be

40 loved. I warned you about her, didn't I, Joe? But you don't

listen to me, why, because you say Roy is smart and Roy's a friend but Roy . . . well, he isn't nice, and you wanna be nice. Right? A nice, nice man!

(*Little pause.*)

You know what my greatest accomplishment was, Joe, in my life, what I am able to look back on and be proudest 45 of? And I have helped make Presidents and unmake them and mayors and more goddam judges than anyone in NYC ever—AND several million dollars, tax-free—and what do you think means the most to me?

You ever hear of Ethel Rosenberg? Huh, Joe, huh? 50

JOE: Well, yeah, I guess I. . . . Yes.

ROY: Yes. Yes. You have heard of Ethel Rosenberg. Yes. Maybe you even read about her in the history books.

If it wasn't for me, Joe, Ethel Rosenberg would be alive today, writing some personal-advice column for *Ms.* mag- 55 azine. She isn't. Because during the trial, Joe, I was on the phone every day, talking with the judge . . .

JOE: Roy . . .

ROY: Every day, doing what I do best, talking on the tele-phone, making sure that timid Yid nebbish on the bench 60 did his duty to America, to history. That sweet unprepos-sessing woman, two kids, boo-hoo-hoo, reminded us all of our little Jewish mamas—she came this close to getting life; I pleaded till I wept to put her in the chair. Me. I did that. I would have fucking pulled the switch if they'd have 65 let me. Why? Because I fucking hate traitors. Because I fucking hate communists. Was it legal? Fuck legal. Am I a nice man? Fuck nice. They say terrible things about me in the *Nation.* Fuck the *Nation.* You want to be Nice, or you want to be Effective? Make the law, or subject to it. 70 Choose. Your wife chose. A week from today, she'll be back. SHE knows how to get what SHE wants. Maybe I ought to send *her* to Washington.

JOE: I don't believe you.

ROY: Gospel. 75

JOE: You can't possibly mean what you're saying.

Roy, you were the Assistant United States Attorney on the Rosenberg case, ex-parte communication with the judge during the trial would be . . . censurable, at least, probably conspiracy and . . . in a case that resulted in exe- 80 cution, it's . . .

ROY: What? Murder?

JOE: You're not well is all.

ROY: What do you mean, not well? Who's not well?

(*Pause.*)

JOE: You said . . . 85

ROY: No I didn't. I said what?

JOE: Roy, you have cancer.

ROY: No I don't.

(*Pause.*)

JOE: You told me you were dying.

ROY: What the fuck are you talking about, Joe? I never said 90 that. I'm in perfect health. There's not a goddam thing wrong with me.

(*He smiles.*)

Shake?

(JOE *hesitates. He holds out his hand to* ROY. ROY *pulls* JOE *into a close, strong clinch.*)

ROY: (*More to himself than to* JOE.) It's OK that you hurt me because I love you, baby Joe. That's why I'm so rough on you.

(ROY *releases* JOE. JOE *backs away a step or two.*)

ROY: Prodigal son. The world will wipe its dirty hands all over you.
JOE: It already has, Roy.
ROY: Now go.

(ROY *shoves* JOE *hard.* JOE *turns to leave.* ROY *stops him, turns him around.*)

ROY: (*Smoothing* JOE's *lapels, tenderly.*) I'll always be here, waiting for you . . .

(*Then again, with sudden violence, he pulls* JOE *close, violently.*)

What did you want from me, what was all this, what do you want, treacherous ungrateful little . . .

(JOE, *very close to belting* ROY, *grabs him by the front of his robe, and propels him across the length of the room. He holds* ROY *at arm's length, the other arm ready to hit.*)

ROY: (*Laughing softly, almost pleading to be hit.*) Transgress a little, Joseph.

(JOE *releases* ROY.)

ROY: There are so many laws; find one you can break.

(JOE *hesitates, then leaves, backing out. When* JOE *has gone,* ROY *doubles over in great pain, which he's been hiding throughout the scene with joe.*)

ROY: Ah, Christ . . .
Andy! Andy! Get in here! Andy!

(*The door opens, but it isn't* ANDY. *A small Jewish Woman dressed modestly in a fifties hat and coat stands in the doorway. The room darkens.*)

ROY: Who the fuck are you? The new nurse?

(*The figure in the doorway says nothing. She stares at* ROY. *A pause.* ROY *looks at her carefully, gets up, crosses to her. He crosses back to the chair, sits heavily.*)

ROY: Aw, fuck. Ethel.
ETHEL ROSENBERG: (*Her manner is friendly, her voice is ice-cold.*) You don't look good, Roy.
ROY: Well, Ethel. I don't feel good.
ETHEL ROSENBERG: But you lost a lot of weight. That suits you. You were heavy back then. Zaftig, mit hips.

ROY: I haven't been that heavy since 1960. We were all heavier back then, before the body thing started. Now I look like a skeleton. They stare.
ETHEL ROSENBERG: The shit's really hit the fan, huh, Roy?

(*Little pause.* ROY *nods.*)

ETHEL ROSENBERG: Well the fun's just started.
ROY: What is this, Ethel, Halloween? You trying to scare me?

(ETHEL *says nothing.*)

ROY: Well you're wasting your time! I'm scarier than you any day of the week! So beat it, Ethel! BOOO! BETTER DEAD THAN RED! Somebody trying to shake me up? HAH HAH! From the throne of God in heaven to the belly of hell, you can all fuck yourselves and then go jump in the lake because I'M NOT AFRAID OF YOU OR DEATH OR HELL OR ANYTHING!
ETHEL ROSENBERG: Be seeing you soon, Roy. Julius sends his regards.
ROY: Yeah, well send this to Julius!

(*He flips the bird in her direction, stands and moves towards her. Half-way across the room he slumps to the floor, breathing laboriously, in pain.*)

ETHEL ROSENBERG: You're a very sick man, Roy.
ROY: Oh God . . . ANDY!
ETHEL ROSENBERG: Hmmm. He doesn't hear you, I guess. We should call the ambulance.

(*She goes to the phone.*)

Hah! Buttons! Such things they got now.
What do I dial, Roy?

(*Pause.* ROY *looks at her, then:*)

ROY: 911.
ETHEL ROSENBERG: (*Dials the phone.*) It sings!
(*Imitating dial tones.*) La la la . . .
Huh.
Yes, you should please send an ambulance to the home of Mister Roy Cohn, the famous lawyer.
What's the address, Roy?
ROY: (*A beat, then.*) 244 East 87th.
ETHEL ROSENBERG: 244 East 87th Street. No apartment number, he's got the whole building.
My name? (*A beat.*) Ethel Greenglass Rosenberg.
(*Small smile.*) Me? No I'm not related to Mr. Cohn. An old friend.

(*She hangs up.*)

They said a minute.
ROY: I have all the time in the world.
ETHEL ROSENBERG: You're immortal.
ROY: I'm immortal. Ethel. (*He forces himself to stand.*)
I have *forced* my way into history. I ain't never gonna die.
ETHEL ROSENBERG: (*A little laugh, then.*) History is about to crack wide open. Millennium approaches.

SCENE VI

Late that night. PRIOR's *bedroom.* PRIOR 1 *watching* PRIOR *in bed, who is staring back at him, terrified. Tonight* PRIOR 1 *is dressed in weird alchemical robes and hat over his historical clothing and he carries a long palm-leaf bundle.*

PRIOR 1: Tonight's the night! Aren't you excited? Tonight she arrives! Right through the roof! Ha–adam, Ha–gadol . . .

PRIOR 2: (*Appearing, similarly attired.*) Lumen! Phosphor! Fluor! Candle! An unending billowing of scarlet and . . .

5   PRIOR: Look. Garlic. A mirror. Holy water. A crucifix. FUCK OFF! Get the fuck out of my room! GO!

PRIOR 1: (*To* PRIOR 2.) Hard as a hickory knob, I'll bet.

PRIOR 2: We all tumesce when they approach. We wax full, like moons.

10 PRIOR 1: Dance.

PRIOR: Dance?

PRIOR 1: Stand up, dammit, give us your hands, dance!

PRIOR 2: Listen . . .

(*A lone oboe begins to play a little dance tune.*)

PRIOR 2: Delightful sound. Care to dance?

15 PRIOR: Please leave me alone, please just let me sleep . . .

PRIOR 2: Ah, he wants someone familiar. A partner who knows his steps. (*To* PRIOR.) Close your eyes. Imagine . . .

PRIOR: I don't . . .

PRIOR 2: Hush. Close your eyes.

(PRIOR *does.*)

20 PRIOR 2: Now open them.

(PRIOR *does.* LOUIS *appears. He looks gorgeous. The music builds gradually into a full-blooded, romantic dance tune.*)

PRIOR: Lou.

LOUIS: Dance with me.

PRIOR: I can't, my leg, it hurts at night . . .
       Are you . . . a ghost, Lou?

25 LOUIS: No. Just spectral. Lost to myself. Sitting all day on cold park benches. Wishing I could be with you. Dance with me, babe . . .

(PRIOR *stands up. The leg stops hurting. They begin to dance. The music is beautiful.*)

PRIOR 1: (*To* PRIOR 2.) Hah. Now I see why he's got no children. He's a sodomite.

30 PRIOR 2: Oh be quiet, you medieval gnome, and let them dance.

PRIOR 1: I'm not interfering, I've done my bit. Hooray, hooray, the messenger's come, now I'm blowing off. I don't like it here.

(PRIOR 1 *vanishes.*)

35 PRIOR 2: The twentieth century. Oh dear, the world has gotten so terribly, terribly old.

(PRIOR 2 *vanishes.* LOUIS *and* PRIOR *waltz happily. Lights fade back to normal.* LOUIS *vanishes.*)

(PRIOR *dances alone.*)

(*Then suddenly, the sound of wings fills the room.*)

SCENE VII

Split scene: PRIOR *alone in his apartment;* LOUIS *alone in the park.*

Again, a sound of beating wings.

PRIOR: Oh don't come in here don't come in . . . LOUIS!! No. My name is Prior Walter, I am . . . the scion of an ancient line, I am . . . abandoned I . . . no, my name is . . . is . . . Prior and I live . . . *here and now,* and . . . in the dark, in the dark, the Recording Angel opens its hundred eyes and snaps the spine of the Book of Life and . . . hush! Hush! I'm talking nonsense, I . . .
       No more mad scene, hush, hush . . .

(LOUIS *in the park on a bench.* JOE *approaches, stands at a distance. They stare at each other, then* LOUIS *turns away.*)

LOUIS: Do you know the story of Lazarus?

JOE: Lazarus?

LOUIS: Lazarus. I can't remember what happens, exactly.

JOE: I don't. . . . Well, he was dead, Lazarus, and Jesus breathed life into him. He brought him back from death.

LOUIS: Come here often?

JOE: No. Yes. Yes.

LOUIS: Back from the dead. You believe that really happened?

JOE: I don't know anymore what I believe.

LOUIS: This is quite a coincidence. Us meeting.

JOE: I followed you.
       From work. I . . . followed you here.

(*Pause.*)

LOUIS: You followed me.
       You probably saw me that day in the washroom and thought: there's a sweet guy, sensitive, cries for friends in trouble.

JOE: Yes.

LOUIS: You thought maybe I'll cry for you.

JOE: Yes.

LOUIS: Well I fooled you. Crocodile tears. Nothing . . . (*He touches his heart, shrugs.*)

(JOE *reaches tentatively to touch* LOUIS's *face.*)

LOUIS: (*Pulling back.*) What are you doing? Don't do that.

JOE: (*Withdrawing his hand.*) Sorry. I'm sorry.

LOUIS: I'm . . . just not . . . I think, if you touch me, your hand might fall off or something. Worse things have happened to people who have touched me.

JOE: Please.
       Oh, boy . . .
       Can I . . .
       I . . . want . . . to touch you. Can I please just touch you . . . um, here?

(*He puts his hand on one side of* LOUIS's *face. He holds it there.*)

       I'm going to hell for doing this.

LOUIS: Big deal. You think it could be any worse than New
   York City?
      (*He puts his hand on* JOE's *hand. He takes* JOE's *hand away
      from his face, holds it for a moment, then.*) Come on.
45 JOE: Where?
LOUIS: Home. With me.
JOE: This makes no sense. I mean I don't know you.
LOUIS: Likewise.
JOE: And what you do know about me you don't like.
50 LOUIS: The Republican stuff?
JOE: Yeah, well for starters.
LOUIS: I don't not like that. I hate that.
JOE: So why on earth should we . . .

(LOUIS *goes to* JOE *and kisses him.*)

LOUIS: Strange bedfellows. I don't know. I never made it with
55   one of the damned before.
      I would really rather not have to spend tonight alone.
JOE: I'm a pretty terrible person, Louis.
LOUIS: Lou.
JOE: No, I really really am. I don't think I deserve being loved.
60 LOUIS: There? See? We already have a lot in common.

(LOUIS *stands, begins to walk away. He turns, looks back at* JOE. JOE
follows. They exit.)

(PRIOR *listens. At first no sound, then once again, the sound of beating wings, frighteningly near.*)

PRIOR: That sound, that sound, it. . . . What is that, like birds
   or something, like a *really* big bird, I'm frightened, I . . . no,
   no fear, find the anger, find the . . . anger, my blood is
   clean, my brain is fine, I can handle pressure, I am a gay
65 man and I am used to pressure, to trouble, I am tough and
   strong and. . . . Oh. Oh my goodness. I . . . (*He is washed*

over by an intense sexual feeling.) Ooohhhh. . . . I'm hot, I'm
. . . so . . . aw Jeez what is going on here I . . . must have a
fever I . . .

(*The bedside lamp flickers wildly as the bed begins to roll forward
and back. There is a deep bass creaking and groaning from the bedroom ceiling, like the timbers of a ship under immense stress, and
from above a fine rain of plaster dust.*)

PRIOR: OH!   70
   PLEASE, OH PLEASE! Something's coming in here, I'm
   scared, I don't like this at all, something's approaching and
   I. . . . OH!

(*There is a great blaze of triumphal music, heralding. The light turns
an extraordinary harsh, cold, pale blue, then a rich, brilliant warm
golden color, then a hot, bilious green, and then finally a spectacular
royal purple. Then silence.*)

PRIOR: (*An awestruck whisper.*) God almighty . . .
   Very Steven Spielberg.   75

(*A sound, like a plummeting meteor, tears down from very, very far
above the earth, hurtling at an incredible velocity towards the bedroom; the light seems to be sucked out of the room as the projectile
approaches; as the room reaches darkness, we hear a terrifying
CRASH as something immense strikes earth; the whole building
shudders and a part of the bedroom ceiling, lots of plaster and lathe
and wiring, crashes to the floor. And then in a shower of unearthly
white light, spreading great opalescent gray-silver wings, the* ANGEL
descends into the room and floats above the bed.)

ANGEL: Greetings, Prophet;
   The Great Work begins:
   The Messenger has arrived.

(*Blackout.*)

Anna Deavere Smith

Anna Deavere Smith (b. 1950) is one of the leading performance artists working in the United States and one of the most prominent African-American women working in the U.S. theater. The eldest of five children, Smith was born and raised in Baltimore; she graduated from Beaver College in 1971 and then took an M.F.A. in acting from the American Conservatory Theatre in 1976. Throughout the 1970s and 1980s, Smith pursued a dual career as a teacher of acting and as a performer. She has taught at Carnegie-Mellon University, Yale University, New York University, the American Conservatory Theatre, the University of Southern California, Stanford University, and Harvard University. Her many stage, television, and film roles include parts in *Mother Courage* (1980) and *Tartuffe* (1983), in "All My Children" (1983), and in the films *Soup for One* (1982), *Dave* (1993), and *Philadelphia* (1993). She has most recently appeared on television in "The West Wing" (2000).

As a playwright and performer, Smith is best known for a series of one-woman shows that form part of an extended series of performances collectively entitled *On the Road: A Search for American Character.* Smith began devising *On the Road* in the early 1980s. The project was inspired by acting exercises she devised for her cast while directing Adrienne Kennedy's play, *A Movie Star Has to Star in Black and White.* To wean her students away from a strictly psychological approach to acting, in which the actor's focus is on the role-as-self, Smith had them watch and then reenact celebrity television talk-show interviews as a way of building a bridge to a "character" as something other. Working with actual interview material gave Smith the working method for much of her subsequent work. For the various *On the Road* performances, Smith interviews a range of subjects who are part of a given event or situation she wants to explore. In fact, she is often invited to colleges and other organizations to use performance to help explore race, gender, and identity issues. After conducting the interviews, Smith devises a performance, using minimal props and costumes, in which she interweaves sections from the interviews, performing all of the roles herself. In 1987, she was invited by San Francisco's Eureka Theater to devise a show concerning racial attitudes in that city; it was performed under the title *From the Outside Looking In.* She also performed a piece on women in San Francisco's theater community, at the invitation of the Bay Area Women in Theater. In 1988 she was invited to conduct an oral history of the Women and Theater Program of the Association for Theatre in Higher Education; *Chlorophyll Postmodernism and the Mother Goddess/A Conversation* was performed at the Women and Theater conference in San Diego that year. She was asked to Princeton University in 1989 to conduct interviews on gender politics among students, faculty, and staff, and performed *Gender Bending;* she has conducted similar workshops and performances for the Five Colleges (Amherst, Hampshire, Mount Holyoke, and Smith colleges, and the University of Massachusetts) in Massachusetts, and for the University of Pennsylvania.

Smith is now known, though, for two performance works that confront recent urban uprisings: *Fires in the Mirror: Crown Heights, Brooklyn and Other Identities* (1992), and *Twilight: Los Angeles 1992* (1993), which concerns the unrest in Los Angeles following the acquittal of four L.A. police officers who were tried for beating an African American man, Rodney King. *Fires in the Mirror,* which earned Smith a 1992 Obie Special Citation, was shown on the Public Broadcasting Service in 1993. Both *Fires in the Mirror* and *Twilight* have been produced for television and are available from PBS. Smith's most recent play, *House Arrest,* investigates the press and the presidency; her work on the play is documented in *Talk to Me: Travels in Media and Politics,* 2000.

Fires in the Mirror concerns racial and ethnic rioting that took place in the Crown Heights neighborhood of Brooklyn, New York, in August 1991. The events that sparked three nights of rioting began on the evening of Monday, August 19, and remain in some dispute. Menachem Schneerson, the Grand Rebbe of the Lubavitcher sect of Hasidic Jews, was returning from his weekly visit to a cemetery; his car was accompanied by an unmarked police escort car and by a third car, driven by Yosef Lifsh and carrying two other Hasidic passengers. At one point Lifsh's car fell behind; apparently accelerating to catch up with the others, Lifsh's car ran a red light, glanced off another car, jumped the curb, and pinned two small African American children to a window grating. Gavin Cato was killed; his cousin Angela Cato was seriously injured.

Crown Heights has a history of racial and ethnic tension, and the accident quickly drew a large and volatile crowd. Within minutes, two ambulances arrived at the scene. The first ambulance to arrive was from a private Hasidic ambulance service; police ordered it to attend to the three Jewish men in the car and to leave the scene immediately. The police later claimed that the city ambulance was also at the scene and that they acted to protect the three men from the crowd and to reduce further confrontation. A city ambulance did attend to the children, but within minutes word that medical attention had been given first to the three white, Jewish men rather than to the two black children ignited a street riot. Three hours later, at 11:30 P.M., a group of black youths a few blocks from the accident surrounded a visiting Australian Hasidic scholar, Yankel Rosenbaum, and stabbed him to death. Lemrick Nelson, Jr., was arrested and held shortly thereafter.

Anna Deavere Smith as Rabbi Shea Hecht in *Fires in the Mirror: Crown Heights, Brooklyn and Other Identities.*

Over the next three days and nights both African American and Jewish groups protested the city's handling of the incident and became involved in a civil uprising. Crown Heights became the scene not only of protests and protest marches, but of widespread arson, looting, and rioting. Police, journalists, and citizens were beaten. Although the rioting broke by the end of the week, several events kept Crown Heights in the public eye: the funerals of Gavin Cato and Yankel Rosenbaum, protest marches led by the Reverend Al Sharpton and Alton Maddox, Yosef Lifsh's sudden trip to Israel, the unsuccessful effort to charge Lifsh with vehicular negligence and arrest him. Indeed, throughout the remainder of 1991 and 1992, Crown Heights remained a flashpoint: in September, the Reverend Al Sharpton flew to Israel to inform Lifsh that the Cato family had brought a civil suit against him; throughout 1992, Lubavitchers demonstrated and ran newspaper ads calling for further police investigation and judicial action in connection with Rosenbaum's death, alleging that the police had handled the riots and the subsequent investigation in a biased and unfair manner; in October 1992, Lemrick Nelson, Jr., was acquitted, provoking a Hasidic rally in protest.

In part, the Crown Heights riots reflected the tensions of an unusually diverse community. The Lubavitch is an Orthodox Jewish sect whose strict religious beliefs make them a close and easily identifiable community in the Crown Heights neighborhood. Many of the black residents of Crown Heights have recently emigrated from the Caribbean and are working to make a place for themselves in the United States. Both groups face overt and subtle discrimination in a number of ways. Moreover, before the riots, Crown Heights had been the scene of several racial incidents. In 1986, a group of young black men had beaten a Hasidic man to death in a subway station; in April 1987, four hundred African Americans marched to protest city favoritism (streets in the neighborhood are regularly closed to traffic during Jewish holidays) and harassment by a Hasidic neighborhood surveillance patrol; in 1989, a crowd of Hasidim surrounded and beat a black teenager they accused of slashing a Hasidic woman and her son.

Rather than providing a "history" of these events, Smith's *Fires in the Mirror* refracts the events through a series of monologues, some by participants—Gavin Cato's father, the Reverend Al Sharpton, Yankel Rosenbaum's brother Norman—and some by more distant observers, such as the playwrights Ntozake Shange and George C. Wolfe (who subsequently directed the television version of *Fires in the Mirror* for PBS). Performing the words of her subjects, Smith carefully weaves an elaborate texture of commentary about race and ethnicity in the United States. Beginning with topics like "identity," "hair," "race," "rhythm," Smith uses the characters' voices to frame the larger issues and attitudes surrounding black-white conflict in the United States and then moves more insistently into the specifics of the Crown Heights uprising. As with some other postmodern works—Norman Mailer's novel *The Executioner's Song,* Don De Lillo's *Libra,* or the Oliver Stone film *JFK*—*Fires in the Mirror* insistently blurs the boundary between the events and their retelling, presenting a kaleidoscopic re-presentation of events rather than a summary that pretends to a specious objectivity. One of the most striking features of *Fires in the Mirror* in performance is the way that Smith plays both white and black characters, men and women, Jews and non-Jews, the powerful and the oppressed, the famous and the unknown. And although Smith carefully observes the details of behavior, dress, and gesture with which her "characters" speak, her performance here is not a kind of mimicry. For instead of effacing identity, Smith's performance shows the challenges of negotiating between "identities." Smith's performance shows the difficulty of grappling with an *other's* identity, an *other's* attitudes, an *other's* orientation to the world.

FIRES IN THE MIRROR
CROWN HEIGHTS, BROOKLYN AND OTHER IDENTITIES

Anna Deavere Smith

THIS BOOK IS DEDICATED TO THE RESIDENTS OF
CROWN HEIGHTS, BROOKLYN, AND IN THE MEMORY
OF GAVIN CATO AND YANKEL ROSENBAUM

CHARACTERS

NTOZAKE SHANGE, *playwright, poet, novelist*
ANONYMOUS LUBAVITCHER WOMAN, *preschool teacher*
GEORGE C. WOLFE, *playwright, director, producing director of the New York Shakespeare Festival*
AARON M. BERNSTEIN, *physicist at Massachusetts Institute of Technology*
ANONYMOUS GIRL, *junior high school black girl of Haitian descent. Lives in Brooklyn near Crown Heights*
REVEREND AL SHARPTON, *well-known New York activist, minister*
RIVKAH SIEGAL, *Lubavitcher woman, graphic designer*
ANGELA DAVIS, *author, orator, activist, scholar. Professor in the History of Consciousness Department at the University of California, Santa Cruz*
MONIQUE "BIG MO" MATTHEWS, *Los Angeles rapper*
LEONARD JEFFRIES, *professor of African American Studies at City University of New York, former head of the department*
LETTY COTTIN POGREBIN, *author* Deborah, Golda, and Me. *One of the founding editors of Ms magazine*
CONRAD MOHAMMED, *New York minister for the Honorable Louis Farrakhan*
ROBERT SHERMAN, *director, Mayor of the City of New York's Increase the Peace Corps*

RABBI JOSEPH SPIELMAN, *spokesperson in the Lubavitcher community*
THE REVEREND CANON DOCTOR HERON SAM, *pastor, St. Mark's, Crown Heights Church*
ANONYMOUS YOUNG MAN #1, *Crown Heights resident*
MICHAEL S. MILLER, *executive director at the Jewish Community Relations Council*
HENRY RICE, *Crown Heights resident*
NORMAN ROSENBAUM, *brother of Yankel Rosenbaum. A barrister from Australia*
ANONYMOUS YOUNG MAN #2, *African American young man, late teens, early twenties. Resident of Crown Heights*
SONNY CARSON, *activist*
RABBI SHEA HECHT, *Lubavitcher rabbi, spokesperson*
RICHARD GREEN, *director, Crown Heights Youth Collective Codirector Project CURE, a Black-Hasidic basketball team that developed after the riots*
ROSLYN MALAMUD, *Lubavitcher resident of Crown Heights*
REUVEN OSTROV, *Lubavitcher male: at the time of the riot, was seventeen years old. Worked as assistant chaplain at Kings County Hospital*
CARMEL CATO, *father of Gavin Cato, Crown Heights resident, originally from Guyana*

IDENTITY
Ntozake Shange

THE DESERT

This interview was done on the phone at about 4:00 P.M. Philadelphia time. The only cue NTOZAKE gave about her physical appearance was that she took one earring off to talk on the phone. On stage we placed her upstage center in an arm chair, smoking. Then we placed her standing, downstage.

Hummmm.
Identity—
it, is, uh . . . in a way it's, um . . . it's sort of, it's uh . . .
it's a psychic sense of place
5   it's a way of knowing I'm not a rock or that tree?
I'm this other living creature over here?
And it's a way of knowing that no matter where I put myself
that I am not necessarily
what's around me.
10   I am part of my surroundings
and I become separate from them
and it's being able to make those differentiations clearly

that lets us have an identity
and what's inside our identity
is everything that's ever happened to us.   15
Everything that's ever happened
to us as well as our responses to it
'cause we might be alone in a trance state,
someplace like the desert
and we begin to feel as though   20
we are part of the desert—
which we are right at that minute—
but we are not the desert,
uh . . .
we are part of the desert,   25
and when we go home
we take with us that part of the desert that the desert gave us,
but we're still not the desert.
It's an important differentiation to make because you don't know
what you're giving if you don't know what you have and you don't   30
know what you're taking if you don't know what's yours and what's
somebody else's.

Anonymous Lubavitcher Woman

STATIC

This interview was actually done on the phone. Based on what she told me she was doing, and on the three visits I had made to her home for other interviews, I devised this physical scene. A LUBA-VITCHER WOMAN, *in a wig, and loose-fitting clothes. She is in her mid-thirties. She is folding clothes. There are several children around. Three boys of different ages are lying together on the couch. The oldest is reading to the younger two. A teen-age girl with long hair, a button-down-collar shirt, and skirt is sweeping the floor.*

> Well,
> it was um,
> 35   getting toward the end of Shabbas,
> like around five in the afternoon,
> and it was summertime
> and sunset isn't until about eight, nine o'clock,
> so there were still quite a few hours left to go
> 40   and my baby had been playing with the knobs on the
>   stereo system
> then all of a sudden he pushed the button—
> the *on* button—
> and all of a sudden came blaring out,
> at full volume,
> 45   sort of like a half station
> of polka music.
> But just like with the static,
> it was blaring, blaring
> and we can't turn off,
> 50   we can't turn off electrical,
> you know electricity, on Shabbas.
> So um,
> uh . . .
> there was—
> 55   we just were trying to ignore it,
> but a young boy that was visiting us,
> he was going nuts already, he said
> it was giving him such a headache could we do
>   something about it,
> couldn't we get a baby
> 60   to turn it off;
> we can't make the baby turn it off but if the baby,
> but if a child under three
> turns something on or turns something off it's not
>   considered against the Torah,
> so we put the baby by it and tried to get the baby to
>   turn it off,
> 65   he just probably made it worse,
> so the guest was so uncomfortable that I said I would go
>   outside
> and see if I can find someone who's not Jewish and see
>   if they would
> like to—
> see if they could turn it off,
> 70   so you can have somebody who's not Jewish do a simple
>   act like
> turning on the light or turning off the light,
> and I hope I have the law correct,
> but you can't ask them to do it directly.

> If they wanna do it of their own free will—
> and hopefully they would get some benefit from it too,   75
> so I went outside
> and I saw
> a little
> boy in the neighborhood
> who I didn't know and didn't know me—   80
> not Jewish, he was black and he wasn't wearing a
>   yarmulke because you can't—
> so I went up to him and I said to him
> that my radio is on really loud and I can't turn it off,
> could he help me,
> so he looked at me a little crazy like,   85
> Well?
> And I said I don't know what to do,
> so he said okay,
> so he followed me into the house
> and he hears this music on so loud   90
> and so unpleasant
> and so
> he goes over to the
> stereo
> and he says, "You see this little button here   95
> that says on and off?
> Push that in
> and that turns it off."
> And I just sort of stood there looking kind of dumb
> and then he went and pushed it,   100
> and we laughed that he probably thought:
> And people say Jewish people are really smart and they
>   don't know
> how to turn off their radios.

George C. Wolfe

101 DALMATIANS

The Mondrian Hotel in Los Angeles. Morning, Sunny. A very nice room. GEORGE *is wearing denim jeans, a light blue denim shirt, and white leather tennis shoes. His hair is in a ponytail. He wears tortoise/wire spectacles. He is drinking tea with milk. The tea is served on a tray, the cups and teapot are delicate porcelain.* GEORGE *is sitting on a sofa, with his feet up on the coffee table.*

> I mean I grew up on a black—
> a one-block street—   105
> that was black.
> My grandmother lived on that street
> my cousins lived around the corner.
> I went to this
> Black—Black—   110
> private Black grade school
> where
> I was extraordinary.
> Everybody there was extraordinary.
> You were told you were extraordinary.   115
> It was very clear
> that I could not go to see *101 Dalmatians* at the Capital
>   Theatre
> because it was segregated.
> And at the same time

120   I was treated like I was the most extraordinary creature
            that had
       been born.
       So I'm on my street in my house,
       at my school—
       and I was very spoiled too—
125   so I was treated like I was this special special creature.
       And then I would go beyond a certain point
       I was treated like I was insignificant.
       Nobody was
       hosing me down or calling me nigger.
130   It was just that I was insignificant.

(*Slight pause.*)

       You know what I mean so it was very clear of

(*Teacup on saucer strike twice on "very clear."*)

       where my extraordinariness lived.
       You know what I mean.
       That I was extraordinary as long as I was Black.
135   But I am—not—going—to place myself

(*Pause.*)

       in relationship to your whiteness.
       I will talk about your whiteness if we want to talk
            about that.
       But I,
       but what,
140   that which,
       what I—
       what am I saying?
       My blackness does not resis—ex—re—
       exist in relationship to your whiteness.

(*Pause.*)

145   You know

(*Not really a question, more like a hum.*)

(*Slight pause.*)

       it does not exist in relationship to—
       it *exists*
       it exists.
       I come—
150   you know what I mean—
       like I said, I, I, I,
       I come from—
       it's a very com*plex,*
       con*fused,*
155   *neu-*rotic,
       at times destructive
       reality, but it is completely
       and totally a reality
       contained and, and,
160   and full unto itself.
       It's complex.
       It's demonic.
       It's ridiculous.

It's absurd.
It's evolved.
It's all the stuff.   165
That's the way I grew up.

(*Slight pause.*)

So that *therefore*—
and then you're White—

(*Quick beat.*)

And then there's a point when,   170
and then these two things come into contact.

MIRRORS
Aaron M. Bernstein
MIRRORS AND DISTORTIONS

Evening, Cambridge, Massachusetts. Fall. He is a man in his fifties, wearing a sweater and a shirt with a pen guard. He is seated at a round wooden table with a low-hanging lamp.

Okay, so a mirror is something that reflects light.
It's the simplest instrument to understand,
okay?
So a simple mirror is just a flat   175
reflecting
substance, like,
for example,
it's a piece of glass which is silvered on the back,
okay?   180
Now the notion of distortion also goes back into
       literature,
okay?
I'm trying to remember from art—
You probably know better than I.
You know you have a pretty young woman and she   185
       looks in a mirror
and she's a witch

(*He laughs.*)

because she's evil on the inside.
That's not a real mirror,
as everyone knows—
you see the inner thing.   190
Now that really goes back in literature.
So everyone understood that mirrors don't distort,
so that was a play
not on words
but a concept.   195
But physicists do
talk about distortion.
It's a big
subject, distortions.
I'll give you an example—   200
if you wanna see the
stars
you make a big
reflecting mirror—

205   that's one of the ways—
you make a big telescope
so you can gather in a lot of light
and then it focuses at a point
and then there's always something called the circle of
   confusion.
210   So if ya don't make the thing perfectly spherical or
   perfectly
parabolic
then,
then, uh, if there are errors in the construction
which you can see, it's easy, if it's huge,
215   then you're gonna have a circle of confusion,
you see?
So that's the reason for making the
telescope as large as you can,
because you want that circle
220   to seem smaller,
and you want to easily see errors in the construction.
So, you see, in physics it's very practical—
you wanna look up in the heavens
and see the stars as well as you can
225   without distortion.
If you're counting stars, for example,
and two look like one,
you've blown it.

HAIR

Anonymous Girl

LOOK IN THE MIRROR

Morning. Spring. A teen-age black GIRL *of Haitian descent. She has hair which is straightened, and is wearing a navy blue jumper and a white shirt. She is seated in a stairwell at her junior high school in Brooklyn.*

When I look in the mirror . . .
230   I don't know.
How did I find out I was Black . . .

(Tongue sound.)

When I grew up and I look in the mirror and saw I was
   Black.
When I look at my parents,
That's how I knew I was Black.
235   Look at my skin.
You Black?
Black is beautiful.
I don't know.
That's what I always say.
240   I think White is beautiful too.
But I think Black is beautiful too.
In my class nobody is White, everybody's Black,
and some of them is Hispanic.
In my class
245   you can't call any of them Puerto Ricans.
They despise Puerto Ricans, I don't know why.
They think that Puerto Ricans are stuck up and
   everything.

They say, Oh my Gosh my nail broke, look at that cute
   guy and everything.
But they act like that themselves.
250   They act just like White girls.
Black girls is not like that.
Please, you should be in my class.
Like they say that Puerto Ricans act like that
and they don't see that they act like that themselves.
255   Black girls, they do bite off the Spanish girls,
they bite off of your clothes.
You don't know what that means? biting off?
Like biting off somebody's clothes
Like cop, following,
260   and last year they used to have a lot of girls like that.
They come to school with a style, right?
And if they see another girl with that style?
Oh my gosh look at her.
What she think she is,
265   she tryin' to bite off of me in some way
no don't be bitin' off of my sneakers
or like that.
Or doin' a hairstyle
I mean Black people are into hairstyles.
270   So they come to school, see somebody with a certain
   style,
they say uh-huh I'm gonna get me one just like that uh-
   huh,
that's the way Black people are
Yea-ah!
They don't like people doing that to them
275   and they do that to other people,
so the Black girls they won't follow the Spanish girls.
The Spanish girls don't bite off of us.
Some of the Black girls follow them.
But they don't mind
280   They don't care.
They follow each other.
Like there's three girls in my class,
they from the Dominican Republic.
They all stick together like glue.
285   They all three best friends.
They don't follow nobody,
like there's none of them lead or anything.
They don't hang around us either.
They're
290   by themselves.

The Reverend Al Sharpton

ME AND JAMES'S THING

Early afternoon. Fall. A small room that is a part of a suite of of-fices in a building on West Fifty-Seventh Street and Seventh Av-enue in New York. A very large man Black man with straightened hair. REVEREND SHARPTON'S *hair is in the style of James Brown's hair. He is wearing a suit, colorful tie, and a gold medallion that was given to him by Martin Luther King, Jr.* REVEREND SHARPTON *has a pinky ring, a very resonant voice even in this small room. There is a very built, very tall man who sits behind me during the interview.* REVEREND SHARPTON'S *face is much younger, and more innocent than it appears to be in the media. His humor is in his*

face. He is very direct. The interview only lasts fifteen minutes be-
cause he had been called out of a meeting in progress to do the in-
terview.

James Brown raised me.
Uh . . .
I never had a father.
My father left when I was ten.
295 James Brown took me to the beauty parlor one day
and made my hair like his.
And made me promise
to wear it like that
'til I die.
300 It's a personal family thing
between me and James Brown.
I always wanted a father
and he filled that void.
And the strength that he's demonstrated—
305 I don't know anybody that reached his heights,
and then had to go as low as he did and come back.
And I think that if anybody I met in life deserved that
  type of
tribute from
somebody
310 that he wanted a kid
to look like him
and be like his son . . .
I just came home from spending a weekend with him
  now,
uh, uh,
315 I think James deserved that.
And just like
he was the father I never had,
his kids never even visited him when he went to jail.
So I was like the kid he never had.
320 And if I had to choose between arguing with people
  about my
hairstyle
or giving him that one tribute
he axed,
I'd rather give him that tribute
325 because he filled a void for me.
And I really don't give a damn
who doesn't understand it.
The press and everybody do
their thing on that.
330 It's a personal thing between me and James Brown.
And just like
in other communities
people do their cultural thing
with who they like,
335 uh,
there's nothing wrong with me doing
that with James.
It's, it's, *us.*
I mean in the fifties it was a slick.
340 It was acting like White folks.
But today
people don't wear their hair like that.
James and I the only ones out there doing that.
So it's certainlih not

a reaction to Whites. 345
It's me and James's thing.

Rivkah Siegal

WIGS

Early afternoon. Spring. The kitchen of an apartment in Crown
Heights. A very pretty Lubavitcher woman, with clear eyes and a di-
rect gaze, wearing a wig and a knit sweater, that looks as though it
might be hand knit. A round wooden table. Coffee mug. Sounds of
children playing in the street are outside. A neighbor, a Lubavitcher
woman with light blond hair who no longer wears the wig, observes
the interview at the table.

Your hair—
It only has to be—
there's different,
uhm, 350
customs in different
Hasidic groups.
Lubavitch
the system is
it should be two inches 355
long.
It's—
some groups
have
the custom 360
to shave their
heads.
There's—
the reason is,
when you go to the mikvah 365
you may, maybe,
it's better if it's short
because of what you—
the preparation
that's involved 370
and that
you have to go under the water.
The hair has a tendency to float
and you have to be completely submerged
including your hair. 375
So . . .
And I got married
when I was a little older,
and I really wanted to be married
and I really wanted to, um . . . 380
In some ways I was eager to cover my head.
Now if I had grown up in a Lubavitch household
and then had to cut it,
I don't know what that would be like.
I really don't. 385
But now that I'm wearing the wig,
you see,
with my hair I can keep it very simple
and I can change it all the time.
So with a wig you have to have like five wigs if you 390
  want to do that.
But I, uh,

I feel somehow like it's fake,
I feel like it's not me.
I try to be as much myself as I can,
395 and it just
bothers me
that I'm kind of fooling the world.
I used to go to work.
People . . .
400 and I would wear a different wig,
and they'd say I like your new haircut
and I'd say it's not mine!
You know,
and it was very hard for me to say it
405 and
it became very difficult.
I mean, I've gone through a lot with wearing wigs and
    not wearing
wigs.
It's been a big issue for me.

Angela Davis

ROPES

*Morning, Spring, Oakland, California. In reality this interview was
done on the phone, with myself and Thulani Davis. Thulani and I
were calling from an office at the Public Theatre. We do not know
exactly what ANGELA was doing or wearing. I believe, from things
she said, that she was sitting on her deck in her home in Oakland,
which overlooks a beautiful panorama of trees.*

410 Race, um—
of course
for many years in the history
of African Americans in this country—
was synonymous with community.
415 As a matter of fact
we were race women and race men.
Billie Holiday for example
called herself a race woman
because she supported the community
420 and as a child growing up in the South
my assumptions were
that if anybody in the race
came under attack
then I had to be there
425 to support that person,
to support the race.
I was saying to my students just the other day,
I said,
if in 1970,
430 when I was
in jail,
someone had told me
that in 1991,
a black man
435 who
said that his, um . . .
hero—

(Increased volume, speed, and energy.)

one of his heroes
was Malcolm X—
would be nominated to the Supreme Court   440
I would have celebrated
and I don't think it would have been possible at that
    time
to convince me
that I would
be absolutely opposed,   445
a black candidate—
I mean like absolutely—

(A new attack, more energy.)

or that if anyone would have told me that
a *woman* . . .
finally be elected to the Supreme Court,   450
it would have been very difficult,
as critical as I am with respect to feminism,
as critical as I have always been with what I used to call,
you know, narrow nationalism?
I don't think   455
it would have been possible to convince me that things
    would have so absolutely
shifted that
someone could have evoked
the specter of lynching
on national television   460
and that specter of lynching would be used to violate
    our history.
And I still feel that we have to point out the racism
    involved
in the razing of a Black man
and a Black woman
in that way.   465
I mean [Ted] Kennedy was sitting right there
and it had never occurred to anyone to bring him up
before
the world,
which is not to say that I don't think it should happen. 470
And it is actually a sign of how we,
in our various oppressed
marginalized communities,
have been able to turn
terrible acts of racism directed against us   475
into victory . . .
And therefore I think
Anita Hill did that,
and so it's very complicated,
but I have no problems aligning myself politically 480
against Clarence Thomas in a real passionate way,
but at the same time I can talk about the racism that led
    to the possibility
of constructing those kinds of hearings
and
the same thing with Mike Tyson.   485
So I guess that would be,
um . . .
the way in which I would begin to look at community,
and would therefore think
that race has become, uh,   490

an increasingly obsolete way
of constructing community
because it is based on unchangeable
immutable biological
495 facts
in a very pseudo-scientific way,
alright?
Now
racism is entirely different
500 because see *racism,*
uh,
actually I think
is
at the origins of this concept of race.
505 It's not—
it's not the other way around,
that there were racists,
and then the racists—
one race came to dominate
510 the others.
As a matter of fact
in order for a European colonialist
to attempt
to conquer the world,
515 to colonize the world,
they had to construct this notion
of,
uh,
the populations of the earth being divided into certain,
520 uh,
firm biological, uh,
communities,
and that's what I think we have to go back and look at.
So when I use the word race now I put it in quotations.
525 Because if we don't transform
this . . . this intransigent
rigid
notion of race,
we will be caught up in this cycle
530 of genocidal
violence
that, um,
is at the origins of our history.
So I think—
535 and I'm
I'm convinced—and this is what I'm working on in my
    political practice right now—
is that we have to find ways of coming together in a
    different way,
not the old notion of coalition in which we anchor
    ourselves very solidly
in our,
540 um,
communities,
and simply voice
our
solidarity with other people.
545 I'm not suggesting that we do not anchor ourselves in
    our communities;
I feel very anchored in,
um,

my various communities,
but I think that,
you know, 550
to use a metaphor, the rope
attached to that anchor should be long enough to allow
    us to move
into other communities
to understand and learn.
I've been thinking a lot about the need to make more 555
    intimate
these connections and associations and to really take on
    the responsibility
of learning.
So I think that we need to—
in order to find ways of working with
and understanding 560
the vastness
of our many cultural heritages
and ways of coming together without
rendering invisible all of that heterogeneity—
I don't have the answer, 565
you know
I don't know.
What I'm interested in is communities
that are not static,
that 570
can change, that can respond to new historical needs.
So I think it's a very exciting moment.

RHYTHM
Monique "Big Mo" Matthews
RHYTHM AND POETRY

*In reality this interview was done on an afternoon in the spring of
1989, while I was in residence at the University of California, Los
Angeles, as a fellow at the Center for Afro-American Studies.* MO
*was a student of mine. We were sitting in my office, which was a nar-
row office, with sunlight. I performed* MO *in many shows, and in the
course of performing her, I changed the setting to a performance setting, with microphone. I was inspired by a performance that I saw of
Queen Latifah in San Francisco, and by* MO's *behavior in my class,
which was performance behavior, to change the setting to one that was
more theatrical, since* MO's *everyday speech was as theatrical as
Latifah's performance speech. Speaking directly to the audience, pacing the stage.*

And she say, "This is for the fellas,"
and she took off all her clothes and she had on a leotard
that had all cuts and stuff in it, 575
and she started doin' it on the floor.
They were like
"Go, girl!"
People like, "That look really stink."
But that's what a lot of female rappers do— 580
like to try to get off,
they sell they body or pimp they body
to, um, get play.
And you have people like Latifah who doesn't, you know,
she talks intelligent. 585

You have Lyte who's just hard and people are scared by
   her hardness,
her strength of her words.
She encompasses that whole, New York–street sound.
It's like, you know, she'll like . . .
590 what's a line?
What's a line
like "Paper Thin,"
"IN ONE EAR AND RIGHT OUT THE OTHUH."
It's like,
595 "I don't care what you have to say,
I'm gittin' done what's gotta be done.
Man can't come across me.
A female she can't stand against me.
I'm just the toughest, I'm just the hardest/You just can't
   come up
600 against me/if you do you get waxed!"
It's like a lot of my songs,
I don't know if I'm gonna get blacklisted for it.
The image that I want is a strong strong African strong
   Black woman
and I'm not down with what's going on, like Big Daddy
   Kane had a song
605 out called "Pimpin Ain't Easy," and he sat there and he
   talk for the
whole song, and I sit there I wanna slap him, I wanna
   slap him so
hard, and he talks about, it's one point he goes, yeah
   um,
"Puerto Rican girls Puerto Rican girls call me Papi and
610 White girls say
even White girls say I'm a hunk!"
I'm like,
"What you mean 'even'?
Oh! Black girls ain't good enough for you huh?"
615 And one of my songs has a line that's like
"PIMPIN' AIN'T EASY BUT WHORIN' AIN'T
   PROPER, RESPECT AND
CHERISH THE ORIGINAL MOTHER."
And a couple of my friends were like,
"Aww, Mo, you good but I can't listen to you 'cause you
   be Men bashin'."
620 I say,
"It ain't men bashin', it's female assertin'."
Shit.
I'm tired of it.
I'm tired of my friends just acceptin'
625 that they just considered to be a ho.
You got a song,
"Everybody's a Hotty."
A "hotty" means you a freak, you a ho,
and it's like Too Short
630 gets up there and he goes,
"B I AYYYYYYYYYYYYE."
Like he stretches "bitch" out for as long as possible,
like you just a ho and you can't be saved,
and 2 Live Crew. . . . "we want some pussy," and the
   girls! "La le la le la le la,"
635 it's like my friends say,
"Mo, if you so bad how come you don't never say
   nothin about Two

Live Crew?"
When I talk about rap,
and I talk about people demeaning rap,
I don't even mention them   640
because they don't understand the fundamentals of rap.
Rap, rap
is basically
broken down
Rhythm   645
and Poetry.
And poetry is expression.
It's just like poetry; you release so much through poetry
   you get
angry, you get it?
Poetry is like   650
intelligence.
You just release it all and if you don't have a complex
   rhyme
it's like,
"I'm goin to the store."
What rhymes with store?   655
More store for more bore
"I'm going to the store I hope I don't get bored,"
it's like,
"WHAT YOU SAYIN', MAN? WHO CARES?"
You have something that flows.   660
You have to be def,
D-E-F.
I guess I have to think of something for you that ain't
   slang.
Def is dope, def is live
when you say somethin's dope   665
it means it is the epitome of the experience
and you have to be def by your very presence
because you have to make people happy.
And we are living in a society where people are not
   happy with their everyday lives.

SEVEN VERSES
Leonard Jeffries

ROOTS

*3:00 P.M. Wednesday, November 20, 1991. A very large confer-
ence room in the African American Studies Department at
CUNY. Drawn venetian blinds, fluorescent lighting.* DR. JEFFRIES
*wears a light, multicolored African top, and a multicolored African
hat. His shoes are black functional shoes, like the shoes to a uniform. He sits facing the table, and often sits back with the chair
back from the table, often touches the table, and often sits back
with the chair on its back legs only. Sometimes he scratches his
head by throwing his hat forward on his head with great ease and
authority. There is a bodyguard, a large heavy-set African American man, present.*

People are asking who is this guy Jeffries?   670
When they find out my background they're gonna be
   surprised.
They are gonna find out that I was even related to Alex
   Haley.
In fact I was a major consultant for *Roots.*

In fact there might not have been a *Roots* without me.
675 Now when I say that,
that's my own personal in-group joke wit' Alex.
He was in Philadelphia
getting his ticket to go down to Jamaica
and
680 *Roots* was lost.
He had it in a duffle bag,
a big duffle bag like this,
the whole manuscript.
It was lost in the airport of Philadelphia.
685 I got on my horse and ran around the airport of
  Philadelphia
and found *Roots.*
So that's my joke.
He had this manuscript,
Alex didn't have anything else but this manuscript.
690 Now if he had lost that, that would have been it.
He didn't have any photocopies.
Alex did everything on a shoestring.
uhm
so for him to deny me now . . .
695 He never even acknowledged
Pat
Alexander
his girlfriend/secretary who he had paid with affection
  and not with
resources.
700 So I didn't expect him to acknowledge me.
He called me to come down.
I called my wife who was working on her Ph.D. at Yale.
I said, "Rosalind, Alex wants us to come down to
  Brunswick, Georgia,
they're filming *Roots.*"
705 She said yes she'd come down and we'd go, then she
  called me back.
She said, "I got too much work," so I went down to
  Brunswick, Georgia.
He introduced me to Margulies,
who was the, um, director
of *Roots,*
710 as the leading expert in America on Africa, and I said,
  "Wow," to
myself, "that's kind of high."
When Margulies said,
"That makes me number two," then I realized what Alex
  was doing to keep *Roots* honest.
So for two weeks I tried to change *Roots.*
715 Alex would say, "Wait a
minute, let's consult the experts."
After two weeks they got tired of me, sat me down
and said, "Dr. Jeffries," at lunch,
"we are very happy to have you here
720 but we just bought the rights to the book *Roots*
and we are under no obligation to maintain the integrity
  of the book
and we certainly don't have to deal with the truth of
  Black history."
Now,
this was a wipeout for me
725 I

I, there's been very few trau*matic*
moments

(*Longest pause in his text.*)

uh, just to think.
Now I wasn't even prepared for this
but Pat had called me before and said,   730
"Len, I'm looking at this document and I don't know
  what to make of it."
I said, "What is it, Pat, what is it?"
and I knew she was nervous, she said,
"I'm reading a contract that says
'*Roots* has been sold to David Wolper and their heirs for 735
  ever and
ever

(*He is thumping his hand on table.*)

and their heirs for ever and ever.'"
Alex had signed the contract for fifty thousand dollars.

(*He is thumping his hand on table.*)

Fifty thousand dollars for paperback *Roots.*
Something that made how much?   740
Three hundred million dollars?
He was suing them for years.
The millions he made out to TV *Roots* he spent a lot of
  it to sue
Doubleday to get a better deal—I don't know if he ever
  got it.
Roots was a devastation.   745
The tens of millions and hundreds of millions made on
  Roots
went to produce,
not to make more Black series,
like *Roots,*
but they went to produce a *series*   750
maybe a dozen mini-series on *Jewish* history
as opposed to Black history.
You can document what was produced in terms of Black
  history
compared to what was produced of Jewish history.
It's a devastation.   755
But the *one* thing that came out of this for me,
was that when these people told me, you know,
"We bought your research
We bought your history
You really have no . . ."   760
I was thrown off
I had to get out of there.
I stayed for another couple of days.
I told Alex I had to make a pilgrimage to my
  grandfather's grave.
Never saw my grandfather.   765
Then I watched one more scene in the Alex Haley thing
and that finished it for me.
A cutaway of a slave ship
that was so real that they had to bring in these high
  school kids,
and once these high school kids played the enslaved 770
  Africans greased

down in simulated vomit
and feces
they couldn't come back,
so they had to continue to get,
775   go take these youngsters,
and some little White woman
who was there sleeping with one of those guys,
they told her, "You cannot take these kids without
    authorization."
But she would drive a bus
780   up to the schoolyard,
put the kids in it, and bring them to the set.
And it almost produced a riot
there.
But anyway this slave scene
785   was so realistic
the trainer's up on a lower deck
and Kunta Kinte's on a bottom deck
and they call down to each other,
and the trainer says,
790   "Kunta Kinte,
Be strong! Be strong!
We may have to fight.
Kill the White man and return to Mother Africa."
This was high drama.
795   All of us grown men over hiding in the shadows in
    tears.
Then
Green rushes out and said, "Break! Break!"
He said he didn't want the scene.
We said, "What?"
800   Even Lou Gossett and them were ready to *fight!*
You know 'cause they had—
a movie script is just
a skeleton,
you have to put your soul in a movie script,
805   and they put their heart and soul into what would have
    been . . .
And with the African—
because the "earth is mother" all over Africa.
So to say to go back to Mother Africa is a very
    meaningful phrase.
But this
810   Englishman refused
to accept it,
and they almost had a physical fight on the set.
They compromised and said,
"We—are—all—from—one—village,"

(*Hitting his hand rhythmically on the desk.*)

815   which is not the same thing.
After that I said, "I have to go."
I said I have to go,
and I rented a—
I flew out with Lorne Greene of all people.
820   He saw me and we had known each other for a couple
    of weeks from
the set,
and he's sitting there drinking his little drinks
talking about "Isn't *Roots* wonderful.

It's everybody's history,"
and I'm dying.   825

(*Pause.*)

Get to Atlanta.
Rent a car. Cut across the Georgia countryside.
came to a fork in the road,
made the right turn,
and there on a bluff   830
was a clapboard church
made by my grandfather
and
four
other trustees.   835
Then when
I went across the cemetery
to see, uh,
the gravesite where he was—
the tallest tombstone in the graveyard was his.   840
Uhm,
It was an obelisk.
On it was a Masonic symbol.
He was the master of the lodge.
On it was his vital statistics: 845
"*Born August the tenth 1868.*"
At the birth of the Fourteenth Amendment.
I later learned that his brother Sam was born
1865 at the birth of the Thirteenth Amendment!
And this is why people say,   850
"Who is he?
What is he?
Why is he?"
If they only know
I've had one of the best educations on the planet.   855
Yeah.
So . . .
When I went to Albany
in July,
I went knowing that you might not have   860
much time,
just like my wife said on the radio today:
"When we speak
we speak as though it is the last speech we're gonna
    make."
But I knew what was at stake   865
ever since they branded me a conspiracy theorist,
February 12, 1990,
two-column editorial in the *New York Times.*
That was,
in the concept of Jewish thinking,   870
the kiss of death.
I knew I had been targeted.
Arthur Schlesinger went and wrote a book
called *The Disuniting of America.*
He has everybody in the margin   875
except a half-page photo of myself
which said to us,
"This is the one they got to kill."
We knew that Schlesinger
and his people had sent out a thousand letters   880

to CEOs around the country
and foundation heads
not to have anything to do with
all of us involved in these studies
885 for multicultural curriculum
so, uh . . .
Knowing that I had taken this beating for two and a half
    years
it was my chance to strike out,
but people don't understand
890 that that was my way of saying,
"You bastids! . . .
for starting this process
of destroying *me*."
That was my striking out.
895 But people don't know the context.
They don't know that for two and a half years
I bore this burden
by myself
and I bore it well.
900 And now they've got a problem.
'Cause after they destroyed me,
here he is resurrected!!!!!
I spoke at Columbia, I spoke at Queens College. . . .

Letty Cottin Pogrebin

NEAR ENOUGH TO REACH

Evening. The day before Thanksgiving, 1991. On the phone. Direct, passionate, confident, lots of volume. She is in a study with a rolltop desk and a lot of books.

I think it's about rank frustration and the old story
905 that you pick a scapegoat
that's much more, I mean Jews and Blacks,
that's manageable,
because we're near,
we're still near enough to each other to reach!
910 I mean, what can you do about the people who voted
    for David Duke?
Are Blacks going to go there and deal with that?
No, it's much easier to deal with Jews who are also
    panicky.
We're the only ones that pay any attention

(*Her voice makes an upward inflection.*)

Do you hear?
915 Well, Jeffries did speak about the Mafia being, um,
    Mafia,
and the Jews in Hollywood.
I didn't see
this tremendous outpouring of Italian
920 reaction.
Only *Jews* listen,
only *Jews* take Blacks seriously,
only *Jews* view Blacks as full human beings that you
    should *address*
925 in their rage
and, um,
people don't seem to notice that.

But Blacks, it's like a little child kicking up against
    Arnold
Schwarzenegger
when they,   930
when they have anything to say about the dominant
    culture
nobody listens! Nobody reacts!
To get a headline,
to get on the evening news,
you have to attack a Jew.   935
Otherwise you're ignored.
And it's a shame.
We all play into it.

Minister Conrad Mohammed

SEVEN VERSES

April 1992, morning. A café/restaurant. Roosevelt Island, New York. We are sitting in the back, in an area that is surrounded by glass floor-to-ceiling windows. MR. MOHAMMED *is impeccably dressed in a suit of an elegant fabric. He wears a blue shirt and a bow tie. He has on fine shoes, designer socks, and a large fancy watch and wedding ring. His hair is closely cropped. He drinks black coffee, and uses a few packs of sugar. He is traveling with another man, also a Muslim, in the clothing of a Muslim, impeccable, who sits at another table and watches us.*

The condition of the Black man in America today is
    part and parcel,
through the devlishment   940
that permitted Caucasian people
to rob us of our humanity,
and put us in the throes of slavery . . .
The fact that our—our Black
parents   945
were actually taken
as cattle
and as, as
animals
and packed into   950
slave ships
like sardines
amid feces
and urine—
and the suffering of our people,   955
for months,
in the middle passage—
Our women,
raped
before our own eyes,   960
so that today
some look like you,
some look like me,
some look like a brother . . .
(indicating his companion)   965
This is a crime of tremendous proportion.
In fact,
no crime in the history of humanity
has before or since
equaled that crime.   970

The Holocaust did not equal it
Oh, absolutely not.
First of all,
that was a horrible crime
975 and that is something that is a disgrace in the eyes of
civilized
people.
That, uh, crime also stinks
in the nostrils of God.
But it in no way compares with the slavery of our
people
980 because we lost over a hundred
and some say two hundred and fifty,
million
in the middle passage
coming from Africa
985 to America.
We were so thoroughly robbed.
We didn't just lose six million.
We didn't just
endure this
990 for, for
five or six years
or from '38 to '45 or '39 to
We endured this for over three hundred years—
the total subjugation of the Black man.
995 You can go into Bangladesh today,
Calcutta,

(*He strikes the table with a sugar packet three or four times.*)

New Delhi,
Nigeria,
some really
1000 so-called underdeveloped nation,
and I don't care how low that person's humanity is

(*He opens the sugar packet.*)

whether they never
had running water,
if they'd never seen a television or anything.
1005 They are in better condition than the Black man and
woman
in America today
right now.
Even at Harvard.
They have a contextual understanding of what their
destiny is.

(*He strikes the table with another sugar packet three or four times
and opens it.*)

1010 But the Black man has no knowledge of that;
he's an amnesia victim

(*Starts stirring his coffee.*)

He has lost knowledge of himself

(*Stirring his coffee.*)

and he's living a beast life.

(*Stirring his coffee.*)

So this proves that it was the greatest
crime. 1015
Because we were cut off from our past.
Not only were we killed and murdered,
not only were our women raped
in front of their own children.
Not only did the slave master stick 1020

(*The spoon drops onto saucer.*)

at times,
daggers into a pregnant woman's stomach,
slice the stomach open
push the baby out on the ground and crush the head of
the baby
to instill fear in the Massas of the plantation. 1025

(*Stirring again.*)

Not only were these things done,
not only were our thumbs

(*Spoon drops.*)

put in, in devices
that would just slowly torture the slave
and tear the thumb off from the root. 1030
Not only were we sold on the auction block
like cattle,
not permitted to marry.
See these are the crimes
of slavery that nobody wants to talk about. 1035
But the most significant crime—
because we could have recovered from all of that—
but the fact that they cut off all knowledge from us,
told us that we were animals,
told us that we were subhuman, 1040
took from us our names,
gave us names like
Smith
and Jones
and today we wear those names 1045
with dignity
and pride,
yet these were the names given to us in one of the
greatest crimes
ever committed on the face of the earth.
So this kind of thing, 1050
Sister,
is what qualifies slavery
as the greatest
crime
ever committed. 1055
They have stolen
our garment.
Stolen our identity.
The Honorable Louis Farrakhan
teaches us 1060
that *we* are the chosen of God.
We are those people

that almighty God Allah
has selected as his chosen,
1065 and they are masquerading in our garment—
the Jews.
We don't have an identity today.
Because we are the people . . .
There are seven verses
1070 in the Bible
seven verses,
I believe it is in Deuteronomy,
that the Jews base
their chosen people, uh, uh,
1075 claim the theology,
the whole theological exegesis
with respect
of being the chosen
is based upon seven verses
1080 in the Scripture that talk
about a covenant
with Abraham.

Letty Cottin Pogrebin

ISAAC

Morning. Spring. On the phone. She is in her office in her home on West 67th Street and Central Park West in Manhattan. Her office has an old-fashioned wooden rolltop desk and bookcases filled with books. She says she was wearing leggings and a loose shirt.

Well,
it's hard for me to do that
1085 because
I think there's a tendency to make hay
with the Holocaust,
to push
all the buttons.
1090 And I mean this story about my uncle Isaac—makes *me* cry
and it's going to make your audience cry
and I'm beginning to worry
that
we're trotting out our Holocaust stories
1095 too regularly and that we're going to inure each other to the truth of
them.
But
I think
maybe if you let me read it,
1100 I would prefer to read it:

(Reading from Deborah, Golda, and Me.*)*

"I remember my mother's cousin
Isaac who came to New York
immediately after the war and lived with us for several months.
Isaac is my connection to dozens of other family members who
1105 were murdered in the concentration camps.
Because he was blond and blue-eyed he had been
chosen as the designated survivor of his town.

That is the Jewish councils had instructed him to do anything
to stay alive and tell the story.
For Isaac   1110
anything turned out to mean this.
The Germans accepted his forged Aryan papers and decided that he
would have to prove by his actions that he was not a Jew.
They put him on a transport train with the Jews of his town
and then gave him the task of herding into the gas chambers   1115
everyone in his train load.
After he had fulfilled that assignment
with patriotic
German efficiency,
the Nazis accepted the authenticity of his identity papers   1120
and let him go.
Among those whom Isaac packed into the gas chambers that day
dispassionately as if shoving a few more items into an overstuffed
closet
were his wife   1125
and
two children.
The designated survivor
arrived in America
at about age forty   1130

(Breathes in.)

with prematurely white hair and a dead gaze within the sky blue
eyes that's helped save his life.
As promised he told his story to dozens of Jewish agencies
and community leaders and to groups of families and friends which
is how I heard the account   1135
translated from his Yiddish
by my mother.
For months he talked,
speaking the unspeakable.
Describing a horror   1140
that American Jews had suspected but could not conceive.
A monstrous tale
that dwarfed the demonology of legend
and gave me the nightmare I still dream to this day.
And as he talked   1145
Isaac seemed to grow older and older
until one night a few months later
when he finished telling everything he knew
he died."

Robert Sherman

LOUSY LANGUAGE

11:00 A.M. Wednesday, November 13, 1991. A very sunny and large, elegant living room in a large apartment near the Brooklyn Museum. MR. SHERMAN *is sitting in an armchair near an enormous bouquet of flowers for the birth of his first child. He wears sweats, and a bright orange long-sleeved tee shirt. Smiles frequently, upbeat, impassioned. Fingers his wedding ring. Each phrase builds on the next, pauses are all sustained intensity, never lets up. Full. Lots of volume, clear enunciation, teeth, and tongue very involved in his speech. Good-humored, seems to like the act of speech.*

1150   Do you have demographic information on Crown
                Heights?
        The important thing to remember is that—
        and I will check these numbers when I get back to the
                office—
        I think the
        Hasidim
1155   comprise only ten percent
        of the population
        of the neighborhood.
        The Crown Heights conflict has been brewing on and
                off for twenty years
        since the Hasidic community
1160   developed some serious numbers
        and some strength in Crown Heights and as African
                Americans and
        Caribbean Americans came to make up the dominant
                culture in
        Crown Heights.
        Very important to remember that
1165   those things that are expressed really as
        bias,
        those things
        that we at the Human Rights Commission
        would consider to be bias,
1170   have the same trappings of bias,
        which is complaints based on a characteristic, not on a
                knowledge of a
        specific person.
        There sort of is a soup
        of bias—prejudice, racism, and discrimination.
1175   I think bias really does relate to
        feelings with a valence,
        feelings with a, uhm,

        (*Breathing in.*)

        feelings that can go in a direction positive or negative
        although we usually use bias to mean a negative.
1180   What it means usually
        is negative attitudes
        that can lead to negative behaviors:
        biased
        acts, biased incidents,
1185   or biased crimes.
        Racism is hatred based on race.
        Discrimination refers to
        acts against somebody . . .
        so that the words
1190   actually tangle up.
        I think in part
        because vocabulary
        follows general awareness. . . .
        I think you know
1195   the Eskimos have seventy words for snow?

We probably have seventy different kinds of bias,
        prejudice, racism, and
discrimination,
but it's not in our mind-set to be clear about it,
so I think that we have
sort of lousy language   1200
on the subject
and that
is a reflection
of our unwillingness
to deal with it honestly   1205
and to sort it out.
I think we have very, very bad language.

CROWN HEIGHTS, BROOKLYN

AUGUST 1991

Rabbi Joseph Spielman

NO BLOOD IN HIS FEET

9:30 A.M. Tuesday, November 12, 1991. A large home on President Street in Crown Heights. Only natural light, not very much light. Dark wood. A darkish dining room with an enormous table, could seat twenty. The RABBI sits at the head of the table. Lots of stuff on the table. He wears Hasidic clothing, a black fedora, black jacket, and reading glasses. As he talks, he slightly slides around the tape-recorder microphone, which is in front of him at the table. The furniture in the dining room including his chair is, for the most part, very old, solid wood. There are children playing quietly in another room, and people come in and out frequently, but always whispering and walking carefully not to make noise, unless they speak to him directly. The children at one point came over and stared at me.

Many people were on the sidewalk,
talking, playing,
drinking   1210
beer or whatever—
being that type of neighborhood.
A car
driven by an individual—
a Hasidic individual—   1215
went through the intersection,
was hit by another car,
thereby causing it to go onto the sidewalk.
The driver on seeing
himself in such a position that he felt he was going to   1220
        definitely hit
someone,
because of the amount of people on the sidewalk,
he steered at the building,
so as to get out of the way of the people.
Obviously, for the most part,   1225
he was successful.
But regrettably,
one child was killed
and another child
was wounded.   1230
Um,
seeing what happened,
he jumped out of the car

and, realizing
1235   there may be a child under the car,
he tried to physically lift
the car
from the child.
Well, as he was doing this
1240   the Afro-Americans were beating him already.
He was beaten so much he needed stitches in the scalp
    and the face,
fifteen or sixteen stitches
and also
there were three other passengers in the car
1245   that were being beaten too.
One of the passengers was calling 911
on the cellular phone.
A Black person
pulled the phone out of his hand and ran.
1250   Just stole the—stole the telephone.
The Jewish community
has a volunteer
ambulance corps
which is funded totally from the nations—
1255   there is not one penny of government funds—
and manned by volunteers—
who many times at their expense—
supplied the equipment that they carry in order to save
    lives.
As one of the EMS ambulances were coming,
1260   one of the Hasidic ambulances or the Jewish ambulances
    came
on the scene.
The EMS responded with three ambulances on the scene.
They were there before
the Jewish ambulance came.
1265   Two or three police cars were already on the scene.
The police saw the potential for violence
and saw that the occupants of the car
were being beaten and were afraid for their safety.
At the same time the EMS asked
1270   the Hasidic ambulances for certain pieces of equipment
    that they
were out of,
that they needed to take care of the Cato kid,
and,
um,
1275   in fact, I was . . .
The Hasidic ambulance left, leaving behind one of the
    passengers.
That passenger had a walkie-talkie and he requested that I
come down to pick him up.
And at that time there was a lot of screaming and shouting
1280   and it was a mixed crowd, Hasidic and Afro-American.
The police said, "Rabbi get your people out of here."
I told them to leave and I left.
Now,
a few hours later,
1285   two and a half hours later,
in a different part of Crown Heights,
a scholar
from Australia,
Yankel Rosenbaum,

who, urr,   1290
I think he had a doctorate or he was working on his
    doctorate,
was walking on the street
on his own—
I mean he was totally oblivious—
and he was accosted by a group of young Blacks   1295
about twenty of them strong
which was being egged on by a Black
male approximately
forty years old and balding,
telling them,   1300
"Kill all Jews—
look what they did to the kid,
kill all Jews,"
and all the epithets that go along with it,
"Heil Hitler" and all of it.   1305
They stabbed him,
which later on the stab wounds were fatal
and he passed away in the hospital.
The Mayor,
hearing about the Cato kid,   1310
came to the Kings County Hospital
to give condolences to the family of the child who had
    regrettably been killed.
At the meantime they had already wheeled in
Mr. Rosenbaum.
He was in the emergency room   1315
and I was at the hospital at the same time,
and the Mayor, seeing me there,
expressed his concern
that a child,
uh, innocent child, had been killed.   1320
Where I explained to him
the fact
that,
whereas the child was killed from an unfortunate
    accident
where there was no malicious intent,   1325
here
there was an individual lying in the emergency room
who had been stabbed with malicious intent
and for the sole reason—
not that he did anything to anyone—   1330
just from the fact that he happened to be Jewish.
And the mayor went with me to the emergency room
to visit Mr. Rosenbaum.
This was approximately one and a half hours before he
    passed away.
I noticed at the time that his feet   1335
were
completely white.
And I complained to the doctor
on the scene,
"He's having a problem with blood circulation   1340
because there's no blood in his feet."
And she gave me some asinine answer.
And the mayor asked her what his condition is:
"Serious but stable."
In the meantime he was screaming and in pain   1345
and they weren't doing anything.

Subsequently they, um,
they started giving him anaesthesia in a time that
they weren't allowed to give him anaesthesia
1350 and while he was under anaesthesia,
he passed away.
So there was totally mismanagement in his case.
So whereas the Mayor,
had been fed . . .
1355 his people got
whatever information he got out of the Black community
        was
that
the driver had run a red light
and also,
1360 and that the ambulance,
the Hasidic ambulance,
refused to take care of the Black child that was dying and
rather took care of their own.
Nenh?
1365 And this is what was fed amongst the Black community.
And it was false,
it was totally false
and it was done maliciously
only with the intent to get the riots,
1370 to start up the resulting riots.

The Reverend Canon Doctor Heron Sam

MEXICAN STANDOFF

November 12, 1991, 4:00 P.M. The rectory office at St. Mark's Church in Crown Heights. A small, short office. Lived in but impeccably ordered. Some light from lamps, some from overhead. Plaques and awards everywhere. THE REVEREND is wearing a yellow shirt, priest's collar, tan summer jacket. He wears spectacles. There are clocks that make noise and sound the hour in his office and outside church bells sound during the interview, loud. Throughout the talk he is trying to get the corner of a calendar to stay down, but it continues to stick up. Finally he uses a paperweight to keep it down.

You can't have that kind of accident
if people are observing the speed limits.
People knew it was the Grand Rebbe.
People have seen the Grand Rebbe
1375 charging through the community.
He is worried
about a threat on his life
from the Satmars.
These Lubavitcher people
1380 are really very,
uh, enigmatic people.
They move so easily between
simplicity and sophistication.
Because
1385 they fear for his life,
because the Satmars
who are their sworn enemies

(*He laughs/chuckles.*)

have threatened to *kill*
the Rebbe.

So whenever he comes out   1390
he's gotta be *whisked!*
You know like a President
or even better than a President.
He says he's an intuhnational figuh
like a Pope!   1395
I say
then, "Why don't you get the Swiss guards
to escort you
rather than using the police
and taxpayers' money?"   1400
He's gotta be
whisked!
Quickly through the neighborhood.
Can't walk around.
He used to walk.   1405
When I first came here.
Now he doesn't walk at all.
They drive him.
And when he walked
you could tell he was in front   1410
because there was,
he was protected all around
and they spilled out onto the streets
and buses had to stop
because this BIG BAND   1415
had to escort
the Rebbe from his house over there
to the synagogue.
So the Rebbe goes to the cemetery.
Every time the Rebbe goes to the cemetery,   1420
which is once a week
to visit his dead wife
and father-in-law,
the police
lead him in escort   1425
charging down the street
at seventy miles an hour in a metropolis—
what do you want?

(*Swift increase in volume and suddenly businesslike.*)

It happened that on this occasion that as they were
        coming back,
uh,   1430
the police car
with its siren,
had gone over a main
intersection with the light
in favor   1435
of the police car.
The Rebbe's Cadillac had passed
when the lights had become amber
and nobody expected the bodyguard van,
uh,   1440
station wagon
to deliberately go through the red light.
So the traffic
that had the right of way kept coming and
BANG!   1445
came the collision and the careening

onto the sidewalk
had to damage whoever was there
and then, um, they were more concerned about licking
    their own
1450 wounds.
Rather than pick
the car off the boy
who died as a result.
And then the ambulance that came—
1455 the Jewish ambulance—
was concerned about the people in the van
while some boy lay dead,
a black boy lay dead on the street.
The people showed their—

(*Increase in volume.*)

1460 they burned and whatever else,
upturned
police cars
and looted,
and as a result,
1465 I think in retaliation, murdered one of the Hasidics.
But that was just the match that lit the powder keg.
It's gonna happen again and again.
There's a Mexican standoff right now
But it's gonna happen again.

Anonymous Young Man #1

WA WA WA

*7:00 or 8:00 P.M. Spring. A recreation room at Ebbets Field apart-
ments. A very handsome young Caribbean American* MAN *with
dreadlocks, in his late teens or early twenties, wearing a bright, loose-
fitting shirt. The room is ill equipped. There are a few pieces of broken furniture. It is poorly lit. A woman, Kym, with dreadlocks and
shells in her hair, is at the interview. It was originally scheduled to
be her interview. The* ANONYMOUS YOUNG MAN #1 *and the
other* ANONYMOUS YOUNG MAN #2 *started by watching the interview from the side of the room but soon approached me and began to join in.* ANONYMOUS YOUNG MAN #1 *was the most vocal.*
ANONYMOUS YOUNG MAN #2 *stood lurking in the shadows. A
third young man, younger than both of them, wearing wire spectacles and a blue Wind-breaker, who looks quite like a young Spike
Lee, sat silent with his hands and head on the table the entire time.
There is a very bad radio or tape recorder playing music in the background.*

1470 What I saw was
she was pushin'
her brother on the bike like
this,
right?
1475 She was pushin'
him
and he kept dippin' around
like he didn't know how
to ride the bike.
1480 So she kept runnin'
and pushin' him to the side.
So she was already runnin'

when the car was comin'.
So I don't know if she was runnin' toward him
because we was watchin' the car   1485
weavin',
and we was goin'
"Oh, yo
it's a Jew, man.
He broke the stop light, they never get arrested."   1490
At first we was laughin', man, we was like
you see they do anything
and get away with it,
and then
we saw that he was out of control,   1495
and den
we started regrettin' laughin',
because then
we saw where he was goin'.
First he hit a car, right,   1500
he tore a whole front fender off a car,
and then we was like
Oh
my god,
man, look at the kids,   1505
you know,
so we was already runnin' over there
by the time the accident happened.
That's how we know he was drinkin'
cause he was like   1510
Wa Wa Wa Wa
and I was like
"Yo, man, he's drunk.
Grab him,
grab him.   1515
Don't let him go anywhere."
I said,
"Grab him."
I didn't want him to limp off
in some apartment somewhere   1520
and come back in a different black jacket.
So I was like,
"Grab him,"
and then I was like, "Is the ambulance comin' for the
    kids?"
'Cause I been in a lot of confrontations with Jews   1525
    before
and I know that when they said an ambulance
is comin'
it most likely meant for them.
And they was like,
"oh, oh."   1530
Jews right?
"Ambulance comin', ambulance comin',
calm down, calm down,
God will help them,
God will help them if you believe."   1535
And he was actin' like he was dyin'.
"Wa Aww,
me too,
I'm hurt, I'm hurt, I'm hurt too."
Wan nothin wrong with him,   1540
wan nothin wrong with him.

They say that we beat up on that man
that he had to have stitches because of us.
You don't come out of an accident like that
    unmarked,
1545 without a scratch.
The most he got from us was slapped
by a little kid.
And here come the ambulance
and I was like, "That's not a city ambulance,"
1550 not like this I was upset right
and I was like,
"YO,
the man is drunk!
He ran a red light!
1555 You all ain't gonna do nothin'."
Everybody started comin' around, right,
'cause I was talkin' about
these kids is dyin' man!
I'm talkin' about the skull of the baby is on the ground
    man!
1560 and he's walking'!
I was like, "Don't let him get into that ambulance!"
And the Jews,
the Jews
was like private, private ambulance
1565 I was like, "Grab him,"
but my buddies was like,
"We can't touch them."
Nobody wanted to grab him,
nobody wanted to touch him,
1570 An' I was breakin' fool, man,
I was goin' mad,
I couldn't believe it.
Everybody just stood
there,
1575 and that made me cry.
I was cryin'
so I left, I went home and watched the rest of it on TV,
it was too lackadazee
so it was like me, man, instigatin' the whole thing.
1580 I got arrested for it
long after
in Queens.
Can't tell you no more about that,
you know.
1585 Hey, wait a minute,
they got eyes and ears everywhere.
What color is the Israeli flag?
And what color are the police cars?
The man was drunk,
1590 I open up his car door,
I was like, when—
I was like, he'd been drinkin'
I know our words don't have no meanin',
as Black people in Crown Heights.
1595 You realize, man,
ain't no justice,
ain't never been no justice,
ain't never gonna be no justice.

Michael S. Miller

HEIL HITLER

A large airy office in Manhattan on Lexington in the fifties. MR.
MILLER *sits behind a big desk in a high-backed swivel chair drinking coffee. He's wearing a yarmulke. Plays with the swizzle stick
throughout. There is an intercom in the office, so that when the re-
ceptionist calls him, you can hear it, and when she calls others in
other offices, you can hear it, like a page in a public place, faintly.*

I was at Gavin Cato's funeral,
at nearly every public event   1600
that was conducted by the Lubavitcher community and
    the Jewish
community as a whole.
Words of comfort
were offered to the family of Gavin Cato.
I can show you a letter that we sent   1605
to the Cato family expressing, uh,
our sorrow over the loss,
unnecessary loss, of their son.
I am not aware of a word
that was spoken at that funeral.   1610
I am not aware of a—
and I was taking notes—
of a word that was uttered
of comfort to the family of Yankel Rosenbaum.
Frankly this was a political rally rather than a funeral.   1615
The individuals you mentioned—
and again,
I am not going to participate in verbal acrimony,
not only
were there cries of, "Kill the Jews"   1620
or,
"Kill the Jew,"
there were cries of, "Heil Hitler."
There were cries of, "Hitler didn't finish the job."
There were cries of,   1625
"Throw them back into the ovens again."
To hear in *Crown Heights*
and Hitler was no lover of Blacks—
"Heil Hitler"?
"Hitler didn't finish the job"?   1630
"We should heat up the ovens"?
From *Blacks*?
Is more inexplicable
or unexplainable
or any other word that I cannot fathom.   1635
The hatred is so
deep seated
and the hatred
knows no boundaries.
There is no boundary   1640
to anti-Judaism.
The anti-*Judaism*—
if people don't want me
to use,
hear me use the word anti-Semitism.   1645

And I'll be damned if,
if preferential treatment is gonna
be the excuse
for every bottle,
1650   rock,
or pellet that's, uh, directed
toward a Jew
or the window of a Jewish home
or a Jewish store.
1655   And, frankly,
I think the response of the Lubavitcher community was
        relatively
passive.

Henry Rice
KNEW HOW TO USE CERTAIN WORDS

*Thursday, November 21, 1991. The Jackson Hole restaurant on
Lexington Avenue in the thirties in Manhattan. Lunchtime, dimly
lit a reddish haze on everything, perhaps from a neon light.* MR.
RICE, *very neatly dressed, is eating a large, messy hamburger and
horizontally chopped pickles. Drinking a Miller Lite. Beer is in a
bottle next to a red plastic glass. He's wearing a baseball cap over very
closely cut hair and a bright, multicolored, expensive-looking colored
nylon jacket. Heavy new Timberland boots. Struggling to eat without making a mess of the food. At some point sits up from food and
has his right hand or fist on his hip a very unaffected but truly authoritative stance. Good-natured, handsome, healthy. Patsy Cline's
"Crazy" is very loud on the jukebox.*

I went back home and got my bike
because I knew I would have to be
1660   illusive.
I was there in body and in spirit
but I didn't participate in any of the violence
because basically I have a lot to lose.
But I was there
1665   and I would have defended myself if it was necessary,
        most definitely.
I weaved around trouble.
When something broke out, I moved back,
when it calmed down, I would move back in on the
        front line.
1670   I was always there.
And Richard Green heard me saying something to a
        bunch of kids
about *voting*
about the power of *vote*
the power of *numbers*
1675   and he said,
uh,
I said, "Get away from me, you're an Uncle Tom,
get away from me.
Get back in your Mercedes-Benz!"
1680   No! I said that to Clarence Norman
and to Richard Green,
both of them.
I was tearing them apart.

Richard Green was very persistent.
He said,   1685
"Look, Mr. Rice,
I like the way you speak.
I need you.
Please help me.
I'm a community activist. . . .   1690
ba, ba, ba, ba, ba."

(He drops some food on his clothes, or so it seems, he looks and grins.)

It didn't get on me.
"I'm a community activist.
I need your help,
please help me,"   1695
and so forth.
Again,
I didn't pay him no mind
but we spoke
some   1600
the next day after that,
after the incidents that took place on that corner
of Albany Avenue.
A brother was beat up—
cops rushing into the Black crowd   1705
didn't rush into the Jewish crowd,
cops rushed into the Black crowd
started beatin' up
Black people.
But the next day Richard came by in a yellow van,   1710
a New York City Department of Transportation van,
with a megaphone,
yellow light flashing,

*(Music segues from Patsy Cline's "Crazy" to Public Enemy's
"Can't Truss It," or Naughty by Nature's "O.P.P.")*

the whole works
and, um,   1715
he said,
"Henry, I need you in this van.
Drive around with me.
Let's keep some of these kids off the street tonight."
I said, "Okay."   1720
He said,
"The blood
of Black men are on your hands tonight!"
I said, "Okay."
We drive around in the van,   1725
"Young people stay in the house!
Mothers keep your children in the house,
please."
So I began fillin'
I began feeling like   1730
I had to do it
after he told me that,
"the blood of the Black man"
were on my hands,
you know.   1735
Richard Green sure know how to use certain words.

(He giggles.)

I remember reaching Albany Avenue—
kids were being chased by the police.
I jump out with a portable megaphone,
1740   I tell them, "Stop running!
The cops won't chase you!
and they won't hit you!"
The next thing I know,
cop grabs my megaphone hits me in the head with a
    stick,
1745   handcuffs me,
and takes the megaphone out of my hand.
So I'm like,
"Wait a minute
I'm doing a community service for the mayor's office."
1750   They don't want to hear it.
Matter of fact,
they still have the megaphone 'til this day.
I'm like,
"Richard Green get me
1755   out of this police car, please!"
So a Black captain came by,
thank God,
and he says, "What's goin' on?"
Richard Green explained it to him.
1760   He said, "Let him go."
Get back in the van,
there's another Brother in van,
starts saying,
"Non violence!"
1765   to the young Brothers.
They begin throwing bottles at the, uh,
at the van.
One guy got so upset
he had a nine-millimeter
1770   fully loaded.
He said, "Get the hell out of this neighborhood!"
The next day
more violence:
fires,
1775   cars being burnt,
stores being broken into,
a perception that Black youth
are going crazy in Crown Heights
like we were angry over
1780   nothing,
understand?

Norman Rosenbaum
MY BROTHER'S BLOOD

A Sunday afternoon. Spring. Crisp, clear, and windy. Across from City Hall in New York City. Crowds of people, predominantly Lubavitcher, with placards. A rally that was organized by Lubavitcher women. All of the speakers were men, but the women stand close to the stage. MR. ROSENBAUM, *an Australian, with a beard, hat, and wearing a pinstripe suit, speaks passionately and loudly from the microphone on a stage with a podium. Behind him is a man in an Australian bush hat with a very large Australian flag which*

blows dramatically in the wind. It is so windy that MR. ROSENBAUM *has to hold his hat to keep it on his head.*

Al do lay achee so achee aylay alo dalmo
My brother's blood cries out from the ground.
Let me make it clear
why I'm here.   1785
In August of 1991,
as you all have heard before today,
my brother was killed in the streets of Crown Heights
for no other reason
than that he was a Jew!   1790
The only miracle was
that my brother was the only victim
who paid for being a Jew with his life.
When my brother was surrounded,
each and every American was surrounded.   1795
When my brother was stabbed four times,
each and every American was stabbed four times
and as my brother bled to death in this city,
while the medicos stood by
and let him bleed   1800
to death, it was the gravest of indictments against this
    country.
One person out of twenty gutless individuals
who attacked my brother has been arrested.
I for one am not convinced that it is beyond the ability
    of the New York police
to arrest others.   1805
Let me tell you, Mayor Dinkins,
let me tell you, Commissioner Brown:
I'm here,
I'm not going home,
until there is justice.   1810

Norman Rosenbaum
SIXTEEN HOURS DIFFERENCE

7:00 A.M. Spring. Newark Airport, Departure Gate, Continental Airlines. MR. ROSENBAUM *is moments before his flight to L.A. and then back to Australia. Wearing a pinstripe suit with an Australian fit. Hat. Suitcase. He has sparkling blue eyes with a twinkle, rosy cheeks, and a large smile throughout the interview.*

There's sixteen hours difference between New York and
    Melbourne
and I had just gotten back to my office
and I had a phone call from my wife,
and she said she wanted me to come home straight away
and I sensed the urgency in her voice.   1815
I said, "are you all right?" She said, "Yeah."
I said, "are the children all right, you know the kids?"
    She says, "yeah."
So I'm driving home and I'm thinking, I wonder what's
    the problem now, you know?
We had some carpenters doing some work, I wonder if
    there has been a disaster,
some sort of domestic problem,   1820
and I thought, oh my God, you know, my parents,
I didn't even ask after them,
how insensitive not to even ask after my parents,

and I've got a grandmother eighty-five years old, same
   sort of thing.
1825 So I get home,
I walk in the door, and a friend of mine was standing
   there,
close friend,
does the same sort of work as me, he's a barrister and an
   academic,
and he sees me and he says,
1830 "There's got a pro—
uh,
we've got a problem. There's a problem."
I thought he was talking about a case we were working
   on together,
he says, "'Z come,
1835 come and sit down."
He goes to me,
"There's been a riot in New York,
been a riot in Crown Heights,
Yankel's been stabbed and he's dead."
1840 And
my brother was the last in the world,
I hadn't even given him a thought.
I mean the fact that my brother
could be attacked
1845 or die,
it just hadn't even entered my mind.
At first I appeared all cool, calm and collected.
I then
started asking questions
1850 like who told you,
how do you know,
are you sure?
I just asked the question,
you know,
1855 are you sure?

Anonymous Young Man #2

BAD BOY

Evening. Spring. The same recreation room as interview with ANONYMOUS YOUNG MAN #1, YOUNG MAN #2 *is wearing a black jacket over his clothes. He has a gold tooth. He has some dreadlocks, and a very odd-shaped multicolored hat. He is soft-spoken, and has a direct gaze. He seems to be very patient with his explanation.*

That youth,
that sixteen-year-old
didn't murder that Jew.

(Pause.)

For one thing,
1860 he played baseball, right?
He was a atha-lete,
right?
A bad boy
does
1865 bad things.
Only a bad boy coulda stabbed the man.
Somebody who

does those type a things,
or who sees
those types a things.   1870
A atha-lete
sees people,
is interested in athletics,
stretchin',
exercisin',   1875
goin' to his football games,
or his baseball games.
He's not interested
in stabbin'
people.   1880
So
it's not in his mind
to stab,
to just jump into somethin',
that he has no idea about   1885
and
sta—
and kill a man.
A bad boy,
somebody who's groomed in badness,   1890
or did badness
before,
stabbed the man.
Because I used to be a atha-lete
and I used to be a bad boy,   1895
and when I was a atha-lete,
I was a atha-lete.
All I thought about was atha-lete.
I'm not gonna jeopardize my athleticism
or my career to do anything   1900
that bad people do.
And when I became a bad boy
I'm not a athalete no more.
I'm a bad boy,
and I'm groomin' myself in things that is bad.   1905
You understand, so
he's a athalete,
he's not a bad boy.
It's a big difference.
Like,   1910
mostly the Black youth in Crown Heights have two
   things to do—
either DJ or be a bad boy, right?
You either
DJ, be a MC, a rapper
or Jamaican rapper,   1915
ragamuffin,
or you be a bad boy,
you sell drugs or you rob people.
What do you do?
I sell drugs.   1920
What do you do?
I rap.
That's how it is in Crown Heights.
I been livin' in Crown Heights mosta my life.
I know for a fact that that youth, that sixteen-year-old, 1925
didn't kill that Jew.
That's between me and my Creator.

Sonny Carson

CHORDS

Lunchtime. Spring. A fancy restaurant in Brooklyn. SONNY *tells me it's where all the judges come for lunch. White linen tablecloths. Light wood walls, lamplight next to the table. Tile floor. He is eating crab cakes. He is dressed in a black turtleneck and a gray jacket. He has on a mud cloth hat. He has an authority stick with him, and it lays on the table. His bodyguard, wearing a black leather jacket, enters in the middle of the interview.* SONNY *chides him for being late.*

It's going to be a long hot summer.
I'm connected up with the young people all over the
    country
1930 and there's a thread
leading to an eruption
and Crown Heights began the whole thing.
And the Jews come second to the police
when it comes to feelings of dislike among Black folks.
1935 The police,
the police,
believe me, the police—
I know the police and the police know me
and they turn that whole place into an occupied camp
1940 with the Seventy-first Precinct as the overseers.
And don't think that everything is OK within that
    precinct among those officers
either.
Don't think that,
don't think that.
1945 You know the media has always painted me as the bad
    guy—
that's OK!
I'm a good guy to pick on.
Their viewers don't like me either,
they really don't like me because I *am* the bad guy,
1950 I am the ultimate bad guy
because of my relationship to the young people in the
    city.
I understand their language.
I respect them as the future.
I speak their language. They don't even engage in long
    dialogue
1955 anymore
just short
"words."
It always amazes me
how the city fathers,
1960 the power brokers,
just continue to deny what's happening.
And it is just getting intolerable for me to continue to
    watch
this small
arrogant
1965 group of people continue to get this kind of preferential
    treatment.
They sit on the school board.
A board of nine
and they have

four members, and their kids don't even go to public
    school.
So that's the kind of arrogance I'm talking about.   1970
I have no reason to be eagerly awaiting the coming
    together of our
people.
They owe me first.
I'm not givin' in just like that,
I don't want it.   1975
You can have it.
Like my grandmother said,
"Help the bear!
If you see me and the bear in a fight,
help the bear—   1980
don't help me,
help the bear."
I don't need any of it from them!
And I'm not gonna advocate any coming together and
    healing of
America   1985
and all that shit.
You kiddin'?
You kiddin'?
Just 'cause I can have the fortune of walking in here
and sitting and talking   1990
and having a drink,
it appear that I have all the same kinds of abilities
of other folks in here.
No, it's not that way.
'Cause tonight   1995
by nighttime it could all change for me.
So I'm always aware of that, and that's what keeps me
    goin'
today
and each day!

(*He eats.*)

I have   2000
this idea
about a film.
See,
these kids, they got
another kinda rhythm now,   2005
there's a whole new kinda
step that they do.
When I first heard rap
I was sittin' in a huge open kinda stadium,
boys and girls high school field,   2010
and I heard these kids come out and start rappin',
and I'm listening
but it's not really clickin',
but I was mesmerized though.
But it was simontaneouis   2015
all around the country
and I said, "Oh shit,"
and everybody I knew who was young was listenin' to it
and I said, "Wow."
Because I have always been involved with young people   2020
and all of a sudden I got it,
I really heard the rhythm,

the chords,
the discord.
2025   There's a whole new sound
that the crackers are tryin' to get, but they can't get it.
I heard it on a television commercial.
One of the most beautiful pieces of art
that I ever witnessed
2030   was a play
called
um,
um,
um,
2035   'bout, 'bout the Puerto Rican gang—
no, no, no, no, no—
the Puerto Rican gang,
the musical
that was on Broad—
2040   yeah,
West Side Story—
the answer should be
a musical.

Rabbi Shea Hecht

OVENS

Morning. Spring. A building on Eastern Parkway. A large room with a very long conference table. There are pictures of Lubavitcher men on the walls. RABBI HECHT *is wearing a shirt, open at the neck. He has several crisp one-dollar bills in his shirt pocket. These are, apparently, dollar bills that the Rebbe has given him. It is the custom that the Rebbe gives out one-dollar bills on Sunday.* RABBI HECHT *has a beard. He wears glasses, traditional Hasidic garb, including tsitses (ceremonial fringes that hang over his belt) and a red yarmulke with gold trim which is ripped. His daughter comes in frequently to get money from him. He keeps telling her to wait until he is finished. She becomes more and more agitated. His brother also enters frequently to ask him questions, and to tell him he's late.*

What is my goal?
2045   My goal is not
to give anybody a message
that we plan on working things out
by integrating
our two
2050   things.
By a person understanding more of their own religion
they will automatically respect another person.
The respect that my religion teaches me has nothing to
       do
with understanding you.
2055   See, there's a problem.
If
the only way I'm going to respect you
is based on how much I understand you,
no matter what it is
2060   in certain circles you're gonna run into problems.
Number one,
we are different,
and we think we should and can be different.
When the Rebbe said to the Mayor
2065   that we were all

one people,
I think
what the Rebbe is talking about is that,
that common denominator that we're all children of
      God, and the
respect we all have to give each other under that banner.   2070
But that does not mean that I have to invite you to my
      house for
dinner,
because I cannot go back to your home for dinner,
because you're not gonna give me kosher food.
And I said,   2075
so, like one Black said,
I'll bring in kosher food.
I said eh-eh.
We can't use your ovens,
we can't use your dishes,   2080
it's, it—
it's not just a question of buying certain food,
it's buying the food,
preparing it a certain way.
We can't use your dishes, we can't use your oven.   2085
The—the higher you go
the more common denominator.
And what the Rebbe was saying,
you as the Mayor
don't get caught up in the differences,   2090
you're—
from your position is—
you have to look at it as one city
and one
human race.   2095
We are all New Yorkers
and therefore I will protect all New Yorkers.
You see
preferential treatment
suggests   2100
that you're giving the person
the police car
not because they need the police car
but because
they are who they are.   2105
You're not gonna
give them the housing
because they
need the housing—
you're giving it because of who they are.   2110
But
just because I'm a Jew
therefore I
shouldn't get the police car.
The question is   2115
a synagogue
that has five thousand Jews
leave
the synagogue
at the same time,   2120
do they have a police car to stop the traffic?
The answer is every—single—synagogue,
temple,
mosque,

2125 in
the
world
stops traffic
when five thousand people have to walk out
2130 at the same time.

Reverend Al Sharpton

RAIN

The D.A.
came back with no indictment.
Uh, so then our only course
was to ask for a special prosecutor
2135 which is appointed by the Governor,
who's been hostile,
and to sue civilly.
When we went into civil court
we went to get an order to show cause.
2140 The judge signed it and gave me a deadline of three days.
The driver left the country. . . .
No one even said, "Why would he run?
If he did no wrong."
If you and I were in an accident we'd have to go to civil
court.
2145 Why is this man
above the law?
So they said, "He's in Israel."
So I said,
"Well, I'll go to Israel to show best effits."
2150 And the deadline
was,
I had to serve him by Tuesday,
which was Yom Kippur—
that was the judge's decision not mine.
2155 So we went.
Alton Maddox and I
got on a plane,
left Monday night,
landed Tuesday morning,
2160 went and served the American embassy, uh,
so that
if this man had any decency at all
he could come to the American embassy and receive
service,
which he has not done to this day.
2165 Come back,
went to court
and showed the judge the receipts,
and the judge said, "You made best effits,
therefore you are now permitted,
2170 by default,
to go ahead
and sue the rabbi or whomever
because you cannot do the driver."
So it wasn't just a media grandstand.
2175 We wanted to show the world
one, this man *ran*
and was *allowed* to run, and, two, we wanted to be able
to legally go

around him,
to sue the people he was working for so that we can
bring them into
court and establish *why* and what happened.   2180
And it came out in the paper the other day
that the driver in the other car didn't even have a
driver's license.
So we're dealing with a *complete* outrage here,
we're dealing with a double standard,
we're dealing with uh, uh, a, a   2185
situation where
Blacks do not have equal protection under the law
and the media is used to castigate us
that merely asked for justice
rather than castigate those that would hit a kid   2190
and walk away like he just stepped on a roach!
Uh,
there also is the media
contention of the young Jewish scholar
that was stabbed that night   2195
and they've even distorted
saying *my words at the funeral*
I *preached* the funeral.
Uh, [the newspaper said I]
helped to, to, uh, uh,   2200
spark or, or, or, or, or *inspire* or *incite* people to kill him
[Yankel Rosenbaum]
when he was dead the day before
I came out there.
He was killed the night
that the young man   2205
was killed with the car accident.
I didn't even get a call
from the family
'til eighteen hours later.
So there's a whole media distortion   2210
to protect them [the Lubavitchers].
Nobody is talking about,
"Why
is this guy
in flight?"   2215
If I was a rabbi
(I am a ministuh)
and my driver hit a kid,
I would not let the driver *leave*
and I certainlih would give my condolences,   2220
or anything else I could,
to the family,
I don't care what race they are.
To this minute the Rebbe has never even uttered a word
of
sympathy   2225
to the family,
not even sent 'em a *card*
a *flower* or *nothing!*
So it's treating us with absolute contempt
and I don't care how controversial it makes us.   2230
I *won't* tolerate being insulted.
If you piss in my face I'm gonna call it *piss.*
I'm not gonna call it rain.

Richard Green

RAGE

2:00 P.M. in a big red van. GREEN is in the front. He has a driver. I am in the back. GREEN wears a large knit hat with reggae colors over long dreadlocks. Driving from Crown Heights to Brooklyn College. He turns sideways to face me in the back, and bends down, talking with his elbow on his knee.

Sharpton, Carson, and Reverend Herbert Daughtry
2235 didn't have any power out there really.
The media gave them power.
But they weren't turning those youfs on and off.
Nobody knew who controlled the switch out there.
Those young people had rage like an oil-well fire
2240 that has to burn out.
All they were doin' was sort of orchestratin' it.
Uh, they were not really the ones that were saying, "Well
stop, go, don't go, stop, turn around, go up."
It wasn't like that.
2245 Those young people had rage out there,
that didn't matter who was in control of that—
that rage had to get out
and that rage
has been building up.
2250 When all those guys have come and gone,
that rage is still out here.
I can show you that rage every day
right up and down this avenue.
We see, sometimes in one month, we see three bodies
2255 in one month. That's rage,
and that's something that nobody has control of.
And I don't know who told you that it was preferential
        treatment for
Blacks that the Mayor kept the cops back. . . .
If the Mayor had turned those cops on?
2260 We would still be in a middle of a battle.
And
I pray on both sides of the fence,
and I tell the people in the Jewish community the same
        thing,
"This is not something that force will hold."
2265 Those youfs were running on cops without nothing in
        their hands,
seven- and eight- and nine- and ten-year-old boys were
        running at
those cops
with nothing,
just running at 'em.
2270 That's rage.
Those young people out there are angry
and that anger has to be vented,
it has to be negotiated.
And they're not angry at the Lubavitcher community
2275 they're just as angry at you and me,
if it comes to that.
They have no
role models,
no guidance

so they're just out there growin' up on their own,   2280
their peers are their role models,
their peers is who teach them how to move
so when they see the Lubavitch
they don't know the difference between "Heil Hitler"
and, uh, and uh, whatever else.   2285
They don't know the difference.
When you ask 'em to say who Hitler was they wouldn't
        even be able
to tell you.

(*Phone rings, RICHARD picks it up, it's a mobile phone.*)

"Richard Green, can I help?
Aw, man I tol' you I want some color   2290
up on that wall. Give me some colors.
Look, I'm in the middle of somethin'."

(*He returns to the conversation.*)

Half them don't even know three quarters of 'em.
Just as much as they don't know who Frederick
        Douglass was.
They know Malcolm   2295
because Malcolm has been played up to such an extent
        now
that they know Malcolm.
But ask who Nat Turner was or Mary McCleod
        Bethune or Booker T.
Because the system has given 'em
Malcolm is convenient and   2300
Spike is goin' to give 'em Malcolm even more.
It's convenient.

Roslyn Malamud

THE COUP

Spring. Midafternoon. The sunny kitchen of a huge, beautiful house on Eastern Parkway in Crown Heights. It's a large, very well-equipped kitchen. We are sitting at a table in a breakfast nook area, which is separated by shelves from the cooking area. There is a window to the side. There are newspapers on the chair at the far side of the table. MRS. MALAMUD offers me food at the beginning of the interview. We are drinking coffee. She is wearing a sweatshirt with a large sequined cat. Her tennis shoes have matching sequined cats. She has on a black skirt and is wearing a wig. Her nails are manicured. She has beautiful eyes that sparkle are very warm, and a very resonant voice. There is a lot of humor in her face.

Do you know what happened in August here?
You see when you read the newspapers.
I mean my son filmed what was going on,   2305
but when you read the newspapers . . .
Of course I was here
I couldn't leave my house.
I only would go out early during the day.
The police were barricading here.   2310
You see,
I wish
I could just like

go on television.

2315 I wanna scream to the whole world.
They said
that the Blacks were rioting against the Jews in Crown
   Heights
and that the Jews were fighting back.
Do you know that the Blacks who came here to riot
   were not my
2320 neighbors?
I don't love my neighbors.
I don't know my Black neighbors.
There's one lady on President Street—
Claire—
2325 I adore her.
She's my girl friend's next-door neighbor.
I've had a manicure
done in her house and we sit and kibbitz
and stuff
2330 but I don't know them.
I told you we don't mingle socially
because of the difference
of food
and religion
2335 and what have you here.
But
the people in this community
want exactly
what I want out of life.
2340 They want to live
in nice homes.
They all go to work.
They couldn't possibly
have houses here
2345 if they didn't
generally—They have
two,
um,
incomes
2350 that come in.
They want to send their kids to college.
They wanna live a nice quiet life.
They wanna shop for their groceries and cook their
   meals and go to
their Sunday picnics!
2355 They just want to have decent homes and decent lives!
The people who came to riot here
were brought here
by this famous
Reverend Al Sharpton,
2360 which I'd like to know who ordained him?
And he brought in a bunch of kids.
I wish you could see the *New York Times,*
unfortunately it was on page twenty,
but,
2365 he brought in a bunch of kids who didn't have jobs in
   the
summertime
when you don't have a job
and you're hanging out all day.
I mean, they interviewed
2370 one of the Black girls on Utica Avenue.

She said,
"The guys will make you pregnant
at night
and in the morning not know who you are."

(*Almost whispering.*)

And if you're sitting on a front stoop and it's very, very   2375
   hot
and you have no money
and you have nothing to do with your time
and someone says, "Come on, you wanna riot?"
You know how kids are.
The fault lies with the police department.   2380
The police department did nothing to stop them.
I was sitting here in the front of the house
when bottles were being thrown
and the sergeant tells five hundred policemen
with clubs and helmets and guns   2385
to duck.
And I said to him,
"You're telling them to duck?
What should I do?
I don't have a club and a gun."   2390
Had they put it—
stopped it on the first night
this kid who came from Australia . . .

(*She sucks her teeth.*)

You know,
his parents were Holocaust survivors, he didn't have to   2395
   die.
He worked,
did a lot of research in Holocaust studies.
He didn't have to die.
What happened on Utica Avenue
was an accident.   2400
JEWISH PEOPLE
DO NOT DRIVE VANS INTO SEVEN-YEAR-OLD
   BOYS.
YOU WANT TO KNOW SOMETHING? BLACK
   PEOPLE DO NOT DRIVE
VANS INTO SEVEN-YEAR-OLD BOYS.
HISPANIC PEOPLE DON'T DRIVE VANS INTO   2405
   SEVEN-YEAR-OLD BOYS.
IT'S JUST NOT DONE.
PEOPLE LIKE JEFFREY DAHMER MAYBE THEY
   DO IT.
BUT AVERAGE CITIZENS DO NOT GO OUT
   AND TRY TO KILL

(*Sounds like a laugh but it's just a sound.*)

SEVEN-YEAR-OLD BOYS.
It was an accident!   2410
But it was allowed to fester and to steam and all that.
When you come here do you see anything that's going
   on, riots?
No.
But Al Sharpton and the likes of him like *Dowerty,*
who by the way has been in prison   2415

and all of a sudden he became Reverend *Dowerty*—
they once did an exposé on him—
but
these guys live off of this,
2420   you understand?
People are not gonna give them money,
contribute to their causes
unless they're out there rabble-rousing
My Black neighbors?
2425   I mean I spoke to them.
They were hiding in their houses just like I was.
We were scared.
I was scared!
I was really frightened.
2430   I had five hundred policemen standing in front of my
        house
every day
I had mounted police,
but I couldn't leave my block,
because when it got dark I couldn't come back in.
2435   I couldn't meet anyone for dinner.
Thank God, I told you my children were all out of
        town.
My son was in Russia.
The coup
was exactly the same day as the riot
2440   and I was very upset about it.
He was in Russia running a camp
and I was very concerned when I had heard about that.
I hadn't heard from him
that night the riot started.
2445   When I did hear from him I told him to stay in Russia,
        he'd be safer
there than here.
And he was.

Reuven Ostrov

POGROMS

*9:00 P.M. November 1991. In a basement of a Crown Heights
house. MR. OSTROV wears a yarmulke. Eating popcorn and sliced
apples. Very low, gentle-sounding nigunim music plays in the background, it almost sounds like New Age music, perhaps because traditional music is played on a modern electronic keyboard instrument.
In the show, I wore a basketball jacket with the team's insignia, and
used a basketball—which MR. OSTROV did not do at this interview,
but previously had at a basketball game. He has no beard, which is
unusual for a man his age who does have a beard if grown. He has
a very rich, deep voice.*

I was working in a hospital.
I work as an assistant chaplain at
2450   Down State Kings County Hospital.
I heard that Yankel Rosenbaum was stabbed and, um,
        they
were gonna give him an *aurtopsy*
and they asked if he had an
aurtopsy
2455   or not because in the Jewish religion a person is not
        allowed to have
an aurtopsy

and I found out later that he did have one
a few days later.
I found a Jewish man in a room,
a Russian man.   2460
His mother committed suicide
because she was, uhm, she was terrified.
She jumped out of the third floor of her apartment
        building,
committed suicide.
The mother originally came from Russia.   2465
I was speaking to her son
in one of the rooms near the morgue
trying to get his mother not to have an aurtopsy
and he was telling me that the mother
came from Russia eleven years ago   2470
and the mother left Russia eleven years ago
because of the hardships that they had over there,
and when they came to America
and when this thing started to happen in Crown
        Heights.
It became painful   2475
and it felt like, like there was no place to go.
It's like you're trapped,
everywhere you go there's Jew haters.
And then he told me she commit suicide,
told me the next morning he woke up   2480
he heard the doorbell ring.
He wasn't,
she wasn't there.
He noticed that the window was open,
which is never open   2485
because she was afraid of the cold
even in the summertime.
And he saw his mother
with blood all over her
landed head first   2490
on the concrete side of the apartment building.
After that we already knew this was getting serious,
because we had,
we had Sonny Carson come down
and we had, um,   2495
Reverend Al Sharpton come down
start making pogroms.

Carmel Cato

LINGERING

*7:00 P.M. The corner where the accident occurred in Crown Heights.
An altar to Gavin is against the wall where the car crashed. Many
pieces of cloth are draped. Some writing in color is on the wall. Candle wax is everywhere. There is a rope around the area. CATO is
wearing a trench coat, pulled around him. He stands very close to me.
Dark outside. Reggae music is in the background. Lights come from
stores on each corner. Busy intersection. Sounds from outside. Traffic.
Stores open. People in and out of shops. Sounds from inside apartments, televisions, voices, cooking, etc. He speaks in a pronounced
West Indian accent.*

In the meanwhile
it was two.
Angela was on the ground   2500

but she was trying to move. Gavin was still.
They was trying to pound him.
I was the father.
I was 'it, chucked, and pushed,
2505 and a lot of
sarcastic words were passed towards me
from the police
while I was trying to explain: It was my kid!
These are my children.
2510 The child was hit you know.
I saw everything, everything,
the guy radiator burst
all the hoses,
the steam,
2515 all the garbage buckets along the building.
And it was very loud,
everything burst.
It's like an atomic bomb,
and that's why all these people comin' round
2520 wanna know what's happening.
Oh it was very outrageous.
Numerous numbers.
All the time the police sayin'
you can't get in,
2525 you can't pass,
and the children laying on the ground.
He was hit at exactly eight-thirty.
Why?
I was standing over there.
2530 There was a little child—
a friend of mine
came up with a little child—
and I lift the child up
and she look at her watch at the same time
2535 and she say it was eight-thirty.
I gave the child back to her.
And then it happen.
Um, Um . . .
My child, these are the things I never dream about.
2540 I take care of my children.
You know it's a funny thing,
if a child get sick and he dies
it won't hurt me so bad,
or if a child run out into the street
2545 it wouldn't hurt me.
That's what's hurtin' me.
And the whole week
that Gavin died
my body was changing,
2550 I was having different feelings.
I stop eating,
I didn't et
nothin',
only drink water,
2555 for two weeks;
and I was very touchy—
any least thing that drop
or any song I hear
it would effect me.

Every time I try to do something   2560
I would have to stop.
I was
lingering, lingering, lingering, lingering,
all the time.
But I can do things,   2565
I can see things,
I know that for a fact.
I was telling myself,
"Something is wrong somewhere,"
but I didn't want to see,   2570
I didn't want to accept,
and it was inside of me,
and even when I go home I tell my friends,
"Something coming I could feel it
but I didn't want to see,"   2575
and all the time I just deny deny deny,
and I never thought it was Gavin,
but I didn't have a clue.
I thought it was one of the other children—
the bigger boys   2580
or the girl,
because she worry me,
she won't et—
but Gavin 'ee was 'ealtee,
and he don't cause no trouble.   2585
That's what's devastating me now.
Sometime it make me feel like it's no justice,
like, uh,
the Jewish people,
they are very high up,   2590
it's a very big thing,
they runnin' the whole show
from the judge right down.
And something I don't understand:
The Jewish people, they told me   2595
there are certain people I can not be seen with
and certain things I can not say
and certain people I can not talk to.
They made that very clear to me—the Jewish people—
they can throw the case out   2600
unless
I go to them with pity.
I don't know what they talkin' about.
So I don't know what kind of crap is that.
And make me say things I don't wanna say   2605
and make me do things I don't wanna do.
I am a special person.
I was born different.
I'm a man born by my foot.
I born by my foot.   2610
Anytime a baby comin' by the foot
they either cut the mother
or the baby dies.
But I was born with my foot.
I'm one of the special.   2615
There's no way they can overpower me.
No there's nothing to hide,
you can repeat every word I say.

Naomi Iizuka

Naomi Iizuka (b. 1965) took her B.A. from Yale University and her M.F.A. in playwriting at the University of California–San Diego, where her most well-known play, *Skin,* an inventive reimagining of Georg Büchner's *Woyzeck,* was produced in 1995, directed by Robert Woodruff. Since then, Iizuka has written a number of plays—including *Polaroid Stories, Language of Angels,* a collaboration with director Anne Bogart and the Saratoga International Theater Institute (SITI) company entitled *War of the Worlds, Aloha Say the Pretty Girls, Tattoo Girl,* and *Scheherazade*—and has won several prestigious awards for playwriting, including the PEN Center USA West Award for Drama. *36 Views* premiered at the Berkeley Repertory Theatre in 2001.

36 VIEWS

36 Views is an elegant meditation on the commodification of authenticity. In the play, Iizuka brings a series of narratives to bear on one another: the art-dealer Darius Wheeler's effort to discover and sell a unique Chinese antiquity, a woman's "pillow book" of erotic literary reminiscences; the journalist Elizabeth Newmann-Orr's attempt to catch and expose Wheeler in the theft of protected Asian antiquities; Setsuko Hearn's implication—as an art-history professor and expert on pillow books—in the savage politics of the art and the academic marketplaces; Claire Tsong's struggle to find a place for her own artwork, and its ambiguous implication in her "day job," restoring Asian masterpieces. Like Hokusai's thirty-six views of Mount Fuji, though, each of these narratives opens several perspectives on the relation between art and money, and the structures of power and representation it sustains. Much as art and money are exchangeable terms—"You spend all your time surrounded by all this 'art,'" Claire points out to Wheeler's assistant John, "and it's affecting your brain. Strip it all away, and all you have is money, jazzed up to make you think its something more than money"—so, too the relationship between the "real" and the "fake," the "authentic" and the

A scene from the 2002 Joseph Papp Public Theater production of Naomi Izuka's *36 Views.*

"forged" (is an original contemporary work of art that's sold as an antiquity necessarily a forgery?) is a convertible one in the play. Indeed, in the world of *36 Views,* everything is convertible, even human identity: as the play proceeds, several of the characters—some willingly, some reluctantly—undergo transformation. Several of these transformations are signaled by one of the play's fascinating formal elements: its use of some of the conventions of **KABUKI** performance. In scene 25, for example, Iizuka calls for a *bakkaeri,* a kabuki costume change in which the upper half of the costume falls over the lower half to reveal a new costume—transforming Claire in an instant. Throughout the play, scene and costume changes are assisted by *kurogo* performers, scene-changers dressed entirely in black, and Iizuka calls for a ritualized clapping of *ki* sticks, which "are used to accompany and highlight the emotional content of certain points in the play." Much as the stage design of the play calls for the projection of various artworks that change before our eyes, so Iizuka seems to imagine a stage that itself embodies the play's interplay of Eastern and Western perspectives, different means of claiming the authoritative reality of performance.

36 VIEWS

Naomi Iizuka

CHARACTERS

DARIUS WHEELER, *a dealer of Asian arts and antiquities*
SETSUKO HEARN, *an Assistant Professor of East Asian Literature*
JOHN BELL, *Darius Wheeler's assistant*
CLAIRE TSONG, *a restorer of Asian artifacts*
ELIZABETH NEWMAN-ORR, *a free agent*
OWEN MATTHIASSEN, *the Chair of an East Asian Studies Department*

"Only a part of what is perceived comes through the senses from the object; the remainder always comes from within."
—Matthew Luckiesh, *Visual Illusions*

The sound of wooden clappers is a convention taken from Kabuki theatre. They are used to accompany and highlight the emotional content of certain points in the play.

ACT ONE

SCENE I

Darkness. Suspended in the darkness is a hanging scroll with a painting of a Japanese woman in formal pose: Kamakura era, gilt background, a portrait of a lady. In the shadows is DARIUS WHEELER. *As he speaks, he becomes more and more visible.*

DARIUS WHEELER: True story. This is a true story.
     I'm in the middle of the Doi Larng mountain range, no-man's land between Thailand and Myanmar—Burma, end of what they call the old Elephant Trail—Kipling country, used to be—Now—well now it's something else.
     I'm talking early eighties, opium in every little village east of Mae Hong Son, opium not even the half of it—sapphires, ivory, pigeon blood rubies from the Mogok Valley—blackmarket all of it, and you could get a bullet in your brain trying to do business with these people. Some hop-head Palang with an M-16, he just blows you away on the spot, 'cause he thinks you're a white devil—
     Or a ghost—

The sound of the bamboo flute begins. SETSUKO HEARN *is revealed in Heian-era kimono, wig and white face paint. She begins to remove her makeup and wig.*

DARIUS WHEELER: 'Cause these tribal people, they hate ghosts—
     Or maybe, maybe he just doesn't like the look in your eye.
     Human nature—
     A little cultural miscommunication—
     And what are you going to do about it, you're in the middle of what they call the Shan state. There are no maps for this part of the world. You disappear and that's it, you're shit out of luck, head on a pole, tiger meat—
     Then again, you go in there, and you meet the right people, and maybe, say, you do some business with these people, and maybe, just maybe you come away with something so beautiful, something so incredibly beautiful, something you'd never find, not in a million years on the outside, and if you're lucky, if you're smart, you get yourself out of there in one piece. So I'm there with my Lahu guide, feeling lucky, tiny Shan village, waiting for my contact, friend of a friend . . .

DARIUS WHEELER continues to speak. His voice grows fainter, a distinct echo. The sound of the bamboo flute is joined by the sound of drums. SETSUKO HEARN *is turning. With each turn, a layer of kimono is removed. The music grows louder, the pace grows faster. The sound of wooden clappers. Silence. The sound of the bamboo flute continues, alone and unadorned.*

DARIUS WHEELER: Unbelievable what I saw that night: Song dynasty temple paintings, Kushan period buddhas almost two thousand years old. He had stuff from Angkor Wat, museum quality, objects there's no way he should've had, and I'm thinking, who are you? Who are you? Because the thing was, this was the thing, I knew, as soon I saw it, as soon as I touched it and held it in my hands, I knew it was real. No question in my mind, it was real, and if I had enough money, it was mine.

The sound of the bamboo flute ends. Hikinuki (a Kabuki costume change in which threads are pulled and the outer kimono falls away revealing a new costume underneath): SETSUKO HEARN *is transformed into an urban, late-twentieth-century Western woman. The sound of wooden clappers.*

SCENE II

Evening. SETSUKO HEARN *and* DARIUS WHEELER *in* WHEELER's *loft space. The space is divided by translucent shoji screens. The Kamakura-era painting, the portrait of the woman in formal pose, is prominently featured. Somewhere else in the space, a party is in progress: voices, music.*

DARIUS WHEELER: Beautiful, isn't it. Everything else I bought that night, I sold, made out like a bandit. This one I never had the heart to sell.
SETSUKO HEARN: Sentimental attachment?
DARIUS WHEELER: Call it an appetite for beauty.
SETSUKO HEARN: Ah. A connoisseur.
DARIUS WHEELER: A lover of beautiful things, absolutely.
SETSUKO HEARN: I see.
DARIUS WHEELER: Is that such a terrible thing to be? Don't we all gravitate towards beauty? Don't we all crave beautiful things? It's second nature, don't you think, an instinct almost. I don't know that we can help ourselves.
SETSUKO HEARN: A philosopher and also quite the renegade, it would seem.
DARIUS WHEELER: Oh, I don't know about that.

1271

SETSUKO HEARN: I think you're being modest, Mr. Wheeler. From what you've told me, I'm guessing you've had more than your share of adventures in the Orient.

DARIUS WHEELER: I have some tales to tell.

20 SETSUKO HEARN: I'm sure you do, all kinds of wild and woolly tales.

DARIUS WHEELER: Very wild, very woolly, yes.

SETSUKO HEARN: Let me guess: rickshaws and opium dens. A rendezvous with some shady characters on the back

25 streets of Hong Kong, Chinese Triad types, practitioners of kung fu. Or perhaps it was on the South China Sea, a foggy night, a sampan full of Malay pirates, inscrutable, ninja-like.

DARIUS WHEELER: Is it my imagination or are you making

30 fun of me?

SETSUKO HEARN: Am I?

DARIUS WHEELER: You know, I think you are.

SETSUKO HEARN: I'm afraid that tales from the Orient, there's this sort of wilted quality to them.

35 DARIUS WHEELER: Ah.

SETSUKO HEARN: I've offended you.

DARIUS WHEELER: No, on the contrary. The ridicule, the skepticism, I find it kinda bracing. So tell me, I'm curious: am I the biggest idiot you've ever met?

40 SETSUKO HEARN: Let's just say, you seem to be a man with a weakness for stereotype.

DARIUS WHEELER: Oh the kindness cut of all. You know, you look very familiar to me.

SETSUKO HEARN: Do I?

45 DARIUS WHEELER: I can't say from where. Maybe you look like someone else.

SETSUKO HEARN: Possibly.

DARIUS WHEELER: Jakarta? Sidney?

SETSUKO HEARN: I've never been.

50 DARIUS WHEELER: Are you sure?

SETSUKO HEARN: Very.

DARIUS WHEELER: Maybe you have an evil twin.

SETSUKO HEARN: Maybe I am an evil twin. People make mistakes, Mr. Wheeler. They misapprehend.

55 DARIUS WHEELER: I don't know why, but I feel as if I know you.

SETSUKO HEARN: You don't. Trust me. We're perfect strangers.

The sound of wooden clappers.

DARIUS WHEELER: Darius Wheeler.

60 SETSUKO HEARN: Setsuko Hearn.

DARIUS WHEELER: Please forgive me. I'm being a terrible host. Here I let you just stand there without any kind of refreshment, parched, no doubt. What are you drinking? I have this wonderful plum wine in honor of Utagawa.

65 Very light, very seasonal. The guy probably prefers single malt scotch, but what the hell. Plum wine? Good stuff.

SETSUKO HEARN: All right.

DARIUS WHEELER: Plum wine it is.

DARIUS WHEELER *prepares drinks, cracking ice with a pick.*

DARIUS WHEELER: Somehow I feel like you know a lot more

70 about me than I know about you.

SETSUKO HEARN: Funny, I feel that way, too.

DARIUS WHEELER: So fill me in, Setsuko. Tell me something about yourself.

SETSUKO HEARN: There's nothing really to tell, I'm afraid. My life is very humdrum compared to yours. Very unevent- 75 ful, very tame.

DARIUS WHEELER'*s hand slips. A cut.*

SETSUKO HEARN: Are you all right?

DARIUS WHEELER: A little cut. It's nothing.

SETSUKO HEARN: Are you sure?

DARIUS WHEELER: Yeah, no, it's fine. 80

SETSUKO HEARN: You know, I actually found your story very entertaining, Mr. Wheeler.

DARIUS WHEELER: Darius, please, and don't be kind. I'll just think you're feeling sorry for me.

SETSUKO HEARN: No, but I did. Truly. It was very, I don't 85 know, very sort of Hunter S. Thompson meets *Apocalypse Now.* I mean that in the best possible sense.

DARIUS WHEELER: Say no more, please. I think I get the picture. (*Handing* SETSUKO HEARN *her drink.*) Dozo.

SETSUKO HEARN: Thank you. 90

The sound of wooden clappers.

SETSUKO HEARN: (*Reapproaching the portrait.*) This really is, it's exquisite. I'm guessing what? Kamakura period?

DARIUS WHEELER: Very good. Takanobu.

SETSUKO HEARN: Rings a bell.

DARIUS WHEELER: Portrait painter. Late twelfth century. 95 Painted on silk. Japanese painting, up to that point, the human face, you know, it was just a mask. A line here, a line there, two dots. Takanobu, he was after this thing, to make something life-like. To create this thing that was real. Their eyes, everything that was going on in their eyes. The way 100 the light hits the skin. The shape of the mouth. Kampai.

DARIUS WHEELER *and* SETSUKO HEARN *drink. Light shift. The objects in* WHEELER'*s loft space are revealed. Objects that look like works of art.*

SETSUKO HEARN: It's good.

DARIUS WHEELER: Umeshu, they call it.

SETSUKO HEARN: Yes, no, I love umeshu. Ume, it means summer plums. By themselves, they're bitter, but once they've 105 aged in the shochu, the spirits, they become very sweet. It's really, it's lovely. Please, I don't want to keep you from all your other guests.

DARIUS WHEELER: Don't worry. I don't know half the people out there. Trust me, I won't be missed. So what did you 110 think of the show tonight? What do you think of Utagawa's work?

SETSUKO HEARN: I like it. I like the sensibility, the painterliness, and the scope, the sheer size of the canvases, the ambition. I like the way he mixes Asian and Western forms, 115 the way he deploys classical techniques, and yet his vision is so unconventional, so contemporary in a way—I'm curious: how do you know Utagawa?

DARIUS WHEELER: I don't. I've never met the man. I'm hosting this little get-together as a favor for an old friend. 120

SETSUKO HEARN: That's nice of you.

DARIUS WHEELER: I have my moments. He, like you, is quite a fan.

SETSUKO HEARN: And you are not.
125 DARIUS WHEELER: No.
SETSUKO HEARN: And why is that do you suppose?
DARIUS WHEELER: Who can say? A question of taste.
SETSUKO HEARN: Not Oriental enough for you?
DARIUS WHEELER: It's just one white man's humble opinion.
130 SETSUKO HEARN: You're a traditionalist?
DARIUS WHEELER: Let's just say I have high standards.

The sound of wooden clappers.

SETSUKO HEARN: (*Approaching an art object.*) Chinese?
DARIUS WHEELER: Liao dynasty. The goddess Guanyin. That's
    an Udayana Buddha, eighth-century Korean, Silla dynasty,
135   gilt bronze. That's a, that's a Muromachi ink painting. Six-
    teenth century, Unkoku school, you can see what they call
    suiboku, or splashed ink technique, very unusual, very ab-
    stract. I got it at a private auction in Kyoto. No catalog, no
    previewing, some of the stuff is in really bad shape, but
140   every so often, you find a gem. I got it for a song. Do you
    like it?
SETSUKO HEARN: Very much.
DARIUS WHEELER: Here, wait, let me show you, I want to
    show you something else.

DARIUS WHEELER *retrieves a jade figure from its case. The sound of
the bamboo flute begins.*

145 DARIUS WHEELER: Jade. Sung dynasty era, over nine hundred
    years old. Very rare. Because the thing about jade, it's
    meant to be held, you see, and what it does, it warms to
    your skin, human touch, it alters the stone, there's a kind
    of chemical reaction, it actually changes the color of the
150   stone. With each touch it changes over time, almost im-
    perceptible, impossible to replicate. Very old jade like this,
    it comes in these translucent colors I can't describe—
    beautiful, unimaginably beautiful.

DARIUS WHEELER *holds out the jade figure.*

DARIUS WHEELER: Here. Feel.

SETSUKO HEARN *touches the jade. Their hands touch.* DARIUS
WHEELER *and* SETSUKO HEARN *recede from view.*

SCENE III

Light on JOHN BELL. *The sound of the bamboo flute continues. As*
JOHN BELL *speaks,* CLAIRE TSONG *is revealed. She's reading from a
transcript.* JOHN BELL *is the voice behind the words she reads:*

JOHN BELL:
    A list of beautiful things:
    The curve of a lover's neck, delicate, white.
    The touch of a lover's finger tips.
5   The weight of a lover's hair, the scent: clove and
        sandalwood.
    The rustle of silk undone,
    Warm breath against one's skin—

The sound of wooden clappers. CLAIRE TSONG *and* JOHN BELL *see
each other from across the space.*

CLAIRE TSONG: John?
JOHN BELL: Claire?   10

The sound of wooden clappers. The sound of the bamboo flute ends.

SCENE IV

*A desk is revealed. The desk is covered with papers, catalogs, slides,
pens, paints, paintbrushes and books.* JOHN BELL *starts sifting
through papers on the desk.* CLAIRE TSONG *approaches him.*

JOHN BELL: What are you doing here?
CLAIRE TSONG: Crashing the party. So where's Utagawa?
JOHN BELL: I don't know, I don't know where he is.
CLAIRE TSONG: Did you see him at the show?
JOHN BELL: No, he was running late. I got a message from his 5
    assistant. He was supposed to come directly here.
CLAIRE TSONG: Looking for something?
JOHN BELL: I wrote his assistant's number on this little piece
    of paper. I thought I left it here. Goddamnit.
CLAIRE TSONG: (*Holding up the transcript she was reading earlier.*) 10
    What's this?
JOHN BELL: Nothing.
CLAIRE TSONG: Where's it from?
JOHN BELL: Nowhere. (*Taking the transcript.*) Can you please
    not touch my stuff please, Claire, thank you.   15
CLAIRE TSONG: John—
JOHN BELL: I have to go.
CLAIRE TSONG: Oh come on, John. John—

JOHN BELL *exits.* ELIZABETH NEWMAN-ORR *enters.*

ELIZABETH NEWMAN-ORR: Cheers.
CLAIRE TSONG: Cheers.   20
ELIZABETH NEWMAN-ORR: It's so crowded out there. I
    needed some air. I was feeling a little flushed. Do you hap-
    pen to know where Mr. Wheeler is by any chance?
CLAIRE TSONG: No, I don't.
ELIZABETH NEWMAN-ORR: I'm an old friend of his.   25
CLAIRE TSONG: He's got a lot of old friends. He's a very
    friendly guy. Make yourself at home. I'm sure he wouldn't
    mind.
ELIZABETH NEWMAN-ORR: Thanks.

ELIZABETH NEWMAN-ORR *scans the works of art.*

ELIZABETH NEWMAN-ORR: So what do you like?   30

CLAIRE TSONG *studies the art objects, then picks one.*

CLAIRE TSONG: I like this. It's nice. A little showy, but nice.
ELIZABETH NEWMAN-ORR: Is it real?
CLAIRE TSONG: I guess it all depends on how you define real.
ELIZABETH NEWMAN-ORR: That's being a little coy, don't you
    think.   35
CLAIRE TSONG: It's old. It's painted by the guy it's supposed
    to be painted by. I guess that makes it real. Most of the
    time with a fake, it's pretty obvious. There's something re-
    ally stupid going on, something that doesn't make sense.
    Wrong materials, shoddy workmanship.   40
ELIZABETH NEWMAN-ORR: What about the fake that looks
    real?
CLAIRE TSONG: Uh-huh. It happens.

ELIZABETH NEWMAN-ORR: I take it you can tell the differ-
45   ence.
CLAIRE TSONG: I can.
ELIZABETH NEWMAN-ORR: How?
CLAIRE TSONG: Because I'm very very good.
ELIZABETH NEWMAN-ORR: And what is it you do?
50   CLAIRE TSONG: I'm an artist actually. Mixed-media.
ELIZABETH NEWMAN-ORR: That's a big, broad category. It
    could mean all kinds of things.
CLAIRE TSONG: Yes.
ELIZABETH NEWMAN-ORR: (*Referring to another art object.*)
55   Real?
CLAIRE TSONG: Iffy.
ELIZABETH NEWMAN-ORR: It looks real.
CLAIRE TSONG: Lots of things look real. You go to a mu-
    seum, it all looks real. And don't get me started on auc-
60   tion houses. What a shell game those guys are running.
    You wouldn't believe the crap that cycles through, third-
    rate counterfeits somebody paid a lot of money for, and
    now they gotta pawn it off on somebody else, or else end
    up eating the loss.
65   ELIZABETH NEWMAN-ORR: You sound like an expert.
CLAIRE TSONG: It's not about expertise. It's all about the eye.
ELIZABETH NEWMAN-ORR: The eye? That sounds so hoodoo.

The sound of the bamboo flute begins. In the foreground SETSUKO
HEARN *and* DARIUS WHEELER *begin to come into view. They reconstruct the pose that they were in last. The pose becomes real,
fleshed out.*

CLAIRE TSONG: It's like it's physical, you know, I'm talking
    about a physical sensation, an instinct. It's like there's an
70   invisible thread between you and this thing—I don't
    know. It's hard to explain, it's not objective, it's irrational,
    it's completely irrational. You can't quantify or predict it.
    You just know, all of a sudden you know.

The sound of wooden clappers.

SCENE V

The sound of the bamboo flute continues. JOHN BELL *and* OWEN
MATTHIASSEN *appear.* JOHN BELL, OWEN MATTHIASSEN, CLAIRE
TSONG, ELIZABETH NEWMAN-ORR, DARIUS WHEELER *and* SET-
SUKO HEARN *are figures in a woodblock print, flesh figures in a
floating world. The sound of wooden clappers.* DARIUS WHEELER
and CLAIRE TSONG *see each other. It's a moment of nagashime (a
sideways glance as seen in old woodblock prints of Kabuki actors).
The sound of wooden clappers. The sound of the bamboo flute ends.*

SCENE VI

The woodblock print suddenly dissolves into movement. CLAIRE
TSONG, ELIZABETH NEWMAN-ORR *and* JOHN BELL *exit in different directions. The sound of a party in progress.*

OWEN MATTHIASSEN: Darius—
DARIUS WHEELER: Owen—
SETSUKO HEARN: Dr. Matthiassen—
OWEN MATTHIASSEN: Setsuko, my dear, I'm so glad you made
5   it. Utagawa should be here any minute now. Darius, what
    are you drinking?

DARIUS WHEELER: Plum wine.
OWEN MATTHIASSEN: Umeshu, how delightful.
DARIUS WHEELER: You're in fine spirits, Owen.
OWEN MATTHIASSEN: I am, I am. I'll have a drop, if it's not   10
    too much of a bother.
DARIUS WHEELER: Not at all.

DARIUS WHEELER *prepares a drink.*

OWEN MATTHIASSEN: Darius, you've outdone yourself. I just
    ran into an old friend of mine from Waseda I haven't seen
    in ages, and some woman from the consulate, turns out I   15
    knew her father. I see you've met my brilliant young col-
    league.
DARIUS WHEELER: I have. I had no idea.
SETSUKO HEARN: Dr. Matthiassen is too kind.
OWEN MATTHIASSEN: Dr. Hearn is a shining star in our de-   20
    partment. We're incredibly lucky to have her join our
    ranks. Almost lost her to Stanford, you know.
SETSUKO HEARN: You are really, really too kind.

DARIUS WHEELER *gives* OWEN MATTHIASSEN *his drink.*

OWEN MATTHIASSEN: What happened to your hand.
DARIUS WHEELER: Nothing.   25
OWEN MATTHIASSEN: Darius, you're hemorrhaging.
DARIUS WHEELER: I'm fine, Owen, I'm fine. (*To* SETSUKO
    HEARN.) So what are you working on exactly?
OWEN MATTHIASSEN: Dr. Hearn's field of expertise is writing
    from the eleventh century, diaries, memoirs, pillow books   30
    written by women of the Heian era. How the writer
    speaks in her most private moments, depictions of her in-
    terior life, the private self.
DARIUS WHEELER: That doesn't sound humdrum at all.

SETSUKO HEARN *turns away, approaching an art object.*

OWEN MATTHIASSEN: Humdrum? Hardly. Where did you get   35
    that idea? One the contrary, it's fascinating, the feminine
    vernacular in the golden age of Japanese literature. Some
    wonderful women writing back then: Sei Shonagon,
    Izumi Shikibu—
DARIUS WHEELER: Lady Murasaki.   40
SETSUKO HEARN: Very good.
OWEN MATTHIASSEN: *The Tale of Genji.* Darius, I'm im-
    pressed. Have you read it?
DARIUS WHEELER: I have not.
OWEN MATTHIASSEN: Oh, but you must.   45
SETSUKO HEARN: You'd like it.
DARIUS WHEELER: Would I?
OWEN MATTHIASSEN: It's very engaging. Romance, intrigue.
    Some fine translations out there—Waley's always good,
    accessible, surprisingly modern, I find.   50
DARIUS WHEELER: Owen, I haven't read a book in over a
    decade.
OWEN MATTHIASSEN: Nonsense.
DARIUS WHEELER: Sad, but true. I'm a philistine, Owen.
    You've just always been too polite to notice. I had no idea 55
    I was conversing with such a shining star. I have to say, I
    feel a little out of my depth in such learned company.
OWEN MATTHIASSEN: Oh you do not. Don't listen to a word
    he says. (*Joining* SETSUKO HEARN.) Breathtaking, isn't it?

Nobody has this kind of stuff anymore. I don't know how
60 he does it. Fantastic pieces, uncanny really. Good eye. I
have to say, I take a little pride in my contribution to all
of it. I've known Darius for ages, you know.
SETSUKO HEARN: You studied with Dr. Matthiassen?
OWEN MATTHIASSEN: Oh no no no. Darius has never been
65   much for the academic life, I'm afraid.
DARIUS WHEELER: I was a lazy bum, dropped out of school,
never made it through my second year.
SETSUKO HEARN: It doesn't seem to have held you back.
OWEN MATTHIASSEN: An understatement, my dear, you have
70   no idea. He's done fabulously well. I always knew he
would.
DARIUS WHEELER: Owen is an eternal optimist.
OWEN MATTHIASSEN: I'm a fantastic judge of human nature.
The man leads a charmed life. I envy you, Darius, I do,
75   surrounded by things most of us only see in picture
books. A nice life. I could think of a lot worse. You have
an eye for beautiful things.
DARIUS WHEELER: I like to think so.
SETSUKO HEARN: You don't care for Utagawa's work, how-
80   ever.
OWEN MATTHIASSEN: Darius despises contemporary art. He's
very contrary, willfully anachronistic.
DARIUS WHEELER: I like his shunga.
OWEN MATTHIASSEN: Ah, yes, his erotic prints.
85 SETSUKO HEARN: And why is that, do you suppose?
OWEN MATTHIASSEN: They're very, very vulgar.
DARIUS WHEELER: Exactly. They're honest. They're getting at
something basic and real.
OWEN MATTHIASSEN: The more graphic, the less beautiful, I
90   find.
DARIUS WHEELER: I don't think Utagawa's about beauty,
Owen. I think that's precisely the problem. I think he's
about making a point. He's about ideas, his art is all about
ideas, ideas about ideas.

Enter JOHN BELL.

95 OWEN MATTHIASSEN: I disagree entirely.
JOHN BELL: Mr. Wheeler—
DARIUS WHEELER: It's just a series of abstractions tarted up to
look like art.
OWEN MATTHIASSEN: I disagree, I have to disagree.
100 JOHN BELL: Mr. Wheeler—
DARIUS WHEELER: I mean the guy's got craft, I'll give him
that. Technically, he's great, but what he has to say—I
wonder why it is that he can't just make a beautiful thing
and leave it at that.
105 SETSUKO HEARN: I wonder what you mean when you say
beautiful.

The sound of wooden clappers.

DARIUS WHEELER: Beautiful means beautiful.
SETSUKO HEARN: That's something of a dead end, don't you
think?
110 DARIUS WHEELER: No, no I don't.
SETSUKO HEARN: It's so absolute.
DARIUS WHEELER: Of course, it is. It has to be. What are you
left with otherwise.

The sound of wooden clappers.

JOHN BELL: Mr. Wheeler—
DARIUS WHEELER: I'm sorry—John, what is it?   115
JOHN BELL: I just spoke with Utagawa san's assistant just now,
and it seems—well, it seems that he won't be able to make
it this evening.
OWEN MATTHIASSEN: What do you mean? I spoke to his assistant on the phone just this afternoon.   120
JOHN BELL: Something came up apparently, some sudden
obligation he couldn't get out of. He sends his sincere
regrets.
OWEN MATTHIASSEN: I see. How disappointing. I was so
looking forward to meeting the man in person. Although   125
I guess I shouldn't be surprised. I hear he's somewhat of a
recluse, you know. Poor Darius, putting this whole
evening together, loathe his work as you do. We should
tell the other guests.
DARIUS WHEELER: I'll take care of it.   130
OWEN MATTHIASSEN: Well, there's nothing to be done. Another time perhaps. Life is full of the unexpected, best to
be flexible, I find. At any rate, what a delight, my dear, to
find you here. Here, let's go this way. I want you to see this
mandala painting—Nepalese, thirteenth century—when I   135
first saw the thing, I was complete stupefied . . .

OWEN MATTHIASSEN *and* SETSUKO HEARN *exit.* DARIUS
WHEELER *and* JOHN BELL *remain. The sound of wooden clappers.*

SCENE VII

The party begins to dissolve. Guests begin to exit into the night.
DARIUS WHEELER *begins to exit after* OWEN MATTHIASSEN *and*
SETSUKO HEARN. *Enter* ELIZABETH NEWMAN-ORR.

DARIUS WHEELER: All right let's wind this up, shall we. John,
can you make an announcement: The guest of honor is a
no-show. Everybody just go home.
JOHN BELL: Mr. Wheeler, one more thing.
DARIUS WHEELER: Yeah, John, what? What is it?   5
ELIZABETH NEWMAN-ORR: Mr. Wheeler, Elizabeth Newman-
Orr. It's a pleasure. You have a beautiful space here, so many
beautiful things.
DARIUS WHEELER: Thank you. Do I know you?
ELIZABETH NEWMAN-ORR: I'm a friend of Utagawa's. I'm ac-   10
tually, I'm more of a friend of a friend, really an acquain-
tance, I'm more of an acquaintance.
DARIUS WHEELER: I see.
ELIZABETH NEWMAN-ORR: I lie.
DARIUS WHEELER: I see.   15
ELIZABETH NEWMAN-ORR: I'm uninvited. I know no one.
You've found me out, I'm afraid.
DARIUS WHEELER: I won't tell. Now if you'll excuse me.
ELIZABETH NEWMAN-ORR: Mr. Wheeler, if I could, I was
speaking just now with your assistant. I was hoping you   20
and I could find a time to meet, tomorrow perhaps. I have
a small matter I was hoping to discuss with you.
DARIUS WHEELER: Tomorrow's kinda tight for me.
ELIZABETH NEWMAN-ORR: I believe you'll find it worth your
while.   25
DARIUS WHEELER: And should I trust your judgment?

ELIZABETH NEWMAN-ORR: I'm a woman of unerring judgment.

DARIUS WHEELER: I'm intrigued. Should I be intrigued?

30 ELIZABETH NEWMAN-ORR: I think so. I'll be glad to explain everything at length. Tomorrow perhaps?

DARIUS WHEELER: So eager. All right, look, why don't you set something up with John. Now if you'll excuse me.

ELIZABETH NEWMAN-ORR: Of course. Good night, Mr.
35 Wheeler.

ELIZABETH NEWMAN-ORR and JOHN BELL exit. The sound of a party breaking up. Kurogo, stage assistants in black over-costumes, remove props and scenery. The sound of wooden clappers. OWEN MATTHIASSEN enters holding a portfolio.

OWEN MATTHIASSEN: Darius, a word with you.

SCENE VIII

Light shift. Late evening. OWEN MATTHIASSEN and DARIUS WHEELER occupy a sliver of light.

DARIUS WHEELER: Where did Dr. Hearn go?

OWEN MATTHIASSEN: She had to leave, the lateness of the hour.

DARIUS WHEELER: What a pity.

5 OWEN MATTHIASSEN: She said to tell you that she had a lovely time. Marvelous girl, isn't she? Very smart, humbling really, and so young. My God, I remember being that young. I remember it vividly. How did I get to be so old?

DARIUS WHEELER: You're not that old.

10 OWEN MATTHIASSEN: I'm ancient. It's ridiculous.

DARIUS WHEELER: You're young at heart.

OWEN MATTHIASSEN: Don't condescend, Darius. It's not nice.

DARIUS WHEELER: What do you have there, Owen? One of Utagawa's sly little "Masterpieces."

15 OWEN MATTHIASSEN: Out of my price range, I'm afraid. No no, something else. Very exciting. More to your taste, I assure you. Stumbled upon it today, private gallery, little hole in the wall, one of those things, at the right place, at the right time. Here take a look.

A woodblock print is revealed. A reproduction of a woodblock print. Larger than life. OWEN MATTHIASSEN and DARIUS WHEELER appear as tiny human figures in the foreground of Hokusai's landscape.

20 OWEN MATTHIASSEN: Hokusai for Chrissakes. When I first saw it, I couldn't believe my eyes. Fuji from Kajikazawa. First edition, not cheap, but fair, more than fair, and all things considered, in pretty good shape, some water damage, it's true, and the colors' faded a bit, but other than
25 that—I mean, good Lord, almost two hundred years old. Paper. Can you imagine. It's a miracle it hasn't sustained worse damage. Survival is a kind of beautiful thing, isn't it. After all these years. Look at the mountain through the mist, the composition. Gorgeous, just gorgeous.

30 DARIUS WHEELER: Owen, this is a fake.

OWEN MATTHIASSEN: What are you talking about?

DARIUS WHEELER: It's good. I mean, whoever did this is pretty good.

OWEN MATTHIASSEN: Well, I know you're the expert, but I
35 like to think I know a thing or two. For God's sakes, I've

been collecting prints for years. Look at the water marks, the publisher's seal. The artist's hand is proof enough, the vigor and delicacy of the lines, the weight of detail. I'm telling you, I've examined this print. I've studied it. I know what it looks like. I know what it should look like. 40

DARIUS WHEELER: It's nice, Owen.

OWEN MATTHIASSEN: Nice? It's not just nice. It's spot on.

DARIUS WHEELER: Whoever the artist is, he knows what he's doing. The only problem is: whoever he is, he's not Hokusai. Look at the color. Look at it, really look. 45

The colors of the woodblock print slowly transform, becoming unnaturally bright and lurid.

DARIUS WHEELER: The color is a dead giveaway. It's all wrong. I don't care how much you distress it, underneath the stain, whatever this is, tea stain, coffee grounds, ash, it's way too bright, way too brassy. Look at these blues. Aniline pigment, artificial, inorganic, imported to Japan 50 from Germany. This print dates—or should date—from the 1830s. This kind of pigment wasn't introduced into Japan until the mid-1850s. We're talking twenty years after the fact. The print's nice, Owen. It just happens to be fake.

OWEN MATTHIASSEN fades away. The sound of wooden clappers. Light on CLAIRE TSONG in a distant corner of the space.

SCENE IX
A Disclaimer in Fine Print

CLAIRE TSONG: The vendor will not be responsible for the correctness of description, authenticity, or any defect or fault in or concerning any article, and makes no warranty whatever, but will sell each object exactly as is, without re- 5 course.

The sound of wooden clappers.

CLAIRE TSONG: Always read the fine print. There is always fine print.

The sound of the bamboo flute begins. CLAIRE TSONG and the woodblock print fade away. DARIUS WHEELER remains.

SCENE X

Pre-dawn light. The sound of the bamboo flute continues. A kurogo enters. His face is wrapped in black fabric. He carries a large rectangular panel covered by a drop cloth. He puts the panel down, then removes the cloth, revealing an Edo-period screen. On the screen is a painting of a garden in autumn.

The sound of wooden clappers.

The kurogo begins removing his black over-costume. DARIUS WHEELER goes to the desk, and notices the transcript that CLAIRE TSONG was looking through earlier. He picks it up and reads. SETSUKO HEARN is revealed in a sliver of light.

DARIUS WHEELER: A list of beautiful things:

The curve of a lover's neck,
The touch of a lover's fingertips,
The weight of a lover's hair, the scent,
5   The rustle of silk undone,
Your tongue, your lips,
The taste: salt and wet,
Warm breath against one's skin.

The kurogo removes the last piece of fabric covering his face. The kurogo is revealed as JOHN BELL. *The sound of wooden clappers. The sound of the bamboo flute ends.* SETSUKO HEARN *vanishes.* DARIUS WHEELER *exits.*

SCENE XI

The day after the party. Mid-morning. WHEELER*'s loft space.* JOHN BELL *is examining the screen that he unwrapped in the previous scene.* CLAIRE TSONG *is packing up, putting away the dropcloth along with various paints and tools.*

CLAIRE TSONG: All right look it, you're not listening, or maybe I'm not making myself clear. I don't care what it looks like, what it seems to be. All this is, at the end of the day, is fine furnishing, bric-a-brac for the leisure class.
5   JOHN BELL: Last I looked, Claire, it was called art.
CLAIRE TSONG: I'm telling you, pal, it's all just capital.
JOHN BELL: Spare me, please.
CLAIRE TSONG: O.K., you know what your problem is? You romanticize this stuff. You spend all your time surrounded
10   by all this "art" and it's affecting your brain. Strip it all away, and all you have is money jazzed up to make you think it's something more than money—which it's not. That it has some kind of deep, spiritual aura because it's "art"—which it doesn't.
15   JOHN BELL: I know you don't believe that.
CLAIRE TSONG: I believe all kinds of things.

The sound of wooden clappers.

CLAIRE TSONG: So? What do you think? How does it look?
JOHN BELL: It's nice, Claire. This is really nice work.
CLAIRE TSONG: Is this a surprise?
20   JOHN BELL: What do you want me to say?
CLAIRE TSONG: That I'm brilliant, a genius, the best.
JOHN BELL: You're brilliant, a genius, the best.
CLAIRE TSONG: Fuck you.
JOHN BELL: You are, Claire. The restorations are really—
25   they're great. I know what this looked like before.
CLAIRE TSONG: Trashed. A lost cause.
JOHN BELL: Pretty much.

JOHN BELL *goes to the desk to cut* CLAIRE *a check.*

JOHN BELL: Listen, Wheeler has some other screens he'd like you to take a look at. Minor stuff: mildew damage, fading,
30   standard wear and tear.
CLAIRE TSONG: Wheeler can kiss my ass. Like I sit around waiting for him to kick down some crap for me to tinker with. Like I don't have better things to do.
JOHN BELL: Claire, it's way too early in the day.
35   CLAIRE TSONG: I don't even know why you still work for that guy. He's like the evil empire.

JOHN BELL: You work for him, too.
CLAIRE TSONG: I'm an independent contractor. There's a difference. I'm my own little business of which I am the boss. I do the work because I choose to.   40
JOHN BELL: Why? I mean, why do you choose to work for Wheeler?
CLAIRE TSONG: (*Taking the check.*) Imp of the perverse. I don't know. Who knows. I'm a masochist, I guess. Besides I'm subsidizing my own art—look, don't change the subject.   45
I'm trying to educate you. Somebody has to. This is about your future. These are economic realities I'm talking about.

CLAIRE TSONG *retrieves a can of spray paint. She begins to shake it.*

CLAIRE TSONG: How much does Wheeler pay you, if you don't mind me asking?   50
JOHN BELL: I don't like talking about money, Claire.
CLAIRE TSONG: Why?
JOHN BELL: It makes me feel awkward.
CLAIRE TSONG: Guilty?
JOHN BELL: No. I don't know. Maybe a little. I don't know.   55
CLAIRE TSONG: You act like it's a dirty word, and it's not. It's just a thing like any other thing. Don't mystify it. Don't do that to yourself. You should've quit a long time ago. It's so stupid. It doesn't make any sense.

CLAIRE TSONG *aims the spray paint can at the screen she has just restored.*

JOHN BELL: Claire—   60
CLAIRE TSONG: Would I be destroying it? Or restoring it?
JOHN BELL: Claire—
CLAIRE TSONG: How would I be affecting its market value? That's what Wheeler'd want to know. But now here's the thing: what if I happened to make it a better painting? Or   65
better yet, what if I made it so that you couldn't tell the difference?
JOHN BELL: Claire, please—
CLAIRE TSONG: Do you really want to spend the rest of your life worrying about market value? Because, frankly, I think   70
you're a lot more interesting than that.
JOHN BELL: Wait—

CLAIRE TSONG *sprays.* JOHN BELL *blocks the screen with his body. A flower of paint blooms on his shirt.*

CLAIRE TSONG: You're brilliant, for one thing. It's like your brain is a very big thing, and it's filled with all this knowledge. You try to hide it, but I'm so onto your game. You   75
know all this stuff, you don't even let on the half of it.
JOHN BELL: Yeah? What stuff do I know?
CLAIRE TSONG: Art, for one. Literature. Languages. You're like fluent in all these languages. What do you speak? No, wait, let me guess: Japanese. Uh-huh. Korean? Right. Chi-   80
nese—how many dialects? No, wait, let me: Mandarin, Hunan, Cantonese—
JOHN BELL: My Cantonese is really, really basic.
CLAIRE TSONG: Oh my God, John, stop it. You're learned. Step to it, buddy, you're really learned.   85
JOHN BELL: I have a masters in East Asian studies and an unfinished thesis that's never going to get finished. I happen

to know a few languages. I also happen to have a drawer-
ful of unfinished novels, and once upon a time, a long
90 time ago, I played the french horn.
CLAIRE TSONG: You're a Renaissance man.
JOHN BELL: Jack of all trades, master of none.
CLAIRE TSONG: John, honey, you gotta work on your self-
esteem. You're withering on the vine here. Wheeler's us-
95 ing you. Cheap, overeducated labor. What are you
anyway?
JOHN BELL: What am I? I don't know, Claire. That's so exis-
tential.
CLAIRE TSONG: What's your title?
100 JOHN BELL: I'm an assistant.
CLAIRE TSONG: And what does that mean exactly?
JOHN BELL: Uh, that I assist. Look, Claire, I like my job. And
I like Wheeler.

Enter DARIUS WHEELER.

JOHN BELL: The guy's like a legend, broke all the rules, and I
105 guess I kinda respect that.
CLAIRE TSONG: Please. Dealers are the scum of the earth, and
Wheeler's in a class all his own.
JOHN BELL: He's complex.
CLAIRE TSONG: He's a prick.
110 JOHN BELL: He's a complicated guy.
CLAIRE TSONG: He's a self-absorbed, narcissistic prick. He's
also a liar, a con artist, and a thief.

Enter ELIZABETH NEWMAN-ORR.

DARIUS WHEELER: I was at this party once in Boston, and this
attractive Asian woman comes up to me from out of
115 nowhere, and she just starts in on me—calls me a liar, a
con artist, and a few other choice names I'm not going to
share in mixed company. And people, you know, they're
starting to turn around and look, and before I know it,
right, she's hurling her drink at me, hard, you know, in my
120 face, and I hear the glass shatter, and the room goes silent,
and I feel a heat and a kind of stinging, and I reach up and
touch my face, and I look at my hand, and I see there's this
red liquid all over my fingers, and I'm thinking to myself,
Jesus Christ, I'm bleeding. Turned out to be tomato juice.
125 But for a second or two, I thought it was blood.

The sound of wooden clappers. JOHN BELL *and* CLAIRE TSONG
exit.

SCENE XII

Late morning. DARIUS WHEELER *and* ELIZABETH NEWMAN-ORR
remain.

DARIUS WHEELER: The world is full of crackpots. Most of
them are harmless, but then again you never know.
ELIZABETH NEWMAN-ORR: So what was the story? Who was
she?
5 DARIUS WHEELER: Who knows. A kook.
ELIZABETH NEWMAN-ORR: Your reputation, I have to say,
precedes you.
DARIUS WHEELER: And what exactly have you heard?
ELIZABETH NEWMAN-ORR: Nothing but praise.

DARIUS WHEELER: Is that right?
ELIZABETH NEWMAN-ORR: Praise tempered by maybe just a 10
little bit of envy.
DARIUS WHEELER: Look, I don't need to tell you, this busi-
ness is full of thwarted souls with nothing good to say
about anyone. I'm a lucky man. Some people have a prob-
lem with that. Don't get me wrong, I'm good at what I 15
do, but I'm also very lucky. That's all it really is, you know.
Dumb luck.
ELIZABETH NEWMAN-ORR: That's very modest of you.
DARIUS WHEELER: It's the God's honest truth.
ELIZABETH NEWMAN-ORR: How homespun. 20

ELIZABETH NEWMAN-ORR *moves toward the screen from the previous scene, the screen that* CLAIRE TSONG *restored.*

ELIZABETH NEWMAN-ORR: This is new.
DARIUS WHEELER: It's a beauty, isn't it? Just came in this
morning. Edo era. Museum quality, in mint condition.
ELIZABETH NEWMAN-ORR: What kind of restorations?
DARIUS WHEELER: Hardly any at all. 25

The sound of wooden clappers.

DARIUS WHEELER: Interested?
ELIZABETH NEWMAN-ORR: Another time perhaps.
DARIUS WHEELER: By then it'll be gone. It never pays to wait.
It's the nature of the business. Things move, they get
traded, they circulate. 30
ELIZABETH NEWMAN-ORR: I guess I'll just have to take my
chances. I'm curious: do you ever find yourself getting at-
tached to a particular object, something very special?
DARIUS WHEELER: Rarely.
ELIZABETH NEWMAN-ORR: I would find that hard, I think. 35
DARIUS WHEELER: Things come and go in this life. It's best
not to get too attached.
ELIZABETH NEWMAN-ORR: That's very Zen of you.
DARIUS WHEELER: What can I say? I'm a Zen kinda guy. Now
what can I do for you today? 40
ELIZABETH NEWMAN-ORR: Suppose there were a painting,
very ancient, very rare, part of a large, private collection in
Hong Kong. A Taiwanese banker and his Austrian wife.
DARIUS WHEELER: Villa on Lugard Road. A smallish collec-
tion, some nice lacquerware, Imari, tasteful, very tasteful. 45
ELIZABETH NEWMAN-ORR: Keeping track of the bodies?
DARIUS WHEELER: I'm a dealer, Ms. Orr. You never know
when someone's going to want to sell.
ELIZABETH NEWMAN-ORR: You know the painting I'm talk-
ing about. 50
DARIUS WHEELER: I might.
ELIZABETH NEWMAN-ORR: Suppose my client'd purchased
this painting in a private sale, and it turned out, unbe-
knownst to either seller or purchaser, that the painting was
a national treasure. 55
DARIUS WHEELER: Ah.
ELIZABETH NEWMAN-ORR: If authorities were to get wind of
the transaction, which they would, if we were to go through
more traditional channels of sale and transfer, the painting
would need to be returned to its country of origin. 60
DARIUS WHEELER: It's tricky these days.
ELIZABETH NEWMAN-ORR: I was given your name.
DARIUS WHEELER: Given my name by whom?

ELIZABETH NEWMAN-ORR: I'd rather not say.

65 DARIUS WHEELER: Ever mysterious. I like that quality in a woman. In a business associate, I like it less so. Now if you'll excuse me.

ELIZABETH NEWMAN-ORR: Can't we be candid with one an-
70 other, Mr. Wheeler? I'd like that so much. It would make everything so much easier.

DARIUS WHEELER: What are we talking about?

ELIZABETH NEWMAN-ORR: I think you have an idea.

DARIUS WHEELER: Why don't you spell it out for me?

ELIZABETH NEWMAN-ORR: The discreet transport of an ob-
75 ject from one place to another.

The sound of wooden clappers.

DARIUS WHEELER: Ah. I see. Well, now OK this is the thing, Ms. Orr, about the part of the world we're dealing with here, because it's all a little Cowboys and Indians, and that can go a lot of ways. You're talking tariffs and tea money,
80 never mind some government type getting a bug up his ass and throwing a wrench in the works. Now it used to be, you could go in, pick up almost anything. Nowadays, it's a different story. These people, they've gotten very touchy about their culture. They see us raiding their tem-
85 ples, pilfering their buddhas, and they get a little pissed off, understandably perhaps, and they confiscate our property, and more than that, they throw people like myself in jail for long and indeterminate prison sentences—have you ever spent time in a third-world jail, Ms. Orr?

90 ELIZABETH NEWMAN-ORR: Ten percent of the purchase price placed in an offshore account.

DARIUS WHEELER: You have got to be kidding me.

ELIZABETH NEWMAN-ORR: Fifteen percent.

DARIUS WHEELER: Twenty percent. Half up front, half upon
95 the object's arrival.

ELIZABETH NEWMAN-ORR: I think—I think that can be arranged.

ELIZABETH NEWMAN-ORR *exits.*

SCENE XIII

The sound of the bamboo flute begins. DARIUS WHEELER *returns to his desk and picks up the transcript he was reading earlier. He scans the pages.* SETSUKO HEARN *appears in a sliver of light. As she speaks, she becomes more visible, more real.*

SETSUKO HEARN:
No rain tonight, no moon, the air is perfectly still
Not even the faintest breeze stirs the leaves.
In the pool in the garden below, carp swim beneath the
5   surface—
Flashes of white in the murky green
Their bellies slick and wet—
The tickle of waterweed
The soft wet moss—
10 The curve of your neck, your fingertips
The rustle of silk undone—
Your mouth, your tongue
Your lips, the taste of your lips: salt, wet
The warmth of your breath against my skin
15 And I am seized with sudden longing.

The sound of wooden clappers. The sound of the bamboo flute ends.
SETSUKO HEARN *vanishes.*

SCENE XIV

Enter JOHN BELL *carrying files.*

DARIUS WHEELER: John?

JOHN BELL: Yes?

DARIUS WHEELER: What's this?

JOHN BELL: What's what?

DARIUS WHEELER: (*Holding up the transcript.*) This. What's this? 5

JOHN BELL: Oh. That. It's a, it's a—

The sound of wooden clappers.

SCENE XV

A History of Origins

JOHN BELL: It's a transcription.
Of a manuscript.
It turned up in a private library, and was sent to us for appraisal just the other day.
I've been meaning to tell you. 5
I've been translating it, looking into its provenance. Japanese, eleventh century. Heian era. A memoir or pillow book.
The author remains nameless, hard biographical data is, as is often the case, scant. The earliest known owner of the 10
document appears to have been a Dutch trader and some-time scholar by the name of Van Rijn, stationed on the is-land of Dejima in the seventeenth century. There's an oblique mention of it in a letter he wrote to his wife (I 15
have it on file). How or why he disposed of it remains un-clear. Regardless of the disposition, the document disap-pears for almost a century, resurfacing again in the first decade of the eighteenth century, when it was transferred along with various other scrolls. To a money lender in Edo. 20
Whose eldest son lost it one night in a single game of chance, to an affluent sake maker by the name of Sato (I found a reference in an article on the redistribution of capital in the Edo period by a French Marxist in the six-ties, his name escapes me). Sato presented the document 25
shortly thereafter to the celebrated courtesan Hanaogi, who kept it until her death, when it was appropriated by the proprietor of a local tea house in satisfaction of out-standing and unspecified debts.
Next we hear of it, it's in the possession of one Con- 30
stance Hooley, the daughter of Methodist missionaries from Buffalo, New York, transplanted to Japan in the 1880s to spread the word of the Lord—she makes passing mention of it in a small, self-published anthology of Japanese literature compiled by her on behalf of her ladies 35
church group. Upon the Reverend Hooley's death, Con-stance Hooley sells the document along with various other Asian antiquities to a Chinese shipping magnate by the name of Liu, who sells it shortly thereafter to a wealthy Englishman and amateur poet, one Thaddeus 40
Biddle, who happened to be touring the Orient on holi-day, in search of souvenirs. Biddle pays an astronomical

price by the standards of the day—he was, he writes "utterly enchanted by the work, besotted by its curious and ineffable beauty" (I'm quoting directly from his journal here.) He took the document along with the rest of his acquisitions back to Europe, where it eventually ended up in the hands of an antiquarian in Lyon, who bought it in the years preceding World War I, and sold it to a Scotsman in the spring of 1952, who bequeathed it to his nephew along with the rest of his private library in the fall of 1979. There is a bill of sale. The original's in pretty bad shape.

That's about the long and the short of it.

I don't know the whole story. I just translated it, that's all.

DARIUS WHEELER? Heian era?

JOHN BELL: Yes. A memoir of sorts. It actually partakes more of the zuihitsu genre, loosely translated: books of miscellany. A hybrid form consisting of lists, poems, memoir fragments and observations. A pillow book, if you will.

DARIUS WHEELER: What do you make of it? Is it authentic?

JOHN BELL: From what I can tell, it appears to be, yes.

DARIUS WHEELER exits with the transcript.

JOHN BELL: Mr. Wheeler, wait—

The sound of wooden clappers. CLAIRE TSONG *appears.*

CLAIRE TSONG: So what exactly did you tell him?

The sound of wooden clappers.

SCENE XVI

Late afternoon. The same day. DARIUS WHEELER's *loft.*

JOHN BELL: I lied. Claire, I lied. I can't believe this. What have I done? What was I thinking? I don't know what came over me. I was totally caught up in something else. I wasn't thinking. He caught me completely off guard. I panicked. I made up this stupid story right on the spot. It was like a reflex. It was like it wasn't even me doing the talking.

CLAIRE TSONG: And Wheeler?

JOHN BELL: He believed me. He believed every word out of my mouth.

CLAIRE TSONG: Wow. That is so—great.

JOHN BELL: What are you? Nuts? Don't you get it. I lied not just once or twice, but over and over and over again, and the thing is, I didn't even mean to do it, even as I was looking this guy right in the eye, this guy I look up to, this guy I like—I know you don't like him, but I do, I like the guy, Claire—and I'm telling him all these facts, except they're not facts, because I'm lying through my teeth, I just happen to be lying with this incredible degree of specificity. I don't know what came over me. This is so unethical. Not to mention illegal.

CLAIRE TSONG: Fraud.

JOHN BELL: Jesus Christ.

CLAIRE TSONG: Look, it's only illegal if he tries to sell it.

JOHN BELL: Oh my God, what have I done? Claire, what have I done? I can't believe this.

CLAIRE TSONG: How was it written?

The sound of wooden clappers.

CLAIRE TSONG: I mean I know it's a "translation," but your original, was it written in kanji or kana or what?

JOHN BELL: Kana, it was written in kana. Or more accurately speaking, onna moji, which is a kind of, it's a kind of, it's a kind of precursor to hiragana. Syllabic, purely syllabic.

CLAIRE TSONG: How close to contemporary Japanese?

JOHN BELL: There are, you know, there are echoes. I mean, the meanings of individual words have changed over time, and the usages, how the language sounds, the spoken language, and the syntax, the syntax is different, archaic, it's archaic, but the strokes, the strokes are pretty much the same, I mean the basic shape is identical, I mean virtually identical, I mean I guess it depends on how you define identical.

CLAIRE TSONG: (*Handing* JOHN BELL *a paintbrush.*) Here.

The sound of wooden clappers.

CLAIRE TSONG: Show me.

The sound of the bamboo flute begins. JOHN BELL *draws Japanese kana (Japanese lettering) with the paintbrush on a panel of the shoji screen. He writes* きれい. *He returns the paintbrush to* CLAIRE TSONG. *She mimics his strokes, and picks up where he left off. She continues to write. She creates the artifact. Darkness.*

SCENE XVII

A Translation

Japanese lettering etches itself into the void, strokes of ink on blank pages. The sound of the bamboo flute continues. SETSUKO HEARN *appears in a sliver of light. As she speaks,* DARIUS WHEELER *emerges from the darkness.*

SETSUKO HEARN: In the evening, I hear a tapping at my screen, like the sound of rain on the eaves, and yet there is no rain tonight. There is no moon. The air is perfectly still. Not even the faintest breeze stirs the leaves. Even the birds are silent in the trees. Within my chambers, the air is dark as ink. No words. Cool hands, warm breath against my skin. I cannot see your face. Is it Lord S. or is it another? In the pool in the garden below, carp swim beneath the water, flashes of alabaster and gold in the murky green, their bellies brush against the cool wet mud, the tickle of waterweed, slick and heavy, the soft wet moss. I hear them breathing in the dark, and I am seized with sudden longing.

DARIUS WHEELER:
A list of beautiful things:
The curve of a lover's neck: delicate, white.
The touch of a lover's fingertips.
The weight of a lover's hair, the scent: clove and
    sandalwood.
The rustle of silk undone—

SETSUKO HEARN:
Your mouth, your tongue, your fingertips,
The hollow of my neck,
The inside of my thigh,
The taste: salt and wet,
Warm breath against one's skin—

The sound of the bamboo flute changes tone. DARIUS WHEELER *recedes from view. Light on the screen that* CLAIRE TSONG *restored. A painting of a garden. It is an autumn scene: bares branches shrouded in mist. The painting of the garden in autumn begins to transform into a painting of a garden in summer: branches in bloom, ripe fruit, fireflies, a summer night.* OWEN MATTHIASSEN *and* ELIZABETH NEWMAN-ORR *become visible in slivers of light.*

OWEN MATTHIASSEN: I hear the ladies whispering of late. So many tongues fluttering all at once. It's as though I live in a nest of starlings. If I could, I would snip each wagging tongue, chop it into little bits, and feed the bits to the carp.

30 ELIZABETH NEWMAN-ORR: A secret not longer secret is like an oyster pried open.
How clumsy the blade, how strange the pearl.

SETSUKO HEARN: I have taken a new lover who is not without charms. Lord S. wonders why I am otherwise engaged
35 this evening. I tell him I am busy chanting sutras.

OWEN MATTHIASSEN:
A list of unsuitable things:
Gossip, slander, accusation.

ELIZABETH NEWMAN-ORR: I hear things, Lord S. says. Do
40 you? Rumors, he says. Do not take me for a fool. Do not tramp filth into my chambers. Lord S. asks if I am seeing another. Bad enough that he suspects and that I lie. Worse that I do not care.

SETSUKO HEARN: At night, my new lover whispers monstrous
45 things to me, too terrifying to imagine. I feel a tingling through my belly, a chill more pleasurable than words.

ELIZABETH NEWMAN-ORR: Who is this new lover? She is a lady of the fifth rank, new to court. I spied her at the moon-viewing, her sleeve spilled over the edge of her ves-
50 sel, and trailed across the water—crimson, vermilion, a sliver of white. Her skill with silk, I have found, is surpassed only by her skill in love. She is very skillful in love.

OWEN MATTHIASSEN: Why do you tell me these things. Why? I do not know.

55 SETSUKO HEARN: Faithless, I am a faithless creature. I received the letter in the morning on violet paper bound with plumeria. So exquisite I could not bear to open it.

The sound of the bamboo flute changes tone. JOHN BELL *becomes visible in a sliver of light.*

JOHN BELL: On the fifteenth day of the eighth month, we catch fireflies in the sleeves of our robes. They glitter
60 through the summer silk. Later, we play games of chance. A visiting sage entertains us with his parrot, a strange green bird who utters bits of wisdom.

OWEN MATTHIASSEN: Lord S. drinks too much rice wine, and comports himself poorly. His wife sends a reproachful
65 note the following morning. Her handwriting, I notice, is very poor.

SETSUKO HEARN: Some women are wives and mothers, I tell him. Some women choose different, less familiar paths. He calls on me several times afterwards. His letters moulder at
70 my door.

JOHN BELL: A list of unsuitable things:

ELIZABETH NEWMAN-ORR: A certain powerful man whose nose turns pink when he drinks. His wife, a well-born woman with the handwriting of a small, slow-witted child.

75 OWEN MATTHIASSEN: You are unreasonable and unkind.

SETSUKO HEARN: Am I? And why is it you may have as many lovers as you wish? Why am I wrong that I would wish to enjoy the same? Foolish to even ask. I wish I had been born a man.

JOHN BELL: But you are not a man. I think sometimes that 80
you forget.

SETSUKO HEARN: I do not forget.

JOHN BELL: Later as I pass her chambers, I hear the sound of weeping.

The sound of the bamboo flute changes tone. OWEN MATTHIASSEN *and* ELIZABETH NEWMAN-ORR *recede from view.* SETSUKO HEARN *and* JOHN BELL *remain. He echoes the italicized lines.*

SETSUKO HEARN: An inauspicious wind. My mood grows 85
worse with each passing day. *I am a terrible person, I think.*

A list of unsuitable things:
Leaving too quickly.
Also, staying too long.
This morning I hear the servants smashing snails with 90
wooden cudgels. *There is something very satisfying* in
the sound.
One night passes. And then a second, and then a third.
No word from Lord S. Another night and not a word.
The sound of footsteps on nightingale floors 95
The echo of the temple bell
All the words I have not spoken—
I dreamt last night, *the taste* of snow, the frozen river
What sleeps beneath the silent ice, *I wonder.*

JOHN BELL: Yesterday I tried to write. All day and night I 100
waited, but still the words would not come.

SETSUKO HEARN: How like an autumn leaf my passion, brittle and unlovely in its passing.

JOHN BELL: A list of unsuitable things:

SETSUKO HEARN: A new lover who is no longer new. 105

JOHN BELL: Hasty action followed by regret.

The sound of the bamboo flute changes tone. JOHN BELL *recedes from view.*

SETSUKO HEARN: We pass each other in the garden.
The blossoms have long been swept away.
The taste of your lips, now bitter as unripe plums.
You are my one heart's truth. Did I ever tell you this? Did 110
I ever speak this out loud? Would you have ever guessed?

The sound of the bamboo flute changes tone. DARIUS WHEELER *emerges from the shadows.*

SETSUKO HEARN: It was summer when I went to sleep last night, yet when I awoke this morning, it was all of a sudden fall. The smell of foxfires at daybreak, ice drops on the branches of the trees. In the hills near Higashiyama, I 115
heard a deer cry. I looked for you by the lake. There was a thick mist, I remember I could not see, and when I emerged from it at last, the leaves had all turned crimson in the night. Strange. Nothing is how it used to be.

The screen returns to its original image: a painting of a garden in autumn—bare branches shrouded in mist. The sound of wooden clappers. The screen vanishes. The sound of the bamboo flute ends. SETSUKO HEARN *and* DARIUS WHEELER *remain.*

SCENE XVIII

Light shift. Late afternoon of the same day. A corridor in the university. SETSUKO HEARN *is looking through the transcript of the pillow book.* DARIUS WHEELER *looks on.*

SETSUKO HEARN: Where did you get this?
DARIUS WHEELER: It was found in a private library. It was sent to us for appraisal by the owner. People send us stuff. Most of the time, it's not worth the cost of shipping, but every
5   so often, something comes your way. You never know.
SETSUKO HEARN: Who did the translation?
DARIUS WHEELER: My assistant.
SETSUKO HEARN: Working from the original?
DARIUS WHEELER: From photos. This whole thing, to be
10   honest, is kinda beyond my ken. My assistant gave me some background, smart guy, but he's a little naive in some ways. I thought I'd run it by you, see what you think.
SETSUKO HEARN: I don't know what to say.
DARIUS WHEELER: Worthless, huh? You know, I gotta say
15   I'm not surprised. I had a feeling. I thought I'd bring it by, what the hell. Look, to tell you the truth, what I really—
SETSUKO HEARN: No, wait. I don't think you understand.

The sound of wooden clappers.

SETSUKO HEARN: There's a quality, something in the voice, in
20   the writing, it's uncanny. The batsubun, the epilogue, the interpolation of standard seasonal metaphors of transformation and loss, something in the syntax, the diction, even in translation—Utamakura, literally poem pillow, or pillow book. Heian era, eleventh century. The number of
25   extant examples in the genre is practically nil. I don't know how I can articulate this to you. For something like this to turn up in this way, it would change everything, everything we thought we knew, all the assumptions we've made—well, it would, it would be premature to
30   speculate.
DARIUS WHEELER: But if it is, I mean if it is what it seems to be—
SETSUKO HEARN: I'd need to see more. I'd love to get my hands on the original, if I could. If I could just, if I could
35   examine the original. In the meantime, if I could take a look at those photos. The sooner the better.
DARIUS WHEELER: I'll get right on it.
SETSUKO HEARN: Forgive me.
DARIUS WHEELER: No, it would be my pleasure. I mean that.
40   SETSUKO HEARN: Thank you.
DARIUS WHEELER: So what are you doing now?
SETSUKO HEARN: I was just, I was going to go back to my office, do a little bit of work.
DARIUS WHEELER: Are you free for dinner? I know this place.
45   It's not far. Just a few blocks away from here. Nothing fancy. How does that sound?
SETSUKO HEARN: That sounds—nice. Listen, why don't you meet me out front. I need to stop by my office on the way out, make a quick call. I'll just be a minute.

The sound of a tape rewinding.

SCENE XIX

Light on ELIZABETH NEWMAN-ORR *removing hidden recording equipment taped to her skin.*

A fragment from a previous scene:

ELIZABETH NEWMAN-ORR: So what was the story? Who was she?

The sound of a tape rewinding.

DARIUS WHEELER: Hardly any at all.

The sound of wooden clappers.

DARIUS WHEELER: Interested?
ELIZABETH NEWMAN-ORR: Another time perhaps.   5
DARIUS WHEELER: By then it'll be gone.

The sound of a tape rewinding.

ELIZABETH NEWMAN-ORR: I was given your name.
DARIUS WHEELER: Given my name by whom?
ELIZABETH NEWMAN-ORR: I'd rather not say.

The sound of a tape rewinding.

ELIZABETH NEWMAN-ORR: Can't we be candid with one an- 10
other, Mr. Wheeler? I'd like that so much. It would make everything so much easier.
DARIUS WHEELER: What are we talking about?
ELIZABETH NEWMAN-ORR: I think you have an idea.
DARIUS WHEELER: Why don't you spell it out for me.   15

A phone begins to ring. ELIZABETH NEWMAN-ORR *exits. Enter* JOHN BELL.

SCENE XX

JOHN BELL *answers the phone in* DARIUS WHEELER's *loft. Light on* OWEN MATTHIASSEN.

JOHN BELL: Hello?
OWEN MATTHIASSEN: John, it's Owen Matthiassen. Is Darius there by any chance?
JOHN BELL: No, Dr. Matthiassen, I'm afraid he's left for the day.   5
OWEN MATTHIASSEN: I see. Well, John, maybe you can help me. I was on the phone just now with my colleague Dr. Hearn, and she mentioned the most fascinating thing. A manuscript that turned up. Japanese. Heian era. Apparently, Darius brought the translation around for her to 10
take a look at. I'm curious how he got a hold of the thing, where it came from, how it came to light. Do you know anything about this? You understand it could be immensely valuable, priceless even. Although I suppose everything eventually has a price.   15

The sound of wooden clappers. A dial tone.

OWEN MATTHIASSEN: Hello? John, are you still there? John?— John?—

The sound of a dial tone transforms into the sound of the bamboo flute. Light on the shoji panel where JOHN BELL *previously drew the Japanese kana. The sound of the flute grows, a single note sustained.* JOHN BELL *smashes his fist through the shoji panel, splitting the word apart. The sound of wooden clappers.*

End of Act One.

ACT TWO

SCENE XXI

Darkness. Scattered pages of paper are suspended in the darkness. The paper is distressed, ancient-seeming. The pages are dyed vermilion, rose, dayflower blue. Some are covered with a sprinkling of gold leaf and tiny Japanese kana. Light on CLAIRE TSONG. *She examines a page, takes a lighter out of her pocket, sets the page on fire, lets it burn, then blows it out. She retrieves a Polaroid camera. She takes a picture of the page. A flash. Darkness.*

SCENE XXII

A university lecture hall. OWEN MATTHIASSEN *and* SETSUKO HEARN *are backstage. The ambient sound of voices in the audience.*

OWEN MATTHIASSEN: I spoke with the dean this morning. Needless to say, he's taken a personal interest in the matter. I have to say I've never seen anything like it. I've been getting calls from all over the States, Europe, Japan. The 5 media interest is overwhelming. When is Darius getting a hold of the original?

SETSUKO HEARN: In the next day or so.

OWEN MATTHIASSEN: Good, good. I have to confess, this whole thing, I'm afraid it's a little beyond my scope of expertise. I'm more of a generalist, as you know. I guess that's 10 what they call us now—rather euphemistically, I suspect. We're a dying breed. We used to call ourselves Orientalists, and we studied the Orient. That's how old I am. It was a different time, I suppose, a different way of doing 15 things. It's exciting, this whole thing, it's all very exciting, and you should be, well, you should be pleased. So then I'll say a few words, and then you can give them a little bit of background, and then we'll take questions. Ready?

SETSUKO HEARN: Yes.

20 OWEN MATTHIASSEN: All right then—

OWEN MATTHIASSEN *goes onstage. The sound of the audience grows louder.* SETSUKO HEARN *remains backstage.*

SCENE XXIII

Light shift. Backstage of a press conference. OWEN MATTHIASSEN *is speaking into a microphone. He is a distant figure.* SETSUKO HEARN *remains in the foreground.*

OWEN MATTHIASSEN: Ladies—gentlemen—please—if I could have your attention—I cannot stress enough the significance of this manuscript. Even in its fragmentary state, its impact on our field of scholarship is immeasurable—

OWEN MATTHIASSEN *continues to speak. His words grow faint. The sound of wooden clappers. Silence.*

SCENE XXIV

A park near the university. Autumn. Crimson leaves, bare branches against the sky. SETSUKO HEARN *and* DARIUS WHEELER *are looking at Polaroids of the original manuscript.*

The middle of a conversation:

DARIUS WHEELER: There's some damage. You can see it, here and here. It's not the end of the world, but the sooner we can get a hold of it, get it in a climatized setting, the better.

SETSUKO HEARN: When do you think that will be?

DARIUS WHEELER: Tomorrow or the day after. Trust me. This 5 part I know.

SETSUKO HEARN: Over a thousand years old—it's like a dream. You dream about this sort of thing, that lightning will strike, and maybe you'll be lucky enough to be there when it does. At least I do. I mean, I have. I guess every- 10 body has at some point or another. Did you know—

DARIUS WHEELER: Tell me.

SETSUKO HEARN: Did you know that men of Heian-era Japan wrote in Chinese, a language not their own, and one in which most gained only, at best, a schoolboy profi- 15 ciency—

DARIUS WHEELER: Is that right—

SETSUKO HEARN: But Heian-era women, by contrast, wrote almost exclusively in their native tongue, allowing them, I think, a kind of emotional clarity, an immediacy, a seam- 20 less correspondence between the inchoate thought and the written word. One might even go so far as to say that because they wrote in their native tongue, they were able to write with a candor and transparency virtually impossible for their male contemporaries. 25

DARIUS WHEELER: Now that seems very, very doctrinaire.

SETSUKO HEARN: Perhaps. Let's say instead that they wrote without artifice. They wrote about their innermost feelings—feelings of restlessness, uncertainty, desire, doubt. Modern, almost modern in their insights, oddly familiar, 30 they wrote in a voice that was singular and unmistakably female—

The sound of wooden clappers.

SETSUKO HEARN: How is your hand?

DARIUS WHEELER *holds out his hand.*

SETSUKO HEARN: I can barely see where it was. What? What is it? 35

DARIUS WHEELER: Nothing. It's just you're so beautiful.

SETSUKO HEARN: I wonder how many women you've said that to. I'm guessing quite a few.

DARIUS WHEELER: What if I told you this was different?

SETSUKO HEARN: I don't think I'd believe you. 40

DARIUS WHEELER: You've got to be the most beautiful skeptic I've ever met.

SETSUKO HEARN: I'm afraid flattery needs to be a little more subtle than that.

DARIUS WHEELER: I know, I know how I sound. I know what 45 you're thinking, and you know what, normally you'd be right.

SETSUKO HEARN: But not now.

DARIUS WHEELER: No, not now. You don't believe me.

50 SETSUKO HEARN: What I believe is that there are words—

DARIUS WHEELER: Yes—

SETSUKO HEARN: And then there are the feelings and thoughts behind the words, and that the relationship between the two is neither reliable nor precise, nor is it

55 maybe meant to be—

DARIUS WHEELER: No?—

SETSUKO HEARN: No, and that maybe the space between what we say and what we do, what we see and what we feel, that it's necessary, the space where anything can hap-

60 pen. Chaos, confusion, terrible, terrible confusion—

DARIUS WHEELER and SETSUKO HEARN kiss.

SETSUKO HEARN: OK, you know what, this is really, this is not a good idea. I don't know you, and you don't know me, and whatever this is, it's based on nothing, a first impression.

65 DARIUS WHEELER: Love at first sight.

SETSUKO HEARN: Please.

DARIUS WHEELER: You don't believe in that.

SETSUKO HEARN: No. No, I don't.

DARIUS WHEELER: It's kinda old-fashioned.

70 SETSUKO HEARN: It's also very convenient.

DARIUS WHEELER: Look all I want—what I want—is for you to entertain, just for a second, the possibility that maybe what I'm saying to you, what I'm trying to say to you, that it's—

75 SETSUKO HEARN: What? The truth?

DARIUS WHEELER: Yes.

SETSUKO HEARN: Ah I see. What if we were truthful? What if we were good? What if desire were the same as love? What if it were all simple and clear?

80 DARIUS WHEELER: Maybe it is. Maybe sometimes it is.

SETSUKO HEARN: You know, I don't think so.

DARIUS WHEELER: How can you know for sure?

SETSUKO HEARN: Because nothing is easy. In the world I live in, nothing is ever that easy.

The sound of wooden clappers.

85 DARIUS WHEELER: I like you so much.

The sound of wooden clappers.

DARIUS WHEELER: Everything I say sounds like a line. I know that. I know that. I'm blowing it, aren't I?

SETSUKO HEARN: It depends on what you're trying to do.

DARIUS WHEELER: Make you like me just a little. Something

90 like that.

SETSUKO HEARN: I like you.

The sound of wooden clappers.

SETSUKO HEARN: It's that I look at you and I don't know what I'm seeing. What am I seeing?

DARIUS WHEELER: A deeply fucked-up individual.

95 SETSUKO HEARN: Is that right?

DARIUS WHEELER: The worst. And the funny thing is—this is the funny thing—he's fallen for this woman who happens to see through all his bullshit, this beautiful, brilliant

woman, and he can barely talk when he's around her, which I know is kinda hard to believe, but it's true, and I 100 know, I know right now he sounds like an idiot and a jerk, probably because he is an idiot and a jerk, and she should probably tell him to just get lost, but I really—I hope she doesn't, I really hope she doesn't.

DARIUS WHEELER and SETSUKO HEARN are very close. The sound of a phone ringing.

SCENE XXV

CLAIRE TSONG's work space. JOHN BELL is studying the pages form the top of the act. They're pages from the "original" manuscript, distressed paper, ancient-seeming, with Japanese lettering, colored paper sprinkled with gold leaf. CLAIRE TSONG is changing out of paint-spattered work clothes into dress clothes. She puts on makeup, fixes her hair, transforming herself. The phone continues to ring.

CLAIRE TSONG: Mulberry paper. Carbon-based ink. A little dirt, a little fire, a little tea—are you going to get that or what?

The phone stops ringing.

JOHN BELL: The calligraphy—

CLAIRE TSONG: Authentic. I know. 5

JOHN BELL: How did you do this?

CLAIRE TSONG: Honey, I'm just the midwife to your genius. Analyze the brushstroke. Hold it up to the light. I'm a very gifted girl. If you didn't know better, if you saw this under Plexiglas in some museum somewhere— 10

JOHN BELL: But it's not real.

CLAIRE TSONG: Isn't it? It looks pretty real to me.

JOHN BELL: It's not about what it looks like. It's about what it is. Eventually somebody's going to figure out the difference.

CLAIRE TSONG: And what if they don't? 15

The sound of wooden clappers.

CLAIRE TSONG: Provenance.

JOHN BELL: Claire—

CLAIRE TSONG: All you need to do is piece together a credible paper trail: a bill of sale, a catalog reference, cut and paste, some signatures— 20

JOHN BELL: It's not that easy. Do you have any idea how many calls we've been getting? Everybody wants to see the original.

CLAIRE TSONG: Good thing we have it.

JOHN BELL: No, Claire, no. We have no original because 25 there is no original, because even the so-called "original" is not an original.

CLAIRE TSONG: I guess it all depends on how you define "original."

JOHN BELL: You know, I define it the way I think most every- 30 body else does. It's the thing that's real as opposed to the thing that's fake. I think it's pretty clear-cut. Jesus Christ, what am I doing, what the hell am I doing? I feel like an imposter.

CLAIRE TSONG: That's because you are. 35

JOHN BELL: No, see, Claire, you're wrong. I'm not. This was not my idea. This was never my idea.

CLAIRE TSONG: No?

JOHN BELL: I didn't want this.

40 CLAIRE TSONG: You didn't want what? You didn't want to write what you wrote? You didn't want to get recognition for doing what you do? You didn't want to take credit for something you did for once in your life? Can you maybe own up, John, can you maybe try?

45 JOHN BELL: We're different, OK, we see things differently. I'm not like you.

CLAIRE TSONG: You know, I think you are. I think you're exactly like me. I just don't think you realize it yet.

The sound of wooden clappers.

CLAIRE TSONG: Just think of it as a little insurance policy.
50 Somebody sniffs it out, you say you were duped, no harm no foul. Look, it's not a crime unless money changes hands, unless you try to sell it.

JOHN BELL: I wish he'd never seen it. I don't know why I left it out in the first place. It was so stupid. I should've seen
55 this coming, I should've known. What was I thinking?

CLAIRE TSONG: What were you thinking?

The sound of wooden clappers.

CLAIRE TSONG: All right look it, Wheeler needs to buy before he can sell. In order to sell the manuscript—the "original," that is—he needs to own it, and he doesn't own it.

60 JOHN BELL: Not yet. He wants me to talk to the guy, a guy who doesn't exist, get him to sell a thing, a thing that doesn't exist. This is insane, this whole thing is insane.

CLAIRE TSONG: Do it. If Wheeler wants to buy it, let him. You pick the price. Just remember, make it steep. The
65 higher the price, the more desirable.

JOHN BELL: I don't believe you, Claire. What kind of person thinks like this? It's like you planned this whole thing from the start.

CLAIRE TSONG: Doll, I couldn't have planned this if I wanted
70 to. I just seized the day is all.

JOHN BELL: What about Wheeler?

CLAIRE TSONG: What about him?

JOHN BELL: I don't know, Claire—call me a nut, but I think he's maybe going to sue us, and then I think he's maybe
75 going to have criminal charges brought against us, and then I think we're maybe going to go to jail.

CLAIRE TSONG: That's not going to happen.

JOHN BELL: How can you be so sure?

The sound of wooden clappers.

CLAIRE TSONG: Because I know him. I know his mind, I
80 know how it works. I know him. He'd rather save face and eat the loss. Trust me. He's not going to say a word.

The sound of wooden clappers. Bukkaeri (a Kabuki costume-change in which the upper half of the costume falls down over the lower half revealing a new pattern.) CLAIRE TSONG's *appearance has completely transformed.*

JOHN BELL: Claire—

CLAIRE TSONG: Look, just talk to him, set it up, call me when you're done. (*Picking up the pages of the "original" manu-*
85 *script.*) Here, we don't want these lying around here, do we—What?

JOHN BELL: I don't know. Nothing. You just, I don't know, you look different.

CLAIRE TSONG: I just changed my clothes. That's all.

The sound of wooden clappers. CLAIRE TSONG *exits. A version of the Kitsune Roppo exit (a kind of Kabuki exit marked by leaps and bounds).* JOHN BELL *vanishes. The sound of the bamboo flute begins.*

SCENE XXVI

A Shunga

Shunga: an erotic woodblock print. The sound of the bamboo flute continues. Light shift. Two lovers in the shadows. Glimpses of naked flesh. The sound of breathing. A disembodied voice, faint and faraway, a recorded echo of what came before.

SETSUKO HEARN:
No rain tonight, no moon, the air is perfectly still
Not even the faintest breeze stirs the leaves.
In the pool in the garden below, carp swim beneath the
    surface—
Flashes of white in the murky green   5
Their bellies slick and wet—
The tickle of waterweed
The soft wet moss—
The curve of your neck, your fingertips
The rustle of silk undone—   10
Your mouth, your tongue
Your lips, the taste of your lips: salt, wet
The warmth of your breath against my skin—

SCENE XXVII

The sound of the bamboo flute continues. Light on OWEN MATTHIASSEN. *Visible behind him is the fake Hokusai print of Mount Fuji.*

OWEN MATTHIASSEN: Footnote number 27: Ibid, opus cit. Prevalent throughout the text is a sensibility the Japanese call "mono no aware," i.e., an awareness of imminent loss, a melancholic perspective one finds prevalent throughout the history of Japanese literature. Loosely translated,   5
"mono no aware" is the phenomenon by which one perceives the beauty of a thing only in the moment of recognizing its essential impermanence. Seasons pass. Flowers wither and die. Indeed, it is precisely this delimited life span which lends an object its beauty, which endows it   10
with value, and renders it precious—no, not precious, not precious—priceless—priceless in our eyes.

The sound of wooden clappers. The sound of the bamboo flute ends. OWEN MATTHIASSEN *and the fake print recede from view.*

SCENE XXVIII

Light on SETSUKO HEARN *and* DARIUS WHEELER. *They dress.*

DARIUS WHEELER: What was she like?

SETSUKO HEARN: We don't really know. The details of her life, the circumstances that brought her to court, her name even are all unknown. Which is often the case.

DARIUS WHEELER: I have this image of her in my mind.   5

SETSUKO HEARN: Do you? Well, we know—what do we know—we know her skin was very white, and that she whitened it further with a cream made from nightingale droppings. We know she plucked the entirety of her eye-
10 brows, and blackened her teeth, as was the fashion of the day, and that she wore multiple layers of kimono—colorful, complicated, coded in a language of symbols, hidden meanings, of which we have only inklings. The Heian-era court in which she lived was a highly literate,
15 highly aestheticized society. Like her peers, she spent her days writing poetry and preparing for the many festivals that marked the passing of the seasons. We know she was unmarried and during her time at court, she engaged in multiple romantic liaisons with both men and women.
20 This alone is a remarkable revelation. As an articulation of transgressive sexuality and a revisioning of gender stereo-types prevalent in a patriarchal culture—you know, I'm talking an awful lot.

DARIUS WHEELER: You have a lot to say.
25 SETSUKO HEARN: Yes. Yes, I co.

DARIUS WHEELER: What do you think happened to her? Af-terwards, I mean.

SETSUKO HEARN: Maybe she left the court and married a provincial lord. Maybe she lived her final years as a Bud-
30 dhist nun, chanting sutras in a temple. The fragment ends abruptly. We won't ever know with any degree of cer-tainty. We can only speculate.

DARIUS WHEELER: Do you think she was happy?

SETSUKO HEARN: I don't know. I'm not sure. Perhaps. I mean
35 I'm not sure I know what happy means.

DARIUS WHEELER: Happy means happy.

SETSUKO HEARN: Happy means happy, beautiful means beau-tiful. Oh to live in the world you live in. What a great world. Everything's so clear-cut, so simple.
40 DARIUS WHEELER: Sometimes things just are what they are, what they seem to be.

SETSUKO HEARN: So I've heard. What? What is it?

DARIUS WHEELER: I want very much, I want to make you happy.

The sound of wooden clappers.

45 SETSUKO HEARN: I need to go. I need to get back to work.

DARIUS WHEELER: What if I say, "I don't want you to."

SETSUKO HEARN: Then I would say, "But I have to."

DARIUS WHEELER: And I would say, "But I won't let you."

SETSUKO HEARN: Would you really say that?
50 DARIUS WHEELER: I might.

SETSUKO HEARN: Then I would say, "Unhand me, sir."

DARIUS WHEELER: "Unhand me"?

SETSUKO HEARN: Yes.

DARIUS WHEELER: I like that. It's quaint.
55 SETSUKO HEARN: I'm quaint.

DARIUS WHEELER: Are you quaint?

SETSUKO HEARN: Very very quaint. You'd be surprised.

SETSUKO HEARN *and* DARIUS WHEELER *kiss.*

SETSUKO HEARN: I have to get back to the office. I've got a stack of work waiting for me and about a million calls to
60 return, and I need to proof the draft of the article, I'm al-most done—

DARIUS WHEELER: Dinner late? What about drinks? How about dinner and drinks, how about a nightcap—

SETSUKO HEARN: I don't know—

DARIUS WHEELER: Say, "Yes." 65

SETSUKO HEARN: I don't know I don't know—

DARIUS WHEELER: I won't let you go until you say yes. Say yes, please say yes.

SETSUKO HEARN: Yes.

The sound of wooden clappers. SETSUKO HEARN *exits.* DARIUS WHEELER *remains. Enter* ELIZABETH NEWMAN-ORR.

SCENE XXIX

The hanging scroll from the top of the play appears. Portrait of a lady: Kamakura era, gilt background. DARIUS WHEELER's *loft space, later that day.*

ELIZABETH NEWMAN-ORR: Mr. Wheeler, you seem dis-tracted.

DARIUS WHEELER: I'm sorry, what were you saying?

ELIZABETH NEWMAN-ORR: Just that I was running a little late. I called, but there was no answer. I got here as fast as 5 I could. I take it there were no problems.

DARIUS WHEELER: No. None.

Enter JOHN BELL *pushing a dolley on which rests a large box. He parks the dolley and begins prying the front lid of the box open with a crowbar. It's a noisy and violent opening up.*

DARIUS WHEELER: Everything went smoothly. It arrived early this morning.

ELIZABETH NEWMAN-ORR: I'm impressed. So efficient. How 10 do you manage it?

DARIUS WHEELER: Piece of cake.

ELIZABETH NEWMAN-ORR: I have to hand it to you. You have a knack, but I wonder if you ever have any qualms.

DARIUS WHEELER: Qualms about what? 15

ELIZABETH NEWMAN-ORR: Breaking the law.

DARIUS WHEELER: I don't think about it that way.

ELIZABETH NEWMAN-ORR: How do you think about it?

DARIUS WHEELER: I don't, Ms. Orr. I think your question is a philosophical one, and I'm not much of a philosopher, 20 I'm afraid.

ELIZABETH NEWMAN-ORR: It's such an interesting business, the business you're in. It's fascinating. You know, I read an item in the paper just this morning. About an ancient manuscript that was sent to you for appraisal. I understand 25 it could be quite valuable.

DARIUS WHEELER: Yes.

ELIZABETH NEWMAN-ORR: But now you don't own it, do you—the original, that is?

DARIUS WHEELER: No. 30

ELIZABETH NEWMAN-ORR: You're just a representative.

DARIUS WHEELER: An interested party, yes.

ELIZABETH NEWMAN-ORR: I wonder how much that manu-script would fetch on the open market—the original, I mean. 35

DARIUS WHEELER: It's an interesting question.

ELIZABETH NEWMAN-ORR: I think so.

DARIUS WHEELER: You're full of interesting questions.

ELIZABETH NEWMAN-ORR: I try.

40 DARIUS WHEELER: I have a few interesting questions of my
       own.
    ELIZABETH NEWMAN-ORR: Oh?
    DARIUS WHEELER: For starters, I wonder who you are and
       why you're here. I have to say, I have an idea.

    JOHN BELL *pries the last nail loose. The front lid of the box crashes
    open. Revealed inside the box is a painting on silk: a portrait of a
    lady seemingly identical to the portrait of a lady already hanging in
    DARIUS WHEELER's loft.*

45 ELIZABETH NEWMAN-ORR: She has a twin.
    DARIUS WHEELER: Not exactly.
    ELIZABETH NEWMAN-ORR: I'm afraid I don't follow.
    DARIUS WHEELER: This is a fake. I saw it once at a party at
       that villa on Lugard Road, had a chance to look at it up
50   close. I didn't need to. I could tell it was a fake from a mile
       away. All you need to do is look at it a while. You'll see
       what I mean. I hope you like it, I really do, because you
       and whoever you work for just paid an awful lot of money
       for it. Is your mike picking me up—this is key—in order
55   for this little exposé of yours to work—and I think that's
       what this was, I may be wrong, it's just a hunch—this
       painting needs to be authentic, an actual antiquity a coun-
       try of origin would hate to see go. Because it's not, you
       have no crime, you barely have an impropriety, all you
60   have is the purchase and transport of a second-rate fake
       for a large, some might say, absurdly large sum of money.
       But who am I to judge. In art, as in life, there's no ac-
       counting for taste. Your line producer didn't do his home-
       work, Ms. Orr. In the future, you and he—forgive me, he
65   or she—are going to have to do better than that.

    The sound of wooden clappers.

    ELIZABETH NEWMAN-ORR: If it's a crime to transport a na-
       tional treasure, surely it's a crime to own one.

    The sound of wooden clappers.

    ELIZABETH NEWMAN-ORR: Oh. I see. Yours is a fake, too.
    DARIUS WHEELER: You know, there are fakes, and then there
70   are fakes. Some fakes are obvious, and some are pretty
       good. Some are so good, in fact, it's hard to be sure one
       way or another without carbon dating, autoradiography,
       all kinds of tests you'd have to get my permission to run.
       She is afterall my property, and last I checked, that still
75   counted for something.
    ELIZABETH NEWMAN-ORR: You're very pleased with yourself,
       aren't you?
    DARIUS WHEELER: I'm actually wracked with self-loathing.
    ELIZABETH NEWMAN-ORR: Somehow I find that hard to
80   believe.
    DARIUS WHEELER: I hide it well. I think you know the way
       out. If not—
    ELIZABETH NEWMAN-ORR: That's quite all right. I think I can
       manage. Thank you for your time, Mr. Wheeler and
85   Mr.—
    JOHN BELL: Bell.
    ELIZABETH NEWMAN-ORR: Mr. Bell. Good day, Mr. Wheeler.
       Mr. Bell.

    The sound of wooden clappers. ELIZABETH NEWMAN-ORR *exits.*

SCENE XXX

JOHN BELL *and* DARIUS WHEELER *study each other from a distance.*

JOHN BELL: It's not a fake.
DARIUS WHEELER: No.
JOHN BELL: I didn't think so. I mean I didn't think it was.
DARIUS WHEELER: I lied, John. People lie. Sometimes they get
   caught, sometimes they don't. It depends on who they're 5
   lying to.
JOHN BELL: No, I understand, I understand completely.
DARIUS WHEELER: So?
JOHN BELL: Yeah?
DARIUS WHEELER: What's the story?   10
JOHN BELL: Sorry?
DARIUS WHEELER: The manuscript. How's it looking?
JOHN BELL: It's looking good, it's looking really good.
DARIUS WHEELER: Good.
JOHN BELL: He wants to sell.   15
DARIUS WHEELER: Great. What's he asking?
JOHN BELL: One million.
DARIUS WHEELER: Dollars.
JOHN BELL: Pounds. Pounds sterling.

The sound of wooden clappers.

JOHN BELL: But I get the sense, from the little bit I know, that 20
   it's just an arbitrary figure, a stab in the dark, because
   frankly I'm not really sure, you know, I'm not really sure
   he knows what he's doing.
DARIUS WHEELER: Tell him we'll have a courier ready with a
   check before the close of business. Or we can do a direct 25
   money transfer, Channel Islands account. It's his call. The
   thing I wonder is why he'd go so low. He could get twice
   that much, if he wanted to, more.
JOHN BELL: Maybe he doesn't realize what he has. You know,
   I don't know. I don't really know him.   30
DARIUS WHEELER: People are mysterious, aren't they, why
   they do what they do.
JOHN BELL: I guess so, yeah.
DARIUS WHEELER: Well, whatever it is, I want you to make
   the call right away, nail it down, last thing I want is cold 35
   feet and a bidding war. Oh and John—

The sound of wooden clappers.

DARIUS WHEELER: Don't think I'm not aware of everything
   you've done. I am. When this is all settled, I want us to sit
   down together and have a talk. I want to talk about your
   future.   40

The sound of wooden clappers. Exit DARIUS WHEELER. JOHN
BELL *picks up the phone and dials. He exits, listening as the phone
rings on the other end of the line.*

SCENE XXXI

Light shift. DARIUS WHEELER's *loft. An hour later. Enter* CLAIRE
TSONG *in the new clothes she changed into earlier. She carries a
package containing the "original" manuscript. She studies the two
paintings, the two portraits of a lady, one real, one fake. Reenter*
ELIZABETH NEWMAN-ORR.

CLAIRE TSONG: Hey.

The sound of wooden clappers.

ELIZABETH NEWMAN-ORR: Hey.
CLAIRE TSONG: Looking for Wheeler?
ELIZABETH NEWMAN-ORR: No, I'm actually, I'm looking for
5   Mr. Bell. Is he in, do you know?
CLAIRE TSONG: He should be. I was just looking for him
     myself.
ELIZABETH NEWMAN-ORR: I'd love to talk to him.
CLAIRE TSONG: He's a very interesting guy.
10 ELIZABETH NEWMAN-ORR: I sense that.
CLAIRE TSONG: He knows all kinds of things.
ELIZABETH NEWMAN-ORR: I sense that, too.
CLAIRE TSONG: More than he lets on.
ELIZABETH NEWMAN-ORR: Do I know you? I do, don't I? We
15   met the other night, at the party for Utagawa. I didn't, I
     didn't recognize you. New outfit. And your hair, it's dif-
     ferent.
CLAIRE TSONG: Yeah, it's—well, yeah, it's different.
ELIZABETH NEWMAN-ORR: I like it.
20 CLAIRE TSONG: Yeah?
ELIZABETH NEWMAN-ORR: No, it's very, it's really, it's pretty.
CLAIRE TSONG: Thanks, thank you. Claire.
ELIZABETH NEWMAN-ORR: Beth.
CLAIRE TSONG: It's nice to see you again.
25 ELIZABETH NEWMAN-ORR: Yeah.
CLAIRE TSONG: Are you OK?
ELIZABETH NEWMAN-ORR: Yeah, no, I'm fine. It's just, it's been
     a really shitty day. You're an artist. I remember. Mixed-
     media.
30 CLAIRE TSONG: Very good. And you? What do you do? I
     don't think you ever said.
ELIZABETH NEWMAN-ORR: I'm a writer, a journalist actually.
     I was working on a piece. It didn't quite pan out the way
     I'd planned. I thought maybe Mr. Bell, I thought maybe
35   he might—well, I don't know what I was thinking.
CLAIRE TSONG: Shouldn't you be asking me why I'm here,
     how I know Wheeler?
ELIZABETH NEWMAN-ORR: How do you know Wheeler? You
     know—never mind. I don't even care anymore. He's a
40   piece of work, that guy.
CLAIRE TSONG: He's a prick.
ELIZABETH NEWMAN-ORR: I'm so glad I'm not the only one
     who thinks so.
CLAIRE TSONG: You're not.

The sound of wooden clappers.

45 CLAIRE TSONG: So you're a journalist, huh?
ELIZABETH NEWMAN-ORR: Not a very good one and proba-
     bly not for long—but yes, in theory, yes.
CLAIRE TSONG: Listen, you want to maybe, you want to go for
     a drink? I have this story. I think you might find it pretty
50   interesting. Besides, you look like you could use a drink.
ELIZABETH NEWMAN-ORR: What about Mr. Bell?
CLAIRE TSONG: John? We'll catch up with him later. After
     you.

CLAIRE TSONG *and* ELIZABETH NEWMAN-ORR *exit. The sound
of wooden clappers.*

SCENE XXXII

OWEN MATTHIASSEN *and* SETSUKO HEARN *in* OWEN MATTHI-
ASSEN'S *office. The fake Hokusai print hangs on the wall.* OWEN
MATTHIASSEN *is holding a xeroxed copy of the transcript.*

OWEN MATTHIASSEN: Have you ever seen Mount Fuji? In
     real life, I mean?
SETSUKO HEARN: Once. Through the window of a passing
     train.
OWEN MATTHIASSEN: You were lucky. Half the time it's cov- 5
     ered in clouds, you can't see a thing. Hokusai was an old
     man when he made his study of the mountain. He came
     up with forty-six views, why they call the series thirty-six
     views—well, things are sometimes more than they seem
     to be, I suppose. Or less. If he'd lived longer, I suspect there 10
     would've been more. The permutations are infinite. How
     we look at the thing itself, which part we're able to see, if
     we're able to see it at all.

The sound of wooden clappers.

SETSUKO HEARN: Dr. Matthiassen—
OWEN MATTHIASSEN: (*Paging through the xeroxed copy.*) In fair- 15
     ness, it wouldn't have even occurred to me, if I hadn't gotten
     the call from the journalist—I've forgotten her name. She's
     apparently seen the actual forgery, interviewed the forger.
     The story will air sometime next week. The text was very
     convincing, I must say. And of course, the photos were a 20
     nice touch. The thing is, though, and this is the awkward
     thing, it was all right here in front of us the whole time.
     Anomalies, inconsistencies. "On the fifteenth day of the
     eighth month, we catch fireflies … A visiting sage entertains
     us with his parrot." The parrot—nonindigenous, virtually 25
     unheard of in Heian-era Japan. "I received your letter in the
     morning on violet paper bound with plumeria." Plumeria.
     Again another nonindigenous species, anomalous, com-
     pletely anomalous. The list goes on. At first I ascribed it to
     flaws in transcription, a certain license taken in translation, 30
     but the sheer volume of discrepancies, it's overwhelming.
     When I look at the text now, all I see are anomalies. Once
     you begin to look, you see, it gives itself away.

The sound of wooden clappers. OWEN MATTHIASSEN *recedes from
view.* SETSUKO HEARN *remains in the foreground.*

SCENE XXXIII

Light shift. DARIUS WHEELER'S *loft. Early evening of the same day.*
SETSUKO HEARN *is looking at two virtually identical paintings of
the lady, one real, one fake.* DARIUS WHEELER *is preparing drinks.
He gives one to* SETSUKO HEARN.

The middle of a conversation:

SETSUKO HEARN: Tell me something about yourself.
DARIUS WHEELER: What do you want to know?
SETSUKO HEARN: I don't know where to begin. Where do I
     begin?
DARIUS WHEELER: Who was your first true love? 5
SETSUKO HEARN: Who was your first true love?
DARIUS WHEELER: Suzanne Henig. I was fifteen. She broke
     my heart.
SETSUKO HEARN: You've had other loves since.

10 DARIUS WHEELER: One.

SETSUKO HEARN: Only one?

DARIUS WHEELER: I've had affections.

SETSUKO HEARN: Which is different?

DARIUS WHEELER: Which is different, yes.

15 SETSUKO HEARN: Were you ever married?

DARIUS WHEELER: No. And you?

SETSUKO HEARN: Once. A long time ago. It lasted less than a
year. I think we were friends more than we were lovers.
We're still friends. We talk on the phone every so often.
20 He's married, a father. I think we wanted different things.

DARIUS WHEELER: What did you want?

SETSUKO HEARN: To be very good at what I do.

DARIUS WHEELER: Ambitious.

SETSUKO HEARN: I used to be embarrassed by that word, but
25 then I stopped. It's pointless to pretend to be something
you're not. We make certain choices, some without even
realizing. Tell me something else. Where are you from?
Where did you grow up?

DARIUS WHEELER: Bellingham, Washington.

30 SETSUKO HEARN: Iowa. Fairfield, Iowa.

DARIUS WHEELER: That's not what I would've guessed.

SETSUKO HEARN: What would you have guessed?

DARIUS WHEELER: Tokyo. Los Angeles. I don't know.

SETSUKO HEARN: My father was a missionary in Japan. When
35 he came back, he wanted to go home. Iowa was home.
Did you have brothers and sisters?

DARIUS WHEELER: A sister.

SETSUKO HEARN: Younger?

DARIUS WHEELER: Older. She lives on Mercer Island. On a
40 clear day, you can see Mount Rainier. It's like a picture.
It's, it's beautiful. And you?

SETSUKO HEARN: Only child.

DARIUS WHEELER: Your mother was Japanese.

SETSUKO HEARN: I was adopted actually. From an orphanage
45 in Hangzhou. I was there until I was almost two. I'm Chinese by birth. My mother, my adopted mother, her family is Japanese.

DARIUS WHEELER: And your father?

SETSUKO HEARN: Scotch-Irish, a little German, you know,
50 mixed. When I was growing up, people saw me, and they
just assumed I was my parents' daughter—which of course,
in almost every way, I am.

DARIUS WHEELER: Do you remember China?

SETSUKO HEARN: No. If no one had told me, I would never
55 have known, I would never have even guessed. My earliest memories are of cornfields and big sky and college
football. My dad was a big college football fan.

DARIUS WHEELER: Hawkeyes?

SETSUKO HEARN: You bet. Huge. Help me.

60 DARIUS WHEELER: What were you like as a little girl?

SETSUKO HEARN: Very studious. Very idealistic. I wanted to
find out things, all kinds of things. And I believed I could.
I think I was, in retrospect, very sheltered.

DARIUS WHEELER: Were you happy?

65 SETSUKO HEARN: Yes. Yes, I was.

DARIUS WHEELER: Listen—

SETSUKO HEARN: No, please. Tell me something, tell me
something else.

DARIUS WHEELER: I don't know what to say. What can I say?

70 SETSUKO HEARN: Who do you look like, your mother or
your father?

DARIUS WHEELER: My father.

SETSUKO HEARN: And are you like him?

DARIUS WHEELER: In a way, I guess. He was an amateur col-
lector. Collected woodblock prints. Got hooked when he 75
was in the navy, stationed in Tokyo right after the war.
He'd keep his prints between sheets of transparent paper.
It gave him great pleasure. When I was eight, he took us
back to Japan. He bought this Hokusai print on that trip,
found it in a little hole-in-the-wall in Shinagawa. Mount 80
Fuji at sunset, crimson sky, seen across the Bay of Kuroda.
He paid a lot of money for it, more than he had to spend.
Ten years later, I remember coming home, and looking at
it and realizing it was a fake.

SETSUKO HEARN: Did you tell him?   85

DARIUS WHEELER: No.

SETSUKO HEARN: But you thought less of him.

DARIUS WHEELER: My father loved the print. He loved it
with a big and undiscerning heart. It didn't matter if it
wasn't what he thought it was.   90

SETSUKO HEARN: Love is blind. Is that the moral of the story?

DARIUS WHEELER: Listen to me—

SETSUKO HEARN: I should've known better. I should've seen
this for what it was. Don't.

The sound of wooden clappers.

SETSUKO HEARN: I tendered my resignation today, I take full 95
responsibility for this, I'm the one to blame, it was my
mistake. The only question I'm left with is what you
stood to gain. What did you stand to gain? Money, I
suppose—

DARIUS WHEELER: You think I knew. You think I'd do that to 100
you—

SETSUKO HEARN: I suppose you needed somebody to certify
the authenticity of your property, to ensure its value prior
to sale—

DARIUS WHEELER: That's not what this is about—   105

SETSUKO HEARN: What is this about? Why don't you tell me
what this is all about.

DARIUS WHEELER: It's not what you think—

SETSUKO HEARN: What I think? How dare you. What do I
think? Tell me, what do I think?   110

DARIUS WHEELER: That I somehow, that I used you. Listen to
me—

SETSUKO HEARN: Don't.

SETSUKO HEARN *drops her glass. It shatters. The clear liquid pools
on the floor. In the light it looks red.*

SETSUKO HEARN: You actually seemed, for a moment, you
seemed sincere. I believed you. I wanted to believe you. 115

The sound of wooden clappers. SETSUKO HEARN *exits.* DARIUS
WHEELER *recedes from view.*

SCENE XXXIV

*A gallery. Thirty-six paintings are revealed hanging in the space.
From a distance each painting looks like a canvas filled with flecks
of color.* CLAIRE TSONG *is cleaning up a broken glass. She sweeps up
the pieces. Enter* ELIZABETH NEWMAN-ORR *with two drinks.*

CLAIRE TSONG: It just slipped.

ELIZABETH NEWMAN-ORR: I got you another.

CLAIRE TSONG: Thanks.

ELIZABETH NEWMAN-ORR: Excited?

CLAIRE TSONG: Nervous.

5 ELIZABETH NEWMAN-ORR: Don't be. Everything looks perfect. (*Giving* CLAIRE TSONG *her drink.*) Here. Cheers.

CLAIRE TSONG: Cheers.

ELIZABETH NEWMAN-ORR *and* CLAIRE TSONG *drink. The sound of wooden clappers.*

CLAIRE TSONG: So?

ELIZABETH NEWMAN-ORR: So?

10 CLAIRE TSONG: How did the interview with Wheeler go?

ELIZABETH NEWMAN-ORR: All right, I guess. Frankly, I don't know why he agreed to do it. I mean, after everything.

CLAIRE TSONG: What did he say?

ELIZABETH NEWMAN-ORR: Lots of things. He claims he
15 didn't know. He claims he didn't know a thing. He says he was fooled like everyone else.

CLAIRE TSONG: Don't tell me you believe him.

ELIZABETH NEWMAN-ORR: You know, I have to say, I kinda do. When we were editing the tape, he seemed—I don't
20 know—I hate to say it, but he seemed kinda truthful.

CLAIRE TSONG: Did he?

The sound of wooden clappers.

CLAIRE TSONG: When you were interviewing him, did he ever tell you about how he got started, in his business, I mean?

25 ELIZABETH NEWMAN-ORR: I don't know. I think he told me a story, some story about his father.

CLAIRE TSONG: That's not the story I'm talking about. It takes money, you know. You need a little nut, some capital to start a business like Wheeler had. He met this girl—he
30 didn't tell you about the girl? Maybe it slipped his mind. This was a while ago. She was very young. She had some stuff, some artwork she'd inherited when her parents died, some scrolls, a screen, what turned out to be a celadon vase. She knew he knew a thing or two about Asian art.
35 She asked him what he thought. He said it was all pretty much worthless, but he'd buy it all from her, if she wanted, for a lump sum, a very modest sum. She was an art student at the time. There were debts. She needed the cash. A year later, she sees this painting that used to be-
40 long to her parents. It's in a Christie's catalog, along with some other stuff he bought from her. The whole lot ended up selling for just under two million. She saw him later at a party in Boston. He said that art and business were two different things. That he hoped she was better
45 at art than she was at business. And that he'd give her a job, if she wanted, doing restoration. She could make good money.

ELIZABETH NEWMAN-ORR: And she threw her drink in his face.

The sound of wooden clappers.

50 CLAIRE TSONG: She may have. She was young and naive.

ELIZABETH NEWMAN-ORR: There are worse things to be. Besides she sounds like an interesting girl.

CLAIRE TSONG: I don't know. I think, at the end of the day, she's just your run-of-the-mill, girl-next-door kinda girl.

ELIZABETH NEWMAN-ORR: You know, somehow I find that 55 hard to believe.

CLAIRE TSONG: I guess she's a lot of things. I guess she's kinda complicated.

ELIZABETH NEWMAN-ORR: I like complicated.

CLAIRE TSONG: Yeah? I'm glad.   60

CLAIRE TSONG *and* ELIZABETH NEWMAN-ORR *kiss. The sound of wooden clappers. They recede from view.*

SCENE XXXV

The ambient sound of voices and laughter can be heard from another room in the gallery. Enter JOHN BELL *in new clothes. Enter* OWEN MATTHIASSEN.

OWEN MATTHIASSEN: John.

JOHN BELL: Dr. Matthiassen. How are you?

OWEN MATTHIASSEN: Well, I'm doing well. I didn't know you were a fan of Utagawa's work.

JOHN BELL: My friend—well, she, she helped put this all to- 5 gether.

OWEN MATTHIASSEN: I see. He's supposed to make an appearance tonight, Utagawa, that is. At least that's what they tell me. You know, I saw your book in the bookstore the other day. There was a big display. I bought a copy, 10 couldn't resist. I should tell you, as a piece of fiction, I rather enjoyed it. I bet you never imagined it would go on and have such a life of its own.

JOHN BELL: No. No, I didn't.

The sound of wooden clappers.

JOHN BELL: I didn't mean for things to go the way they did. 15 That wasn't my intent.

OWEN MATTHIASSEN: You know, some of my colleagues, they become very skeptical when the author begins talking about intent, what he intended to do. They suspect the author's a bit of a liar in the first place. Why should they 20 listen to him after the fact?

JOHN BELL: I don't remember writing what I wrote. It's like it was written by another person.

OWEN MATTHIASSEN: I've heard people say that. A speculative leap. But now you see, one always hears that fiction is 25 based on real life. Of course, that would mean you'd have to be a Japanese woman going on a thousand years old, by my reckoning, give or take a few decades. As far as I can tell, you are not.

JOHN BELL: Maybe in a past life.   30

OWEN MATTHIASSEN: Come now. You can do better than that.

JOHN BELL: I just wrote what I wrote. I don't know where it came from. Maybe I was inspired.

OWEN MATTHIASSEN: The muse descended from the ether, 35 and whispered in your ear. And you, humble scribe, you just jotted it all down.

JOHN BELL: Something like that, yes.

OWEN MATTHIASSEN: It's fascinating, isn't it, how the human mind works, how it spins yarns, its infinite capacity for 40 fabrication. Such literary talent, such business acumen.

You surprise me, John, how far you've come. I never
would have guessed you had it in you.

JOHN BELL: You don't really know me. You don't know me
45 at all.

OWEN MATTHIASSEN: No. No, I suppose I don't. You know,
there's something about his new work, I don't know what
to make of it. There's something I don't quite understand.
Perhaps, it's generational. Or perhaps it's just me. Just a dif-
50 ferent way of seeing things. Either way, it's late, it's been a
long day, and I should, I should get going. You must tell
me if Utagawa shows up this time around. I'll be curious
to hear.

JOHN BELL: Good night, Dr. Matthiassen.

55 OWEN MATTHIASSEN: Good night.

OWEN MATTHIASSEN *exits. The sound of wooden clappers.* JOHN
BELL *recedes from view.*

SCENE XXXVI

The thirty-six paintings remain. Light on DARIUS WHEELER. *Light
on* SETSUKO HEARN.

SETSUKO HEARN: He was your assistant, wasn't he.

DARIUS WHEELER: Yes.

SETSUKO HEARN: Funny, I don't remember him.

DARIUS WHEELER: He was one of those people, he kinda
5 blended in.

SETSUKO HEARN: I can't believe you didn't read his book.

DARIUS WHEELER: I'm not much of a reader, as you know. So
was it a fake? The original, I mean.

SETSUKO HEARN: You mean the one you paid an obscene
10 amount of money for?

DARIUS WHEELER: That one, yes.

SETSUKO HEARN: Yes and no. It was a fake Heian-era manuscript. It was also an original work by a contemporary
artist, a very popular, if somewhat reclusive painter—

15 DARIUS WHEELER: Ah. And did Utagawa, did he ever show
up that night, in that second to last scene?

SETSUKO HEARN: Yes, in fact.

DARIUS WHEELER: What was he like?

SETSUKO HEARN: She. Utagawa turned out to be a she, a
20 woman, a young woman. She'd been making her living
restoring masterworks. She'd picked up quite a few techniques along the way. She'd actually, oddly enough,
worked for Darius Wheeler at one point. They knew each
other, in passing. So tell me, what's Darius Wheeler up to
25 these days?

DARIUS WHEELER: He's been doing some traveling.

SETSUKO HEARN: Whereabouts?

DARIUS WHEELER: Southeast Asia. The Doi Larng mountain
range, no-man's-land between Thailand and Myanmar,
30 Burma.

SETSUKO HEARN: Rings a bell. Is it like you remembered it?

DARIUS WHEELER: No. It's different. Or maybe he's different.
It's hard to say. I hear you ended up in Palo Alto after all.

SETSUKO HEARN: Yes.

35 DARIUS WHEELER: How is it?

SETSUKO HEARN: It's good.

DARIUS WHEELER: You know, I didn't expect, I didn't think
I'd see you here.

SETSUKO HEARN: I come back a few times a year. I have
work, it brings me back. I saw in the paper, I saw Utagawa 40
was having a show. I had a little time to kill, I thought I'd
stop by. You know, I was teaching an undergraduate seminar last semester on Orientalism. I actually included the
book in the syllabus.

DARIUS WHEELER: What did your students think?   45

SETSUKO HEARN: They questioned the motives of the antiquities dealer, his desire to own and appropriate a culture
outside his own. They wondered why the professor, why
she would fall for someone like him, how she could be so
blind in a way.   50

DARIUS WHEELER: What did you tell them?

SETSUKO HEARN: I said that desire was a complicated thing.
That attraction to something, or someone, is, on some
level, completely irrational. And that when you find yourself desiring something, or someone, that the things you 55
feel in that moment, there's a kind of truth to them, however flawed, however incomplete. That maybe it's unfair
to judge.

DARIUS WHEELER: Tell me, in the book, at the end, did the
dealer, did he and that lady professor, did they ever?— 60

SETSUKO HEARN: No.

DARIUS WHEELER: That's too bad.

SETSUKO HEARN: I don't know. I think it's realistic. He did
just fine. She did just fine, too. It's just one version of the
story. I'm sure there are others.   65

DARIUS WHEELER: Do you think they're happy?

SETSUKO HEARN: Happy enough.

DARIUS WHEELER: So what are you doing now?

SETSUKO HEARN: What are my options?

DARIUS WHEELER: Drinks? A nightcap? I know this place, it's 70
not far, it's just a few blocks away, nothing fancy.

SETSUKO HEARN: You're unbelievable.

DARIUS WHEELER: Is that a yeas or a no?

SETSUKO HEARN: I'm afraid that's a no.

DARIUS WHEELER: Next time. Maybe next time. When you're 75
back in the city. If you have time. I'd like that. I'd like that
very much.

SETSUKO HEARN: Maybe. I'll give you a call and then, and
then we'll see.

SETSUKO HEARN *exits.* DARIUS WHEELER *returns to where he
stood at the start of the play. The sound of the bamboo flute begins.
The lights begin to fade. The thirty-six paintings begin to shift their
positions. Together all thirty-six paintings form a larger picture, like
individual tiles of a larger mosaic. The image they form is of a
woman, a portrait of a lady. An echo of the lady from the top of the
play, but different—part ancient, part contemporary, part Japanese
woodblock print, part anime.*

Bright light on the image.

The sound of wooden clappers.

Darkness.

END OF PLAY

Suzan-Lori Parks

Suzan-Lori Parks (b. 1963) is among the best known African American playwrights writing today; her work is characterized by brilliant language and elegant and powerful imagery on-stage. She is the author of *Betting on the Dust Commander* (1987), *Imperceptible Mutabilities in the Third Kingdom* (1989), *The Death of the Last Black Man in the Whole Entire World* (1990), *The America Play* (1994), *Venus* (1995), *In the Blood* (1999), *Fucking A* (2000), and *Topdog/Underdog,* for which she won the Pulitzer Prize in Drama in 2002. She has won a range of awards for her playwriting, collaborated on the script for the Spike Lee film *Girl 6,* and currently teaches at the California School of the Arts.

TOPDOG/UNDERDOG *Topdog/Underdog* is in many ways Parks's least experimental play, staging a realistic conflict between two African American brothers. At the same time, though, the realistic surface of the play is complicated by its sharp outlining of a larger historical and cultural frame of reference. For the play's two brothers—Lincoln and Booth—develop the cultural conceit of Parks's earlier *America Play,* in which a character (there called The Foundling Father) performs a "Lincoln Act" in a theme park, in which visitors pay for the pleasure of reenacting John Wilkes Booth's assassination of the president at Ford's Theater. Parks's elaborate allegory of the evacuation and persistence of history in *The America Play*—the theme park is evocatively named "The Great Hole of History"—stands behind the rivalry between Booth and Lincoln in *Topdog/Underdog,* and implies that this drama of dispossession is part of a longer historical trajectory. Here, too, Lincoln works in a seedy arcade, playing—in whiteface—the role of Lincoln as he is assassinated by paying customers. The play's murderous finale is, of course, foretold not only by the characters' names, but even in the opening moments of the play, as Booth is surprised by the entrance of Lincoln—in his full costume—and nearly shoots him.

Don Cheadle as Booth in the 2002 Joseph Papp Public Theater production of Suzan-Lori Parks's *Topdog/Underdog*.

Parks has frequently compared her dramatic writing to the "rep and rev" of jazz, the repetition and revision of a phrase of music, and "rep and rev" also provides an image of her use of history as well. While *Topdog/Underdog* is in many respects a play of fraternal rivalry not unlike Sam Shepard's *True West,* the racial and cultural specificity of the drama is deepened by Parks's deft layering of verbal and visual images of racial violence. How do we read Booth's final murder of his brother Lincoln? Is it the historical consequence of slavery, in which the only roles left for African American men are impersonating white fantasies ("dressing up like some crackerass white man," as Booth puts it) as Lincoln does, playing a petty thief (a different kind of fantasy about black men) as Booth does, or a different—though equally dubious—deception, playing the seductive patter of the three-card monte dealer? The cycles of "rep and rev" that lead to Booth's gunshot echo through personal and national history: Booth kills Lincoln, Lincoln conned Booth to bet his inheritance on the cards, Booth seduced Lincoln's wife, Lincoln was given a secret inheritance by their father Pops (with instructions to hide it from Booth), Booth was given a secret inheritance by their mother Moms (with instructions to hide it from Lincoln), Pops deserts the family, Moms deserts the family, Pops betrays Moms with his various lovers, Moms betrays Pops with her "Thursday man," Booth kills Lincoln. Parks's genius in this evocative play is, finally, the way that she honors, in the physical action of the drama, the "rep and rev" of jazz: the repetitions and revisions echo against one another, without resolving into a single, synthetic melody.

TOPDOG/UNDERDOG

Suzan-Lori Parks

THE PLAYERS

LINCOLN, *the topdog*
BOOTH (*aka 3-Card*), *the underdog*

I am God in nature;
I am a weed by the wall.

> Ralph Waldo Emerson
> From "Circles"
> *Essays: First Series* (1841)

AUTHOR'S NOTES: *From the "Elements of Style"*

I'm continuing the use of my slightly unconventional theatrical elements. Here's a road map.

(Rest)

Take a little time, a pause, a breather; make a transition.

A Spell

An elongated and heightened (Rest). *Denoted by repetition of figures' names with no dialogue. Has sort of an architectural look:*

LINCOLN
BOOTH
LINCOLN
BOOTH

This is a place where the figures experience their pure true simple state. While no action or stage business is necessary, directors should fill this moment as they best see fit.

[*Brackets in the text indicate optional cuts for production.*]

(*Parentheses around dialogue indicate softly spoken passages* (*asides; sotto voce*)).

SCENE ONE

Thursday evening. A seedily furnished rooming house room. A bed, a reclining chair, a small wooden chair. Some other stuff but not much else. BOOTH, *a black man in his early 30s, practices his 3-card monte scam on the classic setup: 3 playing cards and the cardboard playing board atop 2 mismatched milk crates. His moves and accompanying patter are, for the most part, studied and awkward.*

BOOTH: Watch me close watch me close now: who-see-thuh-red-card-who-see-thuh-red-card? I-see-thuh-red-card. Thuh-red-card-is-thuh-winner. Pick-thuh-red-card-you-pick-uh-winner. Pick-uh-black-card-you-pick-uh-loser.
5 Theres-thuh-loser, yeah, theres-thuh-black-card, theres-thuh-other-loser-and-theres-thuh-red-card, thuh-winner.

(*Rest.*)

Watch me close watch me close now: 3-Card-throws-thuh-cards-lightning-fast. 3-Card-that's-me-and-Ima-last. Watch-me-throw-cause-here-I-go. One-good-pickll-get-
10 you-in, 2-good-picks-and-you-gone-win. See-thuh-red-card-see-thuh-red-card-who-see-thuh-red-card?

(*Rest.*)

Dont touch my cards, man, just point to thuh one you want. You-pick-that-card-you-pick-a-loser, yeah, that-cards-a-loser. You-pick-that-card-that's-thuh-other-loser.
15 You-pick-that-card-you-pick-a-winner. Follow that card. You gotta chase that card. You-pick-thuh-dark-deuce-thats-a-loser-other-dark-deuces-thuh-other-loser, red-deuce, thuh-deuce-of-heartsll-win-it-all. Follow thuh red card.

(*Rest.*)

20 Ima show you thuh cards: 2 black cards but only one heart. Now watch me now. Who-sees-thuh-red-card-who-knows-where-its-at? Go on, man, point to thuh

card. Put yr money down cause you aint no clown. No? Ah you had thuh card, but you didnt have thuh heart.

(*Rest.*)

You wanna bet? 500 dollars? Shoot. You musta been 25 watching 3-Card real close. Ok. Lay the cash in my hand cause 3-Cards thuh man. Thank you, mister. This card you say?

(*Rest.*)

Wrong! Sucker! Fool! Asshole! Bastard! I bet yr daddy heard how stupid you was and drank himself to death just 30 cause he didnt wanna have nothing to do witchu! I bet yr mama seen you when you comed out and she walked away from you with thuh afterbirth still hanging from out twixt her legs, sucker! Ha Ha Ha! And 3-Card, once again, wins all thuh money!! 35

(*Rest.*)

What? Cops looking my way? Fold up thuh game, and walk away. Sneak outa sight. Set up on another corner.

(*Rest.*)

Yeah.

(*Rest.*)

Having won the imaginary loot and dodged the imaginary cops, BOOTH *sets up his equipment and starts practicing his scam all over again.* LINCOLN *comes in quietly. He is a black man in his later 30s. He is dressed in an antique frock coat and wears a top hat and fake beard, that is, he is dressed to look like Abraham Lincoln. He surreptitiously walks into the room to stand right behind* BOOTH, *who, engrossed in his cards, does not notice* LINCOLN *right away.*

BOOTH: Watch me close watch me close now; who-see-thuh-red-card-who-see-thuh-red-card? I-see-thuh-red-card. 40

Thuh-red-card-is-thuh-winner. Pick-thuh-red-card-you-
pick-uh-winner. Pick-uh-black-card-you-pick-uh-loser.
Theres-thuh-loser-yeah-theres-thuh-black-card, theres-
thuh-other-loser-and-theres-thuh-red-card, thuh-winner.
45   Don't touch my cards, man, don't—

(Rest.)

Dont do that shit. Dont do that shit. Dont do that shit!

BOOTH, *sensing someone behind him, whirls around, pulling a gun
from his pants. While the presence of* LINCOLN *doesnt surprise him,
the Lincoln costume does.*

BOOTH: And woah, man dont *ever* be doing that shit! Who
thuh fuck you think you is coming in my shit all spooked
out and shit. You pull that one more time I'll shoot you!
50   LINCOLN: I only had a minute to make the bus.
BOOTH: Bullshit.
LINCOLN: Not completely. I mean, its either bull or shit, but
not a complete lie so it aint bullshit, right?

(Rest.)

Put yr gun away.
55   BOOTH: Take off the damn hat at least.

LINCOLN *takes off the stovepipe hat.* BOOTH *puts his gun away.*

LINCOLN: Its cold out there. This thing kept my head warm.
BOOTH: I dont like you wearing that bullshit, that shit that
bull that disguise that getup that motherdisfuckinguise
anywhere in the vicinity of my humble abode.
60   LINCOLN: Better?
BOOTH: Take off the damn coat too. Damn, man. Bad enough
you got to wear that shit all day you come up in here
wearing it. What my women gonna say?
LINCOLN: What women?
65   BOOTH: I got a date with Grace tomorrow. Shes in love with
me again but she dont now it yet. Aint no man can love
her the way I can. She sees you in that getup its gonna reflect bad on me. She coulda seen you coming down the
street. Shit. Could be standing outside right now taking
70   her ring off and throwing it on the sidewalk.

BOOTH *takes a peek out the window.*

BOOTH: I got her this ring today. Diamond. Well, diamond-
esque, but it looks just as good as the real thing. Asked her
what size she wore. She say 7 so I go boost a size 6 and a
half, right? Show it to her and she loves it and I shove it
75   on her finger and its a tight fit right, so she cant just take
it off on a whim, like she did the last one I gave her.
Smooth, right?

BOOTH *takes another peek out the window.*

LINCOLN: She out there?
BOOTH: Nope. Coast is clear.
80   LINCOLN: You boosted a ring?
BOOTH: Yeah. I thought about spending my inheritance on it
but—take off that damn coat, man, you make me nervous
standing there looking like a spook, and that damn face

paint, take it off. You should take all of it off at work and
leave it there.   85
LINCOLN: I dont bring it home someone might steal it.
BOOTH: At least *take it off* there, then.
LINCOLN: Yeah.

(Rest.)

LINCOLN *takes off the frock coat and applies cold cream, removing
the whiteface.*

LINCOLN: I was riding the bus. Really I only had a minute to
make my bus and I was sitting in the arcade thinking,   90
should I change into my street clothes or should I make the
bus? Nobody was in there today anyway. Middle of week
middle of winter. Not like on weekends. Weekends the
place is packed. So Im riding the bus home. And this kid
asked me for my autograph. I pretended I didnt hear him   95
at first. I'd had a long day. But he kept asking. Theyd just
done Lincoln in history class and he knew all about him,
he'd been to the arcade but, I dunno, for some reason he
was tripping cause there was Honest Abe right beside him
on the bus. I wanted to tell him to go fuck hisself. But then 100
I got a look at him. A little rich kid. Born on easy street,
you know the type. So I waited until I could tell he really
wanted it, the autograph, and I told him he could have it
for 10 bucks. I was gonna say 5, cause of the Lincoln connection but something in me made me ask for 10.   105
BOOTH: But he didnt have a 10. All he had was a penny. So
you took the penny.
LINCOLN: All he had was a *20*. So I took the 20 and told him
to meet me on the bus tomorrow and Honest Abe would
give him the change.   110
BOOTH: Shit.
LINCOLN: Shit is right.

(Rest.)

BOOTH: Whatd you do with thuh 20?
LINCOLN: Bought drinks at Luckys. A round for everybody.
They got a kick out of the getup.   115
BOOTH: You shoulda called me down.
LINCOLN: Next time, bro.

(Rest.)

You making bookshelves? With the milk crates, you making bookshelves?
BOOTH: Yeah, big bro, Im making bookshelves.   120
LINCOLN: Whats the cardboard part for.
BOOTH: Versatility.
LINCOLN: Oh.
BOOTH: I was thinking we dont got no bookshelves we dont
got no dining room table so Im making a sorta modular   125
unit you put the books in the bottom and the table top
on top. We can eat and store our books. We could put the
photo album in there.

BOOTH *gets the raggedy family photo album and puts it in the milk
crate.*

BOOTH: Youd sit there, Id sit on the edge of the bed. Gathered around the dinner table. Like old times.   130

LINCOLN: We just gotta get some books but thats great, Booth, thats real great.

BOOTH: Dont be calling me Booth no more, K?

LINCOLN: You changing yr name?

135   BOOTH: Maybe.

LINCOLN

BOOTH

LINCOLN: What to?

BOOTH: Im not ready to reveal it yet.

140   LINCOLN: You already decided on something?

BOOTH: Maybe.

LINCOLN: You gonna call yrself something african? That be cool. Only pick something thats easy to spell and pronounce, man, cause you know, some of them african

145   names, I mean, ok, Im down with the power to the people thing, but, no ones gonna hire you if they cant say yr name. And some of them fellas who got they african names, no one can say they names and they cant say they names neither. I mean, you dont want yr new handle to

150   obstruct yr employment possibilities.

BOOTH

LINCOLN

BOOTH: You bring dinner?

LINCOLN: "Shango" would be a good name. The name of the

155   thunder god. If you aint decided already Im just throwing it in the pot. I brought chinese.

BOOTH: Lets try the table out.

LINCOLN: Cool.

They both sit at the new table. The food is far away near the door.

LINCOLN

160   BOOTH

LINCOLN: I buy it you set it up. Thats the deal. Thats the deal, right?

BOOTH: You like this place?

LINCOLN: Ssallright.

165   BOOTH: But a little cramped sometimes, right?

LINCOLN: You dont hear me complain. Although that recliner sometimes Booth, man—no Booth, right—man, Im too old to be sleeping in that chair.

BOOTH: Its my place. You dont got a place. Cookie, she threw

170   you out. And you cant seem to get another woman. Yr lucky I let you stay.

LINCOLN: Every Friday you say *mi casa es su casa.*

BOOTH: Every Friday you come home with yr paycheck. Today is Thursday and I tell you brother, its a long way from

175   Friday to Friday. All kinds of things can happen. All kinds of bad feelings can surface and erupt while yr little brother waits for you to bring in yr share.

(Rest.)

I got my Thursday head on. Link. Go get the food.

LINCOLN *doesnt budge.*

LINCOLN: You dont got no running water in here, man.

180   BOOTH: So?

LINCOLN: You dont got no toilet you dont got no sink.

BOOTH: Bathrooms down the hall.

LINCOLN: You living in thuh Third World, fool! Hey, I'll get thuh food.

LINCOLN *goes to get the food. He sees a stray card on the floor and examines it without touching it. He brings the food over, putting it nicely on the table.*

LINCOLN: You been playing cards?   185

BOOTH: Yeah.

LINCOLN: Solitaire?

BOOTH: Thats right. Im getting pretty good at it.

LINCOLN: Thats soup and thats sauce. I got you the meat and I got me the skrimps.   190

BOOTH: I wanted the skrimps.

LINCOLN: You said you wanted the meat. This morning when I left you said you wanted the meat.

(Rest.)

Here man, take the skrimps. No sweat.

They eat. Chinese food from styrofoam containers, cans of soda, fortune cookies. LINCOLN *eats slowly and carefully.* BOOTH *eats ravenously.*

LINCOLN: Yr getting good at solitaire?   195

BOOTH: Yeah. How about we play a hand after eating.

LINCOLN: Solitaire?

BOOTH: Poker or rummy or something.

LINCOLN: You know I dont touch thuh cards, man.

BOOTH: Just for fun.   200

LINCOLN: I dont touch thuh cards.

BOOTH: How about for money?

LINCOLN: You dont got no money. All the money you got I bring in here.

BOOTH: I got my inheritance.   205

LINCOLN: Thats like saying you dont got no money cause you aint never gonna do nothing with it so its like you dont got it.

BOOTH: At least I still got mines. You blew yrs.

LINCOLN   210

BOOTH

LINCOLN: You like the skrimps?

BOOTH: Ssallright.

LINCOLN: Whats yr fortune?

BOOTH: "Waste not want not." Whats yrs?   215

LINCOLN: "Your luck will change!"

BOOTH *finishes eating. He turns his back to* LINCOLN *and fiddles around with the cards, keeping them on the bed, just out of* LINCOLNs *sight. He mutters the 3-card patter under his breath. His moves are still clumsy. Every once and a while he darts a look over at* LINCOLN *who does his best to ignore* BOOTH.

BOOTH: ((((Watch me close watch me close now: who-see-thuh-red-card-who-see-thuh-red-card? I-see-thuh-red-card. Thuh-red-card-is-thuh-winner. Pick-thuh-red-card-you-pick-uh-winner. Pick-uh-black-card-and-you-   220

pick-uh-loser. Theres-thuh-loser, yeah, theres-thuh-black-card, theres-thuh-other-loser-and-theres-thuh-red-card, thuh-winner! Cop C, Stick, Cop C! Go on—))))

LINCOLN: ((Shit.))

BOOTH: (((((((One-good-pickll-get-you-in, 2-good-picks-   225

and-you-gone-win. Dont touch my cards, man, just point to thuh one you want. You-pick-that-card-you-pick-uh-loser, yeah, that-cards-uh-loser. You-pick-that-card-thats-thuh-other-loser. You-pick-that-card-you-pick-uh-win-ner. Follow-that-card. You-gotta-chase-that-card!))))))) 230

LINCOLN: You wanna hustle 3-card monte, you gotta do it right, you gotta break it down. Practice it in smaller bits. Yr trying to do the whole thing at once thats why you keep fucking it up.

BOOTH: Show me. 235

LINCOLN: No. Im just saying you wanna do it you gotta do it right and if you gonna do it right you gotta work on it in smaller bits, thatsall.

BOOTH: You and me could team up and do it together. We'd clean up, Link. 240

LINCOLN: I'll clean up—bro.

LINCOLN cleans up. As he clears the food, BOOTH *goes back to using the "table" for its original purpose.*

BOOTH: My new names 3-Card. 3-Card, got it? You wanted to know it so now you know it. 3-card monte by 3-Card. Call me 3-Card from here on out.

LINCOLN: 3-Card. Shit. 245

BOOTH: Im getting everybody to call me 3-Card. Grace likes 3-Card better than Booth. She says 3-Cards got some-thing to it. Anybody not calling me 3-Card gets a bullet.

LINCOLN: Yr too much, man.

BOOTH: Im making a point. 250

LINCOLN: Point made, 3-Card. Point made.

LINCOLN picks up his guitar. Plays at it.

BOOTH: Oh, come on, man, we could make money you and me. Throwing down the cards. 3-Card and Link: look out! We could clean up you and me. You would throw the cards and I'd be yr Stickman. The one in the crowd who 255 looks like just an innocent passerby, who looks like just another player, like just another customer, but who gots intimate connections with you, the Dealer, the one throwing the cards, the main man. I'd be the one who brings in the crowd, I'd be the one who makes them want 260 to put they money down, you do yr moves and I do mines. You turn yr head and I turn the card—

LINCOLN: It aint as easy as all that. Theres—

BOOTH: We could be a team, man. Rake in the money! Sure thered be some cats out there with fast eyes, some broth- 265 ers and sisters who would watch real close and pick the right card, and so thered be some days when we would lose money, but most of the days we would come out on top! Pockets bulging, plenty of cash! And the ladies would be thrilling! You could afford to get laid! Grace would be 270 all over me again.

LINCOLN: I thought you said she was all over you.

BOOTH: She is she is. Im seeing her tomorrow but today we gotta solidify the shit twixt you and me. Big Brother Link and little brother Booth— 275

LINCOLN: 3-Card.

BOOTH: Yeah. Scheming and dreaming. No one throws the cards like you, Link. And with yr moves and my magic, and we get Grace and a girl for you to round out the posse. We'd be golden, bro! Am I right? 280

LINCOLN

LINCOLN

BOOTH: Am I right?

BOOTH: I dont touch thuh cards, 3-Card. I dont touch thuh cards no more. 285

LINCOLN

BOOTH

LINCOLN

BOOTH

BOOTH: You know what Mom told me when she was pack- 290 ing to leave? You was at school motherfucker you was at school. You got up that morning and sat down in yr reg-ular place and read the cereal box while Dad read the sports section and Mom brought you yr dick toast and then you got on the damn school bus cause you didnt 295 have the sense to do nothing else you was so into yr own shit that you didnt have the sense to feel nothing else go-ing on. I had the sense to go back cause I was feeling something going on man, I was feeling something chang-ing. So I— 300

LINCOLN: Cut school that day like you did almost every day—

BOOTH: She was putting her stuff in bags. She had all them nice suitcases but she was putting her stuff in bags.

(Rest.)

Packing up her shit. She told me to look out for you. I 305 told her I was the little brother and the big brother should look out after the little brother. She just said it again. That I should look out for you. Yeah. So who gonna look out for me. Not like you care. Here I am interested in an eco-nomic opportunity, willing to work hard, willing to take 310 risks and all you can say you shiteating motherfucking pa-thetic limpdick uncle tom, all you can tell me is how you dont do no more what I be wanting to do. Here I am try-ing to earn a living and you standing in my way. YOU STANDING IN MY WAY, LINK! 315

LINCOLN: Im sorry.

BOOTH: Yeah, you sorry all right.

LINCOLN: I cant be hustling no more, bro.

BOOTH: What you do all day aint no hustle?

LINCOLN: Its honest work. 320

BOOTH: Dressing up like some crackerass white man, some dead president and letting people shoot at you sounds like a hustle to me.

LINCOLN: People know the real deal. When people know the real deal it aint a hustle. 325

BOOTH: We do the card game people will know the real deal. Sometimes we will win sometimes they will win. They fast they win, we faster we win.

LINCOLN: I aint going back to that, bro. I aint going back.

BOOTH: You play Honest Abe. You aint going back but you 330 going all the way back. Back to way back then when folks was slaves and shit.

LINCOLN: Dont push me.

BOOTH

LINCOLN 335

BOOTH: You gonna have to leave.

LINCOLN: I'll be gone tomorrow.

BOOTH: Good. Cause this was only supposed to be a tempo-rary arrangement.

LINCOLN: I will be gone tomorrow. 340

BOOTH: Good.

BOOTH *sits on his bed.* LINCOLN, *sitting in his easy chair with his guitar, plays and sings.*

LINCOLN:
  My dear mother left me, my fathers gone away
  My dear mother left me and my fathers gone away
345 I dont got no money, I dont got no place to stay.

  My best girl, she threw me out into the street
  My favorite horse, they ground him into meat
  Im feeling cold from my head down to my feet.

  My luck was bad but now it turned to worse
350 My luck was bad but now it turned to worse
  Dont call me up a doctor, just call me up a hearse.

BOOTH: You just made that up?
LINCOLN: I had it in my head a few days.
BOOTH: Sounds good.
355 LINCOLN: Thanks.

(*Rest.*)

  Daddy told me once why we got the names we do.
BOOTH: Yeah?
LINCOLN: Yeah.

(*Rest.*)

  He was drunk when he told me, or maybe I was drunk
360 when he told me. Anyway he told me, may not be true,
  but he told me. Why he named us both. Lincoln and
  Booth.
BOOTH: How come. How come, man?
LINCOLN: It was his idea of a joke.

Both men relax back as the light fades.

SCENE TWO

Friday evening. The very next day. BOOTH *comes in looking like he is bundled up against the cold. He makes sure his brother isnt home, then stands in the middle of the room. From his big coat sleeves he pulls out one new shoe then another, from another sleeve come two more shoes. He then slithers out a belt from each sleeve. He removes his coat. Underneath he wears a very nice new suit. He removes the jacket and pants revealing another new suit underneath. The suits still have the price tags on them. He takes two neckties from his pockets and two folded shirts from the back of his pants. He pulls a magazine from the front of his pants. Hes clearly had a busy day of shoplifting. He lays one suit out on* LINCOLNs *easy chair. The other he lays out on his own bed. He goes out into the hall returning with a folding screen which he sets up between the bed and the recliner creating 2 separate spaces. He takes out a bottle of whiskey and two glasses, setting them on the two stacked milk crates. He hears footsteps and sits down in the small wooden chair reading the magazine.* LINCOLN, *dressed in street clothes, comes in.*

LINCOLN: Taaaaadaaaaaaaa!
BOOTH: Lordamighty, Pa, I smells money!
LINCOLN: Sho nuff, Ma. Poppas brung home thuh bacon.
BOOTH: Bringitherebringitherebringithere.

With a series of very elaborate moves LINCOLN *brings the money over to* BOOTH.

BOOTH: Put it in my hands, Pa!   5
LINCOLN: I want ya tuh smells it first, Ma!
BOOTH: Put in neath my nose then, Pa!
LINCOLN: Take yrself a good long whiff of them greenbacks.
BOOTH: Oh lordamighty Ima faint, Pa! Get me muh med-sin!

LINCOLN *quickly pours two large glasses of whiskey.*

LINCOLN: Dont die on me, Ma!   10
BOOTH: Im fading fast, Pa!
LINCOLN: Thinka thuh children, Ma! Thinka thuh farm!
BOOTH: 1-2-3.

Both men gulp down their drinks simultaneously.

LINCOLN **and** BOOTH: AAAAAAAAAAAAAAAAAAAAAAH!

Lots of laughing and slapping on the backs.

LINCOLN: Budget it out man budget it out.   15
BOOTH: You in a hurry?
LINCOLN: Yeah. I wanna see how much we got for the week.
BOOTH: You rush in here and dont even look around. Could
  be a fucking A-bomb in the middle of the floor you
  wouldnt notice. Yr wife, Cookie—   20
LINCOLN: X-wife—
BOOTH: —could be in my bed you wouldnt notice—
LINCOLN: She was once—
BOOTH: Look the fuck around please.

LINCOLN *looks around and sees the new suit on his chair.*

LINCOLN: Wow.   25
BOOTH: Its yrs.
LINCOLN: Shit.
BOOTH: Got myself one too.
LINCOLN: Boosted?
BOOTH: Yeah, I boosted em. Theys stole from a big-ass de- 30
  partment store. That store takes in more money in one
  day than we will in our whole life. I stole and I stole gen-
  erously. I got one for me and I got one for you. Shoes belts
  shirts ties socks in the shoes and everything. Got that
  screen too.   35
LINCOLN: You all right, man.
BOOTH: Just cause I aint good as you at cards dont mean I
  cant do nothing.
LINCOLN: Lets try em on.

They stand in their separate sleeping spaces, BOOTH *near his bed,* LINCOLN *near his recliner, and try on their new clothes.*

BOOTH: Ima wear mine tonight. Gracell see me in this and 40
  she gonna ask me tuh marry *her.*

(*Rest.*)

  I got you the blue and I got me the brown. I walked in
  there and walked out and they didnt as much as bat an
  eye. Thats how smooth lil bro be, Link.
LINCOLN: You did good. You did real good, 3-Card.   45
BOOTH: All in a days work.

LINCOLN: They say the clothes make the man. All day long I wear that getup. But that dont make me who I am. Old black coat not even real old just fake old. Its got worn
50 spots on the elbows, little raggedy places thatll break through into holes before the winters out. Shiny strips around the cuffs and the collar. Dust from the cap guns on the left shoulder where they shoot him, where they shoot me I should say but I never feel like they shooting me.
55 The fella who had the gig before I had it wore the same coat. When I got the job they had the getup hanging there waiting for me. Said thuh fella before me just took it off one day and never came back.

(Rest.)

Remember how Dads clothes used to hang in the closet?
60 BOOTH: Until you took em outside and burned em.

(Rest.)

He had some nice stuff. What he didnt spend on booze he spent on women. What he didnt spend on them two he spent on clothes. He had some nice stuff. I would look at his stuff and calculate thuh how long it would take till I was
65 big enough to fit it. Then you went and burned it all up.
LINCOLN: I got tired of looking at em without him in em.

(Rest.)

They said thuh fella before me—he took off the getup one day, hung it up real nice, and never came back. And as they offered me thuh job, saying of course I would have
70 to wear a little makeup and accept less than what they would offer a—another guy—
BOOTH: Go on, say it. "White." Theyd pay you less than theyd pay a white guy.
LINCOLN: I said to myself thats exactly what I would do: wear
75 it out and then leave it hanging there and not come back. But until then, I would make a living at it. But it dont make me. Worn suit coat, not even worn by the fool that Im supposed to be playing, but making fools out of all those folks who come crowding in for they chance to play
80 at something great. Fake beard. Top hat. Dont make me into no Lincoln. I was Lincoln on my own before any of that.

The men finish dressing. They style and profile.

BOOTH: Sharp, huh?
LINCOLN: Very sharp.
85 BOOTH: You look sharp too, man. You look like the real you. Most of the time you walking around all bedraggled and shit. You look good. Like you used to look back in thuh day when you had Cookie in love with you and all the women in the world was eating out of yr hand.
90 LINCOLN: This is real nice, man. I dont know where Im gonna wear it but its real nice.
BOOTH: Just wear it around. Itll make you feel good and when you feel good yll meet someone nice. Me I aint interested in meeting no one nice, I mean, I only got eyes
95 for Grace. You think she'll go for me in this?
LINCOLN: I think thuh tie you gave me'll go better with what you got on.

BOOTH: Yeah?
LINCOLN: Grace likes bright colors dont she? My ties bright, yrs is too subdued. 100
BOOTH: Yeah. Gimmie yr tie.
LINCOLN: You gonna take back a gift?
BOOTH: I stole the damn thing didnt I? Gimmie yrs! I'll give you mines.

They switch neckties. BOOTH *is pleased.* LINCOLN *is more pleased.*

LINCOLN: Do thuh budget. 105
BOOTH: Right. Ok lets see: we got 314 dollars. We put 100 aside for the rent. 100 a week times 4 weeks makes the rent and—
LINCOLN **and** BOOTH: —we dont want thuh rent spent.
BOOTH: That leaves 214. We put aside 30 for the electric 110 leaving 184. We put aside 50 for thuh phone leaving 134.
LINCOLN: We dont got a phone.
BOOTH: We pay our bill theyll turn it back on.
LINCOLN: We dont need no phone.
BOOTH: How you gonna get a woman if you dont got a 115 phone? Women these days are more cautious, more waddacallit, more circumspect. You go into a club looking like a fast daddy, you get a filly to give you her numerophono and gone is the days when she just gives you her number and dont ask for yrs. 120
LINCOLN: Like a woman is gonna call me.
BOOTH: She dont wanna call you she just doing a preliminary survey of the property. Shit, Link, you dont know nothin no more.

(Rest.)

She gives you her number and she asks for yrs. You give 125 her yr number. The phone number of yr home. Thereby telling her 3 things: 1) you got a home, that is, you aint no smooth talking smooth dressing *homeless* joe; 2) that you is in possession of a telephone and a working telephone number which is to say that you got thuh cash and thuh 130 wherewithal to acquire for yr self the worlds most revolutionary communication apparatus and you together enough to pay yr bills!
LINCOLN: Whats 3?
BOOTH: You give her yr number you telling her that its cool 135 to call if she should so please, that is, that you aint got no wife or wife approximation on the premises.

(Rest.)

50 for the phone leaving 134. We put aside 40 for "medsin."
LINCOLN: The price went up. 2 bucks more a bottle. 140
BOOTH: We'll put aside 50, then. That covers the bills. We got 84 left. 40 for meals together during the week leaving 44. 30 for me 14 for you. I got a woman I gotta impress tonight.
LINCOLN: You didnt take out for the phone last week. 145
BOOTH: Last week I was depressed. This week things is looking up. For both of us.
LINCOLN: Theyre talking about cutbacks at the arcade. I only been there 8 months, so—
BOOTH: Dont sweat it man, we'll find something else. 150

LINCOLN: Not nothing like this. I like the job. This is sit down, you know, easy work. I just gotta sit there all day. Folks come in kill phony Honest Abe with the phony pistol. I can sit there and let my mind travel.

135 BOOTH: Think of women.

LINCOLN: Sometimes.

(*Rest.*)

All around the whole arcade is buzzing and popping. Thuh whirring of thuh duckshoot, baseballs smacking the back wall when someone misses the stack of cans, some

140 woman getting happy cause her fella just won the ring toss. The Boss playing the barker talking up the fake freaks. The smell of the ocean and cotton candy and rat shit. And in thuh middle of all that, I can just sit and let my head go quiet. Make up songs, make plans. Forget.

(*Rest.*)

145 You should come down again.

BOOTH: Once was plenty, but thanks.

(*Rest.*)

Yr Best Customer, he come in today?

LINCOLN: Oh, yeah, he was there.

BOOTH: He shoot you?

150 LINCOLN: He shot Honest Abe, yeah.

BOOTH: He talk to you?

LINCOLN: In a whisper. Shoots on the left whispers on the right.

BOOTH: Whatd he say this time?

155 LINCOLN: "Does thuh show stop when no ones watching or does thuh show go on?"

BOOTH: Hes getting deep.

LINCOLN: Yeah.

BOOTH: Whatd he say, that one time? "Yr only yrself—"

160 LINCOLN: "—when no ones watching," yeah.

BOOTH: Thats deep shit.

(*Rest.*)

Hes a brother, right?

LINCOLN: I think so.

BOOTH: He know yr a brother?

165 LINCOLN: I dunno. Yesterday he had a good one. He shoots me, Im playing dead, and he leans in close then goes: "God aint nothing but a parasite."

BOOTH: Hes one *deep* black brother.

LINCOLN: Yeah. He makes the day interesting.

170 BOOTH

(*Rest.*)

Thats a fucked-up job you got.

LINCOLN: Its a living.

BOOTH: But you aint living.

LINCOLN: Im alive aint I?

(*Rest.*)

175 One day I was throwing the cards. Next day Lonny died. Somebody shot him. I knew I was next, so I quit. I saved my life.

(*Rest.*)

The arcade gig is the first lucky break Ive ever had. And Ive actually grown to like the work. And now theyre talking about cutting me. 180

BOOTH: You was lucky with thuh cards.

LINCOLN: Lucky? Aint nothing lucky about cards. Cards aint luck. Cards is work. Cards is skill. Aint never nothing lucky about cards.

(*Rest.*)

I dont wanna lose my job. 185

BOOTH: Then you gotta jazz up yr act. Elaborate yr moves, you know. You was always too stiff with it. You cant just sit there! Maybe, when they shoot you, you know, leap up flail yr arms then fall down and wiggle around and shit so they gotta shoot you more than once. Blam Blam Blam! 190 Blam!

LINCOLN: Help me practice. I'll sit here like I do at work and you be like one of the tourists.

BOOTH: No thanks.

LINCOLN: My paychecks on the line, man. 195

BOOTH: I got a date. Practice on yr own.

(*Rest.*)

I got a rendezvous with Grace. Shit she so sweet she makes my teeth hurt.

(*Rest.*)

Link, uh, howbout slipping me an extra 5 spot. Its the biggest night of my life. 200

LINCOLN

BOOTH

LINCOLN *gives* BOOTH *a 5er.*

BOOTH: Thanks.

LINCOLN: No sweat.

BOOTH: Howabout I run through it with you when I get 205 back. Put on yr getup and practice till then.

LINCOLN: Sure.

BOOTH *leaves.* LINCOLN *stands there alone. He takes off his shoes, giving them a shine. He takes off his socks and his fancy suit, hanging it neatly over the little wooden chair. He takes his getup out of his shopping bag. He puts it on, slowly, like an actor preparing for a great role: frock coat, pants, beard, top hat, necktie. He leaves his feet bare. The top hat has an elastic band which he positions securely underneath his chin. He picks up the white pancake makeup but decides against it. He sits. He pretends to get shot, flings himself on the floor and thrashes around. He gets up, considers giving the new moves another try, but instead pours himself a big glass of whiskey and sits there drinking.*

SCENE THREE

Much later that same Friday evening. The recliner is reclined to its maximum horizontal position and LINCOLN *lies there asleep. He wakes with a start. He is horrific, bleary eyed and hungover, in his full* LINCOLN *regalia. He takes a deep breath, realizes where he is and reclines again, going back to sleep.* BOOTH *comes in full of swag-*

ger. He slams the door trying to wake his brother who is dead to the world. He opens the door and slams it again. This time LINCOLN *wakes up, as hungover and horrid as before.* BOOTH *swaggers about, his moves are exaggerated, rooster-like. He walks round and round* LINCOLN *making sure his brother sees him.*

LINCOLN: You hurt yrself?

BOOTH: I had me "an evening to remember."

LINCOLN: You look like you hurt yrself.

BOOTH: Grace Grace Grace. *Grace.* She wants me back. She
5   wants me back so bad she wiped her hand over the past
       where we wasn't together just so she could say we aint
       never been apart. She wiped her hand over our breakup.
       She wiped her hand over her childhood, her teenage
       years, her first boyfriend, just so she could say that she
10   been mine since the dawn of time.

LINCOLN: Thats great, man.

BOOTH: And all the shit I put her through; she wiped it clean.
       And the women I saw while I was seeing her—

LINCOLN: Wiped clean too?

15 BOOTH: Mister Clean, Mister, Mister Clean!

LINCOLN: Whered you take her?

BOOTH: We was over at her place. I brought thuh food.
       Stopped at the best place I could find and stuffed my coat
       with only the best. We had candlelight, we had music we
20   had—

LINCOLN: She let you do it?

BOOTH: Course she let me do it.

LINCOLN: She let you do it without a rubber?

BOOTH: —Yeah.

25 LINCOLN: Bullshit.

BOOTH: I put my foot down—and she *melted.* And she was—
       huh—she was something else. I dont wanna get you jeal-
       ous, though.

LINCOLN: Go head, I dont mind.

30 BOOTH

       (*Rest.*)

       Well, you know what she looks like.

LINCOLN: She walks on by and the emergency room fills up
       cause all the guys get whiplash from lookin at her.

BOOTH: Thats right thats right. Well—she comes to the door
35   wearing nothing but her little nightie, eats up the food I'd
       brought like there was no tomorrow and then goes and
       eats on me.

       (*Rest.*)

LINCOLN: Go on.

BOOTH: I dont wanna make you feel bad, man.

40 LINCOLN: Ssallright. Go on.

BOOTH

       (*Rest.*)

       Well, uh, you know what she likes. Wild. Goodlooking.
       So sweet my teeth hurt.

LINCOLN: Sexmachine.

45 BOOTH: Yeah.

LINCOLN: Hotsy-Totsy.

BOOTH: Yeah.

LINCOLN: Amazing Grace.

BOOTH: Amazing Grace! Yeah. Thats right. She let me do her
       how I wanted. And no rubber.   50

(*Rest.*)

LINCOLN: Go on.

BOOTH: You dont wanna hear the mushy shit.

LINCOLN: Sure I do.

BOOTH: You hate mushy shit. You always hated thuh mushy
       shit.   55

LINCOLN: Ive changed. Go head. You had "an evening to re-
       member," remember? I was just here alone sitting here.
       Drinking. Go head. Tell Link thuh stink.

(*Rest.*)

       Howd ya do her?

BOOTH: Dogstyle.   60

LINCOLN: Amazing Grace.

BOOTH: In front of a mirror.

LINCOLN: So you could see her. Her face her breasts her back
       her ass. Graces got a great ass.

BOOTH: Its all right.   65

LINCOLN: Amazing Grace!

BOOTH *goes into his bed area and takes off his suit, tossing the clothes on the floor.*

BOOTH: She said next time Ima have to use a rubber. She let
       me have my way this time but she said that next time I'd
       have to put my boots on.

LINCOLN: Im sure you can talk her out of it.   70

BOOTH: Yeah.

(*Rest.*)

       What kind of rubbers you use, I mean, when you was
       with Cookie.

LINCOLN: We didnt use rubbers. We was married, man.

BOOTH: Right. But you had other women on the side. What   75
       kind you use when you was with them?

LINCOLN: Magnums.

BOOTH: Thats thuh kind I picked up. For next time. Grace
       was real strict about it.

While BOOTH *sits on his bed fiddling with his box of condoms,* LIN-
COLN *sits in his chair and resumes drinking.*

LINCOLN: Im sure you can talk her out of it. You put yr foot 80
       down and she'll melt.

BOOTH: She was real strict. Sides I wouldnt wanna be taking
       advantage of her or nothing. Putting my foot down and
       her melting all over thuh place.

LINCOLN: Magnums then.   85

(*Rest.*)

       Theyre for "the larger man."

BOOTH: Right. Right.

LINCOLN *keeps drinking as* BOOTH, *sitting in the privacy of his bedroom, fiddles with the condoms, perhaps trying to put one on.*

LINCOLN: Thats right.

BOOTH: Graces real different from them fly-by-night gals I
       was making do with. Shes in school. Making something of 90

herself. Studying cosmetology. You should see what she can do with a womans hair and nails.

LINCOLN: Too bad you aint a woman.

BOOTH: What?

95 LINCOLN: You could get yrs done for free, I mean.

BOOTH: Yeah. She got this way of sitting. Of talking. Everything she does is. Shes just so hot.

(*Rest.*)

We was together 2 years. Then we broke up. I had my little employment difficulty and she needed time to think.

100 LINCOLN: And shes through thinking now.

BOOTH: Thats right.

LINCOLN

BOOTH

LINCOLN: Whatcha doing back there?

105 BOOTH: Resting. That girl wore me out.

LINCOLN: You want some med-sin?

BOOTH: No thanks.

LINCOLN: Come practice my moves with me, then.

BOOTH: Lets hit it tomorrow, K?

110 LINCOLN: I been waiting. I got all dressed up and you said if I waited up—come on, man, they gonna replace me with a wax dummy.

BOOTH: No shit.

LINCOLN: Thats what theyre talking about. Probably just talk,

115 but—come on, man, I even lent you 5 bucks.

BOOTH: Im tired.

LINCOLN: You didnt get shit tonight.

BOOTH: You jealous, man. You just jail-us.

LINCOLN: You laying over there yr balls blue as my boosted

120 suit. Laying over there waiting for me to go back to sleep or black out so I wont hear you rustling thuh pages of yr fuck book.

BOOTH: Fuck you, man.

LINCOLN: I was over there looking for something the other

125 week and theres like 100 fuck books under yr bed and theyre matted together like a bad fro, bro, cause you spunked in the pages and didnt wipe them off.

BOOTH: Im hot. I need constant sexual release. If I wasnt taking care of myself by myself I would be out there running

130 around on thuh town which costs cash that I dont have so I would be doing worse: I'd be out there doing who knows what, shooting people and shit. Out of a need for unresolved sexual release. I'm a hot man. I aint apologizing for it. When I dont got a woman, I gotta make do. Not like

135 you, Link. When you dont got a woman you just sit there. Letting yr shit fester. Yr dick, if it aint falled off yet, is hanging there between yr legs, little whiteface shriveled-up blank-shooting grub worm. As goes thuh man so goes thuh mans dick. Thats what I say. Least my shits intact.

(*Rest.*)

140 You a limp dick jealous whiteface motherfucker whose wife dumped him cause he couldnt get it up and she told me so. Came crawling to me cause she needed a man.

(*Rest.*)

I gave it to Grace good tonight. So goodnight.

LINCOLN

(*Rest.*)

Goodnight.   145

LINCOLN

BOOTH

LINCOLN

BOOTH

LINCOLN   150

BOOTH

LINCOLN *sitting in his chair.* BOOTH *lying in bed. Time passes.* BOOTH *peeks out to see if* LINCOLN *is asleep.* LINCOLN *is watching for him.*

LINCOLN: You can hustle 3-card monte without me you know.

BOOTH: Im planning to.

LINCOLN: I could contact my old crew. You could work with 155 them. Lonny aint around no more but theres the rest of them. Theyre good.

BOOTH: I can get my own crew. I dont need yr crew. Buncha hasbeens. I can get my own crew.

LINCOLN: My crews experienced. We usedta pull down a 160 thousand a day. Thats 7 G a week. That was years ago. They probably do twice, 3 times that now.

BOOTH: I got my own connections, thank you.

LINCOLN: Theyd take you on in a heartbeat. With my say. My say still counts with them. They know you from before, 165 when you tried to hang with us but—wernt ready yet. They know you from then, but I'd talk you up. I'd say yr my bro, which they know, and I'd say youd been working the west coast. Little towns. Mexican border. Taking tourists. I'd tell them you got moves like I dreamed of 170 having. Meanwhile youd be working out yr shit right here, right in this room, getting good and getting better every day so when I did do the reintroductions youd have some marketable skills. Youd be passable.

BOOTH: I'd be more than passable, I'd be the be all end all. 175

LINCOLN: Youd be the be all end all. And youd have my say. If yr interested.

BOOTH: Could do.

LINCOLN: Youd have to get a piece. They all pack pistols, bro.

BOOTH: I *got* a piece.   180

LINCOLN: Youd have to be packing something more substantial than that pop gun, 3-Card. These hustlers is upper echelon hustlers they pack upper echelon heat, not no Saturday night shit, now.

BOOTH: Whata you know of heat? You aint hung with those 185 guys for 6, 7 years. You swore off em. Threw yr heat in thuh river and you "Dont touch thuh cards." I know more about heat than you know about heat.

LINCOLN: Im around guns every day. At the arcade. Theyve all been reworked so they only fire caps but I see guns 190 every day. Lots of guns.

BOOTH: What kinds?

LINCOLN: You been there, you seen them. Shiny deadly metal each with their own deadly personality.

BOOTH: Maybe I *could* visit you over there. I'd boost one of 195 them guns and rework it to make it shoot for real again. What kind you think would best suit my personality?

LINCOLN: You aint stealing nothing from the arcade.

BOOTH: I go in there and steal if I want to go in there and
200   steal I go in there and steal.

LINCOLN: It aint worth it. They dont shoot nothing but
blanks.

BOOTH: Yea, like you. Shooting blanks.

(*Rest.*)

(*Rest.*)

You ever wonder if someones gonna come in there with
205   a real gun? A real gun with real slugs? Someone with uh
axe tuh grind or something?

LINCOLN: No.

BOOTH: Someone who hates you come in there and guns
you down and gets gone before anybody finds out.

210 LINCOLN: I dont got no enemies.

BOOTH: Yr X.

LINCOLN: Cookie dont hate me.

BOOTH: Yr Best Customer? Some miscellaneous stranger?

LINCOLN: I cant be worrying about the actions of miscella-
215   neous strangers.

BOOTH: But there they come day in day out for a chance to
shoot Honest Abe.

(*Rest.*)

Who are they mostly?

LINCOLN: I dont really look.

220 BOOTH: You must see something.

LINCOLN: Im supposed to be staring straight ahead. Watching a play, like Abe was.

BOOTH: All day goes by and you never ever take a sneak peek
at who be pulling the trigger.

Pulled in by his own curiosity, BOOTH *has come out of his bed area
to stand on the dividing line between the two spaces.*

225 LINCOLN: Its pretty dark. To keep thuh illusion of thuh
whole thing.

(*Rest.*)

But on thuh wall opposite where I sit theres a little electrical box, like a fuse box. Silver metal. Its got uh dent in
it like somebody hit it with they fist. Big old dent so
230   everything reflected in it gets reflected upside down. Like
yr looking in uh spoon. And thats where I can see em.
The assassins.

(*Rest.*)

Not behind me yet but I can hear him coming. Coming
in with his gun in hand, thuh gun he already picked out
235   up front when he paid his fare. Coming on in. But not behind me yet. His dress shoes making too much noise on
the carpet, the carpets too thin, Boss should get a new one
but hes cheap. Not behind me yet. Not behind me yet.
Cheap lightbulb just above my head.

(*Rest.*)

And there he is. Standing behind me. Standing in position. 240
Standing upside down. Theres some feet shapes on the
floor so he knows just where he oughta stand. So he wont
miss. Thuh gun is always cold. Winter or summer thuh
gun is always cold. And when the gun touches me he can
feel that Im warm and he knows Im alive. And if Im alive 245
then he can shoot me dead. And for a minute, with him
hanging back there behind me, its real. Me looking at him
upside down and him looking at me looking like Lincoln.
Then he shoots.

(*Rest.*)

I slump down and close my eyes. And he goes out thuh 250
other way. More come in. Uh whole day full. Bunches of
kids, little good for nothings, in they school uniforms.
Businessmen smelling like two for one martinis. Tourists
in they theme park t-shirts trying to catch it on film.
Housewives with they mouths closed tight, shooting more 255
than once.

(*Rest.*)

They all get so into it. I do my best for them. And now
they talking bout replacing me with uh wax dummy. Itll
cut costs.

BOOTH: You just gotta show yr boss that you can do things a 260
wax dummy cant do. You too dry with it. You gotta add
spicy shit.

LINCOLN: Like what.

BOOTH: Like when they shoot you, I dunno, scream or something.   265

LINCOLN: Scream?

BOOTH *plays the killer without using his gun.*

BOOTH: Try it. I'll be the killer. Bang!

LINCOLN: Aaaah!

BOOTH: Thats good.

LINCOLN: A wax dummy can scream. They can put a voice- 270
box in it and make it like its screaming.

BOOTH: You can curse. Try it. Bang!

LINCOLN: Motherfucking cocksucker!

BOOTH: That's good, man.

LINCOLN: They aint going for that, though.   275

BOOTH: You practice rolling and wiggling on the floor?

LINCOLN: A little.

BOOTH: Lemmie see. Bang!

LINCOLN *slumps down, falls on the floor and silently wiggles
around.*

BOOTH: You look more like a worm on the sidewalk. Move
yr arms. Good. Now scream or something.   280

LINCOLN: Aaaah! Aaaaah! Aaaah!

BOOTH: A little tougher than that, you sound like yr fucking.

LINCOLN: Aaaaaah!

BOOTH: Hold yr head or something, where I shotcha. Good.
And look at me! I am the assassin! *I am Booth!!* Come on 285
man this is life and death! Go all out!

LINCOLN *goes all out.*

BOOTH: Cool, man thats cool. Thats enough.

LINCOLN: Whatdoyathink?

BOOTH: I dunno, man. Something about it. I dunno. It was looking too real or something.

LINCOLN: They dont want it looking too real. I'd scare the customers. Then I'd be out for sure. Yr trying to get me fired.

BOOTH: Im trying to help. Cross my heart.

LINCOLN: People are funny about they Lincoln shit. Its historical. People like they historical shit in a certain way. They like it to unfold the way they folded it up. Neatly like a book. Not raggedy and bloody and screaming. You trying to get me fired.

(*Rest.*)

I am uh brother playing Lincoln. Its uh stretch for anyones imagination. And it aint easy for me neither. Every day I put on that shit, I leave my own shit at the door and I put on that shit and I go out there and I make it work. I make it look easy but its hard. That shit is hard. But it works. Cause I work it. And you trying to get me fired.

(*Rest.*)

I swore off them cards. Took nowhere jobs. Drank. Then Cookie threw me out. What thuh fuck was I gonna do? I seen that "Help Wanted" sign and I went up in there and I looked good in the getup and agreed to the whiteface and they really dug it that me and Honest Abe got the same name.

(*Rest.*)

Its a sit down job. With benefits. I dont wanna get fired. They wont give me a good reference if I get fired.

BOOTH: Iffen you was tuh get fired, then, well—then you and me could—hustle the cards together. We'd have to support ourselves somehow.

(*Rest.*)

Just show me how to do the hook part of the card hustle, man. The part where the Dealer looks away but somehow he sees—

LINCOLN: I couldnt remember if I wanted to.

BOOTH: Sure you could.

LINCOLN: No.

(*Rest.*)

Night, man.

BOOTH: Yeah.

LINCOLN *stretches out in his recliner.* BOOTH *stands over him waiting for him to get up, to change his mind. But* LINCOLN *is fast asleep.* BOOTH *covers him with a blanket then goes to his bed, turning off the lights as he goes. He quietly rummages underneath his bed for a girlie magazine which, as the lights fade, he reads with great interest.*

SCENE FOUR

Saturday. Just before dawn. LINCOLN *gets up. Looks around.* BOOTH *is fast asleep, dead to the world.*

LINCOLN: No fucking running water.

He stumbles around the room looking for something which he finally finds: a plastic cup, which he uses as a urinal. He finishes peeing and finds an out of the way place to stow the cup. He claws at his Lincoln getup, removing it and tearing it in the process. He strips down to his t-shirt and shorts.

LINCOLN: Hate falling asleep in this damn shit. Shit. Ripped the beard. I can just hear em tomorrow. Busiest day of the week. They looking me over to make sure Im presentable. They got a slew of guys working but Im the only one they look over every day. "Yr beards ripped, pal. Sure, we'll getcha new one but its gonna be coming outa yr pay." Shit. I should quit right then and there. I'd yank off the beard, throw it on the ground and stomp it, then go strangle the fucking boss. Thatd be good. My hands around his neck and his bug eyes bugging out. You been ripping me off since I took this job and now Im gonna have to take it outa *yr* pay, motherfucker. Shit.

(*Rest.*)

Sit down job. With benefits.

(*Rest.*)

Hustling. Shit, I was good. I was great. Hell I was the be all end all. I was throwing cards like throwing cards was made for me. Made for me and me alone. I was the best anyone ever seen. Coast to coast. Everybody said so. And I never lost. Not once. Not one time. Not never. Thats how much them cards was mines. I was the be all end all. I was that good.

(*Rest.*)

Then you woke up one day and you didnt have the taste for it no more. Like something in you knew.—Like something in you knew it was time to quit. Quit while you was still ahead. Something in you was telling you.—But hells no. Not Link thuh stink. So I went out there and threw one more time. What thuh fuck. And Lonny died.

(*Rest.*)

Got yrself a good job. And when the arcade lets you go yll get another good job. I dont gotta spend my whole life hustling. Theres more to Link than that. More to me than some cheap hustle. More to life than cheating some idiot out of his paycheck or his life savings.

(*Rest.*)

Like that joker and his wife from out of town. Always wanted to see the big city. I said you could see the bigger end of the big city with a little more cash. And if they was fast enough, faster than me, and here I slowed down my moves I slowed em way down and my Lonny, my right hand, my Stickman, spanish guy who looked white and could draw a customer in like nothing else, Lonny could draw a fly from fresh shit, he could draw Adam outa Eve just with that look he had, Lonny always got folks playing.

(*Rest.*)

Somebody shot him. They dont know who. Nobody knows nobody cares.

(*Rest.*)

We took that man and his wife for hundreds. No, thou-
45   sands. We took them for everything they had and everything they ever wanted to have. We took a father for the
money he was gonna get his kids new bike with and he
cried in the street while we vanished. We took a mothers
welfare check, she pulled a knife on us and we ran. She
50   threw it but her aim werent shit. People shopping. Greedy.
Thinking they could take me and they got took instead.

(*Rest.*)

Swore off thuh cards. Something inside me telling me—.
But I was good.
LINCOLN
55   LINCOLN

*He sees a packet of cards. He studies them like an alcoholic would
study a drink. Then he reaches for them, delicately picking them up
and choosing 3 cards.*

LINCOLN: Still got my moves. Still got my touch. Still got my
chops. Thuh feel of it. And I aint hurting no one, God.
Link is just here hustling hisself.

(*Rest.*)

Lets see whatcha got.

*He stands over the monte setup. Then he bends over it placing the
cards down and moving them around. Slowly at first, aimlessly, as if
hes just making little ripples in water. But then the game draws him
in. Unlike* BOOTH, LINCOLNs *patter and moves are deft, dangerous,
electric.*

60   LINCOLN: (((Lean in close and watch me now: who see thuh
black card who see thuh black card I see thuh black card
black cards thuh winner pick thuh black card thats thuh
winner pick thuh red card thats thuh loser pick thuh
other red card thats thuh other loser pick thuh black card
65   you pick thuh winner. Watch me as I throw thuh cards.
Here we go.)))

(*Rest.*)

(((Who see thuh black card who see thuh black card? You
pick thuh red card you pick a loser you pick that red card
you pick a loser you pick thuh black card thuh deuce of
70   spades you pick a winner who sees thuh deuce of spades
thuh one who sees it never fades watch me now as I
throw thuh cards. Red losers black winner follow thuh
deuce of spaces chase thuh black deuce. Dark deuce will
get you thuh win.)))

Even though LINCOLN *speaks softly,* BOOTH *wakes and, unbe-
knownst to* LINCOLN, *listens intently.*

(*Rest.*)

LINCOLN: ((10 will get you 20, 20 will get you 40.))   75

(*Rest.*)

((Ima show you thuh cards: 2 red cards but only one
spade. Dark winner in thuh center and thuh red losers
on thuh sides. Pick uh red card you got a loser pick
thuh other red card you got a loser pick thuh black card
you got a winner. One good pickll get you in, 2 good   80
picks and you gone win. Watch me come on watch me
now.))

(*Rest.*)

((Who sees thuh winner who knows where its at? You do?
You sure? Go on then, put yr money where yr mouth is.
Put yr money down you aint no clown. No? Ah, you had   85
thuh card but you didnt have thuh heart.))

(*Rest.*)

((Watch me now as I throw thuh cards watch me real
close. Ok, man, you know which card is the deuce of
spades? Was you watching Links lighting fast express? Was
you watching Link cause he the best? So you sure, huh?   90
Point it out first, then place yr bet and Linkll show you yr
winner.))

(*Rest.*)

((500 dollars? You thuh man of thuh hour you thuh man
with thuh power. You musta been watching Link real
close. You must be thuh man who know thuh most. Ok.   95
Lay the cash in my hand cause Link the man. Thank you,
mister. This card you say?))

(*Rest.*)

((Wrong! Ha!))

(*Rest.*)

((Thats thuh show. We gotta go.))

LINCOLN *puts the cards down. He moves away from the monte
setup. He sits on the edge of his easy chair, but he can't take his eyes
off the cards.*

Intermission

SCENE FIVE

Several days have passed. Its now Wednesday night. BOOTH *is sitting in his brand-new suit. The monte setup is nowhere in sight. In
its place is a table with two nice chairs. The table is covered with a
lovely tablecloth and there are nice plates, silverware, champagne
glasses and candles. All the makings of a very romantic dinner for
two. The whole apartment in fact takes its cue from the table. Its been
cleaned up considerably. New curtains on the windows, a doily-like
object on the recliner.* BOOTH *sits at the table darting his eyes
around, making sure everything is looking good.*

BOOTH: Shit.

He notices some of his girlie magazines visible from underneath his bed. He goes over and nudges them out of sight. He sits back down. He notices that theyre still visible. He goes over and nudges them some more, kicking at them finally. Then he takes the spread from his bed and pulls it down, hiding them. He sits back down. He gets up. Checks the champagne on much melted ice. Checks the food.

BOOTH: Foods getting cold, Grace!! Dont worry man, she'll get here, she'll get here.

He sits back down. He goes over to the bed. Checks it for springiness. Smoothes down the bedspread. Double-checks 2 matching silk dressing gowns, very expensive, marked "His" and "Hers." Lays the dressing gowns across the bed again. He sits back down. He cant help but notice the visibility of the girlie magazines again. He goes to the bed, kicks them fiercely, then on his hands and knees shoves them. Then he begins to get under the bed to push them, but he remembers his nice clothing and takes off his jacket. After a beat he removes his pants and, in this half-dressed way, he crawls under the bed to give those telltale magazines a good and final shove. LINCOLN comes in. At first BOOTH, still stripped down to his underwear, thinks its his date. When he realizes its his brother, he does his best to keep LINCOLN from entering the apartment. LINCOLN wears his frock coat and carries the rest of his getup in a plastic bag.

LINCOLN: You in the middle of it?
BOOTH: What the hell you doing here?
5   LINCOLN: If yr in thuh middle of it I can go. Or I can just be real quiet and just—sing a song in my head or something.
BOOTH: The casas off limits to you tonight.
LINCOLN: You know when we lived in that 2-room place with the cement backyard and the frontyard with nothing
10   but trash in it, Mom and Pops would do it in the middle of the night and I would always hear them but I would sing in my head, cause, I dunno, I couldnt bear to listen.
BOOTH: You gotta get out of here.
LINCOLN: I would make up all kinds of songs. Oh, sorry, yr
15   all up in it. No sweat, bro. No sweat. Hey, Grace, howyadoing?!
BOOTH: She aint here yet, man. Shes running late. And its a good thing too cause I aint all dressed yet. Yr gonna spend thuh night with friends?
20   LINCOLN: Yeah.

BOOTH *waits for* LINCOLN *to leave.* LINCOLN *stands his ground.*

LINCOLN: I lost my job.
BOOTH: Hunh.
LINCOLN: I come in there right on time like I do every day and that motherfucker gives me some song and dance
25   about cutbacks and too many folks complaining.
BOOTH: Hunh.
LINCOLN: Showd me thuh wax dummy—hes buying it right out of a catalog.

(*Rest.*)

I walked out still wearing my getup.

(*Rest.*)

30   I could go back in tomorrow. I could tell him I'll take another pay cut. Thatll get him to take me back.

BOOTH: Link. Yr free. Dont go crawling back. Yr free at last! Now you can do anything you want. Yr not tied down by that job. You can—you can do something else. Something that pays better maybe.   35
LINCOLN: You mean Hustle.
BOOTH: Maybe. Hey, Graces on her way. You gotta go.

LINCOLN *flops into his chair.* BOOTH *is waiting for him to move.* LINCOLN *doesnt budge.*

LINCOLN: I'll stay until she gets here. I'll act nice. I wont embarrass you.
BOOTH: You gotta go.   40
LINCOLN: What time she coming?
BOOTH: Shes late. She could be here any second.
LINCOLN: I'll meet her. I met her years ago. I'll meet her again.

(*Rest.*)

How late is she?
BOOTH: She was supposed to be here at 8.   45
LINCOLN: Its after 2 a.m. Shes—shes late.

(*Rest.*)

Maybe when she comes you could put the blanket over me and I'll just pretend like Im not here.

(*Rest.*)

I'll wait. And when she comes I'll go. I need to sit down. I been walking around all day.   50
BOOTH
LINCOLN

BOOTH *goes to his bed and dresses hurriedly.*

BOOTH: Pretty nice, right? The china thuh silver thuh crystal.
LINCOLN: Its great.

(*Rest.*)

Boosted?   55
BOOTH: Yeah.
LINCOLN: Thought you went and spent yr inheritance for a minute, you had me going I was thinking shit, Booth—3-Card—that 3-Cards gone and spent his inheritance and the gal is—late.   60
BOOTH: Its boosted. Every bit of it.

(*Rest.*)

Fuck this waiting bullshit.
LINCOLN: She'll be here in a minute. Dont sweat it.
BOOTH: Right.

BOOTH *comes to the table. Sits. Relaxes as best he can.*

BOOTH: How come I got a hand for boosting and I dont got   65
a hand for throwing cards? Its sorta the same thing—you gotta be quick—and slick. Maybe yll show me yr moves sometime.
LINCOLN
BOOTH   70

LINCOLN
BOOTH

LINCOLN: Look out the window. When you see Grace coming, I'll go.

75 BOOTH: Cool. Cause youd jinx it, youd really jinx it. Maybe you being here has jinxed it already. Naw. Shes just a little late. You aint jinxed nothing.

BOOTH sits by the window, glancing out, watching for his date. LINCOLN sits in his recliner. He finds the whiskey bottle, sips from it. He then rummages around, finding the raggedy photo album. He looks through it.

LINCOLN: There we are at the house. Remember when we moved in?
80 BOOTH: No.
LINCOLN: You were 2 or 3.
BOOTH: I was 5.
LINCOLN: I was 8. We all thought it was the best fucking house in the world.
85 BOOTH: Cement backyard and a frontyard full of trash, yeah, dont be going down memory lane man, yll jinx thuh vibe I got going in here. Gracell be walking in here and wrinkling up her nose cause you done jinxed up thuh joint with yr raggedy recollections.
90 LINCOLN: We had some great times in that house, bro. Selling lemonade on thuh corner, thuh treehouse out back, summers spent lying in thuh grass and looking at thuh stars.
BOOTH: We never did none of that shit.
LINCOLN: But we had us some good times. That row of nails
95 I got you to line up behind Dads car so when he backed out the driveway to work—
BOOTH: He came back that night, only time I ever seen his face go red, 4 flat tires and yelling bout how thuh white man done sabotaged him again.
100 LINCOLN: And neither of us flinched. Neither of us let on that itd been us.
BOOTH: It was at dinner, right? What were we eating?
LINCOLN: Food.
BOOTH: We was eating pork chops, mashed potatoes and
105 peas. I remember cause I had to look at them peas real hard to keep from letting on. And I would glance over at you, not really glancing not actually turning my head, but I was looking at you out thuh corner of my eye. I was sure he was gonna find us out and then he woulda whipped us
110 good. But I kept glancing at you and you was cool, man. Like nothing was going on. You was cooooool.

(*Rest.*)

What time is it?
LINCOLN: After 3.

(*Rest.*)

You should call her. Something mighta happened.
115 BOOTH: No man, Im cool. She'll be here in a minute. Patience is a virtue. She'll be here.
LINCOLN: You look sad.
BOOTH: Nope. Im just, you know, Im just—
LINCOLN: Cool.
120 BOOTH: Yeah, Cool.

BOOTH comes over, takes the bottle of whiskey and pours himself a big glassful. He returns to the window looking out and drinking.

BOOTH: They give you a severance package, at thuh job?
LINCOLN: A weeks pay.
BOOTH: Great.
LINCOLN: I blew it. Spent it all.
BOOTH: On what?   125
LINCOLN: — Just spent it.

(*Rest.*)

It felt good, spending it. Felt really good. Like back in thuh day when I was really making money. Throwing thuh cards all day and strutting and rutting all night. Didnt have to take no shit from no fool, didnt have to worry 130 about getting fired in favor of some damn wax dummy. I was thuh shit and they was my fools.

(*Rest.*)

Back in thuh day.

(*Rest.*)

(*Rest.*)

Why you think they left us, man?
BOOTH: Mom and Pops? I dont think about it too much.   135
LINCOLN: I dont think they liked us.
BOOTH: Naw. That aint it.
LINCOLN: I think there was something out there that they liked more than they liked us and for years they was struggling against moving towards that more liked something. 140 Each of them had a special something that they was struggling against. Moms had hers. Pops had his. And they was struggling. We moved out of that nasty apartment into a house. A whole house. I wernt perfect but it was a house and theyd bought it and they brought us there and every- 145 thing we owned, figuring we could be a family in that house and them things, them two separate things each of them was struggling against, would just leave them be. Them things would see thuh house and be impressed and just leave them be. Would see thuh job Pops had and how 150 he shined his shoes every night before he went to bed, shining them shoes whether they needed it or not, and thuh thing he was struggling against would see all that and just let him be, and thuh thing Moms was struggling against, it would see the food on the table every night and 155 listen to her voice when she'd read to us sometimes, the clean clothes, the buttons sewed on all right and it would just let her be. Just let us all be, just regular people living in a house. That wernt too much to ask.
BOOTH: Least we was grown when they split.   160
LINCOLN: 16 and 13 aint grown.
BOOTH: 16s grown. Almost. And I was ok cause you were there.

(*Rest.*)

Shit man, it aint like they both one day both, together packed all they shit up and left us so they could have fun 165 in thuh sun on some tropical island and you and me would have to grub in thuh dirt forever. They didnt leave together. That makes it different. She left, 2 years go by. Then he left. Like neither of them couldnt handle it no more. She split then he split. Like thuh whole family mortgage bills going to work thing was just too much. And I dont blame them. You dont see me holding down a steady job. Cause its bullshit and I know it. I seen how it cracked them up and I aint going there.

(Rest.)

It aint right me trying to make myself into a one woman man just because she wants me like that. One woman rubber-wearing motherfucker. Shit. Not me. She gonna walk in here looking all hot and shit trying to see how much she can get me to sweat, how much she can get me to give her before she gives me mines. Shit.

LINCOLN

BOOTH

LINCOLN: Moms told me I shouldnt never get married.

BOOTH: She told me thuh same thing.

LINCOLN: They gave us each 500 bucks then they cut out.

BOOTH: Thats what Im gonna do. Give my kids 500 bucks then cut out. Thats thuh way to do it.

LINCOLN: You dont got no kids.

BOOTH: Im gonna have kids then Im gonna cut out.

LINCOLN: Leaving each of yr offspring 500 bucks as yr split-ting.

BOOTH: Yeah.

(Rest.)

Just goes to show Mom and Pops had some agreement between them.

LINCOLN: How so.

BOOTH: Theyd stopped talking to eachother. Theyd stopped *screwing* eachother. But they had an agreement. Some-where in there when it looked like all they had was hate they sat down and did thuh "split" budget.

(Rest.)

When Moms splits she gives me 5 hundred-dollar bills rolled up and tied up tight in one of her nylon stock-ings. She tells me to put it in a safe place, to spend it only in case of an emergency, and not to tell nobody I got it, not even you. 2 years later Pops splits and before he goes—

LINCOLN: He slips me 10 fifties in a clean handkerchief: "Hide this somewheres good, dont go blowing it, dont tell no one you got it, especially that Booth."

BOOTH: Theyd been scheming together all along. They left separately but they was in agreement. Maybe they arrived at the same place at the same time, maybe they renewed they wedding vows, maybe they got another family.

LINCOLN: Maybe they got 2 new kids. 2 boys. Different than us, though. Better.

BOOTH: Maybe.

Their glasses are empty. The whiskey bottle is empty too. BOOTH *takes the champagne bottle from the ice tub. He pops the cork and pours drinks for his brother and himself.*

BOOTH: I didnt mind them leaving cause you was there. Thats why Im hooked on us working together. If we could work together it would be like old times. They split and we got that room downtown. You was done with school and I stopped going. And we had to run around doing odd jobs just to keep the lights on and the heat go-ing and thuh child protection bitch off our backs. It was you and me against thuh world, Link. It could be like that again.

LINCOLN

BOOTH

LINCOLN

BOOTH

LINCOLN: Throwing thuh cards aint as easy as it looks.

BOOTH: I aint stupid.

LINCOLN: When you hung with us back then, you was just on thuh sidelines. Thuh perspective from thuh sidelines is thuh perspective of a customer. There was all kinds of things you didnt know nothing about.

BOOTH: Lonny would entice folks into thuh game as they walked by. Thuh 2 folks on either side of ya looked like they was playing but they was only pretending tuh play. Just tuh generate excitement. You was moving thuh cards as fast as you could hoping that yr hands would be faster than yr customers eyes. Sometimes you won sometimes you lost what else is there to know?

LINCOLN: Thuh customer is actually called the "Mark." You know why?

BOOTH: Cause hes thuh one you got yr eye on. You mark him with yr eye.

LINCOLN

LINCOLN

BOOTH: Im right, right?

LINCOLN: Lemmie show you a few moves. If you pick up these yll have a chance.

BOOTH: Yr playing.

LINCOLN: Get thuh cards and set it up.

BOOTH: No shit.

LINCOLN: Set it up set it up.

In a flash, BOOTH *clears away the romantic table setting by gather-ing it all up in the tablecloth and tossing it aside. As he does so he reveals the "table" underneath: the 2 stacked monte milk crates and the cardboard playing surface.* LINCOLN *lays out the cards. The brothers are ready.* LINCOLN *begins to teach* BOOTH *in earnest.*

LINCOLN: Thuh deuce of spades is thuh card tuh watch.

BOOTH: I work with thuh deuce of hearts. But spades is cool.

LINCOLN: Theres thuh Dealer, thuh Stickman, thuh Sides, thuh Lookout and thuh Mark. I'll be thuh Dealer.

BOOTH: I'll be thuh Lookout. Lemmie be thuh Lookout, right? I'll keep an eye for thuh cops. I got my piece on me.

LINCOLN: You got it on you right now?

BOOTH: I always carry it.

LINCOLN: Even on a date? In yr own home?

BOOTH: You never know, man.

(Rest.)

So Im thuh Lookout.

LINCOLN: Gimmie yr piece.

BOOTH *gives* LINCOLN *his gun.* LINCOLN *moves the little wooden chair to face right in front of the setup. He then puts the gun on the chair.*

LINCOLN: We dont need nobody standing on the corner watching for cops cause there aint none.

BOOTH: I'll be thuh Stickman, then.

270 LINCOLN: Stickman knows the game inside out. You aint there yet. But you will be. You wanna learn good, be my Sideman. Playing along with the Dealer, moving the Mark to lay his money down. You wanna learn, right?

BOOTH: I'll be thuh Side.

275 LINCOLN: Good.

(*Rest.*)

First thing you learn is what is. Next thing you learn is what aint. You dont know what is you dont know what aint, you dont know shit.

BOOTH: Right.

280 LINCOLN

BOOTH

BOOTH: Whatchu looking at?

LINCOLN: Im sizing you up.

BOOTH: Oh yeah?!

285 LINCOLN: Dealer always sizes up thuh crowd.

BOOTH: Im yr Side, Link, Im on yr team, you dont go sizing up yr own team. You save looks like that for yr Mark.

LINCOLN: Dealer always sizes up thuh crowd. Everybody out there is part of the crowd. His crew is part of the crowd,

290 he himself is part of the crowd. Dealer always sizes up thuh crowd.

LINCOLN *looks* BOOTH *over some more then looks around at an imaginary crowd.*

BOOTH: Then what then what?

LINCOLN: Dealer dont wanna play.

BOOTH: Bullshit man! Come on you promised!

295 LINCOLN: Thats thuh Dealers attitude. He *acts* like he dont wanna play. He holds back and thuh crowd, with their eagerness to see his skill and their willingness to take a chance, and their greediness to win his cash, the larceny in their hearts, all goad him on and push him to throw his

300 cards, although of course the Dealer has been wanting to throw his cards all along. Only he dont never show it.

BOOTH: Thats some sneaky shit, Link.

LINCOLN: It sets thuh mood. You wanna have them in yr hand before you deal a hand, K?

305 BOOTH: Cool.—K.

LINCOLN: Right.

LINCOLN

BOOTH

BOOTH: You sizing me up again?

310 LINCOLN: Theres 2 parts to throwing thuh cards. Both parts are fairly complicated. Thuh moves and thuh grooves, thuh talk and thuh walk, thuh patter and thuh pitter pat, thuh flap and thuh rap: what yr doing with yr mouth and what yr doing with yr hands.

315 BOOTH: I got thuh words down pretty good.

LINCOLN: You need to work on both.

BOOTH: K.

LINCOLN: A goodlooking walk and a dynamite talk captivates their entire attention. The Mark focuses with 2 organs primarily: his eyes and his ears. Leave one out you lose yr 320 shirt. Captivate both, yr golden.

BOOTH: So them times I seen you lose, them times I seen thuh Mark best you, that was a time when yr hands werent fast enough or yr patter werent right.

LINCOLN: You could say that.   325

BOOTH: So, there was plenty of times—

LINCOLN *moves the cards around.*

LINCOLN: You see what Im doing? Dont look at my hands, man, look at my eyes. Know what is and know what aint.

BOOTH: What is?

LINCOLN: My eyes?   330

BOOTH: What aint?

LINCOLN: My hands. Look at my eyes not my hands. And you standing there thinking how thuh fuck I gonna learn how tuh throw thuh cards if I be looking in his eyes? Look into my eyes and get yr focus. Dont think about 335 learning how tuh throw thuh cards. Dont think about nothing. Just look into my eyes. Focus.

BOOTH: Theyre red.

LINCOLN: Look into my eyes.

BOOTH: You been crying?   340

LINCOLN: Just look into my eyes, fool. Now. Look down at thuh cards. I been moving and moving and moving them around. Ready?

BOOTH: Yeah.

LINCOLN: Ok, Sideman, thuh Marks got his eye on you. Yr 345 gonna show him its easy.

BOOTH: K.

LINCOLN: Pick out thuh deuce of spades. Dont pick it up just point to it.

BOOTH: This one, right?   350

LINCOLN: Dont ask thuh Dealer if yr right, man, point to yr card with confidence.

BOOTH *points.*

BOOTH: That one.

(*Rest.*)

Flip it over, man.

LINCOLN *flips over the card. It is in fact the deuce of spades.* BOOTH *struts around gloating like a rooster.* LINCOLN *is mildly crestfallen.*

BOOTH: Am I right or am I right?! Make room for 3-Card! 355 Here comes thuh champ!

LINCOLN: Cool. Stay focused. Now we gonna add the second element. Listen.

LINCOLN *moves the cards and speaks in a low hypnotic voice.*

LINCOLN: Lean in close and watch me now: who see thuh black card who see thuh black card I see thuh black card 360 black cards thuh winner pick thuh black card thats thuh winner pick thuh red card thats thuh loser pick thuh other red card thats thuh other loser pick thuh black card you pick thuh winner. Watch me as I throw thuh cards. Here we go.   365

(*Rest.*)

Who see thuh black card who see thuh black card? You pick thuh red card you pick a loser you pick that red card you pick a loser you pick thuh black card thuh deuce of spades you pick a winner who sees thuh deuce of spades
370   thuh one who sees it never fades watch me now as I throw thuh cards. Red losers black winner follow thuh deuce of spades chase thuh black deuce. Dark deuce will get you thuh win. One good pickll get you in 2 good picks you gone win. 10 will get you 20, 20 will get you 40.

(*Rest.*)

375   Ima show you thuh cards: 2 red cards but only one spade. Dark winner in thuh center and thuh red losers on thuh sides. Pick uh red card you got a loser pick thuh other red card you got a loser pick thuh black card you got a winner. Watch me watch me watch me now.

(*Rest.*)

380   Ok, 3-Card, you know which cards thuh deuce of spade?
      BOOTH: Yeah.
      LINCOLN: You sure? Yeah? You sure you sure or you just think you sure? Oh you sure you sure huh? Was you watching
385   Links lighting fast express? Was you watching Link cause he the best? So you sure, huh? Point it out. Now, place yr bet and Linkll turn over yr card.
      BOOTH: What should I bet?
      LINCOLN: Dont bet nothing man, we just playing. Slap me 5
390   and point out thuh deuce.

BOOTH *slaps* LINCOLN *5, then points out a card which* LINCOLN *flips over. It is in fact again the deuce of spades.*

      BOOTH: Yeah, baby! 3-Card got thuh moves! You didnt know lil bro had thuh stuff, huh? Think again, Link, think again.
      LINCOLN: You wanna learn or you wanna run yr mouth?
      BOOTH: Thought you had fast hands. Wassup? What hap-
395   pened tuh "Links Lightning Fast Express"? Turned into uh local train looks like tuh me.
      LINCOLN: Thats yr whole motherfucking problem. Yr so busy running yr mouth you aint never gonna learn noth-ing! You think you something but you aint shit.
400   BOOTH: I aint shit, I am *The* Shit. Shit. Wheres thuh dark deuce? Right there! Yes, baby!
      LINCOLN: Ok, 3-Card. Cool. Lets switch. Take thuh cards and show me whatcha got. Go on. Dont touch thuh cards too heavy just—its a light touch. Like yr touching
405   Graces skin. Or, whatever, man, just a light touch. Like uh whisper.
      BOOTH: Like uh whisper.

BOOTH *moves the cards around, in an awkward imitation of his brother.*

      LINCOLN: Good.
      BOOTH: Yeah. All right. Look into my eyes.

BOOTHs *speech is loud and his movements are jerky. He is doing worse than when he threw the cards at the top of the play.*

BOOTH: Watch-me-close-watch-me-close-now: who-see-   410
      thuh-dark-card-who-see-thuh-dark-card? I-see-thuh-dark-card. Here-it-is. Thuh-dark-card-is-thuh-winner. Pick-thuh-dark-card-and-you-pick-uh-winner. Pick-uh-red-card-and-you-pick-uh-loser. Theres-thuh-loser-yeah-theres-thuh-red-card, theres-thuh-other-loser-and-   415
      theres-thuh-black-card, thuh-winner. Watch-me-close-watch-me-close-now: 3-Card-throws-thuh-cards-light-ning-fast. 3-Card-thats-me-and-Ima-last. Watch-me-throw-cause-here-I-go. See thuh black card? Yeah? Who see I see you see thuh black card?   420
LINCOLN: Hahahahhahahahahahahahah!

LINCOLN *doubles over laughing.* BOOTH *puts on his coat and pockets the gun.*

BOOTH: What?
LINCOLN: Nothing, man, nothing.
BOOTH: *What?!*   425
LINCOLN: Yr just, yr just a little wild with it. You talk like that on thuh street cards or no cards and theyll lock you up, man. Shit. Reminds me of that time when you hung with us and we let you try being thuh Stick cause you wanted to so bad. Thuh hustle was so simple. Remember? I told   430
      you that when I put my hand in my left pocket you was to get thuh Mark tuh pick thuh card on that side. You got to thinking something like Links left means my left some dyslexic shit and turned thuh wrong card. There was 800 bucks on the line and you fucked it up.   435

(*Rest.*)

But it was cool, little bro, cause we made the money back. It worked out cool.

(*Rest.*)

So, yeah, I said a light touch, little bro. Throw thuh cards light. Like uh whisper.
BOOTH: Like Graces skin.   440
LINCOLN: Like Graces skin.
BOOTH: What time is it?

LINCOLN *holds up his watch.* BOOTH *takes a look.*

BOOTH: Bitch. *Bitch!* She said she was gonna show up around 8. 8-a-fucking-clock.
LINCOLN: Maybe she meant 8 *a.m.*   445
BOOTH: Yeah. She gonna come all up in my place talking bout how she *love* me. How she cant stop *thinking* bout me. Nother mans shit up in her nother mans thing in her nother mans dick on her breath.
LINCOLN: Maybe something happened to her.   450
BOOTH: Something happened to her all right. She trying to make a chump outa me. I aint her chump. I aint nobodys chump.
LINCOLN: Sit. I'll go to the payphone on the corner. I'll—
BOOTH: Thuh world puts its foot in yr face and you dont   455
      move. You tell thuh world tuh keep on stepping. But Im my own man, Link. I aint you.

BOOTH *goes out, slamming the door behind him.*

LINCOLN: You got that right.

After a moment LINCOLN *picks up the cards. He moves them around fast, faster, faster.*

SCENE SIX

Thursday night. The room looks empty, as if neither brother is home. LINCOLN *comes in. Hes fairly drunk. He strides in, leaving the door slightly ajar.*

LINCOLN: Taaadaaaa!

(*Rest.*)

(*Rest.*)

　Taadaa, motherfucker. Taadaa!

(*Rest.*)

　Booth—uh, 3-Card—you here? Nope. Good. Just as well. Ha Ha *Ha Ha Ha*!

He pulls an enormous wad of money from his pocket. He counts it, slowly and luxuriously, arranging and smoothing the bills and sounding the amounts under his breath. He neatly rolls up the money, secures it with a rubber band and puts it back in his pocket. He relaxes in his chair. Then he takes the money out again, counting it all over again, but this time quickly, with the touch of an expert hustler.

LINCOLN: You didnt go back, Link, you got back, you got it back you got yr shit back in thuh saddle, man, you got back in business. Walking in Luckys and you seen how they was looking at you? Lucky starts pouring for you
5　when you walk in. And the women. You see how they was looking at you? Bought drinks for everybody. Bought drinks for Lucky. Bought drinks for Luckys damn dog. Shit. And thuh women be hanging on me and purring. And I be feeling that old call of thuh wild calling. I got
10　more phone numbers in my pockets between thuh time I walked out that door and thuh time I walked back in than I got in my whole life. Cause my shit is *back*. And back better than it was when it left too. Shoot. Who thuh man? Link. Thats right. Purrrrring all up on me and letting me
15　touch them and promise them shit. 3 of them sweethearts in thuh restroom on my dick all at once and I was *there* my shit was there. And Cookie just went out of my mind which is cool which is very cool. 3 of them. Fighting over it. Shit. Cause they knew I'd been throwing thuh cards.
20　Theyd seen me on thuh corner with thuh old crew or if they aint seed me with they own eyes theyd heard word. Links thuh stink! Theyd heard word and they seed uh sad face on some poor sucker or a tear in thuh eye of some stupid fucking tourist and they figured it was me whod
25　just took thuh suckers last dime, it was me who had all thuh suckers loot. They knew. They knew.

BOOTH *appears in the room. He is standing behind the screen, unseen all this time. He goes to the door, soundlessly, just stands there.*

LINCOLN: And they was all in Luckys. Shit. And they was waiting for me to come in from my last throw. Cant take too many fools in one day, its bad luck, Link, so they was all waiting in there for me to come in thuh door and let 30 thuh liquor start flowing and thuh music start going and let thuh boys who dont have thuh balls to get nothing but a regular job and uh weekly paycheck, let them crowd around and get in somehow on thuh excitement, and make way for thuh ladies, so they can run they hands on 35 my clothes and feel thuh magic and imagine thuh man, with plenty to go around, living and breathing underneath.

(*Rest.*)

　They all thought I was down and out! They all thought I was some NoCount HasBeen LostCause motherfucker. 40 But I got my shit back. Thats right. They stepped on me and kept right on stepping. Not no more. Who thuh man?! Goddamnit, who thuh—

BOOTH *closes the door.*

LINCOLN
BOOTH　　　　　　　　　　　　　　　　　　　　　　　　45

(*Rest.*)

LINCOLN: Another evening to remember, huh?
BOOTH

(*Rest.*)

　Uh—yeah, man, yeah. Thats right, thats right.
LINCOLN: Had me a memorable evening myself.
BOOTH: I got news.　　　　　　　　　　　　　　　　　50

(*Rest.*)

　What you been up to?
LINCOLN: Yr news first.
BOOTH: Its good.
LINCOLN: Yeah?
BOOTH: Yeah.　　　　　　　　　　　　　　　　　　55
LINCOLN: Go head then.
BOOTH

(*Rest.*)

　Grace got down on her knees. Down on her knees, man. Asked *me* tuh marry *her*.
LINCOLN: Shit.　　　　　　　　　　　　　　　　　60
BOOTH: Amazing Grace!
LINCOLN: Lucky you, man.
BOOTH: And guess where she was, I mean, while I was here waiting for her. She was over at her house watching tv. I'd told her come over Thursday and I got it all wrong and 65 was thinking I said Wednesday and here I was sitting waiting my ass off and all she was doing was over at her house just watching tv.
LINCOLN: Howboutthat.
BOOTH: She wants to get married right away. Shes tired of 70 waiting. Feels her clock ticking and shit. Wants to have a

baby. But dont look so glum man, we gonna have a boy
and we gonna name it after you.
LINCOLN: Thats great, man. Thats really great.
75 BOOTH
LINCOLN
BOOTH: Whats yr news?
LINCOLN

(Rest.)

Nothing.
80 BOOTH: Mines good news, huh?
LINCOLN: Yeah. Real good news, bro.
BOOTH: Bad news is—well, shes real set on us living together.
And she always did like this place.

(Rest.)

Yr gonna have to leave. Sorry.
85 LINCOLN: No sweat.
BOOTH: This was only a temporary situation anyhow.
LINCOLN: No sweat man. You got a new life opening up for
you, no sweat. Graces moving in today? I can leave right
now.
90 BOOTH: I dont mean to put you out.
LINCOLN: No sweat. I'll just pack up.

LINCOLN *rummages around finding a suitcase and begins to pack his
things.*

BOOTH: Just like that, huh? "No sweat"?! Yesterday you lost yr
damn job. You dont got no cash. You dont got no friends,
no nothing, but you clearing out just like that and its "no
95 sweat"?!
LINCOLN: Youve been real generous and you and Grace need
me gone and its time I found my own place.
BOOTH: No sweat.
LINCOLN: No sweat.

(Rest.)

100 K. I'll spill it. I got another job, so getting my own place
aint gonna be so bad.
BOOTH: You got a new job! Doing what?
LINCOLN: Security guard.
BOOTH

(Rest.)

105 Security guard. Howaboutthat.

LINCOLN *continues packing a few things he has. He picks up a
whiskey bottle.*

BOOTH: Go head, take thuh med-sin, bro. You gonna need it
more than me. I got, you know, I got my love to keep me
warm and shit.
LINCOLN: You gonna have to get some kind of work, or are
110 you gonna let Grace support you?
BOOTH: I got plans.
LINCOLN: She might want you now but she wont want you
for long if you dont get some kind of job. Shes a smart
chick. And she cares about you. But she aint gonna let you

treat her like some pack mule while shes out working her 115
ass off and yr laying up in here scheming and dreaming to
cover up thuh fact that you dont got no skills.
BOOTH: Grace is very cool with who I am and where Im at,
thank you.
LINCOLN: It was just some advice. But, hey, yr doing great just 120
like yr doing.
LINCOLN
BOOTH
LINCOLN
BOOTH 125
BOOTH: When Pops left he didnt take nothing with him. I al-
ways thought that was fucked-up.
LINCOLN: He was a drunk. Everything he did was always half
regular and half fucked-up.
BOOTH: Whyd he leave his clothes though? Even drunks 130
gotta wear clothes.
LINCOLN: Whyd he leave his clothes whyd he leave us? He
was uh drunk, bro. He—whatever, right? I mean, you aint
gonna figure it out by thinking about it. Just call it one of
thuh great unsolved mysteries of existence. 135
BOOTH: Moms had a man on thuh side.
LINCOLN: Yeah? Pops had side shit going on too. More than
one. He would take me with him when he went to visit
them. Yeah.

(Rest.)

Sometimes he'd let me meet the ladies. They was all very 140
nice. Very polite. Most of them real pretty. Sometimes
he'd let me watch. Most of thuh time I was just outside on
thuh porch or in thuh lobby or in thuh car waiting for
him but sometimes he'd let me watch.
BOOTH: What was it like? 145
LINCOLN: Nothing. It wasnt like nothing. He made it seem
like it was this big deal this great thing he was letting me
witness but it wasnt like nothing.

(Rest.)

One of his ladies liked me, so I would do her after he'd
done her. On thuh sly though. He'd be laying there, spent 150
and sleeping and snoring and her and me would be sneak-
ing it.
BOOTH: Shit.
LINCOLN: It was alright.
BOOTH 155
LINCOLN

LINCOLN *takes his crumpled Abe Lincoln getup from the closet. Isnt
sure what to do with it.*

BOOTH: Im gonna miss you coming home in that getup. I
dont even got a picture of you in it for the album.
LINCOLN

(Rest.)

Hell, I'll put it on. Get thuh camera get thuh camera. 160
BOOTH: Yeah?
LINCOLN: What thuh fuck, right?
BOOTH: Yeah, what thuh fuck.

BOOTH *scrambles around the apartment and finds the camera.* LIN-
COLN *quickly puts on the getup, including 2 thin smears of white
pancake makeup, more like war paint than whiteface.*

LINCOLN: They didnt fire me cause I wasnt no good. They
165   fired me cause they was cutting back. Me getting dis-
      missed didnt have no reflection on my performance. And
      I was a damn good Honest Abe considering.
BOOTH: Yeah. You look great man, really great. Fix yr hat.
      Get in thuh light. Smile.
170 LINCOLN: Lincoln didnt never smile.
BOOTH: Sure he smiled.
LINCOLN: No he didnt, man, you seen thuh pictures of him.
      In all his pictures he was real serious.
BOOTH: You got a new job, yr having a good day, right?
175 LINCOLN: Yeah.
BOOTH: So smile.
LINCOLN: Snapshots gonna look pretty stupid with me—

BOOTH *takes a picture.*

BOOTH: Thisll look great in thuh album.
LINCOLN: Lets take one together, you and me.
180 BOOTH: No thanks. Save the film for the wedding.
LINCOLN: This wasnt a bad job. I just outgrew it. I could put
      in a word for you down there, maybe when business picks
      up again theyd hire you.
BOOTH: No thanks. That shit aint for me. I aint into pre-
185   tending Im someone else all day.
LINCOLN: I was just sitting there in thuh getup. I wasnt pre-
      tending nothing.
BOOTH: What was going on in yr head?
LINCOLN: I would make up songs and shit.
190 BOOTH: And think about women.
LINCOLN: Sometimes.
BOOTH: Cookie.
LINCOLN: Sometimes.
BOOTH: And how she came over here one night looking for
195   you.
LINCOLN: I was at Luckys.
BOOTH: She didnt know that.
LINCOLN: I was drinking.
BOOTH: All she knew was you couldnt get it up. You couldnt
200   get it up with her so in her head you was tired of her and
      had gone out to screw somebody new and this time
      maybe werent never coming back.

(Rest.)

She had me pour her a drink or 2. I didnt want to. She
      wanted to get back at you by having some fun of her own
205   and when I told her to go out and have it, she said she
      wanted to have her fun right here. With me.

(Rest.)

[And then, just like that, she changed her mind.

(Rest.)

But she'd hooked me. That bad part of me that I fight
down everyday. You beat yrs down and its stays there dead

but mine keeps coming up for another round. And she   210
hooked the bad part of me. And the bad part of me
opened my mouth and started promising her things.
Promising her things I knew she wanted and you couldnt
give her. And the bad part of me took her clothing off and
carried her into thuh bed and had her, Link, yr Cookie. It   215
wasnt just thuh bad part of me it was all of me, man,] I
had her. Yr damn wife. Right in that bed.
LINCOLN: I used to think about her all thuh time but I dont
      think about her no more.
BOOTH: I told her if she dumped you I'd marry her but I   220
      changed my mind.
LINCOLN: I dont think about her no more.
BOOTH: You dont go back.
LINCOLN: Nope.
BOOTH: Cause you cant. No matter what you do you cant get   225
      back to being who you was. Best you can do is just pre-
      tend to be yr old self.
LINCOLN: Yr outa yr mind.
BOOTH: Least Im still me!
LINCOLN: Least I work. You never did like to work. You bet-   230
      ter come up with some kinda way to bring home the ba-
      con or Gracell drop you like a hot rock.
BOOTH: I got plans!
LINCOLN: Yeah, you gonna throw thuh cards, right?
BOOTH: Thats right!   235
LINCOLN: You a double left-handed motherfucker who dont
      stand a chance in all get out out there throwing no cards.
BOOTH: You scared.
LINCOLN: Im gone.

LINCOLN *goes to leave.*

BOOTH: Fuck that!   240
LINCOLN: Yr standing in my way.
BOOTH: You scared I got yr shit.
LINCOLN: The only part of my shit you got is the part of my
      shit you think you got and that aint shit.
BOOTH: Did I pick right them last times? Yes. Oh, I got yr   245
      shit.
LINCOLN: Set up the cards.
BOOTH: Thought you was gone.
LINCOLN: Set it up.
BOOTH: I got yr shit and Ima go out there and be thuh man   250
      and you aint gonna be nothing.
LINCOLN: Set it up!

BOOTH *hurriedly sets up the milk crates and cardboard top.* LIN-
COLN *throws the cards.*

LINCOLN: Lean in close and watch me now: who see thuh
      black card who see thuh black card I see thuh black card
      black cards thuh winner pick thuh black card thats thuh   255
      winner pick thuh red card thats thuh loser pick thuh
      other red card thats thuh other loser pick thuh black card
      you pick thuh winner. Who see thuh black card who see
      thuh black card? You pick thuh red card you pick a loser
      you pick that red card you pick a loser you pick thuh   260
      black card thuh deuce of spades you pick a winner who
      sees thuh deuce of spades thuh one who sees it never fades
      watch me now as I throw thuh cards. Red losers black
      winner follow thuh deuce of spades chase thuh black

265 deuce. Dark deuce will get you thuh win. 10 will get you 20, 20 will get you 40. One good pickll get you in 2 good picks and you gone win.

(*Rest.*)

Ok, man, wheres thuh black deuce?

BOOTH *points to a card.* LINCOLN *flips it over. It is the deuce of spades.*

BOOTH: Who thuh man?!

LINCOLN *turns over the other 2 cards, looking at them confusedly.*

270 LINCOLN: Hhhhh.
BOOTH: Who thuh man, Link?! Huh? Who thuh man, Link?!?!
LINCOLN: You thuh man, man.
BOOTH: I got yr shit down.
275 LINCOLN: Right.
BOOTH: "Right"? All you saying is "right"?

(*Rest.*)

You was out on the street throwing. Just today. Werent you? You wasnt gonna tell me.
LINCOLN: Tell you what?
280 BOOTH: That you was out throwing.
LINCOLN: I was gonna tell you, sure. Cant go and leave my little bro out thuh loop, can I? Didnt say nothing cause I thought you heard. Did all right today but Im still rusty, I guess. But hey—yr getting good.
285 BOOTH: But I'll get out there on thuh street and still fuck up, wont I?
LINCOLN: You seem pretty good, bro.
BOOTH: You gotta do it for real, man.
LINCOLN: I am doing it for real. And yr getting good.
290 BOOTH: I dunno. It didnt feel real. Kinda felt—well it didnt feel real.
LINCOLN: We're missing the essential elements. The crowd, the street, thuh traffic sounds, all that.
BOOTH: We missing something else too, thuh thing thatll re-
295 ally make it real.
LINCOLN: Whassat, bro?
BOOTH: Thuh cash. Its just bullshit without thuh money. Put some money down on thuh table then itd be real, then youd do it for real, then I'd win it for real.

(*Rest.*)

300 And dont be looking all glum like that. I know you got money. A whole pocketful. Put it down.
LINCOLN
BOOTH
BOOTH: You scared of losing it to thuh man, chump? Put it
305 down, less you think thuh kid who got two left hands is gonna give you uh left hook. Put it down, bro, put it down.

LINCOLN *takes the roll of bills from his pocket and places it on the table.*

BOOTH: How much you got there?

LINCOLN: 500 bucks.
BOOTH: Cool.

(*Rest.*)

Ready? 310
LINCOLN: Does it feel real?
BOOTH: Yeah. Clean slate. Take it from the top. "One good pickll get you in 2 good picks and you gone win."

(*Rest.*)

Go head.
LINCOLN: Watch me now: 315
BOOTH: Woah, man, woah.

(*Rest.*)

You think Ima chump.
LINCOLN: No I dont.
BOOTH: You aint going full out.
LINCOLN: I was just getting started. 320
BOOTH: But when you got good and started you wasnt gonna go full out. You wasnt gonna go all out. You was gonna do thuh pussy shit, not thuh real shit.
LINCOLN: I put my money down. Money makes it real.
BOOTH: But not if I dont put no money down tuh match it. 325
LINCOLN: You dont got no money.
BOOTH: I got money!
LINCOLN: You aint worked in years. You dont got shit.
BOOTH: I got money.
LINCOLN: Whatcha been doing, skimming off my weekly 330
paycheck and squirreling it away?
BOOTH: I got money.

(*Rest.*)

They stand there sizing eachother up. BOOTH *breaks away, going over to his hiding place from which he gets an old nylon stocking with money in the toe, a knot holding the money secure.*

LINCOLN
BOOTH
BOOTH: You know she was putting her stuff in plastic bags? 335
She was just putting her stuff in plastic bags not putting but shoving. She was shoving her stuff in plastic bags and I was standing in thuh doorway watching her and she was so busy shoving thuh shit she didnt see me. "I aint made of money," thats what he always saying. The guy she had on 340
the side. I would catch them together sometimes. Thuh first time I cut school I got tired of hanging out so I goes home—figured I could tell Mom I was sick and cover my ass. Come in thuh house real slow cause Im sick and mov- ing slow and quiet. He had her bent over. They both had 345
all they clothes on like they was about to do something like go out dancing cause they was dressed to thuh 9s but at thuh last minute his pants had fallen down and her dress had flown up and theyd ended up doing something else.

(*Rest.*)

They didnt see me come in, they didnt see me watching 350
them, they didnt see me going out. That was uh Thurs-

day. Something told me tuh cut school thuh next Thursday and sure enough.—He was her Thursday man. Every
Thursday. Yeah. And Thursday nights she was always all
355 cleaned up and fresh and smelling nice. Serving up dinner.
And Pops would grab her cause she was all bright and she
would look at me, like she didnt know that I knew but she
was asking me not to tell nohow. She was asking me to—
oh who knows.

(Rest.)

360 She was talking with him one day, her sideman, her Thursday dude, her backdoor man, she needed some money for
something, thered been some kind of problem some kind
of mistake had been made some kind of mistake that
needed cleaning up and she was asking Mr. Thursday for
365 some money to take care of it. "I aint made of money," he
says. He was putting his foot down. And then there she
was 2 months later not showing yet, maybe she'd got rid
of it maybe she hadnt maybe she'd stuffed it along with all
her other things in them plastic bags while he waited out-
370 side in thuh car with thuh motor running. She musta
known I was gonna walk in on her this time cause she had
my payoff—my *inheritance*—she had it all ready for me.
500 dollars in a nylon stocking. Huh.

He places the stuffed nylon stocking on the table across from LIN-
COLN*s money roll.*

BOOTH: Now its real.
375 LINCOLN: Dont put that down.
BOOTH: Throw thuh cards.
LINCOLN: I dont want to play.
BOOTH: Throw thuh fucking cards, man!!
LINCOLN

(Rest.)

380 2 red cards but only one black. Pick thuh black you pick
thuh winner. All thuh cards are face down you point out
thuh cards and then you move them around. Now watch
me now, now watch me real close. Put thuh winning
deuce down in the center put thuh loser reds on either
385 side then you just move thuh cards around. Move them
slow or move them fast, Links thuh king he gonna last.

(Rest.)

Wheres thuh deuce of spades?

BOOTH *chooses a card and chooses correctly.*

BOOTH: HA!
LINCOLN: One good pickll get you in 2 good picks and you
390 gone win.
BOOTH: I know man I know.
LINCOLN: Im just doing thuh talk.
BOOTH: Throw thuh fucking cards!

LINCOLN *throws the cards.*

LINCOLN: Lean in close and watch me now: who see thuh
395 black card who see thuh black card I see thuh black card

black cards thuh winner pick thuh black card thats thuh
winner pick thuh red card thats thuh loser pick thuh
other red card thats thuh other loser pick thuh black card
you pick thuh winner. Watch me as I throw thuh cards.
Here we go.   400

(Rest.)

Ima show you thuh cards: 2 red cards but only one spade.
Dark winner in thuh center and thuh red losers on thuh
sides. Pick up red card you got a loser pick thuh other red
card you got a loser pick thuh black card you got a winner. Watch me watch me watch me now.   405

(Rest.)

Who see thuh black card who see thuh black card? You
pick thuh red card you pick a loser you pick that red card
you pick a loser you pick thuh black card thuh deuce of
spades you pick a winner who sees thuh deuce of spades
thuh one who sees it never fades watch me now as I   410
throw thuh cards. Red losers black winner follow thuh
deuce of spades chase thuh black deuce. Dark deuce will
get you thuh win.

(Rest.)

Ok, 3-Card, you know which cards thuh deuce of spades?
This is for real now, man. You pick wrong Im in yr wad 415
and I keep mines.
BOOTH: I pick right I got yr shit.
LINCOLN: Yeah.
BOOTH: Plus I beat you for real.
LINCOLN: Yeah.   420

(Rest.)

You think we're really brothers?
BOOTH: Huh?
LINCOLN: I know we *brothers,* but is we really brothers, you
know, blood brothers or not, you and me, whatduhya-
think?   425
BOOTH: I think we're brothers.
BOOTH
LINCOLN
BOOTH
LINCOLN   430
BOOTH
LINCOLN
LINCOLN: Go head man, wheres thuh deuce?

In a flash BOOTH *points out a card.*

LINCOLN: You sure?
BOOTH: Im sure!   435
LINCOLN: Yeah? Dont touch thuh cards, now.
BOOTH: Im sure.

The 2 brothers lock eyes. LINCOLN *turns over the card that* BOOTH
selected and BOOTH, *in a desperate break of concentration, glances
down to see that he has chosen the wrong card.*

LINCOLN: Deuce of hearts, bro. Im sorry. Thuh deuce of
spades was this one.

(*Rest.*)

440   I guess all this is mines.

He slides the money toward himself.

LINCOLN: You were almost right. Better luck next time.

(*Rest.*)

Aint yr fault if yr eyes aint fast. And you cant help it if you got 2 left hands, right? Throwing cards aint thuh whole world. You got other shit going for you. You got Grace.
445   BOOTH: Right.
LINCOLN: Whassamatter?
BOOTH: Mm.
LINCOLN: Whatsup?
BOOTH: Nothing.
450   LINCOLN

(*Rest.*)

It takes a certain kind of understanding to be able to play this game.

(*Rest.*)

I still got thuh moves, dont I?
BOOTH: Yeah you still got thuh moves.

LINCOLN *cant help himself. He chuckles.*

455   LINCOLN: I aint laughing at you, bro, Im just laughing. Shit there is so much to this game. This game is—there is just so much to it.

LINCOLN, *still chuckling, flops down in the easy chair. He takes up the nylon stocking and fiddles with the knot.*

LINCOLN: Woah, she sure did tie this up tight, didnt she?
BOOTH: Yeah. I aint opened it since she gived it to me.
460   LINCOLN: Yr kidding. 500 and you aint never opened it? Shit. Sure is tied tight. She said heres 500 bucks and you didnt undo thuh knot to get a look at the cash? You aint needed to take a peek in all these years? Shit. I woulda opened it right away. Just a little peek.
465   BOOTH: I been saving it.

(*Rest.*)

Oh, dont open it, man.
LINCOLN: How come?
BOOTH: You won it man, you dont gotta go opening it.
LINCOLN: We gotta see whats in it.
470   BOOTH: We *know* whats in it. Dont open it.
LINCOLN: You are a chump, bro. There could be millions in here! There could be nothing! I'll open it.
BOOTH: Dont.
LINCOLN
475   BOOTH

(*Rest.*)

LINCOLN: Shit this knot aint coming out. I could cut it, but that would spoil the whole effect, wouldnt it? Shit. Sorry.

I aint laughing at you Im just laughing. Theres so much about those cards. You think you can learn them just by watching and just by playing but there is more to them 480 cards than that. And—. Tell me something, Mr. 3-Card, she handed you this stocking and she said there was money in it and then she split and you say you didnt open it. Howd you know she was for real?
BOOTH: She was for real.   485
LINCOLN: How you know. She coulda been jiving you, bro. Jiving you that there really *was* money in this thing. Jiving you big time. Its like thuh cards. And ooooh you certainly was persistent. But you was in such a hurry to learn thuh last move that you didnt bother learning thuh first one.   490 That was yr mistake. Cause its thuh first move that separates thuh Player from thuh Played. And thuh first move is to know that there aint no winning. It may look like you got a chance but the only time you pick right is when thuh man lets you. And when its thuh real deal, when its   495 thuh real fucking deal, bro, and thuh moneys on thuh line, thats when thuh man wont want you picking right. He will want you picking wrong so he will make you pick wrong. Wrong wrong wrong. Ooooh, you thought you was finally happening, didnt you? You thought yr ship had   500 come in or some shit, huh? Thought you was uh Player. But I played you, bro.
BOOTH: Fuck you. Fuck you FUCK YOU *FUCK YOU!!*
LINCOLN: Whatever, man. Damn this knot is tough. Ima cut it.

LINCOLN *reaches in his boot, pulling out a knife. He chuckles all the while.*

LINCOLN: Im not laughing at you, bro, Im just laughing.   505

BOOTH *chuckles with him.* LINCOLN *holds the knife high, ready to cut the stocking.*

LINCOLN: Turn yr head. You may not wanna look.

BOOTH *turns away slightly. They both continue laughing.* LINCOLN *brings the knife down to cut the stocking.*

BOOTH: I popped her.
LINCOLN: Huh?
BOOTH: Grace. I popped her. Grace.

(*Rest.*)

Who thuh fuck she think she is doing me like she done?   510 Telling me I dont got nothing going on. I showed her what I got going on. Popped her good. Twice. 3 times. Whatever.

(*Rest.*)

She aint dead.

(*Rest.*)

She werent wearing my ring I gived her. Said it was too   515 small. Fuck that. Said it hurt her. Fuck that. Said she was into bigger things. *Fuck* that. Shes alive not to worry, she aint going out that easy, shes alive shes shes—
LINCOLN: Dead. Shes—

520 BOOTH: Dead.

LINCOLN: Ima give you back yr stocking, man. Here, bro—

BOOTH: Only so long I can stand that little brother shit. Can only take it so long. Im telling you—

LINCOLN: Take it back, man—

525 BOOTH: That little bro shit had to go—

LINCOLN: Cool—

BOOTH: Like Booth went—

LINCOLN: Here, 3-Card—

BOOTH: That Booth shit is over. 3-Cards thuh man now—

530 LINCOLN: Ima give you yr stocking back, 3-Card—

BOOTH: Who thuh man now, huh? Who thuh man now?! Think you can fuck with me, motherfucker think again motherfucker think again! Think you can take me like Im just some chump some two lefthanded pussy dickbreath

535 chump who you can take and then go laugh at. Aint laughing at me you was just laughing bunch uh bullshit and you know it.

LINCOLN: Here. Take it.

BOOTH: I aint gonna be needing it. Go on. You won it you

540 open it.

LINCOLN: No thanks.

BOOTH: Open it open it open it open it. _OPEN IT!!!_

(*Rest.*)

Open it up, bro.

LINCOLN

545 BOOTH

LINCOLN *brings the knife down to cut the stocking. In a flash,* BOOTH *grabs* LINCOLN *from behind. He pulls his gun and thrusts it into the left side of* LINCOLNs *neck. They stop there poised.*

LINCOLN: Dont.

BOOTH *shoots* LINCOLN. LINCOLN *slumps forward, falling out of his chair and onto the floor. He lies there dead.* BOOTH *paces back and forth, like a panther in a cage, holding his gun.*

BOOTH: Think you can take my shit? My shit. That shit was mines. I kept it. Saved it. All this while. Through thick and through thin. Through fucking thick and through fucking thin, motherfucker. And you just gonna come up 550 in here and mock my shit and call me two lefthanded talking bout how she coulda been jiving me then go steal from me? My *inheritance.* You stole my *inheritance,* man. That aint right. That aint right and you know it. You had yr own. And you blew it. You *blew it,* motherfucker! I 555 saved mines and you blew yrs. Thinking you all that and blew yr shit. And I *saved* mines.

(*Rest.*)

You aint gonna be needing yr fucking money-roll no more, dead motherfucker, so I will pocket it thank you.

(*Rest.*)

Watch me close watch me close now: Ima go out there 560 and make a name for myself that dont have nothing to do with you. And 3-Cards gonna be in everybodys head and in everybodys mouth like Link was.

(*Rest.*)

Ima take back my inheritance too. It was mines anyhow. Even when you stole it from me it was still mines cause 565 she gave it to me. She didnt give it to you. And I been saving it all this while.

He bends to pick up the money-filled stocking. Then he just crumples. As he sits beside LINCOLNs *body, the money-stocking falls away.* BOOTH *holds* LINCOLNs *body, hugging him close. He sobs.*

BOOTH: *AAAAAAAAAAAAAAAAAAAAAH!*

END OF PLAY

CRITICAL CONTEXTS

ARTHUR MILLER

from "Tragedy and the Common Man" (1949)

Arthur Miller wrote this essay for the New York Times *shortly after the opening of* Death of a Salesman. *In the essay, Miller develops a reading of the tragic hero that both contests and modifies Aristotle's description of the form and style of tragic drama. He also identifies his own presiding interests in the dynamics of tragic character. How important is it to Miller to be able to retain Aristotle's categories? Why? How do the different social, political, and cultural circumstances of Greek tragedy force Miller to redefine Aristotle's understanding of the function, purpose, and meaning of tragedy, particularly his understanding of tragic "character"?*

In this age few tragedies are written. It has often been held that the lack is due to a paucity of heroes among us, or else that modern man has had the blood drawn out of his organs of belief by the skepticism of science, and the heroic attack on life cannot feed on an attitude of reserve and circumspection. For one reason or another, we are often held to be below tragedy—or tragedy above us. The inevitable conclusion is, of course, that the tragic mode is archaic, fit only for the very highly placed, the kings or the kingly, and where this admission is not made in so many words it is most often implied.

I believe that the common man is as apt a subject for tragedy in its highest sense as kings were. On the face of it this ought to be obvious in the light of modern psychiatry, which bases its analysis upon classic formulations, such as the Oedipus and Orestes complexes, for instances, which were enacted by royal beings, but which apply to everyone in similar emotional situations.

More simply, when the question of tragedy in art is not at issue, we never hesitate to attribute to the well-placed and the exalted the very same mental processes as the lowly. And finally, if the exaltation of tragic action were truly a property of the high-bred character alone, it is inconceivable that the mass of mankind should cherish tragedy above all other forms, let alone be capable of understanding it.

As a general rule, to which there may be exceptions unknown to me, I think the tragic feeling is evoked in us when we are in the presence of a character who is ready to lay down his life, if need be, to secure one thing—his sense of personal dignity. From Orestes to Hamlet, Medea to Macbeth, the underlying struggle is that of the individual attempting to gain his "rightful" position in his society.

Sometimes he is one who has been displaced from it, sometimes one who seeks to attain it for the first time, but the fateful wound from which the inevitable events spiral is the wound of indignity, and its dominant force is indignation. Tragedy, then, is the consequence of a man's total compulsion to evaluate himself justly.

In the sense of having been initiated by the hero himself, the tale always reveals what has been called his "tragic flaw," a failing that is not peculiar to grand or elevated characters. Nor is it necessarily a weakness. The flaw, or crack in the character, is really nothing—and need be nothing—but his inherent unwillingness to remain passive in the face of what he conceives to be a challenge to his dignity, his image of his rightful status. Only the passive, only those who accept their lot without active retaliation, are "flawless." Most of us are in that category.

But there are among us today, as there always have been, those who act against the scheme of things that degrades them, and in the process of action everything we have accepted out of fear or insensitivity or ignorance is shaken before us and examined, and from this total onslaught by an individual against the seemingly stable cosmos surrounding us—from this total examination of the "unchangeable" environment—comes the terror and the fear that is classically associated with tragedy.

More important, from this total questioning of what has previously been unquestioned, we learn. And such a process is not beyond the common man. In revolutions around the world, these past thirty years, he has demonstrated again and again this inner dynamic of all tragedy.

Insistence upon the rank of the tragic hero, or the so-called nobility of his character, is really but a clinging to the outward forms of tragedy. If rank or nobility of character was indispensable, then it would follow that the problems of those with rank were the particular problems of tragedy. But surely the right of one monarch to capture the domain from another no longer raises our passions, nor are our concepts of justice what they were to the mind of an Elizabethan king.

The quality in such plays that does shake us, however, derives from the underlying fear of being displaced, the disaster inherent in being torn away from our chosen image of what and who we are in this world. Among us today this fear is as strong, and perhaps stronger, than it ever was. In fact, it is the common man who knows this fear best.

Now, if it is true that tragedy is the consequence of a man's total compulsion to evaluate himself justly, his destruction in the attempt posits a wrong or an evil in his environment. And this is precisely the morality of tragedy and its lesson. The discovery of the moral law, which is what the enlightenment of tragedy consists of, is not the discovery of some abstract or metaphysical quantity.

The tragic right is a condition of life, a condition in which the human personality is able to flower and realize itself. The wrong is the condition which suppresses man, perverts the flowing out of his love and creative instinct. Tragedy enlightens—and it must, in that it points the heroic finger at the enemy of man's freedom. The thrust for freedom is the quality in tragedy which exalts. The revolutionary questioning of the stable environment is what terrifies. In no way is the common man debarred from such thoughts or such actions.

Seen in this light, our lack of tragedy may be partially accounted for by the turn which modern literature has taken toward the purely psychiatric view of life, or the purely sociological. If all our miseries, our indignities, are born and bred within our minds, then all action, let alone the heroic action, is obviously impossible.

And if society alone is responsible for the cramping of our lives, then the protagonist must needs be so pure and faultless as to force us to deny his validity as a character. From neither of these views can tragedy derive, simply because neither represents a balanced concept of life. Above all else, tragedy requires the finest appreciation by the writer of cause and effect.

No tragedy can therefore come about when its author fears to question absolutely everything, when he regards any institution, habit or custom as being either everlasting, immutable or inevitable. In the tragic view the need of man to wholly realize himself is the only fixed star, and whatever it is that hedges his nature and lowers it is ripe for attack and examination. Which is not to say that tragedy must preach revolution.

The Greeks could probe the very heavenly origin of their ways and return to confirm the rightness of laws. And Job could face God in anger, demanding his right and end in submission. But for a moment everything is in suspension, nothing is accepted, and in this stretching and tearing apart of the cosmos, in the very action of so doing, the character gains "size," the tragic stature which is spuriously attached to the royal or the highborn in our minds. The commonest of men may take on that stature to the extent of his willingness to throw all he has into the contest, the battle to secure his rightful place in his world.

There is a misconception of tragedy with which I have been struck in review after review, and in many conversations with writers and readers alike. It is the idea that tragedy is of necessity allied to pessimism. Even the dictionary says nothing more about the word than that it means a story with a sad or unhappy ending. This impression is so firmly fixed that I almost hesitate to claim that in truth tragedy implies more optimism in its author than does comedy, and that its final result ought to be the reinforcement of the onlooker's brightest opinions of the human animal.

For, if it is true to say that in essence the tragic hero is intent upon claiming his whole due as a personality, and if this struggle must be total and without reservation, then it automatically demonstrates the indestructible will of man to achieve his humanity.

The possibility of victory must be there in tragedy. Where pathos rules, where pathos is finally derived, a character has fought a battle he could not possibly have won. The pathetic is achieved when the protagonist is, by virtue of his witlessness, his insensitivity or the very air he gives off, incapable of grappling with a much superior force.

Pathos truly is the mode for the pessimist. But tragedy requires a nicer balance between what is possible and what is impossible. And it is curious, although edifying, that the plays we revere, century after century, are the tragedies. In them, and in them alone, lies the belief—optimistic, if you will, in the perfectibility of man.

It is time, I think, that we who are without kings, took up this bright thread of our history and followed it to the only place it can possibly lead in our time—the heart and spirit of the average man.

AMIRI BARAKA / LEROI JONES
from "The Revolutionary Theatre" (1966)

In "The Revolutionary Theatre," Amiri Baraka describes the challenges posed by an emerging African- American theater. How does Baraka's understanding of the necessity of "revolution"—what does Baraka mean by "revolution"—sustain his sense of what theater can and should do?

The Revolutionary Theatre should force change; it should be change. (All their faces turned into the lights and you work on them black nigger magic, and cleanse them at having seen the ugliness. And if the beautiful see themselves, they will love themselves.) We are preaching virtue again, but by that to mean NOW, toward what seems the most constructive use of the world.

The Revolutionary Theatre must EXPOSE! Show up the insides of these humans, look into black skulls. White men will cower before this theatre because it hates them. Because they themselves have been trained to hate. The Revolutionary Theatre must hate them for hating. For presuming with their technology to deny the supremacy of the Spirit. They will all die because of this.

The Revolutionary Theatre must teach them their deaths. It must crack their faces open to the mad cries of the poor. It must teach them about silence and the truths lodged there. It must kill any God anyone names except Common Sense. The Revolutionary Theatre should flush the fags and murderers out of Lincoln's face.

It should stagger through our universe correcting, insulting, preaching, spitting craziness—but a craziness taught to us in our most rational moments. People must be taught to trust true scientists (knowers, diggers, oddballs) and that the holiness of life is the constant possibility of widening the consciousness. And they must be incited to strike back against any agency that attempts to prevent this widening.

The Revolutionary Theatre must Accuse and Attack anything that can be accused and attacked. It must Accuse and Attack because it is a theatre of Victims. It looks at the sky with the victims' eyes, and moves the victims to look at the strength in their minds and their bodies.

Clay in *Dutchman*, Ray in *The Toilet*, Walker in *The Slave*, are all victims. In the Western sense they could be heroes. But the Revolutionary Theatre, even if it is Western, must be anti-Western. It must show horrible coming attractions of The Crumbling of the West. Even as Artaud designed *The Conquest of Mexico*, so we must design *The Conquest of White Eye*, and show the missionaries and wiggly liberals dying under blasts of concrete. For sound effects, wild screams of joy, from all the peoples of the world.

The Revolutionary Theatre must take dreams and give them a reality. It must isolate the ritual and historical cycles of reality. But it must be food for all those who need food, and daring propaganda for the beauty of the Human Mind. It is a political theatre, a weapon to help in the slaughter of these dimwitted fatbellied white guys who somehow believe that the rest of the world is here for them to slobber on.

This should be a theatre of World Spirit. Where the spirit can be shown to be the most competent force in the world. Force. Spirit. Feeling. The language will be anybody's, but tightened by the poet's backbone. And even the language must show what the facts are in this consciousness epic, what's happening. We will talk about the world, and the preciseness with which we are able to summon the world will be our art. Art is method. And art, "like any ashtray or senator," remains in the world. Wittgenstein said ethics and aesthetics are one. I believe this. So the Broadway theatre is a theatre of reaction whose ethics, like its aesthetics, reflect the spiritual values of this unholy society, which sends young crackers all over the world blowing off colored people's heads. (In some of these flippy Southern towns they even shoot up the immigrants' Favorite Son, be it Michael Schwerner or JFKennedy.)

The Revolutionary Theatre is shaped by the world, and moves to reshape the world, using as its force the natural force and perpetual vibrations of the mind in the world. We are history and desire, what we are, and what any experience can make us.

It is a social theatre, but all theatre is social theatre. But we will change the drawing rooms into places where real things can be said about a real world, or into smoky rooms where the destruction of Washington can be plotted. The Revolutionary Theatre must function like an incendiary pencil planted in Curtis Lemay's cap. So that when the final curtain goes down brains are splattered over the seats and the floor, and bleeding nuns must wire SOS's to Belgians with gold teeth.

Our theatre will show victims so that their brothers in the audience will be better able to understand that they are the brothers of victims, and that they themselves are victims if they are blood brothers. And what we show must cause the blood to rush, so that pre-revolutionary temperaments will be bathed in this blood, and it will cause their deepest souls to move, and they will find themselves tensed and clenched, even ready to die, at what the soul has been taught. We will scream and cry, murder, run through the streets in agony, if it means some soul will be moved, moved to actual life understanding of what the world is, and what it ought to be. We are preaching virtue and feeling, and a natural sense of the self in the world. All men live in the world, and the world ought to be a place for them to live.

What is called the imagination (from image, magi, magic, magician, etc.) is a practical vector from the soul. It stores all data, and can be called on to solve all our "problems." The imagination is the projection of ourselves past our sense of ourselves as "things." Imagination (Image) is all possibility, because from the image, the initial circumscribed energy, any use (idea) is possible. And so begins that image's use in the world. Possibility is what moves us.

The popular white man's theatre like the popular white man's novel shows tired white lives, and the problems of eating white sugar, or else it herds bigcaboosed blondes onto huge stages in rhinestones and makes believe they are dancing or singing. WHITE BUSINESSMEN OF THE WORLD, DO YOU WANT TO SEE PEOPLE REALLY DANCING AND SINGING??? ALL OF YOU GO UP TO HARLEM AND GET YOURSELF KILLED. THERE WILL BE DANCING AND SINGING, THEN, FOR REAL!! (In *The Slave,* Walker Vessels, the black revolutionary, wears an armband, which is the insignia of the attacking army—a big red-lipped minstrel, grinning like crazy.)

The liberal white man's objection to the theatre of the revolution (if he is "hip" enough) will be on aesthetic grounds. Most white Western artists do not need to be "political," since usually, whether they know it or not, they are in complete sympathy with the most repressive social forces in the world today. There are more junior birdmen fascists running around the West today disguised as Artists than there are disguised as fascists. (But then, that word, *Fascist,* and with it, *Fascism,* has been made obsolete by the words *America,* and *Americanism.*) The American Artist usually turns out to be just a super-Bourgeois, because, finally, all he has to show for his sojourn through the world is "better taste" than the Bourgeois—many times not even that.

Americans will hate the Revolutionary Theatre because it will be out to destroy them and whatever they believe is real. American cops will try to close the theatres where such nakedness of the human spirit is paraded. American producers will say the revolutionary plays are filth, usually because they will treat human life as if it were actually happening. American directors will say that the white guys in the plays are too abstract and cowardly ("don't get me wrong . . . I mean aesthetically . . .") and they will be right.

The force we want is of twenty million spooks storming America with furious cries and unstoppable weapons. We want actual explosions and actual brutality: AN EPIC IS CRUMBLING and we must give it the space and hugeness of its actual demise. The Revolutionary Theatre, which is now peopled with victims, will soon begin to be peopled with new kinds of heroes—not the weak Hamlets debating whether or not they are ready to die for what's on their minds, but men and women (and minds) digging out from under a thousand years of "high art" and weak-faced dalliance. We must make an art that will function so as to call down the actual wrath of world spirit. We are witch doctors and assassins, but we will open a place for the true scientists to expand our consciousness. This is a theatre of assault. The play that will split the heavens for us will be called THE DESTRUCTION OF AMERICA. The heroes will be Crazy Horse, Denmark Vesey, Patrice Lumumba, and not history, not memory, not sad sentimental groping for a warmth in our despair; these will be new men, new heroes, and their enemies most of you who are reading this.

PERFORMANCE IN HISTORY

AUGUST WILSON   "The Ground on Which I Stand"
ROBERT BRUSTEIN   "Subsidized Separatism" (1996)

In 1996, the celebrated playwright August Wilson delivered an address entitled "The Ground on Which I Stand" to the Theatre Communications Group National Conference; shortly thereafter, Robert Brustein—a distinguished critic, founder of the Yale Repertory Theatre, and at the time director of the American Repertory Theatre—published a response, entitled "Subsidized Separatism." In this discussion—which was subsequently staged as a live debate between Brustein and Wilson, moderated by Anna Deavere Smith—two of the American theater's most eminent and provocative artists take on the issue that has vexed the stage since the founding of the republic: the relationship between "race" and representation.

AUGUST WILSON
The Ground on Which I Stand

I have come here today to make a testimony, to talk about the ground on which I stand and all the many grounds on which I and my ancestors have toiled, and the ground of theatre on which my fellow artists and I have labored to bring forth its fruits, its daring and its sometimes lacerating, and often healing, truths.

I wish to make it clear from the outset, however, that I do not have a mandate to speak for anyone. There are many intelligent blacks working in the American theatre who speak in loud and articulate voices. It would be the greatest of presumptions to say I speak for them. I speak only for myself and those who may think as I do.

In one guise, the ground I stand on has been pioneered by the Greek dramatists—by Euripides, Aeschylus and Sophocles—by William Shakespeare, by Shaw and Ibsen, and by the American dramatists Eugene O'Neill, Arthur Miller and Tennessee Williams. In another guise, the ground that I stand on has been pioneered by my grandfather, by Nat Turner, by Denmark Vesey, by Martin Delaney, Marcus Garvey and the Honorable Elijah Muhammad. That is the ground of the affirmation of the value of one being, an affirmation of his worth in the face of society's urgent and sometimes profound denial. It was this ground as a young man coming into manhood searching for something to which to dedicate my life that I discovered the Black Power movement of the '60s. I felt it a duty and an honor to participate in that historic moment, as the people who had arrived in America chained and malnourished in the hold of a 350-foot Portuguese, Dutch or English sailing ship, were now seeking ways to alter their relationship to the society in which they lived— and, perhaps more important, searching for ways to alter the shared expectations of themselves as a community of people.

The Black Power movement of the '60s: I find it curious but no small accident that I seldom hear those words "Black Power" spoken, and when mention is made of that part of black history in America, whether in the press or in conversation, reference is made to the Civil Rights Movement as though the Black Power movement—an important social movement by America's ex-slaves—had in fact never happened. But the Black Power movement of the '60s was a reality; it was the kiln in which I was fired, and has much to do with the person I am today and the ideas and attitudes that I carry as part of my consciousness.

I mention this because it is difficult to disassociate my concerns with theatre from the concerns of my life as a black man, and it is difficult to disassociate one part of my life from another. I have strived to live it all seamless . . . art and life together, inseparable and indistinguishable. The ideas I discovered and embraced in my youth when my idealism was full blown I have not abandoned in middle age when idealism is something less then blooming, but wisdom is starting to bud. The ideas of self-determination, self-respect and self-defense that governed my life in the '60s I find just as valid and self-urging in 1996. The need to alter our relationship to the society and to alter the shared expectations of ourselves as a racial group I find of greater urgency now than it was then.

I am what is known, at least among the followers and supporters of the ideas of Marcus Garvey, as a "race man." That is simply that I believe that race matters—that is the largest, most identifiable and most important part of our personality. It is the largest category of identification because it is the one that most influences your perception of yourself, and it is the one to which others in the world of men most respond. Race is also an important part of the American landscape, as America is made up of an amalgamation of races from all parts of the globe. Race is also the product of a shared gene pool that allows for group identification, and it is an organizing principle around which cultures are formed. When I say culture I am speaking about the behavior patterns, arts, beliefs, institutions and all other products of human work and thought as expressed in a particular community of people.

There are some people who will say that black Americans do not have a culture—that cultures are reserved for other people, most notably Europeans of various ethnic groupings, and that black Americans make up a sub-group of American culture that is derived from the European origins of its majority population. But black Americans are Africans, and there are many histories and many cultures on the African continent.

Those who would deny black Americans their culture would also deny them their history and the inherent values that are a part of all human life.

Growing up in my mother's house at 1727 Bedford Ave. in Pittsburgh, Pa., I learned the language, the eating habits, the religious beliefs, the gestures, the notions of common sense, attitudes towards sex, concepts of beauty and justice, and the responses to pleasure and pain, that my mother had learned from her mother, and which you could trace back to the first African who set foot on the continent. It is this culture that stands solidly on these shores today as a testament to the resiliency of the African-American spirit.

The term black or African-American not only denotes race, it denotes condition, and carries with it the vestige of slavery and the social segregation and abuse of opportunity so vivid in our memory. That this abuse of opportunity and truncation of possibility is continuing and is so pervasive in our society in 1996 says much about who we are and much about the work that is necessary to alter our perceptions of each other and to effect meaningful prosperity for all.

The problematic nature of the relationship between white and black for too long led us astray from the fulfillment of our possibilities as a society. We stare at each other across a divide of economics and privilege that has become an encumbrance on black Americans' ability to prosper and on the collective will and spirit of our national purpose.

In terms of economics and privilege, one significant fact affects us all in the American theatre: Of the 66 LORT theatres, there is only one that can be considered black. From this it could be falsely assumed that there aren't sufficient numbers of blacks working in the American theatre to sustain and support more theatres.

If you do not know, I will tell you that black theatre in America is alive . . . it is vibrant . . . it is vital . . . it just isn't funded. Black theatre doesn't share in the economics that would allow it to support its artists and supply them with meaningful avenues to develop their talent and broadcast and

disseminate ideas crucial to its growth. The economics are reserved as privilege to the overwhelming abundance of institutions that preserve, promote and perpetuate white culture.

That is not a complaint. That is an advertisement. Since the funding sources, both public and private, do not publicly carry avowed missions of exclusion and segregated support, this is obviously either a glaring case of oversight, or we the proponents of black theatre have not made our presence or our needs known. I hope here tonight to correct that.

I do not have the time in this short talk to reiterate the long and distinguished history of black theatre—often accomplished amid adverse and hostile conditions—but I would like to take the time to mark a few high points.

There are and have always been two distinct and parallel traditions in black art: that is, art that is conceived and designed to entertain white society, and art that feeds the spirit and celebrates the life of black America by designing its strategies for survival and prosperity.

An important part of black theatre that is often ignored but is seminal to its tradition is its origins on the slave plantations of the South. Summoned to the "big house" to entertain the slave owner and his guests, the slave began a tradition of theatre as entertainment for whites that reached its pinnacle in the heyday of the Harlem Renaissance. This entertainment for whites consisted of whatever the slave imagined or knew that his master wanted to see and hear. This tradition has its present life counterpart in the crossover artists that slant their material for white consumption.

The second tradition occurred when the African in the confines of the slave quarters sought to invest his spirit with the strength of his ancestors by conceiving in his art, in his song and dance, a world in which he was the spiritual center and his existence was a manifest act of the creator from whom life flowed. He then could create art that was functional and furnished him with a spiritual temperament necessary for his survival as property and the dehumanizing status that was attendant to that.

I stand myself and my art squarely on the self-defining ground of the slave quarters, and find the ground to be hallowed and made fertile by the blood and bones of the men and woman who can be described as warriors on the cultural battlefield that affirmed their self-worth. As there is no idea that cannot be contained by black life, these men and women found themselves to be sufficient and secure in their art and their instructions.

It was this high ground of self-definition that the black playwrights of the '60s marked out for themselves. Ron Milner, Ed Bullins, Philip Hayes Dean, Richard Wesley, Lonne Elder III, Sonia Sanchez, Barbara Ann Teer and Amiri Baraka were among those playwrights who were particularly vocal and where remain indebted to them for their brave and courageous forays into an area that is marked with land mines and the shadows of snipers—those who would reserve the territory of arts and letters and the American theatre as their own special province and point blacks toward the ball fields and the bandstands.

That black theatre today comes under such assaults should surprise no one, as we are on the verge of reclaiming and reexamining the purpose and pillars of our art and laying out new directions for its expansion. As such we make a target for cultural imperialists who seek to empower and propagate their ideas about the world as the only valid ideas, and see blacks as woefully deficient not only in arts and letters but in the abundant gifts of humanity.

In the 19th century, the lack of education, the lack of contact with different cultures, the expensive and slow methods of travel and communication fostered such ideas, and the breeding ground of ignorance and racial intolerance promoted them.

The King's English and the lexicon of a people given to such ignorance and intolerance did not do much to dispel such obvious misconceptions, but provided them with a home. I cite Webster's *Third New International Dictionary*:

"BLACK: outrageously wicked, dishonorable, connected with the devil, menacing, sullen, hostile, unqualified, illicit, illegal, violators of public regulations, affected by some undesirable condition, etc.

"WHITE: free from blemish, moral stain or impurity; outstandingly righteous, innocent, not marked by malignant influence, notably auspicious, fortunate, decent, a sterling man."

Such is the linguistic environment that informs the distance that separates blacks and whites in America and which the cultural imperialist, who cannot imagine a life existing and flourishing outside his benevolent control, embraces.

Robert Brustein, writing in an article/review titled "Unity from Diversity" [*The New Republic,* July 19–26, '93] is apparently disturbed that "there is a tremendous outpouring of work by minority artists" which he attributes to cultural diversity. He writes that the practice of extending invitations to a national banquet from which a lot of hungry people have long been excluded is a practice that can lead to confused standards. He goes on to establish a presumption of inferiority of the work of minority artists: "Funding agencies have started substituting sociological criteria for aesthetic criteria in their grant procedures, indicating that 'elitist' notions like quality and excellence are no longer functional." He goes on to say, "It's disarming in all senses of the word to say that we don't share common experiences that are measurable by common standards. But the growing number of truly talented

artists with more universal interests suggests that we may soon be in a position to return to a single value system."

Brustein's surprisingly sophomoric assumption that this tremendous outpouring of work by minority artists leads to confusing standards and that funding agencies have started substituting sociological for aesthetic criteria, leaving aside notions like quality and excellence, shows him to be a victim of 19th-century thinking and the linguistic environment that posits blacks as unqualified. Quite possibly this tremendous outpouring of works by minority artists may lead to a *raising* of standards and a *raising* of the levels of excellence, but Mr. Brustein cannot allow that possibility.

To suggest that funding agencies are rewarding inferior work by pursuing sociological criteria only serves to call into question the tremendous outpouring of plays by white playwrights who benefit from funding given to the 66 LORT theatres.

Are those theatres funded on sociological or aesthetic criteria? Do we have 66 excellent theatres? Or do those theatres benefit from the sociological advantage that they are run by whites and cater to largely white audiences?

The truth is that often where there are aesthetic criteria of excellence, there are also sociological criteria that have traditionally excluded blacks. I say raise the standards and remove the sociological consideration of race as privilege, and we will meet you at the crossroads, in equal numbers, prepared to do the work of extending and developing the common ground of the American theatre.

We are capable of work of the highest order; we can answer to the high standards of world-class art. Anyone who doubts our capabilities at this late stage is being intellectually dishonest.

We can meet on the common ground of theatre as a field of work and endeavor. But we cannot meet on the common ground of experience.

Where is the common ground in the horrifics of lynching? Where is the common ground in the maim of a policeman's bullet? Where is the common ground in the hull or the deck of a slave ship with its refreshments of air and expanse?

We will not be denied our history.

We have voice and we have temper. We are too far along this road from the loss of our political will, we are too far along the road of reassembling ourselves, too far along the road to regaining spiritual health to allow such transgression of our history to go unchallenged.

The commonalties we share are the commonalities of culture. We decorate our houses. That is something we do in common. We do it differently because we value different things. We have different manners and different values of social intercourse. We have different ideas of what a party is.

There are some commonalities to our different ideas. We both offer food and drink to our guests, but because we have different culinary values, different culinary histories, we offer different food and drink. In our culinary history, we have learned to make do with the feet and ears and tails and intestines of the pig rather than the loin and the ham and the bacon. Because of our different histories with the same animal, we have different culinary ideas. But we share a common experience with the pig as opposed to say Muslims and Jews, who do not share that experience.

We can meet on the common ground of the American theatre.

We cannot share a single value system if that value system consists of the values of white Americans based on their European ancestors. We reject that as Cultural Imperialism. We need a value system that includes our contributions as Africans in America. Our agendas are as valid as yours. We may disagree, we may forever be on opposite sides of aesthetics, but we can only share a value system that is inclusive of all Americans and recognizes their unique and valuable contributions.

The ground together. We must develop the ground together. We reject the idea of equality among equals, but we say rather the equality of all men.

The common values of the American theatre that we can share are plot . . . dialogue . . . characterization . . . design. How we both make use of them will be determined by who we are—what ground we are standing on and what our cultural values are.

Theatre is part of art history in terms of its craft and dramaturgy, but it is part of social history in terms of how it is financed and governed. By making money available to theatres willing to support colorblind casting, the financiers and governors have signaled not only their unwillingness to support black theatre but their willingness to fund dangerous and divisive assaults against it. Colorblind casting is an aberrant idea that has never had any validity other than as a tool of the Cultural Imperialists who view American culture, rooted in the icons of European culture, as beyond reproach in its perfection. It is inconceivable to them that life could be lived and enriched without knowing Shakespeare or Mozart. Their gods, their manners, their being, are the only true and correct representations of humankind. They refuse to recognize black conduct and manners as part of a system that is fueled by its own philosophy, mythology, history, creative motif, social organization and ethos. The idea that blacks have their own way of responding to the world, their own values, style, linguistics, religion and aesthetics, is unacceptable to them.

For a black actor to stand on the stage as part of a social milieu that has denied him his gods, his culture, his humanity, his mores, his ideas of himself and the world he lives in, is to be in league with a thousand nay-sayers who wish to corrupt the vigor and spirit of his heart.

To cast us in the role of mimics is to deny us our own competence.

Our manners, our style, our approach to language, our gestures, and our bodies are not for rent. The history of our bodies—the maimings . . . the lashings . . . the lynchings . . . the body that is capable of inspiring profound rage and pungent cruelty—is not for rent.

To mount an all-black production of a *Death of a Salesman* or any other play conceived for white actors as an investigation of the human condition through the specifics of white culture is to deny us our own humanity, our own history, and the need to make our own investigations from the cultural ground on which we stand as black Americans. It is an assault on our presence, our difficult but honorable history in America; it is an insult to our intelligence, our playwrights, and our many and varied contributions to the society and the world at large.

The idea of colorblind casting is the same idea of assimilation that black Americans have been rejecting for the past 380 years. For the record, we reject it again. We reject any attempt to blot us out, to reinvent history and ignore our presence or to maim our spiritual product. We must not continue to meet on this path. We will not deny our history, and we will not allow it to be made to be of little consequence, to be ignored or misinterpreted.

In an effort to spare us the burden of being "affected by an undesirable condition" and as a gesture of benevolence, many whites (like the proponents of colorblind casting) say, "Oh, I don't see color." We want you to see us. We are black and beautiful. We are not patrons of the linguistic environment that has us as "unqualified, and violators of public regulations." We are not a menace to society. We are not ashamed. We have an honorable history in the world of men. We come from a long line of honorable people with complex codes of ethics and social discourse, people who devised myths and systems of cosmology and systems of economics. We are not ashamed, and do not need you to be ashamed for us. Nor do we need the recognition of our blackness to be couched in abstract phases like "artist of color." Who are you talking about? A Japanese artist? An Eskimo? A Filipino? A Mexican? A Cambodian? A Nigerian? An African American? Are we to suppose that if you put a white person on one side of the scale and the rest of humanity lumped together as nondescript "people of color" on the other side, that it would balance out? That whites carry that much spiritual weight? We reject that. We are unique, and we are specific.

We do not need colorblind casting; we need some theatres to develop our playwrights. We need those misguided financial resources to be put to better use. We cannot develop our playwrights with the meager resources at our disposal. Why is it difficult to imagine 9 black theatres but not 66 white ones? Without theatres we cannot develop our talents. If we cannot develop our talents, then everyone suffers: our writers; the theatre; the audience. Actors are deprived of material, and our communities are deprived of the jobs in support of the art—the company manager, the press coordinator, the electricians, the carpenters, the concessionaires, the people that work in wardrobe, the box-office staff, the ushers and the janitors. We need some theatres. We cannot continue like this. We have only one life to develop our talent, to fulfill our potential as artists. One life, and it is short, and the lack of the means to develop our talent is an encumbrance on that life.

We did not sit on the sidelines while the immigrants of Europe, through hard work, skill, cunning, guile and opportunity, built America into an industrial giant of the 20th century. It was our labor that provided the capital. It was our labor in the shipyards and the stockyards and the coal mines and the steel mills. Our labor built the roads and the railroads. And when America was challenged, we strode on the battlefield, our boots strapped on and our blood left to soak into the soil of places whose names we could not pronounce, against an enemy whose only crime was ideology. We left our blood in France and Korea and the Philippines and Vietnam, and our only reward has been the deprivation of possibility and the denial of our moral personality.

It cannot continue. The ground together: The American ground on which I stand and which my ancestors purchased with their perseverance, with their survival, with their manners and with their faith.

It cannot continue, as other assaults upon our presence and our history cannot continue: When the *New York Times* publishes an article on pop singer Michael Bolton and lists as his influences four white singers, then as an afterthought tosses in the phrase "and the great black rhythm and blues singers," it cannot be anything but purposeful with intent to maim. These great black rhythm and blues singers are reduced to an afterthought on the edge of oblivion—one stroke of the editor's pen and the history of American music is revised, and Otis Redding, Jerry Butler and Rufus Thomas are consigned to the dustbin of history while Joe Cocker, Mick Jagger and Rod Stewart are elevated to the status of the originators and creators of a vital art that is a product of our spiritual travails; the history of music becomes a fabrication, a blatant forgery which under the hallowed auspices of the *New York Times* is presented as the genuine article.

We cannot accept these assaults. We must defend and protect our spiritual fruits. To ignore these assaults would be to be derelict in our duties. We cannot accept them. Our political capital will not permit them.

So much of what makes this country rich in art and all manners of spiritual life is the contributions that we as African Americans have made. We cannot allow others to have authority over our cultural and spiritual products. We reject, without reservation, any attempts by anyone to rewrite our history so as to deny us the rewards of our spiritual labors, and to become the cultural custodians of our art, our literature and our lives. To give expression to the spirit that has been shaped and fashioned by our history is of necessity to give voice and vent to the history itself.

It must remain for us a history of triumph.

The time has come for black playwrights to confer with one another, to come together to meet each other face to face, to address questions of aesthetics and ways to defend ourselves from the nay-sayers who would trumpet our talents as insufficient to warrant the same manner of investigation and exploration as the majority. We need to develop guidelines for the protection of our cultural property, our contributions and the influence they accrue. It is time we took responsibility for our talents in our own hands. We cannot depend on others. We cannot depend on the directors, the managers or the actors to do the work we should be doing for ourselves. It is our lives and the pursuit of our fulfillment that are being encumbered by false ideas and perceptions.

It is time to embrace the political dictates of our history and answer the challenge to our duties. I further think we should confer in a city in our ancestral homeland in the southern part of the United States in 1998, so that we may enter the millennium united and prepared for a long future of prosperity.

From the hull of a ship to self-determining, self-respecting people. That is the journey we are making.

We are robust in spirit, we are bright with laughter, and we are bold in imagination. Our blood is soaked into the soil and our bones lie scattered the whole way across the Atlantic Ocean, as Hansel's crumbs, to mark the way back home.

We are no longer in the House of Bondage, and soon we will no longer be victims of the counting houses who hold from us ways to develop and support our talents and our expressions of life and its varied meanings. Assaults upon the body politic that demean and ridicule and depress the value and worth of our existence, that seek to render it immobile and to extinguish the flame of freedom lit eons ago by our ancestors upon another continent—these must be met with a fierce and uncompromising defense.

If you are willing to accept it, it is your duty to affirm and urge that defense, that respect and that determination.

I must mention here, with all due respect to W. E. B. DuBois, that the concept of a "talented tenth" creates an artificial superiority. It is a fallacy and a dangerous idea that only serves to divide us further. I am not willing to throw away as untalented 90 percent of my blood; I am not willing to dismiss the sons and daughters of those people who gave more than lip service to the will to live and made it a duty to prosper in spirit, if not in provision. All God's children got talent. It is a dangerous idea to set one part of the populace above and aside from the other. We do a grave disservice to ourselves not to seek out and embrace and enable all of our human resources as a people. All blacks in America, with very few exceptions—no matter what our status, no matter the size of our bank accounts, no matter how many and what kind of academic degrees we can place beside our names, no matter the furnishings and square footage of our homes, the length of our closets and the quality of the wool and cotton that hangs there—we all in America originated from the same place: the slave plantations of the South. We all share a common past, and despite how some us might think and how it might look, we all share a common present and will share a common future.

We can make a difference. Artists, playwrights, actors— we can be the spearhead of a movement to reignite and re-unite our people's positive energy for a political and social change that is reflective of our spiritual truths rather than economic fallacies. Our talents, our truth, our belief in ourselves is all in our hands. What we make of it will emerge as a baptismal spray that names and defines. What we do now becomes history by which our grandchildren will judge us.

We are not off on a tangent. The foundation of the American theatre is the foundation of European theatre that begins with the great Greek dramatists; it is based on the proscenium stage and the poetics of Aristotle. This is the theatre that we have chosen to work in. We embrace the values of that theatre but reserve the right to amend, to explore, to add our African consciousness and our African aesthetic to the art we produce.

To pursue our cultural expression does not separate us. We are not separatists, as Mr. Brustein asserts. We are Americans trying to fulfill our talents. We are not the servants at the party. We are not apprentices in the kitchens. We are not the stableboys to the King's huntsmen. We are Africans. We are Americans. The irreversible sweep of history has decreed that. We are artists who seek to develop our talents and give expression to our personalities. We bring advantage to the common ground that is the American theatre.

All theatres depend on an audience for its dialogue. To the American theatre, subscription audiences are its life blood. But the subscription audience holds the seats of our theatres hostage to the mediocrity of its tastes, and serves to impede the further development of an audience for the work that we do. While intentional or not, it serves to keep blacks out of the theatre where they suffer no illusion of welcome anyway. A subscription thus becomes not a support system but makes the patrons members of a club to which the theatre serves as a clubhouse. It is an irony that the people who can most afford a full-price ticket get discounts for subscribing, while the single-ticket buyer who cannot afford a subscription is charged the additional burden of support to offset the subscription-buyer's discount. It is a system that is in need of overhaul to provide not only a more equitable access to tickets but access to influence as well.

I look for and challenge students of arts management to be bold in their exploration of new systems of funding theatres, including profit-making institutions and ventures, and I challenge black artists and audiences to scale the walls erected by theatre subscriptions to gain access to this vital area of spiritual enlightenment and enrichment that is the theatre.

All theatregoers have opinions about the work they witness. Critics have an informed opinion. Sometimes it may be necessary for them to gather more information to become more informed. As playwrights grow and develop, as the theatre changes, the critic has an important responsibility to guide and encourage that growth. However, in the discharge of their duties, it may be necessary for them to also grow and develop. A stagnant body of critics, operating from the critical criteria of 40 years ago, makes for a stagnant theatre without the fresh and abiding influence of contemporary ideas. It is the critics who should be in the forefront of developing new tools for analysis necessary to understand new influences.

The critic who can recognize a German neo-romantic influence should also be able to recognize an American influence from blues or black church rituals, or any other contemporary American influence.

The true critic does not sit in judgment. Rather he seeks to inform his reader, instead of adopting a posture of self-conscious importance in which he sees himself a judge and final arbiter of a work's importance or value.

We stand on the verge of an explosion of playwriting talent that will challenge our critics. As American playwrights absorb the influence of television and use new avenues of approach to the practice of their craft, they will prove to be wildly inventive and imaginative in creating dramas that will guide and influence contemporary life for years to come.

Theatre can do that. It can disseminate ideas, it can educate even the miseducated, because it is art—and all art reaches across that divide that makes order out of chaos, and embraces the truth that overwhelms with its presence, and connects man to something larger than himself and his imagination.

Theatre asserts that all of human life is universal. Love, Honor, Duty, Betrayal belong and pertain to every culture or race. The way they are acted out on the playing field may be different, but betrayal is betrayal whether you are a South Sea Islander, a Mississippi farmer or an English baron. All of human life is universal, and it is theatre that illuminates and confers upon the universal the ability to speak for all men.

The ground together: We have to do it together. We cannot permit our lives to waste away, our talents unchallenged. We cannot permit a failure to our duty. We are brave and we are boisterous, our mettle is proven, and we are dedicated.

The ground together: the ground of the American theatre on which I am proud to stand . . . the ground which our artistic ancestors purchased with their endeavors . . .with their pursuit of the American spirit and its ideals.

I believe in the American theatre. I believe in its power to inform about the human condition, its power to heal, its power to hold the mirror as 'twere up to nature, its power to uncover the truths we wrestle from uncertain and sometimes unyielding realities. All of art is a search for ways of being, of living life more fully. We who are capable of those noble pursuits should challenge the melancholy and barbaric, to bring the light of angelic grace, peace, prosperity and the unencumbered pursuit of happiness to the ground on which we all stand.

ROBERT BRUSTEIN
Subsidized Separatism

August Wilson's keynote address at the TCG (Theatre Communications Group) Conference in late June 1996, later published as "The Ground on Which I Stand," was greeted with a standing ovation by the various resident theatre people attending, though some found it divisive and disturbing. Since I was not present at the conference, I was hardly in a position to express my own reactions, though word leaked back to me that chief among the malefactors identified in Wilson's broadside—his "snipers" and "naysayers" and "cultural imperialists"—was myself.

Wilson's rambling jeremiad is essentially an effort to accentuate the achievements of black theatre, which he claims to be supreme today though "often accomplished amid adverse and hostile conditions." "Black theatre is alive, it is vibrant, it is vital," he says. But not all its practitioners are following the proper path. In the same speech Wilson manages to express his disdain for black "crossover artists" who, "like house slaves entertaining the white master and his guests," manage to "slant their material for white consumption." He rebukes white foundations for failing to create and subsidize black theatre companies. And he characterizes the idea of "color-blind casting" as "a tool of the Cultural Imperialists"—"the same idea of assimilation that black Americans have been rejecting for the past 300 years."

If you hear echoes in this of 1960s radicalism, particularly the language of black nationalism, your ears are not deceiving you. And Wilson is hardly reluctant to admit his militant inheritance. Testifying that the black power movement was "the kiln in which I was fired," he proclaims that its concern with "self-determination, self-respect and self-defense" are the values that govern his life. He claims that "I am what is known, at least among the followers and supporters of Marcus Garvey, as a 'race man.'" He announces that the ground on which he stands was pioneered "by Nat Turner, by Denmark Vesey, by Martin Delaney, Marcus Garvey and the Honorable Elijah Muhammad"—rebels or separatists all, some proponents of a return to Africa. Conspicuous by its absence is the name of Martin Luther King, among many other honored black Americans for whom the idea of integration has not been considered anathema.

The foundation of this long tirade is Wilson's insistence on black culture, particularly black theatre, not only as an unparalleled achievement but also a singular and discrete experience of life. It is an experience that cannot be fully absorbed or understood by white people, much less criticized by them: "We cannot allow others to have authority over our cultural and spiritual products," he says. "We need to develop guidelines of the protection of our cultural property, our contributions and the influence they accrue." Whites and blacks can occupy the same country, but they cannot occupy the same ground. "Where is the common ground in the horrifics of lynching? Where is the common ground in the policeman's bullet? Where is the common ground in the hull or the deck of a slave ship . . . ?" He describes "black conduct and manners as part of a system that is fueled by its own philosophy, mythology, history, creative motif, social organization and ethos." He deplores the presence of a black actor in a non-black play, standing on the stage "as part of a social milieu that has denied him his gods, his humanity, his mores, his ideas of himself and the world he lives in. . . ." Indeed, he considers the very idea of an all-black production of *Death of a Salesman* to be "an assault on our presence . . . an insult to our intelligence."

This is the language of self-segregation. At times, it is true, Wilson is willing to concede that blacks and whites breathe the same air and partake of certain "commonalities" of culture. Among these "commonalities" he mentions food, though even that admission is weirdly exclusionary. Black people have had to be satisfied with the leavings of the pig. Yet blacks and whites "share a common experience with the pig as opposed to say Muslims and Jews, who do not share that experience." (Black Muslims? Reform Jews?) It is also true that, in the rolling cadences that bring his speech to its climax, Wilson concedes the American theatre's power to "inform about the human condition, its power to heal, its power to hold the mirror as 'twere up to nature, its power to uncover the truths we wrestle from uncertain and sometimes unyielding realities." Even this boiler-plate rhetoric, however, for all its afterthought references to the unifying nature of the theatre, fails to compensate for the divisive nature of his remarks. Perhaps some future student of syntax will analyze how Wilson's vacillating use of the word "we" in the same paragraph (first inclusive: "We have to do it together," then exclusive: "We are brave and we are boisterous") betrays his ambivalent sense of American identity. This ambivalence makes for some confusing assertions. "We are black and beautiful. . . . We are not separatists. . . . We are Africans. We are Americans."

Furthermore, Wilson's insistence on the strength and uniqueness of a proud black culture is oddly inconsistent with his notion that blacks are "victims of the counting houses who hold from us ways to develop and support our talents." This inconsistency grows more glaring when Wilson directs his biblical fury toward some of these "counting houses" (his name for the funding agencies) and concludes that "the economics are reserved as privilege to the overwhelming abundance of institutions that promote and perpetrate white culture." He notes that of the sixty-six League of Resident Theatres (LORT) only one can be considered black. And in an impassioned if curious appeal for subsidized separatism, he sees no contradiction in demanding that white foundations take the responsibility for founding as well as funding black theatres, as if theatre companies were the creation of philanthropic agencies rather than the indigenous outgrowths of dedicated artists and supporting communities.

I'm not at all certain any more what constitutes a "black" or "white" theatre. Both the precarious Negro Ensemble Company and the thriving Crossroads Theater fit Wilson's exclusive definition clearly enough. But how does one describe the New York Public Theater and Atlanta Alliance Theater under their black directors George C. Wolfe and Kenneth Leon? Or the Yale Repertory Theatre and Syracuse Stage when they were led by such black directors as Lloyd Richards and Tazewell Thompson? Most American theatres today, like many American cities—indeed like many Americans—are racially mixed. Are black actors now to perform only black parts writ-ten by black playwrights? Will James Earl Jones no longer have a chance to play Judge Brack or Darth Vader? Must we bar Andre Braugher and Denzel Washington from enacting the Shakespearean monarchs? Is Othello to be an unacceptable opportunity for Morgan Freeman or Laurence Fishburne? Will Athol Fugard be told he cannot take a colored role in his own plays? No more voodoo *Macbeths* or all-black *Godots?* No more efforts on behalf of nontraditional casting and integrated theatre companies? Must history be rolled back to the days of segregated theatres?

I fear Wilson is displaying a failure of memory—I hesitate to say a failure of gratitude—when he charges nonprofit resident theatres with using "sociological criteria" in choosing plays that "traditionally exclude blacks." All of his own plays were originated and produced by a large consortium of mainstream institutions, including the Yale Repertory Theatre, the Huntington, the American Conservatory Theater, the Goodman, the Mark Taper, and others. Wilson's pervasive tone of victimization, in fact, is oddly inappropriate for a playwright whose six LORT-generated plays, after completing the resident theatre circuit, all found their way to Broadway, where they won two Pulitzer Prizes, five New York Drama Critics Circle awards, and I don't know how many Tonys, besides generating enormous box office income for the playwright (from white and black audiences alike). Is a man who has garnered such extraordinary media attention (not to mention every conceivable playwriting fellowship) really in a position to say that blacks are being excluded from the American theatre or that these institutions only "preserve, promote, and perpetuate white culture"? Has he read any foundation reports lately? Does he have any idea of the proportion of grants, both public and private, that are exclusively reserved for inner-city audience development and multicultural activities in resident theatres?

I am the only villain identified by name in Wilson's speech. He makes reference to my article "Diversity and Unity," but there are also hidden allusions to what I wrote in "The Options of Multiculturalism," my unfavorable review of his play *The Piano Lesson,* and my *Times* op-ed piece on coercive foundation funding. Wilson specifically attacks what he calls my "surprisingly sophomoric assumption" that the present funding climate is characterized by confused standards and sociological rather than aesthetic criteria. I confess to believing that most foundations (by their own admission) no longer make artistic quality their primary consideration. But I categorically deny I ever said that "the practice of extending invitations to a national banquet from which a lot of hungry people have been excluded" (my phrase, uncredited) establishes (his phrase) "a presumption of inferiority of the work of minority artists."

Wilson's charge, with its nasty imputations of racism, is intended to characterize a review of two minority playwrights who, in my estimation, met the highest standards, and without being exclusionary. "Drenched in their own cultural juices," I wrote, "they are nevertheless capable of telling stories that include us all, thus proving again that the theatre works best as a unifying rather than a segregating medium." I was talking about transcendence, about recognizing that the greatest art embraces a common humanity. Although Wilson might dismiss such playwrights—the younger generation of black writers like Anna Deavere Smith and OyamO and Suzan-Lori Parks—as "crossover artists" entertaining the slave owner and his guests, my article was a plea to minority playwrights like himself to acknowledge, without any loss of racial consciousness, that they belong, as artists, to the same human family as everyone else.

Some people may remember that, almost alone among white critics, I have expressed reservations about Wilson's plays. This was an aesthetic judgment, not a racial one. While I admire Wilson's control of character and dialogue, a lot of his writing has seemed to me weakly structured, badly edited, prosaic, and overwritten. Consider, for instance, *Seven Guitars*, which I didn't review (I left after four guitars). I don't think it exposes "the values of white Americans based on their European ancestors" to believe that a conventionally realistic play needs an animating event, and that, however colorful its subject matter, it cannot ramble willy-nilly for one act lasting two and a half hours without establishing a line of action. My less technical objection has been that, by choosing to chronicle the oppression of black people through each of the decades, Wilson has fallen into a monotonous tone of victimization which happens to be the leitmotif of his TCG speech.

I am also disturbed by other attitudes reflected in that speech, notably that only the black experience inspires the work of black artists. In "The Options of Multiculturalism," I suggested that, while Wilson has announced he will never allow a white director to stage his plays, a backyard drama like his *Fences* shows the considerable influence of white playwrights, particularly Arthur Miller's *All My Sons*. (It may be that Wilson's anger over this conjecture ricochets into his ferocious attack on the *New York Times* for allegedly underplaying the influence of black singers on Michael Bolton—something he calls an "intent to maim.")

It is perfectly possible that I am wrong in my assessments. And I can understand how a playwright, no matter how highly praised by mainstream critics, can smart under adverse criticism, even in a relatively small-circulation periodical such as *The New Republic*. It is also no doubt painful to him that *Seven Guitars* lost the Tony this year to *Master Class*. But that is no justification for wheeling out the creaky juggernaut of black power to roll over anyone who makes a negative judgment on his plays. Indeed, Wilson seems to suggest occasionally that the only true critical function is boosterism. For at the same time Wilson is questioning the very idea of critical opinions ("The true critic does not sit in judgment . . . the critic has an important responsibility to guide and encourage . . . growth"), he is announcing that every African American, contrary to Du Bois's idea of "the talented tenth," is artistically gifted: "All God's children got talent." This is progressive-school nonsense. The greatest tribute that a critic can pay to a playwright such as Wilson is to judge and analyze his work by the same criteria as anybody else's work.

Wilson writes: "I stand myself and my art squarely on the self-defining ground of the slave quarters." Isn't it time to acknowledge that, for all the grim uncompleted racial business in this country, those quarters have long been razed to the ground? Isn't there some kind of statute of limitations on white guilt and white reparations? Isn't it possible to recognize that there is a difference between losing your freedom and losing a Tony, between toting a bale of cotton and bearing the burden of an unfavorable review? To say that whites can't understand black culture because their ancestors were not enslaved is almost as problematical as saying that Wilson can't understand the writings of a Jew because he hasn't experienced life under the pharaohs. Many brilliant black artists and intellectuals—Albert Murray, Ralph Ellison, Henry Louis Gates, Shelby Steele, and others—have repudiated the "ethnographic fallacy" that one writer's peculiar experiences can represent a whole social category. This tribalist approach, as Diane Ravitch has written, "confuses race with culture, as though everyone with the same skin color had the same culture and history."

August Wilson is more comfortable writing plays than apostolic decrees. His speech is melancholy testimony to the rabid identity politics and poisonous racial consciousness that have been infecting our country in recent years. Although Wilson would deny it, such sentiments represent a reverse form of the old politics of division, an appeal for socially approved and foundation-funded separatism. I don't think Martin Luther King ever imagined an America where playwrights such as August Wilson would be demanding, under the pretense of calling for healing and unity, an entirely separate stage for black theatre artists. What next? Separate schools? Separate washrooms? Separate drinking fountains?

A DESIGNER'S PERSPECTIVE

ARNOLD ARONSON

"Design for *Angels in America*: Envisioning the Millennium" (1997)

Arnold Aronson is well known for his writing on theater design; he is the author of American Set Design, *and currently teaches at Columbia University. In this essay, Aronson considers the twofold work of design in the theater: how set, costume, and lighting provide a specific interpretation of the play in production, and how they help to orient the audience to the play through its physical stage milieu. Aronson discusses the different ways in which the "idea of 'America'" was expressed by the design of three productions of Tony Kushner's* Angels in America, *and how design for that play is part of an ongoing tradition of American stage design.*

There are two essential questions to be answered in considering the scenography of *Angels in America*. One is a fundamental scenographic question for any play: where are we? (and how do we, as an audience, know where we are?). The other is a practical one: how can the sheer magnitude of the play be dealt with? *Angels in America* unfolds through two parts, eight acts, and an epilogue, consisting of some sixty scenes, a significant number of which are "split"—presenting two locales simultaneously. Some, such as the Brooklyn apartment of Joe and Harper, Prior's bedroom, or the hospital room of Roy Cohn, are recurring, but many are seen only once, resulting in a dizzying array of settings through which the spectators must be led on their theatrical journey. The practical question is a daunting one because the visual landscape must have a unity that provides an overall structure for the production while at the same time providing enough specificity to allow the audience to locate itself within the ever-changing geography of the play. Yet, from a practical point of view, the sixty scene changes must not be allowed to become time-consuming or disruptive to the emotional and narrative progression of the play; they must flow with the ineluctable logic and fluidity of a dream.

The solution to the practical problems will ultimately be determined by the approach to the more philosophical question of location. If we begin with "where," the answer is, on the surface, relatively simple: we are in America. More precisely, we are in various specified locations in New York City in the latter half of the 1980s as well as in apparently hallucinatory images and fantasies of various characters. It is from these simple observations that the visual environment—the world—of *Angels* must be drawn.

How does one present the idea of "America"? Is there an obvious imagistic or emblematic representation? Is there a single icon, perhaps, that will provide the audience with a sense of time, place, tone, and point of view? The British production, for example, directed by Declan Donnellan and designed by Nick Ormerod at the Royal National Theatre in

London, attempted to do so by transforming the stage into a "stars and stripes" background against which the play unfolded quite simply. But it is much easier to convey the concept of a foreign nation to an audience than to confront spectators with their own culture and heritage. For a British audience (indeed, for any non-American audience) the mere sight of the emblem of the United States is sufficient to evoke a vast array of associations; the simple environment suggested that all the characters and their actions were enmeshed in America, whatever that might mean for each individual spectator. Tony Kushner, himself, plays with that sort of iconography when he calls for a "great red flag" behind Prelapsarianov at the start of *Perestroika*. But in the United States the subtleties, contradictions, and even violently opposing concepts of America make such simple emblematic scenography problematic, if not impossible.

In fact, at least part of the play's theme is wrapped up in the epic struggle to come to terms with what America means as the millennium approaches. Just as Prior wrestles with the Angel, so must the scenographer contend with the landscape of the play. At the start of part 1 the Rabbi, talking to the mourners of Sarah Ironson (though addressing the audience in the theater) states: "You do not live in America. No such place exists."[1] America is a fantasy, a chimera, made up of the individual perceptions, expectations, and projections of hundreds of millions of individuals whose true roots are elsewhere. How remarkable to be told in the first moments of the play that the very location identified in the title is nonexistent—a state of mind. It is, perhaps, not unlike Alfred Jarry's siting of *Ubu Roi* in Poland—"that is to say," as Jarry explained in his address to the audience at the first performance,

---

[1] Tony Kushner, *Angels in America: A Gay Fantasia on National Themes. Part One: Millennium Approaches* (New York: Theatre Communications Group, 1993), 10. All subsequent references to part 1 will be indicated in parentheses in the text.

"nowhere."[2] Jarry's Poland was "nowhere" because it was a country that, historically, existed more often as a concept of nationhood in the souls of its people than as a political entity. America, on the other hand, has been a political entity for over two centuries, yet it consists of such a commingling of disparate peoples that its identity as a nation has always been a subject of debate, never more so than now. Kushner's dramatis personae contains a veritable catalogue of individuals who fly in the face of the Reaganite image of America. It is not that Kushner's image has more truth than any other; it simply emphasizes the difficulty of arriving at a unified coherent image. There is no landscape that easily will provide the world of Kushner's vision.

In the production at the Mark Taper Forum in Los Angeles, director Oskar Eustis and set designer John Conklin nonetheless sought a unifying image that would evoke Americana without overly specifying or imposing a narrow view. The back wall of Conklin's set was the façade of a house that combined elements of a New England meetinghouse with Jeffersonian classicism. The meetinghouse was evoked largely by a geometrically square floor of natural wood planks set on gray boulders suggestive of a Maine or California coast. The image suggested simplicity, sturdiness, and a connection with the continent itself—all elements of American mythology. The façade was a pastiche of windows, doors, and cornices based on the designs of Thomas Jefferson, the towering intellect of the American Revolution. The total effect, though obviously a theatricalized amalgamation, was of distinctly American architecture. It created, according to Conklin, a "civilized public space."[3] The choice was inspired: the American home, as developed over the last three centuries, has been considered the country's most original contribution to architecture. Jefferson's classicism, of course, was based on European Renaissance models, which, in turn, were drawn from ancient Roman and Greek sources. So the visual imagery echoed the Eurocentric foundation of America that is depicted in the play. Here was a visual iconography that evoked the idea of America without being overly symbolic or trite.

But Conklin took the concept of the house-as-metaphor one step further by creating a large jagged split down the center of the façade to create, as he noted, "an ideal that was cracked."[4] The Angel flew in through this crack in the wall, rather than through the ceiling, which did not exist in this production.

[2]Alfred Jarry, "Preliminary Address at the First Performance of Ubu Roi, December 10, 1896," in Selected Works of Alfred Jarry, ed. Roger Shattuck and Simon Watson Taylor (New York: Grove Press, 1980), 78.

[3]John Conklin, personal interview, 2 January 1996.

[4]Ibid.

The Broadway production, directed by George C. Wolfe and designed by Robin Wagner, opted for neutrality rather than visual metaphor. Unity was achieved by the proscenium arch itself and ever-changing configurations of black velour flats in chrome frames. Perhaps the production's very presence in New York City, the center of the American theater world, the place where Kushner developed as a playwright, a center of gay culture and consciousness, and a place where much of the audience would know firsthand the sites referred to in the text, mitigated the need for some other visual element as a unifying image.

Interestingly, the Los Angeles production never sought to suggest New York City as a locale nor to use images of the city in an iconographic way. It would not be unreasonable for a designer to use the visual iconography of New York City as a unifying framework, but, other than, perhaps, Bethesda Fountain in Central Park, Kushner sets none of the play in a recognizable locale. (There are many specific locations, such as the Mormon Visitor's Center, but they are not instantly recognizable landmarks as is, say, the Empire State Building, which was the locale for the conclusion of Perestroika in an early draft of the script.) The play ranges through unremarkable apartments, offices, and streetscapes that carry no particular resonance except what is bestowed upon them by their occupants. And that is as it should be. New York City is vital to the play because it is the historical point of entry to America for immigrants on their journey to a new land, and it is still the destination for those from within the country who seek refuge from their own bleak landscape; it is a place for those who do not fit elsewhere. It is a city of the displaced, the outsiders, the adventurers, the seekers and searchers. In its diversity and lack of apparent cohesion, in its gaudy excess as well as decay, it seems to defy the standard images of America. It is the place of the "other," and thus it serves as America's other. But, as the home for everyone and a repository of history, it embodies all that is America and makes it the quintessential emblem of America at the millennium. This is an "everytown," which is to say "our town."

If Angels in America has a precedent in American theater history, it is surely Thornton Wilder's Our Town, and a comparison of the two is instructive. Wilder combined aspects of Italian futurism, German expressionism, other European vanguard movements, and the ideas of Gertrude Stein with American sensibilities, especially emotional realism, to create not only innovative forms of drama but also a new way of physical presentation. Though Wilder did not invent the bare stage or emblematic scenery, he popularized them as a means of economic staging while inviting a wider audience imagination—a kind of radio for the eyes. Wilder's play is both a reading of the geography of America in the first third of the American century as well as a teleological explication of human existence. At the end of act 1 of Wilder's play, Rebecca Gibbs remarks on a letter her friend had received that was addressed to "Jane Crofut; The Crofut Farm; Grover's Corners; Sutton County; New Hampshire; United States of America . . . Continent of North America; Western Hemisphere; the Earth; the Solar System; the Universe; the Mind of God."[5] Just as Wilder provides a few scenic items "for those who think they have to have scenery,"[6] he also provides this simple explanation of the microcosm within the macrocosm for those who might need an explanation. Tony Kushner's version of "our town" is not as idyllic as Wilder's world, and God, we are told, has been missing since the San Francisco earthquake of 1906, but the play unfolds, nonetheless, in Heaven as well as on earth and in the minds of the characters, who—given the Judeo-Christian matrix of the play—were created in God's image. And, if anyone doubts the connection to *Our Town,* it is made at the very end of the play, in the epilogue, as several of the characters sit around Bethesda Fountain. Prior, like a latter-day stage manager, approaches the audience and says:

> They'll be at it for hours. It's not that what they're saying isn't important, it's just . . .
>
> This is my favorite place in New York City. No, in the whole universe. The parts of it I have seen.
>
> On a day like today. A sunny winter's day, warm and cold at once. The sky's a little hazy, so the sunlight has a physical presence, a character. In autumn, those trees across the lake are yellow, and the sun strikes those most brilliantly. Against the blue of the sky, that sad fall blue, those trees are more light than vegetation. They are Yankee trees, New England transplants. They're barren now. It's January 1990. I've been living with AIDS for five years.[7]

Just as Wilder realized that the best setting for his play was the bare signifying stage, so Kushner places his play on an essentially empty stage with minimal emblematic elements to guide us. A reading of the stage directions reveals almost no description. The first time we see the Pitt apartment in Brooklyn the stage directions read only: "*Harper at home, alone. She is listening to the radio and talking to herself, as she often does. She speaks to the audience*" (1:16). No description of ground plan, furniture, light, atmosphere, bric-a-brac; no adjectives. Somewhat like the captured sol-

dier's recitation of name, rank, and serial number, Kushner gives us only place, character, and basic action. In the case of Joe and Harper Pitt we discover all we need to know about them through dialogue, action, response to other characters, and, in the case of Harper, her hallucinations and fantasies. The style of furniture, the color of the walls, the decorations, and the relative tidiness of the apartment—the sort of information often vital to our understanding of characters in O'Neill, Odets, Williams, Miller, or even Shepard or Mamet—is irrelevant here and would be distracting and limiting even if it were practical to provide such complete and illusionistic settings. Kushner's landscape, like Wilder's, is the stage, which takes us directly from the individual characters to the "mind of God" with only a bench, a chair, a bed, or "*an impressive desk, bare except for a very elaborate phone system*" (1:11). It is worth noting, though, that Wilder provides one of the most evocative elements possible in his settings: sound. His scenes are enhanced by specific aural effects that, to paraphrase *Hamlet,* allow us to see with the mind's ear. Kushner rarely indicates sound.

But there are, nonetheless, clues about the look of this landscape to be found in his text. When settings *are* described or when characters talk of locales, they tend to describe barren and bleak sites. Most obvious is Harper's recurring hallucination of Antarctica, though a confused Antarctica with Eskimos. Mr. Lies describes it as "a retreat, a vacuum, its virtue is that it lacks everything; deep-freeze for feelings" (1:102). Harper is a person at odds with the given landscape of New York City. As an agoraphobic, she remains in her apartment envisioning her own private Antarctica. When she does venture outside she rarely remains in perceived reality; she interacts with the inanimate diorama of Mormon history, and even in Prospect Park she fights the surroundings to maintain her vision of Antarctica:

> For a moment, the magical antarctic light begins to dim, replaced by the glare of sodium park lights; the sea sounds and wind are drowned out by the sound of traffic as heard from the middle of a city park at night; Harper looks about, and as she does, Antarctica is restored a bit, though the city lights and sounds do not retreat entirely (2:19).

The arrival of Hannah Pitt occurs in the South Bronx, and it is one of the few scenes with any sort of physical description of location: "*An abandoned lot in the South Bronx. A homeless Woman is standing near an oil drum in which a fire is burning. Snowfall. Trash around*" (1:103). It is a scene of desolation and urban blight—a vision of Hell. This vision is echoed in part 2, when Belize describes Heaven to Roy Cohn:

> Big city, overgrown with weeds, but flowering weeds. On every corner a wrecking crew and something new and crooked going up

---

[5] Thornton Wilder, *Our Town,* act 1, in *Three Plays* (New York: Avon Books, 1976), 28.

[6] Ibid., 6.

[7] Tony Kushner, *Angels in America: A Gay Fantasia on National Themes. Part Two: Perestroika* (New York: Theatre Communications Group, 1994), 146. All subsequent references to part 2 will be indicated in parentheses in the text.

catty-corner to that. Windows missing in every edifice like broken teeth, fierce gusts of gritty wind, and a gray high sky full of ravens. . . . Piles of trash, but lapidary like rubies and obsidian, and diamond-colored cowspit streamers in the wind (2:77).

This diction elevates aspects of *Angels* to the poetic, but it would be a mistake to use these tonal clues as a guide for literal scenography. The magic of the scene with Harper in the park is created through sound and light and is made possible by the essentially neutral canvas of the stage. As appropriate as any overriding image may be metaphorically, it becomes an inflexible and immutable landscape that, when realized onstage, can never fulfill the grand canvas of the text. The stage has the remarkable power to transform any object that is placed upon it; these objects acquire, said Russian folklorist Petr Bogatyrev, "special features, qualities and attributes that they do not have in real life."[8] The moment anything specific is placed on the stage, be it a bed, a living room, or a trash heap, its details begin to acquire special significance that starts a process, however subconscious, of interpretation on the part of the spectator. This is a play in which light, sound, and suggestion become crucial.

Ultimately, any production is faced with the overwhelming question of practicality. How are transitions made from one scene to the next? The answer will be informed in part by the way in which the director and designer interpret the structure of the play. Is the structure seen in terms of a Shakespearean or possibly Brechtian model? Is it perhaps seen as an example of the episodic structure of medieval or Expressionist drama? Or is it conceived of as cinematic—that is, a series of cross-fades, jump cuts, and montage among related but disparate scenes? Since the 1930s many critics have seen the inevitable influence of movies upon the theater and have designated almost any play that moves through multiple scenes as cinematic. Though *Angels* clearly has affinities to all these forms and undoubtedly draws from them—consciously or not—I would suggest that the play's organization and scenic movement derive from something else. Its structure is inevitably informed by contemporary sensibilities and perceptions of the world, and film is no longer the defining mode of perception. Neither, needless to say, is a medieval or Renaissance or early-twentieth-century perspective. Unless Kushner were to say that his play was based upon one of these theatrical forms, to attempt to solve the scenographic problems posed by the play by utilizing historical models will result in a clash of sensibilities.

Ours is a paradoxical world of isolation and interconnection. Certainly, the audiences of Tony Kushner's generation are comfortable with rapidly shifting barrages of images and sounds presented in overlapping, incongruent, dissociated juxtaposition. The world of computers, VCRs, and fax machines allows unfathomable amounts of information and imagery—virtually all knowledge and culture—to be accessible almost on demand. Significantly, it is no longer necessary to go to the concert hall, the museum, the movie house, or even the library in order to consume these products of culture. They can be brought into the private realm, freed from the temporal constraints of exhibition or performance. They can be fragmented, deconstructed, juxtaposed. All this has contributed to our transformation into a society of isolated individuals, both producing and consuming all this information in the privacy of homes or offices away from the life of cities. Television has produced the anomaly of audiences of one hundred million or more, each at his or her own private screen. This is the generation that has produced the neologism *cyberspace* to define a location, occupied by millions, that does not exist. We are, to quote Michel Foucault, in

the epoch of space. We are in the epoch of simultaneity: we are in the epoch of juxtaposition, the epoch of the near and far, of side-by-side, of the dispersed. We are at a moment, I believe, when our experience of the world is less that of a long life developing through time than that of a network that connects points and intersects with its own skein. One could perhaps say that certain ideological conflicts animating present-day polemics oppose the pious descendants of time and the determined inhabitants of space.[9]

It would be absurd to suggest that *Angels in America* is some sort of cyber-tech futuristic play or a theatrical analogue to the Internet. Far from it. Spiritually, the play and its characters are closer to the sociopolitical dramas of the 1930s than to the avant-garde, and it remains a piece of theater abiding by relatively well-established conventions of theatrical presentation. But it is in its *structure* and *spatial sensibility* that it reflects most definitely the dominant forces of our time. The philosopher Henri Lefebvre, in his major work *The Production of Space,* points out that "every society . . . produces a space, its own space. The city of the ancient world cannot be understood [merely] as a collection of people and things in space. . . . Each society offers up its own peculiar space, as it were, as an 'object' for analysis and overall theoretical explication."[10]

Our space is, as Foucault suggests, nonlinear, nongeometric, disjointed, juxtapositional; one moves not from one

[8]Quoted in Keir Elam, *The Semiotics of Theatre and Drama* (New York and London: Methuen, 1980, 1983), 7.

[9]Michel Foucault, "Of Other Spaces," *diacritics* 16(1986): 22.
[10]Henri Lefebvre, *The Production of Space,* trans. Donald Nicholson-Smith (Oxford, U.K., and Cambridge, Mass.: Blackwell Publishers, 1991), 31.

contiguous space to another but across disparate spatial and temporal boundaries. Ours is the space of hypertext. In the age of computers and fiber-optic technology it seems unexceptional to be able to connect any two or more points regardless of their seeming disparity; in cyberspace the laws of geometry do not prevail. With the click of a button, words, symbols, and images can be connected in an almost infinite string of associations. In hypertext, just as in dreams and imagination, key words or images can transport us from one locale to another, from one world to another. This is the driving logic of *Angels in America*. It is a way of thinking, seeing, and conceptualizing the world that has surreptitiously entered the consciousness of contemporary culture and utterly transformed the society.

A pervasive computer culture is a recent phenomenon. But before hypertext was a familiar concept Foucault described what he called "heterotopias." "We do not live inside a void that could be colored with diverse shades of light," he wrote, "we live inside a set of relations that delineates sites which are irreducible to one another and absolutely not superimposable on one another. . . . The heterotopia is capable of juxtaposing in a single real place several spaces, several sites that are in themselves incompatible."[11] While Foucault was using the *heterotopia* to analyze such varied societal institutions as churches, vacation villages, fairgrounds, and brothels, the term works superbly as a description of theater. The stage, after all, is a single real space that can hold a multitude of places.

This heterotopic/hypertextual idea is not a recent phenomenon in theater. The simultaneous stage of the Middle Ages, the split scenes and vision scenes of melodrama, the flashback (credited to playwright Elmer Rice), and Sergei Eisenstein's idea of montage all predate in practice what Foucault described in theory. As a result, *Angels* can seem part of an old theatrical tradition, but Kushner pushes it further. Act 3, scene 5, of *Perestroika,* for instance, begins on the Brooklyn Heights Promenade with Harper talking to the Mormon Mother seen earlier as part of the diorama of the Mormon Visitor's Center. But the characters from the previous two scenes remain onstage. This means that Joe and Louis are at Jones Beach, while Roy Cohn and Belize are in Cohn's hospital room. During this scene Prior becomes visible in his bedroom; Louis leaves Joe and is suddenly at a pay phone in Manhattan calling Prior. This layering of scenes and transpositions of characters resemble "windows" on a computer screen: multiple locations, some hidden behind others, but any one available to foreground at any moment and in any sequence. Kushner has interwoven seven characters (one a hal-

lucination) and five locations and has collapsed time. Another slightly different example of this hypertextual space can be found in the interconnection of Harper's Valium-induced hallucination with Prior's dream in part 1, one of the wonderful conceits of this play. In this scene not only are the conventions of theatrical fantasy transcended, but mental space is bridged as well. The scene almost suggests the reconciliation between conceptual space and social space discussed by Lefebvre. The scene is an initially comic reconciliation, with echoes of the narrative and structural logic of Buster Keaton films. But, again, there is a more contemporary resonance in this strange dislocation.

But the practical considerations still haunt the designer. There is, after all, no button to click that will take the viewer from screen to screen, leaping through cyberspace in milliseconds. The stage is still bound by the laws of physics, Euclidean geometry, linear time, and the limitations of human actors. And, even if it were possible somehow to recreate the speed and spatiality of hypertext, to do so would subvert the spirit of the play, which is based on fundamental human relationships. Kushner is fairly clear about the type of production he desires in his note on staging, and it sounds very much like the *Our Town* school of theater:

> The play benefits from a pared-down style of presentation, with minimal scenery and scene shifts done rapidly (no blackouts!), employing the cast as well as stagehands—which makes an actor-driven event, as this must be. The moments of magic . . . are to be fully realized, as bits of wonderful *theatrical* illusion—which means it's OK if the wires show (1:5).

One reads Kushner's injunction with vigorous agreement, but it is not as easy to achieve as it may seem. There are a limited number of ways to accomplish Kushner's goal, and all of them have certain drawbacks. If one were to make a list of the minimum set pieces required to produce the play (as some scholars have done for Shakespeare), the list would be fairly short—an amazingly iconographic collection of elements: a bed, a park bench, a hospital bed, a chair, a desk. Other than the unique scenes such as the diorama in the Mormon Visitor's Center, very little else is needed. Does Prior's bed need to be different from Louis's? Does his hospital bed need to be different from Cohn's? Does one park bench need to be different from another? If there is a willingness to use emblematic furniture and stick to the bare minimum, it could be possible to set at least the recurrent scenes more or less permanently on the stage so that scene shifts might be achieved largely through lighting changes and actor movement. This, indeed, was the original intent of Conklin and Eustis at the Taper: to place essential scenic pieces against the cracked façade of the background. During the develop-

[11]Foucault, "Of Other Spaces," 25.

ment process more specific scenery was added, and the final product was, as so many theater pieces are, a compromise among several visions. The more elements that need to move on and off the stage, the more one is dependent on actors or stage hands to do the moving. In a play with so many changes this parade of furniture-toting figures ultimately adds not simply an encumbrance or distraction but also another level of text—a secondary play about furniture moving that exists in the interstices of the primary text.

The Broadway production had the resources—and perhaps the temptation—to employ technology for fluidity. The relatively small stage of the Walter Kerr Theatre was fitted with an elaborate winch system that allowed wagons (movable stage platforms) to glide on and off the stage with seeming ease as other units flew in or out. This is a different kind of magic, though. It is the slickness and trickery of Broadway musicals that "wows" an audience with scenery that is as choreographed as the dancers. Nevertheless, there is no question that, once the decision had been made to depict each room, park, hospital room, and office with individualized scenic units, then Wagner's solution to the problem of scene shifts was the most efficient one possible. Action or dialogue could start as one wagon rolled on while another rolled off; scenes could overlap, intersect, and recombine. The proscenium stage, however, imposes a limitation on movement: wagons can roll on from stage right or stage left, and there is only so much variety possible. A certain repetitive monotony was inevitable with such a scheme. *Village Voice* critic Michael Feingold may have summed it up best when he noted that the set, "too elaborate for the pared-down version Kushner's notes request, yet too sparing of its

effects to drown the play in glitz . . . gets the many scenes on and off with a flat, neat efficiency."[12]

Since the play's New York staging, productions of *Angels* have proliferated. The approaches to design have used some variant or combination of the approaches described here: unifying, metaphorical environment or neutral space; multiple scene changes or some sort of simultaneous setting. Most have sought some way visually to encapsulate the idea of America. Interestingly, discussions with several individuals who had seen more than one production suggested that the most emotionally powerful ones were those that, because of necessity or choice, were utterly simple and even had a "rough theater" quality to them. Notable were the production by graduate acting students at New York University and a reading of *Millennium Approaches* at the Taper as a prelude to the theater's first production of *Perestroika*. Some of the response, of course, may have to do with audience expectations and production context. We neither want nor expect production values in a reading; we come to focus on the text. But it does suggest that Kushner is right in asking for a pared-down production, and perhaps the play, somewhat like Marc Blitzstein's opera *The Cradle Will Rock,* benefits from a dramatic equivalent of a concert performance. It also suggests that the play's depth and power is such that, like most good theater, it not only tolerates but demands scenographic exploration and experimentation. There is no one correct way to design *Angels.*

[12]Michael Feingold, "Building the Monolith," review of *Angels in America* by Tony Kushner, *Village Voice,* 18 May 1993, 218–19.

PERFORMANCE REVIEW

Brothers in a Game Where the Hand Is Faster Than the Eye

BEN BRANTLEY
Review of *Topdog/Underdog*

NEW YORK TIMES, JULY 27, 2001
DIRECTED BY GEORGE C. WOLFE, AT THE JOSEPH PAPP PUBLIC THEATER, NEW YORK, 27 JULY 2001.

Even the most untrusting New Yorker won't be able to resist Jeffrey Wright's invitation to a little game of three-card monte. Mr. Wright is portraying a retired master of that most basic and complex of sidewalk scams in "Topdog/Underdog," Suzan-Lori Parks's vibrant comic drama of shifting identity and betrayal, which opened last night at the Joseph Papp Public Theater.

When Mr. Wright finally picks up the cards toward the end of the evening's first act, his magnetic pull feels strong enough to suck the cars off Lafayette Street. His eyes glitter with both confrontational challenge and childlike supplication; his hands float over the cards with the casual arrogance of a concert pianist doing scales. "Watch me now," Mr. Wright commands. As if we could possibly do otherwise.

There are many levels of deception practiced in "Topdog/Underdog," which also stars the estimable Don Cheadle and has been directed with high wit and flair by George C. Wolfe. As its title promises, the play divides the world into a seesawing population of hustlers and victims, the corners and the conned.

Indeed, this latest offering from the ferociously talented author of "The America Play" and "In the Blood" goes so far as to suggest that any human exchange involves sham, that a person can be himself only when no one else is watching. And when the person is a black man in the history lesson that is Ms. Parks's United States, the existential lies multipy. Then again, not being yourself can be a very fine art. Especially when it's demonstrated by actors as skilled as Mr. Wright and Mr. Cheadle.

The first act of this lively tale of belligerent brothers in close quarters is as exciting as any new play from a young American since Tony Kushner's "Angels in America." Certainly, it's the most exhilarating fraternal stand-off since Philip Seymour Hoffman and John C. Reilly took on Sam Shepard's "True West" last year.

"Topdog," it should be noted, doesn't sustain the momentum of "West." After the teasing dazzle of the first act, the second often feels like conventional melodrama, thematically apt but emotionally unsatisfying. You badly want it to pay off in richer dividends.

Nonetheless, you'll probably still feel like raising a glass of the expensive (stolen) Champagne the brothers share in a fleeting moment of domestic harmony. For there remains a lot to celebrate. "Topdog," its author's most consumer friendly and outright entertaining work to date, should establish an expanded audience for Ms. Parks, who has often been regarded as overly opaque.

Then there's the return of Mr. Wolfe, the artistic director of the Public, to the top of his form, combining showmanship and subversion as few directors can. And Mr. Wright, who teamed with Mr. Wolfe for "Angels in America" and "Bring in da Noise, Bring in da Funk," gives the kind of multi-dimensional performance that leaves you dizzy.

Mr. Cheadle is also excellent, but it's Mr. Wright who has the more intricate role, and he runs with it. Better known in recent years for his work in film ("Basquiat," "Shaft"), he emerges here as one of the finest American stage actors of

his generation, a match for Liev Schreiber and Kevin Spacey.

As she demonstrated with "In the Blood" last year, Ms. Parks shares Mr. Shepard's gift for locating the state of a nation in a single family. Here she gives us the ominously named Lincoln (Mr. Wright) and Booth (Mr. Cheadle), whose parents walked out on them when they were teenagers for reasons they still can't understand.

As a consequence, they are forever on the qui vive, hoping to cheat before they are cheated. They both manipulate and fall into the traps of how they are perceived as members of an underclass. Consciously or unconsciously, they tend to wear their personae lopsided, and it seems fitting that they are often seen only half dressed.

Lincoln, the older, was once a whiz at three-card monte, but he has traded that profession for an honest job, which happens to be in an arcade shooting booth, impersonating Abraham Lincoln (in white face), awaiting his assassination at Ford's Theater. (This exotic form of employment, by the way, was the center of Ms. Parks's cryptic allegory, "The America Play.") The slower-witted Booth longs to command his brother's former trade but in the meantime is an agile shoplifter.

Uncomfortably lodged in a single boardinghouse room, a simple wonder of sepia-toned decrepitude by Riccardo Hernández, Booth and Lincoln regard even each other with wary eyes as the fraternal balance of power keeps changing. And don't doubt their capacity for wounding. They aren't named Lincoln and Booth for nothing.

There is, thank heaven, much joy in this mortal battle of wills. And that has everything to do with its being presented in the context of that most deliciously deceitful of art forms, the theater, something that Ms. Parks and Mr. Wolfe obviously both love to distraction.

They have generously provided both actors with terrific set pieces in which to strut their characters' wiles. There are, of course, those memorable presentations of the right and wrong ways to run a monte game. But there is also the delightful, barbed spectacle of the brothers' corn pone celebration of Lincoln's weekly paycheck, sending up the homey, rustic family they never had.

In a similar vein is Mr. Cheadle's shoplifter's striptease, in which he wriggles out of the day's loot (including two new suits), to James Brown singing "Papa's Got a Brand New Bag." (The dead-on costumes are by Emilio Sosa.) It is also a pleasure to watch Booth trying to put one over on the more subtle Lincoln, who responds by furtively puncturing his brother's pretenses, even when he has lost the round.

Ms. Parks has given each a resonant language of his own. "I stole and I stole generously," Booth says in a typically direct but eloquent assertion. Lincoln's speech is more elaborately devious and often more introspective, reaching a lyrical high point in his monologue about the different clients in the shooting gallery.

"I'm looking at him upside down and him looking at me looking like Lincoln," he says, describing the reflected image of a shooter behind him. Throughout the first act, Ms. Parks plays with this sense of distorting perceptions with commanding intelligence and indirection.

In the second act, the masks fall for more naked confrontations, and so does some of our sense of an original, self-contained theatrical world. In talking about impersonating the president for whom he was named, Lincoln says, "People like their historical information in a certain way. They like to unfold it the way they folded it up. Neatly like a book." Somehow "Topdog" itself succumbs to such an unfolding.

Part of Ms. Parks's point seems to be that social identity, even when it's impersonation, is destiny, and of course Booth and Lincoln are fated to act upon their names. But the concluding tragedy has far less impact than the unforgettable image of Mr. Wright all alone, in stove-pipe hat, false beard and boxer shorts, pretending to be Abe Lincoln.

The weighted stillness with which he begins the scene, hauntingly underscored by Scott Zielinski's first-rate lighting, is as disturbing as a death mask. In the succeeding moments, Lincoln pantomimes President Lincoln's imagined responses—from guffaws to sobs—to "Our American Cousin." But when he simulates being shot, he always slides to the ground in the same way.

There's a chill of inevitability as he realizes how little room death allows for variation. It's a stark, brilliant moment of implicit prophecy, a shivery reminder that these men are trapped in a game in which the rules and the outcome are predetermined.

John and Winston rehearse *Antigone* in John Kani, Winstona Ntshona, and Athol Fugard's *The Island,* produced at the Market Theater of Johannesburg.

Historic social, political, and technological changes have reshaped the world since 1950, with a consequential impact on the theater. The aftermath of World War II has seen the remapping of the planet: the independence of India, Pakistan, and many Asian and African nations from colonial rule; the founding of Israel and the displacement of the Palestinians; and wars in Korea, Indochina, the Middle East, Africa, the Persian Gulf, and Afghanistan. Those decades also witnessed bitter civil strife and the glimmering of peace in Northern Ireland, Argentina, Chile, the United States, Europe, and elsewhere; the Cuban missile crisis, the death of Francisco Franco in Spain, and the dismantling of the Berlin Wall; independence movements in the former Soviet Union and throughout Eastern Europe; the collapse of Yugoslavia and protracted war in Bosnia; the civil rights movement in the United States, the waning of apartheid in South Africa, the failure of peace in the Middle East.

With the rise of global communications, a global economy, and global political and military interests, such social and political revolutions immediately become the world's business. They reshape the world we live in even as we watch the changes unfold on our television screens. Fortunately, television has not really transformed the world's diverse cultures into a single "global village," but local cultures all feel the impact of events around the world. Think of the global effects of environmental disasters such as the Chernobyl, Ukraine, nuclear power plant meltdown in 1986 and the deforestation of the rain forests of the Amazon; of medical advances such as vaccination; of epidemics like AIDS; of the international effects of social movements like nuclear disarmament, human rights, Amnesty International, feminism, and the peace movement, or, more horrifyingly, of anti-Semitism, racism, homophobia, and "ethnic cleansing."

Drama requires the collaboration of playwrights, actors, and audiences; the public structure of a theater site or building; and the social and political incentives and protections that make theatergoing attractive—it is an art deeply woven into the social fabric of a given culture and its history. Although we can still speak of the "London theater" or of "American drama," these terms have become in our era a critical convenience for reducing the dynamic variety of contemporary theater to the fictional boundaries of a single "national" culture. Although the theater still requires the support, work, and energy of its local community, today's dramatic repertoire is a global one. American playwright Sam Shepard first produced several of his plays in London. British playwright Edward Bond is more widely produced in Germany than in the United Kingdom. Many Eastern European and Latin American playwrights have been forced by censorship and political persecution to smuggle their plays to Europe or the United States to be staged. South African playwright Athol Fugard has premiered several plays in the United States. Nigerian Wole Soyinka is regularly produced throughout the world. These playwrights are deeply implicated in the working of their native cultures, but their plays have rapidly become part of the world repertoire.

Unit VII presents a different perspective on drama and theater than other units in this book. Earlier units have been organized around a distinctive moment in the history of a relatively discrete culture: Athens in the fifth century BCE, Japan in the early shogunate; late medieval England and Renaissance London; late seventeenth-century London, Paris, and Madrid; and twentieth-century Europe and the United States. In many respects, this book is organized around undergraduate college teaching in the United States today, which emphasizes the historical development of Western theater practices and dramatic literatures. This unit takes a broadly "postcolonial" perspective on contemporary drama, establishing some continuities with Western traditions while bringing other traditions of world theater and drama into view.

POSTCOLONIAL PERSPECTIVES

In the past several decades all areas of the humanities and cultural studies have come to challenge a narrowly Eurocentric vision of the contemporary world. These challenges have arisen from a wide range of causes: worldwide national independence movements, such as those in India in 1947, on the African continent throughout the 1950s and 1960s, and in Eastern Europe and the Baltic states in the 1990s; international involvement in South Africa's struggle with apartheid; global media and economic interconnections, that make business activity in Asia have an immediate impact on Wall Street; the fall of the Berlin wall in 1989, the breakup of the Soviet Union, and of the new relations between Eastern and Western Europe, and between the republics of formerly Soviet Central Asia; the return of Islam as a political, social, and military force in the West; oil crises and the war in the Persian Gulf; the challenges to "national" identity reflected in Québec's ongoing separatist movement in Canada; the various anxieties about language and immigration in the United States; racial tensions in Britain, France, Germany, and elsewhere in Europe; the ongoing political and social crisis in Northern Ireland; the emergence of Japan, South Korea, and China as economic powers; the struggles of many Latin American countries—often against both local military dictatorships and the international finance they receive—to achieve the promise of their nineteenth-century wars of liberation. In many places, these changes have not only had to overcome the military and political power of European governments—the Latin American revolutions against Spain; African and Indian independence movements—but have forced crucial challenges to the model of European culture itself, dramatizing the often oppressive entailments of the culture of "enlightenment" that was imposed on much of the world in the "civilizing" process of colonization.

In 1900, the sun never set on Britain's colonies around the world, and the legacy of three centuries of European expansion are still felt throughout the world: England, France, Spain, Portugal, the Netherlands, Italy, and Belgium all had extensive colonial holdings in Africa, Asia, and the New World. In many cases, of course, colonization was undertaken largely as a means of extracting wealth, in the form of slaves, precious metals, and/or raw materials, that could be sent back to enrich the capital: this was the model of Spanish colonization in the New World, in which Spain prevented trading between colonial cities in Mexico, Peru, Argentina, and elsewhere to have all trade proceed directly to Madrid. Even though very different patterns of colonization were practiced throughout the world, colonization always brought with it European institutions, such as Catholic and Protestant churches, legal practices and courts, schools and universities, and other aspects of European culture as well—sports and games, fashion and foods, and literature, drama, and theater. In many places, the colonial language was rapidly imposed as the language of government, education, and the law. Much as England banned Gaelic in Ireland in the eighteenth century (Gaelic is now taught in school in the Republic of Ireland, but not in state-supported schools in Northern Ireland), so in the twentieth century, postcolonial politics are often centered in the politics of language. In Latin America, for example, there has been a significant movement to reestablish various native languages—Quechua in Peru, Nahua in Mexico—as part of literary and public discourse; in Mexico, for example, many pre-Columbian architectural sites have guide materials in at least one native language, as well as in Spanish. Writers like Aimé Césaire, in French-speaking Martinique, or Wole Soyinka, growing up in preindependence Nigeria, were schooled on European writers such as Molière and Shakespeare and have used this education as part of their critical representation of the cultural politics of colonial and postcolonial rule: Césaire in his adaptation of Shakespeare's *The Tempest* to a Caribbean setting; Soyinka in the dialogue between English and Yoruba culture that informs many of his plays, including *Death and the King's Horseman*.

Language is never neutral; as Stephen Dedalus notices when talking to an English clergyman in James Joyce's *A Portrait of the Artist as a Young Man,* language encodes an entire system of social and political values—the words "Christ," "ale," and "master" mean something different to the English than they do to the Irish, much as terms like "white," "free," "citizen," or "nation" are obvious flashpoints, places where words reveal the political work language performs. Like language itself, the values exported to the colonies often have traced within them a powerfully oppressive dynamic. For in regarding itself as bearing "civilization" into the wilderness—as though North and South America, Africa, and parts of Asia were not only uninhabited, but as though the highly developed cultures the Europeans found there were negligible—European culture often regards the colonized as "other," and as inferior. The indigenous cultures of Africa, Latin America, and Asia were usually defined in antithesis to the values that justified the brutalities of occupation and exploitation: in opposition to the values of civilization, of a rich literary language, of an important and dynamic culture, indigenous cultures were seen as noncivil, their languages nonliterary, their cultures noncultivated, their (nonwhite) peoples nonpeople. Given this history, the cultural sphere—the sphere of theater and drama, of music and the visual arts, of literature, of film—has also been an important area of revolution as well. As the Kenyan novelist and playwright Ngũgĩ wa Thiong'o has argued, the practices of culture are in many ways more forceful than the more visible structures of the law or politics in maintaining a sense of "colonized" identity. He suggests that "decolonizing the mind" means decolonizing the tools that the mind thinks with, language, visual imagery, patterns of narrative and storytelling, everything used to make sense of the world:

> The oppressed and the exploited of the earth maintain their defiance: liberty from theft. But the biggest weapon wielded and actually daily unleashed by imperialism against that collective defiance is the cultural bomb. The effect of a cultural bomb is to annihilate a people's belief in their names, in their languages, in their environment, in their heritage of struggle, in their unity, in their capacities and ultimately in themselves. It makes them see their past as one wasteland of nonachievement and it makes them want to distance themselves from that wasteland. It makes them want to identify with that which is farthest removed from themselves; for instance, with other peoples' languages rather than their own.[1]

In their introduction to British postcolonial literatures, *The Empire Writes Back,* Bill Ashcroft, Gareth Griffiths, and Helen Tiffin "use the term 'post-colonial' . . . to cover all the culture affected by the imperial process from the moment of colonization to the present day."[2] Although several of the playwrights and theaters presented here—Wole Soyinka from Nigeria, Maishe Maponya and Athol Fugard from South Africa, Aimé Césaire from the French island of Martinique—are readily understood within the context of national liberation movements, others point to a different, though analogous, understanding of the global politics of culture today. The Northern Irish playwright Brian Friel writes in a place where the politics of "nation"—Northern Ireland is physically part of Ireland, but politically a province of the United Kingdom—are still unresolved. Beyond that, in the twentieth century the dynamics of a kind of imperialism are not restricted to politics: a former colony— the United States—has emerged as a prodigiously powerful influence on many areas of economic and cultural life around the world, in ways that are frequently experienced as a kind of colonialism. While France, for instance, continues to struggle with the legacy of its colonization of North Africa, it also is engaged in a protracted trade controversy with the

---

[1] Ngũgĩ wa Thiong'o, *Decolonising the Mind: The Politics of Language in African Literature* (Portsmouth: Heinemann, 1986), 3.

United States, protecting the French film industry—and, by extension, "French" culture—by sharply limiting the distribution of American films. This sense that American culture, American values, American money, and American military power have become so pervasive as to threaten the political, economic, and cultural autonomy even of powerful countries—like France or Canada—informs a broader resistance to "imported" or Western or American culture. This resistance to a form of cultural imperialism animates some aspects of contemporary Asian theater, especially in plays like Manjula Padmanabhan's *Harvest;* it is also a theme in contemporary Canadian arts, in Mexico, and elsewhere. Finally, many indigenous peoples—the aboriginal peoples of Australia, the native peoples of North and South America—were not really "colonized"; instead they were both decimated and isolated on reservations, and often stand in a quite different relationship to cultural formation in the state.

POSTCOLONIAL DRAMA IN PERFORMANCE AND HISTORY

The remainder of this introduction briefly traces some connections between the dramatic, theatrical, and cultural history informing the work of playwrights presented later in the unit. This discussion—like the collection of plays assembled here—is by no means "representative": Japan's role in Asia, and the theater traditions that have developed there are very different from the energetic performance traditions of Indonesia, or Malaysia, and from both the traditional and contemporary theater of India; although their histories are quite different, the energetic theatrical life of South Africa and Nigeria in the past four decades hardly spans the range of African dramatic and nondramatic performance, especially the performance traditions of North African countries like Algeria or Egypt; Argentina's orientation toward northern Europe, and the relatively sparse population of indigenous peoples in Argentina during the conquest period make its theater quite different from the flourishing theaters of Mexico and Brazil. In each of these places, however, drama and theater have come to be one of the ways in which public discourse is conducted, an esthetic engagement with the changing status of the "nation" and its peoples.

Argentina

Argentina's historical and cultural development is hardly "representative" of the diverse histories of Latin American countries. Unlike Peru or Mexico, for example, Argentina was never a source of gold or silver, and throughout the seventeenth century the vast region that comprises much of present day Argentina, Paraguay, and Uruguay was a backwater of the viceroyalty of Peru. Puerto Nuestra Señora Santa María del Buen Aire was first established by Pedro de Mendoza in 1535. But although his expedition of 1,600 men was three times the size of the contingent that accompanied Hernan Cortés in conquering Mexico, the expedition arrived late in the summer, with little time to plant crops and harvest them for winter, and in a swampy region that was not well suited to agriculture in any case. The Spaniards established bad relations with the indigenous population, who soon began to lay siege to the settlement. The settlers finally—after slaughtering their cattle—resorted to cannibalism to survive the winter. Although the original settlement of Buenos Aires held on until 1541, it was abandoned as the settlers moved north to the thriving city of Asunción.

When Buenos Aires was reestablished in 1580, the central city of Córdoba was the dominant city of the viceroyalty, but by the seventeenth century the port city of Buenos Aires—whose people still refer to themselves today as "porteños"—emerged as the center of power in the region. The economy of Argentina depended on agriculture, and plantations were run by *encomienda,* the forced servitude of the native populations, licensed by the church. Throughout the eighteenth century, Buenos Aires was the center of military development, as well as of the burgeoning cattle ranching of the *pampas* stretching to the west and south of the city. Until 1776, the region was part of the viceroyalty of Peru and ruled from Lima; when Spain reformed the trade, administrative, and legal structure of its South American colonies in 1776, Buenos Aires became the capital of the viceroyalty of the Rió de la Plata. Argentina's independence was part of the continental struggle for liberation of the first decades of the nineteenth century, precipitated by Napoleon's intervention in Spain in 1808. Although the Congress declared the independence of the United Provinces of the Rió de la Plata on July 9, 1816, various civil and revolutionary wars would traverse the territory for the next thirty years. Argentina lost much of its viceregal territory in the wars of independence—parts of Peru in 1814, of Bolivia in 1825, of Uruguay in 1828. Beyond that, the revolution established two patterns that would afflict Argentina for a century. First, the *caudillos*—rural ranchers and landholders, with their own private armies—wanted the new nation organized as a loose federations of provinces, not as a centralized government emanating from Buenos Aires; much of the political conflict of nineteenth-century Argentina can be understood as a struggle between the federalist and central-government forces. Second, the wars drew a generation of British traders—some of whom fought with distinction in the revolution—to Argentina; they capitalized on the rich resources and weak economy of the new country, establishing lucrative trade relations with the United States, the United Kingdom, and Europe.

In some respects, Argentina's economic growth in the early twentieth century parallels that of the United States: several waves of European immigration in the 1880s and 1890s provided the labor power to transform Argentina into a manufacturing and agricultural power (in the early decades of the twentieth century, it was a cliché to be "as rich as an Argentine"). At the same time, however, Argentina's economy was drained by outside investment: by the Bank of England in the nineteenth century, and by American and European concerns in the twentieth. This situation was exploited by the charismatic Colonel Juan Perón, who was first elected president in 1946 on the promise of better wages and social programs for workers; Perón succeeded both in reducing foreign debt and in restoring the control of major industries—railroads and communications—to Argentine corporations. But Perón's economy also produced considerable inflation, and social unrest led to a series of military *juntas,* which typically used the excuse of Communist insurgency, the familiar bogeyman of the post-Castro era in the Americas, to justify the suspension of civil law.

In 1976, General Jorge Rafael Videla led a *junta* that inaugurated seven years of state terrorism, the "Dirty War" (1976-1983) in which brutal torture was routinely practiced, and thousands of Argentine citizens (*los desaparecidos*) were made to disappear by federal, state, and local government officials. This regime and its successors frequently collaborated with European and U.S. governments—on the eve of the disastrous Falklands War, General Leopoldo Galtieri attempted to gain U.S. government investment by offering military support to the United States in its military conflicts in Central America—and received both government and private investment. The Falklands conflict proved disastrous for the *junta,* and by January 1983 General Ramón J. Camps, the Buenos Aires chief of police in the Videla government admitted that the mass graves that had been discovered were those of *desaparecidos* (the "disappeared"), and that none were alive. Dissension in the military, a more activist prosecution of military crimes by the courts, and a widening sense that the *junta* could be ousted— typified around the world by Las Madres de la Plaza de Mayo—led to the election of Raúl Alfonsín in 1983, to the promise of trials, and then to the election of Carlos Menem.

Argentina has a long and distinguished theatrical tradition; plays were performed at the Jesuit missions in Córdoba in the early 1600s, and the first theater was built in Buenos Aires in 1757; the Teatro de la Ranchería was built in 1783. Throughout the seventeenth and eighteenth centuries, most of the plays performed in Argentina—in theaters in Santiago del Estero, Catamarca, Santa Fe, Corrientes, as well as Córdoba and Buenos Aires—were either Spanish *loas* or adaptations of French and Spanish dramas. By the nineteenth century, however, Argentine theater began to develop a more local flavor: in the romanticized dramas of *gaucho* (the famous Argentine cowboy) life typified by the anonymous *El amor de la estanciera* (1814); in plays of Argentine history, such as the independence play *25 de Mayo* and the play about the Peruvian native uprising *Tupac Amaru* (1817), both written by Luis Ambrosia Morante (1775–1837); and in a variety of short, sometimes satirical plays—called *SAINETES*—on political figures, and on the typical "characters" of Argentine life. This "local color" movement—*costumbrismo*—led to several popular genres, notably the *sainete gauchesco* and the *sainete criollo.*

The magnificent Teatro Colón opera house was built in 1857, at the early edge of Buenos Aires's development as a major metropolitan area; by 1900, Buenos Aires was known as the Paris of the New World for its fashionable elegance, and supported a wide range of theaters; 1900–1910 is regarded in Buenos Aires as the "golden decade" of its theaters, and many of Argentina's best-known playwrights—such as Florencio Sánchez (1875–1910), author of *La gringa* (1904) and *Barranca abajo* ("Down the Gully," 1905)—date from this era. As in Europe and the United States, an independent theater movement—El Teatro del Pueblo (1933) and La Máscara (1939)—arose, emphasizing (on the eve of Perón's mobilization of *los descamisados,* the shirtless workers) a more political, realistic, and Marxist orientation toward the staging of social life. Given the European orientation of Buenos Aires, it's not surprising that the various modes of European theatrical experimentation of the 1950s and after—Artaud's "theater of cruelty," theater of the absurd, Brechtian epic theater—have made their impact on Argentine drama, notably in the celebrated plays of Osvaldo Dragún (b. 1929); in the turbulence of the Perón and succeeding eras, the theater has often been a place of protest, and frequently subject to implicit or explicit censorship. This is especially true of the "dirty war" period. When the Teatro Abierto was founded in 1981, its building mysteriously burned to the ground within its first week of operation. Nonetheless, although many writers and intellectuals left Argentina, many remained, and their work often traces the connections between state terrorism and the diffuse nature of cultural and economic imperialism. Though written just before the "dirty war," Griselda Gambaro's play, *Information for Foreigners,* makes a direct assault on the authoritarian state; at the same time, by treating its audience as foreign tourists, the play implicates that larger world whose social and economic support helped to maintain the terror in Argentina.

Australia

Some have argued that the American independence—British convicts were transported to the American colonies before the Revolution—played a direct role in the British settlement of Australia as a penal colony in the eighteenth century. For although Portuguese, Dutch, Spanish, and British ships had all explored the Australian coastline, European settlement of Australia dates from 1788: the First Fleet—carrying 530 male prisoners, 160 female prisoners, and 250 freemen—sailed from England on May 13, 1787, and arrived in Botany Bay in January of 1788. The settlement at Sydney was soon followed by penal colonies at Newcastle in 1804, Moreton Bay in 1824, and other colonies: by 1830, 58,000 convicts (nearly 50,000 were men) had been transported to Australia. Most were relatively petty urban criminals, and the life they found in Australia could be very hard: conditions in many of the prisons were nightmarish, and prison life was for many nearly enslavement. Yet many convicts served their time outside prison—as something like indentured servants—and many remained to settle permanently. In the early nineteenth century Australia's economy was driven by sheep ranching and mining, and by the 1860s four relatively autonomous states had been formed, which moved toward federalization in the 1880s.

Western theater was brought to Australia in much the way Timberlake Wertenbaker dramatizes it in her play *Our Country's Good:* as a performance of George Farquhar's comedy *The Recruiting Officer* in 1789, in honor of the king's birthday, one year after the establishment of the British penal colony at Sydney in 1788. Beyond the slice of theater staged in Wertenbaker's play, though, the penal colonies were in many ways responsible for stimulating the importation of theater to Australia in the eighteenth century. Robert Sideway—one of the convicts in the Farquhar production—went on to open a theater in Sydney in

1796, which was opened to convicts and freemen until he was forced to close it in 1798; theaters were also operated in the penal colonies on Norfolk Island, in the Sydney Gaol, and in the colony on the Emu Plains.

By the mid-nineteenth century, the major cities of Australia—Melbourne and Sydney—had large theaters on the model of the major London houses, theaters seating upwards of two thousand patrons offering a repertoire of classical and contemporary European plays. Given the large population of recently released convicts, censorship was widespread in Australia, though many convicts—like Robert Sideway—made their way into the theater: David Burn's play, *The Bushrangers* (1828) was based on the life of a Tasmanian convict; and Edward Geoghegan, a convict, wrote or adapted ten plays for the Sydney Royal Victoria Theater. The major theaters received international tours—by Janet Achurch in the English production of Ibsen's *A Doll House* in 1889, and by Sarah Bernhardt in 1891—and developed in many ways along the lines of commercial theaters in England or the United States. Indeed, until the 1950s, the theater scene in Australia was similar to that of Canada or the United States: large commercial theaters devoted principally to popular drama and entertainment; a small smattering of amateur or independent theaters exploring various "new" dramatic and theatrical styles.

In 1954, in commemoration of the visit of Elizabeth II to Australia, the Governors of the Commonwealth Bank established the Australian Elizabethan Theatre Trust, with the purpose of establishing a national theater. It was a propitious moment; in 1956, Ray Lawler's (b. 1921) vivid working-class play about cane cutters who take an annual visit to the city, *The Summer of the Seventeenth Doll,* opened and soon became celebrated throughout Australia and the world. In an important act of nation building, the Theatre Trust used its subsidy for a number of purposes, not only to establish a National Theatre Company (1956), an Australian Ballet (1962), and an Australian Opera (1969), but to establish and support professional theater in each of the state capital cities: companies in Melbourne and Sydney in 1960, in Adelaide in 1965, in Brisbane in 1969, in Hobart, Tasmania, 1973.

As a result, even despite a conservative sense of Australian propriety that led to the censorship of playwrights like Patrick White (1912-1990) in the 1960s, Australia today has an energetic theater scene, both in subsidized and self-sustaining companies. In 1973 the Australian National Playwrights' Conference provided a means to support emerging writers, and a range of experimental companies—The Australian Performance Group, Nimrod—stimulated a new burst of playwriting, in plays like David Williamson's (b. 1942) *The Removalists* (1971), or the plays of Louis Nowra (b. 1950), Alma De Groen (b. 1941), or Michael Gow (b. 1955).

The Black Theatre Group was also organized in the 1970s, as part of an urgent desire to sustain traditional and new performance by Australia's Aborigine peoples. The various Aborigine tribes—estimated at about 500 tribes or smaller groups, numbering about 300,000 in 1788—mainly populated the northern and eastern areas of Australia. When the British began to establish colonies, they were put under the protection of the Colonial Office in London, but to little avail: the Aborigines did not integrate well into the British colonies (as a docile labor force, for example), and most were either killed outright, died from disease, or were driven into small "mission" areas. By the 1920s and 1930s, the overwhelming majority of Aboriginal peoples were "half-caste," and many were herded into squalid settlements, such as the Moore River Settlement that provides the setting for Jack Davis's play *No Sugar.* During this period, Aborigine infants were often taken to be raised by white families, in the hope that the "Aborigine problem" would gradually disappear through intermarriage (until 1966, Australia had an unofficial "whites only" immigration policy; only "white" immigrants were allowed to settle permanently). A 1967 referendum established Aboriginal Australians as part of the national population, to be counted in the census and therefore given parliamentary representation; in 1976 the Aborigine Rights Act granted 139,000 acres in the Northern Territory to Aborigine claimants as freehold property; South Australia made a similar grant to the Pitjantjatjara people. The National Aborigine Conference was formed in 1977, elected from Aborigine and Torres Strait Islander peoples, and in the 1980s, the Aboriginal Playwright's Conference was established to further the aims of aboriginal playwrights, and to protect native traditions. Given the distinctive beliefs of the Aborigine peoples—"The Dreaming," a mythic creation time when world and its peoples were formed, and whose spirits persist in the material world—and the dance-storytelling-musical *corroboree,* it is perhaps not surprising that a number of companies devoted to developing and preserving these arts have arisen, such as the Aborigine and Islander Dance Theater Company of Sydney.

Canada   Theater in Canada, like the culture of Canada itself, has been largely defined by its two dominant European settler cultures—English and French. Until the American Revolution, much of the eastern third of North America was contested by English and French explorers and traders: Jacques Cartier sailed down the St. Lawrence River, past the sites of Québec and Montréal in the 1530s; Samuel de Champlain's extensive explorations in the first quarter of the seventeenth century helped to define important fur-trading routes. By the mid-seventeenth century, however, Louis XIV declared New France a royal province, and throughout the remainder of the seventeenth and eighteenth centuries, France and Britain vied for control of Canada. The British had several strongholds in the maritime provinces, and to the west, in present-day Ontario; the exodus of British loyalists from the American colonies during the revolution—many of whom went into French Canada—enabled Britain to gain control of Canada; the 1791 Constitutional Act recognizes British legal and civil institutions, and the increasing British dominance of the important fur trade as well. In 1841, the United Provinces of Canada, in an effort to "assimilate" French Canada more effectively, gave a plurality of seats in the parliament to the British provinces. Although Canada was united as a Dominion in 1867, and gained its autonomy in 1931, the tensions between British and French Canada remain very much alive today: the separatist Parti Québécois and its charismatic leader René Levesque came to prominence in the early 1970s, and in several recent plebiscites, the citizens of Québec have voted to remain in Canada by only a narrow margin.

Although there are records of garrison performances in English Canada—an English version of Molière's *The Misanthrope* in January of 1744, in Nova Scotia—the earliest European performances in Canada are in French Canada. At Port-Royal, in Arcadia, Marc Lescarbot's aquatic pageant *Le Théâtre de Neptune en la Nouvelle-France* was performed (in war canoes!) to honor visiting French dignitaries in November 1606, and until a production of Molière's *Tartuffe* aroused the ire of the Catholic bishop—who forbade public theater in Québec in 1694—many performances of neoclassical French playwrights, including Corneille, Racine, and Molière were given in Québec. By the early nineteenth century, however, the Amateur Canada Dramatic Society had formed in Montréal (1835), and the church came to see that modest and moral stage performance could promote Catholic values. In 1898 it sanctioned the first lay company of actors, *Les Soirées de Famille* ("Family Evenings"). By this time, however, two permanent French-speaking theaters had been built in Montréal: the Monument National (1894) and Le Théâtre des Nouveautés (1898), serving a thriving trade in both touring companies from France and in the work of French-Canadian playwrights, such as Louis-Honoré Fréchette (1839–1908), whose sensational patriotic drama *Félix Porré* opened in 1862.

Theatre in English Canada was stimulated in part by the American Revolution; many British loyalists fled the revolution to the eastern provinces of Canada. The 500–seat Grand Playhouse was built in Halifax in 1789, and by the early nineteenth century, Toronto and other cities had major theaters on the European model. Nonetheless, much of the theatrical activity in the nineteenth century was by touring companies. However, much as in Europe, several smaller amateur companies developed, both to stage the new drama, and to support Canadian playwrights. The most significant of these companies was founded in 1919 by Roy Mitchell, at the University of Toronto—the Hart House Theatre. The Hart House was responsible for importing a number of experimental European playwrights, as well as for supporting the production of Canadian playwrights, including Dora Smith Conover, and Marjorie Price; Herman Voaden's expressionistic plays of the 1930s were produced at the Play Workshop. Other art theaters were formed in other cities as well; Martha Allan returned from working at the Pasadena Playhouse to her native Montréal to found the Montréal Repertory theater in 1930; the Toronto Workers Theater was active in the 1930s as well; and the establishment of the Canadian Broadcasting Company in 1936 brought radio drama throughout the nation.

The postwar period was the first real period for the growth of Canadian drama and theater. In part spurred by the Vincent Massey Report on the Arts of 1951 and the development of the Canada Council in 1957, both English and French Canada witnessed a flowering of new theater in the 1960s and 1970s. Several institutions—notably the Dora Mavor Moore New Play Society of Toronto (1946)—worked to develop Canadian plays and playwrights, like John Coulter's epic of the Métis rebellion in western Canada, *Riel* (1950); the founding in 1960 of a National Theatre School in Montréal. Both the Stratford Festival (established in 1953) and the Shaw Festival (1962) became showcases for Canadian actors, and by the mid-1960s a range of important theaters often working with new Canadian material had been founded: the Jupiter Theatre (1951); Tarragon Theatre (1971) in Toronto; L'équipe (1943), the Rideau Vert (1948), the Théâtre du Nouveau Monde (1961), the Théâtre des Cuisines (1973) and the Théâtre Expérimental des Femmes (1979) in Montréal; the Manitoba Theatre Center (1958), the Vancouver Playhouse (1962), the Neptune Theatre in Halifax (1962).

Although Gratien Gélinas (b. 1908) is usually described as the instigator of postwar French-Canadian drama—his play *Tit-Coq* (1948) about a soldier returning to Québec after the war is a modern classic—the drama of contemporary Canada was given an important impetus by the 1967 Dominion Drama Festival. Within the year a series of important plays were produced throughout Canada as part of its Centennial celebrations—Gélinas's *Yesterday the Children Were Dancing* (in English Translation), George Ryga's (1932-1967) *The Ecstasy of Rita Joe* among them. In 1968 Michel Tremblay's (b. 1942) groundbreaking play of working-class life in Québec, *Les Belles Soeurs* was produced; the play is also notable for being written in *joual,* the characteristic dialect of the city. Many plays, such as Sharon Pollock's *Walsh* (1973) attempt to reinterpret Canadian history; this play dramatizes the relation-ship between Major James Walsh, who commanded the North West Mounted Police in the 1870s and Sitting Bull, chief of the Hunkpapa Sioux. Since throughout much of the history of Canada the French-speaking minority of Québec has been dominated by an English-speaking majority, it's not surprising that the agitation in support of Québécois independence is reflected in a variety of plays as well. Indeed, the past three decades have seen a range of plays interrogating the Québec situation—not only the well-known plays of Michel Tremblay, but plays like Jean Barbeau's *Le chemin de lacroix* (1970) about a bill permitting Anglophone Québec parents to send their children to English-language schools in violation of Québec's bilingual policy, or Jean-Claude Germain's *A Canadian Play/Une plaie canadienne* (1979) about the mythology of a unified Canada. More recently, Marianne Ackerman's *L'Affaire Tartuffe, or, The Garrison Officers Rehearse Molière* (1993) takes a production of *Tartuffe* at the moment of Québec's incorporation into English Canada in 1774 as a turning point in the imagining of a nation. Much as Canadian drama—in different ways in English and French plays, in English and French theaters—considers the dynamics of Canadian nationalism, so the more recent work of Native playwrights like Tomson Highway, Monique Mojica—author of *Princess Pocahontas and the Blue Spots* (1990)—and others engage the position and representation of Native Canadians today. In the 1990s, Canadian theater continued in a period of artistic richness characteristic of Canada's official policy of multiculturalism. Robert Lepage not only directed landmark productions of Shakespeare's *A Midsummer Night's Dream* (at Britain's Royal National Theatre, 1992) but developed a stunning series of multimedia meditations—*Needles and Opium* (1994), *Elsinore* (1995), and *The Far Side of the Moon* (2000)—at his Theater Ex Machina in Quebec City. Guillermo Verdecchia's brilliant performance piece exploring *latinidad* in a wider North American context, *Fronteras Americanas* opened in 1993. Canadian drama continues to have an increasingly pronounced impact on world theater, and several plays—notably the plays of Judith Thompson, Ann-Marie MacDonald's *Good Night Desdemona, Good Morning Juliet* (1988), and several of George Walker's plays—*Zastrossi* (1981) and *Escape from Happiness* (1991)—have found mainstream audiences in the United States and in Europe.

China

The most populous country on the planet, China has a long and magnificently diverse theatrical tradition. The first records of theater in China date from the Shang Dynasty, roughly 1500 BCE, and the history of China is studded with important landmarks in the development of performance. The Han period (206 BCE–221 AD) witnessed China's first important artistic flowering, and the characteristically complex blending of spoken language, acting, music, mime, and acrobatics that distinguishes Chinese theater dates from this period as well. The first training school, "The Pear Garden," was established during the T'ang dynasty (618–904), and the earliest surviving plays date from the succeeding the Sung dynasty (960-1279), plays which only began to be rediscovered in the 1920s. Although the Mongol conquest of the later thirteenth century put China under foreign rule, in the Yuan dynasty (1279–1368), seven hundred titles survive from this period, including several plays that have had an impact on the Western theater, including Chi Chun-hsiang's *The Orphan of the House of Chao*, adapted in 1775 by Voltaire, and Li Hsing-tao's *The Story of the Chalk Circle*, which provides the foundation for Bertolt Brecht's *Caucasian Chalk Circle*. While these plays typically use music and theatrical elements, they are considerably shorter than the "southern drama" that developed in southern China after the ejection of the Mongols in the Ming dynasty (1368–1644). The "southern drama" typically has more than fifty acts; it was mastered by playwrights such as T'ang Hsien Tsu (1550–1616), whose *Peony Pavilian* (recently adapted by the American director Peter Sellars) is today perhaps the most familiar of these plays. It is only in the Ch'ing period (1644–1912) that the most familiar form of traditional theater—Beijing Opera—began to take shape. Beijing Opera is a dynamic theatrical genre, using a scenario that sets the acting, singing, acrobatic, and musical skills of the performers on a narrative framework. Although there have always been a number of regional versions of this form, in 1790 the best performers from throughout China were brought to Beijing to celebrate the eightieth birthday of the Emperor Chi'ien-lung, and Beijing Opera is conventionally dated from this event.

With the increasing opening of China to the West in the nineteenth century, and after the revolution that established the Republic of China in 1912, Western culture came to have a more direct influence on the arts in China. Usually termed "spoken drama," to distinguish it from the musical conventions of traditional Chinese theater, the first Western play—Alexandre Dumas's (*fils*) *La Dame aux camélias*—produced in China was staged by the Spring Willow Drama Society in 1907, and in the decades following, several important playwrights wrote and adapted plays in the Western style for Chinese audiences, under the rubric of the New Cultural Movement: Tian Han (1898-1968) at the Nan Guo Drama Society, Hong Shen (1894–1955) for the Theatre Association, Xia Lan (1900–1995) for the Shanghai Art and Drama Association. Perhaps the most influential playwright of the prewar period is Ts'ao Yu (1902), whose plays *Thunderstorm* (1933) and *Sunrise* (1935) continue to be read and produced. "Spoken drama," mainly in the mode of Western realism, thrived in China, and was given additional impetus by the victory of the Communists and the founding of the People's Republic of China in 1949. The new government was at once concerned to preserve traditional Chinese theater and to promote theater that would more dynamically reflect contemporary life. The Traditional Theater Research Institute (now part of the China Arts Research Institute) was founded in 1950, and within a decade had revived hundreds of theater forms: by 1960, China had over 3,000 companies performing over 50,000 traditional plays. At the same time, companies worked to update the subject matter of traditional theater forms, using, for example, Beijing Opera to address more contemporary social issues, often in the "model plays" that trained the Beijing Opera (or related styles, such as Kun Opera or Chuan Opera) on historical subjects with a revolutionary perspective. The new government also established a National Theater Festival in 1956, which supported the work of postwar "spoken drama" playwrights, notably Lao She (1899–1966), whose play *Tea House* has become a modern Chinese classic, as well as Lao Yu (1910–1997), and the work of the Shanghai People's Art Theatre, which adapted Brecht's for Chinese audiences.

In 1966, the wife of China's leader Mao Zedong, Jiang Qing—helped by Kang Sheng and two others, becoming the notorious "Gang of Four"—instituted a decade-long Cultural Revolution. The purpose of the Cultural Revolution was at once to purge China of foreign influences, and also to institute a massive program of reeducation to the proletarian ideals of Maoist communism. The decade-long Cultural Revolution forced a generation of artists, professionals, and intellectuals—regarded by the Gang of Four as their principal political opposition—out of the major cities and into rural areas, where they would be reeducated into revolutionary culture through manual labor. Since the traditions of Chinese theater descended from aristocratic patronage, and the modern "spoken drama" theater was so clearly influenced by the West, it's perhaps not surprising that Chinese theater stagnated during the Cultural Revolution. Most theater companies disbanded during this period, and with the exception of plays specifically developed under Jiang's guidance, plays were heavily censored or prohibited altogether; only eight new "model" productions were developed, five in traditional theater forms. In 1976, however, the Gang of Four were removed from power; Deng Xiaoping inaugurated a period of new openness to the west, and allowed considerably greater latitude to artists and writers, Although previous regimes had insisted on Mao's "revolutionary realism" in the theater, in the 1980s, playwrights and performers experimented more widely: Gao Xingjian's *Absolute Signal,* a fluid hallucinatory drama, was performed briefly by the Beijing People's Art Theater in 1982, the same theater that invited Arthur Miller to direct a Chinese production of *Death of a Salesman* the following year. A Shakespeare Festival was staged in both Beijing and Shanghai in 1986, followed by Festivals of Experimental Theater in 1989 and 1993. The 1980s saw the rise of a number of important younger playwrights, including Gao Xingjian and Sha Ye Xing (b. 1939), whose satirical *Major Chen* (1980) was rivaled in controversy only by his *Confucius, Jesus Christ, and John Lennon* (1988); produced by the Shanghai People's Art Theater while he was Artistic Director. Zong Fu Xian (b. 1947) uses a rally in Tianamen Square to indict the Gang of Four in *In the Depth of Silence* (1978).

Theater in China has a tradition of patronage, both by the aristocracy and by the state. With the rise of a market economy in the 1990s, subsidies for theaters have declined, sometimes to as little as thirty percent of operating expenses. Moreover, after the Tiananmen Square protests in 1989 theater has been subject to somewhat more censorship than in the immediately preceding decade.

India

The second-most populous nation on the planet, with seventeen official languages, India has an immensely rich cultural and theatrical history. The earliest literary writing—the epic poems *Ramayana* and *Mahabharata*—date from between the tenth and fifteenth centuries BCE, and provide the narrative sources for much of the diverse range of traditional Indian per-

formance. The oldest dramatic traditions date to the Sanskrit plays first written and performed during the Gupta empire in northern India, beginning about 100 AD; the aesthetic
animating this theater is systematically explored in Bharata's *Natyasastra* (150 AD) (on Sanskrit Theater and Drama, see Unit II). Although Sanskrit has an important dramatic tradition—including King Sudraka's *The Clay Cart* and Khalidasa's *Shakuntala* (fifth century),
Sanskrit—like Latin in Europe—gradually split into a range of vernacular languages; the invasion and rise of the Muslims to power after the seventh century restricted theatrical performance, and Sanskrit theater was believed until quite recently to have ceased, being
replaced throughout India with an astonishingly diverse range of folk performance. As in
other Asian performance forms, "theater" is not restricted to the spoken enactment of
scripted plays: instead, the great majority of Indian folk theater forms use a brilliant interplay of story-telling, singing, dance, and music; there are also important forms of puppet theater as well. In the northern states of India, for instance, there is a 400-year tradition of
performing the *Ramlila* and *Raslila* plays: cycle-dramas concerning events in the lives of Krishna, and Vishnu Rama. These performances often take place over three or four weeks, and
involve the audiences in various kinds of religious ritual; they also mark one of the features
of many Indian theater forms, the discrimination of actors from singers. In the *Ramlila,* the
singer narrates the action, while the actors perform. A more recently developed form, the
JATRA, is a staple of performance in Bengal, in eastern India. *Jatra* performances—like most
Indian folk theater—do not take place in a theater, but in the open air, with the audience
surrounding the performers. Unlike *Ramlila,* though, *jatra* tend to address contemporary
concerns rather than the lives of mythic heroes. Indeed, the central figure of the *jatra* is always called Vivek, or "conscience": Traditionally, there is music in the *jatra,* and the actors
sing; the performers are all male, and there are now professional *jatra* companies. Perhaps the
most familiar form of traditional Indian performance in the West is *kathakali,* a dance-drama
form from the southern state of Kerala. Performed in Malayalam—the language of Kerala—
kathakali nonetheless preserves important elements of Sanskrit drama. In *kathakali,* the actors learn an elaborate and refined set of stylized bodily movements and detailed
hand-gestures, each of which is codified as part of the *Natyasastra* tradition; having learned
these techniques over many decades, the actors (all of whom are male) do not rehearse: they
simply perform one of the 500 plays in the *kathakali* repertoire. Although it would be difficult to say that any form—or any three forms—can represent the range of traditional theater in India—there are literally hundreds of distinct theater and dance forms in this vast
nation's rich folk and ritual traditions—what these forms share is a popular tradition of performance in village squares, at temples, or other open spaces, a complex involvement of music, acting, and dance, and a vigorously disciplined performance training.

While folk theater remains the dominant experience for the majority of Indians today,
it remains in a now-productive tension with "modern" Indian theater. India has had a long
history of contact with Europe: the Persians invaded northwest India in the sixth century
BCE; Alexander the Great invaded again in 326 AD; the Portuguese explorer Vasco da Gama
landed in India in 1498. British involvement with India was handled by the East India Company throughout the seventeenth and eighteenth centuries, but in 1858 the British government took over the Company, and in 1877 Queen Victoria became the Empress of India,
and India became the "jewel" in her colonial "crown." Even before India was incorporated
into the Empire, there were strong nationalist movements, and the British recognized the
need for an Indian administrative class: universities were established in 1857 in the principal colonial cities, Calcutta (now Kolkata), Bombay (now Mumbai), and Madras to produce
a "native" population educated to British values. In line with Thomas Babington Macaulay's
infamous "Minute" to the House of Lords on Indian education, education was sustained by
the teaching of English history and literature, the plays of Shakespeare and of eighteenth-
century dramatists in particular. The British also produced English-language plays, and built

theaters to accommodate touring companies. In the late nineteenth century, several Indian playwrights began to write plays—often in native languages such as Hindi or Urdu—in imitation of European drama; Wajid Ali Shah wrote several musical dance dramas, notably *The Tale of Radha and Krishna* (1851) and *Tale of Love* (1853); the Urdu poet Agha Hasan Amanat's *The Court of Lord Indra* (1854) was widely produced and translated. Moreover, the mid-nineteenth century also saw the rise of a new form of theater for India, profit-making companies. This kind theater, usually called Parsi Theater because these theaters were operated by Parsi businessmen (though usually employing Hindu and Muslim actors and playwrights), became the principal venue for "modern drama" in India, as the Parsi theaters often built new theater buildings on the model of Victorian proscenium theaters—such as the Victoria Theater and the Alfred Theater in 1871—and financed stage productions. Some of these plays adapted Western drama, as Agha Hashra Kashmiri (1879-1931) did in *White Blood* (1906), his adaptation of Shakespeare's *King Lear;* in the main, though, the Parsi theater was known for large-cast musical dramas, such as K.P. Khadikar's *Self Respect and Insult* (1911), a Marathi play arguing against the practice of child marriage. While the Parsi theater was extremely popular, particularly in the major urban areas, it seems finally to have been extinguished by the rise of film: indeed, many of the first Indian movie theaters were adapted from Parsi theater buildings.

While the Parsi theater represents one side of the "modernization" of Indian theater—turning it into a profit-making enterprise—there were other theater currents animating Indian theater in the later nineteenth-century. Bharatendu Harishchandra (1850–1885), for example, wrote plays in Hindi on pressing social issues—*The Sorry State of Bharat* (1880), *The Truthful King* (1975)—which were produced in public spaces. In Bengal, several playwrights used drama for specifically nationalistic purposes. Dinbandhu Mitra's *Neel Darpan* (*Indigo Mirror*) (1860) protested the plight of indigo workers, and was produced by the fledgling National Theater Company of Calcutta. When this company split into a Hindu National Theater and a Bengali National Theater, it retained this oppositional edge. The Bengali National Theater revived *Neel Darpan,* not only summoning agricultural workers to rebel against the British, but also showing the rape of a peasant woman by her British landlord. Largely due to the celebrity of this production, the government instigated the Dramatic Performances Control Act of 1876, in which local police were obliged to censor all new drama being produced in their jurisdiction. Perhaps for this reason, India's most famous poet and playwright of the colonial period—Rabindranath Tagore (1861-1941)—worked away from the realism of other playwrights, attempting to revive the mythological orientation of Sanskrit literature, and indeed to adapt it to critical purposes; Tagore won the Nobel Prize for Literature in 1913. Of course, the nationalist movement was given critical impetus by the work of Gandhi (1869–1948) and Jawaharlal Nehru (1899–1864), and "modern theater" in the twentieth century was strategically advanced by the Indian People's Theater, which opened branches in every Indian state in 1943, in many places bringing women to the stage for the first time.

India gained its independence from Britain on August 15, 1947; partition was established dividing Pakistan as an Islamic nation to the north at the same time, and in 1971 East Pakistan separated from Pakistan as Bangladesh. In the 1950s the Indian government established a range of cultural institutions, including the Cultural Academy of Performing Arts and the National School of Drama in 1959. The School's second director, Ebrahim Alkazi (b. 1925)—who had trained at the Royal Academy of Dramatic Art in London—was responsible at once for developing training in modern Western dramatic and theatrical traditions as well as for training performers in traditional Indian forms; his staging of Kalidasa's *Abhijnana Shakuntalam* (a Sanskrit play dating from 6 AD) at the Congress of Orientalists in New Delhi in 1964 is said to have inaugurated a revival of interest in exploring and preserving classical forms. In the aftermath of independence, Indian culture struggled at once to define a specifically "Indian" identity, and to modernize along the lines of Western culture: this tension governs the theater as well. The "theater of roots" movement sought to explore and experiment with traditional theater forms, sometimes using traditional tribal performers as well. One of the leading playwrights of modern India, Girish Karnad (b. 1938), writes in the Kannada language; his *Hayavadana* (1971) uses music, mime, dancing and costume of traditional theater; his *Naga Mandala* is the first modern Indian play to be produced in the U.S. (Guthrie Theater, Minneapolis, 1993). Vijay Tendulkur (b. 1928) Several other playwrights and directors have worked in traditional forms, which have also been applied to Western dramas—as in the Annette Leday/Keli Theatre Company *Kathakali King Lear* (1989). While the "theater of roots" continues to work with traditional forms, street theater has become an increasingly popular form of theater and protest; one prominent playwright, Safdar Hashimi of Delhi produced an extensive series of street production in support of the rights of the urban poor: he was murdered in 1989 during a street performance of his play *Attack!,* beaten to death by the members of a rival political organization.

The major playwrights of modern India write in a range of languages—Hindi, Kannada, Marathi, Bengali—and for a variety of theatrical traditions. There is also an emerging dramatic literature in English. Writing in the colonial language has posed a problem for writers from Joyce to Ngũgĩ, and it is controversial as well in India. At the same time, English is one of the nation's official languages; it provides the *lingua franca* for citizens from different regions, who may not speak one another's language, and when plays from one region are translated for performance in another region, they are translated into English.

Ireland and Northern Ireland

English involvement in Ireland dates to the twelfth-century "conquest" of Ireland—Henry VIII assumed the title of "King of Ireland" in 1541—and the relationship between England and Ireland has been contested ever since. In the late sixteenth and early seventeenth century, Hugh O'Neill led a series of uprisings against English immigrants, who were establishing plantations in the northern areas of Ulster; later, during the English Civil War (1641–1642), the forces that Charles I raised in Ireland were eventually defeated, and Oliver Cromwell enacted a series of brutal massacres in Ireland in retribution, confiscating lands as well. When Charles II took the English throne in 1660, the Act of Settlement confirmed the landowning claims then in place in Ireland: Catholics who had been evicted from their property were unable to regain it. In 1688 the Catholic heir, James II, ascended the English throne; when Parliament invited William of Orange (who was married to Mary Stuart, a Protestant heir) to assume the throne, James fled to Ireland: his forces were defeated at the Battle of the Boyne in 1690 and he fled to France; his Irish supporters were defeated in 1691 at Aughrim.

William's victories inaugurated a prolonged period of Irish misery: the displacement of Catholics from land and property, restrictions of their rights to education, to bear arms, to pass property to their heirs, or to vote. Although some of these laws lost force in the later eighteenth century, they provided the backdrop for political unrest in the period, particularly Wolfe Tone's mobilization of the Dublin United Irishmen in support of a French-supplied invasion. Although the French did send naval forces, and rebellions in Leinster, Ulster, and elsewhere looked promising, Tone was captured in 1798 and committed suicide in prison. In 1809, the Act of Union brought Ireland into the United Kingdom, effectively ending aspirations to nationhood. Nonetheless, throughout the nineteenth century, several movements worked for independence: Daniel O'Connell fought to repeal the Union, and Michael Davitt won security for tenants following the crop failures of 1879. Yet famine and immigration cut the Irish population in half between 1840 and 1900, and the Union's free-trade legislation turned Ireland into an impoverished supplier of raw material and labor to English factories. In the later nineteenth century, nationalism was pursued on two fronts: by the desire for "home rule" led by Charles Stewart Parnell, and by a new sense of Irish cultural identity, fostered by the Gaelic League and other cultural institutions.

Although Dublin and Ulster had supported theaters, these theaters were driven by an English repertoire: the only Irish characters to play on the stage were comic, drunken, buffoons—"Stage Irishmen." It was this sense of cultural nationalism that gave rise to the first burst of Irish theater, the founding of the Irish Literary Theater—later the Abbey Theatre—in 1899 by the poet/playwright W.B. Yeats (1865–1939), and the playwrights Lady Augusta Gregory (1852–1932) and John Millington Synge (1871–1909). The ambition of this company was to "build up a Celtic and Irish school of dramatic literature," and in the next thirty years, the Abbey succeeded not only in producing a wide range of plays on national subjects—peasant dramas about rural life like Synge's *The Playboy of the Western World* (1907); plays exhuming Irish mythology, like Yeats's cycle on Cuchulain; or realistic dramas of working-class urban life like Sean O'Casey's *The Plough and the Stars* (1926)—but establishing both an Irish style of performance, and the materials of a national theater as well. The Abbey remains a leading theater in the Republic of Ireland, and several leading playwrights have had major productions there: Tom Murphy, Ann Devlin, and Frank McGuinness among many others.

The aborted revolution of Easter 1916 was a precursor of sweeping political change by 1917, Eamonn De Valera was elected president of Sinn Féin and campaigned for an independent Ireland rather than merely achieving Home Rule as a province of Britain; in 1919, Ireland's war of independence was under way. In 1922, Sinn Féin succeeded in negotiating a treaty with the United Kingdom for independence, but the Free State was not to include the counties of Northern Ireland, which remained a British province. There have been various periods of tension between Northern Ireland and the Republic of Ireland and between Ireland and the United Kingdom; these tensions came to a head in the late 1960s. In Northern Ireland, sharp divisions between rich and poor, the politically powerful and the oppressed have often fallen across religious divisions as well, separating Protestant Anglo-Irish from Catholics. Throughout the 1960s, Catholic and Protestant groups rioted in the Northern cities of Belfast and Derry (then, Londonderry); British soldiers were summoned to protect Protestant marchers. In 1972, the "Bloody Sunday" riots resulted in thirteen deaths, and a newly mobilized Provisional Irish Republican Army (IRA) began a series of retaliatory campaigns; the British Embassy was burned in Dublin, and the British secretary of state suspended the Northern Irish parliament and instigated direct rule.

The history of Northern Ireland for the past thirty years is the history of this conflict: the hunger strikes by Catholic prisoners in the Maze prison who claimed the right to be treated as political prisoners rather than criminals; the increasing insurgency of Protestant paramilitary forces, inspired by the nationalist rhetoric of Ian Paisley; Gerry Adams and Sinn Féin's efforts to gain and remain in a position to be part of the bargaining for peace. The IRA cease-fire of 1994 was part of that bargain, and although violence has erupted since then, the current round of peace talks seems promising.

One of the most difficult aspects of the situation in Northern Ireland is the challenge to ideas of "national identity." Although Northern Ireland is physically part of Ireland, many of its citizens—even those who do not wish to be part of the United Kingdom—feel distinct from the Republic of Ireland; similarly, the long traditions of English rule have instilled a feeling of identification with England, one strengthened (for some) by the pro-Irish violence of the IRA. In many respects the theater of Northern Ireland has had to negotiate this vexed sense of nationalism. For example, the Field Day Theatre Company was founded in 1980 by the playwright Brian Friel, the poet Tom Paulin, the actor Stephen Rea, and the poet Seamus Heaney: the purpose of the company was to develop a new theater, a new dramatic literature of the North, one that attempted to identify the distinctiveness of Northern Ireland. In plays such as Friel's *Translations* or Thomas Kilroy's (b. 1934) *The Double Cross* (1986), or even in translations like Tom Paulin's version of *Antigone, The Riot Act,* Field Day attempted to bring a specifically Northern Irish culture into dialogue with a wider world.

But the work of Field Day should be seen in the context of other playwrights, some of whom, such as Christina Reid (b. 1942), see the problems of contemporary urban life in cities like Belfast to be "political" in ways that extend well beyond the problems of national identification, into areas of gender and economic exploitation. While Frank McGuinness was born in Donegal (part of the Republic of Ireland), his brilliant play *Observe the Sons of Ulster Marching Toward the Somme* (1985) uses the situation of Irish soldiers during the First World War (before the independence of the Republic and the partitioning of the northern counties) to explore the complex personal politics of Unionism. Although Field Day—which toured its productions throughout Northern Ireland—has ceased producing plays, it has published a widely read anthology of Irish writing and has sponsored a series of essays on questions of national and postcolonial art and culture.

Japan   The introductory essay of Unit II traced the development of the classical forms of Japanese theater—Noh, Kabuki, and Doll Theater—through the period of the Tokugawa shogunate (1603–1868). In 1868, the last of the Tokugawa shoguns was defeated and replaced by the Meiji Emperor, who wanted to open political, social, and cultural relations with the West, while at the same time disentangling Japan from a series of restrictive and exploitative trade relations with Europe. Indeed, throughout the 1880s and 1890s, Japan developed an aggressive military presence throughout the northern Asian Pacific, and both fought with China over the control of Korea and skirmished with Russia over the control of several of its islands. By the 1930s, Japan was a major military presence in the region. Taking advantage of political disorganization in China, Japan invaded Manchuria, and by 1938 had occupied parts of Mongolia and Kiangsu. Before drawing the United States into the Pacific theater with the bombing of its naval base at Pearl Harbor in Hawai'i, Japan had gained control of a huge territory, including all of Southeast Asia, Burma, the Philippines, and parts of New Guinea. Although the Western allies were unprepared for a Pacific war—after Pearl Harbor, the Japanese Navy greatly outnumbered the U.S. Navy—and suffered great casualties, the tide of the war was turned by one of the decisive events of the twentieth century: dropping the first atomic bombs on Hiroshima and Nagasaki. It is fair to say that life in Japan—and in different ways, in the rest of the world—was forever changed in that instant.

The new Meiji cultural connections to the West put different kinds of pressure on the traditional forms of Japanese theater. The Noh theater had been the special province of the *samurai* classes, and in the newly competitive theater marketplace was rapidly threatened with extinction. Several Noh actors—notably Umewaka Minoru (1828–1909)—worked to establish the Noh as a special part of Japan's cultural inheritance, an elite entertainment funded by the state (something like the "state opera" in many Western countries today), and today there are five Noh and two kyogen schools operating in Japan. Kabuki and Bunraku (the only form of Doll Theater still active) were more readily assimilated by the more open Japanese culture of the late nineteenth and early twentieth centuries, in large part because they had always been popular entertainments. Although there has been considerable modernization of Kabuki in the past century—contemporary Kabuki is not usually the daylong affair of the eighteenth-century theater; and to some extent Kabuki's reputation for lasciviousness has been replaced by a more "classical" orientation—the Kabuki and Bunraku theaters did not need to look for a new audience after 1868, and in many respects are a continuous performance tradition.

The history of modern Japanese theater is the history of Japan's negotiation of Western modes of playwriting and performance. The *SHIMPA* theater of the turn of the century adapted Western plays—Shakespearean tragedies and popular melodramas alike—to Japanese settings; it was a significant also for introducing actresses to the stage. Of greater consequence was the *SHINGEKI* theater. *Shingeki* ("new theater") imported both European plays in the realistic mode—Ibsen, Chekhov, Gorky, for example—and stimulated a new "realistic" style of drama among Japanese playwrights of the 1920s, 1930s, and 1940s. As it had in Europe in the 1880s, and in the United States in the 1910s and 1920s, this new dramaturgy was associated with a little theater movement. The most influential theater—the Tsukiji Little Theater of Tokyo—produced only Western playwrights in its first two years of operation, under the influence of its director Osanai Kaoru (1881–1928), who admired the work of Stanislavski and the Moscow Art Theater. Thereafter, the Tsukiji and other theaters like it tended toward social realism, plays such as Kubo Sakae's (1900–1958) splendid Marxist-inspired drama, *The Land of Volcanic Ash,* which traces the social and economic upheaval of the 1930s in a rural Japanese village on the colonial island of Hokkaido, was first performed by the Shinyo Troupe at the Tsukiji Little Theater in 1938. Although *shingeki* performance was banned during World War II, it became the predominant movement of the immediate postwar period, and Kubo's play was not only among the first plays to be staged after the war, but the play—and especially its central character, the radical agricultural scientist Kubo Amamiya—provided a model for postwar playwrights as well.

After World War II, the rebuilding of Japan was heavily financed by the United States, which also exerted considerable censorship control as well. Yet while "modern" Japanese theater had developed largely through the importation of European dramatic models, after the war, many writers worked to revive more traditional Japanese literary, dramatic, and theatrical forms. In some cases—Mishima Yukio (1925–1970) is a good example—this revival was part of an intense and conservative nationalist movement, the sense that "true" Japan was embodied in the prewar values of an imperial culture; but in other cases, it was part of a broader resistance to being culturally absorbed by the United States. A more experimental approach to blending foreign and indigenous dramatic modes arose, for instance, as part of the energetic protest against the U.S.–Japan Mutual Security Treaty in 1960. Many Japanese refused to participate in a "nuclear umbrella" agreement with the United States after the bombings of Hiroshima and Nagasaki (nearly a million demonstrated in Tokyo alone in 1959–1960), and the demonstrations around the treaty catalyzed a new introspection into the shape and meaning of Japanese culture, with its unique, deeply scarred relation to the postnuclear era. Hotta Kiyomi's (b. 1922) *The Island* (1955) was the first play about the bombings, and in the wake of the 1960 protests, a range of new kinds of theater and drama emerged: the backlash against Western dominance of Japan in the postwar period often appeared as a rejection of *shingeki* and of the Marxist politics that sustained its socialist realist esthetics. Kobo Abe's (1924–1993) plays, for example, often resonate with the **THEATER OF THE ABSURD,** but develop—as in the play *Slave Hunting* (1955)—a critique of spiritual poverty of postwar Japan. As David Goodman argues in his book *Japanese Drama and Culture in the 1960s: The Return of the Gods* (Armonk, NY: East Gate, 1988), playwrights like Fukuda Yoshiyuki (b. 1931) and Satoh Makoto (b. 1943) responded to the social and spiritual crisis of the post-1960 period in two ways: departing from *shingeki* conventions, they tend to use at least one godlike or archetypal character, and develop plays concerned "with the interrelated questions of personal redemption (salvation of the individual) and social revolution (salvation of the world)."[10]

This new style of playwriting demanded a new style of performance, and some of the most powerful innovations of the Japanese theater in the past twenty years have involved performance style. The director Suzuki Tadashi (b. 1939) has been very influential in this regard. Suzuki's production of Satoh's play *The Black Tent* seemed to call for a "new realism"; Suzuki formed an experimental company, Suzuki Company of Toga (SCOT), in which he developed some exercises from Noh training toward a kind of performance emphasizing the actor's physicality. Suzuki's work has become well known to American audiences through his collaborations with Anne Bogart and the Saratoga International Theater Institute's productions (see Unit VI). The spiritual scars of Hiroshima and Nagasaki are perhaps more literally visible in the emergence of *BUTOH* (the word means simply "dance") performance. In *butoh,* the dancers are naked, shaven, and dusted with a white powder; their performance style demands a ferocious discipline, for their movements are exceptionally slow. Devised originally by Ohno Kazuo (b. 1966) and Tatsumi Hijikata (1928–1986), *butoh* is famous for the sense of ghostly apparitions that its dancers become onstage, enacting what Tatsumi called "the gestures of the dead."

Martinique

Christopher Columbus stopped at the island of Martinique in 1502; it was an inhospitable island, dominated by the fierce Caribs. Although both Spain and England briefly established outposts on the island, it was settled in 1658 as a French colony, soon of some six thousand settlers. As happened throughout the Caribbean, the native population was exterminated by violence and disease. But the Compagnie de Sénégal, a French slave-trading company, made frequent stops at Martinique on its way to the larger island of Guadeloupe; the French imported slaves to the island, especially after the introduction of coffee in 1723. But a series of slave uprisings (1789, 1815, 1822), and an ongoing conflict with the English over the slave trade, led France to abolish slavery in Martinique in 1848; as a result, plantation owners frequently had to import workers from India and China, and the population of Martinique today is descended from these various groups. Martinique was made a crown colony in 1674; control of the island passed briefly to the English several times in the late eighteenth and early nineteenth century. Since the 1840s, however, Martinique has been governed by France: first as a colony, then as a *département* (1946), and since 1974 as a region.

All of the colonial powers brought theaters to the Caribbean—the first theater was built in Jamaica in 1682, and a production of John Gay's *The Beggar's Opera* was staged there in 1733. Since the 1950s, Aimé Césaire—Martinique's most famous poet, playwright, and essayist—has been critical to the public life of Martinique, and indeed to the theory of postcolonial development more widely. For Césaire has played an important part in the public life of Martinique, beginning a long term of service as a deputy to the French National Assembly in 1945, and then leading his Progressive party into power in 1957, and establishing several national institutions in support of the arts and theater. In part due to his efforts and those of his followers—training performers in traditional Caribbean forms of masking, drumming, and dancing, as well as inviting celebrated playwrights and directors such as Ariane Mnouchkine and Wole Soyinka to work in Martinique—Martinique now has a thriving theater culture.

Nigeria

With ninety million people, Nigeria is Africa's most populous country; of its twenty language groups, four—Yoruba, Ibo, Hausa, and Fulani—predominate, and the histories of the Yoruba, Ibo, and Hausa peoples are entwined in Nigeria's precolonial, colonial, and postcolonial history. In the precolonial period, Nigeria was home to several rich cultures. In the northern region adjacent to Lake Chad, ninth-century Arab writers described a flourishing culture, organized around a series of walled cities along Saharan trade routes between Egypt and western Africa. With the introduction of Islam from Mali in the fourteenth century, the Hausa and Fulani peoples became Muslim; in the nineteenth century, several emirs led a massive *jihad* or holy war against religious and civil authorities, and established a new center of power in Sokoto. Yoruba culture emanated from the southwestern region of Nigeria, centered around the city of Ife (eleventh through the fifteenth centuries); this Old Oyo culture—from which contemporary Yoruba culture descends—was a complex monarchial society, spread through several important cities; this is the kingdom that the Portuguese discovered when they arrived in the city of Benin in the fifteenth century. Ibo culture was less centrally organized, and stretched in a series of villages through the southeastern part of Nigeria.

European colonization of Nigeria began around the slave trade. The Portuguese slave trade of the seventeenth and eighteenth centuries was centered in Benin; the Portuguese transported slaves to their New World colonies, and deep strains of Yoruba can be found in many

New World–African cultures, particularly in Brazil. The expansion of Islamic Fulani emirates in northern Nigeria in the nineteenth century intruded into the Old Oyo empire, driving the Yoruba south, instigating a series of wars, and—by displacing a large population—stimulating the slave trade.

The British Royal Niger Company established trade with various Ibo and Yoruba leaders in the 1840s, but only established an administrative headquarters in Lagos in 1886. Although initially making contact as traders, the British presence rapidly developed from trade and missionary work into a more conventional colonial profile: consolidating territory, developing a legal apparatus, deporting local leaders who resisted, including the northern emirs, who were conquered in 1903. Originally divided into northern and southern colonies, Britain formed the Colony and Protectorate of Nigeria under a governor-general in 1914. Nigeria gained independence in 1960, but the strains between various regions and ethnic groups have not been readily resolved; in 1967 General Odumegwu Ojukwu declared a secession of the eastern states (Biafra), and despite marching successfully on Benin City, and nearly taking Lagos, surrendered in 1970. Although an initial constitution placed a legislature in each region, Nigeria has been beset by a series of brutal military regimes—the first coup in 1966 established a pattern for the 1970s, 1980s, and 1990s. In 1999, the government of Nigeria was returned to civilian control, with free elections.

The area now known as Nigeria was the home of a variety of cultures prior to becoming a British colony, and many of the performance practices of these cultures are visible in contemporary Nigerian theater and drama. Best known is the festival of *EGUNGEN;* this festival, which has been performed at least since the fourteenth century, attempts to establish a communion between the living and the dead. In it, masked and costumed celebrants proceed to a sacred grove, where the accumulated troubles of the village are removed by a "carrier." The persistence of this ritual is acknowledged by Wole Soyinka's play *Death and the King's Horseman,* which in various direct and indirect ways engages with the *egungen* narrative. Yoruba ritual is also known for the dynamic character of its gods—Obatala, the god of creation; Ogun, the god of creativity; Sango, the god of lightning—and for the use of masquerade as a central feature of ritual. One of the most popular theatrical forms in Nigeria is the Yoruba Traveling Theater; first developed by Hubert Ogunde (1916–1990), these performances generally concern a contemporary social issue, such as the exploitation of workers in his 1945 *Strike and Hunger.* Rather than a formal "drama," though, this form of theater takes the shape of a series of short skits, involving both dialogue and song, framed by a musical opening and closing number. In part because his company frequently satirized the colonial government (and was censored), Ogunde's work became widely known and imitated, and gave rise to a large number of companies practicing this narrative/dramatic/musical genre. Recently, Yoruba Traveling Theater has become almost exclusively a film genre.

In part because of the English presence—an English-language theater first opened in Lagos in 1899—in education, drama and theater played a large part in colonial Nigeria. D.A. Oloyede's play *King Elejigbo and Princess Abeje* (1904)—the first play in English by a Nigerian author—was written for a church group, and both reading and playing in the plays of the European tradition—Shakespeare, Molière, Shaw, Chekhov—formed part of the education of the generation of Nigerian writers and intellectuals who came of age with the independence. Wole Soyinka's plays often stage a rich dialogue between colonial and indigenous culture, drawing on the ritual and religious beliefs of the Yoruba. An Ibo playwright, John Pepper Clark (b. 1936) has dramatized the tales of the *ozidi* sagas—long stories that required several years to prepare and were performed by an entire village—and since the 1980s has directed his own professional theater. Femi Osofisan (b. 1946) is well known for taking a more critical, and politically engaged view of the problems of contemporary Nigerian society.

South Africa

Contemporary theater and drama in South Africa has been marked, as have all areas of South African life, by the imposition of racial *apartheid*—the legal separation and discrimination of various "racial" and ethnic groups—in 1948, laws which were only lifted with the election of Nelson Mandela as president in 1994. Apartheid can be seen as a politically conservative response to the social and racial situation that has developed in South Africa over the past four hundred years, in which the Portuguese, British, and Dutch vied with one another for control of the land, while at the same time being hugely outnumbered—South Africa today has about five million white inhabitants and thirty million black inhabitants—by an oppressed indigenous population.

In 1487, Bartholomeu Dias, a Portuguese explorer, reached Mossel Bay, opening a sea route from Europe to Asia. Over the course of the next three centuries, the port at the Cape of Good Hope gained enormous strategic and military value. In 1652, the Dutch East India Company established a station there to supply water, food, and supplies to trade ships. Dutch settlers—called "Afrikaners" (or "Boers")—expanded from the immediate Cape region, conquering the Khoisan tribes, and importing slaves from Indonesia, India, Ceylon, Madagascar, and Mozambique. Throughout the eighteenth century, however, important colonies of British settlers developed in the region as well: after a series of battles and broken treaties, Britain gained control of the Cape Colony in 1806. Yet by gaining control of the region, the British were faced with two opponents: the indigenous tribes, and the Afrikaners, who resisted the imposition of British rule. The nineteenth century then witnessed two kinds of struggle. The conflict between British and Afrikaner settlers intensified when the British emancipated the colonial slaves in 1834. The years 1835-40 saw the "Great Trek," the departure of Afrikaners and their "clients"—slaves—from the Cape Colony northward, where they settled the Transvaal and Orange Free State as independent republics in 1852 and 1854 (the Trek is part of the consciousness of Afrikaner culture, and is frequently reenacted). However, the discovery of diamonds in 1867 and of gold in 1886 led to renewed conflict, as Britain attempted to annex the Afrikaner republics. The "War Between the Whites"—the Boer War of 1899–1902—led to British control of all three republics, which were united in 1910 as the Union of South Africa. The Union gained its independence from Britain in 1931, and became the Republic of South Africa in 1961, when it left the British Commonwealth.

Competing with one another for land and resources, the British and Afrikaners also had large and powerful indigenous populations to contend with, and despite the British policy against slavery, both parties systematically subjugated the black populations of South Africa. The most important of these groups were the Zulu; their leader Shaka defeated other African tribes, organized the Zulu as a kingdom in the 1820s, and was killed in 1828. In a series of conflicts—the British war with the Xhosa in 1834–1840, the Afrikaner defeat of a Zulu force at the Battle of Blood River in 1838, and the final British defeat of the Zulu in 1879—the white population gained control of the land and its people.

In many respects, the political history of modern South Africa is the history of the white minority's efforts to subordinate and control this populace. The discovery of gold and diamonds led—after the Boer War—to an increasing demand for mine laborers; although 64,000 Chinese workers were imported in 1904–1907, most of these laborers were Africans, who were increasingly segregated from the white population. When the Union of South Africa was formed in 1910, only whites were enfranchised; in 1911, the Mine and Works Act, the first of a series of laws restricting African workers to laboring work stipulated that skilled labor in the mines could only be performed by whites; in 1913, the Natives Land Act enacted the first of a series of segregation laws, by limiting African land ownership to certain reserves. Eventually, Africans were restricted to "townships," large, impoverished cities close enough to major cities to provide a constant labor supply. Moreover, the conflicts between British and Afrikaner South Africans were hardly resolved by the Union. Although South Africa participated in World War I as a dominion of the British Empire, the rise of

Afrikaner nationalism in the 1930s led not only to considerable support for Germany in the country, but finally to the election of the Afrikaner National party in 1948.

The Afrikaner government installed apartheid as the law of the land in South Africa. Based on the notion that South Africa was comprised of four "racial" groups—White, Colored, Indian, and African—these laws legitimated White South Africans as the "nation," with the power to govern all other groups. Apartheid legislation was rapidly passed, and pervasive in its structuring of South African society: the Pass Laws of 1948 required one to carry a passbook at all times; the Population Registration Act of 1950 classified each person by race; the Group Areas Act forced people to live in racially segregated areas; in 1949 the Prohibition of Mixed Marriages Act passed; and in 1950 the Immorality Amendment Act prohibited sex between white and "nonwhite" persons. Property once "reserved" for ownership by Africans was claimed by whites: the segregated area of Sophiatown west of Johannesburg—where, since 1923, some African and Colored people owned land—was summarily converted into a White area, "Triomf" ("Triumph"). In the 1953 Bantu Education Act, the government assumed control of all schools—including missionary schools and colleges that had formerly educated Africans—and prohibited any instruction counter to the aims of the government; the 1959 Extension of University Education Act prohibited universities from admitting African students except with the permission of a cabinet minister.

The South African Native National Congress was founded in 1912 to advance the cause of Africans in South Africa: renamed the African National Congress, it responded swiftly to the imposition of apartheid: it organized a passive resistance campaign in 1952, and other acts of resistance throughout the 1950s. In 1959 a more radical group—the Pan African Congress, which included only Africans as members—split from the ANC; both were banned by the State of Emergency declared in 1960, after an uprising in Sharpeville when sixty Africans were shot by police during a peaceful protest. Although national and international opposition to apartheid was intense, it remained in force throughout the tumult of the 1960s, 1970s, and 1980s: the imprisonment of Nelson Mandela in 1962; the rise of the Black Consciousness Movement sponsored by Steve Biko and Barney Pityana in the late 1960s; the 1976 uprising in Soweto, a black township of one million people; the government's efforts to release the pressure on apartheid by forming black "homelands" in Transkei, Bophuthatswana, Venda, and Ciskei. By the mid-1980s, however, South Africa's isolation led to some political change: A new constitution in 1984 giving Colored, Asian, and Indian populations separate houses of parliament; the repeal of some pass laws in 1986; the release of Mandela in 1990, and the negotiations for a new constitution.

In all respects, theater in South Africa has been marked by this history. As a rough-and-tumble port, Cape Town did not support a legitimate theater until 1801, with the building of the African Theater, though performances of plays were given occasionally elsewhere (Beaumarchais's *Barber of Seville* was performed in Cape Town in 1783). By the early twentieth century, though, diamonds and gold were able to finance theater building, and every large city had several good theaters, performing European plays to white audiences. Since there was no repertory in Afrikaans, Afrikaners were particularly concerned to develop a "literary" culture: the first Afrikaans play was *Magrita Prinslo,* written by S.J. du Toit in 1897. Afrikaner theater flourished in the 1920s and 1930s, and continues today. Indeed, because the English-language theaters could rely on the traditional repertoire and touring companies, dramatic writing in English emerged much later in South Africa. Although the traditional forms of performance predate the colonial period, black theater in South Africa originates with Herbert Dhlomo (1903–1956), who studied at a mission school and became a teacher and journalist, and the author of twenty-four plays. In 1933 the Bantu Drama Society at the Bantu Men's Social Center performed his play *The Girl Who Killed to Save,* the first play by a black South African to be published in English, in 1936. Nonetheless, despite producing Dhlomo's play, the repertoire of the Bantu Drama Society was very much a European repertoire: Dhlomo himself played in Sheridan's comedy *She Stoops to Conquer.* Throughout the 1920s and 1930s, several companies—the Lucky Stars, the Syco Fans—worked to develop black drama.

The production of theater, like everything else in South African society, was segregated. In 1947 the government began funding a National Theater. Although the theater supported two companies—one in English, one in Afrikaans—they used no black actors, and included South African plays in their European repertoire only if they were written by white authors. In the 1940s, Es'kia Mphahlele and Khoti Mngoma founded the Syndicate of African Artists, but were refused government funding as long as they insisted on performing to mixed racial audiences: they were disbanded in 1956 after years of police harassment. The Union of South African Artists was organized in the 1950s to protect black artists' royalties, and engineered the production of the massively successful musical review about a boxer, *King Kong,* in 1959. Although the organization was white run, and showcased black talent to white audiences, it also performed successfully to mixed audiences, and sponsored mixed-cast shows: the Union produced Athol Fugard's *No-Good Friday* in 1958, at the Bantu Men's Social Center in Johannesburg, with a cast including Fugard, Zakes Mokae, Bloke Modisane, and Stephen Moloi. When the show moved to the Brooke Theater, however, Fugard had to be replaced by a black actor—Lewis Nkosi—because segregated venues (the Brooke was an all-white theater) required segregated casts.

The principal challenge to resistant theater offered by the apartheid laws in the 1960s was the Group Areas Act, which prohibited the association of different races in clubs, cinemas, and restaurants; while mixed casts could perform to these segregated audiences, this loophole was closed in 1965: segregated audiences, segregated casts. In 1961, Fugard's *The Blood Knot*—about half brothers, one black (played by Mokae), one passing as white (played by Fugard)—could not be played in a legitimate theater, but gained good audiences in Dorkay House, and was shortly produced in London and New York. In 1963, Fugard began to work with the Serpent Players of Port Elizabeth, a black company, on adaptations of European playwrights—Büchner, Chekhov, Brecht, and Sophocles' *Antigone.* At the same time, however, a more improvisational, storytelling mode of theater was being developed in the townships, in plays such as Gibson Kente's *Manana, the Jazz Prophet* (1963). Kente's performances were popular and influential; in their use of narrative, mime, music, and dance to dramatize township life, they provided the form for later works like Barney Simon, Mbongeni Ngema, and Percy Mtwa's *Woza Albert!* (1981). Despite their popularity, these township playwrights had difficulty getting published; the South African Performing Arts Councils received large subsidies, but produced European plays mainly for white audiences, while the township theaters performed under poor circumstances to huge audiences, often sponsored by the Union.

The 1970s saw the real flowering of resistance theater in South Africa: Athol Fugard's collaboration with John Kani and Winston Ntshona (from the Serpent Players) led to *Sizwe Bansi Is Dead* (1972), which they performed (while the police looked on) as a mixed cast; subsequent performances were canceled. When they attempted to perform the play at the University of Witwatersrand, the security police arrested both the cast and the audience. Kente's performances became more politically inflected, in township plays like *How Long* (1973) and *Too Late* (1981), and inspired many other township works: Sol Rachilos's *The Township Wife* (1972), Sidney Sepamia's *Cry Yesterday* (1972), the Theater Workshop of Durban's *Umabatha* (the Zulu *Macbeth,* revived in London and the U.S. in 1997). The 1970s also saw the forming of several influential theater groups, including the Market Theater of Johannesburg in 1976, which produced Kente's *Mama and the Load* in 1980; Simon, Ngema, and Mtwa's *Woza Albert!* in 1981; Maishe Maponya's *Gangsters* in 1984; Ngema's *Asinamali;* and Mtwa's *Bhopa!* in 1985. The Market Theater has been influential outside South Africa as well, as many of its plays have been exported to Europe and the United States, and many of its playwrights—Fugard and Maponya, for instance—have since produced plays outside South Africa. With the lifting of apartheid, race emerges as a different kind of issue in South African drama, and has been explored by a number of playwrights, including Ismail Mahomed (b. 1959), Reza de Wet (b. 1955), Brett Bailey (b. 1967) and many others. The Grahamstown National Arts Festival continues as the premiere annual theater festival in South Africa.

ANALYZING POSTCOLONIAL THEATER AND DRAMA

In part because postcolonial drama emerges out of the complex historical dynamics of global expansion, intercultural contact, political controversy, and sometimes unfamiliar artistic traditions, analyzing and discussing this material presents unique challenges. One approach to postcolonial culture attempts to develop a "national" or "regional" model, isolating themes (apartheid in South Africa, for instance), historical questions (plays that respond to the 1960 treaty controversy in Japan), or local features of dramatic style (the prevalence of domestic realism in American drama; the use of a trickster figure by Native Canadian playwrights) to assess the relationship between theater and the place of its production. This model can also lead to productive kinds of comparative study: in what ways does it make sense to frame a dialogue, say, between the writing of Aboriginal Australian writers like Jack Davis, and Native Canadian writers like Tomson Highway?

A second model recognizes the importance that ideas of "race" have had in mapping literary study, in drawing out political affinities between African, African-American, and Caribbean writers, for example. This model interrogates the ways in which "race" informs ideas of identity across national boundaries; it might place the ideas of W.E.B. DuBois or Amiri Baraka (see Unit VI) alongside the writings of Aimé Césaire and the Senegalese poet Leopold Senghor or the black Algerian psychiatrist Frantz Fanon's incendiary and brilliant book, *The Wretched of the Earth* (1961). In these writings, "race" emerges often as a cultural construct rather than a biological "fact," though its consequences are nonetheless powerful; and theorists of the production of "race" have often found a searching model in dramatic performance, both in plays in which "race" is a conscious issue—Soyinka's *Death and the King's Horseman,* or Baraka's *Dutchman*—as well as those in which it seems to be part of the play's unconscious politics, O'Neill's *The Hairy Ape,* for example, or Pinter's *The Homecoming.* Indeed, the constructedness of "race" or "ethnicity" can be a powerful weapon for *forging* a political consciousness: while the term "Latino" or "Latina" is relatively meaningless outside the Anglo-affiliated cultures of North America (people from Latin American countries tend to identify *nationally,* much as North Americans do; they think of themselves as Mexicans, Peruvians, or Cubans), it has become an important way for people experiencing *ethnic* discrimination in the United States to organize in a common effort.

One of the most powerful ways of considering postcolonial culture—its art, music, literature, drama, and performance—is to consider the formal properties of its artworks. Postcolonial critics, however, have resisted merely imposing the critical categories of Western literary study—tragic and comic form, for example, or verbal as opposed to music drama—on postcolonial arts, largely because such works often seem designed both to resist those categories, and to dramatize their implication in a wider politics. Wole Soyinka's early play *The Lion and the Jewel,* for example, is at once a play using the familiar stereotypes of Western comedy since Plautus—a pedantic schoolteacher, a cantankerous aging king, a pretty young girl—and interrogating them as well. As the play proceeds, it seems to ask whether this way of representing African village life—comedy—is complicit with the other ways that African village life is represented in the play: in magazine pictures, as a site for a railroad station, as the "dark continent" of the schoolteacher's textbooks. In other words, the play brings about a collision between the Western dramatic traditions Soyinka learned in Lagos, Leeds, and London, and the indigenous traditions—the social routines of the village, the songs, the marriage rituals—he blends into the texture of the play. This practice of blending both "indigenous" and "colonizing" literary or performance styles is generally called **HYBRIDIZATION,** and considering plays, poems, novels, films, and music in terms of their "hybrid" blending of cultural traditions is an important way of recognizing the cultural work that artworks do. Some writers (Ngũgĩ might be an example) call for postcolonial art to resist and replace the inauthentic and oppressive means of "colonial" art—writing in the colonial language, using colonial forms, like tragedy, the novel, the pop song—as a way to locate a new and authentic space of liberation. Others (Soyinka and Homi Bhabha, for example) tend to see hybrid forms as a useful tool, an instrument for exposing the dynamics of oppression at the heart of the colonizing culture itself. Reading or listening for hybridity—the collision between the tragedy of Steve Biko and Samuel Beckett's absurdist play *Catastrophe* in Maponya's *Gangsters* for instance—involves the subtle and delicate task of putting these forms into dialogue with one another, listening for how they shape and qualify one another, open the possibility of new meanings.

One of the most challenging aspects of performance today has to do with the relative ease with which cultures now come into contact with one another, use—or steal—one another's forms of art and this hybridizing tendency is often visible in the plays in Unit VII. The interpenetration of different musical idioms has become a standard aspect of contemporary pop music; for instance, reggae and ska and mambo and tango and high-life and many other musical languages once local to a given culture now filter in and out of many American pop songs. And while the music industry has worked to sell this variety by copying the restaurant industry—as "World Music"—we might wonder whether the analogy with the variety of "ethnic" or "international" cuisine in the pricey restaurant districts of major cities (or even the new interest in Asian and Mexican foods shown by McDonald's and Burger King) isn't more to the point: have the products of other cultures, their music, their food, their plays, become empty commodities, consumed by a kind of global consumer elite?

In the past two decades, this kind of controversy has animated "intercultural performance," a kind of performance that attempts to bridge the differences between two different cultures not so much by erasing or occluding them as by concocting artworks in which these boundaries become visible and meaningful. Ari-ane Mnouchkine's productions of Shakespearean or classical Greek dramas using Eastern movement and dance techniques is one well-known example; another is Peter Brook's famous staging of the Indian epic, *The Mahabharata* at the Avignon Festival in 1985, and then on tour in the following years, which used fundamentally Western theatrical techniques to stage the narrative. In 1989, David McRuvie and Annette Leday collaborated with the Kerala State Arts Academy on a production of Shakespeare's *King Lear,* adapted to the extraordinarily complex conventions of the *kathakali*—an Indian form of masked dance-drama. Unlike the hybrid works of playwrights like Maponya or Luis Valdez, this intercultural strategy does not arise from the blending of cultural materials already present in a given culture—in the way Luis Valdez's *actos* draw from both Mexican and Anglo performance traditions visible in California in the 1960s. Instead, they work to bring about a dialogue between cultures that are distant from one another in space and time.

As Marvin Carlson suggests in a careful anatomy of contemporary intercultural performances, there is not only a long tradition of intercultural performance, but a variety of ways of imagining the relationship between cultural forms that performance brings about.[1] He lists seven possibilities: a performance in a tradition foreign to the audience, such as a Noh company or the Comédie Française visiting New York; the complete assimilation of foreign elements (does anyone really hear a reggae beat as "foreign" to American pop any-more?); the assimilation of an entire foreign structure, such as Yeats's writing of Noh plays, or Maponya's work with Brechtian epic theater; making the foreign into a new blend with familiar elements (Molière's absorption of Italian *commedia dell' arte*); assimilating an entire foreign genre, such as Westerns in Japan; using some foreign elements within familiar structures, such as the dance sequences in Hwang's *M. Butterfly*, or perhaps the *egungen* costumes in Soyinka's *Death and the King's Horseman*; and importing an entire performance from another culture as something distinctly unfamiliar, such as *butoh*.

This list clarifies the extent to which intercultural performance is a highly charged, contestatory activity: Brook was widely criticized, despite the evident elegance of *The Mahabharata,* for transforming something like the national conscience of India into a piece of slick theater; similarly, while McRuvie and Leday's *Kathakali King Lear* framed an ambitious attempt to chart how far one kind of theater might be translated into the traditions of another culture, its reception was often relatively simplistic: British reviewers complained that the "true" *King Lear* was lost in the translation. As we move into the next millennium, we can certainly expect kind of theatrical and dramatic experimentation to continue, and to be challenged to think about the kind of cultural work it performs.

[1]Marvin Carlson, "Brook and Mnouchkine: Passages to India?" *The Intercultural Performance Reader,* ed. Patrice Pavis (London: Routledge, 1996), 82–83.

READING THE MATERIAL THEATER

From the perspective of theater research, modern students of theater and drama live in an era of extraordinary privilege: generations of scholars have worked to assemble the primary and secondary materials that document earlier theaters; the amount of information available in archives, libraries, and on the internet is nearly overwhelming; and, of course, performances now can be recorded on film or videotape, or for digital media. Yet we should not be seduced into thinking that a recording of a performance is the same thing as the live performance. First, of course, the camera's perspective governs everything we see on the screen, and makes it possible to achieve effects not possible in the theater; at the same time, it also transforms the performance from an actor's medium to the camera's. Viewers of the PBS versions of Anna Deavere Smith's *Fires in the Mirror* or *Twilight* can't help noticing the role played by the camera work, which brings Smith and her characters into a sharp close-up not possible onstage, to say nothing of the many scene changes, which—while they are handled seamlessly on television—point to a distracting "realism" that betrays Smith's open theatricality in performance.

Different kinds of documents—paintings, memoirs, reviews, illustrations, promptbooks, videotapes—tell us different kinds of things about the evanescent, always-lost performance onstage. One of the most useful documents for assessing the producers' original purposes in staging a play is the program, which often contains extensive program notes. With the rise of the director since the late nineteenth-century, theater companies have often found it important to have a second "conceptual" voice in the production process: the dramaturg. Dramaturgs play a wide variety of functions. In European theater, they often have a central

role in imagining the production and work in close cooperation with the director and cast throughout the development of the play. Under these circumstances, a company might use a dramaturg not only to conduct research into the historical background of the play and its author (and even—say, in the case of Shakespeare—into the play's language), but also to help articulate a critical perspective on the play for the performance in daily dialogue with the director and actors. In other circumstances—and more commonly in the United States—the dramaturg might function both as a literary manager, helping to acquire and develop new plays, as well as a kind of researcher, providing background information to the director and to the cast, as well as playing a central part in writing program information. As theatrical production has been understood to be an art independent of the narrowly literary meanings of dramatic writing, the theatrical program has become a place to inform and educate the audience about the play, both to provide historical information and to help develop a useful perspective on the production.

In 1980, the Field Day Theatre Company premiered Brian Friel's *Translations*. In writing the play, Friel had conducted considerable research into two important events in the history of Northern Ireland in the nineteenth century: the Ordnance Survey mapping of Ireland, and the transformation of the educational system. While Friel clearly worked to incorporate the information needed to understand the play *into* the play, the Field Day Company clearly felt that a greater understanding of the historical background would help readers to understand the play, and their production of it. What follows here are extracts from the program notes of *Translations*. It's important, of course, to train a skeptical eye on such efforts to explain the work of the production: how do these notes work to structure the audience's response to the play? Do the notes provide the kinds of information you think

is needed? Do the notes tend to emphasize some elements in the play as essential for understanding the play, and overlook other, perhaps other important, elements? How do these notes provide a perspective on the playwright's work in writing the play.

FIELD DAY THEATRE COMPANY PROGRAM NOTES FOR *TRANSLATIONS*[1] (1980)

Extract from *The Hedge Schools of Ireland* by P.J. Dowling The Hedge Schools owed their origin to the suppression of all the ordinary legitimate means of education, first during the Cromwellian regime and then under the Penal Code introduced in the reign of William III and operating from that time till within less than twenty years from the opening of the nineteenth century . . .

"The Hedge Schools were clearly of peasant institution. They were maintained by the people who wanted their children educated; and they were taught by men who came from the people . . .

"The poorest and humblest of the schools gave instruction in reading, writing and arithmetic; Latin, Greek, Mathematics and other subjects were taught in a great number of schools; and in many cases the work was done entirely through the medium of the Irish language. Though the use of the vernacular was rapidly falling into decay during the eighteenth century, it was owing to the greater value of English on the fair and market rather than to any shifting of ground on the part of the schools . . .

"The Hedge Schools were the most vital force in popular education in Ireland during the eighteenth century. They emerged in the nineteenth century more vigorous still, outnumbering all other schools, and so profoundly national as to hasten the introduction of a State system of education in 1831 . . ."

Extract from *The Autobiography of William Carleton* (born in County Tyrone, 1794) "The only place for giving instruction was a barn. The barn was a loft over a cowshed and stable . . . It was one of the largest barns in the parish.

"(At the age of fourteen) I had only got as far as Ovid's *Metamorphoses,* Justin, and the first chapter of John in the Greek Testament."

Extract from the memoirs of the Reverend Mr Alexander Ross, Rector, Dungiven, County Derry. 1814 "Even in the wildest districts, it is not unusual to meet with good classical scholars; and there are several young mountaineers of the writer's acquaintance, whose knowledge and taste in the Latin poets, might put to the blush many who have all the advantages of established schools and regular instruction."

Extract from *A History of Ireland* by Edmund Curtis "In 1831 Chief Secretary Stanley introduced a system of National Education . . . The system became a great success as an educational one but it had fatal effects on the Irish language and the old Gaelic tradition. According to Thomas Davis, at this time the vast majority of the people living west of a line drawn from Derry to Cork spoke nothing but Irish daily and east of it a considerable minority. It seems certain that at least two millions used it as their fireside speech . . . But the institution of universal elementary schools where English was the sole medium of instruction, combined with the influence of O'Connell, many of the priests, and other leaders who looked on Irish as a barrier to progress, soon made rapid inroads on the native speech . . ."

Extract from *Ordnance Survey of Ireland* by Thomas Colby, Colonel, Royal Engineers (1835) "To carry on a minute Survey of all Ireland no collection of ready instructed surveyors would have sufficed. It, therefore, became indispensable to train and organise a completely new department for the purpose. Officers and men from the corps of Royal Engineers formed the basis for this new organisation, and very large numbers of other persons possessing various qualifications, were gradually added to them to expedite the great work . . .

"The mode of spelling the names of places was peculiarly vague and unsettled, but on the maps about to be constructed it was desirable to establish a standard orthography, and for future reference, to identify the several localities with the names by which they had formerly been called . . ."

Extract from the Spring Rice Report (advocating a general survey of Ireland) to the British Government; 21 June 1824 "The general tranquility of Europe, enables the state to devote the abilities and exertions of a most valuable corps of officers to an undertaking, which, though not unimportant in a military point of view, recommends itself more directly as a civil measure. Your committee trust that the survey will be carried on with energy, as well as with skill, and that it will, when completed, be creditable to the nation, and to the scientific acquirements of the present age. In that portion of the Empire to which it more particularly applies, it cannot but be received as a proof of the disposition of the legislature to adopt all measures calculated to advance the interests of Ireland."

Extracts from the letters of John O'Donovan, a civilian employee with the Ordnance Survey, later Professor of Celtic Studies, Queen's College, Belfast
Buncrana
23 August 1835
"On Friday we travelled through the Parish of Clonmany and ascended the Hill of Beinnin. Clonmany is the most Irish Parish I have yet visited; the men only, who go to markets and fairs, speak a little English, the women and children speak Irish only. This arises from their distance from Villages and Towns and from their being completely environed by mountains, which form a gigantic barrier between them and the more civilized and less civil inhabitants of the lower country."
Dun Fionnchada? Dun Fionnchon?
Dunfanaghy
9 September 1835
"I am sick to death's door of the names on the coast, because the name I get from one is denied by another of

equal intelligence and authority to be correct. The only way to settle these names would be to summon a Jury and order them to say and present 'upon ther Oathes' what these names are and ought to be. But there are several of them such trifling places that it seems to me that it matters not which of two or three appelations we give them. For example, the name Timlin's Hole is not of thirty years standing and will give way to another name as soon as that dangerous hole shall have swallowed a fisherman of more illustrious name than Tim Lyn."
Glenties
15 October 1835
"Yesterday being a fair-day at Dunglow we were obliged to leave it in consequence of the bustle and confusion. We directed our course southwards through the Parish of the Templecroan, keeping Traigh Eunach (a name which I find exceedingly difficult to Anglicise) to the right . . . On the road we met crowds of the women of the mountains who were loaded with stockings going to the stocking fair of Dunglow and who bore deep graven on their visages the effects of poverty and smoke, of their having been kept alive by the potatoe only . . . I have seen several fields of oats on this coast, some prostrated and rotting, others with the grain completely blown off the stalk—and some so green in October as to preclude the possibility of ripening at all."
Ballyshanny
1 November 1835
"I have met in this town a fine old man named Edward Quin, from whom I have received a good deal of information. He has been employed by Lieutenant Vickers to give the Irish names of places about Ballyshannon, and has saved me a good deal of trouble—I wish you could induce Mr Vickers to take him to his next district, and keep him employed writing in the Name Books, and taking down the names from the pronunciation of the country people."

———————————

[1]Courtesy Field Day Theatre Company

Satoh Makoto

Satoh Makoto was born in 1943 and studied philosophy at Waseda University before leaving to join the Actors' Theater school. As with many writers and artists of his generation, Satoh was outraged at the prospect of Japan joining a nuclear defense alliance sponsored by the United States, and he participated in the national demonstrations of 1960–1961. And while a persistent note of social critique is heard in his plays, it is only one strain in a deeper harmony, combining with Satoh's investment in the recovery of a more authentic sense of Japanese identity and a spiritual orientation based on his reading of philosophy, both early Christian writings and existential writers such as Kierkegaard. From 1968 to 1971, Satoh was playwright and director of the Black Tent Theater. Several of his best-known plays were written and produced at this time, including *My Beatles* (1969), *The Rat* (1969), and *The Subway* (1967). Satoh remains a prominent playwright in Japan; his later plays include *The World of Showa*.

MY BEATLES

My Beatles is a brilliant pastiche of the alienated dramaturgy of postwar absurdism and a summons to recognize a social and spiritual crisis. In his fine collection, *Japanese Drama and Culture in the 1960s: The Return of the Gods* (Armonk, NY: East Gate, 1988), David Goodman notes that the action of *My Beatles* is based on the rooftop rape and murder of a Japanese teenage girl by a Japanese-born Korean boy at the Komatsugawa High School in Tokyo in 1958. The details of the Komatsugawa Incident were widely known—indeed, Goodman reports Satoh commenting that "the Komatsugawa Incident is a living wound that will never heal." The incident reveals the deep animosity between Koreans and Japanese and the deep social discrimination faced by Koreans in Japan. The boy, Li Jin-wu, grew up in the Korean ghetto of Tokyo and was a very good student; he took the Japanese name Kaneko Shizuo in school and "passed" as Japanese until he began looking for a job. Corporations refused to hire him because of his Korean background, and he bounced around through a series of factory jobs in frustration. On August 17, 1958, Li found Ōta Yoshie on the roof of Komatsugawa High School and threatened her with a knife; when she screamed, Li choked her into silence. He then raped and strangled her. He was later convicted of murdering another young woman the previous year.

The Komatsugawa Incident represented to many Japanese Japan's exploitation of Korea; Imperial Japan had seized Korea in 1910, forcing Korean men into military service and Korean women into prostitution as "comfort women," compelling Koreans to work in Japanese factories; Japan seized large areas of land as well. At the end of the war, there were nearly two million Koreans living in Japan, where they had to live in specified Korean ghettoes, and were brutally discriminated against in all areas of public life.

Satoh's play, *My Beatles,* is less a direct response to the Komatsugawa Incident than a meditation on the Korean-Japanese relations. The play opens with Chong and Katsura rehearsing a play that resembles the Incident; in the play, Chong rapes and murders Katsura, who is then avenged by "The Japanese," clearly a figure of Japanese popular attitudes toward Koreans. The play's logic is deftly complicated by the arrival of The Quartet, four characters who come onstage as movers, but rapidly claim to be "the Beatles": Sundown Lennon, McCartney the Stripe, Side-Street Harrison, and Twinkle Starr. The Quartet, in other words, present a kind of fusion of attitudes: they are at once movers and *the* Beatles; they are the Beatles, and Katsura's fantasy of the Beatles, *my* Beatles; and they are something like powerful gods who descend into the action, and the popular stereotypes of the Fab Four. What's striking about the action of the play is that despite its violence—at various points the Beatles seem to observe the play, to enter into directing the play, and actually to intervene in it—*My Beatles* begins and ends with Chong and Katsura longing for the peaceful emerald peninsula, a kind of fantasy of escape to Korea. In *My Beatles,* the history of Japan's rape of Korea, and its reversed reenactment in the Korean's rape of a Japanese girl, outline a scene of social injustice that even the gods—the sacred or the pop-culture projections of our desires—can't really help to bring about change.

MY BEATLES

Satoh Makoto

TRANSLATED BY DAVID G. GOODMAN

CHARACTERS

THREE YOUNG PEOPLE	THE QUARTET

CHONG, *young husband; plays the guitar*

KATSURA, *young wife*

THE JAPANESE, *dressed in black and carries a pistol, an onion, and something resembling a bomb*

SUNDOWN LENNON, *soft-spoken, intense leader of the group; dresses formally and has long hair*

MC CARTNEY THE STRIPE, *wears a knit shirt and small square sunglasses*

SIDE-STREET HARRISON, *bearded and wears a "Make Love Not War" button*

TWINKLE STARR, *smokes a pipe and wears flowered slacks with a man's white shirt*

A room the size and description of a cheap flat, the home that CHONG *and* KATSURA *call their castle. There is one door and one window, both carelessly painted green. A naked light bulb swings just above the floor on a cord that is much too long. There is a record player and a stack of records, but otherwise the room is bare. The ceiling is low and the floor slopes gently. The overall impression is less of a room than the inside of a large crate.*

It is one o'clock in the morning.

It is dark. The voices of several young people can be heard: "Bird!" "God!" "My Bird!" "My God!" The alternating voices of men and women repeat: "Oh my bird!"

The strains of a Beatles' song are also audible.

The naked light bulb brightens slowly. KATSURA *is seated in the center of the room.* CHONG *pokes his head in through the window from outside. Beneath the light bulb a record revolves on a cheap phonograph.*

CHONG: Bird?

*(*KATSURA *shakes her head.)*

CHONG: But it seemed as if. . . .

*(*KATSURA *nods. A woman's voice is heard. It is* TWINKLE STARR. *Half stoned, she sounds like a child.)*

STARR: (*Voice only.*) Maybe I should throw it away.

CHONG: It was a bird, I'm sure of it.

*(*KATSURA *shakes her head again.)*

5 LENNON: (*Voice only.*) Why are you crying?

HARRISON: (*Voice only.*) Dear Lord, we beseech you to accept these, your humble servants, and grant eternal rest. We. . . .

(Suddenly the QUARTET *breaks into raucous laughter.* KATSURA *slowly gets to her feet.)*

CHONG: It was a bird. What are you getting up for? Sit down.

10 *(He notices the commotion and looks up.)*

*(*KATSURA *smiles briefly to herself.)*

LENNON: (*Voice only.*) Answer my question. Why are you crying?

STARR: (*Voice only.*) None of your business.

HARRISON: (*Voice only.*) Oh, lay off her. She doesn't have to have a reason. Hail Mary. . . .

LENNON: (*Voice only.*) That's no answer. There's got to be a 15
reason.

STARR: (*Voice only.*) I guess I will throw it away.

MC CARTNEY: (*Voice only, simply.*) All right.

(A red high-heeled shoe falls into the room from above.)

KATSURA: Whirling around. A bird?

CHONG: No. 20

STARR: (*Voice only, discordantly.*) Our Father who art in Heaven. . . .

MC CARTNEY: (*Voice only.*) Like Elvis, man!

HARRISON: (*Voice only.*) It is our fervent hope that you will judge our departed. . . . 25

STARR: (*Voice only.*) Our departed and deceased!

CHONG: Sit down, will you? You're reading a book. Just as we rehearsed it. All right?

*(*KATSURA *seats herself lethargically on the floor with both legs folded to one side and pretends to read.)*

CHONG: There's only one light on the roof. It's the lamp over the emergency exit. It's very dim, so you've pasted yourself 30
to the wall, trying to get enough light to read by. The last light of evening fades. All of a sudden the chimney that soars up before you seems somehow different. You don't look up, but you notice the change all the same. Until a few minutes ago it was dusk—until a few minutes ago the sky 35
was orange and the chimney stood bold and inorganic before you. But now it is night. Against the darkened sky, the chimney's silhouette begins to expand; its contours diffuse into the darkness.

KATSURA: That's not the way it was at all. 40

CHONG: As a matter of fact you don't notice the end of evening. You're too engrossed in your book. But you notice the change in the chimney all the same.

KATSURA: No, there was no chimney. You couldn't see any chimney from that roof. 45

CHONG: Listen, it's a factory district. There have to be chimneys in a factory district. Now look, Katsura, you're still not doing as I said. The light on the roof is dim. You'd never be able to read like that.

(KATSURA *moves to the wall opposite the window and presses herself up against it. She continues to pore over her imaginary book.*)

50 CHONG: That's better.

KATSURA: There was no chimney. But a river was flowing nearby, a thick, lazy river, a river like a swamp.

KATSURA: (*Reading.*) "I was waiting for the ship."

CHONG: (*Sharply.*) No!

55 KATSURA: "I was waiting for the ship."

CHONG: Katsura, that's all wrong! There's nothing about a ship written there.

KATSURA: (*Not too insistently.*) I'm reading my diary. There are bound to be things in it Chong doesn't know.

60 CHONG: Listen, I made up this play! . . .

KATSURA: You decided that I should be reading, that I should be engrossed in a book. (*She touches the wall of the room.*) This is a concrete wall on the roof. There's an emergency exit lamp attached to it. The lamp is red. That's right, isn't it?

65

CHONG: Yes, that's right.

KATSURA: I'm just part of the setting. I'm leaning against the wall and reading. But I only need to pretend I'm reading. The play has only just begun; nothing really happens until Chong appears on the roof.

70

CHONG: You just don't understand!

KATSURA: (*Paying no attention, reading.*) "I was waiting for the ship." If you don't like it we'll forget the whole thing.

CHONG: All right, have it your way. Keep reading. I just won't listen, that's all.

75

KATSURA: (*Reading.*) "I was waiting for the ship. I have a bicycle, but a bicycle won't do. I can't go by bicycle. The Beatles are on the ship. I will board the ship and set off. Two of the Beatles will carry me on board, while the other two load my bicycle and rocking chair: the bicycle on the deck, the rocking chair in my cabin. I'll ask them to help me. And when they're finished, I'll thank them one by one. I'll let them feel my smooth, even tummy."

80

CHONG: (*Interrupting.*) The canal flowing into the night sky symbolizes Katsura's presentiment, the presentiment that a sinister change is taking place in the vicinity of the river, a change that terrifies her. And yet her presentiment is mistaken, for the danger lurks in an entirely different direction. . . . (*Shouting unexpectedly.*) Who's there?

85

(*Unnoticed,* THE JAPANESE *has arrived and is standing in the doorway.*)

90 JAPANESE: It's me, "The Japanese." Just go ahead with what you were doing.

(*The record ends.*)

CHONG: You see, this is what always happens—we never get to the end!

(KATSURA *no longer pretends to read but remains sitting on her haunches.*)

KATSURA: Are we going on, Chong?

CHONG: (*To* JAPANESE.) Come on in. (CHONG *also enters the room* 95 *through the window.*) Which direction was the canal?

(KATSURA *is silent but points toward the audience.*)

CHONG: Over there? Then Chong would approach from the direction of The Japanese. (*He sits down and picks up his guitar.*)

KATSURA: I wind up as usual, don't I, just reading my book and waiting? 100

JAPANESE: (*Still standing in the doorway.*) It's the same old story, isn't it? The same old story.

KATSURA: I wonder if things would go as you say?

CHONG: (*Strumming his guitar.*) What do you mean?

KATSURA: If we got any farther. 105

CHONG: There's no way to tell. There's always the chance we'll flop.

JAPANESE: Don't worry. Things will go just fine. They have to.

CHONG: Listen, you're not even supposed to be here yet! And anyway, how do you know? We'll just have to try and see 110 what happens.

JAPANESE: Things had better go well. Otherwise I'm the odd man out.

CHONG: Then the first thing to do is avoid arriving so damned early! You show up prematurely and I have to quit right in 115 the middle of everything. Every night it's the same way. I never get far enough to see how things will turn out. How can you stand there and tell me not to worry?

JAPANESE: I just haven't been able to find a good way to kill the time, that's all. 120

CHONG: Sure.

JAPANESE: But I know everything will go fine.

CHONG: Do you think Chong will show up, though? Will he really appear there, in your place?

JAPANESE: Will he show up? You mean, will you show up? Yes, 125 you'll show up. You have to.

KATSURA: Let's have something to drink. It looks like we've gotten as far as we're going to tonight, anyway.

CHONG: All right.

JAPANESE: I'd just like a glass of water. I'm hot. 130

KATSURA: Okay, I'll be right back.

(KATSURA *exits.* JAPANESE *enters the room and sits with his back to the wall like* CHONG.)

CHONG: You're always so easy-going. I can count on you, can't I? Are you certain you can handle your part?

JAPANESE: That depends entirely on you. I'm ready whenever you are. I've made all the necessary preparations, and start- 135 ing tomorrow I'll make it a point to plan the time of my arrival more precisely. What I'm most afraid of is that you'll lose your nerve.

CHONG: If we could just get through it once, I'm sure there'd be nothing to it. We were doing pretty well tonight, too, as 140 a matter of fact. Did you hear the part about the canal?

JAPANESE: Just half. (*He takes an onion from his bag and begins to eat it without peeling it, as if it were an apple.*)

CHONG: (*Singing half to himself.*)

All men will be equal, 145
On an even plane.

JAPANESE: Do you have everything you need?

CHONG: What do you mean?

150 JAPANESE: Weapons and such. I was just wondering how you expect to go about it.

CHONG: I don't need anything. I'll just have my hands in the pockets of my trench coat.

JAPANESE: And then?

CHONG: "Hey!" I'll yell, but I won't look at her. This first
155 "Hey!" will be more to reassure myself than anything else. "Hey!" I'll be practicing, see? I'll be asking myself if I can really take her, take her properly, like a man.

JAPANESE: "Hey"?

CHONG: I'll be tired—being tired's good, don't you think? It's
160 appropriate for a man performing his duty to be tired. A weary man in a trench coat, dispensing justice.

JAPANESE: Justice . . . interesting.

CHONG: (*Again singing half to himself.*)

165 Mountains will be leveled,
Seas their waters drained.

I'll appear before her without saying a word. I won't say a word, but I'll grab the book she's reading. She'll look up at me . . . or perhaps she won't. If she does, I'll smile at her with as much affection as I can. If she just looks at the
170 ground, I'll say, "It's not good for a man to smile alone," and then I'll ask her if she'd like an apple. How does that sound?

JAPANESE: I suppose it will do. There's no reason you have to force yourself on her right away. Just so you don't miss your
175 chance. It's probably as good a way as any.

CHONG: She'll probably refuse the apple and ask for her book back.

JAPANESE: Perhaps.

CHONG: Why not?

180 JAPANESE: I don't think she'll say anything. She'll be silent. She won't respond to your question or ask for her book back.

CHONG: She won't say anything?

JAPANESE: Much better that way, I should think. More realistic. You're the one who does the talking. The only thing that
185 matters about her is that she's there. She'll just remain passive until you've finished your part in the play.

CHONG: Yes, when you show up I'll probably act the same way. I'll just be passive until you've finished your part in the play. I can understand that. My role is very much like hers.
190 You're the assailant and I'm your victim. But Katsura and I have to be more than that. We have to be more like accomplices. She talks to me, just a bit. We need that moment of intimacy, of warmth, before anything else happens.

JAPANESE: I was only offering my opinion. I didn't mean you
195 have to follow my advice.

(KATSURA *returns. She carries two cups and a glass on a tray.*)

KATSURA: (*Handling the glass to* JAPANESE.) You were just kidding about feeling hot. You don't really want water, do you?

CHONG: Just then she says, "I don't care for an apple. Please re-
200 turn my book."

(CHONG *is absorbed in his own thoughts.* JAPANESE *and* KATSURA *take advantage of their moment of privacy to kiss quickly on the lips.*)

KATSURA: (*Handling* CHONG *his cup.*) I would like an apple, thank you. In return you can keep the book!

(JAPANESE *chuckles, drinks his water, and eats his onion.*)

CHONG: (*Annoyed.*) "You can't have it. You'll catch cold from eating apples."

KATSURA: Chong is ashamed because his apple is so small. Men 205 with small apples hate themselves.

(JAPANESE *laughs again.*)

CHONG: (*To* JAPANESE.) Are you going to kill me with a knife? I don't think I could take a poisoned apple.

JAPANESE: Are you kidding?

KATSURA: (*Interrupting her imagination sparked.*) Death by hang- 210 ing, of course!

JAPANESE: (*Ignoring her.*) The trouble with a knife is that the chances of failure are so great. It requires a certain amount of skill, don't you think?

CHONG: But that's the way it's supposed to happen, isn't it? I'll 215 do everything I can to cooperate. I'll only start writhing and struggling once I'm drenched in my own blood, tottering on the brink of death.

JAPANESE: I suppose a knife isn't entirely out of the question.

KATSURA: Poison would be pretty awful, too, wouldn't it? 220

CHONG: Of course, but there's no blood.

KATSURA: There must be a little bleeding from the nose.

CHONG: I don't want a bloody nose, I want to bleed!

KATSURA: Of course you do, dear.

CHONG: Bleed, you hear! (*To* JAPANESE.) Right? 225

JAPANESE: I suppose. Here, look what I made. (*He removes a bomb from his pocket. It is small, round, and black.*) I don't know whether it'll do the job or not.

CHONG: How does it work?

JAPANESE: There's really nothing to it. You just light this fuse 230 and in five seconds, bang! I tested it on a mouse—blew the beast to smithereens!

CHONG: Smithereens. . . .

KATSURA: Did you throw it?

JAPANESE: No. I had the mouse trapped in a box back in the 235 woods. The bomb made quite a noise when it went off; even sent up a column of flame in the air.

KATSURA: Sounds terrific!

CHONG: Isn't it overdoing things a bit?

JAPANESE: Don't you like the idea of using explosives? 240

CHONG: No, explosives are all right, I suppose.

JAPANESE: (*Relieved.*) Well, I'm glad to hear that! (*He returns the bomb to his pocket.*)

KATSURA: This is really going to be fun!

CHONG: You think so? 245

KATSURA: Is there anything wrong with that?

CHONG: No, I'm glad it makes you happy. It's just that I had no idea he'd use a bomb, that's all. I always assumed he'd use a knife. You know: the dark of night, a narrow alley, a knife in the back. With a bomb an alley's out of the ques- 250 tion, and daylight would be better, too. A major thorough-fare in broad daylight, that's it.

JAPANESE: Right: broad daylight, a beautiful, wide boulevard. I'll blow you to kingdom come!

CHONG: I'm beginning to see what you mean! 255

JAPANESE: I'll wait for you to climb the stairs out of the subway. You'll squint as you emerge into the daylight, and that will be my signal. The bomb will land exactly six inches in front of you. I'll have dropped it from the roof of a building.

260 CHONG: Have you given it a run-through already?

JAPANESE: No, I'm still in the planning stages.

KATSURA: Don't you think we ought to give it a trial, though? It would be awfully embarrassing to fail.

JAPANESE: Yes, there always is that possibility.

265 CHONG: (*Singing.*)

> All the world will be afire,
> Turned to flame and heat.

KATSURA: Failure would mean Chong would be the sole survivor.

270 CHONG: When I come out of the subway, I could walk real slowly. I could even stand still. You just can't count on "The Japanese": they might spoil the whole thing. If I'm not dead when this is over, it will all have been for nothing.

KATSURA: You could lose a leg and still survive, you know.

275 That's what happened to my father.

JAPANESE: (*Chanting.*) Smithereens . . . smithereens . . . smi-ther-eens!

CHONG: That's right. Just like the mouse in your experiment. I'm counting on you. Blow me to bits!

280 JAPANESE: Leave it to me. One fine day you can be sure you'll be blown as high as the clear, blue sky. A cloudless Sunday would be ideal.

CHONG: Sunday.

KATSURA: The day after tomorrow!

285 CHONG: I wonder if it'll clear up by then.

JAPANESE: (*Noticing something.*) Did somebody just come in? (*He looks at the door.*)

KATSURA: Did you hear something?

JAPANESE: I thought so.

(KATSURA *stands up, goes to the door, opens it, and looks out.*)

290 KATSURA: Nobody there now.

JAPANESE: (*Deliberately.*) The Beatles. (*He begins to laugh.*)

CHONG: Nonsense! (*To* KATSURA.) Right?

KATSURA: Sure. (*Laughing, she closes the door and returns to her place.*)

CHONG: Listen, the Beatles aren't coming. The whole idea's

295 ridiculous.

KATSURA: Maybe they won't come. Then again, maybe they will. Either way it's too early to tell.

CHONG: They're not coming, I said.

KATSURA: Yes, they will! They'll come to take me back to the

300 Emerald Peninsula, where the air is fresh and the grass is green.

JAPANESE: They'll come by ship . . . won't they?

KATSURA: A fabulous yacht!

CHONG: It's a lie! I've told you a hundred times—all this talk

305 about the Emerald Peninsula is a pack of lies. It isn't green and it isn't fresh. It's a land of wasted soil and mountains stripped of foliage. It's a parched land, and the only time the wind isn't filled with dust is when it's whipping the snow into drifts.

310 KATSURA: My father told me there are gentle, rolling hills, and pastures where herds of horses graze.

CHONG: (*Sarcastically.*) And where's your father now?

KATSURA: He's gone. He went back.

JAPANESE: Back? (*Making a ditty of the words.*) He went back. 315 He went back. He went back-a-back-a-back!

CHONG: He went back all right. He headed back to the Emerald Peninsula as fast as he could go. But he didn't go by yacht. He took the rusty, mottled ferry that came for him.

KATSURA: (*Urgently.*) You don't understand!

CHONG: And did you get letters from the pastures and the 320 hills? Did your father write you about the blue sky and the fresh air?

KATSURA: The letters came from a tiny shanty built in the shadow of a forest of chimneys. My father wrote that he would walk around the corner with his crutch under his 325 arm and hear a baby crying.

CHONG: Even so, he's pretty damn happy, isn't he? He dishes hot vittles onto a tin plate and it's enough to make him weep with joy. If you ask me, I think your old man crossed the straits all right, but when he got to the other side he 330 didn't find what he expected. He was rotten with years, and he filled your head with a pack of fairy tales and lies.

JAPANESE: Who knows? Maybe he never made it after all.

CHONG: Katsura's old man got where he was going, all right. But it wasn't green. I know. I've known for a long time. 335 Katsura shouldn't waste her time dreaming about the Beatles and their peninsula. There isn't a chance in a million we'll ever get there.

KATSURA: You're not going. The Beatles are coming for me alone. 340

CHONG: We'll see how things go when and if the Beatles get here. Until then. . . . Listen, you haven't been good for anything around here lately. You couldn't even read with enthusiasm. It's half your fault I never get anywhere.

KATSURA: I read just as I was told. Maybe I'm just sick and 345 tired of play-acting. Sometimes I think I am. But who cares? Either way. . . .

CHONG: You have no choice but to be here, to go on being here, to go on play-acting with me.

(*Pause.*)

STARR: (*Voice only.*) Bye-bye, my God! 350

MC CARTNEY: (*Voice only.*) Like Elvis Presley!

STARR: (*Voice only.*) God? Bird?

JAPANESE: (*Looking up.*) What's all the noise about?

CHONG: Somebody's grandmother died. They must be having a wake. 355

JAPANESE: Grandmother?

CHONG: Used to live up there. I never met her, though. Seems like they're going a little overboard, doesn't it?

JAPANESE: For a wake, yes.

KATSURA: Under her breath. "Bye-bye, my God." . . . 360

CHONG: What?

KATSURA: Nothing. What sort of people are they?

CHONG: You mean upstairs? Let me see. They're a strange bunch, certainly not ordinary. There are four of them.

KATSURA: Four? 365

CHONG: Yes.

(*Pause.*)

CHONG: Well, what shall we do? Is tonight going to be like all the others?

JAPANESE: We don't have much choice, do we?

370 KATSURA: The nights certainly are long, though.

JAPANESE: Yes.

CHONG: If you'd like to go home. . . .

JAPANESE: No, there's nothing to do at home but sleep and mess around. But if you'd like me to. . . .

375 CHONG: No, it doesn't matter. In fact, I'd rather have you here. The nights are so damn long, sometimes I wonder if I'll last till morning. I thought maybe we were keeping you, that's all.

JAPANESE: Don't worry about me. I'm all right.

380 KATSURA: There's no part in the play for you at this point anyway. But your name, "The Japanese," don't you think it's funny?

JAPANESE: Not particularly. The avenging Japanese, that's my role, after all. I take the necessary reprisals for what Chong

385 does.

CHONG: You'll bury me in a hole and cover me over with sand so that no trace remains. You'll bury the wretched Korean who's raped Katsura and strangled her to death. Then I'll return to life! Glorious revenge, my blood's atonement! I'll

390 die and thus gain new life. You see, I'll be murdered by "The Japanese," by their rage, and so I'll be able to die smiling and satisfied. I'll die proud that I could be murdered in just revenge. That will be my resurrection. "The Japanese" will see me through my resurrection and then quietly bury

395 my remains.

JAPANESE: I understand. Perfectly. I'll do just as you say. You don't have to worry.

CHONG: Tomorrow we're going to run through the whole thing. And then on Sunday. . . .

400 JAPANESE: Yes.

KATSURA: Tomorrow? Really?

CHONG: Yes, tomorrow. We'll play this thing out to the very end.

KATSURA: The Beatles won't make it, will they?

405 CHONG: Not a chance. Okay, you'd better get back to rehearsing.

(KATSURA *stands, walks over to the window, takes out her imaginary book, and begins to read aloud.* JAPANESE *takes out his pistol and polishes it.* CHONG *is strumming his guitar.*)

KATSURA: (*Reading.*) "My father was lame. He had a pair of red high heels. I wanted to try them on. I wanted to try them on for the longest time. Father was generally grumpy, and I was afraid of him, but once I told my brother. We were

410 standing up on top of this mountain of cinders, and I screwed up the courage to tell him that I wanted to try on Father's red high heels. He laughed, and as he laughed he hit me. He hit me again and again; he hit me until my cheeks were red and swollen. But all the time, even as he

415 was hitting me, I couldn't think of anything but the red high heels placed so carefully on that dark shelf in our house. My brother's first hurt me terribly, and I could have cursed him, but for some reason I didn't cry. He hit me for a long time and then suddenly left me alone on the moun-

420 tain of cinders. As I watched him disappear into the darkness at the foot of the cinder mountain I was struck by how

grown-up he seemed. It was just a year later that he hanged himself. We found a letter of acceptance from a university somewhere in his pocket. Afterward Father and I took the

425 red high heels and the letter out back to the garbage dump and burned them. Somehow it seemed like a terrible waste to burn those things, but I was afraid of what Father might do if I said anything, so I kept quiet. I helped him carry books and newspapers and our battered old desk out of the

430 house to feed the fire. Somehow, though, our kindling wouldn't burn, and for a long time it sputtered and smoked without catching fire. Eventually we burned everything in the house. Then Father boarded the ship and left."

(*While* KATSURA *is speaking the door opens and* LENNON *and* HARRISON *look in.* KATSURA, CHONG, *and* JAPANESE *do not notice them.* LENNON *and* HARRISON *examine the room carefully, then look at each other and nod.*)

LENNON: (*Deliberately, oppressively, just as* KATSURA *finishes speaking.*) Guitar. . . .   435

(CHONG *notices the intruders and swings around.* KATSURA *and* JAPANESE *also notice.*)

LENNON: (*Continuing.*) . . . girl, pistol. Three people in all. No mistake, this is the place.

(CHONG, KATSURA, *and* JAPANESE *are silent.*)

LENNON: (*Looking around the room.*) The room is swaying. Maybe it's the wind.

HARRISON: (*Sniffing.*) Smells like sweat and cum in here.   440

JAPANESE: What do you want? Who are you?

LENNON: We're movers. Officially, that is.

JAPANESE: Movers?

LENNON: We have a truck, a tarpaulin, ropes, and all the necessary gear. Moving, packing, transport, that's our line.   445 "You groove it, we'll move it!"

(HARRISON *enters and approaches* KATSURA.)

HARRISON: (*Turning to* LENNON.) Nice piece, eh?

JAPANESE: (*To* LENNON.) What business do movers have here at this time of night?

LENNON: We've brought some packages for you.   450

JAPANESE: Well why didn't you say so? Bring them in and be on your way. (*Worrying about* HARRISON.) There's no need to barge in here like this.

HARRISON: Button up, buddy. (*Indicating the pistol.*) And let's have a look at that six-shooter.   455

JAPANESE: What right do you have to make demands? This is my pistol. There's no reason I should hand it over to you. If you're movers, then you should act like movers and be about your business.

LENNON: It may not seem like it, but we're acting as much like   460 movers as we can. It'd just be better if you'd hand the gun over, that's all. In order to avoid any unpleasantness. You see what I mean?

JAPANESE: Unpleasantness? Listen, you force your way in here. . . .   465

LENNON: I told you, we've brought something for you.

JAPANESE: Then for heaven's sake hurry up with it!

HARRISON: In our own sweet time, baby. We don't need you to tell us how to do our job. Just keep your trap shut and hand over the gun.

JAPANESE: No.

LENNON: It would be best if you'd obey orders. Nothing's going to happen to you. We'll give it back as soon as we're finished.

JAPANESE: There's no reason I should take orders from you.

CHONG: Let them have it.

JAPANESE: You know them?

CHONG: They're the ones from upstairs. They said they wouldn't do anything.

JAPANESE: But. . . .

(HARRISON, *seeing his chance, grabs the pistol from* JAPANESE. JAPANESE, *in turn, moves to attack* HARRISON, *but he is subdued by* LENNON, *who pins him with more than amateur dexterity.*)

LENNON: All right, now relax! Just take it easy. We aren't going to be the first to resort to violence, but we do reserve the right to defend ourselves.

JAPANESE: Let me go!

HARRISON: Hey, the bastard's carrying a bomb!

LENNON: (*To* HARRISON.) Never mind about that. It's only the pistol that's an immediate danger. Put it away so it won't get broken.

HARRISON: Right. (*He turns it over two or three times in the palm of his hand and then puts it in his pocket.*)

LENNON: (*To* JAPANESE.) You're not going to cause any more trouble, now, are you?

HARRISON: It's loaded, isn't it? (*He places his hand menacingly over his pocket.*)

(LENNON *releases* JAPANESE, *who sits smoldering.*)

KATSURA: Uh. . . .

LENNON: Yes?

KATSURA: Are there only two of you?

LENNON: No, four. The other two'll be here in a minute— McCartney the Stripe and Twinkle Starr.

HARRISON: I'm Side-Street Harrison and this is Sundown Lennon. Glad to meet you.

KATSURA: You're a quartet, then?

(MC CARTNEY *and* STARR *enter.* STARR *walks uncertainly and is supported by* MC CARTNEY.)

MC CARTNEY: Good evening.

LENNON: We're the Beatles.

STARR: Bea-tles! Don't you guys have any music around here?

(HARRISON *quickly spies the record player and puts on a record. This, too, is a* BEATLES *number.*)

KATSURA: The Beatles!

JAPANESE: You said you were movers.

LENNON: There's no reason we can't be the Beatles and movers at the same time. The fact of the matter is we're both!

HARRISON: We were having a wake. Couldn't you hear us? "Our Father who art in heaven." . . .

STARR: Departed and deceased! (*She dances to the music.*)

CHONG: Did somebody die?

LENNON: Good thinking! The fact that we were having a wake means that somebody died!

CHONG: Your grandmother?

LENNON: That's one way of putting it.

(HARRISON *guffaws.*)

LENNON: (*To* HARRISON.) It was my grandmother!

HARRISON: Yes, yes. Your grandmother. Your grandmother, of course.

MC CARTNEY: (*To* LENNON.) Come on, let's ask them.

LENNON: Oh, yeah! Listen, we seem to have started off on the wrong foot, but we've got a favor to ask.

CHONG: A favor?

LENNON: Yes, we were wondering if you wouldn't do it for us.

HARRISON: We're bored.

STARR: Just like Elvis Presley!

MC CARTNEY: Shut up, stupid!

CHONG: Do it for you? You mean our play?

MC CARTNEY: That's right. We've come all the way down here now. You wouldn't mind, would you?

CHONG: No, it's out of the question.

LENNON: Plays require an audience. That's the way it works.

CHONG: It's not that kind of play—it's not a play to be shown to anyone. It's . . . it's a play for the acting out.

HARRISON: We're not going to do anything. We'll just sit here quietly and watch, that's all.

LENNON: Of course you're still rehearsing, but that doesn't matter. We realize it's not finished yet.

CHONG: Please leave.

KATSURA: Let's do it! Come on, Chong!

HARRISON: Chong?

STARR: What's a "chong"?

LENNON: It's his name, I guess.

HARRISON: (*Looking at* CHONG.) Ah, a Korean. A diarrhean Korean.

CHONG: Katsura!

KATSURA: It won't make any difference. We were just rehearsing, anyway. (*To* LENNON.) We'll be glad to do the play for you.

CHONG: Katsura!

STARR: Hurray! (*She claps her hands gleefully.*)

CHONG: Katsura!

KATSURA: Please come and sit over here, will you? (*To* JAPANESE.) You, too. (*She arranges* THE QUARTET *and* JAPANESE *against the wall near the window.*)

JAPANESE: (*Changing his tone, unusually familiar.*) Are we really going through with it?

HARRISON: You bet! And you're going to sit with us right here and watch.

CHONG: Not me!

KATSURA: If you don't like it you can just stand there and be quiet. I want the Beatles to see our play.

CHONG: Katsura, these aren't the Beatles! The Beatles you're waiting for. . . .

LENNON: We're the Beatles all right. There's no mistake.

KATSURA: (*To* THE QUARTET.) The play begins. We're on the roof. It's winter. (*She looks at* CHONG, *but he remains expressionless.*) Or perhaps it's autumn, I don't remember exactly. I'm wearing a middy blouse and a thin cotton skirt. It's

570 been two hours since the siren from the factories signaled
the end of the day. I'm alone on the roof of the school, reading. (*She goes to the wall opposite* THE QUARTET, *leans against it
and pretends to read.*) "Do you know the lollipop song?"

(STARR, *who is embracing* MC CARTNEY *as she watches, suddenly
breaks into song.*)

MC CARTNEY: Shhh!
575 STARR: (*Singing.*)

> Lollipop, lollipop, beautiful lollipop.
> Lollipop ponies pink and marching
> Lollipop stops and lollipop starting
> Pop a lolli pill, pop a lolli Polly.

580 LENNON: (*Interested in* STARR's *song, but turning back to* KATSURA.)
And then?
KATSURA: (*Reading.*) "Do you know the lollipop song? . . . I
loved that basement room. There was always a party going
on down there, where everyone danced and bodies touched
585 one another. The place was called Chester, and every evening
I spent three hours there, doing nothing but feeling alive.
Everyone in the place was unsure, unsure of something.
Hardly anyone could afford a cup of coffee; everyone seemed
weary somehow; and everyone carried with him a lonely
590 secret. . . . After everyone had politely shaken hands, we
formed a circle and sang the lollipop song at the top of our
lungs. We passed the multicolored capsules around the circle, popping one, two, three, then sank slowly into our rainbow lollipop whirlpool." (*No longer reading but explaining the
595 play.*) All of a sudden he is standing in front of me....
HARRISON: Who?

(KATSURA *indicates* CHONG.)

HARRISON: Hey, you're on, buster!
KATSURA: He speaks to me, gently.
MC CARTNEY: (*To* CHONG.) Come on, be a sport. Look how hard
600 she's trying.

(CHONG *moves toward* KATSURA *almost unconsciously. Perhaps he
was intending to stop the play.*)

LENNON: (*Forcefully.*) Speak to her!
CHONG: (*Unenthusiastically.*) Hey. (*Apparently resigned, he goes
through the motions of taking* KATSURA's *book away from her.*)

(KATSURA *looks up and smiles.* CHONG *tries to smile back, but his
face assumes a cramped, unhappy expression instead. He looks at*
LENNON, *who returns the look with a friendly wink.*)

MC CARTNEY: Not bad, not bad!
605 CHONG: Here's an apple.
STARR: That's the spirit!
KATSURA: Please return my book.
CHONG: It's green and hard and sour.... The two of us used to
take apples out of a paper bag and eat them in this room. It
610 hasn't been such a long time since we started doing that and
came to live together.
HARRISON: I'll return your book. I'm sorry I took it. If you
don't mind, though, I'd like to talk to you.

LENNON: (*To* HARRISON.) The audience seems to know the lines
better than the actors. 615
KATSURA: (*To both* CHONG *and* HARRISON.) Who are you?
CHONG: I'm....
HARRISON: Katsura, forgive me, I'm....
KATSURA: How do you know my name?
HARRISON: I've been admiring you from afar for some time. I'm 620
sure you've noticed.
CHONG: I've been watching you, you and your friends, sitting
there nearly every day at the back of the coffee shop, mixing cheap whisky, sleeping pills, barbies and bennies. I've
seen your faces contorted in the shadow of a grin. I've 625
looked at you and wondered if your wandering eyes had
pierced the white walls to gaze at some distant landscape.
HARRISON: Why do you run from me? Yesterday it was like
this, and the day before.
CHONG: Come with me, and let's perform a little play I have in 630
mind. I've been looking for someone to work with, and you
seem perfect for the part.
LENNON: (*To* JAPANESE.) You have a smoke?

(JAPANESE *silently hands him a cigarette and lights one for himself.*)

MC CARTNEY: I know where you live. It's the brick house with the
little garden. It's at the top of the hill. Every night I stand in 635
front of your house and look up at the window on the second
floor. The window facing the road is yours, isn't it?
CHONG: If you're waiting for the Beatles, that's all right. Come
with me and we'll wait together. We can even have an apple as we wait. 640
HARRISON: Last Sunday you went out, didn't you? Do you remember? I didn't recognize you at first. You were wearing
makeup and a pair of red high heels.
CHONG: Your mother had already left by the time your father
got home. You'd cried yourself to sleep and were lying in 645
the middle of the room, rolled into a little ball. On the
table were a cardboard box and a letter. Inside the box was
a pair of high-heeled shoes. They were the keepsake your
mother had left for you.
MC CARTNEY: You didn't notice me. Clutching your handbag, 650
your nose in the air, you walked down the hill. I watched
you until you disappeared into the distance.
CHONG: (*To* KATSURA.) I'll work hard and buy you everything
you want. Our room will be our castle, and our castle will
be our reason for living. No matter how hard the day has 655
been, your smile will make it all worthwhile.
HARRISON: Please say something. Your silence makes me feel as
if I were doing something wrong.
KATSURA: I want to go home. Please . . . let me go home.
CHONG: Home? Where is that? 660
KATSURA: Home....
CHONG: What are you talking about? This is your home. This
is our castle. You have no place else.
KATSURA: Mother will be worried. It's late, and....
CHONG: Your mother ran away. You don't remember her, and 665
you never want to see her. You said so yourself.
HARRISON: I'll see you home, and I'll explain to your mother,
so stay just a few minutes more.
KATSURA: Home is neither here nor at the top of the hill. It's
somewhere else, somewhere far away. 670

CHONG: Somewhere else?

KATSURA: You've been very kind to me. You're one of the nicest people I've ever met. But I can't go on. I don't understand what you want me to do. I have to wait for the Beatles. I'm
675   tired. I want to sleep. Suddenly I feel very cold.

HARRISON: I've captured you at last. I'll never let you go. Come with me to the . . . .

CHONG: (*Almost simultaneously.*) Come with me. . . .

KATSURA: Thank you. Thank you very much, but I can't. . . .

680 MC CARTNEY: (*Changing his attitude.*) You feel cold because it's going to snow. But don't worry. It won't be much longer. You can close your eyes. It'll be all right. Soon you'll be where the wind never blows.

KATSURA: I'm afraid. You're so . . . I'm going home. I can find
685   my way alone. Good-bye. Please, don't follow me. (*She starts to get up.*)

MC CARTNEY: Wait!

CHONG: Wait!

(KATSURA *attempts to move toward the door, but* HARRISON *shoves her in* MC CARTNEY's *direction.* MC CARTNEY *wraps his arms roughly around her.*)

(HARRISON *attacks* CHONG. *Grabbing him in a double arm-lock, he forces him into a corner of the room opposite* KATSURA *and her captor.*)

LENNON: (*To* CHONG.) It's a play, that's all, just a play. You
690   understand.

CHONG: Katsura! (*He tries desperately to resist, but* HARRISON *is much too strong for him. To* JAPANESE.) Do something!

HARRISON: I wouldn't count on him if I were you. What good do you think he'll be?

695 CHONG: Hurry up! Help Katsura!

(JAPANESE *remains immobile. Inhaling his cigarette, he calmly observes the two struggling groups of people. Before long both* MCCARTNEY *and* HARRISON *have their adversaries helplessly pinned to the ground.*)

CHONG: Cut it out! Please! What are you trying to do? This is our castle. Get out! The play is over. Get out of here! Get out!

LENNON: No, the play's not over yet. We'll see it through to the
700   end.

HARRISON: What are you so afraid of? We aren't going to do anything. We're just trying to lend a hand, that's all. (*To* JAPANESE.) That's right, isn't it?

(JAPANESE *puts out his cigarette, drinks his water, and eats his onion. Ignoring* HARRISON *and* CHONG, STARR *approaches* MC CARTNEY *and speaks softly to* KATSURA.)

STARR: There's a song about a whorehouse in New Orleans called the House of the Rising Sun. Unless I'm mistaken,
705   the name of your house on the hill was the Hotel Fuji. You remember, don't you? But of course, that was no brothel, was it? It was just an ordinary hotel. Everyone knew that. There was a maid in the Hotel Fuji. Her name was O'Tsune and she used to climb into bed wearing a pair of red high
710   heels. She was small, dark, and a little scrawny. Did the rising sun shine on the Hotel Fuji? It was high on a hill, so the sun must have shone through its windows. Please don't struggle.

(MC CARTNEY *removes* KATSURA's *blouse and throws it to* HARRISON.)

STARR: O'Tsune used to say she'd become a maid at the Hotel Fuji after she ran away from a one-legged coal miner. Of 715 course you can't believe women like that tell you. She also claimed that she had two children. You remember, don't you? Now you see? That wasn't your house. You just felt like it was, that's all. The Hotel Fuji seemed more like a mansion to you than a house of ill repute. To tell the 720 truth, I have no idea where you belong.

HARRISON: (*To* CHONG.) Boy, do you guys stink! What is that smell?

STARR: I can't understand it. I can't understand why you have to run away. O'Tsune never tried to run away. 725

MC CARTNEY: During the summer I worked part time for the iceman. I pulled a heavy wagon loaded with ice.

JAPANESE: A white short-sleeved blouse and white socks. (*Abstractly, to* CHONG.) Do you really think it'll clear up by Sunday? Do you think everything will go all right? 730

MC CARTNEY: The minute I saw you my summer seemed long and hot. Let me tell you about my long, hot summer.

JAPANESE: Will you really appear out of the subway as we planned?

CHONG: (*To* MC CARTNEY.) Please, leave her alone! Leave us both 735 in peace! You're spoiling everything!

LENNON: (*To* CHONG.) Do you really understand what we're doing? How about being a bit quieter?

MC CARTNEY: I saved my money. I read books. I had hopes for my summer. It was easy to live from one day to the next. 740

LENNON: You're the one who was supposed to act this out. Instead, look at the mess you made of it. You couldn't even speak your lines properly. We're here to finish what you've begun. Believe me, we're doing this out of the goodness of our hearts. 745

CHONG: It's all wrong. We were trying to do something different. We . . . .

HARRISON: Then why don't you do it? (*Indicating* MC CARTNEY.) It's not much, but at least he's trying. If you think you can do better, go ahead. Nobody's stopping you. 750

STARR: Suddenly I felt as if an icy wind had blown through my heart. I thought at first that I'd been out in the sun too long.

JAPANESE: (*To* CHONG.) My bomb is perfect. You're the one I'm worried about. 755

CHONG: I thought we agreed to run through the whole thing tomorrow night. You said so yourself!

HARRISON: What's wrong with tonight?

CHONG: Who asked you anyway? We're the ones who have to do it. 760

LENNON: That's right, you are.

STARR: Suddenly my summer seemed hot and oppressive. I had never given much thought to my empty stomach, but suddenly it began to bother me. I came to curse the piercing rays of the sun. 765

MC CARTNEY: You glanced in my direction. I was halfway up the hill and had put down the handle of the wagon to wipe the sweat off my forehead. You remember, don't you?

CHONG: Of course she doesn't remember. That nonsense has nothing to do with our play. 770

HARRISON: If you're so damned smart, get up and do it yourself!

JAPANESE: Yeah, go ahead.

CHONG: Fuck off!

HARRISON: As you like. You couldn't do it anyway. Just keep your trap shut, that's all.

JAPANESE: You're not going to chicken out on me, are you?

(CHONG *remains silent with eyes downcast.*)

JAPANESE: That's what I was afraid of. You're the one who came up with this idea. We knew the story, but the story had no ending. You said you'd go give it one. You're the one who suggested the whole thing. Now I've gone and made this bomb and everything. What do you expect me to do?

CHONG: It's all Katsura's. . . .

LENNON: She'll do whatever you say. Isn't that the way it's always been?

CHONG: She's waiting for the Beatles. She didn't really want to go through with this in the first place.

(*All of a sudden* JAPANESE *begins to participate in the play. Roughly, almost violently, he covers* KATSURA's *body with his own and begins to speak as if he were* CHONG.)

JAPANESE: Listen. This is a play. From now on you have to play your part in it. Okay, now look at me. I'm Chong. Chong. Chong. Chong. Chong. Chong! A Korean. And you're Katsura. You are a Japanese girl named Katsura. I'm Korean and you're Japanese. That's why your father isn't going back to the peninsula. Why should he? He's having a nice cup of hot tea with your mother and waiting for you to come home. But your old man's in for a surprise, because Chong's going to murder you. Rape you and then murder you. Next Chong will be murdered by the Japanese. That's the play. We have to act it out. We have to see it through. Yes, we have to act the play out to the end. We have to be faithful to its pattern until the curtain falls and the house lights come up.

STARR: You passed me by. You didn't even know I existed. Yes, perhaps that's the way it happened. You didn't see that as I watched you walk down that narrow, dusty road I imagined myself jumping you from behind.

HARRISON: You hate me, don't you? You hate me! You hate me, I can tell. But maybe that's why. Maybe I try so hard to hold you because you try so hard to get away. Maybe someone else might have done as well, someone else who pretended I didn't exist.

STARR: Hate me! It doesn't matter. Hate me! I'm going to kill you. Struggle! Try to run away. Try as if your life depended upon it!

JAPANESE: She ran away. My mother and the others tried to run away. But your old man . . . your old man! He sits smoking his pipe in that big house on the hill. He's waiting for his daughter to come home, and he's beginning to get worried because it's late. That's your old man today. But in the yellow distance of an all but forgotten past, it was your old man who dragged my mother by the hair from her hut and did just what I'm doing! (*He fondles* KATSURA's *thighs, and his tone changes suddenly.*) Is that the way it was, Katsura? Can you believe it? Can you perform a play like this and really believe it? Don't you think it's ridiculous? Chong? The very idea that he could ever be a Korean! Katsura, you understand, don't you? You've understood for a long time. He failed. Failed! He brought you here and tried to make you play opposite his imitation Korean. But as luck would have it . . . (*He laughs convulsively.*) . . . as luck would have it, your father, bless his soul, your father really was a Korean! (*His laughter grows louder.*) That really threw him for a loop. Like some idiot he tried to reconcile his fantasies with the facts. His little play got all caught up in itself! What a mess! Can you believe it? Fantastic! Katsura, can you believe it?

(JAPANESE *goes on laughing. He buries his face in* KATSURA's *crotch, his whole body shaking with laughter. His hands move spasmodically over* KATSURA's *body.* KATSURA *groans quietly, pleasurably, her body responding to the stimulation, increasingly . . .*)

JAPANESE: (*Lifting his head, in a small voice.*) Katsura, keep your eyes closed. There's nothing to see. There's no such person as Chong. It was only make-believe. Stupid play-acting. A common . . . ordinary . . . KATSURA!!!

(KATSURA *draws a sudden, deep breath. It sounds like a cry of anguish.*)

KATSURA: Beatles! I've been waiting so long! Finally . . . finally! . . .

CHONG: Katsura! . . .

KATSURA: I knew it. I just knew that someday I'd have a wonderful dinner with John, George, Paul, and Ringo in the dining room of the ship, with freshly caught fish and sweet wine. That was all I wanted. I'd sleep with you in turn and have your children one by one. But by that time you'd be gone. I'd be satisfied with just one dinner and a night on the high seas, sleeping with one of you and then another. Then smiling, wearing a long, white dress, I'd take our four children out for a stroll. I'd be proud of my soft, gentle, tummy, and I'd sing the song I made in it.

(KATSURA *greedily embraces* JAPANESE.)

JAPANESE: (*To* CHONG.) It was on the beach. You never knew. The two of us looked far out to sea for a long time. "It's a yacht. It may arrive here any minute," she said and invited me to join her.

STARR: (*Disappointed.*) You're not going to try to escape after all! You're not going to hate me, are you!

LENNON: (*To* CHONG.) You strangle Katsura.

MC CARTNEY: I murder you.

HARRISON: Let me at the son of a bitch!

STARR: Get him!

JAPANESE: Please understand. I really don't care what happens to you. The reason I've worked so hard to help you with this play has had nothing to do with the little crime you hoped to mimic.

LENNON: (*Laughing.*) Crime? The murder of a schoolgirl? Chickenshit!

CHONG: Katsura! You've been after Katsura from the first!

HARRISON: Big deal!

(THE QUARTET *moves away from* KATSURA, *apparently having lost interest in her.*)

KATSURA: Hold me, Paul. Hold me, John. Hold me, George
870   and Ringo!
JAPANESE: I touched her tummy. You're listening, aren't you?
    Her tummy taught me how to make my bomb. I'm afraid
    it won't do for you to be stabbed to death. It wouldn't do
    for you to die peacefully, reassured by the blood flowing
875   from your body. You have to be blown limb from limb. Be-
    cause it's all your fault!
CHONG: Yes, the bomb . . . the bomb will be fine. Now!
JAPANESE: I knew from the first. I knew you wouldn't be able
    to go through with it. You couldn't even take Katsura. Do
880   you deny it? You've never even held her!
KATSURA: (*Murmuring.*) Come to me . . . come . . . come to me,
    everyone. Touch my tummy . . . listen to its song.
CHONG: Katsura. . . .

(CHONG *leaps at* JAPANESE. JAPANESE, *however, is unresisting; he
gives* KATSURA *up without a struggle.*)

JAPANESE: Too late, my friend. Much, much too late.

(CHONG *straddles* KATSURA. MC CARTNEY, HARRISON, LENNON,
and STARR *once again turn their attention to the play.*)

885   KATSURA: Who is it? Who are you?
CHONG: It's me.
KATSURA: Chong?
CHONG: Yes, it's me.
LENNON: (*Coolly.*) You have to do things in order. You mustn't
890   kill her yet.
HARRISON: First you have to rape her.
CHONG: This is my revenge for what your father. . . .
JAPANESE: (*Scornfully.*) Her feet are cold inside her white
    bobby-socks.
895   STARR: (*Angrily.*) I was bored beyond words. I want my sum-
    mer back!
CHONG: (*Suppressing his emotions as much as possible.*) I've been
    cold every summer of my life.
KATSURA: I wrote in my diary. . . .
900   LENNON: Invisible diary . . . nonexistent diary. Say it! Say you
    hate me! I'm a Korean!
QUARTET: Diarrhean Korean smells like shit! Not worth a
    penny or his weight in spit!
KATSURA: I mustn't wear the red high heels. I mustn't wait for
905   the Beatles, either. That's what you said. You made an aw-
    ful face. Every night I read my old diary and try not to sing
    the lollipop song. I'm just a simple girl with a wandering
    glance and a soft tummy . . . a girl like any other, that's all.
    But I knew. I knew, because I'm the type who thinks with
910   her tummy, that you'd never be able to touch me. The
    Japanese bit my shoulder. It hurt terribly, but that's his way
    of being kind. He tries hard to set me afire with his flicker-
    ing flame. That's his way of being kind. But you're differ-
    ent. You have no flame of your own. You're lame. You came
915   limping to me out of loneliness. You spoke to me self-con-
    sciously of a murder I'd heard about long ago. Before I
    knew it you had things arranged so that on a certain Sun-
    day, you and the Japanese and I would march out of the sub-
    way arms locked and whistling, onto a broad avenue. And
920   a bomb would come floating down almost like a joke and
    land in front of us. . . . But it's too late. You didn't make it.

This is where our paths part. They have to. The Beatles are
    coming for me!
CHONG: The velocity of the falling bomb . . . a back alley . . . a
    knife . . . the peninsula . . . noise, laughing voices. . . .   925

(*The stage goes black for an instant. Out of the darkness* STARR's
*voice: "Departed and deceased!" A Beatles song begins, and then the
lights come up again.*)

(CHONG *lies with a knife in his chest. He is dead.* KATSURA *is beside* CHONG. THE QUARTET *and* JAPANESE *stand around them.*)

KATSURA: Reading an imaginary book. "'Chong' leaves on a
    lonely journey. 'Chong' doesn't ride a bicycle or take a boat.
    He turns his back on the others and walks toward a kind-
    ness of his own at the speed of clotting blood."

(THE QUARTET *claps enthusiastically.*)

LENNON: Wonderful! Really marvelous!   930
HARRISON: (*Mimicking.*) "This is where our paths part. They
    have to. The Beatles are coming for me." Ha-ha-ha-ha!
LENNON: (*To* JAPANESE.) Looks like you've lost your part.
HARRISON: You don't have to take revenge anymore.
KATSURA: Take me with you.   935
LENNON: Where?
KATSURA: To Liverpool, my Liverpool, to the Emerald
    Peninsula.
HARRISON: Sorry. We're the Beatles, all right, but I'm afraid
    we're not your Beatles. (*Realizing.*) That's right, I almost   940
    forgot!

(HARRISON *looks over his shoulder at* LENNON, *who nods.*)

HARRISON: We'll introduce you to your Beatles. We'll intro-
    duce you right away. Wait one second.

(LENNON *and* HARRISON *exit.*)

JAPANESE: (*To* CHONG's *lifeless form.*) "The Japanese." It seems
    the time has come to return your role. You were "The   945
    Japanese" all along. It would have been better if you'd
    played your own part from the first. (*He produces a flag, red
    sun on white field, and carefully covers the corpse. Pointing.*) He
    looks like a hero, dying like this.
KATSURA: Yes.   950
JAPANESE: You must be tired. You'd better rest.
KATSURA: They weren't the ones, were they?
JAPANESE: It doesn't look like it.

(MC CARTNEY *and* STARR *start to hum a funeral march. Picking up
the tune,* LENNON *and* HARRISON *enter carrying four white coffins.*)

KATSURA: Are . . . are those the Beatles?
HARRISON: I'm afraid they're no longer with us.   955
JAPANESE: Don't believe them, Katsura. They're lying. Those
    coffins are empty.

(JAPANESE *approaches the coffins and is about to open their lids.*)

KATSURA: (*Firmly.*) Don't!
JAPANESE: But. . . .
KATSURA: Please, just leave them as they are.   960

HARRISON: Now you see, we're movers. Are you satisfied? We've brought these four parcels, just as we said.

KATSURA: You've come at last. But you're dead! Why? Why? (*She bursts into tears over the coffins.*)

965   HARRISON: (*Staring at* KATSURA.) What's she bawling about? Maybe it's that onion.

KATSURA: Why did they have to die?

LENNON: It's hard to say, actually. It was a cold night. All four of them went at once.

970   JAPANESE: That's ridiculous! You're back to playing games.

KATSURA: They were my Beatles. I'd waited for them so long!

HARRISON: Of course.

KATSURA: They came from the peninsula, didn't they?

LENNON: Couldn't be sure, actually. Perhaps.

975   KATSURA: Was the peninsula emerald-colored?

LENNON: Perhaps.

KATSURA: Were there open pastures at the foot of rolling hills?

LENNON: Perhaps.

KATSURA: And horses grazing?

980   LENNON: Perhaps.

KATSURA: Grass with flowers?

LENNON: Perhaps!! (THE QUARTET *exchange glances and burst out laughing.*)

KATSURA: Oh.

STARR: (*Still laughing.*) Come on, everybody, let's have a funeral, a double funeral for Chong and the Beatles, how about it?   985

(MC CARTNEY *puts on a record.*)

STARR: Let's dance!

LENNON: That's the ticket! (*To* JAPANESE.) Come on, you too! (*To* KATSURA.) You, too! We'll have a wild funeral for our departed friends!   990

KATSURA: (*Softly.*) Wait.

(*Everyone looks at* KATSURA.)

KATSURA: Just now . . . there was something there. It looked like a bird.

(*Everyone stares at* KATSURA *for a moment, then goes back to dancing. The song is "A Hard Day's Night" by the Beatles.*)

(*Curtain.*)

Aimé Césaire

Aimé Césaire, one of the most prominent and influential theorists of postcolonial culture, was born in Martinique, West Indies, in 1913; he was educated there, and in Paris at L'École Normale Supérieur, and in 1934 began *L'Étudiant Noir* with Leopold Senghor and Léon Damas. Since 1946, Césaire has served as deputy from Martinique in the French National Assembly, and was a founding member of the Parti Progressiste Martiniquais, which came to power in 1950; he served as the mayor of the capital city, Fort-de-France from 1945 to 1993. Throughout the 1950s and 1960s, Césaire laid the foundations for the theory of post-colonial culture and was closely associated with the Négritude movement—the assertion of black history, culture, and identity in the face of oppressive European culture—and he used his political influence to establish cultural institutions, such as the Service Minicipale d'Action Culturelle, a school offering training in traditional Caribbean performing arts, in 1976, that would extend this understanding of Caribbean identity. Césaire's cultural criticism—*Discourse on Colonialism* (1950), *Toussaint L'Ouverture: The French Revolution and the Colonial Problem* (1960), *Culture and Colonization* (1978)—were accompanied by several volumes of poetry and four plays: *And the Dogs Were Quiet* (1956), *The Tragedy of King Christophe* (1964), *A Season in the Congo* (1966), and *A Tempest* (1969).

A TEMPEST

Césaire's *A Tempest* is one of many works written in the past forty years taking Shakespeare's play as a site for revising colonial experience: O. Mannoni's psychoanalytic study, *Prospero and Caliban: The Psychology of Colonization* (1950); Max Dorsinville's *Caliban Without Prospero* (1974); the Cuban critic Roberto Fernández Retamar's brilliant essay, *Caliban* (1974); and David Malouf's dramatic resetting of the play to contemporary Australia, *Blood Relations* (1987), to name only a few. Shakespeare's *The Tempest* was based in part on accounts of a shipwreck in the Americas (see Unit III), and although Prospero's island seems to be at once in the Bermudas and the Mediterranean, most commentators have seen in *The Tempest* Shakespeare's representation of contact between European and New World peoples. Prospero, for example, both exploits Caliban's knowledge of the island and enslaves him and Ariel, a clear symmetry with European behavior throughout Africa and the Americas. For this reason, invoking Caliban as a kind of guiding spirit, or rewriting *The Tempest* to bring this dynamic more to the surface, has become an important strategy for evoking the relations between colonizer and colonized.

Aimé Césaire's *A Tempest* makes several uses of Shakespeare's play, taking both a more colloquial and a more clearly political perspective on the action. When Prospero is forced into exile by his brother and the Inquisition, he is trying to conceal a secret "empire" that he has discovered, ripe for conquest; when Alonso sets sail to find it, Prospero uses his magic to divert him to the island, so as to save the empire for later exploitation. We also get some idea of what kind of king Prospero might be from his treatment of Caliban and Ariel, who themselves demonstrate a range of attitudes held by colonized subjects. While Caliban refuses, like many African Americans, to continue using his "slave name" and wants to be called simply "X," like a man "whose name has been stolen," Ariel serves Prospero as a kind of overseer and identifies his interests with him.

Césaire develops a resistant reading of Shakespeare in a number of ways: showing how Prospero's power divides rather than unites Ariel and Caliban; depicting how manual labor is fit only for the indigenous Caliban, not for the European Ferdinand; summoning Eshu to invade Prospero's masque of the classical goddesses; staging Caliban's overwhelming desire for revolution. Césaire's rewriting of Shakespeare, and his critique of European colonial representation, is focused in the final scene of *A Tempest,* which enacts a striking reversal of *The Tempest.* In Césaire's version, Prospero finds the pleasures of colonial rule so irresistible, he refuses to return to Europe.

Translator's Note

The translation of Aimé Césaire's *Une Tempête* presented more challenges than usually arise in the transfer of a play from one language into another (differences in cultural background, tone, milieu, and so on). Although Césaire has denied attempting any linguistic echo of Shakespeare, the transposition of his play into English inevitably calls up such echoes, for the literate English/American playgoer cannot help but "hear," behind the language of the play, the original text resounding in all its well-known beauty, its familiarity. For the translator, therefore, the temptation to quote the Ariel songs, for example, or to paraphrase them, was strong. When Césaire has his Ariel sing of something "proche et étrange," for example, Shakespeare's "rich and strange" must, inevitably, sound in the translator's mind.

I have attempted to avoid temptation (there is, if I recall, only one instance of direct quotation in the prose text, but it fell so aptly into place that I was unable to resist); in the main I have left the (slightly altered) song for Ariel with its Shakespearean references unchanged. In an appendix I have now added a "literal" translation of Césaire's text to give a better notion of the imagery he uses for the character. As for the other songs in the text, the options indicated are extremely free adaptations or indications of what I felt to be the substance of the originals or (as in the case of "Oh, Susannah" and "Blow the Man Down") songs familiar to an English-speaking audience that I thought reflected something of the spirit and possible familiarity of the originals.

For this revised edition, I have also included, as an appendix, a "literal" translation of these songs as they occur in French.

Then there is the question of overall tone of voice, taken for granted in *The Tempest,* where social classes, the real and the spirit worlds, are a given. In *A Tempest,* with its Caribbean (and therefore colonial) setting and its consecration to a black theater, it is essential, I feel, for the director and the actors to decide what accents, what "classes," they wish the various characters to reflect. In my own head, I have heard Ariel's song, for example, as vaguely calypso; others will have other ideas. The director may also wish to emphasize the "political" aspects of the play, in which case the accents employed by the actors would tend to serve that purpose. In any event, in translating the play I have not tried to indicate accent (other than in the Ariel song) and where slang or obscenities have been employed, the emphasis to be given will be set by the director or actor in the way that will best reflect and enhance the tone and style of the particular production.

—Richard Miller

A TEMPEST

Aimé Césaire

TRANSLATED BY RICHARD MILLER

CHARACTERS

ARIEL	FERDINAND	GODS *and* GODDESSES (CERES, JUNO)
TRINCULO/CAPTAIN	ALONSO	BOATSWAIN
CALIBAN	ESHU/MASTER OF CEREMONIES	SAILORS
STEPHANO	MIRANDA	THE FRIAR
GONZALO	SEBASTIAN	ELVES
PROSPERO	ANTONIO	NYMPHS

Ambiance of a psychodrama. The actors enter singly, at random, and each chooses for himself a mask at his leisure.

MASTER OF CEREMONIES: Come gentlemen, help yourselves. To each his character, to each character his mask. You, Prospero? Why not? He has reserves of will power he's not even aware of himself. You want Caliban? Well, that's re-
5 vealing. Ariel? Fine with me. And what about Stephano, Trinculo? No takers? Ah, just in time! It takes all kinds to make a world.

And after all, they aren't the worst characters. No problem about the juvenile leads, Miranda and Ferdinand. You,
10 okay. And there's no problem about the villains either: you, Antonio; you, Alonso, perfect! Oh, Christ! I was forgetting the Gods. Eshu will fit you like a glove. As for the other parts, just take what you want and work it out among yourselves. But make up your minds . . . Now, there's one part I
15 have to pick out myself: you! It's for the part of the Tempest, and I need a storm to end all storms . . . I need a really big guy to do the wind. Will you do that? Fine! And then someone strong for Captain of the ship. Good, now let's go. Ready? Begin. Blow, winds! Rain and lightning *ad lib!*

ACT ONE

SCENE I

GONZALO: Of course, we're only straws tossed on the raging sea . . . but all's not lost, Gentlemen. We just have to try to get to the eye of the storm.
ANTONIO: We might have known this old fool would nag us
5 to death!
SEBASTIAN: To the bitter end!
GONZALO: Try to understand what I'm telling you: imagine a huge cylinder like the chimney of a lamp, fast as a galloping horse, but in the center as still and unmoving as Cy-
10 clop's eye. That's what we're talking about when we say "the eye of the storm" and that's where we have to get.
ANTONIO: Oh, great! Do you really mean that the cyclone or Cyclops, if he can't see the beam in his own eye, will let us escape! Oh, that's very illuminating!
15 GONZALO: It's a clever way of putting it, at any rate. Literally false, but yet quite true. But what's the fuss going on up there? The Captain seems worried. (*Calling.*) Captain!
CAPTAIN: (*With a shrug.*) Boatswain!
BOATSWAIN: Aye, sir!

CAPTAIN: We're coming round windward of the island. At this 20 speed we'll run aground. We've got to turn her around. Heave to! (*Exits.*)
BOATSWAIN: Come on, men! Heave to! To the topsail; man the ropes. Pull! Heave ho, heave ho!
ALONSO: (*Approaching.*) Well, Boatswain, how are things go- 25 ing? Where are we?
BOATSWAIN: If you ask me, you'd all be better off below, in your cabins.
ANTONIO: *He* doesn't seem too happy. We'd better ask the Captain. Where's the Captain, Boatswain? He was here just a 30 moment ago, and now he's gone off.
BOATSWAIN: Get back below where you belong! We've got work to do!
GONZALO: My dear fellow, I can quite understand your being nervous, but a man should be able to control himself in any 35 situation, even the most upsetting.
BOATSWAIN: Shove it! If you want to save your skins, you'd better get yourselves back down below to those first-class cabins of yours.
GONZALO: Now, now, my good fellow, you don't seem to know 40 to whom you're speaking. (*Making introductions.*) The King's brother, the King's son and myself, the King's counsellor.
BOATSWAIN: King! King! Well, there's someone who doesn't give a fuck more about the kind that he does about you or 45 me, and he's called the Gale. His Majesty the Gale! And right now, he's in control and we're all his subjects.
GONZALO: He might just as well be pilot on the ferry to hell . . . his mouth's foul enough!
ANTONIO: In a sense, the fellow *r*egales me, as you might say. 50 We'll pull through, you'll see, because he looks to me more like someone who'll end up on the gallows, not beneath the billows.
SEBASTIAN: The end result is the same. The fish will get us and the crows will get him. 55
GONZALO: He did irritate me, rather. However, I take the attenuating circumstances into account . . . and, you must admit, he lacks neither courage nor wit.
BOATSWAIN: (*Returning.*) Pull in the stud sails. Helmsman, into the wind! Into the wind! 60

(*Enter* SEBASTIAN, ANTONIO, GONZALO.)

BOATSWAIN: You again! If you keep bothering us and don't get below and say your prayers I'll give up and let you sail the ship! You can't expect me to be the go-between for your souls and Beelzebub!

65 ANTONIO: It's really too much! The fellow is taking advantage of the situation . . .

BOATSWAIN: Windward! Windward! Heave into the wind!

(*Thunder, lightning.*)

SEBASTIAN: Ho! Ho!

GONZALO: Did you see that? There, at the top of the masts, in
70   the rigging, that glitter of blue fire, flashing, flashing? They're right when they call these magic lands, so different from our homes in Europe . . . Look, even the lightning is different!

ANTONIO: Maybe its a foretaste of the hell that awaits us.

75 GONZALO: You're too pessimistic. Anyway, I've always kept myself in a state of grace, ready to meet my maker.

(SAILORS *enter.*)

SAILORS: Shit! We're sinking!

(*The passengers can be heard singing "Nearer, my God, to Thee . . ."*)

BOATSWAIN: To leeward! To leeward!

FERDINAND: (*Entering.*) Alas! There's no one in hell . . . all the
80   devils are here!

(*The ship sinks.*)

SCENE II

MIRANDA: Oh God! Oh God! A sinking ship! Father, help!

PROSPERO: (*Enters hurriedly carrying a megaphone.*) Come daughter, calm yourself! It's only a play. There's really nothing wrong. Anyway, everything that happens is for our own
5   good. Trust me, I won't say any more.

MIRANDA: But such a fine ship, and so many fine, brave lives sunk, drowned, laid waste to wrack and ruin . . . A person would have to have a heart of stone not to be moved . . .

PROSPERO: Drowned . . . hmmm. That remains to be seen. But
10   draw near, dear Princess. The time has come.

MIRANDA: You're making fun of me, father. Wild as I am, you know I am happy—like a queen of the wildflowers, of the streams and paths, running barefoot through thorns and flowers, spared by one, caressed by the other.

15 PROSPERO: But you are a Princess . . . for how else does one address the daughter of a Prince? I cannot leave you in ignorance any longer. Milan is the city of your birth, and the city where for many years I was the Duke.

MIRANDA: Then how did we come here? And tell me, too, by
20   what ill fortune did a prince turn into the reclusive hermit you are now, here, on this desert isle? Was it because you found the world distasteful, or through the perfidy of some enemy? Is our island a prison or a hermitage? You've hinted at some mystery so many times and aroused my curiosity,
25   and today you shall tell me all.

PROSPERO: In a way, it is because of all the things you mention. First, it is because of political disagreements, because of the intrigues of my ambitious younger brother. Antonio is his name, your uncle, and Alonso the name of the envious King
30   of Naples. How their ambitions were joined, how my

brother became the accomplice of my rival, how the latter promised the former his protection and my throne . . . the devil alone knows how all that came about. In any event, when they learned that through my studies and experiments I had managed to discover the exact location of these
35   lands for which many had sought for centuries and that I was making preparations to set forth to take possession of them, they hatched a scheme to steal my as-yet-unborn empire from me. They bribed my people, they stole my charts and documents and, to get rid of me, they denounced
40   me to the Inquisition as a magician and sorcerer. To be brief, one day I saw arriving at the palace men to whom I had never granted audience: the priests of the Holy Office.

(*Flashback: Standing before* PROSPERO, *who is wearing his ducal robes, we see a* FRIAR *reading from a parchment scroll.*)

THE FRIAR: The Holy Inquisition for the preservation and integrity of the Faith and the pursuit of heretical perversion,
45   acting through the special powers entrusted to it by the Holy Apostolic See, informed of the errors you profess, insinuate and publish against God and his Creation with regard to the shape of the Earth and the possibility of discovering other lands, notwithstanding the fact that the Prophet
50   Isaiah stated and taught that the Lord God is seated upon the circle of the Earth and in its center is Jerusalem and that around the world lies inaccessible Paradise, convinced that it is through wickedness that you support your heresy you quote Strabus, Ptolemy and the tragic author Seneca, thereby lend-
55   ing credence to the notion that profane writings can aspire to an authority equal to that of the most profound of the Holy Scriptures, given your notorious use by both night and day of Arabic calculations and scribblings in Hebrew, Syrian and other demonic tongues and, lastly, given that you have
60   hitherto escaped punishment owing to your temporal authority and have, if not usurped, then transformed that authority and made it into a tyranny, doth hereby strip you of your titles, positions and honors in order that it may then proceed against you according to due process through a full
65   and thorough examination, under which authority we require that you accompany us.

PROSPERO: (*Back in the present.*) And yet, the trial they said they were going to hold never took place. Such creatures of darkness are too much afraid of the light. To be brief: instead of
70   killing me they chose—even worse—to maroon me here with you on this desert island.

MIRANDA: How terrible, and how wicked the world is! How you must have suffered!

PROSPERO: In all this tale of treason and felony there is but one
70   honorable name: Gonzalo, counsellor to the King of Naples and fit to serve a better master. By furnishing me with food and clothing, by supplying me with my books and instruments, he has done all in his power to make my exile in this disgusting place bearable. And now, through a singular
80   turn, Fortune has brought to these shores the very men involved in the plot against me. My prophetic science had of course already informed me that they would not be content merely with seizing my lands in Europe and that their greed would win out over their cowardice, that they would
85   confront the sea and set out for those lands my genius had

discovered. I couldn't let them get away with that, and since I was able to stop them, I did so, with the help of Ariel. We brewed up the storm you have just witnessed,
90 thereby saving my possessions overseas and bringing the scoundrels into my power at the same time.

(*Enter* ARIEL.)

PROSPERO: Well, Ariel?
ARIEL: Mission accomplished.
PROSPERO: Bravo; good work! But what seems to be the mat-
95 ter? I give you a compliment and you don't seem pleased? Are you tired?
ARIEL: Not tired; disgusted. I obeyed you but—well, why not come out with it?—I did so most unwillingly. It was a real pity to see that great ship go down, so full of life.
100 PROSPERO: Oh, so you're upset, are you! It's always like that with you intellectuals! Who cares! What interests me is not your moods, but your deeds. Let's split: I'll take the zeal and you can keep your doubts. Agreed?
ARIEL: Master, I must beg you to spare me this kind of labour.
105 PROSPERO: (*Shouting.*) Listen, and listen good! There's a task to be performed, and I don't care how it gets done!
ARIEL: You've promised me my freedom a thousand times, and I'm still waiting.
PROSPERO: Ingrate! And who freed you from Sycorax, may I
110 ask? Who rent the pine in which you had been imprisoned and brought you forth?
ARIEL: Sometimes I almost regret it . . . After all, I might have turned into a real tree in the end . . . Tree: that's a word that really gives me a thrill! It often springs to mind: palm
115 tree—springing into the sky like a fountain ending in non-chalant, squid-like elegance. The baobab—twisted like the soft entrails of some monster. Ask the calao bird that lives a cloistered season in its branches. Or the Ceiba tree—spread out beneath the proud sun. O bird, o green mansions
120 set in the living earth!
PROSPERO: Stuff it! I don't like talking trees. As for your free-dom, you'll have it when I'm good and ready. In the mean-while, see to the ship. I'm going to have a few words with Master Caliban. I've been keeping my eye on him, and he's
125 getting a little too emancipated. (*Calling.*) Caliban! Cal-iban! (*He sighs.*)

(*Enter* CALIBAN.)

CALIBAN: Uhuru!
PROSPERO: What did you say?
CALIBAN: I said, Uhuru!
130 PROSPERO: Mumbling your native language again! I've already told you, I don't like it. You could be polite, at least; a sim-ple "hello" wouldn't kill you.
CALIBAN: Oh, I forgot . . . But make that as froggy, waspish, pustular and dung-filled "hello" as possible. May today has-
135 ten by a decade the day when all the birds of the sky and beasts of the earth will feast upon your corpse!
PROSPERO: Gracious as always, you ugly ape! How can anyone be so ugly?
CALIBAN: You think I'm ugly . . . well, I don't think you're so
140 handsome yourself. With that big hooked nose, you look

just like some old vulture. (*Laughing.*) An old vulture with a scrawny neck!
PROSPERO: Since you're so fond of invective, you could at least thank me for having taught you to speak at all. You, a sav-age . . . a dumb animal, a beast I educated, trained, dragged 145
up from the bestiality that still clings to you.
CALIBAN: In the first place, that's not true. You didn't teach me a thing! Except to jabber in your own language so that I could understand your orders: chop the wood, wash the dishes, fish for food, plant vegetables, all because you're too 150
lazy to do it yourself. And as for your learning, did you ever impart any of *that* to me? No, you took care not to. All your science you keep for yourself alone, shut up in those big books.
PROSPERO: What would you be without me?   155
CALIBAN: Without you? I'd be the king, that's what I'd be, the King of the Island. The king of the island given me by my mother, Sycorax.
PROSPERO: There are some family trees it's better not to climb! She's a ghoul! A witch from whom—and may God be 160
praised—death has delivered us.
CALIBAN: Dead or alive, she was my mother, and I won't deny her! Anyhow, you only think she's dead because you think the earth itself is dead . . . It's so much simpler that way! Dead, you can walk on it, pollute it, you can tread 165
upon it with the steps of a conqueror. I respect the earth, because I know that it is alive, and I know that Sycorax is alive.
Sycorax. Mother.
Serpent, rain, lightning.   170
And I see thee everywhere!
In the eye of the stagnant pool which stares back at me, through the rushes,
in the gesture made by twisted root and its awaiting thrust.
In the night, the all-seeing blinded night,   175
the nostril-less all-smelling night!
    . . . Often, in my dreams, she speaks to me and warns me . . . Yesterday, even, when I was lying by the stream on my belly lapping at the muddy water, when the Beast was about to spring upon me with that huge stone in his 180
hand . . .
PROSPERO: If you keep on like that even your magic won't save you from punishment!
CALIBAN: That's right, that's right! In the beginning, the gentle-man was all sweet talk: dear Caliban here, my little Cal– 185
iban there! And what do you think you'd have done with-out me in this strange land? Ingrate! I taught you the trees, fruits, birds, the seasons, and now you don't give a damn . . . Caliban the animal, Caliban the slave! I know that story! Once you've squeezed the juice from the orange, 190
you toss the rind away!
PROSPERO: Oh!
CALIBAN: Do I lie? Isn't it true that you threw me out of your house and made me live in a filthy cave. The ghetto!
PROSPERO: It's easy to say "ghetto"! It wouldn't be such a 195
ghetto if you took the trouble to keep it clean! And there's something you forgot, which is that what forced me to get rid of you was your lust. Good God, you tried to rape my daughter!

200 CALIBAN: Rape! Rape! Listen, you old goat, you're the one that
put those dirty thoughts in my head. Let me tell you something: I couldn't care less about your daughter, or about
your cave, for that matter. If I gripe, it's on principle, because I didn't like living with you at all, as a matter of fact.
205 Your feet stink!

PROSPERO: I did not summon you here to argue. Out! Back to
work! Wood, water, and lots of both! I'm expecting company today.

CALIBAN: I've had just about enough. There's already a pile of
210 wood that high . . .

PROSPERO: Enough! Careful, Caliban! If you keep grumbling
you'll be whipped. And if you don't step lively, if you keep
dragging your feet or try to strike or sabotage things, I'll
beat you. Beating is the only language you really under-
215 stand. So much the worse for you: I'll speak it, loud and
clear. Get a move on!

CALIBAN: All right, I'm going . . . but this is the last time. It's
the last time, do you hear me? Oh . . . I forgot: I've got
something important to tell you.

220 PROSPERO: Important? Well, out with it.

CALIBAN: It's this: I've decided I don't want to be called Caliban
any longer.

PROSPERO: What kind of rot is that? I don't understand.

CALIBAN: Put it this way: I'm *telling* you that from now on I
225 won't answer to the name Caliban.

PROSPERO: Where did you get that idea?

CALIBAN: Well, because Caliban *isn't* my name. It's as simple as
that.

PROSPERO: Oh, I suppose it's mine!

230 CALIBAN: It's the name given me by your hatred, and everytime
it's spoken it's an insult.

PROSPERO: My, aren't we getting sensitive! All right, suggest
something else . . . I've got to call you something. What
will it be? Cannibal would suit you, but I'm sure you
235 wouldn't like that, would you? Let's see . . . what about
Hannibal? That fits. And why not . . . they all seem to like
historical names.

CALIBAN: Call me X. That would be best. Like a man without
a name. Or, to be more precise, a man whose name has been
240 stolen. You talk about history . . . well, that's history, and
everyone knows it! Every time you summon me it reminds
me of a basic fact, the fact that you've stolen everything
from me, even my identity! Uhuru! (*He exits.*)

(*Enter* ARIEL *as a sea-nymph.*)

PROSPERO: My dear Ariel, did you see how he looked at me,
245 that glint in his eye? That's something new. Well, let me tell
you, Caliban is the enemy. As for those people on the boat,
I've changed my mind about them. Give them a scare,
but for God's sake don't touch a hair of their heads! You'll
answer to me if you do.

250 ARIEL: I've suffered too much myself for having made them suffer not to be pleased at your mercy. You can count on me,
Master.

PROSPERO: Yes, however great their crimes, if they repent you
can assure them of my forgiveness. They are men of my race,
255 and of high rank. As for me, at my age one must rise above
disputes and quarrels and think about the future. I have a

daughter. Alonso has a son. If they were to fall in love, I
would give my consent. Let Ferdinand marry Miranda, and
may their marriage bring us harmony and peace. That is my
plan. I want it executed. As for Caliban, does it matter what 260
that villain plots against me? All the nobility of Italy,
Naples and Milan henceforth combined, will protect me
bodily. Go!

ARIEL: Yes, Master. Your orders will be fully carried out.

(ARIEL *sings.*)

Sandy seashore, deep blue sky, 265
Surf is rising, sea birds fly
Here the lover finds delight,
Sun at noontime, moon at night.
Join hands lovers, join the dance,
Find contentment, find romance. 270

Sandy seashore, deep blue sky,
Cares will vanish . . . so can I . . .

FERDINAND: What is this music? It has led me here and now it
stops . . . No, there it is again . . .

ARIEL: (*Singing.*) 275

Waters move, the ocean flows,
Nothing comes and nothing goes . . .
Strange days are upon us . . .

Oysters stare through pearly eyes
Heart-shaped corals gently beat 280
In the crystal undersea

Waters move and ocean flows,
Nothing comes and nothing goes . . .
Strange days are upon us . . .

FERDINAND: What is this that I see before me? A goddess? A 285
mortal?

MIRANDA: I know what *I'm* seeing: a flatterer. Young man, your
ability to pay compliments in the situation in which you
find yourself at least proves your courage. Who are you?

FERDINAND: As you see, a poor shipwrecked soul. 290

MIRANDA: But one of high degree!

FERDINAND: In other surroundings I might be called "Prince,"
"son of the King" . . . But, no, I was forgetting . . . not
"Prince" but "King," alas . . . "King" because my father has
just perished in the shipwreck. 295

MIRANDA: Poor young man! Here, you'll be received with hospitality and we'll support you in your misfortune.

FERDINAND: Alas, my father . . . Can it be that I am an unnatural son? Your pity would make the greatest of sorrows
seem sweet. 300

MIRANDA: I hope you'll like it here with us. The island is
pretty. I'll show you the beaches and the forests, I'll tell you
the names of fruits and flowers, I'll introduce you to a whole
world of insects, of lizards of every hue, of birds . . . Oh, you
cannot imagine! The birds! . . . 305

PROSPERO: That's enough, daughter! I find your chatter irritating . . . and let me assure you, it's not at all fitting. You are
doing too much honor to an impostor. Young man, you are
a traitor, a spy, and a woman-chaser to boot! No sooner has
he escaped the perils of the sea than he's sweet-talking the 310

first girl he meets! You won't get round me that way. Your
arrival is convenient, because I need more manpower: you
shall be my house servant.

FERDINAND: Seeing the young lady, more beautiful than any
315 wood-nymph, I might have been Ulysses on Nausicaa's isle.
But hearing you, Sir, I now understand my fate a little
better . . . I see I have come ashore on the Barbary Coast and
am in the hands of a cruel pirate. (*Drawing his sword.*) However, a gentleman prefers death to dishonor! I shall defend
320 my life with my freedom!

PROSPERO: Poor fool: your arm is growing weak, your knees are
trembling! Traitor! I could kill you now . . . but I need the
manpower. Follow me.

ARIEL: It's no use trying to resist, young man. My master is a
325 sorcerer: neither your passion nor your youth can prevail
against him. Your best course would be to follow and obey
him.

FERDINAND: Oh God! What sorcery is this? Vanquished, a captive—yet far from rebelling against my fate, I am finding
330 my servitude sweet. Oh, I would be imprisoned for life if
only heaven will grant me a glimpse of my sun each day, the
face of my own sun. Farewell, Nausicaa.

(*They exit.*)

ACT TWO

SCENE I

CALIBAN's *cave.* CALIBAN *is singing as he works when* ARIEL *enters.*
He listens to him for a moment.

CALIBAN: (*Singing.*)

> May he who eats his corn heedless of Shango
> Be accursed! May Shango creep beneath
> His nails and eat into his flesh!
> 5   Shango, Shango ho!
>
> Forget to give him room if you dare!
> He will make himself at home on your nose!
>
> Refuse to have him under your roof at your own risk!
> He'll tear off your roof and wear it as a hat!
> 10   Whoever tries to mislead Shango
> Will suffer for it!
> Shango, Shango ho!

ARIEL: Greetings, Caliban. I know you don't think much of me,
but after all we *are* brothers, brothers in suffering and slav-
15   ery, but brothers in hope as well. We both want our freedom. We just have different methods.

CALIBAN: Greetings to you. But you didn't come to see me just
to make that profession of faith. Come on, Alastor! The old
man sent you, didn't he? A great job: carrying out the Mas-
20   ter's fine ideas, his great plans.

ARIEL: No, I've come on my own. I came to warn you. Prospero
is planning horrible acts of revenge against you. I thought
it my duty to alert you.

CALIBAN: I'm ready for him.

25   ARIEL: Poor Caliban, you're doomed. You know that you aren't
the stronger, you'll never be the stronger. What good will
it do you to struggle?

CALIBAN: And what about you? What good has your obedience
done you, your Uncle Tom patience and your sucking up to
him. The man's just getting more demanding and despotic   30
day by day.

ARIEL: Well, I've at least achieved one thing: he's promised me
my freedom. In the distant future, of course, but it's the
first time he's actually committed himself.

CALIBAN: Talk's cheap! He'll promise you a thousand times and   35
take it back a thousand times. Anyway, tomorrow doesn't
interest me. What I want is (*Shouting.*) "Freedom now!"

ARIEL: Okay. But you know you're not going to get it out of
him "now," and that he's stronger than you are. I'm in a
good position to know just what he's got in his arsenal.   40

CALIBAN: The stronger? How do you know that? Weakness always has a thousand means and cowardice is all that keeps
us from listing them.

ARIEL: I don't believe in violence.

CALIBAN: What *do* you believe in, then? In cowardice? In giv-   45
ing up? In kneeling and groveling? That's it, someone
strikes you on the right cheek and you offer the left.
Someone kicks you on the left buttock and you turn the
right . . . that way there's no jealousy. Well, that's not
Caliban's way . . .   50

ARIEL: You know very well that that's not what I mean. No violence, no submission either. Listen to me: Prospero is the
one we've got to change. Destroy his serenity so that he's
finally forced to acknowledge his own injustice and put an
end to it.   55

CALIBAN: Oh sure . . . that's a good one! Prospero's conscience!
Prospero is an old scoundrel who has no conscience.

ARIEL: Exactly—that's why it's up to us to give him one. I'm
not fighting just for *my* freedom, for *our* freedom, but for
Prospero too, so that Prospero can acquire a conscience.   60
Help me, Caliban.

CALIBAN: Listen, kid, sometimes I wonder if you aren't a little
bit nuts. So that Prospero can acquire a conscience? You
might as well ask a stone to grow flowers.

ARIEL: I don't know what to do with you. I've often had this in-   65
spiring, uplifting dream that one day Prospero, you, me, we
would all three set out, like brothers, to build a wonderful
world, each one contributing his own special thing: patience, vitality, love, will-power too, and rigor, not to mention the dreams without which mankind would perish.   70

CALIBAN: You don't understand a thing about Prospero. He's
not the collaborating type. He's a guy who only feels something when he's wiped someone out. A crusher, a pul-
veriser, that's what he is! And you talk about brotherhood!

ARIEL: So then what's left? War? And you know that when it   75
comes to that, Prospero is invincible.

CALIBAN: Better death than humiliation and injustice. Anyhow,
I'm going to have the last word. Unless nothingness has it.
The day when I begin to feel that everything's lost, just let
me get hold of a few barrels of your infernal powder and as   80
you fly around up there in your blue skies you'll see this island, my inheritance, my work, all blown to smithereens
. . . and, I trust, Prospero and me with it. I hope you'll like
the fireworks display—it'll be signed Caliban.

ARIEL: Each of us marches to his own drum. You follow yours.   85
I follow the beat of mine. I wish you courage, brother.

CALIBAN: Farewell, Ariel, my brother, and good luck.

SCENE II

GONZALO: A magnificent country! Bread hangs from the trees and the apricots are bigger than a woman's full breast.

SEBASTIAN: A pity that it's so wild and uncultivated . . . here and there.

5 GONZALO: Oh, that's nothing. If there were anything poisonous, an antidote would never be far away, for nature is intrinsically harmonious. I've even read somewhere that guano is excellent compost for sterile ground.

SEBASTIAN: Guano? What kind of animal is that? Are you sure
10 you don't mean iguana?

GONZALO: Young man, if I say guano, I mean guano. Guano is the name for bird-droppings that build up over centuries, and it is by far the best fertilizer known. You dig it out of caves . . . If you want my opinion, I think we should inves-
15 tigate all the caves on this island one by one to see if we find any, and if we do, this island, if wisely exploited, will be richer than Egypt with its Nile.

ANTONIO: Let me understand: your guano cave contains a river of dried bird-shit.

20 GONZALO: To pick up your image, all we need to do is channel that river, use it to irrigate, if I may use the term, the fields with this wonderful fecal matter, and everything will bloom.

SEBASTIAN: But we'll still need manpower to farm it. Is the is-
25 land even inhabited?

GONZALO: That's the problem, of course. But if it is, it must be by wonderful people. It's obvious: a wondrous land can only contain wonderful creatures.

ANTONIO: Yes!

30   Men whose bodies are wiry and strong
        And women whose eyes are open and frank . . .
        creatures in it! . . .

GONZALO: Something like that! I see you know your literature. But in that case, watch out: it will all mean new responsi-
35 bilities for us!

SEBASTIAN: How do you get that?

GONZALO: I mean that if the island is inhabited, as I believe, and if we colonize it, as is my hope, then we have to take every precaution not to import our shortcomings, yes, what
40 we call civilization. They must stay as they are: savages, noble and good savages, free, without any complexes or complications. Something like a pool granting eternal youth where we periodically come to restore our aging, citified souls.

45 ALONSO: Sir Gonzalo, when will you shut up?

GONZALO: Ah, Your Majesty, if I am boring you, I apologize. I was only speaking as I did to distract you and to turn our sad thoughts to something more pleasant. There, I'll be silent. Indeed, these old bones have had it. Oof! Let me sit
50 down . . . with your permission, of course.

ALONSO: Noble Old Man, even though younger than you, we are all in the same fix.

GONZALO: In other words, dead tired and dying of hunger.

ALONSO: I have never pretended to be above the human
55 condition.

(*A strange, solemn music is heard.*)

. . . Listen, listen! Did you hear that?

GONZALO: Yes, it's an odd melody!

(PROSPERO *enters invisible. Other strange figures enter as well, bearing a laden table. They dance and graciously invite the* KING *and his company to eat, then they disappear.*)

ALONSO: Heaven protect us! Live marionettes!

GONZALO: Such grace! Such music! Hum. The whole thing is most peculiar. 60

SEBASTIAN: Gone! Faded away! But what does that matter, since they've left their food behind! No meal was ever more welcome. Gentlemen, to table!

ALONSO: Yes, let us partake of this feast, even though it may be our last. 65

(*They prepare to eat, but* ELVES *enter and, with much grimacing and many contortions, carry off the table.*)

GONZALO: Ah! that's a fine way to behave!

ALONSO: I have the distinct feeling that we have fallen under the sway of powers that are playing at cat and mouse with us. It's a cruel way to make us aware of our dependent status.

GONZALO: The way things have been going it's not surprising, 70 and it will do us no good to protest.

(*The* ELVES *return, bringing the food with them.*)

ALONSO: Oh no, this time I won't bite!

SEBASTIAN: I'm so hungry that I don't care, I'll abandon my scruples.

GONZALO: (*To* ALONSO.) Why not try? Perhaps the Powers 75 controlling us saw how disappointed we were and took pity on us. After all, even though disappointed a hundred times, Tantalus still tried a hundred times.

ALONSO: That was also his torture. I won't touch that food.

PROSPERO: (*Invisible.*) Ariel, I don't like his refusing. Harass 80 them until they eat.

ARIEL: Why should we go to any trouble for them? If they won't eat, they can die of hunger.

PROSPERO: No, I *want* them to eat.

ARIEL: That's despotism. A while ago you made me snatch it 85 away just when they were about to gobble it up, and now that they don't want it you are ready to force feed them.

PROSPERO: Enough hairsplitting! My mood has changed! They insult me by not eating. They must be made to eat out of my hand like chicks. That is a sign of submission I insist 90 they give me.

ARIEL: It's evil to play with their hunger as you do with their anxieties and their hopes.

PROSPERO: That is how power is measured. I am Power.

(ALONSO *and his group eat.*)

ALONSO: Alas, when I think . . . 95

GONZALO: That's your trouble, Sire: you think too much.

ALONSO: And thus I should not even think of my lost son! My throne! My country!

GONZALO: (*Eating.*) Your son! What's to say we won't find him again! As for the rest of it . . . Look, Sire, this filthy hole is 100 now our entire world. Why seek further? If your thoughts are too vast, cut them down to size.

(*They eat.*)

ALONSO: So be it! But I would prefer to sleep. To sleep and to forget.

105 GONZALO: Good idea! Let's put up our hammocks!

(*They sleep.*)

SCENE III

ANTONIO: Look at those leeches, those slugs! Wallowing in their slime and their snot: Idiots, slime—they're like beached jellyfish.

SEBASTIAN: Shhh! It's the King. And that old graybeard is his
5   venerable counsellor.

ANTONIO: The King is he who watches over his flock when they sleep. That one isn't watching over anything. Ergo, he's not the King. (*Brusquely.*) You're really a bloodless lily-liver if you can see a king asleep without getting certain ideas . . .

10 SEBASTIAN: I mustn't have any blood, only water.

ANTONIO: Don't insult water. Every time I look at myself I think I'm more handsome, more *there*. My inner juices have always given me my greatness, my true greatness . . . not the greatness men grant me.

15 SEBASTIAN: All right, so I'm stagnant water.

ANTONIO: Water is never stagnant. It works, it works in us. It is what gives man his dimension, his true one. Believe me, you're mistaken if you don't grab the opportunity when it's offered you. It may never come again.

20 SEBASTIAN: What are you getting at? I have a feeling I can guess.

ANTONIO: Guess, guess! Look at that tree swaying in the wind. It's called a coconut palm. My dear Sebastian, in my opinion it's time to shake the coconut palm.

SEBASTIAN: Now I really don't understand.

25 ANTONIO: What a dope! Consider my position: I'm Duke of Milan. Well, I wasn't always . . . I had an older brother. That was Duke Prospero. And if I'm now Duke Antonio, it's because I knew when to shake the coconut palm.

SEBASTIAN: And Prospero?

30 ANTONIO: What do you mean by that? When you shake a tree, someone is bound to fall. And obviously it wasn't me who fell, because here I am: to assist and serve you, Majesty!

SEBASTIAN: Enough! He's my brother! My scruples won't allow me to . . . You take care of him while I deal with the old
35   Counsellor.

(*They draw their swords.*)

ARIEL: Stop, ruffians! Resistance is futile: your swords are enchanted and falling from your hands!

ANTONIO, SEBASTIAN: Alas! Alas!

ARIEL: Sleepers, awake! Awake, I say! Your life depends on it.
40   With these fine fellows with their long teeth and swords around, anyone who sleeps too soundly risks sleeping forever.

(ALONSO *and* GONZALO *awaken.*)

ALONSO: (*Rubbing his eyes.*) What's happening? I was asleep, and I was having a terrible dream!

ARIEL: No, you were not dreaming. These fine lords here are
45   criminals who were about to perpetrate the most odious of crimes upon you. Yes, Alonso, you may well marvel that a god should fly to your aid. Were to heaven you deserved it more!

ALONSO: I have never been wanting in respect for the divinity . . .

ARIEL: I don't know what effect my next piece of news will have 50 on you: The name of him who has sent me to you is Prospero.

ALONSO: Prospero! God save us! (*He falls to his knees.*)

ARIEL: I understand your feelings. He lives. It is he who reigns over this isle, as he reigns over the spirits of the air you 55 breathe . . . But rise . . . You need fear no longer. He has not saved your lives to destroy them. Your repentance will suffice, for I can see that it is deep and sincere. (*To* ANTONIO *and* SEBASTIAN.) As for you, Gentlemen, my master's pardon extends to you as well, on the condition that you renounce 60 your plans, knowing them to be vain.

SEBASTIAN: (*To* ANTONIO.) We could have got worse!

ANTONIO: If it were men we were up against, no one could make me withdraw, but when it's demons and magic there's no shame in giving in. (*To* ARIEL.) . . . We are the Duke's 65 most humble and obedient servants. Please beg him to accept our thanks.

GONZALO: Oh, how ignoble! How good of you to just wipe the slate clean! No surface repentance . . . not only do you want attrition, you want contrition as well! Why look at me as 70 though you didn't know what I was talking about? *Attrition*: A selfish regret for offending God, caused by a fear of punishment. *Contrition*: An unselfish regret growing out of sorrow at displeasing God.

ARIEL: Honest Gonzalo, thank you for your clarification. Your 75 eloquence has eased my mission and your pedagogical skill has abbreviated it, for in a few short words you have expressed my master's thought. May your words be heard! Therefore, let us turn the page. To terminate this episode, I need only convoke you all, on my master's behalf, to the cel- 80 ebrations that this very day will mark the engagement of his daughter, Miranda. Alonso, that's good news for you . . .

ALONSO: What—my son?

ARIEL: Correct. Saved by my master from the fury of the waves.

ALONSO: (*Falling to his knees.*) God be praised for this blessing 85 more than all the rest. Rank, fortune, throne, I am prepared to forgo all if my son is returned to me . . .

ARIEL: Come, Gentlemen, follow me.

ACT THREE

SCENE I

FERDINAND: (*Hoeing and singing.*)

> How life has changed
> Now, hoe in hand
> I work away all day . . .   5
>
> Hoeing all the day,
> I go my weary way . . .

CALIBAN: Poor kid! What would he say if he was Caliban! He works night and day, and when he sings, it's

> Oo–en–day, Oo–en–day, Oo–en–day, Macaya . . .   10

And no pretty girl to console him! (*Sees* MIRANDA *approaching.*) Aha! Let's listen to this!

FERDINAND: (*Singing.*)

How life has changed
Now, hoe in hand
15   I work away all day . . .

MIRANDA: Poor young man! Can I help you? You don't look
like you were cut out for this kind of work!

FERDINAND: One word from you would be more help to me
than anything in the world.

20 MIRANDA: One word? From me? I must say, I . . .

FERDINAND: Your name—that's all: What is your name?

MIRANDA: That, I cannot do! It's impossible. My father has expressly forbidden it!

FERDINAND: It is the only thing I long for.

25 MIRANDA: But I can't, I tell you; it's forbidden!

CALIBAN: (*Taking advantage of* MIRANDA*'s momentary distraction,
he whispers her name to* FERDINAND.) Mi–ran–da!

FERDINAND: All right then, I shall christen you with a name of
my own. I will call you Miranda.

30 MIRANDA: That's too much! What a low trick! You must have
heard my father calling me . . . Unless it was that awful Caliban who keeps pursuing me and calling out my name in
his stupid dreams!

FERDINAND: No, Miranda . . . I had only to allow my eyes to
35   speak, as you your face.

MIRANDA: Sssh! My father's coming! He'd better not catch you
trying to sweet talk me . . .

FERDINAND: (*Goes back to work, singing.*)

But times have changed
40   Now, hoeing all the day,
I go my weary way . . .

PROSPERO: That's fine, young man! You've managed to accomplish a good deal for a beginning! I see I've misjudged you.
But you won't be the loser if you serve me well. Listen, my
45 young friend, there are three things in life: Work, Patience,
Continence, and the world is yours . . . Hey, Caliban, I'm
taking this boy away with me. He's done enough for one
day. But since the job is urgent, see that it gets finished.

CALIBAN: Me?

50 PROSPERO: Yes, you! You've cheated me enough with your
loafing and fiddling around, so you can work a double shift
for once!

CALIBAN: I don't see why I should do someone else's job!

PROSPERO: Who's the boss here? You or me? Listen, monster: if
you don't like work, I'll see to it you change your mind!

(PROSPERO *and* FERDINAND *move away.*)

55 CALIBAN: Go on, go on . . . I'll get you one day, you bastard!
(*He sets to work, singing.*)

"O–o–en–day, Oo–en–day, Oo–en–day, Macaya . . ."

Shit, now it's raining! As if things weren't bad enough . . .
(*Suddenly, at the sound of a voice,* CALIBAN *stiffens.*) Do you hear
60 that, boy? That voice through the storm. Bah! It's Ariel. No,
that's not his voice. Whose, then? With an old coot like Prospero . . . One of his cops, probably. Oh, fine! Now, I'm for it.
Men and the elements both against me. Well, the hell with it
. . . I'm used to it. Patience! I'll get them yet. In the meantime
65 better make myself scarce! Let Prospero and his storm and
his cops go by . . . let the seven maws of Malediction bay!

SCENE II

Enter TRINCULO.

TRINCULO: (*Singing.*)

Oh Susannah . . . oh don't you cry for me . . . (*Etc.*)

You can say that again! My dearest Susannah . . . trust Trinculo, we've had all the roaring storms we need, and more! I
swear: the whole crew wiped out, liquidated . . . Nothing! 5
Nothing left . . . ! Nothing but poor wandering and wailing
Trinculo! No question about it, it'll be a while before anyone persuades me to depart from affectionate women and
friendly towns to go off to brave roaring storms! How it's raining! (*Notices* CALIBAN *underneath the wheelbarrow.*) Ah, an In- 10
dian! Dead or alive? You never know with these tricky races.
Yukkk! Anyhow, this will do me fine. If he's dead, I can use
his clothes for shelter, for a coat, a tent, a covering. If he's alive
I'll make him my prisoner and take him back to Europe and
then, by golly, my fortune will be made! I'll sell him to a car- 15
nival. No! I'll show him myself at fairs! What a stroke of luck!
I'll just settle in here where it's warm and let the storm rage!
(*He crawls under cover, back to back with* CALIBAN.)

(*Enter* STEPHANO.)

STEPHANO: (*Singing.*)

Blow the man down, hearties,   20
Blow the man down . . . (*Etc.*)

(*Takes a swig of his bottle and continues.*)

Blow, blow, blow the man down . . . (*Etc.*)

Fortunately, there's still a little wine left in this bottle . . .
enough to give me courage! Be of good cheer, Stephano,
where there's life there's thirst . . . and vice versa! (*Suddenly* 25
spies CALIBAN*'s head sticking out of the cover.*) My God, on
Stephano's word, it looks like a Nindian! (*Comes nearer.*)
And that's just what it is! A Nindian. That's neat. I really
am lucky. There's money to be made from a Nindian like
that. If you showed him at a carnival . . . along with the 30
bearded lady and the flea circus, a real Nindian! An authentic Nindian from the Caribbean! That means real
dough, or I'm the last of the idiots! (*Touching* CALIBAN.) But
he's ice cold! I don't know what the body temperature of a
Nindian is, but this one seems pretty cold to me! Let's hope 35
he's not going to croak! How's that for bad luck: You find a
Nindian and he dies on you! A fortune slips through your
fingers! But wait, I've got an idea . . . a good swig of this
booze between his lips, that'll warm him up. (*He gives* CAL-
IBAN *a drink.*) Look . . . he's better already. The little glutton 40
even wants some more! Just a second, just a second! (*He*
walks around the wheelbarrow and sees TRINCULO*'s head sticking*
out from under the covering.) Jeez! I must be seeing things! A
Nindian with two heads! Shit! If I have to pour drink down
two gullets I won't have much left for myself! Well, never 45
mind. It's incredible . . . your everyday Nindian is already
something, but one with two heads . . . a Siamese-twin Nindian, a Nindian with two heads and eight paws, that's really
something! My fortune is made. Come on, you wonderful
monster, you . . . let's get a look at your other head! (*He draws* 50

nearer to TRINCULO.) Hello! That face reminds me of something! That nose that shines like a lighthouse . . .

TRINCULO: That gut . . .

STEPHANO: That nose looks familiar . . .

55 TRINCULO: That gut—there can't be two of them in this lousy world!

STEPHANO: Oh-my-gawd, oh-my-gawd, oh-my-gawd . . . *that's* it . . . it's that crook Trinculo!

TRINCULO: Good lord! It's Stephano!

60 STEPHANO: So, Trinculo, you were saved too . . . It almost makes you believe God looks after drunks . . .

TRINCULO: Huh! God . . . Bacchus, maybe. As a matter of fact, I reached these welcoming shores by floating on a barrel . . .

STEPHANO: And I by floating on my stomach . . . it's nearly the
65 same thing. But what kind of creature is this? Isn't it a Nindian?

TRINCULO: That's just what I was thinking . . . Yes, by God, it's a Nindian. That's a piece of luck . . . he'll be our guide.

STEPHANO: Judging from the way he can swill it down, he doesn't
70 seem to be stupid. I'll try to civilize him. Oh . . . not too much, of course. But enough so that he can be of some use.

TRINCULO: Civilize him! Shee-it! Does he even know how to talk?

STEPHANO: I couldn't get a word out of him, but I know a way
75 to loosen his tongue. (*He takes a bottle from his pocket.*)

TRINCULO: (*Stopping him.*) Look here, you're not going to waste that nectar on the first savage that comes along, are you?

STEPHANO: Selfish! Back off! Let me perform my civilizing mission. (*Offering the bottle to* CALIBAN.) Of course, if he was
80 cleaned up a bit he'd be worth more to both of us. Okay? We'll exploit him together? It's a deal? (*To* CALIBAN.) Drink up, pal. You. Drink . . . Yum-yum botty botty! (CALIBAN *drinks.*) You, drink more. (CALIBAN *refuses.*) You no more thirsty? (STEPHANO *drinks.*) Me always thirsty! (STEPHANO
85 *and* TRINCULO *drink.*)

STEPHANO: Trinculo, you know I used to be prejudiced against shipwrecks, but I was wrong. They're not bad at all.

TRINCULO: That's true. It seems to make things taste better afterwards . . .

90 STEPHANO: Not to mention the fact that it's got rid of a lot of old farts that were always keeping the world down! May they rest in peace! But then, you liked them, didn't you, all those kings and dukes, all those noblemen! Oh, I served them well enough, you've got to earn your drink some-
95 how . . . But I could never stand them, ever—understand? Never. Trinculo, my friend, I'm a long-time believer in the republic . . . you might as well say it: I'm a died-in-the-wool believer in the people first, a republican in my guts! Down with tyrants!

100 TRINCULO: Which reminds me . . . If, as it would seem, the King and the Duke are dead, there's a crown and a throne up for grabs around here . . .

STEPHANO: By God, you're right! Smart thinking, Trinculo! So, I appoint myself heir . . . I crown myself king of the island.

105 TRINCULO: (*Sarcastically.*) Sure you do! And why you, may I ask? I'm the one who thought of it first, that crown!

STEPHANO: Look, Trinculo, don't be silly! I mean, really: just take a look at yourself! What's the first thing a king needs? Bearing. Presence. And if I've got anything, it's that.
110 Which isn't true for everyone. So, I am the King!

CALIBAN: Long live the King!

STEPHANO: It's a miracle . . . he can talk! And what's more, he talks sense! O brave savage! (*He embraces* CALIBAN.) You see, my dear Trinculo, the people has spoken! Vox populi, vox Dei . . . But please, don't be upset. Stephano is magnanimous and will 115 never abandon his friend Trinculo, the friend who stood by him in his trials. Trinculo, we've eaten rough bread together, we've drunk rot-gut wine together. I want to do something for you. I shall appoint you Marshal. But we're forgetting our brave savage . . . It's a scientific miracle! He can talk! 120

CALIBAN: Yes, Sire. My enthusiasm has restored my speech. Long live the King! But beware the usurper!

STEPHANO: Usurper? Who? Trinculo?

CALIBAN: No, the other one . . . Prospero!

STEPHANO: Prospero? Don't know him. 125

CALIBAN: Well, you see, this island used to belong to me, except that a man named Prospero cheated me of it. I'm perfectly willing to give you my right to it, but the only thing is, you'll have to fight Prospero for it.

STEPHANO: That is of no matter, brave savage. It's a bargain! I'll 130 get rid of this Prospero for you in two shakes.

CALIBAN: Watch out, he's powerful.

STEPHANO: My dear savage, I eat a dozen Prosperos like that for breakfast every day. But say no more, say no more! Trinculo, take command of the troops! Let us march upon the foe! 135

TRINCULO: Yes, forward march! But first, a drink. We will need all our strength and vigor.

CALIBAN: Let's drink, my new-found friends, and let us sing. Let us sing of winning the day and of an end to tyranny.

(*Singing.*)

> Black pecking creature of the savannas 140
> The quetzal measures out the new day
> solid and lively
> in its haughty armor.
> Zing! the determined hummingbird
> revels in the flower's depths, 145
> going crazy, getting drunk,
> a lyrebird gathers up our ravings,
> Freedom hi-day! Freedom hi-day!

STEPHANO *and* TRINCULO: (*Together.*) Freedom hi-day! Freedom hi-day! 150

CALIBAN:

> The ringdove dallies amid the trees,
> wandering the islands, here it rests—
> The white blossoms of the miconia
> Mingle with the violet blood of ripe berries 155
> And blood stains your plumage,
> traveller!
> Lying here after a weary day
> We listen to it:
> Freedom hi-day! Freedom hi-day! 160

STEPHANO: Okay, monster . . . enough crooning. Singing makes a man thirsty. Let's drink instead. Here, have some more . . . spirits create higher spirits . . . (*Filling a glass.*) Lead the way, O bountiful wine! Soldiers, forward march! Or rather . . . no: At ease! Night is falling, the fireflies twin- 165 kle, the crickets chirp, all nature makes its brek-ke-ke-kek!

And since night has fallen, let us take advantage of it to gather our forces and regain our strength, which has been sorely tried by the unusually . . . copious emotions of the
170 day. And tomorrow, at dawn, with a new spring in our step, we'll have the tyrant's hide. Good night, gentlemen. (*He falls asleep and begins to snore.*)

SCENE III

PROSPER*'s cave.*

PROSPERO: So then, Ariel! Where are the gods and goddesses? They'd better get a move on! And all of them! I want all of them to take part in the entertainment I have planned for our dear children. Why do I say "entertainment"? Because
5 starting today I want to inculcate in them the spectacle of tomorrow's world: logic, beauty, harmony, the foundations for which I have laid down by my own will-power. Unfortunately, alas, at my age it's time to stop thinking of deeds and to begin thinking of passing on . . . Enter, then!

(GODS *and* GODDESSES *enter.*)

10 JUNO: Honor and riches to you! Long continuance and increasing long life and honored issue! Juno sings to you her blessings!
CERES: May scarcity and want shun you! That is Ceres' blessing on you.
15 IRIS: (*Beckoning to the* NYMPHS.) Nymphs, come help to celebrate here a contact of true love.

(NYMPHS *enter and dance.*)

PROSPERO: My thanks, Goddesses, and my thanks to you, Iris. Thank you for your good wishes.

(GODS *and* GODDESSES *continue their dance.*)

FERDINAND: What a splendid and majestic vision! May I be so
20 bold to think these spirits?
PROSPERO: Yes, spirits which by my art I have from their confines called to greet you and to bless you.

(*Enter* ESHU.)

MIRANDA: But who is that? He doesn't look very benevolent! If I weren't afraid of blaspheming, I'd say he was a devil
25 rather than a god.
ESHU: (*Laughing.*) You are not mistaken, fair lady. God to my friends, the Devil to my enemies! And lots of laughs for all!
PROSPERO: (*Softly.*) Ariel must have made a mistake. Is my magic getting rusty? (*Aloud.*) What are you doing here?
30 Who invited you? I don't like such loose behavior, even from a god!
ESHU: But that's just the point . . . no one invited me . . . And that wasn't very nice! Nobody remembered poor Eshu! So poor Eshu came anyway. Hihihi! So how about something
35 to drink? (*Without waiting for a reply, he pours a drink.*) . . . Your liquor's not bad. However, I must say I prefer dogs! (*Looking at* IRIS.) I see that shocks the little lady, but to each his own. Some prefer chickens, others prefer goats. I'm not too fond of chickens, myself. But if you're talking about a
40 black dog . . . think of poor Eshu!

PROSPERO: Get out! Go away! We will have none of your grimaces and buffoonery in this noble assembly. (*He makes a magic sign.*)
ESHU: I'm going, boss, I'm going . . . But not without a little 45 song in honor of the bride and the noble company, as you say.

> Eshu can play many tricks,
> Give him twenty dogs!
> You will see his dirty tricks.
>
> Eshu plays a trick on the Queen 50
> And makes her so upset that she runs
> Naked into the street
>
> Eshu plays a trick on a bride,
> And on the day of the wedding
> She gets into the wrong bed! 55
>
> Eshu can throw a stone yesterday
> And kill a bird today.
> He can make a mess out of order and vice-versa.
> Ah, Eshu is a wonderful bad joke.
> Eshu is not the man to carry a heavy load. 60
> His head comes to a point. When he dances
> He doesn't move his shoulders . . .
> Oh, Eshu is a merry elf!
>
> Eshu is a merry elf,
> And he can whip you with his dick, 65
> He can whip you,
> He can whip you . . .

CERES: My dear Iris, don't you find that song quite obscene?
JUNO: It's disgusting! It's quite intolerable . . . if he keeps on, I'm leaving! 70
IRIS: It's like Liber, or Priapus!
JUNO: Don't mention that name in my presence!
ESHU: (*Continuing to sing.*)

> . . . with his dick
> He can whip you, whip you . . . 75

JUNO: Oh! Can't someone get rid of him? I'm not staying here!
ESHU: Okay, okay . . . Eshu will go. Farewell, my dear colleagues!

(GODS *and* GODDESSES *exit.*)

PROSPERO: He's gone . . . what a relief! But alas, the harm is done! I am perturbed . . . My old brain is confused. Power! Power! Alas! All this will one day fade, like foam, like a 80 cloud, like all the world. And what is power, if I cannot calm my own fears? But come! My power has gone cold. (*Calling.*) Ariel!
ARIEL: (*Runs in.*) What is it, Sire?
PROSPERO: Caliban is alive, he is plotting, he is getting a guer- 85 rilla force together and you—you don't say a word! Well, take care of him. Snakes, scorpions, porcupines, all stinging poisonous creatures, he is to be spared nothing! His punishment must be exemplary. Oh, and don't forget the mud and mosquitoes! 90
ARIEL: Master, let me intercede for him and beg your indulgence. You've got to understand: he's a rebel.
PROSPERO: By his insubordination he's calling into question the whole order of the world. Maybe the Divinity can afford to let him get away with it, but I have a sense of responsibility! 95

ARIEL: Very well, Master.

PROSPERO: But a thought: arrange some glass trinkets, some trumpery and some second-hand clothes too ... but colorful ones ... by the side of the road along which General
100 Caliban and his troops are travelling. Savages adore loud, gaudy clothes ...

ARIEL: Master ...

PROSPERO: You're going to make me angry. There's nothing to understand. There is a punishment to be meted out. I will
105 not compromise with evil. Hurry! Unless you want to be the next to feel my wrath.

SCENE IV

In the wild; night is drawing to a close; the murmurings of the spirits of the tropical forest are heard.

VOICE I: Fly!

VOICE II: Here!

VOICE I: Ant!

VOICE II: Here.

5   VOICE I: Vulture!

VOICE II: Here.

VOICE I: Soft-shelled crab, calao, crab, hummingbird!

VOICES: Here. Here. Here.

VOICE I: Cramp, crime, fang, opossum!

10 VOICE II: Kra. Kra. Kra.

VOICE I: Huge hedgehog, you will be our sun today. Shaggy, taloned, stubborn. May it burn! Moon, my fat spider, my big dreamcat, go to sleep, my velvet one.

VOICES: (*Singing.*)

15   King-ay
                        King-ay
                        Von-von
                        Maloto
                        Vloom-vloom!

(*The sun rises.* ARIEL'*s band vanishes.* CALIBAN *stands for a moment, rubbing his eyes.*)

20 CALIBAN: (*Rises and searches the bushes.*) Have to think about getting going again. Away, snakes, scorpions, porcupines! All stinging, biting, sticking beasts! Sting, fever, venom, away! Or if you really want to lick me, do it with a gentle tongue, like the toad whose pure drool soothes me with
25 sweet dreams of the future. For it is for you, for all of us, that I go forth today to face the common enemy. Yes, hereditary and common. Look, a hedgehog! Sweet little thing ... How can any animal—any natural animal, if I may put it that way—go against me on the day I'm setting forth to conquer
30 Prospero! Unimaginable! Prospero is the Anti-Nature! And I say, down with Anti-Nature! And does the porcupine bristle his spines at that? No, he smoothes them down! That's nature! It's kind and gentle, in a word. You've just got to know how to deal with it. So come on, the way is clear! Off
35 we go!

(*The band sets out.* CALIBAN *marches forward singing his battle song:*)

                Shango carries a big stick,
                He strikes and money expires!

He strikes and lies expire!

He strikes and larceny expires!

Shango, Shango ho!   40

Shango is the gatherer of the rain,

He passes, wrapped in his fiery cloak,

His horse's hoofs strike lighting

On the pavements of the sky!

Shango is a great knight!   45

Shango, Shango ho!

(*The roar of the sea can be heard.*)

STEPHANO: Tell me, brave savage, what is that noise? It sounds like the roaring of a beast at bay.

CALIBAN: Not a bay ... more like on the prow! ... Don't worry, it's a pal of mine.   50

STEPHANO: You are very closemouthed about the company you keep.

CALIBAN: And yet it helps me breathe. That's why I call it a pal. Sometimes it sneezes, and a drop falls on my forehead and cools me with its salt, or blesses me ...   55

STEPHANO: I don't understand. You aren't drunk, are you?

CALIBAN: Come on! It's that howling impatient thing that suddenly appears in a clap of thunder like some God and hits you in the face, that rises up out of the very depths of the abyss and smites you with its fury! It's the sea!   60

STEPHANO: Odd country! And an odd baptism!

CALIBAN: But the best is still the wind and the songs it sings ... its dirty sigh when it rustles through the bushes, or its triumphant chant when it passes by breaking trees, remnants of their terror in its beard.   65

STEPHANO: The savage is delirious, he's raving mad! Tough luck, Trinculo, our savage is playing without a full deck!

TRINCULO: I'm kind of shuffling myself ... In other words, I'm exhausted. I never knew such hard going! Savage, even your mud is muddier.   70

CALIBAN: That isn't mud ... it's something Prospero's dreamed up.

TRINCULO: There's a savage for you ... everything's always caused by someone. The sun is Prospero's smile. The rain is the tear in Prospero's eye ... And I suppose the mud is   75
Prospero's shit. And what about the mosquitoes? What are they, may I ask? Zzzzzz, Zzzzzz ... do you hear them? My face is being eaten off!

CALIBAN: Those aren't mosquitoes. It's some kind of gas that stings your nose and throat and makes you itch. It's another   80
of Prospero's tricks. It's part of his arsenal.

STEPHANO: What do you mean by that?

CALIBAN: I mean his anti-riot arsenal! He's got a lot of gadgets like these ... gadgets to make you deaf, to blind you, to make you sneeze, to make you cry ...   85

TRINCULO: And to make you slip! Shit! This is some fix you've got us in! I can't take anymore ... I'm going to sit down!

STEPHANO: Come on, Trinculo, show a little courage! We're engaged in a mobile ground manoeuvre here, and you know what that means: drive, initiatives, split-second decisions to   90
meet new eventualities, and—above all—mobility. Let's go! Up you get! Mobility!

TRINCULO: But my feet are bleeding!

STEPHANO: Get up or I'll knock you down! (TRINCULO *begins to walk again.*) But tell me, my good savage, this usurper of   95 yours seems very well protected. It might be dangerous to attack him!

CALIBAN: You mustn't underestimate him. You mustn't overestimate him, either . . . he's showing his power, but he's do-
100 ing it mostly to impress us.

STEPHANO: No matter. Trinculo, we must take precautions. Axiom: never underestimate the enemy. Here, pass me that bottle. I can always use it as a club.

(*Highly colored clothing is seen, hanging from a rope.*)

TRINCULO: Right, Stephano. On with the battle. Victory
105 means loot. And there's a foretaste of it . . . look at that fine wardrobe! Trinculo, my friend, methinks you are going to put on those britches . . . they'll replace your torn trousers.

STEPHANO: Look out, Trinculo . . . one move and I'll knock you down. As your lord and master I have the first pick, and
110 with those britches I'm exercising my feudal rights . . .

TRINCULO: I saw them first!

STEPHANO: The King gets first pick in every country in the world.

TRINCULO: That's tyranny, Stephano. I'm not going to let you get away with it.

(*They fight.*)

115 CALIBAN: Let it alone, fool. I tell you about winning your dignity, and you start fighting over hand-me-downs! (*To himself.*) To think I'm stuck with these jokers! What an idiot I am! How could I ever have thought I could create the Revolution with swollen guts and fat faces! Oh well! History
120 won't blame me for not having been able to win my freedom all by myself. It's you and me, Prospero! (*Weapon in hand, he advances on* PROSPERO *who has just appeared.*)

PROSPERO: (*Bares his chest to him.*) Strike! Go on, strike! Strike your Master, your benefactor! Don't tell me you're going to
125 spare him!

(CALIBAN *raises his arm, but hesitates.*)

Go on! You don't dare! See, you're nothing but an animal . . . you don't know how to kill.

CALIBAN: Defend yourself! I'm not a murderer.

PROSPERO: (*Very calm.*) The worse for you. You've lost your
130 chance. Stupid as a slave! And now, enough of this farce. (*Calling.*) Ariel! (*To* ARIEL.) Ariel, take charge of the prisoners!

(CALIBAN, TRINCULO, *and* STEPHANO *are taken prisoners.*)

SCENE V

PROSPERO'*s cave.* MIRANDA *and* FERDINAND *are playing chess.*

MIRANDA: Sir, I think you're cheating.

FERDINAND: And what if I told you that I would not do so for twenty kingdoms?

MIRANDA: I would not believe a word of it, but I would forgive
5 you. Now, be honest . . . you did cheat!

FERDINAND: I'm pleased that you were able to tell. (*Laughing.*) That makes me less worried at the thought that soon you will be leaving your innocent flowery kingdom for my less-innocent world of men.

MIRANDA: Oh, you know that, hitched to your star, I would 10 brave the demons of hell!

(*The* NOBLES *enter.*)

ALONSO: My son! This marriage! The thrill of it has struck me dumb! The thrill and the joy!

GONZALO: A happy ending to a most opportune shipwreck!

ALONSO: A unique one, indeed, for it can legitimately be de- 15 scribed as such.

GONZALO: Look at them! Isn't it wonderful! I've been too choked up to speak, or I would have already told these children all the joy my old heart feels at seeing them living love's young dream and cherishing each other so tenderly. 20

ALONSO: (*To* FERDINAND *and* MIRANDA.) My children, give me your hands. May the Lord bless you.

GONZALO: Amen! Amen!

(*Enter* PROSPERO.)

PROSPERO: Thank you, Gentlemen, for having agreed to join in this little family party. Your presence has brought us com- 25 fort and joy. However, you must now think of getting some rest. Tomorrow morning, you will recover your vessels— they are undamaged—and your men, who I can guarantee are safe, hale and hearty. I shall return with you to Europe, and I can promise you—I should say: promise us—a rapid 30 sail and propitious winds.

GONZALO: God be praised! We are delighted . . . delighted and overcome! What a happy, what a memorable day! With one voyage Antonio has found a brother, his brother has found a dukedom, his daughter has found a husband. 35 Alonso has regained his son and gained a daughter. And what else? . . . Anyway, I am the only one whose emotion prevents him from knowing what he's saying . . .

PROSPERO: The proof of that, my fine Gonzalo, is that you are forgetting someone: Ariel, my loyal servant. (*Turning to* 40 ARIEL.) Yes, Ariel, today you will be free. Go, my sweet. I hope you will not be bored.

ARIEL: Bored! I fear that the days will seem all too short! There, where the Cecropia gloves its impatient hands with silver,
Where the ferns free the stubborn black stumps 45
from their scored bodies with a green cry—
There where the intoxicating berry ripens the visit of the wild ring-dove
through the throat of that musical bird
I shall let fall 50
one by one,
each more pleasing than the last
four notes so sweet that the last
will give rise to a yearning
in the heart of the most forgetful slaves 55
yearning for freedom!

PROSPERO: Come, come. All the same, you are not going to set my world on fire with your music, I trust!

ARIEL: (*With intoxication.*) Or on some stony plane
perched on an agave stalk 60
I shall be the thrush that launches
its mocking cry
to the benighted field-hand

"Dig, nigger! Dig, nigger!"
65 and the lightened agave will
straighten from my flight,
a solemn flag.
PROSPERO: That is a very unsettling agenda! Go! Scram! Before
I change my mind!

(*Enter* STEPHANO, TRINCULO, CALIBAN.)

70 GONZALO: Sire, here are your people.
PROSPERO: Oh no, not all of them! Some are yours.
ALONSO: True. There's that fool Trinculo and that unspeakable
Stephano.
STEPHANO: The very ones, Sire, in person. We throw ourselves
75 at your merciful feet.
ALONSO: What became of you?
STEPHANO: Sire, we were walking in the forest—no, it was in
the fields—when we saw some perfectly respectable clothing blowing in the wind. We thought it only right to col-
80 lect them and we were returning them to their rightful
owner when a frightful adventure befell us . . .
TRINCULO: Yes, we were mistaken for thieves and treated accordingly.
STEPHANO: Yes, Sire, it is the most dreadful thing that could
85 happen to an honest man: victims of a judicial error, a mis-
carriage of justice!
PROSPERO: Enough! Today is a day to be benevolent, and it will
do no good to try to talk sense to you in the state you're
in . . . Leave us. Go sleep it off, drunkards. We raise sail
90 tomorrow.
TRINCULO: Raise sail! But that's what we do all the time, Sire,
Stephano and I . . . at least, we raise our glasses, from dawn
till dusk till dawn. The hard part is putting them down,
landing, as you might say.
95 PROSPERO: Scoundrels! If only life could bring you to the safe
harbors of Temperance and Sobriety!
ALONSO: (*Indicating* CALIBAN.) That is the strangest creature
I've ever seen!
PROSPERO: And the most devilish too!
100 GONZALO: What's that? Devilish! You've reprimanded him,
preached at him, you've ordered and made him obey and
you say he is still indomitable!
PROSPERO: Honest Gonzalo, it is as I have said.
GONZALO: Well—and forgive me, Counsellor, if I give
105 counsel—on the basis of my long experience the only
thing left is exorcism. "Begone, unclean spirit, in the
name of the Father, of the Son and of the Holy Ghost."
That's all there is to it!

(CALIBAN *bursts out laughing.*)

GONZALO: You were absolutely right! And more so that you
110 thought . . . He's not just a rebel, he's a real tough customer! (*To* CALIBAN.) So much the worse for you, my
friend. I have tried to save you. I give up. I leave you to the
secular arm!
PROSPERO: Come here, Caliban. Have you got anything to say
115 in your own defence? Take advantage of my good humor.
I'm in a forgiving mood today.
CALIBAN: I'm not interested in defending myself. My only regret is that I've failed.

PROSPERO: What were you hoping for?
CALIBAN: To get back my island and regain my freedom.   120
PROSPERO: And what would you do all alone here on this island, haunted by the devil, tempest tossed?
CALIBAN: First of all, I'd get rid of you! I'd spit you out, all your
works and pomps! Your "white" magic!
PROSPERO: That's a fairly negative program . . .   125
CALIBAN: You don't understand it . . . I say I'm going to spit
you out, and that's very positive . . .
PROSPERO: Well, the world is really upside down . . . We've
seen everything now: Caliban as a dialectician! However, in
spite of everything I'm fond of you, Caliban. Come, let's   130
make peace. We've lived together for ten years and worked
side by side! Ten years count for something, after all! We've
ended up by becoming compatriots!
CALIBAN: You know very well that I'm not interested in peace.
I'm interested in being free! Free, you hear?   135
PROSPERO: It's odd . . . no matter what you do, you won't suc-
ceed in making me believe that I'm a tyrant!
CALIBAN: Understand what I say, Prospero:
For years I bowed my head
for years I took it, all of it—   140
your insults, your ingratitude . . .
and worst of all, more degrading than all the rest,
your condescension.
But now, it's over!
Over, do you hear?   145
Of course, at the moment
You're still stronger than I am.
But I don't give a damn for your power
or for your dogs or your police or your inventions!
And do you know why?   150
It's because I know I'll get you.
I'll impale you! And on a stake that you've sharpened
yourself!
You'll have impaled yourself!
Prospero, you're a great magician:
you're an old hand at deception.   155
And you lied to me so much,
about the world, about myself,
that you ended up by imposing on me
an image of myself:
underdeveloped, in your words, undercompetent   160
that's how you made me see myself!
And I hate that image . . . and it's false!
But now I know you, you old cancer,
And I also know myself!
And I know that one day   165
my bare fist, just that,
will be enough to crush your world!
The old world is crumbling down!

Isn't it true? Just look!
It even bores you to death.   170

And by the way . . . you have a chance to get it over with:
You can pick up and leave.
You can go back to Europe.
But the hell you will!   175
I'm sure you won't leave.
You make me laugh with your "mission"!

Your "vocation"!
Your vocation is to hassle me.
And that's why you'll stay,
180 just like those guys who founded the colonies
and who now can't live anywhere else.
You're just an old addict, that's what you are!
PROSPERO: Poor Caliban! You know that you're headed towards
your own ruin. You're sliding towards suicide! You know I
185 will be the stronger, and stronger all the time. I pity you!
CALIBAN: And I hate you!
PROSPERO: Beware! My generosity has its limits.
CALIBAN: (*Shouting.*)

190   Shango marches with strength
          along his path, the sky!
          Shango is a fire-bearer,
          his steps shake the heavens
          and the earth
          Shango, Shango, ho!

195 PROSPERO: I have uprooted the oak and raised the sea,
I have caused the mountain to tremble and have bared my
chest to adversity.
With Jove I have traded thunderbolt for thunderbolt.
Better yet—from a brutish monster I have made man!
But ah! To have failed to find the path to man's heart . . .
200 if that be where man is.
(*To* CALIBAN.) Well, I hate you as well!
For it is you who have made me
doubt myself for the first time.
(*To the* NOBLES.) . . . My friends, come near. We must say
205 farewell . . . I shall not be going with you. My fate is here:
I shall not run from it.
ANTONIO: What, Sire?
PROSPERO: Hear me well.
I am not in any ordinary sense a master,
210 as this savage thinks,
but rather the conductor of a boundless score:
this isle,
summoning voices, I alone,
and mingling them at my pleasure,
215 arranging out of confusion
one intelligible line.
Without me, who would be able to draw music from all that?
This isle is mute without me.
My duty, thus, is here,
220 and here I shall stay.

GONZALO: Oh day full rich in miracles!
PROSPERO: Do not be distressed. Antonio, be you the lieutenant
of my goods and make use of them as procurator until that
time when Ferdinand and Miranda may take effective possession of them, joining them with the Kingdom of Naples. 225
Nothing of that which has been set for them must be postponed: Let their marriage be celebrated at Naples with all
royal splendor. Honest Gonzalo, I place my trust in your word.
You shall stand as father to our princess at this ceremony.
GONZALO: Count on me, Sire. 230
PROSPERO: Gentlemen, farewell.

(*They exit.*)

And now, Caliban, it's you and me!
What I have to tell you will be brief:
Ten times, a hundred times, I've tried to save you,
above all from yourself. 235
But you have always answered me with wrath
and venom,
like the opossum that pulls itself up by its own tail
the better to bite the hand that tears it from the darkness.
Well, my boy, I shall set aside my indulgent nature 240
and henceforth I will answer your violence
with violence!

(*Time passes, symbolized by the curtain's being lowered halfway and
reraised. In semi-darkness* PROSPERO *appears, aged and weary. His
gestures are jerky and automatic, his speech weak, toneless, trite.*)

PROSPERO: Odd, but for some time now we seem to be overrun
with opossums. They're everywhere. Peccarys, wild boar, all
this unclean nature! But mainly opossums. Those eyes! The 245
vile grins they have! It's as though the jungle was laying
siege to the cave . . . But I shall stand firm . . . I shall not let
my work perish! (*Shouting.*) I shall protect civilization! (*He
fires in all directions.*) They're done for! Now, this way I'll be
able to have some peace and quiet for a while. But it's cold. 250
Odd how the climate's changed. Cold on this island . . .
Have to think about making a fire . . . Well, Caliban, old fellow, it's just us two now, here on the island . . . only you and
me. You and me. You-me . . . me-you! What in the hell is
he up to? (*Shouting.*) Caliban! 255

(*In the distance, above the sound of the surf and the chirping of birds,
we hear snatches of* CALIBAN'*s song:*)

FREEDOM HI-DAY, FREEDOM HI-DAY!

1395 _____

APPENDIX

LITERAL TRANSLATIONS OF SONGS
ARIEL'S SONG
1400   **(Act I, Scene 2)**

Chestnut horses of the sand
They bite out the place
Where the waves expire in
Pure languor.

Where the waves die
Here come all,
Join hands
And dance.

Blond sands,
What fire!
Languorous waves,
Pure expiration.
Here lips lick and lick again
Our wounds.

The waves make a waterline . . .
Nothing is, all is becoming . . .
The season is close and strange

The eye is a fine pearl
The heart of coral, the bone of coral,
There, at the waterline
As the sea swells within us.

TRINCULO'S SONG
(Act III, Scene 2)

Virginia, with tears in my eyes
I bid you farewell.
We're off to Mexico,
Straight into the setting sun.

With sails unfurled, my dear love,

It torments me to leave you,
A tempest is brewing
Some storm is howling
That will carry off the entire crew!

STEPHANO'S SONG
(Act III, Scene 2)

(*Obviously an old sea chanty or Césaire's adaptation of one.*)

Bravely on, guys, step it lively,
bravely on, farewell Bordeaux,
To Cape Horn, it won't be hot,
Off to hunt the whale.

More than one of us will lose his skin
Farewell misery, farewell ship.
The ones who return with all flags flying
Will be the first-rate sailors . . .

Griselda Gambaro

Griselda Gambaro is one of the most distinguished writers of contemporary Argentina. Born in Buenos Aires in 1928, Gambaro's career as a writer has been deeply intertwined with the history and politics of her country. Argentina has a long history of repressive military rule, and Gambaro's career as a playwright began during a period of exceptional crisis, inaugurated by Juan Carlos Onganía's brutal military coup in 1966. Gambaro's plays from this period—*The Walls* (1963), *The Blunder* (1965), *The Siamese Twins* (1965), *The Camp* (1967)—concern the progressive deterioration of the fabric of society. But as the political repression of the 1960s gave way to state terrorism in the 1970s—especially the "Dirty War" (1976–1983), in which the military government systematically imprisoned and/or murdered hundreds of thousands of civilians, the "disappeared"—Gambaro's fiction and drama became increasingly engaged, making her situation in Argentina even more precarious. Her plays of the 1970s—including *Saying Yes* (1972), *Strip* (1972), *The Name* (1976), and *Information for Foreigners* (1973)—depict a world totally slipped from its moorings, in which murder, torture, and execution seem part of the horizon of everyday life.

Gambaro has written several novels as well, including *Nothing to Do with Another Story* (1972), *To Earn One's Death* (1976), *God Does Not Want Us Happy* (1979), and *Impenetrable* (1984). In 1977, *To Earn One's Death* was banned and Gambaro left Argentina to live in Spain and France. She returned to Argentina in 1980, where she continued her career as a playwright, with *Royal Gambit* (1980), *Bitter Blood* (1981), *From the Rising Sun* (1983), *Antígona Furiosa* (1986), *Fear* (1989), and *Worthless Trouble* (1990). Gambaro has lectured extensively in the United States and is currently living in Buenos Aires.

INFORMATION FOR FOREIGNERS

Griselda Gambaro's *Information for Foreigners* uses the participatory element of environmental theater to enact a sophisticated political process as theater. Ideally performed in a house, the play divides the audience into four groups, each led through the play's scenes in a different order, and then reassembled as a single audience for the final scene, scene 20.

Information for Foreigners forces its audience to engage the subtle interinvolvement between theater and the theater of state terrorism, between fiction and fact, a blurring of boundaries between the simulated and the "real" typical of postmodern art. For throughout the play, the audience is repeatedly confronted by two kinds of "performance": overtly "theatrical" or "staged" scenes—like scene 14, where the audience observes a reenactment of a scene of police violence—and "backstage" or "offstage" scenes where the "disappeared"—the man in his underwear in scene 1, the girl who is tortured with the "submarine" (held under water in a bathtub of filthy water)—accidentally come into the audience's view. The play forces its audience both to connect these two spheres of performance and to question its own role in each. The Guide repeatedly provides "Information for Foreigners" to the audience, which articulates the historical background of state violence in the 1970s, and implicitly addresses that wider, European and North American audience whose tacit or financial support kept the regime in power. The audience is, in a sense, incriminated for adopting this "tourist" role.

In many respects, *Information for Foreigners* is a play about its audience. Scene 4 reenacts the famous Milgram experiment, in which the participant's willingness to follow orders and please authority figures leads him to kill (or, in the original versions of the experiment, to believe he has killed) the "student." The Milgram experiment provides a kind of metaphor for the audience's function in *Information for Foreigners,* in that observation repeatedly involves the audience in a kind of deference to authority. The silent willingness to participate as spectators of the violence makes the audience responsible for the violence, becoming its silent authors. This implied assault on the audience's moral freedom is the point of the play's final scene, where the line between theater and torture is finally suspended, and the "stage" of torture is one the audience is explicitly shown to authorize. Having brought the audience to witness a final execution, the Guide turns to us: "Ladies and gentlemen, what are you waiting for? The show is over." As he suggests in his final, ritual chant, "Theater imitates life"; but the boundaries between theater and life, between what we see and what we know, have been forever broken:

> Who once said: here the ken
> of men and women
> here the bounds?

INFORMATION FOR FOREIGNERS

A CHRONICLE IN TWENTY SCENES

Griselda Gambaro

TRANSLATED BY MARGUERITE FEITLOWITZ

CHARACTERS

GUIDES, *number contingent on number of audience groups*
VOICES, *heard at intervals throughout*

MAN IN ROOM

GIRL, *with wet clothes*
MAN, *with pistol*

COORDINATOR
MATURE MAN/TEACHER
YOUNG MAN/PUPIL

MOTHER
FATHER

GROUP OF MEN, *attack* MAN IN AUDIENCE
MAN, *defends attacked man*

SOMEONE FROM THE AUDIENCE, *number contingent on number of audience groups*
USHERETTE

THREE MEN, *carry table*
GROUP OF MEN, *surround* GIRL
TWO WORKMEN

MOTHER (*Sara Palacio de Verdt*)
FATHER (*Marcelo Verdt*)
TWO CHILDREN (*Verdt girl and boy*)
CHIEF
TWO POLICEMEN

MAN IN LOINCLOTH

MAN (*Robert Quieto*)

NEIGHBOR #1
NEIGHBOR #2
FIRST GROUP OF MEN, *tied together*
NEIGHBOR #3
SECOND GROUP OF MEN, *tied together*
OFFICIAL
JUDGE
GUARD

GIRL, *with long hair* (HERMENEGILDA)
FOUR MEN, *on skates*
HUSBAND OF HERMENEGILDA
MOTHER OF HERMENEGILDA
NEIGHBORS

MAN (*Juan Pablo Maestre*)
WOMAN (*Miera Elena Misetich*)
TWO POLICEMEN
GROUP OF POLICEMEN, *dressed as sweepers*

GAME PLAYERS
POLICEMEN, *with clubs*

ACTOR #1
TWO MEN, *in box*

ACTRESS #1
ACTRESS #2
ACTOR #1
POLICEMAN #1
POLICEMAN #2

CHILD MONSTER

CHILDREN, *play Anton Pirulero*
FIRST MAN
SECOND MAN
THIRD MAN
YOUNG WOMAN

TWO GUARDS
PRISONERS
VISITORS TO PRISON
PRETTY GIRL

GROUP OF GUARDS, *attack* PRETTY GIRL
LITTLE OLD LADY
OUTLANDISH-LOOKING PRISONER

PROSTITUTES
MAN #1
MAN #2
MAN #3
MAN #4

The theater space can be a spacious, residential house, preferably two stories, with corridors and empty rooms, some of which interconnect. A larger space is needed for the final scene.

Situated in the passageways, propped against the walls, are two or three vertical rectangular boxes, each with a door and air holes.

In a different area, chosen by the director, sits an additional box, larger but otherwise the same as those in the passageways.

Some of the corridors are dark, while others, in obvious contrast, are crudely lit.

The audience will be divided into groups, the number and size of which will depend on the space. A particular number or color can serve to identify each group.

Group 1 will mark one possible development of the action.

Guides 1, 2, 3, 4, etc., lead their respective groups. The order in which the scenes are observed by these groups is left to the director's discretion until the last scene, scene 20, when all groups converge.

In certain scenes, actors play audience members and are actually part of the audience. Audience members, however, are never forced to participate in the action.

The groups cross in the passageways and may watch the same scene— perhaps one taking place in the passageway—when the director considers it necessary.

Excerpts introduced by the guides as "Explanation: For Foreigners" come from Argentine newspapers of the period 1971–72.

GUIDES: Organize the groups.
GUIDE: Ladies and gentlemen: Admission is ———, for adults. If you've already paid, you can't repent. The cost is already incurred. Better to enjoy yourself. No one under eigh-
5 teen will be admitted. Or under thirty-five or over thirty-six. Everyone else can attend with no problem. No obscenity or strong words. The play speaks to our way of life: Argentine, Western, and Christian. We are in 1971. I ask that you stay together and remain silent. Careful on the
10 stairs.

SCENE ONE

The GUIDE leads the group toward one of the rooms. The room is completely in shadow. The door closes. We hear a shrill, metallic signal. Then, we hear many voices, indistinct and juxtaposed, carrying on an incomprehensible conversation.

GUIDE: One moment . . . I don't find my flashlight. Remember, opportunity makes the thief. Watch your pocketbooks! (*Light comes up on a dark and wrinkled wall.*) Only the naked

walls are left. (*The light travels. A man is seated on a chair,*
wearing only faded underwear. He raises his head, surprised and
frightened. He covers his sex with his hands. To the audience.) Excuse me. I've got the wrong room.

SCENE TWO

The GUIDE, *lighting the way with his flashlight, leads the group out of*
the room. He tries to open the door of another room. Behind the door
a sweet voice sings

VOICE:

"Carnation, sleep and dream,
the horse won't drink from the stream . . ."

GUIDE: (*Shrugging his shoulders, turns to the group.*) It's locked.
(*He knocks. Nicely.*) May I? I've brought a group of spectators. And they're getting anxious.
VOICE: (*Very rudely.*) What's it to me? Beat it! I'm rehearsing.

SCENE THREE

GUIDE: (*To the group.*) Sorry. People should be brought up better, don't you think? (*Tries the latch on the next door. It gives.*)
Good. Here. Go ahead. (*The group enters this other dark room.*
Against the wall, some chairs. The GUIDE *shines his light on them.*
Then, nicely.) You can position yourselves wherever you like.
There are chairs for everyone. (*He looks.*) No, not enough to
go around. (*Arranges them, offers.*) Ladies first . . . !

(*Lights on in the middle of the room. A young* GIRL *sits on a chair*
wearing clothes that are soaking wet. A MAN *stands next to her, ob-*
serving her with a tender smile. The GUIDE *waits for people to get com-*
fortable, points out places. Then, with a finger on his lips, he signals
for silence and turns, like one more spectator, toward the characters who
begin the action.)

MAN: (*Always speaks softly, tenderly.*) Why didn't you dry yourself? You're getting the floor all wet. (*He bends down and*
dries the floor with a rag.) Lucky it's not waxed. (*The* GIRL
shivers with cold. The MAN *takes off his jacket, puts it on her*
shoulders. The GIRL *looks at it, wraps herself in the jacket.*) Why
didn't you dry yourself? Wasn't there a towel?
GIRL: No.
MAN: (*Drying the floor.*) What a mess! They fill the tub but don't
put any towels. What about the water? Was it warm? (*The*
GIRL *doesn't answer. He shakes her, gently.*) Was it warm?
GIRL: No.

---

ii. 2 **"Carnation, sleep and dream,"** sung by a "sweet" female
Voice, the Mother in scene 5, and other voices elsewhere, is from
García Lorca's *Bodas de sangre,* or *Blood Wedding,* scene 2. I use the
translation by James Graham-Luján and Richard L. O'Connell in
Three Tragedies of Federico García Lorca: Blood Wedding, Yerma,
Bernarda Alba (New York: New Directions, 1955). In the original,
Gambaro used only "Nana, niño, nana, del caballo grande que no
quiso el agua," repeated over and over. For the English version, I
chose to use many more fragments of the lullabye over the course
of the play. Gambaro approved this choice in her letter to me of
March 28, 1986

MAN: (*He pulls a pistol from his belt and cleans it with a rag.*) Ah!
This department isn't worth shi . . . (*The* GUIDE *says some-*
thing. The MAN *shoots him a quick look.*) Right. (*He shows her*
his weapon.) Do you like it? It isn't loaded. (*She looks at it but*
doesn't answer. The MAN *begins loading the gun.*) Why so sad?
(*Points to the group.*) Nothing will happen to you. There are
lots of people. They're watching us. (*Puts the pistol back in*
his belt.) You're not pretty with your hair all wet. But that's
not too serious. (*He leans toward her, curious.*) Tell me, do you
dye your hair? (*Still studying her.*) You're getting my jacket
all wet. Sorry, it's the only one I have . . . (*He takes it gently,*
shakes it, and puts it on. With a shiver.) It's damp. (*Pointing to*
the pistol.) Do you want it?
GIRL: No.
MAN: I'm leaving it for you. I have another. The jacket I can't,
I swear to you.
GIRL: (*Shaking her head.*) No.
MAN: (*Surreptitiously.*) Speak up! They can't hear a thing!
GUIDE: Louder! Louder!
MAN: What did I tell you? (*The* GIRL *doesn't answer.*) Look at me.
(*She obeys. He holds out the gun.*) Take it!
GIRL: No . . . I don't want to.
MAN: Why are you squeezing your legs together? Do you want
to go to the bathroom?
GIRL: (*Nods her head.*) Yes.
MAN: Then go!
GIRL: They're . . . watching me.
MAN: So? We're all adults, aren't we? They at least are watching. What are you doing, always looking over there? What
do you see that's so pretty? (*Puts his cheek against hers. Looks*
in the same direction.) Nothing! (*Separates from her.*) I like to
see people's eyes when I talk to them. (*Gently, he turns her*
head.) Look at me. (*He points to the pistol.*) Do you want it?
GIRL: No, no! Leave me alone!
MAN: (*Anxious.*) Would you like some stockings? (*He puts his*
hand on her foot.)
GIRL: No!
MAN: Always no! Why? My intentions are good. Take it. Don't
you get bored all alone? (*Insists.*) Take it, it doesn't bite. But
don't squeeze the trigger. Unless . . .
GIRL: (*Barely audible.*) Unless . . .
MAN: If you squeeze, it's all over. Do you have a boyfriend?
GIRL: No.
MAN: Well then? Take it! I'm leaving it here, on the floor. All
you have to do is lean down.
GIRL: For what? I don't want . . . to lean down, I don't want . . .
anything.
MAN: The heart and the forehead . . . are sure. I mean, so you
don't suffer . . .
GIRL: No . . .
MAN: (*Caresses her cheek.*) Of course, no. There's a sun outside.
It's hot as hell. So you don't have a boyfriend? Well
then . . . ? (*He goes toward the door. Turns. Smiles.*) I'm going
to tell them to heat the water! (*He goes out. The* GIRL *looks*
at the pistol on the floor, leans down, trembling, stretches her hand.
Freezes in the act.)
GUIDE: Ladies and gentlemen, if it bothers you. (*He opens the*
door. Leading the group into the hallway, he explains.) In March
1970, at the Max Planck Institute in Munich, Germany,
they began an interesting experiment. Careful on the stairs.

SCENE FOUR

The group enters a white room that adjoins another, also painted white, but that may be smaller. In the first room, a small table with a cage full of white rats. On another table, a metal box outfitted with buttons and a microphone. Carefully folded on an ordinary chair, a white coat.

Through the half-open door one can see in the other room a chair whose armrests are outfitted with side straps attached to electric cables. Cables to tie down a person's legs. A microphone hangs down from the ceiling.

In the first room are the COORDINATOR, *dressed in a white coat, and two others in street clothes, a* MATURE MAN *and a* YOUNG MAN. *The* MATURE MAN *lingers in front of the cage, putting his fingers through the bars, trying to attract the rats and get them to play.*

COORDINATOR: (*To the group, in a professional tone.*) Gentlemen: The subject of our experiment is to determine the pedagogical effect of punishment. To what degree does punishment accelerate the learning process? Imagine. If with one
5 slap a child learns to behave, we waste years teaching and persuading only with nice words. We don't have time to lose. Soon he will be an adult; soon he will be molded. Molded for destruction, when one slap, two or three electrical jolts at the right moment could put things in place.
10 (*He begins observing the* MATURE MAN *playing with the rats.*) The gentlemen will help us to clarify...unclear...details... Please, sir, stop pestering those rats! Idiot! (*He goes toward him and kicks him away from the cage.*)

MATURE MAN: Okay, okay. I'm sorry. They're so cute that . . .
15 COORDINATOR: (*Calm.*) Of course they're cute. (*Becoming irritated.*) Shall we begin?

MATURE MAN: At your orders, sir!

COORDINATOR: (*Happy.*) One kick . . . and acquiescence. You, sir, emotionally more mature, will be the teacher.
20 MATURE MAN: Yes, delighted.

COORDINATOR: (*To the* YOUNG MAN.) You will be the pupil.

YOUNG MAN: (*He speaks with a metallic voice, like a parrot.*) I will be the pupil.

GUIDE: (*To the group, surreptitiously.*) Everyone's a researcher,
25 even the mule.

COORDINATOR: (*Drily.*) Silence! (*He takes money and some papers out of his pocket.*) Help yourself. Twenty-five marks, or thirty-six dollars for your trouble. If you would be so kind as to sign the receipt and the release. (*They sign, take their*
30 *money. The* COORDINATOR *hands the* TEACHER *a white coat.*) This is for you. (*Cordially, the* COORDINATOR *helps him on with the coat, adjusts the collar.*) There, now. Right this way, please. (*He leads them into the other room. The* GUIDE *follows with his group.* COORDINATOR *to the* PUPIL.) Please be seated.
35 Don't be afraid, it's an experiment, remember that.

PUPIL: Happy to please
I sit with the greatest of ease!

COORDINATOR: I made a mistake. Take off your jacket, roll up your sleeves. (*The* PUPIL *does so.*) Thank you. We have to
40 strap you in. If you would like to resign . . .

PUPIL No! For the sake of science
Let us commence!

COORDINATOR: (*Strapping him. To the* TEACHER.) Will you help me?

TEACHER: (*With dispatch.*) Yes, of course! 45

COORDINATOR: (*From a pocket of his coat, he takes a tube of cream and starts smearing the* PUPIL's *forearms.*) The cream facilitates the passage of current and prevents burns. (*Winking at him.*) It's an experiment, don't be frightened. It's like . . . talking to hear yourself talk. 50

PUPIL: I'm not afraid
I'm not afraid
I really feel I have it made.

COORDINATOR: (*Attaches electrodes to the* PUPIL's *forearms. The* TEACHER *helps diligently.*) How obliging! Thank you. 55

PUPIL: It's . . . very tight.

COORDINATOR: Let's loosen this a bit. (*He does.*) You—the Teacher—are going to station yourself at the microphone in the next room. (*To the* PUPIL.) You pay attention. He will read out a group of words, such as *day-sun, night-moon,* 60 *mother-love,* etc. Then he will repeat the word *day* followed by four others. You must remember which of these four words was associated with *day.* If you make a mistake, you'll receive an electric shock as punishment.

TEACHER: And then you'll learn. 65

PUPIL: Why will punishment teach me?

COORDINATOR: The shock won't be strong.

TEACHER: Never?

COORDINATOR: No! Unless he really blunders. But it's impossible. They're very obvious associations. For idiots. (*To the* 70 TEACHER.) Let's go! (*They go into the adjoining room. The* GUIDE *settles his group. The* COORDINATOR *hands the* TEACHER *a sheet of paper.*) Here is the list of words. A clean game: read slowly, with good pronunciation. Wait! Roll up your sleeve.

TEACHER: Me? What for? 75

COORDINATOR: I want to give you a charge of forty-five volts.

TEACHER: (*Surprised.*) Me? I'm the teacher!

COORDINATOR: Don't be afraid. I'm doing it so that you'll appreciate the intensity of the punishment. Otherwise, you might have a heavy hand. (*He puts an electrode on the* 80 TEACHER's *arm, pushes a button.*)

TEACHER: (*Jumps, frightened.*) That's strong!

COORDINATOR: No, no. You'll start with fifteen volts. You won't have to increase it much. Be seated. Read. Slowly, in a clear voice. 85

TEACHER: (*He sits in front of the metal box, clears his throat, reads haltingly.*) Day-sun, night-moon, mother-love, water-ship, plague-war, house-forest, child-innocence, prison-bars, window-freedom, blue-sky, bird-flight, nation-Germany, torture-dissuasion. (*He finishes, looks at the* COORDINATOR 90 *like a child awaiting instructions.*)

COORDINATOR: (*Claps him on the shoulder.*) Very good! Now you must read one word, then four more, so that the pupil will pick the correct association. If he makes a mistake, say "Error," press the first button, and tell the pupil the voltage 95 with which you're punishing him. Then read the right answer. Punishments start at 15 volts and end at 450. (*He makes a horizontal gesture with his hand.*) As you see, it couldn't be easier. Begin.

TEACHER: (*Clears his throat.*) Sun! Day, forest, mother, water. 100

VOICE OF THE PUPIL: Day!

COORDINATOR: Very good! (*Encouraging the* TEACHER.) Let's go on! Do you like it?

TEACHER: (*Like a child.*) Yes! It's terrific!

105   COORDINATOR: Continue.

TEACHER: Night! Plague, forest, moon, child.

VOICE OF THE PUPIL: Moon!

TEACHER: (*Enthused.*) Correct! (*To the* COORDINATOR, *laughing.*) This is like a drug!

110   COORDINATOR: Ssshh! Go on!

TEACHER: Mother! Day, water, child, love. (*Silence from the* PUPIL.) But this is bread in your belly! What memories do you have of your mother?

COORDINATOR: (*With bonhomie.*) Now, don't help! It's not

115   scientific!

VOICE OF THE PUPIL: Chi . . .

TEACHER: (*Advises.*) No!

COORDINATOR: (*Drily.*) Excuse me, sir. This is an experiment, not a game.

120   VOICE OF THE PUPIL: We can't repeat? (*The* TEACHER *looks at the* COORDINATOR.)

COORDINATOR: Just this once. You've got to follow the rules.

TEACHER: Just this once, not again. Mother: day, water, child, love. (*Silence from the* PUPIL.) Well?

125   VOICE OF THE PUPIL: Love!

TEACHER: Very good! But faster. (*The* COORDINATOR *nods approval.*) Blue: ship, bird, sky, house. (*Silence from the* PUPIL.) I'm waiting.

VOICE OF THE PUPIL: Want to repeat?

130   TEACHER: I won't repeat. How can you not remember? What a fool. (*Looks at the* COORDINATOR, *who assents.*) Answer, I won't wait any longer.

VOICE OF THE PUPIL: Bird!

TEACHER: (*Pleased.*) He made a mistake! Now what do I do?

135   COORDINATOR: (*He points to the box. The* TEACHER *vacillates in his choice among the buttons.*) The first. Fifteen volts.

TEACHER: (*Smiles timidly. Pushes the button.*) Here we go! Take that. (*Through the door, we see that the* PUPIL *is jolted but cries out more in surprise than pain. His cries are always in a parrot-voice,*

140   *stereotyped like those of someone who, as a joke, coarsely imitates moans, groans, and pain. To the* COORDINATOR.) I didn't do anything! (*Into the microphone.*) Now remember. (*He reads.*) Plague: child, innocence, love, night.

COORDINATOR: (*Very low.*) You forgot war.

145   TEACHER: I did?

COORDINATOR: Plague-war. It's all right, let it go. It doesn't matter.

TEACHER: (*Low.*) Should I repeat? (*The* COORDINATOR *shrugs.*) Well? (*The* PUPIL *is silent.*) Come on. Quick. Otherwise it's

150   boring, I get tired.

VOICE OF THE PUPIL: Night.

TEACHER: (*Pleased.*) He made a mistake! Thirty volts! (*Instantly presses the second button. A louder groan from the* PUPIL.) Moving right along. Child: love, mother, innocence, bird.

155   VOICE OF THE PUPIL: (*Quickly.*) Love!

TEACHER: He made a mistake! You were dreaming! Forty-five volts! (*He pushes another button. Howling loudly, the* PUPIL *arches his back. Surprised by the howling, the* TEACHER *looks into the other room. To the* COORDINATOR, *disturbed.*) A bit strong, wasn't it?

160   COORDINATOR: (*Soothingly.*) No. This is a scientific experiment, and I am in charge. What experiment? Just as I told you: simply to determine the effectiveness of punishment in learning. If from the beginning we doubt, we'll never arrive at a conclusion.

TEACHER: Yes, that's right. The associations are easy.   165

COORDINATOR: And it's not so much. I gave you forty-five volts, remember?

TEACHER: I didn't shout. What a weakling! (*To the* PUPIL.) Listen to me. Don't scream. Pay attention. Sky: mother, child, innocence, blue.   170

VOICE OF THE PUPIL: Blue!

TEACHER: Goooood!

COORDINATOR: Magnificent. We're already getting results.

TEACHER: It's no time to stop, then. Plague: prison, house, forest, war. Well? (*Slowly, the* COORDINATOR *closes the door con-*   175 *necting the rooms.*) Repeat. (*The* COORDINATOR *shakes his head.*) I can't. (*Silence from the* PUPIL.) Well? (*To the* COORDINATOR.) Can I repeat? Just this once. He's not very intelligent. (*The* COORDINATOR *snorts, accedes with a gesture.*)

TEACHER: Listen. Don't let your mind wander. Plague: prison,   180 house, forest, war.

VOICE OF THE PUPIL: Prison.

TEACHER: He's an idiot!

COORDINATOR: (*Exasperated.*) You must say, "Error," and press the button. That is your job! Save the commentary!   185

TEACHER: And now he's growling at me! (*He presses the button.*)

VOICE OF THE PUPIL: (*Screams.*) No, no! I didn't think I'd be in so much pain!

TEACHER: A smart aleck! Well, he better hold up! (*Into the microphone.*) Pupil: Pay attention. You think I like pushing   190 these little buttons? Try to remember. Blue: bird, flight, sky, freedom. (*Waits, nervous.*) Out with it!

VOICE OF THE PUPIL: I don't remember!

TEACHER: How can you not remember?

VOICE OF THE PUPIL: I don't!   195

TEACHER: (*Furious, pushes the button.*) If you don't remember, take this.

VOICE OF THE PUPIL: (*A scream.*) Sky! (*He whimpers.*)

TEACHER: Very good! (*He wipes the sweat from his face.*) You see? With a little determination, you hit it! Okay! Here we go.   200 Flight: bird, blue, forest, night. You gotta be quick. Answer.

VOICE OF THE PUPIL: I won't play! No matter what you say!

COORDINATOR: Youth today! Now he refuses!

TEACHER: What's the matter with him? He's howling.   205

COORDINATOR: He signed the release. He can't give up. The results are important, aren't they? You're not screaming. You can be counted on.

TEACHER: Pupil? Pay attention. I am going to read you the words.

VOICE OF THE PUPIL: Go to hell! Let's change places!   210

TEACHER: Change places? That's crazy. It'll be worse for you, if you don't answer. Bird: flight, blue, plague, war. And I'm repeating the words. And it isn't allowed! Who do you think you are? Answer!

VOICE OF THE PUPIL: I'll make a mistake!   215

TEACHER: Answer! (*He pushes the button. A scream. To* COORDINATOR.) He's screaming.

COORDINATOR: He feels a bit jolted. You have just one thing to watch out for: 450 volts—kaput. Otherwise, after a week, there isn't a mark.   220

TEACHER: Listen good. Are you listening?

VOICE OF THE PUPIL: Are you listening?

TEACHER: We'll see who's listening. Bird: night, flight, house, plague.

225 VOICE OF THE PUPIL: I don't remember!

TEACHER: Don't be such an ass!

VOICE OF THE PUPIL: Don't be such an ass! Plague!

TEACHER: (*Furious.*) Imbecile! Bird-plague! (*To the* COORDI-NATOR.) See how he answers! (*The* COORDINATOR, *under-*
230 *standing, shrugs his shoulders.*) He's jerking me around! (*He pushes a button. The* PUPIL *screams, weeps. Disconcerted, to the* COORDINATOR.) And now he's crying! What do I do?

COORDINATOR: Keep going. Don't worry about it.

TEACHER: Listen, kid, answer right, or I'll blow you away. Win-
235 dow: prison, flight, torture, fr . . . freedom.

VOICE OF THE PUPIL: Torture! Torture!

TEACHER: What did you say? Tortoise! Idiot! You're making fun of me! (*He pushes the button. The* PUPIL *howls.*)

COORDINATOR: (*Checking.*) One hundred eighty volts. (*Smiles*
240 *approvingly.*) It's moving right along.

VOICE OF THE PUPIL: Let me go, you're hurting me! Oh, my belly!

TEACHER: Do we stop?

COORDINATOR: No.

245 TEACHER: He doesn't remember anything!

COORDINATOR: He'll remember now.

TEACHER: You think so? He burst into tears. If he doesn't an-swer, this is useless!

COORDINATOR: It isn't useless! If we don't succeed in getting
250 concrete results, all this suffering will be useless. Besides, you have to.

TEACHER: *I* do?

COORDINATOR: Of course. The tears, the screams. Think about it.

255 TEACHER: I'm not exactly sucking my thumb!

COORDINATOR: Of course not. Go ahead.

TEACHER: Nation: prison, bars, Germany, torture.

VOICE OF THE PUPIL: I don't know!

TEACHER: (*His finger on the button.*) Out with it!

260 VOICE OF THE PUPIL: Argentina!

TEACHER: (*Beside himself.*) Germany, idiot! (*He pushes the button. The* PUPIL *howls.*)

COORDINATOR: Planck Institute, Munich.

TEACHER: (*Furious.*) Prison: nation, plague, war, bars.

265 VOICE OF THE PUPIL: I don't know, let me go! I want to go home!

TEACHER: (*Screams.*) Out with it!

VOICE OF THE PUPIL: Nation!

TEACHER: You made a mistake! (*He pushes button after button.*
270 *The* PUPIL *howls.*)

COORDINATOR: (*Stops him.*) Slow! One at a time.

TEACHER: He's fucking with me! Why doesn't he answer right?

COORDINATOR: Make him.

TEACHER: I don't like doing this to you. Is that clear? You
275 signed. Don't count your lost sheep. Concentrate! Here's another. Do you hear me? (*Silence.*) Do you hear?

VOICE OF THE PUPIL: (*Lifeless.*) Vultures fly near . . .

TEACHER: Moon: night, prison, window, flight. (*To the* COOR-DINATOR.) He'll get this one. It's easy. (*Low.*) If he doesn't
280 answer, what do I do?

COORDINATOR: (*Gently.*) I told you.

TEACHER: (*Puts his hand on the last button. Closes his eyes.*) He doesn't answer. Why doesn't he answer?

COORDINATOR: (*Softly.*) Laziness. Low level.

285 TEACHER: Moon.

VOICE OF THE PUPIL: Ni . . . Niii . . . ght . . .

TEACHER: (*Without consulting the list.*) He made a mistake. He made a mistake . . . again. (*He opens his eyes.*) It's deliberate. He can't not know. Still . . . it hurts me . . . (*He slowly*
290 *pushes the last button. Silence. He smiles with relief.*) He didn't scream.

COORDINATOR: No. (*Changes his tone. Exultantly.*) Very good! Four hundred fifty volts! Excellent! Your help has been in-valuable.

295 TEACHER: Why didn't he help?

COORDINATOR: Look . . . we choose the risks we take! Some-times we're not so lucky. (*Removes the* TEACHER's *lab coat.*)

TEACHER: It was his fault. Wasn't it?

COORDINATOR: Yes, yes. Your work was magnificent!

300 TEACHER: He didn't even make an effort. A baby at the breast could have answered right. Some people like to fuck with you!

COORDINATOR: Yes, yes! You were splendid. (*He shakes his hand.*) Thank you ever so much. Don't worry. An unforget-
305 table performance.

TEACHER: (*Flattered.*) It was nothing. I did what I could!

COORDINATOR: (*Seeing him to the door.*) No, no, you were quick, concise, sure. Thanks ever so much! (*Again he shakes his hand. The* TEACHER *exits. The* COORDINATOR *turns toward*
310 *the audience, professional.*) This experiment, with recorded screams and simulated tortures, was repeated 180 times. Unfortunately, this teacher who continued his punish-ments to the lethal 450 volts was no exception. Eighty-five percent of the teachers proceeded in the same way. The
315 same test was done in 1960 in the United States. The re-sults? Sixty-six percent. They were obeying rules and weren't responsible. Curious, isn't it? Surprised?

GUIDE: Okay, enough. Don't wear out the audience. (*To his group.*) The experiment was done in Germany and the
320 United States. Here among ourselves, it would be unthink-able, absurd. Ladies and gentlemen, let's look for something more amusing. (*He leads his group out of the room.*) This way, this way. If you would be so kind . . . Ladies and gentlemen . . .

SCENE FIVE

The GUIDE *leads the group to the room that in scene two was locked.*

GUIDE: (*He knocks.*) May I?

VERY SILLY VOICE: (*From inside the room.*) Yeeeess.

(*The group enters the room. Seated on a chair is a woman [*MOTHER*] made up like a doll, wearing a white dress that reaches to her feet and holding a baby in her arms. The baby, swaddled in tulle and lace, is obviously a doll. Sitting on the floor, at the woman's feet, a young man [*FATHER*] watches them with an enraptured expression. The group is enveloped in a beam of rosy light. The acting is frankly crude.*)

GUIDE: (*Pleased.*) Ah! Finally something coherent!

MOTHER: (*Rocking the child.*)

---

iv. 319 Stanley Milgram describes this experiment in his book, *Obedience to Authority* (New York: Harper & Row, 1974).

"My rose, asleep now lie
the horse is starting to cry
His poor hooves were . . ."

GUIDE: What a picture! (*To his group.*) Make yourselves comfortable. Can you see? Madam . . . (*Helps her get comfortable. Then, rapidly, drily.*) Explanation: For Foreigners. Seven P.M., Wednesday, December 16, 1970. Nestor Martins, attorney, defender of political prisoners and trade unions, consults with his client Nildo Zenteno. They take leave of one another in the street. Six men surround Martins, violently force him into a white Peugeot. Nildo Zenteno rushes back, manages momentarily to free the lawyer. A karate chop to the back of his neck brings Zenteno down as well. The car speeds off. A black Chevrolet escorts it. That car had pulled out of a nearby parking lot of the Federal Police. *Desaparecidos.* (*From newspaper.*) Nestor Martins, thirty-three. Nildo Zenteno, thirty-seven.

MOTHER:

" . . . bleeding,
his long mane was frozen,
and deep in his eyes
stuck a silvery dagger."

(*She suddenly stops. Distorting her voice as though she were a ventriloquist speaking for the little one.*) Stop it, Mama. That's old. Daddy, tell me a story.

FATHER: (*Very sweet.*) Yes, darling.

MOTHER: (*Idiotic voice.*) Daddy, it has to be modern! No morals, Daddy!

FATHER: Yes, darling.

MOTHER: (*Impatient.*) Come on, Daddy, start!

FATHER: (*Enraptured.*) Precious!

MOTHER: (*In the voice of a ferocious little child.*) I know I'm precious! Why do you go round and around, Daddy?

FATHER: Now, now . . . This child is in such a hurry! Daddy has to think!

MOTHER: Enough horsing around, Daddy. Well?

FATHER: (*Laughs confusedly. Then, grossly exaggerating the traditional tone in which one tells a story.*) Once upon a time . . .

MOTHER: (*In the voice of a fierce, exasperated little child.*) Yeeeess . . .

FATHER: (*In the same tone.*) Once upon a time there was a tall man, ugly, ugly, ugly . . . (*With disgust.*) Bolivian. (*Resuming the story.*) He had a pile of children. (*Drily.*) They procreate a lot. Then they send the kids here.

MOTHER: What happened to the little kids?

FATHER: (*Sweetly.*) They were in the street, begging, stealing . . .

MOTHER: And what happened to the tall man?

FATHER: The tall man met another man. This one was a shorty. They talked and talked . . .

MOTHER: (*Voice of a stupid baby.*) About what?

FATHER: Well . . . ! Ugly things! And when they were tired of talking, the tall man walked him to his car.

5–7 **My rose . . . were** the Mother sings fragments from the *Blood Wedding* lullabye   20–21 **Nestor . . . Zenteno** the disappearance of Nestor Martins and his client Nildo Zenteno was in fact one of the first. It happened during the term of de facto president General Levingston, who had come to power in a coup d'état, unseating the previous de facto president, General Onganía

MOTHER: Who?

FATHER: The shorty. The short one was bad, bad. And then some men came, and since he was bad, they put him in another car to punish him. Because he was bad, bad. And what did the tall man do?

MOTHER: I don't know!

FATHER: He didn't want them to punish him!

MOTHER: Stupid!

FATHER: He ran and ran and hit the good guys. And then, the good guys put him into the car as well.

MOTHER: The good guys took them for a ride! 'Cause they're so good!

FATHER: So very good!

MOTHER: And then what happened, Daddy?

FATHER: Nothing more was ever known!

MOTHER: Yea, yea, yea!

GUIDE: What horrible acting. So sorry. Let's look for something else. (*He pushes the people toward the door.*) The whole show's not like this. I hope.

MOTHER: (*Same voice of a stupid baby.*) Did they punish them a lot, Daddy?

FATHER: Nothing more was ever known!

MOTHER and FATHER: Yea, yea, yea!

GUIDE: (*Cutting it.*) Let's go. Let's go, gentlemen. They need at least another month of rehearsal. What dunces!

SCENE SIX

GUIDE: Let's go upstairs, see if we have better luck. He who searches finds. They say. (*The group goes up the stairs, or down, if the preceding scene took place on the upper level. Natural lighting. When the group reaches the landing of the upper level.*) No, I made a mistake. I had you climb to the . . . (*Stops.*) In vain. Let's go down.

(*They go down. Suddenly, a group of men burst in, hurling themselves at a person in the audience who is talking with someone else. This other person is for a second paralyzed with astonishment. Then shouting, he throws himself into the fray.*)

MAN: Let him go! Let him go!

(*He succeeds in freeing him. The two make it down a few stairs, but the group of men rush them, surround them, and drag them down the stairs. Over the loudspeaker a distressed voice is heard.*)

VOICE: My God, why did I run? (*Almost instantaneously, the scene breaks out in another place with other characters. The groups may cross at this moment. Again the voice is heard.*) My God, why did I run? (*The scene is repeated in another spot.*) My God, why did I run?

GUIDE: (*Meanwhile.*) If we search carefully, we'll find remains in the catacombs. There aren't many, but we can still hope for surprises. Careful please. Don't wander off now. That's it, all together. Careful on the stairs. Look over here! (*Matter of factly.*) A brutish people! Yes, we will find remains. Sometimes discoveries come about by chance. (*He examines the door to a room. Opens it. The room is lit.*) Oh, this one has good light. Imagine, ladies and gentlemen, the faith, the heroism of the first Christians. To pray in these pigsties. It gives me claustrophobia. (*He spots a form covered with canvas in a corner, on the floor.*) Here's something. Finally! (*He draws near.*) Stand back a little, ladies and gentlemen. (*With curiosity.*)

25 What is it? (*He lifts an edge of the canvas, immediately lets it fall and steps back.*) Puah! What a shitty surprise!

VOICE: My God, why did I run?

GUIDE: Sssh! (*Turns toward the audience, with a big feigned smile, gives the form a kick.*)

30 VOICE: My God, why did I run?

(*The* GUIDE *jumps on the form, tramples it, inflamed. In the doorway to the room, another* GUIDE *appears. He claps his hands loudly.*)

GUIDE #2: Ladies and gentlemen! Please leave. Out, everyone out! Sorry. We have a few like machines without an off button. If you would be so kind as to follow me. (*The light in the room fades out.*)

SCENE SEVEN

GUIDE #2: What was the other one telling you?

SOMEONE FROM THE AUDIENCE: About the catacombs.

GUIDE #2: (*Glib.*) Oh, yes! The remains of the first Christians in the catacombs . . . ! Impressive!

(*He opens a room. The* GIRL *from scene 3 is crawling on all fours toward a corner. Weak light on her. The rest of the room is in shadow. The pistol still lies abandoned on the floor.*)

5 GUIDE #2: What do we have here? What is she sniffing at like a dog? (*Goes closer. Joking, gives her a slap on the rear. Suddenly he changes expression, helps her to get up.*) What is this? Composure. Pull yourself together.

GIRL: (*Lost.*) He told me to wait. They keep my head underwa-

10 ter, until . . .

GUIDE #2: (*Interrupts.*) Who threw water on you? This isn't Carnival. Excuse me, I have to go back to work. (*Resumes his professional tone. To the group.*) The paintings are fantastic, a little deteriorated, but still . . . (*He shines a light on the*

15 *walls.*) Jesus, there's nothing! (*He sees a graffito in a corner, crouches, shines a light on it.*) Gentlemen, come closer! (*Looks more closely.*) What kind of filth is this? (*Stands.*) Please, ladies, no! Excuse me, but the ladies may not look! (*He gestures them away.*) Gentlemen, if you like, but . . . (*To the*

20 GIRL, *very surprised.*) You did this? Your idea of fun? It was a saint's head and they put a . . . (*He finishes with an expressive gesture.*) Let go, let go of the pencil!

GIRL: No. It wasn't me.

GUIDE #2: (*Spots the pistol on the floor.*) What's this? Just a mo-

25 ment, gentlemen. (*He picks it up.*) How strange!

GIRL: He left it so that, so that . . .

GUIDE #2: So that you could bullshit me. (*He raises his arm as though to hit her. Remembers the audience. Smiles.*) What negligence. (*Referring to the gun.*) I have to take care of everything

30 around here.

GIRL: I'm thirsty.

GUIDE #2: Then you'll pee and be even wetter. (*He shines his light on the walls.*) There's nothing here either. But I swear there was. And not this filth! (*He slaps her skirt.*) No way you're a virgin!

GIRL: I'm thirsty. 35

GUIDE #2: (*Looking around.*) Isn't there any water? In the other room, there's a bathtub filled to overflowing.

GIRL: No! No, damn you!

GUIDE #2: What did I tell you? Does anyone understand women? A difficult bunch. As you see, ladies and gentle- 40 men, there's nothing here either. Only the walls. And this filth. (*To the* GIRL.) You weren't getting discouraged, were you? He left you the pistol? How strange. Who am I to . . . ? (*He shrugs.*) But don't touch it. If you squeeze the trigger, it's all over. The baths and . . . (*He smiles.*) I'm meddling in 45 something that's none of my business. This is the safety. I'm leaving it up. Careful with the trigger. Sit down.

GIRL: (*She sits, shakes her head.*) I don't want it.

GUIDE #2: There's no danger, stupid! The slightest touch and it goes off. 50

GIRL: Take it!

GUIDE #2: (*Surprised.*) Why? Soaking and thirsty, it's not a good combination. (*He puts the pistol on her lap, takes her hand and places it on the weapon.*) Do you have a boyfriend? Touch this and it's all over, done with. 55

GIRL: I'm thirsty. (*She raises her hands.*)

GUIDE #2: Right. Sorry. I forgot: Ladies and gentlemen, forgive us for the . . . (*He points to the wall.*) How mortifying! If you would be so kind as to follow me . . . (*He opens the door, indicates the exit. At this moment an* USHERETTE *arrives* 60 *carrying a tray. She invites the group to have a glass of wine.*) Help yourselves, ladies and gentlemen. It's on the house. There's no reason to be scared: you won't have to pay for it. It's all included. Then we'll go on with our visit. (*A scream is heard. To the audience.*) Who screamed? Who is the imbe- 65 cile who screamed?

SCENE EIGHT

The USHERETTE *steps close to the* GUIDE *and whispers a few words in his ear.*

GUIDE: (*Making amends.*) Forgive me. In room 3 we are going to find something interesting. "Finally!" you must be saying to yourselves. "We should have stayed home." (*He laughs.*) Ah, theater's a risky business! What do you think? TV's a better bet, isn't it? But no, gentlemen. All is not 5 lost. Please, gentlemen. I'm swallowing the "ladies" so I can go faster. With so many "ladies and gentlemen, ladies and gentlemen," I can't go on to anything else. (*He leads the group through the passageway. The group is shunted aside by three men carrying a long, half-finished table. It is missing a few strips* 10 *of wood on the surface. It is an ordinary table except that it has a strap nailed to one end. One of the men carries a tool box.*) The first Christians were very persecuted. They were fed to the lions. (*The men put the table on the floor.*) Until San Martín. What would the Spanish say about San Martín? "That son 15 of a bitch traitor. That black shit." (*The men start to saw and drive nails, as though they were alone. They are blocking the passageway.*) Can't you work somewhere else? (*The men don't answer.*) This way, gentlemen. Here's a little path. (*They*

---

vii. 1 this Guide is different from the Guide in scene 6. Since the order of the scenes is up to the director, however, this Guide will be called Guide #2 only in scene 7, where the shift occurs

---

viii. 14 **San Martín** General José de San Martín, the liberator (El Libertador) of the southern part of South America, is an Argentine national hero

20   *can't get through. The men move the table, forcing the group to-*
     ward the GIRL'*s room.*)
  WOMAN'S VOICE:

> "Down he went to the river,
> Oh, down he went down!"

25 GUIDE: What a pain in the ass she is with that lullabye! (*He looks
    at the door.*) Here we are again. We may as well ... Through
    here. Sooner or later we'll see a whole scene. (*He opens. Jok-
    ing.*) Well? Have you dried yourself? How's ... (*There are some
    men surrounding the* GIRL. *The* GUIDE *quickly closes the door,*
30   *shoos the people away. With a false smile.*) No, I made a mistake.
    Room 3, they told me. Careful on the stairs. This way, ladies
    and gentlemen. Ladies, once again. It's nicer ...
  WOMAN'S VOICE:

> "And his blood was running,
35 > Oh, more than the water."

(*The* GUIDE *snorts. Two men have positioned the table against the
wall, clearing the passage way. They are smoking cigarettes, like two
workers taking a break.*)

  GUIDE: (*To the* WORKMEN.) Room 3? This one here? (*The men
    nod yes.*) Thank you!

SCENE NINE

*The room is lit with rosy light. Four chairs. There is a group com-
prising a man, a woman, and two other adults disguised as children,
a girl and a boy. Their makeup is exaggerated, and their clothes are
cheap, vulgar. The* MOTHER *is sewing, the* FATHER *is seated a little
apart, and the* CHILDREN *are playing at throwing a hoop.*

On the far side of the room are the CHIEF *and two* POLICEMEN. *They
sit very erect with their arms crossed over their chests. The characters act
very broadly, a little like marionettes. The tone is grossly exaggerated.*

  GUIDE: (*In a professional tone, dry and rapid.*) Explanation: For
    Foreigners. July 2, 1971. Marcelo Verdt and his wife, Sara
    Palacio de Verdt, were kidnapped by a group of eight men.
    Desaparecidos. Both were members of RAF, Revolutionary
5   Armed Forces. According to information in the newspa-
    pers, the wife, before disappearing, brought the children to
    her sister for protection.
  MOTHER: (*Moving her hand as though sewing.*) Children, I'm
    making a little outfit for the one who is best behaved!
10 CHILDREN: (*Playing.*) Thank you, Mommy!
  POLICEMEN: (*Coming forward.*) Hands up, in the name of the law!
  MOTHER: (*Raising her arm, protecting her face like the heroine in a
    silent movie.*) Oh! (*The* FATHER *doesn't move.*)
  CHILDREN: Mommy, Mommy, who are they?
15 MOTHER: Don't be afraid, my darlings! No one is hurting your
    mother!
  CHILDREN: Blessed Mommy!
  POLICEMAN: (*Comes close, snatches at her clothes.*) You're dis-
    guised! (*Shoving her violently.*)

---

viii. 23–24 **Down ... down** the Woman's Voice in this scene sings
from the Blood Wedding lullabye   **ix. 4–5 RAF, or Revolutionary Armed Forces,** is the translation of the name of FAR,
Fuerza Armada Revolucionaria, a left-wing guerilla group

CHILDREN: Mommy, Mommy, who are they?   20
  POLICEMEN: Where's your husband?
  MOTHER: I don't know!
  CHILDREN: What do you mean, you don't know, Mommy! In
    the bathroom! Making caca! (*They call.*) Daddy! Daddy!
    They're looking for you!   25
  FATHER: (*Gets up, comes forward, wide-eyed.*) Who? What's
    happening?
  POLICEMAN: This is what's happening! It's all over! (*Screams.*)
    Silence everyone! Let's get out of this hole! The car's out
    front!   30
  MOTHER: Not the children! They don't know anything about it!
  POLICEMAN: Them too!
  MOTHER: Have pity!
  POLICEMAN: Silence! Let's go! Everyone!

(*They put the chairs together to make the car. All squeeze in. One of
the* POLICEMEN *holds the hoop between his hands and handles it as
though it were a steering wheel. He imitates the sound of a motor.
The children wave. The* POLICEMAN *brakes suddenly. The others
fall backward. They get out of the car, their gestures exaggeratedly
frightened.*)

  CHIEF: They fell!   35
  MOTHER: (*On her knees.*) Pity!
  POLICEMAN: What should we do with the kids?
  CHILDREN: Daddy!
  FATHER: (*Dignified.*) I'll protect you, don't be afraid. (*Puts his
    arms around them.*)   40
  CHIEF: (*To the* POLICEMAN.) Idiot! Why did you bring the
    kids?
  POLICEMAN: You said everyone, Chief.
  MOTHER: They're innocent!
  CHIEF: I'll see if they're not already lost. Kids: Who created the   45
    flag?
  MOTHER: (*Begging them.*) Answer right, answer right!
  CHILDREN: (*In unison.*) Manuel Belgrano!
  CHIEF: When?
  CHILDREN: February 27, 1812.   50
  CHIEF: Where?
  CHILDREN: On the banks of the Paraná. He had it blessed right
    there, beneath a blue and white sky, blue and white sky,
    blue and white ...
  CHIEF: Exactly! Very good! (*Kisses them.*) Here's a prize. (*Gives   55
    them each a piece of candy.*)
  CHILDREN: Thank you, sir!
  CHIEF: (*To the* MOTHER.) Take them home. And don't be long.
  POLICEMAN: Chief, what if she doesn't return?
  CHIEF: (*With an exaggeratedly sinister laugh, pointing to the*   60
    FATHER.) This one stays here. It's in his interest that she
    return. (*To the* MOTHER.) Take my advice: be discreet. I'm
    doing you a favor. Don't be long. Take a taxi.
  MOTHER: What are you going to do to him?
  CHIEF: Nothing! From his eye to his sex. But only if I'm   65
    vexed.
  MOTHER: Marcelo!
  FATHER: My love!
  CHIEF: Take them home. We don't have any small sacks.
    They're only in the way. Move it.   70
  MOTHER: Come, children! Give Daddy a kiss. (*The* FATHER
    kisses them.) Don't be afraid. We're going home.

CHILDREN: (*Happy.*) The men are nice, Mama!

MOTHER: (*Moves off with the* CHILDREN. *Picks up the outfit she was sewing. To one of them.*) Tell Grandma that the hem was turned here. Will you remember?

CHILD: Yes, Mama.

MOTHER: There's soup in the pot. Have it for supper.

CHILDREN: If you're not there, we won't eat any soup! We won't eat any soup!

MOTHER: Be good!

CHILDREN: Where are you going, Mama?

MOTHER: I'm going with Daddy. You behave. (*Hugs them.*)

CHILDREN: Mommy! Mommy!

GUIDE: (*Choked up.*) It gets to you, doesn't it?

(*The* MOTHER *separates from the* CHILDREN *and returns toward the* CHIEF. *During the good-bye scene the* POLICEMEN *were trying various sacks—as though they were items of clothing—on the* FATHER. *They have found the right one. Then they take him out of the room.*)

CHILDREN: (*Singing in a round.*) We won't eat any soup! We won't eat any soup!

MOTHER: Here I am. Where's my husband?

CHIEF: Husband? What husband? Take off your clothes.

GUIDE: (*Quickly.*) Let's go! Let's get out of here! (*Claps his hands.*) Out! Where's "Carnation, sleep and dream"? Who wants more wine? (*Pushes the group toward the door.*) Follow me! Quick! No dawdling! (*The group goes out. The* GUIDE *closes the door, leans against it.*) Ouf!

SCENE TEN

GUIDE: A little wine! Careful . . . on the . . . stairs. (*The* USHERETTE *brings him a glass of water.*) Water? For me? What for? (*Remembers.*) Oh, right. She's waiting for water! Come, gentlemen, this way. We're almost there. Just another little minute. No reason to fret. (*Again they enter the room of the* GIRL *from scenes 3, 7, and 8. Her clothes are drenched. The* GIRL *is breathing anxiously. She's seated, with the pistol, which is dry, in her lap. To the group.*) Come in. Careful on the stairs. Or rather: fasten your seatbelts, no smoking. (*He laughs. To the* GIRL, *very amiably.*) May I? (*He puts the glass and the pistol on the floor. Takes the chair on which she is sitting. Offers it to a woman in the audience.*) Sit, madam, sit. She may have wet it, but she didn't piss on it! (*He dries the chair with a hankie. To the woman.*) Please, have a seat! (*To the* GIRL.) They paid admission. Are you thirsty? (*The* GIRL, *lost, doesn't answer. The* GUIDE *shakes her gently.*) Hey! Wake up. I'm asking you if you're thirsty. (*The* GIRL, *shakes her head no.*) Oh, no? I brought you water. Drink it. (*He takes the glass, brings it to her lips. The* GIRL *resists.*) And now, what do I do with the glass? I need my hands free. I'm working. This can't be! Drink, little girl, drink. The water flowed . . . (*Forcing her.*) There. There, that's good. So capricious! Well, I don't like people pulling my leg. You're all wet. (*Puts his hand under her skirt.*) Even your little firecracker. (*He laughs. Turns toward the audience.*) Oh, excuse me. (*Takes the pistol.*) Shall I take it? No? Freedom is within your grasp. No? (*He puts the

---

ix. 75–76 **Tell Grandma that the hem was turned here** is an encoded way of communicating the arrest

barrel against her breast.*) How stupid. I can't. (*He cleans the weapon, puts it in the* GIRL's *lap.*) I don't know why they trust you so . . . It's loaded. If you had a boyfriend, old girl . . . But like this. Idiot, why endure so much? (*Another* GUIDE *appears in the doorway.*)

OTHER GUIDE: (*Shouting.*) What are you doing here? It's about to start there! And they're giving out wine! It's not to be missed. I saw it! Exceptional! You can understand everything!

GUIDE: Really? Step on it, fellas, let's go! Move it, girls!

OTHER GUIDE: (*Teases.*) Don't you mean ladies and gentlemen?

GUIDE: (*To* OTHER GUIDE.) There's wine? For sure? (OTHER GUIDE *affirms it and leaves.*) If you would be so kind, ladies and gentlemen . . . (*He holds open the door so the group can pass through. Before closing the door, in a friendly way.*) Think about it, little girl.

SCENE ELEVEN

In the passageway, one of the vertical wooden boxes.

GUIDE: Wait! This has always intrigued me . . . (*Tries to see through the peephole.*) I can't see a thing. How about you, sir? (*Someone from the audience has a look.*) It's very dark. (*He knocks at the door. Jokingly.*) Is anyone home? *Hay alguien?* (*Curious, he opens the door. There's a heavily madeup man inside, dressed in a loincloth, staring fixedly. Matter of factly.*) Hi. (*He closes the door, turns toward the audience with an uncomfortable smile. As though it were not so strange.*) What a surprise! To me this is very curious . . .

OTHER GUIDE: (*Shouts from the doorway of the other room.*) Well? What are you waiting for? A carriage? If you don't get there at the beginning, they won't understand anything!

GUIDE: (*Annoyed, referring to the vertical box.*) What about this? Does anyone understand this? (*To the* OTHER GUIDE.) I give the orders in my group! And if they don't get it, too bad for them! This way, gentlemen! (*He leads them in the opposite direction.*) Follow me! (*A panting death rattle is heard through the door of a room they pass.*)

SCENE TWELVE

GUIDE: (*He lingers in front of the door, listening to the death rattle inside.*) What could this be? (*A* MAN *passes by, whistling.*)

MAN: (*To* GUIDE.) Good day!

GUIDE: Good day! (*Surprised.*) Well, he's happy! Let's follow him. (*Referring to the death rattle in the room.*) Sounds like that and we've really got a mess on our hands! We can check it out later. (*He and the group follow the* MAN. *The* MAN *walks along, whistling. He meets another man who is coming from the opposite direction.*)

MAN: Good day!

NEIGHBOR #1: Hello! How's it going, doctor?

(*They shake hands. They continue walking together. The group follows them. They enter a large room, where* NEIGHBOR #2 *is sweeping the floor. Two chairs stacked in a corner, against the wall.*)

NEIGHBOR #2: Hello, doctor!

GUIDE: (*To his group.*) Watch out for the cars! Stay on the sidewalk, please!

(*He situates them. He hasn't finished doing so when the* FIRST GROUP OF MEN *enters at a trot, one behind the other, tied together at their waists.*)

15 FIRST GROUP OF MEN: Let us through! Let us through!

(*They come forward, trot through the room, then suddenly halt in front of the* MAN *and surround him, forming a closed circle.*)

MAN: Excuse me.
FIRST GROUP OF MEN: Quieto! Quieto!
MAN: Are you calling me? What do you want? (*The men acceler-
    ate, tightening their circular movement, forming two closed rings.*)
20   Excuse me. Let me through.
NEIGHBOR #1: What's going on, doctor?
NEIGHBOR #2: (*Stops sweeping.*) Hey! Let him go!
NEIGHBOR #3: (*From the audience.*) What the hell is going on?
    (*Comes forward to help the* MAN.)
25 MAN: Let me go! Enough fooling around!

(*He pushes, tries to get through the circle. Hits, struggles. The men try to drag him toward the door.*)

NEIGHBORS: Let him go! Let him go!

(*They try to break up the group,* NEIGHBOR #2 *hitting out with his broom. The* SECOND GROUP OF MEN *enters, also at a trot and tied together at their waists. They sing.*)

SECOND GROUP OF MEN:

        Peace and security
        That is our domain
30   With a little authority
        Order will be maintained!

(*Observing the tumult, they linger.*)

OFFICIAL: (*Heading the* SECOND GROUP OF MEN.) What's going
    on here? This is scandalous! Halt! Separate!

(*The fight freezes.*)

NEIGHBORS: (*All at the same time.*) Sir, they were pushing him!
35   (*Alternating.*)
    —Over here.
    —Over there.
    —They tied him up.
    —They dragged him down!
40 OFFICIAL: One at a time, magpies. Who asked you anything?
    (*To the group in the fight.*) And you, you're prisoners in the
    name of the law. (*He "aims" at them, with his finger. The* SEC-
    OND GROUP OF MEN *"handcuffs" them. They're all, including
    the* MAN *put into a line and tied together at the wrists.*)
45 NEIGHBORS: Officer, sir:
        Why the arrest?
        He's one of the best!

---

17 **Quieto!** Roberto Quieto, whose surname in fact means
"quiet," was a prominent, highly respected liberal lawyer. Unbe-
knownst to most, he was also a powerful member of the Mon-
toneros, the premier left-wing guerrilla organization

OFFICIAL: It doesn't matter, my esteemed citizens
    Have faith
    Justice is there for a reason   50
    To prevent baseness, which is treason.
NEIGHBORS: But we saw . . .
OFFICIAL: What you saw is of no consequence
    If there's offense
    Rest assured   55
    The man's secure . . .
SECOND GROUP OF MEN: Sure!

(*They "take aim" at the* NEIGHBORS.)

OFFICIAL: In my providence.

(*The* NEIGHBORS *mix in with the audience. The* OFFICIAL *moves off to the side, crosses his arms, his expression serious. The* FIRST GROUP OF MEN *and the* MAN *attacked in the first place draw near. One of the men from the second group arranges the chairs.*)

OFFICIAL: (*Seating himself. To the* MAN.) Name.
MAN: Quieto.   60
GUIDE: (*Shouts.*) Sí, Quieto! (*To his group.*) Quieto means quiet.
    (*Smiles.*) Stop a moment. (*Gestures toward the group.*) So they'll
    understand. Otherwise, they'll miss the point. (*The others stop
    the action. In a dry, professional tone.*) Explanation: For Foreign-
    ers. July 7, 1971. Robert Quieto, attorney, defender of politi- 65
    cal prisoners, resists a kidnapping attempt. Fortunately, the
    neighbors intervene and call a police squad. The kidnappers
    turn out to be policemen. Dr. Quieto was put at the disposi-
    tion of the executive power. Subsequently he was accused of
    having been implicated in an auto theft and of having par-   70
    ticipated, after his detention, in various subversive acts. He
    was transferred to Rawson Prison, 730 miles from Buenos
    Aires. What happened then? I don't remember. Lost in the
    night of time. (*Smiles.*) But he wasn't so innocent. High up in
    the Montoneros, the son of a b——. It's not my responsibil- 75
    ity. Although when you have the truth, I don't know why it
    should be hidden. Go on. I'm done.
OFFICIAL: (*To the* MAN.) Name.
MAN: Quieto.
OFFICIAL: Quieto! That's what I'm telling *you!* Now what is   80
    your name?
MAN: Blame.
OFFICIAL: (*Suspicious.*) Ohhhh? (*To the* FIRST GROUP OF MEN.)
    And you? What are your names?
FIRST GROUP OF MEN: (*They sing.*)   85

        Peace and security
        That is our domain
        With a little authority
        Order will be maintained!

SECOND GROUP OF MEN: 90

        If you're lying
        You'll get bruised!

OFFICIAL: Explain what happened
    I'm confused!
FIRST GROUP OF MEN: 95

        Boca will never lose!
        Boca's the team we choose!

OFFICIAL: (*Very pleased.*) For this, you are excused. But who began . . .

100 FIRST GROUP OF MEN: That man!

OFFICIAL: No more rhyming! (*To the* MAN.) Don't you know that it's a crime to incite a riot in the street? (*To the* SECOND GROUP OF MEN.) Did they stop traffic?

SECOND GROUP OF MEN: Yes, sir! They delayed it!

105 OFFICIAL: For how long?

SECOND GROUP OF MEN: For three minutes!

OFFICIAL: Re-create it!

SECOND GROUP OF MEN:

> In their cars the men grew irritated
110 > At the office work accumulated.

OFFICIAL: (*To the first group, fiercely.*) I want a confession. (*Sweetly.*) What team are you from?

FIRST GROUP OF MEN:

> Boca will never lose
115 > Boca . . .

OFFICIAL: Fine, fine, no need to repeat! (*The* FIRST GROUP OF MEN "*free*" *their hands, which had been "cuffed." To the* MAN.) What about you?

MAN: What about me?

120 OFFICIAL: What team are you from?

MAN: I nurse the same illusion.

OFFICIAL: I smell collusion. Why aren't you from San Lorenzo?

MAN: Because I'm not?

OFFICIAL: Don't be a wise guy! (*The* SECOND GROUP OF MEN
125 *hit* MAN. *To the others.*) And you, what are you waiting for? Get going!

MAN: You can't let them go! They attacked me! I want to see my attorney!

OFFICIAL: The one who gives the orders here is me. (*To the others.*)
130 And you, once again, (*Sweetly.*) why don't you do your work?

FIRST GROUP OF MEN: (*Tied together at their waists, they trot out, singing.*)

> For us it was a sad event
> That ended to our detriment
135 > Of this our song's a testament!
> For us it was a sad event
> That ended to our detriment
> Of this our song's a testament!

OFFICIAL: (*To the* MAN.) Justice will be done.

(*One of the men in the second group puts on a judge's robe and comes closer. Another moves in a chair and has him sit. Becoming the* GUARD, *he remains standing behind the* JUDGE's *back.*)

140 JUDGE: (*To the* MAN.) You're free. Being from Boca's no crime. But next time . . .

114–115 **Boca** the Boca Juniors are one of the most important Argentine soccer teams. Their home stadium is in the Buenos Aires neighborhood of La Boca, traditionally an Italian working-class section. San Lorenzo is another team from Greater Buenos Aires. Soccer is by far the most passionately followed sport in Argentina

(*The* MAN *frees his hands and stands up. The* JUDGE *turns halfway around and grabs him from behind. No sooner has he done so when the* GUARD *leans into the* MAN *and pushes him roughly down by the shoulders, forcing him to sit. The* MAN *again joins his hands as though they were handcuffed.*)

OFFICIAL: (*To the* MAN.) You stole a car. Your trial's pending. Your sentence could be unending!

MAN: I need defending!

OFFICIAL: Superintending! (*To the* JUDGE.) He stole a car. 145

JUDGE: He did not steal a car!

MAN: Am I absolved? Can I go?

JUDGE: Why not? Go ahead!

(*He turns so that his back is to the* MAN. *The previous scene is repeated: the* MAN *frees his hands, the* GUARD *forces him to sit down again, etc.*)

OFFICIAL: He robbed a bank!

MAN: I was in prison! 150

JUDGE: (*It starts again.*) Absolved!

MAN: Thank you. Can I go?

JUDGE: Why not? Go ahead. (*Again. The rhythm speeds up.*)

OFFICIAL: He robbed a station!

JUDGE: (*Over his shoulder.*) What kind of station? 155

OFFICIAL: Service station. Five old wrecks.

MAN: (*Forced to sit.*) How? I was in prison!

OFFICIAL: (*With pretended fury.*) Guards, you let him go?

JUDGE: (*Turns.*) Why can't you see? There is no case. Let him go free! (*Turns his back.*) 160

OFFICIAL: He robbed a commissary, several stores, and several dairies!

MAN: (*Forced to sit.*) If I'd been seized How could I be eating cheese?

JUDGE: He is innocent 165
> Surely
> I declare it
> Firmly.

MAN: (*Stands up, etc.*) Thank you. Can I go?

JUDGE: Naturally. Why not. (*It starts again. The action accelerates* 170 *to the point of dislocation but always remains precise. The speeches are transferred but not the actions, which remain a constant with each character.*)

OFFICIAL: Don't move. I've heard a little story!

JUDGE: He murdered a canary. 175

MAN: That isn't fair!
> I love all canaries
> Everywhere!

OFFICIAL: You love them, but you kill them!

JUDGE: Guards, you let him go? 180

OFFICIAL: Your Honor, you're the witness Of this bad faith.

MAN: I only want to live!

JUDGE: Guards, you let him go?

OFFICIAL: If he'd been seized 185

MAN: How could I've been eating cheese?

JUDGE: Thank you.

OFFICIAL: Beat it! I can't stand you anymore!

MAN: I'm going back to my city!

JUDGE: Can I go? 190

OFFICIAL: Beat it!

MAN: (*Resisting those who are making him sit.*) No, no, I was in prison!

JUDGE: He's free! Oh, such obsession!

OFFICIAL: He's free! What fascination!

195 MAN: But I'm not!

JUDGE: Yes, you are! So you better shut up! (*Turns his back, covers his ears.*)

OFFICIAL: Enough already! He's hard to handle. All that screaming. What a scandal!

(*Gestures to the guards to take the* MAN *away. To the audience.*)

200   The idiots they send me, it's outrageous!
        The courts
        aren't beneficial
        Unless they're
        sacrificial!

(*Lights out.*)

GUIDE: Shit! What happened? They turned out the light with-
205   out telling me! Cretins! (*Take out his flashlight, switches it on.*) Where is the door? Luckily I know the house. (*Opens door. The passageway is lit.*) This way, gentlemen. There aren't any stairs. But be careful all the same. You only get to stumble once, like the tango says. Hey, hey. Everyone make it? (*He
210   leads the group through the passageway. They pass the door to the room where the death rattle was heard. It is heard again. The* GUIDE *puts his ear to the door. Admiringly.*) Persistent! We go in? We don't go in? What do you want to do? Free choice. At my orders! We go in!

SCENE THIRTEEN

The GUIDE *opens the door. The labored breathing stops. There is a* GIRL *with long hair laid out on a stretcher, with a sheet carefully folded under her feet.*

GUIDE: (*Advancing on tiptoe.*) Don't make any noise. She's sleep-ing. (*He approaches, looks at her. The* GIRL *smiles at him. Sweetly.*) How're you doing?

GIRL: (*Sits up, brushes her hair off her face, folds her hands in her lap.*
5   *She looks at the group with a semismile. Silence. Then, very simply, colloquially.*)
        I would like to die
        as softly as possible
        So that my friends will think
10   she is sleeping
        in the earth
        become a worm
        digging in the earth
        so that in spring
15   the flowers blossom
        After my death
        I want my children
        to sit at the table
        and say
20   at her age
        Mama
        ran off with some guy
        What a shame
        poor old Dad

staring at the tablecloth   25
his cup of coffee
searching for her
This is how I want to die
as simply
as though I had never lived   30
What a lovely thought
to leave like that
not causing any pain
The cup of coffee
that no one drinks   35
absent . . .

(*Silently, a character mixed in with the audience goes up to the* GIRL. *He puts his hand over her mouth and nose. The* GIRL *offers desperate, mute resistance. She dies. The man gently lays her out, covers her with the sheet. Then he moves off and mixes in with the crowd, like one more spectator.*)

GUIDE: (*Amazed.*) How about that? (*Looks at the man.*) And now he's so calm! But what a feat! Phenomenal! (*He lifts the sheet. Matter of factly.*) She's dead. Poor creature! Really, with-out so much as a moan. Discreet. And in the bloom of   40
youth! (*Lets the sheet fall.*) She spoke of children, a husband. We'll have to go find them. Nice news I've got. What a bad deal. (*Hopefully.*) Anyone want to go? Of course, for this there are no volunteers. (*Furious.*) The son of a bitch. (*He goes to the door, leaving the audience.*) Excuse me. (*He opens the   45
door, yells out.*) I need someone from the family! Quick! Someone from the family! (*He comes back inside.*) She didn't move, did she? What with the advances of medicine, for a moment I thought that . . .

(FOUR MEN *enter, two-by-two, each pair moving as one. They are wearing white smocks down to their feet, very loose, belted at the waist. They come in on skates. Their faces are painted with large red smiling mouths. One pair beats pot lids; the other pair waves a white sack.*)

FOUR MEN: (*Singing.*)   50

        Tachín, tachín, tachín
        She died as she would have ordained
        Without causing any pain.

GUIDE: What about the family? I've got to tell them . . . It's so unfortunate . . . My heartfelt sympathy. (*Extending his   55
hand.*)

FOUR MEN: (*They pay no attention to the* GUIDE. *They approach the stretcher, lift the sheet. Sing.*)

        The jokester
        Coaxed her   60

GUIDE: (*Very confused.*) Choked her . . . A son of a bitch who . . . (*Searches with his eyes. The* MEN *start putting the* GIRL *into the sack. Surprised.*) What are you doing? But . . .

FOUR MEN: (*Sing.*)

        But nothing   65
        But nothing
        Just doing our bit
        Ashes to ashes
        Shit to shit

GUIDE: (*Indignant.*) That's gross! Don't you see there's people?   70
You must have been raised in a barn! Ladies, your forgive-

ness. I knew nothing … The modern theater is like this. No respect for the ladies!

FOUR MEN:

(*They finish putting the* GIRL *into the sack, leaving her head out. They tie the end of the sack around her neck. It is evident that the* GIRL *is playing dead: though her head is bent over, she is able to support it. The* FOUR MEN *hold the bundle, swing it hammocklike. They sing.*)

75   If you don't like this Tin Pan band
    Because it hasn't any flair
    Because it just gave you a scare
    Swing high, swing well
    You can go to hell!

80 GUIDE: Go on!
FOUR MEN:

    Tachín, tachín, tachín,
    Tachín, tachín, tachín!
    Pran-pran-pran!
85   T333á-ta-ta!

(*They near the door. The* HUSBAND *and* MOTHER *enter. The* HUSBAND *is wearing threadbare clothing. His hair is long and all over the place. The* MOTHER *is the typical little old lady—black clothes, shawl over her head. Both act crudely, like prototypes of desperate people.*)

HUSBAND: What happened? I heard screams!
MOTHER: Sirs, have pity! Where is my daughter? Darling! Darling!
GUIDE: Oh my God, the family's here!
90 MOTHER and HUSBAND: (*Together.*) We've come to look for our poor Hermenegilda.
FOUR MEN:

(*They come back, set the corpse down; it supports itself against the stretcher. Horrified.*)

That name she inherited
She certainly merited!
95 MOTHER and HUSBAND: (*Together.*) We're here to find out What she finally merited!
GUIDE: Oh no! If these two speak in verse, I'm leaving! Although the language may be terse, I can't bear
100 so much pain. I'm leaving! (*He pushes away from the crowd, but upon hearing the* HUSBAND, *he stops, comes back.*)
HUSBAND: Where is she?
FOUR MEN: (*They shake the corpse in front of the* HUSBAND's *face.*)
105 We don't know! We don't know! She was never here!
HUSBAND: What do you mean? She came here to buy wine!
FOUR MEN: (*They turn the corpse facedown on the stretcher, look underneath.*) She bought her bread and went away, evaporated … Surely it was fated! (*They look at the ceiling. The* HUSBAND *and*
110 MOTHER *imitates them. The men point.*) Look sir. That moth …
HUSBAND: She wasn't a moth! At dawn …
FOUR MEN: She was a moth. At dawn Before the sun came up full we found her eating
115 wool

MOTHER: It's not true! She didn't like wool!
FOUR MEN: Was she a woman or a moth? The question's far from risible. Lady, lady don't be miserable. Don't be upset 120 We'll give you your daughter yet.

(*They approach an interior door. They call the* HUSBAND *and* MOTHER *as one would a dog.*)

Tch, tch, tch …

(*The* HUSBAND *and* MOTHER *advance, their smiles exaggeratedly hopeful. The others open the door. The interior is dark. The* HUSBAND *and* MOTHER *look in.*)

FOUR MEN: You'll find her here, here! So be of good cheer, cheer! (*Moving in unison, the* FOUR MEN *push them inside with kicks in* 125 *the rump.*) And stop mugging! (*They close the door. They sway.*) Ladies, Gentlemen, dearest friends Our show is over, Curtains!

(*They take the corpse. They lead the way to the exit, singing.*)

    Tachín, tachín, tachín!
    Tachín, tachín, tachín! 130
    Tarará-ta-ta!
    Tarará-ta-ta!

GUIDE: (*Enthused.*) Let's go, let's go! Let's follow them! See what happens! They're entertaining! (*The group follows the* FOUR MEN *and* GUIDE. *The* FOUR MEN *enter a contiguous room* 135 *and close the door. An actor, pretending to be part of the audience, opens it. The interior is dark. An enormous club comes out and hits the actor over the head. He falls. The* GUIDE *leans over him.*) Why did he butt in? I'm the Guide here! One to a group! (*He pokes him. The man doesn't move. He then lifts him by the armpits* 140 *and puts him into one of the vertical boxes. He talks all the while, completely dissociated from his actions.*) That's how it is. In they all go but … who takes the potatoes out of the fire? The son of a bitch. If he was part of the audience, why did he make like an actor? Vanity, vanity will be the end of us all! … 145 (*He closes the door.*) Now what were we going to see?
SOMEONE FROM THE AUDIENCE: The catacombs.
GUIDE: Right. Thank you. The first Christians really had a hard time of it. Just thinking about how the lions loved to chew them up … Human meat, they say, is sweet. Sweet, bit- 150 ter, what could be stupider. (*They cross with another group. To the* OTHER GUIDE.) Where's there something good? We went in here, and it's all fucked up. (*Without stopping, the* OTHER GUIDE *points to a door.*)

SCENE FOURTEEN

The GUIDE *leads the group into the designated room. Inside is a group of* NEIGHBORS *all crowded together, some looking over the heads of others. On the far side, two* POLICEMEN *crouch, their expressions very attentive. In the center are the* MAN *and* WOMAN, *both heavily made-up. Their clothes are cheap, flashy; the* WOMAN *wears very high heels. All the acting is crude, infantile, and exaggerated.*

GUIDE: Attention. Ladies and gentlemen, this is the main course. So they tell me. Hope it's true. Make yourselves

comfortable. If you find a chair, be seated. Silence, please. The story of a BM, or bad marriage. (*His tone is professional,*
5 *dry and quick.*) Explanation: For Foreigners. On the afternoon of July 13, 1971, Juan Pablo Maestre and his wife, Mirta Elena Misetich, were kidnapped by a group of men. Juan Pablo Maestre managed to run a few yards but then was shot. Mirta Elena Misetich ran in the opposite direc-
10 tion, losing a shoe. She was captured and pushed into one car; her husband was thrown into another. Shortly afterward, a police squad sent to the scene recovered the shoe and ordered the doorman of an apartment building to wash the blood from the pavement. The body of Juan Pablo
15 Maestre appeared days later in Escobar. Of Mirta Elena Misetich there was no further news. Both belonged to the RAF, or Revolutionary Armed Forces. Juan Pablo Maestre, twenty-eight years old. Mirta Elena Misetich, the same age.

MAN: (*With a conspiratorial air.*) Let's plant a bomb here
20 WOMAN: (*With a conspiratorial air.*) And a bomb over there!

MAN: When these go off

WOMAN: No one will be spared!

MAN and WOMAN: (*Taking bombs with fuses out from under their clothes.*) Subversion, subversion,
all rise up!
25 in revolution!

MAN: (*Looking around.*) Let's go, all clear!

WOMAN: Nothing will be left here! (*They take a few cautious steps.*)

POLICEMAN: (*Comes forward, arm extended.*) Hands up! In the
30 name of the law!

MAN: We're caught! Run! (*They drop their bombs and run in opposite directions.*)

POLICEMAN: (*Aims with his finger and shoots.*) Pum!

(*The MAN falls. His blood is obviously fake. The other POLICEMAN runs after the WOMAN.*)

WOMAN: (*Stops.*) Darling!
35 POLICEMAN: Hey, hey! Justice always triumphs! Olé!

(*The two POLICEMEN drag the MAN and WOMAN away. The WOMAN loses her shoe. They exit. Slowly, the NEIGHBORS untangle themselves and come forward.*)

NEIGHBORS: The ass must be judged
Not broken!

(*The two POLICEMEN reenter. The NEIGHBORS immediately reform their group.*)

POLICEMEN: Of our respect
Here's a token!

(*They're carrying the MAN, dragging him along. The NEIGHBORS watch, timidly come forward. Romantic music is heard. More POLICEMEN enter, smiling and wearing sweepers jackets. They swing long-handled brooms, dance as in a musical comedy.*)

---

xiv. 38–39 **"Of our respect / Here's a token"** is the couplet substituted for "violín, violón / es la mejor razón." See "Crisis, Terror, Disappearance"

GROUP OF POLICEMEN: (*They sing.*)   40

> We're here to clean!
> We're here to clean!
> The filth is gone
> Your street is clean!
> Let mothers pray   45
> let children play
> in celebration!

(*Smiling, they sweep. They lift the shoe. They sing.*)

> Little shoe, little shoe
> Whom might you belong to?
> Why, to Snow White   50
> or to her mother.

GUIDE: What do you mean, fellas! The little lost shoe was Cinderella's!

POLICEMAN: (*Emphatically.*) I say it's Snow White's or her mother's. (*Recovering his smile.*) Whose little shoe is this?   55 Madam, is it yours? Say yes. A Prince Charming awaits you in the wings.

GUIDE: No, no! Error! It's the prince, the prince who searches for the owner of the shoe, not a cop! Didn't you read the story?   60

POLICEMAN: Calm down! It's a free interpretation. (*Smiling.*) Doesn't it belong to anyone? Neighbors? (*He shows them the shoe. The NEIGHBORS immediately deny ownership, shaking their heads in unison.*) So we'll look in another neighborhood. It'll belong to someone. (*He repeats, frowning in the* 65 *GUIDE's direction.*) It's Snow White's or her mother's.

GUIDE: (*Servile.*) Yes, of course, her mother's. Well, let's get going. We can follow you, can't we? (*To his group.*) We'll just stroll along. If you get tired, let me know.

GROUP OF POLICEMEN: (*They go out with the shoe. Asking.*)   70 Madam, is this yours? Is this yours? Young man? (*The group follows them. They enter another room. The WOMAN, wearing no makeup, is seated on a chair. Sitting nearby on the floor, with her legs crossed, is a GIRL, who may be the same as the one from scene 13.*)

POLICEMAN: (*To the WOMAN.*) Madam, excuse me. We found a   75 little shoe. Is it yours? Prince Charming will marry you. Cash in a flash! You'll live in a palace! Let's see. (*He puts the shoe on her foot.*) She's Cinderella! It fits! Perfect! What luck, old girl! You win! A royal flush! (*Bows.*) Princess! My respects! (*The WOMAN stares ahead, immobile. Surprised.*) Aren't   80 you happy? What's the matter?

WOMAN: My darling!

POLICEMAN: Your darling was stopped by a cop. (*The POLICEMEN exit arm-in-arm, tap dancing.*)

WOMAN: I was at home, eating my bread. I was   85
    making love. I was kissing my children.
And you will be the only one who knows
where and how my body was lost,
how my voice became unstrung
Only you will know   90
    how to know
the voices of fear and the faces of
    desperation
My God, what did the brave ones become?
I will speak   95

Only you will know
this tongue.

(*A shot is heard.*)

GUIDE: What's going on? Did you hear that? It was a shot.
(*Looks at the* WOMAN *and the* GIRL.) But why so quiet! It's
100   over. Gentlemen, follow me. Did you like that? (*He leads his
group out of the room.*) A bit mixed up, wasn't it? Me . . . well,
what do you like . . . I'm old-fashioned. I prefer something
else. If this was the main course, what will the others be?
(*They enter the adjoining room. The* GIRL *of scenes 3, 7, and 8 lies
105   on the floor, shot, the pistol in her hand. The* GUIDE *looks at her,
surprised. Then, matter of factly, pushing them toward the exit.*)
Oh, sorry! Shall we? The jug may as well go to the fountain
as . . . (*Happy music is heard.*) How about that music! So
there is a little happiness in this world! Enough drama!
110   Let's go. Move along. A little gaiety, dammit!

(*The poem spoken by the* WOMAN *was written by Marina, a Greek
girl, who was captured and tortured.*)

SCENE FIFTEEN

*As the group leaves, the music fades and after a few minutes disappears.
Through the passageway comes a group holding hands. They sing.*

GAME PLAYERS:
   —Martin Fisherman, will you let me pass?
   —Pass, pass, but the last one stays with me!

(*The group starts playing Martin Fisherman, a singing game somewhat like London Bridge Is Falling Down. Two children make a
bridge with their arms; the others run underneath, single file, holding
each other by the waist. The line of children sings for permission to pass
through; the last one is taken prisoner. In another version, the children
making the bridge ask questions. Those who answer correctly pass
through; the others do not. Two lines form, one comprising the "free,"
the other "prisoners." After everyone has had a question, the longer line
wins, and the game may start again.*)

GUIDE: Ladies and gentlemen, you're welcome to participate.
5   That's not coercion, only if you want to. Grotowsky used to
say: The more physical distance, the more spiritual closeness. What nonsense! Don't be afraid to join in, ladies and
gentlemen!

(*The game continues. Suddenly one of the men forming Martin Fisherman's bridge yells.*)

GAME PLAYERS: (*Alternately.*)
10   —I know that one! Don't let him go!
   —Me?

(*The latter tries to get off the bridge.*)

   —I know that one! Don't let him go!
   —Don't fight!
   —Just answer right!
15   —I don't have to! No!

(*He whistles over his shoulder for help. Those in his line start to push.
The others shout.*)

—Don't push! Hold tight!
—Wait!

(*Nevertheless they react. The shorter line becomes crooked. A man
forming the bridge yells.*)

—They're shooting! Hold tight!

(*The sound of a police whistle.* POLICEMEN *arrive, dressed like the cops
in Charlie Chaplin's The Kid, with large, prehistoric-type clubs.
Music is heard. Their acting is crude. They immediately start hitting
those in the longer line over the head. The sound of the clubs: Plac!
Plac! Plac! Those hit fall into artificially distorted poses. The men
rush the bridge of Martin Fisherman, crushing the captured player,
who screams.*)

GUIDE: Kids today! They don't know how to play peacefully!
   Let's get out of the way. I wonder if they'll tie them up. 20
   (*Warns a* POLICEMAN.) Not the audience! (*The* POLICEMAN
   *moves his head like Harpo Marx. He spins around like an acrobat,
   beating on actors mixed in with the public, acting as audience
   members. Very confused.*) On the double, ladies and gentlemen, quickly! Let's go! No stragglers! My group this way! 25
   Forward! Toward the music! (*Music floats in the air, disappears.*) Now what? (*He opens his hands in a gesture of incomprehension. Taking advantage of the* GUIDE's *position, someone comes
   forward and puts a tin plate full of garbage in his hands. To this
   person, absolutely astonished.*) What is this? (*Protests.*) Not to 30
   me you don't! This is not what I get paid for! Who do they
   think they are?

(*Meanwhile, the game of Martin Fisherman has stopped. The* PO-
LICEMEN *and* ACTORS *from the shorter line carry off those who were
knocked unconscious and throw them into a room.*)

GUIDE: (*To the group.*) With so much confusion, I forgot about the
   catacombs. You'll end up leaving without seeing anything.
WOMAN'S VOICE: 35

         "The water was black there
         under the branches.
         When it reached the bridge
         it stopped and sang."

GUIDE: (*Pleased.*) Her again! What persistence! You want to 40
   risk it? Sooner or later it's got to improve!

(*He opens the door. The people inside won't let him in.*)

SCENE SIXTEEN

ACTOR #1: Sorry, old man. You can't come in. Off-limits.
GUIDE: Why not? I'm bringing people.
ACTOR #1: No, old man. We're rehearsing.
GUIDE: So what? Aren't you getting tired?
ACTOR #1: No! (*He closes the door.*)   5
GUIDE: (*Outraged.*) What balls. Sorry. (*He remembers something,
   smiles.*) They're not gonna fuck with me. Psss! This way!
   There's another entrance! (*He leads them along a passageway.*

---

xv. 36–39 **"The water . . . sang"** the Woman's Voice sings lines
from the *Blood Wedding* lullabye

They pass a vertical box like the others, only bigger. Naturally.)
10 Just a moment. (*He opens the door of the box. Inside, two men are plastered together. The* GUIDE *puts the tin plate on their shoulders. They stretch their necks desperately, trying to suck up what's on the plate. It falls. Matter of factly, to the audience.*) They let it fall! What idiots! (*He closes the door.*)

SCENE SEVENTEEN

GUIDE: Don't make a sound. Walk on tiptoe. Don't say a word. (*They enter a room. Folding screens around an illuminated central space.*) Sssh . . . Silence . . . (*The group watches the scene through the folding screens. Two* ACTORS *and two* ACTRESSES *are rehearsing* Othello, *in rehearsal clothes.* ACTRESS #1, *as Desdemona, is already dead on the floor.*)
5
ACTOR #1: (*As Iago.*) Villainous whore!
ACTRESS #2: (*As Emilia.*) She give it Cassio? No, alas, I found it, And I did give't my husband.
10 ACTOR #1: Filth, thou liest!
GUIDE: Such language!
ACTRESS #2: (*As Emilia.*) By heaven, I do not, I do not, gentlemen.
    O murd'rous coxcomb! What should such a fool
15   Do with so good a wife?
ACTOR #2: (*As Othello.*) Are there no stones in heaven
    But what serves for the thunder?—Precious villain!

(*Othello runs at Iago. Iago strikes Emilia and leaves.* ACTOR #1 *marks his exit and sits off to one side. A* POLICEMAN *enters in Isabel-lesque attire.*)

POLICEMAN #1: (*To* ACTOR #2.) You killed those two women! Villain! Viper!

(*The* ACTRESSES *get up, go sit down. They watch calmly, a bit surprised.*)

20 ACTOR #1: Who told this guy to come in?
POLICEMAN #1: (*Acting, calling his men.*) Over here, men. Here!
ACTOR #1: Go act for the other side. Who called you. Get out of here!
POLICEMAN #1: Thou hast no weapon, and perforce must
25   suffer. They are dead.
ACTRESS #1: (*Joking.*) I am dead!
ACTRESS #2: (*Sings.*)

    Willow, willow, willow.
    Moor, she was chaste. She loved thee, cruel Moor!

30 ACTOR #1: Stop! (*To the* POLICEMAN.) Will you beat it!
POLICEMAN #1: To raise your sword against a woman!
ACTOR #2: What are you talking about?
ACTOR #1: The guy's a mental case. Beat it! (*He pushes him toward the door.*) Out! (*Returns.*) Better keep the door locked.
35   There's no telling who could walk in. Let's go, girls. That guy stank worse than a pig. (*Claps his hands.*) One more time!
POLICEMAN #1: (*Draws his sword.*) No, traitor!

---

xvii. 7 **Villainous whore!** lines from *Othello* are taken from act 5, scene 2, lines 229–235, 248–249, 256, 287, 306–307, 317, 367–371. All are found on pages 1239–1240 of *The Riverside Shakespeare* (Boston: Houghton Mifflin, 1974)

ACTOR #2: (*Returns. In spite of himself, in character.*) Wrench his sword from him.   40
POLICEMAN #1: Torments will ope your lips.
ACTOR #2: Well, thou dost best.
ACTOR #1: Cut! Right there!
POLICEMAN #1: Officers, come here! (*Another* POLICEMAN *enters, dressed in the same style.*)   45
POLICEMAN #2: What's happening, sir?
POLICEMAN #1: (*He shows him the vial he's just taken from his own pocket.*) Trotyl! And the women are dead! Oh my! O thou pernicious caitiff!
POLICEMAN #2: (*With his sword, rounds up the* ACTORS, *who* 50 *move into a corner.*) Move it, or I'll take a slice! (*The* ACTRESSES *let out an inappropriate laugh.*)
POLICEMAN #1: Take them, too, for having laughed at the wrong time! (*In a dramatic voice.*)
    To you, Lord Governor,   55
    Remains the censure of this hellish villain,
    The time, the place, the torture, O, enforce it!
    Myself will straight aboard, and to the state
    This heavy act with heavy heart relate.

(*He takes a gun from his pocket, forces the* ACTORS *to exit.*)

GUIDE: (*To his group.*) A bit confusing, the way that happened, 60 don't you think? So you understand. (*He walks into the light. In a professional, dry and rapid voice.*) Explanation: For Foreigners. (*Fierce and rude.*) Does anyone really need an explanation? If you want to act like actors, just go into a tenement and howl like dogs, throw a good scare into people. If 65 you don't have money, people will be even more afraid. Why scream? Why pretend? When no one can open his mouth, why would anyone scream gratuitously? (*He waits for a response, which he doesn't get.*) Okay then! (*Resumes his professional tone.*) August 6, 1971. The police burst into an 70 old house with many rooms, like this one, in the city of Santa Fe. In one of the rooms they find eight hundred grams of trotyl. They say. One journalist and three members of the Grupo 67 theater are arrested. They're taken to Buenos Aires on suspicion of subversive actions. The district attor- 75 ney recommended they be absolved on the benefit of doubt. They were absolved May 24, 1972. (*Change of tone.*) Few are called, many are chosen. Nine months in the cage. In misery. Well, that's life! (*He leaves the illuminated space, goes back to his group.*) Wait! The show goes on!   80

SCENE EIGHTEEN

A sort of deformed CHILD-MONSTER, *dressed in a floor-length white shirt with lots of lace and frills. He is heavily made-up. Others disguised as* CHILDREN *follow. The* CHILD-MONSTER *clutches a club. They sing.*

CHILDREN:

    Anton, Anton Pirulero
    each one, each one
    attends to his game
    and he who does not   5
    he who does not
    will suffer the blame.

(*The* CHILDREN *sit in a circle around the* CHILD-MONSTER, *who calls to one of the bigger children and gives him the club. The latter stays outside the ring. They play Anton Pirulero, in which the child playing Anton is in the center of the circle, turning around and around, his arms extended like wings. The others keep singing and pretend to play musical instruments—guitar, cornet, violin, etc. They have to be very alert, for if Anton Pirulero stops and points at one of them with his arm and that child isn't moving his own arms like Anton, then that child loses. He who loses three times is out. The game is played singing, and very fast.*)

CHILD-MONSTER: (*He is Anton Pirulero. In an out-of-tune sing-song.*)

> Anton, Anton Pirulero
> 10   each one, each one
> attends to his game
> and he who does not
> he who does not
> will suffer the blame.

(*Now they play only guitar. The child with the club goes to the one who has changed places with Anton and hits him. The child falls. The game continues, faster every time. The* CHILD-MONSTER *never finishes his song, the game falls apart, and the child with the club hits out indiscriminately. Finally, the only ones left unharmed are the* CHILD-MONSTER *and the character with the club. They wave their arms and sing. The* CHILD-MONSTER *glares at the other one, more and more menacingly. He aims with his finger as though it were a revolver and kills the other child. Pum! He plays alone, his gestures increasingly spastic. The song "Anton Pirulero" becomes unintelligible. The lights go out.*)

15 GUIDE: What now? Why did they kill the lights?
VOICES: (*Singing.*)

> Anton, Anton Pirulero
> each one
> 20   each one
> attends to his game.

(*Lights up. In the same space,* THREE MEN *and a* YOUNG WOMAN. *The* CHILD-MONSTER *laughs in his labored way, waves his arms, stutters.*)

CHILD-MONSTER: D-d-d-ow-ow-n-n-n! S-s-s-i-i-i-t-t-t-d-d-d-ow-n-n-n-n!

(*He aims his hand like a revolver. The* MEN *and* WOMAN *don't seem to notice his presence. They sit of their own volition.*)

FIRST MAN: What is your game?
SECOND MAN: Fear.
25 FIRST MAN: And yours?
THIRD MAN: Fear.
FIRST MAN: (*To the* YOUNG WOMAN.) What is your game?
YOUNG WOMAN: Fear. (*Pause.*) And the question.
FIRST MAN: What question?
30 YOUNG WOMAN: Why fear? My name is Marina. I am twenty years old. I am Greek, a prisoner, and I have been tortured. (*The* CHILD-MONSTER *stutters low, furiously. He keeps playing, getting all tangled up in his own movements.*)
Time is altered, the years to come are altered

You know where you will find me   35
I, fear, I, death
I, the memory beyond reach
I, the recollection of the tenderness of your hands
I, the sadness of our broken life
I will defeat "it's not my concern" with my   40
   anguish
blast their alien sleep with fireworks,
   horrible and indecent
with countless shootings I will fall on the indifference
of those who pass by   45
until they begin to ask, to ask themselves
THREE MEN: (*In an even tone.*) Why fear?
Why torture?
Why deaths?

(*Stuttering and autistic, the* CHILD-MONSTER *plays.*)

THREE MEN: Who set limits?   50
Who once said: this much thirst
this much water?
Who once said: this much air
this much fire?
Who once said: here the ken   55
of men and women
here the bounds?
Only hope has sharp knees.
They are bleeding.

(*Darkness.*)

(*The poem spoken by the* YOUNG WOMAN *was written by Marina. The poem spoken by the* THREE MEN *is Juan Gelman's.*)

GUIDE: Now what? There they go again cutting the light 60 without warning me! I understand less and less. We're the ones who bear the brunt of this show. I shit on poetry! Watch your wallets! And I left my flashlight. This way, this way. It's so dark! Don't touch each other! Whose little ass is this?   65

(*He laughs. Opens the door. The passageway is illuminated.*)

Ah! Light, more light! What a phrase! Only a genius could come up with that one, eh?
WOMAN'S VOICE:

> "Ay-y-y, for the big horse
> who didn't like water"   70

GUIDE: Still at it! Now that's perseverance! (*Baroque music is heard. The* GUIDE *puts his ear to the door. Unsure.*) Do we go in here? I don't remember. Oh well, let's do it! Come along, gentlemen! You're almost there!

---

59 s.d. **The poem . . . Gelman's** Gelman's lines are: "Quien puso limites? / Quien dijo alguna vez: hasta aquí la sed? hasta aquí el agua? / Quien dijo alguna vez: hasta aquí el aire, hasta aquí el fuego? / Quien dijo alguna vez: hasta aquí el hombre, hasta aquí, no? / Solo la esperanza tiene las rodillas nitidas. / Sangran." 69–70 **"Ay-y-y . . . water"** the Woman's Voice sings from the *Blood Wedding* lullabye

SCENE NINETEEN

They enter another room. Two GUARDS *are dressing a group of squalid-looking characters who are handcuffed to the wall, heavily made-up, with false eyelashes and lots of rouge. Some are half-undressed, wearing only jackets and underwear. Others wear bras and costume jewelry. The* GUARDS *move around busily. They bring chairs. Make the prisoners sit. They arrange them artistically, crossing their legs, raising their arms as though they were holding cigarettes between their fingers. The prisoners stay in these poses. During the development of this scene, one* GUARD— *seated apart—recites with a melancholy air.*

GUARD: You, who come from the shores of the Tagus
    Every day sing of my death
    Only this do I ask
      with my dying breath
5   Every day sing of my death
    You, who come from the shores of the Tagus.

(A signal is heard. A line of frightened men and women enter. Some carry small packages in their hands, obviously clothing or food. The GUARD *watches them.)*

GUARD: No one enters without being checked. (*He turns his face away. Raises and lowers his index finger mechanically, while the people pass in front of him and go out. Recites rapidly.*)
10   With pants, no. With skirts, no. With stockings, no. With packages, no. With children, no. With faces, no. (*A* PRETTY GIRL *passes. He looks at her. His finger stops. Very nicely.*)
    Twenty little hard ones, twenty little hard ones
15   all in a roll, all in a roll
    twenty little hard ones
    in your little asshole.
    May I?
PRETTY GIRL: (*Stupidly.*) What?
20 GUARD: (*Wiggles his finger obscenely.*) May I?
PRETTY GIRL: No!
GUARD: (*Pulls himself up, undiscouraged.*) To arms! To arms against the little asshole! Right over here!

---

xix. 1 **"You, who come from the shores of the Tagus"** is from a poem of Garcilaso de la Vega. The Tagus River flows through western Spain and Portugal. In her letter to me of March 28, 1986, Gambaro brought up "substituting an English-language poem about death, provided of course it's by a Master." I decided against this option since I felt that Gambaro's appropriation of Garcilaso was important as a reference to a specific age, place, and literary tradition. One of the greatest poets of the Spanish Golden Age, Garcilaso influenced not only San Juan de la Cruz, Lope de Vega, and Cervantes but also Rafael Alberti, Pedro Salinas, Miguel Hernández, and other twentieth-century Spanish and Latin American poets. The original reads: "Vosotros, los del Tajo en su ribera / Cantáreis mi muerte cada día / Este descanso llevaré nunque muera / Que cada día cantáreis mi muerte, / Vosotros, los del Tajo en su ribera." 13 **"Twenty little hard ones"** is from García Lorca's *Los titeres de cachiporra.* The original reads: "Veinte duritos y veinte duritos / y un rollito de veinte duritos / en el agujero del culito."

(A group of guards enters at a trot. They rush the PRETTY GIRL *and fling themselves on her as though she were the ball in a game of baseball. They roll with her out of the room.)*

GUARD: (*Moves off, uninterested. Starts again with a melancholy air.*) You, who come from the shores of the Tagus . . .   25
LITTLE OLD LADY: (*The last of the visitors. She brings a sandwich wrapped in a handkerchief.*) I've come to see my little son. He misbehaved.
GUARD: (*Deflated.*) Ah . . . Why didn't you bring him up better, madam?   30
LITTLE OLD LADY: He was always my wayward one!
GUARD: A good beating is what they need. They don't learn unless they bleed.
LITTLE OLD LADY: At ten years old, he was looking up the girls' skirts.   35
GUARD: (*Dumbfounded.*) Filthy!
LITTLE OLD LADY: (*Plaintive.*) I cut his little whistle, but it did no good!
GUARD: It's late to repent. Show me what you've brought!
LITTLE OLD LADY: (*Unwraps her handkerchief.*) A sandwich.   40
GUARD: (*Lifts the top of the bread.*) Ah! Extra testicles. No, madam! Here they only lose them. And for us that's work! Confiscated! (*He takes the sandwich.*) Out!
LITTLE OLD LADY: I want to see my son! Just once! Be generous! You have a mother too!   45
GUARD: Yeah, but she's not an old whore like you.
LITTLE OLD LADY: Why are you insulting me?
GUARD: (*With disgust.*) You're old! (*In another tone.*) All right. Go see him. I'm doing this for my mother. Sentimentality will be the end of me! (*Gestures toward one of the seated prisoners.*) There he is.   50
LITTLE OLD LADY: (*Goes toward an* OUTLANDISH-LOOKING PRISONER *and embraces him.*) Son! (*She separates, looks at him.*) No, this isn't him. (*Hugs another.*) Son! (*Looks.*) No, this one either.   55
OUTLANDISH-LOOKING PRISONER: (*Opening his arms.*) Da-da-da-da!
GUARD: Choose already. Take this one. What's the difference.
LITTLE OLD LADY: (*Leaning toward the prisoner. Timidly.*) Juan?
OUTLANDISH-LOOKING PRISONER: Da!
LITTLE OLD LADY: Son!   60
OUTLANDISH-LOOKING PRISONER: Da!
GUIDE: (*To the group.*) Pretty depressing, wouldn't you say?
GUARD: What about you all? Over here, young men!
GUIDE: (*Raises his hands.*) No! Out, quick! (*The sound of music.*) We were going to go dancing. We got the wrong room.   65 (*Very distressed.*) Let's go dancing! Dancing! Move it! Let's beat it! Let's go, gentlemen. Let's go! (*They exit.*)

SCENE TWENTY

GUIDE: Ouf! A narrow escape! (*He listens. The music gets louder. It's happy, catchy.*) That's it. Come. (*He leads his group to a large space, where at this moment all the other groups converge.*) Leave the space open, ladies and gentlemen! If you would be so kind   5 as to stand against the wall. That's it. Thank you, everyone.

(On one side of the performing space is a semitranslucent folding screen, behind which can be seen a long table. In the center, a group of women, dressed like stereotypical prostitutes, execute the gestures conventionally attributed to them: they smoke, show their legs, swing their

purses, put on makeup. A man roughly pushes in two more PROSTI-
TUTES. *They look at him with a mixture of fear and outrage. The
other women observe the new arrivals curiously, then one offers each of
the new women a cigarette. The music suddenly stops. One of the*
PROSTITUTES *starts dancing, moving slowly, singing a blues number
in a gravelly voice. A line of* FOUR MEN *enter at a trot, leading a prisoner with his eyes bandaged, to the center. They sing.*)

FOUR MEN:

> We have come, we have come
> To have some fun!

(*The* PROSTITUTES *watch them. The one dancing gradually slows
down the rhythm until she is moving in place, singing inaudibly. The
men spin the prisoner around until he becomes completely disoriented.*)

10   MAN #1: Let's play the Little Blind Cock!
MAN #2: Cockadoodledoo!

(*They play, rapidly poking and moving away from the prisoner, who
searches for them with his arms outstretched.*)

MAN #1: Play! Head down!
MAN #3: There are beams!
MAN #4: You could break your head open!

(*They play, yell "Cockadoodledoo!" One of the* PROSTITUTES *comes
forward. She first starts to join in the game, then stretches her hand toward the prisoner's bandage.*)

15   MAN #1: (*Pushes her away.*) Get out of here! This is our game!
       In your place, whore!
MAN #2: (*Poking the prisoner.*) He's sweating! He's hot!
MEN #1, #3, AND #4: (*In a chorus.*) Make him strip! Make him
       strip!

(*Maintaining an ambiguous air of play and violence, they take off his
jacket, his pants, his shirt; they throw his clothes, which flutter around.*)

20   MAN #1: Hard-boiled egg! Let's play hard-boiled egg!

(*They fight like children.*)

MAN #2: Me! Me!
MAN #3: Get out! Me!

(*They play. The prisoner holds his body rigid while the others rush
him, tie him up. Finally, one of the* MEN *hits him on the head. The
prisoner falls.*)

MAN #4: We warned you!
MAN #1: A beam, idiot!

MAN #2: We told you to keep your head down!   25

(*They drag the prisoner behind the screen. Through the screen, one can
see fuzzily that they are strapping him down on the table. A scream.
Instantaneously, the volume of the music shoots up; two of the men
come out from behind the screen.*)

TWO MEN: Girls, if you want to sing,
       it's not prohibited!

(*They clap. The* PROSTITUTES *don't move.*)

Sing!

(*The* PROSTITUTES, *forced into it, clap and sing. Again the music gets
louder.*)

> Girls, if you want to dance,
> it's not prohibited!   30

(*The* PROSTITUTES *dance. Behind the screen, one can see the shadow
of the two* MEN *moving away from the table. The hand of the prisoner
falls softly. At the same time, the* PROSTITUTES *freeze in a musical
comedy finale. The music stops. The lights go out, then come up again.
The actors disperse, naturally. They take down the screen. The dead
man gets up from the table, gathers his clothes, and begins to dress.
Only the prisoners seated against the wall remain immobile.*)

GUIDE: (*Drily.*) Ladies and gentlemen, what are you waiting
       for? The show is over. (*House lights come up.*)
GUIDE 2: (*Resentfully.*) If you clap enthusiastically in all good
       haste your hands won't go to waste!

(*He claps, and the* GUIDES *and actors present imitate him.*)

GUIDE: Theater imitates life   35
> If you don't clap
> It means that life is rotten to the core
> And we may as well just head for the door.

(*He moves the audience out toward the door. From far away can be heard
police sirens. Even when the audience is near the exit, they can hear.*)

> Who once said: here the ken
> of men and women
> here the bounds?   40

(*After a moment, repeat.*)

> Who once said: here the ken
> of men and women
> here the bounds?

Athol Fugard, John Kani, and Winston Ntshona

Born in 1932, the South African playwright Athol Fugard began his career in the theater in the 1950s, working with the Circle Players in Cape Town. As a mixed-race company, the Circle Players worked in violation of South Africa's apartheid laws. They brought the issue of apartheid to a head when Fugard—a white man—collaborated with the black actor Zakes Mokae in the play *The Blood Knot* (1961), a play about two brothers, one of whom is light-skinned enough to "pass" for white. The play's powerful indictment of apartheid and the fine performances of Fugard and Mokae were widely admired, and gained Fugard a reputation as a dramatist outside South Africa. Yet, despite its notoriety, the play could hardly remove apartheid itself; Fugard and Mokae were still forced to travel separately, and the government passed new laws limiting interracial theater. In 1963, Fugard began his long association with The Serpent Players, a black company. This association was made nearly impossible, however, by the 1965 extension of the Group Areas Act, one of the principal apartheid statutes: both racially mixed casts and racially mixed audiences were forbidden. By June of 1965, Fugard was denied a permit to enter the black township of New Brighton for the dress rehearsal of Sophocles' *Antigone,* which he had adapted and produced with The Serpent Players.

By the early 1970s, Fugard had written several of his best-known plays—*Hello and Goodbye* (1965), *Boesman and Lena* (1969)—when he became frustrated with his method of writing plays and decided to work more collaboratively with The Serpent Players. Fugard had worked with John Kani (b. 1944) on the 1965 *Antigone,* and Kani and Winston Ntshona (b. 1941) had performed another absurdist two-hander about convicts—Jean Genet's *Death-watch*—with the Serpent company in 1968. Both Kani and Ntshona were recognized performers in their own right when they agreed to collaborate with Fugard in the early 1970s. These collaborations were different from Fugard's earlier adaptations of European classics for The Serpent Players, for in this work Kani and Ntshona supplied information, dialogue, and performance tropes which were scripted and shaped in dialogue with Fugard. The plays they devised—*Sizwe Bansi Is Dead* (1972) and *The Island* (1973)—are fully collaborative, for the three men improvised a variety of possible performances before setting them down in a final design; the opening monologue with the newspaper in *Sizwe Bansi Is Dead,* for instance, is based on Kani's usual stand-up performance routines. Fugard has gone on to write a number of plays about the effects of apartheid and racism on South African life, including *A Lesson from Aloes* (1980), *Master Harold . . . and the boys* (1982) *My Children! My Africa!* (1989), *Playland* (1993), and *Valley Song* (1996). Kani and Ntshona have come to enjoy considerable success in the theater and in films; Kani collaborated on an important interracial production of Shakespeare's *Othello* with Janet Suzman at the Market Theater in Johannesburg, where he has served as Associate Director.

THE ISLAND

Although accounts of the collaboration between Fugard, Kani, and Ntshona differ somewhat, John Kani has remarked that Fugard's role in the composition of *Sizwe Bansi Is Dead* was that of an "overseer," while in the writing of *The Island,* the three worked together more directly. The play is set on Robben Island, a prison-island off the shore of South Africa, which could not be named onstage when the play was first written and produced. It centers on two prisoners—John and Winston—who open the play performing a mime of back-breaking routine labor. But as the play proceeds, John and Winston undertake a form of resistance: they devise a production of Sophocles' *Antigone*. Although Winston is uncomfortable with playing a woman, they use *Antigone* to gain a voice; protesting against Creon's unreasonable law, John and Winston speak out against their own entombment by the state.

As prisoners, John and Winston produce *Antigone* in the mode of "poor theater" elaborated by Jerzy Grotowski, as Fugard suggests in his introduction to *Statements*. But while Grotowski's "poor theater" refers to a chosen poverty of means, a reduction of theater to its essence in acting, in the political context of contemporary South African theater, "poverty" has different causes and consequences. John and Winston fashion their performance—their meager costumes, their brief text—from an imposed poverty, one that lends the Grotowskian actor's "total act," his immediate presence to the audience a different register of meaning. For the production of *Antigone* that John and Winston enact is not only an allegory of their own condition and of the injustice of apartheid, but it has immediate consequences on them, on their bodies. Taking the role of Antigone, Winston insures his apparently interminable punishment.

Finally, *The Island* raises the question of intercultural authority. Although it's possible to read the production of *Antigone* as an act of brave resistance, it's also true that *Antigone* is what keeps Winston in jail. To what extent is this use of one of the classic texts of Western drama also being shown to be an *ineffective* strategy of resistance, the replaying of part of the cultural inheritance that continues to imprison John and Winston, a culture of which both *Antigone* and apartheid are a part? The play's simple, open—perhaps even Beckettian—structure doesn't resolve such questions, but it does help us to entertain them.

John and Winston in *The Island*.

THE ISLAND

Athol Fugard, John Kani, and Winston Ntshona

CHARACTERS

JOHN
WINSTON   *two prisoners*

This play was given its first performance on 2 July 1973, directed by Athol Fugard with John Kani as John and Winston Ntshona as Winston.

SCENE I

Centre stage: a raised area representing a cell on Robben Island. Blankets and sleeping-mats—the prisoners sleep on the floor—are neatly folded. In one corner are a bucket of water and two tin mugs.

The long drawn-out wail of a siren. Stage-lights come up to reveal a moat of harsh, white light around the cell. In it the two prisoners— JOHN *stage-right and* WINSTON *stage-left—mime the digging of sand. They wear the prison uniform of khaki shirt and short trousers. Their heads are shaven. It is an image of back-breaking and grotesquely futile labour. Each in turns fills a wheelbarrow and then with great effort pushes it to where the other man is digging, and empties it. As a result, the piles of sand never diminish. Their labour is interminable. The only sounds are their grunts as they dig, the squeal of the wheel-barrows as they circle the cell, and the hum of Hodoshe, the green carrion fly.*

A whistle is blown. They stop digging and come together, standing side by side as they are handcuffed together and shackled at the ankles. Another whistle. They start to run . . . JOHN *mumbling a prayer,* WINSTON *muttering a rhythm for their three-legged run.*

They do not run fast enough. They get beaten . . . WINSTON *receiving a bad blow to the eye and* JOHN *spraining an ankle. In this condition they arrive finally at the cell door. Handcuffs and shackles are taken off. After being searched, they lurch into their cell. The door closes behind them. Both men sink to the floor.*

A moment of total exhaustion until slowly, painfully, they start to explore their respective injuries . . . WINSTON *his eye, and* JOHN *his ankle.* WINSTON *is moaning softly and this eventually draws* JOHN's *attention away from his ankle. He crawls to* WINSTON *and examines the injured eye. It needs attention.* WINSTON's *moaning is slowly turning into a sound of inarticulate outrage, growing in volume and violence.* JOHN *urinates into one hand and tries to clean the other man's eye with it, but* WINSTON's *anger and outrage are now uncontrollable. He breaks away from* JOHN *and crawls around the cell, blind with rage and pain.* JOHN *tries to placate him . . . the noise could bring back the warders and still more trouble.* WINSTON *eventually finds the cell door but before he can start banging on it* JOHN *pulls him away.*

WINSTON: (*Calling.*) Hodoshe!

JOHN: Leave him, Winston. Listen to me, man! If he comes now we'll be in bigger shit.

WINSTON: I want Hodoshe. I want him now! I want to take him to the office. He must read my warrant. I was sentenced to Life brother, not bloody Death! 5

JOHN: Please, Winston! He made us run. . . .

WINSTON: I want Hodoshe!

JOHN: He made us run. He's happy now. Leave him. Maybe he'll let us go back to the quarry tomorrow. . . . 10

(WINSTON *is suddenly silent. For a moment* JOHN *thinks his words are having an effect, but then he realizes that the other man is looking at his ear.* WINSTON *touches it. It is bleeding. A sudden spasm of fear from* JOHN *who puts a hand to his ear. His fingers come away with blood on them. The two men look at each other.*)

WINSTON: *Nyana we Sizwe!*

(*In a reversal of earlier roles* WINSTON *now gets* JOHN *down on the floor of the cell so as to examine the injured ear. He has to wipe blood and sweat out of his eyes in order to see clearly.* JOHN *winces with pain.* WINSTON *keeps restraining him.*)

WINSTON: (*Eventually.*) It's not too bad. (*Using his shirt-tail he cleans the injured ear.*)

JOHN: (*Through clenched teeth as* WINSTON *tends his ear.*) Hell, *ons was gemoer vandag!* (*A weak smile.*) News bulletin and 15 weather forecast! Black Domination was chased by White Domination. Black Domination lost its shoes and collected a few bruises. Black Domination will run barefoot to the quarry tomorrow. Conditions locally remain unchanged—thunderstorms with the possibility of cold 20 showers and rain. Elsewhere, fine and warm!

(WINSTON *has now finished tending* JOHN's *ear and settles down on the floor beside him. He clears his nose, ears, and eyes of sand.*)

WINSTON: Sand! Same old sea sand I used to play with when I was young. St. George's Strand. New Year's Day. Sand dunes. Sand castles . . .

JOHN: *Ja,* we used to go there too. Last. . . . (*Pause and then a* 25 *small laugh. He shakes his head.*) The Christmas before they arrested me, we were down there. All of us. Honeybush. My little Monde played in the sand. We'd given her one of those little buckets and spades for Christmas.

---

11 **nyana we sizwe** brother of the land   15 **ons was gemoer vandag** we were fucked up today   25 **ja** yes

1421

30   WINSTON: *Ja.*

JOHN: Anyway, it was Daddy's turn today. (*Shaking his head ruefully.*) *Haai,* Winston, this one goes on the record. 'Struesgod! I'm a man, brother. A man! But if Hodoshe had kept
us at those wheelbarrows five minutes longer . . . ! There
35   would have been a baby on the Island tonight. I nearly
cried.

WINSTON: *Ja.*

JOHN: There was no end to it, except one of us!

WINSTON: That's right.

40   JOHN: This morning when he said: "You two! The beach!" . . .
I thought, Okay, so it's my turn to empty the sea into a
hole. He likes that one. But when he pointed to the
wheelbarrows, and I saw his idea . . . ! (*Shaking his head.*) I
laughed at first. Then I wasn't laughing. Then I hated
45   you. You looked so stupid, *broer!*

WINSTON: That's what he wanted.

JOHN: It was going to last forever, man! Because of *you.* And
for *you,* because of *me. Moer!* He's cleverer than I thought.

WINSTON: If he was God, he would have done it.

50   JOHN: What?

WINSTON: Broken us. Men get tired. Hey! There's a thought.
We're still alive because Hodoshe got tired.

JOHN: Tomorrow?

WINSTON: We'll see.

55   JOHN: If he takes us back there . . . If I hear that wheelbarrow
. . . of yours again, coming with another bloody load of . . .
eternity!

WINSTON: (*With calm resignation.*) We'll see.

(*Pause.* JOHN *looks at* WINSTON.)

JOHN: (*With quiet emphasis, as if the other man did not fully un-
60   derstand the significance of what he had said.*) I *hated* you
Winston.

WINSTON: (*Meeting* JOHN's *eyes.*) I *hated* you.

(JOHN *puts a hand on* WINSTON's *shoulder. Their brotherhood is
intact. He gets slowly to his feet.*)

JOHN: Where's the *lap?*

WINSTON: Somewhere. Look for it.

65   JOHN: Hey! You had it last.

(*Limping around the cell looking for their washrag.*)

WINSTON: *Haai,* man! You got no wife here. Look for the rag
yourself.

JOHN: (*Finding the rag beside the water bucket.*) Look where it
is. Look! Hodoshe comes in here and sees it. "Whose *lap-
70   pie* is that?" Then what do you say?

WINSTON: "It's his rag, sir."

JOHN: Yes? Okay. "It's my rag, sir." When you wash, use your
shirt.

WINSTON: Okay, okay! "It's our rag, sir!"

75   JOHN: That will be the bloody day!

---

32 **haai; hai** exclamation of surprise   45 **broer** brother   48
moer literally, womb; used as a swear-word equivalent to "fuck,"
"fucking"   63 **lap, lappie** rag

(JOHN, *getting ready to wash, starts to take off his shirt.* WINSTON
*produces a cigarette butt, matches, and flint from their hiding-place
under the water bucket. He settles down for a smoke.*)

Shit, today was long. Hey, Winston, suppose the watch of
the chap behind the siren is slow! We could still be there,
man! (*He pulls out three or four rusty nails from a secret pocket
in his trousers. He holds them out to* WINSTON.) Hey there.

WINSTON: What?   80

JOHN: With the others.

WINSTON: (*Taking the nails.*) What's this?

JOHN: Necklace, man. With the others.

WINSTON: Necklace?

JOHN: Antigone's necklace.   85

WINSTON: *Ag,* shit, man!

(*Slams the nails down on the cell floor and goes on smoking.*)

Antigone! Go to hell, man, John.

JOHN: Hey, don't start any nonsense now. You promised.
(*Limps over to* WINSTON's *bed-roll and produces a half-
completed necklace made of nails and string.*) It's nearly fin-   90
ished. Look. Three fingers, one nail . . . three fingers, one
nail . . . (*Places the necklace beside* WINSTON *who is shaking his
head, smoking aggressively, and muttering away.*) Don't start
any nonsense now, Winston. There's six days to go to the
concert. We're committed. We promised the chaps we'd   95
do something. This *Antigone* is just right for us. Six more
days and we'll make it.

(*He continues washing.*)

WINSTON: Jesus, John! We were down on the beach today.
Hodoshe made us run. Can't you just leave a man . . . ?

JOHN: To hell with you! Who do you think ran with you? I'm   100
also tired, but we can't back out now. Come on! Three
fingers. . . .

WINSTON: . . . one nail! (*Shaking his head.*) *Haai . . . haai . . .
haai!*

JOHN: Stop moaning and get on with it. Shit, Winston! What   105
sort of progress is this? (*Abandoning his wash.*) Listen. Listen! Number 42 is practising the Zulu War Dance. Down
there they're rehearsing their songs. It's just in this *moer*
cell that there's always an argument. Today you want to do
it, tomorrow you don't want to do it. How the hell must   110
I know what to report to the chaps tomorrow if we go
back to the quarry?

(WINSTON *is unyielding. His obstinacy gets the better of* JOHN, *who
eventually throws the wash-rag at him.*)

There! Wash!

(JOHN *applies himself to the necklace while* WINSTON, *still muttering away in an undertone, starts to clean himself.*)

How can I be sure of anything when you carry on like
this? We've still got to learn the words, the moves. Shit! It   115
could be so bloody good, man.

(WINSTON *mutters protests all the way through this speech of*
JOHN's. *The latter holds up the necklace.*)

Nearly finished! Look at it! Three fingers. . . .

WINSTON: . . . one nail.

JOHN: *Ja!* Simple. Do you still remember all I told you yes-
120   terday? Bet you've bloody forgotten. How can I carry on
like this? I can't move on, man. Over the whole bloody lot
again! Who Antigone is . . . who Creon is . . .

WINSTON: Antigone is mother to Polynices . . .

JOHN: *Haai, haai, haai* . . . shit, Winston! (*Now really exasper-*
125   *ated.*) How many times must I tell you that Antigone is the
sister to the two brothers? Not the mother. That's another
play.

WINSTON: Oh.

JOHN: That's all you know! "Oh." (*He abandons the necklace and*
130   *fishes out a piece of chalk from a crack in the floor.*) Come here.
This is the last time. 'Struesgod. The last time.

WINSTON: *Ag,* no, John.

JOHN: Come! I'm putting this plot down for the last time! If
you don't learn it tonight I'm going to report you to the
135   old men tomorrow. And remember, *broer,* those old men
will make Hodoshe and his tricks look like a little boy.

WINSTON: Jesus Christ! Learn to dig for Hodoshe, learn to
run for Hodoshe, and what happens when I get back to
the cell? Learn to read *Antigone!*

140 JOHN: Come! And shut up! (*He pulls the reluctant* WINSTON
down beside him on the floor. WINSTON *continues to clean himself with the rag while* JOHN *lays out the "plot" of Antigone.*)
If you would just stop moaning, you would learn faster.
Now listen!

145 WINSTON: Okay, do it.

JOHN: Listen! It is the Trial of Antigone. Right?

WINSTON: So you say.

JOHN: First, the accused. Who is the accused?

WINSTON: Antigone.

150 JOHN: Coming from you that's bloody progress. (*Writing away
on the cell floor with his chalk.*) Next the State. Who is the
State?

WINSTON: Creon.

JOHN: King Creon. Creon is the State. Now . . . what did
155   Antigone do?

WINSTON: Antigone buried her brother Eteocles.

JOHN: No, no, no! Shit, Winston, when are you going to remember this thing? I told you, man, Antigone buried
Polynices! The traitor! The one who I said was on *our*
160   side. Right?

WINSTON: Right.

JOHN: Stage one of the Trial. (*Writing on the floor.*) The State
lays its charges against the Accused . . . and lists counts . . .
you know the way they do it. Stage two is Pleading. What
165   does Antigone plead? Guilty or Not Guilty?

WINSTON: Not Guilty.

JOHN: (*Trying to be tactful.*) Now look, Winston, we're not going to argue. Between me and you, in this cell, we know
she's Not Guilty. But in the play she pleads Guilty.

170 WINSTON: No, man, John! Antigone is Not Guilty. . . .

JOHN: In the play. . . .

WINSTON: (*Losing his temper.*) To hell with the play! Antigone
had every right to bury her brother.

JOHN: Don't say "To hell with the play." We've got to do the
175   bloody thing. And in the play she pleads Guilty. Get that
straight. Antigone pleads. . . .

WINSTON: (*Giving up in disgust.*) Okay, do it your way.

JOHN: It's not my way! In the play. . . .

WINSTON: Guilty!

JOHN: Yes, Guilty!   180

(*Writes furiously on the floor.*)

WINSTON: Guilty.

JOHN: Stage three, Pleading in Mitigation of Sentence. Stage
four, Sentence, State Summary, and something from you
. . . Farewell Words. Now learn that.

WINSTON: Hey?   185

JOHN: (*Getting up.*) Learn that!

WINSTON: But we've just done it!

JOHN: *I've* just done it. Now *you* learn it.

WINSTON: (*Throwing aside the wash-rag with disgust before applying himself to learning the "plot".*) Learn to run, learn to 190
read. . . .

JOHN: And don't throw the rag there! (*Retrieving the rag and
placing it in its correct place.*) Don't be so bloody difficult,
man. We're nearly there. You'll be proud of this thing
when we've done it.   195

(*Limps to his bed-roll and produces a pendant made from a jam-
tin lid and twine.*) Look. Winston, look! Creon's medallion.
Good, hey! (*Hangs it around his neck.*) I'll finish the necklace while you learn that.

(*He strings on the remaining nails.*) Jesus, Winston! June 200
1965.

WINSTON: What?

JOHN: This, man. *Antigone.* In New Brighton. St. Stephen's
Hall. The place was packed, man! All the big people. Front
row . . . dignitaries. Shit, those were the days. Georgie was 205
Creon. You know Georgie?

WINSTON: The teacher?

JOHN: That's him. He played Creon. Should have seen him,
Winston. Short and fat, with big eyes, but by the time the
play was finished he was as tall as the roof.   210

(*Onto his legs in an imitation of Georgie's Creon.*)

"My Councillors, now that the Gods have brought our
City safe through a storm of troubles to tranquility. . . ."
And old Mulligan! Another short-arsed teacher. With a
beard! He used to go up to the Queen. . . . (*Another imitation.*) "Your Majesty, prepare for grief, but do not weep." 215

(*The necklace in his hands.*)

Nearly finished!
Nomhle played Antigone. A bastard of a lady that one, but
a beautiful bitch. Can't get her out of my mind tonight.

WINSTON: (*Indicating the "plot".*) I know this.

JOHN: You sure?   220

WINSTON: This! . . . it's here. (*Tapping his head.*)

JOHN: You're not bullshitting, hey? (*He rubs out the "plot" and
then paces the cell.*) Right. The Trial of Antigone. Who is
the Accused?

WINSTON: Antigone.   225

JOHN: Who is the State?

WINSTON: King Creon.

JOHN: Stage one.

WINSTON: (*Supremely self-confident.*) Antigone lays charges. . . .

JOHN: NO, SHIT, MAN, WINSTON!!!   230

(WINSTON *pulls* JOHN *down and stifles his protests with a hand over his mouth.*)

WINSTON: Okay . . . okay . . . listen, John . . . listen. . . . The State lays charges against Antigone.

(*Pause.*)

JOHN: Be careful!
WINSTON: The State lays charges against Antigone.
235 JOHN: Stage two.
WINSTON: Pleading.
JOHN: What does she plead? Guilty or Not Guilty?
WINSTON: Guilty.
JOHN: Stage three.
240 WINSTON: Pleading in Mitigation of Sentence.
JOHN: Stage four.
WINSTON: State Summary, Sentence, and Farewell Words.
JOHN: (*Very excited.*) He's got it! That's my man. See how easy it is, Winston? Tomorrow, just the words.

(WINSTON *gets onto his legs,* JOHN *puts away the props. Mats and blankets are unrolled. The two men prepare for sleep.*)

245 JOHN: Hell, I hope we go back to the quarry tomorrow. There's still a lot of things we need for props and costumes. Your wig! The boys in Number Fourteen said they'd try and smuggle me a piece of rope from the jetty.
WINSTON: *Ja*, I hope we're back there. I want to try and get
250   some tobacco through to Sipho.
JOHN: Sipho?
WINSTON: Back in solitary.
JOHN: Again!
WINSTON: *Ja.*
255 JOHN: Oh hell!
WINSTON: Simon passed the word.
JOHN: What was it this time?
WINSTON: Complained about the food I think. Demanded to see the book of Prison Regulations.
260 JOHN: Why don't they leave him alone for a bit?
WINSTON: Because he doesn't leave them alone.
JOHN: You're right. I'm glad I'm not in Number Twenty-two with him. One man starts getting hard-arsed like that and the whole lot of you end up in the shit.

(WINSTON'*s bed is ready. He lies down.*)

265   You know what I'm saying?
WINSTON: *Ja.*
JOHN: What?
WINSTON: What "What"?
JOHN: What am I saying?
270 WINSTON: *Haai*, Johnny, man! I'm tired now! Let a man. . . .
JOHN: I'm saying Don't Be Hard-Arsed! You! When Hodoshe opens that door tomorrow say *"Ja, Baas"* the right way. I don't want to be back on that bloody beach tomorrow just because you feel like being difficult.
275 WINSTON: (*Wearily.*) Okay, man, Johnny.
JOHN: You're not alone in this cell. I'm here too.
WINSTON: Jesus, you think I don't know that!
JOHN: People must remember their responsibilities to others.

WINSTON: I'm glad to hear you say that, because I was just going to remind you that it is your turn tonight.   280
JOHN: What do you mean? Wasn't it my turn last night?
WINSTON: (*Shaking his head emphatically.*) *Haai, haai.* Don't you remember? Last night I took you to bioscope.
JOHN: Hey, by the way! So you did. Bloody good film too. "Fastest Gun in the West." Glenn Ford.   285

(*Whips out a six-shooter and guns down a few bad-men.*)

You were bullshitting me a bit though. How the hell can Glenn Ford shoot backwards through his legs. I tried to work that one out on the beach.

(*He is now seated on his bed-roll. After a moment's thought he holds up an empty mug as a telephone-receiver and starts to dial.* WINSTON *watches him with puzzlement.*)

Operator, put me through to New Brighton, please . . . yes, New Brighton, Port Elizabeth. The number is   290
414624. . . . Yes, mine is local . . . local. . . .
WINSTON: (*Recognizing the telephone number.*) The Shop!

(*He sits upright with excitement as* JOHN *launches into the telephone conversation.*)

JOHN: That you Scott? Hello, man! Guess who! . . . You got it! You bastard! Hell, shit, Scott, man . . . how things with you? No, still inside. Give me the news, man . . . you don't say!   295
No, we don't hear anything here . . . not a word. . . . What's that? Business is bad? . . . You bloody undertaker! People aren't dying fast enough! No, things are fine here. . . .

(WINSTON, *squirming with excitement, has been trying unsuccessfully to interrupt* JOHN'*s torrent of words and laughter. He finally succeeds in drawing* JOHN'*s attention.*)

WINSTON: Who else is there? Who's with Scott?
JOHN: Hey, Scott, who's there with you? . . . Oh no! . . . call   300
him to the phone, man. . . .
WINSTON: Who's it?
JOHN: (*Ignoring* WINSTON.) Just for a minute, man, please, Scott. . . .

(*Ecstatic response from* JOHN *as another voice comes over the phone.*)

Hello there, you beautiful bastard . . . how's it, man? . . .   305
WINSTON: Who the hell is it, man?
JOHN: (*Hand over the receiver.*) Sky!

(WINSTON *can no longer contain his excitement. He scrambles out of his bed to join* JOHN, *and joins in the fun with questions and remarks whispered into* JOHN'*s ear. Both men enjoy it enormously.*)

How's it with Mangi? Where's Vusi? How are the chaps keeping, Sky? Winston? . . . All right, man. He's here next to me. No, fine, man, fine, man . . . small accident today   310
when he collided with Hodoshe, but nothing to moan about. His right eye bruised, that's all. Hey, Winston's asking how are the punkies doing? (*Big laugh.*) You bloody lover boy! Leave something for us, man!

---

283 **bioscope** cinema

(JOHN *becomes aware of* WINSTON *trying to interrupt again: to* WINSTON.)

315   Okay . . . okay. . . .
       (*Back to the telephone.*) Listen, Sky, Winston says if you get a chance, go down to Dora Street, to his wife. Tell V. Winston says he's okay, things are fine. Winston says she must carry on . . . nothing has happened . . . tell her to take care
320   of everything and everybody. . . . *Ja.* . . .

(*The mention of his wife guillotines* WINSTON'S *excitement and fun. After a few seconds of silence he crawls back heavily to his bed and lies down. A similar shift in mood takes place in* JOHN.)

       And look, Sky, you're not far from Gratten Street. Cross over to it, man, drop in on number thirty-eight, talk to Princess, my wife. How is she keeping? Ask her for me. I haven't received a letter for three months now. Why aren't
325   they writing? Tell her to write, man. I want to know how the children are keeping. Is Monde still at school? How's my twin baby, my Father and Mother? Is the old girl sick? They mustn't be afraid to tell me. I want to know. I know it's an effort to write, but it means a lot to us here. Tell her
330   . . . this was another day. They're not very different here. We were down on the beach. The wind was blowing. The sand got in our eyes. The sea was rough. I couldn't see the mainland properly. Tell them that maybe tomorrow we'll go to the quarry. It's not so bad there. We'll be
335   with the others. Tell her also . . . it's starting to get cold now, but the worst is still coming.

(*Slow fade to blackout.*)

SCENE II

The cell, a few days later.

JOHN *is hidden under a blanket.* WINSTON *is in the process of putting on Antigone's wig and false breasts.*

JOHN: Okay?
WINSTON: (*Still busy.*) No.
JOHN: Okay?
WINSTON: No.
5 JOHN: Okay?
WINSTON: No.

(*Pause.*)

JOHN: Okay?

(WINSTON *is ready. He stands waiting.* JOHN *slowly lifts the blanket and looks. He can't believe his eyes.* WINSTON *is a very funny sight.* JOHN's *amazement turns into laughter, which builds steadily. He bangs on the cell wall.*)

       Hey, Norman. Norman! Come this side, man. I got it here. *Poes!*

---

9 **poes** cunt

(JOHN *launches into an extravagant send-up of* WINSTON's *Antigone. He circles "her" admiringly, he fondles her breasts, he walks arm in arm with her down Main Street, collapsing with laughter between each "turn." He climaxes everything by dropping his trousers.*)

       Speedy Gonzales! Here I come!   10

(*This last joke is too much for* WINSTON *who has endured the whole performance with mounting but suppressed anger. He tears off the wig and breasts, throws them down on the cell floor, and storms over to the water bucket where he starts to clean himself.*)

WINSTON: It's finished! I'm not doing it. Take your Antigone and shove it up your arse!
JOHN: (*Trying to control himself.*) Wait, man. Wait. . . .

(*He starts laughing again.*)

WINSTON: There is nothing to wait for, my friend. I'm not doing it.   15
JOHN: Please, Winston!
WINSTON: You can laugh as much as you like, my friend, but just let's get one thing straight, I'm *not* doing Antigone. And in case you want to know why . . . I'm a man, not a bloody woman.   20
JOHN: When did I say otherwise?
WINSTON: What were you laughing at?
JOHN: I'm not laughing now.
WINSTON: What are you doing, crying?

(*Another burst of laughter from* JOHN.)

       There you go again, more laughing! Shit, man, you want 25
me to go out there tomorrow night and make a bloody fool of myself? You think I don't know what will happen after that? Every time I run to the quarry . . . "Nyah . . . nyah . . . Here comes Antigone! . . . Help the poor lady! . . ." Well, you can go to hell with your Antigone. 30
JOHN: I wasn't laughing at you.
WINSTON: Then who were you laughing at? Who else was here that dressed himself as a lady and made a bloody fool of himself?
JOHN: (*Now trying very hard to placate the other man.*) Okay 35
Winston, Okay! I'm not laughing any more.
WINSTON: You can go to hell with what you're saying.
JOHN: Look, Winston, try to understand, man, . . . this is Theatre.
WINSTON: You call laughing at me Theatre? Then go to hell 40
with your Theatre!
JOHN: Please, Winston, just stop talking and listen to me.
WINSTON: No! You get this, brother, . . . I am not doing your Antigone! I would rather run the whole day for Hodoshe. At least I know where I stand with him. All *he* wants is to 45
make me a "boy" . . . not a bloody woman.
JOHN: Okay, okay. . . .
WINSTON: Nothing you can say. . . .
JOHN: (*Shouting the other man down.*) Will you bloody listen!
WINSTON: (*Throwing the wash-rag down violently.*) Okay. I'm 50
listening.

JOHN: Sure I laughed. *Ja . . . I laughed.* But can I tell you why I laughed? I was preparing you for . . . stage fright! You think I don't know what I'm doing in this cell? This is
55   preparation for stage fright! I know those bastards out there. When you get in front of them, sure they'll laugh . . . Nyah, nyah! . . . they'll laugh. But just remember this brother, nobody laughs forever! There'll come a time when they'll stop laughing, and that will be the time
60   when our Antigone hits them with her words.
WINSTON: You're day-dreaming, John. Just get it into your head that I'm not doing Antigone. It's as simple as that.
JOHN: (*Realizing for the first time that* WINSTON *needs to be handled very carefully.*) Hey, Winston! Hold on there, man.
65   We've only got one more day to go! They've given us the best spot in the programme. We end the show! You can't back out now.
WINSTON: You think I can't? Just wait and see.
JOHN: Winston! You want to get me into trouble? Is that what
70   you want?
WINSTON: Okay, I won't back out.
JOHN: (*Delighted with his easy victory.*) That's my man!
WINSTON: (*Retrieving the wig and false breasts off the floor and slamming them into* JOHN's *hands.*) Here's Antigone . . . take
75   these titties and hair and play Antigone. I'm going to play Creon. Do you understand what I'm saying? Take your two titties. . . . I'll have my balls and play Creon. (*Turns his back on a flabbergasted* JOHN, *fishes out a cigarette-butt and matches from under the water bucket, and settles down for a*
80   *smoke.*)
JOHN: (*After a stunned silence.*) You won't make it! I thought about that one days ago. It's too late now to learn Creon's words.
WINSTON: (*Smoking.*) I hate to say it, but that is just too bad.
85   I am not doing Antigone.

(JOHN *is now furious. After a moment's hesitation he stuffs on the wig and false breasts and confronts* WINSTON.)

JOHN: Look at me. Now laugh.

(WINSTON *tries, but the laugh is forced and soon dies away.*)

Go on.

(*Pause.*)

Go on laughing! Why did you stop? Must I tell you why? Because behind all this rubbish is me, and you know it's
90   me. You think those bastards out there won't know it's you? Yes, they'll laugh. But who cares about that as long as they laugh in the beginning and listen at the end. That's all we want them to do . . . listen at the end!
WINSTON: I don't care what you say John. I'm not doing
95   Antigone.
JOHN: Winston . . . you're being difficult. You promised. . . .
WINSTON: Go to hell, man. Only last night you tell me that this Antigone is a bloody . . . what you call it . . . legend! A Greek one at that. Bloody thing never even happened.
100   Not even history! Look, brother, I got no time for bullshit. Fuck legends. Me? . . . I live my life here! I know why I'm here, and it's history, not legends. I had my chat with

a magistrate in Cradock and now I'm here. Your Antigone is a child's play, man.
JOHN: Winston! That's Hodoshe's talk.   105
WINSTON: You can go to hell with that one too.
JOHN: Hodoshe's talk, Winston! That's what he says all the time. What he wants us to say all our lives. Our convictions, our ideals . . . that's what he calls them . . . child's play. Everything we fucking do is "child's play" . . . when we   110
ran that whole day in the sun and pushed those wheelbarrows, when we cry, when we shit . . . child's play! Look, brother, . . . I've had enough. No one is going to stop me doing Antigone. . . .

(*The two men break apart suddenly, drop their trousers, and stand facing the wall with arms outstretched. Hodoshe calls* JOHN.)

Yes, sir!   115

(*He then pulls up his trousers and leaves the cell. When he has left,* WINSTON *pulls up his trousers and starts muttering with savage satisfaction at the thought of* JOHN *in Hodoshe's hands.*)

WINSTON: There he goes. Serves him right. I just hope Hodoshe teaches him a lesson. Antigone is important! Antigone this! Antigone that! Shit, man. Nobody can sleep in this bloody cell because of all that bullshit. Polynices! Eteocles! The other prisoners too. Nobody gets   120
any peace and quiet because of that bloody Antigone! I hope Hodoshe gives it to him.

(*He is now at the cell door. He listens, then moves over to the wig on the floor and circles it. He finally picks it up. Moves back to the cell door to make sure no one is coming. The water bucket gives him an idea. He puts on the wig and, after some difficulty, manages to see his reflection in the water. A good laugh, which he cuts off abruptly. He moves around the cell trying out a few of Antigone's poses. None of them work. He feels a fool. He finally tears off the wig and throws it down on the floor with disgust.*)

Ag voetsek!

(*Hands in pockets he paces the cell with grim determination.*)

I'm not going to do it. And I'm going to tell him. When he comes back. For once he must just shut that big bloody   125
mouth of his and listen. To me! I'm not going to argue, but 'struesgod that . . . !

(*The wig on the floor. He stamps on it.*)

Shit, man! If he wants a woman in the cell he must send for his wife, and I don't give a damn how he does it. I didn't walk with those men and burn my bloody passbook   130
in front of that police station, and have a magistrate send me here for life so that he can dress me up like a woman and make a bloody fool of me. I'm going to tell him. When he walks through that door.

(JOHN *returns.* WINSTON *is so involved in the problem of Antigone that at first he does not register* JOHN's *strangely vacant manner.*)

---

123 **ag voetsek** go to hell

135   Listen, *broer,* I'm not trying to be difficult but this
      Antigone! No! Please listen to me, John. 'Struesgod I can't
      do it. I mean, let's try something else, like singing or some-
      thing. You always got ideas. You know I can sing or
      dance. But not Antigone. Please, John.
140 JOHN: (*Quietly.*) Winston . . .
   WINSTON: (*Still blind to the other man's manner.*) Don't let's ar-
      gue, man. We've been together in this cell too long now
      to quarrel about rubbish. But you know me. If there's one
      thing I can't stand it's people laughing at me. If I go out
145   there tomorrow night and those bastards start laughing I'll
      fuck up the first one I lay my hands on. You saw yourself
      what happened in here when you started laughing. I
      wanted to *moer* you, John. I'm not joking. I really wanted
      to. . . . Hey, are you listening to me? (*Looking squarely at*
150   JOHN.)
   JOHN: Winston . . . I've got something to tell you.
   WINSTON: (*Registering* JOHN's *manner for the first time.*) What's
      the matter? Hodoshe? What happened? Are we in shit?
      Solitary?
155 JOHN: My appeal was heard last Wednesday. Sentence re-
      duced. I've got three months to go.

(*Long silence.* WINSTON *is stunned. Eventually. . . .*)

   WINSTON: Three. . . .
   JOHN: . . . months to go.
   WINSTON: Three. . . .
160 JOHN: *Ja.* That's what Prinsloo said.
   WINSTON: John!

(WINSTON *explodes with joy. The men embrace. They dance a jig
in the cell.* WINSTON *finally tears himself away and starts to hammer on the cell walls so as to pass on the news to other prisoners.*)

      Norman! Norman!! John. Three months to go. *Ja.* . . . Just
      been told. . . .

(WINSTON's *excitement makes* JOHN *nervous. He pulls* WINSTON
away from the wall.)

   JOHN: Winston! Not yet, man. We'll tell them at the quarry
165   tomorrow. Let me just live with it for a little while.
   WINSTON: Okay okay. . . . How did it happen?

(*He pulls* JOHN *down to the floor. They sit close together.*)

   JOHN: Jesus, I'm so mixed up, man! *Ja* . . . the door opened
      and I saw Hodoshe. Ooo God, I said to myself. Trouble!
      Here we go again! All because of me and the noise you
170   were making. Went down the corridor straight to Num-
      ber Four . . . Solitary and Spare Diet!! But at the end, in-
      stead of turning right, we turned left into the main block,
      all the way through it to Prinsloo's office.
   WINSTON: Prinsloo!
175 JOHN: I'm telling you. Prinsloo himself, man. We waited out-
      side for a little bit, then Hodoshe pushed me in. Prinsloo
      was behind his desk, busy with some papers. He pulled
      out one and said to me: "You are very lucky. Your lawyers
      have been working on your case. The sentence has been
180   reduced from ten years, to three."
   WINSTON: What did Hodoshe say?

JOHN: Nothing. But he looked unhappy.

(*They laugh.*)

      Hey, something else. Hodoshe let me walk back here by
      myself! He didn't follow me.
   WINSTON: Of course. You are free.   185
   JOHN: *Haai,* Winston, not yet. Those three months . . . ! Or
      suppose it's a trick.
   WINSTON: What do you mean?
   JOHN: Those bastards will do anything to break you. If the
      wheelbarrows and the quarry don't do it, they'll try some-   190
      thing else. Remember that last visit of wives, when they
      lined up all the men on the other side. . . . "Take a good
      look and say goodbye! Back to the cells!"
   WINSTON: You say you saw Prinsloo?
   JOHN: Prinsloo himself. Bastard didn't even stand up when I   195
      walked in. And by the way . . . I had to sign. *Ja!* I had to
      sign a form to say that I had been officially told of the re-
      sult of my appeal . . . that I had three months to go. *Ja.* I
      signed!
   WINSTON: (*Without the slightest doubt.*) It's three months,   200
      John.
   JOHN: (*Relaxing and living with the reality for the first time.*) Hell,
      Winston, at the end of those three months, it will be three
      years together in this cell. Three years ago I stood in front
      of that magistrate at Kirkwood—bastard didn't even look   205
      at me: "Ten years!" I watched ten years of my life drift
      away like smoke from a cigarette while he fidgeted and
      scratched his arse. That same night back in the prison van
      to the cells at Rooihel. First time we met!
   WINSTON: *Ja.* We had just got back from our trial in   210
      Cradock.
   JOHN: You, Temba, . . .
   WINSTON: Sipho. . . .
   JOHN: Hell, man!
   WINSTON: First time we got close to each other was the next   215
      morning in the yard, when they lined us up for the
      vans. . . .
   JOHN: And married us!

(*They lock left and right hands together to suggest handcuffs.*)

   WINSTON: Who was that old man . . . remember him? . . . in
      the corner handcuffed to Sipho?   220
   JOHN: Sipho?
   WINSTON: *Ja,* the one who started the singing.
   JOHN: (*Remembering.*) Peter. Tatu Peter.
   WINSTON: That's him!
   JOHN: Hell, it comes back now, man! Pulling through the big   225
      gates, wives and mothers running next to the vans, trying
      to say goodbye . . . all of us inside fighting for a last look
      through the window.
   WINSTON: (*Shaking his head.*) Shit!
   JOHN: Bet you've forgotten the song the old man started?   230

(WINSTON *tries to remember.* JOHN *starts singing softly. It is one of
the Defiance Campaign songs.* WINSTON *joins in.*)

   WINSTON: (*Shaking his head ruefully.*) By the time we reach
      Humansdorp though, nobody was singing.

JOHN: Fuck singing. I wanted to piss. Hey! I had my one free
hand on my balls, holding on. I'd made a mistake when we
235   left the Rooihel. Drank a gallon of water thinking of
those five hundred miles ahead. Jesus! There was the
bucket in the corner! But we were packed in so tight, remember, we couldn't move. I tried to pull you but it was
no bloody good. So I held on—Humansdorp, Storms
240   River, Blaaukrantz . . . held on. But at Knysna, to hell with
it, I let go!

(Gesture to indicate the release of his bladder. WINSTON *finds this
enormously funny.* JOHN *joins in.)*

    You were also wet by then!
WINSTON: Never!
JOHN: Okay, let's say that by George nobody was dry. Re-
245   member the stop there?
WINSTON: *Ja.* I thought they were going to let us walk
around a bit.
JOHN: Not a damn! Fill up with petrol and then on. Hey, but
what about those locals, the Coloured prisoners, when we
250   pulled away. Remember? Coming to their cell windows
and shouting . . . "Courage, Brothers! Courage!" After
that . . . ! Jesus, I was tired. Didn't we fall asleep? Standing
like that?
WINSTON: What do you mean standing? It was impossible to
255   fall.
JOHN: Then the docks, the boat. . . . It was my first time on
one. I had nothing to vomit up, but my God I tried.
WINSTON: What about me?
JOHN: Then we saw this place for the first time. It almost
260   looked pretty, hey, with all the mist around it.
WINSTON: I was too sick to see anything, *broer.*
JOHN: Remember your words when we jumped off onto the
jetty?

(Pause. The two men look at each other.)

    Heavy words, Winston. You looked back at the mountains
265   . . . "Farewell Africa!" I've never forgotten them. That was
three years ago.
WINSTON: And now, for you, it's three months to go.

(Pause. The mood of innocent celebration has passed. JOHN *realizes
what his good news means to the other man.)*

JOHN: To hell with everything. Let's go to bed.

*(*WINSTON *doesn't move.* JOHN *finds Antigone's wig.)*

    We'll talk about Antigone tomorrow.

*(*JOHN *prepares for bed.)*

270   Hey, Winston! I just realized. My family! Princess and the
children. Do you think they've been told? Jesus, man,
maybe they're also saying . . . three months! Those three
months are going to feel as long as the three years. Time
passes slowly when you've got something . . . to wait
275   for. . . .

(Pause. WINSTON *still hasn't moved.* JOHN *changes his tone.)*

    Look, in this cell we're going to forget those three
months. The whole bloody thing is most probably a trick
anyway. So let's just forget about it. We run to the quarry
tomorrow. Together. So let's sleep.

SCENE III

The cell, later the same night. Both men are in bed. WINSTON *is apparently asleep.* JOHN, *however, is awake, rolling restlessly from side
to side. He eventually gets up and goes quietly to the bucket for a
drink of water, then back to his bed. He doesn't lie down, however.
Pulling the blanket around his shoulders he starts to think about the
three months. He starts counting the days on the fingers of one hand.
Behind him* WINSTON *sits up and watches him in silence for a few
moments.*

WINSTON: *(With a strange smile.)* You're counting!
JOHN: *(With a start.)* What! Hey, Winston, you gave me a
fright, man. I thought you were asleep. What's the matter?
Can't you sleep?
WINSTON: *(Ignoring the question, still smiling.)* You've started 5
counting the days now.
JOHN: *(Unable to resist the temptation to talk, moving over to* WIN-
STON's *bed.)* Ja.
WINSTON: How many?
JOHN: Ninety-two.   10
WINSTON: You see!
JOHN: *(Excited.)* Simple, man. Look . . . twenty days left in this
month, thirty days in June, thirty-one in July, eleven days
in August . . . ninety-two.
WINSTON: *(Still smiling, but watching* JOHN *carefully.)* Tomor- 15
row?
JOHN: Ninety-one.
WINSTON: And the next day?
JOHN: Ninety.
WINSTON: Then one day it will be eighty!   20
JOHN: *Ja!*
WINSTON: Then seventy.
JOHN: Hey, Winston, time doesn't pass so fast.
WINSTON: Then only sixty more days.
JOHN: That's just two months here on the Island.   25
WINSTON: Fifty . . . forty days in the quarry.
JOHN: Jesus, Winston!
WINSTON: Thirty.
JOHN: One month. Only one month to go.
WINSTON: Twenty . . . *(Holding up his hands.)* then ten . . . five, 30
four, three, two . . . tomorrow!

(The anticipation of that moment is too much for JOHN.*)*

JOHN: NO! Please, man, Winston. It hurts. Leave those three
months alone. I'm going to sleep!

*(Back to his bed where he curls up in a tight ball and tries deter-
minedly to sleep.* WINSTON *lies down again and stares up at the ceiling. After a pause he speaks quietly.)*

WINSTON: They won't keep you here for the full three
months. Only two months. Then down to the jetty, into 35
a ferry-boat . . . you'll say goodbye to this place . . . and
straight to Victor Verster Prison on the mainland.

(*Against his will* JOHN *starts to listen. He eventually sits upright and completely surrenders himself to* WINSTON'*s description of the last few days of his confinement.*)

Life will change for you there. It will be much easier. Because you won't take Hodoshe with you. He'll stay here
40 with me, on the Island. They'll put you to work in the vineyards at Victor Verster, John. There are no quarries there. Eating grapes, oranges . . . they'll change your diet . . . Diet C, and exercises so that you'll look good when they let you out finally. At night you'll play games . . .
45 Ludo, draughts, snakes and ladders! Then one day they'll call you into the office, with a van waiting outside to take you back. The same five hundred miles. But this time they'll let you sit. You won't have to stand the whole way like you did coming here. And there won't be handcuffs.
50 Maybe they'll even stop on the way so that you can have a pee. Yes, I'm sure they will. You might even sleep over somewhere. Then finally Port Elizabeth. Rooihel Prison again, John! That's very near home, man. New Brighton is next door! Through your cell window you'll see people
55 moving up and down in the street, hear the buses roaring. Then one night you won't sleep again, because you'll be counting. Not days, as you are doing now, but hours. And the next morning, that beautiful morning, John, they'll take you straight out of your cell to the Discharge Office
60 where they'll give you a new khaki shirt, long khaki trousers, brown shoes. And your belongings! I almost forgot your belongings.
JOHN: Hey, by the way! I was wearing a white shirt, black tie, grey flannel trousers . . . brown Crockett shoes . . . socks?
65 (*A little laugh.*) I can't remember my socks! A check jacket . . . and my watch! I was wearing my watch!
WINSTON: They'll wrap them up in a parcel. You'll have it under your arm when they lead you to the gate. And outside, John, outside that gate, New Brighton will be wait-
70 ing for you. Your mother, your father, Princess and the children . . . and when they open it. . . .

(*Once again, but more violently this time,* JOHN *breaks the mood as the anticipation of the moment of freedom becomes too much for him.*)

JOHN: Stop it, Winston! Leave those three months alone for Christ's sake. I want to sleep.

(*He tries to get away from* WINSTON, *but the latter goes after him.* WINSTON *has now also abandoned his false smile.*)

WINSTON: (*Stopping* JOHN *as he tries to crawl away.*) But it's not
75 finished, John!
JOHN: Leave me alone!
WINSTON: It doesn't end there. Your people will take you home. Thirty-eight, Gratten Street, John! Remember it? Everybody will be waiting for you . . . aunts, uncles,
80 friends, neighbours. They'll put you in a chair, John, like a king, give you anything you want . . . cakes, sweets, cooldrinks . . . and then you'll start to talk. You'll tell them about this place, John, about Hodoshe, about the quarry, and about your good friend Winston who you left behind.
85 But you still won't be happy, hey. Because you'll need a fuck. A really wild one!

JOHN: Stop it, Winston!
WINSTON: (*Relentless.*) And that is why at ten o'clock that night you'll slip out through the back door and make your way to Sky's place. Imagine it, man! All the boys waiting 90 for you . . . Georgie, Mangi, Vusumzi. They'll fill you up with booze. They'll look after you. They know what it's like inside. They'll fix you up with a woman. . . .
JOHN: NO!
WINSTON: Set you up with her in a comfortable joint, and 95 then leave you alone. You'll watch her, watch her take her clothes off, you'll take your pants off, get near her, feel her, feel it. . . . *Ja,* you'll feel it. It will be wet. . . .
JOHN: WINSTON!
WINSTON: Wet *poes,* John! And you'll fuck it wild! 100

(JOHN *turns finally to face* WINSTON. *A long silence as the two men confront each other.* JOHN *is appalled at what he sees.*)

JOHN: Winston? What's happening? Why are you punishing me?
WINSTON: (*Quietly.*) You stink, John. You stink of beer, of company, of *poes,* of freedom. . . . Your freedom stinks, John, and it's driving me mad.
JOHN: No, Winston! 105
WINSTON: Yes! Don't deny it. Three months time, at this hour, you'll be wiping beer off your face, your hands on your balls, and *poes* waiting for you. You will laugh, you will drink, you will fuck and forget.

(JOHN'*s denials have no effect on* WINSTON.)

Stop bullshitting me! We've got no time left for that. 110 There's only two months left between us. (*Pause.*) You know where I ended up this morning, John? In the quarry. Next to old Harry. Do you know old Harry, John?
JOHN: Yes.
WINSTON: Yes what? Speak, man! 115
JOHN: Old Harry, Cell Twenty-three, seventy years, serving Life!
WINSTON: That's not what I'm talking about. When you go to the quarry tomorrow, take a good look at old Harry. Look into his eyes, John. Look at his hands. They've 120 changed him. They've turned him into stone. Watch him work with that chisel and hammer. Twenty perfect blocks of stone every day. Nobody else can do it like him. He loves stone. That's why they're nice to him. He's forgotten himself. He's forgotten everything . . . why he's here, 125 where he comes from. That's happening to me John. I've forgotten why I'm here.
JOHN: No.
WINSTON: Why am I here?
JOHN: You put your head on the block for others. 130
WINSTON: Fuck the others.
JOHN: Don't say that! Remember our ideals. . . .
WINSTON: Fuck our ideals. . . .
JOHN: No Winston . . . our slogans, our children's freedom. . . .
WINSTON: Fuck slogans, fuck politics . . . fuck everything, 135 John. Why am I here? I'm jealous of your freedom, John. I also want to count. God also gave me ten fingers, but what do I count? My life? How do I count it, John? One . . . one . . . another day comes . . . one. . . . Help me, John! . . . Another day . . . one . . . one . . . Help me, brother! . . . one. . . . 140

(JOHN *has sunk to the floor, helpless in the face of the other man's torment and pain.* WINSTON *almost seems to bend under the weight of the life stretching ahead of him on the Island. For a few seconds he lives in silence with his reality, then slowly straightens up. He turns and looks at* JOHN. *When he speaks again, it is the voice of a man who has come to terms with his fate, massively compassionate.*)

    Nyana we Sizwe!

(JOHN *looks up at him.*)

    Nyana we Sizwe . . . it's all over now. All over. (*He moves over to* JOHN.) Forget me. . . .

(JOHN *attempts a last, limp denial.*)

    No, John! Forget me . . . because I'm going to forget you.
145   Yes, I will forget you. Others will come in here, John, count, go, and I'll forget them. Still more will come, count like you, go like you, and I will forget them. And then one day, it will all be over.

(*A lighting change suggests the passage of time.* WINSTON *collects together their props for Antigone.*)

    Come. They're waiting.
150 JOHN: Do you know your words?
WINSTON: Yes. Come, we'll be late for the concert.

SCENE IV

The two men convert their cell-area into a stage for the prison concert. Their blankets are hung to provide a makeshift backdrop behind which WINSTON *disappears with their props.* JOHN *comes forward and addresses the audience. He is not yet in his Creon costume.*

JOHN: Captain Prinsloo, Hodoshe, Warders, . . . and Gentlemen! Two brothers of the House of Labdacus found themselves on opposite sides in battle, the one defending the State, the other attacking it. They both died on the
5   battlefield. King Creon, Head of the State, decided that the one who had defended the State would be buried with all religious rites due to the noble dead. But the other one, the traitor Polynices, who had come back from exile intending to burn and destroy his fatherland, to
10   drink the blood of his masters, was to have no grave, no mourning. He was to lie on the open fields to rot, or at most be food for the jackals. It was a law. But Antigone, their sister, defied the law and buried the body of her brother Polynices. She was caught and arrested. That is
15   why tonight the Hodoshe Span, Cell Forty-two, presents for your entertainment: "The Trial and Punishment of Antigone."

(*He disappears behind the blankets. They simulate a fanfare of trumpets. At its height the blankets open and he steps out as Creon. In addition to his pendant, there is some sort of crown and a blanket draped over his shoulders as a robe.*)

    My People! Creon stands before his palace and greets you! Stop! Stop! What's that I hear? You, good man, speak up.
20   Did I hear "Hail the King"? My good people, I am your *servant* . . . a happy one, but still your servant. How many times must I ask you, implore you to see in these symbols of office nothing more, or less, than you would in the uniform of the humblest menial in your house. Creon's crown is as simple, and I hope as clean, as the apron 25 Nanny wears. And even as Nanny smiles and is your happy servant because she sees her charge . . . your child! . . . waxing fat in that little cradle, so too does Creon— your obedient servant!—stand here and smile. For what does he see? Fatness and happiness! How else does one 30 measure the success of a state? By the sumptuousness of the palaces built for its king and princes? The magnificence of the temples erected to its gods? The achievements of its scientists and technicians who can now send rockets to the moon? No! These count for nothing beside 35 the fatness and happiness of its people.

    But have you ever paused to ask yourself whose responsibility it is to maintain that fatness and happiness? The answer is simple, is it not? . . . your servant the king! But have you then gone on to ask yourself what does the 40 king need to maintain this happy state of affairs? What, other than his silly crown, are the tools with which a king fashions the happiness of his people? The answer is equally simple, my good people. The law! Yes. The law. A three-lettered word, and how many times haven't you glibly 45 used it, never bothering to ask yourselves, "What then is the law?" Or if you have, then making recourse to such clichés as "the law states this . . . or the law states that." The law states or maintains nothing, good people. The law defends! The law is no more or less than a shield in your 50 faithful servant's hand to protect YOU! But even as a shield would be useless in one hand, to defend, without a sword in the other, to strike . . . so too the law has its edge. The penalty! We have come through difficult times. I am sure it is needless for me to remind you of the constant 55 troubles on our borders . . . those despicable rats who would gnaw away at our fatness and happiness. We have been diligent in dealing with them. But unfortunately there are still at large subversive elements . . . there are still amongst us a few rats that are not satisfied and to them I 60 must show this face of Creon . . . so different to the one that hails my happy people! It is with a heavy heart, and you shall see why soon enough, that I must tell you that we have caught another one. That is why I have assembled you here. Let what follows be a living lesson for those 65 among you misguided enough still to harbour sympathy for rats! The shield has defended. Now the sword must strike!

    Bring in the accused.

(WINSTON, *dressed as Antigone, enters. He wears the wig, the necklace of nails, and a blanket around his waist as a skirt.*)

    Your name!   70
WINSTON: Antigone, daughter of Oedipus, sister of Eteocles and Polynices.
JOHN: You are accused that, in defiance of the law, you buried the body of the traitor Polynices.
WINSTON: I buried the body of my brother Polynices.   75
JOHN: Did you know there was a law forbidding that?
WINSTON: Yes.
JOHN: Yet you defied it.

WINSTON: Yes.

80 JOHN: Did you know the consequences of such defiance?

WINSTON: Yes.

JOHN: What did you plead to the charges laid against you? Guilty or Not Guilty?

WINSTON: Guilty.

85 JOHN: Antigone, you have pleaded guilty. Is there anything you wish to say in mitigation? This is your last chance. Speak.

WINSTON: Who made the law forbidding the burial of my brother?

90 JOHN: The State.

WINSTON: Who is the State?

JOHN: As King I am its manifest symbol.

WINSTON: So you made the law.

JOHN: Yes, for the State.

95 WINSTON: Are you God?

JOHN: Watch your words, little girl!

WINSTON: You said it was my chance to speak.

JOHN: But not to ridicule.

WINSTON: I've got no time to waste on that. Your sentence
100 on my life hangs waiting on your lips.

JOHN: Then speak on.

WINSTON: When Polynices died in battle, all that remained was the empty husk of his body. He could neither harm nor help any man again. What lay on the battlefield wait-
105 ing for Hodoshe to turn rotten, belonged to God. You are only a man, Creon. Even as there are laws made by men, so too there are others that come from God. He watches my soul for a transgression even as your spies hide in the bush at night to see who is transgressing your laws. Guilty
110 against God I will not be for any man on this earth. Even without your law, Creon, and the threat of death to who-ever defied it, I know I must die. Because of your law and my defiance, that fate is now very near. So much the bet-ter. Your threat is nothing to me, Creon. But if I had let
115 my mother's son, a Son of the Land, lie there as food for the carrion fly, Hodoshe, my soul would never have known peace. Do you understand anything of what I am saying, Creon?

JOHN: Your words reveal only that obstinacy of spirit which
120 has brought nothing but tragedy to your people. First you break the law. Now you insult the State.

WINSTON: Just because I ask you to remember that you are only a man?

JOHN: And to add insult to injury you gloat over your deeds!
125 No, Antigone, you will not escape with impunity. Were you my own child you would not escape full punishment.

WINSTON: Full punishment? Would you like to do more than just kill me?

JOHN: That is all I wish.

WINSTON: Then let us not waste any time. Stop talking. I 130
buried my brother. That is an honourable thing, Creon.
All these people in your state would say so too, if fear of
you and another law did not force them into silence.

JOHN: You are wrong. None of my people think the way
you do. 135

WINSTON: Yes they do, but no one dares tell you so. You will
not sleep peacefully, Creon.

JOHN: You add shamelessness to your crimes, Antigone.

WINSTON: I do not feel any shame at having honoured my
brother. 140

JOHN: Was he that died with him not also your brother?

WINSTON: He was.

JOHN: And so you honour the one and insult the other.

WINSTON: I shared my love, not my hate.

JOHN: Go then and share your love among the dead. I will 145
have no rats' law here while yet I live.

WINSTON: We are wasting time, Creon. Stop talking. Your
words defeat your purpose. They are prolonging my life.

JOHN: (*Again addressing the audience.*) You have heard all the
relevant facts. Needless now to call the state witnesses 150
who would testify beyond reasonable doubt that the accused is guilty. Nor, for that matter, is it in the best interests of the State to disclose their identity. There was a law.
The law was broken. The law stipulated its penalty. My
hands are tied. Take her from where she stands, straight to 155
the Island! There wall her up in a cell for life, with enough
food to acquit ourselves of the taint of her blood.

WINSTON: (*To the audience.*) Brothers and Sisters of the Land!
I go now on my last journey. I must leave the light of day
forever, for the Island, strange and cold, to be lost between 160
life and death. So, to my grave, my everlasting prison, condemned alive to solitary death.

(*Tearing off his wig and confronting the audience as* WINSTON, *not
Antigone.*)

Gods of Our Fathers! My Land! My Home!
Time waits no longer. I go now to my living death, because I honoured those things to which honour belongs. 165

(*The two men take off their costumes and then strike their "set."
They then come together and, as in the beginning, their hands come
together to suggest handcuffs, and their right and left legs to suggest
ankle-chains. They start running . . .* JOHN *mumbling a prayer, and*
WINSTON *a rhythm for their three-legged run.*)

(*The siren wails.*)

(*Fade to blackout.*)

Wole Soyinka

Wole Soyinka was born in 1934 in Abeokuta, Nigeria. Educated at Government College in Ibadan, Soyinka then studied at Leeds University in England, where he worked with the notable Shakespearian scholar and actor G. Wilson Knight and took his B.A. in English in 1957. He remained in England working as play reader for the Royal Court Theater before returning to Nigeria in 1959, where his first play, *The Lion and the Jewel,* was produced. In the course of the next decade, Soyinka wrote an important body of dramatic work, including the plays *The Invention* (1959), *A Dance of the Forests* (1960), *The Trials of Brother Jero* (1960), *Camwood on the Leaves* (radio play, 1960), *The Strong Breed* (1964), *Kongi's Harvest* (1964), and *The Road* (1965). He also taught at the universities of Ibadan, Ife, and Lagos, and founded two important theaters, the Orisun Theater (1964) and the Masks Theater (1960). Much of Soyinka's work is critical of authoritarian politics; he was arrested in 1967 and held as a political prisoner until 1969. Soyinka's memoir of imprisonment, *The Man Died,* was published in 1972 and was cited for excellence by Amnesty International. In the 1970s, Soyinka continued to write plays examining the tensions of tribal life in modern Africa: *Madmen and Specialists* (1970) and *Death and the King's Horseman* (1976). He also wrote plays more directly examining contemporary African politics: his rewriting of Brecht's *Threepenny Opera* as *Opera Wonyosi* (1977), and *A Play of Giants* (1985). He also wrote an adaptation of Euripides' *The Bacchae* (1973), placing the Greek narrative in a more explicitly tribal and ritualistic setting. Soyinka was awarded the Nobel Prize in 1986, the first African writer to receive the prize for literature.

Elesin faces the accusatory body of his son Olunde in Wole Soyinka's *Death and the King's Horseman* in this 1990 production at the New Rose Theatre, Portland.

DEATH AND THE KING'S HORSEMAN

Soyinka is sometimes criticized by other African writers for being too oriented toward Europe. Not only are some of his plays adaptations or imitations of European works, but Soyinka has continued to write in English—the language of the colonial power, after all—rather than writing in his native language, Yoruba. It is precisely this tension between village and metropolis, between Africa and Europe, that provides the springboard for some of Soyinka's greatest work and dramatizes the challenges of cross-cultural interaction in the complex contemporary political environment.

Death and the King's Horseman is based on events that took place in the Yoruba city of Oyo in 1946. The play opens on the day the local African king is to be buried. According to custom, his Horseman, Elesin Oba, will die on this day as well, following his master in death as he followed him in life. It is clear from the scene in the marketplace that this ritual death is, however, a celebration. The village enacts a festive and playful marriage between Elesin and a new, young bride, so that he can procreate before he dies, bringing new life into the world even as he passes out of it, but fatefully delaying his required sacrifice.

In *Death and the King's Horseman,* indigenous African culture operates within the more restricted sphere of Britain's colonial values, laws, and institutions. The region's colonial administrator, Simon Pilkings, who is on his way to a masquerade to celebrate the arrival of the Prince, acts to stop Elesin's death. However, Pilkings and his wife are wearing African ceremonial costumes of the dead to the English masquerade, a decision that is not only offensive and irreligious to the Africans they meet, but that marks their complete incomprehension of the complex situation in which they find themselves. Wearing the costume also marks the Pilkingses, and the colonial British as a whole, as figures of death, in contrast to the paradoxical life celebrated by Elesin.

Pilkings "saves" Elesin and brings about the play's tragic catastrophe. Elesin's son Olunde—studying medicine in Britain—returns to perform funeral rites for his father. However, when Elesin is prevented from dying, it becomes clear that colonial intervention has destroyed what it attempted to protect. Olunde, too, is dishonored when his father remains alive and takes the only possible course of action.

In his note to the play, Soyinka criticizes the phrase "clash of cultures" to describe his work, for it "presupposes a potential equality in *every given situation* of the alien culture and the indigenous." In *Death and the King's Horseman,* the power vested in the colonial administration signals its ability to destroy the indigenous culture it claims, ironically, to govern.

Author's Note

This play is based on events which took place in Oyo, ancient Yoruba city of Nigeria, in 1946. That year, the lives of Elesin (Olori Elesin), his son, and the Colonial District Officer intertwined, with the disastrous results set out in the play. The changes I have made are in matters of detail, sequence and of course characterisation. The action has also been set back two or three years to while the war was still on, for minor reasons of dramaturgy.

The factual account still exists in the archives of the British Colonial Administration. It has already inspired a fine play in Yoruba (Oba Wàjà) by Duro Ladipo. It has also misbegotten a film by some German television company.

The bane of themes of this genre is that they are no sooner employed creatively than they acquire the facile tag of "clash of cultures," a prejudicial label which, quite apart from its frequent misapplication, presupposes a potential equality *in every given situation* of the alien culture and the indigenous, on the actual soil of the latter. (In the area of misapplication, the overseas prize for illiteracy and mental conditioning undoubtedly goes to the blurb-writer for the American edition of my novel *Season of Anomy* who unblushingly declares that this work portrays the "clash between old values and new ways, between western methods and

African traditions"!) It is thanks to this kind of perverse mentality that I find it necessary to caution the would-be producer of this play against a sadly familiar reductionist tendency, and to direct his vision instead to the far more difficult and risky task of eliciting the play's threnodic essence.

One of the more obvious alternative structures of the play would be to make the District Officer the victim of a cruel dilemma. This is not to my taste and it is not by chance that I have avoided dialogue or situation which would encourage this. No attempt should be made in production to suggest it. The Colonial Factor is an incident, a catalytic incident merely. The confrontation in the play is largely metaphysical, contained in the human vehicle which is Elesin and the universe of the Yoruba mind—the world of the living, the dead and the unborn, and the numinous passage which links all: transition. *Death and the King's Horseman* can be fully realised only through an evocation of music from the abyss of transition.

Wole Soyinka

DEATH AND THE KING'S HORSEMAN
Wole Soyinka

CHARACTERS

PRAISE-SINGER
ELESIN, *Horseman of the King*
IYALOJA, *'Mother' of the market*
SIMON PILKINGS, *District Officer*
JANE PILKINGS, *his wife*
SERGEANT AMUSA
JOSEPH, *houseboy to the Pilkingses*
BRIDE

H.R.H. THE PRINCE
THE RESIDENT
AIDE-DE-CAMP
OLUNDE, *eldest son of Elesin*
DRUMMERS, WOMEN, YOUNG GIRLS, DANCERS AT THE BALL

The play should run without an interval. For rapid scene changes, one adjustable outline set is very appropriate.

ACT ONE

A passage through a market in its closing stages. The stalls are being emptied, mats folded. A few women pass through on their way home, loaded with baskets. On a cloth-stand, bolts of cloth are taken down, display pieces folded and piled on a tray. ELESIN OBA *enters along a passage before the market, pursued by his* DRUMMERS *and* PRAISE-SINGERS. *He is a man of enormous vitality, speaks, dances and sings with that infectious enjoyment of life which accompanies all his actions.*

PRAISE-SINGER: Elesin O! Elesin Oba! Howu! What tryst is this the cockerel goes to keep with such haste that he must leave his tail behind?

ELESIN: (*Slows down a bit, laughing.*) A tryst where the cockerel
5 needs no adornment.

PRAISE-SINGER: O-oh, you hear that my companions? That's the way the world goes. Because the man approaches a brand-new bride he forgets the long faithful mother of his children.

ELESIN: When the horse sniffs the stable does he not strain at
10 the bridle? The market is the long-suffering home of my spirit and the women are packing up to go. That Esu-harassed day slipped into the stewpot while we feasted. We ate it up with the rest of the meat. I have neglected my women.

15 PRAISE-SINGER: We know all that. Still it's no reason for shedding your tail on this day of all days. I know the women will cover you in damask and *alari* but when the wind blows cold from behind, that's when the fowl knows his true friends.

20 ELESIN: Olohun-iyo!

PRAISE-SINGER: Are you sure there will be one like me on the other side?

ELESIN: Olohun-iyo!

PRAISE-SINGER: Far be it for me to belittle the dwellers of that
25 place but, a man is either born to his art or he isn't. And I don't know for certain that you'll meet my father, so who is going to sing these deeds in accents that will pierce the deafness of the ancient ones. I have prepared my going— just tell me: Olohun-iyo, I need you on this journey and I
30 shall be behind you.

Note to this edition: Certain Yoruba words which appear in italics in the text are explained in a brief glossary at the end of the play.

ELESIN: You're like a jealous wife. Stay close to me, but only on this side. My fame, my honour are legacies to the living; stay behind and let the world sip its honey from your lips.

PRAISE-SINGER: Your name will be like the sweet berry a child places under his tongue to sweeten the passage of food. The 35 world will never spit it out.

ELESIN: Come then. This market is my roost. When I come among the women I am a chicken with a hundred mothers. I become a monarch whose palace is built with tenderness and beauty. 40

PRAISE-SINGER: They love to spoil you but beware. The hands of women also weaken the unwary.

ELESIN: This night I'll lay my head upon their lap and go to sleep. This night I'll touch feet with their feet in a dance that is no longer of this earth. But the smell of their flesh, 45 their sweat, the smell of indigo on their cloth, this is the last air I wish to breathe as I go to meet my great forebears.

PRAISE-SINGER: In their time the world was never tilted from its groove, it shall not be in yours.

ELESIN: The gods have said No. 50

PRAISE-SINGER: In their time the great wars came and went, the little wars came and went; the white slavers came and went, they took away the heart of our race, they bore away the mind and muscle of our race. The city fell and was rebuilt; the city fell and our people trudged through mountain and forest to 55 found a new home but—Elesin Oba do you hear me?

ELESIN: I hear your voice Olohun-iyo.

PRAISE-SINGER: Our world was never wrenched from its true course.

ELESIN: The gods have said No. 60

PRAISE-SINGER: There is only one home to the life of a river-mussel; there is only one home to the life of a tortoise; there is only one shell to the soul of man: there is only one world to the spirit of our race. If that world leaves its course and smashes on boulders of the great void, whose world will 65 give us shelter?

ELESIN: It did not in the time of my forebears, it shall not in mine.

PRAISE-SINGER: The cockerel must not be seen without his feathers. 70

ELESIN: Nor will the Not-I bird be much longer without his nest.

PRAISE-SINGER: (*Stopped in his lyric stride.*) The Not-I bird, Elesin?

ELESIN: I said, the Not-I bird. 75

1435

PRAISE-SINGER: All respect to our elders but, is there really such
a bird?

ELESIN: What! Could it be that he failed to knock on your door?

PRAISE-SINGER: (*Smiling.*) Elesin's riddles are not merely the nut
80 in the kernel that breaks human teeth; he also buries the
kernel in hot embers and dares a man's fingers to draw it out.

ELESIN: I am sure he called on you, Olohun-iyo. Did you hide in
the loft and push out the servant to tell him you were out?

(ELESIN *executes a brief, half-taunting dance. The* DRUMMER *moves
in and draws a rhythm out of his steps.* ELESIN *dances towards the
market-place as he chants the story of the Not-I bird, his voice changing dexterously to mimic his characters. He performs like a born raconteur, infecting his retinue with his humour and energy. More women
arrive during his recital, including* IYALOJA.)

Death came calling.
85 Who does not know his rasp of reeds?
A twilight whisper in the leaves before
The great araba falls? Did you hear it?
'Not I!' swears the farmer. He snaps
His fingers round his head, abandons
90 A hard-won harvest and begins
A rapid dialogue with his legs.

'Not I,' shouts the fearless hunter, 'but—
It's getting dark, and this night-lamp
Has leaked out all its oil. I think
95 It's best to go home and resume my hunt
Another day.' But now he pauses, suddenly
Lets out a wail: 'Oh foolish mouth, calling
Down a curse on your own head! Your lamp
Has leaked out all its oil, has it?'
100 Forwards or backwards now he dare not move.
To search for leaves and make *etutu*
On that spot? Or race home to the safety
Of his hearth? Ten market-days have passed
My friends, and still he's rooted there
105 Rigid as the plinth of Orayan.

The mouth of the courtesan barely
Opened wide enough to take a ha' penny *robo*
When she wailed: 'Not I.' All dressed she was
To call upon my friend the Chief Tax Officer.
110 But now she sends her go-between instead:
'Tell him I'm ill: my period has come suddenly
But not—I hope—my time.'

Why is the pupil crying?
His hapless head was made to taste
115 The knuckles of my friend the Mallam:
'If you were then reciting the Koran
Would you have ears for idle noises
Darkening the trees, you child of ill omen?'
He shuts down school before its time
120 Runs home and rings himself with amulets.
And take my good kinsman Ifawomi.
His hands were like a carver's, strong
And true. I saw them
Tremble like wet wings of a fowl
125 One day he cast his time-smoothed *opele*
Across the divination board. And all because

The suppliant looked him in the eye and asked,
'Did you hear that whisper in the leaves?'
'Not I,' was his reply; 'perhaps I'm growing deaf—
Good-day.' And Ifa spoke no more that day   130
The priest locked fast his doors,
Sealed up his leaking roof—but wait!
This sudden care was not for Fawomi
But for Osanyin, courier-bird of Ifa's
Heart of wisdom. I did not know a kite   135
Was hovering in the sky
And Ifa now a twittering chicken in
The brood of Fawomi the Mother Hen.

Ah, but I must not forget my evening
Courier from the abundant palm, whose groan   140
Became 'Not I,' as he constipated down
A wayside bush. He wonders if Elegbara
Has tricked his buttocks to discharge
Against a sacred grove. Hear him
Mutter spells to ward off penalties   145
For an abomination he did not intend.
If any here
Stumbles on a gourd of wine, fermenting
Near the road, and nearby hears a stream
Of spells issuing from a crouching form.   150
Brother to a *sigidi,* bring home my wine,
Tell my tapper I have ejected
Fear from home and farm. Assure him,
All is well.

PRAISE-SINGER: In your time we do not doubt the peace of   155
farmstead and home, the peace of road and hearth, we do
not doubt the peace of the forest.

ELESIN: There was fear in the forest too.
Not-I was lately heard even in the lair
Of beasts. The hyena cackled loud 'Not I,'   160
The civet twitched his fiery tail and glared:
Not I. Not-I became the answering-name
Of the restless bird, that little one
Whom Death found nesting in the leaves
When whisper of his coming ran   165
Before him on the wind. 'Not-I'
Has long abandoned home. This same dawn
I heard him twitter in the gods' abode.
Ah, companions of this living world
What a thing this is, that even those   170
We call immortal
Should fear to die.

IYALOJA: But you, husband of multitudes?

ELESIN: I, when that Not-I bird perched
Upon my roof, bade him seek his nest again,   175
Safe, without care or fear. I unrolled
My welcome mat for him to see. Not-I
Flew happily away, you'll hear his voice
No more in this lifetime—You all know
What I am.   180

PRAISE-SINGER: That rock which turns its open lodes
Into the path of lightning. A gay
Thoroughbred whose sudden disdains
To falter though an adder reared
Suddenly in his path.   185

ELESIN: My rein is loosened.
    I am master of my Fate. When the hour comes
    Watch me dance along the narrowing path
    Glazed by the soles of my great precursors.
190   My soul is eager. I shall not turn aside.
WOMEN: You will not delay?
ELESIN: Where the storm pleases, and when, it directs
    The giants of the forest. When friendship summons
    Is when the true comrade goes.
195 WOMEN: Nothing will hold you back?
ELESIN: Nothing. What! Has no one told you yet?
    I go to keep my friend and master company.
    Who says the mouth does not believe in
    'No, I have chewed all that before?' I say I have.
200   The world is not a constant honey-pot.
    Where I found little I made do with little.
    Where there was plenty I gorged myself.
    My master's hands and mine have always
    Dipped together and, home or sacred feast,
205   The bowl was beaten bronze, the meats
    So succulent our teeth accused us of neglect.
    We shared the choicest of the season's
    Harvest of yams. How my friend would read
    Desire in my eyes before I knew the cause—
210   However rare, however precious, it was mine.
WOMEN: The town, the very land was yours.
ELESIN: The world was mine. Our joint hands
    Raised houseposts of trust that withstood
    The siege of envy and the termites of time.
215   But the twilight hour brings bats and rodents—
    Shall I yield them cause to foul the rafters?
PRAISE-SINGER: Elesin Oba! Are you not that man who
    Looked out of doors that stormy day
    The god of luck limped by, drenched
220   To the very lice that held
    His rags together? You took pity upon
    His sores and wished him fortune.
    Fortune was footloose this dawn, he replied,
    Till you trapped him in a heartfelt wish
225   That now returns to you. Elesin Oba!
    I say you are that man who
    Chanced upon the calabash of honour
    You thought it was palm wine and
    Drained its contents to the final drop.
230 ELESIN: Life has an end. A life that will outlive
    Fame and friendship begs another name.
    What elder takes his tongue to his plate,
    Licks it clean of every crumb? He will encounter
    Silence when he calls on children to fulfill
235   The smallest errand! Life is honour.
    It ends when honour ends.
WOMEN: We know you for a man of honour.
ELESIN: Stop! Enough of that!
WOMEN: (*Puzzled, they whisper among themselves, turning mostly*
240   *to* IYALOJA.) What is it? Did we say something to give of-
    fense? Have we slighted him in some way?
ELESIN: Enough of that sound I say. Let me hear no more in that
    vein. I've heard enough.
IYALOJA: We must have said something wrong. (*Comes forward*
245   *a little.*) Elesin Oba, we ask forgiveness before you speak.

ELESIN: I am bitterly offended.
IYALOJA: Our unworthiness has betrayed us. All we can do is
    ask your forgiveness. Correct us like a kind father.
ELESIN: This day of all days . . .
IYALOJA: It does not bear thinking. If we offend you now we 250
    have mortified the gods. We offend heaven itself. Father of
    us all, tell us where we went astray. (*She kneels, the other*
    women follow.)
ELESIN: Are you not ashamed? Even a tear-veiled
    Eye preserves its function of sight.   255
    Because my mind was raised to horizons
    Even the boldest man lowers his gaze
    In thinking of, must my body here
    Be taken for a vagrant's?
IYALOJA: Horseman of the King, I am more baffled than ever. 260
PRAISE-SINGER: The strictest father unbends his brow when
    the child is penitent, Elesin. When time is short, we do not
    spend it prolonging the riddle. Their shoulders are bowed
    with the weight of fear lest they have marred your day be-
    yond repair. Speak now in plain words and let us pursue the 265
    ailment to the home of remedies.
ELESIN: Words are cheap. 'We know you for
    A man of honour.' Well tell me, is this how
    A man of honour should be seen?
    Are these not the same clothes in which   270
    I came among you a full half-hour ago?

(*He roars with laughter and the* WOMEN, *relieved, rise and rush into*
stalls to fetch rich cloths.)

WOMAN: The gods are kind. A fault soon remedied is soon for-
    given. Elesin Oba, even as we match our words with deed,
    let your heart forgive us completely.
ELESIN: You who are breath and giver of my being   275
    How shall I dare refuse you forgiveness
    Even if the offence were real.
IYALOJA: (*Dancing round him. Sings.*)
                    He forgives us. He forgives us.
                    What a fearful thing it is when   280
                    The voyager sets forth
                    But a curse remains behind.
WOMEN: For a while we truly feared
    Our hands had wrenched the world adrift
    In emptiness.   285
IYALOJA: Richly, richly, robe him richly
    The cloth of honour is *alari*
    Sanyan is the band of friendship
    Boa-skin makes slippers of esteem.
WOMEN: For a while we truly feared   290
    Our hands had wrenched the world adrift
    In emptiness.
PRAISE-SINGER: He who must, must voyage forth
    The world will not roll backwards
    It is he who must, with one   295
    Great gesture overtake the world.
WOMEN: For a while we truly feared
    Our hands had wrenched the world
    In emptiness.
PRAISE-SINGER: The gourd you bear is not for shirking. 300
    The gourd is not for setting down

At the first crossroad or wayside grove.
Only one river may know its contents.
WOMEN: We shall all meet at the great market
305   We shall all meet at the great market
He who goes early takes the best bargains
But we shall meet, and resume our banter.

(ELESIN *stands resplendent in rich clothes, cap, shawl, etc. His sash is
of a bright red alari cloth. The* WOMEN *dance round him. Suddenly,
his attention is caught by an object off-stage.*)

ELESIN: The world I know is good.
WOMEN: We know you'll leave it so.
310 ELESIN: The world I know is the bounty
Of hives after bees have swarmed.
No goodness teems with such open hands
Even in the dreams of deities.
WOMEN: And we know you'll leave it so.
315 ELESIN: I was born to keep it so. A hive
Is never known to wander. An anthill
Does not desert its roots. We cannot see
The still great womb of the world—
No man beholds his mother's womb—
320   Yet who denies it's there? Coiled
To the navel of the world is that
Endless cord that links us all
To the great origin. If I lose my way
The trailing cord will bring me to the roots.
325 WOMEN: The world is in your hands.

(*The earlier distraction, a beautiful young girl, comes along the passage through which* ELESIN *first made his entry.*)

ELESIN: I embrace it. And let me tell you, women—
I like this farewell that the world designed,
Unless my eyes deceive me, unless
We are already parted, the world and I,
330   And all that breeds desire is lodged
Among our tireless ancestors. Tell me friends,
Am I still earthed in that beloved market
Of my youth? Or could it be my will
Has outleapt the conscious act and I have come
335   Among the great departed?
PRAISE-SINGER: Elesin-Oba why do your eyes roll like a bush-
rat who sees his fate like his father's spirit, mirrored in the
eye of a snake? And all these questions! You're standing on
the same earth you've always stood upon. This voice you
340   hear is mine, Oluhun-iyo, not that of an acolyte in heaven.
ELESIN: How can that be? In all my life
As Horseman of the King, the juiciest
Fruit on every tree was mine. I saw,
I touched, I wooed, rarely was the answer No.
345   The honour of my place, the veneration I
Received in the eye of man or woman
Prospered my suit and
Played havoc with my sleeping hours.
And they tell me my eyes were a hawk
350   In perpetual hunger. Split an iroko tree
In two, hide a woman's beauty in its heartwood
And seal it up again—Elesin, journeying by,
Would make his camp beside that tree
Of all the shades in the forest.

PRAISE-SINGER: Who would deny your reputation, snake-on-   355
the-loose in dark passages of the market! Bed-bug who
wages war on the mat and receives the thanks of the vanquished! When caught with his bride's own sister he
protested—but I was only prostrating myself to her as becomes a grateful in-law. Hunter who carries his powder-horn   360
on the hips and fires crouching or standing! Warrior who
never makes that excuse of the whining coward—but how
can I go to battle without my trousers?—trouserless or shirtless it's all one to him. Oka-rearing-from-a-camouflage-of-
leaves, before he strikes the victim is already prone! Once   365
they told him, Howu, a stallion does not feed on the grass
beneath him: he replied, true, but surely he can roll on it!
WOMEN: Ba-a-a-ba O!
PRAISE-SINGER: Ah, but listen yet. You know there is the leaf-
knibbling grub and there is the cola-chewing beetle; the   370
leaf-nibbling grub lives on the leaf, the cola-chewing bee-
tle lives in the colanut. Don't we know what our man feeds
on when we find him cocooned in a woman's wrapper?
ELESIN: Enough, enough, you all have cause
To know me well. But, if you say this earth   375
Is still the same as gave birth to those songs,
Tell me who was that goddess through whose lips
I saw the ivory pebbles of Oya's river-bed.
Iyaloja, who is she? I saw her enter
Your stall; all your daughters I know well.   380
No, not even Ogun-of-the-farm toiling
Dawn till dusk on his tuber patch
Not even Ogun with the finest hoe he ever
Forged at the anvil could have shaped
That rise of buttocks, not though he had   385
The richest earth between his fingers.
Her wrapper was no disguise
For thighs whose ripples shamed the river's
Coils around the hills of Ilesi. Her eyes
Were new-laid eggs glowing in the dark.   390
Her skin . . .
IYALOJA: Elesin Oba . . .
ELESIN: What! Where do you all say I am?
IYALOJA: Still among the living.
ELESIN: And that radiance which so suddenly   395
Lit up this market I could boast
I knew so well?
IYALOJA: Has one step already in her husband's home. She is
betrothed.
ELESIN: (*Irritated.*) Why do you tell me that?   400

(IYALOJA *falls silent. The* WOMEN *shuffle uneasily.*)

IYALOJA: Not because we dare give you offence Elesin. Today
is your day and the whole world is yours. Still, even those
who leave town to make a new dwelling elsewhere like to
be remembered by what they leave behind.
ELESIN: Who does not seek to be remembered?   405
Memory is Master of Death, the chink
In his armour of conceit. I shall leave
That which makes my going the sheerest
Dream of an afternoon. Should voyagers
Not travel light? Let the considerate traveller   410
Shed, of his excessive load, all
That may benefit the living.

WOMEN: (*Relieved.*) Ah Elesin Oba, we knew you for a man of honour.

415 ELESIN: Then honour me. I deserve a bed of honour to lie upon.

IYALOJA: The best is yours. We know you for a man of honour. You are not one who eats and leaves nothing on his plate for children. Did you not say it yourself? Not one who blights the happiness of others for a moment's pleasure.

420 ELESIN: Who speaks of pleasure? O women, listen!
Pleasure palls. Our acts should have meaning.
The sap of the plantain never dries.
You have seen the young shoot swelling
Even as the parent stalk begins to wither.
425 Women, let my going be likened to
The twilight hour of the plantain.

WOMEN: What does he mean Iyaloja? This language is the language of our elders, we do not fully grasp it.

IYALOJA: I dare not understand you yet Elesin.

430 ELESIN: All you who stand before the spirit that dares
The opening of the last door of passage,
Dare to rid my going of regrets! My wish
Transcends the blotting out of thought
In one mere moment's tremor of the senses.
435 Do me credit. And do me honour.
I am girded for the route beyond
Burdens of waste and longing.
Then let me travel light. Let
Seed that will not serve the stomach
440 On the way remain behind. Let it take root
In the earth of my choice, in this earth
I leave behind.

IYALOJA: (*Turns to* WOMEN.) The voice I hear is already touched by the waiting fingers of our departed. I dare not refuse.

445 WOMAN: Buy Iyaloja ...

IYALOJA: The matter is no longer in our hands.

WOMAN: But she is betrothed to your own son. Tell him.

IYALOJA: My son's wish is mine. I did the asking for him, the loss can be remedied. But who will remedy the blight of
450 closed hands on the day when all should be openness and light? Tell him, you say! You wish that I burden him with knowledge that will sour his wish and lay regrets on the last moments of his mind. You pray to him who is your intercessor to the other world—don't set this world adrift in
455 your own time; would you rather it was my hand whose sacrilege wrenched it loose?

WOMAN: Not many men will brave the curse of a dispossessed husband.

IYALOJA: Only the curses of the departed are to be feared. The
460 claims of one whose foot is on the threshold of their abode surpasses even the claims of blood. It is impiety even to place hindrances in their ways.

ELESIN: What do my mothers say? Shall I step
Burdened into the unknown?

465 IYALOJA: Not we, but the very earth says No. The sap in the plantain does not dry. Let grain that will not feed the voyager at his passage drop here and take root as he steps beyond this earth and us. Oh you who fill the home from hearth to threshold with the voices of children, you who now bestride the hid-
470 den gulf and pause to draw the right foot across and into the resting-home of the great forebears, it is good that your loins be drained into the earth we know, that your last strength be ploughed back into the womb that gave you being.

PRAISE-SINGER: Iyaloja, mother of multitudes in the teeming market of the world, how your wisdom transfigures you! 475

IYALOJA: (*Smiling broadly, completely reconciled.*) Elesin, even at the narrow end of the passage I know you will look back and sigh a last regret for the flesh that flashed past your spirit in flight. You always had a restless eye. Your choice has my blessing. (*To the* WOMEN.) Take the good news to our 480 daughter and make her ready. (*Some* WOMEN *go off.*)

ELESIN: Your eyes were clouded at first.

IYALOJA: Not for long. It is those who stand at the gateway of the great change to whose cry we must pay heed. And then, think of this—it makes the mind tremble. The fruit of such 485 a union is rare. It will be neither of this world nor of the next. Nor of the one behind us. As if the timelessness of the ancestor world and the unborn have joined spirits to wring an issue of the elusive being of passage ... Elesin!

ELESIN: I am here. What is it? 490

IYALOJA: Did you hear all I said just now?

ELESIN: Yes.

IYALOJA: The living must eat and drink. When the moment comes, don't turn the food to rodents' droppings in their mouth. Don't let them taste the ashes of the world when 495 they step out at dawn to breathe the morning dew.

ELESIN: This doubt is unworthy of you Iyaloja.

IYALOJA: Eating the awusa nut is not so difficult as drinking water afterwards.

ELESIN: The waters of the bitter stream are honey to a man 500 Whose tongue has savoured all.

IYALOJA: No one knows when the ants desert their home; they leave the mound intact. The swallow is never seen to peck holes in its nest when it is time to move with the season. There are always throngs of humanity behind the leave- 505 taker. The rain should not come through the roof for them, the wind must not blow through the walls at night.

ELESIN: I refuse to take offence.

IYALOJA: You wish to travel light. Well, the earth is yours. But be sure the seed you leave in it attracts no curse. 510

ELESIN: You really mistake my person Iyaloja.

IYALOJA: I said nothing. Now we must go prepare your bridal chamber. Then these same hands will lay your shrouds.

ELESIN: (*Exasperated.*) Must you be so blunt? (*Recovers.*) Well, weave your shrouds, but let the fingers of my bride seal my 515 eyelids with earth and wash my body.

IYALOJA: Prepare yourself Elesin.

(*She gets up to leave. At that moment the women return, leading the* BRIDE. ELESIN'*s face glows with pleasure. He flicks the sleeves of his agbada with renewed confidence and steps forward to meet the group. As the girl kneels before* IYALOJA, *lights fade out on the scene.*)

ACT TWO

The verandah of the District Officer's bungalow. A tango is playing from an old hand-cranked gramophone and, glimpsed through the wide windows and doors which open onto the forestage verandah are the shapes of SIMON PILKINGS *and his wife,* JANE, *tangoing in and out of shadows in the living-room. They were wearing what is immediately apparent as some form of fancy-dress. The dance goes on for some moments and then the figure of a 'Native Administration' policeman emerges and climbs up the steps onto the verandah. He peeps through and observes the dancing couple, reacting with what is obviously a long-standing bewilderment. He stiffens suddenly, his expression changes to one of disbelief and horror. In his excitement he upsets a flower-pot and attracts the attention of the couple. They stop dancing.*

PILKINGS: Is there anyone out there?

JANE: I'll turn off the gramophone.

PILKINGS: (*Approaching the verandah.*) I'm sure I heard something fall over. (*The constable retreats slowly, open-mouthed as*

5   PILKINGS *approaches the verandah.*) Oh it's you Amusa. Why didn't you just knock instead of knocking things over?

AMUSA: (*Stammers badly and points a shaky finger at his dress.*) Mista Pirinkin . . . Mista Pirinkin . . .

PILKINGS: What is the matter with you?

10 JANE: (*Emerging.*) Who is it dear? Oh, Amusa . . .

PILKINGS: Yes it's Amusa, and acting most strangely.

AMUSA: (*His attention now transferred to* MRS PILKINGS.) Mammadam . . . you too!

PILKINGS: What the hell is the matter with you man!

15 JANE: Your costume darling. Our fancy dress.

PILKINGS: Oh hell, I'd forgotten all about that. (*Lifts the face mask over his head showing his face. His wife follows suit.*)

JANE: I think you've shocked his big pagan heart bless him.

PILKINGS: Nonsense, he's a Moslem. Come on Amusa, you

20   don't believe in all this nonsense do you? I thought you were a good Moslem.

AMUSA: Mista Pirinkin, I beg you sir, what you think you do with that dress? It belong to dead cult, not for human being.

PILKINGS: Oh Amusa, what a let down you are. I swear by you

25   at the club you know—thank God for Amusa, he doesn't believe in any mumbo-jumbo. And now look at you!

AMUSA: Mista Pirinkin, I beg you, take it off. Is not good for man like you to touch that cloth.

PILKINGS: Well, I've got it on. And what's more Jane and I have

30   bet on it we're taking first prize at the ball. Now, if you can just pull yourself together and tell me what you wanted to see me about . . .

AMUSA: Sir, I cannot talk this matter to you in that dress. I no fit.

35 PILKINGS: What's that rubbish again?

JANE: He is dead earnest too Simon. I think you'll have to handle this delicately.

PILKINGS: Delicately my. . . ! Look here Amusa, I think this little joke has gone far enough hm? Let's have some sense. You

40   seem to forget that you are a police officer in the service of His Majesty's Government. I order you to report your business at once or face disciplinary action.

AMUSA: Sir, it is a matter of death. How can man talk against death to person in uniform of death? Is like talking against

45   government to person in uniform of police. Please sir, I go and come back.

PILKINGS: (*Roars.*) Now! (AMUSA *switches his gaze to the ceiling suddenly, remains mute.*)

JANE: Oh Amusa, what is there to be scared of in the costume?

50   You saw it confiscated last month from those *egungun* men who were creating trouble in town. You helped arrest the cult leaders yourself—if the juju didn't harm you at the time how could it possibly harm you now? And merely by looking at it?

55 AMUSA: (*Without looking down.*) Madam, I arrest the ringleaders who make trouble but me I no touch *egungun*. That

egungun itself, I no touch. And I no abuse 'am. I arrest ringleader but I treat *egungun* with respect.

PILKINGS: It's hopeless. We'll merely end up missing the best part of the ball. When they get this way there is nothing 60 you can do. It's simply hammering against a brick wall. Write your report or whatever it is on that pad Amusa and take yourself out of here. Come on Jane. We only upset his delicate sensibilities by remaining here.

(AMUSA *waits for them to leave, then writes in the notebook, somewhat laboriously. Drumming from the direction of the town wells up.* AMUSA *listens, makes a movement as if he wants to recall* PILKINGS *but changes his mind. Completes his note and goes. A few moments later* PILKINGS *emerges, picks up the pad and reads.*)

PILKINGS: Jane!   65

JANE: (*From the bedroom.*) Coming darling. Nearly ready.

PILKINGS: Never mind being ready, just listen to this.

JANE: What is it?

PILKINGS: Amusa's report. Listen. 'I have to report that it come to my information that one prominent chief, namely, the 70 Elesin Oba, is to commit death tonight as a result of native custom. Because this is criminal offence I await further instruction at charge office. Sergeant Amusa.'

(JANE *comes out onto the verandah while he is reading.*)

JANE: Did I hear you say commit death?

PILKINGS: Obviously he means murder.   75

JANE: You mean a ritual murder?

PILKINGS: Must be. You think you've stamped it all out but it's always lurking under the surface somewhere.

JANE: Oh. Does it mean we are not getting to the ball at all?

PILKINGS: No-o. I'll have the man arrested. Everyone remotely 80 involved. In any case there may be nothing to it. Just rumours.

JANE: Really? I thought you found Amusa's rumours generally reliable.

PILKINGS: That's true enough. But who knows what may have been giving him the scare lately. Look at his conduct 85 tonight.

JANE: (*Laughing.*) You have to admit he had his own peculiar logic. (*Deepens her voice.*) How can man talk against death to person in uniform of death? (*Laughs.*) Anyway, you can't go into the police station dressed like that.   90

PILKINGS: I'll send Joseph with instructions. Damn it, what a confounded nuisance!

JANE: But don't you think you should talk first to the man, Simon?

PILKINGS: Do you want to go to the ball or not?   95

JANE: Darling, why are you getting rattled? I was only trying to be intelligent. It seems hardly fair just to lock up a man—and a chief at that—simply on the er . . . what is that legal word again?—uncorroborated word of a sergeant.

PILKINGS: Well, that's easily decided. Joseph!   100

JOSEPH: (*From within.*) Yes master.

PILKINGS: You're quite right of course, I am getting rattled. Probably the effect of those bloody drums. Do you hear how they go on and on?

JANE: I wondered when you'd notice. Do you suppose it has 105 something to do with this affair?

PILKINGS: Who knows? They always find an excuse for making a noise ... (*Thoughtfully.*) Even so ...
JANE: Yes Simon?
110 PILKINGS: It's different Jane. I don't think I've heard this particular—sound—before. Something unsettling about it.
JANE: I thought all bush drumming sounded the same.
PILKINGS: Don't tease me now Jane. This may be serious.
JANE: I'm sorry. (*Gets up and throws her arms around his neck.*
115 *Kisses him. The houseboy enters, retreats and knocks.*)
PILKINGS: (*Wearily.*) Oh, come in Joseph! I don't know where you pick up all these elephantine notions of tact. Come over here.
JOSEPH: Sir?
PILKINGS: Joseph, are you a christian or not?
120 JOSEPH: Yessir.
PILKINGS: Does seeing me in this outfit bother you?
JOSEPH: No sir, it has no power.
PILKINGS: Thank God for some sanity at last. Now Joseph, answer me on the honour of a christian—what is supposed to
125 be going on in town tonight?
JOSEPH: Tonight sir? You mean that chief who is going to kill himself?
PILKINGS: What?
JANE: What do you mean, kill himself?
130 PILKINGS: You do mean he is going to kill somebody don't you?
JOSEPH: No master. He will not kill anybody and no one will kill him. He will simply die.
JANE: But why Joseph?
JOSEPH: It is native law and custom. The King die last month.
135 Tonight is his burial. But before they can bury him, the Elesin must die so as to accompany him to heaven.
PILKINGS: I seem to be fated to clash more often with that man than with any of the other chiefs.
JOSEPH: He is the King's Chief Horseman.
140 PILKINGS: (*In a resigned way.*) I know.
JANE: Simon, what's the matter?
PILKINGS: It would have to be him!
JANE: Who is he?
PILKINGS: Don't you remember? He's that chief with whom I
145 had a scrap some three or four years ago. I helped his son get to a medical school in England, remember? He fought tooth and nail to prevent it.
JANE: Oh now I remember. He was that very sensitive young man. What was his name again?
150 PILKINGS: Olunde. Haven't replied to his last letter come to think of it. The old pagan wanted him to stay and carry on some family tradition or the other. Honestly I couldn't understand the fuss he made. I literally had to help the boy escape from close confinement and load him onto the next
155 boat. A most intelligent boy, really bright.
JANE: I rather thought he was much too sensitive you know. The kind of person you feel should be a poet munching rose petals in Bloomsbury.
PILKINGS: Well, he's going to make a first-class doctor. His
160 mind is set on that. And as long as he wants my help he is welcome to it.
JANE: (*After a pause.*) Simon.
PILKINGS: Yes?
JANE: This boy, he was his eldest son wasn't he?
165 PILKINGS: I'm not sure. Who could tell with that old ram?
JANE: Do you know, Joseph?

JOSEPH: Oh yes madam. He was the eldest son. That's why Elesin cursed master good and proper. The eldest son is not supposed to travel away from the land.
JANE: (*Giggling.*) Is that true Simon? Did he really curse you 170 good and proper?
PILKINGS: By all accounts I should be dead by now.
JOSEPH: Oh no, master is white man. And good christian. Black man juju can't touch master.
JANE: If he was his eldest, it means that he would be the 175 Elesin to the next king. It's a family thing isn't it, Joseph?
JOSEPH: Yes madam. And if this Elesin had died before the King, his eldest son must take his place.
JANE: That would explain why the old chief was so mad you took the boy away. 180
PILKINGS: Well it makes me all the more happy I did.
JANE: I wonder if he knew.
PILKINGS: Who? Oh, you mean Olunde?
JANE: Yes. Was that why he was so determined to get away? I wouldn't stay if I knew I was trapped in such a horrible 185 custom.
PILKINGS: (*Thoughtfully.*) No, I don't think he knew. At least he gave no indication. But you couldn't really tell with him. He was rather close you know, quite unlike most of them. Didn't give much away, not even to me. 190
JANE: Aren't they all rather close, Simon?
PILKINGS: These natives here? Good gracious. They'll open their mouths and yap with you about their family secrets before you can stop them. Only the other day ...
JANE: But Simon, do they really give anything away? I mean, 195 anything that really counts. This affair for instance, we didn't know they still practised that custom did we?
PILKINGS: Ye-e-es, I suppose you're right there. Sly, devious bastards.
JOSEPH: (*Stiffly.*) Can I go now master? I have to clean the kitchen. 200
PILKINGS: What? Oh, you can go. Forgot you were still here.

(JOSEPH *goes.*)

JANE: Simon, you really must watch your language. Bastard isn't just a simple swear-word in these parts, you know.
PILKINGS: Look, just when did you become a social anthropologist, that's what I'd like to know. 205
JANE: I'm not claiming to know anything. I just happen to have overheard quarrels among the servants. That's how I know they consider it a smear.
PILKINGS: I thought the extended family system took care of all that. Elastic family, no bastards. 210
JANE: (*Shrugs.*) Have it your own way.

(*Awkward silence. The drumming increases in volume.* JANE *gets up suddenly, restless.*)

That drumming Simon, do you think it might really be connected with this ritual? It's been going on all evening.
PILKINGS: Let's ask our native guide. Joseph! Just a minute Joseph. (JOSEPH *re-enters.*) What's the drumming about? 215
JOSEPH: I don't know master.
PILKINGS: What do you mean you don't know? It's only two years since your conversion. Don't tell me all that holy water nonsense also wiped out your tribal memory.

220 JOSEPH: (*Visibly shocked.*) Master!
JANE: Now you've done it.
PILKINGS: What have I done now?
JANE: Never mind. Listen Joseph, just tell me this. Is that drum-
ming connected with dying or anything of that nature?
225 JOSEPH: Madam, this is what I am trying to say: I am not sure.
It sounds like the death of a great chief and then, it sounds
like the wedding of a great chief. It really mix me up.
PILKINGS: Oh get back to the kitchen. A fat lot of help you are.
JOSEPH: Yes master. (*Goes.*)
230 JANE: Simon . . .
PILKINGS: Alright, alright. I'm in no mood for preaching.
JANE: It isn't my preaching you have to worry about, it's the
preaching of the missionaries who preceded you here.
When they make converts they really convert them. Calling
235 holy water nonsense to our Joseph is really like insulting
the Virgin Mary before a Roman Catholic. He's going to
hand in his notice tomorrow you mark my word.
PILKINGS: Now you're being ridiculous.
JANE: Am I? What are you willing to bet that tomorrow we are
240 going to be without a steward-boy? Did you see his face?
PILKINGS: I am more concerned about whether or not we will
be one native chief short by tomorrow. Christ! Just listen to
those drums. (*He strides up and down, undecided.*)
JANE: (*Getting up.*) I'll change and make up some supper.
245 PILKINGS: What's that?
JANE: Simon, it's obvious we have to miss this ball.
PILKINGS: Nonsense. It's the first bit of real fun the European
club has managed to organise for over a year, I'm damned if
I'm going to miss it. And it is a rather special occasion.
250 Doesn't happen every day.
JANE: You know this business has to be stopped Simon. And
you are the only man who can do it.
PILKINGS: I don't have to stop anything. If they want to throw
themselves off the top of a cliff or poison themselves for the
255 sake of some barbaric custom what is that to me? If it were
ritual murder or something like that I'd be duty-bound to
do something. I can't keep an eye on all the potential suicides in this province. And as for that man—believe me it's
good riddance.
260 JANE: (*Laughs.*) I know you better than that Simon. You are going to have to do something to stop it—after you've finished blustering.
PILKINGS: (*Shouts after her.*) And suppose after all it's only a
wedding. I'd look a proper fool if I interrupted a chief on
265 his honeymoon, wouldn't I? (*Resumes his angry stride, slows
down.*) Ah well, who can tell what those chiefs actually do
on their honeymoon anyway? (*He takes up the pad and scribbles rapidly on it.*) Joseph! Joseph! Joseph! (*Some moments later
JOSEPH puts in a sulky appearance.*) Did you hear me call you?
270 Why the hell didn't you answer?
JOSEPH: I didn't hear master.
PILKINGS: You didn't hear me! How come you are here then?
JOSEPH: (*Stubbornly.*) I didn't hear master.
PILKINGS: (*Controls himself with an effort.*) We'll talk about it in
275 the morning. I want you to take this note directly to
Sergeant Amusa. You'll find him at the charge office. Get
on your bicycle and race there with it. I expect you back in
twenty minutes exactly. Twenty minutes, is that clear?
JOSEPH: Yes master. (*Going.*)

PILKINGS: Oh er . . . Joseph. 280
JOSEPH: Yes master?
PILKINGS: (*Between gritted teeth.*) Er . . . forget what I said just
now. The holy water is not nonsense. I was talking nonsense.
JOSEPH: Yes master. (*Goes.*)
JANE: (*Pokes her head round the door.*) Have you found him? 285
PILKINGS: Found who?
JANE: Joseph. Weren't you shouting for him?
PILKINGS: Oh yes, he turned up finally.
JANE: You sounded desperate. What was it all about?
PILKINGS: Oh nothing. I just wanted to apologise to him. As- 290
sure him that the holy water isn't really nonsense.
JANE: Oh? And how did he take it?
PILKINGS: Who the hell gives a damn! I had a sudden vision of
our Very Reverend Macfarlane drafting another letter of
complaint to the Resident about my unchristian language 295
towards his parishioners.
JANE: Oh I think he's given up on you by now.
PILKINGS: Don't be too sure. And anyway, I wanted to make
sure Joseph didn't 'lose' my note on the way. He looked sufficiently full of the holy crusade to do some such thing. 300
JANE: If you've finished exaggerating, come and have something to eat.
PILKINGS: No, put it all way. We can still get to the ball.
JANE: Simon . . .
PILKINGS: Get your costume back on. Nothing to worry 305
about. I've instructed Amusa to arrest the man and lock
him up.
JANE: But that station is hardly secure Simon. He'll soon get
his friends to help him escape.
PILKINGS: A-ah, that's where I have out-thought you. I'm not 310
having him put in the station cell. Amusa will bring him
right here and lock him up in my study. And he'll stay with
him till we get back. No one will dare come here to incite
him to anything.
JANE: How clever of you darling. I'll get ready. 315
PILKINGS: Hey.
JANE: Yes darling.
PILKINGS: I have a surprise for you. I was going to keep it until
we actually got to the ball.
JANE: What is it? 320
PILKINGS: You know the Prince is on a tour of the colonies
don't you? Well, he docked in the capital only this morning
but he is already at the Residency. He is going to grace the
ball with his presence later tonight.
JANE: Simon! Not really. 325
PILKINGS: Yes he is. He's been invited to give away the prizes
and he has agreed. You must admit old Engleton is the best
Club Secretary we ever had. Quick off the mark that lad.
JANE: But how thrilling.
PILKINGS: The other provincials are going to be damned envious. 330
JANE: I wonder what he'll come as.
PILKINGS: Oh I don't know. As a coat-of-arms perhaps. Any-
way it won't be anything to touch this.
JANE: Well that's lucky. If we are to be presented I won't have
to start looking for a pair of gloves. It's all sewn on. 335
PILKINGS: (*Laughing.*) Quite right. Trust a woman to think of
that. Come on, let's get going.
JANE: (*Rushing off.*) Won't be a second. (*Stops.*) Now I see
why you've been so edgy all evening. I thought you weren't

340   handling this affair with your usual brilliance—to begin
    with that is.
PILKINGS: (*His mood is much improved.*) Shut up woman and get
    your things on.
JANE: Alright boss, coming.

(PILKINGS *suddenly begins to hum the tango to which they were dancing before. Starts to execute a few practice steps. Lights fade.*)

ACT THREE

*A swelling, agitated hum of women's voices rises immediately in the
background. The lights come on and we see the frontage of a converted
cloth stall in the market. The floor leading up to the entrance is covered in rich velvets and woven cloth. The* WOMEN *come on stage, borne
backwards by the determined progress of Sergeant* AMUSA *and his two
constables who already have their batons out and use them as a pressure against the* WOMEN. *At the edge of the cloth-covered floor however
the* WOMEN *take a determined stand and block all further progress of
the* MEN. *They begin to tease them mercilessly.*

AMUSA: I am tell you women for last time to commot my road.
    I am here on official business.
WOMAN: Official business you white man's eunuch? Official
    business is taking place where you want to go and it's a
5   business you wouldn't understand.
WOMAN: (*Makes a quick tug at the constable's baton.*) That doesn't
    fool anyone you know. It's the one you carry under your
    government knickers that counts. (*She bends low as if to peep
    under the baggy shorts. The embarrassed constable quickly puts his
10   knees together. The* WOMEN *roar.*)
WOMAN: You mean there is nothing there at all?
WOMAN: Oh there was something. You know that handbell
    which the white man uses to summon his servants . . . ?
AMUSA: (*He manages to preserve some dignity throughout.*) I hope
15   you women know that interfering with officer in execution
    of his duty is criminal offence.
WOMAN: Interfere? He says we're interfering with him. You
    foolish man we're telling you there's nothing there to inter-
    fere with.
20 AMUSA: I am order you now to clear the road.
WOMAN: What road? The one your father built?
WOMAN: You are a Policeman not so? Then you know what
    they call trespassing in court. Or—(*Pointing to the cloth-lined
    steps.*)—do you think that kind of road is built for every
25   kind of feet.
WOMAN: Go back and tell the white man who sent you to
    come himself.
AMUSA: If I go I will come back with reinforcement. And we
    will all return carrying weapons.
30 WOMAN: Oh, now I understand. Before they can put on those
    knickers the white man first cuts off their weapons.
WOMAN: What a cheek! You mean you come here to show
    power to women and you don't even have a weapon.
AMUSA: (*Shouting above the laughter.*) For the last time I warn
35   you women to clear the road.
WOMAN: To where?
AMUSA: To that hut. I know he dey dere.
WOMAN: Who?
AMUSA: The chief who call himself Elesin Oba.

WOMAN: You ignorant man. It is not he who calls himself 40
    Elesin Oba, it is his blood that says it. As it called out to his
    father before him and will to his son after him. And that
    is in spite of everything your white man can do.
WOMAN: Is it not the same ocean that washes this land and the
    white man's land? Tell your white man he can hide our son 45
    away as long as he likes. When the time comes for him, the
    same ocean will bring him back.
AMUSA: The government say dat kin' ting must stop.
WOMAN: Who will stop it? You? Tonight our husband and fa-
    ther will prove himself greater than the laws of strangers. 50
AMUSA: I tell you nobody go prove anyting tonight or anytime.
    Is ignorant and criminal to prove dat kin' prove.
IYALOJA: (*Entering, from the hut. She is accompanied by a group of*
    YOUNG GIRLS *who have been attending the* BRIDE.) What is it
    Amusa? Why do you come here to disturb the happiness of 55
    others.
AMUSA: Madame Iyaloja, I glad you come. You know me. I no
    like trouble but duty is duty. I am here to arrest Elesin for
    criminal intent. Tell these women to stop obstructing me in
    the performance of my duty. 60
IYALOJA: And you? What gives you the right to obstruct our
    leader of men in the performance of his duty.
AMUSA: What kin' duty be dat one Iyaloja.
IYALOJA: What kin' duty? What kin' duty does a man have to
    his new bride? 65
AMUSA: (*Bewildered, looks at the* WOMEN *and at the entrance to the
    hut.*) Iyaloja, is it wedding you call dis kin' ting?
IYALOJA: You have wives haven't you? Whatever the white man
    has done to you he hasn't stopped you having wives. And if
    he has, at least he is married. If you don't know what a mar- 70
    riage is, go and ask him to tell you.
AMUSA: This no to wedding.
IYALOJA: And ask him at the same time what he would have
    done if anyone had come to disturb him on his wedding
    night. 75
AMUSA: Iyaloja, I say dis no to wedding.
IYALOJA: You want to look inside the bridal chamber? You want
    to see for yourself how a man cuts the virgin knot?
AMUSA: Madam . . .
WOMAN: Perhaps his wives are still waiting for him to learn. 80
AMUSA: Iyaloja, make you tell dese women make den no insult
    me again. If I hear dat kin' insult once more . . .
GIRL: (*Pushing her way through.*) You will do what?
GIRL: He's out of his mind. It's our mothers you're talking to,
    do you know that? Not to any illiterate villager you can 85
    bully and terrorise. How dare you intrude here anyway?
GIRL: What a cheek, what impertinence!
GIRL: You've treated them too gently. Now let them see what
    it is to tamper with the mothers of this market.
GIRLS: Your betters dare not enter the market when the women 90
    say no!
GIRL: Haven't you learnt that yet, you jester in khaki and
    starch?
IYALOJA: Daughters . . .
GIRL: No no Iyaloja, leave us to deal with him. He no longer 95
    knows his mother, we'll teach him.

(*With a sudden movement they snatch the batons of the two constables.
They begin to hem them in.*)

GIRL: What next? We have your batons? What next? What are you going to do?

(With equally swift movements they knock off their hats.)

100 GIRL: Move if you dare. We have your hats, what will you do about it? Didn't the white man teach you to take off your hats before women?

IYALOJA: It's a wedding night. It's a night of joy for us. Peace . . .

GIRL: Not for him. Who asked him here?

GIRL: Does he dare go to the Residency without an invitation?

105 GIRL: Not even where the servants eat the left-overs.

GIRLS: *(In turn. In an 'English' accent.)* Well well it's Mister Amusa. Were you invited? *(Play-acting to one another. The older* WOMEN *encourage them with their titters.)*

—Your invitation card please?

110 —Who are you? Have we been introduced?

—And who did you say you were?

—Sorry, I didn't quite catch your name.

—May I take your hat?

—If you insist. May I take yours? *(Exchanging the policeman's hats.)*

115 —How very kind of you.

—Not at all. Won't you sit down?

—After you.

—Oh no.

120 —I insist.

—You're most gracious.

—And how do you find the place?

—The natives are alright.

—Friendly?

125 —Tractable.

—Not a teeny-weeny bit restless?

—Well, a teeny-weeny bit restless.

—One might even say, difficult?

—Indeed one might be tempted to say, difficult.

130 —But you do manage to cope?

—Yes indeed I do. I have a rather faithful ox called Amusa.

—He's loyal?

—Absolutely.

—Lay down his life for you what?

135 —Without a moment's thought.

—Had one like that once. Trust him with my life.

—Mostly of course they are liars.

—Never known a native tell the truth.

—Does it get rather close around here?

140 —It's mild for this time of the year.

—But the rains may still come.

—They are late this year aren't they?

—They are keeping African time.

—Ha ha ha ha

145 —Ha ha ha ha

—The humidity is what gets me.

—It used to be whisky.

—Ha ha ha ha

—Ha ha ha ha

150 —What's your handicap old chap?

—Is there racing by golly?

—Splendid golf course, you'll like it.

—I'm beginning to like it already.

—And a European club, exclusive.

155 —You've kept the flag flying.

—We do our best for the old country.

—It's a pleasure to serve.

—Another whisky old chap?

—You are indeed too too kind.

160 —Not at all sir. Where is that boy? *(With a sudden bellow.)* Sergeant!

AMUSA: *(Snaps to attention.)* Yessir!

(The WOMEN *collapse with laughter.)*

GIRL: Take your men out of here.

AMUSA: *(Realising the trick, he rages from loss of face.)* I'm give you warning . . .

165 GIRL: Alright then. Off with his knickers! *(They surge slowly forward.)*

IYALOJA: Daughters, please.

AMUSA: *(Squaring himself for defence.)* The first woman wey touch me . . .

170 IYALOJA: My children, I beg of you . . .

GIRL: Then tell him to leave this market. This is the home of our mothers. We don't want the eater of white left-overs at the feast their hands have prepared.

IYALOJA: You heard them Amusa. You had better go. 175

GIRLS: Now!

AMUSA: *(Commencing his retreat.)* We dey go now, but make you no say we no warn you.

GIRL: Before we read the riot act—you should know all about that. 180

AMUSA: Make we go. *(They depart, more precipitately.)*

(The WOMEN *strike their palms across in the gesture of wonder.)*

WOMEN: Do they teach you all that school?

WOMAN: And to think I nearly kept Apinke away from the place.

WOMAN: Did you hear them? Did you see how they mimicked 185 the white man?

WOMAN: The voices exactly. Hey, there are wonders in this world!

IYALOJA: Well, our elders have said it: Dada may be weak, but he has a younger sibling who is truly fearless. 190

WOMAN: The next time the white man shows his face in this market I will set Wuraola on his tail.

(A WOMAN *bursts into song and dance of euphoria—'Tani l'awa o l'ogbeja? Kayi! A l'ogbeja. Omo Kekere l'ogbeja.' ['Who says we haven't a defender? Silence! We have our defenders. Little children are our champions.'] The rest of the* WOMEN *join in, some placing the* GIRLS *on their back like infants, other dancing round them. The dance becomes general, mounting in excitement.* ELESIN *appears, in wrapper only. In his hands a white velvet cloth folded loosely as if it held some delicate object. He cries out.)*

ELESIN: Oh you mothers of beautiful brides! *(The dancing stops. They turn and see him, and the object in his hands.* IYALOJA *approaches and gently takes the cloth from him.)* Take it. It is no 195 mere virgin stain, but the union of life and the seeds of passage. My vital flow, the last from this flesh is intermingled with the promise of future life. All is prepared. Listen! *(A*

200 *steady drum-beat from the distance.*) Yes. It is nearly time. The King's dog has been killed. The King's favourite horse is about to follow his master. My brother chiefs know their task and perform it well. (*He listens again.*)

(*The* BRIDE *emerges, stands shyly by the door. He turns to her.*)

Our marriage is not yet wholly fulfilled. When earth and passage wed, the consummation is complete only when
205 there are grains of earth on the eyelids of passage. Stay by me till then. My faithful drummers, do me your last service. This is where I have chosen to do my leave-taking, in this heart of life, this hive which contains the swarm of the world in its small compass. This is where I have known love
210 and laughter away from the palace. Even the richest food cloys when eaten days on end; in the market, nothing ever cloys. Listen. (*They listen to the drums.*) They have begun to seek out the heart of the King's favourite horse. Soon it will ride in its bolt of raffia with the dog at its feet. Together
215 they will ride on the shoulders of the King's grooms through the pulse centres of the town. They know it is here I shall await them. I have told them. (*His eyes appear to cloud. He passes his hand over them as if to clear his sight. He gives a faint smile.*) It promises well; just then I felt my spirit's ea-
220 gerness. The kite makes for wide spaces and the wind creeps up behind its tail; can the kite say less than—thank you, the quicker the better? But wait a while my spirit. Wait. Wait for the coming of the courier of the King. Do you know friends, the horse is born to this one destiny, to
225 bear the burden that is man upon its back. Except for this night, this night alone when the spotless stallion will ride in triumph on the back of man. In the time of my father I witnessed the strange sight. Perhaps tonight also I shall see it for the last time. If they arrive before the drums beat for me,
230 I shall tell him to let the Alafin know I follow swiftly. If they come after the drums have sounded, why then, all is well for I have gone ahead. Our spirits shall fall in step along the great passage. (*He listens to the drums. He seems again to be falling into a state of semi-hypnosis; his eyes scan the
235 sky but it is in a kind of daze. His voice is a little breathless.*) The moon has fed, a glow from its full stomach fills the sky and air, but I cannot tell where is that gateway through which I must pass. My faithful friends, let our feet touch together this last time, lead me into the other market with sounds
240 that cover my skin with down yet make my limbs strike earth like a thoroughbred. Dear mothers, let me dance into the passage even as I have lived beneath your roofs. (*He comes down progressively among them. They make a way for him, the* DRUMMERS *playing. His dance is one of solemn, regal motions,
245 each gesture of the body is made with a solemn finality. The* WOMEN *join him, their steps a somewhat more fluid version of his. Beneath the* PRAISE-SINGER*'s exhortations the* WOMEN *dirge 'Alę lę, awo mi lǫ'.*)
PRAISE-SINGER: Elesin Alafin, can you hear my voice?
250 ELESIN: Faintly, my friend, faintly.
PRAISE-SINGER: Elesin Alafin, can you hear my call?
ELESIN: Faintly my king, faintly.
PRAISE-SINGER: Is your memory sound Elesin?
Shall my voice be a blade of grass and
255 Tickle the armpit of the past?

ELESIN: My memory needs no prodding but
What do you wish to say to me?
PRAISE-SINGER: Only what has been spoken. Only what concerns
The dying wish of the father of all.
ELESIN: It is buried like seed-yam in my mind   260
This is the season of quick rains, the harvest
Is this moment due for gathering.
PRAISE-SINGER: If you cannot come, I said, swear
You'll tell my favourite horse. I shall
Ride on through the gates alone.   265
ELESIN: Elesin's message will be read
Only when his loyal heart no longer beats.
PRAISE-SINGER: If you cannot come Elesin, tell my dog.
I cannot stay the keeper too long
At the gate.   270
ELESIN: A dog does not outrun the hand
That feeds it meat. A horse that throws its rider
Slows down to a stop. Elesin Alafin
Trusts no beasts with messages between
A king and his companion.   275
PRAISE-SINGER: If you get lost my dog will track
The hidden path to me.
ELESIN: The seven-way crossroads confuses
Only the stranger. The Horseman of the King
Was born in the recesses of the house.   280
PRAISE-SINGER: I know the wickedness of men. If there is
Weight on the loose end of your sash, such weight
As no mere man can shift; if your sash is earthed
By evil minds who mean to part us at the last . . .
ELESIN: My sash is of the deep purple *alari;*   285
It is no tethering-rope. The elephant
Trails no tethering-rope; that king
Is not yet crowned who will peg an elephant—
Not even you my friend and King.
PRAISE-SINGER: And yet this fear will not depart from me   290
The darkness of this new abode is deep—
Will your human eyes suffice?
ELESIN: In a night which falls before our eyes
However deep, we do not miss our way.
PRAISE-SINGER: Shall I now not acknowledge I have stood   295
Where wonders met their end? The elephant deserves
Better than that we say 'I have caught
A glimpse of something.' If we see the tamer
Of the forest let us say plainly, we have seen
An elephant.   300
ELESIN: (*His voice is drowsy.*) I have freed myself of earth and now
It's getting dark. Strange voices guide my feet.
PRAISE-SINGER: The river is never so high that the eyes
Of a fish are covered. The night is not so dark
That the albino fails to find his way. A child   305
Returning homewards craves no leading by the hand.
Gracefully does the mask regain his grove at the end of
    the day . . .
Gracefully. Gracefully does the mask dance
Homeward at the end of day, gracefully . . .

(ELESIN*'s trance appears to be deepening, his steps heavier.*)

IYALOJA: It is the death of war that kills the valiant,   310
Death of water is how the swimmer goes

It is the death of markets that kills the trader
And death of indecision takes the idle away
The trade of the cutlass blunts its edge
315   And the beautiful die the death of beauty.
It takes an Elesin to die the death of death . . .
Only Elesin . . . dies the unknowable death of death . . .
Gracefully, gracefully does the horseman regain
The stables at the end of day, gracefully . . .

320   PRAISE-SINGER: How shall I tell what my eyes have seen? The
Horseman gallops on before the courier, how shall I tell
what my eyes have seen? He says a dog may be confused by
new scents of beings he never dreamt of, so he must precede
the dog to heaven. He says a horse may stumble on strange
325   boulders and be lamed, so he races on before the horse to
heaven. It is best, he says, to trust no messenger who may
falter at the outer gate; oh how shall I tell what my ears
have heard? But do you hear me still Elesin, do you hear
your faithful one?

(ELESIN *in his motions appears to feel for a direction of sound, subtly,
but he only sinks deeper into his trance-dance.*)

330   Elesin Alafin, I no longer sense your flesh. The drums are
changing now but you have gone far ahead of the world. It
is not yet noon in heaven; let those who claim it is begin
their own journey home. So why must you rush like an impatient bride: why do you race to desert your Olohun-iyo?

(ELESIN *is now sunk fully deep in his trance, there is no longer sign of
any awareness of his surroundings.*)

335   Does the deep voice of *gbedu* cover you then, like the passage of royal elephants? Those drums that brook no rivals,
have they blocked the passage to your ears that my voice
passes into wind, a mere leaf floating in the night? Is your
flesh lightened Elesin, is that lump of earth I slid between
340   your slippers to keep you longer slowly sifting from your
feet? Are the drums on the other side now tuning skin to
skin with ours in *osugbo*? Are there sounds there I cannot
hear, do footsteps surround you which pound the earth like
gbedu, roll like thunder round the dome of the world? Is the
345   darkness gathering in your head Elesin? Is there now a
streak of light at the end of the passage, a light I dare not
look upon? Does it reveal whose voices we often heard,
whose touches we often felt, whose wisdoms come suddenly into the mind when the wisest have shaken their
350   heads and murmured: It cannot be done? Elesin Alafin,
don't think I do not know why your lips are heavy, why
your limbs are drowsy as palm oil in the cold of harmattan. I
would call you back but when the elephant heads for the
jungle, the tail is too small a handhold for the hunter that
355   would pull him back. The sun that heads for the sea no
longer heeds the prayers of the farmer. When the river begins to taste the salt of the ocean, we no longer know what
deity to call on, the river-god or Olokun. No arrow flies
back to the string, the child does not return through the
360   same passage that gave it birth. Elesin Oba, can you hear me
at all? Your eye-lids are glazed like a courtesan's, is it that you
see the dark groom and master of life? And will you see my
father? Will you tell him that I stayed with you to the last?
Will my voice ring in your ears awhile, will you remember

Olohun-iyo even if the music on the other side surpasses his   365
mortal craft? But will they know you over there? Have they
eyes to gauge your worth, have they the heart to love you,
will they know what thoroughbred prances towards them
in caparisons of honour? If they do not Elesin, if any there
cuts your yam with a small knife, or pours you wine in a   370
small calabash, turn back and return to welcoming hands. If
the world were not greater than the wishes of Olohun-iyo, I
would not let you go . . .

(*He appears to break down.* ELESIN *dances on, completely in a trance.
The dirge wells up louder and stronger.* ELESIN's *dance does not lose its
elasticity but his gestures become, if possible, even more weighty. Lights
fade slowly on the scene.*)

ACT FOUR

*A Masque. The front side of the stage is part of a wide corridor around
the great hall of the Residency extending beyond vision into the rear
and wings. It is redolent of the tawdry decadence of a far-flung but key
imperial frontier. The couples in a variety of fancy-dress are ranged
around the walls, gazing in the same direction. The guest-of-honour is
about to make an appearance. A portion of the local police brass band
with its white conductor is just visible. At last, the entrance of Royalty. The band plays 'Rule Britannia', badly, beginning long before
he is visible. The couples bow and curtsey as he passes by them. Both
he and his companions are dressed in seventeenth century European
costume. Following behind are the* RESIDENT *and his partner similarly
attired. As they gain the end of the hall where the orchestra dais begins the music comes to an end. The* PRINCE *bows to the guests. The
band strikes up a Viennese waltz and the* PRINCE *formally opens the
floor. Several bars later the* RESIDENT *and his companion follow suit.
Others follow in appropriate pecking order. The orchestra's waltz rendition is not of the highest musical standard.*

Some time later the PRINCE *dances again into view and is settled into
a corner by the* RESIDENT *who then proceeds to select couples as they
dance past for introduction, sometimes threading his way through the
dancers to tap the lucky couple on the shoulder. Desperate efforts from
many to ensure that they are recognised in spite of, perhaps, their costume. The ritual of introductions soon takes in* PILKINGS *and his wife.
The* PRINCE *is quite fascinated by their costume and they demonstrate
the adaptations they have made to it, pulling down the mask to demonstrate how the* egungun *normally appears, then showing the various
press-button controls they have innovated for the face flaps, the sleeves,
etc. They demonstrate the dance steps and the guttural sounds made by
the* egungun, *harass other dancers in the hall,* MRS PILKINGS *playing the 'restrainer' to* PILKINGS' *manic darts. Everyone is highly entertained, the Royal Party especially who lead the applause.*

*At this point a liveried footman comes in with a note on a salver and
is intercepted almost absent-mindedly by the* RESIDENT *who takes the
note and reads it. After polite coughs he succeeds in excusing the* PILK-
INGSES *from the* PRINCE *and takes them aside. The* PRINCE *consider-
ately offers the* RESIDENT's *wife his hand and dancing is resumed.*

On their way out the RESIDENT *gives an order to his* AIDE-DE-CAMP.
They come into the side corridor where the RESIDENT *hands the note
to* PILKINGS.

RESIDENT: As you see it says 'emergency' on the outside. I took
the liberty of opening it because His Highness was obvi-

ously enjoying the entertainment. I didn't want to interrupt unless really necessary.

5 PILKINGS: Yes, yes of course sir.

RESIDENT: Is it really as bad as it says? What's it all about?

PILKINGS: Some strange custom they have sir. It seems because the King is dead some important chief has to commit suicide.

RESIDENT: The King? Isn't it the same one who died nearly a
10 month ago?

PILKINGS: Yes sir.

RESIDENT: Haven't they buried him yet?

PILKINGS: They take their time about these things sir. The pre-burial ceremonies last nearly thirty days. It seems tonight is
15 the final night.

RESIDENT: But what has it got to do with the market women? Why are they rioting? We've waived that troublesome tax haven't we?

PILKINGS: We don't quite know that they are exactly rioting yet
20 sir. Sergeant Amusa is sometimes prone to exaggerations.

RESIDENT: He sounds desperate enough. That comes out even in his rather quaint grammar. Where is the man anyway? I asked my aide-de-camp to bring him here.

PILKINGS: They are probably looking in the wrong verandah.
25 I'll fetch him myself.

RESIDENT: No no you stay here. Let your wife go and look for them. Do you mind my dear ...?

JANE: Certainly not, your Excellency. (*Goes.*)

RESIDENT: You should have kept me informed Pilkings. You
30 realise how disastrous it would have been if things had erupted while His Highness was here.

PILKINGS: I wasn't aware of the whole business until tonight sir.

RESIDENT: Nose to the ground Pilkings, nose to the ground. If we all let these little things slip past us where would the
35 empire be eh? Tell me that. Where would we all be?

PILKINGS: (*Low voice.*) Sleeping peacefully at home I bet.

RESIDENT: What did you say Pilkings?

PILKINGS: It won't happen again sir.

RESIDENT: It mustn't Pilkings. It mustn't. Where is that
40 damned sergeant? I ought to get back to His Highness as quickly as possible and offer him some plausible explanation for my rather abrupt conduct. Can you think of one Pilkings?

PILKINGS: You could tell him the truth sir.

45 RESIDENT: I could? No no no no no Pilkings, that would never do. What! Go and tell him there is a riot just two miles away from him? This is supposed to be a secure colony of His Majesty, Pilkings.

PILKINGS: Yes sir.

50 RESIDENT: Ah, there they are. No, these are not our native po-lice. Are these the ring-leaders of the riot?

PILKINGS: Sir, these are my police officers.

RESIDENT: Oh, I beg your pardon officers. You do look a little ... I say, isn't there something missing in their uni-
55 forms? I think they used to have some rather colourful sashes. If I remember rightly I recommended them myself in my young days in the service. A bit of colour always ap-peals to the natives, yes. I remember putting that in my re-port. Well well well, where are we? Make your report man.

60 PILKINGS: (*Moves close to* AMUSA, *between his teeth.*) And let's have no more superstitious nonsense from you Amusa or I'll throw you in the guardroom for a month and feed you pork!

RESIDENT: What's that? What has pork to do with it?

PILKINGS: Sir, I was just warning him to be brief. I'm sure you are most anxious to hear his report.
65

RESIDENT: Yes yes yes of course. Come on man, speak up. Hey, didn't we give them some colourful fez hats with all those wavy things, yes, pink tassells ...

PILKINGS: Sir, I think if he was permitted to make his report we might find that he lost his hat in the riot.
70

RESIDENT: Ah yes indeed. I'd better tell His Highness that. Lost his hat in the riot, ha ha. He'll probably say well, as long as he didn't lost his head. (*Chuckles to himself.*) Don't forget to send me a report first thing in the morning young Pilkings.

PILKINGS: No sir.
75

RESIDENT: And whatever you do, don't let things get out of hand. Keep a cool head and—nose to the ground Pilkings. (*Wanders off in the general direction of the hall.*)

PILKINGS: Yes sir.

AIDE-DE-CAMP: Would you be needing me sir?
80

PILKINGS: No thanks Bob. I think His Excellency's need of you is greater than ours.

AIDE-DE-CAMP: We have a detachment of soldiers from the capital sir. They accompanied His Highness up here.

PILKINGS: I doubt if it will come to that but, thanks, I'll bear
85 it in mind. Oh, could you send an orderly with my cloak.

AIDE-DE-CAMP: Very good sir. (*Goes.*)

PILKINGS: Now Sergeant.

AMUSA: Sir ... (*Makes an effort, stops dead. Eyes to the ceiling.*)

PILKINGS: Oh, not again.
90

AMUSA: I cannot against death to dead cult. This dress get power of dead.

PILKINGS: Alright, let's go. You are relieved of all further duty Amusa. Report to me first thing in the morning.

JANE: Shall I come Simon?
95

PILKINGS: No, there's no need for that. If I can get back later I will. Otherwise get Bob to bring you home.

JANE: Be careful Simon ... I mean, be clever.

PILKINGS: Sure I will. You two, come with me. (*As he turns to go, the clock in the Residency begins to chime.* PILKINGS *looks at his
100 watch then turns, horror-stricken, to stare at his wife. The same thought clearly occurs to her. He swallows hard. An* ORDERLY *brings his cloak.*) It's midnight. I had no idea it was that late.

JANE: But surely ... they don't count the hours the way we do. The moon, or something.
105

PILKINGS: I am ... not so sure.

(*He turns and breaks into a sudden run. The two constables follow, also at a run.* AMUSA, *who has kept his eyes on the ceiling throughout waits until the last of the footsteps has faded out of hearing. He salutes suddenly, but without once looking in the direction of the woman.*)

AMUSA: Goodnight madam.

JANE: Oh. (*She hesitates.*) Amusa ... (*He goes off without seeming to have heard.*) Poor Simon ... (*A figure emerges from the shad-ows, a young black man dressed in a sober western suit. He peeps
110 into the hall, trying to make out the figures of the dancers.*) Who is that?

OLUNDE: (*Emerging into the light.*) I didn't mean to startle you madam. I am looking for the District Officer.

JANE: Wait a minute ... don't I know you? Yes, you are
115 Olunde, the young man who ...

OLUNDE: Mrs Pilkings! How fortunate. I came here to look for your husband.

JANE: Olunde! Let's look at you. What a fine young man you've become. Grand but solemn. Good God, when did you return? Simon never said a word. But you do look well Olunde. Really!

OLUNDE: You are . . . well, you look quite well yourself Mrs Pilkings. From what little I can see of you.

JANE: Oh, this. It's caused quite a stir I assure you, and not all of it very pleasant. You are not shocked I hope?

OLUNDE: Why should I be? But don't you find it rather hot in there? Your skin must find it difficult to breathe.

JANE: Well, it is a little hot I must confess, but it's all in a good cause.

OLUNDE: What cause Mrs Pilkings?

JANE: All this. The ball. And His Highness being here in person and all that.

OLUNDE: (*Mildly.*) And that is the good cause for which you desecrate an ancestral mask?

JANE: Oh, so you are shocked after all. How disappointing.

OLUNDE: No I am not shocked Mrs Pilkings. You forget that I have now spent four years among your people. I discovered that you have no respect for what you do not understand.

JANE: Oh. So you've returned with a chip on your shoulder. That's a pity Olunde. I am sorry.

(*An uncomfortable silence follows.*)

I take it then that you did not find your stay in England altogether edifying.

OLUNDE: I don't say that. I found your people quite admirable in many ways, their conduct and courage in this war for instance.

JANE: Ah yes the war. Here of course it is all rather remote. From time to time we have a black-out drill just to remind us that there is a war on. And the rare convoy passes through on its way somewhere or on manoeuvres. Mind you there is the occasional bit of excitement like that ship that was blown up in the harbour.

OLUNDE: Here? Do you mean through enemy action?

JANE: Oh no, the war hasn't come that close. The captain did it himself. I don't quite understand it really. Simon tried to explain. The ship had to be blown up because it had become dangerous to the other ships, even to the city itself. Hundreds of the coastal population would have died.

OLUNDE: Maybe it was loaded with ammunition and had caught fire. Or some of those lethal gases they've been experimenting on.

JANE: Something like that. The captain blew himself up with it. Deliberately. Simon said someone had to remain on board to light the fuse.

OLUNDE: It must have been a very short fuse.

JANE: (*Shrugs.*) I don't know much about it. Only that there was no other way to save lives. No time to devise anything else. The captain took the decision and carried it out.

OLUNDE: Yes . . . I quite believe it. I met men like that in England.

JANE: Oh just look at me! Fancy welcoming you back with such morbid news. Stale too. It was at least six months ago.

OLUNDE: I don't find it morbid at all. I find it rather inspiring. It is an affirmative commentary on life.

JANE: What is?

OLUNDE: That captain's self-sacrifice.

JANE: Nonsense. Life should never be thrown deliberately away.

OLUNDE: And the innocent people round the harbour?

JANE: Oh, how does one know? The whole thing was probably exaggerated anyway.

OLUNDE: That was a risk the captain couldn't take. But please Mrs Pilkings, do you think you could find your husband for me? I have to talk to him.

JANE: Simon? Oh. (*As she recollects for the first time the full significance of* OLUNDE's *presence.*) Simon is . . . there is a little problem in town. He was sent for. But . . . when did you arrive? Does Simon know you're here?

OLUNDE: (*Suddenly earnest.*) I need your help Mrs Pilkings. I've always found you somewhat more understanding than your husband. Please find him for me and when you do, you must help me talk to him.

JANE: I'm afraid I don't quite . . . follow you. Have you seen my husband already?

OLUNDE: I went to your house. Your houseboy told me you were here. (*He smiles.*) He even told me how I would recognise you and Mr Pilkings.

JANE: Then you must know what my husband is trying to do for you.

OLUNDE: For me?

JANE: For you. For your people. And to think he didn't even know you were coming back! But how do you happen to be here? Only this evening we were talking about you. We thought you were still four thousand miles away.

OLUNDE: I was sent a cable.

JANE: A cable? Who did? Simon? The business of your father didn't begin till tonight.

OLUNDE: A relation sent it weeks ago, and it said nothing about my father. All it said was, Our King is dead. But I knew I had to return home at once so as to bury my father. I understood that.

JANE: Well, thank God you don't have to go through that agony. Simon is going to stop it.

OLUNDE: That's why I want to see him. He's wasting his time. And since he has been so helpful to me I don't want him to incur the enmity of our people. Especially over nothing.

JANE: (*Sits down open-mouthed.*) You . . . you Olunde!

OLUNDE: Mrs Pilkings, I came home to bury my father. As soon as I heard the news I booked my passage home. In fact we were fortunate. We travelled in the same convoy as your Prince, so we had excellent protection.

JANE: But you don't think your father is also entitled to whatever protection is available to him?

OLUNDE: How can I make you understand? He *has* protection. No one can undertake what he does tonight without the deepest protection the mind can conceive. What can you offer him in place of his peace of mind, in place of the honour and veneration of his own people? What would you think of your Prince if he had refused to accept the risk of losing his life on this voyage? This . . . showing-the-flag tour of colonial possessions.

JANE: I see. So it isn't just medicine you studied in England.

OLUNDE: Yet another error into which your people fall. You believe that everything which appears to make sense was learnt from you.

235 JANE: Not so fast Olunde. You have learnt to argue I can tell that, but I never said you made sense. However cleverly you try to put it, it is still a barbaric custom. It is even worse— it's feudal! The king dies and a chieftain must be buried with him. How feudalistic can you get!

240 OLUNDE: (*Waves his hand towards the background. The* PRINCE *is dancing past again—to a different step—and all the guests are bowing and curtseying as he passes.*) And this? Even in the midst of a devastating war, look at that. What name would you give to that?

245 JANE: Therapy, British style. The preservation of sanity in the midst of chaos.

OLUNDE: Others would call it decadence. However, it doesn't really interest me. You white races know how to survive; I've seen proof of that. By all logical and natural laws this
250 war should end with all the white races wiping out one another, wiping out their so-called civilisation for all time and reverting to a state of primitivism the like of which has so far only existed in your imagination when you thought of us. I thought all that at the beginning. Then I
255 slowly realised that your greatest art is the art of survival. But at least have the humility to let others survive in their own way.

JANE: Through ritual suicide?

OLUNDE: Is that worse than mass suicide? Mrs Pilkings, what
260 do you call what those young men are sent to do by their generals in this war? Of course you have also mastered the art of calling things by names which don't remotely describe them.

JANE: You talk! You people with your long-winded, round-
265 about way of making conversation.

OLUNDE: Mrs Pilkings, whatever we do, we never suggest that a thing is the opposite of what it really is. In your newsreels I heard defeats, thorough, murderous defeats described as strategic victories. No wait, it wasn't just on your news-
270 reels. Don't forget I was attached to hospitals all the time. Hordes of your wounded passed through those wards. I spoke to them. I spent long evenings by their bedside while they spoke terrible truths of the realities of that war. I know now how history is made.

275 JANE: But surely, in a war of this nature, for the morale of the nation you must expect . . .

OLUNDE: That a disaster beyond human reckoning be spoken of as a triumph? No. I mean, is there no mourning in the home of the bereaved that such blasphemy is permitted?

280 JANE: (*After a moment's pause.*) Perhaps I can understand you now. The time we picked for you was not really one for seeing us at our best.

OLUNDE: Don't think it was just the war. Before that even started I had plenty of time to study your people. I saw
285 nothing, finally, that gave you the right to pass judgement on other peoples and their ways. Nothing at all.

JANE: (*Hesitantly.*) Was it the . . . colour thing? I know there is some discrimination.

OLUNDE: Don't make it so simple, Mrs Pilkings. You make it
290 sound as if when I left, I took nothing at all with me.

JANE: Yes . . . and to tell the truth, only this evening, Simon and I agreed that we never really knew what you left with.

OLUNDE: Neither did I. But I found out over there. I am grateful to your country for that. And I will never give it up.

295 JANE: Olunde, please . . . promise me something. Whatever you do, don't throw away what you have started to do. You want to be a doctor. My husband and I believe you will make an excellent one, sympathetic and competent. Don't let anything make you throw away your training.

300 OLUNDE: (*Genuinely surprised.*) Of course not. What a strange idea. I intend to return and complete my training. Once the burial of my father is over.

JANE: Oh, please . . . !

OLUNDE: Listen! Come outside. You can't hear anything
305 against that music.

JANE: What is it?

OLUNDE: The drums. Can you hear the change? Listen.

(*The drums come over, still distant but more distinct. There is a change of rhythm, it rises to a crescendo and then, suddenly, it is cut off. After a silence, a new beat begins, slow and resonant.*)

There. It's all over.

JANE: You mean he's . . .

310 OLUNDE: Yes Mrs Pilkings, my father is dead. His will-power has always been enormous; I know he is dead.

JANE: (*Screams.*) How can you be so callous! So unfeeling! You announce your father's own death like a surgeon looking down on some strange . . . stranger's body! You're just a
315 savage like all the rest.

AIDE-DE-CAMP: (*Rushing out.*) Mrs Pilkings. Mrs Pilkings. (*She breaks down, sobbing.*) Are you alright, Mrs Pilkings?

OLUNDE: She'll be alright. (*Turns to go.*)

AIDE-DE-CAMP: Who are you? And who the hell asked your
320 opinion?

OLUNDE: You're quite right, nobody. (*Going.*)

AIDE-DE-CAMP: What the hell! Did you hear me ask you who you were?

OLUNDE: I have business to attend to.

325 AIDE-DE-CAMP: I'll give you business in a moment you impudent nigger. Answer my question!

OLUNDE: I have a funeral to arrange. Excuse me. (*Going.*)

AIDE-DE-CAMP: I said stop! Orderly!

JANE: No no, don't do that. I'm alright. And for heaven's sake
330 don't act so foolishly. He's a family friend.

AIDE-DE-CAMP: Well he'd better learn to answer civil questions when he's asked them. These natives put a suit on and they get high opinions of themselves.

OLUNDE: Can I go now?

335 JANE: No no don't go. I must talk to you. I'm sorry about what I said.

OLUNDE: It's nothing Mrs Pilkings. And I'm really anxious to go. I couldn't see my father before, it's forbidden for me, his heir and successor to set eyes on him from the moment of
340 the king's death. But now . . . I would like to touch his body while it is still warm.

JANE: You will. I promise I shan't keep you long. Only, I couldn't possibly let you go like that. Bob, please excuse us.

AIDE-DE-CAMP: If you're sure . . .

345 JANE: Of course I'm sure. Something happened to upset me just then, but I'm alright now. Really.

(*The* AIDE-DE-CAMP *goes, somewhat reluctantly.*)

OLUNDE: I mustn't stay long.

JANE: Please, I promise not to keep you. It's just that . . . oh
you saw yourself what happens to one in this place. The
350   Resident's man thought he was being helpful, that's the
way we all react. But I can't go in among that crowd just
now and if I stay by myself somebody will come looking
for me. Please, just say something for a few moments and
then you can go. Just so I can recover myself.

355   OLUNDE: What do you want me to say?

JANE: Your calm acceptance for instance, can you explain that?
It was so unnatural. I don't understand that at all. I feel a
need to understand all I can.

OLUNDE: But you explained it yourself. My medical training
360   perhaps. I have seen death too often. And the soldiers who
returned from the front, they died on our hands all the
time.

JANE: No. It has to be more than that. I feel it has to do with
the many things we don't really grasp about your people.
365   At least you can explain.

OLUNDE: All these things are part of it. And anyway, my father
has been dead in my mind for nearly a month. Ever since I
learnt of the King's death. I've lived with my bereavement
so long now that I cannot think of him alive. On that jour-
370   ney on the boat, I kept my mind on my duties as the one
who must perform the rites over his body. I went through
it all again and again in my mind as he himself had taught
me. I didn't want to do anything wrong, something which
might jeopardise the welfare of my people.

375   JANE: But he had disowned you. When you left he swore publicly you were no longer his son.

OLUNDE: I told you, he was a man of tremendous will. Sometimes that's another way of saying stubborn. But among our
people, you don't disown a child just like that. Even if I had
380   died before him I would still be buried like his eldest son.
But it's time for me to go.

JANE: Thank you. I feel calmer. Don't let me keep you from
your duties.

OLUNDE: Goodnight Mrs Pilkings.

385   JANE: Welcome home. (She holds out her hand. As he takes it footsteps are heard approaching the drive. A short while later a
woman's sobbing is also heard.)

PILKINGS: (Off.) Keep them here till I get back. (He strides into
view, reacts at the sight of OLUNDE but turns to his wife.)
390   Thank goodness you're still here.

JANE: Simon, what happened?

PILKINGS: Later Jane, please. Is Bob still here?

JANE: Yes, I think so. I'm sure he must be.

PILKINGS: Try and get him out here as quietly as you can. Tell
395   him it's urgent.

JANE: Of course. Oh Simon, you remember . . .

PILKINGS: Yes yes. I can see who it is. Get Bob out here. (She
runs off.) At first I thought I was seeing a ghost.

OLUNDE: Mr Pilkings, I appreciate what you tried to do. I want
400   you to believe that. I can only tell you it would have been a
terrible calamity if you'd succeeded.

PILKINGS: (Opens his mouth several times, shuts it.) You . . . said
what?

OLUNDE: A calamity for us, the entire people.

405   PILKINGS: (Sighs.) I see. Hm.

OLUNDE: And now I must go. I must see him before he turns
cold.

PILKINGS: Oh ah . . . em . . . but this is a shock to see you. I
mean er thinking all this while you were in England and
thanking God for that.   410

OLUNDE: I came on the mail boat. We travelled in the Prince's
convoy.

PILKINGS: Ah yes, a-ah, hm . . . er well . . .

OLUNDE: Goodnight. I can see you are shocked by the whole
business. But you must know by now there are things you   415
cannot understand—or help.

PILKINGS: Yes. Just a minute. There are armed policemen that
way and they have instructions to let no one pass. I suggest
you wait a little. I'll er . . . yes, I'll give you an escort.

OLUNDE: That's very kind of you. But do you think it could be   420
quickly arranged.

PILKINGS: Of course. In fact, yes, what I'll do is send Bob over
with some men to the er . . . place. You can go with them.
Here he comes now. Excuse me a minute.

AIDE-DE-CAMP: Anything wrong sir?   425

PILKINGS: (Takes him to one side.) Listen Bob, that cellar in the
disused annexe of the Residency, you know, where the
slaves were stored before being taken down to the coast . . .

AIDE-DE-CAMP: Oh yes, we use it as a storeroom for broken
furniture.   430

PILKINGS: But it's still got the bars on it?

AIDE-DE-CAMP: Oh yes, they are quite intact.

PILKINGS: Get the keys please. I'll explain later. And I want a
strong guard over the Residency tonight.

AIDE-DE-CAMP: We have that already. The detachment from   435
the coast . . .

PILKINGS: No, I don't want them at the gates of the Residency.
I want you to deploy them at the bottom of the hill, a long
way from the main hall so they can deal with any situation
long before the sound carries to the house.   440

AIDE-DE-CAMP: Yes of course.

PILKINGS: I don't want His Highness alarmed.

AIDE-DE-CAMP: You think the riot will spread here?

PILKINGS: It's unlikely but I don't want to take a chance. I made
them believe I was going to lock the man up in my house,   445
which was what I had planned to do in the first place. They
are probably assailing it by now. I took a roundabout route
here so I don't think there is any danger at all. At least not
before dawn. Nobody is to leave the premises of course—
the native employees I mean. They'll soon smell something 450
is up and they can't keep their mouths shut.

AIDE-DE-CAMP: I'll give instructions at once.

PILKINGS: I'll take the prisoner down myself. Two policemen
will stay with him throughout the night. Inside the cell.

AIDE-DE-CAMP: Right sir. (Salutes and goes off at the double.)   455

PILKINGS: Jane. Bob is coming back in a moment with a detachment. Until he gets back please stay with Olunde.

(He makes an extra warning gesture with his eyes.)

OLUNDE: Please Mr Pilkings . . .

PILKINGS: I hate to be stuffy old son, but we have a crisis on our
hands. It has to do with your father's affair if you must   460
know. And it happens also at a time when we have His
Highness here. I am responsible for security so you'll simply have to do as I say. I hope that's understood. (Marches off
quickly, in the direction from which he made his first appearance.)

465 OLUNDE: What's going on? All this can't be just because he
failed to stop my father killing himself.

JANE: I honestly don't know. Could it have sparked off a riot?

OLUNDE: No. If he'd succeeded that would be more likely to
start the riot. Perhaps there were other factors involved.

470 Was there a chieftaincy dispute?

JANE: None that I know of.

ELESIN: (*An animal bellow from off.*) Leave me alone! Is it not
enough that you have covered me in shame! White man,
take your hand from my body!

(OLUNDE *stands frozen on the spot.* JANE *understanding at last, tries
to move him.*)

475 JANE: Let's go in. It's getting chilly out here.

PILKINGS: (*Off.*) Carry him.

ELESIN: Give me back the name you have taken away from me
you ghost from the land of the nameless!

PILKINGS: Carry him! I can't have a disturbance here. Quickly!

480 stuff up his mouth.

JANE: Oh God! Let's go in. Please Olunde. (OLUNDE *does not move.*)

ELESIN: Take your albino's hand from me you . . .

(*Sounds of a struggle. His voice chokes as he is gagged.*)

OLUNDE: (*Quietly.*) That was my father's voice.

JANE: Oh you poor orphan, what have you come home to?

(*There is a sudden explosion of rage from off-stage and powerful steps
come running up the drive.*)

485 PILKINGS: You bloody fools, after him!

(*Immediately* ELESIN, *in handcuffs, comes pounding in the direction of*
JANE *and* OLUNDE, *followed some moments afterwards by* PILKINGS
and the constables. ELESIN *confronted by the seeming statue of his son,
stops dead.* OLUNDE *stares above his head into the distance. The constables try to grab him.* JANE *screams at them.*)

JANE: Leave him alone! Simon, tell them to leave him alone.

PILKINGS: All right, stand aside you. (*Shrugs.*) Maybe just as
well. It might help to calm him down.

(*For several moments they hold the same position.* ELESIN *moves a few
steps forward, almost as if he's still in doubt.*)

ELESIN: Olunde? (*He moves his head, inspecting him from side to*

490 *side.*) Olunde! (*He collapses slowly at* OLUNDE's *feet.*) Oh son,
don't let the sight of your father turn you blind!

OLUNDE: (*He moves for the first time since he heard his voice, brings
his head slowly down to look on him.*) I have no father, eater of
left-overs.

(*He walks slowly down the way his father had run. Light fades out
on* ELESIN, *sobbing into the ground.*)

ACT FIVE

*A wide iron-barred gate stretches almost the whole width of the cell in
which* ELESIN *is imprisoned. His wrists are encased in thick iron
bracelets, chained together; he stands against the bars, looking out.
Seated on the ground to one side on the outside is his recent* BRIDE, *her*

*eyes bent perpetually to the ground. Figures of the two guards can be
seen deeper inside the cell, alert to every movement* ELESIN *makes.*
PILKINGS *now in a police officer's uniform enters noiselessly, observes
him for a while. Then he coughs ostentatiously and approaches. Leans
against the bars near a corner, his back to* ELESIN. *He is obviously trying to fall in mood with him. Some moments' silence.*

PILKINGS: You seem fascinated by the moon.

ELESIN: (*After a pause.*) Yes, ghostly one. Your twin-brother up
there engages my thoughts.

PILKINGS: It is a beautiful night.

ELESIN: Is that so?   5

PILKINGS: The light on the leaves, the peace of the night . . .

ELESIN: The night is not at peace, District Officer.

PILKINGS: No? I would have said it was. You know, quiet . . .

ELESIN: And does quiet mean peace for you?

PILKINGS: Well, nearly the same thing. Naturally there is a   10
subtle difference . . .

ELESIN: The night is not at peace ghostly one. The world is not
at peace. You have shattered the peace of the world for ever.
There is no sleep in the world tonight.

PILKINGS: It is still a good bargain if the world should lose one   15
night's sleep as the price of saving a man's life.

ELESIN: You did not save my life District Officer. You destroyed
it.

PILKINGS: Now come on . . .

ELESIN: And not merely my life but the lives of many. The end   20
of the night's work is not over. Neither this year nor the
next will see it. If I wished you well, I would pray that you
do not stay long enough on our land to see the disaster you
have brought upon us.

PILKINGS: Well, I did my duty as I saw it. I have no regrets.   25

ELESIN: No. The regrets of life always come later.

(*Some moments' pause.*)

You are waiting for dawn white man. I hear you saying to
yourself: only so many hours until dawn and then the danger
is over. All I must do is keep him alive tonight. You don't
quite understand it all but you know that tonight is when   30
what ought to be must be brought about. I shall ease your
mind even more, ghostly one. It is not an entire night but a
moment of the night, and that moment is past. The moon
was my messenger and guide. When it reached a certain
gateway in the sky, it touched that moment for which my   35
whole life has been spent in blessings. Even I do not know
the gateway. I have stood here and scanned the sky for a
glimpse of that door but, I cannot see it. Human eyes are useless for a search of this nature. But in the house of *osugbo*,
those who keep watch through the spirit recognised the   40
moment, they sent word to me through the voice of our sacred drums to prepare myself. I heard them and I shed all
thoughts of earth. I began to follow the moon to the abode
of gods . . . servant of the white king, that was when you
entered my chosen place of departure on feet of desecration. 45

PILKINGS: I'm sorry, but we all see our duty differently.

ELESIN: I no longer blame you. You stole from me my first-
born, sent him to your country so you could turn him into
something in your own image. Did you plan it all beforehand? There are moments when it seems part of a larger   50

plan. He who must follow my footsteps is taken from me, sent across the ocean. Then, in my turn, I am stopped from fulfilling my destiny. Did you think it all out before, this plan to push our world from its course and sever the cord
55 that links us to the great origin?

PILKINGS: You don't really believe that. Anyway, if that was my intention with your son, I appear to have failed.

ELESIN: You did not fail in the main thing ghostly one. We know the roof covers the rafters, the cloth covers blemishes;
60 who would have known that the white skin covered our future, preventing us from seeing the death our enemies had prepared for us. The world is set adrift and its inhabitants are lost. Around them, there is nothing but emptiness.

PILKINGS: Your son does not take so gloomy a view.

65 ELESIN: Are you dreaming now white man? Were you not present at my reunion of shame? Did you not see when the world reversed itself and the father fell before his son, asking forgiveness?

PILKINGS: That was in the heat of the moment. I spoke to him
70 and . . . if you want to know, he wishes he could cut out his tongue for uttering the words he did.

ELESIN: No. What he said must never be unsaid. The contempt of my own son rescued something of my shame at your hands. You may have stopped me in my duty but I know
75 now that I did give birth to a son. Once I mistrusted him for seeking the companionship of those my spirit knew as enemies of our race. Now I understand. One should seek to obtain the secrets of his enemies. He will avenge my shame, white one. His spirit will destroy you and yours.

80 PILKINGS: That kind of talk is hardly called for. If you don't want my consolation . . .

ELESIN: No white man, I do not want your consolation.

PILKINGS: As you wish. Your son anyway, sends his consolation. He asks your forgiveness. When I asked him not to despise
85 you his reply was: I cannot judge him, and if I cannot judge him, I cannot despise him. He wants to come to you to say goodbye and to receive your blessing.

ELESIN: Goodbye? Is he returning to your land?

PILKINGS: Don't you think that's the most sensible thing for
90 him to do? I advised him to leave at once, before dawn, and he agrees that is the right course of action.

ELESIN: Yes, it is best. And even if I did not think so, I have lost the father's place of honour. My voice is broken.

PILKINGS: Your son honours you. If he didn't he would not ask
95 your blessing.

ELESIN: No. Even a thoroughbred is not without pity for the turf he strikes with his hoof. When is he coming?

PILKINGS: As soon as the town is a little quieter. I advised it.

ELESIN: Yes white man, I am sure you advised it. You advise all
100 our lives although on the authority of what gods, I do not know.

PILKINGS: (*Opens his mouth to reply, then appears to change his mind. Turns to go. Hesitates and stops again.*) Before I leave you, may I ask just one thing of you?

105 ELESIN: I am listening.

PILKINGS: I wish to ask you to search the quiet of your heart and tell me—do you not find great contradictions in the wisdom of your own race?

ELESIN: Make yourself clear, white one.

110 PILKINGS: I have lived among you long enough to learn a saying or two. One came to my mind tonight when I stepped

into the market and saw what was going on. You were surrounded by those who egged you on with song and praises. I thought, are these not the same people who say: the elder grimly approaches heaven and you ask him to bear your 115
greetings yonder; do you really think he makes the journey willingly? After that, I did not hesitate.

(*A pause.* ELESIN *sighs. Before he can speak a sound of running feet is heard.*)

JANE: (*Off.*) Simon! Simon!
PILKINGS: What on earth . . . ! (*Runs off.*)

(ELESIN *turns to his new wife, gazes on her for some moments.*)

ELESIN: My young bride, did you hear the ghostly one? You sit 120
and sob in your silent heart but say nothing to all this. First I blamed the white man, then I blamed my gods for deserting me. Now I feel I want to blame you for the mystery of the sapping of my will. But blame is a strange peace offering for a man to bring a world he has deeply wronged, and to its 125
innocent dwellers. Oh little mother, I have taken countless women in my life but you were more than a desire of the flesh. I needed you as the abyss across which my body must be drawn, I filled it with earth and dropped my seed in it at the moment of preparedness for my crossing. You 130
were the final gift of the living to their emissary to the land of the ancestors, and perhaps your warmth and youth brought new insights of this world to me and turned my feet leaden on this side of the abyss. For I confess to you, daughter, my weakness came not merely from the abomination of 135
the white man who came violently into my fading presence, there was also a weight of longing on my earth-held limbs. I would have shaken it off, already my foot had begun to lift but then, the white ghost entered and all was defiled.

(*Approaching voices of* PILKINGS *and his wife.*)

JANE: Oh Simon, you will let her in won't you? 140
PILKINGS: I really wish you'd stop interfering.

(*They come in view.* JANE *is in a dressing-gown.* PILKINGS *is holding a note to which he refers from time to time.*)

JANE: Good gracious, I didn't initiate this. I was sleeping quietly, or trying to anyway, when the servant brought it. It's not my fault if one can't sleep undisturbed even in the Residency. 145

PILKINGS: He'd have done the same if we were sleeping at home so don't sidetrack the issue. He knows he can get round you or he wouldn't send you the petition in the first place.

JANE: Be fair Simon. After all he was thinking of your own interests. He is grateful you know, you seem to forget that. 150
He feels he owes you something.

PILKINGS: I just wish they'd leave this man alone tonight, that's all.

JANE: Trust him Simon. He's pledged his word it will all go peacefully. 155

PILKINGS: Yes, and that's the other thing. I don't like being threatened.

JANE: Threatened? (*Takes the note.*) I didn't spot any threat.

PILKINGS: It's there. Veiled, but it's there. The only way to prevent serious rioting tomorrow—what a cheek! 160

JANE: I don't think he's threatening you Simon.

PILKINGS: He's picked up the idiom alright. Wouldn't surprise me if he's been mixing with commies or anarchists over there. The phrasing sounds too good to be true. Damn! If
165 only the Prince hadn't picked this time for his visit.

JANE: Well, even so Simon, what have you got to lose? You don't want a riot on your hands, not with the Prince here.

PILKINGS: (*Going up to* ELESIN.) Let's see what he has to say. Chief Elesin, there is yet another person who wants to see
170 you. As she is not a next-of-kin I don't really feel obliged to let her in. But your son sent a note with her, so it's up to you.

ELESIN: I know who that must be. So she found out your hiding-place. Well, it was not difficult. My stench of shame is so strong, it requires no hunter's dog to follow it.

175 PILKINGS: If you don't want to see her, just say so and I'll send her packing.

ELESIN: Why should I not want to see her? Let her come. I have no more holes in my rag of shame. All is laid bare.

PILKINGS: I'll bring her in. (*Goes off.*)

180 JANE: (*Hesitates, then goes to* ELESIN.) Please, try and understand. Everything my husband did was for the best.

ELESIN: (*He gives her a long strange stare, as if he is trying to understand who she is.*) You are the wife of the District Officer?

JANE: Yes. My name is Jane.

185 ELESIN: That is my wife sitting down there. You notice how still and silent she sits? My business is with your husband.

(PILKINGS *returns with* IYALOJA.)

PILKINGS: Here she is. Now first I want your word of honour that you will try nothing foolish.

ELESIN: Honour? White one, did you say you wanted my word
190 of honour?

PILKINGS: I know you to be an honourable man. Give me your word of honour you will receive nothing from her.

ELESIN: But I am sure you have searched her clothing as you would never dare touch your own mother. And there are
195 these two lizards of yours who roll their eyes even when I scratch.

PILKINGS: And I shall be sitting on that tree trunk watching even how you blink. Just the same I want your word that you will not let her pass anything to you.

200 ELESIN: You have my honour already. It is locked up in that desk in which you will put away your report of this night's events. Even the honour of my people you have taken already; it is tied together with those papers of treachery which make you masters in this land.

205 PILKINGS: Alright. I am trying to make things easy but if you must bring in politics we'll have to do it the hard way. Madam, I want you to remain along this line and move no nearer to that cell door. Guards! (*They spring to attention.*) If she moves beyond this point, blow your whistle. Come on
210 Jane. (*They go off.*)

IYALOJA: How boldly the lizard struts before the pigeon when it was the eagle itself he promised us he would confront.

ELESIN: I don't ask you to take pity on me Iyaloja. You have a message for me or you would not have come. Even if it is
215 the curses of the world, I shall listen.

IYALOJA: You made so bold with the servant of the white king who took your side against death. I must tell your brother chiefs when I return how bravely you waged war against him. Especially with words.

ELESIN: I more than deserve your scorn.   220

IYALOJA: (*With sudden anger.*) I warned you, if you must leave a seed behind, be sure it is not tainted with the curses of the world. Who are you to open a new life when you dared not open the door to a new existence? I say who are you to make so bold? (*The* BRIDE *sobs and* IYALOJA *notices her. Her* 225
contempt noticeably increases as she turns back to ELESIN.) Oh you self-vaunted stem of the plantain, how hollow it all proves. The pith is gone in the parent stem, so how will it prove with the new shoot? How will it go with that earth that bears it? Who are you to bring this abomination on us!   230

ELESIN: My powers deserted me. My charms, my spells, even my voice lacked strength when I made to summon the powers that would lead me over the last measure of earth into the land of the fleshless. You saw it, Iyaloja. You saw me struggle to retrieve my will from the power of the stranger   235
whose shadow fell across the doorway and left me floundering and blundering in a maze I had never before encountered. My senses were numbed when the touch of cold iron came upon my wrists. I could do nothing to save myself.

IYALOJA: You have betrayed us. We fed you sweetmeats such   240
as we hoped awaited you on the other side. But you said No, I must eat the world's left-overs. We said you were the hunter who brought the quarry down; to you belonged the vital portions of the game. No, you said, I am the hunter's dog and I shall eat the entrails of the game and the faeces of   245
the hunter. We said you were the hunter returning home in triumph, a slain buffalo pressing down on his neck, you said wait, I first must turn up this cricket hole with my toes. We said yours was the doorway at which we first spy the tapper when he comes down from the tree, yours was the blessing   250
of the twilight wine, the purl that brings night spirits out of doors to steal their portion before the light of day. We said yours was the body of wine whose burden shakes the tapper like a sudden gust on his perch. You said, No, I am content to lick the dregs from each calabash when the   255
drinkers are done. We said, the dew on earth's surface was for you to wash your feet along the slopes of honour. You said No, I shall step in the vomit of cats and the droppings of mice; I shall fight them for the left-overs of the world.

ELESIN: Enough Iyaloja, enough.   260

IYALOJA: We called you leader and oh, how you led us on. What we have no intention of eating should not be held to the nose.

ELESIN: Enough, enough. My shame is heavy enough.

IYALOJA: Wait. I came with a burden.

ELESIN: You have more than discharged it.   265

IYALOJA: I wish I could pity you.

ELESIN: I need neither your pity nor the pity of the world. I need understanding. Even I need to understand. You were present at my defeat. You were part of the beginnings. You brought about the renewal of my tie to earth, you helped in   270
the binding of the cord.

IYALOJA: I gave you warning. The river which fills up before our eyes does not sweep us away in its flood.

ELESIN: What were warnings beside the moist contact of living earth between my fingers? What were warnings beside the   275
renewal of famished embers lodged eternally in the heart of man. But even that, even if it overwhelmed one with a thousandfold temptations to linger a little while, a man could overcome it. It is when the alien hand pollutes the source of will, when a stranger force of violence shatters the   280

mind's calm resolution, this is when a man is made to commit the awful treachery of relief, commit in his thought the unspeakable blasphemy of seeing the hand of the gods in this alien rupture of his world. I know it was this thought
285 that killed me, sapped my powers and turned me into an infant in the hands of unnamable strangers. I made to utter my spells anew but my tongue merely rattled in my mouth. I fingered hidden charms and the contact was damp; there was no spark left to sever the life-strings that should stretch
290 from every finger-tip. My will was squelched in the spittle of an alien race, and all because I had committed this blasphemy of thought—that there might be the hand of the gods in a stranger's intervention.

IYALOJA: Explain it how you will, I hope it brings you peace of
295 mind. The bush-rat fled his rightful cause, reached the market and set up a lamentation. 'Please save me!'—are these fitting words to hear from an ancestral mask? 'There's a wild beast at my heels' is not becoming language from a hunter.

300 ELESIN: May the world forgive me.

IYALOJA: I came with a burden I said. It approaches the gates which are so well guarded by those jackals whose spittle will from this day on be your food and drink. But first, tell me, you who were once Elesin Oba, tell me, you who know
305 so well the cycle of the plantain: is it the parent shoot which withers to give sap to the younger or, does your wisdom see it running the other way?

ELESIN: I don't see your meaning Iyaloja?

IYALOJA: Did I ask you for a meaning? I asked a question.
310 Whose trunk withers to give sap to the other? The parent shoot or the younger?

ELESIN: The parent.

IYALOJA: Ah. So you do know that. There are sights in this world which say different Elesin. There are some who
315 choose to reverse this cycle of our being. Oh you emptied bark that the world once saluted for a pith-laden being, shall I tell you what the gods have claimed of you?

(*In her agitation she steps beyond the line indicated by* PILKINGS *and the air is rent by piercing whistles. The two* GUARDS *also leap forward and place safe-guarding hands on* ELESIN. IYALOJA *stops, astonished.* PILKINGS *comes racing, followed by* JANE.)

PILKINGS: What is it? Did they try something?

GUARD: She stepped beyond the line.
320 ELESIN: (*In a broken voice.*) Let her alone. She meant no harm.

IYALOJA: Oh Elesin, see what you've become. Once you had no need to open your mouth in explanation because evil-smelling goats, itchy of hand and foot had lost their senses. And it was a brave man indeed who dared lay hands on you
325 because Iyaloja stepped from one side of the earth onto another. Now look at the spectacle of your life. I grieve for you.

PILKINGS: I think you'd better leave. I doubt you have done him much good by coming here. I shall make sure you are not
330 allowed to see him again. In any case we are moving him to a different place before dawn, so don't bother to come back.

IYALOJA: We foresaw that. Hence the burden I trudged here to lay beside your gates.

PILKINGS: What was that you said?

335 IYALOJA: Didn't our son explain? Ask that one. He knows what it is. At least we hope the man we once knew as Elesin remembers the lesser oaths he need not break.

PILKINGS: Do you know what she is talking about?

ELESIN: Go to the gates, ghostly one. Whatever you find there,
340 bring it to me.

IYALOJA: Not yet. It drags behind me on the slow, weary feet of women. Slow as it is Elesin, it has long overtaken you. It rides ahead of your laggard will.

PILKINGS: What is she saying now? Christ! Must your people
345 forever speak in riddles?

ELESIN: It will come white man, it will come. Tell your men at the gates to let it through.

PILKINGS: (*Dubiously.*) I'll have to see what it is.

IYALOJA: You will. (*Passionately.*) But this is one oath he cannot
350 shirk. White one, you have a king here, a visitor from your land. We know of his presence here. Tell me, were he to die would you leave his spirit roaming restlessly on the surface of earth? Would you bury him here among those you consider less than human? In your land have you no ceremonies
355 of the dead?

PILKINGS: Yes. But we don't make our chiefs commit suicide to keep him company.

IYALOJA: Child, I have not come to help your understanding. (*Points to* ELESIN.) This is the man whose weakened understanding holds us in bondage to you. But ask him if you
360 wish. He knows the meaning of a king's passage; he was not born yesterday. He knows the peril to the race when our dead father, who goes as intermediary, waits and waits and knows he is betrayed. He knows when the narrow gate was opened and he knows it will not stay for laggards who drag
365 their feet in dung and vomit, whose lips are reeking of the left-overs of lesser men. He knows he has condemned our king to wander in the void of evil with beings who are enemies of life.

PILKINGS: Yes er ... but look here ...
370 IYALOJA: What we ask is little enough. Let him release our King so he can ride on homewards alone. The messenger is on his way on the backs of women. Let him send word through the heart that is folded up within the bolt. It is the least of all his oaths, it is the easiest fulfilled.
375

(*The* AIDE-DE-CAMP *runs in.*)

PILKINGS: Bob?

AIDE-DE-CAMP: Sir, there's a group of women chanting up the hill.

PILKINGS: (*Rounding on* IYALOJA.) If you people want trouble ...

JANE: Simon, I think that's what Olunde referred to in his letter.
380 PILKINGS: He knows damned well I can't have a crowd here! Damn it, I explained the delicacy of my position to him. I think it's about time I got him out of town. Bob, send a car and two or three soldiers to bring him in. I think the sooner he takes his leave of his father and gets out the better.
385 IYALOJA: Save your labour white one. If it is the father of your prisoner you want, Olunde, he who until this night we knew as Elesin's son, he comes soon himself to take his leave. He has sent the women ahead, so let them in.

(PILKINGS *remains undecided.*)

390   AIDE-DE-CAMP: What do we do about the invasion? We can still
      stop them far from here.
    PILKINGS: What do they look like?
    AIDE-DE-CAMP: They're not many. And they seem quite peaceful.
    PILKINGS: No men?
395   AIDE-DE-CAMP: Mm, two or three at the most.
    JANE: Honestly, Simon, I'd trust Olunde. I don't think he'll de-
      ceive you about their intentions.
    PILKINGS: He'd better not. Alright, let them in Bob. Warn
      them to control themselves. Then hurry Olunde here.
400   Make sure he brings his baggage because I'm not returning
      him into town.
    AIDE-DE-CAMP: Very good sir. (*Goes.*)
    PILKINGS: (*To* IYALOJA.) I hope you understand that if anything
      goes wrong it will be on your head. My men have orders to
405   shoot at the first sign of trouble.
    IYALOJA: To prevent one death you will actually make other
      deaths? Ah, great is the wisdom of the white race. But have
      no fear. Your Prince will sleep peacefully. So at long last will
      ours. We will disturb you no further, servant of the white
410   king. Just let Elesin fulfil his oath and we will retire home
      and pay homage to our King.
    JANE: I believe her Simon, don't you?
    PILKINGS: Maybe.
    ELESIN: Have no fear ghostly one. I have a message to send my
415   King and then you have nothing more to fear.
    IYALOJA: Olunde would have done it. The chiefs asked him to
      speak the words but he said no, not while you lived.
    ELESIN: Even from the depths to which my spirit has sunk, I
      find some joy that this little has been left to me.

(*The* WOMEN *enter, intoning the dirge 'Alẹ lẹ lẹ' and swaying from side
to side. On their shoulders is borne a longish object roughly like a cylin-
drical bolt, covered in cloth. They set it down on the spot where*
IYALOJA *had stood earlier, and form a semicircle round it. The*
PRAISE-SINGER *and* DRUMMER *stand on the inside of the semicircle
but the drum is not used at all. The* DRUMMER *intones under the*
PRAISE-SINGER*'s invocations.*)

420   PILKINGS: (*As they enter.*) What is *that*?
    IYALOJA: The burden you have made white one, but we bring it
      in peace.
    PILKINGS: I said *what* is it?
    ELESIN: White man, you must let me out. I have a duty to per-
425   form.
    PILKINGS: I most certainly will not.
    ELESIN: There lies the courier of my King. Let me out so I can
      perform what is demanded of me.
    PILKINGS: You'll do what you need to do from inside there or
430   not at all. I've gone as far as I intend to with this business.
    ELESIN: The worshipper who lights a candle in your church to
      bear a message to his god bows his head and speaks in a whis-
      per to the flame. Have I not seen it ghostly one? His voice
      does not ring out to the world. Mine are no words for any-
435   one's ears. They are not words even for the bearers of this
      load. They are words I must speak secretly, even as my father
      whispered them in my ears and I in the ears of my first-born.
      I cannot shout them to the wind and the open night-sky.
    JANE: Simon . . .
440   PILKINGS: Don't interfere. Please!

IYALOJA: They have slain the favourite horse of the king and slain
    his dog. They have borne them from pulse to pulse centre of
    the land receiving prayers for their king. But the rider has
    chosen to stay behind. Is it too much to ask that he speak his
    heart to heart of the waiting courier? (PILKINGS *turns his back* 445
    on her.) So be it. Elesin Oba, you see how even the mere leav-
    ings are denied you. (*She gestures to the* PRAISE-SINGER.)
PRAISE-SINGER: Elesin Oba! I call you by that name only this
    last time. Remember when I said, if you cannot come, tell
    my horse. (*Pause.*) What? I cannot hear you? I said, if you 450
    can-not come, whisper in the ears of my horse. Is your
    tongue severed from the roots Elesin? I can hear no re-
    sponse. I said, if there are boulders you cannot climb, mount
    my horse's back, this spotless black stallion, he'll bring you
    over them. (*Pauses.*) Elesin Oba, once you had a tongue that 455
    darted like a drummer's stick. I said, if you get lost my dog
    will track a path to me. My memory fails me but I think you
    replied: My feet have found the path, Alafin.

(*The dirge rises and falls.*)

    I said at the last, if evil hands hold you back, just tell my
    horse there is weight on the hem of your smock. I dare not 460
    wait too long.

(*The dirge rises and falls.*)

    There lies the swiftest ever messenger of a king, so set me
    free with the errand of your heart. There lie the head and
    heart of the favourite of the gods, whisper in his ears. Oh my
    companion, if you had followed when you should, we would 465
    not say that the horse preceded its rider. If you had followed
    when it was time, we would not say the dog has raced be-
    yond and left his master behind. If you had raised your will to
    cut the thread of life at the summons of the drums, we would
    not say your mere shadow fell across the gateway and took its 470
    owner's place at the banquet. But the hunter, laden with a
    slain buffalo, stayed to root in the cricket's hole with his toes.
    What now is left? If there is a dearth of bats, the pigeon must
    serve us for the offering. Speak the words over your shadow
    which must now serve in your place. 475
ELESIN: I cannot approach. Take off the cloth. I shall speak my
    message from heart to heart of silence.
IYALOJA: (*Moves forward and removes the coverings.*) Your courier
    Elesin, cast your eyes on the favoured companion of the King.

(*Rolled up in the mat, his head and feet showing at either end is the
body of* OLUNDE.)

    There lies the honour of your household and of our race. 480
    Because he could not bear to let honour fly out of doors, he
    stopped it with his life. The son has proved the father
    Elesin, and there is nothing left in your mouth to gnash but
    infant gums.
PRAISE-SINGER: Elesin, we placed the reins of the world in your 485
    hands yet you watched it plunge over the edge of the bitter
    precipice. You sat with folded arms while evil strangers
    tilted the world from its course and crashed it beyond the
    edge of emptiness—you muttered, there is little that one
    man can do, you left us floundering in a blind future. Your 490
    heir has taken the burden on himself. What the end will be,

we are not gods to tell. But this young shoot has poured its sap into the parent stalk, and we know this is not the way of life. Our world is tumbling in the void of strangers, Elesin.

(ELESIN *has stood rock-still, his knuckles taut on the bars, his eyes glued to the body of his son. The stillness seizes and paralyses everyone, including* PILKINGS *who has turned to look. Suddenly* ELESIN *flings one arm round his neck, once, and with the loop of the chain, strangles himself in a swift, decisive pull. The guards rush forward to stop him but they are only in time to let his body down.* PILKINGS *has leapt to the door at the same time and struggles with the lock. He rushes within, fumbles with the handcuffs and unlocks them, raises the body to a sitting position while he tries to give resuscitation. The* WOMEN *continue their dirge, unmoved by the sudden event.*)

495   IYALOJA: Why do you strain yourself? Why do you labour at tasks for which no one, not even the man lying there would give you thanks? He is gone at last into the passage but oh, how late it all is. His son will feast on the meat and throw him bones. The passage is clogged with droppings from the
500   King's stallion; he will arrive all stained in dung.
      PILKINGS: (*In a tired voice.*) Was this what you wanted?
      IYALOJA: No child, it is what you brought to be, you who play with strangers' lives, who even usurp the vestments of our

dead, yet believe that the stain of death will not cling to you. The gods demanded only the old expired plantain but   505 you cut down the sap-laden shoot to feed your pride. There is your board, filled to overflowing. Feast on it. (*She screams at him suddenly, seeing that* PILKINGS *is about to close* ELESIN'S *staring eyes.*) Let him alone! However sunk he was in debt he is no pauper's carrion abandoned on the road. Since when   510 have strangers donned clothes of indigo before the bereaved cries out his loss?

(*She turns to the* BRIDE *who has remained motionless throughout.*)

Child.

(*The girl takes up a little earth, walks calmly into the cell and closes* ELESIN'S *eyes. She then pours some earth over each eyelid and comes out again.*)

Now forget the dead, forget even the living. Turn your mind only to the unborn.   515

(*She goes off, accompanied by the* BRIDE. *The dirge rises in volume and the* WOMEN *continue their sway. Lights fade to a black-out.*)

GLOSSARY

alari, a rich, woven cloth, brightly coloured
egungun, ancestral masquerade
etutu, placatory rites or medicine
gbedu, a deep-timbred royal drum
opele, string of beads used in Ifa divination
osugbo, secret 'executive' cult of the Yoruba; its meeting place

robo, a delicacy made from crushed melon seeds, fried in tiny balls
sanyan, a richly valued woven cloth
sigidi, a squat, carved figure, endowed with the powers of an incubus

Brian Friel

Brian Friel (b. 1929) is perhaps the most prominent living Irish playwright, the heir of Ireland's brilliant modern dramatic tradition, the tradition of William Butler Yeats, John Millington Synge, and Sean O'Casey. Unlike these predecessors, who worked for the independence of the Republic of Ireland, Friel works in Northern Ireland, still a part of the United Kingdom. Educated in Derry and Belfast, Friel's concerns as a playwright have spanned the "troubles" of Northern Ireland, the poverty and depression of Derry in the 1930s, 1940s, and 1950s, and the installation of a British military presence and the open street warfare of the 1960s, 1970s, and 1980s. From his earliest success, *Philadelphia, Here I Come!* (1964), about a man's divided feelings concerning his emigration to the United States, Friel's drama has centered on the problems of Irish identity in the face of British rule. Many of his early plays and stories—*The Loves of Cass McGuire* (1966), *The Lovers* (1967)— are portraits of Irish life in the manner of Synge, and Friel's dramatization of the personal consequences of contemporary Irish life remains a prominent feature of fine plays like *Living Quarters* (1977) and *Faith Healer* (1979). However, Friel's drama has increasingly become more satirical—in *The Mundy Scheme* (1969) and *The Gentle Island* (1971)—and more politically concerned. In *The Freedom of the City* (1973), Friel dramatizes the fate of three people caught and killed by British soldiers in the 1972 "Bloody Sunday" riots in Derry. In *Volunteers* (1975), a crew of political prisoners are forced to work on an archaeological site, recovering the history of Celtic Ireland even as they are oppressed by British rule. In *Making History* (1988), Friel returns to the origins of Ireland's subjection to the British in the seventeenth and eighteenth centuries. In 1980, Friel and Stephen Rea founded the Field Day Theatre Company in Derry, and its first production was the play generally taken to be

The 1993 Donmar Warehouse production of Brian Friel's *Translations*.

1458   UNIT VII · WORLD STAGES

Friel's masterpiece, *Translations*. Friel's more recent plays include *Dancing at Lughnasa* (1990), *Wonderful Tennessee* (1992), and *Give Me Your Answer, Do!* (1997). Friel has also adapted several plays—Turgenev's *A Month in the Country* (1992) and *London Vertigo*, by the eighteenth-century actor Charles Macklin (1992)—and has specialized in adapting Chekhov's drama to Irish English, in versions of *Three Sisters* (2001) and *Uncle Vanya* (1995).

TRANSLATIONS

Translations is set in early nineteenth-century Ireland and concerns the mapping—both actual and cultural—of Ireland by the British. The play takes place at a local hedge-school, a subscription school run by a local master and attended by a variety of children and adults. This Ireland is already threatened by the British culture to the east: a national school—where, presumably, English will be the required language—is about to open, and the British army surveyors have arrived to map the region, part of the 1833 Ordnance Survey of Ireland.

The play's politics are largely conveyed through the politics of language. Jimmy's Homeric Greek, for example, draws a parallel between Ireland and another lost civilization. The romance between Yolland and Maire bridges the barrier of language. They learn to communicate across this barrier, while the British army works to tear it down and destroy Irish cultural identity in the process. In mapping Ireland, the British convert local place names into English, either by translating them directly or by inventing some equivalent. As the relationship between the Irish Owen and his British officers makes clear, English is the language of power; to map the landscape with English names is a figure for rewriting Ireland and its culture into submission and, finally, into nonexistence.

Although *Translations* may seem only indirectly about contemporary Irish politics, it dramatizes a struggle for national and cultural identity that continues to embroil Northern Ireland today. Throughout the play, for example, the mysterious and unseen Donnelly twins move around the edges of the action, guerrillas hindering the British progress through the country. Finally, when Yolland is missing, we learn the true consequences of the British mapping of Ireland. Mapping the land in English is the prelude to its occupation, as the army systematically destroys the village and countryside that they have made their own. At the play's close, we scent the sickly sweet smell of blighted potatoes, the sign of the impending famine that would weaken and disperse rural Ireland.

TRANSLATIONS

Brian Friel

CHARACTERS

MANUS	BRIDGET
SARAH	HUGH
JIMMY JACK	OWEN
MAIRE	CAPTAIN LANCEY
DOALTY	LIEUTENANT YOLLAND

Act I   An afternoon in late August 1833.
Act II   A few days later.
Act III   The evening of the following day.
One interval—between the two scenes in Act Two.

The action takes place in a hedge-school in the townland of Baile Beag/Ballybeg, an Irish-speaking community in County Donegal.

ACT ONE

The hedge-school is held in a disused barn or hay-shed or byre. Along the back wall are the remains of five or six stalls—wooden posts and chains—where cows were once milked and bedded. A double door left, large enough to allow a cart to enter. A window right. A wooden stairway without a banister leads to the upstairs living-quarters (off) of the schoolmaster and his son. Around the room are broken and forgotten implements: a cart-wheel, some lobster-pots, farming tools, a battle of hay, a churn, etc. There are also the stools and bench-seats which the pupils use and a table and chair for the master. At the door a pail of water and a soiled towel. The room is comfortless and dusty and functional—there is no trace of a woman's hand.

When the play opens, MANUS *is teaching* SARAH *to speak. He kneels beside her. She is sitting on a low stool, her head down, very tense, clutching a slate on her knees. He is coaxing her gently and firmly and—as with everything he does—with a kind of zeal.*

MANUS *is in his late twenties/early thirties; the master's older son. He is pale-faced, lightly built, intense, and works as an unpaid assistant—a monitor—to his father. His clothes are shabby; and when he moves we see that he is lame.*

SARAH's *speech defect is so bad that all her life she has been considered locally to be dumb and she has accepted this: when she wishes to communicate, she grunts and makes unintelligible nasal sounds. She has a waiflike appearance and could be any age from seventeen to thirty-five.*

JIMMY JACK CASSIE—*known as the Infant Prodigy—sits by himself, contentedly reading Homer in Greek and smiling to himself. He is a bachelor in his sixties, lives alone, and comes to these evening classes partly for the company and partly for the intellectual stimulation. He is fluent in Latin and Greek but is in no way pedantic—to him it is perfectly normal to speak these tongues. He never washes. His clothes—heavy top coat, hat, mittens, which he wears now—are filthy and he lives in them summer and winter, day and night. He now reads in a quiet voice and smiles in profound satisfaction. For* JIMMY *the world of the gods and the ancient myths is as real and as immediate as everyday life in the townland of Baile Beag.*

MANUS *holds* SARAH's *hands in his and he articulates slowly and distinctly into her face.*

MANUS: We're doing very well. And we're going to try it once more—just once more. Now—relax and breathe in . . . deep . . . and out . . . in . . . and out . . .

(SARAH *shakes her head vigorously and stubbornly.*)

MANUS: Come on, Sarah. This is our secret.

(*Again vigorous and stubborn shaking of* SARAH's *head.*)

MANUS: Nobody's listening. Nobody hears you.   5
JIMMY: '*Ton d'emeibet epeita thea glaukopis Athene . . .*'
MANUS: Get your tongue and your lips working. 'My name—' Come on. One more try. 'My name is—' Good girl.
SARAH: My . . .
MANUS: Great. 'My name—'   10
SARAH: My . . . my . . .
MANUS: Raise your head. Shout it out. Nobody's listening.
JIMMY: '. . . *alla hekelos estai en Atreidao domois* . . .'
MANUS: Jimmy, please! Once more—just once more—'My name—' Good girl. Come on now. Head up. Mouth open.   15
SARAH: My . . .
MANUS: Good.
SARAH: My . . .
MANUS: Great.
SARAH: My name . . .   20
MANUS: Yes?
SARAH: My name is . . .
MANUS: Yes?

(SARAH *pauses. Then in a rush.*)

SARAH: My name is Sarah.
MANUS: Marvellous! Bloody marvellous!   25

(MANUS *hugs* SARAH. *She smiles in shy, embarrassed pleasure.*)

Did you hear that, Jimmy?—'My name is Sarah'—clear as a bell. (*To* SARAH.) The Infant Prodigy doesn't know what we're at. (SARAH *laughs at this.* MANUS *hugs her again and stands up.*) Now we're really started! Nothing'll stop us now! Nothing in the wide world!   30

I. 6 *Ton . . . Athene* But the grey-eyed goddess Athene then replied to him (from Homer, *Odyssey*, 13.420)   **13 *alla . . . domois*** . . . but he sits at ease in the halls of the Sons of Athens . . . (from Homer, *Odyssey*, 13.423–24)

(JIMMY, *chuckling at his text, comes over to them.*)

JIMMY: Listen to this, Manus.

MANUS: Soon you'll be telling me all the secrets that have been in that head of yours all these years. Certainly, James—what is it? (*To* SARAH.) Maybe you'd set out the stools?

(MANUS *runs up the stairs.*)

35 JIMMY: Wait till you hear this, Manus.

MANUS: Go ahead. I'll be straight down.

JIMMY: '*Hos ara min phamene rabdo epemassat Athene*—' 'After Athene had said this, she touched Ulysses with her wand. She withered the fair skin of his supple limbs and destroyed
40 the flaxen hair from off his head and about his limbs she put the skin of an old man . . .'! The divil! The divil!

(MANUS *has emerged again with a bowl of milk and a piece of bread.*)

JIMMY: And wait till you hear! She's not finished with him yet!

(*As* MANUS *descends the stairs he toasts* SARAH *with his bowl.*)

JIMMY: '*Knuzosen de oi osse*—' 'She dimmed his two eyes that were so beautiful and clothed him in a vile ragged cloak be-
45 grimed with filthy smoke . . .'! D'you see! Smoke! Smoke! D'you see! Sure look at what the same turf-smoke has done to myself! (*He rapidly removes his hat to display his bald head.*) Would you call that flaxen hair?

MANUS: Of course I would.

50 JIMMY: 'And about him she cast the great skin of a filthy hind, stripped of the hair, and into his hand she thrust a staff and a wallet'! Ha-ha-ha! Athene did that to Ulysses! Made him into a tramp! Isn't she the tight one?

MANUS: You couldn't watch her, Jimmy.

55 JIMMY: You know what they call her?

MANUS: '*Glaukopis Athene.*'

JIMMY: That's it! The flashing-eyed Athene! By God, Manus, sir, if you had a woman like that about the house, it's not stripping a turf-bank you'd be thinking about—eh?

60 MANUS: She was a goddess, Jimmy.

JIMMY: Better still. Sure isn't our own Grania a class of a god- dess and—

MANUS: Who?

JIMMY: Grania—Grania—Diarmuid's Grania.

65 MANUS: Ah.

JIMMY: And sure she can't get her fill of men.

MANUS: Jimmy, you're impossible.

JIMMY: I was just thinking to myself last night: if you had the choosing between Athene and Artemis and Helen of
70 Troy—all three of them Zeus's girls—imagine three powerful-looking daughters like that all in the one parish of Athens!—now, if you had the picking between them, which would you take?

MANUS: (*To* SARAH.) Which should I take, Sarah?

JIMMY: No harm to Helen; and no harm to Artemis; and indeed 75 no harm to our own Grania, Manus. But I think I've no choice but to go bull-straight for Athene. By God, sir, them flashing eyes would fair keep a man jigged up constant!

(*Suddenly and momentarily, as if in spasm,* JIMMY *stands to attention and salutes, his face raised in pained ecstasy.* MANUS *laughs. So does* SARAH. JIMMY *goes back to his seat, and his reading.*)

MANUS: You're a dangerous bloody man, Jimmy Jack.

JIMMY: 'Flashing-eyed'! Hah! Sure Homer knows it all, boy. 80 Homer knows it all.

(MANUS *goes to the window and looks out.*)

MANUS: Where the hell has he got to?

(SARAH *goes to* MANUS *and touches his elbow. She mimes rocking a baby.*)

MANUS: Yes, I know he's at the christening; but it doesn't take them all day to put a name on a baby, does it?

(SARAH *mimes pouring drinks and tossing them back quickly.*)

MANUS: You may be sure. Which pub? 85

(SARAH *indicates.*)

MANUS: Gracie's?

(*No. Further away.*)

MANUS: Con Connie Tim's?

(*No. To the right of there.*)

MANUS: Anna na mBreag's?

(*Yes. That's it.*)

MANUS: Great. She'll fill him up. I suppose I may take the class then. 90

(MANUS *begins to distribute some books, slates and chalk, texts, etc., beside the seats.* SARAH *goes over to the straw and produces a bunch of flowers she has hidden there. During this:*)

JIMMY: '*Autar o ek limenos prosebe*—''But Ulysses went forth from the harbour and through the woodland to the place where Athene had shown him he could find the good swineherd who—'*o oi biotoio malista kedeto*'—what's that, Manus?

MANUS: 'Who cared most for his substance.' 95

JIMMY: That's it! 'The good swineherd who cared most for his substance above all the slaves that Ulysses possessed . . .'

---

37 **Hos . . . Athene** as she spoke Athene touched him with her ᵥand (from Homer, *Odyssey*, 13.429) 43 **Knuzosen . . . osse** she ⁿed his eyes (from Homer, *Odyssey*, 13.433) 56 **Glaukopis** ᵈashing-eyed Athene

91 **Autar . . . prosebe** but he went forth from the harbour (from Homer, *Odyssey*, 14.1) 94 **o . . . kedeto** he cared very much for his substance (from Homer, *Odyssey*, 14.3–4)

(SARAH *presents the flowers to* MANUS.)

MANUS: Those are lovely, Sarah.

(*But* SARAH *has fled in embarrassment to her seat and has her head buried in a book.* MANUS *goes to her.*)

MANUS: Flow-ers.

(*Pause.* SARAH *does not look up.*)

100 MANUS: Say the word: flow-ers. Come on—flow-ers.
SARAH: Flowers.
MANUS: You see?—you're off!

(MANUS *leans down and kisses the top of* SARAH*'s head.*)

MANUS: And they're beautiful flowers. Thank you.

(MAIRE *enters, a strong-minded, strong-bodied woman in her twenties with a head of curly hair. She is carrying a small can of milk.*)

MAIRE: Is this all's here? Is there no school this evening?
105 MANUS: If my father's not back, I'll take it.

(MANUS *stands awkwardly, having been caught kissing* SARAH *and with the flowers almost formally at his chest.*)

MAIRE: Well now, isn't that a pretty sight. There's your milk. How's Sarah?

(SARAH *grunts a reply.*)

MANUS: I saw you out at the hay.

(MAIRE *ignores this and goes to* JIMMY.)

MAIRE: And how's Jimmy Jack Cassie?
110 JIMMY: Sit down beside me, Maire.
MAIRE: Would I be safe?
JIMMY: No safer man in Donegal.

(MAIRE *flops on a stool beside* JIMMY.)

MAIRE: Ooooh. The best harvest in living memory, they say; but I don't want to see another like it. (*Showing* JIMMY *her*
115 *hands.*) Look at the blisters.
JIMMY: *Esne fatigata?*
MAIRE: *Sum fatigatissima.*
JIMMY: *Bene! Optime!*
MAIRE: That's the height of my Latin. Fit me better if I had
120 even that much English.
JIMMY: English? I thought you had some English?
MAIRE: Three words. Wait—there was a spake I used to have off by heart. What's this it was? (*Her accent is strange because she is speaking a foreign language and because she does not understand*
125 *what she is saying.*) 'In Norfolk we besport ourselves around the maypoll.' What about that!

───────────

116 *Esne fatigata?* are you tired?   117 *Sum fatigatissima* I am very tired   118 *Bene! Optime!* good! Excellent!

MANUS: Maypole.

(*Again* MAIRE *ignores* MANUS.)

MAIRE: God have mercy on my Aunt Mary—she taught me that when I was about four, whatever it means. Do you know what it means, Jimmy? 130
JIMMY: Sure you know I have only Irish like yourself.
MAIRE: And Latin. And Greek.
JIMMY: I'm telling you a lie: I know one English word.
MAIRE: What?
JIMMY: Bo-som. 135
MAIRE: What's a bo-som?
JIMMY: You know—(*He illustrates with his hands.*)—bo-som—bo-som—you know—Diana, the huntress, she has two powerful bosom.
MAIRE: You may be sure that's the one English word you would 140
know. (*Rises.*) Is there a drop of water about?

(MANUS *gives* MAIRE *his bowl of milk.*)

MANUS: I'm sorry I couldn't get up last night.
MAIRE: Doesn't matter.
MANUS: Biddy Hanna sent for me to write a letter to her sister in Nova Scotia. All the gossip of the parish. 'I brought the 145
cow to the bull three times last week but no good. There's nothing for it now but Big Ned Frank.'
MAIRE: (*Drinking.*) That's better.
MANUS: And she got so engrossed in it that she forgot who she was dictating to: 'The aul drunken schoolmaster and that 150
lame son of his are still footering about in the hedge-school, wasting people's good time and money.'

(MAIRE *has to laugh at this.*)

MAIRE: She did not!
MANUS: And me taking it all down. 'Thank God one of them new national schools is being built above at Poll na 155
gCaorach.' It was after midnight by the time I got back.
MAIRE: Great to be a busy man.

(MAIRE *moves away.* MANUS *follows.*)

MANUS: I could hear music on my way past but I thought it was too late to call.
MAIRE: (*To* SARAH.) Wasn't your father in great voice last night? 160

(SARAH *nods and smiles.*)

MAIRE: It must have been near three o'clock by the time you got home?

(SARAH *holds up four fingers.*)

MAIRE: Was it four? No wonder we're in pieces.
MANUS: I can give you a hand at the hay tomorrow.
MAIRE: That's the name of a hornpipe, isn't it?—'The Scholar 165
In The Hayfield'—or is it a reel?
MANUS: If the day's good.
MAIRE: Suit yourself. The English soldiers below in the tents, them sapper fellas, they're coming up to give us a hand. I don't know a word they're saying, nor they me; but sure 170
that doesn't matter, does it?

MANUS: What the hell are you so crabbed about?!

(DOALTY *and* BRIDGET *enter noisily. Both are in their twenties.* DOALTY *is brandishing a surveyor's pole. He is an open-minded, open-hearted, generous and slightly thick young man.* BRIDGET *is a plump, fresh young girl, ready to laugh, vain, and with a countrywoman's instinctive cunning.* DOALTY *enters doing his imitation of the master.*)

DOALTY: Vesperal salutations to you all.

BRIDGET: He's coming down past Carraig na Ri and he's as full
175   as a pig!

DOALTY: *Ignari, stulti, rustici*—pot-boys and peasant whelps—semi-literates and illegitimates.

BRIDGET: He's been on the batter since this morning; he sent the wee ones home at eleven o'clock.

180   DOALTY: Three questions. Question A—Am I drunk? Question B—Am I sober? (*Into* MAIRE's *face.*) *Responde—responde!*

BRIDGET: Question C, Master—When were you last sober?

MAIRE: What's the weapon, Doalty?

BRIDGET: I warned him. He'll be arrested one of these days.

185   DOALTY: Up in the bog with Bridget and her aul fella, and the Red Coats were just across at the foot of Croc na Mona, dragging them aul chains and peeping through that big machine they lug about everywhere with them—you know the name of it, Manus?

190   MAIRE: Theodolite.

BRIDGET: How do you know?

MAIRE: They leave it in our byre at night sometimes if it's raining.

JIMMY: Theodolite—what's the etymology of that word, Manus?

195   MANUS: No idea.

BRIDGET: Get on with the story.

JIMMY: *Theo—theos*—something to do with a god. Maybe *thea*—a goddess! What shape's the yoke?

DOALTY: 'Shape!' Will you shut up, you aul eejit you! Anyway,
200   every time they'd stick one of these poles into the ground and move across the bog, I'd creep up and shift it twenty or thirty paces to the side.

BRIDGET: God!

DOALTY: Then they'd come back and stare at it and look at their
205   calculations and stare at it again and scratch their heads. And cripes, d'you know what they ended up doing?

BRIDGET: Wait till you hear!

DOALTY: They took the bloody machine apart!

(*And immediately he speaks in gibberish—an imitation of two very agitated and confused sappers in rapid conversation.*)

BRIDGET: That's the image of them!

210   MAIRE: You must be proud of yourself, Doalty.

DOALTY: What d'you mean?

MAIRE: That was a very clever piece of work.

MANUS: It was a gesture.

MAIRE: What sort of gesture?

MANUS: Just to indicate . . . a presence.   215

MAIRE: Hah!

BRIDGET: I'm telling you—you'll be arrested.

(*When* DOALTY *is embarrassed—or pleased—he reacts physically. He now grabs* BRIDGET *around the waist.*)

DOALTY: What d'you make of that for an implement, Bridget? Wouldn't that make a great aul shaft for your churn?

BRIDGET: Let go of me, you dirty brute! I've a headline to do   220
before Big Hughie comes.

MANUS: I don't think we'll wait for him. Let's get started.

(*Slowly, reluctantly they begin to move to their seats and specific tasks.* DOALTY *goes to the bucket of water at the door and washes his hands.* BRIDGET *sets up a hand-mirror and combs her hair.*)

BRIDGET: Nellie Ruadh's baby was to be christened this morning. Did any of yous hear what she called it? Did you, Sarah?

(SARAH *grunts:* No.)

BRIDGET: Did you, Maire?   225

MAIRE: No.

BRIDGET: Our Seamus says she was threatening she was going to call it after its father.

DOALTY: Who's the father?

BRIDGET: That's the point, you donkey you!   230

DOALTY: Ah.

BRIDGET: So there's a lot of uneasy bucks about Baile Beag this day.

DOALTY: She told me last Sunday she was going to call it Jimmy.

BRIDGET: You're a liar, Doalty.   235

DOALTY: Would I tell you a lie? Hi, Jimmy, Nellie Ruadh's aul fella's looking for you.

JIMMY: For me?

MAIRE: Come on, Doalty.

DOALTY: Someone told him . . .   240

MAIRE: Doalty!

DOALTY: He heard you know the first book of the Satires of Horace off by heart . . .

JIMMY: That's true.

DOALTY: and he wants you to recite it for him.   245

JIMMY: I'll do that for him certainly, certainly.

DOALTY: He's busting to hear it.

(JIMMY *fumbles in his pockets.*)

JIMMY: I came across this last night—this'll interest you—in Book Two of Virgil's *Georgics*.

DOALTY: Be God, that's my territory alright.   250

BRIDGET: You clown you! (*To* SARAH.) Hold this for me, would you? (*Her mirror.*)

JIMMY: Listen to this, Manus. '*Nigra fere et presso pinguis sub vomere terra . . .*'

DOALTY: Steady on now—easy, boys, easy—don't rush me, boys—   255

---

⁷⁶ *Ignari, stulti, rustici* ignoramuses, fools, peasants   181 *Re-*
⸻responde! answer—answer   197 *theos* a god   198 *thea*

253–54 *Nigra . . . terra* land that is black and rich beneath the
pressure of the plough

(He mimes great concentration.)

JIMMY: Manus?
MANUS: 'Land that is black and rich beneath the pressure of the plough ...'
DOALTY: Give *me* a chance!
260 JIMMY: 'And with *cui putre*—with crumbly soil—is in the main best for corn.' There you are!
DOALTY: There you are.
JIMMY: 'From no other land will you see more wagons wending homeward behind slow bullocks.' Virgil! There!
265 DOALTY: 'Slow bullocks'!
JIMMY: Isn't that what I'm always telling you? Black soil for corn. *That's* what you should have in that upper field of yours—corn, not spuds.
DOALTY: Would you listen to that fella! Too lazy be Jasus to
270 wash himself and he's lecturing me on agriculture! Would you go and take a running race at yourself, Jimmy Jack Cassie! *(Grabs SARAH.)* Come away out of this with me, Sarah, and we'll plant some corn together.
MANUS: All right—all right. Let's settle down and get some
275 work done. I know Sean Beag isn't coming—he's at the salmon. What about the Donnelly twins? *(To DOALTY.)* Are the Donnelly twins not coming any more?

(DOALTY shrugs and turns away.)

Did you ask them?
DOALTY: Haven't seen them. Not about these days.

(DOALTY begins whistling through his teeth. Suddenly the atmosphere is silent and alert.)

280 MANUS: Aren't they at home?
DOALTY: No.
MANUS: Where are they then?
DOALTY: How would I know?
BRIDGET: Our Seamus says two of the soldiers' horses were
285 found last night at the foot of the cliffs at Machaire Buidhe and ... *(She stops suddenly and begins writing with chalk on her slate.)* D'you hear the whistles of this aul slate? Sure nobody could write on an aul slippery thing like that.
MANUS: What headline did my father set you?
290 BRIDGET: 'It's easier to stamp out learning than to recall it.'
JIMMY: Book Three, the *Agricola* of Tacitus.
BRIDGET: God but you're a dose.
MANUS: Can you do it?
BRIDGET: There. Is it bad? Will he ate me?
295 MANUS: It's very good. Keep your elbow in closer to your side. Doalty?
DOALTY: I'm at the seven-times table. I'm perfect, skipper.

(MANUS moves to SARAH.)

MANUS: Do you understand those sums?

(SARAH nods: Yes. MANUS leans down to her ear.)

_____

260 *cui putre* crumbly soil

MANUS: My name is Sarah.

(MANUS goes to MAIRE. While he is talking to her the others swop books, talk quietly, etc.)

MANUS: Can I help you? What are you at?   300
MAIRE: Map of America. *(Pause.)* The passage money came last Friday.
MANUS: You never told me that.
MAIRE: Because I haven't seen you since, have I?
MANUS: You don't want to go. You said that yourself.   305
MAIRE: There's ten below me to be raised and no man in the house. What do you suggest?
MANUS: Do you want to go?
MAIRE: Did you apply for that job in the new national school?
MANUS: No.   310
MAIRE: You said you would.
MANUS: I said I might.
MAIRE: When it opens, this is finished: nobody's going to pay to go to a hedge-school.
MANUS: I know that and I ... *(He breaks off because he sees SARAH,*   315 *obviously listening, at his shoulder. She moves away again.)* I was thinking that maybe I could ...
MAIRE: It's £56 a year you're throwing away.
MANUS: I can't apply for it.
MAIRE: You *promised* me you would.   320
MANUS: My father has applied for it.
MAIRE: He has not!
MANUS: Day before yesterday.
MAIRE: For God's sake, sure you know he'd never—
MANUS: I couldn't—I can't go in against him.   325

(MAIRE looks at him for a second. Then:—)

MAIRE: Suit yourself. *(To BRIDGET.)* I saw your Seamus heading off to the Port fair early this morning.
BRIDGET: And wait till you hear this—I forgot to tell you this. He said that as soon as he crossed over the gap at Cnoc na Mona—just beyond where the soldiers are making the   330 maps—the sweet smell was everywhere.
DOALTY: You never told me that.
BRIDGET: It went out of my head.
DOALTY: He saw the crops in Port?
BRIDGET: Some.   335
MANUS: How did the tops look?
BRIDGET: Fine—I think.
DOALTY: In flower?
BRIDGET: I don't know. I think so. He didn't say.
MANUS: Just the sweet smell—that's all?   340
BRIDGET: They say that's the way it snakes in, don't they? First the smell; and then one morning the stalks are all black and limp.
DOALTY: Are you stupid? It's the rotting stalks makes the sweet smell for God's sake. That's what the smell is—rotting   345 stalks.
MAIRE: Sweet smell! Sweet smell! Every year at this time somebody comes back with stories of the sweet smell. Sweet God, did the potatoes ever fail in Baile Beag? Well, did they ever—ever? Never! There was never blight here.   350 Never. Never. But we're always sniffing about for it, aren't

we?—looking for disaster. The rents are going to go up again—the harvest's going to be lost—the herring have gone away for ever—there's going to be evictions. Honest to God, some of you people aren't happy unless you're mis-erable and you'll not be right content until you're dead!

355

DOALTY: Bloody right, Maire. And sure St Colmcille prophe-sied there'd never be blight here. He said:

> The spuds will bloom in Baile Beag
> Till rabbits grow an extra lug.

360

And sure that'll never be. So we're all right. Seven threes are twenty-one; seven fours are twenty-eight; seven fives are forty-nine—Hi, Jimmy, do you fancy my chances as boss of the new national school?

365   JIMMY: What's that?—what's that?

DOALTY: Agh, g'way back home to Greece, son.

MAIRE: You ought to apply, Doalty.

DOALTY: D'you think so? Cripes, maybe I will. Hah!

BRIDGET: Did you know that you start at the age of six and you

370   have to stick at it until you're twelve at least—no matter how smart you are or how much you know.

DOALTY: Who told you that yarn?

BRIDGET: And every child from every house has to go all day, every day, summer or winter. That's the law.

375   DOALTY: I'll tell you something—nobody's going to go near them—they're not going to take on—law or no law.

BRIDGET: And everything's free in them. You pay for nothing except the books you use; that's what our Seamus says.

DOALTY: 'Our Seamus.' Sure your Seamus wouldn't pay any-

380   way. She's making this all up.

BRIDGET: Isn't that right, Manus?

MANUS: I think so.

BRIDGET: And from the very first day you go, you'll not hear one word of Irish spoken. You'll be taught to speak English

385   and every subject will be taught through English and everyone'll end up as cute as the Buncrana people.

(SARAH *suddenly grunts and mimes a warning that the master is com-ing. The atmosphere changes. Sudden business. Heads down.*)

DOALTY: He's here, boys. Cripes, he'll make yella meal out of me for those bloody tables.

BRIDGET: Have you any extra chalk, Manus?

390   MAIRE: And the atlas for me.

(DOALTY *goes to* MAIRE *who is sitting on a stool at the back.*)

DOALTY: Swop you seats.

MAIRE: Why?

DOALTY: There's an empty one beside the Infant Prodigy.

MAIRE: I'm fine here.

395   DOALTY: Please, Maire. I want to jouk in the back here.

(MAIRE *rises.*)

God love you. (*Aloud.*) Anyone got a bloody table-book? Cripes, I'm wrecked.

(SARAH *gives him one.*)

I'm dying about you.

(*In his haste to get to the back seat,* DOALTY *bumps into* BRIDGET *who is kneeling on the floor and writing laboriously on a slate resting on top of a bench-seat.*)

BRIDGET: Watch where you're going, Doalty!

(DOALTY *gooses* BRIDGET. *She squeals. Now the quiet hum of work:* JIMMY *reading Homer in a low voice;* BRIDGET *copying her headline;* MAIRE *studying the atlas;* DOALTY, *his eyes shut tight, mouthing his tables;* SARAH *doing sums. After a few seconds:—*)

BRIDGET: Is this 'g' right, Manus? How do you put a tail on it?   400

DOALTY: Will you shut up! I can't concentrate!

(*A few more seconds of work. Then* DOALTY *opens his eyes and looks around.*)

False alarm, boys. The bugger's not coming at all. Sure the bugger's hardly fit to walk.

(*And immediately* HUGH *enters. A large man, with residual dignity, shabbily dressed, carrying a stick. He has, as always, a large quan-tity of drink taken, but he is by no means drunk. He is in his early sixties.*)

HUGH: *Adsum*, Doalty, *adsum*. Perhaps not in *sobrietate perfecta* but adequately *sobrius* to overhear your quip. Vesperal saluta-   405 tions to you all.

(*Various responses.*)

JIMMY: *Ave*, Hugh.

HUGH: James. (*He removes his hat and coat and hands them and his stick to* MANUS, *as if to a footman.*) Apologies for my late ar-rival: we were celebrating the baptism of Nellie Ruadh's   410 baby.

BRIDGET: (*Innocently.*) What name did she put on it, Master?

HUGH: Was it Eamon? Yes, it was Eamon.

BRIDGET: Eamon Donal from Tor! Cripes!

HUGH: And after the *caerimonia nominationis*—Maire?   415

MAIRE: The ritual of naming.

HUGH: Indeed—we then had a few libations to mark the occa-sion. Altogether very pleasant. The derivation of the word 'baptize'?—where are my Greek scholars? Doalty?

DOALTY: Would it be—ah—ah—   420

HUGH: Too slow. James?

JIMMY: 'Baptizein'—to dip or immerse.

HUGH: Indeed—our friend Pliny Minor speaks of the 'baptis-terium'—the cold bath.

DOALTY: Master.   425

HUGH: Doalty?

DOALTY: I suppose you could talk then about baptizing a sheep at sheep-dipping, could you?

(*Laughter. Comments.*)

---

404 ***adsum*** I am present; ***sobrietate perfecta*** with complete so-briety   405 ***sobrius*** sober   407 ***Ave*** hail   415 ***caerimonia nominationis*** ceremony of naming   422 ***baptizein*** to dip or im-merse   423 ***baptisterium*** a cold bath, swimming pool

HUGH: Indeed—the precedent is there—the day you were appropriately named Doalty—seven nines?

DOALTY: What's that, Master?

HUGH: Seven times nine?

DOALTY: Seven nines—seven nines—seven times nine—seven times nine are—cripes, it's on the tip of my tongue, Master—I knew it for sure this morning—funny that's the only one that foxes me—

BRIDGET: (*Prompt.*) Sixty-three.

DOALTY: What's wrong with me: sure seven nines are fifty-three, Master.

HUGH: Sophocles from Colonus would agree with Doalty Dan Doalty from Tulach Alainn: 'To know nothing is the sweetest life.' Where's Sean Beag?

MANUS: He's at the salmon.

HUGH: And Nora Dan?

MAIRE: She says she's not coming back any more.

HUGH: Ah. Nora Dan can now write her name—Nora Dan's education is complete. And the Donnelly twins?

(*Brief pause. Then:—*)

BRIDGET: They're probably at the turf. (*She goes to* HUGH.) There's the one-and-eight I owe you for last quarter's arithmetic and there's my one-and-six for this quarter's writing.

HUGH: *Gratias tibi ago.* (*He sits at his table.*) Before we commence our *studia* I have three items of information to impart to you—(*To* MANUS.) A bowl of tea, strong tea, black—

(MANUS *leaves.*)

Item A: on my perambulations today—Bridget? Too slow. Maire?

MAIRE: *Perambulare*—to walk about.

HUGH: Indeed—I encountered Captain Lancey of the Royal Engineers who is engaged in the ordnance survey of this area. He tells me that in the past few days two of his horses have strayed and some of his equipment seems to be mislaid. I expressed my regret and suggested he address you himself on these matters. He then explained that he does not speak Irish. Latin? I asked. None. Greek? Not a syllable. He speaks—on his own admission—only English; and to his credit he seemed suitably verecund—James?

JIMMY: *Verecundus*—humble.

HUGH: Indeed—he voiced some surprise that we did not speak his language. I explained that a few of us did, on occasion—outside the parish of course—and then usually for the purposes of commerce, a use to which his tongue seemed particularly suited—(*Shouts.*) and a slice of soda bread—and I went on to propose that our own culture and the classical tongues made a happier conjugation—Doalty?

DOALTY: *Conjugo*—I join together.

(DOALTY *is so pleased with himself that he prods and winks at* BRIDGET.)

HUGH: Indeed—English, I suggested, couldn't really express us. And again to his credit he acquiesced to my logic. Acquiesced—Maire?

(MAIRE *turns away impatiently.* HUGH *is unaware of the gesture.*)

Too slow. Bridget?

BRIDGET: *Acquiesco.*

HUGH: *Procede.*

BRIDGET: *Acquiesco, acquiescere, acquievi, acquietum.*

HUGH: Indeed—and Item B . . .

MAIRE: Master.

HUGH: Yes?

(MAIRE *gets to her feet uneasily but determinedly. Pause.*)

Well, girl?

MAIRE: We should all be learning to speak English. That's what my mother says. That's what I say. That's what Dan O'Connell said last month in Ennis. He said the sooner we all learn to speak English the better.

(*Suddenly several speak together.*)

JIMMY: What's she saying? What? What?

DOALTY: It's Irish he uses when he's travelling around scrounging votes.

BRIDGET: And sleeping with married women. Sure no woman's safe from that fella.

JIMMY: Who-who-who? Who's this? Who's this?

HUGH: *Silentium!* (*Pause.*) Who is she talking about?

MAIRE: I'm talking about Daniel O'Connell.

HUGH: Does she mean that little Kerry politician?

MAIRE: I'm talking about the Liberator, Master, as you well know. And what he said was this: 'The old language is a barrier to modern progress.' He said that last month. And he's right. I don't want Greek. I don't want Latin. I want English.

(MANUS *reappears on the platform above.*)

I want to be able to speak English because I'm going to America as soon as the harvest's all saved.

(MAIRE *remains standing.* HUGH *puts his hand into his pocket and produces a flask of whiskey. He removes the cap, pours a drink into it, tosses it back, replaces the cap, puts the flask back into his pocket. Then:—*)

HUGH: We have been diverted—*diverto*—*divertere*—Where were we?

DOALTY: Three items of information, Master. You're at Item B.

HUGH: Indeed—Item B—Item B—yes—On my way to the christening this morning I chanced to meet Mr George Alexander, Justice of the Peace. We discussed the new national school. Mr Alexander invited me to take charge of it when it opens. I thanked him and explained that I could do

---

451 ***Gratias tibi ago*** I thank you   452 ***studia*** studies   456 ***perambulare*** to walk through   466 ***verecundus*** shame-faced, modest   474 ***conjugo*** I join together

480 ***Procede*** proceed   481 ***acquiesco, acquiescere*** to rest, to find comfort in   496 ***Silentium!*** silence!   505 ***diverto, divertere*** to turn away

that only if I were free to run it as I have run this hedge-school for the past thirty-five years—filling what our friend Euripides calls the 'aplestos pithos'—James?
JIMMY: 'The cask that cannot be filled.'
HUGH: Indeed—and Mr. Alexander retorted courteously and emphatically that he hopes that is how it will be run.

(MAIRE *now sits.*)

Indeed. I have had a strenuous day and I am weary of you all. (*He rises.*) Manus will take care of you.

(HUGH *goes towards the steps.* OWEN *enters.* OWEN *is the younger son, a handsome, attractive young man in his twenties. He is dressed smartly—a city man. His manner is easy and charming: everything he does is invested with consideration and enthusiasm. He now stands framed in the doorway, a travelling bag across his shoulder.*)

OWEN: Could anybody tell me is this where Hugh Mor O'Donnell holds his hedge-school?
DOALTY: It's Owen—Owen Hugh! Look, boys—it's Owen Hugh!

(OWEN *enters. As he crosses the room he touches and has a word for each person.*)

OWEN: Doalty! (*Playful punch.*) How are you, boy? *Jacobe, quid agis?* Are you well?
JIMMY: Fine. Fine.
OWEN: And Bridget! Give us a kiss. Aaaaaah!
BRIDGET: You're welcome, Owen.
OWEN: It's not—? Yes, it *is* Maire Chatach! God! A young woman.
MAIRE: How are you, Owen?

(OWEN *is now in front of* HUGH. *He puts his two hands on his* FATHER's *shoulders.*)

OWEN: And how's the old man himself?
HUGH: Fair—fair.
OWEN: Fair? For God's sake you never looked better! Come here to me. (*He embraces* HUGH *warmly and genuinely.*) Great to see you, Father. Great to be back.

(HUGH's *eyes are moist—partly joy, partly the drink.*)

HUGH: I—I'm—I'm—pay no attention to—
OWEN: Come on—come on—come on—(*He gives* HUGH *his handkerchief.*) Do you know what you and I are going to do tonight? We are going to go up to Anna na mBreag's . . .
DOALTY: Not there, Owen.
OWEN: Why not?
DOALTY: Her poteen's worse than ever.
BRIDGET: They say she puts frogs in it!
OWEN: All the better. (*To* HUGH.) And you and I are going to get footless drunk. That's arranged.

---

aplestos pithos unfillable cask   525–526 *Jacobe, quid agis?* ... are you?

(OWEN *sees* MANUS *coming down the steps with tea and soda bread. They meet at the bottom.*)

And Manus!
MANUS: You're welcome, Owen.
OWEN: I know I am. And it's great to be here. (*He turns round, arms outstretched.*) I can't believe it. I come back after six years and everything's just as it was! Nothing's changed! Not a thing! (*Sniffs.*) Even that smell—that's the same smell this place always had. What is it anyway? Is it the straw?
DOALTY: Jimmy Jack's feet.

(*General laughter. It opens little pockets of conversation round the room.*)

OWEN: And Doalty Dan Doalty hasn't changed either!
DOALTY: Bloody right, Owen.
OWEN: Jimmy, are you well?
JIMMY: Dodging about.
OWEN: Any word of the big day?

(*This is greeted with 'ohs' and 'ahs.'*)

Time enough, Jimmy. Homer's easier to live with, isn't he?
MAIRE: We heard stories that you own ten big shops in Dublin—is it true?
OWEN: Only nine.
BRIDGET: And you've twelve horses and six servants.
OWEN: Yes—that's true. God Almighty, would you listen to them—taking a hand at me!
MANUS: When did you arrive?
OWEN: We left Dublin yesterday morning, spent last night in Omagh and got here half an hour ago.
MANUS: You're hungry then.
HUGH: Indeed—get him food—get him a drink.
OWEN: Not now, thanks; later. Listen—am I interrupting you all?
HUGH: By no means. We're finished for the day.
OWEN: Wonderful. I'll tell you why. Two friends of mine are waiting outside the door. They'd like to meet you and I'd like you to meet them. May I bring them in?
HUGH: Certainly. You'll all eat and have . . .
OWEN: Not just yet, Father. You've seen the sappers working in this area for the past fortnight, haven't you? Well, the older man is Captain Lancey . . .
HUGH: I've met Captain Lancey.
OWEN: Great. He's the cartographer in charge of this whole area. Cartographer—James?

(OWEN *begins to play this game—his father's game—partly to involve his classroom audience, partly to show he has not forgotten it, and indeed partly because he enjoys it.*)

JIMMY: A maker of maps.
OWEN: Indeed—and the younger man that I travelled with from Dublin, his name is Lieutenant Yolland and he is attached to the toponymic department—Father?—*responde—responde!*
HUGH: He gives names to places.
OWEN: Indeed—although he is in fact an orthographer—Doalty?—too slow—Manus?

MANUS: The correct spelling of those names.   595

OWEN: Indeed—indeed!

(OWEN *laughs and claps his hands. Some of the others join in.*)

Beautiful! Beautiful! Honest to God, it's such a delight to be back here with you all again—'civilized' people. Anyhow—may I bring them in?

HUGH: Your friends are our friends.   600

OWEN: I'll be straight back.

(*There is general talk as* OWEN *goes towards the door. He stops beside* SARAH.)

OWEN: That's a new face. Who are you?

(*A very brief hesitation. Then:—*)

SARAH: My name is Sarah.

OWEN: Sarah who?

SARAH: Sarah Johnny Sally.   605

OWEN: Of course! From Bun na hAbhann! I'm Owen—Owen Hugh Mor. From Baile Beag. Good to see you.

(*During this* OWEN—SARAH *exchange.*)

HUGH: Come on now. Let's tidy this place up. (*He rubs the top of his table with his sleeve.*) Move, Doalty—lift those books off the floor.   610

DOALTY: Right, Master; certainly, Master; I'm doing my best, Master.

(OWEN *stops at the door.*)

OWEN: One small thing, Father.

HUGH: *Silentium!*

OWEN: I'm on their pay-roll.   615

(SARAH, *very elated at her success, is beside* MANUS.)

SARAH: I said it, Manus!

(MANUS *ignores* SARAH. *He is much more interested in* OWEN *now.*)

MANUS: You haven't enlisted, have you?!

(SARAH *moves away.*)

OWEN: Me a soldier? I'm employed as a part-time, underpaid, civilian interpreter. My job is to translate the quaint, archaic tongue you people persist in speaking into the King's good English.   620

(*He goes out.*)

HUGH: Move—move—move! Put some order on things! Come on, Sarah—hide that bucket. Whose are these slates? Somebody take these dishes away. *Festinate! Festinate!*

(MANUS *goes to* MAIRE *who is busy tidying.*)

---

624 **Festinate!** hurry!

MANUS: You didn't tell me you were definitely leaving.   625

MAIRE: Not now.

HUGH: Good girl, Bridget. That's the style.

MANUS: You might at least have told me.

HUGH: Are these your books, James?

JIMMY: Thank you.   630

MANUS: Fine! Fine! Go ahead! Go ahead!

MAIRE: You talk to me about getting married—with neither a roof over your head nor a sod of ground under your foot. I suggest you go for the new school; but no—'My father's in for that.' Well now he's got it and now this is finished and now you've nothing.   635

MANUS: I can always . . .

MAIRE: What? Teach classics to the cows? Agh—

(MAIRE *moves away from* MANUS. OWEN *enters with* LANCEY *and* YOLLAND. CAPTAIN LANCEY *is middle-aged; a small, crisp officer, expert in his field as cartographer but uneasy with people—especially civilians, especially these foreign civilians. His skill is with deeds, not words.* LIEUTENANT YOLLAND *is in his late twenties/early thirties. He is tall and thin and gangling, blond hair, a shy, awkward manner. A soldier by accident.*)

OWEN: Here we are. Captain Lancey—my father.

LANCEY: Good evening.   640

(HUGH *becomes expansive, almost courtly, with his visitors.*)

HUGH: You and I have already met, sir.

LANCEY: Yes.

OWEN: And Lieutenant Yolland—both Royal Engineers—my father.

HUGH: You're very welcome, gentlemen.   645

YOLLAND: How do you do.

HUGH: *Gaudeo vos hic adesse.*

OWEN: And I'll make no other introductions except that these are some of the people of Baile Beag and—what?—well you're among the best people in Ireland now. (*He pauses to allow* LANCEY *to speak.* LANCEY *does not.*) Would you like to say a few words, Captain?   650

HUGH: What about a drop, sir?

LANCEY: A what?

HUGH: Perhaps a modest refreshment? A little sampling of our *aqua vitae*?   655

LANCEY: No, no.

HUGH: Later perhaps when—

LANCEY: I'll say what I have to say, if I may, and as briefly as possible. Do they speak *any* English, Roland?   660

OWEN: Don't worry. I'll translate.

LANCEY: I see. (*He clears his throat. He speaks as if he were addressing children—a shade too loudly and enunciating excessively.*) You may have seen me—seen me—working in this section—section?—working. We are here—here—in this place—   665
you understand?—to make a map—a map—a map and—

JIMMY: *Nonne Latine loquitur?*

---

647 **Gaudeo . . . adesse** welcome   667 **Nonne Latine loquitur?** does he not speak Latin?

(HUGH *holds up a restraining hand.*)

HUGH: James.
LANCEY: (*To* JIMMY.) I do not speak Gaelic, sir.

(*He looks at* OWEN.)

670 OWEN: Carry on.
LANCEY: A map is a representation on paper—a picture—you understand picture?—a paper picture—showing, representing this country—yes?—showing your country in miniature—a scaled drawing on paper of—of—of—

(*Suddenly* DOALTY *sniggers. Then* BRIDGET. *Then* SARAH. OWEN *leaps in quickly.*)

675 OWEN: It might be better if you *assume* they understand you—
LANCEY: Yes?
OWEN: And I'll translate as you go along.
LANCEY: I see. Yes. Very well. Perhaps you're right. Well. What we are doing is this. (*He looks at* OWEN. OWEN *nods reassur-*
680 *ingly.*) His Majesty's government has ordered the first ever comprehensive survey of this entire country—a general triangulation which will embrace detailed hydrographic and topographic information and which will be executed to a scale of six inches to the English mile.
685 HUGH: (*Pouring a drink.*) Excellent—excellent.

(LANCEY *looks at* OWEN.)

OWEN: A new map is being made of the whole country.

(LANCEY *looks to* OWEN: *Is that all?* OWEN *smiles reassuringly and indicates to proceed.*)

LANCEY: This enormous task has been embarked on so that the military authorities will be equipped with up-to-date and accurate information on every corner of this part of the Empire.
690 OWEN: The job is being done by soldiers because they are skilled in this work.
LANCEY: And also so that the entire basis of land valuation can be reassessed for purposes of more equitable taxation.
OWEN: This new map will take the place of the estate agent's
695 map so that from now on you will know exactly what is yours in law.
LANCEY: In conclusion I wish to quote two brief extracts from the white paper which is our governing charter: (*Reads*) 'All former surveys of Ireland originated in forfeiture and vio-
700 lent transfer of property; the present survey has for its object the relief which can be afforded to the proprietors and occupiers of land from unequal taxation.'
OWEN: The captain hopes that the public will cooperate with the sappers and that the new map will mean that taxes are
705 reduced.
HUGH: A worthy enterprise—*opus honestum!* And Extract B?
LANCEY: 'Ireland is privileged. No such survey is being undertaken in England. So this survey cannot but be received as

_____
strum an honourable task

proof of the disposition of this government to advance the interests of Ireland.' My sentiments, too.   710
OWEN: This survey demonstrates the government's interest in Ireland and the captain thanks you for listening so attentively to him.
HUGH: Our pleasure, Captain.
LANCEY: Lieutenant Yolland?   715
YOLLAND: I—I—I've nothing to say—really—
OWEN: The captain is the man who actually makes the new map. George's task is to see that the place-names on this map are . . . correct. (*To* YOLLAND.) Just a few words—they'd like to hear you. (*To class.*) Don't you want to hear 720
George, too?
MAIRE: Has he anything to say?
YOLLAND: (*To* MAIRE.) Sorry—sorry?
OWEN: She says she's dying to hear you.
YOLLAND: (*To* MAIRE.) Very kind of you—thank you . . . (*To 725
class.*) I can only say that I feel—I feel very foolish to—to—to be working here and not to speak your language. But I intend to rectify that—with Roland's help—indeed I do.
OWEN: He wants me to teach him Irish!
HUGH: You are doubly welcome, sir.   730
YOLLAND: I think your countryside is—is—is—is very beautiful. I've fallen in love with it already. I hope we're not too—too crude an intrusion on your lives. And I know that I'm going to be happy, very happy, here.
OWEN: He is already a committed Hibernophile—   735
JIMMY: He loves—
OWEN: All right, Jimmy—we know—he loves Baile Beag; and he loves you all.
HUGH: Please . . . May I . . . ?

(HUGH *is now drunk. He holds on to the edge of the table.*)

OWEN: Go ahead, Father. (*Hands up for quiet.*) Please—please. 740
HUGH: And we, gentlemen, we in turn are happy to offer you our friendship, our hospitality, and every assistance that you may require. Gentlemen—welcome!

(*A few desultory claps. The formalities are over. General conversation. The soldiers meet the locals.* MANUS *and* OWEN *meet down stage.*)

OWEN: Lancey's a bloody ramrod but George's all right. How are you anyway?   745
MANUS: What sort of a translation was that, Owen?
OWEN: Did I make a mess of it?
MANUS: You weren't saying what Lancey was saying!
OWEN: 'Uncertainty in meaning is incipient poetry'—who said that?   750
MANUS: There was nothing uncertain about what Lancey said: it's a bloody military operation, Owen! And what's Yolland's function? What's 'incorrect' about the place-names we have here?
OWEN: Nothing at all. They're just going to be standardized.   755
MANUS: You mean changed into English?
OWEN: Where there's ambiguity, they'll be Anglicized.
MANUS: And they call you Roland! They both call you Roland!
OWEN: Shhhhh. Isn't it ridiculous? They seemed to get it wrong from the very beginning—or else they can't pronounce 760
Owen. I was afraid some of you bastards would laugh.

MANUS: Aren't you going to tell them?

OWEN: Yes—yes—soon—soon.

MANUS: But they . . .

765 OWEN: Easy, man, easy. Owen—Roland—what the hell. It's only a name. It's the same me, isn't it? Well, isn't it?

MANUS: Indeed it is. It's the same Owen.

OWEN: And the same Manus. And in a way we complement each other. (*He punches* MANUS *lightly, playfully and turns to*
770 *join the others. As he goes.*) All right—who has met whom? Isn't this a job for the go-between?

(MANUS *watches* OWEN *move confidently across the floor, taking* MAIRE *by the hand and introducing her to* YOLLAND. HUGH *is trying to negotiate the steps.* JIMMY *is lost in a text.* DOALTY *and* BRIDGET *are reliving their giggling.* SARAH *is staring at* MANUS.)

ACT TWO

SCENE I

The sappers have already mapped most of the area. YOLLAND's *official task, which* OWEN *is now doing, is to take each of the Gaelic names— every hill, stream, rock, even every patch of ground which possessed its own distinctive Irish name—and Anglicize it, either by changing it into its approximate English sound or by translating it into English words. For example, a Gaelic name like Cnoc Ban could become Knockban or—directly translated—Fair Hill. These new standardized names were entered into the Name-Book, and when the new maps appeared they contained all these new Anglicized names.* OWEN's *official function as translator is to pronounce each name in Irish and then provide the English translation.*

The hot weather continues. It is late afternoon some days later.

Stage right: an improvised clothes-line strung between the shafts of the cart and a nail in the wall; on it are some shirts and socks.

A large map—one of the new blank maps—is spread out on the floor. OWEN *is on his hands and knees, consulting it. He is totally engrossed in his task which he pursues with great energy and efficiency.*

YOLLAND's *hesitancy has vanished—he is at home here now. He is sitting on the floor, his long legs stretched out before him, his back resting against a creel, his eyes closed. His mind is elsewhere. One of the reference books—a church registry—lies open on his lap.*

Around them are various reference books, the Name-Book, a bottle of poteen, some cups, etc.

OWEN *completes an entry in the Name-Book and returns to the map on the floor.*

OWEN: Now. Where have we got to? Yes—the point where that stream enters the sea—that tiny little beach there. George!

YOLLAND: Yes. I'm listening. What do you call it? Say the Irish name again?

5 OWEN: Bun na hAbhann.

YOLLAND: Again.

OWEN: Bun na hAbhann.

YOLLAND: Bun na hAbhann.

OWEN: That's terrible, George.

10 YOLLAND: I know. I'm sorry. Say it again.

OWEN: Bun na hAbhann.

YOLLAND: Bun na hAbhann.

OWEN: That's better. Bun is the Irish word for bottom. And Abha means river. So it's literally the mouth of the river.

YOLLAND: Let's leave it alone. There's no English equivalent 15 for a sound like that.

OWEN: What is it called in the church registry?

(*Only now does* YOLLAND *open his eyes.*)

YOLLAND: Let's see . . . Banowen.

OWEN: That's wrong. (*Consults text.*) The list of freeholders calls it Owenmore—that's completely wrong: Owenmore's the 20 big river at the west end of the parish. (*Another text.*) And in the grand jury lists it's called—God!—Binhone!—wherever they got that. I suppose we could Anglicize it to Bunowen; but somehow that's neither fish nor flesh.

(YOLLAND *closes his eyes again.*)

YOLLAND: I give up. 25

OWEN: (*At map.*) Back to first principles. What are we trying to do?

YOLLAND: Good question.

OWEN: We are trying to denominate and at the same time describe that tiny area of soggy, rocky, sandy ground where 30 that little stream enters the sea, an area known locally as Bun na hAbhann . . . Burnfoot! What about Burnfoot?

YOLLAND: (*Indifferently.*) Good, Roland, Burnfoot's good.

OWEN: George, my name isn't . . .

YOLLAND: B-u-r-n-f-o-o-t? 35

OWEN: Are you happy with that?

YOLLAND: Yes.

OWEN: Burnfoot it is then. (*He makes the entry into the Name-Book.*) Bun na hAbhann—B-u-r-n-

YOLLAND: You're becoming very skilled at this. 40

OWEN: We're not moving fast enough.

YOLLAND: (*Opens eyes again.*) Lancey lectured me again last night.

OWEN: When does he finish here?

YOLLAND: The sappers are pulling out at the end of the week. 45 The trouble is, the maps they've completed can't be printed without these names. So London screams at Lancey and Lancey screams at me. But I wasn't intimidated.

(MANUS *emerges from upstairs and descends.*)

'I'm sorry, sir,' I said, 'But certain tasks demand their own tempo. You cannot rename a whole country overnight.' 50 Your Irish air has made me bold. (*To* MANUS.) Do you want us to leave?

MANUS: Time enough. Class won't begin for another half-hour.

YOLLAND: Sorry—sorry?

OWEN: Can't you speak English? 55

(MANUS *gathers the things off the clothes-line.* OWEN *returns to the map.*)

OWEN: We now come across that beach . . .

YOLLAND: Tra—that's the Irish for beach. (*To* MANUS.) I'm picking up the odd word, Manus.

MANUS: So.

60 OWEN: . . . on past Burnfoot; and there's nothing around here that has any name that I know of until we come down here to the south end, just about here . . . and there should be a ridge of rocks there . . . Have the sappers marked it? They have. Look, George.

65 YOLLAND: Where are we?

OWEN: There.

YOLLAND: I'm lost.

OWEN: Here. And the name of that ridge is Druim Dubh. Put English on that, Lieutenant.

70 YOLLAND: Say it again.

OWEN: Druim Dubh.

YOLLAND: Dubh means black.

OWEN: Yes.

YOLLAND: And Druim means . . . what? a fort?

75 OWEN: We met it yesterday in Druim Luachra.

YOLLAND: A ridge! The Black Ridge! (*To* MANUS.) You see, Manus?

OWEN: We'll have you fluent at the Irish before the summer's over.

80 YOLLAND: Oh, I wish I were. (*To* MANUS *as he crosses to go back upstairs.*) We got a crate of oranges from Dublin today. I'll send some up to you.

MANUS: Thanks. (*To* OWEN.) Better hide that bottle. Father's just up and he'd be better without it.

85 OWEN: Can't you speak English before your man?

MANUS: Why?

OWEN: Out of courtesy.

MANUS: Doesn't he want to learn Irish? (*To* YOLLAND.) Don't you want to learn Irish?

90 YOLLAND: Sorry—sorry? I—I—

MANUS: I understand the Lanceys perfectly but people like you puzzle me.

OWEN: Manus, for God's sake!

MANUS: (*Still to* YOLLAND.) How's the work going?

95 YOLLAND: The work?—the work? Oh, it's—it's staggering along—I think—(*To* OWEN.)—isn't it? But we'd be lost without Roland.

MANUS: (*Leaving.*) I'm sure. But there are always the Rolands, aren't there?

(*He goes upstairs and exits.*)

100 YOLLAND: What was that he said?—something about Lancey, was it?

OWEN: He said we should hide that bottle before Father gets his hands on it.

YOLLAND: Ah.

105 OWEN: He's always trying to protect him.

YOLLAND: Was he lame from birth?

OWEN: An accident when he was a baby: Father fell across his cradle. That's why Manus feels so responsible for him.

YOLLAND: Why doesn't he marry?

110 OWEN: Can't afford to, I suppose.

YOLLAND: Hasn't he a salary?

OWEN: What salary? All he gets is the odd shilling Father throws him—and that's seldom enough. I got out in time, didn't I?

(*pouring a drink.*)

Easy with that stuff—it'll hit you suddenly.

115 YOLLAND: I like it.

OWEN: Let's get back to the job. Druim Dubh—what's it called in the jury lists? (*Consults texts.*)

YOLLAND: Some people here resent us.

OWEN: Dramduff—wrong as usual.

120 YOLLAND: I was passing a little girl yesterday and she spat at me.

OWEN: And it's Drimdoo here. What's it called in the registry?

YOLLAND: Do you know the Donnelly twins?

125 OWEN: Who?

YOLLAND: The Donnelly twins.

OWEN: Yes. Best fishermen about here. What about them?

YOLLAND: Lancey's looking for them.

OWEN: What for?

130 YOLLAND: He wants them for questioning.

OWEN: Probably stolen somebody's nets. Dramduffy! Nobody ever called it Dramduffy. Take your pick of those three.

YOLLAND: My head's addled. Let's take a rest. Do you want a drink?

135 OWEN: Thanks. Now, every Dubh we've come across we've changed to Duff. So if we're to be consistent, I suppose Druim Dubh has to become Dromduff.

(YOLLAND *is now looking out the window.*)

You can see the end of the ridge from where you're standing. But D-r-u-m- or D-r-o-m-? (*Name-Book.*) Do you remember—which did we agree on for Druim Luachra?

140 YOLLAND: That house immediately above where we're camped—

OWEN: Mm?

YOLLAND: The house where Maire lives.

145 OWEN: Maire? Oh, Maire Chatach.

YOLLAND: What does that mean?

OWEN: Curly-haired; the whole family are called the Chatachs. What about it?

YOLLAND: I hear music coming from that house almost every night.

150 OWEN: Why don't you drop in?

YOLLAND: Could I?

OWEN: Why not? We used D-r-o-m then. So we've got to call it D-r-o-m-d-u-f-f—all right?

YOLLAND: Go back up to where the new school is being built 155 and just say the names again for me, would you?

OWEN: That's a good idea. Poolkerry, Ballybeg—

YOLLAND: No, no; as they still are—in your own language.

OWEN: Poll na gCaorach,

(YOLLAND *repeats the names silently after him.*)

Baile Beag, Ceann Balor, Lis Maol, Machaire Buidhe, Baile 160 na gGall, Carraig na Ri, Mullach Dearg—

YOLLAND: Do you think I could live here?

OWEN: What are you talking about?

YOLLAND: Settle down here—live here.

OWEN: Come on, George. 165

YOLLAND: I mean it.

OWEN: Live on what? Potatoes? Buttermilk?

YOLLAND: It's really heavenly.

OWEN: For God's sake! The first hot summer in fifty years and
170   you think it's Eden. Don't be such a bloody romantic. You
       wouldn't survive a mild winter here.
YOLLAND: Do you think not? Maybe you're right.

(DOALTY *enters in a rush.*)

DOALTY: Hi, boys, is Manus about?
OWEN: He's upstairs. Give him a shout.
175 DOALTY: Manus! The cattle's going mad in that heat—Cripes,
       running wild all over the place. (*To* YOLLAND.) How are you
       doing, skipper?

(MANUS *appears.*)

YOLLAND: Thank you for—I—I'm very grateful to you for—
DOALTY: Wasting your time. I don't know a word you're saying.
180   Hi, Manus, there's two bucks down the road there asking
       for you.
MANUS: (*Descending.*) Who are they?
DOALTY: Never clapped eyes on them. They want to talk to you.
MANUS: What about?
185 DOALTY: They wouldn't say. Come on. The bloody beasts'll end
       up in Loch an Iubhair if they're not capped. Good luck, boys!

(DOALTY *rushes off.* MANUS *follows him.*)

OWEN: Good luck! What were you thanking Doalty for?
YOLLAND: I was washing outside my tent this morning and he
       was passing with a scythe across his shoulder and he came
190   up to me and pointed to the long grass and then cut a path-
       way round my tent and from the tent down to the road—so
       that my feet won't get wet with the dew. Wasn't that kind of
       him? And I have no words to thank him . . . I suppose you're
       right: I suppose I couldn't live here . . . Just before Doalty
195   came up to me this morning, I was thinking that at that mo-
       ment I might have been in Bombay instead of Ballybeg.
       You see, my father was at his wits end with me and finally he
       got me a job with the East India Company—some kind of a
       clerkship. That was ten, eleven months ago. So I set off for
200   London. Unfortunately I—I—I missed the boat. Literally.
       And since I couldn't face Father and hadn't enough money
       to hang about until the next sailing, I joined the army. And
       they stuck me into the Engineers and posted me to Dublin.
       And Dublin sent me here. And while I was washing this
205   morning and looking across the Tra Bhan, I was thinking
       how very, very lucky I am to be here and not in Bombay.
OWEN: Do you believe in fate?
YOLLAND: Lancey's so like my father. I was watching him last
       night. He met every group of sappers as they reported in.
210   He checked the field kitchens. He examined the horses. He
       inspected every single report—even examining the texture
       of the paper and commenting on the neatness of the hand-
       writing. The perfect colonial servant: not only must the job
       be done—it must be done with excellence. Father has that
215   drive, too; that dedication; that indefatigable energy. He
       builds roads—hopping from one end of the Empire to the
       other. Can't sit still for five minutes. He says himself the
       longest time he ever sat still was the night before Waterloo
       when they were waiting for Wellington to make up his
220   mind to attack.

OWEN: What age is he?
YOLLAND: Born in 1789—the very day the Bastille fell. I've of-
       ten thought maybe that gave his whole life its character. Do
       you think it could? He inherited a new world the day he
       was born—The Year One. Ancient time was at an end. The 225
       world had cast off its old skin. There were no longer any
       frontiers to man's potential. Possibilities were endless and
       exciting. He still believes that. The Apocalypse is just
       about to happen . . . I'm afraid I'm a great disappointment
       to him. I've neither his energy, nor his coherence, nor his 230
       belief. Do I believe in fate? The day I arrived in Ballybeg—
       no, Baile Beag—the moment you brought me in here, I had
       a curious sensation. It's difficult to describe. It was a mo-
       mentary sense of discovery; no—not quite a sense of dis-
       covery—a sense of recognition, of confirmation of some- 235
       thing I half knew instinctively; as if I had stepped . . .
OWEN: Back into ancient time?
YOLLAND: No, no. It wasn't an awareness of *direction* being
       changed but of experience being of a totally different order.
       I had moved into a consciousness that wasn't striving nor 240
       agitated, but at its ease and with its own conviction and as-
       surance. And when I heard Jimmy Jack and your father
       swapping stories about Apollo and Cuchulainn and Paris
       and Ferdia—as if they lived down the road—it was then
       that I thought—I knew—perhaps I could live here . . . 245
       (*Now embarrassed.*) Where's the pot-een?
OWEN: Poteen.
YOLLAND: Poteen—poteen—poteen. Even if I did speak Irish
       I'd always be an outsider here, wouldn't I? I may learn the
       password but the language of the tribe will always elude 250
       me, won't it? The private core will always be . . . hermetic,
       won't it?
OWEN: You can learn to decode us.

(HUGH *emerges from upstairs and descends. He is dressed for the road.
Today he is physically and mentally jaunty and alert—almost self-
consciously jaunty and alert. Indeed, as the scene progresses, one has the
sense that he is deliberately parodying himself. The moment* HUGH
gets to the bottom of the steps YOLLAND *leaps respectfully to his feet.*)

HUGH: (*As he descends.*)
       Quantumvis cursum longum fessumque moratur 255
       Sol, sacro tandem carmine vesper adest.
       I dabble in verse, Lieutenant, after the style of Ovid. (*To*
       OWEN.) A drop of that to fortify me.
YOLLAND: You'll have to translate it for me.
HUGH: Let's see— 260
       No matter how long the sun may linger on his long and
       weary journey
       At length evening comes with its sacred song.
YOLLAND: Very nice, sir.
HUGH: English succeeds in making it sound . . . plebeian.
OWEN: Where are you off to, Father? 265

II.i. 255–256 ***Quantumvis . . . adest*** no matter how long the sun
delays on his long weary course / At length evening comes with its
sacred song

HUGH: An *expeditio* with three purposes. Purpose A: to acquire a testimonial from our parish priest—(*To* YOLLAND.) a worthy man but barely literate; and since he'll ask me to write it myself, how in all modesty can I do myself justice? (*To*
270 OWEN.) Where did this [*drink*] come from?

OWEN: Anna na mBreag's.

HUGH: (*To* YOLLAND.) In that case address yourself to it with circumspection. (*And* HUGH *instantly tosses the drink back in one gulp and grimaces.*) Aaaaaagh! (*Holds out his glass for a re-*
275 *fill.*) Anna na mBreag means Anna of the Lies. And Purpose B: to talk to the builders of the new school about the kind of living accommodation I will require there. I have lived too long like a journeyman tailor.

YOLLAND: Some years ago we lived fairly close to a poet—well,
280 about three miles away.

HUGH: His name?

YOLLAND: Wordsworth—William Wordsworth.

HUGH: Did he speak of me to you?

YOLLAND: Actually I never talked to him. I just saw him out
285 walking—in the distance.

HUGH: Wordsworth? . . . No. I'm afraid we're not familiar with your literature, Lieutenant. We feel closer to the warm Mediterranean. We tend to overlook your island.

YOLLAND: I'm learning to speak Irish, sir.

290 HUGH: Good.

YOLLAND: Roland's teaching me.

HUGH: Splendid.

YOLLAND: I mean—I feel so cut off from the people here. And I was trying to explain a few minutes ago how remarkable
295 a community this is. To meet people like yourself and Jimmy Jack who actually converse in Greek and Latin. And your place names—what was the one we came across this morning?—Termon, from Terminus, the god of boundaries. It—it—it's really astonishing.

300 HUGH: We like to think we endure around truths immemorially posited.

YOLLAND: And your Gaelic literature—you're a poet yourself—

HUGH: Only in Latin, I'm afraid.

YOLLAND: I understand it's enormously rich and ornate.

305 HUGH: Indeed, Lieutenant. A rich language. A rich literature. You'll find, sir, that certain cultures expend on their vocabularies and syntax acquisitive energies and ostentations entirely lacking in their material lives. I suppose you could call us a spiritual people.

310 OWEN: (*Not unkindly; more out of embarrassment before* YOLLAND.) Will you stop that nonsense, Father.

HUGH: Nonsense? What nonsense?

OWEN: Do you know where the priest lives?

HUGH: At Lis na Muc, over near . . .

315 OWEN: No, he doesn't. Lis na Muc, the Fort of the Pigs, has become Swinefort. (*Now turning the pages of the Name-Book—a page per name.*) And to get to Swinefort you pass through Greencastle and Fair Head and Strandhill and Gort and Whiteplains. And the new school isn't at Poll na gCaorach—it's at Sheepsrock. Will you be able to find your way?

⸌ an expedition

(HUGH *pours himself another drink. Then:—*)

HUGH: Yes, it is a rich language, Lieutenant, full of the mythologies of fantasy and hope and self-deception—a syntax opulent with tomorrows. It is our response to mud cabins and a diet of potatoes; and our only method of reply- 325 ing to . . . inevitabilities. (*To* OWEN.) Can you give me the loan of half-a-crown? I'll repay you out of the subscriptions I'm collecting for the publication of my new book. (*To* YOLLAND.) It is entitled: 'The Pentaglot Preceptor or Elementary Institute of the English, Greek, Hebrew, Latin and 330 Irish Languages; Particularly Calculated for the Instruction of Such Ladies and Gentlemen as may Wish to Learn without the Help of a Master.'

YOLLAND: (*Laughs.*) That's a wonderful title!

HUGH: Between ourselves—the best part of the enterprise. 335 Nor do I, in fact, speak Hebrew. And that last phrase—'without the Help of a Master'—that was written before the new national school was thrust upon me—do you think I ought to drop it now? After all you don't dispose of the cow just because it has produced a magnificent calf, do you? 340

YOLLAND: You certainly do not.

HUGH: The phrase goes. And I'm interrupting work of moment. (*He goes to the door and stops there.*) To return briefly to that other matter, Lieutenant. I understand your sense of exclusion, of being cut off from a life here; and I trust you 345 will find access to us with my son's help. But remember that words are signals, counters. They are not immortal. And it can happen—to use an image you'll understand—it can happen that a civilization can be imprisoned in a linguistic contour which no longer matches the landscape 350 of . . . fact. Gentlemen. (*He leaves.*)

OWEN: 'An *expeditio* with three purposes': the children laugh at him: he always promises three points and he never gets beyond A and B.

YOLLAND: He's an astute man. 355

OWEN: He's bloody pompous.

YOLLAND: But so astute.

OWEN: And he drinks too much. Is it astute not to be able to adjust for survival? Enduring around truths immemorially posited—hah! 360

YOLLAND: He knows what's happening.

OWEN: What is happening?

YOLLAND: I'm not sure. But I'm concerned about my part in it. It's an eviction of sorts.

OWEN: We're making a six-inch map of the country. Is there 365 something sinister in that?

YOLLAND: Not in—

OWEN: And we're taking place-names that are riddled with confusion and—

YOLLAND: Who's confused? Are the people confused? 370

OWEN: —and we're standardizing those names as accurately and as sensitively as we can.

YOLLAND: Something is being eroded.

OWEN: Back to the romance again. All right! Fine! Fine! Look where we've got to. (*He drops on his hands and knees and stabs* 375 *a finger at the map.*) We've come to this crossroads. Come here and look at it, man! Look at it! And we call that crossroads Tobair Vree. And why do we call it Tobair Vree? I'll tell you why. Tobair means a well. But what does Vree

380 mean? It's a corruption of Brian—(*Gaelic pronunciation.*)
Brian—an erosion of Tobair Bhriain. Because a hundred-
and-fifty years ago there used to be a well there, not at the
crossroads, mind you—that would be too simple—but in a
field close to the crossroads. And an old man called Brian,
385 whose face was disfigured by an enormous growth, got it
into his head that the water in that well was blessed; and
every day for seven months he went there and bathed his
face in it. But the growth didn't go away; and one morning
Brian was found drowned in that well. And ever since that
390 crossroads is known as Tobair Vree—even though that well
has long since dried up. I know the story because my grandfather told it to me. But ask Doalty—or Maire—or Bridget—even my father—even Manus—why it's called Tobair
Vree; and do you think they'll know? I know they don't
395 know. So the question I put to you, Lieutenant, is this: what
do we do with a name like that? Do we scrap Tobair Vree altogether and call it—what?—The Cross? Crossroads? Or
do we keep piety with a man long dead, long forgotten, his
name 'eroded' beyond recognition, whose trivial little story
400 nobody in the parish remembers?
     YOLLAND: Except you.
     OWEN: I've left here.
     YOLLAND: You remember it.
     OWEN: I'm asking you: what do we write in the Name-Book?
405 YOLLAND: Tobair Vree.
     OWEN: Even though the well is a hundred yards from the ac-
     tual crossroads—and there's no well anyway—and what the
     hell does Vree mean?
     YOLLAND: Tobair Vree.
410 OWEN: That's what you want?
     YOLLAND: Yes.
     OWEN: You're certain?
     YOLLAND: Yes.
     OWEN: Fine. Fine. That's what you'll get.
415 YOLLAND: That's what you want, too, Roland.

(*Pause.*)

     OWEN: (*Explodes.*) George! For God's sake! My name is not
     Roland!
     YOLLAND: What?
     OWEN: (*Softly.*) My name is Owen.

(*Pause.*)

     YOLLAND: Not Roland?
420 OWEN: Owen.
     YOLLAND: You mean to say—?
     OWEN: Owen.
     YOLLAND: But I've been—
     OWEN: O-w-e-n.
425 YOLLAND: Where did Roland come from?
     OWEN: I don't know.
     YOLLAND: It was never Roland?
     OWEN: Never.
     YOLLAND: O my God!

(*Pause. They stare at one another. Then the absurdity of the situation
strikes them suddenly. They explode with laughter.* OWEN *pours
drinks. As they roll about, their lines overlap.*)

430 YOLLAND: Why didn't you tell me?
     OWEN: Do I look like a Roland?
     YOLLAND: Spell Owen again.
     OWEN: I was getting fond of Roland.
     YOLLAND: O my God!
435 OWEN: O-w-e-n.
     YOLLAND: What'll we write—
     OWEN: —in the Name-Book?!
     YOLLAND: R-o-w-e-n!
     OWEN: Or what about Ol-
440 YOLLAND: Ol-what?
     OWEN: Oland!

(*And again they explode.* MANUS *enters. He is very elated.*)

     MANUS: What's the celebration?
     OWEN: A christening!
     YOLLAND: A baptism!
445 OWEN: A hundred christenings!
     YOLLAND: A thousand baptisms! Welcome to Eden!
     OWEN: Eden's right! We name a thing and—bang!—it leaps
     into existence!
     YOLLAND: Each name a perfect equation with its roots.
450 OWEN: A perfect congruence with its reality. (*To* MANUS.) Take
     a drink.
     YOLLAND: Poteen—beautiful.
     OWEN: Lying Anna's poteen.
     YOLLAND: Anna na mBreag's poteen.
455 OWEN: Excellent, George.
     YOLLAND: I'll decode you yet.
     OWEN: (*Offers drink.*) Manus?
     MANUS: Not if that's what it does to you.
     OWEN: You're right. Steady—steady—sober up—sober up.
460 YOLLAND: Sober as a judge, Owen.

(MANUS *moves beside* OWEN.)

     MANUS: I've got good news! Where's Father?
     OWEN: He's gone out. What's the good news?
     MANUS: I've been offered a job.
     OWEN: Where? (*Now aware of* YOLLAND.) Come on, man—
465 speak in English.
     MANUS: For the benefit of the colonist?
     OWEN: He's a decent man.
     MANUS: Aren't they all at some level?
     OWEN: Please.

(MANUS *shrugs.*)

     He's been offered a job.
470 YOLLAND: Where?
     OWEN: Well—tell us!
     MANUS: I've just had a meeting with two men from Inis Mead-
     hon. They want me to go there and start a hedge-school.
     They're giving me a free house, free turf, and free milk; a
475 rood of standing corn; twelve drills of potatoes; and—

(*He stops.*)

     OWEN: And what?
     MANUS: A salary of £42 a year!

OWEN: Manus, that's wonderful!

480 MANUS: You're talking to a man of substance.

OWEN: I'm delighted.

YOLLAND: Where's Inis Meadhon?

OWEN: An island south of here. And they came looking for you?

485 MANUS: Well, I mean to say . . .

(OWEN *punches* MANUS.)

OWEN: Aaaaagh! This calls for a real celebration.

YOLLAND: Congratulations.

MANUS: Thank you.

OWEN: Where are you, Anna?

490 YOLLAND: When do you start?

MANUS: Next Monday.

OWEN: We'll stay with you when we're there. (*To* YOLLAND.) How long will it be before we reach Inis Meadhon?

YOLLAND: How far south is it?

495 MANUS: About fifty miles.

YOLLAND: Could we make it by December?

OWEN: We'll have Christmas together. (*Sings.*) 'Christmas Day on Inis Meadhon . . .'

YOLLAND: (*Toast.*) I hope you're very content there, Manus.

500 MANUS: Thank you.

(YOLLAND *holds out his hand.* MANUS *takes it. They shake warmly.*)

OWEN: (*Toast.*) Manus.

MANUS: (*Toast.*) To Inis Meadhon.

(*He drinks quickly and turns to leave.*)

OWEN: Hold on—hold on—refills coming up.

MANUS: I've got to go.

505 OWEN: Come on, man; this is an occasion. Where are you rushing to?

MANUS: I've got to tell Maire.

(MAIRE *enters with her can of milk.*)

MAIRE: You've got to tell Maire what?

OWEN: He's got a job!

510 MAIRE: Manus?

OWEN: He's been invited to start a hedge-school in Inis Meadhon.

MAIRE: Where?

MANUS: Inis Meadhon—the island! They're giving me £42 a

515 year and . . .

OWEN: A house, fuel, milk, potatoes, corn, pupils, what-not!

MANUS: I start on Monday.

OWEN: You'll take a drink. Isn't it great?

MANUS: I want to talk to you for—

520 MAIRE: There's your milk. I need the can back.

(MANUS *takes the can and runs up the steps.*)

...JS: (*As he goes.*) How will you like living on an island? You know George, don't you?

... wave to each other across the fields.

... orry-sorry?

... you wave to each other across the fields.

YOLLAND: Yes, we do; oh, yes; indeed we do.

MAIRE: What's he saying?

OWEN: He says you wave to each other across the fields.

MAIRE: That's right. So we do.

YOLLAND: What's she saying? 530

OWEN: Nothing—nothing—nothing. (*To* MAIRE.) What's the news?

(MAIRE *moves away, touching the text books with her toe.*)

MAIRE: Not a thing. You're busy, the two of you.

OWEN: We think we are.

MAIRE: I hear the Fiddler O'Shea's about. There's some talk of 535 a dance tomorrow night.

OWEN: Where will it be?

MAIRE: Maybe over the road. Maybe at Tobair Vree.

YOLLAND: Tobair Vree!

MAIRE: Yes. 540

YOLLAND: Tobair Vree! Tobair Vree!

MAIRE: Does he know what I'm saying?

OWEN: Not a word.

MAIRE: Tell him then.

OWEN: Tell him what? 545

MAIRE: About the dance.

OWEN: Maire says there may be a dance tomorrow night.

YOLLAND: (*To* OWEN.) Yes? May I come? (*To* MAIRE.) Would anybody object if I came?

MAIRE: (*To* OWEN.) What's he saying? 550

OWEN: (*To* YOLLAND.) Who would object?

MAIRE: (*To* OWEN.) Did you tell him?

YOLLAND: (*To* MAIRE.) Sorry-sorry?

OWEN: (*To* MAIRE.) He says may he come?

MAIRE: (*To* YOLLAND.) That's up to you. 555

YOLLAND: (*To* OWEN.) What does she say?

OWEN: (*To* YOLLAND.) She says—

YOLLAND: (*To* MAIRE.) What—what?

MAIRE: (*To* OWEN.) Well?

YOLLAND: (*To* OWEN.) Sorry-sorry? 560

OWEN: (*To* OLLAND.) Will you go?

YOLLAND: (*To* MAIRE.) Yes, yes, if I may.

MAIRE: (*To* OWEN.) What does he say?

YOLLAND: (*To* OWEN.) What is she saying?

OWEN: Oh for God's sake! (*To* MANUS *who is descending with the* 565 *empty can.*) You take on this job, Manus.

MANUS: I'll walk you up to the house. Is your mother at home? I want to talk to her.

MAIRE: What's the rush? (*To* OWEN.) Didn't you offer me a drink?

OWEN: Will you risk Anna na mBreag? 570

MAIRE: Why not.

(YOLLAND *is suddenly intoxicated. He leaps up on a stool, raises his glass and shouts.*)

YOLLAND: Anna na mBreag! Baile Beag! Inis Meadhon! Bombay! Tobair Vree! Eden! And poteen—correct, Owen?

OWEN: Perfect.

YOLLAND: And bloody marvellous stuff it is, too. I love it! 575 Bloody, bloody, bloody marvellous!

(*Simultaneously with his final 'bloody marvellous' bring up very loud the introductory music of the reel. Then immediately go to black. Retain the music throughout the very brief interval.*)

SCENE II

The following night.

This scene may be played in the schoolroom, but it would be preferable to lose—by lighting—as much of the schoolroom as possible, and to play the scene down front in a vaguely 'outside' area.

The music rises to a crescendo. Then in the distance we hear MAIRE *and* YOLLAND *approach—laughing and running. They run on, hand-in-hand. They have just left the dance. Fade the music to distant background. Then after a time it is lost and replaced by guitar music.* MAIRE *and* YOLLAND *are now down front, still holding hands and excited by their sudden and impetuous escape from the dance.*

MAIRE: O my God, that leap across the ditch nearly killed me.
YOLLAND: I could scarcely keep up with you.
MAIRE: Wait till I get my breath back.
YOLLAND: We must have looked as if we were being chased.

(They now realize they are alone and holding hands—the beginnings of embarrassment. The hands disengage. They begin to drift apart. Pause.)

5 MAIRE: Manus'll wonder where I've got to.
YOLLAND: I wonder did anyone notice us leave.

(Pause. Slightly further apart.)

MAIRE: The grass must be wet. My feet are soaking.
YOLLAND: Your feet must be wet. The grass is soaking.

(Another pause. Another few paces apart. They are now a long distance from one another.)

YOLLAND: *(Indicating himself.)* George.

*(*MAIRE *nods: Yes-yes. Then:—)*

10 MAIRE: Lieutenant George.
YOLLAND: Don't call me that. I never think of myself as Lieutenant.
MAIRE: What-what?
YOLLAND: Sorry-sorry? *(He points to himself again.)* George.

*(*MAIRE *nods: Yes-yes. Then points to herself.)*

15 MAIRE: Maire.
YOLLAND: Yes, I know you're Maire. Of course I know you're Maire. I mean I've been watching you night and day for the past—
MAIRE: *(Eagerly.)* What-what?
20 YOLLAND: *(Points.)* Maire. *(Points.)* George. *(Points both.)* Maire and George.

*(*MAIRE *nods: Yes-yes-yes.)*

I—I—I—
MAIRE: Say anything at all. I love the sound of your speech.
YOLLAND: *(Eagerly.)* Sorry-sorry?

(In acute frustration he looks around, hoping for some inspiration that will provide him with communicative means. Now he has a thought:

he tries raising his voice and articulating in a staccato style and with equal and absurd emphasis on each word.)

Every-morning-I-see-you-feeding-brown-hens-and-giving-   25
meal-to-black-calf—*(The futility of it.)*—Oh my God.

*(*MAIRE *smiles. She moves towards him. She will try to communicate in Latin.)*

MAIRE: *Tu es centurio in—in—in exercitu Britannico—*
YOLLAND: Yes-yes? Go on—go on—say anything at all—I love the sound of your speech.
MAIRE: *—et es in castris quae—quae—quae sunt in agro—(The fu-*   30
tility of it.)—O my God. (YOLLAND *smiles. He moves towards her. Now for her English words.)* George—water.
YOLLAND: 'Water'? Water! Oh yes—water—water—very good— water—good—good.
MAIRE: Fire.   35
YOLLAND: Fire—indeed—wonderful—fire, fire, fire—splen-did—splendid!
MAIRE: Ah . . . ah . . .
YOLLAND: Yes? Go on.
MAIRE: Earth.   40
YOLLAND: 'Earth'?
MAIRE: Earth. Earth. (YOLLAND *still does not understand.* MAIRE *stoops down and picks up a handful of clay. Holding it out.)* Earth.
YOLLAND: Earth! Of course—earth! Earth. Earth. Good Lord,   45
Maire, your English is perfect!
MAIRE: *(Eagerly.)* What-what?
YOLLAND: Perfect English. English perfect.
MAIRE: George—
YOLLAND: That's beautiful—oh, that's really beautiful.   50
MAIRE: George—
YOLLAND: Say it again—say it again—
MAIRE: Shhh. *(She holds her hand up for silence—she is trying to remember her one line of English. Now she remembers it and she delivers the line as if English were her language—easily, fluidly,*   55
conversationally.) George, 'In Norfolk we besport ourselves around the maypoll.'
YOLLAND: Good God, do you? That's where my mother comes from—Norfolk. Norwich actually. Not exactly Norwich town but a small village called Little Walsingham close be-   60
side it. But in our own village of Winfarthing we have a maypole too and every year on the first of May—*(He stops abruptly, only now realizing. He stares at her. She in turn misunderstands his excitement.)*
MAIRE: *(To herself.)* Mother of God, my Aunt Mary wouldn't   65
have taught me something dirty, would she?

(Pause. YOLLAND *extends his hand to* MAIRE. *She turns away from him and moves slowly across the stage.)*

YOLLAND: Maire.

II.ii. 27 *Tu . . . Britannico* you are a centurion in the British Army   30 *et . . . agro* and you are in the camp in the field

(*She still moves away.*)

Maire Chatach.

(*She still moves away.*)

70   Bun na hAbhann? (*He says the name softly, almost privately, very tentatively, as if he were searching for a sound she might respond to. He tries again.*) Druim Dubh?

(MAIRE *stops. She is listening.* YOLLAND *is encouraged.*)

Poll na gCaorach. Lis Maol.

(MAIRE *turns towards him.*)

Lis na nGall.
MAIRE: Lis na nGradh.

(*They are now facing each other and begin moving—almost imperceptibly—towards one another.*)

75   MAIRE: Carraig an Phoill.
YOLLAND: Carraig na Ri. Loch na nEan.
MAIRE: Loch an Iubhair. Machaire Buidhe.
YOLLAND: Machaire Mor. Cnoc na Mona.
MAIRE: Cnoc na nGabhar.
80   YOLLAND: Mullach.
MAIRE: Port.
YOLLAND: Tor.
MAIRE: Lag.

(*She holds out her hands to* YOLLAND. *He takes them. Each now speaks almost to himself/herself.*)

YOLLAND: I wish to God you could understand me.
85   MAIRE: Soft hands; a gentleman's hands.
YOLLAND: Because if you could understand me I could tell you how I spend my days either thinking of you or gazing up at your house in the hope that you'll appear even for a second.
MAIRE: Every evening you walk by yourself along the Tra Bhan
90   and every morning you wash yourself in front of your tent.
YOLLAND: I would tell you how beautiful you are, curly-headed Maire. I would so like to tell you how beautiful you are.
MAIRE: Your arms are long and thin and the skin on your shoulders is very white.
95   YOLLAND: I would tell you . . .
MAIRE: Don't stop—I know what you're saying.
YOLLAND: I would tell you how I want to be here—to live here—always—with you—always, always.
MAIRE: 'Always'? What is that word—'always'?
100   YOLLAND: Yes-yes; always.
MAIRE: You're trembling.
YOLLAND: Yes, I'm trembling because of you.
MAIRE: I'm trembling, too.

(*She holds his face in her hand.*)

YOLLAND: I've made up my mind . . .
105   MAIRE: Shhhh.
YOLLAND: I'm not going to leave here . . .
MAIRE: Shhhh—listen to me. I want you, too, soldier.

YOLLAND: Don't stop—I know what you're saying.
MAIRE: I want to live with you—anywhere—anywhere at all—always—always.
110
YOLLAND: 'Always'? What is that word—'always'?
MAIRE: Take me away with you, George.

(*Pause. Suddenly they kiss.* SARAH *enters. She sees them. She stands shocked, staring at them. Her mouth works. Then almost to herself.*)

SARAH: Manus . . . Manus!

(SARAH *runs off. Music to crescendo.*)

ACT THREE

The following evening. It is raining.

SARAH *and* OWEN *alone in the schoolroom.* SARAH, *more waif-like than ever, is sitting very still on a stool, an open book across her knee. She is pretending to read but her eyes keep going up to the room upstairs.* OWEN *is working on the floor as before, surrounded by his reference books, map, Name-Book, etc. But he has neither concentration nor interest; and like* SARAH *he glances up at the upstairs room.*

After a few seconds MANUS *emerges and descends, carrying a large paper bag which already contains his clothes. His movements are determined and urgent. He moves around the classroom, picking up books, examining each title carefully, and choosing about six of them which he puts into his bag. As he selects these books:—*

OWEN: You know that old limekiln beyond Con Connie Tim's pub, the place we call The Murren?—do you know why it's called The Murren?

(MANUS *does not answer.*)

I've only just discovered: it's a corruption of Saint Muranus. It seems Saint Muranus had a monastery somewhere about 5 there at the beginning of the seventh century. And over the years the name became shortened to the Murren. Very unattractive name, isn't it? I think we should go back to the original—Saint Muranus. What do you think? The original's Saint Muranus. Don't you think we should go back to that? 10

(*No response.* OWEN *begins writing the name into the Name-Book.* MANUS *is now rooting about among the forgotten implements for a piece of rope. He finds a piece. He begins to tie the mouth of the flimsy, overloaded bag—and it bursts, the contents spilling out on the floor.*)

MANUS: Bloody, bloody, bloody hell!

(*His voice breaks in exasperation: he is about to cry.* OWEN *leaps to his feet.*)

OWEN: Hold on. I've a bag upstairs.

(*He runs upstairs.* SARAH *waits until* OWEN *is off. Then:—*)

SARAH: Manus . . . Manus, I . . .

(MANUS *hears* SARAH *but makes no acknowledgement. He gathers up his belongings.* OWEN *reappears with the bag he had on his arrival.*)

OWEN: Take this one—I'm finished with it anyway. And it's supposed to keep out the rain. 15

(MANUS *transfers his few belongings.* OWEN *drifts back to his task. The packing is now complete.*)

MANUS: You'll be here for a while? For a week or two anyhow?
OWEN: Yes.
MANUS: You're not leaving with the army?
OWEN: I haven't made up my mind. Why?
20 MANUS: Those Inis Meadhon men will be back to see why I haven't turned up. Tell them—tell them I'll write to them as soon as I can. Tell them I still want the job but that it might be three or four months before I'm free to go.
OWEN: You're being damned stupid, Manus.
25 MANUS: Will you do that for me?
OWEN: Clear out now and Lancey'll think you're involved somehow.
MANUS: Will you do that for me?
OWEN: Wait a couple of days even. You know George—he's a
30 bloody romantic—maybe he's gone out to one of the islands and he'll suddenly reappear tomorrow morning. Or maybe the search party'll find him this evening lying drunk somewhere in the sandhills. You've seen him drinking that poteen—doesn't know how to handle it. Had he drink on
35 him last night at the dance?
MANUS: I had a stone in my hand when I went out looking for him—I was going to fell him. The lame scholar turned violent.
OWEN: Did anybody see you?
40 MANUS: (*Again close to tears.*) But when I saw him standing there at the side of the road—smiling—and her face buried in his shoulder—I couldn't even go close to them. I just shouted something stupid—something like, 'You're a bastard, Yolland.' If I'd even said it in English . . . 'cos he kept saying
45 'Sorry-sorry?' The wrong gesture in the wrong language.
OWEN: And you didn't see him again?
MANUS: 'Sorry?'
OWEN: Before you leave tell Lancey that—just to clear yourself.
MANUS: What have I to say to Lancey? You'll give that message
50 to the islandmen?
OWEN: I'm warning you: run away now and you're bound to be—
MANUS: (*To* SARAH.) Will you give that message to the Inis Meadhon men?
55 SARAH: I will.

(MANUS *picks up an old sack and throws it across his shoulders.*)

OWEN: Have you any idea where you're going?
MANUS: Mayo, maybe. I remember Mother saying she had cousins somewhere away out in the Erris Peninsula. (*He picks up his bag.*) Tell Father I took only the Virgil and the
60 Caesar and the Aeschylus because they're mine anyway—I bought them with the money I got for that pet lamb I reared—do you remember that pet lamb? And tell him that Nora Dan never returned the dictionary and that she still owes him two-and-six for last quarter's reading—he always
65 forgets those things.
OWEN: Yes.
MANUS: And his good shirt's ironed and hanging up in the press and his clean socks are in the butter-box under the bed.
OWEN: All right.

MANUS: And tell him I'll write.   70
OWEN: If Maire asks where you've gone . . . ?
MANUS: He'll need only half the amount of milk now, won't he? Even less than half—he usually takes his tea black. (*Pause.*) And when he comes in at night—you'll hear him; he makes a lot of noise—I usually come down and give him   75
a hand up. Those stairs are dangerous without a banister. Maybe before you leave you'd get Big Ned Frank to put up some sort of a handrail. (*Pause.*) And if you can bake, he's very fond of soda bread.
OWEN: I can give you money. I'm wealthy. Do you know what   80
they pay me? Two shillings a day for this—this—this—

(MANUS *rejects the offer by holding out his hand.*)

Goodbye, Manus.

(MANUS *and* OWEN *shake hands. Then* MANUS *picks up his bag briskly and goes towards the door. He stops a few paces beyond* SARAH, *turns, comes back to her. He addresses her as he did in Act One but now without warmth or concern for her.*)

MANUS: What is your name? (*Pause.*) Come on. What is your name?
SARAH: My name is Sarah.   85
MANUS: Just Sarah? Sarah what? (*Pause.*) Well?
SARAH: Sarah Johnny Sally.
MANUS: And where do you live? Come on.
SARAH: I live in Bun na hAbhann.

(*She is now crying quietly.*)

MANUS: Very good, Sarah Johnny Sally. There's nothing to stop   90
you now—nothing in the wide world. (*Pause. He looks down at her.*) It's all right—it's all right—you did no harm—you did no harm at all.

(*He stoops over her and kisses the top of her head—as if in absolution. Then briskly to the door and off.*)

OWEN: Good luck, Manus!
SARAH: (*Quietly.*) I'm sorry . . . I'm sorry . . . I'm so sorry,   95
Manus . . .

(OWEN *tries to work but cannot concentrate. He begins folding up the map. As he does:—*)

OWEN: Is there a class this evening?

(SARAH *nods: Yes.*)

I suppose Father knows. Where is he anyhow?

(SARAH *points.*)

Where?

(SARAH *mimes rocking a baby.*)

I don't understand—where?   100

(SARAH *repeats the mime and wipes away tears.* OWEN *is still puzzled.*)

It doesn't matter. He'll probably turn up.

(BRIDGET *and* DOALTY *enter, sacks over their heads against the rain. They are self-consciously noisier, more ebullient, more garrulous than ever—brimming over with excitement and gossip and brio.*)

DOALTY: You're missing the crack, boys! Cripes, you're missing the crack! Fifty more soldiers arrived an hour ago!

BRIDGET: And they're spread out in a big line from Sean Neal's
105   over to Lag and they're moving straight across the fields towards Cnoc na nGabhar!

DOALTY: Prodding every inch of the ground in front of them with their bayonets and scattering animals and hens in all directions!

110 BRIDGET: And tumbling everything before them—fences, ditches, haystacks, turf-stacks!

DOALTY: They came to Barney Petey's field of corn—straight through it be God as if it was heather!

BRIDGET: Not a blade of it left standing!

115 DOALTY: And Barney Petey just out of his bed and running after them in his drawers: 'You hoors you! Get out of my corn, you hoors you!'

BRIDGET: First time he ever ran in his life.

DOALTY: Too lazy, the wee get, to cut it when the weather was
120   good.

(SARAH *begins putting out the seats.*)

BRIDGET: Tell them about Big Hughie.

DOALTY: Cripes, if you'd seen your aul fella, Owen.

BRIDGET: They were all inside in Anna na mBreag's pub—all the crowd from the wake—

125 DOALTY: And they hear the commotion and they all come out to the street—

BRIDGET: Your father in front; the Infant Prodigy footless behind him!

DOALTY: And your aul fella, he sees the army stretched across
130   the countryside—

BRIDGET: O my God!

DOALTY: And Cripes he starts roaring at them!

BRIDGET: 'Visigoths! Huns! Vandals!'

DOALTY: '*Ignari! Stulti! Rustici!*'

135 BRIDGET: And wee Jimmy Jack jumping up and down and shouting, 'Thermopylae! Thermopylae!'

DOALTY: You never saw crack like it in your life, boys. Come away on out with me, Sarah, and you'll see it all.

BRIDGET: Big Hughie's fit to take no class. Is Manus about?

140 OWEN: Manus is gone.

BRIDGET: Gone where?

OWEN: He's left—gone away.

DOALTY: Where to?

OWEN: He doesn't know. Mayo, maybe.

145 DOALTY: What's on in Mayo?

OWEN: (*To* BRIDGET.) Did you see George and Maire Chatach leave the dance last night?

BRIDGET: We did. Didn't we, Doalty?

OWEN: Did you see Manus following them out?

150 BRIDGET: I didn't see him going out but I saw him coming in by himself later.

OWEN: Did George and Maire come back to the dance?

BRIDGET: No.

OWEN: Did you see them again?

BRIDGET: He left her home. We passed them going up the back   155
road—didn't we, Doalty?

OWEN: And Manus stayed till the end of the dance?

DOALTY: We know nothing. What are you asking us for?

OWEN: Because Lancey'll question me when he hears Manus's gone. (*Back to* BRIDGET.) That's the way George went   160
home? By the back road? That's where you saw him?

BRIDGET: Leave me alone, Owen. I know nothing about Yolland. If you want to know about Yolland, ask the Donnelly twins.

(*Silence.* DOALTY *moves over to the window.*)

(*To* SARAH.) He's a powerful fiddler, O'Shea, isn't he? He told our Seamus he'll come back for a night at Hallowe'en.   165

(OWEN *goes to* DOALTY *who looks resolutely out the window.*)

OWEN: What's this about the Donnellys? (*Pause.*) Were they about last night?

DOALTY: Didn't see them if they were.

(*Begins whistling through his teeth.*)

OWEN: George is a friend of mine.

DOALTY: So.   170

OWEN: I want to know what's happened to him.

DOALTY: Couldn't tell you.

OWEN: What have the Donnelly twins to do with it? (*Pause.*) Doalty!

DOALTY: I know nothing, Owen—nothing at all—I swear to   175
God. All I know is this: on my way to the dance I saw their boat beached at Port. It wasn't there on my way home, after I left Bridget. And that's all I know. As God's my judge. The half-dozen times I met him I didn't know a word he said to me; but he seemed a right enough sort ... (*With sud-*   180
den excessive interest in the scene outside.) Cripes, they're crawling all over the place! Cripes, there's millions of them! Cripes, they're levelling the whole land!

(OWEN *moves away.* MAIRE *enters. She is bareheaded and wet from the rain; her hair in disarray. She attempts to appear normal but she is in acute distress, on the verge of being distraught. She is carrying the milk-can.*)

MAIRE: Honest to God, I must be going off my head. I'm halfway here and I think to myself, 'Isn't this can very   185
light?' and I look into it and isn't it empty.

OWEN: It doesn't matter.

MAIRE: How will you manage for tonight?

OWEN: We have enough.

MAIRE: Are you sure?   190

OWEN: Plenty, thanks.

MAIRE: It'll take me no time at all to go back up for some.

OWEN: Honestly, Maire.

MAIRE: Sure it's better you have it than that black calf that's ... that ... (*She looks around.*) Have you heard anything?   195

OWEN: Nothing.

MAIRE: What does Lancey say?

OWEN: I haven't seen him since this morning.

MAIRE: What does he *think*?

200 OWEN: We really didn't talk. He was here for only a few seconds.

MAIRE: He left me home, Owen. And the last thing he said to me—he tried to speak in Irish—he said, 'I'll see you yesterday'—he meant to say 'I'll see you tomorrow.' And I laughed that much he pretended to get cross and he said
205 'Maypoll! Maypoll!' because I said that word wrong. And off he went, laughing—laughing, Owen! Do you think he's all right? What do *you* think?

OWEN: I'm sure he'll turn up, Maire.

MAIRE: He comes from a tiny wee place called Winfarthing.
210 (*She suddenly drops on her hands and knees on the floor—where* OWEN *had his map a few minutes ago—and with her finger traces out an outline map.*) Come here till you see. Look. There's Winfarthing. And there's two other wee villages right beside it; one of them's called Barton Bendish—it's there; and
215 the other's called Saxingham Nethergate—it's about there. And there's Little Walsingham—that's his mother's townland. Aren't they odd names? Sure they make no sense to me at all. And Winfarthing's near a big town called Norwich. And Norwich is in a county called Norfolk. And
220 Norfolk is in the east of England. He drew a map for me on the wet strand and wrote the names on it. I have it all in my head now: Winfarthing—Barton Bendish—Saxingham Nethergate—Little Walsingham—Norwich—Norfolk. Strange sounds, aren't they? But nice sounds; like Jimmy Jack recit-
225 ing his Homer. (*She gets to her feet and looks around; she is almost serene now. To* SARAH.) You were looking lovely last night, Sarah. Is that the dress you got from Boston? Green suits you. (*To* OWEN.) Something very bad's happened to him, Owen. I know. He wouldn't go away without telling
230 me. Where is he, Owen? You're his friend—where is he? (*Again she looks around the room; then sits on a stool.*) I didn't get a chance to do my geography last night. The master'll be angry with me. (*She rises again.*) I think I'll go home now. The wee ones have to be washed and put to bed and
235 that black calf has to be fed . . . My hands are that rough; they're still blistered from the hay. I'm ashamed of them. I hope to God there's no hay to be saved in Brooklyn. (*She stops at the door.*) Did you hear? Nellie Ruadh's baby died in the middle of the night. I must go up to the wake. It didn't
240 last long, did it?

(MAIRE *leaves. Silence. Then:*)

OWEN: I don't think there'll be any class. Maybe you should . . .

(OWEN *begins picking up his texts.* DOALTY *goes to him.*)

DOALTY: Is he long gone?—Manus?

OWEN: Half an hour.

DOALTY: Stupid bloody fool.

245 OWEN: I told him that.

DOALTY: Do they know he's gone?

OWEN: Who?

DOALTY: The army.

OWEN: Not yet.

250 DOALTY: They'll be after him like bloody beagles. Bloody, bloody fool, limping along the coast. They'll overtake him before night for Christ's sake.

(DOALTY *returns to the window.* LANCEY *enters—now the commanding officer.*)

OWEN: Any news? Any word?

(LANCEY *moves into the centre of the room, looking around as he does.*)

LANCEY: I understood there was a class. Where are the others?

OWEN: There was to be a class but my father—
255
LANCEY: This will suffice. I will address them and it will be their responsibility to pass on what I have to say to every family in this section.

(LANCEY *indicates to* OWEN *to translate.* OWEN *hesitates, trying to assess the change in* LANCEY'*s manner and attitude.*)

I'm in a hurry, O'Donnell.

OWEN: The captain has an announcement to make. 260

LANCEY: Lieutenant Yolland is missing. We are searching for him. If we don't find him, or if we receive no information as to where he is to be found, I will pursue the following course of action. (*He indicates to* OWEN *to translate.*)

OWEN: They are searching for George. If they don't find him— 265

LANCEY: Commencing twenty-four hours from now we will shoot all livestock in Ballybeg.

(OWEN *stares at* LANCEY.)

At once.

OWEN: Beginning this time tomorrow they'll kill every animal in Baile Beag—unless they're told where George is. 270

LANCEY: If that doesn't bear results, commencing forty-eight hours from now we will embark on a series of evictions and levelling of every abode in the following selected areas—

OWEN: You're not—!

LANCEY: Do your job. Translate. 275

OWEN: If they still haven't found him in two days time they'll begin evicting and levelling every house starting with these townlands.

(LANCEY *reads from his list.*)

LANCEY: Swinefort.

OWEN: Lis na Muc. 280

LANCEY: Burnfoot.

OWEN: Bun na hAbhann.

LANCEY: Dromduff.

OWEN: Druim Dubh.

LANCEY: Whiteplains. 285

OWEN: Machaire Ban.

LANCEY: Kings Head.

OWEN: Cnoc na Ri.

LANCEY: If by then the lieutenant hasn't been found, we will proceed until a complete clearance is made of this entire 290 section.

OWEN: If Yolland hasn't been got by then, they will ravish the whole parish.

LANCEY: I trust they know exactly what they've got to do. (*Pointing to* BRIDGET.) I know you. I know where you live. 295 (*Pointing to* SARAH.) Who are you? Name!

(SARAH'*s mouth opens and shuts, opens and shuts. Her face becomes contorted.*)

What's your name?

(*Again* SARAH *tries frantically.*)

OWEN: Go on, Sarah. You can tell him.

(*But* SARAH *cannot. And she knows she cannot. She closes her mouth. Her head goes down.*)

OWEN: Her name is Sarah Johnny Sally.
300   LANCEY: Where does she live?
OWEN: Bun na hAbhann.
LANCEY: Where?
OWEN: Burnfoot.
LANCEY: I want to talk to your brother—is he here?
305   OWEN: Not at the moment.
LANCEY: Where is he?
OWEN: He's at a wake.
LANCEY: What wake?

(DOALTY, *who has been looking out the window all through* LANCEY's *announcements, now speaks—calmly, almost casually.*)

DOALTY: Tell him his whole camp's on fire.
310   LANCEY: What's your name? (*To* OWEN.) Who's that lout?
OWEN: Doalty Dan Doalty.
LANCEY: Where does he live?
OWEN: Tulach Alainn.
LANCEY: What do we call it?
315   OWEN: Fair Hill. He says your whole camp is on fire.

(LANCEY *rushes to the window and looks out. Then he wheels on* DOALTY.)

LANCEY: I'll remember you, Mr Doalty. (*To* OWEN.) You carry a big responsibility in all this.

(*He goes off.*)

BRIDGET: Mother of God, does he mean it, Owen?
OWEN: Yes, he does.
320   BRIDGET: We'll have to hide the beasts somewhere—our Seamus'll know where. Maybe at the back of Lis na nGradh— or in the caves at the far end of Tra Bhan. Come on, Doalty! Come on! Don't be standing about there!

(DOALTY *does not move.* BRIDGET *runs to the door and stops suddenly. She sniffs the air. Panic.*)

The sweet smell! Smell it! It's the sweet smell! Jesus, it's the
325   potato blight!
DOALTY: It's the army tents burning, Bridget.
BRIDGET: Is it? Are you sure? Is that what it is? God, I thought we were destroyed altogether. Come on! Come on!

(*She runs off.* OWEN *goes to* SARAH *who is preparing to leave.*)

OWEN: How are you? Are you all right?

(SARAH *nods:* Yes.)

330   OWEN: Don't worry. It will come back to you again.

(SARAH *shakes her head.*)

OWEN: It will. You're upset now. He frightened you. That's all's wrong.

(*Again* SARAH *shakes her head, slowly, emphatically, and smiles at* OWEN. *Then she leaves.* OWEN *busies himself gathering his belongings.* DOALTY *leaves the window and goes to him.*)

DOALTY: He'll do it, too.
OWEN: Unless Yolland's found.
DOALTY: Hah!   335
OWEN: Then he'll certainly do it.
DOALTY: When my grandfather was a boy they did the same thing. (*Simply, altogether without irony.*) And after all the trouble you went to, mapping the place and thinking up new names for it. (OWEN *busies himself. Pause.* DOALTY *almost*   340
dreamily.) I've damned little to defend but he'll not put me out without a fight. And there'll be others who think the same as me.
OWEN: That's a matter for you.
DOALTY: If we'd all stick together. If we knew how to defend   345
ourselves.
OWEN: Against a trained army.
DOALTY: The Donnelly twins know how.
OWEN: If they could be found.
DOALTY: If they could be found. (*He goes to the door.*) Give me a   350
shout after you've finished with Lancey. I might know something then.

(*He leaves.*)

(OWEN *picks up the Name-Book. He looks at it momentarily, then puts it on top of the pile he is carrying. It falls to the floor. He stoops to pick it up—hesitates—leaves it. He goes upstairs. As* OWEN *ascends,* HUGH *and* JIMMY JACK *enter. Both wet and drunk.* JIMMY *is very unsteady. He is trotting behind* HUGH, *trying to break in on* HUGH's *declamation.* HUGH *is equally drunk but more experienced in drunkenness: there is a portion of his mind which retains its clarity.*)

HUGH: There I was, appropriately dispositioned to proffer my condolences to the bereaved mother . . .
JIMMY: Hugh—   355
HUGH: and about to enter the *domus lugubris*—Maire Chatach?
JIMMY: The wake house.
HUGH: Indeed—when I experience a plucking at my elbow: Mister George Alexander, Justice of the Peace. 'My tidings   360
are infelicitous,' said he—Bridget? Too slow. Doalty?
JIMMY: *Infelix*—unhappy.
HUGH: Unhappy indeed. 'Master Bartley Timlin has been appointed to the new national school.' 'Timlin? Who is Timlin?' 'A schoolmaster from Cork. And he will be a major as-   365
set to the community: he is also a very skilled bacon-curer!'
JIMMY: Hugh—
HUGH: Ha-ha-ha-ha-ha! The Cork bacon-curer! *Barbarus hic ego sum quia non intelligor ulli*—James?

III. 356 *domus lugubris* house of mourning   362 *infelix* unlucky, unhappy   368–369 *Barbarus . . . ulli* I am a barbarian here because I am not understood by anyone

370   JIMMY: Ovid.
       HUGH: *Procede.*
       JIMMY: 'I am a barbarian in this place because I am not under-
           stood by anyone.'
       HUGH: Indeed—(*Shouts.*) Manus! Tea! I will compose a satire
375   on Master Bartley Timlin, schoolmaster and bacon-curer.
           But it will be too easy, won't it? (*Shouts.*) Strong tea! Black!

(*The only way* JIMMY *can get* HUGH's *attention is by standing in front
of him and holding his arms.*)

       JIMMY: Will you listen to me, Hugh!
       HUGH: James. (*Shouts.*) And a slice of soda bread.
       JIMMY: I'm going to get married.
380   HUGH: Well!
       JIMMY: At Christmas.
       HUGH: Splendid.
       JIMMY: To Athene.
       HUGH: Who?
385   JIMMY: Pallas Athene.
       HUGH: *Glaukopis Athene?*
       JIMMY: Flashing-eyed, Hugh, flashing-eyed!

(*He attempts the gesture he has made before: standing to attention, the
momentary spasm, the salute, the face raised in pained ecstasy—but
the body does not respond efficiently this time. The gesture is grotesque.*)

       HUGH: The lady has assented?
       JIMMY: She asked *me*—I assented.
390   HUGH: Ah. When was this?
       JIMMY: Last night.
       HUGH: What does her mother say?
       JIMMY: Metis from Hellespont? Decent people—good stock.
       HUGH: And her father?
395   JIMMY: I'm meeting Zeus tomorrow. Hugh, will you be my
           best man?
       HUGH: Honoured, James; profoundly honoured.
       JIMMY: You know what I'm looking for, Hugh, don't you? I
           mean to say—you know—I—I—I joke like the rest of
400   them—you know?—(*Again he attempts the pathetic routine
           but abandons it instantly.*) You know yourself, Hugh—don't
           you?—you know all that. But what I'm really looking for,
           Hugh—what I really want—companionship, Hugh—at
           my time of life, companionship, company, someone to talk
405   to. Away up in Beann na Gaoithe—you've no idea how
           lonely it is. Companionship—correct, Hugh? Correct?
       HUGH: Correct.
       JIMMY: And I always liked her, Hugh. Correct?
       HUGH: Correct, James.
410   JIMMY: Someone to talk to.
       HUGH: Indeed.
       JIMMY: That's all, Hugh. The whole story. You know it all now,
           Hugh. You know it all.

(*As* JIMMY *says those last lines he is crying, shaking his head, trying
to keep his balance, and holding a finger up to his lips in absurd gestures of secrecy and intimacy. Now he staggers away, tries to sit on a
stool, misses it, slides to the floor, his feet in front of him, his back
against the broken cart. Almost at once he is asleep.* HUGH *watches all
of this. Then he produces his flask and is about to pour a drink when
he sees the Name-Book on the floor. He picks it up and leafs through*

it, pronouncing the strange names as he does. Just as he begins, OWEN
emerges and descends with two bowls of tea.)

       HUGH: Ballybeg. Burnfoot. King's Head. Whiteplains. Fair
           Hill. Dunboy. Green Bank.   415

(OWEN *snatches the book from* HUGH.)

       OWEN: I'll take that. (*In apology.*) It's only a catalogue of names.
       HUGH: I know what it is.
       OWEN: A mistake—my mistake—nothing to do with us. I
           hope that's strong enough [*tea*]. (*He throws the book on the
           table and crosses over to* JIMMY.) Jimmy. Wake up, Jimmy.   420
           Wake up, man.
       JIMMY: What—what-what?
       OWEN: Here. Drink this. Then go on away home. There may
           be trouble. Do you hear me, Jimmy? There may be trouble.
       HUGH: (*Indicating Name-Book.*) We must learn those new   425
           names.
       OWEN: (*Searching around.*) Did you see a sack lying about?
       HUGH: We must learn where we live. We must learn to make
           them our own. We must make them our new home.

(OWEN *finds a sack and throws it across his shoulders.*)

       OWEN: I know where I live.   430
       HUGH: James thinks he knows, too. I look at James and three
           thoughts occur to me: A—that it is not the literal past, the
           'facts' of history, that shape us, but images of the past em-
           bodied in language. James has ceased to make that dis-
           crimination.   435
       OWEN: Don't lecture me, Father.
       HUGH: B—we must never cease renewing those images; be-
           cause once we do, we fossilize. Is there no soda bread?
       OWEN: And C, Father—one single, unalterable 'fact': if Yolland
           is not found, we are all going to be evicted. Lancey has is-   440
           sued the order.
       HUGH: Ah. *Edictum imperatoris.*
       OWEN: You should change out of those wet clothes. I've got to
           go. I've got to see Doalty Dan Doalty.
       HUGH: What about?   445
       OWEN: I'll be back soon.

(*As* OWEN *exits.*)

       HUGH: Take care, Owen. To remember everything is a form of
           madness. (*He looks around the room, carefully, as if he were about
           to leave it forever. Then he looks at* JIMMY, *asleep again.*) The
           road to Sligo. A spring morning. 1798. Going into battle.   450
           Do you remember, James? Two young gallants with pikes
           across their shoulders and the *Aeneid* in their pockets.
           Everything seemed to find definition that spring—a con-
           gruence, a miraculous matching of hope and past and pre-
           sent and possibility. Striding across the fresh, green land.   455
           The rhythms of perception heightened. The whole enter-
           prise of consciousness accelerated. We were gods that
           morning, James; and I had recently married *my* goddess,

---

442 ***edictum imperatoris*** the decree os the commander

460 Caitlin Dubh Nic Reactainn, may she rest in peace. And to leave her and my infant son in his cradle—that was heroic, too. By God, sir, we were magnificent. We marched as far as—where was it?—Glenties! All of twenty-three miles in one day. And it was there, in Phelan's pub, that we got home-sick for Athens, just like Ulysses. The *desiderium*
465 *nostrorum*—the need for our own. Our *pietas,* James, was for older, quieter things. And that was the longest twenty-three miles back I ever made. (*Toasts* JIMMY.) My friend, confusion is not an ignoble condition.

(MAIRE *enters.*)

MAIRE: I'm back again. I set out for somewhere but I couldn't
470 remember where. So I came back here.
HUGH: Yes, I will teach you English, Maire Chatach.
MAIRE: Will you, Master? I must learn it. I need to learn it.
HUGH: Indeed you may well be my only pupil.

(*He goes towards the steps and begins to ascend.*)

MAIRE: When can we start?
475 HUGH: Not today. Tomorrow, perhaps. After the funeral. We'll begin tomorrow. (*Ascending.*) But don't expect too much. I will provide you with the available words and the available grammar. But will that help you to interpret between privacies? I have no idea. But it's all we have. I have no idea at all.

(*He is now at the top.*)

480 MAIRE: Master, what does the English word 'always' mean?
HUGH: *Semper—per omnia saecula.* The Greeks called it *'aei.'* It's not a word I'd start with. It's a silly word, girl.

(*He sits.* JIMMY *is awake. He gets to his feet.* MAIRE *sees the Name-Book, picks it up, and sits with it on her knee.*)

MAIRE: When he comes back, this is where he'll come to. He told me this is where he was happiest.

(JIMMY *sits beside* MAIRE.)

JIMMY: Do you know the Greek word *endogamein?* It means to 485 marry within the tribe. And the word *exogamein* means to marry outside the tribe. And you don't cross those borders casually—both sides get very angry. Now, the problem is this: Is Athene sufficiently mortal or am I sufficiently god-like for the marriage to be acceptable to her people and to 490 my people? You think about that.
HUGH: *Urbs antiqua fuit*—there was an ancient city which, 'tis said, Juno loved above all the lands. And it was the goddess's aim and cherished hope that here should be the capital of all nations—should the fates perchance allow that. 495 Yet in truth she discovered that a race was springing from Trojan blood to overthrow some day these Tyrian towers—a people *late regem belloque superbum*—kings of broad realms and proud in war who would come forth for Libya's downfall—such was—such was the course—such 500 was the course ordained—ordained by fate . . . What the hell's wrong with me? Sure I know it backwards. I'll begin again. *Urbs antiqua fuit*—there was an ancient city which, 'tis said, Juno loved above all the lands.

(*Begin to bring down the lights.*)

And it was the goddess's aim and cherished hope that here 505 should be the capital of all nations—should the fates perchance allow that. Yet in truth she discovered that a race was springing from Trojan blood to overthrow some day these Tyrian towers—a people kings of broad realms and proud in war who would come forth for Libya's downfall . . . 510

(*Blackout.*)

464–465 *desiderium nostrorum* longing/need for our things/ people 465 *pietas* piety 481 *Semper . . . saecula* always—for all time; *aei* always

485 *endogamein* to marry within the tribe 486 *exogamein* to marry outside the tribe 492 *Urbs antiqua* *fuit* there was an ancient city 498 *late . . . superbum* kings of broad realms and proud in war, from Virgil's *Aeneid,* book I.

Maishe Maponya

Maishe Maponya (b. 1951) is one of South Africa's best-known playwrights. Born in the Alexandra township near Johannesburg, Maponya moved to Soweto when his family was forcibly resettled there in 1962. He worked as an insurance clerk, writing plays in his spare time; he also worked with the Medupi Writers Association (banned in 1977), and was co-founder of the Bahumutsi Drama Group in 1977. The Bahumutsi Group produced many of his plays, but Maponya is also an accomplished poet and oral performer, and worked with the Allahpoets in the townships as well. Maponya had written two plays—*The Cry* (1976) and *Peace and Forgive* (1978)—when he won a British Council grant to study in England. There he read Bertolt Brecht's classic "learning play," *The Measures Taken* (see Unit V), which inspired his own play, *The Hungry Earth,* about labor conditions in South Africa (1978). Brecht emphasized a socially engaged drama, episodic in structure and revealing its characters' social implications through a dramatic gesture, the *gest*. Maponya adapts, extends, and redirects these principles in several plays, notably *Umongikazi* (1982), a play about the working conditions of nurses, *Dirty Work* (1984), about the security police, and *Gangsters* (1984), about the detention and murder of activists like Steve Biko. Maponya teaches in the Drama Department of Witwatersrand University and has written several other plays, including *Jika* (1986) and *Valley of the Blind* (1987).

GANGSTERS

Although it's possible to read *Gangsters* as a purely political allegory—on the model of Samuel Beckett's play *Catastrophe,* which it both invokes and challenges—the play in fact responds to a series of laws that came into force in South Africa in the 1980s. As Ian Steadman remarks in "The Theatre of Maishe Maponya," the play engages the South African

Maishe Maponya as Rasechaba (the character's name when the role is male; Masechaba is the name when the role is female) in this 1985 production of Maponya's *Gangsters* at the Market Theater of Johannesburg.

Internal Security Act of 1982, which allowed the minister of Justice to detain individuals suspected of supporting communism or otherwise endangering the state.[1] The minister was given broad powers, and could seize any publication (and its author) that appeared to challenge "law and order," to advocate communism, to be published by or agree with the views of any banned organization, or appearing to "encourage or foment feelings of hostility between different population groups." The character Masechaba—in the original version of *Gangsters* a male poet named Rasechaba and played by Maponya—is detained under the act and subjected to a series of increasingly brutal interrogations, until she is killed.

Much as Brecht's *The Measures Taken* provided a kind of inspiration for *The Hungry Earth*, *Gangsters* clearly invokes—indeed, literally transcribes—the action of Beckett's *Catastrophe*. Beckett's play, which was written to protest the incarceration of Czech playwright—later, president of the Czech Republic—Vaclav Havel, is a kind of metadramatic allegory: a nameless Protagonist is put on a pedestal, while a Director orders his Assistant to pose and re-pose the figure, whitening his flesh, revealing his skin, bowing his head, in order to provide a kind of perfect image of the suffering victim. Maponya had been asked by the novelist Nadine Gordimer to direct *Catastrophe,* but he found the play not only too abstract from his own experience, but too remote from the more concrete experience of apartheid. In this sense, then, as in Césaire's *A Tempest,* we might consider *Gangsters* as a kind of resistant writing, a play that invokes a familiar document of European culture—here, both Beckett's play and perhaps the entire absurdist tradition it embodies—to suggest its role in the politics of oppression. Is there a sense, for example, in which "the absurd" is something like the condition of arbitrary violence that was the condition of everyday life for black South Africans before the ending of apartheid? Is there a sense in which "the absurd" is not only the instrument of apartheid, but in some way part of its rationale, its justification?

When *Gangsters* was to be produced at Johannesburg's Market Theater in 1984, the theater was notified that the play verged on violating the 1974 Publications Act. Yet rather than censoring the play outright, the government merely stipulated that it could only be performed in small theaters, and that any future productions in a different venue would need to be approved. Since 1984, however, *Gangsters* has been performed successfully not only in South Africa, but throughout the world.

---

[1] In Maishe Maponya, *Doing Plays for a Change* (Johannesburg: Witwatersrand UP, 1995).

GANGSTERS

Maishe Maponya

CHARACTERS

MAJOR WHITEBEARD, *a white Security Police Officer*
JONATHAN, *a black Security Policeman*
MASECHABA, *a poet*

SETTING: *The stage is divided into two acting areas, stage left and stage right, by lighting or other means. Stage right is a security cell. Stage left represents Major Whitebeard's office and various settings. Additional lighting needed is a blue cover (for the recitation of poems) and a special, used twice only. The transitions between these states are marked in the text.*

PROPS: *Slab or stretcher, table, two chairs, cell window bars, blanket (black), rope (two metres), two tape recorders (one small, one large), note pad and pen, one Bible, a briefcase, books, papers, two photographs, a gun and holster, handcuffs. Uniforms for Jonathan and Whitebeard, veil for Masechaba, clothes and gown (mourning) for Masechaba.*

SOUND: *A taped hymn.*

PROLOGUE

House lights off. Stage lights off. House lights slowly come up to 50 per cent as MASECHABA *enters the auditorium.*

The recitation of the first three poems should take place in the auditorium suggesting a public performance by the poet. The reading must not be in a rigid stationary position, the poet must move in any direction she wishes, through the seats of the auditorium, walking and sometimes running, depending on the mood in each poem. It is also important to note that the tempo varies from one poem to the other and therefore requires the poet to be flexible.

MASECHABA: Kutheni na mawethu
    that you leave the evil fires
    from Europe to spread through Afrika!

    Sisi Phithiphithi!
5   Our children lie dead in the streets
    whilst their fathers die
    digging the gold
    they will never smell.

    Sisi Wiliwili!
10   Gugulethu is no longer ours
    Sophiatown is no more
    e-Mgababa ziya phel'izindlu ngo mlilo

    There are no roads e-Crossroads
    And our heroes
15   Are buried in Sharpeville.

    Izwe liya nyikima!
    Zi ya phel'ingane nga-mabhunu
    They still refuse to swallow Bantu Education
    Ncedani Mawethu
20   They are your children.

    Izwe liya shukuma!
    Nobody can buy apartheid
    Rent is going up!
    Food is also expensive
25   Asinamali we cannot afford it.

(Lights come up to 30 per cent on Major WHITEBEARD's *office revealing* WHITEBEARD *on a chair at a table and* JONATHAN *adjacent to* WHITEBEARD. *They are both reading newspapers.)*

    Kutheni na mawethu
    That you leave the stranger
    To beat the drums of war
    In your own backyards!
    Hlanganani mawethu!   30
    Lelethu!

(She pauses as she contemplates the audience and then continues with another poem.)

    Ugly brown canvas uniform
    Have you had lunch today?
    I have seen
    Your contorted face   35
    Behind an ugly brown truck
    In Sharpeville again

    Ugly brown canvas uniform
    I thought I saw your cousin
    Behind an ugly brown truck   40
    That roams the streets
    By day in Mamelodi

    My brother wrote me a letter
    And told me about a mean looking face
    In Nyanga   45
    Behind an ugly brown truck
    And I bet you
    It sounds like your brother

    Other people too
    In Katlehong   50
    In Huhudi
    In Leandra
    Say they live in fear of
    Ugly brown canvas uniforms
    Behind ugly brown trucks   55

    And when at night
    I smell cyanide in the air
    I twitch my nose
    Helplessly acknowledging
    The announcement of the air   60
    'Life must be short for others'

    And in the morning
    When I walk the same streets

In Sharpeville again
65 I see mothers kneeling beside bodies
Riddled with bullets
And I mutter to myself
The ugly brown truck
Drives a maneater
70 Dressed in ugly brown canvas uniform

(She pauses, then continues with a third poem.)

You puzzle me Mister Gunslinger
To think you will be strong enough
To rid your conscience
Of the days you made our lives ugly

75 With torture
With blood
With massacre

Mister Gunslinger
Are you really sure
80 You understand why you suppress
Our aspirations
And our dreams
Into nightmares

Mister Gunslinger
85 Are you aware of the deeds
Of your settler-forebears
With their wagon-wheels
Running
And crushing
90 The blooming lives
Cuddled with hope

You with your brown bombers
Ugly as ever
Parading the streets
95 Like it is the bush
Instilling fears into old folks
Cannot do the same
To the young determined
Azanians

100 Grandmothers!
Daughters of the living cradle
Summon your gods
In all Afrika
And let it be known
105 The realities of history are today

Settler child
You defended your
Vile interests
With the blood of my brother
110 You broom-flying witch
Afrika knows your kind

All ye black shadows
Very darkness of
The gunslingers' high noon
115 Awake and break open
The gates of the Azanian morning

Grope dear children
Waggle your fingers
Grab the pole
And raise the flag 120
Drenched in blood
And give us a song
For this victory!

(With her hands raised and fists clenched in a black power salute she shouts her last lines as she walks backwards out of the auditorium.)

Amandla to the people!
Amandla to the people! 125

FIRST ENCOUNTER

Lights at full on WHITEBEARD'*s office.* WHITEBEARD *and* JONATHAN *are still seated in the same positions.*

WHITEBEARD: Jonathan!
JONATHAN: Yes sir.
WHITEBEARD: Has someone gone to fetch the poet?
JONATHAN: Yes sir, Sergeant Ngobese has gone to fetch her.
WHITEBEARD: All right. *(Pause. He pages through the newspaper to* 5
the end.)
I see Kaizer Chiefs are playing Orlando Pirates on
Saturday—who do you think is going to win?
JONATHAN: Of course it goes without saying, it will be Orlando
Pirates all the way—it's like I see it happening again. Ex- 10
actly what happened in 1973 when they collected all the
titles. They are the darlings of our soccer in black and white.
(He throws down the paper, excitedly and mimics.) Nang'u Rhee!
Nang'u Jomo Sono! There's Rhee and Jomo Sono is close
behind him . . . Rhee dribbles past two defenders . . . one 15
man lies sprawling on the ground! Rhee passes the ball to
Jomo Sono . . . walibamba umfana wa likhahlela! *(Kicks with
one leg.)* Laduma! It's a goal!
WHITEBEARD: *(Interrupting.)* Jonathan!
JONATHAN: *(Freezes, leg still in the air.)* Yes sir! 20
WHITEBEARD: Fetch the poet.
JONATHAN: Yes sir! *(Shouts out* MASECHABA'*s name.* MASECHABA
walks in slowly. She notes the tape recorder on WHITEBEARD'*s
desk. She stops.)*
WHITEBEARD: *(Folds the newspaper and stands up.)* Miss Masechaba? 25
(He mispronounces the name.)
MASECHABA: *(Correcting him.)* Masechaba is my name.
WHITEBEARD: Oh, I'm sorry Miss Masechaba—Major Whitebeard
is my name . . . security. *(Produces an identification document.)*
MASECHABA: Yes, what can I do for you? 30
WHITEBEARD: Miss Masechaba, we in the branch are a little
worried about your poetry. We feel it's inflammatory.
MASECHABA: Can you explain yourself? What do you mean?
WHITEBEARD: I don't have to explain myself. All I have to do is
to play one of the cassettes that we've got of you reciting 35
those poems—particularly the one called . . . *(Recalling.)*
"The Spirit of Nation." All I have to do is play one of the
video tapes we've made of you doing your poetry at Regina
Mundi commemorative services. That's explanation enough
of what I mean. Oh, I'm forgetting my manners, please sit 40
down. *(Offers her a seat.)* Let me get one thing clear for myself. Do you write as well as perform these poems?
MASECHABA: Yes I do.

WHITEBEARD: Don't you feel they are inflammatory?

45 MASECHABA: They're not.

WHITEBEARD: They're not inflammatory?

MASECHABA: No.

WHITEBEARD: So Miss Masechaba, when you stand in front of a hall full of people, and you've just recited one of your po-
50 ems and the people start screaming and waving their fists in the air . . . you don't feel it's your poetry that's caused them to react like that?

MASECHABA: No.

WHITEBEARD: That interests me. It interests me . . . (*He looks at*
55 JONATHAN.) I don't think we need you any longer Jonathan. Why don't you get yourself a cup of coffee. (JONATHAN *leaves.* WHITEBEARD *switches off the tape.*)

MASECHABA: So you have been taping all this?

WHITEBEARD: Regulations, I'm afraid. That's why I got rid of
60 Jonathan. I wanted to have an off-the-record chat with you and I didn't want him to report me upstairs for breaking the rules.

But Miss Masechaba, it really interests me that a woman as obviously intelligent and sensitive as you, can actually
65 believe that your poetry and the reaction it evokes are un-related? How does the whole thing work?

MASECHABA: You see Major, the manner in which I write my po-etry is decided by the situation and inspiration at a given time. Major, when a poet pens anything on paper and the
70 spirit of nature moves within her, she will write about nature. If the spirit of the nation moves within her, she will write about the nation. She will talk about botho, humanness, she'll talk about pain and she'll talk about that which moves the people at a given time. If her people live in happiness,
75 this happiness will be seen in her works; and that will be evidence to the world of how marvellous the lives of her peo-ple are. If I don't feel anything, I don't write anything.

WHITEBEARD: Very interesting Miss Masechaba, but that doesn't explain the militant style that you've chosen.

80 MASECHABA: Major, a poet sees things not in the manner that you and your colleagues see them. You may regard their world as fantasy, but it is in that abstract frame of mind that things start to take a certain shape and form, and that shape is influenced by the material that inspires the poet; hence
85 the manner that I express myself in my poetry.

WHITEBEARD: Very good and very informative. (*Sighs.*) But un-fortunately as you yourself put it, my colleagues and I see things differently from you and your people. We live in a different world; far from your abstract frames of mind. So
90 what interests us is not so much the creative process as the effect that your poetry has on ordinary people; people who don't have the insight and understanding that you and I have, and therefore there can be no doubt Miss Masechaba that your poems have made a lot of people feel very angry,
95 even violent and it is my job to put a stop to that sort of thing. So I called you in to have a friendly chat with you and to warn you . . .

MASECHABA: But you talk about violence! I think it's your frame of mind. Maybe it's guilt.

100 WHITEBEARD: But your poetry is responsible for the creation of a violent frame of mind in the people who hear it . . .

MASECHABA: I am not responsible for the creation of the squat-ters. I am not responsible for the starvation of millions of children because their parents have been forced into arid homelands. I did not create the humiliating laws, and I 105 never created the racial barriers in this land. Who do you expect me to blame when life becomes unfair to a black soul?

(*No response. Lights fade leaving* MASECHABA *covered by blue light for poem.*)

When life becomes unfair to a black soul
Who is to blame? 110
When a child leaves home for school never to come back
When a mother hides the cracks on her face created by years of crying.
When a brother dashes in fear to seek refuge in the wilderness
We are all taken by surprise!
When life becomes unfair to a black soul 115
Who is to blame?
When a child throws a stone in anger and dies!
When a family takes a brazier into a shack and dies!
We are all taken by surprise.
But God is not at all taken by surprise! 120

(*Blue light fades as general lights come up.* MASECHABA *turns chal-lengingly to the major.*)

Who do you expect me to blame?

WHITEBEARD: Okay, Miss Masechaba, for the purposes of this discussion I will agree that things are not perfect with your people, and this government is doing everything within re-alistic terms to improve their situation. But you as a poet 125 have a responsibility to your people. I don't know why you choose to depress them by concentrating on the negative as-pects of their life. Why don't you cheer them up by talking about the good things that surround them—by telling them of the natural beauty that surrounds them. I'm not an 130 expert of course but I had to learn one poem at school which has stuck in my mind. It goes something like this:

(*He recites any Afrikaans poem about flowers or nature. At the end of his recitation, he goes to lean on the table directly opposite* MASECHABA *and challenges her.*)

Now that sort of poem Miss Masechaba has a beautiful melody to it and it makes me feel good inside not violent and angry. 135

MASECHABA: Of course I could write about flowers. But where are the flowers in Winterveld for me to write about? What kind of flowers will ever grow in Crossroads? (*Daringly walks to the table, leans on it in the same position as his.*)

If that poet of yours lived in Alexandra he would write 140 about the stagnant pools of water and the smell of shit fil-tering through the streets at night because there is no drainage system! He would write about the buckets of faeces placed in the streets at night as if families are brag-ging which family eats more to shit more! 145

WHITEBEARD: I don't think we need that kind of language Miss Masechaba!

MASECHABA: And my people don't need that kind of life Major Whitebeard.

(*There is tension as they look each other in the eye.*)

150 WHITEBEARD: All right. Let's get back to your poetry. (MASECHABA *goes back to her seat.*)

Can't you see that you are inciting people to violence with your poetry. When you use lines like "the barbed wire mentality of a good-looking Afrikaner" you are insulting
155 the Afrikaner people. When you write about the "trigger-happy fingers" it shouldn't surprise you when the people respond by raising their fists in the air and shouting "Amandla Ngawethu!"

MASECHABA: (*Standing to make her point.*) But you have just
160 directed your . . .

WHITEBEARD: Yes Miss Masechaba! (*Points to the chair. Then softer.*) It's been a very interesting discussion. But the fact remains that I have a job to do and that job is to warn you. (*Goes to stand behind the chair on which* MASECHABA *is seated.*)
165 You are playing with fire. And remember my friend that people who play with fire must expect to get burned. If you want to continue playing with fire, don't blame anyone when you get those poetry-writing fingers of yours burned. Well, thank you very much for coming to this chat with
170 me. You may go.

(*There is tension as* MASECHABA *stands to leave the room.*)

WHITEBEARD: (*Calls out.*) Jonathan!

JONATHAN: (*Comes in.*) Yes sir!

WHITEBEARD: Give me the tape. (JONATHAN *goes to some corner in the office and produces a small tape recorder which he passes to him.*
175 WHITEBEARD *makes a mark on the tape and puts it away.*)

I want you to keep an eye on Masechaba. This means, Jonathan, that you do not go to Ellis Park to watch the soccer match on Saturday. I want you to do a good job. Do you hear me Jonathan?

180 JONATHAN: (*Disappointed.*) Yes sir.

(*The church. A hymn. Suggest that Bach or Mozart should be played softly during this scene. Suggest the acting area should be downstage centre.* MASECHABA *enters dressed for church. She crosses herself, finds a place and goes to kneel down. Hymn continues.* JONATHAN *enters, Bible in hand. Finds a place and kneels. Crosses himself and looks about. He sees her and shuffles about to get closer to her. She sees him. He kneels immediately behind her. A little later she challenges him. They talk in whispers.*)

MASECHABA: Jonathan, is there anywhere one can go without you following one?

JONATHAN: (*Sarcastically.*) Yes. The toilet.

MASECHABA: No Jonathan, this is serious. I am getting irritated
185 at the manner in which you keep following me. What is it you want from me?

JONATHAN: (*Amused.*) You must be exaggerating. What makes you such an expert on the Special Branch? Anyway, what would I find to do here besides attending the church
190 service?

MASECHABA: You should be ashamed of yourself coming to church every Sunday and knowing that your job is to help the white man preserve an ungodly status quo.

JONATHAN: Remember Masechaba that I'm doing a job like
195 any other person who wakes up in the morning to go to

work for a white man in town. On Friday when that person gets his salary I also get my salary.

MASECHABA: But the difference is that your salary is dirty. It is enveloped with the blood of your own brothers!

BOTH: (*Responding loudly to the priest at the altar.*) Amen!   200

(*Different hymn, softer.* MASECHABA *rises to go to the front to receive the sacrament. As she kneels,* JONATHAN *follows her and kneels beside her. She opens her mouth.*)

MASECHABA: Amen! (*Crosses herself.*)

JONATHAN: (*Receives the communion.*) Amen!

(*She goes back to her previous position. A little later he follows. Then he challenges her as the hymn goes softer.*)

JONATHAN: How many children die of malnutrition because their parents cannot find jobs? I have mouths to feed. (*Makes sure he is not heard by other congregants.*) I have my   205
children's school fees to attend to. Do you know that since I took up this job things have changed for the better for me. I'm also convinced that we must stand aloof from politics. We are servants of God and God does not wish us to enter the political arena.   210

MASECHABA: I've had enough of this senseless talk. The sermon delivered by the priest is enough. I'm not going to listen to a sell-out sermon from you Jonathan, you are a bloodsucker. You have no conscience. You are dead inside.

JONATHAN: What do you mean I'm dead? I'm alive. I've the   215
same feelings as you.

MASECHABA: (*Shifting away from him slightly.*) I knew you wouldn't understand me.
By dead (*Blue light comes up, simultaneously general light fades down.*)
I mean the smile you put on when the enemy grins at you.   220
Death is when the colour of your skin turns against you and you don't know where you stand as others decide your fate.
Death is the smile you put on when the enemy grins at you.
Death is when you stop being you! And above all,

(*General lights come up whilst the blue fades down.*)

Death, is when you start to hate to be black!

(*A closing hymn.*)

JONATHAN: Masechaba you are too hasty to condemn me before   225
you understand my situation better. Maybe we are not so different after all.

MASECHABA: Ag fuck off you are a sellout! (*She moves away.*)

JONATHAN: (*Humiliated and disregarding the congregants.*) Hey Masechaba you ridicule me in the presence of all these   230
people—that is nice for you.

(MASECHABA *heads for the door and he calls after her.*)

But one day you'll know who I am. Then you'll know what death is. Mcundu wakho! Lentombi iyandigezela, masemb'akho! Shit! Bastard! (*Realises the Bible is still in his hand. Quickly crosses himself as he exits.*)   235

Oh! I'm sorry Lord!

(*Blackout.*)

SECOND ENCOUNTER

WHITEBEARD *is sorting out some documents at the table.*

WHITEBEARD: Jonathan, where are those poems of Masechaba's that the Soweto Business Association is complaining about?

JONATHAN: Which ones are those sir?

WHITEBEARD: The ones I gave you to photostat.

5 JONATHAN: (*To himself as he goes through his bag.*) My driver's licence, my insurance contract. O sir look, my daughter turned two years yesterday, this is her picture taken last night.

WHITEBEARD: (*Businesslike.*) Later Jonathan. Bring me the
10 poems. (JONATHAN *gives him the poems.*)
Now call the poet inside.

JONATHAN: (*Opens the door and calls out.*) Masechaba!

(*She walks in and stops.* JONATHAN *stands at the door.*)

WHITEBEARD: Miss Masechaba, you disappoint me. When I had you in here the last time I thought we'd come to some un-
15 derstanding. But when I read these poems I'm not sure. Sit down please, and listen objectively to these poems of yours. I'm going to read them the way you do …

MASECHABA: No. If they have to be read I'll read them for you, I wrote them.

20 WHITEBEARD: No! I want you to hear the way they sound.

(MASECHABA *stands to take the page from* WHITEBEARD *but* JONATHAN *quickly steps in and looks at her threateningly.* MASECHABA *stops, realises the risk and sits down.* JONATHAN *walks back to his previous position.* WHITEBEARD *starts to read the poem out loud with agitation.*)

Look deep into the ghetto
And see the modernised graves,
Where only the living-dead exist
Manacled with chains
25 So as not to resist.
Look deep into the ghetto
And see streets dividing the graves
Streets with pavements
Dyed with blood
30 Blood of the innocent.
Look deep into the ghetto
And see yourself silenced
By a ninety-nine year lease
Thus creating a class struggle
35 Within a struggle for survival
Look the ghetto over
You will see smog hover
And dust choking the lifeless living dead
Can you hear the beasts hell
40 And creatures evil
Howling and brawling
As they rush to devour you
and suck the last drop of blood

From your emaciated corpse …

MASECHABA: That is not the way the poem is …   45
WHITEBEARD: I haven't finished yet. (*Pause.*) Now, "class struggle," that is Marxist talk. It is dangerous talk Miss Masechaba. Don't you feel that Marxism and Africanism are contradictory?
MASECHABA: No. They are not contradictory.   50
WHITEBEARD: Oh! So you admit that you are a Marxist.
MASECHABA: I didn't say that.
WHITEBEARD: I'm glad you didn't say that. Because if you had you wouldn't be here with me. Miss Masechaba you're fortunate that you're here with me tonight because some of my   55
colleagues would have dealt with you firmly.

(*Slight pause.*)

You puzzle me Miss Masechaba. You claim to be an Africanist and yet when one of your people goes out to improve his or her living conditions and when some of them participate in the political organs made available to them   60
you attack them.
Can't you see that places like Crossroads and Mogopa are a health hazard? Can't you see that the proliferation of shacks and shanties in the townships are a drawback to those blacks who want to live a better life? What is your   65
Black Consciousness motto? "Black man you are on your own." Why then do you try and belittle the black men who are trying to go on their own by owning businesses and improving their living conditions? It seems you in your poetry attack them.   70
MASECHABA: You have spoken about two groups of people. Besides you know that I am not attacking those who are caught in the capitalists' spider's web …
WHITEBEARD: Who do you attack then? You go about attacking your own people and then you tell me there are two   75
groups. I want you to tell me here and now who your attack is aimed at? (*No response.*)
I asked you a question. Who do you attack?

(*General lights fade, blue comes up.*)

MASECHABA: (*Standing on a chair.*) On the wings of the storm
            of liberation
Waving black tickets in their hands   80
Degrees hanging like monuments of heroes
In their glass houses
Sit the cheese and wine drinkers
Of our struggle.

Others are undegreed   85
Unread, underpaid
And deprived of the right to quench
Their education thirst.
Pity, they too are caught in the web.

The motto reads thus!   90
"Divide and rule"
A new dispensation
Is the name of the game.
The ghetto is fast becoming a suburb
Beverly Hills   95
Selection Park

Prestige Park
Monument Park

100 "Who cares
"It's my sweat
"It's my money
"You're just wasting your time
"Damn it. I'm going out
"To have a swim."

105 Hats off for the Master's plan!
We salute you Soweto Homemakers' Festival!
Thank you Urban Foundation!
Thank you Gough Cooper!
Thank you Mr Constructive Engagement!
110 Thank you "Iron Lady"
Voetsek! You have messed up our struggle!

(*General lights come up, blue light fades.*)

WHITEBEARD: I asked you a question—who do you attack?
MASECHABA: (*Seemingly inattentive and still seated.*) The cheese and wine drinkers of our struggle.
115 WHITEBEARD: Always a poet. That rings a bell—here in this poem you write "silenced by a ninety-nine year lease . . . Selection Park, Monument Park . . ." It seems to me Miss Masechaba that these people who go and live in these better suburbs are worthy of your contempt?
120 MASECHABA: Everything I feel is in the poem and the poem says it all . . .
WHITEBEARD: Would I be correct in assuming that organisations like for example the Soweto Business Association are targets of your attack?
125 MASECHABA: You can make up your mind on that.
WHITEBEARD: (*Tension as their eyes lock. Pause.*) I'll do that! You may go. (*Before* MASECHABA *reaches the door.*)
One more thing before you go. (MASECHABA *stops.*) It might interest you Miss Masechaba, to know that a lot of
130 people give us information. Normally we don't want to share it but sometimes we do. Every Thursday night for the past four weeks you've been going to these rent boycott meetings and reciting your poetry in support of those leaders of yours who've been saying to the people "Don't
135 go and live in Selection Park, don't go to that petit-bourgeois place." It might interest you to know that those very same people have applied for bigger and better houses in Beverley Hills and Prestige Park. Would you like to see their names? (*He tries to pass a book to her. She is*
140 *not interested.*)
I thought not. What about those Black Consciousness, Afrika for the Africans leaders of yours who send their children secretly to white schools to get a white education—would you like to see their names?
145 MASECHABA: Every struggle has its betrayers. My leader is the people.
WHITEBEARD: The people? (*Disappointed.*) I'll try and remember that. (*Gestures with finger to dismiss her and then remembers something. This action is intended deliberately to torment her.*)
150 Oh, just before you go, I have a poem of yours which seems to be written in some ethnic language. Would you tell me what it means? It's called Hoy, Hoy, Hoy-in-a-Hoyini . . .

(*General light fades. Blue light comes up.*)

MASECHABA: Hoyina!!
Nivile nga maculo
Esizwe sintsundu e-Azania 155
Ethetha ngokuthi asifikanga apha
We have no history of arrival
Kuya mangalisa
Asihlalanga ngoxolo ezweni lethu
Simile kodwa ngomlenz'omnye 160
Siphandliwe simana siyalila
Sovuthelwa ngubanina
Namhlanje siyagxothwa
Ngomso siyabotshwa
Hayi ngenyimini siyazilwela 165
We fight back
Unzima lomthwalo womzabalazo

Abanye bayathengisa
Abanye bayathengiswa
Kuvuthumlilo 170
Ithayela lityumtu
Kwenze njanina sizwe' sintsundu
Aqhubeka njalo
Amaculo esizwe sintsundu e-Azania
Igcwele imigaqo ngabasebenzi 175
Bayazabalaza nabo
Baqhubeka phambili
Abantwana bayalishukumisa ilizwe
Baculela phezulu
Bazama ngapha nangapha 180
Bayalinyikimisa
Bayalizongomisa
Ngomso ngenene sophumelela

Abasetyhini bayalilizela
Sengathi kumnandi kowethu 185
Kanti thina siyazi
It is the African
Way of doing things
Even the revolution!

(*Blue light fades, general light comes up.*)

WHITEBEARD: It's called "Hoyina." Would you care to tell me 190 what it means?
MASECHABA: (*Immediately.*) No! I'm sure you have translators in here who would be happy to do it for you.

(*She walks out angrily. As she pulls the door open, she's pushed back into the room by* JONATHAN *who's been standing outside the door. He walks a few steps towards her as she steps backwards.*)

WHITEBEARD: (*Angrily.*) Masechaba. (*Points to a chair.* MASECHABA *sits down.*) 195
Jonathan, it seems you are going to get a chance to read this after all. (*Hands him a written page.*) Read clauses four, five and six out loud.
JONATHAN: Clause Four: You are to report at your nearest police station daily before eight o'clock every evening. Clause Five: 200
You are not to attend any gathering and note that talking to more than one person at a time will be a contravention of

your banning order. Clause Six: This banning order is imposed on you for the next three years.

205 WHITEBEARD: I warned you, and you chose to ignore my friendly advice. You asked for it. Jonathan explain the full implications of that document to our Soweto poet laureate.

(*He makes a move for the door.*)

MASECHABA: (*Standing.*) Just before you go, Major! (WHITEBEARD
210 *returns and stands in front of her. He is obviously shocked at her nerve in calling him back as he called her back. There is more tension as she addresses him.*) Mr William Shakespeare wrote some very wonderful lines about you which go:

Man proud man,
Dressed in a little brief authority
215 Plays such fantastic tricks before high heaven
As makes the angels weep.

WHITEBEARD: (*Chuckling.*) You really amuse me. What did you expect me to answer? Who is this Shakespeare? What political organisation does he belong to? (*Softer, but hard.*) We
220 are not as stupid as you might think. (*He leaves.* MASECHABA *sits down. She is obviously shattered by the banning order.*)
JONATHAN: Ya Masechaba, poet of the people! Where are all the people you were preaching poetry to? Do you think the people will eat your poetry when they starve? Let me tell you
225 something. I can't be led by a bastard like you! I know your kind. Showing off all the time with your name on the front pages of newspapers. All you know is jet-setting from time to time, and then you think you can fool us with your petty politics. Ha! You think we are impressed by your behaviour
230 in your two-piece costumes—carrying an executive bag when you go and talk to the same white people that you criticise. Ah! but when you read your poetry you put on African dresses, use revolutionary language and then you think you can fool everybody. (*Laughs.*) Bigmouth, I'm talking to you.
235 Talk! You've just earned yourself a banning order!
MASECHABA: (*Grabs the banning order, crumples it and throws it away.*) This is just a piece of paper—I'm still myself. My conscience is clear … The people out there are waiting for me—Masechaba, Mother of the Nation … That's what the
240 name means if you don't know. If they have to wait for you, it will only be to tear you apart! They will scorn you, they'll reject you!
JONATHAN: C'mon enjoy yourself for this is your last poetry session …
245 MASECHABA: Yes, they can ban me here but they won't ban the spirit of the nation. For as long as those millions of people are still thirsty the march will continue. I respect the convictions of my people and they respect my beliefs. I will help them carry the cross …
250 JONATHAN: Don't give me this shit about "your people." I know your kind …
MASECHABA: You don't know for you have no conscience.
JONATHAN: It's easy for you because you get your money from the World Council of Churches. You have nothing to lose,
255 because you have no mouths to feed …
MASECHABA: And so that is what makes you sell your people out? Why don't you stand up and pull up your pants and tell the white man it's enough—your face against his; tell him you've had enough …

JONATHAN: You are dreaming, for the white man is in power—   260
can't you see?
MASECHABA: (*Changes mood.*) Jonathan, you don't understand. You are black and I'm black …
JONATHAN: And then?
MASECHABA: In the beginning it was you and me. The land be-   265
longed to us. We tilled it. We shared everything equally. Then came the white man with his own thoughts. He put us asunder; put us against each other and while this was going on, he fenced us around and then moved about freely declaring our land his land—no man's land. Did you not   270
seen those boards along the road as you came from home this morning, saying: "In front of you, behind you and all around you is a Rand Mines Property?" Have you bothered to ask yourself "where did Rand Mines get our land from? Who did he buy it from?" He took it with the gun. Do you   275
know what the white man is doing today? He is sharing every little bit of our soil equally with his own brother. (JONATHAN *is torn apart.*)
The system is so planned that we don't realise these tricks easily. (*Her voice builds up.*) Why should we let the   280
white man decide our fate? Are we not matured to know and understand the world around us? (*She hoists his hand and fits her palm into his.*) The white man is aware that your clenched fist together with mine is the dawning of a new era. And when that dawn comes, no amount of machinery   285
will put us apart. This is the spirit of the nation! And this is what moves the people today!
WHITEBEARD: (*Bursting in.*) Masechaba! (JONATHAN *pulls his hand away and stands a distance away from her.*) You have overstayed your welcome! (*Picks up the crumpled banning or-*   290
der and puts it into MASECHABA's *pocket.* MASECHABA *exits.*)
JONATHAN: (*Guilty.*) Major, what she was saying to me—there is sense in her talk …
WHITEBEARD: Do you think she makes sense?
JONATHAN: I … I … I think …   295
WHITEBEARD: Let me make some sense to you. How many children have you got?
JONATHAN: Four, Major.
WHITEBEARD: Where are they being educated?
JONATHAN: Waterford, in Swaziland.   300
WHITEBEARD: And who pays for their education?
JONATHAN: You do, sir, as a benefit for me.
WHITEBEARD: Am I making sense Jonathan. Am I making sense?
JONATHAN: (*Embarrassed.*) Yes Sir!   305
WHITEBEARD: Now, I'm detaching you from normal duties. I want you to organise a team of four men to follow her wherever she goes. I want to know who she meets. I want her telephone tapped and mail screened. I have a suspicion that since the bastard is banned she is going to pursue her ac-   310
tivities underground. I want you to do a good job … Hear me Jonathan?
JONATHAN: Yes sir. (*Slight pause.*) By the way Major, you promised that I could take the blue Mercedes Benz home for the weekend.   315
WHITEBEARD: Yes. The keys are in the key-box.
JONATHAN: (*Excited.*) Thank you sir!

(*Blackout.*)

(*Back in the township* MASECHABA *continues to read her poetry in public, defying the banning order. The following poem can be read from any part of the stage as long as the position will not confuse the location. Blue light comes on.*)

MASECHABA: Apartheid!
    You maintained yourself
320   By keeping us separate
    You were father of many
    Like Suppression of Communism Act

    Who killed many
    Who hanged many
325   Who maimed many

    And when later you realised
    He was not doing you good
    You killed him

    Amongst your sons
330   Bantu Education
    Stripped many
    Of their brains

    Made them docile
    Killed many
335   Maimed many
    Jailed many

    And now you realise
    He is not doing you good
    You want to kill him
340   I remember your other son
    Old and notorious
    Pass-Law
    Never smiled
    Just locked millions
345   And I heard yesterday
    He died
    And millions are beginning to smile
    I hope he is not resurrected underground
    As for you
350   I heard your bodyguard Botha say
    You are outdated
    And wants to send you to the grave
    But he defended you
    By sending many of us to their graves

355   I think we must bring him to trial
    Like all Nazi war criminals
    How's that?

(*Blue light fades.*)

THIRD ENCOUNTER

MASECHABA *is arrested. Special light comes up on* MASECHABA'*s face behind bars. She is dressed in her nightgown and her feet are bare. This part can also be depicted by light—no specific stage area.*

MASECHABA: They broke one window first
    Then on all windows played sounds
    Made by the drums of wars
    Both doors joined the chorus

The front emitting quick soprano notes   5
The back a slow dub-dub-dub

It all happened in minutes
The vocalists shouted
The notes one after the other
Like they'd never rehearsed before   10
Vula! Vula! Bulang man!
Open up! The lyrics went
The timing was bad.

This is the music
That has become notorious   15
It plays at the first hour of the day
When your name rings
To be registered in the books
Of those messengers of darkness
You jump to your feet   20

Try to say something you think makes sense
You take all your poems
Hide all manuscripts
Throw some into the stove
To destroy the creation   25
rather than see it defiled by them
With their dirty hands.

If you are the poet's sister
"Don't open they are thugs!"
And then the poet will follow   30
"We won't open you are thugs!"
To give herself time to destroy
Everything and quickly relay messages
To the family.

But then the door has to be opened   35
Delaying tactics won't last forever
You saw it in Zimbabwe
The back door is kicked open
While you open the front
Within seconds   40

The musicians spit their songs into every room
While others guard the doors for escapers.
Torches flashing all over!
And the poet is taken.

(JONATHAN *comes to take her out of the cell and pushes her into the interrogation room. She falls on her knees.*)

MASECHABA: (*Exhausted and still handcuffed.*) I could not say no   45
    to them. Does the impala say no to the lion? Could the Star
    of David say no to the jackboot? I could not say no.

(JONATHAN *walks behind her.* WHITEBEARD *bursts in. He switches on the tape. Tension.* MASECHABA *stands up to challenge him.*)

    And why do all this to me . . .
WHITEBEARD: Shut up! If I want you to talk I'll order you! Miss
    Masechaba, spirit of the nation, poet, word merchant, what   50
    is the protector of the state? (*No response.*) I asked you a
    question. What is the protector of the state? Jonathan, will
    you tell Miss Masechaba what the protector of the state is?

JONATHAN: Yes. The law.

55 WHITEBEARD: And you Miss Masechaba have chosen to break that law . . .

MASECHABA: I have not . . .

WHITEBEARD: Shut up! Six months ago I had you in my office, I talked to you person-to-person. One intelligence to what
60 I thought was another intelligence. I said to you Miss Masechaba, your poetry is inciting the people. Please, I said to you, you are a woman of reason, stop this! You are treading on a dangerous path. You wouldn't listen to me. Three months later, I bring you in here again. I say to you, I'm
65 sorry, justice has to prevail everywhere. I don't want to do this to you, I respect you, but the law has decided, here is your banning order for your own protection. That too is not good enough for Miss Masechaba . . .

MASECHABA: But . . .

70 WHITEBEARD: Shut up! Miss Masechaba has to ignore the provisions of her banning order. She has to go out into the halls and she has to say to the people, "you see my banning order. This is what I do to my banning order!" (*He raises his hand and shows his palm to the audience. He spits on it.*) I could live
75 with that Miss Masechaba, I could just live with it. But then yesterday something happened. I have a press release which is going out this afternoon . . . (*First he goes to wipe his hand on her shoulder, then goes to his table, produces a document and reads it out to her.*)
80   "Yesterday evening patrol police spotted four men who they suspected were part of the fifty cadres that crossed the border into the country and when the terrorists realised they were being followed they opened fire on the police who responded by killing all four men. None of the police was
85 injured. Large quantities of arms and ammunition and literature were captured."
         Now Miss Masechaba, amongst the AK47s, Scorpions and limpet mines; among the T5s and T7s; amongst those instruments of terror that were going to sow discord and
90 violence among your people as well as mine, among them was a book of your poetry with the inscription inside (*He produces the book.*) "To LMA—solidarity and strength my comrades—Masechaba."

MASECHABA: I have signed lots of autographs in my poetry
95 books. When people bring them to me to sign what do I do? Do I refuse? As for LMA, I don't know who he is . . .

WHITEBEARD: Who is LMA?

MASECHABA: I said I do not know.

WHITEBEARD: (*Going closer to her and punching her in the stomach.*)
100 I asked you a question. Who is LMA?

MASECHABA: (*Writhing in pain.*) How must I talk to convince you that I do not know? Are you ever going to understand my language?

WHITEBEARD: (*Making as if to punch her again.*) I have no desire
105 to understand your language. (*Sarcastic assurance.*) You don't need to be scared of me, remember we are friends. (*He rushes to the table.*) I have a confession to make to a friend. Yes, Miss Masechaba, you have been followed night and day. Yes you have been watched. (*Indicating from a list in his hands.*) This
110 is a known terrorist hideout, that is a known terrorist hideout. That is a shebeen where terrorists are known to congregate. Is it coincidence that you visited these places on your poetic pilgrimage? What organisation do you belong to?

MASECHABA: I do not belong to any organisation.

WHITEBEARD: Isn't the African Poets of Azania an organisation? 115 Is that not an organisation?

MASECHABA: It is a cultural body. It's a traditional African ensemble . . .

WHITEBEARD: Is it not an organisation?

MASECHABA: Yes it is.   120

WHITEBEARD: Are you not their member?

MASECHABA: Yes I am.

(WHITEBEARD *presses the tape to play back* MASECHABA's *denials: "I do not belong to any organisation."*)

WHITEBEARD: Now you tell me you do. Do you know what that means Miss Masechaba? That means my friend that you are lying to me and I don't like that. You've just told me one 125 lie, how do I know how many other lies you have told me? I think I must give you a chance to decide whether you want to continue lying to me. (*He pulls her by the handcuffs.*) Jonathan, will you teach Miss Masechaba what we do to people who tell lies. (*Walks out.*)   130

(JONATHAN *takes out a rope and hooks it to the handcuffed hands and then orders her to squat while he relaxes. This continues until he falls asleep. The lights fade to a blackout. She continues to squat until she falls down. Lights come up.*)

(WHITEBEARD *comes back.* JONATHAN *jumps to his feet.*)

WHITEBEARD: Poor Miss Masechaba has been treated so badly. Jonathan, what have you done? (JONATHAN *does not respond. He knows* WHITEBEARD's *tricks during interrogations.* WHITEBEARD *changes moods.*)
         Weren't you taught manners, kaffir, that when you're in 135 the presence of the white man you must stand up? (*He kicks her.*) Up! Up! I can't talk to a grown woman on the floor. Up! (MASECHABA *stands.*) Who is LMA?

MASECHABA: I said I do not know.

WHITEBEARD: (*Taking some documents from the drawers of his table.*) 140 These are all the names and addresses of people you communicated with regularly—have you anything to say?

MASECHABA: I have communicated with lots of friends in the past, some of them are fellow writers. Do you expect me to live in isolation? I'm human.   145

WHITEBEARD: There you are, agreeing that you have something in common with the people on our lists.

MASECHABA: Whatever my friends do because of their convictions has nothing to do with me. I'm a simple poet.

WHITEBEARD: Yes, a poet you are, but I don't think you are that 150 simple. I have here photographs of two of your best friends who've skipped the country and received training in Moscow and in Africa. How do you respond to your friends doing that?

MASECHABA: Your government sells diamonds to Moscow. It is 155 known to be getting arms from Bulgaria. How do you respond to your friends doing that?

WHITEBEARD: Did you hear that Jonathan? Our poet friend fancies herself as a foreign policy analyst. Now you listen very carefully. You see these hands. They are clean, unsoiled and 160 they look friendly. Every day when these hands get home, they lift up a one-year-old bundle called David and they

throw him into the air and they catch him, they tickle him
and hold him steady as he threatens to fall over with pure
165 enjoyment. But Miss Masechaba, in order to protect that
little boy from you and your Marxist friends, to stop your
violence and terror from changing that little boy's joy to
tears, these hands will do anything, (*Hits her with both
hands.*) anything! And the blood will wash off very easily.
170 Do you understand me? I asked you a question. Do you understand me? Well my friend, seeing that you don't understand my words maybe you'll understand my actions. (*He
throttles her and throws her to the floor.* MASECHABA *falls and
writhes in pain. He kicks her in the stomach. Pause.*) Is there
175 anything that you don't understand?
MASECHABA: (*On her knees boldly faces* WHITEBEARD.) So deep is
my love for my land that those who fail to understand seek
to destroy me.

(*She stands up slowly.*)

Perhaps, finally at the very end
180 When the curtain falls
On the last act of your pillage
You will come to understand
How deeply
We loved this land
185 And cared for all its people

(*Upright and facing forward.*)

White and black
Free and unfree

(*There is silence and tension.*)

WHITEBEARD: Jonathan, will you deal with Masechaba as you
deem fit and if you have to teach her that electricity has
190 other uses than providing light you must do it!
JONATHAN: (*In a dilemma.*) But sir, it seems from the look of
things she does not know who this LMA is. Besides, she's
an ordinary poet.
WHITEBEARD: (*Angrily.*) Do I have to start wondering where
195 your loyalties lie Jonathan?
JONATHAN: No sir!
WHITEBEARD: Then do it! (WHITEBEARD *exits leaving the two
behind. A little later* JONATHAN *takes off his jacket to start the
torture of* MASECHABA *as lights fade to blackout.*)

FOURTH ENCOUNTER

Lights come up instantly on the cell area. MASECHABA's *body is lying
on a slab covered with a blanket. A hood covers her head.* WHITEBEARD
stands to the left of the slab with JONATHAN *opposite him. The atmosphere is tense.* JONATHAN *puts on his jacket.* WHITEBEARD *begins to
walk nervously round the slab.* JONATHAN *does the same to make way
for* WHITEBEARD.

WHITEBEARD: So, this is what you did?
JONATHAN: Yes my lord.
WHITEBEARD: How long has she been like this?
JONATHAN: My lord knows.
5 WHITEBEARD: I forget!
JONATHAN: One week!

WHITEBEARD: So, so! (*Pause.*) This is serious! I'll have to see
what I can do. Why the slab?
JONATHAN: So that you can see her well!
WHITEBEARD: Why the blanket? 10
JONATHAN: To have her covered!
WHITEBEARD: Why the hood?
JONATHAN: To help hide the head!
WHITEBEARD: What?
JONATHAN: It is common practice my lord that when detainees 15
are in this state, we cover their heads.
WHITEBEARD: It is a stupid procedure to have them covered all
the time! She was healthier when I last saw her!

(*Blackout.*)

FIFTH ENCOUNTER

In the cell a few hours later. The slab is positioned in a different place.
WHITEBEARD *and* JONATHAN *walk round it.*

WHITEBEARD: How's the head?
JONATHAN: As before.
WHITEBEARD: I forget! (JONATHAN *moves towards* MASECHABA *to
show her head.*)
Say it! (JONATHAN *stops.*) 5
JONATHAN: Septic.
WHITEBEARD: Colour?
JONATHAN: Red and pink.
WHITEBEARD: Put calamine lotion on head.
JONATHAN: Okay my lord. I make a note. Calamine lotion on 10
head.

(*He takes out pad and pencil and makes notes. A piece of rope protrudes
from his pocket.*)

WHITEBEARD: And why the rope?
JONATHAN: Used during interrogation.
WHITEBEARD: Unnecessary evidence!
JONATHAN: I make a note. 15
(*Writes again.*) Rope to discard. (*Slowly, with a sad look on
his face.*) Rope to discard.
WHITEBEARD: What is wrong now Jonathan?
JONATHAN: I remember seeing her hands many times in
church. 20
WHITEBEARD: Remember, you had a job to do.
JONATHAN: Yes my lord.

SIXTH ENCOUNTER

In the cell a few hours later. The slab has been removed. MASECHABA's
body lies sprawled on the floor.

WHITEBEARD: What will you tell the court?
JONATHAN: I'll say she threw herself out of the window in an
attempt to escape . . .
WHITEBEARD: No good. The interrogation room is on the
ground floor! 5
JONATHAN: No, no, it's simple. We called her in to have breakfast with us—she was so hungry that she ate her food so fast
that it choked her . . .

WHITEBEARD: Not convincing. We never have breakfast with
10   detainees in our rooms.
JONATHAN: (*Tries again.*) All right, I'll say she was on a hunger
      strike since we took her in.
WHITEBEARD: No! Jonathan when last did you check your
      record books? We gave that excuse some time ago!
15 JONATHAN: (*Still panicking.*) How about saying she hanged her-
      self with her gown-strap, that's right! (*Exited.*) Suicide!
WHITEBEARD: Not convincing. There's nothing in the cell to
      hang herself from!
JONATHAN: (*A bit hopeless but tries . . . to himself.*) Seems like
20   nothing is convincing. I'll try one more time . . . (*Hilarious
      with excitement.*) She slipped on a piece of soap . . . !
WHITEBEARD: You can't fool the public with that one again!
JONATHAN: (*Defeated.*) My lord knows all . . .
WHITEBEARD: Maybe we should look back at our history with
25   her. Maybe that will give us a clue.
JONATHAN: Yes my lord. Maybe that will give us an idea.
      (JONATHAN *exits.*)

(*Blackout.*)

SEVENTH ENCOUNTER

In the cell one day later. WHITEBEARD *and* JONATHAN *are among
huge piles of files.* MASECHABA'*s body is in the same position as before.*
JONATHAN *drops the files on the floor one after the other.*

JONATHAN: (*Apologetic.*) Some pages are missing sir . . .
WHITEBEARD: (*Authoritative.*) Confidential to The Party!

(*A pause as* JONATHAN *continues his search through the files.*)

JONATHAN: When will the pathologist see her sir?
WHITEBEARD: That too is confidential to The Party. Be here on
5   Sunday. Eight o'clock. Write your statement in full.
JONATHAN: Should I make up anything?
WHITEBEARD: No! That's important. He has to know what di-
      rection to channel his finding. Let him know it. What hap-
      pened. Where. When it happened and who was present.
10 JONATHAN: I'll remember. I make a note. (*Louder.*) Details of
      torture in full . . . !
WHITEBEARD: Shhh! Walls have ears. I pray they don't have a
      private pathologist.
JONATHAN: Will you allow it sir . . . ?
15 WHITEBEARD: Sometimes we have to show off our democratic
      processes. Now let's take a closer look at her.
JONATHAN: Why my lord?
WHITEBEARD: Don't be stupid we must make our own study.
JONATHAN: Fine. Orders taken.
20 WHITEBEARD: Remove the hood, the blanket. (JONATHAN *is slow.*)
      Snap to it! I have a meeting with the pathologist!
JONATHAN: Like to see her naked?
WHITEBEARD: (*Irritated.*) Quick! The court will order it. This
      looks horrible—cover her up!
25   (JONATHAN *covers the body.*) Calamine all visible wounds.
WHITEBEARD: The gown, why did you do it when she had it on?
JONATHAN: She refused to change into different clothes when I
      ordered her to.

(*Another long pause.*)

WHITEBEARD: Now bring back the slab. Move it to the right.
      (JONATHAN *does as instructed.*) More. Pick up the body   30
      and put it back on the slab. Higher. Make sure that we
      see all parts of her body before we make the first press
      statements.
JONATHAN: Why my lord?
WHITEBEARD: Don't be stupid, the family may order a public   35
      enquiry!
JONATHAN: Fine. Orders taken.
WHITEBEARD: Remove the blanket again. Bare the chest.
      (JONATHAN *unbuttons the gown and steps back.*) Now let's go
      to the legs. (*He rolls the gown up.*) Higher. Put calamine on   40
      chest and legs.
JONATHAN: I make a note. Calamine chest and legs.

(WHITEBEARD *and* JONATHAN *take a final look at* MASECHABA *as
in the opening scene.*)

JONATHAN: What if we were to clothe her in prison attire?
WHITEBEARD: That's stupid! This is detention. She hasn't been
      to prison yet.   45
JONATHAN: (*Humiliated.*) My lord knows everything.

(*More contemplation of* MASECHABA.)

WHITEBEARD: That's enough for the day and remember what-
      ever happens DON'T PANIC! You've proved your loyalty
      and I'll do everything to protect you!

(*He puts his arm around* JONATHAN *as they walk away and freeze
at some point with their faces looking down as if shying away from the
public eye.*)

(*General lights fade as Special comes up on* MASECHABA'*s head
and shoulders. Slow fade to semi-darkness on* WHITEBEARD *and*
JONATHAN *so that their shadows can be seen.* MASECHABA'*s voice can
be heard reciting her last poem.*)

EPILOGUE

(*On tape:*)

When the parricidal mania
That grips the uncrowned villains
Roams free
And the streets are
Dyed with blood   5
They would seek me out to pray together
At the altar
For they would have come to realise
That I was against their own destruction
And clung frantically   10
On the frail hope
That they would be brought to sanity

Perhaps finally
They would be calling me out
To rebuke the storms   15
But all hope and understanding
Shall have gone by then

(*Slow fade both positions to blackout.*)

Jack Davis

Jack Davis was born in Perth, Australia, in 1917 and raised in Yarloop; his mother—a Nyoongah (often Anglicized to "Nyungar"; nyoongah means "man" or "person"), one of the Aboriginal peoples of Western Australia—had been raised by whites and was uneducated, and Davis taught himself to read and write by studying an English-language dictionary. His family was moved to the Moore River Settlement in 1931, and he later lived on the Brookton Aboriginal Reserve, where he learned the Nyoongah language and history. He worked at a variety of trades while becoming an influential political figure; he served as director of the Aboriginal Center in Perth (1969–1971), as chairman of the Aboriginal Lands Trust in Western Australia (1971), as managing editor of the Aboriginal Publications Foundation (1972–1977), and as a member of the Institute for Aboriginal Studies in Canberra. He received the British Empire medal for his services in 1977.

Davis is best known in Australia for several fine volumes of poetry: *The First Born and Other Poems* (1976), *Jagardoo: Poems from Aboriginal Australia* (1978), *John Pat and Other Poems* (1988), and *Black Life* (1992). He has also written a memoir, *A Boy's Life* (1991). Davis's interest in documenting and preserving Nyoongah culture is visible throughout his plays, many of which record the history of English settlement and its effects: *Kullark* (1979), written to mark the sesquicentennial of Western Australia; *The Dreamers* (1982); *No Sugar* (1985), about the relocations to Moore River; *Bargunin: Smell the Wind* (1988); *In Our Town* (1992); and *The Honey Spot* (1987), a children's play. Davis's plays have been performed throughout Australia and in Europe and North America, and Davis has occasionally acted in them as well: he took the role of Billy in the 1986 revival of *No Sugar*.

NO SUGAR

No Sugar dramatizes life in the 1930s at the Moore River Settlement, where Davis's family had been forcibly moved in 1931. In 1800, 6,000 to 12,000 Nyoongah lived in the south-

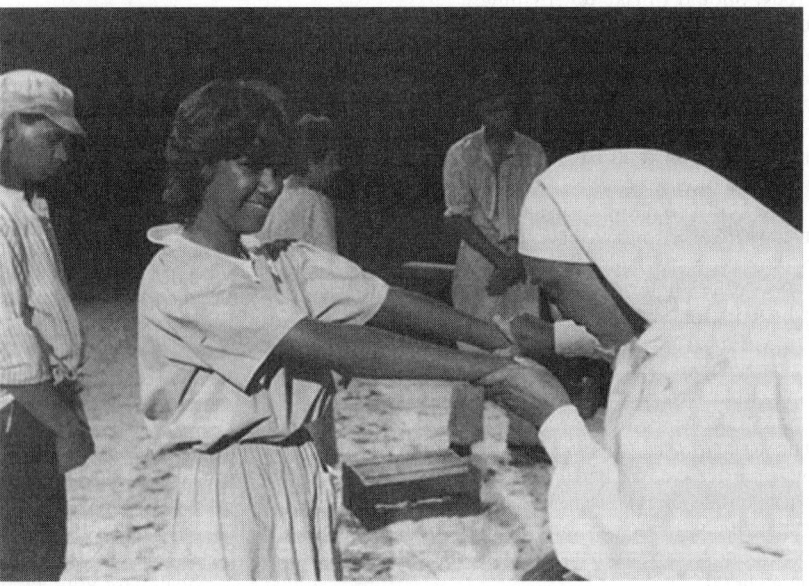

In the Playhouse Company production of Jack Davis's *No Sugar* (1985), Matron Neal inspects the Millimurra family in the Moore River Native Settlement.

western part of Australia, dispersed throughout a large geographical area and maintaining about a dozen language and social groups. Throughout the early nineteenth century, they made several attacks on settlers, their crops, and cattle, but by the 1840s little direct resistance remained, and the measles epidemic of the 1880s further decimated their numbers. Ultimately, the Nyoongah were simply dispossessed, to the extent that by 1900 there were few truly indigenous settlements or people remaining. At the turn of the century, white Australians found the "half-caste" population its principal concern and adopted a concerted strategy of "absorption": taking Aborigine children to be raised in white families, forcing families onto the settlements, where their children were raised in dormitories apart from the family, and other measures. W.O. Neville was appointed Chief Protector of Aborigines in 1915, and founded the Moore River Settlement a year later. In succeeding years, Aborigines from throughout Western Australia were forced to live there. As on American Indian reservations, conditions at Moore River were brutal: the Aborigines were prisoners in a hard landscape, with shanties for shelter, little food and clothing, and were punished for leaving. As Davis shows in *No Sugar,* Neville was both sympathetic to the need to resolve the "Native Question"—the title of a paper he delivered to the Australasian Association for the Advancement of Science in 1926—and responsible for implementing a destructive program of racial purification.

In Act Four of the play, during the 1934 Australia Day celebrations, the interned Aborigines of Moore River parody a verse of the hymn "There Is a Happy Land":

> There is a happy land,
> Far, far away.
> No sugar in our tea,
> Bread and butter we never see.
> That's why we're gradually
> Fading away.

No Sugar uses an open staging to document the direct consequences of the administrative attitudes and practices of the settlement program on the lives of the Aborigines the settlement is supposed to "protect," the ways it encourages the Aborigines to fade away. The play opens by showing Neville coping with the sharply decreasing budgets given to the settlement during the Depression, and deciding not to offer rations of soap or meat; at the same time, he's concerned to educate the Aborigines in European sanitation practices, teaching them to sew handkerchiefs and use toilet paper. The extent to which the government's "protection" of the Aborigines amounts to the systematic elimination of their way of life is everywhere evident in the play: the Millimurra family is rounded up for transport to the Moore River settlement without the time to gather their belongings or animals; the families are separated, and Joe is sent off to prison labor merely for challenging his captors' authority; the superintendent of Moore River deliberately assigns young Aborigine women to hospital duty and rapes them; the Aborigines are even prevented from learning to read and write in English, so that they could document their history. Yet the play also demonstrates the Millimurra family's unwillingness to disappear, the urgency with which they confront the "protection" system in order to escape it. And when Joe and Mary—the Biblical echo is intentional—finally do receive permission to leave Moore River, it's only on the condition that they never return to Northam, indeed that they remain outside the boundaries of institutional civic life in Western Australia. It is an opportunity they seize immediately.

NO SUGAR

Jack Davis

CHARACTERS

JIMMY MUNDAY
GRAN MUNDAY, *Jimmy's mother*
MILLY MILLIMURRA, *Jimmy's sister*
SAM MILLIMURRA, *Milly's husband*
JOE MILLIMURRA, *their eldest son*
CISSIE MILLIMURRA, *their daughter*
DAVID MILLIMURRA, *their younger son*
FRANK BROWN, *an unemployed farmer*
SERGEANT CARROL, *sergeant of police at Northam*
CONSTABLE KERR, *of the Northam Police*
JUSTICE OF THE PEACE, *a Northam cocky farmer*
AUBER OCTAVIUS NEVILLE, *Chief Protector of Aborigines*
MISS DUNN, *his secretary*
MR N.S. NEAL, *Superintendent of the Moore River Settlement*
MATRON NEAL, (*Koodjie*), *his wife, matron in charge of the Settlement hospital*
TOPSY, *a Settlement girl, assisting Matron*

SISTER EILEEN, *a missionary*
MARY DARGURRU, *a young girl from the Kimberley region*
BILLY KIMBERLEY, *a black tracker*
BLUEY, *a black tracker*

SETTING: *The play is designed for a dispersed setting on an open stage. On one side is the Avon Valley town of Northam, including the Police Station with two cells, a main street and the Government Well Aboriginal Reserve. Also on this side should be the office, in Murray Street, Perth, of the Chief Protector of Aborigines, with an entrance front and rear for whites and blacks respectively. The scene on the other side is the Moore River Native Settlement, near Mogumber in the Victoria Plains district. The areas include the Superintendent's office, the Millimurra tent and camp at Long Pool, a clearing in the pine plantation and a dais and flagpole. Other parts of the stage serve as an area by the railway line at Moolumbeenee and a meeting room of the Western Australian Historical Society.*

ACT ONE

Northam

SCENE I

Government Well Aboriginal Reserve, Northam, morning, 1929. SAM MILLIMURRA *prepares mugs of tea, lacing them generously with sugar. He passes one to* JOE *who is absorbed in the special centenary edition of the* Western Mail. GRAN *and* MILLY *sort clothes for washing.* DAVID *and* CISSIE *play cricket with a home-made bat and ball.* JIMMY *sharpens an axe, bush fashion.*

DAVID: Bowl overarm!
CISSIE: I can't.
DAVID: Well, try.

(*She does, clumsily.* JOE *bashes the paper into shape and reads aloud falteringly. His father,* SAM, *listens with great interest.*)

JOE: 'The—blood—was stirred . . . as if by a trumpet . . . by
5   the histor-ical . . .

(CISSIE *bowls again.* DAVID *bashes the ball out of sight.*)

DAVID: *Woolah!* Don Bradman.

(DAVID *and* CISSIE *scamper after the ball.*)

JOE: '. . . Headed by a tab-leau . . .
MILLY: David, where you goin'? Gimme that shirt, it's filthy.

(DAVID *removes it and inspects it but continues after the ball He and* CISSIE *exit.*)

JOE: '. . . Commemorating the pioneers whose lives . . .
10 GRAN: (*To* JIMMY.) James, you put that bucket a' water on?
JIMMY: Yeah, Mum, boilin' and waitin' for you by now.
JOE: '. . . Were a steadfast performance of duty in the face of difficulty and danger. With them was a reminder of the dan-

gers they faced, in the shape of three lorries . . . carrying Aborigines.   15

(*They all stop what they are doing and listen.*)

. . . Aborigines, incong . . . incongruously . . .
SAM: Come on.
JOE: All right! '. . . Dancing . . . to a brass-band.'

(SAM *laughs.*)

SAM: *Koorawoorung!* Nyoongahs corroboreein' to a *wetjala's* brass band!   20
JIMMY: Ah! That beats everythin': stupid bloody blackfellas.
GRAN: Ay! You . . . *dawarra* you *mirri* up and get them clothes down the soak, go on!

(JIMMY *gets up, but can't resist the final word.*)

JIMMY: You fellas, you know why them *wetjalas* marchin' down the street, eh? I'll tell youse why. 'Cause them bastards took   25 our country and them blackfellas dancin' for 'em. *Bastards!*

(*He nicks his finger with the axe and watches the blood drip to the ground.* GRAN *gives him a piece of cloth for it.*)

MILLY: Don't worry, if you woulda been there you woulda been right with 'em.
JIMMY: No bloody fear I wouldn't have.

(*He drives the axe savagely into a log.*)

GRAN: Eh! Now you take them clothes down the soak, you   30 'ear me?

(JIMMY *reluctantly obeys,* DAVID *and* CISSIE *return with the bat but no ball.* DAVID *wears his shirt inside out.*)

DAVID: You're the fielder; you're supposed to chase it.

CISSIE: Well, you shouldn't hit it so hard.

DAVID: Yeah, well it's lost now.

35 MILLY: Come on, you two, get to school. (*Reaching into a pocket.*) Here's twopence, you can buy an apple each for lunch.

(*She gives it to them.*)

DAVID: Aw, can't I have enough for a pie?

MILLY: It's all the money I got.

CISSIE: Aw mum, Old Tony the ding always sells us little shriv-
40   elled ones and them *wetjala* kids big *fat* ones.

JOE: Here's thrippence each.

(JOE *flips them sixpence.*)

DAVID: Aw, thanks, Brudge.

MILLY: Where's that shirt?

DAVID: (*Tapping his chest.*) 'Ere.

45 MILLY: Take it off.

DAVID: But it's clean on this side.

MILLY: Come 'ere.

(*She tugs it off him and swaps it for a clean one.*)

And you go straight down the soak after school. (*To* SAM *and* JOE.) And you fellas, we got no meat for dinner or supper;
50   you'll have to go out and get a couple of rabbits.

(GRAN *and* MILLY *exit.* JOE *continues to read to himself.*)

SAM: Ba, ba, what else?

JOE: 'The pag . . . page . . . page-ant pre-sented a picture of Western Australia's pre-sent condition of hopeful opti-mum-optimis-tic prosperity, and gave some idea of
55   what men mean when they talk about the soul of the nation.'

SAM: Sounds like bullshit to me. Come on, let's get these rabbits.

(JOE *springs to his feet and walks off. Dogs bark.*)

Bring Ruffy and Moonie; don't bring Spring, he's too slow.

(JOE *returns with a dowak. He picks up the camp oven.*)

60 JOE: *Allewah wilbra, gnuny barminy barkiny.*

(*He mimes throwing the dowak at a rabbit and runs off after his father.*)

SCENE II

A street in Northam, day. FRANK BROWN *rolls a cigarette from stoop-ers.* SERGEANT CARROL *enters from the police station and approaches him.*

SERGEANT: Hey, just a moment you!

FRANK: Yes?

SERGEANT: How long you been in Northam?

FRANK: About a fortnight.

5 SERGEANT: Where are you camped?

FRANK: Down near the saleyards.

SERGEANT: By yourself?

FRANK: No, there's about ten other blokes.

SERGEANT: White blokes?

FRANK: What?   10

SERGEANT: Not abos or half-castes?

FRANK: No, why?

SERGEANT: Your name Francis Brown?

FRANK: Yes.

SERGEANT: You've been seen hangin' about with natives.   15

FRANK: It's not against the law.

SERGEANT: No, Mr Brown, it's not, but it is an offence to sup-ply liquor to an Aboriginal native under the Aboriginal Act.

FRANK: Thanks for the information.   20

SERGEANT: Oh I've got plenty of information, mate. Last Friday, James Munday, a native, took a bundle of fox scalps to the Shire Office and collected a bounty of three pounds.

FRANK: Very interesting. And?

SERGEANT: And, on Friday night he was apprehended drunk in   25
    Bernard Park after you were seen purchasing two bottles of port wine in the Shamrock Hotel.

FRANK: I'm a wine connoisseur.

SERGEANT: (*Intimately.*) Listen, mate, don't try being smart. This time I sent Munday back to his camp with a warning;   30
    next time I'll nail him and the bloke that buys wine for him. The last bloke I nabbed for supplying is doing three months hard labour in Fremantle.

FRANK: Thanks for the tip.

SERGEANT: Why don't you think about movin' on?   35

FRANK: Where to? I been on the road already for six months. Kondinin, Merredin, Kalgoorlie: no work. Headed up the Murchison, Mullewa, Northampton: nothing. I got a wife and two kids staying with her parents in Leederville. I can't even raise a train fare to Perth to go and see them.   40

(*The* SERGEANT *takes out a packet of cigarettes and gives a couple to* FRANK.)

SERGEANT: Look, mate, I understand; I hear it every day a' the week, but I got a job to do, so don't forget what I said.

FRANK: Thanks.

SERGEANT: Natives best left to keep to themselves.

FRANK: I was only tryin' to do—   45

SERGEANT: (*Interrupting.*) You might think your doin' 'em a good turn, but your not. Take it from me, I been dealin' with 'em for years. I got nothin' against 'em, but I know exactly what they're like.

(FRANK *carefully puts the cigarettes away as the* SERGEANT *enters the police station.* MISS DUNN *enters an office with a sign displayed, reading 'Government of Western Australia, Fisheries, Forestry, Wildlife and Aborigines'. There are two desks, each with a tele-phone. She goes immediately to one, takes a note from her handbag and dials.* FRANK *exits. The* SERGEANT *settles behind his desk and busies himself.*)

MISS DUNN: (*Into the receiver.*) Hell . . . Hello, good morning. Is   50
    that the *West*? Yes, thankyou . . . I'd like to place an adver-tisement, 'Wanted to Sell'.

(NEVILLE *enters. He takes some files from his briefcase and settles down at his desk with the West Australia.*)

NEVILLE: Good Morning, Miss Dunn.

MISS DUNN: (*Into the receiver.*) A motor cycle. (*To* NEVILLE.) Good
55   morning, Mr Neville. I'm sorry, it's a personal . . . (*Into the
      receiver.*) sorry. Twelve pounds, in, Douglas, 1923 Model,
      one forty-eight Stirling Street, Highgate . . . Please . . . (*To*
      NEVILLE.) Sorry, Mr Neville, it's a personal call . . . (*Into the
      receiver.*) Thank you . . . Dunn . . . Miss E.

60   NEVILLE: I didn't know you were a motor cyclist.

MISS DUNN: No, it's my brother's. He's down the South-West,
      looking for work, and his wife and children are with me.

NEVILLE: Couldn't find anything in Perth.

MISS DUNN: No, and not for want of trying. He eventually got
65   work selling wirelesses. Door to door.

NEVILLE: Doesn't sound very suitable.

MISS DUNN: He only sold one in three weeks, didn't even cover
      the cost of the petrol.

NEVILLE: Well, he's certainly not on his own. Unemploy-
70   ment's hit thirty per cent according to the *West*.

MISS DUNN: There's some mail for you, and an urgent internal
      one from the Minister's Office and one from the Northam
      Town Clerk.

NEVILLE: Goodness me, the *West*'s scraping the barrel for a bit
75   of good news. Results of the 'Most Economical Housewife
      Contest' . . . What next? . . . I'm afraid you're not the lucky
      winner, Miss Dunn.

(*He shows her the paper.*)

MISS DUNN: 'Mrs Hill of Greenmount on two pounds five
      shillings a week . . .' Rent, seven shillings; light, one and
80   threepence.

(MISS DUNN *reads to herself.*)

NEVILLE: She's ingenious, alright: makes tap washers out of old
      car tyres.

MISS DUNN: Yes, and slippers from her husband's old felt hats.

(NEVILLE *picks up the mail and starts to read it.*)

NEVILLE: Perhaps the *West* could run a contest for the most fru-
85   gal civil servant . . . Could you get me Sergeant Carrol in
      Northam on the line, please?

(*He gets out files and makes notes while* MISS DUNN *dials the exchange.*)

MISS DUNN: Trunks please . . . Hello . . . Northam nine please
      . . . Yes, BM nine seven oh seven . . . Thank you operator.

(*She hangs up.*)

NEVILLE: Can you take down a note for the Minister, please?
90   (*He shuffles through the files and documents.*) My dear Minister,
      herewith the information requested. I know I don't need to
      remind your good self of the extreme budgetry constraints
      under which this Department operates. Item one: the native
      weekly ration currently costs this Department two shillings
95   and fourpence per week. Perhaps this bears comparison
      with the sustenance paid to white unemployed which I be-
      lieve is seven shillings per week.

(*The phone rings in the Northam Police Station.* SERGEANT CARROL
answers it.)

SERGEANT: Hello, Northam Police Station. Thanks, Sybil.

NEVILLE: Item two: off the cuff, the proposed budget cut of
      three thousand one hundred and thirty-four pounds could   100
      be met by discontinuing the supply of meat in native ra-
      tions. Soap was discontinued this financial year. Item Three:
      of eighty girls from the Moore River Native Settlement
      who went out into domestic service last year, thirty
      returned—   105

(*The phone rings in* NEVILLE'*s office.* MISS DUNN *picks up the receiver.*)

MISS DUNN: Excuse me, Mr Neville . . . (*Into the receiver.*) Hello,
      Chief Protector of Aborigines Office . . . Thank you, opera-
      tor. (*To* NEVILLE.) Northam.

(NEVILLE *takes the call and* MISS DUNN *hangs up.*)

NEVILLE: Sergeant Carrol. Neville, Aborigines.

SERGEANT: Hello, Northam Police . . . Hello.   110

NEVILLE: It's an awful line, Sergeant. Are you on the line?

SERGEANT: Yes, I can hear you.

NEVILLE: Good. We seem to have encountered a few obstacles
      with the new reserve. The Guilford Road site isn't accept-
      able to the Council. Apparently the adjoining landholders   115
      have lodged objections.

SERGEANT: I thought they might. What grounds? Did they say?

NEVILLE: (*Looking at his letter.*) A Mr Smith . . .

SERGEANT: Oh, yeah . . .

NEVILLE: . . . Claims he wouldn't be able to go out and leave his   120
      wife home alone at night.

SERGEANT: And he's generally down the Shamrock Hotel till
      stumps.

(GRAN *and* MILLY *approach the Police Station.*)

NEVILLE: Well, the upshot of it is that the Lands Department
      won't be able to gazette it, so you as the local Protector of   125
      Aborigines will have to recommend an alternative site . . .
      The Council's concerned that it's well away from any
      residences.

GRAN: Chergeant! . . . Chergeant!

NEVILLE: What's that terrible racket?   130

GRAN: Chergeant!

SERGEANT: (*To* NEVILLE.) Ration day.

GRAN: Chergeant.

NEVILLE: All right, letter to follow, I'll leave you to it.

SERGEANT: Thanks, Mr Neville.   135

NEVILLE: Cheerio.

(*The* SERGEANT *and* NEVILLE *hang up.*)

SERGEANT: Alright Gran, come in.

NEVILLE: Where was I?

MISS DUNN: Of eighty who went out in the domestic service last
      year . . .   140

NEVILLE: Thirty returned to the settlement in pregnant condi-
      tion, yours etcetera . . . If you could type that straight away
      I'll run it up to the Office myself.

(*The* SERGEANT *places flour, sugar and two small packages on the
bench and marks them off in his ration book.*)

SERGEANT: Flour, sugar, tea . . . And how you been keepin',
145   Granny?

GRAN: I'm awright.

SERGEANT: Been behavin' yourself?

GRAN: Have you?

SERGEANT: There's your butcher's order, meat and dripping.

150 MILLY: (*Inspecting the small packages.*) You got two cream a tartar 'ere.

SERGEANT: Right, let's change 'em.

GRAN: Damper won't rise without no bicarbonate.

SERGEANT: That shouldn't worry you, Granny, you should remember when you used to grind up jam and wattle seeds.

155 GRAN: More better than white man's flour, no weevils in jam
and wattle seeds.

SERGEANT: Good tucker, eh?

GRAN: When I was that high we go and get 'em and smash 'em
up and get a bag full, that much!

160 SERGEANT: You can still collect 'em, nothin' stoppin' you.

GRAN: Where? *Wetjala* cut all the trees down.

MILLY: Haven't got any soap yet.

SERGEANT: I'm afraid that soap is no longer included as a ration
item.

165 MILLY: What do you mean, we got no more soap?

SERGEANT: That's right.

MILLY: But why? What am I gonna wash with? How can I keep
my kids clean and sen 'em to school?

SERGEANT: You could buy some.

170 MILLY: What with?

GRAN: What about *gnummarri*? You stop that too?

SERGEANT: No, Granny, you still get your stick of nigger twist.

(*He gives it to her.*)

MILLY: Whose idea was it to stop the soap?

SERGEANT: The idea, as you call it, came from the Aboriginal
175   Department in Perth.

GRAN: Mister Neville?

MILLY: I just can't believe it: no soap!

SERGEANT: Your trouble, Milly, is you got three healthy men
bludging off you, too lazy to work.

180 MILLY: Where they gonna get work?

SERGEANT: They're afraid to look for it in case they find it.

MILLY: Cockies want 'em to work for nothin'.

GRAN: They not slaves, Chergeant!

SERGEANT: Well, they'll have to work if you want luxury items
185   like soap.

MILLY: Look, last week my Joe cut a hundred posts for old
Skinny Martin and you know what he got? A pair of
second-hand boots and a piece of stag ram so tough even
the dawgs couldn't eat it; skinnier than old Martin 'imself.

190 GRAN: And we couldn't eat the boots.

MILLY: You wait till brother Jimmy hears about this no soap
business. He'll make you fellas jump.

SERGEANT: Yeah, and you tell that bush lawyer brother of
yours, if he comes here arguing I'll make him jump:
195   straight inside.

(*They turn to go. As they leave he raises his voice after them.*)

You hear me?

MILLY: (*Calling.*) Yeah, I hear you. Can't help hearin' you.

(*They walk down the street.*)

GRAN: (*Calling.*) You don't want to shout like that, Chergeant.
You'll 'ave a fit, just like a dingo when he gets bait.

MILLY: (*Calling.*) Seein' you're drinkin down the Federal every 200
night, Sergeant, you can tell old Skinny Martin to stick his
stag ram right up his skinny *kwon*!

GRAN: (*Calling.*) Yeah, an' the boots too.

(*They exit, laughing and hooting Nyoongah fashion. The* SERGEANT
*returns to the police station, puts the ration book away and settles down
to reading the newspaper.* MISS DUNN *finishes typing the letter. She
hands it to* NEVILLE, *who reads it quickly.*)

NEVILLE: (*Signing it.*) Thank you, Miss Dunn. We'd better get
a thank you note off to Mr Neal. 205

MISS DUNN: I can do it straight away for you.

NEVILLE: All right; Mr N.S. Neal, Superintendent, Moore
River Native Settlement, etcetera.

    Dear Mr Neal, just a short note to thank you for your . . .
thank you and Matron for your hospitality on our recent visit 210
to the Settlement. The Settlement is looking splendid, considering, obviously a credit to you both. The conduct of the
ceremony was a tribute to your military precision, and the
afternoon tea, especially Matron's homemade lemonade, was
splendid on such a hot day. As I mentioned, I was a little con- 215
cerned to see so many dirty little noses amongst the children.
I'm a great believer that if you provide the native the basic
accoutrements of civilisation you're half way to civilising
him. I'd like to see each child issued with a handkerchief and
instructed on its use. Funds as always are short so I've taken 220
the liberty of ordering several bolts of cloth from Government stores. I'm sure the girls in the sewing room could run
up the handkerchiefs. I take your point about losing them
and suggest attaching them to their sleeves by way of a tape.
Likewise, as discussed, the stores branch will henceforth be 225
supplying limited supplies of toilet paper for use in the dormitory lavatories. I think some practical training from yourself and Matron in its correct usage would be appropriate. If
you can successfully inculcate such basic but essential details
of civilised living you will have helped them along the road 230
to taking their place in Australian society. Again, many
thanks to Matron and yourself. Australia Day at the settlement is something I'll always look forward to.

    Yours, etcetera.

    I'd better get this off to the Minister. I'll be back after 235
lunch.

SCENE III

Government Well, dusk. Magpies are carolling. CISSIE *is preparing a
damper.* JOE *and* DAVID *play two-up with bottle tops.* DAVID *has the
headers.*

DAVID: Come on, set me up. Not beer tops, wine tops.

CISSIE: (*Calling.*) Joe! Make a place for the damper for me.

JOE: (*Laughing, to* DAVID.) Don't make no difference.

DAVID: It does.

JOE: Why? 5

DAVID: Wine cost more than beer.

CISSIE: Joe! Joe, come on.

JOE: Okay, Okay.

(CISSIE *calls impatiently. The dough is beginning to fall apart.*)

CISSIE: Joe, hurry up!
10 JOE: Awright.
CISSIE: Joe, come on!

(CISSIE *stands by the fire holding the dough.* JOE *uses his dowak to make an impression in the ashes.* CISSIE *puts the damper in and covers it with ashes.*)

DAVID: (*Spinning.*) *Woolah!* Heads!
JOE: Let's have a look.
DAVID: *Moorditj, unna?*

(*The dogs bark.*)

15 CISSIE: David, git me some more wood.

(DAVID *spins.*)

    David!

DAVID: Wait till I've finished spinnin'.
CISSIE: *Shoo-i,* tail them.

(DAVID *spins them high.*)

DAVID: Have a look at them, Ciss.

(*He looks. They're tails.*)

20   See what you made me do.

(*He goes for the wood.*)

CISSIE: Joe, better chop some more wood up.
JOE: Yeah, okay.

(*He spins.*)

    Bastard.

(*He picks up the axe and goes to the woodpile.* DAVID *returns with a load of wood. He puts it down and begins to count his bottle tops.*)

DAVID: Boy, look at my *boondah.*

(JIMMY *enters.*)

25 JIMMY: Wait till I see him tomorrow. I'll give him no soap.

(SAM *and* BILLY *follow* JIMMY *on.* FRANK *follows them. The men are slightly drunk. Finally,* GRAN *and* MILLY *enter.*)

CISSIE: About time.
DAVID: Took youse long enough, got any boiled lollies?
GRAN: No. No lollies.
MILLY: Ain't even got no soap.
30 JOE: (*Indicating* FRANK.) *Gneean baal?*
JIMMY: He's our friend.
SAM: Ay! Mate! That's me eldest boy Joe, and that's Cissie and
    that's the youngest, David.
FRANK: Hello.

(*The children don't reply.*)

CISSIE: Ay, Mum? Why isn't there any soap? I wanna wash my   35
    hair tomorrow.
GRAN: What you got in the camp oven?

(*She looks.*)

MILLY: Don't git soap in the rations no more.
GRAN: (*Peering into the camp oven.*) No onions or taters.
CISSIE: Why? What for?   40

(*She feels her hair.*)

MILLY: Just what I said, darlin', Sergeant ain't giving no soap
    any more.
GRAN: Don't worry, we can use *tjeerung* bush. I know where
    some growin'.
JIMMY: Don't worry about Sergeant, I'll give him a piece of my   45
    mind.
GRAN: You know what he'll give you? Six months.

(JIMMY *takes a drink.*)

JIMMY: Six months.

(*He laughs.*)

Mother, I can do that standing on my head.

(*He passes the bottle to* FRANK.)

    Here, mate.   50
DAVID: Ay, Dad, fixed my bike today. Wanna see it?
SAM: Yeah.

(DAVID *runs off, followed by* CISSIE.)

DAVID: It's goin' real good.

(GRAN *puts onions and potatoes in the camp oven.* JIMMY *produces turnips from his pocket.*)

JIMMY: Here, Mum, chuck them in.
MILLY: Ay! Where d'you git them from?   55
JOE: He never growed 'em and I bet he never bought 'em.

(MILLY *takes them, prepares them and adds them to the rabbit stew.* JIMMY *produces a mouth organ.*)

MILLY: You lookin' for gaol awright!
JIMMY: (*To* FRANK.) You been inside?
FRANK: Inside? Inside where?
JIMMY: Gaol. You been in Freeo?   60
FRANK: No.
GRAN: You'll be in gaol if Chergeant catch you here.
SAM: Ne'mine 'bout Sergeant, Mother-In-Law; give him a feed.
MILLY: Won't be long; stew ain't proper cooked yet.

(JIMMY *takes a drink.*)

JIMMY: Ay *wetjala.* You know how many time I been in gaol?   65
    (*Holding up four fingers.*) That many times.
FRANK: (*Shyly.*) What for?

JIMMY: Aw, drinkin', fightin' and snowdroppin'.

SAM: You know what snowdroppin' is?

70 MILLY: Pinchin' things off other people's clothes lines.

JIMMY: Hey, *wetjala*, mate, you know when I was a little fella, 'bout twelve, thirteen years old . . .

JOE: Aw, here we go . . .

JIMMY: Shut up, you. (*To* FRANK.) You know what I was?

75 FRANK: Ah, no.

JIMMY: Choir boy. I tell you I was the leadin' choir boy at New Norcia Mission; wasn't I, Mother?

SAM: Didn't do you much good.

MILLY: He used to sing 'Ave Maria' solo, real good.

80 JIMMY: Yeah! (*To* SAM.) 'Ow do you know? You wasn't even there.

SAM: 'Course I was there. (*To* FRANK.) That's where I met her, *unna* Mill?

FRANK: Did you get married at New Norcia?

85 SAM: Too right.

GRAN: In the church too.

JIMMY: An' engaged under a Government blanket.

MILLY: Shut up! *Dawarra, nitja wetjala.*

GRAN: (*Clicking her tongue.*) *Choo, kienya.*

90 JIMMY: I'm only jokin'. Anyways, who wants to 'ear a song?

(JIMMY *produces a mouth organ and plays 'Springtime in the Rockies'.* MILLY *begins to remove the damper from the ashes and dust it off.*)

MILLY: Cissie! David! Mum, see if the stew's cooked . . . Cissie! David!

(GRAN *checks the stew.*)

GRAN: Yeah, it's cooked.

(CISSIE *and* DAVID *return with the bike.* JOE *spreads a wogga on the ground.*)

Cissie, plates, plates. David, put the billy on.

95 DAVID: Me bike's *moorditj;* we went right down the rubbish dump.

CISSIE: Yeah, an' I had to push you back through the sand.

(DAVID *lays the bike on its side and they sit and serve the food.* SAM *breaks up the damper.*)

SAM: (*To* FRANK.) You eat this before?

FRANK: Damper? Plenty a' times.

100 SAM: Cooked in the ashes?

FRANK: No.

JOE: You eat underground mutton before?

(MILLY *gives him a plate of stew.*)

FRANK: What? Oh, thanks, missus.

JIMMY: Underground mutton!

105 JOE: Rabbit.

JIMMY: You try that, dip the damper, *moorditj!*

FRANK: Yeah, we used to live on 'em when we was on the farm.

GRAN: James, you come an' get your supper.

JIMMY: No, leave it, I'll get it dreckly.

(*He takes a long drink of wine as the others eat.*)

(*To* GRAN *and* MILLY, *indicating* FRANK.) You see that fella 110
there, Mum, Mill? He had his own farm once. You wouldn't believe it, eh?

JOE: (*To* FRANK.) Yeah? Where?

FRANK: Out Lake Yealering.

JOE: What happened? 115

FRANK: Aw, between the rabbits and a couple of bad seasons and the bank, the bloody bank, I lost it; the lot, even the crop in the ground.

JIMMY: (*Drunken.*) Yeah, fuckin' gubmet. Fucks everybody up; everybody, eh? Eh? You allowed to walk down the street 120
after sundown? Eh?

FRANK: Yeah, don't see why not.

JIMMY: Well I'm not. None of us are; you know we're not allowed in town, not allowed to go down the soak, not allowed to march . . . ? 125

(*He mimes handcuffs and gaol by first putting his wrists together and then placing a hand downwards over his forehead with the fingers spread over his eyes.*)

Manatj grab us like that. Bastards . . .

FRANK: Who?

GRAN: Politjmans.

JIMMY: They can shoot our dawgs, anytime they want to. Bastards. They shot Streak. (*To* SAM *and* MILLY.) Eh, you 'member 130
Streak. Kill and show dawg, used to catch meat for every blackfella in Northam and they shot him. (*Miming.*) Just like that. (*Maudlin, almost in tears.*) Ay, Mill, he's married; got three kids and a wife.

MILLY: (*Sympathetically.*) *Nyorn, winyarn.* 135

GRAN: (*To* FRANK.) Where they now?

FRANK: When we walked off I sent 'em to Perth, stayin' with her parents.

(JIMMY *drags a wallet out of* FRANK'S *pocket.*)

JIMMY: Show 'em that photo. Go on, mate, show 'em.

(JIMMY *gives* FRANK *the wallet and stands.*)

(*Wandering off.*) Go on, show 'em. 140

SAM: Where you goin'?

JIMMY: I'm gonna strain the spuds.

(FRANK *takes out the photo and passes it around.*)

MILLY: All girls, eh?

GRAN: *Nyorn, winyarn,* pretty *koolangah* too.

SAM: Nice lookin' *yorgah.* 145

CISSIE: She come from Lake Yealering?

FRANK: No, met her at a dancin' contest; Charleston, at the Lux, in Perth.

SAM: How long since you seen your kids?

FRANK: Six months; haven't even sent 'em any money. 150

(JIMMY *returns and falls over the bike in the dark.*)

JIMMY: Oh, Jesus, me bloody leg! Fuck that bike!

(JIMMY *kicks at the bike savagely.*)

DAVID: Oh, Uncle Jimmy, don't do that; I just fixed it up.

JOE: (*Jumping up.*) Eh, *Kongi,* David's been workin' on it all day. *Kienya.*

(*He runs to rescue the bike, but collects an accidental blow from* JIMMY.)

155 Ow! me nose!

(SAM *jumps up, runs to* JIMMY *and pushes him.*)

SAM: You cut that out, you hear me?
JIMMY: You git!

(*He swings an ineffectual punch at* SAM.)

SAM: Just stop it, awright?

(JIMMY *attacks and they engage in a ragged brawl. After a moment they separate and circle one-another.* JIMMY *takes his coat off.*)

JIMMY: Awright, come on, come on.
160 SAM: Stop it, you hear me? And none of your bitin'.
FRANK: I'd better go, Mrs Millimurra.
MILLY: Yeah, awright.

(FRANK *stands.*)

FRANK: And thanks for the really nice meal.
MILLY: That's all right. Eh! Cut it out, you two.
165 FRANK: Tooroo!

(FRANK *leaves.* JIMMY *and* SAM *are locked together, cursing each other.* CISSIE *and* DAVID *rescue the bike from under their feet.* JOE *blows his nose and looks for blood on his sleeve.*)

GRAN: Don't you hit him, Sam.
SAM: I will if he bites me.
GRAN: I'll stop you two fellas.

(*She charges at them, grabbing both by the hair and pulling viciously. They separate and she falls on her backside.* MILLY *laughs.*)

MILLY: Aw, Mum, you're cruel.

(JOE *goes and tries to pick her up.* SAM *seizes his chance and sits on* JIMMY, *who thrashes about helplessly.*)

170 JOE: Granny, git up, you're getting dirt all over you.

(GRAN *gets up with help from* JOE.)

JIMMY: Who do you think you are, fuckin' Jack Johnston?
SAM: You think you're fuckin' Jack Dempsey.
GRAN: I'll stop youse, I'll stop youse.

(*She takes her wahna stick and gives them both a solid poke in the ribs. They separate and get up, reluctantly.*)

(*To* SAM.) Now git off him. You know he's *weern koort minditj.*
175 SAM: He ain't sick in the chest, he's sick in the bloody head.

(JIMMY *crawls for his coat, then for the bottle.* MILLY *beats him to it.*)

MILLY: This is real fightin' stuff, eh? Real fightin' stuff.

(*She pours it onto the ground.* JIMMY *sits, head between his knees, and groans.*)

SCENE IV

The Police Station and lock-up, Northam, night. Two separate cells imprison JIMMY *and* SAM. *The* SERGEANT *and* CONSTABLE *put possessions into drawstring bags and record their contents. Beside them stands a bottle of port, nearly empty.*

SERGEANT: Munday, James Emmanuel.
CONSTABLE: One mouth organ, one length of binder twine; tobacco tin, Wild Woodbine; one book, *Lasseter's Last Ride,* eightpence halfpenny.
SERGEANT: (*Inspecting the bottle.*) Port. Who got it for 'em? 5
CONSTABLE: (*Laughing.*) They're not sayin'.

(JIMMY *takes out a mouth organ and plays 'Home, Sweet Home'.*)

SERGEANT: Be that bloke camped down the goods yard. I'll check with publicans and pick him up in the morning . . . (*Nodding at* JIMMY.) Thought you took that thing off him.
CONSTABLE: (*Picking up a bag.*) I did, it's here. 10
SERGEANT: Musta had two of 'em. Get it off him.

(*The* CONSTABLE *walks down to* JIMMY's *cell.*)

CONSTABLE: Give me that instrument.
JIMMY: This ain't a hinstrument, it's a mouth organ.
CONSTABLE: Hand it over.
JIMMY: You already got one. 15
CONSTABLE: Give it here.
JIMMY: I gave you me other one.
CONSTABLE: Just bloody-well hand it over.
SAM: Give it to him, *Gnoolya, baal nooniny barminy.*

(JIMMY *relents and pokes it through the door. The* CONSTABLE *returns and puts it in the bag.*)

JIMMY: Bastard. 20
CONSTABLE: Two mouth organs. Wish I knew how to play one of these.

(JIMMY *picks up the toilet bucket.*)

JIMMY: (*Calling.*) Eh, Sergeant! Sergeant!
SERGEANT: (*To the* CONSTABLE.) See what he wants.

(*The* CONSTABLE *walks to the cellblock doorway.*)

JIMMY: (*Calling.*) Sergeant! 25
CONSTABLE: What do you want?
JIMMY: Tell your boss the *koomp* bucket's got a hole in it.
CONSTABLE: (*To the* SERGEANT.) He reckons the piss bucket's got a hole in it.
SERGEANT: Bullshit; he can't aim straight. 30
CONSTABLE: There's nothing wrong with it, you not aimin' straight.

(*The* CONSTABLE *returns to the bench.*)

JIMMY: (*Calling.*) I'm aiming straight, all right. I'm a good shot. I can knock a rabbit's eye out at a hundred yards, and

35   I *could* blow the sergeant's head off with a three-oh-three at
     six hundred, bloody oath.
SAM: Eh, *Gnoolya, dubakieny.*
SERGEANT: Listen, Munday, if you know what's good for you,
     you'll shut up.
40 JIMMY: Him, he don't care. He's happy he's got us here. Fuck
     'em! Fuck 'em! Fuck 'em all!

(He hurls the bucket against the wall.)

SAM: *Gnoolya,* you flamin' idiot.
SERGEANT: *(To the* CONSTABLE.*)* That's government property.
     Stop him.

(The CONSTABLE *goes to* JIMMY*'s cell carrying a baton.)*

45 CONSTABLE: Put that down!
SAM: Stop it, Gnoolya, steady down, steady down!

*(*JIMMY *puts the bucket down and turns around as if to urinate in it.
The* CONSTABLE *returns to the bench.)*

SERGEANT: Damage to government property, to whit, one shit
     bucket. Add it to the charge sheet.

(The CONSTABLE *gets out the charge sheet. Silence.)*

JIMMY: *(Calling.)* I don't give two hoots of a lamb's tail. Never
50   mind, Serge, I'll sing you a song. I'll sing you a hymn, if
     you like. *(Singing.)*

        'Hail, Queen of Heaven, the ocean star,
        Guide of the wanderer here below,
        Thrown on life's surge, we claim thy care:
55   Save us from peril and from woe.
        Mother of Christ, star of the sea,
        Pray for the wanderer, pray for—'

(He stops abruptly.)

     No hymns. No good to you, you're a proper *mummari.*
     Proper *Mummari,* fuckin' both of youse . . . *(Singing.)*

60   'When its springtime in the Rockies,
        I'm comin' back to you . . .'

SERGEANT: I think I preferred the mouth organ.
SAM: See you gettin' six months tomorrow, *gnoolya.*
JIMMY: *(Calling.)* Six months! I can do that on me fuckin' head.
65 SERGEANT: I'll see what we can do.
JIMMY: *(Calling.)* Yeah, you would. *(Singing.)*

        Mammy, Mammy,
        How I love you, How I love you,
        My dear old Mammy . . .

70 SERGEANT: Oh, gawd!
JIMMY: *(Singing.)*

        I'd walk a million miles
        For one of your smiles,
        My Ma-a-a-ammy.

75   *(Calling.)* Hey Serge, Serge.
SERGEANT: *(To the* CONSTABLE.*)* Ignore him.

JIMMY: *(Calling.)* I seen that talkin' picture at the Palace, sit-
     tin' right up the front, the roped off section for blackfellas.
     Al Jolson makin' out he was black, poor white bastard.
SAM: Eh, *dubakieny, wahnginy.*   80
JIMMY: *(Calling.)* Sergeant! Sergeant!
CONSTABLE: *(To the* SERGEANT.*)* Jesus, I wish he'd shut up.
JIMMY: *(Calling.)* Eh, Sergeant! You bin, you bin out to Gub-
     ment Well and told Mum and Milly me and Sam in here?
     . . . Eh? No, you wouldn't think of that.   85
SERGEANT: *(Standing, to the* CONSTABLE.*)* I'll leave you to it. I'm
     going to interview a few publicans.
CONSTABLE: Had enough?

(The SERGEANT *exits towards the main street.)*

JIMMY: *(Calling.)* Fuck you, you white bastard, fuck you.
     (Singing feebly.)   90
        I don't give a damn for any damn man,
        That don't give a damn for me.

SCENE V

The court house at Northam, morning. The SERGEANT *stands near the*
JP, *a local cocky, who sits at the bench.*

JP: What have we got?
SERGEANT: Not much.
JP: Good, I'm in a hurry.
SERGEANT: Two natives. One supplying.
JP: All right, let's get moving. I've got to get to a bank auction   5
     in Wongamine; tryin' to pick up a cheap binder.
SERGEANT: *(Calling.)* Francis James Brown.

*(*FRANK *enters and goes to the dock. The* SERGEANT *passes the* JP *a paper bag. The* JP *pulls the port bottle out of it and looks at it curiously.)*

     Evidence.

(The JP *examines it and sniffs it.)*

JP: Are Munday and, ah, what's-his-name, natives within the
     meaning of the Aborigines Act?   10
SERGEANT: Yes, sir.
JP: What do you plead?
FRANK: Guilty with an explanation, sir.
JP: If you're guilty I can't see much point in an explanation.
FRANK: I'd still like to say something, sir.   15
SERGEANT: The accused has been warned on two previous occa-
     sions about associating with natives.
JP: All right, make it brief.
FRANK: I arrived in Northam a few days ago, and I was broke
     and I didn't have anything to eat for two days and I ran into   20
     Jimmy in the park and he—
JP: *(Interrupting, to the* SERGEANT.*)* Who?
SERGEANT: James Munday. He was one of the natives arrested
     along with the accused.
JP: *(To* FRANK.*)* All right, get on with it.   25
FRANK: Well, he was a real mate to me. He took me to his
     home and gave me a meal of
JP: *(Interrupting, to the* SERGEANT.*)* His what?
SERGEANT: His camp at Government Well.

30 FRANK: He gave me a meal of—
JP: (*Interrupting.*) Look, I'm not interested in what you had for dinner. If you've got an explanation, just tell me what it is.
FRANK: (*Nervously.*) And he even lent me a razor; I hadn't had a shave in several days. He and his family were very kind to
35 me and when he asked me to pick up a bottle of wine for him, I felt obliged to do it.
JP: Were you aware that you were breaking the law?
FRANK: Yes sir, but I didn't—
JP: (*Interrupting.*) Is there any previous record?
40 SERGEANT: No.
FRANK: I've never been in trouble before. I am an ex-service-man and I settled at Lake Yealering.
JP: All right, I don't need your life story. I understand the difficulty of the situation you were in, but it's my duty to
45 protect natives and half-castes from alcohol. In view of this, I sentence you to six weeks imprisonment with hard labour.

(FRANK *steps down.*)

SERGEANT: (*Calling.*) Samuel Nathaniel Millimurra and James Emanuel Munday.

(*Pause. No one appears.*)

50 (*Calling.*) Samuel Nathaniel Millimurra and James Emanuel Munday.

(*The* JP *looks at his fob watch.* SAM *enters alone.*)

JP: (*To the* SERGEANT.) Where's the other one?
SERGEANT: Don't know. (*Yelling.*) James Emanuel Munday. Come on, Jimmy. Get a move on.

(JIMMY *enters, tying a bit of binder twine around his trousers, and stands next to* SAM.)

55 JP: I hope you're not making a mockery of the court by delaying proceedings.
JIMMY: Sorry, sir, I was on the shit bucket . . . toilet . . . Got a guts ache, sir.

(SAM *nudges him.*)

SERGEANT: The two accused were apprehended in Bernard Park
60 yesterday at approximately nine-twenty P.M. They were both under the influence of liquor. Munday was in possession of one bottle of wine, three parts empty. (*Indicating.*) That is the bottle there, sir. Upon being placed in separate cells, Munday became noisy and abusive. At one stage he
65 damaged a toilet bucket. He threatened me and used indecent language. He threatened to 'blow my head off'.
JIMMY: I did not.
SERGEANT: Silence in the court.
JIMMY: (*To the* JP.) What I said was that if I had a—
70 SERGEANT: (*Interrupting.*) Silence!
JIMMY: (*To the* JP.) But he's telling it wrong. What I said was, that—
JP: (*Interrupting.*) Order, order. Now you be quiet, Munday, you'll get your chance shortly.
75 JIMMY: But all I was gunna say was that what—

JP: (*Interrupting.*) Shut up, you bloody idiot, or I'll charge you with contempt of court.
SAM: Yes, sir.
JP: (*Indicating* JIMMY.) Not you, him. (*To the* SERGEANT.) Are there any previous records? 80
SERGEANT: Munday has several previous convictions for the same offence and one of unlawful disposal of government rations.
JP: And Millimurra?
SERGEANT: One, drinking, when in the company of Munday. 85
JP: Are they related?
SAM: He's my *gnoolya*, sir.
JP: He's your what?
SERGEANT: They're brothers-in-law. Millimurra's married to—
JP: (*Interrupting.*) All right. I see this is your sixth offence re- 90 lated to alcohol. On the last occasion you were sentenced to fourteen days imprisonment. This time your sentence is three months imprisonment with hard labour.

(*He stands.*)

All right . . .
SERGEANT: What about Millimurra, sir?
JP: Ah, fine of twenty-five shillings. Any costs? 95
SERGEANT: Two and sixpence.
JP: And two and six costs, in default seven days imprisonment.
SERGEANT: He'll need time to pay.
JP: All right, fourteen days. Stand down. 100

(*The* JP *hurries out.*)

SCENE VI

Government Well, Northam, early morning. It is winter, GRAN *builds a fire.* SAM *carries water and* DAVID *gets ready for school.* CISSIE *huddles near the fire, wrapped in a blanket.* MILLY *fries fat in a camp oven.*

MILLY: Cissie, I want you to write that letter to Uncle Jimmy 'fore you go.
SAM: What's to eat?
CISSIE: Oh, Mumma.
MILLY: (*To* SAM.) Damper there, dip in the camp oven. 5
SAM: Me *gnoolya's* better off than I am, bet he's not eating bread 'n fat for breakfast.
GRAN: Joe be back directly with a *wilbra*.
DAVID: (*To* CISSIE.) You want to hurry up. I ain't waitin' for you.

(CISSIE *doesn't move.* JOE *appears, wet and dejected, with empty rabbit traps.*)

GRAN: Rabbits *wah?* 10
JOE: Open. These ain't worth settin'. Bloody rabbits only look at 'em and they snap off.
SAM: Well, grab a bit of breakfast, I want you to help me cut the rest of them posts today.

(JOE *eats damper and dip.* GRAN *gives him a cup of tea.*)

MILLY: Cissie, come on, hurry up. 15
CISSIE: (*Weakly.*) Mum, I feel worse.

(*She coughs.* DAVID *stuffs a piece of damper in his pocket and grabs his bike.*)

MILLY: You wait for your sister.

DAVID: Come on, Cissie.

GRAN: What's wrong with you?

20 MILLY: What's the matter, you *minditj?*

(*She feels* CISSIE's *forehead.* CISSIE *coughs and her mother rubs her back. They all gather around her with increasing concern.*)

God, she's burnin' up.

CISSIE: (*Holding her throat.*) Hurts, Mum, here; hurts when I cough.

MILLY: Well, no school for you today, my girl. (*To* SAM.) You

25 ain't goin' post cuttin' today, and David, you walk to school.

DAVID: Aw, Mum!

MILLY: Don't, 'Aw Mum' me. Joe, you git on that bike and go and ask Uncle Herbie for a lend of his horse and cart. We

30 takin' her to the doctor straight away.

(JOE *takes the bike from* DAVID.)

SAM: Aw Mill, can't you and Mum take her? I only want another hundred posts and I'll have enough *boondah* to pay me fine.

(GRAN *grabs* JOE *before he rides off.*)

GRAN: Ask him for some *gnummarri* for me.

MILLY: You can go this afternoon.

35 JOE: Okay, Gran.

SAM: What doctor you takin' her to?

(DAVID *gets on the bike behind* JOE *and they ride off together towards the main street.*)

GRAN: More better take her straight to the hospital.

SAM: (*Calling after* JOE *and* DAVID.) We'll wait down the road for you.

40 JOE: Okay!

(JOE *and* DAVID *exit.*)

MILLY: (*To* SAM.) You better ask Skinny for a couple of dozen bags.

SAM: He'll want me to cut an extra one hundred and fifty posts for that.

45 MILLY: Well, cut 'em then, and get a lend of some bag needles and don't forget binder twine.

SAM: Another twenty posts.

MILLY: You an' Joe can patch up the sides, then go down the dump an' see if you can find more tin for the roof. Bloody

50 place is colder than the North Pole. And that old baldy had better cough up with some more blankets.

SAM: Come on girlie, I'll carry you.

(SAM *picks up* CISSIE *and they all leave. The dogs bark.*)

SCENE VII

The Police Station, Northam, winter's morning, 1932. SERGEANT CARROL *walks into the station and sits down to read the local newspaper, the Northam Advertiser. Outside the Chief Protector's office,* JIMMY *waits around.* MR NEVILLE *briskly approaches his office.*

JIMMY: Mr Neville, Mr Neville! I wanna see you.

NEVILLE: The office opens at nine o'clock.

JIMMY: Can't wait, gotta train to catch.

NEVILLE: The native's entrance is around the back.

JIMMY: I'm not waitin' 'round there all day.   5

NEVILLE: (*Affronted.*) I beg your pardon?

JIMMY: I only wanna train fare to Northam.

NEVILLE: You can wait around the back and you'll be attended to in due course.

JIMMY: I'm not sittin' down there all bloody day.   10

NEVILLE: What's your name?

JIMMY: Jimmy Munday.

NEVILLE: Munday, Northam . . . Oh yes, I've got a good fat file of police reports on you. What are you doing in Perth?

JIMMY: Mindin' me own bloody business.   15

NEVILLE: Munday, let me give you a piece of advice: sugar catches more flies than vinegar.

(NEVILLE *storms into his office, sits at his desk, and starts to read his mail as* CONSTABLE KERR *limps into the police station.*)

SERGEANT: Afternoon.

CONSTABLE: Sorry, had to walk, got a crook leg playin' footy.

SERGEANT: When was that?   20

CONSTABLE: Sat'dy . . . You were there.

SERGEANT: It's all right, I just wasn't sure whether you were on the field.

(MISS DUNN *arrives at the office.*)

JIMMY: Missus! Hey, Missus!

MISS DUNN: Good morning.   25

JIMMY: Missus, I wanna see Mr Neville.

MISS DUNN: I'm not sure if he's in yet.

JIMMY: He's in there, all right. I seen 'im, an asked 'im for a train fare.

MISS DUNN: And what did he say?   30

JIMMY: Sometin' about catchin' flies.

MISS DUNN: All right, I'll mention it to him. There's a bench on the back verandah, if you'd like to wait there.

(MISS DUNN *enters the office.*)

SERGEANT: (*To the* CONSTABLE.) Oh yeah, you rated a mention in the 'Tiser.   35

CONSTABLE: I know.

MISS DUNN: (*Seating herself.*) Good morning, Mr Neville.

NEVILLE: Morning, Miss Dunn.

MISS DUNN: There's a native outside, wants to see you about a train fare.   40

NEVILLE: (*Abruptly.*) I know. He can wait.

(NEVILLE *continues to read as* JIMMY *ambles around the back of the office and sits on the waiting bench.* MISS DUNN *opens the rest of the mail.*)

SERGEANT: (*Reading.*) 'Towards the end of the first quarter, Kerr marked in front of goal . . . but kicked out of bounds. Towns eight: twenty-two; seventy points to Federals ten: twelve; seventy-two points.'   45

CONSTABLE: I know the score.

(SERGEANT CARROL *continues reading and chuckles to himself.* NEVILLE *lays an open letter on the desk in front of him.*)

NEVILLE: Miss Dunn, would you mind getting Sergeant Carrol in Northam on the line?

(MISS DUNN *picks up the phone and dials.*)

SERGEANT: (*To the* CONSTABLE.) And you got another mention.
50 MISS DUNN: (*Into the receiver.*) Hello, operator; Northam nine please . . . Thank you.
SERGEANT: (*Reading.*) 'In front of goal, Gillet put Kerr in possession who . . . kicked out of bounds . . .' Sea breeze in, was it?

(JIMMY *ventures into* MISS DUNN'*s part of the office.*)

JIMMY: S'cuse me, Missus.
55 CONSTABLE: (*To the* SERGEANT.) I kicked a couple of goals.
JIMMY: (*To* MISS DUNN.) I wanna see him.
MISS DUNN: All right, what's your name?
JIMMY: Jimmy Munday. I wanna train fare; mixed goods leaves at eleven o'clock.
60 MISS DUNN: All right, I'll ask him . . .

(*She goes to* NEVILLE'*s desk.*)

That native, Jimmy Munday, is waiting to see you. He wants a train fare.
NEVILLE: Well, he'll just have to wait.
MISS DUNN: (*Returning to her desk.*) I'm afraid he's very busy at
65 the moment.

(*The phone rings in Northam.*)

He'll see you later on.

(*The* CONSTABLE *answers the phone.*)

CONSTABLE: } (*Together.*) Hello, Northam Police . . . Yes.
JIMMY: } (*To* MISS DUNN.) Look, Missus. I just got outa gaol an' I wanna train fare back home.

(*The phone rings in the Chief Protector's Office.*)

70 CONSTABLE: (*To the* SERGEANT.) Niggers' Department.

(*The* SERGEANT *takes the phone.*)

MISS DUNN: (*To* NEVILLE.) He says he's just been released from gaol. (*Into the receiver.*) Hello, Aborigines Department.
NEVILLE: Then he should have the price of a train fare.
MISS DUNN: (*Into the receiver.*) Yes, hold the line please. (*To*
75 NEVILLE.) Northam.
SERGEANT: Hello.
NEVILLE: (*To* MISS DUNN.) Oh, he can have a travel voucher if he comes back after two.

(*He picks up the phone.* MISS DUNN *hangs up and relays* NEVILLE'*s message to* JIMMY.)

SERGEANT: Hello.
80 NEVILLE: Sergeant Carrol . . . Neville. Sergeant, we seem to be running into problems again. I've received correspondence

from the Town Clerk to the effect that they are opposing the gazetting of the Guilford Road site as a native reserve. They consider it unsuitable.
SERGEANT: It's got a water supply and a couple acres of grazing 85 land.

(MILLY *and* GRAN *approach the police station.*)

NEVILLE: Apparently the Council has plans to develop it.
SERGEANT: What as?
NEVILLE: (*Reading.*) As a 'recreation park, for boy scouts and picnic parties'. 90
SERGEANT: Pretty recent plans.
GRAN: (*Shouting.*) Chergeant! Chergeant!
SERGEANT: (*To the* CONSTABLE.) For Christ's sake, see who that is.
NEVILLE: Sorry, Sergeant.
SERGEANT: Between you and me and the gatepost, the Council'd 95 prefer it if you sent 'em to Moore River or somewhere.
GRAN: Chergeant!

(*The* CONSTABLE *goes to the door.*)

NEVILLE: Most councils would prefer that, Sergeant, but the place is bursting at the seams.
GRAN: (*To the* CONSTABLE.) I wanna see him. 100
CONSTABLE: He's on the phone.
NEVILLE: You can only do your best, but I'm afraid you'll have to come up with another alternative.
CONSTABLE: (*To* GRAN.) You'll have to come back later on.
GRAN: You ain't the boss . . . Chergeant! 105
NEVILLE: I'll be in touch soon.
SERGEANT: 'Bye, Mr. Neville.
CONSTABLE: (*To* GRAN.) I don't want any lip from you.
NEVILLE: Better leave you to it.

(NEVILLE *and the* SERGEANT *hang up.*)

GRAN: (*To the* CONSTABLE.) And I don't want any from you. (*To* 110 *the* SERGEANT, *shouting.*) Hey, Chergeant, your man gettin' cheeky out 'ere.
SERGEANT: (*To the* CONSTABLE.) For God's sake, let 'em in.
MILLY: *Choo, choo.* Mum, don't shout.
SERGEANT: They can be heard all the way down the bloody 115 street . . .

(*They enter.* JIMMY *barges into the Chief Protector's Office.*)

JIMMY: Mr Neville.
NEVILLE: I thought you were told to wait outside.
JIMMY: I only want a train fare.
NEVILLE: I distinctly heard Miss Dunn tell you to come back 120 after two.
JIMMY: Too late, mixed goods leaves at eleven.
NEVILLE: You can catch the Kalgoorlie train at five.
JIMMY: I don't want to go to Kalgoorlie.
SERGEANT: (*To* GRAN *and* MILLY, *taking out the ration book.*) Why 125 weren't youse here yesterday?
NEVILLE: (*To* JIMMY, *exploding.*) Wait outside, then.
GRAN: (*To the* SERGEANT.) Had to go t'ospital.
NEVILLE: A travel voucher please, Miss Dunn.
MILLY: (*To the* SERGEANT.) My gel's sick in 'ospital. 130

(JIMMY *ambles out and stretches out on the bench.*)

SERGEANT: (*Taking out packets of rations.*) Sugar, tea.
MILLY: We need blankets.
SERGEANT: (*To the* CONSTABLE.) See if you can find some bicarb. There. Here's your stick of nigger twist, Gran.
135 MILLY: What about blankets?
SERGEANT: (*Taking out a packet.*) Flour . . . What?
MILLY: Blankets. My girl's in 'ospital with 'monia and pleurisy.
GRAN: An' we want blankets.
SERGEANT: Sorry, blankets not here yet, Milly.
140 GRAN: Her name Mrs Millimurra. Proper church married, New Norcia, white dress an' all.
MILLY: Got paper to prove it, and birth 'tificate.
GRAN: (*At the approaching* CONSTABLE.) Not like some people, I bet.
145 CONSTABLE: Here's your bi-carb.
GRAN: What about them *wanbru?*
CONSTABLE: What?
MILLY: Blankets!
SERGEANT: Look, there's nothin' I can do about it except put in
150   a reminder to the Department in Perth. Why don't youse go around to St John's and ask the vicar?
MILLY: For blankets? He'll give us nothin', he's like that.
GRAN: (*Adopting a praying attitude.*) Yeah, when he come to Gubment Well he goes like that with his eyes closed and
155   he says the Lord will help you, and now he prays with his eyes open, 'cause time 'fore last Wow Wow bit him on the leg . . . musta wanted a bit a' holy meat.
MILLY: You forgot our meat order.
SERGEANT: No meat this week.
160 MILLY: What?
SERGEANT: Finished; in future no meat is included in rations.
GRAN: Why?
CONSTABLE: There's a bloody depression on.
MILLY: What are we gunna do for meat?
165 CONSTABLE: There's plenty of roos and rabbits.
GRAN: What about *tjirrung?*
CONSTABLE: What about what?
MILLY: Fat!
SERGEANT: Fat is classified as meat. I'll see what I can do about
170   the blankets for youse.
MILLY: I want 'em 'fore Cissie gits outa hospital.
SERGEANT: I can't promise anything, but I'll check with the Department.
GRAN: An' you're supposed to be native 'tector.

(GRAN *and* MILLY *take their rations and exit.*)

175 SERGEANT: Looks like I'm the one needs protectin'.
CONSTABLE: Should put a pinch of strychnine in the flour.
SERGEANT: Too late to adopt the Tasmanian solution.
NEVILLE: (*Yelling.*) Munday!

(JIMMY *stands and enters the office.*)

The eleven o'clock mixed goods, make sure you're on it.

(*He hands* JIMMY *the voucher.*)

180   And try to keep out of trouble for a while.

(JIMMY *shuffles off at a snail's pace.*)

You'd better get a move on if you're going to catch that train.
JIMMY: Don't think I'll worry about the mixed goods, catch the five o'clock Kalgoorlie train instead. Haven't been down in the big smoke for a few weeks, might have a bit of a look 185 around.
NEVILLE: You get on that train—
JIMMY: (*Interrupting.*) You know one thing about Fremantle Gaol? Even some of them screws are polite—not like this place. (*Walking off.*) Native Protector, couldn't protect my 190 dog from fleas.
NEVILLE: (*Returning to his office.*) Cheeky, too bloody cheeky.

SCENE VIII

Government Well, day. JIMMY *is mending a pair of shoes.* GRAN *and* MILLY *sew bags together.* SAM *enters with buckets of water and sits down, exhausted.* JOE *enters with a sugar bag slung over his back.*

JIMMY: There y'are, Joe, good as new.
JOE: *Woolah! Moorditj!*
JIMMY: Learnt me trade well, in Freeo.
MILLY: (*To* JOE.) What did you get?
JOE: Fat, taters, onions.   5
SAM: You get meat?
MILLY: No *boondah* for meat.
JIMMY: Wish I'd known the meat ration was cut out when I saw Mr bloody Neville the other day.
GRAN: He take no notice of you.   10
JOE: Cissie ready to come home from hospital.
MILLY: How do you know?
JOE: Sergeant told me. Saw him at the Post Office.
SAM: When, today?
JOE: She's waiting there now.   15
MILLY: Why didn't you ask him to give youse a lift 'ome?
JOE: Him? Hah!
JIMMY: Only time blackfellas git a ride off him is when he's takin' you to gaol.
MILLY: Well, she ain't walkin' home, anyways. Sam, you better 20 get a lend of Herbie's cart.
JOE: It's got the wheel broke, Mum.
MILLY: Then you'll have to get a lend of old Skinny Martin's.
SAM: Another hundred posts, I bet.
MILLY: Ne'mine the posts, long as we git her home.   25
JIMMY: Yeah, go and ask him, *Gnoolya,* and I'll solve the meat problem at the same time.
MILLY: What you talkin' about?
JOE: Yeah, *Kongi,* I know where his wethers runnin'.
JIMMY: Him, I know that bastard's farm like the back a me 30 hand.
JOE: Old Skinny might be bony but his sheep are cruel fat.
GRAN: You wanna watch out. Chergeant catch you, he give you six months just like that.
JIMMY: Oh, bugger old baldy.   35

(JOE *takes a knife and starts to sharpen it.*)

JOE: *Woolah,* sheep guts and lo-o-o-vely hot damper.
GRAN: Don't git *tjeuripiny,* you ain't got the horse and cart yet.

SAM: Don't worry 'bout that, Mother-In-Law, as long as he reckons he's gettin' somethin' for nothin' he'll be in it, *kwonna tjuellara.*

JOE: Come on, let's get goin', I'm hungry.

JIMMY: Well, he ain't gitten it for nothin' this time.

SAM: Better bring Wow Wow, help round the sheeps up.

GRAN: Put them shoes on, Joe.

JOE: Don't need no dawg. Don't need no shoes either, Granny, I can run better barefoot and faster than Wow Wow.

JIMMY: Come on, *Gnoolya,* we'll git one of the skinny old bastard's sheep and bring it home on his own cart.

MILLY: Me and Mum, we'll wait for youse in the park, all right?

GRAN: Youse be careful now, you hear me?

MILLY: Come on, Gran.

JIMMY: (*Miming slitting the sheep's throat.*) Mirri-up, mirri-up. Allewah koorkantjerri gnuny nooniny dininy, woort dininy.

SCENE IX

The Chief Protector of Aborigines' Office, Perth, day. MISS DUNN *types while* MR NEVILLE *dictates from a list of warrants.* SERGEANT CARROL *approaches.*

NEVILLE: Munday, Herbert Williams and wife Wooleen. Munday, James Emanuel. Munday, May Alice. Millimurra, Samuel … wife Millicent and three children: Joseph, Cecilia and David.

(*There is a knock on the door.* MISS DUNN *rises to answer it.*)

SERGEANT: Sergeant Carrol, Northam. I'm meant to be seeing—

NEVILLE: Sergeant, I wasn't expecting you until later. Train on time?

SERGEANT: (*Entering.*) Not exactly, sir, I caught the seven-twenty mixed goods.

NEVILLE: When are you returning? Come through, sit down.

(*They sit at* NEVILLE'*s desk.*)

SERGEANT: On the five-fifteen Kalgoorlie train.

NEVILLE: Right, I don't want to delay you, so we'll deal with the matter in hand. Miss Dunn, would you bring the Northam file, please, and the warrants?

(MISS DUNN *locates the file, collects the warrants and brings them to* NEVILLE.)

Sergeant, as I mentioned on the phone, Doctor Aberdeen examined the natives camped at Government Well.

(*He goes through the file and finds the doctor's report.*)

And found them to be … 'rotten with scabies', and as a result of—ah, well, various submissions, it's been decided to transfer the entire native population to the Moore River Settlement.

SERGEANT: Yes sir. We can give up looking for a site for a new reserve, then.

NEVILLE: The transfer is a temporary measure, Sergeant. Well, I've got all the warrants, following your own census, Sergeant; a total of eighty-nine natives.

(*He hands over the warrants.*)

If that list changes at all, let me know and I'll obtain any additional warrants. It's essential that the town and shire are quite devoid of natives after the seventeenth.

SERGEANT: Yes, sir.

NEVILLE: I've arranged with the railway authorities for an AR coach and brake van to be at your disposal on the seven-twenty A.M. train on the seventeenth. It will arrive, I am assured, at ten-twenty-nine A.M. at Midland and I've arranged for the Midland Railway Company to attach both to a train to leave immediately for Mogumber. Should arrive at three P.M. You'll be met and proceed on foot to a quarantine camp at Long Pool, just east of the settlement. (*Handing him an order form.*) I've authorised expenditure of one and sixpence per native for food en route to be purchased in Northam, and for buckets of tea to be available at Chidlows and Muchea. Following your recommendation, Sergeant, no native will need to leave the train at any stage of the journey. I'll leave it to your discretion what personal luggage is to accompany your charges, preferably as little as possible.

SERGEANT: What about conveyances? There's a couple of sulkies and a spring cart.

NEVILLE: I'm afraid if they don't fit in the brake van they don't go.

SERGEANT: What about horses and dogs?

NEVILLE: They certainly can't go. You'll have to make arrangements to store the property and look after the livestock left behind.

SERGEANT: How long is that likely to be?

NEVILLE: Well, your guess is as good as mine. Until the scabies are cleared up and a new reserve is gazetted.

SERGEANT: Or until after the election.

NEVILLE: I wouldn't know about that.

SERGEANT: They won't leave their dogs behind.

NEVILLE: No, but the superintendent won't have any dogs coming with them to the settlement.

SERGEANT: What about a small road party to go with the conveyances and horses?

NEVILLE: Personally, I'd prefer to see them go in one operation.

SERGEANT: One officer could handle it, and it would avoid a lot of problems at my end, sir.

NEVILLE: All right, you're in the front line. But I want as many as possible on the train, and definitely no dogs.

SERGEANT: No, I'll attend to the dogs when I clean up the camp.

NEVILLE: (*Standing.*) Good, I don't need to impress upon you the absolute confidentiality of the matter.

SERGEANT: Yes, sir.

NEVILLE: Well, I won't keep you. You've got a couple of hours before your train.

SERGEANT: Yes, I'm going down to Boan's to pick a few presents for the Mrs and the kids.

NEVILLE: Good, thank you for your co-operation. And don't forget, no dogs.

SERGEANT: (*Standing.*) Thank you, Mr Neville. All the best for Christmas.

NEVILLE: And to you and yours.

(*The* SERGEANT *moves past* MISS DUNN'*s desk.*)

MISS DUNN: Goodbye, Sergeant. Have a happy Christmas.

SERGEANT: Same to you, madam.

(*The* SERGEANT *exits.*)

SCENE X

Government Well, Northam, day. CISSIE *with the aid of a knife is looking for lice in* DAVID's *hair.* MILLY *and* GRAN *sew. A car approaches.*

CISSIE: Keep still!

DAVID: Well stop diggin' a hole in me head.

CISSIE: Hold still, I got a big one.

GRAN: (*Looking up at the car.*) Gneean nitja koorling?

5 MILLY: *Allewah, manatj!*

CISSIE: They got Dad and Joe and Uncle Jimmy.

MILLY: Gawd, hope they haven't been caught stealin' a sheep.

(*Everyone is silent. The three men are escorted to the camp by the* SERGEANT *and* CONSTABLE.)

What's up?

JIMMY: (*Nodding at the* SERGEANT.) Just listen to him.

10 SAM: We're all goin'.

(*He gestures Nyoongah fashion as the* CONSTABLE *goes through a pile of warrants.*)

SERGEANT: Millimurra and Munday.

GRAN: Goin'? Where?

SERGEANT: I've got warrants here for the arrest and apprehension of all of youse.

15 MILLY: What for? We ain't done nothin'.

SERGEANT: I never said you did. You're bein' transferred, every native in Northam's goin'!

MILLY: Goin' where?!

SAM: Mogumber.

20 CONSTABLE: You're being transferred to the Moore River Native Settlement.

GRAN: I ain't goin'.

CONSTABLE: You're all goin'. You're under arrest.

GRAN: What for? We done nothin' wrong.

25 SERGEANT: It's for health reasons. Epidemic of skin disease.

JIMMY: Bullshit, I'll tell you why we're goin'.

CONSTABLE: You wouldn't know.

JIMMY: You reckon blackfellas are bloody mugs. Whole town knows why we're goin'. 'Coz *wetjalas* in this town don't
30 want us 'ere, don't want our kids at the school, with their kids, and old Jimmy Mitchell's tight 'coz they reckon Bert 'Awke's gonna give him a hidin' in the election.

CONSTABLE: What the hell would you know? You don't even vote.

35 JIMMY: I know more about *wetjala's* gubment than you do, and what I'm tellin' you's the truth.

CONSTABLE: Bullshit.

SERGEANT: Shut up, will you? I don't know whose idea it is, it's got nothin' to do with me.

40 CONSTABLE: You barkin' up the wrong tree, Munday.

JIMMY: Bullshit, Jimmy Mitchell's—

SERGEANT: (*Interrupting.*) Look, I know this much; Jimmy Mitchell's got nothin' against blackfellas, or anybody else, for that matter.

45 JIMMY: No, he's got nothin' against 'em. Not worth losin' a bloody election over, that's all. I'll tell youse somethin': you're wastin' your fuckin' time.

CONSTABLE: Hey, all right.

JIMMY: 'Coz *wetjalas* aren't gonna vote for 'im. You know why?
50 'Coz he's got all them Chinamen workin' on his farm at Grass Valley and *wetjalas* don't like that. He's gunna get rida the blackfellas, he should get rid of them Chinamen too.

SERGEANT: Oh, Jesus, shut up will youse? You're all goin' and
55 that's that, an' if you don't co-operate you'll just go along for resisting arrest and escaping legal custody.

SAM: When are we supposed to be leavin'?

SERGEANT: On the seven-twenty mixed goods train in the morning. You'll be camping in the goods shed overnight.

60 MILLY: What about all our things?

SERGEANT: You can pack personal things belonging to you. Herbert Munday is too old to go by road, Sam and his family will be going on the road party, with his horse and spring cart. Jimmy and Gran can go on the train.

65 GRAN: I ain't goin' on no train, I'm goin' with Sam and Milly. You're not makin' me go on no train.

CONSTABLE: You'll get pretty hot walkin'.

SERGEANT: Listen, Granny, the road trip will take four days. You'll be better off on the train.

70 GRAN: Chergeant, I ain't goin' on no train. You can put me in gaol if you want to.

(*She begins to wail and cry.*)

I'm not goin' by train; what we leaving Gubment Well for? *Wetjala warrah, warrahmut,* oooh!

SERGEANT: All right, all right, Gran, you can go by road if you
75 want to.

GRAN: (*Recovering instantly.*) I am, too.

CONSTABLE: It's her funeral if she doesn't make it.

JIMMY: It'll be your funeral.

SERGEANT: That's enough. Jimmy, you're comin' with us. The rest of you better start packin' and go and get Herbie's
80 horse and cart.

SAM: What about our kangaroo dogs?

SERGEANT: I'm under strict orders that no dogs are allowed to go.

SAM: What, leave the dogs behind?

85 JIMMY: Come off it, Sergeant, how are they gonna get meat on the way?

CONSTABLE: You won't need to worry, you'll be on the train.

SERGEANT: There's plenty of rabbits.

JOE: What, are you gonna run 'em down?

90 SERGEANT: According to Dr Aberdeen you've got a serious heart condition, so you'll be going on the train, Jimmy.

JIMMY: I'm not goin' on no fuckin' train.

GRAN: Chergeant, I'm not leavin' Wow Wow behind. If I can't take him, I'm not goin'.

95 MILLY: Who's gonna look after our dogs?

CONSTABLE: We'll attend to them.

MILLY: Yeah, we know that.

JIMMY: With a police bullet.

GRAN: (*Frantically.*) You're not gonna shoot Wow, you're not gonna shoot Wow Wow. You hear me, Chergeant? I'm not
100 goin'.

(GRAN *is frantic now. She tears her hair and throws plates and mugs about.*)

SERGEANT: Oh Jesus, take your bloody mangy Wow Wow, whatever you call it. Take the bloody lot, just remember to be ready to move out tomorrow morning.

(*The police escort* JIMMY *away. The family looks on in stunned silence.* CISSIE *clings to her mother and cries.*)

ACT TWO
Moore River

SCENE I

The track to Moore River, day. The family enters. They are laden with possessions, hot, dusty and tired. In a clearing at the Long Pool Camp. Moore River Native Settlement, JIMMY *erects a bush shade over a tent. The family is approached by a tracker,* BILLY KIMBERLEY. *He smokes a clay pipe and carries a whip.*

BILLY: Mornin', mornin'.
SAM: Gawd, who the fuckin' hell are you?
BILLY: I'm a politjman, name Billy Kimberley.
DAVID: (*Amazed, to* CISSIE.) He's a policeman!
5 SAM: More like Tom Mix.

(BILLY *holds out his pipe.*)

BILLY: You got *killarla*?
CISSIE: He might be Buck Jones.
SAM: Ain't got none.
GRAN: You ain't politjman, you just black tracker.
10 BILLY: All right, you fella follow me, now. I show you where your camp. Come on now, this way.

(*They follow* BILLY *towards the clearing.*)

CISSIE: (*To* DAVID, *nodding at* BILLY.) Gawd, he's black.
DAVID: He ain't black, he's purple!
GRAN: Choo, you fellas want to *dubakieny wahnginy*. He might
15 be *boolyaduk*.
JOE: Ah, Granny, he's *yuart*. (*Making an open gesture.*) He's like that.

(*They approach* JIMMY.)

JIMMY: 'Ullo! 'Ullo! How's everybody?
SAM: Tired, bloody tired.

(*They start to unload their possessions.*)

20 BILLY: Now, you fellas sit down along this place, you hear me? Matron comin' bye and bye.
MILLY: Who?
JIMMY: Matron, Superintendent's Missus. She runs the hospital.
MILLY: When's she comin'?
25 BILLY: Dunno, 'morrow, must be next day. She comin' you fella all wait this place now.

(BILLY *exits.*)

JOE: Gawd strewth!

(*The children laugh at the departed* BILLY.)

JIMMY: Anyway, how you, Mill? Joe and you kids? Mum?
MILLY: We're all right, I s'pose.
JIMMY: And how you, Mother?   30
GRAN: I'm *warrah, gnuny tjenna minditj*; and I got no *gnummarri*.
JIMMY: Never mind, Mother, here.

(JIMMY *takes some tobacco from his pocket and gives it to her.*)

GRAN: *Winjar kaep?*
JIMMY: Straight down the pad, there.
MILLY: You kids get a billy each and go and get some water.   35
DAVID: Oh boy, I'm gonna have a swim.
MILLY: No, you ain't. Might be *bilbarl, dugaitj,* anything down there.
DAVID: Aw, Mum.
MILLY: I said no!   40
JOE: I'll come with youse.
MILLY: All right, you can if Joe's with youse.
DAVID: Come on, Cissie!
MILLY: Take the water bag.

(*They take it and run off.*)

JIMMY: Kimberley tell youse where to get the tucker tonight? 45
MILLY: No.
JIMMY: Down the kitchen.
SAM: Where?
JIMMY: Soup Kitchen.
SAM: Good tucker?   50
JIMMY: More like three-course bloody pig swill. Treacle and bread or bread and fat, take your pick.
SAM: What about *daitj*?
JIMMY: Meat? You gotta be jokin'.
MILLY: What about a sheet of iron for the fireplace?   55
JIMMY: Don't worry, I know where I can get one. Come on, Sam, I'll knock it off, you can watch.

(JIMMY *exits, followed by* SAM.)

GRAN: Cooo, cooo! You come back now, Jimmy, you hear? Cooo!

(MILLY *unrolls a blanket. She and* GRAN *are left alone.*)

MILLY: Come on, Mum, lay down and have a rest.   60

SCENE II

A clearing near the Moore River, day. JOE, DAVID *and* CISSIE *fill a water bag from billy cans.*

JOE: Don't spill it.
CISSIE: I'm tryin' not to.

(DAVID *tries the water.*)

JOE: Good *kaep*.
CISSIE: Don't spit in it.
DAVID: I ain't.   5

(*Unseen, two girls approach:* TOPSY *and* MARY, *who carries a bag of meat.* DAVID *takes his shirt off.*)

Where we gonna swim?

CISSIE: Dunno, let's find a place.

(DAVID *sees the girls.*)

DAVID: *Tjinung, yorgahs!*

(*They all look.*)

JOE: Gidday.

10   MARY: Hello.

TOPSY: You fellas amongst the Northam lot?

JOE: Yeah, that's Cissie, and that's David. I'm Joe, Joe Mil-
        limurra. We're all Millimurras.

TOPSY: I'm Topsy, that's Mary.

15   She's from up North.

JOE: They grow 'em pretty up there.

(DAVID, CISSIE *and* TOPSY *giggle.*)

What you got in the bag?

TOPSY: *Yonga,* we're takin' it up to Uncle Herbie.

CISSIE: Uncle Herbie's our uncle too.

20   JOE: How come he's your uncle?

TOPSY: His cousin is our grandfather—I think, on our mum's
        side. How come he's your uncle?

CISSIE: He's married to our aunt. You know, not really married.

(*She and* DAVID *dissolve into the giggles.*)

JOE: (*To* MARY.) Are you related too?

25   MARY: No.

(DAVID *and* CISSIE *laugh.*)

DAVID: Eh, *Gnoon,* you're cruel!

JOE: Shut up. Take the water back, you two.

DAVID: What about our swim?

JOE: I'll take youse later, get goin'!

(CISSIE *and* DAVID *run off.*)

30   CISSIE: ⎱
     DAVID: ⎰ (*Together.*) Joe's got a girlfriend, Joe's got a girlfriend.

(*They exit.*)

TOPSY: I got to get goin' to set the tables for supper.

(TOPSY *exits.*)

JOE: (*To* MARY.) I can take the meat for you if you like.

(MARY *approaches with the bag of meat.*)

What's your name?

MARY: Mary.

35   JOE: I know that. Your full name?

MARY: Mary Dargurru.

(*She runs after* TOPSY, *still carrying the meat.*)

JOE: Mary!

MARY: (*Stopping.*) Yeah?

JOE: The *daitj.*

MARY: Oh, yeah.   40

(*She returns to him with it.*)

JOE: (*Taking the meat.*) When will I see you again?

MARY: Dunno.

JOE: Can you be here tomorrow?

MARY: I'll try.

JOE: Don't say 'try', say you will be.   45

MARY: All right.

JOE: Same time.

MARY: I'll try, I mean, yes.

JOE: I'm glad we're not related.

MARY: So am I.   50

(*She runs off.* JOE *watches her into the distance.*)

SCENE III

Long Pool Camp, Moore River, a hot day. CISSIE *and* DAVID *play
knuckle bones.* MILLY *and* JOE *enter with water.* GRAN *sits in the
shade. The dogs bark.* BILLY *trudges on, followed at a distance by*
MATRON NEAL, TOPSY *and* MARY.

BILLY: (*Calling.*) You fella got them *doothoo* tied up?

SAM: (*Calling.*) Yeah.

BILLY: Come on, Missus, come on.

SAM: (*To* JOE.) Nothin' to bite on him, he's all skin and bone.

JOE: Plenty of meat on the matron.   5

BILLY: You fella stand up straight, now.

DAVID: Hey, that's them girls.

BILLY: (*Poking his whip at* DAVID.) You shut up now.

JOE: Hey, old man, *dubakieny.*

MATRON: Good morning, good morning. Now, all the family   10
        here?

GRAN: My boy Jimmy ain't.

MATRON: (*Checking her list.*) Munday, James Emanuel. Oh, yes,
        with the train party. It's all right, we've seen him. Now let's
        see. Samuel, Millicent, Joseph, David and Cecilia, and the   15
        grandmother. Good. Now I'm the matron, Matron Neal,
        and I'm in charge of the hospital and Topsy here is help-
        ing me.

DAVID: We already seen her.

JOE: Shut up, *gnoon.*   20

MATRON: Now, seeing you came here for health reasons, I'd just
        like to examine you.

GRAN: What for?

MATRON: For any skin complaints, Granny.

GRAN: Scabies? We ain't got it.   25

SAM: Even the dogs ain't got it.

BILLY: You be quiet now, Matron make you no more sick fella.

JOE: What's he yakkin' about? We ain't sick.

(BILLY *threatens* JOE *nervously with the whip.*)

MATRON: All right, Billy. Now David, you first. Come on.

(*He doesn't move.* BILLY *prods him with the whip.*)

Billy!   30

DAVID: I ain't takin' me pants off.

JOE: Me either.

(TOPSY *giggles*.)

MATRON: Just your shirt will do for a start.

(*She begins to take* DAVID's *shirt off.* TOPSY *moves to help him but he jumps away and does it himself.*)

DAVID: Git!
35 MILLY: David.

(MATRON *examines his hands, elbows and knees, ankles and abdomen.*)

MATRON: Good boy. Now you, Cecilia.

(*She checks her much the same way.*)

MILLY: None of us got it.

(MATRON *checks her and* SAM.)

MATRON: No, they're a healthy lot, a credit to you, Millicent. All right Joe, take your shirt off.
40 JOE: There's nothin' wrong with me.
MATRON: No, I'm sure there's not. I just want to check.

(*She checks him in the same way.*)

How old are you, Joe?
JOE: Dunno.
MILLY: He's seventeen next burnin' season.
45 MATRON: He's a strapping lad.

(GRAN *gets up.*)

No need to get up, Gran, I'm sure you're all right.
GRAN: Joe, show Matron your belly button, go on.

(*She pulls* JOE's *shirt up.*)

What do you think of that, Matron?
JOE: Aw Gran, *kienya.*
50 GRAN: Isn't that the neatest belly button you seen? Have a look, Matron. I brought him into the world with me own two hands.
SAM: (*Laughing.*) Mumma!
MATRON: You did a very good job, Granny.
55 GRAN: I brought plenty *kooloongah* into this world, Matron.
MATRON: Well, there doesn't seem to be anything wrong with your family, Millicent. I won't bother putting you on the sulphur, but I want you all to use the washing facilities every day before every meal and after you've been to the toi-
60 let. Now, look at those fingernails, David; perhaps you could set an example by going off and scrubbing them.

(DAVID *exits reluctantly.*)

Well, Milly, here are a few more cakes of Lysol soap and some handkerchiefs for the children. Well, busy, busy. Topsy, one more family visit. 'Bye for the present. Goodbye,
65 Gran.

(*She goes to leave, then stops.*)

Oh, how many dogs have you got in the camp?

(*They look at each other in silence, then:*)

SAM: A couple of kangaroo dogs, and Granny's dog.

(MATRON *strides off, followed by* BILLY, *who stops her some distance away.*)

BILLY: They got that many, missus.

(*He holds up seven fingers.*)

JOE, DAVID and CISSIE: *Wahrdung, wahrdung,* black crow!

(MATRON *exits.* BILLY *glares at the children.*)

SCENE IV

Moore River Native settlement, a clearing in the pine plantation, night. JOE *creeps on and lets out a mopoke call. Pause. He calls again, and the call is returned.* MARY *approaches, carrying a crumpled parcel.*

JOE: You got here all right.
MARY: I brought you a present.

(*She hands him the crumpled parcel and they sit on a log.*)

JOE: What is it?
MARY: Damper, oven cooked, mixed with emu fat and they're real raisins, not weevils.   5

(*They giggle and eat.*)

JOE: You comfortable? Sit closer. How long you been here?
MARY: About five minutes.
JOE: I know that, I mean how long you been here at the settlement?
MARY: This was my third Christmas . . . I wish I was back   10 home. I hate this place, I hate everything in it.
JOE: Even me?
MARY: No, I don't hate you.
JOE: Them *wetjalas* treat you all right?
MARY: *Gudeeahs?* Matron and Sister Eileen are all right. They   15 try to be nice, but I don't like Mr Neal. He scares me.
JOE: He don't scare me.
MARY: I don't like the way he looks at me.
JOE: Well, you got me now, for what I'm worth.

(*He laughs.*)

MARY: He's always hangin' around where the girls are workin';   20 in the cookhouse, in the sewin' room. And he's always carryin' that cat-o'-nine tails and he'll use it, too.
JOE: Bastard, better not use it on you or any of my lot.
MARY: He reckoned he was gunna belt me once.
JOE: What for?   25
MARY: 'Coz I said I wasn't gunna go and work for *guddeeah* on a farm.
JOE: Why not? Be better than this place.
MARY: No! (*With shame.*) Some of them *guddeeahs* real bad. My friend went last Christmas and then she came back *bood-*   30 *jarri.* She reckons the boss's sons used to belt her up and,

you know, force her. Then they kicked her out. And when
she had that baby them trackers choked it dead and buried
it in the pine plantation.

35 JOE: What? You dinkum?

MARY: That's true.

JOE: (*Stunned.*) The bastards. The fuckin' bastards.

(MARY *starts to cry.*)

Come on, Mary, stop that. You know somethin'?

MARY: What?

40 JOE: I don't like you.

(*She draws away.*)

I love you.

(*They embrace.*)

MARY: I have to go back, Matron will find out.

JOE: Stay a bit longer.

(*She kisses him.*)

MARY: I have to go now, or she won't let me out again.

45 JOE: When will I see you again?

MARY: Tomorrow.

JOE: Same time?

MARY: Yeah.

JOE: Same log?

50 MARY: Yeah. Joe, I don't like you either.

(*They laugh and embrace.* MARY *runs away.* JOE *watches after her.*)

SCENE V

The Moore River Settlement, a hot morning. JIMMY *ambles about outside the Superintendent's office.* MR NEAL *approaches. He has a hangover.*

NEAL: Hey, you, you're with the Northam lot, aren't you? What
are you doing here?

JIMMY: What's it look like I'm doing?

NEAL: You're supposed to be up in the quarantine camp.

5 JIMMY: Quarantine camp, me arse.

NEAL: You're out of bounds and you know it.

JIMMY: Come off it, you know that quarantine camp is a load of
bullshit, so don't try and tip it over me.

NEAL: I'll attend to you later.

(*He heads for his office.*)

10 JIMMY: You know, if fertiliser was in short supply you'd make
a bloody fortune.

(*He sniggers.*)

NEAL: (*Mumbling.*) Another bloody troublemaker.

(*He sits at his desk.* MARY *brings him tea on a tray. He leers at her body.* MATRON *enters, almost catching him.*)

MATRON: Where did you get to yesterday?

NEAL: You know very well I had to go to Moora to see about—

MATRON: (*Interrupting.*) To spend the day in the hotel drinking.   15
Don't imagine no one sees you come in, the condition you
were in—fine example.

NEAL: I've got to get away from the place now and again.

MATRON: What about me? I was at the quarantine camp from
dawn till dusk again yesterday.   20

NEAL: Done them all?

MATRON: Yes, eventually.

NEAL: How many have got it?

MATRON: Scabies? Mrs Mason and her three youngsters.

NEAL: Yes.   25

MATRON: That's all, just the four of them. I've isolated them,
put them on sulphur and regular bathing.

NEAL: Four of 'em, only cases of skin disease? Only four?

MATRON: Yes, Alf. I can recognise a case of scabies when I see
one.   30

NEAL: And you've examined the lot of them?

MATRON: Yes, I haven't been going up the Long Pool for a picnic.

NEAL: Are you telling me out of eighty-nine dumped on me,
only four of them have got the bloody disease?

(*She puts the record book in front of him.*)

Good God, woman, what's the bloody game? Eighty-nine   35
natives in a bloody quarantine camp I've just busted me gut
to get ready on time, and there's nothing bloody well wrong
with 'em?

MATRON: Alf, there's no need to lose your temper and no need
for bad language. They should be cleared up in a few days.   40

NEAL: The whole job's a waste of time. They could have been
treated in Northam.

MATRON: The only health hazard in the camp are the dogs.

NEAL: What dogs?

MATRON: There's about fifty of them, and a good many in less   45
than healthy condition.

NEAL: How did the dogs get here?

MATRON: With the road party, apparently.

NEAL: No one told me anything about dogs.

MATRON: One per family.   50

(*She exits.*)

NEAL: That's one too many. (*Calling.*) Billy! Billy!

(*He unlocks the armoury cupboard and gets a rifle and ammunition.*)

BILLY: (*Off.*) Yeah, comin' boss.

(NEAL *counts out the ammunition.* BILLY *enters.*)

Yeah, Boss?

NEAL: Get the horses and a length of rope, Billy.

BILLY: Yeah, boss.   55

(NEAL *takes a rifle and ammunition. They exit.*)

SCENE VI

A clearing in the pine plantation. Moore River Native Settlement, night. A camp fire burns. JIMMY *and* SAM *are painted for a corroboree.* JIMMY *mixes wilgi in tobacco tin lids, while* SAM *separates inji sticks from clapsticks.* JOE *arrives with an armful of firewood and pokes at the fire.*

JOE: They comin' now.

BILLY: (*Off.*) Get no rain this place summertime.

(BILLY *and* BLUEY *enter and remove their shirts.*)

JIMMY: Eh? Where you fellas been?

BLUEY: Aw, we been pushing truck for Mr Neal.

5   BILLY: He goin' Mogumber.

BLUEY: (*Miming taking a drink.*) Doin' this fella.

JOE: He'll be *minditj* tomorrow.

(BLUEY *and* BILLY *paint themselves with wilgi.*)

BILLY: My word you fellas pr-retty fellas.

BLUEY: *Wee-ah,* plenty *wilgi.*

10 BILLY: Eh? You know my country, must be walk two, three days
       for this much. Your country got plenty.

(JIMMY *strikes up a rhythm on the clapsticks.* BLUEY *joins him.*)

JIMMY: (*Singing.*)
       Tjinnung nitjakoorliny?
       Karra, karra, karra, karra,
15   *Moyambat a-nyinaliny a-nyinaliny,*
       Baal nitja koorliny moyambat a-moyambat moyambat,
       Moyambat nitja koorliny moyambat.
       Kalkanna yirra nyinny kalkanna,
       Yirra nyinniny, yirra nyinniny,
20   *Moyambat a-kalkanna moyambat a-kilkanna*
       Yirra nyinniny, yirra nyinniny, yirra nyinniny,
       Karra koorliny kalkanna karra karra koorliny kalkanna.
       Karra koorliny, karra koorliny, karra koorliny,
       Woolah!
25 BLUEY: Eh, what that one?

JIMMY: That's my grandfather song. (*Miming with his hands.*)
       He singin' for the *karra,* you know, crabs, to come up the
       river and for the fish to jump up high so he can catch them
       in the fish traps.

30 SAM: (*Pointing to* BILLY'*s body paint.*) Eh! Eh! Old man, what's
       that one?

BILLY: This one *bungarra,* an' he lookin' for berry bush. But he
       know that fella eagle watchin' him and he know that fella
       is cunnin' fella. He watchin' and lookin' for that eagle, that
35   way, this way, that way, this way.

(*He rolls over a log, disappearing almost magically.* BLUEY *plays the
didgeridoo and* BILLY *appears some distance away by turning quickly
so the firelight reveals his painted body. He dances around, then seems
to disappear suddenly. He rolls back over the log and drops down,
sealed by the fire.*)

BLUEY, SAM *and* JIMMY: *Yokki! Moorditj! Woolah!*

JIMMY: Eh? That one dance come from your country?

BILLY: Nah. That one come from that way, lo-o-ong way. *Wanmulla*
       country. Proper bad fellas.

40 SAM: Well, I won't be goin' there.

JOE: Me either!

(JIMMY, *joe and* SAM *laugh.* SAM *jumps to his feet with the clapsticks.*)

SAM: This one *yahllarah! Everybody! Yahllarah!*

(*He starts a rhythm on the clapsticks.* BLUEY *plays didgeridoo.* JIMMY,
and then JOE, *join him dancing.*)

Come on! Come on!

(*He picks up inji sticks. The Nyoongahs,* SAM, JIMMY *and* JOE, *dance
with them.* BILLY *joins in. They dance with increasing speed and energy, stamping their feet, whirling in front of the fire, their bodies appearing and disappearing as the paint catches the firelight. The dance
becomes faster and more frantic until finally* SAM *lets out a yell and
they collapse, dropping back to their positions around the fire.* JIMMY
coughs and pants painfully.)

(*To* JIMMY.) Eh! Eh! (*Indicating his heart.*) You wanta
dubakieny, you know your *koort minditj.*   45

BILLY: This country got plenty good dance, eh?

BLUEY: *Wee-ah!*

JIMMY: Ah, *yuart,* not too many left now. Nearly all finish.

BILLY: No, no, no. You song man, you fella dance men. This
       still your country. (*Flinging his arms wide.*) You, you, you,   50
       you listen! *Gudeeah* make 'em fences, windmill, make 'em
       road for motor car, big house, cut 'em down trees. Still
       your country! Not like my country, finish . . . finish.

(*He sits in silence. They watch him intently.* JOE *puts wood on the fire.
He speaks slowly.*)

BILLY: *Kuliyah.* (*Miming pulling a trigger, grunting.*) *Gudeeah* bin
       kill 'em. Finish, kill 'em. Big mob, 1926, kill 'em big mob   55
       my country.

(*Long pause.*)

SAM: *Nietjuk?*

BILLY: I bin stop Liveringa station and my brother, he bin run
       from Oombulgarri. (*Holding up four fingers.*) That many
       days. Night time too. He bin tell me 'bout them *gudeeah.*   60
       They bin two, three stockman *gudeeah.* Bin stop along that
       place, Juada Station, and this one *gudeeah* Midja George, he
       was ridin' and he come to this river and he see these two old
       womans, *koories,* there in the water hole. He says, what you
       doin' here? They say they gettin' *gugja.*   65

(*He mimes pulling lily roots and eating.*)

Midja George say, where the mans? They over by that tree
sleepin', and Midja George, he get off his horse, and he bin
belt that old man with the stockwhip. He bin flog 'em, flog
'em, till that *gudeeah,* he get tired. Then he break the bottle glass spear, and he break the *chubel* spear.   70

(*He grunts and mimes this.*)

And that old man, he was bleedin', bleedin' from the eyes,
and he get up and he pick up that one *chubel* spear, and he
spear that one *Midja George.*

(*He demonstrates violently.*)

And that *gudeeah,* he get on his horse, he go little bit way
and he fall off . . . finish . . . dead.   75

JIMMY: Serve the bastard right.

BILLY: No, no, no bad for my mob. Real bad. That old man and his two *koories*, they do this next day.

(*He indicates running away.*)

Two *gudeeah* come looking for Midja George. They bin find 80 him dead.

(*Silence.*)

(*Holding up a hand.*) Must be that many day. Big mob gudeeah. Big mob politjmans, and big mob from stations, and shoot 'em everybody means, *koories,* little *yumbah.*

(*He grunts and mimes pulling a trigger.*)

They chuck 'em on a big fire, chuck 'em in river.

(*They sit in silence, mesmerized and shocked by* BILLY*'s gruesome story.*)

85 JIMMY: Anybody left, your mob?
BILLY: Not many, gid away, hide. But no one stop that place now, they all go 'nother country.
JOE: Why?
BILLY: You go there, night time you hear 'em. I bin bring cattle 90 that way for Wyndham Meat Works. I hear 'em. Mothers cryin' and babies cryin', screamin'. *Waiwai! Wawai! Wawai!*

(*They sit in silence staring at* BILLY *who stares into the fire. Suddenly a night hawk screeches.*)

SAM: Gawd, I'm getting out of here.
JIMMY: Me too!
BLUEY: Hm, hm, hm, hm, *wee-ah, wee-ah!*

(*They quickly pick up their things and leave.* JOE *remains alone.*)

95 SAM: You comin'?
JOE: Go on, I'll catch you up. Go on!
JIMMY: You watch out.

(*He pinches his throat with thumb and forefinger.*)

JOE: I'll be all right.
SAM: Don't forget the *kaal.*
100 JOE: Okay.

(*They exit.* JOE *looks around, pokes the fire, stands and waits. The moon begins to rise. There is a low mopoke call. He replies with a similar call and gets a reply.* MARY *runs into the clearing. They embrace.*)

I didn't think you were gunna get here.
MARY: I bin watchin' youse for nearly half an hour.
JOE: *Kienya!*
MARY: I mean listenin', not watchin'.
105 JOE: It's all right, wasn't man's business. Did you have any trouble gettin' away?
MARY: Nah. Topsy's coverin' up for me. I'll just walk in the dinin' room in the mornin'. They won't miss me.
JOE: (*Nervously.*) Where you gunna sleep tonight?

(*They kiss.* MARY *withdraws from him and sits on the log. She begins to cry. He checks that they are alone and sits close beside her on the log.*)

JOE: Eh? What's up? Come on, tell me what's up. You been 110 fightin' with someone?

(*She shakes her head.*)

Come on! Tell me what's the matter.
MARY: Mr Neal.
JOE: Yeah, what about him?
MARY: He's tryin' to make me go and work at the hospital. 115
JOE: Well, what's wrong with that?
MARY: Everything.
JOE: You get better tucker.
MARY: It's more than that, Joe.
JOE: What d'ya mean? 120
MARY: When Mr Neal sends a girl to work at the hospital, it usually means . . .
JOE: Means what?
MARY: That he wants that girl . . . for himself.
JOE: *What?* 125
MARY: Everyone know, even the *wetjalas.*
JOE: Rotten, stinkin', lowdown bastard. I'll kill him!
MARY: Joe . . .
JOE: I'll smash his head in with a *doak!*
MARY: Joe, listen! 130
JOE: Filthy pig. You not goin' anywhere near that hospital!
MARY: If I don't, he reckons he'll send me back home.
JOE: Home? Where?
MARY: Wyndham. He reckons he send me up home 'coz I'm a give girl. 135
JOE: Like hell you are.
MARY: I don't want to go up there to marry no old man.
JOE: You're meant to be gettin' married to me.
MARY: Mr Neal not gonna let us get married.
JOE: (*Exploding.*) Jesus! (*Indicating running.*) We're doin' this 140 tonight, right this fuckin' minute.
MARY: Joe, you'll get in big trouble!
JOE: I'll get in bigger trouble if I have to chip that walrus-faced bastard. I'll kill him.
MARY: Joe, listen! Where we gunna go? 145
JOE: Home, Northam.
MARY: What about your mum and dad?
JOE: We'll tell 'em now, come on, come on.

(MARY *just stands there.*)

Come on. I'm gunna show you my country. Got a big river, swans, beautiful white swans. 150

(JOE *picks up his shirt and a billy of water, which he tips on the fire. He leads* MARY *off into the darkness.*)

SCENE VII

Long Pool Camp, Moore River, night. Dogs bark. JOE *and* MARY *appear as shapes in the darkness.* JOE *tries to quieten the dogs. He approaches the tent.*

JOE: Mum, Dad? You wake?

(*He looks back at* MARY, *who stands alone.*)

Mum, Dad!

MILLY: Hmm, who is it?

JOE: It's only me.

5 MILLY: It's Joe.

(*The tent lights up as a match is struck and a hurricane lamp lit.*)

SAM: What's he want?

(*He crawls out.*)

Where you bin? We been home for hours.

(MILLY *appears behind him.*)

JOE: Mary's with me.

(MILLY *takes the lamp and goes to* MARY.)

MILLY: Mary! You should be in the compound.

10 JOE: She ain't goin' back there.

(JIMMY *appears, sleepy and dazed.*)

JIMMY: What's goin' on?

JOE: It's only me, *Kongi!*

MILLY: She can't stay here, Joe, she's a compound girl.

JOE: I know, Mum, we're runnin' away—tonight!

15 SAM: Now? What for?

JOE: 'Cause Neal's givin' Mary a bad time.

SAM: Can't be all that bad.

JOE: Neal's after her for himself. He's tryin' to make her work in the hospital and he keeps sayin' he's gonna send her back

20 to her lot to marry some old man—and he won't give no permission for us to get married.

MILLY: (*Comforting* MARY.) There's gotta be some other way than clearin' out.

JOE: Only other way's to stiffen that bastard in the dark.

(*He goes to* MARY.)

25 MILLY: They'll catch you sooner or later, son, and you'll go to gaol.

JIMMY: That right, Neph, you clear out. Gaol's *yuart,* only a *wetjala* thing. Don't worry about it.

MILLY: No, I'll do the worryin'.

30 SAM: Where's Granny?

MILLY: She's stoppin' with Aunty Wooleen.

(*She picks up a camp oven and breaks damper and crams it into a billy.*)

There's a bit of *merrang,* it's all we got.

(*She gives it to* MARY. SAM *gives* JOE *a blanket. He begins to roll it.*)

Where will you go?

JOE: (*Smiling.*) Northam. I'm gonna show Mary the swans.

35 Well, 'bye Dad, Uncle Jimmy! Say goodbye to Gran.

(*He moves towards the tent. His mother stops him.*)

MILLY: Don't wake the kids. Less they know the better.

JOE: (*Kissing her.*) Bye, Mum.

(MARY *kisses* MILLY, *then she and* JOE *walk away swiftly. They look back and wave, then vanish into the darkness.* MILLY *cries quietly.*)

JIMMY: (*Calling after them.*) You can jump the rattler 'bout half a mile outside a' Mogumber. Keep to the gravel country. Trackers won't find your tracks. 40

SCENE VIII

The Superintendant's Office, Moore River Native Settlement, day. MR NEAL *is sitting at his desk reading the* West Australian, *10 April 1933. The headlines read, 'Government Routed', 'Three Ministers Defeated', 'Labor Majority of Ten', 'Premier Loses Northam Seat', 'Two To One For Secession'.* MATRON *enters.*

MATRON: I've got some news for you.

NEAL: I know. I've read it, a bloody massacre.

(MATRON *is pleased, almost gloating.*)

Premier's gone in Northam . . . Looks like a majority of about ten . . . A bloody Labor Government.

MATRON: That's the good news . . . Two natives appear to— 5

NEAL: (*Interrupting.*) The only good news is the referendum: two to one.

MATRON: Beg your pardon, but I thought you might—

NEAL: (*Interrupting.*) The bloody secession referendum. In favour, one hundred and sixty three thousand six hundred and fifty 10 three, against seventy thousand seven hundred and six.

(*He stands and walks to the door, thrusting the paper at* MATRON.)

MATRON: Where are you going?

NEAL: Moora.

MATRON: What, holding a wake?

NEAL: I'm not staying here to listen to you gloat all bloody day. 15

MATRON: Well, before you go off to commiserate with your cronies in the hotel, you'd better do something about the runaways.

NEAL: What bloody runaways?

MATRON: (*Looking him in the eye.*) Mary Dargurru, and Joe 20 Millimurra.

NEAL: Since when?

JIMMY: Mary wasn't in the dormitory last night, or at breakfast this morning.

NEAL: Jesus, they'll be miles away. Why didn't you say some- 25 thing last night?

MATRON: I thought she might have been somewhere else.

NEAL: (*Yelling.*) Billy!

MATRON: Apparently you told her she was going to work at the hospital and stay in the nurses' quarters. 30

NEAL: Who told you that? (*Yelling.*) Billy!

BILLY: (*Off.*) Comin', boss.

MATRON: It seems she was terrified at the prospect of working in the hospital.

NEAL: They're all scared of the dead. 35

MATRON: I think she was scared of the living.

(BILLY *enters, buttoning up his jacket.*)

NEAL: Two runaways, Billy! You know Joe Millimurra, Northam native?

BILLY: Yeah, boss.
40 NEAL: And Mary Dargurru?
BILLY: That one Dargurru, my countryman. (*Pointing with his chin.*) She got go back Oombulgarri.
NEAL: You better get movin'! They'll be at the railway line by now.
BILLY: Ne'mine boss. I find 'em. Take 'em whip?
45 NEAL: Yes, take your whip, and pick up some tucker from the store. Here!

(*He throws a stick of tobacco onto the floor.* BILLY *picks it up.*)

BILLY: Thanks, boss.

(BILLY *exits.* MATRON *turns to follow him.*)

MATRON: As matron in charge of the hospital, I thought it was my job to allocate nursing aides.
50 NEAL: I was only trying to help you.
MATRON: Or yourself.

(*She exits.* NEAL *collapses into his chair.*)

SCENE IX

A clearing near the railway line at Mooloombeeni, early morning. MARY *is curled up asleep under a blanket.* JOE *appears with a billy can of water and his hat full of quandongs. He gently wakes* MARY. *She wakes in fright.*

JOE: Look, quandongs.
MARY: Oooh, my feet still hurt.
JOE: Let's have a look.

(JOE *washes and rubs her feet. She flinches.*)

They're a bit skinned. (*Nodding at the quandongs.*) Eat 'em.
5 MARY: Oh, that feels good. (*She bites into a quandong.*) Aagh! They're sour!
JOE: They're nice with sugar on 'em.

(MARY *jumps up and begins to vomit.* JOE *supports her. A magpie warbles.*)

You all right?
MARY: Gawd! Oh! I've never been sick like that in my life before.

(*She retches again.*)

10 JOE: You'll be all right once we get on the rattler. We'll get a nice cosy truck.

(JOE *sits her down and puts a blanket around her. She rests against him and recovers. A magpie squawks and* JOE, *immediately on his guard, jumps up and grabs his doak.* BILLY KIMBERLEY *appears and rushes at him with a stockwhip in one hand and handcuffs in the other.* JOE *dodges him.* MARY *is sick again as* BILLY *advances slowly and menacingly on* JOE.)

BILLY: You two fella, silly fella. Everyone run away. Wait here for the choo choo. (*Swinging the whip at* JOE.) Choo, choo, choo, choo.

(JOE *dodges the whip and threatens him with the doak.*)

JOE: Go back, old man. I don't want to hurt you. 15
BILLY: (*Pointing with his chin to* MARY.) She got to come back, she my countryman.

(MARY *vomits.* BILLY *drops the handcuffs and the two men crouch and circle each other.*)

JOE: She's comin' with me.
BILLY: She give girl. Mitjer Neal says she gotta come back.
JOE: Fuck Mr Neal! 20
BILLY: You bad boy, *Tjenna Guppi* gunna git you!
JOE: And fuck the *Tjenna Guppi* too!

(JOE *grabs the end of the whip and wrenches it from* BILLY, *sending him tumbling forward.* JOE *leaps on him and twists the whip around his neck.* MARY *staggers across to them. The train whistle blows in the distance.*)

MARY: Joe, Joe you choking him!
JOE: I'll kill the old bastard!
MARY: Get up off him. Please! Please, for my sake! 25
JOE: Gimme them handcuffs! Handcuffs, quick!

(MARY *throws him the handcuffs.* JOE *handcuffs* BILLY'S *hands in front of him, releases the whip and throws it down. He starts to go through* BILLY'S *pockets.*)

(*To* MARY.) You run, run, ru-un flat out to the hill! I'll catch you up!

(MARY *starts to pick up their possessions.*)

Leave them! Just run . . . Run!

(MARY *runs, hopping painfully on bruised and lacerated feet.* JOE *finds the keys to the handcuffs and throws them away. He picks up their gear.*)

You shouldn't fight young fella, old man. Here, tucker. 30

(JOE *thrusts quandongs into* BILLY'S *pockets, pushes his hat down over his head, and runs after* MARY.)

BILLY: Thas awright, thas awright. *Gudeeah* politjman git you bye and bye, you see.

(BILLY *picks up his whip with his handcuffed hands, pokes it in his belt and walks off slowly. The train thunders past.*)

SCENE X

The Superintendent's Office, Moore River, day. BILLY, *still handcuffed, limps past the Long Pool Camp followed by* DAVID, CISSIE *and* TOPSY, *all shouting 'Black crow, black crow'.* MR NEAL *reads the paper at his desk as* BILLY *approaches.*

BILLY: Mitjer Neal, Mitjer Neal! Eh boss!
NEAL: Come in.

(BILLY *enters.*)

Jesus, what the bloody hell happened?!
BILLY: He bin chuck me off my 'orse and he bin knock me silly fella with a *waddi*. 5

(MATRON *walks in briskly with an arm full of linen. She stops in her tracks when she sees* BILLY.)

MATRON: Goodness me, what happened?

NEAL: Well, he never caught Millimurra, Millimurra caught him.

MATRON: (*Putting the linen on* NEAL'*s desk.*) Oh, you poor man, where's the keys?

NEAL: Listen, Billy, where did you catch up with them?

BILLY: I bin find 'em Moolambeenee.

NEAL: Where were they heading?

BILLY: And that fella bin say he gunna hang me from Christmas tree like that.

(*He demonstrates.*)

Eh boss, you bin take 'em off handcuffs now?

MATRON: Where are the keys?

NEAL: All right, which way did they go?

BILLY: They bin run along train line. Train comin', whoo, whoo!

NEAL: All right, which—way—was—the—train—going?

BILLY: Goin' along train line.

NEAL: I know that, you blithering stone-age idiot!

MATRON: (*Pointing left and then right.*) Billy, was the train going that way or that way?

BILLY: (*Pointing with his chin to her left.*) He bin go that way, Kaggardu.

NEAL: You bloody fool of a man! What did you let him jump the bloody train for?

BILLY: He bin knock me silly fella, with a big stone. (*Indicating his back and then ribs.*) He bin kill 'em me here, here, and in the guts. Aw, he bad fella. (*Desperately, almost in tears.*) Eh boss, you bin take 'em off handcuffs now?

NEAL: (*To* MATRON.) Get the keys out of his pocket.

BILLY: No key, boss.

NEAL: Where are they?

(MATRON *starts to find quandongs.*)

BILLY: Dunno, boss . . . that one, he bin—

NEAL: (*Interrupting.*) You bloody incompetent savage. Where are the fuckin' keys?

BILLY: He bin chuck 'em away. He bad boy that one!

(MATRON *has a handful of quandongs but no keys.* NEAL *puts his hat on and prepares to leave.*)

NEAL: Come on, looks like a blacksmith's job.

MATRON: Then you'd better send him down to the hospital. I'll examine him and give him some dinner.

(MATRON *looks at them and at the quandongs.*)

BILLY: They good tucker, missus.

(*She laughs.*)

NEAL: I can't see anything funny about this.

MATRON: I know you can't.

(NEAL *and* BILLY *walk off.* MATRON *bites on a quandong but it's bitterly sour. She picks up the linen and leaves.*)

ACT THREE
Northam

SCENE I

Government Well Aboriginal Reserve, Northam, day. A few burnt out relics of the camp remain. JOE *and* MARY *stare about blankly.*

JOE: Grass ain't burnt.

MARY: What d'ya mean?

JOE: *Manatj* . . . (*Bitterly.*) Burned everything, those bastards!

(*He looks at the rubble.*)

We camped just 'ere.

(*He leads* MARY *to the spot.*)

(*Pointing up and off.*) See them rocks up there? Me and Cissie used to slide down them on pieces of tin when we was little. Magpies used to nest in that white gum tree.

MARY: Probably still do.

JOE: Yeah, s'pose so.

(*He sifts through the rubble and unearths a rabbit trap.*)

One a' Dad's.

(*He finds a wine bottle.*)

One of Uncle Jimmy's.

(*He puts it down carefully and continues the search.*)

MARY: Where did you get water?

JOE: Soak, down the creek.

MARY: Good *kaep*?

JOE: Sometimes. Mum used to always growl about it. She used to reckon it was harder than Uncle Jimmy's head. She'd be real upset if she saw the place now. Gran too. 'Specially Gran.

(*He sees something, off.*)

Oh, no!

(*He drags on the burnt remains of* DAVID'*s bike.*)

MARY: Whose was that?

JOE: Bastards! They reckon they was gunna look after everything we left behind.

MARY: Never mind, it's all over now.

JOE: It'll never be over!

(*He throws the bike down viciously.*)

MARY: Come on, *dubakieny*.

(JOE *picks up a rabbit trap and inspects it. He is pleased with it and they walk off.*)

SCENE II

A street in Northam, day. JOE *and* MARY *carry their swag,* BILLY *can and the rabbit trap.* SERGEANT CARROL *approaches.*

SERGEANT: Hey . . . You're one of the Millimurras, aren't you? . . . Joe?

JOE: Yeah.

SERGEANT: What are you doin' back in Northam?

5 JOE: We're livin' here.

SERGEANT: Who's this?

JOE: Me missus.

SERGEANT: Where are you staying?

JOE: Not at the Shamrock, that's for sure!

10 SERGEANT: You can't camp at Government Well.

JOE: What did you burn everything for?

SERGEANT: We're simply following orders.

JOE: What, to burn a push bike? I thought you were meant to look after our stuff till we come back.

15 SERGEANT: Look! I don't know nothing about no push bike.

JOE: What about rations?

SERGEANT: I can't help you there. Since all the natives have shifted out, Northam is no longer a ration depot.

JOE: We never shifted out, we was booted out. Anyway, what
20 happened to the horses?

SERGEANT: They were in terrible nick. We had to shoot one, the other one's down at Martin's, I think.

JOE: Trust him to grab one.

SERGEANT: He didn't grab it, it just wandered onto his property.

(MARY *grabs* JOE's *sleeve and tries to lead him away.*)

25 MARY: Come on, Joe!

SERGEANT: Where's the rest of your lot? Not here, I hope.

JOE: You oughta know where they are, you dragged 'em there.

SERGEANT: All right, all right. Look, I don't care where they are
so long as they're not here. Just make yourself scarce and
30 don't go campin' anywhere you're not s'posed to be—and
that includes Government Well.

JOE: Yeah, you made sure of that!

(*The policeman exits.* JOE *watches him go.* MARY *tugs at him and they exit.*)

SCENE III

Northam Police Station, day. SERGEANT CARROL *enters. At the Protector of Aborigines' Office, Perth,* MISS DUNN *steps in briskly and settles to typing.* SERGEANT CARROL *picks up the phone.*

SERGEANT: Hello. Hello, operator, a Perth number: B-M-nine-seven-o-seven. Nine-seven-o-seven. Yes, thanks Sybil, can't complain. Yourself?

(*He hangs up as* MR NEVILLE *enters his office, carrying a briefcase.*)

NEVILLE: Good morning, Miss Dunn. You're bright and early.

5 MISS DUNN: Good morning, Mr Neville. I thought I'd get a few pages of your Royal Commission submission typed before the telephone starts for the day.

(*Her telephone rings. She answers it.*)

Hello, Aborigines Department . . . yes . . . (*To* NEVILLE.) It's Sergeant Carrol, Northam.

(*The phone rings in the police station.* SERGEANT CARROL *answers it.*)

NEVILLE: Thank you. Would you mind having a look at the 10 mail when you have a moment?

(NEVILLE *goes to his desk and takes the call.* MISS DUNN *hangs up.*)

SERGEANT: Hello, Northam Police. Hello.

NEVILLE: Hello. Hello, Sergeant. Neville, Aborigines.

SERGEANT: Hello.

NEVILLE: Hello, Sergeant. Are you on the line? 15

SERGEANT: Hello, Mr Neville. It's a crook line.

NEVILLE: There's an appalling cracking noise, but I can hear you. Did you find out how many—

SERGEANT: (*Interrupting.*) As far as I can ascertain, the only natives here are Joe Millimurra and girl who he claims is his 20 wife—Mary, I think. They're not actually camped in the town.

NEVILLE: Dargurru.

SERGEANT: Pardon?

NEVILLE: The girl. Mary Dargurru. Rhymes with kangaroo. 25 D-A-R-G-U-double R-U.

(*The* SERGEANT *fumbles for a pencil and writes on the desk.*)

SERGEANT: . . . Double R, U. Yeah . . . Haven't had any bother with them. Millimurra's working at Lockyers, they're not collecting rations.

NEVILLE: Well, I've had two letters from the Town Clerk. The 30 Council's still adamant that no natives remain in the Northam area.

SERGEANT: I know, I had a yarn with the Town Clerk last week; they're putting something into this Royal Commission, apparently. 35

NEVILLE: Well, you'd better apprehend them, anyway.

SERGEANT: What about warrants?

NEVILLE: Dargurru's a minor, and Millimurra's guilty of absconding with her: it carries a mandatory six months. You can hold him on the existing warrant; the girl can be sent 40 down here under escort. I'll organise to have her met at Midland. Can you pick them up today?

SERGEANT: Yeah, I suppose so.

NEVILLE: Good, and let me know if any more natives return to the district. I've written to the Town Clerk letting him know 45 that any Northam natives released from the settlement have undertaken not to return to the Northam District.

SERGEANT: Good-oh, Mr Neville.

NEVILLE: And let me know which train you're putting the girl on.

SERGEANT: Good-oh, sir. 50

NEVILLE: Thank you, Sergeant.

(*They hang up as* MISS DUNN *puts a thick pile of typing on* NEVILLE's *desk.*)

MISS DUNN: That's the section on settlements completed.

NEVILLE: (*Taking a pile of notes from his briefcase.*) Oh thank you. Here's the next lot, keep you busy for a while. Did you get a chance to do the mail? 55

MISS DUNN: Yes; a couple of accounts and a letter from the Western Australian Historical Association.

NEVILLE: What do they want?

MISS DUNN: They'd like you to present a paper at their next meeting. Shall I write and tell them you're too busy at present? 60

NEVILLE: No, I'm very interested; I'll reply myself.

(*He begins drafting a reply while she commences typing.* CONSTABLE KERR *enters the police station and begins to remove his hat and coat.*)

SERGEANT: Leave them on, your coming with me.
CONSTABLE: Where's the fire?
SERGEANT: Picking up a couple of natives, Joe Millimurra and
65   Mary . . .

(*He reads the desk and copies the name onto a scrap of paper.*)

    Darg . . . something.
CONSTABLE: What for?
SERGEANT: Absconding. Council, George Withnall and Ray
    Brew and so on have been getting on the Chief Protector's
70   back. (*Starting to search.*) Do you know where those warrants
    for their removal are?
CONSTABLE: Haven't seen them for months. What's the panic?
    They've been here for weeks.
SERGEANT: Oh, you know all this Royal Commission business.
75   Some mob of do-gooder women are kicking up about them
    being shifted out before the election.

(*He finds the warrants.*)

    You can stop looking now, Constable . . . (*Reading.*)
    'Lawrence' . . . 'Lawson' . . . 'Millimurra'. Come on. Royal
    Commission on Natives; they had one about thirty years
80   ago. A waste of bloody time, like the bloody referendum;
    they'll just stick it in some government filing cabinet and
    forget about it.

SCENE IV

A street in Northam, day. JOE *is approached by* SERGEANT CARROL *and* CONSTABLE KERR.

SERGEANT: G'day, Joe. Where's the girl?
JOE: What girl?
CONSTABLE: Don't be smart, just answer the question.
JOE: Don't have to be smart to answer your questions.
5   SERGEANT: Where is she?
JOE: What do you want her for?
CONSTABLE: Listen, you cheeky bla—
SERGEANT: (*Interrupting.*) I'll handle this. Come on, Joe, where
    is she?
10   JOE: Out at Lockyers.
SERGEANT: You are under arrest under Section Twelve of the
    Aborigines Act for absconding from the Moore River Set-
    tlement with, um . . .

(*He takes the piece of paper out of his pocket and peruses it.*)

JOE: What for? We're not livin' in town.
15   SERGEANT: . . . With Mary Dargurru.
JOE: Why are youse worryin' about us now? We been back in
    Northam for nearly two months.
SERGEANT: Because Mr Neville only contacted me this morning.
JOE: What about Mary?
20   SERGEANT: The girl? She'll be returned to the settlement.
JOE: Back to that bastard.

SERGEANT: What do you mean by that?
JOE: It's my business.
CONSTABLE: Hold out your hands.

(*He produces handcuffs.*)

JOE: You ain't puttin' them on me.   25
CONSTABLE: Are you resisting arrest?
JOE: No I'm not . . . I just don't want them things on me.
SERGEANT: (*To the* CONSTABLE.) Don't worry about them. If he
    runs he'll only get an extra couple of months.
JOE: I'm not gunna run.   30
SERGEANT: Take him down the lock-up.
JOE: Sergeant, will you tell Mary where I am? She's out at Lock-
    yers, on the York Road.
SERGEANT: Yeah, I know. I'll tell her.

(*The* SERGEANT *exits.*)

CONSTABLE: Come on, get movin'.   35

(JOE *doesn't move.*)

    Get movin'!
JOE: I'm not walkin' in front of you.
CONSTABLE: Why not?
JOE: You're not the sort of bloke I want to turn me back to.

(*They walk off slowly, side by side.*)

SCENE V

AUBER OCTAVIUS NEVILLE, *groomed and dressed smartly, addresses the Royal Western Australian Historical Society. Behind him is a por-trait of the King, the Union Jack and the Western Australian flag. He nears the end of a long speech.*

NEVILLE: Ladies and gentlemen of the Historical Society, it has
    been a great privilege and pleasure to address you here
    tonight at a time when, with Mr Mosley's Royal Commis-
    sion, the welfare of our Aboriginal and coloured folk is
    somewhat more than usually in the public arena. If I may   5
    beg your indulgence for a few more minutes, I shall con-
    clude with a brief word about those early years when that
    little band of pioneers, fewer than one hundred souls, led by
    Captain Stirling, laid anchor in the Swan River, little know-
    ing that they faced in the fertile valleys of the south-   10
    west alone some thirteen thousand savages.
        Stirling's first acts was to issue a proclamation regard-
    ing the treatment of the native inhabitants.

(*He reads:*)

    'And whereas the protection of the law doth of right be-
    long to all people whatsoever who may come or be found   15
    within the territory aforesaid, I do hereby give notice that
    if any person or persons shall be, convicted of behaving in
    a fraudulent, cruel, or felonious manner towards the abo-
    riginal race of inhabitants of this country, such a person
    or persons will be liable to be prosecuted and tried for   20
    the offence as if the same had been committed against any
    others of His Majesty's subjects.' In the same proclamation,

all male persons between the ages of fifteen and fifty were required to enrol in the militia, to secure the safety of the
25 territory from invasion and from the attacks of hostile native tribes as might be necessary.

(*Pause.*)

From the beginning the natives provided the settlers with bush food and assisted exploring parties, and a happy relationship between settlers and blacks continued for some eigh
30 teen months. The newcomers were yet to impress the blacks with the significance of their invasion. In November of that year, an Aborigine was shot while stealing flour. That was the beginning of the end. Constant pressure from the whites drove back the erstwhile native inhabitants, depriving them
35 of their water and food supplies. Naturally enough, the bolder spirits among the blacks resented this, and we cannot wonder that the murder of isolated whites occurred during this period, with a heavy toll of black life being exacted in reprisal. On the twenty-seventh of October, 1834, Governor Stirling
40 led a detachment of soldiers and civilians to the Murray River at Pinjarra. In the early morning they came across a camp of some sixty or seventy natives. The detachment took up positions on both sides of the river. Rain, which had been threatening for some time, began to fall heavily. The party opened
45 fire and more natives appeared from shelters. The men defended themselves with spears, while the women and children sought shelter in the river. For one hour they were subjected to crossfire from twenty-four guns from both banks. The official estimate was fifteen to twenty dead, but only eight
50 women and several children were finally rounded up.

(*He pauses and takes a drink of water.*)

One more word and I shall have finished. When referring to Australia's treatment of her Aborigines we are apt to refer somewhat scathingly to Tasmania's harshness in ridding herself of her natives within the first seventy years of settle
55 ment. In that time some six thousand natives disappeared and only one was left alive. Yet here, in the south-west of our State, within an area about twice the size of Tasmania between 1829 and 1901—seventy-two years—a people estimated to number thirteen thousand were reduced to one
60 thousand four hundred and nineteen, of whom nearly half were half-caste.

ACT FOUR
Moore River

SCENE I

Moore River outdoor Sunday School, a hot day. SISTER EILEEN, CISSIE *and* TOPSY *sit in a group.* SISTER EILEEN *is telling a story from memory. Next to her are several sheets of paper.*

SISTER: After the shepherds had visited the baby Jesus in the manger, Mary and Joseph and the Holy Jesus had three very special visitors. Can anyone tell me who they were?
TOPSY: The Three Wise Men, Sister Eileen.
5 SISTER: Yes, very good, Topsy. And the Three Wise Men brought the Holy Jesus gifts of gold, frankincense and

myrrh. But on the way to visit Jesus the Three Wise Men spoke to the King of Judea. Who can tell me the name of the King of Judea?

(TOPSY's *hand goes up.*)

Well, do you know, Cissie?   10
CISSIE: No, Sister.
SISTER: Topsy, can you tell us?
TOPSY: King Herod, Sister.

(CISSIE *notices* DAVID *enter at a distance.* BILLY *enters behind* DAVID *and sees him.*)

SISTER: That's right, King Herod. And when the Three Wise Men heard that a Saviour was born to be King of the Jews, he 15 wasn't pleased at all, because he was king and he didn't want any other king. So what did he do? Can anybody tell me?

(BILLY *puts a hand on* DAVID's *shoulder.* CISSIE *puts up her hand.*)

BILLY: Eh, boy, where you goin'?
DAVID: Swimmin'.
SISTER: (*Surprised.*) Yes, Cecilia.   20

(BILLY *belts* DAVID *on the legs with his whip.*)

CISSIE: Look, Sister Eileen, look.
BILLY: (*To* DAVID.) You s'posed to be Chunday School. *Gudeeah* waitin' for you.
TOPSY: Billy Kimberley's belting one of the boys.
BILLY: (*To* DAVID.) Now you git to Sunday School, straight away 25 now, git, git, git.
CISSIE: It's David.

(*She jumps up and picks up a stone, and runs to* DAVID.)

SISTER: Cecilia, wait. Cecilia!

(SISTER EILEEN *jumps up and runs after her.*)

CISSIE: You leave him alone, old man.
SISTER: Billy, Billy!   30

(CISSIE *prepares to throw the stone.*)

Cecilia, don't you dare!

(*She grabs* CISSIE's *arm.*)

Billy, what are you hitting that boy for?
BILLY: Him cheeky fella, missus. He goin' swimmin', don't wanna go Chunday school. He bad boy, that one.
SISTER: All right, Billy, but we don't hit people to make them 35 do God's will.
DAVID: (*To* BILLY.) Black crow, black crow.
SISTER: David, that's enough of that! Come on, now.
BILLY: (*To* DAVID.) You bad boy.

(*He exits.*)

SISTER: Did he hurt you?   40
DAVID: I'm all right.

CISSIE: Rotten stinkin' mongrel.

SISTER: That's enough! David, in one way it's your own fault.

DAVID: It's not.

45 SISTER: If you'd been at Sunday School that wouldn't have happened, so remember that … All right, now where were we?

(*She gives* DAVID *a humbug and they go back to the others.*)

TOPSY: King Herod, Sister Eileen.

SISTER: Now, King Herod was very angry and very wicked and you know what he did? He ordered his soldiers to kill every

50 first-born baby boy under two years old. So Mary and Joseph didn't want them to kill the baby Jesus, so they had to flee from Bethlehem. They wrapped the baby in a blanket and crept away in the middle of the night. They travelled all night and by sunrise they were far away and safe.

55 TOPSY: Where did they go, Sister?

SISTER: They went to Egypt until King Herod died and there was a new King of Judea. And then they returned to Jesus' home in Nazareth, where Jesus grew up to be a man. Now wasn't that a splendid story? Did you like it, David?

60 DAVID: S'all right.

(SISTER EILEEN *hands out a sheet of paper to each.*)

SISTER: Now, here are the hymn sheets for today. It's a hymn I'm sure you all know, and want you to sing in your very best voice, because this is the hymn we'll be singing for Mr Neville in the Australia Day celebrations.

65 ALL: (*Singing.*)

> There is a happy land,
> Far, far away,
> Where saints in glory stand,
> Bright, bright as day:
70 > Oh, how they sweetly sing,
> 'Worthy is our Saviour King!'
> Loud, let His praises ring,
> Praise, praise for aye!

> Bright in that happy land,
75 > Beams every eye:
> Kept by a Father's hand
> Love cannot die.
> Oh, then, to glory run,
> Be a Crown and Kingdom won
80 > And, bright above the sun,
> Reign, reign for aye!

Amen.

(*They gather around for their humbugs.* DAVID *holds out his hand.*)

CISSIE: You've already had one.

DAVID: Shut up.

(SISTER EILEEN *gives him a humbug.*)

SCENE II

The Superintendent's Office, Moore River, day. MR NEAL *reads at his desk.* MATRON *enters while* BILLY *and* MARY, *now very pregnant, wait outside.*

MATRON: She's here.

NEAL: Dargurru?

MATRON: Yes.

NEAL: Oh, good. Aren't you needed down the hospital?

MATRON: Just remember, that girl is pregnant, and unwell. 5

NEAL: Don't worry, I won't touch her.

(MATRON *exits.*)

NEAL: Billy? Billy?

BILLY: Yes, boss.

NEAL: Bring her in.

(BILLY *brings* MARY *into the office.*)

You wait, all right? Don't go walkabout. 10

(BILLY *goes outside to wait.*)

Dargurru, you finally got caught, eh? And you got yourself pregnant? Well, you'll be all right here. You can stay in the nurses' quarters.

MARY: No, I wanta stay with Joe's Mum and Dad.

NEAL: Don't be stupid, girl: you're meant to be pregnant and 15 sick, so you can stay in the nurses' quarters and do a bit of light work in the hospital.

MARY: I don't want to work in the hospital.

NEAL: You'll work where I think fit, digging graves if I say so.

MARY: I'm not gunna work in the hospital. 20

NEAL: You'll do as I say, do you understand?

MARY: No.

NEAL: So you intend to defy me, do you? Billy!

(*He takes the cat-o'-nine-tails from his desk.*)

Do you know what that is?

(BILLY *enters.*)

MARY: I don't care. You can belt me if you like, I'm not workin' 25 in the hospital.

BILLY: Boss talkin' to you.

MARY: Go to hell!

BILLY: Don't be cheeky, now.

NEAL: (*To* MARY.) What did you say? 30

(*Silence.*)

BILLY: Boss talkin' to you.

NEAL: What—did—you—say?

MARY: Go to hell! Fuck youse!

NEAL: Millimurra seems to have learnt her well. Well, I'm going to unlearn you. 35

(NEAL *grabs her.* BILLY *holds her outstretched over a pile of flour bags.* NEAL *raises the cat-o'-nine-tails. Blackout. A scream.*)

SCENE III

Long Pool Camp, Moore River. MILLY *sorts clothes for washing.* SAM *and* JIMMY *drink tea.* GRAN *sits in the shade.* MILLY *looks up as* MARY *enters.*

MILLY: Mary! Oh, gawd, Mary . . .

(MILLY *runs to her, takes the flour and helps her to the camp.*)

Come on, Mary, sit down.

(MARY *sits painfully.*)

You all right?
MARY: Yeah.

(*The others gather around as* MILLY *carefully lifts the back of* MARY's *galatea blouse to reveal huge welts.* GRAN *fetches some medicinal leaves.*)

5   SAM: Oh, my gawd.
JIMMY: The bastard. I'll kill him.
GRAN: Ne'mine, ne'mine, put these *jeerung meear* on your back. Fix up quick and make you better.
MILLY: Baby all right?
10 MARY: Yeah. He's kickin' like a Kimberley camel.
SAM: I think we better take her to the hospital.
MARY: No. No, I'm not goin' to no hospital. I'll die first.
MILLY: But you'll have to go to have the baby.
MARY: No, I'm havin' it 'ere. I can 'ave it 'ere, can't I?
15 GRAN: You can have it right 'ere, darlin'. I brought Joe into this world and, by crikey, I'll bring his baby.

(*The sound of the shrill voices of* DAVID *and* CISSIE *are heard, off.*)

DAVID:
CISSIE: (*Together.*)   Mum, Dad . . .

(*The kids run on.* DAVID *carries a letter.*)

CISSIE: Mary, a letter from Brother Joe.

(MARY *takes the letter and reads.*)

DAVID: Willy Knapp give it to me. He just came back from
20   gaol, and Joe give it to him.
CISSIE: *Gave* it to him, not 'give'.
DAVID: That's what I said.
CISSIE: *Nyummi.*
DAVID: . . . Give it him to gave to youse so Mr Neal wouldn't
25   read it and tear it up or something.
JIMMY: Bastard reads everybody's mail.
MILLY: How is he?
MARY: Good, reckons the tucker's all right. Here, you read it, Cissie.

(CISSIE *takes the letter and reads in silence.*)

30 DAVID: Out loud, *nyummi!*
CISSIE: 'I'm giving this to Willie to give to youse 'coz if . . .'

(*Pause.*)

(*Spelling.*) 'F-U-C-K F-A-C-E gets it, he'll most likely tear it up. How is everyone? Mum and Dad and Gran and the kids and Uncle Jimmy . . . And my little brother and sister? But
35   really, how are you and the baby? I've only got eight weeks to go and I'm counting them days, every one of them. We

are getting married when I get out. If the Aborigines Department give us permission. I am going to ask Mister Neville myself. I'd sooner we got married at New Norcia like Mum and Dad. Though I ain't really a Catholic. You 40 know, I don't know what you are, I forgot to ask you. It not too bad here, plenty of Nyoongahs and some from up North. Tucker's not too bad, better than the Settlement. At least they don't give us bread and fat, and we get real bacca, not nigger twist. Tell Willy to behave himself now he's out 45 and not to go hitting any more policemen. Well, darling, I'll close.

(CISSIE *sniggers.*)

'I love you and I think of you day and night.

(*She laughs.*)

'I even dream about you. Lots of love and kisses to you and Baby. Joe.' 50
MILLY: Come on, Mary, you come and lie down.

SCENE IV

The Superintendent's Office, Moore River. MR NEAL *works at his desk.* SISTER EILEEN *approaches and knocks. He ignores it. She knocks again.*

NEAL: Who is it?
SISTER: Me, Sister Eileen.

(*He continues working, head down.* SISTER EILEEN *enters the office.*)

Matron said you wanted to see me.
NEAL: Yeah.

(*He continues working. Pause.*)

Yeah, now . . . Australia Day, the ceremony. Mr Neville 5 likes to have the agenda in advance. I'd like you to say a few words yourself and an appropriate hymn.
SISTER: We've been practising 'There Is a Happy Land' . . . I thought it would be . . .
NEAL: Good. 10
SISTER: I thought it might be nice if Mr Neville announced the hymn.
NEAL: Yeah, all right. What was it again?
SISTER: 'There Is a Happy Land'.

(NEAL *writes it down and shuffles his papers. He ignores her. Pause.*)

Is that all, Mr Neal? 15
NEAL: Just a moment . . . There's another matter I'd like to discuss with you. I believe you've been lending books— novels—to some of the natives.
SISTER: Yes, I have.
NEAL: There's a sort of unofficial directive on this; it's the sort 20 of thing which isn't encouraged by the Department.
SISTER: What do you mean? That you don't encourage the natives to read?
NEAL: That's right
SISTER: (*Incredulously.*) But why? I'd intended to ask your per- 25 mission to start a small library.

NEAL: I'm sorry, Sister, but—

SISTER: (*Interrupting.*) It won't cost the Department a penny, I can get the books donated. Good books.

30 NEAL: It's quite out of the question.

SISTER: But why?

NEAL: Look, my experience with natives in South Africa and here has taught—led me to believe that there's a lot of wisdom in the old adage that 'a little knowledge is a danger-

35 ous thing'.

SISTER: I can't believe what you're saying.

NEAL: Look Sister, I've got a big mob here, over seven hundred—you know that—and there's enough troublemakers without giving them ideas.

40 SISTER: But Mr Neal—

NEAL: (*Interrupting.*) I don't think there's anything more to be said on the subject.

SISTER: Well, I'd like to say something on another subject.

NEAL: Yes?

45 SISTER: The use of violence by your native policemen to enforce attendance at my religious instruction classes.

NEAL: If I didn't make attendance compulsory, you'd have none of them there.

SISTER: I'd prefer that they come of their own free will.

50 NEAL: Look, Sister, if you're not happy here, I could arrange a transfer for you to another settlement; perhaps Mulla Bulla, on the edge of the Gibson Desert.

(*She goes to leave, but stops by the door.*)

SISTER: Getting back to the books, what do you classify the Bible as?

(*She exits.*)

55 NEAL: (*To himself.*) Bloody do-gooders.

SCENE V

Moore River Native Settlement, Australia Day, 1934, a very hot afternoon. MR NEVILLE, MR NEAL *and* MATRON *are seated on a dais.* BILLY KIMBERLEY *and* BLUEY, *dressed in new but absurdly ill-fitting uniforms, stand beside a flag pole with a flag furled ready to raise.* SISTER EILEEN *addresses the assembled population of the settlement, including the Millimurra family.* JOE *is still absent.*

SISTER: It gives me great pleasure to be with you all on this very special day, when we gather together to pledge our allegiance to the King and to celebrate the birth of this wonderful young country that we are so fortunate to be living

5 in. We must remember today not just our country and King, but the King of kings, the Prince of princes, and to give thanks to God for what He has provided for us because our sustenance in life is provided by Him. Even we here today, Mr Neal, Matron Neal and myself, are but His humble

10 servants, sent by Him to serve your needs. The Lord Jesus Christ has sent His servant, Mr Neville, Chief Protector of Aborigines, to speak to us on this special day. Mr Neville is going to say a few words before leading us in a song of praise to our Lord and Saviour, Jesus Christ.

(NEVILLE *rises. The whites clap while the Aborigines remain silent.*)

NEVILLE: Today we are gathered here to celebrate the birth of 15 this nation of Australia one hundred and forty-six years ago at Sydney Cove in the Eastern States. As I was driving up, I remembered that it is only a hundred and four years since the British flag was first raised on our West Australian shores. As I drove through Guildford, Midland and Bulls- 20 brook, I saw men on the road, hundreds of men, and I was reminded that the world is in the grip of depression and that many people are suffering from hunger and deprivation of many of the essential elements which make for a contented existence. But you, in this small corner of the Em- 25 pire, are fortunate in being provided for with adequate food and shelter.

JIMMY: (*Muttering.*) Yeah, weevily flour.

NEVILLE: . . . And to be with family and friends. Occasionally some of you might ponder why you are here— 30

JIMMY: (*A little louder.*) Too bloody right.

SAM: (*To* JIMMY.) *Dubakieny wahnginy, gnoolya.*

NEVILLE: . . . It doesn't hurt to remind yourselves that you are preparing yourselves here to take your place in Australian society, to live as other Australians live, and to live along- 35 side other Australians; to learn to enjoy the privileges and to shoulder the responsibilities of living like the white man, to be treated equally, not worse, not better, under the law.

(*Pause. He looks around at the others on the dais.*)

SAM: What's he talkin' about? 40

JIMMY: He's talkin' outa his *kwon.*

SISTER: (*Aside, to* NEVILLE.) The hymn.

NEVILLE: We are now going to sing the song . . . ah, hymn.

NEAL: (*Aside to* NEVILLE.) The hymn, then the flag raising.

NEVILLE: Sing the hymn before we raise the flag and sing the 45 national anthem. (*To* SISTER EILEEN.) Sorry, I've forgotten.

SISTER: 'There is a Happy Land'.

NEVILLE: 'There is a Happy Land'.

(SISTER EILEEN *stands.*)

ALL: (*Singing.*)

There is a happy land, 50
Far, far away,
Where saints in glory stand,
Bright, bright as day:
Oh, how they sweetly sing,
'Worthy is our Saviour King!' 55
Loud let His praises ring,
Praise, praise for aye!

(*As the whites continue, the Aborigines break into full clear voice with a parody of the words.*)

There is a happy land,
Far, far away.
No sugar in our tea, 60
Bread and butter we never see.
That's why we're gradually
Fading away.

NEVILLE: Stop, stop. Stop that immediately.

(*The Aborigines repeat the parody even louder.*)

65   Stop it. Stop this nonsense immediately. Never in my life
     have I witnessed such a disgraceful exhibition.

(*The song stops.*)

     I'm appalled by this disgraceful demonstration of ingrati-
     tude. I can tell you that you will live to rue this day. There
     will be no privileges from now on.
70   JIMMY: (*Calling out.*) Rotten spuds and onions?
     NEVILLE: Be quiet! And there will be no Christmas this year!
     No Christmas!
     JIMMY: What, a dried up orange and a puddin'?
     NEVILLE: Will you be quiet? Who is it, who is that fellow?
75   Munday, isn't it? Northam. I've got police reports on you.
     You're a troublemaker, and a ringleader. You must listen
     to me.
     JIMMY: (*Approaching* NEVILLE.) No, you listen to me Mr A.O.
     You come an' eat supper with us, tonight, right? B'read and
80   drippin' and black tea. Are you game to try it?

(NEAL *stands to leave, then turns back.*)

NEAL: Look, Munday, what's your bloody game?
JIMMY: Did you vote for Jimmy **Mit**chell's lot?

(*Silence.* JIMMY *sniggers.* SISTER EILEEN *stands and starts to sing
'God Save the King'. The other whites join in. The Aborigines
laugh.*)

     Yeah, you musta done, eh?

(NEAL *stares at him in disbelief. The blacks, with the exception of the
Millimurra family, gradually disperse.* BILLY *and* BLUEY *remain by
the flag.*)

     Nothin' to do with bloody scabies. And that's why we got
85   dragged 'ere; so them *wetjalas* vote for him.

(JIMMY *is left alone, shouting.* SAM *looks on.*)

     So he could have a nice, white little town, a nice, white lit-
     tle fuckin' town.

(JIMMY *runs out of breath, heaves and clutches his chest.* SAM
*catches him as he collapses, clutching at the flagpole. The official
party continues to sing 'God Save the King'.* JIMMY*'s family rushes
to him.*)

MARY: Matron, Matron, help! Help us!
NEAL: (*To the whites.*) Ah! He's only fainted.

(*The singing stops.* MATRON *breaks ranks and rushes to* JIMMY*'s aid,
loosens his clothing, checks his breathing and pulse.*)

90   MATRON: He's got a heart condition. Billy, Bluey, pick him up.
     Bring him to the hospital. Come on, come on. Easy now.

(MATRON *and the Millimurras exit with* BILLY *and* BLUEY. NEVILLE
and NEAL *exit in the other direction.* SISTER EILEEN *remains, unsure
which way to go.*)

SCENE VI

The Superintendant's Office, day. NEAL *reads the* West Australian,
Monday 30 January 1934. MATRON *enters.*

MATRON: What's the latest?
NEAL: A cool change tomorrow.

(*He looks at the date on the paper.*)

     That's today.
MATRON: Not much sign of it.
NEAL: Pictures of cars stuck in the bitumen on Crawley Drive   5
     . . . Hmm, a truck load of eggs in Fremantle hatched out
     chickens . . . Hot, all right.
MATRON: No news from Kalgoorlie?
NEAL: Oh, yeah . . . Three dead.
MATRON: Oh, dear.   10
NEAL: Yeah, besides Jordan. One of us stabbed—typical—and
     one a them shot. The foreigners have dug themselves in
     around Ding Flat . . . They're recruiting specials.
MATRON: Who?
NEAL: Volunteers, special constables. A man with a military   15
     background has a responsibility to volunteer in an emer-
     gency like this.
MATRON: Why don't you?
NEAL: Can't leave this place.

(MILLY *and* SAM *approach the office.*)

MATRON: Got your own civil war?   20
NEAL: Don't be stupid, woman, I can handle a mob of unruly
     niggers.
MATRON: Yes? Yes, Milly? Hello, Sam.
MILLY: (*Pointing inside.*) We want to see him.

(MATRON *beckons them in.*)

NEAL: (*To* SAM *and* MILLY.) What do you want?   25
SAM: We want to know if you can get Joe out for the funeral.
NEAL: Who?
MATRON: Joe Millimurra.
NEAL: Impossible.
MILLY: Why? Other Nyoongahs get out when the 'lations die.   30
SAM: You could ring up Mr Neville and ask him.
NEAL: Too late. Funeral's tomorrow.
SAM: Well, hold it the day after.
NEAL: What, in this weather?
MILLY: You could if you wanted to.   35

(MILLY *starts to cry.*)

MATRON: Don't get upset; there's nothing we can do about it.
MILLY: And don't you go wrappin' him up in the gubment
     blanket. You put him in a proper box.
MATRON: Don't worry, he'll receive a proper burial.
SAM: Will you ring the prison and tell 'em to tell Joe?   40
NEAL: As a member of the family you can write to him yourself.
MILLY: You scared to tell him. You scared to tell him.

(SAM *puts his hands on her shoulders and tries to steer her to the door.*
MILLY *struggles against him.*)

You're scared to tell him. You're scared at what he'll do when he gets out. You're *wayarniny*. *Wayarniny bridaira,*
45   you're *wayarniny*.

SAM: Come on, Milly, we get Cissie to write to him. Come on, Milly. Come on, come on now.

MILLY: I'll tell him all about it when he gits out, you hear me? You hear me?

50 SAM: Come on, Mil, *dubakieny*.

MILLY: An' Matron, you don't forget put him in a proper coffin box, Matron. Matron, coo-cooo, cooh.

(They exit.)

NEAL: (*To* MATRON.) A classic case of emotion comes in through the door and reason goes out the window.

55 MATRON: (*Exiting.*) I couldn't agree more. Seems to be happening frequently in this office lately.

SCENE VII

Long Pool Camp, Moore River, night. The campfire is blazing. DAVID *is asleep.* MARY, GRAN *and* MILLY *are silhouetted inside the tent.* MARY *suffers a contraction.*

MARY: Help, help! Joe! I want Joe!

(The contraction continues.)

Don't let them take Baby. Don't let them take Baby.

(She cries in panic.)

GRAN: Nobody's goin' to take Baby, darlin'. Nobody. You'll be all right, darling, Matron comin' to see you directly.

5 MARY: I don't want her to come here. Granny, tell her to go away. Please, I don't want to see her.

GRAN: You shut up, now. What will Joe say if anythin' happens to you and Baby, eh? We gotta look after youse.

MARY: I wish Joe was here.

(Another contraction starts and she yells.)

10 GRAN: (*To* MILLY.) Gawd, I think it's comin'. (*To* MARY.) Come on darlin', push down. Come on, breathe deep.

(The contraction continues.)

(*To* MILLY.) Git the water and the rags. (*To* MARY.) Come on darlin', you doin' good. Joe'd be real *tjeuripiny* for you. Breathe deep, eh? (*To* MILLY.) Git me clean ashes, make sure
15 there's no lumps.

*(*MARY *cries out while* MILLY *collects ashes on a sugar bag, picking out the pieces of charcoal. She takes the ashes, water and rags back to the tent.*)*

Come on, darlin', breathe deep. Push down, keep pushin', keep pushin'. Hurry up, Milly, come on. (*To* MARY.) Come on, darlin', you doin' good.

*(*MARY *yells and sighs.)*

Firestick! Firestick, live one, quick!

*(*MILLY *races to the fire and takes a burning stick back into the tent.)*

I got you a little Nyoongah. Now I cut your cord and tie it, 20
make a real pretty belly button for you, just like your daddy's. Now cover you in ashes. More better than Johnson's Baby Powder, eh?

(The baby cries.)

You got a great big handsome Nyoongah boy. Come on, darlin', one more push, come on . . . 25

*(*MARY *pushes.)*

Keep pushin', eh? Good, it's all over.

*(*DAVID *wakes.)*

GRAN: There you are, darlin'. He's yours for life.

DAVID: Hey? What's goin' on?

MILLY: You're an uncle now.

DAVID: What? Dinkum? 30

*(*DAVID *rushes to the tent and looks in.)*

Geez, look at him. Why don't he open his *meeowl*?

MILLY: 'Coz he's just been born, son. He's only five minutes old.

*(*SAM *appears, breathless.)*

Where's Matron?

SAM: They comin'.

DAVID: We don't need her, everything's all right. 35

SAM: Dinkum?

GRAN: That's what David said.

SAM: Here's Matron comin' now.

*(*MATRON *appears with a hurricane lamp and a satchel followed by* CISSIE *and* TOPSY.)*

MATRON: Hello, Granny. Hello everybody.

MARY: No! Don't let Matron see Baby. Granny, go and hide 40
him. Please, please, don't let Matron take him away.

(The three approach the tent.)

MATRON: Well, well. How is she? Hello, Mary.

GRAN: Baby boy.

CISSIE: Oh, he's beautiful.

MATRON: Come on, Mary, don't be a silly girl. I just want to 45
check him over.

MARY: No, don't touch him! You're not havin' my baby, leave him alone!

MATRON: But Mary, it's for your own good and the baby's and I only want to help. 50

MARY: No, don't take him to hospital. The trackers will get him and kill him.

MATRON: What on earth is she talking—

MARY: (*Interrupting.*) . . . And bury him in the pine plantation.

MATRON: I think she's delirious. 55

MARY: Like Lillian's baby. Mr Neal tell them to do it, to kill Baby.

MATRON: She's delirious.

SAM: No she ain't.

60 MARY: Gran, Gran, don't let 'em take him.

GRAN: (*Soothingly.*) No one's takin' Baby, darlin'. You're all right, you're all right. (*To* MATRON.) She's all right. Better go.

MATRON: Gran evidently seems to have done a good job.

GRAN: I brought plenty of babies into this world, Matron.

65 MATRON: (*Reaching into her satchel.*) Well, here's plenty of clean cotton wool and baby powder and Lysol soap.

GRAN: Don't need powder, use me own.

MATRON: All right, see you tomorrow when she's calmed down. (*To* MARY.) Bye, dear. You have a good sleep now.

70 MARY: Yes, Matron.

(MATRON *and* TOPSY *leave the tent and vanish into the darkness with the hurricane lamp.*)

SCENE VIII

Long Pool Camp, Moore River, day. GRAN *seems to have aged suddenly. She sits and stares into the smouldering fire, quietly grumbling and singing.* CISSIE *and* DAVID *play knucklebones.* MILLY *and* SAM *play cards.* MARY *watches over the baby who sleeps in a kerosene tin. A loud whistle is heard in the distance.*

SAM: Who the hell is that?

DAVID: Boys whistling at girls, I bet.

MARY: No.

(*The whistle is heard again.*)

I know that whistle, that's Joe. It's Joe, it's Joe!

(CISSIE *and* DAVID *start to run.*)

5 MILLY: Come back, you two! Come back!

DAVID: It's Joe, Mum. It's Joe.

(*The kids run off.*)

JOE: (*Off.*) Hey! Where are all you blackfellas?

(JOE *enters carrying a sugar bag and with* DAVID *on his back. They are followed by* CISSIE. *He sees* MARY *and they embrace. He swings her around and around.* DAVID *falls off, laughing and yelling.* JOE *wears a yellow shirt and black pants.*)

How's everybody? Gawd, it's good to be back.

SAM: Yeah, son, we wasn't expectin' you for another two weeks.

10 DAVID: (*Yelling, pointing to the tin.*) Your baby in there! (*Quietly.*) Sleepin'.

JOE: How are you, Gran?

GRAN: Bit crook. (*Rubbing her leg.*) Me leg git tired, little bit, this one.

15 MARY: Come and see baby.

(*They walk to where the baby sleeps.*)

JOE: Gawd.

(*Pause.*)

Can he sit up?

MARY: Give him time. He's only ten weeks old.

JOE: What did you call him?

SAM: We call him *koolbardi*, Nyoongah name. 20

GRAN: Magpie.

MARY: We waited for you to come home to give him a *wetjala* name.

(*Silence.*)

JOE: I wanna call him Jimmy.

(*Silence.*)

MARY: Yeah. 25

(GRAN *begins to wail and cry.*)

JOE: Eh, Gran, got somethin' here for you.

(*He dives his hand into the sugar bag and produces a wooden pipe and a tin of tobacco.*)

Here y'are, Gran, real pipe and real *gnummarri*, not nigger twist.

GRAN: *Woolah, kwobiduk, cooo-ooh.*

JOE: (*Pulling out coloured ribbons.*) Here y'are, Cissie, ribbons for 30 your hair.

CISSIE: Oh thanks, brother, they're *moorditj*.

(*She ties yellow and red ribbons in her hair.*)

JOE: Here y'are, *gnoon*.

(*He gives* DAVID *a pocket knife.*)

Here y'are, Mum.

(*He produces a needle and cotton.*)

And Dad. 35

(*He produces tobacco and papers.*)

SAM: Hey, real papers. Rizlas. Good on ya, son.

MILLY: Didn't you git nothin' for Mary?

JOE: Course I did, Mum.

(*He pulls out a larger parcel and gives it to her.*)

Go on, open it.

(*She tears the paper off: it's a red dress.*)

MILLY: Go and try it on, dear. 40

SAM: Hey, son, where did you git the *boondah*?

JOE: Wages. Earned a few bob and they give it to me when I got out. Not like this place.

(*He takes out a packet of cigarettes.*)

Had enough left for a packet of Luxor!

(*They share them.* MARY *returns with the dress on, unbuttoned down the back. She goes to* JOE *to do it up.*)

Geez, what happened to your back? 45

MILLY: Neal belted her.

DAVID: With the cat-'o-nine-tails. Tracker held her down over the flour bags.

CISSIE: And she was seven months *bootjari*.

50 JOE: Dinkum?

GRAN: *Kunarn, kunarn!*

JOE: Bloody stinkin' walrus-faced bastard. I'm gunna kick his teeth down his fuckin' throat.

(*He starts to run off, but* MARY *stops him.*)

MARY: Joe, please, please, please, don't go near him. Please
55   think of Baby and me. He'll put you in gaol again.

JOE: But why did he have to belt you?

MARY: 'Cause I told him to go to hell.

JOE: Dinkum?

MARY: Yeah.

(*They embrace and laugh.*)

60   He got wild 'coz I wouldn't knuckle under to him. Don't go, Joe, not now. Go on Monday and ask him if we can leave the Settlement. *Koodjie'll* be there, an' he's scared a' her.

JOE: Who?

MARY: *Koodjie.* Matron. He's frightened a' her. Come an' see
65   Uncle Herbie before Baby wakes; he's cruel hungry and he's got a cruel loud voice.

(*They exit.*)

SCENE IX

Superintendent's Office, Moore River, day. TOPSY *brings* NEAL *a cup of tea on a tray in exact repetition of Scene Five.* JOE *waits outside as* NEAL *rummages through drawers until he finds a piece of paper. He reads it, adds a few words, and places it on his desk.*

NEAL: (*Yelling.*) Millimurra!

(*JOE walks in, stands and stares at him in silence.*)

   Sign this.

JOE: What is it?

NEAL: Read it.

(*JOE takes the paper and reads it slowly to himself.*)

5   Oh, Jesus, give it to me.

(*He snatches it from* JOE.)

   I want you to understand this. Are you listening?

JOE: I'm listenin'.

NEAL: 'I, Joseph Millimurra, undertake not to domicile in the town of Northam, nor anywhere in the Northam Shire. I
10   fully understand that if I return to Northam I am liable to be returned under warrant to the Moore River or other Government Native Settlement.'

JOE: You mean if I put me name on this, me and Mary can take off?

NEAL: That's what I mean.

15 JOE: Right, give us the pen.

NEAL: Hold your horses. Billy! Billy!

BILLY: (*Off.*) Comin', boss. Comin'.

(BILLY *enters the office.*)

NEAL: (*To* JOE.) Witness.

JOE: Gawd, some witness.

BILLY: Yeah, boss?   20

NEAL: I want you to watch him sign this.

(NEAL *picks up the paper and shows it to* BILLY.)

   You can understand this?

BILLY: No, boss.

NEAL: Good. (*To* JOE.) Go on, sign it.

JOE: (*Signing.*) Gawd, you *wetjalas* funny fellas.   25

NEAL: Good, now get out. The sooner you leave, the better.

JOE: (*Leaving.*) I'll see you one day, in hell. And you won't have your cat-o'-nine-tails.

(*He laughs and walks out with* BILLY.)

BILLY: Hey, what that one *milly milly*?

JOE: Me an' Mary clearin' out, an' that one say we not allowed 30
   to go to Northam.

BILLY: Augh, *gudeeah*, silly fella.

JOE: If I go back to Northam he put me this one.

(*He puts his fingers across his face, indicating gaol.*)

BILLY: That your country. You back sit down that place.

(MARY *enters with some baby clothes.*)

MARY: Everything all right?   35

JOE: Couldn't be better.

MARY: What happened?

JOE: He told us to get outa the Settlement.

MARY: When?

JOE: Tomorrow, next day, soon as we like.   40

MARY: Why?

JOE: 'Coz the bastard's scared of us.

BILLY: You watch this one, she go Kargudda but she still Oom-boolgari girl.

JOE: She'll be all right.   45

BILLY: You want this one?

(*He hands him his whip.*)

   Kill rabbit, snake, bungarra.

JOE: No, Billy, that's yours.

BILLY: Ne'mine, ne'mine.

MARY: Take it, it's a gift.   50

JOE: Thanks, old man.

(JOE *walks off, leaving* BILLY *and* MARY *together.*)

MARY: Goodbye, *dumbart*.

JOE: (*Returning to* BILLY.) Here, *gnummari*.

(*He gives* BILLY *the rest of his packet of Luxor.* BILLY *breaks one up and puts it in his pipe. He gazes at them as they walk off.*)

NEAL: (*Off.*) Billy!

BILLY: Comin' boss. Comin'.   55

(*He exits.*)

SCENE X

Long Pool Camp, Moore River, morning. The fire is burning. JOE *rolls a swag.* MILLY *gives* MARY *a sugar bag. The others stand around.*

MILLY: There's enough flour there for three dampers, a fryin' pan, billy can and two mugs. A bit of drippin', too, and a spud and a couple a' onions.

MARY: Thanks, Mum.

5 SAM: Where will you go, son?

JOE: Back to Northam.

GRAN: You wanna watch them *manatj*, they *warrah* there now.

JOE: Yeah, Gran. Don't worry, if they git rough we just move on.

*(*MARY *straps the baby to her chest.)*

GRAN: Just as well you a good milker, girl. Least he won't go

10   'ungry.

CISSIE: You got him right next to the tit.

DAVID: Eh, brother, you want my pocket knife? You might need it.

JOE: No, Brudge, I can use glass if I wanna gut a rabbit.

*(*SAM *hands* JOE *a home-made knife.)*

SAM: Here, son, take this one.

JOE: No, I'll be all right.   15

SAM: Take it. I can git another bit of steel and make another one. Here, take it.

(Magpies squawk. GRAN *begins to sing. They farewell each member of the family, then walk off into the distance.)*

GRAN:

> Weert miny, jinna koorling, weert miny.
> Jinna koorling   20
> Wayanna, wayanna, wayanna,
> Weert, miny, weert miny, weert miny.
> Jinna koorling
> Jinna koorling
> Jinna koorling   25
> Yay, yay, yay
> Coo-oo-ooo-ooh.

THE END

TRANSLATION OF SONGS

Jimmy's Song

Look, who is this coming?
Crabs, crabs, crabs, crabs
In the river mouth,
They are coming in the river mouth, river mouth,
Coming in the river mouth.
Fish coming up the river,
Up the river, up the river,
Fish in the river mouth,
Fish in the river mouth,
Coming up, coming up, coming up,
Fish and crabs, fish and crabs, fish and crabs,
Shout of praise!

Gran's Song

Woe, woe, woe.
My boy and girl and baby
Going a long way walking,
That way walking,
That way walking.
Pity, pity, pity,
Hungry, walking, hungry,
Pity, pity, pity,
Hungry, hungry,
Walking, walking, walking,
Yay, yay, yay,
Cooo-ooo-ooo-oooh.

NOTES AND GLOSSARY OF ABORIGINAL TERMS

The Aboriginal language used in these plays is usually called *Nyoongah* but occasionally referred to as *Bibbulumun*. *Nyoongah* literally means 'man', but has become a general term denoting Aboriginality in the South-West of Western Australia. *Bibbulumun* is one of the fourteen South-West languages that have combined over the last 152 years to create the modern *Nyoongah* spoken in the play.

   Nyoongah words here are spelt phonetically, however the pronunciations of certain sounds are as follows:

NG has a silent 'g', as in 'sing'
Y is always short, as in 'yet'
A is always long, as in 'raft'
R is rolled, as with a Scottish burr
TJ is pronounced 'ch', as in 'change'
B is pronounced 'p', as in 'pit'

allewah, watch out
baal nooniny barminy, he'll hit you

barkiny, bite
barminy, strike
bilbarl, black goanna
boolyaduk, magic man
boondah, money
bootjarri, pregnant
bridaira, boss
brudge, brother (from the English)
bungarru, goanna
choo, shame
chubel, spear
clapsticks, two short sticks which, when struck together give a musical beat for the corroborree
daitj, meat
dawarra, bad mouth
dawarra, nitja wetjala, bad mouth, this is a white man
ding, Italian (W.A. slang)
doak, throwing stick
doothoo, dogs
dubakieny, steady, slowly
dubakieny wahnginy, talk steady
dugaitj, dugite snake
dumbart, people of the same tribe
freeo, Fremantle, Fremantle Gaol (W.A. slang)
gneean baal?, Who's he?
gneean nitja koorling?, Who's coming there?
gnuny, me, I
gnuny tjenna minditj, my feet hurt
gnoolya, brother-in-law
gnoon, brother
gnummarri, tobacco
gudeeah, white people, white person
gugja, lilyroot (North-West language)
inji sticks, decorated sticks used in the corroborree
jeerung meear, medicinal leaves
kaal, fire
kaep, water
kargudda, south
kia, yes
kienya, shame
killarla, tobacco (North-West language)
kongi, uncle
koodjie, bony, the Sister and Matron's nickname
koolangah, children
koolbardi, magpie
koomp, urine
koorawooroong, an expression of disbelief
koories, women (North-West language)
koort, weak
koort minditj, weak heart
kuliya, yes (North-West language)
kunarn, true
kwombinyarn, excellent
kwon, arse
kwonna tjuellara, bony arse

manatj, police, black cockatoo
meeowl, eyes
merrang, flour, bread
minditj, sick
mirri–up, hurry
mirri–up, mirri–up, allewah koorkanjerri gnuny nooniny woort dininy, woort dininy, Hurry, hurry. Watch out sheep, I'm going to cut your throat
moorditj, good
mummari, little spirit beings
nemine, corruption of 'never mind'
nietjuk, why
nitja bridair yorgah koorling, The boss's woman is coming
nyoongah, Aboriginal, literally 'man' in the languages of the South-West. Some time after 1829 it entered common usage as a term denoting Aboriginality, similar to *Wongai* in the eastern goldfields, *Yamatji* in the Murchison and *Koori* and *Murri* in the eastern states.
nyorn, pity
nyorn, winyarn, pity, poor fellow
nyummi, slow learner
rizla's, a brand of cigarette papers
shoo-i, a shout or warning of evil
tjenna, feet
tjenna gubbi, an Aboriginal secret executioner
tjeuripiny, glad
tjinung, look
tjirrung, fat
tjuellara, bony
Unna?, Isn't it?
waddi, club
wah, where
wahnging, talk
wanbru, blankets
wanmulla, cannibals
warrah, warrahmut, bad
wayarniny, frightened
wee-ah, cry of grief, yes
weerny, weak
wetjala, white person, a corruption of the English 'white fellow'
wilbra, rabbit
wilgi, specially prepared paint for ceremonies
winjar, where, which way
winjar kaep?, Where's water?
winyarn, poor fellow, weak-willed person
wogga, (coll.) a blanket made up of four or six wheat sacks sewn together.
woolah, shout of praise
yahllarah, group dance
yokki, shout of praise
yonga, yongarah, kangaroo
yorgah, woman, girl
yuart, nothing, no
yumbah, children (North-West language)

Gao Xingjian

The first Chinese writer to win the Nobel Prize for Literature, Gao Xingjian (b. 1940), was raised in provincial Ganzhou after the Communist revolution in China. His mother was an amateur actress, and when he went to Beijing in 1958 to study at the Beijing Foreign Languages Institute, he not only studied French literature, but became involved in theater as well. He was working as a translator when the Cultural Revolution (1967–1977) forced the "reeducation" of intellectuals and professionals by exiling them to rural areas to work in agriculture; he was working as a schoolteacher in southwestern China when he published his first novel, *Stars on a Cold Night* in 1980. The following year, during Deng Xiaoping's easing of cultural restrictions, he published a critical essay, "Preliminary Explorations into the Techniques of Modern Fiction," which attempted—as Brecht had done earlier in relation to Soviet realism—to articulate the purpose and power of "modernist" formal and theoretical experimentation in the face of the state-supported demands of Maoist "revolutionary realism." Though the essay proved controversial, Gao was soon appointed as playwright to the Beijing People's Art Theater; several of the plays he wrote for the company proved controversial in a climate in which formal "experimentation" signaled a departure from Party doctrines. *Bus Stop* (1981) was not produced by the company, and *Absolute Signal* was shown in a few public rehearsals before being closed after only thirteen performances: Gao was prohibited from writing for publication for a year and went into exile in southwestern China.

Returning to Beijing in 1984, he wrote *Wilderness Man,* which updates and innovates the episodic and mythological structure of traditional Chinese theater, and *The Other Shore* (1985). Insistently framing a conflict between individual characters and the Crowd, *The Other Shore* was closed during rehearsal, and Gao fled to France in 1987. In France, Gao has written a number of his most celebrated works, including *Exile* (1989)—which concerns the flight of dissidents from the Tiananmen Square uprising in 1989—and the plays *Between Life and Death* (1991), *Dialogue and Rebuttal* (1992), *Nocturnal Wanderer* (1993), *Weekend Quartet* (1995), and the novel *Spiritual Mountain* (1990). Although Gao's work is not well known in the United States, a collection of plays (to which I am indebted here) *The Other Shore: Plays by Gao Xingjian,* edited and translated by Gilbert C.F. Fong, was published in 1999. Gao's plays have, however, become part of the international theatrical repertoire, and have been produced professionally in China, Sweden, England, Austria, Germany, France, Australia, Poland, Japan, and Taiwan, as well as in the United States. Gao won the Nobel Prize for Literature in 2000.

THE OTHER SHORE

The Other Shore witnesses Gao's deep investment in theatrical experimentation, particularly his desire to investigate the means of acting in the theater. As he suggests in his notes to the play, *The Other Shore* attempts to fuse the physical elements of acting ("somatics"), language, and psychology in "a kind of emotive abstraction through performance, i.e., a non-philosophical abstraction." Noting his indebtedness to the work of Polish director Jerzy Grotowski—whose **POOR THEATER,** like Gao's, dispensed with elaborate sets, costumes, and lighting to focus attention on acting as the essence of theater—Gao also makes a significant departure: while Grotowski used physical discipline to force the actor's "sacrifice" of himself, a kind of "exposure" of his innermost identity to himself and to the audience, Gao's theater "helps the actor to ascertain his own self through the process of discovering his partners."

The tension between the demands of the self and of its relation to others animates the action of the play, which takes the shape of an allegorical journey, in the mode of plays from *Everyman* to Strindberg's *A Dream Play*. Gao suggests that the play should be performed environmentally, in an open space shared by actors and audience, and the play opens with a series of acting exercises and games, in which the performers use ropes to explore and define their group identity. This exercise demands a high level of physical training and responsiveness from the performers, as the actors work to embody the different "identities" that emerge from different relationships. The actors also use the rope exercises to begin their narrative, traveling to "the other shore," a nonexistent realm that nonetheless evokes the state of Buddhist enlightenment (sometimes called "the other shore"). But *The Other Shore* is hardly doctrine-disguised-as-allegory. Rather than a banal or a politicized vision of individual or collective peace, the play imagines a dynamic and conflictual journey, centered on a series of confrontations between individuated characters like The Woman, The Man, The Young Girl, The Card Player, The Mad Woman, and the Crowd (in a way reminiscent of the history of Greek drama, Gao's actor/protagonists emerge from and blend back into the choral Crowd). Many of the scenes revolve around The Man, who resists the Crowd's often self-deluded efforts toward conformity. Yet much of the power of this elegant play depends on the tension between Gao's lyrical language and the actors' lyrical physicality, their ability to individuate and transform the Crowd itself. Arriving at "the other shore," the actors seem both to discover and to explore their bodies, and discover and explore language as well; having discovered their instrument, the use it throughout the play to transform the Crowd—into a vengeful mob, a throng of pilgrims, a host of demented automatons, a monstrous forest. In this sense, the Crowd is not a monolithic and regimented opponent of the individual, but the network within which the individual discovers his or her identity; as Gao suggests in one of his notes, the Crowd should not be understood as a regimented entity—its "performance must be fresh, regenerating, and improvisational."

THE OTHER SHORE

Gao Xingjian

CHARACTERS

An actor playing with ropes
CARD PLAYER
"DOGSKIN" PLASTER SELLER
WOMAN
YOUNG GIRL
MAD WOMAN
MODEL
MAN
YOUNG MAN
SHADOW
HEART
MOTHER
FATHER
ZEN MASTER

OLD LADY
STABLE KEEPER
ACTORS
CROWD

TIME: *The time cannot be defined or stated precisely.*

LOCATION: *From the real world to the nonexistent other shore.*

The play can be performed in a theatre, a living room, a rehearsal room, an empty warehouse, a gymnasium, the hall of a temple, a circus tent, or any empty space as long as the necessary lighting and sound equipment can be properly installed. Lighting can be dispensed with if the play is performed during the day. The actors may be among the audience, or the audience among the actors. The two situations are the same and will not make any difference to the play.

ACTOR PLAYING WITH ROPES: Here's a rope. Let's play a game, but we've got to be serious, as if we're children playing their game. Our play starts with a game.

Okay, I want you to take hold of this end of the rope.
5 You see, this way a relationship is established between us. Before that you were you and I was I, but with this rope between us we're tied to each other and it becomes you and I.

Let's try running in opposite directions. See, now you're pulling me, but then again I'm also holding you
10 back, like two locusts tied to the same string, neither of us can get away from each other. Of course, we're also like husband and wife. (*Pauses.*) But that's not a good metaphor. If I were to pull the rope real hard towards me, then we'd have to see who's stronger. The stronger one
15 pulls and the weaker is being pulled. It becomes a tug-of-war, a competition of strength, and there'll be a winner and a loser, victory and defeat.

Now if I carry this rope on my back like this and pull even harder, you'll be like a dead dog; likewise if you man-
20 age to gain control of this rope, I'll be like a horse or a cow, and you'll be able to drive me around like cattle. In other words, you'll be running the show. So you see, our relationship is not at all constant, it's not at all unchanging.

Or we can establish an even more complex relation-
25 ship. For instance if you revolve around me, I'll be the centre of your orbit, and you'll become my satellite. But if you don't wish to revolve around me, I can rotate on my own, thinking that all of you are revolving around me. Are you revolving or am I the one who's revolving? I could be
30 revolving around you or you could be revolving around me. Who knows? Perhaps we're both turning at the same time, or maybe we're both revolving around other people, or maybe those other people are revolving around us both or maybe all of us are revolving around God—maybe
35 there isn't a God after all, maybe there's only a universe rotating by itself like a millstone—now we're touching on philosophy. Never mind, we'll leave philosophy to the philosophers, let's just continue to play our game.

Everyone of you can pick up a rope and play different kinds of games, the possibilities are endless. Playing with 40 ropes is such a game, that it can be a manifestation of all kinds of interpersonal relationships.

(*The actors each choose a partner to play the game, using a piece of rope. They can switch partners or briefly make contact with other pairs of players, but the contacts are soon broken. The game becomes increasingly lively, tense, and exciting, accompanied by all kinds of salutations and screams.*)

ACTOR PLAYING WITH ROPES: Okay everybody, let's knock it off for a moment. Let's make this game bigger and more complex. Now I want all of you to hold on to one end of 45 your rope and give me the other end. This way you'll be able to establish all kinds of relationships with me, some tense, some lax, some distant, and some close, and soon your individual attitudes will have a strong impact on me. Society is complex and ever-changing, we're constantly 50 pulling and being pulled. (*Pauses.*) Just like a fly that's fallen into a spider's web. (*Pauses.*) Or just like a spider. (*Pauses.*)

The rope is like our hands. (*He lets go one rope and his partner also lets go. The rope falls on the ground.*) Or like an 55 extended antenna. (*He lets go another and his partner follows.*) Or like the language we use, for instance when we say "Good Morning" or "How are you!" (*Another rope falls to the ground.*) Or perhaps it's like looking at each other, (*Replaces another rope.*) or like the thoughts in our minds. (*His 60 back is against his current partner, but the two sides are still communicating.*) Either you're thinking of her, or she's thinking of someone else. (*He brushes past her shoulders. She and someone else are gazing into each other's eyes.*) In this way the rope is pulling all of us, binding us together. 65

We look—

(*The actors are communicating with one another through pieces of imaginary ropes.*)

We observe—
We stare—
Then there's temptation and attraction—
70 Orders and obedience—

(*In the following, the performance is accompanied by all kinds of sighs and screams but without resorting to the use of language.*)

Conflicts—
Intimacy—
Exclusion—
Entanglement—
75 Abandonment—
Emulation—
Evasion—
Repulsion—
Pursuit—
80 Encirclement—
Congregation—
Fragmentation
Dismiss!
At ease!
85 Now there is a river in front of us, not a piece of rope.
Let's cross the river and try to reach the other shore.

ACTORS: (*One after another.*) Yes, to the other shore! To the other shore!
The other shore! To the other shore! To the other shore!
90 The other shore!
Oh—Oh—Oh
The water in the river is so clear!
So cool!
Watch out, the stones are killing my feet!
95 How nice!

(*Gradually there comes the sound of running water.*)

My skirt's soaking wet!
Is the river deep?
Let's swim across to the other shore!
Don't go by yourself!
100 Look at the water spray, how it sparkles in the sunshine!
What fun, just like a waterfall.
A dam, a river flowing gently down the dam.
Form a line in the middle of the river.
Further down the water's dark blue, it's got to be really
105 deep there.
I've got some fish wriggling between my legs . . .
So exciting!
I'm going to fall.
Don't worry, hold on to me.
110 There's an eddy over there—
Look after one another, hold hands.
To the rapid waters.
To the other shore!
No one can see the other shore.
115 Cut the poetry crap! I'm falling.
Hold tight, one after another now.
Over there the water is deep blue . . .
Aahh! The water's over my waist all of a sudden!
I'm getting dizzy.
120 Close your eyes for a while.

Look in front of you, look ahead, keep your eyes open!
All looking at the other shore.
How come I can't see it?
We'll drown, all of us.
We'll all be fish food. 125
If we're going to die, let's die together.
Girls, stop blabbing, try to concentrate.
The current is very strong, tread in the shallows, try going up stream!
I can't make it across, I'm sure I can't make it. 130
Where's the other shore?
Sometimes it's dark, sometimes it's bright.
Are there lights on the other shore?
There are flowers, lots of flowers on the other shore, it's a world of flowers. 135
I'm afraid I can't make it, please don't leave me behind.

(*Sobs.*)

Can you feel it? We're drifting in the river.
Like corks on a string.
And like water weed.
Why are we going to the other shore? I really don't un- 140
derstand.
Right, why do we want to go to the other shore?
The other shore is the other shore, you'll never reach it.
But you still want to go, to see what it's like over there.
I can't see anything. 145
No oasis, and no light.
In total darkness.
It's like this . . .
No, I can't make it.
We haven't been there before. 150
We must get there.
But why?
To make a long-time wish come true, the other shore, the other shore.
No, I can't make it, I want to go home! 155
None of us can.
Can't go back at all.
O—!
Who is it?
Don't know. 160

(*Silence, only the sound of water gurgling.*)

Was somebody screaming? Did you hear it?
You must have heard it, but nobody answered.

(*Silence. Sound of sobbing.*)

This is a ditch of dead water.
There's only oblivion.

(*Bewildered, the* CROWD *slowly walk out of the dead water. Music is faintly heard. The* CROWD *gradually reach the shore and lie down totally exhausted on the ground.* WOMAN *appears in darkness. Like a strand of light mist, she walks around to inspect the people who have lost their memories. She drifts among them, touching and waking them up one by one. They lazily open their eyes and look up, turning their bodies and staring at her. They try to speak but in vain.*)

165 WOMAN: (*Raises her hand.*) Look here, this is a hand.

(*The* CROWD *utter muddled sounds from their throat.*)

WOMAN: This is a hand.
CROWD: (*Still mumbling.*) Th . . . The . . . This . . . ee . . . ha . . . han . . . hand.
WOMAN: Hand—
170 CROWD: Hand—band—sand—hand—
WOMAN: This is a foot.
CROWD: Th . . . Th . . . This . . . ee . . . fo . . . foo . . . foot.
WOMAN: (*Pointing to her eye.*) Eye.
CROWD: Ee . . . ee . . . eye . . . eye . . .
175 WOMAN: (*Gesturing.*) Your eyes are looking at your foot!
CROWD: (*Totally confused.*) Eyes . . . cook . . . cook your . . . own . . . coot . . .

(WOMAN *laughs, and the* CROWD *join in the laughter with her, giggling.*)

WOMAN: (*Stops laughing, somewhat sad.*) This is a hand—
CROWD: This is a hand, this is a band, this is a sand, this is a
180 hand . . .
WOMAN: This is a foot—
CROWD: This is a boot, this is a hoot, this is a root, this is a foot . . .
WOMAN: This is a body—your body—
185 CROWD: This is a body, this is a body, this is a body your body, this is your body is a body is a body is your body your . . .
WOMAN: (*Shakes her head, gesturing more slowly and still being patient.*) My hand—my body—my foot—this is me.
CROWD: My band, my hand, my body, my coot, my hand's
190 body's foot's my coot's hand's foot's body this is my hand's foot's body is meat!
WOMAN: Say, me—
CROWD: Say me say me say me say me say me!
WOMAN: (*Shakes her head and points to herself, from her eyes to
195 her mouth, and from her body to her feet.*) Me.
CROWD: (*Together at last.*) Me.
WOMAN: Good!
CROWD: Food! Hood! Good! Wood!
WOMAN: (*At once she waves her hand in disagreement. After
200 thinking for a moment, she points at one person among the crowd.*) You.
CROWD: (*All pointing at* THE PERSON.) You!
THE PERSON: (*He looks around him and then points at himself.*) You!
205 WOMAN: (*Shakes her head and helps him to point his finger at someone else.*) You.
CROWD: You.
WOMAN: (*Gesturing.*) Me and you.
CROWD: Me and you.
210 WOMAN: (*Laughs.*) Good!
CROWD: (*Also laugh.*) Good!

(*Music. Gradually the tempo of the music becomes faster.*)

WOMAN: Me and him!
CROWD: Me and him!
WOMAN: Them and me.
215 CROWD: Them and me.
WOMAN: Me and you.

CROWD: Me and you.
WOMAN: You and us.
CROWD: You and us.
WOMAN: Now follow me when you're seeing with your 220
eyes—
CROWD: See—
WOMAN: Tell me, who do you see?
CROWD: (*One after another.*) See him, see you, see me, see them, they see you, you see us, we see them . . . 225
WOMAN: Now say touch, give, like, and love, and you won't feel lonely any more.
CROWD: (*Becoming active.*) I touch you, you give me, I like him, he loves you, you touch me, I give him, he likes you, you love me . . . 230

(MAN *comes out from among the* CROWD.)

MAN: Who are you?
WOMAN: I'm one of you.
MAN: Where are we now?
WOMAN: The other shore, which we wanted to reach but couldn't. 235
MAN: Are you the same person who drowned while we were crossing the river? (WOMAN *shakes her head.*) Are you her soul? (WOMAN *still shakes her head.*) Have you been hiding in our thoughts, do you appear only when we think of you? Or are you something like a kind of consciousness? 240 Did you guide us to the other shore so that we wouldn't get lost?
CROWD: (*At the same time.*) I detest you.
You touched me!
I'll beat you up! 245
You hate me?
I'll torture her.
He cheats on me.
You're swearing at him!
I'll tell on you. 250
You punish him!
He plots against me!
I hate you!
You curse him!
I'll kill you . . . 255
MAN: (*To* WOMAN.) You're so kind.
CROWD: (*Turn to face* WOMAN *one after another, playing with words.*)
You're so generous.
You're so lovely. 260
You're so despicable.
He's a bastard.
You don't say what you mean, you're a crook.
You're a double-dealing no-good tramp!
She butters you up, but she's actually jealous of you. 265
You're snaky, you teach us words so that you can talk to our men and seduce them!
You may look so kind and gentle, but who knows if you're a whore or not?
She's trying to seduce our husbands! 270
Stirring up trouble among our brothers.
A buttered bun, look, just look at her—
Keep the girls away from her, she'll turn them into whores.

275 She may look prim and proper, but she's really more corrupt than a common whore.
She's the one, she makes people panic, there'll be no more peace in this world.

(WOMAN *draws back as the* CROWD *surrounds her from all sides. They are excited by their own increasingly venomous language. She cannot escape from the stares of the* CROWD, *so she turns to* MAN *for help and hangs on to him.*)

CROWD: (*Getting more angry.*)
280 Whore!
Venomous snake!
Witch!
Shameless slut!

(WOMAN *holds on to* MAN *and pleads for his protection. The* CROWD *go wild.*)

CROWD: Look, go and take a look!
285 Pooh!
Dump her!
Drag her away!
Get a hold of her!
Strip her!
290 Wring her neck! The shameless whore!

(*The* CROWD *drag her away from* MAN *and jump on her. In the confusion they strangle her to death. When* MAN *pushes his way into the* CROWD *and shakes her body, there is no response.*) (*Witnessing this, the* CROWD *is stunned.*)

CROWD: Dead.
Dead?
Dead?
She's dead!

(*The* CROWD *disperse in a hurry.*)

295 Was she strangled to death?
It's you—
No, he started it.
You shouted first!
I was only following you, you were all shouting.
300 Who shouted first? Who?
Who shouted first to grab her, strip her and strangle her?
Who?
We all shouted.
I shouted because you did.
305 I shouted because all of you were shouting.
But she's dead! Strangled alive!
I didn't kill her.
I didn't kill her.
I didn't kill her.
310 I didn't kill her.
I didn't kill her.
I didn't.
I didn't.
Didn't.
315 Didn't.
Didn't.

But she's dead for sure, so lovely even when she's dead.
So beautiful, nobody could help loving her.
Her skin is like jade, it's got no blemishes, it's so pure.
Look at her pretty little hands, they've got her endless 320 tenderness in them.
My, she's like a statue of the Bodhisattva!
So pure, so prim and proper.
She gave us language, she brought us wisdom, but she was murdered! 325
This is the greatest sin of all, you despicable lot!
Who are you talking about?
Murderers! You, all of you!
How dare you smear me? You bastard!
You're a thug! 330
You're a rascal!

(*The* CROWD *fight among themselves.*)

MAN: Are you finished? We killed her, there's no question about it. It's you, it's him, it's me, and it's all of us. We're all in it together! On this desolate other shore, she gave us language, but we didn't know how to cherish it; she gave 335 us wisdom, but we didn't know how to use it! We ought to be shocked by what we did, but we're cowards, we're too spineless to feel any shame.
CROWD: What do you think we should do?
We need a leader, a flock of sheep also needs a leader. 340 We'll follow you.
MAN: I detest you, I detest myself. It's better for us to go our separate ways.
CROWD: No, don't abandon us.
We've made up our mind to follow you, and you want to 345 leave us?
MAN: Follow me where? Where can I lead you? (*He leaves by himself. The* CROWD *follow behind.*) Don't follow me! (*Troubled.*) I don't even know where I want to go myself. (*Stops and tries to figure out where to go. The* CROWD *still follow him* 350 *at a distance.*)

(MOTHER *appears in front of him.*)

MOTHER: Do you still remember me?
MAN: Yes, mother.
MOTHER: You've almost forgotten me, haven't you?
MAN: (*On his knees.*) Yes, mother. 355
MOTHER: (*Stroking his head.*) Find yourself a girl, you really should start a family.
MAN: But I want to make something of myself.
MOTHER: You're too ambitious.
MAN: (*Looks down.*) I'm still your son. 360
MOTHER: Are they all following you? Where are you going to take them?
MAN: I don't know. I only know we should go forward, is that right, mother?
MOTHER: My good son. (*Embraces his head.*) 365
MAN: Your hands are cold! (*Shocked by his discovery.*) Mother, is this the world of the dead? Am I in another dimension?
MOTHER: There's nothing to be scared of, son. It's just a bit dark, a bit cold and damp, that's all.
MAN: (*Leaves her.*) How do I get out of here? Mother, I 370 haven't lived long enough!

(MOTHER *turns and disappears. He hesitates for a moment and then follows in a hurry. A* YOUNG GIRL *blocks his way.*)

MAN: Who are you? I've seen you somewhere, but I can't recall your name. It seems like we used to live on the same
street or something, many years ago. Every day on my way
375 to school I always hoped that I could catch a glimpse of
you, even if it's only your back. My heart would keep on
pounding whenever I saw your long ponytail and your
crimson red dress, you seemed to be wearing that crimson
dress all that time. . . . I used to follow you, follow you
380 right to your doorsteps, hoping that when you turned
around to close the door, you'd at least say one word to
me before you went inside, or smile at me just once. But
every time you'd only look at me, saying nothing. Oh, I
can see those eyes of yours again . . . (*He rubs his eyes and*
385 *looks more closely, but she has disappeared into the dark shadows*
of the CROWD.)
   (*To the* CROWD.) We've got to get out of this ghastly
place. Once we're away from this darkness we'll find light
ahead of us. With the light there'll be houses, and we'll be
390 able to dry our clothes around the stove and drink some
hot tea. (*Incitingly.*) We'd be able to return to our homes,
see our families, our wives and husbands, our children and
parents, and all our loved ones and those who love us!
(YOUNG GIRL *appears again from behind the* CROWD.)
395 Who are you?
   (*Blocking her way.*) Wait, your name is on the tip of my
tongue! It seems like I used to write poetry for you, that
we used to go to the movies together and I held your
hand in the dark, those tiny frail hands of yours . . . (*She*
400 *turns and gets away from his grasp. She is now behind him, be-*
coming more illusory. He turns around but cannot see her, no
matter how hard he tries.)
   She always appeared in my dreams to torment me
whenever I was worried and couldn't set my mind free. I
405 couldn't recall her name, I couldn't see her face clearly, I
couldn't even get hold of her presence in any way, but she
still kept on tormenting me.
   (*Speaking to the shadowy* CROWD.) Why do you keep following me? I need some peace and quiet, I need to be
410 alone! I don't need to be stared at by a crowd, I don't need
you, just as you don't need me. What you need is someone
who can guide you, to show you the way, even though
once you've found a way out, or think you have, you'd put
on a spurt, darting away faster than rabbits. And you'd
415 abandon your guide without even taking a second look,
just like throwing away a worn-out shoe. I understand, I
understand it only too well. You've all experienced loving
and being loved, possessing and being possessed. I, too, have
a right to be in love, to love a woman and to possess a
420 woman, and to be loved and possessed by her. I'm human
just like you are, so full of desires and ambitions, I'm what
you may call a career-minded man, a man who is competitive yet extremely weak sometimes, and a man who is
righteous, compassionate, willing to sacrifice himself and
425 . . . (*He rolls on the ground and wails loudly like a fretting and*
self-indulgent child.)

(*The* CROWD *is stunned. When* MAN *has had enough wailing and*
is totally exhausted, he settles down and gets up from the floor. He

continues *his way forward and the* CROWD *follow silently behind*
him. A faint light in the dark becomes brighter. A man is seen drink-
ing and playing cards alone under an oil lamp. MAN *mimes knock-*
ing on the door. The CROWD *clap their hands three times.*)

MAN: Sorry to bother you.
CARD PLAYER: (*Without lifting his head.*) Come in. Take a seat.
MAN: May I ask—
CARD PLAYER: (*Tosses a card from his hand. Looks up.*) You play 430
cards?
MAN: I've played before.

(*The* CROWD *try to squeeze in through the door.*)

CARD PLAYER: Come in, come in. Do you all want to play
cards? Close the door for me. I hate draughts, they make
the light flicker, which is bad for a card player's eyes. Al- 435
right, let's form a circle, I'll be the banker here. All of you
will each take a card, and I'll take one myself, only one,
just like you. That's only fair. The card in my hand will
be the trump, there's got to be a trump, right? And it's better if I choose the trump card instead of you, it's more 440
convenient that way. (*Turns over his card.*) My card is the
two of spades. I'm not trying to fly low, luck is all you
need when you're playing cards. Now if you pick a spade,
any spade, you'd have a higher number than mine and I'd
be the loser and you'd be the winner. But if you didn't 445
pick a spade, you'd lose no matter what, it doesn't matter
which card you've picked. You got me?
MAN: What happens if one wins or loses?
CARD PLAYER: The winner gets to drink the wine in this pot.
MAN: And the loser? 450
CARD PLAYER: There'll be a penalty.
MAN: I have no money, no land, no property, and no wife.
CARD PLAYER: But you do have a face, haven't you?
MAN: I don't get it.
CARD PLAYER: You'll find out soon enough. All of you, any- 455
one who loses will stick a piece of paper on his face for me.
CROWD: That's easy enough.
   How big is the paper?
   Any paper?
   The thing is, have you really got wine in your pot? 460
CARD PLAYER: Have a taste first.
CROWD: It's good.
   What aroma!
   Of course, it's the real thing.
   Let me have a sip. 465
   It's worth playing for.
CARD PLAYER: In a moment you'll pick your cards. I've
shown you my card, all of you have seen it, right? Now
you can only look at your own card, no ganging up, that's
a no-no. 470
CROWD: (*Eager to pick their cards.*)
   That's nothing, it's fine with me.
   We should play our own games.
   Don't worry, I won't look even if you let me.
   Me, I'm honesty personified. 475
   Integrity comes first, winning and losing second.
   Hear! Hear!

(*Those who have picked their cards are silent.*)

CARD PLAYER: (*To the person who picks first.*) Show me your
 card. You lose.
480 THIS PERSON: (*Nods.*) What's the penalty?

(CARD PLAYER *takes a piece of paper and spits on it. He sticks the paper
onto the cheek of* THIS PERSON, *who mutters something. The* CROWD
watch and laugh. THIS PERSON *is relieved and laughs with them.*)

CARD PLAYER: (*Turns to another person.*) My friend, how about
 you? (THAT PERSON *shows his card.*) You lose too.
THAT PERSON: Well, give it to me.
CARD PLAYER: Stick it under your chin.

(THAT PERSON *takes a piece of paper, spits on it, and sticks it under his chin. He is somewhat embarrassed, but when he sees the*
CROWD *laughing, he is himself again.*)

485 THIRD PERSON (FEMALE): It's fun.
CARD PLAYER: (*Turns towards her.*) And you? (*She shows her card
 and hurriedly takes it back.*)
CROWD: Did you win?
 You won!
490 Did you really win?
 (*She frets demurely and shakes her head.*)
 Why aren't you sticking the paper on your face?
 Stick the paper on, stick it on!
 Come on, it's the rule, no exceptions allowed.
495 If you don't stick it on, we won't either.
THIRD PERSON (FEMALE): It's too embarrassing.
CROWD: You think we're not?
 That won't do. Stick it on the ear.
 Right, on the ear.
500 Stick it on the nose!
 It must be different with everybody, okay? No repetitions.
 Everybody gets one.

(*When the* CARD PLAYER *looks at someone, the person will show
his card and then obediently stick a piece of paper on his face.*)

CROWD: (*Sticking paper to their own faces.*)
 Fair and square.
505 No doubt about that.
 Nobody tells you to lose, but when you do, you've got to
 take what comes.
 Everyone gets a penalty, everyone sticks a paper on their
 face.
510 If you haven't got a paper on your face, you'll look odd
 and out of place, and people will be afraid of you.

(*The strange-looking, papered faces all turn towards* MAN.)

CARD PLAYER: My friend, it's your turn now.
MAN: I don't play.
CARD PLAYER: Everybody plays, why don't you?
515 MAN: I find the whole thing very silly. What's more, I've got
 to go.
CROWD: Yes, that's right. We should all be going.
 Don't go by yourself.
 Where are we going?
520 Right, where exactly are we going?
MAN: In any case I've got to go.
CARD PLAYER: I've got the whole place lit up and I've pre-
 pared wine. I went through all these troubles just to play

cards with you people. I've never heard of anyone who
comes here and leaves without playing. You shouldn't 525
have come in the first place!
CROWD: (*Stopping Man.*) Play!
 Come on, be a good sport. Don't be such a party popper.
 Just play one game. Just one.
 Play once and then we'll go. 530
MAN: Don't you understand? You're not really playing cards,
 he's playing a trick on you. You can't win. Your card,
 yours, and yours are all no trumps, including all the cards
 still in the deck. The only spade in the deck is in his hand!
 (CARD PLAYER *giggles.*) Let's go! Why waste our time on 535
 this guy.
CARD PLAYER: There is no such thing as time here. (*He blows
 on the oil lamp and the light flickers, and it gradually turns
 brighter again.*) There is only eternal light. (*He takes the lamp
 and shines on everyone from below the chin. The papered faces* 540
 look like gargoyles.) I'm a sucker for big crowds. You're
 scared, aren't you?
MAN: You're a devil.
CARD PLAYER: Why don't you try feeling their arses? They've
 all got a bristly tail down there! (*He points to the* CROWD's 545
 *bottoms and laughs out loud. Then he pushes a deck of cards in
 front of* MAN.) Take a card! Let everyone see if it's a spade
 or no trumps? (*Turns over a no trump card and flashes it in
 front of the* CROWD.) What is it, is it a spade or not?
PERSON A: I can't really tell. 550
CARD PLAYER: What'd you say?
PERSON B: It looked like—
CARD PLAYER: You must have seen it clearly.
PERSON C: I think I saw a—spade.
CARD PLAYER: That's right! Young lady, what do you think? 555
OBEDIENT GIRL: Spades.
CARD PLAYER: That a girl. You've made my day. Old Sir, how
 about you?
PERSON D: Spades, how can it not be spades?
CARD PLAYER: Bless you. (*Suddenly explodes.*) How can we let 560
 him bullshit us like this and tell us that they're all no
 trumps? Huh?
CROWD: It's spades.
 Of course it's spades. It can't be anything else.
 No mistake about it. 565
 We all saw it.
 We're all witnesses!
CARD PLAYER: You heard what they said, didn't you? Why did
 you lie, why did you insist that a spade is no trump? You're
 scared, aren't you? Have you ever tried eating rat meat? A 570
 bouncing baby rat, its hair not fully grown and its eyes unopened, the little creature still squeaking when you dip it
 in the sauce and put it in your mouth, ready for a bite? If
 you had, then you'd be brave enough to tell the truth. My
 friend, I'm gonna give you one more chance to tell the 575
 truth. Tell me, was it spades or a no trump?
MAN: I think . . . that's still a no trump.
CARD PLAYER: You're no fun, you make people miserable.
 Tell me, people, is this guy bad or what?
CROWD: (*Passing the wine pot and taking sips one after another.*) 580
 Bad, bad, bad, bad, bad, bad, bad, bad . . .
CARD PLAYER: (*Takes the wine from them.*) What shall we do
 with this bad guy?
CROWD: (*Surround* MAN.) Throw him out!

585   Tell him to get out of here!
       Trouble-maker.
       A real pest.
       When he's here, we've got no wine to drink.
       Teach him a lesson!
590   Spank him!
       Strip him!
       Take off his pants!

(*The* CROWD *try to take off* MAN's *pants.*)

CARD PLAYER: I'm gonna give you a second chance. Think
       clearly. Think again!
595 MAN: (*Holding up his pants.*) But I remember . . . it looked like
       a . . . no trump.

(CARD PLAYER *tucks the wine pot under his arm and turns away.*
The CROWD *pull at* MAN *as if they were teasing a bird.*)

CROWD: Tell him to fly!
       What? What did you say?
       Fly like a bird!
600   Men are not birds, why should they learn to fly like birds?
       Wow, it's so fun!
       Fly!
       Lower your head, let your arms fly!
CARD PLAYER: My friend, I refuse to believe that you're a
605   stubborn man.
OBEDIENT GIRL: (*Takes pity on* MAN.) You can't turn a spade
       into a no trump. What's with you? Please, try to take hold
       of yourself.
MAN: Maybe it was really a spade . . .
610 OBEDIENT GIRL: Then why did you say it was a no trump?
MAN: I think it should be . . .
OBEDIENT GIRL: But what should be is not necessarily the
       truth.
CARD PLAYER: You're a loser because you're a pighead. What
615   do you mean by "should be"? It either is or isn't. To hell
       with "should be."
MAN: But why can't we have "should be"?
CARD PLAYER: (*Irritated.*) Should be my foot! What do you
       say, should be or not should be?
620 CROWD: (*Immediately tear at* MAN.) We don't want any "should
       be"!
       We want "yes" or "no"!
       We want spades, not no trumps!
       Down with no trumps!
625   Spades are the best!
MAN: It . . . seemed . . . like a . . . sp . . .
CROWD: (*Beating their chests and stamping their feet.*) Speak up!
       Louder!
       Can't hear you!
630   You've got to clear this up!
MAN: Sp . . . Spa . . . It's spades . . . (*On his knees and collapses.*)

(*The* CROWD *surround* CARD PLAYER *and perform a strange and
awkward dance. They exit.*

A woman dressed in a white cotton skirt appears. She covers MAN
*with her skirt, bends down and wraps herself in it as well. The two
form a white object which disappears with the gradually approaching
drumbeat. The drumbeat builds up into a heart-thumping bang. A*

*scrawny monk comes out jumping and beating a gigantic drum with
his fingers, palms, elbows, and knees as if he were bewitched.* ZEN
MASTER *enters, dressed in a Buddhist robe of kasaya, his hands
clasped together and his right shoulder bare. Other monks and nuns,
all cloaked in grey kasaya, follow* ZEN MASTER *onto the stage. The*
CROWD *enter in a single file, chanting "Amitabha" as they come.
Their chanting is not in any particular order, each singing their own
tune and at their own pitch. The chanting comes and goes, combining with the drumbeat into a cacophony of intersecting sounds.* MAN
is following the CROWD; *he also chants and looks around him at
times. The* CROWD *all put down a futon, on which they sit with
their legs crossed.* MAN *does same. The drum stops, followed by the
sound of a wooden fish★ and an inverted bell.*)

ZEN MASTER: (*Recites the Vajraccedika prajna paramita sutra,
       his palms clasped together and his right knee on the ground.*)
       ". . . How much the Bodhisattvas, the great beings, have
       been helped with the greatest help by the Tathagata, the   635
       Fully Enlightened One. It is wonderful, O Lord, how
       much the Bodhisattvas, the great beings, have been
       favoured with the highest favour by the Tathagata, the
       Fully Enlightened One. How then, O Lord, should good
       men and women stand, who seek the supreme wisdom,   640
       how progress, how control their thoughts?"
       After these words the Lord said to the Venerable Sub-
       huti: "Well said, well said, Subhuti! So it is, Subhuti, so it
       is as you say! The Tathagata has helped the Bodhisattvas,
       the great beings with the greatest help, and he has   645
       favoured them with the highest favour. Therefore, Sub-
       huti, listen well, and attentively! . . ."

(*Incense smoke permeates the whole place during the chanting. The*
CROWD *close their eyes in meditation, and* MAN *gradually does so
as well.* YOUNG GIRL *appears, her eyes slightly closed. She is squatting in a corner and doing her mental exercise, like a baby who is
sleeping not too tightly in a transparent egg shell, its hands and feet
pressed against the four walls of the shell.* YOUNG MAN, *who has
been hiding behind her, gets up slowly and walks towards* YOUNG
GIRL *in gingerly steps. The chanting gradually fades. The* CROWD
disappear.)

ZEN MASTER: (*The sound of chanting can still be heard faintly.*)
       "Monks of the Buddha, nuns of the Buddha, I will teach
       you how they should stand, who seek the supreme wis-   650
       dom, how progress, how control their thoughts."
       "So be it, O Lord. With a joyful heart we long to
       hear," the Venerable Subhuti replied to the Lord.
       The Lord said: "Here, Subhuti, someone who seeks
       supreme wisdom should produce a thought in this man-   655
       ner . . ."

(YOUNG MAN *stretches his hand to touch* YOUNG GIRL's *fingers.
Surprised, she wakes and withdraws her hand immediately.*)

YOUNG GIRL: Stop it!
YOUNG MAN: Are you doing your mental exercise?
YOUNG GIRL: Yes.
YOUNG MAN: May I ask what kind of exercise are you doing?   660

★A percussion instrument made of a hollow wooden block, used
by Buddhist priests to make rhythm while chanting scriptures.

YOUNG GIRL: They say it's called Small Circular Heaven.

YOUNG MAN: Is there a Big Circular Heaven as well?

YOUNG GIRL: I don't know.

665 YOUNG MAN: You're doing something you don't know anything about?

YOUNG GIRL: (*Nervously.*) Stop interrogating me! Just stop it!

YOUNG MAN: (*Mischievously.*) Then perhaps you don't know what's the use of this exercise? (*Grabs her hand.*)

YOUNG GIRL: No, don't, you can't do that—

670 YOUNG MAN: Why not?

YOUNG GIRL: I'm scared . . .

YOUNG MAN: What's there to be scared of?

YOUNG GIRL: Don't touch me!

YOUNG MAN: What if I do?

675 YOUNG GIRL: Then I'd feel the pain.

YOUNG MAN: So you don't feel any pain right now?

YOUNG GIRL: (*Painfully.*) I can't say for sure . . .

YOUNG MAN: (*Grabs her hand by force.*) Then for once I'll let you feel the pain!

680 YOUNG GIRL: (*Begging him and trying to struggle free.*) Oh no, don't . . . (FATHER *enters carrying an umbrella. The chanting* ZEN MASTER *and the meditating* CROWD *have all disappeared. Only* MAN *is left sitting on the futon with his eyes closed.*)

YOUNG MAN: Father!

685 FATHER: Don't get into trouble. Come home with me, now!

(FATHER *drags* YOUNG MAN *along.*)

(YOUNG GIRL *disappears.*)

YOUNG MAN: (*Turns back to look. Nonchalantly.*) Why? It's not raining.

FATHER: I tell you it will.

YOUNG MAN: But it's not raining now.

690 FATHER: It'll be too late if it does.

YOUNG MAN: What if it doesn't.

FATHER: It's going to rain sooner or later! Look, what do you think I've brought my umbrella for?

YOUNG MAN: You've brought it because you have nothing

695 else to do.

FATHER: I've been carrying an umbrella all my life!

YOUNG MAN: You've brought it upon yourself.

FATHER: How dare you talk to your father like that?

YOUNG MAN: Fine, I won't say anything then.

700 FATHER: Get away from me! Go as far as you possibly can! Don't even bother coming back to see me. I don't have a son like you! (*Exits angrily.*)

(YOUNG MAN *is bewildered.* MAN *is still sitting on the futon meditating. The sound of chanting approaches, but there is no sign of* ZEN MASTER.)

CHANTING SOUND: The Buddha said: Here, subhuti, someone who seeks supreme wisdom should produce a thought in

705 this manner: "As many beings as there are in the universe of beings, comprehended under the term 'beings'—egg-born, born from a womb, moisture-born, or miraculously born; with or without form; with perception, without perception,—as far as any conceivable form of beings is

710 conceived: all these I must lead to Nirvana, into that Realm of Nirvana which leaves nothing behind. . . ."

(YOUNG MAN *turns and finds a wall of people behind him. He tries unsuccessfully to find a way to get over it.* OLD LADY *comes out from a crack in the "wall.")*

OLD LADY: Young man, do you want to go over there?

YOUNG MAN: I just want to take a look.

OLD LADY: Look, look. Everybody wants to take a look. Do you have any money? 715

YOUNG MAN: (*He searches all his pockets and finally takes out a coin.*) Here.

OLD LADY: (*Laughs out loud.*) You want to take care of me with this? Don't you have anything valuable on you at all? Something your mother gave you, for example? 720

YOUNG MAN: (*Suddenly understands.*) I've got this fountain pen, it has a gold nib, my mother gave it to me for my birthday. (*Takes the pen out and hands it over to her.*)

OLD LADY: (*Takes the pen and inspects it carefully.*) Hmm, this is quite nice. (*Stuffs the pen into her waist bag and steps aside to* 725 *reveal a crack in the "wall.*") Now you can go ahead.

YOUNG MAN: (*Hesitating.*) I'm afraid my mother might find out . . .

OLD LADY: Will she beat you?

YOUNG MAN: I . . . I can't say . . . 730

OLD LADY: You'll just have to lie to her, tell her that you've lost it. Don't you know how to lie?

YOUNG MAN: Mother wouldn't allow it.

OLD LADY: That's why you're still such a kid. I'm telling you, there's no adult who doesn't lie, and you know, without 735 lying there'd be no more happy days. All right, just go right through.

(*Crawling,* YOUNG MAN *goes through the crack of the wall of people. When he looks up he sees* YOUNG GIRL *sobbing quietly on the other side, her hands covering her face. He tries to get up, but two thugs approach and take turns beating him up.* YOUNG GIRL *and the sound of chanting disappear at the same time. Only* MAN *is left sitting on the futon and meditating with his eyes closed.*)

PLASTER SELLER: Dogskin Plasters! Dogskin Plasters! Thirteen generations in the family. Give me internal wounds, external wounds, fractures, strains and contusions, give me 740 rabies, heart-attacks, infant convulsions, geriatric strokes, lovesick young men and women, unspeakable depravity and the possessed, stick one on and you'll be as good as new. The first don't work, the second will. . . . Dogskin Plasters! Dogskin Plasters! Taken junky home remedy? 745 Swallowed the wrong drug? No problem! Infertile women, impotent men, sinners and delinquents? Sure thing! Oh yes, and the stutterers, the crooked mouthed, jealous women, avenging men, fathers who love not the mothers, sons who listen not to their old men, pock- 750 marked faces, tinea feet, one plaster cures all. The first don't work, the second will. Satisfaction guaranteed or your money gladly refunded. . . . Dogskin Plasters! Come and get the miracle Dogskin Plasters! Don't miss this golden opportunity! Your chance in a life time! 755

(YOUNG MAN, *on the outside of the* CROWD's *circle, finally manages to get up from his feet.* MAD WOMAN *enters.*)

MAD WOMAN: (*Approaching* YOUNG MAN.) They say I'm a whore, but they didn't say anything when they sneaked

into my bed to sleep with me. They say I'm bad as if they
haven't been bad before, as if they haven't had fun with a
760   woman's body before!

(YOUNG MAN *retreats and hides himself from her. The* CROWD
turn to face them.)

CROWD: Here comes the mad woman.
    The mad woman's here!
    The mad woman's here!
MAD WOMAN: You're mad!
765 CROWD: Look, look at her.
    She's talking crazy again.
MAD WOMAN: You're talking crazy.

(*The* CROWD *happily break out in laughter.*)

PLASTER SELLER: (*At the same time.*) If you've got money, give
    me money, if you don't, stay and watch the show! Dogskin
770   Plasters for sale! (*Throws a bundle of plasters on the ground.*)
    Big sacrifice! Everything must go! Pay what you will.
    Cheap! Cheap! Cheap! . . . Pooh! You stinking whore!
    (*Puts away plasters and exits.*)
MAD WOMAN: You're cheap! (*The* CROWD *laugh at her again.*)
775   What are you laughing at? Go laugh at yourselves! What
    things you wouldn't do to get into a woman's pants! You
    all look like you're human, but actually you're all dogs,
    dogs, dirty dogs.
MEN IN CROWD: (*To women in the* CROWD.) Stop her wagging
780   tongue.
    Take her away.
MAD WOMAN: Why? You're scared because I'll tell on you,
    right? You're hiding something, aren't you? Right, keep
    away from me, as far away as you can. I know exactly what's
785   going on in those shitty little heads of yours. (*Snickers.*)
MEN IN CROWD: Take her away! Take her away!

(WOMEN *in the* CROWD *come forward to drag* MAD WOMAN *away.*)

MAD WOMAN: You're afraid too, aren't you? You're afraid I'll
    say that all of your husbands, every single one of them,
    have slept with me? Afraid because you'll become like me,
790   dumped by your men after they've gotten their rocks off?
    Afraid your husbands will know you've screwed other
    men? Afraid people will find out you'd lost your cherry
    before you got married?
CROWD: Gag her!
795   With horse shit!
    With bull shit!
    Shut her big mouth!
MAD WOMAN: (*Grappling with* WOMEN *in the* CROWD.)
    Haven't you got off with a man before? You're like me,
800   you can't take your hands off your men after they've
    screwed you . . .

(*The* CROWD *move forward to tie up* MAD WOMAN *with ropes and
gag her mouth. Crying and wailing, she becomes hysterical, but is finally dragged away by the* CROWD. YOUNG MAN *watches in astonishment and leaves with the* CROWD. MAN, *who has been sitting
and meditating on the futon, also disappears at the same time. Immediately afterwards, he returns from the other side with his
SHADOW. SHADOW is dressed in black and has on black headgear*

which covers his face. MAN *and* SHADOW *do not look at each other.
They talk only to themselves, but their steps and movements are synchronized.*)

MAN: A seed falls on to the soil—
SHADOW: A child is born onto the world—
MAN: A gust of wind blows through the forest—
SHADOW: A horse gallops on the plateau—   805
MAN: A grain of sand falls into the eye—
SHADOW: An eye is crying tears—
MAN: The tears fall on the parched desert—
SHADOW: Like entering a bustling marketplace—
MAN: People squashing people, but their eyes can't be seen— 810
SHADOW: Seeing dead fish one by one—
MAN: That's a lonely city—
SHADOW: Pop singers are yelling and screaming to exhaus-
    tion—
MAN: Only the stars can hear the wind chimes ringing— 815
SHADOW: It is not our hearts that are ringing—
MAN: It's the electric guitars picking your nerves—
SHADOW: You jump three times, nine times, eight times, seven
    times and you're out of breath—
MAN: Just because you're no hero— 820
SHADOW: More like a popular and low-minded farce—
MAN: An out-of-tune trumpet blows, blows, blows, blows and
    blows—
SHADOW: The conductor has to be right—
MAN: Everyone says he's 180% painful— 825
SHADOW: Only one minute's happiness—
MAN: It's not the time for drinking beer—
SHADOW: Chicago Nuremberg—
MAN: Once there was a war—
SHADOW: Only sparrows were killed— 830
MAN: Soldiers didn't fight, they only stood on guard—
SHADOW: And those standing on guard got to wear medals—
MAN: Who is the person speaking to me?
SHADOW: It is your shadow, your thoughts spoken out loud—
MAN: You're always following me— 835
SHADOW: When you have lost your self—
MAN: You'll come and remind me and double my trouble?
SHADOW: What are you looking for so desperately?
MAN: Now that you've reminded me! I've definitely lost
    something, can you tell me where to look for it? 840
SHADOW: (*Sarcastically.*) You probably do not know what you
    are looking for?
MAN: It appears to be . . . isn't everyone looking for it?

(*The* CROWD *enter. They form a circle and bend down to look for
something in the circle, like children at play.*)

SHADOW: It would not hurt to ask them what you are look-
    ing for. (*Takes the chance to leave and disappear.*) 845
MAN: Excuse me, are you looking for—
PERSON A: A needle, they say you can lead a camel through
    the eye of this needle.
MAN: (*To another person.*) Excuse me, can you tell me what
    you're looking for? 850
PERSON B: Looking for a place where I can sit comfortably
    and securely. Once I'm there, I won't leave the seat ever
    again. (*Whispering.*) I have haemorrhoids, I can't sit on any
    wooden bench.

855 MAN: And, what are you looking for?
PERSON C: (*Stuttering.*) I . . . I . . . I am . . . looking for a . . . a . . . mouth . . . which can . . . s . . . s . . . peak . . . for me. I . . . I . . . have to s . . . s . . . speak a lot . . . of . . . of . . . words ev . . . every . . . every day.
860 MAN: And you, young man?
PERSON D: I'm looking for a rice bowl! You have everything, but I don't even have a rice bowl!
MAN: Of course, I know, I know it's very important to have a rice bowl. Go for it. Keep looking. (*To another person.*)
865   Excuse me, I didn't do it on purpose. (*Removes his foot.*) What are you looking for?
PERSON E: I'm looking for a pair of shoes that fits. I don't know why my shoes pinch. I want to know—
MAN: I'm also looking for—
870 PERSON E: Do your shoes pinch too?
MAN: My shoes don't pinch, but I don't know where my feet should be going.
PERSON E: You just have to follow other people's footsteps.
MAN: Are you also looking for other people's footsteps?
875 PERSON F: (*Laughing playfully.*) I'm looking for a hole I can sneak through without anyone noticing me. And then I'll come out on the other side swaggering.
MAN: How about you, my friend? You don't look like the sneaky type.
880 PERSON G: You're right.
MAN: Can you tell me what are you looking for?
PERSON G: Looking for my childhood dream.
MAN: It must be a very beautiful dream. (*To another.*) And you? Are you looking for a dream too?
885 PERSON H: No, I'm looking for a sentence.
MAN: Are you writing a poem?
PERSON H: Everybody can write poetry, just like everybody knows how to make love.
MAN: Then you're—
890 PERSON H: Thinking! Everyone's got a mind, but not everyone can think.
MAN: You're right. What you're looking for must be an epigram.
PERSON H: I'm not sure if it's an epigram. The problem is, if
895   I didn't find this sentence my thoughts would be cut off, and thoughts which have been cut off are like a cut-off kite, you'll never be able to retrieve it again. Without a sentence you just can't think, because thinking is like a chain, each ring is linked to the next one. You under-
900   stand?
MAN: Young lady, how about you? What are you looking for?
YOUNG LADY: Take a guess.
MAN: It must be something to do with love.
YOUNG LADY: You're so right! I'm waiting for a pair of eyes,
905   tender, profound, and burning with passion—

(*He avoids the young lady, but he bumps into another person.*)

PERSON I: Don't step on my toes!
MAN: Oh, I beg your pardon.
PERSON I: Never seen anyone who walks like you.
MAN: Neither have I. I'm going that way.
910 PERSON I: Everyone's looking here, what are you going to do over there?
MAN: There is nothing I want here.

PERSON I: What are you looking for?
MAN: (*Troubled.*) I don't know what I'm looking for.
PERSON I: Everybody, look! The man is a weirdo, he doesn't 915 know what he's looking for!
PERSON J: He must have found it already.

(*The* CROWD *surround* MAN.)

MAN: No, I haven't. Really I haven't. (*Walks away.*)
STABLE KEEPER: (*Coming out from the* CROWD.) Where are you going? 920
MAN: Over there.
STABLE KEEPER: You haven't found anything yet, right? How come you're going over there?
MAN: I'm not going to look for anything any more. I just want to go over there. 925
STABLE KEEPER: We're all looking here, but you insist on going there.
EVERYBODY: Shall we let him?
CROWD: No!
    Absolutely not! 930
    He can't go.
    Just wait until we've all found it, then you can go.
MAN: Let me explain.
CROWD: There's no need, we already know.
    We've been looking, you've been looking, everybody's 935 been looking, but no one's found anything. Why do you want to go there now?
    It won't do.
    When we say no, we mean no.
    If you quit looking and we quit looking, then you can 940 go there. But everybody's still looking right now and you insist on going, of course we won't let you. How can you? If we're going to quit, we should all quit. So if we're going to look, we should all be looking, right?
MAN: I don't have anything to do with you. 945
STABLE KEEPER: My friend, we're treating you like a friend, don't you see? (*To the* CROWD.) Try again to make him understand. Okay, let's start from the beginning.
CROWD: (*One after the other.*) That's to say, yes, no, everybody looks or nobody looks, even if nobody looks or every- 950 body looks, not looking is not the same as not wanting to look, the question is whether we can look and find it—
MAN: What if I don't want to look?
CROWD: You don't want to look, sure, okay, we can't force you to if you don't want to, if you don't want to look, it 955 doesn't mean nobody should look, and if everybody looks then you can't be not looking, nobody looks you don't look no more, everybody wants to look and you don't look, everybody looks for everybody, you don't look for everybody, you don't look and everybody looks, you look 960 or not you don't look everybody looks you look or not nobody looks you look everybody looks—
MAN: (*Can't control himself.*) I'm going my way! I'm not bothering anybody, and nobody's going to bother me, okay?
STABLE KEEPER: I'll give it to you straight: No way! You've 965 found it but we haven't, it just won't wash!
MAN: But I haven't found anything!
STABLE KEEPER: Then keep looking.
MAN: I'm not looking here any more. I—want—to—go— there. 970

STABLE KEEPER: Don't you know the rules here'? We've told you over and over again, why can't you admit that you're wrong and change your ways?

CROWD: What's happening?

975 What's happening?

Son of a bitch, he's looking for trouble!

STABLE KEEPER: Wait, this is no good, it's so uncivilized. If he doesn't want to repent, let him. We won't make it difficult for him. Just tell him to crawl through here. (*Pointing to his*

980 *crotch.*) What do you say?

CROWD: (*Bursting into laughter.*) Wonderful!

(*Silence. Surprisingly,* MAN *crawls through* STABLE KEEPER*'s crotch. The* CROWD *is shocked and disappears.* MAN *picks up a key while he is crawling.* SHADOW *enters immediately.*)

SHADOW: A key? That is correct. You must have been looking for a key like this one. Yes, yes, the key is what you have been looking for!

(MAN *is on his knees, inspecting the key in his hand. He then stands up and walks to centre stage and uses the key to open an imaginary door. He pulls hard on the big and heavy door and manages to open it. He walks inside.* SHADOW *exits. Silence everywhere.*)

985 MAN: (*Inquiring.*) Hello—(Echo: Hello—hello—hello—hello . . . hello . . .) Ah—(Ah—Ah—Ah—Ah . . . Ah . . . Ah . . . *The echoes seem to make the room more hollow and deserted.*) Anybody home? (Echo: Anybody home? Anybody home? Anybody home? Anybody home? Anybody home? . . .) Nobody has ever

990 set foot in here before for sure . . . (*Echolike murmuring: so lonely, so lonely, so lonely, so lonely.*)

(MAN *looks around and finds that some objects are hidden under the cover of a piece of black cloth. He carefully pulls out a bare woman's arm from under the black cloth.*)

MAN: (*Shocked.*) O—

(*Simulated female voice sighs, echoing: O . . . O . . . O . . . O . . . O. . . . The voice seems to make him more enthusiastic. He begins to clear out what lies beneath the black cloth more diligently, and he pulls out a woman's leg.*)

MAN: (*Excited.*) Ah!

(*There is another series of simulated female voice calling urgently: Ah! Ah! Ah! Ah! Ah! Ah! . . . Finally* MAN *discovers a female mannequin hidden under the black cloth. He lifts the mannequin out and lays it down carefully. He admires it and then starts to move its hands and feet. And with increasing passion and energy, he fiddles with its shoulders, arms and the whole body, bringing it to a rather awkward forward leaning position. He turns the head around, and groping and touching, he manages to create various facial expressions. Every change he makes on the mannequin is accompanied by a simulated female voice akin to mechanical sound. The different expressions on the mannequin's face, including joy, pain, bewilderment, and peaceful staring, are also accompanied by music expressing the same sentiments in a simulated female voice. He puts the head straight so that it is staring at a not-so-distant place in front. . . . Then he stops and tries to figure out what to do next.*

He becomes more excited now. One by one he pulls out more male and female mannequins and arranges them into a kind of pattern. After thinking for a while, he decides to put a piece of headgear on the first model. He keeps rearranging the pattern, his feet dancing to the beat of the increasingly loud music. The pattern changes according to one or more rules of his own making and at a speed which can only be observed in an instant. Gradually he finds himself hemmed in by the pattern and becomes one of its composite parts, and he crawls busily back and forth in between the mannequins. The process is a sustained and intense consumption of will power and strength.

Now the mannequins form a gigantic collective pattern using the first mannequin as its centre. As they move about, the pattern keeps changing slowly yet unstoppably. MAN *runs around in a hurry, jumping, moving, and rolling among his own creations. Highly excited, he calls out and responds to the mannequins in all kinds of non-language shouts and screams. This is a process of constant discovery, renewal, rediscovery, and further renewal. But gradually the objects no longer obey his commands and the sounds they make begin to overwhelm his shouts. As he is totally drawn in among them, he gradually becomes weaker, and it becomes difficult for him to get out. After a long while he finally manages to crawl out like a worm, utterly exhausted. His creations roaringly gyrate past him and slowly disappear.*)

(SHADOW *appears again, keeping a certain distance front him.*)

SHADOW: (*Narrates in a serene voice.*) Then winter came along. It was snowing hard that day, and you walked barefoot on 995 the ice to experience the bone-chilling cold. You seemed to feel that you were Jesus Christ, that you were the loneliest person, the only person who was suffering in this world. You felt that you were pervaded by the spirit of self-sacrifice, even though you were not sure for whom 1000 you would be sacrificing yourself. Yes, you did leave your footprints in the snow, and in the distance was a hazy, misty forest.

(*Totally worn out,* MAN *walks into a simulated forest made of human bodies.*)

SHADOW: (*Following him.*) You walked into the dark and shady forest. The trees, every one of them, had already 1005 shed their leaves, stretching out their shaven branches like naked women. Somberly they stood in the snow, lonely and speechless. You could not help wanting to tell them about your sorrows and torments. You recalled the time of your youth, when you waited for her on the roadside 1010 for a long long time. That day it was also snowing, and you were determined to tell her that you loved her. You want to say that at the time you were still young and innocent, but now you have sinned deeply, and you will never be able to go back to those early days any more. 1015 You have long lost your faith in people, your heart has grown old and it will not love again. Your only wish is to go walking among the trees in the forest until you are totally exhausted. Then you will collapse somewhere, hoping never to be found. 1020

(*Finally* MAN *leans against a tree to take a breath.* SHADOW *comes closer and closer, observing him.*)

1546 UNIT VII · WORLD STAGES

SHADOW: In fact it is nothing more than a kind of self-pity.
     You are unwilling to end like this, you are so vain. (*Exits.*)

(*The tree* MAN *has been leaning against bends down its trunk and speaks in a human-like voice: "Oh, here you are." Then all the trees in the forest move slowly towards him like monsters. They reveal their human forms and become the* CROWD, *all dressed in mourning clothes.*)

CROWD: (*They speak and move, but they are unfeeling and expressionless.*)
1025   We've been looking all over for you.
     Come on, take us to the pub to have a drink.
     You're our host, how come you're here in the snow?
     You're a giant, and we have to look up to see you.
     You're famous, so famous that we're scared of you.
1030   We admire you, but we don't want to idolize you.
     You're no more than a crook, only we don't have your
     tricks.
     Get up and come with us.
     You should donate money to our charities for children,
1035   you must know that children need money the most.
     You went through the forest alone, a forest even the devil
     fears to tread, you're number one.
     You're a pathfinder, you've walked out a road nobody
     wants to walk on, you've led people astray.
1040   You're lucky, not everyone is as lucky as you are.
     It's not that you're more talented than the others, it's only
     that they don't get the chance to show what they've got.
     You're the tops, let's us give him a pat on the behind!

(*The* CROWD *laugh coldly and sinisterly. Some start to pull at him and grapple with him.*)

CROWD: (*Suddenly.*) Here he comes!
1045   Talk of the devil.
     Make way.

(SHADOW *backs in as the* CROWD *step aside to make way for him.*)

MAN: (*Weakly.*) Who are you?
SHADOW: Your heart.

(*As the* CROWD *watch the drooping, blind, and deaf heart slouching past them,* SHADOW *quietly drags* MAN *away. The* CROWD *slowly follow behind the heart which is extremely old and actually invisible. All exit.*)

(*One by one the* ACTORS *enter from the other side.*)

ACTORS: We set off before dawn. The morning dew was
     thick, and in the dark we heard the cows breathing while   1050
     they were chewing grass on a small hill nearby. In the dis-
     tance, the river bend was enveloped in a shade of deep
     blue light brighter than the sky.
     He told us a fable.
     I dreamed that there's a piece of ivory in my stomach, it   1055
     scared me to death!
     Have you thought of becoming a bird?
     Why a bird? I'm happy with the way I am, and he says he
     loves me.
     Faulkner.   1060
     I like "Roses for Emily."
     I called you up many times.
     Do you know how to read palms?
     No need for any explanations, you don't have to explain
     any more!   1065
     This kitten is so cute.
     I think I've seen you somewhere.
     I have a sweet tooth, and I'm also a sucker for sour milk.
     Your hair looks so nice, is it real?

(*The sound of a baby crying.*)

     Sweetie, oh, sorry, I forgot to change your diapers!   1070

(*The sound of a car engine starting.*)

     How are you going to get back?
     It's so bad, what kind of stupid play is this anyway?
     Are you doing anything tomorrow? Shall we have dinner
     together?

(*Sounds of a baby crying, a car engine starting and running, bicycle bells and the trickle of running water from a tap, and in the distance, the siren of an ambulance.*)

The End

Some Suggestions on Producing *The Other Shore*

1. The so-called "spoken drama" (*huaju*) tends to emphasize and highlight the art of language; in order to free drama from its constraints and to revive drama in all its functions as a performing art, we have to provide training for a new breed of modern actors. As with the actors in traditional operas, these new actors must be versatile, and their skills should include singing, the martial arts, stylized movements and delivering dialogues. They should also be able to perform Shakespeare, Ibsen, Chekov, Aristophanes, Racine, Lao She, Cao Yu, Guo Moruo, Goethe, Brecht, Pirandello, Beckett, and even mimes and musicals. The present play is written with the intention of providing an all-around training for the actors.

2. An ideal performance should be a unity of somatics, language, and psychology. Our play is an attempt to pursue this unified artistic expression and to assist the actors to achieve this goal. In other words, we should allow the actors the chance for linguistic expression in their search for suitable somatic movements, so that language and somatics are able to evoke psychological process at the same time. For this reason, during rehearsals and actual performances, it is not advisable to separate dialogue from movement, i.e., to memorize only the dialogue, to do reading as in common practice, or to strip the language and transform the play into a mime. Certain scenes in the play do not feature dialogue, but there are still other aural expressions, which could be regarded as a kind of sound language.

3. Even though our play is abstract, the performance should not aim at sheer conceptualization in the stark fashion of the play of ideas. Our aspiration is to achieve a kind of emotive abstraction through performance, i.e., a non-philosophical abstraction. The play seeks to set up the performance on the premise of non-reality, and to fully mobilize the imagination of the actors before evoking abstraction through emotion. Therefore the performance requires not only the unity of language and somatics but also the unity of thought and psychology.

4. Except for a few simple props, the performance does not require any scenery. The characters' relationships with their surroundings and other objects are contingent upon life-like dialogue and communicative exchanges in the play. In the case of monologues or in the absence of dialogue, music, sound effects, movement, the look of the eyes and changes in posture could also take on performing roles, so that the props and surroundings will not be relegated to being inanimate objects or mere adornments.

5. The play highlights the performance's ability to ascertain in the mind of the audience the existence of non-existing objects, for instance a decrepit heart, a concrete or abstract river. We may say that this is the inherent difference between a film and a theatrical performance. Even though the play itself relies heavily upon imaginary surroundings, relationships and acting partners, real and life-like objects can be deployed as stage props at the beginning of the performance. For instance, an interpersonal relationship could be established through a piece of rope. Once an actor is equipped with the capability to relate with others, he can easily communicate with his non-existent partners anytime, anywhere. He can also materialize his non-existent partners through his power of imagination, making them come to life and communicate with them, even though they have been created through his own imagination and are actually non-existent.

6. Grotowski's training method aims at helping the actor to discover his own self and to release its potential through big-movement exercises which also relax both body and mind. Thus he calls this type of performance a form of sacrifice. Our play's performance helps the actor to ascertain his own self through the process of discover-

ing his partners. If the actor, without being obsessed with his own self, is consistently able to find a partner to communicate with him, his performance will always be positive and lively, and he will be able to gain a real sense of his own self, which has been awakened by action, and which is alert and capable of self-observation.

7. The play demands that the actors abandon completely the kind of performance dependent upon logic and semantic thinking. The liveliest performances are exactly those which are intuitive, improvisational, and on the spur of the moment. On the stage as in real life, the actor sees with his eyes, hears with his ears, and captures his partners' reactions with his free-moving body. In other words, a performance can only be lively without the use of intellect. Therefore it is best not to resort to literary analysis outside of theatrical performance or to uncover hidden meanings in the text in performing the play.

8. Our play aims at training actors who can be as versatile as the actors in Chinese traditional operas, but it is not our intention to create a new set of conventions for modern drama, because the latter aspires to the kind of acting which is non-formulaic, unregulated, and flexible. Before the actual performance, the actor should enter into a state of competitiveness similar to that of an athlete before a game, or of a cock preparing to slug it out in a cock-fight, ready to provoke as well as to receive his partners' reactions. Thus the performance must be fresh, regenerating, and improvisational, which is essentially different from gymnastic or musical performances.

9. The play's performance strives to expand and not to reduce the expressiveness of language in drama. The language in a play is voiced language, but it is not limited to beautifully written dialogue. In this play, all the sounds uttered by the actor in the prescribed circumstances are also voiced language. If an actor has learned to communicate using fragmented language which features unfinished sentences, disjointed phonetic elements, and ungrammatical constructions, he will be better able to make the unspoken words in the script come to life as voiced language.

The above suggestions are for reference only.

Tomson Highway

Since the production of his two most celebrated plays, *The Rez Sisters* (1986) and *Dry Lips Oughta Move to Kapuskasing* (1989), Tomson Highway has become perhaps the best-known of the many Native playwrights now working in North America. Tomson Highway was born in 1951, the eleventh of twelve children, on a trapline in a Native reserve (the Canadian term for what is called a "reservation" in the United States) in northern Manitoba, Canada. Until the age of six, Highway lived a nomadic life with his family. His first language was Cree, and he did not begin to learn English until he was sent to a Roman Catholic boarding school. Like many Native children, Highway attended boarding school, visiting his family only during the summer. After graduating from high school in Winnipeg, Highway studied piano at the University of Manitoba Faculty of Music, and then studied in London before returning to Canada. He graduated with a bachelor's degree in music from the University of Western Ontario in 1975 and is an accomplished concert pianist. He remained at the university for an additional year, however, to complete a bachelor's degree in English.

After college, Highway worked at The Native Peoples' Resource Centre in London, Ontario, and at the Ontario Federation of Indian Friendship Centres in Toronto. Highway traveled to reserves across Canada, working with Native people in schools, prisons, and other institutions. He also began writing plays about Native life, many of which were performed on reserves and in Native community centers. He first worked on *The Rez Sisters* with the De-ba-jeh-mu-jig Theatre Company of Manitoulin Island, Ontario, in 1986. Like many Native theater companies, De-ba-jeh-mu-jig is devoted to the production of new plays by Native playwrights and produces an increasing number of its plays in Native languages. As artistic director of the Native Earth Performing Arts Company, Highway produced *The Rez*

Big Joey in the 1989 Theatre Passe Muraille production of Tomson Highway's *Dry Lips Oughta Move to Kapuskasing*.

Sisters again in Toronto in December of 1986, where it won the Dora Mavor Moore Award for the best new play of the season and was runner-up for outstanding Canadian play of the year. The play was produced in 1993 in New York by the American Indian Community House and the New York Theater Workshop.

Highway's next play, *Dry Lips Oughta Move to Kapuskasing* was first produced in Toronto in 1989 by the Native Earth Performing Arts Company. It was later moved to the Royal Alexandra Theatre in Toronto, one of the very few Canadian plays—and the first by a Native playwright—to receive a full-scale production by a commercial theater. Highway continues to work as artistic director of Native Earth Performing Arts, one of many important Native theater companies now working in Canada and the United States (others include Four Winds Theatre, Native Theatre School, Ondinnok, Takwakin Theatre, Awasikan Theatre, and A-Maize Theatre in Canada; Spiderwoman Theater, Institute of American Indian Arts, American Indian Theater Company, Minneapolis American Indian AIDS Task Force, and Off the Beaten Path in the United States). Though Highway is gay, his central aims as a playwright to date have been to make Native narrative and mythological traditions more central to contemporary Native—and non-Native—arts.

DRY LIPS OUGHTA MOVE TO KAPUSKASING

Like *The Rez Sisters, Dry Lips Oughta Move to Kapuskasing* concerns life on the fictional Wasaychigan Hill reserve and is written in a mixture of English, Cree, and Ojibway. However, while *The Rez Sisters* concerns a group of Native women who travel to Toronto for the "World's Biggest Bingo," *Dry Lips* is a much darker and more violent play, concerning the men of the reserve. In some respects, the poverty of life on the reserve is made evident in the play's opening scene, the run-down living room of the reserve house shared by Big Joey and Gazelle Nataways, and is developed through the men's interrupted plans to improve life on the "rez." While the women have formed a hockey team (the importance of hockey is epitomized in Pierre's mantra, "Hockey. Life. Hockey. Life."), the men squabble about their plans: Zachary Jeremiah Keechigeesik's bakery, Big Joey's radio station, and Pierre St. Pierre's new job as referee for the women's games. In some ways, the men seem threatened by the women's independence and by their brash appropriation of hockey, and this anxiety seems to imply a more generalized impotence: seedy Creature Nataways does Big Joey's bidding, even though his wife Gazelle has moved in with Big Joey; Simon Starblanket is absorbed in an endlessly aborted effort at cultural revival; Dickie Bird Halked, born with fetal alcohol syndrome, is at once shy and explosive, violently raping Patsy Pegahmagahbow with a crucifix. Even Pierre St. Pierre has a hard time finding his other skate.

Hanging around, drinking beer, complaining about the women—in many ways the Native men seem to epitomize "Canadian hoser culture," in the words of one Native critic of the play. Yet the men continually blame the women for the state of their lives, as Big Joey does in act 2: "I hate them fuckin' bitches. Because they—our own women—took the fuckin' power away from us faster than the FBI ever did." Big Joey's tirade points up the play's most controversial element, which centers on the performance of the Trickster figure Nanabush. The play begins and ends with Zachary awakening on the floor of Big Joey's house; we don't discover until the end of the play that the action has been a kind of dream, maybe a nightmare. Throughout, Nanabush occupies an elevated stage, sometimes watching the action, sometimes participating in it. In Native mythology, Nanabush is capable of changing shape and gender; neither explicitly male nor female, the Trickster uses his/her wiles in a range of legendary escapades. In *Dry Lips,* however, Nanabush takes "female" shape in a number of ways—assuming outsized breasts to play Gazelle Nataways, a large rear-end to play Patsy ("Big-Bum") Pegahmagahbow, and so on. In one reading of the play—a dream play, after all—Nanabush here enacts the men's phobias and fantasies about women, and so offers an implied critique of their sexist attitudes. From another perspective, though, one shared by many Native women who saw the play, the way Nanabush is characterized as a woman—her appearance (a version of the derogatory "squaw" stereotype), the "stripper" scene, the rape scene, the loss of the hockey puck in Gazelle/Nanabush's enormous breasts—merely reinforces the fundamentally misogynistic attitudes of the men in the play. In this sense, *Dry Lips Oughta Move to Kapuskasing* seems poised on the razor's edge of political theater: readers, audiences, and producers of the play must consider whether it criticizes the sexist and possibly misogynist ways women are presented in the play, or whether it merely reinforces such attitudes.

Production Notes

The set for the original production of *Dry Lips Oughta Move to Kapuskasing* contained certain elements which I think are essential to the play.

First of all, it was designed on two levels, the lower of which was the domain of the "real" Wasaychigan Hill. This lower level contained, on stage-left, Big Joey's living room/kitchen, with its kitchen counter at the back and, facing down-stage, an old brown couch with a television set a few feet in front of it. This television set could be made to double as a smaller rock for the forest scenes. Stage-right had Spooky Lacroix's kitchen, with its kitchen counter (for which Big Joey's kitchen counter could double) and its table and chairs.

In front of all this was an open area, the floor of which was covered with Teflon, a material which looks like ice and on which one can actually skate, using real ice skates; this was the rink for the hockey arena scenes. With lighting effects, this area could also be turned into "the forest" surrounding the village of Wasaychigan Hill, with its leafless winter trees. The only other essential element here was a larger jutting rock beside which, for instance, Zachary Jeremiah Keechigeesik and Simon Starblanket meet, a rock which could be made to glow at certain key points. Pierre's "little boot-leg joint" in Act Two, with its "window," was also created with lighting effects.

The upper level of the set was almost exclusively the realm of Nanabush. The principal element here was her perch, located in the very middle of this area. The perch was actually an old jukebox of a late 60's/early 70's make, but it was semi-hidden throughout most of the play, so that it was fully revealed as this fabulous jukebox only at those few times when it was needed; the effect sought after here is of this magical, mystical jukebox hanging in the night air, like a haunting and persistent memory, high up over the village of Wasaychigan Hill. Over and behind this perch was suspended a huge full moon whose glow came on, for the most part, only during the outdoor scenes, which all take place at nighttime. All other effects in this area were accomplished with lighting. The very front of this level, all along its edge, was also utilized as the "bleachers" area for the hockey arena scenes.

Easy access was provided for between the lower and the upper levels of this set.

The "sound-scape" of *Dry Lips Oughta Move to Kapuskasing* was mostly provided for by a musician playing, live, on harmonica, off to the side. It is as though the "dream-scape" of the play were laced all the way through with Zachary Jeremiah Keechigeesik's "idealized" form of harmonica playing, permeated with a definite "blues" flavor. Although Zachary ideally should play his harmonica, and not too well, in those few scenes where it is called for, the sound of this harmonica is most effectively used to underline and highlight the many magical appearances of Nanabush in her various guises.

Spooky Lacroix's baby, towards the end of Act Two, can, and should, be played by a doll wrapped in a blanket. But for greatest effect, Zachary's baby, at the very end of the play, should be played by a real baby, preferably about five months of age.

Finally, both Cree and Ojibway are used freely in this text for the reasons that these two languages, belonging to the same linguistic family, are very similar and that the fictional reserve of Wasaychigan Hill has a mixture of both Cree and Ojibway residents.

A Note on Nanabush

The dream world of North American Indian mythology is inhabited by the most fantastic creatures, beings and events. Foremost among these beings is the "Trickster," as pivotal and important a figure in our world as Christ is in the realm of Christian mythology. "Weesageechak" in Cree, "Nanabush" in Ojibway, "Raven" in others, "Coyote" in still others, this Trickster goes by many names and many guises. In fact, he can assume any guise he chooses. Essentially a comic, clownish sort of character, his role is to teach us about the nature and the meaning of existence on the planet Earth; he straddles the consciousness of man and that of God, the Great Spirit.

The most explicit distinguishing feature between the North American Indian languages and the European languages is that in Indian (e.g., Cree, Ojibway), there is no gender. In Cree, Ojibway, etc., unlike English, French, German, etc., the male-female-neuter hierarchy is entirely absent. So that by this system of thought, the central hero figure from our mythology—theology, if you will—is theoretically neither exclusively male nor exclusively female, or is both simultaneously. Therefore, where in *The Rez Sisters,* Nanabush was male, in this play—"flip-side" to *The Rez Sisters*—Nanabush is female.

Some say that Nanabush left this continent when the white man came. We believe she/he is still here among us—albeit a little the worse for wear and tear—having assumed other guises. Without the continued presence of this extraordinary figure, the core of Indian culture would be gone forever.

Tomson Highway

DRY LIPS OUGHTA MOVE TO KAPUSKASING

Tomson Highway

CHARACTERS

NANABUSH (*as the spirit of Gazelle Nataways, Patsy Pegahma-gahbow and Black Lady Halked*)
ZACHARY JEREMIAH KEECHIGEESIK—*41 years old*
BIG JOEY—*39*
CREATURE NATAWAYS—*39*
DICKIE BIRD HALKED—*17*
PIERRE ST. PIERRE—*53*

SPOOKY LACROIX—*39*
SIMON STARBLANKET—*20*
HERA KEECHIGEESIK—*39*

TIME: *Between Saturday, February 3, 1990, 11 P.M., and Saturday, February 10, 1990, 11 A.M.*
PLACE: *The Wasaychigan Hill Indian Reserve, Manitoulin Island, Ontario*

ACT ONE

The set for this first scene is the rather shabby and very messy living room/kitchen of the reserve house BIG JOEY and GAZELLE NATAWAYS currently share. Prominently displayed on one wall is a life-size pin-up poster of Marilyn Monroe. The remains of a party are obvious. On the worn-out old brown couch, with its back towards the entrance, lies ZACHARY JEREMIAH KEECHIGEESIK, a very handsome Indian man. He is naked, passed out. The first thing we see when the light comes up—a very small "spot," precisely focussed—is ZACHARY's bare, naked bum. Then, from behind the couch, we see a woman's leg, sliding languorously into a nylon stocking and right over Zachary's bum. It is NANABUSH, as the spirit of GAZELLE NATAWAYS, dressing to leave. She eases herself luxuriously over the couch and over Zachary's bum and then reaches under Zachary's sleeping head, from where she gently pulls a gigantic pair of false, rubberized breasts. She proceeds to put these on over her own bare breasts. Then NANABUSH/GAZELLE NATAWAYS sashays over to the side of the couch, picks a giant hockey sweater up off the floor and shimmies into it. The sweater has a huge, plunging neck-line, with the capital letter "W" and the number "1" prominently sewn on. Then she sashays back to the couch and behind it. Pleasurably and mischievously, she leans over and plants a kiss on Zachary's bum, leaving behind a gorgeous, luminescent lip-stick mark. The last thing she does before she leaves is to turn the television on. This television sits facing the couch that ZACHARY lies on. NANABUSH/GAZELLE does not use her hand for this, though; instead, she turns the appliance on with one last bump of her voluptuous hips. "Hockey Night in Canada" comes on. The sound of this hockey game is on only slightly, so that we hear it as background "music" all the way through the coming scene. Then NANABUSH/GAZELLE exits, to sit on her perch on the upper level of the set. The only light left on stage is that coming from the television screen, giving off its eery glow. Beat.

The kitchen door bangs open, the "kitchen light" flashes on and BIG JOEY and CREATURE NATAWAYS enter, CREATURE carrying a case of beer on his head. At first, they are oblivious to ZACHARY's presence. Also at about this time, the face of DICKIE BIRD HALKED emerges from the shadows at the "kitchen window." Silently, he watches the rest of the proceedings, taking a particular interest—even fascination—in the movements and behavior of BIG JOEY.

BIG JOEY: (*Calling out for GAZELLE who, of course, is not home.*) Hey, bitch!

Keechigeesik means "heaven" or "great sky" in Cree **Wasaychigan** means "window" in Ojibway

CREATURE: (*As he, at regular intervals, bangs the beer case down on the kitchen counter, rips it open, pops bottles open, throws one to BIG JOEY, all noises that serve to "punctuate" the rat-a-tat rhythm of his frenetic speech.*) Batman oughta move to Kapuskasing, nah, Kap's too good for Batman, right, Big Joey? I tole you once I tole you twice he shouldna done it he shouldna done what he went and did goddawful Batman Manitowabi the way he went and crossed that blue line with the puck, man, he's got the flippin' puck right in the palm of his flippin' hand and only a minute-and-a-half to go he just about gave me the shits the way Batman Manitowabi went and crossed that blue line right in front of that brick shithouse of a whiteman why the hell did that brick shit-house of a white-man have to be there . . .

ZACHARY: (*Talking in his sleep.*) No!

CREATURE: Hey!

(BIG JOEY *raises a finger signaling* CREATURE *to shut up.*)

ZACHARY: I said no!

CREATURE: (*In a hoarse whisper.*) That's not a TV kind of sound.

BIG JOEY: Shhh!

ZACHARY: . . . goodness sakes, Hera, you just had a baby . . .

CREATURE: That's a real life kind of sound, right, Big Joey? (BIG JOEY *and* CREATURE *slowly come over to the couch.*)

ZACHARY: . . . women playing hockey . . . damn silliest thing I heard in my life . . .

BIG JOEY: Well, well . . .

CREATURE: Ho-leee! (*Whispering.*) Hey, what's that on his arse look like lip marks.

ZACHARY: . . . Simon Starblanket, that's who's gonna help me with my bakery . . .

CREATURE: He's stitchless, he's nude, he's gonna pneumonia . . .

BIG JOEY: Shut up.

CREATURE: Get the camera. Chris'sakes, take a picture.

(CREATURE *scrambles for the Polaroid, which he finds under one end of the couch.*)

ZACHARY: . . . Simon! (*Jumps up.*) What the?!

CREATURE: Surprise! (*Camera flashes.*)

ZACHARY: Put that damn thing away. What are you doing here? Where's my wife? Hera!

(*He realizes he's naked, grabs a cast iron frying pan and slaps it over his crotch, almost castrating himself in the process.*)

Ooof!

40   BIG JOEY: (*Smiling.*) Over easy or sunny side up, Zachary Jeremiah Keechigeesik?

ZACHARY: Get outa my house.

CREATURE: This ain't your house. This is Big Joey's house, right, Big Joey?

45   BIG JOEY: Shut up.

ZACHARY: Creature Nataways. Get outa here. Gimme that camera.

CREATURE: Come and geeeet it!

(*Grabs* ZACHARY's *pants from the floor.*)

ZACHARY: Cut it out. Gimme them goddamn pants.

50   CREATURE: (*Singing.*) Lipstick on your arshole, tole da tale on you-hoo.

ZACHARY: What? (*Straining to see his bum.*) Oh lordy, lordy, lordy gimme them pants.

(*As he tries to wipe the stain off.*)

CREATURE: Here doggy, doggy. Here poochie, poochie woof
55   woof! (ZACHARY *grabs the pants. They rip almost completely in half.* CREATURE *yelps.*) Yip!

(*Momentary light up on* NANABUSH/GAZELLE, *up on her perch, as she gives a throaty laugh.* BIG JOEY *echoes this,* CREATURE *tittering away in the background.*)

ZACHARY: Hey, this is not my doing, Big Joey. (*As he clumsily puts on what's left of his pants.* CREATURE *manages to get in one more shot with the camera.*) We were just having a nice quiet drink
60   over at Andy Manigitogan's when Gazelle Nataways shows up. She brought me over here to give me the recipe for her bannock apple pie cuz, goodness sakes, Simon Starblanket was saying it's the best, that pie was selling like hot cakes at the bingo and he knows I'm tryna establish this reserve's first
65   pie-making business gimme that camera.

(BIG JOEY *suddenly makes a lunge at* ZACHARY *but* ZACHARY *evades him.*)

CREATURE: (*In the background, like a little dog.*) Yah, yah.

BIG JOEY: (*Slowly stalking* ZACHARY *around the room.*) You know, Zach, there's a whole lotta guys on this rez been slippin' my old lady the goods but there ain't but a handful been stupid
70   enough to get caught by me. (*He snaps his fingers and, as always,* CREATURE *obediently scurries over. He hands* BIG JOEY *the picture of* ZACHARY *naked on the couch.* BIG JOEY *shows the picture to* ZACHARY, *right up to his face.*) Kinda em-bare-ass-in' for a hoity-toity educated community pillar like you, eh
75   Zach?

(ZACHARY *grabs for the picture but* BIG JOEY *snaps it away.*)

ZACHARY: What do you want?

BIG JOEY: What's this I hear about you tellin' the chief I can wait for my radio station?

ZACHARY: (*As he proceeds with looking around the room to collect and
80   put on what he can find of his clothes.* BIG JOEY *and* CREATURE *follow him around, obviously enjoying his predicament.*) I don't know where the hell you heard that from.

BIG JOEY: Yeah, right. Well, Lorraine Manigitogan had a word or two with Gazelle Nataways the other night. When you presented your initial proposal at the band office, you said: 85
"Joe can wait. He's only got another three months left in the hockey season."

ZACHARY: I never said no such thing.

BIG JOEY: Bullshit.

ZACHARY: W-w-w-what I said was that employment at this bak-   90
ery of mine would do nothing but add to those in such places as those down at the arena. I never mentioned your name once. And I said it only in passing reference to the fact . . .

BIG JOEY: . . . that this radio idea of mine doesn't have as much long-term significance to the future of this community as   95
this fancy bakery idea of yours, Mr. Pillsbury dough-boy, right?

ZACHARY: If that's what you heard, then you didn't hear it from Lorraine Manigitogan. You got it from Gazelle Nataways and you know yourself she's got a bone to pick with . . .   100

BIG JOEY: You know, Zach, you and me, we work for the same cause, don't we?

ZACHARY: Never said otherwise.

BIG JOEY: We work for the betterment and the advancement of this community, don't we? And seeing as we're about the   105
only two guys in this whole hell-hole who's got the get-up-and-go to do something . . .

ZACHARY: That's not exactly true, Joe. Take a look at Simon Starblanket . . .

BIG JOEY: . . . we should be working together, not against.   110
What do you say you simply postpone that proposal to the Band Council . . .

ZACHARY: I'm sorry. Can't do that.

BIG JOEY: (*Cornering* ZACHARY.) Listen here, bud. You turned your back on me when everybody said I was responsible for   115
that business in Espanola seventeen years ago and you said nothin'. I overlooked that. Never said nothin'. (ZACHARY *re-members his undershorts and proceeds, with even greater despera-tion, to look for them, zeroing in on the couch and under it.* BIG
JOEY *catches the drift and snaps his fingers, signaling* CREATURE   120
to look for the shorts under the couch. creature *jumps for the couch. Without missing a beat,* BIG JOEY *continues.*) You turned your back on me when you said you didn't want nothin' to do with me from that day on. I overlooked that. Never said nothin'. You gave me one hell of a slap in the face when   125
your wife gave my Gazelle that kick in the belly. I over-looked that. Never said nothin'. (CREATURE, *having found the shorts among the junk under the couch just split seconds before* ZACHARY *does, throws them to* BIG JOEY. BIG JOEY *holds the shorts up to* ZACHARY, *smiling with satisfaction.*) That, how-   130
ever, was the last time . . .

ZACHARY: That wasn't my fault, Joe. It's that witch woman of yours Gazelle Nataways provoked that fight between her and Hera and you know yourself Hera tried to come and sew up her belly again . . .   135

BIG JOEY: Zach. I got ambition . . .

ZACHARY: Yeah, right.

BIG JOEY: I aim to get that radio station off the ground, start-ing with them games down at my arena.

ZACHARY: Phhhh!   140

BIG JOEY: I aim to get a chain of them community radio sta-tions not only on this here island but beyond as well . . .

ZACHARY: Dream on, Big Joey, dream on . . .

145 BIG JOEY: . . . and I aim to prove this broadcasting of games among the folks is one sure way to get some pride . . .

ZACHARY: Bullshit! You're in it for yourself.

BIG JOEY: . . . some pride and dignity back so you just get your ass on out of my house and you go tell that Chief your Band Council Resolution can wait until next fiscal year or
150 else . . .

ZACHARY: I ain't doing no such thing, Joe, no way. Not when I'm this close.

BIG JOEY: (*As he eases himself down onto the couch, twirling the shorts with his fore-finger.*) . . . or else I get my Gazelle Nataways to
155 wash these skivvies of yours, put them in a box all nice and gussied up, your picture on top, show up at your door-step and hand them over to your wife. (*Silence.*)

ZACHARY: (*Quietly, to* BIG JOEY.) Gimme them shorts. (*No answer. Then to* CREATURE.) Gimme them snapshots. (*Still no*
160 *response.*)

BIG JOEY: (*Dead calm.*) Get out.

ZACHARY: (*Seeing he can't win for the moment, prepares to exit.*) You may have won this time, Joe, but . . .

BIG JOEY: (*Like a steel trap.*) Get out.

(*Silence. Finally* ZACHARY *exits, looking very humble. Seconds before* ZACHARY's *exit,* DICKIE BIRD HALKED, *to avoid being seen by* ZACHARY, *disappears from the "window." The moment* ZACHARY *is gone,* CREATURE *scurries to the kitchen door, shaking his fist in the direction of the already-departed* ZACHARY.)

165 CREATURE: Damn rights! (*Then strutting like a cock, he turns to* BIG JOEY.) Zachary Jeremiah Keechigeesik never shoulda come in your house, Big Joey. Thank god, Gazelle Nataways ain't my wife no more . . . (BIG JOEY *merely has to throw a glance in* CREATURE's *direction to intimidate him. At once,* CREATURE
170 *reverts back to his usual nervous self.*) . . . not really, she's yours now, right, Big Joey? It's you she's livin' with these days, not me.

BIG JOEY: (*As he sits on the couch with his beer, mostly ignoring* CREATURE *and watching the hockey game on television.*) Don't make
175 her my wife.

CREATURE: But you live together, you sleep together, you eat ooops!

BIG JOEY: Still don't make her my wife.

CREATURE: (*As he proceeds to try to clean up the mess around the*
180 *couch, mostly shoving everything back under it.*) I don't mind, Big Joey, I really don't. I tole you once I tole you twice she's yours now. It's like I loaned her to you, I don't mind. I can take it. We made a deal, remember? The night she threw the toaster at me and just about broke my skull, she tole
185 me: "I had enough, Creature Nataways, I had enough from you. I had your kids and I had your disease and that's all I ever want from you, I'm leavin'." And then she grabbed her suitcase and she grabbed the kids, no, she didn't even grab the kids, she grabbed the TV and she just sashayed herself
190 over here. She left me. It's been four years now, Big Joey, I know, I know. Oh, it was hell, it was hell at first but you and me we're buddies since we're babies, right? So I thought it over for about a year . . . then one day I swallowed my pride and I got up off that chesterfield and I walked over
195 here, I opened your door and I shook your hand and I said:

"It's okay, Big Joey, it's okay." And then we went and played darts in Espanola except we kinda got side-tracked, remember, Big Joey, we ended up on that three-day bender?

BIG JOEY: Creature Nataways?

200 CREATURE: What?

BIG JOEY: You talk too much.

CREATURE: I tole you once I tole you twice I don't mind . . .

(*But* PIERRE ST. PIERRE *comes bursting in, in a state of great excitement.*)

PIERRE: (*Addressing the case of beer directly.*) Hallelujah! Have you heard the news?

205 CREATURE: Pierre St. Pierre. Chris'sakes, knock. You're walkin' into a civilized house.

PIERRE: The news. Have you heard the news?

CREATURE: I'll tell you a piece of news. Anyways, we come in the door and guess who . . .

210 BIG JOEY: (*To* CREATURE.) Sit down.

PIERRE: Gimme a beer.

CREATURE: (*To* PIERRE.) Sit down.

PIERRE: Gimme a beer.

BIG JOEY: Give him a fuckin' beer. (*But* PIERRE *has already*
215 *grabbed, opened and is drinking a beer.*)

CREATURE: Have a beer.

PIERRE: (*Talking out the side of his mouth, as he continues drinking.*) Tank you.

BIG JOEY: Talk.

220 PIERRE: (*Putting his emptied bottle down triumphantly and grabbing another beer.*) Toast me.

BIG JOEY: Spit it out.

CREATURE: Chris'sakes.

PIERRE: Toast me.

225 CREATURE: Toast you? The hell for?

PIERRE: Shut up. Just toast me.

CREATURE/BIG JOEY: Toast.

PIERRE: Tank you. You just toasted "The Ref."

CREATURE: (*To* PIERRE.) The ref? (*To* BIG JOEY.) The what?

230 PIERRE: "The Ref!"

CREATURE: The ref of the what?

PIERRE: The ref. I'm gonna be the referee down at the arena. Big Joey's arena. The Wasaychigan Hill Hippodrome.

CREATURE: We already got a referee.

235 PIERRE: Yeah, but this here's different, this here's special.

BIG JOEY: I'd never hire a toothless old bootlegger like you.

PIERRE: They play their first game in just a coupla days. Against the Canoe Lake Bravettes. And I got six teeth left so you just keep your trap shut about my teeth.

240 CREATURE: The Canoe Lake Bravettes?

BIG JOEY: Who's "they"?

PIERRE: Haven't you heard?

BIG JOEY: Who's "they"?

PIERRE: I don't believe this.

245 BIG JOEY: Who's "they"?

PIERRE: I don't believe this. (BIG JOEY *bangs* PIERRE *on the head.*) Oww, you big bully! The Wasaychigan Hill Wailerettes, of course. I'm talkin' about the Wasy Wailerettes, who else geez.

250 CREATURE: The Wasy Wailerettes? Chris'sakes . . .

PIERRE: Dominique Ladouche, Black Lady Halked, that terrible Dictionary woman, Fluffy Sainte-Marie, Dry Lips

Manigitogan, Leonarda Lee Starblanket, Annie Cook, June Bug McLeod, Big Bum Pegahmagahbow, all twenty-seven of 'em. Them women from right here on this reserve, a whole batch of 'em, they upped and they said: "Bullshit! Ain't nobody on the face of this earth's gonna tell us us women's got no business playin' hockey. That's bullshit!" That's what they said: "Bullshit!" So. They took matters into their own hands. And, holy shit la marde, I almost forgot to tell you my wife Veronique St. Pierre, she went and made up her mind she's joinin' the Wasy Wailerettes, only the other women wouldn't let her at first on account she never had no babies—cuz, you see, you gotta be pregnant or have piles and piles of babies to be a Wasy Wailerette—but my wife, she put her foot down and she says: "Zhaboonigan Peterson may be just my adopted daughter and she may be retarded as a doormat but she's still my baby." That's what she says to 'em. And she's on and they're playin' hockey and the Wasy Wailerettes, they're just a-rarin' to go, who woulda thunk it, huh?

CREATURE: Ho-leee!

PIERRE: God's truth . . .

BIG JOEY: They never booked the ice.

PIERRE: Ha! Booked it through Gazelle Nataways. Sure as I'm alive and walkin' these treacherous icy roads . . .

BIG JOEY: Hang on.

PIERRE: . . . god's truth in all its naked splendor. (*As he pops open yet another beer.*) I kid you not, gentlemen, not for one slippery goddamn minute. Toast!

BIG JOEY: (*Grabbing the bottle right out of* PIERRE's *mouth.*) Where'd you sniff out all this crap?

PIERRE: From my wife, who else? My wife, Veronique St. Pierre, she told me. She says to me: "Pierre St. Pierre, you'll eat your shorts but I'm playin' hockey and I don't care what you say. Or think." And she left. No. First, she cleaned out my wallet, (*Grabs his beer back from* BIG JOEY's *hand.*) grabbed her big brown rosaries from off the wall. Then she left. Just slammed the door and left. Period. I just about ate my shorts. Toast!

CREATURE: Shouldn't we . . . shouldn't we stop them?

PIERRE: Phhht! . . . (CREATURE *just misses getting spat on.*)

CREATURE: Ayoah!

PIERRE: . . . Haven't seen hide nor hair of 'em since. Gone to Sudbury. Every single last one of 'em. Piled theirselves into seven cars and just took off. Them back wheels was squealin' and rattlin' like them little jinger bells. Just past tea-time. Shoppin'. Hockey equipment. Phhht! (*Again,* CREATURE *just misses getting spat on.*)

CREATURE: Ayoah! It's enough to give you the shits every time he opens his mouth.

PIERRE: And they picked me. Referee.

BIG JOEY: And why you, may I ask?

PIERRE: (*Faking humility.*) Oh, I don't know. Somethin' about the referee here's too damn perschnickety. That drum-bangin' young whipperschnapper, Simon Starblanket, (*Grabbing yet another beer.*) he's got the rules all mixed up or somethin' like that, is what they says. They kinda wanna play it their own way. So they picked me. Toast me.

CREATURE: Toast.

PIERRE: To the ref.

CREATURE: To the ref.

PIERRE: Tank you. (*They both drink.*) Ahhh. (*Pause. To* BIG JOEY.) So. I want my skates.

CREATURE: Your skates?

PIERRE: My skates. I want 'em back.

CREATURE: The hell's he talkin' about now?

PIERRE: They're here. I know they're here. I loaned 'em to you, remember?

BIG JOEY: Run that by me again?

PIERRE: I loaned 'em to you. That Saturday night Gazelle Nataways came in that door with her TV and her suitcase and you and me we were sittin' right there on that old chesterfield with Lalala Lacroix sittin' between us and I loaned you my skates in return for that forty-ouncer of rye and Gazelle Nataways plunked her TV down, marched right up to Lalala Lacroix, slapped her in the face and chased her out the door. But we still had time to make the deal whereby if I wanted my skates back you'd give 'em back to me if I gave you back your forty-ouncer, right? Right. (*Produces the bottle from under his coat.*) Ta-da! Gimme my skates.

BIG JOEY: You sold them skates. They're mine.

PIERRE: Never you mind, Big Joey, never you mind. I want my skates. Take this. Go on. Take it.

(BIG JOEY *fishes one skate out from under the couch.*)

CREATURE: (*To himself, as he sits on the couch.*) Women playin' hockey. Ho-leee!

(BIG JOEY *and* PIERRE *exchange bottle and skate.*)

PIERRE: Tank you. (*He makes a triumphant exit.* BIG JOEY *merely sits there and waits knowingly. Silence. Then* PIERRE *suddenly re-enters.*) There's only one. (*Silence.*) Well, where the hell's the other one? (*Silence.* PIERRE *nearly explodes with indignation.*) Gimme back my bottle! Where's the other one?

BIG JOEY: You got your skate. I got my bottle.

PIERRE: Don't talk backwards at me. I'm your elder.

CREATURE: It's gone.

PIERRE: Huh?

CREATURE: Gone. The other skate's gone, right, Big Joey?

PIERRE: Gone? Where?

CREATURE: My wife Gazelle Nataways . . .

PIERRE: . . . your ex-wife . . .

CREATURE: . . . she threw it out the door two years ago the night Spooky Lacroix went crazy in the head and tried to come and rip Gazelle Nataways' door off for cheatin' at the bingo. Just about killed Spooky Lacroix too, right, Big Joey?

PIERRE: So where's my other skate?

CREATURE: At Spooky Lacroix's, I guess.

PIERRE: Aw, shit la marde, you'se guys don't play fair.

BIG JOEY: You go over to Spooky Lacroix's and you tell him I told you you could have your skate back.

PIERRE: No way, José. Spooky Lacroix's gonna preach at me.

BIG JOEY: Preach back.

PIERRE: You come with me. You used to be friends with Spooky Lacroix. You talk to Spooky Lacroix. Spooky Lacroix likes you.

BIG JOEY: He likes you too.

PIERRE: Yeah, but he likes you better. Oh, shit la marde! (*As he takes another beer out of the case.*) And I almost forgot to tell you they decided to make Gazelle Nataways captain of the Wasy Wailerettes. I mean, she kind of . . . decided on her own, if you know what I mean.

BIG JOEY: Spooky Lacroix's waitin' for you.

PIERRE: How do you know?

BIG JOEY: God told me.

PIERRE: (*Pause.* PIERRE *actually wonders to himself. Then:*) Aw, bullshit.

(*Exits. Silence. Then* BIG JOEY *and* CREATURE *look at each other, break down and laugh themselves into prolonged hysterical fits. After a while, they calm down and come to a dead stop. They sit and think. They look at the hockey game on the television. Then, dead serious, they turn to each other.*)

CREATURE: Women . . . Gazelle Nataways . . . hockey? Ho-leee . . .

BIG JOEY: (*Still holding* PIERRE*'s bottle of whiskey.*) Chris'-sakes . . .

(*Fade-out.*)

(*From this darkness emerges the sound of* SPOOKY LACROIX*'s voice, singing with great emotion. As he sings, the lights fade in on his kitchen, where* DICKIE BIRD HALKED *is sitting across the table from* SPOOKY LACROIX. DICKIE BIRD *is scribbling on a piece of paper with a pencil.* SPOOKY *is knitting [pale blue baby booties]. A bible sits on the table to the left of* SPOOKY, *a knitting pattern to his right. The place is covered with knitted doodads: knitted doilies, tea cozy, a tacky picture of "The Last Supper" with knitted frame and, on the wall, as subtly conspicuous as possible, a crucifix with pale blue knitted baby booties covering each of its four extremities. Throughout this scene,* SPOOKY *periodically consults the knitting pattern, wearing tiny little reading glasses, perched "just so" on the end of his nose. He knits with great difficulty and, therefore, with great concentration, sometimes, in moments of excitement, getting the bible and the knitting pattern mixed up with each other. He has tremendous difficulty getting the "disturbed"* DICKIE BIRD *to sit still and pay attention.*)

SPOOKY: (*Singing.*) Everybody oughta know. Everybody oughta know. Who Jesus is. (*Speaking.*) This is it. This is the end. Igwani eeweepoonaskeewuk. (*"The end of the world is at hand."*) Says right here in the book. Very, very, very important to read the book. If you want the Lord to come into your life, Dickie Bird Halked, you've got to read the book. Not much time left. Yessiree. 1990. The last year. This will be the last year of our lives. Clear as a picture. The end of the world is here. At last. About time too, with the world going crazy, people shooting, killing each other left, right and center. Jet planes full of people crashing into the bushes, lakes turning black, fish choking to death. Terrible. Terrible. (DICKIE BIRD *shoves a note he's been scribbling over to* SPOOKY.) What's this? (SPOOKY *reads, with some difficulty.*) "How . . . do . . . you . . . make . . . babies?" (*Shocked.*) Dickie Bird Halked? At your age? Surely. Anyway. That young Starblanket boy who went and shot himself. Right here. Right in the einsteins. Bleeding from the belly, all this white mushy stuff come oozing out. Yuch! Brrr! I guess there's just nothing better to do for the young people on this reserve these days than go around shooting their einsteins out from inside their bellies. But the Lord has had

enough. He's sick of it. No more, he says, no more. This is it. (DICKIE BIRD *shoves another note over.* SPOOKY *pauses to read. And finishes.*) Why, me and Lalala, we're married. And we're gonna have a baby. Period. Now. When the world comes to an end? The sky will open up. The clouds will part. And the Lord will come down in a holy vapor. And only those who are born-again Christian will go with him when he goes back up. And the rest? You know what's gonna happen to the rest? They will die. Big Joey, for instance, they will go to hell and they will burn for their wicked, whorish ways. But we will be taken up into the clouds to spend eternity surrounded by the wondrous and the mystical glory of god. Clear as a picture, Dickie Bird Halked, clear as a picture. So I'm telling you right now, you've got to read the book. Very, very, very important. (DICKIE BIRD *shoves a third note over to* SPOOKY. SPOOKY *reads and finishes.*) Why, Wellington Halked's your father, Dickie Bird Halked. Don't you be asking questions like that. My sister, Black Lady Halked, that's your mother. Right? And because Wellington Halked is married to Black Lady Halked, he is your father. And don't you ever let no one tell you different.

(*Black-out. From the darkness of the theater emerges the magical flickering of a luminescent powwow dancing bustle. As it moves gradually towards the downstage area, a second—and larger—bustle appears on the upper level of the set, also flickering magically and moving about. The two bustles "play" with each other, almost affectionately, looking like two giant fire flies. The smaller bustle finally reaches the downstage area and from behind it emerges the face of* SIMON STARBLANKET. *He is dancing and chanting in a forest made of light and shadows. The larger bustle remains on the upper level; behind it is the entire person of* NANABUSH *as the spirit of* PATSY PEGAHMAGAHBOW, *a vivacious young girl of eighteen with a very big bum (i.e., an over-sized prosthetic bum). From this level,* NANABUSH/PATSY *watches and "plays" with the proceedings on the lower level. The giant full moon is in full bloom behind her. From the very beginning of all this, and in counterpoint to* SIMON*'s chanting, also emerges the sound of someone playing a harmonica, a sad, mournful tune. It is* ZACHARY JEREMIAH KEECHIGEESIK, *stuck in the bush in his embarrassing state, playing his heart out. Then the harmonica stops and, from the darkness, we hear* ZACHARY*'s voice.*)

ZACHARY: Hey. (SIMON *hears this, looks behind, but sees nothing and continues his chanting and dancing.* SIMON *chants and dances as though he were desperately trying to find the right chant and dance. Then:*) Pssst!

SIMON: Awinuk awa? (*"Who's this?"*)

ZACHARY: (*In a hoarse whisper.*) Simon Starblanket.

SIMON: Neee, Zachary Jeremiah Keechigeesik. Awus! ("Go away!") Katha peeweestatooweemin. ("Don't come bothering me [with your words].")

(*Finally,* ZACHARY *emerges from the shadows and from behind a large rock, carrying his harmonica in one hand and holding his torn pants together as best he can with the other.* SIMON *ignores him and continues with his chanting and dancing.*)

I. 428 **Neee** probably the most common Cree expression, meaning something like "Oh, you," or "My goodness"

ZACHARY: W-w-w-what's it cost to get one of them dough-making machines?

SIMON: (*Not quite believing his ears.*) What?

ZACHARY: Them dough-making machines. What's it cost to
435 buy one of them?

SIMON: A Hobart?

ZACHARY: A what?

SIMON: Hobart. H-O-B-A-R-T. Hobart.

ZACHARY: (*To himself.*) Hobart. Hmmm.

440 SIMON: (*Amused at the rather funny-looking* ZACHARY.) Neee, machi ma-a, ("Oh you, but naturally,") Westinghouse for refrigerators, Kellogg's for corn flakes igwa ("and") Hobart for dough-making machines. Kinsitootawin na? ("Get it?") Brand name. Except we used to call it "the pig" because it
445 had this . . . piggish kind of motion to it. But never mind. Awus. Don't bother me.

ZACHARY: What's it cost to get this . . . pig?

SIMON: (*Laughing.*) Neee, Zachary Jeremiah, here you are, one of Wasy's most respected citizens, standing in the middle of
450 the bush on a Saturday night in February freezing your buns off and you want to know how much a pig costs?

ZACHARY: (*Vehemently.*) I promised Hera I'd have all this information by tonight we were supposed to sit down and discuss the budget for this damn bakery tonight and here I went and
455 messed it all up thank god I ran into you because now you're the only person left on this whole reserve who might have the figures I need what's this damn dough-making machine cost come on now tell me!

SIMON: (*A little cowed.*) Neee, about four thousand bucks.
460 Maybe five.

ZACHARY: You don't know for sure? But you worked there.

SIMON: I was only the dishwasher, Zachary Jeremiah, I didn't own the place. Mama Louisa was a poor woman. She had really old equipment, most of which she dragged over herself
465 all the way from Italy after the Second World War. It wouldn't cost the same today.

ZACHARY: Five thousand dollars for a Mobart, hmmm . . .

SIMON: Hobart.

ZACHARY: I wish I had a piece of paper to write all this down,
470 sheesh. You got a piece of paper on you?

SIMON: No. Just . . . this. (*Holding the dancing bustle up.*) Why are you holding yourself like that?

ZACHARY: I was . . . standing on the road down by Andy Manigitogan's place when this car came by and wooof!
475 My pants ripped. Ripped right down the middle. And my shorts, well, they just . . . took off. How do you like that, eh?

SIMON: Nope. I don't like it. Neee, awus. Kigithaskin. ("You're lying to me.")

480 ZACHARY: W-w-w-why would I pull your leg for? I don't really mind it except it is damn cold out here.

(*At this point,* NANABUSH/PATSY, *on the upper level, scurries closer to get a better look, her giant powwow dancing bustle flickering magically in the half-light.* SIMON's *attention is momentarily pulled away by this fleeting vision.*)

SIMON: Hey! Did you see that?

(*But* ZACHARY, *too caught up with his own dilemma, does not notice.*)

ZACHARY: I'm very, very upset right now . . .

SIMON: . . . I thought I just saw Patsy Pegahmagahbow . . . with this . . . 485

ZACHARY: (*As he looks, perplexed, in the direction* SIMON *indicates.*) . . . do you think . . . my two ordinary convection ovens . . .

SIMON: (*Calling out.*) Patsy? . . . (*Pause. Then, slowly, he turns back to* ZACHARY.) . . . like . . . she made this for me, eh? (*Referring to the bustle.*) She and her step-mother, Rosie Kakapetum, 490 back in September, after my mother's funeral. Well, I was out here thinking, if this . . . like, if this . . . dance didn't come to me real natural, like from deep inside of me, then I was gonna burn it. (*Referring to the bustle.*) Right here on this spot. Cuz then . . . it doesn't mean anything real to me, does it? 495 Like, it's false . . . it's driving me crazy, this dream where Indian people are just dropping off like flies . . .

(NANABUSH/PATSY *begins to "play" with the two men, almost as if with the help of the winter night's magic and the power of the full moon, she were weaving a spell around* SIMON *and* ZACHARY.)

ZACHARY: (*Singing softly to himself.*) Hot cross buns. Hot cross buns. One a penny, two a penny, hot cross buns . . .

SIMON: . . . something has to be done . . . 500

ZACHARY: (*Speaking.*) . . . strawberry pies . . .

SIMON: . . . in this dream . . .

ZACHARY: . . . so fresh and flakey they fairly bubble over with the cream from the very breast of Mother Nature herself . . .

SIMON: . . . the drum has to come back, mistigwuskeek ("the 505 drum") . . .

ZACHARY: . . . bran muffins, cherry tarts . . .

SIMON: . . . the medicine, the power, this . . .

(*Holding the bustle up in the air.*)

ZACHARY: . . . butter tarts . . .

SIMON: . . . has to come back. We've got to learn to dance again. 510

ZACHARY: . . . tarts tarts tarts upside-down cakes cakes cakes and not to forget, no, never, ever to forget that Black Forest Cake . . .

SIMON: . . . Patsy Pegahmagahbow . . .

ZACHARY: . . . cherries jubilee . . . 515

SIMON: . . . her step-mother, Rosie Kakapetum, the medicine woman . . .

ZACHARY: . . . lemon meringue pie . . .

SIMON: . . . the power . . .

ZACHARY: . . . baked Alaska . . . 520

SIMON: . . . Nanabush! . . .

ZACHARY: (*Then suddenly, with bitterness.*) . . . Gazelle Nataways. K'skanagoos! ("The female dog!")

(*All of a sudden, from the darkness of the winter night, emerges a strange, eery sound; whether it is wolves howling or women wailing, we are not sure at first. And whether this sound comes from somewhere deep in the forest, from the full moon or where, we are not certain. But there is definitely a "spirit" in the air. The sound of this wailing is under-cut by the sound of rocks hitting boards, or the sides of houses, echoing, as in a vast empty chamber. Gradually, as* SIMON *speaks,* ZACHARY—*filled with confusing emotion as he is—takes out his harmonica, sits down on the large rock and begins to play, a sad, mournful melody, tinged, as always, with a touch of the blues.*)

SIMON: I have my arms around this rock, this large black rock sticking out of the ground, right here on this spot. And then I hear this baby crying, from inside this rock. The baby is crying out my name. As if I am somehow responsible for it being caught inside that rock. I can't move. My arms, my whole body, stuck to this rock. Then this . . . eagle . . . lands beside me, right over there. But this bird has three faces, three women. And the eagle says to me: "the baby is crying, my grand-child is crying to hear the drum again." (NANABUSH/PATSY, *her face surrounded by the brilliant feathers of her bustle, so that she looks like some fantastic, mysterious bird, begins to wail, her voice weaving in and out of the other wailing voices.*) There's this noise all around us, as if rocks are hitting the sides of houses—echoing and echoing like in a vast empty room—and women are wailing. The whole world is filled with this noise. (*Then* SIMON, *too, wails, a heart-searing wail. From here on, all the wailing begins to fade.*) Then the eagle is gone and the rock cracks and this mass of flesh, covered with veins and blood, comes oozing out and a woman's voice somewhere is singing something about angels and god and angels and god . . .

(*The wailing has now faded into complete silence.* ZACHARY *finally rises from his seat on the rock.*)

ZACHARY: I dreamt I woke up at Gazelle Nataways' place with no shorts on. And I got this nagging suspicion them shorts are still over there. If you could just go on over there now . . . I couldn't have been over there. I mean, there's my wife Hera. And there's my bakery. And this bakery could do a lot for the Indian people. Economic development. Jobs. Bread. Apple pie. So you see, there's an awful lot that's hanging on them shorts. This is a good chance for you to do something for your people, Simon, if you know what I mean . . .

SIMON: I'm the one who has to bring the drum back. And it's Patsy's medicine power, that stuff she's learning from her step-mother Rosie Kakapetum that . . . helps me . . .

ZACHARY: I go walking into my house with no underwear, pants ripped right down the middle, not a shred of budget in sight and wooof! . . .

(PIERRE ST. PIERRE *comes bursting in on the two men with his one skate in hand, taking them completely by surprise.* NANABUSH/PATSY *disappears.*)

ZACHARY: Pierre St. Pierre! Just the man . . .

PIERRE: No time. No time. Lalala Lacroix's having a baby any minute now so I gotta get over to Spook's before she pops.

SIMON: I can go get Rosie Kakapetum.

PIERRE: Too old. Too old. She can't be on the team.

SIMON: Neee, what team? Rosie Kakapetum's the last mid-wife left in Wasy, Pierre St. Pierre, of course she can't be on a team.

ZACHARY: (*To* PIERRE.) You know that greasy shit-brown chesterfield over at Gazelle Nataways?

SIMON: (*To* ZACHARY.) Mind you, if there was a team of mid-wives, chee-i? ("eh?") Wha!

PIERRE: Gazelle Nataways? Hallelujah, haven't you heard the news?

ZACHARY: What? . . . you mean . . . it's out already?

PIERRE: All up and down Wasaychigan Hill . . .

ZACHARY: (*Thoughtfully, to himself, as it dawns on him.*) The whole place knows.

PIERRE: clean across Manitoulin Island and right to the outskirts of Sudbury . . .

ZACHARY: Lordy, lordy, lordy . . .

PIERRE: Gazelle Nataways, Dominique Ladouche, Black Lady Halked, that terrible Dictionary woman, Fluffy Sainte-Marie, Dry Lips Manigitogan, Leonarda Lee Starblanket, Annie Cook, June Bug McLeod, Big Bum Pegahmagahbow . . .

SIMON: Patsy Pegahmagahbow. Get it straight . . .

PIERRE: Quiet! I'm not finished . . . all twenty-seven of 'em . . .

SIMON: Neee, Zachary Jeremiah, your goose is cooked.

PIERRE: Phhht! Cooked and burnt right down to a nice crispy pitch black cinder because your wife Hera Keechigeesik is in on it too.

(ZACHARY, *reeling from the horror of it all, finally sits back down on the rock.*)

SIMON: Patsy Pegahmagahbow is pregnant, Pierre St. Pierre. She can't go running around all over Manitoulin Island with a belly that's getting bigger by the . . .

SIMON: Aw, they're all pregnant, them women, or have piles and piles of babies and I'll be right smack dab in the middle of it all just a-blowin' my whistle and a-throwin' that dirty little black thingie around . . .

ZACHARY: (*Rising from the rock.*) Now you listen here, Pierre St. Pierre. I may have lost my shorts under Gazelle Nataways' greasy shit-brown chesterfield not one hour ago and I may have lost my entire life, not to mention my bakery, as a result of that one very foolish mistake but I'll have you know that my shorts, they are clean as a whistle, I change them every day, my favorite color is light blue and black and crusted with shit my shorts most certainly are not!

SIMON: (*Surprised and thrilled at* ZACHARY's *renewed "fighting" spirit.*) Wha!

PIERRE: Whoa! Easy, Zachary Jeremiah, easy there. Not one stitch of your shorts has anything whatsoever to do with the revolution.

SIMON: Pierre St. Pierre, what revolution are you wheezing and snorting on about?

PIERRE: The puck. I'm talkin' about the puck.

ZACHARY: The puck?

SIMON: The puck?

PIERRE: Yes, the puck. The puck, the puck, the puck and nothin' but the goddam puck they're playin' hockey, them women from right here on this reserve, they're playin' hockey and nothin', includin' Zachary Jeremiah Keechigeesik's bright crispy undershorts, is gonna stop 'em.

SIMON: Women playing hockey. Neee, watstagatch! ("Good grief!")

PIERRE: "Neee, watstagatch" is right because they're in Sudbury, as I speak, shoppin' for hockey equipment, and I'm the referee! Outa my way! Or the Lacroixs will pop before I get there.

(*He begins to exit.*)

ZACHARY: Pierre St. Pierre, get me my shorts or I'll report your bootleg joint to the police.

630   PIERRE: No time. No time.

(*Exits.*)

ZACHARY: (*Calling out.*) Did Hera go to Sudbury, too? (*But
       PIERRE is gone.*)
SIMON: (*Thoughtfully to himself, as he catches another glimpse of
       NANABUSH/PATSY and her bustle.*) . . . rocks hitting boards . . .
635   ZACHARY: (*To himself.*) What in God's name is happening to
       Wasaychigan Hill . . .
SIMON: women wailing . . .
ZACHARY: (*With even greater urgency.*) Do you think those two or-
       dinary convection ovens are gonna do the job or should I
640   get one of them great big pizza ovens right away?
SIMON: . . . pucks . . .
ZACHARY: Simon, I'm desperate!
SIMON: (*Finally, snapping out of his speculation and looking straight
       into ZACHARY's face.*) Neee, Zachary Jeremiah. Okay. Goes
645   like this. (*Then, very quickly:*) It depends on what you're
       gonna bake, eh? Like if you're gonna bake bread and, like,
       lots of it, you're gonna need one of them great big ovens but
       if you're gonna bake just muffins . . .
ZACHARY: (*In the background.*) . . . muffins, nah, not just
650   muffins . . .
SIMON: . . . then all you need is one of them ordinary little
       ovens but like I say, I was only the dishwasher . . .
ZACHARY: How many employees were there in your bakery?
SIMON: . . . it depends on how big a community you're gonna
655   serve, Zachary Jeremiah . . .
ZACHARY: . . . nah, Wasy, just Wasy, to start with . . .
SIMON: . . . like, we had five, one to make the dough—like,
       mix the flour and the water and the yeast and all that—
       like, this guy had to be at work by six A.M., that's gonna
660   be hard here in Wasy, Zachary Jeremiah, I'm telling you
       that right now . . .
ZACHARY: . . . nah, I can do that myself, no problem . . .
SIMON: . . . then we had three others to roll the dough and
       knead and twist and punch and pound it on this great big
665   wooden table . . .
ZACHARY: . . . I'm gonna need a great big wooden table? . . .
SIMON: . . . hard wood, Zachary Jeremiah, not soft wood. And
       then one to actually bake the loaves, like, we had these long
       wooden paddles, eh? . . .
670   ZACHARY: . . . paddles . . .
SIMON: . . . yeah, paddles, Zachary Jeremiah, real long ones. It
       was kinda neat, actually . . .
ZACHARY: . . . go on, go on . . .
SIMON: Listen here, Zachary Jeremiah, I'm going to Sudbury
675   next Saturday, okay? And if you wanna come along, I can
       take you straight to Mama Louisa's Pasticceria myself. I'll
       introduce you to the crusty old girl and you can take a good
       long look at her rubbery old Hobart, how's that? You can
       even touch it if you want, neee . . .
680   ZACHARY: . . . really? . . .
SIMON: Me? I'm asking Patsy Pegahmagahbow to marry me . . .
ZACHARY: . . . Simon, Simon . . .
SIMON: . . . and we're gonna hang two thousand of these
       things (*Referring to his dancing bustle.*) all over Manitoulin
685   Island, me and Patsy and our baby. And me and Patsy and
       our baby and this Nanabush character, we're gonna be

dancing up and down Wasaychigan Hill like nobody's
business cuz I'm gonna go out there and I'm gonna bring
that drum back if it kills me.
ZACHARY: (*Pause. Then, quietly.*) Get me a safety pin.   690
SIMON: (*Pause.*) Neee, okay. And you, Zachary Jeremiah
       Keechigeesik, you're gonna see a Hobart such as you have
       never seen ever before in your entire life!
SIMON/ZACHARY: (*Smiling, almost laughing, at each other.*) Neee . . .

(*Black-out.*)

(*Lights up on the upper level, where we see this bizarre vision of
NANABUSH, now in the guise of BLACK LADY HALKED, nine months
pregnant [i.e., wearing a huge, out-sized prosthetic belly]. Over this,
she wears a maternity gown and, pacing the floor slowly, holds a huge
string of rosary beads. She recites the rosary quietly to herself. She is
also drinking a beer and, obviously, is a little unsteady on her feet because of this.*)

(*Fade-in on the lower level into SPOOKY LACROIX's kitchen. DICKIE
BIRD HALKED is on his knees, praying fervently to this surrealistic,
miraculous vision of "the Madonna" [i.e., his own mother], which he
actually sees inside his own mind. Oblivious to all this, SPOOKY
LACROIX sits at his table, still knitting his baby booties and preaching away.*)

SPOOKY: Dickie Bird Halked? I want you to come to heaven   695
       with me. I insist. But before you do that, you take one of
       them courses in sign language, help me prepare this reserve
       for the Lord. Can't you just see yourself, standing on that
       podium in the Wasaychigan Hill Hippodrome, talking
       sign language to the people? Talking about the Lord and   700
       how close we are to the end? I could take a break. And these
       poor people with their meaningless, useless . . .

(*PIERRE ST. PIERRE comes bursting in and marches right up to SPOOKY.
The vision of NANABUSH/BLACK LADY HALKED disappears.*)

PIERRE: Alright. Hand it over.
SPOOKY: (*Startled out of his wits.*) Pierre St. Pierre! You went and
       mixed up my booty!   705
PIERRE: I know it's here somewhere.
SPOOKY: Whatever it is you're looking for, you're not getting it
       until you bring the Lord into your life.
PIERRE: My skate. Gimme my skate.
SPOOKY: I don't have no skate. Now listen to me.   710
PIERRE: My skate. The skate Gazelle Nataways threw at you
       and just about killed you.
SPOOKY: What the hell are you gonna do with a skate at this
       hour of the night?
PIERRE: Haven't you heard the news?   715
SPOOKY: (*Pauses to think.*) No, I haven't heard any news.

(*DICKIE BIRD gets up and starts to wander around the kitchen. He
looks around at random, first out the window, as if to see who has been
chanting, then, eventually, he zeroes in on the crucifix on the wall and
stands there looking at it. Finally, he takes it off the wall and plays
with its cute little booties.*)

PIERRE: The women. I'm gonna be right smack dab in the mid-
       dle of it all. The revolution. Right here in Wasaychigan Hill.

SPOOKY: The Chief or the priest. Which one are they gonna
720   revolution?

PIERRE: No, no, no. Dominique Ladouche, Black Lady Halked, that terrible Dictionary woman, that witch Gazelle Nataways, Fluffy Sainte-Marie, Dry Lips Manigitogan, Leonarda Lee Starblanket, Annie Cook, June Bug McLeod, Big Bum
725   Pegahmagahbow, all twenty-seven of 'em. Even my wife, Veronique St. Pierre, she'll be right smack dab in the middle of it all. Defense.

SPOOKY: Defense? The Americans. We're being attacked. Is the situation that serious?

730 PIERRE: No, no, no, for Chris'sakes. They're playin' hockey. Them women are playin' hockey. Dead serious they are too.

SPOOKY: No.

PIERRE: Yes.

SPOOKY: Thank the Lord this is the last year!

735 PIERRE: Don't you care to ask?

SPOOKY: Thank the Lord the end of the world is coming this year!

(*Gasping, he marches up to* DICKIE BIRD.)

PIERRE: I'm the referee, dammit.

SPOOKY: Watch your language.

(*Grabbing the crucifix from* DICKIE BIRD.)

740 PIERRE: That's what I mean when I say I'm gonna be right smack dab in the middle of it all. You don't listen to me.

SPOOKY: (*As he proceeds to put the little booties back on the crucifix.*) But you're not a woman.

PIERRE: You don't have to be. To be a referee these days, you can
745   be anything, man or woman, don't matter which away. So gimme my skate.

SPOOKY: What skate?

PIERRE: The skate Gazelle Nataways just about killed you with after the bingo that time.

750 SPOOKY: Oh, that. I hid it in the basement. (PIERRE *opens a door, falls in and comes struggling out with a mouse trap stuck to a finger.*) Pierre St. Pierre, what the hell are you doing in Lalala's closet?

PIERRE: Well, where the hell's the basement?

(*He frees his finger.*)

755 SPOOKY: Pierre St. Pierre, you drink too much. You gotta have the Lord in your life.

PIERRE: I don't need the Lord in my life, for god's sake, I need my skate. I gotta practice my figure eights.

SPOOKY: (*As he begins to put the crucifix back up on the wall.*) You
760   gotta promise me before I give you your skate.

PIERRE: I promise.

SPOOKY: (*Unaware, he threatens* PIERRE *with the crucifix, holding it up against his neck.*) You gotta have the Lord come into your life.

765 PIERRE: Alright, alright.

SPOOKY: For how long?

PIERRE: My whole life. I promise I'm gonna bring the Lord into my life and keep him there right up until the day I die just gimme my goddamn skate.

770 SPOOKY: Cross my heart.

PIERRE: Alright? Cross your heart.

(*Neither man makes a move, until* SPOOKY, *finally catching on, throws* PIERRE *a look.* PIERRE *crosses himself.*)

SPOOKY: Good.

(*Exits to the basement.*)

PIERRE: (*Now alone with* DICKIE BIRD, *half-whispering to him. As* PIERRE *speaks,* DICKIE BIRD *again takes the crucifix off the wall and returns with it to his seat and there takes the booties off in* 775 *haphazard fashion.*) Has he been feedin' you this crappola, too? Don't you be startin' that foolishness. That Spooky Lacroix's so fulla shit he wouldn't know a two thousand year-old Egyptian Sphinxter if he came face to face with one. He's just preachifyin' at you because you're the one 780 person on this reserve who can't argue back. You listen to me. I was there in the same room as your mother when she gave birth to you. So I know well who you are and where you come from. I remember the whole picture. Even though we were all in a bit of a fizzy . . . I remember. Do 785 you know, Dickie Bird Halked, that you were named after that bar? Anyone ever tell you that? (DICKIE BIRD *starts to shake.* PIERRE *takes fright.*) Spooky Lacroix, move that holy ass of yours, for fuck's sakes! (DICKIE BIRD *laughs.* PIERRE *makes a weak attempt to laugh along.*) And I'll never forgive 790 your father, Big Joey oops . . . (DICKIE BIRD *reacts.*) . . . I mean, Wellington Halked, for letting your mother do that to you. "It's not good for the people of this world," I says to him "it's not good for 'em to have the first thing they see when they come into the world is a goddamn jukebox." 795 That's what I says to him. Thank god, you survived, Dickie Bird Halked, thank god, seventeen years later you're sittin' here smack-dab in front of me, hail and hearty as cake. Except for your tongue. Talk, Dickie Bird Halked, talk. Say somethin'. Come on. Try this: "Daddy, daddy, daddy." 800 (DICKIE BIRD *shakes his head.*) Come on. Just this once. Maybe it will work. (*Takes* DICKIE BIRD *by the cheeks with one hand.*) "Daddy, daddy, daddy, daddy." (DICKIE BIRD *jumps up and attacks* PIERRE, *looking as though he were about to shove the crucifix down* PIERRE's *throat.* PIERRE *is genuinely terrified. Just* 805 *then,* SPOOKY *reenters with the skate.*) Whoa, whoa. Easy. Easy now, Dickie Bird. Easy.

SPOOKY: (*Gasping again at the sight of* DICKIE BIRD *man-handling the crucifix, he makes a bee-line for the boy.*) Dickie Bird Halked? Give me that thing. (*And grabs the crucifix with a* 810 *flourish. Then he turns to* PIERRE *and holds the skate out with his other hand.*) Promise.

PIERRE: Cross my heart. (*Crosses himself.*)

SPOOKY: (*Replacing the crucifix on the wall and pointing at* PIERRE.) The Lord. 815

PIERRE: The Lord.

(SPOOKY *hands the skate over to* PIERRE. *Just then,* CREATURE NAT-AWAYS *stumbles in, now visibly drunk.*)

CREATURE: The Lord!

(*Picking on the hapless* DICKIE BIRD, CREATURE *roughly shoves the boy down to a chair.*)

PIERRE: (*Holding up both his skates.*) I got 'em both. See? I got 'em.

820 CREATURE: Hallelujah! Now all you gotta do is learn how to skate.

SPOOKY: Creature Nataways, I don't want you in my house in that condition. Lalala is liable to pop any minute now and I don't want my son to see the first thing he sees when he 825 comes into the world is a drunk.

PIERRE: Damn rights!

SPOOKY: . . . you too, Pierre St. Pierre.

CREATURE: Aw! William Lacroix, don't give me that holier than-me, poker-up-the-bum spiritual bull crap . . .

830 SPOOKY: . . . say wha? . . .

CREATURE: Are you preachin' to this boy, William Lacroix? Are you usin' him again to practice your preachy-preachy? Don't do that, William, the boy is helpless. If you wanna practice, go practice on your old buddy, go preach on Big 835 Joey. He's the one who needs it.

SPOOKY: You're hurting again, aren't you, Creature Nataways.

CREATURE: Don't listen to Spooky Lacroix, Dickie Bird. You follow Spooky Lacroix and you go right down to the dogs, I'm tellin' you that right now. Hair spray, Lysol, vanilla ex-840 tract, shoe polish, Xerox machine juice, he's done it all, this man. If you'd given William Lacroix the chance, he'd have sliced up the Xerox machine and ate it . . .

PIERRE: (*Mockingly, in the background.*) No!

CREATURE: . . . He once drank a Kitty Wells record. He lied 845 to his own mother and he stole her record and he boiled it and swallowed it right up . . .

PIERRE: Good heavens!

(BIG JOEY *enters and stands at the door unseen.*)

CREATURE: Made the Globe and Mail, too. He's robbed, he's cheated his best friend . . .

850 SPOOKY: Alphonse Nataways? Why are you doing this, may I ask?

CREATURE: Oh, he was bad, Dickie Bird Halked, he was bad. Fifteen years. Fifteen years of his life pukin' his guts out on sidewalks from here to Sicamous, B.C., this man . . .

SPOOKY: Shush!

855 CREATURE: and this is the same man . . .

BIG JOEY: (*Speaking suddenly and laughing, he takes everyone by surprise. They gasp. And practically freeze in their tracks.*) . . . who's yellin' and preachin' about "the Lord!" They oughta retire the beaver and put this guy on the Canadian nickel, 860 he's become a national goddamn symbol, that what you're sayin', Creature Nataways? This the kind of man you wanna become, that what you're sayin' to the boy, Creature Nataways? (*Close up to* DICKIE BIRD.) A man who couldn't get a hard-on in front of a woman if you paid him a two 865 dollar bill?

SPOOKY: (*Stung to the quick.*) And is this the kind of man you wanna become, Dickie Bird Halked, this MAN who can't take the sight of blood least of all woman's blood, this MAN who, when he sees a woman's blood, chokes up, 870 pukes and faints, how do you like that?

(PIERRE, *sensing potential violence, begins to sneak out.*)

BIG JOEY: (*Pulls a bottle out of his coat.*) Spooky Lacroix, igwani eeweepoonaskeewuk. ("The end of the world is at hand.")

(PIERRE, *seeing the bottle, retraces his steps and sits down again, grabbing a tea-cup en route, ready for a drink.*)

SPOOKY: (*Shocked.*) Get that thing out of my house!

BIG JOEY: Tonight, we're gonna celebrate my wife, Spooky Lacroix, we're gonna celebrate because my wife, the fabu-875 lous, the incredible Gazelle Delphina Nataways has been crowned Captain of the Wasy Wailerettes. The Rez is makin' history, Spooky Lacroix. The world will never be the same. Come on, it's on me, it's on your old buddy, the old, old buddy you said you'd never, ever forget. 880

SPOOKY: I told you a long time ago, Big Joey, after what you went and done to my sister, this here boy's own mother, you're no buddy of mine. Get out of my house. Get!

BIG JOEY: (*Handing the bottle of whiskey to* CREATURE.) Creature Nataways, celebrate your wife. 885

CREATURE: (*Raising the bottle in a toast.*) To my wife!

PIERRE: (*Holding his cup out to the bottle.*) Your ex-wife.

BIG JOEY: (*Suddenly quiet and intimate.*) William. William. You and me. You and me, we used to be buddies, kigiskisin? ("Remember?") Wounded Knee. South Dakota. Spring of 890 '73. We parked my van over by that little lake, we swam across, you almost didn't make it and nothin' could get you to swim back. Kigiskisin? So here we're walkin' back through the bush, all the way around this small lake, nothin' on but bare feet and wet undershorts and this black 895 bear come up behind you, kigiskisin? And you freaked out.

(*Laughs.* PIERRE *tries, as best he can, to create a party atmosphere, to little avail.* CREATURE *nervously watches* BIG JOEY *and* SPOOKY. DICKIE BIRD *merely sits there, head down, rocking back and forth.*)

SPOOKY: (*Obviously extremely uncomfortable.*) You freaked out too, ha-ha, ha-ha.

BIG JOEY: That bear gave you a real spook, huh? (*Pause. Then, suddenly, he jumps at the other men.*) Boo! (*The other men, in-900 cluding* SPOOKY, *jump, splashing whiskey all over the place.* BIG JOEY *laughs. The other men pretend to laugh.*) That's how you got your name, you old Spook . . .

SPOOKY: You were scared too, ha-ha, ha-ha.

BIG JOEY: . . . we get back to the camp and there's Creature 905 and Eugene and Zach and Roscoe, bacon and eggs all ready for us. Christ, I never laughed so hard in my life. But here you were, not laughin' and we'd say: "What's the matter, Spook, you don't like our jokes? And you'd say: "That's good, yeah, that's good." I guess you were laughin' from a 910 different part of yourself, huh? You were beautiful . . .

SPOOKY: That's good, yeah, that's good.

BIG JOEY: (*Getting the bottle back from* CREATURE *and* PIERRE.) So tonight, Bear-who-went-and-gave-you-a-real-Spooky Lacroix, we're gonna celebrate another new page in our lives. 915 Wounded Knee Three! Women's version!

PIERRE: Damn rights.

BIG JOEY: (*Raising the bottle up in a toast.*) To my wife!

SPOOKY: Ha! Get that thing away from me.

PIERRE: Spooky Lacroix, co-operate. Co-operate for once. The 920 women, the women are playin' hockey.

CREATURE: To my wife!

PIERRE: Your ex-wife.

CREATURE: Shut up you toothless old bugger.

SPOOKY: Big Joey, you're not my friend no more. 925

BIG JOEY: (*Finally grabbing* SPOOKY *roughly by the throat.* CREATURE *jumps to help hold* SPOOKY *still.*) You never let a friend for life go, William Hector Lacroix, not even if you turn your back on your own father, Nicotine Lacroix's spiritual teachings

930   and pretend like hell to be this born-again Christian.

SPOOKY: Let go, Creature Nataways, let go of me! (*To* BIG JOEY.) For what you did to this boy at that bar seventeen years ago, Joseph Jeremiah McLeod, you are going to hell. To hell!

935   (BIG JOEY *baptizes* SPOOKY *with the remainder of the bottle's contents. Breaking free,* SPOOKY *grabs* DICKIE BIRD *and shoves him toward* BIG JOEY.) Look at him. He can't even talk. He hasn't talked in seventeen years! (DICKIE BIRD *cries out, breaks free, grabs the crucifix from off the wall and runs out the door, crying.* SPOOKY *breaks down, falls to the floor and weeps.* BIG JOEY *at-*

940   *tempts to pick him up gently, but* SPOOKY *kicks him away.*) Let go of me! Let go!

CREATURE: (*Lifting the empty bottle, laughing and crying at the same time.*) To my wife, to my wife, to my wife, to my wife, to my wife . . .

(BIG JOEY *suddenly lifts* SPOOKY *off the floor by the collar and lifts a fist to punch his face. Black-out.*)

(*Out of this black-out emerges the eery, distant sound of women wailing and pucks hitting boards, echoing and echoing as in a vast empty chamber. The lights come up on* DICKIE BIRD HALKED *and* SIMON STARBLANKET, *standing beside each other in the "bleachers" of the hockey arena, watching the "ice" area (i.e., looking out over the audience). The "bleachers" area is actually on the upper level of the set, in a straight line directly in front of* NANABUSH's *perch.* DICKIE BIRD *is still holding* SPOOKY's *crucifix and* SIMON *is still holding his dancing bustle.*)

945 SIMON: Your grandpa, Nicotine Lacroix, was a medicine man. Hell of a name, but he was a medicine man. Old priest here, Father Boucher, years ago—oh, he was a terrible man—he went and convinced the people old Nicotine Lacroix talked to the devil. That's not true. Nicotine Lacroix was a good

950   man. That's why I want you for my best man. Me and Patsy are getting married a couple of months from now. It's decided. We're gonna have a baby. Then we're going down to South Dakota and we're gonna dance with the Rosebud Sioux this summer. (*Sings as he stomps his foot in the rhythm of*

955   *a powwow drum.*) " . . . and me I don't wanna go to the moon, I'm gonna leave that moon alone. I just wanna dance with the Rosebud Sioux this summer, yeah, yeah, yeah . . . "

(*And he breaks into a chant.* DICKIE BIRD *watches, fascinated, particularly by the bustle* SIMON *holds up in the air.*)

(*At this point,* ZACHARY JEREMIAH KEECHIGEESIK *approaches timidly from behind a beam, his pants held flimsily together with a huge safety pin. The sound of women wailing and pucks hitting boards now shifts into the sound of an actual hockey arena, just before a big game.*)

ZACHARY: (*To* SIMON.) Hey! (*But* SIMON *doesn't hear and continues chanting.*) Pssst!

960 SIMON: Zachary Jeremiah. Neee, watstagatch!

ZACHARY: Is Hera out there?

SIMON: (*Indicating the "ice."*) Yup. There she is.

ZACHARY: Lordy, lordy, lordy . . .

SIMON: Just kidding. She's not out there . . .

ZACHARY: Don't do that to me!   965

SIMON: . . . yet.

ZACHARY: (*Finally coming up to join the young men at the "bleachers."*) You know that Nanabush character you were telling me about a couple of nights ago? What do you say I give his name over to them little gingerbread cookie men I'm   970 gonna be making? For starters. Think that would help any?

SIMON: Neee . . .

(*Just then,* BIG JOEY *enters and proceeds to get a microphone stand ready for broadcasting the game.* ZACHARY *recoils and goes to stand as far away from him as possible.*)

ZACHARY: (*Looking out over the "ice."*) It's almost noon. They're late getting started.

BIG JOEY: (*Yawning luxuriously.*) That's right. Me and Gazelle   975 Nataways . . . slept in.

(CREATURE NATAWAYS *comes scurrying in.*)

CREATURE: (*Still talking to himself.*) . . . I tole you once I tole you twice . . . (*Then to the other men.*) Chris' sakes! Are they really gonna do it? Chris'sakes!

(SPOOKY LACROIX *enters wearing a woolen scarf he obviously knitted himself. He is still knitting, this time a pale blue baby sweater. He also now sports a black eye and band-aide on his face. All the men, except* PIERRE ST. PIERRE, *are now in the "bleachers," standing in a straight line facing the audience, with* DICKIE BIRD *in the center area,* SIMON *and* SPOOKY *to his immediate right and left, respectively.*)

SPOOKY: It's bad luck to start late. I know. I read the interview   980 with Gay Lafleur in last week's Expositor. They won't get far. (*He sees* GAZELLE NATAWAYS *entering the "rink," unseen by the audience.* [*All the hockey players on the "ice" are unseen by the audience; it is only the men who can actually "see" them.*]) Look! Gazelle Nataways went and got her sweater trimmed in the   985 chest area!

(*Wild cat calls from the men.*)

CREATURE: Trimmed it? She's got it plunging down to her ootsee. ("belly button.")

ZACHARY: Ahem. Smokes too much. Lung problems.

BIG JOEY: Nah. More like it's got somethin' to do with the un-   990 dershorts she's wearin' today.

ZACHARY: (*Fast on the up-take.*) Fuck you!

BIG JOEY: (*Blowing* ZACHARY *a kiss.*) Poosees. ("Pussy cat." [*Zachary's childhood nickname.*])

SPOOKY: Terrible. Terrible. Tsk, tsk, tsk.   995

(PIERRE ST. PIERRE *enters on the lower level, teetering dangerously on his skates towards the "ice" area downstage. He wears a referee's top and a whistle around his neck.*)

PIERRE: (*Checking the names off as he reads from a clipboard.*) Dominique Ladouche, Black Lady Halked, Annie Cook, June Bug McLeod, Big Bum Pegahmagahbow . . .

SIMON: (*Calling out.*) Patsy Pegahmagahbow, turkey.

1000 PIERRE: Shut up. I'm workin' here. . . . Leonarda Lee Starblan-ket, that terrible Dictionary woman, Fluffy Sainte-Marie, Chicken Lips Pegahmagahbow, Dry Lips Manigitogan, Lit-tle Hand Manigitogan, Little Girl Manitowabi, Victoria Manitowabi, Belinda Nickikoosimeenicaning, Martha
1005 Two-Axe Early-in-the-Morning, her royal highness Gazelle Delphina Nataways, Delia Opekokew, Barbra Nahwegah-bow, Gloria May Eshkibok, Hera Keechigeesik, Tall Mary Ann Patchnose, Short Mary Ann Patchnose, Queen Eliza-beth Patchnose, the triplets Marjorie Moose, Maggie May
1010 Moose, Mighty Moose and, of course, my wife, Veronique St. Pierre. Yup. They're all there, I hope, and the world is about to explode!
   SPOOKY: That's what I've been trying to tell you!

(PIERRE ST. PIERRE, *barely able to stand on his skates, hobbles about, obviously getting almost trampled by the hockey players at various times.*)

   BIG JOEY: (*Now speaking on the microphone. The other men watch the women on the "ice"; some are cheering and whistling, some calling
1015 down the game.*) Welcome, ladies igwa gentlemen, welcome one and all to the Wasaychigan Hill Hip-hip-hippodrome. This is your host for the big game, Big Joey—and they don't call me Big Joey for nothin'—Chairman, CEO and Proprietor of the Wasaychigan Hill Hippodrome, bringin'
1020 you a game such as has never been seen ever before on the ice of any hockey arena anywhere on the island of Manitoulin, anywhere on the face of this country, anywhere on the face of this planet. And there . . .
   CREATURE: . . . there's Gazelle Nataways, number one . . .
1025 BIG JOEY: . . . they are, ladies . . .
   SPOOKY: . . . terrible, terrible . . .
   BIG JOEY: . . . igwa gentlemen . . .
   CREATURE: . . . Chris'sakes, that's my wife, Chris'sakes . . .
   BIG JOEY: . . . there they are, the most beautiful . . .
1030 SIMON: . . . give 'em hell, Patsy Pegahmagahbow, give 'em hell . . .
   BIG JOEY: . . . daring, death- . . .
   SIMON: (*To* ZACHARY.) . . . there's Hera Keechigeesik, number nine . . .
1035 BIG JOEY: . . . defying Indian women . . .
   SPOOKY: . . . terrible, terrible . . .
   BIG JOEY: . . . in the world . . .
   ZACHARY: . . . that's my wife . . .
   BIG JOEY: . . . the Wasy Wailerettes . . .

(*Clears his throat and tests the microphone by tapping it gently.*)

1040 ZACHARY: . . . lordy, lordy, lordy . . .
   CREATURE: Hey, Gazelle Nataways and Hera Keechigeesik are lookin' at each other awful funny. Something bad's gonna happen, I tole you once I tole you twice, something bad's gonna happen . . .
1045 SPOOKY: This is sign from the Lord. This is THE sign . . .
   BIG JOEY: Number One Gazelle Nataways, Captain of the Wasy Wailerettes, facing off with Number Nine, Flora McDon-ald, Captain of the Canoe Lake Bravettes. And referee Pierre St. Pierre drops the puck and takes off like a herd of wild
1050 turtles . . .
   SIMON: Aw, Spooky Lacroix, eat my shitty shorts, neee . . .

BIG JOEY: . . . Hey, aspin Number Six Dry Lips Manigitogan, right-winger for the Wasy Wailerettes . . .
   ZACHARY: . . . look pretty damn stupid, if you ask me. Fifteen thousand dollars for all that new equipment . . .
   BIG JOEY: . . . eemaskamat Number Thirteen of the Canoe 1055 Lake Bravettes anee-i puck . . .
   CREATURE: . . . Cancel the game! Cancel the game! Cancel the game! . . .

(*Etc.*)

   BIG JOEY: . . . igwa aspin sipweesinskwataygew. Hey, k'see 1060 goochin! (*Off microphone.*) Creature Nataways. Shut up. (*To the other men.*) Get this asshole out of here. . . .
   SIMON: Yay, Patsy Pegahmagahbow! Pat-see! Pat-see! Pat-see! . . .

(*Etc.*)

   BIG JOEY: (*Back on microphone.*) . . . How, Number Six Dry Lips Manigitogan, right-winger for the Wasy Wailerettes, 1065 soogi pugamawew igwa anee-i puck igwa aspin center-line ispathoo ana puck . . .
   CREATURE: (*To* SIMON.) Shut up. Don't encourage them . . .
   BIG JOEY: . . . ita Number Nine Hera Keechigeesik, left-winger for . . . 1070
   SIMON: (*To* CREATURE.) Aw, lay off! Pat-see! Pat-see! Pat-see! . . . (*Etc.*)
   BIG JOEY: . . . the Wasy Wailerettes, kagatchitnat. How, Num-ber Nine Hera Keechigeesik . . .

(*He continues uninterrupted.*)

   CREATURE: . . . Stop the game! Stop the game! Stop the 1075 game! . . . (*Etc.*)
   ZACHARY: Goodness sakes, there's gonna be a fight out there!

(CREATURE *continues his "stop the game,"* ZACHARY *repeats "goodness sakes, there's gonna be a fight out there,"* SIMON's *"Pat-see!" has now built up into a full chant, his foot pounding on the floor so that it sounds like a powwow drum, his dancing bustle held aloft like a shield.* SPOOKY *finally grabs the crucifix away from* DICKIE BIRD, *holds it aloft and begins to pray, loudly, as in a ceremony.* DICKIE BIRD, *caught between Simon's chanting and* SPOOKY's *praying, blocks his ears with his hands and looks with growing consternation at "the game."* PIERRE *blows his whistle and skates around like a puppet gone mad.*)

   SPOOKY: The Lord is my shepherd; I shall not want. He maketh me to lie down in green pastures; he leadeth me beside the still waters. He restoreth my soul; he leadeth me 1080 in the paths of righteousness for his name's sake. Yea, though I walk through the valley of the shadow of death, I will fear no evil; for thou art with me. Yea, though I walk through the valley of the shadow of death, I will fear no evil; for thou art with me . . . 1085

(*He repeats this last phrase over and over again. Finally,* DICKIE BIRD *freaks out, screams and runs down to the "ice" area.*)

1052 . . . **Hey,** . . . The following hockey commentary by Big Joey (pp. 1564–1565) is translated on p. 1577.

BIG JOEY: (*Continuing uninterrupted above all the other men's voices.*) …igwa ati-ooteetum blue line ita Number One Gazelle Nataways, Captain of the Wasy Wailerettes, kagagweemaskamat anee-i puck, ma-a Number Nine Hera Keechigeesik mawch

1090 weemeethew anee-i puck. Wha! "Hooking," itwew referee Pierre St. Pierre, Gazelle Nataways isa keehookiwatew her own team-mate Hera Keechigeesikwa, wha! How, Number One Gazelle Nataways, Captain of the Wasy Wailerettes, face-off igwa meena itootum asichi Number Nine Flora

1095 McDonald, Captain of the Canoe Lake Bravettes igwa Flora McDonald soogi pugamawew anee-i puck, ma-a Number Thirty-seven Big Bum Pegahmagahbow, defense-woman for the Wasy Wailerettes, stops the puck and passes it to Number Eleven Black Lady Halked, also defense-woman for the

1100 Wasy Wailerettes, but Gazelle Nataways, Captain of the Wasy Wailerettes, soogi body check meethew her own teammate Black Lady Halked woops! She falls, ladies igwa gentlemen, Black Lady Halked hits the boards and Black Lady Halked is singin' the blues, ladies igwa gentlemen, Black

1105 Lady Halked sings the blues. (*Off microphone, to the other men.*) What the hell is goin' on down there? Dickie Bird, get off the ice! (*Back on microphone.*) Wha! Number Eleven Black Lady Halked is up in a flash igwa seemak n'taymaskamew Gazelle Nataways anee-i puck, holy shit! The ailing but very,

1110 very furious Black Lady Halked skates back, turns and takes aim, it's gonna be a slap shot, ladies igwa gentlemen, slap shot keetnatch taytootum Black Lady Halked igwa Black Lady Halked shootiwoo anee-i puck, wha! She shoots straight at her very own captain, Gazelle Nataways and holy shit, holy

1115 shit, holy fuckin' shit!

(*All hell breaks loose; it is as though some bizarre dream has entered the arena. We hear the sound of women wailing and pucks hitting boards, echoing and echoing as in a vast empty chamber. The men are all screaming at the same time, from the "bleachers," re-calling* BLACK LADY HALKED's *legendary fall of seventeen years ago.*)

BIG JOEY: (*Dropping his microphone in horror.*) Holy Christ! If there is a devil in this world, then he has just walked into this room. Holy Christ! … (*He says this over and over again.*)
ZACHARY: Do something about her, goodness sakes, I told you

1120 guys to do something about her seventeen years ago, but you wouldn't do fuck-all. So go out there now and help her … (*Repeated.*)
CREATURE: Never mind, Chris'sakes, don't bother her. Let me out of here. Chris'sakes, let me out of here! … (*Repeated.*)

1125 SPOOKY: Yea, though I walk through the valley of the shadow of death, I will fear no evil; for thou art with me …

(*Repeated. While* SIMON *continues chanting and stomping.*)

PIERRE: (*From the "ice" area.*) Never you mind, Zachary Jeremiah, never you mind. She'll be okay. No she won't. Zachary Jeremiah, go out there and help her. No. She'll be okay. No she

1130 won't. Yes. No. Yes. No. Help! Where's the puck? Can't do nothin' without the goddamn puck. Where's the puck?! Where's the puck?! Where's the puck?! …

(*He repeats this last phrase over and over again. Center- and down-stage, on the "ice" area,* DICKIE BIRD *is going into a complete "freak-out," breaking into a grotesque, fractured version of a Cree chant. Gradually,* BIG

JOEY, ZACHARY *and* CREATURE *join* PIERRE's *refrain of "where's the puck?!", with which they all, including the chanting* SIMON *and the praying* SPOOKY, *scatter and come running down to the "ice" area. As they reach the lower level and begin to approach the audience, their movements break down into slow motion, as though they were trying to run through the sticky, gummy substance of some horrible, surrealistic nightmare.*)

PIERRE/BIG JOEY/ZACHARY/CREATURE: (*Slower and slower, as on a record that is slowing down gradually to a stop.*) Where's the puck?! Where's the puck?! Where's the puck?! … (*Etc.*)   1135

(SIMON *continues chanting and stomping,* SPOOKY *continues intoning the last phrase of his prayer and* DICKIE BIRD *continues his fractured chant. Out of this fading "sound collage" emerges the sound of a jukebox playing the introduction to Kitty Wells' "It Wasn't God Who Made Honky Tonk Angels," as though filtered through memory. At this point, on the upper level, a giant luminescent hockey stick comes seemingly out of nowhere and, in very slow motion, shoots a giant luminescent puck. On the puck, looking like a radiant but damaged "Madonna-with-child," sits* NANABUSH, *as the spirit of* BLACK LADY HALKED, *naked, nine months pregnant, drunk almost senseless and barely able to hold a bottle of beer up to her mouth. All the men freeze in their standing positions facing the audience, except for* DICKIE BIRD *who continues his fractured chanting and whimpering, holding his arms up towards* NANABUSH/BLACK LADY HALKED. *The giant luminescent puck reaches and stops at the edge of the upper level.* NANABUSH/BLACK LADY HALKED *struggles to stand and begins staggering toward her perch. She reaches it and falls with one arm on top of it. The magical, glittering lights flare on and, for the first time, the jukebox is revealed.* NANABUSH/BLACK LADY HALKED *staggers laboriously up to the top of the jukebox and stands there in profile, one arm lifted to raise her beer as she pours it over her belly. Behind her, the full moon begins to glow, blood red. And from the jukebox, Kitty Wells sings.*)

As I sit here tonight, the jukebox playing,
That tune about the wild side of life;
As I listen to the words you are saying,
It brings memories when I was a trusting wife.

It wasn't God who made honky tonk angels,   1140
As you said in the words of your song;
Too many times married men think they're still single,
That has caused many a good girl to go wrong.

(*During the "instrumental break" of the song here,* DICKIE BIRD *finally explodes and shrieks out towards the vision of* NANABUSH/BLACK LADY HALKED.)

DICKIE BIRD: Mama! Mama! Katha paksini. Katha paksini. Kanawapata wastew. Kanawapataw wastew. Michimina.   1145
Michimina. Katha pagitina. Kaweechee-ik nipapa. Kaweechee-ik nipapa. Nipapa. Papa. Papa. Papa. Papa. Papa. Papa! Mommy! Mommy! Don't fall. Don't fall. Look at the light. Look at the light. Hold on to it. Hold on to it. Don't let it go. My daddy will help you. My daddy will   1150
help you. My daddy. Daddy. Daddy. … (*Etc.*)

(*He crumples to the floor and freezes. Kitty Wells sings.*)

It's a shame that all the blame is on us women,
It's not true that only you men feel the same;
From the start most every heart that's ever broken,
Was because there always was a man to blame.   1155

It wasn't God who made honky tonk angels;
As you said in the words of your song;
Too many times married men think they're still single,
That has caused many a good girl to go wrong.

(*As the song fades, the final tableau is one of* DICKIE BIRD *collapsed on the floor between* SIMON, *who is holding aloft his bustle, and* SPOOKY, *who is holding aloft his crucifix, directly in front of and at the feet of* BIG JOEY *and, above* BIG JOEY, *the pregnant* NANABUSH/BLACK LADY HALKED, *who is standing on top of the flashing jukebox, in silhouette against the full moon, bottle held up above her mouth.* ZACHARY, CREATURE *and* PIERRE *are likewise frozen, standing off to the side of this central grouping. Slow fade-out.*)

ACT TWO

When the lights come up, DICKIE BIRD HALKED *is standing on a rock in the forest, his clothes and hair all askew. He holds* SPOOKY'S *crucifix, raised with one hand up to the night sky; he is trying, as best he can, to chant, after* SIMON STARBLANKET'S *fashion. As he does,* NANABUSH *appears in the shadows a distance behind him (as the spirit of* GAZELLE NATAWAYS, *minus the gigantic breasts, but dressed, this time, as a stripper). She lingers and watches with interest. Slowly,* DICKIE BIRD *climbs off the rock and walks off-stage, his quavering voice fading into the distance. The full moon glows. Fade-out.*

Fade-in on SPOOKY LACROIX'S *kitchen, where* SPOOKY *is busy pinning four little pale blue baby booties on the wall where the crucifix used to be, the booties that, in Act One, covered the four extremities of the crucifix. At the table are* PIERRE ST. PIERRE *and* ZACHARY JEREMIAH KEECHIGEESIK. PIERRE *is stringing pale blue yarn around* ZACHARY'S *raised, parted hands. Then* SPOOKY *joins them at the table and begins knitting again, this time, a baby bonnet, also pale blue.* ZACHARY *sits removed through most of this scene, pre-occupied with the problem of his still missing shorts, his bakery and his wife. The atmosphere is one of fear and foreboding, almost as though the men were constantly resisting the impulse to look over their shoulders. On the upper level, in a soft, dim light,* NANABUSH/GAZELLE *can be seen sitting up on her perch, waiting impatiently for "the boys" to finish their talk.*

PIERRE: (*In a quavering voice.*) The Wasy Wailerettes are dead. Gentlemen, my job is disappeared from underneath my feet.
SPOOKY: And we have only the Lord to thank for that.
5 PIERRE: Gazelle Nataways, she just sashayed herself off that ice, behind swayin' like a walrus pudding. That game, gentlemen, was what I call a real apostrophe . . .
ZACHARY: Catastrophe.
PIERRE: That's what I said, dammit. . . .
10 SPOOKY: . . . tsk . . .
PIERRE: . . . didn't even get to referee more than ten minutes. But you have to admit, gentlemen, that slap shot . . .
SPOOKY: . . . that's my sister, Black Lady Halked, that's my sister . . .
15 PIERRE: . . . did you see her slap shot? Fantastic! Like a bullet, like a killer shark. Unbelievable!
ZACHARY: (*Uncomfortable.*) Yeah, right.
PIERRE: When Black Lady Halked hit Gazelle Nataways with that puck. Them Nataways eyes. Big as plates!
20 SPOOKY: Bigger than a ditch!

PIERRE: Them mascara stretch marks alone was a perfectly frightful thing to behold. Holy shit la marde! But you know, they couldn't find that puck.
SPOOKY: (*Losing his cool and laughing, falsely and nervously.*) Did you see it? It fell . . . it fell . . . that puck went splat on her 25 chest . . . and it went . . . it went . . . plummety plop . . .
PIERRE: . . . plummety plop to be sure . . .
SPOOKY: . . . down her . . . down her . . .
PIERRE: Down the crack. Right down that horrendous, scarifyin' Nataways bosom crack. 30

(*The "kitchen lights" go out momentarily and, to the men, inexplicably. Then they come back on. The men look about them, perplexed.*)

SPOOKY: Serves . . . her . . . right for trimming her hockey sweater in the chest area, is what I say.
PIERRE: They say that puck slid somewhere deep, deep into the folds of her fleshy, womanly juices . . .
ZACHARY: . . . there's a lot of things they're saying about that 35 puck . . .
PIERRE: and it's lost. Disappeared. Gone. Phhht! Nobody can find that puck.

(*At this point,* SPOOKY *gets up to check the light switch. The lights go out.*)

ZACHARY: (*In the darkness.*) Won't let no one come near her, is what they say. Not six inches. 40
PIERRE: I gotta go look for that puck. (*Lights come back on.* PIERRE *inexplicably appears sitting in another chair.*) Gentlemen, I gotta go jiggle that woman.

(*Lights out again.*)

ZACHARY: (*From the darkness.*) What's the matter, Spook?
SPOOKY: (*Obviously quite worried.*) Oh, nothing, nothing . . . 45 (*Lights come back on.* PIERRE *appears sitting back in his original chair. The men are even more mystified, but try to brighten up anyway.*) . . . just . . . checking the lights . . . Queen of the Indians, that's what she tried to look like, walking off that ice. 50
PIERRE: Queen of the Indians, to be sure. That's when them women went and put their foot down and made up their mind, on principle, no holds barred . . .

(*A magical flash of lavender light floods the room very briefly, establishing a connection between* SPOOKY'S *kitchen and* NANABUSH'S *perch, where* NANABUSH/GAZELLE *is still sitting, tapping her fingers impatiently, looking over her shoulder periodically, as if to say: "come on, boys, get with it."* PIERRE'S *speech momentarily goes into slow motion.*)

. . . no . . . way . . . they're . . . takin' up . . . them hockey sticks again until that particular puck is found. "The par- 55 ticular puck," that's what they call it. Gentlemen, the Wasy Wailerettes are dead. My job is disappeared. Gone. Kaput kaput. Phhht!
SPOOKY: Amen.

(*Pause. Thoughtful silence for a beat or two.*)

ZACHARY: W-w-w-where's that nephew of yours, Spook? 60
SPOOKY: Dickie Bird Halked?

PIERRE: My wife, Veronique St. Pierre, she informs me that Dickie Bird Halked, last he was seen, was pacin' the bushes in the general direction of the Pegahmagahbow acreage
65 near Buzwah, lookin' for all the world like he had lost his mind, poor boy.

ZACHARY: Lordy, lordy, lordy, I'm telling you right now, Spooky Lacroix, if you don't do something about that nephew of yours, he's liable to go out there and kill some-
70 one next time.

SPOOKY: I'd be out there myself pacing the bushes with him except my wife Lalala's liable to pop any minute now and I gotta be ready to zip her up to Sudbury General.

PIERRE: Bah. Them folks of his, they don't care. If it's not
75 hockey, it's bingo she's out playin' every night of the week, that Black Lady of a mother of his.

ZACHARY: Went and won the jackpot again last night, Black Lady Halked did. All fifty pounds of it . . .

PIERRE: Beat Gazelle Nataways by one number!

80 ZACHARY: . . . if it wasn't for her, I'd have mastered that apple pie recipe by now. I was counting on all that lard. Fifty pounds, goodness sakes.

SPOOKY: This little old kitchen? It's yours, Zachary Jeremiah, anytime, anytime. Lalala's got tons of lard.

85 PIERRE: Ha! She better have. Zachary Jeremiah hasn't dared go nowhere near his own kitchen in almost a week.

ZACHARY: Four nights! It's only Wednesday night, Pierre St. Pierre. Don't go stretching the truth just cuz you were too damn chicken to go get me my shorts.

90 PIERRE: Bah!

SPOOKY: (*To* ZACHARY.) Your shorts?

ZACHARY: (*Evading the issue.*) I just hope that Black Lady Halked's out there looking after her boy cuz if she isn't, we're all in a heap of trouble, I have a funny feeling. (*Suddenly, he*
95 *throws the yarn down and rises.*) Achh! I've got to cook!

(*He goes behind the kitchen counter, puts an apron on and begins the preparations for making pie pastry.*)

SPOOKY: (*To* PIERRE, *half-whispering.*) His shorts?

(PIERRE *merely shrugs, indicating* ZACHARY's *pants, which are still held together with a large safety pin.* SPOOKY *and* PIERRE *laugh nervously.* SPOOKY *looks concernedly at the four little booties on the wall where the crucifix used to be. Beat.*)

(*Suddenly,* PIERRE *slaps the table with one hand and leans over to* SPOOKY, *all set for an argument, an argument they've obviously had many times before. Through all this,* ZACHARY *is making pie pastry at the counter and* SPOOKY *continues knitting. The atmosphere of "faked" jocular camaraderie grows, particularly as the music gets louder later on.* NANABUSH/GAZELLE *is now getting ready for her strip in earnest, standing on her perch, spraying perfume on, stretching her legs, etc. The little tivoli lights in the jukebox begin to twinkle little by little.*)

PIERRE: Queen of Hearts.
100 SPOOKY: Belvedere.
PIERRE: Queen of Hearts.
SPOOKY: The Belvedere.
PIERRE: I told you many times, Spooky Lacroix, it was the Queen of Hearts. I was there. You were there. Zachary Jeremiah, Big Joey, Creature Nataways, we were all there.

(*From here on, the red/blue/purple glow of the jukebox (i.e.,* NANABUSH's *perch) becomes more and more apparent.*)

SPOOKY: And I'm telling you it was the Belvedere Hotel, before it was even called the Belvedere Hotel, when it was still 105 called . . .

PIERRE: Spooky Lacroix, don't contribute your elder. Big Joey, may he rot in hell, he was the bouncer there that night, he was right there the night it happened.

ZACHARY: Hey, Spook. Where do you keep your rolling pin? 110

SPOOKY: Use my salami.

PIERRE: (*To* SPOOKY.) He was there.

ZACHARY: Big Joey was never the bouncer, he was the janitor.

SPOOKY: At the Belvedere Hotel.

PIERRE: Never you mind, Spooky Lacroix, never you mind. 115 Black Lady Halked was sittin' there in her corner of the bar for three weeks . . .

SPOOKY: Three weeks?! It was more like three nights. Aw, you went and mixed up my baby's cap. (*Getting all tangled up with his knitting.*) 120

ZACHARY: Got any cinnamon?

SPOOKY: I got chili powder. Same color as cinnamon.

(*Faintly, the strip music from the jukebox begins to play.*)

PIERRE: . . . the place was so jam-packed with people drinkin' beer and singin' and smokin' cigarettes and watchin' the dancin' girl . . . 125

SPOOKY: . . . Gazelle Nataways, she was the dancing girl . . .

(*The music is now on full volume and* NANABUSH/GAZELLE's *strip is in full swing. She dances on top of the jukebox, which is now a riot of sound and flashing lights.* SPOOKY's *kitchen is bathed in a gorgeous lavender light.* BIG JOEY *and* CREATURE NATAWAYS *appear at* SPOOKY's *table, each drinking a bottle of beer. The strip of seventeen years ago is fully recreated, the memory becoming so heated that* NANABUSH/GAZELLE *magically appears dancing right on top of* SPOOKY's *kitchen table. The men are going wild, applauding, laughing, drinking, all in slow motion and in mime. In the heat of the moment, as* NANABUSH/GAZELLE *strips down to silk tassels and G-string, they begin tearing their clothes off.*)

(*Suddenly,* SIMON STARBLANKET *appears at* SPOOKY's *door:* NANABUSH/GAZELLE *disappears, as do* BIG JOEY *and* CREATURE. *And* SPOOKY, PIERRE *and* ZACHARY *are caught with their pants down. The jukebox music fades.*)

SIMON: Spooky Lacroix. (*The lavender light snaps off, we are back to "reality" and* SPOOKY, PIERRE *and* ZACHARY *stand there, embarrassed. In a panic, they begin putting their clothes back on and reclaim the positions they had before the strip.* 130 SPOOKY *motions* SIMON *to take a seat at the table.* SIMON *does so.*) Spooky Lacroix. Rosie Kakapetum expresses interest in coming here to birth Lalala's baby when the time comes.

SPOOKY: Rosie Kakapetum? No way some witch is gonna come 135 and put her witchy little fingers on my baby boy.

SIMON: Rosie Kakapetum's no witch, Spooky Lacroix. She's Patsy Pegahmagahbow's step-mother and she's Wasy's only surviving medicine woman and mid-wife . . .

SPOOKY: Hogwash! 140

PIERRE: Ahem. Rosie Kakapetum says it's a cryin' shame the Wasy Wailerettes is the only team that's not in the Ontario Hockey League.

ZACHARY: Ontario Hockey League?

145 PIERRE: Absolutely. The OHL. Indian women's OHL. All the Indian women in Ontario's playin' hockey now. It's like a fever out there.

ZACHARY: Shoot. (*Referring to his pastry.*) I hope this new recipe works for me.

150 PIERRE: Well, it's not exactly new without the cinnamon.

SPOOKY: (*To* SIMON.) My son will be born at Sudbury General Hospital . . .

SIMON: You know what they do to them babies in them city hospitals?

155 SPOOKY: . . . Sudbury General, Simon Starblanket, like any good Christian boy . . .

PIERRE: (*Attempting to diffuse the argument.*) Ahem. We got to get them Wasy Wailerettes back on that ice again.

SIMON: (*Refusing to let go of* SPOOKY.) They pull them away right

160 from their own mother's breast the minute they come into this world and they put them behind these glass cages together with another two hundred babies like they were some kind of scientific specimens . . .

PIERRE: . . . like two hundred of them little monsters . . .

165 ZACHARY: Hamsters!

PIERRE: . . . that's what I said dammit . . .

SPOOKY: . . . tsk . . .

PIERRE: . . . you can't even tell which hamster belongs to which mother. You take Lalala to Sudbury General,

170 Spooky Lacroix, and your hamster's liable to end up stuck to some French lady's tit.

SIMON: . . . and they'll hang Lalala up in metal stirrups and your baby's gonna be born going up instead of dropping down which is the natural way. You were born going up in-

175 stead of dropping down like you should have . . .

PIERRE: Yup. You were born at Sudbury General, Spooky Lacroix, that's why you get weirder and weirder as the days get longer, that's why them white peoples is so weird they were all born going up . . .

180 SIMON: . . . instead of dropping down . . .

ZACHARY: (*Sprinkling flour in* SPOOKY's *face, with both hands, and laughing.*) . . . to the earth, Spooky Lacroix, to the earth . . .

SPOOKY: Pooh!

PIERRE: . . . but we got to find that puck, Simon Starblanket,

185 them Wasy Wailerettes have got to join the OHL . . .

SPOOKY: (*To* SIMON.) If Rosie Kakapetum is a medicine woman, Simon Starblanket, then how come she can't drive the madness from my nephew's brain, how come she can't make him talk, huh?

190 SIMON: Because the medical establishment and the church establishment and people like you, Spooky Lacroix, have effectively put an end to her usefulness and the usefulness of people like her everywhere, that's why Spooky Lacroix.

SPOOKY: Phooey!

195 SIMON: Do you or your sister even know that your nephew hasn't been home in two days, since that incident at the hockey game, Spooky Lacroix? Do you even care? Why can't you and that thing . . . (*Pointing at the bible that sits beside* SPOOKY.) and all it stands for cure your nephew's

200 madness, as you call it, Spooky Lacroix? What has this

thing . . . (*The bible again.*) done to cure the madness of this community and communities like it clean across this country, Spooky Lacroix? Why didn't "the Lord" as you call him, come to your sister's rescue at that bar seventeen years ago, huh, Spooky Lacroix? (*Pause. Tense silence.*) Rosie 205 Kakapetum is gonna be my mother-in-law in two months, Spooky Lacroix, and if Patsy and I are gonna do this thing right, if we're gonna work together to make my best man, Dickie Bird Halked, well again, then Rosie Kakapetum has got to birth that baby. (*He begins to exit.*) 210

SPOOKY: (*In hard, measured cadence.*) Rosie Kakapetum works for the devil.

(SIMON *freezes in his tracks. Silence. Then he turns, grabs a chair violently, bangs it down and sits determinedly.*)

SIMON: Fine. I'll sit here and I'll wait.

SPOOKY: Fine. You sit there and you wait.

(*Silence.* SIMON *sits silent and motionless, his back to the other men.*)

PIERRE: Ahem. Never you mind, Spooky Lacroix, never you 215 mind. Now as I was sayin', Black Lady Halked was nine months pregnant when she was sittin' in that corner of the Queen of Hearts.

SPOOKY: The Belvedere!

PIERRE: Three weeks, Black Lady Halked was sittin' there 220 drinkin' beer. They say she got the money by winnin' the jackpot at the Espanola bingo just three blocks down the street. Three weeks, sure as I'm alive and walkin' these treacherous icy roads, three weeks she sat there in that dark corner by herself. They say the only light you could see her 225 by was the light from the jukebox playin' "Rim of Fire" by Johnny Cash . . .

ZACHARY: "Rim of Fire." Yeah, right, Pierre St. Pierre.

SPOOKY: Kitty Wells! Kitty Wells!

(*The sound of the jukebox playing "It Wasn't God Who Made Honky Tonk Angels" can be heard faintly in the background.*)

PIERRE: . . . the place was so jam-packed with people drinkin' 230 and singin' and smokin' cigarettes and watchin' the dancin' girl . . .

SPOOKY: . . . Gazelle Nataways, she was the dancing girl, Lord save her soul . . .

PIERRE: . . . until Black Lady Halked collapsed . . . 235

(SPOOKY, PIERRE *and* ZACHARY *freeze in their positions, looking in horror at the memory of seventeen years ago.*)

(*On the upper level,* NANABUSH, *back in her guise as the spirit of* BLACK LADY HALKED, *sits on the jukebox, facing the audience, legs out directly in front. Nine months pregnant and naked, she holds a bottle of beer up in the air and is drunk almost senseless. The song, "It Wasn't God Who Made Honky Tonk Angels," rises to full volume, the lights from the jukebox flashing riotously. The full moon glows blood red. Immediately below* NANABUSH/BLACK LADY HALKED, DICKIE BIRD HALKED *appears, kneeling, naked, arms raised toward his mother.* NANABUSH/BLACK LADY HALKED *begins to writhe and scream, laughing and crying hysterically at the same time and, as she does, her water breaks.* DICKIE BIRD, *drenched, rises slowly from the floor, arms still raised, and screams.*)

DICKIE BIRD: Mama! Mama!

(*And from here on, the lights and the sound on this scene begin to fade slowly, as the scene on the lower level resumes.*)

PIERRE: ...she kind of oozed down right then and there, right down to the floor of the Queen of Hearts Tavern. And Big Joey, may he rot in hell, he was the bouncer there that night, when he saw the blood, he ran away and puked over on the other side of the bar, the sight of all that woman's blood just scared the shit right out of him. And that's when Dickie Bird Halked, as we know him, came ragin' out from his mother's womb, Spooky Lacroix, in between beers, right there on the floor, under a table, by the light of the juke-box, on a Saturday night, at the Queen of Hearts ...

SPOOKY: They went and named him after the bar, you crusted old fossil! That bar, which is now called the Belvedere Hotel, used to be called the Dickie Bird Tavern ...

SIMON: (*Suddenly jumping out of his chair and practically lunging at* SPOOKY.) It doesn't matter what the fuck the name of that fucking bar was! (*The lights and sound on* NANABUSH *and the jukebox have now faded completely.*) The fact of the matter is, it never should have happened, that kind of thing should never be allowed to happen, not to us Indians, not to any-one living and breathing on the face of God's green earth. (*Pause. Silence. Then, dead calm.*) You guys have given up, haven't you? You and your generation. You gave up a long time ago. You'd rather turn your back on the whole thing and pretend to laugh, wouldn't you? (*Silence.*) Well, not me. Not us. (*Silence.*) This is not the kind of Earth we want to inherit. (*He begins to leave, but turns once more.*) I'll be back. With Patsy. And Rosie.

(*He exits. Another embarrassed silence.*)

SPOOKY: (*Unwilling to face up to the full horror of it, he chooses, in-stead, to do exactly what* SIMON *said: turn his back and pretend to laugh.*) That bar, which is now called the Belvedere Hotel, used to be called the Dickie Bird Tavern. That's how Dickie Bird Halked got his name. And that's why he goes hay-wire every now and again and that's why he doesn't talk. Fetal Al-cohol something-something, Pierre St. Pierre ...

ZACHARY: (*From behind the counter, where he is still busy making pie crust.*) Fetal Alcohol Syndrome.

SPOOKY: ... that's the devil that stole the baby's tongue be-cause Dickie Bird Halked was born drunk and very, very mad. At the Dickie Bird Tavern in downtown Espanola sev-enteen years ago and that's a fact.

PIERRE: Aw, shit la marde. Fuck you, Spooky Lacroix, I'm gonna go get me my rest.

(*Throws the yarn in* SPOOKY's *face, jumps up and exits.* SPOOKY *sits there with a pile of yarn stuck to his face, caught on his glasses.*)

ZACHARY: (*Proudly holding up the pie crust in its plate.*) It worked!

(*Black-out*)

(*On the upper level, in a dim light away from her perch,* NANABUSH/ BLACK LADY HALKED *is getting ready to go out for the evening, combing her hair in front of a mirror, putting on her clothes, etc.* DICKIE BIRD *is with her, naked, getting ready to go to bed.* SPOOKY's *crucifix sits on a night-table to his side. In* DICKIE BIRD's *mind, he is at home with his mother.*)

DICKIE BIRD: Mama. Mama. N'tagoosin. ("I'm sick.")

NANABUSH/BLACK LADY: Say your prayers.

DICKIE BIRD: Achimoostawin nimoosoom. ("Tell me about my grandpa.")

NANABUSH/BLACK LADY: Go to bed. I'm going out soon.

DICKIE BIRD: Mawch. Achimoostawin nimoosoom. ("No. Tell me about my grandpa.")

NANABUSH/BLACK LADY: You shouldn't talk about him.

DICKIE BIRD: Tapweechee eegeemachipoowamit nimoosoom? ("Is it true my grandpa had bad medicine?")

NANABUSH/BLACK LADY: They say he met the devil once. Your grandpa talked to the devil. Don't talk about him.

DICKIE BIRD: Eegeemithoopoowamit nimoosoom, eetweet Simon Starblanket. ("Simon Starblanket says he had good medicine.")

NANABUSH/BLACK LADY: Ashhh! Simon Starblanket.

DICKIE BIRD: Mawch eemithoosit awa aymeewatik keetnanow kichi, eetweet Simon Starblanket. ("Simon Starblanket says that this cross is not right for us.") (*He grabs the crucifix from the night-table and spits on it.*)

NANABUSH/BLACK LADY: (*Grabbing the crucifix from* DICKIE BIRD, *she attempts to spank him but* DICKIE BIRD *evades her.*) Dickie Bird! Kipasta-oon! ("You're committing a mortal sin!") Say ten Hail Marys and two Our Fathers.

DICKIE BIRD: Mootha apoochiga taskootch nimama keetha. Mootha apoochiga m'tanawgatch kisagee-in. ("You're not even like my mother. You don't even love me at all.")

NANABUSH/BLACK LADY: Dickie Bird. Shut up. I'll say them with you. "Hail Mary, full of grace, the Lord is with thee ... "Hurry up. I have to go out. (*As* NANABUSH/BLACK LADY HALKED *now prepares to leave.*) "Hail Mary, full of grace, the Lord is with thee ... "(*She gives up.*) Ashhh! Your father should be home soon. (*Exits.*)

DICKIE BIRD: (*Speaking out to the now absent* NANABUSH/BLACK LADY.) Mootha nipapa ana. ("He's not my father.") (*He grabs his clothes and the crucifix and runs out, down to the lower level and into the forest made of light and shadows.*) Tapwee anima ka–itweechik, chee-i? Neetha ooma kimineechagan, chee-i? ("It's true what they say, isn't it? I'm a bastard, aren't I?") (*He is now sitting on the rock, where* SIMON *and* ZACHARY *first met in Act One.*) Nipapa ana ... Big Joey ... (*To himself, quietly.*) ... nipapa ana ... Big Joey ... ("My father is ... Big Joey.")

(*Silence.*)

(*A few moments later,* NANABUSH *comes bouncing into the forest, as the spirit of the vivacious, young* PATSY PEGAHMAGAHBOW, *complete with very large, oversized bum. The full moon glows.*)

NANABUSH/PATSY: (*To herself, as she peers into the shadows.*) Oooh, my poor bum. I fell on the ice four days ago, eh? And it still hurts, oooh. (*She finally sees* DICKIE BIRD *huddling on the rock, barely dressed.*) There you are. I came out to look for you. What happened to your clothes? It's freezing out here. Put them on. Here. (*She starts to help dress him.*) What happened

at the arena? You were on the ice, eh? You feel like talking?
330   In Indian? How, weetamawin. ("Come on, tell me.")

(BIG JOEY *and* CREATURE NATAWAYS *enter a distance away. They
are smoking a joint and* BIG JOEY *carries a gun. They stop and watch
from the shadows.*)

CREATURE: Check her out.
NANABUSH/PATSY: Why do you always carry that crucifix? I
      don't believe that stuff. I traded mine in for sweetgrass.
      Hey. You wanna come to Rosie's and eat fry bread with me?
335   Simon will be there, too. Simon and me, we're getting mar-
      ried, eh? We're gonna have a baby . . .
CREATURE: What's she trying to do?
NANABUSH/PATSY: . . . Rosie's got deer meat, too, come on, you
      like my Mom's cooking, eh? (*She attempts to take the crucifix*
340   *away from* DICKIE BIRD.) But you'll have to leave that here
      because Rosie can't stand the Pope . . .

(DICKIE BIRD *grabs the crucifix back.*)

CREATURE: What's he trying to do?
NANABUSH/PATSY: . . . give it to me . . . Dickie . . . come on . . .
CREATURE: He's weird, Big Joey, he's weird.
345   NANABUSH/PATSY: . . . leave it here . . . it will be safe here . . .
      we'll bury it in the snow . . .

(*Playfully, she tries to get the crucifix away from* DICKIE BIRD.)

CREATURE: Hey, don't do that, don't do that, man, he's ticklish.
NANABUSH/PATSY: (*As* DICKIE BIRD *begins poking her playfully
      with the crucifix and laughing,* NANABUSH/PATSY *gradually
350   starts to get frightened.*) . . . don't look at me that way . . .
      Dickie Bird, what's wrong? . . . ya, Dickie Bird, awus . . .

(DICKIE BIRD *starts to grab at* NANABUSH/PATSY.)

CREATURE: Hey, don't you think, don't you think . . . he's get-
      ting kind of carried away?
NANABUSH/PATSY: . . . awus . . .
355   CREATURE: We gotta do something, Big Joey, we gotta do
      something. (BIG JOEY *stops* CREATURE.) Let go! Let go!
NANABUSH/PATSY: (*Now in a panic.*) . . . Awus! Awus! Awus! . . .

(DICKIE BIRD *grabs* NANABUSH/PATSY *and throws her violently to the
ground, he lifts her skirt and shoves the crucifix up against her.*)

BIG JOEY: (*To* CREATURE.) Shut up.
NANABUSH/PATSY: (*Screams and goes into hysteria.*) . . . Simon! . . .

(DICKIE BIRD *rapes* NANABUSH/PATSY *with the crucifix. A heartbreaking, very slow, sensuous tango breaks out on off-stage harmonica.*)

360   CREATURE: (*To* BIG JOEY.) No! Let me go. Big Joey, let me go,
      please! (BIG JOEY *suddenly grabs* CREATURE *violently by the collar.*)
BIG JOEY: Get out. Get the fuck out of here. You're nothin' but
      a fuckin' fruit. Fuck off. (CREATURE *collapses.*) I said fuck off.

(CREATURE *flees.* BIG JOEY *just stands there, paralyzed, and watches.*)

(NANABUSH/PATSY, *who has gradually been moving back and back,
is now standing up on her perch again (i.e., the "mound"/jukebox
which no longer looks like a jukebox). She stands there, facing the*

*audience, and slowly gathers her skirt, in agony, until she is holding
it up above her waist. A blood stain slowly spreads across her panties
and flows down her leg. At the same time, Dickie Bird stands downstage beside the rock, holding the crucifix and making violent jabbing
motions with it, downward. All this happens in slow motion. The crucifix starts to bleed. When* DICKIE BIRD *lifts the crucifix up, his arms
and chest are covered with blood. Finally,* NANABUSH/PATSY *collapses
to the floor of her platform and slowly crawls away. Lights fade on her.
On the lower level,* BIG JOEY, *in a state of shock, staggers, almost
faints and vomits violently. Then he reels over to* DICKIE BIRD *and,
not knowing what else to do, begins collecting his clothes and calming
him down.*)

BIG JOEY: How, Dickie Bird, How, astum. Igwa. Mootha nan-
      tow. Mootha nantow. Shhh. Shhh. ("Come on, Dickie Bird.   365
      Come. Let's go. It's okay. It's okay. Shhh. Shhh . . . ") (*Barely
      able to bring himself to touch it, he takes the crucifix from* DICKIE
      BIRD *and drops it quickly on the rock. Then he begins wiping the
      blood off* DICKIE BIRD.) How, mootha nantow. Mootha nan-
      tow. How, astum, keeyapitch upisees ootee. Igwani. Igwani.   370
      Poonimatoo. Mootha nantow. Mootha nantow. ("Come on,
      it's okay. It's okay. Come on, a little more over here. That's
      all. That's all. Stop crying. It's okay. It's okay . . .") (DICKIE
      BIRD, *shaking with emotion, looks questioningly into* BIG JOEY*'s
      face.*) Eehee. Nigoosis keetha. Mootha Wellington Halked   375
      kipapa. Neetha . . . kipapa. ("Yes. You are my son. Wellington
      Halked is not your father. I'm . . . your father.")

(*Silence. They look at each other.* DICKIE BIRD *grabs* BIG JOEY *and
clings to him,* BIG JOEY *reacting tentatively, at first, and then passionately, with* DICKIE BIRD *finally bursting out into uncontrollable
sobs. Fade-out.*)

(*Out of this darkness, gunshots explode. And we hear a man's voice
wailing, in complete and utter agony. Then comes violent pounding at
a door. Finally, still in the darkness, we hear* SIMON STARBLANKET*'s
speaking voice.*)

SIMON: Open up! Pierre St. Pierre, open up! I know you're in
      there!
PIERRE: (*Still in the darkness.*) Whoa! Easy now. Easy on that   380
      goddamn door. Must you create such a carpostrophe smack
      dab in the middle of my rest period? (*When the lights come
      up, we are outside the "window" to* PIERRE ST. PIERRE*'s little boot-
      leg joint.* PIERRE *pokes his head out, wearing his night clothes,
      complete with pointy cap.*) Go home. Go to bed. Don't be dis-   385
      turbin' my rest period. My wife, Veronique St. Pierre, she
      tells me there's now not only a OHL but a NHL, too. In-
      dian women's National Hockey League. All the Indian
      women on every reserve in Canada, all the Indian women in
      Canada is playin' hockey now. It's like a fever out there.   390
      That's why I gotta get my rest. First thing tomorrow
      mornin', I go jiggle that puck out of Gazelle Nataways. Lis-
      ten to me. I'm your elder.

(SIMON *shoots the gun into the house, just missing* PIERRE*'s head.*)

SIMON: (*Dead calm.*) One, you give me a bottle. Two, I report
      your joint to the Manitowaning police. Three, I shoot your   395
      fucking head off.

PIERRE: Alright. Alright. (*He pops in for a bottle of whiskey and hands it out to* SIMON.) Now you go on home with this. Go have yourself a nice quiet drink. (SIMON *begins to exit.* PIERRE *calls out.*) What the hell are you gonna do with that gun?

SIMON: (*Calling back.*) I'm gonna go get that mute. Little bastard raped Patsy Pegahmagahbow. (*Exits.*)

(*Pause.*)

PIERRE: Holy shit la marde! (*Pause.*) I gotta warn him. No. I need my rest. No. I gotta warn that boy. No. I gotta find that puck. No. Dickie Bird's life. No. The puck. No. Dickie Bird. No. Hockey. No. His life. No. Hockey. No. Life. Hockey. Life. Hockey. Life. Hockey. Life. Hockey. Life . . .

(*Fade-out.*)

(*Lights up on* SPOOKY LACROIX*'s kitchen.* CREATURE NATAWAYS *is sitting at the table, silent, head propped up in his hands.* SPOOKY *is knitting, with obvious haste, a white christening gown, of which a large crucifix is the center-piece.* SPOOKY*'s bible still sits on the table beside him.*)

SPOOKY: Why didn't you do something? (*Silence.*) Creature. (*Silence. Finally,* SPOOKY *stops knitting and looks up.*) Alphonse Nataways, why didn't you stop him? (*Silence.*) You're scared of him, aren't you? You're scared to death of Big Joey. Admit it.

(*Silence.*)

CREATURE: (*Quietly and calmly.*) I love him, Spooky.

SPOOKY: Say wha?!

CREATURE: I love him.

SPOOKY: You love him? What do you mean? How? How do you love him?

CREATURE: I love him.

SPOOKY: Lord have mercy on Wasaychigan Hill!

CREATURE: (*Rising suddenly.*) I love the way he stands. I love the way he walks. The way he laughs. The way he wears his cowboy boots . . .

SPOOKY: You're kidding me.

CREATURE: . . . the way his tight blue jeans fall over his ass. The way he talks so smart and tough. The way women fall at his feet. I wanna be like him. I always wanted to be like him, William. I always wanted to have a dick as big as his.

SPOOKY: Creature Alphonse Nataways? You know not what you say.

CREATURE: I don't care.

SPOOKY: I care.

CREATURE: I don't care. I can't stand it anymore.

SPOOKY: Shut up. You're making me nervous. Real nervous.

CREATURE: Come with me.

SPOOKY: Come with you where?

CREATURE: To his house.

SPOOKY: Whose house?

CREATURE: Big Joey.

SPOOKY: Are you crazy?

CREATURE: Come with me.

SPOOKY: No.

CREATURE: Yes.

SPOOKY: No.

CREATURE: (*Suddenly and viciously grabbing* SPOOKY *by the throat.*) Cut the goddamn bull crap, Spooky Lacroix! (SPOOKY *tries desperately to save the christening gown.*) I seen you crawl in the mud and shit so drunk you were snortin' like a pig.

SPOOKY: I changed my ways, thank you.

CREATURE: Twenty one years. Twenty one years ago. You, me, Big Joey, Eugene Starblanket, that goddamn Zachary Jeremiah Keechigeesik. We were eighteen. We cut our wrists. Your own father's huntin' knife. We mixed blood. Swore we'd be friends for life. Frontenac Hotel. Twenty one years ago. You got jumped by seven white guys. Broken beer bottle come straight at your face. If it wasn't for me, you wouldn't be here today, wavin' that stinkin' bible in my face like it was a slab of meat. I'm not a dog. I'm your buddy. Your friend.

SPOOKY: I know that.

(CREATURE *tightens his hold on* SPOOKY*'s throat. The two men are staring straight into each other's eyes, inches apart. Silence.*)

CREATURE: William. Think of your father. Remember the words of Nicotine Lacroix.

(*Finally,* SPOOKY *screams, throwing the christening gown, knitting needles and all, over the bible on the table.*)

SPOOKY: You goddamn, fucking son-of-a-bitch!

(*Black-out. Gunshots in the distance.*)

(*Lights up on* BIG JOEY*'s living room/kitchen.* BIG JOEY *is sitting, silent and motionless, on the couch, staring straight ahead, as though he were in a trance. His hunting rifle rests on his lap.* DICKIE BIRD HALKED *stands directly in front of and facing the life-size pin-up poster of Marilyn Monroe, also as though he were in a trance. Then his head drops down in remorse.* BIG JOEY *lifts the gun, loads it and aims it out directly in front. When* DICKIE BIRD *hears the snap of the gun being loaded, he turns to look. Then he slowly walks over to* BIG JOEY, *kneels down directly in front of the barrel of the gun, puts it in his mouth and then slowly reaches over and gently, almost lovingly, moves* BIG JOEY*'s hand away from the trigger, caressing the older man's hand as he does.* BIG JOEY *slowly looks up at* DICKIE BIRD*'s face, stunned.* DICKIE BIRD *puts his own thumb on the trigger and pulls. Click. Nothing. In the complete silence, the two men are looking directly into each other's eyes. Complete stillness. Fade-out. Split seconds before complete black-out, Marilyn Monroe farts, courtesy of* MS. NANABUSH*: a little flag reading "poot" pops up out of Ms. Monroe's derrier, as on a play gun. We hear a cute little "poot" sound.*)

(*Out of this black-out emerges the sound of a harmonica; it is* ZACHARY JEREMIAH KEECHIGEESIK *playing his heart out. Fade-in on* PIERRE ST. PIERRE, *still in his night-clothes but also wearing his winter coat and hat over them, rushing all over the "forest" ostensibly rushing to* BIG JOEY*'s house to warn* DICKIE BIRD HALKED *about the gun-toting* SIMON STARBLANKET. *He mutters to himself as he goes.*)

PIERRE: Hockey. Life. Hockey. Life. Hockey. Life . . .

(ZACHARY *appears in the shadows and sees* PIERRE.)

ZACHARY: Hey!

PIERRE: (*Not hearing* ZACHARY.) . . . Hockey. Life. Hockey. Life . . .

ZACHARY: Pssst!

PIERRE: (*Still not hearing* ZACHARY.) . . . Hockey. Life. Hockey. Life. (*Pause.*) Hockey life!

ZACHARY: (*Finally yelling.*) Pierre St. Pierre!

(PIERRE *jumps.*)

470 PIERRE: Hallelujah! Have you heard the news?

ZACHARY: The Band Council went and okayed Big Joey's radio station.

PIERRE: All the Indian women in the world is playin' hockey now! World Hockey League, they call themselves. Aborigi-

475 nal Women's WHL. My wife, Veronique St. Pierre, she just got the news. Eegeeweetamagoot fax machine. ("Fax machine told her.") It's like a burnin', ragin', blindin' fever out there. Them Cree women in Saskatchewan, them Blood women in Alberta, them Yakima, them Heidis out in the

480 middle of your Specific Ocean, them Kickapoo, Chickasaw, Cherokee, Chipewyan, Choctaw, Chippewa, Wichita, Kiowa down in Oklahoma, them Seminole, Navajo, Onondaga, Tuscarora, Winnebago, Mimac-paddy-wack-why-it's-enough-to-give-your-dog-a-bone! . . .

(*As, getting completely carried away, he grabs his crotch.*)

485 ZACHARY: Pierre. Pierre.

PIERRE: . . . they're turnin' the whole world topsy-turkey right before our very eyes and the Prime Minister's a-shittin' grape juice . . . (*A gunshot explodes in the near distance.* PIERRE *suddenly lays low and changes tone completely.*) Holy shit la

490 marde! He's after Dickie Bird. There's a red-eyed, crazed devil out there and he's after Dickie Bird Halked and he's gonna kill us all if we don't stop him right this minute.

ZACHARY: Who? Who's gonna kill us?

PIERRE: Simon Starblanket. Drunk. Power mad. Half-crazed on

495 whiskey and he's got a gun.

ZACHARY: Simon?

PIERRE: He's drunk and he's mean and he's out to kill. (*Another gunshot.*) Hear that?

ZACHARY: (*To himself.*) That's Simon? I thought . . .

500 PIERRE: When he heard about the Pegahmagahbow rape . . .

ZACHARY: Pegahmagahbow what?

PIERRE: Why, haven't you heard? Dickie Bird Halked raped Patsy Pegahmagahbow in most brutal fashion and Simon Starblanket is out to kill Dickie Bird Halked so I'm on my

505 way to Big Joey's right this minute and I'm takin' that huntin' rifle of his and I'm sittin' next to that Halked boy right up until the cows come home.

(*Exits.*)

ZACHARY: (*To himself.*) Simon Starblanket. Patsy . . .

(*Black-out.*)

(*Out of this black-out come the gunshots, much louder this time, and* SIMON's *wailing voice.*)

SIMON: Aieeeeee-yip-yip! Nanabush! . . . (*Fade-in on* SIMON, *in*

510 *the forest close by the large rock, still carrying his hunting rifle.* SIMON *is half-crazed by this time, drunk out of his skull. The full moon glows.*) . . . Weesageechak! Come back! Rosie!

Rosie Kakapetum, tell him to come back, not to run away, cuz we need him . . .

(NANABUSH/PATSY PEGAHMAGAHBOW's *voice comes filtering out of the darkness on the upper level. It is as though* SIMON *were hearing a voice from inside his head.*)

NANABUSH/PATSY: . . . her . . .   515

SIMON: . . . him . . .

NANABUSH/PATSY: . . . her . . .

(*Slow fade-in on* NANABUSH/PATSY, *standing on the upper level, looking down at* SIMON. *She still wears her very large bum.*)

SIMON: . . . weetha ("him/her"—i.e., no gender) . . . Christ! What is it? Him? Her? Stupid fucking language, fuck you, da Englesa. Me no speakum no more da goodie Englesa, in   520 Cree we say "weetha," not "him" or "her" Nanabush, come back! (*Speaks directly to* NANABUSH, *as though he/she were there, directly in front of him; he doesn't see* NANABUSH/PATSY *standing on the upper level.*) Aw, boozhoo how are ya? Me good. Me berry, berry good. I seen you! I just seen you jumping jack-   525 ass thisa away . . .

NANABUSH/PATSY: (*As though she/he were playing games behind* SIMON's *back.*) . . . and thataway . . .

SIMON: . . . and thisaway and . . .

NANABUSH/PATSY: . . . thataway . . .   530

SIMON: . . . and thisaway and . . .

NANABUSH/PATSY: . . . thataway . . .

SIMON: . . . and thisaway and . . .

NANABUSH/PATSY: . . . thataway . . .

SIMON: . . . etcetra, etcetra, etcetra . . .   535

NANABUSH/PATSY: . . . etcetERA. (*Pause.*) She's here! She's here!

SIMON: . . . Nanabush! Weesageechak! . . . (NANABUSH/PATSY *peals out with a silvery, magical laugh that echoes and echoes.*) . . . Dey shove dis . . . whach-you-ma-call-it . . . da crucifix up your holy cunt ouch, eh? Ouch, eh? (SIMON *sees the bloody*   540 *crucifix sitting on the rock and slowly approaches it. He kneels directly before it.*) Nah . . . (*Laughs a long mad, hysterical laugh that ends with hysterical weeping.*) . . . yesssss . . . noooo . . . oh, noooo! Crucifix! (*Spits violently on the crucifix.*) Fucking goddamn crucifix yesssss . . . God! You're a man. You're a   545 woman. You're a man? You're a woman? You see, nineethoo-wan poogoo neetha ("I speak only Cree") . . .

NANABUSH/PATSY: . . . ohhh . . .

SIMON: . . . keetha ma-a? ("How about you?") . . . Nah. Da En-glesa him . . .   550

NANABUSH/PATSY: . . . her . . .

SIMON: . . . him . . .

NANABUSH/PATSY: . . . her . . .

SIMON: . . . him! . . .

NANABUSH/PATSY: . . . her! . . .   555

SIMON: all da time . . .

NANABUSH/PATSY: . . . all da time . . .

SIMON: . . . tsk, tsk, tsk . . .

NANABUSH/PATSY: . . . tsk, tsk, tsk.

SIMON: If God, you are a woman/man in Cree but only a man   560 in da Englesa, then how come you still got a cun . . .

NANABUSH/PATSY: . . . a womb.

(*With this,* SIMON *finally sees* NANABUSH/PATSY. *He calls out to her.*)

SIMON: Patsy! Big Bum Pegahmagahbow, you flying across da ice on world's biggest puck. Patsy, look what dey done to your
565 puss . . . (NANABUSH/PATSY *lifts her skirt and displays the blood stain on her panties. She then finally takes off the prosthetic that is her huge bum and holds it in one arm.*) Hey! (*And* NANABUSH/PATSY *holds an eagle feather up in the air, ready to dance.* SIMON *stomps on the ground, rhythmically, and sings.*) " . . .
570 and me I don't wanna go to the moon, I'm gonna leave that moon alone. I just wanna dance with the Rosebud Sioux this summer, yeah, yeah, yeah . . . " (SIMON *chants and he and* NANABUSH/PATSY *dance, he on the lower level with his hunting rifle in the air, she on the upper level with her eagle feather.*) How, astum,
575 Patsy, kiam. N'tayneemeetootan. ("Come on, Patsy, never mind. Let's go dance.")

(*We hear* ZACHARY JEREMIAH KEECHIGEESIK's *voice calling from the darkness a distance away.*)

ZACHARY: Hey!

(*But* SIMON *and* NANABUSH/PATSY *pay no heed.*)

NANABUSH/PATSY: n'tayneemeetootan South Dakota? . . .
SIMON: how, astum, Patsy. N'tayneemeetootan South
580 Dakota. Hey, Patsy Pegahmagahbow. . . .

(*As he finally approaches her and holds his hand out.*)

NANABUSH/PATSY: (*As she holds her hand out toward his.*) . . . Simon Starblanket . . .
SIMON/NANABUSH/PATSY: . . . eenpaysagee-itan ("I love you to death") . . .

(ZACHARY *finally emerges tentatively from the shadows. He is holding a beautiful, fresh pie.* NANABUSH/PATSY *disappears.*)

585 ZACHARY: (*Calling out over the distance.*) Hey! You want some pie?
SIMON: (*Silence. Calling back.*) What?!

(*Not seeing* ZACHARY, *he looks around cautiously.*)

ZACHARY: I said. You want some pie?
SIMON: (*Calling back, after some confused thought.*) What?
ZACHARY: (*He approaches* SIMON *slowly.*) Do you want some pie?
590 SIMON: (*Silence. Finally, he sees* ZACHARY *and points the gun at him.*) What kind?
ZACHARY: Apple. I just made some. It's still hot.
SIMON: (*Long pause.*) Okay.

(*Slowly,* NANABUSH/PATSY *enters the scene and comes up behind* SIMON, *holding* SIMON's *dancing bustle in front of her, as in a ceremony.*)

ZACHARY: Okay. But you gotta give me the gun first. (*The gun*
595 *goes off accidentally, just missing* ZACHARY's *head.*) I said, you gotta give me the gun first.

(*Gradually, the dancing bustle begins to shimmer and dance in* NANABUSH/PATSY's *hands.*)

SIMON: Patsy. I gotta go see Patsy.
ZACHARY: You and me and Patsy and Hera. We're gonna go have some pie. Fresh, hot apple pie. Then, we go to Sud-
600 bury and have a look at that Mobart, what do you say?

(*The shimmering movements of the bustle balloon out into these magical, dance-like arches, as* NANABUSH/PATSY *maneuvers it directly in front of* SIMON, *hiding him momentarily. Behind this,* SIMON *drops the base of the rifle to the ground, causing it to go off accidentally. The bullet hits* SIMON *in the stomach. He falls to the ground.* ZACHARY *lets go of his pie and runs over to him. The shimmering of the bustle dies off into the darkness of the forest and disappears,* NANABUSH/PATSY *maneuvering it.*)

ZACHARY: Simon! Simon! Oh, lordy, lordy, lordy . . . Are you alright? Are you okay? Simon. Simon. Talk to me. Goodness sakes, talk to me Simon. Ayumi-in! ("Talk to me!")
SIMON: (*Barely able to speak, as he sinks slowly to the ground beside the large rock.*) Kamoowanow . . . apple . . . pie . . . patima . . . 605 neetha . . . igwa Patsy . . . n'gapeetootanan . . . patima . . . apple . . . pie . . . neee. ("We'll eat . . . apple . . . pie . . . later . . . me . . . and Patsy . . . we'll come over . . . later . . . apple . . . pie . . . neee.")

(*He dies.*)

ZACHARY: (*As he kneels over* SIMON's *body, the full moon glowing even* 610 *redder.*) Oh, lordy, lordy . . . Holy shit! Holy shit! What's happening? What's become of this place? What's happening to this place? What's happening to these people? My people. He didn't have to die. He didn't have to die. That's the goddamn most stupid . . . no reason . . . this kind of 615 living has got to stop. It's got to stop! (*Talking and then just shrieking at the sky.*) Aieeeeeee-Lord! God! God of the Indian! God of the Whiteman! God-Al-fucking-mighty! Whatever the fuck your name is. Why are you doing this to us? Why are you doing this to us? Are you up there at all? 620 Or are you some stupid, drunken shit, out-of-your-mind-passed out under some great beer table up there in your stupid fucking clouds? Come down! Astum oota! ("Come down here!") Why don't you come down? I dare you to come down from your high-falutin' fuckin' shit-throne up 625 there, come down and show us you got the guts to stop this stupid, stupid, stupid way of living. It's got to stop. It's got to stop. It's got to stop. It's got to stop. It's got to stop. It's got to stop . . .

(*He collapses over* SIMON's *body and weeps. Fade-out. Towards the end of this speech, a light comes up on* NANABUSH. *Her perch (i.e., the jukebox) has swivelled around and she is sitting on a toilet having a good shit. He/she is dressed in an old man's white beard and wig, but also wearing sexy, elegant women's high-heeled pumps. Surrounded by white, puffy clouds, she/he sits with her legs crossed, nonchalantly filing his/her fingernails. Fade-out.*)

(*Fade-in on* BIG JOEY's *living room/kitchen.* BIG JOEY, DICKIE BIRD HALKED, CREATURE NATAWAYS, SPOOKY LACROIX *and* PIERRE ST. PIERRE *are sitting and standing in various positions, in complete silence. A hush pervades the room for about twenty beats.* DICKIE BIRD *is holding* BIG JOEY's *hunting rifle. Suddenly,* ZACHARY JEREMIAH KEECHIGEESIK *enters; in a semi-crazed state.* DICKIE BIRD *starts and points the rifle straight at* ZACHARY's *head.*)

CREATURE: Zachary Jeremiah! What are you doing here? 630
BIG JOEY: Lookin' for your shorts, Zach?

(*From his position on the couch, he motions* DICKIE BIRD *to put the gun down.* DICKIE BIRD *does so.*)

ZACHARY: (*To* BIG JOEY.) You're unbelievable. You're fucking unbelievable. You let this young man, you let your own son get away with this inconceivable act . . .

635 CREATURE: Don't say that to him, Zachary Jeremiah, don't say that . . .

ZACHARY: (*Ignoring* CREATURE.) You know he did it and you're hiding him what in God's name is wrong with you?

SPOOKY: Zachary Jeremiah, you're not yourself . . .

640 PIERRE: Nope. Not himself. Talkin' wild.

(*Sensing potential violence, he sneaks out the door.*)

BIG JOEY: (*To* ZACHARY.) He don't even know he done anything.

ZACHARY: Bull shit! They're not even sure the air ambulance will get Patsy Pegahmagahbow to Sudbury in time. Simon Starblanket just shot himself and this boy is responsible . . .

(SIMON *rises slowly from the ground and "sleep walks" right through this scene and up to the upper level, towards the full moon. The men are only vaguely aware of his passing.*)

645 BIG JOEY: He ain't responsible for nothin'.

ZACHARY: Simon Starblanket was on his way to South Dakota where he could have learned a few things and made something of himself, same place you went and made a total asshole of yourself seventeen years ago . . .

650 CREATURE: Shush, Zachary Jeremiah, that's the past . . .

SPOOKY: . . . the past . . .

CREATURE: . . . Chris'sakes . . .

ZACHARY: What happened to all those dreams you were so full of for your people, the same dreams this young man just 655 died for?

SPOOKY: (*To* BIG JOEY, *though not looking at him.*) And my sister, Black Lady Halked, seventeen years ago at that bar, Big Joey, you could have stopped her drinking, you could have sent her home and this thing never would have happened. 660 That was your son inside her belly.

CREATURE: He didn't do nothing. He wouldn't let me do nothing. He just stood there and watched the whole thing . . .

SPOOKY: Creature Nataways!

CREATURE: I don't care. I'm gonna tell. He watched this little 665 bastard do that to Patsy Pegahmagahbow . . .

BIG JOEY: (*Suddenly turning on* CREATURE.) You little cocksucker!

(DICKIE BIRD *hits* CREATURE *on the back with the butt of the rifle, knocking him unconscious.*)

SPOOKY: Why, Big Joey, why did you do that?

(*Silence.*)

ZACHARY: Yes, Joe. Why?

(*Long silence. All the men look at* BIG JOEY.)

BIG JOEY: (*Raising his arms, as for a battle cry.*) "This is the end 670 of the suffering of a great nation!" That was me. Wounded Knee, South Dakota, Spring of '73. The FBI. They beat us to the ground. Again and again and again. Ever since that spring, I've had these dreams where blood is spillin' out from my groin, nothin' there but blood and emptiness. It's 675 like . . . I lost myself. So when I saw this baby comin' out

of Caroline, Black Lady . . . Gazelle dancin' . . . all this blood . . . and I knew it was gonna come . . . I . . . I tried to stop it . . . I freaked out. I don't know what I did . . . and I knew it was mine . . .

ZACHARY: Why? Why did you let him do it? Why? Why did 680 you let him do it? Why? Why did you let him do it? Why? Why did you let him do it? (*Finally grabbing* BIG JOEY *by the collar.*) Why?! Why did you let him do it?!

BIG JOEY: (*Breaking free from* ZACHARY's *hold.*) Because I hate them! I hate them fuckin' bitches. Because they—our own 685 women—took the fuckin' power away from us faster than the FBI ever did.

SPOOKY: (*Softly, in the background.*) They always had it.

(*Silence.*)

BIG JOEY: There. I said it. I'm tired. Tired.

(*He slumps down on the couch and cries.*)

ZACHARY: (*Softly.*) Joe. Joe.   690

(*Fade-out.*)

(*Out of this darkness emerges the sound of* SIMON STARBLANKET's *chanting voice. Away up over* NANABUSH's *perch, the moon begins to glow, fully and magnificently. Against it, in silhouette, we see* SIMON *wearing his powwow bustle.* SIMON STARBLANKET *is dancing in the moon. Fade-out.*)

(*Fade-in on the "ice" at the hockey arena, where* PIERRE ST. PIERRE, *in full referee regalia, is gossiping with* CREATURE NATAWAYS *and* SPOOKY LACROIX. CREATURE *is knitting, with great difficulty, pink baby booties.* SPOOKY *is holding his new baby, wrapped in a pale blue knit blanket. We hear the sound of a hockey arena, just before a big game.*)

PIERRE: . . . she says to me: "did you know, Pierre St. Pierre, that Gazelle Nataways found Zachary Jeremiah Keechigeesik's undershorts under her chesterfield and washed them and put them in a box real nice, all folded up and even sprinkled her perfume all over them and sashayed 695 herself over to Hera Keechigeesik's house and handed the box over to her? I just about had a heart attack," she says to me. "And what's more," she says to me, "when Hera Keechigeesik opened that box, there was a picture sittin' on top of them shorts, a color picture of none other than our 700 very own Zachary Jeremiah Keechigeesik . . . (*Unseen by* PIERRE, ZACHARY *approaches the group, wearing a baker's hat and carrying a rolling pin.*) . . . wearin' nothin' but the suit God gave him. That's when Hera Keechigeesik went wild, like a banshee tigger, and she tore the hair out of Gazelle 705 Nataways which, as it turns out, was a wig . . ." Imagine. After all these years. " . . . and she beat Gazelle Nataways to a cinder, right there into the treacherous icy door-step. And that's when 'the particular puck' finally came squishin' out of them considerable Nataways bosoms." And gentle- 710 men? The Wasy Wailerettes are on again!

CREATURE: Ho-leee!

SPOOKY: Holy fuck!

PIERRE: And I say shit la ma . . . (*Finally seeing* ZACHARY, *who is standing there, listening to all this.*) . . . oh my . . . (PIERRE 715 *turns quickly to* SPOOKY'*s baby.*) . . . hello there, koochie-koochie-koo, welcome to the world!

SPOOKY: It's not koochie-koochie-koo, Pierre St. Pierre. Her name's "Kichigeechacha." Rhymes with Lalala. Ain't she
720 purdy?

(*Up in the "bleachers,"* BIG JOEY *enters and prepares his microphone stand.* DICKIE BIRD *enters with a big sign saying: "WASY-FM" and hangs it proudly up above the microphone stand.*)

PIERRE: Aw, she'll be readin' that ole holy bible before you can go:"Phhht! Phhht!"

(PIERRE *accidentally spits in the baby's face.* SPOOKY *shoos him away.*)

SPOOKY: "Phhht! Phhht!" to you too, Pierre St. Pierre.

CREATURE: Spooky Lacroix. Lalala. They never made it to
725 Sudbury General.

SPOOKY: I was busy helping Eugene Starblanket out with Simon . . .

SPOOKY/PIERRE: . . . may he rest in peace . . .

ZACHARY: Good old Rosie Kakapetum. "Stand and deliver,"
730 they said to her. And stand and deliver she did. How's the knitting going there, Creature Nataways?

CREATURE: Kichigeechacha, my **god**-daughter, she's wearin' all the wrong colors. I gotta work like a dog.

PIERRE: (*Calling up to* DICKIE BIRD HALKED.) Don't you worry a
735 wart about that court appearance, Dickie Bird Halked. I'll be right there beside you tellin' that ole judge a thing or two about that goddamn jukebox.

SPOOKY: (*To* CREATURE.) Come on. Let's go watch Lalala play her first game.

(*He and* CREATURE *go up to the "bleachers" on the upper level, directly in front of* NANABUSH'*s perch, to watch the big "game."*)

740 PIERRE: (*Reading from his clip-board and checking off the list.*) Now then, Dominique Ladouche, Black Lady Halked, Annie Cook, June Bug Mcleod . . .

(*He stops abruptly for* BIG JOEY'*s announcement, as do the other men.*)

BIG JOEY: (*On the microphone.*) Patsy Pegahmagahbow, who is re-cuperating at Sudbury General Hospital, sends her love and
745 requests that the first goal scored by the Wasy Wailerettes be dedicated to the memory of Simon Starblanket . . .

(CREATURE *and* SPOOKY, *with knitting and baby, respectively, are now up in the "bleachers" with* DICKIE BIRD *and* BIG JOEY, *who are standing beside each other at the microphone stand.* PIERRE ST. PIERRE *is again skating around on the "ice" in his own inimitable fashion, "warming up."* ZACHARY JEREMIAH KEECHIGEESIK, *meanwhile, now has his apple pie, as well as his rolling pin, in hand, still wearing his baker's hat. At this point, the hockey arena sounds shift abruptly to the sound of women wailing and pucks hitting boards, echoing and echoing as in a vast empty chamber. As this "hockey game sequence" progresses, the spectacle of the men watching, cheering, etc., becomes more and more dream-like, all the men's movements imperceptibly breaking down into slow motion, until they fade, later, into the darkness.* ZACHARY *"sleep walks" through the whole lower level of the set, almost as though he were retracing his steps back through the whole*

play. Slowly, he takes off his clothes item by item, until, by the end, he is back lying naked on the couch where he began the play, except that, this time, it will be his own couch he is lying on. BIG JOEY *continues uninterrupted.*)

. . . And there they are, ladies igwa gentlemen, there they are, the most beautiful, daring, death-defying Indian women in the world, the Wasy Wailerettes! How, Number Nine Hera Keechigeesik, CAPTAIN of the Wasy Wailerettes, face-off   750
igwa itootum asichi Number Nine Flora McDonald, Captain of the Canoe Lake Bravettes. Hey, soogi pagichee-ipinew "particular puck" referee Pierre St. Pierre . . .

CREATURE: Go Hera go! Go Hera go! Go Hera go! . . .

(*Repeated all the way through—and under—*BIG JOEY'*s commentary.*)

BIG JOEY: igwa seemak wathay g'waskootoo like a herd of   755
wild turtles . . .

SPOOKY: Wasy once. Wasy twice. Holy jumping Christ! Rim ram. God damn. Fuck, son-of-a-bitch, shit!

(*Repeated in time to* CREATURE'*s cheer, all the way through—and under—*BIG JOEY'*s commentary.*)

BIG JOEY: . . . Hey, aspin Number Six Dry Lips Manigitogan, right-winger for the Wasy Wailerettes, eemaskamat Num-   760
ber Thirteen of the Canoe Lake Bravettes anee-i "particular puck" . . . (DICKIE BIRD *begins chanting and stomping his foot in time to* CREATURE'*s and* SPOOKY'*s cheers. Bits and pieces of* NANABUSH/GAZELLE NATAWAYS' *"strip music" and Kitty Wells'* "It Wasn't God Who Made Honky Tonk Angels" *begin to weave*   765
in and out of this "sound collage," a collage which now has a definite "pounding" rhythm to it. Over it all soars the sound of ZACHARY'*s harmonica, swooping and diving brilliantly, recalling many of* NANABUSH'*s appearances throughout the play.* BIG JOEY
continues uninterrupted.) . . . igwa aspin sipweesin-   770
skwataygew. Hey, k'seegoochin! How, Number Six Dry Lips Manigitogan igwa soogi pugamawew anee-i "particular puck" ita Number Twenty-six Little Girl Manitowabi, left-winger for the Wasy Wailerettes, katee-ooteetuk blue line ita Number Eleven Black Lady Halked, wha! defense-   775
woman for the Wasy Wailerettes, kagatchitnat anee-i "particular puck" igwa seemak kapassiwatat Captain Hera Keechigeesikwa igwa Hera Keechigeesik mitooni eepimithat, hey, kwayus graceful Hera Keechigeesik, mitooni Russian ballerina eesinagoosit. Captain Hera   780
Keechigeesik bee-line igwa itootum straight for the Canoe Lake Bravettes' net igwa shootiwatew anee-i "particular puck" igwa she shoots, she scores . . . almost! Wha! Close one, ladies igwa gentlemen, kwayus close one. But Number Six Dry Lips Manigitogan, right-winger for the Wasy   785
Wailerettes, accidentally tripped and blocked the shot . . . (BIG JOEY'*s voice begins to trail off as, at this point,* CREATURE
NATAWAYS *marches over and angrily grabs the microphone away from him.*) . . . How, Number Nine Flora McDonald, Cap-tain of the Canoe Lake Bravettes, igwa ooteetinew anee-i   790
"particular puck" igwa skate-oo-oo behind the net igwa

---

747 **. . . And . . .** The following hockey commentary by Big Joey (pp. 1575–1576) is translated on p. 1577.

soogi heading along the right side of the rink ita Number Twenty-one Annie Cook ...

CREATURE: (*Off microphone, as he marches over to it.*) Aw shit! Aw
795   shit! ... (*He grabs the microphone and, as he talks into it, the sound of all the other men's voices, including the entire "sound collage," begins to fade.*) ... That Dry Lips Manigitogan, she's no damn good, Spooky Lacroix, I tole you once I
800   tole you twice she shouldna done it she shouldna done what she went and did goddawful Dry Lips Manigitogan they shouldna let her play, she's too fat, she's gotten positively blubbery lately, I tole you once I tole you twice that Dry Lips Manigitogan oughta move to Kapuskasing, she re-
805   ally oughta, Spooky Lacroix. I tole you once I tole you twice she oughta move to Kapuskasing, Dry Lips oughta move to Kapuskasing! Dry Lips oughta move to Kapuskasing! Dry Lips oughta move to Kapuskasing Dry Lips oughta move to Kapuskasing Dry Lips oughta move to Kapuskasing Dry Lips oughta move to
810   Kapuskasing Dry Lips oughta move to Kapuskasing Dry Lips oughta move to Kapuskasing ...

(*And this, too, fades into, first a whisper, magnified on tape to "otherworldly" proportions, then into a slow kind of heavy breathing. On top of this we hear* SPOOKY's *baby crying. Complete fade-out on all this [lights and sound], except for the baby's crying and the heavy breathing, which continue in the darkness. When the lights come up again, we are in* ZACHARY's *own living room [i.e., what was all along* BIG JOEY's *living room/kitchen, only much cleaner]. The couch* ZACHARY *lies on is now covered with a "starblanket" and over the pin-up poster of Marilyn Monroe now hangs what was, earlier on,* NANABUSH's *large powwow dancing bustle. The theme from "The Smurfs" television show bleeds in.* ZACHARY *is lying on the couch face down, naked, sleeping and snoring. The television in front of the couch comes on and "The Smurfs" are playing merrily away.* ZACHARY's *wife, the "real"* HERA KEECHIGEESIK, *enters carrying their baby, who is covered completely with a blanket.* HERA *is soothing the crying baby.*)

ZACHARY: (*Talking in his sleep.*) ... Dry Lips ... oughta move to ... Kapus ...
HERA: Poosees.
815   ZACHARY: ... kasing ... damn silliest thing I heard in my life ...
HERA: Honey.

(*Bends over the couch and kisses* ZACHARY *on the bum.*)

ZACHARY: ... goodness sakes, Hera, you just had a baby ... (*Suddenly, he jumps up and falls off the couch.*) Simon!
820   HERA: Yoah! Keegatch igwa kipageecheep'skawinan. ("Yoah! You almost knocked us down.")
ZACHARY: Hera! Where's my shorts?!

HERA: Neee, kigipoochimeek awus-chayees. ("Neee, just a couple of inches past the rim of your ass-hole.")
ZACHARY: Neee, chimagideedoosh. ("Neee, you unfragrant   825
kozy": Ojibway.)

(*He struggles to a sitting position on the couch.*)

HERA: (*Correcting him and laughing.*) "ChimagideeDEESH." ("You unfragrant KOOZIE.")
ZACHARY: Alright. "ChimagideeDEESH."
HERA: And what were you dreaming abou ...   830
ZACHARY: (*Finally seeing the television.*) Hey, it's the Smurfs! And they're not playing hockey de Englesa.
HERA: Neee, machi ma-a tatoo-Saturday morning Smurfs. Mootha meena weegatch hockey meetaweewuk weethawow Smurfs. ("Well, of course, the Smurfs are on every Saturday   835
morning. But they never play hockey, those Smurfs.") Here, you take her. (*She hands the baby over to* ZACHARY *and goes to sit beside him.*) Boy, that full moon last night. Ever look particularly like a giant puck, eh? Neee ...

(*Silence.* ZACHARY *plays with the baby.*)

ZACHARY: (*To* HERA.) Hey, cup-cake. You ever think of playing   840
hockey?
HERA: Yeah, right. That's all I need is a flying puck right in the left tit, neee ... (*But she stops to speculate.*) ... hockey, hmmm ...
ZACHARY: (*To himself.*) Lordy, lordy, lordy ... (HERA *fishes*   845
ZACHARY's *undershorts, which are pale blue in color, from under a cushion and hands them to him.* ZACHARY *gladly grabs them.*) Neee, magawa nipeetawitoos ... ("Neee, here's my sharts ... ")
HERA: (*Correcting him and laughing.*) "NipeetawiTAS." ("My   850
SHORTS")
ZACHARY: Alright. "NipeetawiTAS." (*Dangles the shorts up to the baby's face with thumb and fore-finger and laughs. Sing-songy, bouncing the baby on his lap:*) Magawa nipeetawitas. Nipeetawitas. Nipeetawitas. Nipeetawitas ...   855

(*The baby finally gets "dislodged" from the blanket and emerges, naked. And the last thing we see is this beautiful naked Indian man lifting his naked baby Indian girl up in the air, his wife sitting beside them watching and laughing. Slow fade-out. Split seconds before complete black-out,* HERA *peals out with this magical, silvery* NANABUSH *laugh, which is echoed and echoed by one last magical arpeggio on the harmonica, from off-stage. Finally, in the darkness, the last sound we hear is the baby's laughing voice, magnified on tape to fill the entire theater. And this, too, fades into complete silence.*)

(*End of play.*)

TRANSLATION OF BIG JOEY'S HOCKEY COMMENTARIES

Translation from the Cree of Big Joey's hockey commentary, Act One, pages 1564–1565.

. . . Hey, and there goes Number Six Dry Lips Manigitogan, right-winger for the Wasy Wailerettes . . . and steals the puck from Number Thirteen of the Canoe Lake Bravettes . . . and skates off. Hey, is she ever flying . . . (*Off microphone.*) Creature Nataways. Shut up. (*To the other men.*) Get this asshole out of here. (*Back on microphone.*) Now, Number Six Dry Lips Manigitogan, right-winger for the Wasy Wailerettes, shoots the puck and the puck goes flying over towards the center-line . . . where Number Nine Hera Keechigeesik, left-winger for . . . the Wasy Wailerettes, catches it. Now, Number Nine Hera Keechigeesik . . . approaching the blue line where Number One Gazelle Nataways, Captain of the Wasy Wailerettes, tries to get the puck off her, but Number Nine Hera Keechigeesik won't give it to her. Wha! "Hooking," says referee Pierre St. Pierre, Gazelle Nataways has apparently hooked her own team-mate Hera Keechigeesik, wha! Now, Number One Gazelle Nataways, Captain of the Wasy Wailerettes, facing off once again with Number Nine Flora McDonald, Captain of the Canoe Lake Bravettes and Flora McDonald shoots the puck, but Number Thirty-seven Big Bum Pegahmagahbow, defense-woman for the Wasy Wailerettes, stops the puck and passes it to Number Eleven Black Lady Halked, also defense-woman for the Wasy Wailerettes, but Gazelle Nataways, Captain of the Wasy Wailerettes, gives a mean body check to her own team-mate Black Lady Halked woops! She falls, ladies and gentlemen, Black Lady Halked hits the boards and Black Lady Halked is singin' the blues, ladies and gentlemen, Black Lady sings the blues. (*Off microphone.*) What the hell is going on down there? Dickie Bird, get off the ice! (*Back on microphone.*) Wha! Number Eleven Black Lady Halked is up in a flash and grabs the puck from Gazelle Nataways, holy shit! The ailing but very, very furious Black Lady Halked skates back, turns and takes aim, it's gonna be a slap shot, ladies and gentlemen, Black Lady Halked is gonna take a slap shot for sure and Black Lady Halked shoots the puck, wha! She shoots straight at her very own captain, Gazelle Nataways and holy shit, holy shit, holy fuckin' shit!

Translation from the Cree of Big Joey's hockey commentary, Act Two, pages 1575–1576.

. . . And there they are, ladies and gentlemen, there they are, the most beautiful, daring, death-defying Indian women in the world, the Wasy Wailerettes! Now, Number Nine HeraKeechigeesik, CAPTAIN of the Wasy Wailerettes, facing off with Number Nine Flora McDonald, Captain of the Canoe Lake Bravettes. Hey, and referee Pierre St. Pierre drops the "particular puck" . . . and takes off like a herd of wild turtles . . . Hey, and there goes Dry Lips Manigitogan, right-winger for the Wasy Wailerettes, and steals the "particular puck" from Number Thirteen of the Canoe Lake Bravettes . . . and skates off. Hey, is she ever flying. Now, Number Six Dry Lips Manigitogan shoots the "particular puck" towards where Number Twenty-six Little Girl Manitowabi, left-winger for the Wasy Wailerettes, is heading straight for the blue line where Number Eleven Black Lady Halked, wha! defense-woman for the Wasy Wailerettes, catches the "particular puck" and straight-way passes it to Captain Hera Keechigeesik and Hera Keechi-geesik is just a-flyin', hey, is she graceful or what, that Hera Keechigeesik, she looks just like a Russian ballerina. Captain Hera Keechigeesik now makes a bee-line straight for the Canoe Lake Bravettes' net and shoots the "particular puck" and she shoots, she scores . . . almost! Wha! Close one, ladies and gentlemen, real close one. But Number Six Dry Lips Manitigotan, right-winger for the Wasy Wailerettes, accidentally tripped and blocked the shot . . . (CREATURE NATAWAYS *grabs the microphone away from* BIG JOEY.) . . . Now, Number Nine Flora McDonald, Captain of the Canoe Lake Bravettes, grabs the "particular puck" and skates behind the net and now heading along the right side of the rink where Number Twenty-one Annie Cook . . .

Judith Thompson

Judith Thompson (b. 1954), is one of Canada's most celebrated playwrights. Born in Montréal and raised both in the United States and in Kingston, Ontario, Thompson took her B.A. at Queen's University (Ontario) and studied acting at the National Theatre School before turning to playwriting. Her first play, *The Crackwalker* (1981), established Thompson's characteristic blend of poetic language and brutal violence. Several of her major plays have won important awards in Canada, including *White Biting Dog* (1985, Governor General's Award for Drama), *I Am Yours* (1987, Chalmers Award), *Tornado* (1988, Nelly Award for Best Radio Drama), and *The Other Side of the Dark* (1989, Governor General's Award). *Lion in the Streets* was first produced at the Tarragon Theatre in Toronto and won a Chalmers Award in 1991. She currently teaches playwriting at the University of Guelph.

LION IN THE STREETS

Lion in the Streets is exemplary of Thompson's violent, verbally dazzling theater. The play is structured as a series of vignettes, scenes of everyday life: children playing in a playground, a wife accusing her cheating husband, a parents' meeting at a daycare center, a woman telling her best friend that she has cancer. So, too, Thompson captures the everyday abrasions of social life, particularly those of class, in the ways the children torment Isobel because she's poor and Portuguese, in working-class Rhonda's anger at the condescension of the other parents, and in the ways the paraplegic Scarlett understands and criticizes the journalist Christine's romanticized view of poverty, disease, and suffering. Yet from the play's opening moment, Thompson rends the delicate surface of everyday life. As the ghost of murdered Isobel leads the audience from scene to scene, violence erupts into the everyday world, ripping through those superficial realities. The viciousness of the children in the opening scene is echoed several times, as the adults—when Sue confronts her husband at the dinner party, the fighting at the parents' meeting—repeatedly enact childish yet irrepressible malevolence. Much as the play is haunted by Isobel, murdered seventeen years earlier, so everyone in the play is haunted by the past, by the memories and fantasies that continue to animate their lives today: Joanna's fantasy of committing Ophelia's suicide; Father Hayes's confession; even Rhonda's hymn to the importance of sweets. These fantasies are deeply personal and often destructive and as the play proceeds, Isobel is joined by characters who seem to materialize memory and desire. The play's action becomes significantly more violent as well, as Christine kills the paralyzed Scarlett, giving her the kiss of death, as Rodney summons and murders the memory of Michael and of childhood sexual guilt, as Edward forces Sherry to reexperience a brutal rape as *his* fantasy of her sexual fulfillment.

   Lion in the Streets closes with Isobel's confrontation of her murderer Ben, and as in many of the previous scenes, the meaning and purpose of this confrontation is ambiguous. Isobel at once wants to kill Ben and to forgive him, to arrive at a moment that transcends the physical, emotional, and psychological violence that motivates daily life. As she puts it, to the audience, "I came back. I take my life. I want you all to take your life. I want you to have your life."

Judith Thompson's *Lion in the Streets,* produced at the University of Newfoundland in 1999.

LION IN THE STREETS

Judith Thompson

CHARACTERS

ISOBEL	ISOBEL'S FATHER	RON	ELLEN
NELLIE	TIMMY	JILL	SCARLETT
RACHEL	LAURA	RHONDA	RODNEY
SCALATO	BILL	JOANNE	MICHAEL
MARTIN	GEORGE	DAVID	SHERRY
SUE	LILY	FATHER HAYES	EDWARD
ROSE	MARIA	CHRISTINE	BEN

The ghost of ISOBEL, *a deranged and very ragged looking nine-year-old Portuguese girl, runs around and around a large circle, to music, terrified of a remembered pursuer, in fact, the man who killed her in this playground seventeen years before the action of the play. There are autumn leaves all over the playground, and the kids who approach her all have large handfuls of leaves, which they throw at her. At this point* ISOBEL *does not know she is a ghost, but she knows that something is terribly wrong. She is terrified.*

ISOBEL: Doan be scare. Doan be scare. (*Turns to audience.*) Doan be scare of this pickshur! This pickshur is niiiice, nice! I looove this pickshur, this pickshur is mine! (*Gesturing behind her.*) Is my house, is my street, is my park, is
5 my people! You know me, you know me very hard! I live next house to you, with my brother and sisters, Maria, Luig, Carla and Romeo we play, we play with your girl, your boy, you know me, you know me very hard. But . . . when did tha be? Tha not be now! Tha not be today! I
10 think tha be very long years ago I think I be old. I think I be very old. Is my house but is not my house is my street but is not my street my people is gone I am lost. I am lost. I AM LOOOOOOOOOST!!

(*Four children—two girls and two boys—laugh and approach* ISOBEL.)

NELLIE: Take a bird why doncha?
15 RACHEL: Go back with the nutties to the nuttyhouse!
SCALATO: She looks like a crazy dog!
MARTIN: (*Barks.*) Hey!

(*All bark.*)

ISOBEL: Peoples! Peoples, little boy little girl peoples! Hey!

(ISOBEL *walks towards them.*)

MARTIN: What's she doin?
20 NELLIE: She's coming over here!
RACHEL: She's gonna get us!
ISOBEL: You, girl, you help to me. I am lost you see! You help!
NELLIE: She smells.
RACHEL: You should dial 911 so the police could help you.
25 SCALATO: Where do you live?
MARTIN: With all the other pork and cheese west of Christie Street?
RACHEL: Martin that's not nice.

ISOBEL: (*Overlapping.*) Portuguese, Portuguese, yes . . . I catch a bus! Is there a bus, bus maybe? To take me to my home? 30 You know a bus?
SCALATO: No buses here.
ISOBEL: Yah, bus right here, bus right here, number ten, eleven, I take with my mother to cleaning job, where this bus? 35
SCALATO: I said there's no buses here you ugly little SNOT.
ISOBEL: (*Points.*) You! YOU bad boy you bad boy say Isobel, BAD.
SCALATO: Why don't you get your ugly little face outa here, snot? 40
MARTIN: Snotface!
ISOBEL: Shut up boy, shut up, I kill you I kill you boy.
SCALATO: Hey she's gonna kill me!
RACHEL: She's a witch.

(ISOBEL *tosses rocks at them.*)

MARTIN: She's throwin rocks! Hey she's throwin rocks! 45
NELLIE: STOP IT.
RACHEL: Stop throwin rocks or we'll tell the police!
ISOBEL: You BAD boy you BAD I will kill you!
SCALATO: (*Jumping off, attacking her.*) You just try it you goddamned faggot!! Faggot! Faggot!! (*Hitting her.*) 50
ISOBEL: (*Growling like a dog.*) G-r-r-r-r-r. G-r-r-r-r-r.

(*They circle one another.*)

MARTIN: What's she doing?
NELLIE: I don't like her.

(ISOBEL *and* SCALATO *scrap and the others join in.* SUE, *a thirty-eight-year-old woman in a grey sweatsuit, walking home from a meeting, spies the fight and rushes up.*)

SUE: Hey! Hey hey hey stop that right now!

(SUE *pries them apart.*)

HEY! Listen! What is going on?? 55
ISOBEL: I KILL YOU BOY!
SCALATO: She started it!
MARTIN: She was throwing rocks at us!
ROSE: She's crazy.

(ISOBEL *leaps towards* SCALATO. SUE *catches her, she falls to the ground.*)

60 SUE: Little girl? Little girl!
    ISOBEL: (*Overlapping.*) I kill that stupid boy.
    SCALATO: She started it, lady.
    MARTIN: I'm getting out of here.
    SCALATO: Me too.
65 NELLIE & ROSE: Wait for me!!
    SCALATO: You chicken, Martin! You suck!
    ISOBEL: I kill that stupid boy! (*Beat.*) I no like those boys.
    SUE: I'm sorry if they hurt you.
    ISOBEL: They no want play with me. Why they no want play
70   with me? Why all the kids no want play with Isobel? Ha?
    SUE: Ohhh . . . sometimes kids are just . . . mean, that way, Iso-
        bel, when I was little kids were mean like that to me once.
    ISOBEL: Kids? Mean no play to you?
    SUE: That's right. We had just moved to a new town, Corn-
75   wall actually, near Montreal? Well my sisters and I went for
        a walk around the neighbourhood and these big boys on
        bikes started firing arrows at us.
    ISOBEL: Boys on bikes?
    SUE: That's right, just like those nasty boys!
80 ISOBEL: Nasty boys, to you, too! Mean to you!!
    SUE: That's right. And those arrows, they hurt! They really
        hurt!! And I was the oldest so I told my sisters, 'Just cry,
        just start to cry and then maybe they'll feel sorry for us,'
        so we all started to cry.
85 ISOBEL: Cry.
    SUE: But you know what? It didn't work! They kept shoot-
        ing those arrows anyways. They were just *mean.*
    ISOBEL: Mean boys shoot arrows. Haaah!
    SUE: AND suddenly, a bigger boy, about sixteen, came along
90   and made them stop, and you know, he was like an angel,
        to us, an angel who came down from the sky on his big
        blue bicycle I've never forgotten that.
    ISOBEL: Never forgetting.
    SUE: Nope. I guess I'm your helper today.
95 ISOBEL: Helper.
    ISOBEL'S FATHER: (*On porch.*) Hey! Is-o-bel.
    SUE: Isobel is that your father?
    ISOBEL: Father. My father. Eu pensava que té tinha perdedo!
    ISOBEL'S FATHER: (*Ordering* ISOBEL *to go around to the back*
100   *door.*) Vai pela porta das traseiras.
    SUE: Hello.

(ISOBEL'S FATHER *grunts.*)

    My name is Sue Winters and I don't know if you're aware
    of it, but some of the boys in the neighbourhood have
    been well I'd say doing some not very nice teasing of your
105 daughter. I just . . . thought . . . you might . . .

(*He goes in, slamming the door.*)

    Poor man probably works all day in construction and then
    all night as a janitor in some Bay Street office building.
    What a life.

(SUE *exits.*)

    ISOBEL: My father? My father is not there. My father is dead.
110   Yes, was killed by a subway many many years; it it breathed
        very hard push push over my father; push over to God. Hi
        my father.

(*Music. Lights come up just a bit.* SUE *is in her son* TIMMY'S *room, in the dark.* TIMMY *is in bed.* ISOBEL *watches.*)

    SUE: And so the giant starfish saved the drowning boy.
    TIMMY: What was the starfish's name?
    SUE: The starfish's name? Uh . . . Joey. It was Joey.   115
    TIMMY: Mummy? Why isn't magic true? I want magic to be
        true.
    SUE: Well. It is true, in a way, it . . .
    TIMMY: Not it's not. It's not true. And ya know what else?
    SUE: What, darling?   120
    TIMMY: I think tonight's the night.
    SUE: That what, Tim?
    TIMMY: That we're all gonna die. Tonight's the night we're
        gonna die.

(*Music. A dinner party, around a table.* ISOBEL *is there, invisible. The conversation is simultaneous.*)

    LAURA: There was nothing to do! Nothing to bloody do but 125
        sing in the church choir!! And go to baked-bean suppers!!
        The snow at one point was actually up to the second-
        floor window.
    BILL: No, she had the *gall* to ask my male students to, 'Please
        leave the room,' for her senior seminar. She did 'not wish 130
        to be dominated by men.' Where did that leave me, I asked
        her?
    LILY: No, no no, you have to pat the dough, pat it for ohh a
        good five minutes then put it in the microwave for one,
        then take it out, then pat it again.   135
    GEORGE: St. Paul said, 'We are as vapour,' what is it? Like
        'vapour vanisheth' or—something. 'We are no more.' So I
        got up this notion of Martians—being these—wisps of
        vapour . . . No, you see your problem is you want the
        aliens to be like you, you are anthropomorphizing, you . . . 140
    LAURA: That's so boring. That's so knee-jerk boring.
    BILL: And she launched into the most savage tirade—

(SUE *rushes in, dressed in her sweatsuit and sneakers. Everyone turns and freezes, except* BILL, *who continues to talk until* SUE'S *third* 'BILL'.)

    SUE: Bill . . . Bill . . . Bill!! We have to talk!
    BILL: Sue! Hi! Who's with the boys?
    SUE: Mum came over, Bill I need to talk, NOW.   145
    LAURA: Would you like a drink, Sue? We have . . .
    GEORGE: Yeah, come in and sit down . . .
    SUE: No, no thank you, I just . . . want to talk to my husband.
    ISOBEL: My helper, Suuuuusan!
    BILL: Oh—okay, Sue, I'll just finish this conversation. Any- 150
        way—
    SUE: He thinks he's going to die.
    BILL: Who?
    SUE: Timmy! Your son! He—
    BILL: What, did he say that tonight? Oh, that's just kids, he's— 155
    SUE: BILL, come home, your son is very depressed his father
        is never there, why are you never never . . .
    BILL: Sue PLEASE, we'll talk about it later, okay? So as I was
        saying, Laura . . .
    SUE: Come with me.   160
    BILL: I'll come in a while. I'll just finish this conversation, and
        then I'll come, okay?

SUE: YOU COME WITH ME NOW!

BILL: Sue.

165   SUE: Bill, I need you, please, why won't you come?

BILL: Why won't I come? Why won't I come? Because . . .

(BILL *walks over to the others.*)

I'm . . . not . . . I am not coming home tonight.

SUE: Bill! Stop it, this is private—

BILL: It is not private, Sue, nothing we do is private for
170   Christ's sake, you tell your friends everything, they all—
know—everything—about us, don't they? How many
times we had sex in the last month.

LAURA: I don't think that's true, Bill.

GEORGE: I haven't heard anything.

175   SUE: Bill, I think you're being very unreasonable.

(*There is an awkward pause in which* BILL *and* SUE *lock eyes.*)

LAURA: (*To* LILY *and* GEORGE.) Well, it's a lovely night out
there. Why don't the three of us go for a walk?

BILL: No.

SUE: You stay and finish up that wonderful looking chocolate
180   paté, Laura, I'm sure you spent a lot of time on it. I'll just
get Bill's coat and we'll go on home.

BILL: There is . . . somebody else, Sue. And I will be going
home with her.

GEORGE: I think we've all had a little too much to drink, why
185   don't we just . . .

SUE: Don't worry guys this isn't real. He's just drunk he's just
trying to scare me because we had this argument about
the new sofa—Come on honey, let's go home. Who is it.
Who is it, Bill? She's not here, is she? You didn't, you didn't
190   bring her to my neighbours', OUR friends' dinner party,
to which I was invited. Laura! Laura for God's sake.

LILY: It's me.

(SUE *laughs.*)

LILY: Why do you think I'm joking?

SUE: (*Looks at* LILY, *looks at* BILL) Bill??

195   BILL: This is—Lily.

LILY: How do you do, Susan?

SUE: Don't you call me by my name you FAT!! Please, I don't
think you know what you're doing. This is not just me,
this is a family, a family, we have two children.

200   LILY: I'm sorry.

SUE: Bill you are not leaving your children.

BILL: Sue, please.

SUE: YOU TOOK A VOW! In a CHURCH in front of a
priest and my mother and your mother and your father
205   and you swore to LOVE and honour and cherish till
DEATH US DO PART till DEATH US DO PART
BILL, it's your WORD your WORD.

BILL: I am breaking my word.

SUE: No!

210   BILL: YOU turned your back on me!! You you—look at you in
that . . . sweatsuit thing you're not—I mean look at her, really, you're you're you're a kind of . . . cartoon now, a . . . cartoon mum a . . . with your day-care meetings and
neighbourhood fairs, you know what I mean Laura! Your
215   face is a drawing your body, lines. The only time, the only

time you are alive, electric again is . . . when you talk on the
phone, to the other mums, there's a flush in your face, excitement, something rushing through your body, you laugh,
loudly, you make all those wonderful female noises, you cry,
your voice, like . . . music, or in the park, with Timmy and   220
John, while they cavort with the other children at the
drinking fountain, spraying the water and you talking and
talking with all the mothers, storming, storming together
your words like crazy swallows, swooping and pivots and . . .
landing . . . softly on a branch, a husband, one of us husbands   225
walk in and it's like walking into . . . a large group of . . .

LILY: You see, I love . . . his body, Sue. I mean, I really love it.
I love to suck it. I love to kiss it his body is my God, okay?
His body—

(SUE *slaps* LILY *twice.*)

SUE: YOU . . . DON'T LIVE ON THIS STREET. You don't   230
belong in this neighbourhood.

(LILY *contains herself from slapping* SUE *back.*)

Where did you meet this . . . woman? On the street?

(*Bill starts to try to answer.*)

In a house of prostitution? I demand to know—

LILY: I fucked him on the telephone, Susan, many many
times.   235

SUE: That is a disgusting . . . lie.

LILY: Come on Suzy, don't you remember? You caught him a
couple of times, on the downstairs phone with his pyjamas around his ankles, he told me!

SUE: (*The wind totally out of her.*) I thought he was making . . .   240
obscene phone calls.

BILL: Hello.

LILY: Hi there.

BILL: You got back to me quickly.

LILY: Fucking right.   245

BILL: Fucking right.

LILY: Your voice makes me crazy.

BILL: My voice.

LILY: I'm wet, Bill, wet just from hearing your voice.

BILL: What are you wearing?   250

LILY: Black silk underwear, red spiked heels, black lace bra.

BILL: Yeah? And what do you want? What do you want?

LILY: I want to suck your big cock, Bill, would you like me
to do that? Would you like me to suck your big cock?

BILL: Oh baby, baby.   255

LILY: And then I want you to fuck me from behind all night
long, can you do that? Can you do that for me, Bill?

BILL: Yes, yes, oh yes! Yes! Yes!

LILY: Oh, Bill!

SUE: BILLLLLLLLLLLLLLLLLLLLL!!!!!!!   260

(SUE *physically attacks* LILY.)

Aghhhh! Listen, you, if you take my husband away from
me and my children I will . . . kill you, I will I will . . .
come when you are sleeping and I will pull your filthy
tongue out of your filthy mouth. And then I will . . . feed
it to our cat.   265

BILL: Susan.

SUE: (*Forced laugh.*) I didn't mean that, I really didn't. I'm sorry everybody, this is all just so ridiculous and embarrassing and I'm sure we'll all laugh about it someday I KNOW we
270   will, but um . . . Bill? Won't you just . . . give me a chance? To show you? That I can? Be sexy? Cause I can, you know, much much more so than THAT creepy shit . . . Don't you remember? Don't you remember before we were married how you loved to watch me dance? Come on, you did!
275   Remember remember that wedding, Kevin and Leslie's? I wore that peach silk that you loved so much that dress drove you crazy! And after after the wedding we were in that room in the Ramada Inn over the water and I danced? You lay on the bed and you just . . . watched me you loved
280   it I . . . whooshed whooshed in that dress, back and forth to this thing on the radio back and oooh and back and you were laughing and and (*Laughs.*) and whoosh.

(*Music beats louder, filling the room, and* SUE *begins a slow striptease.*)

And whoosh . . . and . . . close to you, you're hard . . . and far away and . . . turn . . . and whooosh . . . and . . . let . . .
285   my . . . hair . . . down . . . you—love my hair whoosh and . . . zipppper . . . whoooo down so slowwwww turn and turn . . . you watching lying on the bed and ease . . . off my shoulders you love my shoulders, elegant ohhh Billy, and down. Over my body the soft silky down and
290   whoooooooooooooooo whooOOOOOOOO Billy. Take me home, Billy, take me home and let's make mad passionate love! Please.

(BILL *and* LILY *leave.* GEORGE *and* LAURA *pick up* SUE's *clothing and bring it to her.* LAURA *dresses her.*)

LAURA: Honey, I'm sorry.

SUE: Aghh don't feel sorry for me it's fine, everything will be
295   fine because . . . his colon cancer's gonna come back, don't you think? Dr. Neville said he had a sixty-forty chance, it will. And she'll drop him, for sure, don't you think? And he will let me nurse him I will . . . feed him broth, with a spoon, like I did my mum, and I will hold, I will hold his
300   sweet head in my chest till till his lips are black and his eyes . . . like bright dead stars and he is dead and I will stay I will stay with his body, in the hospital room because I did love that body . . . oh I did love—that—body once.

ISOBEL: Susan, Susan, Susan. The boy with the arrow ha *killed*
305   you, ha? Where's your helper now? Oh Susan, you can't help me now you can't take me home. (*To the audience.*) Hey! Who gonna take me home? You? You gotta car? What kinda car you got? Trans-Am? What about bus tickets? You gotta bus tickets? C'mon. Come on. COME ON.
310   SOMEBODY. What I'm sposed to do, ha? Who gonna take me home? Who gonna take me home?

(ISOBEL *finds a watching place. A few hours later, at* LAURA *and* GEORGE's, LAURA *clears the table.*)

LAURA: Poor Suzy. Poor poor Suzy.

GEORGE: (*Half asleep.*) Yeahh. Chee.

LAURA: God, that is the worst thing I have ever seen happen
315   to anybody.

(GEORGE *and* LAURA *laugh hysterically and imitate* SUE *in the previous scene.*)

GEORGE: Whoosh! That peach silk, oh baby take me home.

LAURA: Take me home, Bill. Let's make mad passionate love. (*Stops imitating* SUE) I don't know, I mean I know she needs a friend badly, I am her friend I mean I love her. George, how can you laugh? This is important. If she calls 320 me tomorrow, what should I say? I'm just going to say, I'm going to say, 'SUZY? I feel really badly for you and I think you're a wonderful person but you will have to look somewhere else for—'

GEORGE: Nice.   325

LAURA: GEORGE, you KNOW—

GEORGE: You always say she's your best friend, Laura, 'my BEST'—

LAURA: She is! But George, are you forgetting Maria? I had a nervous breakdown because of that woman and her 330 problem how could you FORGET?

GEORGE: I was on the book tour, Loo.

LAURA: I told you about it a hundred times, how could you forget?

GEORGE: I was on the book tour—Loo.   335

LAURA: George, you are so insensitive, I can't believe this. I told you about it one hundred times. How can you forget?

(GEORGE *grabs a tablecloth and wraps it around his head, like a shawl, speaking in a Portuguese accent.*)

GEORGE: How could I forget, how could I forget?

LAURA: George.

GEORGE: Looka this. Me? I donta forget nothing.   340

LAURA: George I'm going to bed, Molly gets up in two hours and it's always me that gets up with her of course.

(*She walks around the circle.*)

GEORGE/MARIA: LAURA.

(*Now he speaks as* MARIA, ISOBEL's *mother.* ISOBEL *recognizes her.*)

LAURA: George! Come to bed.

GEORGE/MARIA: LAURA.   345

LAURA: Maria.

MARIA: I am . . . so sorry to be coming to your house, maybe you busy, I don't know—

LAURA: No, no, please come in Maria, I'm just—reading the paper the kids are at school and—   350

(MARIA *starts shaking violently and keening. She looks like she is in shock.*)

Maria? . . . uh . . . Maria? Are you alright? You look—why don't you sit down. Here. Sit down. Can I get you a drink of water?

(MARIA *starts to keen with grief, quite quietly.*)

MARIA: Eeeeeeee

LAURA: Maria? Maria . . . are you alright? Maria, Maria please 355 tell me . . . what's . . .

MARIA: . . . I think . . . I think . . . Antonio—

LAURA: Your husband? Something happened to your husband?

(MARIA *continues to keen.*)

It's okay, Maria, you don't have to tell me if you don't—
360 MARIA: Five o'clock in the morning I cook: smelt and three
scramble eggs, nice bread, coffee. For Antony must work
long day, construction on highway, long day in the sun, he
come from his shower to kitchen, but he don't want. He
365 gotta rat in his stomach that day he say, make a joke, don't
want my cooking eat a little bitta bread and just small glass
of milk and he go, catch his subway. I fold. I fold clothes
one pile for Antony, one pile for me, one for Maria,
Romeo, ISOBEL and Luig, my hands fold the clothes but
my . . . (*Gesture indicating self or soul.*)
370 LAURA: Sure, you go on automatic—I—
MARIA: Like I fold myself too, and I go in his body, maybe,
you know, his . . . hand to, wipe off his face when he hot
and too sweat I am there;

(*She walks operatically down-stage and delivers the rest of the
speech, which should be like an aria.*)

I am foldin a light sheet of blue then and sudden, I can see
375 through his eye, am at subway, in him, he stands on the
platform, is empty, empty and I am his head, circles and
circles like red birds flying around and around I am his
throat, tight, cannot breathe enough air in my body the
floor the floor move, and sink in, rise up rise like a wall
380 like a killin wave turn turn me in circles with teeth in circles and under and over I fall!

(ISOBEL *falls on an imaginary track in front of her mother.*)

I fall on the silver track nobody move I hearing the sound.
The sound of the rats in the tunnel their breath like a basement these dark rats running running towards me I am
385 stone I am earth cannot scream cannot move the rats tramp
. . . trample my body flat-ten and every bone splinter like . . .

(*We hear the sound of a strong wind as the 'Sugar Meeting' is being set up on the stage. By the end of the wind,* LAURA *is at her
table, addressing the meeting.*)

LAURA: Good evening everybody.
GEORGE: Good evening.
RON: Hi Laura.
390 LAURA: I uh might as well get straight down to business. As
head and sole member of the menu research committee, I
have spent some three weeks doing . . . a great deal . . . of
. . . research, and even a little detective work . . .

(RON *and* GEORGE *are talking to one another.*)

. . . and I would like to make my presentation tonight
395 without too much interruption, thank you.
GEORGE: Go for it.
RON: No problem.
LAURA: POINT ONE. Sugar: I strongly recommend that we
make a concerted effort to eradicate all sugar from the
400 children's diet. Sugar is an overstimulant, sugar is empty
calories, sugar rots . . .
RON: Uh, I have to say, that, while I agree, sure, too much
sugar is not a good thing, that once in a while . . .

LAURA: Would you let your four-year-old smoke 'once in a
while'? 405

(*A murmur from the crowd.*)

RON: (*With a little laugh.*) I don't really think you can equate . . .

(ISOBEL *rises and walks into the meeting.*)

LAURA: Sugar is a known carcinogen, Ron, I have a study
right here . . .
JILL: Lettuce is a known carcinogen, for God's sake!
ISOBEL: Hey! Boys! Girls! Looka this! I think tha they can't 410
see me! They no see Isobel! Wha happen? Wha happen?
JILL: Okay as chairperson, I say—let's cut the comments and
raise our hands for questions. Laura? You want to go
ahead?
LAURA: Yes, thank you, Jill. Uh. (*Clears throat.*) It has come to 415
my attention . . .

(GEORGE *groans.*)

Excuse me, I have to ask you why you groaned like that,
George, did I say something wrong?
JILL: George, penalty for groaning out of turn, just kidding.
GEORGE: No, no, I'm sorry, I just, I don't know, I just . . . have 420
a kind of a hard time with 'meeting . . . talk' . . . 'it has come
to my attention.'
LAURA: Well, I'm very sorry, George, if you have a better way
of—
JILL: That was uncalled for George, really. 425
RON: George, your mother's calling you.

(*General laughter.*)

JILL: Let's let Laura continue please, so we can get out of here . . .
ISOBEL: I think I invisible!
LAURA: Thank you Jill. I have NOTICED, if you don't like 'it
has come to my attention.' I have noticed that in this nurs- 430
ery school they are . . . subtly, and I'm sure unwittingly, en-
couraging an addiction to sugar in our children.
RHONDA: Hey, that's not true.
LAURA: Rhonda, I'm SAYING it's not intentional . . .
RHONDA: The kids are not . . . 435
LAURA: PLEASE LET ME TALK.
JILL: Go ahead, Laura, please.
LAURA: I have noticed that sugar is used as a reward. If you're
good we'll make cookies tomorrow. If you tidy up you get
chocolate cake as a reward. You are creating . . . unwit- 440
tingly, I concede, you are creating TOMORROW'S
COKE ADDICTS . . . TO—
RHONDA: EXCUSE ME I HAVE TO SAY THAT, AS THE
CAREGIVER, I RESENT THIS.
LAURA: Rhonda, I'm not accusing just you, I think you are 445
fabulous with the kids, it's our whole society . . .
RHONDA: I am not creating drug addicts.
JILL: Rhonda, Laura does not mean any of this personally, I
think that's . . .
LAURA: I'm saying it's a small step from sugar addiction to— 450
RON: Excuse me, I have to say, all food is sugar . . .
LAURA: REFINED SUGAR IS FAST-ACTING, RON, IT
BURDENS THE PANCREAS.

GEORGE: I think you are taking this a little too seriously, Laura, we're just talking about a few cookies now and then for heaven's sake.

LAURA: WE ARE TALKING ABOUT A LIFETIME ADDICTION AND I DON'T THINK IT SHOULD BE TAKEN LIGHTLY.

JILL: Laura, are you willing to listen to a response from Rhonda.

LAURA: Sure.

RHONDA: I would just . . . like to say that I, also have done . . . a great deal of studying diet and menu and that, and I fully agree with Laura that sugar is . . . something to be avoided, IF YOU CAN. Listen, if I'm giving the kids yoghurt, they won't eat it without honey they won't, so I figure, a bit of honey is worth getting the yoghurt down em . . .

LAURA: BULLSHIT THAT IS ABSOLUTE UNADULTERATED BULLSHIT.

RHONDA: I beg your pardon, Laura?

LAURA: You don't know what you're saying, Rhonda.

RHONDA: If you don't trust me, Laura . . .

LAURA: Rhonda . . .

RHONDA: I do not encourage sugar, I do not hold it up as a reward, ever, I have never done that.

LAURA: You're lying, Rhonda.

RON: WAIT A MINUTE HOLD ON JUST A . . .

LAURA: SHUT UP RON. LISTEN. LISTEN TO ME RHONDA. I FOUND OUT THAT JUST LAST FRIDAY, LAST FRIDAY, AS A REWARD, YOU TOOK SIX KIDS, INCLUDING MY TWINS, TO A DOUGHNUT SHOP. YOU TOOK THEM TO A DOUGHNUT SHOP AND BOUGHT THEM EACH A JELLY DOUGHNUT. I think I screamed for five minutes when the twins told me that I just couldn't believe it they started harassing me every five minutes, 'Mum, if we're good, can we have a jelly doughnut?' I don't think they'd ever HEARD OF JELLY DOUGHNUTS BEFORE THAT!! I find it unconscionable, UNCONSCIONABLE that a jelly doughnut would be the sole purpose of an excursion.

RHONDA: Um, I can explain that. It was a Friday, right, and I happen to get severe cramps with my period, right? And I was very sick that day and the kids had bad bad cabin fever, well . . .

LAURA: (Overlapping.) And the Friday before that it was popsicles, Rhonda, I'm not blaming you I'm saying you need to be re-educated, we all do, smelling the flowers is a reason to go for a walk, not getting a poisonous body-destroying drug . . .

RHONDA: LET MEEEEE TALLLLLK. LET ME TALK LET ME TALLLLLLLLLLLLK!! I feel . . . nailed to the wall by you lady, nailed right to the fucking wall. I have to say and something else I have to say is that I think you are . . . are very . . . inconsiderate . . . of feelings! I brought up two kids on what I feed your kids, and they turned out just fine, are you telling me what I feed my kids isn't good enough for your kids? You know the funny thing is, Laura, you may be a bitch on wheels, but lookin at all the rest of you, Laura? at least you're honest you are. Youse others, what you're thinkin is . . . it really doesn't matter what they get at the day care the real learning is at home, that's where youse teach your kids to become—huh. Here I am saying 'youse' I haven't said that since I was a kid! that's how flustered I am—at home you teach your kids . . . to be . . . higher kind of people, higher kind of people don't eat Kraft slices and tuna casserole, I've seen that kind a laugh in your voices, all of you, when you say, 'Oh, they had "tuna casserole," ' I seen, I have seen the roll in your eyes at the grace before meals, or the tidy-up song, or the stars we give out for citizen of the week, you think, oh well the kid is happy, well cared for, we can undo all that and we can make the kids high people like ourselves better people, more better people than the poor little teacher who reads ROMANCE, yes, yes, JILL MATHINS, I saw you showin my book, my novel to RON there and Cathy and havin a big giggle, you think I didn't see that? You think the books you read are deeper more . . . higher, well it's the same story, don't you see that? What's makin me cry in my book is, when ya come right down to it, is exactly the same thing that's makin you cry in your book, oh yes, oh yes and I'll tell you something, I'll tell all of you I GREW UP ON THAT. I grew up on jelly doughnuts and butter tarts, and chocolate ice-cream, and I happen to think they're a wonderful thing. I happen to agree with the mice and the cockroaches and the horses and birds that treats are a wonderful thing, you need treats, you need treats in this life, each bit of a treat can wipe out a nasty word, every bite of a jelly doughnut cleans out your soul it is a gift from GOD, a wonderful gift from GOD and I for one . . . I for one . . . I . . . for . . . your eyes, eh? Your eyes are all the same colour and shape like a picture, a . . . freaky art picture all the same in a row like dark soldiers raisin your . . .

(ISOBEL *shoots everybody there except* RHONDA *with her finger. There are real shot sounds although* ISOBEL *is imagining this.*)

ISOBEL: (*Big laugh. Struts.*) Rho-HONDA! Bebbe! Beautiful belle! I have killed those dirty bastards, babe, I have killed them dirty dead. I am your harmy, Rhohonda! And you! You gonna take me home!

(ISOBEL *falls and wraps herself around* RHONDA's *feet. Music. A restaurant.* DAVID *takes his place behind the bar, another person is sitting alone at a table.* RHONDA *and her friend* JOANNE *meet for drinks. They are laughing.* ISOBEL *watches.*)

RHONDA: Oh man is this Singapore Sling fantastic.

JOANNE: My Fuzzy Navel is warm. Hot!

RHONDA: SEND it back! We're paying through the teeth for these drinks. Waiter, take this thing back!

JOANNE: No, I like it this way, honest, Rhonda, I do.

DAVID: Is there a problem with your cocktail?

JOANNE: No no no no please . . .

DAVID: I could take it back—

JOANNE: No.

RHONDA: Are you sure?

JOANNE: I'm sure.

DAVID: Okaaay.

RHONDA: Ohhh Christ, I'd like to just sit and drink all afternoon to tell you the truth.

JOANNE: I thought you quit heavy drinkin.

RHONDA: I did. I'm just . . . down in the dumps.

JOANNE: Why, ya on your time?

ISOBEL: Is this my home? This is not my home!

RHONDA: No no no, I get happy then, no, it's just . . . work.

JOANNE: Yeah, Jeez I'm glad I'm not workin it made me crazy, what's goin on? the kids at the day care gettin to ya?

570 RHONDA: No no it's not the kids, the kids are great, it's the parents.

JOANNE: Uh oh. That same B-I-T-C-H?

RHONDA: No, she was quite good this time, strangely enough, it's another one.

JOANNE: They all look like bitches to me in their leather
575 pants. Stuck up, puttin their kids in forty-five-dollar shoes, I looked at the price of them REEboks for kids—the other day when I picked you up I saw three of those kids had those shoes on I couldn't believe my eyes.

RHONDA: Yeah, well, they're pretty well-off, but I don't hold
580 that against them, I mean, who wouldn't be if they had the chance, right?

JOANNE: Well that's a good point SO . . .

RHONDA: We had this meeting, okay?

JOANNE: RHONDA. Excuse Me!

585 RHONDA: What?

JOANNE: (Intake of breath.) . . . I don't know.

RHONDA: What do you mean?

JOANNE: I mean . . . no, I don't know.

RHONDA: Joanne.

590 JOANNE: I mean . . . Oh God, I wasn't going to tell nobody—

RHONDA: You're pregnant again?

JOANNE: No no no no, if only, I . . .

RHONDA: JOANNE, I'M YOUR BEST FRIEND.

JOANNE: YOU'RE MY BEST FRIEND?

595 RHONDA: Yes, you know that!

JOANNE: THEN SWEAR ON YOUR MOTHER'S LIFE.

RHONDA: What?

JOANNE: That you will do what I'm gonna ask you.

RHONDA: Joanne, what is this?

600 JOANNE: Just . . . swear.

RHONDA: I'm not swearing on my mother's life without knowing what it is, she's got enough problems . . .

JOANNE: Okay, your husband's life.

RHONDA: Okay, I swear on the asshole's life. There. Now
605 what?

JOANNE: You remember . . . I had this pain in my back?

RHONDA: Yeah, for the last few months, every time ya bend down.

JOANNE: SEARING pain, every time I moved . . .

610 RHONDA: . . . Okay . . .

JOANNE: Well remember I told you I went to that specialist and he said he was gonna do some tests?

RHONDA: Right, uh-huh.

JOANNE: Well—

615 RHONDA: You gotta go in and have an operation and you want me to take your kids, no problem of COURSE I'll take them Jo, for God's—

JOANNE: (Overlapping.) No. No, I mean, you might have to take the kids but that's only . . . part of it.

620 RHONDA: Joanne, I really don't like guessing games.

JOANNE: Shadows . . . that's what they call them, and . . . it is . . . the very worst thing it could be, and the . . . kind, the kind is of the bone.

RHONDA: Oh boy.

625 JOANNE: Yeah.

RHONDA: (Whispers.) Jo . . .

JOANNE: Don't . . . don't touch me. I'll go hysterical please.

RHONDA: YOU . . . want a cigarette?

JOANNE: Yeah.

(RHONDA lights one and gives it to her.)

630 Ya know, I have to go to the bathroom, like, real bad but I'm not gonna go, ya know why? Cause every time . . . I sit down to pee I feel my whole life drainin out of me, just draining out with the pee, goin . . . outa me, into the water down in the pipes, and under the . . . friggin . . .
635 GROUND. That's where I'll be, Rho, that's where I'm gonna . . . (Fights to regain her composure.) I'll come home with the groceries? Like after dark? and I'll see Frank and the kids through the window, in the livin-room, right? Watchin TV, or drawing on paper, cuttin out stuff, what-
640 ever, and I'll stand on the porch and watch em, just . . . playing . . . on the floor, and I think . . . that's life, that's life goin on without me, it'll be just like that, only I won't be here with the groceries, I'll be under the ground under the ground with my flesh fallin off a my face and I just
645 can't take it. You know in that picture? That picture I had in my bedroom growing up?

RHONDA: UHH—

JOANNE: My aunt and uncle sent me that from England, the poster it's OPHELIA, from this play by Shakespeare, right?
650 And she she—got all these flowers, tropical flowers, wild flowers, white roses, violets and buttercups, everything she loved and she kinda weaved them all together. Then she got the heaviest dress she could find . . . you know how dresses in the olden days were so long and heavy, with pet-
655 ticoats and that? And she got this heavy heavy blue dress, real . . . blue and then she wrapped all these pretty pretty flowers round and round her body, round her head, and her hair, she had this golden, wavy hair, long, and then she steps down the bank, and she lies, on her back, in the
660 stream. She lies there, but the stream runs so fast she's on her back and she goes. It pulls her along so fast and she's lookin at the sky and the clouds, and she's singing little songs—'I'm lookin over a four-leaf clover'—and being pulled so fast by a clear cold water pulled along and she's
665 not scared, she's not scared at all, she's calm, so happy! And just ever so slowly her dress, gets heavier, right? Then, then, she gets caught on a stick, like a branch, of a willow tree, and her dress pulls her down, soft, she's still singin down deep deep deep to the bottom of the stream and
670 with all these 'fantastic garlands,' these beautiful flowers all around her—'one's for the roses that blew down the lane'—she dies, Rhon, she dies . . . good. She dies good.

RHONDA: That's . . . something.

JOANNE: I want to die like that. But . . . I don't . . . want to do
675 it all alone, I mean, I want you to help me, with the flow-ers, and with the dress, and my hair, I want you to make sure the willow branch is there, and the stream is right, and maybe . . . maybe that . . . Frank . . . sees I . . . wouldn't mind him seein . . . me in that stream, with the flowers,
680 and the heavy blue dress . . . I wouldn't mind if you took maybe some pictures of me like that and then you could have them printed and given out at the funeral, something like that . . . just, you know, two by four, colour, whatever, it's the one thing that would make it alright—it's the one
685 thing . . .

RHONDA: I just . . . I don't know, Jo, you know I'd do anything to make it alright . . .

JOANNE: Well this is what I want, Rhonda, it's really really really what I want. Are you going to help me?

690 RHONDA: I uh—think you need to see a counsellor, Jo, you
know they have counsellors that . . . specialize in these . . .
situations I'm surprised your doctor didn't . . .

JOANNE: You think I'm crazy.

RHONDA: No no, Joanne, I just think that . . . your situation is
695   so hard that you are not quite yourself, I mean this is not . . .
you, the Joanne I know is practical she . . . you should believe in the treatments, Jo, they do work sometimes, they
really do, and the Joanne I know—would never ask a friend
to help . . . her . . . is one of the most thoughtful people that
700   I know, of other people and how the hell, how the hell do
you think that I could live with that after, eh?? I mean it's
all very lovely and that, your picture, in your room but
that's a picture, that's a picture, you dimwit! The real of it
would be awful, the stalks of the flowers would be chokin
705   you, and the smells of them would make you sick, all those
smells comin at you when you're feelin so sick to begin
with, and the stream, well if you're talking about the Humber River or any stream in this country you're talkin filth,
in the Humber River you're even talkin sewage, Jo, you're
710   talkin cigarette packages and used condoms and old tam-
pons floating by you're talking freezin, you'd start shakin
from head to toe you're talkin rocks gashin your head
you're talkin a bunch of longhairs and goofs on the banks
yellin at you callin you whorebag sayin what they'd like to
715   do to you, you're talkin . . . and where would you get a dress
like that, eh? You'd never find the one in the picture, Jo, it'd
be too tight at the neck and the waist, it'd be a kind of material that itches your skin, even worse wet, drives you nut-
crazy, the blue would be off, wouldn't look right your shoes
720   wouldn't match you could never find the same colour,
Joanne. You can't become a picture, do you know what I
mean? I mean you can't . . . BE . . . a picture, okay?

(They freeze. ISOBEL *runs from her watching place, around the circle
screaming; she has realized, listening to* JOANNE, *that she is not lost,
but dead, murdered seventeen years before.)*

ISOBEL: AAHHHHHHHHHHH!! I am dead! I have been
bones for seventeen years, missing, missing, my face in the
725   TV and newspapers, posters, everybody lookin for, nobody find, I am gone, I am dead, I AM DEADLY DEAD!
Down! It was night, was a lion, roar!! with red eyes: he
come closer *(Silent scream.)* come closer *(Silent scream.)*
ROAR tear my throat out ROAR tear my eyes out . . .
730   ROAR I am kill! I am kill! I am no more!

(Music.)

(To JOANNE.) We are both pictures now. WHO WILL
TAKE US? WHO WILL TAKE US TO HEAVEN, HA?

(Lights down. Cathedral bells ring. DAVID *is outside, walking down
the street.)*

DAVID: God, that customer dying of bone cancer. I didn't
even want to touch her glass. I don't know she had that
735   look, that dead look. I mean I almost felt hostile.

ISOBEL: *(Inside the cathedral.)* I WANT TO GO TO HEAVEN
NOW!

(She sees a life-size statue of the Virgin Mary and approaches it.)

Holy Mary Mother of God. Will you take Isobel to
heaven now, please?

*(She lies at the base of the statue, her hand touching the statue's
foot.)*

DAVID: God that cathedral is beautiful, funny, I've passed it   740
every day on my way out from work and I've never really
looked at it. Look at the stonework, those *spires*—

(He opens the church doors and enters. The doors slam behind him.)

Oh I love this it's so . . . the air is so . . . holy it IS, look at
those bird-bath things full of holy water, I love it it's so
primitive. *(He splashes some on his face.)* In the name of the   745
Father . . . the Son, and the Holy—

FATHER HAYES: Good evening.

(DAVID shrieks, startled. His shriek echoes.)

It's alright, it's alright. Have you come for . . .

DAVID: Confession. I've come for confession, 8:30, yes? I'm
not too late, am I, see, I just finished work, and . . .   750

FATHER HAYES: Not too late, of course not.

(FATHER HAYES goes into his part of the confessional.)

DAVID: *(To himself.)* I guess just—God I don't remember a
THING about what to do!!

*(We hear the wooden barrier being opened, and the priest begins the
Latin prayer.)*

FATHER HAYES: In the name of the Father, and the Son, and
the Holy Spirit.   755

DAVID: *(Overlapping.)* Oh God he's saying something—

FATHER HAYES: May the Lord be in your heart and help you
to confess your sins with true sorrow. Let us listen to the
Lord as he speaks to us: I will give them a new heart and
put a new spirit within them; I will remove the strong   760
heart from their bodies and replace it with a natural heart,
so that they will live according to my statutes, and observe
and carry out my ordinances; thus they shall be my people and I will be their God.

DAVID: *(Overlapping.)* I think it's Latin, isn't that against Papal   765
Law? I should report him to the Vatican and have him de-
frocked here goes nothing—

(FATHER HAYES finishes the prayer.)

AHH—FORGIVE ME FATHER FOR I have sinned. It
has been . . . four weeks since my last confession. These are
my sins? . . . OKAY, told Barb I'd be there last night for din-   770
ner with her and the niece and nephew—didn't show up
didn't phone nothing, was in a mad PASH with my hockey
player. I was very cruel to Daniel Thursday, saw him at
Billy's—the club? And I don't know, the way he was looking
at me drove me CRAZY CRAZY he was mooning! Well I   775

walked up to him and told him to 'quit mooning I'd rather see your hairy ass than that pathetic face, face it!' I said, 'Face it you old fag, you have been dumped, DUMPED!' That was really mean, that's gotta be more than a venial sin, AND 780 THEN, then, yesterday, I walked through a park? And I saw a large group of poor children playing, and I just thought they were trouble; I wondered why God had put them in the world, really, isn't that unkind? THEN today I saw a fat lady eating an ice-cream cone and I said, I think quite audi- 785 bly I said 'disgusting' oh AND I did not stand up in the sub- way the incredibly packed subway, for a hugely pregnant lady and her kid, I just didn't feel like it. Quite the catalogue, eh? Oh and another thing, I've lied to you already. I haven't been to confession in fifteen years, haven't stepped in a 790 church in fifteen years, just . . . did it on a whim, don't ask me why I was passing by on my way . . .

FATHER HAYES: AND you felt the hand of GOD?

DAVID: Well . . . it was just a whim—really . . .

FATHER HAYES: David.

795 DAVID: How do you know my name?

FATHER HAYES: David I know your name better than I know my own.

DAVID: Wait a minute, wait a minute, I think maybe this is some odd coincidence because although my name is 800 DAVID, I don't actually know you at all, so . . .

FATHER HAYES: There's nothing odd about it, David, you were an altar boy for me, two years, for two years you served, in 1957 and 1958 at St. Bernard's in Moncton, New Brunswick. Remember?

805 DAVID: Moncton? We were around there for a couple of years—

FATHER HAYES: You were a believer, David, the other boys were just forced into it by their parents, you believed in every statue every—

810 DAVID: Father Hayes? You—are Father Hayes?

FATHER HAYES: I am.

DAVID: You're still alive?

FATHER HAYES: I think.

DAVID: But you were so old even way back then!

815 FATHER HAYES: Not really.

DAVID: I remember you now. I remember you did look old, because you stooped, and you had white hair already didn't you?

FATHER HAYES: Indeed, I was prematurely white . . .

820 DAVID: White hair and . . . and . . . red eyes.

FATHER HAYES: I . . . suffered from allergies, hay fever. I'm sorry if it frightened you.

DAVID: I guess maybe it did frighten me a bit, Father, but you know how young boys are—

825 FATHER HAYES: I am sorry, but, but . . .

DAVID: No no, I . . . look, I uh—

FATHER HAYES: David, I want . . .

DAVID: . . . don't mean to be impolite but I'd like you to be honest with me, sort of man to man I . . . I always got the 830 impression that you were looking at me much more than you looked at the other boys am I right?

FATHER HAYES: Well . . .

DAVID: I felt . . . I felt as though your eyes were devouring me.

FATHER HAYES: No, no, no . . .

835 DAVID: No?? I'm gay, Father, you can be honest with me. I'll forgive you, I mean you never actually did anything, you

never even touched me, you just . . . looked. You kept looking at me—tell me, tell me the truth.

FATHER HAYES: It was not what you think, no, no please—

DAVID: Confess to me Father, come on, come on . . .   840

FATHER HAYES: I make my confessions on a regular . . .

DAVID: Have you confessed this sin?

FATHER HAYES: No, no I haven't, but—

DAVID: God loves sinners who confess, Father, you taught me that, as long as you speak up and you're sorry as hell, you're 845 okay, you still got your ticket to heaven, but you won't you won't Father, if you don't tell me, you'll wither in LIMBO! I suffered, I need you to tell me! CONFESS . . .

FATHER HAYES: I'm due to a christening. I have to shave first, there's a big party, I—   850

DAVID: You would christen a baby with this sin, bobbing on the surface, bobbing? Confess, you son of a bitch. Con—

FATHER HAYES: Forgive me Father for I have sinned.

DAVID: Alright.

FATHER HAYES: I looked at you, David, because . . . I . . . be- 855 cause . . . I wanted . . . to . . . remember . . . you.

DAVID: Remember me?

FATHER HAYES: Because . . . of what was to happen, in the water: oh OH when the day arrived, when the picnic came round, in July, that Canada Day picnic? I had a bad 860 feeling, I had . . . a very bad feeling indeed. We all piled out of the cars: families, priests, nuns, altar boys, piled out and lugged all those picnic baskets to tables under trees. The grownups all fussed with food and drink while the kids, all of you children, ran ran in your white bare feet to 865 the water, throwing stones and balls, and a warning sound a terrible, the sound of deep nausea filled my ears and I looked up and saw you, dancing on the water, and I saw a red circle, a red, almost electric circle, dazzling round and round like waves, spinning round your head and body. I 870 thought watch, watch that boy, on this day he will surely drown, he *will*. David, *I knew that you would die*. And all be- cause of the chicken. The twenty-nine-pound chicken brought there by Mrs. Henry grown on her brother's farm, everyone had talked and talked about that chicken, 875 who would carve that chicken, Mrs. Henry took it out you skipped along the shore, she laid it on the table, 'FA- THER HAYES, YOU GO AHEAD AND CARVE, AND DON'T MAKE A MESS OF IT OR YOU WON'T SEE ME AT MASS NEXT SUNDAY.' Everyone laughed 880 laughed the men, the men drinking beer, watching me, sure they're thinking, 'Watch him carve like a woman,' most men hate priests, you know this is a fact, I could see them thinking cruel thoughts under hooded eyes and practised grins; my sin was the sin of pride! The sin of 885 pride David, I started to carve, didn't want to look up, lest I wreck the bird. You see at that moment that chicken was worth more, indeed worth more . . . than your LIFE, David I SHUT OUT the warning voice and I—carved. I carved and carved and ran into trouble, real trouble I re- 890 member thinking, 'Damn how does any person do it, it's a terrible job,' people behave as if it's nothing, but it's ter- rible, I kept at it, I wouldn't give up, I wouldn't look up till I'd finished, and I finished carving, and I had made a massacre. The men turned away the women . . . mur- 895 mured comfort, and before I looked up I had a hope, a hard hope, that you were still skipping on the rocks and

shouting insults to your pals all hands reached for chicken
and bread, potato salad, chocolate cake I looked I looked
900 up and your hand from the sea, your hand, far away, was
reaching, reaching for me far away . . . oh no! I ran, and
tripped, fell on my face ran again, I could not speak ran to
the water and shouted as loud as I could but my voice was
so tiny; I saw your hand, ran to the fisherman close, he
905 wasn't home his fat daughter and I, in the skiff; not
enough wind no wind, paddling paddling, you a small
spot nothing then nothing the sun burns our faces our red
red faces.

DAVID: And I . . . was . . . never found?

910 FATHER HAYES: And now . . . you have come!! You have finally come!!

DAVID: And what have I come for?

(FATHER HAYES *is sleeping.*)

DAVID: Uh . . . Father? Uh—listen . . . I'm sorry. I'm sorry but
I never died. You got the wrong guy I knew you . . . some
915 other time—I mean, shit, I wish I had died, I only wish, it
would have made my life so much more interesting . . . I
grew up, I grew up. Listen if I had drowned in the sea, in
Moncton, New Brunswick a beautiful perfect young boy,
if I was . . . pulled by the sea if I reached and was lost, and
920 all those people felt this loss, a loss all their lives, mother
father brothers and sister friends a dark ache, somewhere
in their chest for what could have been, they could all
imagine, you see, what could have been Father Father? I
forgive you, I forgive you Father, it was nice on the wa-
925 ter, you know? It was neat, so calm, as I slipped underneath I wasn't scared, I'll tell ya. I wasn't scared a bit. The
water was so . . . nice!!

(*Music.* ISOBEL *dances, joined by the cast one by one until they are
all dancing fully. Cast dance off one by one leaving* ISOBEL, *who
freezes. Blackout.*)

ACT II

Sounds of kids playing in a park, a group of mothers chat. ISOBEL
watches

CHRISTINE: How's your pregnancy going, dear?

(*Lion roar.*)

ISOBEL: I hear the LION, I hear the Lion ROAR!!

ELLEN: Wonderful! I finally feel . . . good for something. LEO,
SHARE IT. Share it please.

5 CHRISTINE: Not me NOT me when I was pregnant I felt as
useful as a cow. A large, stupid . . .

ELLEN: Christine!!

CHRISTINE: EMMA! Five more minutes honey! Mummy's
got to go to work! Well, considering I despised the man
10 whose child I was carrying—

ELLEN: I suppose that would . . . alter things—GOOD
CATCH, Leo!

SUE: Hi guys. Timmy, just five minutes. Remember, your father's coming to get you at five.

15 CHRISTINE: Sue, I love that blouse! Really suits you!

ELLEN: Gorgeous!

SUE: Thank you, I'm organizing a bake sale, if you can believe
it, for the community centre over on Ash Street. PLEASE
say you'll bake, or sell tickets, even a promise to buy—

ISOBEL: I must tell these peoples, I must tell them now!   20

ELLEN: Forget me, I'm a diabetic! I can't even look at the
stuff!

SUE: Tim! Why don't you try the swing? You love swings.

CHRISTINE: Okay, put me down for fudge brownies, *if* my
kids don't eat them first.   25

(GEORGE *enters with a kid's bicycle.*)

George! How's the book going?

GEORGE: Well, well, very well indeed!! And how's the busiest
freelancer in town? Bradley, don't push so hard!

CHRISTINE: Overworked and underpaid.

GEORGE: What else is new?   30

(RON *enters.*)

Ron! Why aren't you at your office?

ELLEN: We're telling!

GEORGE: Good, Bradley!

SUE: Tim? Why don't you try the swing?

CHRISTINE: RON did you get my note? EMMA PUT IT   35
BACK!

RON: Yes, I did, I—I—I—

ISOBEL: (*Hitting them.*) Shut up Boy! Shut up Girl! I say I say
it's time!! He's in the streets get them out he's in the streets
save your children take their hand take their leg.   40

SUE: Isobel! I saw this girl before, she—

ISOBEL: I say shut up! I say LISTEN TO ME NOW! Can you
no hear? Listen! Can you nooo—

(*All freeze except* SUE, *who crosses slowly towards the children.*)

SUE: Timmy?

ISOBEL: (*Goes to her.*) The lion is here, in your streets. He is   45
trying to kill you, to kill all of your children. He really really is.

(*She picks up a great crooked stick which she will carry until she says
'I love you' to* BEN *in the final scene.*)

Watch me! (*Laughs.*) I am your HARMY! (*Laughs.*) I am
your SAINT! I am your HARMY! Watch me, watch me,
(*A war cry.*) I WILL KILL THE LION NOW!!   50

(*Thunderstorm as* SUE *shouts* 'TIMMMYY!!' *and the others ad lib
to their children, e.g.,* 'Quick, you don't want to get wet!' *All exit. A
kid's bike is left on-stage. Blackout. Lights up on* CHRISTINE *walking towards* SCARLETT's *basement apartment, 'tracked' by* ISOBEL.)

ISOBEL: This girl, Christine, Christine, this girl, SHE will take
me to the lion, yes, for she . . . she is very hard. Harrrrd.
HARRRRRRRD!!

CHRISTINE: 116 Carlisle. Lord what a stench. What could
that be?   55

(*knocks.*)

SCARLETT: Come in!

CHRISTINE: Scarlett Deer?

SCARLETT: That's my name, don't wear it out, has to last a lifetime!!

60 CHRISTINE: I'm Christine Pierce from the *Telegraph*. We
talked on the phone.

SCARLETT: Have a seat.

CHRISTINE: Thank you. Nice place.

SCARLETT: What, this hole? Sorry if it stinks, I cooked
65 chicken today an ever since I ate it I been fartin up a
storm. Dead chicken farts, that's what my brother always
said.

CHRISTINE: Scarlett, I don't have a lot of time, so is it all right
if I ask you some questions?

70 SCARLETT: Sure, How does it feel to be an ugly geek? Fine
thank you, fuck you very much.

CHRISTINE: Scarlett, advanced cerebral palsy is a serious
handicap. Don't you feel that living on your own is dangerous?

75 SCARLETT: Would you like to live in a freakhouse?

CHRISTINE: Well, Scarlett, I—

SCARLETT: Freedom, freedom girl, I'd rather fuckin rot on
the floor of my own home than be well-fed and cared for
in a freakhouse.

80 CHRISTINE: What you're saying, then, is that above all things,
you cherish freedom. That you would rather risk—

SCARLETT: Once when my volunteers were sick? All of em
were sick, right? And I just wanted to see what the hell I
would do? I lay in my own shit and piss for three days.

85 CHRISTINE: Good Lord, what—

SCARLETT: I coulda phoned somebody, my parents live down
the street, but I just wanted to see . . . I wanted to see how
long I'd survive, I wanted to see if I could do it.

CHRISTINE: Well, who did you eventually—

90 SCARLETT: My mother, my poor mother. And it makes me
sick, sick, because what will I do when they die? They're
old you know, they're gonna die soon.

CHRISTINE: What will you do?

SCARLETT: I'll die on the floor in my shit and piss.

95 CHRISTINE: Scarlett, do you have any hobbies; that is, what do
you do between volunteers, do you have favourite soap
operas or game shows, or—

SCARLETT: I screw my brains out.

CHRISTINE: (*A weak laugh.*) No, seriously, Scarlett.

100 SCARLETT: You think I'm kiddin? You think I sit around and
watch game shows and uh stare out the window waitin
for the next volunteer? No way, girlie, I git it ONNN.

CHRISTINE: You're . . . sexually active, then?

SCARLETT: Shocked, aren't you, pretty pea?

105 CHRISTINE: No.

SCARLETT: YOU ARE TOO YOU LYING BITCH!!

CHRISTINE: Alright, I will admit, I am . . . surprised. I suppose
the public perception of handicapped people is somewhat—skewered.

110 SCARLETT: You think you're bettern me, dontcha?

CHRISTINE: Oh Scarlett, really I . . .

SCARLETT: Well I'll tell you somethin, Christine, my
boyfriend wouldn't rub your tittie. And you think he's
handicapped? No way, babe, I'm not fucking a freak.

115 CHRISTINE: Well, I'm very happy for you, really Scarlett.

SCARLETT: Bullshit, you think it's sick.

CHRISTINE: No, honestly Scarlett, I don't! I think everybody
deserves to—have a happy sex life.

SCARLETT: Yeah? Wanna hear more?

CHRISTINE: Sure! 120

SCARLETT: But don't print this part in your article, right, just
the crap about how noble I am copin on my own and that
shit, and how good the United Church is helpin me out,
all that shit right?

CHRISTINE: Scarlett, I won't print anything that you don't 125
want me to. I despise journalists that do that kind of thing.
I want you to think of me as a friend. Maybe we could
even go out sometime, catch a movie, or go to dinner . . .

SCARLETT: Sure, if you like.

CHRISTINE: So! How did it all start with your boyfriend? 130

SCARLETT: It all started one night, I'd just been watching TV
for sixteen hours straight, from eight in the morning,
right? And that's hard on the eyes, I was bone tired. So I
go to bed, I look out the window and there's no moon,
right? And I lie there for hours, can't sleep, itchy, bored, 135
just wishin I was dead, as usual, when I hear, my door
open.

CHRISTINE: Were you frightened?

SCARLET: I couldnta cared. I thought it was, you know, a guy
with a knife, come to carve me up. I thought good, great, 140
whata way to go. I laughed thinkin a Monica, she's my
morning volunteer, thinkin a her comin in findin me
dead—so I wait to be cut, but I don't hear nothin, nothin,
I figure he's in his socks, not a sound then . . . he sits on
the edge of my bed, and and and, and then he start . . . he 145
start . . . he start . . . touchin my foot just touchin my foot
so soft, and nice, and I . . . laugh. I laugh and laugh, and
Christine, I don't think I ever laughed so long and so long
in my life.

CHRISTINE: Who was it? 150

SCARLETT: That's the question, isn't it Chris? Who the hell is it?

CHRISTINE: Did he . . . ever come again?

SCARLETT: He come every time there isn't no moon, in like
a big cat sit on the bed, and me, like a big piece of fruit,

(*Dance music starts.* SCARLETT *gets up.*)

explodin in the heat, exploding up and out the whole 155
night, I can MOVE when my boy comes, (*She twirls.*) I am
movin, I know I am, I am turnin and swishin and holdin,

(*A* MAN *enters. He and* SCARLETT *dance romantically around the
set. He leaves her back in her chair, immobile, and exits.*)

like eels, you ever seen eels? Lamprey eels, brilliant light
moving fast fast they swim from the Saint John River
down to Montego Bay to spurt their young, I swim like 160
that coloured-up, bright and fast when my boy comes,
swirlin and movin in the dark no moon . . .

CHRISTINE: Hey, is he handsome?

SCARLETT: I tole you there's no moon.

CHRISTINE: You mean you haven't— 165

SCARLETT: He's my midnight man, you dick! My midnight
man he is my midnight man, get it? You can't SEE night,
you can't SEE when there's no moon why? Why do you
think it's so big to see your boyfriend two eyes, nose, a
mouth, what the diff, what the hell is the— 170

CHRISTINE: I must go, I . . . have an appointment.

SCARLETT: You're not gonna print that.

CHRISTINE: I have a job, Scarlett, I have a child to support . . .
SCARLETT: I'll slit your throat if ya print that.
175 CHARLOTTE: Goodbye.

(SCARLETT *grabs* CHRISTINE's *clothing.*)

SCARLETT: PLEASE!! PLEASE!! Please, Christine, my old
    lady and old man, they're old, my mum's had a stroke, my
    dad's got MS, this'd kill em, please!!
CHRISTINE: That is not my business, Scarlett, Scarlett, let go
180   of me, LET GO!
SCARLETT: Reverend Pete and everybody down the church,
    they'd think I was a slut, they'd send me to the freakhouse.

(*They struggle.*)

CHRISTINE: Let me go!!

(SCARLETT *falls on top of* CHRISTINE.)

SCARLETT: You're gonna kill me, you're gonna kill me.

(CHRISTINE *rolls her off and onto the floor.*)

185 CHRISTINE: You are trying to obstruct the freedom of the
    press, lady.
SCARLETT: You can't do this you can't do this!
CHRISTINE: (*Frees herself, gets away.*) I'm sorry. I'm doing it.
SCARLETT: I'll see you in hell!!

(*This stops* CHRISTINE.)

190 CHRISTINE: What?
SCARLETT: I said you'll go right to hell for this!!
CHRISTINE: I don't believe in hell.
SCARLETT: Joke's on you, girl, cause I'm in it, right now, live
    from hell, and if you do this, you're gonna be burning here
195   with me, maybe not today, maybe not tomorrow but soon,
    soon, you'll be whizzing down the highway with a large
    group of handsome friends to some ski resort or other,
    and your male driver will decide to pass on the right, you
    will turn over and over, knocking into each other's skulls
200   breaking each other's necks like eggs in a bag, falling
    through windshields it's gonna rain blood and I will open
    my big jaws and swallow youuuu! YOU will spend the rest
    of eternity inside me. Inside my . . . body and ooooh time
    goes slowwwwwwe . . .
205 CHRISTINE: You're crazy.
SCARLETT: I am waiting for you Chrissy, I'm waiting for you
    Chrissy, I am waiting for you Chrissy, I am . . .
CHRISTINE: STOP THAT. Stop that craziness NOW there is
    no such thing, there is no such thing as any of that ANY
210   of it. You live and you die in your own body and you go
    up to heaven or just nowhere.
SCARLETT: Into the middle of Scarlett . . .
CHRISTINE: You don't know ANYTHING.
SCARLETT: Inside my big wet behind . . .
215 CHRISTINE: Stop It. Stop saying those things.
SCARLETT: In the bummy of a big dead fish . . .
CHRISTINE: Stop it, I said stop it now.
SCARLETT: Your left arm and your head too, Chrissy, gonna
    be severed you'll be all over the highway and your mean
220   little soul will . . .

CHRISTINE: (*Beats* SCARLETT *to the ground, screaming*) STOP
    IT! STOP IT! (*Kicking her.*) STOP IT! STOP IT! (CHRIS-
    TINE *collapses.*)

(SCARLETT *breathes with difficulty.*)

Oh no. Oh no. Scarlett, are you okay? You're okay. You're
okay. Your mother will be by soon or a volunteer and, and   225
I'll call, I, I, I'll call an ambulance. You shouldn't have
made me do that, Scarlett. You shouldn't have made me
kick you like that. The way you, you, you talked to me
like that. Like, like, like you belong. In the world. As if you
belong. Where did you get that feeling? I want it. I need   230
it. (*Pause, about to exit.*) I need it.
SCARLETT: OOOOOOH! Come down and kiss me, put
    your tongue in my mouth!! Come on, NOW, RIGHT
    now, there's no one around, right now, on the ground, do
    me, kiss me, come down and kiss me, like a lion, so hot   235
    right here right now, swirl, swirl me twirl, twirl me, make
    me light, light exploding into . . . (*Laughs.*)

(CHRISTINE *returns, swooping down like a condor, gives* SCARLETT
the kiss of death. SCARLETT, *thinking it is her lover, responds passionately and then, without air, dies.*)

ISOBEL: (*To* CHRISTINE, *touching her.*) SLAVE! *You* are a slave
    of the lion! You lie with him you laugh you let him bite
    your neck, you spread your legs. You will take me to him   240
    now.

(*Music, blackout. Lights up on* CHRISTINE's *office. She is moving
things in an angry way.*)

ISOBEL: Shhh. I wait for the lion!!

(RODNEY, *an early-middle-aged man with a stoop,* CHRISTINE's *research assistant, comes in and waits until she addresses him. He has
an armload of papers.*)

CHRISTINE: Yes, Rodney, what is it?
RODNEY: I've . . . uh . . . brought the research material you
    asked for.   245
CHRISTINE: Good. Great. Thank you . . . How was your
    weekend?
RODNEY: Quiet.
CHRISTINE: Rodney. Rodney—Rodney I told you I wanted
    stats on CP, cerebral palsy, not just 'handicapped people.' I   250
    wanted information on cerebral palsy!
RODNEY: You did NOT specify cerebral palsy, Christine.
CHRISTINE: Oh yes I most certainly did, I said—
RODNEY: I have it on tape, Christine!
CHRISTINE: Rodney! Are you or are you not a professional   255
    researcher?
RODNEY: Yes.
CHRISTINE: Well then start doing professional work! NOW!
    Or you are out. Is that understood? IS THAT UNDER-
    STOOD?   260
RODNEY: . . . of . . . course . . .

(CHRISTINE *exits.* RODNEY *is at his desk.*)

You will NOT EVER SPEAK TO ME THAT WAY AGAIN CHRISTINE YOU WILL NOT TREAT ME AS AN OBJECT do you understand? Is that understood?
265   IS THAT UNDERSTOOD??

(*Knock on the door.*)

Yes? Hello. May I help you?

MICHAEL: Yes, I'm looking for a Rodney LeHavre—I was directed to this office.

RODNEY: I . . . am . . . Mr. LeHavre.

270   MICHAEL: Rodney?

RODNEY: Do I know you?

MICHAEL: Michael . . . Lind . . . from St. George's, '60 to '64. How are you? You remember me, don't you?

RODNEY: Michael . . . Lind? No. No, I'm afraid I don't, I'm
275   sorry. Were you in my class?

MICHAEL: Yeah, yeah, we were good friends for a while even; don't you remember? Come on. We played chess. You were a great player. You taught me . . . how to play. You must remember.

280   RODNEY: Chess.

MICHAEL: I guess you don't remember. I'm sorry. I was sure that you'd remember. I . . . I . . . (*Backing out.*)

RODNEY: Would you like to come in and sit down? I can take ten minutes I think. Would you like to sit down?

285   MICHAEL: Oh, oh, okay, if you don't mind . . .

RODNEY: No. A cup of coffee . . . I could—get the secretary—Sherry—to—

MICHAEL: (*Laughs.*) You've got to remember the fly collection. It was really hot. July, I think. We caught it must have
290   been fifty house flies, and, and we stuck them with Elmer's glue, to a piece of Bristol board. To a big piece of Bristol board. And labelled them in Latin. Don't you remember? You must remember.

RODNEY: Wait a minute . . . wait a minute . . . yeah, yeah, and
295   we even *named* them, didn't we? Didn't we name each one?

MICHAEL: Yeah, yeah . . . I'll never forget. You even named one Clarence. I thought it was brilliant.

RODNEY: Right! And yours were all names like Fred, Joe, Cindy, weren't they? Right!

300   MICHAEL: And yours were all royalty—Elizabeth, Margaret, Clarence. God!

RODNEY: God. A fly collection. So what did we *do* with it?

MICHAEL: I think . . . we had it arranged . . . to show someone. A colleague of my father's. Someone in insect . . .

305   RODNEY: Entomology.

MICHAEL: Yeah, that's it. And it was raining or something . . .

RODNEY: Pouring, yes, pouring, and all the flies—

RODNEY & MICHAEL: FELL OFF THE BRISTOL BOARD!

RODNEY: God. Michael Lind. Michael LIND! I'm sorry.

310   CHRISTINE: (*Off.*) Rodney I need that material *as soon as possible,* please!

MICHAEL: Well I see that you have to get back to work, I'd better go . . . Ahhh . . . just before I go, there's one thing. I uh . . . this is going to sound strange, but . . . I've been
315   having . . . sort of . . . dreams . . . about . . . back then, I . . . have them a lot—

RODNEY: Oh?

MICHAEL: Yes, only . . . I always wake up at the same spot, fairly distressed, actually, and . . . I just . . . wondered . . . if

you could . . . help me . . . remember . . . what actually hap- 320
pened. Back then . . . When we were . . . kids. Do you think you could—

RODNEY: Sure, I could try . . .

MICHAEL: Okay, let's start at the beginning. It was something to do with chess. 325

RODNEY: Chess.

MICHAEL: You loved to play chess you . . . brought me to your house after school, it was a Tuesday, I think, cold, we went through a short cut it said 'Pedestrians Only' I thought it said 'Protestants Only' and I was terrified. 330

(RODNEY *laughs.*)

And we went to your room, with all the paper airplanes hanging from the ceiling all over the room! And we lay on the floor. Do you remember? You remember lying on the floor? Rodney, your carpet. Your carpet was brown and orange, sort of circles or something. There was the sound 335 of a snowblower outside. My queen. You took my queen. And then, and then, Rodney, didn't we laugh, or or or or . . . some touch some touch Rodney and you made a strange sound. What was that sound. Please help me! I need to go back there. I need to go back there, you see? 340 You were the only—friend that I—we saw the world the same way. Remember? We saw the world the same way. I want to go back there. (*Caresses his shoulder.*) I want to go back there . . .

RODNEY: I want to go back there, too. I want to go back 345 there, too.

(MICHAEL *and* RODNEY *embrace.* RODNEY *makes the sound.* MICHAEL *pulls him back and throws him to the ground.*)

MICHAEL: QUEER!! Queer queer queer queer queer queer QUEER! FAIRY SISSY LITTLE CREEP!! DON'T YOU EVER ever remember again. YOU have WRECKED my life, your slimy memory, using me over 350 and over and over again like an old porno magazine you will RELINQUISH that memory you will wipe it out, you understand?

RODNEY: You're crazy, you need psychiatric . . .

MICHAEL: You will NOT remember me again because if you 355 do, if you do, I will feel it, oh yes, and I will come and I will kill you. I could feel you remembering, almost daily, I would be in the middle, the middle of a crucial business meeting all the way in Vancouver and suddenly I would feel you . . . holding my memory, turning it over and over, 360 folding it, caressing it, reliving it, SPEWING, spewing your filth all over me. How how I always wondered how could you do it in the middle of the day? Did you do it here, at work, at this desk is this where you—

RODNEY: Anywhere I can, Michael. You see, my life has been 365 terribly disappointing.

MICHAEL: You will . . . free me—

RODNEY: Of course. I'll try, but memory . . . does seem to have a will of its own, I can't really help what—

(MICHAEL *hits him, they fight, rolling and punching, and end up on the floor. Very, very slowly* MICHAEL *raises his head, extends his tongue,* RODNEY *does the same. They come together and their tongues touch. It is an ecstatic moment for both of them.* MICHAEL *pulls out a knife,* RODNEY *takes it from him and cuts his throat.* MICHAEL *dies. Music. The actor playing* MICHAEL *gets up and exits.* ISOBEL *goes to* RODNEY *and touches him, then* RODNEY *gets up, straightens himself.*)

370 RODNEY: 'Hello, welcome to St. George's. My name is Rodney LeHavre, grade seven, and you're . . .? Michael Lind! Welcome! You just came from Vancouver? I have a cousin there! Do you play chess?' Chess, every day . . . chess, Monday, Tuesday, Wednesday, Thursday, chess, with . . . Michael
375 . . . at school, at my house at his house in his room, lying on our stomachs staring at the chess board, he sticks his tongue out at me because he had just captured my queen and then I stuck my tongue out back at him and he moved forward just a bit till his tongue was touching mine, and my whole
380 life jumped into my tongue we didn't move just lay there touching tongues, 'Would you boys like some tuna sandwiches?' his mother the best mother in the world with her red bangles and bourbon sour at six, 'Okay Mrs. Lind, thanks!' And we had a secret, an atomic secret nobody else
385 in the whole entire world knew that we had touched tongues oh OH wrote his name, MICHAEL, over and over one thousand times one thousand times; on the fifth day, the fifth day after, I'm at the blackboard doing math, very good at math, superb mind for mathematics the other boys
390 jealous, always been jealous of my superior brain throwing spitballs, used to that, yelling 'Froggy, froggy frog' because of my francophone name, used to that, I turn, I catch his face white darkened so quickly like a sky, he caught, he knew, suddenly he knew, Michael, that he had been play-
395 ing chess with the loser 'FROGGY, HEY FROGGY' they scream 'HEY FROG.' He stands up! They look expectantly, is the new kid going to defend his friend? What's he going to say, I to myself, 'Oh thank you, Michael, thank you thank you the first to ever defend me oh what what are you
400 going to say to defend me?' He takes a breath, I'm holding mine, he smiles he speaks he says: 'Is he a frog . . . OR A TOAD!!' They laugh and laugh and laugh screaming their laughter slapping their desks shaking their fists triumphing a new member of the PACK!! Is he a frog, or a toad—Am
405 I a frog or am I a toad?

(SHERRY *enters.*)

SHERRY: RODDEE! RODDEEE!! Baby Bunny.
ISOBEL: She!
SHERRY: You'll never guess what I have! Milk chocolate bar with lots of gushy cream in it. Two squares for you, and
410 two squares for me.
ISOBEL: She!
SHERRY: One hundred and forty calories a square who gives a shit. I heard Christine chewin ya out, what a fuckin cow.
ISOBEL: She . . . I see, I smell the spray, the Lion's spray . . .
415 SHERRY: (*Notices that* RODNEY *is very upset.*) What happened?

(SHERRY *runs from* RODNEY's *office back home to the apartment she shares with her boyfriend of two years,* EDWARD, *an out-of-work actor. When she comes in he is practising a tap routine for an audition. Newspapers all over the floor.*)

SHERRY: JeSUS I'm peed off—I'm standing on the escalator, right? Goin down to the subway? My back hurts, I don't

feel like takin the stairs? So I'm standin there when this woman shoves by me right into the wall and goes, 'Can't you move? Some people are in a hurry!' And I just 420 STAND there like a fucking WETWIPE with my mouth open FUCK if I see that bitch again—
EDWARD: That's very interesting, Sherry.
SHERRY: Whatcha workin on that dance try-out thing?
EDWARD: Uh, no. I'm fixing the faulty wiring with my feet, 425 it's magic, Sherry, really! Right through the—
SHERRY: Ah Jeez, you're not mad at me again are ya? Whad I do now?
EDWARD: I don't know, Sherry, what did you do now?
SHERRY: I get off work at five thirty, Ed, it's ten to six what 430 the hell am I supposed to do? Fly home?
EDWARD: I phoned work at four o'clock, Sherry, and Arlene said that you had left for the day.
SHERRY: Oh well THAT—I was havin a coffee and a piece of cake with Rodney, he— 435
EDWARD: Don't lie, please.
SHERRY: I was, Eddie, ask Rodney, ask—
EDWARD: You've rehearsed them all.
SHERRY: Listen to me! Rodney had some kind of fit today, Christine just about called the cops he was yelling and 440 screaming at nobody all afternoon—he's right nuts.
EDWARD: It is a skilful liar it is.
SHERRY: *Don't call me 'it'.*
EDWARD: I beg your pardon?
SHERRY: Have you been drinking? Or doin coke or some 445 shit? You have, haven't you? You—
EDWARD: We're out of toilet paper.
SHERRY: No, there's more right under the—
EDWARD: No there's NOT!
SHERRY: Alright, I'll go and get some now— 450
EDWARD: YOU'LL stay right where you are, Sherry. Please. PLEASE I'm asking you. Don't leave me alone—here—I don't want to be alone.
SHERRY: Aww Eddie, you know I love you, don't you.
EDWARD: If—if you're not happy with my performance in 455 bed . . . I wish you'd just . . . tell me and—and—
SHERRY: Honey, I love your performance in bed.
EDWARD: You don't really, do you?
SHERRY: Listen I was just tellin Arlene today you got the best hands of I bet any guy there is on the whole fuckin planet! 460
EDWARD: You were?
SHERRY: The way you touch me, Eddie, Christ, I feel like a whole bouquet, you know? A bouquet of red flowers just . . . poppin open, poppop pop pop pop just like on one of them nature specials. I love makin love with you, I 465 think about it all day, half the time my pants are wet thinkin about you.
EDWARD: They're not, really?
SHERRY: They are. Feel . . . feel that (*Puts his hand under her dress.*) Oh honey I want you to make love to me. Please? 470
EDWARD: (*Kissing her.*) Oh! Oh! I've been thinking about you too, all day, every day.
SHERRY: Oh Eddie, I want you.
EDWARD: You want me . . .?
SHERRY: Did you not get that part in the TV series? About 475 the runaway kid or whatever? Is that why you're—Eddie what's wrong? Did I say something wrong?
EDWARD: YOU ARE A FLAMING ASSHOLE!

SHERRY: Eddie!

480 EDWARD: Who are you dreaming about every night?

SHERRY: What?

EDWARD: Every night you're moaning like an animal in heat, who?

SHERRY: What?

485 EDWARD: Who are you dreaming about, Sherry?

SHERRY: Nobody! I'm not dreaming about—nobody.

EDWARD: WHO ARE YOU DREAMING ABOUT?

SHERRY: Just forget it, I'm going over to Arlene's I'll see you later.

490 EDWARD: You tell me who you are dreaming about or I will cancel the wedding.

SHERRY: Eddie.

EDWARD: I will . . . TODAY, if you don't stop lying to me treating me like a fucking maggot—

495 SHERRY: I'm not lying to you Ed, please, just—

EDWARD: I'll cancel the wedding! I'll phone up Father Hayes and I'll cancel the whole fucking thing.

SHERRY: I paid nine hundred dollars for that dress, Eddie.

EDWARD: I don't give a flying fuck what you paid for it.

500 SHERRY: EDDIE my mum's got her ticket from Florida, my sisters—

EDWARD: I don't give a hot damn miss—

SHERRY: OKAY OKAY OKAY OKAY you're right, you're right. There is someone I'm dreaming about; it's . . . uh . . .

505 EDWARD: It's him, isn't it?

SHERRY: Him? Who?

EDWARD: The rape from six years ago—

SHERRY: (*She throws the telephone book at him.*) Eddie THAT is not fair!

510 EDWARD: It's him, isn't it?

SHERRY: I think I'm going to be sick!

EDWARD: That was the best fuck you ever had, wasn't it? It was the only fuck you ever respected, wasn't it? WASN'T IT, SHERRY?

(SHERRY *cries.*)

515 WASN'T IT? WASN'T IT?

SHERRY: NO!

EDWARD: Listen to me. You don't tell me the truth right now and I cancel the wedding. RIGHT now, I'll call up Father Hayes and I'll cancel the whole thing for good.

520 SHERRY: Eddie, please!

(*He goes to the phone, flips through the telephone book.*)

EDWARD: St. Paul's Cathedral, St. Paul's—532—

SHERRY: (*She grabs the phone book.*) Okay! Okay okay okay!

EDWARD: You admit?

(SHERRY *nods.*)

What? To what do you admit, Sherry?

525 SHERRY: That . . .

EDWARD: Come on, tell the truth, the truth, truth, truth.

SHERRY: THAT . . .

(EDWARD *picks up the phone.*)

That he's the best fuck I ever had.

EDWARD: NOW we are cooking with GAS. This is what I always knew in my heart never DARED with all this feminist shit going down. Come on, come on tell me if I'm going to be your husband I want to know it all. 530

SHERRY: But what should I—

EDWARD: The truth!! I know how hard it is for you after a lifetime of female . . . conniving and guile but let's do it! Come on! Tell me, tell me how you led him on. 535

SHERRY: Led . . . him . . . on??

EDWARD: HOW YOU LAID YOUR TRAP! Come on, what was it you were wearing? Wasn't it those sex shorts, those, pink . . . what are they called? Sherry, what are they called? 540

(SHERRY *is saying what she thinks he wants to hear because she is scared, but it is like excrement in her mouth, and* EDWARD *is gratified and ripped apart at the same time by what she hears.*)

SHERRY: Pink . . . hot pants?

EDWARD: That's it! And what else, what else?

SHERRY: Ahhh . . .

EDWARD: Come on!

SHERRY: No—underwear? 545

EDWARD: Yes? YES?

SHERRY: I was a real—cocktease with that guy?

EDWARD: Good, good Sherry, the truth is good. And . . . AND.

SHERRY: Ahh—One—one—time I dropped—dropped my 550 smokes uh—cause I knew the—the sight of my ass in those shorts bending over would make him—him—him—come right in his pants.

EDWARD: Yes?

SHERRY: See— 555

EDWARD: YES? YES?

SHERRY: I—hated—him, I hated him because . . .

EDWARD: YES?

SHERRY: . . . because that . . . hunger . . . I seen when he looked at me I fuckin hated that . . . hunger in his 560 eyes. And his fucking mouth always open like a fuckin baby bird reachin reachin for the fuckin worm all the fuckin—

EDWARD: So you tortured him!

SHERRY: I fuckin hated him— 565

(*Lines simultaneous:.*)

EDWARD: Tell me, tell me what happened.

SHERRY: Wa—walkin to the subway, about ten o'clock at night, somethin grabs my arm, it's him, the guy I seen, he asks me if I want to go to the show, the porno show down the street. 570

EDWARD: You look at him like garbage.

SHERRY: I tell him, 'No, asshole.'

EDWARD: Like a piece of filth. And?

SHERRY: And . . . like I told you before, I take off, fast, but—but my heels are givin me trouble, I can't run in them. 575

EDWARD: You let him catch up.

SHERRY: And . . . and . . . he throws me between two houses, on the cement, near the trash.

EDWARD: Where were all the people, Sherry?

580 SHERRY: I guess they thought we were married, they thought
       it was okay.
     EDWARD: You were very aroused.
     SHERRY: (*She very obviously was not.*) I was . . .?
     EDWARD: And he—pushed you back to the cement?
585 SHERRY: When I tried to get up.
     EDWARD: And? And?
     SHERRY: He starts . . . smashin my head against the cement!
     EDWARD: You're so frightened, breathing fast, like an animal!
     SHERRY: I'm bleeding, and I'm throwing up, and he rips off
590   my blouse, and my skirt, he—he—he kept telling me that
       he was going to kill me.
     EDWARD: And you're very aroused!
     SHERRY: He was going to smash my head in and leave me for
       dead!
595 EDWARD: And then . . . he penetrated you?
     SHERRY: He—he—
     EDWARD: Inside you?
     SHERRY: He couldn't get it up, so he used . . . he used . . .
     EDWARD: You're moaning with ecstasy.
600 SHERRY: 'I'm gonna kill you, bitch,' he kept sayin, 'I'm gonna
       kill you, bitch.'
     EDWARD: The hottest sex you ever had!
     SHERRY: And . . . and . . . I lie there for hours, passed out, all
       my blood pouring out onto the cement.
605 EDWARD: But happy, right? You finally got it GOOD.
     SHERRY: Until the lady's puttin out her garbage!
     EDWARD: And you told her the truth, didn't you?
     SHERRY: What?
     EDWARD: That it was all your fault.
610 SHERRY: What?
     EDWARD: That you teased the poor guy, that you wanted him
       to power you, it was the sexiest hottest sex ever you
       wanted to be HAD.
     SHERRY: The lady, she helped me up, she—she gave me a
615   Kleenex, and a glass of water, she—
     EDWARD: You told her, of course, that you are the snake.
     SHERRY: I . . . am . . . the snake?
     EDWARD: Because SATAN tempts OTHERS to sin, right?
     SHERRY: Satan tempts others to sin?
620 EDWARD: You were the snake with the diamond back,
       glittering!
     SHERRY: I . . . am . . . the snake.
     EDWARD: It was all your fault.
     SHERRY: It was . . . all . . . my fault.
625 EDWARD: You ARE the snake.
     SHERRY: I am the snake. I am the snake. I AM the snake. I AM
       THE SNAKE. I AM THE SNAKE! I AM THE SNAKE!
       I AM THE SNAKE! I AM THE SNAKE! I AM THE
       SNAAAAAAAAKE!!

(SHERRY *breaks down in tears. She collapses on the floor.* EDWARD *cleans up and then sits down.*)

630 Eddie? Will you come with me tomorrow then to Ashley's
       to pick out a pattern? Like I've made the appointment and
       everything Ed, and after all, you are going to have to live
       with the dishes. I mean, I know guys hate goin in there,
       all guys do, but everyone that gets married goes to Ash-
635   ley's, everyone that gets married—

EDWARD: Alright. But nothing with flowers on it. I just want
       something clean, maybe—white, with a black stripe.

(ISOBEL *enters the room, and offers her hand to* SHERRY, *who takes it, gratefully. Arm in arm, they walk away from* SHERRY *and* EDWARD's *apartment to a graveyard. At first* ISOBEL *is helping* SHERRY, *but by the time they reach the graveyard it is* SHERRY *who helps* ISOBEL *find her grave, and gently lays her down, and disappears. In the graveyard, sitting on another tombstone, is* BEN, *the man who killed* ISOBEL *seventeen years before.*)

BEN: There's one thing, you know. There's one thing that I
       always . . . wanted to tell somebody and that is that . . . I
       done her a favour. I was—kindly—yeah, see, I pull her 640
       outa the car and throw her on the cement in front of the
       warehouse there's a streetlight and . . . and she says to me
       she says, 'Please,' she says, 'Please no strangle, I so . . . scared
       of strangle,' in this voice of breath just . . . purely of breath
       so I stopped, eh? I did. I stepped out of the twister cause 645
       that's what it's like, when you're doin something like that,
       you're inside a twister and to step out, is like . . . liftin a
       dishwasher, eh, but I did. So I go back of the warehouse
       and I picked up a brick and I hit her—cause she touched
       me okay? She touched me, right?   650

(ISOBEL *approaches with her weapon.*)

ISOBEL: BEN . . . ja . . . men.

(BEN *looks.*)

  Ben ja men BEN ja men.
BEN: Who the fuck are you?
ISOBEL: Is . . . o . . . bel.
BEN: Isobel.   655
ISOBEL: Isobel in July July the one, CANADA day day for
       CANADA Birthday. I selling tickets on a Chrysler car, for
       boys' and girls' club, one dollar fifty for a ticket. I have five
       tickets left. I see you in park. It is raining on park. Don't
       you remember? I ask you, 'You want to buy ticket on a 660
       Chrysler car?' You say, 'Yes, yes, I buy all five all five tick-
       ets. Come into my car, come into my silver car with dark
       red meat, come into my car. I will give you the money for
       the tickets I have the money in my car,' you said . . .
BEN: I'm hallucinatin.   665
ISOBEL: I'm Isobel.
BEN: You're a picture.
ISOBEL: I'm Isobel.
BEN: What . . . do you want?
ISOBEL: I have come.   670
BEN: What do you want?
ISOBEL: I am here.
BEN: WELL GO AWAY! You hear me? GO AWAY.
ISOBEL: (*She is about to kill him with the stick, the forces of
       vengeance and forgiveness warring inside her—forgiveness wins.*) 675
       I love you.
BEN: NO!!
ISOBEL: *You took my last breath!*
BEN: Christ I'm sick, I'm so sick.
ISOBEL: *I want back my life. Give me back my life!*   680

(*Players enter singing a religious-sounding chorale with a sense of sadness and triumph. They place a veil on* ISOBEL's *head, the actor playing* BEN *joining them.*)

ISOBEL: (*An adult now.*) I want to tell you now a secret. I was dead, was killed by lion in long silver car, starving lion, maul maul maul me to dead, with killing claws over and over my little young face and chest, over my chest my blood running out he take my heart with. He take my heart with, in his pocket deep, but my heart talk. Talk and talk and never be quiet never be quiet. I came back. I take my life. I want you all to take your life. I want you all to have your life. 685

(*Players sing a second, joyful chorale, walking off.* ISOBEL *ascends, in her mind, into heaven. The last thing we see is her veil. End.*)

Manjula Padmanabhan

Well-known as a cartoonist in Delhi, Manjula Padmanabhan (b. 1953), has worked as a journalist and fiction writer, as well as writing for television and the stage; she has also written several children's books. After completing her university studies abroad, Padmanabhan returned to India and began a career in journalism. She wrote several plays—including *Lights Out!* (1984), *The Artist's Model* (1995), and *Sextet* (1996)—and a well-known book of short stories, *Hot Death, Cold Soup* (1995). *Harvest* won the first Onassis Prize for Theater, and premiered in Greece in 1999; it has also been produced in India. Her most recent novel is *Getting There* (2000).

HARVEST

Written in the lineage of plays like Vaclav Havel's *The Memorandum* or Slawomir Mrozek's *Tango,* Manjula Padmanabhan's *Harvest* develops an absurd narrative of the structure of representation and power in the contemporary globalized culture. For *Harvest* brilliantly allegorizes the relationship between the First and Third Worlds, literalizing the fundamental practices of globalization as its central dramatic situation: the Third World provides the raw materials that the First World consumes for its own survival and expansion.

In the play, Om has sold his body—through the aptly named InterPlanta Services company—to an American "Receiver." According to the terms of his contract, he and his immediate family (his wife Jaya, who is forced by the contract to pretend to be his sister, his

The family confronts Ginni in Manjula Padmanabhan's *Harvest,* in the 1999 production of the play at the Teatro Texnis, Greece.

brother Jeetu, and his mother, Ma) will enjoy a First World standard of living and lifestyle—they'll be clean, well-fed, entertained, and wealthy—until such time as his Receiver demands Om's organs for his own survival. As the play develops, however, the economic motives driving Om's sacrifice are gradually inflected by the mediatized relations of global culture. His family is consulted (on a giant-screen Contact Module that drops from the ceiling) by the Receiver, Virginia—or "Ginni," whose name recalls the demonic *djinni,* or "genies" of Indian folktales—a "blonde and white-skinned epitome of an American-style youth goddess" whose image floats above the room, and increasingly demands obedience from the family. Ma comes nearly to worship Ginni, but truly idolizes her new television, finally choosing to entomb herself inside a video sarcophagus—called the Video Paradise—where she will remain for the rest of her "life." When the InterPlanta agents come to take Om, however, they mistakenly take his wastrel brother Jeetu, removing his eyes and replacing them with a contraption that projects Ginna's sexy image directly into his brain. Although Jeetu had been the most critical of the organ-donation scheme, now that all he can see is Ginni's sultry image, he's seduced, and this virtual relationship leads him finally to "donate" his entire body.

The play's brilliant satire fully takes in First World attitudes toward India, its fear of disease, its anxiety about sanitation, its incomprehension of family and social life, its ignorance of Third World reality altogether. Replacing the family's food with "goat-shit" pellets, installing a toilet and shower in the middle of its one-room apartment, dumping the family's possessions and replacing them with Western clothes and housewares, InterPlanta at once appears to improve the family's standard of living while cutting it off from real life altogether. Yet the final scenes seem to suggest a strategy of resistance. Once Ginni has harvested Jeetu's body, she reveals that "Ginni" had only been a computer-animation after all: Jeetu had been seduced to give up his body by the empty image of youthful, sexy America, an image projected to the world to conceal that the First World paradise is aging and impotent, supporting "the poorer sections of the world, while gaining fresh bodies for ourselves." Virgil—the real Ginni—proposes that he (in the body of Jeetu) and Jaya have children to repopulate the First World; he even makes an insemination gadget appear outside the apartment while he's trying to close the deal. But if the body is, finally, what the Third World has to sell, it may still be possible to withhold it, to insist on a real rather than a mediated relationship with First World power. At the play's close, Jaya seals herself inside the apartment, with its endless food supply and television, telling Virgil that if he wants to repopulate the First World, he will have to come to her, in the flesh.

HARVEST
Manjula Padmanabhan

CHARACTERS
DONORS

OM *Twenty years old, he has been laid off from his job as a clerk and is the bread-earner of his small family. He is of medium height, nervy and thin. He would be reasonably good-looking if not for his anxious expression.*

JAYA OM's *wife. Thin and haggard at the outset, she looks older than her nineteen years, but is passionate and spirited. Her bright cotton sari has faded with repeated washing, to a meek pink. Like the others, she is barefoot at the outset. She wears glass bangles, a tiny nose-ring, ear-studs, a slender chain around her neck. No make-up aside from the kohl around her eyes and the red bindi on her forehead.*

MA OM's *mother. She is sixty years old, stooped, scrawny and crabby, wears a widow's threadbare white-on-white sari. Her hair is a straggly white.*

JEETU OM's *younger brother, seventeen and handsome. The same height as* OM, *he is wiry and conscious of his body. He works as a male prostitute and has a dashing, easy-going likeable personality.*

BIDYUT BAI *An elderly neighbour, very similar in appearance to* MA, *but timid and self-effacing.*

Also URCHINS *and the crowd outside the door. The crowd is audible rather than visible.*

GUARDS and AGENTS

GUARDS *The* GUARDS *are a group of three commando-like characters who bear the same relationship to each other whenever they appear.* GUARD 1 *is the leader of the team, a man in his mid forties, of military bearing.* GUARD 2 *is a young and attractive woman, unsmiling and efficient.* GUARD 3 *is a male clone of* GUARD 2. *Only* GUARD 1 *interacts with* DONORS.

AGENTS *The* AGENTS *are space-age delivery persons and their uniforms are fantastical verging on ludicrous, like the costumes of waiters in exotic restaurants. Their roles are interchangeable with the* GUARDS, *though it must be clear that they do not belong to the same agency.*

RECEIVERS

GINNI *We see only her face and hear her voice. She is the blonde and white-skinned epitome of an American-style youth goddess. Her voice is sweet and sexy.*

VIRGIL *He is never seen. He has an American cigarette-commercial accent—rich and smoky, attractive and rugged.*

ACT ONE

SCENE I

The sound of inner city traffic: grimy, despairing, poison-fumed. It wells up before the curtains open, then cuts out to a background rumble as . . . the lights reveal a single-room accommodation in a tenement building. It is bare but cluttered. In the foreground, stage left, is a board-bed across the tops of three steel trunks. MA *sits on the bed, her ear straining towards the wall, listening intently. Near her is the front door.* JAYA *stands by the window stage right, looking out, her face drained. To the rear is the kitchen area.*

MA: (*Grunts.*) Ho! (*Turns to look at* JAYA.) Ho—you! Come here a moment—

JAYA: (*Listlessly.*) What is it?

MA: Come here and tell me what they're saying—

5 JAYA: It's none of your business—

MA: Eh?

JAYA: What they say in their room—none of your business!

MA: The cheek of the thing! (*Turns around in indignation.*) As if she knows what my business is! Why—I'm her mother-

10 in-law! And what is she? A dry stick!

JAYA: Leave me out of it. I'm not interested.

MA: Oh of course not, your majesty! So high and mighty she is—staring out of her precious window! Stare all you like but it's useless. There's no chance he'll get the job.

15 JAYA: (*Quickly.*) I'm not the one hoping!

MA: Oh—I forgot! Missie Madam *isn't* hoping the best for her husband—like she should, like any dutiful, sane, reasonable, respectable wife—oh no! Missie Madam has her own sweet thoughts, doesn't she!

JAYA: (*Briefly enlivened.*) Oh! There—I think I see him— 20

MA: Well—well—job or not, he's not got wings, *that* I can tell you. He'll *still* have to climb four floors getting up here. But—what does he look like?

JAYA: (*Straining to see.*) He's—no—yes . . . that's him—

MA: Is his face shining? Are his footsteps sweet? A songbird 25 on his shoulder?

JAYA: It's a bit far to see such details—

MA: Pah! As if you can see them even when he's right in front of you. Now I—I can see it even without looking at him. Just from the sound of his feet. His little feet! Like flowers 30 they were—

JAYA: (*Frustrated.*) Oh—please! The way you go on—!

MA: Jealous!

JAYA: You'd like to think that—

MA: And rude, my arse. Why, you're hardly human! You must 35 have grown up in a jungle!

JAYA: Leave me alone—

MA: Alone, alone! Have you seen your neighbours? Ten in that room, twenty in the other! And harmonious, my dear! Harmonious as a TV show! But you? An empty room 40 would be too crowded for you!

JAYA: That's because I live in a room in which two people think the other two don't exist—

MA: Two and . . . two—four? Have you forgotten how to
45   count?

JAYA: Not at all! You're the one who never counts Jeetu—

MA: Huh! That pimping rascal! That soul's disgrace!

JAYA: You like to pretend he's not there—but *I'm* the one
who has to cook for him, worry about him—

50   MA: You worry far too much about that one, if you ask me—

JAYA: Yet he's *your* son.

MA: Nah. The gods left a jackal in my belly by mistake when
they made him—maybe that's why *you* like him—he's just
like you, rude, insolent, ungrateful—

55   JAYA: I! *Like* him!

MA: Think I don't see the way you wet yourself when he
walks in the door. Yes! Your brother-in-law—oh the sin
of it, the sin! You'll suffer in your next life. See if you
don't! You'll be made into a cockroach and I'll have to
60   smash you—(*Lifts her bare foot and stamps hard.*) just like
this one. (*Shows* JAYA *the underside of the foot.*) See? Do you
see your fate?

JAYA: (*Paying no attention, her ear cocked to the door.*) There!
That's Om—

(*Goes quickly to the door, stage left. Opens it, looks out, steps out,
shutting the door behind her.*)

65   MA: (*Makes a face behind her back.*) Yah, yah! Go on—running
out to meet him, like some idiot schoolgirl! Think I'm
fooled by it! I'm not fooled! I see everything! Even inside
your head! I—

(*The door opens.* OM *walks in.*)

MA: (*Half rising, her face is transformed.*) Ah, my son! My own
70   boy! What news?

(OM, *carrying a bulky parcel, his face set tight, as if too dazed to
know whether to be glad or sad.* JAYA *comes in behind him and shuts
the door.* OM *loosens the collar of his shirt.*)

MA: What? No hope? Nothing at all?

(JAYA *stands uncertainly at centre stage.*)

MA: They are fools, that's all! Don't recognize a diamond
when they see one! It's their loss. Still . . . it would have
been nice. A change. A godsend. How'll we manage now?

75   JAYA: (*Carefully.*) What is it? What happened?

OM: (*Looks up.*) I got it. (*Puts the package down on the bed.*)

(JAYA *stifles a sob, spins around and back to her window.*)

MA: (*As if unable to believe him.*) What? Say that again?

OM: I got it. I got the job.

MA: (*Painfully fierce intake of breath.*) Hhhhhh! Hhhhh! Oh!
80   Say it again! Say the blessed words again! (*Rises shakily to
her feet, declaiming to the world.*) Never stop saying it! "I—
have—got—the—job!" (*Turns to him holding out her arms.*)
Ah my soul, my heartbeat! Come, kiss me! Let me hold
you, fondle your ears! Why am I surprised? You deserve
85   every success.

OM: (*Starts to remove his shirt.*) Yes. It was quite easy, in the end.

MA: (*To* JAYA's *back.*) Bring him a glass of milk! Bring him two
glasses! (*To* OM.) Come here, my darling boy! My only delight! Let your old mother hug you to her belly! (*She goes
to him.*)   90

OM: (*His shirt off, tucked into the waistband of his trousers.*) There
were six thousand men—

MA: Six thousand! Waiting in the sun!

OM: No. Inside a building like a big machine. They had—like
iron bars—snaking around and around (*His hands describe*   95
a narrow looping channel.)—we could only stand one behind the other—like goats at the slaughterhouse—

MA: Shoo! Where has my son seen a slaughterhouse!

OM: And everywhere there were guards—

MA: Police, you mean?   100

OM: Guards in grey uniforms—you'll see them for yourself
any minute now—they're coming—

JAYA: (*From where she stands.*) They're coming now?

OM: They have to check. They have to set it all up.

MA: What? What are you talking about?   105

JAYA: You mean it's not certain yet?

OM: They're just checking the building.

MA: For what—

JAYA: (*Bitterly.*) Better train your mother to tie her tongue
down!   110

MA: Hear that? How your wife speaks of your mother?

OM: Ma—when the men come, you *must keep quiet.*

MA: As if I ever get a chance to speak!

JAYA: She can pretend she doesn't understand!

MA: (*Starting up indignantly.*) What—   115

OM: Yes, Ma. It's the best way. Behave as if you don't understand, when they ask.

MA: But why? What's there to hide? Have you done something wrong?

OM: No—but—but—there's no time to explain! And you'll   120
know for yourself any minute now—

MA: But what's the trouble! Has something gone wrong?
What did they say to you?

OM: They have to check, you see. So that the arrangements
are—are—all right. They're very particular—   125

JAYA: And for how long is the job?

OM: They didn't say—

MA: And what will they pay you?

OM: A lot.

MA: Huh! That's how paupers talk—"a lot". Listen to the   130
rich? They're on first name terms with all the leading
numbers—hundreds, thousands, hundred-thousand . . .

OM: (*His voice is hushed.*) We'll have more money than you
and I have names for! (*Shakes his head in wonderment.*)
Who'd believe there's so much money in the world?   135

MA: Ho!

JAYA: Can we be sure?

MA: You met with the top men? They spoke to you themselves?

OM: No . . .

MA: Pooh! Then you've got nothing!   140

OM: We were standing all together in that line. And the line
went on—and on not just on one floor, but slanting up,
up, forever. All in iron bars and grills. It was like being in
a cage shaped like a tunnel. All around, up, down, sideways, there were men—   145

JAYA: Doing what?

OM: Slowly moving. All the time. I couldn't understand it. . . .
Somewhere there must be a place to stop, to write a form?
Answer questions? But no. Just—forward, forward, for-

150 ward. One person fainted but the others pushed him onward. And at the corners, a—a sort of pipe was kept . . .

MA: For what?

JAYA: To make water, what else!

MA: Even while moving?

155 OM: You had to be quick. Other men would squeeze past behind the fellow who was doing his business. Sometimes
there was no place and he'd have to move on before he
finished. Still dripping.

MA: Shee!

160 OM: What could we do? As for those who had more solid de-
posits to make—! Foo! It was terrible!

JAYA: And then?

OM: The stench! The heat!

MA: But what happened?

165 OM: I don't know for how long we moved. Then there was
a door. Inside it was dark, like being in heaven! So cool,
so fresh! I too fainted then, with pleasure, I don't know.
(*Stands up, reliving his movements.*) I wake up to find now
the ground is moving under me—

170 MA: What? How's that?

OM: I don't know. But the floor is moving. Then there's a
sign: "REMOVE CLOTHING"—

MA: Whaaat?

OM: So we do that. Still moving. Then each man gets a bag.
175 To put the clothes inside.

JAYA: . . . *naked?*

OM: (*Nods.*) Then—a sort of—rain burst. (*He laughs shakily.*)
I wonder if I am dreaming! The water is hot, scented.
Then cold. Then hot air. Then again the water. It stings a
180 little, this second water. Smells like some medicine. Then
air again. Then we pass through another place . . . I don't
know what is happening. Ahead of me a man screams and
cries, but we are in separate little cages now, can't move.
At one place, something comes to cover the eyes. There's
185 no time to think, just do. Put your arm here, get one
prick, put your arm there, get another prick—*pissshhh!*—
pissshhh!—Sit here, stand here, take your head this side,
look at a light that side. On and on. Finally at the end
there's another tunnel, with pretty pictures and some mu-
190 sic. And the sign comes: RESUME CLOTHING. I just do
what I have to do. All the time, the ground keeps moving. Then at the end, the ground stops, we are back on
our feet, there are steps. It must be the other side of the
building. And as we come down, guards are standing
195 there, waiting for us. And to me they say, "You, come—"
(*Pause.*) And that was it!

MA: What!

JAYA: What?

OM: That's all. Some other men were also with me, all look-
200 ing like me, I suppose. Blank. They told us we had been
selected. They wrote down our names, addresses . . . (*He
hesitates.*) and . . . this-that. All details. Then they gave us
these packets (*Indicates the package.*), told us not to open
them and said we must go home, the guards would come
205 with us for final instructions.

MA: But what is the work? The pay-packet? The hours?

OM: (*Looking distracted.*) I—I'll be in the house . . .

MA: What?! All the time?

JAYA: (*Staring intensely at him.*) . . . you don't really know what
210 it's going to be like, do you?

MA: What kind of job pays a man to sit at home?

OM: Oh—there was some pamphlet they gave us to read,
right in the beginning. Just to tell us to be relaxed and to
do whatever we were told. In that it said that once we
were selected, each man would get special instructions. 215
That we would be monitored carefully. Not just us but
our . . . lives. To remain employed, we have to keep ourselves exactly as they tell us.

JAYA: But—but *who* will tell us—how'll we afford it—

(*There is an excited tapping on the door which was left unbolted. A*
CHILD *bursts in.*)

CHILD: Auntie! Auntie! They're coming to your house! Police! 220

(*From the corridor, approaching footsteps.* JAYA *shoos the child from
the door as she stands by it. The footsteps come to a halt. A small
crowd has collected out on the corridor (out of sight, but audible) to
whom* JAYA *pays no attention.*)

JAYA: Yes?

MA: (*Remaining seated.*) Let him in, let him in—

GUARD 1: (*Out of sight.*) InterPlanta Services wishes to confirm that this is the residence of Om Prakash?

JAYA: It is—(*And she stands aside.*)   225

GUARD 1: (*Entering officiously.*) Thank you—(*Looks around.*)
Ah. Yes. Am I addressing Mr Om Prakash?

(*As he talks, enter* GUARD 2 *and* GUARD 3. *They are both carrying equipment which they set down and immediately begin to ready
for installation.* GUARD 3 *produces collapsible cartons which he begins to set up.* GUARD 2 *starts to install a device onto the window
frame.*)

MA: Who are these people? What are they doing?

GUARD 1: (*To* OM.) Ready? We can start.

OM: What do I have to do?   230

GUARD 1: Just listen. (*He consults his clipboard and begins to read
in a loud formal voice.*) Congratulations! InterPlanta Services is proud and honoured to welcome Mr Om Prakash
to its programme! (*To* OM.) Sir, you have received the
Starter Kit? (*Doesn't wait, sights the package* OM *brought with* 235
him, nods, ticks.) Yes. There it is. Sir: you are directed to
open the kit and make it operational after our departure.
Instructions are provided within. Any questions? (OM
shakes his head. GUARD 1 *nods and ticks.*) All right.

(*In the background,* GUARD 3 *has got two cartons set up. He wears
large plastic mitts over his existing skin-tight gloves and starts dumping all the items on the kitchen counter into the cartons. Meanwhile
two or three urchins have come into the room and are goggling at the
goings-on. Just beyond the door, a crowd of onlookers is standing out
of sight, doing likewise.*)

JAYA: (*To* GUARD 1.) Hi! What're you doing! (*Turns to* OM.) 240
See—see what's happening! (*Back to* GUARD 3, *who goes
ahead.*) Who said you can touch my things? (*Tugs at his arm
but he pays her no heed.*) Hi! Stop that!

GUARD 1: (*To* OM, *who is distracted.*) Sir: we will set up the
Contact Module. It will start functioning in approxi- 245
mately two hours.

OM: I—I'm sorry, but I must—

GUARD 1: Sir: pay no attention! About the Contact Module, all details will be found in the Starter Kit.

(*Meanwhile, downstage,* JAYA *struggles with* GUARD 3.)

250 JAYA: Who told you to do that! No! (*She attempts hitting* GUARD 3, *but he continues relentlessly dumping everything into the cartons.*) You can't do this! It's my house! No! Oh! Stop it, you monster, you beast! (*She tries to return items to the counter, but he is much faster than her.*) Stop it, stop it, stop it!
255 Don't you understand what I'm saying? Are you a machine? Answer me! Oh! (*She abruptly turns in on herself and succumbs to a fit of stormy weeping.*)

(GUARD 3 *continues with his job unperturbed in the course of the other events at stage front. After removing everything but the counter top and shelf, he cleans and swabs the entire area, then sprays it with attention to corners. After that he reaches into his kit and brings out a cooking device and bottles full of multi-coloured pellets.*)

(GUARD 2 *continues her installation without interruption.*)

GUARD 1: (*Regardless of the commotion behind him.*) At the time of first contact, you and your Receiver will exchange per-
260 sonal information. Your physical data has been sent for matching and we are confident that you will both be well satisfied. Any questions?
OM: Uhh uhh but what about . . . I mean, when will I actually have to—
265 GUARD 1: Sir: Any questions to the information received so far?
OM: (*Uncertainly.*) No . . . I mean—
GUARD 1: (*Nods and ticks.*) Right. When we have confirmed that the Contact Unit is functioning, you will not be re-
270 sponsible for anything but the maintainance of your personal resources. Any questions?
OM: But what about
GUARD 1: Sir! Any questions?
OM: (*Subdued.*) No.
275 GUARD 1: (*Nods and ticks.*) Right. All implements of personal fuel preparation will be supplied exclusively by Inter-Planta Services. Henceforward, you and your domestic unit will consume only those fuels which will be made available to you by InterPlanta. We will provide more
280 than enough for the unit described in your data sheet, but will forbid you from sharing, selling or by any means whatsoever, commercially exploiting this facility. Any questions?
OM: No.
285 GUARD 1: (*Nods and ticks.*) We are providing a remote-source electrical connection. It will be adequate for the systems currently being used by you and your domestic unit, as well as for the equipment which we ourselves will install. But on no account must it bear any additional loads, nor
290 must it be used by any agencies other than yourselves, loaned out, rented out, sold or put to any use other than the one just described. Any questions?
OM: No.
GUARD 1: (*Nods and ticks.*) Good. Now if I can just interview
295 the members of your domestic unit—
JAYA: (*From the rear.*) I have a question!

GUARD 1: (*Doesn't acknowledge her.*)—beginning with the oldest member—
JAYA: (*Desperately.*) Your—your man has thrown my stove into his bag and broken it! Who is going to replace that?   300
OM: (*Hissed aside.*) Not now, Jaya! Just be patient—

(GUARD 1 *is shuffling papers till he gets the relevant sheet.*)

JAYA: Be patient! While my house is broken up! (*But she turns herself aside and weeps, even as she shoos the bystanders away from the door. She is not able to do this easily or efficiently because she is crying too bitterly, so her actions have little impact.*   305
The urchins who are inside wriggle aside and continue to stand where they are.)
GUARD 1: (*Approaching* MA *and addressing her.*) Madam: Full name?
OM: (*Interceding.*) She doesn't understand your speech. Her   310
name's Indumati. Missiz Indumati Prakash.
GUARD 1: (*Continuing to address* MA *who looks genuinely bewildered.*) Missiz Indumati Prakash. (*Ticks.*) Relationship with Donor?
OM: Mother.   315
GUARD 1: (*Ticks.*) Have you understood all that has been said so far?
OM: Yes.
GUARD 1: (*His hand wavers. He looks up at* OM. *A flicker of normal communication.*) You will explain to her?   320
OM: (*Woodenly.*) Yes.
GUARD 1: (*Ticks.*) Right. Good. Now—(*He turns.*) next relative (*He sees her.*) Missiz—Missiz—(*He consults the sheet.*)

(JAYA, *who knows that it will now be her turn, shoves the children out roughly, anxiety lending determination to her movements. She slams the door shut against resistance from the other side and with some difficulty pushes the bolt home.*)

GUARD 1: —Kumar. Missiz Kumar come this way, please—
JAYA: (*Moves across to centre-stage.*) Yes—yes.   325
GUARD 1: (*Consulting his clip-board.*) Full name?
JAYA: Jaya. Mrs Jaya Kumar. (*She begins to weep anew.*)

(MA *stirs at this and looks over to where* JAYA *stands, a frown on her face.* OM *holds his head in his hands, his eyes on the floor.*)

GUARD 1: Relationship with Donor?
JAYA: (*Lifts her head. In a barely audible voice.*) Sister.

(MA *registers a shock. Her hand to her mouth, she seems to hold in her words manually. Then her hand goes to her heart.*)

GUARD 1: (*Neutral.*) Madam: please repeat response.   330
JAYA: Sister. He's my sister—I —I mean, I'm his—(*She is about to say, "brother" but succumbs to a fit of silent sobbing. Regains control.*) Sister. I'm . . . his . . . sister.

(MA's *face and limbs perform a dumb charade of her feelings, as she fights against the urge to react because she's not supposed to understand the exchange, yet she cannot make sense of what's going on.*)

GUARD 1: (*Ticks.*) Right. (*Looks around cursorily, merely to confirm what he already knows.*) Husband?   335
JAYA: (*Nods.*) At work.
GUARD 1: (*Ticks.*) Full name?

JAYA: Jeetu—Jeeten. Jeeten Kumar.

(MA's *body jerks like a puppet. She reins in her comments with ferocious effort.*)

GUARD 1: (*Ticks, nods.*) Right. (*He looks up and around.*) In-
340 terPlanta recommends that those members absent at this
briefing make themselves available at the nearest collection centre not later than twenty-four hours from the
time of our departure, failing which such member will
lose all rights to the facilities provided by us. Any ques-
345 tions? (*He does not wait for confirmation before ticking off, then
looks up.*) Good. (*Turns to the other two* GUARDS.) Briefing
complete, initiate departure procedure.

(*Behind him,* GUARD 2 *and* GUARD 3 *have both completed their
tasks and are standing stiffly "at ease" at their stations, awaiting orders. Whatever is visible of their faces is completely blank.*)

(*Hanging from the ceiling is a white, faceted globe, at least three feet
in diameter. It looks like a Japanese lantern, unlit.*)

(*In the course of the following action,* JAYA *wanders towards the window,* OM *remains seated on the bed,* MA's *physical movements sub-
side.*)

GUARD 1: (*Moving towards them, checking off his list as he inspects
and is responded to.*) Officer Contact Module Installation,
350 activity report: Installation complete?
GUARD 2: Yessir.
GUARD 1: Remote Power Reception cable in place?
GUARD 2: Yessir.
GUARD 1: Cable check complete?
355 GUARD 2: Yessir.
GUARD 1: Contact Module in operational mode?
GUARD 2: Yessir.
GUARD 1: Good. Initialize for contact.

(GUARD 2 *moves swiftly over to the* CONTACT MODULE *which is
roughly at centre stage and points a remote at it. As* GUARD 2
*works, there are musical notes and clicks. The polygon stirs alight.
Random facets light up. A screen-saver pattern appears. The entire
polygon moves in a slow, smooth circle, then is lowered to ground level
and up again.* GUARD 1 *steps back, satisfied.*)

GUARD 1: (*Paying no further attention to* GUARD 2's *activities, ad-
360 dresses* GUARD 3, *who is ready with two neat cartons prepared
for transport.*) Officer Fuel Supplies and Installation: activity report: sanitization of supply area complete?
GUARD 3: Yessir.
GUARD 1: Installation of fuel preparation equipment com-
365 plete?
GUARD 3: Yessir.
GUARD 1: Delivery of one month's fuel supplies for family of
four complete?
GUARD 3: Yessir.
370 GUARD 1: Good. Proceed with departure.

(GUARD 2 *and* GUARD 3 *station themselves by the door.*)

GUARD 1: (*Approaching* OM, *holding out his clipboard for signing
with a pen offered in the same motion.*) Mr Om Prakash, I am
pleased to inform you that the installation and initializa-

tion procedures have been completed satisfactorily. Thank
you for your cooperation. Please sign the following activ-   375
ity report after confirming that the observations contained herein are true and accurate to the best of your
knowledge. (*Hands him the clipboard.*)
OM: (*He stands up as* GUARD 1 *approaches him: Takes the clipboard, glances at it cursorily.*) Yes. I agree. (*Signs, hands the*   380
board back.)
JAYA: (*Over her shoulder.*) You don't need any confirmation
from us?
GUARD 1: All further queries will be satisfied by the Starter
Kit. (*He tucks the clipboard under his arm.*) Thank you for   385
your cooperation and valuable time! I and my colleagues
deeply appreciate the contribution you are about to make
towards creating a healthier, happier and longer-lived
world!

(*Clicks his heels together and turns smartly towards the others.*
GUARD 3 *immediately opens the latch on the door which is buffeted
open by the listeners on the other side, who immediately fall back and
away at the sight of* GUARD 3. GUARD 1 *exits and the other two
follow suit. The door is left open and the original one or two urchins
poke their noses inside, darting quick glances around.* JAYA *sees them
and moves across to shoo them away again. They dart out again with
no further urging from her. She shuts the door once more.*)

MA: (*To no-one in particular*) What sort of job makes a wife into   390
a sister?
OM: (*Subsides onto the bed again, head in his hands.*) Don't get
confused, Ma. What they write in their reports doesn't
change our lives.
MA: But what *is* she, really? A wife? Or a sister?   395
JAYA: (*Has come back and is standing at centre stage.*) How shall
I cook now? They've taken all our things! Every last grain!
MA: Who is Jeetu, now? Is he a son? Or a son-in-law?
OM: Nothing's changed! The words are different, that's all.
MA: But these aren't words! They're people!   400
JAYA: Are you listening to me, (*Mocking.*) brother? (OM *looks
up.*) What are we to do for food?
MA: (*Whispers.*) How can my daughter be married to my son?
What will people think?
JAYA: (*Louder.*) Tell me, brother!—   405
OM: (*Stirring.*) It's in this package. Whatever we need to
know.
JAYA: (*Hard.*) Even about food?
OM: (*Wearily.*) Even food.

(*Lights snap out.*)

SCENE II

The same room. OM *and* MA *are sitting upstage centre. A mat is spread
on the floor and they are eating the coloured pellets of their new food.*
JAYA *is leaning her head and shoulders against the side of the bed.*

*The package is open. Its contents are strewn about. There are
brightly coloured instruction leaflets, elaborately devised containers for
pills and powders and a number of small gadgets similar in size and
shape to a slide-viewing device but of obscure purpose.*

MA: Tell me again: all you have to do is sit at home and stay
healthy?

OM: Well—not *sit* necessarily—

MA: And they'll pay you?

5 OM: Yes.

MA: Even if you do nothing but pick your nose all day?

OM: They'll pay me.

MA: And what about off-days?

OM: (*Shrugs.*) Well. *Every* day is off, in one sense—

10 JAYA: (*Suddenly.*) Why don't you tell her the truth?

MA: Isn't this the truth?

OM: Jaya—

JAYA: (*Swinging herself around, to face them.*) Tell her. Tell your mother what you've really done—

15 MA: Shoo! Don't speak to your husband in that voice—

OM: The walls are thin. Everyone can hear. When you talk like this—

JAYA: Everyone knows already! D'you think you're the only one with this—this *job*? D'you think everyone doesn't

20 know what it means . . . when the grey guards come? (*Tears in her voice.*) All that remains to be known is which part of you's been given away!

MA: (*Mystified.*) What's this, what's this? Who's giving away parts of whom?

25 JAYA: Which goes first, the brain or the heart, that's what I want to know—

MA: (*To* OM.) I'm sorry to say, your wife has gone mad. Your sister, I mean—

OM: She's just trying to make trouble—

30 JAYA: (*Bitter laugh.*) Huh!

MA: Who cares about her? Wife or sister, Mother comes first! So tell me—these people, your employers, who exactly are they?

OM: It's—it's well, actually it's just one person.

35 MA: Just one person! With so much money to give away!

JAYA: It's a foreigner. That's why it's so much—

MA: What?

OM: (*Sighs.*) The money comes from abroad—

MA: Really! (*A sudden doubt.*) But . . . doesn't that mean you'll

40 have to go there? Abroad?

OM: Ma—no-one goes abroad these days . . .

JAYA: Not whole people, anyway!

OM: (*Warningly.*) I'm warning you now, Jaya—

MA: What's that? What's that? Knot-hole people? What d'you

45 mean—shorties?

JAYA: (*Patiently.*) Not his whole body. Just parts of it—

MA: (*To* OM.) What's your wife saying—not your body, but your what?

(JAYA *curls herself more tightly into herself.*)

OM: (*To* JAYA's *back.*) Why're you doing this? Why're you mak-

50 ing trouble?

JAYA: (*Over her shoulder.*) You said it wouldn't affect us—but see what it's done already!

OM: So *tell* me—what? In exchange for your old kitchen you have a new modern one—

55 JAYA: (*Swivelling round.*) You call this food? This—(*She indicates the pellets they have been eating.*) this—this goat-shit?

MA: It's better than what you make—

JAYA: And calling me your sister—what's that? (*Sobs.*) If I'm your sister, what does that make you? (*Hysterical edge.*) Sis-

ter, huh! My forehead burns, when I say that word, "sis- 60 ter"! (*She smears the red kumkum on her forehead in her torment and succumbs to her tears.*)

MA: Shoo! Are you a street woman? To speak in such a voice?

OM: You think I did it lightly. You think it's a heavy price. 65 But at the cost of calling you my sister . . . we'll be *rich*! Very rich! Insanely rich! What're you saying? (*He gets up to wash his hands and mouth at the kitchen sink, stopping to make his point along the way.*) But you'd rather live in this one small room, I suppose! Think it's such 70 a fine thing (*Washes his mouth, spits.*) living day in, day out, like monkeys in a hot-case—(*Washes mouth again and spits again, wipes face, mouth.*) lulled to sleep by our neighbours' rhythmic farting! Dancing to the tune of the melodious traffic! And starving. Yes—you'd prefer 75 this to being called my sister on a stupid slip of paper no-one we know will ever see!

MA: Why fight over what is finished? Tell me about this rich foreigner, your employer! Who is he? Why does he love you so much? That's what I don't understand—where did 80 he meet you?

JAYA: (*Half-sob/laugh.*) Ohh—just tell her, tell her!

OM: (*Coming back to centrestage.*) We've never met, Ma . . .

MA: What!

OM: He's rich—and old. That's all I know about him. Prob- 85 ably suffering from some illness—

MA: Then why's he paying you so much!

JAYA: Oh *Ma!*—don't you see it? Isn't it obvious?

MA: (*To* JAYA.) You're so smart that you can hear the Holy Father himself thinking but I, I need to hear with my ears— 90 (*Turns to* OM.) Tell me, my son—

OM: (*Irritated.*) Oh, you won't understand, Ma—

JAYA: I'll tell you! He's sold the rights to his organs! His skin. His eyes. His arse. (*Sobs again.*) Sold them! (*Holds her head.*) Oh God, oh God! What's the meaning of this nightmare! 95 (*Sobs. To* OM.) How can I hold your hand, touch your face, knowing that at any moment it might be snatched away from me and flung across the globe! (*Sobs.*) If you were dead I could shave my head and break my bangles— but this? To be a widow by slow degrees? To mourn you 100 piece by piece? (*Sobs.*) Should I shave half my head? Break my bangles one at a time? (*Succumbs to her tears.*)

MA: (*Only half-comprehending. Turns to* OM *who stands with his back to the women.*) How is it possible?

OM: (*Looking up at* JAYA.) If you weren't so busy feeling sorry 105 for yourself, you'd have read what they say about respecting the donor—

JAYA: (*Bitterly.*) Of course! They bathe him in praise while gutting him like a chicken!

MA: But why must they come to us? 110

OM: (*Holds up a pamphlet.*) Look? In this paper it says that one third of all donors are left absolutely intact!

MA: Don't they have enough of their own people?

JAYA: And where does that leave you? Two thirds a man? Half a wit? 115

OM: (*To* MA, *distractedly.*) They don't have people to spare.

JAYA: And we do, of course. Spare lives! We grow on trees, in the bushes! *What are we, teacher? Oh just some spare lives!*

120 MA: (*Uncertainly.*) Well. So long as they don't hurt you . . .

(*At this moment, a loud tone sounds. All three react, looking immediately at the globe.*)

MA: Hai! What's that sound! I must wash my hands! (*She gets up.*)

(*The polygon flickers to life. Each face displays one view of a young woman's face, unmistakeably blonde and white-skinned. She is beautiful in a clear-eyed, unequivocal manner, exuding a youthful innocence and radiant purity.*)

MA: (*She sees the globe head-on.*) Ahhh! Who is this angel?

(*The room fills abruptly with the pip! of an international phone call about to commence. There is a crackling sound and an audible pause.*)

GINNI: . . . hello? Hello?

125 OM: (*Stepping forward self-consciously.*) Yes—!

GINNI: I see you!—oh, my Gad! I see you! Is that really you? Auwm? Praycash?

OM: Yes! Yes—it's me, Om! (*He's grinning wide.* MA *looks bewildered.* JAYA *looks awe-struck.*)

130 GINNI: Well—hi! That's really great! This is Virginia—Ginni—speaking! Can you see me? How's your reception?

OM: Quite good—quite perfect, I should say! Fantastic!

GINNI: Wow! Yeah . . . well it's pretty wonderful for me too, you know! I mean, I can't tell you . . . (*Her voice grows*

135 *breathy with emotion.*) I can't *tell* you how much this means to me—

MA: (*To* JAYA.) What's it saying? I can't understand when they speak so fast—

OM: No, no, Madam! It's our pleasure! Our duty, I mean!

140 Anything we can do to help—

JAYA: (*To* MA.) She's saying that she's happy—

GINNI: It's the most beautiful day of my life! I feel I've got hope, at last! And all because of you—

OM: No, no, Madam, it is my—our—pleasure.

145 GINNI: Is it—I mean, can you see me clearly, Auwm?

OM: Perfectly clear.

GINNI: Okay—okay—now you've got to tell me—I'm just switching screens here—okay—there we are—okay! I can see . . . is that your . . . your mother? In the pink— (JAYA

150 *flinches; she is wearing a pink sari.*) whatdyacallit—sarong?

OM: We call it—*sari*—

GINNI: (*Sings an old tune.*) "Who's sari now? Who's sari now?!!" (*Laughs to herself.*) Hehheh—It's magical, it's wonderful! I'm talking to India—this is really happen-

155 ing! Okay! And your sister—let's see—

JAYA: (*Stirring to life.*) No! *I*'m his sister!

OM: (*Flustered and confused.*) She's my wife—

GINNI: Excuse me?

JAYA: (*Hissing to* OM.) Sister. I'm your sister.

160 GINNI: You said just now—

OM: (*Still smiling woodenly.*) I mean, she is my sister, you see—

GINNI: Auwm—it says here on your form, you're not married.

OM: I'm not. She's my sister.

165 GINNI: You're sure you're not kidding me or anything?

OM: Sure, sure, of course I'm sure!

GINNI: Because it's important for us to trust one another. I mean, one little slip like that one—and I dunno. I mean, it's hard for me to tell, from so far away—

OM: No, no! I'm telling the truth! I swear on my God! 170

ginni: Okay. I mean, 'coz I've gotta know, you know. If you're married—

JAYA: (*Suddenly.*) Why?

GINNI: What's that?

JAYA: Why does it matter? 175

GINNI: Uhh—I'll get back to you on that, okay? Just now . . . lemme see . . . there's two more people in your household, am I right, Auwm? There's (*As if checking a list.*) . . . your mother and your brother-in-law. S'right?

JAYA: That is right. 180

GINNI: Just a moment—uhh—Zhaya? (*The* CONTACT MODULE *swivels towards* JAYA, *who nods.*) Is that your name? Yeah—okay, now honey: I can't handle two people at a time, okay? I mean, it's just this dumb camera, you know, can't look at two people at a time, okay? So—I'm talking 185 to Auwm, well I can't talk to you as well, okay? I mean, no offence—

JAYA: Okay.

OM: My mother is also here—

GINNI: Yes. Okay. I'm turning the scanner around (*The* CON- 190 TACT MODULE *turns.*) . . . I'm panning across the room . . . Jeeezus! It's not very much, is it? I mean—oh! Okay! I see her. Hi! Mrs Praycash? Hi! This is Ginni! Can you hear me?

MA: (*Shielding her eyes against the light.*) What? 195

GINNI: I said, this is Virginia! I'm—uh, well just look up, if you can—

OM: Ma—just take your hand down—

GINNI: Look towards the Contact Module! You know the thing hanging in the room? 200

MA: (*To* JAYA.) What's happening?

JAYA: Ma—just look at that light—

OM: The light! The light!

MA: (*Getting annoyed, straightens up to snap back at* OM.) Stop shouting! 205

GINNI: Ahhright! I see you! Mrs Praycash, glad to meet you!

MA: I can't understand a word of what that thing is saying! Is it a man or a woman?

GINNI: What do I look like to you, Mrs Praycash?

MA: (*Cupping her ear.*) Ehh? 210

JAYA: Ma—she wants to know, what she looks like—

OM: Come on, Ma! You've seen foreigners before—

GINNI: Please—Auwm—your mother can answer my questions herself—

OM: She can't understand, you see— 215

JAYA: (*To* MA.) Ma—look up at that light and say what you see—

MA: (*Looks up.*) I see an angel.

GINNI: (*Laughing.*) Ha! I look good to you?

MA: Good, bad, I don't know. All I know is I've got to take a 220 leak—(*Turns around.*)

GINNI: (*Embarrassed laugh.*) Heh! Mm. But—wait! I'm not through yet!

OM: (*As* MA *continues moving away, slowly.*) Don't go yet, Ma— she's not finished— 225

MA: Since when did I need anyone's permission to take a leak?

GINNI: I'm sorry, Mrs Praycash, this won't take a minute—

MA: Nothing doing. I'll piss myself if I don't go right away— 230 (*She moves to the door.*)

GINNI: Hey! I didn't let you go!

OM: She has some problem, you see—

MA: Wait till you're my age! (*Grunts with the effort of opening the door.*) Why they can't keep a bathroom on each floor I 235 don't know—

(*Exit* MA.)

OM: (*Apologetically.*) The toilet is two floors down, you see—

GINNI: Hmmm. Your mother's some character, Auwm. (*She doesn't sound pleased.*) I don't know if I can handle it. I mean—walking out on me like that!

240 OM: She takes a long time to get there. Old people, you know!

GINNI: Wait a minute—did you say two floors down? What about in your house? There's no toilet in your house?

JAYA: (*Bitter laugh.*) Huh!

245 OM: No-one has a toilet in the house. Forty families share one. And my mother walks so slowly—

GINNI: Forty families! (*Hushed voice.*) My Gad. Well that's— that's—(*She seems at a loss for words.*) I'm sorry, Auwm. But that's shocking. Shocking! I can't accept that!

250 OM: (*Embarrassed laugh.*) Well—I—

GINNI: No! It's wrong! It's disgusting! And I—well, I'm going to change that. I can't accept that. I mean, it's unsanitary!

OM: (*Muttering.*) Of course, of course.

GINNI: We'll just have to install one in your house.

255 JAYA: (*Startled out of her silence.*) What? In this—this room?

GINNI: Is that you again, Zhaya?

OM: (*To* JAYA.) Shh!

JAYA: I'm sorry—but we *can't!* There's no place for a toilet!

GINNI: Excuse me, but you'll have to find the space. It's inex-260 cusable not to have your own toilet! Forty families—! It's a wonder you're all not dead of the plague years ago!

JAYA: There's only this one room!

GINNI: Look—there's enough place for a married couple and two others—you! You're married, right, Zhaya?

265 JAYA: (*Helplessly.*) Yes, but—

GINNI: (*Firmly.*) Then there's place for a toilet. I'm sorry, Zhaya, but there's no way around this one. What d'you do for baths?

JAYA: (*Close to tears.*) I—we—

270 GINNI: You—you *do* bathe, don't you? I mean, at least once a day?

JAYA: (*Overcome by the humiliation, bends her head and sobs.*)

GINNI: (*Instantly contrite.*) Hey—wait! No, please! Don't cry! I didn't mean to upset you—oh Jeez—stop, please! Look—275 it's not your fault, okay?

OM: It's all right, she'll be all right—(*Goes over to* JAYA *and thumps her on the back.*) She's fine!

GINNI: Okay—okay—look, Zhaya—I'll make it up to you, okay? I'll send you something, okay? Just tell me what you 280 like and it's yours, okay? Jewellery, perfume, you name it— flowers?

OM: (*Bending down to speak to* JAYA.) Come on, now, come on! It'll be all right—that's enough now—

GINNI: Okay—I tell you what, I'll send you some chocolate, okay? I love candy myself. Okay? I'll send you my 285 favourite candy and—tell you what? I'll sign off now. Okay? It's been a big day for all of us, we're all tired, aren't we? Auwm? Could you look here for a moment?

OM: (*Standing up.*) Me?

GINNI: Okay—look, I'll get back to you, okay? And I'm sorry 290 about Zhaya. Really.

OM: No, no—she's not used to this—this—

GINNI: Yeah. Well—the first contact is always a little . . . ah, intense, you know? And I meant that about . . . the toilet, okay? It'll be with you in about an hour. 295

OM: An hour—!

GINNI: Oops! Time's up—Byeeee!

(*The tone sounds again. The light fades from the* CONTACT MOD-ULE. OM *sits down, suddenly, next to* JAYA *who is wiping her eyes.*)

OM: (*Shakily.*) My god! That was something! (*Puts his arm around* JAYA.) Imagine—a woman!

JAYA: Not old, not sick, nothing— 300

OM: Oh, she must be sick—or else why spend all this money?

JAYA: (*Tiredly.*) It's too late to ask questions now!

OM: But what can be her problem?

JAYA: Maybe there's no problem. Maybe she just likes to suck the life out of young men, like a vampire! 305

OM: Sometimes you talk rubbish—

JAYA: At least I only talk.

OM: It feels strange. To think that . . . that some part of me will be—might be, some day—inside *her*—(*Stops abruptly.*) I mean— 310

JAYA: (*Numbly.*) I know what you mean.

OM: (*Holds her a little tighter.*) I did it, all of it, for us—

JAYA: (*Moving delicately, to loosen his hold.*) Careful. I'm your sister, remember?

OM: (*Jerks his arm away.*) Oh! Sorry. 315

JAYA: (*Bitterly.*) Me too.

(*Lights fade out.*)

SCENE III

Moonlit night, on the roof of the tenement building. City skyline in the backdrop. Clotheslines, watertanks, TV antennas and water pipes snaking in all directions. There is a sense of shadowy figures, move-ments in the background, murmured conversations.

JAYA *appears, holding a small torch to her face.*

JAYA: (*Looking afraid but determined.*) Jeetu? Are you there? Jeetu—it's me, Jaya!

(*Quick steps, two shadows move away, one shadow materializes in front of* JAYA.)

JEETU: (*He does not look pleased to see her.*) Who told you to come? This is not the right time—

JAYA: I had to. Jeetu—you don't know what's happened— 5

JEETU: Huh! I know everything—

JAYA: So—so you've heard?

JEETU: Which part? That my brother's sold himself to the for-eigners? Or that you're my wife? (*Shrugs.*) The second one

10 is hardly . . . news! (*Looks back at her.*) Is it? (*Reaches to tweak her plait.*) Is it?

JAYA: But you must come—they're asking for you!

JEETU: (*Frowning.*) They? Who—

JAYA: The grey guards. They came again in the evening. To
15 install the toilet—

JEETU: In the room?!

JAYA: And a bath-shower as well, imagine! We have our own water supply now, as much as we want—and there's no place to sneeze any more!

20 JEETU: (*Sardonically.*) Or . . . anything else, no doubt?

JAYA: (*Lowered tone.*) That . . . there never was.

JEETU: (*Leering.*) Didn't bother us, though, did it? (*He caresses her chin—but she whips her face away.*)

JAYA: And now there won't be any reason for Ma to go
25 downstairs! We'll never be alone in the room again, never!

JEETU: So what? If we can shit in public, we can just as well screw in public too—especially since you're now officially my wife!

JAYA: (*Pained*) Don't joke about it—

30 JEETU: Why not? I joke about everything else—

JAYA: My throat bulges with the lies trapped within it!

JEETU: Here—let me kiss it—

JAYA: (*Pushes him away.*) Get away! That's all finished now!

JEETU: (*He lets her go.*) As you wish.

35 JAYA: (*Gasps in indignation.*) So easy! Won't you protest a little at least?

JEETU: Make up your mind! D'you want me or not?

JAYA: You are all I have, now that my husband has become my brother . . .

40 JEETU: According to you he was never much else!

JAYA: (*Troubled.*) Still. He would come to me now and then—

JEETU: (*Shrugs.*) Maybe incest is more his style!

JAYA: No! He's too afraid! Before it was his mother. Now it's this . . . *job.*

45 JEETU: Ahh—forget him! You waste your time thinking of my brother!

JAYA: But what about me!

JEETU: Why? Now that you have a new . . . (*Mockingly.*) husband! (*Reaches for her shoulder.*)

50 JAYA: (*Slipping out of reach.*) Oh you—! You're a free-lancer—

JEETU: (*Laughing.*) No! My lance costs money! (*Squats down on a low ledge and starts to roll himself a joint.*) Had you forgotten?

JAYA: And anyway—I'm looking for a plough, not a lance—

JEETU: Oops—sorry! Wrong number! I can't afford any . . .
55 crops!

JAYA: As if I don't know that! I know that. And in any case . . . I feel guilty. I feel soiled—

JEETU: My, my! Such delicacy! Don't worry—I'll tell the world that I forced my attentions on you—routinely, in
60 phase with my mother's bowel movements!

JAYA: Oh stop—! (*Swats at him, playfully.*) You always make such a joke of everything!

JEETU: That's all that life is, one long joke. The only trick is in learning when to laugh.

65 JAYA: Easy for you to laugh! What do you care of my needs, my desires?

JEETU: I thought I was the *only* one who cared about your desires! (*Lights his joint.*)

JAYA: You care—you care—but not enough! A woman wants
70 more than just . . . (*Breaks off.*) satisfaction.

JEETU: Ah—get off my case! You women are gluttons for satisfaction—that's the bare fact of it! You cry when you don't get it—and when you do, you cry that it's not often enough!

JAYA: I cry because—because you awaken one hunger while 75 satisfying the other!

JEETU: (*Darkly.*) That other hunger is insatiable. A man has to protect himself against that hunger or he will find himself sucked dry by new little mouths, screaming "Papa! Papa!"—little mouths with big, big appetites—oh no! I'm 80 afraid of that other hunger! Mortally afraid!

JAYA: (*Acidly.*) I suppose that's why so many of your "clients" are men!

JEETU: (*Coolly.*) Not really. It's just that there are more men with money to spare on services such as mine— 85

JAYA: You should be ashamed of yourself! A man—behaving like a vagrant bull!

JEETU: Why? I'm not fussy—cows, pigs, horses, I'll service all—for a price.

JAYA: You don't need to sell yourself anymore. There'll be 90 enough money in the house now!

JEETU: But not for me—

JAYA: Yes—for all of us. For the whole building—

JEETU: No. I don't mind being bought—but I won't be *owned!*

(*There is a space of silence.*)

JAYA: (*Fidgeting.*) Well—I suppose I should go— 95

JEETU: Yes—yes—run home before the grey guards come to fetch you!

JAYA: Jeetu—

JEETU: (*Looking lazily up at her.*) . . . unless you had something else in mind. 100

JAYA: No . . . no . . . (*She can't face him.*) I mean . . . I—didn't bring any food.

JEETU: (*A faintly twisted smile.*) Ah . . . so we're asking for credit, are we?

JAYA: (*Her voice is husky.*) There's no food in the house any 105 more! Only those goat-shit pills and some strange powders. (*Tears in her voice.*) And—and—it's all measured out, you see! I couldn't take a portion without having to explain—

JEETU: (*Looking steadily at her.*) Never mind. As a long-time 110 client, you are permitted certain liberties. Come here— (*It's a short distance, barely afoot. He is seated on a step, leaning back against a tank. She doesn't move.*) I said, come here—

JAYA: (*As if drawn by an irresistible force.*) Jeetu—there are other people around! 115

JEETU: Turn the other way. (*She turns her back to him.*) Your left foot up on this step—(*He pats the narrow ledge on which he sits. She rests the heel of her left foot there. He puts his arm up her sari unobtrusively, barely shifting his position, looking steadily up at her. She looks straight ahead.*) Now tell me about this 120 food. I'm told that it's quite tasty?

JAYA: (*Her voice is thick and strangled.*) Yes! It looks like plastic beads but . . . it's *quite tasty!*

JEETU: And filling too, they say—

JAYA: (*Gasping slightly.*) Filling, yes. It . . . is. But it's not . . . 125 natural—it's not real food—(*She has no place to keep her hands and arms. She clutches her neck, her face, knotting the loose end of her sari around her mouth.*)

JEETU: (*Mildly.*) But it must be, don't you think? And healthy?
130   I mean, isn't that the point? To keep us . . . healthy?
JAYA: Yes . . . yes, of course. . . . but (*She's finding it difficult to concentrate on what she says.*) . . . but . . . who knows if it's . . . *good* for us! . . . (*Gasps.*)
JEETU: Everything's good that tastes good and feels right—
135   JAYA: (*She's desperate to lean on something but the closest is a ventilation pipe. She clings to it with both hands, eyes shut tight, breathing in gasps.*) No . . . no . . . that's *not* true. . . . it's *false* food—uhh!—like it's a *false* marriage—Uhh!—false—false (*Her voice wobbles and ends on a squeak. She gasps/sobs once,*
140   *twice*—.) False. (*Breathes out, shudderingly.*) False . . . *life.* (*She catches her breath, wiping her face with the end of her sari-pallav.*) It's not really a life any more. We're just spare parts in someone else's garage—
JEETU: (*Removing his arm and wiping his fingers on the hem of her*
145   *sari.*) My brother, yes. But not you—
JAYA: (*Her voice is normal again.*) No! All of us. If we get sick, he might get sick too. So we all have to eat this excuse for food and live like virgin brides—
JEETU: (*Snorts.*) Good! Now there's no reason at all for me to
150   come home!
JAYA: (*Distraught.*) No! You have to, Jeetu—
JEETU: Are you mad? When they find out what I do for a living they won't be pleased! They won't be pleased with you either—
155   JAYA: (*Pleading.*) They've asked for you twice now—they'll cancel your permit if they can't confirm your presence—
JEETU: Too bad! My brother will have to find some dummy to take my place—
JAYA: Please, Jeetu! Please . . . think of me—
160   JEETU: I can't afford to think of you. Thinking of you causes too many problems for me. I'll have to go away—
JAYA: What'll I do! You can't leave me—
JEETU: I can if I must. Don't worry—your grey guards will probably have a cure for the disease of dissatisfaction as
165   well—just ask them?
JAYA: But why! Why when there's enough money for all of us, to do whatever we want!
JEETU: Because no employer pays his staff to do as they please. At least when I sell my body, I decide which part
170   of me goes into where and whom! But it's the money in the end, isn't it? I don't want to get used to the kind of money that can make stud bulls into milk cows. (*Shakes his head.*) My poor brother. Thought he was so pure. But he's like everyone else after all! Only as pure as the price of his
175   rice.

(*Lights dim out.*)

ACT TWO

SCENE I

Two months later. The same room, but transformed into a sleek residence, gleaming surfaces, chrome steel and glass. The furniture is largely of the convertible kind (Bed-cum-sofa, etc), in keeping with the restricted space. In addition, there are the gadgets—TV set, computer terminal, mini-gym, an air-conditioner, the works. To the rear and right, there are two cubicles containing the bathroom and toilet. The changes are functional rather than cosmetic. In the middle of the space is a low, Japanese-style dining table.

JAYA *is sitting on the sofa and and doing her nails. She looks over-dressed, her face is heavily made-up, jewellery winking from her ears, wrists, ankles and throat.* MA *is wearing a quilted dressing gown and is watching TV, upstage, right.* OM *is wearing a fluorescent Harlequin track-suit and sits at the computer terminal. All sport new footwear.* JAYA *in heels,* MA *in fluffy bedroom slippers,* OM *in inflatable track shoes with blinking rear lights.*

Suddenly OM *leaps up.*

OM: Look at the time!—Ma!
MA: (*Not turning around, but addressing her remark to* JAYA.) Don't call me—it's your wife's turn to do the food.
JAYA: (*Waving her hands in the air.*) Why didn't you tell me earlier? Now my nails are wet—   5
MA: And now—I'm watching my programme!
OM: (*Rushing over to dining area. He starts to set it up.*) Come on, come on! Ginni will be with us—
MA: Better get Bidyut-bai out first—
OM: (*Stops what he's doing.*) Out? Out of where?   10
MA: (*Barely looking up.*) Out of the toilet. Didn't you see her going in? She's been there all morning!
OM: Why! Who let her use it!
MA: She can't stay away from it, she says! Gets cramps, poor thing, from waiting for the one downstairs—   15
OM: Who cares about her cramps—I want to know how she got into the habit of using our toilet at all!
MA: (*Shrugs, but aiming her rebuke in* JAYA's *direction.*) Who knows what happens when my back is turned?
JAYA: (*Aggrieved, blowing on her nails.*) Huh! Look who's talk-   20
ing! The Empress of the Bath-house herself? (*To* OM.) If your mother had her way, half this building would be bathing up here—(*Blowing on her nails.*) But how would you know? You never bother to talk to us any more!
MA: (*Placatory whine.*) We have so much! Can't we share a lit-   25
tle at least? As it is, my former friends tell me I've put on airs—
OM: (*Standing with his hands on his hips.*) Ma, I've told you. When we have our own place, that'll be another thing— but now, when we're still struggling—   30

(*At this moment there is the sound of the flush.* BIDYUT-BAI *comes out of the cubicle, trying to look inconspicuous.*)

BIDYUT-BAI: Oh . . . I hope I'm not intruding—
OM: I'm sorry, Bidyut-maasi—but who invited you to use our toilet?
BIDYUT-BAI: (*Instantly on the defensive.*) No, no! Please! I was just passing this way—   35
OM: But you used our toilet, didn't you?
BIDYUT-BAI: Toilet? What toilet? Is there a toilet in this room? My! That must be a wonder! May I see it?
OM: (*Sighing.*) Oh just go on, go on!
MA: (*Speaking up for her friend.*) How can she go on when the   40
door's been barricaded?
OM: (*Woodenly.*) She's your friend, you can let her out yourself.
MA: (*Peevishly.*) But I'm watching my programme—
JAYA: Your eyes'll be stuck to that screen from staring at it   45
twenty-four hours of the day!
MA: And why can't our busybody open it? Worn out from the tension of painting her nails, I suppose?

BIDYUT-BAI: Is anyone going to let me out?

50 JAYA: Oh! For god's sake! (*Gets up and flings herself across the room.*) I might as well apply for a job as a doorkeeper!

MA: And you'd make a bad one—

(*The warning tone sounds.*)

OM: Oh my God—Ginni's call-sound!

JAYA: (*Struggling to open the door with her nails still wet.*) Tell her

55 it's because your mother can't control her generosity—

MA: See how your sister insults me! Her own mother!

OM: (*Frantic.*) Hurry up! Hurry up!

JAYA: (*Throws the door open—*BIDYUT-BAI*wriggles past her and out.*) All right, all right—(*Slams the door shut and moves

60 quickly over to the "kitchen" to snatch up a few items from the "oven". *OM *is almost done setting the table up.*) Anyway it only takes a few minutes—

OM: (*Sitting down, as* JAYA *brings a few things from the "kitchen" area.*) You know how she hates it when we're late to eat!

65 JAYA: (*Setting things down.*) Tell your mother to come along—

MA: (*Whiningly.*) It's just about to end—

JAYA: (*Sitting down herself.*) One of these days, when this dream comes to an end, it'll be because you were too busy watching your damned TV—

70 OM: It isn't going to end—

(*The warning tone sounds a third time and the* CONTACT MOD-ULE *springs to life.*)

OM: Ahh—

(MA *scrambles to her feet and scurries over, leaving the TV on.*)

GINNI: Hello-oo! Guess who-oo!

OM: (*He has a falsely beaming expression on his face and affects a nasal twang.*) Hello, Ginni! Hi! Howdy!

(MA *settles hurriedly into place.*)

75 GINNI: Hey—whatcha doing—eating again?

OM: No! We're just having lunch—why don't you join us?

GINNI: Lunch! Hey, that's too late—for lunch!

JAYA: No, no, Ginni! (*To* OM.) Tell her it is only ten minutes—

GINNI: I'm sorry Auwm—but I insist: you *must eat at regular*

80 *hours*—okay? We've had this problem before!

OM: Yes—yes—you see we just had some visitor—heh-heh—these people, you know! Don't understand what it means to keep to a strict schedule—

GINNI: Ah-ah! No excuses, now! That's another bad habit you

85 have, Auwm. You don't confront your booboos. Now—you've gotta learn to control it, okay? You can't help it, I know, it's a part of your culture—it's what your people do when they want to Avoid Conflict and it's even got a name: it's called "face saving". But we can't go through the

90 whole of our lives Avoiding Conflict, now can we, Auwm? You do see that?

OM: (*His smile is strained.*) Yes—yes—of course, Ginni! It is perfectly clear—

GINNI: Good! That's what I like about you, Auwm! You learn

95 real fast.

OM: (*Modestly.*) Thank you, Ginni!

GINNI: And now—let's look at how your family's doing—Mrs Praycash? I can see the food's suiting you, huh? You're putting on weight!

MA: (*Holding her hand to her ear, but beaming nevertheless.*) What's   100
that? What's that?

GINNI: And Zhaya—how're you doin'? I don't see a smile on your face!

JAYA: (*Instantly pasting a smile on.*) Oh—no, no! I'm fine!

GINNI: It's a scientific fact that people who smile longer live   105
longer—

JAYA: I'm smiling!

GINNI: But not enough, Zhaya. You see, it's important to smile all through the day. After all, if you're not smiling, it means you're not happy. And if you're not happy, you   110
might affect your brother's mood—and then where would we be?

JAYA: (*Grinning wide.*) I understand, Ginni.

GINNI: If I've said it once, I've said it a hundred times: The Most Important Thing is to keep *Auwm* smiling. Coz if   115
Auwm's smiling, it means his body's smiling and if his body's smiling, it means his organs are smiling. And that's the kind of organs that'll survive a transplant best, smiling organs—I mean, God forbid that it should ever come to that, right? But after all, we can't let ourselves forget what   120
this programme is about! I mean, if I'm going to need a transplant—then by God, let's make it the best damn transplant that we can manage! Are you with me?

JAYA: Yes, Ginni, of course, Ginni.

(*From the door, there is now a knocking sound.* JAYA *looks around.*)

GINNI: (*Reacting at once, and the* CONTACT MODULE *swivels.*)   125
What's that? What're you looking at?

OM: (*Nervously.*) Oh nothing—just—it's nothing!

GINNI: Now—Zhaya—I saw you look—

JAYA: Really, Ginni—it's probably just the wind—

(*The knocking sound again.*)

MA: (*Loud whisper.*) There's someone at the door—   130

GINNI: What's that you said, Mrs Praycash? Someone at the door?

JAYA: (*Unable to control an exasperated sound.*) Oh—for God's sake! She treats us like children—

GINNI: What? Zhaya—Look! All of you—I've told you once,   135
I've told you a zillion times! I hate it when y'all speak at once!

JAYA: (*Now faking a sneeze.*) Chhoo!—sorry, Ginni, sorry—

GINNI: (*Sounding very excited.*) That was a sneeze! Don't deny it—you have a cold, Zhaya, don't you? Come on, con-   140
fess—

JAYA: No, Ginni, no—it wasn't—it wasn't—

GINNI: Don't lie to me, Zhaya—I know a sneeze when I hear one—

JAYA: It was the—the *pepper*—   145

GINNI: I'll have to ask Auwm—tell me the truth, Auwm—does your sister have a cold? Does she?

OM: Cold? Oh—no, no, no! No cold, Ginni—it was only the—

JAYA: —pepper. It's this foreign pepper. I'm not really used to it.   150

GINNI: Then—why haven't you reacted before this?

(The knocking sounds again, more like a thump.)

MA: *(Looking around.)* That Bidyut-bai is really shameless—

GINNI: What? What was that?

JAYA: Nothing. She was just—

155 GINNI: You're keeping something from me! I just know it—you're all keeping something from me!

JAYA: Oh god, Ginni—we are *not*! Really!

GINNI: Yes you *are*, Zhaya! I can see it in your lying scheming little face! You think you're such an cutie-pie, Zhaya—

160 but you don't fool me! Not for one instant! Now *tell me*—

OM: *(Raising his voice and leaning into the viewing field of the* CONTACT MODULE.*)* No—Ginni—please! You trust me—see, look at me—are you looking? Would I tell you a lie?

GINNI: We-e-e-ell. I don't know! What was all that about?

165 Why did Zhaya sneeze? You know how terrified I am of colds, Auwm! Ever since we eradicated colds from here, where I live, it's like—like having the plague!

OM: Ginni—it's not a cold. I promise you that.

GINNI: If you get a cold, Auwm, I can't take your transplant!

170 You'll be quarantined! This whole program will go to waste!

OM: Ginni—Ginni—believe me. I will never risk your health.

GINNI: *(Calming down slightly.)* Though—I guess—they

175 screen everything that comes in. Even if you did have a cold, they'd never let your organs through—

OM: I live only for your benefit. You know that—

GINNI: All right, I believe you. I'll make myself believe you. I

180 mean it's been hard to read your faces, you know? You people don't use facial expressions, not like us, anyhow. But what *was* that your mother said just now? It sounded like . . . like . . .

JAYA: She was praying, taking the name of god—

GINNI: Oh. Yeah. Well, I don't know—sometimes I just get

185 the feeling—

OM: Please, Ginni—trust me. I would not do anything to harm our—our relationship. We have known each other only for two months, but from the first day itself, I have felt that you are just like my sister! Yes! I would not keep

190 anything from you—

GINNI: *(A touch sardonic.)* Is that right? You wouldn't keep anything from your sister—is that right, Zhaya? *(To* JAYA.*)* You're his sister, so you should know—does he keep anything from you?

195 OM: I mean—

JAYA: No, he doesn't. He would never tell a lie. He is pure like fresh cotton.

GINNI: *(Childlike glee.)* Pure like fresh cotton! Haha! That's quaint! That's really quaint! You know what? Even if I

200 didn't need transplants and if I wasn't so sick and all—I'd get the kick of my life from these conversations! It's like—it's like—I dunno. Human goldfish bowls, you know? I mean, I just look in on you folks every now and then and it just like—blows my mind. Better than TV. Better than

205 CyberNet. Coz this is Real Life—and don't think I don't appreciate it! You get to be my age and you really appreciate human companionship—

JAYA: You look very young—

GINNI: —what I meant, people in my country, at my age, they

210 just don't have any worthwhile friends, you know? Noth-

ing to hold on to—nothing precious. Nothing like . . . this. I get to give you things you'd never get in your lifetime and you get to give me, well . . . Maybe my life. *(Voice goes husky.)* You know? That's a special bond. Don't think I don't appreciate it. 215

OM: We know you do, Ginni—

GINNI: And now I'm feeling tired, real tired. You just don't know how tired I get sometimes—

JAYA: *(Carefully.)* Is it—is it your illness?

GINNI: I guess you could say so, Zhaya, in a manner of speak- 220 ing, yes. It's my illness. But now I've gotta go. Okay? *(The tone sounds.)* Byeeee—

OM: Good-bye, Ginni—

(Knocking sounds again.)

OM: *(Ignoring the knocking.)* See you soo-oon—

(The CONTACT MODULE *goes dead. Instantly,* JAYA *leaps up to go to the door.)*

JAYA: We've got to do something about the door! We can't 225 have people knocking whenever they like!

MA: Oh? Now you're going to have special times for knocking as well?

*(*JAYA *gets to the door and opens it easily because she didn't have time to lock it completely before lunch.)*

JAYA: *(Opening the door.)* Now look—*(Stops dead and exclaims.)* Huhhhhhh! 230

*(*MA *and* OM *look up in alarm, just in time to see* JAYA *step back quickly, as* JEETU *makes a dramatic entrance—almost falling in at the door. His condition is terrible, his clothes in tatters, his hair wild, covered in solid muck and grime. Only his spirit seems undiminished.)*

JAYA: Oh my God—*(She bolts the door, her face grim and frowning.)*

MA: What—? *(She is momentarily speechless.)* Who is it—what is it—

JEETU: *(Staggering forward, till he can support himself on a chair* 235 *back.)* Only . . . your beloved son, Jeetu. Yes, I can see how delighted you are to see me—*(Mock concern.)* Oh—wait! Sorry! I'm your son-in-law, now, right?

OM: *(Has risen slowly to his feet.)* My god. What have you done to yourself? 240

JEETU: Don't bother breaking coconuts at my feet! *(His tone is sarcastic but good-humoured despite all.)* Yes, yes—your arms are wide open with welcome! Thank you for inviting me to share the comforts of your modest home with me, your younger brother! *(Comes forward across to stage right. Sits on* 245 *the silky white sofa, which receives his grimy presence with an audible flinch.)* And yes, I'd love to sit in this comfortable sofa—*(Succumbing to the sensuous embrace of the cushions, becoming slightly delirious.)* Ahh! Ahhh!

JAYA: *(Concerned.)* What's the matter—are you in pain? 250

JEETU: Is it possible to know such ease? It feels so good that it hurts! Ahh! Ahh . . . ah. You know—it's a strange thing with the pavements: no matter how long you sleep on them, they never grow soft!

255 JAYA: (*Haltingly.*) You've been on the pavements!

JEETU: (*Gesturing to* JAYA.) Come, come sit by me, my darling wife! Or have you reverted to being my sister-in-law again? Come—

(JAYA *flees downstage.*)

JEETU: Well! No words to express your delight? Strange . . . at
260   one time, she used to fight for my attention—

OM: (*Trying to regain control of the situation.*) Jeetu—you owe us an explanation—

JEETU: I owe no-one anything—

OM: Where have you been these many weeks?

265 JEETU: Careful—you might go deaf to hear the things I'd tell you—

OM: But . . . are you here to stay?

JAYA: What else? You can't turn him out!

MA: (*Hard.*) Maybe we don't have a choice!

270 JEETU: Ah my loving mother speaks at last! And what does she say? What music does she pour into my parched ears?

OM: (*Sternly.*) Stop it! Things have changed around here—

JEETU: Really? I'd never have noticed—

OM: And the fact is—your permit to live with us was
275   surrendered!

(*There is a silence as* JEETU *processes this idea.*)

OM: Yes. I'm sorry—you had your chance. You chose to leave. We had to make our excuses to the guards. To explain why the fourth member of the family wasn't here. Now it's too late to take you back in—and in any case,
280   you're undoubtedly a health hazard—

JEETU: (*Getting up slowly.*) A "health hazard" did you say? (*He stands unsteadily.*) Heh! That's rich! (*Laughs.*) Me—a health "hazard"! My brother—I'm not a health hazard, I'm a walking, talking, health CATASTROPHE! (*Goes towards*
285   OM, *grinning.*) Oh, yes! I'm so unhealthy that even even my germs have germs . . . yes. My lice are dying on my skull—see? (*He offers his head for examination, to* OM, *who shrinks away.*) They're just lying in little black heaps—

JAYA: Stop! Stop it—why make things worse for yourself—

290 JEETU: Ah those honeyed words of love! How they soothe my running sores!

JAYA: What do you expect? You're the one who left. And now you come back looking like Death's first cousin—is that our fault?

295 OM: We'll have no choice—

JEETU: (*Turning towards* MA.) And you, my mother? I hear your love for me has been bought for the price of a flush toilet?

MA: When you reach my age you'll know that a peaceful shit
300   is more precious than money in the bank!

JEETU: Thank goodness I won't live long enough to be rich—

JAYA: What d'you mean—

JEETU: I'm ill. I'm going to die soon—

OM: Oh God—(*He starts to pace.*)

305 JAYA: Don't be foolish—

OM: This is serious, very serious—

MA: Of what?

JEETU: An overdose—

JAYA: Some drug?

JEETU: Called freedom. (*He sinks to the floor.*) I've been over- 310
dosing on freedom. Spent my hoard of years—splurged them all, for a few weeks of freedom on the streets. (*Lies flat.*) Freedom to lie in the filth of the open road and to drink from the open sewer! Yes. Freedom to eat the choicest servings from the garbage dump—shared only with 315
crows, flies and pigs! Ah, such freedom as you newly-rich people never know! (*He is slightly delirious. He attempts a laugh, but his voice is cracked.*) But expensive. For all that it looks so cheap, each mouthful of garbage costs a handful of years off your life. And I gorged myself! So I'm . . . 320
gone. Flat broke. Burnt out . . .

(*He turns weakly on his side and starts to throw up.*)

OM: Quick—stop him—

JAYA: (*Kneeling quickly.*) A towel—cloth, anything—

(*She uses the loose end of her sari to cover her hand as she holds his head, then wipes his face with it with the other corner—*OM *hands her disposable towels and fetches a mug of water.*)

OM: (*His face showing revulsion.*) What a mess! You'll have to
incinerate your sari—   325

MA: And what about the carpet?

(JAYA *places* JEETU's *head on her lap.*)

OM: We can disinfect the whole room—and better wear the nose guard—

MA: But the lice—the lice can get into everything—then
we're finished—   330

OM: Oh! (*In exasperation.*) It would have been better if—

JAYA: (*Quietly, stroking* JEETU's *dishevelled hair.*) Don't say it.

MA: What?

OM: (*Ignoring* MA.) How can we keep him! What will we tell
the guards—   335

JAYA: (*With finality.*) We're not going to turn him out.

MA: There's no place for him now!

JAYA: We've managed before—

OM: (*Fretting.*) Ginni won't like it—she'll forbid it—

JAYA: (*Weakly.*) Who?   340

MA: She'll chuck him out!

OM: She'll be so angry, so angry—

JAYA: (*To* JEETU.) Shhhh, don't talk—

OM: Just think of the risk! We've gone so far—given up so
much and to lose it! Just because of—of—   345

JAYA: (*Looking steadily up at him.*) Your brother. Whatever's written on paper, that's what he really is—

OM: But—(*Frets, pacing.*)

MA: What'll we do for food? There won't be enough for
him—   350

JEETU: Uhhhh . . . if I could just have a little water—

(JAYA *wets one of the disposable towels, soaks it in water and drib-bles water into his mouth.*)

JAYA: Don't sit up yet.

OM: It's starting to stink! Ginni'll be furious, *furious*—

JAYA: Look, we'll wrap him up in a sheet and keep him to one side till he's better. Then when he can sit up and talk, 355
we'll just tell Ginni that's he's come back. My husband's come back from his—his business trip—

JEETU: (*Weakly, his head lolling.*) Who's this . . . Ginni . . . (*Rolls back down.*)

360 JAYA: Shhh . . . shhh—don't talk—(*She whispers to him, as if to a child.*)

MA: See how she treats him—her brother-in-law!

OM: (*Fretfully.*) How long can we keep him wrapped up! And what if Ginni finds out—

365 JAYA: (*Looking up.*) There's no point getting frantic—

OM: And who'll believe that this . . . this . . . *wreck* was away on business!

MA: (*Maliciously.*) Look how she holds him—her darling!

JAYA: We'll have to fix him up, of course. Shave his hair, give

370 him some clothes—

OM: (*Clutching his head.*) But the diseases—the diseases—

JAYA: (*Calmly.*) Clean water and strong food will cure him of whatever he has—

(*Lights dim.*)

SCENE II

The same scene, a couple of hours later. JEETU's *wasted and scab-scarred body lies in the centre. He has been shaved and visibly grows cleaner, as* JAYA *tenderly washes him and attends to the wounds puckering his skin. He is conscious and groans only occasionally.* MA *is sitting to one side, her expression blank.* OM *is at stage front right, standing, occasionally pacing. He and* JAYA *have both changed their clothes.* OM *is trying to master the emotions tearing at his face.*

OM: Any minute now—any minute!—she's going to call!

JAYA: Just try and relax—

MA: I don't understand how we plan to hide him—

JAYA: Look—look at these sores!

5 OM: (*To* JAYA.) How can you touch him with your bare hands? He must be oozing with disease—

MA: —and he! Her brother-in-law!

JAYA: (*Exasperated.*) How can I leave him to rot!

OM: Wear rubber gloves, for pity's sake!

10 JAYA: We abandoned him to the streets. The least we can do is to risk our own skin when we touch him—

OM: It's like Ginni says—the curse of the Donor World is sentimentality—

MA: (*To* JAYA.) Ginni will throw him out—just you see!

15 OM: Here I am, willing to give my whole body to improve our lives—and what're you doing? Endangering the whole project by feeling up your brother-in-law—

JAYA: (*At this she stops.*) Who switched roles with his brother? Who turned this family inside out?

20 OM: All I'm saying is—leave him till we can disinfect him at least! Show him to the guards—they'll know what to do—

JAYA: (*Resumes her task.*) What faith you have in them! They don't care about any of us, not as people, not as human beings—

25 OM: What're you saying? You don't talk enough to Ginni. If you did, you wouldn't feel this way—

MA: Oh she's jealous of our Ginni-angel! Look at her face? Pinched with envy!

OM: Ginni really cares for us—

30 JAYA: Oh yes, she *cares*—just as much as she cares about the chicken she eats for dinner—that's all you are for her, another kind of dinner—

OM: (*Contemptuously.*) How little you understand of Western-ers! They are not small, petty people—like us!

MA: Oh she's just jealous, jealous! Can't bear to think of you 35 being inside that foreign angel. After all, who wouldn't want to be inside such a divine being? Why—it would be indecent to object—

OM: (*Moderately.*) Now, now, Ma—

MA: Who knows? Maybe she'll even want you for a husband 40 some day—why not? If my son's kidneys are good enough for her why not his—

OM: Ma—!

MA: Why not his children, I was going to say! Now that's what I want to know! What a miracle—grandchildren! 45 And with an angel for a daughter-in-law!

JAYA: Huh! An angel who shares her bed with her dinner—now that *would* be a miracle!

OM: Would she spend so much money on me, then? If I am just—a—a chicken to her? Answer me that! Do you know 50 how much she's spent on us? Our comfort?

JAYA: Never mind chicken—have you seen how their beef cattle live? Air-conditioned! Individual potties! Music from loudspeakers—why, they even have their own psychiatrists! All to ensure that their meat, when it finally gets 55 to Ginni's table, will be the freshest, purest, sanest, *happi-est*—

OM: (*Steps towards* JAYA.) I'll slap you if you're not careful!

JAYA: (*Unimpressed.*) Mind that you wear your rubber gloves— 60

(*There's knocking at the door.*)

MA: Hear that?

OM: Who is it—who!

MA: The right-hand neighbours. Wanting to borrow a bucket of water.

OM: Well, they're not getting it— 65

MA: Yesterday they offered me money—

OM: Tell them to ask the muncipality to increase their supply.

MA: I told them—

OM: Then why don't they shut up?

MA: They told me I'd forgotten what it was like before we got 70 this external connection—they started to scream and cry—

OM: Ahh . . . ! These people! No wonder foreigners think so little of us! We have no pride, no shame!

(*Knocking increases in volume.*)

JAYA: (*To* MA.) How can you be sure that it's the neighbours? 75

OM: Who else can it be?

MA: Listen carefully. There's a code, you see—

JAYA: Supposing it's the guards?

OM: Why should they come?

(*Sustained knocking.*)

JAYA: What kind of code— 80

MA: Three knocks means it's the next-door-right-side. Two knocks means it's the next-door-left-side—

OM: There's no reason for the guards to come!

JAYA: What does loud thumping with no pattern mean?

(Thumping on the door.)

85 OM: (*Looking suddenly grey.*) You're right—it could be the guards!

MA: No, no! It's the neighbours I tell you!

(Violent thumping.)

JAYA: (*A touch of malice.*)—it's been two months, you know! Time to collect their fattened broiler!

90 MA: Shouldn't you just open the door and find out?

OM: I—I—(*Looking panicked.*) What about—what about Jeetu! What'll we do about hiding him!

JAYA: If they've come for you, they won't have eyes for any-one else—

(Knocking, knocking, knocking.)

95 OM: (*Sweating.*) But—Ginni looked fine at lunch-time—she looked perfectly normal—

JAYA: Her condition is such that she can deteriorate sud-denly—

OM: But she would tell us herself! Not just send the guards—

(Rhythmic thumping.)

100 JAYA: Maybe she doesn't have the strength?

OM: My god. My god—you're right! It's not happened so far, this knocking!

JAYA: Why not just open the door and find out?

OM: I always hoped, you see, that it would never actually

105 come to this—

JAYA: A vain hope. Answer the door—

OM: (*Querulous.*) A dutiful wife would open it for me!

JAYA: You forget—I'm your sister—

MA: That knocking's getting on my nerves now!

(Knocking, knocking, knocking.)

110 OM: My legs! My legs refuse to move!

JAYA: Such a hero, my man.

(Hammering, thumping, knocking.)

OM: At least she could have let us enjoy the illusion for a lit-tle longer—

JAYA: It's in God's will, when your time is up—

115 MA: What'll they think—this delay?

OM: Another month—another week, another day, even—

JAYA: But in the end it would always come to this—the bill collector at the door—

OM: Do it for me—please! I order you—you're still my wife!

(Knock, thump, knock, thump. A pleasing rhythm.)

120 MA: I'll be driven mad!

OM: Would you prefer to see your son dead?

JAYA: Maybe they just want one of your finger-nails—your hair—something unimportant—

OM: The smallest pimple on my chin is more precious to me

125 at this moment than a diamond mine in someone else's fist! Oh—how could I have done this to myself? What sort of fool am I?

(Knocknocknock.)

MA: If you don't open the door, I will—

OM: And if you move even one muscle, I'll kill you with my bare hands— 130

JAYA: Your mother!

OM: Whoever opens that door is my murderer, my assassin—

JAYA: I'm sorry, I cannot live with this—(*She's completed* JEETU's *cleaning and starts to get up.*)

(Thumpthumpthump. JEETU *gingerly rolls over onto one elbow. Looks up and around him. Then collapses gently onto his belly and lies still, as if ready to sleep.)*

OM: No!! I beg of you—please! Please! Leave that cursed 135 door alone! Seal it with cement and fire! I cannot bear to see its gape, admitting those vile, those cruel, those vicious guards! (*Groans.*) Ahhhh . . .

JAYA: Till just a moment ago they were your dearest friends— (*Gets up.*) 140

OM: NO! Sit still! Don't stir! Or I'll—I'll—

(He rushes to the door, holds himself against it.)

JAYA: How can I respect you? Move aside!

OM: (*Wildly.*) I don't care! So long as you keep the guards from the door—

JAYA: I'll offer myself in exchange— 145

OM: They won't take you—they're very selective—

(Knockthumpknockthump.)

JAYA: (*Exasperated.*) They'll break the door down in a mo-ment!

OM: (*Sinks to the floor. Voice barely audible.*) Yes. I never thought of that. They could do that—and then what'll happen? 150 Where'll I hide? (*Starts to crawl away from the door.*) In the fridge. That's where. I'll just crawl along here, all the way to the fridge and I'll sit there, yes—

JAYA: (*As soon as* OM *moves away from the door,* JAYA *starts to un-lock the bolts.*) Ohhh—this bravery makes my heart sick— 155

MA: (*To* OM, *as he crawls past her.*) Why are you on the floor?

OM: I'm hiding.

*(*JAYA *gets the bolts on the door open. Opens the door.*)*

JAYA: (*Off-stage.*) Yes? What d'you want?

(There is an indistinct mumble.)

JAYA: (*Re-enters looking bewildered.*) Ma—it's for you—

MA: (*Getting to her feet.*) What? Already? 160

JAYA: There must be some mistake—

MA: (*Coming forward briskly.*) It's very prompt, I must say!

JAYA: (*Mystified.*) You ordered something?

MA: (*She is already at the door.*) Yes. (*Moves out of sight, off-stage.*) Yes?—Yes! That's right! But where is it? You haven't 165 brought it? It hasn't come? You'll bring it tomorrow? When? Ah . . . Okay. No—no, I'll be at home—and—sign here? No . . . payment? Oh. Okay. Right. I'll be waiting— (*She re-enters and shuts the door behind her.*)

JAYA: (*She heard this exchange with no comprehension.*) Ma? What 170 was all that?

MA: (*Airily.*) Oh . . . Just something I've ordered—

JAYA: (*Astounded.*) Ordered!

MA: Something I saw on TV—

175 JAYA: But . . . how did you place the order?

MA: That thing, the remote—you press some buttons and you can buy things, do things—and they bring it right to the door! But Madam wouldn't know, would she! Too high and mighty to watch TV!

180 OM: (*He has reached as far upstage as he can comfortably go. He stops there, his hands over his head.*) I'm hiding.

JAYA: (*She locks the door.*) But what have you ordered? How much will it cost?

MA: (*Philosophically.*) You'll see, when it comes!

(*Lights dim.*)

SCENE III

OM *is lying in a foetal position on the floor, stage front right.* JEETU *is sitting at the table eating slowly, carefully. He has had a bath and is wearing* OM's *track suit.* JAYA *and* MA *are sitting beside* OM.

JAYA: He doesn't seem to hear anything I say.

MA: He's a good boy. He's just tired, that's all—

JAYA: But what'll we do! Ginni notices everything!

MA: She'll understand.

5 JAYA: Huh!

MA: You're just jealous of her. You don't see what a good, kind, generous, loving person she really is. It's a reflection on you, but of course, you're too fancy to care—

JAYA: Please! This is no time to be criticising me!

10 MA: Who's criticising? I'm just pointing out some simple truths.

JAYA: Come on, Om—get up! This'll never do—

MA: Want to watch TV? There's something good on in twenty minutes—

15 JAYA: (*Looks at* OM.) It's so typical. He can't face things. He never could.

MA: You should watch more TV. You could learn so much—

JAYA: It's amazing that he got this job at all.

MA: On *Happy Families* you can see it, the exact same situa-

20 tion. The mother has one son and one daughter—and the son gets an expensive job—

JAYA: Ma—you have two sons!

MA: But the daughter is jealous! She can't bear to see her brother succeeding, getting all the praise from the mother!

25 The poor mother was widowed in early life and has to struggle—but then one day the father comes back!

JAYA: I thought you just said he was dead?

MA: No, I never! I said the mother was widowed—meaning, she just thought the husband was dead—

30 JAYA: (*Snapping in irritation.*) Oh—it's all so pointless! Any moment now, you won't have a TV to watch!

MA: What!

JAYA: —this whole dream will come crashing down around us! The grey guards will come and take everything back!

35 MA: No!

JAYA: What d'you think—it's your birthright? To have all this water, these gadgets? The moment Ginni finds out what's happened to her little pet, she'll have the place emptied—

MA: Shoo! Such dirty lies!

JAYA: (*Quieter.*) And then how'll I cook without a stove? 40

MA: I'll slap you if you talk like that! Why, my son said so himself—we'll be rich for ever and ever—

JAYA: (*Raising her voice.*) Look at your son, Ma! Look! He's been reduced to a cabbage!

MA: At least a cabbage doesn't talk back! 45

JAYA: (*Frustrated.*) Oh! (*Angry tears.*) At least before there was nothing to lose!

JEETU: (*Suddenly.*) Why? You used to have a smile before. You've certainly lost that—

JAYA: Oh shut up, shut up! Who are you to talk! You're just a 50 waster! Drifting about the streets, not caring what happened to yourself, not caring about any of us, but when you're ready to die, where d'you come? To us of course! Yes! It's so easy for you to talk—you who can't even lose yourself competently! You've come back to make sure that 55 we lose ourselves as well!

MA: Don't speak to your husband like that—

JAYA: He's *not* my husband! He's my brother-in-law!

JEETU: And your lover—

(OM *reacts to this—his limbs twitch, but he does not participate in the conversation.*)

MA: What's this? 60

JAYA: (*Broken.*) Ohh! Not now! Not this!

JEETU: How strange it is, to be here. Talking to all of you . . .

MA: (*Indifferently.*) Not that I'm surprised. Nothing from this slut surprises me. She's capable of anything—

JAYA: Doesn't it matter to you that you're trampling on my 65 life? Doesn't it matter what harm you cause to others?

JEETU: When you've lost everything, when you're so weak you can't even eat the cockroaches who walk into your mouth, that's when your life's desire breathes in your ear— 70

JAYA: And? It tells you to torment your family?

MA: She always was shameless—

JEETU: That I should see you again. You, Jaya. (*Leans back and smiles lazily, wincing slightly.* OM *listens.*) Lying there, covered in shit and dirt, ready to die—*dying* to die!—hearing the 75 engine, roaring in my ears, ready to take me away—I thought of you.

MA: I should have thrown her out from the moment she started making eyes at him—her brother-in-law!

JAYA: (*This is the closest thing to a compliment she has ever been 80 paid. She is overwhelmed with conflicting emotions, trying to cover it with sarcasm.*) And then? Some goddess picked you up?

JEETU: (*Lolling back.*) Huh! Yes. Some goddess! A dog . . .

JAYA: What? (*Uncomprehending.*) A dog?

JEETU: Came and peed on me. Straight into my mouth, 85 cheeky bastard! (JAYA *shudders in disgust and pity.*) But he revived me all right. Lucky for him he ran off—or I would have sucked him dry! Life is a strange thing. When your pockets are full with it, you throw it away like rich whores buying silk bedsheets. But the moment you've emptied 90 your purse of days, your throat begins to scream of its own accord, like a beggar in the streets—(*He imitates a beggar's cry.*) Help me, oh God!—please! Just another five minutes—that's all I ask—just another five minutes to drink a last cup of tea—just two minutes! Just one minute, one! 95 One . . . *please* God, help this dying shithead one more time—(*Looks at her, reverts to his normal voice.*) That's when I thought of you. I knew you would revive me. (*Shuts his eyes.*) Just the smell of your hair—just the touch of your fingernails—

JAYA: (*Biting her lip.*) Hush! These are not things to be said!

MA: And it's too late, anyway. She's already married. To your elder brother—

OM: (*Suddenly.*) Who's a cabbage.

JAYA: (*Uncertainly.*) Om . . .

JEETU: That's all right. We don't need anyone. We don't need this fancy prison. We managed before. We'll manage again —

MA: (*Suddenly jumping up.*) What's the time? Look at the time! It's late—Ginni'll be angry at us—

(*From the corridor, the sound of booted steps.*)

JAYA: (*Tiredly.*) Ohh. I don't care, I don't care any more—

JEETU: That's what I say—

(*From the corridor, the sound of booted steps, closer.*)

MA: Listen! What's that sound?

(OM *hears and reacts immediately, before the others notice him, by crawling off, stage right.*)

JAYA: What's the worst they can do? Take away what was never ours to begin with—

(*From the door, a couple of sharp loud raps.*)

GUARD 1: InterPlanta Services! Open this door, please!

MA: It's the guards!

JAYA: (*Looking blankly.*) So they *have* come for him, after all.

JEETU: (*Holding out his hand.*) Come. Let me kiss your hand. Then you can go and open the door. Tell them to bugger off and take all their goodies with them.

GUARD 1: (*From outside.*) InterPlanta Services—we know you're in there! Open up!

JAYA: (*Raising her voice.*) Coming! (*She gets up.*) I might as well get it over with. (*To the door.*) Wait! It takes a while to unlock the door—

(*Works at the bolts.*)

GUARD 1: (*From outside.*) Resistance is useless! We are authorised to break down this barrier if you do not comply with our request in ten seconds exactly—(*Starts a count down.*) Ten! Nine! Eight!—

(JAYA *gets the door open.*)

GUARD 1: (*Breaking off in mid-stride.*) Sev- . . . ah! (*Enters, pushing* JAYA *aside as* GUARD 2 *and* GUARD 3 *take up defensive positions at the door, holding a fold-up stretcher between them.*) Right—where is the Donor? Come on, quickly now—(*He plunges straight for* JEETU.) The penalty for resistance is—

JAYA: (*In sudden alarm.*) But that's not—

(JEETU, *who has got to his feet, starts to back away*—)

MA: (*Suddenly, pointing to* JEETU.) Go on! Take him—before he runs!

(JEETU *panics and runs,* GUARD 1 *pounces for him, chasing him around the room, while the other two guards stand like goal-keepers at the door.*)

GUARD 1: Ah! He's running, is he? I'll show him—I'll show the cowardly little shit—

JAYA: (*Screaming.*) But he's not the one you want!

JEETU: (*As he runs—though he's really in no condition to make the effort and tires almost instantly.*) You fools! Can't you see I'm not your man?

GUARD 1: (*Panting in pursuit, dodging around the others, even around* OM *lying inert on the floor.*) Always the same story—no-one wants to pay their dues—come on, come on! It's hopeless to run away—

(GUARD 1 *catches him.* JAYA *screams.*)

GUARD 1: There—there—(*As* JEETU *struggles, grunting,* GUARD 1 *holds him in a cruel arm-lock.*) I've got you now—

JAYA: Don't hurt him—don't hurt him—oh he's sick! Please!

GUARD 1: Resistance is useless—(*Starts to lift/drag* JEETU *kicking and struggling, but losing strength.*) we'll have you knocked out in a second—

JEETU: (*Weakly.*) Jaya! Uhh—tell them . . . tell them—

JAYA: (*She darts forward.*) You fools! You maniacs—

MA: (*Reaches out, grabs* JAYA's *ankle and forces her to fall.*) Let him go—slut!

JAYA: (*Paying no attention to* MA.)—He's not the one you want! My husband is there—(*She points from her ungainly position on the floor.*) There!

GUARD 1: Ohh! That's what they all say when we come to take them! (*In a falsetto, as he subdues* JEETU.) "Not me! Not me! It's my brother you want! My uncle! My son" Huh! Lying scum—(*To the other two guards.* GUARD 2 *helps him to wrestle* JEETU *to the ground, while* GUARD 3 *gets the stretcher ready.*) We have no time to spare!

(*Beyond the door interested by-standers have started to collect.*)

JAYA: How can you take the wrong man! Can't you see? Don't you have eyes in your head?

GUARD 1: —(*To the other two.*) Officer! Ready hypo!

MA: Hurry up, you fools—how long d'you think I can hold her?

GUARD 2: (*Holding a gun-shaped hypo-syringe.*) Ready, sir!

JEETU: (*Weakly.*) Jaya—Jaya—help me!

GUARD 1: Prepare to administer hypo—

JAYA: (*Struggling now with* MA *who has her ankle in a vice-like grip.*) Lemme go—lemme go! Don't you care about your own son—

MA: Your lover, you mean! Slut! Serves him right if he goes in place of my only darling—

GUARD 3: (*Holding* JEETU *in a suffocating lock.*) Yes sir—(JEETU *starts to struggle, grunting.*)

JAYA: No! (*Panicking.*) You're killing him! He's not strong enough—

GUARD 1: (*Ignoring her.*) Administer hypo—(*He aids in holding* JEETU *down.*)

(GUARD 2 *is unable to gain access to* JEETU *because he is now struggling so wildly.* JAYA *and* MA *are also struggling but* MA *is practically lying on top of* JAYA *to hold her down.*)

JAYA: They're hurting him! They'll kill him—oh! I can't bear to watch—I can't!

GUARD 1: Officer—I said, administer hypo—

190 GUARD 2: I'm trying sir—I—(*She gets in a shot.*)

JEETU: (*Howls.*) Ahhhhh! Ahhhhh!

GUARD 2: —Damn! Missed the muscle—

JEETU: Ahhhhh!

JAYA: (*In tears.*) Oh what's the use, what's the use! After all
195   we've gone through—

GUARD 1: Ready fresh hypo, officer—and hurry! He's getting out of control—

JAYA: (*No longer able to struggle.*) Oh—please, no, no! He wanted nothing—he had no part to play in this—

(GUARD 2 *fiddles with her kit, discarding one cartridge and fitting another on.*)

200 JAYA: Don't hurt him, don't hurt him—please! Oh! Oh! They'll make mincemeat out of him—

GUARD 2: (*Calmly.*) Hypo ready, sir—

GUARD 1: Administer hypo—

JEETU: (*Hollering as* GUARD 1 *and* GUARD 3 *lean with all their*
205   *weight on him.*) AHHHHHHHHHHHH! AHHHH-
HHH!

GUARD 2 *holds down* JEETU'*s shoulder with her knee and delivers a punch with the muzzle of the hypo.* JEETU'*s body arcs up in a convulsion—he seems to hover in mid-air—*JAYA *screams—Then all is still.* JEETU *is limp and inert on the stretcher. The three guards get to their feet, returning as quickly as possible to their professional composure.* JAYA *remains clutched within* MA'*s savage embrace, though she strains towards the tableau.*)

GUARD 1: Officers—initiate departure.

(GUARD 2 *and* GUARD 3 *quickly spread an opaque shield over the stretcher so that* JEETU *is completely hidden from sight.*)

JAYA: (*In a dull voice, knowing that she won't be answered.*) He's dead, isn't he? They've killed him. I feel it in my
210   bones.

GUARD 2: Donor secured for departure.

GUARD 1: Proceed with departure—

(GUARD 2 *and* GUARD 3 *hoist the stretcher up and exit. From beyond the door, the sound of the wondering crowd.* JAYA *holds out her hand helplessly in the direction of the door.*)

GUARD 1: (*Turning to* JAYA *as the other two officers vanish, removing his clipboard from his belt.*) InterPlanta Services thank
215   you for your cooperation. Your family member is about to fulfil the solemn and noble contract into which he entered. We, on our part, offer you our sincerest assurance that we will do everything in our power to ensure that he will come to no avoidable harm and will suffer no dis-
220   comforts other than what is deemed normal under the circumstances—(*He pauses.* JAYA *is looking dully at the floor, still lying half prone, though* MA *has now backed off and is straightening her clothes.*) Any questions?

JAYA: (*Not looking up.*) When will he be back?

225 GUARD 1: (*Patiently.*) Madam! Any questions?

JAYA: (*Not looking up.*) No.

GUARD 1: (*Ticking off his clipboard.*) Right. Donor will remain in our custody until such time as he is ready to be returned. This can be any period from two hours onwards and upto one week—   230

JAYA: (*Jerks her head up.*) One week! What'll be left of him!

GUARD 1: —depending on the nature of the transplant required, the availability of artificial substitutes for the organs that the Donor has, of his own free will, made available to the Receiver and the Donor's own speed of 235 recovery. Any questions?

JAYA: (*Gets slowly to her feet.*) Yes! What part of him is going to be removed?

GUARD 1: I'm sorry, Madam, I am not free to discuss such details.   240

JAYA: You're going to cut him up and you're not even going to tell his wife what you're going to do with him?

GUARD 1: Excuse me, Madam—relationship with Donor is . . . ?

JAYA: (*Gives her head a guilty little shake.*) I—I meant, his fam- 245 ily—

GUARD 1: Madam: Full details will be furnished once the formalities have been completed—

JAYA: And can I see him? In the hospital, the clinic, wherever?

GUARD 1: Security and health regulations prohibit any con- 250 tact between Donors and their families—

JAYA: Why ask if we have questions when you don't want to answer any of them?

GUARD 1: (*Imperturbably ticking off his clipboard.*) Right. (*Handing her the clipboard.*) And now, if you would be so kind as 255 to sign the despatch voucher—

JAYA: (*Grabs the pen and signs violently.*) There—there—your stupid forms, your—papers—your—questions . . . (*She would like to throw the pen at the floor, but it is attached to the clip-board.*)   260

GUARD 1: (*Retrieving the clip-board.*) Thank you, Madam. We are grateful for your kind cooperation and assure you—

JAYA: Just get out! Take your lying, insincere face away from my door—(*Makes as if to push him.*)

GUARD 1: (*Moving nimbly out of her range, as he continues his 265 spiel.*)—assure you that we will do everything in our power to return your beloved one to you in as short a time as possible—(*He leans inwards on the door handle.*) On behalf of our clients—

JAYA: (*Rushes at him, shouting.*) GET OUT! (*Pushes the door 270 shut in his face.*)

GUARD 1: (*He pushes back, completing his parting message through the door.*)—we at InterPlanta Services extend our heartfelt gratitude for your family's support and compassion! (*This last bit is shouted from behind the closed door.*)   275

(*Sound of boots marching away.*)

JAYA: Ahhh! (*Venting her fury against the door.*) How I hate them!

MA: (*She has been silent all along.*) Good. They've gone at last.

JAYA: (*Leaning against the door, her head against her fists.*) He's gone! They've taken him—and I could do nothing to pre- 280 vent it!

MA: Can I switch on my TV?

JAYA: (*Yelling at her.*) Your son goes off to the slaughterhouse and you're just worried about your TV!

285 MA: (*Mustering as much dignity as she can.*) If you watched more TV you wouldn't dare talk to your mother-in-law that way—

JAYA: (*Coming back towards her.*) Oh! So I've gone back to being your daughter-in-law, have I?

(*Stands threateningly in front of* MA, *who is facing the TV with the remote raised in readiness in her hand.*)

290 MA: I'm your mother-in-law, that's your brother-in-law on the floor there, your husband's gone to work at the spare parts factory. And you? You're just a slut who happens to be standing between me and my TV!

(*Lights dim.*)

SCENE IV

Night. The only difference between daytime and night-time is the spotlight illumination. MA *is snoring in her corner upstage and left.* JAYA *is standing uneasily in a pool of light, upstage left, near the gym equipment. She is wearing an expensive nightgown with matching robe, in satin and lace. Her face gleams with night-cream.*

OM *lies in his corner, on a sleeping pallet near the TV, apparently asleep.*

JAYA *pacing restlessly, finally comes over to where* OM *lies.*

JAYA: (*Shaking him.*) Om! Om—wake up!

(*He does not respond.*)

JAYA: Om—come on—I know you're not asleep—wake up!

OM: (*In a disembodied voice.*) Why? What's the point?

JAYA: We've got to talk. To decide what to do—

5 OM: About what?

JAYA: When they bring Jeetu back—when they realize they've got the wrong man—

OM: They've not realized that. They've used him instead of me.

10 JAYA: No! No—they *can't*—they can't be that stupid!

OM: Then why haven't they brought him back?

JAYA: Because they're . . . interrogating him. Because he collapsed, maybe, and now they're treating him—

OM: You yourself said they don't give a damn about us—why

15 should they care about him? (*He raises himself slowly.*) No. They've used him, take my word for it. Or else they'd have brought him back—

JAYA: —But—but don't they *check*? Don't they bother?

OM: (*Shrugs.*) Maybe they were in too much of a hurry?

20 JAYA: Maybe the part they've taken from him doesn't need to be so special—maybe they've just taken something small, something insignificant—

OM: Then they would have come back by now.

JAYA: It's been six hours. Six hours! They can't remove any-

25 thing of much consequence in six hours! Why—they've probably just taken his—his front teeth! His toe-nails!

OM: Then why hasn't he come back?

JAYA: (*In a small voice.*) You're right. It must be something bigger. More crucial. (*Pause.*) What d'you think it is? His stom-

30 ach? His intestines? Maybe he won't come back for a week!

OM: Or maybe they've found out he's not me and they've just done away with him!

JAYA: (*Cries out.*) No! That would be murder! They can't be allowed to murder people!

OM: (*Coldly.*) Who'd notice? We don't have the right to com- 35 plain. Technically, anyone who isn't claimed by his family within twenty-four hours of going missing can be terminated without attracting legal attention.

JAYA: All these weeks he's been away—he could've been dead! And we'd never even have known! 40

OM: It's a wonder he's alive at all. I've heard that the street gangs eat derelicts these days—

JAYA: No!

OM: Cook them and eat them. Why not? There's no law to prevent it— 45

JAYA: How did he survive!

OM: He was protected by his friends on the street. But they couldn't do it indefinitely. They forced him to come back.

JAYA: Oh. 50

OM: Whatever he says—that's the real reason he's here.

JAYA: (*Pause.*) D'you think he's really ill?

OM: Must be.

JAYA: (*With finality.*) Then it's better if he dies in their hands. They'd be humane, they wouldn't hurt him— 55

OM: Why? They could use him for research—

JAYA: No!

OM: He's not officially on their records—they can do whatever they like—

JAYA: (*Covering her ears.*) No! I don't want to think of it— 60

OM: —give him drugs and sell him to those game sanctuaries—

JAYA: Don't! Oh—please—

OM: —where the rich have licenses to hunt socially disadvantaged types—yes! That's what they've done with your 65 Jeetu! Turned him loose to become a trophy for some industrialist's daughter—

JAYA: You're—you're—(*She calms down.*) It's just your jealousy speaking, isn't it? (*She insists.*) Tell me—isn't it?

OM: What's it to you? 70

JAYA: (*Tiredly.*) I'm still your wife.

OM: Not really. On paper, you're my sister. In reality, you're nothing to me. If not for Ginni I'd throw you out like a shot. Onto the streets. To be hunted. What do I care? You betrayed me. Seduced my brother. I feel nothing but con- 75 tempt.

JAYA: You never cared for me. You never wanted me—

OM: Wanting—not wanting—what meaning do these words have in our world? What choices do we have? Was it my choice that I signed up for this programme? 80

JAYA: —Yes! You went of your own accord!

OM: No. I went because there wasn't anything left to do. I went because I lost my job in the company. And why did I lose it? Because nobody needs clerks any more! There are no new jobs now, from here till next week! It's all over! 85 The factories are all closing! There was nothing *left* for people like us! Don't you know that? There's us—and there's the street gangs—and then the rich.

JAYA: But—the village—

OM: The village is just another kind of factory now. To live 90 there you have to be born there—or you have to be an in-

dustrialist. I'm not an industrialist. I'm just a clerk. What choices do I have? I didn't even choose *this* job—I stood in queue and I was chosen! And if I hadn't got this one,
95 there would have been other queues—but they are all just another kind of lottery in the end. It was just my fate! Like it is my fate to have a faithless tart for a wife—

JAYA: Then why didn't you go with the grey guards when they came! Why did you lie down like a corpse!

100 OM: I don't know what came over me. That too was my fate. It was my fate to lie down in a trance and my brother to take my place. It was his fate to face the scalpel—

JAYA: —even though he may never return?

OM: Nothing matters. Whatever happens, it's fate.

(There's a sound, indistinct.)

105 JAYA: Wait!—What's that?

(The sound of boots in the corridor, accompanied by a shuffling.)

JAYA: Oh! (*Turning excitedly towards the door.*) Hear that? It sounds like boots—

(She runs to the door.)

OM: It doesn't matter what they've done to him—he didn't care about his life anyway—he didn't take any responsi-
110 bility for anything—

*(*JAYA *flings the door open, leans out into the corridor—and freezes where she stands. The footsteps come to a halt. The shuffling continues.* OM *looks straight ahead, affecting unconcern. The shuffling draws close.* JAYA *stands aside, her face blank, watching as* JEETU *enters the room, shuffling slowly, his arms half-raised in front of him, being steered by* GUARD 2, *impassively.* GUARD 1 *enters as well.*)*

OM *does not look around.* JAYA *slowly re-enters, shutting the door behind her, never taking her stricken eyes off the silent, pathetic figure of* JEETU.)

(He is wearing silk pajamas white on white and a wine-red brocade robe and velvet bedroom slippers. Across his eyes, and wrapped around his head, heavy bandages.)

*(*JAYA *remains where she is, by the door, her hands over her mouth, staring. In the foreground,* MA *snores lightly.*)*

GUARD 1: (*Clears his throat, takes out his memo pad.*) Donor Prakash, we have no words with which to express our deep and sincere appreciation of your generosity towards your Receiver . . .

(Lights fade as he drones on.)

115 GUARD 1: You will be glad to hear that the transplant has been a tremendous success and that henceforward you will receive every benefit and consideration due to you under the terms of your contract . . .

(Lights out and curtain.)

ACT THREE

SCENE I

Little has changed in the room. JEETU *sits on the floor with his head between his knees, facing stage front.* MA *is watching TV wearing head phones.* JAYA *and* OM *are sitting on either side of* JEETU.

JAYA: Jeetu—Jeetu speak to me—(*She tries to put her arm over his back.*)

JEETU: (*Throwing her arm off violently, not lifting up his head.*) Don't touch me!

OM: What does he care what happens to us? He's only think- 5 ing of himself—

JAYA: Jeetu, you've already paid the price—now why not live with the reward?

JEETU: (*He is silent for a beat. Then he lifts his head. In the place of his eyes are enormous goggles, created to look like a pair of im- 10 itation eyes. They fit flush with his skin, without ear pieces and cannot be removed. His voice is a hoarse whisper.*) This . . . is my *reward*?

JAYA: Jeetu—Jeetu—if you would only listen a moment—

JEETU: No! (*He gets to his feet.*) I won't listen! Because listen- 15 ing brings acceptance. (*He moves, but warily. He never bumps into anything but he "looks" around himself like a first-time vis- itor from Mars.*) And I will never accept. I will never live with this—this—

OM: Selfish, that's what he is— 20

JAYA: No, Jeetu, no!

JEETU: I don't need your permission to step off the bus! I make my own decisions—

OM: —only thinks of himself. Look at me?

JEETU: Yes, my brother! Look at you? Look at you with these 25 eyes that were meant for you? (*Makes a croaking, sobbing sound, hitting his eyes with his hands.*) These eyes—these blind eyes, this sightless sight—

JAYA: But Jeetu—if they think you're Om, then we need you! Without you, they won't maintain us— 30

JEETU: I don't care! I'm not the one who got this job—and I'm not going to be the one to suffer the consequences—

OM: He was always selfish. Always lived just for himself—

JAYA: Jeetu—just wait till we can ask Ginni—she'll listen at least, maybe even help— 35

JEETU: Ginni, huh!—Ginni only helps herself—

JAYA: No, Jeetu—(*But she herself sounds uncertain.*) That's not true . . .

JEETU: You show me a rich woman who plucks a poor man's eyes out of his body and I'll show you a she-demon! 40

JAYA: But Jeetu, without you . . .

OM: Just wait till Ginni finds out whose eyes are in her head! Just wait!

JAYA: (*To* OM.) Why tell her? If she goes on thinking Jeetu is you then maybe— 45

OM: Fat chance! It's the guards who made the mistake! The moment she sees me here she'll know what happened— and she'll be mad! She'll be furious! She'll probably have the guards court-martialled—

JAYA: You heard what they said—the transplant was a success. 50 So maybe . . . maybe it *is* all right? Maybe Jeetu's eyes are good enough?

OM: It's not so easy as you think—remember all those injec- tions I had in the beginning? They were to prepare my

55   body, to change it so that it could match Ginni's body perfectly. But now they've taken the wrong pair of eyes—
who knows what it'll do to Ginni? And what about Jeetu's
infections, all the poisons and germs he's had circulating
inside him—what about them? Ginni's scared about
60   catching your cold! What'll she catch from Jeetu?

JAYA: But they *said*—

OM: It takes time to know that a transplant has been a success!

JAYA: How long—

65   OM: I don't know. I'm not a doctor. Not less than a week, I
think—

JEETU: Good. I'll be dead long before then—

JAYA: Jeetu—I'm not going to let you die! I don't care what
she says—I'm not going to lose you again—

70   JEETU: You don't know what you're asking of me. You don't
know what it's like to walk around with a nightmare
wrapped around your head—

JAYA: Jeetu—

OM: (*To* JAYA.) Why waste your breath? Neither will he listen,
75   nor will it make the slightest difference to the outcome.
What will be, will be, regardless of what we try to do
about it—

JAYA: But *why*—when it doesn't *have* to be! Why—when all
he has to do is to pretend—just for a couple of hours in a
80   day—

JEETU: Why? (*Pause.*) Because I am in place beyond death. I
am in a place worse than death.

JAYA: There's no place worse than death—

JEETU: Yet I know such a place, now. (*Painfully.*) A bleached
85   and pitted place. Scars and slashes, no stillness, no dimensions. No here, no there—(*He moves his head about, "looking" at his visions.*) I see in molten bars and blinding shapes,
I see symmetries and confused fragments—sparks, shadows, water on mad glass, heat dreams, trains flying on fever
90   tracks—

JAYA: But can you see me, Jeetu?

JEETU: (*Looking there.*) Yes. I see you. And through you. (*Looks
around.*) And through the floor. And through all the gadgets, pulsing with electric gold, liquid atoms sizzling down
95   infinite mineshafts . . . (*He turns his gaze.*) my brother
standing there, a blaze of fried nerves and straining bones,
his eyes like ping-pong balls jittering in their orbits.
(*Turns.*) And I can see Ma—a dim bundle of red desires
bathed in a blue haze of radiation. (*Turns.*) And I can see
100   you, Jaya, my Jaya . . . I can see your purple blood, I can
see your thoughts sparkling like stars through the pearly
cloud of your brain, I can see your heart twitching like an
epileptic kitten—yes, I can see all these things, but who
would want to see them? Who can bear to see them? (*He
105   sits down, on his haunches.*) And yet . . . I can't even turn
them off. I can't shut these freakish eyes of mine. I can't
turn my head away, I can't end this poison-vision. I can't
sleep, I can't dream, I can't even cry. (*He looks at her.*) This
is what you want from me?

(*There is a silence.*)

110   JEETU: Well? You're not saying anything.

JAYA: I—(*She holds her forehead.*)

JEETU: Is it selfish to want to end this?

OM: I was willing to accept anything for my family—

JEETU: Oh yes!—And what happened when the guards came?

OM: (*Mustering what dignity he can.*) That was different. It was   115
the shock, the lack of warning—

JEETU: It was cowardice!

JAYA: (*Carefully.*) Jeetu—we've not asked anything of you so
far—

JEETU: This is no time to start!   120

JAYA: Maybe you'll get used to it in time—maybe they'll be
able to improve it—

JEETU: (*He clutches his head.*) Let me die before I'm too maddened by visions to make the effort!

OM: Just wait, just wait—when Ginni comes, she'll make all   125
the effort for all of us!

JAYA: Don't be so cocksure! You think she'll take your side—

OM: Of course she will. And she'll throw the two of you out,
I wouldn't be surprised! For fooling her. For fooling
around. For being dirty, filthy fornicators—   130

JAYA: We haven't! Not . . . not since you got the job—

OM: Ah but he hasn't been here has he! Now that he's back
it'll start again, won't it? Don't think I don't know how it
is with people like you! You'd do it right in front of me if
you got half a chance—   135

(*The warning tone sounds.*)

JAYA: Oh my God—

OM: (*Looking relieved.*) Ah! Just let me do the talking—I'll explain everything—

JEETU: (*His whole body jerks.*) Ah! What's that? I—I—I *saw*
something—   140

(*The second tone sounds.*)

JAYA: What's the matter Jeetu?

OM: You shut up, both of you! I'll explain it—and don't
worry, I won't leave you two out of the picture. But if she
asks me, I'll tell her—

JEETU: (*Breathlessly.*) Something's . . . happening. The blackness   145
is lifting . . . I can see . . . some sort, some sort of . . . pattern—

(*The third tone sounds.*)

GINNI: Well—hellooo-oo! Guess whoo-ooo!

JEETU: Ahh! (*He falls silent, with his mouth open in wonder,
breathing heavily.*) Ahh . . .

OM: Hello! Howdy! Hi, Ginni—   150

GINNI: Hello-ooo? Is anybody home—(*The* CONTACT MOD-
ULE *swivels.*) Auwm? (*The* CONTACT MODULE *has swivelled
around to find* JEETU, *who doesn't respond.*) Isn't that you,
Auwm?

OM: (*Running around to get in front of the* CONTACT MODULE.)   155
No! No—this is me! I'm here! Here!

(*The* CONTACT MODULE *flips up and out of* OM's *reach.*)

GINNI: Come in, Auwm! Can you see me? Auwm?

JEETU: (*In a strange, strangled voice, not looking at the* CONTACT
MODULE.) My God! My God—I can see!

GINNI: (*Sounding extremely cheerful.*) Sure you can see Auwm!   160
That's what we gave you eyes for! And I'm sure you're real
glad to know that *I* can see better now! And with your eyes!

OM: (*Screaming.*) NO!! It's a mistake! There's been a terrible mistake!

(*But* JAYA *intercepts him.*)

165 JAYA: (*In a loud whisper.*) Wait—don't disturb them—

JEETU: (*Gesturing directly in front of him, in a wondering voice.*) And that . . . and you must be . . .

OM: (*He is almost in tears.*) She's wrong! She's wrong! (*But* JAYA *silences him by dragging him sharply aside.*) It's—

170 JAYA: (*Holds* OM *back.*) Shhhhh—!

GINNI: —Ginni! That's right, Auwm—it's me you're seeing 'coz I'm beaming my video image straight into your mind! So you can see me right in front of you, all of me, for once, not just my face . . . (*In a seductive voice.*) well?

175 What do you think?

(*There is a silence in the room as* JEETU *moves slowly around, looking at something that no-one else in the room with him can see. What little of his face is visible shows wonder.*)

JEETU: It's—you're—beautiful. Like . . . magic.

GINNI: You like me, Auwm? You like what you see?

JEETU: (*Shakily.*) Yes. And—and the room! What is this place?

GINNI: Oh . . . it's just where I live, Auwm, it's one of the

180 rooms in my little house—

JEETU: (*Breathing out.*) It's a palace—

GINNI: I'm glad you like it Auwm—

JEETU: I can't help but like it! Who wouldn't? (*He points around him.*) That—that—(*He has no words.*) Those . . .

185 plants! That . . . light! What are those things there? It's . . . (*Hushed.*) beautiful. Beautiful. I've never seen anything like this. Never.

OM: (*In anguish.*) But it's mine, what he's seeing—MINE!

JAYA: (*Watching carefully.*) Can't you hush?

190 OM: (*In tears.*) It's all a mistake! She'll find out and then what'll happen? What'll happen to us?

JAYA: Shhh—

JEETU: (*Wonderingly.*) And you . . . is that really . . . you?

GINNI: Yup! It's me, Ginni! You look like you're seeing me for

195 the first time, Auwm!

JEETU: I—I am! I never realized this is what you looked like—I mean, when the others talked about you—

GINNI: Well—now. I'm glad you like me so well, 'coz you know what? Now that the transplants have started, it's

200 time that we talked about the next phase—

JEETU: (*Still dazed.*) "Next phase"?

OM: (*Shouting.*) But he's the wrong man!

(JAYA *holds* OM *back.*)

(JEETU *is facing the* CONTACT MODULE, *which now rises above him and glows white as the rest of the stage lights dim.* JEETU *is bathed in the light, sealed into the vision that is projected into him.*)

GINNI: The next phase of the transplants. You see, we have to progress rapidly now and I need all your support. Until we

205 reached this platform of contact, we couldn't be sure. But now that we're sure, we've got to move really fast. Are you with me?

JEETU: (*Uncertainly.*) Yes . . .

GINNI: Because you have to be willing, for what we want to do now. You have to be really willing, Auwm— 210

JEETU: Tell me, Ginni, tell me what you want—(*He moves towards the illusion he sees.*)

GINNI: Ah-ah—can't touch me Auwm! (*He reacts by jerking his hand away.*) Well . . . you'll have to go back to the clinic and they'll prepare you— 215

JEETU: (*He continues to behave as if he is standing very close to someone, following her around as she moves out of his reach.*) You need some more parts of me?

GINNI: Well, yes—I mean, that's one way of looking at it but I—I think you should understand that time is kind of 220 short, Auwm and we really have to get a move on—

JEETU: (*He moves his body seductively, winningly.*) Just tell me what you want of me Ginni—

GINNI: The guards will come for you and they'll request you to follow them away— 225

JEETU: Anything, Ginni, anything—

GINNI: The sooner you can go the better it'll be for you—

JEETU: Whatever you say, Ginni—

GINNI: I mean, really, Auwm, if it's okay with you, I can tell the guards to come for you right now— 230

JAYA: No . . . (*But she says it softly, shaking her head, knowing that it's futile.*)

JEETU: That's fine with me, Ginni—

OM: (*Hoarsely.*) Ask her what she wants from you!

JEETU: Anything you want is fine, Ginni— 235

GINNI: Okay, Auwm, I'm turning this video session off for the moment and I'm going to ask you to wait for the guards—

JEETU: (*He holds his arms out forlornly.*) You're—you're going?

GINNI: But I'll be back, Auwm, closer than you'd ever believe . . . (*The* CONTACT MODULE *moves high, as its light starts to* 240 *dim.*)

JEETU: (*Stretching his arms up.*) Don't—don't—(*He drops his arms.*) Ahh—! (*Strikes his eyes.*) AHHHH!

GINNI: The guards will come, Auwm, you don't have long to wait—we'll talk again when you're in the clinic, okay? 245

JEETU: NO!! Don't leave me in this blindness—

GINNI: Remember to keep smiling Auwm—

JEETU: (*Brokenly.*) No!

GINNI: —byeeee!

(*The* CONTACT MODULE *snaps off.*)

JEETU: (*Softly.*) Ah—no! She's gone—she's gone! 250

(JAYA *and* OM *come forward around him.*)

JAYA: Jeetu—Jeetu—do you know what you've said?

JEETU: All I know is that I'm going to her—I'm going—

OM: You didn't even find out what they're going to take from you this time—

JEETU: You don't understand! I was blind! And now I have the 255 chance to see again—

JAYA: But . . . it's not *real*, what you see—I—I mean, we could watch you moving like a madman, waving your arms about, pointing to things that weren't there—

(OM, *having listened so far, begins to move away, towards the door.*)

JEETU: Ah—but they're *somewhere*, aren't they? And that's all 260 that matters to me.

n the remote.) I won't—I won't—

t up and is flailing at JAYA *with her thin arms.*)
uffalo! Give it back or I'll—I'll shit in the wa-

uldn't dare—(*She has not managed to break the re-*

as enough force to push JAYA *off her balance.*) I'll mi-
e your entrails!—(*Pushes* JAYA *down.*) Ah! (*Snatches*
remote.)

ackling MA *from the ground, hanging onto her from behind*
trying to claw the remote out of her hands. She is panting
the effort.) I'm sick of being the only one to make de-
ions around here! There's nothing wrong with you—
ou're not sick—or busy—

ll the while OM *has been listening, like a dog for its master, by the*
or. Now the sounds that he has been listening for are audible: boots
n the corridor. He readies himself by flattening himself alongside the
door as the footsteps come to a halt. A pause and the bolt is opened
from outside.)

MA: Let me go, you barren dog—mmmh! Mmmmh! (*She
pulls her arm up so that she can gnaw at* JAYA'*s hand where it's
clamped to her wrist.*) LET ME GO!

(*At this moment the door is flung open.* JAYA *and* MA *fall apart and
turn to the door just as* OM *wriggles out almost the same instant.*
AGENT I *enters, paying no attention to* OM.)

370 AGENT I: Madam Indumati? Who is Madam Indumati?
MA: Me! I'm Madam Indumati! (*She starts to move towards the
door.*)
JAYA: (*Craning her neck.*)—Om! Om—where are you?
AGENT I: (*Salutes, announcing loudly.*) VideoCouch Enterprises,
375 Ma'm—please—(*He stands aside to open the door a little
wider and leans out in anticipation. Sounds of something being
wheeled along.*)
JAYA: (*Flabbergasted.*) Wh-what is this? Who're you!
MA: (*To the* AGENT.) Have you brought it?
380 AGENT I: Yes, Ma'm—

(AGENT II *and* AGENT III *wheel in a long gleaming case. It is reminiscent of Tutankhamen's sarcophagus, encrusted with electronic dials
and circuitry in the place of jewels. The* AGENTS *wheel it into the
centre of the room, move the dining platform aside and install the device in its place.*)

AGENT I: (*Coming forward to where* MA *stands.*) Please, Ma'm,
sign here—
JAYA: (*To* MA.) Ma—who are these people—what's going on—
MA: (*Ignoring* JAYA.) What about this insti—instig—?
385 AGENT I: Installation. (*Patiently.*) Just sign this form, Ma'm, to
confirm receipt of the unit—
MA: (*Taking the form and the pen.*) How do I know you won't
just run away after I've signed this, eh?
AGENT I: (*Shrugs.*) As you wish, Ma'm—(*To the other two
390 AGENTS, *expressionlessly.*) Proceed with installation.

(*The other two* AGENTS *open the case, revealing an equally ornate
interior, filled with tubes, switches, circuitry. Inside are a number of
containers.* AGENTS II *and* III *set about attaching the containers to
various parts of the case while* AGENT I *explains to* MA.)

AGENT I: This is the SuperDeluxe VideoCouch model XL
5000! We are certain it will provide you, our valued customer, with every satisfaction! This is the nourishment
panel—the hydration filter—the pangrometer! Here you
see the Lexus Phantasticon which is programmed to receive 395
seven hundred and fifty video channels from all over the—
JAYA: (*Shaking him.*) Stop this at once! Explain to me what's
going on!
AGENT I: (*Stops, baffled.*) Ma'm—
MA: (*To* JAYA.) Can't you shut up? It's my VideoCouch! It's 400
what I ordered the other day!
JAYA: But—
AGENT I: Ma'm—
MA: (*To the* AGENT.) Proceed!
AGENT I: (*He is off-stride.*) Uhh—This is the SuperDeluxe 405
VideoCouch model XL 5000! We are certain it will provide you, our valued customer, with every satisfaction!
This is the nourishment panel—the hydration filter—the
pangrometer! Here you see the Lexus Phantasticon which
is programmed to receive seven hundred and fifty video 410
channels from all over the world! There are ten modes,
seventeen frequencies, three sub-strate couplers, extra-
sensory feedback impulses and cross-net capturing faci-
tilies! All media access—satellite, bio-tenna, visitelly and
radiogonad. Manual control panel, neuro-stimulator and 415
full-body processing capacities—all other queries will be
answered on-line from within the VideoCouch self-
training program. (*He ends abruptly.*) Any questions, Ma'm?
MA: (*She has heard very little of this.*) Hanh?
AGENT I: Ma'm—if you sign the delivery voucher we can 420
complete installation—
MA: But I haven't understood a word you've said—
JAYA: (*Standing between the VideoCouch and* MA.) Ma—You
MUST explain what this is about—
MA: (*To the* AGENT.) Stop her! She'll destroy it—she'll dam- 425
age it—
JAYA: (*Frustrated.*) Oh—! (*She moves away.*)

(*The* AGENT *moves to get closer to the VideoCouch.*)

JAYA: Just do it, do it! (*From stage right, watching the proceedings.*)
But make sure I'm not held responsible for anything—
MA: (*To the* AGENT.) If I sign this . . . no-one can take if from 430
me, can they?
AGENT I: No, Ma'm—
MA: And your people won't go till I've got into it? (*She signs
the voucher and hands it back, not glancing at the many pages of
forms.*) 435
AGENT I: No, Ma'm—thank you, Ma'm—If you'll just come
this way, Ma'm—

(*The other two* AGENTS *have attached a power-line to the unit and at
this moment activate the system. It twinkles with small LCDs. It looks
like a tiny space-module.* AGENT II *delinks the power connection and
the lights continue to twinkle. She detaches the cable from the couch.*)

COUCH: (*A fruity voice issues from the VideoCouch.*) Wel-
Video Paradiso! You will not regret your ch-
ask our authorized representative to settl-
customized, contour-gel, fully automa-
(*Appropriate music plays.*)

JAYA: Yes—but—(*She looks dissatisfied and worried.*) she's taken your *eyes*—
JEETU: —and left me something even better! I can't tell you
265 what things I saw—
JAYA: Really? So much?
JEETU: (*Reverentially.*) Yes—oh, yes! (*Then he pauses.*) Of course, I can't see what's directly around me. But maybe they'll find a way to change that—
270 JAYA: You should have asked her—
JEETU: I'd not seen her, you see, till just now! I thought she was an old woman! You never told me she was so—so *young!* (*Hushed.*) And beautiful. (*Accusingly.*) Why didn't you tell me, Jaya?
275 JAYA: (*Shrugs.*) You didn't seem interested—we hardly discussed Ginni at all—
JEETU: Well. It would have made all the difference if I had known. I saw all of her, you know! Standing there (*He draws her with his arms.*), all of her . . . wearing . . . almost
280 nothing! (JAYA *bites her lip, frowning.*) And she kept . . . (*He moves his body sensuously.*) moving, like this, like that . . . wah! I could have had her, right there and then!
JAYA: (*Bitterly.*) But she wasn't real!
JEETU: She exists. That's enough for me. She's a goddess and
285 she exists. I would do anything for her—anything!
JAYA: (*Looks depressed.*) Yes. I can see that—
JEETU: (*A touch of guilt.*) Don't hold it against me, Jaya—think of her as just another client—you were always good at that—
290 JAYA: Yes . . . but your other clients wanted only your services. Not your . . . body itself!
JEETU: You should be happy for me—and anyway, you've got your wish, now. I'll stay alive, and they'll go on looking after all of us—

(*There is a knocking at the door.*)

295 GUARD 1: (*From outside.*) InterPlanta Services!—

(*But* before *he can say "open up",* OM *has thrown the door open.*)

OM: Yes! Take me! Take me! I'm ready to go!

(*Several things happen at once.* JEETU *and* JAYA *turn towards the door, as* GUARD 1 *and* GUARD 2 *roughly shove* OM *aside, entering the room.*)

JEETU: Yes—
GUARD 1: Mr Om Prakash—we have been intimated of your willingness to participate in the second phase of our trans-
300 plant service!
OM: (*Screaming.*) No! Not him—take ME!! I'm Om Prakash! Check your records—

(GUARD 3 *entering behind the other two, quickly grabs* OM *and holds him pinned to the wall, struggling.*)

JEETU: Yes—I am Om Prakash—
OM: (*From his pinned position, bellowing.*) NOOO!!! He's lying!
05 A lying, scheming swine!!! He's my brother, I tell you— my younger brother—
GUARD 1: All right sir, if you would just follow us—we're ready to leave—

JEETU: Let's go—

(GUARD 1 *star*

JAYA: (*Dar*
JEETU: (*Swive*
JAYA: (*She is su* too soon, they never be the sam
JEETU: (*He grabs her qui* away, into the waiting gras band to look after—he ne and exits.)
JAYA: (*Losing all restraint.*) Jeetu! Je her and exits.) What happened to doms! Your pride! (*She sinks to her k* ily gone—

(GUARD 3 *has a brief struggle disengaging himsel* too slips out, slamming the door behind him—then the outside.)

OM: (*Hollering.*) AHHHHHHHHHH! You've locked you bastards! You've locked us in! (*He roars and poun* the door.) You can't do this to us! We've not signed a consent forms! You've not taken any permissions! AHH-HHHHHHH! You've locked us in here! AAAAAHHH-HHHH! And you've taken the wrong man—you'll regret it—you'll suffer for it—AAAAAAHHHHHHH!—

(*He subsides onto the floor, moaning.* JAYA *looks at the door, too shocked and defeated even to cry. She turns and walks slowly till she is near her place at the dining area. She sits, seeming distracted. Looks across at* MA, *who is totally absorbed by the TV programme she's watching.*)

330 JAYA: Ma? Ma—(*Goes across to stage right, where* MA *sits.*) listen to me—(*But* MA *can't hear her. She shakes* MA *by the shoulder.*) Ma! Listen to me!
MA: (*Irritated, holding one of her ear phones up from her ear.*) What is it!
335 JAYA: Ma—do you realize they've taken Jeetu?
MA: What?
JAYA: (*In a raised voice.*) Jeetu—they've taken him away!
MA: (*Indifferently.*) So? (*Starts to replace the ear-piece.*) He was never here to begin with—
340 JAYA: No! You *can't* be so indifferent—
MA: (*Shaking off her hand.*) Tch! Let me be! Why should I care what happens to Jeetu? I'm through caring about anybody—(*She replaces the ear-piece and turns back to her set.*)
JAYA: (*For a second she is nonplussed. Then she loses control.*) That's—too much! (MA *can't hear her.*) You hear me, Ma? 345 (*She screams.*) It's just TOO MUCH! (*She darts forward and snatches the TV remote from* MA's *hand—.*) You can't do this—(*Smashes it on the floor, the TV abruptly goes off, as* MA's *reaction sets in.*) you've got be involved with what's going on around you— 350
MA: (*Removing headphones and getting up as fast as her old limbs will let her.*) You—GIVE THAT BACK TO ME—

(*They do not notice that* OM *is sitting up alertly, by the door. He is listening to something.*)

(*As the* COUCH *begins speaking,* MA *is helped into it by the* AGENTS. *She lies down and the* AGENTS *huddle around her, connecting her up to various pouches and tubes. They do this very quickly and she gasps and grunts once or twice. There is a breathing mask on her face. Soon they are ready to close the lid.*)

COUCH: Thank you for being cooperative! Your fully automatic Video Paradiso unit is now ready for operation! Just relax and let your guide show you the way to an experience of ultimate bliss—

445

(*The* AGENTS *gently shut the lid. There is a faint hiss, a thin vapour escapes as the two edges nest one within the other—and it is closed. The* AGENTS *secure the edges, seal them and lock them. They work extremely fast. The muted sound of the* COUCH *voice continues but becomes a constant unintelligible background hum.*)

JAYA: (*She has been craning her neck to get a view of the proceedings.*) But—how will she breathe!

AGENT I: (*Turning to her, as the other two* AGENTS *collapse the undercarriage and lower the unit to floor level. They replace the dining platform over the* COUCH. *It is efficiently concealed, aside from occasional blinks of light.*) Ma'm—it's a total-comfort unit Ma'm—

450

JAYA: Won't she have to—to—

AGENT I: We have a full-recycling and bio-feed-in processor! Your relative will have no further need of the outside world from now till—(*He coughs delicately.*) till she chooses to delink.

455

JAYA: Does she—how will she—

AGENT I: (*Smoothly.*) Everything is now in the customer's operation, Ma'm—the unit is fully self-sufficient—

460

JAYA: Won't I have to . . . switch it on or off? No . . . food? Water?

AGENT I: Total self-sufficiency, Ma'm! There is nothing to be done!

465

(*The other two* AGENTS *are ready to leave.*)

AGENT I: Ma'm—installation is complete—

JAYA: No—wait—who's paying for this thing—

AGENT I: (*Impatient to leave, walking towards the door.*) Debited from the customer's InterPlanta account Ma'm—(*As an afterthought he brings out his card.*) but in case you have any queries Ma'm, please get in touch with our local representative—

470

(*He hands her the card, salutes smartly but unseen, as she stares at the card. The* AGENT *turns on his heel and has left the room before she registers that he's gone.*)

JAYA: (*Startled by the sound of the door shutting.*) No—you've not explained anything—(*Runs to the door.*) what happens if there's a malfunction—(*Opens the door, leans out, steps out. After a moment, comes back in, looking bewildered.*) Alone! I can't believe it—they've left me alone! Every one!

475

(*From the* COUCH *a friendly mumble trills out.*)

JAYA: (*Leans, exhausted, against the door.*) But not at peace.

(*Lights start to fade.*)

JAYA: (*Slides to the floor.*) Not yet at peace.

(*Lights out.*)

SCENE II

Five days later. The room is unchanged. It is night. JAYA *has fallen asleep at the table-cum-sarcophagus. There are occasional hums of sound from the VideoCouch underneath.*

She is looking worn out, unslept. With jarring suddenness the warning tone sounds. JAYA *startles awake.*

The CONTACT MODULE *is ablaze. It no longer has any face on its facets. It hovers over* JAYA.

VOICE: (*A rich, gravelly male voice.*) Zhaya . . .

JAYA: (*She is badly shocked, recoils away from the* CONTACT MODULE, *her hand to her mouth.*) Ahhh!

VOICE: Don't be frightened, Zhaya—

JAYA: (*Crawling backwards towards stage right.*) No—please—   5

VOICE: (*The* CONTACT MODULE *follows her.*) There's nothing to be afraid of, Zhaya—

JAYA: Who are you! What d'you want—

VOICE: Calm down, honey, be easy—shh, shhh—

JAYA: (*More frightened than ever, wriggling along the floor, away from the light which follows her nevertheless.*) Who told you my name—how did you—   10

VOICE: Easy, girl, easy—don't keep moving, it's no use—

(JAYA *continues to back away.*)

JAYA: (*Almost screaming.*) NO! . . . please! Leave me alone— I've done nothing—nothing!   15

VOICE: Zhaya—I can't harm you, honey—

JAYA: (*She is backed up against the wall stage right and can go no further.*) Please—please—(*She shields her eyes from the glare.*)

VOICE: Zhaya —Zhaya—just listen to me—

JAYA: (*Straining away from the light.*) Go away! Leave me alone!   20

VOICE: Zhaya—

JAYA: (*The accumulated tension, despair and solitude combine forces to break her. She subsides on her side in heaving sobs.*) Leave me . . . just leave me . . . please, please . . . just leave me!

VOICE: (*Abruptly the* CONTACT MODULE *moves up and away from her.*) All right, Zhaya—if that's what you really want—   25

(*The* CONTACT MODULE *moves a comfortable distance away from her. It dims down till it looks like a Japanese paper-lantern. The rest of the stage is in darkness. Slowly, cautiously,* JAYA *raises her head, looks around herself, warily. There is a pregnant silence.*)

JAYA: Have you—gone?

VOICE: No.

JAYA: (*She is startled but waits. There's no further communication.*) Hello?   30

VOICE: I'm here, Zhaya, if you're ready to speak to me—

JAYA: (*Warily.*) Who are you?

VOICE: Let's just say . . . I'm a friend.

JAYA: But I don't know you!   35

VOICE: Still—I'm a friend.

JAYA: How can you be—if we've never met?

VOICE: I've seen you. Heard your voice—

JAYA: How?

40   VOICE: Oh . . . we have our ways—

JAYA: (*Pause.*) You mean, you're a friend of Ginni's?

VOICE: A friend? Yeah. Sort of.

JAYA: You live where she lives?

VOICE: Sort of, yeah.

45   JAYA: How is she? Is she well?

VOICE: Oh—! (*Nonchalantly.*) Fine, she's fine—

JAYA: (*Gusts a laugh that sounds like tears.*)

VOICE: What's the matter?

JAYA: (*Parodying his tone.*) "Fine"! "Fine"!—

50   VOICE: I don't understand—

JAYA: —Ginni might be "fine, fine"—but what has happened
    to my life?—She's taken Om, she's taken Jeetu! And where
    is she? Now that she's "fine, fine"?

VOICE: Well, I was just getting around to that—

55   JAYA: (*Whispers.*) It's madness. Talking to a lighted ball. Send-
    ing eyes across the ocean—(*Indicates the sarcophagus.*) lock-
    ing Ma into a trunk—it's all madness!

VOICE: Why don't I tell you my name?

JAYA: (*She shakes her head.*) It's not *natural*, any of it—

60   VOICE: Virgil. That's my name, Zhaya—

JAYA: I don't know you, I don't even know if you really ex-
    ist, but here we are, talking! Pretending we're friends—

VIRGIL: Not pretending—

JAYA: I was pretending—with Ginni, I mean. Om said he
65   liked her, but what did he know about her, really? What
    did any of us know? We saw only her face. When she
    chose to show it to us. That's not a friend! That's not even
    a human being!

VIRGIL: I can show you myself, Zhaya—

70   JAYA: I don't want to see you. I don't want to start thinking
    of you as a real person, when all the time you're just a
    voice in the air—

VIRGIL: Not just my face. All of me—

JAYA: (*She looks up suspiciously.*) You'll come *here*? In *person*?

75   VIRGIL: Sort of. A version of me—

JAYA: (*Shakes her head resolutely.*) No! I'm not interested in *ver-
    sions.* I'm not like Jeetu—

VIRGIL: Tell you what. I'll show you what I look like. Then
    you decide—

80   JAYA: No! I'll never pluck my eyes out or get into a box—

VIRGIL: Nothing like that. You'll see me here, with your own
    eyes—

JAYA: How? (*Sarcastically.*) You'll send a statue with the
    guards?

85   VIRGIL: Just come to the Module—no, wait. I'll move to you.

(*The* CONTACT MODULE *moves till it's within her reach. She
flinches back.*)

JAYA: This? You'll come from this?

VIRGIL: Don't worry! It can't harm you—

JAYA: (*Warily.*) No, but—

VIRGIL: It's very simple. Just do as I say. Reach under the
90   Module—that's right, hold the Module, it's not hot—
    reach under it and push the, the uh lower panel, the flat
    one right underneath—okay, gently push it—push it up—
    you'll hear a click—

JAYA *follows these instructions, kneeling as she does so, touching the
glowing globe gingerly, squinting against the light. There is a click,
and she releases the* MODULE. *Falls back.*)

VIRGIL: Ah—okay! Good girl!

JAYA: Now—?   95

VIRGIL: Now . . . just wait . . . (*The* MODULE *grows bright again
    and sinks to almost floor level.*) keep watching this space . . .
    underneath . . . keep watching . . .

(JAYA *complies. A bright light issues from under the* CONTACT
MODULE. *Slowly it rises, creating a projection with the motion of its
ascent. A figure is revealed. A young man's bare legs, well-formed
. . . his shorts, bright and brassy . . . a bare torso—*JAYA *gasps. . . .*)

JAYA: . . . Jeetu!

(JEETU *stands there, smiling, his face no longer obscured by the goggles. He looks happy and healthy, but his expression is unfamiliar.
He looks like someone else. He seems to glow very slightly.*)

VIRGIL: (*The voice comes from the* CONTACT MODULE *though*   100
    JEETU's *mouth moves.*) Well? What d'you say now?

JAYA: (*She wants to move forward.*) Jeetu . . . (*Her hand moves to
    her mouth.*) Is it—you?

VIRGIL: Of course it's me, Zhaya!

JAYA: But . . . you're not—where's the (*She means the gog-*   105
    gles.)—you can't be—no! It can't be—it *can't* be! (*To the*
    CONTACT MODULE.) What have you done! It can't be him!

VOICE: (*Distressed.*) Oh! You're not happy? Don't you like the
    way I look?

JAYA: What is this! What is this thing in front of me! What   110
    have you done with—JEETU! (*She screams.*) JEETUUU-
    UUU! What have they done to you! Where have you
    gone!!

(*The figure walks forward.*)

VIRGIL: This *is* me, Zhaya—don't you recognize me? I'm
    your Jittoo now—   115

JAYA: Oh! (*Doubles over, sinks to the ground, sobbing heartily.*)
    What have you done, what have you done!

VIRGIL: (*The figure walks over to where* JAYA *kneels, kneels down
    himself.*) I thought you'd be happy to see me!

JAYA: (*Refuses to look at him.*) How can I be happy with a   120
    ghost!

VIRGIL: I'm not a ghost—

JAYA: You *can't* be who you look like!

VIRGIL: But I am—in one sense.

JAYA: (*She looks up.*) You can't be. It's all just another mad-   125
    ness—

VIRGIL: Why, Zhaya? Trust your eyes—

JAYA: But *you're* not here! And *he's* . . . dead, isn't he? The one
    to whom this . . . this . . . *body* belonged?

VIRGIL: (*Gazes meaningfully but with an entirely non-*JEETU *ex-*   130
    pression on his face.) Depends. On how you define death.

JAYA: There's only one way to define death!

VIRGIL: (*Softly.*) Not where I live. (*Pause.*) We have some new
    definitions. (*Pause.*) We speak of a body-death and a self-
    death. (*Pause.*) The body you knew is . . . still alive. (*Waits.*)   135
    Come! Doesn't that count for anything?

JAYA: (*Whispers.*) And . . . the self?

VIRGIL: (*Briskly.*) The self you knew is also alive.

JAYA: Huh—! Without his body?

140 VIRGIL: He was willing to sell, I was willing to buy—

JAYA: And you paid him in—(*She stops, realizing her mistake.*) But . . . it *wasn't* you! It was . . . Ginni! (*Staring at him.*) *Ginni?*

VIRGIL: What do *you* think, Zhaya?

145 JAYA: Ginni . . . Ginni . . . wasn't *real?*

VIRGIL: Ginni was . . . me.

JAYA: You?

VIRGIL: Me. Just a minute—(*A faint buzz, then the voice that issues is in* GINNI's *cloying tones.*) Hello, Zhaya! Recognize me

150 now? This is what I sound like when my voice is a few decibels higher—

JAYA: (*She leaps to her feet.*) But then . . . but then Jeetu was paid in phantoms!

VIRGIL: (*Standing as well.*) He sees what he wants to see. He

155 lives what he wants to live.

JAYA: And he has no body!

VIRGIL: He has a—casing.

JAYA: —but no body!

VIRGIL: He is happy, Zhaya. He made his choice—

160 JAYA: (*Shouting.*) I saw his choosing! With his mind bandaged in dreams!

VIRGIL: Was it any different than his life? Any worse? When he was lying on the streets—was that better?

JAYA: When he was lying in the streets at least he knew what

165 he was! He was—he was—(*She stops.*) But you don't know this—

VIRGIL: I do.

JAYA: You can't! We never told Ginni!

VIRGIL: But I know.

170 JAYA: *He* . . . told you?

VIRGIL: *You* told me—

JAYA: I? (*Frowns.*) Never!

VIRGIL: Always. I listened in to you, Zhaya. I heard every word said in the room—even when the Module was off,

175 it recorded—

JAYA: (*She is shocked.*) HHhhh! (*Starts to pace about in agitation.*)

VIRGIL: I know Jittoo's not Auwm and that Auwm's your husband.

JAYA: And about—about Jeetu being—

180 VIRGIL: Diseased. Yes—but he was more available than his brother. So we took him.

JAYA: And it doesn't matter! It makes no difference!

VIRGIL: Do I look unwell? Do I look disabled? (*Smiles ironically.*) There's no scalpel as keen as youth! His body healed

185 in hours.

JAYA: And you heard . . . every, every thing?

VIRGIL: Saw, too. I know about the toilet being loaned out to half the city! About the water being sold! About the food being shared! Every sneeze, every belch. And you

190 Zhaya—I knew when you bled and when you passed wind. I even saw you . . . pleasure yourself, Zhaya, lying there, alone. I even knew that.

JAYA: (*Humiliated.*) No! You must have slept—

VIRGIL: —and played it back when I awoke!

195 JAYA: And Ginni! Who is Ginni?

VIRGIL: Nothing. Nobody. A computer-animated wet-dream.

JAYA: What?

VIRGIL: There's a joke we have, back at the agency—well, it's not a great joke— 200

JAYA: What joke—

VIRGIL: "For every fish, a dish—"

JAYA: (*Shaking her head in despair.*) That's all we are to you—a game to play with—

VIRGIL: No, no—I just meant Ginni was something we 205 needed to bait the hook—

JAYA: Hook! Fish!

VIRGIL: You misunderstand—

JAYA: You would eat us if you could—(*Painful pause.*) Maybe you . . . do? 210

VIRGIL: Do I look like someone who would eat another human being?

JAYA: You look like Jeetu but . . . you're not him. (*Slowly.*) So I don't know what you look like. I don't know what you are. 215

VIRGIL: This is what I look like, now.

JAYA: How can I believe you?

VIRGIL: Zhaya, *you've* lied to me—but *I've* told you only the truth.

JAYA: No!—they said you'd be old! And sick! 220

VIRGIL: I am old and I was sick until I got into this young body—

JAYA: They said you were a man—

VIRGIL: And I am! Always have been—

JAYA: But then you *looked* like a woman! You *spoke* like a 225 woman—

VIRGIL: Without being one. Without ever saying I was one—

JAYA: You said you wanted Om!

VIRGIL: No, I didn't ask for Auwm. He came to us.

JAYA: You said you wanted a healthy body— 230

VIRGIL: Yes, Zhaya—yours!

JAYA: (*Stops dead.*) Mine! But it was *Om* who got the job . . .

VIRGIL: He's part of the job, but not the job itself. (*Pause.*) We're interested in women where I live, Zhaya. Child-bearing women. 235

JAYA: But . . .

VIRGIL: So we look for young couples, without children—

JAYA: . . . Om said he wasn't married!

VIRGIL: His polygraph showed he lied. All donors lie. They think we need singles. We let them think that. That way 240 only the very desperate apply. That suits us. We search for skin and blood matches. Auwm matched mine.

JAYA: Yet you've taken *Jeetu's* body!

VIRGIL: Jittoo is Auwm's brother. He was an even better match— 245

JAYA: —and now you say that all the while you've wanted me! (*Shakes her head.*) What can I believe? You sew a crooked seam and call it straight!

(*There is a silence while he looks at her.*)

VIRGIL: But this seam now is true. We look for young men's bodies to live in and young women's bodies in which to 250 sow their children—

JAYA: Why! Don't you have your own?

VIRGIL: We . . . lost the art of having children.

JAYA: How can that be?

VIRGIL: We began to live longer and longer. And healthier 255 each generation. And more demanding—soon there was competition between one generation and the next—old against young, parent against child. (*Shrugs.*) We older ones had the advantage of experience. We prevailed. But our victory was bitter. We secured Paradise—at the cost of birds and flowers, bees and snakes! We were determined to make our amends. So we designed this programme. In exchange for the life support we offer poorer sections of the world, we gain fresh bodies for ourselves.

JAYA: (*Incredulous.*) And it works? You live forever?

VIRGIL: Not all of us—every year there are fewer of us. We fixed the car, but not the driver! Time comes when the driver just wanders off and (*Shrugs.*) . . . merges with the statistics. I'm one of the stubborn ones! This is my fourth body in fifty years.

JAYA: Fourth!

VIRGIL: Two were not successful. My first wife ran away. The third one kept her child. I saw him but never held him. Still . . . I'm willing to keep trying.

JAYA: (*She stares at him.*) I have never been with child.

VIRGIL: I know I can fill your belly.

(*There is a silence.*)

JAYA: (*Drops her gaze. Hushed.*) No . . .

VIRGIL: You have longed for a child. Your arms cry out for that sweet burden. To hold it in your arms, cuddle and crush it with kisses —it is your destiny as a woman—

JAYA: (*Tormented.*) NO! (*Wrings her hands.*) It was never meant to be! Years ago a seer told me—my stars denied it—

VIRGIL: Yet I sanction it, now, I. With Jittoo's body—

JAYA: (*In panic.*) No! Jeetu's dead and you're—you're a stranger's phantom—

VIRGIL: I am real and warm and willing. (*Pats himself.*) This body is hot with life and heavy with desire! This body aches for you and to give you what you yearn for—

JAYA: (*Covers her head against his words but pleased in spite of herself.*) No! A married woman must not hear such words from a stranger's mouth—

VIRGIL: But this mouth is no stranger to you, Zhaya!

JAYA: (*Whispering.*) No, no!

VIRGIL: This voice is but the latest tenant in a house that you have known—

JAYA: No—no—

VIRGIL: You deny the truth that is humming in my newly commissioned veins—

JAYA: Please—ohh . . . it's sinful—sinful!

VIRGIL: (*Bending to look in her face.*)—but . . . echoed in your pulse?

JAYA: (*Covering her face.*) It's madness you're offering me—madness!

VIRGIL: Is it madness to offer you your heart's desire?

JAYA: I had stopped hoping—I had ceased to dream—

VIRGIL: But you can start again. I am here to make it possible.

JAYA: But (*Her voice softens.*) whose child would it be . . . Jeetu's? Or . . . yours?

VIRGIL: (*Smiles.*) This is Jittoo's body!

JAYA: Yes—but—

VIRGIL: It would belong to this body—it would belong to Jittoo's body—

JAYA: But—would it be Jeetu's *child?* Would it look like him? Have his voice?

VIRGIL: No-one can say for certain which parent a child will take after—It could look like you, after all, have your voice.

JAYA: (*Looking perplexed she extends a hand wonderingly towards the apparition.*) Yes—but—(*Her hand passes through it and she recoils in horror.*)

VIRGIL: Ah-ah! Can't touch!

JAYA: Then—how . . . how—?

(*There is a knocking at the door.*)

GUARD 1: (*Indistinctly from the door.*) InterPlanta Services! Request permission to make contact!

JAYA: Ah!

VIRGIL: Don't—don't be frightened! It's just the agency. I can tell them to wait, if you want—(*He discreetly touches a small device at his waistband.*)

JAYA: Wait! Wait for what!

VIRGIL: For you to decide if you want to proceed—

JAYA: I don't understand! What are you saying—

VIRGIL: The guards will make the child possible Zhaya. It's just a formality; a device—

JAYA: What device!

VIRGIL: —an implant. Something I sent for you, which they're ready to deliver. But you can take your time. About two or three days are still within your fertile cycle—

JAYA: (*Shouting.*) What are you talking about! I told you—no more madness! Either you are here or—

VIRGIL: (*Patiently.*) Zhaya—I'd love to travel to be with you—

JAYA: Then do it! You who are so powerful—you who can travel from body to body—

VIRGIL: —but the risks of travelling across the world are too great! The world you live in is too dangerous for me, Zhaya—

JAYA: (*Outraged.*) Then you *are* a phantom after all! (*She raises her hands to strike the figure, then whirls towards the* CONTACT MODULE.) An illusion come to mock me—again! Again!

(*The* CONTACT MODULE *flicks easily out of her reach.*)

VIRGIL: I'll show you what to do, step by step. It's simple and it's painless—

JAYA: No! (*Leaping futilely at the globe, as the figure of* JEETU *watches tranquilly, at a distance.*) The pain tells me I'm alive! I want the pain!

VIRGIL: Then you can have all the pain you want, Zhaya—just as you want. It can take the usual nine months if you want, with diet and exercise and medical personnel to monitor you—

JAYA: (*She leaps at the globe, roaring in frustration.*) AR-RRHHH!

VIRGIL: —and I'll be with you, all the way—

JAYA: I believed you! I trusted you! (*In one of her leaps she jumps from a slight height and comes fractionally closer to the globe.*) But it was just one more of your crooked truths!

VIRGIL: Nothing I have said is untrue. I can set it up so that we can be together—go places—anywhere you want—right inside your room—

370 JAYA: I don't want your make-believe travels! I don't want your tricking comforts! (*She has stopped jumping and is looking around for something with which to strike the* CONTACT MODULE.)

375 VIRGIL: Zhaya we can even be . . . intimate, too! Really. But I thought you'd like to get to know me first—

JAYA: (*She starts to throw things up at the globe. Glasses, cushions, slippers, bottles, pill-boxes, gadgets.*) I don't want to know a ghost! (*The* CONTACT MODULE *moves, so her task isn't easy.*)
380 I want real hands touching me! I want to feel a real weight upon me! Hear your breath in my ear—feel my hair being pulled, sweat running in my mouth—

VIRGIL: And it's all possible—

JAYA: (*Sharply.*) No! Not without risking your skin! (*Shouting.*) Never! Do you hear me, whoever you are, wherever
385 you are? Never! Never! NEVER! (*With this, she strikes a direct hit.*) There is no closeness without risk!

(*There is a shower of sparks and a crack of electric light. Then the* CONTACT MODULE *goes dim. For a few seconds the lights in the whole room flicker, purple and blue. Then they stabilize.* JAYA *stands panting in the centre of the stage.* JEETU's *figure has vanished.*)

JAYA: (*Looking up, towards the darkened globe.*) You! Can you hear me?

(*From the door, a knocking.*)

GUARD 1: (*Through the door.*) InterPlanta Services! Request
390 permission to gain entry!

JAYA: (*To the* CONTACT MODULE.) Can you you hear me, You? I've forgotten your name—but it doesn't matter! You never bothered to say mine correctly anyway!

GUARD 1: (*Knocking.*) I repeat! Request permission to enter!
395 JAYA: (*To the* CONTACT MODULE.) Look: I'm not stupid, you know? I know you're stronger than me, you're richer than me. You'll get me in the end—I know you will. But I want you to risk your skin for me. Even though it's really Jeetu's skin—I want you to risk it. For me.
400 GUARD 1: (*Hammering at the door.*) Madam! Madam! We have an urgent message for you from your Receiver!

JAYA: Either that or—

GUARD 1: (*Sounds of mechanical activity at the door.*)—attaching external speaker—(*There is a scraping sound, a crackle.*)
405 JAYA: (*She grabs up a piece of broken glass.*)—you won't have me at all! In any sense!

GUARD 1: Speaker installed. Begin transmission . . .

VIRGIL: (*His voice is strained and crackled, but loud and clear enough that he is once more a presence in the room.*) Zhaya—
410 listen to me—*you can't hope to win this one!*

JAYA: I've discovered a new definition for winning. Winning by losing. I win if you lose.

VIRGIL: Zhaya, this is craziness—

JAYA: I'm sorry, you-whose-name-I-have-forgot—
415 VIRGIL: Virgil—

JAYA: It's your fault. If you want to play games with people, you should be careful not to push them off the board. You pushed me too far. Now there's nothing left for me to lose—
420 VIRGIL: —but your life, Zhaya! You still have your life ahead of you!

JAYA: What do I care about my life? You've shown me that it's not really mine any more. It's yours. I'm not willing to caretake *my* body for *your* sake! The only thing I have left
425 which is still mine is my death. My death and my pride—

VIRGIL: Zhaya—Zhaya—pride is nothing. Pride is a poor man's fancy dress—

JAYA: And if I let you take it from me, I will be naked as well as poor! Do you think I haven't understood you by now? You'll never let me have what you have, you're only will-
430 ing to share your electronic shadows with me, your night-visions, your "virtual" touch! No, no—if the only clothes I can afford are these rags of pride then let me have those! Unlike Om—unlike Ma—and Jeetu—

VIRGIL: Zhaya—don't make me tell the guards to force the
435 door—if you want respect, then open the door yourself

JAYA: You can't see me, can you? I'm holding a piece of glass against my throat. If you force the door, you will push this glass into my throat.

VIRGIL: Zhaya—the food you take contains anti-suicide drugs.
440 You are physically *incapable* of taking your own life—

JAYA: Test the strength of your drugs. Force that door.

VIRGIL: Zhaya—please! We've got this far—I love your spirit—I really do. In these months and weeks, I have come to admire you and care for you. Don't let me down now!
445 JAYA: Then risk your skin.

VIRGIL: (*Pause.*) You're being unreasonable—

JAYA: Is it unreasonable to ask one who has cheated death, to cross the oceans?

VIRGIL: Zhaya—
450 JAYA: I'm bored of this argument! Don't you understand? This game is over! Either you have to erase me and start again or . . . you must accept a new set of rules.

VIRGIL: (*Sulkily.*) This is ridiculous! This is blackmail—

JAYA: What use do I have for words like "blackmail" when I
455 hold my death in the palm of my hands?

VIRGIL: You're not so stupid as to think you can win against me, Zhaya—

JAYA: Stupid or not, if I lose my life, I win this game.

VIRGIL: You won't be alive to savour that victory—
460 JAYA: —but I'll die knowing that you, who live only to win, will have lost to a poor, weak and helpless woman. And I'll get more pleasure out of that first moment of death than I've had in my entire life so far!

VIRGIL: Zhaya, this is childish—
465 JAYA: You still can't see me?

VIRGIL: (*Pause.*) No—but I can get a camera—

JAYA: No, don't. I'll tell you what I'm doing (*Matches her actions to her words.*). I'm collecting all the pills and medicines I can find. I'm going to take the ones for staying awake,
470 until I run out of them. If I don't hear the sound of your own hand on my door before that time, I'll take my life. If the guards cause me any discomfort whatsoever—I'll take my life. If you do anything at all other than come here in person—I'll take my life!
475 VIRGIL: Zhaya—

JAYA: And in the meantime, I want you to practise saying my name correctly: It's Jaya—"j" as in "justice", "j" as in "jam"—
480 VIRGIL: Zhaya—

JAYA: I won't talk to you unless you say it right!

VIRGIL: (*Pause.*) Zh . . . Jaya. Jaya. Jaya—listen to me—

JAYA: No! You listen to me! I want to be left alone—truly
alone. I don't want to hear any sounds, I don't want any
485 disturbances. I'm going to take my pills, watch TV, have a
dozen baths a day, eat for three instead of one. For the first
time in my life and maybe the last time of my life, I'm going to enjoy myself, all by myself. I suggest you take some
rest. You have a long journey ahead of you and it's sure to
490 be a hard one.

(*Lights dim out as* JAYA *settles down comfortably in front of the television, bolstered by cushions. She looks happy and relaxed. She
points the remote and turns the sound up loud. Rich, joyous music
fills the room.*)

FINAL CURTAIN

CRITICAL CONTEXTS

FRANTZ FANON (1925–1961)

"The Fact of Blackness" (1952)

Frantz Fanon was perhaps the seminal theoretician of postcolonial politics, culture, and identity; his two major books, Black Skin, White Masks *(1952) and* The Wretched of the Earth *(1961), have been widely read and have provided an important inspiration for liberation movements around the world. Born in Martinique, Fanon studied medicine in Paris and became a psychiatrist in Algeria during its wars of liberation from France. "The Fact of Blackness" is Fanon's celebrated essay describing the consciousness of "black" subjects in a world of "white" power.*

"Dirty nigger!" Or simply, "Look, a Negro!"

I came into the world imbued with the will to find a meaning in things, my spirit filled with the desire to attain to the source of the world, and then I found that I was an object in the midst of other objects.

Sealed into that crushing objecthood, I turned beseechingly to others. Their attention was a liberation, running over my body suddenly abraded into nonbeing, endowing me once more with an agility that I had thought lost, and by taking me out of the world, restoring me to it. But just as I reached the other side, I stumbled, and the movements, the attitudes, the glances of the other fixed me there, in the sense in which a chemical solution is fixed by a dye. I was indignant; I demanded an explanation. Nothing happened. I burst apart. Now the fragments have been put together again by another self.

As long as the black man is among his own, he will have no occasion, except in minor internal conflicts, to experience his being through others. There is of course the moment of "being for others," of which Hegel speaks, but every ontology is made unattainable in a colonized and civilized society. It would seem that this fact has not been given sufficient attention by those who have discussed the question. In the *Weltanschauung* of a colonized people there is an impurity, a flaw that outlaws any ontological explanation. Someone may object that this is the case with every individual, but such an objection merely conceals a basic problem. Ontology—once it is finally admitted as leaving existence by the wayside—does not permit us to understand the being of the black man. For not only must the black man be black; he must be black in relation to the white man. Some critics will take it on themselves to remind us that this proposition has a converse. I say that this is false. The black man has no ontological resistance in the eyes of the white man. Overnight the Negro has been given two frames of reference within which he has had to place himself. His metaphysics, or, less pretentiously, his customs and the sources on which they were based, were

wiped out because they were in conflict with a civilization that he did not know and that imposed itself on him.

The black man among his own in the twentieth century does not know at what moment his inferiority comes into being through the other. Of course I have talked about the black problem with friends, or, more rarely, with American Negroes. Together we protested, we asserted the equality of all men in the world. In the Antilles there was also that little gulf that exists among the almost-white, the mulatto, and the nigger. But I was satisfied with an intellectual understanding of these differences. It was not really dramatic. And then. . . .

And then the occasion arose when I had to meet the white man's eyes. An unfamiliar weight burdened me. The real world challenged my claims. In the white world the man of color encounters difficulties in the development of his bodily schema. Consciousness of the body is solely a negating activity. It is a third-person consciousness. The body is surrounded by an atmosphere of certain uncertainty. I know that if I want to smoke, I shall have to reach out my right arm and take the pack of cigarettes lying at the other end of the table. The matches, however, are in the drawer on the left, and I shall have to lean back slightly. And all these movements are made not out of habit but out of implicit knowledge. A slow composition of my *self* as a body in the middle of a spatial and temporal world—such seems to be the schema. It does not impose itself on me; it is, rather, a definitive structuring of the self and of the world—definitive because it creates a real dialectic between my body and the world.

For several years certain laboratories have been trying to produce a serum for "denegrification"; with all the earnestness in the world, laboratories have sterilized their test tubes, checked their scales, and embarked on researches that might make it possible for the miserable Negro to whiten himself and thus to throw off the burden of that corporeal malediction. Below the corporeal schema I had sketched a historico-racial schema. The elements that I used had been provided for me not by "residual sensations and perceptions primarily of a tactile, vestibular, kinesthetic, and visual character,"[1] but by the other, the white man, who had woven me out of a thousand details, anecdotes, stories. I thought that what I had in hand was to construct a physiological self, to balance space, to localize sensations, and here I was called on for more.

"Look, a Negro!" It was an external stimulus that flicked over me as I passed by. I made a tight smile.

"Look, a Negro!" It was true. It amused me.

"Look, a Negro!" The circle was drawing a bit tighter. I made no secret of my amusement.

"Mama, see the Negro! I'm frightened!" Frightened! Frightened! Now they were beginning to be afraid of me. I made up my mind to laugh myself to tears, but laughter had become impossible.

I could no longer laugh, because I already knew that there were legends, stories, history, and above all *historicity*, which I had learned about from Jaspers. Then, assailed at various points, the corporeal schema crumbled, its place taken by a racial epidermal schema. In the train it was no longer a question of being aware of my body in the third person but in a triple person. In the train I was given not one but two, three places. I had already stopped being amused. It was not that I was finding febrile coordinates in the world. I existed triply: I occupied space. I moved toward the other . . . and the evanescent other, hostile but not opaque, transparent, not there, disappeared. Nausea. . . .

I was responsible at the same time for my body, for my race, for my ancestors. I subjected myself to an objective examination, I discovered my blackness, my ethnic characteristics; and I was battered down by tom-toms, cannibalism, intellectual deficiency, fetishism, racial defects, slave-ships, and above all else, above all: "Sho' good eatin'."

On that day, completely dislocated, unable to be abroad with the other, the white man, who unmercifully imprisoned me, I took myself far off from my own presence, far indeed, and made myself an object. What else could it be for me but an amputation, an excision, a hemorrhage that spattered my whole body with black blood? But I did not want this revision, this thematization. All I wanted was to be a man among other men. I wanted to come lithe and young into a world that was ours and to help to build it together.

But I rejected all immunization of the emotions. I wanted to be a man, nothing but a man. Some identified me with ancestors of mine who had been enslaved or lynched: I decided

to accept this. It was on the universal level of the intellect that I understood this inner kinship—I was the grandson of slaves in exactly the same way in which President Lebrun was the grandson of tax-paying, hard-working peasants. In the main, the panic soon vanished.

In America, Negroes are segregated. In South America, Negroes are whipped in the streets, and Negro strikers are cut down by machine-guns. In West Africa, the Negro is an animal. And there beside me, my neighbor in the university, who was born in Algeria, told me: "As long as the Arab is treated like a man, no solution is possible."

"Understand, my dear boy, color prejudice is something I find utterly foreign. . . . But of course, come in, sir, there is no color prejudice among us. . . . Quite, the Negro is a man like ourselves. . . . It is not because he is black that he is less intelligent than we are. . . . I had a Senegalese buddy in the army who was really clever. . . ."

Where am I to be classified? Or, if you prefer, tucked away?

"A Martinican, a native of 'our' old colonies."

Where shall I hide?

"Look at the nigger! . . . Mama, a Negro! . . . Hell, he's getting mad. . . . Take no notice, sir, he does not know that you are as civilized as we. . . ."

My body was given back to me sprawled out, distorted, re-colored, clad in mourning in that white winter day. The Negro is an animal, the Negro is bad, the Negro is mean, the Negro is ugly; look, a nigger, it's cold, the nigger is shivering, the nigger is shivering because he is cold, the little boy is trembling because he is afraid of the nigger, the nigger is shivering with cold, that cold that goes through your bones, the handsome little boy is trembling because he thinks that the nigger is quivering with rage, the little white boy throws himself into his mother's arms: Mama, the nigger's going to eat me up.

All round me the white man, above the sky tears at its navel, the earth rasps under my feet, and there is a white song, a white song. All this whiteness that burns me. . . .

I sit down at the fire and I become aware of my uniform. I had not seen it. It is indeed ugly. I stop there, for who can tell me what beauty is?

Where shall I find shelter from now on? I felt an easily identifiable flood mounting out of the countless facets of my being. I was about to be angry. The fire was long since out, and once more the nigger was trembling.

"Look how handsome that Negro is! . . ."

"Kiss the handsome Negro's ass, madame!"

Shame flooded her face. At last I was set free from my rumination. At the same time I accomplished two things: I identified my enemies and I made a scene. A grand slam. Now one would be able to laugh.

---

[1] Jean Lhermitte, *L'Image de notre corps* (Paris: Nouvelle Revue critique, 1939), p. 17.

The field of battle having been marked out, I entered the lists.

What? While I was forgetting, forgiving, and wanting only to love, my message was flung back in my face like a slap. The white world, the only honorable one, barred me from all participation. A man was expected to behave like a man. I was expected to behave like a black man—or at least like a nigger. I shouted a greeting to the world and the world slashed away my joy. I was told to stay within bounds, to go back where I belonged.

They would see, then! I had warned them, anyway. Slavery? It was no longer even mentioned, that unpleasant memory. My supposed inferiority? A hoax that it was better to laugh at. I forgot it all, but only on condition that the world not protect itself against me any longer. I had incisors to test. I was sure they were strong. And besides. . . .

What! When it was I who had every reason to hate, to despise, I was rejected? When I should have been begged, implored, I was denied the slightest recognition? I resolved, since it was impossible for me to get away from an *inborn complex*, to assert myself as a BLACK MAN. Since the other hesitated to recognize me, there remained only one solution: to make myself known.

In *Anti-Semite and Jew* (p. 95), Sartre says: "They [the Jews] have allowed themselves to be poisoned by the stereotype that others have of them, and they live in fear that their acts will correspond to this stereotype. . . . We may say that their conduct is perpetually overdetermined from the inside."

All the same, the Jew can be unknown in his Jewishness. He is not wholly what he is. One hopes, one waits. His actions, his behavior are the final determinant. He is a white man, and, apart from some rather debatable characteristics, he can sometimes go unnoticed. He belongs to the race of those who since the beginning of time have never known cannibalism. What an idea, to eat one's father! Simple enough, one has only not to be a nigger. Granted, the Jews are harassed—what am I thinking of? They are hunted down, exterminated, cremated. But these are little family quarrels. The Jew is disliked from the moment he is tracked down. But in my case everything takes on a *new* guise. I am given no chance. I am overdetermined from without. I am the slave not of the "idea" that others have of me but of my own appearance.

I move slowly in the world, accustomed now to seek no longer for upheaval. I progress by crawling. And already I am being dissected under white eyes, the only real eyes. I am *fixed*. Having adjusted their microtomes, they objectively cut away slices of my reality. I am laid bare. I feel, I see in those white faces that it is not a new man who has come in, but a new kind of man, a new genus. Why, it's a Negro!

I slip into corners, and my long antennae pick up the catch-phrases strewn over the surface of things—nigger underwear smells of nigger—nigger teeth are white—nigger feet are big—the nigger's barrel chest—I slip into corners, I remain silent, I strive for anonymity, for invisibility. Look, I will accept the lot, as long as no one notices me!

"Oh, I want you to meet my black friend. . . . Aimé Césaire, a black man and a university graduate. . . . Marian Anderson, the finest of Negro singers. . . . Dr. Cobb, who invented white blood, is a Negro. . . . Here, say hello to my friend from Martinique (be careful, he's extremely sensitive). . . ."

Shame. Shame and self-contempt. Nausea. When people like me, they tell me it is in spite of my color. When they dislike me, they point out that it is not because of my color. Either way, I am locked into the infernal circle.

I turn away from these inspectors of the Ark before the Flood and I attach myself to my brothers, Negroes like myself. To my horror, they too reject me. They are almost white. And besides they are about to marry white women. They will have children faintly tinged with brown. Who knows, perhaps little by little. . . .

I had been dreaming.

"I want you to understand, sir, I am one of the best friends the Negro has in Lyon."

The evidence was there, unalterable. My blackness was there, dark and unarguable. And it tormented me, pursued me, disturbed me, angered me.

Negroes are savages, brutes, illiterates. But in my own case I knew that these statements were false. There was a myth of the Negro that had to be destroyed at all costs. The time had long since passed when a Negro priest was an occasion for wonder. We had physicians, professors, statesmen. Yes, but something out of the ordinary still clung to such cases. "We have a Senegalese history teacher. He is quite bright. . . . Our doctor is colored. He is very gentle."

It was always the Negro teacher, the Negro doctor; brittle as I was becoming, I shivered at the slightest pretext. I knew, for instance, that if the physician made a mistake it would be the end of him and of all those who came after him. What could one expect, after all, from a Negro physician? As long as everything went well, he was praised to the skies, but look out, no nonsense, under any conditions! The black physician can never be sure how close he is to disgrace. I tell you, I was walled in: No exception was made for my refined manners, or my knowledge of literature, or my understanding of the quantum theory.

I requested, I demanded explanations. Gently, in the tone that one uses with a child, they introduced me to the existence of a certain view that was held by certain people, but,

I was always told, "We must hope that it will very soon disappear." What was it? Color prejudice.

> It [colour prejudice] is nothing more than the unreasoning hatred of one race for another, the contempt of the stronger and richer peoples for those whom they consider inferior to themselves and the bitter resentment of those who are kept in subjection and are so frequently insulted. As colour is the most obvious outward manifestation of race it has been made the criterion by which men are judged, irrespective of their social or educational attainments. The light-skinned races have come to despise all those of a darker colour, and the dark-skinned peoples will no longer accept without protest the inferior position to which they have been relegated.[2]

I had read it rightly. It was hate; I was hated, despised, detested, not by the neighbor across the street or my cousin on my mother's side, but by an entire race. I was up against something unreasoned. The psychoanalysts say that nothing is more traumatizing for the young child than his encounters with what is rational. I would personally say that for a man whose only weapon is reason there is nothing more neurotic than contact with unreason.

I felt knife blades open within me. I resolved to defend myself. As a good tactician, I intended to rationalize the world and to show the white man that he was mistaken.

In the Jew, Jean-Paul Sartre says, there is

> a sort of impassioned imperialism of reason: for he wishes not only to convince others that he is right; his goal is to persuade them that there is an absolute and unconditioned value to rationalism. He feels himself to be a missionary of the universal; against the universality of the Catholic religion, from which he is excluded, he asserts the "catholicity" of the rational, an instrument by which to attain to the truth and establish a spiritual bond among men.[3]

And, the author adds, though there may be Jews who have made intuition the basic category of their philosophy, their intuition

> has no resemblance to the Pascalian subtlety of spirit, and it is this latter—based on a thousand imperceptible perceptions—which to the Jew seems his worst enemy. As for Bergson, his philosophy offers the curious appearance of an anti-intellectualist doctrine constructed entirely by the most rational and most critical of intelligences. It is through argument that he establishes the existence of pure duration, of philosophic intuition; and that very intuition which discovers duration or life, is itself universal, since anyone may practice it, and it leads toward the universal, since its objects can be named and conceived.[4]

With enthusiasm I set to cataloguing and probing my surroundings. As times changed, one had seen the Catholic religion at first justify and then condemn slavery and prejudices. But by referring everything to the idea of the dignity of man, one had ripped prejudice to shreds. After much reluctance, the scientists had conceded that the Negro was a human being; *in vivo* and *in vitro* the Negro had been proved analogous to the white man: the same morphology, the same histology. Reason was confident of victory on every level. I put all the parts back together. But I had to change my tune.

That victory played cat and mouse; it made a fool of me. As the other put it, when I was present, it was not; when it was there, I was no longer. In the abstract there was agreement: The Negro is a human being. That is to say, amended the less firmly convinced, that like us he has his heart on the left side. But on certain points the white man remained intractable. Under no conditions did he wish any intimacy between the races, for it is a truism that "crossings between widely different races can lower the physical and mental level. . . . Until we have a more definite knowledge of the effect of race-crossings we shall certainly do best to avoid crossings between widely different races."[5]

For my own part, I would certainly know how to react. And in one sense, if I were asked for a definition of myself, I would say that I am one who waits; I investigate my surroundings, I interpret everything in terms of what I discover, I become sensitive.

In the first chapter of the history that the others have compiled for me, the foundation of cannibalism has been made eminently plain in order that I may not lose sight of it. My chromosomes were supposed to have a few thicker or thinner genes representing cannibalism. In addition to the *sex-linked*, the scholars had now discovered the *racial-linked*.[6] What a shameful science!

But I understand this "psychological mechanism." For it is a matter of common knowledge that the mechanism is only psychological. Two centuries ago I was lost to humanity, I was a slave forever. And then came men who said that it all had gone on far too long. My tenaciousness did the rest; I was saved from the civilizing deluge. I have gone forward.

Too late. Everything is anticipated, thought out, demonstrated, made the most of. My trembling hands take hold of nothing; the vein has been mined out. Too late! But once again I want to understand.

---

[2]Sir Alan Burns, *Colour Prejudice* (London: Allen and Unwin, 1948), p. 16.

[3]*Anti-Semite and Jew* (New York: Grove Press, 1960), pp. 112–13.

[4]Ibid., p. 115.

[5]Jon Alfred Mjoen, "Harmonic and Disharmonic Race-crossings," *The Second International Congress of Eugenics* (1921), *Eugenics in Race and State*, vol. 2, p. 60, quoted in Sir Alan Burns, op. cit., p. 120.

[6]In English in the original (*Translator's note*).

Since the time when someone first mourned the fact that he had arrived too late and everything had been said, a nostalgia for the past has seemed to persist. Is this that lost original paradise of which Otto Rank speaks? How many such men, apparently rooted to the womb of the world, have devoted their lives to studying the Delphic oracles or exhausted themselves in attempts to plot the wanderings of Ulysses! The pan-spiritualists seek to prove the existence of a soul in animals by using this argument: A dog lies down on the grave of his master and starves to death there. We had to wait for Janet to demonstrate that the aforesaid dog, in contrast to man, simply lacked the capacity to liquidate the past. We speak of the glory of Greece, Artaud says; but, he adds, if modern man can no longer understand the *Choephoroi* of Aeschylus, it is Aeschylus who is to blame. It is tradition to which the anti-Semites turn in order to ground the validity of their "point of view." It is tradition, it is that long historical past, it is that blood relation between Pascal and Descartes, that is invoked when the Jew is told, "There is no possibility of your finding a place in society." Not long ago, one of those good Frenchmen said in a train where I was sitting: "Just let the real French virtues keep going and the race is safe. Now more than ever, national union must be made a reality. Let's have an end of internal strife! Let's face up to the foreigners (here he turned toward my corner) no matter who they are."

It must be said in his defense that he stank of cheap wine; if he had been capable of it, he would have told me that my emancipated-slave blood could not possibly be stirred by the name of Villon or Taine.

An outrage!

The Jew and I: Since I was not satisfied to be racialized, by a lucky turn of fate I was humanized. I joined the Jew, my brother in misery.

An outrage!

At first thought it may seem strange that the anti-Semite's outlook should be related to that of the Negro-phobe. It was my philosophy professor, a native of the Antilles, who recalled the fact to me one day: "Whenever you hear anyone abuse the Jews, pay attention, because he is talking about you." And I found that he was universally right—by which I meant that I was answerable in my body and in my heart for what was done to my brother. Later I realized that he meant, quite simply, an anti-Semite is inevitably anti-Negro.

You come too late, much too late. There will always be a world—a white world—between you and us. . . . The other's total inability to liquidate the past once and for all. In the face of this affective *ankylosis* of the white man, it is understandable that I could have made up my mind to utter my Negro cry. Little by little, putting out pseudopodia here and there, I secreted a race. And that race staggered under the burden of a basic element. What was it? *Rhythm!* Listen to our singer, Léopold Senghor:

> It is the thing that is most perceptible and least material. It is the archetype of the vital element. It is the first condition and the hallmark of Art, as breath is of life: breath, which accelerates or slows, which becomes even or agitated according to the tension in the individual, the degree and the nature of his emotion. This is rhythm in its primordial purity, this is rhythm in the masterpieces of Negro art, especially sculpture. It is composed of a theme—sculptural form—which is set in opposition to a sister theme, as inhalation is to exhalation, and that is repeated. It is not the kind of symmetry that gives rise to monotony; rhythm is alive, it is free. . . . This is how rhythm affects what is least intellectual in us, tyrannically, to make us penetrate to the spirituality of the object; and that character of abandon which is ours is itself rhythmic.[7]

Had I read that right? I read it again with redoubled attention. From the opposite end of the white world a magical Negro culture was hailing me. Negro sculpture! I began to flush with pride. Was this our salvation?

I had rationalized the world and the world had rejected me on the basis of color prejudice. Since no agreement was possible on the level of reason, I threw myself back toward unreason. It was up to the white man to be more irrational than I. Out of the necessities of my struggle I had chosen the method of regression, but the fact remained that it was an unfamiliar weapon; here I am at home; I am made of the irrational; I wade in the irrational. Up to the neck in the irrational. And now how my voice vibrates!

> Those who invented neither gunpowder nor the compass
> Those who never learned to conquer steam or electricity
> Those who never explored the seas or the skies
> But they know the farthest corners of the land of anguish
> Those who never knew any journey save that of abduction
> Those who learned to kneel in docility
> Those who were domesticated and Christianized
> Those who were injected with bastardy. . . .

Yes, all those are my brothers—a "bitter brotherhood" imprisons all of us alike. Having stated the minor thesis, I went overboard after something else.

> . . . But those without whom the earth would not be the earth
> Tumescence all the more fruitful
> than
> the empty land
> still more the land
> Storehouse to guard and ripen all
> on earth that is most earth
> My blackness is no stone, its deafness
> hurled against the clamor of the day

---

[7]"Ce que l'homme noir apporte," in Claude Nordey, *L'Homme de couleur* (Paris: Plon, 1939), pp. 309–310.

My blackness is no drop of lifeless water
on the dead eye of the world
My blackness is neither a tower nor a cathedral
It thrusts into the red flesh of the sun
It thrusts into the burning flesh of the sky
It hollows through the dense dismay of its own pillar of
patience.[8]

Eyah! the tom-tom chatters out the cosmic message. Only the Negro has the capacity to convey it, to decipher its meaning, its import. Astride the world, my strong heels spurring into the flanks of the world, I stare into the shoulders of the world as the celebrant stares at the midpoint between the eyes of the sacrificial victim.

But they abandon themselves, possessed, to the essence of all things, knowing nothing of externals but possessed by the movement of all things
uncaring to subdue but playing the play of the world
truly the eldest sons of the world
open to all the breaths of the world
meeting-place of all the winds of the world
undrained bed of all the waters of the world
spark of the sacred fire of the World
flesh of the flesh of the world, throbbing with the very movement of the world.[9]

Blood! Blood! . . . Birth! Ecstasy of becoming! Three-quarters engulfed in the confusions of the day, I feel myself redden with blood. The arteries of all the world, convulsed, torn away, uprooted, have turned toward me and fed me.

"Blood! Blood! All our blood stirred by the male heart of the sun."[10]

Sacrifice was a middle point between the creation and myself—now I went back no longer to sources but to The Source. Nevertheless, one had to distrust rhythm, earth-mother love, this mystic, carnal marriage of the group and the cosmos.

In *La vie sexuelle en Afrique noire,* a work rich in perceptions, De Pédrals implies that always in Africa, no matter what field is studied, it will have a certain magico-social structure. He adds:

All these are the elements that one finds again on a still greater scale in the domain of secret societies. To the extent, moreover, to which persons of either sex, subjected to circumcision during adolescence, are bound under penalty of death not to reveal to the uninitiated what they have experienced, and to the extent to which initiation into a secret society always excites to acts of *sa-*

cred love, there is good ground to conclude by viewing both male and female circumcision and the rites that they embellish as constitutive of minor secret societies.[11]

I walk on white nails. Sheets of water threaten my soul on fire. Face to face with these rites, I am doubly alert. Black magic! Orgies, witches' sabbaths, heathen ceremonies, amulets. Coitus is an occasion to call on the gods of the clan. It is a sacred act, pure, absolute, bringing invisible forces into action. What is one to think of all these manifestations, all these initiations, all these acts? From very direction I am assaulted by the obscenity of dances and of words. Almost at my ear there is a song:

First our hearts burned hot
Now they are cold
All we think of now is Love
When we return to the village
When we see the great phallus
Ah how then we will make Love
For our parts will be dry and clean.[12]

The soil, which only a moment ago was still a tamed steed, begins to revel. Are these virgins, these nymphomaniacs? Black Magic, primitive mentality, animism, animal eroticism, it all floods over me. All of it is typical of peoples that have not kept pace with the evolution of the human race. Or, if one prefers, this is humanity at its lowest. Having reached this point, I was long reluctant to commit myself. Aggression was in the stars. I had to choose. What do I mean? I had no choice. . . .

Yes, we are—we Negroes—backward, simple, free in our behavior. That is because for us the body is not something opposed to what you call the mind. We are in the world. And long live the couple, Man and Earth! Besides, our men of letters helped me to convince you; your white civilization overlooks subtle riches and sensitivity. Listen:

Emotive sensitivity. *Emotion is completely Negro as reason is Greek.*[13] Water rippled by every breeze? Unsheltered soul blown by every wind, whose fruit often drops before it is ripe? Yes, in one way, the Negro today is richer *in gifts than in works.*[14] But the tree thrusts its roots into the earth. The river runs deep, carrying precious seeds. And, the Afro-American poet, Langston Hughes, says:
I have known rivers
ancient dark rivers

---

[8]Aimé Césaire, *Cahier d'un retour au pays natal* (Paris: Présence Africaine, 1956), pp. 77–78.

[9]Ibid., p. 78.

[10]Ibid., p. 79.

[11]De Pédrals, *La vie sexuelle en Afrique noire* (Paris: Payot), p. 83.

[12]A. M. Vergiat, *Les rites secrets des primitifs de l'Oubangui* (Paris: Payot, 1951), p. 113.

[13]My italics—F.F.

[14]My italics—F.F.

my soul has grown deep
like the deep rivers.
The very nature of the Negro's emotion, of his sensitivity, furthermore, explains his attitude toward the object perceived with such basic intensity. It is an abandon that becomes need, an active state of communion, indeed of identification, however negligible the action—I almost said the personality—of the object. A rhythmic attitude: The adjective should be kept in mind.[15]

So here we have the Negro rehabilitated, "standing before the bar," ruling the world with his intuition, the Negro recognized, set on his feet again, sought after, taken up, and he is a Negro—no, he is not a Negro but the Negro, exciting the fecund antennae of the world, placed in the foreground of the world, raining his poetic power on the world, "open to all the breaths of the world." I embrace the world! I am the world! The white man has never understood this magic substitution. The white man wants the world; he wants it for himself alone. He finds himself predestined master of this world. He enslaves it. An acquisitive relation is established between the world and him. But there exist other values that fit only my forms. Like a magician, I robbed the white man of "a certain world," forever after lost to him and his. When that happened, the white man must have been rocked backward by a force that he could not identify, so little used as he is to such reactions. Somewhere beyond the objective world of farms and banana trees and rubber trees, I had subtly brought the real world into being. The essence of the world was my fortune. Between the world and me a relation of coexistence was established. I had discovered the primeval One. My "speaking hands" tore at the hysterical throat of the world. The white man had the anguished feeling that I was escaping from him and that I was taking something with me. He went through my pockets. He thrust probes into the least circumvolution of my brain. Everywhere he found only the obvious. So it was obvious that I had a secret. I was interrogated; turning away with an air of mystery, I murmured:

Tokowaly, uncle, do you remember the nights gone by
When my head weighed heavy on the back of your patience or
Holding my hand your hand led me by shadows and signs
The fields are flowers of glowworms, stars hang on the bushes, on the trees
Silence is everywhere
Only the scents of the jungle hum, swarms of reddish bees that overwhelm the crickets' shrill sounds,
And covered tom-tom, breathing in the distance of the night.

You, Tokowaly, you listen to what cannot be heard, and you explain to me what the†ancestors are saying in the liquid calm of the constellations,
The bull, the scorpion, the leopard, the elephant, and the fish we know,
And the white pomp of the Spirits in the heavenly shell that has no end,
But now comes the radiance of the goddess Moon and the veils of the shadows fall.
Night of Africa, my black night, mystical and bright, black and shining.[16]

I made myself the poet of the world. The white man had found a poetry in which there was nothing poetic. The soul of the white man was corrupted, and, as I was told by a friend who was a teacher in the United States, "The presence of the Negroes beside the whites is in a way an insurance policy on humanness. When the whites feel that they have become too mechanized, they turn to the men of color and ask them for a little human sustenance." At last I had been recognized, I was no longer a zero.

I had soon to change my tune. Only momentarily at a loss, the white man explained to me that, genetically, I represented a stage of development: "Your properties have been exhausted by us. We have had earth mystics such as you will never approach. Study our history and you will see how far this fusion has gone." Then I had the feeling that I was repeating a cycle. My originality had been torn out of me. I wept a long time, and then I began to live again. But I was haunted by a galaxy of erosive stereotypes: the Negro's *sui generis* odor . . . the Negro's *sui generis* good nature . . . the Negro's *sui generis* gullibility. . . .

I had tried to flee myself through my kind, but the whites had thrown themselves on me and hamstrung me. I tested the limits of my essence; beyond all doubt there was not much of it left. It was here that I made my most remarkable discovery. Properly speaking, this discovery was a rediscovery.

I rummaged frenetically through all the antiquity of the black man. What I found there took away my breath. In his book *L'abolition de l'esclavage* Schoelcher presented us with compelling arguments. Since then, Frobenius, Westermann, Delafosse—all of them white—had joined the chorus: Ségou, Djenné, cities of more than a hundred thousand people; accounts of learned blacks (doctors of theology who went to Mecca to interpret the Koran). All of that, exhumed from the past, spread with its insides out, made it possible for me to find a valid historic place. The white man was wrong, I was not a primitive, not even a half-man, I belonged to a race

---

[15]Léopold Senghor, "Ce que l'homme noir apporte," in Nordey, op. cit., p. 205.

[16]Léopold Senghor, *Chants d'ombre* (Paris: Editions du Seuil, 1945).

that had already been working in gold and silver two thousand years ago. And too there was something else, something else that the white man could not understand. Listen:

What sort of men were these, then, who had been torn away from their families, their countries, their religions, with a savagery unparalleled in history?

Gentle men, polite, considerate, unquestionably superior to those who tortured them—that collection of adventurers who slashed and violated and spat on Africa to make the stripping of her the easier.

The men they took away knew how to build houses, govern empires, erect cities, cultivate fields, mine for metals, weave cotton, forge steel.

Their religion had its own beauty, based on mystical connections with the founder of the city. Their customs were pleasing, built on unity, kindness, respect for age.

No coercion, only mutual assistance, the joy of living, a free acceptance of discipline.

Order—Earnestness—Poetry and Freedom.

From the untroubled private citizen to the almost fabulous leader there was an unbroken chain of understanding and trust. No science? Indeed yes; but also, to protect them from fear, they possessed great myths in which 'the most subtle observation and the most daring imagination were balanced and blended. No art? They had their magnificent sculpture, in which human feeling erupted so unrestrained yet always followed the obsessive laws of rhythm in its organization of the major elements of a material called upon to capture, in order to redistribute, the most secret forces of the universe. . . .[17]

Monuments in the very heart of Africa? Schools? Hospitals? Not a single good burgher of the twentieth century, no Durand, no Smith, no Brown even suspects that such things existed in Africa before the Europeans came. . . .

But Schoelcher reminds us of their presence, discovered by Caillé, Mollien, the Cander brothers. And, though he nowhere reminds us that when the Portuguese landed on the banks of the Congo in 1498, they found a rich and flourishing state there and that the courtiers of Ambas were dressed in robes of silk and brocade, at least he knows that Africa had brought itself up to a juridical concept of the state, and he is aware, living in the very flood of imperialism, that European civilization, after all, is only one more civilization among many—and not the most merciful.[18]

I put the white man back into his place; growing bolder, I jostled him and told him point-blank, "Get used to me, I am not getting used to anyone." I shouted my laughter to the stars. The white man, I could see, was resentful. His reaction time lagged interminably. . . . I had won. I was jubilant.

"Lay aside your history, your investigations of the past, and try to feel yourself into our rhythm. In a society such as ours, industrialized to the highest degree, dominated by scientism, there is no longer room for your sensitivity. One must be tough if one is to be allowed to live. What matters now is no longer playing the game of the world but subjugating it with integers and atoms. Oh, certainly, I will be told, now and then when we are worn out by our lives in big buildings, we will turn to you as we do to our children—to the innocent, the ingenuous, the spontaneous. We will turn to you as to the childhood of the world. You are so real in your life—so funny, that is. Let us run away for a little while from our ritualized, polite civilization and let us relax, bend to those heads, those adorably expressive faces. In a way, you reconcile us with ourselves."

Thus my unreason was countered with reason, my reason with "real reason." Every hand was a losing hand for me. I analyzed my heredity. I made a complete audit of my ailment. I wanted to be typically Negro—it was no longer possible. I wanted to be white—that was a joke. And, when I tried, on the level of ideas and intellectual activity, to reclaim my negritude, it was snatched away from me. Proof was presented that my effort was only a term in the dialectic:

But there is something more important: The Negro, as we have said, creates an anti-racist racism for himself. In no sense does he wish to rule the world: He seeks the abolition of all ethnic privileges, wherever they come from; he asserts his solidarity with the oppressed of all colors. At once the subjective, existential, ethnic idea of *negritude* "passes," as Hegel puts it, into the objective, positive, exact idea of proletariat. "For Césaire," Senghor says, "the white man is the symbol of capital as the Negro is that of labor. . . . Beyond the black-skinned men of his race it is the battle of the world proletariat that is his song."

That is easy to say, but less easy to think out. And undoubtedly it is no coincidence that the most ardent poets of negritude are at the same time militant Marxists.

But that does not prevent the idea of race from mingling with that of class: The first is concrete and particular, the second is universal and abstract; the one stems from what Jaspers calls understanding and the other from intellection; the first is the result of a psychobiological syncretism and the second is a methodical construction based on experience. In fact, negritude appears as the minor term of a dialectical progression: The theoretical and practical assertion of the supremacy of the white man is its thesis; the position of negritude as an antithetical value is the moment of negativity. But this negative moment is insufficient by itself, and the Negroes who employ it know this very well; they know that it is intended to prepare the synthesis or realization of the human in a society without races. Thus negritude is the root of its own destruction, it is a transition and not a conclusion, a means and not an ultimate end.[19]

When I read that page, I felt that I had been robbed of my last chance. I said to my friends, "The generation of the younger black poets has just suffered a blow that can never

[17]Aimé Césaire, Introduction to Victor Schoelcher, *Esclavage et colonisation* (Paris: Presses Universitaires de France, 1948), p. 7.

[18]Ibid., p. 8.

[19]Jean-Paul Sartre, *Orphée Noir*, preface to *Anthologie de la nouvelle poésie nègre et malgache* (Paris: Presses Universitaires de France, 1948), pp. xl ff.

be forgiven." Help had been sought from a friend of the colored peoples, and that friend had found no better response than to point out the relativity of what they were doing. For once, that born Hegelian had forgotten that consciousness has to lose itself in the night of the absolute, the only condition to attain to consciousness of self. In opposition to rationalism, he summoned up the negative side, but he forgot that this negativity draws its worth from an almost substantive absoluteness. A consciousness committed to experience is ignorant, has to be ignorant, of the essences and the determinations of its being.

Orphée Noir is a date in the intellectualization of the *experience* of being black. And Sartre's mistake was not only to seek the source of the source but in a certain sense to block that source:

> Will the source of Poetry be dried up? Or will the great black flood, in spite of everything, color the sea into which it pours itself? It does not matter: Every age has its own poetry; in every age the circumstances of history choose a nation, a race, a class to take up the torch by creating situations that can be expressed or transcended only through Poetry; sometimes the poetic impulse coincides with the revolutionary impulse, and sometimes they take different courses. Today let us hail the turn of history that will make it possible for the black men to utter "the great Negro cry with a force that will shake the pillars of the world" (Césaire).[20]

And so it is not I who make a meaning for myself, but it is the meaning that was already there, pre-existing, waiting for me. It is not out of my bad nigger's misery, my bad nigger's teeth, my bad nigger's hunger that I will shape a torch with which to burn down the world, but it is the torch that was already there, waiting for that turn of history.

In terms of consciousness, the black consciousness is held out as an absolute density, as filled with itself, a stage preceding any invasion, any abolition of the ego by desire. Jean-Paul Sartre, in this work, has destroyed black zeal. In opposition to historical becoming, there had always been the unforeseeable. I needed to lose myself completely in negritude. One day, perhaps, in the depths of that unhappy romanticism. . . .

In any case I *needed* not to know. This struggle, this new decline had to take on an aspect of completeness. Nothing is more unwelcome than the commonplace: "You'll change, my boy; I was like that too when I was young . . . you'll see, it will all pass."

The dialectic that brings necessity into the foundation of my freedom drives me out of myself. It shatters my unreflected position. Still in terms of consciousness, black consciousness is immanent in its own eyes. I am not a poten-

tiality of something, I am wholly what I am. I do not have to look for the universal. No probability has any place inside me. My Negro consciousness does not hold itself out as a lack. It is. It is its own follower.

But, I will be told, your statements show a misreading of the processes of history. Listen then:

> Africa I have kept your memory Africa
> you are inside me
> Like the splinter in the wound
> like a guardian fetish in the center of the village
> make me the stone in your sling
> make my mouth the lips of your wound
> make my knees the broken pillars of your abasement
> AND YET
> I want to be of your race alone
> workers peasants of all lands . . .
> . . . white worker in Detroit black peon in Alabama
> uncountable nation in capitalist slavery
> destiny ranges us shoulder to shoulder
> repudiating the ancient maledictions of blood taboos
> we roll away the ruins of our solitudes
> If the flood is a frontier
> we will strip the gully of its endless
> covering flow
> If the Sierra is a frontier
> we will smash the jaws of the volcanoes
> upholding the Cordilleras
> and the plain will be the parade ground of the dawn
> where we regroup our forces sundered
> by the deceits of our masters
> As the contradiction among the features
> creates the harmony of the face
> we proclaim the oneness of the suffering
> and the revolt
> of all the peoples on all the face of the earth
>   and we mix the mortar of the age of brotherhood
>   out of the dust of idols.[21]

Exactly, we will reply, Negro experience is not a whole, for there is not merely one Negro, there are *Negroes*. What a difference, for instance, in this other poem:

> The white man killed my father
> Because my father was proud
> The white man raped my mother
> Because my mother was beautiful
> The white man wore out my brother in the hot sun of the roads
> Because my brother was strong
> Then the white man came to me
> His hands red with blood
> Spat his contempt into my black face
> Out of his tyrant's voice:
> "Hey boy, a basin, a towel, water."[22]

---

[20]Ibid., p. xliv.

[21]Jacques Roumain, "Bois d'Ebène," *Prelude*, in *Anthologie de la nouvelle poésie nègre et malgache*, p. 113.

[22]David Diop, "Le temps du martyre," ibid., p. 174.

Or this other one:

> My brother with teeth that glisten at the compliments of hypocrites
> My brother with gold-rimmed spectacles
> Over eyes that turn blue at the sound of the Master's voice
> My poor brother in dinner jacket with its silk lapels
> Clucking and whispering and strutting through the drawing rooms of Condescension
> How pathetic you are
> The sun of your native country is nothing more now than a shadow
> On your composed civilized face
> And your grandmother's hut
> Brings blushes into cheeks made white by years of abasement and Mea culpa
> But when regurgitating the flood of lofty empty words
> Like the load that presses on your shoulders
> You walk again on the rough red earth of Africa
> These words of anguish will state the rhythm of your uneasy gait
> I feel so alone, so alone here![23]

From time to time one would like to stop. To state reality is a wearing task. But, when one has taken it into one's head to try to express existence, one runs the risk of finding only the nonexistent. What is certain is that, at the very moment when I was trying to grasp my own being, Sartre, who remained The Other, gave me a name and thus shattered my last illusion. While I was saying to him

> My negritude is neither a tower nor a cathedral,
> it thrusts into the red flesh of the sun,
> it thrusts into the burning flesh of the sky,
> it hollows through the dense dismay of its own pillar of patience . . .

while I was shouting that, in the paroxysm of my being and my fury, he was reminding me that my blackness was only a minor term. In all truth, in all truth I tell you, my shoulders slipped out of the framework of the world, my feet could no longer feel the touch of the ground. Without a Negro past, without a Negro future, it was impossible for me to live my Negrohood. Not yet white, no longer wholly black, I was damned. Jean-Paul Sartre had forgotten that the Negro suffers in his body quite differently from the white man.[24] Between the white man and me the connection was irrevocably one of transcendence.[25]

---

[23]David Diop, "Le Renégat."

[24]Though Sartre's speculations on the existence of The Other may be correct (to the extent, we must remember, to which *Being and Nothingness* describes an alienated consciousness), their application to a black consciousness proves fallacious. That is because the white man is not only The Other but also the master, whether real or imaginary.

[25]In the sense in which the word is used by Jean Wahl in *Existence humaine et transcendance* (Neuchâtel: La Baconnière, 1944).

But the constancy of my love had been forgotten. I defined myself as an absolute intensity of beginning. So I took up my negritude, and with tears in my eyes I put its machinery together again. What had been broken to pieces was rebuilt, reconstructed by the intuitive lianas of my hands.

My cry grew more violent: I am a Negro, I am a Negro, I am a Negro. . . .

And there was my poor brother—living out his neurosis to the extreme and finding himself paralyzed:

> THE NEGRO: I can't, ma'am.
> LIZZIE: Why not?
> THE NEGRO: I can't shoot white folks.
> LIZZIE: Really! That would bother them, wouldn't it?
> THE NEGRO: They're white folks, ma'am.
> LIZZIE: So what? Maybe they got a right to bleed you like a pig just because they're white?
> THE NEGRO: But they're white folks.

A feeling of inferiority? No, a feeling of nonexistence. Sin is Negro as virtue is white. All those white men in a group, guns in their hands, cannot be wrong. I am guilty. I do not know of what, but I know that I am no good.

> THE NEGRO: That's how it goes, ma'am. That's how it always goes with white folks.
> LIZZIE: You too? You feel guilty?
> THE NEGRO: Yes, ma'am.[26]

It is Bigger Thomas—he is afraid, he is terribly afraid. He is afraid, but of what is he afraid? Of himself. No one knows yet who he is, but he knows that fear will fill the world when the world finds out. And when the world knows, the world always expects something of the Negro. He is afraid lest the world know, he is afraid of the fear that the world would feel if the world knew. Like that old woman on her knees who begged me to tie her to her bed:

"I just know, Doctor: Any minute that thing will take hold of me."

"What thing?"

"The wanting to kill myself. Tie me down, I'm afraid."

In the end, Bigger Thomas acts. To put an end to his tension, he acts, he responds to the world's anticipation.[27]

So it is with the character in *If He Hollers Let Him Go*[28]—who does precisely what he did not want to do. That big blonde who was always in his way, weak, sensual, offered, open, fearing (desiring) rape, became his mistress in the end.

---

[26]Jean-Paul Sartre, *The Respectful Prostitute,* in *Three Plays* (New York: Knopf, 1949), pp. 189, 191. Originally, *La Putain respectueuse* (Paris: Gallimard, 1947). See also *Home of the Brave,* a film by Mark Robson.

[27]Richard Wright, *Native Son* (New York: Harper, 1940).

[28]By Chester Himes (Garden City: Doubleday, 1945).

The Negro is a toy in the white man's hands; so, in order to shatter the hellish cycle, he explodes. I cannot go to a film without seeing myself. I wait for me. In the interval, just before the film starts, I wait for me. The people in the theater are watching me, examining me, waiting for me. A Negro groom is going to appear. My heart makes my head swim.

The crippled veteran of the Pacific war says to my brother, "Resign yourself to your color the way I got used to my stump; we're both victims."[29]

Nevertheless with all my strength I refuse to accept that amputation. I feel in myself a soul as immense as the world, truly a soul as deep as the deepest of rivers, my chest has the power to expand without limit. I am a master and I am advised to adopt the humility of the cripple. Yesterday, awakening to the world, I saw the sky turn upon itself utterly and wholly. I wanted to rise, but the disemboweled silence fell back upon me, its wings paralyzed. Without responsibility, straddling Nothingness and Infinity, I began to weep.

---

[29] *Home of the Brave*, op. cit.

HOMI K. BHABHA

"Of Mimicry and Man: The Ambivalence of Colonial Discourse" (1984)

Homi K. Bhabha is a leading theorist of postcolonial literature and culture, and is the author of The Location of Culture *(1994) and editor of* Nation and Narration *(1990). In "Of Mimicry and Man," Bhabha considers how notions of imitation and performance structure the relations of power and legitimation between colonized peoples and their colonizers. Although Bhabha makes a very dense argument here and uses a specialized critical vocabulary, several of his key terms and principles emerge clearly, particularly the ways in which "mimicry" can be seen to have a resistant force. How does Bhabha adapt the discourse of psychoanalysis to a critique of the formation of political subjects? What are the dynamics of mimicry in the colonial state? Do they operate in the same ways in the imperial metropole? Is it possible to use Bhabha's dynamic model to discuss the "interpellation" of characters in contemporary drama—Owen in Friel's* Translations, *for example, or even Om in Padmanabhan's* Harvest?

Mimicry reveals something insofar as it is distinct from what might be called an itself that is behind. The effect of mimicry is camouflage.... It is not a question of harmonizing with the background, but against a mottled background, of becoming mottled—exactly like the technique of camouflage practised in human warfare.

Jacques Lacan,
"The Line and Light," *Of the Gaze*

It is out of season to question at this time of day, the original policy of conferring on every colony of the British Empire a mimic representation of the British Constitution. But if the creature so endowed has sometimes forgotten its real insignificance and under the fancied importance of speakers and maces, and all the paraphernalia and ceremonies of the imperial legislature, has dared to defy the mother country, she has to thank herself for the folly of conferring such privileges on a condition of society that has no earthly claim to so exalted a position. A fundamental principle appears to have been forgotten or overlooked in our system of colonial policy—that of colonial dependence. To give to a colony the forms of independence is a mockery; she would not be a colony for a single hour if she could maintain an independent station.

Sir Edward Cust,
"Reflections on West African Affairs . . .
Addressed to the Colonial Office,"
Hatchard, London 1839

The discourse of post-Enlightenment English colonialism often speaks in a tongue that is forked, not false. If colonialism takes power in the name of history, it repeatedly exercises its authority through the figures of farce. For the epic intention of the civilizing mission, "human and not wholly human" in the famous words of Lord Rosebery, "writ by the finger of the Divine"[1] often produces a text rich in the traditions of *trompe l'oeil*, irony, mimicry, and repetition. In this comic turn from the high ideals of the colonial imagination to its low mimetic literary effects, mimicry emerges as one of

---

This paper was first presented as a contribution to a panel on "Colonialist and Post-Colonialist Discourse," organized by Gayatri Chakravorty Spivak for the Modern Language Association Convention in New York, December 1983. I would like to thank Professor Spivak for inviting me to participate on the panel and Dr. Stephan Feuchtwang for his advice in the preparation of the paper.

[1] Cited in Eric Stokes, *The Political Ideas of English Imperialism* (Oxford: Oxford University Press, 1960), pp. 17–18.

the most elusive and effective strategies of colonial power and knowledge.

Within that conflictual economy of colonial discourse which Edward Said[2] describes as the tension between the synchronic panoptical vision of domination—the demand for identity, stasis—and the counter-pressure of the diachrony of history—change, difference—mimicry represents an *ironic* compromise. If I may adapt Samuel Weber's formulation of the marginalizing vision of castration,[3] then colonial mimicry is the desire for a reformed, recognizable Other, as *a subject of a difference that is almost the same, but not quite.* Which is to say, that the discourse of mimicry is constructed around an *ambivalence:* in order to be effective, mimicry must continually produce its slippage, its excess, its difference. The authority of that mode of colonial discourse that I have called mimicry is therefore stricken by an indeterminacy: mimicry emerges as the representation of a difference that is itself a process of disavowal. Mimicry is, thus, the sign of a double articulation; a complex strategy of reform, regulation, and discipline, which "appropriates" the Other as it visualizes power. Mimicry is also the sign of the inappropriate, however, a difference or recalcitrance which coheres the dominant strategic function of colonial power, intensifies surveillance, and poses an immanent threat to both "normalized" knowledges and disciplinary powers.

The effect of mimicry on the authority of colonial discourse is profound and disturbing. For in "normalizing" the colonial state or subject, the dream of post-Enlightenment civility alienates its own language of liberty and produces another knowledge of its norms. The ambivalence which thus informs this strategy is discernible, for example, in Locke's *Second Treatise* which *splits* to reveal the limitations of liberty in his double use of the word "slave": first simply, descriptively as the locus of a legitimate form of ownership, then as the trope for an intolerable, illegitimate exercise of power. What is articulated in that distance between the two uses is the absolute, imagined difference between the "Colonial" State of Carolina and the Original State of Nature.

It is from this area between mimicry and mockery, where the reforming, civilizing mission is threatened by the displacing gaze of its disciplinary double, that my instances of colonial imitation come. What they all share is a discursive process by which the excess or slippage produced by the *ambivalence* of mimicry (almost the same, *but not quite*) does

not merely "rupture" the discourse, but becomes transformed into an uncertainty which fixes the colonial subject as a "partial" presence. By "partial" I mean both "incomplete" and "virtual." It is as if the very emergence of the "colonial" is dependent for its representation upon some strategic limitation or prohibition *within* the authoritative discourse itself. The success of colonial appropriation depends on a proliferation of inappropriate objects that ensure its strategic failure, so that mimicry is at once resemblance and menace.

A classic text of such partiality is Charles Grant's "Observations on the State of Society among the Asiatic Subjects of Great Britain" (1792)[4] which was only superseded by James Mills's *History of India* as the most influential early nineteenth-century account of Indian manners and morals. Grant's dream of an evangelical system of mission education conducted uncompromisingly in English was partly a belief in political reform along Christian lines and partly an awareness that the expansion of company rule in India required a system of "interpellation"—a reform of manners, as Grant put it, that would provide the colonial with "a sense of personal identity as we know it." Caught between the desire for religious reform and the fear that the Indians might become turbulent for liberty, Grant implies that it is, in fact the "partial" diffusion of Christianity, and the "partial" influence of moral improvements which will construct a particularly appropriate form of colonial subjectivity. What is suggested is a process of reform through which Christian doctrines might collude with divisive caste practices to prevent dangerous political alliances. Inadvertently, Grant produces a knowledge of Christianity as a form of social control which conflicts with the enunciatory assumptions which authorize his discourse. In suggesting, finally, that "partial reform" will produce an empty form of the *imitation* of English manners which will induce them [the colonial subjects] to remain under our protection,[5] Grant mocks his moral project and violates the Evidences of Christianity—a central missionary tenet—which forbade any tolerance of heathen faiths.

The absurd extravagance of Macaulay's *Infamous Minute* (1835)—deeply influenced by Charles Grant's *Observations*—makes a mockery of Oriental learning until faced with the challenge of conceiving of a "reformed" colonial subject. Then the great tradition of European humanism seems capable only of ironizing itself. At the intersection of European learning and colonial power, Macaulay can conceive of noth-

[2]Edward Said, *Orientalism* (New York: Pantheon Books, 1978), p. 240.

[3]Samuel Weber, "The Sideshow, Or: Remarks on a Canny Moment," *Modern Languages Notes,* vol. 88, no. 6 (1973), p. 112.

[4]Charles Grant, "Observations on the State of Society among the Asiatic Subjects of Great Britain," *Sessional Papers,* vol. 10, no. 282 (1812–13), East India Company.

[5]Ibid., chap. 4, p. 104.

ing other than "a class of interpreters between us and the millions whom we govern—a class of persons Indian in blood and colour, but English in tastes, in opinions, in morals and in intellect"[6]—in other words a mimic man raised "through our English School," as a missionary educationist wrote in 1819, "to form a corps of translators and be employed in different departments of Labour."[7] The line of descent of the mimic man can be traced through the works of Kipling, Forester, Orwell, Naipaul, and to his emergence, most recently, in Benedict Anderson's excellent essay on nationalism, as the anomalous Bipin Chandra Pal.[8] He is the effect of a flawed colonial mimesis, in which to be Anglicized, is *emphatically* not to be English.

The figure of mimicry is locatable within what Anderson describes as "the inner incompatibility of empire and nation."[9] It problematizes the signs of racial and cultural priority, so that the "national" is no longer naturalizable. What emerges between mimesis and mimicry is a *writing*, a mode of representation, that marginalizes the monumentality of history, quite simply mocks its power to be a model, that power which supposedly makes it imitable. Mimicry *repeats* rather than *re-presents* and in that diminishing perspective emerges Decoud's displaced European vision of Sulaco as:

> the endlessness of civil strife where folly seemed even harder to bear than its ignominy . . . the lawlessness of a populace of all colours and races, barbarism, irremediable tyranny. . . . America is ungovernable.[10]

Or Ralph Singh's apostasy in Naipaul's *The Mimic Men:*

> We pretended to be real, to be learning, to be preparing ourselves for life, we mimic men of the New World, one unknown corner of it, with all its reminders of the corruption that came so quickly to the new.[11]

Both Decoud and Singh, and in their different ways Grant and Macaulay, are the parodists of history. Despite their intentions and invocations they inscribe the colonial text erratically, eccentrically across a body politic that refuses to be representative, in a narrative that refuses to be representational. The desire to emerge as "authentic" through mimicry—through a process of writing and repetitio—is the final irony of partial representation.

What I have called mimicry is not the familiar exercise of *dependent* colonial relations through narcissistic identification so that, as Fanon has observed,[12] the black man stops being an actional person for only the white man can represent his self-esteem. Mimicry conceals no presence or identity behind its mask: it is not what Césaire describes as "colonialization-thingification."[13] behind which there stands the essence of the *présence Africaine*. The *menace* of mimicry is its *double* vision which in disclosing the ambivalence of colonial discourse also disrupts its authority. And it is a double-vision that is a result of what I've described as the partial representation/recognition of the colonial object. Grant's colonial as partial imitator, Macaulay's translator, Naipaul's colonial politician as play-actor, Decoud as the scene setter of the *opéra bouffe* of the New World, these are the appropriate objects of a colonialist chain of command, authorized versions of otherness. But they are also, as I have shown, the figures of a doubling, the part-objects of a metonymy of colonial desire which alienates the modality and normality of those dominant discourses in which they emerge as "inappropriate" colonial subjects. A desire that, through the repetition of *partial presence,* which is the basis of mimicry, articulates those disturbances of cultural, racial, and historical difference that menace the narcissistic demand of colonial authority. It is a desire that reverses "in part" the colonial appropriation by now producing a partial vision of the colonizer's presence. A gaze of otherness, that shares the acuity of the genealogical gaze which, as Foucault describes it, liberates marginal elements and shatters the unity of man's being through which he extends his sovereignty.[14]

I want to turn to this process by which the look of surveillance returns as the displacing gaze of the disciplined, where the observer becomes the observed and "partial" representation rearticulates the whole notion of *identity* and alienates it from essence. But not before observing that even an exemplary history like Eric Stokes's *The English Utilitarians*

[6]T. B. Macaulay, "Minute on Education," in *Sources of Indian Tradition*, vol. II, ed. William Theodore de Bary (New York: Columbia University Press, 1958), p. 49.

[7]Mr. Thomason's communication to the Church Missionary Society, September 5, 1819, in *The Missionary Register*, 1821, pp. 54–55.

[8]Benedict Anderson, *Imagined Communities* (London: Verso, 1983), p. 88.

[9]Ibid., pp. 88–89.

[10]Joseph Conrad, *Nostromo* (London: Penguin, 1979), p. 161.

[11]V. S. Naipaul, *The Mimic Men* (London: Penguin, 1967), p. 146.

[12]Frantz Fanon, *Black Skin, White Masks* (London: Paladin, 1970), p. 109.

[13]Aimé Césaire, *Discourse on Colonialism* (New York: Monthly Review Press, 1972), p. 21.

[14]Michel Foucault, "Nietzsche, Genealogy, History," in *Language, Counter-Memory, Practice,* trans. Donald F. Bouchard and Sherry Simon (Ithaca: Cornell University Press, 1977), p. 153.

in India acknowledges the anomalous gaze of otherness but finally disavows it in a contradictory utterance:

> Certainly India played *no* central part in fashioning the distinctive qualities of English civilisation. In many ways it acted as a disturbing force, a magnetic power placed at the periphery tending to distort the natural development of Britain's character. . . .[15]

What is the nature of the hidden threat of the partial gaze? How does mimicry emerge as the subject of the scopic drive and the object of colonial surveillance? How is desire disciplined, authority displaced?

If we turn to a Freudian figure to address these issues of colonial textuality, that form of difference that is mimicry—*almost the same but not quite*—will become clear. Writing of the partial nature of fantasy, caught *inappropriately*, between the unconscious and the preconscious, making problematic, like mimicry, the very notion of "origins," Freud has this to say:

> Their mixed and split origin is what decides their fate. We may compare them with individuals of mixed race who taken all round resemble white men but who betray their coloured descent by some striking feature or other and on that account are excluded from society and enjoy none of the privileges.[16]

Almost the same but not white: the visibility of mimicry is always produced at the site of interdiction. It is a form of colonial discourse that is uttered *inter dicta:* a discourse at the crossroads of what is known and permissible and that which though known must be kept concealed; a discourse uttered between the lines and as such both against the rules and within them. The question of the representation of difference is therefore always also a problem of authority. The "desire" of mimicry, which is Freud's *striking feature* that reveals so little but makes such a big difference, is not merely that impossibility of the Other which repeatedly resists signification. The desire of colonial mimicry—an interdictory desire—may not have an object, but it has strategic objectives which I shall call the *metonymy of presence.*

Those inappropriate signifiers of colonial discourse—the difference between being English and being Anglicized; the identity between stereotypes which, through repetition, also become different; the discriminatory identities constructed across traditional cultural norms and classifications, the Simian Black, the Lying Asiatic—all these are metonymies of presence. They are strategies of desire in discourse that make the anomalous representation of the colonized something

other than a process of "the return of the repressed," what Fanon unsatisfactorily characterized as collective catharsis.[17] These instances of metonymy are the nonrepressive productions of contradictory and multiple belief. They cross the boundaries of the culture of enunciation through a strategic confusion of the metaphoric and metonymic axes of the cultural production of meaning. For each of these instances of "a difference that is almost the same but not quite" inadvertently creates a crisis for the cultural priority given to the *metaphoric* as the process of repression and substitution which negotiates the difference between paradigmatic systems and classifications. In mimicry, the representation of identity and meaning is rearticulated along the axis of metonymy. As Lacan reminds us, mimicry is like camouflage, not a harmonization or repression of difference, but a form of *resemblance* that differs/defends presence by displaying it in part, metonymically. Its threat, I would add, comes from the prodigious and strategic production of conflictual, fantastic, discriminatory "identity effects" in the play of a power that is elusive because it hides no essence, no "itself." And that form of *resemblance* is the most terrifying thing to behold, as Edward Long testifies in his *History of Jamaica* (1774). At the end of a tortured, negrophobic passage, that shifts anxiously between piety, prevarication, and perversion, the text finally confronts its fear; nothing other than the repetition of its resemblance "in part":

> (Negroes) are represented by all authors as the vilest of human kind, to which they have little more pretension of resemblance *than what arises from their exterior forms* (my italics).[18]

From such a colonial encounter between the white presence and its black semblance, there emerges the question of the ambivalence of mimicry as a problematic of colonial subjection. For if Sade's scandalous theatricalization of language repeatedly reminds us that discourse can claim "no priority," then the work of Edward Said will not let us forget that the "ethnocentric and erratic will to power from which texts can spring"[19] is itself a theater of war. Mimicry, as the metonymy of presence is, indeed, such an erratic, eccentric strategy of authority in colonial discourse. Mimicry does not merely destroy narcissistic authority through the repetitious slippage of difference and desire. It is the process of the *fixation* of the colonial as a form of cross-classificatory, discriminatory knowledge in the defiles of an interdictory

[15]Eric Stokes, *The English Utilitarians and India* (Oxford, Oxford University Press, 1959), p. xi.

[16]Sigmund Freud, "The Unconscious" (1915), SE, XIV, pp. 190–91.

[17]Fanon, p. 103.

[18]Edward Long, *A History of Jamaica,* 1774, vol. 2, p. 353.

[19]Edward Said, "The Text, the World, the Critic," in *Textual Strategies,* ed. J.V. Harari (Ithaca: Cornell University Press, 1979), p. 184.

discourse, and therefore necessarily raises the question of the *authorization* of colonial representations. A question of authority that goes beyond the subject's lack of priority (castration) to a historical crisis in the conceptuality of colonial man as an *object* of regulatory power, as the subject of racial, cultural, national representation.

"This culture . . . fixed in its colonial status," Fanon suggests, "(is) both present and mummified, it testified against its members. It defines them in fact without appeal."[20] The ambivalence of mimicry—almost but not quite—suggests that the fetishized colonial culture is potentially and strategically an insurgent counter-appeal. What I have called its "identity-effects," are always crucially *split*. Under cover of camouflage, mimicry, like the fetish, is a part-object that radically revalues the normative knowledges of the priority of race, writing, history. For the fetish mimes the forms of authority at the point at which it deauthorizes them. Similarly, mimicry rearticulates presence in terms of its "otherness," that which it disavows. There is a crucial difference between this *colonial* articulation of man and his doubles and that which Foucault describes as "thinking the unthought"[21] which, for nineteenth-century Europe, is the ending of man's alienation by reconciling him with his essence. The colonial discourse that articulates an *interdictory* "otherness" is precisely the "other scene" of this nineteenth-century European desire for an authentic historical consciousness.

The "unthought" across which colonial man is articulated is that process of classificatory confusion that I have described as the metonymy of the substitutive chain of ethical and cultural discourse. This results in the *splitting* of colonial discourse so that two attitudes towards external reality persist; one takes reality into consideration while the other disavows it and replaces it by a product of desire that repeats, rearticulates "reality" as mimicry.

So Edward Long can say with authority, quoting variously, Hume, Eastwick, and Bishop Warburton in his support, that:

> Ludicrous as the opinion may seem I do not think that an orangutang husband would be any dishonour to a Hottentot female.[22]

Such contradictory articulations of reality and desire—seen in racist stereotypes, statements, jokes, myths—are not caught in the doubtful circle of the return of the repressed. They are the effects of a disavowal that denies the differences of the other but produces in its stead forms of authority and multiple belief that alienate the assumptions of "civil" discourse. If, for a while, the ruse of desire is calculable for the uses of discipline soon the repetition of guilt, justification, pseudoscientific theories, superstition, spurious authorities, and classifications can be seen as the desperate effort to "normalize" *formally* the disturbance of a discourse of splitting that violates the rational, enlightened claims of its enunciatory modality. The ambivalence of colonial authority repeatedly turns from *mimicry*—a difference that is almost nothing but not quite—to *menace*—a difference that is almost total but not quite. And in that other scene of colonial power, where history turns to farce and presence to "a part," can be seen the twin figures of narcissism and paranoia that repeat furiously, uncontrollably.

In the ambivalent world of the "not quite/not white," on the margins of metropolitan desire, the *founding objects* of the Western world become the erratic, eccentric, accidental *objects trouvés* of the colonial discourse—the part-objects of presence. It is then that the body and the book lose their part-objects of presence. It is then that the body and the book lose their representational authority. Black skin splits under the racist gaze, displaced into signs of bestiality, genitalia, grotesquerie, which reveal the phobic myth of the undifferentiated whole white body. And the holiest of books—the Bible—bearing both the standard of the cross and the standard of empire finds itself strangely dismembered. In May 1817 a missionary wrote from Bengal:

> Still everyone would gladly receive a Bible. And why?—that he may lay it up as a curiosity for a few pice; or use it for waste paper. Such it is well known has been the common fate of these copies of the Bible. . . . Some have been bartered in the markets, others have been thrown in snuff shops and used as wrapping paper.[23]

[20] Frantz Fanon, "Racism and Culture," trans. H. Chevalier, in *Toward the African Revolution* (London: Pelican, 1967), p. 44.

[21] Michel Foucault, *The Order of Things* (New York: Pantheon, 1970), part 2, chap. 9.

[22] Long, p. 364.

[23] *The Missionary Register*, May 1817, p. 186.

PERFORMANCE IN HISTORY

HELEN GILBERT AND JOANNE TOMPKINS,
from *Post-Colonial Drama* (1996)

Helen Gilbert and Joanne Tompkins are both well known for their studies of postcolonial theater and drama, and teach at the University of Queensland, Australia. In this selection from their recent book Post-Colonial Drama, *Gilbert and Tompkins discuss the ways in which the body can be made to represent the impact of gender, racial, or sexualizing ideologies, and so become a site for social critique in performance. In their wide-ranging discussion of the formation of gendered and racialized bodies onstage, Gilbert and Tompkins take in many of the plays and playwrights represented in this Unit. How does this discussion of embodiment relate to the treatment of bodies in the texts of modern plays, or in the staging of bodies in the modern theater? How does the notion of "inscription"—treating the body as though it were always a signifier, already "written" with meanings—help us to understand the relationships between colonized and colonizing subjects in contemporary drama? Is it possible to use this critique of racialized and gendered bodies to read against the grain of earlier playwrights?*

> The body is the inscribed surface of events (traced by language and dissolved by ideas), the locus of a dissociated self (adopting the illusion of substantial unity), and a volume of disintegration.
> —Foucault (1977): 148

Foucault's definition of the body omits a crucial performative fact: the body also *moves*. In the theatre, the actor's body is the major physical symbol; it is distinguished from other such symbols by its capacity to offer a multifarious complex of meanings. The body signifies through both its appearance and its actions. As well as indicating such categories as race and gender, the performing body can also express place and narrative through skilful mime and/or movement. Moreover, it interacts with all other stage signifiers—notably costume, set, and dialogue—and, crucially, with the audience. It is not surprising, then, that the body functions as one of the most charged sites of theatrical representation.

The colonised subject's body, as Elleke Boehmer explains, has been an object of the coloniser's fascination and repulsion (and, in effect, possession) in sexual, pseudo-scientific, and political terms:

> In colonial representation, exclusion or suppression can often literally be seen as 'embodied'. From the point of view of the colonizer specifically, fears and curiosities, sublimated fascinations with the strange or the 'primitive', are expressed in concrete physical and anatomical images. . . . [T]he Other is cast as corporeal, carnal, untamed, instinctual, raw, and therefore also open to mastery, available for use, for husbandry, for numbering, branding, cataloging, description or possession.

Paying attention to the body can be a highly useful (and even essential) strategy for reconstructing post-colonial subjectivity because imperialist discourse has been both insidious and persuasive in its construction of the colonised

subject as an inscribed object of knowledge. As Elizabeth Grosz argues, the body is never simply a passive object upon which regimes of power are played out:

> If the body is the strategic target of systems of codification, supervision and constraint, it is also because the body and its energies and capacities exert an uncontrollable, unpredictable threat to a regular, systematic mode of social organisation. As well as being the site of knowledge-power, the body is thus a site of *resistance,* for it exerts a recalcitrance, and always entails the possibility of a counter-strategic reinscription, for it is capable of being self-marked, self-represented in alternative ways.

The ways in which the reinscription and self-representation of colonised bodies translate into performative strategies is obviously a key issue for post-colonial theatre. Hence, current movements towards cultural decolonisation involve not just a verbal/textual counter-discourse but a reviewing of the body and its signifying practices. Whereas narrative writing tends to erase the gender and race of its authors and protagonists through its production as an artefact of predominantly western cultures, performance centralises the physical and socio-cultural specificities of its participants. It follows that post-colonial theatre (much like feminist theatre) finds in the body more than mere 'actor function' or 'actor vehicle'. The body's ability to move, cover up, reveal itself, and even 'fracture' on stage provides it with many possible sites for decolonisation.

In general, the post-colonial body disrupts the constrained space and signification left to it by the colonisers and becomes a site for resistant inscription. For instance, the Kathakali actor's stylised facial expressions signify the history of specific Indian acting traditions and communicate the carefully preserved systems of meaning through the actor's body. The colonial subject's body contests its stereotyping and representation by others to insist on self-representation by its physical presence on the stage. Corporeal signifiers quickly become politicised when a black actor appears in a traditionally 'white' role, or when a West Indian cast stages, say, a Shakespearian play; such choices, as well as colour-blind casting, contribute to the development of an identity independent from the imposed colonial one of inadequacy, subordination, and often barbarity. Because the body is open to multifarious inscriptions which produce it as a dialogic, ambivalent, and unstable signifier rather than a single, inde-pendent, and discrete entity, it is not surprising that the pro-duction of some sort of personal or cultural subjectivity via the body is complex indeed.

The post-colonial subject is often preoccupied with re-fusing colonially determined labels and definitions, espe-cially those which operate in the name of race and gender. Part of the project of redefining staged identity is to affix the *colonised's* choice of signification to the body rather than to maintain the limited tropes traditionally assigned to it. This oppositional process of *embodiment* whereby the colonised creates his/her own subjectivity ascribes more flexible, cul-turally laden, and multivalent delineations to the body, rather than circumscribing it within an imposed, imperialist calculation of otherness. The post-colonial stage offers op-portunities to recuperate the colonised subject's body—es-pecially when it has been maimed or otherwise rendered 'incomplete'—and to transform its signification and its sub-jectivity. This chapter explores the process of recuperation by examining some of the basic performative elements of the post-colonial body: how it looks, what it does, how it is seen, and, most importantly, how it presents itself.

As *visual* markers of 'identity', race and gender are par-ticularly significant in theatrical contexts even if their con-notations are sometimes highly unstable. It is crucial to remember, however, that such markers are inscribed on the body through discourse—visual, verbal, or otherwise—rather than simply being unmediated or objectively given. In other words, the perceived (constructed) binary categories of male/female and white/black are never merely biologically determined but are also historically and ideologically condi-tioned. Moreover, as our earlier discussion of various femi-nisms indicates, race and gender are distinct, albeit sometimes intersecting and/or overlapping, factors which cannot be collapsed under the conceptual umbrella of mar-ginalisation. It follows, then, that there can be neither an unproblematically essentialised 'black', 'female', or any other kind of body nor, conversely, can there be a universalised body which categorically avoids these markers of difference. If post-colonial theory has long rejected the idealised undif-ferentiated body of the other that is characteristic of imperi-alist discourse, representational practice—especially in largely iconic art-forms such as theatre—still faces the prob-lem of how to avoid essentialist constructions of race and gender while recognising the irreducible specificity of their impact on subject formation. One possible solution is to con-ceptualise all markers of identity/difference as partial, provi-sional, and likely to change depending upon the context or the signifying system in which they operate at any particular time. This notion avoids a single (biological) origin for race or gender but leaves open the possibility of what Spivak calls 'strategic essentialism—'the foregrounding of 'pure' differ-ence for particular political purposes.

RACE

Since one of the key features of colonialism has been the ex-ertion of European authority over non-white peoples, it is not surprising that an emphasis on race is widespread in post-colonial drama, particularly when the projected audi-ence includes a high proportion of white (or otherwise dom-inant) viewers. Two parallel, if apparently contradictory, strategies are evident: to emphasise racial difference as part of a 'scrupulously visible political interest' (Spivak) designed to recuperate marginalised subjects, or, alternatively, to dismantle all racial categories by showing their constructed-ness. Some plays adopt both of these approaches simultane-ously, a manoeuvre which often results in a dialectical tension that further destabilises 'race' as a signifying code. A case in point is Chi and Kuckles's *Bran Nue Dae*, which high-lights the presence of a large cast of Australian Aboriginal characters/ actors while at the same time insisting that race is less a colour than an attitude. In this context, it becomes artistically plausible that even several 'white' characters (played by non-Aborigines) eventually discover their Aborig-inality. The play participates in current debates in Australia about the construction of Aboriginal identity and notions of authenticity based primarily on skin colour.

The physical stage presence of black, indigenous, or oth-erwise 'coloured' actors cannot be undervalued in discussing the counter-discursive possibilities of the body in perfor-mance, even if what constitutes race is neither fixed nor ob-jectively measurable. On one level, staging the visibility of imperialism's racial other is in itself a subversive act since Anglo-European theatre has a long history of excluding non-white actors while maintaining *representations* of racial dif-ference, usually constructed through costume, make-up, and/or mask. The Othello of Shakespeare's day, for example, was played by a white actor who 'blacked up' and donned a curly-haired wig, a tradition which varied little for centuries. Not just a trope in popular entertainment (epitomised by Al Jolson's blackface performances in the early part of this century), blackface was used by Sir Laurence Olivier's version of *Othello* even as recently as the 1960s. When racially marked characters are played in this way, the resistance potential of the fictionalised black/coloured body is compromised by the 'wayward signification' of the actor's whiteness (Goldie). Matching the race (and/or gender) of the actor with that of the character does not mean, however, that the performing body completely escapes the web of imperial inscription. Rather, the body is inevitably 'read' through multiple codes and contexts and shaped not only by the narrative structures of a play itself but also by its audience. Historically, this has meant that when the nonwhite actor performed on western stages, his/her body generally carried a kind of mystique that both heightened and detracted from its significance. Another mode of *mis*representation consistent with colonial attempts to figure racial others as inferior and/or subordinate was thus conventionalised.

Whereas much western culture constructs the female body on stage as a passive to-be-looked-at object rather than as an active subject, the racially distinct body is often designed to be *overlooked* (in two senses of the word: to be examined more fully than other signifiers as an object of curiosity *and* to be rendered invisible as an object of disregard). Until quite recently, many post-colonial plays devised by whites fell into this representational trap by depicting sentimentalised or exoticised versions of racial difference. Terry Goldie's study of settler drama in Canada, Australia, and New Zealand demonstrates the ways in which images of the indigene have been circumscribed by a semiotic field that is limited to seven signifiers: orality, mysticism, violence, nature, sexuality, historicity, and an imitation of indigenous 'forms' of communication. Often moved on or off stage to create a particular atmosphere and/or elicit laughter, indigenous characters have functioned as stage properties, as fragments of the setting, and, at times, as foils against which the normative values of white society can be defined. Likewise, roles for blacks in the wider field of western drama have been constituted within racist discourses, with perhaps even more emphasis on their supposed violence and sexuality. In these prescribed spaces, imperialism's colonised subject is denied its full humanity; it performs an imposed representational function rather than being a focal point in its own right. And while some roles can be subverted in performance, there is little scope in such plays for significant interrogation of dominant assumptions about race.

When indigenous and black playwrights depict themselves on stage, the body is one of the first theatrical elements to take on new iconic possibilities. One text that manipulates the body's signification for political purposes is Monique Mojica's *Princess Pocahontas and the Blue Spots*, which deconstructs the semiotic field of 'Indianness'—to use Daniel Francis's concept of the term (1992)—by staging its common inscriptions in juxtaposition to alternative (and generally more empowering) expressions of native North American subjectivity. Conflicting images/identities are held in tension through the performing body of Contemporary Woman #1, who plays (with) the white-defined stereotypes presented, as well as transforming herself into various native characters. In this way, Mojica provides a critical rereading of the ways in which indigenous women have characteristically been coded and constrained by North and South American history, culture, and literature. The women's bodies contort to create images of imposed signifying codes; they also depict the scenery, including a volcano, thereby critiquing the conventional use of indigenous bodies to suggest the geographical landscape and/or to provide an apparently authentic atmosphere. The play employs an overabundance of clichéd Hollywood and explorer/ pioneer depictions of the 'Indian' in order to demonstrate their emptiness as representations: the sheer number of represented 'Indian' and 'native' bodies destabilises the power of the imposed depictions. Such figures as the Cigar Store Squaw, the Storybook Princess, and Princess Buttered-on-Both-Sides are effectively meaningless, having been overdetermined by and within white discourse. More specifically, Pocahontas, Christianised and re-named Lady Rebecca, is 'stuck [and] girdled' in the costume of the 'good Indian' even if it is clearly an uncomfortable fit. These 'museum exhibits' contrast sharply with the two contemporary women and with others recuperated from the margins of imperial representation: Matoaka (the younger persona of Pocahontas), Malinche, and the three Métis women who demand that their stories be told. The Storybook Princess and the Cigar Store Squaw are predictably wooden in personality and in their movements on the stage, whereas Matoaka and Malinche, in particular, embody sexualities that cannot be contained within the virgin/whore paradigm imposed upon them by the British and the Spaniards.

Mojica's interest in countering the semiotic codes of cinema and television is shared by other native Canadian writers such as Margo Kane, Daniel David Moses, and Tomson Highway, all of whom have dramatised characters/events that rework the stereotype of the Hollywood Indian. In Australia, the project of reconstructing an indigenous subjectivity is slightly different in so far as Aborigines have been less often mythologised in/ through popular representation than simply ignored, especially in visual media. In some ways, then, the conventional Aboriginal body is underdetermined because of its systematic erasure, rather than overdetermined as a result of repeated exposure. This is not to suggest that

Aborigines escape the designation of 'other', but to argue that this particular other is often less well-delineated in imperial discourse than is the 'Indian'. Nevertheless, Aboriginal inscriptions of corporeality—as opposed to European constructions of Aboriginality or a generic and even less specific otherness—function to embody in Aborigines on stage a different, more culturally accurate, subjectivity. Jack Davis's plays address the blind spots of settler history and literature on a number of levels, bringing the black body into acute visibility via individual characters (often dancers) and also through group interaction (especially across colour lines). *Kullark,* for example, inverts imperialism's racial norms in a comic depiction of first contact when Mitjitjiroo responds to Captain Stirling's proffered hand by rubbing its skin vigorously to see if the white stain can be removed. This gesture, along with the Aborigines' astonishment at the strange appearance of the Europeans, denaturalises the white body as the dominant sign of humanity. In a related manoeuvre, the play points to the *in*humanity of the invaders when they decapitate Yagan and skin him in order to remove his tribal markings for a souvenir. Here, Davis suggests that the mutilated black body functions within the colonising culture as a fetishised object. His overall project is to reinstate the corporeal presence of the Aborigines in history—and, on a metatheatrical level, in theatre—at the same time as he details the colonisers' attempts to annihilate all signs of difference. Reference to such atrocities does not mean, however, that *Kullark* simply stereotypes its characters according to race, reassigning the connotations of 'black' and 'white' in the process; rather, this play, like Davis's other works, carefully stages the misunderstandings brought about by discourses of racial otherness in a context where it is possible for conceptual gaps to be bridged. . . .

GENDER

The South African plays discussed demonstrate the constructedness of racial categories at the same time as they attempt to (re)claim strategic, if negotiable, race-inflected identities. For many post-colonial dramatists, particularly women, a parallel project is to recuperate female subjectivities while showing that gender is an ideology mapped across the body in and through representation. It seems, however, that the imperative is less to deconstruct the category of female (or male) than to intervene in the discourses that naturalise gender hierarchies. This pattern is possibly related to the perceived fixity of the gender binary. White/black classifications are quickly broken down by racial hybridity—indeed the threat of miscegenation is precisely that it produces visible signs of the permeability of racial boundaries. Gender classifications, in contrast, most often admit androgyny as

merely as hypothetical category which can be dissolved into male *or* female when the biological markers of sex are known. Some writers and practitioners do share Anglo-American feminism's interest in destabilising gender binaries, whether through 'sex-radical' performance or through visually recorded (transvestite) bodies, but most are more concerned with demarcating areas of women's subjugation under imperialism. Accordingly, gender is less likely to function alone as a category of discrimination in post-colonial plays than in combination with other factors such as race, class, and/or cultural background. An additional factor complicating the delineation of a gender-specific body politics is the metaphorical link between woman and the land, a powerful trope in imperial discourse and one which is reinforced, consciously or not, in much post-colonial drama, particularly by male writers. In some instances, women's bodies are not only exploited by the colonisers but also reappropriated by the colonised patriarchy as part of a political agenda which may not fully serve the interests of the women in question.

Rape is a prominent signifier in a number of plays, particularly in countries where settlers' annexation of so-called 'unoccupied territories' disrupted not only the culture but also the livelihoods of indigenous peoples. Both native and non-native dramatists have featured inter-racial rape as an analogue for the colonisers' violation of the land, and also for related forms of economic and political exploitation. Often such representations are designed to reveal less about the experiences of the oppressed than about the rape mentality of the oppressors. In the chilling final moments of Canadian George Ryga's *The Ecstasy of Rita Joe,* for example, the rape and murder of the central protagonist by three white men provides a graphic depiction of the widespread brutality of the colonial/judicial system. This play figures Rita Joe as the site on and through which the disciplinary inscriptions of imperial patriarchy are played out as her body is progressively marked by capture, assault, and sexual penetration. Politically, she functions less as an individual than as an emblem of native cultures in Canada; hence, her death signals the grim triumph of the imperial project. As Gary Boire argues, Ryga's text can be read as a 'Foucaultian allegory' which foregrounds the sexually fragmented body of Rita Joe in order to chart the systems of power that instigate and maintain the settler/invader society's dominance over indigenous groups.

Depending on how they are staged, theatrical images of sexual violence can have more than merely illustrative functions; in some instances, they also challenge the voyeuristic gaze of the white spectator, inviting him/her to admit complicity in that violence. Janis Balodis's *Too Young for Ghosts* critiques white invasion of indigenous land/

culture in Australia in a complex 'cross-over' scene in which the same actors play Aboriginal and Latvian women almost simultaneously. The scene collapses the rapes of two Aboriginal women with the sexual assault of their Latvian counterparts in a displaced persons camp after World War Two. This visual conflation—achieved through doubling roles and overlaying theatrical time and space—is a performative technique intended to elicit both empathy for the Aboriginal women and outrage against the colonial regime, here constructed as a more local 'war' for control over native land/bodies. Throughout the composite rape scene, the audience's perspective is further manipulated by the presence of Karl, whose position as a callous observer reminds the viewers of their own non-intervention. By collapsing chronological and spatial frameworks, Balodis is able to use the bodies of white characters/actors to stand in for black ones without appropriating Aboriginal figures in service of a narrative about migrant experience. Instead, by refusing to display the violation of the black women, the performance text frustrates the libidinal economy of inter-racial rape while still harnessing this trope's metaphorical power to express the colonisers' attitudes and actions. Using different strategies for a similar effect, Dorothy Hewett's *The Man From Mukinupin* (1979) stages the 'rape' of Aboriginal women through a savagely ironic song which details the settlers' attempts to conquer the recalcitrant landscape, a project explicitly figured as the male penetration of female space. Hewett's call for the doubling of her one Aboriginal character with the female heroine, presumably played by a white actor, effectively highlights the ways in which all women have been discursively merged with each other and with the landscape.

The treatment of rape in texts by native dramatists who recognise the significant intersections of race and gender takes on slightly different inflections, especially when local mythologies inform the wider play. Tomson Highway's *The Rez Sisters*, for example, stages rape as a violation not only of the land but also of the very spirit of native culture. In a brief but visually haunting scene, the mentally disabled Zhaboonigan reveals that a gang of white boys penetrated her vagina with a screwdriver. While she details the event with the casual disinterest of a child who has only limited understanding of what has happened, the Ojibway trickster spirit, Nanabush, *embodies* her trauma by performing the 'agonising contortions' of the rape victim. Zhaboonigan's assault thus accrues wider significance, though her own body remains relatively unmarked because the trickster absorbs and transforms her experience. Moreover, the conventional gender paradigms of such a scene are somewhat complicated by the fact that Nanabush—a spirit, who adopts

the forms of either and both genders simultaneously—is played by a male dancer. In what is to some extent a mirror image of *The Rez Sisters'* rape scene, Highway's controversial companion play, *Dry Lips Oughta Move to Kapuskasing*, enacts a native youth's sexual assault of a young native woman, Patsy Pegahmagahbow. That the rape is performed with a crucifix by a victim of foetal alcohol syndrome suggests that Christian imperialism is at least partly responsible for the current schism between native men and women. On a performative level, this scene also points to the desecration of indigenous land/culture by the colonising forces, a resonance achieved in a series of stylised movements in which Dickie Bird Halked repeatedly stabs his crucifix into the earth while Nanabush, here played by a woman, lifts her skirt to reveal the blood which slowly spreads down her legs. In *Dry Lips*, Nanabush and Patsy are embodied by the same ever-transforming actor who variously functions as the *idea* of the 'real' women referred to in the play *and* as the female trickster who again absorbs Patsy's experience. Although Highway has been accused of displaying sexism and gratuitous violence, it could be argued that *Dry Lips*, like *The Rez Sisters*, actually refuses the power of rape by subsuming it within the mythological frameworks invoked, since Nanabush is, above all, the great survivor and healer. Once again, the trickster's body—operating in this text as a sign of native women/culture/land that refigures the imperial collapsing of these categories—absorbs and transforms the forces which would leave it vulnerable and degraded. After the rape, Nanabush is visibly marked but still all-powerful as she reappears in various guises throughout the rest of the dream play, and then enters the 'real' action in a final triumphant moment with the baby that foreshadows a hopeful future for the Rez.

As all these images of sexual violence suggest, women's bodies often function in post-colonial theatre as the spaces on and through which larger territorial or cultural battles are being fought. In a similar fashion, representations of fertility, pregnancy, and motherhood frequently take on political inflections, a fact which is not surprising, given that imperialism's will to power over its (female) subjects also extended to the control of many aspects of reproduction. The slave trade, in which women were bought and sold for their 'breeding' capacities, is the most obvious example of a political economy based on the institutionalised commodification of the female body. Dennis Scott takes up this particular subject in one of the historical scenes of *An Echo in the Bone*, foregrounding the processes by which slavery reduced the female body to its sexual and reproductive functions. The setting is an early nineteenth-century auctioneer's office where three slaves are being inspected by a regular customer while the black middleman lists their attributes in turn, lingering over the two women:

> Now this—(To BRIGIT.) please make note, the wide hips, the breasts just filling out. No offspring yet. Do you wish to see proof of virginity—perhaps you'll wish to see for yourself—indeed, that's hardly necessary, we have a long association of trust, don't we, sir. Calves well muscled, exceedingly well turned, you will notice. . . . The other. . . . Here is the doctor's certificate, equally untouched. Notice the nipples. Fire in this one sir, you'll forgive my saying so. But the clear eyes show how easily she can be taught. All kinds of things.

With their bodies anatomised by the imperial gaze, the women are positioned as merchandise and are thus denied all sense of subjectivity. At the same time, they are constructed as sex objects *and* as passive children ripe for the expert tutelage (read exploitation) of the white master. Further degradation follows when Stone puts on a glove to examine the 'goods', inspecting one of the women's teeth and then running his hand up between her thighs, as if at a livestock sale. While the male slave is also commodified, he is not described in corporeal terms; indeed, his best selling feature is that he 'can read, write and reckon like a schoolmaster'. This scene exemplifies gender's impact on slavery: women's bodies are marked for consumption within imperialism's particular brand of patriarchy. The added focus on the middleman's ingratiating 'sales talk' also gives weight to the theory that in patriarchal systems women function in a symbolic exchange which cements the relationships between men—in this case between the white slave owner and the black agent who acts as proxy for the buyer.

Whereas the bodies of black women were commandeered in some colonies to breed a slave class to fulfil the demands of imperialism's labour market, white women's bodies were often appropriated to preserve the racial (and moral) integrity of the ruling class. In Africa and India, as well as in the Caribbean, the colonial woman/wife was expected, indeed compelled, to offer her sexual, social, and reproductive labours in the service of the Empire. Where the goal was settlement rather than rule, white women were even more crucial to the imperial project because of the imperative to (re)populate newly conquered lands. Jill Shearer's quasi-historical play, *Catherine* (1978), demonstrates how the body of the Australian settler woman functioned as part of the physical terrain upon which colonial expansion was mapped, both literally and symbolically. A large section of this metatheatrical text details the shipment of the first convict women to Botany Bay and makes abundantly clear the fact that such 'cargo' was designed to 'balance the imbalance' of the colony—that is, to prevent the male settlers' deviant sexual behaviour (with indigenous women or other men) and to provide progeny for the successful peopling of the nation. The main character, Catherine, becomes pregnant by the ship's surgeon but will not be allowed to keep her child, who has been earmarked as the first of a new generation of Australians whose ignominious heritage must be suppressed. The proposed management of Catherine's pregnancy—she will be taken care of only until she can safely deliver the baby into its father's hands—highlights the transplanted society's complete disregard for women themselves. While much of the play's narrative content critiques the convict system by exposing the ways in which it facilitated institutional control over the female body, the performance text insists on staging women's subjectivity: its structure as a play-within-a-play enables the recuperation of Catherine's body as a group of contemporary actors continually rehearse and re-interpret the fragments of her history to provide a wider comment on gender oppression.

If the settler woman's reproductive labour was harnessed in the interests of expanding the Empire, the indigenous woman's fertility presented a threat to the colonisers and was often suppressed. Eva Johnson's *Murras* (1988) addresses this issue in Australia by referring to the deliberate and systematic sterilisation of pubescent Aboriginal girls who are duped into taking medication that renders them infertile. *Murras* illustrates ways in which native women's bodies become sites of conquest in the imperial regime and how they are permanently marked by its various administrative systems, even those which purport to be benevolent. As Ruby says of her daughter in the closing scene, 'She carries the scars of the *wudjella's* [whitefellow's] medicine'. While generally much less harmful than the enforced sterilisation detailed in *Murras,* medical management of pregnancy and childbirth also has the effect, if not the intention, of bringing the bodies of indigenous women under control. Sistren Theatre Collective's *Bellywoman Bangarang* (1978) takes up the issue of western medicine as part of its focus on teenage pregnancy in Jamaica, and attempts to reclaim the birthing process through the use of African-based rituals which emphasise female power. The play's opening image features three masked interlocking figures as the mother-woman, a healer and protector who mimes a traditional labour before transforming herself into a modern-day doctor in a movement which indicates the medicalisation of childbirth. After the stories of the four pregnant girls have been told, the mother-woman returns at the end of the play to oversee the births. She guides Marie through a difficult labour and also frees her from the ropes (symbols of fear and self-loathing) which have entangled her since her rape. Like the trickster in Highway's plays, the mother-woman is a regenerative force/spirit who disperses the effects of trauma, restoring the colonised body to physical and spiritual health.

Imperialism's attempt to exercise authority over the reproductive processes of its female subjects is sometimes paralleled with more local tendencies to reduce women to functions of gender and/or fertility. Some post-colonial drama invests female fertility with great symbolic importance but none the less subordinates women to the interests of the colonised patriarchy. In India and Africa in particular, male writers are inclined to image the land as a mother and to present the truly-fecund woman as a signifier of nationhood. Giving birth thus becomes largely metaphorical, particularly in plays concerning independence from colonial rule, where the birth of a child mirrors the birth of the new nation. This trope, also common to Caribbean drama, occurs in Michael Gilkes's *Couvade* (1972) which invokes an Amerindian birthing ritual to articulate the play's complex dream-vision of a unified post-independent Guyana. The custom of *couvade* requires the father-to-be to undertake a trial or ordeal while his wife is in labour. This tradition is designed to affirm the connection between the unborn child and its father and to ensure a successful birth. *Couvade,* recently revised for Guyana's 1993 independence anniversary celebrations, uses the ritual to chart the psychological and spiritual 'rebirth' of the protagonist, Lionel, who, along with his newborn child, becomes emblematic of the nation. While the choice of ritual is apt for Gilkes's political vision, it shifts the focus of the birth from the woman (and the child) to the man and the community. Such paradigms figure the paternal body as much more significant than the maternal counterpart; thus, possible representations of the female post-colonial subject are often limited to the merely practical.

The maternal body is also compromised by her child in several plays when, for instance, stalled or uncertain progress towards decolonisation is figured by some kind of failure in the reproductive process. The unborn, stillborn, or otherwise incomplete child has special significance in this respect and often features in several signifying capacities: as well as representing the specific and local community, this child also acts as a site of struggle between competing political groups, especially in cultures that acknowledge the presence of ancestral spirits. The *abiku* or Half-Child in Soyinka's *A Dance of the Forests* (1960), a play about and for Nigeria's independence, represents the contemporary Nigerian world of spiritual transition, matching the political and social transition of the country. *A Dance of the Forests* is a cautionary rather than a purely celebratory play in so far as it recognises the difficulties inherent in attempts to unite the variety of forces that would impact on an independent Nigeria. The uncertain location of the *abiku* in this text also points to some of the dilemmas Nigerians would face in the following decades. Just as the *abiku* is neither living nor dead, neither

body nor spirit, neither recognised nor forgotten, Nigeria's independence augurs an ambivalent future. A more hopeful treatment of the spirit child occurs in Walcott's *Ti-Jean and His Brothers* where the *bolum,* a disfigured foetus who represents the Caribbean people under the tyranny of colonialism, is eventually wrested from the clutches of the devil/plantation owner and reborn into full human life. In both of these plays, the female body is once again completely removed from the (potential) birthing process: the *abiku's* 'mother', the Dead Woman, has no say in the life or role of her half-child while the *bolum* is restored to the human world as a result of Ti-Jean's victory over the devil. On a performative level, the incomplete child-figure simply transforms from the spirit state as if birthing itself independently of any mother figure. This process was imaged through costuming codes in one recent video production of *Ti-Jean* where the *bolum* was encased in a huge egg-shell which it broke upon 'hatching'.

Examples such as these suggest that male playwrights are primarily interested in childbirth as a symbolic, often unifying trope. Women, on the other hand, have a vested interest in refusing the gender-specific roles/images that circumscribe their representation. One of the most important achievements of recent women's post-colonial writing is its refusal to endorse the traditional signifiers of gender, particularly those linked to reproduction and mothering. When motherhood is invoked, it frequently becomes a very mixed 'blessing', much as it is in Buchi Emecheta's ironically titled novel, *The Joys of Motherhood.* Interestingly, with a few exceptions, post-colonial plays by women tend not to centralise birth, perhaps in an attempt to fracture the concept of 'Mother Earth', an idealistic notion that denies women full humanity and compromises their ability to change, to choose, and to be individuated. The Canadian playwright, Judith Thompson, *does* frequently foreground pregnancies—in *The Crackwalker* (1980), *Tornado* (1987), and *I am Yours* (1987)—but these imminent births tend not to represent a bright hope for the future. Instead, they symbolise evil or a social cancer; regardless of the baby's health, pregnancy is a metaphor for disease in Thompson's work. Likewise, Sistren's *Bellywoman Bangarang* and Shearer's *Catherine* construct the pregnant body in terms of disorder and/or pathology rather than invoking traditional images of fruition.

Our discussion of the gendered body supports Ketu Katrak's argument that 'the traditions most oppressive for women [in colonised societies] are specifically located within the arena of female sexuality: fertility/infertility, motherhood and the sexual division of labour'. While women as narrative subjects are characteristically erased in imperial and patriarchal discourses, their corporeal presence is often intensified through a focus on factors such as sexuality and reproduction. This habit can be just as limiting as the neglect of gender-specific issues. As Peggy Phelan argues, 'In excessively marking the boundaries of the woman's *body,* in order to make it thoroughly visible, patriarchal culture subjects it to legal, artistic, and psychic surveillance. This, in turn, reinforces the idea that she *is* her body'. The challenge for postcolonial dramatists—both male and female—is to refuse such body politics while re-inscribing all theatricalised bodies with more enabling markers of gender. Yet, as Monique Mojica makes clear in *Princess Pocahontas and the Blue Spots,* women as a group cannot claim a collective victim status when they have been—and continue to be—complicit in the colonisation, appropriation, and denigration of other women. In this play, Contemporary Woman #1 refuses the feminist label because its collectivity tries to override her individuality as a subject who happens to be native and who happens to be female. The contemporary characters (and actors) present to their audience transforming, individuated bodies that refuse collectivity of any type if it does not also recognise the rights of the singular subject. Contemporary Woman #1 rejects the International Women's Day march until 'feminist shoes' manage to accommodate her 'wide, square, brown feet' and so allow her to 'feel the earth through their soles'. Refusing to be both the token 'Indian' and to represent all natives, this woman demands, in Gloria Anzaldua's words, 'the freedom to carve and chisel [her] own face', thus maintaining the individuality of her body *among* groups (mis)identified solely by race or gender. . . .

A PLAYWRIGHT'S PERSPECTIVE

ATHOL FUGARD

from *Notebooks: 1960–1977* (1983)

In the Notebooks *that he published in 1983, Athol Fugard makes available his working diary from the period of his first notoriety as a playwright in South Africa. In this selection, covering the year 1973 in which he was collaborating with John Kani and Winston Ntshona on short, experimental pieces like* Sizwe Bansi is Dead *and* The Island, *Fugard documents the range of thoughts, experiences, and reflections that came together in* The Island.

1973
January

Dawn on the mudflats after night filming *Boesman and Lena,* then the drive past New Brighton beach along the freeway and back to S'kop as the sun rose; the bay calm with ships at anchor. Moments of real serenity. Similarly a few sunsets and early evenings as we packed up after a day's filming. I was glad when we finally gave the mudflats, and the Island in particular, back to itself. We never related to it other than as an occupation force. The same at Missionvale.

The Island—a shrinking, dying world, with each spring-tide a few more inches of the bank crumbling away. Its men, women and children, the young man I got talking to and who said, 'Ons geslag is verkeerd.'

An oasis of privacy and safety—the only trouble that could ford the spruit at high water, or struggle through the mud at lowtide, is what they carry with them. But dying. A spirit of bitter and brooding resentment when the bottle of Golden Mustang or sherry is half-way down. The outside world is not as far away as it used to be—Mr Ackerman, the Nature Conservation Officer, has a boat; the men who come there over weekends to fish are not allowed to dig for prawn any more—spades and tackle are confiscated; the African ranger on Ackerman's staff goes out on patrol with a pair of binoculars.

The connection between the slow death of the Island, the bulldozers and evictions at South End, Korsten, Salisbury Park, Missionvale, and the new housing schemes such as Salt Lake, on the other side of the saltpan behind Missionvale. Five men were certified insane last week in places like Salt Lake. In each case, after a period of abnormal behaviour—hearing voices, etc.—the men had erupted into violence then been tied down to a chair or locked in an empty room until the police came and took them away to the cells. Then an examination by two doctors and certification.

And, always, for all of them, the dream of a big fish.

Mr Ackerman, his uniform, binoculars and patrol boat, as totally corrosive of that place and its meaning as the tides eating it away.

A walk from Salt Lake to the Island in the lurid light of a sky filled with smoke from veldfires. Past the graveyard at Veeplaas. Past the saltpans with their 'ripening' red water. Salt Lake itself—the water seen as sweat.

The Island—'This is our place, hey.' 'Ja . . . this is our place.'

The camaraderie of nameless strangers made brothers by a common fate. Yet again . . . a camaraderie of the damned. 'Ons geslag is verkeerd.'
Lena's song:

> Daar's 'n klokkie wat die waarheid vertel,
> That Lena goes to heaven, and Boesman goes to hel.
> Daar's 'n klokkie wat die waarheid vertel.
> And it's too late to change de troef ou pel.

February

A long dry and now drought-stricken summer has culminated in an outbreak of bad veldfires in the Eastern Cape. Times during our filming at Missionvale when I couldn't look in any direction without seeing a tell-tale pall of smoke on the horizon. Heat and desperation. Euphorbias wilting in the veld; thorntrees dying. Starting about ten days ago a series of fires deep in the drift-sands area between S'kop and Summerstrand. Watched safely from a distance until the day before yesterday when a gale-force South-Easter suddenly swept one right up to the village.

Near-panic. The smoke was so thick outside you could barely see your hand; inside the house was grey with ash and smoke. At the height of the pandemonium buck were running around like mad-dogs; fire-engines, teams of African beaters, people evacuating houses in a catastrophic twilight.

Five African men spent the night sleeping on the sand in front of a neighbour's house, all with pangas, ready in case the fire swept down again—ashen-grey men, cold, utterly exhausted, hungry—while we slept in our houses. A fleeing buck was chased by a group of African men, armed with spades and pangas, and these followed by a motley collection of white children trying to save the buck from hungry New Brighton stomachs.

A summer that reminded me of the story from Piet: the terrible drought when he was a young man in the Alexandria district, trying to run the family farm. He tore down the half-completed milking shed to provide for a coffin for his African friend. Piet buried him . . . 'here lies a man . . .' then walked away into the veld and cried.

Fishing again. Twice into the Reserve in the past week. Caught nothing. Yesterday afternoon's spell—all of what fishing is about to me. Simple relationship between self, rocks and the sea. Warm sun, blue sea and the rocks black and wet as the tide went out. So active as compared with the stillness, the silent rhythm of the river. Dart as far down the rocks to a safe point, there to wait, thumb and forefinger of the left hand on the line, a small lump of expectation in the throat . . . a small repetitive dance between the limits of Life and Death, Yin and Yang, the active and the passive . . . black rock, white sea . . . known and unknown . . . the fishing line, with its baited barb unreeling from one into the other.

The Ashram suddenly and unexpectedly provides us with a small lesson in the harsh realities of Boesman and Lena and Sizwe Banzi. Melton's two pondoks in the bush on the Ashram have been 'discovered' by the Divisional Council. A notice from them the day before yesterday demanding the demolition of 'said illegal structures' within fourteen days. Melton? God alone knows. On to the road with his wife and two children to look for somewhere else to stay, possibly back to the drought and poverty of the Alexandria district where he appears to come from.

'Sardinia Bay is rapidly becoming a much sought-after area. We are not going to let it become a slum.'—Secretary of the Divisional Council.

On the face of it there is absolutely nothing I can do to help Melton and prevent his eviction. I thought it was 'our land'!

And Daan in the garden, drinking himself to death . . . two bottles of Lieberstein just about every day.

For the moment I can't see past the appalling wreckage of human lives that our society is creating. A dumb and despairing rage at what we are doing.

'We, all of us, *are* a mistake.'

Oscar Lewis's Sanchez family. Mexico City slum = Missionvale. What we most probably lack, and fatally so, is a real prophet of doom.

The fusing of Hopelessness (metaphysical predicament) and Hope (historical predicament) . . . the reality, the Truth that is both, even as a coin is both heads and tails. Maybe that is what the Robben Island idea must be about. A dialogue, encounter, opposition and then resolution between Hopelessness (life sentence) and Hope (. . . 'my appeal has succeeded; I've only got six months to go').

Finally: When we run to the quarry tomorrow, and they chase us and the dogs snarl . . .

Second chapter in the story of Melton's eviction from the Ashram—Setting, the lounge, into which Melton has never before been invited ('Different now because of the suffering involved'). Present also, John and Winston, an hour or so back in P.E. after another 'full-house' run of *Sizwe Banzi* down in Cape Town. After discussing our business I introduce them, with much embarrassment (because I can't speak Xhosa), to the problem of Melton. Note the phrasing . . . my sense, personal, was of 'the problem of Melton', not 'Melton's problem'. I explain to Johnny my, the, abysmal lack of communication between us. I need somebody to 'translate', 'talk'. Winston watches; Johnny talks; I talk; Melton listens. And, as I say . . . Melton sitting on the sofa in a room he has never before been invited into. Melton playing nervously with an old eye-patch in his hands. Sore eye, I think. A few drops of Eyegene when we've finished talking. (Complacent sense of 'helping'.) Right at the end, Melton mentions the sore eye himself and says something about being frightened of losing it, of going blind. When I look, I see that an evil-looking film (cataract?) has already almost covered the pupil. So much for Eyegene.

Anyway, the conversation proceeds something like this:
Self: Let's start right at the beginning. I'm not so sure how much he understands. I have received a notice from the . . .
Johnny: (in Xhosa) . . . Melton listens. Nods.
Self: Tell him that I tried . . .
Johnny: (in Xhosa) . . . Melton listens.
Self: Explain to him . . .
Johnny: (in Xhosa) . . . Melton listens.
Etc. etc.

Melton is younger than me. Wife and three children. He was wearing a shirt, trousers, battered shoes, no socks. When I watched him talk and listen to Johnny a most remarkable transformation took place in a face that I have at times hated because of my inability to reach it, communicate with it meaningfully. I can only describe watching Melton's face as he communicated with Johnny on the basis of total reciprocity—let me start again: I saw the beauty of life, of value, of a sense of self infuse something that circumstances had trapped me into relating to as 'dead'.

All he wants to do is live his life.

We dropped him off at the Ashram and he walked away from us in a lull in the rain which had started last night and which promises, if it continues a little longer, to break the terrible drought we are now experiencing.

Grey sky.

Melton's courage.

And, a second later, Lisa on the side of the road on her horse, Seaweed, radiant, stunned with happiness.

March

Robben Island: the two men arrived on the Island handcuffed together. Their friendship forged in the long trip down, standing hand-cuffed together all the time, from the Rooi Hel to the Cape Town docks.

Somewhere tonight, two men—shackled together—have started that journey. They will stand for all the 500 miles, pressed close together in the over-crowded prison van. There is a bucket in the dark suffocating cabin, but there are so many of them they cannot use it; they shit and piss as they stand, together. In the first grey light of tomorrow morning they will crawl out of the van at the Cape Town docks and be herded on board a tugboat and taken to Robben Island.

Somewhere tonight the same two men confront each other, shocked over the simple fact that one has had his sentence reduced through a legal appeal, and can start to count days, while the other . . .

Somehow and somewhere tonight B. is wiping his mouth after a good drink of beer . . . and A. is running to the quarry.

Who are they?

As always—was, is and will ever be—somebody must ask the question that can't be answered.

Dream images: a naked white pilot, standing strapped to his tiller in a harness, ferrying a load of people to their death by hanging—the images as remote and 'grainy' as old photographs. The people executed were survivors of a wreck; their 'crime' was never revealed. The photograph of the hanging bodies was too 'long' a shot for any details of pain and suffering.

A large, strange tree in the middle of a forest. Enormous bole. The impossibility of explaining or knowing anything about it because '. . . its branches start where the mists begin'. Not even climbing would have helped. The inevitable was not 'ignorance', but 'acceptance'. All categories of 'knowing' were defied.

The small shark—twenty to thirty pounds—on the rocks at Cape St. Francis; lying on its back, a heavy rock on its body just below the jaws, presumably so that it would suffocate to death. I had seen the angler catch it, recognised a shark, but had thought it one of the harmless sandsharks. When the angler packed up and left that particular rock, I took it over and found the shark. Far from being one of the harmless variety it had a mouthful of the most terrible-looking teeth—possibly ragged-tooth. Setting sun; rough white sea; strong South-Easter. The appalling intolerance and savagery of man when he encounters anything that does not fit into 'his' scheme of things. The vanity and vicious pride that is blind to the possibility of a pattern larger than 'his' needs and convenience. Out of the shark's terrible maws the voices of Jews in gas-ovens, the condemned in death cells, the thin spiral of 'time' on Robben Island.

Nothing is as deadly as ignorance combined with fear.

My thinking about the complex of Robben Island ideas and images reached a point yesterday where it suddenly occurred to me that they require a style and a form very different from the four plays of the past ten years. Words like 'distance', 'elevation', 'objectivity' occur to me. 'Classical' in the sense of a cool detachment, is another.

A large canvas as opposed to the intimate miniature.

At a distance of ten paces the pondok I built for Boesman at Swartkops looked like nothing. The only significant relationship to it was from inside . . . the room in Valley Road; the shack at Korsten.

Rain tonight—listening to it here in the shed where I'm writing. Like a firm and sure hand on something that is troubled. A mother's hand on her son's shoulder. And the wind like the neglected sister agitating—agitating in the dark. Still by herself—even though she touches so much.

One of those nights when the sea was giving bad advice.

The earth—Protestant. Sea—Catholic. Sky—Buddhist.

Daan: his walk from, and at the end of the day, back to Walmer location. Eight kilometres each way. Not the sort of man many stop to give a lift to. The weather of that walk—wind sun rain darkness.

The gardens he looks after here in the village.

Animals—the monkey he found in the bush, paralysed from the waist down. Fed it with his own bread. Tortoises. Snakes. The dogs of S'kop.

His friends—Sophie, Anna, Emily, John, Simon, Paulus Olifant, James at the pump station. The first time I ever heard Anna laugh was because of something Daan said. He was weeding, she was hanging up washing, they were talking.

His Reference Book—he deliberately lost it because it didn't have the right stamp.

His constant curiosity about people and what they were doing. Twisting his head off in the back seat of the car whenever I gave him a lift.

Dialogue:

Of Paulus Olifant, he says: Paulus catches snakes with his hands. You believe that? His hands. I seen him. Skaapsteker—just so . . . and in the bag. One bite and you're dead.

May

Vivid series of dreams involving guns and violence and torture and any number of incidents and images which involved other people, and myself feeling self-conscious and foolish. One seemed to suggest my inability to destroy evil in myself, another to warn against the potential to hurt what I love.

One dream of violence involved a gun. I was in Parliament and—during a lot of shooting, in the course of which two MPs were killed—I tried to assassinate the Prime Minister. I only succeeded in wounding him. I turned out to be a member of Vorster's staff. After the attempted assassination—he did not suspect my part in it—I continued in a disgusting, toadying relationship with him (almost as if I were parasitic and dependent on a powerful and hated 'father' figure). A second important relationship—I seemed to be looking after her—with a crippled woman—the State President's wife. Occasionally I spoke Afrikaans in the dream.

1. I am ineffective against what I know to be evil.

2. (because of this) I am a threat to what I love.

3. ? the reason for 1 and 2 . . . That I am still looking for the 'effective' father I never had as a child? Trying to destroy this undermining 'need'.

A powerful sense of the unconscious trying to talk . . . improvising, making a vocabulary of the externals that impinge on my life each day . . . re-assembled, loaded each night so as to convey meaning.

Then why was a knife not the central image—why repeatedly, a gun? To kill, destroy, *accidentally* with a knife is not really feasible. Guns, on the other hand, have got *triggers,* are loaded (unreleased—the dangerous potential). Also: I have got knives. I do not have a gun.

Dream: more important than 'what do they mean' is to let them really 'happen' to you . . . to live with them consciously as a decisive, formative experience.

Johnny's description of a shebeen scene with Norman: the latter drinking compulsively in a violent silence while a brash youngster talked loosely about the need for militant action and courage. Norman finally erupted and, as Johnny put it, 'rubbed that kid's face in the shit'. What it amounted to was Norman just talking, talking about Robben Island: his arrival at the prison and being thrown into the corridor that led to his cell—the little window in one of the cell doors opened and the face of a well-known New Brighton man appeared there briefly, 'Norman! It is an honour to be here.' It was another six months before their paths crossed on the Island. 'It will be another six years before I see him here in New Brighton!'

The tree, a big one, which he and five others were told to uproot bare-handed. For six months, every day except weekends, they were led out to it. The six of them, their foreheads pressed against the bole, pushing, the whole day. Waking at night with a neck so sore it was impossible to find a comfortable position on his blanket on the floor. 'And let me tell you, little man, young man, with your big mouth, we uprooted it finally!'

The young man was a member of the Black People's Convention—highly critical of what seemed to him to be the prevailing spirit of acceptance and resignation in the township.

The informers that gave evidence against him in his trial in Cradock. He named them, their addresses . . . he sees them every day. They look the other way. What drives him mad is not that they were weak, and broke under pressure and told what they knew, but that they told *lies.*

Johnny went on to describe the scene at the Labour Bureau—the large cement-floored room full of work-seekers and the white man behind the counter. The men wait, reference books ready; the white man waits . . . short, aggressive little Afrikaner who, as Johnny puts it, had learnt the 'bad-half of the Xhosa language'. The telephone rings, the Afrikaner answers. Somebody wants a 'good boy'. Then a scene so awful, so degrading it is almost unbelievable: the white man stands on a chair and addresses the desperate throng '. . . Baas who wants a good boy.' The crowd goes mad. Eighty to a hundred men jumping around like monkeys waving their 'clean' books in the air. The white man drags it out; he knows a lot of the men by sight: 'You! I know you . . . sent you to a job last week. Why you back here? Unreliable kaffir, hey. Go to hell! . . . (to another one) you too old . . . (another one) . . . I told you not to come back . . .'

While the men, ravenous for work, continue to prance around like idiots, waving their reference books in an attempt to attract his attention.

He finally selects one from the forest. Again a drawn-out game . . . examines the reference book to see where the man worked, how long in each job, etc. etc. Decides the man is a thief, throws the book down. While the owner is down on the floor trying to retrieve his book, the crowd goes mad again. Four or five games like this before somebody finally gets the job. White man closes the hatch, sits down and waits for the next telephone call. The crowd settles down and waits for the next chance. The man who was rolling a zol just before the pandemonium broke loose tries to scrape together the shreds of tobacco he spilt on the floor, etc. Most of them standing, leaning against the wall; a few bring along apple-boxes and sit on these.

Even the opening of the gate into the yard of the Labour Bureau at the start of the day is a game. Two or three hundred people—men, women and children—pressing against it. The white man almost opens, then closes, almost opens, then closes . . . finally throws it open and then the mad scramble to form the two queues—men one side, women the other.

The Island

1. *Space:* Restricted.
    The Island itself.
    The straight line from the prison to the quarry.
    The cell
    and—most savage of all—the solitary confinement cell.
    Locked doors.
2. *Time:* The taking away of a portion, or all of a man's life.
    Sentenced to so many 'years' of nothing.
    Experienced as a loss of Life, as a Living Death. You are no more.
    The grave of the Living.
3. *Meaningless Absurd Labour:* Punishment. Sisyphus.
    The loss of Freedom that imprisonment involves.
    What is 'Freedom'?
    Two men in a cell on the Island.
    Two men in New Brighton.
    What is the difference?

July

Shells of demolished houses and shacks at Salisbury Park— the coloured area which has been bulldozed as a result of Group Areas ruling. Roofs torn off, gaping, blind holes that were doors and windows, graffiti on the walls. In some cases all that remains is the bakoond and chimney, the house itself was made of corrugated iron and was torn down in a few minutes by the demolition gang. The mission school likewise—all that remains is a derelict waste space with weeds already slowly obliterating the groundplan of classrooms. The unbelievable sacrilege of taking the destruction of a thing just so far (tearing off the roof and ripping out windows and doors) so that it cannot be used again. A world of ghosts— windswept and unbearably lonely. Exactly what I had tried to imagine, and understand in trying to write the Fairview play: 'A man without scenery'.

The splendid *Aloe ciliaris* I admired every time I drove past it when taking Lisa to school, is in bloom again.

Faces I shall never see again: the school principal— middle-aged, dapper little man; his pipe in his mouth. The young school teachers, trudging up the hill with their loads of exercise books. The four poor-white children who slunk out of the location every morning to go to the white school in Green Shields Park. Little Trevor, waiting for a lift from the pump station to the mission school.

PERFORMANCE REVIEW

Native Grace—An Indian Reserve Struggles for Salvation

JOHN BEMROSE

Review of *Dry Lips Oughta Move to Kapuskasing*

DIRECTED BY LARRY LEWIS, AT THE ROYAL ALEXANDRIA THEATRE, TORONTO, 29 APRIL 1991.

John Bemrose's review of Tomson Highway's Dry Lips Oughta Move to Kapuskasing *documents the play's remounting at the prestigious Royal Alexandria Theatre in Toronto. As Bemrose notes, the play had opened originally in 1989 at Toronto's Theatre Passe Muraille, a venue long associated with new and experimental drama; here, it is the first play by a Canadian playwright to open at the Royal Alexandria in eight years. Beyond that, however, Bemrose's review illustrates the different function of a review in a weekly—this review appeared in* Maclean's, *a weekly newsmagazine—than in a daily. Rather than merely highlighting aspects of the production and providing a quick evaluation, Bemrose undertakes to educate his audience about the importance of Highway's play, both for Canadian theater and as a document in the history of Canadian society in the 1990s.*

Last summer, as armed Mohawks stood guard at their barricades in Oka, Que., a new image of Canada's native people forced itself on the national consciousness. But such defiance is only one aspect of the current Indian struggle for greater self-determination. Early this month at Toronto's Royal Alexandra Theatre, native people staged a different kind of event—the production of Tomson Highway's award-winning play, *Dry Lips Oughta Move to Kapuskasing.* The bitter tragicomedy first appeared at the city's Theatre Passe Muraille two years ago. But its remounting at the plush Royal Alex—where it is the first Canadian play in eight years—marks a special triumph for an Indian cultural community determined to raise the profile of its concerns and its achievements.

Pride in those achievements was in evidence at the theatre earlier this month as native people in formal evening attire mingled under the television lights with the well-to-do opening-night crowd. In part, the celebrity atmosphere was a carryover from last month's Academy Awards show when one of the stars of *Dry Lips,* Toronto actor Graham Greene, was an Oscar nominee for his role in Kevin Costner's *Dances With Wolves.* The glitter contrasted starkly with the events portrayed onstage. For all its broad humor, Highway's vision of life on Wasaychigan Hill, a fictional Manitoulin Island reserve,

is as bleak as the morning after a weeklong binge. Like so many native communities, Wasaychigan Hill is destroying itself in a black orgy of substance abuse and violence. Only its frayed links to traditional values and a kind of gamy courage hold it back from complete disintegration.

Highway's earlier hit play, *The Rez Sisters,* focused on Wasaychigan Hill's women, who made an epic comedy of their journey to a big-city bingo game. In *Dry Lips,* Highway turns his attention to the men. They are a pathetic if oddly endearing lot. Of the seven native males in the play, five are drunks, fools or both. The remaining two, Dickie Bird Halked (Kennetch Charlette) and Simon Starblanket (Dwayne Manitowabi), are youths struggling to escape the community's collective nightmare. But Simon is killed in a pointless accident, while Dickie Bird's inner demons—he has been left speechless by a mysterious childhood trauma—drive him to commit a brutal rape.

All the men of Wasaychigan Hill are caught in a vortex of angry passivity. Even the authority figure, Big Joey (Ben Cardinal), is a bully obsessed with past memories. By contrast, the women of the reserve—who appear mostly through the eyes of the men—positively brim with creativity and initiative. That has helped inspire a deep strain of misogyny. When Big Joey is pressed to

explain why he stands by passively during Dickie Bird's attack on Simon Starblanket's fiancée, Patsy Pegahmagahbow (Doris Linklater), he blurts out that he hates all women for taking power away from the men.

Fortunately, Highway, a Cree born 39 years ago in Brochet, Man., leavens Wasaychigan's anguish with humor of a very high order. The chief vehicle of the play's comedy is a loquacious bootlegger named Pierre St. Pierre, played by Greene. The gap-toothed, jut-jawed drunk is the utter antithesis of dignity: he shamelessly cadges beer and chugalugs it a bottle at a time. Greene is simply brilliant in the role. When he appears as the referee for an all-women's hockey game, his physical comedy has the stumbling insouciance of Buster Keaton. St. Pierre is also, in his way, the poet of the reserve, as he sums up with wonderful exaggeration and malapropisms the exploits of the women hockey players. His repeated recitation of their outlandish names, including Big Bummed Pegahmagahbow and Dry Lips Manatawagan, grows more deliciously funny every time.

While all the comic sections of the production have an engaging buoyancy, a certain heaviness creeps in elsewhere. Much of the play concerns Dickie Bird's search to discover his true father and understand the causes of his dumb-ness. It is a tedious quest, unable to bear the dramatic importance that Highway places on it. Part of the problem is Charlette's too-frenetic performance. Even more critically, Highway has not found a language adequate to his characters' rage and pain. That makes the climactic rape scene—which involves the brutal use of a crucifix—a bloody but emotionally unaffecting affair.

The result of those failures is that *Dry Lips* breaks in half between beguiling comedy and less effective tragedy. Still, much of the production soars above that split, including Carlos del Junco's haunting accompaniment on the blues harp. Also successful is the use of the Ojibwa trickster figure, Nanabush (Linklater), who hovers like Puck in the background, an invisible influence on the characters. In one scene, she waggles an enormous pair of false buttocks and causes the reserve's baker, Zachary (Gary Farmer), to break into a chorus—he has no idea why—of *Hot Cross Buns*.

The drama's earthiness and gallows humor are important gifts from native people to a society that has all too often lost sight of such qualities. *Dry Lips* is also a warning. Wasaychigan Hill's predicament can be seen as being symbolic of the larger society that surrounds it—a society that may itself be bent on self-destruction in more subtle or socially acceptable ways. In that sense, *Dry Lips Oughta Move to Kapuskasing* is more than just a play about conditions on Canada's Indian reserves. It is a reminder that when the cultural underpinnings of a society crumble, chaos is not far behind.

Appendix: Writing About Drama and Theater

In most ways, writing about drama and theater is like other kinds of analytical and argumentative writing. The best work is clear in its claims, tenacious in its analysis, rich and skillful in its discussion of detail. This section presents a brief outline of some of the techniques and practices of effective writing and some of the special concerns particular to writing about drama.

WHY WRITE?

On one level, the question, Why write? is easy to answer. You are writing because the instructor has assigned a paper as one of the requirements of the class. Most instructors assign papers—rather than merely assigning quizzes or examinations—because they believe that writing plays a unique role in teaching and in learning. Writing is active, a means of producing learning. When you write, you explore a particular problem or issue: thinking about it in a variety of ways, and teaching yourself something about it in the process. By writing, you also present an argument that attempts to persuade your audience to view the problem in the way that you do. In effect, you become a teacher yourself. Writing forces you to make the subject your own. It forces you to explore it and to consider how you can best represent the results of your thinking. Indeed, in the act of writing you may well discover what it is you have to say.

THE WRITING PROCESS

Most college-level writing about drama asks you to construct an interpretation of some aspect of a play or plays. The kind of interpretation you will perform, though, has much in common with persuasive argument—your paper should make an assertion about the play, a **claim** that you will develop in the course of the essay. First, a good claim is not simply a description of the work, a statement of what's already self-evident. To say, for example, that Ibsen's play *A Doll House* is about conflicted gender and marital relations is merely to state the obvious; it leaves you nothing to argue. Nor is a good claim merely a personal opinion about the work, a statement that invites agreement without persuasion or evidence. To say that *A Doll House* is a bad play, or that Nora is an unbelievable character, is an opinion-statement of this kind. Argumentative writing requires you to consider a fundamentally **problematic** issue, a question about which there could be some important disagreement— disagreement regarding the interpretation of the play itself. Writing is, after all, a form of communication. It is important that you have something worthwhile to say and that your way of saying it can be made persuasive to others.

For most people, writing an effective analytical argument has three basic phases that work to transform thoughts into an effective piece of writing. The first phase is the **invention** phase, when you consider the issues you want to raise. This is the time to ask yourself very general and stimulating questions that will lead to a commitment—a **claim**—about the work. If the choice of the paper is up to you, you might ask which of the plays you have read you liked the most. What aspects of the play seem most important, impressive, or unusual to you? If a paper topic has been assigned, you still need to make it your own. You might ask yourself how the topic seems to interpret the play, what problems or questions the topic seems to raise about your understanding of the play. It is at this point that most students come up with the **topic** of their papers, but a topic is only a first step. In order for a topic to be transformed into an argumentative claim, you have to think about it as a **problem.** A topic is inert while a problem is controversial—an idea about which there can be disagreement. For example, this is a topic: "Nora Helmer is a good mother in *A Doll House.*" Although this statement does make a claim, the claim is vague and underdeveloped. Its importance and consequences are not yet made clear. To transform the topic into a problem, we might ask how this claim could be seen as controversial, to involve us in a specific kind of interpretation of the play. One way to transform this topic into a problem is to imply an alternative perspective as part of the claim: "Although Nora Helmer leaves her children at the end of the play, she is really a good mother." This is a more problematic claim, precisely because it raises the possibility that Nora could be seen in two ways. This claim could be made more effective by suggesting how resolving this problem is central to an understanding of the play: "Although Nora Helmer leaves her children at the end of *A Doll House,* the play presents her as a good mother. Nora herself must become a free adult, must discover who she really is, before she can raise her children." This claim raises several complex issues and suggests a particular perspective on them. Your audience would expect you to discuss Nora's accomplishments as a mother in the play and relate those accomplishments to her difficult decision to leave her family at the end of the play.

This process—transforming a topic into a problem—usually marks the end of the first phase of writing, at which you come up with the major claim of your paper, a provisional **thesis.** This claim is still only provisional, because you will probably have to modify it in the next phase of the writing process: organizing your argument, developing your evidence, and drafting the paper. Now that you have a sense of what you want to claim in the essay, you will want to consider how to present your claim effectively. This usually means choosing some elements of the play to examine in detail. In this case, for instance, you might choose to discuss the scenes in which Nora interacts with her children; or the scenes in which she refuses to see them; or the scenes in which she discusses her children with others, like Mrs. Linde and Torvald. Of course, none of these scenes explicitly answers your claim: Ibsen never tells his audience "Nora is a good mother in this scene." It's your task to **interpret** the scene, suggest how we—your audience—should look at it in order to see it as you do. Generating detail of this kind—scenes, characters, speeches, language—to discuss is often one of the most challenging parts of the writing process. One way to help yourself here (and as a writer) is to take some notes on the play after you have read it. What scenes do you think are important or memorable? Why? What do you make of the major characters? These notes can help to provide some of the initial material you will discuss as part of your drafting of the essay.

Having considered what aspects of the play you want to address, you will want to make an outline, a map of your approach. Most students learn to make a formal outline—with major headings, subheadings, and so on—in high school, and some college and university classes require you to submit the outline as part of your writing process. Most writers use a more informal outlining strategy; they make a list of the issues or evidence they want to treat in the paper, as a way of putting main points and main pieces of evidence in order. Once you begin writing, you may well need to revise your outline, as what you have already written suggests new directions for the rest of the essay. Having outlined your approach, the next step is the writing itself. Instead of trying to get everything right in the first draft, most writers use the writing process to generate ideas and develop some prose. There will be plenty of opportunity to shape, develop, and revise the writing later. So, when you begin the paper, do your best to get your argument into a clear order. Write as much as it occurs to you to say on each point, giving yourself a lot of leeway to improvise ideas that may need to be clarified in revision. If important new evidence occurs to you, put it down in the draft, making a note to return to it. The important factor at this stage is to get as many of your thoughts down in order as you can.

The final phase—or phases, since most good papers take several revisions—is the process of revision. Revising is where the process of your thinking is transformed into an effective argument. Through revision your thinking is reshaped to become effective written communication. Written communication is sequential; your audience can only process information one piece at a time. For that reason, it's important to clarify your claims at the outset, tell your audience where the argument is going, and why. It's also important to tell the audience how each section of the argument is helping to substantiate that claim, and why it is important that we've accompanied you so far. A major objective of revision is to make the outlines of the argument—its major phases—explicit in this way. When revising, one useful trick is to read over your text—a paragraph, for instance—and then ask yourself, "What's the point of this paragraph? How does it contribute to my overall argument?" If you cannot answer that question, then you need to consider whether the paragraph—in this form—belongs in the paper at all. If you can answer it, then look to see that your answer is actually written down in the paragraph somewhere, made explicit to your readers, who, after all, are probably not thinking about the problem in exactly the way that you are.

Of course, these are the large-scale revisions; you will also want to ask similar questions of more local matters. Have I presented enough evidence on this point? Have I interpreted the evidence fully for the reader? How are my mechanics—sentence clarity, structure, variety, spelling?

APPROACHES TO WRITING

Writing about drama and theater is not essentially different from writing about other literary, historical, or cultural subjects, and the skills and habits of effective writing will serve well in writing about drama, too. However, writing about drama and theater also follows some of its own conventions. First, papers are generally written in the present verb tense, as though the play were actually taking place now, in front of us. It's up to you, of course, whether you want to write from the point of view of the reader or the point of view of the theater audience, but you will have to adopt a consistent perspective throughout and recognize that each perspective can help to make certain features of the play more clearly visible.

Second, many papers about drama begin by taking issue with one of Aristotle's categories of dramatic structure: the play's plot (how does its sequence of events contribute to its overall meaning?), its characters (how are the characters constructed; how do the conventions of characterization represent "real" people?), its thought or themes (how does the play generate its "themes"?), its language (are there patterns of language, images, or ways of speaking that contribute to your sense of its action?), and its spectacle (are there explicit features of its action onstage that help to realize the play's meaning?). These topics can be expanded through reference to the specific forms of drama in a given period or theater. To talk about the plot structure of a Shakespearean play, after all, is to talk about something very different from the plot of a Beckett play. It's important to realize that these features of the drama can provide a good starting point for your discussion, but that each will need to be specified in terms of your particular argument.

Another approach that's often useful in thinking about drama is to consider the play's staging, either in terms of effects that are described or made explicit in the text (the times that Prospero appears "aloft" in *The Tempest*; the confining single room of *A Doll House*), or in terms of the actual production choices made in a given staging. Thinking about how a production you have seen interpreted the text and how it used acting, movement, set design, and costuming to provide the audience with a given perspective on the play is another standard approach to writing about drama and theater.

CITATION AND DOCUMENTATION

There are a few mechanical conventions specific to writing about drama. As you can see from the essays included in this volume, there are several forms you can use for citing secondary sources. The two main approaches are to use footnotes for all citations (see Sue-Ellen Case's article in Unit 1), or to put the page numbers in parentheses in the text and add a list of Works Cited at the end of the paper, saving notes only for further explanation. Your instructor may well have a preference here and will help you to use secondary citations. The purpose of citing secondary works you may use in writing your essay is twofold: first, to give credit to your sources, to the other writers whose work you may have used in coming to your own conclusions; second, to direct your readers to other material that may be interesting or helpful to them. At most colleges and universities, plagiarism—submitting someone else's work as your own—is an extremely serious offense, and careful attention to citations protects you as well as informing your readers.

Writing about drama uses several conventions to identify quotations from plays. Classical Greek plays are usually cited by line number, and the citation follows the quotation:

Clytaemnestra's effect on Agamemnon is complete when he steps on to the blood-red-carpet, saying, "I feel such shame / to tread the life of the house" (ll. 945–946).

Notice that "ll." is the abbreviation for the word "lines" and is used to identify the line numbers of the quotation, and that the citation follows the close-quotation mark and precedes the period. The citation is part of the sentence, so it's included inside the sentence, before the period.

A different convention is followed for plays from the Renaissance, Restoration, and Neoclassical periods, which are commonly written in verse and usually are divided into acts and scenes. Here, the citation includes act, scene, and line numbers, separated by a period. Some people prefer using Roman numerals (IV.iii.21–22) for act 4, scene 3, lines 21–22, but many people now use Arabic numerals (4.3.21–22) as follows:

Prospero finally accepts his own role in creating Caliban at the end of *The Tempest*, when he says, "this thing of darkness I / Acknowledge mine" (5.1.278–279).

When the play is written in verse, the lineation of the original text is preserved with a slash (/) between the lines, and the capitalization of each new line is preserved as above. Usually, quotations of more than three lines are set off as a separate quotation.

Since modern plays are not consistently divided into acts and scenes and are usually not written in verse lines, it's common to identify the section (act and scene) of the play you are discussing as part of your prose, and then to cite the page number:

The most chilling moment in Shaw's *Major Barbara* occurs at the end of the second act of the play, when Cusins claims, "Dionysus Undershaft has descended. I am possessed!" (687).

The mechanics of quotation are easy to learn and lend your work an air of competence and credibility. For additional information, ask your instructor to recommend a handbook, or consult *The MLA Handbook for Writers of Research Papers*. It contains extensive material on how and when to use footnotes, the preparation of works cited, and more specialized questions of style and mechanics.

STUDENT WRITING ABOUT DRAMA AND THEATER

Although many literature and theater students tend to write about the action, characters, language, or themes of plays as literary works, different kinds of issues often emerge when a play is considered in performance. While a more "literary" essay necessarily focuses considerable attention on developing evidence suggestively from the text of the play, writing about performance negotiates between the prescriptions of the text and their engagement by live performers, actual men and women onstage, moving and behaving in a specific environment.

Two papers written by university students dramatize some of the consequences of writing about drama- as-literature or drama-in-the-theater. Both papers are about Caryl Churchill's play, Cloud Nine, in which questions of text-and-performance are central to thinking about the play's action. The first paper, written by Kimberly Gordon, a Theater major at Northwestern University, considers the play's representation of women, and particularly its characterization of Betty, as part of its critique of the effects of the sexual revolution on the lives of women today. The second paper, written by Charles Heath, an English and Political Science major at the University of California at Davis, responds directly to a performance of Cloud Nine, staged by the Department of Theater and Dance at UC Davis in 1998. Heath concentrates his attention on the ways different roles were performed in this production, and comes to some surprising conclusions about how this production represented the play's sexual politics. Both Kimberly Gordon and Charles Heath graduated in 1998.

Kimberly Gordon   Gordon 1

Professor Worthen

Introduction to Modern Drama

BETTY IN BONDAGE

Choices, respect, and new possibilities were all to have been characteristic of the post-sexual revolution. Many people believed that an entirely new place in history for women would be born. Caryl Churchill, England's most noted feminist playwright, would laugh at such a notion. In all her works, she portrays women as "stuck" and unsatisfied. The relationships of Churchill's women and their positions in them, have been pre-defined by their male counterparts. A woman's adherence to these man-made molds forces her to give precedence to society's demands over her own desires; this trap is exemplified in Churchill's play, Cloud Nine. In this play Churchill employs the character Betty to illustrate the subordinate role of the woman in a male-dominated world. This "subordination" is addressed by the character's desire for something more, her views on marriage, her ingrained, warped perception that a woman must be "bad" in order to be happy, and the punishment she faces if she dares to disobey man's guidelines.

Cloud Nine opens in Victorian Africa with the colonist Clive's introduction of his family. When he speaks of Betty, his wife, he admits, "My wife is all I dreamt a wife to be / and everything she is she owes to me" (Churchill 810). The first words Betty utters confirm Clive's remark: "I live for Clive. The whole aim of my life / Is to be what he looks for in a wife. / I am

Gordon 2

a man's creation as you see, / And what men want is what I want to be" (810). Betty has become a "man's creation" by patterning her behavior and actions to fit her husband's desires. Churchill emphasizes the inequalities in this relationship by using role reversal. In the first act of the play, Betty and others are portrayed by actors of the opposite sex. This information layers the interpretation of the first scene. The audience watches a man play Betty, literalizing the idea that a man helped create her role; the viewer witnesses Betty through the male creator's eyes.

Regarding the issue of cross-dressing, Elin Diamond reminds the reader, "The point is not that the male is feminized but that the female is absent" (97). Betty, who in thought and action is represented as the "token female," is presented, not as a woman, but rather as the illusion of one. A man in a woman's costume produces a greater presence of masculinity and reduction of physical femininity. The absence Diamond speaks of also reflects on women's character—they must be content with being discontent, with having their desires denied. This attitude is established by the male characters and later fostered through the women. When Betty acknowledges her dissatisfaction with the expectations imposed upon her, for example, Harry, an old friend of the family, proves discouraging:

> HARRY: . . . I need you, and I need you where you are, I need you to be Clive's wife. I need to
> go up rivers and know that you are still here thinking of me.
>
> BETTY: I want more than that. Is that wicked of me?
>
> HARRY: Not wicked Betty, silly. (816)

Betty's wanting more is irrelevant. Harry trivializes her plea by calling her "silly," an adjective implying a lack of power more frequently used to describe women and children than men.

Perhaps more damaging than the implications made by the men, are the ways in which they are passed down by the women. This masculine legacy occurs frequently in the mother-daughter relationship, and is seen in the following dialogue between Betty and Maud:

> MAUD: Young women are never happy.
>
> BETTY: Mother, what a thing to say.
>
> MAUD: Then when they're older they look back and see that comparatively speaking they were
> ecstatic. (812)

In this scene, a mother is guilty of perpetuating the void and emptiness in her daughter. As Betty hints of interests outside the domestic range, Maud smothers this curiosity by instructing Betty of

Gordon 3

her place as a wife and daughter. When Betty asks for information about the tribes and floggings taking place on their property, Maud reminds her, "I don't think it's up to us to wonder. . . . You would not want to be told about it, Betty. It is enough for you to know that Clive knows what is happening. Clive will know what to do. Your father always knew what to do" (818). Betty is not taught to be a self-sufficient woman. Maud helps to create and reinforce Betty's dependency on men. As with any mother, Maud means no malice. In act 2, Maud lets her daughter know that all her actions were out of love. She confesses, "I know we have our little differences but I always want what is best for you" (833). Betty's mother, like all mothers, wants her daughter to fit the mold of society. Unfortunately, following Maud's advice robs Betty of her identity as an independent woman.

Betty has been taught to understand the protection she receives by conforming to society's ideals, and reproduces those ideals in her own relationships with other women. She convinces the governess of her children, Ellen, to disregard her own desires and marry for the sole purpose of fulfilling her obligations as a woman:

> BETTY: If you go back to England you might get married, Ellen. You're quite pretty, you should-
> n't despair of getting a husband.
> ELLEN: I don't want a husband. I want you.
> BETTY: Children of your own, Ellen, think.
> ELLEN: I don't want children . . .
> BETTY: . . . Women have their duties as soldiers have. You must be a mother if you can. (821)

Ellen agrees to marry Harry, and just moments after the wedding, Betty reminds her friend that she is, ". . . not getting married to enjoy herself" (822).

Not only are the women portrayed as inferior, and prevented from living life as they please, they are also made to feel "bad" and "weak." In the exchange between Betty and Harry, Betty questions whether she is innately "wicked." Betty refers to being made "better," implying that she feels there is something wrong with her present condition. Churchill reinforces the widespread acceptance of these qualities in women when Clive confronts Betty about her kissing Harry. Betty automatically finds fault in her actions and confesses:

> BETTY: There is something wicked in me, Clive.
> CLIVE: I have never thought of you as having the weakness of your sex, only good qualities.

Gordon 4

> **BETTY:** I am bad, bad, bad
>
> **CLIVE:** You are thoughtless, Betty, that's all. Women can be treacherous and evil. They are darker and more dangerous than men . . . It was a moment of passion such as women are too weak to resist. (819)

The key words "bad," "wicked," "weak," and "treacherous" become not merely the ways in which the men perceive the women, but more dangerously, the characteristics women attribute to themselves. Betty learns to equate sin with happiness, and is punished accordingly.

When women stray from the alleged "social norm" in thought or behavior, the men discipline them to correct their actions. After Clive blames the female sex for Betty's weakness with Harry, he goes on to explain the severe consequences that might have followed had he not shown his wife mercy. He threatens, ". . . It would hurt me to cast you off. That would be my duty . . . If I shot you every British man and woman would applaud me . . ." (819). Clive's warning carries with it a double standard. He reprimands Betty for being an unfaithful wife while he is currently having an affair with the widow Mrs. Saunders.

As act 2 of Cloud Nine begins, the audience encounters an entirely new setting and an entirely new Betty. Act 2 jumps seventy-five years into the future (although the characters age only twenty-five years) and Churchill switches continents as well. It is London, 1979, and Betty has undergone an enormous transformation. During the transition she has become more comfortable with her own sexuality and herself, and her role is now appropriately played by an actress.

The Betty of act 2 leaves her husband, seeks and finds employment, and starts to define herself as her own person. As she begins to disregard her conventional definitions of the roles of wife and mother, she is able to escape her self-implemented boundaries. Betty comes to the realization, "You appreciate the weekend when you're working . . . And the money, I feel like a child with the money, Clive always paid everything but I do understand it perfectly well" (832). She enjoys work and the strength derived from the ability to support herself.

Betty's new self-possession is complemented by her rediscovery of her sexuality at the end of the show. She confides:

> I touched my face, it was there, my arm, my breast and my hand went down where I thought it shouldn't, and I thought well there is somebody there . . . and I felt angry with Clive and angry with my mother and I went on defying them . . . Afterwards I thought I'd betrayed Clive. My mother would kill me. But then I felt triumphant because I was a separate person from them. And

I cried because I didn't want to be. But I don't cry anymore. Sometimes I do it three times in one night and it really is great fun. (833)

Where Betty finds success in living alone, the adjustment is not an easy one. It is hard to break old habits, such as making tea for two. She discovers that, "It's strange not having a man in the house. You don't know how to do things for yourself" (828). The Betty in act 2 is still lonely and struggles with some reluctance to accept the new ideals and lifestyles presented by the generations of her children and grandchildren.

By the play's close, Betty does begin to embrace a more independent future. This action is visually demonstrated as Churchill instructs that the Bettys from each act appear on stage together and embrace as the last action of the play. This hug implies both a sympathetic understanding of their shared past, and an appreciation for the genuine efforts to ensure a happier future. Betty is on the right path to freeing herself from remaining "stuck" in the outline man has provided her. But she has just begun the challenge. For now, Betty and all of Churchill's women, are still a long way from being on "Cloud Nine."

Works Cited

Churchill, Caryl. "Cloud Nine." In *The Harcourt Brace Anthology of Drama*. 3rd ed. Ed. W.B. Worthen. Fort Worth: Harcourt, 2000. 810–834.

Diamond, Elin. "Refusing the Romanticism of Identity." *Performing Feminisms: Feminist Critical Theory and Theatre*. Ed. Sue-Ellen Case. Baltimore: Johns Hopkins UP, 1990. 92–105.

Charles Heath

Professor Worthen

Modern Drama

THE VALUE OF SUBTLE CROSS-DRESSING

What everyone remembers after seeing a performance of <u>Cloud Nine</u> are the cross-dressing characters and the stark difference between the first and second acts. The performance of the cross-dressing characters and the staging changes between acts can be manipulated to produce a multitude of effects on the audience. If the director opts to have the cross-dressing characters of Betty, Edward, and Cathy be flamboyant and exaggerated in their portrayal of the opposite sex, a highly funny yet probing production ensues. This performance choice produces a strong Brechtian alienation effect on the audience. The flamboyant performance examines what outwardly expressed symbols define us as men and women. Seeing a woman playing a man clearly delineates between actor and character, drawing out the methodology employed by the actor to perform the "stock male," drawing the audience's attention to how speech, physical movements, interaction among characters, construct "masculine" behavior. When the audience sees these gestures performed in an exaggerated way, it becomes possible to recognize that they too employ this socially constructed system to label themselves "male" or "female." Witnessing exaggerated gender construction alienates audience members from their own practices of gender construction and the identities that accompany those constructions. Once alienated, having stepped back from this "identity," the spectator can scrutinize and examine it. The flamboyant method of performing <u>Cloud Nine</u> is visually appetizing, producing a colorful spectacle on stage as it communicates what Churchill clearly wants us to take from the play: that our identities are a social construction, and that construction is inextricably linked to the power hierarchies of our society and history.

The current production of <u>Cloud Nine</u> at UC Davis accomplishes very different goals. To say it accomplishes different goals is not to say it does not embody the themes of a more flamboyant production, but that it emphasizes a different set of effects available to a director of Churchill's rich text. The cross-dressing Davis actors are far from flamboyant in their portrayals of the opposite sex; they at times seem gender neutral, almost to "disappear" in a realistic way into the roles they play. Despite Craig Swogger's elevated voice and occasional fluttering of a Victorian-era fan, he rarely makes overtly feminine gestures in his performance of Betty in act 1. Similarly, he never adds masculine gestures to the performance. Rather than highlighting his own gender, or flamboyantly exaggerating Betty's, Swogger instead remains gender neutral, allowing the wig, dress, and Churchill's brilliant lines to convey the character's femininity and trapped masculinity. Similarly, Nancy Stone's portrayal of Edward is not flamboyantly masculine, nor does she allow her femininity to show through. Again Churchill's dialogue and the young Victorian boy's outfit contrast against her clearly female appearance to stage a problem of frustrated identity in a low-key, realistic manner.

While this way of performing Cloud Nine takes away from the audience's examination of the socially constructed male and female as exaggerated by an actor, it does allow the audience to see Churchill's characters in more psychological terms, struggling between their inner selves and their social circumstances. The theme of this production is entrapment. The inner self, as symbolized by the gender of the actor playing the role, is not allowed to express itself because it is trapped inside the social role of the character, be it Betty, Edward, or Cathy. Instead of commenting on what it means to be a man or a woman in some essential way, this production looks more at what it means to want to live the socially constructed life of a man or woman, and the consequences that arise from the imposed conformity to norms of gender and sexuality.

What we find out through the course of the play is that men and women are quite capable of crossing gender barriers, once oppressive males are out of the way. Mrs. Saunders in act 1 seemingly lives the life Betty desires: to break out of the constricted female role of a Victorian wife and satisfy her desires for sexual and personal independence. Mrs. Saunders is liberated because her husband is dead. Betty, too, is able to dislodge the yoke of patriarchy by leaving her husband in act 2, and subsequently satisfies her own needs. Edward seems to come to terms with his sexuality once on his own, out from under the scrutinizing and demanding reign of his father. In act 2, with a sense of liberation, Edward's repressed homosexuality (construed as femininity in act 1) flourishes; even the "male," self-determining side of Betty appears. In act 2 Betty and Edward are no longer confined in the roles their characters were subjected to in act 1. Liberated from repression, the innate person and his or her outward identity are reconciled, which is the point of having actors play same-sex characters in act 2.

What the Davis performance does particularly well is to emphasize Cloud Nine as metatheater, as a play that examines the practice of drama. Act 1 is a more or less realist Victorian drama. The stage has an elaborate Victorian verandah with white wicker furniture and a Union Jack flying above. The characters wear elaborate period costumes and even though the theater has a thrust stage (surrounded on three sides by the audience), the stage is brightly lit, marking out the familiar, proscenium-like "realistic" division between stage and audience. The story of act 1 unfolds organically as we learn about the characters' pasts in order to understand the present conflict that drives the drama. When the audience returns from the intermission, though, they find a dimly lit stage with the Victorian plantation home removed. In the plantation's place is an ominous wrought iron fence and some children's play furniture. The dark stage blends almost seamlessly with the auditorium, providing no buffer between drama onstage, and the world of the audience. Further breaking down the space between the characters and the audience, the characters often speak directly to the audience, in addition to using traditional methods of dialogue at other times. The plot of the play becomes very fragmented and episodic. The links between the individual episodes are left to be made by the audience. Despite the over-130-year gap between Victorian colonialism and late 1970s London, the characters have only aged twenty-five years. This deconstruction of time compresses modern English history into a short representative mode that conveys the process of modernization in a single setting.

The multitude of marked changes between act 1 and act 2 shows the evolution of theater from the conventional Victorian stage, contemporary with the act 1 characters, to the postmodern stage contemporary with the act 2 characters and the audience. David Moon's scenic and lighting design accentuate the period-specific differences between the acts to make the audience member aware of the dramatic methodology being employed. Nancy Stone and Jon Jackson, as Betty and Gerry, respectively, deliver highly provocative monologues describing their sexual liberation, leaving the audience member convinced that the modern dramatic conventions applied in Cloud Nine are the only suitable means of representation for the contemporary world. A more traditional realistic rendering could not adequately convey the intimate details of Betty and Gerry's sex lives that the intimate dialogue between character and audience made clear. The "realistic" separation of stage and audience in act 1 both protects the audience and provides a feeling of omniscience; breaking down the proscenium in act 2 puts the audience more into the middle of the action, where we look for our bearings in the confusion of the present, much like the characters. The production's synthesis of history becomes overtly clear when certain characters of act 1 come onto the modern stage and clash with act 2 characters who remain in contemporary apparel, and clash with the dark and sparse set. The contrast looks unnatural and the characters of the past look foreign or alien.

Heath 4

The production shows at once how alien Victorian England is within the realm of modernity, and how those characters nonetheless form the past's very presence on the modern stage, demonstrating how that colonial and patriarchal history lingers and influences the modern day.

A production of <u>Cloud Nine</u> forces actors, director, and designers to make many very important decisions. The impressions of the audience can be swayed immensely by the handling of the play's abundant complexities. The UC Davis production uses a rather conservative production style for a potentially outrageous play. The conservative line does compromise the play's spectacular qualities. However, to downplay the visual feast is to evoke the more subtle qualities in Churchill's text. What the play loses in flamboyant performance it recovers in simplicity. Costuming, scenery and lighting are dead-on throughout the play, picking up on and exploiting Churchill's toying with notions of time, modernization and representation. Churchill's text is meant to reach out and probe each audience member's conception of his or her identity; the UC Davis performance aptly violates its viewing audience.

Glossary

Absurd *See* **Theater of the Absurd.**

Académie Française An academy founded by Cardinal Richelieu in 1635 to resolve the critical debate surrounding Corneille's play *The Cid* and to regularize the French language.

actos Short satirical plays devised by Luis Valdez and El Teatro Campesino in the late 1960s to dramatize the conditions of farmworkers in California.

afterpiece A short play—usually a pantomime or farce—that followed the main play on the evening's bill; common in England in the eighteenth and nineteenth centuries.

agora The marketplace in ancient Greek towns; the *agora* was often used for dramatic performance.

alienation effect A stage technique developed by Bertolt Brecht in the 1920s and 1930s for "estranging" the action of the play. By making characters and their actions seem re-markable, alien, or unusual, Brecht encouraged the audience to question the social real-ities that produced such events, the political and ideological background of the drama and of its stage production.

allegory A literary or dramatic technique that uses actual characters, places, and actions to represent more abstract political, moral, or religious ideas. *See Everyman.*

alojería The tavern at the rear of the *patio* in a Spanish Golden Age theater, or *corral*.

amphitheater A semicircular theater design, consisting of a playing area faced by rising tiers of seats; often used outdoors, this was the design of classical Greek theaters.

anachronism Using people, places, or things that are chronologically out of keeping with the rest of the fictive world of a play or narrative; for example, using medieval English shepherds to attend the birth of Christ in medieval **cycle plays.**

anagnorisis Greek term for a character's "recognition" of something previously not known in the play. In *The Poetics,* Aristotle links *anagnorisis* with **peripeteia,** the "reversal" in the action of the play.

antagonist The force or character that opposes the main character **(protagonist)** of a play.

antimasque A scene of misrule, usually involving witches, goblins, demons, or savages, who are transformed magically into princes, gods and goddesses, or virtues in a Jacobean **masque.**

antiphonal performance Alternative or responsive singing between individuals or groups; in the Middle Ages, it commonly involved two choirs.

archon A magistrate in classical Athens; each year, an *archon* was assigned the responsibility for organizing the **City Dionysia.**

apron The section of the stage that extends toward the auditorium beyond the **proscenium.**

Atellan farce Improvised comic skits featuring stock characters performed by masked ac-tors in ancient Rome.

atoza Upstage area in a **Noh** theater in which the musicians are seated.

auto sacramentale Elaborate Spanish religious dramas originally devised as part of the feast of Corpus Christi. *Autos* continued to be performed in Spain until 1765.

avant-garde Literally, the "advance guard"; the term usually refers to the most innovative, experimental, or unorthodox artists in a given historical period. Used almost exclusively of late nineteenth- and twentieth-century movements.

backcloth A painted cloth lowered at the rear of the stage to represent a dramatic location.

Beijing Opera Elaborate form of Chinese theater involving an onstage orchestra, ornate costumes, music, and dance.

benefit In the English theater of the seventeenth, eighteenth, and nineteenth centuries, a performance whose profits were assigned to a single performer or to the playwright.

biomechanics An experimental technique for actor training and performance devised by the Russian director Vsevolod Meyerhold after the Russian Revolution (1917). The technique emphasized the actor's physical training, stressing acrobatic and choreographic elements in production.

bhava A stageable emotion in **Sanskrit drama,** related to the play's principal *rasa,* or mood.

biwa Four-stringed, plucked instrument used to accompany spoken narration in medieval Japan.

blank verse An English verse meter consisting of unrhymed **iambic pentameter** lines (ten syllables with alternating stress, the first stress falling on the second syllable).

box Box seating first appeared in theaters in the late seventeenth century; boxes were arranged around the side of the stage and the sides of the auditorium for the private accommodation of small numbers of people. Boxes were more expensive than **pit** or **gallery** seats.

box set First devised in the 1830s, a set consisting of three practical walls enclosing the stage in a roomlike way.

bunraku The term used for modern Japanese **doll theater,** derived from the eighteenth-century master Uemura Bunrakuken.

butai The acting area, or stage proper, of a **Noh** theater.

butoh A powerful form of dance developed in the post-Hiroshima era in Japan; it features nude actors, covered in white powder, whose movements are slow and ethereal.

cabaret performance Stage performances in restaurants serving food and drink; especially popular in Europe after World War I, cabarets often were used for innovative kinds of performance.

canon An authorized body of texts, such as the *canon* of Shakespeare's known plays; also commonly used to mean a "traditional" body of texts.

capa y espada Literally, "cape and sword" plays, swashbuckling romances in the Spanish Golden Age theater.

Capitano The braggart soldier of *commedia dell' arte.*

carro Wagon used for performance of Spanish *auto sacramentale.*

catastrophe The turning point in the plot of a classical **tragedy.**

catharsis Literally, the "purging" that Aristotle discusses as the effect of **tragedy** in his *The Poetics.* Catharsis has been variously described as an emotional release on the part of the spectators, or as the recognition and purging of wrongdoing in the action of the play.

cazuela The women's **gallery** above the *alojería* in a Spanish Golden Age theater, or *corral.*

character A fictional "person" appearing in a play or other work of fiction; usually conventionalized to some degree.

chonin Japanese term for townsmen.

choregos An important citizen in ancient Athens given the responsibility for financing, assembling, and training the chorus of Greek **tragedy.**

chorus A masked group of young men who sang and danced as a group in Greek **tragedy** and **comedy;** larger choruses also performed **dithyrambs.**

City Dionysia Annual spring festival honoring the god Dionysus; one of four festivals held between December and April. Sometimes called the *Great Dionysia,* it was the site of dramatic competitions and other public displays and rituals.

comedia nueva Mixed mode form of drama associated with Lope de Vega.

Comédie Française   The official national theater of France, devoted to the staging of the classics. Founded and chartered by Louis XIV in 1680, when Molière's company and the Marais company were united.

comedy   Traditionally a humorous literary form, comedy typically concerns the trials of love, and/or ridicules the failings of certain members of society. *See* **comedy of manners, new comedy, old comedy, romantic comedy.**

comedy of manners   Comic drama that takes the manners of high society as its subject; in comedy of manners, the dialogue is often witty or epigrammatic.

commedia dell' arte   Improvised comic plays performed by itinerant companies; it originated in Italy in the sixteenth century and then spread throughout Europe. Actors each played a stock character type and improvised the action according to a shared outline plot.

constructivist theater   A movement in the Soviet theater after World War I, and often associated with the director Vsevolod Meyerhold. Adapted from the visual arts, constructivist theater resisted the use of representational sets, using more abstract "constructions" onstage.

corral   Open-air Spanish theater of the sixteenth and seventeenth centuries, constructed within an open courtyard.

cross-dressing   One of the conventions of cross-gendered acting, in which women play male characters in male costume, and men play female characters in women's clothing.

cycle plays   A series of plays dramatizing Christian history from the Creation to the Last Judgment, devised and performed in the Middle Ages by craft guilds called *mysteries;* the cycles are sometimes also called *mystery cycles* or *mystery plays.* Performed outside the church on the Feast of Corpus Christi.

Dada   A nonsense term adopted as the name of a literary and theatrical movement in Europe after World War I; Dada developed an esthetic of random and irrational art. Dada performances became popular in cabarets of Paris, Zurich, and Berlin in the 1920s.

daimyo   Feudal lord of Japan, member of the *samurai* class of warriors, and owing duty to the *shogun.*

decorum   The concept, associated with **neoclassicism,** that the action and subject matter (idealized), language (heightened), and moral propriety (elevated), should be stylistically integrated and unified.

deme   A neighborhood in classical Athens; the root of the modern word "democracy."

demonstration   Describing the *alienation effect,* Bertolt Brecht urged his actors to "demonstrate" the roles they played, rather than identifying with them in the mode of Stanislavskian acting. Acting-as-demonstration keeps the audience aware of both the actor *and* the "character" at the same time.

dengaku-no   Form of dance, role-playing, and acrobatics popular in Japan in the eleventh and twelfth centuries; said to be one of the progenitors of **Noh** theater.

desvanes   Small open galleries on the third and fourth **stories** in a Spanish Golden Age theater, or *corral.*

deus ex machina   Literally, the "god from the machine"; the term refers to the practice of using a crane to lower the character of a god to the stage at the end of a classical Greek **tragedy,** usually to resolve the action of the play. In modern usage the term refers to any dramatic device that suddenly resolves the action of a play.

dithyramb   Choral hymns sung and danced to honor Dionysus as part of the **City Dionysia.** Choruses of fifty men or fifty boys drawn from each tribe performed *dithyrambs* prior to the tragedy competition; Aristotle thought **tragedy** to have originated in these dithyrambic performances.

dokekata   Comic roles in **Kabuki** theater.

doll theater   Form of Japanese theater originating in the seventeenth century; doll theater uses elaborate dolls, operated by three visible puppeteers, and combines music and narration. The most prominent form of doll theater today is called *bunraku.*

Dottore   The "doctor" or old pedant of *commedia dell' arte;* usually a friend of **Pantalone.**

drama   A literary composition, usually in dialogue form, and centering on the actions of fictional characters.

Egungen   Festival common among the Yoruba peoples of Nigeria involving masks and costumes for communication with the dead.

ekkyklema   A low platform used to roll objects or bodies from the *skene* doors onto the stage in classical Greek theater.

emotion memory   A term developed by the Russian director Constantin Stanislavski to describe an actor's "work on himself" in acting. After considering a character's circumstances in the play and his past life leading up to the action of the play, the actor tries to connect the character's situation with important events in his or her own life: this emotional or affectual connection can make the character's display of emotion onstage seem realistic and immediate.

entremeses   Short plays performed as interludes between acts of Golden Age dramas.

environmental theater   A term coined by Richard Schechner in the late 1960s to describe performances that do not distinguish between the playing area and the audience; the performance takes place throughout the theatrical environment.

epic theater   A term associated with the German director Erwin Piscator and theorized by Bertolt Brecht in the late 1920s and 1930s, epic theater uses episodic dramatic action, nonrepresentational staging, and the **alienation effect,** to demonstrate the political, social, and economic factors governing the lives of the dramatic characters. In the theater, Brecht advocated the use of placards to announce the action, visible lighting, filmscreens on the stage, and other devices to produce this epic effect.

episode   Originally, a dramatic scene in a classical Greek **tragedy,** as distinct from the choral odes; now, usually refers to any incident or event in a play. Plays that are episodic tend not to subordinate episodes to a causal plot, but simply to arrange them in a series.

exodos   The final scene and exit of the characters and chorus in a classical Greek play.

expressionist theater   An early twentieth-century movement challenging the **verisimilitude** of realistic theater by staging individual emotional, unconscious states of mind directly. In expressionist plays, the action is usually abrupt and intense; the characters are usually generalized; the plot is typically symbolic or allegorical.

extravaganza   Visual spectacle popular in nineteenth-century theater.

Fabian society   A late nineteenth-century English socialist political society; Marxist in its orientation to social change, the Fabian society advocated a policy of gradual reform rather than revolution.

farce   Usually a short comic play, often relying on a highly coincidental plot.

film noir   A **genre** of black-and-white detective films popular in the 1940s, which frequently used shadowy, nighttime settings to establish an aura of menace and foreboding.

folio   A large-format printed volume, in which only four pages (two per side) are printed on each sheet of paper; the paper is folded once to form four pages.

fourth wall   Refers to the style of realistic theater since the late nineteenth century, in which the stage is treated as a room with one wall missing. The audience is not acknowledged or addressed by the actors, but overlooks the scene as a silent, invisible observer.

fuebashira   Flute-player's pillar in a **Noh** theater, the upstage right pillar where the flute-player is positioned during the performance.

gallery   In seventeenth-, eighteenth-, and nineteenth-century theaters, ascending rows of bench seating, usually located opposite the stage on the third level of the auditorium; generally the most inexpensive seats in the theater.

geisha   In Japan, a hired female companion valued for artistic accomplishment; legally not classed as a prostitute.

genre   Literally, "kind" or "type"; *genre* in literary and dramatic studies refers to the main types of literary form, principally tragedy and comedy. The term can also refer to forms that are more specific to a given historical era, such as **revenge tragedy** or to more specific subgenres of **tragedy** and **comedy,** such as **comedy of manners.**

given circumstances   Term used by Constantin Stanislavski to describe the situation a character finds himself or herself in at the opening of the play, which the actor must construct as his first step in building the character toward performance.

gracioso   The comic fool of Spanish Golden Age drama, popularized in part by Lope de Vega.

gradas   The steeply raked side seats along the side of the patio in a Spanish Golden Age theater, or *corral.*

grave trap   A trap door in the floor of the stage, often in the center.

hamartia   A term used by Aristotle in *The Poetics* to describe the tragic hero's decisive act, the "error" or "mistake" that brings about the **tragedy.** Sometimes mistranslated as "tragic flaw," a translation that mistakenly changes the meaning of the term from the description of an action to a feature of the character's moral makeup or personality.

hanamichi   Elevated gangway extending from the rear of **Kabuki** theater to the stage; major characters use this bridge for their entrances and some scenes are played here as well.

Harlequin   The main character of *commedia dell' arte,* and later of English pantomime. Usually a wily schemer, Harlequin was originally played in a patched costume, which became conventionalized as the familiar diamond-covered costume. Harlequin was usually masked and carried a flat bat or paddle.

hashigakari   The long bridge from the **mirror room** to the stage of a **Noh** theater.

heroic tragedy   A seventeenth-century **genre**, usually on the theme of love vs. honor; associated with Dryden in England, Corneille in France, and Calderón de la Barca in Spain.

hon kyōgen   The main play of a **Kabuki** performance, originally lasting from about 7 A.M. until dusk when the theater closed.

hurry door   The small door leading offstage from the *atoza,* or upstage area of a **Noh** theater; used by the chorus, the stage assistants, and by dead characters.

hybridization   In the theory of **postcolonial** literatures, the use of several styles—typically elements of indigenous or colonized and colonial cultures—in one work, typically to dramatize the cultural politics engrained in colonial habits of representation.

iambic pentameter   English verse meter consisting of ten-syllable lines with alternating stressed and unstressed syllables, the first stress falling on the second syllable.

ideology   A complex term first used in the eighteenth century to categorize political beliefs and attitudes. Used to mean (1) a body of beliefs, a doctrine; (2) a body of illusory beliefs, a false doctrine; or (3) a socially grounded system for producing beliefs and values, a way of producing meanings or doctrines.

Independent Theater Movement   A late-nineteenth-century movement in Europe, in which small theaters gambled on the production of new and unconventional plays—by Ibsen, Shaw, Chekhov—to a small audience, usually outside the theatrical mainstream.

Innamorata/o   The attractive young lovers of *commedia dell' arte;* played without masks.

interlude   A short play, usually comic, performed during courtly feasts at the English court in the sixteenth century.

jatra   A form of Indian folk theater popular in Bengal, traditionally involving music and singing; the jatra typically centers on the adventures of a central character—Vivek, or "conscience"—and can treat contemporary social issues

jidaimono   The four- to six-act "history" section of a **Kabuki** performance.

jōruri   Performance of narrative and dialogue to the accompaniment of a samisen in Japanese theater; these elements absorbed into **doll theater.**

Kabuki   Form of Japanese popular theater originating in the early seventeenth century. Kabuki tends to encompass both comic and serious elements in elaborate and conventional performances that originally lasted from ten to twelve hours; it includes live acting, narration, music, and singing.

kamyonguk   Dance-drama form practiced in Korea, using colorful costumes, masked actors, and musical accompaniment.

katakiyaku   Villain role in **Kabuki** theater.

kathakali   An elaborate form of music and dance drama that originated in the Kerala province of southern India in the sixteenth century; kathakali uses highly conventionalized movements and hand gestures and has preserved some of the dramatic forms of classical **Sanskrit** theater.

komos   A procession and dance in ancient Greece, sometimes thought to be the origin of comic drama.

kyōgen   Brief farcical play performed as interludes between **Noh** plays.

language   One of the six constituent elements of drama defined by Aristotle in *The Poetics.*

line of business   A conventional or stock "character" type that is the specialty of a given actor; his or her "line of business" might be old men, heavy villains, comic heroines, etc.

Little Negro Theater Movement   A movement in U.S. theater in the 1920s to develop theaters owned and operated by African Americans, playing a dramatic repertory by African American writers.

Little Theater Movement   A movement in the American theater in the early twentieth century akin to the **Independent Theater Movement** in Europe. Little Theaters offered new or noncommercial plays to smaller audiences.

liturgical drama   Short dramatized sections of the Catholic Mass performed as part of the service; may have inspired the more elaborate, nonliturgical **cycle plays.**

loa   A short, typically allegorical play used to introduce a **comedy** or religious play in Spanish Golden Age theater.

machina   The Greek term for the crane used in the ancient theater to raise and lower characters, particularly the gods.

machine plays   Term used principally in seventeenth-century French theater to describe spectacular special-effects extravaganzas, in which the dramatic action—usually drawn from mythological subjects—was merely a pretext for the use of stage machinery.

magic if   Term developed by Constantin Stanislavski to describe the actor's attitude toward a role; to play "as if I were in this situation."

mansions   Structures placed at several locations inside medieval churches as settings for liturgical plays.

masque   A brief, usually symbolic, mythological, or allegorical play, with elaborate scenic effects performed at the English court during the sixteenth and seventeenth centuries; performed both by actors and by courtiers.

melodrama   First used in the late eighteenth century, the term originally referred to highly charged, popular plays using music to reinforce their clear-cut moral action; now refers more generally to plays with a schematic opposition between good and evil, in which good usually prevails.

metatheater   A term used to describe plays that self-consciously comment on the process of theater, or treat the process of theater as a metaphor for off-stage reality. Such plays sometimes use the play-within-the-play device.

Method acting   A technique of acting developed by Constantin Stanislavski at the turn of the twentieth century, which teaches actors to use **emotion memory** to enact the character's feelings persuasively and realistically in performance; method acting became especially popular in the United States in the 1930s, 1940s, and 1950s.

metsukebashira   The "gazing pillar" in a **Noh** theater, where the *shite* looks when delivering his first speech. It is the downstage right pillar.

mie   Exaggerated pose struck for expressive effect by actors in **Kabuki** theater.

mimesis   Greek word for "imitation" used by Aristotle in *The Poetics* to describe the function of art.

mirror room   The waiting room of a **Noh** theater, where actors in costume contemplate their characterization.

mise-en-scène   The "putting onstage" of a play, including the setting, scenery, direction, and action.

mitos   Lyrical plays on Mexican American life devised by Luis Valdez and El Teatro Campesino in the late 1960s and 1970s.

monopoly   The right to exclusive production of the drama.

montage   A technique used in film consisting of a rapid sequence of images.

morality drama   A late-medieval dramatic form using allegorical characters to dramatize moral and ethical problems involved in leading a Christian life.

music   A constituent element of drama as defined by Aristotle in *The Poetics;* Aristotle refers to the flute music that accompanied performance in the ancient Greek theater.

mystery cycles   *See* **cycle plays.**

naturalism   A late nineteenth-century movement that attempted to achieve an objective **verisimilitude** in art—chiefly in theater and literature—by adopting a "scientific" attitude toward its subject matter. Thematically, naturalism emphasizes the role of society, history, and personality in determining the actions of its characters, usually expressed as a conflict between the characters and their environment.

nautical shows   A type of **melodrama** popular in England in the eighteenth and nineteenth centuries on seafaring subjects; in aquatic dramas, the stage was actually flooded.

neoclassical drama   Drama written under the influence of **neoclassicism.**

neoclassicism   A movement throughout Europe in the sixteenth to eighteenth centuries to revive the forms and values of art exemplified by ancient literature; associated with the recovery of Aristotle's *The Poetics* and its translation into prescriptions for the stage.

new comedy   A form originating in the fourth and third centuries BCE, first in Greece and then in Rome. In the plays of Plautus, for instance, new comedy generally concerns a romantic plot involving a conflict between young lovers, an old man, and a tricky servant.

Noh   Japanese classical theater dating from the fourteenth century; the plays are highly poetic dramas given extremely formal production onstage. Noh drama was admired by Yeats and by other modern playwrights.

ode   In Greek drama, a song performed by the chorus while dancing.

old comedy   Satiric social comedy of fifth-century BCE Athens; Aristophanes' plays are the only surviving examples.

onnagata   Women's roles in **Kabuki** theater, all of which are played by men.

onna kabuki   Literally, "women's Kabuki," an early name for **Kabuki** companies, which were composed mainly of women.

orchestra   Literally, the "dancing place," the circular area before the **skene** where the **chorus** performed in ancient Greek theater.

pageant master The guild officer responsible for gathering funds to finance medieval mystery pageants.

pageant wagons Wagons carrying the sets for productions of medieval **cycle plays,** on which the plays were performed.

Pantalone Foolish old man in *commedia dell' arte;* played masked.

pantomime In general, silent acting using gesture and facial expression. English pantomime—or "panto"—is a spoken form, in which spectacular fairy-tale extravaganzas are performed with music and dance during the Christmas holidays.

parabasis A choral speech in ancient Greek **comedy** in which the **chorus** comments on contemporary social issues.

parodos The entrance song of the **chorus** in Greek tragedy.

parterre The standing area in the auditorium of late seventeenth-century Parisian theaters; the **pit.**

pastiche Term used by Fredric Jameson to describe the toneless quotation of earlier artistic styles in contemporary (or postmodern) works.

patents Licenses given by the crown permitting a company to give dramatic performances; often, a patent would give a company or a small number of companies a **monopoly** on dramatic performance.

patent theaters Theaters given **patents** (or licenses) by the crown for dramatic performance, sometimes holding a monopoly on performance. Charles II of England granted two patents and gave their owners a monopoly on dramatic performance.

patio The flat central courtyard of a Spanish Golden Age theater, or *corral.*

peripeteia A term used by Aristotle in *The Poetics* to describe the "reversal" in the action of a **tragedy.**

phallus A leather phallus worn by male characters in Greek **comedy.**

pit Floor area immediately in front of the stage in seventeenth- and eighteenth-century theaters.

plot The sequence of events in a play or narrative; differs from the "story," which encompasses earlier events. Some works have several plots.

pointing Common practice in the eighteenth-century theater of delivering a famous speech directly to the audience from a downstage position; to "make a point."

polis A city-state in ancient Greece.

political theater In conventional usage, theater that seems to question the inequities and injustices of contemporary society. Bertolt Brecht developed a more searching critique of political theater, however, in which the ideology of theatrical representation itself could be seen as the theater's "politics."

postcolonial While referring specifically to the cultures of a nation that has gained independence, the term *postcolonial* is generally applied more broadly, referring to cultures still negotiating for political freedom, to internally colonized cultures, and to cultures that experience economic or cultural imperialism, even though they may be part of an independent nation-state.

postmodern A term used to characterize the complex relationship between some contemporary works of art and their modernist forebears. Postmodern works are generally characterized by stylistic "quotation," an invocation and disengagement from history, and the fragmentation of artistic surface.

Prakit The everyday, prose dialect spoken in **Sanskrit drama,** usually reserved for comic characters, women, and children.

private theaters In Renaissance England, indoor theaters serving a more privileged audience. Often located on lands within the city limits that were not under city jurisdiction, such as Blackfriars.

prologue In Greek **drama,** an introductory scene preceding the entrance of the **chorus.** In later usage, an introductory scene not directly part of the main action.

proscenium An arch over the front of the stage. First used in European theaters in the Renaissance; throughout the eighteenth and nineteenth centuries, theater design gradually eliminated the **apron** that extended in front of the proscenium and decorated the proscenium arch itself, emphasizing its framelike quality.

protagonist Literally, the "first contestant" in the ancient Greek theater, the term referred to the "first" or main actor competing for a prize. In modern usage, refers to the play's main character.

public theaters In Renaissance England, large outdoor theaters, usually polygonal in shape, consisting of three-story galleries surrounding an open standing pit and a thrust stage.

quarto A small-size book format, in which eight pages are printed on a single sheet of paper; the paper is folded twice to make eight pages.

raked stage A stage that is elevated in the back and lower in the front; common in Europe after the seventeenth century. The raked stage gave rise to the terms "upstage" (toward the back, which was higher) and "downstage" (toward the front, which was lower).

Ramlila and **Raslila** Forms of traditional found in northern India, Ramlila and Raslila performances generally last several weeks and concern events from the *Ramayana* and *Mahabharata* epic poems.

rasa An impersonal mood or attitude of contemplation in Hindu philosophy; in **Sanskrit drama,** the play is designed to produce one of eight *rasas* in the audience: erotic, comic, pathetic, furious, heroic, terrible, odious, or marvelous. The basic *rasa* of each play is related to its bhava, or stageable emotion.

realism A literary and theatrical practice valuing direct imitation or **verisimilitude.** Often associated with **naturalism,** modern realism is sometimes described as the inheritor of naturalism. In practice, realism is usually more concerned with psychological motives, the "inner reality," and less committed to achieving a superficial **verisimilitude** alone.

repertory A company that performs several plays in rotation throughout a season is a repertory company; the term also refers to a set of plays.

revenge tragedy A tragic **genre** popular in English Renaissance, usually involving a complicated intrigue plot in which the hero is force to commit murder in order to avenge himself; madness and supernatural agents (ghosts) are also a common feature. Shakespeare's *Hamlet* is the best-known example.

role-doubling The practice of using one actor to play more than one part.

romance A modern term used to define idealized narratives and sometimes applied to the idealized comedies written by Shakespeare late in his career, especially *The Winter's Tale* and *The Tempest.*

romantic comedy Comic form centering on the romance between two lovers, or between several sets of lovers. Romantic comedy typically begins with some unreasonable impediment to the lovers' union, and when after a complicated series of events the obstacle is overcome, the play ends in marriage.

rōnin *Samurai* warriors who have been disgraced and outcast from society; "men adrift."

ruido A "noise" play or violent **comedy** in Spanish Golden Age theater.

Rupaka The "major drama" of classical **Sanskrit** theater.

sainete Deriving from the *genero chico* of Spain, a short, sometimes satirical play often used for interludes or ***entremeses,*** it was widely used for plays on regional or local-color themes in Argentina in the nineteenth century.

samisen Three-stringed instrument that is both plucked and struck as accompaniment to narration in *jōruri.* In the late sixteenth century, became instrumental in the **doll theater.**

samurai Warrior class of feudal Japan; *samurai* lords both patronized **Noh** playwrights and companies, and provided the code of conduct informing many **Noh, doll theater,** and **Kabuki** plays.

Sanskrit An ancient Indo-European language; once a spoken language, by the modern era it had become mainly a written language reserved for academic and religious purposes. In **Sanskrit drama,** Sanskrit is reserved for elevated scenes and characters, while **Prakrit,** the everyday dialect, is spoken by other characters.

Sanskrit drama The **drama** of ancient India, particularly the plays of its "Golden Age" (second to ninth centuries).

sarugaku-no Form of dance, role-playing, and acrobatics popular in Japan in the eleventh and twelfth centuries; said to be the progenitor of **Noh** theater.

saruwaka Comic roles in **Kabuki** theater, performed by men.

satyr play A brief, rugged **comedy** performed by actors in satyr costumes (half-man, half-goat) after the performance of a tragic **trilogy** at the **City Dionysia;** usually on mythological subjects.

scaena Three-story stage house behind the stage in the Roman theater, facing the audience. Elaborately decorated with columns, panels, and porticos.

scenic unity The practice of harmonizing acting style, costumes, and sets to create the illusion of a single, unified environment on the stage.

sewamono "Domestic plays" of the Japanese **doll theater.**

sharers Actors and playwrights in the English Renaissance theater who, as investors in the company, took a share of the profits; they were responsible for building or leasing a theater and were legally liable for the company's actions.

shimpa A movement in Japanese theater beginning in the late nineteenth century to adapt European **drama** to Japanese style and subject matter.

shingeki A movement in twentieth-century Japanese theater to import the style and techniques of European realistic theater into the Japanese theater.

shite Principal actor in **Noh** theater.

shitebashira The upstage right pillar in a **Noh** theater, near the *hashigakari,* where the *shite* delivers his opening speech.

shogun Hereditary military leader of Japan from the twelfth through the nineteenth centuries; the *shogun* was the most important of the *samurai* (warrior) class, composed of *daimyo* (feudal lords) and lesser *samurai.*

skene A low building behind the **orchestra** in the Greek theater facing the audience; possibly used for changing costumes or storage.

social realism A form of modern realistic **drama** emphasizing social messages and themes; social realism was the official **genre** approved by the Communist party in the Soviet Union after the revolution.

sociétaires Leading actors and shareholders in the Comédie Française; upon serving twenty years, *sociétaires* were entitled to a pension.

soliloquy A speech delivered by a character alone onstage, speaking to himself or herself, or to the audience.

soubrette A stock character in **drama:** a young, pert female character.

spectacle Aristotle's term for the visual element of theatrical performance in *The Poetics.*

subtext A term first elaborated by Constantin Stanislavski, *subtext* refers to the unspoken motive for a given line or speech, what the character wants to get or to do by saying the line. It is sometimes now used more generally to suggest a text's underlying sense or meaning.

surrealist theater   A movement originating in Paris in the 1920s attempting to represent subconscious experience directly in art.

symbolist theater   A European movement of the later nineteenth and early twentieth centuries in reaction to **realism** and **naturalism.** Symbolist theater attempted to dramatize more poetic or metaphorical situations, often using unusual stage settings and ethereal dramatic action and language.

Syndicate   A group of investors who developed a massive organization for theatrical production in the United States in the late nineteenth century.

tableau/tableaux   (pl.) A motionless grouping of actors to represent a "picture" of a dramatic scene; sometimes called *tableau vivant,* a "living picture."

tableaux vivants   See **tableau;** *tableaux vivants* is the plural form of *tableau vivant.*

taburetes   The raised and fenced rows of benches near the stage in a Spanish Golden Age theater, or *corral.*

tachiyaku   Leading male role in **Kabuki** theater.

tertulia   An upper **gallery** occupied by church officials and intellectuals in a Spanish Golden Age theater, or *corral.*

theater   A structure built for the performance of drama; also refers to the institution of dramatic performance.

theater in the round   The presentation of a play in an arena setting, in which the audience sits on all sides of the stage area, but is separate from the playing space itself.

Theater of Cruelty   Term used by Antonin Artaud to describe his nonrepresentational, mystical, mythological theater.

Theater of the Absurd   A type of late twentieth-century **theater** and **drama,** characterized by a relatively abstract setting, and arbitrary and illogical action. It is sometimes said to express the "human condition" in a basic or "existential" way. The term was first coined by Martin Esslin.

theme   A term used to describe a consistent kind of meaning asserted by a work of literature.

tiring house   A structure at the rear of the stage in the Renaissance English **public theater,** where actors would change costumes (attire themselves), and from which they would enter the stage.

tragedy   Originating in the classical Greek theater, tragedy generally refers to serious drama, taking a central character's conflict with himself or herself, with society, or with god as its subject. Aristotle first described tragedy in his *The Poetics,* and tragedy has undergone almost continual redefinition.

tragicomedy   In the English Renaissance, a term describing a dramatic form: a play beginning like a **tragedy,** but ending happily, like a **comedy.** In modern usage, the term refers most often to a play's tone or attitude: a play that is ironic, both serious and absurd, leaning toward black comedy or tragic farce.

traveling song   Song sung in **Noh** theater by the *waki* during his first entrance; it announces who the *waki* is and where he is going.

trilogy   Three tragedies produced in sequence as part of the tragic competition in the **City Dionysia** of ancient Greece. Plays were not necessarily on the same subject.

trope   An enlargement on Catholic liturgy, through song or dramatic performance.

tsure   Followers of the *shite* and *waki* in **Noh** theater.

Upa-rupaka   The "minor drama" of classical **Sanskrit** theater.

verisimilitude   Refers to the extent to which the drama or stage setting appears to copy the superficial appearance of life offstage.

villancicos   Religious songs, like English carols, performed in Spain and its colonies.

wakashugata   Adolescent male roles in **Kabuki** theater.

wakashu kabuki   Literally, "boys' Kabuki"; the term refers to **Kabuki** companies composed mainly of adolescent boys, many of whom were prostitutes; banned by the Tokugawa shogunate in 1652.

waki   The secondary actor in **Noh** theater, who responds to the *shite.*

wakibashira   The downstage left pillar in a **Noh** theater, where the *waki* is usually positioned at the opening of the play.

waki-za   A narrow stage area along the stage-left side of a **Noh** theater stage used for seating the chorus.

wayang kulit   Shadow-puppet theater of Java concerning characters and events drawn from the *Ramayana* and *Mahabharata,* the epic poems of classical India. Performances generally begin early in the evening and last until dawn; audiences sit on both sides of a screen, against which puppeteers cast the shadows of elaborate, flat puppets, whose actions are accompanied by dialogue, narration, song, and music.

well-made play   A form of drama popularized in the nineteenth century, especially in France. The plot usually turns on the revelation of a secret and includes a character who explains and moralizes the action of the play to others; the plot is often relentlessly coincidental, often mechanically so.

wings and backdrop   Scenic practice developed in Italy and exported to France and England in the seventeenth century, using staggered painted flats in a receding series, and a painted central backcloth to depict the setting of the play.

yaro kabuki   The "adult male Kabuki" common in Japan today; the yaro kabuki replaced the boys' and women's **Kabuki** that were popular before such companies were banned in the early seventeenth century.

yugen   The Japanese term for the mysterious beauty, grace, and repose that are the goal of **Noh** performance.

yūgo   Professional prostitute in classical Japan; distinct from *geisha,* a hired companion valued for artistic accomplishment.

yūgo kabuki   Literally, "prostitutes' Kabuki," an early term for **Kabuki** companies, which were composed mainly of women.

Zanni   Wily and clever comic characters, usually clowns or servants, in *commedia dell' arte;* played masked.

zen   Term in Buddhist thought for a contemplative attitude that is disengaged from worldly desire.

Bibliography

Many of the books and articles listed here were consulted in writing the introductory essays in this anthology. Both students and teachers using *The Wadsworth Anthology of Drama* should find them a useful starting point for research into general questions of the history of drama and theater, as well as into specific playwrights.

Barish, Jonas. *The Antitheatrical Prejudice.* Berkeley, CA: U of California P, 1981.

Beckerman, Bernard. *Dynamics of Drama.* New York: Drama Book Specialists, 1979.

Bennett, Susan. *Theatre Audiences: A Theory of Production and Reception.* London: Routledge, 1990.

Bentley, Eric. *The Life of the Drama.* New York: Atheneum, 1964.

Brockett, Oscar G. *History of the Theatre.* Boston: Allyn & Bacon, 1987.

Carlson, Marvin. *Performance: A Critical Introduction.* London: Routledge, 1996

———. *Theories of the Theatre: A Historical and Critical Survey, from the Greeks to the Present.* Ithaca, NY: Cornell UP, 1984.

Case, Sue-Ellen. *Feminism and Theatre.* New York: Methuen, 1988.

———, ed. *Performing Feminisms: Feminist Critical Theory and Theatre.* Baltimore: Johns Hopkins UP, 1990.

Clark, Barrett H. *European Theories of the Drama.* New York: Crown, 1965.

Dukore, Bernard F. *Dramatic Theory and Criticism: Greeks to Grotowski.* New York: Holt, Rinehart & Winston, 1974.

Elam, Keir. *The Semiotics of Theatre and Drama.* London: Methuen, 1980.

Frye, Northrop. *Anatomy of Criticism.* Princeton, NJ: Princeton UP, 1957.

Goldman, Michael. *The Actor's Freedom.* New York: Viking, 1975.

———. *On Drama: Boundaries of Genre, Borders of Self.* Ann Arbor, MI: University of Michigan P, 2000.

Leacroft, Richard, and Helen Leacroft. *Theatre and Playhouse: An Illustrated Survey of Theatre Building from Ancient Greece to the Present Day.* New York: Methuen, 1984.

Nagler, Alois M. *Sources of Theatrical History.* New York: Dover, 1952.

Peters, Julie Stone. *Theatre of the Book 1480-1880: Print, Text, and Performance in Europe.* Oxford, England: Oxford UP, 2000.

Phelan, Peggy. *Mourning Sex: Performing Public Memories.* London: Routledge, 1997.

———. *Unmarked: The Politics of Performance.* London: Routledge, 1993.

Roach, Joseph. *Cities of the Dead: Circum-Atlantic Performances.* New York: Columbia UP, 1996.

Rubin, Don. *The World Encyclopedia of Contemporary Theatre.* 6 vols. London: Routledge, 1999.

States, Bert O. Great *Reckonings in Little Rooms: On the Phenomenology of Theater.* Berkeley, CA: U of California P, 1985.

———. *Irony and Drama.* Ithaca, NY: Cornell UP, 1971.

Turner, Victor. *From Ritual to Theatre: The Human Seriousness of Play.* New York: Performing Arts Journal Publications, 1982.

Worthen, William B. *The Idea of the Actor: Drama and the Ethics of Performance.* Princeton, NJ: Princeton UP, 1984.

READINGS ON DRAMA AND THEATER

Arnott, Peter D. *Greek Scenic Conventions in the Fifth Century,* B.C. Oxford, England: Oxford UP, 1962.

UNIT 1: CLASSICAL ATHENS

Bassi, Karen. *Acting Like Men: Gender, Drama, and Nostalgia in Ancient Greece.* Ann Arbor, MI: U of Michigan P, 1998.

Beare, William. *The Roman Stage.* London: Methuen, 1969.

Bieber, Margarete. *The History of the Greek and Roman Theatre.* Princeton, NJ: Princeton UP, 1961.

Csapo, Eric, and William J. Slater. *The Context of Ancient Drama.* Ann Arbor, MI: U of Michigan P, 1995.

Else, Gerald F. *The Origin and Early Form of Greek Tragedy.* New York: Norton, 1972.

Griffith, Mark. "The King and Eye: The Rule of the Father in Greek Tragedy." *Proceedings of the Cambridge Philological Society* 44 (1998): 20-84.

Hamilton, Edith. *The Greek Way.* New York: Norton, 1983.

Knox, Bernard M. *Word and Action: Essays on the Ancient Theater.* Baltimore: Johns Hopkins UP, 1979.

Konstan, David. *Roman Comedy.* Ithaca, NY: Cornell UP, 1983.

McClure, Laura. *Spoken Like a Woman: Speech and Gender in Athenian Drama.* Princeton, NJ: Princeton UP, 1999.

McDonald, Marianne. *Ancient Sun, Modern Light: Greek Drama on the Modern Stage.* New York: Columbia UP, 1992.

Mills, Sophie. *Theseus, Tragedy and the Athenian Empire.* Oxford, England: Clarendon, 1997.

Pickard-Cambridge, A.W. *Dithyramb, Tragedy, and Comedy.* Oxford, England: Oxford UP, 1962.

———. *The Dramatic Festivals of Athens.* Oxford, England: Oxford UP, 1968.

———. *The Theatre of Dionysus in Athens.* Oxford, England: Oxford UP, 1945.

Segal, Erich, ed. *Greek Tragedy: Modern Essays in Criticism.* New York: Harper & Row, 1983.

Taplin, Oliver. *Greek Tragedy in Action.* Berkeley, CA: U of California P, 1978.

Vince, Ronald W. *Ancient and Medieval Theatre: A Historiographical Handbook.* Westport, CT: Greenwood, 1984.

Webster, T.B.L. *Greek Theater Production.* London: Methuen, 1970.

Wiles, David. *Tragedy in Athens.* Cambridge, England: Cambridge UP, 1997.

Winkler, John J., and Froma I. Zeitlin, eds. *Nothing to Do with Dionysus? Athenian Drama in Its Social Context.* Princeton, NJ: Princeton UP, 1990.

Zeitlin, Froma. *Playing the Other: Gender and Society in Classical Greek Literature.* Chicago: U of Chicago P, 1996.

———. *Before Sexuality: The Construction of Erotic Experience in the Ancient Greek World.* Princeton, NJ: Princeton UP, 1990.

Aeschylus

Gagarin, Michael. *Aeschylean Drama.* Berkeley, CA: U of California P, 1976.

Knox, B.M.W., "Aeschylus and the Third Actor." *Word and Action: Essays on the Ancient Theater.* Ed. Bernard M. Knox. Baltimore: Johns Hopkins UP, 1979.

Lloyd-Jones, Hugh. "The Guilt of Agamemnon." *Greek Tragedy: Modern Essays in Criticism.* Ed. Erich Segal. New York: Harper & Row, 1983.

Rosenmeyer, Thomas G. *The Art of Aeschylus.* Berkeley, CA: U of California P, 1982.

Taplin, Oliver. *The Stagecraft of Aeschylus.* Oxford, England: Oxford UP, 1977.

Aristophanes

Deardon, C.W. *The Stage of Aristophanes.* London: Athlone, 1976.

Dover, K.J. *Aristophanic Comedy.* Berkeley, CA: U of California P, 1972.

Harriott, Rosemary. *Aristophanes: Poet and Dramatist.* Baltimore: Johns Hopkins UP, 1986.

Ussher, Robert Glenn. *Aristophanes.* Oxford, England: Oxford UP, 1979.

Euripides

Dodds, E.R. *The Greeks and the Irrational.* Berkeley, CA: U of California P, 1951.

Foley, Helene P. *Ritual Irony: Poetry and Sacrifice in Euripides.* Ithaca, NY: Cornell UP, 1985.

Michelini, Ann N. *Euripides and the Tragic Tradition.* Madison, WI: U of Wisconsin P, 1987.

Dodds, E.R., "On Misunderstanding the *Oedipus Rex*." *Greek Tragedy: Modern Essays in Criticism.* Ed. Erich Segal. New York: Harper & Row, 1983.

Fergusson, Francis. *The Idea of a Theater.* Princeton, NJ: Princeton UP, 1947.

Knox, B.M.W. *Oedipus at Thebes.* New York: Norton, 1971.

Ringer, Mark. *Electra and the Empty Urn: Metatheater and Role Playing in Sophocles.* Chapel Hill, NC: U of North Carolina P, 1998.

Segal, Charles. *Tragedy and Civilization: An Interpretation of Sophocles.* Cambridge, MA: Harvard UP, 1981.

Whitman, C.H. *Sophocles: A Study in Heroic Humanism.* Cambridge, England: Cambridge UP, 1951.

Winnington-Ingram, R. P. *Sophocles: An Interpretation.* New York: Cambridge UP, 1980.

Sophocles

Arnott, Peter D. *The Theatres of Japan.* New York: St. Martin's P, 1969.

Bowers, Faubion. *Japanese Theatre.* New York: Hermitage House, 1952.

Brandon, James R. *Theatre in Southeast Asia.* Cambridge, MA: Harvard UP, 1967.

———, ed. *Traditional Asian Plays.* New York: Hill & Wang, 1972.

Dunn, Charles James, and Bunzo Torigoe, trans. and eds. *The Actors' Analects: Yakusha Rongo.* New York: Columbia UP, 1969.

Malm, William P. *Japanese Music and Musical Instruments.* Rutland, VT: Tuttle, 1963.

Samson, G.B. *A Short Cultural History of Japan.* London: Cresset P, 1952.

UNIT 2: CLASSICAL JAPAN

Brandon, James R., ed. *Chūshingura: Studies in Kabuki and the Puppet Theater.* Honolulu: U of Hawai'i P, 1982.

———, trans. *Kabuki: Five Classic Plays.* Cambridge, MA: Harvard UP, 1975.

Ernst, Earle. *The Kabuki Theatre.* Rev. ed. Honolulu: U of Hawai'i P, 1974.

Halford, Aubrey S. and Giovanna M. Halford. *The Kabuki Handbook.* Tokyo: Tuttle, 1952.

Kawatake Toshio. *A History of Japanese Theatre, II: Bunraku and Kabuki.* Tokyo: Kokusai Bunka Shinkokai, 1971.

Keene, Donald. *Chūshingura: The Treasury of Loyal Retainers.* New York: Columbia UP, 1971.

———, trans. *Major Plays of Chikamatsu.* New York: Columbia UP, 1961.

Rimer, J. Thomas, and Yamazaki Masakazu, trans. *On the Art of the Now Drama: The Major Treatises of Zeami.* Princeton, NJ: Princeton UP, 1984.

Scott, Adolphe Clarence. *The Kabuki Theatre of Japan.* London: George Allen & Unwin, 1955.

Doll Theater and Kabuki Theater

Araki, James T. *The Ballad-Drama of Medieval Japan.* Berkeley, CA: U of California P, 1964.

Brower, Robert H., and Earl Miner. *Japanese Court Poetry.* Stanford, CA: Stanford UP, 1961.

Ernst, Earle. *Three Japanese Plays from the Traditional Theatre.* London: Oxford UP, 1959.

Fenollosa, Ernest, and Ezra Pound. *The Classic Noh Theatre of Japan.* New York: New Directions, 1959.

Keene, Donald. *Nō, the Classical Theatre of Japan.* Tokyo and Palo Alto, CA: Kodansha International, 1966.

———, ed. *Twenty Plays of the Nō Theatre.* New York: Columbia UP, 1970.

Komparo Kunio. *The Noh Theater: Principles and Perspectives.* Trans. Jane Corddry and Stephen Comeo. Tokyo/New York: Weatherhill, 1983.

Waley, Arthur. *The Nō Plays of Japan.* London: George Allen & Unwin, 1921.

Yasuda, Kenneth. Masterworks of the Now Theater. *Masterworks of the Nō Theater.* Bloomington, IN: Indiana UP, 1989.

Noh Theater

Baumer, Rachel V., and James R. Brandon. *Sanskrit Drama in Performance.* Honolulu: University of Hawai'i P, 1981.

Sanskrit Theater and Drama

Bharata. *Natyasastra.* Trans. P.S.R. Appa Rao. Hyderabad, India: Naatyd Maala, 1967.

Keith, A.B. *Sanskrit Drama: Its Origins, Development, Theory and Practice.* Oxford, England: Oxford UP, 1924.

Tarlekar, G.H. *Studies in the Natyasastra, with Special Reference to the Sanskrit Drama in Performance.* Delhi, India, 1975.

Wells, Henry W. *Six Sanskrit Plays.* London/Bombay: Asia Publishing House, 1964.

UNIT 3: MEDIEVAL AND RENAISSANCE ENGLAND

Aughterson, Kate. *The English Renaissance: An Anthology of Sources and Documents.* London: Routledge, 1998.

Bentley, Gerald Eades. *The Jacobean and Caroline Stage.* 5 vols. Oxford, England: Oxford UP, 1941-1956.

———. *The Profession of Dramatist in Shakespeare's Time, 1590-1642.* Princeton, NJ: Princeton UP, 1971.

———. *The Profession of Player in Shakespeare's Time, 1590-1642.* Princeton, NJ: Princeton UP, 1984.

Bevington, David. *From Mankind to Marlowe: Growth in Structure in the Popular Drama of Tudor England.* Cambridge, MA: Harvard UP, 1962.

———. *Medieval Drama.* Boston: Houghton, 1975.

Chambers, E.K. *The Elizabethan Stage.* 4 vols. Oxford, England: Oxford UP, 1923.

———. *The Medieval Stage.* 2 vols. London: Oxford UP, 1967.

Cox, John D., and David Scott Kastan, eds. *A New History of Early English Drama.* New York: Columbia UP, 1997.

Enders, Jody. *The Medieval Theater of Cruelty: Rhetoric, Memory, Violence.* Ithaca, NY: Cornell UP, 1999.

Graves, R.B. *Lighting the Shakespearean Stage, 1567-1642.* Carbondale: Southern Illinois UP, 1999.

Greenblatt, Stephen, ed. *Representing the English Renaissance.* Berkeley, CA: U of California P, 1988.

Gurr, Andrew. *The Shakespearean Stage, 1574-1642.* Cambridge, England: Cambridge UP, 1970.

Hardison, O.B., Jr. *Christian Rite and Christian Drama in the Middle Ages.* Baltimore: Johns Hopkins UP, 1965.

Kobialka, Michal. *This Is My Body: Representational Practices in the Early Middle Ages.* Ann Arbor, MI: U of Michigan P, 1999.

Kolve, V.A. *The Play Called Corpus Christi.* Stanford, CA: Stanford UP, 1966.

Orgel, Stephen. *The Illusion of Power: Political Theatre in the English Renaissance.* Berkeley, CA: U of California P, 1975.

Vince, Ronald W. *Ancient and Medieval Theatre: A Historiographical Handbook.* Westport, CT: Greenwood, 1984.

Wells, Stanley, and Catherine M.S. Alexander. *Shakespeare and Sexuality.* Cambridge, England: Cambridge UP, 2001.

Wickham, Glynne. *The Medieval Theatre.* New York: Cambridge UP, 1987.

Woolf, Rosemary. *The English Mystery Plays.* Berkeley, CA: U of California P, 1972.

Everyman

Bevington, David. *From Mankind to Marlowe: Growth in Structure in the Popular Drama of Tudor England.* Cambridge, MA: Harvard UP, 1962.

Garner, Stanton B., Jr. "Theatricality in *Mankind* and *Everyman.*" *Studies in Philology,* 84 (1987): 272-85.

Christopher Marlowe

Bevington, David. *From Mankind to Marlowe: Growth in Structure in the Popular Drama of Tudor England.* Cambridge, MA: Harvard UP, 1962.

Cole, Douglas. *Suffering and Evil in the Plays of Christopher Marlowe*. Princeton, NJ: Princeton UP, 1962.

Kernan, Alvin B., ed. *Two Renaissance Mythmakers: Christopher Marlowe and Ben Jonson*. Baltimore: Johns Hopkins UP, 1977.

Leech, Clifford, ed. *Marlowe: A Collection of Critical Essays*. Englewood Cliffs, NJ: Prentice-Hall, 1964.

Levin, Harry. *The Overreacher: A Study of Christopher Marlowe*. Boston: Beacon, 1964.

William Shakespeare

Barber, C.L. *Shakespeare's Festive Comedy*. Princeton, NJ: Princeton UP, 1968.

Barker, Francis, and Peter Hulme. "Nymphs and Reapers Heavily Vanish: The Discursive Contexts of *The Tempest.*" *Alternative Shakespeares*. Ed. John Drakakis. New York: Methuen, 1985.

Bennett, Susan. *Performing Nostalgia: Shifting Shakespeare and the Contemporary Past*. London: Routledge, 1996.

Boose, Lynda E., and Richard Burt, eds. *Shakespeare the Movie: Popularizing the Plays on Film, TV, and Video*. London: Routledge, 1997.

Booth, Stephen. "On the Value of *Hamlet.*" *Reinterpretations of Elizabethan Drama: Selected Papers from the English Institute*. Ed. Norman Rabkin. New York: Columbia UP, 1969: 137-176.

Brown, Paul. "This Thing of Darkness I Acknowledge Mine: *The Tempest* and the Discourse of Colonialism." *Political Shakespeare: New Essays in Cultural Materialism*. Ed. Jonathan Dollimore and Alan Sinfield. Ithaca, NY: Cornell UP, 1985.

Bullough, Geoffrey, ed. *Narrative and Dramatic Sources of Shakespeare*. 8 vols. New York: Columbia UP, 1957-75.

Bulman, James, ed. *Shakespeare, Theory, and Performance*. London: Routledge, 1996.

Callaghan, Dympna, ed. *A Feminist Companion to Shakespeare*. Oxford, England: Blackwell, 2000.

Cerasano, S.P., and Marion Wynne-Davies, eds. *Renaissance Drama by Women: Texts and Documents*. London: Routledge, 1996.

Dollimore, Jonathan, and Alan Sinfield, eds. *Political Shakespeare: New Essays in Cultural Materialism*, Ithaca, NY: Cornell UP, 1985.

Drakakis, John, ed. *Alternative Shakespeares*. New York: Methuen, 1985.

Fergusson, Francis. *The Idea of a Theatre*. Princeton, NJ: Princeton UP, 1947.

Forker, Charles R. "Shakespeare's Theatrical Symbolism and Its Function in *Hamlet.*" *Shakespeare Quarterly* 14 (1963): 215-229.

Goldman, Michael. *Shakespeare and the Energies of Drama*. Princeton, NJ: Princeton UP, 1970.

Greenblatt, Stephen. *Hamlet in Purgatory*. Princeton, NJ: Princeton UP, 2001.

———. *Shakespearean Negotiations*. Berkeley, CA: U of California P, 1988.

Hendricks, Margo, and Patricia Parker, eds. *Women, "Race," and Writing in the Early Modern Period*. London: Routledge, 1994.

Howard, Jean E., and Marion F. O'Connor, eds. *Shakespeare Reproduced: The Text in History and Ideology*. London: Methuen, 1987.

Jardine, Lisa. *Still Harping on Daughters: Women and Drama in the Age of Shakespeare*. Totowa, NJ: Barnes & Noble, 1983.

Kastan, David, ed. *A Companion to Shakespeare*. Oxford, England: Blackwell, 1999.

Kernan, Alvin B., ed. *Modern Shakespeare Criticism*. New York: Harcourt, Brace & World, 1970.

———. *The Playwright as Magician*. New Haven, CT: Yale UP, 1979.

Mack, Maynard. "The World of *Hamlet.*" *Yale Review* 41 (1952): 502-23.

Orgel, Stephen. "Prospero's Wife." *Representing the English Renaissance*. Ed. Stephen Greenblatt. Berkeley, CA: U of California P, 1988.

Parker, Patricia, and Geoffrey Hartmenn, eds. *Shakespeare and the Question of Theory*. London: Methuen, 1985.

Schoenbaum, S. *Shakespeare: A Documentary Life.* New York: Oxford UP, 1975.

Schwartz, Murray M., and Coppèlia Kahn, eds. *Representing Shakespeare: New Psychoanalytic Essays.* Baltimore: Johns Hopkins UP, 1981.

Thompson, Marvin, and Ruth Thompson, eds. *Shakespeare and the Sense of Performance.* Newark, DE: U of Delaware P, 1989.

Worthen, W.B. *Shakespeare and the Authority of Performance.* Cambridge, England: Cambridge UP, 1997.

———. *Shakespeare and the Force of Modern Performance.* Cambridge, England: Cambridge UP, 2003.

Wakefield Mystery Cycle

Helterman, Jeffrey. *Symbolic Action in the Plays of the Wakefield Master.* Athens, GA: U of Georgia P, 1981.

Lepow, Lauren. *Enacting the Sacrament—Counter-Lollardy in the Towneley Cycle.* Rutherford, NJ: Fairleigh Dickinson UP, 1990.

Robinson, J. W. *Studies in Fifteenth Century Stagecraft.* Kalamazoo, MI: The Medieval Institute, 1991.

UNIT 4: EARLY MODERN EUROPE

Allen, John. *The Reconstruction of a Spanish Golden Age Playhouse: El Corral del Principe, 1583-1744.* Gainesville, FL: U of Florida P, 1983.

Holland, Norman N. *The First Modern Comedies: The Significance of Etheredge, Wycherly, and Congreve.* Cambridge, MA: Harvard UP, 1959.

Kirsch, Arthur C. *Dryden's Heroic Drama.* Princeton, NJ: Princeton UP, 1965.

Lancaster, H.C. *A History of French Dramatic Literature in the Seventeenth Century.* 5 vols. Baltimore: Johns Hopkins UP, 1929-42.

Loftis, John. *The Politics of Drama in Augustan England.* Oxford, England: Oxford UP, 1963.

Loftis, John, Richard Southern, Marion Jones, and A. H. Scouten, eds. *The Revels History of Drama in English.* Vol. 5: 1660-1750. London: Methuen, 1976.

McKendrick, Melveena. *Theatre in Spain, 1490-1700.* Cambridge, England: Cambridge UP, 1989.

Staves, Susan. *Players' Scepters: Fictions of Authority in the Restoration.* Lincoln, NE: U of Nebraska P, 1979.

Styan, J.L. *Restoration Comedy in Performance.* Cambridge, England: Cambridge UP, 1986.

Waith, Eugene, *The Herculean Hero.* New York: Columbia UP, 1962.

———. *Ideas of Greatness.* London: Routledge & Kegan Paul, 1971.

Wiley, W.L. *The Early Public Theatre in France.* Cambridge, MA: Harvard UP, 1920.

Wilson, Margaret. *Spanish Drama of the Golden Age.* New York, 1989.

Aphra Behn

Diamond, Elin. "Gestus and Signature in Aphra Behn's *The River.*" *ELH* 56 (1989): 519-39.

Duffy, Maureen. *The Passionate Shepherdess: Aphra Behn, 1640-1689.* London: Methuen, 1977.

Goreau, Angeline. *Reconstructing Aphra: A Social Biography of Aphra Behn.* New York: Dial, 1980.

Pedro Calderón de la Barca

Armas, F. A., D. M. Gitlitz, J. A. Madrigal, eds. *Critical Perspectives on Calderón de la Barca.* Lincoln, NE: U of Nebraska P, 1981.

Honig, Edwin. *Calderón and the Seizures of Honor.* Cambridge, MA: Harvard UP, 1972.

Maraniss, James A. *On Calderón.* Columbia, MO: U of Missouri P, 1977.

Sor Juana Inés de la Cruz

Arenal, Electa, and Amanda Powell, trans. *The Answer/La Repuesta, Including a Selection of Poems.* New York: Feminist Press, 1994.

Campion, John, trans. *El Sueño.* Austin: Thorp Springs, 1983.

Flores, Angel, and Kate Flores, eds. *The Defiant Muse: Hispanic Feminist Poems from the Middle Ages to the Present, A Bilingual Anthology*. New York: Feminist Press, 1986.

Paz, Octavio. *Sor Juana, or, The Traps of Faith*. Trans. Margaret Sayers Peden. Cambridge, MA: Harvard UP, 1988.

Peden, Margaret, trans. *Sor Juana Inés de la Cruz: Poems*. Binghamton, NY: Bilingual Review Press, 1985.

Peters, Patricia, and Renée Domeier, O.S.B., trans. *The Divine Narcissus/El Divino Narciso*. Albuquerque, NM: U of New Mexico P, 1998.

Plancarte, Alfonso Méndez, and Alberto G. Salceda, eds. *Obras Completas de Sor Juana Inés de la Cruz*. 4 vols. Mexico City: Fondo de Cultura Económica, 1976.

Tavard, George H, and Lawrence A. Hoffman. *Juana Inés de la Cruz and the Theology of Beauty: The First Mexican Theology*. Notre Dame, IN: U of Notre Dame P, 1991.

Trueblood, Alan S., ed. and trans. *A Sor Juana Anthology*. Cambridge, MA: Harvard UP, 1988.

Molière

Gaines, James F. *Molière's Theater*. Columbus, OH: Ohio State UP, 1984.

Gossman, L. *Men and Masks: A Study of Molière*. Baltimore: Johns Hopkins UP, 1963.

Gross, Nathan. *From Gesture to Idea: Esthetics and Ethics in Molière's Comedy*. New York: Columbia UP, 1982.

Guicharnaud, Jacques. *Molière: A Collection of Critical Essays*. Englewood Cliffs, NJ: Prentice-Hall, 1964.

Scott, Virginia. *Molière: A Theatrical Life*. Cambridge, England: Cambridge UP, 2000.

Jean Racine

Barthes, Roland. *On Racine*. Trans. Richard Howard. New York: Hill & Wang, 1964.

Cook, A.S. *French Tragedy: The Power of Enactment*. Chicago: U of Chicago P, 1980.

Goldmann, Lucien. *Racine*. Trans. Alastair Hamilton. London: Writers and Readers, 1981.

UNIT 5: MODERN EUROPE

Antoine, André. *Memories of the Théâtre Libre*. Trans. Marvin Carlson. Coral Gables FL: U of Miami P, 1964.

Artaud, Antonin. *The Theater and Its Double*. Trans. Mary Caroline Richards. New York: Grove, 1958.

Bennett, Benjamin. *Modern Drama and German Classicism: Renaissance from Lessing to Brecht*. Ithaca, NY: Cornell UP, 1979.

————. *Theater as Problem: Modern Drama and Its Place in Literature*. Ithaca, NY: Cornell UP, 1990.

Bentley, Eric. *The Playwright as Thinker: A Study of Drama in Modern Times*. New York: Harcourt Brace, 1946.

Bigsby, C.W.E. "The Language of Crisis in British Theatre: The Drama of Cultural Pathology." *Contemporary English Drama*. Ed. C.W.E. Bigsby. New York: Holmes & Meier, 1981.

Blau, Herbert. *Eye of the Prey: Subversions of the Postmodern*. Bloomington, IN: Indiana UP, 1987.

Bradby, David. *Modern French Drama, 1940-1980*. New York: Grove, 1984.

Brater, Enoch, ed. *Feminine Focus: The New Women Playwrights*. New York: Oxford UP, 1989.

Braun, Edward. *Meyerhold on Theater*. New York: Hill & Wang, 1969.

Brockett, Oscar G., and Robert R. Findlay. *Century of Innovation: A History of European and American Theatre and Drama Since 1870*. Englewood Cliffs, NJ: Prentice-Hall, 1973.

Brook, Peter. *The Empty Space*. New York: Avon, 1968.

Brustein, Robert. *The Theater of Revolt*. Boston: Little, Brown, 1964.

Chaudhuri, Una. *Staging Place: The Geography of Modern Drama*. Ann Arbor, MI: U of Michigan P, 1995.

Cohn, Ruby. *From Desire to Godot: Pocket Theater of Postwar Paris*. Berkeley, CA: U of California P, 1987.

Cole, Toby, ed. *Directors on Directing.* Indianapolis: Bobbs-Merrill, 1963.

———. *Playwrights on Playwriting.* New York: Hill & Wang, 1960.

Davis, Tracy C. *Actresses as Working Women: Their Social Identity in Victorian Culture.* London: Routledge, 1991.

Dolan, Jill. *The Feminist Spectator as Critic.* Ann Arbor, MI: UMI Research Press, 1988.

Driver, Tom. *Romantic Quest and Modern Query: A History of Modern Theatre.* New York: Delacorte, 1970.

Elsom, John. *Post-War British Theatre.* London: Routledge & Kegan Paul, 1976.

Esslin, Martin. *The Theatre of the Absurd.* Garden City, NJ: Doubleday, 1969.

Finney, Gail. *Women in Modern Drama: Freud, Feminism, and European Theater at the Turn of the Century.* Ithaca, NY: Cornell UP, 1989.

Garner, Stanton B., Jr. *Bodied Spaces: Phenomenology and Performance in Contemporary Drama.* Ithaca, NY: Cornell UP, 1994.

Gilman, Richard. *The Making of Modern Drama.* New York: Farrar, Straus & Giroux, 1974.

Grotowski, Jerzy. *Towards a Poor Theatre.* New York: Simon & Schuster, 1968.

Hunt, Hugh, et al. *The Revels History of Drama in English.* Vol. 7: 1880 to the Present Day. London: Methuen, 1979.

Jones, David Richard. *Great Directors at Work.* Berkeley, CA: U of California P, 1986.

Kelly, Katherine E., ed. *Modern Drama by Women 1880s-1930s: An International Anthology.* London: Routledge, 1996.

Peter, John. *Vladimir's Carrot: Modern Drama and the Modern Imagination.* Chicago: U of Chicago P, 1987.

Quigley, Austin. *The Modern Stage and Other Worlds.* London: Methuen, 1985.

Rebellato, Dan. *1956 And All That: The Making of Modern British Drama.* London: Routledge, 1999.

Rosen, Carol. *Plays of Impasse: Contemporary Drama Set in Confining Institutions.* Princeton, NJ: Princeton UP, 1983.

Schechner, Richard. *Environmental Theater.* New York: Hawthorn, 1973.

Seltzer, Daniel, ed. *The Modern Theatre: Readings and Documents.* Boston: Little, Brown, 1967.

Stanislavski, Constantin. *An Actor Prepares.* Trans. Elizabeth Reynolds Hapgood. New York: Theatre Arts, 1936.

———. *Building a Character.* Trans. Elizabeth Reynolds Hapgood. New York: Theatre Arts, 1949.

———. *Creating a Role.* Trans. Elizabeth Reynolds Hapgood. New York: Theatre Arts, 1961.

———. *My Life in Art.* Trans. J.J. Robbins. Boston: Little, Brown, 1924.

Styan, J.L. *The Dark Comedy.* Cambridge, England: Cambridge UP, 1968.

———. *Modern Drama in Theory and Practice.* 3 vols. Cambridge, England: Cambridge UP, 1980.

Taylor, John Russell. *Anger and After.* London: Methuen, 1969.

———. *The Second Wave: British Drama of the Sixties.* London: Eyre Methuen, 1978.

Whitaker, Thomas R. *Fields of Play in Modern Drama.* Princeton, NJ: Princeton UP, 1977.

Wiles, Timothy J. *The Theater Event: Modern Theories of Performance.* Chicago: U of Chicago P, 1980.

Williams, Raymond. *Drama from Ibsen to Brecht.* London: Hogarth, 1987.

———. *Modern Tragedy.* Stanford, CA: Stanford UP, 1966.

The World Encyclopedia of Contemporary Theatre. Ed. Don Rubin. Vol. 1: Europe. London: Routledge, 1999.

Worth, Katharine. *Revolutions in Modern English Drama.* London: G. Bell & Sons, 1972.

Worthen, W.B. *Modern Drama and the Rhetoric of Theater.* Berkeley, CA: U of California P, 1992.

Samuel Beckett

Acheson, James, and Kateryna Arthur, eds. *Beckett's Later Fiction and Drama: Texts for Company.* New York: St. Martin's Press, 1987.

Bair, Deirdre. *Samuel Beckett: A Biography.* New York: Harcourt Brace Jovanovich, 1978.

Beckett, Samuel. *Happy Days: The Production Notebook of Samuel Beckett.* Ed. James Knowlson. New York: Grove, 1985.

Ben-Zvi, Linda, ed. *Women in Beckett.* Chicago: U of Chicago P, 1990.

Brater, Enoch, ed. *Beckett at 80/Beckett in Context.* Oxford, England: Oxford UP, 1986.

———. *Beyond Minimalism: Beckett's Late Style in the Theater.* Oxford, England: Oxford UP, 1987.

Cohn, Ruby. *Just Play: Beckett's Theater.* Princeton, NJ: Princeton UP, 1980.

———. *Samuel Beckett: The Comic Gamut.* New Brunswick, NJ: Rutgers UP, 1962.

Gontarski, S.E. *On Beckett: Essays and Criticism.* New York: Grove, 1986.

Graver, Lawrence, and Raymond Federman, eds. *Samuel Beckett: The Critical Heritage.* London: Routledge & Kegan Paul, 1979.

Kalb, Jonathan. *Beckett in Performance.* Cambridge, England: Cambridge UP, 1989.

Kenner, Hugh. *Samuel Beckett.* Berkeley, CA: U of California P, 1968.

Knowlson, James. *Damned to Fame: The Life of Samuel Beckett.* New York: Simon and Schuster, 1996.

Worth, Katharine. *The Irish Drama of Europe from Yeats to Beckett.* London: Athlone, 1978.

Bertolt Brecht

Benjamin, Walter. *Understanding Brecht.* Trans. Anna Bostock. London: NLB, 1973.

Bentley, Eric. *The Brecht Commentaries 1943-1980.* New York: Grove, 1981.

Brecht, Bertolt. *Brecht on Theatre: The Development of an Aesthetic.* Ed. and trans. John Willett. New York: Hill & Wang, 1964.

———. *The Messingkauf Dialogues.* Trans. John Willett. London: Methuen, 1965.

Dickson, Keith A. *Towards Utopia: A Study of Brecht.* Oxford, England: Oxford UP, 1978.

Eddershaw, Margaret. *Performing Brecht: Firty-Five Years of British Performance.* London: Routledge, 1996.

Esslin, Martin. *Brecht: The Man and His Work.* Garden City, NJ: Doubleday, 1971.

Ewen, Frederick. *Bertolt Brecht: His Life, His Art and His Times.* New York: Citadel, 1967.

Fuegi, John. *Bertolt Brecht: Chaos According to Plan.* Cambridge, England: Cambridge UP, 1987.

———. *Brecht and Company.* New York: Grove, 1994.

Lyon, James K. *Bertolt Brecht in America.* Princeton, NJ: Princeton UP, 1980.

Wright, Elizabeth. *Postmodern Brecht: A Re-Presentation.* London: Routledge, 1989.

Anton Chekhov

Chekhov, Anton. *Letters of Anton Chekhov.* Trans. Michael Henry Heim and Simon Karlinsky. New York: Harper & Row, 1973.

Gottleib, Vera. *Chekhov and the Vaudeville.* Cambridge, England: Cambridge UP, 1982.

———, and Paul Allain, eds. *The Cambridge Companion to Chekhov.* Cambridge, England: Cambridge UP, 2000.

Hingley, Ronald. *Chekhov: A Biographical and Critical Study.* New York: Barnes & Noble, 1966.

Magarshack, David. *Chekhov the Dramatist.* New York: Hill & Wang, 1960.

Peace, Richard. *Chekhov: A Study of the Four Major Plays.* New Haven, CT: Yale UP, 1983.

Pitcher, Henry. *The Chekhov Play.* London: Chatto & Windus, 1973.

Rayfield, Donald. *Chekhov: The Evolution of His Art.* London: Paul Elek, 1975.

Senelick, Laurence. *The Chekhov Theatre: A Century of the Plays in Performance.* Cambridge, England: Cambridge UP, 1997.

Styan, J.L. *Chekhov in Performance.* Cambridge, England: Cambridge UP, 1971.

Caryl Churchill

Aston, Elaine. *Caryl Churchill.* Plymouth: Northcote House, 1997.

Churchill, Caryl. "The Common Imagination and the Individual Voice." *New Theatre Quarterly* 4 (February 1988): 316.

Diamond, Elin. "Brechtian Theory/Feminist Criticism: Toward a Gestic Feminist Criticism." *TDR—The Drama Review* 32.1 (1988): 82-94.

————. "(In)Visible Bodies in Churchill's Theatre." *Theatre Journal* 40 (1988): 188-204.

————. "Refusing the Romanticism of Identity: Narrative Interventions in Churchill, Benmussa, Duras." *Theatre Journal* 37 (1985): 273-86.

Harding, James M. "Cloud Cover: (Re)Dressing Desire and Comfortable Subversions in Caryl Churchill's *Cloud Nine*." *PMLA* 113 (1998): 258-72

Quigley, Austin E. "Stereotype and Prototype: Character in the Plays of Caryl Churchill." *Feminine Focus: The New Women Playwrights*. Ed. Enoch Brater. New York: Oxford UP, 1989.

Randall, Phyllis R., ed. *Caryl Churchill: A Casebook*. New York: Garland, 1989.

Marguerite Duras

Adler, Laure. *Marguerite Duras: A Life*. Trans. Anne-Marie Glasheen. Chicago: U of Chicago P, 2000.

Cody, Gabrielle H. *Impossible Performances: Duras as Dramatist*. New York: Peter Lang, 2000.

Loufti, Martine. "Duras's India." *Literature/Film Quarterly* 14.3 (1986): 151-53.

Papin, Lilian. "Staging Writing or the Ceremony of the Text in Marguerite Duras." *Modern Drama* 34 (1981): 128-37.

Selous, Trista. *The Other Woman: Feminism and Femininity in the Work of Marguerite Duras*. New Haven: Yale UP, 1988.

Struebig, Patricia. "*India Song / The Vice Consul* of Marguerite Duras: Comparative Techniques in Film and Novel." *Apocalyptic Visions Past and Present*. Ed. JoAnn James and William Cloonan. Tallahassee, FL: Florida State UP, 1988.

David Edgar

Carney, Sean. "Capitalism's *Pharmakos*: David Edgar's *Destiny* and *Pentecost*." *Études Théâtrales/ Essays in Theatre* 18.2 (2000): 131-49.

Garner, Stanton. "Rewriting Europe: *Pentecost* and the Crossroads of Migration." *Études Théâtrales/ Essays in Theatre* 16.1 (1997): 3-14.

Reinelt, Janelle. "Rewriting Europe: Identity Formations for a 'New' Europe." *Theatre Journal* 53 (2001): 365-87.

Swain, Elizabeth. *David Edgar: Playwright and Politician*. New York: Peter Lang, 1986.

Henrik Ibsen

Cima, Gay Gibson. "Discovering Signs: The Emergence of the Critical Actor in Ibsen." *Theatre Journal* 35 (1983): 522.

Egan, Michael, ed. *Ibsen: The Critical Heritage*. London: Routledge & Kegan Paul, 1972.

Hardwick, Elizabeth. "A Doll's House." *Seduction and Betrayal*. New York: Random House, 1970.

Lyons, Charles R. *Henrik Ibsen: The Divided Consciousness*. Carbondale, IL: Southern Illinois UP, 1972.

Marker, Frederick J., and Lise-Lone Marker. *Ibsen's Lively Art: A Performance Study of the Major Plays*. Cambridge, England: Cambridge UP, 1989.

Meyer, Michael. *Henrik Ibsen: A Biography*. Garden City, NJ: Doubleday, 1971.

Northam, John. *Ibsen: A Critical Study*. Cambridge, England: Cambridge UP, 1973.

————. *Ibsen's Dramatic Method: A Study of the Prose Dramas*. London: Faber & Faber, 1953.

Shaw, Bernard. *The Quintessence of Ibsenism*. New York: Hill & Wang, 1957.

Sprinchorn, Evert, ed. *Ibsen: Letters and Speeches*. New York: Hill & Wang, 1964.

Templeton, Joan. *Ibsen's Women*. Cambridge, England: Cambridge UP, 2000.

Heiner Müller

Bathrick, David, and Andreas Huyssen. "Producing Revolution: Heiner Müller's *Mauser* as a Learning Play." *New German Critique* 3.2 (1976): 110-21.

Dudley, Robert M. "Being and Non-Being: The Other and Heterotopia in *Hamletmachine*." *Modern Drama* 35 (1992): 562-70.

Fehervay, Helen. "Enlightenment or Entanglement: History and Aesthetics in Bertolt Brecht and Heiner Müller." *New German Critique* 3.8 (1976): 80-109.

Girshausen, Theo. "'Reject It, in Order to Possess It': On Heiner Müller and Bertolt Brecht." *Modern Drama* 23 (1981): 404-21.
Rouse, John. "Heiner Müller and the Politics of Memory." *Theatre Journal* 45 (1993): 65-74.

Harold Pinter

Diamond, Elin. *Pinter's Comic Play*. Lewisburg, PA: Bucknell UP, 1985.
Esslin, Martin. *Pinter*. New York: Norton, 1976.
Ganz, Arthur, ed. *Pinter: A Collection of Critical Essays*. Englewood Cliffs, NJ: Prentice-Hall, 1972.
Lahr, John, ed. *A Casebook on Harold Pinter's The Homecoming*. New York: Grove, 1971.
Postlewait, Thomas. "Pinter's *The Homecoming*: Displacing and Repeating Ibsen." *Comparative Drama* 15 (1981).
Quigley, Austin E. *The Pinter Problem*. Princeton, NJ: Princeton UP, 1975.

Luigi Pirandello

Bassnet-McGuire, Susan. *Luigi Pirandello*. New York: Grove, 1983.
Bentley, Eric. *The Pirandello Commentaries*. Evanston, IL: Northwestern UP, 1986.
Guidice, Gaspare. *Pirandello: A Biography*. Trans. Alastair Hamilton. Oxford, England: Oxford UP, 1975.
Kennedy, Andrew K. "*Six Characters*: Pirandello's Last Tape." *Modern Drama* 12 (1969): 19.
Oliver, Roger W. *Dreams of Passion: The Theater of Luigi Pirandello*. New York: New York UP, 1979.
Paolucci, Anne. *Pirandello's Theater*. Carbondale, IL: Southern Illinois UP, 1974.
Pirandello, Luigi. *On Humor*. Trans. Antonio Illiano and Daniel P. Testa. Chapel Hill, NC: U of North Carolina P, 1974.
Sogliuzzo, A. Richard. *Luigi Pirandello, Director: The Playwright in the Theatre*. Metuchen, NJ: Scarecrow, 1982.

Elizabeth Robins

Farfan, Penny. "From *Hedda Gabler* to *Votes for Women*: Elizabeth Robins's Early Feminist Critique of Ibsen." *Theatre Journal* 48 (1996): 59-78.
Gates, Joanna E, "Elizabeth Robins and the 1891 Production of *Hedda Gabler*." *Modern Drama* 28 (1985): 610-19.
Marcus, Jane Connor. "Elizabeth Robins." Dissertation, Northwestern University, 1973.
Wiley, Catherine. "'The Matter with Manners': The New Woman and the Problem Play." *Themes in Drama* 11 (1989): 100-27.
Worthen, W.B. *Modern Drama and the Rhetoric of Theater*. Berkeley, CA: U of California P, 1992.

Bernard Shaw

Bentley, Eric. *Bernard Shaw*. New York: Norton, 1976.
Berst, Charles A. *Bernard Shaw and the Art of Drama*. Urbana, IL: U of Illinois P, 1973.
Compton, Louis. *Shaw the Dramatist*. Lincoln, NE: U of Nebraska P, 1969.
Evans, T. F., ed. *Shaw: The Critical Heritage*. London: Routledge & Kegan Paul, 1976.
Goldman, Michael. "Shaw and the Marriage in Dionysus." *The Play and Its Critic: Essays for Eric Bentley*. Ed. Michael Bertin. New York: UP of America, 1986.
Holroyd, Michael. *Bernard Shaw*. 3 vols. New York: Random House, 1988-91.
Innes, Christopher. *The Cambridge Companion to George Bernard Shaw*. Cambridge, England: Cambridge UP, 1998.
Meisel, Martin. *Shaw and the Nineteenth-Century Theater*. Princeton, NJ: Princeton UP, 1963.
Peters, Margot. *Bernard Shaw and the Actresses*. Garden City, NJ: Doubleday, 1980.
Turco, Alfred, Jr. *Shaw's Moral Vision: The Self and Salvation*. Ithaca, NY: Cornell UP, 1976.
Wisenthal, J.L. *The Marriage of Contraries: Bernard Shaw's Middle Plays*. Cambridge, MA: Harvard UP, 1974.

August Strindberg

Carlson, Harry G. *Strindberg and the Poetry of Myth*. Berkeley, CA: U of California P, 1982.
Lucas, F.L. *The Drama of Ibsen and Strindberg*. London: Cassell, 1962.
Reinert, Otto, ed. *Strindberg: A Collection of Critical Essays*. Englewood Cliffs, NJ: Prentice-Hall, 1971.

Sprinchorn, Evert. *Strindberg as Dramatist*. New Haven, CT: Yale UP, 1982.

Strindberg, August. *From an Occult Diary*. Trans. Mary Sandbach. New York: Hill & Wang, 1965.

———. *Open Letters to the Intimate Theater*. Trans. Walter Johnson. Seattle: U of Washington P, n.d.

Tórnqvist, Egil. *Strindbergian Drama*. Atlantic Highlands, NJ: Humanities Press, 1982.

UNIT 6: THE UNITED STATES

Arrizón, Alicia. *Latina Performance: Traversing the Stage*. Bloomington, IN: Indiana UP, 1999.

Bean, Annemarie. *A Sourcebook of African American Performance*. London: Routledge, 1999.

Betsko, Kathleen, and Rachel Koenig, eds. *Interviews with Contemporary Women Playwrights*. New York: Beech Tree, 1987.

Bigsby, C.W.E. *Contemporary American Playwrights*. Cambridge, England: Cambridge UP, 1999.

———. *A Critical Introduction to Twentieth-Century American Drama*. 3 vols. Cambridge, England: Cambridge UP, 1982-85.

Bronner, Edwin, ed. *The Encyclopedia of the American Theatre 1900-1975*. New York: A.S. Barnes, 1980.

Case, Sue-Ellen. "Toward a Butch-Femme Aesthetic." *Making a Spectacle: Feminist Essays on Contemporary Women's Theatre*. Ed. Lynda Hart. Ann Arbor, MI: U of Michigan P, 1989.

Case, Sue-Ellen, Philip Brett, and Susan Leigh Foster, eds. *Cruising the Performative: Interventions into the Representation of Ethnicity, Nationality, and Sexuality*. Bloomington, IN: Indiana UP, 1995.

Chinoy, Helen Krich, and Linda Walsh Jenkins, eds. *Women in American Theatre*. New York: Crown, 1981.

Clurman, Harold. *The Fervent Years: The Story of the Group Theatre and the Thirties*. New York: Knopf, 1945.

Cohn, Ruby. *New American Dramatists, 1960-1980*. New York: Grove, 1982.

Coven, Brenda, ed. *American Women Dramatists of the Twentieth Century: A Bibliography*. Metuchen, NJ: Scarecrow, 1982.

Diamond, Elin. *Unmaking Mimesis: Essays on Feminism and Theater*. London: Routledge, 1997.

Downer, Alan S. *American Drama and Its Critics*. Chicago: U of Chicago P, 1965.

Elam, Harry J., Jr. *Taking It to the Streets: The Social Protest Theater of Luis Valdez and Amiri Baraka*. Ann Arbor, MI: U of Michigan P, 1997.

Flanagan, Hallie. *Arena*. New York: Duell, Sloan & Pearce, 1949.

Garza, Roberto, ed. *Contemporary Chicano Theatre*. Notre Dame, IN: U of Notre Dame P, 1996.

Harrison, Paul Carter. *The Drama of Nommo*. New York: Grove, 1972.

Hart, Lynda, ed. *Making a Spectacle: Feminist Essays on Contemporary Women's Theatre*. Ann Arbor, MI: U of Michigan P, 1989.

Hatch, James V., ed. *Black Theatre USA: Forty-Five Plays by Black Americans, 1847-1974*. New York: Macmillan, 1974.

Hay, James. *African American Theatre: A Historical and Critical Analysis*. Cambridge, England: Cambridge UP, 1994.

Hill, Errol, ed. *The Theatre of Black Americans*. 2 vols. Englewood Cliffs, NJ: Prentice-Hall, 1980.

Houston, Velina Hasu, ed. *But Still, Like Air, I'll Rise: New Asian American Plays*. Philadelphia: Temple UP, 1997.

Huerta, Jorge A. *Chicano Drama: Performance, Society, and Myth*. Cambridge, England: Cambridge UP, 2000.

———. *Chicano Theater: Themes and Forms*. Ypsilanti, MI: Bilingual Press, 1982.

Kanellos, Nicolás. *Hispanic Theatre in the United States*. Houston: Arte Público Press, 1984.

Krasner, David. *Resistance, Parody, and Double Consciousness in African American Theatre, 1895-1910*. New York: St. Martin's, 1997.

Lee, Josephine. *Performing Asian America: Race and Ethnicity and the Contemporary Stage*. Philadelphia: Temple UP, 1997.

Marker, Lise-Lone. *David Belasco: Naturalism in the American Theatre*. Princeton, NJ: Princeton UP, 1975.

Marranca, Bonnie, ed. *The Theatre of Images*. New York: Drama Book Specialists, 1977.

Perkins, Kathy A. *Black Female Playwrights: An Anthology of Plays before 1950*. Bloomington, IN: Indiana UP, 1989.

Perkins, Kathy A., and Roberta A. Uno, eds. *Contemporary Plays by Women of Color*. London: Routledge, 1996.

Phelan, Peggy. *Mourning Sex: Performing Public Memories*. London: Routledge, 1997.

———. *Unmarked: The Politics of Performance*. London: Routledge, 1993.

Rabkin, Gerald. *Drama and Commitment: Politics in the American Theatre of the Thirties*. Bloomington, IN: Indiana UP, 1964.

Roach, Joseph. *Cities of the Dead: Circum-Atlantic Performances*. New York: Columbia UP, 1996.

Savran, David. *Taking It Like a Man: White Masculinity, Masochism, and Contemporary American Culture*. Princeton, NJ: Princeton UP, 1998.

Schneider, Rebecca. *The Explicit Body in Performance*. London: Routledge, 1997.

Shank, Ted. *American Alternative Theatres*. New York: Grove, 1982.

Shewey, Don, ed. *Out Front: Contemporary Gay and Lesbian Plays*. New York: Grove, 1988.

Amiri Baraka/ LeRoi Jones

Baraka, Imamu Amiri. *The Autobiography of LeRoi Jones/Amiri Baraka*. New York: Freundlich, 1984.

———. "Exaugural Address." *Kulchur* 3.3 (1964).

———. *Selected Plays and Prose of Amiri Baraka/LeRoi Jones*. New York: William Morrow, 1979.

Bentson, Kimberly W., ed. *Imamu Amiri Baraka (LeRoi Jones): A Collection of Critical Essays*. Englewood Cliffs, NJ: Prentice-Hall, 1978.

Richards, Sandra. "Negative Forces and Positive Non-Entities: Images of Women in the Drama of Amiri Baraka." *Theatre Journal* 32 (1985): 233-40.

Smith, David. "Amiri Baraka and the Politics of Popular Culture." *Politics and the Muse: Studies in the Politics of Recent American Literature*. Ed. Adam Sorkin. Bowling Green, OH: Popular, 1989.

Sollors, Werner. *Amiri Baraka/LeRoi Jones: The Quest for a "Populist Modernism."* New York: Columbia UP, 1978.

Dion Boucicault

Boltwood, Scott. "'The Ineffable Curse of Cain': Race, Miscegenation, and the Victorian Staging of Irishness." *Victorian Literature and Culture* 29 (2001): 383-96.

Brody, Jennifer De Vere. "The Yankee Hugging the Creole: Reading Dion Boucicault's *The Octoroon*." *Creole*. Ed. Kein Sibil. Baton Rouge, LA: Louisiana State UP, 2000.

Erdman, Harley. "Caught in the 'Eye of the Eternal': Justice, Race, and the Camera from *The Octoroon* to Rodney King." *Theatre Journal* 45 (1993): 333-41.

Fawkes, Richard. *Dion Boucicault: A Biography*. New York: Quartet, 1981.

Hogan, Robert. *Dion Boucicault*. New York: Twayne, 1969.

Parkin, Andrew, ed. *Selected Plays of Dion Boucicault*. Washington, DC: Catholic UP, 1987.

Susan Glaspell

Ben-Zvi, Linda. "Susan Glaspell's Contributions to Contemporary Women Playwrights." *Feminine Focus: The New Women Playwrights*. Ed. Enoch Brater. New York: Oxford UP, 1989.

Dymkowski, Christine. "On the Edge: The Plays of Susan Glaspell." *Modern Drama* 31 (1988): 91-105.

Kolodny, Annette. "A Map for Rereading: Gender and the Interpretation of Literary Texts." *The New Feminist Criticism: Essays on Women, Literature, and Theory*. Ed. Elaine Showalter. New York: Pantheon, 1985.

Makowsky, Veronica. "Glaspell and Modernism." *Cambridge Companion to American Women Playwrights*. Ed. Brenda Murphy. Cambridge, England: Cambridge UP, 1999.

———. *Susan Glaspell's Century of American Women: A Critical Interpretation of Her Work*. Oxford, England: Oxford UP, 1993.

Stein, Karen F. "The Women's World of Glaspell's *Trifles.*" *Women in American Theatre.* Ed. Helen Krich Chinoy and Linda Walsh Jenkins. New York: Crown, 1981.

Angelina Weld Grimké

Bradley, Gerald. "Goodby, Mister Bones." *Drama Critique* 7 (1964): 83.

Davis, Arthur Paul. *From the Dark Tower: Afro-American Writers.* Washington DC: Howard UP, 1974.

Grimké, Angelina Weld. *Selected Works of Angelina Weld Grimké.* Ed. Carolivia Herron. Oxford, England: Oxford UP, 1991.

Hull, Gloria T. *Color, Sex, and Poetry: Three Women Writers of the Harlem Renaissance.* Bloomington, IN: Indiana UP, 1987.

Lerner, Gerda. *The Grimke Sisters from South Carolina: Pioneers for Women's Rights and Abolition.* New York: Oxford UP, 1998.

Perkins, Kathy A., ed. *Black Female Playwrights: An Anthology of Plays before 1930.* Bloomington, IN: Indiana UP, 1989.

David Henry Hwang

Cheng, Anne. *The Melancholy of Race.* Oxford, England: Oxford UP, 2001.

Garber, Majorie. *Vested Interests: Cross-Dressing and Cultural Anxiety.* London: Routledge, 1992.

Hwang, David Henry. Afterword. *M. Butterfly.* New York: New American Library, 1988.

———. *F.O.B.* in *New Plays USA 1.* New York: Theatre Communications Group, 1982.

Moy, James S. "David Henry Hwang's *M. Butterfly* and Philip Kan Gotanda's *Yankee Dawg You Die*: Repositioning Chinese American Marginality on the American Stage." *Theatre Journal* 42 (1990): 48-56.

Naomi Iizuka

Benson, Misha. "Naomi Iizuka: Raising the Stakes." *American Theatre* 15.7 (1998): 56-7.

IIzuka, Naomi. "What Myths May Come." *American Theatre* 16.7 (1999): 78-80.

Tony Kushner

Cheever, Susan. Interview with Tony Kushner. *New York Times*, September 13, 1992: II, 7.

Geis, Deborah R., and Steven F. Kruger, eds. *Approaching the Millennium: Essays on Angels in America.* Ann Arbor, MI: U of Michigan P, 1997.

Savran, David. "Ambivalence, Utopia, and a Queer Sort of Materialism: How Angels in America Reconstructs the Nation." *Theatre Journal* 47 (1995): 207-28.

Arthur Miller

Bigsby, C. W. E., ed. *The Cambridge Companion to Arthur Miller.* Cambridge: Cambridge UP, 1997.

———. *Confrontation and Commitment: A Study of Contemporary American Drama 1959-1966.* London: Methuen, 1967.

———. *A Critical Introduction to Twentieth-Century American Drama,* volume 2. Cambridge: Cambridge UP, 1984.

———. Ed. *File on Miller.* London: Methuen, 1988.

Gussow, Mel. *Conversations with Miller.* New York: Applause, 2002.

Martin, Robert, ed. *The Theater Essays of Arthur Miller.* Harmondsworth: Penguin, 1978.

Miller, Arthur. *Salesman in Beijing.* New York: Viking, 1984.

Murphy, Brenda, and Susan C. W. Abbotson. *Understanding Death of a Salesman: A Student Casebook to Issues, Sources, and Historical Documents.* Westport CT: Greenwood, 1999.

Savran, David. *Cowboys, Communists, and Queers: The Politics of Masculinity in the Work of Arthur Miller and Tennessee Williams.* Minneapolis: U of Minnesota P, 1992.

Schleuter, June. *Dramatic Closure: Reading the End.* Madison NJ: Fairleigh Dickinson UP, 1995.

Eugene O'Neill

Bogard, Travis. *Contour in Time: The Plays of Eugene O'Neill.* Oxford, England: Oxford UP, 1988.

Cargill, Oscar, N. Bryllion Fagin, and William J. Fisher, eds. *O'Neill and His Plays: Four Decades of Criticism.* New York: New York UP, 1961.

Chothia, Jean. *Forging a Language: A Study of the Plays of Eugene O'Neill.* Cambridge, England: Cambridge UP, 1979.

Floyd, Virginia, ed. *Eugene O'Neill at Work: Newly Released Ideas for Plays*. New York: Ungar, 1981.

Gelb, Arthur, and Barbara Gelb. *O'Neill*. New York: Harper & Row, 1973.

Sheaffer, Louis. *O'Neill: Son and Playwright*. Boston: Little, Brown, 1968.

Wainscott, Ronald H. *Staging O'Neill: The Experimental Years, 1920-1934*. New Haven, CT: Yale UP, 1988.

Suzan-Lori Parks

Diamond, Liz. "Perceptible Mutability in the Word Kingdom." *Theatre* 24.3 (1993): 86-7.

Druckman, Steven. "Suzan-Lori Parks and Liz Diamond: Doo-a-diddly-dit-dit." *TDR—The Drama Review* 39.3 (1995): 56-75.

Parks, Suzan-Lori. *The America Play and Other Works*. New York: Theatre Communications Group, 1995.

Pearce, Michele. "Alien Nation: An Interview with the Playwright Suzan-Lori Parks." *American Theatre* March 1994: 26-8.

Rayner, Alice, and Harry J. Elam, Jr. "Unfinished Business: Reconfiguring History in Suzan-Lori Parks's *The Death of the Last Black Man in the Whole Entire World*." *Theatre Journal* 46 (1994): 447-62.

Worthen, W.B. "Citing History: Textuality and Performativity in the Plays of Suzan-Lori Parks." *Essays in Theatre/Études Théâtrales* 18.1 (1999): 3-22.

Sam Shepard

King, Kimball. *Sam Shepard: A Casebook*. New York: Garland, 1988.

Marranca, Bonnie, ed. *American Dreams: The Imagination of Sam Shepard*. New York: Performing Arts Journal Publications, 1981.

Mottram, Ron. *Inner Landscapes: The Theater of Sam Shepard*. Columbia, MO: U of Missouri P, 1984.

Oumano, Ellen. *Sam Shepard: The Life and Work of an American Dreamer*. New York: St. Martin's, 1986.

Anna Deavere Smith

Case, Sue-Ellen. "Introduction to *Chlorophyll Postmodernism and the Mother Goddess/A Conversation*." *Women and Performance* 4.8 (1989): 20-5.

Cheng, Anne. *The Melancholy of Race*. Oxford, England: Oxford UP, 2001.

Dolan, Jill, "Staking Claims and Positions: The Women and Theatre Program, San Diego, and the Danger Zone." *Women and Performance* 4.8 (1989): 46-57.

Richards, Sandra L. "Caught in the Act of Social Definition: *On the Road* with Anna Deavere Smith." *Acting Out: Feminist Performances*. Eds. Lynda Hart and Peggy Phelan. Ann Arbor: U of Michigan P, 1993. 35-53.

Luis Valdez

Broyles-Gonzàlez, Yolanda. *El Teatro Campesino: Theater in the Chicano Movement*. Austin, Texas, U of Texas P, 1994.

———. "Toward a Re-Vision of Chicano Theatre History: The Women of El Teatro Campesino." *Making a Spectacle: Feminist Essays on Contemporary Women's Theatre*. Ed. Lynda Hart. Ann Arbor, MI: U of Michigan P, 1989.

Huerta, Jorge A. *Chicano Theater: Themes and Forms*. Ypsilanti, MI: Bilingual Press, 1982.

Kanellos, Nicolás. *Hispanic Theatre in the United States*. Houston: Arte Público, 1984.

Morton, Carlos. "The Teatro Campesino." *Tulane Drama Review* 18.4 (1974): 71-6.

Valdez, Luis. *Pensamiento Serpentino*. El Centro Campesino Cultural, CA: Cucaracha, 1973.

Valdez, Luis, and El Teatro Campesino. *Actos*. San Juan Bautista, CA: Menyah Productions, 1971.

von Bardeleben, Renate, ed. *Missions in Conflict: Essays on U.S.-Mexican Relations and Chicano Culture*. Tübingen, Germany: G. Narr, 1986.

Tennessee Williams

Boxill, Roger. *Tennessee Williams*. New York: St. Martin's, 1987.

Devlin, Albert J., ed. *Conversations with Tennessee Williams*. Jackson, MS: U of Mississippi P, 1986.

Leavitt, Richard Freeman, ed. *The World of Tennessee Williams*. New York: Putnam, 1978.

Spoto, Donald. *The Kindness of Strangers: The Life of Tennessee Williams*. Boston: Little, Brown, 1985.

Stanton, Stephen, ed. *Tennessee Williams: A Collection of Critical Essays*. Englewood Cliffs, NJ: Prentice-Hall, 1977.

Williams, Tennessee. *Memoirs*. Garden City, NJ: Doubleday, 1975.

August Wilson

Ching, Mei-Ling. "Wrestling against History." *Theater/Yale* 19.3 (1988): 70-1.

Elam, Harry. "August Wilson, Doubling, Madness, and Modern African American Drama." *Modern Drama* 43 (2000): 611-32.

Henderson, Heather. "Building Fences: An Interview with Mary Alice and James Earl Jones." *Theater/Yale* 16.3 (1985): 67-70.

Shannon, Sandra G. "The Long Wait: August Wilson's *Ma Rainey's Black Bottom*." *Black American Literature Forum* 25.1 (1991): 135-45.

Wilde, Lisa. "Reclaiming the Past: Narrative and Memory in August Wilson's *Two Trains Running*." *Theatre/Yale* 22.1 (1991): 73-4.

UNIT 7: WORLD STAGES

Allison, H. *Sistren Song: Popular Theatre in Jamaica*. London: War on Want, 1986.

Alston, J. B. *Yoruba Drama in English: Interpretation and Production*. Lewiston, NY: Mellen, 1989.

Appiah, Kwame Anthony. "Is the Post- in Postmodernism the Post- in Postcolonial?" *Critical Inquiry* 17 (1991): 336-357.

———. *In My Father's House: Africa in the Philosophy of Culture*. London: Methuen, 1992.

Ashcroft, Bill, Gareth Griffiths, and Helen Tiffin. *The Empire Writes Back: Theory and Practice in Post-Colonial Literatures*. London: Routledge, 1989.

———. *The Post-Colonial Studies Reader*. London: Routledge, 1995.

Bennett, Susan. "Who Speaks? Representations of Native Women in Some Canadian Plays." *Canadian Journal of Drama and Theatre* 1.2 (1991): 13-25.

Bhabha, Homi K. *The Location of Culture*. London: Routledge, 1993.

Bharucha, Rustom. *Theatre and the World: Performance and the Politics of Culture*. London: Routledge, 1993.

Bhatia, Nandi. "Staging Resistance: The Indian People's Theatre Association." *The Politics of Culture and the Shadow of Capital*. Ed. Lisa Lowe. Durham: Duke UP, 1997.

———. "Women, Homelands and the Indian Diaspora." *Centennial Review* 32.3 (1997): 511-525.

Black, S. "'What Kind of Society Can Develop Under Corrugated Iron?': Glimpses of New Zealand History in New Zealand Plays." *Australasian Drama Studies* 3.1 (1984): 31-52.

Boal, Augusto. *The Theatre of the Oppressed*. Trans. C.A. McBride and M.L. McBride. New York Theatre Communications Group, 1979.

Boon, Richard, and Jane Plaistow, eds. *Theatre Matters: Performance and Culture on the World Stage*. Cambridge, England: Cambridge UP, 1998.

Carroll, Dennis. *Australian Contemporary Drama*. Sydney: Currency P, 1995.

Chatterjee, Sudipto. "The Nation Staged: Nationalist Drama in Late Nineteenth-Century Bengali Theatre." *Post-Colonial Stages: Cultural and Creative Voices on Drama, Theatre, and Performance*. Ed. Helen Gilbert. London: Dangeroo, 1999.

———. "Mise-en-(Colonial) Scéne: Theatre of the Bengali Renaissance." *Imperialism and Theatre*. Ed. J. Ellen Gainor. London: Routledge, 1995.

Chinwezu, Onwuchekwa Jemie, and Ihechukwu Madubuike. *Toward the Decolonization of African Literature*. Vol. 1. Washington, DC: Howard UP, 1983.

Coplan, David. *In Township Tonight! South Africa's Black City Music and Theatre*. London: Longman, 1985.

Crow, Brian, and Chris Canfield. *An Introduction to Post-Colonial Theatre*. Cambridge, England: Cambridge UP, 1996.

Dasgupta, H. N. *The Indian Theatre*. Delhi: Gian Publishing House, 1988.

Drewal, Margaret T. *Yoruba Ritual: Performers, Play, Agency*. Bloomington, IN: Indiana UP, 1992.

Dunton, C. *"Make Man Talk True": Nigerian Drama in English Since 1970*. London: Hans Zell, 1992.

Emberley, J.V. *Thresholds of Difference: Feminist Critique, Native Women's Writing, Postcolonial Theory*. Toronto: U of Toronto P, 1993.

Fanon, Frantz. *Black Skin, White Masks*. Trans. C.L. Markmann. New York: Grove, 1967.

Filewod, Alan. "Between Empires: Post-Imperialism and Canadian Theatre." *Essays in Theatre/Études Théâtrales*. 11.1 (1992): 3-15.

Fuchs, A. *Playing the Market: The Market Theatre, Johannesburg 1976-1980*. London: Harwood, 1990.

Gargi, B. *Folk Theater of India*. Calcutta: Rupa, 1991.

Gilbert, Helen, ed. *Postcolonial Plays: An Anthology*. London: Routledge, 2001.

————. *Sightlines: Race, Gender, and Nation in Contemporary Australian Theatre*. Ann Arbor, MI: U of Michigan P, 1998.

Gilbert, Helen, and Joanne Tompkins. *Post-Colonial Drama: Theory, Practice, Politics*. London: Routledge, 1996.

Glissant, Edouard. *Caribbean Discourse: Selected Essays*. Charlottesville: UP of Virginia, 1989.

Goldie, T. *Fear and Temptation: The Image of the Indigene in Canadian, Australian, and New Zealand Literatures*. Kingston, Ontario: McGill-Queen's UP, 1989.

Graver, David, ed. *Drama for a New South Africa*. Bloomington, IN: Indiana UP, 1999.

Hauptfleisch, Temple. *Theatre and Society in South Africa: Some Reflections in a Fractured Mirror*. Pretoria: J.L. Van Schaik Academic, 1997.

Holloway, P., ed. *Contemporary Australian Drama: Perspectives Since 1955*. Sydney: Currency P, 1987.

Hulme, Peter. *Colonial Encounters: Europe and the Native Caribbean 1492-1797*. London: Routledge, 1986.

Kavangh, Robert Mshengu. *Theatre and Cultural Struggle in South Africa*. London: Zed, 1985.

Knowles, Ric. *The Theatre of Form and the Production of Meaning: Contemporary Canadian Dramaturgies*. Toronto: ECW, 1999.

Kruger, Loren. *The Drama of South Africa: Plays, Pageants and Publics since 1910*. London: Routledge, 1999.

Mead, P., and Campbell, M., eds. *Shakespeare's Books: Contemporary Cultural Politics and the Persistence of Empire*. Melbourne: U of Melbourne English Department, 1993.

Mee, Erin, ed. *Drama Contemporary: India*. Baltimore: Johns Hopkins UP, 1998.

Mulryne, J.R., Margaret Rulryne, and Takashi Sasayama. *Shakespeare and the Japanese Stage*. Cambridge, England: Cambridge UP, 1998.

Narayan, Birendra. *Hindi Drama and Stage*. Delhi: Bansal, 1981.

Ndlovu, Duma. *Woza Afrika! An Anthology of South African Plays*. New York: Braziller, 1986.

Ngũgĩ wa Thiong'o. *Decolonising the Mind: The Politics of Language in African Literature*. London: James Currey, 1986.

Olaniyan, Tejumola. *Scars of Conquest/Masks of Resistance*. New York: Oxford UP, 1995.

Ortolani, Benito. *The Japanese Theatre from Shamanistic Ritual to Contemporary Pluralism*. Princeton, NJ: Princeton UP, 1995.

Orkin, Martin. *Drama and the South African State*. Manchester, England: Manchester UP, 1991.

Pavis, Patrice, ed. *The Intercultural Performance Reader*. London: Routledge, 1996.

Peterson, Bhekizizwe. *Monarchs, Missionaries, and African Intellectuals: African Theater and the Unmaking of Colonial Marginality*. Trenton: Africa World Press, 2000.

Rahu, Kironmoy. *Bengali Theatre*. New Delhi: National Book Trust, 1978.

Retamar, Roberto Fernández. *Caliban and Other Essays*. Trans. E. Baker. Minneapolis: U of Minnesota P, 1989.

Rock, David. *Argentina, 1516-1987: From Spanish Colonization to Alfonsin*. Berkeley, CA: U of California P, 1987.

Rubin, Don. *The World Encyclopedia of Contemporary Theatre.*Vol. 1: *Europe.*Vol. 2: *The Americas.*Vol. 3: *Africa.*Vol. 4: *The Arab World.*Vol. 5: *Asia and the Pacific.*Vol. 6: *Bibliography and Cumulative Index.* London: Routledge, 1999.

Said, Edward. *Culture and Imperialism.* London: Chatto & Windus, 1993.

Salter, Denis. "On Native Ground: Canadian Theatre Historiography and the Postmodernism/Postcolonial Axis." *Theatre Research in Canada.* 13.12 (1992): 134-43.

Savigliano, Marta E. *Tango and the Political Economy of Passion.* Boulder, CO: Westview, 1995.

Sheng, Gao Wen, ed. *History of Chinese Contemporary Dramatic Literature.* Nan Ning: Guang Xi People's Publishing House, 1990.

Solberg, Rolf. *Alternative Theatre in South Africa: Talks with Prime Movers Since the 1970s.* Pietermartizburg: Hadeda Books, 1999.

Solomon, Rakesh H. "Culture, Imperialism and Nationalist Reszistance: Performance in Colonial India." *Theatre Journal* 46 (1994): 323-347

Spivak, Gayatri Chakravorty. *In Other Worlds: Essays in Cultural Politics.* New York: Methuen, 1988.

Taylor, Diana. *Disappearing Acts: Spectacles of Gender and Nationalism in Argentina's "Dirty War."* Durham, NC: Duke UP, 1997.

————. *Theatre of Crisis: Drama and Politics in Latin America.* Lexington, KY: University of Kentucky P, 1991.

Taylor, Diana, and Juan Villegas, eds. *Negotiating Performance: Gender, Sexuality, and Theatricality in Latino America.* Durham, NC: Duke UP, 1994.

Trinh, T. Minh-ha. *Woman, Native, Other.* Bloomington, IN: Indiana UP, 1989.

Versényi, Adam. *Theatre in Latin America: Religion, Politics and Culture from Cortés to the 1980s.* Cambridge, England: Cambridge UP, 1993.

Wade, Bonnie. *Performing Arts in India: Essays on Music, Dance, and Drama. University of California Centre for South and Southeast Asia Studies Monograph Series* 21 (1983).

Wu, Yan Zhe ed. *History of the Education of Modern Spoken Drama in China.* Shanghai: East China Normal University Publishing House, 1986.

Zarrilli, Phillip. *The Kathakali Complex: Actor, Performance and Structure.* New Delhi: Abhinav, 1984.

Aimé Césaire

Arnold, A. James. *Modernism and Negritude: The Poetry and Poetics of Aimé Césaire.* Cambridge, MA: Harvard UP, 1981.

Davis, Gregson. *Aimé Césaire.* Cambridge, England: Cambridge UP, 1997.

Dawborn, Charles. *Makers of New France.* New York: Pott, 1951.

Frutkin, Susan. *Aimé Césaire: Black between Worlds.* Coral Gables, FL: University of Miami P, 1973.

Jack Davis

Balme, Chris. "The Aboriginal Theater of Jack Davis: Prolegomena to a Theory of Syncretic Theatre." *Crisis and Creativity in New Literatures in English.* Eds. G. Davis and H. Maes-Jelinek. Amsterdam: Rodopi, 1990.

Chesson, Keith. *Jack Davis: A Life-Story.* Melbourne: Dent, 1988.

Davis, Jack. *A Boy's Life.* Broome: Magabala Books, 1991.

Harrison, Hank. *The Art of Jack Davis.* Detroit: Stabir, 1987.

Brian Friel

Dantanus, Ulf. *Brian Friel: A Study.* London: Faber & Faber, 1988.

Deane, Seamus. *Celtic Revivals: Essays in Modern Irish Literature, 1880-1900.* Winston-Salem, NC: Wake Forest UP, 1987.

Delaney, Pauyl. *Brian Friel in Conversation.* Ann Arbor, MI: University of Michigan P, 2000.

Grene, Nicholas. *The Politics of Irish Drama: Plays in Context from Boucicault to Friel.* Cambridge, England: Cambridge UP, 1999.

Maxwell, D. E. S. *Brian Friel.* Lewisburg, PA: Bucknell UP, 1973.

Mcrath, F. C. *Brian Friel's (Post)Colonial Drama: Language, Illusion, and Politics.* Syracuse: Syracuse UP, 1999.

O'Brien, Lance. *Brian Friel*. Boston: Twayne, 1990.

Pine, Richard. *The Diviner: The Art of Brian Friel*. Mullingar, Ireland: Lilliput P, 1988.

Richtarik, Marilyn. *Acting Between the Lines: The Field Day Company and Irish Cultural Politics, 1980-1984*. Oxford, England: Clarendon, 1994.

Athol Fugard

Benson, Mary. *Athol Fugard and Barney Simon*. Randburg: Ravan, 1997.

Fuchs, Anne. *Playing the Market: The Market Theatre, Johannesburg, 1976-1986*. New York: Harwood, 1990.

Fugard, Athol. *Notebooks 1960-1977*. Johannesburg: Ad. Donker, 1983.

Gray, Stephen. *Athol Fugard*. New York: McGraw-Hill, 1992.

———. *File on Fugard*. London: Methuen, 1991.

Vandenbroucke, Russell. *Truths the Hand Can Touch: The Theatre of Athol Fugard*. New York: TCG, 1985.

Walder, Dennis. *Athol Fugard*. New York: Grove, 1995.

Wertheim, Albert. *The Dramatic Art of Athol Fugard: From South Africa to the World*. Bloomington, IN: Indiana UP, 2000.

Worthen, W. B. "Convicted Reading: *The Island,* Hybridity, Performance." *Crucibles of Crisis: Performance and Social Change*. Ed. Janelle Reinelt. Ann Arbor, MI: University of Michigan P, 1996, 165-184.

Griselda Gambaro

Contreras, Marta. *Griselda Gambaro: Teatro de la Descomposicion*. Cóncepcion, Chile: Ediciones Universidad de la Cóncepcion, 1994.

Cypress, Sandra Messerger. "The Plays of Griselda Gambaro." *Dramatists in Revolt: The New Latin American Theatre*. Eds. Leon F. Lyday and George F. Woodyard. Austin, TX: University of Texas P, 1976: 95-109.

Postma, Rosslea. "Space and Spectator in the Theatre of Griselda Gambero: *Información para extranjeros.*" *Latin American Theatre Review* 14.1 (1980): 35-45.

Taylor, Diana. "Theatre and Terrorism: Griselda Gambaro's *Information for Foreigners.*" *Theatre Journal* 43 (1990): 165-182.

Gao Xingjian

Fong, Gilbert C. F. *The Other Shore: Plays by Gao Xingjian*. Hong Kong: Chinese UP, 1999.

Tam, Kwok-kan. *Soul of Chaos: Critical Perspectives on Gao Xingjian*. Hong Kong: Chinese UP, 2001.

Tomson Highway

Baker, Marie Annharte. "An Old Indian Trick Is to Laugh." *Canadian Theatre Review* 68 (Fall 1991): 48-49.

———. "Angry Enough to Spit But with *Dry Lips* It Hurts More Than You Know." *Canadian Theatre Review* 68 (Fall 1991): 88-89.

Dahlquist, Gordon. "I Did It—Highway." *Native Playwrights' Newsletter* (Winter 1994): 22-23.

Filewod, Alan. "Receiving Aboriginality: Tomson Highway and the Crisis of Cultural Authenticity." *Theatre Journal* 46 (1994): 363-73.

Loucks, Bryan. "Another Glimpse: Excerpts from a Conversation with Tomson Highway." *Canadian Theatre Review* 68 (Fall 1991): 9-11.

Rabillard, Sheila. "Absorption, Elimination, and the Hybrid: Some Impure Questions of Gender and Culture in the Trickster Drama of Tomson Highway." *Essays in Theatre/Études Théàtrales* 12.1 (1993): 3-27.

Wilson, Ann. "Tomson Highway." *Other Solitudes: Canadian Multicultural Fictions*. Eds. Linda Hutcheon and Marion Richmond. Toronto: Oxford UP, 1990.

Manjula Padmanabhan

Frow, J. "Bodies in Pieces." *The Body in the Library*. Ed. L. Dale and S. Ryan. Amsterdam: Rodopi, 1998, 35-53.

Padmanabhan, Manjula. "A Government of India undertaking. . ." *Critical Quarterly* 35 (1993): 66–79.

Satoh Makoto

Mishima, Yukio. *Five Modern Noh Plays.* Trans. Donald Keene. New York: Knopf, 1957.

Goodman, David G. *After Apocalypse: Four Japanese Plays of Hiroshima and Nagasaki.* New York: Columbia UP, 1986.

———. *Japanese Drama and Culture in the 1960s: The Return of the Gods.* Armonk, NY: East Gate, 1988.

Wole Soyinka

Gibbs, James. *Wole Soyinka.* London: Macmillan, 1986.

———, ed. *Critical Perspectives on Wole Soyinka.* Washington, DC: Three Continents, 1980.

Gibbs, James, Ketu H. Katrak, and Henry Louis Gates Jr., eds. *Wole Soyinka: A Bibliography of Primary and Secondary Sources.* Westport, CT: Greenwood, 1986.

Gugelberger, Georg M., ed. *Marxism and African Literature.* London: James Currey, 1985.

Jones, Eldred Durosimi. *The Writings of Wole Soyinka.* London: James Currey, 1988.

Nazareth, Peter. *An African View of Literature.* Evanston, IL: Northwestern UP, 1974.

Ogunba, Oyin. *The Movement of Transition: A Study of the Plays of Wole Soyinka.* Ibadan, Nigeria: Ibadan UP, 1975.

Soyinka, Wole. "The Fourth Stage." *The Morality of Art: Essays Presented to G. Wilson Knight by his Colleagues and Friends.* Ed. D. W. Jefferson, New York: Barnes & Noble, 1969.

———. *The Man Died.* London: Rex Collings, 1972.

Judith Thompson

Filewod, Alan. "Casebook on Judith Thompson." *Canadian Theatre Review* 89 (1996): 3–44.

Fletche, Jennifer. "The Last Things in the Sled: An Interview with Judith Thompson," *Canadian Theatre Review* 89 (1996): 39–44.

Harvie, Jennifer. "Constructing Fictions of an Essential Reality, or 'This Pickshur is Nice': Judith Thompson's *Lion in the Streets.*" *Theatre Research in Canada / Recherches Théâtrales au Canada* 13 (1992): 81–93.

Knowles, Ric. *The Theatre of Form and the Production of Meaning: Contemporary Canadian Dramaturgies.* Toronto: ECW, 1999.

Lane, Harry. "Redefining the Comfort Zone: Nancy Palk on Acting Judith Thompson." *Canadian Theatre Review* 89 (1996): 19–21.

Appendix: Video, Film, and Sound Recordings of Plays

Aeschylus, *The Oresteia*

VHS. 1983. National Theatre of Great Britain production. Director: Peter Hall. Films for Humanities.

VHS. 1991. Video/Film Associates.

Aristophanes, *Lysistrata*

VHS. 1986. Greek Video Records and Tapes. Distributed by New York Film Annex.

VHS. 1987. Distributed by Insight Media.

Sound Recording. 1966. Director: Howard Sackler. Cast includes Hermione Gingold and Stanley Holloway. Caedmon Records.

Euripides, *Medea*

VHS. 1970. Director: Pier Paolo Passolini. Cast includes Maria Callas, Guiseppi Gentile, and Laurent Tarzieff.

VHS. 1979. Cast includes Marina Goderdzishvili and Vladimir Julukhadze.

VHS. 1979. Director: Pier Paolo Passolini. Cast includes Maria Callas and Guiseppi Gentile.

VHS. 1982. Cast includes Zoe Caldwell and Judith Anderson. Films for the Humanities.

VHS. 1986. New York Greek Drama Company.

VHS. 1990. Adapted by Robinson Jeffers. Princeton: Films for the Humanities, 1990.

Sound Recording. Cast includes Judith Anderson and Anthony Quayle. Caedmon Records.

Sophocles, *Oedipus the King*

VHS. 1957. Deaf actors' performance. Gallaudet University Library.

VHS. 1957. Director: Tyrone Guthrie. Cast includes Douglas Campbell, Douglas Rain, Eric House, and Eleanor Stuart.

VHS. 1959. *Oedipus Rex: Age of Sophocles*, I. Distributed by Encyclopedia Britannica Educational Corp.

VHS. 1967. Director: Philip Saville. Cast includes Donald Sutherland, Christopher Plummer, Lilli Palmer, Orson Welles, and Cyril Cusack.

VHS. 1975. *The Rise of Greek Tragedy*. Director: Howard Mantell. Cast includes James Mason, Claire Bloom. Set in outdoor amphitheater, using masks. Films for the Humanities, 1982.

VHS. 1987. Cast includes John Gielgud, Michael Pennington, and Claire Bloom. Films for the Humanities.

Sound Recording. Cast includes Douglas Campbell and Eric House. Caedmon Records.

Sound Recording. Cast includes Bernard Mayes. Mind's Eye.

Japanese Classical Theater

VHS. 1980. *Noh: The Classical Theatre of Japan*. Michigan State University.

VHS. 1980. *The Style of Classical Noh Theatre*. Institute for Advanced Studies in Theater Arts

VHS. 1984. *Noh Drama*. Japan Information Center.

VHS. 1992. *The Art of Kabuki*. Films for the Humanities.

VHS. 2000. *Theater in Japan*. Films for the Humanities.

UNIT III

Wakefield Master, *Second Shepherds' Play*
VHS. 1975. *Early English Drama*. Films for the Humanities.

Anonymous, *Everyman*
Film. 1971. Distributed by Paul Lewison.
VHS. 1991. Distributed by Insight Media.
Sound Recording. Cast includes Burgess Meredith. Caedmon Records.

Christopher Marlowe, *Doctor Faustus*
Film. 1950. *Faust and the Devil*. Cast includes Italo Tajo and Nelly Corradi.
VHS. 1968. Cast includes Richard Burton and Elizabeth Taylor.

William Shakespeare, *Hamlet*
Film. 1948. Director: Laurence Olivier. Cast includes Olivier.
Film. 1954. *Prince of Players*. Cast includes Richard Burton and Eva LeGallienne.
Film. 1963. *The Bad Sleep Well*. Director: Akira Kurosawa.
Film. 1966. Russian with English subtitles. Cast includes Innokenti Smoktunovsky and Mikhail
      Nazvanov.
VHS. 1969. Director: Tony Richardson. Cast includes Nicol Williamson.
Film. 1969. Cast includes Nicol Williamson, Gordon Jackson, Judy Parfitt, and Marianne Faithful.
VHS. 1979. Director: Derek Jacobi. Time-Life Video.
VHS. 1980. Director: Rodney Bennett. BBC.
Film. 1982. Director: Robert Nelson.
VHS. 1983. The BBC-TV Shakespeare Plays. Cast includes Derek Jacobi.
VHS. 1985. Director: Douglas Fisher. Classics on Video series.
VHS. 1989. Director: Melvyn Bragg.
VHS. 1990. Director: Franco Zeffirelli. Cast includes Mel Gibson and Glenn Close.
VHS. 1996. Director: Kenneth Branagh. Cast includes Branagh, Derek Jacobi, Julie Christie, and
      Kate Winslet.
VHS. 2001. Director: Michael Almereyda. Cast includes Ethan Hawke, Julia Stiles, Sam Shepard
Sound Recording. Cast includes John Gielgud. Durkin Hayes Publishing.
Sound Recording. 1985. Michael Redgrave.
Sound Recording. 1988. Cast includes Ronald Pickup and Angela Pleasance. BBC Audio
      Collection.

William Shakespeare, *The Tempest*
VHS. 1999. *Silent Shakespeare*. Milestone Film and Video.
Film. 1959. Cast includes Van Heflin and Silvano Mangano.
VHS. 1960. Hallmark Hall of Fame. Cast includes Richard Burton.
Film. 1961. Michigan Media.
VHS. 1963. Director: George Schaefer. Cast includes Maurice Evans, Roddy McDowall, Richard
      Burton, and Lee Remick. Films for the Humanities.
Film. 1968. Director: Peter Brook.
Film. 1969. *Tempest: O Brave New World*. National Broadcasting Company.
VHS. 1973. Yale Repertory Theatre production recorded for Television. LCL TOFT.
VHS. 1979. Director: Derek Jarman. Zeitgeist Films.
VHS. 1980. Director: Derek Jarman. Cast includes Heathcote Williams and Karl Johnson. World
      Northal.
VHS. 1980. Director: Audrey E. Stanley. Berkeley Shakespeare Festival.

VHS. 1982. Director: Paul Mazursky. Cast includes John Cassavetes, Gena Rowlands, Susan Sarandon, Vittorio Gassman, and Raul Julia.

VHS. 1983. The BBC-TV Shakespeare Plays. Cast includes Michael Hordern.

VHS. 1983. Director: William Woodman. Cast includes Efrem Zimbalist Jr., William H. Basset, Ted Sorrel, and Kay E. Kuter.

VHS. 1986. Director: Julie Taymor. Theatre for a New Audience.

VHS. 1992. *Prospero's Books*. Director: Peter Greenaway. Cast includes John Gielgud, Erland Josephson, and Michael Clark.

Sound Recording. Cast includes Michael Redgrave and Vanessa Redgrave. Caedmon Records.

UNIT IV

Pedro Calderón de la Barca, *Life Is a Dream*

Film. 1988. Director: Raul Ruiz. Cast includes Sylvain Thirolle and Roch Leibovici. French with English subtitles.

Moliére, *Tartuffe*

VHS. *Moliére and the Comédie Française*. Director: Jacques Charon.

VHS. 1997. Films for the Humanities.

VHS. 1986. Films for the Humanities.

VHS. 1978. Great Performances, Public Broadcasting Service.

Sound Recording. 1968. Director: Jean Gascon. Stratford National Theatre of Canada. Caedmon Records.

Jean Racine, *Phaedra*

Film. 1962. Cast includes Melina Mercouri and Anthony Perkins.

VHS. 1968. Films for the Humanities.

UNIT V

Marguerite Duras, *India Song*

VHS. 1974. Films de l'Atalante, 1992.

Henrik Ibsen, *A Doll House*

VHS. 1959. Director: Barry A. Brown. Cast includes Christopher Plummer, Julie Harris, and Richard Thomas.

VHS. 1973. Director: Joseph Losey. Cast includes Jane Fonda and Trevor Howard.

VHS. 1973. Director: Patrick Garland. Cast includes Claire Bloom and Anthony Hopkins.

VHS. 1977. Cast includes Claire Bloom.

Sound Recording. Cast includes Claire Bloom and Donald Madden. Caedmon Records.

Harold Pinter, *The Homecoming*

Film. 1973. Director: Peter Hall. Cast includes Cyril Cusak, Ian Holm, and Vivian Merchant.

Luigi Pirandello, *Six Characters in Search of an Author*

VHS. 1976. Cast includes Joseph Heller. Films for the Humanities.

VHS. 1978. Miami Dade Community College.

Bernard Shaw, *Major Barbara*

VHS. 1941. Director: Gabriel Pascal, in consultation with George Bernard Shaw. Cast includes Wendy Hiller, Rex Harrison, and Sybil Thorndike.

Sound Recording. Cast includes Maggie Smith and Robert Morley. Caedmon Records.

August Strindberg, *The Father*
VHS. 1998. Films for the Humanities.

UNIT VI   Amiri Baraka (LeRoi Jones) *Dutchman*
VHS. 1966. Director: Anthony Harvey. Cast includes Al Freeman Jr., and Shirley Knight.

David Henry Hwang, *M. Butterfly*
VHS. 1993. Director: David Cronenberg. Cast includes Jeremy Irons, John Lone, and Barbara
    Sukowa.

Arthur Miller, *Death of a Salesman*
VHS. 1986. Director: Volker Schlondorf. Karl Lorimar Home Video.
VHS. 1966. Director: Alex Segal. Cast includes members of original cast. Broadway Theatre
    Archives, 2001.

Eugene O'Neill, *The Hairy Ape*
VHS. 1944 Director: Alfred Santell.

Sam Shepard, *True West*
VHS. 1984. Director: Allan Goldstein. Cast includes John Malkovich and Gary Sinise.
Anna Deavere Smith, *Fires in the Mirror: Crown Heights, Brooklyn and Other Identities*
VHS. 1992. Director: George Wolfe. Broadcast by "American Playhouse," Public Broadcasting
    Service.
VHS. 2000. Director: George Wolfe. Broadcast by "American Playhouse" Public Broadcasting
    Service.

Tennessee Williams, *The Glass Menagerie*
Film. 1950. Director: Irving Rippen. Cast includes Jane Wyman, Kirk Douglas, and Arthur
    Kennedy.
Film. 1973. Director: Anthony Harvey. Cast includes Katharine Hepburn, Sam Waterston, Joanna
    Miles, and Michael Moriarty.
VHS. 1987. Director: Paul Newman. Cast includes John Malkovich, Joanne Woodward, and
    Karen Allen.
Sound Recording. 1980. Cast includes Helen Hayes and Montgomery Clift. Mind's Eye.
Sound Recording. Cast includes Montgomery Clift and Julie Harris. Caedmon Records.
Sound Recording. *Tennessee Williams Reads "The Glass Menagerie" and Others.* Cast includes
    Tennessee Williams. Caedmon Records.